·1993·

FAR EAST CHINESE-ENGLISH DICTIONARY

遠東漢英大辭典

(原主編人　梁實秋)

簡明本

主　編

張　芳　杰

總審定 朱良箴　總編輯 鄧樂然

遠東圖書公司印行

部　首　表

部 首 表

目　　錄

六畫

七畫

八　畫

九　畫

巂 ············6676
韙 ············6770
馥 ············6919
魏 ············7055

十九　畫

單字　字號

嚮 ············769
龐 ············1403
爇 ············3279
瓣 ············3520
疆 ············3584
藺 ············4453
羆 ············4508
羅 ············4509
羹 ············4533
羸 ············4534
蠃 ············5336
覈 ············5477
賾 ············5810
辭 ············6044
靡 ············6730
韻 ············6778
麗 ············7228
麴 ············7239
黼 ············7274

二十　畫

單字　字號

嚴 ············772
矍 ············3821
競 ············4084
耀 ············4567
贏 ············5814
辮 ············6045
馨 ············6920
騰 ············6965

廿一　畫

單字　字號

囂 ············777
羼 ············4535
臝 ············4754
藥 ············5168
譽 ············5690
辯 ············6046
飜 ············6848
魔 ············7058
鷇 ············7184
齎 ············7305

廿二　畫

單字　字號

囊 ············780
懿 ············1746
疊 ············3586
糴 ············4272
羇 ············4510
聽 ············4612
轡 ············6034
響 ············6779
鬻 ············7047
龔 ············7326
龕 ············7327

廿三　畫

單字　字號

糵 ············4273
蠱 ············5348
蠲 ············5349
變 ············5695
讎 ············5697
靨 ············6734
黴 ············7268
齏 ············7306

廿四　畫

單字　字號

矗 ············3823
纛 ············4473
羈 ············4511
蠶 ············5351
衢 ············5373
贛 ············5820
靆 ············6719

廿五　畫

單字　字號

糶 ············4274
釁 ············6300
靉 ············6721
鹽 ············7215
黌 ············7246

廿六　畫

單字　字號

鬮 ············7043
黶 ············7270

廿七　畫

單字　字號

鑾 ············6526

廿八　畫

單字　字號

豔 ············5721
鑿 ············6527

廿九　畫

單字　字號

爨 ············3283
鬱 ············7045

卅二　畫

單字　字號

籲 ············4232

梁 序

這一部漢英辭典是爲適應現代大衆需要而編的，所以單字收入雖不太多，包括常見常用的字約八千字之數，但是收入短辭、成語卻不在少數。過於典雅的與過於粗鄙的詞語，以及過於專門性的術語，則均割愛。深信在資料的選擇上，這部辭典可以滿足一般讀者的要求。

單字排列沒有萬全的辦法，我們採取部首的編排是因爲這可能是最大多數讀者所熟習的。附有索引，或以筆畫部首爲準，或以國語注音符號爲準，或以威妥瑪式羅馬拼音爲準，以增加讀者檢字的便利。

單字與詞一概加注注音符號，這是我們特別致力的項目之一，讀者於檢求英文解釋之餘，可以因此得到正確的讀音。爲篇幅所限，只能以國語注音符號爲主。事實上國語注音符號是最簡便而又最準確的一套工具，欲求發音正確，讀者無分中外，皆宜通曉國語注音符號。

這樣一部辭典之最重要的一部分，當然是在英文解釋方面。我們使用的英文是現代流行的淺顯的英文。這些字詞，無妨一字對一字的直譯；有些只能以意義相當的字詞譯之；更有些不能不出於較冗長之解釋。我們的主旨是盡力使讀者在理解上得到便利。

我們編輯這部辭典，參考了我們所能獲得的不少的中外辭典，尤其是坊間早已出版的幾種類似的漢英辭典。在取材上、在翻譯上、在編排上，見仁見智，各有其獨特之處，我們不敢自詡後來居上，但是我們能從前此已有之成就汲取經驗，轉益多師，卻是不能不表示感激的。凡是字典均需隨時修訂，方能延長其壽命。我們誠懇的歡迎讀者指示其疏誤，以便陸續補正。

這部辭典的編輯，中文部分是由鍾露昇先生主其事，英文部分由朱良箴先生、董昭輝先生、邵廓清先生分別擔任之。而全稿之綜閱、校覈、修改，則由朱良箴先生獨任其艱巨。稿成之後，遠東圖書公司編輯部同人除悉心校對外，亦常提供意見，使這部辭典減少缺陷。這都是我們應該表示謝意的。

梁實秋

六十年五月

張　序

遠東圖書公司敦請梁實秋先生主編的最新實用漢英辭典，於一九七一年五月問世後，行銷中外，深受歡迎。十餘年來中英新詞語不斷增加。外人學習中文者日多，國人從事中譯英工作者亦衆。隨時代演變，中外讀者莫不殷切期待一部內容更新、更豐富的漢英辭典。遠東圖書公司主人浦家麟先生有鑑於此，遂於一九八四年初就商於梁實秋先生擬將最新實用漢英辭典擴編並增加新詞、新義等以應讀者需要，後經約集編審委員會同仁數度商議，研討擴編細則，由余綜理其事，並聘請遠東英漢大辭典總編輯兼英文中國日報總主筆朱良箴先生爲總審定，聘請鄧樂然先生爲總編輯，成立擴編小組。計畫旣定，立即展開工作。

擴編小組主要成員包括張振生、謝文男、鄭明哲、范國生、嚴偉行等諸位教授外並約請台大、師大、政大、輔大、東吳、淡江、文化等校優秀同學（名單另詳於後）及蘇全福老師等百餘位參加查證、核對、審訂工作，並參考各種中英文辭典、英漢辭典、百科全書、專用名詞辭典、中國歷代名著英譯本、當代中英文刊物，據以擴充詞語，增加例句。凡字詞適用於白話者，以白話爲例句；適用於文言者，以文言者爲例句；可用於白話亦可用於文言者，酌加白話例句及文言例句，並儘量納入科技新詞語、流行的口語、俚語等。一九八七年十一月梁實秋先生逝世後，浦家麟先生將擴編小組擴大爲編審小組，加速進行。其後增聘海峽兩岸及留美十餘位學者專家參加審訂工作以資妥善。

整個擴編過程中，我們特別感謝鄧樂然先生的奉獻，他督導先後一百餘位成員，鍥而不捨，日夜加班，倍極辛勞。他們逐字逐詞複查原稿後，尙須查證辭句出處，故而每字每詞皆經過二十餘次核校，始可發排，工作至艱至鉅。此外，擴編工作歷經六載，其間物價波動，經費較原訂計畫超出數倍，幸賴遠東圖書公司經理部鼎力支援，一一克服遭遇到的諸多困難，其堅毅不撓，精益求精的精神，令人欽佩。

本辭典經擴編後，堪稱規模最大的一部漢英辭典，計彙集常用單字約八千之數，短詞、成語達十餘萬條，例句數萬條。取材標準著重現代化與實用性。爲求儘量幫助讀者，本辭典採用三種注音符號，備有五種索引。惟近來科技發展迅速，中文電腦排版逐漸取代手工排版。漢字若干字體、字彙正用俗用在電腦系統中筆畫體例在技術上仍未臻完善，電腦磁片輸入尙待克服，故在本書中有若干字彙正用俗用互相調用。儘管如此，由於工作量浩瀚，動員了百餘位專業人士，同仁等雖竭盡所能，猶恐力有未逮，疏漏之處難免，尙祈海內外學者、專家、以及所有讀者不吝指正。

張其杰 謹識
一九九一年十月

本辭典編審委員會編校小組

助　理

林淑華

王惠英　　陳佩玟

劉梅珍　　江怡靚

校　對

吳鳳琴	張敏慧	蔡麗香	林雅慧
王麗君	楊純慧	趙蓉慧	張嘉桓
林　錦	謝淑慎	林斐卿	吳幸姬
楊雙鳳	蕭蔓萱	李冬梅	王潁惠
陳淑誼	李清美	宋瓊玲	江幸珍
高皓純	王淑貞	陳麗萍	謝金治
林姿燕	席美欣	張淑芳	屠智萍
蔡美慧	楊淑慧	張文玉	吳玉萍
林靜明	游少嫻	龐士珍	林惠卿
曹眞眞	曾健芬	王瓊芬	王麗英
朱世文	張玉芳	黎靜怡	楊永潁
柯慧霞	陳慧敏	黃櫻芳	陳偉莉
林靜雯	周美燕	杜文慧	林純慧
莊玉花	徐淑媛	陳姿靜	黃惠敏
黃秀英	陳丹荔	李友士	黃素卿
葉秋蘭	羅美玲	楊雅玲	黃智詠
邱瑞珍	陳淑華	呂惠玲	王丹青
費雅琴	方美鈴	羅明麗	李默君
廖俊傑	王麗貞	陳志端	凌澤仁
歐玉芬	楊思涵	昌淑鈴	葉秋杏
葉玉珠	林珍如	葉粟珍	張玉芝
陳玉秀	高麗珍	洪禎玟	劉珍秀

體　例

一、字彙：本辭典收集常用單字七千三百餘字，短詞、成語達十二萬餘條。取材範圍包括中英文辭典、中國經典、新舊文藝作品、報章雜誌及日常談話。取材標準著重現代化與實用性，典雅的、俚俗的、以及常見的科學詞語，一併收羅，深信足供一般中外讀者參考之用。

二、字體：本辭典所列單字，以正體爲準。俗寫與訛體則加註於本字之後，或單獨列入並加註本字正體。

三、排列：

（甲）單字的排列是根據部首（見部首表），同一部首之單字，則依筆畫多寡排列。每一單字均編列號碼，以便檢字，如單字「一」的號碼是「1」，單字「中」的號碼是「21」。

一個單字如有二種或二種以上的讀音，且意義因而變異的，則分開排列。如「中」字在「中間」ㄓㄨㄥ ㄐㄧㄢ與「中毒」ㄓㄨㄥˋ ㄉㄨˊ兩個詞語裏讀音不同，解釋也不同，故分列爲「中」ㄓㄨㄥ與「中」ㄓㄨㄥˋ，但其編號則同爲一個號碼，即「中」ㄓㄨㄥ與「中」ㄓㄨㄥˋ均爲「21」號。

一個單字如果祇是讀音不同而不影響其意義時，則不分列，僅在變異的讀音後註明「又讀」字樣。

（乙）詞語的排列是按照國語注音符號的順序來決定先後。例如「打鼓」與「打草驚蛇」兩個詞語，是按「鼓」ㄍㄨˇ與「草」ㄘㄠˇ在注音符號表上的順序來決定排列的先後。

每一個單字下的詞語，一律以該單字開始。例如在「文」字下的每一個詞語的第一個字，一律是「文」。讀者如果要查「以文會友」這個成語，不要查「文」字，而要查「以」字。

四、注音：本辭典計採用三種注音符號：國語注音符號、國語羅馬字、聯合國華語注音符號（漢語拼音）。每一個單字與每一個詞語的後面都加注國語注音符號，後兩者則僅列於單字之後以節省篇幅。

五、英解：本辭典之英文解釋，可分別爲兩大類：1.直接翻譯，2.解釋。前者適用於中英文可以直接對譯的情形（如：跑—to run，書—a book 等），後者則在無法對譯時使用（如：旦角—a female role in Chinese opera）。本辭典英解方面之體例如下：

1.一個詞語如有兩個或兩個以上截然不同的解釋，它的英文解釋是分開排列而冠以阿拉伯數字。例如「歲暮」的英解是 ① the late season of a year ② the closing years of one's life。

2.許多中文成語、諺語的英解方式，是先直譯爲英文，然後在破折號後面再加引伸的意義。目的是使外國讀者對這些成語、諺語有較深切的體味。

3.書名與拉丁文的專門名詞，一律用斜體字排印。

六、索引：本辭典共有五種索引：1.部首索引。2.筆畫索引。3.國語注音符號索引。4.國語羅馬字索引。5.聯合國注音符號（漢語拼音）索引。

七、附錄：詳見本辭典目錄表。

INTRODUCTION

Vocabulary Between the covers of this dictionary are collected 7,331 Chinese characters, under which are to be found some 120,000 entries. They were selected from a vast wealth of source materials, including dictionaries, Chinese classics, works of old and modern literature, newspapers, periodicals, legal documents and daily conversations. Inasmuch as this dictionary is intended as a useful tool for present-day readers seeking general but not encyclopedic information, the selection of the entries was made with the emphasis on *wide application* and *current usage.* Language being what it is, a lexicographer would be faulted for allowing his personal preference to influence his judgment in this respect. Among the entries of this dictionary one will find, side by side with what is "classic" or "highbrow", scientific and technological terms, familiar journalistic expressions, idioms and even slang, which may appear slightly repulsive to those with a refined taste.

Form of Characters Many characters in the Chinese language are interchangeable. Some characters have a standard form and a popular form. In addition, there are simplified forms and corrupt forms. The problem is further compounded by the fact that many "standard forms" have sunk into oblivion, while what were originally considered "corrupt forms" have been accepted as legitimate through long usage. To solve this problem, the compilers of this dictionary have chosen for inclusion those forms that are treated as "standard" by the majority of Chinese dictionaries in circulation. Popular forms and the most commonly seen corrupt forms are also listed, either separately or right beside the pertinent standard forms, and are included in the Radical Index for easy reference.

Arrangement of Entries Individual characters in this dictionary are arranged according to their radicals in keeping with Chinese tradition. Each radical is shown in the Radical Table with a page number. Characters with the same radical are arranged according to the number of strokes in the ascending order.

Some Chinese characters have more than one pronunciation, with each pronunciation representing a totally different meaning. Characters of the category are listed separately. For example, the character "中" is pronounced ㄓㄨㄥ in "中間" (in the middle) and ㄓㄨㄥˋ in "中毒" (to be poisoned). Therefore, the same character "中" is treated as two separate characters. No such distinction is made with those characters whose meaning is not affected by difference in pronunciation. For example, the character "微" can be pronounced ㄨㄟ or ㄨㄟˊ without change in meaning. Characters of this nature are treated as a single entity with the different pronunciations indicated behind each.

Entries under each character are arranged according to the order of the Mandarin Phonetic Symbols (國語注音符號). For example, the expression "打草驚蛇" ㄉㄚˇ ㄘㄠˇ ㄐㄧㄥ ㄕㄜˊ is listed after

"打鼓" ㄉㄚˇ ㄍㄨˇ.

All entries under each character begin with that particular character. For example, the entries under the character "文" all begin with "文". If one wants to find the expression "以文會友", he must look for it under the character "以".

Pronunciation Guide Three kinds of pronunciation guide are adopted in this dictionary. They are the Mandarin Phonetic Symbols (國語注音符號), the Gwoyeu Romatzyh (國語羅馬字), and the United Nations Mandarin Phonetic Symbols (HAN YU PIN YIN) (聯合國華語注音符號[漢語拼音]).

English Definitions Woe to those who attempt to make a *perfect* translation between Chinese and English, two languages that have few common denominators. The primary objective of this dictionary is to give the Chinese characters and phrases their *equivalent* meaning in English, on the assumption that the majority of them have English counterparts with identical or similar meaning. In cases where this is not true, the Chinese character or phrase in question is merely *explained* in English with no equivalent given. The late Mr. Yen Fu laid down three cardinal principles for the guidance of translators: *fidelity, readability* and *literary elegance*. The compilers of this dictionary have done their best to meet at least the first two of the three requirements, hoping that the deficiency in the last will be made up by the learned user himself.

The following rules are observed in giving the English definitions.

1. If one entry has two or more definitions totally different, they are listed separately and introduced by Arabic numerals in the ascending order with the more popular ones placed first. For example, the phrase "歲暮" has two definitions: (1) the late season of a year and (2) the closing years of one's life.
2. To enable non-Chinese speaking readers to savor the beauty of some Chinese proverbs and expressions, this dictionary usually gives a literal translation first and then the inferred meaning after a dash.
3. Latin words and titles of books which appear in the English definitions are printed in italics.

Indices Five indices are attached to this dictionary. They are: (1) Radical Index, (2) Stroke Number Index, (3) Mandarin Phonetic Symbol Index, (4) Gwoyeu Romatzyh Index, and (5) United Nations Mandarin Phonetic Symbol (HAN YU PIN YIN) Index. With these indices no one can fail to find in this dictionary the character or any of the entries he is looking for.

Appendix See the Table of Contents.

部首筆畫與索引頁碼對照表

部首筆畫索引

編　法：本索引係按單字之部首編列。其屬同一部首者，再以單字筆畫多寡爲序。單字後註明單字編號。

用　法：檢查時先查出單字所屬之部首，按筆畫（除去部首筆畫數）在索引中查出單字，再根據單字編號，查出書內單字及這一單字爲首所組成的詞語。

RADICAL INDEX

In this index the characters are listed under their respective radicals. Characters with the same radical are arranged in the ascending order according to the number of strokes used in writing them. The figure to the right of each character is its identification number under which the character can be found in the body of the dictionary.

The first step in looking for a character is to find out the radical under which it is listed. The next step is to look for the character in the index according to the number of strokes (i.e. the total number of strokes used in writing the whole character minus the number of strokes used in writing the radical) which is indicated with Chinese numerals in the column to the left of the characters. With the identification number as a guide, one can locate in the dictionary the character and the entries beneath it.

筆畫	單字	字號
	削	389
	剋	390
	刺	391
	前	392
八	剔	393
	剖	394
	剚	395
	剛	396
	剜	397
	剝	398
九	副	399
	剪	400
一〇	剩	401
	割	402
	剴	403
	創	404
一一	剿	405
	劃	406
	剽	407
一二	劄	408
	劃	409
一三	劇	410
	劈	411
	劉	412
	劊	413
	劍	414
一四	劑	415
	劓	416

力

筆畫	單字	字號
	力	417
三	功	418
	加	419
四	劣	420
五	助	421
	努	422
	劫	423
	劬	424
	劭	425
六	劾	426
	効	2123
	(效)	
七	勁	427
	勃	428
	勅	429
	勇	430
	勉	431
九	勒	432
	動	433
	勗	434
	勖	434
	(勗)	
	勘	435
	務	436
一〇	勝	437
	勞	438
一一	勦	405
	(剿)	
	勢	439
	募	440
	勤	441
	勠	442
一三	勰	443
一四	勳	444
一五	勵	445
一八	勸	446

勹

筆畫	單字	字號
一	勺	447
二	勻	448
	勾	449
	勿	450
三	包	451
	匆	1549
	(忽)	
四	匈	452
七	匍	453
九	匏	454
	匐	455

匕

筆畫	單字	字號
	匕	456
二	化	457
三	北	458
九	匙	459

匚

筆畫	單字	字號
三	匜	460
	匝	461
四	匠	462
	匡	463
五	匣	464
八	匪	465
九	匭	466
一一	匯	467
一二	匱	468
一三	匳	469

匸

筆畫	單字	字號
二	匹	470
九	匾	471
	匿	472
	區	473

十

筆畫	單字	字號
	十	474
一	千	475
二	升	476
	午	477
	卅	478
三	半	479
	卌	480
	卉	481
	(卉)	
四	卉	481
六	卑	482
	卒	483
	卓	484
	協	485
七	南	486
一〇	博	487

卜

筆畫	單字	字號
	卜	488
二	卞	489
三	占	490
	卡	491
五	卣	492
六	卦	493

卩

筆畫	單字	字號
三	卮	494
	卯	495
四	印	496
	危	497
五	卵	498
	却	503
	(卻)	
	即	504
	(卽)	
六	卷	499
	卸	500
	卹	501
	卺	502
七	卻	503
	卽	504
十	卿	505

厂

筆畫	單字	字號
二	厄	506
七	厖	507
	厚	508
八	原	509
	厝	510
一〇	厥	511
一二	厭	512
一三	厲	513

厶

筆畫	單字	字號
三	去	514
九	參	515

又

筆畫	單字	字號
	又	516
一	叉	517
二	及	518
	友	519
	反	520
六	叔	521
	取	522
	受	523
七	叛	524
	叙	2125
	(敍)	
八	叟	525
一一	叠	3586
	(疊)	
一六	叢	526

口

筆畫	單字	字號
	口	527
二	叨	528
	叼	529
	古	530
	句	531
	另	532
	叩	533
	只	534
	叫	535
	召	536
	叭	537
	叮	538
	可	539
	台	540
	叱	541
	史	542
	右	543
	叵	544
	叶	545
	司	546
三	合	547
	吁	548
	吃	549
	各	550
	吉	551
	吋	552
	同	553
	吆	554
	吒	555
	名	556
	后	557
	吐	558
	向	559
	吏	560
	吊	1420
	(弔)	
四	君	561
	吝	562
	吞	563
	吟	564
	吠	565
	否	566
	吩	567
	含	568
	吮	569
	呈	570
	吳	571

囗

筆畫	單字	字號
	匫	789
	囫	790
五	困	791
	圀	792
	固	793
六	囿	794
七	圃	795
	圄	796
八	國	797
	圇	798
	圈	799
九	圍	800
一〇	園	801
	圓	802
一一	圖	803
	團	804

土

筆畫	單字	字號
	土	805
三	在	806
	圬	807
	圭	808
	圯	809
	地	810
四	坊	811
	圾	812
	址	813
	坂	814
	均	815
	坍	816
	坎	817
	坐	818
	坑	819
五	坡	820
	坤	821
	坦	822
	坷	823
	坼	824
	坳	825
	垂	826
	垃	827
	坪	828
六	垠	829
	垓	830
	垢	831
	型	832
	垮	833
七	埋	834
	城	835
	埂	836
	埃	837
	埔	838
八	培	839
	域	840
	埠	841
	埤	842
	執	843
	基	844
	堂	845
	堅	846
	堆	847
	埽	1912
	(掃)	
九	報	848
	堡	849
	堪	850
	堯	851
	堰	852
	場	853
	堵	854
	堙	6624
	(陻)	
	堤	6626
	(隄)	
一〇	塊	855
	塋	856
	塌	857
	塚	858
	塑	859
	塔	860
	塗	861
	塘	862
	塞	863
	塡	864
	塢	865
一一	墓	866
	塵	867
	塹	868
	塾	869
	境	870
	墅	871
	墉	872
	墊	873
	塼	3530
	(甎)	
	墁	6486
	(鏝)	
一二	墟	874
	墀	875
	墜	876
	增	877
	墨	878
	墩	879
	墮	880
一三	墳	881
	壁	882
	墾	883
	壅	884
	壇	885
	墻	3300
	(牆)	
一四	壓	886
	壎	887
	壑	888
	壕	889
一五	壙	890
	壘	891
一六	壟	892
	壞	893
一七	壤	894
二一	壩	895

士

筆畫	單字	字號
	士	896
一	壬	897
四	壯	898
	壳	2719
	(殼)	
九	壻	899
	壹	900
	壺	901
一〇	壼	902
一一	壽	903

夂

筆畫	單字	字號
七	夏	904
一一	夐	905
一八	夔	906

夕

筆畫	單字	字號
	夕	907
二	外	908
三	多	909
	夙	910
五	夜	911
八	夠	912
	夥	912
	(夠)	
一一	夢	913
	夤	914
	夥	915

大

筆畫	單字	字號
	大	916
一	天	917
	太	918
	夫	919
	夬	920
	夭	921
二	失	922
	央	923
	夯	924
三	夷	925
	夸	926
四	夾	927
五	奄	928
	奇	929
	奈	930
	奉	931
	奔	932
六	奔	932
	(奔)	
	奎	933
	奏	934
	奐	935
	契	936
	奕	937
七	奘	938
	套	939
	畚	940
	奚	941
九	奠	942
	奢	943
一〇	奧	944
一一	奩	469
	(匳)	
	奪	945
	獎	946
一二	奭	947
一三	奮	948

女

筆畫	單字	字號
	女	949
二	奴	950
	奶	951
三	奸	952
	她	953
	好	954
	妁	955
	如	956
	妃	957
	妄	958
	奼	997
	(姹)	
四	妓	959
	妊	960
	妒	961
	妖	962
	妞	963
	妙	964
	妝	965
	妣	966
	妤	967
	妥	968
	妨	969
	妍	996
	(姸)	
五	妬	961
	(妒)	
	妲	970
	妮	971
	妯	972
	妹	973
	妻	974
	妾	975
	姆	976
	姊	977
	姉	977
	(姊)	
	始	978
	姍	979
	姐	980

	姑	981
	姒	982
	姓	983
	委	984
	妳	985
六	姚	986
	姜	987
	姝	988
	姣	989
	姤	990
	姥	991
	姦	992
	姨	993
	姪	994
	姱	995
	姸	996
	姹	997
	姻	998
	姿	999
	威	1000
	娃	1001
	姘	1018
	(姘)	
七	娓	1002
	娉	1003
	娌	1004
	姬	1005
	娑	1006
	娘	1007
	娛	1008
	娜	1009
	娟	1010
	娠	1011
	娣	1012
	娥	1013
	娩	1014
八	婆	1015
	婀	1016
	娶	1017
	姘	1018
	婁	1019
	婉	1020
	婕	1021
	婚	1022
	婢	1023
	婦	1024
	婪	1025
	娼	1026
	婭	1027
	婊	1028
	娬	1029
九	婿	899
	(壻)	
	婷	1030
	婺	1031
	媒	1032
	媚	1033
	媛	1034
	媧	1035
	媖	1036
一〇	嫁	1037
	嫂	1038
	媳	1039
	媵	1040
	媸	1041
	媼	1042
	媽	1043
	媾	1044
	嫉	1045
	嫌	1046
	嫋	1065
	(嬝)	
	媿	1654
	(愧)	
一一	嫠	1047
	嫖	1048
	嫗	1049
	嫚	1050
	嫡	1051
	嫣	1052
	嫦	1053
	嫩	1054
一二	嫵	1029
	(娬)	
	嬉	1055
	嫺	1056
	嫻	1056
	(嫺)	
	嬋	1057
	嬌	1058
一三	嬖	1059
	嬗	1060
	嬙	1061
	嬛	1062
	嬡	1063
	嬴	1064
	嬝	1065
一四	嬰	1066
	嬲	1067
	嬪	1068
一五	嬸	1069
一七	孃	1007
	(娘)	
	孀	1070
	孅	1071
十九	孌	1072

子

筆畫	單字	字號
	子	1073
	孑	1074
	孓	1075
一	孔	1076
二	孕	1077
三	字	1078
	存	1079
四	孚	1080
	孛	1081
	孜	1082
	孝	1083
五	孟	1084
	季	1085
	孥	1086
	孤	1087
六	孩	1088
七	孫	1089
八	孰	1090
九	孱	1091
	孳	1092
一一	孵	1093
一三	學	1094
一四	孺	1095
一六	孽	1096
	(孼)	
	孼	5161
	(孽)	
一七	孽	1096
一九	孿	1097

宀

筆畫	單字	字號
二	宄	1098
	它	1099
	宁	1100
	宂	1101
三	宅	1102
	宇	1103
	守	1104
	安	1105
四	宋	1106
	完	1107
	宏	1108
五	宕	1109
	宓	1110
	宗	1111
	官	1112
	宙	1113
	定	1114
	宛	1115
	宜	1116
六	客	1117
	宣	1118
	室	1119
	宥	1120
	宦	1121
七	宮	1122
	宰	1123
	害	1124
	宴	1125
	宵	1126
	家	1127
	宸	1128
	容	1129
八	寃	330
	(冤)	
	密	1130
	宿	1131
	寂	1132
	寄	1133
	寅	1134
	寇	1135
九	富	1136
	寐	1137
	寒	1138
	寓	1139
一〇	寘	1140
一一	寞	1141
	察	1142
	寧	1143
	寡	1144
	寢	1145
	寤	1146
	寥	1147
	實	1148
	寨	1149
一二	審	1150
	寫	1151
	寬	1152
	寮	1153
一三	寰	1154
一六	寵	1155
	寶	1156
	(寶)	
十七	寶	1156

寸

筆畫	單字	字號
	寸	1157
三	寺	1158
六	封	1159
七	射	1160
八	專	1161
	將	1162
	尉	1163
九	尊	1164
	尋	1165
一一	對	1166
一三	導	1167

小

筆畫	單字	字號
	小	1168
一	少	1169
三	尖	1170
五	尚	1171
九	尞	1172
一〇	尠	1173
	尟	1173
	(尠)	

尢

筆畫	單字	字號
一	尤	1174
四	尨	1175
	尬	1176
九	就	1177
一四	尷	1178

尸

尸

筆畫	單字	字號
	尸	1179
一	尺	1180
	尹	1181
二	尻	1182
	尼	1183
四	尾	1184
	尿	1185
	局	1186
	屁	1187
五	居	1188
	屆	1189
	屈	1190
	屄	1191
	屉	1199
	(屜)	
六	屋	1192
	屍	1193
	屎	1194
七	展	1195
	屐	1196
	屑	1197
八	屏	1198
	屜	1199
	屙	1200
九	屠	1201
一一	屢	1202
	屣	1203
一二	層	1204
	履	1205
一四	屨	1206
一八	屬	1207

屮

筆畫	單字	字號
一	屯	1208

山

筆畫	單字	字號
	山	1209
三	屹	1210
	屺	1211
四	岔	1212
	岌	1213
	岐	1214
	岑	1215
五	岡	1216
	岫	1217
	岬	1218
	岭	1219
	岱	1220
	岳	1221
	岷	1222
	岸	1223
	岩	1224
六	峋	1225
	峒	1226
	峙	1227
七	峨	1228
	峭	1229
	峯	1230
	峴	1231
	島	1232
	峻	1233
	峽	1234
	峪	1235
八	崇	1236
	崎	1237
	崑	1238
	崔	1239
	崖	1240
	崗	1241
	崙	1242
	崛	1243
	崢	1244
	崤	1245
	崧	1246
	崩	1247
	崍	1248
	崌	1249
	崡	1250
	崦	1251
九	崴	1252
	嵑	1253
	崽	1254
	嵇	1255
	嵋	1256
	嵌	1257
	嵐	1258
	嵎	1259
	崿	1260
一〇	嵩	1261
	嵬	1262
	嵊	1263
	嵯	1264
一一	嶇	1265
	嶂	1266
	嶄	1267
一二	嶙	1268
	嶒	1269
	嶓	1270
	嶝	1271
	嶠	1272
	嶢	1273
	嶔	1274
一三	嶧	1275
	嶮	1276
一四	嶸	1277
	嶺	1278
	嶼	1279
	嶽	1280
一七	巇	1281
	巉	1282
	巋	1283
一八	巍	1284
一九	巒	1285
	巔	1286
二〇	巖	1287
	巘	1288

巛

筆畫	單字	字號
	川	1289
三	州	1290
	廵	1291
	(巡)	
	廵	6053
	(巡)	
四	巡	1291
八	巢	1292

工

筆畫	單字	字號
	工	1293
二	左	1294
	巧	1295
	巨	1296
四	巫	1297
七	差	1298

己

筆畫	單字	字號
	己	1299
	已	1300
	巳	1301
一	巴	1302
六	巷	1303
九	巽	1304

巾

筆畫	單字	字號
	巾	1305
二	市	1306
	布	1307
三	帆	1308
	帆	1308
	(帆)	
四	希	1309
五	帔	1310
	帑	1311
	帕	1312
	帖	1313
	帗	1314
	帘	1315
	帙	1316
	帚	1317
	帛	1318
六	帥	1319
	帝	1320
七	帨	1321
	師	1322
	席	1323
	帮	1345
	(幫)	
八	帳	1324
	帶	1325
	帷	1326
	常	1327
九	幅	1328
	帽	1329
	幀	1330
	幃	1331
	幄	1332
一〇	幌	1333
一一	幔	1334
	幕	1335
	幗	1336
	幘	1337
	幛	1338
一二	幟	1339
	幞	1340
	幡	1341
	幢	1342
	幣	1343
一四	幬	1344
	幫	1345
	幪	1346
一五	幮	1347

干

筆畫	單字	字號
	干	1348
二	平	1349
三	年	1350
五	幷	1351
	幸	1352
一〇	幹	1353

幺

筆畫	單字	字號
	幺	1354
一	幻	1355
二	幼	1356
六	幽	1357
九	幾	1358

广

筆畫	單字	字號
二	庀	1359
三	庄	1360
四	庇	1361
	庋	1362
	序	1363
	床	3297
	(牀)	
五	底	1364
	庖	1365
	店	1366
	庚	1367
	府	1368
六	度	1369
	庠	1370
	庥	1371
七	座	1372
	庫	1373
	庭	1374
八	庵	1375
	庶	1376

筆畫	單字	字號
	康	1377
	庸	1378
	庹	1379
九	庾	1380
	廁	1381
	廂	1382
一〇	廈	1383
	廉	1384
	廊	1385
	廋	1386
一一	廏	1387
	廖	1388
	廑	1389
	廓	1390
	廕	1391
一二	廚	1392
	廛	1393
	廝	1394
	廟	1395
	廠	1396
	廡	1397
	廢	1398
	廣	1399
一三	廨	1400
	廩	1401
一六	廬	1402
	龐	1403
一八	廱	1404
二二	廳	1405

廴

筆畫	單字	字號
三	廵	1291
	(巡)	
	廵	6053
	(巡)	
四	延	1406
	廷	1407
五	廸	6067
	(迪)	
	廹	6068
	(迫)	
六	建	1408
	廻	6072
	(迴)	

廾

筆畫	單字	字號
一	廿	1409
二	弁	1410
四	弄	1411
	弃	2476
	(棄)	
六	弇	1412
	弈	1413
一二	弊	1414

弋

筆畫	單字	字號
	弋	1415
三	式	1416
一〇	弒	1417

弓

筆畫	單字	字號
	弓	1418
一	引	1419
	弔	1420
二	弗	1421
	弘	1422
三	弛	1423
四	弟	1424
五	弦	1425
	弧	1426
	弨	1427
	弩	1428
六	弭	1429
	弮	1430
七	弰	1431
	弱	1432
八	張	1433
	強	1434
九	强	1434
	(強)	
	弼	1435
一〇	彀	1436
一二	彈	1437
	彆	1438
一三	彊	1434
	(強)	
一四	彌	1439
一九	彎	1440

彐

筆畫	單字	字號
五	彔	1441
六	彖	1442
八	彗	1443
九	彘	1444
一〇	彙	1445
一三	彝	1446
	(彝)	
一五	彝	1446

彡

筆畫	單字	字號
四	彤	1447
	形	1448
六	形	1448
	(形)	
	彥	1449
七	彧	1450
八	彫	1451
	彩	1452
	彬	1453
	彪	1454
九	彭	1455
一一	彰	1456
一二	影	1457

彳

筆畫	單字	字號
	彳	1458
四	彷	1459
	役	1460
五	彼	1461
	往	1462
	征	1463
	徂	1464
	彿	1465
六	待	1466
	徇	1467
	很	1468
	徉	1469
	徊	1470
	律	1471
	後	1472
七	徐	1473
	徑	1474
	徒	1475
八	得	1476
	徘	1477
	徜	1478
	徙	1479
	從	1480
	徠	1481
	御	1482
九	徧	1483
	徨	1484
	復	1485
	循	1486
一〇	徬	1487
	徭	1488
	徯	1489
	微	1490
一二	徵	1491
	徹	1492
	德	1493
一三	徼	1494
一四	徽	1495

心

筆畫	單字	字號
	心	1496
一	必	1497
二	忉	1498
三	忌	1499
	忍	1500
	忒	1501
	忐	1502
	忑	1503
	志	1504
	忘	1505
	忙	1506
	忖	1507
四	忡	1508
	忤	1509
	快	1510
	忮	1511
	忭	1512
	忱	1513
	忸	1514
	忻	1515
	忪	1516
	忠	1517
	念	1518
	忽	1519
	忿	1520
	忞	1521
	忝	1522
五	怍	1523
	怏	1524
	怖	1525
	怕	1526
	怙	1527
	怛	1528
	怦	1529
	怡	1530
	性	1531
	怩	1532
	怫	1533
	怯	1534
	怪	1535
	怳	1536
	怔	1537
	怜	1538
	怓	1539
	怗	1540
	怵	1541
	怎	1542
	怒	1543
	思	1544
	怠	1545
	急	1546
	怨	1547
	怹	1548
	怱	1549
六	恂	1550
	恆	1551
	恒	1551
	(恆)	
	恃	1552
	恌	1553
	恓	1554
	恍	1555
	恟	1556
	恢	1557
	恨	1558
	恤	1559
	恪	1560
	恫	1561
	恇	1562
	恬	1563
	恰	1564
	恊	1565
	恁	1566
	恐	1567
	恕	1568
	恚	1569

戈

戶

	所	1782
五	扁	1783
	扃	1784
六	扆	1785
	扇	1786
七	扈	1787
八	扉	1788

手

筆畫	單字	字號
	手	1789
	才	1790
一	扎	1791
二	扑	1792
	扒	1793
	打	1794
	扔	1795
三	扞	1796
	扣	1797
	扛	1798
	托	1799
	扦	1800
	扠	1801
四	扭	1802
	扮	1803
	扶	1804
	扯	1805
	扳	1806
	扱	1807
	批	1808
	找	1809
	抃	1810
	技	1811
	抄	1812
	抉	1813
	抆	1814
	抒	1815
	抓	1816
	抔	1817
	把	1818
	投	1819
	抗	1820
	抖	1821
	折	1822
	抑	1823
	扼	1824
	承	1825
	抛	1840
	(拋)	
五	扼	1824
	(扼)	
	抱	1826
	抨	1827
	披	1828
	抵	1829
	抹	1830
	抽	1831
	押	1832
	拄	1833
	拂	1834
	拇	1835
	拈	1836
	拆	1837
	拉	1838
	拊	1839
	拋	1840
	拌	1841
	拐	1842
	拑	1843
	拍	1844
	拎	1845
	拒	1846
	拓	1847
	拔	1848
	拗	1849
	拖	1850
	拕	1850
	(拖)	
	拙	1851
	拘	1852
	拚	1853
	抿	1854
	招	1855
	拜	1856
	拏	1874
	(拿)	
	担	2059
	(擔)	
	抬	2073
	(擡)	
六	拭	1857
	拮	1858
	拯	1859
	括	1860
	拱	1861
	拴	1862
	拶	1863
	拾	1864
	持	1865
	按	1866
	指	1867
	挑	1868
	拽	1869
	挖	1870
	拷	1871
	挓	1872
	拳	1873
	拿	1874
	挈	1875
	拼	1924
	(拼)	
	挂	1928
	(掛)	
七	挨	1876
	挪	1877
	挱	1878
	挫	1879
	振	1880
	挼	1881
	挹	1882
	挽	1883
	挺	1884
	捃	1885
	捆	1886
	捋	1887
	捉	1888
	挾	1889
	捍	1890
	捌	1891
	捕	1892
	捐	1893
	捎	1894
	捏	1895
	挶	1896
八	捨	1897
	捧	1898
	捩	1899
	捭	1900
	捫	1901
	据	1902
	捱	1903
	捵	1904
	捺	1905
	捽	1906
	捲	1907
	捻	1908
	捷	1909
	掂	1910
	掀	1911
	掃	1912
	授	1913
	掇	1914
	掄	1915
	掎	1916
	掏	1917
	掐	1918
	掊	1919
	掉	1920
	排	1921
	掘	1922
	掖	1923
	拼	1924
	掙	1925
	掞	1926
	掠	1927
	掛	1928
	採	1929
	探	1930
	控	1931
	接	1932
	推	1933
	措	1934
	掩	1935
	掮	1936
	掬	1937
	捶	1938
	掫	1939
	掌	1940
	掣	1941
	掰	1942
	掔	1943
	掽	3879
	(碰)	
九	揑	1895
	(捏)	
	㨗	1909
	(捷)	
	揀	1944
	揄	1945
	揆	1946
	掾	1947
	揉	1948
	描	1949
	揍	1950
	提	1951
	揕	1952
	揖	1953
	插	1954
	揷	1954
	(插)	
	揚	1955
	揜	1956
	揠	1957
	換	1958
	握	1959
	揣	1960
	揩	1961
	揪	1962
	揫	1962
	(揪)	
	揮	1963
	揭	1964
	援	1965
	揲	1966
	揸	1967
	揶	1968
	揞	1969
	揹	1970
	揎	1971
一〇	搉	1972
	搊	1973
	搋	1974
	損	1975
	搆	1976
	搏	1977
	搔	1978
	搾	1979
	搓	1980
	搽	1981
	搗	1982
	搖	1983
	搢	1984
	搘	1985
	搥	1986
	搜	1987
	搭	1988
	搶	1989
	搦	1990
	搧	1991
	搨	1992

筆畫	單字	字號
	搬	1993
	搪	1994
	搐	1995
	搯	1996
	摁	1997
	搵	1998
	搠	1999
	搗	2000
	搌	2001
	搴	2002
	搞	2003
	携	2100
	(攜)	
一一	摘	2004
	摑	2005
	摜	2006
	摟	2007
	摒	2008
	摛	2009
	摔	2010
	摭	2011
	摧	2012
	摶	2013
	摳	2014
	摎	2015
	摺	2016
	摸	2017
	摽	2018
	摬	2019
	摴	2020
	摻	2021
	摩	2022
	摹	2023
	摯	2024
	擘	2025
一二	撅	2026
	撐	2027
	撑	2027
	(撐)	
	撈	2028
	撒	2029
	撤	2030
	撥	2031
	撳	2032
	撏	2033
	撇	2034
	撓	2035
	撙	2036
	撚	2037
	撕	2038
	撞	2039
	撟	2040
	撦	2041
	撫	2042
	播	2043
	撩	2044
	撬	2045
	撲	2046
	撰	2047
	撮	2048
	撝	2049
	撢	2050
	撣	2050
	(撢)	
一三	撻	2051
	撼	2052
	撾	2053
	擂	2054
	擄	2055
	擁	2056
	擅	2057
	操	2058
	擔	2059
	擇	2060
	擋	2061
	擒	2062
	據	2063
	擗	2064
	擀	2065
	擐	2066
	撿	2067
	擓	2068
	擊	2069
	擎	2070
	擘	2071
	擕	2100
	(攜)	
	擕	2100
	(攜)	
一四	擠	2072
	擡	2073
	擢	2074
	擣	2075
	擬	2076
	擯	2077
	擦	2078
	擱	2079
	擭	2080
	擤	2081
	擰	2082
	擪	2083
	擥	2111
	(攬)	
	擧	4784
	(舉)	
一五	擲	2084
	擷	2085
	擴	2086
	擺	2087
	擾	2088
	擿	2089
	攉	2090
	攄	2091
	攆	2092
	攀	2093
一六	攏	2094
一七	攔	2095
	攖	2096
	攘	2097
	攙	2098
一八	攛	2099
	攜	2100
	攝	2101
一九	攢	2102
	攤	2103
	攞	2104
	攧	2105
	攣	2106
二〇	攩	2107
	攪	2108
	攫	2109
	攥	2110
二一	攬	2111
二二	攮	2112

支

筆畫	單字	字號
	支	2113
八	攲	2114

攴

筆畫	單字	字號
二	收	2115
	攷	4569
	(考)	
三	攸	2116
	改	2117
	攻	2118
四	放	2119
	攽	2120
五	政	2121
	故	2122
六	效	2123
	敉	2124
七	啟	660
	(啓)	
	敍	2125
	敘	2125
	(敍)	
	教	2126
	敏	2127
	救	2128
	敕	2129
	敖	2130
	敗	2131
	敔	2132
八	敝	2133
	敞	2134
	敠	2135
	敢	2136
	散	2137
	敦	2138
九	敬	2139
一〇	敲	2140
一一	敵	2141
	敷	2142
	數	2143
	敺	2144
一二	整	2145
一三	斁	2146
	斂	2147
一四	斃	2148
一六	斅	2149

文

筆畫	單字	字號
	文	2150
六	斋	7304
	(齋)	
八	斌	2151
	斐	2152
	斑	2153
九	斒	2154
一七	斕	2155

斗

筆畫	單字	字號
	斗	2156
六	料	2157
七	斛	2158
	斜	2159
八	斝	2160
九	斟	2161
一〇	斡	2162
	斢	2163

斤

筆畫	單字	字號
	斤	2164
一	斥	2165
四	斧	2166
五	斫	2167
七	斬	2168
八	斮	2169
	斯	2170
九	新	2171
一〇	斲	2172
一三	斵	2172
	(斲)	
一四	斷	2173

方

筆畫	單字	字號
	方	2174
四	於	2175
	㫄	2178
	(旁)	
五	施	2176
	斿	2177
六	旁	2178
	旂	2179
	旃	2180
	旆	2181
	旄	2182
	旅	2183
七	旋	2184
	旌	2185
	旎	2186
	族	2187
八	旒	2188

	柔	2397		案	2435		梳	2473		(碗)			槔	2543		樟	2577
	柑	2398		桌	2436		桿	2474	九	楠	2367		榭	2544		樗	2578
	柳	2399		桑	2437		梨	2475		(枏)			榫	2545		樊	2579
	柘	2400		栽	2438		(棃)			椶	2507		榨	2546		樓	2580
	柙	2401		桂	2439	八	棃	2475		(棕)			榜	2547		標	2581
	柚	2402		桃	2440		棄	2476		椹	2508		榱	2548		樛	2582
	柜	2403		桄	2441		棉	2477		椳	2509		榻	2549		樞	2583
	柞	2404		桅	2442		棋	2478		椷	2510		榴	2550		模	2584
	柝	2405		框	2443		棊	2478		椽	2511		榮	2551		樣	2585
	柢	2406		桎	2444		(棋)			椰	2512		槃	2552		樠	2586
	柩	2407		桐	2445		棍	2479		椿	2513		槊	2553	一二	樸	2587
	柯	2408		桓	2446		棒	2480		楂	2514		槁	2554		樵	2588
	柱	2409		桔	2447		棗	2481		楓	2515		槀	2554		樺	2589
	柬	2410		栘	2448		棘	2482		楊	2516		(槁)			樨	2590
	査	2411		栢	2449		棖	2483		楔	2517		構	2555		橄	2591
	柰	2412		栱	2450		棧	2484		楙	2518		槌	2556		樾	2592
	柴	2413		梳	2473		棟	2485		楛	2519		槍	2557		樽	2593
	柷	2414		(梳)			棚	2486		楞	2520		槐	2558		橐	2594
	柮	2415	七	桴	2451		棣	2487		楡	2521		槎	2559		樹	2595
	柵	2416		桫	2452		棠	2488		楝	2522		槙	2560		橇	2596
	柶	2417		梧	2453		棨	2489		楢	2523		榷	2561		橈	2597
	柁	2418		桶	2454		棻	2490		楰	2524		榧	2562		橋	2598
	枰	2419		桷	2455		棐	2491		楚	2525		榾	2563		橙	2599
	枱	2420		梁	2456		棼	2492		業	2526		槅	2564		橘	2600
	栀	2461		梃	2457		森	2493		楣	2527	一一	槨	2504		橡	2601
	(梔)			梅	2458		椒	2494		楨	2528		(椁)			橢	2602
六	栓	2421		梓	2459		棫	2495		楫	2529		槥	2565		橦	2603
	栻	2422		梏	2460		棬	2496		楬	2530		槭	2566		[illegible]	2604
	栖	2423		梔	2461		棲	2497		極	2531		樜	2567		機	2605
	栝	2424		梗	2462		棺	2498		楮	2532		槪	2568		橫	2606
	栩	2425		條	2463		棵	2499		楷	2533		槩	2568		橱	2633
	栗	2426		梟	2464		植	2500		楸	2534		(概)			(櫥)	
	株	2427		梵	2465		椎	2501		楹	2535		槧	2569	一三	檀	2607
	核	2428		梯	2466		棹	2502		楯	2536		槳	2570		檄	2608
	校	2429		械	2467		椅	2503		楩	2537		樂	2571		檐	2609
	栲	2430		梲	2468		椁	2504	一〇	榕	2538		槲	2572		檔	2610
	根	2431		梠	2469		椏	2505		榔	2539		槿	2573		檉	2611
	桁	2432		梢	2470		椓	2506		榛	2540		槽	2574		檜	2612
	格	2433		梭	2471		棕	2507		榦	2541		樁	2575		檎	2613
	桀	2434		梆	2472		椀	3886		榖	2542		樅	2576		檟	2614

筆畫	單字	字號
	檢	2615
	檣	2616
	、檁	2617
	檥	2618
	檝	2619
	榜	2630
	(櫓)	
一四	櫈	350
	(凳)	
	檸	2620
	檬	2621
	檮	2622
	檻	2623
	櫃	2624
	檯	2625
	檳	2626
	櫂	2627
	櫈	3691
	(凳)	
一五	櫚	2628
	櫟	2629
	櫓	2630
	櫛	2631
	櫝	2632
	櫥	2633
一六	櫪	2634
	櫬	2635
	櫨	2636
	櫳	2637
	櫳	2637
	(櫳)	
	檗	2638
	櫱	2639
一七	櫺	2640
	欄	2641
	櫻	2642
	欅	2643
	欃	2644
	欂	2645
	[illegible]	2646
一八	權	2647
一九	欒	2648
二一	欖	2649

欠

筆畫	單字	字號
	欠	2650
二	次	2651
四	欣	2652
六	欬	2653
七	欲	2654
	欸	2655
	欷	2656
	欵	2657
	(款)	
八	款	2657
	欽	2658
	欺	2659
	欻	2660
	欿	2661
	欹	2662
九	歇	2663
	歆	2664
	歃	2665
一〇	歉	2666
	歌	2667
一一	歎	2668
	歐	2669
	歑	2670
	歙	2671
一二	歛	2672
	歔	2673
	歗	2674
一三	歜	2675
	歟	2676
	歛	2677
一四	歝	2678
一五	歠	2679
一八	歡	2680

止

筆畫	單字	字號
	止	2681
一	正	2682
二	此	2683
三	步	2684
四	歧	2685
	武	2686
五	歪	2687
九	歲	2688
一二	歷	2689
一四	歸	2690

歹

筆畫	單字	字號
	歹	2691
	歺	2691
	(歹)	
二	死	2692
四	歿	2693
	殁	2693
	(歿)	
五	殀	2694
	殆	2695
	殄	2696
	殃	2697
	殂	2698
六	殉	2699
	殊	2700
七	殍	2701
八	殖	2702
	殘	2703
九	殛	2704
一〇	殞	2705
一一	殣	2706
	殤	2707
	殢	2708
一二	殪	2709
	殫	2710
一三	殭	2711
	殮	2712
一四	殯	2713
一七	殲	2714

殳

筆畫	單字	字號
	殳	2715
五	段	2716
六	殷	2717
	殻	2719
	(殼)	
七	殺	2718
八	殼	2719
	殽	2720
九	殿	2721
	毀	2722
一一	毅	2723
	毆	2724

毋

筆畫	單字	字號
	毋	2725
一	母	2726
三	每	2727
	毒	2728
四	毒	2729
九	毓	2730

比

筆畫	單字	字號
	比	2731
五	毖	2732
	毗	2733
一三	毚	2734

毛

筆畫	單字	字號
	毛	2735
五	毡	2745
	(氈)	
六	毧	2736
七	毫	2737
	毬	2738
八	毯	2739
	毳	2740
九	毽	2741
一一	氂	2742
一二	氅	2743
	氄	2744
一三	氈	2745
	氊	2745
	(氈)	

氏

筆畫	單字	字號
	氏	2746
一	氐	2747
	民	2748
四	氓	2749

气

筆畫	單字	字號
二	氖	2750
四	氛	2751
五	氟	2752
六	氣	2753
	氤	2754
	氧	2755
	氦	2756
七	氫	2757
八	氯	2758
	氮	2759
一〇	氳	2760

水

筆畫	單字	字號
	水	2761
一	永	2762
二	氽	2763
	氾	2764
	汁	2765
	汀	2766
	求	2767
三	汊	2768
	汎	2769
	汕	2770
	汐	2771
	汗	2772
	池	2773
	汜	2774
	汝	2775
	江	2776
	汛	2777
	汞	2778
	汚	2779
	汙	2779
	(污)	
	污	2779
	(汚)	
四	汨	2780
	汩	2781
	汭	2782
	汰	2783
	汪	2784
	汲	2785
	決	2786
	汶	2787
	汴	2788
	汾	2789
	沁	2790
	沂	2791
	沅	2792
	沃	2793
	汽	2794
	沇	2795
	沆	2796
	沌	2797
	沈	2798
	沉	2798

	(濕)	
一一	滬	3029
	滌	3030
	滯	3031
	滲	3032
	滴	3033
	滹	3034
	滸	3035
	滾	3036
	滿	3037
	漁	3038
	漈	3039
	漉	3040
	漂	3041
	漆	3042
	漏	3043
	漓	3044
	漑	3045
	漚	3046
	演	3047
	漕	3048
	漠	3049
	漣	3050
	漪	3051
	漩	3052
	漢	3053
	漫	3054
	漬	3055
	漯	3056
	漱	3057
	漵	3058
	漳	3059
	漲	3060
	漾	3061
	漸	3062
	滮	3063
	滷	3064
	漗	3065
	漦	3066
	漿	3067
	潁	3068
	漻	3069
一二	潾	3070
	潔	3071
	潑	3072
	潛	3073
	潘	3074
	潟	3075
	潞	3076
	潢	3077
	澗	3078
	潦	3079
	潤	3080
	潭	3081
	潮	3082
	潯	3083
	潼	3084
	潺	3085
	潸	3086
	潰	3087
	澄	3088
	澈	3089
	澎	3090
	澍	3091
	澆	3092
	潲	3093
	澇	3094
	潙	3095
	澌	3096
	潡	3097
	澔	3098
	澂	3099
	澁	3121
	(澀)	
一三	澠	3100
	澥	3101
	澡	3102
	澧	3103
	澮	3104
	澨	3105
	澤	3106
	澱	3107
	澳	3108
	澼	3109
	澹	3110
	澶	3111
	激	3112
	濁	3113
	濂	3114
	濃	3115
	濊	3116
	澟	3117
	澣	3118
一四	濘	3119
	濛	3120
	澀	3121
	濠	3122
	濟	3123
	濤	3124
	濡	3125
	濫	3126
	濯	3127
	濮	3128
	濬	3129
	濰	3130
	濱	3131
	濩	3132
	濕	3133
一五	濺	3134
	濼	3135
	瀆	3136
	濾	3137
	瀑	3138
	瀉	3139
	瀋	3140
	瀏	3141
	瀅	3142
	瀌	3143
	瀁	3144
一六	瀘	3145
	瀕	3146
	瀚	3147
	瀝	3148
	瀟	3149
	瀛	3150
	瀨	3151
	瀧	3152
	瀊	3153
	瀦	3154
	瀠	3155
一七	瀰	3156
	瀹	3157
	瀾	3158
	瀲	3159
一八	灋	2832
	(法)	
	灉	3160
	灃	3161
	灌	3162
一九	灑	3163
	灘	3164
二一	灝	3165
	灞	3166
二二	灣	3167
二三	灤	3168
二四	灨	3169
	灧	3170
	(灩)	
二八	灩	3170

火

筆畫	單字	字號
	火	3171
二	灰	3172
三	灸	3173
	灼	3174
	災	3175
	灾	3175
	(災)	
	灶	4071
	(竈)	
四	炎	3176
	炊	3177
	炕	3178
	炖	3179
	炘	3180
	炙	3181
	炒	3182
五	炫	3183
	炬	3184
	炮	3185
	炰	3185
	(炮)	
	炯	3186
	炳	3187
	炷	3188
	炸	3189
	炭	3190
	炤	3191
	為	3192
	烖	3175
	(災)	
六	烏	3193
	烈	3194
	烝	3195
	烊	3196
	烘	3197
	烤	3198
	烟	3199
	烙	3200
七	焗	3186
	(炯)	
	烽	3201
	烹	3202
	焄	3203
	焉	3204
	烺	3205
	烷	3206
	烯	3207
八	焙	3208
	焮	3209
	焯	3210
	焚	3211
	焱	3212
	焦	3213
	無	3214
	然	3215
	焰	3216
九	煌	3217
	煉	3218
	煒	3219
	煖	3220
	煜	3221
	煙	3222
	煤	3223
	煥	3224
	煨	3225
	煩	3226
	煬	3227
	煮	3228
	煑	3228
	(煮)	
	煎	3229
	煞	3230
	煦	3231
	照	3232
	煢	3233
	煅	6441
	(鍛)	
一〇	熙	3234
	熊	3235
	熏	3236
	熄	3237
	熗	3238
	煽	3239
	熔	3240
	熒	3241
一一	熠	3242
	熟	3243

筆畫	單字	標號
	粵	4243
	粧	4244
七	粲	4245
	粱	4246
	粮	4247
	粳	4248
八	精	4249
	粹	4250
	粺	4251
	粽	4253
	(糉)	
九	糊	4252
	糉	4253
	糅	4254
一〇	糗	4255
	糒	4256
	糕	4257
	糖	4258
一一	糜	4259
	糞	4260
	糙	4261
	糝	4262
	糟	4263
	糠	4264
	糢	4265
	糨	4266
	⿰米竟	4266
	(糨)	
一二	糧	4267
一三	糪	4268
一四	糯	4269
	糰	4270
一五	糲	4271
一六	糴	4272
	糱	4273
	(糵)	
一七	糵	4273
一九	糶	4274

糸

筆畫	單字	標號
一	系	4275
	糺	4276
二	糾	4277
三	紀	4278
	紂	4279
	紃	4280
	紆	4281
	約	4282
	紅	4283
	紇	4284
	紈	4285
	紉	4286
四	紋	4287
	納	4288
	紐	4289
	純	4290
	紓	4291
	紕	4292
	紘	4293
	紗	4294
	紙	4295
	紜	4296
	紝	4297
	級	4298
	紛	4299
	紡	4300
	紊	4301
	素	4302
	索	4303
	紥	4304
	(紮)	
五	紮	4304
	絇	4305
	紫	4306
	累	4307
	紬	4308
	細	4309
	紱	4310
	紳	4311
	紹	4312
	紼	4313
	紾	4314
	絀	4315
	紵	4316
	紺	4317
	絃	4318
	終	4319
	組	4320
	絆	4321
	絅	4322
	紽	4323
	紩	4324
	絁	4325
	紲	4329
	(絏)	
六	絍	4297
	(紝)	
	結	4326
	絓	4327
	絕	4328
	絏	4329
	絞	4330
	絡	4331
	絢	4332
	給	4333
	絨	4334
	絪	4335
	絰	4336
	統	4337
	絳	4338
	絲	4339
	絮	4340
	絜	4341
	絝	5399
	(袴)	
七	絛	4342
	絹	4343
	絺	4344
	綁	4345
	綃	4346
	綈	4347
	綆	4348
	綏	4349
	經	4350
	綑	4351
	綖	4352
	緐	4428
	(繁)	
	綉	4444
	(繡)	
八	綜	4353
	綠	4354
	綢	4355
	綣	4356
	綬	4357
	維	4358
	綰	4359
	綱	4360
	網	4361
	綴	4362
	綵	4363
	綹	4364
	綸	4365
	綺	4366
	綻	4367
	綽	4368
	綾	4369
	緇	4370
	緅	4371
	綿	4372
	綦	4373
	綮	4374
	緊	4375
	緋	4376
	緌	4377
	綫	4378
	緍	4386
	(緡)	
	綳	4433
	(繃)	
九	緒	4379
	緘	4380
	線	4381
	緞	4382
	緝	4383
	緗	4384
	締	4385
	緡	4386
	緦	4387
	緣	4388
	編	4389
	緩	4390
	緲	4391
	緬	4392
	緯	4393
	緱	4394
	練	4395
	緹	4396
	緻	4397
	緶	4398
	緙	4399
	緜	4400
一〇	縈	4401
	縣	4402
	縠	4403
	縋	4404
	縐	4405
	縑	4406
	縗	4407
	縛	4408
	縉	4409
	縕	4410
	縞	4411
	縝	4412
	縟	4413
	縢	4414
	縊	4415
一一	縫	4416
	縭	4417
	縱	4418
	縮	4419
	縵	4420
	縲	4421
	綘	4422
	縷	4423
	縹	4424
	總	4425
	縶	4426
	縻	4427
	繁	4428
	繄	4429
	繇	4430
	績	4431
	繅	4432
	繃	4433
	繆	4434
	縧	4435
一二	繒	4436
	織	4437
	繕	4438
	繚	4439
	繖	4440
	繙	4441
	繞	4442
	繢	4443
	繡	4444
一三	繩	4445
	繪	4446
	繮	4447
	繯	4448
	繳	4449
	繨	4450
	繹	4451
	繫	4452
	繭	4453
	繰	4454
一四	辮	4455
	纂	4456
	繻	4457

	繽	4458
	繼	4459
	纉	4460
	纏	4461
一五	纈	4462
	纊	4463
	續	4464
	纆	4465
	纍	4466
	纇	4467
一六	纑	4468
一七	纔	4469
	纓	4470
	纕	4471
	纖	4472
一八	纛	4473
一九	纘	4474
二一	纜	4475

缶

筆畫	單字	字號
	缶	4476
三	缸	4477
四	缺	4478
五	缽	6353
	(鉢)	
八	缾	4479
一〇	罃	4480
一一	罄	4481
	罅	4482
一二	罇	4483
	罈	4484
一三	罋	4485
一四	罌	4486
一五	罍	4487
一六	罏	4488
	罏	4489
一八	罐	4490

网

筆畫	單字	字號
三	罔	4491
	罕	4492
四	罘	4493
五	罡	4494
	罟	4495
	罝	4496
六	罣	4497
八	罩	4498
	罪	4499
	置	4500
九	罰	4501
	署	4502
	罳	4503
一〇	罵	4504
	罷	4505
一一	罹	4506
一二	罽	4507
一四	羆	4508
	羅	4509
一七	羇	4510
一九	羈	4511

羊

筆畫	單字	字號
	羊	4512
	羋	4513
二	羌	4514
三	美	4515
	羑	4516
	羗	4517
四	羗	4514
	(羌)	
	羔	4518
	羖	4519
	羓	4520
	羒	4521
五	羝	4522
	羚	4523
	羞	4524
六	羢	4525
七	羣	4526
	群	4526
	(羣)	
	羨	4527
	義	4528
九	羯	4529
一〇	羲	4530
一二	羴	4531
一三	羶	4532
	羹	4533
	羸	4534
一五	羼	4535

羽

筆畫	單字	字號
	羽	4536
三	羿	4537
四	翁	4538
	翅	4539
	翃	4540
五	翊	4541
	翎	4542
	翌	4543
	習	4544
六	翔	4545
	翕	4546
八	翟	4547
	翠	4548
	翣	4549
	翡	4550
九	翦	4551
	翥	4552
	翬	4553
	翩	4554
	翫	4555
一〇	翱	4556
	翮	4557
	翰	4558
一一	翳	4559
	翼	4560
一二	翹	4561
	翻	4562
	翺	4563
一三	翾	4564
	翽	4565
一四	翿	4566
	耀	4567

老

筆畫	單字	字號
	老	4568
	考	4569
四	耄	4570
	耆	4571
五	者	4572
	耇	4573
	耉	4573
	(耇)	
六	耋	4574

而

筆畫	單字	字號
	而	4575
三	耐	4576
	耍	4577
	耑	4578

耒

筆畫	單字	字號
	耒	4579
三	耔	4580
四	耙	4581
	耕	4582
	耘	4583
	耗	4584
五	耜	4585
七	耡	4586
九	耦	4587
一〇	耨	4588
一五	耰	4589

耳

筆畫	單字	字號
	耳	4590
三	耶	4591
	耷	4592
四	耽	4593
	耿	4594
	聃	4595
	耻	4596
五	聃	4595
	(聃)	
	聆	4597
	聊	4598
六	聒	4599
七	聖	4600
	聘	4601
八	聚	4602
	聞	4603
	聝	6917
	(馘)	
一一	聯	4604
	聰	4605
	聲	4606
	聳	4607
	聱	4608
一二	職	4609
	聵	4610
	聶	4611
一六	聽	4612
	聾	4613

聿

筆畫	單字	字號
	聿	4614
七	肄	4615
	肆	4616
	肅	4617
八	肇	4618

肉

筆畫	單字	字號
	肉	4619
一	肊	4620
二	肋	4621
	肌	4622
	肎	4637
	(肯)	
三	肖	4623
	肘	4624
	肓	4625
	肚	4626
	肛	4627
	肝	4628
	肐	4629
	肜	4630
四	股	4631
	肢	4632
	肥	4633
	肩	4634
	肪	4635
	肫	4636
	肯	4637
	肻	4637
	(肯)	
	肱	4638
	育	4639
	肴	4640
	肣	4641
五	肺	4642
	胥	4643
	胃	4644
	胄	4645
	背	4646
	胎	4647
	胖	4648
	胙	4649
	胛	4650
	胚	4651

筆畫	單字	字號
	胞	4652
	胠	4653
	胡	4654
	胤	4655
	胸	4656
	胗	4657
	胝	4658
	脉	4671
	(脈)	
	胆	4736
	(膽)	
六	胭	4659
	胯	4660
	胰	4661
	胱	4662
	胴	4663
	胸	4664
	胷	4664
	(胸)	
	脁	4665
	能	4666
	胾	4667
	脂	4668
	脆	4669
	脃	4669
	(脆)	
	脅	4670
	脈	4671
	脊	4672
	脄	4673
	胳	4674
	胼	4689
	(胼)	
七	脘	4675
	脛	4676
	脣	4677
	脩	4678
	脫	4679
	脯	4680
	脝	4681
	脰	4682
	脞	4683
	脤	4684
	脖	4685
	脗	4686
	脚	4687
八	脹	4688
	腁	4689
	腆	4690
	腋	4691
	腌	4692
	腔	4693
	腎	4694
	腐	4695
	腑	4696
	腔	4697
	腕	4698
	脾	4699
	腊	4700
	腓	4701
九	腠	4702
	腥	4703
	腦	4704
	腫	4705
	腰	4706
	腳	4707
	腱	4708
	腴	4709
	腸	4710
	腹	4711
	腩	4712
	腺	4713
	腼	4714
	膀	4715
	腮	4716
一〇	腿	4717
	膀	4718
	膂	4719
	膈	4720
	膏	4721
	膆	4722
	膊	4723
一一	膚	4724
	膜	4725
	膝	4726
	滕	4727
	膠	4728
	膛	4729
	膣	4730
	膘	4751
	(臕)	
一二	膵	4693
	(膵)	
	膨	4731
	膩	4732
	膳	4733
	膰	4734
一三	膿	4735
	膽	4736
	膾	4737
	膺	4738
	臀	4739
	臂	4740
	臃	4741
	臆	4742
	臉	4743
	臊	4744
	臌	4745
	臏	4746
	臐	4747
一四	臏	4748
	臍	4749
一五	臘	4750
	臕	4751
一六	臚	4752
	臙	4753
一七	臝	4754
一八	臟	4755
一九	臠	4756
	臢	4757
	臡	4758

臣

筆畫	單字	字號
	臣	4759
一	臣	4760
二	臥	4761
八	臧	4762
一一	臨	4763

自

筆畫	單字	字號
	自	4764
四	臬	4765
	臭	4766
六	臯	4767
一〇	齅	4768

至

筆畫	單字	字號
	至	4769
三	致	4770
四	致	4770
	(致)	
八	臺	4771
一〇	臻	4772

臼

筆畫	單字	字號
	臼	4773
一	臼	4774
二	臾	4775
三	臿	4776
四	舁	4777
	舀	4778
五	舂	4779
六	舄	4780
	舃	4780
	(舄)	
七	舅	4781
	與	4782
九	興	4783
一〇	舉	4784
一二	舊	4785

舌

筆畫	單字	字號
	舌	4786
二	舍	4787
四	舐	4788
六	舒	4789
八	舔	4790
九	舖	4791
一〇	舘	4792

舛

筆畫	單字	字號
	舛	4793
六	舜	4794
七	舝	4795
八	舞	4796

舟

筆畫	單字	字號
	舟	4797
二	舠	4798
三	舢	4799
	舡	4800
四	航	4801
	般	4802
	舫	4803
	舨	4804
五	舲	4805
	舳	4806
	舴	4807
	舵	4808
	舶	4809
	舷	4810
	舸	4811
	船	4812
七	艇	4813
	艄	4814
八	艋	4815
一〇	艘	4816
	艙	4817
一二	艟	4818
一三	艤	4819
一四	艦	4820
	艨	4821
一六	艫	4822

艮

筆畫	單字	字號
	艮	4823
一	良	4824
一一	艱	4825

色

筆畫	單字	字號
	色	4826
五	艴	4827
一八	豔	4828

艸

筆畫	單字	字號
	艸	4829
二	艾	4830
	艿	4831
三	芃	4832
	芄	4833
	芊	4834
	芋	4835
	芍	4836
	芎	4837
	芒	4838
四	芙	4839
	芝	4840
	芟	4841
	芡	4842

	芣	4843		茈	4882		茜	4922		菊	4958		萬	4996		蒙	5034
	芥	4844		苻	4883		茭	4923		菌	4959		萱	4997		蒜	5035
	芧	4845		苾	4884		荃	4924		棻	4960		萵	4998		蒯	5036
	芩	4846		茁	4885		荇	4925		菑	4961		萼	4999		蒱	5037
	芫	4847		茂	4886		荐	4926		菔	4962		落	5000		蒲	5038
	芬	4848		范	4887		荆	4994		菖	4963		葉	5001		蒸	5039
	芚	4849		茄	4888		(荆)			菜	4964		葑	5002		蒹	5040
	芭	4850		茅	4889	七	荷	4927		菠	4965		著	5003		蒺	5041
	芯	4851		茆	4890		荽	4928		華	4966		葚	5004		蒼	5042
	芮	4852		茌	4891		莅	4929		菇	4967		葛	5005		蒿	5043
	芰	4853		苙	4892		荻	4930		菰	4968		葡	5006		蓀	5044
	花	4854		苣	4893		荼	4931		菁	4969		葠	5007		蓁	5045
	芳	4855		苺	4894		莕	4932		菲	4970		董	5008		蓄	5046
	芷	4856		苐	4895		莊	4933		菸	4971		葦	5009		蓆	5047
	芸	4857		茇	4896		莒	4934		菹	4972		葰	5010		蓉	5048
	芹	4858		茉	4897		莓	4935		菽	4973		葩	5011		蓋	5049
	芼	4859		苟	4898		莖	4936		萁	4974		葫	5012		蓐	5050
	芽	4860		茎	4899		莘	4937		萃	4975		葬	5013		蓑	5051
	芾	4861		苽	4900		莞	4938		萄	4976		葭	5014		蓓	5052
	芻	4862		苢	4901		莠	4939		萇	4977		菙	5015		蒔	5053
五	苑	4863	六	茗	4902		莢	4940		菿	4978		葳	5016		蒨	5054
	苒	4864		荔	4903		莧	4941		萊	4979		葵	5017		蒻	5055
	苓	4865		茼	4904		莩	4942		萋	4980		葷	5018		蓊	5056
	苔	4866		茨	4905		莪	4943		萌	4981		葸	5019		蓍	5057
	苕	4867		茫	4906		莫	4944		萍	4982		葺	5020		蓇	5058
	苗	4868		茯	4907		莆	4945		萎	4983		葽	5021		蒓	5059
	苛	4869		茱	4908		莉	4946		菡	4984		葆	5022		蒞	5060
	苜	4870		茲	4909		莽	4947		萏	4985		葒	5023		蓖	5061
	苞	4871		茴	4910		莎	4948		菩	4986		萸	5024		蓩	5062
	苡	4872		茵	4911		莏	4949		菱	4987		萹	5025		蔑	5068
	若	4873		茶	4912		荸	4950		菴	4988		葖	5026		(蔑)	
	苦	4874		茸	4913		莔	4951		萆	4989		葱	5027	一一	蓬	5063
	苧	4875		茹	4914		莝	4952		菉	4990		蒂	5028		蓮	5064
	苫	4876		荀	4915		莨	4953		葹	4991		葢	5029		蔻	5065
	英	4877		荄	4916		荳	4954		菏	4992		葯	5030		蔘	5066
	苴	4878		草	4917	八	莽	4947		菫	4993		葅	5031		蓿	5067
	苶	4879		荏	4918		(莽)			荊	4994		韮	5032		蔑	5068
	苯	4880		荑	4919		莬	4955		菓	4995	一〇	蓡	5007		蔓	5069
	苹	4881		荒	4920		菀	4956	九	菑	4961		(葠)			蔕	5070
				茛	4921		菅	4957		(菑)			蒐	5033		蔗	5071

四	觖	5502
五	觚	5503
	觝	5504
六	解	5505
	觥	5506
七	觫	5507
八	觭	5508
九	觱	5509
一〇	觳	5510
一一	觴	5511
一三	觸	5512
一八	觿	5513

言

筆畫	單字	字號
	言	5514
二	計	5515
	訂	5516
	訆	5517
	訃	5518
	訇	5519
三	討	5520
	訐	5521
	訊	5522
	訌	5523
	訓	5524
	訕	5525
	訖	5526
	託	5527
	記	5528
	訑	5529
	訒	5530
	訏	5531
四	訟	5532
	訛	5533
	訝	5534
	訢	5535
	訣	5536
	訥	5537
	訩	5538
	訪	5539
	設	5540
	許	5541
五	訴	5542
	訶	5543
	診	5544
	註	5545
	訾	5546
	詁	5547
	詆	5548
	詈	5549
	詠	5550
	詎	5551
	詐	5552
	詒	5553
	詔	5554
	評	5555
	詖	5556
	詛	5557
	詞	5558
	詘	5559
	訿	5560
	証	5561
六	詣	5562
	詡	5563
	詢	5564
	試	5565
	詩	5566
	詫	5567
	詬	5568
	詭	5569
	詮	5570
	詰	5571
	話	5572
	該	5573
	詳	5574
	詹	5575
	詼	5576
	誄	5577
	誅	5578
	誇	5579
	詵	5580
	誆	5581
	詿	5582
七	認	5583
	誌	5584
	誑	5585
	誓	5586
	誕	5587
	誘	5588
	誚	5589
	誡	5590
	語	5591
	誠	5592
	誣	5593
	誤	5594
	誥	5595
	誦	5596
	誨	5597
	說	5598
	誒	5599
八	課	5600
	誰	5601
	誶	5602
	誹	5603
	誼	5604
	調	5605
	諂	5606
	諄	5607
	談	5608
	諉	5609
	請	5610
	諍	5611
	諏	5612
	諑	5613
	諒	5614
	論	5615
	諗	5616
	諆	5617
九	諡	5618
	諭	5619
	諼	5620
	諵	5621
	諛	5622
	諜	5623
	諞	5624
	諠	5625
	諢	5626
	諤	5627
	諦	5628
	諧	5629
	諫	5630
	諮	5631
	諱	5632
	諳	5633
	諝	5634
	諶	5635
	諷	5636
	諸	5637
	諺	5638
	諾	5639
	謀	5640
	謁	5641
	謂	5642
	諲	5643
	諰	5644
	諴	5645
	諟	5646
	謔	5647
一〇	謎	5648
	謄	5649
	謊	5650
	謅	5651
	謇	5652
	謖	5653
	謐	5654
	謗	5655
	謙	5656
	講	5657
	謝	5658
	謠	5659
	謏	5660
	謟	5661
	謚	5662
一一	謾	5663
	謷	5664
	謦	5665
	謨	5666
	謫	5667
	謬	5668
	謳	5669
	謹	5670
	謰	5671
一二	譏	5672
	譁	5673
	證	5674
	譎	5675
	譖	5676
	識	5677
	譙	5678
	譚	5679
	譊	5680
	譜	5681
	譌	5682
一三	議	5683
	譟	5684
	警	5685
	譬	5686
	譯	5687
一四	護	5688
	譴	5689
	譽	5690
一五	譾	5691
	讀	5692
	讅	5693
	讁	5694
一六	變	5695
	讌	5696
	讎	5697
	讐	5697
	(讎)	
一七	讕	5698
	讒	5699
	讓	5700
	讖	5701
一八	讙	5702
一九	讚	5703
二〇	讞	5704
	讜	5705

谷

筆畫	單字	字號
	谷	5706
一〇	豁	5707
	谿	5708
	豀	5709

豆

筆畫	單字	字號
	豆	5710
三	豇	5711
	豈	5712
四	豉	5713
六	豋	5714
	豊	5715
八	豌	5716
	豎	5717
一〇	豏	5718
一一	豐	5719
一七	豔	5720
二一	豓	5721

豕

筆畫	單字	字號
	豕	5722
四	豚	5723
	豝	5724
五	象	5725
	豠	5726
六	豢	5727

	蹶	5940
一三	躄	5941
	躁	5942
	躅	5943
	躇	5944
	躉	5945
	躂	5946
	躃	5947
一四	躊	5948
	躋	5949
	躍	5950
一五	躐	5951
	躑	5952
	躓	5953
	躕	5954
一六	躚	5955
一七	躞	5956
一八	躡	5957
	躥	5958
二〇	躝	5959

身

筆畫	單字	字號
	身	5960
三	躬	5961
四	躭	5962
六	躱	5963
八	躺	5964
一一	軀	5965

車

筆畫	單字	字號
	車	5966
一	軋	5967
二	軌	5968
	軍	5969
三	軒	5970
	軔	5971
	軓	5972
四	軛	5973
	軟	5974
五	軫	5975
	軨	5976
	軸	5977
	軺	5978
	軹	5979
	軻	5980
	軼	5981
	軲	5982
六	較	5983
	軾	5984
	輅	5985
	輈	5986
	載	5987
	輊	5988
七	輒	5989
	輓	5990
	輔	5991
	輕	5992
八	輜	5993
	輗	5994
	輘	5995
	輛	5996
	輝	5997
	輞	5998
	輟	5999
	輦	6000
	輧	6001
	輩	6002
	輪	6003
	輬	6004
	輙	6005
九	輯	6006
	輳	6007
	輶	6008
	輸	6009
	輻	6010
	輮	6011
	輭	6012
	輹	6013
一〇	輾	6014
	輿	6015
	轂	6016
	轄	6017
	轅	6018
	轀	6019
一一	轉	6020
	轆	6021
	轇	6022
一二	轍	6023
	轎	6024
	轔	6025
一三	轘	6026
	轕	6027
	轙	6028
	轗	6029
一四	轟	6030
	轝	6031
	轞	6032
一五	轢	6033
	轡	6034
一六	轤	6035
	轣	6036

辛

筆畫	單字	字號
	辛	6037
五	辜	6038
六	辟	6039
	辠	6040
七	辣	6041
九	辨	6042
	辦	6043
一二	辭	6044
一三	辮	6045
一四	辯	6046

辰

筆畫	單字	字號
	辰	6047
三	辱	6048
六	農	6049

辵

筆畫	單字	字號
三	迂	6050
	迄	6051
	迅	6052
	巡	6053
	迆	6054
四	迎	6055
	近	6056
	迓	6057
	返	6058
	迕	6059
	迍	6060
	迒	6061
五	迢	6062
	迤	6063
	迥	6064
	迦	6065
	迨	6066
	迪	6067
	迫	6068
	迭	6069
	述	6070
	迮	6071
六	迴	6072
	迷	6073
	迹	6074
	追	6075
	退	6076
	送	6077
	适	6078
	逃	6079
	逅	6080
	逆	6081
	迻	6082
	逄	6083
	逈	6084
	迺	6085
	迸	6106
	(迸)	
七	逍	6086
	逝	6087
	逋	6088
	透	6089
	逐	6090
	逑	6091
	逕	6092
	途	6093
	逖	6094
	逗	6095
	這	6096
	通	6097
	逛	6098
	逞	6099
	速	6100
	造	6101
	逡	6102
	逢	6103
	連	6104
	逌	6105
八	迸	6106
	逮	6107
	週	6108
	進	6109
	逵	6110
	逶	6111
	逸	6112
	逭	6113
	逯	6114
九	逾	6115
	逼	6116
	遁	6117
	遂	6118
	遄	6119
	遇	6120
	遊	6121
	運	6122
	遍	6123
	過	6124
	遏	6125
	遑	6126
	遐	6127
	遒	6128
	道	6129
	達	6130
	違	6131
一〇	遜	6132
	遘	6133
	遙	6134
	遛	6135
	遝	6136
	遞	6137
	遠	6138
	遡	6139
	遢	6140
	遣	6141
一一	遭	6142
	遨	6143
	適	6144
	遮	6145
	遯	6146
一二	遲	6147
	遴	6148
	遵	6149
	遶	6150
	遷	6151
	選	6152
	遹	6153
	遺	6154
	遼	6155
一三	避	6156
	遽	6157
	邀	6158
	邁	6159
	邂	6160
	還	6161

筆畫	單字	字號
	邅	6162
一四	邇	6163
	邃	6164
	邈	6165
一五	邊	6166
一九	邏	6167
	邐	6168

邑

筆畫	單字	字號
	邑	6169
三	邙	6170
	邛	6171
	邕	6172
四	邠	6173
	那	6174
	邦	6175
	邪	6176
	邢	6177
	邨	6178
五	邵	6179
	邯	6180
	邰	6181
	邱	6182
	邲	6183
	邳	6184
	邶	6185
	邴	6186
	邸	6187
六	郁	6188
	郉	6189
	郅	6190
	郇	6191
	郊	6192
	郃	6193
	邽	6194
	邾	6195
七	郛	6196
	郜	6197
	郝	6198
	郎	6199
	郟	6200
	郡	6201
	郢	6202
	郗	6203
	郤	6204
	郕	6205
八	部	6206
	郫	6207
	郭	6208
	郯	6209
	郴	6210
	郪	6211
	郲	6212
	郵	6213
九	都	6214
	郿	6215
	鄂	6216
	鄆	6217
	郾	6218
	鄄	6219
一〇	鄗	6220
	鄉	6221
	鄒	6222
	鄔	6223
一一	鄙	6224
	鄢	6225
	鄘	6226
	鄜	6227
	鄞	6228
	鄣	6229
一二	鄧	6230
	鄭	6231
	鄯	6232
	鄰	6233
	鄱	6234
	鄲	6235
	鄦	6236
一三	鄴	6237
	鄶	6238
一四	鄹	6239
一五	鄺	6240
一七	酃	6241
一八	酆	6242
一九	酈	6243
	酇	6244

酉

筆畫	單字	字號
	酉	6245
二	酊	6246
	酋	6247
三	酌	6248
	配	6249
	酒	6250
四	酖	6251
	酗	6252
五	酢	6253
	酣	6254
	酤	6255
	酥	6256
六	酩	6257
	酪	6258
	酯	6259
	酬	6260
	酮	6261
七	酲	6262
	酵	6263
	酷	6264
	酸	6265
	酹	6266
	酺	6267
	酴	6268
八	醃	6269
	醅	6270
	醇	6271
	醉	6272
	醊	6273
	醋	6274
	醁	6275
九	醒	6276
	醍	6277
	醐	6278
一〇	醜	6279
	醞	6280
	醚	6281
	醛	6282
	醣	6283
	醢	6284
一一	醫	6285
	醨	6286
	醪	6287
	醬	6288
	醯	6289
一二	醭	6290
	醮	6291
	醱	6292
一三	醴	6293
	醲	6294
	醵	6295
一四	醺	6296
一七	釀	6297
	醹	6298
	醾	6299
一八	釁	6300
二〇	釅	6301

釆

筆畫	單字	字號
一	采	6302
五	釉	6303
一三	釋	6304

里

筆畫	單字	字號
	里	6305
二	重	6306
四	野	6307
五	量	6308
一一	釐	6309

金

筆畫	單字	字號
	金	6310
一	釓	6311
	釔	6312
二	釘	6313
	釜	6314
	釗	6315
	針	6316
	釙	6317
	釕	6318
三	釩	6319
	釣	6320
	釷	6321
	釹	6322
	釦	6323
	釧	6324
	釵	6325
	釤	6326
	釬	6411
	(銲)	
四	鈧	6327
	欽	6328
	鈀	6329
	鈦	6330
	鈔	6331
	鈇	6332
	鈉	6333
	鈍	6334
	鈐	6335
	鈕	6336
	鈞	6337
	鈣	6338
	鈎	6339
五	鈸	6340
	鈴	6341
	鈿	6342
	鉀	6343
	鉧	6344
	鉅	6345
	鉉	6346
	鉋	6347
	鉏	6348
	鉑	6349
	鉗	6350
	鉛	6351
	鉞	6352
	鉢	6353
	鉤	6354
	鉦	6355
	鉟	6356
	鈾	6357
	鈷	6358
	鉈	6359
	鈰	6360
	鉍	6361
	鈹	6362
	鉬	6363
	鉭	6364
	鉰	6365
	鉯	6366
	鉮	6367
六	銀	6368
	鉸	6369
	銃	6370
	銅	6371
	銑	6372
	銓	6373
	銖	6374
	銘	6375
	銚	6376
	銛	6377
	銜	6378
	銍	6379
	銬	6380
	銥	6381
	鉺	6382
	銠	6383

筆畫	單字	字號
	銪	6384
	鉿	6385
	銦	6386
	銫	6387
	銩	6388
	鉻	6389
	銣	6390
七	銳	6391
	銷	6392
	銻	6393
	鉽	6394
	鋇	6395
	鋰	6396
	鋯	6397
	鋨	6398
	鋁	6399
	鋃	6400
	鋅	6401
	鋌	6402
	鋏	6403
	鋒	6404
	鋦	6405
	鋙	6406
	鋤	6407
	鋩	6408
	銼	6409
	鋪	6410
	銲	6411
	銹	6412
八	鋸	6413
	鋼	6414
	[illegible]	6415
	錸	6416
	錒	6417
	錄	6418
	錋	6419
	錐	6420
	錘	6421
	錙	6422
	錚	6423
	錠	6424
	錡	6425
	錢	6426
	錦	6427
	錫	6428
	錕	6429
	錮	6430
	錯	6431
	錳	6432
	錶	6433
	錛	6434
九	鍊	6435
	錨	6436
	鍋	6437
	鍍	6438
	鍔	6439
	鍘	6440
	鍛	6441
	鍥	6442
	鍪	6443
	鍫	6444
	鍰	6445
	鍵	6446
	鍼	6447
	鍾	6448
	鎂	6449
	鍺	6450
	鍶	6451
	鎃	6452
	鍇	6453
	鍬	6454
一〇	鎖	6455
	鎡	6456
	鎊	6457
	鎋	6458
	鎔	6459
	鎗	6460
	鎚	6461
	鎛	6462
	鎧	6463
	鎬	6464
	鎮	6465
	鎰	6466
	鎳	6467
	鎢	6468
	鎓	6469
	鎌	6470
	鎷	6471
	鎘	6472
	鎵	6473
一一	鏃	6474
	鏇	6475
	鎩	6476
	鏦	6477
	鏈	6478
	鏊	6479
	鏑	6480
	鏖	6481
	鏗	6482
	鏘	6483
	鏹	6484
	鏜	6485
	鏝	6486
	鏠	6487
	鏡	6488
	鏢	6489
	鏤	6490
	鏨	6491
	鏁	6492
一二	鐘	6493
	鐃	6494
	鐐	6495
	鐙	6496
	鏽	6497
	鐗	6498
	鐠	6499
	鐂	6500
一三	鐲	6501
	鐫	6502
	鐮	6503
	鐵	6504
	鐶	6505
	鐸	6506
	鐺	6507
	鐳	6508
	鐿	6509
一四	鑊	6510
	鑄	6511
	鑑	6512
	鑒	6513
一五	鑤	6347
	(鉋)	
	鑠	6514
	鑌	6515
	鑛	6516
	鑞	6517
	鑣	6518
一六	鑪	6519
	鑫	6520
一七	鑰	6521
	鑲	6522
一八	鑷	6523
一九	鑼	6524
	鑽	6525
	鑾	6526
二〇	鑿	6527

長

筆畫	單字	字號
	長	6528

門

筆畫	單字	字號
	門	6529
一	閂	6530
二	閃	6531
三	閉	6532
四	開	6533
	間	6534
	閎	6535
	閏	6536
	閑	6537
	閒	6538
	閔	6539
五	閘	6540
	閟	6541
六	閣	6542
	閡	6543
	閤	6544
	閥	6545
	閨	6546
	閩	6547
七	閫	6548
	閬	6549
	閭	6550
	閱	6551
八	閼	6552
	閶	6553
	閽	6554
	閹	6555
	閻	6556
	閾	6557
九	闃	6558
	闇	6559
	闈	6560
	闉	6561
	闊	6562
	闋	6563
	闌	6564
	闆	6565
	闍	6566
一〇	闐	6567
	闑	6568
	闒	6569
	闓	6570
	闔	6571
	闕	6572
	闖	6573
一一	關	6574
	闚	6575
一二	闞	6576
	闠	6577
	闡	6578
一三	闢	6579
	闤	6580
	闥	6581

阜

筆畫	單字	字號
	阜	6582
三	阡	6583
	阢	6584
四	阬	6585
	阨	6586
	阪	6587
	阮	6588
	阱	6589
	防	6590
	阯	6591
五	阻	6592
	阼	6593
	阿	6594
	陀	6595
	陂	6596
	附	6597
	阸	6598
六	陋	6599
	陌	6600
	降	6601
	限	6602
	陔	6603
七	陘	6604
	陛	6605
	陞	6606
	陟	6607
	陡	6608
	院	6609
	陣	6610
	除	6611
	陜	6612

筆畫	單字	字號
	頯	6811
九	額	6812
	顋	6813
	題	6814
	顎	6815
	顏	6816
	顒	6817
	顓	6818
一〇	顗	6819
	願	6820
	顙	6821
	顛	6822
	類	6823
	顋	6824
一一	顢	6825
一二	顧	6826
	顤	6827
	顥	6828
	顦	6829
一三	顫	6830
一四	顯	6831
	顰	6832
一五	顰	6833
一六	顱	6834
一八	顴	6835
	顳	6836

風

筆畫	單字	字號
	風	6837
五	颯	6838
	颱	6839
六	颳	6840
八	颶	6841
九	颺	6842
一〇	颼	6843
	飀	6844
一一	飄	6845
一二	飆	6846
	飇	6846
	(飆)	

飛

筆畫	單字	字號
	飛	6847
一二	飜	6848

食

筆畫	單字	字號
	食	6849
二	飢	6850
	飣	6851
	飡	6852
三	飧	6853
四	飱	6853
	(飧)	
	飩	6854
	飪	6855
	飭	6856
	飲	6857
	飫	6858
	飯	6859
五	飼	6860
	飴	6861
	飽	6862
	飾	6863
六	餂	6864
	餃	6865
	餈	6866
	餉	6867
	養	6868
	餌	6869
	餁	6870
	餅	6871
七	餐	6872
	餑	6873
	餒	6874
	餓	6875
	餔	6876
	餖	6877
	餗	6878
	餘	6879
八	餠	6880
	餚	6881
	餛	6882
	餞	6883
	餡	6884
	餧	6885
	館	6886
	餜	6887
	餟	6888
九	餮	6889
	餱	6890
	餬	6891
	餳	6892
	餵	6893
一〇	餿	6894
	餼	6895
	餾	6896
	餻	6897
	餽	6898
一一	饅	6899
	饈	6900
	饉	6901
	饃	6913
	(饝)	
一二	饋	6902
	饌	6903
	饑	6904
	饒	6905
	饍	6906
	饇	6907
一三	饗	6908
	饔	6909
	饕	6910
	饘	6911
一四	饜	6912
一六	饝	6913
一七	饞	6914

首

筆畫	單字	字號
	首	6915
二	馗	6916
八	馘	6917

香

筆畫	單字	字號
	香	6918
九	馥	6919
一一	馨	6920

馬

筆畫	單字	字號
	馬	6921
二	馭	6922
	馮	6923
三	馱	6924
	馳	6925
	馴	6926
	彝	6927
四	駁	6928
	駃	6929
五	駐	6930
	駑	6931
	駒	6932
	駔	6933
	駕	6934
	駘	6935
	駙	6936
	駛	6937
	駝	6938
	駟	6939
六	駭	6940
	駱	6941
	駬	6942
	駮	6943
	駢	6944
七	騁	6945
	駿	6946
	騂	6947
	騃	6948
	騌	6949
	騀	6950
八	騎	6951
	騈	6952
	騏	6953
	騄	6954
	騅	6955
	騐	6956
九	騖	6957
	騙	6958
	騣	6959
	騤	6960
	騠	6961
	騞	6962
一〇	騫	6963
	騭	6964
	騰	6965
	騷	6966
	騶	6967
	騮	6968
一一	騾	6969
	驁	6970
	驀	6971
	驂	6972
	驃	6973
	驄	6974
	驅	6975
一二	驕	6976
	驊	6977
	驍	6978
	驎	6979
	驑	6980
一三	驗	6981
	驚	6982
	驛	6983
一四	驟	6984
一六	驢	6985
	驥	6986
一七	驤	6987
一八	驩	6988
一九	驪	6989

骨

筆畫	單字	字號
	骨	6990
三	骭	6991
	骫	6992
四	骰	6993
	骯	6994
五	骷	6995
六	骻	6996
	骸	6997
	骼	6998
七	骾	6999
八	髀	7000
	髁	7001
一一	髏	7002
一三	髒	7003
	髓	7004
	體	7005
	髑	7006
一四	髕	7007

高

筆畫	單字	字號
	高	7008

髟

筆畫	單字	字號
三	髡	7009
	髦	7010
四	髣	7011
	髯	7012
	髦	7013
五	髫	7014
	髮	7015
	髴	7016

筆畫	單字	字號
	髯	7017
	髭	7018
六	髻	7019
	髹	7020
七	鬁	7021
	髽	7022
八	鬆	7023
	鬈	7024
	鬃	7025
九	鬎	7026
	鬍	7027
一〇	鬑	7028
	鬐	7029
	鬒	7030
一一	鬘	7031
一二	鬚	7032
一三	鬟	7033
一四	鬢	7034
一五	鬣	7035

鬥

筆畫	單字	字號
	鬥	7036
四	鬦	7037
五	鬧	7038
六	鬨	7039
八	鬩	7040
一〇	鬪	7041
一四	鬬	7042
一六	鬮	7043

鬯

筆畫	單字	字號
	鬯	7044
一九	鬱	7045

鬲

筆畫	單字	字號
	鬲	7046
一二	鬻	7047

鬼

筆畫	單字	字號
	鬼	7048
四	魁	7049
	魂	7050
五	魄	7051
	魅	7052
八	魍	7053
	魎	7054
	魏	7055
	魋	7056
一一	魑	7057
	魔	7058
一四	魘	7059

魚

筆畫	單字	字號
	魚	7060
三	魟	7061
四	魷	7062
	魯	7063
	魴	7064
五	鮎	7065
	鮑	7066
	鮒	7067
六	鮫	7068
	鮪	7069
	鮭	7070
	鮮	7071
	鮝	7072
七	鯀	7073
	鯇	7074
	鯁	7075
	鯉	7076
	鯊	7077
八	鯤	7078
	鯡	7079
	鯖	7080
	鯛	7081
	鯨	7082
	鯪	7083
	鯫	7084
九	鯽	7085
	鰈	7086
	鯿	7087
	鰌	7088
	鰒	7089
	鰍	7090
	鰓	7091
一〇	鰥	7092
	鰜	7093
	鰮	7094
	鰭	7095
	鰣	7096
	鰩	7097
一一	鰻	7098
	鱈	7099
	鰲	7100
	鰱	7101
	鰾	7102
	鱅	7103
	鰹	7104
一二	鱔	7105
	鱖	7106
	鱗	7107
	鱘	7108
	鱉	7281
	(鼈)	
一三	鱟	7109
	鱣	7110
一五	鱵	7111
一六	鱸	7112
	鱷	7113
二二	鱻	7114

鳥

筆畫	單字	字號
	鳥	7115
二	鳧	7116
	鳩	7117
三	鳲	7118
	鳳	7119
	鳴	7120
	鳶	7121
四	鴆	7122
	鴇	7123
	鴉	7124
	鴂	7125
	鴃	7125
	(鴂)	
	鴈	7126
五	鴒	7127
	鴕	7128
	鴛	7129
	鴞	7130
	鴟	7131
	鴣	7132
	鴦	7133
	鴨	7134
	鴥	7135
	鴝	7136
六	鴿	7137
	鵁	7138
	鴻	7139
	鴳	7140
	鵃	7141
	鴽	7142
	鴷	7143
	鴰	7144
	鵂	7145
七	鵒	7146
	鵑	7147
	鵚	7148
	鵓	7149
	鵌	7150
	鵜	7151
	鵝	7152
	鵞	7152
	(鵝)	
	䳘	7152
	(鵝)	
	鵠	7153
	鵡	7154
八	鵬	7155
	鵩	7156
	鵪	7157
	鵰	7158
	鵾	7159
	鵲	7160
	鵷	7161
	鵮	7162
	鶉	7163
	鶄	7164
	鶊	7165
九	鶘	7166
	鶩	7167
	鶚	7168
	鶡	7169
	鶖	7170
	鶒	7171
	鶗	7172
一〇	鶴	7173
	鶬	7174
	鶯	7175
	鷀	7176
	鶿	7176
	(鷀)	
	鶺	7177
	鶻	7178
	鶼	7179
	鷁	7180
	鶹	7181
	鷂	7182
	鶵	7183
	鷇	7184
	鷄	7185
一一	鷓	7186
	鷖	7187
	鷗	7188
	鷙	7189
	鷟	7190
一二	鷥	7191
	鷦	7192
	鷯	7193
	鷩	7194
	鷸	7195
	鷲	7196
	鷊	7197
	鷺	7198
一三	鷽	7199
	鸀	7200
	鸂	7201
	鸇	7202
	鷹	7203
一六	鸕	7204
一七	鸚	7205
一八	鸛	7206
	鸜	7207
一九	鸝	7208
	鸞	7209

鹵

筆畫	單字	字號
	鹵	7210
九	鹹	7211
一〇	鹺	7212
	鹻	7213
一三	鹼	7214
一四	鹽	7215

鹿

筆畫	單字	字號
	鹿	7216
二	麀	7217
	麂	7218
四	麃	7219
五	麈	7220
	麅	7221
六	麋	7222

筆畫	單字	字號
七	麐	7223
	麔	7224
八	麑	7225
	麒	7226
	麓	7227
	麗	7228
	麕	7229
一〇	麝	7230
一一	麞	7231
一二	麟	7232
二二	麤	7233

麥

筆畫	單字	字號
	麥	7234
四	麩	7235
	麪	7236
六	麯	7237
	麰	7238
八	麴	7239
九	麵	7240

麻

筆畫	單字	字號
	麻	7241
三	麼	7242
	麽	7242
	(麼)	
四	麾	7243

黃

筆畫	單字	字號
	黃	7244
五	黈	7245
一三	黌	7246

黍

筆畫	單字	字號
	黍	7247
三	黎	7248
五	黏	7249

黑

筆畫	單字	字號
	黑	7250
三	黓	7251
四	黔	7252
	默	7253
五	點	7254
	黛	7255
	黜	7256
	黝	7257
六	黠	7258
	黟	7259
八	黥	7260
	黧	7261
	黨	7262
	黦	7263
	黤	7264
九	黯	7265
	黮	7266
一一	黲	7267
	黴	7268
一三	黵	7269
一四	黶	7270
一五	黷	7271

黹

筆畫	單字	字號
	黹	7272
五	黻	7273
七	黼	7274

黽

筆畫	單字	字號
	黽	7275
四	黿	7276
五	鼂	7277
六	鼃	7278
八	鼅	7279
一一	鼈	7280
一二	鼇	7281
	鼉	7282

鼎

筆畫	單字	字號
	鼎	7283
二	鼐	7284
	鼏	7285
三	鼒	7286

鼓

筆畫	單字	字號
	鼓	7287
五	鼕	7288
六	鼗	7289
八	鼙	7290

鼠

筆畫	單字	字號
	鼠	7291
五	鼬	7292
	鼪	7293
七	鼯	7294
九	鼴	7295
一〇	鼷	7296
	鼹	7297

鼻

筆畫	單字	字號
	鼻	7298
三	鼾	7299
五	齁	7300
一〇	齅	7301
一三	齈	7302

齊

筆畫	單字	字號
	齊	7303
三	齋	7304
七	齎	7305
九	齏	7306

齒

筆畫	單字	字號
	齒	7307
二	齔	7308
三	齕	7309
四	齗	7310
五	齟	7311
	齠	7312
	齡	7313
	齣	7314
	齜	7315
六	齦	7316
	齧	7317
	齩	7318
七	齪	7319
	齬	7320
九	齷	7321
	齲	7322
	齶	7323
一〇	齹	7324

龍

筆畫	單字	字號
	龍	7325
六	龔	7326
	龕	7327

龜

筆畫	單字	字號
	龜	7328

龠

筆畫	單字	字號
	龠	7329
五	龢	7330
九	龥	7331

筆畫部首索引

編　法：本索引係按單字筆畫多寡編列。其筆畫相同者，再按部首順序。單字後註明單字編號。

用　法：檢字時先計算單字筆畫，按筆畫在索引中查出單字，再根據單字編號，查出書內單字及這一單字爲首所組成的詞語。

STROKE NUMBER INDEX

In this index the characters are arranged in the ascending order according to the number of strokes used in writing them. Characters with the same number of strokes and under the same radical are grouped together, the radicals being indicated in the column to the left of the characters. The figure to the right of each character is its identification number under which the character can be found in the body of the dictionary.

The first step in looking for a character is to count the number of strokes used in writing it. The next step is to find the character in the index according to its number of strokes. With the identification number as a guide, one can locate in the dictionary the character and the entries beneath it.

部首	單字	字號
	召	536
	叭	537
	叮	538
	可	539
	台	540
	叱	541
	史	542
	右	543
	叵	544
	叶	545
	司	546
囗	囚	782
	四	783
夕	外	908
大	失	922
	央	923
	夯	924
女	奴	950
	奶	951
子	孕	1077
宀	宄	1098
	它	1099
	宁	1100
	宂	1101
尸	尻	1182
	尼	1183
工	左	1294
	巧	1295
	巨	1296
巾	市	1306
	布	1307
干	平	1349
幺	幼	1356
广	庀	1359
廾	弁	1410
弓	弗	1421
	弘	1422
心	必	1497
	忉	1498
戈	戊	1752

部首	單字	字號
	戉	1753
戶	戹	1778
手	扑	1792
	扒	1793
	打	1794
	扔	1795
斤	斥	2165
无	无	2196
日	旦	2199
木	未	2331
	末	2332
	本	2333
	札	2334
	朮	2335
止	正	2682
歹	歺	2691
	(歹)	
毋	母	2726
氏	氐	2747
	民	2748
水	永	2762
	氾	2764
	汁	2765
	汀	2766
犬	犮	3339
	犯	3340
玄	玄	3406
玉	玉	3408
瓜	瓜	3516
瓦	瓦	3522
甘	甘	3536
生	生	3539
用	用	3545
	甩	3546
田	田	3551
	由	3552
	甲	3553
	申	3554
疋	疋	3587
白	白	3692

部首	單字	字號
皮	皮	3709
皿	皿	3714
目	目	3739
矛	矛	3826
矢	矢	3829
石	石	3841
示	示	3923
禾	禾	3978
穴	穴	4038
立	立	4073
肉	肊	4620

六畫

部首	單字	字號
一	丞	17
	丟	18
丶	乓	27
丿	乒	34
乙	乩	42
二	亙	56
亠	交	62
	亥	63
	亦	64
人	仰	96
	仲	97
	仳	98
	件	99
	件	100
	任	101
	仿	102
	企	103
	伉	104
	伊	105
	伋	106
	伍	107
	伎	108
	伏	109
	伐	110
	休	111
	伙	112

部首	單字	字號
	充	292
	(充)	
儿	兆	293
	兇	294
	先	295
	光	296
入	全	308
八	共	315
冂	再	324
冫	冰	335
	决	2786
	(決)	
	冲	2801
	(沖)	
刀	刎	363
	刑	364
	划	365
	刓	366
	刖	367
	列	368
力	劣	420
勹	匈	452
匚	匠	462
	匡	463
十	卉	481
卩	印	496
	危	497
口	合	547
	吁	548
	吃	549
	各	550
	吉	551
	吋	552
	同	553
	吆	554
	吒	555
	名	556
	后	557
	吐	558
	向	559

部首	單字	字號
	吏	560
	吊	1420
	(弔)	
囗	回	784
	囟	785
	因	786
土	在	806
	圩	807
	圭	808
	圯	809
	地	810
夕	多	909
	夙	910
大	夷	925
	夸	926
女	奸	952
	她	953
	好	954
	妁	955
	如	956
	妃	957
	妄	958
	妊	997
	(姙)	
子	字	1078
	存	1079
宀	宅	1102
	宇	1103
	守	1104
	安	1105
寸	寺	1158
小	尖	1170
山	屹	1210
	屺	1211
巛	州	1290
	巡	1291
	(巡)	
	廵	6053
	(巡)	
巾	帆	1308

部首	單字	字號
	帆	1308
	(帆)	
干	年	1350
广	庄	1360
廴	巡	1291
	(巡)	
	廵	6053
	(巡)	
弋	式	1416
弓	弛	1423
心	忙	1506
	忖	1507
戈	戍	1754
	戌	1755
	戎	1756
手	扞	1796
	扣	1797
	扛	1798
	托	1799
	扦	1800
	扠	1801
攴	收	2115
	攷	4569
	(考)	
日	旨	2200
	早	2201
	旬	2202
	旭	2203
	旮	2204
	旯	2205
曰	曲	2302
	曳	2303
月	有	2315
木	朱	2336
	朴	2337
	朽	2338
	朵	2339
	朶	2339
	(朵)	
欠	次	2651

部首	單字	字號
止	此	2683
歹	死	2692
气	氛	2750
水	汆	2763
	汊	2768
	汎	2769
	汕	2770
	汐	2771
	汗	2772
	池	2773
	汜	2774
	汝	2775
	江	2776
	汛	2777
	污	2779
	汙	2779
	(汚)	
	污	2779
	(汙)	
火	灰	3172
牛	牝	3311
	牟	3312
犬	犴	3341
王	玎	3410
白	百	3693
竹	竹	4085
米	米	4233
缶	缶	4476
羊	羊	4512
羽	羽	4536
老	老	4568
	考	4569
而	而	4575
耒	耒	4579
耳	耳	4590
聿	聿	4614
肉	肉	4619
	肋	4621
	肌	4622
	肎	4637
	(肯)	
臣	臣	4759
自	自	4764
至	至	4769
臼	臼	4773
舌	舌	4786
舛	舛	4793
舟	舟	4797
艮	艮	4823
色	色	4826
艸	艸	4829
	艾	4830
	艿	4831
血	血	5356
行	行	5360
衣	衣	5374
襾	西	5473
邑	邙	6170
	邛	6171
阜	阡	6583
	阢	6584

七畫

部首	單字	字號
丨	串	23
二	些	57
亠	亨	65
人	伯	113
	估	114
	你	115
	伴	116
	伶	117
	伸	118
	伺	119
	似	120
	伽	121
	佃	122
	但	123
	佇	124
	佈	125
	位	126
	低	127
	住	128
	佐	129
	佑	130
	佔	131
	何	132
	佗	133
	佘	134
	余	135
	佚	136
	佛	137
	作	138
	佞	139
	佟	140
儿	克	297
	兌	298
	免	299
	兎	301
	(兔)	
八	兵	316
冫	冶	336
	冷	337
	况	2821
	(況)	
刀	初	369
	刪	370
	判	371
	別	372
	刨	373
	利	374
力	助	421
	努	422
	劫	423
	劬	424
	劭	425
匚	匣	464
卜	卣	492
卩	卵	498
	却	503
	(卻)	
	即	504
	(卽)	
口	君	561
	吝	562
	吞	563
	吟	564
	吠	565
	否	566
	吩	567
	含	568
	吮	569
	呈	570
	吳	571
	吵	572
	吶	573
	吸	574
	吹	575
	吻	576
	吼	577
	吱	578
	吾	579
	告	580
	呀	581
	呃	582
	呂	583
	呆	584
	呎	585
	吧	586
囗	困	787
	囤	788
	囪	789
	囫	790
土	坊	811
	圾	812
	址	813
	坂	814
	均	815
	坍	816
	坎	817
	坐	818
	坑	819
士	壯	898
	壳	2719
	(殼)	
大	夾	927
女	妓	959
	妊	960
	妒	961
	妖	962
	妞	963
	妙	964
	妝	965
	妣	966
	妤	967
	妥	968
	妨	969
	姸	996
	(妍)	
子	孚	1080
	孛	1081
	孜	1082
	孝	1083
宀	宋	1106
	完	1107
	宏	1108
尢	尨	1175
	尬	1176
尸	尾	1184
	尿	1185
	局	1186
	屁	1187
山	岔	1212
	岌	1213
	岐	1214
	岑	1215
巛	巡	1291
工	巫	1297
巾	希	1309
广	庇	1361
	庋	1362
	序	1363
	床	3297
	(牀)	
廴	延	1406
	廷	1407
廾	弄	1411
	弃	2476
	(棄)	
弓	弟	1424
彡	彤	1447
	形	1448
彳	彷	1459
	役	1460
心	忌	1499
	忍	1500
	忒	1501
	忐	1502
	忑	1503
	志	1504
	忘	1505
	忡	1508
	忤	1509
	快	1510
	忮	1511
	忭	1512
	忱	1513
	忸	1514
	忻	1515
	忪	1516
戈	成	1757
	戒	1758
	我	1759
手	扭	1802
	扮	1803
	扶	1804
	扯	1805
	扳	1806
	扱	1807
	批	1808
	找	1809
	抃	1810
	技	1811
	抄	1812
	抉	1813

八畫

九畫

	麻	1371		恰	1564		昴	2231		柱	2409		泇	2867		珈	3428
廴	建	1408		恊	1565		昶	2232		柬	2410		洲	2868	甘	甚	3537
	廻	6072		恉	1578		昫	2233		查	2411		洮	2869	用	甭	3549
	(迴)		戶	扁	1783		昳	2234		柰	2412		洵	2870	田	界	3560
廾	弇	1412		扃	1784		昝	2235		柴	2413		洶	2871		畏	3561
	弈	1413	手	拜	1856		昪	2236		柷	2414		洽	2872		畋	3562
弓	弭	1429		拭	1857		昺	2237		柮	2415		活	2873		畎	3563
	弮	1430		拮	1858		昞	2237		柵	2416		派	2874	疒	疤	3595
彐	彖	1442		拯	1859		(昺)			柶	2417		流	2875		疥	3596
彡	形	1448		括	1860		昜	2238		柁	2418		洏	2876		疫	3597
	(形)			拱	1861		昵	2278		枰	2419		洸	2877		疣	3598
	彥	1449		拴	1862		(暱)			枱	2420	火	炫	3183	癶	癸	3688
彳	待	1466		拶	1863	曰	曷	2305		栀	2461		炬	3184	白	皆	3697
	徇	1467		拾	1864	月	朏	2318		(梔)			炮	3185		皇	3698
	很	1468		持	1865	木	枯	2380	止	歪	2687		炰	3185		皈	3699
	徉	1469		按	1866		枳	2381	歹	殆	2695		(炮)		皿	盅	3716
	徊	1470		指	1867		枴	2382		殄	2696		炯	3186		盆	3717
	律	1471		挑	1868		柺	2383		殃	2697		炳	3187		盈	3718
	後	1472		拽	1869		枲	2384		殂	2698		炷	3188		盃	3719
心	怎	1542		挖	1870		架	2385	殳	段	2716		炸	3189	目	相	3744
	怒	1543		拷	1871		枷	2386	比	毖	2732		炭	3190		盻	3745
	思	1544		挓	1872		柿	2387		毗	2733		炤	3191		盼	3746
	怠	1545		拏	1874		枸	2388	毛	毡	2745		為	3192		眪	3747
	急	1546		(拿)			枹	2389		(氈)		爪	爰	3287		眇	3748
	怨	1547		拼	1924		柒	2390	气	氟	2752	爿	牁	3298		眈	3749
	怹	1548		(拼)			枻	2391	水	泉	2848	牛	牯	3318		眊	3750
	怱	1549		挂	1928		柎	2392		洄	2850		牲	3319		盹	3751
	恂	1550		(掛)			柄	2393		洎	2851		牴	3320		盾	3752
	恆	1551	攴	政	2121		柏	2394		洑	2852	犬	狠	3352		省	3753
	恒	1551		故	2122		某	2395		洌	2853		狡	3353		眉	3754
	(恆)		斤	斫	2167		染	2396		洋	2854		狩	3354		看	3755
	恃	1552	方	施	2176		柔	2397		洒	2855	玉	珏	3416	矛	矜	3827
	恌	1553		斿	2177		柑	2398		洗	2856		(玨)		矢	矧	3832
	恓	1554	无	既	2197		柳	2399		洙	2857		玲	3418		矦	3833
	恍	1555		(既)			柘	2400		洟	2858		玷	3419	石	砉	3844
	恟	1556	日	星	2223		柙	2401		洞	2859		玳	3420		砂	3845
	恢	1557		映	2224		柚	2402		洛	2860		珉	3421		砌	3846
	恨	1558		春	2225		柜	2403		津	2861		珂	3422		砍	3847
	恤	1559		昧	2226		柞	2404		洧	2862		玭	3423		砒	3848
	恪	1560		昨	2227		柝	2405		洫	2863		珊	3424		研	3864
	恫	1561		昭	2228		柢	2406		洩	2864		珍	3425		(硏)	
	恇	1562		是	2229		柩	2407		洪	2865		玻	3426	示	祆	3928
	恬	1563		昱	2230		柯	2408		洱	2866		珀	3427		祅	3929

十畫

土	埋	834		峪	1235	手	拳	1873		晒	2300		(殼)			烘	3197
	城	835	工	差	1298		拿	1874		(曬)		毛	毬	2736		烤	3198
	埂	836	巾	帨	1321		挈	1875	曰	書	2306	气	氣	2753		烟	3199
	埃	837		師	1322		挨	1876	月	朔	2319		氤	2754		烙	3200
	埔	838		席	1323		挪	1877		朕	2320		氧	2755	父	爹	3292
夂	夏	904		帮	1345		挱	1878		朓	2321		氦	2756	爿	牂	3299
大	奘	938		(幫)			挫	1879	木	栓	2421	水	泰	2849	牛	特	3321
	套	939	广	座	1372		振	1880		栻	2422		浙	2878		牷	3322
	奋	940		庫	1373		挼	1881		栖	2423		浚	2879		牸	3323
	奚	941		庭	1374		挹	1882		栝	2424		浜	2880	犬	狴	3355
女	娓	1002	弓	弰	1431		挽	1883		栩	2425		浡	2881		狼	3356
	娉	1003		弱	1432		挺	1884		栗	2426		浣	2882		狽	3357
	娌	1004	彡	彧	1450		捃	1885		株	2427		浩	2883		狷	3358
	姬	1005	彳	徐	1473		捆	1886		核	2428		浥	2884		狸	3359
	娑	1006		徑	1474		捋	1887		校	2429		浦	2885		狹	3360
	娘	1007		徒	1475		捉	1888		栲	2430		浬	2886		狺	3361
	娛	1008	心	恁	1566		挾	1889		根	2431		浪	2887	玉	珙	3429
	娜	1009		恐	1567		捍	1890		桁	2432		浭	2888		珥	3430
	娟	1010		恕	1568		捌	1891		格	2433		浴	2889		珞	3431
	娠	1011		恚	1569		捕	1892		桀	2434		浮	2890		珠	3432
	娣	1012		恝	1570		捐	1893		案	2435		海	2891		珩	3433
	娥	1013		恙	1571		捎	1894		桌	2436		浸	2892		班	3434
	娩	1014		恣	1572		捏	1895		桑	2437		浼	2893		珪	3435
子	孫	1089		恩	1573		捣	1896		栽	2438		涇	2894		珣	3436
宀	宮	1122		恧	1574	支	效	2123		桂	2439		涅	2895		珮	3437
	宰	1123		息	1575		敉	2124		桃	2440		涉	2896		琉	3438
	害	1124		恭	1576	文	斋	7304		桄	2441		消	2897	瓜	瓞	3517
	宴	1125		恥	1577		(齋)			桅	2442		涑	2898	瓦	瓴	3523
	宵	1126		悃	1579	斗	料	2157		框	2443		涓	2899	生	甡	3540
	家	1127		悁	1580	方	旁	2178		桎	2444		涎	2900	田	畔	3564
	宸	1128		悄	1581		旂	2179		桐	2445		涔	2901		畛	3565
	容	1129		悅	1582		旃	2180		桓	2446		涕	2902		畚	3566
寸	射	1160		悌	1583		旆	2181		桔	2447		洚	2903		畜	3567
尸	展	1195		悔	1584		旄	2182		桫	2448		涖	2904		畝	3568
	屐	1196		悒	1585		旅	2183		栢	2449		浞	2905		留	3569
	屑	1197		悍	1586	日	晏	2239		栱	2450		浯	2906	疒	疲	3599
山	峨	1228		悚	1587		時	2240		梳	2473		涌	2907		疳	3600
	峭	1229		悛	1588		晉	2241		(梳)		火	烖	3175		疸	3601
	峯	1230		悖	1589		晋	2241	欠	欬	2653		(災)			疴	3602
	峴	1231		悟	1590		(晉)		歹	殉	2699		烏	3193		疹	3603
	島	1232		悝	1591		晁	2242		殊	2700		烈	3194		疽	3604
	峻	1233	戶	扆	1785		晃	2243	殳	殷	2717		烝	3195		疼	3605
	峽	1234		扇	1786		晌	2244		殸	2719		烊	3196		疾	3606

	郛	6196		假	216		啡	652		婕	1021		帷	1326		惛	1614
	郜	6197		偈	217		啁	653		婚	1022		常	1327		惝	1615
	郝	6198		偉	218		啄	654		婢	1023	广	庵	1375		惦	1616
	郎	6199		偌	219		商	655		婦	1024		庶	1376		惜	1617
	郟	6200		偎	220		問	656		婪	1025		康	1377		惟	1618
	郡	6201		偏	221		啊	657		娼	1026		庸	1378	戈	戚	1763
	郢	6202		偓	222		啤	658		婭	1027		庹	1379		戛	1764
	郗	6203		偕	223		啐	659		婊	1028	弓	張	1433	戶	扈	1787
	郤	6204		做	224		啓	660		娬	1029		強	1434	手	捨	1897
	郕	6205		停	225		啖	661	子	孰	1090	彐	彗	1443		捧	1898
酉	酌	6248		健	226		啣	662	宀	冤	330	彡	彫	1451		捩	1899
	配	6249		偬	227		唷	663		(寃)			彩	1452		捭	1900
	酒	6250		側	228		啦	664		密	1130		彬	1453		捫	1901
金	釘	6313		偵	229		啞	665		宿	1131		彪	1454		据	1902
	釜	6314		偶	230		啃	666		寂	1132	彳	得	1476		捱	1903
	釗	6315		偷	231		唬	667		寄	1133		徘	1477		捵	1904
	針	6316	儿	兜	304		唪	668		寅	1134		徜	1478		捺	1905
	釙	6317	冂	冕	328		唸	669		寇	1135		徒	1479		捽	1906
	釕	6318	冫	凑	2977		啥	670	寸	專	1161		從	1480		捲	1907
門	閃	6531		(湊)			啜	671		將	1162		徠	1481		捻	1908
阜	陘	6604	几	凰	348	口	國	797		尉	1163		御	1482		捷	1909
	陛	6605	刀	副	399		圇	798	尸	屏	1198	心	悠	1592		掂	1910
	陞	6606		剪	400		圈	799		屝	1199		悉	1593		掀	1911
	陟	6607	力	勒	432	土	培	839		屙	1200		患	1594		掃	1912
	陡	6608		動	433		域	840	山	崇	1236		悤	1595		授	1913
	院	6609		勗	434		埠	841		崎	1237		您	1596		掇	1914
	陣	6610		勖	434		埤	842		崑	1238		悱	1597		掄	1915
	除	6611		(勗)			執	843		崔	1239		悵	1598		掎	1916
	陝	6612		勘	435		基	844		崖	1240		悸	1599		掏	1917
隹	隻	6655		務	436		堂	845		崗	1241		悻	1600		掐	1918
	隼	6656	勹	匏	454		堅	846		崙	1242		悴	1601		掊	1919
馬	馬	6921		匐	455		堆	847		崛	1243		悼	1602		掉	1920
骨	骨	6990	匕	匙	459		埽	1912		崢	1244		悾	1603		排	1921
高	高	7008	匚	匭	466		(掃)			崤	1245		悽	1604		掘	1922
鬥	鬥	7036	匸	匾	471	夕	夠	912		崧	1246		惆	1605		掖	1923
鬯	鬯	7044		匿	472		够	912		崩	1247		情	1606		拼	1924
鬲	鬲	7046		區	473		(夠)			崍	1248		惇	1607		掙	1925
鬼	鬼	7048	厶	參	515	女	婆	1015		崌	1249		惋	1608		掞	1926
			口	售	647		婀	1016		崡	1250		惕	1609		掠	1927
十一畫				唯	648		娶	1017		崦	1251		惓	1610		掛	1928
部首	單字	字號		唱	649		姘	1018	巛	巢	1292		惘	1611		採	1929
乙	乾	44		唳	650		婁	1019	巾	帳	1324		惚	1612		探	1930
人	偃	215		唾	651		婉	1020		帶	1325		惙	1613		控	1931

十二畫

	詆	5548		跖	5855		鈐	6335	黹	黹	7272		嗜	714		嵊	1263
	詈	5549		跗	5856		鈕	6336		十三畫			嗝	715		嵯	1264
	詠	5550		跚	5857		鈞	6337					嗯	716	巾	幌	1333
	詎	5551		跛	5858		鈣	6338	部首	單字	字號		嗟	717	干	幹	1353
	詐	5552		距	5859		鈎	6339	乙	亂	45		嗣	718	广	廈	1383
	詒	5553	車	軫	5975	門	開	6533	人	傕	241		嗤	719		廉	1384
	詔	5554		軨	5976		間	6534		傭	242		嗡	720		廊	1385
	評	5555		軸	5977		閎	6535		傲	243		嗑	721		廋	1386
	詖	5556		軺	5978		閏	6536		傳	244	口	園	801	弋	弑	1417
	詛	5557		軹	5979		閑	6537		傴	245		圓	802	弓	彀	1436
	詞	5558		軻	5980		閒	6538		債	246	土	塊	855	彐	彙	1445
	詘	5559		軼	5981		閔	6539		傷	247		塋	856	彳	徬	1487
	訿	5560		軲	5982	阜	陽	6623		傺	248		塲	857		徭	1488
	証	5561	辛	辜	6038		陻	6624		傾	249		塚	858		徯	1489
豕	象	5725	辵	迸	6106		隃	6625		僂	250		塑	859		微	1490
	[illegible]	5726		逮	6107		隄	6626		僅	251		塔	860	心	想	1644
豸	貂	5738		週	6108		隅	6627		僉	252		塗	861		惹	1645
貝	貯	5759		進	6109		隆	6628		僇	253		塘	862		愁	1646
	貰	5760		逵	6110		隈	6629		傻	276		塞	863		愍	1647
	貲	5761		逶	6111		隉	6630		(傻)			塡	864		愆	1648
	貳	5762		逸	6112		隋	6631	刀	剿	405		塢	865		愈	1649
	貴	5763		逭	6113		隊	6632		剷	406	士	壼	902		意	1650
	貶	5764		逯	6114		階	6633		剽	407	大	奧	944		愚	1651
	買	5765	邑	都	6214	隹	雄	6658	力	勦	405	女	嫁	1037		感	1652
	貸	5766		鄁	6215		雁	6659		(剿)			嫂	1038		愛	1653
	貺	5767		鄂	6216		雅	6660		勢	439		媳	1039		愧	1654
	費	5768		鄆	6217		集	6661		募	440		媵	1040		愴	1655
	貼	5769		郾	6218		雇	6662		勤	441		媸	1041		愫	1656
	貽	5770		鄄	6219	雨	雯	6684		勠	442		媼	1042		慍	1657
	賀	5771	酉	酢	6253		雰	6685	匚	匯	467		媽	1043		愷	1658
	貿	5772		酣	6254		雱	6686	又	疊	3586		媾	1044		愾	1659
	賁	5773		酤	6255		雲	6687		(疊)			嫉	1045		慄	1660
赤	赧	5823		酥	6256	韋	韌	6766	口	嗄	703		嫌	1046		慎	1661
走	趁	5832	釆	釉	6303	頁	項	6783		嗅	704		嫋	1065		慊	1662
	趂	5832	里	量	6308		順	6784		嗆	705		(嬝)			慌	1663
	(趁)		金	鈧	6327		頊	6785		嗇	706		媿	1654		慆	1664
	趄	5833		欽	6328		須	6786		嗉	707		(愧)			慉	1665
	超	5834		鈀	6329	食	飧	6853		嗊	708	宀	寘	1140		慖	1670
	越	5835		鈦	6330	馬	馭	6922		嗎	709	小	尠	1173		(恩)	
足	跋	5851		鈔	6331		馮	6923		嗒	710		尟	1173		惷	5345
	跌	5852		鈇	6332	黃	黃	7244		嗓	711		(尠)			(蠢)	
	跎	5853		鈉	6333	黍	黍	7247		嗔	712	山	嵩	1261	戈	戡	1766
	跑	5854		鈍	6334	黑	黑	7250		嗚	713		嵬	1262		戢	1767

十六畫

十七畫

	燠	3266
	燦	3267
	燬	3268
	燥	3269
	燴	3270
	燭	3271
	燮	3272
爿	牆	3300
犬	獲	3394
	獮	3395
	獯	3396
	獰	3397
玉	璦	3502
	環	3504
	璨	3505
	璫	3506
	璩	3507
瓦	甑	3532
疒	瘤	3658
	(癅)	
	療	3665
	癃	3666
	癌	3667
	癆	3668
	癇	3669
	癉	3670
	癍	3671
白	皤	3708
皿	盩	3736
	盪	3737
目	瞬	3807
	瞰	3808
	瞳	3809
	瞪	3810
	瞭	3811
	瞶	3812
	瞧	3813
	瞵	3814
	瞥	3815
矢	矯	3838
	矰	3839
石	磯	3908
	磴	3909

	磷	3910
	磺	3911
	磽	3912
	礁	3913
示	禧	3967
	禪	3968
	禨	3969
禾	穉	4009
	(稚)	
	穗	4031
穴	窾	4066
	窿	4067
竹	篠	4180
	篳	4181
	篼	4182
	篾	4183
	篷	4184
	簌	4185
	簏	4186
	簇	4187
	簃	4188
	簀	4189
	簋	4190
	簉	4191
	簒	4192
	簍	4193
	篰	4194
	簎	4195
	篺	4196
	篿	4197
米	糜	4259
	糞	4260
	糙	4261
	糝	4262
	糟	4263
	糠	4264
	糢	4265
	糨	4266
	糡	4266
	(糨)	
糸	縫	4416
	縭	4417
	縱	4418

	縮	4419
	縵	4420
	縲	4421
	縴	4422
	縷	4423
	縹	4424
	總	4425
	縶	4426
	縻	4427
	繁	4428
	繄	4429
	繇	4430
	績	4431
	繅	4432
	繃	4433
	繆	4434
	縧	4435
缶	罄	4481
	罅	4482
网	罽	4507
羽	翳	4559
	翼	4560
耳	聯	4604
	聰	4605
	聲	4606
	聳	4607
	聱	4608
肉	膿	4735
	膽	4736
	膾	4737
	膺	4738
	臀	4739
	臂	4740
	臃	4741
	臆	4742
	臉	4743
	臊	4744
	臌	4745
	臏	4746
	膻	4747
臣	臨	4763
艮	艱	4825
艸	薄	5111

	薅	5112
	蕷	5113
	蕾	5114
	薆	5115
	薇	5116
	薈	5117
	薊	5118
	薌	5119
	薏	5120
	薐	5121
	薑	5122
	薔	5123
	薙	5124
	薛	5125
	蕹	5126
	薦	5127
	薨	5128
	薪	5129
	蕺	5130
	薜	5131
虍	虧	5191
虫	螯	5301
	螬	5302
	螭	5303
	螮	5304
	螫	5305
	螳	5306
	螺	5307
	螻	5308
	螽	5309
	蟞	5310
	蟀	5311
	蟄	5312
	蟆	5313
	蟈	5314
	蟋	5315
	蟑	5316
	蟊	5317
衣	褻	5453
	襁	5454
	(襁)	
	襄	5455
	褺	5456

	褺	5456
	(褻)	
	襇	5458
見	覯	5491
	覬	5492
角	觳	5510
言	謎	5648
	謄	5649
	謊	5650
	謅	5651
	謇	5652
	謏	5653
	謐	5654
	謗	5655
	謙	5656
	講	5657
	謝	5658
	謠	5659
	謖	5660
	謟	5661
	謚	5662
谷	豁	5707
	谿	5708
	豀	5709
豆	豏	5718
豕	豳	5733
豸	貔	5744
貝	賺	5801
	賻	5802
	購	5803
	賽	5804
	賸	5805
	賷	7305
	(齎)	
走	趨	5842
足	蹈	5907
	蹇	5908
	蹉	5909
	蹊	5910
	蹋	5911
	蹌	5912
	蹐	5913
	蹏	5914

車	輾	6014
	輿	6015
	轂	6016
	轄	6017
	轅	6018
	轀	6019
辵	避	6156
	遽	6157
	邀	6158
	邁	6159
	邂	6160
	還	6161
	邅	6162
邑	鄹	6239
酉	醜	6279
	醞	6280
	醚	6281
	醛	6282
	醣	6283
	醢	6284
金	鍊	6435
	錨	6436
	鍋	6437
	鍍	6438
	鍔	6439
	鍘	6440
	鍛	6441
	鍥	6442
	鍪	6443
	鍫	6444
	鍰	6445
	鍵	6446
	鍼	6447
	鍾	6448
	鎂	6449
	鍺	6450
	鍶	6451
	鎃	6452
	鍇	6453
	鍬	6454
門	闃	6558
	闇	6559
	闌	6560

十八畫

十九畫

	蹭	5931
	蹯	5932
	蹴	5933
	蹶	5934
	蹺	5935
	蹻	5936
	蹼	5937
	蹵	5938
	躈	5939
	蹰	5940
車	轍	6023
	轎	6024
辛	辭	6044
辵	邊	6166
酉	醭	6290
	醮	6291
	醱	6292
金	鏃	6474
	鏇	6475
	鎩	6476
	鏦	6477
	鏈	6478
	鏊	6479
	鏑	6480
	鏖	6481
	鏗	6482
	鏘	6483
	鏹	6484
	鏜	6485
	鏝	6486
	鏠	6487
	鏡	6488
	鏢	6489
	鏤	6490
	鏨	6491
	鏁	6492
門	關	6574
	闚	6575
阜	隴	6652
隹	離	6679
	難	6680
雨	霧	6707
	霪	6708

非	靡	6730
革	鞲	6756
	鞳	6757
	鞴	6758
	鞶	6759
韋	韜	6771
	韞	6772
音	韻	6778
頁	顗	6819
	願	6820
	顙	6821
	顚	6822
	類	6823
	顖	6824
風	颼	6843
	颻	6844
食	餿	6894
	餼	6895
	餾	6896
	餻	6897
	餽	6898
馬	騖	6957
	騙	6958
	騣	6959
	騤	6960
	騠	6961
	䮟	6962
髟	鬀	7026
	鬍	7027
魚	鯤	7078
	鯡	7079
	鯖	7080
	鯛	7081
	鯨	7082
	鯪	7083
	鯫	7084
鳥	鵬	7155
	鵩	7156
	鶁	7157
	鵰	7158
	鵾	7159
	鶓	7160
	鵷	7161

	鵒	7162
	鶉	7163
	鵲	7164
	鶊	7165
鹿	麑	7225
	麒	7226
	麓	7227
	麗	7228
	麕	7229
麥	麴	7239
黹	黼	7274
黽	鼃	7278
鼓	鼗	7289
鼻	齁	7300
齒	齗	7310

二十畫

部首	單字	字號
力	勸	446
口	嚴	772
	嚷	773
土	壤	894
女	孃	1007
	(娘)	
	孀	1070
	孅	1071
子	孽	1096
宀	寶	1156
山	巇	1281
	巉	1282
	巋	1283
心	懸	1742
	懺	1743
	懿	1746
	(懿)	
手	攔	2095
	攖	2096
	攘	2097
	攙	2098
攴	斆	2149
方	旟	2194
日	曦	2297
	曨	2298

月	朧	2329
木	櫪	2634
	櫬	2635
	櫨	2636
	櫫	2637
	龒	2637
	(櫳)	
	櫱	2638
	櫭	2639
水	瀰	3156
	瀹	3157
	瀾	3158
	瀲	3159
火	爐	3280
牛	犧	3336
	犨	3337
犬	獻	3402
	獼	3403
玉	瓏	3513
	瓌	3514
疒	癢	3677
	癤	3678
	癥	3679
目	矍	3821
石	礫	3916
	礪	3917
	礬	3918
	礦	3919
穴	竇	4070
立	競	4084
竹	籃	4217
	籌	4218
	籍	4219
米	糯	4269
	糰	4270
糸	辮	4455
	纂	4456
	繻	4457
	繽	4458
	繼	4459
	繾	4460
	纁	4461
缶	罌	4486

羽	翿	4566
	耀	4567
肉	臚	4752
	臙	4753
舟	艦	4820
	艨	4821
艸	藺	5152
	蘑	5153
	蘄	5154
	藹	5155
	藻	5156
	藿	5157
	蘀	5158
	蘅	5159
	蘆	5160
	蘖	5161
	蘇	5162
	蘊	5163
	蘋	5164
	藷	5165
	蘢	5166
虫	蠐	5337
	蠑	5338
	蠓	5339
	蠔	5340
	蠕	5341
	蠖	5342
衣	襪	5466
	襬	5467
見	覷	5494
	(覰)	
	覺	5496
角	觸	5512
言	議	5683
	譟	5684
	警	5685
	譬	5686
	譯	5687
貝	贍	5813
	贏	5814
足	躄	5941
	躁	5942
	躅	5943

	躇	5944
	躉	5945
	躂	5946
	躃	5947
車	轔	6025
	轘	6026
	轕	6027
	轙	6028
	轗	6029
辛	辯	6045
邑	酃	6241
酉	醴	6293
	醲	6294
	醵	6295
釆	釋	6304
金	鐘	6493
	鐃	6494
	鐐	6495
	鐙	6496
	鏽	6497
	鐧	6498
	鐠	6499
	鐳	6500
門	闞	6576
	闡	6577
	闥	6578
雨	霰	6709
	霤	6710
	露	6711
革	鞺	6760
頁	顢	6825
風	飄	6845
食	饅	6899
	饎	6900
	饉	6901
	饃	6913
	(饝)	
香	馨	6920
馬	騫	6963
	騭	6964
	騰	6965
	騷	6966
	騶	6967

二十一畫

二十二畫

車	轢	6033
	轡	6034
邑	酈	6243
	酇	6244
金	鑊	6510
	鑄	6511
	鑑	6512
	鑒	6513
雨	霽	6715
	霾	6716
革	韃	6761
	韁	6762
音	響	6779
頁	顫	6830
食	饗	6908
	饔	6909
	饕	6910
	饘	6911
馬	驕	6976
	驊	6977
	驍	6978
	驎	6979
	驑	6980
髟	鬚	7032
鬲	鬻	7047
魚	鰻	7098
	鰽	7099
	鰵	7100
	鰱	7101
	鰾	7102
	鱅	7103
	鰹	7104
鳥	鷓	7186
	鷖	7187
	鷗	7188
	鷙	7189
	鷟	7190
鹿	麞	7231
鼠	鼴	7295
齒	齪	7319
	齬	7320
龍	龔	7326
	龕	7327
龠	龢	7330

二十三畫

部首	單字	字號
山	巖	1287
	巘	1288
心	戀	1748
	戄	1749
手	攣	2106
	攩	2107
	攪	2108
	攫	2109
	攥	2110
日	曬	2300
木	欒	2648
犬	玁	3405
疒	癰	3684
	癯	3685
竹	籤	4226
	籥	4227
	籧	4228
米	糵	4273
糸	纔	4469
	纓	4470
	纕	4471
	纖	4472
肉	臢	4757
艸	蘸	5174
	蘼	5175
	蘪	5176
	蘿	5177
	蘲	5178
虫	蠱	5348
	蠲	5349
	蠭	5350
衣	襶	5471
襾	覊	5479
言	變	5695
	讌	5696
	讎	5697
	讐	5697
	(讎)	
足	躩	5955
車	轤	6035
	轣	6036
辵	邏	6167
	邐	6168
金	鑤	6347
	(鉋)	
	鑠	6514
	鑕	6515
	鑛	6516
	鑞	6517
	鑣	6518
面	靨	6734
頁	顯	6831
	顬	6832
食	饜	6912
馬	驗	6981
	驚	6982
	驛	6983
骨	髒	7003
	髓	7004
	體	7005
	髑	7006
髟	鬟	7033
魚	鱔	7105
	鱖	7106
	鱗	7107
	鱒	7108
	鱉	7281
	(鼈)	
鳥	鷲	7191
	鷦	7192
	鷯	7193
	鷩	7194
	鷳	7195
	鷻	7196
	鷸	7197
	鷺	7198
鹿	麟	7232
黑	黲	7267
	黴	7268
鼠	鼷	7296
	鼹	7297
齊	齏	7306

二十四畫

部首	單字	字號
口	囑	781
	囓	7317
	(齧)	
土	壩	895
手	攬	2111
水	灝	3165
	灞	3166
疒	癲	3686
	癱	3687
目	矗	3823
糸	纛	4473
缶	罐	4490
网	羈	4511
色	艷	4828
虫	蠶	5351
	蠵	5352
	蠹	5353
行	衢	5373
衣	襻	5472
言	讕	5698
	讒	5699
	讓	5700
	讖	5701
豆	豔	5720
貝	贛	5820
足	躞	5956
酉	釀	6297
	醽	6298
	醾	6299
金	鑪	6519
	鑫	6520
雨	靂	6717
	靄	6718
	靆	6719
	靈	6720
革	韆	6763
頁	顰	6833
馬	驟	6984
骨	髕	7007
髟	鬢	7034
鬥	鬭	7042
鬼	魘	7059
魚	鱟	7109
	鱣	7110
鳥	鸑	7199
	鸊	7200
	鸂	7201
	鸇	7202
	鷹	7203
鹵	鹼	7214
黽	鼇	7280
鼻	齅	7301
齒	齷	7321
	齲	7322
	齶	7323

二十五畫

部首	單字	字號
广	廳	1405
木	欖	2649
手	攮	2112
水	灣	3167
目	矙	3824
竹	籩	4229
	籬	4230
	籮	4231
米	糶	4274
糸	纘	4474
肉	臠	4756
	臡	4758
艸	蘖	5179
虫	蠻	5354
襾	覉	5480
見	觀	5499
角	觿	5513
言	讙	5702
豕	貛	5746
	(貛)	
豸	貛	5746
足	躡	5957
	躥	5958
酉	釁	6300
金	鑰	6521
	鑲	6522
雨	靉	6721
頁	顱	6834
食	饞	6913
髟	鬣	7035
鹵	鹽	7215
黃	黌	7246
黑	黶	7269
黽	鼈	7281
	鼉	7282
齒	齹	7324

二十六畫

部首	單字	字號
水	灤	3168
目	矚	3825
虫	蠼	5355
言	讚	5703
走	趲	5843
酉	釃	6301
金	鑷	6523
革	韉	6764
食	饟	6914
馬	驢	6985

部首	單字	字號
馬	驥	6986
鬥	鬮	7043
魚	鱵	7111
黑	黶	7270
龠	龥	7331

二十七畫

部首	單字	字號
水	灨	3169
	灧	3170
	(灩)	
糸	纜	4475
言	讞	5704
	讜	5705
金	鑼	6524
	鑽	6525
	鑾	6526
足	躪	5959
頁	顴	6835
	顳	6836

二十八畫

部首	單字	字號
心	戇	1750
馬	驤	6987
魚	鱸	7112
	鱷	7113
鳥	鸕	7204
黑	黷	7271
鼻	齉	7302

二十九畫

部首	單字	字號
火	爨	3283
疒	癵	3675
	(癵)	
豆	豔	5721
金	鑿	6527
馬	驩	6988
鳥	鸚	7205
馬	驪	6989
鬯	鬱	7045
鳥	鸛	7206
	鸜	7207

三十畫

部首	單字	字號
鳥	鸝	7208
	鸞	7209

三十一畫

部首	單字	字號
水	灩	3170

三十二畫

部首	單字	字號
竹	籲	4232

三十三畫

部首	單字	字號
魚	鱻	7114
鹿	麤	7233

一部
ㄧ i yī

【一】 1 ㄧ yī (變調 ㄧˊ yi yí; ㄧˋ yih yì)

1. union; uniformity; uniform
2. one; unit
3. single; alone
4. whole; all; throughout
5. a; an; the
6. to unify; to unite
7. once; as soon as: 他一聽到消息就立刻動身了。He started as soon as he received the news.
8. each; per; every time

一巴掌(ㄧˋ ㄅㄚ ˙ㄓㄤ)
(to give someone) a slap

一把(ㄧˋ ㄅㄚˇ)
a handful; a bundle; a bunch

一把抓(ㄧˋ ㄅㄚˇ ㄓㄨㄚ)
to grasp all the power or authority (of an organization); authoritarian; dictatorial

一把手(ㄧˋ ㄅㄚˇ ㄕㄡˇ)
a good hand; an expert: 他幹農活可眞是一把手。He is really good at farm work.

一波三折(ㄧˋ ㄅㄛ ㄙㄢ ㄓㄜˊ)
meeting repeated difficulties; hitting one snag after another

一波未平一波又起(ㄧˋ ㄅㄛ ㄨㄟˋ ㄆㄧㄥˊ ㄧˋ ㄅㄛ ㄧㄡˋ ㄑㄧˇ)
Hardly has one wave subsided when another rises.—One trouble follows another.

一百(ㄧˋ ㄅㄞˇ)
one hundred

一百週年(ㄧˋ ㄅㄞˇ ㄓㄡ ㄋㄧㄢˊ)
a centenary; a centennial

一敗塗地(ㄧˊ ㄅㄞˋ ㄊㄨˊ ㄉㄧˋ)
a crushing defeat; a complete failure

一杯(ㄧˋ ㄅㄟ)
a cup of; a glass of

一輩(ㄧˊ ㄅㄟˋ)
a generation

一輩子(ㄧˊ ㄅㄟˋ ˙ㄗ)
throughout one's life; as long as one lives; a lifetime: 我一輩子也忘不了。I won't forget as long as I live.

一包(ㄧˋ ㄅㄠ)
a parcel; a package; a pack

一抱(ㄧˊ ㄅㄠˋ)
an armful

一班(ㄧˋ ㄅㄢ)
a class (of students); a squad (of foot soldiers)

一般(ㄧˋ ㄅㄢ)
① common; general; commonly; generally; as a rule ② same as; just like: 這倆兄弟一般高。The two brothers are of the same height.

一般見識(ㄧˋ ㄅㄢ ㄐㄧㄢˋ ㄕˋ)
to hold the same kind of view (usually in a derogatory sense)

一般性(ㄧˋ ㄅㄢ ㄒㄧㄥˋ)
a common quality; generality

一板一眼(ㄧˋ ㄅㄢˇ ㄧˋ ㄧㄢˇ)
①(to sing) in an expert manner ② methodically ③ following a prescribed pattern in speech or action

一半(ㄧˊ ㄅㄢˋ)or 一半兒(ㄧˊ ㄅㄚˋㄦ)
a half; half; in part

一本(ㄧˋ ㄅㄣˇ)
a copy; a volume

一本正經(ㄧˋ ㄅㄣˇ ㄓㄥˋ ㄐㄧㄥ)
① in a serious manner ② (irony) sanctimonious: 他看起來一本正經的樣子。He looks sanctimonious.

一本萬利(ㄧˋ ㄅㄣˇ ㄨㄢˋ ㄌㄧˋ)
to gain enormous profit out of small capital investment; to make handsome profits with a small capital

一幫(ㄧˋ ㄅㄤ)
a gang; a clique; a group of people devoted to a common cause (usually an unworthy one)

一榜(ㄧˋ ㄅㄤˇ)
(imperial China) a group of scholars who passed the same government-administered civil service examination and whose names were announced in the same official notice

一蹦一跳(ㄧˊ ㄅㄥˋ ㄧˊ ㄊㄧㄠˋ)
skipping and hopping

一鼻孔出氣(ㄧˋ ㄅㄧˊ ㄎㄨㄥˇ ㄔㄨ ㄑㄧˋ)
to hold identical opinions; to conspire or be in league with somebody; to sing the same tune: 他們一個鼻孔出氣。They say exactly the same thing.

一鼻子灰(ㄧˋ ㄅㄧˊ ˙ㄗ ㄏㄨㄟ)
to meet rejection, humiliation or frustration

一筆(ㄧˋ ㄅㄧˇ)
① one stroke (in Chinese painting or calligraphic work) ② a sum (of money); a (debt, account, etc.)

一筆抹殺(ㄧˋ ㄅㄧˇ ㄇㄛˇ ㄕㄚ)
to blot out at one stroke; to condemn out of hand; totally negate

一筆勾消(ㄧˋ ㄅㄧˇ ㄍㄡ ㄒㄧㄠ)
① to undo something by a single stroke; all cancelled ② to settle an account once (and) for all

一臂之力(ㄧˊ ㄅㄧˋ ㄓ ㄌㄧˋ)
help; assistance: 請助我們一臂之力。Please lend us a hand.

一碧萬頃(ㄧˊ ㄅㄧˋ ㄨㄢˋ ㄑㄧㄥˇ)
(said of vast lakes, seas or oceans) boundless; vast; watery blue reaching far beyond the horizon

一表人材(ㄧˋ ㄅㄧㄠˇ ㄖㄣˊ ㄘㄞˊ)
handsome or dashing

一邊(ㄧˋ ㄅㄧㄢ)or 一邊兒(ㄧˋ ㄅㄧㄚㄦ)
on one side; by the side

一邊倒(ㄧˋ ㄅㄧㄢ ㄉㄠˇ)
① to fall on one side; to side with somebody without reservation ② to predominate; to enjoy overpowering superiority

一併(ㄧˊ ㄅㄧㄥˋ)
all; wholly; at the same time; together with

一病不起(ㄧˊ ㄅㄧㄥˋ ㄅㄨˋ ㄑㄧˇ)
to die of illness

一不做二不休(ㄧˋ ㄅㄨˋ ㄗㄨㄛˋ ㄦˋ ㄅㄨˋ ㄒㄧㄡ)
① to do something by hook or by crook ② not to stop half way once a thing is started

一部(ㄧˊ ㄅㄨˋ)
a (book, motion picture, etc.); a volume

一部分 or 一部份(ㄧˊ ㄅㄨˋ ㄈㄣˋ)
a part; a portion; partially

一步登天(ㄧˊ ㄅㄨˋ ㄉㄥ ㄊㄧㄢ)
a meteoric rise to fame; fast advancement in one's career, etc.

一拍即合(ㄧˋ ㄆㄞ ㄐㄧˊ ㄏㄜˊ)
to become good friends or partners after brief contact

一派(ㄧˊ ㄆㄞˋ)
a school (of thought, etc.); a faction; a group of people sharing the same ideals or interests

一派胡言(ㄧˊ ㄆㄞˋ ㄏㄨˊ ㄧㄢˊ)
complete nonsense

一砲而紅(ㄧˊ ㄆㄠˋ ㄦˊ ㄏㄨㄥˊ)
to have a meteoric rise to fame; to become famous all at once

一抔黃土(ㄧˋ ㄆㄡˊ ㄏㄨㄤˊ ㄊㄨˇ)
a handful of yellow earth—a grave

一盤散沙(ㄧˋ ㄆㄢˊ ㄙㄢˇ ㄕㄚ)
a plate of loose sand—utterly lacking cohesion; disunited

一盆(ㄧˋ ㄆㄣˊ)
a plate or tray (of food); a pot (of flower); a basin (of water)

一旁(ㄧˋ ㄆㄤˊ)
one side; on the sideline

一捧(ㄧˋ ㄆㄥˇ)
the amount held by two half-stretched hands linked together with palms up

一匹
①(ㄧˋ ㄆㄧ) a (horse, etc.)
②(ㄧˋ ㄆㄧˇ)參看「一疋」

一批(ㄧˋ ㄆㄧ)
a batch; a shipment (of goods)

一疋 or 一匹(ㄧˋ ㄆㄧˇ)
a roll (of cloth about 100 feet in length)

一瞥(ㄧˋ ㄆㄧㄝ)
a glimpse; a glance

一篇(ㄧˋ ㄆㄧㄢ)
a literary article; a chapter (of a book)

一偏之見(ㄧˋ ㄆㄧㄢ ㄓ ㄐㄧㄢˋ)
a one-sided view

一片(ㄧˊ ㄆㄧㄢˋ)
a denominative adjective for any object which is flat and thin

一片痴心(ㄧˊ ㄆㄧㄢˋ ㄔ ㄒㄧㄣ)
strong affection, usually one-sided, for a member of the opposite sex

一貧如洗(ㄧˋ ㄆㄧㄣˊ ㄖㄨˊ ㄒㄧˇ)
as poor as a church mouse; penniless; in utter destitution

一顰一笑(ㄧˋ ㄆㄧㄣˊ ㄧˊ ㄒㄧㄠˋ)
① every facial expression of a VIP ② affected coquetry of a prostitute

一品(ㄧˋ ㄆㄧㄣˇ)
the highest rank in officialdom in feudal Chinese courts (usually the prime minister)

一品夫人(ㄧˋ ㄆㄧㄣˇ ㄈㄨ ㄖㄣˊ)
the wife of the highest-ranking official in ancient China

一品紅(ㄧˋ ㄆㄧㄣˇ ㄏㄨㄥˊ)
a poinsettia 亦作「聖誕紅」

一暴十寒(ㄧˊ ㄆㄨˋ ㄕˊ ㄏㄢˊ)
to do something by fits and starts

一馬當先(ㄧˋ ㄇㄚˇ ㄉㄤ ㄒㄧㄢ)
to be the first to take on the enemy or to do work

一抹(ㄧˋ ㄇㄛˇ)
a faint trace of something

一脈相傳(ㄧˊ ㄇㄛˋ ㄒㄧㄤ ㄔㄨㄢˊ)
(said of lineage, philosophy, etc.) derived from the same origin

一枚(ㄧˋ ㄇㄟˊ)
a (coin, medal, etc.)

一毛(ㄧˋ ㄇㄠˊ)
① a hair ② one dime or ten cents ③ an insignificant thing

一毛不拔(ㄧˋ ㄇㄠˊ ㄅㄨˋ ㄅㄚˊ)
(literally) unwilling to sacrifice even a single hair (for the sake of others)—parsimonious; very stingy

一門(ㄧˋ ㄇㄣˊ)
① a course in a curriculum ② a family (of patriotic people, heroes, etc.) ③ a (big gun); a (cannon)

一面(ㄧˊ ㄇㄧㄢˋ)
① one side; an aspect ② a (mirror) ③ at the same time

一面倒(ㄧˊ ㄇㄧㄢˋ ㄉㄠˇ)
excessively dependent upon something or somebody

一面之交(ㄧˊ ㄇㄧㄢˋ ㄓ ㄐㄧㄠ)or 一面之緣(ㄧˊ ㄇㄧㄢˋ ㄓ ㄩㄢˊ)
to have met but once; a nodding acquaintance

一面之詞(ㄧˊ ㄇㄧㄢˋ ㄓ ㄘˊ)
one-sided statements

一鳴驚人(ㄧˋ ㄇㄧㄥˊ ㄐㄧㄥ ㄖㄣˊ)
to become famous overnight; to achieve enormous success at the very first try

一命歸陰(ㄧˊ ㄇㄧㄥˋ ㄍㄨㄟ ㄧㄣ)
to die 亦作「一命歸西」

一命嗚呼(ㄧˊ ㄇㄧㄥˋ ㄨ ㄏㄨ)
to die

一模一樣(ㄧˋ ㄇㄨˊ ㄧˊ ㄧㄤˋ)
exactly the same; identical

一木難支(ㄧˊ ㄇㄨˋ ㄋㄢˊ ㄓ)
(literally) A single post cannot support a mansion.—One person alone cannot accomplish a difficult task.

一目了然(ㄧˊ ㄇㄨˋ ㄌㄧㄠˇ ㄖㄢˊ)
(said of clarity in presentation) to understand fully at a glance

一目十行(ㄧˊ ㄇㄨˋ ㄕˊ ㄏㄤˊ)
(said of the ability to read very fast) to read ten lines at one glance

一發(ㄧ ㄈㄚ)
① a round (of ammunition)
② outbreak (of crisis, etc.)

一髮千鈞(ㄧˋ ㄈㄚˇ ㄑㄧㄢ ㄐㄩㄣ)
(literally) A thing which weighs one thousand chiun (鈞) hangs on a hair.—a desperate or critical situation; a close shave

一番(ㄧ ㄈㄢ)
① a kind, type, style, etc. ② once ③ a (silver dollar)

一番好意(ㄧ ㄈㄢ ㄏㄠˇ ㄧˋ)
good will; well-intentioned

一帆風順(ㄧˋ ㄈㄢ ㄈㄥ ㄕㄨㄣˋ)
(literally) May you have favorable winds in your sails!—to proceed smoothly without a hitch

一反常態(ㄧ ㄈㄢˇ ㄔㄤˊ ㄊㄞˋ)
to act out of one's normal behavior; to act out of one's character

一飯千金(ㄧˊ ㄈㄢˋ ㄑㄧㄢ ㄐㄧㄣ)
to reward a benefactor handsomely for the favor or help one has received from him

一分高下(ㄧˋ ㄈㄣ ㄍㄠ ㄒㄧㄚˋ)

to decide who is the better or stronger of two individuals or groups

一分耕耘，一分收穫(ㄧˋ ㄈㄣ ㄍㄥ ㄩㄣˊ, ㄧˋ ㄈㄣ ㄕㄡ ㄏㄨㄛˋ)
One reaps no more than what he has sown. 或 As a man sows, so shall he reap.

一分(價)錢，一分貨(ㄧˋ ㄈㄣ (ㄐㄧㄚˋ) ㄑㄧㄢˊ, ㄧˋ ㄈㄣ ㄏㄨㄛˋ)
The higher the price, the better the quality of the merchandise.

一分爲二(ㄧˋ ㄈㄣ ㄨㄟˊ ㄦˋ)
(philosophy) one dividing into two

一份(兒)(ㄧˊ ㄈㄣˋ(ㄦ))
a part, portion or share

一方(ㄧˋ ㄈㄤ)
① an area or region ② a party (in contract, etc.)

一方面(ㄧ ㄈㄤ ㄇㄧㄢˋ)
① one side ② on the one hand…, on the other hand…; for one thing…, for another …

一方之寄(ㄧˋ ㄈㄤ ㄓ ㄐㄧˋ)or 一方之任(ㄧˋ ㄈㄤ ㄓ ㄖㄣˋ)
a responsible government position which carries considerable authority

一封(ㄧˋ ㄈㄥ)
a (letter)

一夫當關(ㄧˋ ㄈㄨ ㄉㄤ ㄍㄨㄢ)
to hold or defend a key position single-handedly

一夫多妻(ㄧˋ ㄈㄨ ㄉㄨㄛ ㄑㄧ)
polygamy

一夫一妻(ㄧˋ ㄈㄨ ㄧˋ ㄑㄧ)
monogamy

一服(ㄧˋ ㄈㄨˊ)
a dose (of medicine)

一幅(ㄧˋ ㄈㄨˊ)
a (painting, scroll, etc.)

一副(ㄧˊ ㄈㄨˋ)
① a pair; a set ② a (facial expression)

一傅衆咻(ㄧˊ ㄈㄨˋ ㄓㄨㄥˋ ㄒㄧㄡ)
Too many detractors can undo the teachings of the wise.

一打(ㄧˋ ㄉㄚˊ)
a dozen

一刀兩斷(ㄧˋ ㄉㄠ ㄌㄧㄤˇ ㄉㄨㄢˋ)
to sever relations by one stroke; to be through with

一道(ㄧˊ ㄉㄠˋ)
① together ② a (problem, etc.) ③ on the same path

一旦(ㄧˊ ㄉㄢˋ)
① once; whenever ② someday ③ a day

一黨專政(ㄧˋ ㄉㄤˇ ㄓㄨㄢ ㄓㄥˋ)
one-party dictatorship

一登龍門，身價百倍(ㄧˋ ㄉㄥ ㄌㄨㄥˊ ㄇㄣˊ, ㄕㄣ ㄐㄧㄚˋ ㄅㄞˇ ㄅㄟˋ)
to rocket into fame after one's literary or artistic work won the praise of a master; to vault into the high society after winning the patronage of an influential or powerful person

一等(ㄧˋ ㄉㄥˇ)
top-notch; first-class; first-rate

一吊(ㄧˊ ㄉㄧㄠˋ)
a string (of coins)

一點(ㄧˋ ㄉㄧㄢˇ)
① a point ② a little bit

一點兒(ㄧˋ ㄉㄧㄚˇㄦ)or 一丁點兒(ㄧˋ ㄉㄧㄥ ㄉㄧㄚˇㄦ)or 一零兒(ㄧˋ ㄌㄧㄥˊㄦ)
① a little bit; small amount ② somewhat

一點一滴(ㄧˋ ㄉㄧㄢˇ ㄧˋ ㄉㄧ)
every drop; every bit; every little bit

一頂(ㄧˋ ㄉㄧㄥˇ)
a (hat, cap, or sedan chair)

一定(ㄧˊ ㄉㄧㄥˋ)
① fixed; specified; regular: 他沒有一定的職業。He has no regular work. ② certainly; surely; necessarily: 我們一定能夠達到我們的目標。Our goal can unquestionably be attained. ③ given; particular; certain: 在一定程度上 to a certain degree

一度(ㄧˊ ㄉㄨˋ)
once; on one occasion; for a time: 我因病一度休學。I stopped going to school for a time on account of illness.

一度燒傷(ㄧˊ ㄉㄨˋ ㄕㄠ ㄕㄤ)
first-degree burn

一肚子(ㄧˊ ㄉㄨˋ ·ㄗ)
a stomachful (of grudge, food, etc.)

一朶(ㄧˋ ㄉㄨㄛˇ)
a (flower or cloud)

一堆(ㄧˋ ㄉㄨㄟ)
a pile or heap

一隊(ㄧˊ ㄉㄨㄟˋ)
a detachment or contingent (of soldiers, policemen, boy scouts, etc.); a (musical band)

一對(ㄧˊ ㄉㄨㄟˋ)or 一對兒(ㄧˊ ㄉㄨㄜˋㄦ)
a pair; a couple; a brace

一對璧人(ㄧˊ ㄉㄨㄟˋ ㄅㄧˋ ㄖㄣˊ)
(said of newlyweds) an ideal couple

一端(ㄧˋ ㄉㄨㄢ)
① one end ② one aspect

一段(ㄧˊ ㄉㄨㄢˋ)or 一段兒(ㄧˊ ㄉㄨㄚˋㄦ)
① one paragraph, passage or stanza ② a section; a length of…

一頓(ㄧˊ ㄉㄨㄣˋ)
① a pause (in reading) ② a (meal) ③ a (beating or dressing down)

一冬(ㄧˋ ㄉㄨㄥ)
one winter season

一動(ㄧˊ ㄉㄨㄥˋ)
① a move; a jerk; a jolt ② to move once

一動不如一靜(ㄧˊ ㄉㄨㄥˋ ㄅㄨˋ ㄖㄨˊ ㄧˊ ㄐㄧㄥˋ)
Unless one is absolutely sure that he can succeed in doing something, he should not try it.

一棟(ㄧˊ ㄉㄨㄥˋ)
a (house or building): 我買了一棟房子。I have bought a house.

一塌糊塗(ㄧˋ ㄊㄚ ㄏㄨˊ ㄊㄨˊ)
in a great mess; topsy-turvy; in an awful state: 他把事情弄得一塌糊塗。He has made a mess of the job.

一榻橫陳(ㄧˊ ㄊㄚˋ ㄏㄥˊ ㄔㄣˊ)
to lie in bed

一臺(ㄧˋ ㄊㄞˊ)
a (theatrical performance)

一套(ㄧˊ ㄊㄠˋ)
① a suit; a set ② phony promise; trick; flattery; insincere gesture, etc.

一頭(ㄧˋ ㄊㄡˊ)or 一頭兒(ㄧˋ ㄊㄡˊㄦ)
① a head (covered with gray hair, dust, skin ailments, etc.) ② (said of cattle, hogs, mules, etc.) a head ③ a jerky motion of the head ④ to come face to face with someone unexpectedly

〔一部〕

〔一部〕

一頭霧水(ㄧˋ ㄊㄡˊ ㄨˋ ㄕㄨㄟˇ)
(slang) in bewilderment or confusion; not knowing what's the matter

一攤(ㄧˋ ㄊㄢ)
a puddle (of water, blood, oil, etc.)

一堂(ㄧˋ ㄊㄤˊ)
in the same hall; under the same roof

一堂課(ㄧˋ ㄊㄤˊ ㄎㄜˋ)
a period of teaching and learning at school

一趟(ㄧˊ ㄊㄤˋ)
a trip; a ride

一體(ㄧˋ ㄊㄧˇ)
① an organic (or integral) whole: 融成一體 to merge into an organic whole ② all people concerned; to a man

一貼(ㄧˋ ㄊㄧㄝ)
① to paste or glue ② a piece (of adhesive balm)

一帖藥(ㄧˋ ㄊㄧㄝ ㄧㄠˋ)
herbal medicines listed in a prescription for a particular ailment

一條(ㄧˋ ㄊㄧㄠˊ)
① a (rope, whip, snake, etc.) ② an article (of a law) ③ a carton (of cigarettes)

一條心(ㄧˋ ㄊㄧㄠˊ ㄒㄧㄣ)
to be of one mind; to be at one

一天(ㄧˋ ㄊㄧㄢ)
① a whole day ② one day (any day in the past or in the future)

一天到晚(ㄧˋ ㄊㄧㄢ ㄉㄠˋ ㄨㄢˇ)
from morning till night; from dawn to dusk; all day long: 他一天到晚無所事事。He has been doing nothing all day long.

一天星斗(ㄧˋ ㄊㄧㄢ ㄒㄧㄥ ㄉㄡˇ)
to exaggerate

一團和氣(ㄧˋ ㄊㄨㄢˊ ㄏㄜˊ ㄑㄧˋ)
full of goodwill toward one another; amicable; good-natured; harmonious, etc.

一團漆黑(ㄧˋ ㄊㄨㄢˊ ㄑㄧ ㄏㄟ)
pitch-dark—utterly hopeless; an utter failure

一團糟(ㄧˋ ㄊㄨㄢˊ ㄗㄠ)
in a hopeless mess

一通(ㄧˋ ㄊㄨㄥ)
a (telegram, etc.)

一通百通(ㄧˋ ㄊㄨㄥ ㄅㄞˇ ㄊㄨㄥ)
Grasp this one thing and you'll grasp everything.

一同(ㄧˋ ㄊㄨㄥˊ)
together with; in the company of

一統(ㄧˋ ㄊㄨㄥˇ)
① unification; unity ② to unify

一統江山(ㄧˋ ㄊㄨㄥˇ ㄐㄧㄤ ㄕㄢ)
territories under one sovereign

一男半女(ㄧˋ ㄋㄢˊ ㄅㄢˋ ㄋㄩˇ)
a few children (connoting one's longing for children after marriage): 他們想要有個一男半女。They wish to have a few children.

一年半載(ㄧˋ ㄋㄧㄢˊ ㄅㄢˋ ㄗㄞˇ)
from six months to a year —a relatively short time

一年到頭(ㄧˋ ㄋㄧㄢˊ ㄉㄠˋ ㄊㄡˊ)
all (the) year round

一年之計在於春(ㄧˋ ㄋㄧㄢˊ ㄓ ㄐㄧˋ ㄗㄞˋ ㄩˊ ㄔㄨㄣ)
Spring is the best time to do the year's work.

一年四季(ㄧˋ ㄋㄧㄢˊ ㄙˋ ㄐㄧˋ)
throughout the four seasons of the year; all the year round

一年一度(ㄧˋ ㄋㄧㄢˊ ㄧˊ ㄉㄨˋ)
once a year; annual(ly)

一念之差(ㄧˊ ㄋㄧㄢˋ ㄓ ㄔㄚ)
a false step (which brings untold woes); a wrong decision made in a moment of weakness

一怒而去(ㄧˊ ㄋㄨˋ ㄦˊ ㄑㄩˋ)
to go away in a temper; to leave in anger

一諾千金(ㄧˊ ㄋㄨㄛˋ ㄑㄧㄢ ㄐㄧㄣ)
a solemn promise: 他們一諾千金。They keep a solemn promise.

一樂也(ㄧˊ ㄌㄜˋ ㄧㄝˇ)
a great delight or blessing

一來(ㄧˋ ㄌㄞˊ)
① on the one hand ② as soon as (someone) arrives

一類(ㄧˊ ㄌㄟˋ)
of the same class, category or species

一勞永逸(ㄧˋ ㄌㄠˊ ㄩㄥˇ ㄧˋ)
to make a great effort to accomplish something once (and) for all

一覽(ㄧˋ ㄌㄢˇ)
a general survey

一覽表(ㄧˋ ㄌㄢˇ ㄅㄧㄠˇ)
a table list, or chart

一覽無餘(ㄧˋ ㄌㄢˇ ㄨˊ ㄩˊ)
(literally) A single glance takes in all.—a panoramic view

一愣(ㄧˊ ㄌㄥˋ)or 一愣兒(ㄧˊ ㄌㄥˋㄦ)
taken aback

一力成全(ㄧˊ ㄌㄧˋ ㄔㄥˊ ㄑㄩㄢˊ)
to spare no effort in helping somebody to accomplish something

一了百了(ㄧˋ ㄌㄧㄠˇ ㄅㄞˇ ㄌㄧㄠˇ)
(literally) The solution of one problem leads to the solution of all other problems.—To solve the key issue will expedite the solution of the whole problem.

一流(ㄧˋ ㄌㄧㄡˊ)
① first-rate ② of the same class

一溜煙(ㄧˊ ㄌㄧㄡˋ ㄧㄢ)or 一溜煙兒(ㄧˊ ㄌㄧㄡˋ ㄧㄚㄦ)
(to vanish) like smoke; (to get away) quickly: 小男孩一溜煙兒就不見了。The little boy disappeared in a flash.

一連(ㄧˋ ㄌㄧㄢˊ)
① successively; consecutively; in a row: 一連下了三天雨。It rained for three days in a row. ② a company (of foot soldiers)

一連串(ㄧˋ ㄌㄧㄢˊ ㄔㄨㄢˋ)
a series of

一鱗半爪(ㄧˋ ㄌㄧㄣˊ ㄅㄢˋ ㄓㄠˇ)
fragments (of antiques, ancient ruins, etc.)

一輛(ㄧˊ ㄌㄧㄤˋ)
a (car, truck, carriage, etc.)

一令(ㄧˊ ㄌㄧㄥˊ)
a ream(of paper)

一路(ㄧˊ ㄌㄨˋ)
① all the way; through the journey: 他們一路上說說笑笑。They chatted cheerfully all the way. ② to go the same way; to take the same route ③ single file

一路貨(ㄧˊ ㄌㄨˋ ㄏㄨㄛˋ)
of the same ilk 亦作「一路貨色」

一落千丈(ㄧˊ ㄌㄨㄛˋ ㄑㄧㄢ ㄓㄤˋ)
(said of prestige, fortune,

etc.) to nose-dive or decline drastically

一輪明月(ㄧˋ ㄌㄨㄣˊ ㄇㄧㄥˊ ㄩㄝˋ)
the full bright moon

一龍一豬(ㄧˋ ㄌㄨㄥˊ ㄧˋ ㄓㄨ)
One is very capable, while the other is extremely incompetent.

一律(ㄧˊ ㄌㄩˋ)
uniformly; equally; without exception (or discrimination)

一個(ㄧˊ ˙ㄍㄜ)
one; a; an

一個巴掌拍不響(ㄧˊ ˙ㄍㄜ ㄅㄚ ㄓㄤˇ ㄆㄞ ㄅㄨˋ ㄒㄧㄤˇ)
One hand alone can't clap. —It takes two to make a quarrel.

一個個(ㄧˊ ˙ㄍㄜ ˙ㄍㄜ)
① one by one ② each and every one

一個夠(ㄧˊ ˙ㄍㄜ ㄍㄡˋ)
to one's heart's content: 他開懷暢飲一個夠。He drinks to his heart's content.

一個勁兒(ㄧˊ ˙ㄍㄜ ㄐㄧㄜˋㄦ)
full of zest or enthusiasm; persistently

一個心眼兒(ㄧˊ ˙ㄍㄜ ㄒㄧㄣ ㄧㄚˇㄦ)
① to have one's heart set on something; devotedly ② to be of one mind

一個樣(ㄧˊ ˙ㄍㄜ ㄧㄤˋ)or一個樣兒(ㄧˊ ˙ㄍㄜ ㄧㄤˋㄦ)
alike; in the same manner; of the same sort

一概(ㄧˊ ㄍㄞˋ)
all; without exception; totally

一概而論(ㄧˊ ㄍㄞˋ ㄦˊ ㄌㄨㄣˋ)
discussed or regarded in the same frame of mind or in an indiscriminating manner

一干人犯(ㄧˋ ㄍㄢ ㄖㄣˊ ㄈㄢˋ)
a bunch of criminals

一乾二淨(ㄧˋ ㄍㄢ ㄦˋ ㄐㄧㄥˋ)
① thoroughly cleaned-up ② completely

一根(ㄧˋ ㄍㄣ)
a (stick, hair, club, flag pole or other objects which are long and slender)

一骨碌(ㄧˋ ㄍㄨˇ ˙ㄌㄨ)
to get up (from bed) hastily (as a result of a fire alarm, exciting news, or the arrival of some important personage or dear one)

一股(ㄧˋ ㄍㄨˇ)
① a streak; a strand ② one share (in stockholding) ③ a band (of bandits): 一股匪徒在我們鎮上出現。A band of robbers appeared in our town. ④ a (strong smell) ⑤ full of (spirit, zest, etc.)

一股傻勁(ㄧˋ ㄍㄨˇ ㄕㄚˇ ㄐㄧㄣˋ)
great enthusiasm; single-mindedness

一古腦兒(ㄧˋ ㄍㄨˇ ㄋㄠˇㄦ)
(dialect) completely; thoroughly

一鼓作氣(ㄧˋ ㄍㄨˇ ㄗㄨㄛˋ ㄑㄧˋ)
to brace oneself (for a challenge, a difficult task, etc.); to get something done in one tremendous effort

一鼓而下(ㄧˋ ㄍㄨˇ ㄦˊ ㄒㄧㄚˋ)
to conquer (a city or strategic point) in an overpowering attack

一國三公(ㄧˋ ㄍㄨㄛˊ ㄙㄢ ㄍㄨㄥ)
too many leaders in a country or organization

一官半職(ㄧˋ ㄍㄨㄢ ㄅㄢˋ ㄓˊ)
one of official positions in general

一貫(ㄧˊ ㄍㄨㄢˋ)
from beginning to end; consistent; unswerving

一貫道(ㄧˊ ㄍㄨㄢˋ ㄉㄠˋ)
a religious sect with a combination of Confucianist, Buddhist and Taoist features

一貫作風(ㄧˊ ㄍㄨㄢˋ ㄗㄨㄛˋ ㄈㄥ)
the consistent way of doing things

一貫作業(ㄧˊ ㄍㄨㄢˋ ㄗㄨㄛˋ ㄧㄝˋ)
(said of factories) integrated operation

一工(ㄧˋ ㄍㄨㄥ)
a day's work done by a laborer

一共(ㄧˊ ㄍㄨㄥˋ)
altogether; in all; all told

一棵(ㄧˋ ㄎㄜ)
a (tree); a head (of cabbage)

一顆(ㄧˋ ㄎㄜ)
a piece (of candy); a (heart, seal, diamond, star, mole, etc.)

一刻(ㄧˊ ㄎㄜˋ)
① fifteen minutes; a quarter ② a moment

一刻千金(ㄧˊ ㄎㄜˋ ㄑㄧㄢ ㄐㄧㄣ)
(literally) One moment is worth a thousand pieces of gold.—(said of newlyweds during their honeymoon) Time is precious. 或 Every minute is precious.

一客不煩二主(ㄧˊ ㄎㄜˋ ㄅㄨˋ ㄈㄢˊ ㄦˋ ㄓㄨˇ)
(literally) One guest should not bother two hosts.—Since you have already helped me, please help me finish the task.

一口(ㄧˋ ㄎㄡˇ)
① a mouthful; a bite ② (to promise or grant a favor) without hesitation ③ to insist (often falsely that somebody has done something bad) ④ a (well or bell) ⑤ an individual

一口答應(ㄧˋ ㄎㄡˇ ㄉㄚ ㄧㄥ)
to promise without hesitation

一口氣(ㄧˋ ㄎㄡˇ ㄑㄧˋ)
① in one breath; without stop ② breath: 讓我鬆一口氣吧! Let me catch my breath. ③ honor, face, etc. 參看「爭一口氣」

一口咬定(ㄧˋ ㄎㄡˇ ㄧㄠˇ ㄉㄧㄥˋ)
to stick to one's statement; to insist on saying something

一塊兒(ㄧˊ ㄎㄨㄚˋㄦ)
together; altogether

一塊(ㄧˊ ㄎㄨㄞˋ)
a piece; a block

一捆(ㄧˋ ㄎㄨㄣˇ)
a bundle of

一匡天下(ㄧˋ ㄎㄨㄤ ㄊㄧㄢ ㄒㄧㄚˋ)
to unite the whole empire under one government

一孔之見(ㄧˋ ㄎㄨㄥˇ ㄓ ㄐㄧㄢˋ)
a very limited outlook; a narrow view

一行(ㄧˋ ㄏㄤˊ)
a row; a line; a single file

一呼百諾(ㄧˋ ㄏㄨ ㄅㄞˇ ㄋㄨㄛˋ)
(said of a wealthy or powerful person with a large number of attendants) One command draws a hundred answers.

一忽兒(ㄧˋ ㄏㄨㄦ)
in a moment

一壺千金(ㄧˋ ㄏㄨˊ ㄑㄧㄢ ㄐㄧㄣ)
Things that are ordinarily worthless become very valuable when they are needed.

一狐之腋(ㄧˋ ㄏㄨˊ ㄓ ㄧㄝˋ)
the best part of something

一夥(ㄧˋ ㄏㄨㄛˇ)
a group; a gang

一會兒(ㄧˋ ㄏㄨㄜˇㄦ)
①a short while; presently; in a moment ②now…now…; one moment…the next…

一揮而就(ㄧˋ ㄏㄨㄟ ㄦˊ ㄐㄧㄡˋ)
to finish writing an article or drawing a painting very quickly

一回(ㄧˋ ㄏㄨㄟˊ)
①an occasion; a round (in boxing) ②once

一回事(ㄧˋ ㄏㄨㄟˊ ㄕˋ)
①one and the same (thing) ②one thing

一回生二回熟(ㄧˋ ㄏㄨㄟˊ ㄕㄥ ㄦˋ ㄏㄨㄟˊ ㄕㄡˊ)
①awkward at first but skilful later on ②strangers at the first meeting but friends at the second

一還一報(ㄧˋ ㄏㄨㄢˊ ㄧˊ ㄅㄠˋ)
tit for tat; an eye for an eye

一晃兒
①(ㄧˊ ㄏㄨㄤˇㄦ) to flash
②(ㄧˊ ㄏㄨㄤˋㄦ) in an instant; a short period

一哄而起(ㄧˋ ㄏㄨㄥ ㄦˊ ㄑㄧˇ)
(said of crowds) to rush headlong into mass action

一哄而散(ㄧˋ ㄏㄨㄥ ㄦˊ ㄙㄢˋ)
(said of crowds) to disperse in a hubbub

一己之私(ㄧˋ ㄐㄧˇ ㄓ ㄙ)
one's own selfish interests

一紀(ㄧˊ ㄐㄧˋ)
twelve years

一技之長(ㄧˊ ㄐㄧˋ ㄓ ㄔㄤˊ)
proficiency in a particular line (or field); professional skill; speciality

一家(ㄧˋ ㄐㄧㄚ)
the same family

一家言(ㄧˋ ㄐㄧㄚ ㄧㄢˊ)
a school of thought; an authority in a certain field (mostly in the humanities)

一甲子(ㄧˋ ㄐㄧㄚˇ ㄗˇ)
a cycle of sixty years

一截(ㄧˋ ㄐㄧㄝˊ)
a section; a length

一節(ㄧˋ ㄐㄧㄝˊ)
a section or passage (of a written work)

一介(ㄧˊ ㄐㄧㄝˋ)
a (scholar, etc.)

一介不取(ㄧˊ ㄐㄧㄝˋ ㄅㄨˋ ㄑㄩˇ)
said of the integrity of a public servant who does not take a single penny unrightfully

一脚(ㄧˋ ㄐㄧㄠˇ)
①a kick ②to take part in something (often unsolicited)

一…就…(ㄧ…ㄐㄧㄡˋ…)
no sooner … than …; the moment…; as soon as; once: 我一接到通知就動身了。I started off as soon as I got the message.

一間(ㄧˋ ㄐㄧㄢ)
a (room)

一肩行李兩袖清風(ㄧˋ ㄐㄧㄢ ㄒㄧㄥˊ ㄌㄧˇ ㄌㄧㄤˇ ㄒㄧㄡˋ ㄑㄧㄥ ㄈㄥ)
(said of an honest official on retirement) to possess nothing but one's personal belongings

一見鍾情(ㄧˊ ㄐㄧㄢˋ ㄓㄨㄥ ㄑㄧㄥˊ)
to fall in love at first sight

一見如故(ㄧˊ ㄐㄧㄢˋ ㄖㄨˊ ㄍㄨˋ)
to become intimate at the first meeting

一箭之地(ㄧˊ ㄐㄧㄢˋ ㄓ ㄉㄧˋ)
(literally) as far as the arrow flies—a short distance

一箭雙鵰(ㄧˊ ㄐㄧㄢˋ ㄕㄨㄤ ㄉㄧㄠ)
(literally) to kill two birds with one arrow—①to win the affection of two beauties at the same time ②to kill two birds with one stone

一斤(ㄧˋ ㄐㄧㄣ)
one catty

一將功成萬骨枯(ㄧˊ ㄐㄧㄤˋ ㄍㄨㄥ ㄔㄥˊ ㄨㄢˋ ㄍㄨˇ ㄎㄨ)
(literally) One general achieves renown over the dead bodies of 10,000 soldiers. —War is cruel.

一局(ㄧˋ ㄐㄩˊ)
①a game (of chess) ②(baseball) an inning

一舉(ㄧˋ ㄐㄩˇ)
with one action; at a blow; at one fell swoop: 他一舉成名。He became famous overnight.

一舉得男(ㄧˋ ㄐㄩˇ ㄉㄜˊ ㄋㄢˊ)
to get a son as one's first child

一舉兩得(ㄧˋ ㄐㄩˇ ㄌㄧㄤˇ ㄉㄜˊ)
to attain two objectives or gain two advantages by a single move; to kill two birds with one stone

一舉一動(ㄧˋ ㄐㄩˇ ㄧˊ ㄉㄨㄥˋ)
every movement and every action; behavior

一絕(ㄧˋ ㄐㄩㄝˊ)
a special skill; a unique talent or accomplishment

一蹶不振(ㄧˋ ㄐㄩㄝˊ ㄅㄨˊ ㄓㄣˋ)
unable to recover from a failure or after a decline

一決雌雄(ㄧˋ ㄐㄩㄝˊ ㄘˊ ㄒㄩㄥˊ)
to fight it out; to compete for championship

一妻多夫(ㄧˋ ㄑㄧ ㄉㄨㄛ ㄈㄨ)
polyandry

一齊(ㄧˋ ㄑㄧˊ)
at the same time; simultaneously; in unison

一起(ㄧˋ ㄑㄧˇ)
①in the same place ②together; in company

一氣(ㄧˊ ㄑㄧˋ)
①without stop; at a stretch ②to get angry

一氣呵成(ㄧˊ ㄑㄧˋ ㄏㄜ ㄔㄥˊ)
①to complete in one breath (said of a literary piece, painting, etc. so that it is characterized by unity in style and coherence in thought) ②to get something done at one go

一氣之下(ㄧˊ ㄑㄧˋ ㄓ ㄒㄧㄚˋ)
in a huff; in a fit of anger

一切(ㄧˊ ㄑㄧㄝˋ)
all; everything: 金錢對他重於一切。Money is everything to him.

一竅不通(ㄧˊ ㄑㄧㄠˋ ㄅㄨˋ ㄊㄨㄥ)
completely ignorant; utterly stupid; very poor (writing)

一秋(ㄧˋ ㄑㄧㄡ)
one autumnal season

一丘之貉(ㄧˋ ㄑㄧㄡ ㄓ ㄏㄜˊ)
people of the same ilk

一錢不值(ㄧˋ ㄑㄧㄢˊ ㄅㄨˋ ㄓˊ)or 一文

不値(ㄧˋ ㄨㄣˊ ㄅㄨˋ ㄓˊ)
not worth a penny; completely worthless; mere trash: 它一文不值。It isn't worth a penny.

一錢如命(ㄧˋ ㄑㄧㄢˊ ㄖㄨˊ ㄇㄧㄥˋ)
niggardly

一親芳澤(ㄧˋ ㄑㄧㄣ ㄈㄤ ㄗㄜˊ)
to caress, kiss, or sleep with a woman

一琴一鶴(ㄧˋ ㄑㄧㄣˊ ㄧˊ ㄏㄜˋ)
(said of a government official) very honest; incorruptible

一曲(ㄧˋ ㄑㄩˇ)
a song

一去不復返(ㄧˊ ㄑㄩˋ ㄅㄨˋ ㄈㄨˋ ㄈㄢˇ)
gone for ever; gone never to return

一去不回(ㄧˊ ㄑㄩˋ ㄅㄨˋ ㄏㄨㄟˊ)
to leave for good

一瘸一拐(ㄧˋ ㄑㄩㄝˊ ㄧˋ ㄍㄨㄞˇ)
to limp; to walk jerkily and unevenly

一圈(ㄧˋ ㄑㄩㄢ)
① a circle ② one round (in a mah-jong game)

一犬吠形，百犬吠聲(ㄧˋ ㄑㄩㄢˇ ㄈㄟˋ ㄒㄧㄥˊ，ㄅㄞˇ ㄑㄩㄢˇ ㄈㄟˋ ㄕㄥ)
to repeat after what others are saying without knowing why

一羣(ㄧˋ ㄑㄩㄣˊ)
a group; a crowd; a herd; a pack; a flock

一窮二白(ㄧˋ ㄑㄩㄥˊ ㄦˋ ㄅㄞˊ)
grinding poverty

一襲(ㄧˋ ㄒㄧˊ)
a piece of (garment)

一席話(ㄧˋ ㄒㄧˊ ㄏㄨㄚˋ)
a speech (usually referring to enlightening statements)

一息尚存(ㄧˋ ㄒㄧˊ ㄕㄤˋ ㄘㄨㄣˊ)
so long as one is alive (often followed by a vow to do something)

一系列(ㄧˊ ㄒㄧˋ ㄌㄧㄝˋ)
a series of

一夕數驚(ㄧˊ ㄒㄧˋ ㄕㄨˋ ㄐㄧㄥ)
(said of people in troubled times) in constant fear

一下(ㄧˊ ㄒㄧㄚˋ)
once

一下子(ㄧˊ ㄒㄧㄚˋ ˙ㄗ)
① at once ② at one stroke

一夏(ㄧˊ ㄒㄧㄚˋ)
a summer season

一些(ㄧˋ ㄒㄧㄝ)or 一些個(ㄧˋ ㄒㄧㄝ ˙ㄍㄜ)
① some; a few ② somewhat

一蟹不如一蟹(ㄧˊ ㄒㄧㄝˋ ㄅㄨˋ ㄖㄨˊ ㄧˊ ㄒㄧㄝˋ)
Each one is worse than the last.

一瀉千里(ㄧˊ ㄒㄧㄝˋ ㄑㄧㄢ ㄌㄧˇ)
① (descriptive of water in a giant river which) flows a thousand *li* at one plunge ② (said of the ability) to write fast and in a fluent style

一小撮(ㄧˋ ㄒㄧㄠˇ ㄘㄨㄛ)
a handful

一笑千金(ㄧˊ ㄒㄧㄠˋ ㄑㄧㄢ ㄐㄧㄣ)
A smile (of a beautiful woman) is worth a thousand pieces of gold.—an enchanting smile

一笑置之(ㄧˊ ㄒㄧㄠˋ ㄓˋ ㄓ)
to dismiss with a laugh; to laugh off

一宿(ㄧˋ ㄒㄧㄡˇ)or 一宿兒(ㄧˋ ㄒㄧㄡˇㄦ)
one night; an overnight stay

一線(ㄧˊ ㄒㄧㄢˋ)
a thread; a ray

一線希望(ㄧˊ ㄒㄧㄢˋ ㄒㄧ ㄨㄤˋ)
a gleam of hope; a silver lining

一新(ㄧˋ ㄒㄧㄣ)
a new look or fresh look

一心(ㄧˋ ㄒㄧㄣ)
① wholeheartedly; heart and soul ②of one mind; at one: 萬衆一心。Millions of people are all of one mind.

一心一意(ㄧˋ ㄒㄧㄣ ㄧˊ ㄧˋ)
① of one heart and mind ② bent on (doing something)

一心一德(ㄧˋ ㄒㄧㄣ ㄧˋ ㄉㄜˊ)
to be of one heart and one mind

一廂情願(ㄧˋ ㄒㄧㄤ ㄑㄧㄥˊ ㄩㄢˋ)
unilateral willingness; wishful thinking

一向(ㄧˊ ㄒㄧㄤˋ)
① hitherto; up to now ② always; consistently: 他一向爲人正直。He is always upright.

一星半點兒(ㄧˋ ㄒㄧㄥ ㄅㄢˋ ㄉㄧㄚˇㄦ)
just a little

一行(ㄧˋ ㄒㄧㄥˊ)
a group of (officials, businessmen, etc. during a trip)

一枝(ㄧˋ ㄓ)
① a (flower, pen, cigarette, etc.); a piece of (chalk) ② a branch

一枝獨秀(ㄧˋ ㄓ ㄉㄨˊ ㄒㄧㄡˋ)
(literally) One branch of the tree is particularly thriving. —to outshine others

一枝之棲(ㄧˋ ㄓ ㄓ ㄑㄧ)
a shelter or a minor position (for people out of luck)

一知半解(ㄧˋ ㄓ ㄅㄢˋ ㄐㄧㄝˇ)
a smack of knowledge; incomplete comprehension

一之爲甚(ㄧˋ ㄓ ㄨㄟˊ ㄕㄣˋ)
One mistake is enough.

一直(ㄧˋ ㄓˊ)
① always; constantly; on end; all along: 我們一直是朋友。We've been friends all along. ②(to go) straight forward

一擲千金(ㄧˊ ㄓˊ ㄑㄧㄢ ㄐㄧㄣ)
to spend money recklessly

一紙(ㄧˋ ㄓˇ)
a (document); a (letter)

一紙具文(ㄧˋ ㄓˇ ㄐㄩˋ ㄨㄣˊ)
(said of a treaty, contract, or law that has been violated) a piece of worthless paper

一致(ㄧˊ ㄓˋ)
unanimously; one and all; consistent

一折(ㄧˋ ㄓㄜˊ)
① a 90 per cent discount ② one fold

一着(ㄧˋ ㄓㄠ)
a move; a gambit

一着不慎，滿盤皆輸(ㄧˋ ㄓㄠ ㄅㄨˊ ㄕㄣˋ，ㄇㄢˇ ㄆㄢˊ ㄐㄧㄝ ㄕㄨ)
A careless move, and the whole game is lost.

一朝(ㄧˋ ㄓㄠ)
① in one day: 他企盼一朝成名。He expects to become famous in one day. ② once

一朝千古(ㄧˋ ㄓㄠ ㄑㄧㄢ ㄍㄨˇ)
to die suddenly

一朝之忿(ㄧˋ ㄓㄠ ㄓ ㄈㄣˋ)

a sudden outburst of anger
一朝一夕(ㄧˋ ㄓㄠ ㄧˊ ㄒㄧˋ)
a short period of time
一週(ㄧˋ ㄓㄡ)
① a week ② a revolution, circle or cycle
一盞(ㄧˋ ㄓㄢˇ)
a (lamp); a (cup)
一針見血(ㄧˋ ㄓㄣ ㄐㄧㄢˋ ㄒㄧㄝˇ)
exactly right; to the point 亦作「一語中的」
一陣(ㄧˊ ㄓㄣˋ)
a sudden gust (of wind, laughter, etc.)
一陣子(ㄧˊ ㄓㄣˋ ·ㄗ)
for a while
一章(ㄧˋ ㄓㄤ)
a chapter (of a book)
一張(ㄧˋ ㄓㄤ)
a sheet (of paper); a (table, desk, painting or calligraphic work)
一張一弛(ㄧˋ ㄓㄤ ㄧˋ ㄕˇ)
① off and on ② tension and lull
一丈(ㄧˊ ㄓㄤˋ)
a unit in Chinese lineal measurement slightly longer than ten feet
一株(ㄧˋ ㄓㄨ)
a (tree, weed, flower, etc.)
一柱擎天(ㄧˊ ㄓㄨˋ ㄑㄧㄥˊ ㄊㄧㄢ)
to lead the nation safely through a crisis single-handed; to be the only man capable of saving the nation in time of trouble
一桌(ㄧˋ ㄓㄨㄛ)
① a (banquet or feast) ② 8 to 12 people (seated around a table partaking of a feast)
一樁(ㄧˋ ㄓㄨㄤ)
an (affair); a (matter)
一種(ㄧˋ ㄓㄨㄥˇ)
① one kind or type ② a species: 在他的花園裏有一種珍貴的玫瑰。There is a rare species of rose in his garden.
一尺(ㄧˋ ㄔˇ)
a unit in Chinese lineal measurement slightly longer than one foot, which equals to one tenth of 一丈
一差二錯(ㄧˋ ㄔㄚ ㄦˋ ㄘㄨㄛˋ)
mistakes or errors which one is likely to make
一剎那(ㄧˊ ㄔㄚˋ ㄋㄚˋ)
in a moment; in the twinkling of an eye: 一剎那，它便完成了。It was done in a moment.
一朝天子一朝臣(ㄧˋ ㄔㄠˊ ㄊㄧㄢ ㄗˇ ㄧˋ ㄔㄠˊ ㄔㄣˊ)
(literally) When a new king is crowned he brings to the court his own favorites and expels those of his predecessor. 或 Every new sovereign brings his own courtiers. —the tenuous nature of official positions
一籌莫展(ㄧˋ ㄔㄡˊ ㄇㄛˋ ㄓㄢˇ)
knowing not what to do; at one's wit's end; helpless
一塵不染(ㄧˋ ㄔㄣˊ ㄅㄨˋ ㄖㄢˇ)
① immaculate; spotless ② (figuratively) uncontaminated
一場(ㄧˋ ㄔㄤˊ)or(ㄧˋ ㄔㄤˇ)
① a performance ② a (long period of association) ③ a (dream) ④ a (period of happiness, grief, etc.)
一場空(ㄧˋ ㄔㄤˊ ㄎㄨㄥ)
all in vain; futile
一倡百和(ㄧˊ ㄔㄤˋ ㄅㄞˇ ㄏㄜˋ)
One person proposes and a hundred others respond.
一唱三歎(ㄧˊ ㄔㄤˋ ㄙㄢ ㄊㄢˋ)
(literally) one singing and three sighs—an expression to describe a deeply touching literary work
一唱一和(ㄧˊ ㄔㄤˋ ㄧˊ ㄏㄜˋ)
(said of two persons on the same side of an argument, etc.) One echoes the other.
一成(ㄧˋ ㄔㄥˊ)
10 percent
一成不變(ㄧˋ ㄔㄥˊ ㄅㄨˊ ㄅㄧㄢˋ)
fixed; conservative; unchangeable; invariable; inflexible
一程(ㄧˋ ㄔㄥˊ)
a short distance
一齣戲(ㄧˋ ㄔㄨ ㄒㄧˋ)
a play; a theatrical performance
一出一入(ㄧˋ ㄔㄨ ㄧˊ ㄖㄨˋ)or 一出一進(ㄧˋ ㄔㄨ ㄧˊ ㄐㄧㄣˋ)
(the difference between) addition and deduction
一觸卽發(ㄧˊ ㄔㄨˋ ㄐㄧˊ ㄈㄚ)
(literally) One slight touch and off it goes.—imminent
一傳十，十傳百(ㄧˋ ㄔㄨㄢˊ ㄕˊ, ㄕˊ ㄔㄨㄢˊ ㄅㄞˇ)
(said of rumors, gossips, etc.) to travel fast
一串(ㄧˊ ㄔㄨㄢˋ)
a string (of coins, pearls, etc.)
一牀(ㄧˋ ㄔㄨㄤˊ)
a (coverlet or comforter)
一失足成千古恨(ㄧˋ ㄕ ㄗㄨˊ ㄔㄥˊ ㄑㄧㄢ ㄍㄨˇ ㄏㄣˋ)
One pitfall leads to endless misery and regret.
一時(ㄧˋ ㄕˊ)
① for a moment ② a period of time: 此一時彼一時。Times have changed. ③ accidentally
一時半刻(ㄧˋ ㄕˊ ㄅㄢˋ ㄎㄜˋ)
a short time; a little while:
一時一刻(ㄧˋ ㄕˊ ㄧˊ ㄎㄜˋ)
for a single moment
一時瑜亮(ㄧˋ ㄕˊ ㄩˊ ㄌㄧㄤˋ)
two equally talented or outstanding contemporaries
一世(ㄧˊ ㄕˋ)
① an epoch; an age ② a lifetime ③ I (used after the name of an emperor such as Napoleon I)
一世之雄(ㄧˊ ㄕˋ ㄓ ㄒㄩㄥˊ)
a great hero of his time
一事無成(ㄧˊ ㄕˋ ㄨˊ ㄔㄥˊ)
to accomplish nothing; to get nowhere
一視同仁(ㄧˊ ㄕˋ ㄊㄨㄥˊ ㄖㄣˊ)
impartial; without discrimination
一手(ㄧˋ ㄕㄡˇ)
① single-handedly; all by oneself ② good at: 他對於數字計算很有一手。He is good at figures.
一手包辦(ㄧˋ ㄕㄡˇ ㄅㄠ ㄅㄢˋ)
① dictatorial; arbitrary ② to do something all by oneself
一手獨拍雖疾無聲(ㄧˋ ㄕㄡˇ ㄉㄨˊ ㄆㄞ ㄙㄨㄟ ㄐㄧˊ ㄨˊ ㄕㄥ)
No matter how capable one is, he needs the help of others to do more or better work.
一手交錢一手交貨(ㄧˋ ㄕㄡˇ ㄐㄧㄠ ㄑㄧㄢˊ ㄧˋ ㄕㄡˇ ㄐㄧㄠ ㄏㄨㄛˋ)
cash on delivery

一手遮天(ㄧˋ ㄕㄡˇ ㄓㄜ ㄊㄧㄢ)
(literally) to shut out the heavens with one hand—to hide the truth from the masses; to hoodwink the public

一手造成(ㄧˋ ㄕㄡˇ ㄗㄠˋ ㄔㄥˊ)
to be solely responsible for (a bad situation, etc.)

一手掩盡天下人耳目(ㄧˋ ㄕㄡˇ ㄧㄢˇ ㄐㄧㄣˋ ㄊㄧㄢ ㄒㄧㄚˋ ㄖㄣˊ ㄦˇ ㄇㄨˋ)
to try to hide from public knowledge mistakes committed by one person or a few persons

一閃念(ㄧˋ ㄕㄢˇ ㄋㄧㄢˋ)
a fleeting thought

一扇(ㄧˊ ㄕㄢˋ)
a (door, window, etc.)

一身(ㄧˋ ㄕㄣ)
① a suit ② the whole body; all over the body ③ a solitary person: 他孑然一身。He is solitary.

一身是病(ㄧˋ ㄕㄣ ㄕˋ ㄅㄧㄥˋ)
to be afflicted by several ailments or diseases

一身是膽(ㄧˋ ㄕㄣ ㄕˋ ㄉㄢˇ)
to have plenty of guts; very brave

一身是債(ㄧˋ ㄕㄣ ㄕˋ ㄓㄞˋ)
(said of individuals) to be deep in debt

一神教(ㄧˋ ㄕㄣˊ ㄐㄧㄠˋ)
monotheism

一晌(ㄧˋ ㄕㄤˇ)
a short moment

一升(ㄧˋ ㄕㄥ)
a unit in Chinese cubic measurement slightly less than a liter

一生(ㄧˋ ㄕㄥ)
a lifetime

一生受用不盡(ㄧˋ ㄕㄥ ㄕㄡˋ ㄩㄥˋ ㄅㄨˋ ㄐㄧㄣˋ)
to enjoy the benefit or reward all one's life

一聲不響(ㄧˋ ㄕㄥ ㄅㄨˋ ㄒㄧㄤˇ)
do not say a word; do not utter a sound

一聲令下(ㄧˋ ㄕㄥ ㄌㄧㄥˋ ㄒㄧㄚˋ)
as soon as the order (to attack) is given (everyone will rush forward to engage the enemy)

一樹百穫(ㄧˊ ㄕㄨˋ ㄅㄞˇ ㄏㄨㄛˋ)
To encourage or patronize the talented will be rewarded manifold.

一說(ㄧˋ ㄕㄨㄛ)
① according to one version, theory, etc. ② brief explanation

一瞬(ㄧˊ ㄕㄨㄣˋ) or 一眨眼(ㄧˋ ㄓㄚˇ ㄧㄢˇ)
the twinkling of an eye; in an instant

一雙(ㄧˋ ㄕㄨㄤ)
a couple; a pair

一日(ㄧˊ ㄖˋ)
one day; such a day: 總有一日你會達到你的目的。There'll be one day when you will achieve your purpose.

一日千里(ㄧˊ ㄖˋ ㄑㄧㄢ ㄌㄧˇ)
(literally) a thousand *li* a day—to make progress or improvement at a tremendous pace

一日之計在於晨(ㄧˊ ㄖˋ ㄓ ㄐㄧˋ ㄗㄞˋ ㄩˊ ㄔㄣˊ)
Morning hours are the best time of the day to work.

一日之長
①(ㄧˊ ㄖˋ ㄓ ㄓㄤˇ) a little older in age
②(ㄧˊ ㄖˋ ㄓ ㄔㄤˊ) slightly superior in learning

一日之雅(ㄧˊ ㄖˋ ㄓ ㄧㄚˇ)
only slightly acquainted with (a person)

一日三秋(ㄧˊ ㄖˋ ㄙㄢ ㄑㄧㄡ)
(literally) A single day seems as long as three years.—longing for loved ones or close friends far away

一日爲師終身爲父(ㄧˊ ㄖˋ ㄨㄟˊ ㄕ ㄓㄨㄥ ㄕㄣ ㄨㄟˊ ㄈㄨˋ)
One should respect his teacher as if the teacher were his own father, even if the teacher-student relationship has existed for only a single day.

一人得道，雞犬升天(ㄧˋ ㄖㄣˊ ㄉㄜˊ ㄉㄠˋ, ㄐㄧ ㄑㄩㄢˇ ㄕㄥ ㄊㄧㄢ)
(literally) When one attains the Tao, even his chickens and dogs ascend to heaven. —When one gets to the highest position, all his friends and relatives get there with him.

一任(ㄧˊ ㄖㄣˋ)
a tour, term, or tenure (of duty)

一仍舊貫(ㄧˋ ㄖㄥˊ ㄐㄧㄡˋ ㄍㄨㄢˋ)
to stick to the old customs; to follow the old routine

一如既往(ㄧˋ ㄖㄨˊ ㄐㄧˋ ㄨㄤˇ)
just as in the past; as before; as always

一字褒貶(ㄧˊ ㄗˋ ㄅㄠ ㄅㄧㄢˇ)
to praise or criticize with a single word

一字千金(ㄧˊ ㄗˋ ㄑㄧㄢ ㄐㄧㄣ)
(said of superb writings) A single word is worth a thousand pieces of gold.

一字之差(ㄧˊ ㄗˋ ㄓ ㄔㄚ)
the change of one word (which would make a great deal of difference)

一字兒(ㄧˊ ㄗˋㄦ)
in a row; in a line

一字一淚(ㄧˊ ㄗˋ ㄧˊ ㄌㄟˋ)
(said of sentimental writings) a teardrop for every word

一則(ㄧˋ ㄗㄜˊ)
① one item ② on the one hand

一再(ㄧˊ ㄗㄞˋ)
repeatedly; over and over; again and again

一早(ㄧˋ ㄗㄠˇ) or 一早兒(ㄧˋ ㄗㄠˇㄦ)
in the early morning

一走了之(ㄧˋ ㄗㄡˇ ㄌㄧㄠˇ ㄓ)
to evade the solution of a problem by walking away from where it exists

一組(ㄧˋ ㄗㄨˇ)
a set; a group

一座(ㄧˊ ㄗㄨㄛˋ)
a (bridge, mountain, statue, etc.)

一尊(ㄧˋ ㄗㄨㄣ)
① a (fieldpiece, or Buddha statue) ② a jug (of wine)

一此爲甚(ㄧˋ ㄘˇ ㄨㄟˊ ㄕㄣˋ)
Once is enough.

一次(ㄧˊ ㄘˋ)
once

一次方程式(ㄧˊ ㄘˋ ㄈㄤ ㄔㄥˊ ㄕˋ)
(mathematics) a linear equation, or an equation of the first degree

一餐(ㄧˋ ㄘㄢ)
a meal

〔一部〕

一層(ㄧˋ ㄘㄥˊ)
①one story or floor (of a multistory building) ②a stratum

一蹴而幾(ㄧˊ ㄘㄨˋ ㄦˊ ㄐㄧ)
to succeed in doing something at the first try

一寸(ㄧˊ ㄘㄨㄣˋ)
a unit in Chinese lineal measurement slightly longer than an inch

一絲不掛(ㄧˋ ㄙ ㄅㄨˋ ㄍㄨㄚˋ)
to have not a stitch on; stark-naked

一絲不苟(ㄧˋ ㄙ ㄅㄨˋ ㄍㄡˇ)
No detail is overlooked. 或 to do things carefully and seriously

一絲一毫(ㄧˋ ㄙ ㄧˋ ㄏㄠˊ)
a tiny bit; an iota; a trace: 沒有一絲一毫的差別 without the least difference

一死了之(ㄧˋ ㄙˇ ㄌㄧㄠˇ ㄓ)
to end one's troubles or worries by death

一色(ㄧˊ ㄙㄜˋ)
①of one color; of the same color: 海天一色。The sea melts into the sky. ②of the same type

一掃而空(ㄧˋ ㄙㄠˇ ㄦˊ ㄎㄨㄥ)
(worries, doubts) completely removed

一所(ㄧˋ ㄙㄨㄛˇ)
a (school, charity institute, etc.)

一索得男(ㄧˋ ㄙㄨㄛˇ ㄉㄜˊ ㄋㄢˊ)
to produce a male heir by a woman in her first childbirth

一而再再而三(ㄧ ㄦˊ ㄗㄞˋ ㄗㄞˋ ㄦˊ ㄙㄢ)
to happen repeatedly; to repeat or try again and again despite failure

一二(ㄧ ㄦˋ)
a little; a few

一一(ㄧ ㄧ)
one by one; each separately; each one

一衣帶水(ㄧˋ ㄧ ㄉㄞˋ ㄕㄨㄟˇ)
a narrow water course; a strip of water

一以當十(ㄧ ㄧˇ ㄉㄤ ㄕˊ)
One fights against ten. (said of brave soldiers taking on an enemy force enjoying overwhelming numerical superiority)

一意孤行(ㄧˊ ㄧˋ ㄍㄨ ㄒㄧㄥˊ)
to do something against the advice of others; self-willed; self-opinionated

一頁(ㄧˊ ㄧㄝˋ)
one page

一葉扁舟(ㄧˊ ㄧㄝˋ ㄆㄧㄢ ㄓㄡ)
a small boat

一葉知秋(ㄧˊ ㄧㄝˋ ㄓ ㄑㄧㄡ)
(literally) A single fallen leaf tells of the oncoming autumn.—any sign foretelling things to come或A small sign can indicate a great trend.

一言不發(ㄧˋ ㄧㄢˊ ㄅㄨˋ ㄈㄚ)
to keep one's mouth shut

一言不合(ㄧˋ ㄧㄢˊ ㄅㄨˋ ㄏㄜˊ)
A single jarring note in conversation (between two persons is immediately followed by a quarrel, fist fight, etc.).

一言難盡(ㄧˋ ㄧㄢˊ ㄋㄢˊ ㄐㄧㄣˋ)
It is a long story.

一言既出駟馬難追(ㄧˋ ㄧㄢˊ ㄐㄧˋ ㄔㄨ ㄙˋ ㄇㄚˇ ㄋㄢˊ ㄓㄨㄟ)
A promise cannot be taken back once it is made.

一言九鼎(ㄧˋ ㄧㄢˊ ㄐㄧㄡˇ ㄉㄧㄥˇ)
a solemn promise or pledge

一言興邦(ㄧˋ ㄧㄢˊ ㄒㄧㄥ ㄅㄤ)
A timely warning may avert a national crisis.

一言喪邦(ㄧˋ ㄧㄢˊ ㄙㄤˋ ㄅㄤ)
A single wrong statement may bring disaster to the nation.

一言以蔽之(ㄧˋ ㄧㄢˊ ㄧˇ ㄅㄧˋ ㄓ)
to sum up; to make a long story short

一言一行(ㄧˋ ㄧㄢˊ ㄧˋ ㄒㄧㄥˊ)
every word and deed

一言爲定(ㄧˋ ㄧㄢˊ ㄨㄟˊ ㄉㄧㄥˋ)
to reach a binding agreement verbally

一眼看去(ㄧˋ ㄧㄢˇ ㄎㄢˋ ㄑㄩˋ)
①to take a sweeping look ②at first glance

一飲而盡(ㄧˋ ㄧㄣˇ ㄦˊ ㄐㄧㄣˋ)
to empty the glass at one gulp

一飲一啄(ㄧˋ ㄧㄣˇ ㄧˋ ㄓㄨㄛˊ)
One does not try to get what is denied him by destiny.

一氧化碳(ㄧˋ ㄧㄤˇ ㄏㄨㄚˋ ㄊㄢˋ)
carbon monoxide (CO)

一樣(ㄧˊ ㄧㄤˋ)
①alike; in the same manner ②an (object, item or article)

一應俱全(ㄧˊ ㄧㄥ ㄐㄩˋ ㄑㄩㄢˊ)
complete with everything

一無是處(ㄧˋ ㄨˊ ㄕˋ ㄔㄨˋ)
without a single redeeming feature; devoid of any merit

一無所得(ㄧˋ ㄨˊ ㄙㄨㄛˇ ㄉㄜˊ)
Nothing is gained.

一無所獲(ㄧˋ ㄨˊ ㄙㄨㄛˇ ㄏㄨㄛˋ)
to achieve or gain nothing (after all the efforts made)

一無所知(ㄧˋ ㄨˊ ㄙㄨㄛˇ ㄓ)
to know nothing at all; completely unaware; not have the least inkling of; to be absolutely ignorant of

一無所長(ㄧˋ ㄨˊ ㄙㄨㄛˇ ㄔㄤˊ)
do not have a single skill or merit; to be a Jack of all trades

一無所有(ㄧˋ ㄨˊ ㄙㄨㄛˇ ㄧㄡˇ)
to own nothing at all

一五一十(ㄧ ㄨˇ ㄧ ㄕˊ)
to enumerate or to narrate in detail; to tell something exactly as it happened

一物降一物(ㄧˊ ㄨˋ ㄒㄧㄤˊ ㄧˊ ㄨˋ)
There is always one thing to conquer another. 或 Everything has its nemesis.

一誤再誤(ㄧˊ ㄨˋ ㄗㄞˋ ㄨˋ)
①to commit one mistake after another ②to make things worse by repeated delays

一窩(ㄧˋ ㄨㄛ)or 一窩兒(ㄧˋ ㄨㄛㄦ)
a nest

一窩蜂(ㄧˋ ㄨㄛ ㄈㄥ)
(literally) a swarm of bees or hornets—①(said of a crowd of people) to swarm ②to follow the herd instinct

一尾(ㄧˋ ㄨㄟˇ)
a (fish)

一味(ㄧˊ ㄨㄟˋ)
habitually; invariably: 他一味地固執成見。He invariably sticks to his own view.

一位(ㄧˊ ㄨㄟˋ)
a (guest, gentleman, lady, hero, VIP, etc.)

一文不值(ㄧˋ ㄨㄣˊ ㄅㄨˋ ㄓˊ)or 一錢不

值(ㄧˋ ㄑㄧㄢˊ ㄅㄨˋ ㄓˊ)
not worth a penny; worthless
一問三不知(ㄧˊ ㄨㄣˋ ㄙㄢ ㄅㄨˋ ㄓ)
to say "I don't know" to every question—① do not know a thing; to be entirely ignorant ② to keep one's mouth tightly shut
一網打盡(ㄧˋ ㄨㄤˇ ㄉㄚˇ ㄐㄧㄣˋ)
(literally) to catch all the fish in one net—to round up all (the criminals, rebels or other undesirable elements)
一往情深(ㄧˋ ㄨㄤˇ ㄑㄧㄥˊ ㄕㄣ)
to fall deeply in love
一往直前(ㄧˋ ㄨㄤˇ ㄓˊ ㄑㄧㄢˊ)
to go ahead bravely without looking back
一望而知(ㄧˊ ㄨㄤˋ ㄦˊ ㄓ)
to know all at a single glance
一望無際(ㄧˊ ㄨㄤˋ ㄨˊ ㄐㄧˋ)
(said of open space or vast plain) to spread out far beyond the horizon
一隅(ㄧˋ ㄩˊ)
a corner
一語破的(ㄧˋ ㄩˇ ㄆㄛˋ ㄉㄧˋ)
to hit the mark with a single comment
一語道破(ㄧˋ ㄩˇ ㄉㄠˋ ㄆㄛˋ)
to hit the nail on the head; to expose someone's ulterior motive or secret design by a single remark
一語成讖(ㄧˋ ㄩˇ ㄔㄥˊ ㄔㄣˋ)
a casual remark that turned out to be prophetic in a tragedy
一雨成秋(ㄧˋ ㄩˇ ㄔㄥˊ ㄑㄧㄡ)
(said of weather in late summer or early autumn) A sudden shower turns the lingering heat into the brisk cool air of autumn.
一月(ㄧˊ ㄩㄝˋ)
① January ② one month
一員(ㄧˋ ㄩㄢˊ)
a member; a (field commander or top lieutenant)
一元方程式(ㄧˋ ㄩㄢˊ ㄈㄤ ㄔㄥˊ ㄕˋ)
the equation with one unknown
一元化(ㄧˋ ㄩㄢˊ ㄏㄨㄚˋ)
centralized; unified
一院制(ㄧˊ ㄩㄢˋ ㄓˋ)
the unicameral system (of a parliament)
一擁而上(ㄧˋ ㄩㄥˇ ㄦˊ ㄕㄤˋ)
to rush up in a crowd

一畫

【丁】 2
1. ㄉㄧㄥ ding dīng

1. the fourth of the Ten Celestial Stems (天干)
2. population
3. attendants
4. fourth: 丁等 grade D
5. small cubes of meat or vegetable
6. a Chinese family name

丁賦(ㄉㄧㄥ ㄈㄨˋ)
poll tax
丁當(ㄉㄧㄥ ㄉㄤ)
the sound of "*ding dang*"
丁點兒(ㄉㄧㄥ ㄉㄧㄚˇㄦ)
(dialect) a tiny bit
丁東(ㄉㄧㄥ ㄉㄨㄥ)
the sound of "*ting tung*"
丁男(ㄉㄧㄥ ㄋㄢˊ)
a male adult
丁年(ㄉㄧㄥ ㄋㄧㄢˊ)
the age of 16 which was the age of adulthood in ancient China
丁寧(ㄉㄧㄥ ㄋㄧㄥˊ)
to give repeated injunctions 亦作「叮嚀」
丁口(ㄉㄧㄥ ㄎㄡˇ)
people; population
丁錢(ㄉㄧㄥ ㄑㄧㄢˊ)or 丁稅(ㄉㄧㄥ ㄕㄨㄟˋ)
poll tax
丁香(ㄉㄧㄥ ㄒㄧㄤ)
a clove
丁香花(ㄉㄧㄥ ㄒㄧㄤ ㄏㄨㄚ)
lilac
丁字鐵(ㄉㄧㄥ ㄗˋ ㄊㄧㄝˇ)
a T-beam; a T-bar
丁字街(ㄉㄧㄥ ㄗˋ ㄐㄧㄝ)
T-shaped road junction
丁字尺(ㄉㄧㄥ ㄗˋ ㄔˇ)
a T-square
丁財兩旺(ㄉㄧㄥ ㄘㄞˊ ㄌㄧㄤˇ ㄨㄤˋ)
to be blessed with many male children and great wealth (a congratulatory expression in old China)
丁役(ㄉㄧㄥ ㄧˋ)
a male adult undergoing labor service for the country or community
丁夜(ㄉㄧㄥ ㄧㄝˋ)
the fourth watch of the night—(i.e. 2:00 AM)
丁徭(ㄉㄧㄥ ㄧㄠˊ)
poll tax; military service
丁憂(ㄉㄧㄥ ㄧㄡ)or 丁艱(ㄉㄧㄥ ㄐㄧㄢ)
bereavement of parents
丁銀(ㄉㄧㄥ ㄧㄣˊ)
poll tax money

【丁】 2
2. ㄓㄥ jeng zhēng

sound: 伐木丁丁，鳥鳴嚶嚶。(詩經・小雅・伐木) On the trees go the blows *jeng-jeng*;/ And the birds cry out *ying-ying*.

【七】 3
ㄑㄧ chi qī
(變調 ㄑㄧˊ chyi qí)

the number seven
七八成(ㄑㄧ ㄅㄚ ㄔㄥˊ)or 七八成兒(ㄑㄧ ㄅㄚ ㄔㄥˊㄦ)
① seventy or eighty per cent ② very likely
七步成詩(ㄑㄧ ㄅㄨˋ ㄔㄥˊ ㄕ)
(said of a literary genius) to compose a poem within the time required for taking seven steps
七拼八湊(ㄑㄧ ㄆㄧㄣ ㄅㄚ ㄘㄡˋ)
① to raise money from different sources (usually implies financial stringency) ② to cannibalize (said of machines when supply of spare parts has run out) ③ to piece together
七平八穩(ㄑㄧ ㄆㄧㄥˊ ㄅㄚ ㄨㄣˇ)
balanced; stable
七大八小(ㄑㄧ ㄉㄚˋ ㄅㄚ ㄒㄧㄠˇ)
objects of various sizes thrown together
七顛八倒(ㄑㄧ ㄉㄧㄢ ㄅㄚ ㄉㄠˇ)
topsy-turvy; in great confusion
七通八達(ㄑㄧ ㄊㄨㄥ ㄅㄚ ㄉㄚˊ)
very erudite; to know everything
七扭八歪(ㄑㄧ ㄋㄧㄡˇ ㄅㄚ ㄨㄞ)
(said of smashed or ruined objects) out of shape
七零八落(ㄑㄧ ㄌㄧㄥˊ ㄅㄚ ㄌㄨㄛˋ)
scattered here and there; in confusion
七律(ㄑㄧ ㄌㄩˋ)

a poem composed of eight seven-character lines with a strict tonal pattern and rhyme scheme

七高八低(ㄑㄧ ㄍㄠ ㄅㄚ ㄉㄧ)
bumpy (roads); rough (terrain)

七國(ㄑㄧ ㄍㄨㄛˊ)or 七雄(ㄑㄧ ㄒㄩㄥˊ)
the seven states—Chin(秦), Chu(楚), Yen(燕), Chao(趙), Han(韓), Wei(魏), Chi(齊)—in the Epoch of Warring States (403-221 B.C.)

七級浮屠(ㄑㄧ ㄐㄧˊ ㄈㄨˊ ㄊㄨˊ)
a seven-storied pagoda

七角形(ㄑㄧ ㄐㄧㄠˇ ㄒㄧㄥˊ)
a heptagon

七件事(ㄑㄧ ㄐㄧㄢˋ ㄕˋ)
the seven necessities—fuel, rice, oil, salt, soy sauce, vinegar and tea

七絕(ㄑㄧ ㄐㄩㄝˊ)
a verse of four lines with seven characters to a line

七七(ㄑㄧ ㄑㄧ)
the seven-week period after a person's death, during which funeral rites are observed

七七事變(ㄑㄧ ㄑㄧ ㄕˋ ㄅㄧㄢˋ)
the Marco Polo Bridge Incident (July 7, 1937), which triggered the War of Resistance Against Japanese Aggression (1937-1945)

七巧板(ㄑㄧ ㄑㄧㄠˇ ㄅㄢˇ)
the seven-pieced puzzle; a tangram; the magic square (The pieces are cut from a square and may be put together to form a large number of shapes and designs.)

七竅(ㄑㄧ ㄑㄧㄠˋ)
the seven apertures in the human head, i.e. eyes, ears, nostrils and mouth

七竅流血(ㄑㄧ ㄑㄧㄠˋ ㄌㄧㄡˊ ㄒㄧㄝˇ)
bleeding from the seven apertures on the head

七竅生煙(ㄑㄧ ㄑㄧㄠˋ ㄕㄥ ㄧㄢ)
(literally) Smoke belches out from the seven apertures on the head.—in a state of great fury

七擒七縱(ㄑㄧ ㄑㄧㄣˊ ㄑㄧ ㄗㄨㄥˋ)
to capture an enemy seven times and release him after each capture (with the intention to win his heart and submission forever)

七情六慾(ㄑㄧ ㄑㄧㄥˊ ㄌㄧㄡˋ ㄩˋ)
(Buddhism) the seven emotions—happiness (喜), anger (怒), sorrow (憂), fear (懼), love (愛), hate (憎), and desire (慾)—and the six sensory pleasures derived from the eyes, ears, nose, tongue, body and mind

七夕(ㄑㄧ ㄒㄧˋ)
the seventh night of the seventh lunar month when the legendary Cowherd and Weaving Maid meet each other for their once-a-year tryst over a bridge formed by sympathetic magpies over the Milky Way (The day is a festival for girls and young lovers.)

七絃琴(ㄑㄧ ㄒㄧㄢˊ ㄑㄧㄣˊ)
a seven-stringed Chinese musical instrument

七折八扣(ㄑㄧ ㄓㄜˊ ㄅㄚ ㄎㄡˋ)
① big discounts (in a bargain sale) ② to make allowance for inaccuracy, exaggeration, etc. in a statement or report

七尺之軀(ㄑㄧ ㄔˇ ㄓ ㄑㄩ)
men's average height (referring to a full-grown man); the human adult body

七長八短(ㄑㄧ ㄔㄤˊ ㄅㄚ ㄉㄨㄢˇ)
of various lengths

七穿八洞(ㄑㄧ ㄔㄨㄢ ㄅㄚ ㄉㄨㄥˋ)
full of holes; riddled with bullets

七重奏(ㄑㄧ ㄔㄨㄥˊ ㄗㄡˋ)
a septet

七十至七十九歲的人(ㄑㄧ ㄕˊ ㄓˋ ㄑㄧ ㄕˊ ㄐㄧㄡˇ ㄙㄨㄟˋ ˙ㄉㄜ ㄖㄣˊ)
a septuagenarian

七十二烈士(ㄑㄧ ㄕˊ ㄦˋ ㄌㄧㄝˋ ㄕˋ)
the 72 martyrs who sacrificed their lives in an abortive uprising against the Manchus which took place in Canton on March 29, 1911

七十二賢人(ㄑㄧ ㄕˊ ㄦˋ ㄒㄧㄢˊ ㄖㄣˊ)
the 72 most prominent scholars among the 3,000 students of Confucius

七手八脚(ㄑㄧ ㄕㄡˇ ㄅㄚ ㄐㄧㄠˇ)
many people doing something simultaneously in a disorganized manner 或 Too many cooks spoil the broth.

七上八下(ㄑㄧ ㄕㄤˋ ㄅㄚ ㄒㄧㄚˋ)
an unsettled state of mind

七聲(ㄑㄧ ㄕㄥ)or 七音(ㄑㄧ ㄧㄣ)
the seven-notes of the scale—five main notes (宮, 商, 角, 徵, 羽) and two modified notes (變徵 *fa* and 變宮 *si*)

七嘴八舌(ㄑㄧ ㄗㄨㄟˇ ㄅㄚ ㄕㄜˊ)
everybody talking at the same time: 老師離開後，大家就七嘴八舌談了起來。After the teacher left, everyone talked freely.

七死八活(ㄑㄧ ㄙˇ ㄅㄚ ㄏㄨㄛˊ)
on the verge of death (after hard work, severe beating, etc.)

七色(ㄑㄧ ㄙㄜˋ)
the seven colors of the spectrum

七言八語(ㄑㄧ ㄧㄢˊ ㄅㄚ ㄩˇ)
gossip; all sorts of opinions

七言詩(ㄑㄧ ㄧㄢˊ ㄕ)
verses with seven characters to a line

七月(ㄑㄧ ㄩㄝˋ)
① July ② the seventh month of the lunar year; the seventh moon

二畫

【丈】 4 ㄓㄤˋ janq zhàng

1. a unit in Chinese lineal measurement slightly longer than 10 feet
2. an elder; a senior
3. to measure; to survey

丈母娘(ㄓㄤˋ ˙ㄇㄨ ㄋㄧㄤˊ)
a mother-in-law

丈夫(ㄓㄤˋ ㄈㄨ)
① a husband ② a man

丈夫氣概(ㄓㄤˋ ㄈㄨ ㄑㄧˋ ㄍㄞˋ)
manly; manliness

丈量(ㄓㄤˋ ㄌㄧㄤˊ)
to measure; to survey

丈人(ㄓㄤˋ ˙ㄖㄣ)
a father-in-law

【三】 5 ㄙㄢ san sān

three; third; thrice: 孟子曰：「諸侯之寶三：土地、人民、政

事。」(孟子・盡心下) Mencius said, "The precious things of a prince are three:—the territory, the people, the government and its business."

三八節(ㄙㄢ ㄅㄚ ㄐㄧㄝˊ)
Women's Day on March the 8th

三八主義(ㄙㄢ ㄅㄚ ㄓㄨˇ ㄧˋ)
the three "8" system under which a 24-hour day is divided into 8 hours of work, 8 hours of recreation and 8 hours of sleep

三百六十行(ㄙㄢ ㄅㄞˇ ㄌㄧㄡˋ ㄕˊ ㄏㄤˊ)
all trades and professions

三胞胎(ㄙㄢ ㄅㄠ ㄊㄞ)
triplets

三寶(ㄙㄢ ㄅㄠˇ)
(Buddhism) Triratna—the triad of the Buddha, the dharma, and the sangha

三保太監(ㄙㄢ ㄅㄠˇ ㄊㄞˋ ㄐㄧㄢˋ)
Cheng Ho (鄭和), a powerful eunuch in the early Ming Dynasty, who led a large fleet to call at the various ports of the South China Sea and the ports on the eastern African coast during seven expeditions between 1405 and 1423

三不幸(ㄙㄢ ㄅㄨˋ ㄒㄧㄥˋ)
the three greatest misfortunes—death of one's father in youth, widowerhood in middle age, and to have no son in old age

三不管(ㄙㄢ ㄅㄨˋ ㄍㄨㄢˇ)
① referring to a lazy man who does not look after his own and his family's clothing, food and housing ② a district not within the jurisdiction of any of the neighboring magistrates

三不朽(ㄙㄢ ㄅㄨˋ ㄒㄧㄡˇ)
the three imperishable —one's virtue, achievements and teachings (立德, 立功, 立言)

三不知(ㄙㄢ ㄅㄨˋ ㄓ)
to be ignorant of the beginning, the middle, and the end of a matter; complete ignorance (sometimes pretended) 參看「一問三不知」

三部曲(ㄙㄢ ㄅㄨˋ ㄑㄩˇ)
a trilogy

三昧(ㄙㄢ ㄇㄟˋ)
① the key to a problem; the best method to do something (originally, in Buddhism, *samadhi* meaning "intent contemplation") ② a secret; a knack: 他深得其中三昧。He has mastered the secrets of the art.

三民主義(ㄙㄢ ㄇㄧㄣˊ ㄓㄨˇ ㄧˋ)
The Three Principles of the People—nationalism (民族), democracy (民權) and livelihood (民生)—by Dr. Sun Yat-sen, father of the Republic of China

三明治(ㄙㄢ ㄇㄧㄥˊ ㄓˋ)
a sandwich

三番五次(ㄙㄢ ㄈㄢ ㄨˇ ㄘˋ)or 三番兩次(ㄙㄢ ㄈㄢ ㄌㄧㄤˇ ㄘˋ)
time and again; over and over again; repeatedly: 我三番兩次告訴他不可這樣。I have told him over and over again not to do that.

三藩(ㄙㄢ ㄈㄢ)
the three princes—Wu San-kuei (吳三桂), Shang Ke-hsi (尙可喜) and Keng Chung-ming (耿仲明)—They were generals of the Ming Dynasty who surrendered to the Manchus when the latter invaded the Ming Empire. The Manchus rewarded them with the title of king for their surrender.

三藩市(ㄙㄢ ㄈㄢˊ ㄕˋ)
San Francisco

三分人材，七分打扮(ㄙㄢ ㄈㄣ ㄖㄣˊ ㄘㄞˊ, ㄑㄧ ㄈㄣ ㄉㄚˇ ㄅㄢˋ)
three-tenths natural figure and seven-tenths make-up

三分鼎足(ㄙㄢ ㄈㄣ ㄉㄧㄥˇ ㄗㄨˊ)
(said of warlords or rivaling princes) to hold the different parts of a country and vie for hegemony in a three-way tie

三伏天(ㄙㄢ ㄈㄨˊ ㄊㄧㄢ)
dog days

三復斯言(ㄙㄢ ㄈㄨˋ ㄙ ㄧㄢˊ)
to think over or ponder on my advice (an expression used in speaking to a junior)

三達德(ㄙㄢ ㄉㄚˊ ㄉㄜˊ)
the three virtues—wisdom, benevolence and courage (智, 仁, 勇)

三大發明(ㄙㄢ ㄉㄚˋ ㄈㄚ ㄇㄧㄥˊ)
the three major inventions by the Chinese—gunpowder, printing and compass

三大洋(ㄙㄢ ㄉㄚˋ ㄧㄤˊ)
the three big oceans—the Pacific Ocean, the Atlantic Ocean and the Indian Ocean

三代(ㄙㄢ ㄉㄞˋ)
① three generations ② the three ancient Chinese dynasties—Hsia, Shang and Chou

三代同堂(ㄙㄢ ㄉㄞˋ ㄊㄨㄥˊ ㄊㄤˊ)
three generations living under the same roof (under the big family system in old China)

三島(ㄙㄢ ㄉㄠˇ)
① the British Isles—England, Scotland and Ireland ② the three major islands of Japan—Honshu, Shikoku and Kyushu

三到(ㄙㄢ ㄉㄠˋ)
to use three organs—ears, eyes and mouth—simultaneously (in study)

三等(ㄙㄢ ㄉㄥˇ)
① three grades or classes ② the third grade; inferior

三點裝(ㄙㄢ ㄉㄧㄢˇ ㄓㄨㄤ)
a bikini suit

三點水(ㄙㄢ ㄉㄧㄢˇ ㄕㄨㄟˇ)
three points which make up the radical "氵" in Chinese characters

三讀(ㄙㄢ ㄉㄨˊ)
the third reading of a bill in a legislative session

三度空間(ㄙㄢ ㄉㄨˋ ㄎㄨㄥ ㄐㄧㄢ)
three-dimensional space: 直綫爲一度空間, 平面爲二度空間, 立體爲三度空間。A line has one dimension, a plane has two dimensions, and a cube has three dimensions.

三多(ㄙㄢ ㄉㄨㄛ)
three abundances—blessing, longevity and male offspring (多福, 多壽, 多男子)—which the people of old China considered the ingredients of a

〔一部〕

〔一部〕

happy life
三對六面(ㄙㄢ ㄉㄨㄟˋ ㄌㄧㄡˋ ㄇㄧㄢˋ)
All the interested parties are present.
三段論法(ㄙㄢ ㄉㄨㄢˋ ㄌㄨㄣˋ ㄈㄚˇ)
syllogism
三態(ㄙㄢ ㄊㄞˋ)
(physics) the three states of matter—solid, liquid and gas
三頭(ㄙㄢ ㄊㄡˊ)
(in phrases) three-headed
三頭馬車(ㄙㄢ ㄊㄡˊ ㄇㄚˇ ㄔㄜ)
a troika 亦作「三駕馬車」
三頭六臂(ㄙㄢ ㄊㄡˊ ㄌㄧㄡˋ ㄅㄟˋ)
a resourceful and capable man who, figuratively speaking, has three heads and six arms to use
三頭政治(ㄙㄢ ㄊㄡˊ ㄓㄥˋ ㄓˋ)
the triumvirate
三潭印月(ㄙㄢ ㄊㄢˊ ㄧㄣˋ ㄩㄝˋ)
a scenic attraction in the West Lake, Hangchow, where the moon leaves three images in the water
三歎(ㄙㄢ ㄊㄢˋ)
deep sighs and regrets (over an unhappy experience, a tragic accidents, etc.)
三天打魚，兩天曬網(ㄙㄢ ㄊㄧㄢ ㄉㄚˇ ㄩˊ, ㄌㄧㄤˇ ㄊㄧㄢ ㄕㄞˋ ㄨㄤˇ)
to go fishing for three days and dry the nets for two—(figuratively) to work off and on
三天兩頭兒(ㄙㄢ ㄊㄧㄢ ㄌㄧㄤˇ ㄊㄡˊㄦ)
frequently; every other day; almost every day
三年蓄艾(ㄙㄢ ㄋㄧㄢˊ ㄒㄩˋ ㄞˋ)
to make thorough preparations beforehand; to stockpile supplies or build up a manpower pool in anticipation of demand
三年有成(ㄙㄢ ㄋㄧㄢˊ ㄧㄡˇ ㄔㄥˊ)
Three years' hard work is crowned with success.
三年五載(ㄙㄢ ㄋㄧㄢˊ ㄨˇ ㄗㄞˇ)
three to five years
三聯單(ㄙㄢ ㄌㄧㄢˊ ㄉㄢ)
three-sectional tax forms, invoices, etc.; triplicate forms
三令五申(ㄙㄢ ㄌㄧㄥˋ ㄨˇ ㄕㄣ)
① to give repeated orders and injunctions ② repeated orders and injunctions

三輪車(ㄙㄢ ㄌㄨㄣˊ ㄔㄜ)or 三輪兒(ㄙㄢ ㄌㄨㄜˊㄦ)
a pedicab; a tricycle
三個臭皮匠，合成一個諸葛亮(ㄙㄢ ˙ㄍㄜ ㄔㄡˋ ㄆㄧˊ ㄐㄧㄤˋ, ㄏㄜˊ ㄔㄥˊ ㄧˊ ˙ㄍㄜ ㄓㄨ ㄍㄜˊ ㄌㄧㄤˋ)
Three cobblers with their wits combined are a match for Chu-Ko Liang the genius.—The wisdom of the masses exceeds that of the wisest individual. 亦作「三個臭皮匠，勝過諸葛亮」
三綱五常(ㄙㄢ ㄍㄤ ㄨˇ ㄔㄤˊ)
the three bonds in human relations (prince and minister, father and son, husband and wife) and the five constant virtues (father's righteousness, mother's benevolence, elder brother's love, younger brother's respect, and son's filial piety)
三更半夜(ㄙㄢ ㄍㄥ ㄅㄢˋ ㄧㄝˋ)
late at night (usually after midnight)
三姑六婆(ㄙㄢ ㄍㄨ ㄌㄧㄡˋ ㄆㄛˊ)
women whose professions are either illegitimate or disreputable such as 尼姑，道姑，卦姑，牙婆，媒婆，師婆，虔婆，藥婆，穩婆 (a reference to despicable women in general)
三顧茅廬(ㄙㄢ ㄍㄨˋ ㄇㄠˊ ㄌㄨˊ)
to make three calls at the thatched cottage—a historical allusion dating back to the Epoch of the Three Kingdoms, now used to describe a man in power who tries to obtain the service of the capable and the virtuous by showing his utmost sincerity and eagerness
三國(ㄙㄢ ㄍㄨㄛˊ)
the Three Kingdoms—Wei (魏), Shu (蜀) and Wu (吳)—which existed in China simultaneously from A.D. 222 to 265
三國志(ㄙㄢ ㄍㄨㄛˊ ㄓˋ)
The History of the Three Kingdoms by Chen Shou (陳壽)
三國演義(ㄙㄢ ㄍㄨㄛˊ ㄧㄢˇ ㄧˋ)
The Romance of the Three Kingdoms by Lo Kuan-chung (羅貫中), a very popular novel mixing facts with fiction about the Epoch of the Three Kingdoms
三跪九叩(ㄙㄢ ㄍㄨㄟˋ ㄐㄧㄡˇ ㄎㄡˋ)
to kneel three times with the head touching the ground nine times, an ancient ritual performed by a subject during an audience with the emperor
三光政策(ㄙㄢ ㄍㄨㄤ ㄓㄥˋ ㄘㄜˋ)
(said of invading troops) to kill all the civilians, to burn down all the houses, and to take away all that is movable — the policy once pursued by the Japanese invaders in China
三公(ㄙㄢ ㄍㄨㄥ)
the three highest-ranking officials in the imperial court of ancient China
三宮六苑(ㄙㄢ ㄍㄨㄥ ㄌㄧㄡˋ ㄩㄢˋ)
the emperor's harem
三K黨(ㄙㄢ ㄎㄟ ㄉㄤˇ)
the Ku Klux Klan
三合板(ㄙㄢ ㄏㄜˊ ㄅㄢˇ)
a three-ply board; plywood
三合土(ㄙㄢ ㄏㄜˊ ㄊㄨˇ)
mortar
三合會(ㄙㄢ ㄏㄜˊ ㄏㄨㄟˋ)
the Triad Society (a secret society during the Ching Dynasty dedicated to the overthrow of the Manchus and the restoration of the Ming Dynasty)
三呼萬歲(ㄙㄢ ㄏㄨ ㄨㄢˋ ㄙㄨㄟˋ)
to shout "Long Live the Emperor" three times
三花臉(ㄙㄢ ㄏㄨㄚ ㄌㄧㄢˇ)
a clown in Chinese opera
三皇五帝(ㄙㄢ ㄏㄨㄤˊ ㄨˇ ㄉㄧˋ)
the three sage kings and five virtuous emperors of China at the dawn of human civilization
三級跳遠(ㄙㄢ ㄐㄧˊ ㄊㄧㄠˋ ㄩㄢˇ)
hop, step (or skip), and jump
三家村(ㄙㄢ ㄐㄧㄚ ㄘㄨㄣ)
a small village
三街六巷(ㄙㄢ ㄐㄧㄝ ㄌㄧㄡˋ ㄒㄧㄤˋ)
the whole town or city
三節(ㄙㄢ ㄐㄧㄝˊ)
the three important festivals

of the year—端午節 the Dragon-Boat Festival, 5th of 5th lunar month, 中秋節 Mid-Autumn Festival, 15th of 8th lunar month, and 新年 the Lunar New Year

三角(ㄙㄢ ㄐㄧㄠˇ)
①trigonometry ②three angles

三角板(ㄙㄢ ㄐㄧㄠˇ ㄅㄢˇ)
a set square

三角貿易(ㄙㄢ ㄐㄧㄠˇ ㄇㄠˋ ㄧˋ)
triangular trade

三角鐵(ㄙㄢ ㄐㄧㄠˇ ㄊㄧㄝˇ)
(construction) angle iron

三角戀愛(ㄙㄢ ㄐㄧㄠˇ ㄌㄧㄢˋ ㄞˋ)
a love triangle

三角褲(ㄙㄢ ㄐㄧㄠˇ ㄎㄨˋ)
panties; briefs

三角函數(ㄙㄢ ㄐㄧㄠˇ ㄏㄢˊ ㄕㄨˋ)
trigonometric function

三角形(ㄙㄢ ㄐㄧㄠˇ ㄒㄧㄥˊ)
a triangle

三角洲(ㄙㄢ ㄐㄧㄠˇ ㄓㄡ)
a delta

三脚貓(ㄙㄢ ㄐㄧㄠˇ ㄇㄠ)
a person who can do many odd things but specializes in nothing

三脚架(ㄙㄢ ㄐㄧㄠˇ ㄐㄧㄚˋ)
a tripod

三教(ㄙㄢ ㄐㄧㄠˋ)
Confucianism, Taoism and Buddhism

三教九流(ㄙㄢ ㄐㄧㄠˋ ㄐㄧㄡˇ ㄌㄧㄡˊ)
(literally) the three religions (Confucianism, Buddhism and Taoism) and the nine schools (Confucianist, Taoist, Astrologist, Legalist, Nominalist, Mohist, Diplomatist, Miscellanist and Agriculturist)—people of all walks of life

三緘其口(ㄙㄢ ㄐㄧㄢ ㄑㄧˊ ㄎㄡˇ)
to remain silent; to be very reluctant to make comments or voice one's opinions: 你最好三緘其口。You had better be silent.

三晉(ㄙㄢ ㄐㄧㄣˋ)
the states of Han (韓), Wei (魏), and Chao (趙) during the Epoch of Warring States, which constituted the state of Tsin in the preceding Spring and Autumn era

三句不離本行(ㄙㄢ ㄐㄩˋ ㄅㄨˋ ㄌㄧˊ ㄅㄣˇ ㄏㄤˊ)
to talk shop frequently when conversing with people outside one's own profession

三軍(ㄙㄢ ㄐㄩㄣ)
the three armies; the armed forces

三七二十一(ㄙㄢ ㄑㄧ ㄦˋ ㄕˊ ㄧ)
① Three sevens are twenty-one. ②the true story of a matter or happening

三七五減租(ㄙㄢ ㄑㄧ ㄨˇ ㄐㄧㄢˇ ㄗㄨ)
the 37.5% rental reduction policy, the first step taken in Taiwan's land reform program in 1949, under which the ceiling of farm rental was fixed at 37.5% of the crop yield

三秋(ㄙㄢ ㄑㄧㄡ)
① three falls—three years ② the three months of autumn

三缺一(ㄙㄢ ㄑㄩㄝ ㄧ)
(mah-jong) one more player still needed

三拳不敵四手(ㄙㄢ ㄑㄩㄢˊ ㄅㄨˋ ㄉㄧˊ ㄙˋ ㄕㄡˇ)
(literally) Three fists are no match for four hands.—outnumbered

三權分立(ㄙㄢ ㄑㄩㄢˊ ㄈㄣ ㄌㄧˋ)
separation of the legislative, executive and judicial functions of a government

三峽(ㄙㄢ ㄒㄧㄚˊ)
the Three Gorges of the Yangtze River on the border of Szechwan and Hupei

三鮮(ㄙㄢ ㄒㄧㄢ)
a Chinese dish composed of any three kinds of fresh delicacies

三絃(ㄙㄢ ㄒㄧㄢˊ)
a Chinese musical instrument with three strings played by fingers

三心二意(ㄙㄢ ㄒㄧㄣ ㄦˋ ㄧˋ)
① hesitating; irresolute; vacillating ② halfhearted

三薰三沐(ㄙㄢ ㄒㄩㄣ ㄙㄢ ㄇㄨˋ)
to show the highest respect to someone

三隻手(ㄙㄢ ㄓ ㄕㄡˇ)
a pickpocket

三朝(ㄙㄢ ㄓㄠ)
① the third day of baby's birth ② a bride's homecoming on the third day after matrimony

三戰兩勝(ㄙㄢ ㄓㄢˋ ㄌㄧㄤˇ ㄕㄥˋ)
the best of three games

三振(ㄙㄢ ㄓㄣˋ)or 三振出局(ㄙㄢ ㄓㄣˋ ㄔㄨ ㄐㄩˊ)
to strike out; a strikeout

三徵七辟(ㄙㄢ ㄓㄥ ㄑㄧ ㄅㄧˋ)
(said of emperors in ancient China) to issue repeated invitations to the virtuous and capable for public service

三尺童子(ㄙㄢ ㄔˇ ㄊㄨㄥˊ ㄗˇ)
a lad

三叉路口(ㄙㄢ ㄔㄚ ㄌㄨˋ ㄎㄡˇ)
a junction where three roads meet

三朝元老(ㄙㄢ ㄔㄠˊ ㄩㄢˊ ㄌㄠˇ)
① a veteran statesman who had served under three emperors in a row ②(in modern usage) the most senior employee in a government organization

三長兩短(ㄙㄢ ㄔㄤˊ ㄌㄧㄤˇ ㄉㄨㄢˇ)
unforeseen disasters or accidents (usually referring to death): 萬一他有個三長兩短，那我們怎麼辦呢? If an unforeseen accident should happen to him, what should we do?

三十六行(ㄙㄢ ㄕˊ ㄌㄧㄡˋ ㄏㄤˊ)
all trades and professions

三十六計，走爲上計(ㄙㄢ ㄕˊ ㄌㄧㄡˋ ㄐㄧˋ，ㄗㄡˇ ㄨㄟˊ ㄕㄤˋ ㄐㄧˋ)
Of the thirty-six stratagems, the best one is to go away. —The best thing to do now is to go away. 亦作「三十六策，走爲上策」

三十六著(ㄙㄢ ㄕˊ ㄌㄧㄡˋ ㄓㄠ)or 三十六計(ㄙㄢ ㄕˊ ㄌㄧㄡˋ ㄐㄧˋ)or 三十六策(ㄙㄢ ㄕˊ ㄌㄧㄡˋ ㄘㄜˋ)
all the possible schemes or stratagems

三十而立(ㄙㄢ ㄕˊ ㄦˊ ㄌㄧˋ)
thirty years of age when a man should stand on his own feet

三十二開(ㄙㄢ ㄕˊ ㄦˋ ㄎㄞ)
thirty-two-mo; 32-mo

三牲(ㄙㄢ ㄕㄥ)
three sacrificial offerings —ox, sheep and hog—used

in worship

三生有幸(ㄙㄢ ㄕㄥ ㄧㄡˇ ㄒㄧㄥˋ)
the greatest fortune in three incarnations (to make friends with worthy persons or to marry a virtuous and beautiful wife, etc.); lucky indeed

三人行必有我師(ㄙㄢ ㄖㄣˊ ㄒㄧㄥˊ ㄅㄧˋ ㄧㄡˇ ㄨㄛˇ ㄕ)
If three of us are walking together, at least one of the other two is good enough to be my teacher. (an expression to show one's open-mindedness)

三人成虎(ㄙㄢ ㄖㄣˊ ㄔㄥˊ ㄏㄨˇ)
A lie, if repeated often enough, will be accepted as truth.

三字經(ㄙㄢ ㄗˋ ㄐㄧㄥ)
① the *Three-Character Classic* or the *Trimetrical Classic,* formerly the first primer in schools ② a four-letter word; an expletive

三災八難(ㄙㄢ ㄗㄞ ㄅㄚ ㄋㄢˋ)
(said of children) to suffer from one ailment after another

三族(ㄙㄢ ㄗㄨˊ)
① parents, brothers, and wife and children ② relatives of father, of mother and of wife ③ three generations of grandfather, father and son ④ paternal uncles, brothers, and sons

三次方程式(ㄙㄢ ㄘˋ ㄈㄤ ㄔㄥˊ ㄕˋ)
an equation of the third degree or a cubic equation

三才(ㄙㄢ ㄘㄞˊ)
the three powers—heaven, earth and man

三餐(ㄙㄢ ㄘㄢ)
three meals—breakfast, lunch and supper

三寸丁(ㄙㄢ ㄘㄨㄣˋ ㄉㄧㄥ)
a very small short person

三寸金蓮(ㄙㄢ ㄘㄨㄣˋ ㄐㄧㄣ ㄌㄧㄢˊ)
three-inch golden lilies (women's feet deformed by foot-binding, which were considered beautiful in ancient China)

三寸之舌(ㄙㄢ ㄘㄨㄣˋ ㄓ ㄕㄜˊ)
the three-inch tongue (said of a persuasive person who can talk others into doing something, about which the listener at first holds reservations)

三從四德(ㄙㄢ ㄘㄨㄥˊ ㄙˋ ㄉㄜˊ)
three obediences and four virtues of women 〔In ancient China a woman was required to obey her father before marriage, her husband during married life, and her sons in widowhood. (在家從父，出嫁從夫，夫死從子) The four virtues are fidelity, physical charm, propriety in speech and efficiency in needlework. (婦德，婦容，婦言，婦工)〕

三思而後行(ㄙㄢ ㄙ ㄦˊ ㄏㄡˋ ㄒㄧㄥˊ)
Think thrice before you act. 或 Look before you leap.

三色(ㄙㄢ ㄙㄜˋ)
the three basic colors—yellow, blue and red

三色版(ㄙㄢ ㄙㄜˋ ㄅㄢˇ)
(printing) a three-color halftone

三色紫羅蘭(ㄙㄢ ㄙㄜˋ ㄗˇ ㄌㄨㄛˊ ㄌㄢˊ)
pansy 亦作「三色菫」

三三兩兩(ㄙㄢ ㄙㄢ ㄌㄧㄤˇ ㄌㄧㄤˇ)
by twos and threes; in twos and threes

三三制(ㄙㄢ ㄙㄢ ㄓˋ)
the education system which prescribes three years for junior high school and three years for senior high school

三三五五(ㄙㄢ ㄙㄢ ㄨˇ ㄨˇ)
small groups of people scattered here and there

三言兩語(ㄙㄢ ㄧㄢˊ ㄌㄧㄤˇ ㄩˇ)
a brief talk, discussion, conversation, description, etc.

三陽開泰(ㄙㄢ ㄧㄤˊ ㄎㄞ ㄊㄞˋ)
a surge of good luck

三五成羣(ㄙㄢ ㄨˇ ㄔㄥˊ ㄑㄩㄣˊ)
in groups of three or five

三圍(ㄙㄢ ㄨㄟˊ)
the vital statistics, or the three measurements, of a woman

三位一體(ㄙㄢ ㄨㄟˋ ㄧˋ ㄊㄧˇ)
the Trinity; three-in-one

三溫暖(ㄙㄢ ㄨㄣ ㄋㄨㄢˇ)
sauna bath 亦作「蒸氣浴」

三月(ㄙㄢ ㄩㄝˋ)
① March ② the third moon of the lunar calendar ③ three months

【上】 6
1. ㄕㄤˋ shanq shàng

1. above
2. upper; upward; up
3. better; superior
4. previous; before
5. top; summit; on
6. to ascend; to mount; to board
7. to go to court

上輩(ㄕㄤˋ ㄅㄟˋ)or 上輩兒(ㄕㄤˋ ㄅㄜˋㄦ)
the earlier generation; one's seniors

上報(ㄕㄤˋ ㄅㄠˋ)
① to be published in newspapers ② to report to a higher body; to report to one's boss

上班(ㄕㄤˋ ㄅㄢ)or 上班兒(ㄕㄤˋ ㄅㄚㄦ)
to go to office; to go on duty

上半天(ㄕㄤˋ ㄅㄢˋ ㄊㄧㄢ)or 上半天兒(ㄕㄤˋ ㄅㄢˋ ㄊㄧㄚㄦ)
the morning; the forenoon

上半場(ㄕㄤˋ ㄅㄢˋ ㄔㄤˇ)
first half (of a game): 上半場比賽哪一隊贏? Which team won at the first half of the game?

上半身(ㄕㄤˋ ㄅㄢˋ ㄕㄣ)
the upper part of the body; above the waist

上半夜(ㄕㄤˋ ㄅㄢˋ ㄧㄝˋ)
before midnight; the first half of the night

上半月(ㄕㄤˋ ㄅㄢˋ ㄩㄝˋ)
the first half of a month

上榜(ㄕㄤˋ ㄅㄤˇ)
to have one's name included in the name list of successful candidates of an examination

上幣(ㄕㄤˋ ㄅㄧˋ)
gold and jade as currency

上臂(ㄕㄤˋ ㄅㄧˋ)
the upper arm

上邊(ㄕㄤˋ ㄅㄧㄢ)
① the upper side ② up there

上賓(ㄕㄤˋ ㄅㄧㄣ)
distinguished guests

上不去(ㄕㄤˋ ㄅㄨˋ ㄑㄩˋ)
cannot ascend it; cannot go up

上不上(ㄕㄤˋ ㄅㄨˋ ㄕㄤˋ)
(said of tools, instruments, etc.) cannot fix it
上不來(ㄕㄤˋ ㄅㄨˋ ㄌㄞˊ)
cannot come up
上部(ㄕㄤˋ ㄅㄨˋ)
① the upper portion; the first part ② the first volume (of a two-volume book)
上坡(ㄕㄤˋ ㄆㄛ)
to climb a slope
上坡路(ㄕㄤˋ ㄆㄛ ㄌㄨˋ)
an ascending road or path; an uphill road; an upward slope
上片(ㄕㄤˋ ㄆㄧㄢ)
to start showing a movie (in a movie theater)
上品(ㄕㄤˋ ㄆㄧㄣˇ)
goods of superior quality
上鋪(ㄕㄤˋ ㄆㄨˋ)
the upper berth
上馬(ㄕㄤˋ ㄇㄚˇ)
to mount a horse
上門(ㄕㄤˋ ㄇㄣˊ)or 上門兒(ㄕㄤˋ ㄇㄜˊㄦ)
to visit; to call
上面(ㄕㄤˋ ·ㄇㄧㄢ)or 上面兒(ㄕㄤˋ ·ㄇㄧㄚㄦ)
① the upper surface; the top; above ② the higher authorities ③ aspect; respect
上發條(ㄕㄤˋ ㄈㄚ ㄊㄧㄠˊ)
to wind a watch, clock, mechanical toy, etc.
上墳(ㄕㄤˋ ㄈㄣˊ)
to visit somebody's grave
上方(ㄕㄤˋ ㄈㄤ)
① the place above ② the celestial realm
上房(ㄕㄤˋ ㄈㄤˊ)
① the position of a lawfully wedded wife—in contrast to the position of the concubines ② main rooms (usually facing south, within a courtyard)
上風(ㄕㄤˋ ㄈㄥ)
① the upper hand; advantage ② windward
上峯(ㄕㄤˋ ㄈㄥ)
the upper echelon; the higher-up
上伏塔(ㄕㄤˋ ㄈㄨˊ ㄊㄚˇ)
Upper Volta
上達(ㄕㄤˋ ㄉㄚˊ)
to reach the higher authorities
上德(ㄕㄤˋ ㄉㄜˊ)
the highest virtue
上代(ㄕㄤˋ ㄉㄞˋ)
the previous generation
上當(ㄕㄤˋ ㄉㄤˋ)
to be taken in; to be a fool; to be fooled: 同這種人打交道，你會上當。Dealing with such a person, you will be taken in.
上燈(ㄕㄤˋ ㄉㄥ)
to light the lamp; to light up
上等(ㄕㄤˋ ㄉㄥˇ)
first-class; superior quality
上等兵(ㄕㄤˋ ㄉㄥˇ ㄅㄧㄥ)
private first class (PFC)
上帝(ㄕㄤˋ ㄉㄧˋ)
God: 願上帝幫助你。God help you!
上弔 or 上吊(ㄕㄤˋ ㄉㄧㄠˋ)
to commit suicide by hanging; to hang oneself
上端(ㄕㄤˋ ㄉㄨㄢ)
the upper end
上臺(ㄕㄤˋ ㄊㄞˊ)
① to go on the stage ②(said of high-ranking officials) to assume office
上套兒(ㄕㄤˋ ㄊㄠˋㄦ)
① to put the bit on a horse ② to be imposed upon
上頭(ㄕㄤˋ ·ㄊㄡ)
① the top; above; up ② the authorities
上膛(ㄕㄤˋ ㄊㄤˊ)
(said of a gun) to be loaded: 子彈上膛了。The gun is loaded.
上天(ㄕㄤˋ ㄊㄧㄢ)
① Heaven; Providence; God ② to go up to the sky
上天下地(ㄕㄤˋ ㄊㄧㄢ ㄒㄧㄚˋ ㄉㄧˋ)
(literally) to ascend the heaven or to descend to earth—① everywhere ② to leave no stone unturned; to spare no efforts
上天無路入地無門(ㄕㄤˋ ㄊㄧㄢ ㄨˊ ㄌㄨˋ ㄖㄨˋ ㄉㄧˋ ㄨˊ ㄇㄣˊ)
There is no road to heaven and no door into the earth. —(figuratively) no way of escape; at the end of the rope; in a desperate situation; at the end of the line; at the end of the road
上哪兒去?(ㄕㄤˋ ㄋㄚˇㄦ ㄑㄩˋ)
Where to go? 或 Where are you going?
上年(ㄕㄤˋ ㄋㄧㄢˊ)
last year
上年紀(ㄕㄤˋ ㄋㄧㄢˊ ·ㄐㄧ)or 上了年紀(ㄕㄤˋ ·ㄌㄜ ㄋㄧㄢˊ ·ㄐㄧ)
getting on in years; getting along in years
上蠟(ㄕㄤˋ ㄌㄚˋ)
(textile and dyeing) waxing
上來(ㄕㄤˋ ·ㄌㄞ)
Come up! 或 Come out!
上壘(ㄕㄤˋ ㄌㄟˇ)
(baseball) to touch the base
上樓(ㄕㄤˋ ㄌㄡˊ)
to go upstairs
上列(ㄕㄤˋ ㄌㄧㄝˋ)
the above-listed; the above-mentioned
上流(ㄕㄤˋ ㄌㄧㄡˊ)
① the upper part of a stream ② belonging to the upper circles
上流社會(ㄕㄤˋ ㄌㄧㄡˊ ㄕㄜˋ ㄏㄨㄟˋ)
the upper class; the high society
上聯(ㄕㄤˋ ㄌㄧㄢˊ)
the first line of a couplet on a scroll
上梁(ㄕㄤˋ ㄌㄧㄤˊ)
(said of buildings) the main beam
上梁不正下梁歪(ㄕㄤˋ ㄌㄧㄤˊ ㄅㄨˋ ㄓㄥˋ ㄒㄧㄚˋ ㄌㄧㄤˊ ㄨㄞ)
When the higher-ups (or parents) do not set a good example, the subordinates (or children) cannot be expected to behave well.
上路(ㄕㄤˋ ㄌㄨˋ)
① to start a journey ② (slang) good; well-behaved
上略(ㄕㄤˋ ㄌㄩㄝˋ)
the above or preceding part omitted
上鉤(ㄕㄤˋ ㄍㄡ)
①(fishing) to be caught by the hook ② to fall into the snare; to be tricked into doing something
上古(ㄕㄤˋ ㄍㄨˇ)
prehistoric times; ancient times
上軌道(ㄕㄤˋ ㄍㄨㄟˇ ㄉㄠˋ)

〔一部〕

〔一部〕

to get on the right track—to begin to work smoothly: 我們的工作已上軌道。Our work goes on smoothly.

上官(ㄕㄤˋ ㄍㄨㄢ)
①one's direct superior in office ② a compound surname

上工(ㄕㄤˋ ㄍㄨㄥ)
to begin work

上供(ㄕㄤˋ ㄍㄨㄥˋ)
①to offer sacrifices in worship ② taxes which went directly to the imperial treasury in the Tang Dynasty

上客(ㄕㄤˋ ㄎㄜˋ)
distinguished or esteemed guests

上課(ㄕㄤˋ ㄎㄜˋ)
(said of students) to attend class; (said of teachers) to conduct class

上口(ㄕㄤˋ ㄎㄡˇ)
easy to speak or read; euphonious

上款(ㄕㄤˋ ㄎㄨㄢˇ)
the address of the recipient, including his given name and position, etc., of a painting or calligraphic work

上空(ㄕㄤˋ ㄎㄨㄥ)
in the sky; overhead

上空裝(ㄕㄤˋ ㄎㄨㄥ ㄓㄨㄤ)
a topless suit

上海(ㄕㄤˋ ㄏㄞˇ)
Shanghai

上好(ㄕㄤˋ ㄏㄠˇ)
superior; excellent; the best

上戶(ㄕㄤˋ ㄏㄨˋ)
a wealthy family

上火(ㄕㄤˋ ㄏㄨㄛˇ)
①(dialect) to get angry ② (Chinese medicine) to suffer from too much internal heat (with such symptoms as constipation, conjunctivitis and inflammation of the nasal and oral cavities)

上貨(ㄕㄤˋ ㄏㄨㄛˋ)
to load (ships, trucks, etc.)

上回(ㄕㄤˋ ㄏㄨㄟˊ)
on a previous occasion; last time

上會(ㄕㄤˋ ㄏㄨㄟˋ)
to attend a temporary association for mutual loan money, decided monthly by the highest bidder for interest, or by dice

上級(ㄕㄤˋ ㄐㄧˊ)
higher-ups; superiors

上計(ㄕㄤˋ ㄐㄧˋ)
the best plan

上街(ㄕㄤˋ ㄐㄧㄝ)
①to go into (or on) the street ②to go shopping

上屆(ㄕㄤˋ ㄐㄧㄝˋ)
the previous (election, congress, conference, tour of duty, etc.)

上界(ㄕㄤˋ ㄐㄧㄝˋ)
heaven

上繳(ㄕㄤˋ ㄐㄧㄠˇ)
to transfer (revenues, etc.) to the higher authorities

上進(ㄕㄤˋ ㄐㄧㄣˋ)
to make progress; to advance

上勁(ㄕㄤˋ ㄐㄧㄣˋ)
energetically; with gusto; with great vigor: 他工作比別人更上勁。He works more energetically than others.

上江(ㄕㄤˋ ㄐㄧㄤ)
the upper Yangtze

上漿(ㄕㄤˋ ㄐㄧㄤ)
to starch (the laundry, etc.); (textile and dyeing) to size; sizing

上將(ㄕㄤˋ ㄐㄧㄤˋ)
(army, marine, and air force) full general; (navy) full admiral

上鏡頭(ㄕㄤˋ ㄐㄧㄥˋ ㄊㄡˊ)
① photogenic ② to appear in a movie

上氣不接下氣(ㄕㄤˋ ㄑㄧˋ ㄅㄨˋ ㄐㄧㄝ ㄒㄧㄚˋ ㄑㄧˋ)
to be out of breath: 他跑得太快，因而上氣不接下氣。He ran so fast that he was out of breath.

上前(ㄕㄤˋ ㄑㄧㄢˊ)
to come forward

上去(ㄕㄤˋ ·ㄑㄩ)
to go up; to ascend

上下(ㄕㄤˋ ㄒㄧㄚˋ)
①above and below; up and down ②superior and inferior; ruler and subjects; senior and junior; high and low ③about; more or less ④heaven and earth ⑤to go up and come down: 山上修了公路，我們上下很方便。With the completion of the freeway up the mountain, we can easily go up and come down.

上下交征利(ㄕㄤˋ ㄒㄧㄚˋ ㄐㄧㄠ ㄓㄥ ㄌㄧˋ)
Everybody (in a country) is greedy.

上下其手(ㄕㄤˋ ㄒㄧㄚˋ ㄑㄧˊ ㄕㄡˇ)
to distort facts to suit one's private ends

上下四方(ㄕㄤˋ ㄒㄧㄚˋ ㄙˋ ㄈㄤ)
in all directions

上下一心(ㄕㄤˋ ㄒㄧㄚˋ ㄧˋ ㄒㄧㄣ)
of one heart and mind 或 The leadership and the rank and file are of one heart and mind. 亦作「上下一條心」

上下文(ㄕㄤˋ ㄒㄧㄚˋ ㄨㄣˊ)
the context

上校(ㄕㄤˋ ㄒㄧㄠˋ)
(army, marine, and air force) colonel; (navy) captain

上弦(ㄕㄤˋ ㄒㄧㄢˊ)
the first quarter of the moon

上限(ㄕㄤˋ ㄒㄧㄢˋ)
the upper limit

上香(ㄕㄤˋ ㄒㄧㄤ)
to offer incense (to ancestors, Buddhist deities or Taoist deities)

上詳(ㄕㄤˋ ㄒㄧㄤˊ)
to report to a superior

上像(ㄕㄤˋ ㄒㄧㄤˋ)
to come out well in a photograph; to be photogenic 參看「上鏡頭」

上刑(ㄕㄤˋ ㄒㄧㄥˊ)
to apply the third degree; to torture

上行(ㄕㄤˋ ㄒㄧㄥˊ)
to go up to the north

上行下效(ㄕㄤˋ ㄒㄧㄥˊ ㄒㄧㄚˋ ㄒㄧㄠˋ)
The doings of superiors are imitated by inferiors. 或 The subordinates will follow the example set by their superiors.

上行車(ㄕㄤˋ ㄒㄧㄥˊ ㄔㄜ)
the up train

上學(ㄕㄤˋ ㄒㄩㄝˊ)
to go to school

上選(ㄕㄤˋ ㄒㄩㄢˇ)
the choicest

上旬(ㄕㄤˋ ㄒㄩㄣˊ)

the first ten days of a month

上肢(ㄕㄤˋ ㄓ)
the upper limbs

上智 or 上知(ㄕㄤˋ ㄓˋ)
the sage; the wisest; the most intelligent

上週(ㄕㄤˋ ㄓㄡ)or 上禮拜(ㄕㄤˋ ㄌㄧˇ ㄅㄞˋ)or 上星期(ㄕㄤˋ ㄒㄧㄥ ㄑㄧˊ)
last week

上陣(ㄕㄤˋ ㄓㄣˋ)
① to pitch into the work ② to go to battle

上漲(ㄕㄤˋ ㄓㄤˇ)
(said of commodity prices or flood waters) to rise: 物價上漲。The prices are going up.

上賬 or 上帳(ㄕㄤˋ ㄓㄤˋ)
to put a purchase on credit; to make an entry in an account book

上裝(ㄕㄤˋ ㄓㄨㄤ)
to make up (for a theatrical performance); to dress up (as an actor or a bride)

上車(ㄕㄤˋ ㄔㄜ)
to get on or into (a car, truck, bus or train)

上朝(ㄕㄤˋ ㄔㄠˊ)
to go to the imperial court

上場(ㄕㄤˋ ㄔㄤˊ)or(ㄕㄤˋ ㄔㄤˇ)
①(drama) to go on stage; to enter ②(sports) to enter the court or field

上船(ㄕㄤˋ ㄔㄨㄢˊ)
to board a ship; to embark

上床(ㄕㄤˋ ㄔㄨㄤˊ)
to go to bed

上士(ㄕㄤˋ ㄕˋ)
(military rank) first sergeant

上市(ㄕㄤˋ ㄕˋ)
(said of seasonal goods or new products) to go on the market

上世(ㄕㄤˋ ㄕˋ)
the primeval times; the prehistoric times

上首(ㄕㄤˋ ㄕㄡˇ)
① the honored one ② the seat of honor 亦作「上座」

上壽(ㄕㄤˋ ㄕㄡˋ)
① advanced age ② to drink a toast for longevity

上山(ㄕㄤˋ ㄕㄢ)
to go up a hill; to go to the mountains

上身(ㄕㄤˋ ㄕㄣ)or 上身兒(ㄕㄤˋ ㄕㄜㄦ)
① the torso; the upper part of the body ② an upper outer garment; a blouse; a jacket ③ to wear ④ to contract a disease; to incur some misfortune

上上(ㄕㄤˋ ㄕㄤˋ)
the very best

上上大吉(ㄕㄤˋ ㄕㄤˋ ㄉㄚˋ ㄐㄧˊ)
most auspicious (a phrase usually used in divination)

上上下下(ㄕㄤˋ ㄕㄤˋ ㄒㄧㄚˋ ㄒㄧㄚˋ)
① above and below; up and down ② all; the whole

上升 or 上昇(ㄕㄤˋ ㄕㄥ)
to soar or rise

上乘(ㄕㄤˋ ㄕㄥˋ)
① a carriage drawn by a team of four horses ②(Buddhism) the Great Conveyance ③ the best in quality

上書(ㄕㄤˋ ㄕㄨ)
to present a petition; to make a presentation in writing

上述(ㄕㄤˋ ㄕㄨˋ)
the aforesaid or aforementioned; what has been mentioned before

上疏(ㄕㄤˋ ㄕㄨˋ)
to submit an appeal or a memorial to the emperor

上水(ㄕㄤˋ ㄕㄨㄟˇ)
① to add water (to a kettle) ② to sail against the current ③ to feed water to a stream engine, radiator (of an automobile) ④ to sprinkle water on vegetables or fruit

上稅(ㄕㄤˋ ㄕㄨㄟˋ)
to levy taxes or duties

上日(ㄕㄤˋ ㄖˋ)
① the first day of the lunar month ② a beautiful or festive day

上人(ㄕㄤˋ ㄖㄣˊ)
(a courteous address) a monk

上任(ㄕㄤˋ ㄖㄣˋ)
to take up an official appointment; to enter upon office

上祖(ㄕㄤˋ ㄗㄨˇ)
remote ancestors

上座(ㄕㄤˋ ㄗㄨㄛˋ)or 上座兒(ㄕㄤˋ ㄗㄨㄜˋㄦ)
the seat at the head of the table reserved for the guest of honor; the seat of honor

上次(ㄕㄤˋ ㄘˋ)
last time; the previous occasion

上策(ㄕㄤˋ ㄘㄜˋ)
the best stratagem; the best plan; the best way

上菜(ㄕㄤˋ ㄘㄞˋ)
① the best dishes ② to place dishes on the table

上操(ㄕㄤˋ ㄘㄠ)
to drill; to do physical exercises

上蒼(ㄕㄤˋ ㄘㄤ)
Heaven; God

上層(ㄕㄤˋ ㄘㄥˊ)
the upper layer, level or stratum

上竄下跳(ㄕㄤˋ ㄘㄨㄢˋ ㄒㄧㄚˋ ㄊㄧㄠˋ)
to run around on sinister errands

上司(ㄕㄤˋ ㄙ)
a boss; a superior official

上駟(ㄕㄤˋ ㄙˋ)
a thoroughbred horse

上色(ㄕㄤˋ ㄙㄜˋ)
① best-quality; top-grade ② to color (a picture, map, etc.)

上訴(ㄕㄤˋ ㄙㄨˋ)
① to appeal to a higher court ② to state one's case to a superior

上鎖(ㄕㄤˋ ㄙㄨㄛˇ)
to lock

上歲數(ㄕㄤˋ ㄙㄨㄟˋ ㄕㄨˋ)
to be getting on in years

上算(ㄕㄤˋ ㄙㄨㄢˋ)
a profitable deal; economical

上顎(ㄕㄤˋ ㄜˋ)
the palate

上衣(ㄕㄤˋ ㄧ)
upper garments; jackets

上議院(ㄕㄤˋ ㄧˋ ㄩㄢˋ)
the Upper House; the Senate

上油(ㄕㄤˋ ㄧㄡˊ)
to apply lubricant; to replenish lubricating oil

上游(ㄕㄤˋ ㄧㄡˊ)
① the upper reaches (of a river) ② advanced position: 他力爭上游。He strived for

〔一部〕

the best.

上言(ㄕㄤˋ ㄧㄢˊ)
to submit (request, etc.) respectfully

上眼(ㄕㄤˋ ㄧㄢˇ)
to be worth looking at

上演(ㄕㄤˋ ㄧㄢˇ)
to perform; to stage (a play)

上癮(ㄕㄤˋ ㄧㄣˇ)
to become addicted to a certain drug or habit; habit-forming 這種藥吃多了會上癮。This medicine is habit-forming.

上映(ㄕㄤˋ ㄧㄥˋ)
to show (a movie)

上午(ㄕㄤˋ ㄨˇ)
forenoon; A.M.

上位(ㄕㄤˋ ㄨㄟˋ)
① a top seat ② a person occupying a leading position

上尉(ㄕㄤˋ ㄨㄟˋ)
(navy) lieutenant; (army, marine and air force) captain

上文(ㄕㄤˋ ㄨㄣˊ)
the foregoing paragraphs or chapters; preceding part of the text; the preceding context

上愚(ㄕㄤˋ ㄩˊ)
the most stupid

上諭(ㄕㄤˋ ㄩˋ)
an imperial edict

上月(ㄕㄤˋ ㄩㄝˋ)or 上個月(ㄕㄤˋ ·ㄍㄜ ㄩㄝˋ)
last month

上元(ㄕㄤˋ ㄩㄢˊ)
the fifteenth of the first lunar month (which is the Lantern Festival in China)

上苑(ㄕㄤˋ ㄩㄢˋ)
the royal garden

【上】 6
2. ㄕㄤˇ shaang shǎng

上聲(ㄕㄤˇ ㄕㄥ)
falling-rising tone, one of the four tones in classical Chinese and the third tone in modern standard Chinese phonetics

【下】 7
ㄒㄧㄚˋ shiah xià

1. to put down
2. to lay
3. to fall
4. to descend
5. to begin
6. below; under: 現在溫度在冰點以下。The temperature is now below freezing point.
7. inferior; lower
8. next

下巴(ㄒㄧㄚˋ ㄅㄚ)or 下巴頦(ㄒㄧㄚˋ ·ㄅㄚ ㄎㄜ)or 下巴頦兒(ㄒㄧㄚˋ ·ㄅㄚ ㄎㄜㄦ)
the chin; the lower jaw

下膊(ㄒㄧㄚˋ ㄅㄛˊ)
the lower arm

下擺(ㄒㄧㄚˋ ㄅㄞˇ)
the lower part of a Chinese gown

下拜(ㄒㄧㄚˋ ㄅㄞˋ)
to bow

下輩(ㄒㄧㄚˋ ㄅㄟˋ)or 下輩兒(ㄒㄧㄚˋ ㄅㄟˋㄦ)
the next generation; the younger generation of a family

下輩子(ㄒㄧㄚˋ ㄅㄟˋ ·ㄗ)
the next life; the next incarnation

下班(ㄒㄧㄚˋ ㄅㄢ)
to leave office (or factory) after working hours; to knock off

下半輩子(ㄒㄧㄚˋ ㄅㄢˋ ㄅㄟˋ ·ㄗ)
the latter half of one's life; the rest of one's life

下半天(ㄒㄧㄚˋ ㄅㄢˋ ㄊㄧㄢ)
the last half day; afternoon

下半旗(ㄒㄧㄚˋ ㄅㄢˋ ㄑㄧˊ)
to fly a flag at half-mast

下半場(ㄒㄧㄚˋ ㄅㄢˋ ㄔㄤˇ)
the second half (of a game)

下半晌(ㄒㄧㄚˋ ㄅㄢˋ ㄕㄤˇ)
afternoon

下半夜(ㄒㄧㄚˋ ㄅㄢˋ ㄧㄝˋ)
after midnight; the wee hours

下半月(ㄒㄧㄚˋ ㄅㄢˋ ㄩㄝˋ)
the last half month; after the 15th of a month

下筆(ㄒㄧㄚˋ ㄅㄧˇ)
to start writing

下筆成章(ㄒㄧㄚˋ ㄅㄧˇ ㄔㄥˊ ㄓㄤ)
to write quickly and skilfully; to have literary acumen

下邊(ㄒㄧㄚˋ ㄅㄧㄢ)or 下邊兒(ㄒㄧㄚˋ ㄅㄧㄚㄦ)
as follows; following; below; under

下部(ㄒㄧㄚˋ ㄅㄨˋ)
① the lower part ② the private parts

下不了臺(ㄒㄧㄚˋ ㄅㄨˋ ㄌㄧㄠˇ ㄊㄞˊ)
① cannot bring to a conclusion ② to put someone in an awkward position; to be put on the spot

下不爲例(ㄒㄧㄚˋ ㄅㄨˋ ㄨㄟˊ ㄌㄧˋ)
This does not constitute a precedent. 或 Don't do it again! 或 Just this once.

下不來(ㄒㄧㄚˋ ·ㄅㄨ ㄌㄞˊ)
① cannot get down ② to be embarrassed

下不去(ㄒㄧㄚˋ ·ㄅㄨ ㄑㄩˋ)
to go against; to harass; to cause someone to lose face

下坡路(ㄒㄧㄚˋ ㄆㄛ ㄌㄨˋ)
a descending road or foot path

下片(ㄒㄧㄚˋ ㄆㄧㄢˋ)
to stop showing a movie (after attendance tapers off)

下品(ㄒㄧㄚˋ ㄆㄧㄣˇ)
low-grade; inferior

下聘(ㄒㄧㄚˋ ㄆㄧㄣˋ)
to present betrothal gifts

下舖(ㄒㄧㄚˋ ㄆㄨˋ)
the lower berth

下馬(ㄒㄧㄚˋ ㄇㄚˇ)
to dismount from a horse

下馬威(ㄒㄧㄚˋ ㄇㄚˇ ㄨㄟ)
to warn against insubordination, etc. by enforcing strict disciplinary action when one first takes office

下麵(ㄒㄧㄚˋ ㄇㄧㄢˋ)
to cook noodles

下面(ㄒㄧㄚˋ ·ㄇㄧㄢ)or 下面兒(ㄒㄧㄚˋ ·ㄇㄧㄚㄦ)
① underneath; below ② following: ③ lower levels; subordinates 請瞭解下面情況。Please find out about how things are at the lower levels.

下命令(ㄒㄧㄚˋ ㄇㄧㄥˋ ㄌㄧㄥˋ)
to give orders 亦作「下令」

下凡(ㄒㄧㄚˋ ㄈㄢˊ)
(said of supernatural beings or gods in mythology) to descend to earth from heaven

下飯(ㄒㄧㄚˋ ㄈㄢˋ)
(said of dishes) to go along with rice

下方(ㄒㄧㄚˋ ㄈㄤ)

①south and west ②below; under ③the earth

下房(ㄒㄧㄚˋ ㄈㄤˊ)
the servant's quarters

下放(ㄒㄧㄚˋ ㄈㄤˋ)
to transfer to a lower level: 他把權力下放。He transferred his power to a lower level.

下風(ㄒㄧㄚˋ ㄈㄥ)
①in an inferior position; at a disadvantage ②leeward

下蛋(ㄒㄧㄚˋ ㄉㄢˋ)
to lay eggs

下等(ㄒㄧㄚˋ ㄉㄥˇ)
①low-grade ②mean; depraved

下地(ㄒㄧㄚˋ ㄉㄧˋ)
①to go to the fields ②to leave a sickbed

下地獄(ㄒㄧㄚˋ ㄉㄧˋ ㄩˋ)
to go to hell

下定(ㄒㄧㄚˋ ㄉㄧㄥˋ)
to send betrothal gifts or money

下定義(ㄒㄧㄚˋ ㄉㄧㄥˋ ㄧˋ)
to define; to give a definition

下毒(ㄒㄧㄚˋ ㄉㄨˊ)
to poison; to put poison into something

下毒手(ㄒㄧㄚˋ ㄉㄨˊ ㄕㄡˇ)
to lay violent hands on someone

下榻(ㄒㄧㄚˋ ㄊㄚˋ)
to take up abode; to stay

下臺(ㄒㄧㄚˋ ㄊㄞˊ)
①to get off stage ②to be relieved from office; to go out of power

下頭(ㄒㄧㄚˋ ˙ㄊㄡ)
as follows; below; under

下堂(ㄒㄧㄚˋ ㄊㄤˊ)
to leave or to be divorced by one's husband

下體(ㄒㄧㄚˋ ㄊㄧˇ)
the privates; the genitals

下帖(ㄒㄧㄚˋ ㄊㄧㄝˇ)
to send an invitation

下條子(ㄒㄧㄚˋ ㄊㄧㄠˊ ˙ㄗ)
to send notes or memos to one's subordinates

下田(ㄒㄧㄚˋ ㄊㄧㄢˊ)
to work on farmland; to cultivate the land

下土(ㄒㄧㄚˋ ㄊㄨˇ)
①the earth; the world ②the countryside

下同(ㄒㄧㄚˋ ㄊㄨㄥˊ)
similarly hereinafter; the same below

下女(ㄒㄧㄚˋ ㄋㄩˇ)
a maid

下來(ㄒㄧㄚˋ ˙ㄌㄞ)
to come down

下樓(ㄒㄧㄚˋ ㄌㄡˊ)
to descend the stairs; to go (or come) downstairs

下禮(ㄒㄧㄚˋ ㄌㄧˇ)
to send gifts

下里巴人(ㄒㄧㄚˋ ㄌㄧˇ ㄅㄚ ㄖㄣˊ)
simple and crude folk songs

下列(ㄒㄧㄚˋ ㄌㄧㄝˋ)or 下開(ㄒㄧㄚˋ ㄎㄞ)
①as follows ②what are listed below: 注意下列幾點。Pay attention to the following points.

下流(ㄒㄧㄚˋ ㄌㄧㄡˊ)
①downstream ②to flow down ③low; nasty; mean; scurrilous

下流話(ㄒㄧㄚˋ ㄌㄧㄡˊ ㄏㄨㄚˋ)
obscene (or dirty, foul) language; obscenities

下聯(ㄒㄧㄚˋ ㄌㄧㄢˊ)
the second line of a couplet

下令(ㄒㄧㄚˋ ㄌㄧㄥˋ)
to give orders; to order

下落(ㄒㄧㄚˋ ㄌㄨㄛˋ)
whereabouts: 有一幅古畫現在下落不明。The whereabouts of one of the ancient paintings is unknown.

下略(ㄒㄧㄚˋ ㄌㄩㄝˋ)
What follows is omitted.

下崗(ㄒㄧㄚˋ ㄍㄤˇ)
to come or go off sentry duty

下國(ㄒㄧㄚˋ ㄍㄨㄛˊ)
my humble country

下跪(ㄒㄧㄚˋ ㄍㄨㄟˋ)
to kneel down: 教堂中每個人都下跪祈禱。Everyone in the church knelt in prayer.

下工(ㄒㄧㄚˋ ㄍㄨㄥ)
to leave when one's work is done; to stop working

下工夫(ㄒㄧㄚˋ ㄍㄨㄥ ˙ㄈㄨ)
to devote much time and energy to a task

下課(ㄒㄧㄚˋ ㄎㄜˋ)
to get out of class; to finish class

下款(ㄒㄧㄚˋ ㄎㄨㄢˇ)
the signature of an artist on a painting or calligraphic work presented to someone as a gift

下海(ㄒㄧㄚˋ ㄏㄞˇ)
①to turn professional (usually referring to show personalities) ②to go to sea

下頷(ㄒㄧㄚˋ ㄏㄢˋ)
the lower jaw; the mandible

下懷(ㄒㄧㄚˋ ㄏㄨㄞˊ)
one's desire; one's concern: 正中下懷 to be exactly what one wants

下回(ㄒㄧㄚˋ ㄏㄨㄟˊ)
next time

下級(ㄒㄧㄚˋ ㄐㄧˊ)
①lower levels ②subordinates

下嫁(ㄒㄧㄚˋ ㄐㄧㄚˋ)
to marry someone beneath her station

下屆(ㄒㄧㄚˋ ㄐㄧㄝˋ)
next (term, election, etc.)

下界(ㄒㄧㄚˋ ㄐㄧㄝˋ)
the earth (in the eyes of supernatural beings who are supposed to dwell in the heavens above); the world of mortals

下脚(ㄒㄧㄚˋ ㄐㄧㄠˇ)
①to get a foothold; to make a short stay ②residual raw materials; scraps

下酒(ㄒㄧㄚˋ ㄐㄧㄡˇ)
(said of food) to go with wine or liquor

下酒菜(ㄒㄧㄚˋ ㄐㄧㄡˇ ㄘㄞˋ)
a dish that goes with wine

下賤(ㄒㄧㄚˋ ㄐㄧㄢˋ)
low; cheap; degrading

下降(ㄒㄧㄚˋ ㄐㄧㄤˋ)
to descend; to drop: 氣溫驟然下降。There was a sudden drop in the temperature.

下決心(ㄒㄧㄚˋ ㄐㄩㄝˊ ㄒㄧㄣ)
to make a resolution

下棋(ㄒㄧㄚˋ ㄑㄧˊ)
to play chess

下旗歸國(ㄒㄧㄚˋ ㄑㄧˊ ㄍㄨㄟ ㄍㄨㄛˊ)
(said of diplomats) to close diplomatic mission and return home after severance or suspension of official ties

下氣(ㄒㄧㄚˋ ㄑㄧˋ)
①calm; to keep calm ②

〔一部〕

(Chinese medicine) to emit gas

下妾(ㄒㄧㄚˋ ㄑㄧㄝˋ)
(formerly, the wife's self-reference) your wife

下情(ㄒㄧㄚˋ ㄑㄧㄥˊ)
the opinion of the masses; the difficulties or problems encountered by a subordinate

下去(ㄒㄧㄚˋ ·ㄑㄩ)
① to go down 到站了，快下去。Here we are. Let's get off at once. ② to go on: 你這樣工作下去必會累垮。If you go on working like this, you'll certainly crack up.

下弦(ㄒㄧㄚˋ ㄒㄧㄢˊ)
the last quarter of the moon usually on the 22nd or 23rd day of a month in the Chinese lunar calendar

下限(ㄒㄧㄚˋ ㄒㄧㄢˋ)
lower limit; prescribed minimum; floor level

下鄉(ㄒㄧㄚˋ ㄒㄧㄤ)
to go to the country; to rusticate

下行(ㄒㄧㄚˋ ㄒㄧㄥˊ)
(train) traveling away from the starting point of a line, usually southward

下行車(ㄒㄧㄚˋ ㄒㄧㄥˊ ㄔㄜ)
the down train

下學(ㄒㄧㄚˋ ㄒㄩㄝˊ)
to leave for home after school

下學期(ㄒㄧㄚˋ ㄒㄩㄝˊ ㄑㄧˊ)
next semester; the coming term

下雪(ㄒㄧㄚˋ ㄒㄩㄝˇ)
to snow

下旬(ㄒㄧㄚˋ ㄒㄩㄣˊ)
the last ten days of a month

下肢(ㄒㄧㄚˋ ㄓ)
the lower limbs

下詔(ㄒㄧㄚˋ ㄓㄠˋ)
to issue imperial orders or instructions

下戰書(ㄒㄧㄚˋ ㄓㄢˋ ㄕㄨ)
to deliver a challenge in writing

下逐客令(ㄒㄧㄚˋ ㄓㄨˊ ㄎㄜˋ ㄌㄧㄥˋ)
to ask an unwelcome guest or visitor to leave; to throw out a guest after he has overstayed his welcome

下注(ㄒㄧㄚˋ ㄓㄨˋ)
to put stake; to stake a wager; to wager

下箸(ㄒㄧㄚˋ ㄓㄨˋ)
to start eating

下墜(ㄒㄧㄚˋ ㄓㄨㄟˋ)
to fall

下裝(ㄒㄧㄚˋ ㄓㄨㄤ)
to take off one's costume (especially referring to performers)

下種(ㄒㄧㄚˋ ㄓㄨㄥˇ)
to sow seed

下茶(ㄒㄧㄚˋ ㄔㄚˊ)
to send a gift of tea as a token of betrothal

下車(ㄒㄧㄚˋ ㄔㄜ)
① to get off (trains or vehicles, etc.) ② to take up new office

下沉(ㄒㄧㄚˋ ㄔㄣˊ)
to sink; to subside; to submerge

下場(ㄒㄧㄚˋ ㄔㄤˇ)or(ㄒㄧㄚˋ ㄔㄤˊ)
① the conclusion; the end: 他的下場可悲。He met with a miserable fate. ② to get to the playground to compete, play ball, etc. ③ an exit on the stage

下廚(ㄒㄧㄚˋ ㄔㄨˊ)
to go to the kitchen; to prepare food

下處(ㄒㄧㄚˋ ·ㄔㄨ)
one's temporary lodging during a trip; a lodging for the night

下垂(ㄒㄧㄚˋ ㄔㄨㄟˊ)
① to hang down; to droop ②(medicine) prolapse

下船(ㄒㄧㄚˋ ㄔㄨㄢˊ)
to go ashore

下牀(ㄒㄧㄚˋ ㄔㄨㄤˊ)
to get up

下士(ㄒㄧㄚˋ ㄕˋ)
①(military rank) corporal ② a fool ③ an ordinary person

下室(ㄒㄧㄚˋ ㄕˋ)
a bedroom

下手(ㄒㄧㄚˋ ㄕㄡˇ)
① to start doing something: 我不知從何處下手。I don't know where to start. ② to commit a crime ③ an inferior attendant; a helper; an assistant

下首(ㄒㄧㄚˋ ㄕㄡˇ)
the right-hand seat

下山(ㄒㄧㄚˋ ㄕㄢ)
to go down a mountain

下身(ㄒㄧㄚˋ ㄕㄣ)or 下身兒(ㄒㄧㄚˋ ㄕㄜㄦ)
① the lower part of the body ② the privates

下書(ㄒㄧㄚˋ ㄕㄨ)
to deliver a letter

下屬(ㄒㄧㄚˋ ㄕㄨˇ)
subordinates

下水
①(ㄒㄧㄚˋ ㄕㄨㄟˇ) to launch a boat: 這艘新船下水了。This new ship was launched. ②(ㄒㄧㄚˋ ·ㄕㄨㄟ) internal organs of animals (especially poultry)

下水道(ㄒㄧㄚˋ ㄕㄨㄟˇ ㄉㄠˋ)
sewers; the sewerage system

下水禮(ㄒㄧㄚˋ ㄕㄨㄟˇ ㄌㄧˇ)
the ceremony of launching a ship

下人(ㄒㄧㄚˋ ㄖㄣˊ)
servants

下葬(ㄒㄧㄚˋ ㄗㄤˋ)
to bury: 他昨天下葬。He was buried yesterday.

下座(ㄒㄧㄚˋ ㄗㄨㄛˋ)
inferior seats or ranks

下作(ㄒㄧㄚˋ ·ㄗㄨㄛ)
① low; vulgar; nasty ② greedy; gluttonous

下罪(ㄒㄧㄚˋ ㄗㄨㄟˋ)
to convict

下次(ㄒㄧㄚˋ ㄘˋ)
next time

下策(ㄒㄧㄚˋ ㄘㄜˋ)
a bad strategy, measure or policy

下層(ㄒㄧㄚˋ ㄘㄥˊ)
① a lower stratum, layer or deck ② low-ranking

下三爛(ㄒㄧㄚˋ ㄙㄢ ㄌㄢˋ)
a bum

下顎(ㄒㄧㄚˋ ㄜˋ)
the lower jaw; the mandible

下意識(ㄒㄧㄚˋ ㄧˋ ㄕˋ)
subconscious

下議院(ㄒㄧㄚˋ ㄧˋ ㄩㄢˋ)
the Lower House

下野(ㄒㄧㄚˋ ㄧㄝˇ)
to quit or resign from official posts or politics (referring to top-ranking offi-

cials)
下藥(ㄒㄧㄚˋ ㄧㄠˋ)
①(said of doctors) to write a prescription ②to put in poison
下游(ㄒㄧㄚˋ ㄧㄡˊ)
downstream
下嚥(ㄒㄧㄚˋ ㄧㄢˋ)
to swallow
下午(ㄒㄧㄚˋ ㄨˇ)
afternoon
下霧(ㄒㄧㄚˋ ㄨˋ)
to mist; foggy
下文(ㄒㄧㄚˋ ㄨㄣˊ)
①the statement that follows; the words that follow ②further development or information; sequel 這案子未了，尚有下文哩。The case is not over; there is still further development.
下問(ㄒㄧㄚˋ ㄨㄣˋ)
to learn from one's inferior
下愚(ㄒㄧㄚˋ ㄩˊ)
a fool; an imbecile
下餘(ㄒㄧㄚˋ ㄩˊ)
the remnant
下雨(ㄒㄧㄚˋ ㄩˇ)
to rain
下雨天(ㄒㄧㄚˋ ㄩˇ ㄊㄧㄢ)
a rainy day
下獄(ㄒㄧㄚˋ ㄩˋ)
to put behind bars; to imprison
下月(ㄒㄧㄚˋ ㄩㄝˋ)
next month
下元(ㄒㄧㄚˋ ㄩㄢˊ)
the 15th day of the 10th month in the Chinese lunar calendar

三畫

【不】 8
ㄅㄨˋ buh bù
(變調 ㄅㄨˊ bwu bú)
no; not; negative: 他不走了。He's not going.
不白之冤(ㄅㄨˋ ㄅㄞˊ ㄓ ㄩㄢ)
①a wrong that has not been righted ②falsely accused
不敗之地(ㄅㄨˋ ㄅㄞˋ ㄓ ㄉㄧˋ)
an invincible position
不卑不亢(ㄅㄨˋ ㄅㄟ ㄅㄨˊ ㄎㄤˋ)
(literally) neither humble nor arrogant—to conduct oneself properly
不備(ㄅㄨˊ ㄅㄟˋ)
not ready; by surprise; unawares; unprepared
不比(ㄅㄨˋ ㄅㄧˇ)
unlike
不必(ㄅㄨˊ ㄅㄧˋ)
not necessary; unnecessary; not have to
不避艱險(ㄅㄨˊ ㄅㄧˋ ㄐㄧㄢ ㄒㄧㄢˇ)
to shrink (or draw back) from no difficulty or danger
不便(ㄅㄨˊ ㄅㄧㄢˋ)
inconvenience; inconvenient:
不辨菽麥(ㄅㄨˊ ㄅㄧㄢˋ ㄕㄨ ㄇㄞˋ)
(said of a person) unable to distinguish beans from wheat—devoid of common sense; ignorant
不怕(ㄅㄨˊ ㄆㄚˋ)
not afraid
不破不立(ㄅㄨˊ ㄆㄛˋ ㄅㄨˊ ㄌㄧˋ)
No destruction, no construction.
不配(ㄅㄨˊ ㄆㄟˋ)
①mismatch; misfit ②unequal to; not qualified
不偏不倚(ㄅㄨˋ ㄆㄧㄢ ㄅㄨˋ ㄧˇ)
①exact; just ②fair; unbiased
不平(ㄅㄨˋ ㄆㄧㄥˊ)
①complaint; a grudge ②unjust
不平等條約(ㄅㄨˋ ㄆㄧㄥˊ ㄉㄥˇ ㄊㄧㄠˊ ㄩㄝ)
an unequal treaty
不平則鳴(ㄅㄨˋ ㄆㄧㄥˊ ㄗㄜˊ ㄇㄧㄥˊ)
Those who are discriminated against will complain.
不美(ㄅㄨˋ ㄇㄟˇ)
unbeautiful; not pretty
不毛之地(ㄅㄨˋ ㄇㄠˊ ㄓ ㄉㄧˋ)
①barren land ②an uncivilized area
不謀而合(ㄅㄨˋ ㄇㄡˊ ㄦˊ ㄏㄜˊ)
to agree without prior consultation; to be coincident
不滿(ㄅㄨˋ ㄇㄢˇ)
discontent; dissatisfaction
不蔓不枝(ㄅㄨˊ ㄇㄢˋ ㄅㄨˋ ㄓ)
(said of writing) succinct and to the point
不忙(ㄅㄨˋ ㄇㄤˊ)
not in a hurry; to take one's time
不妙(ㄅㄨˊ ㄇㄧㄠˋ)
Something is wrong or going badly.
不眠不休(ㄅㄨˋ ㄇㄧㄢˊ ㄅㄨˋ ㄒㄧㄡ)
without rest; tireless; indefatigable
不免(ㄅㄨˋ ㄇㄧㄢˇ)
have to; must; invariably; unavoidable: 人不免一死。Man must die.
不敏(ㄅㄨˋ ㄇㄧㄣˇ)
not intelligent (a modest term referring to oneself)
不明(ㄅㄨˋ ㄇㄧㄥˊ)
not clear; nebulous; unknown
不明飛行物體(ㄅㄨˋ ㄇㄧㄥˊ ㄈㄟ ㄒㄧㄥˊ ㄨˋ ㄊㄧˇ)
unidentified flying object (UFO)亦作「幽浮」
不明底蘊(ㄅㄨˋ ㄇㄧㄥˊ ㄉㄧˇ ㄩㄣˋ)
ignorant of the true picture
不名一錢(ㄅㄨˋ ㄇㄧㄥˊ ㄧˋ ㄑㄧㄢˊ)
penniless亦作「不名一文」
不名譽(ㄅㄨˋ ㄇㄧㄥˊ ㄩˋ)
disreputable; scandalous
不乏(ㄅㄨˋ ㄈㄚˊ)
there is no lack of; not rare: 不乏先例。There is no lack of precedents
不法(ㄅㄨˋ ㄈㄚˇ)
unlawful; illegal
不法之徒(ㄅㄨˋ ㄈㄚˇ ㄓ ㄊㄨˊ)
lawless elements
不費吹灰之力(ㄅㄨˊ ㄈㄟˋ ㄔㄨㄟ ㄏㄨㄟ ㄓ ㄌㄧˋ)
as easy as blowing dust off—do not need the slightest effort
不凡(ㄅㄨˋ ㄈㄢˊ)
extraordinary; outstanding; unusual
不分彼此(ㄅㄨˋ ㄈㄣ ㄅㄧˇ ㄘˇ)
exchange of goods and services between close friends without asking for payment
不分高下(ㄅㄨˋ ㄈㄣ ㄍㄠ ㄒㄧㄚˋ)
a draw; a tie; well-matched
不分青紅皂白(ㄅㄨˋ ㄈㄣ ㄑㄧㄥ ㄏㄨㄥˊ ㄗㄠˋ ㄅㄞˊ)
indiscriminately 參看「不分皂白」
不分軒輊(ㄅㄨˋ ㄈㄣ ㄒㄩㄢ ㄓˋ)
a draw; a tie; well-matched
不分晝夜(ㄅㄨˋ ㄈㄣ ㄓㄡˋ ㄧㄝˋ)
(to work) day and night
不分畛域(ㄅㄨˋ ㄈㄣ ㄓㄣˇ ㄩˋ)

〔一部〕

〔一部〕

regardless of geographical difference
不分首從(ㄅㄨˋ ㄈㄣ ㄕㄡˇ ㄘㄨㄥˊ)
(All offenders will be punished) whether they are ringleaders or accomplices.
不分勝負(ㄅㄨˋ ㄈㄣ ㄕㄥˋ ㄈㄨˋ)
to tie; to draw; to come out even
不分皂白(ㄅㄨˋ ㄈㄣ ㄗㄠˋ ㄅㄞˊ)
impetuous; indiscriminately
不妨(ㄅㄨˋ ㄈㄤˊ)
no harm in (trying, doing, etc.); might as well
不防(ㄅㄨˋ ㄈㄤˊ)
by surprise; not ready or prepared; unawares
不符(ㄅㄨˋ ㄈㄨˊ)
do not tally; to be inconsistent
不服(ㄅㄨˋ ㄈㄨˊ)
to recalcitrate; to rebel; to disobey; to resist; to refuse to accept
不服氣(ㄅㄨˋ ㄈㄨˊ ㄑㄧˋ)
recalcitrant; unwilling to submit; rebellious; disobedient
不服輸(ㄅㄨˋ ㄈㄨˊ ㄕㄨ)
to refuse to concede defeat
不服水土(ㄅㄨˋ ㄈㄨˊ ㄕㄨㄟˇ ㄊㄨˇ)
(said of a stranger) not get used to the climate of a new place; not acclimatized
不孚衆望(ㄅㄨˋ ㄈㄨˊ ㄓㄨㄥˋ ㄨㄤˋ)
not popular with the masses
不負所託(ㄅㄨˋ ㄈㄨˋ ㄙㄨㄛˇ ㄊㄨㄛ)
to merit someone's trust
不打不相識(ㄅㄨˋ ㄉㄚˇ ㄅㄨˋ ㄒㄧㄤ ㄕˋ)
Friendship results from an exchange of blows. 或 No discord, no concord.
不打緊(ㄅㄨˋ ㄉㄚˇ ㄐㄧㄣˇ)
do not matter; not important
不打自招(ㄅㄨˋ ㄉㄚˇ ㄗˋ ㄓㄠ)
to make a confession without being pressed
不得(ㄅㄨˋ ㄉㄜˊ)
don't; no; must not
不得不(ㄅㄨˋ ㄉㄜˊ ㄅㄨˋ)
to have to; must
不得了(ㄅㄨˋ ㄉㄜˊ ㄌㄧㄠˇ)
①Good heavens! ②It's serious! ③ disastrous ④ extremely
不得勁(ㄅㄨˋ ㄉㄜˊ ㄐㄧㄣˋ)or 不得勁兒(ㄅㄨˋ ㄉㄜˊ ㄐㄧㄜˋㄦ)
listless; uncomfortable
不得其法(ㄅㄨˋ ㄉㄜˊ ㄑㄧˊ ㄈㄚˇ)
do not know the right way (to do something)
不得人心(ㄅㄨˋ ㄉㄜˊ ㄖㄣˊ ㄒㄧㄣ)
not enjoy popular support; to be unpopular
不得而知(ㄅㄨˋ ㄉㄜˊ ㄦˊ ㄓ)
do not know; still unknown
不得已(ㄅㄨˋ ㄉㄜˊ ㄧˇ)
cannot help but…; no alternative but…
不得要領(ㄅㄨˋ ㄉㄜˊ ㄧㄠˋ ㄌㄧㄥˇ)
① cannot get the gist; pointless; irrelevant ② don't know the right way (to do something)
不待說(ㄅㄨˋ ㄉㄞˋ ㄕㄨㄛ)
needless to say; it goes without saying
不導體(ㄅㄨˋ ㄉㄠˇ ㄊㄧˇ)
a nonconductor
不倒翁(ㄅㄨˋ ㄉㄠˇ ㄨㄥ)
① a tumbler ② a politician who deftly manages to survive many political crises; a political tightrope walker
不道德(ㄅㄨˋ ㄉㄠˋ ㄉㄜˊ)
immoral; unethical
不到(ㄅㄨˊ ㄉㄠˋ)
insufficient; less than
不到黃河心不死(ㄅㄨˊ ㄉㄠˋ ㄏㄨㄤˊ ㄏㄜˊ ㄒㄧㄣ ㄅㄨˋ ㄙˇ)
not stop until one reaches the Yellow River—to refuse to give up until one reaches one's goal
不丹(ㄅㄨˋ ㄉㄢ)
Bhutan
不單(ㄅㄨˋ ㄉㄢ)
① not the only ② not merely; not simply
不但(ㄅㄨˊ ㄉㄢˋ)
not only…
不憚煩(ㄅㄨˊ ㄉㄢˋ ㄈㄢˊ)
to spare no effort; do not shrink from trouble
不當(ㄅㄨˊ ㄉㄤˋ)
unsuitable; improper; inappropriate:這件案子他們處理不當。They handled this case improperly.
不登大雅之堂(ㄅㄨˋ ㄉㄥ ㄉㄚˋ ㄧㄚˇ ㄓ ㄊㄤˊ)
do not appeal to refined taste; to be unpresentable
不等(ㄅㄨˋ ㄉㄥˇ)
not uniform; to vary
不敵(ㄅㄨˋ ㄉㄧˊ)
no match for; to be defeated
不抵抗主義(ㄅㄨˋ ㄉㄧˇ ㄎㄤˋ ㄓㄨˇ ㄧˋ)
the principle of nonresistance
不第(ㄅㄨˊ ㄉㄧˋ)
① to fail in a civil service examination ② not only
不定(ㄅㄨˊ ㄉㄧㄥˋ)
① not certain; uncertain ② indefinite
不定冠詞(ㄅㄨˊ ㄉㄧㄥˋ ㄍㄨㄢˋ ㄘˊ)
indefinite article
不定期(ㄅㄨˊ ㄉㄧㄥˋ ㄑㄧˊ)
without a fixed schedule; irregular
不獨(ㄅㄨˋ ㄉㄨˊ)
not only
不對(ㄅㄨˊ ㄉㄨㄟˋ)
not right; wrong
不對頭(ㄅㄨˊ ㄉㄨㄟˋ ㄊㄡˊ)
① incorrect; wrong ② amiss; abnormal
不對勁(ㄅㄨˊ ㄉㄨㄟˋ ㄐㄧㄣˋ)or 不對勁兒(ㄅㄨˊ ㄉㄨㄟˋ ㄐㄧㄜˋㄦ)
not in harmony; feeling not up to par; listless
不端(ㄅㄨˋ ㄉㄨㄢ)
improper; dishonorable: 品行不端 dishonorable behavior
不短(ㄅㄨˋ ㄉㄨㄢˇ)
not lacking; just right
不斷(ㄅㄨˊ ㄉㄨㄢˋ)
unceasing; uninterrupted; continuous; constant
不動(ㄅㄨˋ ㄉㄨㄥˋ)
motionless
不動腦筋(ㄅㄨˊ ㄉㄨㄥˋ ㄋㄠˇ ㄐㄧㄣ)
don't use one's brain(s); do not take the trouble to think
不動心(ㄅㄨˊ ㄉㄨㄥˋ ㄒㄧㄣ)
showing no interest
不動產(ㄅㄨˊ ㄉㄨㄥˋ ㄔㄢˇ)
real estate; immovable assets
不動聲色(ㄅㄨˊ ㄉㄨㄥˋ ㄕㄥ ㄙㄜˋ)
not showing any feeling or emotion; with composure
不凍港(ㄅㄨˊ ㄉㄨㄥˋ ㄍㄤˇ)
an ice-free port; an open port
不透明(ㄅㄨˊ ㄊㄡˋ ㄇㄧㄥˊ)
opaque
不透風(ㄅㄨˊ ㄊㄡˋ ㄈㄥ)

stuffy
不透氣(ㄅㄨˊ ㄊㄡˋ ㄑㄧˋ)
hermetic; airtight
不透水(ㄅㄨˊ ㄊㄡˋ ㄕㄨㄟˇ)
waterproof; watertight; impermeable
不透熱(ㄅㄨˊ ㄊㄡˋ ㄖㄜˋ)
athermanous
不腆之儀(ㄅㄨˋ ㄊㄧㄢˇ ㄓ ㄧˊ)
(my) small gift or negligible present
不停(ㄅㄨˋ ㄊㄧㄥˊ)
without stop
不圖(ㄅㄨˋ ㄊㄨˊ)
① contrary to one's expectation; unexpectedly ② do not intend
不妥(ㄅㄨˋ ㄊㄨㄛˇ)
not the right way; improper; not proper; amiss: 我覺得有點不妥。I feel that something is amiss.
不通(ㄅㄨˋ ㄊㄨㄥ)
① (said of writings) poor; illogical; inarticulate ② blocked; not passable: 管子不通。The pipe is blocked.
不同(ㄅㄨˋ ㄊㄨㄥˊ)
different; distinct
不同凡響(ㄅㄨˋ ㄊㄨㄥˊ ㄈㄢˊ ㄒㄧㄤˇ)
extraordinary; remarkable
不同意(ㄅㄨˋ ㄊㄨㄥˊ ㄧˋ)
to disagree
不痛不癢(ㄅㄨˋ ㄊㄨㄥˋ ㄅㄨˋ ㄧㄤˇ)
① not grasping the main points; pointless; playing with words ② indecisive ③ superficial; perfunctory
不耐煩(ㄅㄨˋ ㄋㄞˋ ㄈㄢˊ)
impatient
不男不女(ㄅㄨˋ ㄋㄢˊ ㄅㄨˋ ㄋㄩˇ)
(a disapproving description of someone's manner, dress, make-up, etc.) neither a male nor a female—grotesque
不能(ㄅㄨˋ ㄋㄥˊ)
cannot; unable
不能不(ㄅㄨˋ ㄋㄥˊ ㄅㄨˋ)
to have to; must; cannot but
不能夠(ㄅㄨˋ ㄋㄥˊ ㄍㄡˋ)
cannot; unable
不念舊惡(ㄅㄨˋ ㄋㄧㄢˋ ㄐㄧㄡˋ ㄜˋ)
to forget past grudges; to let bygones be bygones
不寧唯是(ㄅㄨˋ ㄋㄧㄥˊ ㄨㄟˊ ㄕˋ)
not only
不佞(ㄅㄨˋ ㄋㄧㄥˋ)
my humble self
不樂仕進(ㄅㄨˋ ㄌㄜˋ ㄕˋ ㄐㄧㄣˋ)
unwilling to enter government service
不賴(ㄅㄨˋ ㄌㄞˋ)
not bad; good; fine
不勞而獲(ㄅㄨˋ ㄌㄠˊ ㄦˊ ㄏㄨㄛˋ)
to gain without effort; to get undeserved credit
不稂不莠(ㄅㄨˋ ㄌㄤˊ ㄅㄨˋ ㄧㄡˇ)or 不郎不秀(ㄅㄨˋ ㄌㄤˊ ㄅㄨˋ ㄒㄧㄡˋ)
(said of a person) good for nothing
不冷不熱(ㄅㄨˋ ㄌㄥˇ ㄅㄨˋ ㄖㄜˋ)
lukewarm
不理(ㄅㄨˋ ㄌㄧˇ)
in disregard of; to ignore; don't pay attention to
不理不睬(ㄅㄨˋ ㄌㄧˇ ㄅㄨˋ ㄘㄞˇ)
to refuse to talk to somebody; to give someone the silent treatment
不理會(ㄅㄨˋ ㄌㄧˇ ㄏㄨㄟˋ)
inattentive; unmindful; to pay no attention to
不力(ㄅㄨˋ ㄌㄧˋ)
(said of the performance of duties) half-heartedly; perfunctorily
不利(ㄅㄨˋ ㄌㄧˋ)
① not going smoothly; unsuccessful ② bad; adverse; harmful
不列顛(ㄅㄨˋ ㄌㄧㄝˋ ㄉㄧㄢ)
Britain
不列顛國協(ㄅㄨˋ ㄌㄧㄝˋ ㄉㄧㄢ ㄍㄨㄛˊ ㄒㄧㄝˊ)
the British Commonwealth of Nations
不了了之(ㄅㄨˋ ㄌㄧㄠˇ ㄌㄧㄠˇ ㄓ)
to conclude without concrete result or decision; to leave in the status quo; to end up with nothing definite
不了解(ㄅㄨˋ ㄌㄧㄠˇ ㄐㄧㄝˇ)
do not understand; not familiar with
不料(ㄅㄨˋ ㄌㄧㄠˋ)
unexpectedly; never thought
不留(ㄅㄨˋ ㄌㄧㄡˊ)
① do not keep ② do not leave behind; do not spare ③ do not stay
不留情面(ㄅㄨˋ ㄌㄧㄡˊ ㄑㄧㄥˊ ㄇㄧㄢˋ)
to be very strict; to disregard another's "face" or feelings
不留意(ㄅㄨˋ ㄌㄧㄡˊ ㄧˋ)or 不留心(ㄅㄨˋ ㄌㄧㄡˊ ㄒㄧㄣ)
careless
不留餘地(ㄅㄨˋ ㄌㄧㄡˊ ㄩˊ ㄉㄧˋ)
① without leaving leeway or elbowroom ② to pursue to the brutal end
不吝(ㄅㄨˋ ㄌㄧㄣˋ)
not stingy; without sparing; do not stint
不吝珠玉(ㄅㄨˋ ㄌㄧㄣˋ ㄓㄨ ㄩˋ)
Please make frank comments (on my performance).
不良(ㄅㄨˋ ㄌㄧㄤˊ)
bad; harmful; unhealthy
不良分子(ㄅㄨˋ ㄌㄧㄤˊ ㄈㄣˋ ㄗˇ)
undesirables; scums
不良導體(ㄅㄨˋ ㄌㄧㄤˊ ㄉㄠˇ ㄊㄧˇ)
a nonconductor
不良適應(ㄅㄨˋ ㄌㄧㄤˊ ㄕˋ ㄧㄥˋ)
maladjustment
不良少年(ㄅㄨˋ ㄌㄧㄤˊ ㄕㄠˋ ㄋㄧㄢˊ)
juvenile delinquents
不良影響(ㄅㄨˋ ㄌㄧㄤˊ ㄧㄥˇ ㄒㄧㄤˇ)
harmful or adverse effects
不良於行(ㄅㄨˋ ㄌㄧㄤˊ ㄩˊ ㄒㄧㄥˊ)
to have difficulty in walking
不量力(ㄅㄨˋ ㄌㄧㄤˋ ㄌㄧˋ)
do not consider one's own strength, ability, resources, etc. in doing a job
不靈(ㄅㄨˋ ㄌㄧㄥˊ)
① awkwardly; ineffectively ② do not work
不露聲色(ㄅㄨˊ ㄌㄨˋ ㄕㄥ ㄙㄜˋ)
do not show one's feelings, intentions, motives, etc.
不落窠臼(ㄅㄨˊ ㄌㄨㄛˋ ㄎㄜ ㄐㄧㄡˋ)
do not follow a beaten track; to have a unique style
不倫不類(ㄅㄨˋ ㄌㄨㄣˊ ㄅㄨˋ ㄌㄟˋ)
grotesque; incongruous; unfit
不論(ㄅㄨˊ ㄌㄨㄣˋ)
no matter; regardless
不苟(ㄅㄨˋ ㄍㄡˇ)
in a serious manner; solemn; strict; upright: 他做事一絲不苟。He works in a serious manner.
不苟言笑(ㄅㄨˋ ㄍㄡˇ ㄧㄢˊ ㄒㄧㄠˋ)
strictly adhere to propriety in one's behavior; serious; not given to talking and

〔一部〕

laughing

不夠(ㄅㄨˋ ㄍㄡˋ)
not enough; insufficient; inadequate

不夠本(ㄅㄨˋ ㄍㄡˋ ㄅㄣˇ)
below cost; unable to cover the cost

不夠資格(ㄅㄨˋ ㄍㄡˋ ㄗ ㄍㄜˊ)
not qualified

不甘(ㄅㄨˋ ㄍㄢ)
unreconciled to; not resigned to; unwilling; dissatisfied; chagrined: 他不甘於自己的厄運。He is unreconciled to his misfortune.

不甘落後(ㄅㄨˋ ㄍㄢ ㄌㄨㄛˋ ㄏㄡˋ)
unwilling to lag behind

不甘寂寞(ㄅㄨˋ ㄍㄢ ㄐㄧˋ ㄇㄛˋ)
unwilling to remain out of the limelight; eager to seek publicity

不甘示弱(ㄅㄨˋ ㄍㄢ ㄕˋ ㄖㄨㄛˋ)
unwilling to let the other fellow hold the center stage; not to be outdone

不甘雌服(ㄅㄨˋ ㄍㄢ ㄘˊ ㄈㄨˊ)
unwilling to lie low; eager to prove one's worth

不乾不淨(ㄅㄨˋ ㄍㄢ ㄅㄨˋ ㄐㄧㄥˋ)
not clean; filthy

不敢(ㄅㄨˋ ㄍㄢˇ)
dare not

不敢當(ㄅㄨˋ ㄍㄢˇ ㄉㄤ)
(a polite expression in reply to a compliment) I don't deserve it. 或 I am flattered. 或 I am unworthy.

不敢領教(ㄅㄨˋ ㄍㄢˇ ㄌㄧㄥˇ ㄐㄧㄠˋ)
too bad to be accepted (bought, etc.)

不敢越雷池一步(ㄅㄨˋ ㄍㄢˇ ㄩㄝˋ ㄌㄟˊ ㄔˊ ㄧˊ ㄅㄨˋ)
dare not go one step beyond the commanded limit

不根之談(ㄅㄨˋ ㄍㄣ ㄓ ㄊㄢˊ)
mere talk; unfounded statements or remarks 參看「不經之談」

不更事(ㄅㄨˋ ㄍㄥ ㄕˋ)
inexperienced

不顧(ㄅㄨˋ ㄍㄨˋ)
in disregard of; don't take into consideration; despite; in spite of; regardless of

不過(ㄅㄨˊ ㄍㄨㄛˋ)
① only; merely ② but; nevertheless

不過如此(ㄅㄨˊ ㄍㄨㄛˋ ㄖㄨˊ ㄘˇ)or 不過爾爾(ㄅㄨˊ ㄍㄨㄛˋ ㄦˇ ㄦˇ)
so-so; tolerably passable; barely acceptable; merely mediocre

不過意(ㄅㄨˊ ㄍㄨㄛˋ ㄧˋ)
to feel that one does not deserve a favor or gift given; to be sorry

不規則(ㄅㄨˋ ㄍㄨㄟ ㄗㄜˊ)
irregular

不規則動詞(ㄅㄨˋ ㄍㄨㄟ ㄗㄜˊ ㄉㄨㄥˋ ㄘˊ)
irregular verbs

不軌(ㄅㄨˋ ㄍㄨㄟˇ)
conspiracy, plots, etc.: 他們圖謀不軌。They are engaging in conspiracy.

不關痛癢(ㄅㄨˋ ㄍㄨㄢ ㄊㄨㄥˋ ㄧㄤˇ)
irrelevant; insignificant

不管(ㄅㄨˋ ㄍㄨㄢˇ)
in disregard of; no matter

不管三七二十一(ㄅㄨˋ ㄍㄨㄢˇ ㄙㄢ ㄑㄧ ㄦˋ ㄕˊ ㄧ)
casting all caution to the winds; regardless of consequences; reckless of results

不公(ㄅㄨˋ ㄍㄨㄥ)
unjust; unfair

不恭(ㄅㄨˋ ㄍㄨㄥ)
disrespectful

不攻自破(ㄅㄨˋ ㄍㄨㄥ ㄗˋ ㄆㄛˋ)
to collapse of itself

不共戴天(ㄅㄨˊ ㄍㄨㄥˋ ㄉㄞˋ ㄊㄧㄢ)
won't live under the same sky (with an archenemy); absolutely irreconcilable

不可(ㄅㄨˋ ㄎㄜˇ)
① no; negative ② not allowed; forbidden ③ cannot

不可磨滅(ㄅㄨˋ ㄎㄜˇ ㄇㄛˊ ㄇㄧㄝˋ)
indelible

不可名狀(ㄅㄨˋ ㄎㄜˇ ㄇㄧㄥˊ ㄓㄨㄤˋ)
indescribable 亦作「不可言狀」

不可多得(ㄅㄨˋ ㄎㄜˇ ㄉㄨㄛ ㄉㄜˊ)
hard to come by; scarce; rare

不可理喻(ㄅㄨˋ ㄎㄜˇ ㄌㄧˇ ㄩˋ)
unreasonable; not subject to reason

不可告人(ㄅㄨˋ ㄎㄜˇ ㄍㄠˋ ㄖㄣˊ)
not to be divulged; hidden; ulterior; confidential; secret or shameful (act, etc.)

不可估量(ㄅㄨˋ ㄎㄜˇ ㄍㄨ ㄌㄧㄤˋ)
inestimable; incalculable

不可抗力(ㄅㄨˋ ㄎㄜˇ ㄎㄤˋ ㄌㄧˋ)
irresistible (natural) force

不可究詰(ㄅㄨˋ ㄎㄜˇ ㄐㄧㄡ ㄐㄧㄝˊ)
cannot explain or find out why (because it's too confused or shifting so fast)

不可救藥(ㄅㄨˋ ㄎㄜˇ ㄐㄧㄡˋ ㄧㄠˋ)
incurable; beyond hope; incorrigible

不可限量(ㄅㄨˋ ㄎㄜˇ ㄒㄧㄢˋ ㄌㄧㄤˋ)
limitless (opportunities); very promising

不可捉摸(ㄅㄨˋ ㄎㄜˇ ㄓㄨㄛ ˙ㄇㄛ)
uncanny; unpredictable; unfathomable

不可收拾(ㄅㄨˋ ㄎㄜˇ ㄕㄡ ㄕˊ)
pandemonium; wild disorder or confusion; hopeless (situation, etc.); out of control

不可勝數(ㄅㄨˋ ㄎㄜˇ ㄕㄥ ㄕㄨˇ)
countless; innumerable

不可思議(ㄅㄨˋ ㄎㄜˇ ㄙ ㄧˋ)
uncanny; mysterious; unimaginable; beyond comprehension; inconceivable

不可一世(ㄅㄨˋ ㄎㄜˇ ㄧˊ ㄕˋ)
to consider oneself unrivaled in the world; to be extremely arrogant

不可以道里計(ㄅㄨˋ ㄎㄜˇ ㄧˇ ㄉㄠˋ ㄌㄧˇ ㄐㄧˋ)
(impossible to make a comparison because) the difference is too great

不可逾越(ㄅㄨˋ ㄎㄜˇ ㄩˊ ㄩㄝˋ)
impassable; insurmountable; insuperable

不克(ㄅㄨˊ ㄎㄜˋ)
① can not; unable: 他不克前來。He can not come. ② unable to win (in a fight, etc.)

不客氣(ㄅㄨˊ ㄎㄜˋ ㄑㄧˋ)
① impolite; rude; blunt: 讓我說句不客氣的話。Let me put it bluntly. ②(a term used in reply to another's "thanks") You are welcome. 或 Don't mention it. 或 Not at all. ③ (a term used in expressing one's gratitude for another's kind act) Please don't bother yourself about it. 或 I'll help myself.

不堪(ㄅㄨˋ ㄎㄢ)
cannot suffer or bear; unendurable

不堪回首(ㄅㄨˋ ㄎㄢ ㄏㄨㄟˊ ㄕㄡˇ)
cannot recall without pain;

cannot bear to look back
不堪設想(ㄅㄨˋ ㄎㄢ ㄕㄜˋ ㄒㄧㄤˇ)
(said of consequences) serious or unthinkable
不堪一擊(ㄅㄨˋ ㄎㄢ ㄧˋ ㄐㄧˊ)
too weak to stand competition or attack; cannot withstand a single blow
不刊之論(ㄅㄨˋ ㄎㄢ ㄓ ㄌㄨㄣˋ)
an imperishable statement
不亢不卑(ㄅㄨˋ ㄎㄤˋ ㄅㄨˋ ㄅㄟ)
with perfect propriety; neither proud nor obsequious; to carry oneself with dignity; neither haughty nor humble
不快(ㄅㄨˋ ㄎㄨㄞˋ)
① unhappy; uncomfortable ② slow
不愧(ㄅㄨˋ ㄎㄨㄟˋ)
to be worthy of; to deserve to be; to prove oneself to be
不愧屋漏(ㄅㄨˋ ㄎㄨㄟˋ ㄨ ㄌㄡˋ)
to be strictly honest under all circumstances
不和(ㄅㄨˋ ㄏㄜˊ)
at loggerheads; not on good terms; do not get along well; to be at odds
不和諧(ㄅㄨˋ ㄏㄜˊ ㄒㄧㄝˊ)
disharmony; discord; incompatibility
不合(ㄅㄨˋ ㄏㄜˊ)
unsuitable; in disagreement with (rules, etc.); not up to (standard, etc.); to disagree: 你的作品不合標準。Your work is not up to standard.
不合邏輯(ㄅㄨˋ ㄏㄜˊ ㄌㄨㄛˊ ㄐㄧˊ)
illogical
不合格(ㄅㄨˋ ㄏㄜˊ ㄍㄜˊ)
not qualified; below standard
不合時宜(ㄅㄨˋ ㄏㄜˊ ㄕˊ ㄧˊ)
bad timing; out of fashion; anachronistic; to be incompatible with present needs
不合適(ㄅㄨˋ ㄏㄜˊ ㄕˋ)
not suitable; improper; inappropriate
不合身(ㄅㄨˋ ㄏㄜˊ ㄕㄣ)
(said of a garment) ill-fitting
不合作(ㄅㄨˋ ㄏㄜˊ ㄗㄨㄛˋ)
non-cooperative
不好(ㄅㄨˋ ㄏㄠˇ)
① not good ② to be spoiled; to become worse
不好過(ㄅㄨˋ ㄏㄠˇ ㄍㄨㄛˋ)
feeling miserable (because of financial difficulties, mental or physical discomforts)
不好惹(ㄅㄨˋ ㄏㄠˇ ㄖㄜˇ)
not to be trifled with; not to be pushed around
不好意思(ㄅㄨˋ ㄏㄠˇ ㄧˋ ˙ㄙ)
① to feel ashamed, shy, bashful or embarrassed ② to find it embarrassing (to do something)
不含糊(ㄅㄨˋ ㄏㄢˊ ˙ㄏㄨ)
①(something) solid; with good foundation; very good ② to mince no words
不寒而慄(ㄅㄨˋ ㄏㄢˊ ㄦˊ ㄌㄧˋ)
trembling with fear; terrified
不惑(ㄅㄨˋ ㄏㄨㄛˋ)
① without doubt; with full self-confidence ② the age of 40: 他已屆不惑之年。He is aged forty.
不懷好意(ㄅㄨˋ ㄏㄨㄞˊ ㄏㄠˇ ㄧˋ)
with evil intention; to harbor evil designs
不諱(ㄅㄨˋ ㄏㄨㄟˋ)
① without concealing anything ② to die; to pass away
不會(ㄅㄨˋ ㄏㄨㄟˋ)
unable; can not; will not; do not know how
不會吧(ㄅㄨˋ ㄏㄨㄟˋ ˙ㄅㄚ)
not necessarily so; may not turn out that way
不歡而散(ㄅㄨˋ ㄏㄨㄢ ㄦˊ ㄙㄢˋ)
to part on bad terms; (said of a meeting, etc.) to break up in disagreement
不慌不忙(ㄅㄨˋ ㄏㄨㄤ ㄅㄨˋ ㄇㄤˊ)
① leisurely; unhurried ② with full composure
不遑(ㄅㄨˋ ㄏㄨㄤˊ)
too busy to…
不羈(ㄅㄨˋ ㄐㄧ)
carefree; not bound by social etiquette, customs, etc.
不及(ㄅㄨˋ ㄐㄧˊ)
not so (good, tall, early, etc.) as…; to be inferior to (someone or something in…)
不及格(ㄅㄨˋ ㄐㄧˊ ㄍㄜˊ)
to fail to pass (examinations); disqualified
不及物動詞(ㄅㄨˋ ㄐㄧˊ ㄨˋ ㄉㄨㄥˋ ㄘˊ)
an intransitive verb
不即不離(ㄅㄨˋ ㄐㄧˊ ㄅㄨˋ ㄌㄧˊ)
to keep someone at arm's length; keeping the right distance
不急之務(ㄅㄨˋ ㄐㄧˊ ㄓ ㄨˋ)
not an urgent matter; a matter of no great urgency
不濟(ㄅㄨˊ ㄐㄧˋ)
unsuccessful; ineffective; not good; not help
不濟於事(ㄅㄨˊ ㄐㄧˋ ㄩˊ ㄕˋ)
to no avail; of no use; no good
不記名投票(ㄅㄨˊ ㄐㄧˋ ㄇㄧㄥˊ ㄊㄡˊ ㄆㄧㄠˋ)
secret ballots; secret votes
不計其數(ㄅㄨˊ ㄐㄧˋ ㄑㄧˊ ㄕㄨˋ)
countless; innumerable
不假辭色(ㄅㄨˋ ㄐㄧㄚˇ ㄘˊ ㄙㄜˋ)
to be very stern; to show no kindness
不假思索(ㄅㄨˋ ㄐㄧㄚˇ ㄙ ㄙㄨㄛˇ)
without thinking; without hesitation; readily 亦作「不加思索」
不假外出(ㄅㄨˋ ㄐㄧㄚˋ ㄨㄞˋ ㄔㄨ)
absent without leave
不結盟(ㄅㄨˋ ㄐㄧㄝˊ ㄇㄥˊ)
nonalignment
不結盟國家(ㄅㄨˋ ㄐㄧㄝˊ ㄇㄥˊ ㄍㄨㄛˊ ㄐㄧㄚ)
nonaligned nations
不櫛進士(ㄅㄨˋ ㄐㄧㄝˊ ㄐㄧㄣˋ ㄕˋ)
a learned woman
不解(ㄅㄨˋ ㄐㄧㄝˇ)
① do not understand ② indissoluble
不解風情(ㄅㄨˋ ㄐㄧㄝˇ ㄈㄥ ㄑㄧㄥˊ)
do not understand implications in love affair
不介意(ㄅㄨˊ ㄐㄧㄝˋ ㄧˋ)
do not mind
不教而誅(ㄅㄨˊ ㄐㄧㄠˋ ㄦˊ ㄓㄨ)
to punish an offender who has not been told what is the right thing to do and what is not
不久(ㄅㄨˋ ㄐㄧㄡˇ)
within a short time; soon; shortly afterward
不咎既往(ㄅㄨˊ ㄐㄧㄡˋ ㄐㄧˋ ㄨㄤˇ)
Let bygones be bygones.
不簡單(ㄅㄨˋ ㄐㄧㄢˇ ㄉㄢ)
① not simple; rather complicated ② remarkable; marvel-

ous
不見得(ㄅㄨˊ ㄐㄧㄢˋ ˙ㄉㄜ)
not likely; not necessarily so; do not think so; to doubt the probability of…
不見天日(ㄅㄨˊ ㄐㄧㄢˋ ㄊㄧㄢ ㄖˋ)
①in total darkness ②injustice
不見了(ㄅㄨˊ ㄐㄧㄢˋ ˙ㄌㄜ)
missing; disappeared
不見棺材不落淚(ㄅㄨˊ ㄐㄧㄢˋ ㄍㄨㄢ ㄘㄞˊ ㄅㄨˊ ㄌㄨㄛˋ ㄌㄟˋ)
One does not shed tears until one sees the coffin.—One refuses to be convinced until one faces the grim reality.
不見可欲使心不亂(ㄅㄨˊ ㄐㄧㄢˋ ㄎㄜˇ ㄩˋ ㄕˇ ㄒㄧㄣ ㄅㄨˊ ㄌㄨㄢˋ)
To avoid temptation helps one retain one's presence of mind.
不見經傳(ㄅㄨˊ ㄐㄧㄢˋ ㄐㄧㄥ ㄓㄨㄢˋ)
①(something) not supported by historical fact ②(somebody) of no consequence; a nobody
不禁(ㄅㄨˋ ㄐㄧㄣ)
cannot help…
不今不古(ㄅㄨˋ ㄐㄧㄣ ㄅㄨˋ ㄍㄨˇ)
neither modern nor ancient—a sarcastic reference to a pedant or pedantry
不矜細行(ㄅㄨˋ ㄐㄧㄣ ㄒㄧˋ ㄒㄧㄥˊ)
to pay no attention to trivial matters
不僅(ㄅㄨˋ ㄐㄧㄣˇ)
not only
不盡然(ㄅㄨˊ ㄐㄧㄣˋ ㄖㄢˊ)
not exactly so; not necessarily so
不近人情(ㄅㄨˊ ㄐㄧㄣˋ ㄖㄣˊ ㄑㄧㄥˊ)
unreasonable; inconsiderate; disregarding others' feelings
不進則退(ㄅㄨˊ ㄐㄧㄣˋ ㄗㄜˊ ㄊㄨㄟˋ)
(said of a boat sailing against the current) either to keep progressing or retrogressing
不經濟(ㄅㄨˋ ㄐㄧㄥ ㄐㄧˋ)
not economical
不經之談(ㄅㄨˋ ㄐㄧㄥ ㄓ ㄊㄢˊ)
an absurd statement; a cock-and-bull story 參看「不根之談」
不經事(ㄅㄨˋ ㄐㄧㄥ ㄕˋ)
inexperienced

不經一事，不長一智(ㄅㄨˋ ㄐㄧㄥ ㄧˊ ㄕˋ，ㄅㄨˋ ㄓㄤˇ ㄧˊ ㄓˋ)
One learns from experience. 或 Wisdom comes from experience.
不經意(ㄅㄨˋ ㄐㄧㄥ ㄧˋ)
inattentive(ly); careless(ly)
不景氣(ㄅㄨˋ ㄐㄧㄥˇ ㄑㄧˋ)
(economics) depression
不脛而走(ㄅㄨˋ ㄐㄧㄥˋ ㄦˊ ㄗㄡˇ)
(said of news, etc.) to travel fast; to spread far and wide
不拘(ㄅㄨˋ ㄐㄩ)
①no limit; not to be bound ②whatever
不拘小節(ㄅㄨˋ ㄐㄩ ㄒㄧㄠˇ ㄐㄧㄝˊ)
to disregard trifles, niceties, etc.
不拘一格(ㄅㄨˋ ㄐㄩ ㄧˋ ㄍㄜˊ)
to follow no set pattern
不具(ㄅㄨˊ ㄐㄩˋ)
①not encompassing or complete enough (usually used at the end of a letter) ②crippled
不覺技癢(ㄅㄨˋ ㄐㄩㄝˊ ㄐㄧˋ ㄧㄤˇ)
cannot suppress the desire to show off one's ability or skill
不絕如縷(ㄅㄨˋ ㄐㄩㄝˊ ㄖㄨˊ ㄌㄩˇ)
(said of a situation) critical
不倦(ㄅㄨˊ ㄐㄩㄢˋ)
tireless; indefatigable
不欺暗室(ㄅㄨˋ ㄑㄧ ㄢˋ ㄕˋ)
to be scrupulously honest even when there is no one around
不期然而然(ㄅㄨˋ ㄑㄧˊ ㄖㄢˊ ㄦˊ ㄖㄢˊ)
It happened naturally and out of one's anticipation. 或 It happened unexpectedly.
不期而遇(ㄅㄨˋ ㄑㄧˊ ㄦˊ ㄩˋ)
to meet by chance; to encounter someone unexpectedly
不起(ㄅㄨˋ ㄑㄧˇ)
①very ill ②to die
不棄葑菲(ㄅㄨˊ ㄑㄧˋ ㄈㄥ ㄈㄟˇ)
do not discard one because of one's inability
不洽輿情(ㄅㄨˊ ㄑㄧㄚˋ ㄩˊ ㄑㄧㄥˊ)
to act against public opinion; not popular with the public
不切實際(ㄅㄨˊ ㄑㄧㄝˋ ㄕˊ ㄐㄧˋ)
impractical

不巧(ㄅㄨˋ ㄑㄧㄠˇ)
unfortunately; as luck would have it
不求甚解(ㄅㄨˋ ㄑㄧㄡˊ ㄕㄣˋ ㄐㄧㄝˇ)
to read casually; do not seek to understand things thoroughly
不求聞達(ㄅㄨˋ ㄑㄧㄡˊ ㄨㄣˊ ㄉㄚˊ)
having no desire to enter government service; to be uninterested in fame or prestige
不遷怒(ㄅㄨˋ ㄑㄧㄢ ㄋㄨˋ)
not blame others for one's own failure, mistake, etc.
不屈(ㄅㄨˋ ㄑㄩ)
unyielding; unbending
不屈不撓(ㄅㄨˋ ㄑㄩ ㄅㄨˋ ㄋㄠˊ)
①not to be bent or cowed; unswerving; indomitable; unyielding ②to fight to the very end; do not give up
不羣(ㄅㄨˋ ㄑㄩㄣˊ)
outstanding; foremost
不惜(ㄅㄨˋ ㄒㄧˊ)
to be ready to go to extreme lengths; do not hesitate to do something
不惜工本(ㄅㄨˋ ㄒㄧˊ ㄍㄨㄥ ㄅㄣˇ)
to spare neither energy nor money; to spare no expense
不惜一戰(ㄅㄨˋ ㄒㄧˊ ㄧˊ ㄓㄢˋ)
to be prepared to go to war (unless demand is met)
不暇(ㄅㄨˋ ㄒㄧㄚˊ)
to have no time (for something); to be too busy (to do something)
不下(ㄅㄨˊ ㄒㄧㄚˋ)
①not less than ②unable to capture (a city or position)
不下於(ㄅㄨˊ ㄒㄧㄚˋ ㄩˊ)
①as many as; no less than ②not inferior to; as good as
不屑(ㄅㄨˊ ㄒㄧㄝˋ)
do not condescend (or deign) to do something (for the sake of one's own dignity); to disdain
不謝(ㄅㄨˊ ㄒㄧㄝˋ)
Don't mention it. 或 Not at all.
不懈(ㄅㄨˊ ㄒㄧㄝˋ)
untiring; indefatigable
不曉得(ㄅㄨˋ ㄒㄧㄠˇ ˙ㄉㄜ)
do not know; ignorant of; to know nothing about

不肖(ㄅㄨˋ ㄒㄧㄠˋ)
①a son who is not so good as his father ②good-for-nothing; unworthy
不孝(ㄅㄨˋ ㄒㄧㄠˋ)
①not in accordance with filial piety ②a term referring to oneself in the obituary announcing the death of one's parent
不孝有三(ㄅㄨˋ ㄒㄧㄠˋ ㄧㄡˇ ㄙㄢ)
There are three major offenses against filial piety. (do not support parents when they are alive, do not give them a decent burial upon their death, and do not produce an heir—the last of which is the gravest offense)
不休(ㄅㄨˋ ㄒㄧㄡ)
endlessly; ceaselessly
不修邊幅(ㄅㄨˋ ㄒㄧㄡ ㄅㄧㄢ ㄈㄨˊ)
do not care about details (especially in clothing); unmindful of social conventions; slovenly; sloppy
不朽(ㄅㄨˋ ㄒㄧㄡˇ)
immortal; immortality
不銹鋼(ㄅㄨˋ ㄒㄧㄡˋ ㄍㄤ)
stainless steel
不先不後(ㄅㄨˋ ㄒㄧㄢ ㄅㄨˋ ㄏㄡˋ)
(It happens) just at the right time
不嫌詞費(ㄅㄨˋ ㄒㄧㄢˊ ㄘˊ ㄈㄟˋ)
to speak voluminously; to dwell on (a topic); to talk at length
不相干(ㄅㄨˋ ㄒㄧㄤ ㄍㄢ)
irrelevant; to have nothing to do with
不相下(ㄅㄨˋ ㄒㄧㄤ ㄒㄧㄚˋ)
(said of two sides engaged in a fight) in a state of stalemate
不相稱(ㄅㄨˋ ㄒㄧㄤ ㄔㄣˋ)
ill-matched; inharmonious
不相識(ㄅㄨˋ ㄒㄧㄤ ㄕˋ)
do not know
不相上下(ㄅㄨˋ ㄒㄧㄤ ㄕㄤˋ ㄒㄧㄚˋ)
about the same (in strength, quality, etc.); equal; equally matched
不相容(ㄅㄨˋ ㄒㄧㄤ ㄖㄨㄥˊ)
incompatible
不相聞問(ㄅㄨˋ ㄒㄧㄤ ㄨㄣˊ ㄨㄣˋ)
not on speaking terms; complete severance of relations (between individuals)
不祥(ㄅㄨˋ ㄒㄧㄤˊ)
ominous; unlucky; inauspicious
不祥之兆(ㄅㄨˋ ㄒㄧㄤˊ ㄓ ㄓㄠˋ)
a bad (or an ill) omen
不詳(ㄅㄨˋ ㄒㄧㄤˊ)
①unknown ②not detailed enough
不想(ㄅㄨˋ ㄒㄧㄤˇ)
do not want
不像話(ㄅㄨˊ ㄒㄧㄤˋ ㄏㄨㄚˋ)
absurd or ludicrous (talks, acts, etc.); unreasonable; too ridiculous
不像樣(ㄅㄨˊ ㄒㄧㄤˋ ㄧㄤˋ)or 不像樣兒(ㄅㄨˊ ㄒㄧㄤˋ ㄧㄤˋㄦ)
①improper (behavior); disreputable (conduct) ②beyond recognition
不行(ㄅㄨˋ ㄒㄧㄥˊ)
①not allowed; nothing doing ②unsuccessful; to no avail ③not qualified ④do not work
不行了(ㄅㄨˋ ㄒㄧㄥˊ ·ㄌㄜ)
on the point of death
不省人事(ㄅㄨˋ ㄒㄧㄥˇ ㄖㄣˊ ㄕˋ)
in a coma; unconscious
不幸(ㄅㄨˊ ㄒㄧㄥˋ)
misfortune; adversity; unfortunate; unfortunately; bad luck; sad
不幸中之大幸(ㄅㄨˊ ㄒㄧㄥˋ ㄓㄨㄥ ㄓ ㄉㄚˋ ㄒㄧㄥˋ)
a lucky occurrence in the course of a disaster, such as a priceless painting saved from a fire
不須(ㄅㄨˋ ㄒㄩ)
need not
不需(ㄅㄨˋ ㄒㄩ)
do not need
不虛此行(ㄅㄨˋ ㄒㄩ ㄘˇ ㄒㄧㄥˊ)
One gains much on the trip. 或 The trip has not been made in vain. 或 It's been a worthwhile trip.
不許(ㄅㄨˋ ㄒㄩˇ)
not allowed; must not; prohibited
不學無術(ㄅㄨˋ ㄒㄩㄝˊ ㄨˊ ㄕㄨˋ)
unlearned; ignorant
不宣而戰(ㄅㄨˋ ㄒㄩㄢ ㄦˊ ㄓㄢˋ)
to fight without a declaration of war; to attack without prior notice
不旋踵(ㄅㄨˋ ㄒㄩㄢˊ ㄓㄨㄥˇ)
(literally) in less time than it takes to turn one's heels—a very brief moment
不遜(ㄅㄨˊ ㄒㄩㄣˋ)
not polite; rude; impertinent
不支(ㄅㄨˋ ㄓ)
unable to hang on; exhausted
不知不覺(ㄅㄨˋ ㄓ ㄅㄨˋ ㄐㄩㄝˊ)
imperceptibly; unnoticed; without knowing it; unconsciously: 不知不覺地四個月已經過去了。Four months has passed imperceptibly.
不知道(ㄅㄨˋ ㄓ ㄉㄠˋ)
do not know; to be unconscious: 他不知道自己的錯誤。He was unconscious of his own mistake.
不知天高地厚(ㄅㄨˋ ㄓ ㄊㄧㄢ ㄍㄠ ㄉㄧˋ ㄏㄡˋ)
do not know the height of the heaven and the thickness of the earth—to think too much of one's abilities
不知甘苦(ㄅㄨˋ ㄓ ㄍㄢ ㄎㄨˇ)
do not know how difficult it is to make a living, to earn money, etc.
不知好歹(ㄅㄨˋ ㄓ ㄏㄠˇ ㄉㄞˇ)
①unable to tell good from bad; unappreciative; do not know what's good for one ②stubborn
不知就裏(ㄅㄨˋ ㄓ ㄐㄧㄡˋ ㄌㄧˇ)
do not know the inside story
不知進退(ㄅㄨˋ ㄓ ㄐㄧㄣˋ ㄊㄨㄟˋ)
do not know whether to advance or retreat; muddled or mixed-up
不知輕重(ㄅㄨˋ ㄓ ㄑㄧㄥ ㄓㄨㄥˋ)
muddled or mixed-up; unable to tell the significance of a situation
不知情(ㄅㄨˋ ㄓ ㄑㄧㄥˊ)
to know nothing about…; to be ignorant of…
不知去向(ㄅㄨˋ ㄓ ㄑㄩˋ ㄒㄧㄤˋ)
to disappear without a trace
不知自量(ㄅㄨˋ ㄓ ㄗˋ ㄌㄧㄤˋ)
to do something beyond one's ability
不知自愛(ㄅㄨˋ ㄓ ㄗˋ ㄞˋ)
to act without self-respect; to behave ungenteelly

〔一部〕

不知足(ㄅㄨˋ ㄓ ㄗㄨˊ)
insatiable; greedy

不知死活(ㄅㄨˋ ㄓ ㄙˇ ㄏㄨㄛˊ)
muddled or mixed-up (characterized by rashness or recklessness)

不知所措(ㄅㄨˋ ㄓ ㄙㄨㄛˇ ㄘㄨㄛˋ)
stunned into inaction or stoppage of mental activity; to be at a loss: 我全然不知所措。I am quite at a loss what to do.

不知所云(ㄅㄨˋ ㄓ ㄙㄨㄛˇ ㄩㄣˊ)
(said of statements) unintelligible; do not know what someone is driving at

不值得(ㄅㄨˋ ㄓˊ ˙ㄉㄜ)
not worth it; unworthy of

不值一錢(ㄅㄨˋ ㄓˊ ㄧ ㄑㄧㄢˊ)
worthless

不值一笑(ㄅㄨˋ ㄓˊ ㄧˊ ㄒㄧㄠˋ)
not worth even a laugh; extremely ridiculous

不止(ㄅㄨˋ ㄓˇ)
① do not stop ② not only… ③ more than…; over

不只(ㄅㄨˋ ㄓˇ)
not only; not merely

不治(ㄅㄨˊ ㄓˋ)
to die of illness or injury despite medical help

不治之症(ㄅㄨˊ ㄓˋ ㄓ ㄓㄥˋ)
an incurable disease

不置可否(ㄅㄨˊ ㄓˋ ㄎㄜˇ ㄈㄡˇ)
without giving an affirmative or negative answer; noncommittal; to make no comment; to hedge; to evade (the point, issue, etc.)

不忮不求(ㄅㄨˊ ㄓˋ ㄅㄨˋ ㄑㄧㄡˊ)
generous to others and lacking greediness

不至於(ㄅㄨˊ ㄓˋ ㄩˊ)
will not go so far as…; will not be so serious as…; to be unlikely: 她不至於連這點道理也不懂。She must have more sense than that.

不折不扣(ㄅㄨˋ ㄓㄜˊ ㄅㄨˊ ㄎㄡˋ)
① without any discount; net cost ② absolute; out-and-out

不周延(ㄅㄨˋ ㄓㄡ ㄧㄢˊ)
(logic) undistributed

不戰而勝(ㄅㄨˊ ㄓㄢˋ ㄦˊ ㄕㄥˋ)
to win without fighting a battle

不長進(ㄅㄨˋ ㄓㄤˇ ㄐㄧㄣˋ)
① without improvement or progress ② good-for-nothing

不爭氣(ㄅㄨˋ ㄓㄥ ㄑㄧˋ)
to submit to defeat or failure without putting up a fight; to be easily discouraged; to fail to live up to one's expectations; to let someone down

不主故常(ㄅㄨˋ ㄓㄨˇ ㄍㄨˋ ㄔㄤˊ)
to be flexible; to be ready to adapt to circumstances

不住(ㄅㄨˊ ㄓㄨˋ)
continuously; incessantly

不著邊際(ㄅㄨˋ ㄓㄨㄛˊ ㄅㄧㄢ ㄐㄧˋ)
far-fetched; far off the beam; totally beside the point

不著痕跡(ㄅㄨˋ ㄓㄨㄛˊ ㄏㄣˊ ㄐㄧ)
without trace; ingeniously secret

不准(ㄅㄨˋ ㄓㄨㄣˇ)
not allowed; forbidden

不中聽(ㄅㄨˋ ㄓㄨㄥˋ ㄊㄧㄥ)
(referring to unpleasant words or remarks) not worth listening; grating

不中意(ㄅㄨˋ ㄓㄨㄥˋ ㄧˋ)
not quite up to one's idea (or expectation); not desirable; not suitable; not to one's liking

不中用(ㄅㄨˋ ㄓㄨㄥ ㄩㄥˋ)
useless; good-for-nothing; without any talent or ability; no good

不齒(ㄅㄨˋ ㄔˇ)
to condemn; to despise; condemnable; to hold a person in contempt

不恥下問(ㄅㄨˋ ㄔˇ ㄒㄧㄚˋ ㄨㄣˋ)
not ashamed to learn (or ask for information) from one's inferiors (or subordinates)

不啻(ㄅㄨˊ ㄔˋ)
① equivalent to ② not less than ③ as; like

不差累黍(ㄅㄨˋ ㄔㄚ ㄌㄟˇ ㄕㄨˇ)or不差毫髮(ㄅㄨˋ ㄔㄚ ㄏㄠˊ ㄈㄚˇ)
exactly the same; to fit like hand in glove; not an iota less or more

不瞅不睬(ㄅㄨˋ ㄔㄡˇ ㄅㄨˋ ㄘㄞˇ)or不理不睬(ㄅㄨˋ ㄌㄧˇ ㄅㄨˋ ㄘㄞˇ)
to give someone a cold shoulder; to ignore completely

不稱意(ㄅㄨˊ ㄔㄣˋ ㄧˋ)
Things do not match one's hope.

不成(ㄅㄨˋ ㄔㄥˊ)
① not going to succeed; will not do ② an expression used at the end of a question

不成體統(ㄅㄨˋ ㄔㄥˊ ㄊㄧˇ ㄊㄨㄥˇ)
(acting or talking) wildly; without regard to common practice or propriety

不成話(ㄅㄨˋ ㄔㄥˊ ㄏㄨㄚˋ)
(acting or talking) wildly; unreasonable; absurd; ridiculous

不成敬意(ㄅㄨˋ ㄔㄥˊ ㄐㄧㄥˋ ㄧˋ)
(an expression used in presenting a gift to a friend or a superior) just a little token to show my respect to you

不成器(ㄅㄨˋ ㄔㄥˊ ㄑㄧˋ)
good-for-nothing; without promise of achievement

不成材(ㄅㄨˋ ㄔㄥˊ ㄘㄞˊ)
useless; good-for-nothing; worthless

不成文法(ㄅㄨˋ ㄔㄥˊ ㄨㄣˊ ㄈㄚˇ)
(law) unwritten law; lex non scripta

不逞之徒(ㄅㄨˋ ㄔㄥˇ ㄓ ㄊㄨˊ)
lawbreakers; lawless elements; outlaws

不出所料(ㄅㄨˋ ㄔㄨ ㄙㄨㄛˇ ㄌㄧㄠˋ)
just as expected

不揣(ㄅㄨˋ ㄔㄨㄞˇ)
ignorant of one's own meager strength (usually used as a self-depreciative expression)

不揣冒昧(ㄅㄨˋ ㄔㄨㄞˇ ㄇㄠˋ ㄇㄟˋ)
to venture; to presume; to take the liberty of

不失時機(ㄅㄨˋ ㄕ ㄕˊ ㄐㄧ)
to take one's opportunity; to lose no time

不失爲(ㄅㄨˋ ㄕ ㄨㄟˊ)
can yet be regarded as; may after all be accepted as

不時(ㄅㄨˋ ㄕˊ)
① frequently; often ② at any time; always

不時之需(ㄅㄨˋ ㄕˊ ㄓ ㄒㄩ)
occasional needs; may be needed any time; a possible period of want

不是(ㄅㄨˊ ㄕˋ)

① no; not right ② if…not ③ in the wrong; to be to blame: 這是我的不是。It's my fault. 或 I'm to blame.

不是玩兒的(ㄅㄨˊ ㄕˋ ㄨㄢˊㄦ ·ㄉㄜ)
no joke

不適(ㄅㄨˋ ㄕˋ)
ill; indisposed; unwell

不識大體(ㄅㄨˋ ㄕˋ ㄉㄚˋ ㄊㄧˇ)
to fail to see the important points; to ignore the whole interest

不識擡舉(ㄅㄨˋ ㄕˋ ㄊㄞˊ ㄐㄩˇ)
unappreciative; ungrateful; to fail to appreciate someone's kindness

不識泰山(ㄅㄨˋ ㄕˋ ㄊㄞˋ ㄕㄢ)
to fail to recognize a famous personage when meeting him face to face

不識相(ㄅㄨˋ ㄕˋ ㄒㄧㄤˋ)
impervious to an obvious situation; unable to see the fitness of things

不識之無(ㄅㄨˋ ㄕˋ ㄓ ㄨˊ)
unable to read and write; illiterate

不識時務(ㄅㄨˋ ㄕˋ ㄕˊ ㄨˋ)
ignorant of the changes of the times or failing to make use of available chances; to show no understanding of times

不識字(ㄅㄨˋ ㄕˋ ㄗˋ)
illiterate; cannot read

不識一丁(ㄅㄨˋ ㄕˋ ㄧˋ ㄉㄧㄥ)
illiterate

不世之才(ㄅㄨˋ ㄕˋ ㄓ ㄘㄞˊ)
a rare talent; a genius

不世出(ㄅㄨˋ ㄕˋ ㄔㄨ)
(said of a man of unusual ability) not to be found in every age

不受理(ㄅㄨˋ ㄕㄡˋ ㄌㄧˇ)
①(law) to reject (a complaint); not entertained ② (diplomacy) to refuse to entertain (a proposal)

不受歡迎的人(ㄅㄨˋ ㄕㄡˋ ㄏㄨㄢ ㄧㄥˊ ·ㄉㄜ ㄖㄣˊ)
(diplomacy) *persona non grata*; a nuisance

不衫不履(ㄅㄨˋ ㄕㄢ ㄅㄨˋ ㄌㄩˇ)
to dress slovenly; to disregard outward appearance

不善(ㄅㄨˋ ㄕㄢˋ)
① bad; ill ② improper(ly); not proper(ly) ③ not good at: 我們的老板是個不善管理的人。Our boss is a man not good at management.

不上不下(ㄅㄨˊ ㄕㄤˋ ㄅㄨˊ ㄒㄧㄚˋ)
① on a spot; in an impasse ② inappropriate

不上算(ㄅㄨˊ ㄕㄤˋ ㄙㄨㄢˋ)
a bad bargain; not profitable

不勝(ㄅㄨˋ ㄕㄥ)
① cannot bear (or stand); to be unequal to ② very; extremely; overwhelmed: 她不勝悲傷。She was overwhelmed by grief.

不勝枚舉(ㄅㄨˋ ㄕㄥ ㄇㄟˊ ㄐㄩˇ)
too numerous to recount; too many to cite; too numerous to mention individually

不勝其煩(ㄅㄨˋ ㄕㄥ ㄑㄧˊ ㄈㄢˊ)
cannot stand the harassment, nuisance, etc.

不聲不響(ㄅㄨˋ ㄕㄥ ㄅㄨˋ ㄒㄧㄤˇ)
stealthily; furtively

不舒服(ㄅㄨˋ ㄕㄨ ·ㄈㄨ)
unwell; not feeling well; uncomfortable; indisposed

不淑(ㄅㄨˋ ㄕㄨˊ)
unprincipled; (said of a mate) ill

不順眼(ㄅㄨˋ ㄕㄨㄣˋ ㄧㄢˇ)
incurring dislike or vexation; disagreeable

不爽(ㄅㄨˋ ㄕㄨㄤˇ)
① out of sorts; in a bad mood ② without discrepancy; accurate

不爽快(ㄅㄨˋ ㄕㄨㄤˇ ㄎㄨㄞˋ)
not frank

不日(ㄅㄨˋ ㄖˋ)
soon; in a few days; within the next few days

不然(ㄅㄨˋ ㄖㄢˊ)
① not so ② otherwise; or

不仁(ㄅㄨˋ ㄖㄣˊ)
① not benevolent; hard-hearted ②paralyzed; numbed

不人道(ㄅㄨˋ ㄖㄣˊ ㄉㄠˋ)
inhuman

不忍(ㄅㄨˋ ㄖㄣˇ)or 不忍心(ㄅㄨˋ ㄖㄣˇ ㄒㄧㄣ)
disturbed (characterized by pity); cannot bear to…; cannot stand the sight of…

不忍之心(ㄅㄨˋ ㄖㄣˇ ㄓ ㄒㄧㄣ)
a heart of mercy

不讓鬚眉(ㄅㄨˋ ㄖㄤˋ ㄒㄩ ㄇㄟˊ)
(in terms of ability, vision, valor, etc.) to compare favorably with men; to be a match for men

不如(ㄅㄨˋ ㄖㄨˊ)or 不若(ㄅㄨˋ ㄖㄨㄛˋ)
① not equal to; can do no better than; inferior to ② might as well; it would be better to

不如歸去(ㄅㄨˋ ㄖㄨˊ ㄍㄨㄟ ㄑㄩˋ)
It's better to retire or quit. —a term connoting frustration, disappointment, etc.

不入虎穴，焉得虎子(ㄅㄨˋ ㄖㄨˋ ㄏㄨˇ ㄒㄩㄝˋ, ㄧㄢ ㄉㄜˊ ㄏㄨˇ ㄗˇ)
(literally) How can one get the cubs without entering the tiger's den?—Nothing venture, nothing gain (or have).

不入耳(ㄅㄨˋ ㄖㄨˋ ㄦˇ)
unpleasant to the ear; not worth listening to

不辱使命(ㄅㄨˋ ㄖㄨˇ ㄕˇ ㄇㄧㄥˋ)
to have succeeded in carrying out an assignment

不容(ㄅㄨˋ ㄖㄨㄥˊ)
① do not tolerate; do not allow; do not brook ② do not welcome

不容分說(ㄅㄨˋ ㄖㄨㄥˊ ㄈㄣ ㄕㄨㄛ)
do not wait for an explanation

不容置喙(ㄅㄨˋ ㄖㄨㄥˊ ㄓˋ ㄏㄨㄟˋ)
to refuse to let others talk, explain, etc.

不貲(ㄅㄨˋ ㄗ)
immeasurable; incalculable

不自量(ㄅㄨˊ ㄗˋ ㄌㄧㄤˋ)
without considering one's own capability; overconfident; to overrate one's own abilities

不自在(ㄅㄨˊ ㄗˋ ·ㄗㄞ)
feeling uneasy or uncomfortable

不自愛(ㄅㄨˊ ㄗˋ ㄞˋ)
(said of a person who acts in total disregard of others) do not have self-respect

不自由，毋寧死(ㄅㄨˊ ㄗˋ ㄧㄡˊ, ㄨˊ ㄋㄧㄥˊ ㄙˇ)
"Give me liberty, or give me death."—Liberty is more important than life.

不擇手段(ㄅㄨˋ ㄗㄜˊ ㄕㄡˇ ㄉㄨㄢˋ)

〔一部〕

by fair means or foul; by hook or by crook; unscrupulously
不在(ㄅㄨˊ ㄗㄞˋ)
① dead ② not in; absent
不在乎(ㄅㄨˊ ㄗㄞˋ ·ㄏㄨ)
do not care; do not mind
不在話下(ㄅㄨˊ ㄗㄞˋ ㄏㄨㄚˋ ㄒㄧㄚˋ)
nothing difficult; an easy thing
不在其位，不謀其政(ㄅㄨˊ ㄗㄞˋ ㄑㄧˊ ㄨㄟˋ, ㄅㄨˋ ㄇㄡˊ ㄑㄧˊ ㄓㄥˋ)
unwilling to comment on something which is not one's own concern
不在此限(ㄅㄨˊ ㄗㄞˋ ㄘˇ ㄒㄧㄢˋ)
not subject to the limits or restrictions
不在意(ㄅㄨˊ ㄗㄞˋ ㄧˋ)
① to take no notice of; to pay no attention to ② inattentive; careless; negligent
不贊一辭(ㄅㄨˋ ㄗㄢˋ ㄧˋ ㄘˊ)
to keep silent; to make no comment
不怎麼(ㄅㄨˋ ㄗㄣˇ ·ㄇㄜ)
not very; not particularly
不怎麼樣(ㄅㄨˋ ㄗㄣˇ ·ㄇㄜ ㄧㄤˋ)
not up to much; very indifferent
不足(ㄅㄨˋ ㄗㄨˊ)
① not deserving ② insufficient; not enough
不足道(ㄅㄨˋ ㄗㄨˊ ㄉㄠˋ)
do not deserve mentioning; insignificant; of no consequence
不足掛齒(ㄅㄨˋ ㄗㄨˊ ㄍㄨㄚˋ ㄔˇ)
(What little I have done for you) does not deserve mentioning. 或 not worth mentioning
不足輕重(ㄅㄨˋ ㄗㄨˊ ㄑㄧㄥ ㄓㄨㄥˋ)
of little value; of little importance; carrying little weight
不足採信(ㄅㄨˋ ㄗㄨˊ ㄘㄞˇ ㄒㄧㄣˋ)
①(law) unacceptable as evidence ② can not be considered as reliable
不足爲奇(ㄅㄨˋ ㄗㄨˊ ㄨㄟˊ ㄑㄧˊ)
nothing strange, extraordinary or remarkable about it; not at all surprising
不足爲訓(ㄅㄨˋ ㄗㄨˊ ㄨㄟˊ ㄒㄩㄣˋ)
not to be taken as a guide; not to be taken as an example; not to be taken as authoritative
不足爲外人道(ㄅㄨˋ ㄗㄨˊ ㄨㄟˊ ㄨㄞˋ ㄖㄣˊ ㄉㄠˋ)
no need to let others know (because it's purely a personal matter)
不作美(ㄅㄨˊ ㄗㄨㄛˋ ㄇㄟˇ)
do not help (a happy occasion or marriage), such as rain on a wedding day
不作第二人想(ㄅㄨˊ ㄗㄨㄛˋ ㄉㄧˋ ㄦˋ ㄖㄣˊ ㄒㄧㄤˇ)
not content with playing second fiddle
不作聲(ㄅㄨˊ ㄗㄨㄛˋ ㄕㄥ)
to keep silence; to say nothing
不作此想(ㄅㄨˊ ㄗㄨㄛˋ ㄘˇ ㄒㄧㄤˇ)
to have no intention or desire to do something
不辭辛苦(ㄅㄨˋ ㄘˊ ㄒㄧㄣ ㄎㄨˇ)
to work with all-out effort; to leave no stone unturned; to make nothing of hardships
不辭而別(ㄅㄨˋ ㄘˊ ㄦˊ ㄅㄧㄝˊ)
to leave without bidding (or saying) goodbye; to take French leave
不測(ㄅㄨˊ ㄘㄜˋ)
① unpredictable; unfathomable ② misfortune; disaster; accident
不才(ㄅㄨˋ ㄘㄞˊ)
(usually a polite, self-depreciative term referring to oneself) without capability
不倸 or 不睬(ㄅㄨˋ ㄘㄞˇ)
to ignore (someone)
不曾(ㄅㄨˋ ㄘㄥˊ)
to have never done something
不錯(ㄅㄨˊ ㄘㄨㄛˋ)
① to be right: 一點也不錯。It is quite right. ② granted that; to be sure that; yes ③ not bad; pretty good
不存芥蒂(ㄅㄨˋ ㄘㄨㄣˊ ㄐㄧㄝˋ ㄉㄧˋ)
do not harbor previous grievances (between good friends)
不存心(ㄅㄨˋ ㄘㄨㄣˊ ㄒㄧㄣ)
not intended; unintentional; do not intend
不存在(ㄅㄨˋ ㄘㄨㄣˊ ㄗㄞˋ)
nonexistent
不死心(ㄅㄨˋ ㄙˇ ㄒㄧㄣ)
unwilling to give up
不三不四(ㄅㄨˋ ㄙㄢ ㄅㄨˊ ㄙˋ)
grotesque; incongruous; neither fish nor fowl
不俗(ㄅㄨˋ ㄙㄨˊ)
original; uncommon; not hackneyed or stereotyped
不速之客(ㄅㄨˊ ㄙㄨˋ ㄓ ㄎㄜˋ)
an uninvited guest; an unexpected guest; an unwelcome person
不遂(ㄅㄨˋ ㄙㄨㄟˋ)
① unsuccessful ② paralyzed
不送(ㄅㄨˊ ㄙㄨㄥˋ)
don't bother to see me out
不礙(ㄅㄨˊ ㄞˋ) or 不礙事(ㄅㄨˊ ㄞˋ ㄕˋ)
It doesn't matter. 或 There is no harm in (trying, etc.)
不安(ㄅㄨˋ ㄢ)
① uneasy; disturbed ② intranquil
不安於室(ㄅㄨˋ ㄢ ㄩˊ ㄕˋ)
(said of women) having extramarital affairs
不安於位(ㄅㄨˋ ㄢ ㄩˊ ㄨㄟˋ)
do not discharge official duties conscientiously
不貳過(ㄅㄨˊ ㄦˋ ㄍㄨㄛˋ)
not to repeat a previous mistake
不二法門(ㄅㄨˊ ㄦˋ ㄈㄚˇ ㄇㄣˊ)
the only way
不二價(ㄅㄨˊ ㄦˋ ㄐㄧㄚˋ)
a uniform price; a fixed price
不二色(ㄅㄨˊ ㄦˋ ㄙㄜˋ)
(said of men) consistent in love; loyal to one woman only
不依(ㄅㄨˋ ㄧ)
① do not comply; do not go along with ② not let off easily; not let somebody get away with it
不一(ㄅㄨˋ ㄧ)
to vary; to differ; to disagree: 這些繩子長短不一。These ropes differ in length.
不一而足(ㄅㄨˋ ㄧ ㄦˊ ㄗㄨˊ)
many; a large variety (used in a contemptuous sense); numerous
不一定(ㄅㄨˋ ㄧˊ ㄉㄧㄥˋ)
uncertain; not sure; not nec-

essarily so

不宜(ㄅㄨˋ ㄧˊ)
not suitable; inadvisable: 不宜操之過急。It's no good being overhasty.

不遺在遠(ㄅㄨˋ ㄧˊ ㄗㄞˋ ㄩㄢˇ)
(an expression used in correspondence) Please don't forget me because I'm far away.

不遺餘力(ㄅㄨˋ ㄧˊ ㄩˊ ㄌㄧˋ)
to spare no effort; to spare no pains; to do one's best (or utmost)

不已(ㄅㄨˋ ㄧˇ)
continuously; endlessly; incessantly

不以爲然(ㄅㄨˋ ㄧˇ ㄨㄟˊ ㄖㄢˊ)
to object to; to take exception to; do not approve

不意(ㄅㄨˊ ㄧˋ)
unexpectedly

不亦樂乎(ㄅㄨˊ ㄧˋ ㄌㄜˋ ㄏㄨ)
① What a delight it would be if… ② extremely; awfully: 我忙得不亦樂乎。I am awfully busy.

不易之論(ㄅㄨˊ ㄧˋ ㄓ ㄌㄨㄣˋ)
a sound or irrefutable statement; unalterable truth

不義之財(ㄅㄨˊ ㄧˋ ㄓ ㄘㄞˊ)
dirty money; loot; wealth acquired illicitly; ill-gotten wealth

不翼而飛(ㄅㄨˊ ㄧˋ ㄦˊ ㄈㄟ)
missing inexplicably; stolen

不雅觀(ㄅㄨˋ ㄧㄚˇ ㄍㄨㄢ)
ungraceful; do not look nice or proper; unbecoming

不亞於(ㄅㄨˊ ㄧㄚˋ ㄩˊ)or 不遜於(ㄅㄨˊ ㄒㄩㄣˋ ㄩˊ)
not worse than; as good as; as well as

不夜城(ㄅㄨˊ ㄧㄝˋ ㄔㄥˊ)
(literally) a city with lights turned on all night—a big city with gay night life

不要(ㄅㄨˊ ㄧㄠˋ)
① don't ② don't want

不要臉(ㄅㄨˊ ㄧㄠˋ ㄌㄧㄢˇ)
shameless; brazen; to have no sense of shame

不要緊(ㄅㄨˊ ㄧㄠˋ ㄐㄧㄣˇ)
① unimportant; not serious ② never mind

不藥而愈(ㄅㄨˊ ㄧㄠˋ ㄦˊ ㄩˋ)
to recover (from illness) without medical help

不由分說(ㄅㄨˋ ㄧㄡˊ ㄈㄣ ㄕㄨㄛ)
not waiting for an explanation; unreasonable

不由得(ㄅㄨˋ ㄧㄡˊ ˙ㄉㄜ)
cannot help; cannot but…

不由自主(ㄅㄨˋ ㄧㄡˊ ㄗˋ ㄓㄨˇ)
can't help; involuntarily

不言而喻(ㄅㄨˋ ㄧㄢˊ ㄦˊ ㄩˋ)
understood; self-evident; to understand without explanation

不厭(ㄅㄨˊ ㄧㄢˋ)
do not mind doing something; do not tire of

不厭其煩(ㄅㄨˊ ㄧㄢˋ ㄑㄧˊ ㄈㄢˊ)
do not mind taking all the trouble; to be very patient

不厭求詳(ㄅㄨˊ ㄧㄢˋ ㄑㄧㄡˊ ㄒㄧㄤˊ)
to omit no details

不揚(ㄅㄨˋ ㄧㄤˊ)
(said of one's looks) plain

不無(ㄅㄨˋ ㄨˊ)
not without

不無可取(ㄅㄨˋ ㄨˊ ㄎㄜˇ ㄑㄩˇ)
more or less laudable or commendable

不無可疑(ㄅㄨˋ ㄨˊ ㄎㄜˇ ㄧˊ)
not above suspicion

不無小補(ㄅㄨˋ ㄨˊ ㄒㄧㄠˇ ㄅㄨˇ)
It might be of some small help.

不務正業(ㄅㄨˊ ㄨˋ ㄓㄥˋ ㄧㄝˋ)
①(said of a playboy, etc.) do not have a legitimate business or profession ② do not attend to one's proper duties

不外(ㄅㄨˊ ㄨㄞˋ)
invariably; most likely; no other than; nothing more than; only

不惟(ㄅㄨˋ ㄨㄟˊ)
not only

不違農時(ㄅㄨˋ ㄨㄟˊ ㄋㄨㄥˊ ㄕˊ)
(said of government measure) do not interfere with farming; do not miss the farming season

不爲已甚(ㄅㄨˋ ㄨㄟˊ ㄧˇ ㄕㄣˋ)
do not push (an advantage, victory, etc.) to the extreme

不爲所動(ㄅㄨˋ ㄨㄟˊ ㄙㄨㄛˇ ㄉㄨㄥˋ)
to remain unmoved (by promises of reward, etc.)

不聞不問(ㄅㄨˋ ㄨㄣˊ ㄅㄨˊ ㄨㄣˋ)
to care nothing about; to cut off all intercourse; indifferent to: 朋友有困難，我們不能不聞不問。We can't remain indifferent when any friend is in difficulty.

不穩(ㄅㄨˋ ㄨㄣˇ)
unsteady; unstable (market, position)

不問(ㄅㄨˊ ㄨㄣˋ)
① to pay no attention to; to disregard; to ignore ② to let go unpunished

不忘溝壑(ㄅㄨˊ ㄨㄤˋ ㄍㄡ ㄏㄨㄛˋ)
do not forget the ditch and the stream—(figuratively) to be determined to die for one's country

不渝(ㄅㄨˋ ㄩˊ)
not to change; to remain faithful

不虞(ㄅㄨˋ ㄩˊ)
① unexpected: 不虞之譽 unexpected praise ② eventuality; contingency ③ do not worry about ④ an untoward event

不予考慮(ㄅㄨˋ ㄩˇ ㄎㄠˇ ㄌㄩˋ)
do not consider

不豫(ㄅㄨˊ ㄩˋ)
① to be unprepared ② displeased

不育(ㄅㄨˊ ㄩˋ)
sterility

不約而同(ㄅㄨˋ ㄩㄝ ㄦˊ ㄊㄨㄥˊ)
to accord without consulting each other

不悅(ㄅㄨˊ ㄩㄝˋ)
unhappy; displeased

不用(ㄅㄨˊ ㄩㄥˋ)
① not necessary ② need not

不用功(ㄅㄨˊ ㄩㄥˋ ㄍㄨㄥ)
do not work or study diligently

不用說(ㄅㄨˊ ㄩㄥˋ ㄕㄨㄛ)or 不待說(ㄅㄨˊ ㄉㄞˋ ㄕㄨㄛ)
it goes without saying; needless to say

【丏】
9
ㄇㄧㄢˇ mean miǎn

1. the curtain to ward off arrows
2. hidden

【丐】
10
ㄍㄞˋ gay gài

1. to beg for alms
2. a beggar

〔一部〕

3. to give
丐頭(ㄍㄞ ㄊㄡˊ)
the leader of (a group of) beggars
丐助(ㄍㄞ ㄓㄨˋ)
to ask for help
丐養(ㄍㄞ ㄧㄤˇ)
to adopt a child or children

【丑】 11
ㄔㄡˇ choou chǒu
1. the second of the twelve "Terrestrial Branches" (地支)
2. the period of the day from 1 to 3 a.m.
3. a clown
4. a Chinese family name
丑表功(ㄔㄡˇ ㄅㄧㄠˇ ㄍㄨㄥ)
to claim an undeserved credit; to brag shamelessly about one's deeds
丑旦(ㄔㄡˇ ㄉㄢˋ)or 丑婆子(ㄔㄡˇ ㄆㄛˊ •ㄗ)
a woman clown or comedienne
丑角(ㄔㄡˇ ㄐㄧㄠˇ)or 丑角兒(ㄔㄡˇ ㄐㄩㄝˊㄦ)or 丑兒(ㄔㄡˇㄦ)
a comedian; a clown; a buffoon

四畫

【且】 12
ㄑㄧㄝˇ chiee qiě
1. moreover; still; further
2. just; for the time being: 且等一下。Just wait a moment.
3. even
4. both…and…
且不(ㄑㄧㄝˇ ㄅㄨˋ)
not for the time being; not going to
且慢(ㄑㄧㄝˇ ㄇㄢˋ)
Hold it! 或 Wait a minute.
且…且…(ㄑㄧㄝˇ…ㄑㄧㄝˇ…)
while; as
且住(ㄑㄧㄝˇ ㄓㄨˋ)
Hold it! 或 Stop it!
且說(ㄑㄧㄝˇ ㄕㄨㄛ)
(usually used at the beginning of a narrative) Let us now talk about....或 moreover

【丕】 13
ㄆㄧ pi pī
1. great; distinguished
2. in observance of (a ruling, etc.)
丕烈(ㄆㄧ ㄌㄧㄝˋ)
unusual achievements, merits or contribution
丕基(ㄆㄧ ㄐㄧ)
the imperial throne; a great heritage
丕績(ㄆㄧ ㄐㄧ)
grand achievements
丕顯(ㄆㄧ ㄒㄧㄢˇ)
great and distinguished; splendid; glorious
丕業(ㄆㄧ ㄧㄝˋ)
(especially referring to the throne) great career

【世】 14
ㄕˋ shyh shì
1. a generation
2. a person's life span
3. an age
4. the world
世伯(ㄕˋ ㄅㄛˊ)
a designation for the male friends of one's father
世面(ㄕˋ ㄇㄧㄢˋ)
the various facets of human activities; state of the world
世法(ㄕˋ ㄈㄚˇ)
① tradition; traditional practices ②(Buddhism) common or ordinary *dharmas,* i.e. truths, laws, things, etc.
世風不古(ㄕˋ ㄈㄥ ㄅㄨˋ ㄍㄨˇ)
Public morals are no longer what they were in the good old days.
世風澆薄(ㄕˋ ㄈㄥ ㄐㄧㄠ ㄅㄛˊ)
There are scarcely public morals to speak of these days.
世風日下(ㄕˋ ㄈㄥ ㄖˋ ㄒㄧㄚˋ)
The moral degeneration of the world is getting worse day by day. 或 The world is declining in its moral values.
世德(ㄕˋ ㄉㄜˊ)
traditional morals; moral principles upheld by one's ancestors
世代(ㄕˋ ㄉㄞˋ)
① a generation ② the times ③ from generation to generation: 世代相傳 to pass on from generation to generation
世代交替(ㄕˋ ㄉㄞˋ ㄐㄧㄠ ㄊㄧˋ)
(biology) metagenesis; alternation of generations
世道(ㄕˋ ㄉㄠˋ)
the ways of the world
世道人心(ㄕˋ ㄉㄠˋ ㄖㄣˊ ㄒㄧㄣ)
the ways of the world and the time; the manners and morals of the time
世弟(ㄕˋ ㄉㄧˋ)
a son of one's father's friend, younger than oneself
世態炎涼(ㄕˋ ㄊㄞˋ ㄧㄢˊ ㄌㄧㄤˊ)
snobbish; inconstancy of human relationships
世路(ㄕˋ ㄌㄨˋ)
the ways and state of the world
世祿(ㄕˋ ㄌㄨˋ)
hereditary honors such as rank and wealth
世故(ㄕˋ ㄍㄨˋ)
① the ways of the world ② shrewd; worldly
世紀(ㄕˋ ㄐㄧˋ)
a century
世家(ㄕˋ ㄐㄧㄚ)
a family holding official ranks for generations
世家子弟(ㄕˋ ㄐㄧㄚ ㄗˇ ㄉㄧˋ)
youngsters of「世家」
世界(ㄕˋ ㄐㄧㄝˋ)
the world
世界博覽會(ㄕˋ ㄐㄧㄝˋ ㄅㄛˊ ㄌㄢˇ ㄏㄨㄟˋ)
a world's fair; a world expo
世界末日(ㄕˋ ㄐㄧㄝˋ ㄇㄛˋ ㄖˋ)
the end of the world; doomsday
世界大同(ㄕˋ ㄐㄧㄝˋ ㄉㄚˋ ㄊㄨㄥˊ)
universal brotherhood
世界大戰(ㄕˋ ㄐㄧㄝˋ ㄉㄚˋ ㄓㄢˋ)
a world war; a global war
世界觀(ㄕˋ ㄐㄧㄝˋ ㄍㄨㄢ)
a philosophical view (or concept) of the world; a world view
世界氣象組織(ㄕˋ ㄐㄧㄝˋ ㄑㄧˋ ㄒㄧㄤˋ ㄗㄨˇ ㄓ)
the World Meteorological Organization (WMO)
世界主義(ㄕˋ ㄐㄧㄝˋ ㄓㄨˇ ㄧˋ)
cosmopolitanism
世界潮流(ㄕˋ ㄐㄧㄝˋ ㄔㄠˊ ㄌㄧㄡˊ)
world trends
世界人權宣言(ㄕˋ ㄐㄧㄝˋ ㄖㄣˊ ㄑㄩㄢˊ ㄒㄩㄢ ㄧㄢˊ)
the Universal Declaration of Human Rights

世界衛生組織(ㄕˋ ㄐㄧㄝˋ ㄨㄟˋ ㄕㄥ ㄗㄨˇ ㄓ)
the World Health Organization (WHO)
世界語(ㄕˋ ㄐㄧㄝˋ ㄩˇ)
Esperanto; the universal language
世交(ㄕˋ ㄐㄧㄠ)
families closely related or associated for generations; long-standing friendship between two families
世間(ㄕˋ ㄐㄧㄢ)
on earth; in the world
世襲(ㄕˋ ㄒㄧˊ)
hereditary (title, rank, etc.)
世系(ㄕˋ ㄒㄧˋ)
a family tree; a pedigree; lineage; a genealogy
世兄(ㄕˋ ㄒㄩㄥ)
a designation for the son of one's father's friend or the son of one's teacher
世姪(ㄕˋ ㄓˊ)
one's close friend's son
世職(ㄕˋ ㄓˊ)
a hereditary official rank
世主(ㄕˋ ㄓㄨˇ)
the ruler of the times
世仇(ㄕˋ ㄔㄡˊ)
① family feud; blood feud ② a mortal enemy in family feud
世傳(ㄕˋ ㄔㄨㄢˊ)
hereditary; to be handed down through generations
世事(ㄕˋ ㄕˋ)
the affairs of the world
世世代代(ㄕˋ ㄕˋ ㄉㄞˋ ㄉㄞˋ)
generation after generation; from generation to generation
世上(ㄕˋ ㄕㄤˋ)
on earth; in the world
世叔(ㄕˋ ㄕㄨˊ)
a younger friend of one's father
世人(ㄕˋ ㄖㄣˊ)
people of the world; (in the Bible) men or women; common people
世子(ㄕˋ ㄗˇ)
the crown prince
世族(ㄕˋ ㄗㄨˊ)
a powerful family that has great political influence for generations
世尊(ㄕˋ ㄗㄨㄣ)
(Buddhism) the Revered One of the World——Buddha
世俗(ㄕˋ ㄙㄨˊ)
① customs and traditions; common practices; social conventions ② secular; worldly
世俗之見(ㄕˋ ㄙㄨˊ ㄓ ㄐㄧㄢˋ)
a very vulgar or commonplace point of view; common views
世誼(ㄕˋ ㄧˊ)
long-standing friendship between two families 亦作「世交」
世業(ㄕˋ ㄧㄝˋ)
trade or property inherited from one's ancestors; hereditary profession in the family
世務(ㄕˋ ㄨˋ)
affairs of the world; worldly affairs
世外桃源(ㄕˋ ㄨㄞˋ ㄊㄠˊ ㄩㄢˊ)
an imaginary, ideal world; a secluded paradise; Shangri-la
世味(ㄕˋ ㄨㄟˋ)
the various phases and tastes of the world
世緣(ㄕˋ ㄩㄢˊ)
(Buddhism) secular ties and affairs
世運(ㄕˋ ㄩㄣˋ)
① the Olympiad; the Olympic Games ② trends or vicissitudes of the world

【丘】 15 ㄑㄧㄡ chiou qiū
1. a hillock or mound
2. big; elder
3. empty
4. first name of Confucius
5. a surname
丘八(ㄑㄧㄡ ㄅㄚ)
an anagram for "soldier" (often used in contemptuous sense)
丘墳(ㄑㄧㄡ ㄈㄣˊ)
a grave in the form of an earthen mound
丘里(ㄑㄧㄡ ㄌㄧˇ)
a native village
丘陵(ㄑㄧㄡ ㄌㄧㄥˊ)
mounds; craggy terrains; hills
丘陵地帶(ㄑㄧㄡ ㄌㄧㄥˊ ㄉㄧˋ ㄉㄞˋ)
the hilly country
丘壑(ㄑㄧㄡ ㄏㄨㄛˋ)
(literary) hills and ravines —a wooded place for retirement
丘墟(ㄑㄧㄡ ㄒㄩ)
empty land; wasteland
丘山(ㄑㄧㄡ ㄕㄢ)
① hills and mountains ② the wild country
丘野(ㄑㄧㄡ ㄧㄝˇ)
the rural country
丘園(ㄑㄧㄡ ㄩㄢˊ)
a garden in the hills

【丙】 16 ㄅㄧㄥˇ biing bǐng
1. the third of the ten "Celestial Stems" (天干)
2. another name for fire
3. the tail of a fish
4. a Chinese family name
丙等(ㄅㄧㄥˇ ㄉㄥˇ)
roughly equivalent to the "C" grade; the third grade
丙酮(ㄅㄧㄥˇ ㄊㄨㄥˊ)
(chemistry) acetone

五畫

【丞】 17 ㄔㄥˊ cherng chéng
1. to aid; to assist
2. a deputy to an official
丞相(ㄔㄥˊ ㄒㄧㄤˋ)
the prime minister (in ancient China)

【丟】 18 ㄉㄧㄡ diou diū
1. to throw: 把球丟給我。Throw me the ball.
2. to lose
3. to put (or lay) aside: 他們把工作丟在一邊。They lay their work aside.
丟面子(ㄉㄧㄡ ㄇㄧㄢˋ ·ㄗ)
to lose face
丟掉(ㄉㄧㄡ ㄉㄧㄠˋ)
① to lose ② to cast away; to throw away
丟臉(ㄉㄧㄡ ㄌㄧㄢˇ)or 丟人(ㄉㄧㄡ ㄖㄣˊ)
to lose face; to disgrace
丟開(ㄉㄧㄡ ㄎㄞ)
① to leave it off; not to mention; to forget for a

while ② to throw away
丟盔卸甲(ㄉㄧㄡ ㄎㄨㄟ ㄒㄧㄝˋ ㄐㄧㄚˇ)
(descriptive of defeated troops) to throw away one's helmet and coat of mail
丟去(ㄉㄧㄡ ㄑㄩˋ)or 丟棄(ㄉㄧㄡ ㄑㄧˋ)
to get rid of; to cast away
丟下(ㄉㄧㄡ ㄒㄧㄚˋ)
to throw down; to lay aside
丟醜(ㄉㄧㄡ ㄔㄡˇ)
to disgrace oneself; to make oneself a laughingstock
丟失(ㄉㄧㄡ ㄕ)
to lose
丟三落四(ㄉㄧㄡ ㄙㄢ ㄌㄚˋ ㄙˋ)
forgetful; scatterbrained; to miss this and that
丟眼色(ㄉㄧㄡ ㄧㄢˇ ㄙㄜˋ)
to give somebody a wink

〔丨部〕

七畫

【並】 19

ㄅㄧㄥˋ binq bìng

1. and; also; at the same time
2. on the same level with; even; equal
3. entirely; completely

並不(ㄅㄧㄥˋ ㄅㄨˋ)
really not
並排(ㄅㄧㄥˋ ㄆㄞˊ)
side by side; in a row; in the same row
並非(ㄅㄧㄥˋ ㄈㄟ)
by no means
並蒂(ㄅㄧㄥˋ ㄉㄧˋ)
① two blossoms on one stalk ② united in love
並立(ㄅㄧㄥˋ ㄌㄧˋ)
① to stand together; to stand side by side ② to exist simultaneously
並列(ㄅㄧㄥˋ ㄌㄧㄝˋ)
to stand side by side; to juxtapose
並聯(ㄅㄧㄥˋ ㄌㄧㄢˊ)
parallel connection: 並聯電路 parallel circuit
並駕齊驅(ㄅㄧㄥˋ ㄐㄧㄚˋ ㄑㄧˊ ㄑㄩ)
to ride bridle to bridle; to keep abreast of; to be equal; to run neck to neck
並肩(ㄅㄧㄥˋ ㄐㄧㄢ)
shoulder to shoulder; side by side; abreast: 他們並肩而行。They walked side by side.
並進(ㄅㄧㄥˋ ㄐㄧㄣˋ)
to advance together; to advance at the same time
並舉(ㄅㄧㄥˋ ㄐㄩˇ)
to develop simultaneously
並且(ㄅㄧㄥˋ ㄑㄧㄝˇ)
moreover; furthermore; and; in addition; to boot
並行不悖(ㄅㄧㄥˋ ㄒㄧㄥˊ ㄅㄨˋ ㄅㄟˋ)
to proceed together or simultaneously without interfering with each other; compatible
並重(ㄅㄧㄥˋ ㄓㄨㄥˋ)
to lay equal stress on; to pay equal attention to: 我們應該經濟與教育並重。We should pay equal attention to both economy and education.
並世無雙(ㄅㄧㄥˋ ㄕˋ ㄨˊ ㄕㄨㄤ)
peerless; foremost
並無不當(ㄅㄧㄥˋ ㄨˊ ㄅㄨˋ ㄉㄤˋ)
There is nothing wrong or improper about it.

丨部

ㄍㄨㄣˇ goen gǔn

二畫

【丫】 20

ㄧㄚ ia yā

something that branches or forks upward
丫頭(ㄧㄚ ·ㄊㄡ)
①(in ancient China) a slave girl; a bought maid; a maid ②(in modern usage) a small girl, especially one's own daughter
丫鬟(ㄧㄚ ·ㄏㄨㄢ)
參看「丫頭①」

三畫

【中】 21

1. ㄓㄨㄥ jong zhōng

1. the middle; among; within; between: 她站在男孩們之中。She stood among the boys.
2. China or Chinese; Sino-

中波(ㄓㄨㄥ ㄅㄛ)
(radio) medium wave
中飽(ㄓㄨㄥ ㄅㄠˇ)
to squeeze; to embezzle; to pocket money to which one has no claim
中班(ㄓㄨㄥ ㄅㄢ)
① the middle shift; the swing shift ② the middle class in a kindergarten
中部(ㄓㄨㄥ ㄅㄨˋ)
the central part; the middle part
中篇小說(ㄓㄨㄥ ㄆㄧㄢ ㄒㄧㄠˇ ㄕㄨㄛ)
a medium-length novel; a novelette
中頻(ㄓㄨㄥ ㄆㄧㄣˊ)
intermediate frequency
中美(ㄓㄨㄥ ㄇㄟˇ)
① Central America ② China and U. S. A.; Sino-American
中美洲(ㄓㄨㄥ ㄇㄟˇ ㄓㄡ)
Central America
中飯(ㄓㄨㄥ ㄈㄢˋ)
lunch; luncheon
中非(ㄓㄨㄥ ㄈㄟ)
① Sino-African ② Central Africa
中非共和國(ㄓㄨㄥ ㄈㄟ ㄍㄨㄥˋ ㄏㄜˊ ㄍㄨㄛˊ)
Central African Republic
中鋒(ㄓㄨㄥ ㄈㄥ)
the center (in basketball, soccer, military operations, etc.)
中道(ㄓㄨㄥ ㄉㄠˋ)
① the middle course ② halfway
中道而廢(ㄓㄨㄥ ㄉㄠˋ ㄦˊ ㄈㄟˋ)
to stop halfway
中等(ㄓㄨㄥ ㄉㄥˇ)
middle-class; medium; mediocre; so-so
中等階級(ㄓㄨㄥ ㄉㄥˇ ㄐㄧㄝ ㄐㄧˊ)or 中產階級(ㄓㄨㄥ ㄔㄢˇ ㄐㄧㄝ ㄐㄧˊ)
the middle class; the bourgeois; white-collar workers
中等教育(ㄓㄨㄥ ㄉㄥˇ ㄐㄧㄠˋ ㄩˋ)
secondary education
中隊(ㄓㄨㄥ ㄉㄨㄟˋ)
① a military unit corresponding to a company; a squadron ② a unit composed of several groups
中斷(ㄓㄨㄥ ㄉㄨㄢˋ)
suspension; interruption; to suspend; to discontinue; to interrupt: 電信中斷了好幾個小

時。Telecommunication was suspended for a few hours.

中東(ㄓㄨㄥ ㄉㄨㄥ)
the Middle East (Asia)

中唐(ㄓㄨㄥ ㄊㄤˊ)
the mid-Tang Dynasty

中堂(ㄓㄨㄥ ㄊㄤˊ)
① a large scroll of painting or calligraphy hung vertically in the parlor ② the Grand Secretary in the Ming and Ching Dynasties

中提琴(ㄓㄨㄥ ㄊㄧˊ ㄑㄧㄣˊ)
a viola

中停(ㄓㄨㄥ ㄊㄧㄥˊ)
to stop in the middle; to interrupt or suspend

中途(ㄓㄨㄥ ㄊㄨˊ)
midway; halfway; on the way: 我們中途停下來用餐。We stopped midway for a meal.

中途島(ㄓㄨㄥ ㄊㄨˊ ㄉㄠˇ)
the Midway Islands

中土(ㄓㄨㄥ ㄊㄨˇ)
① China; Cathay ② the Central Plains—the downstream regions of the Yellow River

中南半島(ㄓㄨㄥ ㄋㄢˊ ㄅㄢˋ ㄉㄠˇ)
Indochina

中年(ㄓㄨㄥ ㄋㄧㄢˊ)
middle age

中欄(ㄓㄨㄥ ㄌㄢˊ)
middle hurdles (in track and field)

中立(ㄓㄨㄥ ㄌㄧˋ)
neutral; neutrality: 他們總是保持中立。They always remain neutral.

中立國(ㄓㄨㄥ ㄌㄧˋ ㄍㄨㄛˊ)
neutral nations

中立區(ㄓㄨㄥ ㄌㄧˋ ㄑㄩ)
a neutral zone

中立主義(ㄓㄨㄥ ㄌㄧˋ ㄓㄨˇ ㄧˋ)
neutralism

中流(ㄓㄨㄥ ㄌㄧㄡˊ)
① the middle of the stream ② middle; average

中流砥柱(ㄓㄨㄥ ㄌㄧㄡˊ ㄉㄧˇ ㄓㄨˋ)
① one who stands firm amid adversities; a man of perseverance or independence ② a main supporter or support; a mainstay

中量級(ㄓㄨㄥ ㄌㄧㄤˋ ㄐㄧˊ)
(sports) middle weight

中落(ㄓㄨㄥ ㄌㄨㄛˋ)
a sudden fall of one's family fortune; to decline

中古(ㄓㄨㄥ ㄍㄨˇ)
the Middle Ages; medieval

中國(ㄓㄨㄥ ㄍㄨㄛˊ)
① China; Cathay ② the Middle Kingdom

中國民主社會黨(ㄓㄨㄥ ㄍㄨㄛˊ ㄇㄧㄣˊ ㄓㄨˇ ㄕㄜˋ ㄏㄨㄟˋ ㄉㄤˇ)
China Democratic Socialist Party

中國電影製片廠(ㄓㄨㄥ ㄍㄨㄛˊ ㄉㄧㄢˋ ㄧㄥˇ ㄓˋ ㄆㄧㄢˋ ㄔㄤˇ)
the China Movie Studio

中國國民黨(ㄓㄨㄥ ㄍㄨㄛˊ ㄍㄨㄛˊ ㄇㄧㄣˊ ㄉㄤˇ)
Kuomingtang (the Chinese Nationalist Party)

中國共產黨(ㄓㄨㄥ ㄍㄨㄛˊ ㄍㄨㄥˋ ㄔㄢˇ ㄉㄤˇ)
Communist Party of China; the Chinese Communist Party

中國海(ㄓㄨㄥ ㄍㄨㄛˊ ㄏㄞˇ)
the China Sea

中國話(ㄓㄨㄥ ㄍㄨㄛˊ ㄏㄨㄚˋ)
the Chinese language; Chinese

中國畫(ㄓㄨㄥ ㄍㄨㄛˊ ㄏㄨㄚˋ)
Chinese painting

中國青年黨(ㄓㄨㄥ ㄍㄨㄛˊ ㄑㄧㄥ ㄋㄧㄢˊ ㄉㄤˇ)
Young China Party

中國城(ㄓㄨㄥ ㄍㄨㄛˊ ㄔㄥˊ)
Chinatown

中國銀行(ㄓㄨㄥ ㄍㄨㄛˊ ㄧㄣˊ ㄏㄤˊ)
Bank of China

中國猿人(ㄓㄨㄥ ㄍㄨㄛˊ ㄩㄢˊ ㄖㄣˊ)
Sinanthropus 參看「北京人」

中共(ㄓㄨㄥ ㄍㄨㄥˋ)
Communist Party of China (中國共產黨)

中饋(ㄓㄨㄥ ㄎㄨㄟˋ)
① the wife's job ② a wife

中饋猶虛(ㄓㄨㄥ ㄎㄨㄟˋ ㄧㄡˊ ㄒㄩ)
(said of men) still unmarried

中和(ㄓㄨㄥ ㄏㄜˊ)
① justice and peace ② (chemistry) to neutralize: 一種毒品常能中和另一種毒品。One poison often neutralizes another. ③ to lessen the effect; to modify ④ Chungho, a suburban district of Taipei

中和作用(ㄓㄨㄥ ㄏㄜˊ ㄗㄨㄛˋ ㄩㄥˋ)
neutralization

中華(ㄓㄨㄥ ㄏㄨㄚˊ)
(originally, the region along the Yellow River where the Chinese people thrived) the Chinese nation; the Chinese people

中華民國(ㄓㄨㄥ ㄏㄨㄚˊ ㄇㄧㄣˊ ㄍㄨㄛˊ)
the Republic of China

中華民族(ㄓㄨㄥ ㄏㄨㄚˊ ㄇㄧㄣˊ ㄗㄨˊ)
a name for the ethnic groups that constitute the Chinese nation; the Chinese nation

中華革命黨(ㄓㄨㄥ ㄏㄨㄚˊ ㄍㄜˊ ㄇㄧㄥˋ ㄉㄤˇ)
Chinese Revolutionary Party (the forerunner of Kuomingtang)

中華日報(ㄓㄨㄥ ㄏㄨㄚˊ ㄖˋ ㄅㄠˋ)
the China Daily News

中級(ㄓㄨㄥ ㄐㄧˊ)
middle rank; intermediate

中繼站(ㄓㄨㄥ ㄐㄧˋ ㄓㄢˋ)
a relay station 亦作「轉播站」

中介(ㄓㄨㄥ ㄐㄧㄝˋ)
intermediary; medium

中堅(ㄓㄨㄥ ㄐㄧㄢ)
① the main force (of an army); crack troops ② a cadre; underpinning; the core; the backbone

中堅分子(ㄓㄨㄥ ㄐㄧㄢ ㄈㄣˋ ㄗˇ)
the hard core; the salt of the earth; the people most concerned at the center of an activity, especially when opposed to some other group

中間(ㄓㄨㄥ ㄐㄧㄢ) or 中間兒(ㄓㄨㄥ ㄐㄧㄚㄦ)
in the middle; in the center

中間派(ㄓㄨㄥ ㄐㄧㄢ ㄆㄞˋ)
the middle-of-the-roaders; the neutral faction; the straddlers or fence-sitters

中間產品(ㄓㄨㄥ ㄐㄧㄢ ㄔㄢˇ ㄆㄧㄣˇ)
intermediate products

中將(ㄓㄨㄥ ㄐㄧㄤˋ)
(army, marine and air force) lieutenant general; (navy) vice-admiral

中距離(ㄓㄨㄥ ㄐㄩˋ ㄌㄧˊ)
middle distance

中絕(ㄓㄨㄥ ㄐㄩㄝˊ)
to stop midway; to perish or

〔丨部〕

vanish before reaching a conclusion

中軍(ㄓㄨㄥ ㄐㄩㄣ)
the central column; the main army

中秋節(ㄓㄨㄥ ㄑㄧㄡ ㄐㄧㄝˊ)
the Mid-Autumn Festival or the Moon Festival (the 15th day of the 8th lunar month)

中西(ㄓㄨㄥ ㄒㄧ)
Chinese and Western

中西合璧(ㄓㄨㄥ ㄒㄧ ㄏㄜˊ ㄅㄧˋ)
a (good) combination or blending of Chinese and Western (fashion, style, etc.)

中西文化(ㄓㄨㄥ ㄒㄧ ㄨㄣˊ ㄏㄨㄚˋ)
Chinese and Western civilizations; Chinese and Western culture

中夏(ㄓㄨㄥ ㄒㄧㄚˋ)
China

中宵(ㄓㄨㄥ ㄒㄧㄠ)
middle of the night; midnight

中校(ㄓㄨㄥ ㄒㄧㄠˋ)
(army, marine and air force) lieutenant colonel; (navy) commander

中線(ㄓㄨㄥ ㄒㄧㄢˋ)
(sports) the center line; half-way line

中心(ㄓㄨㄥ ㄒㄧㄣ)
① center ② central point ③ persons holding important positions

中心人物(ㄓㄨㄥ ㄒㄧㄣ ㄖㄣˊ ㄨˋ)
the central figure; the key figure

中心思想(ㄓㄨㄥ ㄒㄧㄣ ㄙ ㄒㄧㄤˇ)
a central idea or thought (of a principle or philosophy); the gist

中興(ㄓㄨㄥ ㄒㄧㄥ)
revival (of a nation or family); to rise after decline; rejuvenation; resurgence

中型(ㄓㄨㄥ ㄒㄧㄥˊ)
medium-sized; middle-sized

中性(ㄓㄨㄥ ㄒㄧㄥˋ)
①(chemistry) neutral or neutrality ②(grammar) the neuter gender

中學(ㄓㄨㄥ ㄒㄩㄝˊ)or 中等學校(ㄓㄨㄥ ㄉㄥˇ ㄒㄩㄝˊ ㄒㄧㄠˋ)
middle school; high school; secondary school

中旬(ㄓㄨㄥ ㄒㄩㄣˊ)
the middle part of a month; the middle ten days of a month

中止(ㄓㄨㄥ ㄓˇ)
to suspend; suspension; to interrupt; interruption

中指(ㄓㄨㄥ ㄓˇ)
the middle finger

中正(ㄓㄨㄥ ㄓㄥˋ)
just; fair; unbiased; impartial; not prejudiced

中裝(ㄓㄨㄥ ㄓㄨㄤ)
traditional Chinese clothing

中產階級(ㄓㄨㄥ ㄔㄢˇ ㄐㄧㄝ ㄐㄧˊ)
the middle class; bourgeois

中程(ㄓㄨㄥ ㄔㄥˊ)
intermediate range; medium-range

中程飛彈(ㄓㄨㄥ ㄔㄥˊ ㄈㄟ ㄉㄢˋ)
an intermediate range missile; a medium-range missile

中輟(ㄓㄨㄥ ㄔㄨㄛˋ)
to stop in the middle of something; to give up halfway

中式(ㄓㄨㄥ ㄕˋ)
the Chinese style or fashion; the Chinese way

中士(ㄓㄨㄥ ㄕˋ)
a sergeant

中世(ㄓㄨㄥ ㄕˋ)or 中世紀(ㄓㄨㄥ ㄕˋ ㄐㄧˋ)
the Middle Ages

中沙群島(ㄓㄨㄥ ㄕㄚ ㄑㄩㄣˊ ㄉㄠˇ)
the Zhongsha Islands

中山(ㄓㄨㄥ ㄕㄢ)
the courtesy name of Dr. Sun Yat-sen(孫逸仙), father of the Republic of China (often used as name of roads, schools, etc.)

中山堂(ㄓㄨㄥ ㄕㄢ ㄊㄤˊ)
any building named after Dr. Sun Yat-sen (often used as a city hall, community center, etc.)

中山樓(ㄓㄨㄥ ㄕㄢ ㄌㄡˊ)
the Chungshan Building (at Yangmingshan near Taipei)

中山狼(ㄓㄨㄥ ㄕㄢ ㄌㄤˊ)
a perfidious person

中山陵(ㄓㄨㄥ ㄕㄢ ㄌㄧㄥˊ)
the Dr. Sun Yat-sen Mausoleum (in Nanking)

中山裝(ㄓㄨㄥ ㄕㄢ ㄓㄨㄤ)or 中山服(ㄓㄨㄥ ㄕㄢ ㄈㄨˊ)
the dress like a military uniform with closed collar; the style of man's jacket with closed collar without tie

中生代(ㄓㄨㄥ ㄕㄥ ㄉㄞˋ)
the Mesozoic (Era)

中樞(ㄓㄨㄥ ㄕㄨ)
① the central administration ②(physiology) the center

中書省(ㄓㄨㄥ ㄕㄨ ㄕㄥˇ)
(the Tang Dynasty) cabinet of ministers

中日戰爭(ㄓㄨㄥ ㄖˋ ㄓㄢˋ ㄓㄥ)
the Sino-Japanese War, 1894; the Sino-Japanese War—the War of Resistance Against Japanese Aggression, 1937-1945

中人(ㄓㄨㄥ ㄖㄣˊ)or 中間人(ㄓㄨㄥ ㄐㄧㄢ ㄖㄣˊ)
a middleman; a go-between; an agent; a mediator

中人之姿(ㄓㄨㄥ ㄖㄣˊ ㄓ ㄗ)
homely

中子(ㄓㄨㄥ ㄗˇ)
neutron

中材(ㄓㄨㄥ ㄘㄞˊ)
a person of ordinary talent

中菜(ㄓㄨㄥ ㄘㄞˋ)
Chinese dishes

中菜西吃(ㄓㄨㄥ ㄘㄞˋ ㄒㄧ ㄔ)
to eat Chinese food in the Western way (by dividing it into shares with one share for each)

中餐(ㄓㄨㄥ ㄘㄢ)
① a midday meal ② Chinese meal; Chinese food

中歐(ㄓㄨㄥ ㄡ)
the central part of Europe

中耳(ㄓㄨㄥ ㄦˇ)
the middle ear

中醫(ㄓㄨㄥ ㄧ)
① a Chinese herb doctor ② traditional Chinese medical science

中亞(ㄓㄨㄥ ㄧㄚˋ)
Central Asia

中葉(ㄓㄨㄥ ㄧㄝˋ)
the middle decades of a century; the middle period (of a dynasty, century, reign)

中藥(ㄓㄨㄥ ㄧㄠˋ)
Chinese medicine (mostly herbs)

中游(ㄓㄨㄥ ㄧㄡˊ)

①middle reaches (of a river) ②the state of being middling: 他甘居中游。He is content to stay middling.
中央(ㄓㄨㄥ ㄧㄤ)
the center; the middle
中央電影公司(ㄓㄨㄥ ㄧㄤ ㄉㄧㄢˋ ㄧㄥˇ ㄍㄨㄥ ㄙ)
Central Motion Picture Corporation
中央通訊社(ㄓㄨㄥ ㄧㄤ ㄊㄨㄥ ㄒㄩㄣˋ ㄕㄜˋ)
Central News Agency (CNA)
中央集權(ㄓㄨㄥ ㄧㄤ ㄐㄧˊ ㄑㄩㄢˊ)
a centralized government; centralization of authority
中央情報局(ㄓㄨㄥ ㄧㄤ ㄑㄧㄥˊ ㄅㄠˋ ㄐㄩˊ)
Central Intelligence Agency (CIA)
中央系統空氣調節(ㄓㄨㄥ ㄧㄤ ㄒㄧˋ ㄊㄨㄥˇ ㄎㄨㄥ ㄑㄧˋ ㄊㄧㄠˊ ㄐㄧㄝˊ)
central system air conditioning
中央信託局(ㄓㄨㄥ ㄧㄤ ㄒㄧㄣˋ ㄊㄨㄛ ㄐㄩˊ)
Central Trust of China
中央政府(ㄓㄨㄥ ㄧㄤ ㄓㄥˋ ㄈㄨˇ)
the Central Government; the National Government
中央日報(ㄓㄨㄥ ㄧㄤ ㄖˋ ㄅㄠˋ)
Central Daily News
中央研究院(ㄓㄨㄥ ㄧㄤ ㄧㄢˊ ㄐㄧㄡˋ ㄩㄢˋ)
Academia Sinica
中央銀行(ㄓㄨㄥ ㄧㄤ ㄧㄣˊ ㄏㄤˊ)
Central Bank of China
中央委員(ㄓㄨㄥ ㄧㄤ ㄨㄟˇ ㄩㄢˊ)
a member of the central committee of a political party
中央預算(ㄓㄨㄥ ㄧㄤ ㄩˋ ㄙㄨㄢˋ)
the central budget
中午(ㄓㄨㄥ ㄨˇ)
noon; high noon; midday
中外(ㄓㄨㄥ ㄨㄞˋ)
Chinese and foreign; in China and abroad
中外一理(ㄓㄨㄥ ㄨㄞˋ ㄧˋ ㄌㄧˇ)
Truth, human nature, and so on are the same everywhere.
中外野手 (ㄓㄨㄥ ㄨㄞˋ ㄧㄝˇ ㄕㄡˇ)
(baseball) a center fielder
中尉(ㄓㄨㄥ ㄨㄟˋ)
(army, marine and air force) first lieutenant; (navy) lieutenant (j.g.)
中文(ㄓㄨㄥ ㄨㄣˊ)
the Chinese language; Chinese
中文打字電報機(ㄓㄨㄥ ㄨㄣˊ ㄉㄚˇ ㄗˋ ㄉㄧㄢˋ ㄅㄠˋ ㄐㄧ)
a Chinese teletype
中文電腦(ㄓㄨㄥ ㄨㄣˊ ㄉㄧㄢˋ ㄋㄠˇ)
a Chinese language programmable computer
中原(ㄓㄨㄥ ㄩㄢˊ)
①the Central Plains—the downstream regions of the Yellow River ②the midst of a plain
中原逐鹿(ㄓㄨㄥ ㄩㄢˊ ㄓㄨˊ ㄌㄨˋ)
to fight for hegemony (among contending princes, warlords, etc.)
中元節(ㄓㄨㄥ ㄩㄢˊ ㄐㄧㄝˊ)
the Ghost Festival on the 15th day of the seventh lunar month
中庸(ㄓㄨㄥ ㄩㄥ)
①the golden mean of the Confucian school ②the *Doctrine of the Mean*—one of the *Four Books* ③of ordinary talent; common; mediocre

【中】 21
2. ㄓㄨㄥˋ jonq zhòng

1. to hit (the target); to attain (a goal)
2. to be hit by; to be affected by: 他被落石擊中。He was hit by a falling stone.

中風(ㄓㄨㄥˋ ㄈㄥ)
to suffer from a stroke of paralysis or apoplexy
中伏(ㄓㄨㄥˋ ㄈㄨˊ)
to be ambushed
中彈(ㄓㄨㄥˋ ㄉㄢˋ)
to be struck by a bullet; to get shot
中的(ㄓㄨㄥˋ ㄉㄧˋ)
to hit the bull's-eye; to hit the right point; to hit the target
中第(ㄓㄨㄥˋ ㄉㄧˋ)
to pass the civil examinations
中毒(ㄓㄨㄥˋ ㄉㄨˊ)
to be poisoned; toxicosis
中聽(ㄓㄨㄥˋ ㄊㄧㄥ)
pleasant to the ear
中看(ㄓㄨㄥˋ ㄎㄢˋ)
good to look at
中肯(ㄓㄨㄥˋ ㄎㄣˇ)
to the point; fair; relevant: 他的回答簡短而中肯。His reply was brief and to the point.
中寒(ㄓㄨㄥˋ ㄏㄢˊ)
to catch cold; to be attacked by cold
中計(ㄓㄨㄥˋ ㄐㄧˋ)
to walk into a trap; to fall into a trap; to be trapped; to be victimized by a scheme
中節(ㄓㄨㄥˋ ㄐㄧㄝˊ)
①in rhythm ②proper and just
中舉(ㄓㄨㄥˋ ㄐㄩˇ)
to pass the provincial civil service examination under the old Chinese examination system
中籤(ㄓㄨㄥˋ ㄑㄧㄢ)
to be chosen by lot
中選(ㄓㄨㄥˋ ㄒㄩㄢˇ)
to be chosen; to be selected
中吃(ㄓㄨㄥˋ ㄔ)
good to eat; tasty
中傷(ㄓㄨㄥˋ ㄕㄤ)
to hurt somebody insidiously; to say damaging things about others before a third party; to malign; to vilify; to slander: 有人在報上中傷他。He was vilified in newspapers.
中暑(ㄓㄨㄥˋ ㄕㄨˇ)
to have (or take) a sunstroke (or heatstroke)
中彩(ㄓㄨㄥˋ ㄘㄞˇ) or 中獎(ㄓㄨㄥˋ ㄐㄧㄤˇ)
to win a (lottery) prize
中意(ㄓㄨㄥˋ ㄧˋ)
to suit one's fancy; agreeable; satisfied; to one's liking: 這些書，我一本也不中意。None of these books is to my liking.
中用(ㄓㄨㄥˋ ㄩㄥˋ)
useful; serviceable

【丰】 22
ㄈㄥ feng fēng

1. good-looking; buxom
2. appearance and carriage of a person

丰標(ㄈㄥ ㄅㄧㄠ)
looks; appearances
丰容(ㄈㄥ ㄖㄨㄥˊ)

(to address a lady) your face

丰姿(ㄈㄥ ㄗ)
appearances of a person (usually indicating grace and charm)

丰采(ㄈㄥ ㄘㄞˇ)
good-looking; dashing appearances

丰韻(ㄈㄥ ㄩㄣˋ)
charming appearances or carriage; graceful poise

六畫

【串】23 ㄔㄨㄢˋ chuann chuàn
1. to string together
2. a string (of coins, etc.)
3. to pour into

串騙(ㄔㄨㄢˋ ㄆㄧㄢˋ)
to swindle; to collaborate for such a purpose

串門子(ㄔㄨㄢˋ ㄇㄣˊ ·ㄗ)or 串門兒(ㄔㄨㄢˋ ㄇㄜˊㄦ)
to visit or gossip from door to door: 她有空就來串門子。She visits from door to door when she's free.

串通(ㄔㄨㄢˋ ㄊㄨㄥ)
to collude or to conspire

串同(ㄔㄨㄢˋ ㄊㄨㄥˊ)
to band together (to do something evil); to gang up

串聯(ㄔㄨㄢˋ ㄌㄧㄢˊ)
series connection

串鈴(ㄔㄨㄢˋ ㄌㄧㄥˊ)
a string of bells used by peddlers to attract customers

串供(ㄔㄨㄢˋ ㄍㄨㄥˋ)
collusion among witnesses or suspects for false confessions; to act in collusion

串戲(ㄔㄨㄢˋ ㄒㄧˋ)
to take part in a play; to act in a play as an amateur

串珠(ㄔㄨㄢˋ ㄓㄨ)or 串珠兒(ㄔㄨㄢˋ ㄓㄨㄦ)
a string of pearls or beads

串演(ㄔㄨㄢˋ ㄧㄢˇ)
to play respective roles in an opera or a play

丶部
ㄓㄨˇ juu zhǔ

二畫

【丸】24 ㄨㄢˊ wan wán
1. a pellet; a small ball; a pill
2. an egg
3. used in Japanese indicating completion or completeness

丸劑(ㄨㄢˊ ㄐㄧˋ)
a medical pill

丸子(ㄨㄢˊ ·ㄗ)
① a meat ball; fish balls ② a medical pill

丸藥(ㄨㄢˊ ㄧㄠˋ)
medicine in pill form

三畫

【丹】25 ㄉㄢ dan dān
1. cinnabar
2. red; scarlet
3. a sophisticated decoction
4. a medical pill, ointment and powder

丹魄(ㄉㄢ ㄆㄛˋ)
amber

丹麥(ㄉㄢ ㄇㄞˋ)
Denmark

丹麥人(ㄉㄢ ㄇㄞˋ ㄖㄣˊ)
a Dane; the Danes

丹麥語(ㄉㄢ ㄇㄞˋ ㄩˇ)
Danish

丹方(ㄉㄢ ㄈㄤ)
a prescription; a folk prescription

丹毒(ㄉㄢ ㄉㄨˊ)
erysipelas; an inflammatory disease with redness of skin

丹田(ㄉㄢ ㄊㄧㄢˊ)
the lower part of abdomen; (Taoism) the region three inches below the navel

丹鉛(ㄉㄢ ㄑㄧㄢ)
a mixture of cinnabar and white lead powder formerly used for writing or painting purpose—the business of proofreading or revision, from practice of using red ink

丹青(ㄉㄢ ㄑㄧㄥ)
① painting ② history; annals

丹闕(ㄉㄢ ㄑㄩㄝˋ)
the red gate of a palace—a palace

丹心(ㄉㄢ ㄒㄧㄣ)
sincere heart; the bottom of one's heart

丹竹(ㄉㄢ ㄓㄨˊ)
the red bamboo

丹忱(ㄉㄢ ㄔㄣˊ)
sincere loyalty

丹誠(ㄉㄢ ㄔㄥˊ)
loyalty; devotion

丹砂(ㄉㄢ ㄕㄚ)
cinnabar; material for red color

丹書(ㄉㄢ ㄕㄨ)or 丹詔(ㄉㄢ ㄓㄠˋ)
the imperial edict written in red

四畫

【主】26 ㄓㄨˇ juu zhǔ
1. a master; a leader; a chief; a host
2. Jesus Christ; God; Lord
3. to officiate at; to preside over; to take charge of
4. main; chief; primary; principal

主辦(ㄓㄨˇ ㄅㄢˋ)
to sponsor; to take charge of

主筆(ㄓㄨˇ ㄅㄧˇ)
an editorial writer of a newspaper

主編(ㄓㄨˇ ㄅㄧㄢ)
a senior editor who edits a specific page or section of a newspaper; an editor-in-chief

主賓席(ㄓㄨˇ ㄅㄧㄣ ㄒㄧˊ)
the head table (at a banquet, etc.); the seat for the guest of honor

主僕(ㄓㄨˇ ㄆㄨˊ)
master and servant

主謀(ㄓㄨˇ ㄇㄡˊ)
①the mastermind; the string-puller ② to head a conspiracy; to be the chief plotter

主犯(ㄓㄨˇ ㄈㄢˋ)
the leader of a racket; the principal criminal; the main

culprit

主峯(ㄓㄨˇ ㄈㄥ)
the main peak of a mountain; the highest peak in a mountain range

主婦(ㄓㄨˇ ㄈㄨˋ)
a housewife; a hostess; the mistress of the house

主導(ㄓㄨˇ ㄉㄠˇ)
leading; dominant; guiding

主動(ㄓㄨˇ ㄉㄨㄥˋ)
to take the initiative; of one's own accord

主動脈(ㄓㄨˇ ㄉㄨㄥˋ ㄇㄞˋ)
(anatomy) the aorta

主動式(ㄓㄨˇ ㄉㄨㄥˋ ㄕˋ)
(grammar) the active voice

主題(ㄓㄨˇ ㄊㄧˊ)
the main theme (of an essay or a musical piece); the main points; the central thought; the gist

主體(ㄓㄨˇ ㄊㄧˇ)
① the subjective (as against the objective) ② the main body or the most important part of something

主腦(ㄓㄨˇ ㄋㄠˇ)
the mastermind; the chief; the leader

主奴(ㄓㄨˇ ㄋㄨˊ)
master and servant

主力(ㄓㄨˇ ㄌㄧˋ)
the main force; the main body of an army

主力艦(ㄓㄨˇ ㄌㄧˋ ㄐㄧㄢˋ)
a battleship; a capital ship

主力軍(ㄓㄨˇ ㄌㄧˋ ㄐㄩㄣ)
the main force; the principal force

主流(ㄓㄨˇ ㄌㄧㄡˊ)
① the mainstream; the main current; the mother current ② the essential or main aspect; the main trend

主糧(ㄓㄨˇ ㄌㄧㄤˊ)
the staple food grain

主格(ㄓㄨˇ ㄍㄜˊ)
(grammar) the subjective case

主稿(ㄓㄨˇ ㄍㄠˇ)
the chief writer; a person who organizes material presented by others for writings

主幹(ㄓㄨˇ ㄍㄢˋ)
① the trunk ② the main force; the mainstay

主顧(ㄓㄨˇ ㄍㄨˋ)
a customer; a client

主觀(ㄓㄨˇ ㄍㄨㄢ)
the subjective point of view

主管(ㄓㄨˇ ㄍㄨㄢˇ)
① the boss; the chief ② to take charge of: 他將主管這件工作。He will be in charge of this job.

主管機關(ㄓㄨˇ ㄍㄨㄢˇ ㄐㄧ ㄍㄨㄢ)
the authorities concerned; the agency which is in charge of (a program, etc.)

主攻(ㄓㄨˇ ㄍㄨㄥ)
the main attack

主客(ㄓㄨˇ ㄎㄜˋ)
the guest of honor

主考(ㄓㄨˇ ㄎㄠˇ)
① to be in charge of a competitive examination ②(in ancient China) the official in charge of a civil service examination

主和(ㄓㄨˇ ㄏㄜˊ)
to advocate peace

主和派(ㄓㄨˇ ㄏㄜˊ ㄆㄞˋ)
the doves

主婚(ㄓㄨˇ ㄏㄨㄣ)
to preside over a wedding ceremony

主婚人(ㄓㄨˇ ㄏㄨㄣ ㄖㄣˊ)
the parents (or guardians) of the marrying couple at a wedding ceremony

主機(ㄓㄨˇ ㄐㄧ)
① the main engine ②(air force) the lead plane; the leader ③ the host computer

主祭(ㄓㄨˇ ㄐㄧˋ)
① to officiate at a religious rite or service ② a person officiating at such a service

主計室(ㄓㄨˇ ㄐㄧˋ ㄕˋ)
the auditing department; the accounting department

主記憶體(ㄓㄨˇ ㄐㄧˋ ㄧˋ ㄊㄧˇ)
(computers) the main memory

主教(ㄓㄨˇ ㄐㄧㄠˋ)
a bishop

主見(ㄓㄨˇ ㄐㄧㄢˋ)
the ideas or thoughts of one's own: 他這人很有主見。He knows his own mind.

主講(ㄓㄨˇ ㄐㄧㄤˇ)
① to lecture; to speak on a special subject ② the main speaker

主將(ㄓㄨˇ ㄐㄧㄤˋ)
① the commanding general ② the most important athlete in a sports team

主句(ㄓㄨˇ ㄐㄩˋ)
a main clause; a principal clause

主角(ㄓㄨˇ ㄐㄩㄝˊ)or 主角兒(ㄓㄨˇ ㄐㄩㄝˊㄦ)
the leading player; the leading role; the main actor or actress; the protagonist; the lead

主權(ㄓㄨˇ ㄑㄩㄢˊ)
① sovereignty ② the right of autonomy

主權國(ㄓㄨˇ ㄑㄩㄢˊ ㄍㄨㄛˊ)
a sovereign state (or country)

主席(ㄓㄨˇ ㄒㄧˊ)
a chairman; a president

主席團(ㄓㄨˇ ㄒㄧˊ ㄊㄨㄢˊ)
the presidium

主修(ㄓㄨˇ ㄒㄧㄡ)
① to specialize (in a subject); to major ② to be responsible for the repair or overhaul (of a machine)

主旨(ㄓㄨˇ ㄓˇ)
the gist, substance, purport, or the main points (of a speech, statement, etc.)

主治(ㄓㄨˇ ㄓˋ)
① the major functions of a drug ② a physician in charge of a patient or patients

主治醫師(ㄓㄨˇ ㄓˋ ㄧ ㄕ)
a physician in charge of a case

主戰(ㄓㄨˇ ㄓㄢˋ)
to advocate war

主戰派(ㄓㄨˇ ㄓㄢˋ ㄆㄞˋ)
the hawks

主張(ㄓㄨˇ ㄓㄤ)
① an opinion or idea ② to hold a view; to advocate: 我主張釋放那犯人。I advocate the release of the prisoner.

主政(ㄓㄨˇ ㄓㄥˋ)
① to head the administration ② the person in charge

主終端機(ㄓㄨˇ ㄓㄨㄥ ㄉㄨㄢ ㄐㄧ)
(computers) the master terminal

〔丿部〕

主持(ㄓㄨˇ ㄔˊ)
to officiate at; to preside over; to take charge of; to supervise: 張先生主持會議。Mr. Chang presided over the meeting.
主持正義(ㄓㄨˇ ㄔˊ ㄓㄥˋ ㄧˋ)
to uphold justice; to champion the cause of justice
主程式(ㄓㄨˇ ㄔㄥˊ ㄕˋ)
(computers) the main program
主食(ㄓㄨˇ ㄕˊ)
the principal food items; staple food
主使(ㄓㄨˇ ㄕˇ)
① a mastermind; a behind-the-scene operator; a ringleader ② to incite; to instigate
主試官(ㄓㄨˇ ㄕˋ ㄍㄨㄢ)
(in ancient China) the official in charge of a civil service examination
主帥(ㄓㄨˇ ㄕㄨㄞˋ)
an address to the commander in chief
主日(ㄓㄨˇ ㄖˋ)
Sunday
主日學校(ㄓㄨˇ ㄖˋ ㄒㄩㄝˊ ㄒㄧㄠˋ)
Sunday school
主人(ㄓㄨˇ ㄖㄣˊ)
① an owner ② a host ③ a master
主人翁(ㄓㄨˇ ㄖㄣˊ ㄨㄥ)
① a respectful term for a host ② a master: 年輕的一代是新社會的主人翁。The younger generation is the master of the new society.
主任(ㄓㄨˇ ㄖㄣˋ)
the head of an office; the person in charge (of an undertaking, committee, etc.)
主子(ㄓㄨˇ ˙ㄗ)
① the emperor ② one's master; one's boss
主宰(ㄓㄨˇ ㄗㄞˇ)
①the man in charge; a man with supreme powers ② a god
主座(ㄓㄨˇ ㄗㄨㄛˋ)
the seat of honor; the person occupying it
主從(ㄓㄨˇ ㄘㄨㄥˊ)
① the master and his servant (or servants) ② the principal and the secondary (criminals)
主詞(ㄓㄨˇ ㄘˊ)
(grammar) the subject
主菜(ㄓㄨˇ ㄘㄞˋ)
entrée; the principal dish
主隨客便(ㄓㄨˇ ㄙㄨㄟˊ ㄎㄜˋ ㄅㄧㄢˋ)
A host respects his guest's wishes.
主意(ㄓㄨˇ ㄧˋ)
an idea; a suggestion: 那眞是個好主意。It's a good idea.
主義(ㄓㄨˇ ㄧˋ)
a principle; a doctrine
主要(ㄓㄨˇ ㄧㄠˋ)
essential; important; major; chief; principal
主祐(ㄓㄨˇ ㄧㄡˋ)
blessed or protected by God
主演(ㄓㄨˇ ㄧㄢˇ)
to star; to play the leading role in a play or a motion picture
主因(ㄓㄨˇ ㄧㄣ)
the major cause; the principal cause
主位(ㄓㄨˇ ㄨㄟˋ)
the seat of the host
主語(ㄓㄨˇ ㄩˇ)
(grammar) the subject of a sentence

五畫

【乒】 27
ㄆㄤ pang pāng
used for the sound 參看「乒乓」: 門在他身後乒然地關上。The door banged after him.

丿部
ㄆㄧㄝˇ piee piě

一畫

【乃】 28
ㄋㄞˇ nae nǎi
1. to be: 需要乃發明之根源。Necessity is the mother of invention.
2. but; however
3. and also; moreover
4. so; therefore
5. you; your
6. then
7. if
乃至(ㄋㄞˇ ㄓˋ)
① so that; so… as to; leading to ② hence; consequently ③ even: 乃至如此。It even came to such a pass.
乃是(ㄋㄞˇ ㄕˋ)
① but ② which is…; to be; really is (are): 失敗乃是成功之母。Failure is the mother of success.
乃祖(ㄋㄞˇ ㄗㄨˇ)
your grandfather
乃翁(ㄋㄞˇ ㄨㄥ)or 乃父(ㄋㄞˇ ㄈㄨˋ)
your father

二畫

【久】 29
ㄐㄧㄡˇ jeou jiǔ
1. long
2. for a long time: 由來久矣! It's been so for a long time.
3. to detain someone long
久別(ㄐㄧㄡˇ ㄅㄧㄝˊ)
long separated; long separation
久病成良醫(ㄐㄧㄡˇ ㄅㄧㄥˋ ㄔㄥˊ ㄌㄧㄤˊ ㄧ)
Long illness makes the patient a good doctor.
久慕(ㄐㄧㄡˇ ㄇㄨˋ)
I have heard of you for a long time.—a conventional phrase for greeting somebody one has just been introduced to
久佃成業(ㄐㄧㄡˇ ㄉㄧㄢˋ ㄔㄥˊ ㄧㄝˋ)
A long-term tenant regards the land he tills as his own.
久歷風塵(ㄐㄧㄡˇ ㄌㄧˋ ㄈㄥ ㄔㄣˊ)
(said of women) to have led a life of sin for a long time
久留(ㄐㄧㄡˇ ㄌㄧㄡˊ)
to stay for a long time
久客(ㄐㄧㄡˇ ㄎㄜˋ)
to be a guest for an extended period of time; to be a wanderer away from home for a long time
久困(ㄐㄧㄡˇ ㄎㄨㄣˋ)
to stay in an unpleasant situation or on a lowly job for a long time
久候(ㄐㄧㄡˇ ㄏㄡˋ)

to wait for a long time

久旱逢甘霖(ㄐㄧㄡˇ ㄏㄢˋ ㄈㄥˊ ㄍㄢ ㄌㄧㄣˊ)
(literally) to have a sweet shower after a long drought—to get something urgently needed after being deprived of it for a long time

久計(ㄐㄧㄡˇ ㄐㄧˋ)
a long-range plan

久假不歸(ㄐㄧㄡˇ ㄐㄧㄚˇ ㄅㄨˋ ㄍㄨㄟ)
to fail to return (something) after having borrowed it for a long time; to put off indefinitely returning something one has borrowed

久久(ㄐㄧㄡˇ ㄐㄧㄡˇ)
for a long, long time

久經風霜(ㄐㄧㄡˇ ㄐㄧㄥ ㄈㄥ ㄕㄨㄤ)
to have experienced all sorts of hardships

久居人下(ㄐㄧㄡˇ ㄐㄩ ㄖㄣˊ ㄒㄧㄚˋ)
to remain in a subordinate position for a long period

久屈(ㄐㄧㄡˇ ㄑㄩ)
(said of a talented person) to occupy a lowly position for a long time

久蟄思動(ㄐㄧㄡˇ ㄓㄜˊ ㄙ ㄉㄨㄥˋ)
to be eager to enter the limelight again after a long period of retirement or inactivity

久長(ㄐㄧㄡˇ ㄔㄤˊ)
for a long time; an extended period of time

久長之策(ㄐㄧㄡˇ ㄔㄤˊ ㄓ ㄘㄜˋ)
a long-range plan

久而久之(ㄐㄧㄡˇ ㄦˊ ㄐㄧㄡˇ ㄓ)
over a long period of time

久仰(ㄐㄧㄡˇ ㄧㄤˇ)
(literally) I have heard of your illustrious name for a long time.—Glad to meet you.

久仰大名(ㄐㄧㄡˇ ㄧㄤˇ ㄉㄚˋ ㄇㄧㄥˊ)
I've heard of your illustrious name for a long time. 亦作「久聞大名」

久違(ㄐㄧㄡˇ ㄨㄟˊ)
the literary form of "Long time no see." 或 I have not seen you for a long time.

久遠(ㄐㄧㄡˇ ㄩㄢˇ)
a long time; forever; long and far-reaching; perpetual; ages ago; remote

三畫

【之】 30 ㄓ jy zhī

1. to go to; to leave for; to arrive at
2. zigzag; winding
3. an expletive
4. third person objective case (it; her; him; them)
5. this; that; these; those
6. (possessive particle) of: 鐘鼓之聲 the sound of drums and bells

之內(ㄓ ㄋㄟˋ)
within; inside; including; included

之後(ㄓ ㄏㄡˋ)
after this; afterward: 他走之後,我們就吃飯。After he goes, we shall eat.

之乎者也(ㄓ ㄏㄨ ㄓㄜˇ ㄧㄝˇ)
① pedantry; archaisms ② auxiliary characters used to embellish the literary style

之前(ㄓ ㄑㄧㄢˊ)
before this; before; prior to: 睡覺之前請服這藥。Please take the medicine before bedtime.

之上(ㄓ ㄕㄤˋ)
above; over; on

之子于歸(ㄓ ㄗˇ ㄩˊ ㄍㄨㄟ)
(said of women) to marry 或 The maiden goes to her future (or new) home.

之字路(ㄓ ㄗˋ ㄌㄨˋ)
a zigzag road (or path); an S-shaped road

之死靡它(ㄓ ㄙˇ ㄇㄧˇ ㄊㄨㄛ)
(said of a widow) to refuse to remarry

之無(ㄓ ㄨˊ)
the simplest and most common characters

之外(ㄓ ㄨㄞˋ)
besides this; in addition

四畫

【乍】 31 ㄓㄚˋ jah zhà

1. at first; for the first time: 乍看起來她很美麗。At first glance she looks beautiful.
2. suddenly; unexpectedly; abruptly; inadvertently

乍富(ㄓㄚˋ ㄈㄨˋ)
from rags to riches; sudden wealth; *nouveau riche*

乍到(ㄓㄚˋ ㄉㄠˋ)
① to arrive at some place unexpectedly and suddenly ② to have just arrived at some place

乍冷乍熱(ㄓㄚˋ ㄌㄥˇ ㄓㄚˋ ㄖㄜˋ)
now cold, now hot (referring to changeable weather): 天氣乍冷乍熱。The temperature changes abruptly.

乍見(ㄓㄚˋ ㄐㄧㄢˋ)
① to meet for the first time ② to see suddenly

乍晴乍雨(ㄓㄚˋ ㄑㄧㄥˊ ㄓㄚˋ ㄩˇ)
sudden change from rain to shine

乍然(ㄓㄚˋ ㄖㄢˊ)
abruptly; unexpectedly

乍聞(ㄓㄚˋ ㄨㄣˊ)
suddenly learn for the first time

【乎】 32 ㄏㄨ hu hū

1. at; in; from; than: 我認爲這不合乎道理。I don't think it's in accord with reason.
2. an interrogative particle
3. an exclamatory particle

【乏】 33 ㄈㄚˊ far fá

1. in want of; deficient; lack
2. exhausted; tired
3. poor; poverty-stricken

乏力(ㄈㄚˊ ㄌㄧˋ)
to feel exhausted; to lack strength or vitality

乏趣(ㄈㄚˊ ㄑㄩˋ)
lacking in interest

乏善可陳(ㄈㄚˊ ㄕㄢˋ ㄎㄜˇ ㄔㄣˊ)
to have nothing good or unusual to report

乏人照應(ㄈㄚˊ ㄖㄣˊ ㄓㄠˋ ㄧㄥˋ)
in need of people to look after

乏味(ㄈㄚˊ ㄨㄟˋ)
monotonous; dull; insipid; tasteless

五畫

【乒】 34 ㄆㄧㄥ ping pīng

used for the sound: 我聽到乒的一聲槍響。I heard the crack of a gun.

〔乙部〕

乒乓(ㄆㄧㄥ ㄆㄤ)
ping-pong (used for the sound)

乒乓球(ㄆㄧㄥ ㄆㄤ ㄑㄧㄡˊ)
① table tennis ② a table tennis ball

七畫

【乖】 35 ㄍㄨㄞ guai guāi

1. to oppose; to contradict; to be at variance
2. perverse; obstinate; untoward; sulky
3. obedient; well-behaved: 他是個乖孩子。He is an obedient child.
4. cunning; artful; crafty; wily

乖僻(ㄍㄨㄞ ㄆㄧˋ)
unreasonable; perverse; eccentric

乖謬(ㄍㄨㄞ ㄇㄧㄡˋ)
absurd; fallacious

乖戾(ㄍㄨㄞ ㄌㄧˋ)
cantankerous; perverse

乖乖(ㄍㄨㄞ ㄍㄨㄞ)or 乖乖兒的(ㄍㄨㄞ ㄍㄨㄚㄦ ˙ㄉㄜ)
① submissive; docile; obedient ② an endearing name for children

乖覺(ㄍㄨㄞ ㄐㄩㄝˊ)
shrewd and capable

乖巧(ㄍㄨㄞ ㄑㄧㄠˇ)
clever; ingenious: 這小孩甚爲乖巧。The child is very clever.

乖張(ㄍㄨㄞ ㄓㄤ)
recalcitrant; stubbornly persisting in doing something wrong

乖異(ㄍㄨㄞ ㄧˋ)
strange; odd; eccentric; intractable: 她的性情乖異。She has an intractable temper.

乖違(ㄍㄨㄞ ㄨㄟˊ)
① contradictory; conflicting ② separate

九畫

【乘】 36 1. ㄔㄥˊ cherng chéng

1. to ride; to mount
2. to avail oneself of; to take advantage of; to seize a chance or an opportunity
3. to multiply

乘便(ㄔㄥˊ ㄅㄧㄢˋ)
① to take advantage of the chance ② at your convenience

乘馬(ㄔㄥˊ ㄇㄚˇ)
to ride a horse

乘冪(ㄔㄥˊ ㄇㄧˋ)or 乘方(ㄔㄥˊ ㄈㄤ)
(mathematics) power

乘法(ㄔㄥˊ ㄈㄚˇ)
(arithmetic) multiplication

乘風破浪(ㄔㄥˊ ㄈㄥ ㄆㄛˋ ㄌㄤˋ)
(literally) to ride the wind and weather the storm—great ambition

乘涼(ㄔㄥˊ ㄌㄧㄤˊ)
to cool oneself in the shade or in the breeze; to enjoy the cool air; to relax in a cool place

乘龍快婿(ㄔㄥˊ ㄌㄨㄥˊ ㄎㄨㄞˋ ㄒㄩˋ)
an ideal son-in-law

乘客(ㄔㄥˊ ㄎㄜˋ)
a passenger

乘空(ㄔㄥˊ ㄎㄨㄥˋ)or 乘空兒(ㄔㄥˊ ㄎㄨㄥˋㄦ)
to do something while one has plenty of time on hand

乘號(ㄔㄥˊ ㄏㄠˋ)
the sign of multiplication

乘積(ㄔㄥˊ ㄐㄧ)
(arithmetic) the product

乘機(ㄔㄥˊ ㄐㄧ)
① to avail oneself of an opportunity; to seize the right time; to embrace a chance ② to ride an airplane

乘堅策肥(ㄔㄥˊ ㄐㄧㄢ ㄘㄜˋ ㄈㄟˊ)
(said of a wealthy person) to ride a sturdy carriage and mount a well-fed horse

乘間(ㄔㄥˊ ㄐㄧㄢˋ)or 乘隙(ㄔㄥˊ ㄒㄧˋ)
to seize a fleeting chance

乘間竊發(ㄔㄥˊ ㄐㄧㄢˋ ㄑㄧㄝˋ ㄈㄚ)
to seize an opportunity to start doing something

乘興(ㄔㄥˊ ㄒㄧㄥˋ)
on the spur of the moment: 我們乘興往海邊走去。We headed for the beach on the spur of the moment.

乘興而往，敗興而歸(ㄔㄥˊ ㄒㄧㄥˋ ㄦˊ ㄨㄤˇ, ㄅㄞˋ ㄒㄧㄥˋ ㄦˊ ㄍㄨㄟ)
to go with great enthusiasm and return disappointed or disillusioned

乘虛而入(ㄔㄥˊ ㄒㄩ ㄦˊ ㄖㄨˋ)
to take advantage of a weak point; to act when somebody is off guard

乘除(ㄔㄥˊ ㄔㄨˊ)
(literally) multiplication and division—wax and wane

乘勢(ㄔㄥˊ ㄕˋ)
to act when a good chance is available; to take advantage of circumstances

乘勝追擊(ㄔㄥˊ ㄕㄥˋ ㄓㄨㄟ ㄐㄧˊ)
to pursue enemy troops in retreat

乘數(ㄔㄥˊ ㄕㄨˋ)
multiplicator or multiplier

乘人之危(ㄔㄥˊ ㄖㄣˊ ㄓ ㄨㄟˊ)
to take advantage of somebody when he is not in a position to resist

【乘】 36 2. ㄕㄥˋ shenq shèng

1. historical records: 這事件記載在史乘中。This event is carried in historical records.
2. an ancient carriage
3. Buddhist teaching—a conveyance to bring the truth to men and help them
4. a team of four horses

乙部 ㄧˇ yii yǐ

【乙】 37 ㄧˇ yii yǐ

1. the second of the Ten Celestial Stems
2. one
3. someone
4. an ancient Chinese family name

乙榜(ㄧˇ ㄅㄤˇ)
the candidate who passed the provincial civil service examination in old China

乙醚(ㄧˇ ㄇㄧˊ)
ether

乙炔(ㄧˇ ㄑㄩㄝ)
acetylene; ethyne

乙烯(ㄧˇ ㄒㄧ)
ethylene

乙種(ㄧˇ ㄓㄨㄥˇ)
Category B

乙醇(ㄧˇ ㄔㄨㄣˊ)

ethanol; alcohol

一畫

【乜】 38
1. ㄇㄧㄝ mhie miē

乜斜(ㄇㄧㄝ ㄒㄧㄝˊ)
to glance sideways: 她乜斜着眼睛看他。She glanced sideways at him.

【乜】 38
2. ㄋㄧㄝ nieh niè

a very rare Chinese family name

【九】 39
ㄐㄧㄡˇ jeou jiǔ

nine; ninth: 他十次有九次忘記。Nine times out of ten he forgot.

九邊形(ㄐㄧㄡˇ ㄅㄧㄢ ㄒㄧㄥˊ)or 九角形(ㄐㄧㄡˇ ㄐㄧㄠˇ ㄒㄧㄥˊ)
a nonagon; nonagonal: 這圖案是九邊形的。The shape of this design is a nonagonal one.

九品(ㄐㄧㄡˇ ㄆㄧㄣˇ)
①(in ancient China) the nine grades of official rank ② the ninth official rank

九大行星(ㄐㄧㄡˇ ㄉㄚˋ ㄒㄧㄥˊ ㄒㄧㄥ)
the nine planets in the solar system—Mercury, Venus, Earth, Mars, Jupiter, Saturn, Uranus, Neptune, and Pluto

九頭鳥(ㄐㄧㄡˇ ㄊㄡˊ ㄋㄧㄠˇ)
a legendary bird with nine heads, now used in reference to a crafty fellow

九天(ㄐㄧㄡˇ ㄊㄧㄢ)
① the highest heavens ② the heaven of the Taoists

九牛二虎(ㄐㄧㄡˇ ㄋㄧㄡˊ ㄦˋ ㄏㄨˇ)
(literally) the combined strength of nine oxen and two tigers—a herculean effort

九牛一毛(ㄐㄧㄡˇ ㄋㄧㄡˊ ㄧˊ ㄇㄠˊ)
(literally) one hair from nine oxen—an iota from a vast quantity

九鍊成鋼(ㄐㄧㄡˇ ㄌㄧㄢˋ ㄔㄥˊ ㄍㄤ)
Mastery is the result of long practice or training.

九宮格(ㄐㄧㄡˇ ㄍㄨㄥ ㄍㄜˊ)
(calligraphy) squares into which each page of a copybook is divided

九九表(ㄐㄧㄡˇ ㄐㄧㄡˇ ㄅㄧㄠˇ)
the multiplication table up to nine times nine

九九歸原(ㄐㄧㄡˇ ㄐㄧㄡˇ ㄍㄨㄟ ㄩㄢˊ)
(said of argument, etc.) to return to where it started

九江(ㄐㄧㄡˇ ㄐㄧㄤ)
Chiuchiang, a city in Kiangsi on the northern bank of the Yangtze

九竅(ㄐㄧㄡˇ ㄑㄧㄠˋ)
the orifices of the body

九泉(ㄐㄧㄡˇ ㄑㄩㄢˊ)
Hades; the underworld

九泉地下(ㄐㄧㄡˇ ㄑㄩㄢˊ ㄉㄧˋ ㄒㄧㄚˋ)
in the grave; the underworld; under the earth; Hades

九霄雲外(ㄐㄧㄡˇ ㄒㄧㄠ ㄩㄣˊ ㄨㄞˋ)
beyond the farthest limits of the sky—far, far away

九州(ㄐㄧㄡˇ ㄓㄡ)
① another name for ancient China ② Kyushu, an island of Japan

九成(ㄐㄧㄡˇ ㄔㄥˊ)
ninety percent

九成宮(ㄐㄧㄡˇ ㄔㄥˊ ㄍㄨㄥ)
① name of a palace in Shensi Province ② a distinctive style of Chinese calligraphy started by Ou-Yang Hsün (歐陽詢), a famous calligrapher of the Tang Dynasty

九重天(ㄐㄧㄡˇ ㄔㄨㄥˊ ㄊㄧㄢ)
① the nine divisions of the celestial sphere, i.e., the four cardinal points, the four intermediate points, and the center ② the Taoist Heaven

九重葛(ㄐㄧㄡˇ ㄔㄨㄥˊ ㄍㄜˊ)
(botany) bougainvillea

九十歲至九十九歲的人(ㄐㄧㄡˇ ㄕˊ ㄙㄨㄟˋ ㄓˋ ㄐㄧㄡˇ ㄕˊ ㄐㄧㄡˇ ㄙㄨㄟˋ ·ㄉㄜ ㄖㄣˊ)
a nonagenarian

九日(ㄐㄧㄡˇ ㄖˋ)
the ninth day of the ninth moon, a festival on the lunar calendar

九族(ㄐㄧㄡˇ ㄗㄨˊ)
the nine degrees of kindred

九死一生(ㄐㄧㄡˇ ㄙˇ ㄧˋ ㄕㄥ)
a very narrow escape from death; grave danger

九一八事變(ㄐㄧㄡˇ ㄧ ㄅㄚ ㄕˋ ㄅㄧㄢˋ)
the Mukden Incident on September 18, 1931, which led to the Japanese occupation of Manchuria and the creation of the puppet Manchukuo

九月(ㄐㄧㄡˇ ㄩㄝˋ)
① September ② the ninth month of the lunar calendar ③ nine months

二畫

【乞】 40
ㄑㄧˇ chii qǐ

to ask for alms; to beg; to entreat; to pray humbly

乞盟(ㄑㄧˇ ㄇㄥˊ)
① to sue for peace ②(said of rulers) to pray before the deity

乞免(ㄑㄧˇ ㄇㄧㄢˇ)
to beg for exception (from taxation, punishment, etc.)

乞命(ㄑㄧˇ ㄇㄧㄥˋ)
to beg for life

乞貸(ㄑㄧˇ ㄉㄞˋ)or 乞借(ㄑㄧˇ ㄐㄧㄝˋ)
to beg for a loan

乞討(ㄑㄧˇ ㄊㄠˇ)
to beg for food, money, etc.

乞憐(ㄑㄧˇ ㄌㄧㄢˊ)
to beg for pity and charity

乞靈(ㄑㄧˇ ㄌㄧㄥˊ)
to seek help (from herbs, divine beings, etc.)

乞丐(ㄑㄧˇ ㄍㄞˋ)
a beggar

乞假(ㄑㄧˇ ㄐㄧㄚˋ)
to ask for a leave of absence

乞巧(ㄑㄧˇ ㄑㄧㄠˇ)
to pray for divine instructions for improvement of needlework on the 7th night of the 7th lunar month when the Weaving Maid meets the Cowherd across the Milky Way (The occasion is a sort of festival to unmarried girls.)

乞求(ㄑㄧˇ ㄑㄧㄡˊ)
to beg for; to supplicate; to implore

乞降(ㄑㄧˇ ㄒㄧㄤˊ)
to negotiate for surrender on the part of the defeated

乞師(ㄑㄧˇ ㄕ)
to ask for military help or troop reinforcements

〔乙部〕

乞兒(ㄑㄧˇ ㄦˊ)
a beggar
乞援(ㄑㄧˇ ㄩㄢˊ)
to ask for assistance; to beg for aid

【也】 41 ㄧㄝˇ yee yě
1. and; also; besides; either; too
2. still
3. even
4. an expletive in Chinese writing
也罷(ㄧㄝˇ ㄅㄚˋ)
Never mind. 或 Let it pass. 或 That's all right. (This expression is used to show the speaker's reluctance.)
也門(ㄧㄝˇ ㄇㄣˊ)
Yemen 亦作「葉門」
也可以(ㄧㄝˇ ㄎㄜˇ ㄧˇ)
① may also ② It makes no difference. 或 It's okay.
也好(ㄧㄝˇ ㄏㄠˇ)
That's fine.
也就(ㄧㄝˇ ㄐㄧㄡˋ)
… and then…
也行(ㄧㄝˇ ㄒㄧㄥˊ)
All right! 或 That will do too.
也許(ㄧㄝˇ ㄒㄩˇ)
perhaps; probably: 也許要下雨。It will probably rain.
也是(ㄧㄝˇ ㄕˋ)
also the same
也有(ㄧㄝˇ ㄧㄡˇ)
① There are in addition.... ② There are others (who or which)....
也未可知(ㄧㄝˇ ㄨㄟˋ ㄎㄜˇ ㄓ)
Who knows but that.... 或 perhaps; maybe

五畫

【乩】 42 ㄐㄧ ji jī
to divine; to resolve doubts by an application to spiritual beings

七畫

【乳】 43 ㄖㄨˇ ruu rǔ
1. breasts; the nipple
2. milk
3. any milk-like liquid
4. the young of animals, birds, etc.
5. to give birth
6. to triturate
乳白(ㄖㄨˇ ㄅㄞˊ)
milky white; cream color
乳哺(ㄖㄨˇ ㄅㄨˇ)
to feed with milk or chewed food
乳糜(ㄖㄨˇ ㄇㄧˊ)
chyle
乳名(ㄖㄨˇ ㄇㄧㄥˊ)
a pet name given to a child
乳母(ㄖㄨˇ ㄇㄨˇ) or 乳娘(ㄖㄨˇ ㄋㄧㄤˊ)
a wet nurse
乳房(ㄖㄨˇ ㄈㄤˊ)
the udders; the breasts
乳頭(ㄖㄨˇ ㄊㄡˊ)
a nipple; a teat
乳糖(ㄖㄨˇ ㄊㄤˊ)
lactose; milk sugar
乳牛(ㄖㄨˇ ㄋㄧㄡˊ)
the dairy cattle; a milch cow
乳牛場(ㄖㄨˇ ㄋㄧㄡˊ ㄔㄤˇ)
a dairy farm
乳酪(ㄖㄨˇ ㄌㄨㄛˋ)
junket; curds
乳化(ㄖㄨˇ ㄏㄨㄚˋ)
emulsification
乳化劑(ㄖㄨˇ ㄏㄨㄚˋ ㄐㄧˋ)
an emulsifying agent; an emulsifier
乳劑(ㄖㄨˇ ㄐㄧˋ)
emulsion: 感光乳劑(photograph) sensitive emulsion
乳膠液(ㄖㄨˇ ㄐㄧㄠ ㄧㄝˋ)
emulsion
乳酒(ㄖㄨˇ ㄐㄧㄡˇ)
milk-white wine
乳氣(ㄖㄨˇ ㄑㄧˋ)
childishness; childish
乳臭未乾(ㄖㄨˇ ㄒㄧㄡˋ ㄨㄟˋ ㄍㄢ)
very young and inexperienced like a sucking child
乳腺(ㄖㄨˇ ㄒㄧㄢˋ)
mammary glands
乳腺炎(ㄖㄨˇ ㄒㄧㄢˋ ㄧㄢˊ)
mastitis
乳香(ㄖㄨˇ ㄒㄧㄤ)
frankincense
乳汁(ㄖㄨˇ ㄓ)
milk
乳脂(ㄖㄨˇ ㄓ)
butter
乳製品(ㄖㄨˇ ㄓˋ ㄆㄧㄣˇ)
dairy products
乳罩(ㄖㄨˇ ㄓㄠˋ)
a brassiere; a bra
乳狀液(ㄖㄨˇ ㄓㄨㄤˋ ㄧㄝˋ)
milklike liquid
乳齒(ㄖㄨˇ ㄔˇ)
milk teeth; deciduous teeth
乳酸(ㄖㄨˇ ㄙㄨㄢ)
lactic acid
乳酸菌(ㄖㄨˇ ㄙㄨㄢ ㄐㄩㄣˋ)
(bacteriology) lactobacillus
乳媼(ㄖㄨˇ ㄠˇ)
a wet nurse
乳兒(ㄖㄨˇ ㄦˊ)
a sucking child
乳癌(ㄖㄨˇ ㄧㄢˊ)
cancer of the breast; mastocarcinoma
乳嫗(ㄖㄨˇ ㄩˋ)
a wet nurse
乳暈(ㄖㄨˇ ㄩㄣˋ)
mammary areola

十畫

【乾】 44 1. (乾) ㄍㄢ gan gān
1. clean: 他的手是乾淨的。His hands are clean.
2. dry; dried: 乾柴可燃。Dry wood will burn.
3. exhausted
乾爸爸(ㄍㄢ ㄅㄚˋ ·ㄅㄚ) or 乾爹(ㄍㄢ ㄉㄧㄝ)
a man whose position is roughly equivalent to a foster father and godfather in Western countries without religious or legal complications
乾巴(ㄍㄢ ·ㄅㄚ) or 乾巴巴的(ㄍㄢ ·ㄅㄚ ㄅㄚ ·ㄉㄜ)
dry; deficient in moisture
乾杯(ㄍㄢ ㄅㄟ)
to toast 或 Bottoms up!
乾貝 or 干貝(ㄍㄢ ㄅㄟˋ)
a dried scallop
乾癟(ㄍㄢ ㄅㄧㄝˇ)
dry and withered; shrunken
乾冰(ㄍㄢ ㄅㄧㄥ)
dry ice
乾媽(ㄍㄢ ㄇㄚ) or 乾娘(ㄍㄢ ㄋㄧㄤˊ)
a woman whose position is roughly equivalent to a foster mother and godmother in Western countries without religious or legal com-

plications

乾麵(ㄍㄢ ㄇㄧㄢˋ)
dry noodles

乾飯(ㄍㄢ ㄈㄢˋ)
cooked rice without gravy

乾粉(ㄍㄢ ㄈㄣˇ)
vermicelli made from flour, not yet soaked in water

乾打雷，不下雨(ㄍㄢ ㄉㄚˇ ㄌㄟˊ, ㄅㄨˋ ㄒㄧㄚˋ ㄩˇ)
thunder without rain—much noise without action

乾瞪眼(ㄍㄢ ㄉㄥˋ ㄧㄢˇ)
to stand by anxiously without doing anything; unable to help; to look on in despair

乾電池(ㄍㄢ ㄉㄧㄢˋ ㄔˊ)
a dry battery or cell

乾女兒(ㄍㄢ ㄋㄩˇ ㄦˊ)
a nominal foster daughter

乾酪(ㄍㄢ ㄌㄠˋ)
cheese

乾冷(ㄍㄢ ㄌㄥˇ)
dry and cold (weather)

乾裂(ㄍㄢ ㄌㄧㄝˋ)
dry and cracked (wood, soil)

乾糧(ㄍㄢ ㄌㄧㄤˊ)
dry provisions; canned or packed food ready to serve

乾果(ㄍㄢ ㄍㄨㄛˇ)
dried or preserved fruit

乾咳(ㄍㄢ ㄎㄜˊ)
to cough without producing sputum

乾枯(ㄍㄢ ㄎㄨ)
dried up; withered

乾涸(ㄍㄢ ㄏㄜˊ)
(said of water) to dry up: 河道乾涸。The river dried up.

乾旱(ㄍㄢ ㄏㄢˋ)
drought

乾貨(ㄍㄢ ㄏㄨㄛˋ)
dried food and nuts (as merchandise)

乾淨(ㄍㄢ ㄐㄧㄥˋ)or 乾乾淨淨(ㄍㄢ ㄍㄢ ㄐㄧㄥˋ ㄐㄧㄥˋ)
① clean ② entirely; all gone

乾淨俐落(ㄍㄢ ㄐㄧㄥˋ ㄌㄧˋ ㄌㄨㄛˋ)
neat and tidy; neat; efficient: 這一仗打得乾淨俐落。The battle was neatly won.

乾親(ㄍㄢ ㄑㄧㄣ)
nominal kinship

乾洗(ㄍㄢ ㄒㄧˇ)
dry cleaning

乾笑(ㄍㄢ ㄒㄧㄠˋ)
to laugh without mirth

乾癬(ㄍㄢ ㄒㄧㄢˇ)
ringworm skin disease, with discolored patches covered with scales

乾薪(ㄍㄢ ㄒㄧㄣ)
a salary for a sinecure

乾著急(ㄍㄢ ㄓㄠˊ ㄐㄧˊ)
to sit fretting and fuming when in trouble, but taking no action (sometimes because nothing can be done)

乾柴烈火(ㄍㄢ ㄔㄞˊ ㄌㄧㄝˋ ㄏㄨㄛˇ)
(literally) a chance meeting between dry firewood and blazing flames—(said of romance between a man and a woman, often illegal liaison) instantaneous response to each other

乾濕表(ㄍㄢ ㄕ ㄅㄧㄠˇ)
a psychrometer

乾熱(ㄍㄢ ㄖㄜˋ)
(weather) dry heat; scorching hot

乾燥(ㄍㄢ ㄗㄠˋ)
dry

乾燥機(ㄍㄢ ㄗㄠˋ ㄐㄧ)
a drier

乾燥劑(ㄍㄢ ㄗㄠˋ ㄐㄧˋ)
a desiccant; a drying agent

乾草(ㄍㄢ ㄘㄠˇ)
hay

乾脆(ㄍㄢ ㄘㄨㄟˋ)
straightforward; clear-cut

乾嘔(ㄍㄢ ㄡˇ)
to retch

乾兒(子)(ㄍㄢ ㄦˊ (•ㄗ))
a nominal foster son

【乾】 44
2. ㄑㄧㄢˊ chyan qián

1. the first of the Eight Diagrams (八卦)
2. heaven; male; a father; a sovereign

乾道(ㄑㄧㄢˊ ㄉㄠˋ)
ways of heaven; natural law

乾隆(ㄑㄧㄢˊ ㄌㄨㄥˊ)
reigning title of Emperor Kao Tsung of the Ching Dynasty, whose reign lasted from 1736 to 1796

乾綱(ㄑㄧㄢˊ ㄍㄤ)
①emperorship ②the authority of a husband to his wife

乾坤(ㄑㄧㄢˊ ㄎㄨㄣ)
two of the Eight Diagrams of the *Book of Changes*—(figuratively) male and female, heaven and earth, sun and moon, etc.

乾象(ㄑㄧㄢˊ ㄒㄧㄤˋ)
celestial phenomena

乾元(ㄑㄧㄢˊ ㄩㄢˊ)
the beginning of the Heaven's creation

十二畫

【亂】 45
ㄌㄨㄢˋ luann luàn

1. chaos; anarchy; distraction; confusion: 地震後這城市甚爲混亂。The city was in great chaos after the earthquake.
2. rebellion; revolt; insurrection: 叛亂很快就被平定了。The insurrection was easily suppressed.
3. confused; perplexed; agitated; disarranged; raveled
4. out of order; out of sorts; to throw into disorder; to confuse; to confound

亂兵(ㄌㄨㄢˋ ㄅㄧㄥ)
rebels; soldiers on the rampage (in the absence of effective control)

亂蓬蓬(ㄌㄨㄢˋ ㄆㄥˊ ㄆㄥˊ)
disheveled; tangled; jumbled

亂民(ㄌㄨㄢˋ ㄇㄧㄣˊ)
rioters; mobsters

亂命(ㄌㄨㄢˋ ㄇㄧㄥˋ)
orders or instructions given when the giver is not in a healthy state of mind due to illness, etc.

亂罰(ㄌㄨㄢˋ ㄈㄚˊ)
to mete out unjustified punishment

亂紛紛(ㄌㄨㄢˋ ㄈㄣ ㄈㄣ)
disorderly; confused; chaotic; tumultuous

亂風(ㄌㄨㄢˋ ㄈㄥ)
degenerate social customs and practices

亂黨(ㄌㄨㄢˋ ㄉㄤˇ)
a rebel party or faction

亂點鴛鴦(ㄌㄨㄢˋ ㄉㄧㄢˇ ㄩㄢ ㄧㄤ)or 亂點鴛鴦譜(ㄌㄨㄢˋ ㄉㄧㄢˇ ㄩㄢ ㄧㄤ ㄆㄨˇ)

〔乙部〕

to cause an exchange of partners by mistake between two couples engaged to marry
亂彈(ㄌㄨㄢˋ ㄊㄢˊ)
name of a dramatic tune played with a few different instruments
亂來(ㄌㄨㄢˋ ㄌㄞˊ)
to act foolishly or recklessly; to do something without following proper procedure or methods
亂離(ㄌㄨㄢˋ ㄌㄧˊ)
involuntary separation in troubled times
亂流(ㄌㄨㄢˋ ㄌㄧㄡˊ)
a turbulent flow
亂倫(ㄌㄨㄢˋ ㄌㄨㄣˊ)
incest
亂搞一氣(ㄌㄨㄢˋ ㄍㄠˇ ㄧˊ ㄑㄧˋ)
to do something without knowing how
亂喊亂叫(ㄌㄨㄢˋ ㄏㄢˇ ㄌㄨㄢˋ ㄐㄧㄠˋ)
to clamor; to talk wildly
亂花亂用(ㄌㄨㄢˋ ㄏㄨㄚ ㄌㄨㄢˋ ㄩㄥˋ)
to spend money recklessly
亂婚(ㄌㄨㄢˋ ㄏㄨㄣ)
incestuous marriage; marriage between blood relatives
亂烘烘(ㄌㄨㄢˋ ㄏㄨㄥ ㄏㄨㄥ)
noisy and disorderly
亂七八糟(ㄌㄨㄢˋ ㄑㄧ ㄅㄚ ㄗㄠ)
in confusion; topsy-turvy: 大城市的交通亂七八糟。Traffic in big cities is in confusion.
亂性(ㄌㄨㄢˋ ㄒㄧㄥˋ)
to upset the presence of mind
亂眞(ㄌㄨㄢˋ ㄓㄣ)
an imitation or forgery so skillfully made that one often takes it as the original or genuine object
亂針繡(ㄌㄨㄢˋ ㄓㄣ ㄒㄧㄡˋ)
a form of embroidery which features overlapping threads in different directions
亂吃(ㄌㄨㄢˋ ㄔ)
to eat without caution
亂臣賊子(ㄌㄨㄢˋ ㄔㄣˊ ㄗㄟˊ ㄗˇ)
ministers or generals who rebel against their monarch or collaborate with the enemy
亂成一團(ㄌㄨㄢˋ ㄔㄥˊ ㄧˋ ㄊㄨㄢˊ)
in great confusion; topsy-turvy
亂世(ㄌㄨㄢˋ ㄕˋ)
times of anarchy and disorder
亂視(ㄌㄨㄢˋ ㄕˋ)
(ophthalmology) astigmatism 亦作「散光」
亂說(ㄌㄨㄢˋ ㄕㄨㄛ)or 亂道(ㄌㄨㄢˋ ㄉㄠˋ)
① to say what should not be said ② to lie
亂嚷(ㄌㄨㄢˋ ㄖㄤˇ)
to clamor
亂子(ㄌㄨㄢˋ ·ㄗ)
disturbance; trouble
亂糟糟(ㄌㄨㄢˋ ㄗㄠ ㄗㄠ)
① chaotic; in a mess ② confused; perturbed

亅部
ㄐㄩㄝˊ jyue jué

一畫

【了】 46
1. ㄌㄧㄠˇ leau liǎo

1. to finish; to end; to complete
2. intelligent; remarkable
3. entirely; wholly
4. to understand

了不得(ㄌㄧㄠˇ ·ㄅㄨ ·ㄉㄜ)
① Wonderful! 或 Excellent! ② at the worst; should the worst come to happen
了不了(ㄌㄧㄠˇ ·ㄅㄨ ㄌㄧㄠˇ)
cannot be brought to an end
了不起(ㄌㄧㄠˇ ·ㄅㄨ ㄑㄧˇ)
Wonderful! 參看「了不得①」
了得(ㄌㄧㄠˇ ·ㄉㄜ)
very good; excellent (said of performance or demonstration of skill)
了得了(ㄌㄧㄠˇ ·ㄉㄜ ㄌㄧㄠˇ)
can be solved or settled
了當(ㄌㄧㄠˇ ㄉㄤˋ)
appropriate
了斷(ㄌㄧㄠˇ ㄉㄨㄢˋ)
① to settle (a case) ② to commit suicide
了了(ㄌㄧㄠˇ ㄌㄧㄠˇ)
intelligent; bright
了結(ㄌㄧㄠˇ ㄐㄧㄝˊ)
to get through with; to bring to conclusion; to settle
了解(ㄌㄧㄠˇ ㄐㄧㄝˇ)
to understand or comprehend
了局(ㄌㄧㄠˇ ㄐㄩˊ)
the end; the result; the final settlement; the conclusion
了卻(ㄌㄧㄠˇ ㄑㄩㄝˋ)
to finish
了債(ㄌㄧㄠˇ ㄓㄞˋ)
to pay off one's debts
了賬(ㄌㄧㄠˇ ㄓㄤˋ)
to settle an account
了事(ㄌㄧㄠˇ ㄕˋ)
to finish up a matter
了然(ㄌㄧㄠˇ ㄖㄢˊ)
to understand clearly
了如指掌(ㄌㄧㄠˇ ㄖㄨˊ ㄓˇ ㄓㄤˇ)
to know something like the palm of one's hand
了此殘生(ㄌㄧㄠˇ ㄘˇ ㄘㄢˊ ㄕㄥ)
to end this miserable life
了案(ㄌㄧㄠˇ ㄢˋ)
to conclude a case; to close a case
了無痕(ㄌㄧㄠˇ ㄨˊ ㄏㄣˊ)
without a trace
了無長進(ㄌㄧㄠˇ ㄨˊ ㄓㄤˇ ㄐㄧㄣˋ)
(said of a good-for-nothing fellow) having made no progress or improvement in the least
了悟(ㄌㄧㄠˇ ㄨˋ)
to comprehend; to understand; to wake up to; to realize

【了】 46
2. ·ㄌㄜ ·le le

an expletive in the Chinese language: 他的病痊癒了。His sickness is wholly cured.

三畫

【予】 47
1. ㄩˊ yu yú

I; me
予取予求(ㄩˊ ㄑㄩˇ ㄩˊ ㄑㄧㄡˊ)
to make repeated demands of somebody
予智自雄(ㄩˊ ㄓˋ ㄗˋ ㄒㄩㄥˊ)
conceited

【予】 47
2. ㄩˇ yeu yǔ

to give: 予人口實 to give people a cause for discussion

七畫

【事】48 ㄕˋ shyh shì
1. an affair; a matter; business
2. a job; an occupation; a task
3. a service: 電話是公用事業。 The telephone is a public service.
4. duties; functions
5. a subject
6. to serve; to attend
7. to manage a business

事倍功半(ㄕˋ ㄅㄟˋ ㄍㄨㄥ ㄅㄢˋ)
to achieve little result despite herculean effort

事半功倍(ㄕˋ ㄅㄢˋ ㄍㄨㄥ ㄅㄟˋ)
half the work with double the result; to achieve maximum results with little effort

事必躬親(ㄕˋ ㄅㄧˋ ㄍㄨㄥ ㄑㄧㄣ)
to attend to everything personally

事變(ㄕˋ ㄅㄧㄢˋ)
an incident

事不宜遲(ㄕˋ ㄅㄨˋ ㄧˊ ㄔˊ)
One must lose no time in doing something.

事非得已(ㄕˋ ㄈㄟ ㄉㄜˊ ㄧˇ)
There is no other choice.

事非經過不知難(ㄕˋ ㄈㄟ ㄐㄧㄥ ㄍㄨㄛˋ ㄅㄨˋ ㄓ ㄋㄢˊ)
One does not realize the difficulty of an undertaking unless he has experienced it before.

事到臨頭(ㄕˋ ㄉㄠˋ ㄌㄧㄣˊ ㄊㄡˊ)
when a thing comes to a critical moment; at the last moment

事到如今(ㄕˋ ㄉㄠˋ ㄖㄨˊ ㄐㄧㄣ)
as things have come to such a pass

事端(ㄕˋ ㄉㄨㄢ)
a trouble

事態(ㄕˋ ㄊㄞˋ)
the state of affairs; the situation

事體(ㄕˋ ㄊㄧˇ)
systems of matters

事理(ㄕˋ ㄌㄧˇ)
the principle of action; facts and principles involved; the way of doing business

事例(ㄕˋ ㄌㄧˋ)
an example; a precedent

事略(ㄕˋ ㄌㄩㄝˋ)
a brief biography

事故(ㄕˋ ㄍㄨˋ)
a troublesome incident; an accident

事過境遷(ㄕˋ ㄍㄨㄛˋ ㄐㄧㄥˋ ㄑㄧㄢ)
Things change with the passage of time.

事後(ㄕˋ ㄏㄡˋ)
after an event; afterward

事迹(ㄕˋ ㄐㄧ)
the trace (of a past event); a vestige

事機(ㄕˋ ㄐㄧ)
① a chance; an opportunity ② a secret or plot

事蹟(ㄕˋ ㄐㄧ)
the accomplishments, exploits, etc. of a person during his or her lifetime

事假(ㄕˋ ㄐㄧㄚˋ)
private affair leave: 他請一天事假。 He asked for one day's private affair leave.

事件(ㄕˋ ㄐㄧㄢˋ)
an individual matter; an incident; an event

事前(ㄕˋ ㄑㄧㄢˊ) or 事先(ㄕˋ ㄒㄧㄢ)
before an event; beforehand: 事先準備一切。 Get everything ready beforehand.

事親至孝(ㄕˋ ㄑㄧㄣ ㄓˋ ㄒㄧㄠˋ)
to treat one's parents with great respect and tender affection

事情(ㄕˋ ˙ㄑㄧㄥ)
a matter; business; circumstances; an event; an affair; an incident

事項(ㄕˋ ㄒㄧㄤˋ)
an individual matter (as part of a whole); an item

事主(ㄕˋ ㄓㄨˇ)
① the principal person concerned in any matter; a client ② the victim in a criminal case

事出有因(ㄕˋ ㄔㄨ ㄧㄡˇ ㄧㄣ)
not entirely devoid of truth

事實(ㄕˋ ㄕˊ)
a fact; truth; reality

事實上(ㄕˋ ㄕˊ ㄕㄤˋ)
in fact; in reality

事實勝於雄辯(ㄕˋ ㄕˊ ㄕㄥˋ ㄩˊ ㄒㄩㄥˊ ㄅㄧㄢˋ)
Facts are more convincing than eloquent theories.

事事(ㄕˋ ㄕˋ)
everything: 他事事親爲。 He does everything himself.

事勢(ㄕˋ ㄕˋ)
the trend of things in general; general course of events

事在人爲(ㄕˋ ㄗㄞˋ ㄖㄣˊ ㄨㄟˊ)
Human effort can achieve everything.

事兒(ㄕˋㄜˊㄦ)
(dialect) an affair, or a matter

事宜(ㄕˋ ㄧˊ)
①affairs; matters ②the necessary arrangements

事已如此(ㄕˋ ㄧˇ ㄖㄨˊ ㄘˇ)
things being so

事業(ㄕˋ ㄧㄝˋ)
① an enterprise; an undertaking ② a career; a pursuit

事由(ㄕˋ ㄧㄡˊ)
① the origin of a matter ② the subject (of a business letter)

事物(ㄕˋ ㄨˋ)
things; articles; objects

事務(ㄕˋ ㄨˋ)
business (in the sense of any serious, often monotonous, work one has to do); work; general affairs (of an office, organization, etc.)

事務官(ㄕˋ ㄨˋ ㄍㄨㄢ)
government officials whose duties require professional expertise

事務所(ㄕˋ ㄨˋ ㄙㄨㄛˇ)
an office (especially of a lawyer, accountant, political candidate, etc.)

事務員(ㄕˋ ㄨˋ ㄩㄢˊ)
an office clerk

事與願違(ㄕˋ ㄩˇ ㄩㄢˋ ㄨㄟˊ)
Things do not turn out as one wishes.

二部
ㄦˋ ell er

【二】 49 ㄦˋ ell èr
two; second; twice

二八年華(ㄦˋ ㄅㄚ ㄋㄧㄢˊ ㄏㄨㄚˊ)
(said of a girl) sixteen years of age

二八佳人(ㄦˋ ㄅㄚ ㄐㄧㄚ ㄖㄣˊ)
a sixteen-year-old beauty

二百五(ㄦˋ ㄅㄞˇ ㄨˇ)
(abuse) a simpleton; a blockhead

二部制(ㄦˋ ㄅㄨˋ ㄓˋ)
the two-shift system (of schools)

二拇指(ㄦˋ ㄇㄨˇ ㄓˇ)
the index finger

二分明月(ㄦˋ ㄈㄣ ㄇㄧㄥˊ ㄩㄝˋ)
the prosperity of Yangchow in former times

二分法(ㄦˋ ㄈㄣ ㄈㄚˇ)
dichotomy

二房(ㄦˋ ㄈㄤˊ)
a concubine

二房東(ㄦˋ ㄈㄤˊ ㄉㄨㄥ)
a person who sublets a house rented from another

二副(ㄦˋ ㄈㄨˋ)
(navigation) a second mate

二等(ㄦˋ ㄉㄥˇ)
(said of trains, ocean liners, etc.) economy class; second grade

二地主(ㄦˋ ㄉㄧˋ ㄓㄨˇ)
a sub-landlord

二度梅(ㄦˋ ㄉㄨˋ ㄇㄟˊ)
(said of women) married for the second time

二度燒傷(ㄦˋ ㄉㄨˋ ㄕㄠ ㄕㄤ)
second-degree burn

二老(ㄦˋ ㄌㄠˇ)
one's father and mother

二郎腿(ㄦˋ ㄌㄤˊ ㄊㄨㄟˇ)
(to sit) cross-legged: 別蹺起二郎腿。Don't sit cross-legged.

二郎神(ㄦˋ ㄌㄤˊ ㄕㄣˊ)
(mythology) a Chinese god who is good at fighting demons

二愣(ㄦˋ ˙ㄌㄥ)
① stunned ② scared stiff

二愣子(ㄦˋ ㄌㄥˋ ˙ㄗ)
a rash fellow

二路兒(ㄦˋ ㄌㄨˋㄦ)
second-rate (goods)

二鍋頭(ㄦˋ ㄍㄨㄛ ㄊㄡˊ)
a kind of strong alcoholic drink usually made from sorghum

二胡(ㄦˋ ㄏㄨˊ)
a two-stringed Chinese musical instrument

二花臉(ㄦˋ ㄏㄨㄚ ㄌㄧㄢˇ)
(Chinese opera) a number two actor with a painted face 亦作「副淨」

二簧(ㄦˋ ㄏㄨㄤˊ)
name of a tune in Peking opera

二級風(ㄦˋ ㄐㄧˊ ㄈㄥ)
force 2 wind; light breeze

二喬(ㄦˋ ㄑㄧㄠˊ)
the Chiao sisters, who were famous beauties in the state of Wu during the Epoch of Three Kingdoms

二親(ㄦˋ ㄑㄧㄣ)
one's father and mother

二心(ㄦˋ ㄒㄧㄣ)
disloyalty; disloyal: 他對主人有二心。He is disloyal to his master.

二姓(ㄦˋ ㄒㄧㄥˋ)
① two families of different clans united in marriage ② two ruling houses of different surnames

二臣(ㄦˋ ㄔㄣˊ)
a turncoat

二程子(ㄦˋ ㄔㄥˊ ㄗˇ)
the Cheng brothers (referring to Cheng Hao (程顥) and Cheng Yi (程頤), both renowned Confucian scholars of the Sung Dynasty)

二重國籍(ㄦˋ ㄔㄨㄥˊ ㄍㄨㄛˊ ㄐㄧˊ)
dual nationality 亦作「雙重國籍」: 他有二重國籍。He has dual nationality.

二重唱(ㄦˋ ㄔㄨㄥˊ ㄔㄤˋ)
(vocal) a duet

二重奏(ㄦˋ ㄔㄨㄥˊ ㄗㄡˋ)
a duet performance on the piano

二重人格(ㄦˋ ㄔㄨㄥˊ ㄖㄣˊ ㄍㄜˊ)
dual personality 亦作「雙重人格」

二十八宿(ㄦˋ ㄕˊ ㄅㄚ ㄒㄧㄡˋ)
(astronomy) the lunar mansions

二十四孝(ㄦˋ ㄕˊ ㄙˋ ㄒㄧㄠˋ)
the 24 examples of filial piety (selected by Kuo Chu-ching (郭居敬) of the Yüan Dynasty)—虞舜, 漢文帝, 曾參, 閔損, 仲由, 董永, 郯子, 江革, 陸績, 唐夫人, 吳猛, 王祥, 郭巨, 楊香, 朱壽昌, 庾黔婁, 老萊子, 蔡順, 黃香, 姜詩, 王裒, 丁蘭, 孟宗, 黃庭堅。

二十四史(ㄦˋ ㄕˊ ㄙˋ ㄕˇ)
The Twenty-Four Books of History (an official history of China up to the end of the Ming Dynasty consisting of 24 books, authorized by Emperor Kao Tsung of the Ching Dynasty)

二十一條(ㄦˋ ㄕˊ ㄧ ㄊㄧㄠˊ)
the Twenty-One Demands, which Japan forced Yüan Shih-kai to accept in 1915

二十五史(ㄦˋ ㄕˊ ㄨˇ ㄕˇ)
The Twenty-Five Books of History (*The Twenty-Four Books of History* plus an additional book, *the New History of Yuan*)

二世(ㄦˋ ㄕˋ)
II (used after the name of an emperor such as 秦二世 or James II)

二手貨(ㄦˋ ㄕㄡˇ ㄏㄨㄛˋ)
a used item; a secondhand commodity

二豎爲害(ㄦˋ ㄕㄨˋ ㄨㄟˊ ㄏㄞˋ)
to suffer from illness

二水貨(ㄦˋ ㄕㄨㄟˇ ㄏㄨㄛˋ)
used goods; secondhand goods 亦作「二手貨」

二次方程式(ㄦˋ ㄘˋ ㄈㄤ ㄔㄥˊ ㄕˋ)
a quadratic equation

二次革命(ㄦˋ ㄘˋ ㄍㄜˊ ㄇㄧㄥˋ)
the Second Revolution (the revolution of the Kuomintang against Yüan Shih-kai in 1913 after the revolution against the Manchu government)

二三其德(ㄦˋ ㄙㄢ ㄑㄧˊ ㄉㄜˊ)
inconsistent

二氧化碳(ㄦˋ ㄧㄤˇ ㄏㄨㄚˋ ㄊㄢˋ)
carbon dioxide

二月(ㄦˋ ㄩㄝˋ)
① February ② the second moon of the lunar calendar ③ two months

二月革命(ㄦˋ ㄩㄝˋ ㄍㄜˊ ㄇㄧㄥˋ)
February Revolution (of February 22-24, 1848) in

French history
二元方程式(ㄦˊ ㄩㄢˊ ㄈㄤ ㄔㄥˊ ㄕˋ)
an equation with two unknowns
二元論(ㄦˊ ㄩㄢˊ ㄌㄨㄣˋ)
dualism

一畫

【亍】50 ㄔㄨˋ chuh chù
a step with the right foot

【于】51 ㄩˊ yu yú
1. (a particle in literary use) in; at; by; to: 光榮歸于勝利者。Glory goes to the victors.
2. (a verb in literary use) to go or proceed; to take
于飛之樂(ㄩˊ ㄈㄟ ㄓ ㄌㄜˋ)
the happiness of a married couple deeply in love
于歸(ㄩˊ ㄍㄨㄟ)
(said of a girl) to enter into matrimony
于今(ㄩˊ ㄐㄧㄣ)
① up to the present; since: 自君別後，于今兩年。It has been two years since you left. ② nowadays
于是(ㄩˊ ㄕˋ)
hence; consequently; thereupon
于思(ㄩˊ ㄙㄞ)
a long and thick beard and mustache (after days without shaving)

二畫

【云】52 ㄩㄣˊ yun yún
to say; to speak: 不要人云亦云。Don't say what everybody says.
云云(ㄩㄣˊ ㄩㄣˊ)
so and so; and so forth; and so on

【互】53 ㄏㄨˋ huh hù
each other; mutually; reciprocally
互保(ㄏㄨˋ ㄅㄠˇ)
to give guarantee for each other
互補角色(ㄏㄨˋ ㄅㄨˇ ㄐㄩㄝˊ ㄙㄜˋ)
(sociology) complementary role
互補色(ㄏㄨˋ ㄅㄨˇ ㄙㄜˋ)
complementary colors
互不侵犯(ㄏㄨˋ ㄅㄨˋ ㄑㄧㄣ ㄈㄢˋ)
to refrain from invading each other
互不侵犯條約(ㄏㄨˋ ㄅㄨˋ ㄑㄧㄣ ㄈㄢˋ ㄊㄧㄠˊ ㄩㄝ)
a nonaggression treaty (or pact)
互訪(ㄏㄨˋ ㄈㄤˇ)
to exchange visits
互通有無(ㄏㄨˋ ㄊㄨㄥ ㄧㄡˇ ㄨˊ)
to give mutual help financially; to supply each other's needs
互利(ㄏㄨˋ ㄌㄧˋ)
mutually beneficial
互惠(ㄏㄨˋ ㄏㄨㄟˋ)
mutually beneficial; reciprocal
互惠條約(ㄏㄨˋ ㄏㄨㄟˋ ㄊㄧㄠˊ ㄩㄝ)
a bilateral treaty in which the signatories grant favored nation status to each other
互惠關稅(ㄏㄨˋ ㄏㄨㄟˋ ㄍㄨㄢ ㄕㄨㄟˋ)
a mutually preferential tariff
互換(ㄏㄨˋ ㄏㄨㄢˋ)
to exchange
互相(ㄏㄨˋ ㄒㄧㄤ)
mutually; reciprocally; each other; one another
互相標榜(ㄏㄨˋ ㄒㄧㄤ ㄅㄧㄠ ㄅㄤˇ)
to eulogize each other
互相切磋(ㄏㄨˋ ㄒㄧㄤ ㄑㄧㄝ ㄘㄨㄛ)
to improve each other by active discussion
互選(ㄏㄨˋ ㄒㄩㄢˇ)
an election in which a voter may elect any other voter
互爭雄長(ㄏㄨˋ ㄓㄥ ㄒㄩㄥˊ ㄓㄤˇ)
to fight for leadership or hegemony
互助(ㄏㄨˋ ㄓㄨˋ)
to help each other; mutual help
互市(ㄏㄨˋ ㄕˋ)
mutual trade
互爲因果(ㄏㄨˋ ㄨㄟˊ ㄧㄣ ㄍㄨㄛˇ)
to interact as both cause and effect

【五】54 ㄨˇ wuu wǔ
five; fifth: 他家裏有五個小孩。There are five children in his family.
五霸(ㄨˇ ㄅㄚˋ)
the Five Powers—Chi (齊), Sung (宋), Tsin (晉), Chin (秦), and Chu (楚)—in the late Chou Dynasty
五倍子(ㄨˇ ㄅㄟˋ ㄗˇ)
gallnuts
五胞胎(ㄨˇ ㄅㄠ ㄊㄞ)
quintuplets
五邊形(ㄨˇ ㄅㄧㄢ ㄒㄧㄥˊ)
a pentagon
五面體(ㄨˇ ㄇㄧㄢˋ ㄊㄧˇ)
a pentahedron
五分(ㄨˇ ㄈㄣ)
fifty percent
五分鐘熱度(ㄨˇ ㄈㄣ ㄓㄨㄥ ㄖㄜˋ ㄉㄨˋ)
short-lived enthusiasm
五方(ㄨˇ ㄈㄤ)
the five directions (east, west, south, north and center)
五服(ㄨˇ ㄈㄨˊ)
the five grades of mourning (according to kinship) —for parents or husbands, three years; for grandparents, twelve months; for brothers, etc., nine months; for uncles, aunts, etc., five months; for distant relatives, three months
五福(ㄨˇ ㄈㄨˊ)
the five blessings—longevity, wealth, health, love of virtue, and natural death (壽，富，康寧，攸好德，考終命)
五大湖(ㄨˇ ㄉㄚˋ ㄏㄨˊ)
Great Lakes
五大洲(ㄨˇ ㄉㄚˋ ㄓㄡ)
the five continents—Asia, Africa, Europe, the Americas, and Oceania
五大洋(ㄨˇ ㄉㄚˋ ㄧㄤˊ)
the five oceans—Pacific, Atlantic, Indian, Arctic and Antarctic
五代(ㄨˇ ㄉㄞˋ)
the (Earlier) Five Dynasties (before the Tang Dynasty), 420-618 A.D.; the (Later) Five Dynasties (after the Tang Dynasty), 907-959 A.D.
五代同堂(ㄨˇ ㄉㄞˋ ㄊㄨㄥˊ ㄊㄤˊ)or 五世同堂(ㄨˇ ㄕˋ ㄊㄨㄥˊ ㄊㄤˊ)
five generations living under the same roof

〔二部〕

五代史(ㄨˇ ㄉㄞˋ ㄕˇ)
The History of the (*Later*) *Five Dynasties*—with two versions, new and old, both included in *The Twenty-Four Books of History*

五斗米折腰(ㄨˇ ㄉㄡˇ ㄇㄧˇ ㄓㄜˊ ㄧㄠ)
to compromise one's principles for some scanty material reward

五等(ㄨˇ ㄉㄥˇ)
the five ranks of the nobility corresponding to duke, marquis, count, viscount, baron (公、侯、伯、子、男)

五帝(ㄨˇ ㄉㄧˋ)
the Five Emperors of the legendary period(太昊, 炎帝, 黃帝, 少昊, 顓頊)

五體投地(ㄨˇ ㄊㄧˇ ㄊㄡˊ ㄉㄧˋ)
① to prostrate oneself ② to admire someone with the utmost sincerity

五內(ㄨˇ ㄋㄟˋ)or 五臟(ㄨˇ ㄗㄤˋ)
the five viscera—the heart, the lungs, the liver, the kidneys, and the spleen

五內如焚(ㄨˇ ㄋㄟˋ ㄖㄨˊ ㄈㄣˊ)
(literally) The five viscera are on fire.—① very anxious ② grief-stricken: 他的失敗使他五內如焚。His failure made him grief-stricken.

五里霧中(ㄨˇ ㄌㄧˇ ㄨˋ ㄓㄨㄥ)
utter bewilderment: 他的話使她如墜五里霧中。His words caused her to fall in utter bewilderment.

五柳先生(ㄨˇ ㄌㄧㄡˇ ㄒㄧㄢ ㄕㄥ)
Mr. Five Willows, a name assumed by poet Tao Chien (陶潛, 365-427 A.D.)

五陵少年(ㄨˇ ㄌㄧㄥˊ ㄕㄠˋ ㄋㄧㄢˊ)
rich and handsome young men

五嶺(ㄨˇ ㄌㄧㄥˇ)
the five mountain ranges (which formed the southern boundary of the empire during the Chin Dynasty)

五倫(ㄨˇ ㄌㄨㄣˊ)
the five human relationships—between sovereign and subjects, father and sons, husband and wife, among brothers, and among friends

五律(ㄨˇ ㄌㄩˋ)
the five-character verse (with five characters to each of the eight lines)

五更(ㄨˇ ㄍㄥ)
the fifth watch of the night which is about 4 a.m. (by the former time system which divided the period from nightfall to daybreak into five watches)

五穀(ㄨˇ ㄍㄨˇ)
(literally) the five major grains (variously listed)—grains of all sorts

五官(ㄨˇ ㄍㄨㄢ)
① the five organs—the ear, the eye, the mouth, the nose and the heart ② the five senses—visual, auditory, olfactory, gustatory and tactile senses

五官端正(ㄨˇ ㄍㄨㄢ ㄉㄨㄢ ㄓㄥˋ)
a pleasant-looking face with the five organs in normal shape and position

五光十色(ㄨˇ ㄍㄨㄤ ㄕˊ ㄙㄜˋ)
resplendent with variegated coloration: 湖面上的風景五光十色。The scenery on the lake is resplendent with variegated coloration.

五口通商(ㄨˇ ㄎㄡˇ ㄊㄨㄥ ㄕㄤ)
the opening of five ports—Shanghai, Canton, Ningpo, Foochow and Amoy—in 1842 to European traders

五口之家(ㄨˇ ㄎㄡˇ ㄓ ㄐㄧㄚ)
a family of five persons

五胡(ㄨˇ ㄏㄨˊ)
the five barbarian tribes from the North (who invaded China in the 5th century A.D.)—匈奴, 鮮卑, 羯, 氐, 羌

五胡亂華(ㄨˇ ㄏㄨˊ ㄌㄨㄢˋ ㄏㄨㄚˊ)
the invasion of China by the northern barbarians (in the 5th century A.D.)

五胡十六國(ㄨˇ ㄏㄨˊ ㄕˊ ㄌㄧㄡˋ ㄍㄨㄛˊ)
the five nomadic tribes(匈奴, 鮮卑, 羯, 氐, 羌)and three Han generals who founded in China 16 states(前涼, 後涼, 南涼, 北涼, 西涼, 前趙(漢), 後趙, 前秦, 後秦, 西秦, 前燕, 後燕, 南燕, 北燕, 夏, 成漢) at one time or another between A.D. 304 and 439

五湖四海(ㄨˇ ㄏㄨˊ ㄙˋ ㄏㄞˇ)
everywhere in the world

五花八門(ㄨˇ ㄏㄨㄚ ㄅㄚ ㄇㄣˊ)
rich in variety; unpredictable as to the variations manifested

五花肉(ㄨˇ ㄏㄨㄚ ㄖㄡˋ)
streaky pork

五加皮(ㄨˇ ㄐㄧㄚ ㄆㄧˊ)
the bark of *Acanthopanax gracilistylus* (used as medicine)

五戒(ㄨˇ ㄐㄧㄝˋ)
the Five Precepts (of Buddhism)—slay not, steal not, lust not, lie not, taste not intoxicants and meat

五角大廈(ㄨˇ ㄐㄧㄠˇ ㄉㄚˋ ㄒㄧㄚˋ)
① the Pentagon, which houses most U. S. Defense Department offices ② the United States Department of Defense

五角形(ㄨˇ ㄐㄧㄠˇ ㄒㄧㄥˊ)
a pentagon

五金(ㄨˇ ㄐㄧㄣ)
① the five metals—gold, silver, copper, iron, and tin ② metals in general ③ hardware

五金店(ㄨˇ ㄐㄧㄣ ㄉㄧㄢˋ)
a hardware store

五經(ㄨˇ ㄐㄧㄥ)
The Five Classics—the Confucian canon comprising *The Book of Changes*(易經), *The Book of Odes*(詩經), *The Book of History*(書經), *The Book of Rites*(禮記), and *The Spring and Autumn Annals*(春秋)

五絕(ㄨˇ ㄐㄩㄝˊ)
a poem of four lines having five characters to each line

五權憲法(ㄨˇ ㄑㄩㄢˊ ㄒㄧㄢˋ ㄈㄚˇ)
the five-power constitution of the Republic of China outlined by Dr. Sun Yat-sen (which provides that the government administration shall be composed of executive, legislative, judiciary, examination and supervisory or control powers)

五線譜(ㄨˇ ㄒㄧㄢˋ ㄆㄨˇ)
(music) a staff; a musical score using the staff notation

五香(ㄨˇ ㄒㄧㄤ)
a kind of blended spice used in Chinese cooking

五項運動(ㄨˇ ㄒㄧㄤˋ ㄩㄣˋ ㄉㄨㄥˋ)
(sports) pentathlon

五星(ㄨˇ ㄒㄧㄥ)
the five planets—Venus, Jupiter, Mercury, Mars, and Saturn

五星上將(ㄨˇ ㄒㄧㄥ ㄕㄤˋ ㄐㄧㄤˋ)
a five-star general or admiral

五刑(ㄨˇ ㄒㄧㄥˊ)
the five penalties—branding, cutting off the nose, cutting off the feet, castration, and death (in ancient classification 古代: 墨, 劓, 剕, 宮, 大辟); or death, life imprisonment, imprisonment for a limited term, detention, and fines (in later classification 現代: 死刑, 無期徒刑, 有期徒刑, 拘留, 罰鍰)

五行(ㄨˇ ㄒㄧㄥˊ)
① the five primary elements—metal, wood, water, fire and earth(金, 木, 水, 火, 土) ② the five constant virtues—benevolence, righteousness, propriety, knowledge, and faith(仁, 義, 禮, 智, 信)

五指(ㄨˇ ㄓˇ)
the five fingers—the thumb, the index finger, the middle finger, the ring finger, the little finger

五常(ㄨˇ ㄔㄤˊ)
the five constant virtues—① benevolence, righteousness, propriety, knowledge and faith (仁, 義, 禮, 智, 信) ② father's righteousness, mother's benevolence, elder brother's love, younger brother's respect, and son's filial piety (父義、母慈、兄友、弟恭、子孝)

五畜(ㄨˇ ㄔㄨˋ)
① the five domestic animals — cattle, sheep, swine, dogs, fowls ② livestock in general

五十步笑百步(ㄨˇ ㄕˊ ㄅㄨˋ ㄒㄧㄠˋ ㄅㄞˇ ㄅㄨˋ)
to deride or denounce another's fault which the denouncer himself also has, though in a smaller degree 或 The pot calls the kettle black.

五十肩(ㄨˇ ㄕˊ ㄐㄧㄢ)
frozen shoulder 亦作「冰凍肩」

五世其昌(ㄨˇ ㄕˋ ㄑㄧˊ ㄔㄤ)
May you be blessed with many children and grandchildren! (The expression is usually used in congratulatory messages to the newlyweds at their wedding.)

五日京兆(ㄨˇ ㄖˋ ㄐㄧㄥ ㄓㄠˋ)
office held for a short time only

五子棋(ㄨˇ ㄗˇ ㄑㄧˊ)
gobang

五臟(ㄨˇ ㄗㄤˋ)
(Chinese medicine) the five internal organs—the heart, liver, spleen, lungs and kidneys

五族(ㄨˇ ㄗㄨˊ)
the five ethnic groups which make up the Chinese nation—Han, Manchu, Mongol, Mohammedan and Tibetan (漢, 滿, 蒙, 回, 藏)

五彩(ㄨˇ ㄘㄞˇ)
blue, yellow, red, white and black

五四運動(ㄨˇ ㄙˋ ㄩㄣˋ ㄉㄨㄥˋ)
The May Fourth Movement (the student demonstrations in Peking on May 4, 1919, in protest of government's surrender to the Twenty-One Demands from Japan, touching off subsequent literary and other reforms)

五卅事件(ㄨˇ ㄙㄚˋ ㄕˋ ㄐㄧㄢˋ)
The May 30 Incident (the incident on May 30, 1925, in which a number of Chinese were shot to death by the British in the International Settlement, Shanghai)

五一勞動節(ㄨˇ ㄧ ㄌㄠˊ ㄉㄨㄥˋ ㄐㄧㄝˊ)
May Day; Labor Day

五顏六色(ㄨˇ ㄧㄢˊ ㄌㄧㄡˋ ㄙㄜˋ)
of variegated colors

五言詩(ㄨˇ ㄧㄢˊ ㄕ)
verse with five characters to each line

五音(ㄨˇ ㄧㄣ)
① the five classes of initials (in ancient Chinese phonology, corresponding to glottals, palatals, dentals, labials and velars in modern phonology) ② the five notes of traditional Chinese music (宮, 商, 角, 徵, 羽)

五味(ㄨˇ ㄨㄟˋ)
the five flavors—sweet, sour, bitter, pungent, salty (甜, 酸, 苦, 辣, 鹹)

五嶽(ㄨˇ ㄩㄝˋ)
the Five Sacred Mountains—the Eastern Mountain located in Shantung, the Southern Mountain in Hunan, the Western Mountain in Shensi, the Northern Mountain in Hopei, and the Central Mountain in Honan (東嶽泰山, 南嶽衡山, 西嶽華山, 北嶽恒山, 中嶽嵩山)

五月(ㄨˇ ㄩㄝˋ)
① May ② the fifth moon of the lunar calendar ③ five months

五月花號(ㄨˇ ㄩㄝˋ ㄏㄨㄚ ㄏㄠˋ)
Mayflower

五月節(ㄨˇ ㄩㄝˋ ㄐㄧㄝˊ)
the Dragon Boat Festival, which comes on the fifth day of the fifth lunar month

五院(ㄨˇ ㄩㄢˋ)
the five yuan (of the government of the Republic of China) —the Executive Yuan, the Judicial Yuan, the Legislative Yuan, the Control Yuan, the Examination Yuan(行政院, 司法院, 立法院, 監察院, 考試院)

【井】 55
ㄐㄧㄥˇ jiing jǐng
a well: 在鄉村中人們掘井取水。In the village people dug wells for water.

井底蛙(ㄐㄧㄥˇ ㄉㄧˇ ㄨㄚ)
(literally) a frog in a well—a person of very limited outlook and experience

井田(ㄐㄧㄥˇ ㄊㄧㄢˊ)
the system of land division in the Chou Dynasty in which a 900-*mu* plot was divided into nine portions like the character 井, with the eight outlying portions separately cultivated and owned by eight families, which jointly cultivated the

〔二部〕

central portion for the state

井欄(ㄐㄧㄥˇ ㄌㄢˊ)
① the railings around a well ② a framework used as a tool for attacking city walls

井臼親操(ㄐㄧㄥˇ ㄐㄧㄡˋ ㄑㄧㄣ ㄘㄠ)
(said of housewives) to do domestic chores personally

井井有條(ㄐㄧㄥˇ ㄐㄧㄥˇ ㄧㄡˇ ㄊㄧㄠˊ)
systematic (in handling things); orderly; methodical

井水不犯河水(ㄐㄧㄥˇ ㄕㄨㄟˇ ㄅㄨˋ ㄈㄢˋ ㄏㄜˊ ㄕㄨㄟˇ)
Well water and river water leave each other alone.—not to interfere with each other's affairs

井然(ㄐㄧㄥˇ ㄖㄢˊ)
orderly

井鹽(ㄐㄧㄥˇ ㄧㄢˊ)
well salt (extracted from brine out of wells, as in Szechwan)

四畫

【亙】 56 ㄍㄣˋ genn gèn
(又讀 ㄍㄥˋ genq gèng)
1. to extend (over space or time)
2. a Chinese family name

亙古未有(ㄍㄣˋ ㄍㄨˇ ㄨㄟˋ ㄧㄡˇ)
unprecedented 或 There has been nothing like it since time immemorial.

五畫

【些】 57 ㄒㄧㄝ shie xiē
a small quantity or number; a little; a few; some

些兒(ㄒㄧㄜㄦ)
① a little while ② a little bit

些個(ㄒㄧㄝ ˙ㄍㄜ)
a little

些些(ㄒㄧㄝ ㄒㄧㄝ)
a little

些須(ㄒㄧㄝ ㄒㄩ)
a little 參看「些個」: 這個他懂得些須。He understands it a little.

些微(ㄒㄧㄝ ㄨㄟˊ)
① very little ② slightly: 他有些微近視。He is slightly near-sighted.

六畫

【亞】 58 ㄧㄚˋ yah yà
(又讀 ㄧㄚˇ yea yǎ)
1. second (in excellence): 他不亞於任何人。He is second to none.
2. Asia

亞伯拉罕(ㄧㄚˋ ㄅㄛˊ ㄌㄚ ㄏㄢˇ)
Abraham, the first patriarch and ancestor of the Hebrews

亞麻(ㄧㄚˋ ㄇㄚˊ)
Linum usitatissimum; flax

亞麻仁油(ㄧㄚˋ ㄇㄚˊ ㄖㄣˊ ㄧㄡˊ)
linseed oil

亞馬遜河(ㄧㄚˋ ㄇㄚˇ ㄒㄩㄣˋ ㄏㄜˊ)
the Amazon River in South America

亞美尼亞(ㄧㄚˋ ㄇㄟˇ ㄋㄧˊ ㄧㄚˋ)
Armenia

亞美利加(ㄧㄚˋ ㄇㄟˇ ㄌㄧˋ ㄐㄧㄚ)
America

亞得里亞海(ㄧㄚˋ ㄉㄜˊ ㄌㄧˇ ㄧㄚˋ ㄏㄞˇ)
the Adriatic Sea

亞當(ㄧㄚˋ ㄉㄤ)
Adam

亞當斯(ㄧㄚˋ ㄉㄤ ㄙ)
transliteration of Adams

亞丁(ㄧㄚˋ ㄉㄧㄥ)
Aden, in southwestern Arabia

亞理斯多德(ㄧㄚˋ ㄌㄧˇ ㄙ ㄉㄨㄛ ㄉㄜˊ)
Aristotle, 384-322 B.C., Greek philosopher

亞歷山大大帝(ㄧㄚˋ ㄌㄧˋ ㄕㄢ ㄉㄚˋ ㄉㄚˋ ㄉㄧˋ)
Alexander the Great, 356-323 B.C.

亞歷山大城(ㄧㄚˋ ㄌㄧˋ ㄕㄢ ㄉㄚˋ ㄔㄥˊ) or 亞力山卓(ㄧㄚˋ ㄌㄧˋ ㄕㄢ ㄓㄨㄛˊ)
Alexandria, a port city in North Africa

亞利桑那州(ㄧㄚˋ ㄌㄧˋ ㄙㄤ ㄋㄚˋ ㄓㄡ)
the state of Arizona, U.S.A.

亞軍(ㄧㄚˋ ㄐㄩㄣ)
the runner-up

亞西司(ㄧㄚˋ ㄒㄧ ㄙ)
Department of West Asia (of the Ministry of Foreign Affairs)

亞洲(ㄧㄚˋ ㄓㄡ) or 亞細亞洲(ㄧㄚˋ ㄒㄧˋ ㄧㄚˋ ㄓㄡ)
Asia

亞洲開發銀行(ㄧㄚˋ ㄓㄡ ㄎㄞ ㄈㄚ ㄧㄣˊ ㄏㄤˊ)
Asian Development Bank

亞聖(ㄧㄚˋ ㄕㄥˋ)
the Lesser Sage—Mencius, next to the Sage Confucius

亞述(ㄧㄚˋ ㄕㄨˋ)
Assyria

亞熱帶(ㄧㄚˋ ㄖㄜˋ ㄉㄞˋ)
the subtropical zone

七畫

【亟】 59 ㄐㄧˊ jyi jí
urgently; pressingly

亟欲(ㄐㄧˊ ㄩˋ)
very anxious to do something

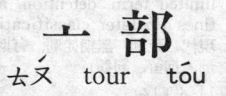

亠部
ㄊㄡˊ tour tóu

一畫

【亡】 60 ㄨㄤˊ wang wáng
1. to perish
2. to flee
3. lost; dead
4. the late (applicable only to deceased blood relatives or friends)

亡命(ㄨㄤˊ ㄇㄧㄥˋ)
to go into exile; to escape (from justice) to a place far away from home

亡命之徒(ㄨㄤˊ ㄇㄧㄥˋ ㄓ ㄊㄨˊ)
lawless elements; criminals

亡故(ㄨㄤˊ ㄍㄨˋ)
dead; died

亡國(ㄨㄤˊ ㄍㄨㄛˊ)
① a conquered country; a subjugated nation ② fall of a nation; national doom

亡國奴(ㄨㄤˊ ㄍㄨㄛˊ ㄋㄨˊ)
subjugated people; conquered people

亡國之音(ㄨㄤˊ ㄍㄨㄛˊ ㄓ ㄧㄣ)
degenerate or decadent music (presaging national ruin)

亡魂(ㄨㄤˊ ㄏㄨㄣˊ)
the spirit of the dead

亡羊補牢(ㄨㄤˊ ㄧㄤˊ ㄅㄨˇ ㄌㄠˊ)
to mend the sheepfold after losing the sheep—to take precaution after suffering a loss: 亡羊補牢，未爲晚也。It is still not too late to mend the sheepfold after a sheep is lost.
亡羊得牛(ㄨㄤˊ ㄧㄤˊ ㄉㄜˊ ㄋㄧㄡˊ)
The gain more than compensates for the loss.

二畫

【亢】 61 ㄎㄤˋ kanq kàng
1. proud
2. indomitable
3. excessive
亢奮(ㄎㄤˋ ㄈㄣˋ)
stimulated; excited
亢旱(ㄎㄤˋ ㄏㄢˋ)
drought
亢直(ㄎㄤˋ ㄓˊ)
righteous(ness)

四畫

【交】 62 ㄐㄧㄠ jiau jiāo
1. to submit; to hand in or over
2. to meet
3. to exchange
4. to intersect
交白卷(ㄐㄧㄠ ㄅㄞˊ ㄐㄩㄢˋ)or 交白卷兒(ㄐㄧㄠ ㄅㄞˊ ㄐㄩㄚˋㄦ)
to turn in a blank examination paper
交拜(ㄐㄧㄠ ㄅㄞˋ)
to exchange bows (especially between bride and bridegroom at the wedding)
交杯酒(ㄐㄧㄠ ㄅㄟ ㄐㄧㄡˇ)
the rite of drinking from nuptial cups by bride and bridegroom in the old-fashioned wedding
交保(ㄐㄧㄠ ㄅㄠˇ)
to release (a suspect) on bail
交班(ㄐㄧㄠ ㄅㄢ)
to hand over to the next shift
交臂(ㄐㄧㄠ ㄅㄧˋ)
very close or near
交兵(ㄐㄧㄠ ㄅㄧㄥ)
to fight (between nations); to wage war
交迫(ㄐㄧㄠ ㄆㄛˋ)
to be pressed from more than one direction; beleaguered; beset
交配(ㄐㄧㄠ ㄆㄟˋ)
①(biology) copulation ②to mate
交鋒(ㄐㄧㄠ ㄈㄥ)
to wage war; to engage in battle
交付(ㄐㄧㄠ ㄈㄨˋ)
①to hand over ②to make payment
交代(ㄐㄧㄠ ㄉㄞˋ)
①to hand over responsibility ②to give an explanation or excuse; the explanation or excuse given
交道(ㄐㄧㄠ ㄉㄠˋ)
social communication; social intercourse
交點(ㄐㄧㄠ ㄉㄧㄢˇ)or 交叉點(ㄐㄧㄠ ㄔㄚ ㄉㄧㄢˇ)
a point of intersection
交桃花運(ㄐㄧㄠ ㄊㄠˊ ㄏㄨㄚ ㄩㄣˋ)
to be successful in romantic affairs
交頭接耳(ㄐㄧㄠ ㄊㄡˊ ㄐㄧㄝ ㄦˇ)or 交耳(ㄐㄧㄠ ㄦˇ)
to whisper in each other's ears
交談(ㄐㄧㄠ ㄊㄢˊ)
to converse
交替(ㄐㄧㄠ ㄊㄧˋ)
to alternate
交通(ㄐㄧㄠ ㄊㄨㄥ)
①traffic ②communication
交通部(ㄐㄧㄠ ㄊㄨㄥ ㄅㄨˋ)
Ministry of Communications
交通大學(ㄐㄧㄠ ㄊㄨㄥ ㄉㄚˋ ㄒㄩㄝˊ)
National Chiao Tung University
交通警察(ㄐㄧㄠ ㄊㄨㄥ ㄐㄧㄥˇ ㄔㄚˊ)
traffic police
交通銀行(ㄐㄧㄠ ㄊㄨㄥ ㄧㄣˊ ㄏㄤˊ)
Bank of Communications
交通網(ㄐㄧㄠ ㄊㄨㄥ ㄨㄤˇ)
a communication network; the communication system
交流(ㄐㄧㄠ ㄌㄧㄡˊ)
to flow across each other
交流道(ㄐㄧㄠ ㄌㄧㄡˊ ㄉㄠˋ)
(traffic) an interchange
交流電(ㄐㄧㄠ ㄌㄧㄡˊ ㄉㄧㄢˋ)
an alternating current or A.C.
交割(ㄐㄧㄠ ㄍㄜ)
a business transaction
交給(ㄐㄧㄠ ㄍㄟˇ)
to hand to; to give to
交媾(ㄐㄧㄠ ㄍㄡˋ)
sexual intercourse; sexual union
交感神經(ㄐㄧㄠ ㄍㄢˇ ㄕㄣˊ ㄐㄧㄥ)
the sympathetic nerve
交口稱讚(ㄐㄧㄠ ㄎㄡˇ ㄔㄥ ㄗㄢˋ)
to praise somebody or something unanimously
交困(ㄐㄧㄠ ㄎㄨㄣˋ)
multiple distress
交好運(ㄐㄧㄠ ㄏㄠˇ ㄩㄣˋ)
to have good luck; lucky
交互(ㄐㄧㄠ ㄏㄨˋ)
mutually; reciprocally
交互作用(ㄐㄧㄠ ㄏㄨˋ ㄗㄨㄛˋ ㄩㄥˋ)
interaction; interplay
交貨(ㄐㄧㄠ ㄏㄨㄛˋ)
to deliver goods; delivery
交歡(ㄐㄧㄠ ㄏㄨㄢ)
to get along with each other very friendly
交還(ㄐㄧㄠ ㄏㄨㄢˊ)
to hand back; to return
交換(ㄐㄧㄠ ㄏㄨㄢˋ)
to exchange
交集(ㄐㄧㄠ ㄐㄧˊ)
(said of different feelings) to be mixed
交際(ㄐㄧㄠ ㄐㄧˋ)
social intercourse
交際費(ㄐㄧㄠ ㄐㄧˋ ㄈㄟˋ)
entertainment fees
交際花(ㄐㄧㄠ ㄐㄧˋ ㄏㄨㄚ)
a derogatory term referring to women who are very active in social functions
交際草(ㄐㄧㄠ ㄐㄧˋ ㄘㄠˇ)
a reference to promiscuous women in general
交際舞(ㄐㄧㄠ ㄐㄧˋ ㄨˇ)
a social dance
交加(ㄐㄧㄠ ㄐㄧㄚ)
to act upon (something) or to hit (someone) simultaneously by two or more forces
交接(ㄐㄧㄠ ㄐㄧㄝ)
①to make contact with each other ②to adjoin each other ③to hand over and to

〔亠部〕

take over (duties)

交結(ㄐㄧㄠ ㄐㄧㄝˊ)
to associate (with a person)

交睫(ㄐㄧㄠ ㄐㄧㄝˊ)
to close eyes

交界(ㄐㄧㄠ ㄐㄧㄝˋ)
a border (between two areas)

交角(ㄐㄧㄠ ㄐㄧㄠˇ)
(mathematics) angle of intersection

交頸(ㄐㄧㄠ ㄐㄧㄥˇ)
to fondle each other; to neck

交卷(ㄐㄧㄠ ㄐㄩㄢˋ)or 交卷兒(ㄐㄧㄠ ㄐㄩㄚˋㄦ)
① to hand in the examination paper ② to complete an assignment

交淺言深(ㄐㄧㄠ ㄑㄧㄢˇ ㄧㄢˊ ㄕㄣ)
intimate in conversation though not intimate in association

交情(ㄐㄧㄠ ㄑㄧㄥˊ)
friendship; association in private life

交卸(ㄐㄧㄠ ㄒㄧㄝˋ)
to leave office to a successor

交心(ㄐㄧㄠ ㄒㄧㄣ)
to lay one's heart bare; to be frank with others

交響樂(ㄐㄧㄠ ㄒㄧㄤˇ ㄩㄝˋ)
a symphony; symphonic music

交響樂團(ㄐㄧㄠ ㄒㄧㄤˇ ㄩㄝˋ ㄊㄨㄢˊ)or 交響樂隊(ㄐㄧㄠ ㄒㄧㄤˇ ㄩㄝˋ ㄉㄨㄟˋ)
an orchestra; a symphony orchestra

交織(ㄐㄧㄠ ㄓ)
to interlace; to interweave

交戰(ㄐㄧㄠ ㄓㄢˋ)
(said of nations) to wage war against each other

交戰國(ㄐㄧㄠ ㄓㄢˋ ㄍㄨㄛˊ)
a belligerent state

交叉(ㄐㄧㄠ ㄔㄚ)
to cross each other; to intersect

交叉火網(ㄐㄧㄠ ㄔㄚ ㄏㄨㄛˇ ㄨㄤˇ)
cross fire

交差(ㄐㄧㄠ ㄔㄞ)
to report what one has done in the line of duty

交出(ㄐㄧㄠ ㄔㄨ)
to surrender; to hand over: 他們交出武器。They surrendered their weapons.

交涉(ㄐㄧㄠ ㄕㄜˋ)
to negotiate; negotiation

交手(ㄐㄧㄠ ㄕㄡˇ)
to exchange blows (in a fight)

交融(ㄐㄧㄠ ㄖㄨㄥˊ)
to blend; to mingle

交錯(ㄐㄧㄠ ㄘㄨㄛˋ)
to interlock

交椅(ㄐㄧㄠ ㄧˇ)
a chair; an armchair

交易(ㄐㄧㄠ ㄧˋ)
a trade; business transaction

交易所(ㄐㄧㄠ ㄧˋ ㄙㄨㄛˇ)
a stock exchange; a bourse

交易物品(ㄐㄧㄠ ㄧˋ ㄨˋ ㄆㄧㄣˇ)
a barter

交誼(ㄐㄧㄠ ㄧˊ)or(ㄐㄧㄠ ㄧˋ)
friendly relations; amity

交遊(ㄐㄧㄠ ㄧㄡˊ)
① to have friendly contact with ② people with whom one has friendly contacts; friends: 他的交遊甚廣。He has a large circle of friends.

交遊不慎(ㄐㄧㄠ ㄧㄡˊ ㄅㄨˋ ㄕㄣˋ)
to be indiscriminate in making friends

交友(ㄐㄧㄠ ㄧㄡˇ)
to make friends

交惡(ㄐㄧㄠ ㄨˋ)
to be on unfriendly terms; to become hostile to each other

交尾(ㄐㄧㄠ ㄨㄟˇ)
(said of birds or fish) to mate

交往(ㄐㄧㄠ ㄨㄤˇ)
to have friendly relations

交運(ㄐㄧㄠ ㄩㄣˋ)
to have everything going one's way; to be favored by Lady Luck

【亥】 63 ㄏㄞˋ hay hài

1. the last of the twelve Terrestrial Branches
2. the hours between 9 and 11 p.m.

亥豕(ㄏㄞˋ ㄕˇ)
errors in handwriting, or typographical errors due to confusion of similar words

【亦】 64 ㄧˋ yih yì

also; too

亦步亦趨(ㄧˋ ㄅㄨˋ ㄧˋ ㄑㄩ)
to follow the example of another person at each move; slavish imitation

亦即(ㄧˋ ㄐㄧˊ)
that is; i.e.; namely; viz.

亦且(ㄧˋ ㄑㄧㄝˇ)
and also; as well

亦然(ㄧˋ ㄖㄢˊ)
also; too; similarly

五畫

【亨】 65 ㄏㄥ heng hēng

to go through smoothly: 他的事業亨通。He runs his business smoothly.

亨利(ㄏㄥ ㄌㄧˋ)
transliteration of Henry

亨通(ㄏㄥ ㄊㄨㄥ)
to go well; to proceed smoothly

六畫

【享】 66 ㄒㄧㄤˇ sheang xiǎng

1. to enjoy; to receive
2. to offer
3. to entertain

享福(ㄒㄧㄤˇ ㄈㄨˊ)
to enjoy happiness and prosperity; to have a blessing

享殿(ㄒㄧㄤˇ ㄉㄧㄢˋ)or 享堂(ㄒㄧㄤˇ ㄊㄤˊ)
a sanctuary (for worship of ancestors or deities)

享年(ㄒㄧㄤˇ ㄋㄧㄢˊ)or 享壽(ㄒㄧㄤˇ ㄕㄡˋ)
the number of years lived (by one who dies old)

享樂(ㄒㄧㄤˇ ㄌㄜˋ)
to seek pleasure; to make merry

享樂主義(ㄒㄧㄤˇ ㄌㄜˋ ㄓㄨˇ ㄧˋ)
hedonism

享國(ㄒㄧㄤˇ ㄍㄨㄛˊ)
the number of years of the reign (by a sovereign)

享受(ㄒㄧㄤˇ ㄕㄡˋ)
to enjoy; to indulge oneself in (some pleasant pursuit)

享有(ㄒㄧㄤˇ ㄧㄡˇ)
to possess; to have in possession: 他享有很多特權。He possesses many privileges.

享用(ㄒㄧㄤˇ ㄩㄥˋ)

to enjoy the use of

【京】 67 ㄐㄧㄥ jing jīng
1. the capital (of a country); a metropolis
2. great; greatness

京派(ㄐㄧㄥ ㄆㄞˋ)
the Peking style or school (as opposed to the Shanghai style)

京調(ㄐㄧㄥ ㄉㄧㄠˋ)
the Peking style (of music in Chinese opera)

京都(ㄐㄧㄥ ㄉㄨ)
① the national capital ② Kyoto, Japan

京官(ㄐㄧㄥ ㄍㄨㄢ)
an official who works in the capital

京胡(ㄐㄧㄥ ㄏㄨˊ)
a Chinese violin

京滬鐵路(ㄐㄧㄥ ㄏㄨˋ ㄊㄧㄝˇ ㄌㄨˋ)
the Nanking-Shanghai Railway

京話(ㄐㄧㄥ ㄏㄨㄚˋ)
Pekinese or Mandarin

京畿(ㄐㄧㄥ ㄐㄧ)
the capital and vicinity

京戲(ㄐㄧㄥ ㄒㄧˋ) or 京劇(ㄐㄧㄥ ㄐㄩˋ)
Peking opera

京兆尹(ㄐㄧㄥ ㄓㄠˋ ㄧㄣˇ)
the mayor of the national capital (in ancient China)

京城(ㄐㄧㄥ ㄔㄥˊ) or 京師(ㄐㄧㄥ ㄕ)
the capital (of the country)

京油子(ㄐㄧㄥ ㄧㄡˊ ·ㄗ)
the oily Pekinese (a derogatory term describing their sophistication)

京韻大鼓(ㄐㄧㄥ ㄩㄣˋ ㄉㄚˋ ㄍㄨˇ)
storytelling in the Peking dialect accompanied by drum-beating

七畫

【亭】 68 ㄊㄧㄥˊ tyng tíng
1. a booth; a pavilion; a garden house or rest house: 公園中有一座八角亭。There is an octagonal pavilion in the park.
2. slim and erect
3. exactly during

亭臺樓閣(ㄊㄧㄥˊ ㄊㄞˊ ㄌㄡˊ ㄍㄜˊ)
a general reference to the elaborate Chinese architecture

亭亭玉立(ㄊㄧㄥˊ ㄊㄧㄥˊ ㄩˋ ㄌㄧˋ)
(said of women, especially young ladies) slim and graceful

亭候(ㄊㄧㄥˊ ㄏㄡˋ)
a military station in ancient China

亭長(ㄊㄧㄥˊ ㄓㄤˇ)
a village constable (of the Chin and Han dynasties)

亭子(ㄊㄧㄥˊ ·ㄗ)
a pavilion

亭午(ㄊㄧㄥˊ ㄨˇ)
high noon

【亮】 69 ㄌㄧㄤˋ lianq liàng
1. bright; lustrous; brilliant; luminous; radiant; clear
2. to display; to show

亮牌(ㄌㄧㄤˋ ㄆㄞˊ)
to lay one's cards on the table—(figuratively) to have a showdown

亮度(ㄌㄧㄤˋ ㄉㄨˋ)
brightness; light intensity; radiance; luminosity

亮光(ㄌㄧㄤˋ ㄍㄨㄤ)
bright light; flash

亮話(ㄌㄧㄤˋ ㄏㄨㄚˋ)
frank remarks; outspoken speech

亮節(ㄌㄧㄤˋ ㄐㄧㄝˊ)
integrity (of character); uprightness

亮晶晶(ㄌㄧㄤˋ ㄐㄧㄥ ㄐㄧㄥ)
bright; brilliant; dazzling; glaring; glistening; glittering; glowing; luminous; lustrous; radiant; resplendent; shining; sparkling; splendid

亮相(ㄌㄧㄤˋ ㄒㄧㄤˋ) or 亮像兒(ㄌㄧㄤˋ ㄒㄧㄤˋㄦ)
to pose for the audience's admiration on the stage (originally said of Peking opera players)

亮察(ㄌㄧㄤˋ ㄔㄚˊ)
to understand (another's difficulty)

八畫

【亳】 70 ㄅㄛˊ boh bó
the seat of government during the Shang Dynasty, located in today's Shangchiu County, Honan Province

人部
ㄖㄣˊ ren rén

【人】 71 ㄖㄣˊ ren rén
a human being; a person; people

人保(ㄖㄣˊ ㄅㄠˇ)
a personal guarantor

人本主義(ㄖㄣˊ ㄅㄣˇ ㄓㄨˇ ㄧˋ) or 人文主義(ㄖㄣˊ ㄨㄣˊ ㄓㄨˇ ㄧˋ)
(philosophy) humanism

人不可貌相(ㄖㄣˊ ㄅㄨˋ ㄎㄜˇ ㄇㄠˋ ㄒㄧㄤˋ)
A man's worth cannot be measured by his looks.

人不知鬼不覺(ㄖㄣˊ ㄅㄨˋ ㄓ ㄍㄨㄟˇ ㄅㄨˋ ㄐㄩㄝˊ)
without the knowledge of anybody else

人不爲己，天誅地滅(ㄖㄣˊ ㄅㄨˋ ㄨㄟˋ ㄐㄧˇ, ㄊㄧㄢ ㄓㄨ ㄉㄧˋ ㄇㄧㄝˋ)
If a person did not look out for himself, Heaven and Earth will destroy him.

人怕出名豬怕肥(ㄖㄣˊ ㄆㄚˋ ㄔㄨ ㄇㄧㄥˊ ㄓㄨ ㄆㄚˋ ㄈㄟˊ)
Men are afraid of becoming famous while pigs of getting fat.—(figuratively) Fame portends trouble for people.

人品(ㄖㄣˊ ㄆㄧㄣˇ)
character (of a person); personality

人馬(ㄖㄣˊ ㄇㄚˇ)
① a person and the horse he rides; a crowd of people and horses ② traffic (consisting of people and horses) ③ troops (consisting of soldiers and horses)

人馬宮(ㄖㄣˊ ㄇㄚˇ ㄍㄨㄥ) or 人馬座(ㄖㄣˊ ㄇㄚˇ ㄗㄨㄛˋ)
(astronomy) Sagittarius

人滿之患(ㄖㄣˊ ㄇㄢˇ ㄓ ㄏㄨㄢˋ)
trouble of overpopulation or overcrowdedness

人面桃花(ㄖㄣˊ ㄇㄧㄢˋ ㄊㄠˊ ㄏㄨㄚ)
① memory of an old sweetheart ② name of a Peking opera play

〔人部〕

人面獅身像(ㄖㄣˊ ㄇㄧㄢˋ ㄕ ㄕㄣ ㄒㄧㄤˋ)
a sphinx

人面獸心(ㄖㄣˊ ㄇㄧㄢˋ ㄕㄡˋ ㄒㄧㄣ)
gentle in appearance but cruel at heart; a wolf in sheep's clothing

人民(ㄖㄣˊ ㄇㄧㄣˊ)
people (as opposed to the ruler or the government)

人民代表大會(ㄖㄣˊ ㄇㄧㄣˊ ㄉㄞˋ ㄅㄧㄠˇ ㄉㄚˋ ㄏㄨㄟˋ)
the National People's Congress in mainland China

人民團體(ㄖㄣˊ ㄇㄧㄣˊ ㄊㄨㄢˊ ㄊㄧˇ)
a civic organization or civic body

人民公社(ㄖㄣˊ ㄇㄧㄣˊ ㄍㄨㄥ ㄕㄜˋ)
people's commune (in mainland China)

人民陣線(ㄖㄣˊ ㄇㄧㄣˊ ㄓㄣˋ ㄒㄧㄢˋ)
the popular front

人命關天(ㄖㄣˊ ㄇㄧㄥˋ ㄍㄨㄢ ㄊㄧㄢ)
Human life is of utmost importance.

人命攸關(ㄖㄣˊ ㄇㄧㄥˋ ㄧㄡ ㄍㄨㄢ)
a matter of life and death

人非木石(ㄖㄣˊ ㄈㄟ ㄇㄨˋ ㄕˊ)
Man is a sentimental creature.

人犯(ㄖㄣˊ ㄈㄢˋ)
a criminal; a suspect (in a criminal case)

人販子(ㄖㄣˊ ㄈㄢˋ ˙ㄗ)
a trader in human beings

人浮於事(ㄖㄣˊ ㄈㄨˊ ㄩˊ ㄕˋ)
There are more job-hunters than there are jobs.

人大心大(ㄖㄣˊ ㄉㄚˋ ㄒㄧㄣ ㄉㄚˋ)
to grow in independence of mind, or insubordination, with growth in body (usually said of girls)

人道(ㄖㄣˊ ㄉㄠˋ)
① humanitarianism; philanthropy; charity; humanity ② sexual union

人地生疏(ㄖㄣˊ ㄉㄧˋ ㄕㄥ ㄕㄨ)
to have trouble getting about in a strange land because of unfamiliarity with the local people and their customs

人丁(ㄖㄣˊ ㄉㄧㄥ)
① an adult ② population: 此村人丁不足一千。The population of this village is less than 1,000.

人定勝天(ㄖㄣˊ ㄉㄧㄥˋ ㄕㄥˋ ㄊㄧㄢ)
Man's determination will conquer nature.

人多嘴雜(ㄖㄣˊ ㄉㄨㄛ ㄗㄨㄟˇ ㄗㄚˊ)
① Agreement is difficult if there are too many people. ② Secrecy is difficult if too many people share it.

人頭稅(ㄖㄣˊ ㄊㄡˊ ㄕㄨㄟˋ)
poll tax

人體(ㄖㄣˊ ㄊㄧˇ)
a human body

人同此心，心同此理(ㄖㄣˊ ㄊㄨㄥˊ ㄘˇ ㄒㄧㄣ, ㄒㄧㄣ ㄊㄨㄥˊ ㄘˇ ㄌㄧˇ)
The sense of justice and rationality is the same with everybody.

人籟(ㄖㄣˊ ㄌㄞˋ)
hubbub or noises of human habitation

人類(ㄖㄣˊ ㄌㄟˋ)
man; mankind; the human race: 一個人應立志為全人類謀幸福。One should make up one's mind to benefit all mankind.

人類學(ㄖㄣˊ ㄌㄟˋ ㄒㄩㄝˊ)
anthropology

人力(ㄖㄣˊ ㄌㄧˋ)
human power, strength or efforts

人力車(ㄖㄣˊ ㄌㄧˋ ㄔㄜ)
a rickshaw, ricksha or jinrikisha

人力資源(ㄖㄣˊ ㄌㄧˋ ㄗ ㄩㄢˊ)
human resources

人倫(ㄖㄣˊ ㄌㄨㄣˊ)
principles of human relationships

人格(ㄖㄣˊ ㄍㄜˊ)
character; personality

人格分裂(ㄖㄣˊ ㄍㄜˊ ㄈㄣ ㄌㄧㄝˋ)
split personality

人工(ㄖㄣˊ ㄍㄨㄥ)
① human labor ② man-made

人工孵化(ㄖㄣˊ ㄍㄨㄥ ㄈㄨ ㄏㄨㄚˋ)
artificial incubation

人工港(ㄖㄣˊ ㄍㄨㄥ ㄍㄤˇ)
an artificial harbor

人工呼吸(ㄖㄣˊ ㄍㄨㄥ ㄏㄨ ㄒㄧ)
artificial respiration

人工湖(ㄖㄣˊ ㄍㄨㄥ ㄏㄨˊ)
an artificial lake

人工受孕(ㄖㄣˊ ㄍㄨㄥ ㄕㄡˋ ㄩㄣˋ)
artificial insemination

人口(ㄖㄣˊ ㄎㄡˇ)
population

人口普查(ㄖㄣˊ ㄎㄡˇ ㄆㄨˇ ㄔㄚˊ)
a population census

人口密度(ㄖㄣˊ ㄎㄡˇ ㄇㄧˋ ㄉㄨˋ)
density of population

人口統計(ㄖㄣˊ ㄎㄡˇ ㄊㄨㄥˇ ㄐㄧˋ)
demographic statistics; population statistics

人口論(ㄖㄣˊ ㄎㄡˇ ㄌㄨㄣˋ)
The Principle of Population by Thomas Robert Malthus

人口過剩(ㄖㄣˊ ㄎㄡˇ ㄍㄨㄛˋ ㄕㄥˋ)
overpopulation

人口學(ㄖㄣˊ ㄎㄡˇ ㄒㄩㄝˊ)
demography

人口政策(ㄖㄣˊ ㄎㄡˇ ㄓㄥˋ ㄘㄜˋ)
population policy

人口問題(ㄖㄣˊ ㄎㄡˇ ㄨㄣˋ ㄊㄧˊ)
population problems

人困馬乏(ㄖㄣˊ ㄎㄨㄣˋ ㄇㄚˇ ㄈㄚˊ)
Both the horse and the rider are exhausted.

人和(ㄖㄣˊ ㄏㄜˊ)
popularity or harmony with the people, colleagues, constituents, etc.

人海(ㄖㄣˊ ㄏㄞˇ)
huge crowds

人海浮沈(ㄖㄣˊ ㄏㄞˇ ㄈㄨˊ ㄔㄣˊ)
the vicissitudes of life

人海戰術(ㄖㄣˊ ㄏㄞˇ ㄓㄢˋ ㄕㄨˋ)
human-sea tactics; human-wave sweep

人話(ㄖㄣˊ ㄏㄨㄚˋ)
reasonable statement (as opposed to nonsense)

人寰(ㄖㄣˊ ㄏㄨㄢˊ)
the world; the earth

人迹(ㄖㄣˊ ㄐㄧ)
signs or traces indicating human presence

人際關係(ㄖㄣˊ ㄐㄧˋ ㄍㄨㄢ ㄒㄧˋ)
human relation

人家(ㄖㄣˊ ㄐㄧㄚ)
① a human abode or residence; a home ② other people

人傑地靈(ㄖㄣˊ ㄐㄧㄝˊ ㄉㄧˋ ㄌㄧㄥˊ)
The birth (or presence) of heroes brings glory to a place.

人間(ㄖㄣˊ ㄐㄧㄢ)
the world of mortals

人間地獄(ㄖㄣˊ ㄐㄧㄢ ㄉㄧˋ ㄩˋ)
pandemonium; a hell away from Hell

人間何世(ㄖㄣˊ ㄐㄧㄢ ㄏㄜˊ ㄕˋ)
What a world is this?!
人見人愛(ㄖㄣˊ ㄐㄧㄢˋ ㄖㄣˊ ㄞˋ)
loved by all; everybody's darling
人盡可夫(ㄖㄣˊ ㄐㄧㄣˋ ㄎㄜˇ ㄈㄨ)
(said of women) promiscuous
人盡其才(ㄖㄣˊ ㄐㄧㄣˋ ㄑㄧˊ ㄘㄞˊ)
No talent is to be wasted.
人君(ㄖㄣˊ ㄐㄩㄣ)
a sovereign; a king
人棄我取(ㄖㄣˊ ㄑㄧˋ ㄨㄛˇ ㄑㄩˇ)
I will take whatever others don't want.
人情(ㄖㄣˊ ㄑㄧㄥˊ)
① human sentiment, emotion or feeling ② favors asked or done ③ good will (expressed in the form of gifts, invitation to dinners, etc.)
人情世故(ㄖㄣˊ ㄑㄧㄥˊ ㄕˋ ㄍㄨˋ)
the ways of the world: 他不懂人情世故。He does not know the ways of the world.
人情味(ㄖㄣˊ ㄑㄧㄥˊ ㄨㄟˋ)
human touch; friendliness; hospitality
人去樓空(ㄖㄣˊ ㄑㄩˋ ㄌㄡˊ ㄎㄨㄥ)
After the occupants are gone, the building is empty. 或 Old sights recall to mind the memory of old friends.
人權(ㄖㄣˊ ㄑㄩㄢˊ)
human rights
人權宣言(ㄖㄣˊ ㄑㄩㄢˊ ㄒㄩㄢ ㄧㄢˊ)
the declaration of human rights
人羣(ㄖㄣˊ ㄑㄩㄣˊ)
a crowd, throng or multitude (of people)
人窮志短(ㄖㄣˊ ㄑㄩㄥˊ ㄓˋ ㄉㄨㄢˇ)
Poverty stifles ambition.
人小鬼大(ㄖㄣˊ ㄒㄧㄠˇ ㄍㄨㄟˇ ㄉㄚˋ)
young but tricky; young but ambitious
人心(ㄖㄣˊ ㄒㄧㄣ)
human heart, will, feeling or emotion; morale
人心不同，各如其面(ㄖㄣˊ ㄒㄧㄣ ㄅㄨˋ ㄊㄨㄥˊ, ㄍㄜˋ ㄖㄨˊ ㄑㄧˊ ㄇㄧㄢˋ)
Individual thinking is as varied as individual looks.
人心不古(ㄖㄣˊ ㄒㄧㄣ ㄅㄨˋ ㄍㄨˇ)
Public morality is not what it used to be. 或 Public morality has degenerated.
人心皇皇(ㄖㄣˊ ㄒㄧㄣ ㄏㄨㄤˊ ㄏㄨㄤˊ)
(said of people in time of war or social upheaval) jittery or panicky
人心思漢(ㄖㄣˊ ㄒㄧㄣ ㄙ ㄏㄢˋ)
The people living under the control of a usurper or foreign invaders long for the return of the legitimate government.
人像(ㄖㄣˊ ㄒㄧㄤˋ)
a portrait; an image
人行道(ㄖㄣˊ ㄒㄧㄥˊ ㄉㄠˋ)
a sidewalk; a footpath
人行穿越道(ㄖㄣˊ ㄒㄧㄥˊ ㄔㄨㄢ ㄩㄝˋ ㄉㄠˋ)
a pedestrian crosswalk; a pedestrian crossing
人性(ㄖㄣˊ ㄒㄧㄥˋ)
human nature; normal human feelings; reason
人選(ㄖㄣˊ ㄒㄩㄢˇ)
candidates (for certain jobs)
人之常情(ㄖㄣˊ ㄓ ㄔㄤˊ ㄑㄧㄥˊ)
the way of the world; what is natural in human relationships
人治(ㄖㄣˊ ㄓˋ)
enlightened government brought about by virtuous rulers or administrators (as distinguished from what results from the rule of law)
人質(ㄖㄣˊ ㄓˋ)
a hostage
人證(ㄖㄣˊ ㄓㄥˋ)
① witnesses ② testimony given by witnesses
人主(ㄖㄣˊ ㄓㄨˇ)
a sovereign; a king
人中(ㄖㄣˊ ㄓㄨㄥ)
(physiognomy) philtrum
人種(ㄖㄣˊ ㄓㄨㄥˇ)
human races
人種學(ㄖㄣˊ ㄓㄨㄥˇ ㄒㄩㄝˊ)
ethnology
人臣(ㄖㄣˊ ㄔㄣˊ)
a vassal
人稱(ㄖㄣˊ ㄔㄥ)
①(grammar) the first, second or third person ② a nickname by which one is known
人稱代名詞(ㄖㄣˊ ㄔㄥ ㄉㄞˋ ㄇㄧㄥˊ ㄘˊ)
a personal pronoun
人師(ㄖㄣˊ ㄕ)
a paragon (of virtue or/and learning)
人士(ㄖㄣˊ ㄕˋ)
personages (usually plural)
人氏(ㄖㄣˊ ㄕˋ)
persons born of a particular place: 他是本地人氏。He is a native here.
人世(ㄖㄣˊ ㄕˋ)
① human life; life ② the world
人事(ㄖㄣˊ ㄕˋ)
① human affairs; human customs ② personnel affairs (of an organization) ③ human endeavors
人事關係(ㄖㄣˊ ㄕˋ ㄍㄨㄢ ㄒㄧˋ)
personal connections
人事管理(ㄖㄣˊ ㄕˋ ㄍㄨㄢˇ ㄌㄧˇ)
personnel administration
人手(ㄖㄣˊ ㄕㄡˇ)
① manpower ② a human hand
人手一册(ㄖㄣˊ ㄕㄡˇ ㄧˊ ㄘㄜˋ)
Everyone has a copy.(referring to a popular book)
人壽保險(ㄖㄣˊ ㄕㄡˋ ㄅㄠˇ ㄒㄧㄢˇ)
life insurance
人山人海(ㄖㄣˊ ㄕㄢ ㄖㄣˊ ㄏㄞˇ)
a large crowd
人身(ㄖㄣˊ ㄕㄣ)
① a human body ②(law) personal (liberty)
人參(ㄖㄣˊ ㄕㄣ)
ginseng
人生(ㄖㄣˊ ㄕㄥ)
human life; life
人生觀(ㄖㄣˊ ㄕㄥ ㄍㄨㄢ)
a view of life; an outlook on life; the philosophy of life
人生朝露(ㄖㄣˊ ㄕㄥ ㄓㄠ ㄌㄨˋ)
Life is ephemeral (like the morning dew).
人生如夢(ㄖㄣˊ ㄕㄥ ㄖㄨˊ ㄇㄥˋ)
Life is but a dream.
人生如寄(ㄖㄣˊ ㄕㄥ ㄖㄨˊ ㄐㄧˋ)
(literally) Man living in the world is like a sojourner in a hotel.—Life is short.
人肉市場(ㄖㄣˊ ㄖㄡˋ ㄕˋ ㄔㄤˊ)or(ㄖㄣˊ ㄖㄡˋ ㄕˋ ㄔㄤˇ)
the sex market; houses of ill fame
人人(ㄖㄣˊ ㄖㄣˊ)
everybody

〔人部〕

〔人部〕

人人自危(ㄖㄣˊ ㄖㄣˊ ㄗˋ ㄨㄟˊ)
Everyone feels insecure.

人瑞(ㄖㄣˊ ㄖㄨㄟˋ)
a very old man or woman, considered a happy omen for the whole human race

人造(ㄖㄣˊ ㄗㄠˋ)
man-made; artificial; imitation

人造寶石(ㄖㄣˊ ㄗㄠˋ ㄅㄠˇ ㄕˊ)
an imitation jewel

人造冰(ㄖㄣˊ ㄗㄠˋ ㄅㄧㄥ)
manufactured ice; artificial ice

人造棉(ㄖㄣˊ ㄗㄠˋ ㄇㄧㄢˊ)
staple rayon

人造肥料(ㄖㄣˊ ㄗㄠˋ ㄈㄟˊ ㄌㄧㄠˋ)
chemical fertilizer

人造奶油(ㄖㄣˊ ㄗㄠˋ ㄋㄞˇ ㄧㄡˊ)or 人造牛油(ㄖㄣˊ ㄗㄠˋ ㄋㄧㄡˊ ㄧㄡˊ)
margarine

人造纖維(ㄖㄣˊ ㄗㄠˋ ㄒㄧㄢ ㄨㄟˊ)
man-made fiber

人造心臟(ㄖㄣˊ ㄗㄠˋ ㄒㄧㄣ ㄗㄤˋ)
an artificial heart

人造絲(ㄖㄣˊ ㄗㄠˋ ㄙ)
synthetic silk; rayon

人造衛星(ㄖㄣˊ ㄗㄠˋ ㄨㄟˋ ㄒㄧㄥ)
an artificial satellite; a satellite

人造雨(ㄖㄣˊ ㄗㄠˋ ㄩˇ)
artificial rain; rain caused by cloud seeding

人造語言(ㄖㄣˊ ㄗㄠˋ ㄩˇ ㄧㄢˊ)
an artificial language

人贓並獲(ㄖㄣˊ ㄗㄤ ㄅㄧㄥˋ ㄏㄨㄛˋ)
(a thief or robber) caught together with the loot

人才(ㄖㄣˊ ㄘㄞˊ)
a man of talent; a talent; a man of ability

人才輩出(ㄖㄣˊ ㄘㄞˊ ㄅㄟˋ ㄔㄨ)
Great talents appear successively (or continuously).

人才濟濟(ㄖㄣˊ ㄘㄞˊ ㄐㄧˇ ㄐㄧˇ)
There is a wealth of talents.

人才外流(ㄖㄣˊ ㄘㄞˊ ㄨㄞˋ ㄌㄧㄡˊ)
the brain drain

人存政舉，人亡政息(ㄖㄣˊ ㄘㄨㄣˊ ㄓㄥˋ ㄐㄩˇ, ㄖㄣˊ ㄨㄤˊ ㄓㄥˋ ㄒㄧˊ)
The policies and regulations of an organization shift with the change of the person in charge.

人一己百(ㄖㄣˊ ㄧ ㄐㄧˇ ㄅㄞˇ)
If others can do it, I must exert myself a hundred times harder (because I am less talented than they are) in order to do the same.

人妖(ㄖㄣˊ ㄧㄠ)
①a man disguised as a woman or vice versa who engages in evil activities under the disguise ②a hermaphrodite

人煙(ㄖㄣˊ ㄧㄢ)
signs of a human settlement; human habitation

人言(ㄖㄣˊ ㄧㄢˊ)
①human speech ②public opinion; the words of people

人言可畏(ㄖㄣˊ ㄧㄢˊ ㄎㄜˇ ㄨㄟˋ)
Criticisms should be feared.

人言嘖嘖(ㄖㄣˊ ㄧㄢˊ ㄗㄜˊ ㄗㄜˊ)
There are plenty of criticisms.

人仰馬翻(ㄖㄣˊ ㄧㄤˇ ㄇㄚˇ ㄈㄢ)
to suffer an utter defeat

人樣兒(ㄖㄣˊ ㄧㄤˋㄦ)
the proper human appearance

人影(ㄖㄣˊ ㄧㄥˇ)or 人影兒(ㄖㄣˊ ㄧㄥˇㄦ)
a human shadow

人無遠慮，必有近憂(ㄖㄣˊ ㄨˊ ㄩㄢˇ ㄌㄩˋ, ㄅㄧˋ ㄧㄡˇ ㄐㄧㄣˋ ㄧㄡ)
Those who do not plan for the future will find trouble at their doorsteps.

人物(ㄖㄣˊ ㄨˋ)
①a personage or figure (usually referring to famous persons) ②people and things

人物畫(ㄖㄣˊ ㄨˋ ㄏㄨㄚˋ)
portrait painting

人微言輕(ㄖㄣˊ ㄨㄟˊ ㄧㄢˊ ㄑㄧㄥ)
(a self-depreciatory expression) Words from a man of lowly position (like me) carry little weight.

人爲(ㄖㄣˊ ㄨㄟˊ)
man-made; artificial

人爲刀俎，我爲魚肉(ㄖㄣˊ ㄨㄟˊ ㄉㄠ ㄗㄨˇ, ㄨㄛˇ ㄨㄟˊ ㄩˊ ㄖㄡˋ)
(literally) to be meat on somebody's chopping board—to be at the mercy of somebody

人爲萬物之靈(ㄖㄣˊ ㄨㄟˊ ㄨㄢˋ ㄨˋ ㄓ ㄌㄧㄥˊ)
The human being is the most intelligent among creatures. 或 Man is the lord of creation.

人文(ㄖㄣˊ ㄨㄣˊ)
①humanities; culture ②human affairs

人文地理(ㄖㄣˊ ㄨㄣˊ ㄉㄧˋ ㄌㄧˇ)
human geography

人文科學(ㄖㄣˊ ㄨㄣˊ ㄎㄜ ㄒㄩㄝˊ)
the humanities; humane studies

人文薈萃(ㄖㄣˊ ㄨㄣˊ ㄏㄨㄟˋ ㄘㄨㄟˋ)
(said of culture centers) gathering of talents

人文主義(ㄖㄣˊ ㄨㄣˊ ㄓㄨˇ ㄧˋ)
humanism

人亡物在(ㄖㄣˊ ㄨㄤˊ ㄨˋ ㄗㄞˋ)
the relics of the dead (heightening the grief of the living)

人望(ㄖㄣˊ ㄨㄤˋ)
popularity

人慾(ㄖㄣˊ ㄩˋ)
desires; passions

人慾橫流(ㄖㄣˊ ㄩˋ ㄏㄥˊ ㄌㄧㄡˊ)
mass indulgence in decadent life

人員(ㄖㄣˊ ㄩㄢˊ)
the personnel; the staff

人猿(ㄖㄣˊ ㄩㄢˊ)
an ape

人緣(ㄖㄣˊ ㄩㄢˊ)or 人緣兒(ㄖㄣˊ ㄩㄚˊㄦ)
relations with others; personality (as an impression upon others)

人云亦云(ㄖㄣˊ ㄩㄣˊ ㄧˋ ㄩㄣˊ)
to parrot what others say; me-tooism; me-too

二畫

【什】 72
1. ㄕˊ shyr shí

1. sundry; miscellaneous
2. ten
3. a squad (of ten soldiers, in former times)

什錦(ㄕˊ ㄐㄧㄣˇ)
multiple ingredients (for a dish); assorted

什器(ㄕˊ ㄑㄧˋ)
miscellaneous utensils

什襲珍藏(ㄕˊ ㄒㄧˊ ㄓㄣ ㄘㄤˊ)
to store away like treasure

什一(ㄕˊ ㄧ)
one tenth

什物(ㄕˊ ㄨˋ)
miscellaneous goods; sundry items

【什】 72
2.(甚) ㄕㄜˊ sher shé
as in 什麽

什麽(ㄕㄜˊ ·ㄇㄜ)
what (used either in question or as an exclamation)

什麽東西(ㄕㄜˊ ·ㄇㄜ ㄉㄨㄥ ·ㄒㄧ)
① What is this (or that)?② What does he think he is?

什麽話(ㄕㄜˊ ·ㄇㄜ ㄏㄨㄚˋ)
How can you say that!? 或 How can you do this!?

【仁】 73
ㄖㄣˊ ren rén
1. benevolence; humanity; mercy; kindness; charity
2. kernel

仁民(ㄖㄣˊ ㄇㄧㄣˊ)
to be benevolent to the common people; to be philanthropic

仁民愛物(ㄖㄣˊ ㄇㄧㄣˊ ㄞˋ ㄨˋ)
to love all people and animals

仁風(ㄖㄣˊ ㄈㄥ)
benevolence (as prevailing effect)

仁德(ㄖㄣˊ ㄉㄜˊ)
benevolence; magnanimity; charity; humanity; kindness

仁弟(ㄖㄣˊ ㄉㄧˋ)
dear little brother (a designation for a younger friend, or one's student)

仁厚(ㄖㄣˊ ㄏㄡˋ)
benevolent and generous

仁君(ㄖㄣˊ ㄐㄩㄣ)
your (or his) lordship

仁心(ㄖㄣˊ ㄒㄧㄣ)
kindheartedness; charity; kindness

仁心仁術(ㄖㄣˊ ㄒㄧㄣ ㄖㄣˊ ㄕㄨˋ)
benevolence entertained at heart and practiced in deeds (usually used as a eulogy to medical practitioners)

仁兄(ㄖㄣˊ ㄒㄩㄥ)
dear elder brother (a designation for a friend of the same standing as oneself)

仁至義盡(ㄖㄣˊ ㄓˋ ㄧˋ ㄐㄧㄣˋ)
Everything to be expected in the light of benevolence and duty has been done.

仁者壽(ㄖㄣˊ ㄓㄜˇ ㄕㄡˋ)
The kind live long.

仁者見仁，智者見智(ㄖㄣˊ ㄓㄜˇ ㄐㄧㄢˋ ㄖㄣˊ, ㄓˋ ㄓㄜˇ ㄐㄧㄢˋ ㄓˋ)
The virtuous see virtue and the wise see wisdom.—Different people have different views.

仁政(ㄖㄣˊ ㄓㄥˋ)
humanitarian rule; good administration

仁人(ㄖㄣˊ ㄖㄣˊ)
a kind-hearted person

仁人君子(ㄖㄣˊ ㄖㄣˊ ㄐㄩㄣ ㄗˇ)
kind-hearted gentlemen; good people; philanthropists

仁人志士(ㄖㄣˊ ㄖㄣˊ ㄓˋ ㄕˋ)
a person with lofty ideals

仁慈(ㄖㄣˊ ㄘˊ)
benevolence; magnanimity; charity; humanity; kindness; love

仁愛(ㄖㄣˊ ㄞˋ)
humanity; philanthropy; kindness; benevolence; love

仁義(ㄖㄣˊ ㄧˋ)
love and justice

仁義道德(ㄖㄣˊ ㄧˋ ㄉㄠˋ ㄉㄜˊ)
benevolence, justice and virtue; virtue and morality

【仂】 74
ㄌㄜˋ leh lè
a fraction (of number)

【仃】 75
ㄉㄧㄥ ding ding
lonely; solitary

【仄】 76
ㄗㄜˋ tzeh zè
1. oblique
2. said of the three tones other than the even tone (in ancient Chinese phonology)
3. narrow
4. uneasy

仄聲(ㄗㄜˋ ㄕㄥ)
an oblique tone (any of the three tones other than the even tone, i.e., rising tone, going tone, and entering tone)

仄韻(ㄗㄜˋ ㄩㄣˋ)
poetry rhyming with the characters of 仄聲

【仆】 77
ㄆㄨ pu pū
(又讀 ㄈㄨˋ fuh fù)
1. to prostrate
2. to fall

【仇】 78
1.(讎) ㄔㄡˊ chour chóu
1. a foe; an enemy; a rival; an adversary
2. hatred; enmity; antagonism; hostility; feud
3. to hate: 她容易仇視別人。She hates easily.

仇敵(ㄔㄡˊ ㄉㄧˊ)
an enemy, a foe, or an antagonist

仇恨(ㄔㄡˊ ㄏㄣˋ)
① hatred; spite; animosity; enmity; hostility; feud; ill will; resentment; bitterness; rancor ② to hate; to bear a grudge against

仇家(ㄔㄡˊ ㄐㄧㄚ)
a personal enemy

仇隙(ㄔㄡˊ ㄒㄧˋ)
a breach (of friendly relations); feud; a quarrel

仇視(ㄔㄡˊ ㄕˋ)
to regard with hostility or enmity

仇殺(ㄔㄡˊ ㄕㄚ)
a murder committed out of grudge or vendetta

仇人(ㄔㄡˊ ㄖㄣˊ)or 仇家(ㄔㄡˊ ㄐㄧㄚ)
an enemy; a foe; a rival; an opponent; an adversary; an antagonist

【仇】 78
2. ㄑㄧㄡˊ chyou qiú
1. a Chinese family name
2. a spouse

仇偶(ㄑㄧㄡˊ ㄡˇ)
one's spouse

【今】 79
ㄐㄧㄣ jin jīn
1. present; recent; modern
2. now; currently; presently; nowadays
3. immediately; right away

今非昔比(ㄐㄧㄣ ㄈㄟ ㄒㄧˊ ㄅㄧˇ)
Time has changed and the good old days are gone.

今體(ㄐㄧㄣ ㄊㄧˇ)
(said of literary works) the modern style

今天(ㄐㄧㄣ ㄊㄧㄢ)or 今兒(ㄐㄧㄜㄦ) or 今兒個(ㄐㄧㄜㄦ ·ㄍㄜ)
today

今年(ㄐㄧㄣ ㄋㄧㄢˊ)
this year

今後(ㄐㄧㄣ ㄏㄡˋ)
hereafter; henceforward;

〔人部〕

henceforth; from now on
今昔(ㄐㄧㄣ ㄒㄧˊ)
the present and the past
今昔之感(ㄐㄧㄣ ㄒㄧˊ ㄓ ㄍㄢˇ)
an expression to convey a sense of loss when the present situation is definitely worse than what it used to be
今朝(ㄐㄧㄣ ㄓㄠ)
today; this morning
今朝有酒今朝醉(ㄐㄧㄣ ㄓㄠ ㄧㄡˇ ㄐㄧㄡˇ ㄐㄧㄣ ㄓㄠ ㄗㄨㄟˋ)
to enjoy while one can; *carpe diem*
今晨(ㄐㄧㄣ ㄔㄣˊ)
this morning
今世(ㄐㄧㄣ ㄕˋ)
① the present era ② life on this side of the grave; this present life
今是昨非(ㄐㄧㄣ ㄕˋ ㄗㄨㄛˊ ㄈㄟ)
(said of repentance and reformation) to step onto the right path as of today and to say good-bye to the wrongdoings of the past
今生(ㄐㄧㄣ ㄕㄥ)
this present life (as distinct from past and future lives by the concept of life and death as a never-ending cycle)
今日(ㄐㄧㄣ ㄖˋ)
① today ② nowadays
今人(ㄐㄧㄣ ㄖㄣˊ)
a now living person; a contemporary
今譯(ㄐㄧㄣ ㄧˋ)
the modern language version
今夜(ㄐㄧㄣ ㄧㄝˋ)or 今夕(ㄐㄧㄣ ㄒㄧˋ) or 今晚(ㄐㄧㄣ ㄨㄢˇ)or 今宵(ㄐㄧㄣ ㄒㄧㄠ)
tonight
今音(ㄐㄧㄣ ㄧㄣ)
modern pronunciation (of words pronounced differently in the past)

【介】 80
ㄐㄧㄝˋ jieh jiè
1. a shelled aquatic animal
2. to lie between
3. (said of one's character) upright
4. great and honorable
5. to aid; to benefit
6. tiny
介弟(ㄐㄧㄝˋ ㄉㄧˋ)
your younger brother (in formal speech)
介殼(ㄐㄧㄝˋ ㄎㄜˊ)
the shell (of an insect or animal)
介居(ㄐㄧㄝˋ ㄐㄩ)
to live in between
介蟲(ㄐㄧㄝˋ ㄔㄨㄥˊ)
a shelled aquatic animal (like the crab, the shrimp, etc.); the crustacean
介士(ㄐㄧㄝˋ ㄕˋ)
a man of principle; an upright man
介紹(ㄐㄧㄝˋ ㄕㄠˋ)
to introduce (a person to another)
介紹人(ㄐㄧㄝˋ ㄕㄠˋ ㄖㄣˊ)
an introducer; a matchmaker
介壽(ㄐㄧㄝˋ ㄕㄡˋ)
to benefit one's longevity—birthday congratulations
介入(ㄐㄧㄝˋ ㄖㄨˋ)
to get involved; to interfere with
介詞(ㄐㄧㄝˋ ㄘˊ)
a preposition
介意(ㄐㄧㄝˋ ㄧˋ)or 介懷(ㄐㄧㄝˋ ㄏㄨㄞˊ)
to mind; to heed: 不要介意他人怎麼說。Don't mind what other people say.
介於(ㄐㄧㄝˋ ㄩˊ)
to lie in between; to be situated between

【仍】 81
ㄖㄥˊ reng réng
still; yet: 我回來的時候，他仍會在這兒嗎? Will he still be here when I get back?
仍舊(ㄖㄥˊ ㄐㄧㄡˋ)or 仍然(ㄖㄥˊ ㄖㄢˊ)
still; yet
仍是(ㄖㄥˊ ㄕˋ)
still is (what it used to be); still was (what it had been): 王小姐仍是學生嗎? Is Miss Wang still a student?

三畫

【仔】 82
1. ㄗˇ tzyy zǐ
careful
仔細(ㄗˇ ㄒㄧˋ)
careful; punctilious; minute; attentive

【仔】 82
2. ㄗㄞˇ tzae zǎi
1. young animals
2. one who tends cattle
仔畜(ㄗㄞˇ ㄔㄨˋ)
a newborn animal; a young animal

【仕】 83
ㄕˋ shyh shì
1. an official
2. to enter government service; to serve the government; to be an official; to fill an office
仕版(ㄕˋ ㄅㄢˇ)
a register of officials
仕途 or 仕塗(ㄕˋ ㄊㄨˊ)
the career in government service; a political career
仕女 or 士女(ㄕˋ ㄋㄩˇ)
① young men and women ② a painting portraying beautiful women
仕路(ㄕˋ ㄌㄨˋ)
an official career
仕宦(ㄕˋ ㄏㄨㄢˋ)
to be an official; to enter government service; to serve the government
仕進(ㄕˋ ㄐㄧㄣˋ)
to advance into government service

【他】 84
ㄊㄚ ta tā
1. he; him
2. other; another
3. future
他們(ㄊㄚ ·ㄇㄣ)
they; them
他們倆(ㄊㄚ ·ㄇㄣ ㄌㄧㄚˇ)
they two; them two: 他們倆是兄弟。They two are brothers.
他方(ㄊㄚ ㄈㄤ)
① the other party (to a transaction, dispute, etc.) ② other places
他動詞(ㄊㄚ ㄉㄨㄥˋ ㄘˊ)
a transitive verb 亦作「及物動詞」
他圖(ㄊㄚ ㄊㄨˊ)
a different scheme or plan; another plot
他年(ㄊㄚ ㄋㄧㄢˊ)
another year; some time in the future
他力(ㄊㄚ ㄌㄧˋ)

somebody else's power (as opposed to one's own)

他故(ㄊㄚ ㄍㄨˋ)
another cause

他國(ㄊㄚ ㄍㄨㄛˊ)
other countries

他計(ㄊㄚ ㄐㄧˋ)
another plan; a different plan

他家(ㄊㄚ ㄐㄧㄚ)
other people's homes; somebody else's home

他就(ㄊㄚ ㄐㄧㄡˋ)
to accept another job

他心(ㄊㄚ ㄒㄧㄣ)
dishonesty; insincerity; treachery; unfaithfulness

他鄉(ㄊㄚ ㄒㄧㄤ)
other lands or strange lands; a land away from home

他鄉遇故知(ㄊㄚ ㄒㄧㄤ ㄩˋ ㄍㄨˋ ㄓ)
to run across an old friend in a distant land

他志(ㄊㄚ ㄓˋ)
other ambitions; other (disloyal) ideas: 他頓萌他志。He suddenly had other (disloyal) ideas.

他處(ㄊㄚ ㄔㄨˋ)
elsewhere

他事(ㄊㄚ ㄕˋ)
other matters, things, or business

他殺(ㄊㄚ ㄕㄚ)
homicide (as opposed to suicide)

他山之石，可以攻玉(ㄊㄚ ㄕㄢ ㄓ ㄕˊ, ㄎㄜˇ ㄧˇ ㄍㄨㄥ ㄩˋ)
The stones of those hills may be used to polish gems. —Advice from others may help one overcome one's defects. 或to remedy one's defects by means of others' good quality or suggestion

他日(ㄊㄚ ㄖˋ)
① another day; some time in the future ② some time in the past

他人(ㄊㄚ ㄖㄣˊ)
others; other people; somebody else; another person

他意(ㄊㄚ ㄧˋ)
another intention (different from the professed one)

【仗】 85 ㄓㄤˋ jang zhàng

1. weaponry
2. to lean upon; to rely upon; to depend on
3. battle; war: 他去打仗。He went to war.

仗氣(ㄓㄤˋ ㄑㄧˋ)
to rely on emotion

仗著本事(ㄓㄤˋ ·ㄓㄜ ㄅㄣˇ ㄕˋ)
to rely on one's own skill or ability

仗恃(ㄓㄤˋ ㄕˋ)
to rely on (an advantage or someone's power)

仗勢欺人(ㄓㄤˋ ㄕˋ ㄑㄧ ㄖㄣˊ)
to bully the weaker on one's strength or power, or connection with powerful people

仗義(ㄓㄤˋ ㄧˋ)
to rely on a sense of justice

仗義執言(ㄓㄤˋ ㄧˋ ㄓˊ ㄧㄢˊ)
to speak in accordance with justice

仗義疏財(ㄓㄤˋ ㄧˋ ㄕㄨ ㄘㄞˊ)
to think little of one's fortune in one's enthusiasm for charity, etc.

【付】 86 ㄈㄨˋ fuh fù

1. to pay (money)
2. to deliver (goods); to consign

付託(ㄈㄨˋ ㄊㄨㄛ)
to entrust; to commission; to charge

付管(ㄈㄨˋ ㄍㄨㄢˇ)
to entrust the care of someone to another

付款(ㄈㄨˋ ㄎㄨㄢˇ)or 付錢(ㄈㄨˋ ㄑㄧㄢˊ)
to make payments; to pay (money); to shell out

付給(ㄈㄨˋ ㄐㄧˇ)
to pay; to deliver

付訖(ㄈㄨˋ ㄑㄧˋ)or 付清(ㄈㄨˋ ㄑㄧㄥ)
(said of a bill, tax, etc.) paid; all paid

付息(ㄈㄨˋ ㄒㄧˊ)
to pay interest

付現(ㄈㄨˋ ㄒㄧㄢˋ)
to pay in cash

付之一炬(ㄈㄨˋ ㄓ ㄧˊ ㄐㄩˋ)or 付丙(ㄈㄨˋ ㄅㄧㄥˇ)
to reduce to ashes; to burn; to burn down

付之一笑(ㄈㄨˋ ㄓ ㄧˊ ㄒㄧㄠˋ)
to laugh it away (or off)

付賬 or 付帳(ㄈㄨˋ ㄓㄤˋ)
to pay a bill

付諸東流(ㄈㄨˋ ㄓㄨ ㄉㄨㄥ ㄌㄧㄡˊ)or 付之流水(ㄈㄨˋ ㄓ ㄌㄧㄡˊ ㄕㄨㄟˇ)
(efforts) wasted; (accomplishments) undone or ruined; (hope) busted; irrevocably lost

付諸實施(ㄈㄨˋ ㄓㄨ ㄕˊ ㄕ)
to put into effect

付出(ㄈㄨˋ ㄔㄨ)
① to pay ② to give

付以重任(ㄈㄨˋ ㄧˇ ㄓㄨㄥˋ ㄖㄣˋ)
to entrust with an important post

付郵(ㄈㄨˋ ㄧㄡˊ)
to post (a letter); to mail (a parcel)

付印(ㄈㄨˋ ㄧㄣˋ)or 付刊(ㄈㄨˋ ㄎㄢ)or 付梓(ㄈㄨˋ ㄗˇ)
① to send to (the) press for publication ② to turn over to the printing shop (after proofreading)

【仙】 87 ㄒㄧㄢ shian xiān

1. a god; an immortal; a fairy
2. divine

仙方兒(ㄒㄧㄢ ㄈㄤㄦ)
a divine prescription—effective medicine

仙風道骨(ㄒㄧㄢ ㄈㄥ ㄉㄠˋ ㄍㄨˇ)
divine poise or bearing

仙丹(ㄒㄧㄢ ㄉㄢ)or 仙藥(ㄒㄧㄢ ㄧㄠˋ)
a divine pill; a panacea; a cure-all; an elixir

仙丹花(ㄒㄧㄢ ㄉㄢ ㄏㄨㄚ)
red ixora

仙桃(ㄒㄧㄢ ㄊㄠˊ)
a divine peach 參看「蟠桃②」

仙童(ㄒㄧㄢ ㄊㄨㄥˊ)
a fairy messenger boy

仙女(ㄒㄧㄢ ㄋㄩˇ)
a fairy; a woman of divine beauty

仙姑(ㄒㄧㄢ ㄍㄨ)
① a fairy; an immortal lady ② a woman Taoist

仙鶴(ㄒㄧㄢ ㄏㄜˋ)
the crane (as a divine bird)

仙界(ㄒㄧㄢ ㄐㄧㄝˋ)
the land of the divine; a paradise; a fairyland

仙境(ㄒㄧㄢ ㄐㄧㄥˋ)
① a fairyland 參看「仙界」② a place of exquisite natural beauty

〔人部〕

仙居(ㄒㄧㄢ ㄐㄩ)
a divine abode

仙鄉(ㄒㄧㄢ ㄒㄧㄤ)
①a fairyland 參看「仙界」② your hometown (an honorific term): 仙鄉何處? Where is your hometown?

仙逝(ㄒㄧㄢ ㄕˋ)or 仙去(ㄒㄧㄢ ㄑㄩˋ)
to die (a euphemistic expression); to pass away

仙山(ㄒㄧㄢ ㄕㄢ)
a mountain inhabited by the immortals

仙術(ㄒㄧㄢ ㄕㄨˋ)
the supernatural feat of the immortals

仙人(ㄒㄧㄢ ㄖㄣˊ)
①an immortal ②a very beautiful woman

仙人跳(ㄒㄧㄢ ㄖㄣˊ ㄊㄧㄠˋ)
a badger game

仙人掌(ㄒㄧㄢ ㄖㄣˊ ㄓㄤˇ)
a prickly pear; a kind of cactus

仙姿(ㄒㄧㄢ ㄗ)
a fairylike look, appearance, or figure

仙子(ㄒㄧㄢ ㄗˇ)
a fairy (in the sense of a beautiful woman); an immortal

【仞】 88
ㄖㄣˋ renn rèn
1. a measure of length (approximately eight feet)
2. to measure depth

【仟】 89
ㄑㄧㄢ chian qiān
1. leader of one thousand men
2. thousand

【仡】 90
ㄧˋ yih yì
1. gallant; valiant
2. stately; majestic
3. upright

仡然(ㄧˋ ㄖㄢˊ)
standing upright

【代】 91
ㄉㄞˋ day dài
1. a generation
2. a dynasty
3. an era
4. to be a substitute or an equivalent; to take the place of

代辦(ㄉㄞˋ ㄅㄢˋ)
①to manage on behalf of another; to act for another ②a chargé d'affaires

代筆(ㄉㄞˋ ㄅㄧˇ)
to write for another; to be a ghost writer

代表(ㄉㄞˋ ㄅㄧㄠˇ)
① to represent (another person, an organization, etc.); to stand for (something) ② a representative; a delegate; a proxy

代表大會(ㄉㄞˋ ㄅㄧㄠˇ ㄉㄚˋ ㄏㄨㄟˋ)
a congress; a representative assembly (or conference)

代表團(ㄉㄞˋ ㄅㄧㄠˇ ㄊㄨㄢˊ)
a delegation (to a conference)

代表權(ㄉㄞˋ ㄅㄧㄠˇ ㄑㄩㄢˊ)
representation

代表作(ㄉㄞˋ ㄅㄧㄠˇ ㄗㄨㄛˋ)
representative works (of art, literature, etc.)

代步(ㄉㄞˋ ㄅㄨˋ)
the means of transportation

代庖(ㄉㄞˋ ㄆㄠˊ)
to work on behalf of another; to act in somebody's place

代名詞(ㄉㄞˋ ㄇㄧㄥˊ ㄘˊ)
a pronoun:「它」是代名詞。"It" is a pronoun.

代打(ㄉㄞˋ ㄉㄚˇ)
to pinch-hit

代電(ㄉㄞˋ ㄉㄧㄢˋ)
correspondence between government agencies which do not have direct connection in the administrative chain of command

代墊(ㄉㄞˋ ㄉㄧㄢˋ)
to advance money for another

代替(ㄉㄞˋ ㄊㄧˋ)
to take the place of; to stand proxy for; to substitute

代勞(ㄉㄞˋ ㄌㄠˊ)
to labor on behalf of another (usually used as a polite expression when asking someone to do something for oneself)

代理(ㄉㄞˋ ㄌㄧˇ)
①an agent (of a business firm, organization, etc.) ② to serve as agent of; to act as the deputy of; to act for

代理貿易(ㄉㄞˋ ㄌㄧˇ ㄇㄠˋ ㄧˋ)
commission agency

代理商(ㄉㄞˋ ㄌㄧˇ ㄕㄤ)
a business agent; an agent

代理人(ㄉㄞˋ ㄌㄧˇ ㄖㄣˊ)
(legal) a representative; an agent; an attorney

代理業務(ㄉㄞˋ ㄌㄧˇ ㄧㄝˋ ㄨˋ)
to act as the deputy of another in charge of business

代溝(ㄉㄞˋ ㄍㄡ)
the generation gap

代購(ㄉㄞˋ ㄍㄡˋ)
to buy on behalf of somebody; to act as a purchasing agent

代管(ㄉㄞˋ ㄍㄨㄢˇ)
to manage, govern, or administer on behalf of another

代課(ㄉㄞˋ ㄎㄜˋ)
to teach on behalf of another teacher

代號(ㄉㄞˋ ㄏㄠˋ)
a code name

代換(ㄉㄞˋ ㄏㄨㄢˋ)
to replace

代價(ㄉㄞˋ ㄐㄧㄚˋ)
price; cost; reward: 我將付出甚麼樣的代價? What will the cost be to me?

代簽(ㄉㄞˋ ㄑㄧㄢ)
(accounting) procuration indorsement

代謝(ㄉㄞˋ ㄒㄧㄝˋ)
①to express thanks to someone on behalf of others ②to metabolize; metabolism

代銷(ㄉㄞˋ ㄒㄧㄠ)
to sell on consignment; to be commissioned to sell something; to act as a commission agent

代銷店(ㄉㄞˋ ㄒㄧㄠ ㄉㄧㄢˋ)
a commission agent

代銷商(ㄉㄞˋ ㄒㄧㄠ ㄕㄤ)
a consignee

代行職權(ㄉㄞˋ ㄒㄧㄥˊ ㄓˊ ㄑㄩㄢˊ)
to do something in an acting capacity

代序(ㄉㄞˋ ㄒㄩˋ)
an article used in lieu of a preface

代售(ㄉㄞˋ ㄕㄡˋ)
to be commissioned to sell something

代書(ㄉㄞˋ ㄕㄨ)
one who writes legal documents for others

代贖(ㄉㄞˋ ㄕㄨˊ)
redemption

代數學(ㄉㄞˋ ㄕㄨˋ ㄒㄩㄝˊ)
algebra

代人受過(ㄉㄞˋ ㄖㄣˊ ㄕㄡˋ ㄍㄨㄛˋ)
to take the blame for others

代罪羔羊(ㄉㄞˋ ㄗㄨㄟˋ ㄍㄠ ㄧㄤˊ)
a scapegoat: 他當他朋友的代罪羔羊。He was made the scapegoat for his friend.

代議制(ㄉㄞˋ ㄧˋ ㄓˋ)
the parliamentary system

代議政治(ㄉㄞˋ ㄧˋ ㄓㄥˋ ㄓˋ)
representative government

代議士(ㄉㄞˋ ㄧˋ ㄕˋ)
a parliamentarian

代有傳人(ㄉㄞˋ ㄧㄡˇ ㄔㄨㄢˊ ㄖㄣˊ)
There are people who carry on in every generation.

代言(ㄉㄞˋ ㄧㄢˊ)
to be a spokesman; to speak in behalf of

代言人(ㄉㄞˋ ㄧㄢˊ ㄖㄣˊ)
a spokesman; a mouthpiece

代爲辦理(ㄉㄞˋ ㄨㄟˊ ㄅㄢˋ ㄌㄧˇ)
to do something for another

代爲說項(ㄉㄞˋ ㄨㄟˊ ㄕㄨㄛ ㄒㄧㄤˋ)
to intercede or intervene for another person; to use one's good office for the sake of another person

代遠年湮(ㄉㄞˋ ㄩㄢˇ ㄋㄧㄢˊ ㄧㄣ)
The exact year (in which a given event took place) cannot be ascertained because it happened long long ago.

代用(ㄉㄞˋ ㄩㄥˋ)
to substitute for something; to use in place of something

代用品(ㄉㄞˋ ㄩㄥˋ ㄆㄧㄣˇ)
a substitute; an ersatz

代用教員(ㄉㄞˋ ㄩㄥˋ ㄐㄧㄠˋ ㄩㄢˊ)
a substitute teacher (who has no teaching certificate)

【令】 92
1. ㄌㄧㄥˋ linq lìng

1. a directive; an order
2. to order
3. to cause; to make
4. nice; good; excellent

令妹(ㄌㄧㄥˋ ㄇㄟˋ)
your younger sister (used in formal speech)

令名(ㄌㄧㄥˋ ㄇㄧㄥˊ)or 令聞(ㄌㄧㄥˋ ㄨㄣˊ)or 令望(ㄌㄧㄥˋ ㄨㄤˋ)or 令譽(ㄌㄧㄥˋ ㄩˋ)
good reputation; fame

令德(ㄌㄧㄥˋ ㄉㄜˊ)
excellent virtue

令弟(ㄌㄧㄥˋ ㄉㄧˋ)
your younger brother (used in formal speech)

令堂(ㄌㄧㄥˋ ㄊㄤˊ)
your mother (used in formal speech)

令郎(ㄌㄧㄥˋ ㄌㄤˊ)or 令嗣(ㄌㄧㄥˋ ㄙˋ)
your son (used in formal speech)

令姊(ㄌㄧㄥˋ ㄐㄧㄝˇ)
your elder sister (used in formal speech)

令箭(ㄌㄧㄥˋ ㄐㄧㄢˋ)
an arrow used as a token of authority (by field commanders in old China)

令親(ㄌㄧㄥˋ ㄑㄧㄣ)
your relative (used in formal speech)

令兄(ㄌㄧㄥˋ ㄒㄩㄥ)
your elder brother (used in formal speech)

令出如山(ㄌㄧㄥˋ ㄔㄨ ㄖㄨˊ ㄕㄢ)
(literally) Every order is as firm as a mountain.—Orders must be obeyed implicitly.

令人噴飯(ㄌㄧㄥˋ ㄖㄣˊ ㄆㄣ ㄈㄢˋ)
(said of clownish acts, witty remarks, etc.) to make people laugh

令人滿意(ㄌㄧㄥˋ ㄖㄣˊ ㄇㄢˇ ㄧˋ)
to make people contented; satisfactory

令人髮指(ㄌㄧㄥˋ ㄖㄣˊ ㄈㄚˇ ㄓˇ)
(said of enemy atrocities, heinous crimes, etc.) to make one's blood boil

令人懷疑(ㄌㄧㄥˋ ㄖㄣˊ ㄏㄨㄞˊ ㄧˊ)
to cause suspicion

令人喜歡(ㄌㄧㄥˋ ㄖㄣˊ ㄒㄧˇ ㄏㄨㄢ)
to be liked by most people

令尊(ㄌㄧㄥˋ ㄗㄨㄣ)
your father (used in formal speech)

令愛(ㄌㄧㄥˋ ㄞˋ)or 令媛(ㄌㄧㄥˋ ㄩㄢˋ)
your daughter (used in formal speech)

令岳(ㄌㄧㄥˋ ㄩㄝˋ)
your father-in-law (used in formal speech)

【令】 92
2. ㄌㄧㄥˊ ling líng

a ream (of paper)

【以】 93
ㄧˇ yii yǐ

by means of; because of

以博一粲(ㄧˇ ㄅㄛˊ ㄧˊ ㄘㄢˋ)
for your entertainment

以備(ㄧˇ ㄅㄟˋ)
to be ready for

以備萬一(ㄧˇ ㄅㄟˋ ㄨㄢˋ ㄧ)
to provide against any accidental happenings

以暴易暴(ㄧˇ ㄅㄠˋ ㄧˋ ㄅㄠˋ)
to displace violence with violence; to replace evil with evil

以便(ㄧˇ ㄅㄧㄢˋ)
① so as to; in order to ② for the convenience of

以不變應萬變(ㄧˇ ㄅㄨˊ ㄅㄧㄢˋ ㄧㄥˋ ㄨㄢˋ ㄅㄧㄢˋ)
to cope with shifting events by sticking to a fundamental principle or policy

以偏概全(ㄧˇ ㄆㄧㄢ ㄍㄞˋ ㄑㄩㄢˊ)
(literally) to take the part for the whole—to make sweeping comments

以貌取人(ㄧˇ ㄇㄠˋ ㄑㄩˇ ㄖㄣˊ)
to judge a person by his appearance or looks

以免(ㄧˇ ㄇㄧㄢˇ)
in order to avoid; so as not to

以大欺小(ㄧˇ ㄉㄚˋ ㄑㄧ ㄒㄧㄠˇ)
to bully the weak

以德報怨(ㄧˇ ㄉㄜˊ ㄅㄠˋ ㄩㄢˋ)
to repay injury with kindness; to return good for evil

以德服人(ㄧˇ ㄉㄜˊ ㄈㄨˊ ㄖㄣˊ)
to win popular following by dint of one's virtue

以毒攻毒(ㄧˇ ㄉㄨˊ ㄍㄨㄥ ㄉㄨˊ)
to fight evil with evil; to use poison as an antidote for poison; to fight fire with fire

以杜後患(ㄧˇ ㄉㄨˋ ㄏㄡˋ ㄏㄨㄢˋ)
to forestall future trouble

以多爲勝(ㄧˇ ㄉㄨㄛ ㄨㄟˊ ㄕㄥˋ)
to crush an enemy by numerical superiority

以太(ㄧˇ ㄊㄞˋ)
(physics) ether

以退爲進(ㄧˇ ㄊㄨㄟˋ ㄨㄟˊ ㄐㄧㄣˋ)
(literally) to retreat in order to advance—to make

concessions in order to gain advantages
以內(ㄧˇ ㄋㄟˋ)
within
以農立國(ㄧˇ ㄋㄨㄥˊ ㄌㄧˋ ㄍㄨㄛˊ)
a nation based on agricultural economy
以來(ㄧˇ ㄌㄞˊ)
since (a given point of time in the past)
以淚洗面(ㄧˇ ㄌㄟˋ ㄒㄧˇ ㄇㄧㄢˋ)
to cry with abandon
以理服人(ㄧˇ ㄌㄧˇ ㄈㄨˊ ㄖㄣˊ)
to convince a person by reasoning
以禮相待(ㄧˇ ㄌㄧˇ ㄒㄧㄤ ㄉㄞˋ)
to treat somebody with due respect
以利民生(ㄧˇ ㄌㄧˋ ㄇㄧㄣˊ ㄕㄥ)
for the benefit of people's livelihood
以鄰爲壑(ㄧˇ ㄌㄧㄣˊ ㄨㄟˊ ㄏㄨㄛˋ)
to profit oneself at the expense of others
以卵投石(ㄧˇ ㄌㄨㄢˇ ㄊㄡˊ ㄕˊ)
to hurl eggs against a stone —to fight a hopeless battle
以古非今(ㄧˇ ㄍㄨˇ ㄈㄟ ㄐㄧㄣ)
to belittle the present by extolling the past
以寡敵衆(ㄧˇ ㄍㄨㄚˇ ㄉㄧˊ ㄓㄨㄥˋ)
to fight a numerically superior enemy
以廣招徠(ㄧˇ ㄍㄨㄤˇ ㄓㄠ ㄌㄞˊ)
in order to promote patronage or sales
以工代賑(ㄧˇ ㄍㄨㄥ ㄉㄞˋ ㄓㄣˋ)
to relieve people in disaster areas by giving them employment instead of outright grant
以攻爲守(ㄧˇ ㄍㄨㄥ ㄨㄟˊ ㄕㄡˇ)
to take the offensive in a basically defensive operation
以匡不逮(ㄧˇ ㄎㄨㄤ ㄅㄨˋ ㄉㄞˋ)
to correct one's mistakes or make up one's shortcomings (usually used when soliciting advice)
以空間爭取時間(ㄧˇ ㄎㄨㄥ ㄐㄧㄢ ㄓㄥ ㄑㄩˇ ㄕˊ ㄐㄧㄢ)
to trade space for time (as a military strategy)
以後(ㄧˇ ㄏㄡˋ)
after (a given point or a period of time); afterward
以及(ㄧˇ ㄐㄧˊ)
and; including; as well as
以己度人(ㄧˇ ㄐㄧˇ ㄉㄨㄛˋ ㄖㄣˊ)
to assume that other people think the same way as oneself
以假亂眞(ㄧˇ ㄐㄧㄚˇ ㄌㄨㄢˋ ㄓㄣ)
to mix the spurious with the genuine
以解倒懸(ㄧˇ ㄐㄧㄝˇ ㄉㄠˋ ㄒㄩㄢˊ)
to save one from a crisis or to help weather a critical situation (usually used in asking for help)
以介眉壽(ㄧˇ ㄐㄧㄝˋ ㄇㄟˊ ㄕㄡˋ)
Many happy returns of the day. (a cliché in offering birthday congratulations)
以救燃眉(ㄧˇ ㄐㄧㄡˋ ㄖㄢˊ ㄇㄟˊ)
to meet a pressing need
以進爲退(ㄧˇ ㄐㄧㄣˋ ㄨㄟˊ ㄊㄨㄟˋ)
to pretend to move ahead in order to hide the intention to retreat
以儆效尤(ㄧˇ ㄐㄧㄥˇ ㄒㄧㄠˋ ㄧㄡˊ)
to warn others against making the same mistake
以竟全功(ㄧˇ ㄐㄧㄥˋ ㄑㄩㄢˊ ㄍㄨㄥ)
to bring a task to a successful conclusion
以其人之道，還治其人之身(ㄧˇ ㄑㄧˊ ㄖㄣˊ ㄓ ㄉㄠˋ, ㄏㄨㄢˊ ㄓˋ ㄑㄧˊ ㄖㄣˊ ㄓ ㄕㄣ)
Pay someone (back) in his own coin. 或 Deal with a man as he deals with you.
以前(ㄧˇ ㄑㄧㄢˊ)
before (a given point or a period of time); previously
以勤補拙(ㄧˇ ㄑㄧㄣˊ ㄅㄨˇ ㄓㄨㄛˊ)
to amend stupidity by diligence
以下(ㄧˇ ㄒㄧㄚˋ)
below (a given point or line)
以饗讀者(ㄧˇ ㄒㄧㄤˇ ㄉㄨˊ ㄓㄜˇ)
to offer to the reader
以直報怨(ㄧˇ ㄓˊ ㄅㄠˋ ㄩㄢˋ)
justice in return for injustice; to repay injustice with justice
以至(ㄧˇ ㄓˋ)
①up to (a given point); until ②so…that
以致(ㄧˇ ㄓˋ)
so that; with the result that
以正視聽(ㄧˇ ㄓㄥˋ ㄕˋ ㄊㄧㄥ)
in order to ensure a right understanding of the facts
以珠彈雀(ㄧˇ ㄓㄨ ㄊㄢˊ ㄑㄩㄝˋ)
to make big investment for small returns
以衆暴寡(ㄧˇ ㄓㄨㄥˋ ㄅㄠˋ ㄍㄨㄚˇ)
to bully the minority
以示公平(ㄧˇ ㄕˋ ㄍㄨㄥ ㄆㄧㄥˊ)
to show fairness or impartiality
以釋群疑(ㄧˇ ㄕˋ ㄑㄩㄣˊ ㄧˊ)
to allay doubt in the public's mind
以手加額(ㄧˇ ㄕㄡˇ ㄐㄧㄚ ㄜˊ)
to exhibit gratification
以身相許(ㄧˇ ㄕㄣ ㄒㄧㄤ ㄒㄩˇ)
(said of girls) to pledge to marry somebody
以身殉職(ㄧˇ ㄕㄣ ㄒㄩㄣˋ ㄓˊ)
to die at one's post
以身試法(ㄧˇ ㄕㄣ ㄕˋ ㄈㄚˇ)
to defy the law; to dare to violate the law
以身作則(ㄧˇ ㄕㄣ ㄗㄨㄛˋ ㄗㄜˊ)
(said of people holding responsible positions or the head of a family) to set examples by one's own action
以上(ㄧˇ ㄕㄤˋ)
above (a given point or line)
以升量石(ㄧˇ ㄕㄥ ㄌㄧㄤˊ ㄉㄢˋ)
A little man cannot understand the ways of a true gentleman.
以柔克剛(ㄧˇ ㄖㄡˊ ㄎㄜˋ ㄍㄤ)
Soft and fair goes far. 或 Willows are weak, yet they bend other wood.
以人廢言(ㄧˇ ㄖㄣˊ ㄈㄟˋ ㄧㄢˊ)
to dismiss someone's statement as untrue or unimportant because of his ill reputation
以子之矛，攻子之盾(ㄧˇ ㄗˇ ㄓ ㄇㄠˊ, ㄍㄨㄥ ㄗˇ ㄓ ㄉㄨㄣˋ)
to attack someone by exploiting his weakness
以奏膚功(ㄧˇ ㄗㄡˋ ㄈㄨ ㄍㄨㄥ)
to complete a monumental task
以詞害意(ㄧˇ ㄘˊ ㄏㄞˋ ㄧˋ)
to sacrifice clarity in the use of wrong words for expression
以此(ㄧˇ ㄘˇ)
for this reason; on this account

以此類推(ㄧˇ ㄘˇ ㄌㄟˋ ㄊㄨㄟ)
The rest can be done in the same manner. 或 The rest can be deduced accordingly.
以此爲戒(ㄧˇ ㄘˇ ㄨㄟˊ ㄐㄧㄝˋ)
to take this as a lesson
以次(ㄧˇ ㄘˋ)
in turn; in due order
以色列(ㄧˇ ㄙㄜˋ ㄌㄧㄝˋ)
Israel
以色列人(ㄧˇ ㄙㄜˋ ㄌㄧㄝˋ ㄖㄣˊ)
Israelis; Israelites
以訛傳訛(ㄧˇ ㄜˊ ㄔㄨㄢˊ ㄜˊ)
(said of rumors) to convey incorrectly what is already incorrect
以一當十(ㄧˇ ㄧ ㄉㄤ ㄕˊ)
to pit one against ten
以一儆百(ㄧˇ ㄧ ㄐㄧㄥˇ ㄅㄞˇ)
to punish one as a warning to the others
以夷制夷(ㄧˇ ㄧˊ ㄓˋ ㄧˊ)
to play off one foreign power against another (so as to prevent them from invading one's own country)
以逸待勞(ㄧˇ ㄧˋ ㄉㄞˋ ㄌㄠˊ)
to wait in comfort for an exhausted enemy; to conserve strength while the enemy tires himself through a long march
以牙還牙(ㄧˇ ㄧㄚˊ ㄏㄨㄢˊ ㄧㄚˊ)
an eye for an eye, a tooth for a tooth; to repay evil with evil
以有易無(ㄧˇ ㄧㄡˇ ㄧˋ ㄨˊ)
to trade what one has in abundance for what one does not have; to barter
以外(ㄧˇ ㄨㄞˋ)
①other than; besides; in addition:除我以外沒人知道。No one knows besides me. ②outside; without; beyond
以爲(ㄧˇ ㄨㄟˊ)
to take …for (or to be); to regard…as; to think; to consider
以文會友(ㄧˇ ㄨㄣˊ ㄏㄨㄟˋ ㄧㄡˇ)
to gather friends together for literary activities
以往(ㄧˇ ㄨㄤˇ)
in the past; formerly
以怨報德(ㄧˇ ㄩㄢˋ ㄅㄠˋ ㄉㄜˊ)
to bite the hand that feeds one

【仨】 94
ㄙㄚ sa sā
three (Peking colloquialism)

【仝】 95
(同) ㄊㄨㄥˊ torng tóng
a Chinese family name

四畫

【仰】 96
ㄧㄤˇ yeang yǎng
1. to look up
2. to adore, admire or revere
3. to lean or rely upon
4. to swallow

仰不愧天(ㄧㄤˇ ㄅㄨˋ ㄎㄨㄟˋ ㄊㄧㄢ)
to feel no shame before God
仰面朝天(ㄧㄤˇ ㄇㄧㄢˋ ㄔㄠˊ ㄊㄧㄢ)
to lie on one's back
仰慕(ㄧㄤˇ ㄇㄨˋ)
to adore; to regard with admiration; to admire and respect
仰毒(ㄧㄤˇ ㄉㄨˊ)or 仰藥(ㄧㄤˇ ㄧㄠˋ)
to swallow or take poison
仰天長歎(ㄧㄤˇ ㄊㄧㄢ ㄔㄤˊ ㄊㄢˋ)
to sigh deeply
仰天長嘯(ㄧㄤˇ ㄊㄧㄢ ㄔㄤˊ ㄒㄧㄠˋ)
to make a long cry into the air
仰能合意(ㄧㄤˇ ㄋㄥˊ ㄏㄜˊ ㄧˋ)
to hope it is what you want
仰賴(ㄧㄤˇ ㄌㄞˋ)
to look to (somebody for help); to rely upon
仰光(ㄧㄤˇ ㄍㄨㄤ)
Rangoon, capital of Burma
仰給(ㄧㄤˇ ㄐㄧˇ)
to depend on
仰角(ㄧㄤˇ ㄐㄧㄠˇ)
(mathematics) an angle of elevation
仰求(ㄧㄤˇ ㄑㄧㄡˊ)
to be dependent on someone; to turn to someone for help, favor, etc.
仰止(ㄧㄤˇ ㄓˇ)
admiration
仰仗(ㄧㄤˇ ㄓㄤˋ)
to rely on (other's influence, power, etc.)
仰食於人(ㄧㄤˇ ㄕˊ ㄩˊ ㄖㄣˊ)
to depend on another person for living
仰事俯畜(ㄧㄤˇ ㄕˋ ㄈㄨˇ ㄒㄩˋ)
to support parents as well as wife and children
仰人鼻息(ㄧㄤˇ ㄖㄣˊ ㄅㄧˊ ㄒㄧˊ)
to rely on others and have to watch their every expression; to be dependent on another's whims and pleasures
仰臥(ㄧㄤˇ ㄨㄛˋ)
to lie on the back
仰臥起坐(ㄧㄤˇ ㄨㄛˋ ㄑㄧˇ ㄗㄨㄛˋ)
(sports) sit-up
仰望(ㄧㄤˇ ㄨㄤˋ)
①to hope ②to rely upon (someone for support, help, etc.)
仰泳(ㄧㄤˇ ㄩㄥˇ)
a backstroke

【仲】 97
ㄓㄨㄥˋ jonq zhòng
1. in the middle; between two entities
2. the second in order of birth

仲冬(ㄓㄨㄥˋ ㄉㄨㄥ)
the second of the winter months (i.e., the eleventh moon); midwinter
仲尼(ㄓㄨㄥˋ ㄋㄧˊ)
another name of Confucius
仲秋(ㄓㄨㄥˋ ㄑㄧㄡ)
the second of the autumn months (i.e., the eighth moon); midautumn
仲夏(ㄓㄨㄥˋ ㄒㄧㄚˋ)
the second of the summer months (i.e., the fifth moon); midsummer
仲春(ㄓㄨㄥˋ ㄔㄨㄣ)
the second of the spring months (i.e., the second moon); midspring
仲裁(ㄓㄨㄥˋ ㄘㄞˊ)
to arbitrate; arbitration

【仳】 98
ㄆㄧˇ pii pǐ
to part company

仳離(ㄆㄧˇ ㄌㄧˊ)
to part (from one's spouse); to divorce

【仵】 99
ㄨˇ wuu wǔ
opposing; wrong

仵作(ㄨˇ ㄗㄨㄛˋ)
a coroner

【件】 100
ㄐㄧㄢˋ jiann jiàn
an auxiliary noun applied to things, clothes, etc.

件件(ㄐㄧㄢˋ ㄐㄧㄢˋ)or 件件兒(ㄐㄧㄢˋ

〔人部〕

ㄐㄧㄚˊㄦ)
all (of the things or items in question)
件數(ㄐㄧㄢˋㄕㄨˋ)or 件數兒(ㄐㄧㄢˋㄕㄨˋㄦ)
the number of things, items, suits, etc.

【任】 101
1. ㄖㄣˋ renn rèn
1. a duty
2. to let (one act at will): 不要任小孩外出。Don't let the child go out.
3. to employ (one for a job): 這女子在郵局任職。This girl is employed at the post office.
4. to bear (a burden)
5. an official post; office
任便(ㄖㄣˋㄅㄧㄢˋ)
as you please; as you see fit: 你來不來任便。You may come or not as you please.
任憑(ㄖㄣˋㄆㄧㄥˊ)
without restriction; (to allow someone to do something) at will; despite
任免(ㄖㄣˋㄇㄧㄢˇ)
hiring and firing; employment and discharge
任命(ㄖㄣˋㄇㄧㄥˋ)
to appoint (someone to an office); appointment
任命狀(ㄖㄣˋㄇㄧㄥˋㄓㄨㄤˋ)
a letter (or certificate) of appointment
任達(ㄖㄣˋㄉㄚˊ)
(said of one's disposition) unrestrained
任勞任怨(ㄖㄣˋㄌㄠˊㄖㄣˋㄩㄢˋ)
to do something without complaint despite hardships and criticisms
任課(ㄖㄣˋㄎㄜˋ)
to teach a course (at school)
任何(ㄖㄣˋㄏㄜˊ)
any; whatever
任期(ㄖㄣˋㄑㄧˊ)
a term of office; the tenure of office; a tour of duty
任俠(ㄖㄣˋㄒㄧㄚˊ)
to be generous and chivalrous
任性(ㄖㄣˋㄒㄧㄥˋ)
doing as one pleases; unrestrained; uninhibited
任職(ㄖㄣˋㄓˊ)
to hold a post; to be in office
任重道遠(ㄖㄣˋㄓㄨㄥˋㄉㄠˋㄩㄢˇ)
The load is heavy, while the way is long.
任人(ㄖㄣˋㄖㄣˊ)
to let people (do something without restriction)
任人唯賢(ㄖㄣˋㄖㄣˊㄨㄟˊㄒㄧㄢˊ)
to appoint a person according to his virtue and ability; to choose a person for an office according to his merits
任從(ㄖㄣˋㄘㄨㄥˊ)
to let (one do something as he pleases)
任意(ㄖㄣˋㄧˋ)
arbitrary; at will
任務(ㄖㄣˋㄨˋ)
duty; responsibility
任用(ㄖㄣˋㄩㄥˋ)
to employ; to hire; to engage

【任】 101
2. ㄖㄣˊ ren rén
a Chinese family name

【仿】 102
(倣) ㄈㄤˇ faang fǎng
to imitate; to copy
仿單(ㄈㄤˇㄉㄢ)
advertising literature attached to merchandise
仿古(ㄈㄤˇㄍㄨˇ)
to imitate the ancient style
仿效(ㄈㄤˇㄒㄧㄠˋ)
to imitate; to copy; to follow the example of
仿製(ㄈㄤˇㄓˋ)or 仿造(ㄈㄤˇㄗㄠˋ)
to manufacture an imitation of something already in market
仿製品(ㄈㄤˇㄓˋㄆㄧㄣˇ)
an imitation
仿照(ㄈㄤˇㄓㄠˋ)
after the example of; to pattern after
仿宋(ㄈㄤˇㄙㄨㄥˋ)
the imitation of the style of Chinese characters prevalent in the Sung Dynasty
仿宋本(ㄈㄤˇㄙㄨㄥˋㄅㄣˇ)
the reprint (of a book) in imitation of the Sung edition
仿宋體(ㄈㄤˇㄙㄨㄥˋㄊㄧˇ)
a kind of printing type in imitation of the style of Chinese characters prevalent during the Sung Dynasty

【企】 103
ㄑㄧˋ chih qì
1. to stand on tiptoe
2. to hope; to long; to expect
企盼(ㄑㄧˋㄆㄢˋ)or 企望(ㄑㄧˋㄨㄤˋ)
to expect or hope with eagerness
企慕(ㄑㄧˋㄇㄨˋ)
to admire greatly
企圖(ㄑㄧˋㄊㄨˊ)
① to intend; to plan; to scheme; to attempt ② an intention; a plan; a scheme
企圖心(ㄑㄧˋㄊㄨˊㄒㄧㄣ)
enterprising spirit; aggressiveness
企管(ㄑㄧˋㄍㄨㄢˇ)
business management
企劃(ㄑㄧˋㄏㄨㄚˋ)
to make a scheme for; to design; to lay out; to plan
企求(ㄑㄧˋㄑㄧㄡˊ)
to desire; to seek for; to hanker for
企踵(ㄑㄧˋㄓㄨㄥˇ)
to stand on tiptoe
企鵝(ㄑㄧˋㄜˊ)
a penguin
企業(ㄑㄧˋㄧㄝˋ)
a business enterprise; an enterprise
企業家(ㄑㄧˋㄧㄝˋㄐㄧㄚ)
an entrepreneur
企望(ㄑㄧˋㄨㄤˋ)
to hope for; to look forward to

【伉】 104
ㄎㄤˋ kanq kàng
a spouse
伉儷(ㄎㄤˋㄌㄧˋ)
a married couple (in formal speech)

【伊】 105
ㄧ i yī
1. he; she
2. a Chinese family name
伊伯利安半島(ㄧㄅㄛˊㄌㄧˋㄢㄅㄢˋㄉㄠˇ)
the Iberian Peninsula
伊凡(ㄧㄈㄢˊ)
transliteration of Ivan
伊底帕斯(ㄧㄉㄧˇㄆㄚˋㄙ)
Oedipus
伊甸樂園(ㄧㄉㄧㄢˋㄌㄜˋㄩㄢˊ)
the Garden of Eden
伊拉克(ㄧㄌㄚㄎㄜˋ)

Iraq
伊拉瓦底江(ㄧ ㄌㄚ ㄨㄚˇ ㄉㄧˇ ㄐㄧㄤ)
the Irawadi River
伊朗(ㄧ ㄌㄤˇ)
Iran
伊犁(ㄧ ㄌㄧˊ)
Ili, an important town in western Sinkiang
伊利諾斯(ㄧ ㄌㄧˋ ㄋㄨㄛˋ ㄙ)
Illinois, U.S.A.
伊利湖(ㄧ ㄌㄧˋ ㄏㄨˊ)
the Erie Lake
伊利莎白(ㄧ ㄌㄧˋ ㄕㄚ ㄅㄞˊ)
transliteration of Elizabeth
伊人(ㄧ ㄖㄣˊ)
that man (in poetry or song)
伊斯坦堡(ㄧ ㄙ ㄊㄢˇ ㄅㄠˇ)
Istanbul, a Turkish city
伊斯蘭(ㄧ ㄙ ㄌㄢˊ)
Islam
伊斯蘭教徒(ㄧ ㄙ ㄌㄢˊ ㄐㄧㄠˋ ㄊㄨˊ)
a Moslem
伊索寓言(ㄧ ㄙㄨㄛˇ ㄩˋ ㄧㄢˊ)
Aesop's Fables
伊于胡底(ㄧ ㄩˊ ㄏㄨˊ ㄉㄧˇ)
(not knowing) when it will stop or where it will lead to
伊鬱(ㄧ ㄩˋ)
melancholy; dejection; depression; despondence; gloom

【伋】 106 ㄐㄧˊ jyi jí

1. deceptive
2. name of Tzu-szu (子思), grandson of Confucius

伋伋(ㄐㄧˊ ㄐㄧˊ)
deceptive

【伍】 107 ㄨˇ wuu wǔ

1. a military unit of five soldiers (in the Chou Dynasty)
2. as in 行伍——the army
3. a Chinese family name
4. to associate (with a person): 大家都不願意與他爲伍。Everyone is unwilling to associate with him.
5. five

伍長(ㄨˇ ㄓㄤˇ)
a leader of a military unit of five soldiers (in former times)

【伎】 108 ㄐㄧˋ jih jì

talent; ability; skill
伎倆(ㄐㄧˋ ㄌㄧㄤˇ)
skill; dexterity; craft
伎藝(ㄐㄧˋ ㄧˋ)
① mechanical arts ② expert skill

【伏】 109 ㄈㄨˊ fwu fú

1. to prostrate; to yield
2. to hide; to lie in ambush

伏筆(ㄈㄨˊ ㄅㄧˇ)
a remark in writing made with a view to preparing the reader for what is to follow
伏兵(ㄈㄨˊ ㄅㄧㄥ)
an ambush
伏法(ㄈㄨˊ ㄈㄚˇ)or 伏誅(ㄈㄨˊ ㄓㄨ)
to plead guilty and be executed
伏地挺身(ㄈㄨˊ ㄉㄧˋ ㄊㄧㄥˇ ㄕㄣ)
push-up
伏特(ㄈㄨˊ ㄊㄜˋ)
(electricity) a volt
伏特計(ㄈㄨˊ ㄊㄜˋ ㄐㄧˋ)
a voltmeter
伏特加(ㄈㄨˊ ㄊㄜˋ ㄐㄧㄚ)
(spirits) vodka
伏貼(ㄈㄨˊ ㄊㄧㄝ)
① comfortable; fitting ② to acknowledge someone's merits, etc. sincerely
伏櫪(ㄈㄨˊ ㄌㄧˋ)
to be in the stable—(figuratively) obedient: 老驥伏櫪，志在千里。The old horse in the stable is yet ambitious to achieve heroic deeds.
伏流(ㄈㄨˊ ㄌㄧㄡˊ)
(geography) subterranean drainage; an underground stream
伏擊(ㄈㄨˊ ㄐㄧˊ)
to attack from ambush
伏祈(ㄈㄨˊ ㄑㄧˊ)
to beg (used in letters to one's elders or superiors)
伏氣(ㄈㄨˊ ㄑㄧˋ)
to yield or submit willingly
伏羲(ㄈㄨˊ ㄒㄧ)
Fu-hsi, a legendary Chinese ruler credited with the introduction of farming, fishing and animal husbandry
伏尸遍野(ㄈㄨˊ ㄕ ㄅㄧㄢˋ ㄧㄝˇ)
The battlefield is littered with the (enemy) dead.
伏輸(ㄈㄨˊ ㄕㄨ)
to concede (an election, a game, etc.); to admit defeat
伏罪(ㄈㄨˊ ㄗㄨㄟˋ)
① to admit guilt ② to be executed
伏藏(ㄈㄨˊ ㄘㄤˊ)
to lie in ambush; to hide
伏案(ㄈㄨˊ ㄢˋ)
absorbed in work at one's desk

【伐】 110 ㄈㄚ fa fā (又讀 ㄈㄚˊ far fá)

1. to cut (wood)
2. to attack; to smite

伐木(ㄈㄚ ㄇㄨˋ)
to fell trees
伐柯(ㄈㄚ ㄎㄜ)
① to hew the wood for an axe-handle ② (figuratively) to be a go-between
伐罪(ㄈㄚ ㄗㄨㄟˋ)
to punish the guilty

【休】 111 ㄒㄧㄡ shiou xiū

1. rest; to rest
2. to stop; to cease
3. happiness; joy; weal: 他們休戚與共。They share weal and woe.

休兵(ㄒㄧㄡ ㄅㄧㄥ)or 休戰(ㄒㄧㄡ ㄓㄢˋ)
① to stop fighting; to cease fire ② a truce; an armistice
休眠(ㄒㄧㄡ ㄇㄧㄢˊ)
(biology) dormancy
休提(ㄒㄧㄡ ㄊㄧˊ)
do not mention
休倫湖(ㄒㄧㄡ ㄌㄨㄣˊ ㄏㄨˊ)
the Huron Lake
休怪(ㄒㄧㄡ ㄍㄨㄞˋ)
① to stop blaming ② to stop wondering
休克(ㄒㄧㄡ ㄎㄜˋ)
shock (in medical science)
休火山(ㄒㄧㄡ ㄏㄨㄛˇ ㄕㄢ)
a dormant volcano
休會(ㄒㄧㄡ ㄏㄨㄟˋ)
to adjourn a meeting; adjournment
休假(ㄒㄧㄡ ㄐㄧㄚˋ)
a holiday; to have a holiday
休咎(ㄒㄧㄡ ㄐㄧㄡˋ)
good fortune and ill
休妻(ㄒㄧㄡ ㄑㄧ)
to divorce one's wife
休戚(ㄒㄧㄡ ㄑㄧ)
weal and woe; for better and worse

〔人部〕

〔人部〕

休戚相關(ㄒㄧㄡ ㄑㄧ ㄒㄧㄤ ㄍㄨㄢ)
to share joys and sorrows with each other
休憩(ㄒㄧㄡ ㄑㄧˋ)
to have a rest; to rest
休息(ㄒㄧㄡ ㄒㄧˊ)
to rest from work; to take a rest; rest
休歇(ㄒㄧㄡ ㄒㄧㄝ)
①to stop for rest; to take a rest ②to take a nap
休閒(ㄒㄧㄡ ㄒㄧㄢˊ)
leisure; relaxation; ease
休閒服(ㄒㄧㄡ ㄒㄧㄢˊ ㄈㄨˊ)
casual wear; sports wear
休想(ㄒㄧㄡ ㄒㄧㄤˇ)
to stop thinking (about something); to stop dreaming: 你休想逃脫。Stop thinking you can get away.
休學(ㄒㄧㄡ ㄒㄩㄝˊ)
a leave of absence (for a considerable period of time) from school
休止(ㄒㄧㄡ ㄓˇ)
to stop; to cease
休止符(ㄒㄧㄡ ㄓˇ ㄈㄨˊ)
a sign of rests in staff notation
休戰(ㄒㄧㄡ ㄓㄢˋ)
to stop fighting; a truce
休書(ㄒㄧㄡ ㄕㄨ)
a divorce paper (signed by the husband in old China)
休業(ㄒㄧㄡ ㄧㄝˋ)
to suspend business; to close the store (for a holiday)
休業式(ㄒㄧㄡ ㄧㄝˋ ㄕˋ)
a semester closing ceremony
休養(ㄒㄧㄡ ㄧㄤˇ)
to rest; to recuperate: 他在病後到海濱休養。He went to the seaside to recuperate after his illness.
休養生息(ㄒㄧㄡ ㄧㄤˇ ㄕㄥ ㄒㄧˊ)
(said of a nation) to recuperate and multiply; to rest and build up strength

【伙】 112 ㄏㄨㄛˇ huoo huǒ
1. a companion; a colleague
2. household goods
伙伴(ㄏㄨㄛˇ ㄅㄢˋ)or 伙伴兒(ㄏㄨㄛˇ ㄅㄚˋㄦ)
a companion; a colleague
伙房(ㄏㄨㄛˇ ㄈㄤˊ)
a kitchen (in a school, factory, etc.)
伙夫(ㄏㄨㄛˇ ㄈㄨ)or 伙頭軍(ㄏㄨㄛˇ ㄊㄡˊ ㄐㄩㄣ)
a cook (in military barracks or troops); kitchen police
伙同(ㄏㄨㄛˇ ㄊㄨㄥˊ)
in league with
伙計(ㄏㄨㄛˇ ·ㄐㄧ)
a shop clerk
伙食(ㄏㄨㄛˇ ㄕˊ)
meals

五畫

【伯】 113 ㄅㄛˊ bor bó (又讀 ㄅㄞˇ bae bǎi)
1. one's father's elder brother; an uncle
2. a rank of the nobility—a count
伯伯(ㄅㄛˊ ·ㄅㄛ)
an uncle (one's father's elder brother)
伯明罕(ㄅㄛˊ ㄇㄧㄥˊ ㄏㄢˇ)
Birmingham, an industrial city in England
伯母(ㄅㄛˊ ㄇㄨˇ)
an aunt (the wife of one's father's elder brother)
伯父(ㄅㄛˊ ㄈㄨˋ)
an uncle (one's father's elder brother)
伯樂(ㄅㄛˊ ㄌㄜˋ)
a man in the Chou Dynasty, who was famous for his being good at examining the qualities of horses
伯勞(ㄅㄛˊ ㄌㄠˊ)
the shrike
伯利恆(ㄅㄛˊ ㄌㄧˋ ㄏㄥˊ)
Bethlehem, a town in Palestine where Jesus Christ was born
伯爵(ㄅㄛˊ ㄐㄩㄝˊ)
a rank of the nobility—a count
伯爵夫人(ㄅㄛˊ ㄐㄩㄝˊ ㄈㄨ ㄖㄣˊ)
a countess
伯仲之間(ㄅㄛˊ ㄓㄨㄥˋ ㄓ ㄐㄧㄢ)
about the same (in terms of competence, quality, etc.)
伯仲叔季(ㄅㄛˊ ㄓㄨㄥˋ ㄕㄨˊ ㄐㄧˋ)
the eldest, second, third and youngest of brothers—order of seniority among brothers
伯爾尼(ㄅㄛˊ ㄦˇ ㄋㄧˊ)
Bern, capital of Switzerland
伯爾格來得(ㄅㄛˊ ㄦˇ ㄍㄜˊ ㄌㄞˊ ㄉㄜˊ)
Belgrade, capital of Yugoslavia

【估】 114 1. ㄍㄨ gu gū
to estimate; to calculate; to evaluate
估量(ㄍㄨ ㄌㄧㄤˊ)or 估計(ㄍㄨ ㄐㄧˋ)
to estimate; to make an estimate; to calculate; to reckon; to conjecture
估價(ㄍㄨ ㄐㄧㄚˋ)
to estimate cost or value; to evaluate; to appraise
估價單(ㄍㄨ ㄐㄧㄚˋ ㄉㄢ)
a list of cost estimate (prepared for the prospective customer, client, etc.)
估稅(ㄍㄨ ㄕㄨㄟˋ)
sales tax 亦作「貨物稅」or「銷售稅」

【估】 114 2. ㄍㄨˋ guh gù
to sell (used clothing)
估衣鋪(ㄍㄨˋ ㄧ ㄆㄨˋ)
a secondhand clothes store

【你】 115 ㄋㄧˇ nii nǐ
you (singular)
你們(ㄋㄧˇ ·ㄇㄣ)
you (plural)
你老(ㄋㄧˇ ㄌㄠˇ)
you (in addressing an elder)
你好(ㄋㄧˇ ㄏㄠˇ)
How do you do? 或 How are you?
你死我活(ㄋㄧˇ ㄙˇ ㄨㄛˇ ㄏㄨㄛˊ)
(to fight) to the bitter end; (to fight) until either of the combatants is killed; to fight *a outrance*

【伴】 116 ㄅㄢˋ bann bàn
1. a companion
2. to accompany
伴娘(ㄅㄢˋ ㄋㄧㄤˊ)
the maid of honor
伴郎(ㄅㄢˋ ㄌㄤˊ)
the best man
伴侶(ㄅㄢˋ ㄌㄩˇ)or 伴兒(ㄅㄚˋㄦ)
a companion; a pal; a buddy; a chum
伴君如伴虎(ㄅㄢˋ ㄐㄩㄣ ㄖㄨˊ ㄅㄢˋ ㄏㄨˇ)
To be in the king's company is tantamount to living with

a tiger (which makes one feel apprehensive all the time).

伴唱(ㄅㄢˋ ㄔㄤˋ)
①a vocal accompaniment ② to accompany (a singer)

伴奏(ㄅㄢˋ ㄗㄡˋ)
to accompany (a soloist); to play an accompaniment

伴宿(ㄅㄢˋ ㄙㄨˋ)
①to keep vigil at a funeral ②(said of a prostitute) to pass the night with a person

伴隨(ㄅㄢˋ ㄙㄨㄟˊ)
to accompany; to follow

伴送(ㄅㄢˋ ㄙㄨㄥˋ)
to escort: 我常伴送她回家。I often escort her home.

伴舞(ㄅㄢˋ ㄨˇ)
to be a dancing partner

【伶】 117
ㄌㄧㄥˊ ling líng

1. a drama performer; a theatrical performer; an actor; an actress
2. lonely; solitary
3. clever; intelligent

伶仃(ㄌㄧㄥˊ ㄉㄧㄥ)
lonely; solitary

伶俐(ㄌㄧㄥˊ ㄌㄧˋ)
clever; intelligent; cute; sharp; bright; smart

伶人(ㄌㄧㄥˊ ㄖㄣˊ)
a theatrical performer; a drama performer; an actor; an actress

伶牙利齒(ㄌㄧㄥˊ ㄧㄚˊ ㄌㄧˋ ㄔˇ)
eloquent

【伸】 118
ㄕㄣ shen shēn

1. to stretch; to extend; to straighten
2. to report

伸頭探腦(ㄕㄣ ㄊㄡˊ ㄊㄢˋ ㄋㄠˇ)
to crane, or stretch the neck in an effort to find out

伸腿(ㄕㄣ ㄊㄨㄟˇ)
①to stretch one's legs ②(figuratively) to die ③ to step in (to gain an advantage)

伸腿瞪眼(ㄕㄣ ㄊㄨㄟˇ ㄉㄥˋ ㄧㄢˇ)
(said of human beings) dead

伸懶腰(ㄕㄣ ㄌㄢˇ ㄧㄠ)
to stretch oneself or one's muscles; to stretch and yawn

伸開(ㄕㄣ ㄎㄞ)
to stretch out; to extend; to spread

伸直(ㄕㄣ ㄓˊ)
to straighten; to stretch out (so as to make straight)

伸志(ㄕㄣ ㄓˋ)
to have one's ambition fulfilled

伸展(ㄕㄣ ㄓㄢˇ)
to stretch; to spread out; to extend

伸展台(ㄕㄣ ㄓㄢˇ ㄊㄞˊ)
a ramp or runway used in a beauty pageant, fashion show, etc.

伸張(ㄕㄣ ㄓㄤ)
to expand (power)

伸張正義(ㄕㄣ ㄓㄤ ㄓㄥˋ ㄧˋ)
to be a champion of justice

伸長(ㄕㄣ ㄔㄤˊ)
to stretch so as to make or become longer; to elongate; to lengthen

伸出(ㄕㄣ ㄔㄨ)
to stretch outward; to stretch out; to reach out; to jut out

伸舌頭(ㄕㄣ ㄕㄜˊ ·ㄊㄡ)
to stick out the tongue (to express horror, often in jest)

伸手(ㄕㄣ ㄕㄡˇ)
to reach out, hold out, or stretch out one's hand

伸訴(ㄕㄣ ㄙㄨˋ)
to present a complaint; to air a grievance

伸縮(ㄕㄣ ㄙㄨㄛ)
to expand and contract; to distend and shrink

伸縮性(ㄕㄣ ㄙㄨㄛ ㄒㄧㄥˋ)
flexibility; elasticity

伸腰兒(ㄕㄣ ㄧㄠㄦ)
①to stretch oneself ②(figuratively) to be successful in one's career

伸冤(ㄕㄣ ㄩㄢ)
to clear up a false charge; to right a wrong

【伺】 119
1. ㄙˋ syh sì

to spy; to reconnoiter; to watch

伺探(ㄙˋ ㄊㄢˋ) or 伺諜(ㄙˋ ㄉㄧㄝˊ)
to investigate secretly; to spy

伺機(ㄙˋ ㄐㄧ)
to wait for one's chance

伺機而動(ㄙˋ ㄐㄧ ㄦˊ ㄉㄨㄥˋ)
to wait for a favorable moment to make a move

伺隙(ㄙˋ ㄒㄧˋ)
to watch for a chance or opening (to do something evil)

伺察(ㄙˋ ㄔㄚˊ)
to spy; to investigate; to trace secretly

【伺】 119
2. ㄘˋ tsyh cì

to serve

伺候(ㄘˋ ·ㄏㄡ)
to wait, or attend upon; to serve

【似】 120
ㄙˋ syh sì

1. to resemble; to seem: 她酷似她的母親。She strongly resembles her mother.
2. like; as if

似的(ㄙˋ ·ㄉㄜ)
to give the impression that

似通非通(ㄙˋ ㄊㄨㄥ ㄈㄟ ㄊㄨㄥ)
(said of writing, argument, etc.) plausible

似乎(ㄙˋ ·ㄏㄨ)
it seems or appears that; it seems, appears, or looks as if or as though

似笑非笑(ㄙˋ ㄒㄧㄠˋ ㄈㄟ ㄒㄧㄠˋ)
(One) looks smiling but (one) actually doesn't smile

似是而非(ㄙˋ ㄕˋ ㄦˊ ㄈㄟ)
seemingly correct but really incorrect; having the semblance of what it is not

【伽】 121
1. ㄑㄧㄝˊ chye qié

(the character is not used alone)

伽藍(ㄑㄧㄝˊ ㄌㄢˊ)
①a Buddhist temple ② a Buddhist deity (*Sangharama or Sanghagara*)

【伽】 121
2. ㄐㄧㄚ jia jiā

伽瑪(ㄐㄧㄚ ㄇㄚˇ)
gamma

伽瑪射線(ㄐㄧㄚ ㄇㄚˇ ㄕㄜˋ ㄒㄧㄢˋ)
(physics) gamma rays

伽利略(ㄐㄧㄚ ㄌㄧˋ ㄌㄩㄝˋ)
Galileo, 1564-1642, Italian physicist, astronomer, and mathematician

〔入部〕

【佃】 122 ㄉㄧㄢˋ diann diàn
1. a tenant farmer
2. to tenant a farm
3. hunting

佃農(ㄉㄧㄢˋ ㄋㄨㄥˊ)
a tenant farmer or sharecropper

佃戶(ㄉㄧㄢˋ ㄏㄨˋ)
a tenant (of a farm)

佃契(ㄉㄧㄢˋ ㄑㄧˋ)
a land lease; a renting contract or agreement (between the tenant farmer and the landlord)

佃租(ㄉㄧㄢˋ ㄗㄨ)
land rent

【但】 123 ㄉㄢˋ dann dàn
but; however; yet

但凡(ㄉㄢˋ ㄈㄢˊ)
whoever; whenever; whatever; all

但丁(ㄉㄢˋ ㄉㄧㄥ)
Dante, 1265-1321, Italian poet

但求無過(ㄉㄢˋ ㄑㄧㄡˊ ㄨˊ ㄍㄨㄛˋ)
Just try to avoid making mistakes.

但是(ㄉㄢˋ ·ㄕ)
but; however; yet

但書(ㄉㄢˋ ㄕㄨ)
a proviso; a condition; a qualifying clause

但說無妨(ㄉㄢˋ ㄕㄨㄛ ㄨˊ ㄈㄤˊ)
Just speak out what is in your mind.

但澤(ㄉㄢˋ ㄗㄜˊ)
Danzig, inlet of the Baltic Sea in northern Poland

但坐無妨(ㄉㄢˋ ㄗㄨㄛˋ ㄨˊ ㄈㄤˊ)
Just sit down as you please.

但願(ㄉㄢˋ ㄩㄢˋ)
to wish; to hope: 但願你成功。I wish you success.

【佇】 124 ㄓㄨˋ juh zhù
1. to stand (for a long time)
2. to hope; to expect

佇立(ㄓㄨˋ ㄌㄧˋ)
to stand still; to stand motionless

佇候(ㄓㄨˋ ㄏㄡˋ)
to stand and wait; to look forward to: 佇候佳音。I look forward to hearing your good message.

【佈】 125 ㄅㄨˋ buh bù
1. to announce; to declare 參看「布」
2. to arrange: 那軍隊佈好陣勢以備戰。The army is arranged for battle.

佈滿(ㄅㄨˋ ㄇㄢˇ)
to be covered with: 野花佈滿了田野。The field is covered with wild flowers.

佈防(ㄅㄨˋ ㄈㄤˊ)
to organize the defense; to deploy troops in anticipation of an enemy attack

佈覆 or 布覆(ㄅㄨˋ ㄈㄨˋ)
to reply (used in letter writing): 謹此佈覆。I hereby reply to your letter.

佈達 or 布達(ㄅㄨˋ ㄉㄚˊ)
to notify: 謹此佈達。I hereby notify you.

佈達式(ㄅㄨˋ ㄉㄚˊ ㄕˋ)
(military) a change-of-command ceremony

佈道(ㄅㄨˋ ㄉㄠˋ)
to preach the gospel; to evangelize

佈雷(ㄅㄨˋ ㄌㄟˊ)
to lay mines

佈告(ㄅㄨˋ ㄍㄠˋ)
① a bulletin ② to make public announcement

佈崗(ㄅㄨˋ ㄍㄤˇ)
to post sentries; to mount guards

佈阱(ㄅㄨˋ ㄐㄧㄥˇ)
to lay a trap

佈景(ㄅㄨˋ ㄐㄧㄥˇ)
scenery (for the stage)

佈局(ㄅㄨˋ ㄐㄩˊ)
the layout (of a literary writing, painting, etc.)

佈置(ㄅㄨˋ ㄓˋ)
① to make arrangement ② to arrange (furniture); to decorate (a living room, convention hall, etc.)

佈施(ㄅㄨˋ ㄕ)
to make a contribution to a relief fund; to give money or materials to the poor

【位】 126 ㄨㄟˋ wey wèi
1. position; rank
2. location

位分(ㄨㄟˋ ㄈㄣˋ)
one's social status

位極人臣(ㄨㄟˋ ㄐㄧˊ ㄖㄣˊ ㄔㄣˊ)
(in ancient China) to become prime minister

位居津要(ㄨㄟˋ ㄐㄩ ㄐㄧㄣ ㄧㄠˋ)
to hold a sensitive post; to occupy a key position

位置(ㄨㄟˋ ㄓˋ)
① position (in space); location ② position (in an organization)

位子(ㄨㄟˋ ·ㄗ)
a seat

位次(ㄨㄟˋ ㄘˋ)
① rank ② seating order

位於(ㄨㄟˋ ㄩˊ)
situated at; located at

位元(ㄨㄟˋ ㄩㄢˊ)
(computers) a bit

【低】 127 ㄉㄧ di dī
1. low
2. to lower

低眉(ㄉㄧ ㄇㄟˊ)
① kindness ② obedience; compliance

低迷(ㄉㄧ ㄇㄧˊ)
(said of the sky, clouds, etc.) turbid

低等動物(ㄉㄧ ㄉㄥˇ ㄉㄨㄥˋ ㄨˋ)
lower animals

低地(ㄉㄧ ㄉㄧˋ)
lowlands

低調(ㄉㄧ ㄉㄧㄠˋ)
(music) low-key

低頭(ㄉㄧ ㄊㄡˊ)
to bow one's head; to lower one's head (in shame): 他們低頭禱告。They bowed their heads in prayer.

低能兒(ㄉㄧ ㄋㄥˊ ㄦˊ)
a mentally retarded child

低欄(ㄉㄧ ㄌㄢˊ)
(sports) low hurdles

低劣(ㄉㄧ ㄌㄧㄝˋ)
poor in quality

低廉(ㄉㄧ ㄌㄧㄢˊ)
cheap; low

低落(ㄉㄧ ㄌㄨㄛˋ)
low; downcast

低估(ㄉㄧ ㄍㄨ)
to underestimate: 不要低估敵人的力量。Don't underestimate the enemy's strength.

低空(ㄉㄧ ㄎㄨㄥ)
the atmosphere near the

earth

低迴(ㄉㄧ ㄏㄨㄟˊ)
to leave, or part reluctantly; to show reluctance to go

低級(ㄉㄧ ㄐㄧˊ)
①elementary; rudimentary ②vulgar; low

低級趣味(ㄉㄧ ㄐㄧˊ ㄑㄩˋ ㄨㄟˋ)
bad taste; vulgar interests

低賤(ㄉㄧ ㄐㄧㄢˋ)
①cheap in price ②low-class

低氣壓(ㄉㄧ ㄑㄧˋ ㄧㄚ)
low atmospheric pressure; atmospheric depression

低下(ㄉㄧ ㄒㄧㄚˋ)
low; lowly

低消耗(ㄉㄧ ㄒㄧㄠ ㄏㄠˋ)
low consumption (of raw materials, fuel, etc.)

低血糖(ㄉㄧ ㄒㄩㄝˇ ㄊㄤˊ)
(medicine) hypoglycemia

低潮(ㄉㄧ ㄔㄠˊ)
a low tide; a low ebb

低產(ㄉㄧ ㄔㄢˇ)
a low yield

低沈(ㄉㄧ ㄔㄣˊ)
low and heavy (spirit, tone, etc.)

低垂(ㄉㄧ ㄔㄨㄟˊ)
to hang low

低濕(ㄉㄧ ㄕ)
(said of places) low and moist; low in elevation and high in humidity

低首(ㄉㄧ ㄕㄡˇ)
to bend one's head

低首下心(ㄉㄧ ㄕㄡˇ ㄒㄧㄚˋ ㄒㄧㄣ)
to submit; to yield; to give oneself up

低聲(ㄉㄧ ㄕㄥ)
in a low voice; under one's breath

低聲下氣(ㄉㄧ ㄕㄥ ㄒㄧㄚˋ ㄑㄧˋ)
to be meek and timid; to be submissive

低姿態(ㄉㄧ ㄗ ㄊㄞˋ)
a low profile

低三下四(ㄉㄧ ㄙㄢ ㄒㄧㄚˋ ㄙˋ)
lowly; mean

低昂(ㄉㄧ ㄤˊ)
rises and falls; fluctuation in height

低壓(ㄉㄧ ㄧㄚ)
①(physics) low pressure ②(electricity) low voltage ③(meteorology) low pressure

低音(ㄉㄧ ㄧㄣ)
①a low-pitched sound ②(female) contralto; (male) bass

低窪(ㄉㄧ ㄨㄚ)
low-lying (ground)

低微(ㄉㄧ ㄨㄟˊ)
①mean; base; menial; ignoble ②humble (origin)

低溫(ㄉㄧ ㄨㄣ)
①low temperature ②(meteorology) microtherm ③(medicine) hypothermia

低溫殺菌(ㄉㄧ ㄨㄣ ㄕㄚ ㄐㄩㄣˋ)
low temperature sterilization

【住】 128 ㄓㄨˋ juh zhù

1. to dwell; to inhabit; to live: 他想居住在鄉間。He wants to live in the country.
2. to stop: 風住了。The wind has stopped.
3. used after verb to complement its meaning: 拿住！Hold it fast!

住不下(ㄓㄨˋ ·ㄅㄨ ㄒㄧㄚˋ)
cannot accommodate (because of limitation of space)

住民(ㄓㄨˋ ㄇㄧㄣˊ)
an inhabitant; a resident

住口(ㄓㄨˋ ㄎㄡˇ)or 住嘴(ㄓㄨˋ ㄗㄨㄟˇ)
①to stop talking ②Shut up!

住戶(ㄓㄨˋ ㄏㄨˋ)
a resident family

住家(ㄓㄨˋ ㄐㄧㄚ)
①a residence; a home ②(said of a married woman) to visit her parents' home

住址(ㄓㄨˋ ㄓˇ)
address: 在信封上寫姓名與住址。Write the name and address on the envelope.

住宅(ㄓㄨˋ ㄓㄞˊ)
a residence; a dwelling; a house

住宅區(ㄓㄨˋ ㄓㄞˊ ㄑㄩ)
a residential area, district or quarter

住持(ㄓㄨˋ ㄔˊ)
an abbot; the head monk (of a temple)

住處(ㄓㄨˋ ㄔㄨˋ)
a residence; a dwelling; lodging; quarters

住手(ㄓㄨˋ ㄕㄡˇ)
①Stop! ②to stop an action; to halt; to hold

住宿(ㄓㄨˋ ㄙㄨˋ)
to stay overnight; to lodge

住所(ㄓㄨˋ ㄙㄨㄛˇ)
a dwelling place; a home; a residence; a domicile

住院(ㄓㄨˋ ㄩㄢˋ)
to be hospitalized

住院總醫師(ㄓㄨˋ ㄩㄢˋ ㄗㄨㄥˇ ㄧ ㄕ)
a chief resident

住院醫師(ㄓㄨˋ ㄩㄢˋ ㄧ ㄕ)
a resident (in a hospital)

【佐】 129 ㄗㄨㄛˇ tzuoo zuǒ

to assist; to aid; to second

佐命(ㄗㄨㄛˇ ㄇㄧㄥˋ)
to help a prince to gain the throne and establish a new dynasty

佐拉(ㄗㄨㄛˇ ㄌㄚ)
Émile Zola, 1840-1902, French novelist

佐理(ㄗㄨㄛˇ ㄌㄧˇ)
to assist

佐證(ㄗㄨㄛˇ ㄓㄥˋ)
the evidence

佐世保(ㄗㄨㄛˇ ㄕˋ ㄅㄠˇ)
Sasebo, a naval base in Japan

佐膳(ㄗㄨㄛˇ ㄕㄢˋ)
side dishes (as distinct from the staple food)

佐餐(ㄗㄨㄛˇ ㄘㄢ)
to be eaten together with rice; to go with rice

【佑】 130 ㄧㄡˋ yow yòu

to help; to protect; to aid; to bless: 求上天保佑這家人。Heaven bless this family.

佑助(ㄧㄡˋ ㄓㄨˋ)
to help; to aid; to assist

【佔】 131 ㄓㄢˋ jann zhàn

to seize; to usurp; to occupy; to take by force: 敵人佔據了我們的堡壘。The enemy occupied our fort.

佔便宜(ㄓㄢˋ ㄆㄧㄢˊ ·ㄧ)
①to be in an advantageous position ②to take advantage (of a person)

佔領(ㄓㄢˋ ㄌㄧㄥˇ)
to occupy (a foreign territory); to capture or take (an enemy position)

〔人部〕

佔領軍(ㄓㄢˋ ㄌㄧㄥˇ ㄐㄩㄣ)
occupation troops
佔據(ㄓㄢˋ ㄐㄩˋ)
to occupy; to take possession of
佔先(ㄓㄢˋ ㄒㄧㄢ)
to lead (in a game or contest)
佔線(ㄓㄢˋ ㄒㄧㄢˋ)
(telephone) The line's busy (or engaged).
佔上風(ㄓㄢˋ ㄕㄤˋ ㄈㄥ)
to have the upper hand (in a struggle or contest)
佔有(ㄓㄢˋ ㄧㄡˇ)
① to own; to possess; to have ② to occupy; to hold: 商業在台灣經濟中佔有重要地位。Commerce occupies an important place in the economy of Taiwan.

【何】 132 ㄏㄜˊ her hé
1. what; how; where; why: 有何不可? Why not?
2. a Chinese family name
何必(ㄏㄜˊ ㄅㄧˋ)or 何須(ㄏㄜˊ ㄒㄩ)
why should; why must; why is it necessary; not necessary …; there is no need: 他只是開個玩笑, 何必當眞? He is only joking. Why take it so seriously?
何不(ㄏㄜˊ ㄅㄨˋ)
why not: 何不早說? Why didn't you say it earlier?
何妨(ㄏㄜˊ ㄈㄤˊ)or(ㄏㄜˊ ㄈㄤˇ)
There is no harm (trying, doing, etc.). 或 might as well: 何妨一試? Why not have a try?
何等(ㄏㄜˊ ㄉㄥˇ)
① how (in exclamatory expressions) ② what sort of; what kind of: 你知道他是何等人物? Do you know what sort of person he is?
何獨(ㄏㄜˊ ㄉㄨˊ)
Why…only?
何樂不爲(ㄏㄜˊ ㄌㄜˋ ㄅㄨˋ ㄨㄟˊ)
Why not do it gladly?
何干(ㄏㄜˊ ㄍㄢ)
What has that got to do with…?
何敢(ㄏㄜˊ ㄍㄢˇ)
How dare…?
何故(ㄏㄜˊ ㄍㄨˋ)
why; for what reason
何可勝數(ㄏㄜˊ ㄎㄜˇ ㄕㄥ ㄕㄨˇ)
countless; numerous
何苦(ㄏㄜˊ ㄎㄨˇ)
Why take the trouble? 或 for what earthly reason
何況(ㄏㄜˊ ㄎㄨㄤˋ)
much less; not to mention; let alone: 他連伙食錢都不夠, 何況娛樂。He hasn't enough money for food, let alone amusements.
何濟於事(ㄏㄜˊ ㄐㄧˋ ㄩˊ ㄕˋ)
Of what avail is it?
何去何從(ㄏㄜˊ ㄑㄩˋ ㄏㄜˊ ㄘㄨㄥˊ)
choice (of action); what course to follow
何須(ㄏㄜˊ ㄒㄩ)
unnecessary; why is it necessary…
何許人(ㄏㄜˊ ㄒㄩˇ ㄖㄣˊ)
who (used to indicate ignorance of someone's background)
何止(ㄏㄜˊ ㄓˇ)
far more than
何至於(ㄏㄜˊ ㄓˋ ㄩˊ)
How could it have turned out (like that)? 或How come?
何者(ㄏㄜˊ ㄓㄜˇ)
which one
何啻(ㄏㄜˊ ㄔˋ)
not different from; to be the same as
何愁(ㄏㄜˊ ㄔㄡˊ)
Why worry about it?
何嘗(ㄏㄜˊ ㄔㄤˊ)
How (could it be an exception)? 或 not that…; never
何處(ㄏㄜˊ ㄔㄨˋ)
where; in what place
何時(ㄏㄜˊ ㄕˊ)
when; at what time
何事(ㄏㄜˊ ㄕˋ)
What (do you want)? 或 What (is the trouble)? 或 for what: 何事令你如此不安? What makes you so anxious?
何首烏(ㄏㄜˊ ㄕㄡˇ ㄨ)
(herb medicine) *Polygonum multiflorum*
何如(ㄏㄜˊ ㄖㄨˊ)
① How about it? ② Wouldn't it be better? ③ What do you think…?
何在(ㄏㄜˊ ㄗㄞˋ)
① Where is (that particular thing)? ② What is (that particular reason)?
何足掛齒(ㄏㄜˊ ㄗㄨˊ ㄍㄨㄚˋ ㄔˇ)
Don't mention it. (used in formal speech)
何曾(ㄏㄜˊ ㄘㄥˊ)
Has it ever happened?
何以(ㄏㄜˊ ㄧˇ)
why; wherefore; how: 何以見得? How do you think so?
何以自處(ㄏㄜˊ ㄧˇ ㄗˋ ㄔㄨˇ)
how to explain (what one has done has caused trouble or harm to others)
何由見得(ㄏㄜˊ ㄧㄡˊ ㄐㄧㄢˋ ㄉㄜˊ)
What makes you think so?
何謂(ㄏㄜˊ ㄨㄟˋ)
what is meant by
何用(ㄏㄜˊ ㄩㄥˋ)
of what use

【佗】 133 1. ㄊㄨㄛˊ two tuó
a load

【佗】 133 2. ㄊㄨㄛ tuo tuō
1. he
2. a Chinese family name

【佘】 134 ㄕㄜˊ sher shé
a Chinese family name

【余】 135 ㄩˊ yu yú
1. (in formal speech) I; me
2. a Chinese family name

【佚】 136 ㄧˋ yih yì
idleness; comfort

【佛】 137 ㄈㄛˊ for fó
1. Buddha (Sakyamuni 釋迦牟尼)
2. of Buddhism
佛門(ㄈㄛˊ ㄇㄣˊ)
Buddhism; the Buddhist faith; the school of Buddhism
佛門弟子(ㄈㄛˊ ㄇㄣˊ ㄉㄧˋ ㄗˇ)
Buddhist monks and nuns; Buddhists
佛法(ㄈㄛˊ ㄈㄚˇ)
the Buddhist doctrines (*Buddhadharma*); the law of Buddha
佛法僧(ㄈㄛˊ ㄈㄚˇ ㄙㄥ)
Buddha-dharma-sangha
佛法無邊(ㄈㄛˊ ㄈㄚˇ ㄨˊ ㄅㄧㄢ)

The greatness of Buddhism is immeasurable.

佛誕日(ㄈㄛˊ ㄉㄢˋ ㄖˋ)
Buddha's Birthday (There are two versions: the 8th day of the 4th moon, and the 8th day of the 2nd moon. The former is preferred in China.)

佛堂(ㄈㄛˊ ㄊㄤˊ)
a Buddhist sanctuary; the hall for worshipping Buddha or with the statue of Buddha

佛徒(ㄈㄛˊ ㄊㄨˊ)
a Buddhist disciple; a Buddhist

佛陀(ㄈㄛˊ ㄊㄨㄛˊ)
Buddha—a title applied by Buddhists to someone regarded as embodying divine wisdom and virtue

佛老(ㄈㄛˊ ㄌㄠˇ)
① Buddha and Lao-tzu ② Buddhism and Taoism

佛蘭克林(ㄈㄛˊ ㄌㄢˊ ㄎㄜˋ ㄌㄧㄣˊ)
Benjamin Franklin, 1706-1790, American statesman, writer and inventor

佛羅里達(ㄈㄛˊ ㄌㄨㄛˊ ㄌㄧˇ ㄉㄚˊ)
Florida, U. S. A.

佛羅倫斯(ㄈㄛˊ ㄌㄨㄛˊ ㄌㄨㄣˊ ㄙ)
Florence, a city in Italy

佛骨(ㄈㄛˊ ㄍㄨˇ)
the remains of Buddha

佛國(ㄈㄛˊ ㄍㄨㄛˊ)
① India, the country where Buddha was born (*Buddhaksetra*) ② the land purified by Buddhism

佛口蛇心(ㄈㄛˊ ㄎㄡˇ ㄕㄜˊ ㄒㄧㄣ)
the mouth of Buddha and the heart of a serpent—(figuratively) descriptive of an evil person who speaks sweet words but does evil things

佛龕(ㄈㄛˊ ㄎㄢ)
a Buddhist altar; a niche for Buddha

佛海(ㄈㄛˊ ㄏㄞˇ)
(the all-encompassing) teachings of Buddha; Buddha's ocean (the realm of Buddha as boundless as the sea)

佛會(ㄈㄛˊ ㄏㄨㄟˋ)
the celebration of Buddhist festivals

佛家(ㄈㄛˊ ㄐㄧㄚ)
a Buddhist; the Buddhist faithful; a Buddhist follower

佛教(ㄈㄛˊ ㄐㄧㄠˋ)
Buddhism; the Buddhist religion

佛經(ㄈㄛˊ ㄐㄧㄥ)
the Sutras; the Buddhist scriptures; the Buddhist canon

佛像(ㄈㄛˊ ㄒㄧㄤˋ)
a figure of Buddha; a statue of Buddha

佛性(ㄈㄛˊ ㄒㄧㄥˋ)
Buddhata; a nature like that of Buddha (believed to be present in every living thing)

佛學(ㄈㄛˊ ㄒㄩㄝˊ)
Buddhistic study; Buddhism

佛事(ㄈㄛˊ ㄕˋ)
Buddhist rituals; Buddhist religious service

佛手(ㄈㄛˊ ㄕㄡˇ)
①(botany) bergamot; *Citrus medica* ② Buddha's hand

佛祖(ㄈㄛˊ ㄗㄨˇ)
① Buddha ② Buddhist patriarchs

佛寺(ㄈㄛˊ ㄙˋ)
a Buddhist temple

佛爺(ㄈㄛˊ ˙ㄧㄝ)
Buddha

【作】 138

1. ㄗㄨㄛˋ tzuoh zuò

1. to do; to make
2. the works (of a writer, etc.)
3. to rise up
4. to pretend; to affect
5. to regard…as; to take… for
6. to write; to compose

作罷(ㄗㄨㄛˋ ㄅㄚˋ)
to drop; to give up

作保(ㄗㄨㄛˋ ㄅㄠˇ)
to guarantee; to vouch for; to be a guarantor; to stand guarantee

作伴(ㄗㄨㄛˋ ㄅㄢˋ)
to keep (someone) company; to serve as a companion for

作弊(ㄗㄨㄛˋ ㄅㄧˋ)
to cheat (especially in examinations); to indulge in corrupt practices

作壁上觀(ㄗㄨㄛˋ ㄅㄧˋ ㄕㄤˋ ㄍㄨㄢ)
to watch (a fight, quarrel, etc.) with detachment

作別(ㄗㄨㄛˋ ㄅㄧㄝˊ)
to bid farewell; to take one's leave

作陪(ㄗㄨㄛˋ ㄆㄟˊ)
to accompany; to escort; to be invited (to a reception, etc.) as company to the guest of honor

作品(ㄗㄨㄛˋ ㄆㄧㄣˇ)
the works (of a writer, artist, etc.); a literary or artistic work

作媒(ㄗㄨㄛˋ ㄇㄟˊ)
to act as a go-between in marriage

作美(ㄗㄨㄛˋ ㄇㄟˇ)
(of weather, etc.) to help; to cooperate; to make things better for somebody: 如果天公作美，我們明天去新公園野餐。If Heaven makes things better for us, we'll go on a picnic in New Park tomorrow.

作夢(ㄗㄨㄛˋ ㄇㄥˋ)
① to dream ② to imagine as in a dream; to have daydreams

作伐(ㄗㄨㄛˋ ㄈㄚˊ)or(ㄗㄨㄛˋ ㄈㄚ)
to be a matchmaker; to act as a go-between in marriage

作法(ㄗㄨㄛˋ ㄈㄚˇ)
① a way of doing or handling things; course of action ② a method of making, preparing, manufacturing, or cooking ③ to exercise magic powers ④ to legislate; to make laws

作法自斃(ㄗㄨㄛˋ ㄈㄚˇ ㄗˋ ㄅㄧˋ)
to get into trouble through one's own scheme; a scheme that boomerangs; to be caught by one's own device

作佛事(ㄗㄨㄛˋ ㄈㄛˊ ˙ㄕ)
(said of Buddhist monks) to recite passages from the Sutras to worship Buddha

作廢(ㄗㄨㄛˋ ㄈㄟˋ)
to nullify; to make void; to cancel; to declare invalid

作風(ㄗㄨㄛˋ ㄈㄥ)
①(literary or artistic) style ② one's way of doing things

作歹(ㄗㄨㄛˋ ㄉㄞˇ)

to do evil; to act criminally

作對(ㄗㄨㄛˋ ㄉㄨㄟˋ)
①to oppose; to act against; to choose to be someone's rival or opponent 亦作「作對頭」②to match with another in marriage

作東(ㄗㄨㄛˋ ㄉㄨㄥ)
to stand treat

作態(ㄗㄨㄛˋ ㄊㄞˋ)
①(especially referring to a woman trying to please a man) to act pretentiously ② to take on a certain expression; to feign; to strike an attitude

作孽(ㄗㄨㄛˋ ㄋㄧㄝˋ)
to do evil; to do something that causes harm to others

作弄(ㄗㄨㄛˋ ㄋㄨㄥˋ)
to tease; to make a fool of; to play a trick on

作樂(ㄗㄨㄛˋ ㄌㄜˋ)
to make merry; to have fun; to enjoy

作亂(ㄗㄨㄛˋ ㄌㄨㄢˋ)
to rebel; to start an uprising; to turn against the authorities

作梗(ㄗㄨㄛˋ ㄍㄥˇ)
to obstruct or to oppose secretly; to impede; to create difficulties; to hamper; to hinder

作古(ㄗㄨㄛˋ ㄍㄨˇ)
to die; to pass away

作怪(ㄗㄨㄛˋ ㄍㄨㄞˋ)
mischievous; to act mischievously; to make trouble; to play tricks: 別作怪。 Don't play dirty tricks on me.

作官(ㄗㄨㄛˋ ㄍㄨㄢ)
to be a government official; to hold a government post

作工(ㄗㄨㄛˋ ㄍㄨㄥ)
to labor; to work

作客(ㄗㄨㄛˋ ㄎㄜˋ)
①to be a guest ②to stay outside of one's hometown; to sojourn in a strange place

作闊(ㄗㄨㄛˋ ㄎㄨㄛˋ)
to show off; to make a vain display: 他愛作闊。He is fond of showing off.

作活(ㄗㄨㄛˋ ㄏㄨㄛˊ)
to work (for one's living)

作家(ㄗㄨㄛˋ ㄐㄧㄚ)
a writer; an author

作假(ㄗㄨㄛˋ ㄐㄧㄚˇ)or 作僞(ㄗㄨㄛˋ ㄨㄟˋ)
to pretend; to be an impostor; to cheat; to make an imitation copy

作嫁(ㄗㄨㄛˋ ㄐㄧㄚˋ)
to sew somebody else's trousseau—to earn a living by working for others: 我們總是爲人作嫁。 We always busy ourselves in helping other people.

作姦犯科(ㄗㄨㄛˋ ㄐㄧㄢ ㄈㄢˋ ㄎㄜ)
to do evil; to break the law; to act criminally

作繭自縛(ㄗㄨㄛˋ ㄐㄧㄢˇ ㄗˋ ㄈㄨˊ)
(said of a silkworm) to spin a cocoon and imprison itself in it—(figuratively) to tie oneself up with duties; to get into trouble by one's own schemes

作曲(ㄗㄨㄛˋ ㄑㄩˇ)
to write a song; to set a song to music; to compose

作曲家(ㄗㄨㄛˋ ㄑㄩˇ ㄐㄧㄚ)
a composer

作秀(ㄗㄨㄛˋ ㄒㄧㄡˋ)
(informal) ①to appear in a stage show ②to grandstand; grandstanding; showboating

作者(ㄗㄨㄛˋ ㄓㄜˇ)
a writer (of a composition, novel, etc.); an author

作戰(ㄗㄨㄛˋ ㄓㄢˋ)
to go to battle; to fight against; to make war

作證(ㄗㄨㄛˋ ㄓㄥˋ)
to act as a witness in court; to bear witness

作主(ㄗㄨㄛˋ ㄓㄨˇ)
to take up responsibility for making a decision; to make the final decision: 這件事由他作主。He made the final decision on this matter.

作長工(ㄗㄨㄛˋ ㄔㄤˊ ㄍㄨㄥ)
to be a regular laborer on a farm; to be a farm hand

作成(ㄗㄨㄛˋ ㄔㄥˊ)
to arrange or complete (a job); to help succeed (in an undertaking, etc.)

作詩(ㄗㄨㄛˋ ㄕ)
to write poems; to versify

作勢(ㄗㄨㄛˋ ㄕˋ)
to put on airs; to pretend

作舍道傍(ㄗㄨㄛˋ ㄕㄜˋ ㄉㄠˋ ㄆㄤˊ)
difficult to succeed

作壽(ㄗㄨㄛˋ ㄕㄡˋ)
to celebrate a birthday

作善(ㄗㄨㄛˋ ㄕㄢˋ)
to do good turns

作聲(ㄗㄨㄛˋ ㄕㄥ)
to make noise; to speak; to break silence

作殊死戰(ㄗㄨㄛˋ ㄕㄨ ㄙˇ ㄓㄢˋ)
to fight to the bitter end

作人(ㄗㄨㄛˋ ㄖㄣˊ)
①to get along with other people ②to be pleasant in manner or personality; to behave oneself properly

作色(ㄗㄨㄛˋ ㄙㄜˋ)
to change facial expression (usually to show anger)

作祟(ㄗㄨㄛˋ ㄙㄨㄟˋ)
①(said of spirits) to haunt ②(said of people) to make mischief; to cause trouble: 這些都是利己主義作祟。All these troubles are caused by egoism.

作惡
①(ㄗㄨㄛˋ ㄜˋ)ⓐ to indulge in evildoings ⓑ gloomy; sullen; melancholy
②(ㄗㄨㄛˋ ㄜˇ)to vomit

作惡多端(ㄗㄨㄛˋ ㄜˋ ㄉㄨㄛ ㄉㄨㄢ)
to indulge in all sorts of evildoing; to commit many crimes

作嘔(ㄗㄨㄛˋ ㄡˇ)
①to nauseate; nauseating (usually referring to poor writings, unflavoring utterances, conceited manner, etc.) ②to feel resentment or detest ③to sicken

作案(ㄗㄨㄛˋ ㄢˋ)
to commit a crime

作押(ㄗㄨㄛˋ ㄧㄚ)
to offer something as a pledge; to mortgage

作業(ㄗㄨㄛˋ ㄧㄝˋ)
①students' homework ②the job of a person ③main fields of operation of a firm, etc.

作業系統(ㄗㄨㄛˋ ㄧㄝˋ ㄒㄧˋ ㄊㄨㄥˇ)
(computers) the operating system

作營生(ㄗㄨㄛˋ ㄧㄥˊ ㄕㄥ)

to work for a living

作物(ㄗㄨㄛˋ ㄨˋ)
①crops ②literary or artistic compositions

作威作福(ㄗㄨㄛˋ ㄨㄟ ㄗㄨㄛˋ ㄈㄨˊ)
bossy; to throw one's weight around freely; to overexert one's power and position by acting impudently

作爲(ㄗㄨㄛˋ ㄨㄟˊ)
①conduct; behavior; action ②to accomplish; a promising future ③to serve as; to look upon as; to regard as

作文(ㄗㄨㄛˋ ㄨㄣˊ)
①to write a composition ②a composition

作樂(ㄗㄨㄛˋ ㄩㄝˋ)
①to play music ②to write scores

作俑(ㄗㄨㄛˋ ㄩㄥˇ)
to make wooden images—to originate an immoral (or vicious) practice

作用(ㄗㄨㄛˋ ㄩㄥˋ)
①functions; uses; usefulness ②effect: 這藥對病人沒有什麼作用。The drug has no effect on patients. ③objective; purpose: 你這麼說有何作用? What is your purpose to have said so?

作用點(ㄗㄨㄛˋ ㄩㄥˋ ㄉㄧㄢˇ)
(physics) a point of application

【作】 138
2. ㄗㄨㄛ tzuo zuō

作坊(ㄗㄨㄛ ˙ㄈㄤ)
a small workshop

作揖(ㄗㄨㄛ ㄧ)
a Chinese gesture in greeting, with the greeter holding his hands together in an up-and-down motion

作寃(ㄗㄨㄛ ㄩㄢ)
to get trapped by oneself

【作】 138
3. ㄗㄨㄛˊ tzwo zuó

作料(ㄗㄨㄛˊ ㄌㄧㄠˋ)or作料兒(ㄗㄨㄛˊ ㄌㄧㄠˋㄦ)
ingredients of a recipe; dressing; seasoning; materials

作踐(ㄗㄨㄛˊ ˙ㄐㄧㄢ)
to abuse; to waste; to ill-use; to trample; to treat harshly

作興(ㄗㄨㄛˊ ˙ㄒㄧㄥ)
①allowable ②to be in good spirits ③in vogue ④to hold in high regard ⑤perhaps; likely

【佞】 139
ㄋㄧㄥˋ ninq nìng

1. eloquent; persuasive; gifted with a glib tongue
2. obsequious; fawning
3. to believe (in superstition)
4. one given to flattery

佞佛(ㄋㄧㄥˋ ㄈㄛˊ)
to worship Buddha ingratiatingly

佞婦(ㄋㄧㄥˋ ㄈㄨˋ)
a glib-tongued woman

佞黨(ㄋㄧㄥˋ ㄉㄤˇ)
a clique of traitors

佞口(ㄋㄧㄥˋ ㄎㄡˇ)
a person who is glib-tongued and good at flattery

佞幸(ㄋㄧㄥˋ ㄒㄧㄥˋ)
flattering

佞臣(ㄋㄧㄥˋ ㄔㄣˊ)
a flattering courtier

佞人(ㄋㄧㄥˋ ㄖㄣˊ)
an obsequious person who flatters others by his glib tongue in order to gain favors; a bootlicker

【佟】 140
ㄊㄨㄥˊ torng tóng

a Chinese family name

六畫

【佩】 141
ㄆㄟˋ pey pèi

1. to wear; to carry: 他腰佩手槍。He carried a pistol in his belt.
2. to admire; to adore
3. to be grateful
4. something worn on a girdle or clothing; a pendant

佩服(ㄆㄟˋ ˙ㄈㄨ)
to admire; to respect: 你的機智勇敢,令我們佩服。We must admire your resourcefulness and courage.

佩帶(ㄆㄟˋ ㄉㄞˋ)
to wear; to carry

佩刀(ㄆㄟˋ ㄉㄠ)
to wear a knife or sword at the waist; a knife thus worn

佩劍(ㄆㄟˋ ㄐㄧㄢˋ)
to wear a sword at the waist; a sword one carries

佩勳章(ㄆㄟˋ ㄒㄩㄣ ㄓㄤ)
to wear medals

佩玉(ㄆㄟˋ ㄩˋ)
a jade ornament

【佯】 142
ㄧㄤˊ yang yáng

1. to pretend; to feign; to sham
2. false; deceitful; feigning

佯病(ㄧㄤˊ ㄅㄧㄥˋ)
to pretend to be ill

佯狂(ㄧㄤˊ ㄎㄨㄤˊ)
to feign madness; feigned madness

佯作不知(ㄧㄤˊ ㄗㄨㄛˋ ㄅㄨˋ ㄓ)
to feign ignorance; to pretend not to know

佯死(ㄧㄤˊ ㄙˇ)
to feign death; to pretend to be dead

【佳】 143
ㄐㄧㄚ jia jiā

1. beautiful; good; fine
2. auspicious
3. distinguished

佳賓(ㄐㄧㄚ ㄅㄧㄣ)
distinguished or honored guests

佳釀(ㄐㄧㄚ ㄋㄧㄤˋ)
excellent wine or liquor

佳麗(ㄐㄧㄚ ㄌㄧˋ)
a beautiful woman; a beauty

佳客(ㄐㄧㄚ ㄎㄜˋ)
a good visitor or guest; an honored guest

佳話(ㄐㄧㄚ ㄏㄨㄚˋ)
①(usually a romance) an interesting story or a story with a happy ending that has been popular for a period of time ②a deed worthy of praising far and wide

佳節(ㄐㄧㄚ ㄐㄧㄝˊ)
a festival; a carnival

佳景(ㄐㄧㄚ ㄐㄧㄥˇ)
beautiful scenery

佳境(ㄐㄧㄚ ㄐㄧㄥˋ)
①delightful regions ②wonderful circumstances; a favorable condition

佳句(ㄐㄧㄚ ㄐㄩˋ)
a quotable quote; a beautiful line; a well-turned verse

佳期(ㄐㄧㄚ ㄑㄧˊ)
①the wedding or nuptial day ②the date of a rendezvous with a beautiful wom-

〔人部〕

an

佳趣(ㄐㄧㄚ ㄑㄩˋ)
(of) a delightful and intriguing flavor; matters of intense interest

佳婿(ㄐㄧㄚ ㄒㄩˋ)
a good or favorite son-in-law

佳城(ㄐㄧㄚ ㄔㄥˊ)
a tomb or a grave

佳士(ㄐㄧㄚ ㄕˋ)
a scholar of virtue and ability

佳人(ㄐㄧㄚ ㄖㄣˊ)
①a beauty; a pretty woman ②a handsome young man

佳作(ㄐㄧㄚ ㄗㄨㄛˋ)
an excellent (literary) work; a fine piece of writing

佳偶(ㄐㄧㄚ ㄡˇ)
a happily married couple; a fine couple

佳偶天成(ㄐㄧㄚ ㄡˇ ㄊㄧㄢ ㄔㄥˊ)
an ideal couple; a wonderful match

佳餚(ㄐㄧㄚ ㄧㄠˊ)
a delicacy

佳餚美酒(ㄐㄧㄚ ㄧㄠˊ ㄇㄟˇ ㄐㄧㄡˇ)
good food and excellent wine—a sumptuous feast

佳言(ㄐㄧㄚ ㄧㄢˊ)
good words; a quotable quote

佳音(ㄐㄧㄚ ㄧㄣ)
good news; welcome news; good tidings

【佻】 144
ㄊㄧㄠˊ tyau tiáo
1. frivolous; imprudent
2. to steal; stealthily; to act in a furtive manner
3. to delay; dilatory; slow
4. to provoke

佻薄(ㄊㄧㄠˊ ㄅㄛˊ)or 佻撻(ㄊㄧㄠˊ ㄊㄚˋ)
frivolous; not dignified

佻脫(ㄊㄧㄠˊ ㄊㄨㄛ)
frivolous and careless

佻巧(ㄊㄧㄠˊ ㄑㄧㄠˇ)
frivolous and tricky

【佼】 145
ㄐㄧㄠˇ jeau jiǎo
1. beautiful; handsome; attractive; charming
2. outstanding

佼好(ㄐㄧㄠˇ ㄏㄠˇ)
pretty; pleasant

佼佼(ㄐㄧㄠˇ ㄐㄧㄠˇ)
①stunningly beautiful; handsome; good-looking ②above the average; remarkable; outstanding

佼佼者(ㄐㄧㄠˇ ㄐㄧㄠˇ ㄓㄜˇ)
an outstanding person

佼人(ㄐㄧㄠˇ ㄖㄣˊ)
a beauty

【佾】 146
ㄧˋ yih yì
a row or file of dancers, especially referring to those in ancient dances at sacrifices or other rites; a dance squad

佾生(ㄧˋ ㄕㄥ)
young boy dancers at the court or temple on ceremonial occasions, etc.

佾舞(ㄧˋ ㄨˇ)
rows of ceremonial dancers; a dance now performed especially on Confucius' birthday at the sage's shrine

【使】 147
1. ㄕˇ shyy shǐ
1. to use; to employ; to apply
2. to make; to act
3. to indulge in
4. to send as diplomatic personnel; diplomatic envoys
5. if

使絆兒(ㄕˇ ㄅㄚˋㄦ)
①(in Chinese wrestling) to trip the opponent with a leg trick ②to injure others by devious (often stealthy) means

使不得(ㄕˇ ·ㄅㄨ ·ㄉㄜ)
①useless; unserviceable: 鋼筆壞了，使不得了。The pen is broken; it is useless. ②impermissible; undesirable

使不慣(ㄕˇ ·ㄅㄨ ㄍㄨㄢˋ)
not used to; not familiar with the use of

使不上(ㄕˇ ·ㄅㄨ ㄕㄤˋ)
not usable; unfit to be used

使脾氣(ㄕˇ ㄆㄧˊ ·ㄑㄧ)
to lose one's temper

使民以時(ㄕˇ ㄇㄧㄣˊ ㄧˇ ㄕˊ)
to employ the people in the proper season (i.e., when they are not busy farming)

使命(ㄕˇ ㄇㄧㄥˋ)
a mission; a job

使命感(ㄕˇ ㄇㄧㄥˋ ㄍㄢˇ)
a sense of calling

使得(ㄕˇ ·ㄉㄜ)
①all right; can be done or used ②to make (somebody mad, sad, happy, etc.); to cause; to render

使得上(ㄕˇ ·ㄉㄜ ㄕㄤˋ)
usable; employable; can be used; useful

使女(ㄕˇ ㄋㄩˇ)
a maidservant; a housemaid; a chambermaid

使壞(ㄕˇ ㄏㄨㄞˋ)
①to be up to mischief; to play a dirty trick ②to destroy

使喚(ㄕˇ ㄏㄨㄢˋ)
①to answer the beck and call of; to run errands for ②to order others to do something

使勁(ㄕˇ ㄐㄧㄣˋ)or 使勁兒(ㄕˇ ㄐㄧㄜˋㄦ)
to use or apply (greater) force; to exert effort; to strain: 他們使勁提高嗓子。They strained their voice.

使氣(ㄕˇ ㄑㄧˋ)
to be influenced by sentiment or emotion in handling things

使性子(ㄕˇ ㄒㄧㄥˋ ·ㄗ)
to lose one's temper; to indulge in one's temper: 不要使性子。Don't indulge in your temper.

使出(ㄕˇ ㄔㄨ)
to exert

使出渾身解數(ㄕˇ ㄔㄨ ㄏㄨㄣˊ ㄕㄣ ㄐㄧㄝˇ ㄕㄨˋ)
to do one's best (in order to please or impress somebody); to bring forth all the talent one has

使眼色(ㄕˇ ㄧㄢˇ ㄙㄜˋ)
to say something with eyes; to make eyes at; to wink: 她向男友使眼色。She made eyes at her boy friend.

使用(ㄕˇ ㄩㄥˋ)
to use; to employ; to resort to: 她使用新的教學法。She employs a new teaching method.

使用年限(ㄕˇ ㄩㄥˋ ㄋㄧㄢˊ ㄒㄧㄢˋ)
the tenure of use

使用價值(ㄕˇ ㄩㄥˋ ㄐㄧㄚˋ ㄓˊ)
①(economics) utility ②the value of something being

utilized

使用權(ㄕˇ ㄩㄥˋ ㄑㄩㄢˊ)
(law) the right of use (or using); the right to use something

147
【使】 2. ㄕˋ shyh shì
(或讀ㄕˇ shyy shǐ)

1. to be appointed as a diplomatic envoy; to be an ambassador to
2. an envoy; an emissary; a minister

使徒(ㄕˇ ㄊㄨˊ)
(in the Bible) the Apostle or Apostles

使團(ㄕˇ ㄊㄨㄢˊ)or 使節團(ㄕˇ ㄐㄧㄝˊ ㄊㄨㄢˊ)
①a diplomatic mission ② the diplomatic corps

使領館(ㄕˇ ㄌㄧㄥˇ ㄍㄨㄢˇ)
embassies and consulates

使館(ㄕˇ ㄍㄨㄢˇ)
a legation; an embassy

使節(ㄕˇ ㄐㄧㄝˊ)
an envoy; an official mission abroad

使君有婦(ㄕˇ ㄐㄩㄣ ㄧㄡˇ ㄈㄨˋ)
a married man

使者(ㄕˇ ㄓㄜˇ)
an envoy; an emissary; a messenger

使臣(ㄕˇ ㄔㄣˊ)
an envoy; a representative of a country abroad

148
【侃】 ㄎㄢˇ kaan kǎn

1. straightforward; frank; bold; open
2. amiable; pleasant
3. with confidence and composure

侃侃而談(ㄎㄢˇ ㄎㄢˇ ㄦˊ ㄊㄢˊ)
to talk with confidence and composure

侃直(ㄎㄢˇ ㄓˊ)
resolute and honest

149
【來】 ㄌㄞˊ lai lái

1. to come; coming; to arrive: 他昨天來這裡。He came here yesterday.
2. used in place of a verb: 讓我自己來吧! Let me do it myself.
3. to return; to come back; returning: 他還沒回來。He has not come back.
4. future; later on; next: 來春 next spring
5. ever since: 別來無恙乎? How have you been since we separated?
6. (used after a number) a little more than; about: 他大約四十來歲。He is about forty years old.
7. used after one, two, to explain: 我很久沒去看她,一來路太遠,二來沒時間。I haven't been to see her for a long time now. For one thing, she lives too far away; for another, I've been rather busy.
8. used after or before a verb to complement its meaning: 大家來想辦法。Let's try our best and see what to do. 我們合不來。We are not able to get along with each other.
9. a Chinese family name

來比錫(ㄌㄞˊ ㄅㄧˇ ㄒㄧˊ)
Leipzig, a city in the east of Germany

來賓(ㄌㄞˊ ㄅㄧㄣ)
①a guest; a visitor ②name of a county in Kwangsi Province

來賓席(ㄌㄞˊ ㄅㄧㄣ ㄒㄧˊ)
seats for guests

來不及(ㄌㄞˊ ·ㄅㄨ ㄐㄧˊ)
unable to make it in time; not enough time left to do it; too late to do something

來犯(ㄌㄞˊ ㄈㄢˋ)
to come to attack us; to invade our territory: 我們決心消滅膽敢來犯的敵人。We resolutely wipe out any enemy that dares to invade our territory.

來訪(ㄌㄞˊ ㄈㄤˇ)
to come to visit; to come to call

來福槍(ㄌㄞˊ ㄈㄨˊ ㄑㄧㄤ)
a rifle

來附(ㄌㄞˊ ㄈㄨˋ)
to flock to; to submit as vassals

來得(ㄌㄞˊ ·ㄉㄜ)
① to be able to; competent: 我父親很能來得一兩杯。My father is able to drink quite a few cups. ② to act or speak with great force: 他這幾句話來得利害。His words are most telling. ③ to happen; to come: 那些事情來得不巧。Those matters happened at the wrong (or unfortunate) moment. ④ to emerge (from a comparison) as; to come out as

來得及(ㄌㄞˊ ·ㄉㄜ ㄐㄧˊ)
① to be able to make it in time; there is time for…: 趕快走還來得及。Go at once while there's (still) time. ② to be able to accomplish or manage

來到(ㄌㄞˊ ㄉㄠˋ)
to arrive; to come: 雨季來到了。The rainy season has come.

來電(ㄌㄞˊ ㄉㄧㄢˋ)
①an incoming telegram (or telephone); your message: 五月五日來電悉。Your message of May 5 received. ② to telephone; to send a telegram here: 請來電告知。Please telephone me.

來頭(ㄌㄞˊ ·ㄊㄡ)or 來頭兒(ㄌㄞˊ ·ㄊㄡㄦ)
① background; personal connections ② fun in doing anything: 這種遊戲還有什麼來頭兒? What's the fun with this kind of game?

來頭大(ㄌㄞˊ ·ㄊㄡ ㄉㄚˋ)or 來頭不小(ㄌㄞˊ ·ㄊㄡ ㄅㄨˋ ㄒㄧㄠˇ)
of an impressive background, connections, etc.; very influential socially or politically; not to be taken lightly: 他們的來頭不小。They have an impressive background.

來年(ㄌㄞˊ ㄋㄧㄢˊ)
the next year; the years to come

來來往往(ㄌㄞˊ ㄌㄞˊ ㄨㄤˇ ㄨㄤˇ)
coming and going in great numbers

來歷(ㄌㄞˊ ㄌㄧˋ)
past history; origin; background

來歷不明(ㄌㄞˊ ㄌㄧˋ ㄅㄨˋ ㄇㄧㄥˊ)
of questionable antecedents, source, origin, background, etc.: 他的來歷不明。He is a man of obscure origin.

〔人部〕

〔人部〕

來臨(ㄌㄞˊ ㄌㄧㄣˊ)
to arrive; to come; to approach

來路(ㄌㄞˊ ㄌㄨˋ)
① source; origin; (personal) background ② incoming road; approach

來路不正(ㄌㄞˊ ㄌㄨˋ ㄅㄨˋ ㄓㄥˋ)or 來路不明(ㄌㄞˊ ㄌㄨˋ ㄅㄨˋ ㄇㄧㄥˊ)
of questionable origin; of dubious background

來路貨(ㄌㄞˊ ㄌㄨˋ ㄏㄨㄛˋ)
imported goods

來龍去脈(ㄌㄞˊ ㄌㄨㄥˊ ㄑㄩˋ ㄇㄛˋ)
the beginning and subsequent development of (an incident, etc.); cause and effect: 我們必須弄清此事的來龍去脈。We must find out the cause and effect of the incident.

來稿(ㄌㄞˊ ㄍㄠˇ)
(often used by newspaper editors or publishing houses) your manuscript; incoming manuscripts

來客(ㄌㄞˊ ㄎㄜˋ)
a visitor; a guest

來函(ㄌㄞˊ ㄏㄢˊ)or 來信(ㄌㄞˊ ㄒㄧㄣˋ) or 來札(ㄌㄞˊ ㄓㄚˊ)or 來翰(ㄌㄞˊ ㄏㄢˋ)
your letter (to me or us)

來亨鷄(ㄌㄞˊ ㄏㄥ ㄐㄧ)
the Leghorn

來貨(ㄌㄞˊ ㄏㄨㄛˋ)
the goods sent here

來回(ㄌㄞˊ ㄏㄨㄟˊ)
① coming and going; to come and go; back and forth; to and fro: 他在房裏來回走動。He paced to and fro the room. ② to make a return journey

來回票(ㄌㄞˊ ㄏㄨㄟˊ ㄆㄧㄠˋ)
a round-trip ticket

來件(ㄌㄞˊ ㄐㄧㄢˋ)
the communication (or the parcel) received

來勁(ㄌㄞˊ ㄐㄧㄣˋ)
(dialect) ① full of enthusiasm; in high spirits ② exciting; thrilling ③ to annoy; to offend: 你別跟我來勁。Don't offend me.

…來…去(…ㄌㄞˊ …ㄑㄩˋ)
back and forth; over and over again: 鳥飛來飛去。Birds fly back and forth.

來信(ㄌㄞˊ ㄒㄧㄣˋ)
① your letter ② to send a letter here: 到了那裏就請來信。Please write to us as soon as you get there.

來之不易(ㄌㄞˊ ㄓ ㄅㄨˋ ㄧˋ)
It has not come easily. 或 It is hard-earned. 我們的勝利來之不易。Our victory was hard-earned.

來者(ㄌㄞˊ ㄓㄜˇ)
① anything in the future ② anyone who has come

來者不拒(ㄌㄞˊ ㄓㄜˇ ㄅㄨˋ ㄐㄩˋ)
to grant favors to whoever asks for it

來者不善，善者不來(ㄌㄞˊ ㄓㄜˇ ㄅㄨˋ ㄕㄢˋ, ㄕㄢˋ ㄓㄜˇ ㄅㄨˋ ㄌㄞˊ)
Those who have come are surely strong. 或 Those who have come, come with ill intentions.

來者可追(ㄌㄞˊ ㄓㄜˇ ㄎㄜˇ ㄓㄨㄟ)
There is still time to mend.

來世(ㄌㄞˊ ㄕˋ)
① later generations ②(Buddhism) the future life

來勢(ㄌㄞˊ ㄕˋ)
oncoming force: 這場雨來勢很猛。The oncoming force of the rainstorm is violent.

來勢洶洶(ㄌㄞˊ ㄕˋ ㄒㄩㄥ ㄒㄩㄥ)
to move threateningly towards

來沙兒(ㄌㄞˊ ㄕㄚ ㄦˊ)or 來沙爾(ㄌㄞˊ ㄕㄚ ㄦˇ)
(medicine) lysol

來生(ㄌㄞˊ ㄕㄥ)
the future life; the next life or incarnation

來日(ㄌㄞˊ ㄖˋ)
① tomorrow ② the future

來日方長(ㄌㄞˊ ㄖˋ ㄈㄤ ㄔㄤˊ)
There is a long time ahead (so there is no need to be in a hurry).

來人(ㄌㄞˊ ㄖㄣˊ)
① the person or persons who came or are coming ② the incoming envoy, messenger, etc.: 收據請交來人帶回。Please give the receipt to the messenger.

來意(ㄌㄞˊ ㄧˋ)
the purpose of a personal call; the objectives of a visit: 他正想說明來意。He is trying to make clear what he has come for.

來由(ㄌㄞˊ ㄧㄡˊ)
reason; cause (of something or some happening): 我在尋思其來由。I'm trying to find out its cause.

來茵河 or 萊茵河(ㄌㄞˊ ㄧㄣ ㄏㄜˊ)
the Rhine

來文(ㄌㄞˊ ㄨㄣˊ)
incoming documents, letters, etc.; document(s) received

來往(ㄌㄞˊ ㄨㄤˇ)
① social intercourse or connection: 我跟他從未有任何來往。I've never had any intercourse with him. ② coming and going: 街上來往的人很多。There are many people coming and going on the streets.

來往存款(ㄌㄞˊ ㄨㄤˇ ㄘㄨㄣˊ ㄎㄨㄢˇ)
a current account

來月(ㄌㄞˊ ㄩㄝˋ)
the following month; months to come

來源(ㄌㄞˊ ㄩㄢˊ)
the source; the origin

【侈】 150 ㄔˇ chyy chǐ

1. wasteful; luxurious; lavish; extravagant
2. to exaggerate; bragging
3. evildoing
4. excessive

侈靡(ㄔˇ ㄇㄧˊ)
extravagance and excesses; extravagant; wasteful

侈論(ㄔˇ ㄌㄨㄣˋ)or 侈談(ㄔˇ ㄊㄢˊ)
① exaggerated talk ② to speak boastingly; to talk glibly about; to prate about

侈言(ㄔˇ ㄧㄢˊ)
① exaggerated talk ② to exaggerate; to swagger

【例】 151 ㄌㄧˋ lih lì

1. a regulation; a rule; a custom; something with which to compare; a practice: 我的慣例是早餐前散步。My rule is to have a walk before breakfast.
2. a precedent: 你要我做的事有前例可援嗎? Is there a precedent for what you want me to do?
3. an example; an instance

4. regular; routine

例題(ㄌㄧˋ ㄊㄧˊ)
(in a textbook) a question or problem for which an answer or a solution is provided for the student; an example

例規(ㄌㄧˋ ㄍㄨㄟ)
regulations; a usual practice

例話(ㄌㄧˋ ㄏㄨㄚˋ)
systematic exemplification of moral teachings

例會(ㄌㄧˋ ㄏㄨㄟˋ)
a regular meeting

例假(ㄌㄧˋ ㄐㄧㄚˋ)
a statutory holiday; a customary holiday; a legal holiday

例句(ㄌㄧˋ ㄐㄩˋ)
a sentence serving as an example (in a textbook, etc.) to show proper structure, arrangement of words, etc.; an illustrative sentence

例行公事(ㄌㄧˋ ㄒㄧㄥˊ ㄍㄨㄥ ㄕˋ)
official routine; routine: 這些不過是例行公事。These are done as a matter of routine.

例證(ㄌㄧˋ ㄓㄥˋ)
an antecedent used to clarify or explain a point; illustration; a case in point; proof of a given proposition or theorem

例如(ㄌㄧˋ ㄖㄨˊ)
for example; for instance; such as

例子(ㄌㄧˋ ˙ㄗ)
an example; an instance

例言(ㄌㄧˋ ㄧㄢˊ)
an introduction to a book; introductory remarks

例外(ㄌㄧˋ ㄨㄞˋ)
an exception: 每一原則都有一些例外。There is no rule without exception.

【侍】 152 ㄕˋ shyh shì

1. to serve; to wait upon
2. to accompany one's elder or superior
3. a designation for oneself when addressing an elder or a senior
4. an attendant

侍婢(ㄕˋ ㄅㄧˋ)
a personal attendant maid; a maidservant

侍奉(ㄕˋ ㄈㄥˋ)
to serve; to attend on

侍女(ㄕˋ ㄋㄩˇ)
a maid; a maidservant

侍候(ㄕˋ ㄏㄡˋ)
to wait upon; to serve; to attend: 他們是侍候國王的。They were in attendance on the king.

侍妾(ㄕˋ ㄑㄧㄝˋ)
a concubine

侍親(ㄕˋ ㄑㄧㄣ)
to attend one's parents (tenderly and dutifully)

侍者(ㄕˋ ㄓㄜˇ)
① attendants, waiters, etc. ② Buddhist monks — as attendants to Buddha

侍臣(ㄕˋ ㄔㄣˊ)
a courtier

侍從(ㄕˋ ㄗㄨㄥˋ)
attendants; servants; retinue

侍應生(ㄕˋ ㄧㄥˋ ㄕㄥ)
an attendant; a waiter or waitress

侍衛(ㄕˋ ㄨㄟˋ)
bodyguards

【侏】 153 ㄓㄨ ju zhū

1. short
2. a pigmy or dwarf

侏儒(ㄓㄨ ㄖㄨˊ)
① a dwarf ② a court jester

【侑】 154 ㄧㄡˋ yow yòu

1. to help
2. to urge (or press) somebody to eat or drink
3. to repay other's kindness

【侘】 155 ㄔㄚˋ chah chà

1. to boast
2. disappointed

侘傺(ㄔㄚˋ ㄔˋ)
disappointed; frustrated

侘傺不安(ㄔㄚˋ ㄔˋ ㄅㄨˋ ㄢ)
uneasy

【供】 156 1. ㄍㄨㄥ gong gōng

to supply; to contribute to

供不應求(ㄍㄨㄥ ㄅㄨˋ ㄧㄥˋ ㄑㄧㄡˊ)
The supply is unable to meet the demand. 或 The demand exceeds the supply.

供電(ㄍㄨㄥ ㄉㄧㄢˋ)
power supply

供過於求(ㄍㄨㄥ ㄍㄨㄛˋ ㄩˊ ㄑㄧㄡˊ)
The supply has outstripped the demand.

供給(ㄍㄨㄥ ㄐㄧˇ)
to supply; to equip; to provide

供求(ㄍㄨㄥ ㄑㄧㄡˊ)
supply and demand

供求律(ㄍㄨㄥ ㄑㄧㄡˊ ㄌㄩˋ)
the law of supply and demand

供銷(ㄍㄨㄥ ㄒㄧㄠ)
supply and marketing

供應(ㄍㄨㄥ ㄧㄥˋ)
① to supply; to furnish ② supply; support: 他出錢供應我讀書。He gave me financial support for my studies.

【供】 156 2. ㄍㄨㄥˋ gonq gòng

1. to give a statement or an account of a criminal act; to give evidence; to confess: 他供出主犯。He gave the name of the chief culprit.
2. to offer in worship
3. articles of sacrifice; offerings
4. testimony of a prisoner; confession
5. supplies

供品(ㄍㄨㄥˋ ㄆㄧㄣˇ)
offerings

供佛(ㄍㄨㄥˋ ㄈㄛˊ)
to make offerings to Buddha

供奉(ㄍㄨㄥˋ ㄈㄥˋ)
① to provide for one's elders (especially parents) ② to offer sacrifices in worshiping

供職(ㄍㄨㄥˋ ㄓˊ)
to hold office

供桌(ㄍㄨㄥˋ ㄓㄨㄛ)
the table on which sacrificial offerings are placed

供狀(ㄍㄨㄥˋ ㄓㄨㄤˋ)
(law) an affidavit

供認(ㄍㄨㄥˋ ㄖㄣˋ)
to confess; a confession

供詞(ㄍㄨㄥˋ ㄘˊ)
a confession to a criminal act; verbal depositions

供養(ㄍㄨㄥˋ ㄧㄤˇ)
① to offer provisions (especially to one's elders) ② to bring up one's children: 他供養三個小孩。He brought up

〔入部〕

three children. ③ provisions offered to one's elders

【依】 157 ㄧ i yī

1. to depend on; to lean to: 他們倆相依爲命。They depend on each other for existence.
2. to follow; to comply with; to consent; to yield to
3. to be tolerant to; to forgive
4. according to; in the light of; judging by: 依我看來，他會贏。According to my opinion, he will win.

依傍(ㄧ ㄅㄤˋ)
①to depend on ②to pattern after; to imitate ; to model after

依憑(ㄧ ㄆㄧㄥˊ)
to rely on; to depend on

依法(ㄧ ㄈㄚˇ)
according to law

依附(ㄧ ㄈㄨˋ)
①to depend on ②to submit to

依託(ㄧ ㄊㄨㄛ)
to trust; to depend on

依賴(ㄧ ㄌㄞˋ)
to depend on

依賴性(ㄧ ㄌㄞˋ ㄒㄧㄥˋ)
the habit of relying upon others

依留申(ㄧ ㄌㄧㄡˊ ㄕㄣ)
Ilyushin (a type of Russian planes)

依戀(ㄧ ㄌㄧㄢˋ)
to be reluctant to leave; to feel attachment to someone

依靠(ㄧ ㄎㄠˋ)
①to rely on; to depend on: 他依靠自己的力量。He depends on his own strength. ②someone or something to fall back on; support; backing: 他尋找依靠。He seeks support.

依舊(ㄧ ㄐㄧㄡˋ)
as usual; as before; in the usual way or manner

依據(ㄧ ㄐㄩˋ)
①according to; in accordance with; on the strength of; based on ②a basis; foundation: 當時我們沒有任何遵循的依據。We didn't have any basis to go by at that time.

依稀(ㄧ ㄒㄧ)
unclear; uncertain; not distinct

依照(ㄧ ㄓㄠˋ)
in accordance with; in compliance with

依仗(ㄧ ㄓㄤˋ)
①someone or something to fall back upon ②to rely on or count on (influence, wealth, etc.): 他依仗權勢。He relies on his power and position.

依順(ㄧ ㄕㄨㄣˋ)
to be obedient

依然(ㄧ ㄖㄢˊ)
as before; as usual; still

依然故我(ㄧ ㄖㄢˊ ㄍㄨˋ ㄨㄛˇ)
I am still what I used to be.

依然如故(ㄧ ㄖㄢˊ ㄖㄨˊ ㄍㄨˋ)
to remain as before; to remain unchanged (as usual)

依此類推(ㄧ ㄘˇ ㄌㄟˋ ㄊㄨㄟ)
The rest may be deduced by analogy. 或 and so on; and so forth

依次(ㄧ ㄘˋ)
in order (in proper sequence or position); one by one

依存(ㄧ ㄘㄨㄣˊ)
interdependent; to depend on somebody or something for existence: 他們相互依存。They are interdependent.

依從(ㄧ ㄘㄨㄥˊ)
to comply with; to follow; to submit or listen to (suggestion, etc.)

依隨(ㄧ ㄙㄨㄟˊ)
to follow (a person, a wish); to comply with

依依不捨(ㄧ ㄧ ㄅㄨˋ ㄕㄜˇ)
unwilling to part (with the loved ones): 他們依依不捨。They are unwilling to part with each other.

依樣(畫)葫蘆(ㄧ ㄧㄤˋ (ㄏㄨㄚˋ) ㄏㄨˊ ㄌㄨˊ)
to imitate others or to follow the beaten path without questioning; to copy mechanically

依違兩可(ㄧ ㄨㄟˊ ㄌㄧㄤˇ ㄎㄜˇ)
shilly-shally; to be undecided; to be unable to make up one's mind

依約(ㄧ ㄩㄝ)
①to follow conventions and traditions ②indistinct; obscure ③in accordance with the promise

【佬】 158 ㄌㄠˇ lao lǎo

1. a fellow; a man; a guy
2. a vulgar person; a hillbilly

七畫

【侮】 159 ㄨˇ wuu wǔ

1. to bully
2. to disgrace; to insult; to humiliate
3. an insult; a bully

侮罵(ㄨˇ ㄇㄚˋ)
to insult with words

侮慢(ㄨˇ ㄇㄢˋ)
①to insult ②haughty and rude

侮蔑(ㄨˇ ㄇㄧㄝˋ)
to disgrace; to slight

侮弄(ㄨˇ ㄋㄨㄥˋ)
to make a fool of

侮辱(ㄨˇ ㄖㄨˋ)
to insult; to humiliate; an insult

【侯】 160 ㄏㄡˊ hour hóu

1. (in ancient China) the second of the five grades of the nobility
2. the target in archery
3. a marquis; a nobleman or a high official
4. a Chinese family name

侯門如海(ㄏㄡˊ ㄇㄣˊ ㄖㄨˊ ㄏㄞˇ)
①(said of women of humble origin married to the nobility) Once inside the marquis's door there's no turning back. ②A rich man's mansion is inaccessible to the common people.

侯國(ㄏㄡˊ ㄍㄨㄛˊ)
a principality

侯爵(ㄏㄡˊ ㄐㄩㄝˊ)
a marquis

侯爵夫人(ㄏㄡˊ ㄐㄩㄝˊ ㄈㄨ ㄖㄣˊ)
a marchioness

【侶】 161 ㄌㄩˇ leu lǚ

1. a companion; a mate
2. to associate with

【侵】 162 ㄑㄧㄣ chin qīn

1. to raid; to aggress; to

invade: 敵人侵略我們的國家。The enemy invaded our country.
2. to encroach upon; to use force stealthily
3. to proceed gradually
4. a bad year; a year of famine or disaster

侵犯(ㄑㄧㄣ ㄈㄢˋ)
(law) to encroach upon other's rights; to violate; to invade; to infringe upon (rights)

侵奪(ㄑㄧㄣ ㄉㄨㄛˊ)
to seize by force

侵吞(ㄑㄧㄣ ㄊㄨㄣ)
to misappropriate (public funds, etc. for private ends); to embezzle; to take by illegal means; to annex: 貪官侵吞公款。Corrupt officials embezzle public funds.

侵陵(ㄑㄧㄣ ㄌㄧㄥˊ)
to raid and humiliate; to intimidate

侵略(ㄑㄧㄣ ㄌㄩㄝˋ)
①to invade ②aggression; encroachment

侵掠(ㄑㄧㄣ ㄌㄩㄝˋ)
to invade; to harass and loot

侵害(ㄑㄧㄣ ㄏㄞˋ)
to infringe or encroach upon (the rights, etc. of another); to violate

侵襲(ㄑㄧㄣ ㄒㄧˊ)
to attack stealthily; to make a sneaking attack on; to encroach upon

侵佔 or 侵占(ㄑㄧㄣ ㄓㄢˋ)
to occupy or take (the land, the property, etc. of another) illegally; misappropriation; to seize

侵佔罪 or 侵占罪(ㄑㄧㄣ ㄓㄢˋ ㄗㄨㄟˋ)
(law) an offense of misappropriation; embezzlement

侵晨(ㄑㄧㄣ ㄔㄣˊ)
early morning

侵蝕(ㄑㄧㄣ ㄕˊ)
erosion; to encroach; to erode; to eat into gradually: 土壤侵蝕 soil erosion

侵擾(ㄑㄧㄣ ㄖㄠˇ)
to trespass and cause disorder or trouble; to harass

侵人犯規(ㄑㄧㄣ ㄖㄣˊ ㄈㄢˋ ㄍㄨㄟ)
(sports) a personal foul

侵入(ㄑㄧㄣ ㄖㄨˋ)
to intrude; to invade; to make incursions into: 他們侵入別國領土。They intruded into another country's territory.

【侷】 163
ㄐㄩˊ jyu jú

narrow; cramped; confined

侷處一隅(ㄐㄩˊ ㄔㄨˇ ㄧ ㄩˊ)
to be confined to a small place or corner

侷促(ㄐㄩˊ ㄘㄨˋ)
①cramped; confined ②fidgeting; restless

侷促不安(ㄐㄩˊ ㄘㄨˋ ㄅㄨˋ ㄢ)
restless; fidgeting; nervous; uneasy

【便】 164
1. ㄅㄧㄢˋ biann biàn

1. expedient; convenient; handy: 這本字典便於帶在口袋中。This dictionary is convenient for carrying in one's pocket.
2. fitting; appropriate
3. in that case; even if: 便有不是，也得原諒他。Even if he is wrong, you shall forgive him.
4. then: 你不去，他便得去。If you do not go, then he has to.
5. advantageous
6. excrement and urine; to relieve oneself
7. informal; at ease; plain; ordinary

便步(ㄅㄧㄢˋ ㄅㄨˋ)
(military drill) to walk at ease as contrasted to goose stepping

便帽(ㄅㄧㄢˋ ㄇㄠˋ) or 便帽兒(ㄅㄧㄢˋ ㄇㄠˋㄦ)
a cap or hat for ordinary wear

便門(ㄅㄧㄢˋ ㄇㄣˊ) or 便門兒(ㄅㄧㄢˋ ㄇㄜˊㄦ)
a side door; a wicket

便祕(ㄅㄧㄢˋ ㄇㄧˋ)
constipation

便民(ㄅㄧㄢˋ ㄇㄧㄣˊ)
to offer greater convenience to the people (by reducing red tape)

便飯(ㄅㄧㄢˋ ㄈㄢˋ)
a meal; potluck; an ordinary meal (as distinguished from a feast); a simple meal

便服(ㄅㄧㄢˋ ㄈㄨˊ)
ordinary clothing; everyday dress; informal dress

便道(ㄅㄧㄢˋ ㄉㄠˋ)
①a shortcut; a snap course ②sidewalks; paths flanking the main road ③to do something on the way

便當
①(ㄅㄧㄢˋ ㄉㄤ) a box lunch one takes to school, office, etc. in the morning
②(ㄅㄧㄢˋ ˙ㄉㄤ) easy; convenient

便條(ㄅㄧㄢˋ ㄊㄧㄠˊ) or 便條兒(ㄅㄧㄢˋ ㄊㄧㄠˊㄦ)
a note; a memo; an informal letter, etc.

便桶(ㄅㄧㄢˋ ㄊㄨㄥˇ)
a deep container for emptying the bowels; a pail for stool

便溺(ㄅㄧㄢˋ ㄋㄧˋ)
to empty the bowels and to urinate

便覽(ㄅㄧㄢˋ ㄌㄢˇ)
a pocket-size book or pamphlet for convenient reading

便利(ㄅㄧㄢˋ ㄌㄧˋ)
convenience; expediency; facility; convenient; expedient

便了(ㄅㄧㄢˋ ㄌㄧㄠˇ)
an expletive used at the end of a sentence (usually found in songs): 這樣做去便了。Just do it like this.

便路(ㄅㄧㄢˋ ㄌㄨˋ)
a shortcut; a bypath

便函(ㄅㄧㄢˋ ㄏㄢˊ)
an informal letter

便壺(ㄅㄧㄢˋ ㄏㄨˊ)
a night-pot for urination; a chamber pot

便捷(ㄅㄧㄢˋ ㄐㄧㄝˊ)
easy and convenient; convenience; facility

便箋(ㄅㄧㄢˋ ㄐㄧㄢ)
notepaper; a memo; a memo pad

便徑(ㄅㄧㄢˋ ㄐㄧㄥˋ)
a quick route; a shortcut

便橋(ㄅㄧㄢˋ ㄑㄧㄠˊ)
a temporary bridge; a makeshift bridge

便鞋(ㄅㄧㄢˋ ㄒㄧㄝˊ)
①cloth shoes ②slippers

便酌(ㄅㄧㄢˋ ㄓㄨㄛˊ)

an informal feast; an informal dinner
便中(ㄅㄧㄢˋ ㄓㄨㄥ)
at (your) convenience
便池(ㄅㄧㄢˋ ㄔˊ)
a urinal
便士(ㄅㄧㄢˋ ㄕˋ)
penny
便菜(ㄅㄧㄢˋ ㄘㄞˋ)
an ordinary dish; an everyday dish
便餐(ㄅㄧㄢˋ ㄘㄢ)
an informal and ordinary meal
便所(ㄅㄧㄢˋ ㄙㄨㄛˇ)
a toilet; a lavatory; a privy; a rest room
便衣(ㄅㄧㄢˋ ㄧ)
① ordinary clothes; plain clothes ② a plainclothesman
便宜行事(ㄅㄧㄢˋ ㄧˊ ㄒㄧㄥˊ ㄕˋ)
to act as circumstances may require without asking for approval from superiors
便於(ㄅㄧㄢˋ ㄩˊ)
easy to; convenient for

〔人部〕

【便】 164
2. ㄆㄧㄢˊ pyan pián
1. cheap; inexpensive
2. a Chinese family name
便嬖(ㄆㄧㄢˊ ㄅㄧˋ)
a sycophant
便辟(ㄆㄧㄢˊ ㄆㄧˋ)
a man of specious airs
便佞(ㄆㄧㄢˊ ㄋㄧㄥˋ)
a glib-tongued man
便宜(ㄆㄧㄢˊ ·ㄧ)
① cheap; inexpensive ② to gain advantage ③ advantage; profit ④ to let someone off lightly

【係】 165
ㄒㄧˋ shih xì
1. to bind; to belong to; to attach to; to connect with
2. relationship; consequences
3. to be
4. a Chinese family name
係數(ㄒㄧˋ ㄕㄨˋ)
(mathematics) coefficient

【促】 166
ㄘㄨˋ tsuh cù
1. close; crowded; near
2. to urge; to hurry; to promote
3. hurried; urgent
促迫(ㄘㄨˋ ㄆㄛˋ)
to urge; to hurry; pressing
促忙(ㄘㄨˋ ㄇㄤˊ)
in a hurry
促進(ㄘㄨˋ ㄐㄧㄣˋ)
to urge to proceed; to press forward; to promote; promotion
促膝談心(ㄘㄨˋ ㄒㄧ ㄊㄢˊ ㄒㄧㄣ)
to talk intimately; to have a heart-to-heart talk; to cross the knees and talk over things as close friends; to sit side by side and talk intimately
促狹鬼(ㄘㄨˋ ㄒㄧㄚˊ ㄍㄨㄟˇ)
a mischievous fellow; a person who likes to play jokes on others; a practical joker; a mean and spiteful fellow
促銷(ㄘㄨˋ ㄒㄧㄠ)
sales promotion
促織(ㄘㄨˋ ㄓ)
another name for the cricket
促成(ㄘㄨˋ ㄔㄥˊ)
to help to materialize; to help to bring about
促使(ㄘㄨˋ ㄕˇ)
to impel; to urge; to spur

【俄】 167
1. ㄜˊ er é
suddenly; sudden; momentarily
俄頃(ㄜˊ ㄑㄧㄥˇ)
shortly afterward; soon; in a short moment; momentarily
俄而(ㄜˊ ㄦˊ)
suddenly; soon

【俄】 167
2. ㄜˋ eh è
俄勒岡(ㄜˋ ㄌㄜˋ ㄍㄤ)
Oregon, U. S. A.
俄羅斯族(ㄜˋ ㄌㄨㄛˊ ㄙ ㄗㄨˊ)
① the Eluosi (Russian) nationality ② the Russians (of the U.S.S.R.)
俄國(ㄜˋ ㄍㄨㄛˊ) or 俄羅斯(ㄜˋ ㄌㄨㄛˊ ㄙ)
Russia
俄國的(ㄜˋ ㄍㄨㄛˊ ·ㄉㄜ)
Russian
俄(國)人(ㄜˋ (ㄍㄨㄛˊ) ㄖㄣˊ)
a Russian
俄亥俄(ㄜˋ ㄏㄞˋ ㄜˋ)
Ohio, U. S. A.
俄語(ㄜˋ ㄩˇ) or 俄文(ㄜˋ ㄨㄣˊ)
Russian (language)

【俊】 168
ㄐㄩㄣˋ jiunn jùn
1. talented; capable; superior; refined; smart; bright
2. handsome; good-looking
3. big; huge
俊拔(ㄐㄩㄣˋ ㄅㄚˊ)
uncommon
俊邁(ㄐㄩㄣˋ ㄇㄞˋ)
excelling in grace and elegance
俊美(ㄐㄩㄣˋ ㄇㄟˇ)
good-looking; handsome
俊傑(ㄐㄩㄣˋ ㄐㄧㄝˊ)
a brave and superior person; a person of extraordinary talent; an individual of distinction and mark
俊俏(ㄐㄩㄣˋ ㄑㄧㄠˋ)
elegant; graceful; good-looking and smart; lovely; charming
俊秀(ㄐㄩㄣˋ ㄒㄧㄡˋ)
talented and superior; handsome and refined
俊才(ㄐㄩㄣˋ ㄘㄞˊ)
a talented person
俊雅(ㄐㄩㄣˋ ㄧㄚˇ)
handsome, elegant and refined
俊偉(ㄐㄩㄣˋ ㄨㄟˇ)
superior and great

【俎】 169
ㄗㄨˇ tzuu zǔ
1. a painted wooden stand used in offering rites
2. a chopping board
3. a small table or stand
4. a Chinese family name
俎豆(ㄗㄨˇ ㄉㄡˋ)
sacrificial stand and pot —sacrificial rites
俎上肉(ㄗㄨˇ ㄕㄤˋ ㄖㄡˋ)
(literally) meat on a chopping board—a helpless victim

【俏】 170
ㄑㄧㄠˋ chiaw qiào
1. like; similar; to resemble; to be like
2. pretty and cute; good-looking; smart; handsome: 她是位俏女郎。She is a pretty girl.
3. (commodities) enjoying brisk sale at higher prices; in great demand
4. (said of stocks) bullish

俏皮(ㄑㄧㄠˋ·ㄆㄧ)
①pretty and cute; winsome: 他年輕又俏皮。He is young and winsome. ②sarcastic; witty; to make sarcastic remarks at

俏皮話(ㄑㄧㄠˋ·ㄆㄧ ㄏㄨㄚˋ)
a wisecrack; a jibe; a clever retort; a witty remark; a sarcastic remark

俏麗(ㄑㄧㄠˋ ㄌㄧˋ)
beautiful; good-looking

俏似(ㄑㄧㄠˋ ㄙˋ)
to resemble; to be like: 人生俏似一場夢。Life is just like a dream.

俏冤家(ㄑㄧㄠˋ ㄩㄢ ·ㄐㄧㄚ)
(my) pretty but naughty lover

【俐】 171 ㄌㄧˋ lih lì

1. facile; easy and quick
2. sharp; clever
3. in good order; tidy; neat

俐落(ㄌㄧˋ ㄌㄨㄛˋ)
well-executed 亦作「利落」

【俑】 172 ㄩㄥˇ yeong yǒng

(in ancient China) wooden or earthen figures of men and women buried with the dead; a tomb figure; a figurine

【俗】 173 ㄙㄨˊ swu sú

1. customs or customary
2. vulgar; unrefined
3. common; popular
4. lay (as distinguished from clerical); worldly; secular
5. tasteless; trite

俗不可耐(ㄙㄨˊ ㄅㄨˋ ㄎㄜˇ ㄋㄞˋ)
unbearably vulgar

俗民文化(ㄙㄨˊ ㄇㄧㄣˊ ㄨㄣˊ ㄏㄨㄚˋ)
folk culture

俗套(ㄙㄨˊ ㄊㄠˋ)
social conventions; conventional patterns

俗念(ㄙㄨˊ ㄋㄧㄢˋ)
worldly thoughts; a layman's ideas

俗累(ㄙㄨˊ ㄌㄟˋ)
worldly troubles

俗例兒(ㄙㄨˊ ㄌㄧㄦˋ)
common practices; customary rules

俗流(ㄙㄨˊ ㄌㄧㄡˊ)
the common lot of people; the layman

俗骨(ㄙㄨˊ ㄍㄨˇ)
(a self-depreciatory expression) vulgar to the bone; vulgar bones

俗話(ㄙㄨˊ ㄏㄨㄚˋ)
a common saying; a proverb: 俗話說時間就是金錢。A proverb says that time is money.

俗家(ㄙㄨˊ ㄐㄧㄚ)
① the layman; the common lot of people ② the home of a monk or nun before taking the tonsure

俗氣(ㄙㄨˊ ·ㄑㄧ)
① vulgarity; vulgar; in poor taste ② hackneyed

俗稱(ㄙㄨˊ ㄔㄥ)
① the secular name of a monk, etc. before consecration ② commonly called…; commonly known as…

俗事(ㄙㄨˊ ㄕˋ)or 俗事兒(ㄙㄨˊ ㄕㄜˋㄦ)
mundane affairs; everyday matters; daily routine; worldly affairs

俗世(ㄙㄨˊ ㄕˋ)
earthly life

俗尚(ㄙㄨˊ ㄕㄤˋ)
customs; customary; common beliefs; common conventions; the current

俗人(ㄙㄨˊ ㄖㄣˊ)
① a layman as opposed to the clergy ② an ordinary person; a vulgarian

俗儒(ㄙㄨˊ ㄖㄨˊ)
a scholar of shallow learning

俗字(ㄙㄨˊ ㄗˋ)
① a non-classical word; a vulgar word ② the popular or simplified form of a Chinese character

俗眼(ㄙㄨˊ ㄧㄢˇ)
(in) the eyes of a commoner, layman, ordinary person, etc.; mortal eyes

俗諺(ㄙㄨˊ ㄧㄢˋ)
a common saying; a popular saying; a proverb 參看「俗語」

俗物(ㄙㄨˊ ㄨˋ)
unrefined persons or things; philistines; a vulgar

俗務(ㄙㄨˊ ㄨˋ)
chores; routines; everyday matters or business; worldly cares

俗謂(ㄙㄨˊ ㄨㄟˋ)
There is a common saying....

俗文學(ㄙㄨˊ ㄨㄣˊ ㄒㄩㄝˊ)
popular literature (ballads, songs, novels, etc.)

俗緣(ㄙㄨˊ ㄩㄢˊ)
worldly relations, ties, obligations, etc. (of a Buddhist monk or nun)

【俘】 174 ㄈㄨˊ fwu fú

1. prisoners of war
2. to capture; to take prisoner: 首領已被俘。The chief was captured.

俘虜(ㄈㄨˊ ㄌㄨˇ)
① to take prisoner: 他被敵人俘虜。He was taken prisoner by the enemy. ② a prisoner of war

俘虜營(ㄈㄨˊ ㄌㄨˇ ㄧㄥˊ)
a concentration camp for prisoners of war

俘獲(ㄈㄨˊ ㄏㄨㄛˋ)
to capture (weapons, documents, etc. from the enemy)

【俚】 175 ㄌㄧˇ lii lǐ

1. vulgar; rustic; unpolished; unrefined
2. a small town or village; a tribe (aborigines, etc.)

俚歌(ㄌㄧˇ ㄍㄜ)
folk songs; country songs

俚俗(ㄌㄧˇ ㄙㄨˊ)
vulgar; unrefined

俚語(ㄌㄧˇ ㄩˇ)
slang; rustic expressions; vulgar expressions

【保】 176 ㄅㄠˇ bao bǎo

1. to guard; to shelter; to protect; to defend: 英勇的軍人保家衛國。Brave soldiers protect our homes and defend our country.
2. to be responsible; to guarantee; to insure
3. a waiter or tender
4. to care for
5. to keep; to maintain
6. to stand guarantor or surety for someone: 我爲他作保。I stand guarantor for him.
7. an official post in ancient

〔人部〕

China

保鏢(ㄅㄠˇ ㄅㄧㄠ)
①a bodyguard; an armed escort (for passengers or cargo) ②to act as a bodyguard

保不住(ㄅㄠˇ ˙ㄅㄨ ㄓㄨˋ)
①cannot be defended ②most likely; more likely than not; may well: 保不住明天會下雨。Most likely it's going to rain tomorrow.

保密(ㄅㄠˇ ㄇㄧˋ)
to keep the secret

保密防諜(ㄅㄠˇ ㄇㄧˋ ㄈㄤˊ ㄉㄧㄝˊ)
to keep the secret and prevent espionage

保姆(ㄅㄠˇ ㄇㄨˇ)
a nurse who looks after small children

保防工作(ㄅㄠˇ ㄈㄤˊ ㄍㄨㄥ ㄗㄨㄛˋ)
security measures

保單(ㄅㄠˇ ㄉㄢ)
①a formal note or document of guaranty ②an insurance policy

保定(ㄅㄠˇ ㄉㄧㄥˋ)
Paoting, a city in Hopeh Province

保留(ㄅㄠˇ ㄌㄧㄡˊ)
①to preserve; to reserve; with reservations; to hold back: 他無保留地同意。He agreed without reservation. ②to defer discussion for the future

保留地(ㄅㄠˇ ㄌㄧㄡˊ ㄉㄧˋ)
①the land reserved for a certain purpose ②a reservation (as the territory set apart for a certain class of people, like aborigines)

保齡球(ㄅㄠˇ ㄌㄧㄥˊ ㄑㄧㄡˊ)
bowling

保齡球場(ㄅㄠˇ ㄌㄧㄥˊ ㄑㄧㄡˊ ㄔㄤˇ)or (ㄅㄠˇ ㄌㄧㄥˊ ㄑㄧㄡˊ ㄔㄤˊ)
a building or enclosed area containing a number of bowling alleys

保羅(ㄅㄠˇ ㄌㄨㄛˊ)
a transliteration of Paul

保管(ㄅㄠˇ ㄍㄨㄢˇ)
①to safeguard; to safekeep; to put something under one's custody ②certainly; surely

保管費(ㄅㄠˇ ㄍㄨㄢˇ ㄈㄟˋ)
storage charges

保管室(ㄅㄠˇ ㄍㄨㄢˇ ㄕˋ)
a storeroom

保護(ㄅㄠˇ ㄏㄨˋ)
to protect; to guard; protection: 我們應保護環境防止污染。We should protect the environment against pollution.

保護貿易政策(ㄅㄠˇ ㄏㄨˋ ㄇㄠˋ ㄧˋ ㄓㄥˋ ㄘㄜˋ)
the policy of protection

保護國(ㄅㄠˇ ㄏㄨˋ ㄍㄨㄛˊ)
a protectorate

保護(關)稅(ㄅㄠˇ ㄏㄨˋ (ㄍㄨㄢ) ㄕㄨㄟˋ)
a protective tariff

保護區 (ㄅㄠˇ ㄏㄨˋ ㄑㄩ)
a protected area

保護主義(ㄅㄠˇ ㄏㄨˋ ㄓㄨˇ ㄧˋ)
protectionism

保護人(ㄅㄠˇ ㄏㄨˋ ㄖㄣˊ)
a guardian

保護組織(ㄅㄠˇ ㄏㄨˋ ㄗㄨˇ ㄓ)
(biology) protected tissue

保護色(ㄅㄠˇ ㄏㄨˋ ㄙㄜˋ)
protective coloration

保皇黨(ㄅㄠˇ ㄏㄨㄤˊ ㄉㄤˇ)
The Royalist Party

保加利亞(ㄅㄠˇ ㄐㄧㄚ ㄌㄧˋ ㄧㄚˋ)
Bulgaria

保家衛國(ㄅㄠˇ ㄐㄧㄚ ㄨㄟˋ ㄍㄨㄛˊ)
to defend the home and the country

保甲(ㄅㄠˇ ㄐㄧㄚˇ)
the Tithing System, devised by Prime Minister Wang An-shih (1021-1086) of the Sung Dynasty to maintain internal security and strengthen national defense

保駕(ㄅㄠˇ ㄐㄧㄚˋ)
①to protect or escort the royalty ②to protect an important person, guest, etc.

保結(ㄅㄠˇ ㄐㄧㄝˊ)
a document signed by one to the authorities to prove or guarantee the identity or good conduct of another person

保薦(ㄅㄠˇ ㄐㄧㄢˋ)
to recommend (somebody for a job, etc.)

保健(ㄅㄠˇ ㄐㄧㄢˋ)
health protection; health care

保健館(ㄅㄠˇ ㄐㄧㄢˋ ㄍㄨㄢˇ)
①a health center ②a gymnasium

保健工作(ㄅㄠˇ ㄐㄧㄢˋ ㄍㄨㄥ ㄗㄨㄛˋ)
public health work

保健箱(ㄅㄠˇ ㄐㄧㄢˋ ㄒㄧㄤ)
a medical kit

保健站(ㄅㄠˇ ㄐㄧㄢˋ ㄓㄢˋ)
a health station (or center)

保全(ㄅㄠˇ ㄑㄩㄢˊ)
to assure the safety of

保全公司(ㄅㄠˇ ㄑㄩㄢˊ ㄍㄨㄥ ㄙ)
a company that offers protection of life and property by rendering such services as guards, patrols and burglar alarms

保修(ㄅㄠˇ ㄒㄧㄡ)
to guarantee to keep something in good repair: 這台收音機保修一年。This radio is guaranteed in good repair for a year.

保險(ㄅㄠˇ ㄒㄧㄢˇ)
①insurance ②to guarantee ③a protective device, especially on a firearm, to prevent accidental discharge ④safe: 開快車可不保險。It's not safe to drive too fast.

保險費(ㄅㄠˇ ㄒㄧㄢˇ ㄈㄟˋ)
the premium of an insurance policy; insurance premiums

保險帶(ㄅㄠˇ ㄒㄧㄢˇ ㄉㄞˋ)
a safety belt 亦作「安全帶」

保險單(ㄅㄠˇ ㄒㄧㄢˇ ㄉㄢ)
an insurance policy

保險套(ㄅㄠˇ ㄒㄧㄢˇ ㄊㄠˋ)
a condom; a sheath

保險槓(ㄅㄠˇ ㄒㄧㄢˇ ㄍㄤˋ)
a bumper (of an automobile)

保險公司(ㄅㄠˇ ㄒㄧㄢˇ ㄍㄨㄥ ㄙ)
an insurance company

保險開關(ㄅㄠˇ ㄒㄧㄢˇ ㄎㄞ ㄍㄨㄢ)
a cut-out switch

保險活門(ㄅㄠˇ ㄒㄧㄢˇ ㄏㄨㄛˊ ㄇㄣˊ)
a safety valve

保險基金(ㄅㄠˇ ㄒㄧㄢˇ ㄐㄧ ㄐㄧㄣ)
an insurance fund

保險金額(ㄅㄠˇ ㄒㄧㄢˇ ㄐㄧㄣ ㄜˊ)
amount insured

保險箱(ㄅㄠˇ ㄒㄧㄢˇ ㄒㄧㄤ)
a safe; a strongbox; a bank's vault

保險事業(ㄅㄠˇ ㄒㄧㄢˇ ㄕˋ ㄧㄝˋ)
insurance business

保險人(ㄅㄠˇ ㄒㄧㄢˇ ㄖㄣˊ)
an insurer; an underwriter

保險絲(ㄅㄠˇ ㄒㄧㄢˇ ㄙ)
a fuse wire

保值(ㄅㄠˇ ㄓˊ)
to preserve the value (of currency)

保障(ㄅㄠˇ ㄓㄤˋ)
to safeguard; to protect; to ensure; to guarantee: 憲法保障人民的言論自由。 The constitution guarantees people's freedom of speech.

保證(ㄅㄠˇ ㄓㄥˋ)
to guarantee; to assure; to assume full responsibility for another person's financial undertaking, etc.; a guaranty

保證金(ㄅㄠˇ ㄓㄥˋ ㄐㄧㄣ)
security deposit; guaranty money

保證書(ㄅㄠˇ ㄓㄥˋ ㄕㄨ)
a deed of security; a letter of guaranty

保證人(ㄅㄠˇ ㄓㄥˋ ㄖㄣˊ)
a guarantor; a guarantee

保重(ㄅㄠˇ ㄓㄨㄥˋ)
(usually used at the end of a letter or when parting) Please take good care (of yourself).

保持(ㄅㄠˇ ㄔˊ)
to maintain; to keep: 這兩國保持友好關係。The two countries maintain friendly relations.

保持現場(ㄅㄠˇ ㄔˊ ㄒㄧㄢˋ ㄔㄤˇ)
to preserve the scene of a crime

保釋(ㄅㄠˇ ㄕˋ)
to release on bail: 他被捕不到十小時就被保釋出來。He was released on bail within ten hours of his arrest.

保釋金(ㄅㄠˇ ㄕˋ ㄐㄧㄣ)
bail

保守(ㄅㄠˇ ㄕㄡˇ)
① conservative: 老年人通常比年輕人保守。Old people are usually more conservative than young people. ② to keep; to guard

保守派(ㄅㄠˇ ㄕㄡˇ ㄆㄞˋ)
an Old Guard 亦作「守舊元老」

保守黨(ㄅㄠˇ ㄕㄡˇ ㄉㄤˇ)
The Conservative Party

保守主義(ㄅㄠˇ ㄕㄡˇ ㄓㄨˇ ㄧˋ)
conservatism

保身(ㄅㄠˇ ㄕㄣ)
to save one's own skin

保稅倉庫(ㄅㄠˇ ㄕㄨㄟˋ ㄘㄤ ㄎㄨˋ)
a bonded godown

保人(ㄅㄠˇ ㄖㄣˊ)
a guarantor

保存(ㄅㄠˇ ㄘㄨㄣˊ)
① to safeguard; safekeeping ② to maintain; to preserve: 這批古畫保存很完整。These ancient paintings are well preserved.

保存期限(ㄅㄠˇ ㄘㄨㄣˊ ㄑㄧˊ ㄒㄧㄢˋ)
① the shelf life of a commodity ② the period for keeping official papers on file

保送(ㄅㄠˇ ㄙㄨㄥˋ)
① to send a student to school or college without an entrance examination, usually for his high scholastic qualifications ② (baseball) to walk; a walk; bases on balls

保安(ㄅㄠˇ ㄢ)
① to ensure local security ② to ensure the workers' safety ③ public security

保安隊(ㄅㄠˇ ㄢ ㄉㄨㄟˋ)
a public security corps, etc.; a unit of public security policemen

保安林(ㄅㄠˇ ㄢ ㄌㄧㄣˊ)
a shelter forest

保安處分(ㄅㄠˇ ㄢ ㄔㄨˇ ㄈㄣˋ)
(law) Peace Preservation Measures

保安人員(ㄅㄠˇ ㄢ ㄖㄣˊ ㄩㄢˊ)
security personnel

保安措施(ㄅㄠˇ ㄢ ㄘㄨㄛˋ ㄕ)
security measures

保有(ㄅㄠˇ ㄧㄡˇ)
possession

保佑(ㄅㄠˇ ㄧㄡˋ)
① to protect or bless ② a blessing

保養(ㄅㄠˇ ㄧㄤˇ)
① maintenance (of a car, ship, etc.) ② to take care (of health) ③ to maintain; to keep in good repair

保養費(ㄅㄠˇ ㄧㄤˇ ㄈㄟˋ)
maintenance cost; upkeep

保衛(ㄅㄠˇ ㄨㄟˋ)
to defend; to guard against

保溫(ㄅㄠˇ ㄨㄣ)
① heat preservation ② to preserve heat; to keep (water, etc.) hot

保溫杯(ㄅㄠˇ ㄨㄣ ㄅㄟ)
a thermos cup or container

保育(ㄅㄠˇ ㄩˋ)
to raise (a kid)

保育院(ㄅㄠˇ ㄩˋ ㄩㄢˋ)
① a nursery ② an orphanage

【俟】 177 ㄙˋ syh sì

1. to wait for; to await
2. until; as soon as

俟候(ㄙˋ ㄏㄡˋ)
to wait for

俟駕(ㄙˋ ㄐㄧㄚˋ)
① to wait for the emperor's arrival ② to wait for your arrival

俟時(ㄙˋ ㄕˊ)
to wait for an opportunity

【俠】 178 ㄒㄧㄚˊ shya xiá

1. a person adept in martial arts and dedicated to helping the poor and weak; one who fights rather than submit to injustice
2. chivalry
3. a Chinese family name

俠盜(ㄒㄧㄚˊ ㄉㄠˋ)
a robber, burglar, bandit, etc. who robs the rich only to help the poor

俠烈(ㄒㄧㄚˊ ㄌㄧㄝˋ)
chivalrous

俠骨(ㄒㄧㄚˊ ㄍㄨˇ)
chivalrous spirit

俠客(ㄒㄧㄚˊ ㄎㄜˋ)or 俠士(ㄒㄧㄚˊ ㄕˋ)
a person dedicated to the cause of justice, fairness, etc. by fighting for the poor and the oppressed; a man who has a strong sense of justice

俠氣(ㄒㄧㄚˊ ㄑㄧˋ)
chivalry

俠義(ㄒㄧㄚˊ ㄧˋ)
chivalry; honor and gallantry; a strong sense of justice

【信】 179 ㄒㄧㄣˋ shinn xìn

1. honesty; truthfulness; faith;

confidence; trust: 政府應取信於民。The government should win the people's confidence (or trust).
2. believing; true
3. to believe or trust
4. an envoy; an emissary; a messenger
5. news; a message; information; word
6. a letter; mail
7. credentials; evidence; a pledge; a token; a sign
8. to let (others do what they choose); free; easy; aimless; at will; at random; without a plan
9. regular periodical appearance

信筆(ㄒㄧㄣˋ ㄅㄧˇ)
to write without much thought; to write freely or aimlessly

信步(ㄒㄧㄣˋ ㄅㄨˋ)
to wander; to stroll aimlessly: 他信步街頭。He wandered the streets.

信不過(ㄒㄧㄣˋ ·ㄅㄨ ㄍㄨㄛˋ)
incredible; to have no trust in

信馬由韁(ㄒㄧㄣˋ ㄇㄚˇ ㄧㄡˊ ㄐㄧㄤ)
to give free rein to (imagination, etc.); to have no fixed opinion; to be easily influenced by the circumstances of the moment

信封(ㄒㄧㄣˋ ㄈㄥ)or 信封兒(ㄒㄧㄣˋ ㄈㄥㄦ)
an envelope

信風(ㄒㄧㄣˋ ㄈㄥ)
trade wind; seasonal wind

信風帶(ㄒㄧㄣˋ ㄈㄥ ㄉㄞˋ)
the trade wind zone

信奉(ㄒㄧㄣˋ ㄈㄥˋ)
to believe in (a religion, etc.)

信服(ㄒㄧㄣˋ ㄈㄨˊ)
to believe in; to trust; to be convinced; to admire

信得過(ㄒㄧㄣˋ ·ㄉㄜ ㄍㄨㄛˋ)
can be believed; credible

信條(ㄒㄧㄣˋ ㄊㄧㄠˊ)
a creed or code; a dogma; a precept

信徒(ㄒㄧㄣˋ ㄊㄨˊ)
a believer (of a religion, etc.); a follower; an adherent: 他是基督教的信徒。He is a believer in Christianity.

信託(ㄒㄧㄣˋ ㄊㄨㄛ)
trust; to trust

信託公司(ㄒㄧㄣˋ ㄊㄨㄛ ㄍㄨㄥ ㄙ)
a trust company

信託局(ㄒㄧㄣˋ ㄊㄨㄛ ㄐㄩˊ)
the Trust Bureau

信筒(ㄒㄧㄣˋ ㄊㄨㄥˇ)
a letter box; a mailbox; a postbox

信念(ㄒㄧㄣˋ ㄋㄧㄢˋ)
a belief; a conviction

信女(ㄒㄧㄣˋ ㄋㄩˇ)
(Buddhism) a female believer

信賴(ㄒㄧㄣˋ ㄌㄞˋ)
trust; to trust

信鴿(ㄒㄧㄣˋ ㄍㄜ)
a carrier pigeon

信稿(ㄒㄧㄣˋ ㄍㄠˇ)
the draft of a letter

信口開河 or 信口開合(ㄒㄧㄣˋ ㄎㄡˇ ㄎㄞ ㄏㄜˊ)
to talk at random (often devoid of truth); to talk without forethought; to brag; to talk irresponsibly

信口胡說(ㄒㄧㄣˋ ㄎㄡˇ ㄏㄨˊ ㄕㄨㄛ)
to talk nonsense

信口雌黃(ㄒㄧㄣˋ ㄎㄡˇ ㄘ ㄏㄨㄤˊ)
to make irresponsible remarks; to criticize without grounds; to criticize wildly

信號(ㄒㄧㄣˋ ㄏㄠˋ)
a signal (with flags, lamps, etc.): 紅燈是危險的信號。A red light is a signal of danger.

信號彈(ㄒㄧㄣˋ ㄏㄠˋ ㄉㄢˋ)
a signal shot; a signal bullet; a flare

信號燈(ㄒㄧㄣˋ ㄏㄠˋ ㄉㄥ)
a semaphore; a signal lamp

信號槍(ㄒㄧㄣˋ ㄏㄠˋ ㄑㄧㄤ)
a signal pistol; a flare pistol

信教(ㄒㄧㄣˋ ㄐㄧㄠˋ)
to believe in a religion

信箋(ㄒㄧㄣˋ ㄐㄧㄢ)
letter paper

信件(ㄒㄧㄣˋ ㄐㄧㄢˋ)
mail or letters (collectively)

信息(ㄒㄧㄣˋ ㄒㄧˊ)
news; information; a message

信心(ㄒㄧㄣˋ ㄒㄧㄣ)
faith; confidence: 我對這計畫的信心不大。I haven't much faith in this plan.

信箱(ㄒㄧㄣˋ ㄒㄧㄤ)
a postbox; a letter box; a post office box (P.O.B.)

信紙(ㄒㄧㄣˋ ㄓˇ)
letter paper

信札(ㄒㄧㄣˋ ㄓㄚˊ)
mail or letters (collectively)

信插(ㄒㄧㄣˋ ㄔㄚ)
a mail rack

信差(ㄒㄧㄣˋ ㄔㄞ)
a mailman; a postman

信實(ㄒㄧㄣˋ ㄕˊ)
good faith; honesty; trustworthiness; reliable

信史(ㄒㄧㄣˋ ㄕˇ)
authentic historical records

信誓(ㄒㄧㄣˋ ㄕˋ)
faithful oaths; faithful pledges

信守(ㄒㄧㄣˋ ㄕㄡˇ)
to abide by; to keep (a promise): 我們必須信守諾言。We must keep our promises.

信手(ㄒㄧㄣˋ ㄕㄡˇ)
without a previous plan; at random: 他信手抽一本書。He picked out a book at random.

信手拈來(ㄒㄧㄣˋ ㄕㄡˇ ㄋㄧㄢ ㄌㄞˊ)
to pick at random; to take without forethought; to get without effort

信賞必罰(ㄒㄧㄣˋ ㄕㄤˇ ㄅㄧˋ ㄈㄚˊ)
to give rewards or punishments strictly and impartially; awards and punishments rigorously carried out

信任(ㄒㄧㄣˋ ㄖㄣˋ)
① to trust; to have faith in
② trust: 你可以信任他。You can put your trust in him.

信任投票(ㄒㄧㄣˋ ㄖㄣˋ ㄊㄡˊ ㄆㄧㄠˋ)
a vote of confidence

信從(ㄒㄧㄣˋ ㄘㄨㄥˊ)
to trust and follow (a person's advice, etc.); to listen to

信義(ㄒㄧㄣˋ ㄧˋ)
honesty

信仰(ㄒㄧㄣˋ ㄧㄤˇ)
(religious or political) belief; to admire; to believe in

信物(ㄒㄧㄣˋ ㄨˋ)
an authenticating object; a token of promise; a pledge

信譽(ㄒㄧㄣˋ ㄩˋ)
credit and reputation

信用(ㄒㄧㄣˋ ㄩㄥˋ)
credit

信用卡(ㄒㄧㄣˋ ㄩㄥˋ ㄎㄚˇ)
a credit card

信用合作社(ㄒㄧㄣˋ ㄩㄥˋ ㄏㄜˊ ㄗㄨㄛˋ ㄕㄜˋ)
a credit cooperative

信用交易(ㄒㄧㄣˋ ㄩㄥˋ ㄐㄧㄠ ㄧˋ)
margin trading or margin transaction

信用狀(ㄒㄧㄣˋ ㄩㄥˋ ㄓㄨㄤˋ)or 信用證(ㄒㄧㄣˋ ㄩㄥˋ ㄓㄥˋ)
a letter of credit

八畫

【修】 180
ㄒㄧㄡ shiou xiū

1. to repair; to mend
2. to adorn; to decorate
3. to construct; to build
4. long; slender
5. to prune; to cut; to sharpen; to trim
6. to study; to cultivate
7. to write; to compile; to edit

修補(ㄒㄧㄡ ㄅㄨˇ)
to repair; to mend: 修補破洞 to repair a puncture

修配(ㄒㄧㄡ ㄆㄟˋ)
to repair and supply replacements

修面(ㄒㄧㄡ ㄇㄧㄢˋ)
to shave one's face

修明(ㄒㄧㄡ ㄇㄧㄥˊ)
(said of political administration) enlightened and orderly

修睦(ㄒㄧㄡ ㄇㄨˋ)
to cultivate friendship with neighbors

修墓(ㄒㄧㄡ ㄇㄨˋ)
to renovate or keep ancestral graves

修福(ㄒㄧㄡ ㄈㄨˊ)
to do good deeds in order to win blessings

修復(ㄒㄧㄡ ㄈㄨˋ)
to complete a repair job; to make as good as new

修復舊觀(ㄒㄧㄡ ㄈㄨˋ ㄐㄧㄡˋ ㄍㄨㄢ)
to restore to original shape and appearance

修道(ㄒㄧㄡ ㄉㄠˋ)
to cultivate oneself according to a religious doctrine; to practice Buddhist or Taoist rules

修道院(ㄒㄧㄡ ㄉㄠˋ ㄩㄢˋ)
① a monastery ② a nunnery; a convent

修訂(ㄒㄧㄡ ㄉㄧㄥˋ)
to revise

修訂版(ㄒㄧㄡ ㄉㄧㄥˋ ㄅㄢˇ)or 修訂本(ㄒㄧㄡ ㄉㄧㄥˋ ㄅㄣˇ)
a revision; the revised edition: 此書的修訂本將於明年出版。A revision of this book will be published next year.

修女(ㄒㄧㄡ ㄋㄩˇ)
a Catholic nun; a sister

修理(ㄒㄧㄡ ㄌㄧˇ)
① to repair; repair; mend: 這部機器正在修理中。The machine is under repair. ② (slang) to torture

修理費(ㄒㄧㄡ ㄌㄧˇ ㄈㄟˋ)
(accounting) repairs

修煉(ㄒㄧㄡ ㄌㄧㄢˋ)
① to practice asceticism ② (Taoism) to cultivate one's physical and mental capabilities according to Taoist rules; to go into religious self-discipline

修路(ㄒㄧㄡ ㄌㄨˋ)
① to repair roads ② to build roads

修路機(ㄒㄧㄡ ㄌㄨˋ ㄐㄧ)
a steam (or gasoline or diesel) roller for surfacing roads; a road-roller

修改(ㄒㄧㄡ ㄍㄞˇ)
to correct; to alter; to revise; to modify

修和(ㄒㄧㄡ ㄏㄜˊ)
to conciliate and unite

修好(ㄒㄧㄡ ㄏㄠˇ)
① to cultivate friendship with other states, etc. ② to do good deeds in order to win blessings

修函(ㄒㄧㄡ ㄏㄢˊ)
to write a letter

修脚(ㄒㄧㄡ ㄐㄧㄠˇ)
to pare toenails (a typical trade in a Chinese bathhouse); pedicure

修脚刀兒(ㄒㄧㄡ ㄐㄧㄠˇ ㄉㄠㄦ)
a tiny blade for paring toenails

修剪(ㄒㄧㄡ ㄐㄧㄢˇ)
to trim, cut, clip, or prune

修建(ㄒㄧㄡ ㄐㄧㄢˋ)
to repair and build

修濬(ㄒㄧㄡ ㄐㄩㄣˋ)
to dredge a river

修葺(ㄒㄧㄡ ㄑㄧˋ)
to repair; to renovate: 此屋修葺一新。This house is completely renovated.

修橋補路(ㄒㄧㄡ ㄑㄧㄠˊ ㄅㄨˇ ㄌㄨˋ)
(literally) to repair bridges and mend roads—to do many good deeds

修修補補(ㄒㄧㄡ ㄒㄧㄡ ㄅㄨˇ ㄅㄨˇ)
to patch up; to tinker

修仙(ㄒㄧㄡ ㄒㄧㄢ)
to train, shape, cultivate oneself to attain divinity; to train by self-discipline to become an immortal

修行(ㄒㄧㄡ ㄒㄧㄥˊ)
① to practice Buddhist or Taoist rules (often strict and ascetic in nature) ② to practice moral teachings

修指甲(ㄒㄧㄡ ㄓ ˙ㄐㄧㄚ)
to manicure fingernails; to trim fingernails

修治(ㄒㄧㄡ ㄓˋ)
to repair and adjust

修整(ㄒㄧㄡ ㄓㄥˇ)
① to repair and maintain ② to prune; to trim

修正(ㄒㄧㄡ ㄓㄥˋ)
to correct

修正主義(ㄒㄧㄡ ㄓㄥˋ ㄓㄨˇ ㄧˋ)
revisionism

修築(ㄒㄧㄡ ㄓㄨˊ)
to build (especially a road or bridge); to construct

修撰(ㄒㄧㄡ ㄓㄨㄢˋ)
① to edit; to compile ② the title of an official in the Tang Dynasty whose job was to revise historical records; a court historian

修長(ㄒㄧㄡ ㄔㄤˊ)
tall and thin; slender

修士(ㄒㄧㄡ ㄕˋ)
a monk; a brother (of the Roman Catholic or Greek Orthodox church); a friar

修飾(ㄒㄧㄡ ㄕˋ)
① to take care of one's appearance; to doll up; to beautify ② to redecorate or

refurnish

修繕(ㄒㄧㄡ ㄕㄢˋ)
to repair; to renovate

修身(ㄒㄧㄡ ㄕㄣ)
to cultivate oneself; to practice moral culture

修身齊家(ㄒㄧㄡ ㄕㄣ ㄑㄧˊ ㄐㄧㄚ)
to cultivate oneself and put family in order

修身自省(ㄒㄧㄡ ㄕㄣ ㄗˋ ㄒㄧㄥˇ)
to look after one's conduct by self-examination

修書(ㄒㄧㄡ ㄕㄨ)
to write a letter

修容(ㄒㄧㄡ ㄖㄨㄥˊ)
to make up one's features

修造(ㄒㄧㄡ ㄗㄠˋ)
to repair and build

修辭(ㄒㄧㄡ ㄘˊ)
rhetoric; diction; the use of proper words

修辭學(ㄒㄧㄡ ㄘˊ ㄒㄩㄝˊ)
rhetoric (as a subject of study)

修業(ㄒㄧㄡ ㄧㄝˋ)
to pursue academic studies; to go to school

修陰功(ㄒㄧㄡ ㄧㄣ ㄍㄨㄥ) or 修陰德(ㄒㄧㄡ ㄧㄣ ㄉㄜˊ)
to do a good deed secretly

修養(ㄒㄧㄡ ㄧㄤˇ)
①to seek perfection in scholastic or ethical pursuits ②man's moral culture as the result of training; possession of profound knowledge and a sense of morality

【俯】 181
ㄈㄨˇ　fuu　fǔ

1. to face down; to come down; to bow down; to stoop
2. to condescend; to deign

俯拜(ㄈㄨˇ ㄅㄞˋ)
to do obeisance to

俯伏(ㄈㄨˇ ㄈㄨˊ)
to prostrate; to make obeisance to

俯念(ㄈㄨˇ ㄋㄧㄢˋ)
Please condescend to consider (my position, situation, etc.).—an expression used in a written request to one's superior

俯瞰(ㄈㄨˇ ㄎㄢˋ)
to look down at; to overlook

俯就(ㄈㄨˇ ㄐㄧㄡˋ)
①to adapt (usually by lowering) oneself to… ②to condescend to accept a job

俯准(ㄈㄨˇ ㄓㄨㄣˇ)
to give (your) gracious approval

俯衝(ㄈㄨˇ ㄔㄨㄥ)
a dive; to dive

俯拾即是(ㄈㄨˇ ㄕˊ ㄐㄧˊ ㄕˋ)
①just to stoop and gather—It's everywhere.或 extremely common ②a very easy thing to do or get

俯視(ㄈㄨˇ ㄕˋ)
to look down at; to overlook

俯首(ㄈㄨˇ ㄕㄡˇ)
to bend one's head; to bow (usually referring to submission or admission of wrongdoing)

俯首帖耳(ㄈㄨˇ ㄕㄡˇ ㄊㄧㄝ ㄦˇ)
servile; submissive

俯首聽命(ㄈㄨˇ ㄕㄡˇ ㄊㄧㄥ ㄇㄧㄥˋ)
to obey submissively

俯首就範(ㄈㄨˇ ㄕㄡˇ ㄐㄧㄡˋ ㄈㄢˋ)
to submit; to surrender

俯首無言(ㄈㄨˇ ㄕㄡˇ ㄨˊ ㄧㄢˊ)
to bend one's head in silence—to admit one's fault or crime without protest

俯仰(ㄈㄨˇ ㄧㄤˇ)
①a bending or lifting of the head ②one's everyday life at home ③(figuratively) a very short time

俯仰之間(ㄈㄨˇ ㄧㄤˇ ㄓ ㄐㄧㄢ)
in the twinkling of an eye; in an instant; a very short time

俯仰由人(ㄈㄨˇ ㄧㄤˇ ㄧㄡˊ ㄖㄣˊ)
to be at somebody's beck and call 亦作「隨人俯仰」

俯仰無愧(ㄈㄨˇ ㄧㄤˇ ㄨˊ ㄎㄨㄟˋ)
to have done nothing to make one feel ashamed

俯允(ㄈㄨˇ ㄩㄣˇ)
to grant (your) gracious permission

【俱】 182
ㄐㄩˋ　jiuh　jù
(又讀 ㄐㄩ　jiu　jū)

1. altogether; all
2. to accompany
3. a Chinese family name

俱備(ㄐㄩˋ ㄅㄟˋ)
all made ready; all complete

俱發罪(ㄐㄩˋ ㄈㄚ ㄗㄨㄟˋ)
concurrent offenses

俱樂部(ㄐㄩˋ ㄌㄜˋ ㄅㄨˋ)
a club (as a country club, golf club, etc.)

俱盡(ㄐㄩˋ ㄐㄧㄣˋ)
all finished; nothing left

俱全(ㄐㄩˋ ㄑㄩㄢˊ)
to be available in all varieties

俱在(ㄐㄩˋ ㄗㄞˋ)
all present

俱已齊備(ㄐㄩˋ ㄧˇ ㄑㄧˊ ㄅㄟˋ)
Everything is ready.

【俳】 183
ㄆㄞˊ　pair　pái

1. a variety show; a vaudeville
2. insincere; not serious
3. to walk to and fro

俳賦(ㄆㄞˊ ㄈㄨˋ)
a light, ornate literary form popular in ancient China

俳體詩(ㄆㄞˊ ㄊㄧˇ ㄕ)
light, comic poetry

俳佪(ㄆㄞˊ ㄏㄨㄞˊ)
to walk to and fro

俳句(ㄆㄞˊ ㄐㄩˋ)
a Japanese form of light poetry consisting of three sentences (17 words in all)

俳諧(ㄆㄞˊ ㄒㄧㄝˊ)
funny talk; comic

俳優(ㄆㄞˊ ㄧㄡ)
①a variety show; a vaudeville ②a player in a variety show; a comedian

【俶】 184
1. ㄔㄨˋ　chuh　chù

1. to begin; a beginning
2. to arrange the baggage for travel
3. to build

【俶】 184
2. ㄊㄧˋ　tih　tì

not bound by conventions

俶儻(ㄊㄧˋ ㄊㄤˇ)
to behave merrily and freely, regardless of conventions

【俸】 185
ㄈㄥˋ　fenq　fèng

emoluments; a salary from the government

俸祿(ㄈㄥˋ ㄌㄨˋ) or 俸給(ㄈㄥˋ ㄐㄧˇ)
emoluments; a government salary

【俺】 186
ㄢˇ　aan　ǎn

the personal pronoun I, used

especially in Shantung Province

俺們(ㄢˇ ・ㄇㄣ)
we

俺家(ㄢˇ ㄐㄧㄚ)
I

俺家的(ㄢˇ ㄐㄧㄚ ・ㄉㄜ)
my husband

【俾】 187
ㄅㄧˋ bih bì

1. to cause; to enable
2. that; so that; in order that

俾倪(ㄅㄧˋ ㄋㄧˋ)
to glance sideways

俾資挹注(ㄅㄧˋ ㄗ ㄧˋ ㄓㄨˋ)
so as to help make both ends meet

俾斯麥(ㄅㄧˋ ㄙ ㄇㄞˋ)
Prince Otto Eduard Leopold von Bismarck (1815-1898), German prime minister

【倀】 188
ㄔㄤ chang chāng

1. (mythology) a ghost controlled by the tiger
2. wild; rash

【併】 189
(并) ㄅㄧㄥˋ binq bìng

1. on a level with; even; equal; to go side by side
2. all; entire
3. together
4. to combine; to annex

併滅(ㄅㄧㄥˋ ㄇㄧㄝˋ)
to destroy

併發(ㄅㄧㄥˋ ㄈㄚ)
to begin, explode, erupt, attack, occur, etc. at the same time

併發症(ㄅㄧㄥˋ ㄈㄚ ㄓㄥˋ)
(medicine) a complication; an epiphenomenon; a syndrome

併呑(ㄅㄧㄥˋ ㄊㄨㄣ)
to swallow up entirely; to annex and absorb (a neighboring country)

併攏(ㄅㄧㄥˋ ㄌㄨㄥˇ)
to draw close to each other

併合(ㄅㄧㄥˋ ㄏㄜˊ)
to unite; to integrate

併肩(ㄅㄧㄥˋ ㄐㄧㄢ)
shoulder to shoulder

併案(ㄅㄧㄥˋ ㄢˋ)
① an arrangement to group similar cases under a single heading for quicker or better processing, treatment, etc. ② a package deal

【倆】 190
1. ㄌㄧㄤˇ leang liǎng

craft; ability

【倆】 190
2. ㄌㄧㄚˇ lea liǎ

two; a pair; a couple

倆口子(ㄌㄧㄚˇ ㄎㄡˇ ・ㄗ)
husband and wife

倆錢兒(ㄌㄧㄚˇ ㄑㄧㄚˊㄦ)
not much money; a little money

倆人(ㄌㄧㄚˇ ㄖㄣˊ)
two persons, usually referring to a couple in love

倆月(ㄌㄧㄚˇ ㄩㄝˋ)
a couple of months

【倉】 191
ㄘㄤ tsang cāng

1. a granary; a storehouse; a warehouse
2. a cabin, as in the ship
3. green
4. a Chinese family name

倉房(ㄘㄤ ㄈㄤˊ)
a storage for food; a granary; a storehouse

倉廩(ㄘㄤ ㄌㄧㄣˇ)
a granary

倉庫(ㄘㄤ ㄎㄨˋ)
a warehouse; a godown; a storehouse

倉皇(ㄘㄤ ㄏㄨㄤˊ)
in haste; hurriedly (especially in panic): 敵人倉皇撤退。The enemy retreated in haste.

倉頡(ㄘㄤ ㄐㄧㄝˊ)
Tsang Chieh, a legendary figure credited with the invention of the written Chinese language

倉儲(ㄘㄤ ㄔㄨˊ)
to keep grain, goods, etc. in a storehouse

倉促 or 倉卒(ㄘㄤ ㄘㄨˋ)
in a hurry: 他倉促下結論。He jumped to a conclusion.

【個】 192
(箇) ㄍㄜˋ geh gè

1. a numerary adjunct: 一個包子 one steamed dumpling
2. piece
3. single
4. roughly
5. an adjunct to an indefinite pronoun, as this, that

個把(ㄍㄜˋ ㄅㄚˇ)
a few; one or two: 多個把人也住得下。There is enough room to put up one or two more people.

個把月(ㄍㄜˋ ㄅㄚˇ ㄩㄝˋ)
a month or two: 再個把月就可做完了。It can easily be finished in a month or two.

個別(ㄍㄜˋ ㄅㄧㄝˊ)
individual; individually; separately: 老師找他個別談話。The teacher had a private talk with him.

個體(ㄍㄜˋ ㄊㄧˇ)
a matter, etc. having an independent and distinct quality; the individual as contrasted with the group; an entity

個體戶(ㄍㄜˋ ㄊㄧˇ ㄏㄨˋ)
an individual business or shop

個個(ㄍㄜˋ ㄍㄜˋ)or 個個兒(ㄍㄜˋ ㄍㄜˋㄦ)
(each and) every one

個性(ㄍㄜˋ ㄒㄧㄥˋ)
personality; individuality

個中(ㄍㄜˋ ㄓㄨㄥ)
within; inside

個人(ㄍㄜˋ ㄖㄣˊ)
① the individual as contrasted with the group ② oneself ③ personal; personally: 我個人認爲他是好人。In my personal opinion he is a good man.

個人主義(ㄍㄜˋ ㄖㄣˊ ㄓㄨˇ ㄧˋ)
individualism; egoism

個子(ㄍㄜˋ ・ㄗ)
physical size of a person; build

個兒(ㄍㄜˋㄦ)
① size; height; stature ② persons or things taken singly

個案(ㄍㄜˋ ㄢˋ)
an individual case; an isolated case; a special case

個位(ㄍㄜˋ ㄨㄟˋ)
(mathematics) a unit; a digit; a unit place

【倌】 193
ㄍㄨㄢ guan guān

1. a boy or an assistant in the employ of a teahouse, tavern or restaurant

〔人部〕

2. a euphemism for a prostitute
3. the groom

倌人(ㄍㄨㄢ ㄖㄣˊ)
①an officer in charge of royal chariots ②(formerly) a prostitute

【倍】 194
ㄅㄟˋ bey bèi
1. double; to double
2. (joined to a numeral) -times; -fold
3. to rebel; to be insubordinate

倍塔(ㄅㄟˋ ㄊㄚˇ)
beta

倍塔射線(ㄅㄟˋ ㄊㄚˇ ㄕㄜˋ ㄒㄧㄢˋ)
a beta ray

倍率(ㄅㄟˋ ㄌㄩˋ)
percentage

倍加(ㄅㄟˋ ㄐㄧㄚ)
to double; double

倍蓰(ㄅㄟˋ ㄒㄧˇ)
one to five times; very many

倍數(ㄅㄟˋ ㄕㄨˋ)
a multiple: 14是7的倍數。Fourteen is a multiple of seven.

倍增(ㄅㄟˋ ㄗㄥ)
double; to double

【倞】 195
1. ㄐㄧㄥˋ jinq jìng
strong

【倞】 195
2. ㄌㄧㄤˋ lianq liàng
1. far
2. to request

【倏】 196
ㄕㄨˋ shuh shù
hastily; suddenly

倏忽(ㄕㄨˋ ㄏㄨ)
all of a sudden; very suddenly; quickly

倏瞬(ㄕㄨˋ ㄕㄨㄣˋ)
a brief glimpse; time for a brief glimpse

【倕】 197
ㄔㄨㄟˊ chwei chuí
name of an expert craftsman in ancient China

【們】 198
ㄇㄣˊ men mén
(語音 ·ㄇㄣ ·men men)
(usually said of persons) an adjunct to a pronoun or noun to indicate plurality: 朋友們 friends 同胞們 fellow citizens

【倒】 199
1. ㄉㄠˇ dao dǎo
to fall down; to lie down

倒班(ㄉㄠˇ ㄅㄢ)
to work in shifts; to work by turns: 我們晝夜倒班。We work in shifts around the clock.

倒閉(ㄉㄠˇ ㄅㄧˋ) or 倒店(ㄉㄠˇ ㄉㄧㄢˋ)
to close down a shop; to go bankrupt or insolvent: 去年有許多企業倒閉。Many enterprises went bankrupt last year.

倒斃(ㄉㄠˇ ㄅㄧˋ)
to fall dead

倒賣(ㄉㄠˇ ㄇㄞˋ)
to resell at a profit

倒楣(ㄉㄠˇ ㄇㄟˊ)
to be out of luck; an unlucky break

倒鳳顛鸞(ㄉㄠˇ ㄈㄥˋ ㄉㄧㄢ ㄌㄨㄢˊ) or 顛鸞倒鳳(ㄉㄧㄢ ㄌㄨㄢˊ ㄉㄠˇ ㄈㄥˋ)
to have sexual intercourse

倒塌(ㄉㄠˇ ㄊㄚ)
(especially said of a building) to collapse; to cave in

倒臺(ㄉㄠˇ ㄊㄞˊ)
to fall from power

倒頭便睡(ㄉㄠˇ ㄊㄡˊ ㄅㄧㄢˋ ㄕㄨㄟˋ)
to fall asleep as soon as one goes to bed (sometimes connoting a sense of carefreeness or indifference)

倒閣(ㄉㄠˇ ㄍㄜˊ)
the resignation of the cabinet (in the face of a political crisis)

倒換(ㄉㄠˇ ㄏㄨㄢˋ)
①to rotate; to take turns ②to exchange; to substitute; to replace

倒嚼(ㄉㄠˇ ㄐㄩㄝˊ)
to chew the cud; to ruminate

倒賬 or 倒帳(ㄉㄠˇ ㄓㄤˋ)
①bad debts ②to refuse to pay loans under various excuses

倒嗓(子)(ㄉㄠˇ ㄙㄤˇ (·ㄗ))
an ailment of the vocal cords caused by over-tensing them with constant singing or shouting

倒胃口(ㄉㄠˇ ㄨㄟˋ ㄎㄡˇ)
to spoil one's appetite

倒運(ㄉㄠˇ ㄩㄣˋ)
to be out of luck; unlucky: 他是個倒運的作家。He is an unlucky writer.

【倒】 199
2. ㄉㄠˋ daw dào
1. to inverse; to place upside down; in reverse order or the wrong direction
2. to pour out; to empty: 倒垃圾 to pour out garbage
3. on the contrary
4. after all: 老師倒底說得不錯。What the teacher said was not wrong after all.
5. but; and yet: 說是她，倒不是她。You think it is she, but it isn't.

倒背如流(ㄉㄠˋ ㄅㄟˋ ㄖㄨˊ ㄌㄧㄡˊ)
can even recite (an article, etc.) backwards fluently—to understand something thoroughly by heart

倒不如(ㄉㄠˋ ·ㄅㄨ ㄖㄨˊ)
①would rather: 倒不如死了乾淨。I would rather die. ②not better than; even worse than

倒賠(ㄉㄠˋ ㄆㄟˊ)
to have to pay—after expecting to receive (usually referring to money)

倒片(ㄉㄠˋ ㄆㄧㄢˋ)
(movie) to rewind

倒飛(ㄉㄠˋ ㄈㄟ)
inverted flight

倒反(ㄉㄠˋ ㄈㄢˇ)
unexpectedly; contrary to what one expects

倒貼(ㄉㄠˋ ㄊㄧㄝ)
(said of an unfaithful wife, wealthy widow or concubine) to pay for the upkeep of a lover

倒退(ㄉㄠˋ ㄊㄨㄟˋ)
①to retreat; to go backwards; to fall back ②to retrospect; to review

倒立(ㄉㄠˋ ㄌㄧˋ)
①to stand upside down ②a handstand

倒流(ㄉㄠˋ ㄌㄧㄡˊ)
to flow backward

倒戈(ㄉㄠˋ ㄍㄜ)
to apostatize or tergiversate; to desert to the enemy camp; mutiny

倒掛(ㄉㄠˋ ㄍㄨㄚˋ)
①to hang upside down ②the lovebird of Taiwan and

Kwangsi Provinces, resembling a parakeet
倒果為因(ㄉㄠˋ ㄍㄨㄛˇ ㄨㄟˊ ㄧㄣ)
to mistake the effect for the cause
倒灌(ㄉㄠˋ ㄍㄨㄢˋ)
(said of a flood which spills over river banks or dikes onto the adjoining land) to flow backward
倒屣(ㄉㄠˋ ㄒㄧˇ)
in a big hurry to welcome a guest
倒行逆施(ㄉㄠˋ ㄒㄧㄥˊ ㄋㄧˋ ㄕ)
to go against commonsense rules; to adopt measures beyond reasonable comprehension; perverse acts
倒敍(ㄉㄠˋ ㄒㄩˋ)
to narrate an incident in inverted order chronologically; the flashback
倒懸(ㄉㄠˋ ㄒㄩㄢˊ)
hanging upside down—great suffering; deep affliction
倒置(ㄉㄠˋ ㄓˋ)
to place (things, etc.) in wrong order; to place emphasis on the wrong point; to put the cart before the horse
倒轉(ㄉㄠˋ ㄓㄨㄢˇ)
① to turn the other way round ② contrary to reason or one's expectation
倒裝(ㄉㄠˋ ㄓㄨㄤ)
① to place things in inverted order ② (rhetoric) hyperbaton
倒持泰阿 or 倒持太阿(ㄉㄠˋ ㄔˊ ㄊㄞˋ ㄜ)
(literally) to hold the sword at the wrong end—to relegate one's power to a subordinate unwisely and suffer the consequences thereof; to allow one's powers to fall into another's hands
倒插(ㄉㄠˋ ㄔㄚ)
① to insert something or plant a tree upside down ② in writing or narration, a reversal of the normal order or sequence of sentences, paragraphs, etc.
倒車(ㄉㄠˋ ㄔㄜ)
to back up a car, locomotive, etc.; to move a vehicle backward
倒抽一口氣(ㄉㄠˋ ㄔㄡ ㄧˋ ㄎㄡˇ ㄑㄧˋ)
to hold one's breath; to give a gasp of astonishment; to be in fear or disappointment, etc.
倒是(ㄉㄠˋ ·ㄕ)
actually; really
倒數(ㄉㄠˋ ㄕㄨˇ)
to count from bottom to top; to count backward; to count from rear to front: 倒數第五行 the fifth line from the bottom
倒數計時(ㄉㄠˋ ㄕㄨˇ ㄐㄧˋ ㄕˊ)
to count down; countdown (as in rocket launching)
倒栽葱(ㄉㄠˋ ㄗㄞ ㄘㄨㄥ)
to fall headlong; to fall head over heels
倒彩(ㄉㄠˋ ㄘㄞˇ)
(Chinese opera) to applaud when a performer slips
倒也罷了(ㄉㄠˋ ㄧㄝˇ ㄅㄚˋ ·ㄌㄜ)
It would have been better if....
倒因為果(ㄉㄠˋ ㄧㄣ ㄨㄟˊ ㄍㄨㄛˇ)
to reverse cause and effect; to take the cause for effect
倒影(ㄉㄠˋ ㄧㄥˇ)
the reflection of something in the water; the upside-down image of an object in the viewfinder of a camera; inverted images

【倔】 200
1. ㄐㄩㄝˊ jyue jué
intransigent; hard; obstinate; stubborn
倔強(ㄐㄩㄝˊ ㄐㄧㄤˋ)
intransigent; intransigence; obstinate; stubborn: 這個老人相當倔強。The old man is as stubborn as a mule.
倔起(ㄐㄩㄝˊ ㄑㄧˇ)
(said of a nation) to rise suddenly

【倔】 200
2. ㄐㄩㄝˋ jiueh juè
gruff; surly; rude in manner or speech

【倖】 201
ㄒㄧㄥˋ shinq xìng
1. good luck; lucky; by luck or chance; fortunate
2. to dote on; to spoil
倖免(ㄒㄧㄥˋ ㄇㄧㄢˇ)
to escape (punishment) by luck; to survive luckily
倖進(ㄒㄧㄥˋ ㄐㄧㄣˋ)
to attain (a position, etc.) by luck; to be promoted by luck
倖臣(ㄒㄧㄥˋ ㄔㄣˊ)
a favorite courtier
倖存(ㄒㄧㄥˋ ㄘㄨㄣˊ)
to survive by good luck

【倘】 202
ㄊㄤˇ taang tǎng
if; supposing; in the event of
倘來之物(ㄊㄤˇ ㄌㄞˊ ㄓ ㄨˋ)
an unexpected or undeserved gain
倘使(ㄊㄤˇ ㄕˇ)
if
倘如(ㄊㄤˇ ㄖㄨˊ)
if
倘若(ㄊㄤˇ ㄖㄨㄛˋ)
if; in the event of; in case

【候】 203
ㄏㄡˋ how hòu
1. to wait; to expect: 請稍候。Please wait a moment.
2. a period; time; a season
3. a situation; a condition
4. to pay (bills); to take care of the bill: 這筆賬他候過鈔了。He has paid the bill.
5. to greet; to inquire after: 他問候你。He inquired after you.
候補(ㄏㄡˋ ㄅㄨˇ)
waiting to fill a vacancy, such as an alternate member of a committee, etc.; to be a candidate
候脈(ㄏㄡˋ ㄇㄛˋ)
to feel the pulse
候鳥(ㄏㄡˋ ㄋㄧㄠˇ)
migratory birds
候光(ㄏㄡˋ ㄍㄨㄤ)
to request (someone's) company at a dinner, etc.; to await the honor of your presence (at a dinner party)
候機室(ㄏㄡˋ ㄐㄧ ㄕˋ)
a lounge or waiting room (at an airport terminal building)
候駕(ㄏㄡˋ ㄐㄧㄚˋ)
to await (your) gracious presence—an expression usually used in an invitation: 隨時候駕。You are welcome

any time.
候教(ㄏㄡˋ ㄐㄧㄠˋ)
to await (your) gracious teaching—a common usage in an invitation, etc.
候選人(ㄏㄡˋ ㄒㄩㄢˇ ㄖㄣˊ)
a candidate (especially in elections)
候診(ㄏㄡˋ ㄓㄣˇ)
to wait to see the doctor
候車亭(ㄏㄡˋ ㄔㄜ ㄊㄧㄥˊ)
a bus stop with an eaves-like roof
候車室(ㄏㄡˋ ㄔㄜ ㄕˋ)
a waiting room (at a railway station or bus terminal)
候示(ㄏㄡˋ ㄕˋ)
to await (your) further instructions
候審(ㄏㄡˋ ㄕㄣˇ)
(law) to await trial

【人部】

【倚】 204 ㄧˇ yii yǐ
1. to rely on; to depend on
2. to lean toward; to rest on
3. biased; partial: 不偏不倚 unbiased; impartial
倚傍(ㄧˇ ㄅㄤˋ)
to pattern after; to emulate
倚馬可待(ㄧˇ ㄇㄚˇ ㄎㄜˇ ㄉㄞˋ)
a writer's ability to write an article very fast
倚門賣笑(ㄧˇ ㄇㄣˊ ㄇㄞˋ ㄒㄧㄠˋ)or 倚門賣俏(ㄧˇ ㄇㄣˊ ㄇㄞˋ ㄑㄧㄠˋ)
(said of coquettish women) to invite attention of passers-by; love for sale; to be a prostitute; to flirt near the door with passers-by
倚門倚閭(ㄧˇ ㄇㄣˊ ㄧˇ ㄌㄩˊ)
to await the return of one's son eagerly
倚托(ㄧˇ ㄊㄨㄛ)
to rely on; to depend on
倚賴(ㄧˇ ㄌㄞˋ)
①to depend on; to rely on (others): 小孩的衣食都倚賴父母。Children depend on their parents for food and clothing. ②to presume on authority to browbeat others
倚老賣老(ㄧˇ ㄌㄠˇ ㄇㄞˋ ㄌㄠˇ)
to presume on age to despise the youth; to take advantage of one's seniority or old age (to ignore manners, regulations, etc.)
倚靠(ㄧˇ ㄎㄠˋ)
①to lean against ②to rely on; to trust to; to depend on; to lean on ③support
倚著(ㄧˇ ·ㄓㄜ)
to count on support; someone or something to depend on
倚仗(ㄧˇ ㄓㄤˋ)
to presume on (one's position, authority, etc.)
倚仗權勢(ㄧˇ ㄓㄤˋ ㄑㄩㄢˊ ㄕˋ)
to rely on one's power and position; to count on one's powerful connections
倚重(ㄧˇ ㄓㄨㄥˋ)
to entrust a person with heavy responsibility
倚恃(ㄧˇ ㄕˋ)
to depend on; to rely on
倚勢凌人(ㄧˇ ㄕˋ ㄌㄧㄥˊ ㄖㄣˊ)or 倚勢欺人(ㄧˇ ㄕˋ ㄑㄧ ㄖㄣˊ)
to take advantage of one's position to bully people

【倜】 205 ㄊㄧˋ tih tì
1. to raise high
2. unrestrained; unoccupied
倜儻 or 俶儻(ㄊㄧˋ ㄊㄤˇ)
elegant in a casual way; free and easy of manner; unconventional
倜儻不羈(ㄊㄧˋ ㄊㄤˇ ㄅㄨˋ ㄐㄧ)
untrammeled; free; unconventional

【借】 206 ㄐㄧㄝˋ jieh jiè
1. to lend: 借我筆好嗎? Could you lend me your pen?
2. to borrow
3. to avail oneself of; to make use of; to resort to
4. to make a pretext of
5. if; supposing
借貸(ㄐㄧㄝˋ ㄉㄞˋ)
①to ask for a loan; to borrow money ②debit and credit sides
借刀殺人(ㄐㄧㄝˋ ㄉㄠ ㄕㄚ ㄖㄣˊ)
to kill one's enemy by another's hands; to instigate (or trick) others to commit a crime to serve one's own purpose
借道(ㄐㄧㄝˋ ㄉㄠˋ)
①(said of an invading army) to reach the target country through the territory of a third nation ②(said of burglars, robbers, etc.) to reach the target house by way of a neighboring residence
借調(ㄐㄧㄝˋ ㄉㄧㄠˋ)
to transfer temporarily; loan
借讀(ㄐㄧㄝˋ ㄉㄨˊ)
to study at a school on a temporary basis
借端(ㄐㄧㄝˋ ㄉㄨㄢ)
on the pretext of
借題發揮(ㄐㄧㄝˋ ㄊㄧˊ ㄈㄚ ㄏㄨㄟ)
to make an issue of; to capitalize on; to seize a pretext (to air one's own complaints, to attack others, etc.)
借古諷今(ㄐㄧㄝˋ ㄍㄨˇ ㄈㄥˇ ㄐㄧㄣ)
to use the past to disparage the present
借故(ㄐㄧㄝˋ ㄍㄨˋ)
to find an excuse
借故推托(ㄐㄧㄝˋ ㄍㄨˋ ㄊㄨㄟ ㄊㄨㄛ)
to find an excuse to refuse
借光(ㄐㄧㄝˋ ㄍㄨㄤ)
①(a polite expression) Please let me pass. 或 Will you please tell me…? ②to be given favors, assistance, help, etc.
借款(ㄐㄧㄝˋ ㄎㄨㄢˇ)
to borrow money; to ask for a loan; a loan
借花獻佛(ㄐㄧㄝˋ ㄏㄨㄚ ㄒㄧㄢˋ ㄈㄛˊ)
(literally) to borrow flowers to offer to Buddha—to get things from another person to entertain one's own guest
借火兒(ㄐㄧㄝˋ ㄏㄨㄛˇㄦ)
Please give me a light. 或 to borrow matches or a lighted cigarette; to ask for a light
借酒澆愁(ㄐㄧㄝˋ ㄐㄧㄡˇ ㄐㄧㄠ ㄔㄡˊ)
to drown one's worries or anxieties by drinking
借鑑(ㄐㄧㄝˋ ㄐㄧㄢˋ)or 借鏡(ㄐㄧㄝˋ ㄐㄧㄥˋ)
to learn a lesson from another person's experience; to benefit by another person's past experience
借據(ㄐㄧㄝˋ ㄐㄩˋ)
an I.O.U.; a written acknowledgment of indebtedness; a certificate of indebtedness
借支(ㄐㄧㄝˋ ㄓ)

to request an advance on one's pay

借債(ㄐㄧㄝˋ ㄓㄞˋ)
to borrow money; to raise a loan

借主(ㄐㄧㄝˋ ㄓㄨˇ)
the creditor

借住(ㄐㄧㄝˋ ㄓㄨˋ)
to stay in another's house

借助(ㄐㄧㄝˋ ㄓㄨˋ)
to have the aid of; to draw support from

借箸代籌(ㄐㄧㄝˋ ㄓㄨˋ ㄉㄞˋ ㄔㄡˊ)
to propose or suggest; to make a plan for others

借重(ㄐㄧㄝˋ ㄓㄨㄥˋ)
to rely on; to seek the assistance (of)

借屍還魂(ㄐㄧㄝˋ ㄕ ㄏㄨㄢˊ ㄏㄨㄣˊ)
①(Chinese folklore) A dead person comes to life again by reposing his or her spirit in the body of another dead person. ②(said of something evil) to revive in a new guise

借書證(ㄐㄧㄝˋ ㄕㄨ ㄓㄥˋ)
a library card

借宿(ㄐㄧㄝˋ ㄙㄨˋ)
to stay overnight in another's place (or hotel, etc.)

借以(ㄐㄧㄝˋ ㄧˇ)
so as to; for the purpose of

借問(ㄐㄧㄝˋ ㄨㄣˋ)
Will you please tell me…?

借喻(ㄐㄧㄝˋ ㄩˋ)
to use an analogy 亦作「比喻」

借用(ㄐㄧㄝˋ ㄩㄥˋ)
to borrow; to use something for another purpose: 借用一下你的字典好嗎? May I use your dictionary?

【倡】 207 1. ㄔㄤ chang chāng

1. a prostitute
2. wild and unrestrained

倡狂(ㄔㄤ ㄎㄨㄤˊ)
profligate

倡優(ㄔㄤ ㄧㄡ)
①a prostitute ②actress (倡) and actor (優); a musician; an entertainer

【倡】 207 2. ㄔㄤˋ chanq chàng

to lead; to introduce; to initiate; to advocate: 首倡 the first to propose or lead

倡導(ㄔㄤˋ ㄉㄠˇ)
to lead; to advocate; to promote

倡議(ㄔㄤˋ ㄧˋ)
to make a motion; to advocate; to advance a cause

倡言(ㄔㄤˋ ㄧㄢˊ)
to be the first to propose or promote publicly; to initiate

【值】 208 ㄓˊ jyr zhí

1. prices of commodities; value; cost; to cost; to be worth
2. at the time of…
3. to meet; to happen: 他上次來訪，正值她外出。She happened to be out when he called.

值班(ㄓˊ ㄅㄢ) or 值班兒(ㄓˊ ㄅㄚㄦ)
to be on duty; to be on the shift

值得(ㄓˊ ˙ㄉㄜ)
to be worth; to be worthy of; to deserve: 這本小說很值得一讀。This novel is well worth reading.

值錢(ㄓˊ ㄑㄧㄢˊ)
valuable; expensive

值勤(ㄓˊ ㄑㄧㄣˊ)
(said of soldiers, policemen, etc.) to be on duty

值星(ㄓˊ ㄒㄧㄥ)
(said of army officers) to be on duty for the week

值日(ㄓˊ ㄖˋ)
to be one's turn to be on duty; to be on duty for the day

值日生(ㄓˊ ㄖˋ ㄕㄥ)
the student on duty

【倦】 209 ㄐㄩㄢˋ jiuann juàn

tired; weary

倦怠(ㄐㄩㄢˋ ㄉㄞˋ)
to be tired; worn out; languor

倦鳥知還(ㄐㄩㄢˋ ㄋㄧㄠˇ ㄓ ㄏㄨㄢˊ)
(literally) The weary bird always returns to its nest. —to return home after years of wandering far away

倦勤(ㄐㄩㄢˋ ㄑㄧㄣˊ)
wanting to resign from a high position; to be tired of work

倦遊(ㄐㄩㄢˋ ㄧㄡˊ)
①to be weary of wandering or traveling ②to be weary of official duties; to be weary of a public life

【倨】 210 ㄐㄩˋ jiuh jù

1. haughty; rude; arrogant
2. slightly bent

倨傲(ㄐㄩˋ ㄠˋ)
haughty; rude; supercilious; conceited

【倩】 211 ㄑㄧㄢˋ chiann qiàn

1. pretty dimples of a smiling woman
2. handsome
3. a son-in-law
4. to ask somebody to do something for oneself; to solicit the service of a ghost writer, etc.

倩兮(ㄑㄧㄢˋ ㄒㄧ)
How graceful she looks!

倩粧(ㄑㄧㄢˋ ㄓㄨㄤ)
beautiful make-up and becoming clothes

倩影(ㄑㄧㄢˋ ㄧㄥˇ)
the beautiful image of a woman

【倪】 212 ㄋㄧˊ ni ní

1. young and weak
2. division
3. a beginning
4. a limit; bounds
5. a Chinese family name

【倫】 213 ㄌㄨㄣˊ luen lún

1. normal relationships among people
2. comparison; a peer; a match: 無與倫比 beyond comparison
3. classification
4. order; logic
5. regular; ordinary
6. to choose; choice

倫比(ㄌㄨㄣˊ ㄅㄧˇ)
comparable; equal

倫敦(ㄌㄨㄣˊ ㄉㄨㄣ)
London

倫理(ㄌㄨㄣˊ ㄌㄧˇ)
moral principles; ethics

倫理學(ㄌㄨㄣˊ ㄌㄧˇ ㄒㄩㄝˊ)
ethics

倫常(ㄌㄨㄣˊ ㄔㄤˊ)
normal and accepted ways and relationships of people

倫次(ㄌㄨㄣˊ ㄘˋ)

〔人部〕

the normal order of things, reasons, evidence, etc.; an orderly presentation of such: 他說話語無倫次。He spoke incoherently.

【倭】214
1. ㄨㄛ uo wō
name of a human race; an old name for Japan

倭奴(ㄨㄛ ㄋㄨˊ)
①(used in ancient times) the Japanese ②(in modern usage, derogatively) the Japs

倭國(ㄨㄛ ㄍㄨㄛˊ)
an ancient name for Japan

倭寇(ㄨㄛ ㄎㄡˋ)
(ancient usage) the dwarf pirates; the Japs; Japanese corsairs (in the Ming Dynasty)

【倭】214
2. ㄨㄟ uei wēi
參看「倭遲」

倭遲(ㄨㄟ ㄔˊ)
winding; circuitous ; meandering

九畫

【偃】215
ㄧㄢˇ yean yǎn
1. to cease; to be at rest; to stop; to suppress; to lay off
2. to lie on one's back
3. an embankment; an earthen bank or dyke
4. a Chinese family name

偃兵(ㄧㄢˇ ㄅㄧㄥ)
to stop a military action

偃仆(ㄧㄢˇ ㄆㄨ)
to fall down flat; to fall on one's back

偃旗息鼓(ㄧㄢˇ ㄑㄧˊ ㄒㄧˊ ㄍㄨˇ)
①to stop the fanfare; to halt the noisy show ②(said of opposing armies) to stop fighting; to lower the banners and muffle the drums—to cease all activities

偃武修文(ㄧㄢˇ ㄨˇ ㄒㄧㄡ ㄨㄣˊ)
(literally) to cease military activities or preparations and promote culture—to emphasize cultural pursuits; (after conquest) to disband troops and attend to civilian affairs

偃臥(ㄧㄢˇ ㄨㄛˋ)
to lie (or sleep) on one's back

偃月刀(ㄧㄢˇ ㄩㄝˋ ㄉㄠ)
a big crescent knife with a long shaft (especially the one used by General Kuan Yü (關羽) in the Epoch of the Three Kingdoms)

【假】216
1. ㄐㄧㄚˇ jea jiǎ
1. false; not real; phoney; artificial; fake; bogus; sham
2. supposing; if
3. to borrow; to avail oneself of
4. a Chinese family name

假扮(ㄐㄧㄚˇ ㄅㄢˋ)
to disguise; to masquerade

假寐(ㄐㄧㄚˇ ㄇㄟˋ)
to sleep without taking off one's clothes; to take a nap; a catnap; a doze; a siesta

假冒(ㄐㄧㄚˇ ㄇㄠˋ)
① to counterfeit ② to assume the identity of somebody else

假面具(ㄐㄧㄚˇ ㄇㄧㄢˋ ㄐㄩˋ)
a mask—a false front

假名(ㄐㄧㄚˇ ㄇㄧㄥˊ)
①a false name; a pseudonym; an alias ② kana (the Japanese syllabary)

假髮(ㄐㄧㄚˇ ㄈㄚˇ)
a wig

假分數(ㄐㄧㄚˇ ㄈㄣ ㄕㄨˋ)
(arithmetic) an improper fraction

假貸(ㄐㄧㄚˇ ㄉㄞˋ)
to borrow (money, etc.)

假貸顏色(ㄐㄧㄚˇ ㄉㄞˋ ㄧㄢˊ ㄙㄜˋ)
to tolerate; to bear

假道(ㄐㄧㄚˇ ㄉㄠˋ)
via; by way of

假道學(ㄐㄧㄚˇ ㄉㄠˋ ㄒㄩㄝˊ)
a sanctimonious person; a hypocrite

假定(ㄐㄧㄚˇ ㄉㄧㄥˋ)
①if; assuming; supposing; a supposition; a hypothesis; an assumption ②(mathematics) a postulate

假動作(ㄐㄧㄚˇ ㄉㄨㄥˋ ㄗㄨㄛˋ)
(sports) dummy play; a deceiving move

假託(ㄐㄧㄚˇ ㄊㄨㄛ)
①an excuse; a pretext; a subterfuge ②by means of ③ under someone else's name

假退役(ㄐㄧㄚˇ ㄊㄨㄟˋ ㄧˋ)
semi-retirement from the military service, which permits the person concerned to take up civilian jobs while still drawing part of his military pay

假老實(ㄐㄧㄚˇ ㄌㄠˇ ㄕˊ)
double-dealing; double-faced

假公濟私(ㄐㄧㄚˇ ㄍㄨㄥ ㄐㄧˋ ㄙ)
to attain private or personal ends in the name of official duties; to gain private ends in public cause or by public money

假扣押(ㄐㄧㄚˇ ㄎㄡˋ ㄧㄚ)
(law) provisional seizure

假花(ㄐㄧㄚˇ ㄏㄨㄚ)
an artificial flower

假話(ㄐㄧㄚˇ ㄏㄨㄚˋ)
a lie; a falsehood

假借(ㄐㄧㄚˇ ㄐㄧㄝˋ)
① to borrow ②"phonetic loan characters"—one of the six classes of the Chinese characters (A character under this category is used with the sense which properly belongs to another of the same sound but different form.)

假借名義(ㄐㄧㄚˇ ㄐㄧㄝˋ ㄇㄧㄥˊ ㄧˋ)
under the guise of; in the name of

假戲眞做(ㄐㄧㄚˇ ㄒㄧˋ ㄓㄣ ㄗㄨㄛˋ)
to do something seriously after starting it as a joke, ruse, etc.

假想(ㄐㄧㄚˇ ㄒㄧㄤˇ)
①an imagination; a hypothesis; a supposition ②imaginary; hypothetical; fictitious

假想敵(ㄐㄧㄚˇ ㄒㄧㄤˇ ㄉㄧˊ)
a hypothetical enemy; an imaginary enemy

假象(ㄐㄧㄚˇ ㄒㄧㄤˋ)
①false appearances or impressions: 他製造假象。He created a false impression. ②(geology) a pseudomorph

假惺惺(ㄐㄧㄚˇ ㄒㄧㄥ ·ㄒㄧㄥ)
to pretend; to shed crocodile tears: 他假惺惺表示願意支持你。He pretended to express his willingness to support

you.
假性天花(ㄐㄧㄚˇ ㄒㄧㄥˋ ㄊㄧㄢ ㄏㄨㄚ)
or 假痘(ㄐㄧㄚˇ ㄉㄡˋ)
varioloid
假性近視(ㄐㄧㄚˇ ㄒㄧㄥˋ ㄐㄧㄣˋ ㄕˋ)
pseudo-myopia
假執行(ㄐㄧㄚˇ ㄓˊ ㄒㄧㄥˊ)
(law) a false execution; to sequestrate
假正經(ㄐㄧㄚˇ ㄓㄥˋ ㄐㄧㄥ)
hypocritical
假裝(ㄐㄧㄚˇ ㄓㄨㄤ)
to pretend; to assume the appearance of
假處分(ㄐㄧㄚˇ ㄔㄨˇ ㄈㄣˋ)
provisional measures
假充(ㄐㄧㄚˇ ㄔㄨㄥ)
to counterfeit; to pretend
假充內行(ㄐㄧㄚˇ ㄔㄨㄥ ㄋㄟˋ ㄏㄤˊ)
to pretend to know what one does not
假使(ㄐㄧㄚˇ ㄕˇ)
if; in case; supposing: 假使他不能來，誰做這項工作? Supposing he can't come, who will do the work?
假釋(ㄐㄧㄚˇ ㄕˋ)
to parole; parole; conditional release; to free (a prisoner) on probation
假設(ㄐㄧㄚˇ ㄕㄜˋ)
a hypothesis; a supposition; an assumption: 科學假設 a scientific hypothesis
假設法(ㄐㄧㄚˇ ㄕㄜˋ ㄈㄚˇ)or 假設語氣(ㄐㄧㄚˇ ㄕㄜˋ ㄩˇ ㄑㄧˋ)
(grammar) the subjunctive mood
假手(ㄐㄧㄚˇ ㄕㄡˇ)
to do something by means of (an agent)
假手他人(ㄐㄧㄚˇ ㄕㄡˇ ㄊㄚ ㄖㄣˊ)
to do something (usually evil) by another's hand; to make somebody else do the work
假山(ㄐㄧㄚˇ ㄕㄢ)
a small artificial hill (used as decoration in a Chinese garden); a rockery
假聲(ㄐㄧㄚˇ ㄕㄥ)
(music) falsetto
假說(ㄐㄧㄚˇ ㄕㄨㄛ)
a postulate; a hypothesis
假仁假義(ㄐㄧㄚˇ ㄖㄣˊ ㄐㄧㄚˇ ㄧˋ)
to be a wolf in sheep's clothing; to shed crocodile tears; pretended benevolence and righteousness; hypocrisy
假如(ㄐㄧㄚˇ ㄖㄨˊ)
supposing; in case; if
假若(ㄐㄧㄚˇ ㄖㄨㄛˋ)
if; supposing; in case
假造(ㄐㄧㄚˇ ㄗㄠˋ)
① to forge; to counterfeit: 那張鈔票是假造的。That bank note is a forgery. ② to invent; to fabricate
假造罪名(ㄐㄧㄚˇ ㄗㄠˋ ㄗㄨㄟˋ ㄇㄧㄥˊ)
to cook up a false charge against; to frame up
假慈悲(ㄐㄧㄚˇ ㄘˊ ㄅㄟ)
pretending to be kindhearted
假死(ㄐㄧㄚˇ ㄙˇ)
①(medicine) suspended animation ② to play dead; to feign death; sham death
假以時日(ㄐㄧㄚˇ ㄧˇ ㄕˊ ㄖˋ)
to give sufficient time
假意(ㄐㄧㄚˇ ㄧˋ)
① false intent; insincerity; hypocrisy ② to pretend
假意奉承(ㄐㄧㄚˇ ㄧˋ ㄈㄥˋ ㄔㄥˊ)
false flattery
假牙(ㄐㄧㄚˇ ㄧㄚˊ)
a false tooth; a denture

【假】 216
2. ㄐㄧㄚˋ jiah jià
a holiday
假條(ㄐㄧㄚˋ ㄊㄧㄠˊ)
① an application for leave ② a leave permit
假期(ㄐㄧㄚˋ ㄑㄧˊ)
a vacation; a holiday
假日(ㄐㄧㄚˋ ㄖˋ)
a holiday

【偈】 217
ㄐㄧㄝˊ jye jié
1. brave; martial
2. hasty; scudding

【偉】 218
ㄨㄟˇ woei wěi
1. extraordinary; great; big; gigantic: 他身體魁偉。He is gigantic in stature.
2. a Chinese family name
偉大(ㄨㄟˇ ㄉㄚˋ)
great; extraordinary: 貝多芬是一個偉大的音樂家。Beethoven was a great musician.
偉績(ㄨㄟˇ ㄐㄧ)
great achievements
偉器(ㄨㄟˇ ㄑㄧˋ)
a man of great capability
偉人(ㄨㄟˇ ㄖㄣˊ)
a great man
偉岸(ㄨㄟˇ ㄢˋ)
tall and robust
偉業(ㄨㄟˇ ㄧㄝˋ)
a great career; monumental accomplishments

【偌】 219
ㄖㄨㄛˋ ruoh ruò
so (used as an adverb to modify an adjective)
偌大(ㄖㄨㄛˋ ㄉㄚˋ)
so big: 你見過偌大的地方? Have you seen such a big place?

【偎】 220
ㄨㄟ uei wēi
1. to cuddle; to embrace
2. intimate; very dear to
3. to lean on
偎傍(ㄨㄟ ㄅㄤˋ)
to stay close together
偎貼(ㄨㄟ ㄊㄧㄝ)
to snuggle close to
偎臉(ㄨㄟ ㄌㄧㄢˇ)
to put cheek and cheek together
偎紅倚翠(ㄨㄟ ㄏㄨㄥˊ ㄧˇ ㄘㄨㄟˋ)
to frequent brothels
偎愛(ㄨㄟ ㄞˋ)
to be intimately in love
偎倚(ㄨㄟ ㄧˇ)or 偎依(ㄨㄟ ㄧ)
to cuddle or curl up; to snuggle up to; to lean close to: 嬰兒偎倚在母親的懷裏。The baby snuggled up in its mother's arms.

【偏】 221
ㄆㄧㄢ pian piān
1. biased; not fair; prejudiced; partial
2. leaning; inclined to one side
3. an auxiliary verb indicating a sense of contrariness or determination
偏頗(ㄆㄧㄢ ㄆㄛ)
partial; biased; not fair
偏旁(ㄆㄧㄢ ㄆㄤˊ)or 偏旁兒(ㄆㄧㄢ ㄆㄤˊㄦ)
a radical on one side of a character
偏僻(ㄆㄧㄢ ㄆㄧˋ)
(said of a place) out-of-the-way; not easily accessible; secluded: 那是一個偏僻的小村莊。That is an out-of-the-way

village.
偏偏(ㄆ丨ㄢ ㄆ丨ㄢ)
①unfortunately it happened that… ②used before a verb to show contrariness or determination: 不該他去，他偏偏要去。He was not supposed to go, but he insisted on going.
偏廢(ㄆ丨ㄢ ㄈㄟˋ)
①crippled ②to emphasize one thing and neglect others
偏方(ㄆ丨ㄢ ㄈㄤ)or 偏方兒(ㄆ丨ㄢ ㄈㄤㄦ)
(Chinese medicine) an informal recipe or prescription; a folk prescription
偏房(ㄆ丨ㄢ ㄈㄤˊ)
a concubine
偏鋒(ㄆ丨ㄢ ㄈㄥ)
①(said of writings or paintings) an oblique stroke of the brush ②(figuratively) an unorthodox way of doing things
偏頭痛(ㄆ丨ㄢ ㄊㄡˊ ㄊㄨㄥˋ)
(medicine) hemicrania; migraine
偏袒(ㄆ丨ㄢ ㄊㄢˇ)
partiality; partial: 做父母的不應偏袒任何一個孩子。A parent should not be partial to any of his children.
偏疼(ㄆ丨ㄢ ㄊㄥˊ)
undue partiality (as of a parent to a child)
偏題(ㄆ丨ㄢ ㄊ丨ˊ)
a catch question (in an examination)
偏聽偏信(ㄆ丨ㄢ ㄊ丨ㄥ ㄆ丨ㄢ ㄒ丨ㄣˋ)
to heed and believe only one side—to favor one side too much; to be prejudiced; to be biased
偏勞(ㄆ丨ㄢ ㄌㄠˊ)
①to let one person take on the work of the whole team: 我們只好偏勞他了。We cannot but let him take on the whole job. ②(usually from a boss to an employee) "Thanks for the good work."
偏離(ㄆ丨ㄢ ㄌ丨ˊ)
to deviate; to diverge: 他的談話偏離論題。His talk deviated from the subject under discussion.
偏枯(ㄆ丨ㄢ ㄎㄨ)
①paralysed on one side ②uneven or unfair distribution of something, such as benefit, etc.③ a theory about calligraphy
偏狂(ㄆ丨ㄢ ㄎㄨㄤˊ)
monomania
偏好(ㄆ丨ㄢ ㄏㄠˋ)
a hobby
偏護(ㄆ丨ㄢ ㄏㄨˋ)
partial; to favor one side against the other; to give undue protection to; to screen or shelter
偏諱(ㄆ丨ㄢ ㄏㄨㄟˋ)
to avoid using either of the two characters in the emperor's or one's parent's name
偏激(ㄆ丨ㄢ ㄐ丨)
extreme; radical: 他的想法偏激。He has radical ideas.
偏激分子(ㄆ丨ㄢ ㄐ丨 ㄈㄣ ㄗˇ)
a radical
偏見(ㄆ丨ㄢ ㄐ丨ㄢˋ)
prejudice; bias: 他對我懷有偏見。He has a prejudice against me.
偏巧(ㄆ丨ㄢ ㄑ丨ㄠˇ)
it so happened; as luck would have it: 那天偏巧是一個晴天。It happened to be a fine day.
偏斜(ㄆ丨ㄢ ㄒ丨ㄝˊ)
to slant
偏心(ㄆ丨ㄢ ㄒ丨ㄣ)
partiality; bias: 她絲毫不偏心。She is free from any bias.
偏向(ㄆ丨ㄢ ㄒ丨ㄤˋ)
to lean or to be inclined toward
偏執(ㄆ丨ㄢ ㄓˊ)
stubbornly biased; strong inclination toward
偏轉(ㄆ丨ㄢ ㄓㄨㄢˇ)
(physics) deflection
偏重(ㄆ丨ㄢ ㄓㄨㄥˋ)
①to give undue emphasis to: 我們研究科學不應只偏重理論而忽視實驗。In studying science, we shouldn't stress theory at the expense of experiment. ②to lean heavily toward; to have extraordinary faith in (somebody)
偏差(ㄆ丨ㄢ ㄔㄚ)
errors; deviation
偏食(ㄆ丨ㄢ ㄕˊ)
(said of children) to eat certain dishes only
偏蝕(ㄆ丨ㄢ ㄕˊ)
a partial eclipse (of the sun or moon)
偏才(ㄆ丨ㄢ ㄘㄞˊ)
clever in petty matters; talents in a petty way
偏私(ㄆ丨ㄢ ㄙ)
biased; favoritism: 受雇者認爲大部分的加薪都偏私。The employees think that most pay raises are based on favoritism.
偏阿(ㄆ丨ㄢ ㄜ)
biased; prejudiced
偏愛(ㄆ丨ㄢ ㄞˋ)
to love someone or something in particular; personal favorites or hobbies: 孩子們常常偏愛糖果。Children love candy in particular.
偏安(ㄆ丨ㄢ ㄢ)
(the authority of the emperor) to be confined to a (usually small) portion of his empire (due to rebellion or foreign invasion)
偏倚(ㄆ丨ㄢ 丨ˇ)
to lean on
偏要(ㄆ丨ㄢ 丨ㄠˋ)
bent on having (in disregard of difficulties involved or others' opposition); to positively choose, take, etc.: 這男孩子偏要惡作劇。The boy is bent on mischief.
偏遠(ㄆ丨ㄢ ㄩㄢˇ)
remote; faraway

【偓】 222
ㄨㄛˋ woh wò
1. narrow-mindedness
2. a Chinese family name

【偕】 223
ㄒ丨ㄝ shye xié
(又讀 ㄐ丨ㄝ jie jiē)
1. to accompany
2. together
偕同(ㄒ丨ㄝ ㄊㄨㄥˊ)
in company with; along with
偕老(ㄒ丨ㄝ ㄌㄠˇ)
to grow old together as man and wife

【做】 224
ㄗㄨㄛˋ tzuoh zuò
1. to work; to make; to do: 她

在做巧克力蛋糕。She is making a chocolate cake.
2. to act as
3. to pretend to be
4. to give (a party, reception, etc.)
5. to enter (a profession)
6. to become: 後來她做了褓姆。Later she became a baby-sitter.

做伴(ㄗㄨㄛˋ ㄅㄢˋ)
to keep somebody company

做不得(ㄗㄨㄛˋ ·ㄅㄨ ·ㄉㄜ)
Don't do it!

做不了(ㄗㄨㄛˋ ·ㄅㄨ ㄌㄧㄠˇ)
cannot do it

做不好(ㄗㄨㄛˋ ·ㄅㄨ ㄏㄠˇ)
cannot do it well

做媒(ㄗㄨㄛˋ ㄇㄟˊ)
to be a matchmaker

做夢(ㄗㄨㄛˋ ㄇㄥˋ)
①to have a dream; to dream: 我昨晚做了個惡夢。I had a bad dream last night. ②to have a pipe dream; to daydream: 她的從影計畫不過是在做夢罷了。Her plans for a movie career are just a pipe dream.

做面子(ㄗㄨㄛˋ ㄇㄧㄢˋ ·ㄗ)
to render eye-service; to put up a pleasant front; to do something for the sake of appearance

做法(ㄗㄨㄛˋ ㄈㄚˇ)
way of doing a thing; practice: 他慣常的做法是利用別人。His usual way of doing things is to take advantage of others.

做飯(ㄗㄨㄛˋ ㄈㄢˋ)
to prepare food; to prepare a meal

做大(ㄗㄨㄛˋ ㄉㄚˋ)
to arrogate to oneself a high rank; to put on airs

做得了(ㄗㄨㄛˋ ·ㄉㄜ ㄌㄧㄠˇ)
can be done

做到(ㄗㄨㄛˋ ㄉㄠˋ)
to accomplish; to achieve: 你應該說到做到。You should accomplish what you promise.

做東(ㄗㄨㄛˋ ㄉㄨㄥ)
to play the host; to host

做頭髮(ㄗㄨㄛˋ ㄊㄡˊ ㄈㄚˇ)
to have one's hair done at a beauty parlor

做禮拜(ㄗㄨㄛˋ ㄌㄧˇ ㄅㄞˋ)
to go to church; to be at church

做弄(ㄗㄨㄛˋ ㄌㄨㄥˋ)
to make fun of; to play jokes upon

做官(ㄗㄨㄛˋ ㄍㄨㄢ)
to become an official; to secure oneself an official position; to join government service: 有些人一旦做官，就想發財。Some people wish to become rich once they become officials.

做工(ㄗㄨㄛˋ ㄍㄨㄥ)
①to work: 他在電算機工廠做工。He works in a computer factory. ②the acting part in Chinese opera, etc.

做客(ㄗㄨㄛˋ ㄎㄜˋ)
to be a guest: 我爸爸昨晚到一個老朋友家裏去做客。My father was a guest at an old friend's last night.

做闊(ㄗㄨㄛˋ ㄎㄨㄛˋ)
to show off one's wealth; to make a display of one's riches

做和尚(ㄗㄨㄛˋ ㄏㄜˊ ㄕㄤˋ)
to become a Buddhist monk

做好事(ㄗㄨㄛˋ ㄏㄠˇ ㄕˋ)
①to do a good deed; to help the needy ②to perform religious rites for the repose of the dead

做好人(ㄗㄨㄛˋ ㄏㄠˇ ㄖㄣˊ)
to play the role of a good guy (often insincerely)

做好做歹(ㄗㄨㄛˋ ㄏㄠˇ ㄗㄨㄛˋ ㄉㄞˇ)
to play the good or crook (to get something done)

做活(ㄗㄨㄛˋ ㄏㄨㄛˊ)or 做活兒(ㄗㄨㄛˋ ㄏㄨㄛˊㄦ)
①to earn a living; to work: 我們一塊兒在田裏做活兒。We worked together in the fields. ②(said of women) to do needlework

做假(ㄗㄨㄛˋ ㄐㄧㄚˇ)
to cheat

做絕(ㄗㄨㄛˋ ㄐㄩㄝˊ)
①to leave no room for a maneuver; to leave no avenue of retreat: 他把事情做絕了。He left himself no avenue of retreat. ②to do to the utmost: 這流氓壞事做絕了。The hoodlum has done villainies to the utmost.

做小(ㄗㄨㄛˋ ㄒㄧㄠˇ)
to be someone's concubine

做主(ㄗㄨㄛˋ ㄓㄨˇ)
to take charge of; to be responsible for; to decide

做莊(ㄗㄨㄛˋ ㄓㄨㄤ)
(gambling) to be the banker

做事(ㄗㄨㄛˋ ㄕˋ)
①to handle affairs; to do a deed; to act: 我們應該熱心為大衆做事。We should handle the public affairs heartily. ②to work; to have a job: 我在鋼廠做事。I work in a steel mill.

做手脚(ㄗㄨㄛˋ ㄕㄡˇ ㄐㄧㄠˇ)
to tamper something with the intention to cheat or to hurt somebody

做聲(ㄗㄨㄛˋ ㄕㄥ)
to make a sound; to speak: 別做聲! Keep quiet! 或Don't speak!

做生日(ㄗㄨㄛˋ ㄕㄥ ㄖˋ)or 做壽(ㄗㄨㄛˋ ㄕㄡˋ)
to give a birthday party; to celebrate one's birthday

做生意(ㄗㄨㄛˋ ㄕㄥ ㄧˋ)
to do business transactions; to be a businessman

做人(ㄗㄨㄛˋ ㄖㄣˊ)
①to conduct oneself; to behave: 他懂得如何做人處世。He knows how to conduct himself in society. ②to be an upright person: 他想要重新做人。He wishes to be an upright person again.

做人情(ㄗㄨㄛˋ ㄖㄣˊ ㄑㄧㄥˊ)
to do something as a favor; to do someone a favor of doing something; to do someone a special favor

做賊心虛(ㄗㄨㄛˋ ㄗㄟˊ ㄒㄧㄣ ㄒㄩ)
(literally) The thief has a guilty conscience.—One who has done something bad secretly cannot look others in the eye. 或 The evildoer has a guilty conscience.

做作(ㄗㄨㄛˋ ㄗㄨㄛˋ)
①affectation; pretentiousness; affected; pretentious ②to affect; to behave unnaturally

[人部]

〔人部〕

做愛(ㄗㄨㄛˋ ㄞˋ)
to make love
做衣服(ㄗㄨㄛˋ ㄧ ㄈㄨˊ)
to tailor; to have a dress made
做一天和尚撞一天鐘(ㄗㄨㄛˋ ㄧˋ ㄊㄧㄢ ㄏㄜˊ ㄕㄤˋ ㄓㄨㄤˋ ㄧˋ ㄊㄧㄢ ㄓㄨㄥ)
to keep tolling the bell as long as one is a monk—to take a passive attitude towards one's duty
做樣子(ㄗㄨㄛˋ ㄧㄤˋ ·ㄗ)
to go through the motion of doing something; to pretend to do something
做文章(ㄗㄨㄛˋ ㄨㄣˊ ㄓㄤ)
①to write an essay ②to make an issue of

【停】 225
ㄊㄧㄥˊ tyng tíng
1. to stop; to pause; to halt; to stay; to park: 雨已經停了。The rain has stopped.
2. to suspend; to delay
3. percentage

停泊(ㄊㄧㄥˊ ㄅㄛˊ)
to anchor; to berth; to dock: 船停泊著。The ship was at anchor.
停擺(ㄊㄧㄥˊ ㄅㄞˇ)
(literally) The pendulum stops.—to suspend work: 鬧鐘停擺了。The alarm clock has stopped.
停辦(ㄊㄧㄥˊ ㄅㄢˋ)
to suspend (a business or school); to stop handling something
停飛(ㄊㄧㄥˊ ㄈㄟ)
the grounding of aircraft: 飛機因霧而停飛。The airplanes were grounded by the fog.
停放(ㄊㄧㄥˊ ㄈㄤˋ)
to park; to place
停付(ㄊㄧㄥˊ ㄈㄨˋ)
to stop payment (of checks, salaries, etc.)
停當(ㄊㄧㄥˊ ㄉㄤˋ)
ready; all set
停電(ㄊㄧㄥˊ ㄉㄧㄢˋ)
①power failure; blackout ② to cut off power supply
停頓(ㄊㄧㄥˊ ㄉㄨㄣˋ)
to grind to a halt; to suspend:罷工使工業逐漸停頓。The strikes brought industry grinding to a halt.
停妥(ㄊㄧㄥˊ ㄊㄨㄛˇ)
①ready; all set; in A-1 condition ②(said of a vehicle, etc.) to have been parked in a proper place
停留(ㄊㄧㄥˊ ㄌㄧㄡˊ)
to stay; to stop or remain (at a certain stage)
停擱(ㄊㄧㄥˊ ㄍㄜ)
to stop and shelve (a project, etc.)
停工(ㄊㄧㄥˊ ㄍㄨㄥ)
to suspend work
停課(ㄊㄧㄥˊ ㄎㄜˋ)
to suspend class: 昨天學校停課了。Classes were suspended yesterday.
停靠(ㄊㄧㄥˊ ㄎㄠˋ)
①(said of a train) to stop ②(said of a ship) to berth
停刊(ㄊㄧㄥˊ ㄎㄢ)
(said of a newspaper, magazine, etc.) to stop publication
停航(ㄊㄧㄥˊ ㄏㄤˊ)
to suspend air or shipping service: 班機因暴風雨而停航。The regular flight is suspended on account of the storm.
停火(ㄊㄧㄥˊ ㄏㄨㄛˇ)
to cease fire
停機坪(ㄊㄧㄥˊ ㄐㄧ ㄆㄧㄥˊ)
an apron (at an airfield)
停經期(ㄊㄧㄥˊ ㄐㄧㄥ ㄑㄧˊ)
menopause
停妻再娶(ㄊㄧㄥˊ ㄑㄧ ㄗㄞˋ ㄑㄩˇ)
to commit bigamy
停息(ㄊㄧㄥˊ ㄒㄧˊ)
to stop; to cease: 暴風雨終於停息了。At last the storm has ceased.
停歇(ㄊㄧㄥˊ ㄒㄧㄝ)
to stop for a rest
停薪(ㄊㄧㄥˊ ㄒㄧㄣ)
to stop or suspend payment to an employee
停學(ㄊㄧㄥˊ ㄒㄩㄝˊ)
to rusticate (a student); rustication
停職(ㄊㄧㄥˊ ㄓˊ)
to suspend a person from office
停止(ㄊㄧㄥˊ ㄓˇ)
to stop; to cease: 比賽因雨停止。The game was stopped by rain.
停滯(ㄊㄧㄥˊ ㄓˋ)
①to stop or be held up (at a certain stage, etc.): 會議停滯不前。The meeting has stopped. ②indigestion
停戰(ㄊㄧㄥˊ ㄓㄢˋ)
①to stop fighting ②a truce; suspension of hostilities: 兩軍之間宣布停戰。A truce was declared between the two armies.
停戰協定(ㄊㄧㄥˊ ㄓㄢˋ ㄒㄧㄝˊ ㄉㄧㄥˋ)
a truce; an armistice
停車(ㄊㄧㄥˊ ㄔㄜ)
to park a car
停車場(ㄊㄧㄥˊ ㄔㄜ ㄔㄤˊ)or(ㄊㄧㄥˊ ㄔㄜ ㄔㄤˇ)
a parking lot
停產(ㄊㄧㄥˊ ㄔㄢˇ)
to stop production
停屍間(ㄊㄧㄥˊ ㄕ ㄐㄧㄢ)
a mortuary
停水(ㄊㄧㄥˊ ㄕㄨㄟˇ)
to cut off the water supply
停業(ㄊㄧㄥˊ ㄧㄝˋ)
to stop doing business; to close down 亦作「歇業」

【健】 226
ㄐㄧㄢˋ jiann jiàn
1. healthy; strong
2. vigorous; capable
3. fond of; inclined to; liable to
4. to strengthen; to toughen

健步(ㄐㄧㄢˋ ㄅㄨˋ)
①to walk fast: 那老人健步如飛。The old man walked as if on wings. ②capable of walking a long way
健美(ㄐㄧㄢˋ ㄇㄟˇ)
①(said of a man) healthy and handsome; tall, dark and handsome ②(said of a woman) healthy and pretty; having a nice figure; beautiful in an athletic way ③vigorous and graceful
健談(ㄐㄧㄢˋ ㄊㄢˊ)
brilliant conversation: 她的健談很令人激賞。Her brilliant conversation is much appreciated.
健康(ㄐㄧㄢˋ ㄎㄤ)
① health: 他身體一向很健康。He has always had good health. ②healthy: 孩子們看起來非常健康。The children

looked very healthy.
健康教育(ㄐㄧㄢˋ ㄎㄤ ㄐㄧㄠˋ ㄩˋ)
health education
健康證明書(ㄐㄧㄢˋ ㄎㄤ ㄓㄥˋ ㄇㄧㄥˊ ㄕㄨ)
a health certificate
健將(ㄐㄧㄢˋ ㄐㄧㄤˋ)
① one who plays a leading role in an activity ② one who is good at a sport or sports; a top-notch player: 他是足球健將。He is a top-notch footballer.
健全(ㄐㄧㄢˋ ㄑㄩㄢˊ)
① in good condition; in good order; flawless (usually referring to a system, an institution, etc.) ② to strengthen; to perfect
健行(ㄐㄧㄢˋ ㄒㄧㄥˊ)
to hike; hiking
健壯(ㄐㄧㄢˋ ㄓㄨㄤˋ)
healthy and robust; strong and vigorous: 他是一位健壯的小伙子。He is a robust young man.
健身房(ㄐㄧㄢˋ ㄕㄣ ㄈㄤˊ)
a gymnasium; a gym
健身操(ㄐㄧㄢˋ ㄕㄣ ㄘㄠ)
calisthenics
健在(ㄐㄧㄢˋ ㄗㄞˋ)
to be in good health; alive
健素糖(ㄐㄧㄢˋ ㄙㄨˋ ㄊㄤˊ)
sugar-coated yeast pills
健兒(ㄐㄧㄢˋ ㄦˊ)
(said of friendly forces) soldiers
健胃散(ㄐㄧㄢˋ ㄨㄟˋ ㄙㄢˇ)
a medicine which expedites food digestion and is consequently conducive to the health of stomach
健旺(ㄐㄧㄢˋ ㄨㄤˋ)
to be in wonderful health; robust and vigorous; energetic: 那老人依然精力健旺有朝氣。The old man is still vigorous and lively.
健忘(ㄐㄧㄢˋ ㄨㄤˋ)
forgetful; liable to forget: 老年人有時很健忘。Old people are sometimes forgetful.
健忘症(ㄐㄧㄢˋ ㄨㄤˋ ㄓㄥˋ)
(pathology) amnesia

【偬】 227 ㄗㄨㄥˇ tzoong zǒng
1. urgent; having no leisure; busy
2. to be in (financial, etc.) straits
偬偬(ㄗㄨㄥˇ ㄗㄨㄥˇ)
in a hurry

【側】 228 ㄘㄜˋ tseh cè
1. the side; sideways: 道路兩側種着楓樹。Maples are planted on both sides of the road.
2. to slant; to incline towards: 我側身和他說話。I was inclining to talk to him.
3. low and narrow-minded; prejudiced
側門(ㄘㄜˋ ㄇㄣˊ)
a side door
側面(ㄘㄜˋ ㄇㄧㄢˋ)
the side; the flank
側面圖(ㄘㄜˋ ㄇㄧㄢˋ ㄊㄨˊ)
a profile
側面消息(ㄘㄜˋ ㄇㄧㄢˋ ㄒㄧㄠ ㄒㄧˊ)
sidelights
側目(ㄘㄜˋ ㄇㄨˋ)
① a sidelong glance; to look askance: 我們全都側目視之。We all looked upon it askance. ② to cause raised eyebrows
側光(ㄘㄜˋ ㄍㄨㄤ)
sidelight; light coming from the side
側擊(ㄘㄜˋ ㄐㄧˊ)
① a flank attack; to make a flank attack ② to make oblique remarks
側重(ㄘㄜˋ ㄓㄨㄥˋ)
to place particular emphasis on; to be partial: 我側重做反污染宣傳工作。My job is to place particular emphasis on anti-pollution propaganda.
側出(ㄘㄜˋ ㄔㄨ)
① to get out (launch, shoot, etc.) from the side ② to be born of a concubine
側身(ㄘㄜˋ ㄕㄣ)
① to live cautiously in apprehension ② to sidle; on one's side; sideways ③ (a modest expression) to be in (a profession, career, etc.)
側耳傾聽(ㄘㄜˋ ㄦˇ ㄑㄧㄥ ㄊㄧㄥ)
to listen attentively; to be all ears
側翼(ㄘㄜˋ ㄧˋ)
(military) a flank
側影(ㄘㄜˋ ㄧㄥˇ)
a silhouette; a profile
側臥(ㄘㄜˋ ㄨㄛˋ)
to lie on the side
側聞(ㄘㄜˋ ㄨㄣˊ)
to learn of something from others

【偵】 229 ㄓㄣ jen zhēn
1. to detect; to spy; to scout: 我們偵探敵人的行動。We spy upon the enemy's movements.
2. a scout; a spy; a detective: 他們派遣偵探到我國來。They sent out a spy to our country.
偵破(ㄓㄣ ㄆㄛˋ)
to bust a crime; to crack a criminal case
偵探(ㄓㄣ ㄊㄢˋ)
① a detective; a private eye ② to investigate
偵探小說(ㄓㄣ ㄊㄢˋ ㄒㄧㄠˇ ㄕㄨㄛ)
detective stories; whodunits
偵聽(ㄓㄣ ㄊㄧㄥ)
(military) to intercept (enemy radio communications); to monitor
偵緝(ㄓㄣ ㄑㄧˋ)
to track down and arrest
偵詢(ㄓㄣ ㄒㄩㄣˊ)
to examine a suspect or someone concerned to gather information
偵查(ㄓㄣ ㄔㄚˊ)
to investigate
偵察(ㄓㄣ ㄔㄚˊ)
reconnaissance; to reconnoiter
偵察敵情(ㄓㄣ ㄔㄚˊ ㄉㄧˊ ㄑㄧㄥˊ)
to gather intelligence about the enemy
偵察機(ㄓㄣ ㄔㄚˊ ㄐㄧ)
a reconnaissance plane

【偶】 230 ㄡˇ oou ǒu
1. an idol; an image
2. coincidentally; accidentally
3. once in a while; occasionally: 他偶一爲之。He does it once in a while.
4. not to be taken for granted
5. an even number
6. a counterpart: 無獨有偶。It is not a unique instance, but has its counterpart.
7. a mate; to mate

8. one's company; fellows; buddies

偶發(ㄡˇ ㄈㄚ)
to happen accidentally; to happen by chance; to happen occasionally

偶犯(ㄡˇ ㄈㄢˋ)
①a casual offense ②a casual offender

偶感(ㄡˇ ㄍㄢˇ)
to feel suddenly; to feel occasionally

偶合(ㄡˇ ㄏㄜˊ)
by coincidence; coincidental; coincidentally; accidental

偶或(ㄡˇ ㄏㄨㄛˋ)
by chance

偶戲(ㄡˇ ㄒㄧˋ)
a marionette show; a puppet show

偶像(ㄡˇ ㄒㄧㄤˋ)
an idol; an image

偶數(ㄡˇ ㄕㄨˋ)
an even number

偶然(ㄡˇ ㄖㄢˊ)
①unexpectedly ②accidentally; by chance: 我偶然遇見一個老朋友。I met an old friend by chance.

偶爾(ㄡˇ ㄦˇ)or 偶而(ㄡˇ ㄦˊ)
occasionally

【偷】 231
ㄊㄡ tou tōu

1. to steal; to filch; to burglarize; to pilfer
2. to do something without others' knowledge; stealthily; surreptitiously
3. to while away time without purpose
4. to have an extra-marital activity

偷盜(ㄊㄡ ㄉㄠˋ)
to steal; stealing; burglary; to pilfer

偷渡(ㄊㄡ ㄉㄨˋ)
to steal into another country by hiding oneself aboard a train, ship, airplane, etc.; to stow away

偷渡者(ㄊㄡ ㄉㄨˋ ㄓㄜˇ)
a stowaway

偷偷(ㄊㄡ ㄊㄡ)or 偷偷地(ㄊㄡ ㄊㄡ ·ㄉㄜ)
stealthily; secretly; covertly; on the sly (or quiet); quietly; without others' knowledge; surreptitiously: 我偷偷告訴他那個秘密。I told him the secret on the sly.

偷偷摸摸(ㄊㄡ ·ㄊㄡ ㄇㄛ ㄇㄛ)
stealthily; surreptitiously; to do something stealthily

偷天換日(ㄊㄡ ㄊㄧㄢ ㄏㄨㄢˋ ㄖˋ)
to steal the sky and put up a sham sun—to perpetrate a gigantic fraud; to commit a big cheat, fraud, etc.; to pull off a monumental hoax

偷聽(ㄊㄡ ㄊㄧㄥ)
to eavesdrop; eavesdropping; to bug; bugging; to tap; tapping

偷懶(ㄊㄡ ㄌㄢˇ)
to loaf on a job; to be lazy

偷工減料(ㄊㄡ ㄍㄨㄥ ㄐㄧㄢˇ ㄌㄧㄠˋ)
to do less work and use less or inferior materials than agreed upon (especially in a building job); to jerry-build; to scamp work and stint material

偷看(ㄊㄡ ㄎㄢˋ)
①to act Peeping Tom; to steal a look; to steal a glance: 他偷看了她一眼。He stole a glance at her. ②to cheat (in an examination)

偷空(ㄊㄡ ㄎㄨㄥˋ)or 偷空兒(ㄊㄡ ㄎㄨㄥˋㄦ)
to avail oneself of a leisure moment; to snatch a moment; to take time off: 他偷空睡了一小時。He snatched an hour's sleep.

偷漢子(ㄊㄡ ㄏㄢˋ ·ㄗ)
(said of a married woman) to have an affair with a man other than her own husband; to have a lover

偷活(ㄊㄡ ㄏㄨㄛˊ)or 偷生(ㄊㄡ ㄕㄥ)
to live without much purpose; to while away one's life span aimlessly; to live in disgrace: 他苟且偷生。He lives without ambition.

偷雞不著賠一把米(ㄊㄡ ㄐㄧ ㄅㄨˋ ㄓㄠˊ ㄆㄟˊ ㄧˋ ㄅㄚˇ ㄇㄧˇ)
(literally) The chicken thief failed to catch a chicken after losing a handful of rice which he used as a bait. —to fail to gain an advantage and incur a loss to oneself in the process; to go for wool and come home shorn

偷雞摸狗(ㄊㄡ ㄐㄧ ㄇㄛ ㄍㄡˇ)
①to steal ②an unprincipled person ③to engage in under-the-table dealings ④a thief

偷竊(ㄊㄡ ㄑㄧㄝˋ)
to steal; to pilfer; to filch; to thieve

偷巧(ㄊㄡ ㄑㄧㄠˇ)
to finesse; to take a shortcut

偷情(ㄊㄡ ㄑㄧㄥˊ)
to make love; to carry on a clandestine love affair

偷襲(ㄊㄡ ㄒㄧˊ)
to attack by surprise; a surprise attack; a sneak attack; a sneak raid

偷閒(ㄊㄡ ㄒㄧㄢˊ)
to steal a moment of leisure; to avail oneself of a leisure moment: 他忙裡偷閒。He snatched a little leisure from a busy life.

偷香竊玉(ㄊㄡ ㄒㄧㄤ ㄑㄧㄝˋ ㄩˋ)
(said of a man) to have illicit relation with a woman

偷生怕死(ㄊㄡ ㄕㄥ ㄆㄚˋ ㄙˇ)
cowardly; to be afraid to die or eager to save one's skin

偷嘴(ㄊㄡ ㄗㄨㄟˇ)
to take food stealthily; to steal food

偷安(ㄊㄡ ㄢ)
①(said of a person) to seek temporary ease; to live in complacency on barely sufficient or insecure means: 他終日苟且偷安。He seeks only temporary ease and comfort all day. ②(said of a state) to exist in precarious peace without trying to improve the situation

偷兒(ㄊㄡㄦ)
a thief

十畫

【傢】 232
ㄐㄧㄚ jia jiā

1. furniture
2. a tool or tools

傢伙(ㄐㄧㄚ ·ㄏㄨㄛ)
(in a comical sense) a character; a jerk; a son of a gun; a fellow; a guy

傢具 or 家具(ㄐㄧㄚ ㄐㄩˋ)
furniture: 床、椅子、書桌皆是傢具。Beds, chairs, and desks are furniture.

【傀】233
1. ㄎㄨㄟˇ koei kuǐ
a puppet

傀儡(ㄎㄨㄟˇ ㄌㄟˇ)
a puppet

傀儡戲(ㄎㄨㄟˇ ㄌㄟˇ ㄒㄧˋ)
a puppet show

【傀】233
2. ㄍㄨㄟ guei guī
great; wonderful

傀異(ㄍㄨㄟ ㄧˋ)
rare and strange

傀偉(ㄍㄨㄟ ㄨㄟˇ)
great and imposing

【傅】234
ㄈㄨˋ fuh fù
1. a teacher; to teach
2. to go together with; to add to; to be attached to
3. a Chinese family name

【傍】235
1. (旁) ㄆㄤˊ parng páng
beside; by the side of

傍邊(ㄆㄤˊ ㄅㄧㄢ)
beside

傍聽(ㄆㄤˊ ㄊㄧㄥ)
to audit (at a college class)

傍聽生(ㄆㄤˊ ㄊㄧㄥ ㄕㄥ)
an auditor (in a school class)

傍觀(ㄆㄤˊ ㄍㄨㄢ)
to watch on the sideline

傍偟(ㄆㄤˊ ㄏㄨㄤˊ)
vacillating

傍敲側擊(ㄆㄤˊ ㄑㄧㄠ ㄘㄜˋ ㄐㄧˊ)
to ask questions slyly (with a view to finding out a secret or an answer to something seemingly having nothing to do with the questions asked); to talk in a roundabout way; to make oblique references

傍系(ㄆㄤˊ ㄒㄧˋ)
blood relatives not on the direct lineal line such as brothers, uncles, nephews, nieces, etc.

傍人(ㄆㄤˊ ㄖㄣˊ)
other people

傍若無人(ㄆㄤˊ ㄖㄨㄛˋ ㄨˊ ㄖㄣˊ)
to act audaciously or uninhibitively as if there were no other persons around

【傍】235
2. ㄅㄤ bang bāng
near; approaching

傍午(ㄅㄤ ㄨˇ)
near noontime; shortly before noon

傍晚(ㄅㄤ ㄨㄢˇ)
dusk; twilight; nightfall: 我將在傍晚時歸來。I shall be back by nightfall.

【傍】235
3. ㄅㄤˋ banq bàng
1. to depend on
2. to draw near; to be close to: 船傍了岸。The boat drew alongside the bank.

傍戶而立(ㄅㄤˋ ㄏㄨˋ ㄦˊ ㄌㄧˋ)
to stand close to the door

傍人門戶(ㄅㄤˋ ㄖㄣˊ ㄇㄣˊ ㄏㄨˋ)
to depend on another or others; to follow in the steps of someone, as a disciple

【傑】236
ㄐㄧㄝˊ jye jié
1. outstanding; remarkable; extraordinary
2. a hero

傑出(ㄐㄧㄝˊ ㄔㄨ)
outstanding; eminent; extraordinary

傑作(ㄐㄧㄝˊ ㄗㄨㄛˋ)
a masterpiece

【傖】237
ㄘㄤ tsang cāng
1. (said of persons) vulgar; cheap; lowly
2. confused; disorderly

傖夫俗子(ㄘㄤ ㄈㄨ ㄙㄨˊ ㄗˇ)
a vulgar person

傖俗(ㄘㄤ ㄙㄨˊ)
vulgar

【傘】238
ㄙㄢˇ saan sǎn
1. an umbrella: 我要帶雨傘以防下雨。I'll take my umbrella in case it rains.
2. a parachute

傘兵(ㄙㄢˇ ㄅㄧㄥ)
paratroopers

傘骨(ㄙㄢˇ ㄍㄨˇ)
the ribs of an umbrella

【備】239
ㄅㄟˋ bey bèi
1. a sense of completeness; perfection
2. to be equipped with
3. to get ready
4. to prepare against
5. fully; in every possible way

備辦(ㄅㄟˋ ㄅㄢˋ)
to prepare; to provide; to get things ready

備補(ㄅㄟˋ ㄅㄨˇ)
awaiting to fill a vacancy (as a runner-up in a contest who will get the top spot if the winner is disqualified, etc.); the next choice; a stand-in or understudy

備馬(ㄅㄟˋ ㄇㄚˇ)
to saddle a horse for riding

備胎(ㄅㄟˋ ㄊㄞ)
a spare tire

備考(ㄅㄟˋ ㄎㄠˇ)
①for reference ② an appendix for reference

備荒(ㄅㄟˋ ㄏㄨㄤ)
to prepare against natural disasters: 他們儲糧以備荒。They store foodstuffs to prepare against natural disasters.

備件(ㄅㄟˋ ㄐㄧㄢˋ)
spare parts

備取(ㄅㄟˋ ㄑㄩˇ)
those candidates who have passed the qualification examination held by a school or organization but are put on the waiting list because the quota of enrollment or recruitment has been filled up by other candidates who score higher marks in the same examination; candidates on the waiting list for admission to a school

備悉(ㄅㄟˋ ㄒㄧ)
to learn completely; to know the whole story

備細(ㄅㄟˋ ㄒㄧˋ)
in detail; all the details (of an incident, etc.)

備至(ㄅㄟˋ ㄓˋ)
to the utmost; in every possible way: 他們對我關懷備至。They are considerate to me in every possible way.

備戰(ㄅㄟˋ ㄓㄢˋ)
①to prepare for war ②to be prepared against war

備註(ㄅㄟˋ ㄓㄨˋ)
①remarks or footnotes ②

〔人部〕

〔人部〕

space reserved for footnotes
備查(ㄅㄟˋ ㄔㄚˊ)
for reference
備嘗辛苦(ㄅㄟˋ ㄔㄤˊ ㄒㄧㄣ ㄎㄨˇ)
to undergo all the hardships
備述(ㄅㄟˋ ㄕㄨˋ)
to narrate or report completely
備案(ㄅㄟˋ ㄢˋ)
to serve as a record; to keep on record; to file or lodge an application and go ahead with a project before formal approval is granted
備而不用(ㄅㄟˋ ㄦˊ ㄅㄨˋ ㄩㄥˋ)
It's better to get ready for nothing than caught unprepared. 或 to have something ready just in case; to keep something for possible future use
備位(ㄅㄟˋ ㄨㄟˋ)
to be a "filler" for an opening
備忘錄(ㄅㄟˋ ㄨㄤˋ ㄌㄨˋ)
a memorandum
備員(ㄅㄟˋ ㄩㄢˊ)
a polite and modest term referring to oneself as just a "filler" for an opening
備用(ㄅㄟˋ ㄩㄥˋ)
reserve; spare; alternate

【傚】240 ㄒㄧㄠˋ shiaw xiào
to model after; to imitate; to emulate; to copy
傚尤(ㄒㄧㄠˋ ㄧㄡˊ)or 傚仿(ㄒㄧㄠˋ ㄈㄤˇ)
emulation (of bad example)

十一畫

【催】241 ㄘㄨㄟ tsuei cuī
to hasten; to urge; to press; to hurry
催逼(ㄘㄨㄟ ㄅㄧ)
to hasten; to press (for payment of a debt)亦作「催迫」
催眠(ㄘㄨㄟ ㄇㄧㄢˊ)
to hypnotize; to mesmerize
催眠術(ㄘㄨㄟ ㄇㄧㄢˊ ㄕㄨˋ)
hypnotism
催命符(ㄘㄨㄟ ㄇㄧㄥˋ ㄈㄨˊ)
a written Taoistic spell which is supposed to hasten a person's death; hence, anything having such an effect
催討(ㄘㄨㄟ ㄊㄠˇ)
to press for repayment of a debt
催淚彈(ㄘㄨㄟ ㄌㄟˋ ㄉㄢˋ)
a tear gas bomb; a tear gas grenade
催趕(ㄘㄨㄟ ㄍㄢˇ)
① to urge someone to come or go ② to hasten to a destination
催化(ㄘㄨㄟ ㄏㄨㄚˋ)
(chemistry) catalysis
催化劑(ㄘㄨㄟ ㄏㄨㄚˋ ㄐㄧˋ)
(chemistry) a catalyst
催請(ㄘㄨㄟ ㄑㄧㄥˇ)
to urge; to urge the guest of honor in a party to be present so that the function can begin in time
催生(ㄘㄨㄟ ㄕㄥ)
① a present from the parental home of the expectant mother usually one month before the childbirth ② a drug to hasten the birth of a child
催生針(ㄘㄨㄟ ㄕㄥ ㄓㄣ)
pituitary extract
催熟(ㄘㄨㄟ ㄕㄨˊ)
(agriculture) to accelerate the ripening (of fruit)
催租(ㄘㄨㄟ ㄗㄨ)
to dun or press for the payment of a rental
催促(ㄘㄨㄟ ㄘㄨˋ)
to hasten; to urge; to press: 他們催促我盡快去紐約。They urged me to go to New York as soon as possible.

【傭】242 ㄩㄥˋ yong yòng (又讀 ㄩㄥ iong yōng)
1. to hire
2. a servant; a domestic help
傭保(ㄩㄥˋ ㄅㄠˇ)
hired labor; an employee
傭兵(ㄩㄥˋ ㄅㄧㄥ)
mercenaries
傭工(ㄩㄥˋ ㄍㄨㄥ)
① to hire laborers ② hired laborers or servants: 傭工們贊成每日工作七小時。Hired laborers favor a seven-hour day.
傭工介紹所(ㄩㄥˋ ㄍㄨㄥ ㄐㄧㄝˋ ㄕㄠˋ ㄙㄨㄛˇ)
an agency handling the hiring of servants for clients at a fee

【傲】243 ㄠˋ aw ào
1. proud; haughty; overbearing
2. to disdain; to despise; to look down upon
3. rash and impatient
傲慢(ㄠˋ ㄇㄢˋ)
haughty and overbearing; impudent: 貴族往往傲慢輕蔑地對待平民。The nobles used to treat the common people with haughty contempt.
傲睨(ㄠˋ ㄋㄧˋ)
to look down upon; to despise
傲骨(ㄠˋ ㄍㄨˇ)
self-esteem; lofty character
傲氣(ㄠˋ ㄑㄧˋ)
an air of arrogance; haughtiness: 他這個人一向傲氣十足。He is always full of arrogance.
傲性(ㄠˋ ㄒㄧㄥˋ)
a proud temperament
傲世(ㄠˋ ㄕˋ)
to look down upon the world; to be lofty-minded
傲視(ㄠˋ ㄕˋ)
to turn up one's nose at; to show disdain for
傲岸(ㄠˋ ㄢˋ)
proud; haughty: 她是個生性傲岸的女人。She is a woman of a haughty nature.
傲物(ㄠˋ ㄨˋ)
overbearing; insolent; rude; haughty

【傳】244 1. ㄔㄨㄢˊ chwan chuán
1. to pass (a ball, an order, learning, etc.) on to
2. to propagate; to disseminate
3. to summon: 債務人被傳出庭。The debtor was summoned to appear in court.
4. to preach
傳播(ㄔㄨㄢˊ ㄅㄛˋ)
to disseminate (news, information, etc.); to spread; dissemination
傳播媒體(ㄔㄨㄢˊ ㄅㄛˋ ㄇㄟˊ ㄊㄧˇ)
a news medium; a mass medium
傳播界 (ㄔㄨㄢˊ ㄅㄛˋ ㄐㄧㄝˋ)
the media; journalistic circles

傳布 or 傳佈(ㄔㄨㄢˊ ㄅㄨˋ)
①to disseminate; to spread ②to preach: 那傳教士去山區傳佈福音。The missionary went to the mountain area to preach the gospel.
傳票(ㄔㄨㄢˊ ㄆㄧㄠˋ)
①(bookkeeping) a voucher ② (law) a summons for appearance in court; a subpoena
傳達(ㄔㄨㄢˊ ㄉㄚˊ)
①to forward (a message) ② to inform, or notify ③ a messenger
傳達室(ㄔㄨㄢˊ ㄉㄚˊ ㄕˋ)
a small office for messengers; an information office at the door of a government organization to announce the arrival of a caller; a reception office; a janitor's room
傳代(ㄔㄨㄢˊ ㄉㄞˋ)
to hand on from generation to generation
傳導(ㄔㄨㄢˊ ㄉㄠˇ)
to conduct (heat, electricity); conduction
傳道(ㄔㄨㄢˊ ㄉㄠˋ)
①to preach a religion (especially Christianity) ② to propagate doctrines of the ancient sages
傳單(ㄔㄨㄢˊ ㄉㄢ)
handbills; leaflets
傳遞(ㄔㄨㄢˊ ㄉㄧˋ)
① to forward (information, letters, etc.); to deliver; to transmit; to transfer: 我們彼此傳遞信息。We transmit messages to each other. ② to cheat by passing slips of paper containing answers in an examination
傳動(ㄔㄨㄢˊ ㄉㄨㄥˋ)
transmission; drive
傳統(ㄔㄨㄢˊ ㄊㄨㄥˇ)
tradition; convention; traditional
傳令(ㄔㄨㄢˊ ㄌㄧㄥˋ)
① to deliver or give orders ② a person delivering orders
傳令兵(ㄔㄨㄢˊ ㄌㄧㄥˋ ㄅㄧㄥ)
a soldier-messenger; a dispatch rider
傳國璽(ㄔㄨㄢˊ ㄍㄨㄛˊ ㄒㄧˇ)
the imperial seal in a hereditary monarchy, handed down by the founder of the dynasty to his heirs as a symbol of royal authority
傳觀(ㄔㄨㄢˊ ㄍㄨㄢ)or 傳閱(ㄔㄨㄢˊ ㄩㄝˋ)
to pass on for a look or reading: 那封信由在座的人傳閱。The letter was passed round the table.
傳話(ㄔㄨㄢˊ ㄏㄨㄚˋ)
to pass on a message
傳喚(ㄔㄨㄢˊ ㄏㄨㄢˋ)
to summon
傳家寶(ㄔㄨㄢˊ ㄐㄧㄚ ㄅㄠˇ)
a family treasure; an heirloom: 我們一定要把中國文化當作傳家寶,世世代代傳下去。We must cherish Chinese culture as our precious heirloom, and hand it on from generation to generation.
傳教(ㄔㄨㄢˊ ㄐㄧㄠˋ)
to preach a religion (especially Christianity)
傳教士(ㄔㄨㄢˊ ㄐㄧㄠˋ ㄕˋ)
a missionary: 那傳教士到非洲去使非洲人改信基督教。The missionary went to Africa to convert people to Christianity.
傳經(ㄔㄨㄢˊ ㄐㄧㄥ)
① to hand down the classics or sacred books ② the exogenous febrile disease passing from one channel to another
傳奇(ㄔㄨㄢˊ ㄑㄧˊ)
a legend, saga, romance, etc.
傳情(ㄔㄨㄢˊ ㄑㄧㄥˊ)
to flirt; to play at love; to coquet
傳習(ㄔㄨㄢˊ ㄒㄧˊ)
to teach and learn
傳寫(ㄔㄨㄢˊ ㄒㄧㄝˇ)
to copy down a masterpiece for study or appreciation
傳薪(ㄔㄨㄢˊ ㄒㄧㄣ)
to pass on the torch of learning
傳信(ㄔㄨㄢˊ ㄒㄧㄣˋ)
① to communicate one's belief to another ② to deliver letters
傳宣(ㄔㄨㄢˊ ㄒㄩㄢ)
to summon someone to the imperial audience
傳訊(ㄔㄨㄢˊ ㄒㄩㄣˋ)
(law) to summon (someone) for interrogation; to command someone to appear in a court of law
傳旨(ㄔㄨㄢˊ ㄓˇ)
(in old China) the transmission of imperial orders or edicts
傳眞(ㄔㄨㄢˊ ㄓㄣ)
① a lifelike portrait by a painter ② to transmit photos, printed matter, etc. (by electronic devices); to facsimile
傳眞機(ㄔㄨㄢˊ ㄓㄣ ㄐㄧ)
a facsimile machine or fax machine
傳種(ㄔㄨㄢˊ ㄓㄨㄥˇ)
① to propagate the species ② to have sons and grandsons to carry on the family name
傳抄(ㄔㄨㄢˊ ㄔㄠ)
to copy privately (a manuscript, document, etc.)
傳示(ㄔㄨㄢˊ ㄕˋ)
to show around
傳世(ㄔㄨㄢˊ ㄕˋ)
①(said of great books, etc.) to pass on to the world ② to hand down from generation to generation
傳授(ㄔㄨㄢˊ ㄕㄡˋ)
to teach; to teach by demonstration (especially in the art of hand-to-hand combat): 大師傳授我們如何攝影。The master teaches us how to take a good picture.
傳神(ㄔㄨㄢˊ ㄕㄣˊ)
a vivid portrayal (of a person or thing by writing or drawing)
傳神之筆(ㄔㄨㄢˊ ㄕㄣˊ ㄓ ㄅㄧˇ)
a vivid touch
傳聲筒(ㄔㄨㄢˊ ㄕㄥ ㄊㄨㄥˇ)
① a person who passes to others remarks supposed to be confidential ② a megaphone
傳說(ㄔㄨㄢˊ ㄕㄨㄛ)
hearsay; legends; unconfirmed reports
傳熱(ㄔㄨㄢˊ ㄖㄜˋ)
① heat conduction ② to communicate heat: 火爐傳熱

〔人部〕

到室內。A stove communicates heat to a room.

傳染(ㄔㄨㄢˊ ㄖㄢˇ)
to infect; to be contagious

傳染病(ㄔㄨㄢˊ ㄖㄢˇ ㄅㄧㄥˋ)
infectious diseases

傳宗接代(ㄔㄨㄢˊ ㄗㄨㄥ ㄐㄧㄝ ㄉㄞˋ)
to continue the family line by producing a male heir: 他的使命就是傳宗接代。His mission is to produce a son to continue the family.

傳送(ㄔㄨㄢˊ ㄙㄨㄥˋ)
to convey; to deliver

傳誦(ㄔㄨㄢˊ ㄙㄨㄥˋ)
① to pass from mouth to mouth (especially good poems): 當地居民傳誦着英雄事跡。The heroic deeds are continually on the lips of the local inhabitants. ② to be admired and appreciated by all; popular

傳訛(ㄔㄨㄢˊ ㄜˊ)
to pass on wrong reports

傳衣鉢(ㄔㄨㄢˊ ㄧ ㄅㄛ)
to hand one's trade on to disciples; to teach one's students all one knows (especially about academic endeavors and the fine arts)

傳言(ㄔㄨㄢˊ ㄧㄢˊ)
① hearsay; rumor: 那只是傳言罷了。It's merely hearsay. ② to pass on a message

傳揚(ㄔㄨㄢˊ ㄧㄤˊ)
to spread (from mouth to mouth): 他的美名已傳揚四方。His good reputation has spread far and wide.

傳爲佳話(ㄔㄨㄢˊ ㄨㄟˊ ㄐㄧㄚ ㄏㄨㄚˋ)
to become a favorite tale or fond memory

傳聞(ㄔㄨㄢˊ ㄨㄣˊ)
hearsay; unconfirmed reports: 據傳聞他已經大學畢業了。According to unconfirmed reports, he has graduated from college.

傳閱(ㄔㄨㄢˊ ㄩㄝˋ)
(said of a public notice or circular) to be passed around for perusal; to be circulated

【傳】 244
2. ㄓㄨㄢˋ juann zhuàn
a biography

傳略(ㄓㄨㄢˋ ㄌㄩㄝˋ)
a brief biography; a biographical sketch

傳記(ㄓㄨㄢˋ ㄐㄧˋ)
a biography

傳記小說(ㄓㄨㄢˋ ㄐㄧˋ ㄒㄧㄠˇ ㄕㄨㄛ)
a saga novel; *roman-fleuve*

傳注(ㄓㄨㄢˋ ㄓㄨˋ)
a remark on a classic

傳疏(ㄓㄨㄢˋ ㄕㄨˋ)
a commentary and further interpretation of a said annotation

傳贊(ㄓㄨㄢˋ ㄗㄢˋ)
commentaries on a biography

傳驛(ㄓㄨㄢˋ ㄧˋ)
a courier station

【傴】 245
ㄩˇ yeu yǔ
hunchbacked

傴僂(ㄩˇ ㄌㄡˊ)
① hunchbacked ② an attitude of reverence

【債】 246
ㄓㄞˋ jay zhài
a debt; an obligation: 我還了債。I paid my debt.

債票(ㄓㄞˋ ㄆㄧㄠˋ)
a bond

債多不愁(ㄓㄞˋ ㄉㄨㄛ ㄅㄨˋ ㄔㄡˊ)
(literally) When debts are too many, one won't worry. —Too many obligations will numb a person's sense of responsibility.

債臺高築(ㄓㄞˋ ㄊㄞˊ ㄍㄠ ㄓㄨˋ)
to be deep in debt; to be up to one's ears in debt; to be heavily in debt; to be debt-ridden

債款(ㄓㄞˋ ㄎㄨㄢˇ)
a loan

債戶(ㄓㄞˋ ㄏㄨˋ)or 債務人(ㄓㄞˋ ㄨˋ ㄖㄣˊ)
a debtor

債券(ㄓㄞˋ ㄑㄩㄢˋ)
bonds issued by a government or debentures issued by a company

債主(ㄓㄞˋ ㄓㄨˇ)or 債權人(ㄓㄞˋ ㄑㄩㄢˊ ㄖㄣˊ)
a creditor

債務(ㄓㄞˋ ㄨˋ)
debt or obligation

【傷】 247
ㄕㄤ shang shāng
1. a cut, wound, or injury
2. to cut or injure: 工作過度傷健康。Overwork injures one's health.
3. grief; to grieve; distressed
4. to impede; an impediment
5. to hurt (feelings)
6. to make sick

傷疤(ㄕㄤ ㄅㄚ)
a scar

傷悲(ㄕㄤ ㄅㄟ)
grief; distress

傷兵(ㄕㄤ ㄅㄧㄥ)
wounded soldiers

傷風(ㄕㄤ ㄈㄥ)
to catch cold; to have a cold

傷風敗俗(ㄕㄤ ㄈㄥ ㄅㄞˋ ㄙㄨˊ)
to act immorally; a breach of morality; to offend public decency; to corrupt public morals

傷悼(ㄕㄤ ㄉㄠˋ)
to mourn over the loss of a dear one

傷天害理(ㄕㄤ ㄊㄧㄢ ㄏㄞˋ ㄌㄧˇ)
to commit crimes

傷痛(ㄕㄤ ㄊㄨㄥˋ)
to mourn

傷腦筋(ㄕㄤ ㄋㄠˇ ㄐㄧㄣ)
① to beat one's brains; to have a nut to crack ② troublesome

傷感(ㄕㄤ ㄍㄢˇ)
distress; distressed; to be deeply moved or touched; to be sick at heart; sentimental

傷感情(ㄕㄤ ㄍㄢˇ ㄑㄧㄥˊ)
① to hurt the feelings ② (colloquial) to have a nut to crack

傷口(ㄕㄤ ㄎㄡˇ)
a wound: 護士清洗那病人的傷口。The nurse bathed that patient's wound.

傷害(ㄕㄤ ㄏㄞˋ)
to hurt; to injure; to harm

傷害罪(ㄕㄤ ㄏㄞˋ ㄗㄨㄟˋ)
(law) injury

傷寒(ㄕㄤ ㄏㄢˊ)
① typhoid fever; typhus ② (Chinese medicine) diseases due to cold factors; the exogenous febrile diseases

傷痕(ㄕㄤ ㄏㄣˊ)
a scar; a bruise

傷痕文學(ㄕㄤ ㄏㄣˊ ㄨㄣˊ ㄒㄩㄝˊ)
scar literature (a body of

literature describing the excesses of the Cultural Revolution Period in Mainland China, which appeared in the early 1980s)

傷懷(ㄕㄤ ㄏㄨㄞˊ)
a distressing mood; grief

傷患(ㄕㄤ ㄏㄨㄢˋ)
the sick and wounded

傷心(ㄕㄤ ㄒㄧㄣ)
① to hurt one's feelings; to break one's heart ② very sad: 她爲她父親的過世而傷心。She is very sad for her father's death.

傷心慘目(ㄕㄤ ㄒㄧㄣ ㄘㄢˇ ㄇㄨˋ)
① to be too ghastly to look at ② tragic (scenes); pitiful (sights)

傷處(ㄕㄤ ㄔㄨˋ)
a wound

傷時感事(ㄕㄤ ㄕˊ ㄍㄢˇ ㄕˋ)
deeply worried about national crises, political corruption, moral decadence, etc.

傷逝(ㄕㄤ ㄕˋ)
to mourn over the loss of a dear person

傷勢(ㄕㄤ ㄕˋ)
the condition of an injury (or a wound)

傷身(ㄕㄤ ㄕㄣ)
to be injurious to health

傷神(ㄕㄤ ㄕㄣˊ)
① to beat one's brains out; to overtax one's nerves; to be nerve-racking ② deeply hurt

傷生(ㄕㄤ ㄕㄥ)
① to bring injury to one's life ② to impair one's vitality

傷人(ㄕㄤ ㄖㄣˊ)
① to hurt people (by verbal attacks, etc.) ② to inflict physical injury on another ③ harmful to health

傷財(ㄕㄤ ㄘㄞˊ)
to lose money; to waste money

傷殘(ㄕㄤ ㄘㄢˊ)
the wounded and disabled

傷亡(ㄕㄤ ㄨㄤˊ)
casualties: 入侵者傷亡慘重。The invaders suffered heavy casualties.

【傺】 248
ㄔˋ chyh chì
1. to hinder
2. to be disappointed

【傾】 249
1. ㄑㄧㄥ ching qīng
1. to slant; to bend: 他身子向前傾。He was bending forward.
2. to collapse; to fall flat; to upset; to subvert
3. to pour out
4. to exhaust (one's wealth, etc.); to exert oneself to do (something)
5. to admire; to be fascinated or intrigued

傾盆大雨(ㄑㄧㄥ ㄆㄣˊ ㄉㄚˋ ㄩˇ)
a pouring rain; to rain hard; to rain cats and dogs; to be pelting with rain: 昨晚一直下著傾盆大雨。It was raining cats and dogs last night.

傾圮(ㄑㄧㄥ ㄆㄧˇ)
(said of buildings) to collapse; in dilapidated condition

傾慕(ㄑㄧㄥ ㄇㄨˋ)
to admire; admiration

傾覆(ㄑㄧㄥ ㄈㄨˋ)
① to topple (a kingdom); the fall of a state ② to overturn; to capsize: 地震使房屋傾覆。The earthquake overturned houses.

傾倒
①(ㄑㄧㄥ ㄉㄠˇ) ⓐ to fall for (a woman); to be infatuated with (a woman); to be overwhelmed with admiration for (a woman) ⓑ to collapse
②(ㄑㄧㄥ ㄉㄠˋ) to dump; to empty the contents of

傾動一時(ㄑㄧㄥ ㄉㄨㄥˋ ㄧˊ ㄕˊ)
to affect the times or generation overwhelmingly ② to have convulsive effect on one's mind

傾談(ㄑㄧㄥ ㄊㄢˊ)
to have a good, heart-to-heart talk

傾聽(ㄑㄧㄥ ㄊㄧㄥ)
to listen carefully; to be all ears for

傾吐(ㄑㄧㄥ ㄊㄨˇ)
to pour out one's heart; to unburden oneself to someone; to get (something) off one's chest

傾囊相助(ㄑㄧㄥ ㄋㄤˊ ㄒㄧㄤ ㄓㄨˋ)
to exhaust (or give) all one has to help; to give one's all to help; to empty one's purse to help; to give generous financial support

傾筐倒篋(ㄑㄧㄥ ㄎㄨㄤ ㄉㄠˋ ㄑㄧㄝˋ)
① to empty the coffers; to exhaust all one has ② to leave no stone unturned; to try one's best

傾家蕩產(ㄑㄧㄥ ㄐㄧㄚ ㄉㄤˋ ㄔㄢˇ)
to exhaust one's wealth—to go bankrupt; to lose a family fortune

傾斜(ㄑㄧㄥ ㄒㄧㄝˊ)
① to slant ② (geology) the angle formed by a stratum with the level; to slope

傾瀉(ㄑㄧㄥ ㄒㄧㄝˋ)
to come down in torrents

傾銷(ㄑㄧㄥ ㄒㄧㄠ)
a cutthroat sale; dumping; to dump

傾心(ㄑㄧㄥ ㄒㄧㄣ)
① to be all for; to admire wholeheartedly ② heart-to-heart: 我們傾心交談。We have a heart-to-heart talk.

傾向(ㄑㄧㄥ ㄒㄧㄤˋ)
① to be inclined to; to side with ② a tendency; a trend

傾注(ㄑㄧㄥ ㄓㄨˋ)
① to pour into: 他將開水傾注到水壺裏。He poured boiled water into a kettle. ② to throw (energy, etc.) into

傾巢(ㄑㄧㄥ ㄔㄠˊ)
(of the enemy or bandits) to turn out in full force: 敵軍傾巢而出。The enemy turned out in full strength.

傾巢來犯(ㄑㄧㄥ ㄔㄠˊ ㄌㄞˊ ㄈㄢˋ)
(said of bandits or enemy forces) to invade in full force

傾城傾國(ㄑㄧㄥ ㄔㄥˊ ㄑㄧㄥ ㄍㄨㄛˊ)
an exceptionally beautiful woman, for whose sake a city is ruined or a country is lost 亦作「傾國傾城」

傾座(ㄑㄧㄥ ㄗㄨㄛˋ)
Everyone present is moved. 或 to win the admiration of all present; to bring the house down

〔人部〕

傾訴(ㄑㄧㄥ ㄙㄨˋ)
to pour out (one's heart, troubles, etc.)
傾訴衷腸(ㄑㄧㄥ ㄙㄨˋ ㄓㄨㄥ ㄔㄤˊ)
to reveal one's innermost feelings
傾耳而聽(ㄑㄧㄥ ㄦˇ ㄦˊ ㄊㄧㄥ)
to listen attentively
傾軋(ㄑㄧㄥ ㄧㄚˋ)
to fight for power; intramural jostling; to jostle against each other
傾危(ㄑㄧㄥ ㄨㄟ)
① mean, treacherous or crooked ② precarious; highly dangerous

【傾】 249
2. ㄎㄥ keng kēng
參看「傾人」
傾人(ㄎㄥ ㄖㄣˊ)
to frame or implicate a person

【僂】 250
ㄌㄡˊ lou lóu
1. hunchbacked; deformed
2. bent
3. a Chinese family name
僂儸(ㄌㄡˊ ㄌㄨㄛˊ)
a bandit's lackey or fellower
亦作「嘍囉」

【僅】 251
ㄐㄧㄣˇ jiin jǐn
1. only: 僅一人出席。Only one is present.
2. barely; scarcely; almost: 他僅免於死。He barely escaped death.
僅夠(ㄐㄧㄣˇ ㄍㄡˋ)
barely enough
僅可(ㄐㄧㄣˇ ㄎㄜˇ)
only for (coping with a specific situation); barely enough for
僅僅(ㄐㄧㄣˇ ㄐㄧㄣˇ)
only; hardly enough; barely: 這僅僅是開始。This is only the beginning.
僅容旋馬(ㄐㄧㄣˇ ㄖㄨㄥˊ ㄒㄩㄢˊ ㄇㄚˇ)
space only big enough for turning a horse—narrow space
僅存(ㄐㄧㄣˇ ㄘㄨㄣˊ)
only (things or persons)
僅以身免(ㄐㄧㄣˇ ㄧˇ ㄕㄣ ㄇㄧㄢˇ)
barely able to escape alive
僅有(ㄐㄧㄣˇ ㄧㄡˇ)
to have only...; there is (or are) only...

【僉】 252
ㄑㄧㄢ chian qiān
all; the whole

【僇】 253
ㄌㄨˋ luh lù
1. to kill; to massacre
2. to disgrace; to shame
3. to collaborate; to pool strength together

十二畫

【像】 254
ㄒㄧㄤˋ shianq xiàng
1. an image; a portrait: 神像 images of gods
2. to resemble; resemblance
3. like; as
像片(ㄒㄧㄤˋ ㄆㄧㄢˋ)
a personal photograph
像貌(ㄒㄧㄤˋ ㄇㄠˋ)
a person's looks
像貌非凡(ㄒㄧㄤˋ ㄇㄠˋ ㄈㄟ ㄈㄢˊ)
a distinguished appearance
像模像樣(ㄒㄧㄤˋ ㄇㄛˊ ㄒㄧㄤˋ ㄧㄤˋ)
①(with) all sincerity ② to look respectable
像話(ㄒㄧㄤˋ ㄏㄨㄚˋ)
to appeal to reason, logic, accepted practice, etc.
像是(ㄒㄧㄤˋ ·ㄕ)
to look like; to seem: 天像是要下雨。It looks like rain.
像煞有介事(ㄒㄧㄤˋ ㄕㄚˋ ㄧㄡˇ ㄐㄧㄝˋ ㄕˋ)
(Shanghai dialect) to act as if one's going to handle a big deal; pretentious; to make a big fuss
像樣(ㄒㄧㄤˋ ㄧㄤˋ)
proper in appearance; presentable; decent

【僑】 255
ㄑㄧㄠˊ chyau qiáo
to sojourn; a sojourn
僑胞(ㄑㄧㄠˊ ㄅㄠ)
overseas Chinese
僑民(ㄑㄧㄠˊ ㄇㄧㄣˊ)
persons who reside in a country other than their own; alien residents
僑聯(ㄑㄧㄠˊ ㄌㄧㄢˊ)
the Federation of Overseas Chinese Associations
僑領(ㄑㄧㄠˊ ㄌㄧㄥˇ)
leaders of overseas Chinese
僑匯(ㄑㄧㄠˊ ㄏㄨㄟˋ)
remittance sent back home by emigrants
僑教(ㄑㄧㄠˊ ㄐㄧㄠˋ)
the education of overseas Chinese
僑居(ㄑㄧㄠˊ ㄐㄩ)
to reside in a town or country other than one's own
僑眷(ㄑㄧㄠˊ ㄐㄩㄢˋ)
dependents of overseas Chinese
僑校(ㄑㄧㄠˊ ㄒㄧㄠˋ)
schools run for overseas Chinese or their children
僑生(ㄑㄧㄠˊ ㄕㄥ)
children of overseas Chinese who attend schools in China; overseas Chinese students in China
僑資(ㄑㄧㄠˊ ㄗ)
overseas Chinese capital
僑務(ㄑㄧㄠˊ ㄨˋ)
affairs concerning nationals living abroad
僑務委員會(ㄑㄧㄠˊ ㄨˋ ㄨㄟˇ ㄩㄢˊ ㄏㄨㄟˋ)
the Overseas Chinese Affairs Commission

【僕】 256
ㄆㄨˊ pwu pú
1. a servant
2. a modest term referring to oneself
3. (formerly) to act as a driver; to drive
僕僕風塵(ㄆㄨˊ ㄆㄨˊ ㄈㄥ ㄔㄣˊ)
to travel around a lot; to be constantly on the run; to be travel-stained; to endure the hardships of a long journey; to be travel-worn and weary
僕人(ㄆㄨˊ ㄖㄣˊ)
① a servant ② a modest term referring to oneself (used in a formal letter or praying to God)
僕從(ㄆㄨˊ ㄗㄨㄥˋ)
retinue; a group of retainers
僕歐(ㄆㄨˊ ㄡ)
a boy or waiter (especially in a restaurant, cabaret)
僕役(ㄆㄨˊ ㄧˋ)
servants

【僖】 257
ㄒㄧ shi xī
1. joy; joyful
2. a Chinese family name

【僚】 258
ㄌㄧㄠˊ liau liáo

1. a companion; a friend
2. a colleague; subordinates
3. officials

僚屬(ㄌㄧㄠˊ ㄕㄨˇ)
subordinates; staff

僚友(ㄌㄧㄠˊ ㄧㄡˇ)
colleagues

【僞】259 ㄨㄟˋ wey wèi (語音 ㄨㄟˇ woei wěi)
1. false; counterfeit
2. simulated; artificial
3. illegal; not legally constituted

僞幣(ㄨㄟˋ ㄅㄧˋ)
①counterfeit money; a spurious coin ②money issued by a puppet government

僞滿(ㄨㄟˋ ㄇㄢˇ)
Manchukuo (a puppet state set up by the Japanese in Manchuria between 1931 and 1945)

僞蒙(ㄨㄟˋ ㄇㄥˊ)
Mongolia when under a puppet rule

僞托(ㄨㄟˋ ㄊㄨㄛ)
①to forge ancient literary or art works ②to pass off counterfeit works as ancient ones

僞國(ㄨㄟˋ ㄍㄨㄛˊ)
an illegal state

僞君子(ㄨㄟˋ ㄐㄩㄣ ㄗˇ)
a hypocrite

僞證(ㄨㄟˋ ㄓㄥˋ)
perjury

僞政府(ㄨㄟˋ ㄓㄥˋ ㄈㄨˇ)
a bogus government; a government dominated by a usurper or traitor

僞裝(ㄨㄟˋ ㄓㄨㄤ)
disguise or camouflage; to disguise or camouflage; to mask

僞鈔(ㄨㄟˋ ㄔㄠ)
a counterfeit bank note

僞善(ㄨㄟˋ ㄕㄢˋ)
hypocrisy; hypocritical

僞造(ㄨㄟˋ ㄗㄠˋ)
to forge; to falsify; to fabricate; to counterfeit

僞造文書(ㄨㄟˋ ㄗㄠˋ ㄨㄣˊ ㄕㄨ)
a forgery; counterfeit documents

僞組織(ㄨㄟˋ ㄗㄨˇ ㄓ)
the quisling government

【僥】260 ㄐㄧㄠˇ jeau jiǎo
luck; lucky

僥倖(ㄐㄧㄠˇ ㄒㄧㄥˋ)
by luck or chance

【僦】261 ㄐㄧㄡˋ jiow jiù
to rent; to hire

僦居(ㄐㄧㄡˋ ㄐㄩ)
to rent (a house)

【僧】262 ㄙㄥ seng sēng
1. a Buddhist; a priest; a monk: 他是一位虔誠的僧人。He is a pious monk.
2. a Chinese family name

僧多粥少(ㄙㄥ ㄉㄨㄛ ㄓㄡ ㄕㄠˇ)
The monks are many and the gruel is meager.—not enough (gifts, positions, etc.) to go around because there are too many people on the waiting list 亦作「粥少僧多」

僧徒(ㄙㄥ ㄊㄨˊ)or 僧侶(ㄙㄥ ㄌㄩˇ)
Buddhist monks; the Buddhist hierarchy; the monks as a group

僧尼(ㄙㄥ ㄋㄧˊ)
Buddhist monks and nuns

僧人(ㄙㄥ ㄖㄣˊ)
a monk

僧寺(ㄙㄥ ㄙˋ)
a Buddhist temple

僧院(ㄙㄥ ㄩㄢˋ)
a monastery

【僭】263 ㄐㄧㄢˋ jiann jiàn
to assume; to usurp; to overstep one's authority

僭號(ㄐㄧㄢˋ ㄏㄠˋ)
usurpation of the title of a king by his subject; to adopt an illegal title

僭竊(ㄐㄧㄢˋ ㄑㄧㄝˋ)
to usurp (the throne, authority, title, etc.)

僭位(ㄐㄧㄢˋ ㄨㄟˋ)
to usurp the throne

僭越(ㄐㄧㄢˋ ㄩㄝˋ)
to assume (a title or powers); to overstep one's authority

【僮】264 1. ㄊㄨㄥˊ torng tóng
1. a servant
2. a boy
3. a Chinese family name

僮僕(ㄊㄨㄥˊ ㄆㄨˊ)
servants

【僮】264 2. ㄓㄨㄤˋ juanq zhuàng
參看「僮族」

僮族(ㄓㄨㄤˋ ㄗㄨˊ)
the name of a small tribe in southwestern China 亦作「壯族」

【僱】265 ㄍㄨˋ guh gù
to hire; to engage; to employ

僱工(ㄍㄨˋ ㄍㄨㄥ)
a hired hand

僱主(ㄍㄨˋ ㄓㄨˇ)
an employer

僱員 or 雇員(ㄍㄨˋ ㄩㄢˊ)
①a government employee who is not on the official payroll of the employing agency and, as such, can be hired or fired without going through the prescribed procedure ②an employee

僱傭(ㄍㄨˋ ㄩㄥ)
a person employed by another

僱用(ㄍㄨˋ ㄩㄥˋ)
to engage (a person): 我僱用了一個學生當嚮導。I engaged a student as a guide.

十三畫

【僵】266 ㄐㄧㄤ jiang jiāng
1. to lie flat
2. to be inactive; stiff; rigid; numb: 我的手指頭幾乎凍僵了。My fingers were nearly numb with cold.
3. to be at a stalemate; deadlocked: 她把事情弄僵了。She's brought things to a deadlock.

僵立(ㄐㄧㄤ ㄌㄧˋ)
to stand rigidly

僵化(ㄐㄧㄤ ㄏㄨㄚˋ)
①heading toward a deadlock ②to become rigid; to ossify

僵局(ㄐㄧㄤ ㄐㄩˊ)
a deadlock; a stalemate; an impasse: 兩派因勢均力敵而陷於僵局。The two parties are at a deadlock.

〔人部〕

僵持(ㄐㄧㄤ ㄔˊ)
to come to a deadlock; to be at a stalemate; to refuse to budge: 雇主和罷工者僵持不下。Employers and strikers have come to a deadlock.
僵屍 or 殭屍(ㄐㄧㄤ ㄕ)
① a stiff corpse ② a vampire
僵死(ㄐㄧㄤ ㄙˇ)
dead; ossified
僵硬(ㄐㄧㄤ ㄧㄥˋ)
rigid; stiff: 他覺得四肢僵硬。He felt stiff in the limbs.
僵臥(ㄐㄧㄤ ㄨㄛˋ)
to lie still at full length

【價】 267
ㄐㄧㄚˋ jiah jià
1. prices; cost; value: 美德乃無價之寶。Virtue is beyond price.
2. (chemistry) valence: 氫是一價的元素。Hydrogen is a one-valence element.
價碼兒(ㄐㄧㄚˋ ㄇㄚˇㄦ)
the price of a commodity
價目(ㄐㄧㄚˋ ㄇㄨˋ)
prices; quotations
價目單(ㄐㄧㄚˋ ㄇㄨˋ ㄉㄢ)
a price (or quotation) list
價廉物美(ㄐㄧㄚˋ ㄌㄧㄢˊ ㄨˋ ㄇㄟˇ)
(literally) excellent quality at low prices—a bargain buy; a good bargain
價格(ㄐㄧㄚˋ ㄍㄜˊ) or 價錢(ㄐㄧㄚˋ ㄑㄧㄢˊ)
prices: 水果價格正在上漲。The prices of fruits are going up.
價值(ㄐㄧㄚˋ ㄓˊ)
①(economics) value: 這項產品的剩餘價值高。The surplus value of this product is plentiful. ② worth; value: 這個線索對我們很有價值。This clue is of great value to us.
價值標準(ㄐㄧㄚˋ ㄓˊ ㄅㄧㄠ ㄓㄨㄣˇ)
standard of value: 每個人都有自己的價值標準。Everybody has his own standard of value.
價值判斷(ㄐㄧㄚˋ ㄓˊ ㄆㄢˋ ㄉㄨㄢˋ)
value judgment
價值連城(ㄐㄧㄚˋ ㄓˊ ㄌㄧㄢˊ ㄔㄥˊ)
invaluable; priceless

【僻】 268
ㄆㄧˋ pih pì
1. biased
2. not easily accessible; out-of-the-way; secluded
3. not common; not ordinary; unusual
僻道(ㄆㄧˋ ㄉㄠˋ)
a seldom-traveled road
僻典(ㄆㄧˋ ㄉㄧㄢˇ)
a quotation of an ambiguous or nebulous source
僻陋(ㄆㄧˋ ㄌㄡˋ)
an out-of-the-way place
僻靜(ㄆㄧˋ ㄐㄧㄥˋ)
out-of-the-way; secluded: 他住在一個僻靜的地方。He lived in a secluded place.
僻巷(ㄆㄧˋ ㄒㄧㄤˋ)
a side-lane; a narrow, out-of-the-way lane
僻處(ㄆㄧˋ ㄔㄨˇ)
to live in an out-of-the-way or secluded place
僻壤(ㄆㄧˋ ㄖㄤˇ)
an out-of-the-way village, town, etc.
僻遠(ㄆㄧˋ ㄩㄢˇ)
distant and out-of-the-way

【儀】 269
ㄧˊ yi yí
1. appearance; deportment; manners; looks; demeanor
2. ceremonies; rites
3. a rule, regulation, form or standard
4. customs
5. instruments; apparatus
6. a Chinese family name
儀表(ㄧˊ ㄅㄧㄠˇ)
① appearance and deportment; a man's personal look: 她的儀表大方。Her appearance is poised and graceful. ② a rule; a model
儀隊(ㄧˊ ㄉㄨㄟˋ)
an honor guard
儀態(ㄧˊ ㄊㄞˋ)
bearing; deportment; demeanor: 這個女孩有一種嫻靜而謙遜的儀態。The girl had a quiet, modest demeanor.
儀態萬方(ㄧˊ ㄊㄞˋ ㄨㄢˋ ㄈㄤ)
(usually said of girls) charming poises and exquisite bearing; regal bearing
儀器(ㄧˊ ㄑㄧˋ)
(laboratory, medical, etc.) instruments; apparatus
儀仗(ㄧˊ ㄓㄤˋ)
flags, weapons, etc. carried by a guard of honor
儀式(ㄧˊ ㄕˋ)
ceremonies; rites: 開幕與閉幕都是以隆重的儀式完成的。Openings and closings were all accomplished with majestic ceremonies.
儀容(ㄧˊ ㄖㄨㄥˊ)
appearance and deportment; looks; demeanor

【儂】 270
ㄋㄨㄥˊ nong nóng
1. (in old usage) I; me
2. (Shanghai dialect) you
3. he; she
4. a Chinese family name

【億】 271
ㄧˋ yih yì
1. a hundred million
2. tranquility; repose
3. (according to) estimates
億兆(ㄧˋ ㄓㄠˋ)
① astronomical in number; countless; numberless ② the people; the masses
億萬(ㄧˋ ㄨㄢˋ)
hundreds of millions; millions upon millions
億萬富翁(ㄧˋ ㄨㄢˋ ㄈㄨˋ ㄨㄥ)
a billionaire

【儆】 272
ㄐㄧㄥˇ jiing jǐng
1. to be on guard; to get ready (for an attack, etc.)
2. to warn; to caution: 死刑用來懲一儆百。Sentence of death is used to punish one to warn a hundred.
儆戒(ㄐㄧㄥˇ ㄐㄧㄝˋ)
to warn; to caution; warning; caution
儆儆(ㄐㄧㄥˇ ㄐㄧㄥˇ)
uneasy; wary

【儈】 273
ㄎㄨㄞˋ kuay kuài
a middleman; a go-between; a broker

【儉】 274
ㄐㄧㄢˇ jean jiǎn
(又讀 ㄐㄧㄢˋ jiann jiàn)
1. frugal; economical; thrift
2. meager
3. a poor harvest
儉薄(ㄐㄧㄢˇ ㄅㄛˊ)
lacking the necessities of life
儉樸(ㄐㄧㄢˇ ㄆㄨˊ)
to be thrifty in daily spend-

ing; simple in dressing: 成功的農夫都是儉樸的。Successful farmers are thrifty.

儉省(ㄐㄧㄢˇ ㄕㄥˇ)
thrift; frugal; economical

儉以養廉(ㄐㄧㄢˇ ㄧˇ ㄧㄤˇ ㄌㄧㄢˊ)
Frugality makes honesty.

儉約(ㄐㄧㄢˇ ㄩㄝ)
thrifty and temperate; practicing austerity

儉用(ㄐㄧㄢˇ ㄩㄥˋ)
to be careful with one's spending; frugal; thrifty; careful in spending

【儋】 275 ㄉㄢ dan dān
1. to shoulder or bear a burden
2. a load of two piculs (especially of rice or grains)

【儍】 276 (傻) ㄕㄚˇ shaa shǎ
1. stupid; foolish; dumb
2. naive
3. stunned; stupefied; terrified
4. to think or work mechanically

儍頭儍腦(ㄕㄚˇ ㄊㄡˊ ㄕㄚˇ ㄋㄠˇ)
① foolish-looking ② muddle-headed

儍裏儍氣(ㄕㄚˇ ·ㄌㄧ ㄕㄚˇ ·ㄑㄧ)
foolish-looking or acting foolishly

儍瓜(ㄕㄚˇ ㄍㄨㄚ)
a fool; a silly; a blockhead; a simpleton: 他很可能是個儍瓜。He's very likely a fool.

儍呵呵(ㄕㄚˇ ㄏㄜ ㄏㄜ)
likable but stupid; silly appearance; simple-minded: 別看他儍呵呵的，他可是滿腹經綸。Maybe he doesn't look very clever, but he is actually very much learned.

儍話(ㄕㄚˇ ㄏㄨㄚˋ)
foolish talk; nonsense

儍勁兒(ㄕㄚˇ ㄐㄧㄣˋㄦ)
① stupidity; foolishness ② sheer enthusiasm; doggedness: 他做事總有股儍勁兒。He always works with doggedness.

儍氣(ㄕㄚˇ ·ㄑㄧ)
silly manners; dumb-looking

儍小子(ㄕㄚˇ ㄒㄧㄠˇ ·ㄗ)
(usually used in a comical sense) a young fool; a silly boy

儍笑(ㄕㄚˇ ㄒㄧㄠˋ)
to smirk; to laugh for no conceivable reason; a silly smile; a smirk: 他對過路的每個人儍笑。He smirked at everyone that passes.

儍子(ㄕㄚˇ ·ㄗ)
a bloody fool; an idiot or imbecile; a nincompoop; a blockhead

儍眼(ㄕㄚˇ ㄧㄢˇ)
to be dumbfounded; to be stunned: 看到此番美景，我們不禁儍眼了。All of us were dumbfounded by the beauty of the scene.

十四畫

【儐】 277 ㄅㄧㄣˋ binn bìn (語音 ㄅㄧㄣ bin bīn)
1. to entertain guests
2. to arrange; to set in order
3. to guide

儐相(ㄅㄧㄣˋ ㄒㄧㄤˋ)
① the best man of a bridegroom ② a bridesmaid

【儒】 278 ㄖㄨˊ ru rú
1. the learned; scholars collectively
2. Confucian; Confucianism
3. weak; shrinking from hardship

儒門(ㄖㄨˊ ㄇㄣˊ)
① scholars following Confucian thoughts; Confucianists ② the name of a fort to the north of Taming County in Hopeh Province

儒風(ㄖㄨˊ ㄈㄥ)
the style, ways, etc. of Confucian scholars

儒林(ㄖㄨˊ ㄌㄧㄣˊ)
① the circle of Confucians ② the circle of scholars

儒林外史(ㄖㄨˊ ㄌㄧㄣˊ ㄨㄞˋ ㄕˇ)
the title of a sarcastic novel lampooning Chinese scholars of the late Ming and early Ching dynasties by Wu Ching-tze (吳敬梓) in the early Ching Dynasty

儒家(ㄖㄨˊ ㄐㄧㄚ)
scholars following Confucian thoughts; Confucianists; the Confucian school

儒教(ㄖㄨˊ ㄐㄧㄠˋ)
Confucianism

儒將(ㄖㄨˊ ㄐㄧㄤˋ)
a general who is also an accomplished scholar

儒學(ㄖㄨˊ ㄒㄩㄝˊ)
① the teachings of Confucius ② (in old China) education officials on various governmental levels

儒生(ㄖㄨˊ ㄕㄥ)
① a scholar ② a scholar of the Confucian school; a Confucian scholar

儒宗(ㄖㄨˊ ㄗㄨㄥ)
one who is admired and respected by the scholastic community

儒雅(ㄖㄨˊ ㄧㄚˇ)
scholarly and refined; elegant; (with) style: 他的舉止溫文儒雅。He has elegant manners.

【儔】 279 ㄔㄡˊ chour chóu
1. a companion or companions
2. a class

儔匹(ㄔㄡˊ ㄆㄧˇ)
a companion

儔類(ㄔㄡˊ ㄌㄟˋ)
① a class ② persons of the same class

【儕】 280 ㄔㄞˊ chair chái
1. a class; company
2. an adjunct to show plurality
3. to match (as man and wife)

儕輩(ㄔㄞˊ ㄅㄟˋ)
persons (especially friends or companions) of the same generation

【儘】 281 ㄐㄧㄣˇ jiin jǐn
1. the utmost; the extreme
2. to let (someone do it)

儘量(ㄐㄧㄣˇ ㄌㄧㄤˋ)
as (much, soon, strong, etc.) as possible: 你年輕時應儘量多讀點書。You should read as many books as possible when young.

儘夠(ㄐㄧㄣˇ ㄍㄡˋ)
quite enough; more than enough

儘管(ㄐㄧㄣˇ ㄍㄨㄢˇ)
①even if; no matter; despite; in spite of ② not hesitate to: 有什麼問題儘管問他。If

you have any questions, don't hesitate to ask him.

儘可能(ㄐㄧㄣˇ ㄎㄜˇ ㄋㄥˊ)
as far as possible; to the best of one's ability: 儘可能快。Be as quick as possible.

儘快(ㄐㄧㄣˇ ㄎㄨㄞˋ)
as quickly (or soon) as possible: 我將儘快來。I will come as soon as I possibly can.

儘其所有(ㄐㄧㄣˇ ㄑㄧˊ ㄙㄨㄛˇ ㄧㄡˇ)
to exhaust all one has

儘情享受(ㄐㄧㄣˇ ㄑㄧㄥˊ ㄒㄧㄤˇ ㄕㄡˋ)
to seek pleasure to one's heart's content

儘先(ㄐㄧㄣˇ ㄒㄧㄢ)
① the very first: 我們應該儘先照顧孩子們。We ought to look after the children first. ②(to give) first priority (to)

儘着(ㄐㄧㄣˇ ·ㄓㄜ)
to the greatest possible extent; to do one's best

儘上頭(ㄐㄧㄣˇ ㄕㄤˋ ·ㄊㄡ)
the uppermost; the highest spot

儘讓(ㄐㄧㄣˇ ㄖㄤˋ)
to let (others try, choose, etc.) first; to be as humble and yielding as possible

儘早(ㄐㄧㄣˇ ㄗㄠˇ)
as early as possible

〔人部〕

十五畫

【償】 282
ㄔㄤˊ charng cháng

1. to repay
2. to compensate; to make restitution
3. to fulfill (a wish): 他得償夙願。He has fulfilled his long-cherished wish.
4. to offset

償命(ㄔㄤˊ ㄇㄧㄥˋ)
a life for a life; to pay with one's life (for a murder)

償付(ㄔㄤˊ ㄈㄨˋ)
to pay back; to pay

償還(ㄔㄤˊ ㄏㄨㄢˊ)
redemption; to repay (what one owes)

償清(ㄔㄤˊ ㄑㄧㄥ)
to clear off: 我已償清我的債務。I have cleared off my debts.

償債(ㄔㄤˊ ㄓㄞˋ)
to repay a debt; to pay (or discharge) a debt

償願(ㄔㄤˊ ㄩㄢˋ)
to fulfill one's wish; to get what one desires

【儡】 283
ㄌㄟˇ leei lěi

1. a puppet: 他們在征服地區建立一傀儡政府。They set up a puppet government in the conquered territory.
2. sickly and thin
3. dilapidated

【優】 284
ㄧㄡ iou yōu

1. good; excellent: 他因英文特優而得獎。He received a prize for excellence in English.
2. abundant; plenty
3. players (as in an opera)
4. victory; winning
5. soft
6. a Chinese family name

優美(ㄧㄡ ㄇㄟˇ)
① good; wonderful; graceful; fine: 我很喜歡優美的風景。I enjoy fine scenery very much. ② anything that inspires a sense of joy

優孟衣冠(ㄧㄡ ㄇㄥˋ ㄧ ㄍㄨㄢ)
to act on the stage

優待(ㄧㄡ ㄉㄞˋ)
favorable treatment; to give special treatment: 我們政府優待軍眷。Our government gives special treatment to servicemen's families.

優待券(ㄧㄡ ㄉㄞˋ ㄑㄩㄢˋ)
① a discount ticket (for shopping in a certain store) ② a free ticket (for a show, etc.); a complimentary ticket

優等(ㄧㄡ ㄉㄥˇ)
an excellent grade; the best class; first-rate

優點(ㄧㄡ ㄉㄧㄢˇ)
① merits: 他的個性有優點和缺點。His character has merits and demerits (or virtues and defects). ② good qualities ③ advantages: 住在大都市裡有許多優點。Living in a big city has many advantages.

優劣(ㄧㄡ ㄌㄧㄝˋ)
① good and bad ② bright and dull ③ fit and unfit

優良(ㄧㄡ ㄌㄧㄤˊ)
fine; good: 他的成績優良。He got good marks.

優伶(ㄧㄡ ㄌㄧㄥˊ)
professional actors or actresses

優厚(ㄧㄡ ㄏㄡˋ)
munificent; liberal; favorable: 這個工作待遇優厚。This job has liberal wages and benefits.

優惠(ㄧㄡ ㄏㄨㄟˋ)
preferential; favorable

優惠待遇(ㄧㄡ ㄏㄨㄟˋ ㄉㄞˋ ㄩˋ)
preferential treatment

優惠國(ㄧㄡ ㄏㄨㄟˋ ㄍㄨㄛˊ)
(international treaty) a favored nation

優惠稅率(ㄧㄡ ㄏㄨㄟˋ ㄕㄨㄟˋ ㄌㄩˋ)
(reduced) import tariff rates for goods imported from a favored nation

優境學(ㄧㄡ ㄐㄧㄥˋ ㄒㄩㄝˊ)
euthenics

優秀(ㄧㄡ ㄒㄧㄡˋ)
outstanding; foremost; remarkable: 她是一個優秀的學生。She is an outstanding student.

優秀份子(ㄧㄡ ㄒㄧㄡˋ ㄈㄣˋ ㄗˇ)
the elite

優先(ㄧㄡ ㄒㄧㄢ)
priority; to have priority; to take precedence

優先股(ㄧㄡ ㄒㄧㄢ ㄍㄨˇ)
preferred stocks; preference shares

優先權(ㄧㄡ ㄒㄧㄢ ㄑㄩㄢˊ)
priority

優閒(ㄧㄡ ㄒㄧㄢˊ)
carefree; leisure; free and content

優質(ㄧㄡ ㄓˋ)
high (or top) quality

優勢(ㄧㄡ ㄕˋ)
supremacy; superiority; advantage; the upper hand

優勢行爲(ㄧㄡ ㄕˋ ㄒㄧㄥˊ ㄨㄟˊ)
dominance behavior

優生學(ㄧㄡ ㄕㄥ ㄒㄩㄝˊ)
eugenics

優勝(ㄧㄡ ㄕㄥˋ)
winning; superior

優勝劣敗(ㄧㄡ ㄕㄥˋ ㄌㄧㄝˋ ㄅㄞˋ)
survival of the fittest

優勝獎(ㄧㄡ ㄕㄥˋ ㄐㄧㄤˇ)

a winning prize

優勝者(ㄧㄡ ㄕㄥˋ ㄓㄜˇ)
a winner; a champion: 他是我們鎮上的網球優勝者。He is the tennis champion of our town.

優柔寡斷(ㄧㄡ ㄖㄡˊ ㄍㄨㄚˇ ㄉㄨㄢˋ)
to be peaceable and easy-going but lacking the strength of making quick decisions

優人(ㄧㄡ ㄖㄣˊ)
an actor

優哉游哉(ㄧㄡ ㄗㄞ ㄧㄡˊ ㄗㄞ)
living a life of ease and leisure; leisurely and carefree

優異(ㄧㄡ ㄧˋ)
excellent; remarkable; extraordinary; brilliant

優游(ㄧㄡ ㄧㄡˊ)
① carefree 亦作「優遊」: 他度過了優游的歲月。He passed his days in carefree leisure. ②indecisive; unable to make decisions ③ to leave one's life to fate

優游林下(ㄧㄡ ㄧㄡˊ ㄌㄧㄣˊ ㄒㄧㄚˋ)
to live in the countryside leisurely and happily after retirement

優渥(ㄧㄡ ㄨㄛˋ)
handsome (pay, gifts, etc.); munificent

優裕(ㄧㄡ ㄩˋ)
well-to-do; wealthy; comfortable (financial standing); excellent (pay); affluent: 他們生活優裕。They lived in affluence.

優遇(ㄧㄡ ㄩˋ)
to treat well

優越(ㄧㄡ ㄩㄝˋ)
superior; outstanding: 他的寫作技巧比我優越。His skill in writing is superior to mine.

優越感(ㄧㄡ ㄩㄝˋ ㄍㄢˇ)
a sense of superiority; superiority complex

十六畫

【儲】285 ㄔㄨˊ chwu chú (又讀 ㄔㄨˇ chuu chǔ)
1. to save; to store; saving
2. a deputy; an alternate
3. a Chinese family name

儲備(ㄔㄨˊ ㄅㄟˋ)
savings and/or reserves

儲量(ㄔㄨˊ ㄌㄧㄤˋ)
(mineral) reserves

儲宮(ㄔㄨˊ ㄍㄨㄥ)
the crown prince 亦作「儲君」or「儲貳」or「儲嗣」

儲款(ㄔㄨˊ ㄎㄨㄢˇ)
to save money (in the bank); savings

儲款以待(ㄔㄨˊ ㄎㄨㄢˇ ㄧˇ ㄉㄞˋ)
to get the money ready

儲戶(ㄔㄨˊ ㄏㄨˋ)
a person or organization that has a savings account in the bank; a depositor

儲積(ㄔㄨˊ ㄐㄧ)
to store; to stockpile; to save up

儲金(ㄔㄨˊ ㄐㄧㄣ)
savings

儲氣(ㄔㄨˊ ㄑㄧˋ)
gas storage

儲蓄(ㄔㄨˊ ㄒㄩˋ)
①to save (money): 我們必須儲蓄,以備不時之需。We must save for a rainy day. ②savings: 她失去了所有的儲蓄。She lost all her savings.

儲蓄銀行(ㄔㄨˊ ㄒㄩˋ ㄧㄣˊ ㄏㄤˊ)
a savings bank

儲藏(ㄔㄨˊ ㄘㄤˊ)
①to store up; to hoard; to save and preserve: 松鼠儲藏堅果過冬。A squirrel hoards nuts for the winter. ② a deposit: 我國有豐富的煤和石油儲藏。Our country abounds in coal and petroleum deposits.

儲藏室(ㄔㄨˊ ㄘㄤˊ ㄕˋ)
a storeroom

儲存(ㄔㄨˊ ㄘㄨㄣˊ)
①storage; saving ②to store or stockpile; to lay in; to lay up

儲油(ㄔㄨˊ ㄧㄡˊ)
(petroleum) oil storage

十九畫

【儷】286 ㄌㄧˋ lih lì
1. a pair; a couple
2. husband and wife; a married couple

儷辭(ㄌㄧˋ ㄘˊ)
a form of literary writing in which sentences or words come in couplets

儷影(ㄌㄧˋ ㄧㄥˇ)
the heart-warming sight of a couple in love; a married couple appearing in a photograph

二十畫

【儼】287 ㄧㄢˇ yean yǎn
1. majestic; respectable
2. (to act, talk, appear) as if; like

儼然(ㄧㄢˇ ㄖㄢˊ)
① dignified-looking; solemn; stern ② neat-looking (house, etc.) ③ just like: 他說起話來儼然是個專家。He speaks just like an expert.

儼如(ㄧㄢˇ ㄖㄨˊ) or 儼若(ㄧㄢˇ ㄖㄨㄛˋ)
just like 參看「儼然③」

儿部
ㄖㄣˊ ren rén

一畫

【兀】288 ㄨˋ wuh wù
1. to cut off the feet
2. high and flat on the top
3. this
4. ignorant-looking

兀立(ㄨˋ ㄌㄧˋ)
to stand rigidly without motion

兀自(ㄨˋ ㄗˋ)
still

兀傲(ㄨˋ ㄠˋ)
proud

兀鷹(ㄨˋ ㄧㄥ)
a vulture (*Gyps fulvus*)

二畫

【允】289 ㄩㄣˇ yeun yǔn
1. to allow; to consent; to grant
2. appropriate; proper

〔儿部〕

3. sincere; loyal; faithful; truly
允當(ㄩㄣˇ ㄉㄤ)
appropriate; suitable; fit; proper; to put just right
允洽(ㄩㄣˇ ㄒㄧㄚˊ)
proper; fair; well settled
允許(ㄩㄣˇ ㄒㄩˇ)or 允諾(ㄩㄣˇ ㄋㄨㄛˋ)
to assent; to consent; to grant; to permit; to give permission; to allow: 請允許我代表全家向你們致謝。Allow me to thank you on behalf of my family.
允准(ㄩㄣˇ ㄓㄨㄣˇ)
to approve; to grant; to consent: 他允准讓他的女兒單獨去旅行。He consented to let his daughter travel alone.
允從(ㄩㄣˇ ㄘㄨㄥˊ)
to follow (one's advice, etc.); to consent to; to comply with; to promise to follow (one's suggestion)
允文允武(ㄩㄣˇ ㄨㄣˊ ㄩㄣˇ ㄨˇ)
to be good at wielding both pen and weapon; to be well versed both in learning and military affairs; both good in civil and in military affairs

【元】 290
ㄩㄢˊ yuan yuán
1. the beginning; the first; original
2. the head
3. a dollar: 一百分等於一元。One hundred cents make a dollar.
4. the eldest; chief; big
5. (Chinese astrology) 60 years
6. the Yüan Dynasty (1279-1367)
7. a Chinese family name
元寶(ㄩㄢˊ ㄅㄠˇ)
① a silver or gold ingot weighing about 55 ounces, used in old China ② a mock ingot of tinfoil paper of similar shape (to be burnt in ancestor-worshipping as an offering)
元本(ㄩㄢˊ ㄅㄣˇ)
① the origin 亦作「原本」② capital (for business) ③ a Yüan Dynasty edition
元配(ㄩㄢˊ ㄆㄟˋ)
a man's first wife
元旦(ㄩㄢˊ ㄉㄢˋ)
New Year's Day
元太祖(ㄩㄢˊ ㄊㄞˋ ㄗㄨˇ)
Genghis Khan, 1162-1227, Mongol conqueror of Central Asia
元年(ㄩㄢˊ ㄋㄧㄢˊ)
the first year of a reign, dynasty, etc.
元老(ㄩㄢˊ ㄌㄠˇ)
an elder person who has held high positions for long period of time and is highly respected by the nation; a veteran statesman; a senior statesman
元老院(ㄩㄢˊ ㄌㄠˇ ㄩㄢˋ)
the Senate (of the Roman Empire)
元氣(ㄩㄢˊ ㄑㄧˋ)
vitality and constitution; stamina; strength; vigor: 一夜的安睡使他恢復元氣。A good night's rest makes him regain his strength.
元曲(ㄩㄢˊ ㄑㄩˇ)
a form of dramatic literature prospered in the Yüan Dynasty
元宵(ㄩㄢˊ ㄒㄧㄠ)
① the Lantern Festival (on the 15th day of the first moon in the Chinese lunar calendar, marking the end of New Year's festivities) ② small rice-flour dumplings eaten on the Lantern Festival
元勳(ㄩㄢˊ ㄒㄩㄣ)
① great achievements ② persons of great achievements; a founding father
元兇(ㄩㄢˊ ㄒㄩㄥ)
the chief culprit; a ringleader (of a crime); an arch-criminal
元世祖(ㄩㄢˊ ㄕˋ ㄗㄨˇ)
Kublai Khan, 1216 - 1294, grandson of Genghis Khan and founder of the Yüan Dynasty
元首(ㄩㄢˊ ㄕㄡˇ)
① the chief of state; the king; the president, etc. ② the beginning
元帥(ㄩㄢˊ ㄕㄨㄞˋ)
a field marshal; a five-star general or admiral; the commander in chief
元戎(ㄩㄢˊ ㄖㄨㄥˊ)
① the commander in chief ② a large war chariot
元素(ㄩㄢˊ ㄙㄨˋ)
(chemistry) the elements
元惡(ㄩㄢˊ ㄜˋ)
the chief culprit
元音(ㄩㄢˊ ㄧㄣ)
the equivalent of vowels in Chinese phonetics
元月(ㄩㄢˊ ㄩㄝˋ)
① the first month of the lunar calendar ② January

三畫

【兄】 291
ㄒㄩㄥ shiong xiōng
1. one's elder brother
2. a term used in addressing a senior of the same generation to show respect: 老兄,這件事就委託你了。And so, brother, I'll leave the matter to you.
兄弟
①(ㄒㄩㄥ ㄉㄧˋ) brothers
②(ㄒㄩㄥ ·ㄉㄧ) ⓐ one's younger brother ⓑ a designation for juniors of the same generation among one's relatives ⓒ I (a modest term): 兄弟不敢推辭。I, your younger brother, dare not decline.
兄弟鬩牆(ㄒㄩㄥ ㄉㄧˋ ㄒㄧˋ ㄑㄧㄤˊ)
brothers fighting among themselves; an intramural fight
兄長(ㄒㄩㄥ ㄓㄤˇ)
an elder brother
兄友弟恭(ㄒㄩㄥ ㄧㄡˇ ㄉㄧˋ ㄍㄨㄥ)
to show love and respect as good brothers should

【充】 292
(充)ㄔㄨㄥ chong chōng
1. full; sufficient: 我們有充分的供應。We have sufficient supplies.
2. to fill
3. to fake; to cheat; to pretend: 你別充內行了。Don't pretend to be an expert.
4. a Chinese family name
充沛(ㄔㄨㄥ ㄆㄟˋ)
brimming (with energy)
充滿(ㄔㄨㄥ ㄇㄢˇ)

to fill up; to resound; full of; filled with; replete with: 她眼中充滿了眼淚。Tears filled her eyes.

充分(ㄔㄨㄥ ㄈㄣˋ)
fully; sufficient; enough

充分條件(ㄔㄨㄥ ㄈㄣˋ ㄊㄧㄠˊ ㄐㄧㄢˋ)
(logic) sufficient condition

充當(ㄔㄨㄥ ㄉㄤ)
to serve as; to act as; to play the part of: 她充當翻譯員。She acted as an interpreter.

充電(ㄔㄨㄥ ㄉㄧㄢˋ)
to recharge (a battery)

充電器(ㄔㄨㄥ ㄉㄧㄢˋ ㄑㄧˋ)
a charger

充公(ㄔㄨㄥ ㄍㄨㄥ)
to confiscate: 政府將所有叛國者的財產充公。The government confiscated the property of all traitors.

充好漢(ㄔㄨㄥ ㄏㄠˇ ㄏㄢˋ)
to play the hero: 你別充好漢。Don't pose as a hero.

充行家(ㄔㄨㄥ ㄏㄤˊ •ㄐㄧㄚ)
to pretend to be a professional or specialist

充飢(ㄔㄨㄥ ㄐㄧ)
to satisfy (or appease) one's hunger (usually with poor food)

充軍(ㄔㄨㄥ ㄐㄩㄣ)
to exile a criminal (or prisoner) to a distant place for military service, as a penalty in old China

充其量(ㄔㄨㄥ ㄑㄧˊ ㄌㄧㄤˋ)
at most; at best: 這點糧食充其量只夠維持十天。The provisions can last ten days at most.

充斥(ㄔㄨㄥ ㄔˋ)
numerous; filled with; rife; everywhere: 走私貨到處充斥。Smuggled goods are everywhere.

充實(ㄔㄨㄥ ㄕˊ)
①rich; substantial; abundant ②to fill out ③(said of knowledge, facilities, etc.) to strengthen or improve

充數(ㄔㄨㄥ ㄕㄨˋ)
(just) to complete the number; to fill a vacancy with an incompetent person; to use a substitute of inferior quality

充任(ㄔㄨㄥ ㄖㄣˋ)
to fill the post of; to hold the position of

充足(ㄔㄨㄥ ㄗㄨˊ)
plenty; abundance; sufficiency; plentiful; abundant; sufficient

充塞(ㄔㄨㄥ ㄙㄜˋ)
full of; filled with

充耳不聞(ㄔㄨㄥ ㄦˇ ㄅㄨˋ ㄨㄣˊ)
to turn a deaf ear to; to ignore what is said

充盈(ㄔㄨㄥ ㄧㄥˊ)
plentiful; full

充裕(ㄔㄨㄥ ㄩˋ)
abundance; sufficiency; abundant; sufficient; rich; substantial

四畫

【兆】 293
ㄓㄠˋ jaw zhào

1. a sign (in fortune-telling)
2. to portend; to foretell: 瑞雪兆豐年。A timely snow portends a good harvest.
3. an omen
4. a trillion (1,000,000,000,000); a billion
5. to begin; beginning
6. a Chinese family name

兆民(ㄓㄠˋ ㄇㄧㄣˊ)
the people; the masses

兆頭(ㄓㄠˋ •ㄊㄡ)
a sign; an omen; a portent

【兇】 294
ㄒㄩㄥ shiong xiōng

1. fierce; violent; cruel; ferocious: 他臉上有兇狠的表情。He has a fierce look on his face.
2. truculent; inhuman

兇暴(ㄒㄩㄥ ㄅㄠˋ)
cruel and violent

兇猛(ㄒㄩㄥ ㄇㄥˇ)
fierce; ferocious: 那隻老虎非常兇猛。The tiger is very ferocious.

兇犯(ㄒㄩㄥ ㄈㄢˋ)
a criminal; a murderer

兇漢(ㄒㄩㄥ ㄏㄢˋ)or 兇徒(ㄒㄩㄥ ㄊㄨˊ)
a hoodlum; a gangster; a violent person

兇悍(ㄒㄩㄥ ㄏㄢˋ)or 兇狠(ㄒㄩㄥ ㄏㄣˇ) or 兇橫(ㄒㄩㄥ ㄏㄥˋ)
truculent, savage, ferocious, fierce, etc.

兇器(ㄒㄩㄥ ㄑㄧˋ)
the murderous weapon

兇險(ㄒㄩㄥ ㄒㄧㄢˇ)
cruel and mean

兇殺(ㄒㄩㄥ ㄕㄚ)
murder; homicide; manslaughter

兇手(ㄒㄩㄥ ㄕㄡˇ)
the murderer; the killer

兇惡(ㄒㄩㄥ ㄜˋ)
evil; wicked; malignant; ferocious: 他是個兇惡的傢伙。He is a ferocious fellow.

【先】 295
ㄒㄧㄢ shian xiān

1. first; foremost: 他首先發言。He spoke first.
2. before; earlier; in advance: 我比他先到。I arrived earlier than he did.
3. the late...; the deceased...
4. one's forebears
5. the abbreviation for Mister or Sir
6. a Chinese family name

先輩(ㄒㄧㄢ ㄅㄟˋ)
the seniors; members of a former generation; the senior generation

先民(ㄒㄧㄢ ㄇㄧㄣˊ)
ancients; the former men

先母(ㄒㄧㄢ ㄇㄨˇ)or 先慈(ㄒㄧㄢ ㄘˊ)or 先妣(ㄒㄧㄢ ㄅㄧˇ)
my late mother

先發制人(ㄒㄧㄢ ㄈㄚ ㄓˋ ㄖㄣˊ)
to attack first (in order to cripple the opponent's defenses); to take the initiative: 他採取先發制人的手段。He took preemptive measures.

先鋒(ㄒㄧㄢ ㄈㄥ)or 先驅(ㄒㄧㄢ ㄑㄩ)
a vanguard; a forerunner; a trailblazer; a pioneer; a harbinger: 知更鳥是春天的先鋒。The robin is a harbinger of spring.

先夫(ㄒㄧㄢ ㄈㄨ)
my late husband

先父(ㄒㄧㄢ ㄈㄨˋ)or 先考(ㄒㄧㄢ ㄎㄠˇ) or 先嚴(ㄒㄧㄢ ㄧㄢˊ)
my late father

先導(ㄒㄧㄢ ㄉㄠˇ)
①to lead the way ②a model; a mentor; a teacher

③a guide; a forerunner; a precursor: 失敗常常是成功的先導。Failure is often the precursor of what is successful.

先帝(ㄒㄧㄢ ㄉㄧˋ)
the late emperor

先睹爲快(ㄒㄧㄢ ㄉㄨˇ ㄨㄟˊ ㄎㄨㄞˋ)
to eagerly await a look at (something) ahead of others; to consider it a pleasure to be among the first to read (a poem, article, etc.)

先頭(ㄒㄧㄢ ㄊㄡˊ)
①ahead; in front; in advance: 我們走在最先頭。We walk ahead of all other people. ②before; formerly; in the past: 他先頭沒說過這事。He didn't mention this before.

先頭部隊(ㄒㄧㄢ ㄊㄡˊ ㄅㄨˋ ㄉㄨㄟˋ)or 先遣部隊(ㄒㄧㄢ ㄑㄧㄢˇ ㄅㄨˋ ㄉㄨㄟˋ)
the vanguard; the advance detachment

先天(ㄒㄧㄢ ㄊㄧㄢ)
①natural physical endowments ②congenital; innate; inherent

先天不足(ㄒㄧㄢ ㄊㄧㄢ ㄅㄨˋ ㄗㄨˊ)
inborn deficiency; inherited weakness

先來後到(ㄒㄧㄢ ㄌㄞˊ ㄏㄡˋ ㄉㄠˋ)
the order of arrival 或 First come, first served.

先禮後兵(ㄒㄧㄢ ㄌㄧˇ ㄏㄡˋ ㄅㄧㄥ)
diplomacy (or courtesy) before the use of force

先例(ㄒㄧㄢ ㄌㄧˋ)
a precedent; a former example: 此事有先例可援。This matter has a precedent to go by.

先烈(ㄒㄧㄢ ㄌㄧㄝˋ)
the national martyrs

先令(ㄒㄧㄢ ㄌㄧㄥˋ)
(the British monetary system) a shilling

先乾爲敬(ㄒㄧㄢ ㄍㄢ ㄨㄟˊ ㄐㄧㄥˋ)
(in toasting someone) I empty my glass first to show my respect to you.

先河(ㄒㄧㄢ ㄏㄜˊ)
the beginning of something; a harbinger; a forerunner

先後(ㄒㄧㄢ ㄏㄡˋ)
①the order (of things placed, narrated, etc.) ②the ins and outs of an incident

先見(ㄒㄧㄢ ㄐㄧㄢˋ)
foresight; forethought; prophetic vision

先見之明(ㄒㄧㄢ ㄐㄧㄢˋ ㄓ ㄇㄧㄥˊ)
the ability to discern what is coming

先進(ㄒㄧㄢ ㄐㄧㄣˋ)
predecessors; seniors

先進國(ㄒㄧㄢ ㄐㄧㄣˋ ㄍㄨㄛˊ)
advanced nations; civilized nations; developed powers

先覺(ㄒㄧㄢ ㄐㄩㄝˊ)
a prophet

先決條件(ㄒㄧㄢ ㄐㄩㄝˊ ㄊㄧㄠˊ ㄐㄧㄢˋ)
a prerequisite; a precondition; an antecedent condition

先決問題(ㄒㄧㄢ ㄐㄩㄝˊ ㄨㄣˋ ㄊㄧˊ)
problems that demand a priority in solution

先君(ㄒㄧㄢ ㄐㄩㄣ)
my late father

先期(ㄒㄧㄢ ㄑㄧˊ)
before the appointed time; beforehand

先前(ㄒㄧㄢ ㄑㄧㄢˊ)
before; previously: 這孩子比先前高多了。The child is much taller than before.

先秦時代(ㄒㄧㄢ ㄑㄧㄣˊ ㄕˊ ㄉㄞˋ)
the era before Shih Huang Ti of the Chin Dynasty (221-207 B.C.) when Chinese culture blossomed

先驅(ㄒㄧㄢ ㄑㄩ)
a vanguard; a forerunner; a pioneer

先下手爲強(ㄒㄧㄢ ㄒㄧㄚˋ ㄕㄡˇ ㄨㄟˊ ㄑㄧㄤˊ)
It's always advantageous to make the first move (or take the initiative).

先小人後君子(ㄒㄧㄢ ㄒㄧㄠˇ ㄖㄣˊ ㄏㄡˋ ㄐㄩㄣ ㄗˇ)
(especially in business negotiations) to specify terms clearly at first and use a good deal of courtesy later

先修班(ㄒㄧㄢ ㄒㄧㄡ ㄅㄢ)
a preparatory class

先賢(ㄒㄧㄢ ㄒㄧㄢˊ)or 先哲(ㄒㄧㄢ ㄓㄜˊ)
ancient saints and sages

先行(ㄒㄧㄢ ㄒㄧㄥˊ)
①to go ahead of the rest; to start off before the others ②beforehand; in advance: 他先行通知我。He let me know it in advance.

先行者(ㄒㄧㄢ ㄒㄧㄥˊ ㄓㄜˇ)
a forerunner: 紀念偉大的革命先行者孫中山先生! Let's pay tribute to our great revolutionary forerunner, Dr. Sun Yat-sen!

先知(ㄒㄧㄢ ㄓ)
①a prophet ②a person of foresight or forethought

先知先覺(ㄒㄧㄢ ㄓ ㄒㄧㄢ ㄐㄩㄝˊ)
①a person of foresight or forethought ②having foresight

先兆(ㄒㄧㄢ ㄓㄠˋ)
an omen; a portent; a sign; an indication: 燕子是夏天的先兆。The swallow is a sign of summer.

先斬後奏(ㄒㄧㄢ ㄓㄢˇ ㄏㄡˋ ㄗㄡˋ)
①(in old China) to order execution of criminals before reporting the case to the emperor ②(in a modern sense) to take action before reporting to one's superior

先師(ㄒㄧㄢ ㄕ)
①Confucius ②my late teacher

先世(ㄒㄧㄢ ㄕˋ)
①the preceding generation ②forebears; ancestors; forefathers

先室(ㄒㄧㄢ ㄕˋ)
my late wife

先手(ㄒㄧㄢ ㄕㄡˇ)
(in chess) on the offensive

先聲(ㄒㄧㄢ ㄕㄥ)
first signs; a herald; a harbinger

先聲奪人(ㄒㄧㄢ ㄕㄥ ㄉㄨㄛˊ ㄖㄣˊ)
to start doing something with such a brilliant performance as to inspire awe among others; with an impressive start; to forestall one's opponent by a show of strength; to overawe others by displaying one's strength

先聖(ㄒㄧㄢ ㄕㄥˋ)
①Confucius ②ancient sages

先生(ㄒㄧㄢ ˙ㄕㄥ)
①an honorable title for a teacher ②a name for the

elderly and learned ③ Mister; Sir ④ a husband

先人(ㄒㄧㄢ ㄖㄣˊ)
① previous generations ② forebears

先入之見(ㄒㄧㄢ ㄖㄨˋ ㄓ ㄐㄧㄢˋ)
a preconception; a preconceived idea; a prejudice

先入爲主(ㄒㄧㄢ ㄖㄨˋ ㄨㄟˊ ㄓㄨˇ)
One is often most impressed by the very first idea entering his mind. 或 One usually favors the very first idea entering his mind. 或 First impressions are most lasting.

先澤(ㄒㄧㄢ ㄗㄜˊ)
kindness and charity from one's ancestors

先意承志(ㄒㄧㄢ ㄧˋ ㄔㄥˊ ㄓˋ)
① to do what one's parents would like one to do ② to anticipate others' intention and do it without being told (in order to please them)

先憂後樂(ㄒㄧㄢ ㄧㄡ ㄏㄡˋ ㄌㄜˋ)
①(said of a capable ruler or statesman) to worry and plan ahead of his subjects and enjoy himself only after they are assured of peace and happiness ② Forethought brings happiness.

先嚴(ㄒㄧㄢ ㄧㄢˊ)
my deceased father

先驗(ㄒㄧㄢ ㄧㄢˋ)
a priori

先務之急(ㄒㄧㄢ ㄨˋ ㄓ ㄐㄧˊ)
first things first

先王(ㄒㄧㄢ ㄨㄤˊ)
① the late king ② ancient sage sovereigns

【光】 296
ㄍㄨㄤ guang guāng

1. light; brightness; light rays
2. glossy; smooth
3. glory; glorious; honor: 我們的棒球隊爲國爭光。Our baseball team won honor for our country.
4. to exhaust; to use up: 他用光了所有的錢。He has used up all the money.
5. alone; only: 光剩下你一人在家。You alone remain at home.
6. bare; to bare; naked
7. a Chinese family name

光被四表(ㄍㄨㄤ ㄅㄟˋ ㄙˋ ㄅㄧㄠˇ)
The benefit (of your enlightened administration) reaches far and wide.

光膀子(ㄍㄨㄤ ㄅㄤˇ ·ㄗ)
stripped to the waist; barebreasted

光波(ㄍㄨㄤ ㄅㄛ)
light waves

光屁股(ㄍㄨㄤ ㄆㄧˋ ·ㄍㄨ)
stark-naked; in the nude; without a single stitch on

光譜(ㄍㄨㄤ ㄆㄨˇ)
a spectrum

光芒(ㄍㄨㄤ ㄇㄤˊ)
rays of light; brilliant rays; radiance

光芒萬丈(ㄍㄨㄤ ㄇㄤˊ ㄨㄢˋ ㄓㄤˋ)
shining in all directions; radiance; radiant; resplendent: 那光芒萬丈的燈塔，照耀着我們勝利前進。The radiant lighthouse guides us in our victorious march forward.

光面(ㄍㄨㄤ ㄇㄧㄢˋ)
a glossy surface

光明(ㄍㄨㄤ ㄇㄧㄥˊ)
① light ② bright; promising: 我們的前途是光明的。Our future is bright. ③ openhearted; guileless

光明磊落(ㄍㄨㄤ ㄇㄧㄥˊ ㄌㄟˇ ㄌㄨㄛˋ)
straightforward and upright; open and aboveboard

光明正大(ㄍㄨㄤ ㄇㄧㄥˊ ㄓㄥˋ ㄉㄚˋ)
honest, just and upright

光復(ㄍㄨㄤ ㄈㄨˋ)
to recover (a lost land); retrocession

光大(ㄍㄨㄤ ㄉㄚˋ)
① glorious and majestic ② to make great; to glorify

光蛋(ㄍㄨㄤ ㄉㄢˋ)
a person reduced to complete poverty

光碟(ㄍㄨㄤ ㄉㄧㄝˊ)
a compact disk

光電(ㄍㄨㄤ ㄉㄧㄢˋ)
photoelectricity

光電子(ㄍㄨㄤ ㄉㄧㄢˋ ㄗˇ)
photoelectrons

光度(ㄍㄨㄤ ㄉㄨˋ)
the intensity of light

光度計(ㄍㄨㄤ ㄉㄨˋ ㄐㄧˋ)
a photometer

光頭(ㄍㄨㄤ ㄊㄡˊ)
a baldhead; baldheaded

光天化日(ㄍㄨㄤ ㄊㄧㄢ ㄏㄨㄚˋ ㄖˋ)
(in) broad daylight; the light of day

光禿禿(ㄍㄨㄤ ㄊㄨ ㄊㄨ)
bare; bald

光年(ㄍㄨㄤ ㄋㄧㄢˊ)
a light-year

光溜溜(ㄍㄨㄤ ㄌㄧㄡ ㄌㄧㄡ)
① bare; naked; bald ② smooth and glossy

光臨(ㄍㄨㄤ ㄌㄧㄣˊ)
(usually used in an invitation) Please grace our place with your presence. 歡迎光臨台灣! Welcome to Taiwan!

光亮(ㄍㄨㄤ ㄌㄧㄤˋ)
brightness; bright; radiance; radiant; light; shiny

光桿兒(ㄍㄨㄤ ㄍㄚˇㄦ)
① a bare trunk or stalk ② a man who has lost his family ③ a person without a following

光顧(ㄍㄨㄤ ㄍㄨˋ)
to patronize; to honor with one's presence: 許多顧客光顧這個新開張的超級市場。Many customers patronize the newly-opened supermarket.

光怪陸離(ㄍㄨㄤ ㄍㄨㄞˋ ㄌㄨˋ ㄌㄧˊ)
grotesque; strange-looking; fantastic

光棍
①(ㄍㄨㄤ ㄍㄨㄣˋ) ⓐ a ruffian; a hoodlum ⓑ a bachelor or unmarried man 亦作「光棍兒」
②(ㄍㄨㄤ ·ㄍㄨㄣ) a tough guy; a brave man: 他總是充光棍。He always pretends to be a brave man.

光光(ㄍㄨㄤ ㄍㄨㄤ)
① radiant ② glossy ③(said of money, goods, etc.) exhausted ④ naked

光合作用(ㄍㄨㄤ ㄏㄜˊ ㄗㄨㄛˋ ㄩㄥˋ)
photosynthesis

光華(ㄍㄨㄤ ㄏㄨㄚˊ)
brilliance; splendor

光滑(ㄍㄨㄤ ㄏㄨㄚˊ)
smooth and glossy

光火(ㄍㄨㄤ ㄏㄨㄛˇ)
① angry ② to anger

光輝(ㄍㄨㄤ ㄏㄨㄟ)
radiance; brightness: 烏雲擋住太陽的光輝。The dark cloud shut out the radiance

of the sun.

光環(ㄍㄨㄤ ㄏㄨㄢˊ)
(astronomy) a corona; a halo

光潔(ㄍㄨㄤ ㄐㄧㄝˊ)
bright and clean

光脚(ㄍㄨㄤ ㄐㄧㄠˇ)
bare feet; barefooted

光景(ㄍㄨㄤ ㄐㄧㄥˇ)
① a situation; circumstances ② about; around: 離這裡大約有十公里光景。It's about 10 kilometers away from here.

光球(ㄍㄨㄤ ㄑㄧㄡˊ)
a photosphere

光前裕後(ㄍㄨㄤ ㄑㄧㄢˊ ㄩˋ ㄏㄡˋ)
(said of one attaining a high position) to glorify the forebears and to provide for the descendants

光圈(ㄍㄨㄤ ㄑㄩㄢ)
the diaphragm of a camera

光鮮(ㄍㄨㄤ ㄒㄧㄢ)
fresh and bright

光線(ㄍㄨㄤ ㄒㄧㄢˋ)
a ray of light

光緒皇帝(ㄍㄨㄤ ㄒㄩˋ ㄏㄨㄤˊ ㄉㄧˋ)
the reigning title of Emperor Te Tsung of the Ching Dynasty, whose reign lasted from 1875 to 1908

光學(ㄍㄨㄤ ㄒㄩㄝˊ)
optics

光學儀器(ㄍㄨㄤ ㄒㄩㄝˊ ㄧˊ ㄑㄧˋ)
optical instruments

光手(ㄍㄨㄤ ㄕㄡˇ)
barehanded

光身人兒(ㄍㄨㄤ ㄕㄣ ㄖㄜˊㄦ)
① a single man ② a person with no valuable possession

光束(ㄍㄨㄤ ㄕㄨˋ)
(physics) a light beam

光潤(ㄍㄨㄤ ㄖㄨㄣˋ)
smooth and glossy

光榮(ㄍㄨㄤ ㄖㄨㄥˊ)
glory; honor; glorious; honorable: 他曾經在戰場上贏得光榮。He had won glory on the field of battle.

光澤(ㄍㄨㄤ ㄗㄜˊ)
luster: 那顆珍珠有美麗的光澤。It is a pearl with beautiful luster.

光宗耀祖(ㄍㄨㄤ ㄗㄨㄥ ㄧㄠˋ ㄗㄨˇ)
to glorify one's forebears (by one's great achievements)

光彩(ㄍㄨㄤ ㄘㄞˇ)
① luster; splendor; radiance: 光彩絢麗的冰雕吸引了許多觀光客。The brilliant luster of the ice carving attracted many tourists. ② honorable; glorious: 我認為做科學家是很光彩的。I think it is honorable to be a scientist.

光彩奪目(ㄍㄨㄤ ㄘㄞˇ ㄉㄨㄛˊ ㄇㄨˋ)
the luster that dazzles the eyes: 她的鑽戒光彩奪目。Her diamond ring dazzled with brilliancy.

光速(ㄍㄨㄤ ㄙㄨˋ)
(physics) the speed of light

光耀(ㄍㄨㄤ ㄧㄠˋ)
① brilliant light; brilliance ② glorious; honorable

光焰(ㄍㄨㄤ ㄧㄢˋ)
radiance; flare

光陰(ㄍㄨㄤ ㄧㄣ)
time

光陰似箭(ㄍㄨㄤ ㄧㄣ ㄙˋ ㄐㄧㄢˋ)
Time passes as fast as a flying arrow.

光源(ㄍㄨㄤ ㄩㄢˊ)
(physics) a light source

五畫

【克】 297 ㄎㄜˋ keh kè

1. to be able to: 他不克分身。He was unable to leave what he was doing at the moment.
2. to win; to overcome; to conquer: 在大戰中他們戰無不克。In the war, they won every battle they were engaged in.
3. love of superiority
4. a gram
5. to limit

克服(ㄎㄜˋ ㄈㄨˊ)
① to overcome (difficulties, etc.): 他克服了許多障礙。He overcame many obstacles. ② to put up with (inconveniences, etc.)

克復(ㄎㄜˋ ㄈㄨˋ)
to recapture or recover (a fallen city, etc.)

克敵致勝(ㄎㄜˋ ㄉㄧˊ ㄓˋ ㄕㄥˋ)
to defeat the enemy and win the battle; to vanquish the enemy

克難(ㄎㄜˋ ㄋㄢˊ)
to overcome difficulties

克拉(ㄎㄜˋ ㄌㄚ)
a carat

克里米亞(ㄎㄜˋ ㄌㄧˇ ㄇㄧˇ ㄧㄚˇ)
Crimea

克里姆林宮(ㄎㄜˋ ㄌㄧˇ ㄇㄨˇ ㄌㄧㄣˊ ㄍㄨㄥ)
the Kremlin

克林威爾(ㄎㄜˋ ㄌㄧㄣˊ ㄨㄟ ㄦˇ)
Oliver Cromwell, 1599-1658, British statesman

克格勃(ㄎㄜˋ ㄍㄜˊ ㄅㄛˊ)
KGB (Soviet State Security Committee)亦作「格別烏」

克己(ㄎㄜˋ ㄐㄧˇ)
① to overcome one's own desires ② reasonable (price)

克己奉公(ㄎㄜˋ ㄐㄧˇ ㄈㄥˋ ㄍㄨㄥ)
to place public interests above one's own; wholehearted devotion to public duty

克勤克儉(ㄎㄜˋ ㄑㄧㄣˊ ㄎㄜˋ ㄐㄧㄢˇ)
diligent and frugal

克制(ㄎㄜˋ ㄓˋ)
to restrain; to control (one's emotions, desires, etc.); to exercise restraint: 我認為你不需克制自己的感情。I think you don't have to restrain your passion.

克什米爾(ㄎㄜˋ ㄕㄜˊ ㄇㄧˇ ㄦˇ)
Kashmir

克紹箕裘(ㄎㄜˋ ㄕㄠˋ ㄐㄧ ㄑㄧㄡˊ)
to be able to follow in the footsteps of one's father; to be able to inherit a business, trade, career, etc. and make good

【兌】 298 ㄉㄨㄟˋ duey duì

1. to exchange; to barter
2. (said of wine, etc.) to water; to weaken by adding water

兌付(ㄉㄨㄟˋ ㄈㄨˋ)
to pay; to advance money; to cash

兌換(ㄉㄨㄟˋ ㄏㄨㄢˋ)
exchange; to exchange (currencies); to convert: 他把英磅兌換成美元。He exchanged pounds for dollars.

兌換率(ㄉㄨㄟˋ ㄏㄨㄢˋ ㄌㄩˋ)
the rate of exchange (between two currencies); exchange rates

兌換紙幣(ㄉㄨㄟˋ ㄏㄨㄢˋ ㄓˇ ㄅㄧˋ)

convertible paper money
兌現(ㄉㄨㄟˋ ㄒㄧㄢˋ)
①to cash (a check, etc.): 我在銀行把支票兌現。I get my checks cashed at the bank. ②to fulfill (a promise); to carry out

【免】 299 (免)ㄇㄧㄢˇ mean miǎn

1. to avoid; to escape; to evade
2. to forego; to spare; to excuse; to exempt
3. to dismiss (from office)

免不了(ㄇㄧㄢˇ ˙ㄅㄨ ㄌㄧㄠˇ)
unavoidable; to have to
免票(ㄇㄧㄢˇ ㄆㄧㄠˋ)
①a free ticket; a free pass ②free of charge
免費(ㄇㄧㄢˇ ㄈㄟˋ)
free of charge; gratuitous; gratis: 美術館在星期六免費開放。The gallery is open free on Saturdays.
免得(ㄇㄧㄢˇ ˙ㄉㄜ)
to save (the trouble of); to avoid; so as not to: 她靜悄悄地走進房間，免得吵醒小孩。She came into the room quietly so that she might not wake her child.
免談(ㄇㄧㄢˇ ㄊㄢˊ)
You might just as well save your breath.
免禮(ㄇㄧㄢˇ ㄌㄧˇ)
(usually ordered by a superior) to forego formalities (especially a salute, etc.)
免官(ㄇㄧㄢˇ ㄍㄨㄢ)
to dismiss from office 參看「免職」
免開尊口(ㄇㄧㄢˇ ㄎㄞ ㄗㄨㄣ ㄎㄡˇ)
You might as well save your breath.
免繳(ㄇㄧㄢˇ ㄐㄧㄠˇ)
to exempt from payment or taxation
免刑(ㄇㄧㄢˇ ㄒㄧㄥˊ)
to be exempted from punishment
免職(ㄇㄧㄢˇ ㄓˊ)
to be dismissed from office (sometimes for a new assignment): 部長受到免職處分。The minister was dismissed from his office in disgrace.
免戰牌(ㄇㄧㄢˇ ㄓㄢˋ ㄆㄞˊ)
a tablet of truce (In old China when one warring party hung the tablet high up the camp, it indicated the party's unwillingness to engage in battle temporarily for some reason which was often respected by the other party.)
免除(ㄇㄧㄢˇ ㄔㄨˊ)
①to prevent; to avoid ②to exempt (from obligations, etc.); to exonerate
免試升學(ㄇㄧㄢˇ ㄕˋ ㄕㄥ ㄒㄩㄝˊ)
to enter a school without taking an entrance examination
免稅(ㄇㄧㄢˇ ㄕㄨㄟˋ)
exemption of tax; free of duty; duty-free; to be exempted from taxation
免稅商店(ㄇㄧㄢˇ ㄕㄨㄟˋ ㄕㄤ ㄉㄧㄢˋ)
a duty-free shop
免罪(ㄇㄧㄢˇ ㄗㄨㄟˋ)
to be acquitted; exonerated; to be exempted from punishment
免俗(ㄇㄧㄢˇ ㄙㄨˊ)
to forego customary routines, formalities, etc.
免役(ㄇㄧㄢˇ ㄧˋ)
exemption from military service
免疫(ㄇㄧㄢˇ ㄧˋ)
immunity (from disease)
免疫性(ㄇㄧㄢˇ ㄧˋ ㄒㄧㄥˋ)
immunity from infection
免驗(ㄇㄧㄢˇ ㄧㄢˋ)
①to forego inspection ②to be exempt from customs examination

六畫

【兒】 300 ㄦˊ erl ér

1. a child; a baby
2. a son: 他有兩個兒子。He has two sons.
3. referring to oneself when addressing parents
4. As a particle after noun, pronoun, adjective, adverb, and verb, 兒 is pronounced (ㄦ). 屋裡有燈兒。There's a lamp in the room.

兒童(ㄦˊ ㄊㄨㄥˊ)
children
兒童電視劇(ㄦˊ ㄊㄨㄥˊ ㄉㄧㄢˋ ㄕˋ ㄐㄩˋ)
children's TV show; a TV show for children
兒童讀物(ㄦˊ ㄊㄨㄥˊ ㄉㄨˊ ㄨˋ)
juvenile publications; children's books; children's reading material
兒童樂園(ㄦˊ ㄊㄨㄥˊ ㄌㄜˋ ㄩㄢˊ)
an amusement park catering to children
兒童廣播劇(ㄦˊ ㄊㄨㄥˊ ㄍㄨㄤˇ ㄅㄛ ㄐㄩˋ)
a radio play for children
兒童節(ㄦˊ ㄊㄨㄥˊ ㄐㄧㄝˊ)
Children's Day (April 4)
兒童節目(ㄦˊ ㄊㄨㄥˊ ㄐㄧㄝˊ ㄇㄨˋ)
children's programs: 所有的兒童節目都很令人愉快。All the children's programs are delightful.
兒童教育(ㄦˊ ㄊㄨㄥˊ ㄐㄧㄠˋ ㄩˋ)
education for children; primary education; children's education: 兒童教育是一件重要的事情。Education for children is an important thing.
兒童戲院(ㄦˊ ㄊㄨㄥˊ ㄒㄧˋ ㄩㄢˋ)
①The Children's Theater (in Taipei) ②a theater for kids
兒童心理學(ㄦˊ ㄊㄨㄥˊ ㄒㄧㄣ ㄌㄧˇ ㄒㄩㄝˊ)
child psychology
兒童醫院(ㄦˊ ㄊㄨㄥˊ ㄧ ㄩㄢˋ)
a children's hospital
兒童文學(ㄦˊ ㄊㄨㄥˊ ㄨㄣˊ ㄒㄩㄝˊ)
literary writings for children; tales for children; children's literature
兒女(ㄦˊ ㄋㄩˇ)
①sons and daughters; children: 他們的兒女都已長大。Their children have all grown up. ②young men and women
兒女情長(ㄦˊ ㄋㄩˇ ㄑㄧㄥˊ ㄔㄤˊ)
Long is the love between a man and a woman.
兒女債(ㄦˊ ㄋㄩˇ ㄓㄞˋ)
the obligations of parents to their children
兒歌(ㄦˊ ㄍㄜ)
children's songs; nursery rhymes
兒科(ㄦˊ ㄎㄜ)
pediatrics

兒媳(ㄦ ㄒㄧˊ)or 兒媳婦(ㄦ ㄒㄧˊ ㄈㄨˋ)
a daughter-in-law
兒戲(ㄦ ㄒㄧˋ)or 兒嬉(ㄦ ㄒㄧ)
① child's play ② a plaything; a trifling matter: 這樣重要的工作可不能當兒戲。Such important work should not be regarded as a trifling matter. ③ to treat lightly
兒時(ㄦ ㄕˊ)
childhood
兒子(ㄦ ㄗˇ)or(ㄦ ·ㄗ)
a son or sons
兒孫(ㄦ ㄙㄨㄣ)
① children and grandchildren ② offspring; descendants
兒孫自有兒孫福(ㄦ ㄙㄨㄣ ㄗˋ ㄧㄡˇ ㄦ ㄙㄨㄣ ㄈㄨˊ)
The children can take care of themselves when they grow up. (Therefore, the parents don't have to work too hard for their children's future.)

【兔】 301
(兎) ㄊㄨˋ tuh tù
1. a hare; a rabbit
2. a young boy kept for sexual perversion
兔脫(ㄊㄨˋ ㄊㄨㄛ)
to escape fast
兔起鶻落(ㄊㄨˋ ㄑㄧˇ ㄏㄨˊ ㄌㄨㄛˋ)
(said of calligraphic works) bold and agile
兔脣(ㄊㄨˋ ㄔㄨㄣˊ)
a harelip, or a cleft lip
兔子(ㄊㄨˋ ·ㄗ)
① a hare; a rabbit ② a young boy kept for sexual perversion
兔子不吃窩邊草(ㄊㄨˋ ·ㄗ ㄅㄨˋ ㄔ ㄨㄛ ㄅㄧㄢ ㄘㄠˇ)
A rabbit doesn't eat the grass near its own burrow. —(figuratively) A villain does not harm his next-door neighbors.
兔崽子(ㄊㄨˋ ㄗㄞˇ ·ㄗ)
a brat; a bastard
兔死狗烹(ㄊㄨˋ ㄙˇ ㄍㄡˇ ㄆㄥ)
(literally) The hounds are killed for cooking food once all the hares are bagged. — Trusted aides are eliminated when they have outlived their usefulness. 或 (usually referring to the first emperor of a dynasty) to get rid of all the brave and meritorious comrades-in-arms after they had helped him win the throne and were no longer useful to him
兔死狐悲(ㄊㄨˋ ㄙˇ ㄏㄨˊ ㄅㄟ)
(literally) When the hare dies, the fox is sad.—sympathy with one of its kind

【兕】 302
ㄙˋ syh sì
a female rhinoceros

七畫

【兗】 303
ㄧㄢˇ yean yǎn
(in ancient China) one of the Nine Divisions of the Empire under Yü the Great including parts of Shantung and Hopeh provinces

九畫

【兜】 304
ㄉㄡ dou dōu
1. a head-covering; a helmet
2. overalls
3. to solicit
4. to go for a drive around; to move around
5. to surround; to wrap up
6. a small pocket in clothes
兜捕(ㄉㄡ ㄅㄨˇ)
to surround and seize
兜風(ㄉㄡ ㄈㄥ)
to go joyriding; to have a drive to enjoy countryside; to take the air; to go for a ride: 坐我的新車去兜風吧! Let's go for a ride in my new car.
兜肚(ㄉㄡ ·ㄉㄨ)
an undergarment covering the chest and abdomen 亦作「兜兜」or「兜子」
兜攬(ㄉㄡ ㄌㄢˇ)
① to befriend another person with a view to winning him over ② to solicit
兜圈子(ㄉㄡ ㄑㄩㄢ ·ㄗ)
①to take a stroll ②to circle: 敵機在我們頭上兜圈子。The enemy's planes circled round and round above our heads. ③ circumlocutory; to beat about the bush
兜紗(ㄉㄡ ㄕㄚ)
(in old China) a head-covering for the bride at a wedding
兜售(ㄉㄡ ㄕㄡˋ)
to peddle
兜兒(ㄉㄡㄦ)
a small pocket

十二畫

【兢】 305
ㄐㄧㄥ jing jīng
to fear; to dread; apprehensive; cautious
兢兢業業(ㄐㄧㄥ ㄐㄧㄥ ㄧㄝˋ ㄧㄝˋ)
with caution and fear; cautious and attentive

入部
ㄖㄨˋ ruh rù

【入】 306
ㄖㄨˋ ruh rù
1. to enter; to come into: 他進入屋子裡。He entered the house.
2. to join; to come into the company of: 他加入了網球俱樂部。He joined a tennis club.
3. to arrive at; to reach: 他已進入成人階段。He has arrived at manhood.
4. to put in: 她打開錢包放入一些錢。She opened her purse and put in some money.
5. receipts; income: 我們必須要量入爲出。We should regulate expenses according to income.
6. to get out of sight; to disappear
7. to get (inside, picked, elected, etc.)
8. to agree with; to conform to
9. one of the four tones of a character 參看「入聲」
入不敷出(ㄖㄨˋ ㄅㄨˋ ㄈㄨ ㄔㄨ)
expenditure exceeding income; cannot make both ends meet; to live beyond

one's means 或 One's income cannot cover one's spending.

入魔(ㄖㄨˋ ㄇㄛˊ)
①to be deeply fascinated; to be captivated; to be infatuated ② bedeviled; bewitched; spellbound

入門(ㄖㄨˋ ㄇㄣˊ)
① to have an elementary knowledge of (a subject); to initiate into; to get ready for more profound study (of a subject) ② a primer (for chess, bridge, etc.)

入夢(ㄖㄨˋ ㄇㄥˋ)
① to fall asleep ② to appear in one's dream

入迷(ㄖㄨˋ ㄇㄧˊ)
to be captivated or fascinated; to be bewitched; to be enchanted: 那美麗的舞者叫我們看得入迷了。We were all bewitched by the pretty dancer.

入木三分(ㄖㄨˋ ㄇㄨˋ ㄙㄢ ㄈㄣ)
①(said of Chinese calligraphy) a forceful style ② (comments, analyses, etc.) incisive; penetrating; sharp; profound: 他的分析眞是入木三分。His analysis was really penetrating.

入黨(ㄖㄨˋ ㄉㄤˇ)
to join a political party; to become a member of a political party

入定(ㄖㄨˋ ㄉㄧㄥˋ)
(Buddhism) to enter into meditation by tranquilizing the body, mouth (i.e. lips), and mind

入肚(ㄖㄨˋ ㄉㄨˋ)
to enter the stomach—to eat

入土(ㄖㄨˋ ㄊㄨˇ)
to bury; to be buried

入列(ㄖㄨˋ ㄌㄧㄝˋ)
to take one's place in the ranks; to fall in

入流(ㄖㄨˋ ㄌㄧㄡˊ)
① to be in fashion ② to attain a certain level ③(in old China) within the Nine Official Ranks

入殮(ㄖㄨˋ ㄌㄧㄢˋ)
to put a corpse in a coffin; to coffin

入閣(ㄖㄨˋ ㄍㄜˊ)
(in old China) to get inside the imperial cabinet; to be appointed a minister

入彀(ㄖㄨˋ ㄍㄡˋ)
to be trapped, harnessed, controlled, etc.

入港(ㄖㄨˋ ㄍㄤˇ)
①to enter a harbor (or port) ② (said of conversation) agreeable, amicable and interesting

入股(ㄖㄨˋ ㄍㄨˇ)
to become a shareholder; to buy a share

入骨(ㄖㄨˋ ㄍㄨˇ)
deep (hatred, love, etc.); to the marrow: 她恨他入骨。She hates him to the marrow.

入貢(ㄖㄨˋ ㄍㄨㄥˋ)
(said of protectorates or tributary nations) to offer tributes to the emperor

入口(ㄖㄨˋ ㄎㄡˇ)
① an entrance ② to import (commodities, etc.) ③ to enter the mouth

入寇(ㄖㄨˋ ㄎㄡˋ)
to invade; intrusion

入扣兒(ㄖㄨˋ ㄎㄡˋㄦ)
to be completely engrossed

入庫(ㄖㄨˋ ㄎㄨˋ)
① to confiscate; to be confiscated ② to enter (cargo) into a public warehouse before shipment to a final destination

入海口(ㄖㄨˋ ㄏㄞˇ ㄎㄡˇ)
an estuary

入畫(ㄖㄨˋ ㄏㄨㄚˋ)
suitable for a painting; picturesque: 花蓮景緻處處可以入畫。Every bit of Hualien scenery is picturesque.

入伙(ㄖㄨˋ ㄏㄨㄛˇ)
① to join in an enterprise (or a gang) ② to join a mess

入夥(ㄖㄨˋ ㄏㄨㄛˇ)
① to join a gang (especially of bandits, etc.) ② to join in an undertaking or enterprise

入會(ㄖㄨˋ ㄏㄨㄟˋ)
to join a society, club, organization, etc.; to become a member

入籍(ㄖㄨˋ ㄐㄧˊ)
to naturalize; to be naturalized

入教(ㄖㄨˋ ㄐㄧㄠˋ)
to become a follower or believer of a religion

入境(ㄖㄨˋ ㄐㄧㄥˋ)
to entry a country

入境證(ㄖㄨˋ ㄐㄧㄥˋ ㄓㄥˋ)
an entry permit

入境問禁(ㄖㄨˋ ㄐㄧㄥˋ ㄨㄣˋ ㄐㄧㄣˋ)
to learn the taboos of the local people after arriving at a strange place; to keep oneself informed of what things are forbidden in the country one is entering

入境問俗(ㄖㄨˋ ㄐㄧㄥˋ ㄨㄣˋ ㄙㄨˊ)
to learn the customs of a new place when one goes there 或 When in Rome, do as the Romans do.

入侵(ㄖㄨˋ ㄑㄧㄣ)
to invade; to intrude; to make an incursion; to make inroads: 敵人再次入侵。The enemy made another intrusion.

入情入理(ㄖㄨˋ ㄑㄧㄥˊ ㄖㄨˋ ㄌㄧˇ)
fair and reasonable

入席(ㄖㄨˋ ㄒㄧˊ)
to be properly seated at a gathering, meeting or feast; to take one's seat at a banquet, ceremony, etc.

入學(ㄖㄨˋ ㄒㄩㄝˊ)
to enter school (usually referring to primary school); to start school: 新生明天入學。The new students will enter school tomorrow.

入學考試(ㄖㄨˋ ㄒㄩㄝˊ ㄎㄠˇ ㄕˋ)
an entrance examination (of a school)

入選(ㄖㄨˋ ㄒㄩㄢˇ)
to be selected; to be chosen

入帳(ㄖㄨˋ ㄓㄤˋ)
to enter an item in an account

入主出奴(ㄖㄨˋ ㄓㄨˇ ㄔㄨ ㄋㄨˊ)
(said of academic schools, political philosophies, etc.) bigotry

入贅(ㄖㄨˋ ㄓㄨㄟˋ)
to marry into the family of one's wife—children thus born will bear her family name

入超(ㄖㄨˋ ㄔㄠ)

〔入部〕

〔入部〕

excess of import; an unfavorable balance of trade

入場(ㄖㄨˋ ㄔㄤˇ)or(ㄖㄨˋ ㄔㄤˊ)
①to enter a meeting place ②to take part in an examination

入場券(ㄖㄨˋ ㄔㄤˇ ㄑㄩㄢˋ)or(ㄖㄨˋ ㄔㄤˊ ㄑㄩㄢˋ)
an admission ticket

入時(ㄖㄨˋ ㄕˊ)
fashionable; to keep up with the times

入室(ㄖㄨˋ ㄕˋ)
to attain profundity in scholastic pursuits; to become a real expert (or specialist)

入室弟子(ㄖㄨˋ ㄕˋ ㄉㄧˋ ㄗˇ)
one who learns an art directly from a master

入室操戈(ㄖㄨˋ ㄕˋ ㄘㄠ ㄍㄜ)
to attack somebody with his own writings or statements

入手(ㄖㄨˋ ㄕㄡˇ)
to begin; to start; to put one's hand to

入山(ㄖㄨˋ ㄕㄢ)
to go to the mountain—to become a hermit; to live the life of a recluse; to decline offers of official ranks, etc.

入神(ㄖㄨˋ ㄕㄣˊ)
with ecstasy; captivated; bewitched; fascinated; spellbound: 他聽音樂聽得入神。He listened to the music with ecstasy.

入聲(ㄖㄨˋ ㄕㄥ)
(traditional Chinese phonetics) the fourth tone

入聖(ㄖㄨˋ ㄕㄥˋ)
(Buddhism) to become an arhat (a saint)

入睡(ㄖㄨˋ ㄕㄨㄟˋ)
to go to sleep; to fall asleep

入座(ㄖㄨˋ ㄗㄨㄛˋ)
properly seated (especially in a feast)

入耳(ㄖㄨˋ ㄦˇ)
①to hear ②pleasing to the ear

入夜(ㄖㄨˋ ㄧㄝˋ)
at night; in the evening; at nightfall: 入夜時分，城裡燈火通明。When night falls, the city is ablaze with light.

入眼(ㄖㄨˋ ㄧㄢˇ)
pleasing to the eye; agreeable to look at; to one's liking

入營(ㄖㄨˋ ㄧㄥˊ)
to enter the barracks—to join the army

入伍(ㄖㄨˋ ㄨˇ)
to become a soldier (usually under the conscription system); to enlist in the armed forces; to join up: 他入伍從軍爲國而戰。He joined up to fight for his country.

入圍(ㄖㄨˋ ㄨㄟˊ)
①to be selected or elected as one of the few; to enter the final contest ②to enter a circle, or a trapped area

入闈(ㄖㄨˋ ㄨㄟˊ)
①(said of a teacher) to enter a tightly guarded building to write test papers and stay there until the examination is over ②(in imperial China) to take the civil service examination in a cubicle of a tightly guarded building

入味(ㄖㄨˋ ㄨㄟˋ)
①tasty: 這湯很入味。The soup is very tasty. ②interesting

入獄(ㄖㄨˋ ㄩˋ)
to be imprisoned; to be put in prison; to be sent to jail; to put behind bars

入院(ㄖㄨˋ ㄩㄢˋ)
①to be hospitalized; to be admitted to hospital: 他昨天入院就醫。He was hospitalized yesterday. ②(Buddhism) to enter a monastery; to become a monk

二畫

【內】 307
ㄋㄟ ney nèi

1. inside; within; inner; interior: 屋子內外都很整潔。The house is clean inside and out.
2. wife
3. the palace of an emperor

內部(ㄋㄟˋ ㄅㄨˋ)
the interior; the internal parts; inside; within: 他油漆房子內部。He painted the inside of the house.

內布拉斯加(ㄋㄟˋ ㄅㄨˋ ㄌㄚ ㄙ ㄐㄧㄚ)
the state of Nebraska, U. S. A.

內蒙古(ㄋㄟˋ ㄇㄥˊ ㄍㄨˇ)
Inner Mongolia (Jehol, Chahar and Suiyüan)

內幕(ㄋㄟˋ ㄇㄨˋ)
an inside story

內幕消息(ㄋㄟˋ ㄇㄨˋ ㄒㄧㄠ ㄒㄧˊ)
inside information; inside skinny 亦作「內幕傳眞」

內犯(ㄋㄟˋ ㄈㄢˋ)
intrusion by (bandits, enemy troops, etc.)

內分泌(ㄋㄟˋ ㄈㄣ ㄇㄧˋ)
glandular excretion; internal secretion; endocrines

內服藥(ㄋㄟˋ ㄈㄨˊ ㄧㄠˋ)
drugs taken orally or internally; drugs for oral administration

內附(ㄋㄟˋ ㄈㄨˋ)
enclosed herewith

內弟(ㄋㄟˋ ㄉㄧˋ)
younger brothers of one's wife

內地(ㄋㄟˋ ㄉㄧˋ)
the hinterland; the inland; a land area behind the border or coast

內地會(ㄋㄟˋ ㄉㄧˋ ㄏㄨㄟˋ)
China Inland Mission

內定(ㄋㄟˋ ㄉㄧㄥˋ)
(said of official appointment) to have already decided, but yet to be officially announced

內動詞(ㄋㄟˋ ㄉㄨㄥˋ ㄘˊ)
linking verbs

內奴外主(ㄋㄟˋ ㄋㄨˊ ㄨㄞˋ ㄓㄨˇ)
(said of a bad government) to treat one's own people as slaves but to regard foreign powers as masters

內陸(ㄋㄟˋ ㄌㄨˋ)
inland; interior

內陸國(ㄋㄟˋ ㄌㄨˋ ㄍㄨㄛˊ)
a landlocked country

內亂(ㄋㄟˋ ㄌㄨㄢˋ)
rebellion; a civil war; civil strife; internal disorders

內亂罪(ㄋㄟˋ ㄌㄨㄢˋ ㄗㄨㄟˋ)
treason

內閣(ㄋㄟˋ ㄍㄜˊ)
the cabinet

內閣制(ㄋㄟˋ ㄍㄜˊ ㄓˋ)
the cabinet system

內閣總理(ㄋㄟˋ ㄍㄜˊ ㄗㄨㄥˇ ㄌㄧˇ)
the premier; the prime minister; the chancellor

內顧(ㄋㄟˋ ㄍㄨˋ)
to look after home or domestic affairs

內顧之憂(ㄋㄟˋ ㄍㄨˋ ㄓ ㄧㄡ)
worries for trouble at home

內功(ㄋㄟˋ ㄍㄨㄥ)
(Chinese boxing) the exercise and training of internal organs to develop uncanny strength, feats, endurance, etc.

內科(ㄋㄟˋ ㄎㄜ)
internal medicine; general medicine

內科醫生(ㄋㄟˋ ㄎㄜ ㄧ ㄕㄥ)
a physician (as distinguished from a surgeon)

內開(ㄋㄟˋ ㄎㄞ)
what is listed therein (used in documents)

內庫(ㄋㄟˋ ㄎㄨˋ)
the treasury within the palace

內河(ㄋㄟˋ ㄏㄜˊ)
rivers in the hinterland; inland rivers

內海(ㄋㄟˋ ㄏㄞˇ)
inland seas; continental seas

內含(ㄋㄟˋ ㄏㄢˊ)
to contain

內涵(ㄋㄟˋ ㄏㄢˊ)
(logic) intension; connotation

內行(ㄋㄟˋ ㄏㄤˊ)
a professional; a specialist; an expert

內華達(ㄋㄟˋ ㄏㄨㄚˊ ㄉㄚˊ)
the state of Nevada, U. S. A.

內訌(ㄋㄟˋ ㄏㄨㄥˋ)
an internal squabble; an intramural fight; internal strife (or dissension)

內角(ㄋㄟˋ ㄐㄧㄠˇ)
(mathematics) an interior angle

內疚(ㄋㄟˋ ㄐㄧㄡˋ)
deep regret; remorse; compunction; a guilty conscience

內奸(ㄋㄟˋ ㄐㄧㄢ)
a spy within; a traitor

內景(ㄋㄟˋ ㄐㄧㄥˇ)
(motion pictures) scenes within the sound stage; studio scenes; indoor scenes (or settings)

內舉不避親(ㄋㄟˋ ㄐㄩˇ ㄅㄨˋ ㄅㄧˋ ㄑㄧㄣ)
to promote or appoint a relative to a post on the basis of personal merit

內眷(ㄋㄟˋ ㄐㄩㄢˋ)
female members of a family

內切圓(ㄋㄟˋ ㄑㄧㄝ ㄩㄢˊ)
(mathematics) an inscribed circle

內親(ㄋㄟˋ ㄑㄧㄣ)
relatives of one's wife

內勤(ㄋㄟˋ ㄑㄧㄣˊ)
desk work; working inside an office

內情(ㄋㄟˋ ㄑㄧㄥˊ)
an inside story

內銷(ㄋㄟˋ ㄒㄧㄠ)
(said of local products) for domestic sale or market

內線(ㄋㄟˋ ㄒㄧㄢˋ)
inside contacts; a stool pigeon

內心(ㄋㄟˋ ㄒㄧㄣ)
heart; the bottom of one's heart: 他是個內心仁慈的人。He is a man with a kind heart.

內詳(ㄋㄟˋ ㄒㄧㄤˊ)
the name and address of the sender enclosed

內向(ㄋㄟˋ ㄒㄧㄤˋ)
introversion; introverted

內省(ㄋㄟˋ ㄒㄧㄥˇ)
self-examination; to search one's own heart

內兄(ㄋㄟˋ ㄒㄩㄥ)
elder brothers of one's wife

內姪(ㄋㄟˋ ㄓˊ)
nephews of one's wife

內姪女(ㄋㄟˋ ㄓˊ ㄋㄩˇ)
nieces of one's wife

內痔(ㄋㄟˋ ㄓˋ)
internal hemorrhoids

內宅(ㄋㄟˋ ㄓㄞˊ)
the inner quarters of a house (usually occupied by the female members)

內債(ㄋㄟˋ ㄓㄞˋ)
internal debts

內戰(ㄋㄟˋ ㄓㄢˋ)
a civil war

內政(ㄋㄟˋ ㄓㄥˋ)
home administration; internal (or domestic) affairs: 他們主張互不干涉內政。They insist on noninterference in each other's internal affairs.

內政部(ㄋㄟˋ ㄓㄥˋ ㄅㄨˋ)
the Ministry of the Interior

內助(ㄋㄟˋ ㄓㄨˋ)
wife (a complimentary term)

內重外輕(ㄋㄟˋ ㄓㄨㄥˋ ㄨㄞˋ ㄑㄧㄥ)
over-concentration of power in the central government

內出血(ㄋㄟˋ ㄔㄨ ㄒㄧㄝˇ)
internal bleeding

內侍(ㄋㄟˋ ㄕˋ)
eunuchs and palace attendants

內傷(ㄋㄟˋ ㄕㄤ)
① internal injury ② (Chinese medicine) disorder of internal organs

內聖外王(ㄋㄟˋ ㄕㄥˋ ㄨㄞˋ ㄨㄤˊ)
sagely within and kingly without—a learning both sound in theory and practice

內燃機(ㄋㄟˋ ㄖㄢˊ ㄐㄧ)
an internal-combustion engine

內人(ㄋㄟˋ ˙ㄖㄣ) or 內子(ㄋㄟˋ ㄗˇ)
my wife

內容(ㄋㄟˋ ㄖㄨㄥˊ)
① content ② the meaning, theme, etc. of a literary or artistic work

內則無虧(ㄋㄟˋ ㄗㄜˊ ㄨˊ ㄎㄨㄟ)
(said of a housewife) dutiful and virtuous

內在(ㄋㄟˋ ㄗㄞˋ)
inherent; intrinsic; internal; inner

內在美(ㄋㄟˋ ㄗㄞˋ ㄇㄟˇ)
inner beauty (as contrasted with physical charms); the beauty of spirit

內臟(ㄋㄟˋ ㄗㄤˋ)
internal organs; viscera

內才(ㄋㄟˋ ㄘㄞˊ)
talent; scholastic achievements; learning

內耳(ㄋㄟˋ ㄦˇ)
the inner ear

內衣(ㄋㄟˋ ㄧ)
underwear; undergarments

內憂外患(ㄋㄟˋ ㄧㄡ ㄨㄞˋ ㄏㄨㄢˋ)
(said of countries) troubles within and without

內應(ㄋㄟˋ ㄧㄥˋ)
an inside help; a planted agent
內務(ㄋㄟˋ ㄨˋ)
① domestic affairs; internal affairs ②(in ancient China) affairs within the palace ③ family affairs
內外(ㄋㄟˋ ㄨㄞˋ)
① inside and outside: 這道牆的內外都是藍色。Both sides of the wall are blue. ② domestic and foreign; home and abroad: 這個國家內外交困。This country is beset with difficulties both at home and abroad. ③ around; about: 他的年紀在六十歲內外。His age is about sixty.
內外夾攻(ㄋㄟˋ ㄨㄞˋ ㄐㄧㄚˊ ㄍㄨㄥ)
to attack (an enemy) simultaneously from within and without; subjected to synchronized attack from within and without
內圓(ㄋㄟˋ ㄩㄢˊ)
(geometry) an internal circle

四畫

【全】308
ㄑㄩㄢˊ chyuan quán
1. perfect
2. complete; whole; total; intact; all; entire; absolute: 上星期我全家人都去台南。My whole family went to Tainan last week.
3. to keep whole or intact
4. a Chinese family name

全豹(ㄑㄩㄢˊ ㄅㄠˋ)
the complete picture; the entire thing: 我們有幸得窺全豹。We are fortunate to see the entire thing.
全班(ㄑㄩㄢˊ ㄅㄢ)
the whole class; the whole squad
全本(ㄑㄩㄢˊ ㄅㄣˇ)
(Chinese opera) the staging of the whole story in a single show
全部(ㄑㄩㄢˊ ㄅㄨˋ)
the whole; completely; fully; total: 他以全部的心力去做這件工作。He did the work with his whole heart.
全盤(ㄑㄩㄢˊ ㄆㄢˊ)
total; overall; all-out; entire; wholesale; complete: 我們將做全盤考慮。We will give overall consideration to it.
全盤計劃(ㄑㄩㄢˊ ㄆㄢˊ ㄐㄧˋ ㄏㄨㄚˋ)
an overall program or plan
全貌(ㄑㄩㄢˊ ㄇㄠˋ)
the overall picture or appearance
全面(ㄑㄩㄢˊ ㄇㄧㄢˋ)
overall; comprehensive; all-round
全面攻擊(ㄑㄩㄢˊ ㄇㄧㄢˋ ㄍㄨㄥ ㄐㄧˊ)
an all-out offensive
全面戰爭(ㄑㄩㄢˊ ㄇㄧㄢˋ ㄓㄢˋ ㄓㄥ)
a total war; a full-scale war
全民(ㄑㄩㄢˊ ㄇㄧㄣˊ)
the whole (or entire) people; all the people
全民皆兵(ㄑㄩㄢˊ ㄇㄧㄣˊ ㄐㄧㄝ ㄅㄧㄥ)
an entire nation in arms; every citizen as a soldier
全民政治(ㄑㄩㄢˊ ㄇㄧㄣˊ ㄓㄥˋ ㄓˋ)
democracy; government by all the people
全副(ㄑㄩㄢˊ ㄈㄨˋ)
the whole set
全副武裝(ㄑㄩㄢˊ ㄈㄨˋ ㄨˇ ㄓㄨㄤ)
to be armed to the teeth; with all the equipment (issued to a soldier such as ammunition, a rifle, a sack, a shovel, etc.); fully armed; in full battle array
全都(ㄑㄩㄢˊ ㄉㄡ)
all; altogether; everyone: 去年栽的花全都開了。All the flowers planted last year have bloomed.
全等(ㄑㄩㄢˊ ㄉㄥˇ)
identically equal; congruent
全套(ㄑㄩㄢˊ ㄊㄠˋ)
the whole set; the complete set: 這實驗室擁有全套設備。This laboratory has a complete set of equipment.
全體(ㄑㄩㄢˊ ㄊㄧˇ)
all; the whole body; everybody; plenary (assembly): 全體贊成他的提議。All approved of his suggestion.
全天候(ㄑㄩㄢˊ ㄊㄧㄢ ㄏㄡˋ)
all-weather; capable of operating under all weather conditions
全能(ㄑㄩㄢˊ ㄋㄥˊ)
① omnipotence ② all-round: 他是個全能運動員。He's an all-round sportsman.
全能運動(ㄑㄩㄢˊ ㄋㄥˊ ㄩㄣˋ ㄉㄨㄥˋ)
(for men) the decathlon; (for women) the pentathlon
全年(ㄑㄩㄢˊ ㄋㄧㄢˊ)
the whole year; throughout the year; all the year round
全壘打(ㄑㄩㄢˊ ㄌㄟˇ ㄉㄚˇ)
(baseball) a home run
全力(ㄑㄩㄢˊ ㄌㄧˋ)
(with) all-out effort; (with) wholehearted dedication
全力以赴(ㄑㄩㄢˊ ㄌㄧˋ ㄧˇ ㄈㄨˋ)
to spare no efforts: 我們全力以赴以挽回局勢。We spared no efforts to save the situation.
全國(ㄑㄩㄢˊ ㄍㄨㄛˊ)
the whole country or nation; national; nationwide; throughout the nation
全國性(ㄑㄩㄢˊ ㄍㄨㄛˊ ㄒㄧㄥˋ)
nationwide; countrywide; national
全國人口普查(ㄑㄩㄢˊ ㄍㄨㄛˊ ㄖㄣˊ ㄎㄡˇ ㄆㄨˇ ㄔㄚˊ)
a nationwide census
全開(ㄑㄩㄢˊ ㄎㄞ)
standard-sized; full-size
全集(ㄑㄩㄢˊ ㄐㄧˊ)
① the complete works of (Shakespeare, etc.) ② the whole set of books of an author dealing with a single subject
全家(ㄑㄩㄢˊ ㄐㄧㄚ)
the whole family
全家福(ㄑㄩㄢˊ ㄐㄧㄚ ㄈㄨˊ)
a family photo
全景(ㄑㄩㄢˊ ㄐㄧㄥˇ)
a panoramic view; a panorama; a full view; a whole scene: 西湖的全景很美。The full view of the West Lake is very beautiful.
全局(ㄑㄩㄢˊ ㄐㄩˊ)
the situation as a whole; the overall situation
全軍(ㄑㄩㄢˊ ㄐㄩㄣ)
the whole (or entire) army
全軍覆沒(ㄑㄩㄢˊ ㄐㄩㄣ ㄈㄨˋ ㄇㄛˋ)
The whole army was lost. 或 The army was totally annihilated.

全球(ㄑㄩㄢˊ ㄑㄧㄡˊ)
around the globe; the globe; the world

全權代表(ㄑㄩㄢˊ ㄑㄩㄢˊ ㄉㄞˋ ㄅㄧㄠˇ)
an envoy plenipotentiary; a representative vested with full authority; a delegate with full powers

全席(ㄑㄩㄢˊ ㄒㄧˊ)
a whole feast; a whole banquet (without omission of any dishes listed in a Chinese menu)

全休(ㄑㄩㄢˊ ㄒㄧㄡ)
a complete rest

全線(ㄑㄩㄢˊ ㄒㄧㄢˋ)
all fronts; the whole line: 我們將全線出擊。We will launch an attack on all fronts.

全心全意(ㄑㄩㄢˊ ㄒㄧㄣ ㄑㄩㄢˊ ㄧˋ)
wholeheartedly: 她決定全心全意爲窮人服務。She decided to serve the poor wholeheartedly.

全脂奶粉(ㄑㄩㄢˊ ㄓ ㄋㄞˇ ㄈㄣˇ)
whole milk powder

全知全能(ㄑㄩㄢˊ ㄓ ㄑㄩㄢˊ ㄋㄥˊ)
omniscient and omnipotent

全場(ㄑㄩㄢˊ ㄔㄤˇ)
① the whole audience; all those present: 全場掌聲雷動。The audience applaused thunderously. ②(basketball) full-court; all-court

全程(ㄑㄩㄢˊ ㄔㄥˊ)
the whole journey; the whole course: 賽車比賽全程五百公里。The whole course of the automobile race is 500 kilometers.

全屍(ㄑㄩㄢˊ ㄕ)
a corpse with no part missing, a reference to execution by hanging or poisoning instead of decapitation or mutilation in imperial China

全蝕(ㄑㄩㄢˊ ㄕˊ)
a total eclipse

全壽(ㄑㄩㄢˊ ㄕㄡˋ)
to live one's full life span; to die of natural cause

全身(ㄑㄩㄢˊ ㄕㄣ)
the whole body

全神貫注(ㄑㄩㄢˊ ㄕㄣˊ ㄍㄨㄢˋ ㄓㄨˋ)
to pay undivided attention to; to concentrate on: 他不能全神貫注於學術工作。He is unable to concentrate on academic work.

全勝(ㄑㄩㄢˊ ㄕㄥˋ)
a total victory; a complete victory

全盛(ㄑㄩㄢˊ ㄕㄥˋ)
flourishing; in full bloom; at the peak of development

全盛時代(ㄑㄩㄢˊ ㄕㄥˋ ㄕˊ ㄉㄞˋ)or 全盛時期(ㄑㄩㄢˊ ㄕㄥˋ ㄕˊ ㄑㄧˊ)
the heyday; the zenith; the prime

全數(ㄑㄩㄢˊ ㄕㄨˋ)
the whole amount; the total number; the sum total

全然(ㄑㄩㄢˊ ㄖㄢˊ)
completely (ignorant, etc.); totally: 他全然不知道這件事。He is totally ignorant of it.

全人(ㄑㄩㄢˊ ㄖㄣˊ)
a sage; a perfect person

全自動化(ㄑㄩㄢˊ ㄗˋ ㄉㄨㄥˋ ㄏㄨㄚˋ)
automation

全才(ㄑㄩㄢˊ ㄘㄞˊ)
an all-round talent; a master of all trades; a versatile person

全速(ㄑㄩㄢˊ ㄙㄨˋ)
full (or maximum) speed: 這部車以全速行駛。The car was running at full speed.

全無心肝(ㄑㄩㄢˊ ㄨˊ ㄒㄧㄣ ㄍㄢ)
totally heartless; totally unconscionable; absolutely ungrateful

全武行(ㄑㄩㄢˊ ㄨˇ ㄏㄤˊ)
a brawl; a free-for-all

全文(ㄑㄩㄢˊ ㄨㄣˊ)
a full text

全愈(ㄑㄩㄢˊ ㄩˋ)
to have completely recovered (from illness, injury, etc.)

六畫

【兩】 309 ㄌㄧㄤˇ leang liǎng

1. two; a pair; a couple: 他們只有兩人沒有通過考試。Only two of them failed in the examination.
2. both; either: 那兩所房子都是白的。Both (the) houses are white.
3. a tael (a unit of weight)
4. (in ancient China) a piece of cloth, etc. of about 44 feet
5. (in ancient China) a group of 25 soldiers

兩敗俱傷(ㄌㄧㄤˇ ㄅㄞˋ ㄐㄩˋ ㄕㄤ)
Both are hurt. 或 Nobody wins.

兩倍(ㄌㄧㄤˇ ㄅㄟˋ)
double; twice: 十是五的兩倍。Ten is the double of five.

兩半(ㄌㄧㄤˇ ㄅㄢˋ)
two halves: 她把蘋果切成兩半。She cut the apple in two.

兩邊(ㄌㄧㄤˇ ㄅㄧㄢ)or 兩旁(ㄌㄧㄤˇ ㄆㄤˊ)
both sides; two sides; two directions: 人群向兩邊散開了。The crowd scattered in two directions.

兩邊倒(ㄌㄧㄤˇ ㄅㄧㄢ ㄉㄠˇ)
(said of fence-sitting opportunists) to lean now to one side, now to the other; to sway; to waver

兩邊討好(ㄌㄧㄤˇ ㄅㄧㄢ ㄊㄠˇ ㄏㄠˇ)
to please both sides by saying bad things about one side in the presence of the other and vice versa

兩便(ㄌㄧㄤˇ ㄅㄧㄢˋ)
① to suit both parties; to be convenient to both; to profit both official and private ends ② to go Dutch

兩碼事(ㄌㄧㄤˇ ㄇㄚˇ ㄕˋ)
two different matters 參看「兩回事」

兩面(ㄌㄧㄤˇ ㄇㄧㄢˋ)or 兩面兒(ㄌㄧㄤˇ ㄇㄧㄚˋㄦ)
① two sides (of a story, etc.) ② straddling; unprincipled; double or dual (character)

兩面夾攻(ㄌㄧㄤˇ ㄇㄧㄢˋ ㄐㄧㄚˊ ㄍㄨㄥ)
to make a pincers drive

兩面作戰(ㄌㄧㄤˇ ㄇㄧㄢˋ ㄗㄨㄛˋ ㄓㄢˋ)
to fight on two fronts

兩黨制(ㄌㄧㄤˇ ㄉㄤˇ ㄓˋ)
the two-party system; the bipartisan system

兩抵(ㄌㄧㄤˇ ㄉㄧˇ)
to balance or cancel each other: 功過兩抵。Merits and demerits balance each other.

兩端(ㄌㄧㄤˇ ㄉㄨㄢ)
① from end to end; from beginning to end; the two extremities ② excess and insufficience ③ vacillation; in-

decision
兩頭蛇(ㄌㄧㄤˇ ㄊㄡˊ ㄕㄜˊ)
①a two-headed snake ② one who tries to hurt or please either of two contending parties when it suits his purpose
兩頭兒(ㄌㄧㄤˇ ㄊㄡˊㄦ)
both ends; either end
兩條心(ㄌㄧㄤˇ ㄊㄧㄠˊ ㄒㄧㄣ)
disagreement between the two; not of one mind
兩難(ㄌㄧㄤˇ ㄋㄢˊ)
(literally) between two difficulties — indecisive; to be in a dilemma
兩立(ㄌㄧㄤˇ ㄌㄧˋ)
to coexist; coexistence
兩姑之間難爲婦(ㄌㄧㄤˇ ㄍㄨ ㄓ ㄐㄧㄢ ㄋㄢˊ ㄨㄟˊ ㄈㄨˋ)
It's difficult to serve under two bosses. 或(said of a small nation) It's difficult to exist between two powers.
兩廣(ㄌㄧㄤˇ ㄍㄨㄤˇ)or 兩粵(ㄌㄧㄤˇ ㄩㄝˋ)
Kwangtung and Kwangsi
兩可(ㄌㄧㄤˇ ㄎㄜˇ)
two alternatives; indecisive; indecision 或 Both (or Either) will do.
兩口子(ㄌㄧㄤˇ ㄎㄡˇ ·ㄗ)or 兩口兒(ㄌㄧㄤˇ ㄎㄡˇㄦ)
①a married couple; husband and wife ②two persons living under the same roof
兩害相權取其輕(ㄌㄧㄤˇ ㄏㄞˋ ㄒㄧㄤ ㄑㄩㄢˊ ㄑㄩˇ ㄑㄧˊ ㄑㄧㄥ)
to accept the lesser of two evils
兩漢(ㄌㄧㄤˇ ㄏㄢˋ)
(history) the Former and Later Han Dynasties
兩湖(ㄌㄧㄤˇ ㄏㄨˊ)
Hunan and Hupeh Provinces
兩虎相鬪必有一傷(ㄌㄧㄤˇ ㄏㄨˇ ㄒㄧㄤ ㄉㄡˋ ㄅㄧˋ ㄧㄡˇ ㄧˊ ㄕㄤ)
When two tigers fight, one is going to get hurt. —When two powers battle, one is going to get hurt.
兩淮(ㄌㄧㄤˇ ㄏㄨㄞˊ)
referring to areas north and south of the Huai River
兩回事(ㄌㄧㄤˇ ㄏㄨㄟˊ ㄕˋ)
two entirely different things; two different matters
兩極(ㄌㄧㄤˇ ㄐㄧˊ)
the opposing poles; two extremes
兩截(ㄌㄧㄤˇ ㄐㄧㄝˊ)or 兩截兒(ㄌㄧㄤˇ ㄐㄧㄝˊㄦ)
two pieces; in two pieces
兩脚規(ㄌㄧㄤˇ ㄐㄧㄠˇ ㄍㄨㄟ)or 圓規(ㄩㄢˊ ㄍㄨㄟ)
compasses; dividers
兩脚書櫥(ㄌㄧㄤˇ ㄐㄧㄠˇ ㄕㄨ ㄔㄨˊ)
①a two-legged bookcase ②a bookworm; a person who cannot profit by what he reads
兩晉(ㄌㄧㄤˇ ㄐㄧㄣˋ)
(history) the Western Tsin and the Eastern Tsin Dynasties
兩江(ㄌㄧㄤˇ ㄐㄧㄤ)
(Ching Dynasty) the area covering the present-day Kiangsu, Anhwei and Kiangsi
兩棲(ㄌㄧㄤˇ ㄑㄧ)
amphibious
兩棲部隊(ㄌㄧㄤˇ ㄑㄧ ㄅㄨˋ ㄉㄨㄟˋ)
amphibious force; amphibious troops; amphibious units
兩棲類(ㄌㄧㄤˇ ㄑㄧ ㄌㄟˋ)
the amphibian
兩棲作戰(ㄌㄧㄤˇ ㄑㄧ ㄗㄨㄛˋ ㄓㄢˋ)
amphibious operations
兩歧(ㄌㄧㄤˇ ㄑㄧˊ)
(said of two things) do not tally
兩訖(ㄌㄧㄤˇ ㄑㄧˋ)or 兩清(ㄌㄧㄤˇ ㄑㄧㄥ)
(said of a purchase) paid and delivered; (said of an account) both sides clear
兩情繾綣(ㄌㄧㄤˇ ㄑㄧㄥˊ ㄑㄧㄢˇ ㄑㄩㄢˇ)
deeply in love with each other
兩全(ㄌㄧㄤˇ ㄑㄩㄢˊ)
to be satisfactory to both parties: 這是個兩全的辦法。This is a measure satisfactory to both sides.
兩全其美(ㄌㄧㄤˇ ㄑㄩㄢˊ ㄑㄧˊ ㄇㄟˇ)
to profit both parties or attain two objectives by a single act
兩權分立(ㄌㄧㄤˇ ㄑㄩㄢˊ ㄈㄣ ㄌㄧˋ)
a political system under which the legislative and executive branches are independent of each other
兩下子(ㄌㄧㄤˇ ㄒㄧㄚˋ ·ㄗ)
①in a few minutes ②a few tricks of the trade
兩小無猜(ㄌㄧㄤˇ ㄒㄧㄠˇ ㄨˊ ㄘㄞ)
(said of a young boy and a little girl) living and playing together in childhood innocence 或 Two innocent ones, a boy and a girl, grew up together.
兩袖清風(ㄌㄧㄤˇ ㄒㄧㄡˋ ㄑㄧㄥ ㄈㄥ)
(usually said of an honest public servant) to attain high official ranks without money in the bank
兩性(ㄌㄧㄤˇ ㄒㄧㄥˋ)
①both sexes ②amphoteric
兩性花(ㄌㄧㄤˇ ㄒㄧㄥˋ ㄏㄨㄚ)
a bisexual flower; a hermaphrodite flower
兩相好(ㄌㄧㄤˇ ㄒㄧㄤ ㄏㄠˇ)
two lovers
兩相情願(ㄌㄧㄤˇ ㄒㄧㄤ ㄑㄧㄥˊ ㄩㄢˋ)
Both parties are willing.
兩浙(ㄌㄧㄤˇ ㄓㄜˋ)
the eastern and western parts of Chekiang Province
兩重(ㄌㄧㄤˇ ㄔㄨㄥˊ)
double; dual; twofold: 他有兩重性格。He has a dual nature.
兩手(ㄌㄧㄤˇ ㄕㄡˇ)
dual tactics
兩造(ㄌㄧㄤˇ ㄗㄠˋ)
the plaintiff and the defendant; parties to a contract or lawsuit
兩側(ㄌㄧㄤˇ ㄘㄜˋ)
two sides
兩耳不聞窗外事(ㄌㄧㄤˇ ㄦˇ ㄅㄨˋ ㄨㄣˊ ㄔㄨㄤ ㄨㄞˋ ㄕˋ)
to care nothing outside one's window—One does not care what is going on beyond one's own surroundings.
兩儀(ㄌㄧㄤˇ ㄧˊ)
the *yin* (陰) and the *yang* (陽), the two polarities
兩翼(ㄌㄧㄤˇ ㄧˋ)
(a military term) two flanks or wings
兩樣(ㄌㄧㄤˇ ㄧㄤˋ)
①two kinds; two different things ②different: 兩樣作法產生兩種結果。Two different

methods produce two different results.
兩院制 (ㄌㄧㄤˇ ㄩㄢˋ ㄓˋ)
the bicameral system (of a parliament)
兩用(ㄌㄧㄤˇ ㄩㄥˋ)
①(said of an instrument, a gadget, etc.) serving two purposes; a dual purpose ②(said of a coat) reversible: 兩用夾克 a reversible jacket

七畫

【俞】 310
ㄩˊ yu yú
1. to answer in the affirmative
2. to make a boat by hollowing the log
3. a Chinese family name
俞允(ㄩˊ ㄩㄣˇ)
to consent; to approve

八部
ㄅㄚ ba bā

【八】 311
ㄅㄚ ba bā
(變調 ㄅㄚˊ bar bá)
eight
八百羅漢(ㄅㄚ ㄅㄞˇ ㄌㄨㄛˊ ㄏㄢˋ)
the eight hundred Buddhist saints
八拜之交(ㄅㄚˊ ㄅㄞˋ ㄓ ㄐㄧㄠ)
sworn brotherhood
八寶飯(ㄅㄚ ㄅㄠˇ ㄈㄢˋ)
rice cooked with eight ingredients
八病(ㄅㄚ ㄅㄧㄥˋ)
the eight taboos of poetry listed by Shen Yüeh (沈約) of the Liang Dynasty
八面體(ㄅㄚˊ ㄇㄧㄢˋ ㄊㄧˇ)
an octahedron
八面玲瓏(ㄅㄚˊ ㄇㄧㄢˋ ㄌㄧㄥˊ ㄌㄨㄥˊ)
to be pleasant all round; well polished and elegant throughout; to be a perfect mixer in any company
八面威風(ㄅㄚˊ ㄇㄧㄢˋ ㄨㄟ ㄈㄥ)
influential in every quarter; having an awe-inspiring reputation everywhere; to make an magnificent appearance
八方(ㄅㄚ ㄈㄤ)or 八區(ㄅㄚ ㄑㄩ)
the eight points of the compass; all directions
八大行星(ㄅㄚˊ ㄉㄚˋ ㄒㄧㄥˊ ㄒㄧㄥ)
the eight major planets of the solar system— Mercury, Venus, Earth, Mars, Jupiter, Saturn, Uranus, and Neptune
八大山人(ㄅㄚˊ ㄉㄚˋ ㄕㄢ ㄖㄣˊ)
the pseudonym of Chu Ta (朱耷), a famous painter of the late Ming Dynasty
八代之衰(ㄅㄚˊ ㄉㄞˋ ㄓ ㄕㄨㄞ)
(literally) the decline of the eight dynasties from Eastern Han (東漢) to Sui(隋) —the dark age in Chinese literature
八斗之才(ㄅㄚ ㄉㄡˇ ㄓ ㄘㄞˊ)
(literally) a person with eight bushels of talent—a very talented or gifted person
八哥(ㄅㄚ ㄍㄜ)or 八哥兒(ㄅㄚ ㄍㄜㄦ)
a mynah
八股(ㄅㄚ ㄍㄨˇ)
corny; lacking in originality
八股文(ㄅㄚ ㄍㄨˇ ㄨㄣˊ)
the eight-legged essay (originally, a style of rigid literary writing during the era of Imperial Examination; hence, writings that reek of pedantry or triteness)
八卦(ㄅㄚˊ ㄍㄨㄚˋ)
the Eight Diagrams, consisting of an arrangement of single and divided lines in eight groups of three lines each as specified in the *Book of Changes*—乾(☰), 兌(☱), 離(☲), 震(☳), 巽(☴), 坎(☵), 艮(☶), 坤(☷)
八國聯軍(ㄅㄚ ㄍㄨㄛˊ ㄌㄧㄢˊ ㄐㄩㄣ)
the joint forces of the eight powers which occupied Peking in the wake of the Boxer Movement in 1900
八開(ㄅㄚ ㄎㄞ)
octavo (books, paper, etc.)
八行書(ㄅㄚ ㄏㄤˊ ㄕㄨ)
a letter of eight lines —a formal letter to recommend someone for a post; a letter of recommendation
八紘一宇(ㄅㄚ ㄏㄨㄥˊ ㄧˋ ㄩˇ)
to unite the whole world under one sovereign by force of arms
八戒(ㄅㄚˊ ㄐㄧㄝˋ)
(Buddhism) the first eight of the Ten Prohibitions
八角(ㄅㄚ ㄐㄧㄠˇ)
Japanese star anise, a kind of spice
八角形(ㄅㄚ ㄐㄧㄠˇ ㄒㄧㄥˊ)
an octagon
八九不離十(ㄅㄚ ㄐㄧㄡˇ ㄅㄨˋ ㄌㄧˊ ㄕˊ)
pretty close; very near; about right
八旗(ㄅㄚ ㄑㄧˊ)
the eight banners (of the Manchu troops identified by the color of the banner —each banner roughly corresponding to a modern division)
八仙(ㄅㄚ ㄒㄧㄢ)
the Eight Immortals of Taoism (namely, 漢鍾離, 張果老, 韓湘子, 曹國舅, 李鐵拐, 藍采和, 呂洞賓, 何仙姑)
八仙桌(ㄅㄚ ㄒㄧㄢ ㄓㄨㄛ)
a square dining table for eight persons
八陣圖(ㄅㄚˊ ㄓㄣˋ ㄊㄨˊ)
a military tactics worked out by Chu-Ko Kung-ming (諸葛孔明), a military genius during the period of the Three Kingdoms
八成(ㄅㄚ ㄔㄥˊ)
(literally) eighty per cent —nearly; almost; very likely; most probably: 事情有了八成了。It's almost settled.
八十至八十九歲的人(ㄅㄚ ㄕˊ ㄓˋ ㄅㄚ ㄕˊ ㄐㄧㄡˇ ㄙㄨㄟˋ ˙ㄉㄜ ㄖㄣˊ)
an octogenarian
八字(ㄅㄚˊ ㄗˋ)or 八字兒(ㄅㄚ ㄗㄜˋㄦ)
a general term for the Celestial Stems and the Terrestrial Branches (干支), denoting the time, date, month and year of a person's birth; now used by fortuneteller as a reference to see if the betrothed are well matched; the horoscope
八字鬍(ㄅㄚˊ ㄗˋ ㄏㄨˊ)
mustaches shaped roughly like the character 八
八音(ㄅㄚ ㄧㄣ)

eight kinds of musical sounds—produced from the calabash, earthenware, stretched hides, wood, stone, metal, silk strings and bamboo

〔八部〕

八音盒(ㄅㄚ ㄧㄣ ㄏㄜˊ)
a music box
八王之亂(ㄅㄚ ㄨㄤˊ ㄓ ㄌㄨㄢˋ)
The Upheaval of the Eight Princes—during the West Tsin Dynasty (265-313 A.D.), when eight feudal lords rose and fought each other
八月(ㄅㄚˊ ㄩㄝˋ)
① August ② eight months ③ the eighth month of the lunar calendar

二畫

【公】 312
ㄍㄨㄥ gong gōng
1. unselfish; unbiased; fair
2. to make public; open to all
3. public
4. the first of old China's five-grades of the nobility; an old Chinese official rank
5. the father of one's husband (one's husband's father); one's father-in-law
6. one's grandfather
7. a respectful salutation
8. the male (of animals)
9. office; official duties: 他因公出差。He took an offical trip.
10. a Chinese family name

公倍數(ㄍㄨㄥ ㄅㄟˋ ㄕㄨˋ)
(mathematics) a common multiple
公保(ㄍㄨㄥ ㄅㄠˇ)
government insurance for public servants
公報(ㄍㄨㄥ ㄅㄠˋ)
an official bulletin; a gazette; a communiqué
公報私仇(ㄍㄨㄥ ㄅㄠˋ ㄙ ㄔㄡˊ)
to avenge oneself on one's enemies in the name of public interests
公布 or 公佈(ㄍㄨㄥ ㄅㄨˋ)
to make public; to promulgate; to announce
公婆(ㄍㄨㄥ ㄆㄛˊ)
the parents of one's husband
公平(ㄍㄨㄥ ㄆㄧㄥˊ)
fair; unbiased; just
公僕(ㄍㄨㄥ ㄆㄨˊ)
a public servant; an official
公馬(ㄍㄨㄥ ㄇㄚˇ)
a stallion (not castrated); a gelding (castrated)
公賣品(ㄍㄨㄥ ㄇㄞˋ ㄆㄧㄣˇ)
a government monopoly
公賣局(ㄍㄨㄥ ㄇㄞˋ ㄐㄩˊ)
a government monopoly bureau
公貓(ㄍㄨㄥ ㄇㄠ)
a tom; a tomcat
公民(ㄍㄨㄥ ㄇㄧㄣˊ)
citizens
公民投票(ㄍㄨㄥ ㄇㄧㄣˊ ㄊㄡˊ ㄆㄧㄠˋ)
the referendum; the plebiscite
公民科(ㄍㄨㄥ ㄇㄧㄣˊ ㄎㄜ)
civics
公民權(ㄍㄨㄥ ㄇㄧㄣˊ ㄑㄩㄢˊ)
civil rights—including election, recall, referendum and initiative
公畝(ㄍㄨㄥ ㄇㄨˇ)
an area of 100 meters square
公墓(ㄍㄨㄥ ㄇㄨˋ)
①a public cemetery ②(in ancient China) tombs or graveyards of kings or the nobility
公法(ㄍㄨㄥ ㄈㄚˇ)
public law
公費(ㄍㄨㄥ ㄈㄟˋ)
public funds; government funds; government scholarships
公分(ㄍㄨㄥ ㄈㄣ)
①a centimeter (cm.) ② a gram (g.)
公分母(ㄍㄨㄥ ㄈㄣ ㄇㄨˇ)
a common denominator
公分子(ㄍㄨㄥ ㄈㄣ ㄗˇ)
a common numerator
公憤(ㄍㄨㄥ ㄈㄣˋ)
public indignation
公德(ㄍㄨㄥ ㄉㄜˊ)
social morality; social ethics
公德心(ㄍㄨㄥ ㄉㄜˊ ㄒㄧㄣ)
regard for public welfare; public-mindedness
公道(ㄍㄨㄥ ㄉㄠˋ)
①justice ②reasonable (prices); just; fair; impartial
公斗(ㄍㄨㄥ ㄉㄡˇ)
a decaliter
公石(ㄍㄨㄥ ㄉㄢˋ)
a hectoliter
公擔(ㄍㄨㄥ ㄉㄢˋ)
a quintal
公敵(ㄍㄨㄥ ㄉㄧˊ)
a public enemy
公牘(ㄍㄨㄥ ㄉㄨˊ)
official documents; official letters or correspondence
公噸(ㄍㄨㄥ ㄉㄨㄣˋ)
a metric ton
公攤(ㄍㄨㄥ ㄊㄢ)
to share (expenditures, capital investment, etc.) equally
公堂(ㄍㄨㄥ ㄊㄤˊ)
a court of law
公天下(ㄍㄨㄥ ㄊㄧㄢ ㄒㄧㄚˋ)
the world belongs to all the people
公聽會(ㄍㄨㄥ ㄊㄧㄥ ㄏㄨㄟˋ)
a public hearing
公兔(ㄍㄨㄥ ㄊㄨˋ)
a buck
公推(ㄍㄨㄥ ㄊㄨㄟ)
to recommend by general acclaim
公牛(ㄍㄨㄥ ㄋㄧㄡˊ)
a bull; a bullock; an ox
公老虎(ㄍㄨㄥ ㄌㄠˇ ㄏㄨˇ)
a tiger
公狼(ㄍㄨㄥ ㄌㄤˊ)
a he-wolf
公釐(ㄍㄨㄥ ㄌㄧˊ)
①a millimeter ② an area of one square meter
公里(ㄍㄨㄥ ㄌㄧˇ)
a kilometer
公理(ㄍㄨㄥ ㄌㄧˇ)
①a universal principle; generally accepted truth; right; justice ②(mathematics) an axiom
公立學校(ㄍㄨㄥ ㄌㄧˋ ㄒㄩㄝˊ ㄒㄧㄠˋ)
public schools
公兩(ㄍㄨㄥ ㄌㄧㄤˇ)
100 grams
公鹿(ㄍㄨㄥ ㄌㄨˋ)
a stag; a hart; a buck
公路(ㄍㄨㄥ ㄌㄨˋ)
a highway
公論(ㄍㄨㄥ ㄌㄨㄣˋ)
public opinion: 是非曲直自有公論。Public opinion is the best judge.
公合(ㄍㄨㄥ ㄍㄜˇ)
a deciliter

公告(ㄍㄨㄥ ㄍㄠˋ)
① a proclamation; a public announcement ② to make an announcement

公告地價(ㄍㄨㄥ ㄍㄠˋ ㄉㄧˋ ㄐㄧㄚˋ)
a government-assessed land price

公狗(ㄍㄨㄥ ㄍㄡˇ)
a dog

公幹(ㄍㄨㄥ ㄍㄢˋ)
an official assignment or duty; official business

公館(ㄍㄨㄥ ㄍㄨㄢˇ)
① an official residence ② a residence (a polite reference to other's residence); a mansion ③ Kungkuan, a suburban district of Taipei ④ Kungkuan in central Taiwan, the site of a big air base

公共(ㄍㄨㄥ ㄍㄨㄥˋ)
public (relations, health, etc.); owned and shared by all

公共電視(ㄍㄨㄥ ㄍㄨㄥˋ ㄉㄧㄢˋ ㄕˋ)
public television

公共投資(ㄍㄨㄥ ㄍㄨㄥˋ ㄊㄡˊ ㄗ)
public investment

公共利益(ㄍㄨㄥ ㄍㄨㄥˋ ㄌㄧˋ ㄧˋ)
public interests

公共關係(ㄍㄨㄥ ㄍㄨㄥˋ ㄍㄨㄢ ㄒㄧˋ)
public relations (PR)

公共汽車(ㄍㄨㄥ ㄍㄨㄥˋ ㄑㄧˋ ㄔㄜ)
a bus; an omnibus

公共行政(ㄍㄨㄥ ㄍㄨㄥˋ ㄒㄧㄥˊ ㄓㄥˋ)
public administration

公共秩序(ㄍㄨㄥ ㄍㄨㄥˋ ㄓˋ ㄒㄩˋ)
public order; public peace and order

公共事業(ㄍㄨㄥ ㄍㄨㄥˋ ㄕˋ ㄧㄝˋ)
public utilities

公共租界(ㄍㄨㄥ ㄍㄨㄥˋ ㄗㄨ ㄐㄧㄝˋ)
the International Settlement in Shanghai

公共財產(ㄍㄨㄥ ㄍㄨㄥˋ ㄘㄞˊ ㄔㄢˇ)
public property

公共衞生(ㄍㄨㄥ ㄍㄨㄥˋ ㄨㄟˋ ㄕㄥ)
public health; public sanitation; public hygiene

公公(ㄍㄨㄥ ˙ㄍㄨㄥ)
① one's grandfather ② the father of one's husband ③ a respectful designation for an elder ④ a eunuch

公克(ㄍㄨㄥ ㄎㄜˋ)
a gram

公開(ㄍㄨㄥ ㄎㄞ)
to make known to the public; to make public; open (letters, etc.); to exhibit; openly; publicly: 他做了公開演講。He gave a public lecture.

公款(ㄍㄨㄥ ㄎㄨㄢˇ)
public funds; public money

公海(ㄍㄨㄥ ㄏㄞˇ)
the high seas

公害(ㄍㄨㄥ ㄏㄞˋ)
social effects of pollution; environmental pollution; a public nuisance

公毫(ㄍㄨㄥ ㄏㄠˊ)
a centigram

公函(ㄍㄨㄥ ㄏㄢˊ)
an official letter

公衡(ㄍㄨㄥ ㄏㄥˊ)
ten kilograms

公會(ㄍㄨㄥ ㄏㄨㄟˋ)
a union, league, society, federation, etc. of a certain trade, as lawyers, medical practitioners, etc.

公雞(ㄍㄨㄥ ㄐㄧ)
a cock; a rooster

公祭(ㄍㄨㄥ ㄐㄧˋ)
a public memorial ceremony

公家(ㄍㄨㄥ ㄐㄧㄚ)
the nation, government, state, public, etc. as distinct from the private

公價(ㄍㄨㄥ ㄐㄧㄚˋ)
an official or controlled price

公教人員(ㄍㄨㄥ ㄐㄧㄠˋ ㄖㄣˊ ㄩㄢˊ)
government employees and staffs of public schools

公斤(ㄍㄨㄥ ㄐㄧㄣ)
a kilogram (kg)

公決(ㄍㄨㄥ ㄐㄩㄝˊ)
a common decision; to decide by majority

公爵(ㄍㄨㄥ ㄐㄩㄝˊ)
a duke

公爵夫人(ㄍㄨㄥ ㄐㄩㄝˊ ㄈㄨ ㄖㄣˊ)
a duchess

公錢(ㄍㄨㄥ ㄑㄧㄢˊ)
a decagram

公卿(ㄍㄨㄥ ㄑㄧㄥ)
(in ancient China) officials of higher ranks; high-ranking officials

公頃(ㄍㄨㄥ ㄑㄧㄥˇ)
a hectare(ha)

公權(ㄍㄨㄥ ㄑㄩㄢˊ)
civil rights; civic rights

公休(ㄍㄨㄥ ㄒㄧㄡ)
① an official holiday ② a holiday for a particular trade

公信力(ㄍㄨㄥ ㄒㄧㄣˋ ㄌㄧˋ)
government credibility

公象(ㄍㄨㄥ ㄒㄧㄤˋ)
a male elephant; a bull elephant

公職(ㄍㄨㄥ ㄓˊ)
government offices; official posts or ranks; (under) government employment

公制(ㄍㄨㄥ ㄓˋ)
the metric system

公債(ㄍㄨㄥ ㄓㄞˋ)
① government bonds ② the public debt

公丈(ㄍㄨㄥ ㄓㄤˋ)
a decameter

公正(ㄍㄨㄥ ㄓㄥˋ)
justice; fairness; just; impartial

公證(ㄍㄨㄥ ㄓㄥˋ)
to legalize an act or document by a notary public; to notarize

公證結婚(ㄍㄨㄥ ㄓㄥˋ ㄐㄧㄝˊ ㄏㄨㄣ)
marriages before the justice of the peace; a court wedding

公證人(ㄍㄨㄥ ㄓㄥˋ ㄖㄣˊ)
a notary public; a witness

公豬(ㄍㄨㄥ ㄓㄨ)
a boar

公諸同好(ㄍㄨㄥ ㄓㄨ ㄊㄨㄥˊ ㄏㄠˋ)
to make (a recipe, manufacturing process, etc.) public for the benefit of kindred spirits; to share what one cherishes with those of the same taste

公主(ㄍㄨㄥ ㄓㄨˇ)
a princess

公轉(ㄍㄨㄥ ㄓㄨㄢˇ)
(said of the earth or other major planets) to revolve around the sun

公忠體國(ㄍㄨㄥ ㄓㄨㄥ ㄊㄧˇ ㄍㄨㄛˊ)
to be loyal to one's country

公衆(ㄍㄨㄥ ㄓㄨㄥˋ)
the public; the general pub-

lic; the community
公尺(ㄍㄨㄥ ㄔˇ)
a meter
公差
①(ㄍㄨㄥ ㄔㄞ)official assignments (usually involving travel)
②(ㄍㄨㄥ ㄔㄚ)(mathematics) common difference
公產(ㄍㄨㄥ ㄔㄢˇ)
government or public property
公娼(ㄍㄨㄥ ㄔㄤ)
a licensed prostitute; licensed prostitution
公出(ㄍㄨㄥ ㄔㄨ)
to be away on official duties or business
公獅(ㄍㄨㄥ ㄕ)
a lion
公使(ㄍㄨㄥ ㄕˇ)
(diplomacy) a minister; an envoy
公使館(ㄍㄨㄥ ㄕˇ ㄍㄨㄢˇ)
a legation
公式(ㄍㄨㄥ ㄕˋ)
a formula
公式化(ㄍㄨㄥ ㄕˋ ㄏㄨㄚˋ)
stereotyped; formulistic; to put in formulas
公事(ㄍㄨㄥ ㄕˋ)
official business; public affairs
公事包(ㄍㄨㄥ ㄕˋ ㄅㄠ)
an attaché case; a briefcase
公事房(ㄍㄨㄥ ㄕˋ ㄈㄤˊ)
an office
公事公辦(ㄍㄨㄥ ㄕˋ ㄍㄨㄥ ㄅㄢˋ)
to discharge official duties strictly according to rules
公示催告(ㄍㄨㄥ ㄕˋ ㄘㄨㄟ ㄍㄠˋ)
(law) a public summons
公示送達(ㄍㄨㄥ ㄕˋ ㄙㄨㄥˋ ㄉㄚˊ)
(law) service by public notification
公社(ㄍㄨㄥ ㄕㄜˋ)
a commune
公設辯護人(ㄍㄨㄥ ㄕㄜˋ ㄅㄧㄢˋ ㄏㄨˋ ㄖㄣˊ)
a public defense counsel
公山羊(ㄍㄨㄥ ㄕㄢ ㄧㄤˊ)
a he-goat
公審(ㄍㄨㄥ ㄕㄣˇ)
a public trial
公升(ㄍㄨㄥ ㄕㄥ)
a liter
公署(ㄍㄨㄥ ㄕㄨˇ)
a government office
公說公有理，婆說婆有理(ㄍㄨㄥ ㄕㄨㄛ ㄍㄨㄥ ㄧㄡˇ ㄌㄧˇ, ㄆㄛˊ ㄕㄨㄛ ㄆㄛˊ ㄧㄡˇ ㄌㄧˇ)
In the presence of a superior, umpire, etc., each of two quarreling parties insists that he is right.
公然(ㄍㄨㄥ ㄖㄢˊ)
openly; in public
公認(ㄍㄨㄥ ㄖㄣˋ)
generally recognized; universally accepted; established
公子(ㄍㄨㄥ ㄗˇ)
①(in ancient China) sons of a duke or a ranking official ②a polite designation for another's son or sons
公子哥兒(ㄍㄨㄥ ㄗˇ ㄍㄜㄦ)
sons of the rich or powerful; dandies; playboys
公子王孫(ㄍㄨㄥ ㄗˇ ㄨㄤˊ ㄙㄨㄣ)
sons of the rich or powerful
公廁(ㄍㄨㄥ ㄘㄜˋ)
a public lavatory
公寸(ㄍㄨㄥ ㄘㄨㄣˋ)
a decimeter
公絲(ㄍㄨㄥ ㄙ)
a milligram
公司(ㄍㄨㄥ ㄙ)
a company; a corporation
公司法(ㄍㄨㄥ ㄙ ㄈㄚˇ)
company law
公私不分(ㄍㄨㄥ ㄙ ㄅㄨˋ ㄈㄣ)
to make no distinction between public and private interests
公私分明(ㄍㄨㄥ ㄙ ㄈㄣ ㄇㄧㄥˊ)
to be scrupulous in separating public from private interests
公私兩便(ㄍㄨㄥ ㄙ ㄌㄧㄤˇ ㄅㄧㄢˋ)
advantageous to both public and private interests
公私合營(ㄍㄨㄥ ㄙ ㄏㄜˊ ㄧㄥˊ)
state and private joint ownership
公訴(ㄍㄨㄥ ㄙㄨˋ)
public prosecution; public indictment
公算(ㄍㄨㄥ ㄙㄨㄢˋ)
the law of probability
公孫(ㄍㄨㄥ ㄙㄨㄣ)
a Chinese family name
公鵝(ㄍㄨㄥ ㄜˊ)
a gander
公安(ㄍㄨㄥ ㄢ)
public security
公安局(ㄍㄨㄥ ㄢ ㄐㄩˊ)
a police department
公案(ㄍㄨㄥ ㄢˋ)
①a case of law ②office desks ③official business
公爾忘私(ㄍㄨㄥ ㄦˇ ㄨㄤˋ ㄙ)or 公而忘私(ㄍㄨㄥ ㄦˊ ㄨㄤˋ ㄙ)
to forget oneself in the discharge of official duties; selfless
公益(ㄍㄨㄥ ㄧˋ)
public interests or welfare; public good; community benefit
公議(ㄍㄨㄥ ㄧˋ)
①public discussion ②discussion of national or public affairs ③open negotiations (for prices, terms, specifications, etc.) as contrasted to a tender
公鴨(ㄍㄨㄥ ㄧㄚ)
a drake
公有(ㄍㄨㄥ ㄧㄡˇ)
publicly owned; public
公有土地(ㄍㄨㄥ ㄧㄡˇ ㄊㄨˇ ㄉㄧˋ)or 公地(ㄍㄨㄥ ㄉㄧˋ)
public land
公演(ㄍㄨㄥ ㄧㄢˇ)
to stage shows for public viewing; to perform in public
公宴(ㄍㄨㄥ ㄧㄢˋ)
to honor a celebrity at a dinner party or luncheon hosted by a club, government organization, etc.
公引(ㄍㄨㄥ ㄧㄣˇ)
a hectometer
公羊(ㄍㄨㄥ ㄧㄤˊ)
①a ram ②a Chinese family name
公羊傳(ㄍㄨㄥ ㄧㄤˊ ㄓㄨㄢˋ)
Spring and Autumn Annals with Commentary by Kung-Yang Kao(公羊高), one of the three expansions of Confucius' *Spring and Autumn Annals*(春秋)
公營(ㄍㄨㄥ ㄧㄥˊ)
publicly owned
公營事業(ㄍㄨㄥ ㄧㄥˊ ㄕˋ ㄧㄝˋ)
public enterprises; govern-

ment-owned enterprises

公物(ㄍㄨㄥ ㄨˋ)
public or government property

公務(ㄍㄨㄥ ㄨˋ)
public business; official matters, business, duties, etc.

公務員(ㄍㄨㄥ ㄨˋ ㄩㄢˊ)
government employees; civil servants

公務員懲誡委員會(ㄍㄨㄥ ㄨˋ ㄩㄢˊ ㄔㄥˊ ㄐㄧㄝˋ ㄨㄟˇ ㄩㄢˊ ㄏㄨㄟˋ)
the Committee on the Discipline of Public Functionaries

公文(ㄍㄨㄥ ㄨㄣˊ)
official documents

公餘(ㄍㄨㄥ ㄩˊ)
after office hours

公寓(ㄍㄨㄥ ㄩˋ)
an apartment house

公約(ㄍㄨㄥ ㄩㄝ)
①a treaty; a covenant; a convention; a pact ②joint pledge

公約數(ㄍㄨㄥ ㄩㄝ ㄕㄨˋ)
(mathematics) a common factor

公元(ㄍㄨㄥ ㄩㄢˊ)
in the year of our Lord…; the Christian era

公園(ㄍㄨㄥ ㄩㄢˊ)
a park; a public garden

公允(ㄍㄨㄥ ㄩㄣˇ)
fair and proper; just and sound

公用(ㄍㄨㄥ ㄩㄥˋ)
public (telephones, etc.); for public use

公用電話(ㄍㄨㄥ ㄩㄥˋ ㄉㄧㄢˋ ㄏㄨㄚˋ)
a public telephone

公用事業(ㄍㄨㄥ ㄩㄥˋ ㄕˋ ㄧㄝˋ)
public utilities

【六】 313 ㄌㄧㄡˋ liow liù (讀音 ㄌㄨˋ luh lù)
six

六邊形(ㄌㄧㄡˋ ㄅㄧㄢ ㄒㄧㄥˊ)
a hexagon

六轡在手(ㄌㄧㄡˋ ㄆㄟˋ ㄗㄞˋ ㄕㄡˇ)
to hold all the trump cards; to have complete power over others

六面體(ㄌㄧㄡˋ ㄇㄧㄢˋ ㄊㄧˇ)
a hexahedron

六法全書(ㄌㄧㄡˋ ㄈㄚˇ ㄑㄩㄢˊ ㄕㄨ)
The Complete Volume of Six Laws—an omnibus of modern Chinese laws

六分儀(ㄌㄧㄡˋ ㄈㄣ ㄧˊ)
a sextant

六大洲(ㄌㄧㄡˋ ㄉㄚˋ ㄓㄡ)
the six continents of the world

六根(ㄌㄧㄡˋ ㄍㄣ)
(Buddhism) the six senses—eyes, ears, nose, tongue, body and mind

六根清淨(ㄌㄧㄡˋ ㄍㄣ ㄑㄧㄥ ㄐㄧㄥˋ)
the purification of the six indriyas or sense organs—(said of a Buddha) free from human desires and passions

六國(ㄌㄧㄡˋ ㄍㄨㄛˊ)
six of the seven major kingdoms during the Warring States Period annexed by the state of Chin (秦)

六宮(ㄌㄧㄡˋ ㄍㄨㄥ)
Six Palaces — a general name for the palaces where the queen and other wives of the emperor lived; the imperial harems

六合(ㄌㄧㄡˋ ㄏㄜˊ)
①the Six Realms (north, south, east, west, up and down)—(in) the whole wide world ②name of a subprefecture in Kiangsu Province

六角形(ㄌㄧㄡˋ ㄐㄧㄠˇ ㄒㄧㄥˊ)
a hexagon

六經(ㄌㄧㄡˋ ㄐㄧㄥ)
the Six Books of Chinese classics—the *Book of Poetry* (詩), the *Book of History* (書), the *Book of Changes* (易), the *Book of Rites* (禮), the *Book of Music* (樂), the *Spring and Autumn Annals* (春秋)

六親(ㄌㄧㄡˋ ㄑㄧㄣ)
the six relations —father, mother, elder brothers, younger brothers, wife, children

六親不認(ㄌㄧㄡˋ ㄑㄧㄣ ㄅㄨˋ ㄖㄣˋ)
not to recognize one's own closest relatives—cold and arrogant

六親無靠(ㄌㄧㄡˋ ㄑㄧㄣ ㄨˊ ㄎㄠˋ)
nobody to turn to

六情(ㄌㄧㄡˋ ㄑㄧㄥˊ)
the six emotions or feelings of a person—joy, anger, sorrow, happiness, love and hatred

六宅不安(ㄌㄧㄡˋ ㄓㄜˊ ㄅㄨˋ ㄢ)
successive family misfortunes

六尺之孤(ㄌㄧㄡˋ ㄔˇ ㄓ ㄍㄨ)
orphaned boys and girls under 15 years of age

六朝(ㄌㄧㄡˋ ㄔㄠˊ)
the Six Dynasties (222–589), which successively made Nanking their capital—Wu (吳), Eastern Tsin (東晉), Sung (宋), Chi (齊), Liang (梁), Chen (陳)

六畜(ㄌㄧㄡˋ ㄔㄨˋ)
the six domestic animals —horse, cattle, sheep, chicken, dog, and hog

六十四開(ㄌㄧㄡˋ ㄕˊ ㄙˋ ㄎㄞ)
sixty-fourmo; 64mo

六神(ㄌㄧㄡˋ ㄕㄣˊ)
the source of energy controlling the six organs(六臟)

六神無主(ㄌㄧㄡˋ ㄕㄣˊ ㄨˊ ㄓㄨˇ)
shocked; stunned out of one's wits; to be in a state of utter stupefaction

六書(ㄌㄧㄡˋ ㄕㄨ)
the six classes into which Chinese characters are divided—pictograph (象形), picture of action (指事), ideograph (會意), figurative extension of meaning (轉注), determinative-phonetics (形聲), making one form stand for another word (假借)

六一居士(ㄌㄧㄡˋ ㄧ ㄐㄩ ㄕˋ)
an alias of Ou-Yang Hsiu (歐陽修), a famous scholar of the Sung Dynasty

六藝(ㄌㄧㄡˋ ㄧˋ)
the six arts — rites (禮), music (樂), archery (射), driving of the chariot (御), learning (書), mathematics (數)—which ancient Chinese scholars were required to master

六問三推(ㄌㄧㄡˋ ㄨㄣˋ ㄙㄢ ㄊㄨㄟ)
to interrogate a criminal

suspect or prisoner of war again and again

六欲 or 六慾(ㄌㄧㄡˋ ㄩˋ)
(Buddhism) the desires originated from the six senses—eyes, ears, nose, tongue, body and mind; the six sexual attractions arising from color, form, carriage, voice, softness, and features 參看「七情六慾」

六月(ㄌㄧㄡˋ ㄩㄝˋ)
① June ② the sixth month of the lunar calendar ③ six months

【兮】 314 ㄒㄧ shi xī

1. an adjunct with no independent meaning, roughly equivalent to "Oh" or "Ah" in English
2. a particle of pause used in ancient poetry and still used in eulogies

四畫

【共】 315 ㄍㄨㄥˋ gonq gòng

1. common; same
2. all; collectively
3. to share; to work together: 我與他們甘苦與共。I shared joys and sorrows with them.
4. together: 我們設法共同來解決這項問題吧! Let's try to get together on this problem.
5. an abbreviation of the word "Communism" or "Communist"

共謀(ㄍㄨㄥˋ ㄇㄡˊ)
to scheme together; to plan together; to collaborate; to collude; collusion

共勉(ㄍㄨㄥˋ ㄇㄧㄢˇ)
to encourage each other: 願共勉之。Let's encourage each other in our endeavors.

共鳴(ㄍㄨㄥˋ ㄇㄧㄥˊ)
①(physics) resonance or sympathetic vibration ②(to inspire) the same feeling in others; sympathetic response or understanding

共犯(ㄍㄨㄥˋ ㄈㄢˋ)
① collusion; collaboration in an act of crime ② a joint offender; an accomplice; a confederate

共赴國難(ㄍㄨㄥˋ ㄈㄨˋ ㄍㄨㄛˊ ㄋㄢˋ)
to work together to save the country in time of a national crisis

共通(ㄍㄨㄥˋ ㄊㄨㄥ)
applicable to both or all

共同(ㄍㄨㄥˋ ㄊㄨㄥˊ)
common; shared by all; to cooperate in (an undertaking, etc.)

共同市場(ㄍㄨㄥˋ ㄊㄨㄥˊ ㄕˋ ㄔㄤˇ)
a common market: 歐洲共同市場 the European Economic Community

共同生活(ㄍㄨㄥˋ ㄊㄨㄥˊ ㄕㄥ ㄏㄨㄛˊ)
to live together; collective life

共管(ㄍㄨㄥˋ ㄍㄨㄢˇ)
(a state, region, etc.) under the joint control of two or more authorities

共和(ㄍㄨㄥˋ ㄏㄜˊ)
a republic; the republican form of government

共和黨(ㄍㄨㄥˋ ㄏㄜˊ ㄉㄤˇ)
the Republican Party

共和國(ㄍㄨㄥˋ ㄏㄜˊ ㄍㄨㄛˊ)
a republic

共計(ㄍㄨㄥˋ ㄐㄧˋ)
the sum total; to come to; to total; to add up to

共襄盛舉(ㄍㄨㄥˋ ㄒㄧㄤ ㄕㄥˋ ㄐㄩˇ)
Let's all work together for this worthy project.

共享(ㄍㄨㄥˋ ㄒㄧㄤˇ)
to enjoy together; to share

共振(ㄍㄨㄥˋ ㄓㄣˋ)
resonance

共產黨(ㄍㄨㄥˋ ㄔㄢˇ ㄉㄤˇ)
the Communist Party

共產國際(ㄍㄨㄥˋ ㄔㄢˇ ㄍㄨㄛˊ ㄐㄧˋ)
the Communist International; the Comintern

共產主義(ㄍㄨㄥˋ ㄔㄢˇ ㄓㄨˇ ㄧˋ)
Communism

共處(ㄍㄨㄥˋ ㄔㄨˇ)
to coexist

共事(ㄍㄨㄥˋ ㄕˋ)
①to work together; to work in the same office; to be colleagues ② (said of women) to share the same husband; to be the wives of one man

共識(ㄍㄨㄥˋ ㄕˋ)
common consensus

共商(ㄍㄨㄥˋ ㄕㄤ)
to discuss together; to hold a joint discussion

共存(ㄍㄨㄥˋ ㄘㄨㄣˊ)
to coexist; coexistent; coexistence

共存亡(ㄍㄨㄥˋ ㄘㄨㄣˊ ㄨㄤˊ)
(to defend a city or place) to the last man; to live or die together

共有(ㄍㄨㄥˋ ㄧㄡˇ)
owned by all; owned by both; common (traits, customs, etc.)

共營(ㄍㄨㄥˋ ㄧㄥˊ)
joint operation

五畫

【兵】 316 ㄅㄧㄥ bing bīng

1. arms; weapons
2. a soldier; a serviceman; the military
3. to strike; to attack
4. a piece in Chinese chess—a pawn

兵變(ㄅㄧㄥ ㄅㄧㄢˋ)
mutiny; troops in mutiny

兵不血刃(ㄅㄧㄥ ㄅㄨˋ ㄒㄩㄝˋ ㄖㄣˋ)
(to achieve military objective) without firing a shot in anger or without bloodshed; to win victory without firing a shot

兵不厭詐(ㄅㄧㄥ ㄅㄨˋ ㄧㄢˋ ㄓㄚˋ)
Trickery is no vice in military operations. 或 All is fair in war.

兵不由將(ㄅㄧㄥ ㄅㄨˋ ㄧㄡˊ ㄐㄧㄤˋ)
disobedient soldiers; troops that do not obey orders

兵馬(ㄅㄧㄥ ㄇㄚˇ)
troops and horses—armaments

兵馬未動,糧草先行(ㄅㄧㄥ ㄇㄚˇ ㄨㄟˋ ㄉㄨㄥˋ, ㄌㄧㄤˊ ㄘㄠˇ ㄒㄧㄢ ㄒㄧㄥˊ)
Provisions and fodder should go before troops and horses.—We should make preparations before we embark on anything.

兵馬俑(ㄅㄧㄥ ㄇㄚˇ ㄩㄥˇ)
wood or clay figures of soldiers and horses buried with the dead

兵法(ㄅㄧㄥ ㄈㄚˇ)or 兵略(ㄅㄧㄥ ㄌㄩㄝˋ)
military tactics and strategy
兵符(ㄅㄧㄥ ㄈㄨˊ)
a commander's seal
兵多將廣(ㄅㄧㄥ ㄉㄨㄛ ㄐㄧㄤˋ ㄍㄨㄤˇ)
(said of military troops) to enjoy numerical superiority
兵團(ㄅㄧㄥ ㄊㄨㄢˊ)
a large (military) unit; corps; a legion
兵力(ㄅㄧㄥ ㄌㄧˋ)
military strength
兵連禍結(ㄅㄧㄥ ㄌㄧㄢˊ ㄏㄨㄛˋ ㄐㄧㄝˊ)
continuous war ravages; constantly ravaged by war
兵臨城下(ㄅㄧㄥ ㄌㄧㄣˊ ㄔㄥˊ ㄒㄧㄚˋ)
The attacking army has reached the city gates.
兵貴神速(ㄅㄧㄥ ㄍㄨㄟˋ ㄕㄣˊ ㄙㄨˋ)
Mobility is the most important thing in fighting a war. 或 Speed is precious in war.
兵工廠(ㄅㄧㄥ ㄍㄨㄥ ㄔㄤˇ)
an arsenal; an ammunition works
兵工署(ㄅㄧㄥ ㄍㄨㄥ ㄕㄨˇ)
the Ordnance Department (under the Logistic Command of the Chinese Army)
兵荒馬亂(ㄅㄧㄥ ㄏㄨㄤ ㄇㄚˇ ㄌㄨㄢˋ)
disorder caused by continuous military operations; the ravages of war; war rapine
兵家(ㄅㄧㄥ ㄐㄧㄚ)
① a person specialized in military operations; a strategist ② military; one of old China's nine categories of professions
兵家常事(ㄅㄧㄥ ㄐㄧㄚ ㄔㄤˊ ㄕˋ)
a commonplace in military operations: 勝敗乃兵家常事。Victory or defeat is a commonplace in military operations.
兵器(ㄅㄧㄥ ㄑㄧˋ)
weapons; arms
兵強馬壯(ㄅㄧㄥ ㄑㄧㄤˊ ㄇㄚˇ ㄓㄨㄤˋ)
strong soldiers and sturdy horses—well-equipped and well-trained troops with high morale; a well-trained and powerful army
兵權(ㄅㄧㄥ ㄑㄩㄢˊ)
authority to make military decisions; military power or leadership
兵燹(ㄅㄧㄥ ㄒㄧㄢˇ)or 兵禍(ㄅㄧㄥ ㄏㄨㄛˋ)
the ravages of soldiery; fire, havoc, disturbance caused by war
兵餉(ㄅㄧㄥ ㄒㄧㄤˇ)
① a soldier's pay ② generally, military expenses and provisions
兵學(ㄅㄧㄥ ㄒㄩㄝˊ)
military science
兵凶戰危(ㄅㄧㄥ ㄒㄩㄥ ㄓㄢˋ ㄨㄟˊ)
In war everybody is a loser.
兵制(ㄅㄧㄥ ㄓˋ)
the military system
兵種(ㄅㄧㄥ ㄓㄨㄥˇ)
intra-service classification of military units according to their equipment and functions
兵士(ㄅㄧㄥ ㄕˋ)
a soldier; a foot soldier
兵書(ㄅㄧㄥ ㄕㄨ)
a book on military strategy
兵戎(ㄅㄧㄥ ㄖㄨㄥˊ)
① arms; weapons ② warfare
兵戎相見(ㄅㄧㄥ ㄖㄨㄥˊ ㄒㄧㄤ ㄐㄧㄢˋ)
to resort to arms; to appeal to force
兵蟻(ㄅㄧㄥ ㄧˇ)
a dinergate; a soldier ant
兵役(ㄅㄧㄥ ㄧˋ)
(compulsory) military service
兵役法(ㄅㄧㄥ ㄧˋ ㄈㄚˇ)
conscription law; military service law
兵營(ㄅㄧㄥ ㄧㄥˊ)or 兵舍(ㄅㄧㄥ ㄕㄜˋ)
barracks; a military camp
兵源(ㄅㄧㄥ ㄩㄢˊ)
manpower as a source of conscription

六畫

【其】 317 ㄑㄧˊ chyi qí

1. a pronoun—he, she, it, they; his, her, its, their
2. this; that; the
3. an interrogative used to introduce a question

其貌不揚(ㄑㄧˊ ㄇㄠˋ ㄅㄨˋ ㄧㄤˊ)
physically unattractive; ugly in appearance
其他(ㄑㄧˊ ㄊㄚ)
the others; the rest
其他費用(ㄑㄧˊ ㄊㄚ ㄈㄟˋ ㄩㄥˋ)
other expenses
其內(ㄑㄧˊ ㄋㄟˋ)
inside
其樂無窮(ㄑㄧˊ ㄌㄜˋ ㄨˊ ㄑㄩㄥˊ)
The joy is boundless.
其來有自(ㄑㄧˊ ㄌㄞˊ ㄧㄡˇ ㄗˋ)
It did not happen by accident. 或 It may be traced to a cause or source.
其間(ㄑㄧˊ ㄐㄧㄢ)
in; among; in between; between
其情可憫(ㄑㄧˊ ㄑㄧㄥˊ ㄎㄜˇ ㄇㄧㄣˇ)
(said of one's conduct, actions, etc.) deserving sympathetic understanding or compassion
其心可誅(ㄑㄧˊ ㄒㄧㄣ ㄎㄜˇ ㄓㄨ)
devious or condemnable in intention
其中(ㄑㄧˊ ㄓㄨㄥ)
in; among; in the midst
其實(ㄑㄧˊ ㄕˊ)
in fact; as a matter of fact; actually
其人其事(ㄑㄧˊ ㄖㄣˊ ㄑㄧˊ ㄕˋ)
the man and his deeds; a biographic sketch
其次(ㄑㄧˊ ㄘˋ)
secondly; the next in order; besides
其一(ㄑㄧˊ ㄧ)
first or firstly
其餘(ㄑㄧˊ ㄩˊ)
the others; the rest; the remainder

【具】 318 ㄐㄩˋ jiuh jù

1. an appliance, implement, utensil, tool, etc.
2. talent; capability
3. to prepare; to equip
4. complete; all; the whole
5. a Chinese family name

具備(ㄐㄩˋ ㄅㄟˋ)or 具足(ㄐㄩˋ ㄗㄨˊ)
① all complete; all ready ② to have (qualifications or advantages): 她具備了當秘書的資格。She has all the qualifications for a secretary.
具保(ㄐㄩˋ ㄅㄠˇ)
(said of a defendant in a lawsuit) to complete all arrangements and proce-

dures for release on bail

具報(ㄐㄩˋ ㄅㄠˋ)
to present or prepare a complete report

具名(ㄐㄩˋ ㄇㄧㄥˊ)
①to sign ②to publish a writing, letter, etc. with a byline

具體(ㄐㄩˋ ㄊㄧˇ)
concrete (measures, results, etc.), as opposed to abstract

具體而微(ㄐㄩˋ ㄊㄧˇ ㄦˊ ㄨㄟˊ)
similar in shape but smaller in proportions

具結(ㄐㄩˋ ㄐㄧㄝˊ)
①to enter into a bond; to submit a pledge or guarantee to a government office for fulfilling of all obligations agreed upon ②(law) to sign a bond to tell the truth; to sign an affidavit

具有(ㄐㄩˋ ㄧㄡˇ)
to be provided with; to be supplied with

具文(ㄐㄩˋ ㄨㄣˊ)
①to prepare a document, etc. for presenting to higher authorities ②(said of agreements, pledges, contracts, etc. which are not carried out) empty words

【典】 319 ㄉㄧㄢˇ dean diǎn

1. a rule; a statute; a law; a canon
2. a tale or story from the classics; an allusion: 他的文章裏用典甚多。His writings are filled with allusions.
3. to pawn; to mortgage
4. to take charge of: 他是典試委員之一。He is a member of the committee in charge of examination affairs.

典舖(ㄉㄧㄢˇ ㄆㄨˋ)
a pawnshop

典賣(ㄉㄧㄢˇ ㄇㄞˋ)
to mortgage

典範(ㄉㄧㄢˇ ㄈㄢˋ)
a model to be followed; an example; a paragon

典當(ㄉㄧㄢˇ ㄉㄤˋ)
①to pawn ②a pawnshop

典禮(ㄉㄧㄢˇ ㄌㄧˇ)
a ceremony; a rite

典故(ㄉㄧㄢˇ ㄍㄨˋ)
an allusion (from history, old classics, etc.); an origin (of a proverb, aphorism, etc.)

典籍(ㄉㄧㄢˇ ㄐㄧˊ)
ancient books, statute-records, etc.

典刑(ㄉㄧㄢˇ ㄒㄧㄥˊ)
laws; penalties

典型(ㄉㄧㄢˇ ㄒㄧㄥˊ)
a model; a pattern; a typical example

典質(ㄉㄧㄢˇ ㄓˋ)
to mortgage; to pawn

典制(ㄉㄧㄢˇ ㄓˋ)or 典章(ㄉㄧㄢˇ ㄓㄤ)
laws and institutions (of a society)

典試委員會(ㄉㄧㄢˇ ㄕˋ ㄨㄟˇ ㄩㄢˊ ㄏㄨㄟˋ)
a committee in charge of examination affairs

典押(ㄉㄧㄢˇ ㄧㄚ)
to mortgage

典雅(ㄉㄧㄢˇ ㄧㄚˇ)
refined (writing); elegant (style)

典要(ㄉㄧㄢˇ ㄧㄠˋ)
①refined and succinct ②a standard; a model

典獄官(ㄉㄧㄢˇ ㄩˋ ㄍㄨㄢ)
prison officials

典獄長(ㄉㄧㄢˇ ㄩˋ ㄓㄤˇ)
the warden (of a penitentiary)

八畫

【兼】 320 ㄐㄧㄢ jian jiān

1. to unite in one; to connect; to annex
2. and; also; together with; both; equally; concurrently

兼備(ㄐㄧㄢ ㄅㄟˋ)
to be in possession of both

兼辦(ㄐㄧㄢ ㄅㄢˋ)
to manage or handle simultaneously

兼併(ㄐㄧㄢ ㄅㄧㄥˋ)
to annex (another country, etc.)

兼祧(ㄐㄧㄢ ㄊㄧㄠ)
to be the heir to two branches of a family

兼顧(ㄐㄧㄢ ㄍㄨˋ)
to look after both sides; to take care of the needs, etc. of both parties

兼管(ㄐㄧㄢ ㄍㄨㄢˇ)
to also look after; to also have charge of

兼課(ㄐㄧㄢ ㄎㄜˋ)
①to do some teaching besides one's main occupation ②to hold two or more teaching jobs concurrently

兼薪(ㄐㄧㄢ ㄒㄧㄣ)
to get pay from two or more employers or organizations

兼旬(ㄐㄧㄢ ㄒㄩㄣˊ)
twenty days: 他別後瞬已兼旬。Very quickly it has been twenty days since he left us.

兼之(ㄐㄧㄢ ㄓ)
furthermore; besides

兼職(ㄐㄧㄢ ㄓˊ)
to take two or more jobs concurrently; to hold a concurrent post; a side job; a part-time job

兼差(ㄐㄧㄢ ㄔㄞ)
to take two or more jobs concurrently; to moonlight; a side job; a part-time job

兼籌並顧(ㄐㄧㄢ ㄔㄡˊ ㄅㄧㄥˋ ㄍㄨˋ)
to plan and care for both duties

兼程(ㄐㄧㄢ ㄔㄥˊ)
to proceed on one's trip on the double

兼善天下(ㄐㄧㄢ ㄕㄢˋ ㄊㄧㄢ ㄒㄧㄚˋ)
to benefit all the people in the world

兼人之量(ㄐㄧㄢ ㄖㄣˊ ㄓ ㄌㄧㄤˋ)
to have the capacity of two persons combined

兼任(ㄐㄧㄢ ㄖㄣˋ)
to serve concurrently as (a secretary, etc.); to have a side job

兼任教師(ㄐㄧㄢ ㄖㄣˋ ㄐㄧㄠˋ ㄕ)
a part-time teacher

兼容並蓄(ㄐㄧㄢ ㄖㄨㄥˊ ㄅㄧㄥˋ ㄒㄩˋ)
tolerant; open-minded

兼愛(ㄐㄧㄢ ㄞˋ)
love without distinction; fraternity

兼而有之(ㄐㄧㄢ ㄦˊ ㄧㄡˇ ㄓ)
to have both (merits and defects, advantages and disadvantages, etc.)

十四畫

【冀】321 ㄐㄧˋ jih jì
1. to hope
2. another name for Hopeh Province
3. a Chinese family name

冂部 ㄐㄩㄥ jiong jiōng

三畫

【冉】322 ㄖㄢˇ raan rǎn
1. gradually
2. tender; weak
3. the outer edge of a turtle's shell
4. a Chinese family name
冉冉(ㄖㄢˇ ㄖㄢˇ)
gradually; imperceptibly
冉冉上升(ㄖㄢˇ ㄖㄢˇ ㄕㄤˋ ㄕㄥ)
to rise gradually

【冊】323 ㄘㄜˋ tseh cè
1. (in ancient China) a register; a book or books in general; volumes
2. a list; statistical tables; to record; records
3. an order to confer nobility titles
冊封(ㄘㄜˋ ㄈㄥ)
(in ancient China) to confer titles of nobility on the emperor's wives or princes
冊立(ㄘㄜˋ ㄌㄧˋ)
to crown an empress
冊子(ㄘㄜˋ ·ㄗ)
a book; a pamphlet

四畫

【再】324 ㄗㄞˋ tzay zài
1. again; repeated
2. still; further; then
再拜(ㄗㄞˋ ㄅㄞˋ)
(literally) to bow twice—a courteous expression in letters, especially those addressed to a superior
再保險(ㄗㄞˋ ㄅㄠˇ ㄒㄧㄢˇ)
reinsurance
再版(ㄗㄞˋ ㄅㄢˇ)
the second printing or edition (of a book)
再發(ㄗㄞˋ ㄈㄚ)
to have a relapse
再犯(ㄗㄞˋ ㄈㄢˋ)
① to repeat an offense ② a second-time offender
再度(ㄗㄞˋ ㄉㄨˋ)
once more; a second time; once again
再談(ㄗㄞˋ ㄊㄢˊ)
to discuss (something) later
再來(ㄗㄞˋ ㄌㄞˊ)
①to come again: 失去的機會不再來。The lost chance will never come again. ② to encore ③ to request for or order a repetition
再過幾天(ㄗㄞˋ ㄍㄨㄛˋ ㄐㄧˇ ㄊㄧㄢ)
in a few more days
再會(ㄗㄞˋ ㄏㄨㄟˋ)
Good-bye. 或 See you again.
再婚(ㄗㄞˋ ㄏㄨㄣ)
to remarry after the annulment of a former marriage; digamy
再嫁(ㄗㄞˋ ㄐㄧㄚˋ)or 再醮(ㄗㄞˋ ㄐㄧㄠˋ)
(usually said of a widow) to remarry
再接再勵 or 再接再厲(ㄗㄞˋ ㄐㄧㄝ ㄗㄞˋ ㄌㄧˋ)
to forge ahead in disregard of obstructions or failures; to make a determined effort undismayed
再見(ㄗㄞˋ ㄐㄧㄢˋ)
Good-bye. 或 See you again. 參看「再會」
再起(ㄗㄞˋ ㄑㄧˇ)
① to rise again; to stage a comeback ② to assume public office again
再娶(ㄗㄞˋ ㄑㄩˇ)
(said of a man) to remarry
再現(ㄗㄞˋ ㄒㄧㄢˋ)
① reappearance ② (geology) the reappearance of an earth stratum or lode ③ reenactment
再製鹽(ㄗㄞˋ ㄓˋ ㄧㄢˊ)
refined salt
再者(ㄗㄞˋ ㄓㄜˇ)
furthermore; in addition
再審(ㄗㄞˋ ㄕㄣˇ)
a retrial
再生(ㄗㄞˋ ㄕㄥ)
① to be a second so-and-so (a well-known figure already dead) ② regeneration; to regenerate
再生父母(ㄗㄞˋ ㄕㄥ ㄈㄨˋ ㄇㄨˇ)
second parents—an expression of deep gratitude to benefactors for great help rendered
再說(ㄗㄞˋ ㄕㄨㄛ)
① please repeat (what you said) ② furthermore; besides
再衰三竭(ㄗㄞˋ ㄕㄨㄞ ㄙㄢ ㄐㄧㄝˊ)
to be nearing exhaustion; to be weakened and demoralized
再造(ㄗㄞˋ ㄗㄠˋ)
born a second time—an expression of gratitude
再次(ㄗㄞˋ ㄘˋ)
once more; a second time; once again: 再次感謝各位的光臨。Thank you once again for your coming.
再三(ㄗㄞˋ ㄙㄢ)
again and again; time and again; repeatedly
再三再四(ㄗㄞˋ ㄙㄢ ㄗㄞˋ ㄙˋ)
repeatedly; over and over again
再議(ㄗㄞˋ ㄧˋ)
to talk about or discuss (a subject, etc.) again or later
再也不(ㄗㄞˋ ㄧㄝˇ ㄅㄨˋ)
never again

七畫

【冒】325 ㄇㄠˋ maw mào
1. incautious; imprudent; rash
2. to risk; to brave; to be exposed to (hardships)
3. to put forth; to issue forth; to go up (as fire, smoke, etc.)
4. a Chinese family name
冒牌(ㄇㄠˋ ㄆㄞˊ)or冒牌兒(ㄇㄠˋ ㄆㄚˊㄦ)
(literally) a product using the brand name or trademark of the same product by another manufacturer—a fake; an imitation; a counterfeit
冒昧(ㄇㄠˋ ㄇㄟˋ)
to make bold; presumptuous;

to presume (usually used as a polite expression)
冒冒失失(ㄇㄠˋ ·ㄇㄠ ㄕ ㄕ)
rash; imprudent; hasty; reckless
冒名(ㄇㄠˋ ㄇㄧㄥˊ)
to assume another's name
冒名頂替(ㄇㄠˋ ㄇㄧㄥˊ ㄉㄧㄥˇ ㄊㄧˋ)
to assume the identity of another person
冒犯(ㄇㄠˋ ㄈㄢˋ)
to offend (a superior, elder, etc.)
冒瀆(ㄇㄠˋ ㄉㄨˊ)
to bother or annoy (a superior)
冒頭(ㄇㄠˋ ㄊㄡˊ)
to begin to crop up
冒天下之大不韙(ㄇㄠˋ ㄊㄧㄢ ㄒㄧㄚˋ ㄓ ㄉㄚˋ ㄅㄨˋ ㄨㄟˇ)
to defy world opinion; to take the chances of universal condemnation; to ignore the will of the people
冒領(ㄇㄠˋ ㄌㄧㄥˇ)
to get or take something by posing as someone else for whom it is intended
冒口(ㄇㄠˋ ㄎㄡˇ)
(machinery) a rising head; a riser
冒號(ㄇㄠˋ ㄏㄠˋ)
the colon
冒火(ㄇㄠˋ ㄏㄨㄛˇ)
to blow one's top; to become angry
冒進(ㄇㄠˋ ㄐㄧㄣˋ)
premature advance; rash advance
冒險(ㄇㄠˋ ㄒㄧㄢˇ)
to take risks; to brave dangers
冒險犯難(ㄇㄠˋ ㄒㄧㄢˇ ㄈㄢˋ ㄋㄢˋ)
to do something despite the dangers and difficulties involved
冒稱(ㄇㄠˋ ㄔㄥ)
to claim falsely; to make false claims
冒充(ㄇㄠˋ ㄔㄨㄥ)
to pretend to be somebody else; to use a substitute (of inferior quality) in place of the genuine item
冒失(ㄇㄠˋ ㄕ)
hasty; reckless; rash: 你這麼做眞是太冒失了。It's rash of you to do so.
冒失鬼(ㄇㄠˋ ㄕ ㄍㄨㄟˇ)
a rash fellow; a reckless guy
冒然(ㄇㄠˋ ㄖㄢˊ)
recklessly; reckless; rashly; rash 參看「貿然」
冒死(ㄇㄠˋ ㄙˇ)
to risk death
冒煙(ㄇㄠˋ ㄧㄢ)
Smoke rises. 或 to belch smoke
冒雨(ㄇㄠˋ ㄩˇ)
to brave the rain: 他們冒雨來訪我們。They braved the rain to visit us.

【冑】 326 ㄓㄡˋ jow jòu
a helmet: 參看肉部「冑」4645
冑甲(ㄓㄡˋ ㄐㄧㄚˇ)
a helmet and armor

八畫

【冓】 327 ㄍㄡˋ gow gòu
a secluded place in a palace; a secret cabinet

九畫

【冕】 328 ㄇㄧㄢˇ mean miǎn
1. a ceremonial cap for high ministers in ancient China
2. a crown

冖部
ㄇㄧˋ mih mì

七畫

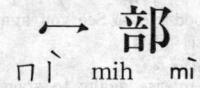

【冠】 329 1. ㄍㄨㄢ guan guān
1. a cap
2. the comb or crest of a bird
3. a Chinese family name
冠冕(ㄍㄨㄢ ㄇㄧㄢˇ)
① the hat ② the high official position
冠冕堂皇(ㄍㄨㄢ ㄇㄧㄢˇ ㄊㄤˊ ㄏㄨㄤˊ)
① elegant and stately; officially or publicly ② high-sounding: 他有冠冕堂皇的理由。His excuses are high-sounding.
冠帶之國(ㄍㄨㄢ ㄉㄞˋ ㄓ ㄍㄨㄛˊ)
a civilized nation; a nation with a highly developed culture
冠蓋相望(ㄍㄨㄢ ㄍㄞˋ ㄒㄧㄤ ㄨㄤˋ)
constant exchange of visits of ranking officials between nations
冠蓋雲集(ㄍㄨㄢ ㄍㄞˋ ㄩㄣˊ ㄐㄧˊ)
(usually said of a meeting or gathering) where ranking officials congregate; a gathering of dignitaries

【冠】 329 2. ㄍㄨㄢˋ guann guàn
1. at 20 when a young man is capped
2. first-rate
3. to wear a cap
冠禮(ㄍㄨㄢˋ ㄌㄧˇ)
(in ancient China) a capping ceremony for a young man when he reaches 20
冠軍(ㄍㄨㄢˋ ㄐㄩㄣ)
a champion; an outstanding person
冠詞(ㄍㄨㄢˋ ㄘˊ)
(grammar) the article ("a", "an", or "the")

八畫

【冤】 330 (寃)ㄩㄢ iuan yuān
1. oppression; injustice; a grievance; a wrong
2. feud; animosity; enmity
3. to cheat; to lie
4. to spend money recklessly; to waste money
5. to make false accusations
冤大頭(ㄩㄢ ㄉㄚˋ ㄊㄡˊ)
a person played for a big fool; a fathead
冤孽(ㄩㄢ ㄋㄧㄝˋ)
a foreordained enemy; a person's stumbling block
冤鬼(ㄩㄢ ㄍㄨㄟˇ)
a wronged soul; the ghost of a person who died of injustice
冤魂(ㄩㄢ ㄏㄨㄣˊ)
the ghost of a person who was wrongly put to death or murdered
冤家(ㄩㄢ ㄐㄧㄚ)

an enemy (but also used for lovers)

冤家路窄(ㄩㄢ ㄐㄧㄚ ㄌㄨˋ ㄓㄞˇ)
(literally) The road is narrow for enemies.—Enemies often cross each other's path.

冤情(ㄩㄢ ㄑㄧㄥˊ)
the details of a grievance or wrong

冤屈(ㄩㄢ ㄑㄩ)
a grievance; a wrong; victimized by a frame-up

冤仇(ㄩㄢ ㄔㄡˊ)
feud; enmity; animus

冤枉(ㄩㄢ ㄨㄤˇ)
to wrong; to accuse a person with a false charge; a wrong; a grievance; to do someone injustice

冤獄(ㄩㄢ ㄩˋ)
miscarriage of justice

冤獄賠償法(ㄩㄢ ㄩˋ ㄆㄟˊ ㄔㄤˊ ㄈㄚˇ)
Law of Compensation for Wrongful Detentions and Executions

【冥】 331 ㄇㄧㄥˊ ming míng
1. dark; obscure; dim; dusk
2. stupidity; stupid: 他秉性冥頑不靈。He has a stupid and stubborn character.
3. far and high
4. deep; profound: 他陷於冥想中。He was deep in thought.
5. the unseen world; Hades
6. night
7. a Chinese family name

冥報(ㄇㄧㄥˊ ㄅㄠˋ)
① a mysterious retribution; a retribution executed by unseen hands ② to return (someone's kindness) in Hades

冥冥之中(ㄇㄧㄥˊ ㄇㄧㄥˊ ㄓ ㄓㄨㄥ)
(said of divine influence) imperceptibly but inexorably

冥府(ㄇㄧㄥˊ ㄈㄨˇ)
the underworld; Hades

冥河(ㄇㄧㄥˊ ㄏㄜˊ)
(mythology) the Styx

冥婚(ㄇㄧㄥˊ ㄏㄨㄣ)
a marriage ceremony for persons already dead

冥器(ㄇㄧㄥˊ ㄑㄧˋ)
paper-made household articles to be burnt for the dead

冥錢(ㄇㄧㄥˊ ㄑㄧㄢˊ)
paper money to be burnt for the dead

冥想(ㄇㄧㄥˊ ㄒㄧㄤˇ)
deep meditation

冥紙(ㄇㄧㄥˊ ㄓˇ)
參看「冥錢」

冥壽(ㄇㄧㄥˊ ㄕㄡˋ)
a birth anniversary of a person already dead

冥思苦想(ㄇㄧㄥˊ ㄙ ㄎㄨˇ ㄒㄧㄤˇ)
to think long and hard; to cudgel one's brains

冥衣(ㄇㄧㄥˊ ㄧ)
paper clothes to be burnt for the dead

冥佑(ㄇㄧㄥˊ ㄧㄡˋ)
protection of the gods

冥頑不靈(ㄇㄧㄥˊ ㄨㄢˊ ㄅㄨˋ ㄌㄧㄥˊ)
stupid and stubborn; foolhardy

冥王星(ㄇㄧㄥˊ ㄨㄤˊ ㄒㄧㄥ)
the planet Pluto

【冢】 332 ㄓㄨㄥˇ joong jhǒng
1. a high grave
2. a peak; a summit
3. the eldest
4. great; supreme; prime (all referring to official ranks)

十四畫

【冪】 333 ㄇㄧˋ mih mì
1. to cover with cloth
2. a cloth cover; a veil
3. (mathematics) power

冫部
ㄅㄧㄥ bing bīng

三畫

【冬】 334 ㄉㄨㄥ dong dōng
1. winter: 有些鳥在南方過冬。Some birds pass the winter in the south.
2. (the lunar calendar) the period from the 10th to the 12th month

冬眠(ㄉㄨㄥ ㄇㄧㄢˊ)
to hibernate; hibernation: 有些熊冬眠。Some bears hibernate.

冬防(ㄉㄨㄥ ㄈㄤˊ)
the winter curfew (imposed annually to guard against undesirable elements)

冬天(ㄉㄨㄥ ㄊㄧㄢ)or 冬令(ㄉㄨㄥ ㄌㄧㄥˋ)
winter

冬暖夏涼(ㄉㄨㄥ ㄋㄨㄢˇ ㄒㄧㄚˋ ㄌㄧㄤˊ)
cool in summer and warm in winter

冬令救濟(ㄉㄨㄥ ㄌㄧㄥˋ ㄐㄧㄡˋ ㄐㄧˋ)
relief of the poor during winter months

冬菇(ㄉㄨㄥ ㄍㄨ)
a mushroom

冬瓜(ㄉㄨㄥ ㄍㄨㄚ)
a white gourd; a wax gourd

冬烘(ㄉㄨㄥ ㄏㄨㄥ)
(used in a contemptuous sense) a pedant or a pedagogue

冬季(ㄉㄨㄥ ㄐㄧˋ)
the winter season

冬青(ㄉㄨㄥ ㄑㄧㄥ)
(botany) holly

冬汛(ㄉㄨㄥ ㄒㄩㄣˋ)
the winter fishing season

冬至(ㄉㄨㄥ ㄓˋ)
the winter solstice, (for the Northern Hemisphere) the time when the sun is farthest south from the equator, on or about December 22

冬至線(ㄉㄨㄥ ㄓˋ ㄒㄧㄢˋ)
the tropic of Capricorn 亦作「南回歸線」

冬裝(ㄉㄨㄥ ㄓㄨㄤ)
winter dress

冬菜(ㄉㄨㄥ ㄘㄞˋ)
preserved, dried cabbages

冬筍(ㄉㄨㄥ ㄙㄨㄣˇ)
winter sprouts of bamboos

四畫

【冰】 335 ㄅㄧㄥ bing bīng
1. ice; icicles
2. cold; frost

冰雹(ㄅㄧㄥ ㄅㄠˊ)
hail; a hailstone

冰棒(ㄅㄧㄥ ㄅㄤˋ)

a flavored popsicle
冰片(ㄅㄧㄥ ㄆㄧㄢˋ)
borneol
冰封(ㄅㄧㄥ ㄈㄥ)
icebound
冰刀(ㄅㄧㄥ ㄉㄠ)
the blades of ice skates
冰島(ㄅㄧㄥ ㄉㄠˇ)
Iceland
冰點(ㄅㄧㄥ ㄉㄧㄢˇ)
the freezing point
冰凍(ㄅㄧㄥ ㄉㄨㄥˋ)
to freeze
冰凍三尺非一日之寒(ㄅㄧㄥ ㄉㄨㄥˋ ㄙㄢ ㄔˇ ㄈㄟ ㄧˊ ㄖˋ ㄓ ㄏㄢˊ)
(literally) Ice sheet of three feet in thickness takes more than one cold day to form. —The grudge or animosity has its deep root.
冰炭(ㄅㄧㄥ ㄊㄢˋ)
as incompatible as ice and burning charcoal
冰糖(ㄅㄧㄥ ㄊㄤˊ)
rock candy
冰天雪地(ㄅㄧㄥ ㄊㄧㄢ ㄒㄩㄝˇ ㄉㄧˋ)
frozen and snow-covered land
冰囊(ㄅㄧㄥ ㄋㄤˊ) or 冰袋(ㄅㄧㄥ ㄉㄞˋ)
an ice bag
冰冷(ㄅㄧㄥ ㄌㄥˇ)
① icy cold; cold as ice ② cold or frosty (expressions, etc.)
冰涼(ㄅㄧㄥ ㄌㄧㄤˊ)
icy cold; very cold
冰輪(ㄅㄧㄥ ㄌㄨㄣˊ) or 冰鏡(ㄅㄧㄥ ㄐㄧㄥˋ) or 冰盤(ㄅㄧㄥ ㄆㄢˊ)
the cool moon
冰菓店(ㄅㄧㄥ ㄍㄨㄛˇ ㄉㄧㄢˋ)
a cold drink shop
冰塊(ㄅㄧㄥ ㄎㄨㄞˋ)
lumps of ice; ice cubes; ice blocks
冰河(ㄅㄧㄥ ㄏㄜˊ)
a glacier
冰河時期(ㄅㄧㄥ ㄏㄜˊ ㄕˊ ㄑㄧˊ)
the glacial epoch; the ice age
冰肌玉骨(ㄅㄧㄥ ㄐㄧ ㄩˋ ㄍㄨˇ)
(literally) flesh of ice and bones of jade—a Chinese description of beautiful women
冰窖(ㄅㄧㄥ ㄐㄧㄠˋ)
an icehouse; a glacial vault
冰淇淋(ㄅㄧㄥ ㄑㄧˊ ㄌㄧㄣˊ)
ice cream
冰橇(ㄅㄧㄥ ㄑㄧㄠ)
a sled; a sledge; a sleigh
冰球(ㄅㄧㄥ ㄑㄧㄡˊ)
(ice hockey) a puck
冰球戲(ㄅㄧㄥ ㄑㄧㄡˊ ㄒㄧˋ)
ice hockey 亦作「冰上曲棍球」
冰清玉潔(ㄅㄧㄥ ㄑㄧㄥ ㄩˋ ㄐㄧㄝˊ)
(said of one's character) incorruptible
冰鞋(ㄅㄧㄥ ㄒㄧㄝˊ)
ice skates
冰消瓦解(ㄅㄧㄥ ㄒㄧㄠ ㄨㄚˇ ㄐㄧㄝˇ)
total dissolution or disintegration like melting ice
冰心(ㄅㄧㄥ ㄒㄧㄣ)
① chaste; chastity; virtuous ② not enthusiastic; to be somewhat indifferent
冰箱(ㄅㄧㄥ ㄒㄧㄤ)
an icebox; a refrigerator
冰雪聰明(ㄅㄧㄥ ㄒㄩㄝˇ ㄘㄨㄥ ㄇㄧㄥˊ)
very clever; remarkably bright; brilliant
冰鎮(ㄅㄧㄥ ㄓㄣˋ)
to preserve on ice; to cool food with ice
冰柱(ㄅㄧㄥ ㄓㄨˋ)
icicles
冰磚(ㄅㄧㄥ ㄓㄨㄢ)
ice blocks; frozen cream
冰川(ㄅㄧㄥ ㄔㄨㄢ) or 冰河(ㄅㄧㄥ ㄏㄜˊ)
a glacier
冰蝕(ㄅㄧㄥ ㄕˊ)
(geology) glacial erosion
冰釋(ㄅㄧㄥ ㄕˋ)
solved; to disappear without a trace
冰山(ㄅㄧㄥ ㄕㄢ)
an iceberg
冰上運動(ㄅㄧㄥ ㄕㄤˋ ㄩㄣˋ ㄉㄨㄥˋ)
ice sports
冰水(ㄅㄧㄥ ㄕㄨㄟˇ)
ice water
冰霜(ㄅㄧㄥ ㄕㄨㄤ)
① cold and severe ② incorruptible
冰人(ㄅㄧㄥ ㄖㄣˊ)
a matchmaker
冰原(ㄅㄧㄥ ㄩㄢˊ)
an ice field

五畫

【冶】 336 ㄧㄝˇ yee yě
1. to smelt; to fuse metals
2. seductive; fascinating
冶煉(ㄧㄝˇ ㄌㄧㄢˋ)
to smelt
冶工(ㄧㄝˇ ㄍㄨㄥ)
a blacksmith
冶金學(ㄧㄝˇ ㄐㄧㄣ ㄒㄩㄝˊ)
metallurgy
冶遊(ㄧㄝˇ ㄧㄡˊ)
to frequent brothels
冶艷(ㄧㄝˇ ㄧㄢˋ)
beautiful; beauty; charms

【冷】 337 ㄌㄥˇ leeng lěng
1. cold
2. (said of business, farming, etc.) off-season
3. a Chinese family name
冷板凳(ㄌㄥˇ ㄅㄢˇ ㄉㄥˋ)
① a post which has little or no authority ② a cold reception
冷冰冰(ㄌㄥˇ ㄅㄧㄥ ㄅㄧㄥ)
icy cold; cold as ice
冷不防(ㄌㄥˇ ㄅㄨˋ ㄈㄤˊ)
a bolt from the blue; unexpectedly
冷盤(ㄌㄥˇ ㄆㄢˊ) or 冷碟(ㄌㄥˇ ㄉㄧㄝˊ)
a dish of assorted cold meats
冷僻(ㄌㄥˇ ㄆㄧˋ)
① out-of-the-way or secluded (places) ② big or hard (words or expressions)
冷漠(ㄌㄥˇ ㄇㄛˋ)
cool and detached; indifferent; apathetic
冷門(ㄌㄥˇ ㄇㄣˊ)
①(said of a commodity, academic course, etc.) not popular or not in great demand ②(said of appointments or nominations) unexpected
冷面(ㄌㄥˇ ㄇㄧㄢˋ)
a poker face
冷鋒(ㄌㄥˇ ㄈㄥ)
a cold front
冷敷(ㄌㄥˇ ㄈㄨ)
(medicine) a cold compress
冷淡(ㄌㄥˇ ㄉㄢˋ)
cold (expressions); indifferent (attitudes)
冷調(ㄌㄥˇ ㄉㄧㄠˋ)
cool color-tone; cool tone
冷凍(ㄌㄥˇ ㄉㄨㄥˋ)

freezing
冷凍庫(ㄌㄥˇ ㄉㄨㄥˋ ㄎㄨˋ)
a freezer
冷凍劑(ㄌㄥˇ ㄉㄨㄥˋ ㄐㄧˋ)
a coolant agent; a refrigerant
冷凍食品(ㄌㄥˇ ㄉㄨㄥˋ ㄕˊ ㄆㄧㄣˇ)
frozen foods
冷凝(ㄌㄥˇ ㄋㄧㄥˊ)
(physics) condensation
冷凝器(ㄌㄥˇ ㄋㄧㄥˊ ㄑㄧˋ)
a condenser
冷暖(ㄌㄥˇ ㄋㄨㄢˇ)
the degree of cold or heat
冷暖自知(ㄌㄥˇ ㄋㄨㄢˇ ㄗˋ ㄓ)
One knows what it's like without being told.
冷冷清清(ㄌㄥˇ ㄌㄥˇ ㄑㄧㄥ ㄑㄧㄥ)
(said of a place) deserted and quiet; desolate; lonely
冷落(ㄌㄥˇ ㄌㄨㄛˋ)
① cold and lonely ② cold reception; to cold-shoulder
冷宮(ㄌㄥˇ ㄍㄨㄥ)
a palace to confine the emperor's concubines after they lost his favor
冷酷(ㄌㄥˇ ㄎㄨˋ)
merciless; heartless
冷汗(ㄌㄥˇ ㄏㄢˋ)
① a cold sweat (as in great fright, etc.) ② (Chinese medicine) clammy perspiration
冷話(ㄌㄥˇ ㄏㄨㄚˋ)
cool, sarcastic remarks
冷箭(ㄌㄥˇ ㄐㄧㄢˋ)
(literally) an arrow shot from an ambush—an unexpected attack or a pot shot
冷靜(ㄌㄥˇ ㄐㄧㄥˋ)
① clear (mind, thinking, etc.); calm or composed: 她冷靜下來回信。She composed herself to answer the letter. ② secluded or quiet (place, etc.)
冷氣(ㄌㄥˇ ㄑㄧˋ)
air conditioning
冷氣機(ㄌㄥˇ ㄑㄧˋ ㄐㄧ)
an air-conditioner
冷氣設備(ㄌㄥˇ ㄑㄧˋ ㄕㄜˋ ㄅㄟˋ)
air-conditioning equipment or facilities
冷槍(ㄌㄥˇ ㄑㄧㄤ)
a sniper's shot

冷清(ㄌㄥˇ ㄑㄧㄥ)
desolate; lonely; deserted
冷却(ㄌㄥˇ ㄑㄩㄝˋ)
to get cold; to cool off
冷却劑(ㄌㄥˇ ㄑㄩㄝˋ ㄐㄧˋ)
a coolant
冷血(ㄌㄥˇ ㄒㄧㄝˋ)
cold-blooded; hardhearted
冷血動物(ㄌㄥˇ ㄒㄧㄝˋ ㄉㄨㄥˋ ㄨˋ)
① cold-blooded animals ② a heartless or ruthless person
冷笑(ㄌㄥˇ ㄒㄧㄠˋ)
a sarcastic smile or grin
冷戰
①(ㄌㄥˇ ㄓㄢˋ) cold war
②(ㄌㄥˇ ·ㄓㄢ) to shiver with cold 亦作「冷顫」
冷嘲熱諷(ㄌㄥˇ ㄔㄠˊ ㄖㄜˋ ㄈㄥˋ)
sarcasm and mockery
冷場(ㄌㄥˇ ㄔㄤˇ)or(ㄌㄥˇ ㄔㄤˊ)
temporary suspension of a show, party, etc. occasioned by inefficient management; a stage wait
冷食(ㄌㄥˇ ㄕˊ)
cold drinks and snacks
冷水(ㄌㄥˇ ㄕㄨㄟˇ)
cold water; unboiled water
冷水澆頭(ㄌㄥˇ ㄕㄨㄟˇ ㄐㄧㄠ ㄊㄡˊ)
(literally) splashing the head with cold water—a sudden and harsh disappointment or discouragement
冷水浴(ㄌㄥˇ ㄕㄨㄟˇ ㄩˋ)
a cold shower; a cold bath
冷霜(ㄌㄥˇ ㄕㄨㄤ)
cold cream
冷熱病(ㄌㄥˇ ㄖㄜˋ ㄅㄧㄥˋ)
① malaria ② sudden waxing and waning of enthusiasm
冷若冰霜(ㄌㄥˇ ㄖㄨㄛˋ ㄅㄧㄥ ㄕㄨㄤ)
(usually said of women) as cold as an iceberg—aloof
冷字(ㄌㄥˇ ㄗˋ)
a rarely used word
冷餐(ㄌㄥˇ ㄘㄢ)
a buffet
冷藏(ㄌㄥˇ ㄘㄤˊ)
to preserve by means of refrigeration
冷色(ㄌㄥˇ ㄙㄜˋ)
cool colors
冷颼颼(ㄌㄥˇ ㄙㄡ ㄙㄡ)
frosty; chilly; cold and windy

冷言冷語(ㄌㄥˇ ㄧㄢˊ ㄌㄥˇ ㄩˇ)
sarcastic remarks
冷眼(ㄌㄥˇ ㄧㄢˇ)
to look at (something) without prejudice; to look on as a disinterested bystander
冷眼旁觀(ㄌㄥˇ ㄧㄢˇ ㄆㄤˊ ㄍㄨㄢ)
① to look on coldly ② to look on with a critical eye
冷飲(ㄌㄥˇ ㄧㄣˇ)
cold drinks

六畫

【冽】 338 ㄌㄧㄝˋ lieh liè
crystal-clear (water or wine)

八畫

【准】 339 ㄓㄨㄣˇ joen zhǔn
1. to approve; to permit; to grant; to authorize
2. in accordance with; accordingly
3. equivalent; equal
准將(ㄓㄨㄣˇ ㄐㄧㄤˋ)
a brigadier general
准許(ㄓㄨㄣˇ ㄒㄩˇ)
to approve; to permit; to allow; approval; permission
准尉(ㄓㄨㄣˇ ㄨㄟˋ)
a warrant officer
准予(ㄓㄨㄣˇ ㄩˇ)
to permit; to authorize

【凊】 340 ㄐㄧㄥˋ jinq jìng
cold; cool; chilly

【凋】 341 ㄉㄧㄠ diau diāo
1. withered; faded
2. exhausted; emaciated
凋敝(ㄉㄧㄠ ㄅㄧˋ)
emaciated; destitute; exhausted; injured; ridden by illness
凋兵(ㄉㄧㄠ ㄅㄧㄥ)
tired and weary soldiers; demoralized troops
凋零(ㄉㄧㄠ ㄌㄧㄥˊ)
① withered ②(said of persons) to pass away
凋落(ㄉㄧㄠ ㄌㄨㄛˋ)or 凋謝(ㄉㄧㄠ ㄒㄧㄝˋ)
① fallen; withered ②(said of

〔冫部〕

persons) to pass away
凋殘(ㄉㄧㄠ ㄘㄢˊ)
①(said of business) declining ②(said of cities) deserted
凋萎(ㄉㄧㄠ ㄨㄟˇ)
①(said of flowers, etc.) withered; faded ②(said of a great person) passing away

【凌】 342 ㄌㄧㄥˊ ling líng
1. accumulated ice
2. to insult; to maltreat; to throw one's weight around
3. to rise; to ride; to soar
4. to traverse
5. a Chinese family name
凌波(ㄌㄧㄥˊ ㄅㄛ)
to ride the waves; to walk over ripples—a term used to describe the grace of a beauty's walking
凌波仙子(ㄌㄧㄥˊ ㄅㄛ ㄒㄧㄢ ㄗˇ)
①fairies walking over ripples ②another name for daffodils
凌厲(ㄌㄧㄥˊ ㄌㄧˋ)
relentless (said of the military offensive, implementation of orders, etc.)
凌亂(ㄌㄧㄥˊ ㄌㄨㄢˋ)
in total disorder or disarray; messy; disheveled; untidy
凌駕(ㄌㄧㄥˊ ㄐㄧㄚˋ)
to ride high; to rise above others; to outstrip
凌霄(ㄌㄧㄥˊ ㄒㄧㄠ)
to ride the clouds; to rise up to the skies; to soar to the skies
凌遲(ㄌㄧㄥˊ ㄔˊ)
(in ancient China) a slow death by torture (usually by dismemberment)
凌晨(ㄌㄧㄥˊ ㄔㄣˊ)
the wee hours; very early in the morning
凌辱(ㄌㄧㄥˊ ㄖㄨˇ)
①to insult; to maltreat ②to assault (a woman)
凌雲(ㄌㄧㄥˊ ㄩㄣˊ)
to ride the high clouds—(usually said of a person's ambition or aspiration) to aim high

【凍】 343 ㄉㄨㄥˋ donq dòng
1. to freeze
2. cold; icy
3. a Chinese family name
凍餒(ㄉㄨㄥˋ ㄋㄟˇ)
to suffer from cold and hunger
凍裂(ㄉㄨㄥˋ ㄌㄧㄝˋ)
to crack as a result of freezing or cold
凍結(ㄉㄨㄥˋ ㄐㄧㄝˊ)
to freeze (an account, etc.)
凍僵(ㄉㄨㄥˋ ㄐㄧㄤ)
to be benumbed with cold; to be frozen stiff
凍瘡(ㄉㄨㄥˋ ㄔㄨㄤ)
frostbite; chilblains
凍傷(ㄉㄨㄥˋ ㄕㄤ)
to suffer injuries or illness as a result of long exposure to cold weather
凍子(ㄉㄨㄥˋ ㄗˇ)
jelly; coagulation (of meat broth, etc.)
凍死(ㄉㄨㄥˋ ㄙˇ)
to freeze to death; to die of frost

十三畫

【凜】 344 ㄌㄧㄣˇ liin lǐn
1. cold; bleak
2. to be apprehensive; to shiver with cold or fear
3. imposing; awe-inspiring
凜冽(ㄌㄧㄣˇ ㄌㄧㄝˋ)
very cold; cold to the marrow
凜凜(ㄌㄧㄣˇ ㄌㄧㄣˇ)
①very cold; icy ②(said of manners) forbidding
凜凜如生(ㄌㄧㄣˇ ㄌㄧㄣˇ ㄖㄨˊ ㄕㄥ)
(said of a portrait) to seem alive
凜然(ㄌㄧㄣˇ ㄖㄢˊ)
a stern, repellent appearance arousing fear, reverence
凜若冰霜(ㄌㄧㄣˇ ㄖㄨㄛˋ ㄅㄧㄥ ㄕㄨㄤ)
(said of a woman) to be cold as ice
凜遵(ㄌㄧㄣˇ ㄗㄨㄣ)
to respectfully comply with; to obey in fear

十四畫

【凝】 345 ㄋㄧㄥˊ ning níng
1. to freeze
2. to congeal; to coagulate
3. to form; to take shape
4. to concentrate; to cohere
凝眸(ㄋㄧㄥˊ ㄇㄡˊ)
to fix one's eyes on
凝凍(ㄋㄧㄥˊ ㄉㄨㄥˋ)
to freeze
凝鍊(ㄋㄧㄥˊ ㄌㄧㄢˋ)
concise; condensed
凝固(ㄋㄧㄥˊ ㄍㄨˋ)
(said of liquid) to congeal; to solidify
凝固點(ㄋㄧㄥˊ ㄍㄨˋ ㄉㄧㄢˇ)
the freezing point; the point of solidification
凝結(ㄋㄧㄥˊ ㄐㄧㄝˊ)
to condense (from gas to liquid); to solidify or congeal (from liquid to solid); to curdle
凝結器(ㄋㄧㄥˊ ㄐㄧㄝˊ ㄑㄧˋ)
a condenser
凝聚(ㄋㄧㄥˊ ㄐㄩˋ)
to concentrate; to curdle
凝聚力(ㄋㄧㄥˊ ㄐㄩˋ ㄌㄧˋ)
cohesion; cohesive force
凝想(ㄋㄧㄥˊ ㄒㄧㄤˇ)
to concentrate one's thought; to meditate; deep in thought
凝脂(ㄋㄧㄥˊ ㄓ)
congealed fat—(usually said of a woman's skin) smooth, soft, and glossy
凝滯(ㄋㄧㄥˊ ㄓˋ)
frozen at a point; delayed; stagnant; stalemated
凝妝(ㄋㄧㄥˊ ㄓㄨㄤ)
(usually said of a woman) to be fully dressed; to dress up; to doll up
凝重(ㄋㄧㄥˊ ㄓㄨㄥˋ)
dignified
凝視(ㄋㄧㄥˊ ㄕˋ)
to gaze (lovingly); to fix one's gaze on; a fixed gaze
凝神(ㄋㄧㄥˊ ㄕㄣˊ)
to concentrate
凝神諦聽(ㄋㄧㄥˊ ㄕㄣˊ ㄉㄧˋ ㄊㄧㄥ)
to listen attentively
凝霜(ㄋㄧㄥˊ ㄕㄨㄤ)
to frost
凝思(ㄋㄧㄥˊ ㄙ)
to concentrate one's thought on; to be deep in thought; meditation; deep thinking

几部
ㄐㄧˇ jii jǐ

【几】 346 ㄐㄧˇ jii jǐ
(語音 ㄐㄧ ji jī)
1. a small table
2. a simplified form of the character "幾"

几席(ㄐㄧˇ ㄒㄧˊ)
a small table with a few mats around it

几案(ㄐㄧˇ ㄢˋ)
① an office desk ② a small table

一畫

【凡】 347 ㄈㄢˊ farn fán
1. common; ordinary; dull: 她是一位平凡的畫家。She is a common painter.
2. worldly; mortal; earthly: 凡人不免死亡。The mortal life has an end.
3. generally; every; whenever; wherever
4. altogether: 全書凡十卷。The set consists of ten volumes altogether.

凡夫俗子(ㄈㄢˊ ㄈㄨ ㄙㄨˊ ㄗˇ)
the masses; ordinary people

凡例(ㄈㄢˊ ㄌㄧˋ)
the introduction of a book

凡骨(ㄈㄢˊ ㄍㄨˇ)
(literally) mortal bones —ordinary endowments; an ordinary person

凡間(ㄈㄢˊ ㄐㄧㄢ)
the material world

凡心(ㄈㄢˊ ㄒㄧㄣ)
worldly desires; desires of the flesh

凡事(ㄈㄢˊ ㄕˋ)
everything

凡是(ㄈㄢˊ ˙ㄕ)
all (who are present, etc.); all (which are black, heavy, etc.)

凡士林(ㄈㄢˊ ㄕˋ ㄌㄧㄣˊ)
Vaseline; petrolatum

凡人(ㄈㄢˊ ㄖㄣˊ)
an ordinary person; one of the masses; a layman

凡爾賽(ㄈㄢˊ ㄦˇ ㄙㄞˋ)
Versailles, French city and site of the Versailles Palace built by Louis XIV

凡眼(ㄈㄢˊ ㄧㄢˇ)
mortal eyes; mortal eyesight

凡庸(ㄈㄢˊ ㄩㄥ)
commonplace; ordinary

九畫

【凰】 348 ㄏㄨㄤˊ hwang huáng
the female phoenix, a legendary bird in Chinese mythology

十畫

【凱】 349 ㄎㄞˇ kae kǎi
1. peace; joy
2. balmy; soothing; tender
3. a victory—a triumphant return of an army

凱風(ㄎㄞˇ ㄈㄥ)
the south wind

凱歌(ㄎㄞˇ ㄍㄜ)
a song of victory or triumph

凱旋(ㄎㄞˇ ㄒㄩㄢˊ)
a triumphant return of an army; to return in triumph

凱旋門(ㄎㄞˇ ㄒㄩㄢˊ ㄇㄣˊ)
① the Arc of Triumph (in Paris, France) ② a triumphal arch

凱撒(ㄎㄞˇ ㄙㄚˋ)
Gaius Julius Caesar

凱樂(ㄎㄞˇ ㄩㄝˋ)
music of triumph

十二畫

【凳】 350 (櫈)ㄉㄥˋ denq dèng
a stool; a bench

凳子(ㄉㄥˋ ˙ㄗ)
a stool; a bench

凵部
ㄑㄩ chiu qū

二畫

【凶】 351 ㄒㄩㄥ shiong xiōng
1. evil; bad
2. famine
3. unlucky; unfortunate
4. fear; fearsome
5. very; excessive; excess

凶暴(ㄒㄩㄥ ㄅㄠˋ)
fierce and brutal

凶猛(ㄒㄩㄥ ㄇㄥˇ)
violent; ferocious

凶夢(ㄒㄩㄥ ㄇㄥˋ)
a bad dream; a nightmare

凶服(ㄒㄩㄥ ㄈㄨˊ)
mourning dress

凶多吉少(ㄒㄩㄥ ㄉㄨㄛ ㄐㄧˊ ㄕㄠˇ)
to bode ill rather than well

凶徒(ㄒㄩㄥ ㄊㄨˊ)
a villain; an evildoer

凶年(ㄒㄩㄥ ㄋㄧㄢˊ) or 凶歲(ㄒㄩㄥ ㄙㄨㄟˋ)
a year of famine; a year of misfortune

凶耗(ㄒㄩㄥ ㄏㄠˋ)
bad news; a death notice

凶悍(ㄒㄩㄥ ㄏㄢˋ)
fierce and tough

凶狠(ㄒㄩㄥ ㄏㄣˇ)
fierce and malicious

凶橫(ㄒㄩㄥ ㄏㄥˊ)
fierce and arrogant

凶氣(ㄒㄩㄥ ㄑㄧˋ)
the fearsome air (of a person)

凶器(ㄒㄩㄥ ㄑㄧˋ)
a tool or weapon for criminal purposes; a lethal weapon

凶險(ㄒㄩㄥ ㄒㄧㄢˇ)
danger; dangerous

凶相(ㄒㄩㄥ ㄒㄧㄤˋ)
ferocious features; fierce looks

凶宅(ㄒㄩㄥ ㄓㄞˊ)
① a house where murders, etc. took place ② a haunted

house
凶兆(ㄒㄩㄥ ㄓㄠˋ)
a bad omen
凶事(ㄒㄩㄥ ㄕˋ)
① unlucky incidents—deaths, killings, etc. ② war; armed clashes
凶殺(ㄒㄩㄥ ㄕㄚ)
homicide; murder
凶煞(ㄒㄩㄥ ㄕㄚˋ)
the evil spirit that causes illness, death, etc.
凶手(ㄒㄩㄥ ㄕㄡˇ)
a murderer; an assassin
凶神惡煞(ㄒㄩㄥ ㄕㄣˊ ㄜˋ ㄕㄚˋ)
devils; fiends
凶殘(ㄒㄩㄥ ㄘㄢˊ)
bloodthirsty; merciless
凶惡(ㄒㄩㄥ ㄜˋ)
brutish; fearful; ferocious

三畫

【凸】 352 ㄊㄨˊ twu tú
1. protuberant; convex
2. to protrude; to jut
凸版(ㄊㄨˊ ㄅㄢˇ)
a relief printing plate
凸面(ㄊㄨˊ ㄇㄧㄢˋ)
convex
凸透鏡(ㄊㄨˊ ㄊㄡˋ ㄐㄧㄥˋ)
a convex lens
凸鏡(ㄊㄨˊ ㄐㄧㄥˋ)or 凸面鏡(ㄊㄨˊ ㄇㄧㄢˋ ㄐㄧㄥˋ)
a convex mirror
凸出(ㄊㄨˊ ㄔㄨ)
bulging out; to protrude

【凹】 353 ㄠ au āo
1. indented; an indention
2. hollow; concave
凹版(ㄠ ㄅㄢˇ)
intaglio; gravure
凹版印刷(ㄠ ㄅㄢˇ ㄧㄣˋ ㄕㄨㄚ)
intaglio printing
凹面(ㄠ ㄇㄧㄢˋ)
concave
凹面鏡(ㄠ ㄇㄧㄢˋ ㄐㄧㄥˋ)
a concave mirror 亦作「凹鏡」
凹地(ㄠ ㄉㄧˋ)
hollow ground
凹透鏡(ㄠ ㄊㄡˋ ㄐㄧㄥˋ)
a concave lens
凹鏡(ㄠ ㄐㄧㄥˋ)
a concave mirror
凹陷(ㄠ ㄒㄧㄢˋ)
(said of a place) a hollow or depression

【出】 354 ㄔㄨ chu chū
1.to go out; to come out: 她出門購物。She went out shopping.
2.to produce; to reproduce: 這工廠出產汽車。This factory produces cars.
3.to beget
4.to happen or occur; to incur
5.to put forth; to bud
6.to divorce (a wife, etc.)
7.to chase away; to banish
8.to expend; to pay out
9.to escape; to leave (one's home, etc.): 我們從敵人手中逃出。We escaped from the enemy.
10.to appear: 他突然出現在我們面前。He suddenly appeared before us.
11.to take office
12.to vent (one's anger, etc.)
出版(ㄔㄨ ㄅㄢˇ)
to publish
出版法(ㄔㄨ ㄅㄢˇ ㄈㄚˇ)
publication law
出版家(ㄔㄨ ㄅㄢˇ ㄐㄧㄚ)or 出版者(ㄔㄨ ㄅㄢˇ ㄓㄜˇ)
a publisher
出版自由(ㄔㄨ ㄅㄢˇ ㄗˋ ㄧㄡˊ)
freedom of publication: 在民主社會中有出版自由。In a democratic society there is freedom of publication.
出版物(ㄔㄨ ㄅㄢˇ ㄨˋ)
publications
出奔(ㄔㄨ ㄅㄣ)
to escape; to leave one's home and live in exile
出榜(ㄔㄨ ㄅㄤˇ)or 放榜(ㄈㄤˋ ㄅㄤˇ)
① to publish or announce the result of successful candidates or examinees ② to put up a notice
出殯(ㄔㄨ ㄅㄧㄣˋ)
to carry a coffin to the grave for burial; a funeral procession
出兵(ㄔㄨ ㄅㄧㄥ)
to dispatch troops; to send military forces: 當局出兵鎮壓叛亂。The authorities dispatched troops to quell the rebellion.
出品(ㄔㄨ ㄆㄧㄣˇ)
products (of a certain company, etc.)
出馬(ㄔㄨ ㄇㄚˇ)
① to go out and face something ② to take office
出沒無常(ㄔㄨ ㄇㄛˋ ㄨˊ ㄔㄤˊ)
(usually said of guerrilla bands or bandits) to appear and disappear at unpredictable places and times
出賣(ㄔㄨ ㄇㄞˋ)
① to sell ② to betray; betrayal
出毛病(ㄔㄨ ㄇㄠˊ ㄅㄧㄥˋ)
to be or go out of order; to go wrong
出門(ㄔㄨ ㄇㄣˊ)or 出門兒(ㄔㄨ ㄇㄜˊㄦ)
to leave one's home; to take a trip
出門子(ㄔㄨ ㄇㄣˊ ˙ㄗ)
(said of a girl) to get married; to leave her parental home for marriage
出面(ㄔㄨ ㄇㄧㄢˋ)
to assume the responsibility (in mediation, negotiations, etc.); to act on someone else's behalf
出名(ㄔㄨ ㄇㄧㄥˊ)
to become famous; famous: 一大群人向那出名的英雄歡呼。A great crowd of people greeted the famous hero.
出發(ㄔㄨ ㄈㄚ)
to set out; to leave for (a destination)
出發點(ㄔㄨ ㄈㄚ ㄉㄧㄢˇ)
① the point from which one sets out; the starting point ②(in argument, discussion, etc.) premises; a basis ③ a motive
出分子(ㄔㄨ ㄈㄣˋ ˙ㄗ)
to offer money as a gift or condolence
出風頭(ㄔㄨ ㄈㄥ ˙ㄊㄡ)
to be in the spotlight; to be very popular; to steal the show; to seek publicity
出婦(ㄔㄨ ㄈㄨˋ)
① a divorced woman ② to divorce one's wife 亦作「出妻」
出點子(ㄔㄨ ㄉㄧㄢˇ ˙ㄗ)
to offer advice

出動(ㄔㄨ ㄉㄨㄥˋ)
to dispatch or send out (especially troops, armored units, reinforcements, etc.)

出頭(ㄔㄨ ㄊㄡˊ)
(said of people of humble origin) to make good or to succeed

出頭露面(ㄔㄨ ㄊㄡˊ ㄌㄡˋ ㄇㄧㄢˋ)
to appear in public

出題(ㄔㄨ ㄊㄧˊ)
① to set a theme (especially in composing poems or writings) ② to set questions (for an examination, etc.)

出天花(ㄔㄨ ㄊㄧㄢ ㄏㄨㄚ)
to have smallpox

出庭(ㄔㄨ ㄊㄧㄥˊ)
to appear in court

出土(ㄔㄨ ㄊㄨˇ)
(said of antiques, etc.) to be unearthed; to come out of earth

出脫(ㄔㄨ ㄊㄨㄛ)
① to vindicate (someone from charges, etc.) ② to sell

出納(ㄔㄨ ㄋㄚˋ)
a teller or treasurer

出來(ㄔㄨ ˙ㄌㄞ)
① to come out; to appear: 星星出來了。The stars came out. ② to make out ③ to bring to pass

出類拔萃(ㄔㄨ ㄌㄟˋ ㄅㄚˊ ㄘㄨㄟˋ)
outstanding; eminent; remarkable

出漏子 or 出婁子(ㄔㄨ ㄌㄡˋ ˙ㄗ) or 出亂子(ㄔㄨ ㄌㄨㄢˋ ˙ㄗ) or 出岔子(ㄔㄨ ㄔㄚˋ ˙ㄗ)
in trouble; to get into trouble

出力(ㄔㄨ ㄌㄧˋ)
to devote one's efforts to (an undertaking, etc.)

出列(ㄔㄨ ㄌㄧㄝˋ)
to leave one's place in the ranks

出獵(ㄔㄨ ㄌㄧㄝˋ)
to go hunting; to hunt

出路(ㄔㄨ ㄌㄨˋ)
① the prospects (of a career, etc.) ② an outlet

出落(ㄔㄨ ㄌㄨㄛˋ)
to grow (prettier, etc.)

出籠(ㄔㄨ ㄌㄨㄥˊ)
to become current; to appear in the market

出格(ㄔㄨ ㄍㄜˊ)
to step out of line; to behave disorderly

出閣(ㄔㄨ ㄍㄜˊ)
(said of a girl) to get married

出港(ㄔㄨ ㄍㄤˇ)
①(said of a vessel) to leave (a) port ② to send (goods) abroad; to export

出國(ㄔㄨ ㄍㄨㄛˊ)
to go abroad

出乖露醜(ㄔㄨ ㄍㄨㄞ ㄌㄡˋ ㄔㄡˇ)
to make oneself a laughingstock in public

出軌(ㄔㄨ ㄍㄨㄟˇ)
① to derail ② to behave contrary to a normal pattern

出恭(ㄔㄨ ㄍㄨㄥ)
to empty the bowels

出口(ㄔㄨ ㄎㄡˇ)
① to export ② to utter; to speak ③ an exit (in a theater, etc.)

出口貿易(ㄔㄨ ㄎㄡˇ ㄇㄠˋ ㄧˋ)
export trade

出口貨(ㄔㄨ ㄎㄡˇ ㄏㄨㄛˋ)
exports; goods for export

出口成章(ㄔㄨ ㄎㄡˇ ㄔㄥˊ ㄓㄤ)
One's tongue is the pen of a ready writer.

出口傷人(ㄔㄨ ㄎㄡˇ ㄕㄤ ㄖㄣˊ)
to make insulting remarks

出口稅(ㄔㄨ ㄎㄡˇ ㄕㄨㄟˋ)
export duties

出海(ㄔㄨ ㄏㄞˇ)
to leave (a) port; to go to sea; to put (out) to sea

出海口(ㄔㄨ ㄏㄞˇ ㄎㄡˇ)
an estuary

出汗(ㄔㄨ ㄏㄢˋ)
to perspire; to sweat

出航(ㄔㄨ ㄏㄤˊ)
① to set out on a voyage; to set sail ② to set out on a flight

出乎(ㄔㄨ ㄏㄨ)
to come from

出乎意外(ㄔㄨ ㄏㄨ ㄧˋ ㄨㄞˋ)
unexpectedly

出貨(ㄔㄨ ㄏㄨㄛˋ)
① to produce goods ② to get delivered goods ③ to contribute money

出擊(ㄔㄨ ㄐㄧˊ)
to leave (a base, camp, position, etc.) to attack or raid (the enemy)

出家(ㄔㄨ ㄐㄧㄚ)
(Buddhism) to leave home and become a monk or nun

出家人(ㄔㄨ ㄐㄧㄚ ㄖㄣˊ)
a monk or nun

出價(ㄔㄨ ㄐㄧㄚˋ)
to bid; to offer a price

出嫁(ㄔㄨ ㄐㄧㄚˋ)
(said of a woman) to get married

出結(ㄔㄨ ㄐㄧㄝˊ)
to guarantee in writing

出界(ㄔㄨ ㄐㄧㄝˋ)
(sports) out-of-bounds; outside

出借(ㄔㄨ ㄐㄧㄝˋ)
to lend

出教(ㄔㄨ ㄐㄧㄠˋ)
to be excommunicated

出尖(ㄔㄨ ㄐㄧㄢ) or 出尖兒(ㄔㄨ ㄐㄧㄚㄦ)
① outstanding; remarkable ② to heap a container (with grains, etc.)

出金(ㄔㄨ ㄐㄧㄣ)
(Japanese) to draw money (from a bank or an investment company)

出進(ㄔㄨ ㄐㄧㄣˋ)
incomings and outgoings; receipts and expenditures

出將入相(ㄔㄨ ㄐㄧㄤˋ ㄖㄨˋ ㄒㄧㄤˋ)
(literally) to be as good a general as a minister—well versed in both politics and military tactics

出境(ㄔㄨ ㄐㄧㄥˋ)
to leave a place or country: 他已辦好出境手續。He has gone through all formalities to leave the country.

出境證(ㄔㄨ ㄐㄧㄥˋ ㄓㄥˋ)
an exit permit

出局(ㄔㄨ ㄐㄩˊ)
(baseball) out

出妻(ㄔㄨ ㄑㄧ)
(in ancient China) to divorce one's wife

出奇(ㄔㄨ ㄑㄧˊ)
① extraordinary; extraordinarily: 今年冬天冷得出奇。It is extraordinarily cold this winter. ② (to win) by sur-

〔凵 部〕

prise

出奇制勝(ㄔㄨ ㄑㄧˊ ㄓˋ ㄕㄥˋ)
to win by surprise

出其不意(ㄔㄨ ㄑㄧˊ ㄅㄨˋ ㄧˋ)
to take (someone) unawares; to take by surprise; to catch (someone) off-guard

出氣(ㄔㄨ ㄑㄧˋ)
to vent one's anger

出氣筒(ㄔㄨ ㄑㄧˋ ㄊㄨㄥˇ)
(in a colloquial expression) one who serves as a vent to somebody's anger and, as such, is often scolded without provocation

出氣口(ㄔㄨ ㄑㄧˋ ㄎㄡˇ)
① a gas outlet ② an air vent

出錢(ㄔㄨ ㄑㄧㄢˊ)
to provide the funds

出勤(ㄔㄨ ㄑㄧㄣˊ)
to take a business trip

出去(ㄔㄨ ˙ㄑㄩ)
① to go out; to be out ② Get out!

出缺(ㄔㄨ ㄑㄩㄝ)
a vacancy created by illness, death, etc.

出席(ㄔㄨ ㄒㄧˊ)
to attend or to be present at (a meeting, etc.): 我必須出席這次的會議。I must attend the meeting.

出息(ㄔㄨ ˙ㄒㄧ)
① promising (kids, etc.) ② profit

出血(ㄔㄨ ㄒㄧㄝˇ)
bleeding; hemorrhage

出現(ㄔㄨ ㄒㄧㄢˋ)
to appear; to emerge: 船出現在水平線上。The ship appeared on the horizon.

出行(ㄔㄨ ㄒㄧㄥˊ)
to leave for a long journey

出巡(ㄔㄨ ㄒㄩㄣˊ)
to go on an inspection trip

出診(ㄔㄨ ㄓㄣˇ)
(said of a physician) to be on house call

出疹子(ㄔㄨ ㄓㄣˇ ˙ㄗ)
to get the measles

出陣(ㄔㄨ ㄓㄣˋ)
(usually said of a general in ancient times) to go out and confront the enemy

出征(ㄔㄨ ㄓㄥ)
to go out to battle

出主意(ㄔㄨ ㄓㄨˇ ㄧˋ)
① to scheme; to cook up something; to provide an idea ② to incite or instigate

出贅(ㄔㄨ ㄓㄨㄟˋ)
(said of a man) to marry into the family of one's wife

出眾(ㄔㄨ ㄓㄨㄥˋ)
outstanding; foremost

出車禍(ㄔㄨ ㄔㄜ ㄏㄨㄛˋ)
to have a car accident

出差(ㄔㄨ ㄔㄞ)
(said of subordinate officials) to go out of town on business

出超(ㄔㄨ ㄔㄠ)
a favorable balance of trade 亦作「貿易順差」

出醜(ㄔㄨ ㄔㄡˇ)
to make a scene; to lose face; to look or sound ridiculous; to make a fool of oneself

出產(ㄔㄨ ㄔㄢˇ)
to produce or grow (especially said of agricultural products)

出塵(ㄔㄨ ㄔㄣˊ)
out-of-the-world

出場(ㄔㄨ ㄔㄤˇ)or(ㄔㄨ ㄔㄤˊ)
①(said of a player) to go on the stage ②(said of an athlete, etc.) to enter the stadium or go on to the playground

出廠(ㄔㄨ ㄔㄤˇ)
(said of a product) to leave the factory

出處
①(ㄔㄨ ㄔㄨˋ) ⓐ background (of a person) ⓑ the source of an allusion or a quotation ② (ㄔㄨ ㄔㄨˇ) to leave and to take office

出師(ㄔㄨ ㄕ)
① to move soldiers forward for attack; to mobilize troops for offensive ② to complete one's apprenticeship in a trade and make a debut as a professional

出師不利(ㄔㄨ ㄕ ㄅㄨˋ ㄌㄧˋ)
① to suffer a defeat at the very first battle ② to meet a setback at the start of an undertaking

出使(ㄔㄨ ㄕˇ)or(ㄔㄨ ㄕˋ)
to be appointed as a diplomatic envoy; to be an ambassador to

出仕(ㄔㄨ ㄕˋ)
to be an official; to take a government position

出世(ㄔㄨ ㄕˋ)
(Buddhism) ① appearance in the world, e.g. the Buddha's appearance ② to leave the mundane world (as a monk or nun) ③ beyond or outside this world; not of this world; of nirvana character ④ to come into the world; to be born

出示(ㄔㄨ ㄕˋ)
to show (something to someone)

出事(ㄔㄨ ㄕˋ)
to be in trouble; to have an accident

出手(ㄔㄨ ㄕㄡˇ)
① to sell; to part with ② to take on a job or work ③ an offer; to offer ④ to reach out with one's hand

出手大方(ㄔㄨ ㄕㄡˇ ㄉㄚˋ ㄈㄤ)
to spend money freely; very generous

出售(ㄔㄨ ㄕㄡˋ)
to sell

出山(ㄔㄨ ㄕㄢ)
to leave retirement and take a government post

出身(ㄔㄨ ㄕㄣ)
(personal) backgrounds; qualifications

出神(ㄔㄨ ㄕㄣˊ)
① absorbed in ② absent-minded

出神入化(ㄔㄨ ㄕㄣˊ ㄖㄨˋ ㄏㄨㄚˋ)
uncanny (feats, skill, etc.); superb; out-of-this-world (performances, etc.)

出聲(ㄔㄨ ㄕㄥ)or 出聲兒(ㄔㄨ ㄕㄥㄦ)
to utter (a sound); to make a sound; to speak

出生(ㄔㄨ ㄕㄥ)
to be born

出生率(ㄔㄨ ㄕㄥ ㄌㄩˋ)
birthrate

出生紙(ㄔㄨ ㄕㄥ ㄓˇ)or 出生證書(ㄔㄨ ㄕㄥ ㄓㄥˋ ㄕㄨ)
a birth certificate

出生入死(ㄔㄨ ㄕㄥ ㄖㄨˋ ㄙˇ)
to risk one's life; to brave untold dangers

出書(ㄔㄨ ㄕㄨ)
to publish books

出人頭地(ㄔㄨ ㄖㄣˊ ㄊㄡˊ ㄉㄧˋ)
to be somebody; to stand out among one's fellows; to make good

出人意表(ㄔㄨ ㄖㄣˊ ㄧˋ ㄅㄧㄠˇ)
beyond expectation; to come as a surprise

出任(ㄔㄨ ㄖㄣˋ)
to take up the post of

出讓(ㄔㄨ ㄖㄤˋ)
to sell; for sale

出入(ㄔㄨ ㄖㄨˋ)
① to come and go ② receipts and expenditures ③ discrepancy; inconsistency

出資(ㄔㄨ ㄗ)
to put up capital (for a business venture, etc.)

出走(ㄔㄨ ㄗㄡˇ)
to run away from one's home; to desert one's family

出租(ㄔㄨ ㄗㄨ)or 出賃(ㄔㄨ ㄌㄧㄣˋ)
to let (a house, equipment, etc.)

出操(ㄔㄨ ㄘㄠ)
to drill; to train (soldiers, etc.): 本隊今天下午出操。Our team will have drill this afternoon.

出錯(ㄔㄨ ㄘㄨㄛˋ)
to make mistakes: 她做事很少出錯。She seldom makes a mistake in her work.

出色(ㄔㄨ ㄙㄜˋ)
outstanding; remarkable

出塞(ㄔㄨ ㄙㄞˋ)
(in ancient China) to go far out of the frontiers; to cross the frontier

出賽(ㄔㄨ ㄙㄞˋ)
to contend with; to contest

出爾反爾(ㄔㄨ ㄦˇ ㄈㄢˇ ㄦˇ)
to renege on one's promise; to act contrary to one's word

出以公心(ㄔㄨ ㄧˇ ㄍㄨㄥ ㄒㄧㄣ)
to do something impartially; to act without any selfish considerations

出芽(ㄔㄨ ㄧㄚˊ)or 出芽兒(ㄔㄨ ㄧㄚˊㄦ)
(said of a plant) to sprout

出遊(ㄔㄨ ㄧㄡˊ)
to go on an excursion

出言不遜(ㄔㄨ ㄧㄢˊ ㄅㄨˋ ㄒㄩㄣˋ)
to utter insulting remarks; to insult

出洋(ㄔㄨ ㄧㄤˊ)
to go abroad

出洋相(ㄔㄨ ㄧㄤˊ ㄒㄧㄤˋ)
to make a fool of oneself (especially in public)

出迎(ㄔㄨ ㄧㄥˊ)
to go or come out to receive

出外(ㄔㄨ ㄨㄞˋ)
to leave for a distant place

出亡(ㄔㄨ ㄨㄤˊ)
to escape; to go into exile

出於 or 出于(ㄔㄨ ㄩˊ)
to start from; to proceed from; to stem from

出於無意(ㄔㄨ ㄩˊ ㄨˊ ㄧˋ)
unintentional; unintentionally

出院(ㄔㄨ ㄩㄢˋ)
to leave the hospital: 他病癒出院了。He left the hospital after recovery.

六畫

【函】 355 ㄏㄢˊ harn hán

1. a letter; correspondence
2. armor
3. to contain; to envelop
4. a sheath, as for a sword or a knife
5. an envelope

函購(ㄏㄢˊ ㄍㄡˋ)
to purchase by mail order

函件(ㄏㄢˊ ㄐㄧㄢˋ)
letters; correspondence

函授(ㄏㄢˊ ㄕㄡˋ)
teaching by mail or correspondence

函授學校(ㄏㄢˊ ㄕㄡˋ ㄒㄩㄝˊ ㄒㄧㄠˋ)
a correspondence school

函數(ㄏㄢˊ ㄕㄨˋ)
(mathematics) function

函索即寄(ㄏㄢˊ ㄙㄨㄛˇ ㄐㄧˊ ㄐㄧˋ)
to send (samples, etc.) upon request by mail

函約(ㄏㄢˊ ㄩㄝ)
to make an appointment by letter

刀部
ㄉㄠ dau dāo

〔刀部〕

【刀】 356 ㄉㄠ dau dāo

1. a knife; a blade; a sword
2. knife-shaped coins of ancient China

刀把兒 or 刀靶兒(ㄉㄠ ㄅㄚˇㄦ)
① the handle of a knife ② power ③ a hold that may be used against somebody 亦作「刀把子」

刀背(ㄉㄠ ㄅㄟˋ)
①the back of a knife ②an occasion on which the money spent is wasted

刀筆吏(ㄉㄠ ㄅㄧˇ ㄌㄧˋ)
(in ancient China) a literary hack who specialized in drawing up indictments and other legal documents for a fee

刀片(ㄉㄠ ㄆㄧㄢˋ)
a razor blade

刀馬旦(ㄉㄠ ㄇㄚˇ ㄉㄢˋ)
(Peking opera) the role of a female warrior

刀鋒(ㄉㄠ ㄈㄥ)
the blade or edge of a knife

刀斧手(ㄉㄠ ㄈㄨˇ ㄕㄡˇ)
an executioner

刀光劍影(ㄉㄠ ㄍㄨㄤ ㄐㄧㄢˋ ㄧㄥˇ)
engaged in hot battle; a heated combat (usually between individual swordsmen)

刀口(ㄉㄠ ㄎㄡˇ)or 刀刃(ㄉㄠ ㄖㄣˋ)
① the blade or edge of a knife ② an occasion on which money can be spent to advantage

刀匠(ㄉㄠ ㄐㄧㄤˋ)
a bladesmith

刀鞘(ㄉㄠ ㄑㄧㄠˋ)
a sheath

刀槍(ㄉㄠ ㄑㄧㄤ)
swords and spears; weapons

刀下留人(ㄉㄠ ㄒㄧㄚˋ ㄌㄧㄡˊ ㄖㄣˊ)
Hold the execution! (The exclamation was used in former times when a criminal about to be beheaded on the

〔刀部〕

execution ground won a last-minute pardon or when the case was suddenly reversed.)

刀叉(ㄉㄠ ㄔㄚ)
knives and forks (used in Western meals)

刀山火海(ㄉㄠ ㄕㄢ ㄏㄨㄛˇ ㄏㄞˇ)
a mountain of swords and a sea of flames—most dangerous places

刀傷(ㄉㄠ ㄕㄤ)
① knife wound ② to inflict a wound or injury with a knife

刀子(ㄉㄠ ˙ㄗ)
a small knife; a dagger

刀俎(ㄉㄠ ㄗㄨˇ)
a knife and chopping board

刀魚(ㄉㄠ ㄩˊ)
Chinese herring

【刁】 357
ㄉㄧㄠ diau diāo

1. low and cunning; crafty; wicked; artful; knavish
2. a Chinese family name

刁蠻(ㄉㄧㄠ ㄇㄢˊ)
obstinate

刁斗(ㄉㄧㄠ ㄉㄡˇ)
a pot made of copper used by the army

刁斗森嚴(ㄉㄧㄠ ㄉㄡˇ ㄙㄣ ㄧㄢˊ)
strict army discipline

刁難(ㄉㄧㄠ ㄋㄢˊ)
to (deliberately) make things difficult for others

刁悍(ㄉㄧㄠ ㄏㄢˋ)
cunning and fierce

刁猾(ㄉㄧㄠ ㄏㄨㄚˊ)
cunning; low and cunning

刁詐(ㄉㄧㄠ ㄓㄚˋ)
knavish; crafty

刁鑽(ㄉㄧㄠ ㄗㄨㄢ)
wily; cunning

刁鑽古怪(ㄉㄧㄠ ㄗㄨㄢ ㄍㄨˇ ㄍㄨㄞˋ)
perverse; mischievous; cranky

一畫

【刃】 358
ㄖㄣˋ renn rèn

1. the blade or edge of a knife
2. to kill

刃兒(ㄖㄜˋㄦ)
the edge or blade of a knife

二畫

【分】 359
1. ㄈㄣ fen fēn

1.to divide
2.to part
3.to share
4.to distribute
5.to distinguish
6.one minute
7.one cent
8.one hundredth of a tael
9.a centimeter
10.located separately; a branch

分貝(ㄈㄣ ㄅㄟˋ)
a decibel

分班(ㄈㄣ ㄅㄢ)
to divide (students) into classes

分謗(ㄈㄣ ㄅㄤˋ)
to share blame; to be the target of the same slander (as that which is directed to another person)

分崩離析(ㄈㄣ ㄅㄥ ㄌㄧˊ ㄒㄧ)
to disintegrate and decompose; to lose unity

分別(ㄈㄣ ㄅㄧㄝˊ)
① to part (from a person) ② to distinguish or tell apart ③ separately; to separate

分辨(ㄈㄣ ㄅㄧㄢˋ)
to distinguish; to tell apart

分辯(ㄈㄣ ㄅㄧㄢˋ)
to make excuses; to explain

分兵進攻(ㄈㄣ ㄅㄧㄥ ㄐㄧㄣˋ ㄍㄨㄥ)
to divide the forces to attack

分布 or 分佈(ㄈㄣ ㄅㄨˋ)
to be scattered (over an area); to spread

分派(ㄈㄣ ㄆㄞˋ)
to assign; to allot; to apportion

分配(ㄈㄣ ㄆㄟˋ)
① to distribute; to portion out; to share out; to deal out; to allocate ② distribution

分批(ㄈㄣ ㄆㄧ)
in batches; in turn

分袂(ㄈㄣ ㄇㄟˋ)
(said of friends) to part; to separate

分門別類(ㄈㄣ ㄇㄣˊ ㄅㄧㄝˊ ㄌㄟˋ)
to classify systematically

分米(ㄈㄣ ㄇㄧˇ)
a decimeter

分泌(ㄈㄣ ㄇㄧˋ)
(biology) to secrete; secretion

分秒必爭(ㄈㄣ ㄇㄧㄠˇ ㄅㄧˋ ㄓㄥ)
to seize every minute and second; to make the best of one's time

分娩(ㄈㄣ ㄇㄧㄢˇ)
to lie in; to give birth; childbirth

分明(ㄈㄣ ㄇㄧㄥˊ)
clear; distinct; unambiguous; unmistakable

分母(ㄈㄣ ㄇㄨˇ)
the denominator of a fraction

分發(ㄈㄣ ㄈㄚ)
① to issue or distribute (articles) ② to assign or appoint (to a post or duty)

分肥(ㄈㄣ ㄈㄟˊ)
to divide or share spoils, embezzled money, etc.

分封(ㄈㄣ ㄈㄥ)
to confer (on each vassal) a title to a feudal state

分付(ㄈㄣ ㄈㄨˋ)
to pay or shell out separately

分赴(ㄈㄣ ㄈㄨˋ)
to leave for different destinations

分道揚鑣(ㄈㄣ ㄉㄠˋ ㄧㄤˊ ㄅㄧㄠ)
① (for two persons) to engage in different pursuits ② to quit partnership, association, etc.

分擔(ㄈㄣ ㄉㄢ)
to undertake different portions of or share the responsibility for (the same task, duty, etc.)

分等(ㄈㄣ ㄉㄥˇ)
to grade; to classify

分隊(ㄈㄣ ㄉㄨㄟˋ)
a unit of soldiers or policemen corresponding to the platoon or squad

分頭辦理(ㄈㄣ ㄊㄡˊ ㄅㄢˋ ㄌㄧˇ)
to manage or handle separately for the same goal

分攤(ㄈㄣ ㄊㄢ)
to share (a financial burden, stocks, etc.)

分庭抗禮(ㄈㄣ ㄊㄧㄥˊ ㄎㄤˋ ㄌㄧˇ)
to function as rivals; to rival each other; to be in competing positions; to compete on equal terms
分途(ㄈㄣ ㄊㄨˊ)
to take different paths; to diverge; to separate
分類(ㄈㄣ ㄌㄟˋ)
① to classify; to sort ② classification; taxonomy
分類廣告(ㄈㄣ ㄌㄟˋ ㄍㄨㄤˇ ㄍㄠˋ)
classified ads
分勞(ㄈㄣ ㄌㄠˊ)
to help someone do work
分離(ㄈㄣ ㄌㄧˊ)
to separate; to part; to divide; to disconnect; to dissociate; to detach; to cut off; to segregate
分離派(ㄈㄣ ㄌㄧˊ ㄆㄞˋ)
secessionists
分力(ㄈㄣ ㄌㄧˋ)
(physics) components of force
分利(ㄈㄣ ㄌㄧˋ)
to share benefit
分裂(ㄈㄣ ㄌㄧㄝˋ)
to break up; to split; to disunite
分路(ㄈㄣ ㄌㄨˋ)
① along separate routes; to take different paths ② (electricity) a shunt
分割(ㄈㄣ ㄍㄜ)
① to divide up; to cut apart ② segmentation
分隔(ㄈㄣ ㄍㄜˊ)
to partition
分光鏡(ㄈㄣ ㄍㄨㄤ ㄐㄧㄥˋ)
a spectroscope
分光儀(ㄈㄣ ㄍㄨㄤ ㄧˊ)
a spectrometer
分工(ㄈㄣ ㄍㄨㄥ)
to divide the work; division of labor
分工合作(ㄈㄣ ㄍㄨㄥ ㄏㄜˊ ㄗㄨㄛˋ)
to share out the work and cooperate with one another
分科(ㄈㄣ ㄎㄜ)
(education) to divide students into groups, each majoring in a different field of studies
分開(ㄈㄣ ㄎㄞ)
to separate; to set apart; to segregate; to isolate
分合(ㄈㄣ ㄏㄜˊ)
union and division; synthesis and analysis; fusion and fission
分毫(ㄈㄣ ㄏㄠˊ)
a modicum; a bit; a trifle; a whit
分號(ㄈㄣ ㄏㄠˋ)
① the semicolon ② a branch store
分行(ㄈㄣ ㄏㄤˊ)
a branch office; a branch store
分化(ㄈㄣ ㄏㄨㄚˋ)
① (biology) differentiation ② to disunite; disunion or dissension; to sow discord
分會(ㄈㄣ ㄏㄨㄟˋ)
a branch association; a chapter (of an organization)
分紅(ㄈㄣ ㄏㄨㄥˊ)
(business) to distribute a dividend
分機(ㄈㄣ ㄐㄧ)
(telephone) an extension
分級(ㄈㄣ ㄐㄧˊ)
to grade; to classify
分家(ㄈㄣ ㄐㄧㄚ)
(for brothers) to divide family property (so as to set up separate households)
分解(ㄈㄣ ㄐㄧㄝˇ)
① to resolve; to decompose ② to dissolve ③ to analyze
分解熱(ㄈㄣ ㄐㄧㄝˇ ㄖㄜˋ)
heat of decomposition
分界(ㄈㄣ ㄐㄧㄝˋ)
① to have as the boundary; to be demarcated by ② a line of demarcation
分界線(ㄈㄣ ㄐㄧㄝˋ ㄒㄧㄢˋ)
a boundary; a borderline; a line of demarcation
分進合擊(ㄈㄣ ㄐㄧㄣˋ ㄏㄜˊ ㄐㄧˊ)
(military) a concerted attack by converging columns
分疆畫界(ㄈㄣ ㄐㄧㄤ ㄏㄨㄚˋ ㄐㄧㄝˋ)
to mark boundaries
分居(ㄈㄣ ㄐㄩ)
to separate without a legal divorce; to live apart
分局(ㄈㄣ ㄐㄩˊ)
a police precinct office
分句(ㄈㄣ ㄐㄩˋ)
(grammar) a clause
分歧(ㄈㄣ ㄑㄧˊ)
① difference; divergence; discrepancy ② to diverge; to differ; to disagree
分期付款(ㄈㄣ ㄑㄧˊ ㄈㄨˋ ㄎㄨㄢˇ)
payment in installments; the installment plan
分區(ㄈㄣ ㄑㄩ)
to divide into districts; to zone
分權(ㄈㄣ ㄑㄩㄢˊ)
division of power or authority
分析(ㄈㄣ ㄒㄧ)
to analyze; to study; to investigate; analysis; study; investigation
分析法(ㄈㄣ ㄒㄧ ㄈㄚˇ)
an analytical method
分析師(ㄈㄣ ㄒㄧ ㄕ)
an analyst
分銷(ㄈㄣ ㄒㄧㄠ)
to retail (goods)
分曉(ㄈㄣ ㄒㄧㄠˇ)
the result (of a developing event); the answer (to a puzzle, riddle, etc.)
分校(ㄈㄣ ㄒㄧㄠˋ)
a branch of a school (away from the school's main campus)
分心(ㄈㄣ ㄒㄧㄣ) or 分神(ㄈㄣ ㄕㄣˊ)
① to give some attention; to give a thought ② to fail to pay full attention; to fail to concentrate oneself ③ distraction
分享(ㄈㄣ ㄒㄧㄤˇ)
to share (joys, rights, etc.); to take part in: 讓我們分享成功的喜悅。Let us share the joys of success.
分支(ㄈㄣ ㄓ)
a branch; a division
分針(ㄈㄣ ㄓㄣ)
the minute hand
分社(ㄈㄣ ㄕㄜˋ)
① a branch office ② a news bureau
分手(ㄈㄣ ㄕㄡˇ)
to part; to separate; to cease associating: 我們是在火車站分手的。We separated at the railway station.
分身(ㄈㄣ ㄕㄣ)
to divide attention; to han-

〔刀部〕

dle more than one thing at the same time
分身乏術(ㄈㄣ ㄕㄣ ㄈㄚˊ ㄕㄨˋ)
unable to show up at all the places where one is needed; unable to do all the things one has to do
分數(ㄈㄣ ㄕㄨˋ)
①a fraction (as distinct from a whole number) ② grades or percentage (in an examination); scores (in sports competitions)
分說(ㄈㄣ ㄕㄨㄛ)
to make excuses; to explain
分水嶺(ㄈㄣ ㄕㄨㄟˇ ㄌㄧㄥˇ)
a watershed (in the sense of a ridge)
分潤(ㄈㄣ ㄖㄨㄣˋ)
to share or have a share of (a fortune, profit, etc.)
分子(ㄈㄣ ㄗˇ)
①(mathematics) a numerator (as opposed to a denominator) ②(physics) a molecule
分子力(ㄈㄣ ㄗˇ ㄌㄧˋ)
molecular force
分子量(ㄈㄣ ㄗˇ ㄌㄧㄤˋ)
molecular weight
分子式(ㄈㄣ ㄗˇ ㄕˋ)
a molecular formula
分贓(ㄈㄣ ㄗㄤ)
to share or get a share of loot or bribes
分組(ㄈㄣ ㄗㄨˇ)
to divide into groups
分詞(ㄈㄣ ㄘˊ)
(grammar) a participle
分冊(ㄈㄣ ㄘㄜˋ)
a fascicle
分層負責(ㄈㄣ ㄘㄥˊ ㄈㄨˋ ㄗㄜˊ)
delegation of the right authority to the right level of officials (as distinct from concentration of authority in the hands of the boss)
分寸(ㄈㄣ ㄘㄨㄣˋ)
judgment for propriety (in speech, behavior, etc.): 說話應有分寸。One should talk with propriety.
分散(ㄈㄣ ㄙㄢˋ)
to scatter; to disperse; to dissipate; to divert
分送(ㄈㄣ ㄙㄨㄥˋ)
to distribute

〔刀部〕

分野(ㄈㄣ ㄧㄝˇ)
demarcation; a borderline; a boundary
分憂(ㄈㄣ ㄧㄡ)
to share sorrows, worries, etc.
分陰(ㄈㄣ ㄧㄣ)
a very short while; a moment
分文不取(ㄈㄣ ㄨㄣˊ ㄅㄨˋ ㄑㄩˇ)
do not charge a single cent

【分】 359
2. (份) ㄈㄣˋ fenn fèn

1. a role or part (played by a person in life)
2. a part or portion (of a whole); a component: 這草稿的一部分不易辨讀。A portion of the manuscript is illegible.

分內之事(ㄈㄣˋ ㄋㄟˋ ㄓ ㄕˋ)
one's due task; a duty
分量(ㄈㄣˋ ㄌㄧㄤˋ)
① an amount ② (said of statements) weight or impact
分子(ㄈㄣˋ ㄗˇ)
a member (of some organization)
分外(ㄈㄣˋ ㄨㄞˋ)
① particularly; especially ② undeserved; beyond the scope of duty or position
分外之物(ㄈㄣˋ ㄨㄞˋ ㄓ ㄨˋ)
undue gain, luxury, etc.

【切】 360
1. ㄑㄧㄝ chie qie

to cut; to mince; to slice; to carve
切片(ㄑㄧㄝ ㄆㄧㄢˋ)
① microtome section ② to cut into slices
切片檢查(ㄑㄧㄝ ㄆㄧㄢˋ ㄐㄧㄢˇ ㄔㄚˊ)
the microscopic examination of the affected tissue cut into very thin pieces
切面(ㄑㄧㄝ ㄇㄧㄢˋ)
a tangent surface or tangent plane
切麵(ㄑㄧㄝ ㄇㄧㄢˋ)
chopped band noodles
切腹自殺(ㄑㄧㄝ ㄈㄨˋ ㄗˋ ㄕㄚ)
to commit hara-kiri (a ritual suicide under the Japanese samurai code of honor)
切斷(ㄑㄧㄝ ㄉㄨㄢˋ)
to sever; to cut asunder: 他用刀子切斷繩子。He cut the rope asunder with a knife.
切開(ㄑㄧㄝ ㄎㄞ)
to cut open
切塊(ㄑㄧㄝ ㄎㄨㄞˋ)
stripping and slicing
切線(ㄑㄧㄝ ㄒㄧㄢˋ)
a tangent (line)
切除(ㄑㄧㄝ ㄔㄨˊ)
① to cut out; to resect ② excision; resection
切磋(ㄑㄧㄝ ㄘㄨㄛ)
to improve oneself through discussions with another; to learn from each other by exchanging views
切圓(ㄑㄧㄝ ㄩㄢˊ)
tangent circles

【切】 360
2. ㄑㄧㄝˋ chieh qiè

to be close to: 譯文需切原意。The translation should be close in meaning to the original.
切莫(ㄑㄧㄝˋ ㄇㄛˋ)
by no means
切脈(ㄑㄧㄝˋ ㄇㄛˋ)
to feel a patient's pulse
切膚(ㄑㄧㄝˋ ㄈㄨ)or 切己(ㄑㄧㄝˋ ㄐㄧˇ)
very close to oneself; keenly felt
切膚之痛(ㄑㄧㄝˋ ㄈㄨ ㄓ ㄊㄨㄥˋ)
① keenly felt pain ② a personal loss
切當(ㄑㄧㄝˋ ㄉㄤˋ)or 切合(ㄑㄧㄝˋ ㄏㄜˊ)
to the point; apposite; appropriate; fitting; apt
切題(ㄑㄧㄝˋ ㄊㄧˊ)
to the point
切骨(ㄑㄧㄝˋ ㄍㄨˇ)
(said of hatred, etc.) strongly felt; deep; intense; bitter
切口(ㄑㄧㄝˋ ㄎㄡˇ)
professional jargons
切忌(ㄑㄧㄝˋ ㄐㄧˋ)
to be sure to avoid; to forbid
切記(ㄑㄧㄝˋ ㄐㄧˋ)
to be sure to remember; to keep in mind; to bear in mind
切近(ㄑㄧㄝˋ ㄐㄧㄣˋ)
close; closely related
切切(ㄑㄧㄝˋ ㄑㄧㄝˋ)
① urgent; important ② pathetic; pathetic sounds ③ soft sounds (or voices)

切切實實(ㄑ丨ㄝ ㄑ丨ㄝ ㄕˊ ㄕˊ)or 切實(ㄑ丨ㄝ ㄕˊ)
① real; sure; certain ② thoroughly; strictly; thorough

切齒(ㄑ丨ㄝ ㄔˇ)
to grind the teeth in anger, with hatred, etc.

切身(ㄑ丨ㄝ ㄕㄣ)
personal (interests); directly affecting a person

切要(ㄑ丨ㄝ 丨ㄠˋ)
very important; of vital importance

切勿(ㄑ丨ㄝ ㄨˋ)
do not by any means: 切勿自以爲是。Do not be presumptuous and opinionated by any means.

【刈】 361 丨ˋ yih yì
to mow; to reap

刈草機(丨ˋ ㄘㄠˇ ㄐ丨)
a lawn mower; a mowing machine; a mower

三畫

【刊】 362 ㄎㄢ kan kān
1. to hew; to cut
2. to engrave
3. a publication
4. to publish

刊本(ㄎㄢ ㄅㄣˇ)
an edition (of a book)

刊謬(ㄎㄢ ㄇ丨ㄡˋ)or 刊誤(ㄎㄢ ㄨˋ)
to correct errors in printing

刊登(ㄎㄢ ㄉㄥ)or 刊載(ㄎㄢ ㄗㄞˇ)
①(for a writer) to publish (an article in a periodical) ②(for a periodical) to carry (an article)

刊頭(ㄎㄢ ㄊㄡˊ)
the masthead of a newspaper or magazine

刊行(ㄎㄢ ㄒ丨ㄥˊ)
to publish for sale

刊印(ㄎㄢ 丨ㄣˋ)
to print for publication

刊物(ㄎㄢ ㄨˋ)
a periodical; a publication

刊誤表 or 勘誤表(ㄎㄢ ㄨˋ ㄅ丨ㄠˇ)
a list of corrections attached to a publication; errata

四畫

【刎】 363 ㄨㄣˇ woen wěn
to cut the throat

刎頸之交(ㄨㄣˇ ㄐ丨ㄥˇ ㄓ ㄐ丨ㄠ)
ties between friends willing to sacrifice even life for each other; profound mutual devotion between friends

【刑】 364 ㄒ丨ㄥˊ shyng xíng
penalty; punishment

刑不上大夫(ㄒ丨ㄥˊ ㄅㄨˋ ㄕㄤˋ ㄉㄞˋ ㄈㄨ)
(in feudal China) High officials are exempt from the penalties prescribed the law.

刑部(ㄒ丨ㄥˊ ㄅㄨˋ)
the Ministry of Justice (one of the six major government branches in former times)

刑名(ㄒ丨ㄥˊ ㄇ丨ㄥˊ)
laws

刑名之學(ㄒ丨ㄥˊ ㄇ丨ㄥˊ ㄓ ㄒㄩㄝˊ)
the philosophy of the Legalist School in the period of Warring States

刑罰(ㄒ丨ㄥˊ ㄈㄚˊ)
penalty; punishment

刑法(ㄒ丨ㄥˊ ㄈㄚˇ)
criminal law; the criminal code; the penal code: 別觸犯刑法。Don't violate criminal law.

刑典(ㄒ丨ㄥˊ ㄉ丨ㄢˇ)
the criminal code; the penal code

刑戮(ㄒ丨ㄥˊ ㄌㄨˋ)
to kill as penalty

刑具(ㄒ丨ㄥˊ ㄐㄩˋ)
an instrument of torture

刑期(ㄒ丨ㄥˊ ㄑ丨ˊ)
a term of imprisonment

刑求(ㄒ丨ㄥˊ ㄑ丨ㄡˊ)
to exact confession by means of torture

刑杖(ㄒ丨ㄥˊ ㄓㄤˋ)
a club, or rod, for torture

刑場(ㄒ丨ㄥˊ ㄔㄤˇ)or(ㄒ丨ㄥˊ ㄔㄤˊ)
an execution ground

刑事(ㄒ丨ㄥˊ ㄕˋ)
criminal; penal

刑事犯(ㄒ丨ㄥˊ ㄕˋ ㄈㄢˋ)
a criminal; a criminal suspect

刑事訴訟法(ㄒ丨ㄥˊ ㄕˋ ㄙㄨˋ ㄙㄨㄥˋ ㄈㄚˇ)
the code of criminal procedure

刑網(ㄒ丨ㄥˊ ㄨㄤˇ)
the criminal code

【划】 365 ㄏㄨㄚˊ hwa huá
to oar; to row

划拳(ㄏㄨㄚˊ ㄑㄩㄢˊ)
① a finger-guessing game—a drinking game at feasts ② to play the finger-guessing game, each putting out one hand and guessing the total of the two parties 亦作「豁拳」

划船(ㄏㄨㄚˊ ㄔㄨㄢˊ)
to row a boat

划子(ㄏㄨㄚˊ ·ㄗ)
a small boat

划算(ㄏㄨㄚˊ ㄙㄨㄢˋ)
①to calculate; to weigh ② profitable; advantageous

【刓】 366 ㄨㄢˊ wan wán
to round off; to trim

【刖】 367 ㄩㄝˋ yueh yuè
to cut off the feet as a punishment

【列】 368 ㄌ丨ㄝˋ lieh liè
1. to arrange in a line; to line up: 將軍整列他的隊伍。The general lined up his troops.
2. to enumerate
3. to display
4. a line; a series: 沿着池塘有一列柳樹。Along the pond there is a line of willows.
5. a Chinese family name

列表(ㄌ丨ㄝˋ ㄅ丨ㄠˇ)
to prepare a list or chart

列名(ㄌ丨ㄝˋ ㄇ丨ㄥˊ)
to appear on a name list

列島(ㄌ丨ㄝˋ ㄉㄠˇ)
a chain of islands; an archipelago

列土分疆(ㄌ丨ㄝˋ ㄊㄨˇ ㄈㄣ ㄐ丨ㄤ)
(said of the first emperor of a dynasty) to award fiefs to the chief lieutenants

列寧(ㄌ丨ㄝˋ ㄋ丨ㄥˊ)
Nikolai Lenin, 1870-1924, Russian revolutionary

列寧格勒(ㄌ丨ㄝˋ ㄋ丨ㄥˊ ㄍㄜˊ ㄌㄜˋ)
Leningrad

列國(ㄌ丨ㄝˋ ㄍㄨㄛˊ)
the various states or nations

列舉(ㄌ丨ㄝˋ ㄐㄩˇ)
to enumerate; to cite or mention item by item

〔刀部〕

列強(ㄌㄧㄝˋ ㄑㄧㄤˊ)
the various powers; an array of powerful nations
列清單(ㄌㄧㄝˋ ㄑㄧㄥ ㄉㄢ)
to list in detail
列席(ㄌㄧㄝˋ ㄒㄧˊ)
to be present (at a meeting as an observer); to attend a meeting with no voting right
列傳(ㄌㄧㄝˋ ㄓㄨㄢˋ)
collected biographies; a collection of biographies
列車(ㄌㄧㄝˋ ㄔㄜ)
a train
列入(ㄌㄧㄝˋ ㄖㄨˋ)
to be included in; to be incorporated in
列子(ㄌㄧㄝˋ ㄗˇ)
a book in philosophy written by Lieh Yü-kou (列禦寇) of the Chou Dynasty, some time right after Confucius, considered as a Taoist classic
列祖列宗(ㄌㄧㄝˋ ㄗㄨˇ ㄌㄧㄝˋ ㄗㄨㄥ)
an array of ancestors
列為(ㄌㄧㄝˋ ㄨㄟˊ)
listed as
列位(ㄌㄧㄝˋ ㄨㄟˋ)
all the ladies and gentlemen present (on this occasion)

五畫

【初】 369
ㄔㄨ chu chū
1. first
2. original: 最初的計畫後來改變了。The original plan was afterwards changed.
3. junior
4. early; initial: 初夏蟬鳴。Cicadas chirp in the early summer.

初版(ㄔㄨ ㄅㄢˇ)
the first edition (of a book)
初步(ㄔㄨ ㄅㄨˋ)
① the first or initial step ② a primer, or the rudimentary knowledge of something
初民(ㄔㄨ ㄇㄧㄣˊ)
primitive people
初犯(ㄔㄨ ㄈㄢˋ)
① first offenses ② a first offender
初等(ㄔㄨ ㄉㄥˇ)
primary or elementary (grade)
初等教育(ㄔㄨ ㄉㄥˇ ㄐㄧㄠˋ ㄩˋ)
elementary education; primary education
初度(ㄔㄨ ㄉㄨˋ)
① one's birthday ② the first time
初冬(ㄔㄨ ㄉㄨㄥ)
early winter
初唐(ㄔㄨ ㄊㄤˊ)
(the poetic style of) the early Tang Dynasty
初露鋒芒(ㄔㄨ ㄌㄡˋ ㄈㄥ ㄇㄤˊ)
to display one's ability for the first time
初戀(ㄔㄨ ㄌㄧㄢˋ)
first love
初稿(ㄔㄨ ㄍㄠˇ)
the first draft (of a poem, play, novel, etc.)
初會(ㄔㄨ ㄏㄨㄟˋ)
the first meeting (between people who are previously strangers)
初婚(ㄔㄨ ㄏㄨㄣ)
the first marriage (of a person who has remarried)
初級(ㄔㄨ ㄐㄧˊ)
elementary; primary
初級小學(ㄔㄨ ㄐㄧˊ ㄒㄧㄠˇ ㄒㄩㄝˊ)or 初小(ㄔㄨ ㄒㄧㄠˇ)
formerly, a primary school which comprises only the first four grades
初級中學(ㄔㄨ ㄐㄧˊ ㄓㄨㄥ ㄒㄩㄝˊ)or 初中(ㄔㄨ ㄓㄨㄥ)
junior middle school (corresponding to the seventh through the ninth grades)
初階(ㄔㄨ ㄐㄧㄝ)
a primer, or the rudimentary knowledge of something
初交(ㄔㄨ ㄐㄧㄠ)
a new friendship; a nodding acquaintance
初更(ㄔㄨ ㄐㄧㄥ)
the first watch (between 7 and 9 p.m.)
初經期(ㄔㄨ ㄐㄧㄥ ㄑㄧˊ)
menarche
初期(ㄔㄨ ㄑㄧˊ)
the first or initial stage; the early or earlier stages
初秋(ㄔㄨ ㄑㄧㄡ)
early autumn; early fall; the first of the autumn months (i.e., the seventh moon)
初夏(ㄔㄨ ㄒㄧㄚˋ)
early summer; the first of the summer months (i.e., the fourth moon)
初學(ㄔㄨ ㄒㄩㄝˊ)
① in the beginning stage of an effort to learn (a subject) ② a beginner
初選(ㄔㄨ ㄒㄩㄢˇ)
a primary election
初旬(ㄔㄨ ㄒㄩㄣˊ)
the first ten days of a month
初志(ㄔㄨ ㄓˋ)
the original ambition (of a youth)
初診(ㄔㄨ ㄓㄣˇ)
① the first visit to a doctor ② to visit a patient for the first time
初衷(ㄔㄨ ㄓㄨㄥ)
the original longing, aspiration, or intention
初產婦(ㄔㄨ ㄔㄢˇ ㄈㄨˋ)
a primiparous woman
初出茅廬(ㄔㄨ ㄔㄨ ㄇㄠˊ ㄌㄨˊ)
still inexperienced
初春(ㄔㄨ ㄔㄨㄣ)
early spring; the first of the spring months (i.e., the first moon)
初創(ㄔㄨ ㄔㄨㄤˋ)
newly founded
初蝕(ㄔㄨ ㄕˊ)or 初虧(ㄔㄨ ㄎㄨㄟ)
(astronomy) the first contact
初試(ㄔㄨ ㄕˋ)
① to try or attempt for the first time; the first trial or attempt ②to make a debut ③a preliminary examination or test
初審(ㄔㄨ ㄕㄣˇ)
① a first hearing (of a case in court) ② a preliminary screening (of applications, entries in a contest, etc.)
初生之犢不畏虎(ㄔㄨ ㄕㄥ ㄓ ㄉㄨˊ ㄅㄨˋ ㄨㄟˋ ㄏㄨˇ)
(literally) A newborn calf doesn't fear the tiger.—Young men fresh from school are uncompromising despite difficulties of pressure from above.
初日(ㄔㄨ ㄖˋ)
the rising sun
初祖(ㄔㄨ ㄗㄨˇ)

the founder of a sect

初次(ㄔㄨ ㄘˋ)
the first time or occasion

初賽(ㄔㄨ ㄙㄞˋ)
a preliminary competition

初葉(ㄔㄨ ㄧㄝˋ)
the early years (of a century): 十八世紀初葉 the early years in the eighteenth century

初夜權(ㄔㄨ ㄧㄝˋ ㄑㄩㄢˊ)
jus primae noctis (the right of a feudal lord to the virginity of a maiden on her wedding night in medieval Europe)

初願(ㄔㄨ ㄩㄢˋ)
one's initial wish

【刪】 370 ㄕㄢ shan shān

to delete; to take out; to erase

刪補(ㄕㄢ ㄅㄨˇ)
to rid superfluities and fill inadequacies (in a writing); to revise

刪繁就簡(ㄕㄢ ㄈㄢˊ ㄐㄧㄡˋ ㄐㄧㄢˇ)
to simplify something by deleting the superfluous

刪訂(ㄕㄢ ㄉㄧㄥˋ)
to revise (an edition)

刪改(ㄕㄢ ㄍㄞˇ)
to remove superfluities and correct errors (in a writing); to revise

刪節(ㄕㄢ ㄐㄧㄝˊ) or 刪減(ㄕㄢ ㄐㄧㄢˇ)
to abridge or condense (a writing)

刪節號(ㄕㄢ ㄐㄧㄝˊ ㄏㄠˋ)
ellipsis (a punctuation mark)

刪削(ㄕㄢ ㄒㄩㄝˋ)
to delete, expunge, strike out, erase, or remove (superfluities from a writing)

刪除(ㄕㄢ ㄔㄨˊ)
to delete; to strike out

刪潤(ㄕㄢ ㄖㄨㄣˋ)
to revise and polish (a writing)

【判】 371 ㄆㄢˋ pann pàn

to judge; to conclude

判別(ㄆㄢˋ ㄅㄧㄝˊ)
to distinguish; to tell apart

判袂(ㄆㄢˋ ㄇㄟˋ)
(said of friends) to separate; to part

判明(ㄆㄢˋ ㄇㄧㄥˊ)
to distinguish

判定(ㄆㄢˋ ㄉㄧㄥˋ)
to judge; to decide

判斷(ㄆㄢˋ ㄉㄨㄢˋ)
① to judge; to decide; to conclude ② judgment, decision or conclusion

判例(ㄆㄢˋ ㄌㄧˋ)
(said of court decisions) a precedent

判官(ㄆㄢˋ ㄍㄨㄢ)
a fierce-looking judge in the afterlife court of law

判決(ㄆㄢˋ ㄐㄩㄝˊ)
a verdict; a sentence

判決書(ㄆㄢˋ ㄐㄩㄝˊ ㄕㄨ)
a verdict or sentence in writing

判處(ㄆㄢˋ ㄔㄨˇ)
to sentence; to condemn

判若兩人(ㄆㄢˋ ㄖㄨㄛˋ ㄌㄧㄤˇ ㄖㄣˊ)
to become a completely different person; to become completely unrecognizable

判罪(ㄆㄢˋ ㄗㄨㄟˋ)
to declare guilty

【別】 372 ㄅㄧㄝˊ bye bié

1. to part
2. to distinguish; to differentiate
3. other; another; different
4. (in imperative expressions) do not: 現在別走。Don't go yet.

別本(ㄅㄧㄝˊ ㄅㄣˇ)
a separate copy; a replica

別忙(ㄅㄧㄝˊ ㄇㄤˊ)
Don't hurry. 或 Don't busy yourself. 或 Take your time.

別苗頭(ㄅㄧㄝˊ ㄇㄧㄠˊ ㄊㄡˊ)
(informal) to match wits; to rival in competition

別名(ㄅㄧㄝˊ ㄇㄧㄥˊ) or 別號(ㄅㄧㄝˊ ㄏㄠˋ)
an alias; a second name

別的(ㄅㄧㄝˊ ˙ㄉㄜ)
other; different

別提(ㄅㄧㄝˊ ㄊㄧˊ)
We needn't mention it. 或 It's not necessary to say.

別體(ㄅㄧㄝˊ ㄊㄧˇ)
a different calligraphic style

別來(ㄅㄧㄝˊ ㄌㄞˊ)
① since parting ② do not

別離(ㄅㄧㄝˊ ㄌㄧˊ)
parting; separation

別管(ㄅㄧㄝˊ ㄍㄨㄢˇ)
no matter (who, what, etc.)

別館(ㄅㄧㄝˊ ㄍㄨㄢˇ)
a villa

別開生面(ㄅㄧㄝˊ ㄎㄞ ㄕㄥ ㄇㄧㄢˋ)
to introduce a novelty or novel feature

別集(ㄅㄧㄝˊ ㄐㄧˊ)
a separate collection or anthology (of literary works published individually)

別解(ㄅㄧㄝˊ ㄐㄧㄝˇ)
a new interpretation; an opinion from a different standpoint

別具隻眼(ㄅㄧㄝˊ ㄐㄩˋ ㄓ ㄧㄢˇ)
to have an original view or opinion

別具一格(ㄅㄧㄝˊ ㄐㄩˋ ㄧˊ ㄍㄜˊ)
having a unique (or distinctive) style

別緒(ㄅㄧㄝˊ ㄒㄩˋ)
the sorrow of parting

別致 or 別緻(ㄅㄧㄝˊ ㄓˋ)
original; fresh; new; novel

別針(ㄅㄧㄝˊ ㄓㄣ) or 別針兒(ㄅㄧㄝˊ ㄓㄜㄦ)
a safety pin; a pin; a brooch

別稱(ㄅㄧㄝˊ ㄔㄥ)
another name; an alternative name

別出心裁(ㄅㄧㄝˊ ㄔㄨ ㄒㄧㄣ ㄘㄞˊ)
(said of art or literary works, craftsmanship, etc.) ingenious; original

別史(ㄅㄧㄝˊ ㄕˇ)
a history compiled privately by someone, as distinguish from an official history

別室(ㄅㄧㄝˊ ㄕˋ)
① a concubine ② another room

別生枝節(ㄅㄧㄝˊ ㄕㄥ ㄓ ㄐㄧㄝˊ)
to have new complications

別墅(ㄅㄧㄝˊ ㄕㄨˋ)
a villa; a country house

別樹一幟(ㄅㄧㄝˊ ㄕㄨˋ ㄧˊ ㄓˋ)
① to become independent; to become one's own master ② to start a business or style of one's own

別人(ㄅㄧㄝˊ ㄖㄣˊ)
other people; others

別字(ㄅㄧㄝˊ ㄗˋ)
①a word which is not correctly written or pronounced ②an alias

別有風味(ㄅㄧㄝˊ ㄧㄡˇ ㄈㄥ ㄨㄟˋ)
to have a unique flavor

別有天地(ㄅㄧㄝˊ ㄧㄡˇ ㄊㄧㄢ ㄉㄧˋ)
a different world (of delight)

別有所本(ㄅㄧㄝˊ ㄧㄡˇ ㄙㄨㄛˇ ㄅㄣˇ)
to be based on another source

別有所指(ㄅㄧㄝˊ ㄧㄡˇ ㄙㄨㄛˇ ㄓˇ)
to imply another thing

別有用心(ㄅㄧㄝˊ ㄧㄡˇ ㄩㄥˋ ㄒㄧㄣ)
to have a hidden purpose (in so doing or saying)

別樣(ㄅㄧㄝˊ ㄧㄤˋ)
of a different kind, sort, type, or fashion

別無所有(ㄅㄧㄝˊ ㄨˊ ㄙㄨㄛˇ ㄧㄡˇ)
to have no other possessions

【刨】 373 ㄆㄠˊ paur páo

to dig; to excavate

刨地(ㄆㄠˊ ㄉㄧˋ)
to dig the ground

刨根兒(ㄆㄠˊ ㄍㄜㄦ)
to dig out the truth

刨坑(ㄆㄠˊ ㄎㄥ)
to dig a pit or hole

刨挖(ㄆㄠˊ ㄨㄚ)
to dig; to excavate

【利】 374 ㄌㄧˋ lih lì

1. profit; benefit; advantage; gain: 這項買賣有利可圖。There are profits to be made in this transaction.
2. sharp: 這女人伶牙利齒。This woman is sharp-tongued.
3. to benefit; to serve: 新鐵路將有利於該地區。The new railway will benefit the district.

利比亞(ㄌㄧˋ ㄅㄧˇ ㄧㄚˇ)
Libya

利弊(ㄌㄧˋ ㄅㄧˋ)or 利病(ㄌㄧˋ ㄅㄧㄥˋ)
advantages and disadvantages

利便(ㄌㄧˋ ㄅㄧㄢˋ)
convenient; handy

利馬竇(ㄌㄧˋ ㄇㄚˇ ㄉㄡˋ)
Matteo Ricci, 1552-1610, Italian Jesuit missionary, who was the first one to introduce Western science to China

利鈍(ㄌㄧˋ ㄉㄨㄣˋ)
①smoothness and ruggedness ②fortune and misfortune; prosperity and adversity

利他主義(ㄌㄧˋ ㄊㄚ ㄓㄨˇ ㄧˋ)
altruism

利尿(ㄌㄧˋ ㄋㄧㄠˋ)
diuresis

利令智昏(ㄌㄧˋ ㄌㄧㄥˋ ㄓˋ ㄏㄨㄣ)
blinded or dulled by greed

利祿(ㄌㄧˋ ㄌㄨˋ)
wealth and position

利落(ㄌㄧˋ ㄌㄨㄛˋ)
neat; orderly 亦作「俐落」

利率(ㄌㄧˋ ㄌㄩˋ)
the interest rate

利國利民(ㄌㄧˋ ㄍㄨㄛˊ ㄌㄧˋ ㄇㄧㄣˊ)
to benefit the nation and the people

利害
①(ㄌㄧˋ ㄏㄞˋ) interest and disinterest; good and harm; advantages and disadvantages
②(ㄌㄧˋ ˙ㄏㄞ) sharp; shrewd

利害關係人(ㄌㄧˋ ㄏㄞˋ ㄍㄨㄢ ㄒㄧˋ ㄖㄣˊ)
the interested party

利己主義(ㄌㄧˋ ㄐㄧˇ ㄓㄨˇ ㄧˋ)
egoism

利器(ㄌㄧˋ ㄑㄧˋ)
①cutting instruments; cutlery ②a very useful and effective tool

利權外溢(ㄌㄧˋ ㄑㄩㄢˊ ㄨㄞˋ ㄧˋ)
the loss of economic rights (especially to foreigners)

利息(ㄌㄧˋ ㄒㄧˊ)
interest 亦作「利錢」

利支敦士登(ㄌㄧˋ ㄓ ㄉㄨㄣ ㄕˋ ㄉㄥ)
Liechtenstein, a small principality in central Europe

利之所在(ㄌㄧˋ ㄓ ㄙㄨㄛˇ ㄗㄞˋ)
something that offers a person the chance to enrich himself

利市三倍(ㄌㄧˋ ㄕˋ ㄙㄢ ㄅㄟˋ)or 利市百倍(ㄌㄧˋ ㄕˋ ㄅㄞˇ ㄅㄟˋ)
to make an enormous profit (in trade)

利上滾利(ㄌㄧˋ ㄕㄤˋ ㄍㄨㄣˇ ㄌㄧˋ)or 利上加利(ㄌㄧˋ ㄕㄤˋ ㄐㄧㄚ ㄌㄧˋ)
the yield of interest by interest; the yield of compound interest

利刃(ㄌㄧˋ ㄖㄣˋ)
a sharp blade; sharp-edged cutlery

利潤(ㄌㄧˋ ㄖㄨㄣˋ)
profit; gain; net profit

利益(ㄌㄧˋ ㄧˋ)
benefit; profit; advantage; good; gain

利益團體(ㄌㄧˋ ㄧˋ ㄊㄨㄢˊ ㄊㄧˇ)
an interest group

利益均霑(ㄌㄧˋ ㄧˋ ㄐㄩㄣ ㄓㄢ)
to let everybody have his hands on the pie

利誘(ㄌㄧˋ ㄧㄡˋ)
to tempt with money or material gain

利物浦(ㄌㄧˋ ㄨˋ ㄆㄨˇ)
Liverpool, a British seaport

利慾(ㄌㄧˋ ㄩˋ)
cupidity

利慾薰心(ㄌㄧˋ ㄩˋ ㄒㄩㄣ ㄒㄧㄣ)
blinded or dulled by greed; lured by profits

利源(ㄌㄧˋ ㄩㄢˊ)
the source of profit

利用(ㄌㄧˋ ㄩㄥˋ)
to utilize; to make use of; to take advantage of; to avail oneself of

利用厚生(ㄌㄧˋ ㄩㄥˋ ㄏㄡˋ ㄕㄥ)
to serve the requirements and to enrich the lives of the people

六畫

【刮】 375 ㄍㄨㄚ gua guā

to pare; to shave; to scrape

刮破(ㄍㄨㄚ ㄆㄛˋ)
to cut or hurt (the face, etc.) in shaving

刮平(ㄍㄨㄚ ㄆㄧㄥˊ)
to pare (so as to make the surface smooth)

刮摩(ㄍㄨㄚ ㄇㄛˊ)
to rub or scrape out

刮目相待(ㄍㄨㄚ ㄇㄨˋ ㄒㄧㄤ ㄉㄞˋ)or 刮目相看(ㄍㄨㄚ ㄇㄨˋ ㄒㄧㄤ ㄎㄢˋ)
to marvel at someone's progress or improvement

刮刀(ㄍㄨㄚ ㄉㄠ)
a scraping cutter; a scraper

刮地皮(ㄍㄨㄚ ㄉㄧˋ ㄆㄧˊ)
(said of corrupt local officials) to exact money from the people

刮臉(ㄍㄨㄚ ㄌㄧㄢˇ)
to shave (the face)

刮刮叫(ㄍㄨㄚ ㄍㄨㄚ ㄐㄧㄠˋ)
splendid; wonderful; tops; very good

刮鬍子(ㄍㄨㄚ ㄏㄨˊ ·ㄗ)
①to shave oneself; to shave ②(colloquial) to meet rejection; to be scolded

刮痧(ㄍㄨㄚ ㄕㄚ)
a popular medical treatment for sunstroke by scraping the patient's neck, chest or back with the fingers or a coin

【券】 376 ㄑㄩㄢˋ chiuann quàn

1. a ticket
2. a certificate
3. a bond

【到】 377 ㄉㄠˋ daw dào

1. to reach; to arrive: 火車何時到達此地? When does the train reach here?
2. a Chinese family name

到達(ㄉㄠˋ ㄉㄚˊ)
to reach; to arrive

到底(ㄉㄠˋ ㄉㄧˇ)
① after all; in the long run; at length; in the end; finally ② to reach the extremity

到頂(ㄉㄠˋ ㄉㄧㄥˇ)
① to reach the summit ② cannot be improved

到頭(ㄉㄠˋ ㄊㄡˊ)
to the end; at an end

到頭來(ㄉㄠˋ ㄊㄡˊ ㄌㄞˊ)
after all; in the long run; in the end

到來(ㄉㄠˋ ㄌㄞˊ)
arrival; coming; the advent

到會(ㄉㄠˋ ㄏㄨㄟˋ)
to be present at a meeting; to attend a meeting

到家(ㄉㄠˋ ㄐㄧㄚ)
① to get home ② to become proficient, or extremely well-versed; thorough

到齊(ㄉㄠˋ ㄑㄧˊ)
Everybody (who is supposed to be here) has come.

到期(ㄉㄠˋ ㄑㄧˊ)
(said of payment, a contract, etc.) to reach the deadline or date of termination; to expire

到職(ㄉㄠˋ ㄓˊ)
to arrive for a new assignment

到差(ㄉㄠˋ ㄔㄞ)
to arrive for a (junior official) post

到場(ㄉㄠˋ ㄔㄤˇ)or(ㄉㄠˋ ㄔㄤˊ)
to show up; to be present

到處(ㄉㄠˋ ㄔㄨˋ)
everywhere; on all sides; far and wide; all about

到處爲家(ㄉㄠˋ ㄔㄨˋ ㄨㄟˊ ㄐㄧㄚ)
Everywhere may be one's home.

到時(ㄉㄠˋ ㄕˊ)
by that time; when that time comes; by then

到手(ㄉㄠˋ ㄕㄡˇ)
to come into one's hands or possession

到任(ㄉㄠˋ ㄖㄣˋ)
to assume a (high official) post

到案(ㄉㄠˋ ㄢˋ)
to appear in court; to answer a court summons

【刳】 378 ㄎㄨ ku kū

1. to cut apart; to carve apart
2. to gouge; to scoop; to hollow

【刹】 379 (剎) ㄔㄚˋ chah chà

a (Buddhist) temple, shrine, monastery or abbey

刹那(ㄔㄚˋ ㄋㄚˋ)or(ㄔㄚˋ ㄋㄨㄛˋ)
a moment; an instant; a split second; (in) the twinkling of an eye

【剁】 380 ㄉㄨㄛˋ duoh duò

to chop; to mince; to hash

剁肉(ㄉㄨㄛˋ ㄖㄡˋ)
to mince or hash meat

剁碎(ㄉㄨㄛˋ ㄙㄨㄟˋ)
to mince; to hash

【制】 381 ㄓˋ jyh zhì

1. to establish; to institute; to set up
2. to prevail; to overpower; to control
3. a system: 學制 the educational system
4. used before the signature in letter writing to indicate the writer is in mourning
5. a Chinese family name

制伏(ㄓˋ ㄈㄨˊ)
to subdue; to subjugate; to prevail over; to overcome; to surmount; to overpower; to put down; to quell

制服(ㄓˋ ㄈㄨˊ)
① a uniform ② formerly, dress of mourning for one's parents

制敵機先(ㄓˋ ㄉㄧˊ ㄐㄧ ㄒㄧㄢ)
to gain an advantage over the enemy by taking steps to forestall him

制定(ㄓˋ ㄉㄧㄥˋ)
to institute; to establish; to set up; to introduce; to initiate; to draw up; to formulate; to work out

制度(ㄓˋ ㄉㄨˋ)
a system; an institution

制動機(ㄓˋ ㄉㄨㄥˋ ㄐㄧ)or 制動器(ㄓˋ ㄉㄨㄥˋ ㄑㄧˋ)
a brake

制禮作樂(ㄓˋ ㄌㄧˇ ㄗㄨㄛˋ ㄩㄝˋ)
to establish rules for ceremonies and to compose appropriate music for different occasions

制空權(ㄓˋ ㄎㄨㄥ ㄑㄩㄢˊ)
air supremacy; air domination

制海權(ㄓˋ ㄏㄞˇ ㄑㄩㄢˊ)
naval supremacy; command of the sea

制衡(ㄓˋ ㄏㄥˊ)
to check and balance

制錢(ㄓˋ ㄑㄧㄢˊ)
coins officially designated for circulation

制限(ㄓˋ ㄒㄧㄢˋ)
① to restrict; to limit; to confine ② a bound; a limit; confines

制憲(ㄓˋ ㄒㄧㄢˋ)
to draw up a national constitution

制止(ㄓˋ ㄓˇ)
to stop by force; to stop; to prevent

制勝(ㄓˋ ㄕㄥˋ)
to be victorious; to prevail; to triumph; to win

制作(ㄓˋ ㄗㄨㄛˋ)
to formulate

制策(ㄓˋ ㄘㄜˋ)
an examination on political topics given by the emperor

〔刀部〕

in old China
制裁(ㄓˋ ㄘㄞˊ)
to restrain, suppress, or hold back by punitive measures; to chasten; to chastise; to sanction; a sanction
制壓(ㄓˋ ㄧㄚ)
①to overpower; to overwhelm; to suppress ②to neutralize (enemy fire)
制約(ㄓˋ ㄩㄝ)
to restrict; to condition: 兩者互相制約。The two condition each other.

【刷】 382
1. ㄕㄨㄚ shua shuā
1. to brush; to scrub; to clean; to daub
2. a brush: 牙刷 a toothbrush
3. to eliminate
刷馬(ㄕㄨㄚ ㄇㄚˇ)
to curry a horse
刷清(ㄕㄨㄚ ㄑㄧㄥ)
to clear (oneself) of a charge
刷洗(ㄕㄨㄚ ㄒㄧˇ)
to scrub: 他將地板刷洗乾淨。He scrubs the floor clean.
刷新(ㄕㄨㄚ ㄒㄧㄣ)
①to make like new (by cleaning, repainting, etc.); to renovate ②to make (a new sports record); to break the records
刷恥(ㄕㄨㄚ ㄔˇ)
to wipe away disgrace
刷子(ㄕㄨㄚ ˙ㄗ)
a brush
刷牙(ㄕㄨㄚ ㄧㄚˊ)
to brush the teeth
刷印(ㄕㄨㄚ ㄧㄣˋ)
to print

【刷】 382
2. ㄕㄨㄚˋ shuah shuà
參看「刷白」、「刷選」
刷白(ㄕㄨㄚˋ ㄅㄞˊ)
(said of face) pale
刷選(ㄕㄨㄚˋ ㄒㄩㄢˇ)
to choose; to pick; to select

【刺】 383
ㄘˋ tsyh cì
1. to pierce; to stab; to prick
2. to irritate; to stimulate
3. a thorn; a splinter; small fishbones; a sting
4. to assassinate
5. a name card
刺鼻(ㄘˋ ㄅㄧˊ)
to irritate the nose
刺目(ㄘˋ ㄇㄨˋ)or 刺眼(ㄘˋ ㄧㄢˇ)
irritating to the eye; dazzling
刺刀(ㄘˋ ㄉㄠ)
a bayonet: 上刺刀 to fix bayonets
刺探(ㄘˋ ㄊㄢˋ)
to spy; to find out secretly
刺桐(ㄘˋ ㄊㄨㄥˊ)
Erythrina variegata orientalis
刺股(ㄘˋ ㄍㄨˇ)
to pierce one's thigh with an awl to prevent oneself from falling asleep, an allusion to Su Chin (蘇秦)—(figuratively) extremely diligent in studying
刺股讀書(ㄘˋ ㄍㄨˇ ㄉㄨˊ ㄕㄨ)
to study hard in defiance of hardships
刺骨(ㄘˋ ㄍㄨˇ)
① (said of cold) bone-chilling ② (said of hatred) bitter or deep
刺客(ㄘˋ ㄎㄜˋ)
an assassin
刺激(ㄘˋ ㄐㄧ)
to stimulate; to provoke; to excite; to irritate; to upset; a stimulus
刺激品(ㄘˋ ㄐㄧ ㄆㄧㄣˇ)or 刺激物(ㄘˋ ㄐㄧ ㄨˋ)
a stimulant; a stimulus
刺激性(ㄘˋ ㄐㄧ ㄒㄧㄥˋ)
stimulativeness; stimulancy; stimulability
刺激作用(ㄘˋ ㄐㄧ ㄗㄨㄛˋ ㄩㄥˋ)
stimulation
刺青(ㄘˋ ㄑㄧㄥ)
to tattoo; a tattoo
刺繡(ㄘˋ ㄒㄧㄡˋ)
to embroider; embroidery
刺史(ㄘˋ ㄕˇ)
(formerly) a provincial governor; a prefectural governor; a district magistrate
刺殺(ㄘˋ ㄕㄚ)
①to assassinate ②(baseball) to put out (a base runner)
刺字(ㄘˋ ㄗˋ)
to tattoo or brand a convict on the face or the arm (usually as a punishment)
刺刺不休(ㄘˋ ㄘˋ ㄅㄨˋ ㄒㄧㄡ)
to chatter without stop; to gabble on and on
刺兒(ㄘㄜˋㄦ)
a thorn
刺耳(ㄘˋ ㄦˇ)
unpleasant to the ear; noisy; harsh; screechy; grating; ear-piercing
刺蝟(ㄘˋ ㄨㄟˋ)
a hedgehog

【刻】 384
1. ㄎㄜˋ keh kè
1. to carve; to engrave; to cut
2. a quarter (of an hour): 三點一刻 a quarter past three
3. cruel; heartless; unfeeling; cutting; harshly; acrimonious; biting
4. moment
刻薄(ㄎㄜˋ ㄅㄛˊ)
cold-hearted; unfeeling; unkind; acrimonious; mean; caustic
刻薄寡恩(ㄎㄜˋ ㄅㄛˊ ㄍㄨㄚˇ ㄣ)
to treat harshly and to give rare generosity
刻板(ㄎㄜˋ ㄅㄢˇ)
①to engrave (for printing) ②monotonous; dull; stereotyped; stiff; mechanical; inflexible
刻本(ㄎㄜˋ ㄅㄣˇ)
a printed copy (printed from engraved blocks)
刻不容緩(ㄎㄜˋ ㄅㄨˋ ㄖㄨㄥˊ ㄏㄨㄢˇ)
most urgent; to brook no delay 或 Not a moment is to be lost.
刻刀(ㄎㄜˋ ㄉㄠ)
a knife used in carving; a burin; a graver
刻毒(ㄎㄜˋ ㄉㄨˊ)
wicked; fiendish; devilish; cruel; venomous; spiteful
刻度(ㄎㄜˋ ㄉㄨˋ)
graduations (on a vessel or an instrument)
刻漏(ㄎㄜˋ ㄌㄡˋ)
a clepsydra; an ancient water clock with hour markings
刻骨(ㄎㄜˋ ㄍㄨˇ)
deeply ingrained
刻骨銘心(ㄎㄜˋ ㄍㄨˇ ㄇㄧㄥˊ ㄒㄧㄣ)
to permanently imprint (another's favor, etc.) on the mind; to remember with

gratitude constantly and forever

刻苦(ㄎㄜˋ ㄎㄨˇ)
① assiduous; hardworking: 他刻苦研讀。He studies assiduously. ② simple and frugal

刻苦耐勞(ㄎㄜˋ ㄎㄨˇ ㄋㄞˋ ㄌㄠˊ)
to endure hardship; to work hard without complaint

刻苦成家(ㄎㄜˋ ㄎㄨˇ ㄔㄥˊ ㄐㄧㄚ)
to build up a family by hard work and frugality

刻畫(ㄎㄜˋ ㄏㄨㄚˋ)
to depict; to portray

刻畫入微(ㄎㄜˋ ㄏㄨㄚˋ ㄖㄨˋ ㄨㄟˊ)
vivid portrayal of details; realistic portrayal of a character

刻己待人(ㄎㄜˋ ㄐㄧˇ ㄉㄞˋ ㄖㄣˊ)
self-sacrificing; self-denial in service to others

刻期(ㄎㄜˋ ㄑㄧˊ)
punctually on a fixed date

刻峭(ㄎㄜˋ ㄑㄧㄠˋ)
①(said of terrain features) rugged ② cruel; relentless; ruthless ③(said of writings) pungency or incisiveness

刻舟求劍(ㄎㄜˋ ㄓㄡ ㄑㄧㄡˊ ㄐㄧㄢˋ)
to carve a mark on the side of one's boat to indicate the place where one's sword has dropped into the water —(figuratively) ridiculous stupidity; to be stubbornly unimaginative; a very stupid way of doing things

刻石(ㄎㄜˋ ㄕˊ)
to engrave (writings) on stone

刻書(ㄎㄜˋ ㄕㄨ)
(in ancient China) to carve the words of a book on wood blocks for printing—to publish a book

刻日(ㄎㄜˋ ㄖˋ)
this very date; a fixed day

刻字(ㄎㄜˋ ㄗˋ)
to engrave words (on stone, blocks, etc.)

刻意(ㄎㄜˋ ㄧˋ)
to do something with intensive attention (in order to achieve perfection or great success); painstakingly

刻意求工(ㄎㄜˋ ㄧˋ ㄑㄧㄡˊ ㄍㄨㄥ)
to strive sedulously for perfection

【刻】 384
2. ㄎㄜ ke kē
to carve; to engrave

刻印(ㄎㄜ ㄧㄣˋ) or 刻圖章(ㄎㄜ ㄊㄨˊ ㄓㄤ)
to make a chop by carving; seal engraving

七畫

【則】 385
ㄗㄜˊ tzer zé
1. a law; a rule; a regulation; a standard; a norm; a criterion
2. a particle indicating consequence (usually used after a supposition) or a reason
3. a numerary particle used before news reports, advertisements, etc.: 那是則有趣的報導。It is an interesting piece of news.
4. but; however: 人皆好名利，我則不然。Others may be fond of fame and wealth, but I am not.
5. to imitate; to follow

則聲(ㄗㄜˊ ㄕㄥ)
to make a sound; to utter a word: 她不敢則聲。She dare not utter a word.

【剃】 386
ㄊㄧˋ tih tì
to shave: 我把我的鬍子剃掉了。I have shaved my beard.

剃髮修行(ㄊㄧˋ ㄈㄚˇ ㄒㄧㄡ ㄒㄧㄥˊ)
(Buddhism) to cut off one's hair and be a monk or nun

剃刀(ㄊㄧˋ ㄉㄠ)
a razor

剃度(ㄊㄧˋ ㄉㄨˋ)
to cut off hair and join a monastery; to tonsure

剃頭(ㄊㄧˋ ㄊㄡˊ)
to shave the head

剃頭店(ㄊㄧˋ ㄊㄡˊ ㄉㄧㄢˋ) or 剃頭鋪(ㄊㄧˋ ㄊㄡˊ ㄆㄨˋ)
a barbershop

【剄】 387
ㄐㄧㄥˇ jiing jǐng
to cut the throat: 自剄 to commit suicide by cutting the throat

【剉】 388
ㄘㄨㄛˋ tsuoh cuò
1. a steel file
2. to file; to smooth (as with a file); to cut; to chop up into fine pieces

剉平(ㄘㄨㄛˋ ㄆㄧㄥˊ)
to smoothen even

剉光(ㄘㄨㄛˋ ㄍㄨㄤ)
to polish fine

剉子(ㄘㄨㄛˋ ·ㄗ)
a file

【削】 389
ㄒㄩㄝˋ shiueh xuè
(語音 ㄒㄧㄠ shiau xiāo)
1. to cut; to pare; to shave; to whittle
2. to deprive

削壁(ㄒㄩㄝˋ ㄅㄧˋ)
a precipice; a cliff

削平(ㄒㄩㄝˋ ㄆㄧㄥˊ)
① to pare; to smooth (with a knife) ② to conquer; to put down; to suppress (a rebellion)

削木爲兵(ㄒㄩㄝˋ ㄇㄨˋ ㄨㄟˊ ㄅㄧㄥ)
(said of a plebeian uprising) to pare wooden poles and use them as weapons

削髮(ㄒㄩㄝˋ ㄈㄚˇ)
to shave the head (so as to become a Buddhist nun or monk)

削奪(ㄒㄩㄝˋ ㄉㄨㄛˊ)
to deprive (someone) of (power, rank, land, etc.); to take by force

削籍(ㄒㄩㄝˋ ㄐㄧˊ)
to dismiss an official from a government post

削價(ㄒㄩㄝˋ ㄐㄧㄚˋ)
to cut price to or below the cost level

削減(ㄒㄩㄝˋ ㄐㄧㄢˇ)
to curtail; to cut down; to slash

削職(ㄒㄩㄝˋ ㄓˊ)
to deprive a person of a position

削趾適履(ㄒㄩㄝˋ ㄓˇ ㄕˋ ㄌㄩˇ)
(literally) to cut the feet to fit the shoes—an impractical solution of a problem 亦作「削足適履」

削除(ㄒㄩㄝˋ ㄔㄨˊ)
to strike out; to take out; to omit

削弱(ㄒㄩㄝˋ ㄖㄨㄛˋ)
to enfeeble; to weaken; to sap; to devitalize

削葱(ㄒㄩㄝ ㄘㄨㄥ)
slender fingers of a lady

【剋】 390
ㄎㄜˋ keh kè
1. to overcome
2. to cut down
3. to limit
4. to engrave; to imprint
5. can; to be able to

剋夫(ㄎㄜˋ ㄈㄨ)
to be fated to mourn one's husband's death

剋扣(ㄎㄜˋ ㄎㄡˋ)
to withhold (military supplies, etc.) for personal gain

剋妻(ㄎㄜˋ ㄑㄧ)
to be fated to mourn one's wife's death

剋期(ㄎㄜˋ ㄑㄧˊ)or 剋日(ㄎㄜˋ ㄖˋ)
① to set a time limit ② on a set date

剋星(ㄎㄜˋ ㄒㄧㄥ)
(literally) a malignant star —a person who always bars another person from success; an unbeatable rival; a jinx

【剌】 391
1. ㄌㄚˋ lah là
to go against; to contradict; perverse; disagreeable; rebellious

剌子(ㄌㄚˋ ·ㄗ)
① a person hard-hearted by nature ② a ruby

【剌】 391
2. ㄌㄚˊ la lá
to slash open

剌破(ㄌㄚˊ ㄆㄛˋ)
to cut

剌開(ㄌㄚˊ ㄎㄞ)
to slash open

【前】 392
ㄑㄧㄢˊ chyan qián
1. front; forward; before
2. previous; former; preceding; past; of earlier times: 前任總統 the former president
3. future: 他是一位很有前途的年輕人。He is a young man with a future.
4. to advance; to proceed; to progress; to precede

前輩(ㄑㄧㄢˊ ㄅㄟˋ)
a senior (in age, standing, length of service, etc.)

前半天(ㄑㄧㄢˊ ㄅㄢˋ ㄊㄧㄢ)
forenoon; morning

前半夜(ㄑㄧㄢˊ ㄅㄢˋ ㄧㄝˋ)
the first half of the night (from nightfall to midnight)

前邊(ㄑㄧㄢˊ ㄅㄧㄢ)or 前邊兒(ㄑㄧㄢˊ ㄅㄧㄚㄦ)
① the front; the front side; the fore part ② ahead; in front; preceding

前怕狼，後怕虎(ㄑㄧㄢˊ ㄆㄚˋ ㄌㄤˊ, ㄏㄡˋ ㄆㄚˋ ㄏㄨˇ)
to fear wolves ahead and tigers behind—to be full of fears

前排(ㄑㄧㄢˊ ㄆㄞˊ)
the front row

前仆後繼(ㄑㄧㄢˊ ㄆㄨ ㄏㄡˋ ㄐㄧˋ)
(usually said of bravery of soldiers in battle) Behind the fallen is an endless column of successors.

前茅(ㄑㄧㄢˊ ㄇㄠˊ)
① a (military) patrol ② the top of the list (of successful candidates in an examination)

前門(ㄑㄧㄢˊ ㄇㄣˊ)or 前門兒(ㄑㄧㄢˊ ㄇㄜˊㄦ)
the front door or gate: 請打開前門。Please open the front door.

前門拒虎，後門進狼(ㄑㄧㄢˊ ㄇㄣˊ ㄐㄩˋ ㄏㄨˇ, ㄏㄡˋ ㄇㄣˊ ㄐㄧㄣˋ ㄌㄤˊ)
to drive the tiger out of the front door and let a wolf in at the back—to fend off one danger only to fall a prey to another

前面(ㄑㄧㄢˊ ㄇㄧㄢˋ)
① the front; the front side ② ahead; in front; preceding: 公園就在前面。The park is right ahead.

前番(ㄑㄧㄢˊ ㄈㄢ)
the last time

前方(ㄑㄧㄢˊ ㄈㄤ)
① the front (in war): 我們必須盡力支援前方。We must do our best to support the front. ② the forward direction

前鋒(ㄑㄧㄢˊ ㄈㄥ)
the vanguard; the van

前夫(ㄑㄧㄢˊ ㄈㄨ)
the former husband (of a woman who has remarried)

前俯後仰(ㄑㄧㄢˊ ㄈㄨˇ ㄏㄡˋ ㄧㄤˇ)
to bend forwards and backwards

前導(ㄑㄧㄢˊ ㄉㄠˇ)or(ㄑㄧㄢˊ ㄉㄠˋ)
the guide or motorcade (of an official party on the road)

前定(ㄑㄧㄢˊ ㄉㄧㄥˋ)
predestined; decided beforehand

前度劉郎(ㄑㄧㄢˊ ㄉㄨˋ ㄌㄧㄡˊ ㄌㄤˊ)
a person who returns to a place he once abandoned

前臺(ㄑㄧㄢˊ ㄊㄞˊ)
the stage; the proscenium

前頭(ㄑㄧㄢˊ ·ㄊㄡ)
① in front; ahead ② before

前膛鎗(ㄑㄧㄢˊ ㄊㄤˊ ㄑㄧㄤ)
a muzzle-loading gun

前提(ㄑㄧㄢˊ ㄊㄧˊ)
① a (logical) premise: 小前提 the minor premise 大前提 the major premise ② the primary consideration; a prerequisite

前天(ㄑㄧㄢˊ ㄊㄧㄢ)
the day before yesterday

前廳(ㄑㄧㄢˊ ㄊㄧㄥ)
an antechamber

前途(ㄑㄧㄢˊ ㄊㄨˊ)
the prospect; promise (in the sense of an indication of a successful prospect or future): 他的事業前途樂觀。He has good prospects in business.

前途茫茫(ㄑㄧㄢˊ ㄊㄨˊ ㄇㄤˊ ㄇㄤˊ)
One's future is indefinite.

前途無量(ㄑㄧㄢˊ ㄊㄨˊ ㄨˊ ㄌㄧㄤˋ)
to have boundless prospects

前腦(ㄑㄧㄢˊ ㄋㄠˇ)
(anatomy) the forebrain

前年(ㄑㄧㄢˊ ㄋㄧㄢˊ)
the year before last

前例(ㄑㄧㄢˊ ㄌㄧˋ)
a precedent: 此事違反所有前例。It is against all precedents.

前列(ㄑㄧㄢˊ ㄌㄧㄝˋ)
the front row; the forefront; the van

前輪(ㄑㄧㄢˊ ㄌㄨㄣˊ)
①(vehicle) the front wheel ②(airplane) the nosewheel

前滾翻(ㄑㄧㄢˊ ㄍㄨㄣˇ ㄈㄢ)
(sports) a forward roll

前功盡棄(ㄑㄧㄢˊ ㄍㄨㄥ ㄐㄧㄣˋ ㄑㄧˋ)
to nullify all the previous efforts; to turn all the previ-

ous labor to nothing 或 All one's previous efforts are wasted.

前科(ㄑㄧㄢˊ ㄎㄜ)
a previous criminal record; a record of previous crime

前科犯(ㄑㄧㄢˊ ㄎㄜ ㄈㄢˋ)
an ex-convict

前款(ㄑㄧㄢˊ ㄎㄨㄢˇ)
(used in legal documents or code of law) the aforesaid clause or item

前後(ㄑㄧㄢˊ ㄏㄡˋ)
① the front and the rear; before and after: 我軍前後受敵。Our troops were attacked by the enemy both front and rear. ② (indicating time) around; about: 中秋節前後 around the Moon Festival ③ from beginning to end; altogether: 這項工程從動工到完成，前後只花了一年。The entire task, from beginning to end, took only one year.

前後矛盾(ㄑㄧㄢˊ ㄏㄡˋ ㄇㄠˊ ㄉㄨㄣˋ)
inconsistent; contradictory: 他對於發生事件的敍述前後矛盾。His account of what happened was inconsistent.

前後左右(ㄑㄧㄢˊ ㄏㄡˋ ㄗㄨㄛˇ ㄧㄡˋ)
on all sides; all around

前漢(ㄑㄧㄢˊ ㄏㄢˋ) or 西漢(ㄒㄧ ㄏㄢˋ)
the Former Han Dynasty (206 B.C.—8 A.D.)

前呼後擁(ㄑㄧㄢˊ ㄏㄨ ㄏㄡˋ ㄩㄥˇ)
(said of VIPs) with a large retinue; with many attendants crowding round

前回(ㄑㄧㄢˊ ㄏㄨㄟˊ)
① last time ② the last chapter (of a novel)

前街後巷(ㄑㄧㄢˊ ㄐㄧㄝ ㄏㄡˋ ㄒㄧㄤˋ)
front streets and back lanes —everywhere

前脚(ㄑㄧㄢˊ ㄐㄧㄠˇ)
the forward foot in a step

前進(ㄑㄧㄢˊ ㄐㄧㄣˋ)
to advance; to proceed; to go forward; to progress: 人群向車站前進。The crowd advanced towards the station.

前經(ㄑㄧㄢˊ ㄐㄧㄥ) or 前已(ㄑㄧㄢˊ ㄧˇ)
(indicating time) already; before

前景(ㄑㄧㄢˊ ㄐㄧㄥˇ)
① a foreground ② the foreground of a painting ③ prospects; vistas; perspectives: 她在繪畫方面有美好的前景。She has good prospects in painting.

前車之鑒(ㄑㄧㄢˊ ㄐㄩ ㄓ ㄐㄧㄢˋ) or 前車之覆，後車之鑒(ㄑㄧㄢˊ ㄐㄩ ㄓ ㄈㄨˋ, ㄏㄡˋ ㄐㄩ ㄓ ㄐㄧㄢˋ)
warning taken from the overturned cart ahead—a lesson from the failure of one's predecessor

前倨後恭(ㄑㄧㄢˊ ㄐㄩˋ ㄏㄡˋ ㄍㄨㄥ)
proud at first but humble afterwards; to change from arrogance to humility —(figuratively) to change one's attitude snobbishly

前妻(ㄑㄧㄢˊ ㄑㄧ)
the former wife (of a man who has remarried)

前愆(ㄑㄧㄢˊ ㄑㄧㄢ)
past errors or faults

前前後後(ㄑㄧㄢˊ ㄑㄧㄢˊ ㄏㄡˋ ㄏㄡˋ)
the whole story; the ins and outs

前情(ㄑㄧㄢˊ ㄑㄧㄥˊ)
① a relevant past event; past affairs ② the past relevant cause

前驅(ㄑㄧㄢˊ ㄑㄩ)
the forerunner; the vanguard; the van; the precursor; the harbinger; the prelude

前夕(ㄑㄧㄢˊ ㄒㄧˋ)
the eve (of an event)

前賢(ㄑㄧㄢˊ ㄒㄧㄢˊ) or 前哲(ㄑㄧㄢˊ ㄓㄜˊ) or 前脩(ㄑㄧㄢˊ ㄒㄧㄡ)
the wise men of the past

前嫌(ㄑㄧㄢˊ ㄒㄧㄢˊ)
a past grudge

前線(ㄑㄧㄢˊ ㄒㄧㄢˋ)
the front line (in war); the front

前項(ㄑㄧㄢˊ ㄒㄧㄤˋ)
the aforesaid or the above-mentioned item; the preceding article or clause (used in legal documents)

前置詞(ㄑㄧㄢˊ ㄓˋ ㄘˊ)
a preposition 亦作「介系詞」

前者(ㄑㄧㄢˊ ㄓㄜˇ)
the former

前兆(ㄑㄧㄢˊ ㄓㄠˋ)
an omen; forewarning; a premonition; an augury; a forerunner; a harbinger: 這是成功的前兆。This is an omen of success.

前站(ㄑㄧㄢˊ ㄓㄢˋ)
the next stop or railway station

前塵(ㄑㄧㄢˊ ㄔㄣˊ)
① (Buddhism) previous impure conditions, influencing the succeeding stage or stages ② what has happened in the past

前程(ㄑㄧㄢˊ ㄔㄥˊ)
① a future; prospects ② a career: 恐怕他前程保不住了。I am afraid his career is finished.

前程似錦(ㄑㄧㄢˊ ㄔㄥˊ ㄙˋ ㄐㄧㄣˇ)
to have brilliant prospects

前程萬里(ㄑㄧㄢˊ ㄔㄥˊ ㄨㄢˋ ㄌㄧˇ)
to have the prospect of a very successful career

前世(ㄑㄧㄢˊ ㄕˋ)
① the previous generation ② the previous life (by the concept of life and death as a cycle)

前事不忘，後事之師(ㄑㄧㄢˊ ㄕˋ ㄅㄨˋ ㄨㄤˋ, ㄏㄡˋ ㄕˋ ㄓ ㄕ)
To remember past errors insures one against repetition of the same errors. 或 If one doesn't forget past experience, it will be a guide for one's future.

前哨(ㄑㄧㄢˊ ㄕㄠˋ)
(military) a sentry; an outpost; an advance guard

前身(ㄑㄧㄢˊ ㄕㄣ)
the forerunner (of a school, organization, etc.)

前生(ㄑㄧㄢˊ ㄕㄥ)
the former life or lives; the previous incarnation

前日(ㄑㄧㄢˊ ㄖˋ)
the day before yesterday

前人(ㄑㄧㄢˊ ㄖㄣˊ)
people of former times; forefathers; predecessors; people of the past

前人種樹，後人乘涼(ㄑㄧㄢˊ ㄖㄣˊ ㄓㄨㄥˋ ㄕㄨˋ, ㄏㄡˋ ㄖㄣˊ ㄔㄥˊ ㄌㄧㄤˊ)
One generation plants the trees under whose shade another generation rests.—

〔刀部〕

to profit from the labor of one's forefathers

前任(ㄑㄧㄢˊ ㄖㄣˋ)
a predecessor

前奏(ㄑㄧㄢˊ ㄗㄡˋ)
a prelude; a harbinger

前此(ㄑㄧㄢˊ ㄘˇ)
prior to that or this; before that or this

前次(ㄑㄧㄢˊ ㄘˋ)
the previous occasion; last time

前思後想(ㄑㄧㄢˊ ㄙ ㄏㄡˋ ㄒㄧㄤˇ)
to turn over (a problem) in one's mind; to ponder; to think over again and again

前所未見(ㄑㄧㄢˊ ㄙㄨㄛˇ ㄨㄟˋ ㄐㄧㄢˋ)
to have never seen before

前所未有(ㄑㄧㄢˊ ㄙㄨㄛˇ ㄨㄟˋ ㄧㄡˇ)
hitherto unknown; unprecedented

前所未聞(ㄑㄧㄢˊ ㄙㄨㄛˇ ㄨㄟˋ ㄨㄣˊ)
to have never heard of before

前額(ㄑㄧㄢˊ ㄜˊ)
the forehead

前夜(ㄑㄧㄢˊ ㄧㄝˋ)
the night before last

前言(ㄑㄧㄢˊ ㄧㄢˊ)
① previous remarks ② the words of past thinkers ③ a foreword; a preface; an introduction

前言不對後語(ㄑㄧㄢˊ ㄧㄢˊ ㄅㄨˋ ㄉㄨㄟˋ ㄏㄡˋ ㄩˇ)
self-contradictory; to talk incoherently

前因(ㄑㄧㄢˊ ㄧㄣ)
an antecedent; a cause

前因後果(ㄑㄧㄢˊ ㄧㄣ ㄏㄡˋ ㄍㄨㄛˇ)
cause and effect; the whole story; the ins and outs: 告訴我這件事的前因後果。Let me know the ins and outs of this incident.

前仰後合(ㄑㄧㄢˊ ㄧㄤˇ ㄏㄡˋ ㄏㄜˊ)
to shake one's sides with laughter; to split one's sides; to stagger forward and back

前無古人(ㄑㄧㄢˊ ㄨˊ ㄍㄨˇ ㄖㄣˊ)
(said of accomplishments) peerless; to have no predecessors; unprecedented

前衛(ㄑㄧㄢˊ ㄨㄟˋ)
① front line troops ② a forward (in basketball, football, etc.) ③ vanguard; avant-garde

前晚(ㄑㄧㄢˊ ㄨㄢˇ)
the evening before last

前往(ㄑㄧㄢˊ ㄨㄤˇ)
to go to (a place); to visit; to leave for

前月(ㄑㄧㄢˊ ㄩㄝˋ)
ultimo; in or of the month preceding the current one

前緣(ㄑㄧㄢˊ ㄩㄢˊ)
predestined ties; predestination (for lovers or enemies)

前院(ㄑㄧㄢˊ ㄩㄢˋ)
the front courtyard

八畫

【剔】 393 ㄊㄧ ti tī

1. to separate bones from meat; to scrape meat off bones
2. to pick out inferior materials; to scrape off
3. a rising stroke in Chinese characters

剔刀(ㄊㄧ ㄉㄠ)
a scraping knife

剔透(ㄊㄧ ㄊㄡˋ)
① (said of writings) well-expressed ② (said of persons) keen and perceptive

剔出去(ㄊㄧ ㄔㄨ ˙ㄑㄩ)
to pick out; to eliminate

剔除(ㄊㄧ ㄔㄨˊ)
to eliminate (undesirable things); to reject

剔牙(ㄊㄧ ㄧㄚˊ)
to pick the teeth

【剖】 394 ㄆㄡˇ poou pǒu

1. to cut, rip or tear open
2. to explain; to analyze; to dissect

剖白(ㄆㄡˇ ㄅㄞˊ)
to dispel suspicion by explanation; to explain oneself; to vindicate oneself; to lay one's heart open

剖辨(ㄆㄡˇ ㄅㄧㄢˋ)
to defend oneself (from a charge) by explanation

剖判(ㄆㄛˇ ㄆㄢˋ)
to give judgment in a case

剖面(ㄆㄡˇ ㄇㄧㄢˋ)
a section (of something cut through at a given plane)

剖分(ㄆㄡˇ ㄈㄣ)
to cut apart at the middle

剖腹(ㄆㄡˇ ㄈㄨˋ)
① to cut the belly open ② to tell one's feelings frankly

剖腹取子手術(ㄆㄡˇ ㄈㄨˋ ㄑㄩˇ ㄗˇ ㄕㄡˇ ㄕㄨˋ)
a Caesarian operation; a Caesarian section 亦作「剖腹產術」

剖腹自殺(ㄆㄡˇ ㄈㄨˋ ㄗˋ ㄕㄚ)
(to commit) *hara-kiri*

剖腹藏珠(ㄆㄡˇ ㄈㄨˋ ㄘㄤˊ ㄓㄨ)
to get killed because of greediness; to sacrifice one's life to gain

剖斷如流(ㄆㄡˇ ㄉㄨㄢˋ ㄖㄨˊ ㄌㄧㄡˊ)
(said of a judge) quick in deciding lawsuits

剖肝泣血(ㄆㄡˇ ㄍㄢ ㄑㄧˋ ㄒㄧㄝˇ)
extremely sad

剖開(ㄆㄡˇ ㄎㄞ)
to cut or rip open

剖解(ㄆㄡˇ ㄐㄧㄝˇ) or 剖析(ㄆㄡˇ ㄒㄧ)
① to dissect; to anatomize ② to analyze

剖心(ㄆㄡˇ ㄒㄧㄣ)
to bare one's heart sincerely

剖字(ㄆㄡˇ ㄗˋ)
to tell fortune from the component parts of written characters 亦作「拆字」or「測字」

剖驗(ㄆㄡˇ ㄧㄢˋ)
to hold an inquest 亦作「驗屍」

【剚】 395 ㄗˋ tzyh zì

to plant on the ground

【剛】 396 ㄍㄤ gang gāng

1. tough; unyielding; inflexible; hard; firm; strong; indomitable: 她的個性柔中有剛。Her character is strong as well as graceful.
2. just now: 她剛走。She has just gone.
3. just; exactly: 這套衣服大小剛好。This dress is just the right size.
4. barely; only

剛愎自用(ㄍㄤ ㄅㄧˋ ㄗˋ ㄩㄥˋ)
stubborn; obstinate; not yielding to reason or advice

剛烈(ㄍㄤ ㄌㄧㄝˋ)
tough and vehement; violent

剛剛(ㄍㄤ ㄍㄤ)

①just now; just a moment ago: 貨剛剛到。The goods came just now. ②just; only

剛果(ㄍㄤ ㄍㄨㄛˇ)
①the Congo (Kinshasa) ②the Congo (Leopoldville)

剛果人(ㄍㄤ ㄍㄨㄛˇ ㄖㄣˊ)
a Congolese

剛果語(ㄍㄤ ㄍㄨㄛˇ ㄩˇ)
Congolese

剛…就…(ㄍㄤ…ㄐㄧㄡˋ…)
as soon as; no sooner... than; immediately

剛健(ㄍㄤ ㄐㄧㄢˋ)
vigorous; energetic; robust

剛勁(ㄍㄤ ㄐㄧㄥˋ)
bold; vigorous; sturdy

剛巧(ㄍㄤ ㄑㄧㄠˇ)or 剛好(ㄍㄤ ㄏㄠˇ)
①exactly; precisely; just: 那剛好是我想說的。That's exactly what I want to say. ②to happen to; it so happened that: 我剛好在公車上碰見她。I happened to meet her in the bus.

剛強(ㄍㄤ ㄑㄧㄤˊ)
tough and strong; indomitable; fortitudinous; firm; staunch

剛直(ㄍㄤ ㄓˊ)
tough and honest; upright

剛正不阿(ㄍㄤ ㄓㄥˋ ㄅㄨˋ ㄜ)
upright and never stooping to flattery

剛柔相濟(ㄍㄤ ㄖㄡˊ ㄒㄧㄤ ㄐㄧˋ)
to properly combine toughness and gentleness (in dealing with people)

剛才(ㄍㄤ ㄘㄞˊ)
just a moment ago; a very short while ago: 他剛才還在這兒。He was here only a moment ago.

剛毅(ㄍㄤ ㄧˋ)
tough and determined; resolute; firm; unwavering

剛毅木訥(ㄍㄤ ㄧˋ ㄇㄨˋ ㄋㄜˋ)
resolute and not eloquent

【剜】 397 ㄨㄢ uan wān

to scoop out; to gouge out; to carve out

剜刀(ㄨㄢ ㄉㄠ)
a reamer

剜空(ㄨㄢ ㄎㄨㄥ)
to gouge hollow

剜空心思(ㄨㄢ ㄎㄨㄥ ㄒㄧㄣ ㄙ)
to exhaust one's wits or ingenuity

剜肉補瘡(ㄨㄢ ㄖㄡˋ ㄅㄨˇ ㄔㄨㄤ)
(literally) to cut out a piece of flesh to patch up a sore—to make do by temporary improvisation without attempting a permanent solution

【剝】 398 1. ㄅㄛ bo bō

to strip; to skin; to make bare; to peel; to peel off; to shell

剝皮(ㄅㄛ ㄆㄧˊ)
to skin; to peel off the skin; to flay

剝膚之痛(ㄅㄛ ㄈㄨ ㄓ ㄊㄨㄥˋ)
the pain of being skinned—what hurts closely

剝得精光(ㄅㄛ ˙ㄉㄜ ㄐㄧㄥ ㄍㄨㄤ)
stripped naked

剝奪(ㄅㄛ ㄉㄨㄛˊ)
to deprive or strip one of (rights, property, etc.)

剝離(ㄅㄛ ㄌㄧˊ)
(said of tissue, skin, covering, etc.) to come off; to be stripped

剝落(ㄅㄛ ㄌㄨㄛˋ)
to come off (as a result of erosion); to be peeled off

剝極必復(ㄅㄛ ㄐㄧˊ ㄅㄧˋ ㄈㄨˋ)
When things are at their worst, they will surely mend.

剝蕉抽繭(ㄅㄛ ㄐㄧㄠ ㄔㄡ ㄐㄧㄢˇ)
peeling a banana plant or unwinding a cocoon—to press an inquiry step by step; to investigate deeper and deeper 亦作「抽絲剝繭」

剝削(ㄅㄛ ㄒㄩㄝ)
to exploit (people)

剝製(ㄅㄛ ㄓˋ)
to make (an animal specimen by removing the meat and entrails from the carcass and stuffing it with something else)

剝啄聲(ㄅㄛ ㄓㄨㄛˊ ㄕㄥ)
a knocking sound; a tap

剝蝕(ㄅㄛ ㄕˊ)
to disintegrate (from erosion or weathering); to decay; to corrode; to ravage

【剝】 398 2. ㄅㄠ bau bāo

to strip

剝開(ㄅㄠ ㄎㄞ)
to strip the covering off

九畫

【副】 399 ㄈㄨˋ fuh fù

1. to assist
2. secondary; auxiliary; subsidiary
3. deputy; assistant; vice-
4. a set

副本(ㄈㄨˋ ㄅㄣˇ)or 副張(ㄈㄨˋ ㄓㄤ)
a duplicate copy; a copy

副標題(ㄈㄨˋ ㄅㄧㄠ ㄊㄧˊ)
a subheading; a subtitle

副末(ㄈㄨˋ ㄇㄛˋ)
(Peking opera) a clown

副代表(ㄈㄨˋ ㄉㄞˋ ㄅㄧㄠˇ)
a deputy representative

副廳長(ㄈㄨˋ ㄊㄧㄥ ㄓㄤˇ)
a deputy commissioner (of a department in a provincial government)

副領事(ㄈㄨˋ ㄌㄧㄥˇ ㄕˋ)
a vice-consul

副官(ㄈㄨˋ ㄍㄨㄢ)
an adjutant; an aide-de-camp

副刊(ㄈㄨˋ ㄎㄢ)
a supplement; a supplementary issue

副會長(ㄈㄨˋ ㄏㄨㄟˋ ㄓㄤˇ)
a vice-president (of an association)

副甲狀腺(ㄈㄨˋ ㄐㄧㄚˇ ㄓㄨㄤˋ ㄒㄧㄢˋ)
the parathyroid

副甲狀腺素(ㄈㄨˋ ㄐㄧㄚˇ ㄓㄨㄤˋ ㄒㄧㄢˋ ㄙㄨˋ)
parathyroid hormone

副駕駛(ㄈㄨˋ ㄐㄧㄚˋ ㄕˇ)
a copilot

副交感神經(ㄈㄨˋ ㄐㄧㄠ ㄍㄢˇ ㄕㄣˊ ㄐㄧㄥ)
the parasympathetic nerve

副教授(ㄈㄨˋ ㄐㄧㄠˋ ㄕㄡˋ)
an associate professor

副啓(ㄈㄨˋ ㄑㄧˇ)
a postscript

副校長(ㄈㄨˋ ㄒㄧㄠˋ ㄓㄤˇ)
a provost (of a university)

副職(ㄈㄨˋ ㄓˊ)
the position of a deputy to the chief of an office, a department, etc.

副州長(ㄈㄨˋ ㄓㄡ ㄓㄤˇ)
a lieutenant governor

副主席(ㄈㄨˋ ㄓㄨˇ ㄒㄧˊ)
a vice-chairman

副產品(ㄈㄨˋ ㄔㄢˇ ㄆㄧㄣˇ)
a by-product

副食(ㄈㄨˋ ㄕˊ)
foods other than the staple food; nonstaple foods

副室(ㄈㄨˋ ㄕˋ)
a concubine

副社長(ㄈㄨˋ ㄕㄜˋ ㄓㄤˇ)
a vice-president or deputy director (of a newspaper, news agency, etc.)

副手(ㄈㄨˋ ㄕㄡˇ)
an assistant; a helper

副傷寒(ㄈㄨˋ ㄕㄤ ㄏㄢˊ)
paratyphoid fever

副署(ㄈㄨˋ ㄕㄨˋ)
to countersign

副熱帶高壓(ㄈㄨˋ ㄖㄜˋ ㄉㄞˋ ㄍㄠ ㄧㄚ)
subtropical anticyclone

副作用(ㄈㄨˋ ㄗㄨㄛˋ ㄩㄥˋ)
(medicine) side effects; by-effects

副總統(ㄈㄨˋ ㄗㄨㄥˇ ㄊㄨㄥˇ)
a vice-president (of a nation)

副總裁(ㄈㄨˋ ㄗㄨㄥˇ ㄘㄞˊ)
①a vice director general (of a political party) ②a vice-governor (of a bank)

副總司令(ㄈㄨˋ ㄗㄨㄥˇ ㄙ ㄌㄧㄥˋ)
a deputy commander-in-chief

副詞(ㄈㄨˋ ㄘˊ)
an adverb that modifies an adjective, a verb or another adverb

副議長(ㄈㄨˋ ㄧˋ ㄓㄤˇ)
a vice-chairman or deputy speaker (of an assembly, council, etc.)

副業(ㄈㄨˋ ㄧㄝˋ)
a side job; on the side

副研究員(ㄈㄨˋ ㄧㄢˊ ㄐㄧㄡˋ ㄩㄢˊ)
an associate research fellow

【剪】 400
(翦) ㄐㄧㄢˇ jean jiǎn

1. to cut or clip with scissors; to shear; to trim: 修剪草坪。Cut the lawn.
2. to annihilate; to destroy completely
3. scissors; shears; clippers

剪報(ㄐㄧㄢˇ ㄅㄠˋ)
a newspaper cutting (or clipping)

剪票(ㄐㄧㄢˇ ㄆㄧㄠˋ)
to punch a ticket

剪毛(ㄐㄧㄢˇ ㄇㄠˊ)
(animal husbandry) shearing; clipping

剪毛機(ㄐㄧㄢˇ ㄇㄠˊ ㄐㄧ)
a shearing machine

剪滅(ㄐㄧㄢˇ ㄇㄧㄝˋ)
to cut away; to cut off; to cut down; to eliminate; to remove; to exterminate

剪伐(ㄐㄧㄢˇ ㄈㄚˊ)
to prune, cut or lop off (branches)

剪髮(ㄐㄧㄢˇ ㄈㄚˇ)
to cut hair

剪刀(ㄐㄧㄢˇ ㄉㄠ)
scissors; shears; clippers
亦作「剪子」

剪貼(ㄐㄧㄢˇ ㄊㄧㄝ)
①to clip and paste (something out of a newspaper, etc.) in a scrapbook or on cards ②cutting out (as a schoolchildren's activity)

剪貼簿(ㄐㄧㄢˇ ㄊㄧㄝ ㄅㄨˋ)
a scrapbook

剪輯(ㄐㄧㄢˇ ㄐㄧˊ)
①(movie) montage; film editing ②editing and rearrangement

剪接(ㄐㄧㄢˇ ㄐㄧㄝ)
to edit or cut a film; film editing

剪徑(ㄐㄧㄢˇ ㄐㄧㄥˋ)
highway robbery; to waylay travelers in order to rob them

剪紙(ㄐㄧㄢˇ ㄓˇ)
(art and crafts) paper-cut; scissor-cut

剪指甲(ㄐㄧㄢˇ ㄓˇ ˙ㄐㄧㄚ)
to trim one's nails

剪燭(ㄐㄧㄢˇ ㄓㄨˊ)
to snuff a candle

剪除(ㄐㄧㄢˇ ㄔㄨˊ)
to remove; to exterminate; to cut off

剪裁(ㄐㄧㄢˇ ㄘㄞˊ)
①to tailor clothing materials for a dress ②to brush up or improve a writing by making additions or deletions; to prune

剪綵(ㄐㄧㄢˇ ㄘㄞˇ)
to cut the ribbon (to inaugurate a building, the opening of an exhibition, etc.)

剪草(ㄐㄧㄢˇ ㄘㄠˇ)
to mow or cut grass

剪草機(ㄐㄧㄢˇ ㄘㄠˇ ㄐㄧ)
a lawn mower

剪草除根(ㄐㄧㄢˇ ㄘㄠˇ ㄔㄨˊ ㄍㄣ)
(literally) to cut the grass and remove the root—to exterminate completely

剪羊毛(ㄐㄧㄢˇ ㄧㄤˊ ㄇㄠˊ)
to shear wool

剪影(ㄐㄧㄢˇ ㄧㄥˇ)
①to cut out a silhouette; ②to outline; to sketch; a silhouette; an outline

十畫

【剩】 401
ㄕㄥˋ shenq shèng

to remain; to be left over; in excess; residues; remainder; surplus; remains: 還剩多少? How much is left (over)?

剩飯(ㄕㄥˋ ㄈㄢˋ)
leftovers from a meal; leftover rice

剩貨(ㄕㄥˋ ㄏㄨㄛˋ)
leftover goods; leftovers

剩錢(ㄕㄥˋ ㄑㄧㄢˊ)
to have money left; money left (in one's possession); the balance

剩下(ㄕㄥˋ ㄒㄧㄚˋ)
to be left over; the remainder

剩餘(ㄕㄥˋ ㄩˊ)
the excess; the surplus; the balance; the remainder

剩餘價值(ㄕㄥˋ ㄩˊ ㄐㄧㄚˋ ㄓˊ)
(economics) residual value; (sociology) surplus value

剩餘物資(ㄕㄥˋ ㄩˊ ㄨˋ ㄗ)
surplus materials

【割】 402
ㄍㄜ ge gē

to cut; to sever; to divide

割包皮(ㄍㄜ ㄅㄠ ㄆㄧˊ)
to shorten prepuce by surgical operation; to circumcise

割刀(ㄍㄜ ㄉㄠ)
a cutter

割地賠款(ㄍㄜ ㄉㄧˋ ㄆㄟˊ ㄎㄨㄢˇ)
to cede territory and pay indemnities (to the victor of

a war)
割斷(ㄍㄜ ㄉㄨㄢˋ)
to cut off; to sever by cutting; apart from
割裂(ㄍㄜ ㄌㄧㄝˋ)
to split; to slash or rip open (by means of a knife); to cut apart; to separate
割股療親(ㄍㄜ ㄍㄨˇ ㄌㄧㄠˊ ㄑㄧㄣ)
to try to cure the illness of one's parent by mixing with medicine a slice of flesh cut from one's own thigh
割開(ㄍㄜ ㄎㄞ)
to cut open
割鷄焉用牛刀(ㄍㄜ ㄐㄧ ㄧㄢ ㄩㄥˋ ㄋㄧㄡˊ ㄉㄠ)
(literally) It's unnecessary to use a butcher's knife to kill a chicken. —A man of less ability can do the job.
割據(ㄍㄜ ㄐㄩˋ)
to exercise sovereign powers in each of the regions of a nation under the control of contending warlords; to set up a separate regime by force of arms
割席(ㄍㄜ ㄒㄧˊ)
to sever friendship
割線(ㄍㄜ ㄒㄧㄢˋ)
(mathematics) a secant
割除(ㄍㄜ ㄔㄨˊ)
to cut off; to cut out; to excise
割勢(ㄍㄜ ㄕˋ)
to castrate
割捨(ㄍㄜ ㄕㄜˇ)
to part with; to give away: 他割捨不下他的雙親。He found it hard to part with his parents.
割曬機(ㄍㄜ ㄕㄞˋ ㄐㄧ)
(agriculture) a swather; a windrower
割讓(ㄍㄜ ㄖㄤˋ)
to cede (land or territory); cession
割草(ㄍㄜ ㄘㄠˇ)
to cut grass; to mow grass
割草機(ㄍㄜ ㄘㄠˇ ㄐㄧ)
a mower
割愛(ㄍㄜ ㄞˋ)
to give up what one treasures; to give up something reluctantly
割與(ㄍㄜ ㄩˇ)
to cede to

【剴】 403 ㄎㄞˇ kae kǎi
1. a sickle
2. thoroughly; clearly
剴切(ㄎㄞˇ ㄑㄧㄝˋ)
(said of statements) clearly; true and pertinent; earnest and sincere

【創】 404 1. ㄔㄨㄤˋ chuanq chuàng
1. to start; to begin; to initiate; to create; to establish; to found
2. original; unprecedented
創辦(ㄔㄨㄤˋ ㄅㄢˋ)
to start (a business, publication, etc.); to found (a school, club, etc.); to set up; to establish: 哈佛大學創辦於1636年。Harvard University was founded in 1636.
創立(ㄔㄨㄤˋ ㄌㄧˋ)
to start, found or establish (an organization)
創刊(ㄔㄨㄤˋ ㄎㄢ)
to put out the first issue (of a periodical); to start publication
創刊號(ㄔㄨㄤˋ ㄎㄢ ㄏㄠˋ)
the first issue (of a periodical)
創獲(ㄔㄨㄤˋ ㄏㄨㄛˋ)
an original finding; a new discovery
創紀錄(ㄔㄨㄤˋ ㄐㄧˋ ㄌㄨˋ)
to set a record; to make a record
創見(ㄔㄨㄤˋ ㄐㄧㄢˋ)
① an original opinion or view; a new idea: 他是有創見的思想家。He is an original thinker. ② an unprecedented thing
創建(ㄔㄨㄤˋ ㄐㄧㄢˋ)
to found; to establish
創舉(ㄔㄨㄤˋ ㄐㄩˇ)
an unprecedented undertaking; pioneering work: 這是了不起的創舉。This is great pioneering work.
創新(ㄔㄨㄤˋ ㄒㄧㄣ)
to bring forth new ideas; to blaze new trails
創制權(ㄔㄨㄤˋ ㄓˋ ㄑㄩㄢˊ)
the right to initiate laws; the initiative
創始(ㄔㄨㄤˋ ㄕˇ)
to start; to begin; to commence
創始人(ㄔㄨㄤˋ ㄕˇ ㄖㄣˊ)
a pioneer or founder
創世紀(ㄔㄨㄤˋ ㄕˋ ㄐㄧˋ)
(Bible) Genesis
創設(ㄔㄨㄤˋ ㄕㄜˋ)
to start or set up (an office, agency, etc.)
創造(ㄔㄨㄤˋ ㄗㄠˋ)
to create; to produce: 神創造了天地。God created the heaven and the earth.
創造力(ㄔㄨㄤˋ ㄗㄠˋ ㄌㄧˋ)
originality; creative ability; the talent to create
創作(ㄔㄨㄤˋ ㄗㄨㄛˋ)
① to write (original works of literature) ② an original work of literature or art
創業(ㄔㄨㄤˋ ㄧㄝˋ)
to be the founder of a business; to start a business

【創】 404 2. ㄔㄨㄤ chuang chuāng
1. a wound
2. same as 瘡—a sore; a boil; an ulcer
創口(ㄔㄨㄤ ㄎㄡˇ)
a wound; a cut
創痕(ㄔㄨㄤ ㄏㄣˊ)
a scar
創鉅痛深(ㄔㄨㄤ ㄐㄩˋ ㄊㄨㄥˋ ㄕㄣ)
The damage is heavy.
創傷(ㄔㄨㄤ ㄕㄤ)
a wound; a cut; a scar
創痍(ㄔㄨㄤ ㄧˊ)
① a wound (with opening lips showing) ② the suffering of the people
創痍滿目(ㄔㄨㄤ ㄧˊ ㄇㄢˇ ㄇㄨˋ)
nothing but ruins and debris (in the wake of a devastating war or a disaster)

十一畫

【剿】 405 (勦) ㄐㄧㄠˇ jeau jiǎo
to exterminate; to stamp out; to destroy; to put down
剿平(ㄐㄧㄠˇ ㄆㄧㄥˊ)
to succeed in suppressing or to put down (a rebellion)
剿滅(ㄐㄧㄠˇ ㄇㄧㄝˋ)

〔刀部〕

to exterminate or destroy (bandits or rebels)

剿匪(ㄐㄧㄠˇ ㄈㄟˇ)
to launch attacks against the bandits

剿撫兼施(ㄐㄧㄠˇ ㄈㄨˇ ㄐㄧㄢ ㄕ)
(to try to suppress a rebellion) by military operations as well as inducements to surrender

【剷】 406 ㄔㄢˇ chaan chǎn
1. a shovel
2. to shovel; to level off; to raze to the ground

剷平(ㄔㄢˇ ㄆㄧㄥˊ)
to level to the ground; to level; to be razed to the ground

剷除(ㄔㄢˇ ㄔㄨˊ)
to root out; to eradicate

【剽】 407 ㄆㄧㄠˋ piaw piào
1. to plunder; to rob; to steal
2. agile; fast

剽掠(ㄆㄧㄠˋ ㄌㄩㄝˋ)or 剽劫(ㄆㄧㄠˋ ㄐㄧㄝˊ)
to plunder; to rob

剽悍(ㄆㄧㄠˋ ㄏㄢˋ)
agile and fierce; warlike

剽悍善戰(ㄆㄧㄠˋ ㄏㄢˋ ㄕㄢˋ ㄓㄢˋ)
swift, daring and skillful at fighting

剽竊(ㄆㄧㄠˋ ㄑㄧㄝˋ)
①to steal; to purloin ②to plagiarize

十二畫

【箚】 408 ㄓㄚˊ jar zhá
1. a letter; a brief note
2. a directive (in former times); an official communication from a superior to an inferior

箚記(ㄓㄚˊ ㄐㄧˋ)
①to take notes in reading ②notes taken in reading; reading notes

箚子(ㄓㄚˊ ·ㄗ)
a directive (in former times); a communication to an official subordinate 參看「札」

【劃】 409 1. ㄏㄨㄚˋ huah huà
1. to unify
2. to lay boundaries
3. to draw a line; to mark; to delineate
4. to plan or design
5. to set aside; to divide
6. a stroke (of a Chinese character)

劃撥(ㄏㄨㄚˋ ㄅㄛ)
to deposit money under the account of a seller in payment of goods purchased; to transfer funds

劃分(ㄏㄨㄚˋ ㄈㄣ)
to divide and delimit; to differentiate

劃定(ㄏㄨㄚˋ ㄉㄧㄥˋ)
to delimit; to define the boundary of; to mark out

劃歸(ㄏㄨㄚˋ ㄍㄨㄟ)or 劃入(ㄏㄨㄚˋ ㄖㄨˋ)
to allot (some revenue, an area, etc. to a government or an organization); to incorporate into

劃界(ㄏㄨㄚˋ ㄐㄧㄝˋ)
to fix boundaries; to define limits; to delimit a boundary

劃清(ㄏㄨㄚˋ ㄑㄧㄥ)
to draw a clear line of demarcation; to make a clear distinction: 我要跟他劃清界線。I want to make a clean break with him.

劃時代(ㄏㄨㄚˋ ㄕˊ ㄉㄞˋ)
epoch-making; epochal: 此舉具有劃時代的意義。The measure has an epoch-making significance.

劃一(ㄏㄨㄚˋ ㄧ)
to make uniform; to give uniformity to something

劃一不二(ㄏㄨㄚˋ ㄧ ㄅㄨˋ ㄦˋ)
uniform (prices), no bargaining or haggling; fixed; unalterable; rigid; hard and fast

【劃】 409 2. ㄏㄨㄚˊ hwa huá
to cut

劃開(ㄏㄨㄚˊ ㄎㄞ)
to cut open; to slash open

十三畫

【劇】 410 ㄐㄩˋ jiuh jù
1. a drama; a theatrical work; a play
2. intense; strenuous; acute; severe
3. to play
4. a Chinese family name

劇本(ㄐㄩˋ ㄅㄣˇ)
a play; a scenario; a script; a libretto

劇評(ㄐㄩˋ ㄆㄧㄥˊ)
a review of a play or an opera; dramatic criticism

劇目(ㄐㄩˋ ㄇㄨˋ)
a list of plays or operas; a repertoire

劇坊(ㄐㄩˋ ㄈㄤ)
a theater workshop

劇盜(ㄐㄩˋ ㄉㄠˋ)
a notorious bandit

劇毒(ㄐㄩˋ ㄉㄨˊ)
deadly poison

劇談(ㄐㄩˋ ㄊㄢˊ)
①to converse enthusiastically ②comments about drama and the theater

劇團(ㄐㄩˋ ㄊㄨㄢˊ)
a theatrical company; an opera troupe; a troupe

劇烈(ㄐㄩˋ ㄌㄧㄝˋ)
strenuous; intense; hard; fierce

劇情(ㄐㄩˋ ㄑㄧㄥˊ)
the plot

劇照(ㄐㄩˋ ㄓㄠˋ)
a stage photo; a still

劇終(ㄐㄩˋ ㄓㄨㄥ)
the end; a curtainfall

劇中人(ㄐㄩˋ ㄓㄨㄥ ㄖㄣˊ)
characters in a play or opera; *dramatis personae*

劇場(ㄐㄩˋ ㄔㄤˇ)or(ㄐㄩˋ ㄔㄤˊ)or 劇院(ㄐㄩˋ ㄩㄢˋ)
a theater

劇作家(ㄐㄩˋ ㄗㄨㄛˋ ㄐㄧㄚ)
a playwright; a dramatist

劇藥(ㄐㄩˋ ㄧㄠˋ)
strong medicine

劇飲(ㄐㄩˋ ㄧㄣˇ)
to drink with abandon; to carouse

劇務(ㄐㄩˋ ㄨˋ)
① stage management ②a stage manager

【劈】 411 1. ㄆㄧ pi pī
1. to cleave; to split; to rive; to rend
2. a wedge

劈刀(ㄆㄧ ㄉㄠ)
①a chopper ②(military) saber fighting
劈頭(ㄆㄧ ㄊㄡˊ)
①straight on the head; right in the face: 我劈頭就給了他一拳。I hit him straight on the head. ②at the very start: 她一進門劈頭就問:「準備好了嗎?」The moment she entered the room she asked, "Are you ready?"
劈哩啪啦(ㄆㄧ ·ㄌㄧ ㄆㄚ ㄌㄚ)
(onomatopoeia) a descriptive sound of firecrackers, guns, etc.: 鞭炮劈哩啪啦地響。The firecrackers were crackling and spluttering.
劈臉(ㄆㄧ ㄌㄧㄢˇ)
right in the face
劈開(ㄆㄧ ㄎㄞ)
①to split open ②do not say the fact that... ③(mining) cleavage
劈胸(ㄆㄧ ㄒㄩㄥ)
right against the chest
劈柴(ㄆㄧ ㄔㄞˊ)
to split or chop firewood
劈手(ㄆㄧ ㄕㄡˇ)
to thrust forth the hand —(figuratively) in a flash; instantly
劈山(ㄆㄧ ㄕㄢ)
to level off hilltops; to blast cliffs
劈刺(ㄆㄧ ㄘˋ)
(military) saber or bayonet fighting

【劈】 411
2. ㄆㄧˇ pii pǐ
to split; to chop
劈柴(ㄆㄧˇ ㄔㄞˊ)
to split or chop firewood

【劉】 412
ㄌㄧㄡˊ liou liú
1. a Chinese family name
2. to kill
劉邦(ㄌㄧㄡˊ ㄅㄤ)
Liu Pang, the founder of the Han Dynasty, whose reign lasted from 206 to 194 B.C.
劉海兒(ㄌㄧㄡˊ ㄏㄞˇㄦ)
bangs; a fringe
劉宋(ㄌㄧㄡˊ ㄙㄨㄥˋ)
the Sung Dynasty under the house of Liu between 420 and 477 (as distinct from the Sung Dynasty under the house of Chao)

【劊】 413
ㄍㄨㄟˋ guey guì
(又讀 ㄎㄨㄞˋ kuay kuài)
to amputate; to cut off
劊子手(ㄍㄨㄟˋ ·ㄗ ㄕㄡˇ)or(ㄎㄨㄞˋ ·ㄗ ㄕㄡˇ)
①an executioner ②a hatchet man; a slaughterman; a butcher

【劍】 414
ㄐㄧㄢˋ jiann jiàn
a sword; a dagger; a saber
劍拔弩張(ㄐㄧㄢˋ ㄅㄚˊ ㄋㄨˇ ㄓㄤ)
(literally) with swords unsheathed and bows drawn —ready to fight; ready to destroy each other; becoming dangerously explosive
劍眉(ㄐㄧㄢˋ ㄇㄟˊ)
straight eyebrows slanting upwards and outwards
劍蘭(ㄐㄧㄢˋ ㄌㄢˊ)
(botany) a gladiolus; a sword lily
劍客(ㄐㄧㄢˋ ㄎㄜˋ)
a swordsman; a fencing master
劍及履及(ㄐㄧㄢˋ ㄐㄧˊ ㄌㄩˇ ㄐㄧˊ)
to perform a task with full vigor and urgency
劍橋(ㄐㄧㄢˋ ㄑㄧㄠˊ)
Cambridge, England
劍俠(ㄐㄧㄢˋ ㄒㄧㄚˊ)
a wandering swordsman (in search of adventures)
劍術(ㄐㄧㄢˋ ㄕㄨˋ)
swordsmanship; fencing: 他擅長劍術。He is good at fencing.

十四畫

【劑】 415
ㄐㄧˋ jih jì
1. a dose (of medicine)
2. prepared medicines or drugs
3. to prepare (medicines and drugs)
劑量(ㄐㄧˋ ㄌㄧㄤˋ)
(pharmaceutics) a dosage; a dose

【劓】 416
ㄧˋ yih yì
to cut off the nose (as a form of punishment in ancient China)

力部
ㄌㄧˋ lih lì

【力】 417
ㄌㄧˋ lih lì
1. strength
2. force; power
3. ability
4. vigor
5. vigorously; earnestly
6. to do one's best: 他辦事不力。He did not do his best in his work.
力臂(ㄌㄧˋ ㄅㄟˋ)
(physics) the lever arm, or the arm of force
力不勝任(ㄌㄧˋ ㄅㄨˋ ㄕㄥ ㄖㄣˋ)
to be unequal to one's task
力不從心(ㄌㄧˋ ㄅㄨˋ ㄘㄨㄥˊ ㄒㄧㄣ)
to have too little power or too few resources to do as much as one wishes; lacking the ability to do what one wishes
力排眾議(ㄌㄧˋ ㄆㄞˊ ㄓㄨㄥˋ ㄧˋ)
to refute the consensus and present a new plan or idea; to prevail over all dissent
力大無比(ㄌㄧˋ ㄉㄚˋ ㄨˊ ㄅㄧˇ)
without a match in physical prowess
力敵萬夫(ㄌㄧˋ ㄉㄧˊ ㄨㄢˋ ㄈㄨ)
able to fight off ten thousand men—(figuratively) very brave
力點(ㄌㄧˋ ㄉㄧㄢˇ)
a point of force (on a lever)
力透紙背(ㄌㄧˋ ㄊㄡˋ ㄓˇ ㄅㄟˋ)
(calligraphy) So forceful are the strokes that the force seems to penetrate the paper.
力田(ㄌㄧˋ ㄊㄧㄢˊ)
to do farming diligently
力圖(ㄌㄧˋ ㄊㄨˊ)
to try hard; to strive to
力量(ㄌㄧˋ ·ㄌㄧㄤ)
strength; force; power
力可拔山(ㄌㄧˋ ㄎㄜˇ ㄅㄚˊ ㄕㄢ)
so strong as to be able to lift a mountain
力疾奔走(ㄌㄧˋ ㄐㄧˊ ㄅㄣ ㄗㄡˇ)

〔力部〕

〔力部〕

to busy oneself in running about (usually doing official duties) despite illness

力疾從公(ㄌㄧˋ ㄐㄧˊ ㄘㄨㄥˊ ㄍㄨㄥ)
to perform official duties in disregard of ailments; to attend to one's duties in spite of illness

力竭聲嘶(ㄌㄧˋ ㄐㄧㄝˊ ㄕㄥ ㄙ)
exhausted and hoarse (as a result of haranguing, crying, etc.)

力薦(ㄌㄧˋ ㄐㄧㄢˋ)
to recommend (someone) strongly

力氣(ㄌㄧˋ ·ㄑㄧ)
① physical strength or power ② an effort

力求(ㄌㄧˋ ㄑㄧㄡˊ)
to make strenuous efforts to; to do one's best to; to strive to

力求上進(ㄌㄧˋ ㄑㄧㄡˊ ㄕㄤˋ ㄐㄧㄣˋ)
to strive vigorously to improve oneself

力請(ㄌㄧˋ ㄑㄧㄥˇ)
to entreat earnestly; to ask with zeal or eagerness

力行(ㄌㄧˋ ㄒㄧㄥˊ)
to practice or perform energetically; to act with might

力行不怠(ㄌㄧˋ ㄒㄧㄥˊ ㄅㄨˋ ㄉㄞˋ)
to do something persistently without a cessation

力學(ㄌㄧˋ ㄒㄩㄝˊ)
① to study with diligence or industry; to study hard ② (physics) mechanics

力戰(ㄌㄧˋ ㄓㄢˋ)
to fight with might or vigor; to fight hard (usually against great odds)

力爭(ㄌㄧˋ ㄓㄥ)
① to struggle hard; to strive with might; to do all one's best ② to argue strongly; to contend vigorously

力爭上流(ㄌㄧˋ ㄓㄥ ㄕㄤˋ ㄌㄧㄡˊ)or 力爭上游(ㄌㄧˋ ㄓㄥ ㄕㄤˋ ㄧㄡˊ)
to try to excel by strenuous efforts; to strive for progress

力士(ㄌㄧˋ ㄕˋ)
a muscleman; a person of great physical strength

力所能及(ㄌㄧˋ ㄙㄨㄛˇ ㄋㄥˊ ㄐㄧˊ)
within one's power

力役(ㄌㄧˋ ㄧˋ)
the exactions of personal service

力挽狂瀾(ㄌㄧˋ ㄨㄢˇ ㄎㄨㄤˊ ㄌㄢˊ)
to make vigorous efforts to turn the tide—(figuratively) to do one's best to reverse the course of events

力與願違(ㄌㄧˋ ㄩˇ ㄩㄢˋ ㄨㄟˊ)
to be unable to do what one wishes

三畫

【功】 418
ㄍㄨㄥ gong gōng

1. a merit; an achievement; an accomplishment; an exploit
2. usefulness; effectiveness
3. a function
4. (physics) work: 機械功 mechanical work

功敗垂成(ㄍㄨㄥ ㄅㄞˋ ㄔㄨㄟˊ ㄔㄥˊ)
to fail within reach of success; to meet with failure when victory is within one's grasp

功不補過(ㄍㄨㄥ ㄅㄨˋ ㄅㄨˇ ㄍㄨㄛˋ)
Demerits outweigh merits.

功不可沒(ㄍㄨㄥ ㄅㄨˋ ㄎㄜˇ ㄇㄛˋ)
The contribution (to success) cannot be left unrecognized.

功名(ㄍㄨㄥ ㄇㄧㄥˊ)
① laurels; glory; distinction; honor ② an official rank or an academic title (in former times)

功夫(ㄍㄨㄥ ·ㄈㄨ)
① time (to do something) ② efforts (devoted to a task) ③ accomplishments ④ skill

功德(ㄍㄨㄥ ㄉㄜˊ)
① merits and virtues ② (Buddhism) charitable and pious deeds; beneficence

功德無量(ㄍㄨㄥ ㄉㄜˊ ㄨˊ ㄌㄧㄤˋ)
(His, your, etc.) kindness knows no bounds; boundless beneficence

功到自然成(ㄍㄨㄥ ㄉㄠˋ ㄗˋ ㄖㄢˊ ㄔㄥˊ)
Constant effort yields sure success.

功能(ㄍㄨㄥ ㄋㄥˊ)
a function: 心臟有很重要的功能。The heart has a very important function.

功勞(ㄍㄨㄥ ㄌㄠˊ)
merits; credit; meritorious deeds; contribution

功力(ㄍㄨㄥ ㄌㄧˋ)
efficacy; effectiveness; potency

功利(ㄍㄨㄥ ㄌㄧˋ)
utility; material gain

功利主義(ㄍㄨㄥ ㄌㄧˋ ㄓㄨˇ ㄧˋ)
utilitarianism

功令(ㄍㄨㄥ ㄌㄧㄥˋ)
orders; decrees; school regulations

功高震主(ㄍㄨㄥ ㄍㄠ ㄓㄣˋ ㄓㄨˇ)
So great is one's achievements as to make one's boss feel uneasy or insecure.

功過(ㄍㄨㄥ ㄍㄨㄛˋ)
merits and demerits

功過相抵(ㄍㄨㄥ ㄍㄨㄛˋ ㄒㄧㄤ ㄉㄧˇ)
One's mistakes or offenses cancel his contributions.

功課(ㄍㄨㄥ ㄎㄜˋ)
schoolwork; homework

功課表(ㄍㄨㄥ ㄎㄜˋ ㄅㄧㄠˇ)
a class schedule (at school)

功虧一簣(ㄍㄨㄥ ㄎㄨㄟ ㄧˊ ㄎㄨㄟˋ)
failure to achieve success or perfection by a very narrow margin

功績(ㄍㄨㄥ ㄐㄧ)
meritorious records; achievements; a contribution

功效(ㄍㄨㄥ ㄒㄧㄠˋ)
effectiveness; efficacy; useful results

功勳(ㄍㄨㄥ ㄒㄩㄣ)
distinctive achievements; an eminent contribution; meritorious services; feats

功臣(ㄍㄨㄥ ㄔㄣˊ)
(in old China) a vassal or subject who distinguished himself by meritorious services; (in a modern sense) one who has made a significant contribution to a specific task; a person who has rendered outstanding services

功成名就(ㄍㄨㄥ ㄔㄥˊ ㄇㄧㄥˊ ㄐㄧㄡˋ)or 功成名遂(ㄍㄨㄥ ㄔㄥˊ ㄇㄧㄥˊ ㄙㄨㄟˋ)
to achieve success and acquire fame; to be successful and famous

功成弗居(ㄍㄨㄥ ㄔㄥˊ ㄈㄨˊ ㄐㄩ)
to achieve success but do

not take credit
功成身退(ㄍㄨㄥ ㄔㄥˊ ㄕㄣ ㄊㄨㄟˋ)or 功遂身退(ㄍㄨㄥ ㄙㄨㄟˋ ㄕㄣ ㄊㄨㄟˋ)
to retire after achieving success; to leave the top post to others after playing the leading role in a successful revolution, movement, etc.
功用(ㄍㄨㄥ ㄩㄥˋ)
use; effect; a function

【加】 419 ㄐㄧㄚ jia jiā
1. plus; to add: 二加三等於五。Two plus three makes five.
2. to increase; to augment
3. to append: 他在箱子上加標籤。He appended a label to that trunk.

加倍(ㄐㄧㄚ ㄅㄟˋ)
to double; to make twice as much; to redouble: 他加倍努力完成他的工作。He redoubled his efforts to finish his work.
加班(ㄐㄧㄚ ㄅㄢ)
to work overtime; to work an extra shift
加鞭(ㄐㄧㄚ ㄅㄧㄢ)
to whip; to apply the whip
加彭(ㄐㄧㄚ ㄆㄥˊ)
Gabon
加盟(ㄐㄧㄚ ㄇㄥˊ)
to join an alliance, a fraternity or a secret society
加冕(ㄐㄧㄚ ㄇㄧㄢˇ)
to crown; to coronate
加勉(ㄐㄧㄚ ㄇㄧㄢˇ)
to make greater exertions
加法(ㄐㄧㄚ ㄈㄚˇ)
(arithmetic) addition
加封(ㄐㄧㄚ ㄈㄥ)
①to bestow a title ②to seal with additional tape
加俸(ㄐㄧㄚ ㄈㄥˋ)
to raise one's pay
加添物(ㄐㄧㄚ ㄊㄧㄢ ㄨˋ)or 加添劑(ㄐㄧㄚ ㄊㄧㄢ ㄐㄧˋ)
an additive
加拿大(ㄐㄧㄚ ㄋㄚˊ ㄉㄚˋ)
Canada
加農砲(ㄐㄧㄚ ㄋㄨㄥˊ ㄆㄠˋ)
a cannon
加勒比海(ㄐㄧㄚ ㄌㄜˋ ㄅㄧˇ ㄏㄞˇ)
the Caribbean Sea
加禮(ㄐㄧㄚ ㄌㄧˇ)
to show more than ordinary civility; to be particularly warm (to a guest)
加里波的(ㄐㄧㄚ ㄌㄧˇ ㄅㄛ ㄉㄧˋ)
Giuseppe Garibaldi, 1807-1882, one of the founders of modern Italy
加利福尼亞(ㄐㄧㄚ ㄌㄧˋ ㄈㄨˊ ㄋㄧˊ ㄧㄚˋ)
the state of California, U.S.A.
加料(ㄐㄧㄚ ㄌㄧㄠˋ)
①to feed raw material into (a container, etc.) ②particular things made of excellent materials
加侖(ㄐㄧㄚ ㄌㄨㄣˊ)
a gallon (a unit of liquid measurement)
加冠(ㄐㄧㄚ ㄍㄨㄢ)
to cap a boy as a symbol of his coming of age (at 20)
加官(ㄐㄧㄚ ㄍㄨㄢ)
①to hold a concurrent post ②(formerly) to be promoted to a higher position
加官晉爵(ㄐㄧㄚ ㄍㄨㄢ ㄐㄧㄣˋ ㄐㄩㄝˊ)
to advance in rank and position; promotion
加工(ㄐㄧㄚ ㄍㄨㄥ)
to process (goods)
加工出口區(ㄐㄧㄚ ㄍㄨㄥ ㄔㄨ ㄎㄡˇ ㄑㄩ)
an export processing zone
加快(ㄐㄧㄚ ㄎㄨㄞˋ)
to speed up; to accelerate
加寬(ㄐㄧㄚ ㄎㄨㄢ)
to broaden; to widen
加害(ㄐㄧㄚ ㄏㄞˋ)
to inflict injury; to do somebody harm
加號(ㄐㄧㄚ ㄏㄠˋ)
the plus symbol (+); a sign of addition
加護(ㄐㄧㄚ ㄏㄨˋ)
①(said of gods) to protect or bless ②to take special care of
加護病房(ㄐㄧㄚ ㄏㄨˋ ㄅㄧㄥˋ ㄈㄤˊ)
an intensive care unit (ICU)
加價(ㄐㄧㄚ ㄐㄧㄚˋ)
to raise or hike the price
加減乘除(ㄐㄧㄚ ㄐㄧㄢˇ ㄔㄥˊ ㄔㄨˊ)
addition, subtraction, multiplication and division
加緊(ㄐㄧㄚ ㄐㄧㄣˇ)
to intensify; to step up
加勁(ㄐㄧㄚ ㄐㄧㄣˋ)
to put more energy into; to make a greater effort
加劇(ㄐㄧㄚ ㄐㄩˋ)
to aggravate; to sharpen; to cause to become worse or more severe
加強(ㄐㄧㄚ ㄑㄧㄤˊ)
to strengthen; to reinforce; to invigorate; to enhance
加權指數(ㄐㄧㄚ ㄑㄩㄢˊ ㄓˇ ㄕㄨˋ)
(stock trading) the weighted index number
加薪(ㄐㄧㄚ ㄒㄧㄣ)
to give a pay raise
加值稅(ㄐㄧㄚ ㄓˊ ㄕㄨㄟˋ)
value-added tax
加重(ㄐㄧㄚ ㄓㄨㄥˋ)
to make heavier; to increase burdens, work loads, etc.
加深(ㄐㄧㄚ ㄕㄣ)
①to deepen: 這條河需要加深河道。The river needed to be deepened the channel. ②to cause to become worse or more severe
加數(ㄐㄧㄚ ㄕㄨˋ)
an addend
加熱(ㄐㄧㄚ ㄖㄜˋ)
to heat; to warm
加入(ㄐㄧㄚ ㄖㄨˋ)
①to join (a group); to accede to ②to add into
加菜(ㄐㄧㄚ ㄘㄞˋ)
to have additional and better foods than the usual fare
加餐(ㄐㄧㄚ ㄘㄢ)
to eat more at meals — to show one's concern
加薩走廊(ㄐㄧㄚ ㄙㄚˋ ㄗㄡˇ ㄌㄤˊ)
the Gaza Strip on the Sinai Peninsula
加速(ㄐㄧㄚ ㄙㄨˋ)
to step up; to quicken the tempo; to accelerate: 他們業已加速開發工業。They have speeded up industrial development.
加速度(ㄐㄧㄚ ㄙㄨˋ ㄉㄨˋ)
acceleration
加爾各答(ㄐㄧㄚ ㄦˇ ㄍㄜˋ ㄉㄚˊ)
Calcutta
加一(ㄐㄧㄚ ㄧ)
to add one tenth (of the original number or quantity)
加意(ㄐㄧㄚ ㄧˋ)
to pay special attention; to make an additional effort

〔力部〕

加油(ㄐㄧㄚ ㄧㄡˊ)
①to oil: 這部機器要加油了。This machine needs oiling. ②to refuel: 飛機要在東京降落加油。The plane will land in Tokyo for refueling. ③to step up effort; to cheer (an athlete in the midst of a sport competition with a view to goading him on for victory): 男孩子們大聲爲他們的足球隊加油。The boys cheered their football team loudly.

加油添醬(ㄐㄧㄚ ㄧㄡˊ ㄊㄧㄢ ㄐㄧㄤˋ)
to exaggerate or give embellishment to a story

加油站(ㄐㄧㄚ ㄧㄡˊ ㄓㄢˋ)
a gas station, or filling station

四畫

【劣】 420 ㄌㄧㄝˋ lieh liè
inferior; mean; bad; of low quality

劣品(ㄌㄧㄝˋ ㄆㄧㄣˇ)
inferior quality

劣馬(ㄌㄧㄝˋ ㄇㄚˇ)
①an inferior horse; an emaciated nag ②a vicious horse

劣等(ㄌㄧㄝˋ ㄉㄥˇ)
of inferior quality; low-grade; poor

劣等貨(ㄌㄧㄝˋ ㄉㄥˇ ㄏㄨㄛˋ)
goods of inferior quality

劣等生(ㄌㄧㄝˋ ㄉㄥˇ ㄕㄥ)
a dull student

劣點(ㄌㄧㄝˋ ㄉㄧㄢˇ)
a defect; a demerit

劣根性(ㄌㄧㄝˋ ㄍㄣ ㄒㄧㄥˋ)
degraded character; a depravity; meanness; innate wickedness; deep-rooted bad habits

劣貨(ㄌㄧㄝˋ ㄏㄨㄛˋ)
goods of poor quality; substandard goods

劣跡(ㄌㄧㄝˋ ㄐㄧ)
the unsavory records (of a person, especially those of a public official); misdeeds; evil-doing

劣質(ㄌㄧㄝˋ ㄓˋ)
of poor (or low) quality; inferior

劣種(ㄌㄧㄝˋ ㄓㄨㄥˇ)
inferior breeds; inferior stock

劣勢(ㄌㄧㄝˋ ㄕˋ)
inferior strength or position

劣紳(ㄌㄧㄝˋ ㄕㄣ)
evil gentry; an unethical intellectual who bullies the less well-educated in the local community

五畫

【助】 421 ㄓㄨˋ juh zhù
to help; to aid; to assist; help; assistance: 天助自助者。God helps those who help themselves.

助跑(ㄓㄨˋ ㄆㄠˇ)
a run-up; an approach

助動詞(ㄓㄨˋ ㄉㄨㄥˋ ㄘˊ)
an auxiliary verb; a helping verb

助聽器(ㄓㄨˋ ㄊㄧㄥ ㄑㄧˋ)
a hearing aid; an audiphone

助理(ㄓㄨˋ ㄌㄧˇ)
①an assistant ②to assist

助力(ㄓㄨˋ ㄌㄧˋ)
help; assistance

助攻(ㄓㄨˋ ㄍㄨㄥ)
(military) a holding (or secondary) attack

助桀爲虐(ㄓㄨˋ ㄐㄧㄝˊ ㄨㄟˊ ㄋㄩㄝˋ)or 助紂爲虐(ㄓㄨˋ ㄓㄡˋ ㄨㄟˊ ㄋㄩㄝˋ)
to help the wicked perpetrate wicked deeds; to help a tyrant to do evil

助教(ㄓㄨˋ ㄐㄧㄠˋ)
a teaching assistant; a TA

助興(ㄓㄨˋ ㄒㄧㄥˋ)
to liven things up; to add to the amusement

助學金(ㄓㄨˋ ㄒㄩㄝˊ ㄐㄧㄣ)
a stipend; a grant-in-aid; a scholarship

助陣(ㄓㄨˋ ㄓㄣˋ)
to cheer or root for (a contestant)

助長(ㄓㄨˋ ㄓㄤˇ)
to encourage (a tendency); to promote the development of; to foster; to nurture

助產士(ㄓㄨˋ ㄔㄢˇ ㄕˋ)
a midwife

助手(ㄓㄨˋ ㄕㄡˇ)
an assistant; a helper; an aide

助人爲快樂之本(ㄓㄨˋ ㄖㄣˊ ㄨㄟˊ ㄎㄨㄞˋ ㄌㄜˋ ㄓ ㄅㄣˇ)
Happiness lies in rendering help to others. 或 Service begets happiness.

助詞(ㄓㄨˋ ㄘˊ)
(grammar) an expletive

助威(ㄓㄨˋ ㄨㄟ)or 助勢(ㄓㄨˋ ㄕˋ)
to encourage (often an evildoer); to goad on; to boost the morale of; to cheer

【努】 422 ㄋㄨˇ nuu nǔ
1. to exert oneself; to make an effort
2. to protrude

努力(ㄋㄨˇ ㄌㄧˋ)
to make efforts; to strive; to endeavor; to work hard: 她努力學好外語。She makes efforts to master a foreign language.

努嘴(ㄋㄨˇ ㄗㄨㄟˇ)or 努嘴兒(ㄋㄨˇ ㄗㄨㄜˇㄦ)
①to move lips (in silent communication); to pout ②to purse up one's lips (to show displeasure)

努爾哈赤(ㄋㄨˇ ㄦˇ ㄏㄚ ㄔˋ)
Nurhachu, 1559-1629, the founder of the Manchu nation and grandfather of Emperor Shunchih (順治), the first monarch of the Ching Dynasty

【劫】 423 (刧) ㄐㄧㄝˊ jye jié
1. to rob; to plunder; to take by force
2. sufferings; disasters; misfortunes

劫道(ㄐㄧㄝˊ ㄉㄠˋ)
to rob travelers on a road

劫盜(ㄐㄧㄝˊ ㄉㄠˋ)
①robbery ②a robber; a bandit

劫奪(ㄐㄧㄝˊ ㄉㄨㄛˊ)
to plunder; to rob; to pillage

劫難(ㄐㄧㄝˊ ㄋㄢˋ)
a destined calamity

劫牢(ㄐㄧㄝˊ ㄌㄠˊ)or 劫獄(ㄐㄧㄝˊ ㄩˋ)
①to free prisoners by force ②jail delivery

劫糧(ㄐㄧㄝˊ ㄌㄧㄤˊ)

to forage; to strip of supplies

劫掠(ㄐㄧㄝˊ ㄌㄩㄝˋ)
to plunder; to rob; to pillage

劫後餘生(ㄐㄧㄝˊ ㄏㄡˋ ㄩˊ ㄕㄥ)
life after surviving a disaster

劫機(ㄐㄧㄝˊ ㄐㄧ)
to skyjack; to hijack a plane

劫寨(ㄐㄧㄝˊ ㄓㄞˋ)
to raid the bandits' mountain fortress

劫持(ㄐㄧㄝˊ ㄔˊ)
① to threaten; to menace ② to hijack: 三個暴徒昨天劫持一架客機。Three mobs hijacked an airliner yesterday.

劫數(ㄐㄧㄝˊ ㄕㄨˋ)or 劫運(ㄐㄧㄝˊ ㄩㄣˋ)
ill luck; ill fortune; fatal calamity

劫案(ㄐㄧㄝˊ ㄢˋ)
a case of robbery

劫餘(ㄐㄧㄝˊ ㄩˊ)
in the wake of a disaster; following a disaster

【劬】 424 ㄑㄩˊ chyu qú

labor; toil; diligent; to labor incessantly

劬勞(ㄑㄩˊ ㄌㄠˊ)
travail; toil (especially said of one's own mother); to labor arduously (as parents for children)

【劭】 425 ㄕㄠˋ shaw shào

1. to encourage; to urge
2. graceful; excellent; admirable; respectable: 年高德劭 of venerable age and respectable character

六畫

【劾】 426 ㄏㄜˊ her hé

to accuse; to charge; to impeach

劾狀(ㄏㄜˊ ㄓㄨㄤˋ)
① archives of charges (against a public official) ② to expose someone's crime

劾奏(ㄏㄜˊ ㄗㄡˋ)
to impeach an official of his crime in a memorandum to the emperor

七畫

【勁】 427 1. ㄐㄧㄥˋ jinq jìng

strong; tough; powerful; sturdy

勁風(ㄐㄧㄥˋ ㄈㄥ)
a gale; a blast

勁敵(ㄐㄧㄥˋ ㄉㄧˊ)
a powerful enemy; a strong adversary

勁旅(ㄐㄧㄥˋ ㄌㄩˇ)
a powerful army; crack troops

勁直(ㄐㄧㄥˋ ㄓˊ)
tough and honest; upright

勁草(ㄐㄧㄥˋ ㄘㄠˇ)
① tough grass ② an indomitable person

【勁】 427 2. ㄐㄧㄣˋ jinn jìn

1. vigor; energy; strength: 這個小孩似乎有用不完的勁。The child seems to have inexhaustible energy.
2. spirit
3. an air; manner

勁兒(ㄐㄧㄜˋㄦ)or 勁頭(ㄐㄧㄣˋ ㄊㄡˊ)
① vigor; drive: 他工作有勁頭。He is full of drive in his work. ② energy; strength ③ manner; expression: 瞧他那股傻勁兒。See how stupid he looks. ④ enthusiasm

【勃】 428 ㄅㄛˊ bor bó

sudden(ly); quick(ly)

勃勃(ㄅㄛˊ ㄅㄛˊ)
flourishing; vigorous; zestful: 生氣勃勃 full of vitality; spirited

勃發(ㄅㄛˊ ㄈㄚ)
① to break out; to begin suddenly ② to thrive; to prosper

勃怒(ㄅㄛˊ ㄋㄨˋ)or 勃然大怒(ㄅㄛˊ ㄖㄢˊ ㄉㄚˋ ㄋㄨˋ)
to lose one's temper suddenly; to break into a rage

勃起(ㄅㄛˊ ㄑㄧˇ)
to have an erection; erection

勃谿(ㄅㄛˊ ㄒㄧ)
to fall to quarreling; a quarrel

勃然變色(ㄅㄛˊ ㄖㄢˊ ㄅㄧㄢˋ ㄙㄜˋ)
to show displeasure or bewilderment all of a sudden

【勅】 429 (敕) ㄔˋ chyh chì

1. an imperial decree
2. orders given to demons and spirits by Taoist priests when they exercise magic powers

勅令(ㄔˋ ㄌㄧㄥˋ)
an imperial decree, edict, command, or ordinance

勅書(ㄔˋ ㄕㄨ)
an imperial message or letter 亦作「勅諭」

【勇】 430 ㄩㄥˇ yeong yǒng

1. brave; courageous; bold; valiant; intrepid; fearless
2. a soldier; a conscript
3. bravery; courage: 他是一個智勇雙全的人。He is a man of wisdom and courage.

勇猛(ㄩㄥˇ ㄇㄥˇ)
brave and fierce: 他勇猛如獅。He is as brave as a lion.

勇退(ㄩㄥˇ ㄊㄨㄟˋ)
to withdraw or retire courageously

勇敢(ㄩㄥˇ ㄍㄢˇ)
brave; courageous: 他們勇敢善戰。They are courageous and skillful in battle.

勇敢善戰(ㄩㄥˇ ㄍㄢˇ ㄕㄢˋ ㄓㄢˋ)
brave and resourceful in battle

勇冠三軍(ㄩㄥˇ ㄍㄨㄢˋ ㄙㄢ ㄐㄩㄣ)
(said of soldiers in combat) peerless or matchless in bravery or valor

勇悍(ㄩㄥˇ ㄏㄢˋ)
brave and fierce

勇將(ㄩㄥˇ ㄐㄧㄤˋ)
a fearless general

勇決(ㄩㄥˇ ㄐㄩㄝˊ)
brave and resolute

勇氣(ㄩㄥˇ ㄑㄧˋ)
courage; bravery; valor; prowess; intrepidity; gallantry; heroism; fearlessness: 他們鼓起最大勇氣。They mustered up all their courage.

勇者不懼(ㄩㄥˇ ㄓㄜˇ ㄅㄨˋ ㄐㄩˋ)
Bravery admits no fear.

勇士(ㄩㄥˇ ㄕˋ)
one who knows no fear; a brave fighter; a warrior

勇武(ㄩㄥˇ ㄨˇ)

brave; daring; valiant; intrepid; courageous
勇往直前(ㄩㄥˇ ㄨㄤˇ ㄓˊ ㄑㄧㄢˊ)
to march fearlessly onward; to go straight ahead
勇於(ㄩㄥˇ ㄩˊ)
to be brave in; to have the boldness to; to have the courage to

力部

【勉】 431 ㄇㄧㄢˇ mean miǎn
1. to urge; to encourage: 他們互勉。They encourage each other.
2. to strive; to make efforts; to exert oneself to
勉勵(ㄇㄧㄢˇ ㄌㄧˋ)
to encourage; to urge; to rouse to action
勉力(ㄇㄧㄢˇ ㄌㄧˋ)
to make efforts; to try hard
勉力爲之(ㄇㄧㄢˇ ㄌㄧˋ ㄨㄟˊ ㄓ)
to do it as best as one can
勉強(ㄇㄧㄢˇ ㄑㄧㄤˇ)or 勉勉強強(ㄇㄧㄢˇ ㄇㄧㄢˇ ㄑㄧㄤˇ ㄑㄧㄤˇ)
① without spontaneity; in a forced manner; involuntarily; reluctantly ② barely (enough, acceptable, etc.) ③ to force ④ unconvincing
勉爲其難(ㄇㄧㄢˇ ㄨㄟˊ ㄑㄧˊ ㄋㄢˊ)
to force oneself to do a hard task; to take on some difficult job reluctantly

九畫

【勒】 432 1. ㄌㄜˋ leh lè
1. to force; to compel
2. to reign or rule; to control; to command
3. to engrave; to carve
4. a bridle
5. (calligraphy) a horizontal stroke
勒逼(ㄌㄜˋ ㄅㄧ)
to force; to compel; to coerce
勒兵(ㄌㄜˋ ㄅㄧㄥ)
① to halt the troops on the march ② to command troops
勒派(ㄌㄜˋ ㄆㄞˋ)
to force somebody to pay levies or do corvée
勒馬(ㄌㄜˋ ㄇㄚˇ)
to stop the horse from going ahead
勒令(ㄌㄜˋ ㄌㄧㄥˋ)
to compel by an order or injunction; to order
勒令退學(ㄌㄜˋ ㄌㄧㄥˋ ㄊㄨㄟˋ ㄒㄩㄝˊ)
suspended indefinitely
勒借(ㄌㄜˋ ㄐㄧㄝˋ)
to borrow by threats or coercion
勒戒所(ㄌㄜˋ ㄐㄧㄝˋ ㄙㄨㄛˇ)
a clinic where addicts are treated and made to kick the habit
勒交(ㄌㄜˋ ㄐㄧㄠ)
to order the surrender of; to force someone to hand over something
勒捐(ㄌㄜˋ ㄐㄩㄢ)
to order contributions
勒限(ㄌㄜˋ ㄒㄧㄢˋ)
to give a time limit to
勒詐(ㄌㄜˋ ㄓㄚˋ)
to defraud
勒住(ㄌㄜˋ ㄓㄨˋ)
to halt by pulling in reins
勒石(ㄌㄜˋ ㄕˊ)or 勒碑(ㄌㄜˋ ㄅㄟ)
to record one's achievements by engraving them on a stone tablet (for posterity)
勒贖(ㄌㄜˋ ㄕㄨˊ)
to kidnap a person for ransom
勒索(ㄌㄜˋ ㄙㄨㄛˇ)
to blackmail; to extort: 他勒索以前的老板。He extorted money from his former employer.

【勒】 432 2. ㄌㄟ lhei lēi
to tighten
勒斃(ㄌㄟ ㄅㄧˋ)
to strangle; to throttle
勒緊褲帶(ㄌㄟ ㄐㄧㄣˇ ㄎㄨˋ ㄉㄞˋ)or 勒緊腰帶(ㄌㄟ ㄐㄧㄣˇ ㄧㄠ ㄉㄞˋ)
to tighten one's belt — to practice parsimony
勒死(ㄌㄟ ㄙˇ)
to strangle; to throttle

【動】 433 ㄉㄨㄥˋ donq dòng
1. to move; to stir: 別動。Don't move.
2. to change; to alter
3. to act
4. to touch (one's heart); to arouse; to excite; to move: 她不爲甜言蜜語所動。She cannot be moved by fine words.
5. to take up: 動筷子 to take up chopsticks; to begin eating
6. to use: 動點腦筋吧! Use your head!
7. to eat or drink: 和尙不動葷腥。Monks never touch meat or fish.
8. movement; action: 他的一舉一動都很怪異。His every movement is very strange.
動筆(ㄉㄨㄥˋ ㄅㄧˇ)
to start writing: 他已動筆寫自傳。He has started writing autobiography.
動兵(ㄉㄨㄥˋ ㄅㄧㄥ)
to send out troops to fight
動不動(ㄉㄨㄥˋ ·ㄅㄨ ㄉㄨㄥˋ)
frequently; susceptible to (certain emotional manifestation such as crying, laughing, etc.); apt (to take certain action); easily: 他動不動就發脾氣。He is apt to lose his temper.
動脈(ㄉㄨㄥˋ ㄇㄞˋ)
an artery
動脈瘤(ㄉㄨㄥˋ ㄇㄞˋ ㄌㄧㄡˊ)
aneurysm
動脈硬化症(ㄉㄨㄥˋ ㄇㄞˋ ㄧㄥˋ ㄏㄨㄚˋ ㄓㄥˋ)
arteriosclerosis
動名詞(ㄉㄨㄥˋ ㄇㄧㄥˊ ㄘˊ)
(grammar) a gerund
動刀動槍(ㄉㄨㄥˋ ㄉㄠ ㄉㄨㄥˋ ㄑㄧㄤ)
to start war
動蕩(ㄉㄨㄥˋ ㄉㄤˋ)
uneasy; unstable; turbulence; unrest: 這個國家局勢動蕩不安。The situation of this country is turbulent.
動電(ㄉㄨㄥˋ ㄉㄧㄢˋ)
dynamic electricity
動態(ㄉㄨㄥˋ ㄊㄞˋ)
① development(s) (of an event or a situation) ② the movement (in a certain sphere of human activity)
動彈(ㄉㄨㄥˋ ㄊㄢˊ)
to budge; to move; to stir
動聽(ㄉㄨㄥˋ ㄊㄧㄥ)
appealing to the ear; fascinating to listen to: 這首歌很動聽。The song sounds fascinating.
動土(ㄉㄨㄥˋ ㄊㄨˇ)

to break ground (for a building project); to start construction work; to start building
動腦筋(ㄉㄨㄥˋ ㄋㄠˇ ㄐㄧㄣ)
①to think ②to secretly plan to get some coveted thing ③to try to obtain the affection of a beautiful woman
動能(ㄉㄨㄥˋ ㄋㄥˊ)
(physics) kinetic energy
動怒(ㄉㄨㄥˋ ㄋㄨˋ)
to lose one's temper; to get angry
動力(ㄉㄨㄥˋ ㄌㄧˋ)
①(physics) power; dynamic force ②driving force; impetus
動量(ㄉㄨㄥˋ ㄌㄧㄤˋ)
(physics) momentum
動亂(ㄉㄨㄥˋ ㄌㄨㄢˋ)
disturbance; disorder; commotion; agitation; unrest; turmoil; upheaval; turbulence: 暴民製造社會動亂。Mobs arouse a social upheaval.
動干戈(ㄉㄨㄥˋ ㄍㄢ ㄍㄜ)
to take up arms
動工(ㄉㄨㄥˋ ㄍㄨㄥ)
to start (construction) work; to begin construction: 這棟房子是去年動工的。They started building the house last year.
動口不動手(ㄉㄨㄥˋ ㄎㄡˇ ㄅㄨˋ ㄉㄨㄥˋ ㄕㄡˇ)
to argue without coming to blows
動滑輪(ㄉㄨㄥˋ ㄏㄨㄚˊ ㄌㄨㄣˊ)
a movable pulley
動火(ㄉㄨㄥˋ ㄏㄨㄛˇ)
to lose one's temper; to get angry; to flare up
動機(ㄉㄨㄥˋ ㄐㄧ)
motives; intentions: 他的動機很明顯。His intentions are clear.
動靜(ㄉㄨㄥˋ ㄐㄧㄥˋ)
①signs of action (being taken) ②in motion or at rest ③the sound of something astir
動氣(ㄉㄨㄥˋ ㄑㄧˋ)
to take offense; to get angry: 不要動氣，聽我解釋。Don't get angry. Let me explain.
動情(ㄉㄨㄥˋ ㄑㄧㄥˊ)
to have more than a fleeting interest in a woman; to have one's (sexual) passions aroused; to be enamored of
動心(ㄉㄨㄥˋ ㄒㄧㄣ)
①to be moved or perturbed mentally ②to show interest
動向(ㄉㄨㄥˋ ㄒㄧㄤˋ)
trends; general directions or tendencies
動刑(ㄉㄨㄥˋ ㄒㄧㄥˊ)
to apply torture; to torture
動輒(ㄉㄨㄥˋ ㄓㄜˊ)
easily; frequently: 他動輒發怒。He easily flew into a rage.
動輒得咎(ㄉㄨㄥˋ ㄓㄜˊ ㄉㄜˊ ㄐㄧㄡˋ)
to draw criticisms at every move
動產(ㄉㄨㄥˋ ㄔㄢˇ)
movable property; movables; personal property 參看「不動產」
動手(ㄉㄨㄥˋ ㄕㄡˇ)
①to start work: 那作家動手寫新作品。The writer started on a new work.② to use hands; to touch; to handle: 請勿動手。No touch, please.③ to raise a hand to strike: 他先動手打人。He struck the first blow.
動手動脚(ㄉㄨㄥˋ ㄕㄡˇ ㄉㄨㄥˋ ㄐㄧㄠˇ)
①to be unrestrained or unreserved (with women); to take liberties (with women) ②to make motions to start a fight
動手術(ㄉㄨㄥˋ ㄕㄡˇ ㄕㄨˋ)
①to operate on a patient; to perform a surgical operation ②to have an operation
動身(ㄉㄨㄥˋ ㄕㄣ)
to set out (on a trip); to depart: 他們在拂曉動身。They set out at dawn.
動人(ㄉㄨㄥˋ ㄖㄣˊ)
①moving; touching; pathetic ②(said of the beauty of a woman) to arouse interest or passion
動容(ㄉㄨㄥˋ ㄖㄨㄥˊ)
to change one's facial expression when one is moved
動作(ㄉㄨㄥˋ ㄗㄨㄛˋ)
motions; movements; actions; gestures: 她的動作敏捷。She is quick in her movement.
動詞(ㄉㄨㄥˋ ㄘˊ)
a verb
動粗(ㄉㄨㄥˋ ㄘㄨ)
to resort to violence
動議(ㄉㄨㄥˋ ㄧˋ)
a motion (at an assembly or a meeting); a proposal: 提出動議 to put forward a motion
動搖(ㄉㄨㄥˋ ㄧㄠˊ)
to waver; to shake
動武(ㄉㄨㄥˋ ㄨˇ)
to resort to violence; to use force; to start a fight
動物(ㄉㄨㄥˋ ㄨˋ)
an animal; a creature
動物界(ㄉㄨㄥˋ ㄨˋ ㄐㄧㄝˋ)
the animal kingdom
動物學(ㄉㄨㄥˋ ㄨˋ ㄒㄩㄝˊ)
zoology
動物誌(ㄉㄨㄥˋ ㄨˋ ㄓˋ)
a fauna—a treatise on the animals of any geographical area or geological period
動物生態學(ㄉㄨㄥˋ ㄨˋ ㄕㄥ ㄊㄞˋ ㄒㄩㄝˊ)
animal-ecology
動物園(ㄉㄨㄥˋ ㄨˋ ㄩㄢˊ)
a zoo; a zoological garden
動問(ㄉㄨㄥˋ ㄨㄣˋ)
to offer a question
動員(ㄉㄨㄥˋ ㄩㄢˊ)
to mobilize; mobilization
動員令(ㄉㄨㄥˋ ㄩㄢˊ ㄌㄧㄥˋ)
a mobilization order
動用(ㄉㄨㄥˋ ㄩㄥˋ)
to use or employ
動用公款(ㄉㄨㄥˋ ㄩㄥˋ ㄍㄨㄥ ㄎㄨㄢˇ)
to use public funds

【勗】 434
(勖) ㄒㄩˋ shiuh xù
to encourage; to stimulate
勗勉(ㄒㄩˋ ㄇㄧㄢˇ)
to encourage; to prompt: 總統勗勉國人更加努力。The president encouraged his countrymen to work harder.

【勘】 435
ㄎㄢ kann kàn
(又讀 ㄎㄢ kan kān)
1. to investigate; to explore; to examine; to check

〔力部〕

〔力部〕

2. to collate; to compare critically

勘探(ㄎㄢ ㄊㄢˋ)
exploration; prospecting: 地震勘探 seismic prospecting

勘察(ㄎㄢ ㄔㄚˊ)
to investigate; to inspect; to examine

勘災(ㄎㄢ ㄗㄞ)
to inspect a disaster area

勘測(ㄎㄢ ㄘㄜˋ)
to survey

勘驗(ㄎㄢ ㄧㄢˋ)
to examine; to check

勘誤(ㄎㄢ ㄨˋ)
to collate; to correct errors

勘誤表(ㄎㄢ ㄨˋ ㄅㄧㄠˇ)
corrigenda; errata

【務】 436
ㄨˋ wuh wù

1. to attend to; to strive after; to be engaged in: 他不務正業。He does not attend to his proper duties.
2. duty; business; affairs: 公務 official business
3. must; necessary
4. a Chinese family name

務本(ㄨˋ ㄅㄣˇ)
to attend to fundamentals: 君子務本。A man of virtue attends to fundamentals.

務必(ㄨˋ ㄅㄧˋ)or 務須(ㄨˋ ㄒㄩ)
to be sure; must; by all means

務農(ㄨˋ ㄋㄨㄥˊ)
to be engaged in farming

務求(ㄨˋ ㄑㄧㄡˊ)
to strive for

務希(ㄨˋ ㄒㄧ)
Please be sure to...

務實(ㄨˋ ㄕˊ)
① to strive for thoroughness ② pragmatism; pragmatic

務使(ㄨˋ ㄕˇ)
to make sure; to ensure

十畫

【勝】 437
1. ㄕㄥˋ shenq shèng

1. to win; to excel; to triumph; to surpass; to get the better of: 你一定會得勝。You are sure to win.
2. victory; success: 他勝不驕，敗不餒。He is not elated by success, nor discouraged by failure.
3. (sports) a win
4. a scenic view; a place of natural beauty: 尋幽覽勝 to visit places of scenic beauty
5. excellent; distinctive; wonderful

勝負(ㄕㄥˋ ㄈㄨˋ)or 勝敗(ㄕㄥˋ ㄅㄞˋ)
victory and defeat; the outcome (of a contest); success or failure: 勝負未定。Victory hangs in the balance.

勝地(ㄕㄥˋ ㄉㄧˋ)
a scenic spot; a vacationland; a place of natural beauty

勝利(ㄕㄥˋ ㄌㄧˋ)
① victory; triumph: 他們充滿了勝利的信心。They are fully confident of victory. ② successfully; triumphantly: 我軍勝利歸來。Our troops triumphantly came back.

勝過(ㄕㄥˋ ㄍㄨㄛˋ)
to be superior to; to excel; to surpass; to prevail over

勝會(ㄕㄥˋ ㄏㄨㄟˋ)
a great, festive occasion

勝迹(ㄕㄥˋ ㄐㄧ)
historical relics

勝家(ㄕㄥˋ ㄐㄧㄚ)
① the winner (in gambling) ② Singer (a manufacturer of sewing machines)

勝景(ㄕㄥˋ ㄐㄧㄥˇ)
scenic beauty

勝之不武(ㄕㄥˋ ㄓ ㄅㄨˋ ㄨˇ)
It brings no honor to the victor in an unequal contest.

勝仗(ㄕㄥˋ ㄓㄤˋ)
a victorious battle; a victory

勝朝(ㄕㄥˋ ㄔㄠˊ)
the preceding dynasty

勝訴(ㄕㄥˋ ㄙㄨˋ)
to win a lawsuit

勝算(ㄕㄥˋ ㄙㄨㄢˋ)
to be sure of success; odds or advantages (in a contest): 我們穩操勝算。We are sure of success.

勝友(ㄕㄥˋ ㄧㄡˇ)
well-known friends

勝於(ㄕㄥˋ ㄩˊ)
better than: 他勝於常人。He is better than the average persons.

【勝】 437
2. ㄕㄥ sheng shēng

to be competent enough (for a task)

勝冠(ㄕㄥ ㄍㄨㄢ)
(said of boys) at the age of 20

勝任(ㄕㄥ ㄖㄣˋ)
competent; qualified; equal to: 她能勝任教職的工作。She is competent for teaching.

勝任愉快(ㄕㄥ ㄖㄣˋ ㄩˊ ㄎㄨㄞˋ)
to be adequate for and happy with a job

【勞】 438
1. ㄌㄠˊ lau láo

1. to labor; to take the toil; to work
2. to trouble; to worry; to bother
3. meritorious deeds; services: 汗馬之勞 distinguished services in battle; war exploits
4. a Chinese family name

勞保(ㄌㄠˊ ㄅㄠˇ)
labor insurance 參看「勞工保險」

勞民傷財(ㄌㄠˊ ㄇㄧㄣˊ ㄕㄤ ㄘㄞˊ)
to tire the people and waste the resources (said of big construction projects of questionable economic value)

勞乏(ㄌㄠˊ ㄈㄚˊ)
fatigued; exhausted

勞費(ㄌㄠˊ ㄈㄟˋ)
to cost much effort and expenditure

勞煩(ㄌㄠˊ ㄈㄢˊ)
(courtesy) to trouble (someone to do something)

勞方(ㄌㄠˊ ㄈㄤ)
labor

勞頓(ㄌㄠˊ ㄉㄨㄣˋ)
fatigue; exhaustion

勞動
①(ㄌㄠˊ ㄉㄨㄥˋ) to labor (physically); to toil; to sweat ②(ㄌㄠˊ ·ㄉㄨㄥ) to trouble (a person with a request)

勞動法(ㄌㄠˊ ㄉㄨㄥˋ ㄈㄚˇ)
labor law; labor legislation

勞動力(ㄌㄠˊ ㄉㄨㄥˋ ㄌㄧˋ)
① labor force; work force; manpower ② capacity or ability for physical labor

勞動量(ㄌㄠˊ ㄉㄨㄥˋ ㄌㄧㄤˋ)

the amount of labor

勞動改造(ㄌㄠˊ ㄉㄨㄥˋ ㄍㄞˇ ㄗㄠˋ)
to reform through forced labor (a Chinese Communist practice as a form of punishment)

勞動階級(ㄌㄠˊ ㄉㄨㄥˋ ㄐㄧㄝ ㄐㄧˊ)
the working class

勞動節(ㄌㄠˊ ㄉㄨㄥˋ ㄐㄧㄝˊ)or 勞工紀念日(ㄌㄠˊ ㄍㄨㄥ ㄐㄧˋ ㄋㄧㄢˋ ㄖˋ)
Labor Day

勞動者(ㄌㄠˊ ㄉㄨㄥˋ ㄓㄜˇ)
a laborer; a workman

勞動日(ㄌㄠˊ ㄉㄨㄥˋ ㄖˋ)
a workday 亦作「工作日」

勞累(ㄌㄠˊ ㄌㄟˋ)
to fatigue, tire or exhaust (a person)

勞力(ㄌㄠˊ ㄌㄧˋ)
①(physical) labor; labor force ②to labor physically

勞力士手錶(ㄌㄠˊ ㄌㄧˋ ㄕˋ ㄕㄡˇ ㄅㄧㄠˇ)
a Rolex watch

勞碌(ㄌㄠˊ ㄌㄨˋ)
to work hard; to toil and moil; to drudge; to busy oneself with drudgery

勞碌命(ㄌㄠˊ ㄌㄨˋ ㄇㄧㄥˋ)
a born laborer

勞改(ㄌㄠˊ ㄍㄞˇ)
(said of criminals) to reform through forced labor 參看「勞動改造」

勞工(ㄌㄠˊ ㄍㄨㄥ)
laborers; workers

勞工保險(ㄌㄠˊ ㄍㄨㄥ ㄅㄠˇ ㄒㄧㄢˇ)
labor insurance 亦作「勞保」

勞苦(ㄌㄠˊ ㄎㄨˇ)
①to work hard; to labor; to toil ②toil; labor; pains: 他將不辭勞苦地幫你。He will spare no pains to help you.

勞苦功高(ㄌㄠˊ ㄎㄨˇ ㄍㄨㄥ ㄍㄠ)
to work hard and make a great contribution (a eulogy for meritorious service)

勞績(ㄌㄠˊ ㄐㄧ)
the fruits of hard work; accomplishment; merits

勞駕(ㄌㄠˊ ㄐㄧㄚˋ)
to be sorry to have to trouble someone to do something

勞心(ㄌㄠˊ ㄒㄧㄣ)
①to labor mentally; to work with one's mind or brains ②to be worried; to be anxious

勞形(ㄌㄠˊ ㄒㄧㄥˊ)
physically fatiguing; tired out

勞師(ㄌㄠˊ ㄕ)
to tire troops

勞師動衆(ㄌㄠˊ ㄕ ㄉㄨㄥˋ ㄓㄨㄥˋ)
①to tire too many troops and people (for unimportant things)—to waste manpower ②to involve too many people

勞神(ㄌㄠˊ ㄕㄣˊ)
①to bother; to trouble ②to be worried; to be concerned

勞人草草(ㄌㄠˊ ㄖㄣˊ ㄘㄠˇ ㄘㄠˇ)
Those who toil physically often have to worry mentally.

勞資(ㄌㄠˊ ㄗ)
labor versus management; labor and management; labor and capital

勞資關係(ㄌㄠˊ ㄗ ㄍㄨㄢ ㄒㄧˋ)
labor-capital relations

勞資爭議(ㄌㄠˊ ㄗ ㄓㄥ ㄧˋ)
labor dispute

勞作(ㄌㄠˊ ㄗㄨㄛˋ)
①manual work or training (at school) ②manual labor

勞損(ㄌㄠˊ ㄙㄨㄣˇ)
(medicine) strain

勞而無功(ㄌㄠˊ ㄦˊ ㄨˊ ㄍㄨㄥ)
to labor to no purpose; to make futile efforts; to plow the sand; to beat the air

勞役(ㄌㄠˊ ㄧˋ)
hard labor (as punishment); forced labor

勞逸不均(ㄌㄠˊ ㄧˋ ㄅㄨˋ ㄐㄩㄣ)
unequal distribution of work with some doing too much while others doing too little

勞燕分飛(ㄌㄠˊ ㄧㄢˋ ㄈㄣ ㄈㄟ)
(said of people) to separate or part (like birds flying in different directions)

勞務(ㄌㄠˊ ㄨˋ)
service

【勞】 438
2. ㄌㄠˋ law lào

to comfort or entertain (the tired)

勞民(ㄌㄠˋ ㄇㄧㄣˊ)
to conciliate the people

勞軍(ㄌㄠˋ ㄐㄩㄣ)
to cheer or entertain troops

十一畫

【勢】 439
ㄕˋ shyh shì

1. power; force; influence: 颱風來勢甚猛。The typhoon came with tremendous force.
2. a tendency: 少年犯罪有增加的趨勢。Juvenile delinquency shows a tendency to increase.
3. the natural features: 山勢 the lie of a mountain
4. a situation; circumstances: 乘勢to take advantage of a situation
5. signs; gestures: 他做了手勢叫我進去。He gave me a sign to come in.
6. male genitals: 去勢to castrate; castration

勢必(ㄕˋ ㄅㄧˋ)
certainly; to be bound to; undoubtedly: 飲酒過度，勢必影響健康。Excessive drinking will certainly affect one's health.

勢不兩立(ㄕˋ ㄅㄨˋ ㄌㄧㄤˇ ㄌㄧˋ)
unable to coexist; unable to live peacefully together; incompatible

勢不可當(ㄕˋ ㄅㄨˋ ㄎㄜˇ ㄉㄤ)
irresistible: 民主的潮流洶湧澎湃，勢不可當。The democracy is surging forward irresistibly.

勢頭(ㄕˋ ㄊㄡˊ)
①impetus; momentum ②a tendency; a situation; a state of affairs

勢頭不對(ㄕˋ ㄊㄡˊ ㄅㄨˊ ㄉㄨㄟˋ)
The situation is unfavorable.

勢難兼顧(ㄕˋ ㄋㄢˊ ㄐㄧㄢ ㄍㄨˋ)
The situation is hard for one to look after both sides simultaneously.

勢難從命(ㄕˋ ㄋㄢˊ ㄘㄨㄥˊ ㄇㄧㄥˋ)
Circumstances make it difficult for me to comply with (or obey) your request.

勢力(ㄕˋ ㄌㄧˋ)
force; power; influence

勢力範圍(ㄕˋ ㄌㄧˋ ㄈㄢˋ ㄨㄟˊ)
the sphere of influence

勢利(ㄕˋ ㄌㄧˋ)

〔力部〕

snobbish

勢利眼(ㄕˋ ㄌㄧˋ ㄧㄢˇ)
①a snob ②a snobbish attitude; snobbishness; snobbery ③to judge people by wealth and power

勢均力敵(ㄕˋ ㄐㄩㄣ ㄌㄧˋ ㄉㄧˊ)
evenly matched; well matched: 雙方勢均力敵。The two sides are well matched.

勢窮力竭(ㄕˋ ㄑㄩㄥˊ ㄌㄧˋ ㄐㄧㄝˊ)
in a terrible plight and powerless

勢如破竹(ㄕˋ ㄖㄨˊ ㄆㄛˋ ㄓㄨˊ)
(said of a victorious army) to advance with irresistible force; to push onward with overwhelming momentum

勢在必行(ㄕˋ ㄗㄞˋ ㄅㄧˋ ㄒㄧㄥˊ)
to be imperative, urgent, or essential (under the circumstances)

勢所必然(ㄕˋ ㄙㄨㄛˇ ㄅㄧˋ ㄖㄢˊ)
(It is) a matter of necessity, a matter of course, a necessary result of the situation, an inevitable outcome, etc.

勢要(ㄕˋ ㄧㄠˋ)
the influential and the mighty

勢燄薰天(ㄕˋ ㄧㄢˋ ㄒㄩㄣ ㄊㄧㄢ)
very influential and powerful

【募】 440 ㄇㄨˋ muh mù

1. to recruit or enlist (personnel): 徵募男子入伍 to enlist men for the army
2. to raise (funds); to collect

募兵(ㄇㄨˋ ㄅㄧㄥ)
to recruit or enlist soldiers; to raise troops

募兵制(ㄇㄨˋ ㄅㄧㄥ ㄓˋ)
a voluntary military service system

募款(ㄇㄨˋ ㄎㄨㄢˇ)
to raise funds

募化(ㄇㄨˋ ㄏㄨㄚˋ)
(said of Buddhist monks or Taoist priests) to beg for alms 亦作「化緣」

募集(ㄇㄨˋ ㄐㄧˊ)
to recruit; to raise; to collect

募捐(ㄇㄨˋ ㄐㄩㄢ)
to solicit or collect contributions; to collect donations

【勤】 441 ㄑㄧㄣˊ chyn qín

1. diligent; industrious; sedulous; hardworking
2. frequently; regularly

勤樸(ㄑㄧㄣˊ ㄆㄨˇ)
industrious and frugal

勤勉(ㄑㄧㄣˊ ㄇㄧㄢˇ)
industrious; diligent; hardworking; sedulous: 勤勉好學 sedulous and eager to learn

勤奮(ㄑㄧㄣˊ ㄈㄣˋ)
diligent; assiduous; industrious: 他工作勤奮。He is diligent in his work.

勤惰(ㄑㄧㄣˊ ㄉㄨㄛˋ)
diligence and negligence; activity and inactivity

勤能補拙(ㄑㄧㄣˊ ㄋㄥˊ ㄅㄨˇ ㄓㄨㄛˊ)
Stupidity can be remedied by diligence.

勤勞(ㄑㄧㄣˊ ㄌㄠˊ)
to toil or labor sedulously; diligent; industrious; hardworking

勤苦(ㄑㄧㄣˊ ㄎㄨˇ)
to work sedulously in defiance of hardships

勤快(ㄑㄧㄣˊ ㄎㄨㄞˋ)
(colloquial) diligent; industrious

勤儉(ㄑㄧㄣˊ ㄐㄧㄢˇ)
hardworking and thrifty; diligent and frugal

勤儉建國(ㄑㄧㄣˊ ㄐㄧㄢˇ ㄐㄧㄢˋ ㄍㄨㄛˊ)
to establish a country through thrift and hard work

勤儉持家(ㄑㄧㄣˊ ㄐㄧㄢˇ ㄔˊ ㄐㄧㄚ)
to be diligent and frugal in managing a household

勤謹(ㄑㄧㄣˊ ㄐㄧㄣˇ)
diligent and prudent

勤學(ㄑㄧㄣˊ ㄒㄩㄝˊ)
to study diligently

勤有功嬉無益(ㄑㄧㄣˊ ㄧㄡˇ ㄍㄨㄥ ㄒㄧ ㄨˊ ㄧˋ)
Reward lies ahead of diligence, but nothing is gained by indolence.

勤務(ㄑㄧㄣˊ ㄨˋ)
①logistic duties (in the armed forces) ②daily duties (of policemen)

勤務兵(ㄑㄧㄣˊ ㄨˋ ㄅㄧㄥ)
an orderly

勤務員(ㄑㄧㄣˊ ㄨˋ ㄩㄢˊ)
①an odd-job man ②a servant

勤王(ㄑㄧㄣˊ ㄨㄤˊ)
to save the throne (by rushing troops to the monarch's rescue in time of crisis)

【勠】 442 ㄌㄨˋ luh lù

1. to unite or join (forces)
2. to kill; to slay

勠力(ㄌㄨˋ ㄌㄧˋ)
to join forces; to unite efforts; to cooperate

勠力同心(ㄌㄨˋ ㄌㄧˋ ㄊㄨㄥˊ ㄒㄧㄣ)
to work together with the same objective in mind

十三畫

【勰】 443 ㄒㄧㄝˊ shye xié

harmonious

十四畫

【勳】 444 ㄒㄩㄣ shiun xūn

merits; honors; meritorious services; achievements

勳勞(ㄒㄩㄣ ㄌㄠˊ)
meritorious contributions; merits

勳貴(ㄒㄩㄣ ㄍㄨㄟˋ)
the nobility and ministers with close connections with the emperor

勳功(ㄒㄩㄣ ㄍㄨㄥ)
meritorious services 亦作「功勳」

勳績(ㄒㄩㄣ ㄐㄧ)
meritorious services; outstanding achievements

勳爵(ㄒㄩㄣ ㄐㄩㄝˊ)
a rank conferred in recognition of merits

勳章(ㄒㄩㄣ ㄓㄤ)
a medal of honor; a decoration

勳臣(ㄒㄩㄣ ㄔㄣˊ)
an official with a record of meritorious services to the country

勳業(ㄒㄩㄣ ㄧㄝˋ)
meritorious achievements or contribution

十五畫

【勵】 445 ㄌㄧˋ lih lì

1. to incite; to encourage; to rouse (to action)
2. to exert oneself

勵精圖治(ㄌㄧˋ ㄐㄧㄥ ㄊㄨˊ ㄓˋ)
(said of a government or a national leader) to pursue the task of a national build-up with determination and dedication

勵行(ㄌㄧˋ ㄒㄧㄥˊ)
to enforce or practice with determination

勵志(ㄌㄧˋ ㄓˋ)
to pursue a goal with determination

勵志社(ㄌㄧˋ ㄓˋ ㄕㄜˋ)
the OMEA, which stands for the Officer's Moral Endeavor Association, a semi-official organization in China created in the early 1930's

十七畫

【勸】 446 ㄑㄩㄢˋ chiuann quàn

to exhort; to urge; to advise; to persuade: 勸他休息一下。Urge him to take a rest.

勸勉(ㄑㄩㄢˋ ㄇㄧㄢˇ)
to exhort to great effort; to encourage; to urge

勸募(ㄑㄩㄢˋ ㄇㄨˋ)
to ask for contributions

勸導(ㄑㄩㄢˋ ㄉㄠˇ)or(ㄑㄩㄢˋ ㄉㄠˋ)
to admonish; to exhort and guide

勸告(ㄑㄩㄢˋ ㄍㄠˋ)
to advise; to counsel; to exhort; advice: 醫生勸告我要好好休息。The doctor advised me to have a good rest.

勸和(ㄑㄩㄢˋ ㄏㄜˊ)
to reconcile a dispute or quarrel

勸化(ㄑㄩㄢˋ ㄏㄨㄚˋ)
① to exhort to conversion; to convert ②(said of monks or nuns) to beg for alms

勸誨(ㄑㄩㄢˋ ㄏㄨㄟˋ)
to advise; to exhort

勸架(ㄑㄩㄢˋ ㄐㄧㄚˋ)
to mediate a quarrel

勸駕(ㄑㄩㄢˋ ㄐㄧㄚˋ)
to urge someone to do something

勸解(ㄑㄩㄢˋ ㄐㄧㄝˇ)
to mediate; to exhort to peace

勸戒(ㄑㄩㄢˋ ㄐㄧㄝˋ)
to admonish; to dissuade; to expostulate

勸酒(ㄑㄩㄢˋ ㄐㄧㄡˇ)
to offer a drink (of wine or liquor)

勸諫(ㄑㄩㄢˋ ㄐㄧㄢˋ)
to remonstrate (with a superior); to plead for rectification

勸進(ㄑㄩㄢˋ ㄐㄧㄣˋ)
(said of sycophants) to persuade (a hypocritical warlord) to ascend to the throne

勸降(ㄑㄩㄢˋ ㄒㄧㄤˊ)
to induce to surrender

勸學(ㄑㄩㄢˋ ㄒㄩㄝˊ)
to urge someone to study hard

勸世(ㄑㄩㄢˋ ㄕˋ)
to give people a sermon; to admonish

勸善規過(ㄑㄩㄢˋ ㄕㄢˋ ㄍㄨㄟ ㄍㄨㄛˋ)
to exhort to reformation and to urge to virtue

勸說(ㄑㄩㄢˋ ㄕㄨㄛ)
to persuade; to advise

勸人爲善(ㄑㄩㄢˋ ㄖㄣˊ ㄨㄟˊ ㄕㄢˋ)or 勸善(ㄑㄩㄢˋ ㄕㄢˋ)
to exhort people to do good

勸阻(ㄑㄩㄢˋ ㄗㄨˇ)or 勸止(ㄑㄩㄢˋ ㄓˇ)
to dissuade someone from; to advise someone against something

勸誘(ㄑㄩㄢˋ ㄧㄡˋ)
to induce; to prevail upon

勸慰(ㄑㄩㄢˋ ㄨㄟˋ)
to console; to soothe

勹部
ㄅㄠ bau bāo

一畫

【勺】 447 ㄕㄠˊ shaur sháo

a ladle; a spoon; a scoop: 飯勺 a ladle for taking rice into bowls

勺子(ㄕㄠˊ・ㄗ)
a ladle; a spoon; a scoop; a dipper

二畫

【匀】 448 ㄩㄣˊ yun yún

uniform; even

匀分(ㄩㄣˊ ㄈㄣ)
to divide equally; to share and share alike

匀調(ㄩㄣˊ ㄊㄧㄠˊ)or 匀停(ㄩㄣˊ・ㄊㄧㄥ)
even; balanced

匀臉(ㄩㄣˊ ㄌㄧㄢˇ)
to powder and paint one's face evenly

匀整(ㄩㄣˊ ㄓㄥˇ)
neat; even and orderly

匀稱(ㄩㄣˊ ㄔㄣˋ)
symmetrical; balanced; even; harmonious

匀出(ㄩㄣˊ ㄔㄨ)
to spare or share something

匀圓(ㄩㄣˊ ㄩㄢˊ)
evenly round

【勾】 449 1. ㄍㄡ gou gōu

1. to mark; to put a check; to mark on
2. to cancel; to cross out (or off)
3. to hook
4. to join; to connect
5. to evoke
6. to entice; to seduce
7. a hook

勾搭(ㄍㄡ・ㄉㄚ)
① to have illegitimate relations (with one of the other sex) ② to conspire with; to gang up ③ to seduce; to entice

勾通(ㄍㄡ ㄊㄨㄥ)
to cooperate secretly; to collaborate or collude

勾勒(ㄍㄡ ㄌㄜˋ)
to draw the outline of; to sketch or delineate the contours of; to give a brief account of; to sketch; to outline

勾欄(ㄍㄡ ㄌㄢˊ)or勾欄院(ㄍㄡ ㄌㄢˊ ㄩㄢˋ)
a brothel

勾留(ㄍㄡ ㄌㄧㄡˊ)
to be detained (by business); to stay; to stop over

勾連(ㄍㄡ ㄌㄧㄢˊ)
to join; to unite; to connect

勾臉(ㄍㄡ ㄌㄧㄢˇ)
to paint the face (in Peking opera)

勾畫(ㄍㄡ ㄏㄨㄚˋ)
to draw the outline of; to delineate; to sketch

勾魂(ㄍㄡ ㄏㄨㄣˊ)
to bewitch; to enchant; to fascinate

勾結(ㄍㄡ ㄐㄧㄝˊ)
to collude or collaborate; collusion or collaboration; to gang up: 你們全部勾結起來對付我一個。You have all ganged up on me.

勾芡(ㄍㄡ ㄑㄧㄢˋ)
to thicken (soup, etc.) by means of starch

勾情(ㄍㄡ ㄑㄧㄥˊ)
to flirt (with someone)

勾消 or 勾銷(ㄍㄡ ㄒㄧㄠ)
to liquidate; to strike out; to cancel; to nullify; to write off

勾心鬥角(ㄍㄡ ㄒㄧㄣ ㄉㄡˋ ㄐㄧㄠˇ)
to intrigue against each other 參看「鉤心鬥角」

勾除(ㄍㄡ ㄔㄨˊ)
to eliminate; to cancel; to delete

勾串(ㄍㄡ ㄔㄨㄢˋ)
to conspire with; to gang up

勾引(ㄍㄡ ㄧㄣˇ)
to entice; to seduce; to tempt; to inveigle: 她勾引他加入另一黨。She seduced him to the other party.

【勾】 449
2. ㄍㄡˋ gow gòu
1. to manage
2. business; affairs

勾當(ㄍㄡˋ ·ㄉㄤ)
an underhand job; a dirty business; a plot; an intrigue; hush-hush activities

【勿】 450
ㄨˋ wuh wù
do not; not; never; a negative word used in formal speech: 勿急。Don't rush. 請勿吸煙。No Smoking.

勿念(ㄨˋ ㄋㄧㄢˋ)
Do not worry.

勿論(ㄨˋ ㄌㄨㄣˋ)
regardless of; to let alone

勿失(ㄨˋ ㄕ)
Do not let (a chance, etc.) slip away.

勿藥(ㄨˋ ㄧㄠˋ)
to recover from illness

三畫

【包】 451
ㄅㄠ bau bāo
1. to wrap: 用紙把書包起來。Wrap (up) a book in a piece of paper.
2. to include; to contain: 他將小費包括在費用的估計中。He included a sum for tips in his estimate of expenses.
3. to surround
4. to guarantee
5. a parcel; a package; a bundle: 郵包 a postal parcel

包辦(ㄅㄠ ㄅㄢˋ)
to assume full responsibility for; to undertake completely: 這事由他包辦。He will be fully responsible for it.

包庇(ㄅㄠ ㄅㄧˋ)
to harbor; to shelter; to shield; to defend someone who does not deserve defense: 他撒謊以包庇他的弟弟。He told a lie to shield his younger brother.

包賠(ㄅㄠ ㄆㄟˊ)
to guarantee to compensate (for loss, injury, etc.)

包皮(ㄅㄠ ㄆㄧˊ)
① a wrapper; a covering ② the prepuce

包票(ㄅㄠ ㄆㄧㄠˋ)
a guaranty; a certificate of guarantee

包飯(ㄅㄠ ㄈㄢˋ)or 包伙(ㄅㄠ ㄏㄨㄛˇ)
to eat meals regularly (at a small restaurant) on a monthly payment basis; to board

包袱(ㄅㄠ ㄈㄨˊ)
① a cloth wrapper ② a bundle in a cloth wrapper ③ a burden; a liability

包賭(ㄅㄠ ㄉㄨˇ)
to protect illegal gambling casinos

包退包換(ㄅㄠ ㄊㄨㄟˋ ㄅㄠ ㄏㄨㄢˋ)
to refund or change for a better one (if the merchandise is defective) 或 Merchandise will be exchanged if found unsatisfactory.

包攬(ㄅㄠ ㄌㄢˇ)
to monopolize; to undertake the whole thing; to take on everything

包攬訟事(ㄅㄠ ㄌㄢˇ ㄙㄨㄥˋ ㄕˋ)or 包攬詞訟(ㄅㄠ ㄌㄢˇ ㄘˊ ㄙㄨㄥˋ)
(said of unethical lawyers) to encourage or instigate litigations with a view to getting the fee; to act as shyster; to engage in pettifoggery

包羅(ㄅㄠ ㄌㄨㄛˊ)
to include; to cover: 音樂種類包羅甚廣。Music covers a wide range.

包羅萬象(ㄅㄠ ㄌㄨㄛˊ ㄨㄢˋ ㄒㄧㄤˋ)
inclusive of everything; all-inclusive; to cover and contain everything

包穀(ㄅㄠ ㄍㄨˇ)
corn

包裹(ㄅㄠ ㄍㄨㄛˇ)
① to wrap up ② a parcel; a bundle; a package

包管(ㄅㄠ ㄍㄨㄢˇ)
to guarantee or assure: 包管沒問題。I guarantee it's all right.

包工(ㄅㄠ ㄍㄨㄥ)
① a job or project awarded to a contractor ② a job for which payment is calculated on the amount of work done (instead of on an hourly or daily basis) 亦作「包活」③ a contractor

包公(ㄅㄠ ㄍㄨㄥ) or 包拯(ㄅㄠ ㄓㄥˇ)
Pao Cheng, 999-1062, an upright official known for his stressing the dignity of law

包括(ㄅㄠ ㄎㄨㄛˋ)or(ㄅㄠ ㄍㄨㄚ)
to include; to comprise

包含(ㄅㄠ ㄏㄢˊ)
to contain; to comprise; to include: 較大者包含較小者。The greater includes the

lesser.
包換(ㄅㄠ ㄏㄨㄢˋ)
to guarantee replacement (of unsatisfactory goods with satisfactory ones)
包機(ㄅㄠ ㄐㄧ)
a chartered airplane
包銷(ㄅㄠ ㄒㄧㄠ)
to assume the responsibility for the sale (of a certain commodity); to be the sole agent for a production unit or a firm
包修(ㄅㄠ ㄒㄧㄡ)
to guarantee the repair of something
包心菜(ㄅㄠ ㄒㄧㄣ ㄘㄞˋ)
a cabbage
包廂(ㄅㄠ ㄒㄧㄤ)
a box (in a theater, stadium, etc.)
包治(ㄅㄠ ㄓˋ)or 包醫(ㄅㄠ ㄧ)
to guarantee a cure; not to receive fees till the patient is cured
包治百病(ㄅㄠ ㄓˋ ㄅㄞˇ ㄅㄧㄥˋ)
to guarantee to cure all diseases
包賺(ㄅㄠ ㄓㄨㄢˋ)
to guarantee profits; profits assured
包准(ㄅㄠ ㄓㄨㄣˇ)
to guarantee (that something is sure to happen, etc.)
包裝(ㄅㄠ ㄓㄨㄤ)
to pack; packing: 這些書容易包裝。These books pack easily.
包車(ㄅㄠ ㄔㄜ)
a chartered bus
包抄(ㄅㄠ ㄔㄠ)
(military) to outflank
包娼(ㄅㄠ ㄔㄤ)
to harbor or protect call girl centers
包場(ㄅㄠ ㄔㄤˇ)
to reserve a whole theater or cinema
包商(ㄅㄠ ㄕㄤ)
a concessionaire (in business); a contractor
包容(ㄅㄠ ㄖㄨㄥˊ)
① to tolerate; to forgive: 他不太能包容批評。He is not very tolerant of criticism. ② to contain; to hold
包子(ㄅㄠ ˙ㄗ)
a steamed pie; a steamed stuffed bun
包紮(ㄅㄠ ㄗㄚ)
to wrap; to bandage; to pack; to tie up; to bind up
包租(ㄅㄠ ㄗㄨ)
① to rent a room or a house for subletting ② a fixed farmland rent one must pay no matter how bad the harvest might be
包藏(ㄅㄠ ㄘㄤˊ)
to contain; to conceal
包藏禍心(ㄅㄠ ㄘㄤˊ ㄏㄨㄛˋ ㄒㄧㄣ)
to harbor evil intentions or malicious intent
包贏(ㄅㄠ ㄧㄥˊ)
to guarantee winning in gambling or in a sports match
包圍(ㄅㄠ ㄨㄟˊ)
to surround; to besiege; to encircle: 一道牆包圍了整個花園。A wall surrounds the garden.
包運(ㄅㄠ ㄩㄣˋ)
to transport; transportation
包用(ㄅㄠ ㄩㄥˋ)
to guarantee serviceability (of an article)

四畫

【匈】 452 ㄒㄩㄥ shiong xiōng
1. the breast; the bosom; the thorax
2. to clamor
匈奴(ㄒㄩㄥ ㄋㄨˊ)
the Huns, an ancient nationality in China
匈牙利(ㄒㄩㄥ ㄧㄚˊ ㄌㄧˋ)
Hungary
匈牙利人(ㄒㄩㄥ ㄧㄚˊ ㄌㄧˋ ㄖㄣˊ)
a Hungarian
匈牙利語(ㄒㄩㄥ ㄧㄚˊ ㄌㄧˋ ㄩˇ)
Hungarian

七畫

【匍】 453 ㄆㄨˊ pwu pú
1. to crawl; to creep
2. to lie prostrate; to prostrate
匍匐 or 匍伏(ㄆㄨˊ ㄈㄨˊ)
① to crawl; to creep ② to prostrate

九畫

【匏】 454 ㄆㄠˊ paur páo
1. a gourd; a bottle gourd; a calabash
2. a kind of wind instrument originally made of a gourd
匏瓜(ㄆㄠˊ ㄍㄨㄚ)
a gourd; a bottle gourd; a calabash
匏尊(ㄆㄠˊ ㄗㄨㄣ)
a gourd shell as a wine cup

【匐】 455 ㄈㄨˊ fwu fú
1. to lie prostrate; to prostrate
2. to crawl; to creep

匕部
ㄅㄧˇ bii bǐ

【匕】 456 ㄅㄧˇ bii bǐ
1. a ladle; a spoon
2. an arrowhead
3. a dagger
匕首(ㄅㄧˇ ㄕㄡˇ)
a dagger; a short sword

二畫

【化】 457 ㄏㄨㄚˋ huah huà
1. to change; to convert; to transform; to influence: 冰在熱天很快化爲水。Ice changes into water rapidly on a hot day.
2. short for "chemistry"
化名(ㄏㄨㄚˋ ㄇㄧㄥˊ)
to assume a pseudonym; a pseudonym
化肥(ㄏㄨㄚˋ ㄈㄟˊ)
chemical fertilizer
化繁爲簡(ㄏㄨㄚˋ ㄈㄢˊ ㄨㄟˊ ㄐㄧㄢˇ)
to simplify what is complicated
化糞池(ㄏㄨㄚˋ ㄈㄣˋ ㄔˊ)
a cesspool or cesspit; a septic tank
化腐朽爲神奇(ㄏㄨㄚˋ ㄈㄨˇ ㄒㄧㄡˇ ㄨㄟˊ

〔匕部〕

ㄕㄣˊ ㄑㄧˊ)
to make the ugly things beautiful; to make use of discarded things; to transform the corruptible into a mysterious life

化敵爲友(ㄏㄨㄚˋ ㄉㄧˊ ㄨㄟˊ ㄧㄡˇ)
to convert an enemy into a friend

化痰止咳(ㄏㄨㄚˋ ㄊㄢˊ ㄓˇ ㄎㄜˊ)
capable of preventing phlegm from forming and stopping coughing (a promotional phrase for medicine)

化膿(ㄏㄨㄚˋ ㄋㄨㄥˊ)
to suppurate; to maturate; to fester

化零爲整(ㄏㄨㄚˋ ㄌㄧㄥˊ ㄨㄟˊ ㄓㄥˇ)
(guerrilla warfare) to concentrate all the forces available in order to deliver a crushing blow to a relatively weak enemy force

化干戈爲玉帛(ㄏㄨㄚˋ ㄍㄢ ㄍㄜ ㄨㄟˊ ㄩˋ ㄅㄛˊ)
to bury the hatchets and work for peace

化工(ㄏㄨㄚˋ ㄍㄨㄥ)
① Nature's work; operations of Nature ② chemical engineering

化開(ㄏㄨㄚˋ ㄎㄞ)
to spread out after being diluted or melted

化合(ㄏㄨㄚˋ ㄏㄜˊ)
to combine (chemically); combination

化合量(ㄏㄨㄚˋ ㄏㄜˊ ㄌㄧㄤˋ)
(chemistry) combining weight

化合物(ㄏㄨㄚˋ ㄏㄜˊ ㄨˋ)
a (chemical) compound

化解(ㄏㄨㄚˋ ㄐㄧㄝˇ)
to bring reconciliation to; to settle (disputes)

化境(ㄏㄨㄚˋ ㄐㄧㄥˋ)
a transcendent or unearthly atmosphere (especially of a work of art); sublimity; perfection

化險爲夷(ㄏㄨㄚˋ ㄒㄧㄢˇ ㄨㄟˊ ㄧˊ)
to turn peril into safety; to head off a disaster

化學(ㄏㄨㄚˋ ㄒㄩㄝˊ)
chemistry

化學變化(ㄏㄨㄚˋ ㄒㄩㄝˊ ㄅㄧㄢˋ ㄏㄨㄚˋ)
chemical change

化學平衡(ㄏㄨㄚˋ ㄒㄩㄝˊ ㄆㄧㄥˊ ㄏㄥˊ)
chemical equilibrium

化學反應(ㄏㄨㄚˋ ㄒㄩㄝˊ ㄈㄢˇ ㄧㄥˋ)
chemical reaction

化學分解(ㄏㄨㄚˋ ㄒㄩㄝˊ ㄈㄣ ㄐㄧㄝˇ)
chemical decomposition

化學分析(ㄏㄨㄚˋ ㄒㄩㄝˊ ㄈㄣ ㄒㄧ)
chemical analysis

化學方程式(ㄏㄨㄚˋ ㄒㄩㄝˊ ㄈㄤ ㄔㄥˊ ㄕˋ)
a chemical equation; a chemical formula

化學工業(ㄏㄨㄚˋ ㄒㄩㄝˊ ㄍㄨㄥ ㄧㄝˋ)
the chemical industry

化學纖維(ㄏㄨㄚˋ ㄒㄩㄝˊ ㄒㄧㄢ ㄨㄟˊ)
synthetic fiber; chemical fiber

化學戰(ㄏㄨㄚˋ ㄒㄩㄝˊ ㄓㄢˋ)
chemical warfare

化學作用(ㄏㄨㄚˋ ㄒㄩㄝˊ ㄗㄨㄛˋ ㄩㄥˋ)
chemical action

化學武器(ㄏㄨㄚˋ ㄒㄩㄝˊ ㄨˇ ㄑㄧˋ)
chemical weapons

化整爲零(ㄏㄨㄚˋ ㄓㄥˇ ㄨㄟˊ ㄌㄧㄥˊ)
(guerrilla warfare) to break up large troops into scattered groups so as to avoid annihilation by a powerful enemy force

化妝(ㄏㄨㄚˋ ㄓㄨㄤ)
to make up; to apply cosmetics

化妝品(ㄏㄨㄚˋ ㄓㄨㄤ ㄆㄧㄣˇ)
cosmetics

化裝(ㄏㄨㄚˋ ㄓㄨㄤ)
to disguise oneself; to masquerade

化裝舞會(ㄏㄨㄚˋ ㄓㄨㄤ ㄨˇ ㄏㄨㄟˋ)
a masquerade

化除(ㄏㄨㄚˋ ㄔㄨˊ)
to dissolve to nothing; to dispel; to remove; to abolish

化除畛域(ㄏㄨㄚˋ ㄔㄨˊ ㄓㄣˇ ㄩˋ)
to eliminate regionalism

化石(ㄏㄨㄚˋ ㄕˊ)
a fossil

化石學(ㄏㄨㄚˋ ㄕˊ ㄒㄩㄝˊ)
petrifactology, or paleontology

化身(ㄏㄨㄚˋ ㄕㄣ)
an incarnation; an embodiment

化生放戰爭(ㄏㄨㄚˋ ㄕㄥ ㄈㄤˋ ㄓㄢˋ ㄓㄥ)
chemical, biological and nuclear warfare

化俗(ㄏㄨㄚˋ ㄙㄨˊ)
to improve customs; to civilize

化暗爲明(ㄏㄨㄚˋ ㄢˋ ㄨㄟˊ ㄇㄧㄥˊ)
to legalize what is illegal

化油器(ㄏㄨㄚˋ ㄧㄡˊ ㄑㄧˋ)
a carburetor

化驗(ㄏㄨㄚˋ ㄧㄢˋ)
to subject to chemical analysis; to put to laboratory examination or test

化驗室(ㄏㄨㄚˋ ㄧㄢˋ ㄕˋ)
a laboratory

化外(ㄏㄨㄚˋ ㄨㄞˋ)
outer fringes of civilization; outside the pale of Chinese civilization

化外之民(ㄏㄨㄚˋ ㄨㄞˋ ㄓ ㄇㄧㄣˊ)
uncivilized people; barbarians

化爲烏有(ㄏㄨㄚˋ ㄨㄟˊ ㄨ ㄧㄡˇ)
to disappear completely; to vanish completely; to come to naught; to vanish into thin air

化雨(ㄏㄨㄚˋ ㄩˇ)
the pervading good influence (of an educator)

化育(ㄏㄨㄚˋ ㄩˋ)
Nature's nourishing

化緣(ㄏㄨㄚˋ ㄩㄢˊ)
to solicit alms (as a means for favorable karma)

三畫

【北】 458
ㄅㄟˇ beei běi
(讀音 ㄅㄛˋ boh bò)

1. north; northern; northerly
2. northward
3. defeated

北半球(ㄅㄟˇ ㄅㄢˋ ㄑㄧㄡˊ)
the Northern Hemisphere

北邊(ㄅㄟˇ ㄅㄧㄢ)or 北邊兒(ㄅㄟˇ ㄅㄧㄚㄦ)
the north; the northern part

北冰洋(ㄅㄟˇ ㄅㄧㄥ ㄧㄤˊ)or 北極海(ㄅㄟˇ ㄐㄧˊ ㄏㄞˇ)
the Arctic Ocean

北平(ㄅㄟˇ ㄆㄧㄥˊ)
Peiping 亦作「北京」

北美洲(ㄅㄟˇ ㄇㄟˇ ㄓㄡ)
North America

北面(ㄅㄟˇ ㄇㄧㄢˋ)
① the north; the northern part ② to have an audience (with the emperor); to pay homage to

北伐(ㄅㄟˇ ㄈㄚˊ)or(ㄅㄟˇ ㄈㄚ)

① the Northward Expedition (the history of the Republic of China) ② to fight north
北非(ㄅㄟˇ ㄈㄟ)
North Africa; North African
北方(ㄅㄟˇ ㄈㄤ)
①the northern region ②the north
北方人(ㄅㄟˇ ㄈㄤ ㄖㄣˊ)
a northerner
北達科塔(ㄅㄟˇ ㄉㄚˊ ㄎㄜ ㄊㄚˇ)
the state of North Dakota, U.S.A.
北大荒(ㄅㄟˇ ㄉㄚˋ ㄏㄨㄤ)
the Great Northern Wilderness in northeast China
北大西洋公約組織(ㄅㄟˇ ㄉㄚˋ ㄒㄧ ㄧㄤˊ ㄍㄨㄥ ㄩㄝ ㄗㄨˇ ㄓ)
North Atlantic Treaty Organization (NATO)
北大西洋航線(ㄅㄟˇ ㄉㄚˋ ㄒㄧ ㄧㄤˊ ㄏㄤˊ ㄒㄧㄢˋ)
North Atlantic Line
北斗星(ㄅㄟˇ ㄉㄡˇ ㄒㄧㄥ)or 北斗七星(ㄅㄟˇ ㄉㄡˇ ㄑㄧ ㄒㄧㄥ)
the Plough; the Big Dipper; the Plow
北瓜(ㄅㄟˇ ㄍㄨㄚ)
a bottle gourd
北卡羅來納州(ㄅㄟˇ ㄎㄚˇ ㄌㄨㄛˊ ㄌㄞˊ ㄋㄚˋ ㄓㄡ)
the state of North Carolina, U. S. A.
北海(ㄅㄟˇ ㄏㄞˇ)
the North Sea
北海道(ㄅㄟˇ ㄏㄞˇ ㄉㄠˋ)
Hokkaido, Japan's northernmost island
北韓(ㄅㄟˇ ㄏㄢˊ)
North Korea
北寒帶(ㄅㄟˇ ㄏㄢˊ ㄉㄞˋ)
the North Frigid Zone
北回歸線(ㄅㄟˇ ㄏㄨㄟˊ ㄍㄨㄟ ㄒㄧㄢˋ)
the Tropic of Cancer
北極(ㄅㄟˇ ㄐㄧˊ)
① the North Pole; the Arctic Pole ② the north magnetic pole
北極光(ㄅㄟˇ ㄐㄧˊ ㄍㄨㄤ)
aurora borealis
北極圈(ㄅㄟˇ ㄐㄧˊ ㄑㄩㄢ)
the Arctic Circle
北極熊(ㄅㄟˇ ㄐㄧˊ ㄒㄩㄥˊ)
a polar bear
北極星(ㄅㄟˇ ㄐㄧˊ ㄒㄧㄥ)
Polaris; the North Star; the polestar
北京(ㄅㄟˇ ㄐㄧㄥ)
Peking
北京狗(ㄅㄟˇ ㄐㄧㄥ ㄍㄡˇ)
a pekingese
北京人(ㄅㄟˇ ㄐㄧㄥ ㄖㄣˊ)
(archaeology) Sinanthropus; the Peking Man
北軍(ㄅㄟˇ ㄐㄩㄣ)
the Union soldiers, or the Union troops (in the American Civil War)
北上(ㄅㄟˇ ㄕㄤˋ)
to proceed northward; to go north
北宋(ㄅㄟˇ ㄙㄨㄥˋ)
the Northern Sung or Earlier Sung Dynasty, 960-1128
北歐(ㄅㄟˇ ㄡ)
northern Europe; northern European
北洋軍閥(ㄅㄟˇ ㄧㄤˊ ㄐㄩㄣ ㄈㄚˊ)
the northern warlords (in the early years of the Republic of China)
北緯(ㄅㄟˇ ㄨㄟˇ)
north latitude; northern latitude
北溫帶(ㄅㄟˇ ㄨㄣ ㄉㄞˋ)
the North Temperate Zone
北嶽(ㄅㄟˇ ㄩㄝˋ)
another name of Mountain Heng (恆山) in Hopeh Province, one of the Five Sacred Mountains

九畫

【匙】 459
1. ㄔˊ chyr chí
a spoon 參看「湯匙」or「茶匙」

【匙】 459
2. ·ㄕ ·shy shi
a key 參看「鑰匙」

匚部
ㄈㄤ fang fāng

三畫

【匝】 460
ㄗㄚ tza zā
to make a revolution round; to encompass; to circle
匝地(ㄗㄚ ㄉㄧˋ)
all over the ground; here, there, and everywhere
匝月(ㄗㄚ ㄩㄝˋ)
a whole month

【匜】 461
ㄧˊ yi yí
a washbasin (of former times)

四畫

【匠】 462
ㄐㄧㄤˋ jianq jiàng
a craftsman; an artisan; a skilled workman: 木匠 a carpenter 石匠 a mason; a stoneman 鐵匠 a blacksmith
匠氣(ㄐㄧㄤˋ ㄑㄧˋ)
commonplaceness or triteness in artistic work
匠心(ㄐㄧㄤˋ ㄒㄧㄣ)or 匠意(ㄐㄧㄤˋ ㄧˋ)
inventiveness; ingenuity; originality; craftsmanship: 這位畫家獨具匠心。This painter has great originality.
匠心經營(ㄐㄧㄤˋ ㄒㄧㄣ ㄐㄧㄥ ㄧㄥˊ)
the original thought in any creation
匠人(ㄐㄧㄤˋ ㄖㄣˊ)
an artisan; a craftsman; a carpenter; a mason; a bricklayer

【匡】 463
ㄎㄨㄤ kuang kuāng
1. to rectify; to correct
2. to deliver from
匡復(ㄎㄨㄤ ㄈㄨˋ)
to restore national prestige or prosperity
匡濟(ㄎㄨㄤ ㄐㄧˋ)
to relieve distress; to help over a difficulty
匡救(ㄎㄨㄤ ㄐㄧㄡˋ)
to deliver from danger or sin; to rescue from disaster or errors
匡正(ㄎㄨㄤ ㄓㄥˋ)
to rectify; to correct; to reform
匡助(ㄎㄨㄤ ㄓㄨˋ)
to assist; to lend a helping hand
匡時(ㄎㄨㄤ ㄕˊ)
to remedy evils of the times; to do things for the good of

〔匚部〕

society

五畫

【匣】 464 ㄒㄧㄚˊ shya xiá
1. a case; a small box
2. a cage 亦作「柙」

匣子(ㄒㄧㄚˊ ·ㄗ)or 匣兒(ㄒㄧㄚˊㄦ)
a case; a small box; a casket

八畫

【匪】 465 ㄈㄟˇ feei fěi
1. bandits; rebels; insurgents
2. not

匪幫(ㄈㄟˇ ㄅㄤ)
a gang of bandits or rebels; a band of robbers

匪徒(ㄈㄟˇ ㄊㄨˊ)
bandits; brigands; robbers; gangsters

匪類(ㄈㄟˇ ㄌㄟˋ)
bandits; brigands; robbers; criminals

匪患(ㄈㄟˇ ㄏㄨㄢˋ)
the evil of bandits; banditry

匪懈(ㄈㄟˇ ㄒㄧㄝˋ)
do not idle or relax; to be diligent

匪巢(ㄈㄟˇ ㄔㄠˊ)
a bandits' lair

匪首(ㄈㄟˇ ㄕㄡˇ)
a bandit chieftain

匪人(ㄈㄟˇ ㄖㄣˊ)
a bandit; a bad person

匪夷所思(ㄈㄟˇ ㄧˊ ㄙㄨㄛˇ ㄙ)
unthinkable; outrageous ideas; bizarre thoughts; unimaginably queer; fantastic

九畫

【匭】 466 ㄍㄨㄟˇ goei guǐ
a box; a casket; a chest: 票匭 a ballot box

十一畫

【匯】 467 ㄏㄨㄟˋ huey huì
1. to remit money: 他每月給父親匯錢。He remits money to his father every month.
2. to converge
3. to flow into

匯撥(ㄏㄨㄟˋ ㄅㄛ)
to transfer a sum of money

匯票(ㄏㄨㄟˋ ㄆㄧㄠˋ)
a money order; a draft; a bill of exchange

匯費(ㄏㄨㄟˋ ㄈㄟˋ)or 匯水(ㄏㄨㄟˋ ㄕㄨㄟˇ)
the remitting charge or fee

匯豐銀行(ㄏㄨㄟˋ ㄈㄥ ㄧㄣˊ ㄏㄤˊ)
Hongkong and Shanghai Banking Corporation

匯付(ㄏㄨㄟˋ ㄈㄨˋ)
to pay to

匯兌(ㄏㄨㄟˋ ㄉㄨㄟˋ)
(commerce) exchange; the transfer of funds; remittance

匯兌銀行(ㄏㄨㄟˋ ㄉㄨㄟˋ ㄧㄣˊ ㄏㄤˊ)
an exchange bank

匯率(ㄏㄨㄟˋ ㄌㄩˋ)or 匯兌率(ㄏㄨㄟˋ ㄉㄨㄟˋ ㄌㄩˋ)
the exchange rate (between currencies)

匯款(ㄏㄨㄟˋ ㄎㄨㄢˇ)
①a remittance ②to remit money

匯合(ㄏㄨㄟˋ ㄏㄜˊ)
to converge; to join: 這兩條河在什麼地方匯合? Where do the two rivers join?

匯集(ㄏㄨㄟˋ ㄐㄧˊ)or 匯聚(ㄏㄨㄟˋ ㄐㄩˋ)
to gather in one place; to converge; to collect

匯價(ㄏㄨㄟˋ ㄐㄧㄚˋ)
the exchange rate; the conversion rate

十二畫

【匱】 468 ㄎㄨㄟˋ kuey kuì
1. to lack; deficient
2. a chest or cabinet
3. exhausted

匱乏(ㄎㄨㄟˋ ㄈㄚˊ)
lack; want; to lack; to be short of: 我的生活不虞匱乏。My life is free from want.

十三畫

【匳】 469 (奩) ㄌㄧㄢˊ lian lián
1. a toilet case; a dressing case
2. as in the following expressions: 香匳 a container for incense 粧匳 a dowry

匳敬(ㄌㄧㄢˊ ㄐㄧㄥˋ)
gifts to a bride

匸部
ㄒㄧˋ shih xì

二畫

【匹】 470 1. ㄆㄧ pi pī
a numerary particle for horses: 他有兩匹馬和一匹騾子。He has two horses and a mule.

匹馬單槍(ㄆㄧ ㄇㄚˇ ㄉㄢ ㄑㄧㄤ)
single-handed; without help; doing something unaccompanied and unaided 亦作「單槍匹馬」

【匹】 470 2. ㄆㄧˇ pii pǐ
1. a bolt (of cloth)
2. to match
3. equal

匹配(ㄆㄧˇ ㄆㄟˋ)
①to match ②(electricity) matching

匹夫(ㄆㄧˇ ㄈㄨ)
①an ordinary man ②every man: 國家興亡,匹夫有責。Every man is responsible for the fate of his country. ③an ignorant person

匹夫匹婦(ㄆㄧˇ ㄈㄨ ㄆㄧˇ ㄈㄨˋ)
common people; commoners

匹夫之勇(ㄆㄧˇ ㄈㄨ ㄓ ㄩㄥˇ)
foolhardiness; reckless courage; mere physical courage

匹敵(ㄆㄧˇ ㄉㄧˊ)
to match or equal (in a contest); to be a match for: 兩隊實力匹敵。The two teams are equally matched.

匹練(ㄆㄧˇ ㄌㄧㄢˋ)
a waterfall

匹儔(ㄆㄧˇ ㄔㄡˊ)
①a spouse ②a worthy match

匹庶(ㄆㄧˇ ㄕㄨˋ)
common people

匹偶 or 匹耦(ㄆㄧˇ ㄡˇ)

a (married) couple

九畫

【匾】 471 ㄅㄧㄢˇ bean biǎn

a (wooden) tablet

匾額(ㄅㄧㄢˇ ㄜˊ)

a (wooden) tablet; a horizontal inscribed board

【匿】 472 ㄋㄧˋ nih nì

to hide; to conceal

匿名信(ㄋㄧˋ ㄇㄧㄥˊ ㄒㄧㄣˋ)

an anonymous letter

匿伏(ㄋㄧˋ ㄈㄨˊ)

to lurk; to hide oneself to escape capture

匿迹銷聲(ㄋㄧˋ ㄐㄧˋ ㄒㄧㄠ ㄕㄥ)

to be in complete hiding

匿情(ㄋㄧˋ ㄑㄧㄥˊ)

to cover up the fact before the law

匿笑(ㄋㄧˋ ㄒㄧㄠˋ)

to laugh in secret

匿影藏形(ㄋㄧˋ ㄧㄥˇ ㄘㄤˊ ㄒㄧㄥˊ)

to hide from public notice

【區】 473 ㄑㄩ chiu qū

1. to distinguish; to discriminate
2. a district; an area; a zone: 這是純粹的農業區。This is a purely agricultural district.
3. a border
4. little; few

區別(ㄑㄩ ㄅㄧㄝˊ)

①to discriminate; to distinguish; to draw a line (between); to differentiate: 他能區別好書與壞書。He can discriminate good books from poor ones. ②difference; distinction: 兩者之間有區別。There is a distinction between the two.

區分(ㄑㄩ ㄈㄣ)

to set apart; to consider to be separate or different; to distinguish; to differentiate: 我無法區分這兩種花。I cannot differentiate the two flowers.

區分部(ㄑㄩ ㄈㄣ ㄅㄨˋ)

district headquarters of a political party

區公所(ㄑㄩ ㄍㄨㄥ ㄙㄨㄛˇ)

a district office

區劃(ㄑㄩ ㄏㄨㄚˋ)

to divide into districts or areas

區間車(ㄑㄩ ㄐㄧㄢ ㄔㄜ)

a bus traveling merely part of its normal route

區區(ㄑㄩ ㄑㄩ)

①small or unimportant (in quantity, amount or size); trifling: 區區小事，何足掛齒。Such a trifling thing is hardly worth mentioning. ②a polite reference to oneself

區長(ㄑㄩ ㄓㄤˇ)

a district magistrate

區宇(ㄑㄩ ㄩˇ)

territory

區域(ㄑㄩ ㄩˋ)

a district; an area; a region; a zone: 本區域已劃爲工業發展之用。This area has been zoned for industrial development.

區域代表制(ㄑㄩ ㄩˋ ㄉㄞˋ ㄅㄧㄠˇ ㄓˋ)

(elections) the regional representation system

區域規劃(ㄑㄩ ㄩˋ ㄍㄨㄟ ㄏㄨㄚˋ)

regional planning

區域性(ㄑㄩ ㄩˋ ㄒㄧㄥˋ)

regional: 那是一場區域性戰爭。That was a regional war.

十部
ㄕˊ shyr shí

【十】 474 ㄕˊ shyr shí

1. ten; the tenth: 他十點鐘來。He will come at ten. 他比你強十倍。He is ten times the man you are. 今天是八月十日。Today's the tenth of August.
2. complete; completely; perfect; perfectly; extremely

十八般武藝(ㄕˊ ㄅㄚ ㄅㄢ ㄨˇ ㄧˋ)

(literally) eighteen weapons and their uses—allegedly devised by Sun Pin (孫臏) and Wu Chi (吳起) in the Epoch of Warring States—(figuratively, said of a person) all skill and knowledge about one's trade, profession, etc.; versatility

十八羅漢(ㄕˊ ㄅㄚ ㄌㄨㄛˊ ㄏㄢˋ)

(Buddhism) the eighteen saints, including 16 disciples of Buddha

十八重地獄(ㄕˊ ㄅㄚ ㄔㄨㄥˊ ㄉㄧˋ ㄩˋ)or 十八層地獄(ㄕˊ ㄅㄚ ㄘㄥˊ ㄉㄧˋ ㄩˋ)

(Buddhism) the eighteen hells where the souls of evil persons are tortured

十邊形(ㄕˊ ㄅㄧㄢ ㄒㄧㄥˊ)or 十角形(ㄕˊ ㄐㄧㄠˇ ㄒㄧㄥˊ)

a decagon

十不得一(ㄕˊ ㄅㄨˋ ㄉㄜˊ ㄧ)

(literally) unable to obtain one out of ten—very hard to find a competent person or something up to the standard

十面體(ㄕˊ ㄇㄧㄢˋ ㄊㄧˇ)

a decahedron

十目所視，十手所指(ㄕˊ ㄇㄨˋ ㄙㄨㄛˇ ㄕˋ, ㄕˊ ㄕㄡˇ ㄙㄨㄛˇ ㄓˇ)

(literally) to be looked at by ten eyes and pointed at by ten fingers—under the glare of the public

十分(ㄕˊ ㄈㄣ)

①complete; completely: 他十分滿意。He was completely satisfied. ②very: 他歌唱得十分好。He sings very well. ③10 points

十方(ㄕˊ ㄈㄤ)

(Buddhism) the ten directions—north, south, east, west, northeast, northwest, southeast, southwest, above and below

十拿九穩(ㄕˊ ㄋㄚˊ ㄐㄧㄡˇ ㄨㄣˇ)

to be very sure of (success, etc.); almost certain; 90 percent sure: 此事我是十拿九穩。I am very sure of success in this matter.

十年九不遇(ㄕˊ ㄋㄧㄢˊ ㄐㄧㄡˇ ㄅㄨˋ ㄩˋ)

hardly occur once in ten years—to be very rare

十年樹木，百年樹人(ㄕˊ ㄋㄧㄢˊ ㄕㄨˋ ㄇㄨˋ, ㄅㄞˇ ㄋㄧㄢˊ ㄕㄨˋ ㄖㄣˊ)

It takes 10 years to grow a tree, while a sound education program may require 10 times as long before it takes root.

十六開(ㄕˊ ㄌㄧㄡˋ ㄎㄞ)

sixteenmo

十戒(ㄕˊ ㄐㄧㄝˋ)
(Buddhism) the Ten Prohibitions

十誡(ㄕˊ ㄐㄧㄝˋ)
the Ten Commandments (in the Bible)

十錦(ㄕˊ ㄐㄧㄣˇ)
multiple ingredients (for a dish)

十進法(ㄕˊ ㄐㄧㄣˋ ㄈㄚˇ)
the denary scale

十全十美(ㄕˊ ㄑㄩㄢˊ ㄕˊ ㄇㄟˇ)
perfect; complete

十項運動(ㄕˊ ㄒㄧㄤˋ ㄩㄣˋ ㄉㄨㄥˋ)
decathlon 亦作「十項全能運動」

十項運動員(ㄕˊ ㄒㄧㄤˋ ㄩㄣˋ ㄉㄨㄥˋ ㄩㄢˊ)
a decathlonist

十之八九(ㄕˊ ㄓ ㄅㄚ ㄐㄧㄡˇ)
eight or nine cases out of ten; most likely

十成(ㄕˊ ㄔㄥˊ) or 十成兒(ㄕˊ ㄔㄥˊㄦ)
very sure; one hundred per cent

十室九空(ㄕˊ ㄕˋ ㄐㄧㄡˇ ㄎㄨㄥ)
(literally) nine out of ten houses are vacant—almost all the villages or cities are deserted, as a result of wars, natural disasters, etc.

十姊妹(ㄕˊ ㄗˇ ㄇㄟˋ) or (ㄕˊ ㄐㄧㄝˇ ㄇㄟˋ)
① *Uroloncha domestica* (a kind of sparrow-size bird with a variety of feather colors) ② *Rosa multiflora* (a kind of plant) ③ ten girls who swear not to get married and stick together (an old fad in Kwangtung)

十字路口(ㄕˊ ㄗˋ ㄌㄨˋ ㄎㄡˇ)
① the junction of crossroads ② a moment or point of decision

十字鎬(ㄕˊ ㄗˋ ㄍㄠˇ)
a pick; a mattock

十字架(ㄕˊ ㄗˋ ㄐㄧㄚˋ)
① the Cross ② a yoke one has to take

十字街頭(ㄕˊ ㄗˋ ㄐㄧㄝ ㄊㄡˊ)
① a road intersection ② a point of decision

十字軍(ㄕˊ ㄗˋ ㄐㄩㄣ)
the Crusaders

十字軍東征(ㄕˊ ㄗˋ ㄐㄩㄣ ㄉㄨㄥ ㄓㄥ)
the Crusade

十字兒(ㄕˊ ㄗˋㄦ)
anything shaped like a cross

十足(ㄕˊ ㄗㄨˊ)
extremely; completely; perfect; perfectly; one hundred per cent; pure (gold); out-and-out; downright

十族(ㄕˊ ㄗㄨˊ)
the ten relations of a person

十四行詩(ㄕˊ ㄙˋ ㄏㄤˊ ㄕ)
(Western poetry) the sonnet

十三點(ㄕˊ ㄙㄢ ㄉㄧㄢˇ)
(slang) silly; acting in a stupid manner which invokes mirth rather than disgust (particularly said of women)

十三太保(ㄕˊ ㄙㄢ ㄊㄞˋ ㄅㄠˇ)
① a gang of 13 juvenile gangsters ② anything that is made up of 13 distinguished members

十三陵(ㄕˊ ㄙㄢ ㄌㄧㄥˊ)
the Ming Tombs (in Peking)

十三經(ㄕˊ ㄙㄢ ㄐㄧㄥ)
the Thirteen Classics of Chinese philosophy and literature—易經, 詩經, 尚書, 禮記, 周禮, 儀禮, 左傳, 公羊傳, 穀梁傳, 論語, 孝經, 爾雅, 孟子 (*Book of Changes, Book of Odes, Historical Records, Book of Rites, Rites of Chou, Book of Etiquettes, Spring and Autumn with Commentary by Tso Chiu-ming, Spring and Autumn with Commentary by Kung-Yang Kao, Spring and Autumn with Commentary by Ku-Liang Chih, Analects of Confucius, Filial Classic, Ancient Dictionary, Works of Mencius*)

十惡不赦(ㄕˊ ㄜˋ ㄅㄨˋ ㄕㄜˋ)
guilty of unpardonable evil

十二碼球(ㄕˊ ㄦˋ ㄇㄚˇ ㄑㄧㄡˊ)
(soccer) a penalty kick

十二分(ㄕˊ ㄦˋ ㄈㄣ)
more than 100 per cent; extremely

十二宮(ㄕˊ ㄦˋ ㄍㄨㄥ)
the twelve constellations of the zodiac

十二肖(ㄕˊ ㄦˋ ㄒㄧㄠˋ) or 十二屬(ㄕˊ ㄦˋ ㄕㄨˇ)
the twelve animals corresponding to the Twelve Terrestrial Branches (地支)—子鼠, 丑牛, 寅虎, 卯兎, 辰龍, 巳蛇, 午馬, 未羊, 申猴, 酉鷄, 戌狗, 亥豬 (Rat, Ox, Tiger, Hare, Dragon, Serpent, Horse, Sheep, Monkey, Cock, Dog and Pig)

十二指腸(ㄕˊ ㄦˋ ㄓˇ ㄔㄤˊ)
a duodenum

十二指腸潰瘍(ㄕˊ ㄦˋ ㄓˇ ㄔㄤˊ ㄎㄨㄟˋ ㄧㄤˊ)
a duodenal ulcer

十二月(ㄕˊ ㄦˋ ㄩㄝˋ)
① December ② the twelfth month of the lunar calendar ③ twelve months

十一月(ㄕˊ ㄧ ㄩㄝˋ)
① November ② the eleventh month of the lunar calendar ③ eleven months

十有八九(ㄕˊ ㄧㄡˇ ㄅㄚ ㄐㄧㄡˇ) or 十之八九(ㄕˊ ㄓ ㄅㄚ ㄐㄧㄡˇ)
eight or nine chances out of ten; most probably; very likely: 十有八九他不會來。 Nine out of ten he won't come.

十羊九牧(ㄕˊ ㄧㄤˊ ㄐㄧㄡˇ ㄇㄨˋ)
(literally) There are nine shepherds tending only ten sheep.—too many government officials; bureaucracy

十位(ㄕˊ ㄨㄟˋ)
(arithmetic) the tens place

十萬八千里(ㄕˊ ㄨㄢˋ ㄅㄚ ㄑㄧㄢ ㄌㄧˇ)
a distance of one hundred and eight thousand *li* — to be poles apart

十萬火急(ㄕˊ ㄨㄢˋ ㄏㄨㄛˇ ㄐㄧˊ)
① to be in posthaste ② Most Urgent (as a mark on dispatches)

十月(ㄕˊ ㄩㄝˋ)
① October ② the tenth month of the lunar calendar ③ ten months

十月革命(ㄕˊ ㄩㄝˋ ㄍㄜˊ ㄇㄧㄥˋ)
the Russian Revolution of 1917

十月十日(ㄕˊ ㄩㄝˋ ㄕˊ ㄖˋ)
October 10 or the Double Tenth, National Day of the Republic of China

一畫

【千】 475
ㄑㄧㄢ chian qiān

1. thousand
2. many; numerous
3. a Chinese family name

千變萬化(ㄑㄧㄢ ㄅㄧㄢˋ ㄨㄢˋ ㄏㄨㄚˋ)
countless changes or variations; ever-changing

千不該萬不該(ㄑㄧㄢ ㄅㄨˋ ㄍㄞ ㄨㄢˋ ㄅㄨˋ ㄍㄞ)
really should not; most emphatically not; a thousand no (usually used in the subjunctive mood to indicate one's regret for having done something); deeply (a thousand times) regret

千篇一律(ㄑㄧㄢ ㄆㄧㄢ ㄧˊ ㄌㄩˋ)
to harp on a single theme; without changes; dull; monotonous; stereotyped: 這些作品千篇一律，沒什麼創意。The works repeat each other and lack for originality.

千門萬戶(ㄑㄧㄢ ㄇㄣˊ ㄨㄢˋ ㄏㄨˋ)
① descriptive of the numerous buildings of a palace ② numerous households

千米(ㄑㄧㄢ ㄇㄧˇ)
a kilometer (km)

千佛洞(ㄑㄧㄢ ㄈㄛˊ ㄉㄨㄥˋ)
the Tunhuang Caves in Kansu Province, where were found in the 1900's countless Buddha statues, Buddhist scriptures and frescoes of the Tang Dynasty

千方百計(ㄑㄧㄢ ㄈㄤ ㄅㄞˇ ㄐㄧˋ)
a thousand schemes—by hook or by crook; by all means at one's command; to use all sorts of wiles and methods

千夫所指(ㄑㄧㄢ ㄈㄨ ㄙㄨㄛˇ ㄓˇ)
to be pointed at by one thousand accusing fingers—to be universally condemned

千刀萬剮(ㄑㄧㄢ ㄉㄠ ㄨㄢˋ ㄍㄨㄚˇ)
to hack someone to pieces

千島羣島(ㄑㄧㄢ ㄉㄠˇ ㄑㄩㄣˊ ㄉㄠˇ)
the Kuril Islands

千叮嚀萬囑咐(ㄑㄧㄢ ㄉㄧㄥ ㄋㄧㄥˊ ㄨㄢˋ ㄓㄨˇ ㄈㄨˋ)
to exhort or enjoin repeatedly

千頭萬緒(ㄑㄧㄢ ㄊㄡˊ ㄨㄢˋ ㄒㄩˋ)
(said of a problem or task) very complicated or confused

千難萬難(ㄑㄧㄢ ㄋㄢˊ ㄨㄢˋ ㄋㄢˊ)
extremely difficult

千年(ㄑㄧㄢ ㄋㄧㄢˊ)
a thousand years

千里(ㄑㄧㄢ ㄌㄧˇ)
a thousand *li*—a long distance: 失之毫釐，差之千里。One false step will make a great difference.

千里馬(ㄑㄧㄢ ㄌㄧˇ ㄇㄚˇ)
a horse with enormous speed and staying power; a winged steed

千里達—托貝哥(ㄑㄧㄢ ㄌㄧˇ ㄉㄚˊ ㄊㄨㄛ ㄅㄟˋ ㄍㄜ)
Trinidad and Tobago, an independent republic in the West Indies

千里迢迢(ㄑㄧㄢ ㄌㄧˇ ㄊㄧㄠˊ ㄊㄧㄠˊ)
thousands of *li* away—from afar

千里駒(ㄑㄧㄢ ㄌㄧˇ ㄐㄩ)
① a horse with enormous speed and staying power ② (figuratively) a young talent

千里之堤，潰于蟻穴(ㄑㄧㄢ ㄌㄧˇ ㄓ ㄊㄧˊ, ㄎㄨㄟˋ ㄩˊ ㄧˇ ㄒㄩㄝˋ)
One ant-hole may lead to the collapse of a thousand-*li* dike.—Slight negligence may result in great disaster.

千里之行，始於足下(ㄑㄧㄢ ㄌㄧˇ ㄓ ㄒㄧㄥˊ, ㄕˇ ㄩˊ ㄗㄨˊ ㄒㄧㄚˋ)
The journey of a thousand *li* starts with the first step.

千里送鵝毛(ㄑㄧㄢ ㄌㄧˇ ㄙㄨㄥˋ ㄜˊ ㄇㄠˊ)
a small gift sent from afar with deep affection: 千里送鵝毛，禮輕情意重。The gift sent from afar may be light in itself, but it conveys deep affection.

千里眼(ㄑㄧㄢ ㄌㄧˇ ㄧㄢˇ)
① farsightedness ② (mythology) name of a god whose eyesight that can reach the heaven ③ another name for telescope or binoculars; field glasses

千慮一得(ㄑㄧㄢ ㄌㄩˋ ㄧˋ ㄉㄜˊ)
One always gets something by thinking constantly. 愚者千慮，必有一得。Even a fool may sometimes have a good idea.

千慮一失(ㄑㄧㄢ ㄌㄩˋ ㄧˋ ㄕ)
Despite careful planning, there will be a slip here and there. 智者千慮，必有一失。Even a wise man sometimes makes a mistake.

千古(ㄑㄧㄢ ㄍㄨˇ)
① a long, long time; through all ages; for all time ② (used in mourning) in eternity

千古奇聞(ㄑㄧㄢ ㄍㄨˇ ㄑㄧˊ ㄨㄣˊ)
a fantastic story; a forever strange tale

千克(ㄑㄧㄢ ㄎㄜˋ)
kilogram (kg)

千赫(ㄑㄧㄢ ㄏㄜˋ)
kilohertz (kHz)

千迴百折(ㄑㄧㄢ ㄏㄨㄟˊ ㄅㄞˇ ㄓㄜˊ) or **千迴百轉**(ㄑㄧㄢ ㄏㄨㄟˊ ㄅㄞˇ ㄓㄨㄢˇ)
(said of the plot of a novel or scenery of a resort) a thousand twists and a hundred turns; innumerable twists and turns

千家詩(ㄑㄧㄢ ㄐㄧㄚ ㄕ)
a collection of poems of the Tang and Sung Dynasties first edited by Liu Ke-chuang (劉克莊) of the Sung Dynasty as an introduction to poetry, usually for youngsters

千嬌百媚(ㄑㄧㄢ ㄐㄧㄠ ㄅㄞˇ ㄇㄟˋ)
the beauty of beauties; the pinnacle of beauty and charms

千斤頂(ㄑㄧㄢ ㄐㄧㄣ ㄉㄧㄥˇ)
a jack

千金(ㄑㄧㄢ ㄐㄧㄣ)
① a courteous expression referring to another's daughter ② a thousand pieces of gold

千金小姐(ㄑㄧㄢ ㄐㄧㄣ ㄒㄧㄠˇ ㄐㄧㄝˇ)
a young lady of a wealthy family

千金市骨(ㄑㄧㄢ ㄐㄧㄣ ㄕˋ ㄍㄨˇ)
very eager and sincere in recruiting talented men

千金一笑(ㄑㄧㄢ ㄐㄧㄣ ㄧˊ ㄒㄧㄠˋ)
A smile of a beautiful lady is worth a thousand taels of gold. 或 A beauty's smile is very valuable.

千金一擲(ㄑㄧㄢ ㄐㄧㄣ ㄧˋ ㄓˋ)
to spend money in a big

way 亦作「一擲千金」

千鈞一髮(ㄑㄧㄢ ㄐㄩㄣ ㄧˋ ㄈㄚˇ)
A thing which weighs one thousand *chiun* (鈞) hangs on a hair.—extremely delicate situation; very precarious (One *chiun* equals to 30 catties.) 亦作「一髮千鈞」

千軍萬馬(ㄑㄧㄢ ㄐㄩㄣ ㄨㄢˋ ㄇㄚˇ)
a large number of mounted and foot soldiers; a large military force; a powerful army; a mighty force

千奇百怪(ㄑㄧㄢ ㄑㄧˊ ㄅㄞˇ ㄍㄨㄞˋ)
numerous strange forms; grotesque or weird shapes

千秋(ㄑㄧㄢ ㄑㄧㄡ)
①a thousand years; centuries ②(polite expression) a kind of birthday congratulations (other than one's own)

千秋萬歲(ㄑㄧㄢ ㄑㄧㄡ ㄨㄢˋ ㄙㄨㄟˋ)
a long, long time; throughout the ages

千辛萬苦(ㄑㄧㄢ ㄒㄧㄣ ㄨㄢˋ ㄎㄨˇ)
to suffer or undergo all conceivable hardships (to accomplish something)

千眞萬確(ㄑㄧㄢ ㄓㄣ ㄨㄢˋ ㄑㄩㄝˋ)
very real; absolutely true

千差萬別(ㄑㄧㄢ ㄔㄚ ㄨㄢˋ ㄅㄧㄝˊ)
to be very different

千錘百鍊(ㄑㄧㄢ ㄔㄨㄟˊ ㄅㄞˇ ㄌㄧㄢˋ)
①(to undergo) severe training and hammering; stringent coaching; to be thoroughly tempered ②(to write) with the utmost care—with countless changes and corrections; to be revised and rewritten many times

千山萬水(ㄑㄧㄢ ㄕㄢ ㄨㄢˋ ㄕㄨㄟˇ)
a thousand mountains and rivers—distant (places, etc.); (a journey from) afar; a long and arduous journey

千日紅(ㄑㄧㄢ ㄖˋ ㄏㄨㄥˊ)
Gomphrena globosa (a small plant which blossoms in fall with spheric flowers of red, purple and white); globe amaranth

千字文(ㄑㄧㄢ ㄗˋ ㄨㄣˊ)
The Thousand-Character Classic, a primer for children authored by Chou Hsing-szu (周興嗣) of the Liang Dynasty

千載一時(ㄑㄧㄢ ㄗㄞˇ ㄧˋ ㄕˊ)or 千載難逢(ㄑㄧㄢ ㄗㄞˇ ㄋㄢˊ ㄈㄥˊ)
once in a thousand years—once in a lifetime; a very rare chance; a golden chance

千絲萬縷(ㄑㄧㄢ ㄙ ㄨㄢˋ ㄌㄩˇ)
①(usually said of the heart of a person in love) a million thoughts — a heart crammed with thoughts and remembrance ② many ramifications—very complicated

千思萬想(ㄑㄧㄢ ㄙ ㄨㄢˋ ㄒㄧㄤˇ)
a million thoughts—to think over and over again

千歲(ㄑㄧㄢ ㄙㄨㄟˋ)
①a thousand years ② Your (His or Her) Highness (when referring to the prince, the princess, the queen, the emperor's brother, etc.)

千恩萬謝(ㄑㄧㄢ ㄣ ㄨㄢˋ ㄒㄧㄝˋ)
a thousand thanks—many thanks

千億(ㄑㄧㄢ ㄧˋ)
(literally) 100,000,000,000 (one hundred thousand million)—myriads

千言萬語(ㄑㄧㄢ ㄧㄢˊ ㄨㄢˋ ㄩˇ)
many, many words in one's heart (but one doesn't know where to begin)

千瓦(ㄑㄧㄢ ㄨㄚˇ)
a kilowatt (kW)

千萬(ㄑㄧㄢ ㄨㄢˋ)
①a huge amount ②an expression used to emphasize an injunction or advice: 千萬要記得。Please do remember.

二畫

【升】 476
ㄕㄥ sheng shēng

1. to rise; to raise; to ascend
2. to advance; to promote
3. a unit of volume measurement (especially for grain)
4. a Chinese family name

升班(ㄕㄥ ㄅㄢ)
(school) to be promoted; to advance to a higher grade

升平 or 昇平(ㄕㄥ ㄆㄧㄥˊ)
peace and prosperity

升斗小民(ㄕㄥ ㄉㄡˇ ㄒㄧㄠˇ ㄇㄧㄣˊ)
those who live from hand to mouth

升等考試(ㄕㄥ ㄉㄥˇ ㄎㄠˇ ㄕˋ)
an examination held to test government employees to determine whether they are qualified for promotion

升堂(ㄕㄥ ㄊㄤˊ)
①to appear in court to conduct a trial ②to ascend to the hall

升堂入室(ㄕㄥ ㄊㄤˊ ㄖㄨˋ ㄕˋ)
(said of scholastic pursuit) to attain mastery

升騰
①(ㄕㄥ ㄊㄥˊ) to fly up; to leap up; to rise: 熱氣升騰。 The hot vapor leapt up.
②(ㄕㄥ ˙ㄊㄥ) to make good progress; to flourish in business

升天(ㄕㄥ ㄊㄧㄢ)
①to ascend to heaven—to die ②(Christianity) the Ascension

升格(ㄕㄥ ㄍㄜˊ)
to promote; to upgrade; to elevate

升官發財(ㄕㄥ ㄍㄨㄢ ㄈㄚ ㄘㄞˊ)
to attain high ranks and acquire great wealth; to be successful in both politics and business

升火待發(ㄕㄥ ㄏㄨㄛˇ ㄉㄞˋ ㄈㄚ)
(said of steamers, trains, etc.) ready to start the journey

升級(ㄕㄥ ㄐㄧˊ)
①(said of an official) to be promoted: 他升級爲上校。He was promoted to the rank of colonel. ② (school) to advance to a higher grade

升降(ㄕㄥ ㄐㄧㄤˋ)
to hoist and lower; to rise and fall

升降機(ㄕㄥ ㄐㄧㄤˋ ㄐㄧ)
an elevator; a lift

升旗(ㄕㄥ ㄑㄧˊ)
to hoist a flag

升遷(ㄕㄥ ㄑㄧㄢ)
to get transferred to a higher position; promotion

升學(ㄕㄥ ㄒㄩㄝˊ)
to enter a higher school; to

advance to a higher school
升學率(ㄕㄥ ㄒㄩㄝˊ ㄌㄩˋ)
the proportion of students entering schools of a higher grade
升學考試(ㄕㄥ ㄒㄩㄝˊ ㄎㄠˇ ㄕˋ)
an entrance examination for a higher school
升學主義(ㄕㄥ ㄒㄩㄝˊ ㄓㄨˇ ㄧˋ)
the attitude of thinking nothing but entering a higher school, paying no attention to the real purpose of education
升值(ㄕㄥ ㄓˊ)
(economics) ① to revalue ② to appreciate
升沈(ㄕㄥ ㄔㄣˊ)
the rise and fall of a public official

【午】477 ㄨˇ wuu wǔ
1. noon; high noon
2. (in old Chinese time measurement) 11 a.m. to 1 p.m.
3. the seventh of the Twelve Terrestrial Branches (地支)
4. a Chinese family name
午砲(ㄨˇ ㄆㄠˋ)
the gun fired at noon
午飯(ㄨˇ ㄈㄢˋ)
lunch; a midday meal
午後(ㄨˇ ㄏㄡˋ)
afternoon
午前(ㄨˇ ㄑㄧㄢˊ)
before noon; the forenoon
午休(ㄨˇ ㄒㄧㄡ)
a noon break; a noontime rest; lunch hour
午時(ㄨˇ ㄕˊ) or 午牌(ㄨˇ ㄆㄞˊ)
the period of the day from 11 a.m. to 1 p.m.
午睡(ㄨˇ ㄕㄨㄟˋ)
an afternoon nap; a siesta; to take a nap after lunch
午日(ㄨˇ ㄖˋ)
the fifth day of the fifth moon; the Dragon Boat Festival
午夜(ㄨˇ ㄧㄝˋ)
midnight
午月(ㄨˇ ㄩㄝˋ)
the fifth moon of the lunar calendar

【卅】478 ㄙㄚˋ sah sà
thirty; 30th (of a month)

三畫

【半】479 ㄅㄢˋ bann bàn
1. half: 一天半 one and a half days 半小時 half an hour; a half hour
2. very little
3. in the middle
4. partly; about half: 大門半開著。The gate was left half open.
半百(ㄅㄢˋ ㄅㄞˇ)
fifty; half a hundred: 王先生年近半百。Mr. Wang's getting on for fifty.
半輩子(ㄅㄢˋ ㄅㄟˋ ·ㄗ)
half a lifetime
半壁江山(ㄅㄢˋ ㄅㄧˋ ㄐㄧㄤ ㄕㄢ)
half of the national territory
半邊(ㄅㄢˋ ㄅㄧㄢ)
half of something; one side of something
半票(ㄅㄢˋ ㄆㄧㄠˋ)
a half-fare ticket; a half-price ticket
半瓶醋(ㄅㄢˋ ㄆㄧㄥˊ ㄘㄨˋ)
(literally) a half bottle of vinegar—a half-educated person; a shallow person
半賣半送(ㄅㄢˋ ㄇㄞˋ ㄅㄢˋ ㄙㄨㄥˋ)
(used by shop owners as a sales gimmick) to sell goods at rock-bottom prices
半明半暗(ㄅㄢˋ ㄇㄧㄥˊ ㄅㄢˋ ㄢˋ)
half-bright and half-shadowy; not very bright
半明不滅(ㄅㄢˋ ㄇㄧㄥˊ ㄅㄨˋ ㄇㄧㄝˋ)
(said of lamps, candlelight, etc.) not very bright
半打(ㄅㄢˋ ㄉㄚˊ)
half a dozen; six
半島(ㄅㄢˋ ㄉㄠˇ)
a peninsula
半導體(ㄅㄢˋ ㄉㄠˇ ㄊㄧˇ)
a semiconductor
半道兒(ㄅㄢˋ ㄉㄠˋㄦ)
midway; halfway
半吊子(ㄅㄢˋ ㄉㄧㄠˋ ·ㄗ)
① a shallow person; a jack of all trades; a dabbler; a smatterer ② a rash person
半點(ㄅㄢˋ ㄉㄧㄢˇ)
the least bit: 職責所在半點也不能輕忽。One should never neglect his own duty.
半透明體(ㄅㄢˋ ㄊㄡˋ ㄇㄧㄥˊ ㄊㄧˇ)
a translucent or subtransparent body
半天(ㄅㄢˋ ㄊㄧㄢ)
① midair; in the air ② half-day; half a day ③ quite a while; a long time: 他已經等了半天。He has already waited for a long time.
半天空(ㄅㄢˋ ㄊㄧㄢ ㄎㄨㄥ)
half of the sky; (in) midair
半途(ㄅㄢˋ ㄊㄨˊ)
halfway; midway: 他們半途拆伙了。They parted company halfway.
半途而廢(ㄅㄢˋ ㄊㄨˊ ㄦˊ ㄈㄟˋ)
to stop (a task) halfway; to give up halfway; to leave something unfinished
半推半就(ㄅㄢˋ ㄊㄨㄟ ㄅㄢˋ ㄐㄧㄡˋ)
to be half willing (at heart) and half unwilling (in appearance)—to yield with a show of reluctance, often referring to price haggling or girls being seduced
半吞半吐(ㄅㄢˋ ㄊㄨㄣ ㄅㄢˋ ㄊㄨˇ)
to hum and haw
半通不通(ㄅㄢˋ ㄊㄨㄥ ㄅㄨˋ ㄊㄨㄥ)
to know or understand a little
半路(ㄅㄢˋ ㄌㄨˋ)
halfway; midway; on the way: 我們走到半路, 天就下雨了。We had got only halfway when it began to rain.
半路出家(ㄅㄢˋ ㄌㄨˋ ㄔㄨ ㄐㄧㄚ)
to switch to a new profession one knows little about; to change one's profession when one is no longer young; to start midway
半官方(ㄅㄢˋ ㄍㄨㄢ ㄈㄤ)
semi-official: 據半官方人士表示物價將會上漲。According to semi-official sources, prices will go up.
半工半讀(ㄅㄢˋ ㄍㄨㄥ ㄅㄢˋ ㄉㄨˊ)
part work, and part study; to work while studying at school
半公開(ㄅㄢˋ ㄍㄨㄥ ㄎㄞ)
semi-overt; more or less open
半開化(ㄅㄢˋ ㄎㄞ ㄏㄨㄚˋ)
semi-civilized (people)
半開眼兒(ㄅㄢˋ ㄎㄞ ㄧㄚˇㄦ)

〔十部〕

〔十部〕

pseudo-professional

半空中(ㄅㄢˋ ㄎㄨㄥ ㄓㄨㄥ)
in midair; in the air: 飛機在半空中互撞了。The airplanes collided in midair.

半飢半飽(ㄅㄢˋ ㄐㄧ ㄅㄢˋ ㄅㄠˇ)
underfed

半價(ㄅㄢˋ ㄐㄧㄚˋ)
half-price; 50 per cent discount

半截(ㄅㄢˋ ㄐㄧㄝˊ)or 半截兒(ㄅㄢˋ ㄐㄧㄝˊㄦ)
half of a body; a half part; half (a section): 他把話只說了半截兒。He finished only half of what he wanted to say.

半斤八兩(ㄅㄢˋ ㄐㄧㄣ ㄅㄚ ㄌㄧㄤˇ)
six of one and half a dozen of the other; tweedledum and tweedledee

半徑(ㄅㄢˋ ㄐㄧㄥˋ)
a radius

半旗(ㄅㄢˋ ㄑㄧˊ)
half-mast: 國王下葬之日，一律下半旗。Flags were at half-mast on the day of the king's funeral.

半球(ㄅㄢˋ ㄑㄧㄡˊ)
a hemisphere

半仙(ㄅㄢˋ ㄒㄧㄢ)
half an immortal—fortune-tellers or medical quacks (who claim the ability to work wonders as immortals are supposed to)

半新不舊(ㄅㄢˋ ㄒㄧㄣ ㄅㄨˋ ㄐㄧㄡˋ)
①half new; used (articles) ②neither modern nor obsolete

半信半疑(ㄅㄢˋ ㄒㄧㄣˋ ㄅㄢˋ ㄧˊ)
between believing and suspicion; half-believing and half-doubting; not quite convinced: 我對他所說的話半信半疑。I was not quite convinced of his words.

半醒半睡(ㄅㄢˋ ㄒㄧㄥˇ ㄅㄢˋ ㄕㄨㄟˋ)
half awake and half asleep; slumberous

半殖民地(ㄅㄢˋ ㄓˊ ㄇㄧㄣˊ ㄉㄧˋ)
a country nominally independent (whose sovereignty is often infringed upon by a great power or powers); a semi-colony

半眞半假(ㄅㄢˋ ㄓㄣ ㄅㄢˋ ㄐㄧㄚˇ)
partly true, partly false: 半眞半假的話不見得比說謊好。A half truth is often no better than a lie.

半中腰(ㄅㄢˋ ㄓㄨㄥ ㄧㄠ)or 半中間(ㄅㄢˋ ㄓㄨㄥ ㄐㄧㄢ)
(colloquial) middle; halfway; midway: 她的講演講到半中間就突然間斷了。She broke off in the middle of her speech.

半嗔半喜(ㄅㄢˋ ㄔㄣ ㄅㄢˋ ㄒㄧˇ)
half-annoyed, half-pleased

半場(ㄅㄢˋ ㄔㄤˇ)
①a half of a game or contest ②half-court

半場緊迫釘人(ㄅㄢˋ ㄔㄤˇ ㄐㄧㄣˇ ㄆㄛˋ ㄉㄧㄥ ㄖㄣˊ)
(basketball) half-court press

半成品(ㄅㄢˋ ㄔㄥˊ ㄆㄧㄣˇ)
semifinished products or articles; half-finished products or goods

半世(ㄅㄢˋ ㄕˋ)
half of a person's life span; (at) middle age

半身不遂(ㄅㄢˋ ㄕㄣ ㄅㄨˋ ㄙㄨㄟˋ)
hemiplegia—paralysis of half of one's body; half-paralyzed

半身像(ㄅㄢˋ ㄕㄣ ㄒㄧㄤˋ)
①a half-length photo or portrait ②a bust

半晌(ㄅㄢˋ ㄕㄤˇ)
(for) quite some time; a long time

半生(ㄅㄢˋ ㄕㄥ)
①half of one's life span ②half-baked; half-raw; not well cooked

半生不熟(ㄅㄢˋ ㄕㄥ ㄅㄨˋ ㄕㄡˊ)
①half-raw; half-cooked; not well cooked ②casual acquaintance

半數(ㄅㄢˋ ㄕㄨˋ)
half the number; half

半日(ㄅㄢˋ ㄖˋ)
①half a day ②half-day

半子(ㄅㄢˋ ㄗˇ)
a son-in-law

半自動(ㄅㄢˋ ㄗˋ ㄉㄨㄥˋ)
semiautomatic

半死不活(ㄅㄢˋ ㄙˇ ㄅㄨˋ ㄏㄨㄛˊ)
①dying; on the verge of death ②listless; lethargic ③half dead; more dead than alive

半夜(ㄅㄢˋ ㄧㄝˋ)
①half a night ②midnight 他工作到半夜。He worked until midnight.

半夜三更(ㄅㄢˋ ㄧㄝˋ ㄙㄢ ㄐㄧㄥ)
in the depth of night; late at night

半音階(ㄅㄢˋ ㄧㄣ ㄐㄧㄝ)
the chromatic scale (in music)

半月刊(ㄅㄢˋ ㄩㄝˋ ㄎㄢ)
a semimonthly; a fortnightly

半圓(ㄅㄢˋ ㄩㄢˊ)
a semicircle

【卌】 480 ㄒㄧˋ shih xì
forty; fortieth

四畫

【卉】 481 (卉) ㄏㄨㄟˋ huey huì
1. a general term for grasses: 這些是奇花異卉。These are rare flowers and grasses.
2. myriads of

六畫

【卑】 482 ㄅㄟ bei bēi
1. low
2. debased; depraved; vile
3. inferior
4. a modest expression referring to oneself 參看「卑職」

卑薄(ㄅㄟ ㄅㄛˊ)
(said of land) poor and barren

卑鄙(ㄅㄟ ㄅㄧˇ)
①(said of a person's character) mean; depraved; crooked; base ②(said of a person's social position) low; inferior

卑鄙手段(ㄅㄟ ㄅㄧˇ ㄕㄡˇ ㄉㄨㄢˋ)
dirty tricks

卑不足道(ㄅㄟ ㄅㄨˋ ㄗㄨˊ ㄉㄠˋ)or 卑卑不足道(ㄅㄟ ㄅㄟ ㄅㄨˋ ㄗㄨˊ ㄉㄠˋ)
too inferior (or contemptible) to be worth mentioning; too insignificant to be worth mentioning

卑陋(ㄅㄟ ㄌㄡˋ)
low; crude; vulgar; inferior

卑劣(ㄅㄟ ㄌㄧㄝˋ)
mean; depraved

卑躬屈節(ㄅㄟ ㄍㄨㄥ ㄑㄩ ㄐㄧㄝˊ)or卑躬曲膝(ㄅㄟ ㄍㄨㄥ ㄑㄩ ㄒㄧ)
obsequious; servile; fawning; to humiliate oneself in serving master

卑賤(ㄅㄟ ㄐㄧㄢˋ)
low; inferior; mean; humble: 他出身卑賤。He is a man of mean birth.

卑親屬(ㄅㄟ ㄑㄧㄣ ㄕㄨˇ)
relatives who are junior to oneself either in age or in generation

卑怯(ㄅㄟ ㄑㄩㄝˋ)
mean and cowardly 參看「卑躬屈膝」

卑下(ㄅㄟ ㄒㄧㄚˋ)
base; mean; humble

卑職(ㄅㄟ ㄓˊ)
①(self-reference) your humble servant ②a low or humble position

卑濕(ㄅㄟ ㄕ)
dampness of low-lying land

卑讓(ㄅㄟ ㄖㄤˋ)
to defer; to yield with courtesy or respect

卑辭厚禮(ㄅㄟ ㄘˊ ㄏㄡˋ ㄌㄧˇ)
sweet words and lavish gifts; humble words and generous (or handsome) gifts

卑污(ㄅㄟ ㄨ)
despicable and filthy

卑微(ㄅㄟ ㄨㄟˊ)
lowly; humble: 他出身卑微。He is a man of humble birth.

【卒】 483
1. ㄗㄨˊ　tzwu　zú

1. a servant; an underling; a lackey
2. a soldier: 士卒 soldiers
3. a unit of one hundred soldiers
4. at last; after all; at long last: 我卒償素願。I had my wishes fulfilled at long last.
5. to complete; to finish: 卒其事 to finish one's job
6. dead; to die
7. a community of 300 families
8. a pawn in Chinese chess

卒子(ㄗㄨˊ·ㄗ)
①a soldier; a private ②a pawn

卒業(ㄗㄨˊ ㄧㄝˋ)
to graduate; to complete study (at an institution, etc.); to finish a course of study

【卒】 483
2. ㄘㄨˋ　tsuh　cù

suddenly; abruptly; hurriedly

卒乍(ㄘㄨˋ ㄓㄚˋ)
suddenly; unexpectedly

卒卒(ㄘㄨˋ ㄘㄨˋ)
hurriedly

【卓】 484
ㄓㄨㄛˊ　jwo　zhuó

1. lofty; high
2. profound; brilliant; eminent
3. (to stand) upright; erect
4. a Chinese family name

卓立(ㄓㄨㄛˊ ㄌㄧˋ)
to stand alone; to stand out; to stand upright

卓犖 or 卓躒(ㄓㄨㄛˊ ㄌㄨㄛˋ)
excellent; unsurpassed; eminent

卓見(ㄓㄨㄛˊ ㄐㄧㄢˋ)
a brilliant idea or view; an excellent or distinguished opinion 亦作「灼見」

卓絕(ㄓㄨㄛˊ ㄐㄩㄝˊ)
① outstanding; eminent; peerless; prominent; brilliant; unsurpassed ②extreme: 艱苦卓絕 extreme hardships and difficulties

卓絕千古(ㄓㄨㄛˊ ㄐㄩㄝˊ ㄑㄧㄢ ㄍㄨˇ)
unmatched past or present

卓著(ㄓㄨㄛˊ ㄓㄨˋ)
prominent; eminent; distinguished; outstanding; well-known

卓卓(ㄓㄨㄛˊ ㄓㄨㄛˊ)
outstanding; distinguished

卓識(ㄓㄨㄛˊ ㄕˋ)
brilliant ideas or views; superior insight or judgment

卓然(ㄓㄨㄛˊ ㄖㄢˊ)
outstanding; distinguished; eminent

卓裁(ㄓㄨㄛˊ ㄘㄞˊ)
(your) esteemed decision; brilliant decision (often used in correspondence)

卓爾(ㄓㄨㄛˊ ㄦˇ)
outstanding; eminent

卓異(ㄓㄨㄛˊ ㄧˋ)
outstanding; towering

卓有成效(ㄓㄨㄛˊ ㄧㄡˇ ㄔㄥˊ ㄒㄧㄠˋ)
fruitful; highly effective

卓文君(ㄓㄨㄛˊ ㄨㄣˊ ㄐㄩㄣ)
Cho Wen-chün, a famous widow who eloped with Ssu-Ma Hsiang-ju (司馬相如) of the Han Dynasty (The elopement has been one of the most celebrated romances among the Chinese literati.)

卓越(ㄓㄨㄛˊ ㄩㄝˋ)
excellent; remarkable; outstanding; foremost; brilliant: 楊先生是位卓越的科學家。Mr. Yang is an outstanding scientist.

【協】 485
ㄒㄧㄝˊ　shye　xié

1. to agree; an agreement
2. to be united; to bring into harmony; to coordinate
3. to assist; to aid; to help

協防(ㄒㄧㄝˊ ㄈㄤˊ)
to help defend (a place)

協定(ㄒㄧㄝˊ ㄉㄧㄥˋ)
an agreement (usually between nations)

協調(ㄒㄧㄝˊ ㄊㄧㄠˊ)
to coordinate; coordination; harmony; to bring to harmony; to adjust; to bring about full coordination

協同(ㄒㄧㄝˊ ㄊㄨㄥˊ)
to work in coordination with; to cooperate with; to work with (others); to join others in (accomplishing an undertaking, etc.)

協理(ㄒㄧㄝˊ ㄌㄧˇ)
① an assistant manager ② an official rank in the Ching Dynasty

協力(ㄒㄧㄝˊ ㄌㄧˋ)
to work in concert; to exert together; in cooperation with: 我們和他協力工作。We worked in cooperation with him.

協和(ㄒㄧㄝˊ ㄏㄜˊ)
harmony; to harmonize

協和醫學院(ㄒㄧㄝˊ ㄏㄜˊ ㄧ ㄒㄩㄝˊ ㄩㄢˋ)
the Union Medical College in Peking (簡稱 PUMC)

協會(ㄒㄧㄝˊ ㄏㄨㄟˋ)
an association; a society

協助(ㄒㄧㄝˊ ㄓㄨˋ)
to assist; to help mutually

協商(ㄒㄧㄝˊ ㄕㄤ)
to negotiate; to discuss; to consult with each other: 我與他們協商此事。I consulted

with them about the matter.
協奏曲(ㄒㄧㄝˊ ㄗㄡˋ ㄑㄩˇ)
(music) a concerto
協議(ㄒㄧㄝˊ ㄧˋ)
①an agreement; a draft agreement ②to discuss; to negotiate
協約(ㄒㄧㄝˊ ㄩㄝ)
an alliance; an agreement
協約國(ㄒㄧㄝˊ ㄩㄝ ㄍㄨㄛˊ)
the Allies (during World War I)
協韻(ㄒㄧㄝˊ ㄩㄣˋ)
to have the same rhyme

七畫

【南】 486
1. ㄋㄚˊ na ná
參看「南無」、「南無阿彌陀佛」
南無(ㄋㄚˊ ㄇㄛˊ)
(Sanskrit) *Namo,* to be converted to (the Buddha, the dharma or the sangha)
南無阿彌陀佛(ㄋㄚˊ ㄇㄛˊ ㄜ ㄇㄧˊ ㄊㄨㄛˊ ㄈㄛˊ)
(Buddhism) *Namo Amitabha* (Homage to Amitabha Buddha.)

【南】 486
2. ㄋㄢˊ nan nán
1. south; southward: 暖和的風從南方吹來。A warm wind was blowing from the south.
2. a type of ancient music played in the south of China
3. a Chinese family name
南北(ㄋㄢˊ ㄅㄟˇ)
①north and south ②from north to south ③(in ancient China) a man
南北貨(ㄋㄢˊ ㄅㄟˇ ㄏㄨㄛˋ)
sundry goods
南北戰爭(ㄋㄢˊ ㄅㄟˇ ㄓㄢˋ ㄓㄥ)
the American Civil War of 1861-65
南北朝(ㄋㄢˊ ㄅㄟˇ ㄔㄠˊ)
(literally) the South and North Dynasties—after the Eastern Tsin, China was divided into the Han-ruled south and the barbarian north (420-589 A.D.)
南北史(ㄋㄢˊ ㄅㄟˇ ㄕˇ)
the history of the South and North Dynasties
南半球(ㄋㄢˊ ㄅㄢˋ ㄑㄧㄡˊ)
the Southern Hemisphere
南邊(ㄋㄢˊ ㄅㄧㄢ) or 南邊兒(ㄋㄢˊ ㄅㄧㄚㄦ)
①the south; the southern side ②the southern provinces of China
南冰洋(ㄋㄢˊ ㄅㄧㄥ ㄧㄤˊ)
the Antarctic Ocean
南部(ㄋㄢˊ ㄅㄨˋ)
southern part; south: 高雄在台灣的南部。Kaohsiung is in the south of Taiwan.
南美洲(ㄋㄢˊ ㄇㄟˇ ㄓㄡ)
South America; Latin America 亦作「拉丁美洲」
南蠻鴃舌(ㄋㄢˊ ㄇㄢˊ ㄐㄩㄝˊ ㄕㄜˊ)
(originally) a sarcastic remark by Mencius about Hsü Hsing (許行), a southerner who spoke a tongue different from others'— a strange language
南面(ㄋㄢˊ ㄇㄧㄢˋ)
①the south 亦作「南面兒」 ②the throne facing south—the monarch
南非(ㄋㄢˊ ㄈㄟ)
South Africa
南非共和國(ㄋㄢˊ ㄈㄟ ㄍㄨㄥˋ ㄏㄜˊ ㄍㄨㄛˊ)
the Republic of South Africa
南方(ㄋㄢˊ ㄈㄤ)
the south; the South: 他住在南方。He lives in the South.
南方大港(ㄋㄢˊ ㄈㄤ ㄉㄚˋ ㄍㄤˇ)
the biggest south China port which Dr. Sun Yat-sen proposed to build at Whampoa near Canton
南方話(ㄋㄢˊ ㄈㄤ ㄏㄨㄚˋ)
the southern dialect
南方人(ㄋㄢˊ ㄈㄤ ㄖㄣˊ)
a southerner
南風(ㄋㄢˊ ㄈㄥ)
①the wind blowing from the south ②a form of ancient Chinese musical composition
南達科他(ㄋㄢˊ ㄉㄚˊ ㄎㄜ ㄊㄚ)
South Dakota, U.S.A.
南丁格爾(ㄋㄢˊ ㄉㄧㄥ ㄍㄜˊ ㄦˇ)
Florence Nightingale, 1820-1910, the founder of modern nursing
南唐(ㄋㄢˊ ㄊㄤˊ)
one of the ten states during the Five Dynasties (lasting from 937 to 975 A.D., and occupying parts of today Kiangsu, Anhwei, Fukie and Kiangsi Provinces
南來北往(ㄋㄢˊ ㄌㄞˊ ㄅㄟˇ ㄨㄤˇ)
①(people) going south an north—descriptive of heav traffic, a busy place or hub of communication ②t hurry along here and there to be always on the move
南瓜(ㄋㄢˊ ㄍㄨㄚ)
a pumpkin; a cushaw
南國(ㄋㄢˊ ㄍㄨㄛˊ)
the southern part of th country; the South
南卡羅來納州(ㄋㄢˊ ㄎㄚˇ ㄌㄨㄛˊ ㄌㄞˊ ㄋㄚˋ ㄓㄡ)
South Carolina, U.S.A.
南柯一夢(ㄋㄢˊ ㄎㄜ ㄧˊ ㄇㄥˋ)
a dream; dreaming; a empty dream (originally, th dream of a person wh thought he was made gover nor of Nanko, a place which did not exist)
南開大學(ㄋㄢˊ ㄎㄞ ㄉㄚˋ ㄒㄩㄝˊ)
The Nankai University a Tientsin
南海(ㄋㄢˊ ㄏㄞˇ)
①name of a county in Kwang tung Province ②the South China Sea, stretching fron the Taiwan Straits to Kwang tung ③(in ancient China) a term for faraway places in the south
南寒帶(ㄋㄢˊ ㄏㄢˊ ㄉㄞˋ)
the Antarctic Zone; the South Frigid Zone
南胡(ㄋㄢˊ ㄏㄨˊ)
the two-stringed Chinese viola 亦作「二胡」
南貨(ㄋㄢˊ ㄏㄨㄛˋ)
①delicacies or products from south China (such as dried bamboo shoots, etc.)② any native product, food stuff, ham, etc.
南回歸線(ㄋㄢˊ ㄏㄨㄟˊ ㄍㄨㄟ ㄒㄧㄢˋ)
the Tropic of Capricorn
南箕北斗(ㄋㄢˊ ㄐㄧ ㄅㄟˇ ㄉㄡˇ)
something which enjoys an empty name but serves no practical purposes
南極(ㄋㄢˊ ㄐㄧˊ)
the South Pole; the Antarctic Pole

南極光(ㄋㄢˊ ㄐㄧˊ ㄍㄨㄤ)
the aurora australis; the southern lights
南極圈(ㄋㄢˊ ㄐㄧˊ ㄑㄩㄢ)
the Antarctic Circle
南極洲(ㄋㄢˊ ㄐㄧˊ ㄓㄡ)
Antarctica; the Antarctic Continent
南京(ㄋㄢˊ ㄐㄧㄥ)
Nanking, capital of the Republic of China
南軍(ㄋㄢˊ ㄐㄩㄣ)
the Confederate soldiers, or the Confederate troops (in the American Civil War)
南腔北調(ㄋㄢˊ ㄑㄧㄤ ㄅㄟˇ ㄉㄧㄠˋ)
a tongue which combines accents of the various spoken dialects in China—to speak with a mixed accent
南曲(ㄋㄢˊ ㄑㄩˇ)
one of the two forms of operas in the Yüan Dynasty
南下(ㄋㄢˊ ㄒㄧㄚˋ)
to go down south
南針(ㄋㄢˊ ㄓㄣ)
① a compass ② a guide or guidance
南征北戰(ㄋㄢˊ ㄓㄥ ㄅㄟˇ ㄓㄢˋ)
to fight up and down the country; to participate in battles everywhere; to fight north and south on many fronts
南朝(ㄋㄢˊ ㄔㄠˊ)
the Southern Dynasties during the South and North Dynasties (420-589 A.D.), the Sung Dynasty(宋), the Chi Dynasty(齊), the Liang Dynasty(梁), the Chen Dynasty(陳)
南昌(ㄋㄢˊ ㄔㄤ)
Nanchang, capital of Kiangsi Province
南沙羣島(ㄋㄢˊ ㄕㄚ ㄑㄩㄣˊ ㄉㄠˇ)
Nansha Chuntao; the Spratly Islands
南山(ㄋㄢˊ ㄕㄢ)
① the Chung-Nan Mountain ② the Chilien Mountain ③ name of a county in Fukien Province
南山壽(ㄋㄢˊ ㄕㄢ ㄕㄡˋ)
(literally) as long-lived as Nan Mountain— many, many happy returns of the day
亦作「壽比南山」
南人(ㄋㄢˊ ㄖㄣˊ)
southerners
南斯拉夫(ㄋㄢˊ ㄙ ㄌㄚ ㄈㄨ)
Yugoslavia
南宋(ㄋㄢˊ ㄙㄨㄥˋ)
the domain of the Sung Dynasty after Emperor Kao Tzung (高宗) withdrew to the south of the Yangtze (1127-1279)
南亞(ㄋㄢˊ ㄧㄚˇ)
South Asia
南洋(ㄋㄢˊ ㄧㄤˊ)
① the area which covers Southeast Asia and Indonesia ②the Chinese coastal region south of Shantung ③ the South Seas
南緯(ㄋㄢˊ ㄨㄟˇ)
latitudes south of the equator
南溫帶(ㄋㄢˊ ㄨㄣ ㄉㄞˋ)
the South Temperate Zone
南嶽(ㄋㄢˊ ㄩㄝˋ)
another name for the Heng Mountain (衡山) in Hunan Province, one of the Five Sacred Mountains
南轅北轍(ㄋㄢˊ ㄩㄢˊ ㄅㄟˇ ㄔㄜˋ)
to try to go south by driving the chariot north—to act in a way that defeats one's purpose; practice diametrically opposed to preaching; to be diametrically opposite

十畫

【博】 487
ㄅㄛˊ bor bó
1. wide; extensive
2. abundant; ample; rich
3. broadly knowledgeable; well-read; learned; erudite
4. to barter for; to exchange
5. to gamble; to play games
6. to win; to gain
7. a Chinese family name

博大精深(ㄅㄛˊ ㄉㄚˋ ㄐㄧㄥ ㄕㄣ)
broad and profound; extensive and profound (knowledge, study, etc.)
博得(ㄅㄛˊ ㄉㄜˊ)or 博取(ㄅㄛˊ ㄑㄩˇ)
to win; to obtain
博徒(ㄅㄛˊ ㄊㄨˊ)
a gambler
博通(ㄅㄛˊ ㄊㄨㄥ)or 博達(ㄅㄛˊ ㄉㄚˊ)
having a broad knowledge of; to possess extensive knowledge of; to be erudite
博覽(ㄅㄛˊ ㄌㄢˇ)
to read extensively; to be well-read
博覽會(ㄅㄛˊ ㄌㄢˇ ㄏㄨㄟˋ)
a trade fair; an exhibition or exposition
博古通今(ㄅㄛˊ ㄍㄨˇ ㄊㄨㄥ ㄐㄧㄣ)
to be acquainted with things ancient and modern; to be well-informed in things past and present; to be well-versed in (or conversant with) ancient and modern learning—erudite and informed
博貫(ㄅㄛˊ ㄍㄨㄢˋ)
to have profound and transcending knowledge of; erudite
博局(ㄅㄛˊ ㄐㄩˊ)
① a gambling session ② a gambling place
博學(ㄅㄛˊ ㄒㄩㄝˊ)
well-read; erudite; well-versed in a wide range of studies or learning; extensively study: 他是位博學的學者。He is a well-read scholar.
博學鴻儒(ㄅㄛˊ ㄒㄩㄝˊ ㄏㄨㄥˊ ㄖㄨˊ)
a rank for great scholars in the reign of Emperor Kang Hsi(康熙)
博施濟衆(ㄅㄛˊ ㄕ ㄐㄧˋ ㄓㄨㄥˋ)
to provide liberal relief to the masses; to relieve the people with liberal aid (especially material); to be interested in charities
博士(ㄅㄛˊ ㄕˋ)
① a doctorate; a doctoral degree ② an official rank, initiated in the Chin Dynasty and conferred upon scholars of profound learning
博斯普魯斯海峽(ㄅㄛˊ ㄙ ㄆㄨˇ ㄌㄨˇ ㄙ ㄏㄞˇ ㄒㄧㄚˊ)
the Bosporus Strait
博愛(ㄅㄛˊ ㄞˋ)
indiscriminate love; fraternity; universal love; love for all
博弈(ㄅㄛˊ ㄧˋ)
playing a game of "go"

〔十部〕

chess

博雅(ㄅㄛˊ ㄧㄚˇ)
① learned and accomplished; well-informed and refined ② erudition

博雅之士(ㄅㄛˊ ㄧㄚˇ ㄓ ㄕˋ)
a scholar of a profound knowledge

博物(ㄅㄛˊ ㄨˋ)
① broadly knowledgeable; well-read; erudite ② natural sciences; nature studies

博物館(ㄅㄛˊ ㄨˋ ㄍㄨㄢˇ)or 博物院(ㄅㄛˊ ㄨˋ ㄩㄢˋ)
a museum

博物學(ㄅㄛˊ ㄨˋ ㄒㄩㄝˊ)
natural history

博聞強記(ㄅㄛˊ ㄨㄣˊ ㄑㄧㄤˊ ㄐㄧˋ)
wide learning and a powerful memory; having an encyclopaedic knowledge

卜部
ㄅㄨˇ buu bǔ

【卜】 488
ㄅㄨˇ buu bǔ
1. to divine; to consult the oracle
2. to foretell; to predict: 勝負難卜。It's difficult to foretell who will win.
3. to choose; to select
4. a Chinese family name

卜鄰(ㄅㄨˇ ㄌㄧㄣˊ)
to choose neighbors

卜卦(ㄅㄨˇ ㄍㄨㄚˋ)
to divine by the Eight Diagrams

卜居(ㄅㄨˇ ㄐㄩ)
to choose a residence; to choose a place for one's home

卜宅(ㄅㄨˇ ㄓㄞˊ)
① to choose a residence ② to choose a tomb site

卜晝卜夜(ㄅㄨˇ ㄓㄡˋ ㄅㄨˇ ㄧㄝˋ)
day and night; around the clock

卜筮(ㄅㄨˇ ㄕˋ)
divination; to divine by the tortoise and by the milfoil

卜辭(ㄅㄨˇ ㄘˊ)
the writings inscribed on oracle bones; oracle inscriptions of the Shang Dynasty on tortoise shells or animal bones

二畫

【卞】 489
ㄅㄧㄢˋ biann biàn
1. hurriedly; rash; impetuous
2. excitable
3. a Chinese family name

卞急(ㄅㄧㄢˋ ㄐㄧˊ)
testy; irascible

三畫

【占】 490
1. ㄓㄢ jan zhān
1. to divine
2. to observe
3. a Chinese family name

占卜(ㄓㄢ ㄅㄨˇ)
to divine; to practice divination

占夢(ㄓㄢ ㄇㄥˋ)
to divine by interpreting dreams

占斷吉凶(ㄓㄢ ㄉㄨㄢˋ ㄐㄧˊ ㄒㄩㄥ)
to find out good or bad luck by divination

占卦(ㄓㄢ ㄍㄨㄚˋ)
to divine by the Eight Diagrams (八卦)

占星(ㄓㄢ ㄒㄧㄥ)
to divine by astrology; to cast a horoscope

占星術(ㄓㄢ ㄒㄧㄥ ㄕㄨˋ)
astrology

占驗(ㄓㄢ ㄧㄢˋ)
the confirmation of an oracle

【占】 490
2. (佔) ㄓㄢˋ jann zhàn
to occupy

占領(ㄓㄢˋ ㄌㄧㄥˇ)
to occupy

占據(ㄓㄢˋ ㄐㄩˋ)
to occupy illegally or by force

占先(ㄓㄢˋ ㄒㄧㄢ)
to occupy before others; to preempt

占有(ㄓㄢˋ ㄧㄡˇ)
to take possession of

【卡】 491
1. ㄎㄚˇ kaa kǎ
1. a card, as a visiting card; cardboard
2. an abbreviated form for "calorie"
3. a guardhouse
4. a customs barrier; a road block; a checkpoint
5. to block; to check

卡賓槍(ㄎㄚˇ ㄅㄧㄣ ㄑㄧㄤ)
a carbine

卡片(ㄎㄚˇ ㄆㄧㄢˋ)
a card; a calling card

卡達(ㄎㄚˇ ㄉㄚˊ)
Qatar or Katar

卡達人(ㄎㄚˇ ㄉㄚˊ ㄖㄣˊ)
a Qatari

卡帶(ㄎㄚˇ ㄉㄞˋ)
a cassette tape

卡通(ㄎㄚˇ ㄊㄨㄥ)
a cartoon (especially a cartoon movie)

卡內基(ㄎㄚˇ ㄋㄟˋ ㄐㄧ)
Andrew Carnegie, 1835-1919, an American steel tycoon

卡農(ㄎㄚˇ ㄋㄨㄥˊ)
(music) canon

卡路里(ㄎㄚˇ ㄌㄨˋ ㄌㄧˇ)
a calorie

卡介苗(ㄎㄚˇ ㄐㄧㄝˋ ㄇㄧㄠˊ)
BCG (Bacillus Calmette-Guerin), a TB vaccine

卡其布(ㄎㄚˇ ㄑㄧˊ ㄅㄨˋ)
khaki

卡車(ㄎㄚˇ ㄔㄜ)
a truck; a lorry

卡式(ㄎㄚˇ ㄕˋ)
cassette

卡氏帶(ㄎㄚˇ ㄕˋ ㄉㄞˋ)
a casparian strip

卡薩布蘭加(ㄎㄚˇ ㄙㄚˋ ㄅㄨˋ ㄌㄢˊ ㄐㄧㄚ)
Casablanca, a seaport in north Africa

【卡】 491
2. ㄑㄧㄚˊ chya qiá
to be squeezed in between; to be sandwiched

【卡】 491
3. ㄑㄧㄚˇ chea qiǎ
to choke; to be choked

卡子(ㄑㄧㄚˇ ˙ㄗ)
① a customs office; a toll-collecting station ② a checkpost; a checkpoint: 下卡子 or 撤卡子 to set checkposts ③ a tool for gripping things (as

a pair of pincers, a clip, a fastener, etc.)
卡鑽(ㄑㄧㄚˇ ㄗㄨㄢˋ)
the jamming of a drilling tool; the sticking of tools

五畫

【卣】 492 ㄧㄡˇ yeou yǒu
(in ancient China) a container or vessel for wine; a Chinese chalice

六畫

【卦】 493 ㄍㄨㄚˋ guah guà
one of the Eight Diagrams of the *Book of Changes*
卦攤兒(ㄍㄨㄚˋ ㄊㄢㄦ)
a fortune-teller's stall

卩部 ㄐㄧㄝˊ jye jié

三畫

【卮】 494 ㄓ jy zhī
a container for holding wine; a goblet with handles

【卯】 495 ㄇㄠˇ mao mǎo
1. the fourth of the 12 Terrestrial Branches
2. the period from 5 to 7 a.m.
3. a roll call
4. a Chinese family name
卯勁兒(ㄇㄠˇ ㄐㄧㄣˋㄦ)
to make a sudden all-out effort
卯時(ㄇㄠˇ ㄕˊ)
the period of the day from 5 a.m. to 7 a.m.

四畫

【印】 496 ㄧㄣˋ yinn yìn
1. a seal; a stamp; a chop
2. to print; to stamp; to imprint
3. an imprint; a mark
4. a Chinese family name
印本(ㄧㄣˋ ㄅㄣˇ)
a printed copy
印譜(ㄧㄣˋ ㄆㄨˇ)
a collection of imprints of seals or chops by famous engravers, ancient and contemporary—appearing first toward the end of the Sung Dynasty
印發(ㄧㄣˋ ㄈㄚ)
to print and distribute
印第安納(ㄧㄣˋ ㄉㄧˋ ㄢ ㄋㄚˋ)
Indiana, U.S.A.
印第安人(ㄧㄣˋ ㄉㄧˋ ㄢ ㄖㄣˊ)
the American Indians
印度(ㄧㄣˋ ㄉㄨˋ)
India
印度半島(ㄧㄣˋ ㄉㄨˋ ㄅㄢˋ ㄉㄠˇ)
the subcontinent of India
印度河(ㄧㄣˋ ㄉㄨˋ ㄏㄜˊ)
the Indus
印度河文化(ㄧㄣˋ ㄉㄨˋ ㄏㄜˊ ㄨㄣˊ ㄏㄨㄚˋ)
Indus culture (3000B.C. — 1500B.C.)
印度教(ㄧㄣˋ ㄉㄨˋ ㄐㄧㄠˋ)
Hinduism
印度支那(ㄧㄣˋ ㄉㄨˋ ㄓ ㄋㄚˋ)
Indochina
印度洋(ㄧㄣˋ ㄉㄨˋ ㄧㄤˊ)
the Indian Ocean
印台(ㄧㄣˋ ㄊㄞˊ)
an ink pad; a stamp pad
印堂(ㄧㄣˋ ㄊㄤˊ)
(physiognomy) the space between the eyebrows
印尼(ㄧㄣˋ ㄋㄧˊ)or 印度尼西亞(ㄧㄣˋ ㄉㄨˋ ㄋㄧˊ ㄒㄧ ㄧㄚˇ)
Indonesia
印泥(ㄧㄣˋ ㄋㄧˊ)or 印色(ㄧㄣˋ ㄙㄜˋ)
ink (usually red) for imprinting of seals
印盒(ㄧㄣˋ ㄏㄜˊ)
a seal box
印花(ㄧㄣˋ ㄏㄨㄚ)
a revenue stamp
印花布(ㄧㄣˋ ㄏㄨㄚ ㄅㄨˋ)
printed cloth; calico
印花稅(ㄧㄣˋ ㄏㄨㄚ ㄕㄨㄟˋ)
stamp tax—a tax imposed on certain legal documents
印加人(ㄧㄣˋ ㄐㄧㄚ ㄖㄣˊ)
an Inca
印鑑(ㄧㄣˋ ㄐㄧㄢˋ)
an imprint or impression of one's chop filed with agencies concerned (especially banks, etc.) for checking purposes
印信(ㄧㄣˋ ㄒㄧㄣˋ)
official seals
印象(ㄧㄣˋ ㄒㄧㄤˋ)
an impression; a mental image
印象派(ㄧㄣˋ ㄒㄧㄤˋ ㄆㄞˋ)
the impressionist school (of the fine arts)
印象主義(ㄧㄣˋ ㄒㄧㄤˋ ㄓㄨˇ ㄧˋ)
impressionism
印行(ㄧㄣˋ ㄒㄧㄥˊ)
to publish
印章(ㄧㄣˋ ㄓㄤ)
a general name for seals, stamps and chops
印證(ㄧㄣˋ ㄓㄥˋ)
to prove; mutual proof
印刷(ㄧㄣˋ ㄕㄨㄚ)
to print
印刷品(ㄧㄣˋ ㄕㄨㄚ ㄆㄧㄣˇ)
printed matter
印刷機(ㄧㄣˋ ㄕㄨㄚ ㄐㄧ)
a printing machine
印刷廠(ㄧㄣˋ ㄕㄨㄚ ㄔㄤˇ)
a printing plant
印染(ㄧㄣˋ ㄖㄢˇ)
printing and dyeing (of textiles)
印子(ㄧㄣˋ ·ㄗ)
a mark; a trace; a print
印歐語系(ㄧㄣˋ ㄡ ㄩˇ ㄒㄧˋ)
Indo-European

【危】 497 ㄨㄟ wei wēi
1. danger; dangerous; precarious; perilous
2. restless
3. to fear; to be upset or afraid
4. lofty; high
5. just; honest; straightforward
6. a Chinese family name
危殆(ㄨㄟ ㄉㄞˋ)
in great danger; in jeopardy; in a critical condition
危篤(ㄨㄟ ㄉㄨˇ)
(said of a patient's condition) critical; dying
危難(ㄨㄟ ㄋㄢˋ)
(in) danger, peril, trouble, disaster or distress
危害(ㄨㄟ ㄏㄞˋ)
to endanger; to harm; to injure; to jeopardize

危害治安(ㄨㄟˊ ㄏㄞˋ ㄓˋ ㄢ)
to jeopardize public security

危機(ㄨㄟˊ ㄐㄧ)
a crisis; a danger point; a critical point; a precarious moment

危機重重(ㄨㄟˊ ㄐㄧ ㄔㄨㄥˊ ㄔㄨㄥˊ)
to bog down in crises; crisis-ridden

危急(ㄨㄟˊ ㄐㄧˊ)
(connoting risk and danger) urgent; pressing; hazardous; (in) a state of emergency; in a desperate situation

危急存亡之秋(ㄨㄟˊ ㄐㄧˊ ㄘㄨㄣˊ ㄨㄤˊ ㄓ ㄑㄧㄡ)
(said of a nation) at the moment of survival and downfall; at the moment of crisis

危局(ㄨㄟˊ ㄐㄩˊ)
a dangerous, critical or desperate situation: 他們已陷危局。They have been in a dangerous situation.

危險(ㄨㄟˊ ㄒㄧㄢˇ)
danger; dangerous; unsafe

危險份子(ㄨㄟˊ ㄒㄧㄢˇ ㄈㄣˋ ㄗˇ)
dangerous elements; undesirable elements

危險物(ㄨㄟˊ ㄒㄧㄢˇ ㄨˋ)
dangerous goods (as poisons, explosives or highly inflammable materials)

危如累卵(ㄨㄟˊ ㄖㄨˊ ㄌㄟˇ ㄌㄨㄢˇ)
(literally) as precarious as a pile of eggs—extremely dangerous

危在旦夕(ㄨㄟˊ ㄗㄞˋ ㄉㄢˋ ㄒㄧˋ)
①(said of a city under enemy attack) may fall at any moment ②(said of a patient critically ill) may die soon; dying

危坐(ㄨㄟˊ ㄗㄨㄛˋ)
to sit rigidly (as on ceremonious occasions or in the presence of superiors)

危言聳聽(ㄨㄟˊ ㄧㄢˊ ㄙㄨㄥˇ ㄊㄧㄥ)
to stir up others with sensational statements; to resort to sensationalism (as news headlines, reporting, etc.)

危亡(ㄨㄟˊ ㄨㄤˊ)
in great danger; in danger of elimination; in peril

五畫

【卵】 498
ㄌㄨㄢˇ loan luǎn

1. an egg; an ovum
2. fish roe
3. the testicles

卵白(ㄌㄨㄢˇ ㄅㄞˊ)
albumen; egg white

卵胎生(ㄌㄨㄢˇ ㄊㄞ ㄕㄥ)
(zoology) ovoviviparity

卵黃(ㄌㄨㄢˇ ㄏㄨㄤˊ)
yolk

卵球(ㄌㄨㄢˇ ㄑㄧㄡˊ)
the egg cell of a plant

卵細胞(ㄌㄨㄢˇ ㄒㄧˋ ㄅㄠ)
an ovum; ova

卵形(ㄌㄨㄢˇ ㄒㄧㄥˊ)
ovoid; oval

卵巢(ㄌㄨㄢˇ ㄔㄠˊ)
ovaries

卵石(ㄌㄨㄢˇ ㄕˊ)
cobbles; pebbles

卵生(ㄌㄨㄢˇ ㄕㄥ)
oviparous

卵子
①(ㄌㄨㄢˇ ㄗˇ) an ovum
②(ㄌㄢˇ ˙ㄗ) testes; testicles

卵翼(ㄌㄨㄢˇ ㄧˋ)
protection; shelter

六畫

【卷】 499
1. ㄐㄩㄢˋ jiuann juàn

1. painting which can be easily folded or rolled up
2. a book: 開卷有益。One will be benefited whenever one opens a book.
3. a division of a book; a volume
4. a test paper
5. filed documents; files

卷紙(ㄐㄩㄢˋ ㄓˇ)
paper for use in examinations

卷帙(ㄐㄩㄢˋ ㄓˋ)
a book; books: 圖書館卷帙繁浩。The library has a great number of books.

卷軸(ㄐㄩㄢˋ ㄓㄡˊ)
a book; books

卷子(ㄐㄩㄢˋ ˙ㄗ)
a test paper; an examination paper

卷宗(ㄐㄩㄢˋ ㄗㄨㄥ)
filed documents, especially in public offices; files; dossiers

【卷】 499
2. (捲) ㄐㄩㄢˇ jeuan juǎn

to roll up

卷土重來(ㄐㄩㄢˇ ㄊㄨˇ ㄔㄨㄥˊ ㄌㄞˊ)
to come back again after defeat; to make another try after failure

【卷】 499
3. ㄑㄩㄢˊ chyuan quán

curly; to curl

卷髮(ㄑㄩㄢˊ ㄈㄚˇ)
①curly hair; hair curling up ②to curl hair

卷曲(ㄑㄩㄢˊ ㄑㄩ)
to curl up

【卸】 500
ㄒㄧㄝˋ shieh xiè

1. to get rid of; to remove
2. to unload (cargoes, etc.)
3. to resign; to retire from office

卸磨殺驢(ㄒㄧㄝˋ ㄇㄛˋ ㄕㄚ ㄌㄩˊ)
to kill the donkey the moment it leaves the millstone—to get rid of someone as soon as he has finished his work

卸貨(ㄒㄧㄝˋ ㄏㄨㄛˋ)
to unload (or discharge) cargoes: 這船正在卸貨。The ship is unloading.

卸肩(ㄒㄧㄝˋ ㄐㄧㄢ)
to lay down responsibilities

卸妝(ㄒㄧㄝˋ ㄓㄨㄤ)
to remove make-up and ornaments

卸除(ㄒㄧㄝˋ ㄔㄨˊ)
to remove; to get rid of

卸任(ㄒㄧㄝˋ ㄖㄣˋ)
to quit a public office

卸責(ㄒㄧㄝˋ ㄗㄜˊ)
①to lay down one's responsibilities ②to shirk one's responsibility

卸載(ㄒㄧㄝˋ ㄗㄞˋ)
to unload cargoes (from a boat or car)

【卹】 501
ㄒㄩˋ shiuh xù

1. pity; to pity; sympathy; to sympathize
2. to give relief

卹金(ㄒㄩˋ ㄐㄧㄣ)

compensation; a pension; an indemnity (especially paid by the government for loss of life on a job, etc.)

卹養(ㄒㄩˋ ㄧㄤˇ)
to raise (orphans, etc.); to aid in the sustenance (of the sick, old, etc.)

【卺】 502 ㄐㄧㄣˇ jiin jǐn
nuptial winecups (made from a gourd split in two)

七畫

【卻】 503 (却) ㄑㄩㄝˋ chiueh què
1. still; but; yet
2. to refuse to accept
3. to retreat; to withdraw

卻病(ㄑㄩㄝˋ ㄅㄧㄥˋ)
to prevent or cure a disease

卻步(ㄑㄩㄝˋ ㄅㄨˋ)
to retreat or withdraw (in fear or in disgust); to shrink back

卻來(ㄑㄩㄝˋ ㄌㄞˊ)
① yet ② in reality

卻立(ㄑㄩㄝˋ ㄌㄧˋ)
to stand back

卻之不恭(ㄑㄩㄝˋ ㄓ ㄅㄨˋ ㄍㄨㄥ)
It's not polite to refuse (an offer, present, etc.).—a modest expression implying that one does not deserve what is offered: 卻之不恭，受之有愧。To refuse would be impolite, but to accept is embarrassing.

卻是(ㄑㄩㄝˋ ㄕˋ)
nevertheless; in fact; the fact is...

卻說(ㄑㄩㄝˋ ㄕㄨㄛ)
Let's resume our story. 或 Now, let's proceed (to tell our story).

卻走(ㄑㄩㄝˋ ㄗㄡˇ)
to run backward; to turn away

卻要(ㄑㄩㄝˋ ㄧㄠˋ)
to want or to want to... (contrary to what others expected)

卻又(ㄑㄩㄝˋ ㄧㄡˋ)
① but again (emphatic "again") ② then...later

【卽】 504 (即) ㄐㄧˊ jyi jí
1. promptly; immediately; now
2. then; accordingly
3. even if—indicating supposition or sequence

卽便(ㄐㄧˊ ㄅㄧㄢˋ)
① at this moment; forthwith ② although; even if; even though

卽令(ㄐㄧˊ ㄌㄧㄥˋ)
① even if; even though ② to order immediately

卽刻(ㄐㄧˊ ㄎㄜˋ)
immediately; promptly; now: 卽刻來這裏。Come here now.

卽或(ㄐㄧˊ ㄏㄨㄛˋ)
even if; even though

卽今(ㄐㄧˊ ㄐㄧㄣ)
right now; at this very moment

卽將(ㄐㄧˊ ㄐㄧㄤ)
to be about to; to be on the point of: 典禮卽將開始。The ceremony is about to begin.

卽景(ㄐㄧˊ ㄐㄧㄥˇ)
to compose poems with the scenery one is looking at as the theme

卽景生情(ㄐㄧˊ ㄐㄧㄥˇ ㄕㄥ ㄑㄧㄥˊ)
the scene arouses a sense (of joy, sorrow, etc.); the scene touches a chord in one's heart

卽席(ㄐㄧˊ ㄒㄧˊ)
on the spot; at once; extempore; impromptu; off the cuff: 我們要求他卽席演講。We asked him to speak extempore.

卽興(ㄐㄧˊ ㄒㄧㄥˋ)
impromptu; extemporaneous

卽興之作(ㄐㄧˊ ㄒㄧㄥˋ ㄓ ㄗㄨㄛˋ)
an improvisation

卽時(ㄐㄧˊ ㄕˊ)
immediately; at once

卽使(ㄐㄧˊ ㄕˇ)
even if

卽事(ㄐㄧˊ ㄕˋ)
① the present affairs ② to do something

卽世(ㄐㄧˊ ㄕˋ)
to leave the world; to die

卽日(ㄐㄧˊ ㄖˋ)
on the very day; immediately; as soon as possible; at once

卽如(ㄐㄧˊ ㄖㄨˊ)
as if

卽速(ㄐㄧˊ ㄙㄨˋ)
instantly; immediately; soon

卽夜(ㄐㄧˊ ㄧㄝˋ)
on the very night; within the night; immediately

卽位(ㄐㄧˊ ㄨㄟˋ)
to ascend the throne

十畫

【卿】 505 ㄑㄧㄥ ching qing
1. (in ancient China) a salutation of an emperor to his ministers
2. used in addressing one's wife—Honey, Darling, Dear, etc.
3. (in ancient China) a nobleman; a high official rank
4. a Chinese family name

卿卿我我(ㄑㄧㄥ ㄑㄧㄥ ㄨㄛˇ ㄨㄛˇ)
to be very much in love

卿雲(ㄑㄧㄥ ㄩㄣˊ)
propitious clouds bringing well-being to all

厂部
ㄏㄢˇ haan hǎn

二畫

【厄】 506 ㄜˋ eh è
1. difficulty; adversity; distress; hardship
2. impeded; cramped

厄難(ㄜˋ ㄋㄢˋ)
distress; difficulty; hardship

厄瓜多爾(ㄜˋ ㄍㄨㄚ ㄉㄨㄛ ㄦˇ)
Ecuador

厄瓜多爾人(ㄜˋ ㄍㄨㄚ ㄉㄨㄛ ㄦˇ ㄖㄣˊ)
an Ecuadorian

厄爾巴(ㄜˋ ㄦˇ ㄅㄚ)
Elba Island in the Mediterranean

厄運(ㄜˋ ㄩㄣˋ)
bad luck; adversity

七畫

厂部

【厖】 507 ㄆㄤˊ parng páng (又讀 ㄇㄤˊ mang máng)
1. bulky; huge
2. confused; disorderly

厖然大物(ㄆㄤˊ ㄖㄢˊ ㄉㄚˋ ㄨˋ)
something which is huge in size

厖雜(ㄆㄤˊ ㄗㄚˊ)
disorderly; messy

【厚】 508 ㄏㄡˋ how hòu
1. thick; thickness
2. deep friendship
3. to treat kindly; generous
4. substantial
5. kind; considerate; virtuous

厚薄(ㄏㄡˋ ㄅㄛˊ)
① thickness and thinness ② munificence and parsimony

厚彼薄此(ㄏㄡˋ ㄅㄧˇ ㄅㄛˊ ㄘˇ)or 厚此薄彼(ㄏㄡˋ ㄘˇ ㄅㄛˊ ㄅㄧˇ)
to favor one more than another; to play favoritism; to treat with partiality

厚貌深情(ㄏㄡˋ ㄇㄠˋ ㄕㄣ ㄑㄧㄥˊ)
kindly in appearance but unfathomable at heart

厚德載福(ㄏㄡˋ ㄉㄜˊ ㄗㄞˋ ㄈㄨˊ)
(used as a eulogy) Great virtue carries happiness with it.

厚待(ㄏㄡˋ ㄉㄞˋ)
to treat kindly and generously

厚道(ㄏㄡˋ ㄉㄠˋ)
kind; virtuous; sincere; considerate; generous

厚度(ㄏㄡˋ ㄉㄨˋ)
thickness

厚禮(ㄏㄡˋ ㄌㄧˇ)
lavish gifts; liberal presents

厚利(ㄏㄡˋ ㄌㄧˋ)
substantial profit

厚臉(ㄏㄡˋ ㄌㄧㄢˇ)or 厚顏(ㄏㄡˋ ㄧㄢˊ)
brazen-faced; shameless

厚祿(ㄏㄡˋ ㄌㄨˋ)
high government pay

厚古薄今(ㄏㄡˋ ㄍㄨˇ ㄅㄛˊ ㄐㄧㄣ)
to emphasize the past, but slight the present

厚今薄古(ㄏㄡˋ ㄐㄧㄣ ㄅㄛˊ ㄍㄨˇ)
to emphasize the present, but slight the past

厚重(ㄏㄡˋ ㄓㄨㄥˋ)
(said of manner) dignified; stately; graceful

厚酬(ㄏㄡˋ ㄔㄡˊ)
handsome reward or remuneration

厚實(ㄏㄡˋ ˙ㄕ)
thick

厚生(ㄏㄡˋ ㄕㄥ)
to improve people's living conditions

厚澤(ㄏㄡˋ ㄗㄜˊ)
great kindness

厚葬(ㄏㄡˋ ㄗㄤˋ)
an elaborate funeral

厚賜(ㄏㄡˋ ㄙˋ)
to reward generously; generous gifts

厚愛(ㄏㄡˋ ㄞˋ)
great kindness; to treat very kindly and generously

厚恩(ㄏㄡˋ ㄣ)
great indebtedness

厚意(ㄏㄡˋ ㄧˋ)
good intention; goodwill

厚誼(ㄏㄡˋ ㄧˊ)
deep friendship or hospitality

厚望(ㄏㄡˋ ㄨㄤˋ)
high hopes; high expectations; great expectations

八畫

【原】 509 ㄩㄢˊ yuan yuán
1. the source; the origin; the beginning
2. original; primary: 原來的計畫後來改變了。The original plan was afterward changed.
3. a steppe; a vast plain; a field: 他曾遊覽過加拿大的廣大平原。He has toured the vast plains of Canada.
4. a graveyard
5. to excuse; to pardon
6. a Chinese family name

原版(ㄩㄢˊ ㄅㄢˇ)
the original print; the original edition; the first print or edition; the edition printed by the original publisher

原本(ㄩㄢˊ ㄅㄣˇ)
① the causes of an incident; the ins and outs of an incident ② the origin of something ③ the author's manuscript; the original draft

原配(ㄩㄢˊ ㄆㄟˋ)
one's first wife 亦作「元配」

原木(ㄩㄢˊ ㄇㄨˋ)
a log

原封不動(ㄩㄢˊ ㄈㄥ ㄅㄨˋ ㄉㄨㄥˋ)
(in) original form; (kept or left) intact or unopened

原底子(ㄩㄢˊ ㄉㄧˇ ˙ㄗ)
① the first script (of a writing); the original script; a manuscript ② originally

原點(ㄩㄢˊ ㄉㄧㄢˇ)
(mathematics) origin; the point of origin

原動力(ㄩㄢˊ ㄉㄨㄥˋ ㄌㄧˋ)
① (mechanics) power ② (physics) action

原動機(ㄩㄢˊ ㄉㄨㄥˋ ㄐㄧ)
(mechanics) a prime mover

原來(ㄩㄢˊ ㄌㄞˊ)
originally or formerly

原來如此(ㄩㄢˊ ㄌㄞˊ ㄖㄨˊ ㄘˇ)
① I see. 或 Now I understand what you mean. 或 So that is what it is! ② It was as it is now. 或 No change has been made.

原理(ㄩㄢˊ ㄌㄧˇ)
principles: 這些機器按照相同的原理運轉。These machines work on the same principles.

原料(ㄩㄢˊ ㄌㄧㄠˋ)
raw materials

原諒(ㄩㄢˊ ㄌㄧㄤˋ)or 原宥(ㄩㄢˊ ㄧㄡˋ)
forgiveness; to forgive; to pardon: 請原諒我這麼說。Please pardon me for saying so.

原稿(ㄩㄢˊ ㄍㄠˇ)
a manuscript: 原稿將於下月初付印。The manuscript will go to press early next month.

原告(ㄩㄢˊ ㄍㄠˋ)
the plaintiff; the appellant; the prosecutor

原故(ㄩㄢˊ ㄍㄨˋ)
a reason; a cause: 告訴我你做這事的原故。Give me the reasons for doing it.

原籍(ㄩㄢˊ ㄐㄧˊ)
hailing from; a native of; originally of (a place); the original domicile: 他原籍上海。He is a native of Shanghai.

原價(ㄩㄢˊ ㄐㄧㄚˋ)

①the original price ② the production cost (of an article, etc.) ③ the price of an article paid by the retailer to the manufacturer or wholesaler
原舊(兒)(ㄩㄢˊ ㄐㄧㄡˋ(ㄦ))
original
原起(ㄩㄢˊ ㄑㄧˇ)
①the origin (of some event) ② originally
原器(ㄩㄢˊ ㄑㄧˋ)
(in the standard of measurements) the prototype
原隰(ㄩㄢˊ ㄒㄧˊ)
plateaus and low, marshy land
原先(ㄩㄢˊ ㄒㄧㄢ)
in the beginning; originally; in the very beginning: 讓我們照原先的計畫進行。 Let us proceed according to our original plan.
原型(ㄩㄢˊ ㄒㄧㄥˊ)
(machinery) the prototype
原形(ㄩㄢˊ ㄒㄧㄥˊ)
①the original form or shape ②one's true colors; the real face or form
原形畢露(ㄩㄢˊ ㄒㄧㄥˊ ㄅㄧˋ ㄌㄨˋ)
completely unmasked or exposed; to reveal the true nature or colors (of a person) completely
原形質(ㄩㄢˊ ㄒㄧㄥˊ ㄓˋ)
(biology) protoplasm
原址(ㄩㄢˊ ㄓˇ)
the former address
原主(ㄩㄢˊ ㄓㄨˇ)
the legal owner; the original owner
原著民(ㄩㄢˊ ㄓㄨˋ ㄇㄧㄣˊ)
an aborigine
原裝(ㄩㄢˊ ㄓㄨㄤ)
made or manufactured by a foreign manufacture
原裝貨(ㄩㄢˊ ㄓㄨㄤ ㄏㄨㄛˋ)
products imported intact (as distinct from those locally assembled or packed)
原狀(ㄩㄢˊ ㄓㄨㄤˋ)
①the original condition: 一切維持原狀。Everything is in its original condition. ②the status quo
原成岩(ㄩㄢˊ ㄔㄥˊ ㄧㄢˊ)
(geology) primary rocks

原處(ㄩㄢˊ ㄔㄨˋ)
the old place; the original place
原始(ㄩㄢˊ ㄕˇ)
①a source; an origin ② primitive; backward
原始分數(ㄩㄢˊ ㄕˇ ㄈㄣ ㄕㄨˋ)
a raw score
原始記錄(ㄩㄢˊ ㄕˇ ㄐㄧˋ ㄌㄨˋ)
original entries
原始價值(ㄩㄢˊ ㄕˇ ㄐㄧㄚˋ ㄓˊ)
original value
原始時代(ㄩㄢˊ ㄕˇ ㄕˊ ㄉㄞˋ)
primeval times or ages
原始社會(ㄩㄢˊ ㄕˇ ㄕㄜˋ ㄏㄨㄟˋ)
a primitive society
原始人(ㄩㄢˊ ㄕˇ ㄖㄣˊ)
a primitive
原始資料(ㄩㄢˊ ㄕˇ ㄗ ㄌㄧㄠˋ)
raw data; firsthand data
原始森林(ㄩㄢˊ ㄕˇ ㄙㄣ ㄌㄧㄣˊ)
a virgin forest
原審(ㄩㄢˊ ㄕㄣˇ)
(law) the first trial
原生動物(ㄩㄢˊ ㄕㄥ ㄉㄨㄥˋ ㄨˋ)
(zoology) a protozoon
原生植物(ㄩㄢˊ ㄕㄥ ㄓˊ ㄨˋ)
a protophyte
原人(ㄩㄢˊ ㄖㄣˊ)
Homo-prigenius (in anthropology)
原任(ㄩㄢˊ ㄖㄣˋ)
①the predecessor ②formerly held the post of...
原子(ㄩㄢˊ ㄗˇ)
an atom
原子筆(ㄩㄢˊ ㄗˇ ㄅㄧˇ)
a ball-point pen
原子炮(ㄩㄢˊ ㄗˇ ㄆㄠˋ)
a cannon firing atomic-tipped shells
原子分裂(ㄩㄢˊ ㄗˇ ㄈㄣ ㄌㄧㄝˋ)
atomic fission
原子彈(ㄩㄢˊ ㄗˇ ㄉㄢˋ)
an atomic bomb
原子能(ㄩㄢˊ ㄗˇ ㄋㄥˊ)
atomic energy
原子量(ㄩㄢˊ ㄗˇ ㄌㄧㄤˋ)
the atomic weight
原子爐(ㄩㄢˊ ㄗˇ ㄌㄨˊ)
an atomic reactor
原子核(ㄩㄢˊ ㄗˇ ㄏㄜˊ)
an atomic nucleus
原子價(ㄩㄢˊ ㄗˇ ㄐㄧㄚˋ)
(chemistry) valences

原子戰爭(ㄩㄢˊ ㄗˇ ㄓㄢˋ ㄓㄥ)
atomic warfare
原子塵(ㄩㄢˊ ㄗˇ ㄔㄣˊ)
atomic fallout
原子時代(ㄩㄢˊ ㄗˇ ㄕˊ ㄉㄞˋ)
the atomic age
原則(ㄩㄢˊ ㄗㄜˊ)
a principle (of handling or doing something)
原作(ㄩㄢˊ ㄗㄨㄛˋ)
the original work; the original
原罪(ㄩㄢˊ ㄗㄨㄟˋ)
(Bible) the original sin
原色(ㄩㄢˊ ㄙㄜˋ)
primary colors
原素(ㄩㄢˊ ㄙㄨˋ)
(chemistry) elements 亦作「元素」
原案(ㄩㄢˊ ㄢˋ)
the original bill; the original documents pertaining to a case at hand; the original records documented
原意(ㄩㄢˊ ㄧˋ)
①original intentions ②original meaning
原議(ㄩㄢˊ ㄧˋ)
the original agreement, resolution, etc.
原野(ㄩㄢˊ ㄧㄝˇ)
the field; a plain
原由(ㄩㄢˊ ㄧㄡˊ)
causes; reasons
原油(ㄩㄢˊ ㄧㄡˊ)
crude oil; crude petroleum
原有(ㄩㄢˊ ㄧㄡˇ)
to possess originally; (what) one had before; (what) was here or there originally
原鹽(ㄩㄢˊ ㄧㄢˊ)
solar salt
原因(ㄩㄢˊ ㄧㄣ)
causes; reasons: 潮汐的原因爲何? What are the causes of the tides?
原物(ㄩㄢˊ ㄨˋ)
①(law) things (as money, land, etc.) from which interest is borne or production of other items is effected ② the very original thing; the very same thing
原委(ㄩㄢˊ ㄨㄟˇ)
the reason why a thing happened; the whole story;

all the details; the ins and outs (of a case, story, etc.)
原文(ㄩㄢˊ ㄨㄣˊ)
the original text
原原本本(ㄩㄢˊ ㄩㄢˊ ㄅㄣˇ ㄅㄣˇ)
the whole (story or thing); in detail

〔厶部〕

【厝】510 ㄘㄨㄛˋ tsuoh cuò
1. to place
2. to place a coffin in a temporary shelter pending burial
3. a gravestone
4. to cut or engrave
厝火積薪(ㄘㄨㄛˋ ㄏㄨㄛˇ ㄐㄧ ㄒㄧㄣ)
(literally) to place fire near piles of fagots—in imminent danger

十畫

【厥】511 ㄐㄩㄝˊ jyue jué
1. to faint
2. same as 撅—to dig
3. a personal and possessive pronoun
厥功甚偉(ㄐㄩㄝˊ ㄍㄨㄥ ㄕㄣˋ ㄨㄟˇ)
to have made great contribution to the successful conclusion of a task
厥後(ㄐㄩㄝˊ ㄏㄡˋ)
after this; afterwards

十二畫

【厭】512 ㄧㄢˋ yann yàn
1. to dislike; to detest; to hate
2. to get tired of
3. satiated; surfeited
厭煩(ㄧㄢˋ ㄈㄢˊ)
bored; wearied; to dislike; to be vexed; to be fed up with
厭故喜新(ㄧㄢˋ ㄍㄨˋ ㄒㄧˇ ㄒㄧㄣ)
to dislike the old and to be fond of the new (often said of love affairs)
厭恨(ㄧㄢˋ ㄏㄣˋ)
to loathe; to hate
厭倦(ㄧㄢˋ ㄐㄩㄢˋ)
to be tired of; to be weary of
厭棄(ㄧㄢˋ ㄑㄧˋ)
to reject; to loathe; to give up; to get rid of: 現代的人厭棄戰爭。Modern people reject war.
厭戰(ㄧㄢˋ ㄓㄢˋ)
to be tired of war; war-weariness; demoralized by war
厭食(ㄧㄢˋ ㄕˊ)
lack of appetite
厭世(ㄧㄢˋ ㄕˋ)
① to be disgusted with the world ② to die ③ misanthropy
厭世主義(ㄧㄢˋ ㄕˋ ㄓㄨˇ ㄧˋ)
pessimism; cynicism
厭惡(ㄧㄢˋ ㄨˋ)
to loathe; to dislike; to detest; to abhor; to abominate; to be disgusted with

十三畫

【厲】513 ㄌㄧˋ lih lì
1. a coarse whetstone
2. harsh; violent; severe; stern; serious
3. to persuade; to urge; to encourage
4. bad; evil
5. a Chinese family name
6. an epidemic
7. to oppress; oppressive; cruel
厲兵秣馬(ㄌㄧˋ ㄅㄧㄥ ㄇㄛˋ ㄇㄚˇ)
to make military preparations; to maintain combat readiness; to remain alert militarily
厲鬼(ㄌㄧˋ ㄍㄨㄟˇ)
a fierce ghost; a malicious spirit
厲害(ㄌㄧˋ ·ㄏㄞ)
① fierceness; ferociousness ② very (ill, etc.); serious (damage, destruction, etc.)
厲階(ㄌㄧˋ ㄐㄧㄝ)
a steppingstone to disorder —(figuratively) disaster; the cause of trouble; a pestilence
厲禁(ㄌㄧˋ ㄐㄧㄣˋ)
strictly prohibited; to ban strictly
厲行(ㄌㄧˋ ㄒㄧㄥˊ)
to enforce; rigorous enforcement; to practice under strong persuasion or discipline
厲聲(ㄌㄧˋ ㄕㄥ)
to talk harshly; to shout angrily
厲色(ㄌㄧˋ ㄙㄜˋ)
to look angry; angry-looking

厶 部
厶 sy sī

三畫

【去】514 ㄑㄩˋ chiuh qù
1. to go away; to depart: 我明天就要離去了。I am going away tomorrow.
2. to get rid of; to remove: 脫去你的帽子。Remove your hat.
3. to be…apart: 兩地相去十英里。The two places are ten miles apart.
4. past; gone: 我們的困難過去了。Our troubles are past.
5. an auxiliary verb: 他早已死去。He died long ago.
6. the fourth of the four tones in Chinese phonetics
7. (Peking opera) to play the part of
去不成(ㄑㄩˋ ㄅㄨˋ ㄔㄥˊ)
unable to go; can not go
去不得(ㄑㄩˋ ·ㄅㄨ ·ㄉㄜ)
① should not go ② should not get rid of (it)
去不了(ㄑㄩˋ ·ㄅㄨ ㄌㄧㄠˇ)
cannot go; unable to go; unable to attend
去不去(ㄑㄩˋ ·ㄅㄨ ㄑㄩˋ)
Are you (or they) going? 或 Is he (or she) going? 或 Will you go?
去得了(ㄑㄩˋ ·ㄉㄜ ㄌㄧㄠˇ) or 去得成(ㄑㄩˋ ·ㄉㄜ ㄔㄥˊ)
able to go; able to attend
去泰去甚(ㄑㄩˋ ㄊㄞˋ ㄑㄩˋ ㄕㄣˋ)
to shun the extremes and to maintain the middle course
去你的(ㄑㄩˋ ㄋㄧˇ ·ㄉㄜ)
Nonsense! 或 Shut up your big mouth!
去年(ㄑㄩˋ ㄋㄧㄢˊ)
last year; the year past
去了(ㄑㄩˋ ·ㄌㄜ)
① already gone ② already

removed
去留(ㄑㄩˋ ㄌㄧㄡˊ)
to go or to stay
去路(ㄑㄩˋ ㄌㄨˋ)
the way along which one is going
去國(ㄑㄩˋ ㄍㄨㄛˊ)
to leave one's country; to leave one's fatherland
去就(ㄑㄩˋ ㄐㄧㄡˋ)
to quit or to stay (on a job)
去取之間(ㄑㄩˋ ㄑㄩˇ ㄓ ㄐㄧㄢ)
between taking and leaving (it); take it or leave it; undecided; a moment of indecision
去向(ㄑㄩˋ ㄒㄧㄤˋ)
the direction one is going; whereabouts
去職(ㄑㄩˋ ㄓˊ)
to be removed from office; to resign from office
去處(ㄑㄩˋ ㄔㄨˋ)
① whereabouts ② the place one is heading for ③ a place; a site
去世(ㄑㄩˋ ㄕˋ)
to die; to leave the world
去勢(ㄑㄩˋ ㄕˋ)
to castrate; castration; to emasculate
去聲(ㄑㄩˋ ㄕㄥ)
the falling tone—the fourth tone in Chinese phonetics
去任(ㄑㄩˋ ㄖㄣˋ)
to resign from a post; to leave a post
去粗取精(ㄑㄩˋ ㄘㄨ ㄑㄩˇ ㄐㄧㄥ)
to discard the dross and select the essential
去惡從善(ㄑㄩˋ ㄜˋ ㄘㄨㄥˊ ㄕㄢˋ)
(said of personal conduct) to reform; to shun the evil and follow the good
去蕪存菁(ㄑㄩˋ ㄨˊ ㄘㄨㄣˊ ㄐㄧㄥ)
(said of editing or compilation work) to keep the good and get rid of the bad
去僞存眞(ㄑㄩˋ ㄨㄟˋ ㄘㄨㄣˊ ㄓㄣ)
to remove the false and retain the true

九畫

【參】 515
1. ㄘㄢ tsan cān

1. to take part in; to get involved in
2. to visit; to interview; to call on
3. to impeach; to censure
4. to recommend
5. to counsel; to consult together
6. to consider; to collate; to compare

參拜(ㄘㄢ ㄅㄞˋ)
formally call on; to pay a courtesy call
參半(ㄘㄢ ㄅㄢˋ)
half; half-and-half: 他毀譽參半。He got both praise and blame. 或 He was as much praised as blamed.
參謀(ㄘㄢ ㄇㄡˊ)
(military) the staff; a staff officer; a counselor or advisor
參訂(ㄘㄢ ㄉㄧㄥˋ)
to revise (a book, etc.) according to one's own ideas or plans
參透(ㄘㄢ ㄊㄡˋ)
① to understand thoroughly; to see through something; to think out ②(Buddhism) to meditate and come to realization
參天(ㄘㄢ ㄊㄧㄢ)
①(usually said of trees, etc.) to reach the sky ② (said of one's scholastic or moral achievements) superb and peerless; profound
參觀(ㄘㄢ ㄍㄨㄢ)
to make a tour; to visit, inspect or tour (a place, a plant, etc.); to watch or witness (military exercises, etc.)
參考(ㄘㄢ ㄎㄠˇ)
① to consult; to collate; to examine and compare ② reference: 這些書籍僅供參考。These books are for reference only.
參考書(ㄘㄢ ㄎㄠˇ ㄕㄨ)
a reference book
參看(ㄘㄢ ㄎㄢˋ)
(please) refer to: 請參看第八頁註解。Please refer to the footnotes on page eight.
參劾(ㄘㄢ ㄏㄜˊ)
to impeach (a person)
參互(ㄘㄢ ㄏㄨˋ)
mixed and confused
參加(ㄘㄢ ㄐㄧㄚ)
① to attend; to participate in; to join; participation ② to give (advice, one's viewpoint, etc.)
參見(ㄘㄢ ㄐㄧㄢˋ)
to call on or to visit (a superior); an audience
參軍(ㄘㄢ ㄐㄩㄣ)
① a military staff officer ② to join the army
參軍長(ㄘㄢ ㄐㄩㄣ ㄓㄤˇ)
a presidential chief military aide
參照(ㄘㄢ ㄓㄠˋ)
please refer to; to consult; in accordance with; with reference to: 他參照規則行事。He acts in accordance with the rules.
參戰(ㄘㄢ ㄓㄢˋ)
to participate in a war; to enter a war
參戰國(ㄘㄢ ㄓㄢˋ ㄍㄨㄛˊ)
a belligerent state
參政(ㄘㄢ ㄓㄥˋ)
to take part in politics or the government
參政權(ㄘㄢ ㄓㄥˋ ㄑㄩㄢˊ)
the right to participate in public affairs
參酌(ㄘㄢ ㄓㄨㄛˊ)
to consult and deliberate
參禪(ㄘㄢ ㄔㄢˊ)
(said of Buddhist monks or nuns) to search for the truth by meditation
參事(ㄘㄢ ㄕˋ)
a councilor
參雜(ㄘㄢ ㄗㄚˊ)
to mix; to add something of the different nature, quality, color, etc.
參贊(ㄘㄢ ㄗㄢˋ)
① to participate in planning; to serve as an advisor ② an attache; a councilor
參議(ㄘㄢ ㄧˋ)
① to participate in planning; to counsel; to advise; counsel; advice ② a counselor
參議會(ㄘㄢ ㄧˋ ㄏㄨㄟˋ)
the local legislature
參議員(ㄘㄢ ㄧˋ ㄩㄢˊ)
members of the local legislature; a senator

〔又部〕

參議院(ㄘㄢ ㄧˋ ㄩㄢˋ)
the upper house of a parliament; the senate
參謁(ㄘㄢ ㄧㄝˋ)
to visit an official of high rank
參驗(ㄘㄢ ㄧㄢˋ)
to verify (the truth) by personal experience; to inspect personally
參伍錯綜(ㄘㄢ ㄨˇ ㄘㄨㄛˋ ㄗㄨㄥˋ)
to mix up; confused; shuffled; variegated
參悟(ㄘㄢ ㄨˋ)
(Zen Buddhism) to get the meaning of (mystery) from meditation; to perceive the truth with one's mind
參預(ㄘㄢ ㄩˋ)
to play a part (in some decision or task)
參與(ㄘㄢ ㄩˋ)
to take part in; to participate in: 我將要參與那個比賽。I will take part in that contest.
參閱(ㄘㄢ ㄩㄝˋ)
to see; to consult; to examine and compare

【參】 515 2. ㄕㄣ shen shēn
1. name of a star
2. a ginseng
參商(ㄕㄣ ㄕㄤ)
① animosity between two brothers ② the morning and evening stars—(figuratively) separated

【參】 515 3. ㄘㄣ tsen cēn
參差(ㄘㄣ ㄘ)
of irregular, different or varied sizes; uneven

【參】 515 4. ㄙㄢ san sān
a formal form of the Chinese character "三"—three, used in accounting to prevent fraud

又部
ㄧㄡˋ yow yòu

【又】 516 ㄧㄡˋ yow yòu
1. also; again; in addition to; and
2. moreover; furthermore
3. and (used in a mixed fraction such as one *and* three fourths)
又打又罵(ㄧㄡˋ ㄉㄚˇ ㄧㄡˋ ㄇㄚˋ)
to beat and curse at the same time
又來了(ㄧㄡˋ ㄌㄞˊ ·ㄌㄜ)
① to have come again ② being repeated again
又聾又啞(ㄧㄡˋ ㄌㄨㄥˊ ㄧㄡˋ ㄧㄚˇ)
deaf-and-dumb; deaf-mute
又哭又笑(ㄧㄡˋ ㄎㄨ ㄧㄡˋ ㄒㄧㄠˋ)
to cry and laugh at the same time
又快又好(ㄧㄡˋ ㄎㄨㄞˋ ㄧㄡˋ ㄏㄠˇ)
(to do something) very fast with excellent results; efficient; efficiently
又紅又專(ㄧㄡˋ ㄏㄨㄥˊ ㄧㄡˋ ㄓㄨㄢ)
(used in mainland China) to be ideologically pure and possess expertise at the same time
又飢又渴(ㄧㄡˋ ㄐㄧ ㄧㄡˋ ㄎㄜˇ)
both hungry and thirsty
又及(ㄧㄡˋ ㄐㄧˊ)
P.S. (a postscript)
又驚又喜(ㄧㄡˋ ㄐㄧㄥ ㄧㄡˋ ㄒㄧˇ)
alarmed and happy at the same time
又稱(ㄧㄡˋ ㄔㄥ)
① also called; also known as: 北平又稱北京。Peiping is also called Peking. ② to say also that...; to say further that...
又是(ㄧㄡˋ ㄕˋ)
① again ② also ③ still another ④ the same as
又是他(ㄧㄡˋ ㄕˋ ㄊㄚ)
It's him again. (implying unwelcomeness, surprise, etc.)
又是老調(ㄧㄡˋ ㄕˋ ㄌㄠˇ ㄉㄧㄠˋ)
(said of clichés, corny statements, etc.) It's the same old tune again.
又是一個(ㄧㄡˋ ㄕˋ ㄧˊ ·ㄍㄜ)
still another one
又要(ㄧㄡˋ ㄧㄠˋ)
① to want to do something which has been done before ② to make additional demands
又問(ㄧㄡˋ ㄨㄣˋ)
to ask again

一畫

【叉】 517 1. ㄔㄚ cha chā
1. to interlace fingers; to cross arms
2. to thrust; to pierce; to stab
3. a prong; a fork (used in catching fish, etc.); a cross
4. to push another's neck with one's hand
叉路(ㄔㄚ ㄌㄨˋ)
the fork of a road: 他們在叉路處離別。They parted at the fork of the road.
叉枝(ㄔㄚ ㄓ)
a forked branch
叉手(ㄔㄚ ㄕㄡˇ)
to fold hands in salute
叉子(ㄔㄚ ·ㄗ)
a fork
叉腰(ㄔㄚ ㄧㄠ)
to stand with arms akimbo (to show defiance, self-satisfaction, etc.); to rest the arms on the hips

【叉】 517 2. ㄔㄚˇ chaa chǎ
叉劈(ㄔㄚˇ ·ㄆㄧ)
(said of the road) divergen

二畫

【及】 518 ㄐㄧˊ jyi jí
1. to reach; to attain; to come up to
2. and; as well as; with
3. just at the moment; timely; when
4. as long as; up to; until
5. to continue; to proceed
6. to extend
及門弟子(ㄐㄧˊ ㄇㄣˊ ㄉㄧˋ ㄗˇ)
a disciple or student who has taken lessons directly from a master (as distinct from 私淑弟子)
及鋒而試(ㄐㄧˊ ㄈㄥ ㄦˊ ㄕˋ)
to seize an opportunity by the forelock
及第(ㄐㄧˊ ㄉㄧˋ)
(in ancient China) to pas

the civil examinations

及齡(ㄐㄧˊ ㄌㄧㄥˊ)
to reach a required age

及格(ㄐㄧˊ ㄍㄜˊ)
to pass an examination (especially in school, etc.); to be qualified

及冠之年(ㄐㄧˊ ㄍㄨㄢˋ ㄓ ㄋㄧㄢˊ)
(said of a young man) to reach the age of 20

及笄之年(ㄐㄧˊ ㄐㄧ ㄓ ㄋㄧㄢˊ)
(said of a girl) 15 years of age—marriageable age

及肩(ㄐㄧˊ ㄐㄧㄢ)
to come up to the shoulder

及期(ㄐㄧˊ ㄑㄧˊ)
to reach the time limit; (said of a bond, etc.) to mature

及至(ㄐㄧˊ ㄓˋ)
until; up to a given point

及長(ㄐㄧˊ ㄓㄤˇ)
(when he or she) grew up; in (his or her) adulthood

及時(ㄐㄧˊ ㄕˊ)
① in time; at the right time or opportune moment; seasonable: 我及時趕上汽船。I was just in time for the steamer. ② promptly; without delay: 我們必須及時糾正錯誤。We must correct a mistake promptly.

及早(ㄐㄧˊ ㄗㄠˇ)
at an early date; as soon as possible; before it is too late

及早回頭(ㄐㄧˊ ㄗㄠˇ ㄏㄨㄟˊ ㄊㄡˊ)
to repent before it is too late; to mend one's ways without delay; to turn back as soon as possible; to extricate oneself (from evil ways) as soon as possible

及物動詞(ㄐㄧˊ ㄨˋ ㄉㄨㄥˋ ㄘˊ)
a transitive verb

【友】 519
ㄧㄡˇ yeou yǒu

1. a friend; friendly; friendship
2. fraternity; fraternal love
3. to befriend

友邦(ㄧㄡˇ ㄅㄤ)
friendly nations; allies

友朋(ㄧㄡˇ ㄆㄥˊ)
friends; companions

友黨(ㄧㄡˇ ㄉㄤˇ)
political parties in coalition; a friendly party; parties sharing the same political aspirations

友悌(ㄧㄡˇ ㄊㄧˋ)
brotherly bonds

友好(ㄧㄡˇ ㄏㄠˇ)
friendly; friendship; amity (treaty, etc.)

友軍(ㄧㄡˇ ㄐㄩㄣ)
friendly forces

友情(ㄧㄡˇ ㄑㄧㄥˊ)
fraternal love; friendship

友善(ㄧㄡˇ ㄕㄢˋ)
friendly

友人(ㄧㄡˇ ㄖㄣˊ)
friends

友愛(ㄧㄡˇ ㄞˋ)
friendship; fraternal love

友誼(ㄧㄡˇ ㄧˊ)
friendship

友于之愛(ㄧㄡˇ ㄩˊ ㄓ ㄞˋ)
brotherly love

【反】 520
ㄈㄢˇ faan fǎn

1. reverse; opposite; contrary
2. to return (something); to turn back; to retreat
3. to introspect; to retrospect
4. to rebel; rebellion; to revolt
5. to infer

反駁(ㄈㄢˇ ㄅㄛˊ)
to refute; to retort

反敗爲勝(ㄈㄢˇ ㄅㄞˋ ㄨㄟˊ ㄕㄥˋ)
to turn defeat into victory

反本(ㄈㄢˇ ㄅㄣˇ)
to search the original meaning of a thing

反比(ㄈㄢˇ ㄅㄧˇ)
(mathematics) inverse ratio

反比例(ㄈㄢˇ ㄅㄧˇ ㄌㄧˋ)
(mathematics) inverse proportion

反辯(ㄈㄢˇ ㄅㄧㄢˋ)
to refute; a rebuttal

反哺(ㄈㄢˇ ㄅㄨˇ)
to repay one's parents when they get old; to show filial piety to one's parents

反派(ㄈㄢˇ ㄆㄞˋ)
a villain (in drama, etc.); a negative character

反叛(ㄈㄢˇ ㄆㄢˋ)
to rebel; to revolt; rebellion; treason

反撲(ㄈㄢˇ ㄆㄨ)
① to pounce on somebody again after being beaten off ② a counterattack

反璞歸眞(ㄈㄢˇ ㄆㄨˊ ㄍㄨㄟ ㄓㄣ)
to return to one's original self and regain truth

反面(ㄈㄢˇ ㄇㄧㄢˋ)or 反面兒(ㄈㄢˇ ㄇㄧㄚˋㄦ)
① the reverse side ② the back side; the other side ③ to turn away from; to be cold towards

反面無情(ㄈㄢˇ ㄇㄧㄢˋ ㄨˊ ㄑㄧㄥˊ)
Old friendship is completely forgotten with the sudden change of facial expression.

反目(ㄈㄢˇ ㄇㄨˋ)
(said of a quarrel between a married couple, etc.) to fight; to squabble

反復 or 反覆(ㄈㄢˇ ㄈㄨˋ)
①(to study or research) carefully ② not dependable ③ to relapse ④ repeatedly; again and again

反覆思量(ㄈㄢˇ ㄈㄨˋ ㄙ ㄌㄧㄤˊ)
to think over and over again

反覆無常(ㄈㄢˇ ㄈㄨˋ ㄨˊ ㄔㄤˊ)
not dependable; always changing; fickle; capricious

反倒(ㄈㄢˇ ㄉㄠˋ)
on the contrary; instead

反定理(ㄈㄢˇ ㄉㄧㄥˋ ㄌㄧˇ)
the inverse theorem

反對(ㄈㄢˇ ㄉㄨㄟˋ)
to oppose; to object; to be against; to disagree

反對黨(ㄈㄢˇ ㄉㄨㄟˋ ㄉㄤˇ)
the opposition party

反對者(ㄈㄢˇ ㄉㄨㄟˋ ㄓㄜˇ)
a dissenter

反動(ㄈㄢˇ ㄉㄨㄥˋ)
reaction; reactionary

反動份子(ㄈㄢˇ ㄉㄨㄥˋ ㄈㄣˋ ㄗˇ)
reactionaries; reactionary elements

反動力(ㄈㄢˇ ㄉㄨㄥˋ ㄌㄧˋ)
reaction; the reaction force

反貪汚(ㄈㄢˇ ㄊㄢ ㄨ)
anti-corruption

反逆(ㄈㄢˇ ㄋㄧˋ)
to rebel against (law, order, or government, etc.)

反老還童(ㄈㄢˇ ㄌㄠˇ ㄏㄨㄢˊ ㄊㄨㄥˊ)
to rejuvenate; rejuvenation; to act like a child when one gets old; to get younger with each passing day

反臉(ㄈㄢˇ ㄌㄧㄢˇ)
to fall out; to turn hostile suddenly 亦作「翻臉」
反亂(ㄈㄢˇ ㄌㄨㄢˋ)
rebellion; revolt; sedition
反戈(ㄈㄢˇ ㄍㄜ)
to revolt; to rebel
反戈一擊(ㄈㄢˇ ㄍㄜ ㄧˋ ㄐㄧˊ)
to turn one's weapon around and strike
反革命(ㄈㄢˇ ㄍㄜˊ ㄇㄧㄥˋ)
counterrevolution
反感(ㄈㄢˇ ㄍㄢˇ)
antipathy
反顧(ㄈㄢˇ ㄍㄨˋ)
to look back; to review; to cast a look behind
反過來(ㄈㄢˇ ㄍㄨㄛˋ ·ㄌㄞ)
①to turn over; to invert ②(to look at something from) the opposite side; (to state something) in another way; contrarily; on the other hand
反光(ㄈㄢˇ ㄍㄨㄤ)
reflection; reflected light
反光鏡(ㄈㄢˇ ㄍㄨㄤ ㄐㄧㄥˋ)
a reflector
反攻(ㄈㄢˇ ㄍㄨㄥ)
to counterattack; a counterattack; a counteroffensive
反躬自問(ㄈㄢˇ ㄍㄨㄥ ㄗˋ ㄨㄣˋ)
to introspect; introspection; to search one's own soul for answers; self-examination
反共(ㄈㄢˇ ㄍㄨㄥˋ)
anticommunism
反客爲主(ㄈㄢˇ ㄎㄜˋ ㄨㄟˊ ㄓㄨˇ)
to exchange the positions of the host and the guest
反抗(ㄈㄢˇ ㄎㄤˋ)
to counter; to rise up against; to resist; to rebel
反話(ㄈㄢˇ ㄏㄨㄚˋ)
statements that are contrary to what the speaker really believes or thinks to be true
反悔(ㄈㄢˇ ㄏㄨㄟˇ)
to renege (on a promise)
反擊(ㄈㄢˇ ㄐㄧˊ)
to fight back; to strike back: 他打我，因此我反擊他。He hit me, so I struck back.
反詰(ㄈㄢˇ ㄐㄧㄝˊ)
to rebut; to refute; a rebuttal
反剪(ㄈㄢˇ ㄐㄧㄢˇ)
①with one's hands behind one's back ②with one's hands tied behind one's back
反間(ㄈㄢˇ ㄐㄧㄢˋ)
to alienate the enemy coalition or alliance; to drive a wedge in the enemy camp
反切(ㄈㄢˇ ㄑㄧㄝˋ)
(old Chinese phonetics) to indicate the pronunciation of a character by quick enunciation of two other characters
反求諸己(ㄈㄢˇ ㄑㄧㄡˊ ㄓㄨ ㄐㄧˇ)
to make self-examination; to search one's own soul
反侵略(ㄈㄢˇ ㄑㄧㄣ ㄌㄩㄝˋ)
antiaggression
反情報(ㄈㄢˇ ㄑㄧㄥˊ ㄅㄠˋ)
counterintelligence
反響(ㄈㄢˇ ㄒㄧㄤˇ)
①a counteraction ②an echo
反向(ㄈㄢˇ ㄒㄧㄤˋ)
the opposite direction; the reverse
反省(ㄈㄢˇ ㄒㄧㄥˇ)
reflection; self-examination; to make soul-searching or self-examination: 我需要時間反省。I want time for reflection.
反宣傳(ㄈㄢˇ ㄒㄩㄢ ㄔㄨㄢˊ)
①counterpropaganda ②a slander campaign
反之(ㄈㄢˇ ㄓ)
on the other hand
反照(ㄈㄢˇ ㄓㄠˋ)
(said of light) to reflect; reflection
反戰者(ㄈㄢˇ ㄓㄢˋ ㄓㄜˇ)
a peacenik
反掌(ㄈㄢˇ ㄓㄤˇ)
a turn of one's hand—an easy task
反正(ㄈㄢˇ ㄓㄥˋ)
①to shift one's loyalty to the side of righteousness; to return to rectitude; to change one's side to the right cause ②in any case; anyway
反證(ㄈㄢˇ ㄓㄥˋ)
the contrary evidence that nullifies the evidence presented by the other party in court; the counter-evidence
反轉(ㄈㄢˇ ㄓㄨㄢˇ)
①to turn inside out ②t return
反襯(ㄈㄢˇ ㄔㄣˋ)
to set off by contrast; t serve as a foil to
反常(ㄈㄢˇ ㄔㄤˊ)
abnormal; not normal; out of-the-ordinary; against com mon practice; abnormality
反芻(ㄈㄢˇ ㄔㄨˊ)
to ruminate; to chew the cu
反芻動物(ㄈㄢˇ ㄔㄨˊ ㄉㄨㄥˋ ㄨˋ)
a ruminant
反串(ㄈㄢˇ ㄔㄨㄢˋ)
①(Peking opera) to play role other than one's spe cialty ②to play the role o the opposite sex (in a movi or a drama)
反脣相稽(ㄈㄢˇ ㄔㄨㄣˊ ㄒㄧㄤ ㄐㄧ)
to rebut or rebuke with sar castic remarks
反時鐘方向(ㄈㄢˇ ㄕˊ ㄓㄨㄥ ㄈㄤ ㄒㄧ
counterclockwise
反噬(ㄈㄢˇ ㄕˋ)
①to implicate others falsel in a criminal act ②t accuse one's benefacto falsely
反舌(ㄈㄢˇ ㄕㄜˊ)
①the mockingbird ②th name of a barbarian state i ancient China
反射(ㄈㄢˇ ㄕㄜˋ)
to reflect; reflection; deflec tion of light or sound waves 鏡子反射出光線。A mirro reflects light.
反射角(ㄈㄢˇ ㄕㄜˋ ㄐㄧㄠˇ)
an angle of reflection
反射行爲(ㄈㄢˇ ㄕㄜˋ ㄒㄧㄥˊ ㄨㄟˊ)
reflex action
反射運動(ㄈㄢˇ ㄕㄜˋ ㄩㄣˋ ㄉㄨㄥˋ)
reflex movement
反手(ㄈㄢˇ ㄕㄡˇ)
(sports) backhand
反坐(ㄈㄢˇ ㄗㄨㄛˋ)
the punishment meted out t one who makes a false accu sation against others i court
反作用(ㄈㄢˇ ㄗㄨㄛˋ ㄩㄥˋ)
①undesirable reactions o results; results contrary t what were expected o

hoped for ②(physics) reaction

反側(ㄈㄢˇ ㄘㄜˋ)
①to turn over and over; restless ②disloyal; treacherous

反訴(ㄈㄢˇ ㄙㄨˋ)
to file a charge against the plaintiff; a countercharge; a crossaction; a counterclaim

反而(ㄈㄢˇ ㄦˊ)
unexpectedly; contrarily

反義字(ㄈㄢˇ ㄧˋ ㄗˋ)
an antonym

反咬一口(ㄈㄢˇ ㄧㄠˇ ㄧˋ ㄎㄡˇ)
to fabricate a countercharge against one's accuser; to make a false countercharge

反游擊戰(ㄈㄢˇ ㄧㄡˊ ㄐㄧˊ ㄓㄢˋ)
counter-guerrilla warfare

反顏相向(ㄈㄢˇ ㄧㄢˊ ㄒㄧㄤ ㄒㄧㄤˋ)
to become hostile (to a friend)

反映(ㄈㄢˇ ㄧㄥˋ)
to reflect (the confusion of the epoch, inner feelings, etc.); a reflection (of one's personality, performance, etc.)

反應(ㄈㄢˇ ㄧㄥˋ)
①response: 我向她求情，她沒有反應。My appeal to her pity met with no response. ②chemical reaction

反應爐(ㄈㄢˇ ㄧㄥˋ ㄌㄨˊ)
(physics) a reactor

反胃(ㄈㄢˇ ㄨㄟˋ)
to upset the stomach; nauseating

反問(ㄈㄢˇ ㄨㄣˋ)
to rebut

反語(ㄈㄢˇ ㄩˇ)
irony

六畫

【叔】 521 ㄕㄨˊ shwu shú

1. younger brothers of one's father; paternal uncles
2. younger brothers of one's husband
3. a general designation for members of one's father's generation who are younger than one's father
4. declining
5. a Chinese family name

叔伯(ㄕㄨˊ ㄅㄛˊ)
①paternal uncles ②a relationship among cousins born of the same grandfather

叔本華(ㄕㄨˊ ㄅㄣˇ ㄏㄨㄚˊ)
Arthur Schopenhauer, 1788-1860, German philosopher

叔婆(ㄕㄨˊ ㄆㄛˊ)
the wife of one's grandfather's younger brother

叔母(ㄕㄨˊ ㄇㄨˇ)
the wife of one's father's younger brother

叔父(ㄕㄨˊ ㄈㄨˋ)
①a younger brother of one's father ②(in ancient China) a term used by the king to address feudal lords bearing his surname

叔公(ㄕㄨˊ ㄍㄨㄥ)
①a granduncle ②a polite term of a woman addressing to her husband's uncle

叔舅(ㄕㄨˊ ㄐㄧㄡˋ)
one's mother's younger brother

叔姪(ㄕㄨˊ ㄓˊ)
uncles and nephews

叔世(ㄕㄨˊ ㄕˋ) or 叔季之世(ㄕㄨˊ ㄐㄧˋ ㄓ ㄕˋ)
(said of a nation) an age of decline

叔嬸(ㄕㄨˊ ㄕㄣˇ)
an aunt; the wife of a junior uncle

叔叔(ㄕㄨˊ ˙ㄕㄨ)
①a younger brother of one's father ②a younger brother of one's husband

叔子(ㄕㄨˊ ˙ㄗ)
one's husband's younger brother 亦作「小叔子」

叔祖(ㄕㄨˊ ㄗㄨˇ)
one's grandfather's younger brother; granduncle

【取】 522 ㄑㄩˇ cheu qǔ

1. to take; to receive; to fetch; to obtain; to take hold of: 他已取得他所要的東西。He has obtained what he wants.
2. to select; to choose
3. to summon; to recall
4. to marry; to take a wife

取保(ㄑㄩˇ ㄅㄠˇ)
to get a guarantor

取便(ㄑㄩˇ ㄅㄧㄢˋ)
①to do as one pleases without restraint ②to promote; to facilitate

取不上(ㄑㄩˇ ˙ㄅㄨ ㄕㄤˋ)
to fail (in an examination, etc.); to be below the standard (set by the selecting board, etc.); unable to get selected

取譬(ㄑㄩˇ ㄆㄧˋ)
to give examples; to cite analogies

取名(ㄑㄩˇ ㄇㄧㄥˊ)
to name; to christen

取法乎上(ㄑㄩˇ ㄈㄚˇ ㄏㄨ ㄕㄤˋ)
to pattern after the first-rate (scholar, performer, etc.) —implying that one would end up a second fiddler

取得(ㄑㄩˇ ㄉㄜˊ)
to gain; to acquire; to obtain

取代(ㄑㄩˇ ㄉㄞˋ)
to replace; to substitute

取道(ㄑㄩˇ ㄉㄠˋ)
to take a route; to go by way of (some place): 他取道香港到台灣。He came to Taiwan by way of Hong Kong.

取締(ㄑㄩˇ ㄉㄧˋ)
to prohibit; to punish the violator (of a police regulation, etc.); to ban

取鬧(ㄑㄩˇ ㄋㄠˋ)
to raise hell; to be unreasonable

取暖(ㄑㄩˇ ㄋㄨㄢˇ)
to warm oneself (by a fire, etc.): 她在爐火旁取暖。She warmed herself by the fire.

取樂(ㄑㄩˇ ㄌㄜˋ)
to make merry; to have a good time: 他們正在舞廳中取樂。They were making merry in the ballroom.

取快一時(ㄑㄩˇ ㄎㄨㄞˋ ㄧˋ ㄕˊ)
to get joy of the moment; to get temporary pleasure (caring little about adverse consequences afterwards)

取款(ㄑㄩˇ ㄎㄨㄢˇ)
to take money or draw money (from a bank, etc.)

取給(ㄑㄩˇ ㄐㄧˇ)
to rely on (someone or something) for supply

取經(ㄑㄩˇ ㄐㄧㄥ)

〔又部〕

①to go on pilgrimage for Buddhist scriptures ②(used in mainland China) to learn or borrow the experience from others

取景(ㄑㄩˇ ㄐㄧㄥˇ)
to find a view (to photograph, paint, etc.)

取決(ㄑㄩˇ ㄐㄩㄝˊ)
It's up to (someone else to make the decision). 是否去買東西,由你取決。It is up to you whether we go shopping or not.

取齊(ㄑㄩˇ ㄑㄧˊ)
①to make even; to even up: 先把兩張紙取齊了再裁。Even up the edges of the two pieces of paper before you cut them. ②to assemble; to meet each other

取巧(ㄑㄩˇ ㄑㄧㄠˇ)
to take a snap course; to use finesse

取消(ㄑㄩˇ ㄒㄧㄠ)
to cancel; to nullify

取笑(ㄑㄩˇ ㄒㄧㄠˋ)
to laugh at; to make fun of

取信於人(ㄑㄩˇ ㄒㄧㄣˋ ㄩˊ ㄖㄣˊ)
to establish credibility among others

取向(ㄑㄩˇ ㄒㄧㄤˋ)
orientation

取之不盡(ㄑㄩˇ ㄓ ㄅㄨˋ ㄐㄧㄣˋ)
The supply is inexhaustible.

取長補短(ㄑㄩˇ ㄔㄤˊ ㄅㄨˇ ㄉㄨㄢˇ)
to learn from others' strong points to make up for one's weaknesses

取士(ㄑㄩˇ ㄕˋ)
to select talented persons for government service

取捨(ㄑㄩˇ ㄕㄜˇ)
to accept or refuse; to make a choice; to choose; to select

取勝(ㄑㄩˇ ㄕㄥˋ)
to win a victory; to score a success

取材(ㄑㄩˇ ㄘㄞˊ)
to select material (for a book, an article, etc.)

取而代之(ㄑㄩˇ ㄦˊ ㄉㄞˋ ㄓ)
to usurp another's (usually higher, and better) position

取義(ㄑㄩˇ ㄧˋ)
to die for the cause of justice and righteousness

取樣(ㄑㄩˇ ㄧㄤˋ)
sampling

取悅(ㄑㄩˇ ㄩㄝˋ)
to please

【受】 523
ㄕㄡˋ show shòu

1. to receive; to accept; to get: 他受過良好教育。He has received a good education.
2. to take; to stand; to suffer; to tolerate; to endure
3. to be pleasant to (the ears, etc.)
4. preceding a verb to form a passive voice

受癟(ㄕㄡˋ ㄅㄧㄝˇ)
to be embarrassed; to be discomfited

受不了(ㄕㄡˋ ·ㄅㄨ ㄌㄧㄠˇ)
①cannot stand it; cannot take it ②very much; too much

受騙(ㄕㄡˋ ㄆㄧㄢˋ)
to be cheated or swindled; to be fooled; to be tricked

受聘(ㄕㄡˋ ㄆㄧㄣˋ)
to accept a job offer

受命(ㄕㄡˋ ㄇㄧㄥˋ)
to accept an order; on the order of; to receive instructions; to receive appointment

受罰(ㄕㄡˋ ㄈㄚˊ)
to be punished or penalized; to be fined

受粉(ㄕㄡˋ ㄈㄣˇ)
(botany) pollination

受封(ㄕㄡˋ ㄈㄥ)
to be appointed with a title

受胎(ㄕㄡˋ ㄊㄞ) or 受精(ㄕㄡˋ ㄐㄧㄥ) or 受孕(ㄕㄡˋ ㄩㄣˋ)
to be impregnated; to conceive; fertilization

受託(ㄕㄡˋ ㄊㄨㄛ)
to be entrusted with: 他受託看房子。He is entrusted with the care of a house.

受難(ㄕㄡˋ ㄋㄢˋ)
to suffer calamities or disasters; to be in distress

受累(ㄕㄡˋ ㄌㄟˋ)
to be involved; to get involved in a trouble (often implying innocence); to be put to much trouble: 讓你受累了。Sorry to have given you so much trouble.

受理(ㄕㄡˋ ㄌㄧˇ)
(said of a legal case) to be accepted by a court for prosecution; to accept (a petition, complaint, etc.)

受禮(ㄕㄡˋ ㄌㄧˇ)
①to receive a salutation ②to receive a gift

受涼(ㄕㄡˋ ㄌㄧㄤˊ)
to catch cold: 我受涼了。I caught cold.

受凌辱(ㄕㄡˋ ㄌㄧㄥˊ ㄖㄨˇ)
to be insulted; to suffer humiliation

受格(ㄕㄡˋ ㄍㄜˊ)
the objective case

受苦(ㄕㄡˋ ㄎㄨˇ)
to suffer (hardships); to have a rough time

受苦受難(ㄕㄡˋ ㄎㄨˇ ㄕㄡˋ ㄋㄢˋ)
to suffer all the hardship there is

受害(ㄕㄡˋ ㄏㄞˋ)
to be victimized; to suffer losses or injuries; to be damaged

受害不淺(ㄕㄡˋ ㄏㄞˋ ·ㄅㄨ ㄑㄧㄢˇ)
badly misguided or ill-advised

受害人(ㄕㄡˋ ㄏㄞˋ ㄖㄣˊ)
the victim; the victimized party

受寒(ㄕㄡˋ ㄏㄢˊ)
to catch cold; to suffer from a cold

受話器(ㄕㄡˋ ㄏㄨㄚˋ ㄑㄧˋ)
a telephone receiver 亦作「聽筒」

受惠(ㄕㄡˋ ㄏㄨㄟˋ)
to be benefited; to receive benefit

受賄(ㄕㄡˋ ㄏㄨㄟˋ)
to be bribed; to receive bribes

受戒(ㄕㄡˋ ㄐㄧㄝˋ)
(Buddhism) to receive ordainment; to be initiated into priesthood; to do penance

受教(ㄕㄡˋ ㄐㄧㄠˋ)
①to receive education ②to receive instructions or guidance; to be benefited by advice

受盡(ㄕㄡˋ ㄐㄧㄣˋ)
to suffer enough from; to suffer all kinds of; to have

one's fill of: 他們受盡帝國主義的壓迫。They have suffered enough from imperialist oppression.

受獎(ㄕㄡˋ ㄐㄧㄤˇ)
①to be cited ②to get a prize; to be rewarded: 立功者受獎。Those who accomplish deeds of merit shall be rewarded.

受驚(ㄕㄡˋ ㄐㄧㄥ)
to be frightened

受精(ㄕㄡˋ ㄐㄧㄥ)
to be fertilized; fertilization

受精卵(ㄕㄡˋ ㄐㄧㄥ ㄌㄨㄢˇ)
a zygote

受窘(ㄕㄡˋ ㄐㄩㄥˇ)
to be embarrassed

受欺侮(ㄕㄡˋ ㄑㄧ ㄨˇ)
to be bullied or maltreated

受氣(ㄕㄡˋ ㄑㄧˋ)
to become an object of another's anger; to be a punching bag; to suffer indignities

受屈(ㄕㄡˋ ㄑㄩ)
to be wronged; to suffer a grievance or indignity

受洗(ㄕㄡˋ ㄒㄧˇ)
to be baptized

受降(ㄕㄡˋ ㄒㄧㄤˊ)
to accept the surrender (of the vanquished enemy)

受刑(ㄕㄡˋ ㄒㄧㄥˊ)
to be tortured; to be punished (by law)

受訓(ㄕㄡˋ ㄒㄩㄣˋ)
to receive training: 他在軍中受訓。He receives training in the army.

受訊(ㄕㄡˋ ㄒㄩㄣˋ)
to face trial in court

受知(ㄕㄡˋ ㄓ)
to be appreciated and well-treated by a superior

受之無愧(ㄕㄡˋ ㄓ ㄨˊ ㄎㄨㄟˋ)
to deserve (a reward, gift, etc.)

受潮(ㄕㄡˋ ㄔㄠˊ)
to be damaged by moisture or humidity; to be affected with damp

受寵若驚(ㄕㄡˋ ㄔㄨㄥˇ ㄖㄨㄛˋ ㄐㄧㄥ)
to receive much more favor than one expected; to be agreeably surprised by the great favor one gets

受審(ㄕㄡˋ ㄕㄣˇ)
to stand trial; to be tried; to be on trial

受傷(ㄕㄡˋ ㄕㄤ)
to be injured; to get hurt; to be wounded

受賞(ㄕㄡˋ ㄕㄤˇ)
to be awarded; to get a reward

受熱(ㄕㄡˋ ㄖㄜˋ)
to be heated: 物體受熱則膨脹。When matter is heated, it expands.

受人擺佈(ㄕㄡˋ ㄖㄣˊ ㄅㄞˇ ㄅㄨˋ)
to be in leading strings

受人之託(ㄕㄡˋ ㄖㄣˊ ㄓ ㄊㄨㄛ)
to be entrusted by someone to do a job

受辱(ㄕㄡˋ ㄖㄨˇ)
to be humiliated

受災(ㄕㄡˋ ㄗㄞ)
to be hit by a natural adversity

受罪(ㄕㄡˋ ㄗㄨㄟˋ)
to suffer hardships; to have a bad time

受詞(ㄕㄡˋ ㄘˊ)
an object

受挫(ㄕㄡˋ ㄘㄨㄛˋ)
to be defeated; to be baffled; to be frustrated; to suffer a setback

受益(ㄕㄡˋ ㄧˋ)
to benefit from; to benefit by

受益費(ㄕㄡˋ ㄧˋ ㄈㄟˋ)
money paid to the government for the benefit derived from public construction projects

受益人(ㄕㄡˋ ㄧˋ ㄖㄣˊ) or 受惠者(ㄕㄡˋ ㄏㄨㄟˋ ㄓㄜˇ)
a beneficiary

受壓迫(ㄕㄡˋ ㄧㄚ ㄆㄛˋ)
to suffer oppression

受業(ㄕㄡˋ ㄧㄝˋ)
①to learn from a master ②your student (used in a letter addressed to a teacher)

受委屈(ㄕㄡˋ ㄨㄟˇ ㄑㄩ)
①to suffer a wrong or humiliation ②to be troubled or inconvenienced

受愚(ㄕㄡˋ ㄩˊ)
to be fooled, duped, tricked, etc.

受援(ㄕㄡˋ ㄩㄢˊ)
to receive aid

受孕(ㄕㄡˋ ㄩㄣˋ)
to become pregnant; to be impregnated

受用
①(ㄕㄡˋ ㄩㄥˋ)to enjoy; enjoyable ②(ㄕㄡˋ ·ㄩㄥ)ⓐto get the benefit ⓑcomfortable; to feel good

受用不盡(ㄕㄡˋ ㄩㄥˋ ㄅㄨˋ ㄐㄧㄣˋ)
to enjoy a benefit forever

七畫

【叛】 524 ㄆㄢˋ pann pàn

to rebel; to revolt

叛變(ㄆㄢˋ ㄅㄧㄢˋ)
a mutiny; an uprising; an insurgence; to revolt; to mutiny

叛兵(ㄆㄢˋ ㄅㄧㄥ)
soldiers in mutiny

叛徒(ㄆㄢˋ ㄊㄨˊ)
a rebel; an insurgent; a turncoat

叛逆(ㄆㄢˋ ㄋㄧˋ)
①to revolt; sedition; a rebellion ②one who rebels against his country or superiors

叛離(ㄆㄢˋ ㄌㄧˊ)
to betray; to desert

叛亂(ㄆㄢˋ ㄌㄨㄢˋ)
a rebellion; revolt; sedition

叛國(ㄆㄢˋ ㄍㄨㄛˊ)
to commit high treason; sedition

叛將(ㄆㄢˋ ㄐㄧㄤˋ)
a turncoat general; a general who mutinies

叛軍(ㄆㄢˋ ㄐㄩㄣ)
the rebellious army; the rebels; the rebellious troops

八畫

【叟】 525 ㄙㄡˇ soou sǒu

an elder; a senior; an old man; the old; venerable sir

十六畫

【叢】 526 ㄘㄨㄥˊ tsorng cóng

1. to crowd together; to meet in large numbers
2. a shrub (plant); a thicket
3. a hideout or den (for robbers, etc.)
4. a Chinese family name

叢莽(ㄘㄨㄥˊ ㄇㄤˇ)
shrubbery

叢木(ㄘㄨㄥˊ ㄇㄨˋ)
underbrush

叢林(ㄘㄨㄥˊ ㄌㄧㄣˊ)
① a dense wood; a jungle; a forest ② a Buddhist monastery

叢刊(ㄘㄨㄥˊ ㄎㄢ)
a series of books; a collection

叢集(ㄘㄨㄥˊ ㄐㄧˊ)
① to crowd together ② to well up: 百感叢集 all sorts of feelings welling up

叢生(ㄘㄨㄥˊ ㄕㄥ)
① lush growth; dense growth ② full of (shortcomings)

叢書(ㄘㄨㄥˊ ㄕㄨ)
a collection of books by an author or on a subject; a library series

叢雜(ㄘㄨㄥˊ ㄗㄚˊ)
motley

口 部
ㄎㄡˇ koou kǒu

【口】 527 ㄎㄡˇ koou kǒu

1. the mouth
2. a person
3. a certain article (as a cistern, a big jar, etc.)
4. the edge or blade of a knife
5. an opening
6. a gate (especially in the Great Wall or city walls)
7. a crack

口碑(ㄎㄡˇ ㄅㄟ)
public praise

口碑載道(ㄎㄡˇ ㄅㄟ ㄗㄞˋ ㄉㄠˋ)
(said of good deeds, expertise, etc.) known widely, known universally, etc.

口不擇言(ㄎㄡˇ ㄅㄨˋ ㄗㄜˊ ㄧㄢˊ)
to talk recklessly; to talk without considering the consequences of what one says

口蜜腹劍(ㄎㄡˇ ㄇㄧˋ ㄈㄨˋ ㄐㄧㄢˋ)
sweet words but a wicked heart; to flatter another while ready to plant a sword in his back; honey-mouthed and dagger-hearted

口伐(ㄎㄡˇ ㄈㄚˊ)
to attack verbally; to launch verbal attacks

口風(ㄎㄡˇ ㄈㄥ)
one's intention or view as revealed in what one says

口服(ㄎㄡˇ ㄈㄨˊ)
① to profess to be convinced: 口服心不服 to pretend to be convinced ② to take orally

口服避孕藥(ㄎㄡˇ ㄈㄨˊ ㄅㄧˋ ㄩㄣˋ ㄧㄠˋ)
an oral contraceptive; the pill

口服疫苗(ㄎㄡˇ ㄈㄨˊ ㄧˋ ㄇㄧㄠˊ)
oral vaccine

口福(ㄎㄡˇ ㄈㄨˊ)
enjoyment of the palate; luck in having good food

口腹(ㄎㄡˇ ㄈㄨˋ)
appetite (for food); indulgence in good food

口腹之慾(ㄎㄡˇ ㄈㄨˋ ㄓ ㄩˋ)
the desire for good food

口德(ㄎㄡˇ ㄉㄜˊ)
propriety in one's remarks; proper restraints in one's utterances

口袋(ㄎㄡˇ ㄉㄞˋ)
a pocket

口頭(ㄎㄡˇ ㄊㄡˊ)
verbally; orally; oral (communication)

口頭禪(ㄎㄡˇ ㄊㄡˊ ㄔㄢˊ)
platitudes; pet phrases; a meaningless phrase which one uses repetitiously

口頭聲明(ㄎㄡˇ ㄊㄡˊ ㄕㄥ ㄇㄧㄥˊ)
an oral statement

口頭語(ㄎㄡˇ ˙ㄊㄡ ㄩˇ)
an expression which one uses regularly or constantly

口糧(ㄎㄡˇ ㄌㄧㄤˊ)
food rations; grain rations

口令(ㄎㄡˇ ㄌㄧㄥˋ)
① a military password ② a verbal instruction; word of command

口蓋(ㄎㄡˇ ㄍㄞˋ)
the palate

口供(ㄎㄡˇ ㄍㄨㄥˋ)
a confession; a thing confessed; a verbal report in court or police station (by a suspect, witness, etc.)

口渴(ㄎㄡˇ ㄎㄜˇ) or 口乾(ㄎㄡˇ ㄍㄢ)
thirsty

口口聲聲(ㄎㄡˇ ㄎㄡˇ ㄕㄥ ㄕㄥ)
to say (or emphasize) repeatedly; to repeat (a statement) over and over again

口快(ㄎㄡˇ ㄎㄨㄞˋ)
① to speak rashly; quick and thoughtless in speech ② to speak frankly or honestly

口號(ㄎㄡˇ ㄏㄠˋ)
① a slogan ②(military) an oral command

口惠(ㄎㄡˇ ㄏㄨㄟˋ)
lip service; empty promises

口紅(ㄎㄡˇ ㄏㄨㄥˊ)
a lipstick 亦作「唇膏」

口吃(ㄎㄡˇ ㄐㄧˊ)
to stammer; to stutter; a stutter: 他說話有點口吃。He speaks with a slight stutter.

口技(ㄎㄡˇ ㄐㄧˋ)
vocal imitation; oral stunts (i.e. the ability to imitate various sounds with the mouth)

口角(ㄎㄡˇ ㄐㄧㄠˇ)
① a quarrel; to quarrel: 他們口角後已經言和了。They have made up their quarrel. ② corners of a mouth

口角春風(ㄎㄡˇ ㄐㄧㄠˇ ㄔㄨㄣ ㄈㄥ)
to say good words about others

口講指畫(ㄎㄡˇ ㄐㄧㄤˇ ㄓˇ ㄏㄨㄚˋ)
to gesticulate

口徑(ㄎㄡˇ ㄐㄧㄥˋ)
① the caliber (of a gun, etc.) ② the diameter (of a round object)

口訣(ㄎㄡˇ ㄐㄩㄝˊ)
a pithy formula (often in rhyme); tables which should be committed to memory for ready use, as the multiplication table, etc.

口氣(ㄎㄡˇ ˙ㄑㄧ)
① the meaning (usually hidden) of words said ② the way of speaking

口琴(ㄎㄡˇ ㄑㄧㄣˊ)
a harmonica
口腔(ㄎㄡˇ ㄑㄧㄤ)
the cavity of the mouth
口腔衛生(ㄎㄡˇ ㄑㄧㄤ ㄨㄟˋ ㄕㄥ)
oral hygiene
口血未乾(ㄎㄡˇ ㄒㄧㄝˇ ㄨㄟˋ ㄍㄢ)
A promise has scarcely been made (before it is broken).
口涎(ㄎㄡˇ ㄒㄧㄢˊ)
saliva
口信(ㄎㄡˇ ㄒㄧㄣˋ)
a verbal message
口香糖(ㄎㄡˇ ㄒㄧㄤ ㄊㄤˊ)
chewing gum: 小孩喜歡口香糖。Kids like chewing gum.
口直心快(ㄎㄡˇ ㄓˊ ㄒㄧㄣ ㄎㄨㄞˋ)
to talk bluntly; to be frank
口罩(ㄎㄡˇ ㄓㄠˋ)
a gauze mask (worn over the nose and the mouth); a mouth-muffle (to prevent infections, etc.)
口占(ㄎㄡˇ ㄓㄢˋ)
to improvise: 他口占一詩。He improvises a poem.
口誅筆伐(ㄎㄡˇ ㄓㄨ ㄅㄧˇ ㄈㄚˊ)
to attack both by speech and in writing; to condemn (a wrongdoer) by the public
口拙(ㄎㄡˇ ㄓㄨㄛˊ)
not good at speaking
口齒留香(ㄎㄡˇ ㄔˇ ㄌㄧㄡˊ ㄒㄧㄤ)
very delicious; delightful to the taste bud
口齒伶俐(ㄎㄡˇ ㄔˇ ㄌㄧㄥˊ ㄌㄧˋ)
glib and suave
口齒清晰(ㄎㄡˇ ㄔˇ ㄑㄧㄥ ㄒㄧ)or 口齒清楚(ㄎㄡˇ ㄔˇ ㄑㄧㄥ ㄔㄨˇ)
to talk distinctly; clear enunciation
口臭(ㄎㄡˇ ㄔㄡˋ)
halitosis; bad breath
口稱(ㄎㄡˇ ㄔㄥ)
to say; to claim
口傳(ㄎㄡˇ ㄔㄨㄢˊ)
① hearsay ② to teach orally
口傳心授(ㄎㄡˇ ㄔㄨㄢˊ ㄒㄧㄣ ㄕㄡˋ)
oral teaching that inspires true understanding within
口瘡(ㄎㄡˇ ㄔㄨㄤ)
an aphtha
口實(ㄎㄡˇ ㄕˊ)
① an excuse; a pretext ② something which makes one to be ridiculed or criticized by others
口試(ㄎㄡˇ ㄕˋ)
an oral test
口是心非(ㄎㄡˇ ㄕˋ ㄒㄧㄣ ㄈㄟ)
to say one thing and mean another; to mean contrary to what is spoken
口舌(ㄎㄡˇ ㄕㄜˊ)
quarrels, bickerings, squabbles, dispute, argument, etc.
口哨(ㄎㄡˇ ㄕㄠˋ)
a whistle
口授(ㄎㄡˇ ㄕㄡˋ)
① to teach orally; oral instruction ② dictate
口述(ㄎㄡˇ ㄕㄨˋ)
to narrate; to make an oral report of something; to dictate: 他口述自己的冒險。He narrated his adventure.
口說無憑(ㄎㄡˇ ㄕㄨㄛ ㄨˊ ㄆㄧㄥˊ)
An oral agreement cannot serve as evidence. 或 An oral promise is not binding.
口水(ㄎㄡˇ ㄕㄨㄟˇ)
saliva
口若懸河(ㄎㄡˇ ㄖㄨㄛˋ ㄒㄩㄢˊ ㄏㄜˊ)
words flowing out like a cataract—glib; eloquent
口子(ㄎㄡˇ ˙ㄗ)
an opening; a hole; a cut
口燥脣乾(ㄎㄡˇ ㄗㄠˋ ㄔㄨㄣˊ ㄍㄢ)
① very thirsty ② to talk (or to persuade another) until one's mouth is rock-dry
口才(ㄎㄡˇ ㄘㄞˊ)
eloquence; eloquent: 他很有口才。He is an eloquent speaker.
口岸(ㄎㄡˇ ㄢˋ)
a harbor; a river port; a trading port
口耳相傳(ㄎㄡˇ ㄦˇ ㄒㄧㄤ ㄔㄨㄢˊ)
to teach orally
口譯(ㄎㄡˇ ㄧˋ)
to interpret; to translate orally; oral interpretation
口音(ㄎㄡˇ ㄧㄣ)
an accent (in speaking a peculiar language or dialect)
口味(ㄎㄡˇ ㄨㄟˋ)
① a person's taste: 各人口味不同。Tastes differ. ② the flavor or taste of food
口吻(ㄎㄡˇ ㄨㄣˇ)
a tone; the connotation of what is being said 亦作「語氣」
口語(ㄎㄡˇ ㄩˇ)
① plain, spoken language ② to slander
口約(ㄎㄡˇ ㄩㄝ)
to make an appointment orally; an oral appointment: 我和他有口約。I had an oral appointment with him.

二畫

【叨】 528
1. ㄉㄠ dau dāo
talkative; garrulous; fond of talking
叨叨(ㄉㄠ ˙ㄉㄠ)
garrulous; a chatterbox; to nag
叨叨念念(ㄉㄠ ˙ㄉㄠ ㄋㄧㄢˋ ㄋㄧㄢˋ)
to mutter and grumble
叨念着(ㄉㄠ ㄋㄧㄢˋ ˙ㄓㄜ)
to chatter incessantly; to nag
叨嘮(ㄉㄠ ˙ㄌㄠ)
① talkative; garrulous; to nag; to chatter ② to complain

【叨】 528
2. ㄊㄠ tau tāo
to be favored with; to get the benefit of
叨陪末座(ㄊㄠ ㄆㄟˊ ㄇㄛˋ ㄗㄨㄛˋ)
to be honored with a seat (usually in a distinguished gathering)
叨光(ㄊㄠ ㄍㄨㄤ)
thanks (for a favor done); to have the honor
叨教(ㄊㄠ ㄐㄧㄠˋ)
to trouble you by requesting your instructions 或 Thank you for favoring (us) with your instructions or advice.
叨擾(ㄊㄠ ㄖㄠˇ)
Thanks for the wonderful entertainment (which has put you to great trouble).
叨在知己(ㄊㄠ ㄗㄞˋ ㄓ ㄐㄧˇ)
Since you are my good friend, (I do not have to look for proper words to express my deep appreciation for the great favor you have done me.)

【叼】 529
ㄉㄧㄠ diau diāo
to hold in the mouth: 貓叼著

〔口部〕

一隻老鼠。The cat held a mouse in its mouth.

【古】 530 ㄍㄨˇ guu gǔ

1. ancient; antiquated; old; antiquity
2. not following current customs or practices
3. a Chinese family name

古巴(ㄍㄨˇ ㄅㄚ)
Cuba

古巴人(ㄍㄨˇ ㄅㄚ ㄖㄣˊ)
a Cuban

古板(ㄍㄨˇ ㄅㄢˇ)
①inactive; dumb ②anachronistic; out of date; old-fashioned; square 亦作「保守」：他很古板。He was real square.

古本(ㄍㄨˇ ㄅㄣˇ)
books of ancient printing

古樸(ㄍㄨˇ ㄆㄨˊ)
kind and simple; simple and unsophisticated

古法(ㄍㄨˇ ㄈㄚˇ)
time-honored methods

古方(ㄍㄨˇ ㄈㄤ)
an ancient medical prescription (believed to be very effective)

古風(ㄍㄨˇ ㄈㄥ)
①ancient practices—usually connoting honesty and simplicity ②ancient-style poetry

古代(ㄍㄨˇ ㄉㄞˋ)
ancient times

古道(ㄍㄨˇ ㄉㄠˋ)
①ancient ways—usually connoting honesty and simplicity ②time-worn roads; ancient paths

古道熱腸(ㄍㄨˇ ㄉㄠˋ ㄖㄜˋ ㄔㄤˊ)
honest and upright, and willing to help

古調(ㄍㄨˇ ㄉㄧㄠˋ)
an ancient tune—anachronistic; outdated

古典(ㄍㄨˇ ㄉㄧㄢˇ)
classics; classical

古典音樂(ㄍㄨˇ ㄉㄧㄢˇ ㄧㄣ ㄩㄝˋ)
classical music

古典文學(ㄍㄨˇ ㄉㄧㄢˇ ㄨㄣˊ ㄒㄩㄝˊ)
classical literature

古都(ㄍㄨˇ ㄉㄨ)
an ancient capital

古董(ㄍㄨˇ ㄉㄨㄥˇ)
antiques; curios: 他是古董鑑賞家。He is a connoisseur of curios.

古體詩(ㄍㄨˇ ㄊㄧˇ ㄕ)
ancient-style poetry

古銅色(ㄍㄨˇ ㄊㄨㄥˊ ㄙㄜˋ)
the color of bronze; brown and healthy

古來(ㄍㄨˇ ㄌㄞˊ)
since ancient times

古老(ㄍㄨˇ ㄌㄠˇ)
old; antiquated; ancient

古怪(ㄍㄨˇ ㄍㄨㄞˋ)
①strange; queer; eccentric; odd ②anachronistic

古柯鹼(ㄍㄨˇ ㄎㄜ ㄐㄧㄢˇ)
cocaine

古話(ㄍㄨˇ ㄏㄨㄚˋ)
an old saying: 古話說，有志者事竟成。As the old saying goes, "Where there's a will, there's a way."

古畫(ㄍㄨˇ ㄏㄨㄚˋ)
ancient paintings

古跡(ㄍㄨˇ ㄐㄧ)
relics; ancient remains

古籍(ㄍㄨˇ ㄐㄧˊ)
ancient books

古今(ㄍㄨˇ ㄐㄧㄣ)
in ancient and modern times

古今中外(ㄍㄨˇ ㄐㄧㄣ ㄓㄨㄥ ㄨㄞˋ)
everywhere and all times; ancient and modern, Chinese and foreign

古今一轍(ㄍㄨˇ ㄐㄧㄣ ㄧˊ ㄔㄜˋ)
(said of principles, reasoning, etc.) to apply in both ancient and modern times; true in all times

古井不波(ㄍㄨˇ ㄐㄧㄥˇ ㄅㄨˋ ㄅㄛ)
impervious to desires and passions

古錢(ㄍㄨˇ ㄑㄧㄢˊ)
ancient money; ancient currency; ancient coins: 他搜集古錢。He collects ancient coins.

古稀(ㄍㄨˇ ㄒㄧ)
70 years of age

古昔(ㄍㄨˇ ㄒㄧˊ)
the time long ago; ancient times

古訓(ㄍㄨˇ ㄒㄩㄣˋ)
①ancient teachings; the lessons of antiquity ②books and works left by a late emperor

古裝 or 古妝(ㄍㄨˇ ㄓㄨㄤ)
ancient costumes

古塚(ㄍㄨˇ ㄓㄨㄥˇ)
ancient graves; ancient mounds

古剎(ㄍㄨˇ ㄔㄚˋ)
an ancient temple

古城(ㄍㄨˇ ㄔㄥˊ)
an ancient city

古詩(ㄍㄨˇ ㄕ)
①ancient-style poetry ②poems composed by ancient scholars

古時候(ㄍㄨˇ ㄕˊ ㄏㄡˋ)
in ancient times; in the olden days

古史(ㄍㄨˇ ㄕˇ)
ancient history: 他研究古史。He studied ancient history.

古事(ㄍㄨˇ ㄕˋ)
an old story; a legend

古生代(ㄍㄨˇ ㄕㄥ ㄉㄞˋ)
(geology) the Paleozoic Era

古生物(ㄍㄨˇ ㄕㄥ ㄨˋ)
ancient, extinct life

古書(ㄍㄨˇ ㄕㄨ)
ancient books: 古書十分珍貴。The ancient books are very precious.

古人(ㄍㄨˇ ㄖㄣˊ)
ancient people

古瓷(ㄍㄨˇ ㄘˊ)
ancient porcelain

古色古香(ㄍㄨˇ ㄙㄜˋ ㄍㄨˇ ㄒㄧㄤ)
(usually said of decor, furniture, etc.) in graceful ancient style

古雅(ㄍㄨˇ ㄧㄚˇ)
(said of buildings, works of art, etc.) graceful and refined

古諺(ㄍㄨˇ ㄧㄢˋ)
ancient proverbs or quotations

古音(ㄍㄨˇ ㄧㄣ)
①the pronunciation of characters in ancient times ②rhyme according to such pronunciation

古物(ㄍㄨˇ ㄨˋ)
antiques; curios; relics things that are ancient

古玩(ㄍㄨˇ ㄨㄢˊ)
curios; antiques

古文(ㄍㄨˇ ㄨㄣˊ)

①ancient written language ② an old Chinese literary style
古文字(ㄍㄨˇ ㄨㄣˊ ㄗˋ)
ancient writing
古往今來(ㄍㄨˇ ㄨㄤˇ ㄐㄧㄣ ㄌㄞˊ)
since time immemorial; from ancient times till today; of all ages; through the ages
古語(ㄍㄨˇ ㄩˇ)
①an archaism ② an old saying
古樂(ㄍㄨˇ ㄩㄝˋ)
ancient music; Chinese classical music; a piece of refined music

【句】 531
1. ㄐㄩˋ jiuh jù
a sentence
句法(ㄐㄩˋ ㄈㄚˇ)
sentence structure; syntax
句讀(ㄐㄩˋ ㄉㄡˋ)
sentences and phrases
句號(ㄐㄩˋ ㄏㄠˋ)or 句點(ㄐㄩˋ ㄉㄧㄢˇ)
a full stop or period
句句實話(ㄐㄩˋ ㄐㄩˋ ㄕˊ ㄏㄨㄚˋ)
Every word said is true.
句句有理(ㄐㄩˋ ㄐㄩˋ ㄧㄡˇ ㄌㄧˇ)
Every word sounds reasonable.
句型(ㄐㄩˋ ㄒㄧㄥˊ)
a sentence pattern
句子(ㄐㄩˋ ·ㄗ)
a sentence

【句】 531
2. (勾) ㄍㄡ gou gōu
a Chinese family name
句踐(ㄍㄡ ㄐㄧㄢˋ)
Kou Chien—the king of Yüeh during the Epoch of Warring States

【另】 532
ㄌㄧㄥˋ linq lìng
1. another; extra; in addition; besides
2. to separate; separation (as of a couple); to divide
另闢蹊徑(ㄌㄧㄥˋ ㄆㄧˋ ㄒㄧ ㄐㄧㄥˋ)
to open or find a new path or snap course
另訂(ㄌㄧㄥˋ ㄉㄧㄥˋ)
to order or arrange (something) separately
另函(ㄌㄧㄥˋ ㄏㄢˊ)
a separate letter; to write another letter
另就(ㄌㄧㄥˋ ㄐㄧㄡˋ)
to leave for a new job; a new position
另起爐灶(ㄌㄧㄥˋ ㄑㄧˇ ㄌㄨˊ ㄗㄠˋ)
①to start a new trade or line of business ②to start all over again; to begin anew
另請高明(ㄌㄧㄥˋ ㄑㄧㄥˇ ㄍㄠ ㄇㄧㄥˊ)
to find someone better qualified (than myself)
另想辦法(ㄌㄧㄥˋ ㄒㄧㄤˇ ㄅㄢˋ ㄈㄚˇ)
to think of some other way or solution
另行安排(ㄌㄧㄥˋ ㄒㄧㄥˊ ㄢ ㄆㄞˊ)
to make separate arrangements
另案辦理(ㄌㄧㄥˋ ㄢˋ ㄅㄢˋ ㄌㄧˇ)
to be handled as a separate case
另議(ㄌㄧㄥˋ ㄧˋ)
to be discussed or negotiated separately
另有他故(ㄌㄧㄥˋ ㄧㄡˇ ㄊㄚ ㄍㄨˋ)
There must be other reasons.
另有高就(ㄌㄧㄥˋ ㄧㄡˇ ㄍㄠ ㄐㄧㄡˋ)
to have found better employment elsewhere (referring to others)
另有企圖(ㄌㄧㄥˋ ㄧㄡˇ ㄑㄧˋ ㄊㄨˊ)
to have other intentions, plans, or ulterior designs
另有事情(ㄌㄧㄥˋ ㄧㄡˇ ㄕˋ ㄑㄧㄥˊ)
to have other fish to fry
另眼看待(ㄌㄧㄥˋ ㄧㄢˇ ㄎㄢˋ ㄉㄞˋ)
to be offered special treatment; to give favored treatment
另外(ㄌㄧㄥˋ ㄨㄞˋ)
besides; another; other; in addition; additionally: 那完全是另外一回事。That's quite another matter.

【叩】 533
ㄎㄡˋ kow kòu
1. to knock; to hit
2. to ask
3. to kowtow
叩門(ㄎㄡˋ ㄇㄣˊ)
to knock at a door
叩頭(ㄎㄡˋ ㄊㄡˊ)or 叩首(ㄎㄡˋ ㄕㄡˇ)
to kowtow—to kneel and touch the ground with the forehead to show great deference, practiced in old China as the highest form of salutation
叩見(ㄎㄡˋ ㄐㄧㄢˋ)or 叩謁(ㄎㄡˋ ㄧㄝˋ)
to call on; to interview or visit a superior
叩謝(ㄎㄡˋ ㄒㄧㄝˋ)
to thank politely
叩安(ㄎㄡˋ ㄢ)
to send greetings
叩問(ㄎㄡˋ ㄨㄣˋ)
to ask; to make inquiries

【只】 534
ㄓˇ jyy zhǐ
1. only; merely
2. but; yet
只不過(ㄓˇ ㄅㄨˋ ㄍㄨㄛˋ)
only; just; merely
只怕(ㄓˇ ㄆㄚˋ)
to be afraid of only one thing; to be afraid of no one (or nothing) except…
只得(ㄓˇ ㄉㄜˊ)
to have to; there is no alternative; to be obliged to
只顧(ㄓˇ ㄍㄨˋ)
①to care about only (the present, etc.); to be absorbed in—implying shortsightedness ②please don't hesitate to…
只管(ㄓˇ ㄍㄨㄢˇ)
①(do anything) as you wish; please don't hesitate to… ② to be responsible for…only
只可(ㄓˇ ㄎㄜˇ)
to be permitted to do this or that only; can only
只好(ㄓˇ ㄏㄠˇ)
the only alternative is to…; the next best thing to do is to…; to have to
只見(ㄓˇ ㄐㄧㄢˋ)
①to see only ②to behold
只消(ㄓˇ ㄒㄧㄠ)
to have only to; to need only (a few minutes, etc.); only; just
只許州官放火，不許百姓點燈
(ㄓˇ ㄒㄩˇ ㄓㄡ ㄍㄨㄢ ㄈㄤˋ ㄏㄨㄛˇ, ㄅㄨˋ ㄒㄩˇ ㄅㄞˇ ㄒㄧㄥˋ ㄉㄧㄢˇ ㄉㄥ)
(literally) The magistrates are free to burn down houses, while the common people are forbidden even to light lamps. —(figuratively) Under tyranny, people can not do anything right while officials are free to do everything wrong.

〔口部〕

只是(ㄓˇ ㄕˋ)
①but; yet ②merely; only; just

只此一家(ㄓˇ ㄘˇ ㄧˊ ㄐㄧㄚ)
This is the only shop of its kind.—There is no branch.

只要(ㄓˇ ㄧㄠˋ)
①to want only… ②all one has to do is to…

只要功夫深，鐵杵磨成針(ㄓˇ ㄧㄠˋ ㄍㄨㄥ ˙ㄈㄨ ㄕㄣ, ㄊㄧㄝˇ ㄔㄨˇ ㄇㄛˊ ㄔㄥˊ ㄓㄣ)
Constant grinding can turn an iron rod into a needle. —Perseverance and diligence make a person successful.

只有(ㄓˇ ㄧㄡˇ)
①to have…only; only; alone ②to have to (do or be)

只因(ㄓˇ ㄧㄣ)
only because; for the simple reason that…

【叫】 535 ㄐㄧㄠˋ jiaw jiào

1. to be called or known as: 這花叫什麼名字? What is this flower called?
2. to cry; to shout; to scream; a shout or scream: 有人向那男孩吼叫。Somebody shouted at the boy.
3. to call; to summon
4. to cause: 他眞叫母親擔心。He really caused a lot of anxiety to his mother.

叫不醒(ㄐㄧㄠˋ ˙ㄅㄨ ㄒㄧㄥˇ)
cannot wake someone up

叫罵(ㄐㄧㄠˋ ㄇㄚˋ)
to scream and use foul language like a fishwife; to shout curses

叫賣(ㄐㄧㄠˋ ㄇㄞˋ)
to peddle goods in the streets by chanting; to hawk

叫門(ㄐㄧㄠˋ ㄇㄣˊ)
to knock at the door; to call someone to open the door from inside

叫姑娘(ㄐㄧㄠˋ ㄍㄨ ˙ㄋㄧㄤ)
to summon a prostitute

叫苦(ㄐㄧㄠˋ ㄎㄨˇ)
to complain of hardship or suffering

叫苦連天(ㄐㄧㄠˋ ㄎㄨˇ ㄌㄧㄢˊ ㄊㄧㄢ)
to be full of complaints; to mouth complaints about hardships

叫好兒(ㄐㄧㄠˋ ㄏㄠˇㄦ)
to cheer; to applaud (Peking opera actors); to utter a bravo 亦作「喝采」

叫喊(ㄐㄧㄠˋ ㄏㄢˇ)
to shout; to yell; to scream; to cry; to call loudly: 不要對我叫喊! Don't shout at me!

叫化子(ㄐㄧㄠˋ ㄏㄨㄚˋ ˙ㄗ)
a beggar 亦作「乞丐」

叫貨(ㄐㄧㄠˋ ㄏㄨㄛˋ)
to order goods

叫喚(ㄐㄧㄠˋ ˙ㄏㄨㄢ)
①to call; to summon ②to shout

叫街的(ㄐㄧㄠˋ ㄐㄧㄝ ˙ㄉㄜ)
a beggar wandering along the streets and crying for pity

叫屈(ㄐㄧㄠˋ ㄑㄩ)
to cry out for justice; to protest against injustice; to complain of unfair treatment

叫囂(ㄐㄧㄠˋ ㄒㄧㄠ)
to shout and yell; vociferation; clamor

叫醒(ㄐㄧㄠˋ ㄒㄧㄥˇ)
to waken; to wake up: 請在明天早晨七點叫醒我。Please wake me up at 7 tomorrow morning.

叫陣(ㄐㄧㄠˋ ㄓㄣˋ)
(in ancient China) to challenge a general of the opposite camp to battle; to challenge the enemy to battle

叫嚷(ㄐㄧㄠˋ ㄖㄤˇ)
to shout; to howl; to clamor

叫子(ㄐㄧㄠˋ ˙ㄗ)
a whistle

叫座(兒)(ㄐㄧㄠˋ ㄗㄨㄛˋ(ㄦ))
(said of performing artists, plays, dramas, etc.) to have appeal to the audience; good box office: 這音樂會並不叫座。This concert isn't good box office.

叫做(ㄐㄧㄠˋ ㄗㄨㄛˋ)
to be called; to be known as: 這種機器叫做起重機。This machine is called a crane.

叫菜(ㄐㄧㄠˋ ㄘㄞˋ)
to order food (in a restaurant); to order dishes: 請替我叫菜。Please order for me.

【召】 536 ㄓㄠˋ jaw zhào

1. to summon; to call up
2. to cause; to invite 參看「召禍」

召募(ㄓㄠˋ ㄇㄨˋ)
to enlist or recruit (soldiers) 亦作「徵募」

召開(ㄓㄠˋ ㄎㄞ)
to convene; to convoke

召禍(ㄓㄠˋ ㄏㄨㄛˋ)
(literary language) to court disaster; to invite disaster

召回(ㄓㄠˋ ㄏㄨㄟˊ)
to recall (a diplomat from abroad)

召喚(ㄓㄠˋ ㄏㄨㄢˋ)
to call; to summon

召集(ㄓㄠˋ ㄐㄧˊ)
①to convene (a meeting, etc.); to summon (a council) ②to call to arms

召見(ㄓㄠˋ ㄐㄧㄢˋ)
to summon a subordinate; to be summoned by a superior

召之即來(ㄓㄠˋ ㄓ ㄐㄧˊ ㄌㄞˊ)
to come as soon as called

召租(ㄓㄠˋ ㄗㄨ)
for rent 亦作「招租」

【叭】 537 ㄅㄚ ba bā

a trumpet

【叮】 538 ㄉㄧㄥ ding dīng

1. the chimes of a bell
2. to exhort or enjoin repeatedly
3. to sting, as a mosquito, etc.

叮噹(ㄉㄧㄥ ㄉㄤ)
dingdong (used for the sound of bells): 我們聽到鐘叮噹地響。We heard the bell dingdonging.

叮嚀 or 丁寧(ㄉㄧㄥ ㄋㄧㄥˊ)
to exhort repeatedly

叮囑(ㄉㄧㄥ ㄓㄨˇ)
to enjoin and urge repeatedly

【可】 539 1. ㄎㄜˇ kee kě

1. may; can; to be able to
2. around; estimated at
3. an auxiliary
4. but; however
5. a Chinese family name

可悲(ㄎㄜˇ ㄅㄟ)
sad; lamentable

可鄙(ㄎㄜˇ ㄅㄧˇ)

contemptible; despicable; mean

可變(ㄎㄜˇ ㄅㄧㄢˋ)
variable

可不得了(ㄎㄜˇ ·ㄅㄨ ㄉㄜˊ ㄌㄧㄠˇ)
What a mess! 或 How disastrous!

可不可以(ㄎㄜˇ ·ㄅㄨ ㄎㄜˇ ㄧˇ)
can; may (used at the beginning of a question): 我可不可以把它交給你? May I leave this with you?

可不是(ㄎㄜˇ ·ㄅㄨ ㄕˋ)or 可不是嗎(ㄎㄜˇ ·ㄅㄨ ㄕˋ ·ㄇㄚ)
really; sure enough

可怕(ㄎㄜˇ ㄆㄚˋ)
dreadful; frightening; fearsome; terrible: 那次地震是可怕的災難。The earthquake was a dreadful disaster.

可佩(ㄎㄜˇ ㄆㄟˋ)
admirable: 他的行爲可佩。His behavior is admirable.

可免(ㄎㄜˇ ㄇㄧㄢˇ)
avoidable; may be exempted from; may avoid; may escape

可否(ㄎㄜˇ ㄈㄡˇ)
① can; may (used at the beginning of a question): 可否一同走呢? Can I go with you? ② an affirmative or negative comment

可分性(ㄎㄜˇ ㄈㄣ ㄒㄧㄥˋ)
(mathematics) divisibility

可風(ㄎㄜˇ ㄈㄥ)
exemplary; worthy to be followed: 他廉潔可風。His honesty is worthy to be followed.

可達(ㄎㄜˇ ㄉㄚˊ)
attainable; accessible; within reach

可大可小(ㄎㄜˇ ㄉㄚˋ ㄎㄜˇ ㄒㄧㄠˇ)
(literally) The size is changeable.—elastic

可多可少(ㄎㄜˇ ㄉㄨㄛ ㄎㄜˇ ㄕㄠˇ)
The amount (or quantity) doesn't matter.

可鍛性(ㄎㄜˇ ㄉㄨㄢˋ ㄒㄧㄥˋ)
(metallurgy) malleability; forgeability

可歎(ㄎㄜˇ ㄊㄢˋ)
Alas! 或 What a pity! 可歎! 他被敵人殺死了。Alas! He was killed by the enemy.

可惱(ㄎㄜˇ ㄋㄠˇ)
irritable; provoking

可能(ㄎㄜˇ ㄋㄥˊ)
probable; possible: 儘可能早來。Come as early as possible.

可能性(ㄎㄜˇ ㄋㄥˊ ㄒㄧㄥˋ)
possibility; probability

可念(ㄎㄜˇ ㄋㄧㄢˋ)
① worthy of remembering ② to be pitied

可蘭經(ㄎㄜˇ ㄌㄢˊ ㄐㄧㄥ)
the Koran

可了不得(ㄎㄜˇ ㄌㄧㄠˇ ·ㄅㄨ ·ㄉㄜ)
How wonderful! 或 How marvelous!

可留則留(ㄎㄜˇ ㄌㄧㄡˊ ㄗㄜˊ ㄌㄧㄡˊ)
If you think you can stay on, then stay on. (Otherwise, you may quit as you please.)

可憐(ㄎㄜˇ ㄌㄧㄢˊ)
pitiful; pitiable; poor; miserable; to have pity on; to be merciful to (a person): 他的處境很可憐。He was in a pitiable condition.

可憐蟲(ㄎㄜˇ ㄌㄧㄢˊ ㄔㄨㄥˊ)
a poor creature; a poor thing; a poor guy; a guy in trouble

可倫坡(ㄎㄜˇ ㄌㄨㄣˊ ㄆㄛ)
Colombo, capital of Sri Lanka

可慮(ㄎㄜˇ ㄌㄩˋ)
worrisome; to be worried

可歌可泣(ㄎㄜˇ ㄍㄜ ㄎㄜˇ ㄑㄧˋ)
(said of bravery or fortitude in serving the nation) very moving; very touching

可耕地(ㄎㄜˇ ㄍㄥ ㄉㄧˋ)
arable land; cultivable land

可怪(ㄎㄜˇ ㄍㄨㄞˋ)
to be strange

可貴(ㄎㄜˇ ㄍㄨㄟˋ)
valuable; praiseworthy; commendable: 這種熱情是很可貴的。Such enthusiasm is highly commendable.

可觀(ㄎㄜˇ ㄍㄨㄢ)
① to be worth seeing ② considerable (sum of money, losses, etc.): 他的收入相當可觀。He has a considerable income.

可攻可守(ㄎㄜˇ ㄍㄨㄥ ㄎㄜˇ ㄕㄡˇ)
equally valuable as a steppingstone for offense or a strong point for defense

可可(ㄎㄜˇ ㄎㄜˇ)
cocoa

可靠(ㄎㄜˇ ㄎㄠˋ)
trustworthy; dependable; reliable (sources, etc.): 該班選出一可靠的男孩做財務股長。The class chose a trustworthy boy for treasurer.

可口(ㄎㄜˇ ㄎㄡˇ)
tasty; pleasant to the palate: 這道菜很可口。This dish is very tasty.

可口可樂(ㄎㄜˇ ㄎㄡˇ ㄎㄜˇ ㄌㄜˋ)
Coca Cola or Coke

可恨(ㄎㄜˇ ㄏㄣˋ)
hateful; detestable; abominable

可嘉(ㄎㄜˇ ㄐㄧㄚ)
commendable; laudable

可加(ㄎㄜˇ ㄐㄧㄚ)
(botany) coca—a South American tree whose dried leaves are used to make cocaine and other alkaloids 亦作「古柯」

可見(ㄎㄜˇ ㄐㄧㄢˋ)
① that can be seen ② to be perceived: 可見他不能達到目的。It is perceived that he can not achieve his goal.

可見度(ㄎㄜˇ ㄐㄧㄢˋ ㄉㄨˋ)
visibility 亦作「能見度」: 在霧中可見度很低。In a fog the visibility is very poor.

可進可退(ㄎㄜˇ ㄐㄧㄣˋ ㄎㄜˇ ㄊㄨㄟˋ)
(where) one can either advance or withdraw—an advantageous position

可驚(ㄎㄜˇ ㄐㄧㄥ)
surprising; startling

可敬(ㄎㄜˇ ㄐㄧㄥˋ)
respectable; admirable: 他是可敬的人。He is a respectable man.

可欺(ㄎㄜˇ ㄑㄧ)
can be imposed upon; can be bullied with impunity

可期(ㄎㄜˇ ㄑㄧ)
can be expected; one may look forward to

可氣(ㄎㄜˇ ㄑㄧˋ)
irritable; disgusting; annoying

可巧(ㄎㄜˇ ㄑㄧㄠˇ)
by a coincidence; coincidently; as luck would have it; luckily: 我們大家正念着她，可

〔口部〕

巧她來了。We were just talking about her when she coincidently turned up.
可親(ㄎㄜˇ ㄑㄧㄣ)
kindly; friendly; amiable
可取(ㄎㄜˇ ㄑㄩˇ)
worth having; recommendable; desirable: 這個方案有可取之處。This plan has something recommendable.
可圈可點(ㄎㄜˇ ㄑㄩㄢ ㄎㄜˇ ㄉㄧㄢˇ)
①(said of a writing) very good ②(said of the manner in doing something) very laudable
可惜(ㄎㄜˇ ㄒㄧˊ)
It's a pity that.... 可惜他不能來。It's a pity that he can not come.
可喜可賀(ㄎㄜˇ ㄒㄧˇ ㄎㄜˇ ㄏㄜˋ)
Congratulations! 或 worth cheering and rejoicing
可笑(ㄎㄜˇ ㄒㄧㄠˋ)
laughable; ridiculous: 你穿這種衣服看起來眞可笑。You look ridiculous in such a dress.
可信度(ㄎㄜˇ ㄒㄧㄣˋ ㄉㄨˋ)
(sociology) the confidence level
可想而知(ㄎㄜˇ ㄒㄧㄤˇ ㄦˊ ㄓ)
to be obvious; one can well imagine
可行(ㄎㄜˇ ㄒㄧㄥˊ)
feasible; can be carried out: 是否可行，請斟酌。Please consider if this is feasible.
可行性(ㄎㄜˇ ㄒㄧㄥˊ ㄒㄧㄥˋ)
feasibility
可知(ㄎㄜˇ ㄓ)
① naturally; obviously; evidently: 他的大衣還在這兒，可知他還沒走。His overcoat is still here; evidently he has not gone yet. ② Don't you know? ③ imaginable
可恥(ㄎㄜˇ ㄔˇ)
shameful: 以勤勞爲光榮，以懶惰爲可恥。It's praiseworthy to work hard, and shameful to idle.
可拆(ㄎㄜˇ ㄔㄞ)
removable; detachable
可長可短(ㄎㄜˇ ㄔㄤˊ ㄎㄜˇ ㄉㄨㄢˇ)
The length is changeable (i.e. collapsible or elastic).
可乘之機(ㄎㄜˇ ㄔㄥˊ ㄓ ㄐㄧ)
an opportunity that can be exploited to somebody's advantage: 我們不給敵人以可乘之機。We give the enemy no opportunity.
可是(ㄎㄜˇ ㄕˋ)
① to be (in a more emphatic sense); will really be ② but; however: 我們工作了一整天，雖然很累，可是都很愉快。Having worked all the day, we are tired out but we feel happy. ③ Is it that…?
可恃(ㄎㄜˇ ㄕˋ)
① to be reliable ② to have the means or resources
可燃性(ㄎㄜˇ ㄖㄢˊ ㄒㄧㄥˋ)
(chemistry) combustibility
可燃物(ㄎㄜˇ ㄖㄢˊ ㄨˋ)
combustible substance
可人(ㄎㄜˇ ㄖㄣˊ)
① enjoyable; lovable; likable ② a person with many admirable qualities; a charming character
可容(ㄎㄜˇ ㄖㄨㄥˊ)
capable of accommodating or holding…: 這旅館可容兩百位客人住宿。This hotel is capable of accommodating 200 guests.
可溶性(ㄎㄜˇ ㄖㄨㄥˊ ㄒㄧㄥˋ)
(chemistry) solubility
可憎(ㄎㄜˇ ㄗㄥ)or 可厭(ㄎㄜˇ ㄧㄢˋ)
abominable; detestable; disgusting or revolting
可操左券(ㄎㄜˇ ㄘㄠ ㄗㄨㄛˇ ㄑㄩㄢˋ)
to have a winning hand; to have an overwhelming chance to win
可塑性(ㄎㄜˇ ㄙㄨˋ ㄒㄧㄥˋ)
plasticity: 兒童的可塑性很高。The plasticity of children is very high.
可哀(ㄎㄜˇ ㄞ)
(it's) a pity that; sorrowful
可愛(ㄎㄜˇ ㄞˋ)
lovable; likable; lovely: 他是個可愛的孩子。He is a lovable child.
可疑(ㄎㄜˇ ㄧˊ)
① suspicious: 這外國人看起來可疑。The foreigner looked suspicious. ② debatable; questionable; doubtful
可以(ㄎㄜˇ ㄧˇ)
① can; may: 你可以這樣說。You may say so. ② Yes, you can. 或 Yes, you may. ③ Okay. That will do.
可以意會，不可以言傳(ㄎㄜˇ ㄧˇ ㄧˋ ㄏㄨㄟˋ, ㄅㄨˋ ㄎㄜˇ ㄧˇ ㄧㄢˊ ㄔㄨㄢˊ)
can be understood but can not be described
可有可無(ㄎㄜˇ ㄧㄡˇ ㄎㄜˇ ㄨˊ)
dispensable; not essential
可惡(ㄎㄜˇ ㄨˋ)
detestable; hateful: 那些人眞可惡！How detestable those people are!
可畏(ㄎㄜˇ ㄨㄟˋ)
awful; awe-inspiring; dreadful; horrible
可謂(ㄎㄜˇ ㄨㄟˋ)
one may well say; it may be said; it may be called
可望而不可即(ㄎㄜˇ ㄨㄤˋ ㄦˊ ㄅㄨˋ ㄎㄜˇ ㄐㄧˊ)
can be looked at but not touched; can be gazed but not approached; will-o'-the-wisp
可遇而不可求(ㄎㄜˇ ㄩˋ ㄦˊ ㄅㄨˋ ㄎㄜˇ ㄑㄧㄡˊ)
(something) considered to be uncertain
可用(ㄎㄜˇ ㄩㄥˋ)
① serviceable; in working order: 牙刷是可用的器具。A toothbrush is a serviceable instrument. ② employable; worth employing

【可】 539 2. ㄎㄜˋ keh kè

參看「可汗」
可汗(ㄎㄜˋ ㄏㄢˊ)
a khan

【台】 540 ㄊㄞˊ tair tái

1. a raised platform 亦作「臺」
2. a polite expression of addressing 參看「台端」

台風(ㄊㄞˊ ㄈㄥ)
stage manners
台甫(ㄊㄞˊ ㄈㄨˇ)
(used in formal speech) your name: 請問台甫? What is your name?
台端(ㄊㄞˊ ㄉㄨㄢ)
you (an honorific in addressing one's equal)
台光(ㄊㄞˊ ㄍㄨㄤ)
your presence (an honorific used in requesting another's presence at a party): 敬請台

光。Your presence is requested.

台駕(ㄊㄞˊ ㄐㄧㄚˋ)
Your Excellency; you (honorific usage)

台階(ㄊㄞˊ ㄐㄧㄝ)
①steps leading up to a building ②a chance to extricate oneself from an awkward position

台教(ㄊㄞˊ ㄐㄧㄠˋ)
your advice

台鑒(ㄊㄞˊ ㄐㄧㄢˋ)or 台照(ㄊㄞˊ ㄓㄠˋ)
a form used after the name in the salutation of a business letter

台啓(ㄊㄞˊ ㄑㄧˇ)
a term used after the name of the addressee on an envelope

台銜(ㄊㄞˊ ㄒㄧㄢˊ)
(formal speech) your title

台柱(ㄊㄞˊ ㄓㄨˋ)
①an important actor in a troupe or cast ②an important person in an organization

台秤(ㄊㄞˊ ㄔㄥˋ)
a platform scale

台詞(ㄊㄞˊ ㄘˊ)
a stage dialogue; the actor's lines

台灣 or 臺灣(ㄊㄞˊ ㄨㄢ)
Taiwan or Formosa: 台灣是個島嶼。Taiwan is an island.

【叱】 541 ㄔˋ chyh chì

to scold; to revile

叱罵(ㄔˋ ㄇㄚˋ)
to scold; to revile; to rail at

叱名請安(ㄔˋ ㄇㄧㄥˊ ㄑㄧㄥˇ ㄢ)
Please give (your elders, parents, etc.) my compliments.

叱令(ㄔˋ ㄌㄧㄥˋ)
to shout an order

叱喝(ㄔˋ ㄏㄜˋ)
to shout or bawl angrily; to yell at

叱咤風雲(ㄔˋ ㄓㄚˋ ㄈㄥ ㄩㄣˊ)
(said of a dictator, conqueror, etc.) to lord it over the world

叱責(ㄔˋ ㄗㄜˊ)
to reproach; to scold; to censure; to blame

【史】 542 ㄕˇ shyy shǐ

1. history; chronicles; annals
2. a Chinese family name

史筆(ㄕˇ ㄅㄧˇ)
①the writing brush of a historiographer ②what a historiographer recorded in history ③the way in which a historiographer faithfully recorded facts in history

史部(ㄕˇ ㄅㄨˋ)
the second section of the *Four Collections of Books*

史不絕書(ㄕˇ ㄅㄨˋ ㄐㄩㄝˊ ㄕㄨ)
History abounds in examples of this.

史評(ㄕˇ ㄆㄧㄥˊ)
criticism on historical events, characters, etc.

史達林(ㄕˇ ㄉㄚˊ ㄌㄧㄣˊ)
Joseph V. Stalin, 1879-1953, Russian dictator

史達林格勒(ㄕˇ ㄉㄚˊ ㄌㄧㄣˊ ㄍㄜˊ ㄌㄜˋ)
Stalingrad (now renamed Volgograd), a city in the Soviet Union in Europe, on the Volga River

史料(ㄕˇ ㄌㄧㄠˋ)
historical data 參看「史話」

史官(ㄕˇ ㄍㄨㄢ)
a historiographer

史可法(ㄕˇ ㄎㄜˇ ㄈㄚˇ)
Shih Ko-fa, a general of the late Ming Dynasty during the Manchu invasion

史話(ㄕˇ ㄏㄨㄚˋ)
a historical story

史蹟 or 史跡(ㄕˇ ㄐㄧ)
①historic events ②historic relics

史記(ㄕˇ ㄐㄧˋ)
the *Historical Records,* by Ssu-Ma Chien(司馬遷)

史家(ㄕˇ ㄐㄧㄚ)
a historian

史前時代(ㄕˇ ㄑㄧㄢˊ ㄕˊ ㄉㄞˋ)
the prehistoric age

史學(ㄕˇ ㄒㄩㄝˊ)
history (as a science)

史詩(ㄕˇ ㄕ)
an epic

史實(ㄕˇ ㄕˊ)
historical facts

史書(ㄕˇ ㄕㄨ)or 史籍(ㄕˇ ㄐㄧˊ)
a book of history; an annal

史册(ㄕˇ ㄘㄜˋ)or 史乘(ㄕˇ ㄕㄥˋ)
a book of history

史無前例(ㄕˇ ㄨˊ ㄑㄧㄢˊ ㄌㄧˋ)
unprecedented in history; without precedent in history

史瓦濟蘭(ㄕˇ ㄨㄚˇ ㄐㄧˋ ㄌㄢˊ)
Swaziland

【右】 543 ㄧㄡˋ yow yòu

1. right (as opposed to left)
2. west
3. to assist; to aid
4. to emphasize

右臂(ㄧㄡˋ ㄅㄟˋ)
①the right arm ②the right-hand man; an important helper 亦作「得力助手」

右邊(ㄧㄡˋ ㄅㄧㄢ)
the right-hand side

右派(ㄧㄡˋ ㄆㄞˋ)
①the right wing ②the rightists; the right-wingers; the conservatives

右面(ㄧㄡˋ ㄇㄧㄢˋ)
the right side; the right-hand side

右舵(ㄧㄡˋ ㄉㄨㄛˋ)
the right standard rudder; the right rudder

右軍(ㄧㄡˋ ㄐㄩㄣ)
①one of the emperor's three armies, i.e. the right army (右軍), the central army (中軍), and the left army (左軍) ②another name of Wang Hsi-chih(王羲之), the most famous calligrapher in Chinese history

右傾(ㄧㄡˋ ㄑㄧㄥ)
right-leaning; conservative

右舷(ㄧㄡˋ ㄒㄧㄢˊ)
the starboard

右心室(ㄧㄡˋ ㄒㄧㄣ ㄕˋ)
the right ventricle

右心耳(ㄧㄡˋ ㄒㄧㄣ ㄦˇ)
the right auricle

右行(ㄧㄡˋ ㄒㄧㄥˊ)
(said of Chinese calligraphy) written from right to left

右職(ㄧㄡˋ ㄓˊ)
an important position

右手(ㄧㄡˋ ㄕㄡˇ)
①the right hand ②the right-hand side

右首(ㄧㄡˋ ㄕㄡˇ)
the right-hand side; the right

〔口部〕

右翼(ㄧㄡˋ ㄧˋ)
① the right wing ② the rightists; the right-wingers; the conservatives ③ the right flank or wing (of an army)
右翼份子(ㄧㄡˋ ㄧˋ ㄈㄣˋ ㄗˇ)
a right-winger; a member of the Right
右武(ㄧㄡˋ ㄨˇ)
giving emphasis to military affairs
右文(ㄧㄡˋ ㄨㄣˊ)
giving emphasis to civil affairs

【叵】 544 ㄆㄛˇ poo pǒ
unable; improbable
叵耐 or 叵奈(ㄆㄛˇ ㄋㄞˋ)
It is an unfortunate fact that....
叵信(ㄆㄛˇ ㄒㄧㄣˋ)
unreliable; not trustworthy
叵測(ㄆㄛˇ ㄘㄜˋ)
unfathomable; unpredictable

【叶】 545 ㄒㄧㄝˊ shye xié
the ancient form of 協
叶韻(ㄒㄧㄝˊ ㄩㄣˋ)
to rime; to put into rime

【司】 546 ㄙ sy sī
1. to have charge of; to preside over: 各司其事。Each presides over his own business.
2. a (government) department

司必靈(ㄙ ㄅㄧˋ ㄌㄧㄥˊ)
(machinery) a spring 亦作「發條」
司馬(ㄙ ㄇㄚˇ)
①(in ancient China) the minister of war ②a Chinese family name
司馬光(ㄙ ㄇㄚˇ ㄍㄨㄤ)
Ssu-Ma Kuang, a conservative writer of the Sung Dynasty
司馬遷(ㄙ ㄇㄚˇ ㄑㄧㄢ)
Ssu-Ma Chien, a famous historian of the Han Dynasty
司馬昭之心，路人皆知(ㄙ ㄇㄚˇ ㄓㄠ ㄓ ㄒㄧㄣ，ㄌㄨˋ ㄖㄣˊ ㄐㄧㄝ ㄓ)
Ssu-Ma Chao's ill intent is known to all.—The villain's design is evident.
司牧(ㄙ ㄇㄨˋ)
the ruler; a king or a local magistrate
司法(ㄙ ㄈㄚˇ)
judicature; judiciary
司法官(ㄙ ㄈㄚˇ ㄍㄨㄢ)
a legal officer; a judge: 司法官必須公正。A judge must be just.
司法機關(ㄙ ㄈㄚˇ ㄐㄧ ㄍㄨㄢ)
judicial organs
司法節(ㄙ ㄈㄚˇ ㄐㄧㄝˊ)
Judicial Day on January 11
司法警察(ㄙ ㄈㄚˇ ㄐㄧㄥˇ ㄔㄚˊ)
judicial police; a judicial policeman
司法行政部(ㄙ ㄈㄚˇ ㄒㄧㄥˊ ㄓㄥˋ ㄅㄨˋ)
the Ministry of Justice
司法院(ㄙ ㄈㄚˇ ㄩㄢˋ)
the Judicial Yuan
司鐸(ㄙ ㄉㄨㄛˊ)
a Roman Catholic priest
司徒(ㄙ ㄊㄨˊ)
①(in ancient China) the minister of education and cultural affairs ②a Chinese family name
司農(ㄙ ㄋㄨㄥˊ)
(in ancient China) the minister of revenue
司令(ㄙ ㄌㄧㄥˋ) or 司令官(ㄙ ㄌㄧㄥˋ ㄍㄨㄢ)
a commander; a commanding officer: 他是遠征隊的司令。He is the commander of an expedition.
司令部(ㄙ ㄌㄧㄥˋ ㄅㄨˋ)
headquarters: 陸軍司令部在那兒呢? Where is the army headquarters?
司令臺(ㄙ ㄌㄧㄥˋ ㄊㄞˊ)
a review stand
司寇(ㄙ ㄎㄡˋ)
(in ancient China) the minister of justice
司空(ㄙ ㄎㄨㄥ)
①(in ancient China) the minister of public works ②a Chinese family name
司空見慣(ㄙ ㄎㄨㄥ ㄐㄧㄢˋ ㄍㄨㄢˋ)
something quite usual; a thing of frequent occurrence; a common thing: 交通事故已是司空見慣。Traffic accidents are of everyday occurrence.
司閽(ㄙ ㄏㄨㄣ)
a doorkeeper; a janitor
司機(ㄙ ㄐㄧ)
a driver; a chauffeur: 那司機車子開太快了。The driver drives too fast.
司長(ㄙ ㄓㄤˇ)
a director of a department under a ministry
司事(ㄙ ㄕˋ)
a clerk performing miscellaneous duties
司儀(ㄙ ㄧˊ)
a master of ceremonies; an M.C.; an emcee

三畫

【合】 547 ㄏㄜˊ her hé
1. to combine; to unite; to gather; to collect: 合則存，分則亡。United, we stand; divided, we fall.
2. to close; to shut: 請把書合起來。Shut your books, please.
3. to suit

合抱(ㄏㄜˊ ㄅㄠˋ)
two or more persons with linked arms to encircle (the trunk of a huge tree)
合板(ㄏㄜˊ ㄅㄢˇ)
plywood
合辦(ㄏㄜˊ ㄅㄢˋ)
to operate, manage, or run jointly
合璧(ㄏㄜˊ ㄅㄧˋ)
• two well-matched objects being put side by side
合併(ㄏㄜˊ ㄅㄧㄥˋ)
to combine; to unite; to conjoin; to consolidate; to merge; to put together
合不來(ㄏㄜˊ ˙ㄅㄨ ㄌㄞˊ)
cannot get along with (somebody): 他與辦公室任何人都合不來。He doesn't get along with anybody in the office.
合浦珠還(ㄏㄜˊ ㄆㄨˇ ㄓㄨ ㄏㄨㄢˊ)
Things lost are regained.
合謀(ㄏㄜˊ ㄇㄡˊ)
to conspire together: 他的敵人合謀毀滅他。His enemies conspired together to ruin him.
合法(ㄏㄜˊ ㄈㄚˇ)
lawful; legal; legitimate
合得來(ㄏㄜˊ ˙ㄉㄜ ㄌㄞˊ)
to get along well; to be con-

genial: 他跟老闆合得來。He gets along well with his boss.

合當(ㄏㄜˊ ㄉㄤ)
should 亦作「該當」

合訂本(ㄏㄜˊ ㄉㄧㄥˋ ㄅㄣˇ)
a bound volume

合度(ㄏㄜˊ ㄉㄨˋ)
of proper length or size

合同(ㄏㄜˊ ㄊㄨㄥˊ)
a contract; an agreement: 他們簽合同。They signed a contract.

合理(ㄏㄜˊ ㄌㄧˇ)
reasonable; logical; rational: 我們要的是合理的解釋。What we want is a rational explanation.

合力(ㄏㄜˊ ㄌㄧˋ)
① to cooperate; to collaborate; to unite efforts; to join forces ② (physics) a resultant (of more than one force)

合流(ㄏㄜˊ ㄌㄧㄡˊ)
① to flow together; to merge ② confluence

合攏(ㄏㄜˊ ㄌㄨㄥˇ)
to close up

合格(ㄏㄜˊ ㄍㄜˊ)
qualified; up to the standard: 他是位合格醫生。He is a qualified doctor.

合該(ㄏㄜˊ ㄍㄞ)
to be fated; to be determined by Heaven

合股(ㄏㄜˊ ㄍㄨˇ)
to pool capital; to enter into partnership

合口(ㄏㄜˊ ㄎㄡˇ)
①palatable; delicious; tasty; savory ②to quarrel; to wrangle; to squabble

合刊(ㄏㄜˊ ㄎㄢ)
a combined issue (of a periodical)

合乎(ㄏㄜˊ ㄏㄨ)
to measure up to; to qualify; to tally with 亦作「符合」: 你的帳目合乎我的帳目。Your account tallies with mine.

合乎情理(ㄏㄜˊ ㄏㄨ ㄑㄧㄥˊ ㄌㄧˇ)
reasonable

合夥(ㄏㄜˊ ㄏㄨㄛˇ)
to enter into partnership

合夥經營(ㄏㄜˊ ㄏㄨㄛˇ ㄐㄧㄥ ㄧㄥˊ)
to run a business in partnership

合夥人(ㄏㄜˊ ㄏㄨㄛˇ ㄖㄣˊ)
(accounting) partners

合會(ㄏㄜˊ ㄏㄨㄟˋ)
a mutual help loan association

合歡(ㄏㄜˊ ㄏㄨㄢ)
①to meet and enjoy together ② a silk tree

合婚(ㄏㄜˊ ㄏㄨㄣ)
to be united in wedlock

合擊(ㄏㄜˊ ㄐㄧˊ)
to make a joint attack on

合計(ㄏㄜˊ ㄐㄧˋ)
a total; to add up to: 合計二十元。It totals up to 20 dollars.

合家(ㄏㄜˊ ㄐㄧㄚ)
the whole family

合家歡(ㄏㄜˊ ㄐㄧㄚ ㄏㄨㄢ)
a family reunion

合金(ㄏㄜˊ ㄐㄧㄣ)
an alloy: 黃銅是銅和鋅的合金。Brass is an alloy of copper and zinc.

合巹酒(ㄏㄜˊ ㄐㄧㄣˇ ㄐㄧㄡˇ)
the wine drunk by bridegroom and bride on the wedding night to signify mutual devotion

合鏡重圓(ㄏㄜˊ ㄐㄧㄥˋ ㄔㄨㄥˊ ㄩㄢˊ)
(said of husband and wife) to reunite after separation

合情合理(ㄏㄜˊ ㄑㄧㄥˊ ㄏㄜˊ ㄌㄧˇ)
fair and reasonable; fair and sensible: 那個計畫合情合理。The plan is fair and reasonable.

合羣(ㄏㄜˊ ㄑㄩㄣˊ)
① to be gregarious ② to get on well with others: 他們不能合羣相處。They don't get on well with each other.

合著(ㄏㄜˊ ㄓㄨˋ)
to write in collaboration with; to coauthor

合衆國(ㄏㄜˊ ㄓㄨㄥˋ ㄍㄨㄛˊ)
① the United States (of America) ② a union of states; a confederacy

合衆國際社(ㄏㄜˊ ㄓㄨㄥˋ ㄍㄨㄛˊ ㄐㄧˋ ㄕㄜˋ)
the United Press International or UPI

合唱(ㄏㄜˊ ㄔㄤˋ)
to sing in chorus

合唱團(ㄏㄜˊ ㄔㄤˋ ㄊㄨㄢˊ)
a chorus; a choir: 那男孩是合唱團指揮。The boy is a chorus master.

合成(ㄏㄜˊ ㄔㄥˊ)
(chemistry) synthesis

合成木材(ㄏㄜˊ ㄔㄥˊ ㄇㄨˋ ㄘㄞˊ)
synthetic wood

合成洗滌劑(ㄏㄜˊ ㄔㄥˊ ㄒㄧˇ ㄉㄧˊ ㄐㄧˋ)
synthetic detergent

合成纖維(ㄏㄜˊ ㄔㄥˊ ㄒㄧㄢ ㄨㄟˊ)
synthetic fibers

合成樹脂(ㄏㄜˊ ㄔㄥˊ ㄕㄨˋ ㄓ)
synthetic resin

合十(ㄏㄜˊ ㄕˊ)or 合掌(ㄏㄜˊ ㄓㄤˇ)
(said of Buddhist monks or nuns) to clasp both hands in salutation

合時(ㄏㄜˊ ㄕˊ)
timely; opportune; seasonable

合式 or 合適(ㄏㄜˊ ㄕˋ)
suitable; fitting; proper; appropriate

合身(ㄏㄜˊ ㄕㄣ)
to fit: 這件襯衫很合身。This shirt fits very well.

合資經營(ㄏㄜˊ ㄗ ㄐㄧㄥ ㄧㄥˊ)
to pool capital for a business

合則留不合則去(ㄏㄜˊ ㄗㄜˊ ㄌㄧㄡˊ ㄅㄨˋ ㄏㄜˊ ㄗㄜˊ ㄑㄩˋ)
to stay if the condition is agreeable and to leave if it's otherwise

合奏(ㄏㄜˊ ㄗㄡˋ)
(music) a united performance of the full number of players

合葬(ㄏㄜˊ ㄗㄤˋ)
to bury (husband and wife) in one grave

合作(ㄏㄜˊ ㄗㄨㄛˋ)
to cooperate; to collaborate; cooperation: 兩位作家合作寫那本書。Two authors collaborated on that book.

合作農場(ㄏㄜˊ ㄗㄨㄛˋ ㄋㄨㄥˊ ㄔㄤˇ)
a cooperative farm

合作金庫(ㄏㄜˊ ㄗㄨㄛˋ ㄐㄧㄣ ㄎㄨˋ)
(Taiwan) Cooperative Bank

合作社(ㄏㄜˊ ㄗㄨㄛˋ ㄕㄜˋ)
a cooperative store or society; a co-op: 他在一家合作社工作。He works in a cooperative society.

合縱(ㄏㄜˊ ㄗㄨㄥ)

the alliance of six states (against the state of Chin during the Epoch of Warring States)

〔口部〕

合算(ㄏㄜˊ ㄙㄨㄢˋ)
①to reckon up ②worthwhile; profitable
合一(ㄏㄜˊ ㄧ)
to unite; to become one: 英格蘭和蘇格蘭在1706年合一。England and Scotland were united in 1706.
合宜(ㄏㄜˊ ㄧˊ)
fitting; suitable; proper
合意(ㄏㄜˊ ㄧˋ)
(said of a thing) to suit one's fancy; to be agreeable; to be to one's liking (or taste): 他沒發現完全合意的領帶。He found no ties completely to his liking.
合議制(ㄏㄜˊ ㄧˋ ㄓˋ)
a joint consultation (as distinct from dictatorship)
合眼(ㄏㄜˊ ㄧㄢˇ)
to close the eyes
合音(ㄏㄜˊ ㄧㄣ)
(music) combination tone
合營(ㄏㄜˊ ㄧㄥˊ)
to run (a business) in partnership
合影留念(ㄏㄜˊ ㄧㄥˇ ㄌㄧㄡˊ ㄋㄧㄢˋ)
to have a group photo taken to mark the occasion
合圍(ㄏㄜˊ ㄨㄟˊ)
to encircle; encirclement
合胃口(ㄏㄜˊ ㄨㄟˋ ㄎㄡˇ)
to suit one's taste; to be to one's taste
合約(ㄏㄜˊ ㄩㄝ)
a contract; an agreement

【吁】 548

ㄒㄩ shiu xū

a sigh
吁吁(ㄒㄩ ㄒㄩ)
the sound of panting

【吃】 549

1. (喫) ㄔ chy chī

1. to eat
2. to sustain: 吃得苦中苦，方爲人上人。Hardship increases stature. 或 No pains, no gains.

吃白相飯(ㄔ ㄅㄞˊ ㄒㄧㄤˋ ㄈㄢˋ)
to loaf; to do no work
吃飽了(ㄔ ㄅㄠˇ ˙ㄌㄜ)
to have had enough food; to be stuffed with food
吃不得(ㄔ ˙ㄅㄨ ㄉㄜˊ)
not good to eat; not edible
吃不來(ㄔ ˙ㄅㄨ ㄌㄞˊ)
not fond of eating (something); unaccustomed to (such food)
吃不了(ㄔ ˙ㄅㄨ ㄌㄧㄠˇ)or 吃不完(ㄔ ˙ㄅㄨ ㄨㄢˊ)
cannot finish (so much food)
吃不了兜着走(ㄔ ˙ㄅㄨ ㄌㄧㄠˇ ㄉㄡ ˙ㄓㄜ ㄗㄡˇ)
to land oneself in serious trouble
吃不開(ㄔ ˙ㄅㄨ ㄎㄞ)
to be unpopular: 這種人到那兒都吃不開。Such a person is unpopular anywhere.
吃不下去(ㄔ ˙ㄅㄨ ㄒㄧㄚˋ ㄑㄩˋ)
cannot eat due to loss of appetite
吃不消(ㄔ ˙ㄅㄨ ㄒㄧㄠ)
cannot stand or bear; too much to take or endure
吃不住(ㄔ ˙ㄅㄨ ㄓㄨˋ)
①to be unable to control ②to be unable to support
吃飯(ㄔ ㄈㄢˋ)
to eat, take, or have a meal
吃飯難(ㄔ ㄈㄢˋ ㄋㄢˊ)
It's difficult to make a living.
吃得來(ㄔ ˙ㄉㄜ ㄌㄞˊ)
to be able to eat; not mind eating
吃得開(ㄔ ˙ㄉㄜ ㄎㄞ)
to be popular; to be much sought after
吃得下(ㄔ ˙ㄉㄜ ㄒㄧㄚˋ)
to be able to eat
吃得消(ㄔ ˙ㄉㄜ ㄒㄧㄠ)
to be able to stand (exertion, fatigue, etc.)
吃得住(ㄔ ˙ㄉㄜ ㄓㄨˋ)
①to be able to support: 再重的卡車，這座橋也能吃得住。This bridge can support the weight of the heaviest truck. ②to be able to control: 這些工人他吃得住。He is able to control these workers.
吃豆腐(ㄔ ㄉㄡˋ ˙ㄈㄨ)
(slang) to make advances to a woman without serious intentions
吃奶(ㄔ ㄋㄞˇ)
to suck the breast: 他只是個吃奶的孩子。He is only a sucking child.
吃老本(ㄔ ㄌㄠˇ ㄅㄣˇ)
to live off one's savings
吃裏扒外(ㄔ ㄌㄧˇ ㄆㄚˊ ㄨㄞˋ)
to work for the interests of an opposing group at the expense of one's own
吃力(ㄔ ㄌㄧˋ)
tired; exhausted; tiring or exhausting (work)
吃力不討好(ㄔ ㄌㄧˋ ㄅㄨˋ ㄊㄠˇ ㄏㄠˇ)
to work laboriously only to earn criticisms; a thankless task
吃利錢(ㄔ ㄌㄧˋ ㄑㄧㄢˊ)
to live on interest
吃糧(ㄔ ㄌㄧㄤˊ)
to be a soldier
吃零食(ㄔ ㄌㄧㄥˊ ㄕˊ)
to eat snacks in small amounts between meals
吃官司(ㄔ ㄍㄨㄢ ˙ㄙ)
to be sued (in a court of law)
吃館子(ㄔ ㄍㄨㄢˇ ˙ㄗ)
to eat at a restaurant
吃光(ㄔ ㄍㄨㄤ)
to eat up; to finish (all the food): 把它吃光吧。Eat it up.
吃苦(ㄔ ㄎㄨˇ)
to suffer hardship; to endure hardship; to bear hardship: 我們應該先吃苦，後享樂。We should be the first to bear hardship and the last to enjoy comfort.
吃苦頭(ㄔ ㄎㄨˇ ˙ㄊㄡ)
to suffer: 我要給他們吃苦頭。I'll make them suffer.
吃苦耐勞(ㄔ ㄎㄨˇ ㄋㄞˋ ㄌㄠˊ)
diligent; hardworking; untiring
吃虧(ㄔ ㄎㄨㄟ)
to be at a disadvantage; to suffer a loss; to take a beating; to be wronged
吃空缺(ㄔ ㄎㄨㄥˋ ㄑㄩㄝ)
to pad the payroll
吃喝嫖賭(ㄔ ㄏㄜ ㄆㄧㄠˊ ㄉㄨˇ)
a dissipated or dissolute life
吃喝玩樂(ㄔ ㄏㄜ ㄨㄢˊ ㄌㄜˋ)
to eat, drink and make merry—to idle away one's time in seeking pleasure
吃花酒(ㄔ ㄏㄨㄚ ㄐㄧㄡˇ)

to drink and eat at a girlie restaurant

吃葷(ㄔ ㄏㄨㄣ)
to eat meat and other food produced by fowls or animals (such as eggs and milk)

吃角子老虎(ㄔ ㄐㄧㄠˇ ·ㄗ ㄌㄠˇ ·ㄏㄨ)
a slot machine

吃緊(ㄔ ㄐㄧㄣˇ)
(usually said of a military situation) hard pressed, critical, or tense: 現在前方情勢吃緊。Now the situation at the front is critical.

吃勁(ㄔ ㄐㄧㄣˋ)
to take much effort to do; to take a lot of strength to do

吃驚(ㄔ ㄐㄧㄥ)
surprised, frightened, startled, or astonished

吃錢(ㄔ ㄑㄧㄢˊ)
①to take a bribe ②to embezzle

吃閒飯(ㄔ ㄒㄧㄢˊ ㄈㄢˋ)
to live like a parasite

吃現成飯(ㄔ ㄒㄧㄢˋ ㄔㄥˊ ㄈㄢˋ)
to enjoy the fruit of somebody else's labor

吃香(ㄔ ㄒㄧㄤ)
to be welcome or valued everywhere; popular; in great demand: 棒球在台灣是很吃香的運動。Baseball is a popular sport in Taiwan.

吃齋(ㄔ ㄓㄞ)or 吃素(ㄔ ㄙㄨˋ)
to practice vegetarianism

吃重(ㄔ ㄓㄨㄥˋ)
to play an important role; to shoulder a heavy responsibility

吃吃喝喝(ㄔ ㄔ ㄏㄜ ㄏㄜ)
interested only in eating and drinking

吃茶(ㄔ ㄔㄚˊ)
①to drink tea ②(said of a girl) to become engaged

吃穿(ㄔ ㄔㄨㄢ)
food and clothing

吃水(ㄔ ㄕㄨㄟˇ)
①to drink water ②to absorb water ③to draw water (as a ship); draft or draught (of a ship)

吃軟不吃硬(ㄔ ㄖㄨㄢˇ ㄅㄨˋ ㄔ ㄧㄥˋ)
yielding to soft approaches but rejecting force, high-handedness, etc.

吃軟飯(ㄔ ㄖㄨㄢˇ ㄈㄢˋ)
to live on the earnings of a prostitute

吃人(ㄔ ㄖㄣˊ)
①man-eating (animals) ②usurious (interest rate)

吃醋(ㄔ ㄘㄨˋ)
to be jealous

吃啞吧虧(ㄔ ㄧㄚˇ ·ㄅㄚ ㄎㄨㄟ)
to be cheated or suffer a loss but unable to talk about it for one reason or another

吃藥(ㄔ ㄧㄠˋ)
to take medicine: 他吃藥吃太多了。He took too much medicine.

吃硬不吃軟(ㄔ ㄧㄥˋ ㄅㄨˋ ㄔ ㄖㄨㄢˇ)
yielding to force but rejecting soft approaches

吃用(ㄔ ㄩㄥˋ)
daily needs or spendings (of a household or an individual)

【吃】 549
2. ㄐㄧˊ jyi jí

to stammer; to stutter

吃吃(ㄐㄧˊ ㄐㄧˊ)
the sound of giggling

【各】 550
ㄍㄜˋ geh gè

1. each; every: 從各方面看，這個都比那個好。This is in every way better than that.
2. all

各半(ㄍㄜˋ ㄅㄢˋ)
half-and-half; fifty-fifty

各奔前程(ㄍㄜˋ ㄅㄣ ㄑㄧㄢˊ ㄔㄥˊ)
Each pursues his own goal (without caring about others' affairs).

各別(ㄍㄜˋ ㄅㄧㄝˊ)
individual; isolated (case); separate; separately; individually

各不相謀(ㄍㄜˋ ㄅㄨˋ ㄒㄧㄤ ㄇㄡˊ)
to proceed without consulting with one another

各得其所(ㄍㄜˋ ㄉㄜˊ ㄑㄧˊ ㄙㄨㄛˇ)
Each person gets his proper position. 或 Each thing finds its proper place.

各地(ㄍㄜˋ ㄉㄧˋ)
various places or localities; everywhere: 他們到各地看看。They visited everywhere.

各條(ㄍㄜˋ ㄊㄧㄠˊ)
various items or clauses

各類(ㄍㄜˋ ㄌㄟˋ)
each or every sort, kind, class, species, or order: 他們賣各類的書。They sell every kind of books.

各個擊破(ㄍㄜˋ ·ㄍㄜ ㄐㄧ ㄆㄛˋ)
to knock out one adversary after another; to defeat enemies by taking on one of them at a time

各個解決(ㄍㄜˋ ·ㄍㄜ ㄐㄧㄝˇ ㄐㄩㄝˊ)
a piecemeal solution

各幹各的(ㄍㄜˋ ㄍㄢˋ ㄍㄜˋ ·ㄉㄜ)
Let each one get on with his job.

各國(ㄍㄜˋ ㄍㄨㄛˊ)
each and every nation (or country); various nations

各管各的(ㄍㄜˋ ㄍㄨㄢˇ ㄍㄜˋ ·ㄉㄜ)
①Everyone minds his own business. ②lacking in coordination

各款(ㄍㄜˋ ㄎㄨㄢˇ)
each and every article (of a document); all the articles; various articles

各行(ㄍㄜˋ ㄏㄤˊ)or 各業(ㄍㄜˋ ㄧㄝˋ)
each and every trade; all professions; various callings

各級(ㄍㄜˋ ㄐㄧˊ)
all or different levels

各界(ㄍㄜˋ ㄐㄧㄝˋ)
all walks of life; all circles: 這本書受到各界的稱讚。The book is praised in all circles.

各就各位(ㄍㄜˋ ㄐㄧㄡˋ ㄍㄜˋ ㄨㄟˋ)
①(military) Man your posts! ②(athletics) On your marks!

各盡所能(ㄍㄜˋ ㄐㄧㄣˋ ㄙㄨㄛˇ ㄋㄥˊ)
Each does his best. 或 from each according to his ability

各取所需(ㄍㄜˋ ㄑㄩˇ ㄙㄨㄛˇ ㄒㄩ)
Each takes what he wants. 或 to each according to his needs

各顯神通(ㄍㄜˋ ㄒㄧㄢˇ ㄕㄣˊ ㄊㄨㄥ)
Each has his own way. 或 Each plays his long suit.

各項(ㄍㄜˋ ㄒㄧㄤˋ)
the various items; each and every item; all the items

各行其是(ㄍㄜˋ ㄒㄧㄥˊ ㄑㄧˊ ㄕˋ)
Each behaves in the ways which he thinks are right. 或

〔口部〕

Each goes his own way.
各執一詞(ㄍㄜˋ ㄓˊ ㄧˊ ㄘˊ)
Each (of the disputants) tells a different story.
各種(ㄍㄜˋ ㄓㄨㄥˇ)
various kinds, species, categories, etc.: 我們談論各種題目。We talked about various subjects.
各持己見(ㄍㄜˋ ㄔˊ ㄐㄧˇ ㄐㄧㄢˋ)
Each sticks to his own view.
各處(ㄍㄜˋ ㄔㄨˋ)
everywhere; various places; all the places: 各處似乎都很安靜。It seemed to be quiet everywhere.
各式各樣(ㄍㄜˋ ㄕˋ ㄍㄜˋ ㄧㄤˋ)or 各色各樣(ㄍㄜˋ ㄙㄜˋ ㄍㄜˋ ㄧㄤˋ)
all sorts, kinds, or varieties; various
各抒己見(ㄍㄜˋ ㄕㄨ ㄐㄧˇ ㄐㄧㄢˋ)
Each airs his own views.
各人(ㄍㄜˋ ㄖㄣˊ)
everybody
各人自掃門前雪，莫管他人瓦上霜(ㄍㄜˋ ㄖㄣˊ ㄗˋ ㄙㄠˇ ㄇㄣˊ ㄑㄧㄢˊ ㄒㄩㄝˇ, ㄇㄛˋ ㄍㄨㄢˇ ㄊㄚ ㄖㄣˊ ㄨㄚˇ ㄕㄤˋ ㄕㄨㄤ)
(literally) Each one sweeps the snow from his own doorstep and doesn't bother about the frost on his neighbor's roof.—(figuratively) Everybody minds his own business only.
各自(ㄍㄜˋ ㄗˋ)
each; respective: 放學後，學生各自回家。After school, students go home respectively.
各自爲政(ㄍㄜˋ ㄗˋ ㄨㄟˊ ㄓㄥˋ)
Each (office) administers its affairs in its own way without coordination with others.
各色俱全(ㄍㄜˋ ㄙㄜˋ ㄐㄩˋ ㄑㄩㄢˊ)or (ㄍㄜˋ ㄙㄜˋ ㄐㄩ ㄑㄩㄢˊ)
Nothing is lacking. 或 complete with everything; of all kinds
各有各的道理(ㄍㄜˋ ㄧㄡˇ ㄍㄜˋ ·ㄉㄜ ㄉㄠˋ ㄌㄧˇ)
Everybody has a point (in his statement). 或 Each (of the disputants) has given a plausible reason.
各有千秋(ㄍㄜˋ ㄧㄡˇ ㄑㄧㄢ ㄑㄧㄡ)
Each shows a unique quality. 或 Each has a unique style.
各有所好(ㄍㄜˋ ㄧㄡˇ ㄙㄨㄛˇ ㄏㄠˋ)
Each has his likes and dislikes. 或 Each has his own taste.
各有所長(ㄍㄜˋ ㄧㄡˇ ㄙㄨㄛˇ ㄔㄤˊ)
Each has a unique merit.
各位(ㄍㄜˋ ㄨㄟˋ)
ladies and gentlemen; gentlemen or ladies (used in addressing a gathering); everybody: 各位請注意! Attention please, everybody.

【吉】 551 ㄐㄧˊ jyi jí
good; lucky; auspicious; propitious; favorable; fortunate
吉卜賽(ㄐㄧˊ ㄅㄨˇ ㄙㄞˋ)or 吉普賽(ㄐㄧˊ ㄆㄨˇ ㄙㄞˋ)
the Gipsies or the Gypsies
吉普車(ㄐㄧˊ ㄆㄨˇ ㄔㄜ)
a jeep
吉房招租(ㄐㄧˊ ㄈㄤˊ ㄓㄠ ㄗㄨ)or 吉屋招租(ㄐㄧˊ ㄨ ㄓㄠ ㄗㄨ)
a house for rent; a house to let
吉他(ㄐㄧˊ ㄊㄚ)
a guitar
吉利(ㄐㄧˊ ㄌㄧˋ)
good luck; propitiousness
吉林(ㄐㄧˊ ㄌㄧㄣˊ)
①Kirin, a province in northeast China ② name of Kirin's provincial capital
吉隆坡(ㄐㄧˊ ㄌㄨㄥˊ ㄆㄛ)
Kuala Lumpur
吉光片羽(ㄐㄧˊ ㄍㄨㄤ ㄆㄧㄢˋ ㄩˇ)
remnants or broken relics (of ancient art works)
吉期(ㄐㄧˊ ㄑㄧˊ)
the wedding day
吉慶(ㄐㄧˊ ㄑㄧㄥˋ)
a happy event; an auspicious occasion
吉祥(ㄐㄧˊ ㄒㄧㄤˊ)
favorable; propitious; auspicious
吉星高照(ㄐㄧˊ ㄒㄧㄥ ㄍㄠ ㄓㄠˋ)
The lucky star shines bright.
吉凶(ㄐㄧˊ ㄒㄩㄥ)
good or bad luck
吉凶未卜(ㄐㄧˊ ㄒㄩㄥ ㄨㄟˋ ㄅㄨˇ)
No one knows how it will turn out.
吉兆(ㄐㄧˊ ㄓㄠˋ)or 吉徵(ㄐㄧˊ ㄓㄥ)
a good omen: 這被視爲吉兆。This is taken as a good omen.
吉事(ㄐㄧˊ ㄕˋ)
ceremonial rites
吉日(ㄐㄧˊ ㄖˋ)or 吉日良辰(ㄐㄧˊ ㄖˋ ㄌㄧㄤˊ ㄔㄣˊ)
① an auspicious day; a lucky day: 今天是吉日。Today is a lucky day. ② the first day of a lunar month
吉人(ㄐㄧˊ ㄖㄣˊ)or 吉士(ㄐㄧˊ ㄕˋ)
a good and virtuous man
吉人天相(ㄐㄧˊ ㄖㄣˊ ㄊㄧㄢ ㄒㄧㄤˋ)
Heaven helps a good man.

【吋】 552 ㄘㄨㄣˋ tsuenn cùn
inch—a unit of length

【同】 553 ㄊㄨㄥˊ torng tóng
1. same; equal; identical; similar; common
2. to share; to agree
3. together
同輩(ㄊㄨㄥˊ ㄅㄟˋ)
one's equal (in seniority); of the same generation; a peer
同胞(ㄊㄨㄥˊ ㄅㄠ)
a compatriot; a fellow countryman
同班(ㄊㄨㄥˊ ㄅㄢ)
a classmate: 他上學期和我同班。He and I were classmates last term.
同伴(ㄊㄨㄥˊ ㄅㄢˋ)
a companion: 我們是好同伴。We are good companions.
同榜(ㄊㄨㄥˊ ㄅㄤˇ)or 同科(ㄊㄨㄥˊ ㄎㄜ)
successful candidates whose names were announced on the same list under the old civil service examination system
同病相憐(ㄊㄨㄥˊ ㄅㄧㄥˋ ㄒㄧㄤ ㄌㄧㄢˊ)
Fellow sufferers have mutual sympathy.
同步(ㄊㄨㄥˊ ㄅㄨˋ)
synchronism; to synchronize; synchronous
同袍(ㄊㄨㄥˊ ㄆㄠˊ)
① comrades in arms ② to share the same robes with
同謀(ㄊㄨㄥˊ ㄇㄡˊ)
to conspire
同門(ㄊㄨㄥˊ ㄇㄣˊ)
a fellow disciple
同門異戶(ㄊㄨㄥˊ ㄇㄣˊ ㄧˋ ㄏㄨˋ)
to be alike except for slight

differences
同盟(ㄊㄨㄥˊ ㄇㄥˊ)
an alliance; a league; a confederacy
同盟國(ㄊㄨㄥˊ ㄇㄥˊ ㄍㄨㄛˊ)
① in World War I, the Central Powers against the Allies ② in World War II, the Allies against the Axis ③ allied nations; an ally
同盟會(ㄊㄨㄥˊ ㄇㄥˊ ㄏㄨㄟˋ)
Tung Meng Hui (an antecedent of Kuomintang)
同名(ㄊㄨㄥˊ ㄇㄧㄥˊ)
a namesake; having the same given name
同名同姓(ㄊㄨㄥˊ ㄇㄧㄥˊ ㄊㄨㄥˊ ㄒㄧㄥˋ)
having the same given name and family name
同命(ㄊㄨㄥˊ ㄇㄧㄥˋ)
to share the same destiny; to be under the influence of the same stars
同房(ㄊㄨㄥˊ ㄈㄤˊ)
to share the same room: 姊妹們同房住。The sisters share the same room.
同父異母(ㄊㄨㄥˊ ㄈㄨˋ ㄧˋ ㄇㄨˇ)
having the same father but different mothers
同道(ㄊㄨㄥˊ ㄉㄠˋ)
the people engaged in the same pursuit; the people with the same ideals
同等(ㄊㄨㄥˊ ㄉㄥˇ)
of the same rank or class; the same (in importance, responsibility, etc.)
同等學力(ㄊㄨㄥˊ ㄉㄥˇ ㄒㄩㄝˊ ㄌㄧˋ)
(said of persons without a diploma in comparison with those who have it) with the same intellectual capacity and scholastic achievements; to have the same educational level
同堂兄弟(ㄊㄨㄥˊ ㄊㄤˊ ㄒㄩㄥ ㄉㄧˋ)
male cousins with the same paternal grandfather
同年(ㄊㄨㄥˊ ㄋㄧㄢˊ)
① of the same age: 他們同年。They are of the same age. ② (in former times) having passed the civil service examination in the same year
同樂晚會(ㄊㄨㄥˊ ㄌㄜˋ ㄨㄢˇ ㄏㄨㄟˋ)
an evening party (held within an organization, school, etc.)
同類(ㄊㄨㄥˊ ㄌㄟˋ)
the same kind, class, species, or family
同類相殘(ㄊㄨㄥˊ ㄌㄟˋ ㄒㄧㄤ ㄘㄢˊ)
(literally) self-extermination by animals of the same species—an intramural fight
同僚(ㄊㄨㄥˊ ㄌㄧㄠˊ)or 同事(ㄊㄨㄥˊ ㄕˋ)
colleagues; a coworker; an associate
同流合污(ㄊㄨㄥˊ ㄌㄧㄡˊ ㄏㄜˊ ㄨ)
to follow the bad example of others: 別與他同流合污。Don't follow the bad example of him.
同量(ㄊㄨㄥˊ ㄌㄧㄤˋ)
the same amount or quantity
同路人(ㄊㄨㄥˊ ㄌㄨˋ ㄖㄣˊ)
a fellow traveler
同甘共苦(ㄊㄨㄥˊ ㄍㄢ ㄍㄨㄥˋ ㄎㄨˇ)
to stick together through thick and thin; to share bliss and adversity together; on shares
同感(ㄊㄨㄥˊ ㄍㄢˇ)
to have the same feeling
同庚(ㄊㄨㄥˊ ㄍㄥ)
of the same age: 他們夫妻同庚。He is of the same age as his wife.
同歸於盡(ㄊㄨㄥˊ ㄍㄨㄟ ㄩˊ ㄐㄧㄣˋ)
to end in death or ruin of both combatants; to die together; to end in common ruin
同工同酬(ㄊㄨㄥˊ ㄍㄨㄥ ㄊㄨㄥˊ ㄔㄡˊ)
to reward the same work with the same pay; to pay employees strictly on the basis of their work; equal pay for equal work
同好(ㄊㄨㄥˊ ㄏㄠˋ)
people with the same hobby
同行
① (ㄊㄨㄥˊ ㄏㄤˊ) in the same trade, line, occupation, or profession
② (ㄊㄨㄥˊ ㄒㄧㄥˊ) to go together
同行相妒(ㄊㄨㄥˊ ㄏㄤˊ ㄒㄧㄤ ㄉㄨˋ)
People in the same profession or line of business are apt to be jealous of one another.
同化(ㄊㄨㄥˊ ㄏㄨㄚˋ)
to assimilate; assimilation
同夥(ㄊㄨㄥˊ ㄏㄨㄛˇ)
a fellow worker in the same company; a member of the same group or gang
同機(ㄊㄨㄥˊ ㄐㄧ)
aboard the same plane
同濟會(ㄊㄨㄥˊ ㄐㄧˋ ㄏㄨㄟˋ)
Kiwanis Club
同進退(ㄊㄨㄥˊ ㄐㄧㄣˋ ㄊㄨㄟˋ)
(said of colleagues taking the same stand over an issue) to advance or withdraw together; to stay on or quit together
同居(ㄊㄨㄥˊ ㄐㄩ)
to cohabit (usually said of an unmarried couple); cohabitation
同氣連枝(ㄊㄨㄥˊ ㄑㄧˋ ㄌㄧㄢˊ ㄓ)
brotherly ties
同氣相求(ㄊㄨㄥˊ ㄑㄧˋ ㄒㄧㄤ ㄑㄧㄡˊ)
People with the same ideals have an affinity for one another.
同衾共枕(ㄊㄨㄥˊ ㄑㄧㄣ ㄍㄨㄥˋ ㄓㄣˇ)
(usually said of a married couple) to share the same comforter and the same pillow
同情(ㄊㄨㄥˊ ㄑㄧㄥˊ)
to sympathize; to be in sympathy with; to have sympathy for
同情心(ㄊㄨㄥˊ ㄑㄧㄥˊ ㄒㄧㄣ)
sympathies; compassion; pity; fellow feeling
同慶(ㄊㄨㄥˊ ㄑㄧㄥˋ)
to celebrate together; universal celebration
同席(ㄊㄨㄥˊ ㄒㄧˊ)
to be seated at the same dining table: 他們同席。They seat themselves at the same table.
同心(ㄊㄨㄥˊ ㄒㄧㄣ)
united at heart or in common purpose
同心同德(ㄊㄨㄥˊ ㄒㄧㄣ ㄊㄨㄥˊ ㄉㄜˊ)
to be of one mind: 我們同心同德。We are all of one mind.
同心協力(ㄊㄨㄥˊ ㄒㄧㄣ ㄒㄧㄝˊ ㄌㄧˋ)
to work in cooperation; to make concerted efforts: 讓我們與朋友同心協力。 Let's

〔口部〕

work in close cooperation with our friends.

同心圓(ㄊㄨㄥˊ ㄒㄧㄣ ㄩㄢˊ)
concentric circles

同鄉(ㄊㄨㄥˊ ㄒㄧㄤ)
the people from the same province, county, town, etc.

同鄉會(ㄊㄨㄥˊ ㄒㄧㄤ ㄏㄨㄟˋ)
a club or association formed by people from the same province, county, city, etc.

同姓(ㄊㄨㄥˊ ㄒㄧㄥˋ)
members of the same clan

同性(ㄊㄨㄥˊ ㄒㄧㄥˋ)
of the same sex

同性戀(ㄊㄨㄥˊ ㄒㄧㄥˋ ㄌㄧㄢˋ) or 同性愛(ㄊㄨㄥˊ ㄒㄧㄥˋ ㄞˋ)
homosexuality; homosexual love

同性戀者(ㄊㄨㄥˊ ㄒㄧㄥˋ ㄌㄧㄢˋ ㄓㄜˇ)
a gay; a homosexual

同學(ㄊㄨㄥˊ ㄒㄩㄝˊ)
a fellow student; a schoolmate 參看「同硯」

同學會(ㄊㄨㄥˊ ㄒㄩㄝˊ ㄏㄨㄟˋ)
an alumni association

同志(ㄊㄨㄥˊ ㄓˋ)
a comrade

同舟共濟(ㄊㄨㄥˊ ㄓㄡ ㄍㄨㄥˋ ㄐㄧˋ)
to show the mutual concern of the people in the same boat

同種(ㄊㄨㄥˊ ㄓㄨㄥˇ)
(people) of the same race

同車(ㄊㄨㄥˊ ㄔㄜ)
to ride on the same train or bus: 他們同車。They rode on the same bus.

同儕(ㄊㄨㄥˊ ㄔㄞˊ)
fellows of the same generation; contemporaries

同仇敵愾(ㄊㄨㄥˊ ㄔㄡˊ ㄉㄧˊ ㄎㄞˋ)
to share the same hatred and fight against a common enemy

同窗(ㄊㄨㄥˊ ㄔㄨㄤ)
a classmate or schoolmate

同牀異夢(ㄊㄨㄥˊ ㄔㄨㄤˊ ㄧˋ ㄇㄥˋ)
① to hide different intentions behind the semblance of accord ② to have different dreams in the same bed (said of a troubled marriage)

同時(ㄊㄨㄥˊ ㄕˊ)
at the same time; simultaneously

同事(ㄊㄨㄥˊ ㄕˋ)
① a colleague ② to serve the same (king, etc.) ③ to marry the same (man)

同室操戈(ㄊㄨㄥˊ ㄕˋ ㄘㄠ ㄍㄜ)
(especially said of brothers) to engage in internal strife

同聲相應(ㄊㄨㄥˊ ㄕㄥ ㄒㄧㄤ ㄧㄥˋ)
to act in unison: 士兵同聲相應。The soldiers act in unison.

同聲一哭(ㄊㄨㄥˊ ㄕㄥ ㄧˋ ㄎㄨ)
to share the same feeling of loss or grief (over the death of a national hero, a great tragedy, etc.)

同日而語(ㄊㄨㄥˊ ㄖˋ ㄦˊ ㄩˇ)
to mention in equal terms

同仁 or 同人(ㄊㄨㄥˊ ㄖㄣˊ)
a colleague; a fellow member (of an organization)

同族(ㄊㄨㄥˊ ㄗㄨˊ)
of the same tribe or clan

同宗(ㄊㄨㄥˊ ㄗㄨㄥ)
of the same clan; having a common ancestor: 我們同宗。We are of the same clan.

同異(ㄊㄨㄥˊ ㄧˋ)
similarities and differences

同意(ㄊㄨㄥˊ ㄧˋ)
to agree; to consent; to concur; agreement; consent; approval: 她同意嫁給他。She consented to marry him.

同意權(ㄊㄨㄥˊ ㄧˋ ㄑㄩㄢˊ)
the right of consent or endorsement

同意書(ㄊㄨㄥˊ ㄧˋ ㄕㄨ)
a written consent; a letter of authorization; a letter of agreement

同義語(ㄊㄨㄥˊ ㄧˋ ㄩˇ)
a synonym: 悲傷與悲哀是同義語。"Sad" and "unhappy" are synonyms.

同業(ㄊㄨㄥˊ ㄧㄝˋ)
the people of the same trade, calling, or occupation

同業公會(ㄊㄨㄥˊ ㄧㄝˋ ㄍㄨㄥ ㄏㄨㄟˋ)
a guild; a trade union

同硯(ㄊㄨㄥˊ ㄧㄢˋ)
schoolmates or classmates

同寅(ㄊㄨㄥˊ ㄧㄣˊ)
(said of government officials in old times) colleagues

同樣(ㄊㄨㄥˊ ㄧㄤˋ)
① in the same way, manner, or fashion; similarly; likewise ② the same; similar

同位角(ㄊㄨㄥˊ ㄨㄟˋ ㄐㄧㄠˇ)
(mathematics) corresponding angles

同位素(ㄊㄨㄥˊ ㄨㄟˋ ㄙㄨˋ)
an isotope

同位語(ㄊㄨㄥˊ ㄨㄟˋ ㄩˇ)
(English grammar) an appositive

同溫層(ㄊㄨㄥˊ ㄨㄣ ㄘㄥˊ)
the stratosphere

同文同種(ㄊㄨㄥˊ ㄨㄣˊ ㄊㄨㄥˊ ㄓㄨㄥˇ)
of the same language and the same race

同源(ㄊㄨㄥˊ ㄩㄢˊ)
homologous

【吆】 554 ㄧㄠ iau yāo
to shout; to cry

吆喝(ㄧㄠ ˙ㄏㄜ)
① to shout; to cry ② to hawk

【吒】 555 ㄓㄚˋ jah zhà
1. to shout with anger
2. to smack in eating

【名】 556 ㄇㄧㄥˊ ming míng
1. a name; a designation; a title; rank
2. position; honor; fame; renown; reputation
3. famous; noted; distinguished; renowned; valuable; precious; noble; rare; great
4. to name; to describe

名簿(ㄇㄧㄥˊ ㄅㄨˋ)
a roster; a roll

名不副實(ㄇㄧㄥˊ ˙ㄅㄨ ㄈㄨˋ ㄕˊ)
The reputation is not supported by fact.

名不虛傳(ㄇㄧㄥˊ ˙ㄅㄨ ㄒㄩ ㄔㄨㄢˊ)
The reputation is well supported by fact.

名不正言不順(ㄇㄧㄥˊ ˙ㄅㄨ ㄓㄥˋ ㄧㄢˊ ˙ㄅㄨ ㄕㄨㄣˋ)
There is no justification to do something without some convincing reason.

名牌(ㄇㄧㄥˊ ㄆㄞˊ)
① a famous brand ② a nameplate

名片(ㄇㄧㄥˊ ㄆㄧㄢˋ) or 名刺(ㄇㄧㄥˊ ㄘˋ) or 名帖(ㄇㄧㄥˊ ㄊㄧㄝ)

〔口部〕

a calling card; a visiting card
名馬(ㄇㄧㄥˊ ㄇㄚˇ) or 名駒(ㄇㄧㄥˊ ㄐㄩ)
a champion horse; a thoroughbred horse
名滿天下(ㄇㄧㄥˊ ㄇㄢˇ ㄊㄧㄢ ㄒㄧㄚˋ)
to enjoy world-wide fame; to be world-famous
名門(ㄇㄧㄥˊ ㄇㄣˊ)
a distinguished family: 她出自名門。 She comes from an eminent family.
名門閨秀(ㄇㄧㄥˊ ㄇㄣˊ ㄍㄨㄟ ㄒㄧㄡˋ)
a daughter of an illustrious family
名目(ㄇㄧㄥˊ ㄇㄨˋ)
a name; a designation
名目繁多(ㄇㄧㄥˊ ㄇㄨˋ ㄈㄢˊ ㄉㄨㄛ)
a multitude of names (or items)
名閥(ㄇㄧㄥˊ ㄈㄚˊ)
an illustrious family of many generations
名分(ㄇㄧㄥˊ ㄈㄣˋ)
a role or duties proper to one's title
名副其實(ㄇㄧㄥˊ ㄈㄨˋ ㄑㄧˊ ㄕˊ)
to be worthy of the name or reputation
名單(ㄇㄧㄥˊ ㄉㄢ)
a name list; a roster; a roll
名堂(ㄇㄧㄥˊ ˙ㄊㄤ)
①a dignified name or designation ②a result that is worth mentioning; a worthwhile result
名女人(ㄇㄧㄥˊ ㄋㄩˇ ㄖㄣˊ)
the women with eminent (or notorious) reputation
名利(ㄇㄧㄥˊ ㄌㄧˋ)
fame and gain; fame and wealth
名利雙收(ㄇㄧㄥˊ ㄌㄧˋ ㄕㄨㄤ ㄕㄡ)
to achieve both fame and wealth
名列前茅(ㄇㄧㄥˊ ㄌㄧㄝˋ ㄑㄧㄢˊ ㄇㄠˊ)
to head the list of successful candidates
名流(ㄇㄧㄥˊ ㄌㄧㄡˊ)
a celebrity; a distinguished personage
名伶(ㄇㄧㄥˊ ㄌㄧㄥˊ)
a renowned actor or actress
名落孫山(ㄇㄧㄥˊ ㄌㄨㄛˋ ㄙㄨㄣ ㄕㄢ)
to fail in an examination
名歌(ㄇㄧㄥˊ ㄍㄜ)
a great or famous song:「快樂頌」是首名歌。"Song of Joy" is a famous song.
名古屋(ㄇㄧㄥˊ ㄍㄨˇ ㄨ)
Nagoya, a Japanese city
名過其實(ㄇㄧㄥˊ ㄍㄨㄛˋ ㄑㄧˊ ㄕˊ)
to have an exaggerated reputation
名貴(ㄇㄧㄥˊ ㄍㄨㄟˋ)
valuable; precious; rare
名花有主(ㄇㄧㄥˊ ㄏㄨㄚ ㄧㄡˇ ㄓㄨˇ)
The beauty has already been won by somebody.
名宦(ㄇㄧㄥˊ ㄏㄨㄢˋ)
a distinguished official
名家(ㄇㄧㄥˊ ㄐㄧㄚ)
①a master (in a branch of art) ②the Nominalist school of philosophy ③an illustrious family
名節(ㄇㄧㄥˊ ㄐㄧㄝˊ)
honor and integrity
名教(ㄇㄧㄥˊ ㄐㄧㄠˋ)
①the body of teachings on morality and ethics ②Confucianism, the body of teachings on social relationships
名酒(ㄇㄧㄥˊ ㄐㄧㄡˇ)
excellent wine or liquor with a famous brand name
名韁利鎖(ㄇㄧㄥˊ ㄐㄧㄤ ㄌㄧˋ ㄙㄨㄛˇ)
to be a slave of fame and wealth
名將(ㄇㄧㄥˊ ㄐㄧㄤˋ)
a great general or admiral
名句(ㄇㄧㄥˊ ㄐㄩˋ)
a famous line or phrase; a well-known phrase; a quotable quote
名脚兒 or 名角兒(ㄇㄧㄥˊ ㄐㄩㄝˊ ㄦ)
a famed actor or actress
名氣(ㄇㄧㄥˊ ㄑㄧˋ)
fame; reputation; renown
名器(ㄇㄧㄥˊ ㄑㄧˋ)
(in ancient China) ranks and proper equipages
名曲(ㄇㄧㄥˊ ㄑㄩˇ)
a great musical composition; a masterpiece in music
名下(ㄇㄧㄥˊ ㄒㄧㄚˋ)
①under (one's) account ②to (one's) account
名正言順(ㄇㄧㄥˊ ㄓㄥˋ ㄧㄢˊ ㄕㄨㄣˋ)
valid in name and in reasoning; to have good reason; to deserve; justified
名著(ㄇㄧㄥˊ ㄓㄨˋ)
a great book; a literary masterpiece: 伊利亞德是本名著。*Iliad* is a great book.
名產(ㄇㄧㄥˊ ㄔㄢˇ)
a noted product or special product (of a place)
名稱(ㄇㄧㄥˊ ㄔㄥ)
the name or designation (of a thing)
名垂青史(ㄇㄧㄥˊ ㄔㄨㄟˊ ㄑㄧㄥ ㄕˇ)
to go down in history; to be crowned with eternal glory
名師(ㄇㄧㄥˊ ㄕ)
a great teacher; a master
名師出高徒(ㄇㄧㄥˊ ㄕ ㄔㄨ ㄍㄠ ㄊㄨˊ)
An accomplished disciple owes his accomplishments to his great teacher.
名實(ㄇㄧㄥˊ ㄕˊ)
name and substance
名實相符(ㄇㄧㄥˊ ㄕˊ ㄒㄧㄤ ㄈㄨˊ)
in deed as well as in name
名氏(ㄇㄧㄥˊ ㄕˋ)
one's name and family name
名世(ㄇㄧㄥˊ ㄕˋ)
to become famous
名士(ㄇㄧㄥˊ ㄕˋ)
a celebrated scholar
名士派(ㄇㄧㄥˊ ㄕˋ ㄆㄞˋ)
a bohemian; an unconventional scholar
名手(ㄇㄧㄥˊ ㄕㄡˇ)
a great player (of a game); a master (in a branch of art)
名山大川(ㄇㄧㄥˊ ㄕㄢ ㄉㄚˋ ㄔㄨㄢ)
famous mountains and mighty streams
名山事業(ㄇㄧㄥˊ ㄕㄢ ㄕˋ ㄧㄝˋ)
writing as a pursuit or occupation
名聲(ㄇㄧㄥˊ ㄕㄥ)
fame; renown; reputation; repute; glory: 他是個名聲很好的人。He is a man of good reputation.
名勝(ㄇㄧㄥˊ ㄕㄥˋ)
a scenic spot; a resort or vacationland
名勝古跡(ㄇㄧㄥˊ ㄕㄥˋ ㄍㄨˇ ㄐㄧ)
places of historic interest and scenic beauty
名數(ㄇㄧㄥˊ ㄕㄨˋ)
(mathematics) a concrete number, or denominate num-

〔口部〕

〔口部〕

ber
名人(ㄇㄧㄥˊ ㄖㄣˊ)
①a notable; a celebrity; a famous person; a man of note ② one of the most coveted titles among professional go players in Japan
名人錄(ㄇㄧㄥˊ ㄖㄣˊ ㄌㄨˋ)
Who's Who: 他的大名在名人錄上出現。 His name appeared in *Who's Who.*
名儒(ㄇㄧㄥˊ ㄖㄨˊ)
a great (Confucian) scholar: 朱熹是位名儒。Chu Hsi was a great scholar.
名字(ㄇㄧㄥˊ ㄗˋ)
the name (of a person, etc.)
名譟一時(ㄇㄧㄥˊ ㄗㄠˋ ㄧˋ ㄕˊ)
(said of artists, writers, etc.) very famous at one time
名作(ㄇㄧㄥˊ ㄗㄨㄛˋ)
a masterpiece: 紅字是霍桑的名作。*The Scarlet Letter* is Nathaniel Hawthorne's masterpiece.
名詞(ㄇㄧㄥˊ ㄘˊ)
①a noun: 鳥是個名詞。"Bird" is a noun. ②a term
名次(ㄇㄧㄥˊ ㄘˋ)
one's position or standing (as compared with others in a contest, a competitive examination, etc.)
名册(ㄇㄧㄥˊ ㄘㄜˋ)
a roster; a roll; a record of names
名存實亡(ㄇㄧㄥˊ ㄘㄨㄣˊ ㄕˊ ㄨㄤˊ)
(said of established institutions) to exist in name only
名額(ㄇㄧㄥˊ ㄜˊ)
the number of openings, or quota (for employees, students, etc.)
名醫(ㄇㄧㄥˊ ㄧ)
a great physician; a famous doctor
名醫束手(ㄇㄧㄥˊ ㄧ ㄕㄨˋ ㄕㄡˇ)
Famed physicians are powerless. (said of grave illnesses or strange ailments)
名義(ㄇㄧㄥˊ ㄧˋ)
①the name (as opposed to the reality or substance) ② the outward reason (for doing something) ③ nominally
名言(ㄇㄧㄥˊ ㄧㄢˊ)
a maxim; an adage:「不浪費,不窮困」是句名言。"Waste not, want not" is a maxim.
名揚四海(ㄇㄧㄥˊ ㄧㄤˊ ㄙˋ ㄏㄞˇ)
to become famous all over the world
名位(ㄇㄧㄥˊ ㄨㄟˋ)
position and title; official rank
名望(ㄇㄧㄥˊ ㄨㄤˋ)
fame; reputation; repute; renown; popularity
名譽(ㄇㄧㄥˊ ㄩˋ)
①honor; repute; reputation: 他是一位名譽很好的醫生。He is a doctor of high reputation. ② honorary
名譽博士(ㄇㄧㄥˊ ㄩˋ ㄅㄛˊ ㄕˋ)
an honorary doctorate
名譽董事長(ㄇㄧㄥˊ ㄩˋ ㄉㄨㄥˇ ㄕˋ ㄓㄤˇ)
the honorary board chairman (of an institution, etc.)
名譽會長(ㄇㄧㄥˊ ㄩˋ ㄏㄨㄟˋ ㄓㄤˇ)
the honorary president or chairman (of an association)
名媛(ㄇㄧㄥˊ ㄩㄢˊ)
a young lady of note

【后】 557
ㄏㄡˋ how hòu
1. an empress
2. the god of the earth
3. after; behind 亦作「後」
后妃(ㄏㄡˋ ㄈㄟ)
the empress and imperial concubines
后土(ㄏㄡˋ ㄊㄨˇ)
the earth; the god of the earth
后冠(ㄏㄡˋ ㄍㄨㄢ)
a tiara
后稷(ㄏㄡˋ ㄐㄧˋ)
the minister of agriculture under Emperor Shun (舜)

【吐】 558
1. ㄊㄨˇ tuu tǔ
to spit; to utter
吐蕃(ㄊㄨˇ ㄈㄢ)
the Tibetan regime in ancient China
吐痰(ㄊㄨˇ ㄊㄢˊ)
to spit phlegm; to spit
吐露(ㄊㄨˇ ㄌㄨˋ)
to confess; to disclose
吐露眞情(ㄊㄨˇ ㄌㄨˋ ㄓㄣ ㄑㄧㄥˊ)
to unbosom oneself; to tell the truth
吐剛茹柔(ㄊㄨˇ ㄍㄤ ㄖㄨˊ ㄖㄡˊ)
to bow to the mighty and powerful but act like a bully toward the weak; to avoid the strong and bully the weak
吐故納新(ㄊㄨˇ ㄍㄨˋ ㄋㄚˋ ㄒㄧㄣ)
①a Taoist art to achieve a long life by breathing out the useless air and breathing in the fresh air ②to get rid of the stale and take in the fresh
吐氣(ㄊㄨˇ ㄑㄧˋ)
to give vent to pent-up feelings
吐棄(ㄊㄨˇ ㄑㄧˋ)
to spurn; to cast aside; to reject
吐出(ㄊㄨˇ ㄔㄨ)
to spit out; to utter

【吐】 558
2. ㄊㄨˋ tuh tù
to vomit; to throw up; to spew
吐沫(ㄊㄨˋ ·ㄇㄛ)
saliva
吐劑(ㄊㄨˋ ㄐㄧˋ)
an emetic
吐血(ㄊㄨˋ ㄒㄧㄝˇ)
to vomit blood; hematemesis; hemoptysis
吐瀉(ㄊㄨˋ ㄒㄧㄝˋ)
vomiting and purging

【向】 559
ㄒㄧㄤˋ shianq xiàng
1. to turn; to face: 這棟建築物向西。This building faces west.
2. a direction; a trend
3. until now
4. a Chinese family name
向背(ㄒㄧㄤˋ ㄅㄟˋ)
the support or opposition (of the people)
向壁虛造(ㄒㄧㄤˋ ㄅㄧˋ ㄒㄩ ㄗㄠˋ)
a gross fabrication; to fabricate
向明(ㄒㄧㄤˋ ㄇㄧㄥˊ)
①toward daybreak ②the bright side of a house
向來(ㄒㄧㄤˋ ㄌㄞˊ)
hitherto; heretofore; until now; always: 向來都是他出主意。He always makes the decisions.

向例(ㄒㄧㄤˋ ㄌㄧˋ)
according to custom; customarily

向光性(ㄒㄧㄤˋ ㄍㄨㄤ ㄒㄧㄥˋ)
(biology) phototropism

向後(ㄒㄧㄤˋ ㄏㄡˋ)
①in the future ②to turn around

向前(ㄒㄧㄤˋ ㄑㄧㄢˊ)
to go forward: 讓我們向前。Let's go forward.

向下(ㄒㄧㄤˋ ㄒㄧㄚˋ)
downward; down: 這條馬路向下傾斜。The road runs downward.

向心力(ㄒㄧㄤˋ ㄒㄧㄣ ㄌㄧˋ)
centripetal force

向學(ㄒㄧㄤˋ ㄒㄩㄝˊ)
to determine or to be inclined to study: 他努力向學。He determined to study hard.

向着(ㄒㄧㄤˋ ˙ㄓㄜ)
toward (an object or direction); to face

向上(ㄒㄧㄤˋ ㄕㄤˋ)
①to turn upward ②to strive upward; to try to improve oneself

向日葵(ㄒㄧㄤˋ ㄖˋ ㄎㄨㄟˊ)
the sunflower: 向日葵向著太陽。Sunflowers turn towards the sun.

向榮(ㄒㄧㄤˋ ㄖㄨㄥˊ)
on the road to prosperity; making progress

向左(ㄒㄧㄤˋ ㄗㄨㄛˇ)
towards the left

向右(ㄒㄧㄤˋ ㄧㄡˋ)
towards the right

向陽(ㄒㄧㄤˋ ㄧㄤˊ)
(said of a house) facing south, or the sunny side: 這屋子向陽。The house faces south.

向無此例(ㄒㄧㄤˋ ㄨˊ ㄘˇ ㄌㄧˋ)
There's no precedent for this.

向外(ㄒㄧㄤˋ ㄨㄞˋ)
①to turn outside ②upwards of, or more (used after a number)

向晚(ㄒㄧㄤˋ ㄨㄢˇ)
toward the evening

向往 or 嚮往(ㄒㄧㄤˋ ㄨㄤˇ)
to admire and try to imitate (a great person, etc.)

向隅(ㄒㄧㄤˋ ㄩˊ)
to miss the opportunity (of seeing a great show, getting a handsome gift, buying a new product, etc.)

【吏】 560 ㄌㄧˋ lih lì

a civil officer

吏部(ㄌㄧˋ ㄅㄨˋ)
(in ancient China) the Ministry of Civil Personnel

吏治(ㄌㄧˋ ㄓˋ)
(said of officials) the achievements of an administration

吏員(ㄌㄧˋ ㄩㄢˊ)
a minor official

四畫

【君】 561 ㄐㄩㄣ jiun jūn

1. a sovereign; a monarch; a king; a lord
2. you (used in addressing a male in formal speech)

君臨萬邦(ㄐㄩㄣ ㄌㄧㄣˊ ㄨㄢˋ ㄅㄤ)
to become an emperor of a vast empire

君權(ㄐㄩㄣ ㄑㄩㄢˊ)
sovereign power; monarchical authority; the royal prerogative

君權神授(說)(ㄐㄩㄣ ㄑㄩㄢˊ ㄕㄣˊ ㄕㄡˋ (ㄕㄨㄛ))
(the theory of) the divine right of kings

君主(ㄐㄩㄣ ㄓㄨˇ)
a sovereign; a monarch; a ruler

君主立憲(ㄐㄩㄣ ㄓㄨˇ ㄌㄧˋ ㄒㄧㄢˋ)
constitutional or limited monarchy

君主國(ㄐㄩㄣ ㄓㄨˇ ㄍㄨㄛˊ)
a monarchy

君主專制(ㄐㄩㄣ ㄓㄨˇ ㄓㄨㄢ ㄓˋ)
absolute or despotic monarchy

君士坦丁堡(ㄐㄩㄣ ㄕˋ ㄊㄢˇ ㄉㄧㄥ ㄅㄠˇ)
Constantinople, the old capital of Turkey

君子(ㄐㄩㄣ ㄗˇ)
①a perfect or true gentleman; a man of virtue: 君子成人之美。A gentleman is always ready to assist others in achieving their objectives. ②a superior

君子國(ㄐㄩㄣ ㄗˇ ㄍㄨㄛˊ)
the (imaginary) land of the virtuous

君子協定(ㄐㄩㄣ ㄗˇ ㄒㄧㄝˊ ㄉㄧㄥˋ)
a gentlemen's agreement: 我與他達成君子協定。I made a gentlemen's agreement with him.

君子之交淡如水(ㄐㄩㄣ ㄗˇ ㄓ ㄐㄧㄠ ㄉㄢˋ ㄖㄨˊ ㄕㄨㄟˇ)
The friendship between gentlemen appears indifferent but is pure like water.

君無戲言(ㄐㄩㄣ ㄨˊ ㄒㄧˋ ㄧㄢˊ)
The king's words are to be taken seriously. 或 A monarch or ruler is expected to honor all his promises.

君王(ㄐㄩㄣ ㄨㄤˊ)
a sovereign; a monarch; a ruler

【吝】 562 ㄌㄧㄣˋ linn lìn

stingy; niggardly; parsimonious

吝惜(ㄌㄧㄣˋ ㄒㄧˊ)
to hold stingily on to; to be stingy about; to stint

吝嗇(ㄌㄧㄣˋ ㄙㄜˋ)
stingy; miserly; niggardly; parsimonious

【吞】 563 ㄊㄨㄣ tuen tūn

to swallow; to engulf; to gulp

吞併(ㄊㄨㄣ ㄅㄧㄥˋ)
to annex (a foreign territory); to take possession of (another's property)

吞沒(ㄊㄨㄣ ㄇㄛˋ)
①to take possession of (another's property); to appropriate ②to engulf

吞滅(ㄊㄨㄣ ㄇㄧㄝˋ)
to conquer and annex (a country)

吞服(ㄊㄨㄣ ㄈㄨˊ)
to swallow or take (medicine)

吞吐(ㄊㄨㄣ ㄊㄨˇ)
①to swallow and spit ②to take in and send out in large quantities

吞吐量(ㄊㄨㄣ ㄊㄨˇ ㄌㄧㄤˋ)
the volume of goods handled at a seaport

吞吞吐吐(ㄊㄨㄣ ㄊㄨㄣ ㄊㄨˇ ㄊㄨˇ)

〔口部〕

trying to hide something while speaking; to hum and haw
吞公款(ㄊㄨㄣ ㄍㄨㄥ ㄎㄨㄢˇ)
to embezzle public funds
吞佔(ㄊㄨㄣ ㄓㄢˋ)
to take possession of land illegally
吞食(ㄊㄨㄣ ㄕˊ)
to swallow; to devour
吞噬(ㄊㄨㄣ ㄕˋ)
①(said of beasts) to swallow or devour (the prey) ②(said of fire, etc.) to devour; to engulf
吞聲(ㄊㄨㄣ ㄕㄥ)
①to suppress complaints or grudges ②to sob
吞雲吐霧(ㄊㄨㄣ ㄩㄣˊ ㄊㄨˇ ㄨˋ)
to puff; to take puffs; to smoke

【吟】 564 ㄧㄣˊ yn yín
1. to chant; to intone; to sing; to recite
2. to moan; to sigh
吟風弄月(ㄧㄣˊ ㄈㄥ ㄋㄨㄥˋ ㄩㄝˋ)
to sing of the wind and toy with the moon (referring to the leisurely abandon of a poet)
吟壇(ㄧㄣˊ ㄊㄢˊ)
the poetic circles: 他在吟壇享有盛名。He was famous in the poetic circles.
吟嘯(ㄧㄣˊ ㄒㄧㄠˋ)
①to sing in freedom; to whistle or shout in freedom ②to lament; to sigh
吟誦(ㄧㄣˊ ㄙㄨㄥˋ)
to recite (a verse); to chant or intone (a verse): 她吟誦李白的詩。She recited Li Po's poems.
吟哦(ㄧㄣˊ ㄜˊ)
to chant or intone (a verse)
吟遊詩人(ㄧㄣˊ ㄧㄡˊ ㄕ ㄖㄣˊ)
a troubadour; a minstrel
吟味(ㄧㄣˊ ㄨㄟˋ)
to enjoy or appreciate (a poem, etc.): 他吟味詩篇。He appreciated a poem.
吟詠(ㄧㄣˊ ㄩㄥˇ)
to chant or intone (a verse)

【吠】 565 ㄈㄟˋ fey fèi
(said of a dog) to bark: 狗對著他吠叫。The dog barks at him.
吠影吠聲(ㄈㄟˋ ㄧㄥˇ ㄈㄟˋ ㄕㄥ)
①to bark at shadows and sounds ②to raise an uproar over an unconfirmed rumor

【否】 566 1. ㄈㄡˇ foou fǒu
1. no; not
2. negative
否定(ㄈㄡˇ ㄉㄧㄥˋ)
①to deny; to negate; to refute: 事實否定他的推論。Facts have refuted his inference. ②denial; negation
否決(ㄈㄡˇ ㄐㄩㄝˊ)
to veto; a veto; to vote down
否決權(ㄈㄡˇ ㄐㄩㄝˊ ㄑㄩㄢˊ)
veto power
否認(ㄈㄡˇ ㄖㄣˋ)
①to deny; to reject; to repudiate; to disown; to disclaim; to gainsay ②denial; rejection; repudiation; disavowal
否則(ㄈㄡˇ ㄗㄜˊ)
otherwise; or else; if not, then…

【否】 566 2. ㄆㄧˇ pii pǐ
evil; bad
否極泰來(ㄆㄧˇ ㄐㄧˊ ㄊㄞˋ ㄌㄞˊ)
Adversity, after reaching its extremity, is followed by felicity. 或 After extreme bad luck comes good luck.

【吩】 567 ㄈㄣ fen fēn
to instruct or direct (someone to do something)
吩咐(ㄈㄣ ·ㄈㄨ)
to instruct or direct (someone to do something); instructions or directions (to do something)

【含】 568 ㄏㄢˊ harn hán
1. to hold in the mouth
2. to contain; to include
3. to bear
含悲(ㄏㄢˊ ㄅㄟ)
to exercise restraint over grief
含苞待放(ㄏㄢˊ ㄅㄠ ㄉㄞˋ ㄈㄤˋ)
①(said of flowers) in a budding condition; in bud ②(said of girls in early teens) in the bud
含怒(ㄏㄢˊ ㄋㄨˋ)
in anger
含淚(ㄏㄢˊ ㄌㄟˋ)
with tears in the eyes
含量(ㄏㄢˊ ㄌㄧㄤˋ)
content
含垢忍辱(ㄏㄢˊ ㄍㄡˋ ㄖㄣˇ ㄖㄨˋ)
to bear shame and indignity; to endure disgrace and humiliations (with a noble purpose in mind)
含恨(ㄏㄢˊ ㄏㄣˋ)
to cherish resentment, disappointment, etc.
含糊(ㄏㄢˊ ·ㄏㄨ)or 含含糊糊(ㄏㄢˊ ㄏㄢˊ ㄏㄨˊ ㄏㄨˊ)or 含混(ㄏㄢˊ ㄏㄨㄣˋ)
(said of a statement, manners, etc.) vague; ambiguous; confusing; befuddling or uncertain
含糊了事(ㄏㄢˊ ㄏㄨˊ ㄌㄧㄠˇ ㄕˋ)
to settle the case carelessly
含糊其詞(ㄏㄢˊ ㄏㄨˊ ㄑㄧˊ ㄘˊ)
to talk ambiguously
含情脈脈(ㄏㄢˊ ㄑㄧㄥˊ ㄇㄛˋ ㄇㄛˋ)
full of tenderness (in silent communication of affection or love, especially said of young girls)
含笑(ㄏㄢˊ ㄒㄧㄠˋ)
①(botany) *Michelia figo* ②to smile; to grin; with a smile; smilingly
含笑九泉(ㄏㄢˊ ㄒㄧㄠˋ ㄐㄧㄡˇ ㄑㄩㄢˊ)or 含笑地下(ㄏㄢˊ ㄒㄧㄠˋ ㄉㄧˋ ㄒㄧㄚˋ)
to be able to smile in Hades—to die with satisfaction
含羞(ㄏㄢˊ ㄒㄧㄡ)
to wear a bashful expression; to blush
含羞草(ㄏㄢˊ ㄒㄧㄡ ㄘㄠˇ)
(botany) mimosa; the sensitive plant
含辛茹苦(ㄏㄢˊ ㄒㄧㄣ ㄖㄨˊ ㄎㄨˇ)
(said of women, especially widows, raising children) to undergo all sorts of hardships and deprivations
含蓄(ㄏㄢˊ ㄒㄩˋ)
with concealed or implied deep meanings
含血噴人(ㄏㄢˊ ㄒㄩㄝˋ ㄆㄣ ㄖㄣˊ)
to bring false accusations against others
含沙射影(ㄏㄢˊ ㄕㄚ ㄕㄜˋ ㄧㄥˇ)
to hurt others maliciously

含辱(ㄏㄢˊ ㄖㄨˇ)
to bear shame
含飴弄孫(ㄏㄢˊ ㄧˊ ㄋㄨㄥˋ ㄙㄨㄣ)
(literally) to eat sweets and play with grandchildren—to lead a carefree life in one's old age
含義(ㄏㄢˊ ㄧˋ)
a meaning; an implication
含英咀華(ㄏㄢˊ ㄧㄥ ㄐㄩˇ ㄏㄨㄚˊ)
to enjoy the beauty of words
含味(ㄏㄢˊ ㄨㄟˋ)
to fully enjoy (food, pleasure, etc.)
含冤(ㄏㄢˊ ㄩㄢ)
to be the victim of an unjust charge
含冤莫白(ㄏㄢˊ ㄩㄢ ㄇㄛˋ ㄅㄞˊ)
unable to clear oneself of a false accusation
含怨(ㄏㄢˊ ㄩㄢˋ)
to bear a grudge

【吮】 569 ㄕㄨㄣˇ shoen shǔn
to suck; to lick: 這個小男孩吮拇指。The little boy sucked his thumb.
吮墨(ㄕㄨㄣˇ ㄇㄛˋ)
to be deep in thought while writing
吮癰舐痔(ㄕㄨㄣˇ ㄩㄥ ㄕˋ ㄓˋ)
to practice sycophancy or servile flattery

【呈】 570 ㄔㄥˊ cherng chéng
1. to submit, present, or hand in (to a superior)
2. to show, manifest, expose, display, disclose, exhibit, etc.
3. a petition or appeal
呈報(ㄔㄥˊ ㄅㄠˋ)
to present or submit a report; to report (to a superior)
呈明(ㄔㄥˊ ㄇㄧㄥˊ)
to state (a case) clearly (to a superior)
呈露(ㄔㄥˊ ㄌㄨˋ)or 呈現(ㄔㄥˊ ㄒㄧㄢˋ)
to expose, disclose , display, exhibit, manifest, or show (something that has been hidden or unobvious); (said of something that has been hidden or unobvious) to become exposed; to come out to the surface
呈核(ㄔㄥˊ ㄏㄜˊ)
to submit (to higher authorities) for review
呈交(ㄔㄥˊ ㄐㄧㄠ)or 呈遞(ㄔㄥˊ ㄉㄧˋ)
to handle or submit (to higher authorities)
呈請(ㄔㄥˊ ㄑㄧㄥˇ)
(a phrase used in official communications to a higher agency to introduce a request) It is requested that....
呈現(ㄔㄥˊ ㄒㄧㄢˋ)
to present (a certain appearance); to appear; to emerge
呈獻(ㄔㄥˊ ㄒㄧㄢˋ)or 呈上(ㄔㄥˊ ㄕㄤˋ)
to present (to a superior)
呈祥(ㄔㄥˊ ㄒㄧㄤˊ)
(the appearance of something or phenomenon which is interpreted as) a sign of auspices
呈正 or 呈政(ㄔㄥˊ ㄓㄥˋ)
to present for correction
呈准(ㄔㄥˊ ㄓㄨㄣˇ)
presented (to a higher agency) for review and approval
呈送(ㄔㄥˊ ㄙㄨㄥˋ)
to forward or send (to a higher agency)
呈文(ㄔㄥˊ ㄨㄣˊ)
an official letter to a higher agency (from a lower agency or from the people); a petition; an appeal
呈閱(ㄔㄥˊ ㄩㄝˋ)
to submit (to a superior or higher agency) for perusal

【吳】 571 ㄨˊ wu wú
1. the name of a state in the Epoch of the Three Kingdoms
2. the name of a state in the Warring States period
3. a Chinese family name
吳鳳(ㄨˊ ㄈㄥˋ)
Wu Feng, (an official who, when head hunting was still common among the aborigines of Taiwan, ended the practice at the cost of his own life in 1768)
吳牛喘月(ㄨˊ ㄋㄧㄡˊ ㄔㄨㄢˇ ㄩㄝˋ)
(literally) The ox of Wu gasps from heat when it mistakes the moon for the sun.—to have an excess fear of something
吳儂軟語(ㄨˊ ㄋㄨㄥˊ ㄖㄨㄢˇ ㄩˇ)
the soft speech spoken by the people in the Shanghai-Soochow area (referring to the soft impression one gets from the Wu dialect)
吳郭魚(ㄨˊ ㄍㄨㄛ ㄩˊ)
a mouth breeder
吳國(ㄨˊ ㄍㄨㄛˊ)
the state of Wu in the Epoch of the Three Kingdoms or the one in the Epoch of Warring States
吳下阿蒙(ㄨˊ ㄒㄧㄚˋ ㄚ ㄇㄥˊ)
an ignorant person: 他已非昔日吳下阿蒙。He is no more an ignorant person.
吳語(ㄨˊ ㄩˇ)
the Wu dialect (of which the main representative is the Shanghai dialect)
吳越同舟(ㄨˊ ㄩㄝˋ ㄊㄨㄥˊ ㄓㄡ)
Even mortal enemies should help each other in the face of common danger.

【吵】 572 ㄔㄠˇ chao chǎo
1. to quarrel; to wrangle; to dispute; to row
2. to disturb; to annoy
吵鬧(ㄔㄠˇ ㄋㄠˋ)or 吵吵鬧鬧(ㄔㄠˇ ㄔㄠˇ ㄋㄠˋ ㄋㄠˋ)
to quarrel noisily; to brawl; noisy
吵架(ㄔㄠˇ ㄐㄧㄚˋ)
to quarrel; to brawl; to argue; to wrangle; to row
吵人(ㄔㄠˇ ㄖㄣˊ)
to disturb others (by noise)
吵嚷(ㄔㄠˇ ㄖㄤˇ)
to quarrel; to dispute; to brawl; to wrangle; to argue; to row
吵嘴(ㄔㄠˇ ㄗㄨㄟˇ)
to dispute; to have a verbal exchange (or quarrel); to wrangle

【吶】 573 ㄋㄚˋ nah nà
1. to shout
2. to speak hesitatingly
吶吶(ㄋㄚˋ ㄋㄚˋ)
to speak haltingly
吶喊(ㄋㄚˋ ㄏㄢˇ)

〔口部〕

〔口部〕

to give a whoop, or to shout (in a battle, etc.)

吶喊助威(ㄋㄚˋ ㄏㄢˇ ㄓㄨˋ ㄨㄟ)
to shout encouragement; to cheer

【吸】 574
ㄒㄧ shi xī
to absorb; to imbibe; to suck in; to attract; to draw; to inhale

吸盤(ㄒㄧ ㄆㄢˊ)
(zoology) sucking disks

吸墨紙(ㄒㄧ ㄇㄛˋ ㄓˇ)
blotting paper

吸附(ㄒㄧ ㄈㄨˋ)
(chemistry) adsorption

吸毒(ㄒㄧ ㄉㄨˊ)
to smoke opium; to become addicted to narcotics

吸毒者(ㄒㄧ ㄉㄨˊ ㄓㄜˇ)
a drug addict

吸鐵石(ㄒㄧ ㄊㄧㄝˇ ㄕˊ)
a loadstone (or lodestone)

吸力(ㄒㄧ ㄌㄧˋ)or 吸引力(ㄒㄧ ㄧㄣˇ ㄌㄧˋ)
① attraction ②(physics) gravitation

吸管(ㄒㄧ ㄍㄨㄢˇ)
① a pipette ② a straw

吸氣(ㄒㄧ ㄑㄧˋ)
to inhale

吸取(ㄒㄧ ㄑㄩˇ)
① to absorb (knowledge) ② to suck (liquids)

吸取教訓(ㄒㄧ ㄑㄩˇ ㄐㄧㄠˋ ㄒㄩㄣˋ)
to draw a lesson

吸血鬼(ㄒㄧ ㄒㄧㄝˇ ㄍㄨㄟˇ)
a vampire

吸塵器(ㄒㄧ ㄔㄣˊ ㄑㄧˋ)
a vacuum cleaner

吸食(ㄒㄧ ㄕˊ)
to suck; to take in

吸收(ㄒㄧ ㄕㄡ)
① to absorb; to take in ② to recruit or enlist

吸收游資(ㄒㄧ ㄕㄡ ㄧㄡˊ ㄗ)
to absorb idle funds

吸吮(ㄒㄧ ㄕㄨㄣˇ)
to suck; to absorb

吸熱(ㄒㄧ ㄖㄜˋ)
absorption of heat

吸二手菸(ㄒㄧ ㄦˋ ㄕㄡˇ ㄧㄢ)
passive smoking

吸煙(ㄒㄧ ㄧㄢ)
to smoke; smoking

吸煙區(ㄒㄧ ㄧㄢ ㄑㄩ)
a smoking area

吸煙室(ㄒㄧ ㄧㄢ ㄕˋ)
a smoking room

吸音(ㄒㄧ ㄧㄣ)
sound-absorbent

吸引(ㄒㄧ ㄧㄣˇ)
to attract; to draw: 磁石吸引鋼鐵。A magnet attracts steel.

吸蠅紙(ㄒㄧ ㄧㄥˊ ㄓˇ)
flypaper

【吹】 575
ㄔㄨㄟ chuei chuī
1. to blow; to puff
2. to brag or boast; to praise in exaggerated words
3. to break up

吹拍(ㄔㄨㄟ ㄆㄞ)or 吹捧(ㄔㄨㄟ ㄆㄥˇ)
to boast (before equals or inferiors) and to flatter (superiors)

吹毛求疵(ㄔㄨㄟ ㄇㄠˊ ㄑㄧㄡˊ ㄘ)
(literally) to blow apart the hair to find defects—to go out of the way to discover another's weak points; to engage in faultfinding

吹法螺(ㄔㄨㄟ ㄈㄚˇ ㄌㄨㄛˊ)
to brag; to boast

吹風(ㄔㄨㄟ ㄈㄥ)
① to be in a draught; to catch a chill ② to dry (hair, etc.) with a blower

吹風機(ㄔㄨㄟ ㄈㄥ ㄐㄧ)
a blower; a drier

吹拂(ㄔㄨㄟ ㄈㄨˊ)
(said of winds, etc.) to move or wave (grass, branches, etc.); to sway

吹打(ㄔㄨㄟ ㄉㄚˇ)or 吹吹打打(ㄔㄨㄟ ㄔㄨㄟ ㄉㄚˇ ㄉㄚˇ)
to make music by blowing and beating; to play music

吹笛(ㄔㄨㄟ ㄉㄧˊ)
to play the flute

吹彈(ㄔㄨㄟ ㄊㄢˊ)
to make music by blowing wind instruments and plucking at string instruments; to play music

吹牛(ㄔㄨㄟ ㄋㄧㄡˊ)
to brag; to boast

吹牛拍馬(ㄔㄨㄟ ㄋㄧㄡˊ ㄆㄞ ㄇㄚˇ)
to boast and flatter

吹喇叭(ㄔㄨㄟ ㄌㄚˇ ˙ㄅㄚ)
to blow the trumpet

吹了(ㄔㄨㄟ ˙ㄌㄜ)
busted; to have failed; to have ended in a flop

吹鼓手(ㄔㄨㄟ ㄍㄨˇ ㄕㄡˇ)
① the trumpeters and drummers (of a band) ② musicians (of small bands of low rating)

吹管(ㄔㄨㄟ ㄍㄨㄢˇ)
a blowpipe

吹口哨(ㄔㄨㄟ ㄎㄡˇ ㄕㄠˋ)
to whistle: 不要在教堂裏吹口哨。Don't whistle in the church.

吹號(ㄔㄨㄟ ㄏㄠˋ)
to blow the bugle: 他很會吹號。He blows his bugle well.

吹呼(ㄔㄨㄟ ㄏㄨ)
to bawl at; to give a scolding

吹鬍子瞪眼(ㄔㄨㄟ ㄏㄨˊ ˙ㄗ ㄉㄥˋ ㄧㄢˇ)
to foam at the mouth and glare with rage

吹灰之力(ㄔㄨㄟ ㄏㄨㄟ ㄓ ㄌㄧˋ)
strength as little as that needed for blowing dust away

吹簫(ㄔㄨㄟ ㄒㄧㄠ)
① to play the vertical flute ② to go begging

吹噓(ㄔㄨㄟ ㄒㄩ)
to recommend or praise (a person) in exaggerated words

吹哨子(ㄔㄨㄟ ㄕㄠˋ ˙ㄗ)
to blow the whistle: 裁判吹哨子。The referee blew his whistle.

吹奏(ㄔㄨㄟ ㄗㄡˋ)
to play (wind instruments)

【吻】 576
ㄨㄣˇ woen wěn
1. the lip
2. the tone of one's speech
3. to kiss; a kiss

吻別(ㄨㄣˇ ㄅㄧㄝˊ)
to kiss someone good-bye

吻合(ㄨㄣˇ ㄏㄜˊ)
(said of two things) to agree, correspond, match, or tally with: 他所說的和事實吻合。His account tallies with the fact.

【吼】 577
ㄏㄡˇ hoou hǒu
(said of beasts) to roar or howl

【吱】 578
ㄗ tzy zī

squeaky cries of an animal
吱喳(ㄗ ㄔㄚ)
chatter (made by birds or animals)
吱吱(ㄗ ㄗ)
(to cry) in a squeak; squeaking sounds (made by insects)

【吾】 579
ㄨˊ wu wú
1. I, me, we, or us (in literary usage)
2. my; our
吾黨(ㄨˊ ㄉㄤˇ)
my fellows
吾弟(ㄨˊ ㄉㄧˋ)
my younger brother
吾兄(ㄨˊ ㄒㄩㄥ)
① my elder brother ②(courteous among friends) you
吾儕(ㄨˊ ㄔㄞˊ)or 吾曹(ㄨˊ ㄘㄠˊ)or 吾輩(ㄨˊ ㄅㄟˋ)or 吾等(ㄨˊ ㄉㄥˇ)
we; us
吾人(ㄨˊ ㄖㄣˊ)
we
吾子(ㄨˊ ㄗˇ)
① you; sir ② my son
吾愛(ㄨˊ ㄞˋ)
my love; my darling
吾友(ㄨˊ ㄧㄡˇ)
my friend

【告】 580
ㄍㄠˋ gaw gào
1. to tell; to inform; to report: 我把我的名字告訴他。I told him my name.
2. to accuse
告白(ㄍㄠˋ ㄅㄞˊ)
a notice; an announcement
告別(ㄍㄠˋ ㄅㄧㄝˊ)
to bid farewell; to say goodbye; to take leave; to announce one's departure
告窆(ㄍㄠˋ ㄅㄧㄢˇ)
a written announcement of a burial
告稟(ㄍㄠˋ ㄅㄧㄥˇ)
to file a petition; to request from a superior
告病(ㄍㄠˋ ㄅㄧㄥˋ)
to resign because of illness; to ask for extended sick leave
告密(ㄍㄠˋ ㄇㄧˋ)
to give a tip, or a piece of secret information (to some authorities); to tip off; to inform against somebody
告廟(ㄍㄠˋ ㄇㄧㄠˋ)
(said of an emperor) to report major state decisions or great events at the imperial ancestral temple
告發(ㄍㄠˋ ㄈㄚ)
to accuse or charge (someone) in a (written or verbal) report to the authorities; to inform against
告乏(ㄍㄠˋ ㄈㄚˊ)
to run out of supply
告貸(ㄍㄠˋ ㄉㄞˋ)
to ask for a loan
告貸無門(ㄍㄠˋ ㄉㄞˋ ㄨˊ ㄇㄣˊ)
to have no one to turn to for a loan
告退(ㄍㄠˋ ㄊㄨㄟˋ)
① to resign ② to withdraw; to leave the scene
告老還鄉(ㄍㄠˋ ㄌㄠˇ ㄏㄨㄢˊ ㄒㄧㄤ)
to retire on account of old age and return to one's native place
告歸(ㄍㄠˋ ㄍㄨㄟ)
to go home on leave; to ask for leave to go home
告急(ㄍㄠˋ ㄐㄧˊ)
in urgent need of help; in a state of emergency; critical; in danger
告假(ㄍㄠˋ ㄐㄧㄚˋ)
to ask for leave of absence
告訐(ㄍㄠˋ ㄐㄧㄝˊ)
to expose (other's secrets)
告捷(ㄍㄠˋ ㄐㄧㄝˊ)
to emerge victorious; to triumph; to win a victory: 他們首戰告捷。They won a victory in the first battle.
告解(ㄍㄠˋ ㄐㄧㄝˇ)
(Catholicism) to confess; confession
告誡(ㄍㄠˋ ㄐㄧㄝˋ)
to admonish; to warn; to caution; to exhort
告警(ㄍㄠˋ ㄐㄧㄥˇ)
to alert; to issue a distress call
告竣(ㄍㄠˋ ㄐㄩㄣˋ)
to be completed; to be ready for inauguration (as a building)
告罄(ㄍㄠˋ ㄑㄧㄥˋ)
(said of a supply) to run out or become exhausted: 瓦斯告罄。Gas has run out.
告知(ㄍㄠˋ ㄓ)
to let know; to notify; to inform
告狀(ㄍㄠˋ ㄓㄨㄤˋ)
① to file a lawsuit ②(colloquial) to say something bad against a colleague, fellow student, etc. before a superior; to speak ill of
告終(ㄍㄠˋ ㄓㄨㄥ)
to come to an end or a close; to end
告成(ㄍㄠˋ ㄔㄥˊ)
to be completed or accomplished
告吹(ㄍㄠˋ ㄔㄨㄟ)
to fizzle out; to fail
告示
①(ㄍㄠˋ ㄕˋ)to make known; to announce; to proclaim; to give notice
②(ㄍㄠˋ ˙ㄕ)an official notice, announcement, or proclamation
告饒(ㄍㄠˋ ㄖㄠˊ)
to seek pardon; to apologize
告擾(ㄍㄠˋ ㄖㄠˇ)
to thank the host for hospitality (after a party, etc.)
告罪(ㄍㄠˋ ㄗㄨㄟˋ)
① to admit a mistake; to apologize for a mistake ② to announce the crimes (of the accused)
告辭(ㄍㄠˋ ㄘˊ)
to take leave; to say goodbye; to bid farewell: 他向朋友們告辭。He took leave of his friends.
告喪(ㄍㄠˋ ㄙㄤ)
to announce a bereavement
告訴
①(ㄍㄠˋ ㄙㄨˋ)to file a lawsuit, or a legal complaint
②(ㄍㄠˋ ˙ㄙㄨ)to tell (a person); to let know
告訴乃論(ㄍㄠˋ ㄙㄨˋ ㄋㄞˇ ㄌㄨㄣˋ)
Prosecution for an offense may be instituted only upon complaint.
告一段落(ㄍㄠˋ ㄧˊ ㄉㄨㄢˋ ㄌㄨㄛˋ)
to draw a conclusion (often referring to a temporary conclusion)
告諭(ㄍㄠˋ ㄩˋ)
to counsel; to advise; to

〔口部〕

〔口部〕

exhort

【呀】 581
1. ㄧㄚ ia yā
a creaking sound

呀然一聲(ㄧㄚ ㄖㄢˊ ㄧˋ ㄕㄥ)
(said of a door) to fling open with a creaking sound

【呀】 581
2. •ㄧㄚ •ia ya

1. a particle used after a phrase for emphasis, expressing surprise, etc.: 她是誰呀? Who is she?
2. to gape (as in surprise): 呀! 毛病在此。Ah! That is the trouble.

【呃】 582
ㄜˋ eh è
to hiccup or hiccough

【呂】 583
ㄌㄩˇ leu lǚ
a Chinese family name

呂宋(ㄌㄩˇ ㄙㄨㄥˋ)
Luzon (the chief island of the Philippines)

【呆】 584
ㄉㄞ dai dāi
(又讀 ㄞˊ air ái)

1. dull; dull-witted; stupid; unintelligent
2. blank; wooden

呆板(ㄉㄞ ㄅㄢˇ)
① boring; dull; monotonous; unvarying ② stiff

呆笨(ㄉㄞ ㄅㄣˋ)or(ㄞˊ ㄅㄣˋ)
stupid; dull-witted; dull; unintelligent

呆頭呆腦(ㄉㄞ ㄊㄡˊ ㄉㄞ ㄋㄠˇ)
stupid; idiot-like

呆滯(ㄉㄞ ㄓˋ)
dull

呆賬 or 呆帳(ㄉㄞ ㄓㄤˋ)
irrecoverable loans or credits; a bad debt

呆若木鷄(ㄉㄞ ㄖㄨㄛˋ ㄇㄨˋ ㄐㄧ)
(literally) as dull as a wooden chicken—very dull or stupid; dumbstruck; transfixed (with fear or amazement); standing like a log

呆子(ㄉㄞ •ㄗ)or 呆人(ㄉㄞ ㄖㄣˊ)
an idiot; a dullard; a mentally retarded person

【呎】 585
ㄔˇ chyy chǐ
the foot (a unit of length in English measure)

呎磅(ㄔˇ ㄅㄤˋ)
a foot-pound

【吧】 586
1. •ㄅㄚ •ba ba
a particle used after an imperative sentence: 我們走吧。Let's go. 不會吧! I don't think it could be that.

【吧】 586
2. ㄅㄚ ba bā
參看「吧吧」

吧吧(ㄅㄚ ㄅㄚ)
loquacious

吧嗒(ㄅㄚ •ㄉㄚ)
① to smack one's lips (in surprise, alarm, etc.) ②(dialect) to pull at (a pipe, etc.)

吧孃(ㄅㄚ ㄋㄧㄤˊ)
a bar girl

五畫

【呢】 587
1. ㄋㄧˊ ni ní

1. a woolen fabric
2. a murmur

呢帽(ㄋㄧˊ ㄇㄠˋ)
a woolen hat

呢喃(ㄋㄧˊ ㄋㄢˊ)
① the chirps of the swallows ② to murmur; to twitter

呢料子(ㄋㄧˊ ㄌㄧㄠˋ •ㄗ)
woolen materials; woolen cloth

呢絨(ㄋㄧˊ ㄖㄨㄥˊ)
a general term for woolen materials; a wool fabric; woolen goods

【呢】 587
2. •ㄋㄜ •ne ne
an interrogative or emphatic particle used after a sentence: 他錯在那兒呢? What has he done wrong? 那人究竟是誰呢? Who in the world is that fellow?

【周】 588
ㄓㄡ jou zhōu

1. the Chou Dynasty
2. a circumference; a circuit: 運動員繞場一周。The athletes made a circuit of the arena.
3. complete
4. all around; everywhere
5. to aid; to provide for
6. a Chinese family name

周報(ㄓㄡ ㄅㄠˋ)or 周刊(ㄓㄡ ㄎㄢ)
a weekly

周邊(ㄓㄡ ㄅㄧㄢ)
a periphery

周遍(ㄓㄡ ㄅㄧㄢˋ)
all round; all over

周末(ㄓㄡ ㄇㄛˋ)
the weekend

周密(ㄓㄡ ㄇㄧˋ)
careful and thorough; attentive to every detail

周到(ㄓㄡ ㄉㄠˋ)or 周至(ㄓㄡ ㄓˋ)
thorough; considerate; thoughtful: 你把他也請去，眞是顧慮周到。You were considerate to invite him too.

周年(ㄓㄡ ㄋㄧㄢˊ)
an anniversary; a full year

周率(ㄓㄡ ㄌㄩˋ)
①(radio) a frequency ②(electricity) a cycle

周公(ㄓㄡ ㄍㄨㄥ)
the Duke of Chou (the brother of King Wu, first ruler of the Chou Dynasty)

周濟 or 賙濟(ㄓㄡ ㄐㄧˋ)
to help the poor with money: 他必須周濟貧困的親戚。He has to help his relatives, who are very poor.

周期(ㄓㄡ ㄑㄧˊ)
a period; a cycle

周期性(ㄓㄡ ㄑㄧˊ ㄒㄧㄥˋ)
periodicity; cyclicity

周全(ㄓㄡ ㄑㄩㄢˊ)
① to aid; to help ② complete with all that is desired

周詳(ㄓㄡ ㄒㄧㄤˊ)
complete and detailed; every detail taken care of or considered

周旋(ㄓㄡ ㄒㄩㄢˊ)
① to attend to guests or friends ② to deal with; to contend with; to fight

周旋到底(ㄓㄡ ㄒㄩㄢˊ ㄉㄠˋ ㄉㄧˇ)
(said of litigation, quarrels, etc.) to fight to the end

周知(ㄓㄡ ㄓ)
generally known; public knowledge: 他是衆所周知的人物。He is known to everybody.

周折(ㄓㄡ ㄓㄜˊ)
a complicated or troublesome course of development; trouble; complication: 這事恐怕要費一番周折。I'm afraid this business will cause us a

good deal of trouble.

周章(ㄓㄡ ㄓㄤ)
①to lose composure; to be confused; to show bewilderment ②trouble: 此事煞費周章。This matter takes a lot of trouble.

周轉不靈(ㄓㄡ ㄓㄨㄢˇ ㄅㄨˋ ㄌㄧㄥˊ)
(said of business firms) to be in financial straits; cash to be not available: 他周轉不靈。He doesn't have enough cash to answer needs.

周長(ㄓㄡ ㄔㄤˊ)
the girth; the circumference; the perimeter

周身(ㄓㄡ ㄕㄣ)
all over the body

周匝(ㄓㄡ ㄗㄚ)
in one round

周遭(ㄓㄡ ㄗㄠ)
around

周歲(ㄓㄡ ㄙㄨㄟˋ)or 周晬(ㄓㄡ ㄗㄨㄟˋ)
one full year of life; the first anniversary of a child

周而復始(ㄓㄡ ㄦˊ ㄈㄨˋ ㄕˇ)
to repeat the process again and again

周易(ㄓㄡ ㄧˋ)
the *Book of Changes,* one of the Five Classics

周遊(ㄓㄡ ㄧㄡˊ)
to make a tour in search of adventures, enjoyments, etc.

周遊列國(ㄓㄡ ㄧㄡˊ ㄌㄧㄝˋ ㄍㄨㄛˊ)
to tour the various states (especially referring to the tour of Confucius)

周圍(ㄓㄡ ㄨㄟˊ)
①surroundings; environment ②the circumference (of a round object): 這棵樹周圍有六英尺。This tree has a circumference of six feet.

【咒】 589
ㄓㄡˋ jow zhòu

1. to curse; to swear: 你在咒什麼? What are you swearing at?
2. words used as charms by Buddhist monks or Taoist priests to exorcize ghosts

咒罵(ㄓㄡˋ ㄇㄚˋ)
to swear at; to curse; to call (a person) names

咒詛(ㄓㄡˋ ㄗㄨˇ)
to curse; to swear at

咒語(ㄓㄡˋ ㄩˇ)
①curses; imprecations ②exorcism; incantation ③hocus-pocus

【咎】 590
ㄐㄧㄡˋ jiow jiù

1. a disaster; a calamity
2. a fault; a mistake
3. to blame; to punish; to censure: 別歸咎他人。Don't lay the blame on anybody else.

咎責(ㄐㄧㄡˋ ㄗㄜˊ)
to be blamed for one's own faults

咎由自取(ㄐㄧㄡˋ ㄧㄡˊ ㄗˋ ㄑㄩˇ)
a trouble of one's own making

咎有應得(ㄐㄧㄡˋ ㄧㄡˇ ㄧㄥ ㄉㄜˊ)
The punishment is well deserved.

【呱】 591
ㄍㄨ gu gū
(語音 ㄨㄚ ua wā)

1. the cries of an infant
2. to wail

呱呱墜地(ㄍㄨ ㄍㄨ ㄓㄨㄟˋ ㄉㄧˋ)
(said of a baby) to come into this world; to raise the first cry of life: 嬰兒呱呱墜地。The baby came into the world with a cry.

呱呱叫(ㄍㄨ ㄍㄨ ㄐㄧㄠˋ) or (ㄨㄚ ㄨㄚ ㄐㄧㄠˋ)
tiptop; topnotch

【味】 592
ㄨㄟˋ wey wèi

1. a taste; a flavor
2. a smell; an odor
3. a delicacy; a dainty

味道(ㄨㄟˋ ㄉㄠˋ)or 味兒(ㄨㄜˋㄦ)
①a taste; a flavor: 我不喜歡這肉的味道。I don't like the taste of this meat. ②a smell ③a feeling: 我心裡有一股說不出的味道。I have an indescribable feeling.

味同嚼蠟(ㄨㄟˋ ㄊㄨㄥˊ ㄐㄩㄝˊ ㄌㄚˋ)
to taste as chewing wax—to be insipid

味蕾(ㄨㄟˋ ㄌㄟˇ)
a taste bud

味精(ㄨㄟˋ ㄐㄧㄥ)
flavor essence; gourmet powder; monosodium glutamate

味覺(ㄨㄟˋ ㄐㄩㄝˊ)
the sense of taste; gustation: 他有敏銳的味覺。He has a keen sense of taste.

【呵】 593
1. ㄏㄜ he hē

1. to scold in a loud voice
2. to yawn

呵呵大笑(ㄏㄜ ㄏㄜ ㄉㄚˋ ㄒㄧㄠˋ)
to roar with laughter; to guffaw; to laugh loudly; to cackle: 每講完一個笑話，老人家就呵呵大笑。The old man cackled after each joke.

呵欠(ㄏㄜ ㄑㄧㄢˋ)
to yawn and to stretch

呵斥 or 呵叱(ㄏㄜ ㄔˋ)or 呵責(ㄏㄜ ㄗㄜˊ)
to scold in a loud voice; to thunder against; to berate

呵手(ㄏㄜ ㄕㄡˇ)
to breathe on one's hands (to warm them)

呵一口氣(ㄏㄜ ㄧˋ ㄎㄡˇ ㄑㄧˋ)
to give a puff

【呵】 593
2. ˙ㄛ ·o o

a particle used after a phrase to express surprise: 這小伙子眞棒呵! Oh, what a fine young boy!

【咕】 594
ㄍㄨ gu gū

1. to murmur
2. (said of hens) a cluck; (said of turtledoves, etc.) a coo

咕嘟着嘴(ㄍㄨ ˙ㄉㄨ ˙ㄓㄜ ㄗㄨㄟˇ)
to keep the mouth firmly closed in anger

咕咚(ㄍㄨ ㄉㄨㄥ)
the sound of impact caused by a falling object; a thumping sound: 他咕咚一聲掉到水裡去了。He fell into the water with a thumping sound.

咕噥(ㄍㄨ ˙ㄋㄨㄥ)
to murmur; to mutter; to whisper

咕嚕(ㄍㄨ ˙ㄌㄨ)
①a mumbled sound or an indistinct utterance ②the rumbling sound in the belly

咕隆(ㄍㄨ ˙ㄌㄨㄥ)
to rumble; to rattle; to roll: 卡車在公路上咕隆咕隆地跑着。The truck rattled along the highway.

咕唧
①(ㄍㄨ ㄐㄧ) to squelch: 農人在稻田裡咕唧地走着。The farmer squelched up and down the paddy fields.

〔口部〕

②(ㄍㄨ ˙ㄐㄧ) to murmur; to whisper: 他們兩人一直在咕唧著。They whispered to each other all the while.

【咂】 595
ㄗㄚ tza zā
to take in food with the tongue; to suck; to sip: 那老人正在咂酒。The old man was sipping at the wine.

咂乾(ㄗㄚ ㄍㄢ)
to suck dry

咂嘴(ㄗㄚ ㄗㄨㄟˇ)or 咂嘴兒(ㄗㄚ ㄗㄨㄜˇㄦ)
to click the tongue (to express admiration or envy)

【咚】 596
ㄉㄨㄥ dong dōng
1. the sound of impact caused by a falling object
2. rub-a-dub
3. rat-tat; rat-a-tat

【呻】 597
ㄕㄣ shen shēn
to groan; to moan

呻吟(ㄕㄣ ㄧㄣˊ)
to groan; to moan: 你們爲什麼無病呻吟? Why do you moan and groan without being ill?

【呼】 598
ㄏㄨ hu hū
1. to call; to cry
2. to exhale: 夜裡植物呼出二氧化碳。At night plants exhale carbon dioxide.

呼朋引類(ㄏㄨ ㄆㄥˊ ㄧㄣˇ ㄌㄟˋ)
to call friends and fellows together (used in a deprecatory sense to indicate bad company)

呼風喚雨(ㄏㄨ ㄈㄥ ㄏㄨㄢˋ ㄩˇ)
①(of immortals with divine power) to summon wind and rain ② to stir up trouble

呼天搶地(ㄏㄨ ㄊㄧㄢ ㄑㄧㄤˇ ㄉㄧˋ)
to cry bitterly and loudly in excessive grief

呼痛(ㄏㄨ ㄊㄨㄥˋ)
to cry out in pain

呼盧喝雉(ㄏㄨ ㄌㄨˊ ㄏㄜˋ ㄓˋ)
(in gambling) to shout for the top number to come up

呼口號(ㄏㄨ ㄎㄡˇ ㄏㄠˋ)
to shout slogans

呼號
①(ㄏㄨ ㄏㄠˊ)to cry; to wail: 風在呼號。The wind wails.
②(ㄏㄨ ㄏㄠˋ)to call the sign (of a message sent by radio)

呼喊(ㄏㄨ ㄏㄢˇ)
to yell; to shout: 他們異口同聲地呼喊。They shouted as with one voice.

呼呼(ㄏㄨ ㄏㄨ)
① the howling of winds ② the regular breathing sound of a heavy sleeper: 他呼呼大睡。He sleeps sound.

呼喚(ㄏㄨ ㄏㄨㄢˋ)
to call; to shout; to cry out: 這小孩的母親在呼喚他。The boy was called by his mother.

呼叫(ㄏㄨ ㄐㄧㄠˋ)
to shout; to cry out; to yell

呼叫器(ㄏㄨ ㄐㄧㄠˋ ㄑㄧˋ)
a pager; a beeper

呼救(ㄏㄨ ㄐㄧㄡˋ)
to cry for help; to call for help; to send out a distress signal: 我聽到呼救聲。I heard a call for help.

呼氣(ㄏㄨ ㄑㄧˋ)
exhalation; expiration; to expire; to exhale

呼吸(ㄏㄨ ㄒㄧ)
① to breathe; to inhale and exhale ② breathing; inhalation and exhalation; breath: 他呼吸急促。He was short of breath.

呼吸道(ㄏㄨ ㄒㄧ ㄉㄠˋ)
the respiratory tract

呼吸器官(ㄏㄨ ㄒㄧ ㄑㄧˋ ㄍㄨㄢ)
the respiratory organs

呼吸系統(ㄏㄨ ㄒㄧ ㄒㄧˋ ㄊㄨㄥˇ)
the respiratory system

呼嘯(ㄏㄨ ㄒㄧㄠˋ)
to roar or howl (like a beast); to whistle; to whiz: 汽車從我們身旁呼嘯而過。The car whizzed past us.

呼之欲出(ㄏㄨ ㄓ ㄩˋ ㄔㄨ)
① obvious; almost certain (said of the identity of a person who remains behind the scene or a criminal suspect against whom no evidence has yet been found) ②(said of lifelike figures in pictures or characters in novels) to seem ready to come out at one's call—to be vividly portrayed

呼叱(ㄏㄨ ㄔˋ)
to shout at (someone): 不要對我呼叱。Don't shout at me.

呼聲(ㄏㄨ ㄕㄥ)
loud cries

呼聲甚高(ㄏㄨ ㄕㄥ ㄕㄣˋ ㄍㄠ)
There are wide speculations (about political candidates, government appointments, etc.).

呼么喝六(ㄏㄨ ㄧㄠ ㄏㄜˋ ㄌㄧㄡˋ)
the noisy shouting in a dice game

呼應(ㄏㄨ ㄧㄥˋ)
to act in coordination with each other; to echo: 他們遙相呼應。They echo each other over a distance.

呼籲(ㄏㄨ ㄩˋ)
to (formally) call for (action, efforts, etc.); to appeal; to petition

【命】 599
ㄇㄧㄥˋ minq mìng
1. life: 醫生救了他的性命。The doctor saved his life.
2. a fate; destiny; a lot
3. the ordinances of Heaven
4. orders; a command

命薄如花(ㄇㄧㄥˋ ㄅㄛˊ ㄖㄨˊ ㄏㄨㄚ)
(said of a woman) to have lived a life as short of blessings as that of an evanescent flower

命不該絕(ㄇㄧㄥˋ ㄅㄨˋ ㄍㄞ ㄐㄩㄝˊ)
(said of one who has had a narrow escape from death) not destined to die

命脈(ㄇㄧㄥˋ ㄇㄛˋ)
(literally) life and artery—(figuratively) a lifeline; lifeblood; a matter of great importance: 外貿是台灣的命脈。Foreign trade is the lifeline of Taiwan.

命名(ㄇㄧㄥˋ ㄇㄧㄥˊ)
to give a name to; to name, christen, baptize, or dub

命婦(ㄇㄧㄥˋ ㄈㄨˋ)
a woman in ancient China who was given a title or rank by the emperor

命定(ㄇㄧㄥˋ ㄉㄧㄥˋ)
predestined; destined: 他命定客死異國。He was predestined to die in a foreign country.

命題(ㄇㄧㄥˋ ㄊㄧˊ)
① a proposition (in logic) ② to prepare examination

questions ③ to name a topic or subject on which the students are asked to write a composition

命途多舛(ㄇㄧㄥˋ ㄊㄨˊ ㄉㄨㄛ ㄔㄨㄢˇ)
Life is full of frustrations.

命令(ㄇㄧㄥˋ ㄌㄧㄥˋ)
a command; orders; an injunction; directions; a directive; to order; to command; to direct; to instruct: 哨兵命令他止步。The sentry commanded him to halt.

命令句(ㄇㄧㄥˋ ㄌㄧㄥˋ ㄐㄩˋ)
an imperative sentence

命該如此(ㄇㄧㄥˋ ㄍㄞ ㄖㄨˊ ㄘˇ)
It's predestined. (an expression of resignation)

命根(ㄇㄧㄥˋ ㄍㄣ)
①the stem (of a plant) ② lifeblood; a life-giver ③one's most beloved (usually said of a favorite child)

命苦(ㄇㄧㄥˋ ㄎㄨˇ)
to suffer from a hard lot; destined to suffer: 他命苦。His lot has been a hard one.

命中註定(ㄇㄧㄥˋ ㄓㄨㄥ ㄓㄨˋ ㄉㄧㄥˋ)
(said of individuals) predestined

命中(ㄇㄧㄥˋ ㄓㄨㄥˋ)
to hit the target

命世之才(ㄇㄧㄥˋ ㄕˋ ㄓ ㄘㄞˊ)
a person whose ability is superior to his contemporaries

命在旦夕(ㄇㄧㄥˋ ㄗㄞˋ ㄉㄢˋ ㄒㄧˋ)
Death may come (to a person) any minute.

命案(ㄇㄧㄥˋ ㄢˋ)
a case of murder or homicide

命運(ㄇㄧㄥˋ ㄩㄣˋ)
a fate; destiny; a lot; fortune: 命運操之在己。Every man is the architect of his own fortune.

【咀】 600
ㄐㄩˇ jeu jǔ
to chew; to masticate

咀嚼(ㄐㄩˇ ㄐㄩㄝˊ)
① to chew; to masticate: 你必須在吞嚥前細細咀嚼。You have to chew thoroughly before swallowing. ② to dwell on (a word, sentence, passage, etc.) in order to fully appreciate or understand its meaning

【咄】 601
ㄉㄨㄛˋ duoh duò
1. an angry cry
2. to scold in a loud voice

咄咄逼人(ㄉㄨㄛˋ ㄉㄨㄛˋ ㄅㄧ ㄖㄣˊ)
① to overwhelm with awe or fear; to browbeat ② overbearing

咄咄怪事(ㄉㄨㄛˋ ㄉㄨㄛˋ ㄍㄨㄞˋ ㄕˋ)
What a queer story! 或 What a strange phenomenon!

【咆】 602
ㄆㄠˊ paur páo
to roar

咆哮(ㄆㄠˊ ㄒㄧㄠ)
①(said of a lion, tiger, etc.) to roar ②(said of winds, waves, etc.) to bluster ③ (said of a person) to rage

【咋】 603
1. ㄓㄚˋ jah zhà
all of a sudden; suddenly

【咋】 603
2. ㄗㄜˊ tzer zé
1. to bite; to gnaw
2. a loud noise

咋舌(ㄗㄜˊ ㄕㄜˊ)
to bite the tongue—to show one's surprise or regret

【和】 604
1. ㄏㄜˊ her hé
1. harmony; harmonious
2. peace; peaceful
3. to be affable
4. the sum or aggregate
5. of Japan
6. and (語音ㄏㄢˋ): 他和我是好友。He and I are good friends.

和盤托出(ㄏㄜˊ ㄆㄢˊ ㄊㄨㄛ ㄔㄨ)
to reveal the whole truth; to disclose the entire fact: 我打算把事實眞相和盤托出。I intend to reveal the whole truth.

和平(ㄏㄜˊ ㄆㄧㄥˊ)
① peace ② peaceful; mild (such as the weather, etc.)

和平條約(ㄏㄜˊ ㄆㄧㄥˊ ㄊㄧㄠˊ ㄩㄝ)
the treaty of peace

和平攻勢(ㄏㄜˊ ㄆㄧㄥˊ ㄍㄨㄥ ㄕˋ)
a peace offensive

和平共存(ㄏㄜˊ ㄆㄧㄥˊ ㄍㄨㄥˋ ㄘㄨㄣˊ)
peaceful coexistence; to coexist peacefully

和平會議(ㄏㄜˊ ㄆㄧㄥˊ ㄏㄨㄟˋ ㄧˋ)
a peace conference

和平主義(ㄏㄜˊ ㄆㄧㄥˊ ㄓㄨˇ ㄧˋ)
pacifism

和鳴(ㄏㄜˊ ㄇㄧㄥˊ)
to sound in harmony

和睦(ㄏㄜˊ ㄇㄨˋ)
to have friendly ties; to be on friendly terms; to be at peace

和風(ㄏㄜˊ ㄈㄥ)
a gentle breeze

和服(ㄏㄜˊ ㄈㄨˊ)
a (Japanese) kimono

和談(ㄏㄜˊ ㄊㄢˊ)
peace talks

和暖(ㄏㄜˊ ㄋㄨㄢˇ)
(said of the weather or climate) mild and warm

和好(ㄏㄜˊ ㄏㄠˇ)
① to be on friendly terms; to maintain friendly relations ② to make up: 他們於爭吵後握手和好。After their quarrel, they shook hands and made it up.

和會(ㄏㄜˊ ㄏㄨㄟˋ)
a peace conference

和解(ㄏㄜˊ ㄐㄧㄝˇ)
to be reconciled; to settle differences; to reach an amiable settlement; reconciliation; a friendly or amicable settlement

和解政策(ㄏㄜˊ ㄐㄧㄝˇ ㄓㄥˋ ㄘㄜˋ)
détente policy

和姦(ㄏㄜˊ ㄐㄧㄢ)
fornication

和局(ㄏㄜˊ ㄐㄩˊ)
(said of a contest) a tie or a draw

和棋(ㄏㄜˊ ㄑㄧˊ)
a chess game that ends in a tie or draw

和氣(ㄏㄜˊ ·ㄑㄧ) or 和和氣氣(ㄏㄜˊ ㄏㄜˊ ㄑㄧˋ ㄑㄧˋ)
gentle; affable; agreeable; friendly; cordial; good-natured

和氣致祥(ㄏㄜˊ ㄑㄧˋ ㄓˋ ㄒㄧㄤˊ)
Good-naturedness leads to propitiousness.

和氣生財(ㄏㄜˊ ㄑㄧˋ ㄕㄥ ㄘㄞˊ)
(literally) Good-naturedness is a source of wealth.—A good-natured person has good chances to get rich.

和洽(ㄏㄜˊ ㄑㄧㄚˋ)

〔口部〕

〔口部〕

congenial; harmonious
和親(ㄏㄜˊ ㄑㄧㄣ)
①to be friendly and intimate with each other ②to make peace by a marriage between the royal families of two opposing states
和協(ㄏㄜˊ ㄒㄧㄝˊ)
to act in concert; to cooperate harmoniously
和諧(ㄏㄜˊ ㄒㄧㄝˊ)
harmonious; in harmony; harmony
和弦(ㄏㄜˊ ㄒㄧㄢˊ)
(music) a chord
和煦(ㄏㄜˊ ㄒㄩˇ)
mild and warm: 天氣和煦。It is mild and warm.
和衷共濟(ㄏㄜˊ ㄓㄨㄥ ㄍㄨㄥˋ ㄐㄧˋ)
to be united and to work in concert
和暢(ㄏㄜˊ ㄔㄤˋ)
agreeable; pleasant; cheery
和事老(ㄏㄜˊ ㄕˋ ㄌㄠˇ)
a mediator; a peacemaker
和善(ㄏㄜˊ ㄕㄢˋ)
kind and gentle; genial
和尚(ㄏㄜˊ ㄕㄤˋ)
a Buddhist monk
和聲(ㄏㄜˊ ㄕㄥ)
(music) harmony
和聲學(ㄏㄜˊ ㄕㄥ ㄒㄩㄝˊ)
harmonics
和聲樂器(ㄏㄜˊ ㄕㄥ ㄩㄝˋ ㄑㄧˋ)
a harmonic instrument
和數(ㄏㄜˊ ㄕㄨˋ)
the sum or aggregate (of an addition in arithmetic)
和順(ㄏㄜˊ ㄕㄨㄣˋ)
civil and obliging; amiable; complaisant; compliant
和菜(ㄏㄜˊ ㄘㄞˋ)
a fixed menu in a restaurant
和藹可親(ㄏㄜˊ ㄞˇ ㄎㄜˇ ㄑㄧㄣ)
gentle and affable; amiable; benign
和衣而臥(ㄏㄜˊ ㄧ ㄦˊ ㄨㄛˋ)
to sleep with clothes on
和議(ㄏㄜˊ ㄧˋ)
a peace accord or agreement (between two states)
和顏悅色(ㄏㄜˊ ㄧㄢˊ ㄩㄝˋ ㄙㄜˋ)
a peaceful and happy look; a kind and pleasant countenance; a smiling face
和約(ㄏㄜˊ ㄩㄝ)
a peace treaty

【和】 604
2. ㄏㄜˋ heh hè
1. to match; to harmonize
2. to write a poem in reply: 我奉和一首。I wrote a poem in reply to yours.
和詩(ㄏㄜˋ ㄕ)
to compose verses to match those by others (as a literary exercise)
和韻(ㄏㄜˋ ㄩㄣˋ)
to adapt rhymes to match those of another poem

【和】 604
3. ㄏㄨㄛˋ huoh huò
to knead (dough, clay, etc.); to mix: 我要在豆沙裡和點兒糖。I'll mix a little sugar into the bean paste.
和麵(ㄏㄨㄛˋ ㄇㄧㄢˋ)
to knead flour
和弄(ㄏㄨㄛˋ ·ㄌㄨㄥ)
①to mix evenly by stirring
②to cause disputes

【咖】 605
1. ㄎㄚ ka kā
a character used in transliterating
咖啡(ㄎㄚ ㄈㄟ)
coffee
咖啡廳(ㄎㄚ ㄈㄟ ㄊㄧㄥ) or 咖啡館(ㄎㄚ ㄈㄟ ㄍㄨㄢˇ)
a café; a coffee house; a coffee shop; a coffee bar
咖啡精(ㄎㄚ ㄈㄟ ㄐㄧㄥ)
instant coffee
咖啡因(ㄎㄚ ㄈㄟ ㄧㄣ)
caffeine 亦作「咖啡鹼」

【咖】 605
2. ㄍㄚ ga gā
a character used in transliterating
咖哩(ㄍㄚ ㄌㄧˇ)
curry
咖哩飯(ㄍㄚ ㄌㄧˇ ㄈㄢˋ)
curry and rice
咖哩牛肉(ㄍㄚ ㄌㄧˇ ㄋㄧㄡˊ ㄖㄡˋ)
curried beef

【咐】 606
ㄈㄨˋ fuh fù
to tell, bid, or instruct (someone to do something): 爸爸吩咐我好好照看小馬。My father told me to take good care of the foal. 他囑咐我們預備去旅行。He bade us prepare for the journey.

六畫

【咧】 607
1. ㄌㄧㄝˇ liee liě
to stretch (the mouth) horizontally
咧着嘴(ㄌㄧㄝˇ ·ㄓㄜ ㄗㄨㄟˇ)
to grin: 他痛得直咧着嘴。He was grinning with pain.

【咧】 607
2. ㄌㄧㄝ lie liē
參看「咧咧」
咧咧
①(ㄌㄧㄝ ·ㄌㄧㄝ) to babble
②(ㄌㄧㄝ·ㄌㄧㄝ) a baby's crying sound

【咤】 608
ㄓㄚˋ jah zhà
to shout with anger

【咦】 609
ㄧˊ yi yí
(an interjection of surprise) well; why; hey: 咦，那是怎麼回事? Hey, what's all that about?

【咨】 610
ㄗ tzy zī
1. to inquire; to consult
2. a very formal official communication between offices of equal rank
咨嗟(ㄗ ㄐㄧㄝ)
to sigh
咨詢(ㄗ ㄒㄩㄣˊ)
to inquire; to consult
咨政(ㄗ ㄓㄥˋ)
a political advisor (to the Chinese presidency)
咨文(ㄗ ㄨㄣˊ)
a very formal official communication between offices of equal rank

【咪】 611
ㄇㄧ mhi mī
1. a meow (meou, miaow, miaou)
2. smiling: 他笑咪咪的。His face was wreathed in smiles. 或 He was all smiles.
咪咪叫(ㄇㄧ ㄇㄧ ㄐㄧㄠˋ)
to meow (meou, miaow, miaou)

【咫】 612
ㄓˇ jyy zhǐ
1. the foot measure of the Chou Dynasty (divided into eight inches)
2. near

咫尺(ㄓˇ ㄔˇ)
very close: 她近在咫尺。She was close at hand.
咫尺天涯(ㄓˇ ㄔˇ ㄊㄧㄢ ㄧㄚˊ)
so near and yet so far

【咬】613 ㄧㄠˇ yeau yǎo
to bite; to gnaw: 狗咬了他的手。The dog bit his hand.
咬破(ㄧㄠˇ ㄆㄛˋ)
① to break by the teeth; to bite through ② to make a revealing remark about something
咬定(ㄧㄠˇ ㄉㄧㄥˋ)
to insist (that someone did such and such a thing)
咬緊牙關(ㄧㄠˇ ㄐㄧㄣˇ ㄧㄚˊ ㄍㄨㄢ)
(literally) to set the teeth firmly—to endure pain or hardships with determination; to persevere
咬住(ㄧㄠˇ ㄓㄨˋ)
① to bite into; to grip with one's teeth ② to grip; to take firm hold of; to refuse to let go of: 追擊部隊咬住敵人不放。The pursuing troops refused to let go of the enemy.
咬扯(ㄧㄠˇ ㄔㄜˇ)
to give vent by angry talking
咬舌(ㄧㄠˇ ㄕㄜˊ)
to speak imperfectly; to lisp; to have a lisp; to speak with a lisp
咬字(ㄧㄠˇ ㄗˋ)
to sing or speak in an elaborate pronunciation (in Chinese opera)
咬耳朵(ㄧㄠˇ ㄦˇ ·ㄉㄨㄛ)
to whisper into another's ear
咬牙(ㄧㄠˇ ㄧㄚˊ)
① to grit (or set, clench, gnash) one's teeth: 他恨得直咬牙。He gnashed his teeth in hatred. ② to grind one's teeth (in sleep)
咬牙切齒(ㄧㄠˇ ㄧㄚˊ ㄑㄧㄝˋ ㄔˇ)
to gnash the teeth (in anger or hatred)
咬文嚼字(ㄧㄠˇ ㄨㄣˊ ㄐㄩㄝˊ ㄗˋ)
to be overcareful or pedantic about the use of each word; to pay excessive attention to wording

【咯】614 1. ㄌㄨㄛˋ luoh luò
to cough; a cough
咯血(ㄌㄨㄛˋ ㄒㄧㄝˇ)
to cough up blood

【咯】614 2. ·ㄌㄛ ·lo lo
a phrase-final particle

【咯】614 3. ㄍㄜ ge gē
參看「咯吱」
咯吱(ㄍㄜ ㄓ)
to creak

【咯】614 4. ㄍㄜˊ ger gé
參看「咯噔」、「咯咯」
咯噔(ㄍㄜˊ ㄉㄥ)
to click
咯咯(ㄍㄜˊ ㄍㄜˊ)
① a low, guttural sound made by a hen when brooding or calling her chicks ② (laughter) a chuckle; a titter

【咱】615 ㄗㄢˊ tzarn zán
I, me (in North China dialect)
咱們(ㄗㄢˊ ·ㄇㄣ)
(inclusive) we; you and I: 咱們是國家的主人翁。We are masters of our country.

【咳】616 1. ㄎㄜˊ ker ké
to cough
咳嗽(ㄎㄜˊ ·ㄙㄡ)
to cough; a cough: 他咳嗽得很厲害。He coughs badly.
咳嗽糖漿(ㄎㄜˊ ·ㄙㄡ ㄊㄤˊ ㄐㄧㄤ)
cough syrup

【咳】616 2. ㄎㄚˇ kaa kǎ
to cough up
咳痰(ㄎㄚˇ ㄊㄢˊ)
to cough up phlegm
咳血(ㄎㄚˇ ㄒㄧㄝˇ)
to cough up blood; to spit blood; hemoptysis

【咳】616 3. ㄏㄞˋ hay hài
an interjection of regret or remorse

【咸】617 ㄒㄧㄢˊ shyan xián
all; completely; fully; wholly
咸信(ㄒㄧㄢˊ ㄒㄧㄣˋ)
generally believed that: 我們咸信他已離開此城。We generally believed that he had left the city.
咸認為(ㄒㄧㄢˊ ㄖㄣˋ ㄨㄟˊ)
generally regarded; generally thought
咸陽(ㄒㄧㄢˊ ㄧㄤˊ)
Hsienyang, the capital of the Chin Dynasty, in northwest Shensi Province

【咽】618 1. ㄧㄢ ian yān
the throat; the larynx; the pharynx; the gullet
咽頭(ㄧㄢ ㄊㄡˊ)
the pharynx; the throat
咽喉(ㄧㄢ ㄏㄡˊ)
① the larynx; the throat ② a narrow, throat-like passage of strategic importance

【咽】618 2. ㄧㄢˋ yann yàn
to swallow; to gulp
咽下去(ㄧㄢˋ ㄒㄧㄚˋ ·ㄑㄩ)
to swallow; to gulp down

【咽】618 3. ㄧㄝˋ yeh yè
to be choked; to weep or speak in a choked voice; to sob

【咿】619 ㄧ i yī
a form used to represent a sound
咿啞(ㄧ ㄧㄚˇ)
① the prattle of a baby ② the creaking sound made by oars
咿啞學語(ㄧ ㄧㄚˇ ㄒㄩㄝˊ ㄩˇ)
(said of a baby) to begin to babble, prattle, or lisp

【哀】620 ㄞ ai āi
1. to grieve; to mourn; to lament
2. to pity; to sympathize; to commiserate; compassion
3. sad; sorrowful; lamentable
4. sadness; sorrow; grief: 哀莫大於心死。There is no grief so great as that for a dead heart.
哀兵必勝(ㄞ ㄅㄧㄥ ㄅㄧˋ ㄕㄥˋ)
An army filled with righteous indignation is bound to win.
哀愍(ㄞ ㄇㄧㄣˇ)
to pity; to commiserate
哀鳴(ㄞ ㄇㄧㄥˊ)
to give mournful cries; to

〔口部〕

wail

哀悼(ㄞ ㄉㄠˋ)
to mourn over, or lament (someone's death); condolence

哀的美頓書(ㄞ ㄉㄧˋ ㄇㄟˇ ㄉㄨㄣˋ ㄕㄨ)
an ultimatum

哀嘆(ㄞ ㄊㄢˋ)
to lament; to bewail; to bemoan

哀痛(ㄞ ㄊㄨㄥˋ)
to feel the anguish of sorrow; to feel the pain of grief

哀樂
①(ㄞ ㄌㄜˋ) grief and joy
②(ㄞ ㄩㄝˋ) funeral music; the music of lament

哀憐(ㄞ ㄌㄧㄢˊ)
to pity; to commiserate; to have sympathy or compassion for

哀歌(ㄞ ㄍㄜ)
a lament; an elegy; a dirge: 樂隊如泣如訴的演奏哀歌。The band was wailing a lament.

哀告(ㄞ ㄍㄠˋ)
to speak about one's grievances (in appealing for help)

哀懇(ㄞ ㄎㄣˇ)
to implore, entreat, or beg (for mercy, help, etc.)

哀號(ㄞ ㄏㄠˊ)
to wail: 風在哀號。The wind wails.

哀毀骨立(ㄞ ㄏㄨㄟˇ ㄍㄨˇ ㄌㄧˋ)
to be consumed away with grief (until nothing but bones and skins are left); to be emaciated by grief

哀鴻遍野(ㄞ ㄏㄨㄥˊ ㄅㄧㄢˋ ㄧㄝˇ)
The wilderness is filled with suffering people. 或 Throngs of famished and homeless people are roaming the country.

哀戚(ㄞ ㄑㄧ)
sorrow; grief; woe; sadness: 他因哀戚而幾至瘋狂。He was nearly driven mad by grief.

哀泣(ㄞ ㄑㄧˋ)
to weep with sorrow

哀求(ㄞ ㄑㄧㄡˊ)
to entreat, implore, beg or appeal pathetically

哀愁(ㄞ ㄔㄡˊ)
sad; sorrowful

哀傷(ㄞ ㄕㄤ)
to feel sorrow or grief; to grieve; to mourn; to be sad

哀榮(ㄞ ㄖㄨㄥˊ)
posthumous honors

哀子(ㄞ ㄗˇ)
a male bereaved of his mother (used in obituary)

哀哉(ㄞ ㄗㄞ)
alas

哀詞 or 哀辭(ㄞ ㄘˊ)
a kind of ancient writing such as a poem that expresses grief over someone's death

哀思(ㄞ ㄙ)
sad feeling about the deceased

哀豔(ㄞ ㄧㄢˋ)
(said of love stories) sadly touching

【品】 621
ㄆㄧㄣˇ piin pǐn

1. personality; character: 他是個品性良好的人。He's a man of fine character.
2. an article; a commodity
3. a rank or grade in the government service in former times: 一品 the highest rank in officialdom in an ancient Chinese court
4. to appraise; to rate
5. to find out

品評(ㄆㄧㄣˇ ㄆㄧㄥˊ)
to determine the quality or worth of; to appraise; to rate: 他以品評的眼光看這幅畫。He looked at the picture appraisingly.

品貌(ㄆㄧㄣˇ ㄇㄠˋ)
one's personality and appearance

品茗(ㄆㄧㄣˇ ㄇㄧㄥˊ) or 品茶(ㄆㄧㄣˇ ㄔㄚˊ)
to drink tea (with critical appreciation of its taste and quality)

品德(ㄆㄧㄣˇ ㄉㄜˊ)
personal character

品第(ㄆㄧㄣˇ ㄉㄧˋ)
① to appraise or rate; to grade ② a rank (as a result of rating); a grade

品頭論足(ㄆㄧㄣˇ ㄊㄡˊ ㄌㄨㄣˋ ㄗㄨˊ)
to make critical remarks about a person's physical appearance: 他對女人品頭論足。He made critical remarks about a woman's appearance.

品題(ㄆㄧㄣˇ ㄊㄧˊ)
to make an appraisal or critical comment (on a person or thing); to rate

品脫(ㄆㄧㄣˇ ㄊㄨㄛ)
a pint

品類(ㄆㄧㄣˇ ㄌㄟˋ)
① to classify ② a class (to which an article belongs)

品格(ㄆㄧㄣˇ ㄍㄜˊ)
one's moral character: 他的品格高雅。He has high character.

品管(ㄆㄧㄣˇ ㄍㄨㄢˇ)
Q.C. (quality control)

品級(ㄆㄧㄣˇ ㄐㄧˊ)
① a grade or rank (in the nine-grade system for government officials in former times) ② the grade of an article (in terms of quality)

品酒(ㄆㄧㄣˇ ㄐㄧㄡˇ)
to taste wine

品鑑(ㄆㄧㄣˇ ㄐㄧㄢˋ)
to criticize; to judge

品行(ㄆㄧㄣˇ ㄒㄧㄥˋ)
one's moral character and performance; behavior: 他的品行端正。He has good behavior.

品性(ㄆㄧㄣˇ ㄒㄧㄥˋ)
one's moral character

品學兼優(ㄆㄧㄣˇ ㄒㄩㄝˊ ㄐㄧㄢ ㄧㄡ)
to excel in morals as well as academic performances; excellent not only morally but also academically; good both in morality and learning: 他眞是一位品學兼優的好學生。He is really a good student in morality and in learning.

品質(ㄆㄧㄣˇ ㄓˋ)
quality (of a commodity, etc.)

品種(ㄆㄧㄣˇ ㄓㄨㄥˇ)
a species or variety (of flora or fauna)

品嘗(ㄆㄧㄣˇ ㄔㄤˊ)
to taste (food) in order to appraise, rate or grade its worth

品味(ㄆㄧㄣˇ ㄨㄟˋ)
taste; a savor

【哂】622
ㄕㄣˇ sheen shěn
to give a sneering smile

哂納(ㄕㄣˇ ㄋㄚˋ)or 哂收(ㄕㄣˇ ㄕㄡ)
Please accept (my small gift).

哂笑(ㄕㄣˇ ㄒㄧㄠˋ)
to laugh at (with contempt)

【哄】623
1. ㄏㄨㄥ hong hōng
(said of a group of people) to make a roaring noise

哄動(ㄏㄨㄥ ㄉㄨㄥˋ)
to create a sensation; to excite (the public)

哄堂(ㄏㄨㄥ ㄊㄤˊ)
(said of a group of people gathered together) to fill the room or house with laughter; to bring down the house (as a result of witty remarks, clownish acts, etc.)

哄堂大笑(ㄏㄨㄥ ㄊㄤˊ ㄉㄚˋ ㄒㄧㄠˋ)
The whole room rocks with laughter.

哄然(ㄏㄨㄥ ㄖㄢˊ)
boisterous; uproarious

【哄】623
2. ㄏㄨㄥˇ hoong hǒng
to beguile; to cheat; to defraud

哄騙(ㄏㄨㄥˇ ㄆㄧㄢˋ)
to defraud; to cheat; to swindle; to take in; to humbug; to hoodwink

哄擡物價(ㄏㄨㄥˇ ㄊㄞˊ ㄨˋ ㄐㄧㄚˋ)
to rig prices; price rigging

哄孩子(ㄏㄨㄥˇ ㄏㄞˊ ·ㄗ)
to coax a child: 她很會哄孩子。She knows how to coax children.

【哆】624
ㄉㄨㄛ duo duō
to shiver; to tremble: 她氣得全身直打哆嗦。She was all of a tremble with rage.

哆嗦(ㄉㄨㄛ ·ㄙㄨㄛ)
to shiver with cold or tremble with fear: 她冷得打哆嗦。She shivered with cold.

【哇】625
1. ㄨㄚ ua wā
1. to vomit
2. the sound of crying by a child: 那小孩哇的一聲哭起來。The child burst out crying.

哇哇大哭(ㄨㄚ ㄨㄚ ㄉㄚˋ ㄎㄨ)
to cry very loudly: 那小男孩痛得哇哇大哭。The little boy could not help crying loudly with pain.

【哇】625
2. ·ㄨㄚ ·ua ·wa
a phrase-final particle: 你好哇? Well, how are you?

【哈】626
1. ㄏㄚ ha hā
1. a form used in transliteration
2. a sound of hearty laughter: 哈哈，我猜着了。Aha, I've guessed it.

哈密瓜(ㄏㄚ ㄇㄧˋ ㄍㄨㄚ)
a honey dew melon; a sweet melon grown in Hami, Sinkiang Province

哈佛大學(ㄏㄚ ㄈㄛˊ ㄉㄚˋ ㄒㄩㄝˊ)
Harvard University

哈得孫河(ㄏㄚ ㄉㄜˊ ㄙㄨㄣ ㄏㄜˊ)
the Hudson River

哈雷彗星(ㄏㄚ ㄌㄟˊ ㄏㄨㄟˋ ㄒㄧㄥ)
(astronomy) Halley's Comet; the Halley Comet

哈哈大笑(ㄏㄚ ㄏㄚ ㄉㄚˋ ㄒㄧㄠˋ)
to roar with laughter; to laugh heartily

哈哈鏡(ㄏㄚ ㄏㄚ ㄐㄧㄥˋ)
a magic mirror (which reflects the distorted image of a person or thing)

哈氣(ㄏㄚ ㄑㄧˋ)
to moisten the surface of an object by exhaling: 眼鏡要哈氣後再擦。Exhale on your glasses before wiping them.

哈欠(ㄏㄚ ㄑㄧㄢˋ)
a yawn: 那枯燥的演講令人連打哈欠。It was a dull speech greeted with yawns.

哈薩克(ㄏㄚ ㄙㄚˋ ㄎㄜˋ)
Kazakh; Kazakhstan

哈爾濱(ㄏㄚ ㄦˇ ㄅㄧㄣ)
Harbin, a city in Northeast China

哈腰(ㄏㄚ ㄧㄠ)
① to bend the body ② to bow (in salutation)

哈瓦那(ㄏㄚ ㄨㄚˇ ㄋㄚˋ)
Havana

【哈】626
2. ㄏㄚˇ haa hǎ
參看「哈巴狗」

哈巴狗(ㄏㄚˇ ·ㄅㄚ ㄍㄡˇ)
① a Pekingese or Pekinese (dog) ② toady; sycophant

【哉】627
ㄗㄞ tzai zāi
a phrase-final particle expressing surprise, admiration, grief, doubt, etc. (a literary form): 嗚呼！哀哉！Alas! 或 What a pity! Alas!

【哎】628
ㄞ ai āi
an interjection of surprise mixed with regret: 哎！我把鑰匙弄丟了。Damn, I've lost the key!

哎呀(ㄞ ·ㄧㄚ)
an interjection of surprise: 哎呀！好大的雨呀！My God! It is pouring!

哎喲(ㄞ ㄧㄠ)
an interjection of surprise or grief: 哎喲，眞辣！Ouch! It's hot!

七畫

【員】629
ㄩㄢˊ yuan yuán
1. a member (of an organization, etc.)
2. a person engaged in some field of activity
3. outer limits (of land, space, etc.)

員工(ㄩㄢˊ ㄍㄨㄥ)
employees (collectively): 這公司擁有二百位員工。The firm has 200 employees.

員額(ㄩㄢˊ ㄜˊ)
the authorized size of a staff; the number of employees

員外(ㄩㄢˊ ㄨㄞˋ)
① a salutation for a rich man in ancient China ② an official title in ancient China

【哥】630
ㄍㄜ ge gē
an elder brother: 我有三個哥哥和一個妹妹。I have three elder brothers and one younger sister.

哥白尼(ㄍㄜ ㄅㄞˊ ㄋㄧˊ)
Nicolaus Copernicus, 1473-1543, Polish astronomer who promulgated the now accepted theory that the earth and the other planets move around the sun

哥本哈根(ㄍㄜ ㄅㄣˇ ㄏㄚ ㄍㄣ)

Copenhagen, capital of Denmark
哥德(ㄍㄜ ㄉㄜˊ)
Johann Wolfgang von Goethe, 1749-1832, a German poet
哥德式(ㄍㄜ ㄉㄜˊ ㄕˋ)
Gothic—a style of architecture of which the characteristics are pointed arches, etc.
哥倫比亞(ㄍㄜ ㄌㄨㄣˊ ㄅㄧˇ ㄧㄚˇ)
① Columbia, an American city ② the Republic of Colombia
哥倫布(ㄍㄜ ㄌㄨㄣˊ ㄅㄨˋ)
Christopher Columbus, 1451-1506, discoverer of America: 哥倫布於1492年發現新大陸。Columbus discovered America in 1492.
哥哥(ㄍㄜ ·ㄍㄜ)
an elder brother
哥斯達黎加(ㄍㄜ ㄙ ㄉㄚˊ ㄌㄧˊ ㄐㄧㄚ)
Costa Rica
哥薩克(ㄍㄜ ㄙㄚˋ ㄎㄜˋ)
the Cossacks
哥兒們(ㄍㄜㄦ ·ㄇㄣ)
① brothers ② buddies; pals
哥兒倆(ㄍㄜㄦ ㄌㄧㄚˇ)
two brothers: 他們哥兒倆長得眞像。The two brothers look alike.

〔口部〕

【哦】 631
1. ㄛˊ or ó
(an interjection) oh; ah: 哦，多麼令人驚奇啊！Oh, what a surprise!

【哦】 631
2. ㄜˊ er é
to recite (verses, etc.): 他能憑記憶吟哦那首詩。He can recite that poem from memory.

【哨】 632
ㄕㄠˋ shaw shào
1. a whistle: 他大聲吹口哨。He gave a loud whistle.
2. to patrol
3. an outpost; a guard station
哨兵(ㄕㄠˋ ㄅㄧㄥ)
a sentinel or sentry: 那哨兵擔任警戒。The sentry is on guard.
哨船(ㄕㄠˋ ㄔㄨㄢˊ)
a patrol boat
哨子(ㄕㄠˋ ·ㄗ)or 哨兒(ㄕㄠˋㄦ)
a whistle
哨所(ㄕㄠˋ ㄙㄨㄛˇ)
a sentry post; a post: 前沿哨所 a forward post; an outpost

【哩】 633
1. ㄌㄧ lhi li
to speak indistinctly
哩哩啦啦(ㄌㄧ · ㄌㄧ ㄌㄚ ㄌㄚ)
① sporadic; off and on ② to straggle along
哩哩囉囉(ㄌㄧ ·ㄌㄧ ㄌㄨㄛ ㄌㄨㄛ)
to speak indistinctly; to utter inarticulate words; verbose and unclear in speech; rambling and indistinct

【哩】 633
2. ㄌㄧˇ lii lǐ
a mile: 我們的學校離海有二哩。Our school is two miles from the sea.

【哭】 634
ㄎㄨ ku kū
to weep; to cry; to sob; to wail; to whimper: 她爲失去的孩子在哭泣。She was wailing for her lost child.
哭哭啼啼(ㄎㄨ ㄎㄨ ㄊㄧˊ ㄊㄧˊ)
to whimper; to blubber; to snivel
哭喊(ㄎㄨ ㄏㄢˇ)
to cry and shout; crying and shouting
哭泣(ㄎㄨ ㄑㄧˋ)
to sob; to weep: 那可憐的男孩哭泣到入睡。The poor boy sobbed himself to sleep.
哭牆(ㄎㄨ ㄑㄧㄤˊ)
the Wailing Wall in Jerusalem
哭窮(ㄎㄨ ㄑㄩㄥˊ)
to tell others how badly one needs money; to complain of one's poverty
哭笑不得(ㄎㄨ ㄒㄧㄠˋ ㄅㄨˋ ㄉㄜˊ)
to be at a loss whether to cry or to laugh; to find oneself in a very embarrassing situation; to be faced with something at once troublesome and ludicrous: 她開的玩笑使他哭笑不得。Her joke made him not know whether to laugh or to cry.
哭喪(ㄎㄨ ㄙㄤ)
to cry aloud at a funeral
哭喪着臉(ㄎㄨ ·ㄙㄤ ·ㄓㄜ ㄌㄧㄢˇ)
to wear a woeful look; to look sad or mournful: 他整天哭喪著臉。He looks mournful all the day.
哭訴(ㄎㄨ ㄙㄨˋ)
to complain tearfully

【哮】 635
1. ㄒㄧㄠˋ shiaw xiào
to cry out in a loud voice

【哮】 635
2. ㄒㄧㄠ shiau xiāo
1. to pant; to wheeze; to gasp; to breathe with difficulty
2. a roar; a howl
哮喘(ㄒㄧㄠ ㄔㄨㄢˇ)
① asthma ② to wheeze

【哲】 636
ㄓㄜˊ jer zhé
1. a sage; a thinker; a philosopher
2. wise; wisdom; sagacious; sagacity: 我要他明哲保身。I demanded that he be wise and keep out of harm.
哲理(ㄓㄜˊ ㄌㄧˇ)
a philosophical principle; a philosophical doctrine; philosophy
哲學(ㄓㄜˊ ㄒㄩㄝˊ)
philosophy (as a field of intellectual pursuit)
哲學家(ㄓㄜˊ ㄒㄩㄝˊ ㄐㄧㄚ)
a philosopher; a thinker
哲人(ㄓㄜˊ ㄖㄣˊ)
a sage; a philosopher: 孔子被視爲中國古代最偉大的哲人。Confucius is considered the greatest of the ancient Chinese sages.
哲人其萎(ㄓㄜˊ ㄖㄣˊ ㄑㄧˊ ㄨㄟ)
The wise man is dead (used as a eulogy to the dead at a funeral service).
哲嗣(ㄓㄜˊ ㄙˋ)
a polite reference to other's son

【哺】 637
ㄅㄨˇ buu bǔ
1. to chew (before swallowing)
2. to feed (a baby, etc.)
哺乳(ㄅㄨˇ ㄖㄨˇ)
to give suck to; to nurse
哺乳類(ㄅㄨˇ ㄖㄨˇ ㄌㄟˋ)or 哺乳動物(ㄅㄨˇ ㄖㄨˇ ㄉㄨㄥˋ ㄨˋ)
mammals; Mammalia
哺養(ㄅㄨˇ ㄧㄤˇ)
to feed; to rear
哺育(ㄅㄨˇ ㄩˋ)

①to feed ② to nurture; to foster

【哼】 638 ㄏㄥ heng hēng

1. to croon; to hum (a melody): 母親哼着歌哄孩子睡覺。The mother crooned the baby to sleep.
2. to groan; to moan: 他痛得直哼哼。He groaned with pain.
3. the grunt of disapproval or contempt: 她輕蔑地哼了一聲。She gave a snort of contempt.

哼哈(ㄏㄥ ㄏㄚ)
to hum and haw

哼哈二將(ㄏㄥ ㄏㄚ ㄦˋ ㄐㄧㄤˋ)
the two sculptured fierce-looking gods usually guarding a temple gate

哼哼(ㄏㄥ·ㄏㄥ)
to groan continually

哼哼唧唧(ㄏㄥ·ㄏㄥ ㄐㄧ ㄐㄧ)
to groan and moan

哼聲(ㄏㄥ ㄕㄥ)
(electricity) hums

【哽】 639 ㄍㄥˇ geeng gěng

to choke; to feel a lump in one's throat

哽塞(ㄍㄥˇ ㄙㄜˋ)
to choke

哽咽(ㄍㄥˇ ㄧㄝˋ)
to be choked with sobs; to sob (with catches and breaks in the voice)

【唁】 640 ㄧㄢˋ yann yàn

to condole with or express sympathy for (the bereaved): 謹致唁慰之忱。Please accept my sincere condolences.

唁電(ㄧㄢˋ ㄉㄧㄢˋ)
a condolatory telegram

唁函(ㄧㄢˋ ㄏㄢˊ)
a letter (or message) of condolence 參看「唁信」

唁信(ㄧㄢˋ ㄒㄧㄣˋ)
a condolatory letter

【唆】 641 ㄙㄨㄛ suo suō

to instigate; to incite

唆使(ㄙㄨㄛ ㄕˇ)
to instigate; to incite

【唉】 642 ㄞ ai āi

(an interjection of regret or disgust) alas; oh; well: 唉，誰能想到啊! Well, who'd have thought of that? 唉，眞可惜! What a pity!

唉聲歎氣(ㄞ ㄕㄥ ㄊㄢˋ ㄑㄧˋ)
to give deploring interjections and sighs; to moan and groan

【唏】 643 ㄒㄧ shi xī

to weep or sob with sorrow; to grieve

唏噓(ㄒㄧ ㄒㄩ)
to sob

【唐】 644 ㄊㄤˊ tarng táng

1. the Tang Dynasty
2. a Chinese family name
3. abrupt; rude; preposterous; impertinent

唐代(ㄊㄤˊ ㄉㄞˋ) or 唐朝(ㄊㄤˊ ㄔㄠˊ)
the Tang Dynasty (618-907 A.D.)

唐太宗(ㄊㄤˊ ㄊㄞˋ ㄗㄨㄥ)
Emperor Tai Tsung, the second emperor of the Tang Dynasty, who laid the groundwork of later prosperity during his reign (627-649 A. D.)

唐唐大國 or 堂堂大國(ㄊㄤˊ ㄊㄤˊ ㄉㄚˋ ㄍㄨㄛˊ)
a great, powerful nation

唐突(ㄊㄤˊ ㄊㄨˊ)
abrupt; rude; brusque; blunt; to be rude or impertinent: 這個小傢伙出言唐突。This little rascal made a blunt remark.

唐努烏梁海(ㄊㄤˊ ㄋㄨˇ ㄨ ㄌㄧㄤˊ ㄏㄞˇ)
Tannu Tuva, in Mongolia

唐璜(ㄊㄤˊ ㄏㄨㄤˊ)
Don Juan, an unfinished epic satire by Byron

唐吉訶德(ㄊㄤˊ ㄐㄧˊ ㄏㄜ ㄉㄜˊ)
Don Quixote

唐玄宗(ㄊㄤˊ ㄒㄩㄢˊ ㄗㄨㄥ)
Emperor Hsüan Tsung, whose preoccupation with the concubine Lady Yang (楊貴妃) in his reign (712-755 A. D.) marked the beginning of the fall of the Tang Dynasty

唐裝(ㄊㄤˊ ㄓㄨㄤ)
①a Chinese dress or garment ② the dresses of the Tang Dynasty

唐詩(ㄊㄤˊ ㄕ)
the poetry of the Tang Dynasty

唐人(ㄊㄤˊ ㄖㄣˊ)
① a Chinese (a term common among the overseas Chinese) ② the people of the Tang Dynasty

唐人街(ㄊㄤˊ ㄖㄣˊ ㄐㄧㄝ)
the Chinatown (of San Francisco, New York, etc.)

唐塞 or 搪塞(ㄊㄤˊ ㄙㄜˋ)
to do things perfunctorily; to reply questions with evasive answers

唐三藏(ㄊㄤˊ ㄙㄢ ㄗㄤˋ)
a high Buddhist priest, known also as Hsüan Tzang (玄奘), who traveled to and back from India to acquire valued Buddhist scriptures for China

唐三彩(ㄊㄤˊ ㄙㄢ ㄘㄞˇ)
(archeology) the tri-colored glazed pottery of the Tang Dynasty

唐宋八大家(ㄊㄤˊ ㄙㄨㄥˋ ㄅㄚ ㄉㄚˋ ㄐㄧㄚ)
the Eight Great Men of Letters of the Tang (Han Yü, Liu Tzung-yüan) and Sung (Ou-Yang Hsiu, Su Hsün, Su Shih, Su Che, Wang An-shih, Tseng Kung) dynasties

唐堯(ㄊㄤˊ ㄧㄠˊ)
Tang Yao, a sage king of over 4,000 years ago who gave the throne to the capable and virtuous minister Shun (舜) instead of his own son

唐虞之世(ㄊㄤˊ ㄩˊ ㄓ ㄕˋ)
the halcyon days of Emperors Yao (堯) and Shun (舜)

【哪】 645 (那)1. ㄋㄚˇ naa nǎ

(an interrogative particle) where; how; what; which: 你講哪一國的話? What foreign language do you speak?

哪怕(ㄋㄚˇ ㄆㄚˋ)
even if

哪門子(ㄋㄚˇ ㄇㄣˊ·ㄗ)
what on earth...; what the devil...: 你說的是哪門子話呀! What the devil are you talking about?

哪能(ㄋㄚˇ ㄋㄥˊ)
how is it possible that...;

〔口部〕

how could it be that...
哪裏(ㄋㄚˇ ·ㄌㄧ)or 哪兒(ㄋㄚˇㄦ)
①(interrogative) where: 你到哪裏去? Where are you going? ② wherever; where
哪個(ㄋㄚˇ ·ㄍㄜ)
① Which one? ② Who is it?
哪些(ㄋㄚˇ ㄒㄧㄝ)
which; who; what: 哪些書是你的? Which books are yours?
哪知(ㄋㄚˇ ㄓ)
who would have foreseen that...
哪樣(ㄋㄚˇ ㄧㄤˋ)
what kind of

【哪】 645 2. ·ㄋㄚ •na nɑ
a phrase-final particle: 我的天哪! My God! 或 O God!

【哶】 646 ㄇㄧㄝ mhie miě
the cries of sheep; to baa; to bleat: 一隻羊, 哶哶叫。 A sheep is baaing.

八畫

【售】 647 ㄕㄡˋ show shòu
to sell
售票(ㄕㄡˋ ㄆㄧㄠˋ)
to sell tickets
售票口(ㄕㄡˋ ㄆㄧㄠˋ ㄎㄡˇ)
a wicket
售票處(ㄕㄡˋ ㄆㄧㄠˋ ㄔㄨˋ)
a ticket office; a box office
售賣(ㄕㄡˋ ㄇㄞˋ)
to sell
售後服務(ㄕㄡˋ ㄏㄡˋ ㄈㄨˊ ㄨˋ)
after service
售貨店(ㄕㄡˋ ㄏㄨㄛˋ ㄉㄧㄢˋ)
a retail store 亦作「零售店」
售貨機(ㄕㄡˋ ㄏㄨㄛˋ ㄐㄧ)
a vending machine 亦作「自動販賣機」
售貨員(ㄕㄡˋ ㄏㄨㄛˋ ㄩㄢˊ)
a shop clerk; a salesclerk; a salesman; a salesgirl
售價(ㄕㄡˋ ㄐㄧㄚˋ)
the (retail) price (of a commodity): 日用品的售價漸漸上漲。The prices of commodities are going up.
售罄(ㄕㄡˋ ㄑㄧㄥˋ)
completely sold out; to sell out: 我們小號的貨品已售罄。We are sold out of small sizes.
售出(ㄕㄡˋ ㄔㄨ)
to sell; to succeed in selling (a car, a house, etc.)

【唯】 648 1. (惟) ㄨㄟˊ wei wéi
only: 唯有他一人留下來。Only he remained.
唯美主義(ㄨㄟˊ ㄇㄟˇ ㄓㄨˇ ㄧˋ)
aestheticism
唯名論(ㄨㄟˊ ㄇㄧㄥˊ ㄌㄨㄣˋ)
(philosophy) nominalism
唯命是從(ㄨㄟˊ ㄇㄧㄥˋ ㄕˋ ㄘㄨㄥˊ)or 唯命是聽(ㄨㄟˊ ㄇㄧㄥˋ ㄕˋ ㄊㄧㄥ)
obsequious; unconditionally obedient; to do whatever is told
唯獨(ㄨㄟˊ ㄉㄨˊ)
only or alone; an exception: 唯獨他一人留下來。Only he remained.
唯利是圖(ㄨㄟˊ ㄌㄧˋ ㄕˋ ㄊㄨˊ)
to be bent solely on profit; to be intent on nothing but profit
唯恐(ㄨㄟˊ ㄎㄨㄥˇ)
for fear that; for fear of: 他唯恐失敗而努力工作。He's working hard for fear that he should fail.
唯恐天下不亂(ㄨㄟˊ ㄎㄨㄥˇ ㄊㄧㄢ ㄒㄧㄚˋ ㄅㄨˋ ㄌㄨㄢˋ)
to be a troublemaker or warmonger; to sow discord to serve private ends
唯心論(ㄨㄟˊ ㄒㄧㄣ ㄌㄨㄣˋ)or 唯心主義(ㄨㄟˊ ㄒㄧㄣ ㄓㄨˇ ㄧˋ)
idealism
唯心史觀(ㄨㄟˊ ㄒㄧㄣ ㄕˇ ㄍㄨㄢ)
the idealistic conception of history
唯一(ㄨㄟˊ ㄧ)
the only one, the only kind, etc.
唯一論(ㄨㄟˊ ㄧ ㄌㄨㄣˋ)
unitarianism
唯有(ㄨㄟˊ ㄧㄡˇ)
only: 唯有白的了。There are white ones only.
唯物辯證法(ㄨㄟˊ ㄨˋ ㄅㄧㄢˋ ㄓㄥˋ ㄈㄚˇ)
materialist dialectics
唯物論(ㄨㄟˊ ㄨˋ ㄌㄨㄣˋ)or 唯物主義(ㄨㄟˊ ㄨˋ ㄓㄨˇ ㄧˋ)
materialism
唯物史觀(ㄨㄟˊ ㄨˋ ㄕˇ ㄍㄨㄢ)
the materialistic conception of history
唯我獨尊(ㄨㄟˊ ㄨㄛˇ ㄉㄨˊ ㄗㄨㄣ)
egoistic; autocratic; bossy
唯我論(ㄨㄟˊ ㄨㄛˇ ㄌㄨㄣˋ)or 唯我主義(ㄨㄟˊ ㄨㄛˇ ㄓㄨˇ ㄧˋ)
solipsism

【唯】 648 2. ㄨㄟˇ woei wěi
yes or no; the words one answers
唯唯否否(ㄨㄟˇ ㄨㄟˇ ㄈㄡˇ ㄈㄡˇ)
yes or no; to have no independent opinion; to echo others
唯唯諾諾(ㄨㄟˇ ㄨㄟˇ ㄋㄨㄛˋ ㄋㄨㄛˋ)
to say yes to a superior's suggestion; to be a yes man

【唱】 649 ㄔㄤˋ chanq chàng
1. to sing; to chant: 他喜歡唱歌。He is fond of singing.
2. to crow; to cry: 雞唱三遍。The cock has crowed for the third time.
3. a song or a singing part of a Chinese opera
唱本(ㄔㄤˋ ㄅㄣˇ)or 唱本兒(ㄔㄤˋ ㄅㄜˇㄦ)
a song book
唱盤(ㄔㄤˋ ㄆㄢˊ)
the turntable of a phonograph
唱票(ㄔㄤˋ ㄆㄧㄠˋ)
to count votes aloud
唱片(ㄔㄤˋ ㄆㄧㄢˋ)or 唱片兒(ㄔㄤˋ ㄆㄧㄚˋㄦ)
a (phonograph) record or a disc
唱名(ㄔㄤˋ ㄇㄧㄥˊ)
to call the roll loudly
唱反調(ㄔㄤˋ ㄈㄢˇ ㄉㄧㄠˋ)
to air an opposing view
唱導(ㄔㄤˋ ㄉㄠˇ)
to lead; to advocate
唱對台戲(ㄔㄤˋ ㄉㄨㄟˋ ㄊㄞˊ ㄒㄧˋ)
to put on a rival show; to enter into rivalry
唱歌(ㄔㄤˋ ㄍㄜ)
to sing songs; to sing: 她很會唱歌。She is a good singer.
唱高調(ㄔㄤˋ ㄍㄠ ㄉㄧㄠˋ)
to make high-sounding statements; to make magnificent but impractical suggestions; to affect a high moral tone
唱工(ㄔㄤˋ ㄍㄨㄥ)

(said of a Peking opera) the art or skill of singing

唱和(ㄔㄤˋ ㄏㄜˋ)
to write verses on the same theme, usually after the same rhyme pattern, as a means of social intercourse; to write and reply in poems between friends

唱機(ㄔㄤˋ ㄐㄧ)
a record player or phonograph

唱腔(ㄔㄤˋ ㄑㄧㄤ)
the music for voices in a Chinese opera

唱戲(ㄔㄤˋ ㄒㄧˋ)or 唱京戲(ㄔㄤˋ ㄐㄧㄥ ㄒㄧˋ)or 唱平劇(ㄔㄤˋ ㄆㄧㄥˊ ㄐㄩˋ)
to sing a Peking opera; to stage a Peking opera show; to play in a theater

唱針(ㄔㄤˋ ㄓㄣ)
a phonograph needle; a stylus

唱籌量沙(ㄔㄤˋ ㄔㄡˊ ㄌㄧㄤˊ ㄕㄚ)
to put up a front in order to fool others

唱詩班(ㄔㄤˋ ㄕ ㄅㄢ)
a choir

唱雙簧(ㄔㄤˋ ㄕㄨㄤ ㄏㄨㄤˊ)
①to give a two-man comic show, in which one person acts according to what the other hiding behind him speaks or sings ②to collaborate with each other

唱詞(ㄔㄤˋ ㄘˊ)
a libretto; the words of a song, ballad, etc.

唱隨之樂(ㄔㄤˋ ㄙㄨㄟˊ ㄓ ㄌㄜˋ)
marital bliss

唱遊(ㄔㄤˋ ㄧㄡˊ)
a recreation class in primary schools during which the children sing and play under the supervision of the teacher

【唳】 650
ㄌㄧˋ lih lì

the cry of a crane, wild goose, etc.: 風聲鶴唳 the whistling of winds and the crying of cranes—a nervous atmosphere of war and turmoil; a fleeing army's suspicion of danger at the slightest sound

【唾】 651
ㄊㄨㄛˋ tuoh tuò

1. saliva
2. to spit: 請不要在公共汽車內唾吐。Please don't spit in the bus.

唾罵(ㄊㄨㄛˋ ㄇㄚˋ)
to spit out; to revile

唾沫(ㄊㄨㄛˋ ·ㄇㄛ)
saliva; spittle

唾沫星子(ㄊㄨㄛˋ ·ㄇㄛ ㄒㄧㄥ ·ㄗ)
particles of saliva

唾面自乾(ㄊㄨㄛˋ ㄇㄧㄢˋ ㄗˋ ㄍㄢ)
(literally) to let the saliva spit in the face dry by itself—to show great forbearance in putting up with an insult; extreme obsequiousness

唾壺(ㄊㄨㄛˋ ㄏㄨˊ)
a spittoon

唾棄(ㄊㄨㄛˋ ㄑㄧˋ)
to spit on or at in contempt; to show contempt for; to throw away in disgust; to cast aside; to spurn

唾腺(ㄊㄨㄛˋ ㄒㄧㄢˋ)
(biology) a salivary gland

唾手可得(ㄊㄨㄛˋ ㄕㄡˇ ㄎㄜˇ ㄉㄜˊ)
very easily obtainable; (to accomplish) with extreme ease 亦作「垂手可得」

唾液(ㄊㄨㄛˋ ㄧㄝˋ)
saliva

【啡】 652
ㄈㄟ fei fēi

a form used in transliterating 參看「咖啡」or「嗎啡」

【啁】 653
ㄓㄡ jou zhōu

the twittering or chirping of a bird

啁啾(ㄓㄡ ㄐㄧㄡ)
to twitter; to chirp: 小鳥在林間啁啾地叫。Birds twittered in the trees.

【啄】 654
ㄓㄨㄛˊ jwo zhuó

(said of a bird) to peck: 小鷄啄米。The chicks are pecking at the rice.

啄木鳥(ㄓㄨㄛˊ ㄇㄨˋ ㄋㄧㄠˇ)
a woodpecker: 啄木鳥把樹啄了一個洞。The woodpecker pecked a hole in the tree.

啄啄(ㄓㄨㄛˊ ㄓㄨㄛˊ)
①the cackling of hens ②the sound of tapping at a door

啄食(ㄓㄨㄛˊ ㄕˊ)
to eat by pecking; to peck: 母鷄啄食穀粒。The hen pecked the corn.

【商】 655
ㄕㄤ shang shāng

1. commerce; trade; business: 他離校後要去經商。He will go to business when he leaves school.
2. a merchant; a trader; a businessman
3. to discuss; to exchange views; to confer: 我有要事相商。I have important matters to discuss with you.
4. (arithmetic) the quotient
5. the Shang Dynasty (c. 1800-1100 B.C.)

商標(ㄕㄤ ㄅㄧㄠ)
a trademark

商標註册(ㄕㄤ ㄅㄧㄠ ㄓㄨˋ ㄘㄜˋ)
trademark registration

商埠(ㄕㄤ ㄅㄨˋ)or 商港(ㄕㄤ ㄍㄤˇ)
a commercial port; a trading port

商品(ㄕㄤ ㄆㄧㄣˇ)
commodities; wares; merchandise; goods

商品展覽會(ㄕㄤ ㄆㄧㄣˇ ㄓㄢˇ ㄌㄢˇ ㄏㄨㄟˋ)or 商展(ㄕㄤ ㄓㄢˇ)
a trade fair; a trade exposition

商品陳列所(ㄕㄤ ㄆㄧㄣˇ ㄔㄣˊ ㄌㄧㄝˋ ㄙㄨㄛˇ)
a commercial museum

商民(ㄕㄤ ㄇㄧㄣˊ)
tradesmen

商法(ㄕㄤ ㄈㄚˇ)
laws governing all kinds of business activities

商店(ㄕㄤ ㄉㄧㄢˋ)
a store; a shop

商定(ㄕㄤ ㄉㄧㄥˋ)
to decide or settle through discussions; to come to a decision as a result of discussions: 他們已商定拆除這棟古老的建築。They had decided to pull down the old building after discussions.

商隊(ㄕㄤ ㄉㄨㄟˋ)
a caravan

商討(ㄕㄤ ㄊㄠˇ)
a discussion; to discuss

商談(ㄕㄤ ㄊㄢˊ)
to exchange views; to con-

fer; to discuss; to negotiate: 你該和律師商談這件事。You should confer with the lawyer about this.
商團(ㄕㄤ ㄊㄨㄢˊ)
a group or society of businessmen
商量(ㄕㄤ ·ㄌㄧㄤ)or 商酌(ㄕㄤ ㄓㄨㄛˊ)
to exchange opinions or views; to hold a discussion; to confer; to put heads together; to go into a huddle: 這事好商量。This can be settled through discussion.
商路(ㄕㄤ ㄌㄨˋ)
a trade route
商旅(ㄕㄤ ㄌㄩˇ)
a traveling merchant
商略(ㄕㄤ ㄌㄩㄝˋ)
to discuss
商港(ㄕㄤ ㄍㄤˇ)
a commercial port; a seaport; a trading port
商股(ㄕㄤ ㄍㄨˇ)
privately owned shares or stock (of a business company, as opposed to state-owned shares or stock)
商賈(ㄕㄤ ㄍㄨˇ)
businessmen
商科(ㄕㄤ ㄎㄜ)
a department of commerce (in a college or university)
商號(ㄕㄤ ㄏㄠˋ)or 商行(ㄕㄤ ㄏㄤˊ)
① name of a shop or firm ② a business firm; a trading company; a commercial firm
商會(ㄕㄤ ㄏㄨㄟˋ)
a chamber of commerce
商家(ㄕㄤ ㄐㄧㄚ)
a business firm
商界(ㄕㄤ ㄐㄧㄝˋ)
the business world, or business circles: 這本書受到商界的稱讚。The book is praised in business circles.
商榷(ㄕㄤ ㄑㄩㄝˋ)
to discuss and consider; to deliberate over
商洽(ㄕㄤ ㄑㄧㄚˋ)
to arrange with somebody; to take up (a matter) with somebody
商情(ㄕㄤ ㄑㄧㄥˊ)
business or market information: 他供給我許多有用的商情。He gave me a lot of useful business information.
商學院(ㄕㄤ ㄒㄩㄝˊ ㄩㄢˋ)
the college of commerce
商戰(ㄕㄤ ㄓㄢˋ)
a trade war
商酌(ㄕㄤ ㄓㄨㄛˊ)
to discuss and consider; to deliberate over: 這個問題尚待商酌。This matter needs further discussion and consideration.
商場(ㄕㄤ ㄔㄤˇ)or(ㄕㄤ ㄔㄤˊ)
a market place; a department store; a bazaar
商船(ㄕㄤ ㄔㄨㄢˊ)
a merchantman; a merchant ship
商事(ㄕㄤ ㄕˋ)
commercial affairs
商事會計(ㄕㄤ ㄕˋ ㄎㄨㄞˋ ㄐㄧˋ)
business accountancy
商數(ㄕㄤ ㄕㄨˋ)
(arithmetic) the quotient: 在26÷2=13中，13是商數。In 26÷2=13, 13 is the quotient.
商人(ㄕㄤ ㄖㄣˊ)
a merchant; a businessman; a trader
商議(ㄕㄤ ㄧˋ)
to discuss and debate
商業(ㄕㄤ ㄧㄝˋ)
commerce; profit-seeking business
商業道德(ㄕㄤ ㄧㄝˋ ㄉㄠˋ ㄉㄜˊ)
business ethics
商業利益(ㄕㄤ ㄧㄝˋ ㄌㄧˋ ㄧˋ)
commercial profit
商業機關(ㄕㄤ ㄧㄝˋ ㄐㄧ ㄍㄨㄢ)
a commercial organization
商業學校(ㄕㄤ ㄧㄝˋ ㄒㄩㄝˊ ㄒㄧㄠˋ)
a vocational school of commerce; a commercial school
商業設計(ㄕㄤ ㄧㄝˋ ㄕㄜˋ ㄐㄧˋ)
commercial design
商業銀行(ㄕㄤ ㄧㄝˋ ㄧㄣˊ ㄏㄤˊ)
a commercial bank
商務(ㄕㄤ ㄨˋ)
commercial affairs; business affairs
商務代表(ㄕㄤ ㄨˋ ㄉㄞˋ ㄅㄧㄠˇ)
a commercial representative; a trade representative
商務代表處(ㄕㄤ ㄨˋ ㄉㄞˋ ㄅㄧㄠˇ ㄔㄨˋ)
a trade representative's office
商務參事(ㄕㄤ ㄨˋ ㄘㄢ ㄕˋ)or 商務專員(ㄕㄤ ㄨˋ ㄓㄨㄢ ㄩㄢˊ)
a commercial attache; a commercial councilor
商約(ㄕㄤ ㄩㄝ)
a business contract; a commercial treaty

【問】 656
ㄨㄣˋ wenn wèn

1. to ask; to inquire: 他們問農人這裡離城有多遠。They ask the farmer how far it is from the city.
2. to interrogate; to examine: 他被法官審問。He was examined by the judge.
3. to ask after; to inquire after: 她常在信裡問起你。She frequently asks after you in her letters.
4. to hold responsible: 出了事唯你是問。You'll be held responsible if anything goes wrong.

問卜(ㄨㄣˋ ㄅㄨˇ)
to consult fortune-tellers (in making a decision); to seek guidance from divination
問明(ㄨㄣˋ ㄇㄧㄥˊ)
to ask for explicit answers; to find out the details
問答(ㄨㄣˋ ㄉㄚˊ)
questions and answers; a dialogue; a conversation
問道於盲(ㄨㄣˋ ㄉㄠˋ ㄩˊ ㄇㄤˊ)
(literally) to ask the blind to show the way—to seek advice from an ignorant person
問鼎(ㄨㄣˋ ㄉㄧㄥˇ)
to inquire about the bronze tripod (which is the symbol of imperial power)—(figuratively) to covet the throne
問鼎中原(ㄨㄣˋ ㄉㄧㄥˇ ㄓㄨㄥ ㄩㄢˊ)
to aspire after the throne; to have an ambition for the throne
問題(ㄨㄣˋ ㄊㄧˊ)
① a problem; a question; an issue: 我可以問個問題嗎? May I ask a question? ② trouble; mishap: 我車子的引擎有問題。My car has engine trouble.
問題行爲(ㄨㄣˋ ㄊㄧˊ ㄒㄧㄥˊ ㄨㄟˊ)
problem behavior
問題少年(ㄨㄣˋ ㄊㄧˊ ㄕㄠˋ ㄋㄧㄢˊ)
a problem youth; a juvenile

delinquent

問題兒童(ㄨㄣˋ ㄊㄧˊ ㄦˊ ㄊㄨㄥˊ)
a problem child

問難(ㄨㄣˋ ㄋㄢˋ)
to ask difficult questions in a debate

問卦(ㄨㄣˋ ㄍㄨㄚˋ)
to consult oracles

問供(ㄨㄣˋ ㄍㄨㄥˋ)
to interrogate a criminal suspect; to examine and take an affidavit

問好(ㄨㄣˋ ㄏㄠˇ)or 問候(ㄨㄣˋ ㄏㄡˋ)
to ask about a person's health or welfare; to inquire after; to ask after; to send one's regards: 請代我向你雙親問好。Please give my regards to your parents.

問號(ㄨㄣˋ ㄏㄠˋ)
①an interrogation mark; a question mark ② an unknown factor; an unsolved problem

問寒問暖(ㄨㄣˋ ㄏㄢˊ ㄨㄣˋ ㄋㄨㄢˇ)
to be solicitous for somebody's health; to show a kind concern for another's comfort

問話(ㄨㄣˋ ㄏㄨㄚˋ)
to ask questions

問疾(ㄨㄣˋ ㄐㄧˊ)
to visit and console a patient

問津(ㄨㄣˋ ㄐㄧㄣ)
①to show interest (in something for sale or intended to arouse public interest) ②to ask for guidance in a new field of endeavor ③to ask in which direction to go

問卷(ㄨㄣˋ ㄐㄩㄢˋ)
a questionnaire

問心有愧(ㄨㄣˋ ㄒㄧㄣ ㄧㄡˇ ㄎㄨㄟˋ)
to feel a twinge of conscience

問心無愧(ㄨㄣˋ ㄒㄧㄣ ㄨˊ ㄎㄨㄟˋ)
to examine oneself and find nothing to be ashamed of; with a clear conscience; to have a clear conscience; to feel no qualms upon self-examination: 我已盡力而爲，因此問心無愧。I had done my best, so I felt no qualms upon self-examination.

問訊(ㄨㄣˋ ㄒㄩㄣˋ)
①to inquire after a person ②to ask; to inquire ③(said of Buddhist monks or nuns) to press the palms together as a salute

問斬(ㄨㄣˋ ㄓㄢˇ)
to execute a prisoner by beheading him

問診(ㄨㄣˋ ㄓㄣˇ)
interrogation, one of the four methods of diagnosis in Chinese medicine

問住(ㄨㄣˋ ˙ㄓㄨ)or 問倒(ㄨㄣˋ ㄉㄠˇ)
to be unable to answer a question asked: 他被問住了。He was unable to answer the difficult question.

問長問短(ㄨㄣˋ ㄔㄤˊ ㄨㄣˋ ㄉㄨㄢˇ)
to ask many questions about other people's affairs; to be inquisitive

問世(ㄨㄣˋ ㄕˋ)
①(said of a new book) to come out: 他的第一部小說將在下個月問世。His first novel will come out next month. ②to participate in public affairs actively

問罪(ㄨㄣˋ ㄗㄨㄟˋ)
to call a person to account; to reprimand; to reprove; to rebuke; to condemn; to denounce

問安(ㄨㄣˋ ㄢ)
(usually to elders) to wish somebody good health; to send greetings

問案(ㄨㄣˋ ㄢˋ)
to try (or hear) a case; to hold court

【啊】657
1. ㄚ a ā

an exclamatory particle: 啊！樹長得眞好哇！Oh, what a wonderful tree! 啊！我們終於到了。Well, here we are at last.

啊哈(ㄚ ˙ㄏㄚ)
"aha" (an exclamation to show irony or mockery)

啊呀(ㄚ ˙ㄧㄚ)
"aya" (an exclamation to show surprise)

啊唷(ㄚ ˙ㄧㄛ)
"ayo" (the sound uttered when suddenly get hurt)

【啊】657
2. ˙ㄚ ·a ɑ

a phrase-final particle: 她唱得多麼好聽啊！How well she sings! 務必珍重啊！Do take care of yourself.

【啤】658
ㄆㄧˊ pyi pí

a character used in transliterating

啤酒(ㄆㄧˊ ㄐㄧㄡˇ)
beer

啤酒花(ㄆㄧˊ ㄐㄧㄡˇ ㄏㄨㄚ)
hops

【啐】659
1. ㄘㄨㄟˋ tsuey cuì

1. to taste; to sip
2. to spit: 我啐他一口。I spat upon him.

啐一口痰(ㄘㄨㄟˋ ㄧˋ ㄎㄡˇ ㄊㄢˊ)
to spit phlegm

【啐】659
2. ˙ㄑ(ㄧ) ·ch(i) q(i)

Fie! (an interjection expressing contempt): 啐！不要臉。Fie, for shame!

【啓】660
(啟) ㄑㄧˇ chii qǐ

1. to open
2. to begin; to start
3. to explain
4. to inform; to state
5. a letter

啓報(ㄑㄧˇ ㄅㄠˋ)
to report to one's superior and ask for instructions

啓蒙(ㄑㄧˇ ㄇㄥˊ)
①to enlighten ②a primer

啓蒙老師(ㄑㄧˇ ㄇㄥˊ ㄌㄠˇ ㄕ)
a child's first tutor or teacher

啓蒙運動(ㄑㄧˇ ㄇㄥˊ ㄩㄣˋ ㄉㄨㄥˋ)
the Enlightenment

啓發(ㄑㄧˇ ㄈㄚ)or 啓迪(ㄑㄧˇ ㄉㄧˊ)
to prompt mental development (of another); to inspire; to teach; to instruct

啓封(ㄑㄧˇ ㄈㄥ)
①to open an envelope ②to remove the labels on impounded goods or property before returning them to the owner

啓動(ㄑㄧˇ ㄉㄨㄥˋ)
to start (a machine, etc.); to switch on

啓開(ㄑㄧˇ ㄎㄞ)
to open

啓航(ㄑㄧˇ ㄏㄤˊ)
to set sail; to weigh anchor

〔口部〕

啓行(ㄑㄧˇ ㄒㄧㄥˊ)or 啓程(ㄑㄧˇ ㄔㄥˊ)
to start on a journey; to set out
啓齒(ㄑㄧˇ ㄔˇ)
to open the mouth to say something: 他難以啓齒。He felt difficult to say it.
啓事(ㄑㄧˇ ㄕˋ)
a notice; an announcement (in writing)
啓示(ㄑㄧˇ ㄕˋ)
revelation; enlightenment; inspiration: 很多詩人和藝術家從大自然中獲得許多啓示。Many poets and artists have drawn a good deal of inspiration from nature.
啓示錄(ㄑㄧˇ ㄕˋ ㄌㄨˋ)
the Revelation (of the New Testament)
啓用(ㄑㄧˇ ㄩㄥˋ)
to start using

【啖】 661
(噉) ㄉㄢˋ dann dàn
1. (a literary expression) to eat
2. to feed

【啣】 662
ㄒㄧㄢˊ shyan xián
the vulgar form of 銜
1. a bridle
2. to hold in the mouth
3. to harbor

【唷】 663
ㄧㄛ io yō
an exclamation expressing surprise or pain: 唷! 好痛! Ouch, it hurts.

【啦】 664
·ㄌㄚ ·la la
a phrase-final particle: 天已不早，你該走啦! You'd better go now; it's getting late. 他早就來啦! Why, he's been here a long time!
啦啦隊(ㄌㄚ ·ㄌㄚ ㄉㄨㄟˋ)
a cheer squad
啦啦隊長(ㄌㄚ ·ㄌㄚ ㄉㄨㄟˋ ㄓㄤˇ)
a cheerleader

【啞】 665
ㄧㄚˇ yea yǎ
1. dumb; mute: 他生來即啞。He has been dumb from birth.
2. hoarse; husky
3. a phrase-final particle
啞巴 or 啞叭(ㄧㄚˇ ·ㄅㄚ)
(a) deaf-mute (person)
啞巴虧(ㄧㄚˇ ·ㄅㄚ ㄎㄨㄟ)
one's grievances which are unable to speak out
啞巴吃黃連(ㄧㄚˇ ·ㄅㄚ ㄔ ㄏㄨㄤˊ ㄌㄧㄢˊ)
to be unable to complain after one suffers a loss, or is unjustly blamed, etc.
啞謎(ㄧㄚˇ ㄇㄧˊ)
a riddle; a puzzling remark; an enigma
啞鈴(ㄧㄚˇ ㄌㄧㄥˊ)
a dumbbell
啞口無言(ㄧㄚˇ ㄎㄡˇ ㄨˊ ㄧㄢˊ)
to be speechless (when a criminal suspect is brought face to face with evidence against him, or when one's argument is completely demolished by the opponent); to be rendered speechless
啞劇(ㄧㄚˇ ㄐㄩˋ)
a pantomime; a dumb show
啞然失笑(ㄧㄚˇ ㄖㄢˊ ㄕ ㄒㄧㄠˋ)
to laugh involuntarily (upon seeing an embarrassing but funny situation); to guffaw
啞然無聲(ㄧㄚˇ ㄖㄢˊ ㄨˊ ㄕㄥ)
Silence reigns.
啞嗓子(ㄧㄚˇ ㄙㄤˇ ·ㄗ)
a hoarse voice

【啃】 666
ㄎㄣˇ keen kěn
to bite; to gnaw; to nibble: 他啃不動甘蔗。He can't bite the sugar cane.
啃骨頭(ㄎㄣˇ ㄍㄨˇ ·ㄊㄡ)
to pick out the residual meat on the bones with teeth
啃書本(ㄎㄣˇ ㄕㄨ ㄅㄣˇ)
to study very hard; to delve into books

【唬】 667
ㄏㄨˇ huu hǔ
1. to intimidate; to scare: 她沒被唬住。She wasn't intimidated.
2. the roar of a tiger
唬人(ㄏㄨˇ ㄖㄣˊ)
to intimidate people; to assume an intimidating air; to bluff: 你別唬人。Quit bluffing.

【唪】 668
ㄈㄥˇ feeng fěng
to chant; to recite
唪經(ㄈㄥˇ ㄐㄧㄥ)
to chant Buddist scriptures

【唸】 669
(念) ㄋㄧㄢˋ niann niàn
to read; to chant; to recite
唸唸有詞(ㄋㄧㄢˋ ㄋㄧㄢˋ ㄧㄡˇ ㄘˊ)
to mumble to oneself

【啥】 670
ㄕㄚˊ shar shá
what: 那有啥關係? What does it matter?
啥事體(ㄕㄚˊ ㄕˋ ㄊㄧˇ)
(Shanghai dialect) What's the matter?
啥人(ㄕㄚˊ ㄖㄣˊ)
(Shanghai dialect) Who are you? 或 Who is it? 或 Who is there?

【啜】 671
ㄔㄨㄛˋ chuoh chuò
1. to drink; to sip
2. to cry in a subdued manner; to sob
啜茗(ㄔㄨㄛˋ ㄇㄧㄥˊ)
to drink tea; to sip tea: 那老人喜歡啜茗。The old man likes to sip tea.
啜泣(ㄔㄨㄛˋ ㄑㄧˋ)
to sob
啜汁(ㄔㄨㄛˋ ㄓ)
to take credit
啜賺(ㄔㄨㄛˋ ㄓㄨㄢˋ)
to make honey promises; to pay lip service
啜菽飲水(ㄔㄨㄛˋ ㄕㄨ ㄧㄣˇ ㄕㄨㄟˇ)
One can be a dutiful son to his parents even in poverty.

九畫

【啻】 672
ㄔˋ chyh chì
1. only; merely
2. as in 不啻—tantamount

【啼】 673
ㄊㄧˊ tyi tí
(especially said of birds) to crow; to cry: 雞啼狗叫。Cocks crow and dogs bark.
啼哭(ㄊㄧˊ ㄎㄨ)
to cry; to weep and wail
啼飢號寒(ㄊㄧˊ ㄐㄧ ㄏㄠˊ ㄏㄢˊ)
to wail with hunger and cold
啼叫(ㄊㄧˊ ㄐㄧㄠˋ)
to scream; to screech; to wail
啼泣(ㄊㄧˊ ㄑㄧˋ)

to wail; to sob
啼笑皆非(ㄊㄧˊ ㄒㄧㄠˋ ㄐㄧㄝ ㄈㄟ)
between tears and laughter; unable to cry or laugh; to choke someone up: 這齣鬧劇令我們啼笑皆非。The farce made us not know whether to laugh or cry.

【啾】674 ㄐㄧㄡ jiou jiū
1. the chirps of birds or insects
2. the wailing of infants
啾啾(ㄐㄧㄡ ㄐㄧㄡ)
the chirps of insects

【喀】675 ㄎㄚˋ kah kà
a character used for transliterating
喀麥隆(ㄎㄚˋ ㄇㄞˋ ㄌㄨㄥˊ)
Cameroon
喀拉蚩(ㄎㄚˋ ㄌㄚ ㄔ)
Karachi, a port city of Pakistan
喀嚓(ㄎㄚˋ ㄔㄚ)
to crack; to snap
喀什米爾(ㄎㄚˋ ㄕˋ ㄇㄧˇ ㄦˇ)
Kashmir

【喁】676 ㄩㄥˊ yong yóng
1. harmony or unison of sounds
2. the state of a fish putting its mouth above the water surface
喁喁(ㄩㄥˊ ㄩㄥˊ)
① the state of people showing unanimous respect for their leader ②(to talk) in whispers: 她們喁喁私語。They talked in whispers.

【喂】677 ㄨㄟˋ wey wèi
(an interjection for calling another's attention) hallo; please; if you please; I say; hey; hullo: 喂！止步！Hey! stop!

【喃】678 ㄋㄢˊ nan nán
1. the cries of a swallow
2. to murmur; to mumble; to mutter
喃喃自語(ㄋㄢˊ ㄋㄢˊ ㄗˋ ㄩˇ)
to murmur to oneself; to mutter to oneself; to mumble to oneself: 那老人喃喃自語。The old man was mumbling to himself.

【善】679 ㄕㄢˋ shann shàn
1. good; virtuous; goodness; virtue; good deeds; benevolent actions
2. to be good at; to be skilled in
3. to perfect; to make a success of: 工欲善其事，必先利其器。A workman must sharpen his tools if he is to do his work well.
4. to remedy; to relieve
5. properly
善罷甘休(ㄕㄢˋ ㄅㄚˋ ㄍㄢ ㄒㄧㄡ)
to stop quarreling, fighting, etc. with others; to leave the matter at that; to let it go at that
善報(ㄕㄢˋ ㄅㄠˋ)
the reward for kindness
善本書(ㄕㄢˋ ㄅㄣˇ ㄕㄨ)
a rare book
善變(ㄕㄢˋ ㄅㄧㄢˋ)
changeable; fickle; capricious
善門難開(ㄕㄢˋ ㄇㄣˊ ㄋㄢˊ ㄎㄞ)
It is difficult to start charity (as it cannot be stopped halfway).
善謀(ㄕㄢˋ ㄇㄡˊ)
①a good scheme ②good at thinking out schemes; quick-minded
善待(ㄕㄢˋ ㄉㄞˋ)
to treat (a person) well; to accord (a person) good treatment
善刀而藏(ㄕㄢˋ ㄉㄠ ㄦˊ ㄘㄤˊ)
do not push one's advantage too far
善男信女(ㄕㄢˋ ㄋㄢˊ ㄒㄧㄣˋ ㄋㄩˇ)
devotees of Buddha; the faithful
善類(ㄕㄢˋ ㄌㄟˋ)
good people
善鄰(ㄕㄢˋ ㄌㄧㄣˊ)
to maintain good relations with neighboring countries
善良(ㄕㄢˋ ㄌㄧㄤˊ)
(said of a person) good; kindhearted; gentle; well-disposed: 她天性很善良。She is very kind at nature.
善果(ㄕㄢˋ ㄍㄨㄛˇ)
the reward of good deeds
善觀風色(ㄕㄢˋ ㄍㄨㄢ ㄈㄥ ㄙㄜˋ)
quick to see which way the wind blows—very shrewd
善後(ㄕㄢˋ ㄏㄡˋ)
rehabilitation (after a disaster, a tragedy, etc.); to make good arrangements for the aftermath
善後救濟(ㄕㄢˋ ㄏㄡˋ ㄐㄧㄡˋ ㄐㄧˋ)
relief measures for rehabilitation
善舉(ㄕㄢˋ ㄐㄩˇ)or 善行(ㄕㄢˋ ㄒㄧㄥˊ)
a good deed; a benevolent action
善心(ㄕㄢˋ ㄒㄧㄣ)
kindness; a compassionate heart
善行足式(ㄕㄢˋ ㄒㄧㄥˊ ㄗㄨˊ ㄕˋ)
a kind deed worthy of emulating
善戰(ㄕㄢˋ ㄓㄢˋ)
brave and skillful in fighting
善終(ㄕㄢˋ ㄓㄨㄥ)
to die a natural death
善始善終(ㄕㄢˋ ㄕˇ ㄕㄢˋ ㄓㄨㄥ)
to begin well and end well; to do something from the beginning to the end
善士(ㄕㄢˋ ㄕˋ)
a benevolent person; a good man; a philanthropist
善事(ㄕㄢˋ ㄕˋ)
good deeds; philanthropic acts; charitable work
善人(ㄕㄢˋ ㄖㄣˊ)
a good Samaritan; a kindhearted and benevolent fellow
善自爲謀(ㄕㄢˋ ㄗˋ ㄨㄟˊ ㄇㄡˊ)
versed in planning or working for one's own interests
善惡(ㄕㄢˋ ㄜˋ)
good and evil; virtue and vice
善惡不分(ㄕㄢˋ ㄜˋ ㄅㄨˋ ㄈㄣ)
to be unable to tell good from evil
善以爲寶(ㄕㄢˋ ㄧˇ ㄨㄟˊ ㄅㄠˇ)
to value virtue as a treasure
善意(ㄕㄢˋ ㄧˋ)
① good or kindly intentions ② well-meaning; sincere criticisms; constructive criticisms
善游者溺(ㄕㄢˋ ㄧㄡˊ ㄓㄜˇ ㄋㄧˋ)
(literally) A good swimmer often gets drowned.—Overconfidence in one's skill may

〔口部〕

bring him disaster.

善有善報(ㄕㄢˋ ㄧㄡˇ ㄕㄢˋ ㄅㄠˋ)
Kind deeds pay rich dividends to the doer. 善有善報，惡有惡報。 Good will be rewarded with good, and evil with evil.

善言(ㄕㄢˋ ㄧㄢˊ)
well-intentioned advice

善忘(ㄕㄢˋ ㄨㄤˋ)
forgetful; weak of memory; to be prone to forget

善於(ㄕㄢˋ ㄩˊ)
good at; skilled in: 她善於歌舞。She is good at singing and dancing.

善緣(ㄕㄢˋ ㄩㄢˊ)
①(Buddhism) the favorable ties resulting from contributions to a temple ② a lucky meeting of good friends

【嗖】 680 ㄙㄡ sou sōu
1. the laughing expression
2. the sound one makes to drive away birds
3. to whiz

嗖嗖(ㄙㄡ ㄙㄡ)
with laughter; laughingly

【喇】 681 1. ㄌㄚˇ laa lǎ
1. a horn; a trumpet; a bugle
2. a lama
3. a character used in transliteration

喇叭(ㄌㄚˇ ˙ㄅㄚ)
① a horn; a trumpet; a bugle ② a loudspeaker

喇叭褲(ㄌㄚˇ ˙ㄅㄚ ㄎㄨˋ)
bell-shaped pants; flared trousers; bell-bottom pants

喇叭花(ㄌㄚˇ ˙ㄅㄚ ㄏㄨㄚ) or 牽牛花(ㄑㄧㄢ ㄋㄧㄡˊ ㄏㄨㄚ)
(botany) morning glory

喇嘛(ㄌㄚˇ ˙ㄇㄚ)
a lama (a priest of Lamaism)

喇嘛教(ㄌㄚˇ ˙ㄇㄚ ㄐㄧㄠˋ)
Lamaism

【喇】 681 2. ㄌㄚ lha lā
a character used for its sound

【喈】 682 ㄐㄧㄝ jie jiē
harmonious sounds

【喉】 683 ㄏㄡˊ hour hóu
the throat; the gullet; guttural: 我喉嚨痛。I have a sore throat.

喉頭(ㄏㄡˊ ㄊㄡˊ)
the larynx

喉頭炎(ㄏㄡˊ ㄊㄡˊ ㄧㄢˊ)
laryngitis; laryngeal catarrh

喉痛(ㄏㄡˊ ㄊㄨㄥˋ)
a sore throat

喉嚨(ㄏㄡˊ ㄌㄨㄥˊ)
the throat; the gullet

喉管(ㄏㄡˊ ㄍㄨㄢˇ)
bronchia

喉科(ㄏㄡˊ ㄎㄜ)
laryngology (usually together with otology and rhinology, known as otorhinolaryngology)

喉急(ㄏㄡˊ ㄐㄧˊ)
desperately anxious

喉結(ㄏㄡˊ ㄐㄧㄝˊ)
Adam's apple

喉舌(ㄏㄡˊ ㄕㄜˊ)
① that which functions as the mechanics of talking ② the mouthpiece or organ of a party, government, etc.

喉音(ㄏㄡˊ ㄧㄣ)
(phonetics) guttural sounds

【喊】 684 ㄏㄢˇ haan hǎn
1. to shout; to scream; to cry; a loud call or cry; a shout or scream: 他把嗓子喊啞了。He shouted himself hoarse.
2. to call (a person): 他從樓上喊我。He called to me from upstairs.

喊打(ㄏㄢˇ ㄉㄚˇ)
to shout "Beat him (her or them)!"

喊痛(ㄏㄢˇ ㄊㄨㄥˋ)
to yell out of pain; to yelp in pain

喊苦(ㄏㄢˇ ㄎㄨˇ)
to complain about hardships loudly; to cry out one's grievances; to bawl out pain or suffering

喊好(ㄏㄢˇ ㄏㄠˇ)
to cheer and applaud (a performer, etc.); to yell "Bravo!"

喊話(ㄏㄢˇ ㄏㄨㄚˋ)
(psychological warfare) to talk to the enemy at close range over a loudspeaker, asking him to surrender, etc.; propaganda directed to the enemy at the front line; to talk to a cornered criminal to effect the same

喊叫(ㄏㄢˇ ㄐㄧㄠˋ)
to shout, scream, or cry loudly; a loud cry, shout, scream, etc.

喊救(ㄏㄢˇ ㄐㄧㄡˋ)
to call for help; to cry for help

喊殺連天(ㄏㄢˇ ㄕㄚ ㄌㄧㄢˊ ㄊㄧㄢ)
The air is filled with shouts of "Kill! Kill!"

喊殺之聲(ㄏㄢˇ ㄕㄚ ㄓ ㄕㄥ)
the voices of soldiers yelling "*Sha! Sha!*"—"Kill! Kill!" (in close-range combat)

喊聲(ㄏㄢˇ ㄕㄥ)
shouts and screams

喊冤(ㄏㄢˇ ㄩㄢ)
to shout out one's grievance in the streets (when a high official is passing) or in court; to demand justice loudly

【喋】 685 ㄉㄧㄝˊ dye dié
to nag; to chatter; to prattle; to babble; to be very talkative; to rattle

喋喋(ㄉㄧㄝˊ ㄉㄧㄝˊ)
talkative; to nag or chatter; to rattle

喋喋不休(ㄉㄧㄝˊ ㄉㄧㄝˊ ㄅㄨˋ ㄒㄧㄡ)
to keep talking; to chatter without stopping; to cackle

喋囁(ㄉㄧㄝˊ ㄋㄧㄝˋ)
to whisper; to converse in a low voice

喋血(ㄉㄧㄝˊ ㄒㄩㄝˋ)
blood flowing; bloodshed; to bleed

【喏】 686 1. ㄖㄜˇ ree rě
an address or greeting of respect when meeting a superior, etc.

【喏】 686 2. ㄋㄨㄛˋ nuoh nuò
a word used to attract other's attention

【喑】 687 ㄧㄣ in yin
1. to lose one's voice—dumb or mute
2. to keep silent—to say noth-

ing
喑聾(ㄧㄣ ㄌㄨㄥˊ)
① deaf-and-mute ② a deaf-mute
喑啞(ㄧㄣ ㄧㄚˇ)
dumb; unable to talk; mute

【喔】 688 1. ㄨㄛˋ woh wò
the crowing of a cock; the cackling of fowls
喔齪 or 齷齪(ㄨㄛˋ ㄔㄨㄛˋ)
in a hurry; in haste; hastily
喔喔(ㄨㄛˋ ㄨㄛˋ)
the crowing of a cock; the cackling of fowls

【喔】 688 2. ㄛ o ō
an exclamation: 喔，原來是你！Oh, so it's you!
喔唷(ㄛ ˙ㄧㄛ)
an exclamation to indicate understanding, surprise, or grief: 喔唷，好痛！Ouch, it hurts!

【喘】 689 ㄔㄨㄢˇ choan chuǎn
1. to pant; to gasp; to breathe hard
2. (pathology) asthma
喘氣(ㄔㄨㄢˇ ㄑㄧˋ)
① to pant; to gasp; to breathe hard ② to take a breather; to take a break
喘息(ㄔㄨㄢˇ ㄒㄧˊ)
① to take breath, or a rest (after strenuous exercise) ② to pant; to gasp for breath
喘息機會(ㄔㄨㄢˇ ㄒㄧˊ ㄐㄧ ㄏㄨㄟˋ)
a breathing spell; a respite
喘噓噓 or 喘吁吁(ㄔㄨㄢˇ ㄒㄩ ㄒㄩ)
breathing very hard; panting; to puff and blow

【喙】 690 ㄏㄨㄟˋ huey huì
1. a beak; a bill; a snout
2. a mouth
喙長三尺(ㄏㄨㄟˋ ㄔㄤˊ ㄙㄢ ㄔˇ)
(literally) to have a beak three feet long—fond of exposing other people's secrets; fond of faultfinding

【喚】 691 ㄏㄨㄢˋ huann huàn
1. to call
2. to summon
3. to arouse
喚起(ㄏㄨㄢˋ ㄑㄧˇ)
① to arouse to action ② to call; to evoke
喚醒(ㄏㄨㄢˋ ㄒㄧㄥˇ)
to arouse; to awaken; to call up: 早晨喚醒我。Call me in the morning.

【喜】 692 ㄒㄧˇ shii xǐ
1. a joyful thing; a happy event
2. joy: 他充滿歡喜。He was filled with joy.
3. to like; to love; to be fond of
4. joyful; happy; delightful; pleasant; auspicious
喜不自勝(ㄒㄧˇ ㄅㄨˋ ㄗˋ ㄕㄥ)
unable to contain oneself for joy; to be delighted beyond measure
喜馬拉雅山(ㄒㄧˇ ㄇㄚˇ ㄌㄚ ㄧㄚˇ ㄕㄢ)
the Himalayas
喜房(ㄒㄧˇ ㄈㄤˊ)
a bridal chamber
喜堂(ㄒㄧˇ ㄊㄤˊ)
a wedding hall
喜帖(ㄒㄧˇ ㄊㄧㄝ)
a wedding invitation: 謝謝你的喜帖。Thank you for your wedding invitation.
喜怒不形於色(ㄒㄧˇ ㄋㄨˋ ㄅㄨˋ ㄒㄧㄥˊ ㄩˊ ㄙㄜˋ)
poker-faced; expressionless; to show no emotion; with a deadpan face
喜怒哀樂(ㄒㄧˇ ㄋㄨˋ ㄞ ㄌㄜˋ)
the feelings of joy, anger, sorrow and delight; different emotions
喜怒無常(ㄒㄧˇ ㄋㄨˋ ㄨˊ ㄔㄤˊ)
having an unpredictable temper
喜樂(ㄒㄧˇ ㄌㄜˋ)
① joy; gladness; great pleasure ② to give a zest to one's joy
喜好(ㄒㄧˇ ㄏㄠˋ)
to be fond of; to delight in; to like; to love: 他喜好運動。He likes sports.
喜歡(ㄒㄧˇ ㄏㄨㄢ)
① to like; to be fond of; to love; to be pleased with: 他很喜歡釣魚。He loves to go fishing. ② happy; joyful; delightful
喜酒(ㄒㄧˇ ㄐㄧㄡˇ)
① a wedding feast ② wine drunk at a wedding feast
喜劇(ㄒㄧˇ ㄐㄩˋ)
a comedy
喜氣洋洋(ㄒㄧˇ ㄑㄧˋ ㄧㄤˊ ㄧㄤˊ)
① a joyful atmosphere; a festival mood ② a cheerful look or expression
喜慶(ㄒㄧˇ ㄑㄧㄥˋ)
auspicious or happy occasions (such as wedding, birth, promotion, etc.)
喜鵲(ㄒㄧˇ ㄑㄩㄝˋ)
the magpie
喜笑顏開(ㄒㄧˇ ㄒㄧㄠˋ ㄧㄢˊ ㄎㄞ)
cheerful; brimming with smiles; an ear-to-ear grin
喜新厭舊(ㄒㄧˇ ㄒㄧㄣ ㄧㄢˋ ㄐㄧㄡˋ)
to like the new and dislike the old (often referring to love affairs)
喜信(ㄒㄧˇ ㄒㄧㄣˋ)
good news; happy tidings
喜形於色(ㄒㄧˇ ㄒㄧㄥˊ ㄩˊ ㄙㄜˋ)
to look pleased; to have an expression of delight: 他喜形於色。He looked visibly pleased. 或 His face lighted up with pleasure.
喜訊(ㄒㄧˇ ㄒㄩㄣˋ)
happy news; good news; glad tidings
喜幛 or 喜帳(ㄒㄧˇ ㄓㄤˋ)
a silk hanging gilded with words of blessing, presented as a wedding gift
喜出望外(ㄒㄧˇ ㄔㄨ ㄨㄤˋ ㄨㄞˋ)
joy over unexpected good luck; unexpected joy
喜事(ㄒㄧˇ ㄕˋ)
an occasion for joy (especially a wedding)
喜孜孜 or 喜滋滋(ㄒㄧˇ ㄗ ㄗ)
joyful; looking pleased
喜色(ㄒㄧˇ ㄙㄜˋ)
a joyful expression; a pleased look
喜愛(ㄒㄧˇ ㄞˋ)
to like; to love; to be fond of; to be keen on: 我們喜愛戶外活動。We are keen on outdoor activities.
喜洋洋(ㄒㄧˇ ㄧㄤˊ ㄧㄤˊ)
beaming with joy; radiant
喜雨(ㄒㄧˇ ㄩˇ)
a timely rainfall; seasonable rain
喜悅(ㄒㄧˇ ㄩㄝˋ)

joy; delight; gratification: 她的臉上洋溢著喜悅。Her face is radiant with joy.

【喝】 693 1. ㄏㄜ he he

to drink

喝墨水兒(ㄏㄜ ㄇㄛˋ ㄕㄨㄟˇ ㄦ)
(literally) to drink ink—to study: 他喝過洋墨水。He has studied abroad.

喝酒(ㄏㄜ ㄐㄧㄡˇ)
to drink (alcoholic beverages)

喝西北風(ㄏㄜ ㄒㄧ ㄅㄟˇ ㄈㄥ)
(literally) to drink the northwest wind—to have nothing to eat; to go hungry; to suffer from hunger

喝醉(ㄏㄜ ㄗㄨㄟˋ)
to get drunk; to become intoxicated

【喝】 693 2 ㄏㄜˋ heh hè

to shout; to call out aloud

喝道(ㄏㄜˋ ㄉㄠˋ)
in imperial China when a ranking official was on tour, the advance party of his retinue would loudly announce his arrival so as to clear a passage and to enable the people to have time to show proper respect

喝倒彩(ㄏㄜˋ ㄉㄠˋ ㄘㄞˇ)
to make catcalls; to hoot; to hiss

喝六呼么(ㄏㄜˋ ㄌㄧㄡˋ ㄏㄨ ㄧㄠ)
to gamble at dice game

喝令(ㄏㄜˋ ㄌㄧㄥˋ)
to shout an order

喝彩(ㄏㄜˋ ㄘㄞˇ)
to shout "Bravo!"; to applaud; to bring down the house; to acclaim; to cheer: 我們齊聲喝彩。 All of us cheer in chorus.

【唧】 694 (唧) ㄐㄧˊ jyi jí (又讀 ㄐㄧ ji jī)

1. a pump
2. the buzzing sound
3. to squirt: 水從管中唧了出來。The water squirted through a tube.

唧筒(ㄐㄧˊ ㄊㄨㄥˇ)
a pump

唧咕(ㄐㄧ ·ㄍㄨ)
to murmur; to whisper; to mutter

唧唧喳喳(ㄐㄧ ㄐㄧ ㄓㄚ ㄓㄚ)
to chirp

唧唧(ㄐㄧˊ ㄐㄧˊ)
to chirp; the buzz (as of cicadas)

【喟】 695 ㄎㄨㄟˋ kuey kuì

to sigh heavily

喟嘆(ㄎㄨㄟˋ ㄊㄢˋ)
to sigh with deep feeling

喟然長嘆(ㄎㄨㄟˋ ㄖㄢˊ ㄔㄤˊ ㄊㄢˋ)
to sigh deeply

【喧】 696 ㄒㄩㄢ shiuan xuan

1. to talk noisily; to clamor
2. noise; hubbub; uproar; noisy

喧賓奪主(ㄒㄩㄢ ㄅㄧㄣ ㄉㄨㄛˊ ㄓㄨˇ)
(literally) a talkative guest usurping the place of the host—to act like a boss where one does not belong; to dominate the show on an occasion when one is supposed to be only a spectator

喧騰(ㄒㄩㄢ ㄊㄥˊ)
noise and excitement; hubbub: 老師進來時，班上一片喧騰。The class was in a hubbub when the teacher came in.

喧天(ㄒㄩㄢ ㄊㄧㄢ)
to fill the air with noise

喧鬧(ㄒㄩㄢ ㄋㄠˋ)
noise from a crowd; hubbub; noisy

喧聒(ㄒㄩㄢ ㄍㄨㄚ)
noisy

喧嘩(ㄒㄩㄢ ㄏㄨㄚˊ)
noise (especially from a brawling crowd); uproar; turmoil: 不要喧嘩。Don't make such a loud noise.

喧囂(ㄒㄩㄢ ㄒㄧㄠ)
noise; din; uproar

喧擾(ㄒㄩㄢ ㄖㄠˇ)
to disturb by noisy talk

喧嚷(ㄒㄩㄢ ㄖㄤˇ)
clamor; hubbub; din; racket

【喨】 697 ㄌㄧㄤˋ liang liàng

a clear, resonant sound

【喻】 698 ㄩˋ yuh yù

1. to liken; to compare; to use a figure of speech; an illustration; a parable
2. to know; to be acquainted with: 他是個家喻戶曉的演員。The actor is known widely.
3. to explain; to make clear; to tell the meaning of; to instruct
4. a Chinese family name

【喪】 699 1. ㄙㄤ sang sāng

1. death; dying
2. to mourn
3. funeral

喪服(ㄙㄤ ㄈㄨˊ)
mourning dress or costume

喪禮(ㄙㄤ ㄌㄧˇ)
funeral rites

喪亂(ㄙㄤ ㄌㄨㄢˋ)
death and disorder

喪祭(ㄙㄤ ㄐㄧˋ)
a funeral service: 我們下星期日要去參加喪祭。We will attend a funeral service next Sunday.

喪家(ㄙㄤ ㄐㄧㄚ)
the bereaved family

喪居(ㄙㄤ ㄐㄩ)
to live in mourning

喪期(ㄙㄤ ㄑㄧˊ)
a mourning period

喪主(ㄙㄤ ㄓㄨˇ)
the eldest son taking charge of a parent's funeral or the eldest grandson in the absence of the eldest son

喪鐘(ㄙㄤ ㄓㄨㄥ)
① a knell; a death knell ② death knell—an action or event presaging death or destruction

喪事(ㄙㄤ ㄕˋ)
funeral affairs

喪葬(ㄙㄤ ㄗㄤˋ)
funeral service and burial

【喪】 699 2. ㄙㄤˋ sanq sàng

1. to lose; to be deprived of
2. to be defeated
3. to decline; to go down

喪敗(ㄙㄤˋ ㄅㄞˋ)
to suffer a downfall; to decline and fall

喪明之痛(ㄙㄤˋ ㄇㄧㄥˊ ㄓ ㄊㄨㄥˋ)
(literally) the pain of losing one's eyesight—the death of one's son

喪命(ㄙㄤˋ ㄇㄧㄥˋ)
to lose one's life; to die

喪夫(ㄙㄤˋ ㄈㄨ)

口部

to be deprived of one's husband

喪膽(ㄙㄤˋ ㄉㄢˇ)
to be much afraid; to be terror-stricken; to lose nerve; to be disheartened

喪國(ㄙㄤˋ ㄍㄨㄛˊ)
to lose one's country to the conqueror

喪家之狗(ㄙㄤˋ ㄐㄧㄚ ㄓ ㄍㄡˇ) or 喪家之犬(ㄙㄤˋ ㄐㄧㄚ ㄓ ㄑㄩㄢˇ)
(literally) a homeless dog; a stray cur—an outcast: 他惶惶如喪家之犬。He felt as frightened as a stray cur.

喪盡天良(ㄙㄤˋ ㄐㄧㄣˋ ㄊㄧㄢ ㄌㄧㄤˊ)
to have no conscience; impervious to the sense of justice; utterly devoid of conscience; conscienceless; heartless

喪妻(ㄙㄤˋ ㄑㄧ)
to be deprived of one's wife

喪氣(ㄙㄤˋ ㄑㄧˋ)
① dejected; despondent; in low spirits; discouraged ② bad luck; to be unlucky; to be out of luck; to have bad luck

喪權辱國(ㄙㄤˋ ㄑㄩㄢˊ ㄖㄨˇ ㄍㄨㄛˊ)
to humiliate the nation and forfeit its sovereignty; to surrender a nation's sovereign rights under humiliating terms

喪心病狂(ㄙㄤˋ ㄒㄧㄣ ㄅㄧㄥˋ ㄎㄨㄤˊ)
out of one's right mind; to act as if one were crazy; seized with crazy ideas; losing the balance of judgment

喪志(ㄙㄤˋ ㄓˋ)
to lose one's determination or ambition; to destroy the mind

喪失(ㄙㄤˋ ㄕ)
to lose; to be deprived of; to be stripped of

喪師(ㄙㄤˋ ㄕ)
to be defeated in battle; to suffer defeat in battle

喪身(ㄙㄤˋ ㄕㄣ)
to lose one's life

喪偶(ㄙㄤˋ ㄡˇ)
to be deprived of one's spouse, especially one's wife

【喬】 700
ㄑㄧㄠˊ chyau qiáo

1. tall
2. to disguise; to pretend
3. a Chinese family name

喬麥(ㄑㄧㄠˊ ㄇㄞˋ)
buckwheat 亦作「蕎麥」

喬木(ㄑㄧㄠˊ ㄇㄨˋ)
a tall tree; a large tree

喬遷(ㄑㄧㄠˊ ㄑㄧㄢ)
to move into a new and better house

喬遷之喜(ㄑㄧㄠˊ ㄑㄧㄢ ㄓ ㄒㄧˇ)
(an expression used in congratulation) Best wishes for your new home.

喬治(ㄑㄧㄠˊ ㄓˋ)
a Chinese transliteration for George

喬治亞(ㄑㄧㄠˊ ㄓˋ ㄧㄚˇ)
Georgia, U.S.A.

喬裝(ㄑㄧㄠˊ ㄓㄨㄤ)
to disguise oneself: 他喬裝成耶誕老人。He disguised himself as Santa Claus.

喬梓(ㄑㄧㄠˊ ㄗˇ)
father and son 亦作「橋梓」

喬松(ㄑㄧㄠˊ ㄙㄨㄥ)
the lofty pine

【單】 701
1. ㄉㄢ dan dān

1. single; individual: 房間中有兩張單人床。There are two single beds in the room.
2. alone; only
3. simple: 這個解釋十分簡單易懂。The explanation was quite simple.
4. of an odd number
5. a slip of paper
6. a list

單薄(ㄉㄢ ㄅㄛˊ)
weak; feeble; flimsy

單幫(ㄉㄢ ㄅㄤ)
a traveling merchant working on his own: 他常跑單幫。He often makes business trip on his own account.

單邊(ㄉㄢ ㄅㄧㄢ)
unilateral

單門獨戶(ㄉㄢ ㄇㄣˊ ㄉㄨˊ ㄏㄨˋ)
a single isolated house

單名(ㄉㄢ ㄇㄧㄥˊ)
one-character given name (instead of the standard two-character name)

單飛(ㄉㄢ ㄈㄟ)
a solo flight

單方(ㄉㄢ ㄈㄤ)
① one-sided ② a prescription or formula; a folk prescription; a home remedy

單方面(ㄉㄢ ㄈㄤ ㄇㄧㄢˋ)
one-sided; unilateral: 他們單方面撕毀協定。They unilaterally tore up an agreement.

單方面行動(ㄉㄢ ㄈㄤ ㄇㄧㄢˋ ㄒㄧㄥˊ ㄉㄨㄥˋ)
a unilateral action

單打(ㄉㄢ ㄉㄚˇ)
(sports) singles: 他只參加單打。He's only playing in the singles.

單刀(ㄉㄢ ㄉㄠ)
① a short-hilted broadsword ②(said of martial arts) a single-broadsword event

單刀直入(ㄉㄢ ㄉㄠ ㄓˊ ㄖㄨˋ)
(said of action, statement, etc.) straightforward; direct; right to the point

單單(ㄉㄢ ㄉㄢ)
alone; only: 別人都來了！單單她沒來。She is the only one absent. Everybody else is here.

單調(ㄉㄢ ㄉㄧㄠˋ)
dull; monotonous; dry; boring: 這是個單調的工作。This is a monotonous job.

單獨(ㄉㄢ ㄉㄨˊ)
independent; alone; solely; singly; individually: 他單獨一個人在家。He was alone in the house.

單獨事件(ㄉㄢ ㄉㄨˊ ㄕˋ ㄐㄧㄢˋ)
isolated incidents

單糖(ㄉㄢ ㄊㄤˊ)
(chemistry) simple sugar; monosaccharide

單利(ㄉㄢ ㄌㄧˋ)
simple interest (as opposed to compound interest)

單戀(ㄉㄢ ㄌㄧㄢˋ)
one-sided love; unrequited love

單個兒(ㄉㄢ ㄍㄜˋㄦ)
① individually; alone ② an odd one

單槓(ㄉㄢ ㄍㄤˋ)
(sports) a horizontal bar

單掛號(ㄉㄢ ㄍㄨㄚˋ ㄏㄠˋ)
registered mail which does not require the post office to deliver the recipient's acknowledgment of receipt

to the sender

單軌(ㄉㄢ ㄍㄨㄟˇ)
single-track (railroad)

單軌鐵路(ㄉㄢ ㄍㄨㄟˇ ㄊㄧㄝˇ ㄌㄨˋ)
①a monorail ②a single-track railroad

單軌火車(ㄉㄢ ㄍㄨㄟˇ ㄏㄨㄛˇ ㄔㄜ)
a monorail (train)

單號(ㄉㄢ ㄏㄠˋ)
odd numbers (of tickets, seats, etc.)

單記投票(ㄉㄢ ㄐㄧˋ ㄊㄡˊ ㄆㄧㄠˋ)
in an election the votes carrying only the candidate's name

單間兒(ㄉㄢ ㄐㄧㄚㄦ)
a separate room; a single room (in a hotel, restaurant, etc.)亦作「單人房」

單價(ㄉㄢ ㄐㄧㄚˋ)
a unit price

單句(ㄉㄢ ㄐㄩˋ)
a simple sentence

單據(ㄉㄢ ㄐㄩˋ)
a receipt; documentary evidence; a voucher; a bill; an invoice: 請給我一張關於此款的單據。Please send me a receipt for the money.

單槍匹馬(ㄉㄢ ㄑㄧㄤ ㄆㄧˇ ㄇㄚˇ)
to take on the enemy alone; to do something unaided; single-handed; all by oneself

單細胞(ㄉㄢ ㄒㄧˋ ㄅㄠ)
unicellular

單線(ㄉㄢ ㄒㄧㄢˋ)
①a single line ②one-way (contact); single-line (links) ③a single track: 單線鐵路 single-track railway

單相思(ㄉㄢ ㄒㄧㄤ ㄙ)
unrequited love; one-sided love

單相電流(ㄉㄢ ㄒㄧㄤˋ ㄉㄧㄢˋ ㄌㄧㄡˊ)
a one-phase, or single-face current

單向(ㄉㄢ ㄒㄧㄤˋ)
one-way; unidirectional

單項(ㄉㄢ ㄒㄧㄤˋ)
(sports) an individual event

單行本(ㄉㄢ ㄒㄧㄥˊ ㄅㄣˇ)
a separate volume (e.g. a novel, etc., originally published in series)

單行法(ㄉㄢ ㄒㄧㄥˊ ㄈㄚˇ)
①laws and regulations that are applicable only in certain districts or regions ②laws each dealing with a single matter

單行道(ㄉㄢ ㄒㄧㄥˊ ㄉㄠˋ)
a one-way street, or a one-way path

單行線(ㄉㄢ ㄒㄧㄥˊ ㄒㄧㄢˋ)
a one-way road

單性花(ㄉㄢ ㄒㄧㄥˋ ㄏㄨㄚ)
a unisexual flower

單循環制(ㄉㄢ ㄒㄩㄣˊ ㄏㄨㄢˊ ㄓˋ)
(sports) a single robin (as distinct from 雙循環制, a round robin)

單張兒(ㄉㄢ ㄓㄤㄦ)
individual sheets

單車(ㄉㄢ ㄔㄜ)
bicycles

單產(ㄉㄢ ㄔㄢˇ)
a per unit area yield

單純(ㄉㄢ ㄔㄨㄣˊ)
①simple; plain: 問題絕不像我們想像的那麼單純。The problem is by no means as simple as we think. ②artless; unpretending; unembellished

單式(ㄉㄢ ㄕˋ)
(bookkeeping) a single entry

單式教學(ㄉㄢ ㄕˋ ㄐㄧㄠˋ ㄒㄩㄝˊ)
single-class teaching (with each class consisting of pupils of the same grade)

單身(ㄉㄢ ㄕㄣ)
①alone; unaccompanied: 他單身在外。He lives alone away from home. ②unmarried; single

單身貴族(ㄉㄢ ㄕㄣ ㄍㄨㄟˋ ㄗㄨˊ)
(colloquial) unmarried gentlemen or ladies

單身漢(ㄉㄢ ㄕㄣ ㄏㄢˋ)
a bachelor: 他還是一個單身漢。He is still a bachelor.

單身宿舍(ㄉㄢ ㄕㄣ ㄙㄨˋ ㄕㄜˋ)
quarters for single men or women

單數(ㄉㄢ ㄕㄨˋ)
①an odd number ②(grammar) singular

單日(ㄉㄢ ㄖˋ)
odd-numbered days (of the month)

單人房(ㄉㄢ ㄖㄣˊ ㄈㄤˊ)
a single-bed room (in a hotel)

單人牀(ㄉㄢ ㄖㄣˊ ㄔㄨㄤˊ)
a single bed

單子
①(ㄉㄢ ㄗˇ)ⓐ(philosophy) monad—any basic metaphysical entity, especially having an autonomous life ⓑthe only son of a family
②(ㄉㄢ ·ㄗ)ⓐpieces of paper with written words on; a list; a bill; a form: 你開個單子。You make out a list. ⓑa bed sheet

單字(ㄉㄢ ㄗˋ)
a single character or word; an individual character

單詞(ㄉㄢ ㄘˊ)
①an individual word; a word; a singular term ②a single-morpheme word

單色(ㄉㄢ ㄙㄜˋ)
monochromatic

單衣(ㄉㄢ ㄧ)
the clothes that have no lining (usually for summer wear)

單一(ㄉㄢ ㄧ)
single; unitary

單眼(ㄉㄢ ㄧㄢˇ)
(zoology) single eye

單眼皮(ㄉㄢ ㄧㄢˇ ㄆㄧˊ)
eyelids that do not have a distinct fold along the edges, a typical feature of most Orientals

單音節(ㄉㄢ ㄧㄣ ㄐㄧㄝˊ)
monosyllabic

單音字(ㄉㄢ ㄧㄣ ㄗˋ)
monosyllabic words

單音詞(ㄉㄢ ㄧㄣ ㄘˊ)
monosyllabic words; monosyllables

單位(ㄉㄢ ㄨㄟˋ)
①a unit (in measurement): 呎是長度的單位; 磅是重量的單位。A foot is a unit of length; a pound is a unit of weight. ②a military unit or organization

單元(ㄉㄢ ㄩㄢˊ)
a unit; a complete entity; a whole

單元劇(ㄉㄢ ㄩㄢˊ ㄐㄩˋ)
a single-episode drama

【單】 701
2. ㄕㄢˋ shann shàn
a Chinese family name

【單】 701
3. ㄔㄢˊ charn chán
the chief of the Huns (a common term during the Han Dynasty)
單于(ㄔㄢˊ ㄩˊ)
the chieftain of the Huns (a common term during the Han Dynasty)

【喳】 702
ㄔㄚ cha chā
the sound of chattering
喳喳(ㄔㄚ ㄔㄚ)
① a chattering sound; jabber ② to whisper

十畫

【嗄】 703
1. ㄕㄚˋ shah shà
(said of voice) hoarse

【嗄】 703
2. ㄚˊ ar á
(interjection) What! 嗄！你又遲到了？ What! Are you late again?

【嗅】 704
ㄒㄧㄡˋ shiow xiù
to smell; to scent; to sniff: 狗會靠其嗅覺而找到賊。The dog can smell out a thief.
嗅覺(ㄒㄧㄡˋ ㄐㄩㄝˊ)
the sense of smell; olfactories; scent: 獵犬嗅覺敏銳。Bloodhounds have a keen scent.
嗅鹽(ㄒㄧㄡˋ ㄧㄢˊ)
smelling salts

【嗆】 705
1. ㄑㄧㄤ chiang qiāng
1. to peck
2. stupid; foolish
嗆哼(ㄑㄧㄤ ㄏㄥ)
stupid

【嗆】 705
2. ㄑㄧㄤˋ chianq qiàng
1. to cough because of a temporary blockade of the nasal passage which sometimes happens during eating or drinking water
2. (said of smoke, smell, etc.) to irritate the throat or nose; to suffocate

【嗇】 706
ㄙㄜˋ seh sè
stingy; parsimonious; miserly
嗇己奉公(ㄙㄜˋ ㄐㄧˇ ㄈㄥˋ ㄍㄨㄥ)
to save money for public welfare by being parsimonious in one's personal spending

【嗉】 707
ㄙㄨˋ suh sù
the crop (of a bird)
嗉囊(ㄙㄨˋ ㄋㄤˊ)
the crop (of a bird)

【嗩】 708
ㄙㄨㄛˇ suoo suǒ
a trumpet-like wind instrument
嗩吶(ㄙㄨㄛˇ ㄋㄚˋ)
a trumpet-like wind instrument

【嗎】 709
1. ㄇㄚˇ maa mǎ
a character used in transliterating
嗎啡(ㄇㄚˇ ㄈㄟ)
morphine
嗎啡針(ㄇㄚˇ ㄈㄟ ㄓㄣ)
a morphine shot or injection
嗎啡中毒(ㄇㄚˇ ㄈㄟ ㄓㄨㄥˋ ㄉㄨˊ)
morphine intoxication

【嗎】 709
2. ·ㄇㄚ ·ma ma
a phrase-final particle used in questions: 你找他有事嗎？Is there something you want to see him about?

【嗒】 710
ㄊㄚˋ tah tà
depressed; dejected; despondent; in low spirits
嗒然(ㄊㄚˋ ㄖㄢˊ)
looking dejected or despondent
嗒喪(ㄊㄚˋ ㄙㄤˋ)
in low spirits; depressed; dejected; despondent

【嗓】 711
ㄙㄤˇ saang sǎng
1. the throat (as the source of one's voice)
2. one's voice: 她的嗓子啞了。She has lost her voice.
嗓門兒(ㄙㄤˇ ㄇㄜˊㄦ)
① one's voice: 他的嗓門兒大。He has a loud voice. ② the vocal organs
嗓子(ㄙㄤˇ ·ㄗ)
① the throat: 我的嗓子痛。I have a sore throat. ② one's voice
嗓音(ㄙㄤˇ ㄧㄣ)
one's voice

【嗔】 712
ㄔㄣ chen chēn
1. to be angry; to take offense; to fly into a temper
2. to be annoyed with
嗔怒(ㄔㄣ ㄋㄨˋ)
to get angry; to be enraged; to be offended; to get or fly into a temper
嗔怪(ㄔㄣ ㄍㄨㄞˋ)
to rebuke; to scold; to reproach; to blame
嗔色(ㄔㄣ ㄙㄜˋ)
angry or sullen looks

【嗚】 713
ㄨ u wū
1. to weep; to sob
2. to toot; to hoot; to zoom
3. Alas!
嗚呼(ㄨ ㄏㄨ)
① Alas! ② to die: 他一命嗚呼。He died.
嗚呼哀哉(ㄨ ㄏㄨ ㄞ ㄗㄞ)
(usually used in lamenting someone's death) What a tragedy! 或 What a tragic loss! 或 All is lost.
嗚咽(ㄨ ㄧㄝˋ)
sobs; to sob; to weep; to whimper: 嗚咽使他們身體抽動。Sobs shook their bodies.
嗚嗚(ㄨ ㄨ)
(descriptive of the sound of trains, whistles, distant horns, etc.) to hoot

【嗜】 714
ㄕˋ shyh shì
to delight in; to be fond of; to relish; to like; to addict: 他嗜好抽煙。He is addicted to smoking.
嗜癖(ㄕˋ ㄆㄧˇ)
a hobby; a special liking for drink, food, etc.
嗜好(ㄕˋ ㄏㄠˋ)
one's liking, hobby, or weakness for something
嗜痂之癖(ㄕˋ ㄐㄧㄚ ㄓ ㄆㄧˇ)
an eccentric taste
嗜酒(ㄕˋ ㄐㄧㄡˇ)
to be addicted to drinking
嗜血(ㄕˋ ㄒㄩㄝˋ)
bloodthirsty; bloodsucking
嗜殺(ㄕˋ ㄕㄚ)
bloodthirsty; fond of killing
嗜慾(ㄕˋ ㄩˋ)
sensual desires

〔口部〕

〔口部〕

【嗝】 715 ㄍㄜˊ ger gé
to hiccup or hiccough; a belch
嗝兒(ㄍㄜˊㄦ)
a hiccup or hiccough; a belch: 他打嗝兒。He has the hiccups.

【嗯】 716 1. ㄣˊ ern én
the nasal sound used to express doubt: 嗯？你說什麼？What? What did you say?

【嗯】 716 2. ㄣˇ een ěn
the nasal sound used when one is surprised or indifferent: 嗯！你怎麼還沒去？What! Haven't you started yet?

【嗯】 716 3. ㄣˋ enn èn
the nasal sound used when one makes a response or promise: 他嗯了一聲，就走了。He merely said, "H'm", and went away.

【嗟】 717 ㄐㄧㄝ jie jiē
an exclamation expressing grief or regret
嗟歎(ㄐㄧㄝ ㄊㄢˋ)
to sigh with grief or regret; to lament; to deplore
嗟來之食(ㄐㄧㄝ ㄌㄞˊ ㄓ ㄕˊ)
① a meal offered from pity mixed with contempt ②(figuratively) a favor done without courtesy
嗟悔無及(ㄐㄧㄝ ㄏㄨㄟˇ ㄨˊ ㄐㄧˊ)
too late for regrets and lamentations

【嗣】 718 ㄙˋ syh sì
1. to inherit; to succeed to
2. a descendant
3. to continue; to follow
嗣立(ㄙˋ ㄌㄧˋ)
to appoint or to be appointed as heir
嗣後(ㄙˋ ㄏㄡˋ)
thereafter; thenceforth; thenceforward; from that time on; after that; afterward
嗣繼(ㄙˋ ㄐㄧˋ)
to inherit; to succeed to
嗣產(ㄙˋ ㄔㄢˇ)
to inherit a fortune
嗣承(ㄙˋ ㄔㄥˊ)
to inherit; to succeed to
嗣子(ㄙˋ ㄗˇ)
① an heir ② an adopted son
嗣歲(ㄙˋ ㄙㄨㄟˋ)
the coming year
嗣業(ㄙˋ ㄧㄝˋ)
to inherit a business or a fortune; to inherit the family estate and continue to carry on one's father's work
嗣位(ㄙˋ ㄨㄟˋ)
to succeed to the throne

【嗤】 719 ㄔ chy chī
to laugh or chuckle sneeringly
嗤鄙(ㄔ ㄅㄧˇ)
to sneer at with contempt
嗤笑(ㄔ ㄒㄧㄠˋ)
to laugh or chuckle sneeringly
嗤之以鼻(ㄔ ㄓ ㄧˇ ㄅㄧˊ)
to pooh-pooh; to give a snicker: 他對那個意見嗤之以鼻。He pooh-poohed the idea.

【嗡】 720 ㄨㄥ ueng wēng
the hum or buzz of insects
嗡嗡叫(ㄨㄥ ㄨㄥ ㄐㄧㄠˋ)
(said of insects) to hum; to buzz: 蜜蜂在花園裏嗡嗡叫。The bees were humming in the garden.

【嗑】 721 ㄎㄜˋ keh kè
to crack something between the teeth
嗑瓜子兒(ㄎㄜˋ ㄍㄨㄚ ㄗㄜˇㄦ)
to crack melon seeds: 他嗑瓜子兒。He cracked melon seeds between his teeth.

十一畫

【嗷】 722 (嗸) ㄠˊ aur áo
a cry of hunger
嗷嗷待哺(ㄠˊ ㄠˊ ㄉㄞˋ ㄅㄨˇ)
crying with hunger; waiting to be fed with cries of hunger; to cry piteously for food

【嗶】 723 ㄅㄧˋ bih bì
a character used in transliterating
嗶嘰(ㄅㄧˋ ㄐㄧ)
serge (a fabric)

【嗽】 724 ㄙㄡˋ sow sòu
to cough; to clear the throat: 他咳嗽得很厲害。He coughs badly.

【嗾】 725 ㄙㄡˇ soou sǒu
1. to give vocal signals to a dog
2. to instigate
嗾使(ㄙㄡˇ ㄕˇ)
to instigate; to incite; to spur on; to urge on; to abet

【嘅】 726 (慨) ㄎㄞˇ kae kǎi
the sound of sighing

【嘈】 727 ㄘㄠˊ tsaur cáo
noisy; clamorous
嘈雜(ㄘㄠˊ ㄗㄚˊ)
noisy and confused; full of confused noises; clamorous: 嘈雜之聲將他驚醒。The clamorous noises woke him up.

【嘉】 728 ㄐㄧㄚ jia jiā
1. to praise; to commend; to admire
2. good; fine; excellent
嘉賓(ㄐㄧㄚ ㄅㄧㄣ)
an honored guest; a respected guest
嘉勉(ㄐㄧㄚ ㄇㄧㄢˇ)
to praise and encourage
嘉南大圳(ㄐㄧㄚ ㄋㄢˊ ㄉㄚˋ ㄗㄨㄣˋ)
the Chia Nan Canal System (a huge irrigation network in southern Taiwan)
嘉年華會(ㄐㄧㄚ ㄋㄧㄢˊ ㄏㄨㄚˊ ㄏㄨㄟˋ)
a carnival
嘉釀(ㄐㄧㄚ ㄋㄧㄤˋ)
quality wine
嘉禮(ㄐㄧㄚ ㄌㄧˇ)
a wedding
嘉陵江(ㄐㄧㄚ ㄌㄧㄥˊ ㄐㄧㄤ)
the Chialing River, which flows from Shensi to Szechwan via Kansu
嘉惠(ㄐㄧㄚ ㄏㄨㄟˋ)
to benefit
嘉惠後學(ㄐㄧㄚ ㄏㄨㄟˋ ㄏㄡˋ ㄒㄩㄝˊ)
to benefit the students of the younger generation
嘉獎(ㄐㄧㄚ ㄐㄧㄤˇ)
to commend or praise (as

an encouragement); to cite
嘉羞(ㄐㄧㄚ ㄒㄧㄡ)or 嘉餚(ㄐㄧㄚ ㄧㄠˊ)
delicacies
嘉許(ㄐㄧㄚ ㄒㄩˇ)
to approve of; to praise: 每個人皆嘉許他的觀點。Everyone approved of his idea.
嘉耦 or 嘉偶(ㄐㄧㄚ ㄡˇ)
an ideal couple; a devoted couple
嘉耦天成(ㄐㄧㄚ ㄡˇ ㄊㄧㄢ ㄔㄥˊ)
an ideal marriage divinely arranged
嘉言懿行(ㄐㄧㄚ ㄧㄢˊ ㄧˋ ㄒㄧㄥˊ)
fine words and deeds (worthy of imitation)
嘉裕關(ㄐㄧㄚ ㄩˋ ㄍㄨㄢ)
The Chiayü Fortress in Kansu, which marks the western end of the Great Wall

【嘍】 729
1. ㄌㄡˊ lou lóu
a bandit's lackey or follower
嘍囉(ㄌㄡˊ ㄌㄨㄛˊ)
①a bandit's lackey or follower; the rank and file of a band of outlaws ②noisy hubbub

【嘍】 729
2. ˙ㄌㄡ ·lou lou
a phrase-final particle: 好嘍。It's ready. 起床嘍。Look, it's time to get up.

【嘏】 730
ㄍㄨˇ guu gǔ
felicity; blessings; happiness; prosperity

【嘔】 731
1.ㄡˇ oou ǒu
to vomit; to throw up
嘔吐(ㄡˇ ㄊㄨˋ)
to vomit; to throw up; to disgorge
嘔心瀝血(ㄡˇ ㄒㄧㄣ ㄌㄧˋ ㄒㄩㄝˋ)
to take infinite pains; to work one's heart out
嘔血(ㄡˇ ㄒㄩㄝˋ)
haematemesis; spitting blood

【嘔】 731
2.ㄡˋ ow òu
to annoy on purpose
嘔氣(ㄡˋ ㄑㄧˋ)
to be angry but refrain from showing it; to feel annoyed or irritated; to feel enraged

【嘖】 732
ㄗㄜˊ tzer zé
1. an interjection of approval or admiration
2. to argue; to dispute
嘖嘖(ㄗㄜˊ ㄗㄜˊ)
①used for the sound to indicate approval or admiration ②the cries of a bird
嘖有煩言(ㄗㄜˊ ㄧㄡˇ ㄈㄢˊ ㄧㄢˊ)
①There are noisy arguments among the people. ②There are complaints from everybody.

【嘗】 733
ㄔㄤˊ charng cháng
1. to taste
2. to try
3. to experience
嘗新(ㄔㄤˊ ㄒㄧㄣ)
to taste a new delicacy
嘗嘗(ㄔㄤˊ ·ㄔㄤ)or 嘗一嘗(ㄔㄤˊ ·ㄧ ·ㄔㄤ)
to taste; to have a taste
嘗試(ㄔㄤˊ ㄕˋ)
to try; a try

十二畫

【嘩】 734
1. ㄏㄨㄚ hua huā
an onomatopoeia, such gurgle, clang, crack, etc.: 河水嘩啦嘩啦地流。The river went gurgling on.
嘩啦(ㄏㄨㄚ ㄌㄚ)
an onomatopoeia, such as crash, rustle, etc.
嘩啦一聲(ㄏㄨㄚ ㄌㄚ ㄧˋ ㄕㄥ)
with a thunderous noise: 這房子嘩啦一聲倒了。The house has crashed down with a thunderous noise.

【嘩】 734
2. ㄏㄨㄚˊ hwa huá
same as 譁—tumult; hubbub; clamor; uproar
嘩衆取寵(ㄏㄨㄚˊ ㄓㄨㄥˋ ㄑㄩˇ ㄔㄨㄥˇ)
to try to please the public with claptrap
嘩然(ㄏㄨㄚˊ ㄖㄢˊ)
in an uproar; an outcry: 觀衆嘩然。The spectators burst into an uproar.

【嘘】 735
ㄒㄩ shiu xū
1.to warm with exhaled air
2.to speak well of (another)
3.a deep sigh
4.to hiss; to boo: 球迷們噓裁判。The fans hissed the umpire.
噓寒問暖(ㄒㄩ ㄏㄢˊ ㄨㄣˋ ㄋㄨㄢˇ)
to show a kind concern for another's comfort; to inquire after somebody's well-being
噓氣(ㄒㄩ ㄑㄧˋ)
to send out breath from the mouth; to blow
噓唏(ㄒㄩ ㄒㄧ)
to sob
噓聲(ㄒㄩ ㄕㄥ)
a hissing or booing sound uttered to show hatred or disapproval; catcalls: 他發噓聲把狗趕出花園。He drove the dog out of the garden by saying "boo!".
噓聲四起(ㄒㄩ ㄕㄥ ㄙˋ ㄑㄧˇ)
to resound with catcalls: 當他演說時觀衆噓聲四起。When he delivered a speech, spectators resound with catcalls.

【嘮】 736
ㄌㄠˊ lau láo
loquacious; garrulous; voluble
嘮叨(ㄌㄠˊ ·ㄉㄠ)or 嘮嘮叨叨(ㄌㄠˊ ㄌㄠˊ ㄉㄠ ㄉㄠ)
to nag; to din; to chatter incessantly

【嘯】 737
ㄒㄧㄠˋ shiaw xiào
1. to whistle
2. to howl; to cry or shout in a sustained voice; to roar
嘯聚(ㄒㄧㄠˋ ㄐㄩˋ)
to band together; to gang up
嘯聚山林(ㄒㄧㄠˋ ㄐㄩˋ ㄕㄢ ㄌㄧㄣˊ)
(said of bandits) to gather in woods or mountains in response to whistles or shouts; to go to the greenwood
嘯傲(ㄒㄧㄠˋ ㄠˋ)
to talk and behave freely without regard for decorum

【嘰】 738
ㄐㄧ ji jī
1. to talk indistinctly in a low voice
2. to chirp: 小鳥嘰嘰叫。Little birds chirp.
嘰哩咕嚕(ㄐㄧ ·ㄌㄧ ㄍㄨ ㄌㄨ)
①to talk in an indistinct manner; to gabble ②(said of bowels) to give forth a roll-

〔口部〕

〔口部〕

ing sound

嘰咕(ㄐㄧ ·ㄍㄨ)

①to grumble; to mumble or mutter complaints ②to gabble; to jabber

嘰嘰喳喳(ㄐㄧ ㄐㄧ ㄓㄚ ㄓㄚ)

①to chirp; to twitter ②to jabber

【嘲】 739 ㄔㄠˊ chaur cháo

to ridicule; to jeer; to sneer; to scoff; to mock; to deride: 他被人嘲弄。He was held up to ridicule.

嘲罵(ㄔㄠˊ ㄇㄚˋ)

to jeer and abuse

嘲風咏月(ㄔㄠˊ ㄈㄥ ㄩㄥˇ ㄩㄝˋ)

(said of poets in former times) to sport with the wind and sing of the moon

嘲諷(ㄔㄠˊ ㄈㄥˋ)

to sneer at; to taunt: 他們嘲諷那男孩膽怯。They taunted the boy with cowardice.

嘲弄(ㄔㄠˊ ㄋㄨㄥˋ)

to mock; to make fun of; to poke fun at

嘲謔(ㄔㄠˊ ㄋㄩㄝˋ)

to make fun of; to poke fun at

嘲戲(ㄔㄠˊ ㄒㄧˋ)

to make fun of; to poke fun at

嘲笑(ㄔㄠˊ ㄒㄧㄠˋ)

to laugh at; to jeer at; to sneer at; to deride; to ridicule; to scoff; to gibe

嘲訕(ㄔㄠˊ ㄕㄢˋ)

to deride; to sneer at; to mock; to scoff: 人人都嘲訕那老人。Everyone sneered at the old man.

【嘴】 740 ㄗㄨㄟˇ tzoei zuǐ

1. the mouth; the bill or beak (of a bird); the snout (of a pig, etc.)
2. a nozzle

嘴巴(ㄗㄨㄟˇ ·ㄅㄚ)

①the mouth: 請張開嘴巴。Open your mouth, please. ②(colloquial) the cheeks

嘴巴不饒人(ㄗㄨㄟˇ ·ㄅㄚ ㄅㄨˋ ㄖㄠˊ ㄖㄣˊ)

fond of making sarcastic remarks; sharp-tongued

嘴笨(ㄗㄨㄟˇ ㄅㄣˋ)

not skilled in talking; inarticulate

嘴皮子(ㄗㄨㄟˇ ㄆㄧˊ ·ㄗ)

the lips (of a glib talker)—a ready tongue

嘴貧 or 嘴頻(ㄗㄨㄟˇ ㄆㄧㄣˊ)

talkative; chatty

嘴甜心苦(ㄗㄨㄟˇ ㄊㄧㄢˊ ㄒㄧㄣ ㄎㄨˇ)

to talk sweetly while harboring evil thoughts

嘴懶(ㄗㄨㄟˇ ㄌㄢˇ)

not inclined to talk much; taciturn; reticence

嘴臉(ㄗㄨㄟˇ ㄌㄧㄢˇ)

the face (usually connoting disgust)

嘴乖(ㄗㄨㄟˇ ㄍㄨㄞ)

given to sweet talking; soft-spoken

嘴快(ㄗㄨㄟˇ ㄎㄨㄞˋ)

rash in speech; incapable of keeping secrets

嘴角(ㄗㄨㄟˇ ㄐㄧㄠˇ)

corners of the mouth

嘴尖舌巧(ㄗㄨㄟˇ ㄐㄧㄢ ㄕㄜˊ ㄑㄧㄠˇ)

to be sharp-tongued; to have a capable tongue; to be gifted with a quick and sharp tongue

嘴緊(ㄗㄨㄟˇ ㄐㄧㄣˇ)

tight-lipped; closemouthed; secretive

嘴強(ㄗㄨㄟˇ ㄑㄧㄤˋ)

①inclined to argue (especially with a superior) ②to talk toughly

嘴直(ㄗㄨㄟˇ ㄓˊ)

to speak frankly; to speak out without reservation

嘴饞(ㄗㄨㄟˇ ㄔㄢˊ)

inclined to eat greedily; gluttonous; fond of good food: 他眞嘴饞。He was really fond of good food.

嘴唇(ㄗㄨㄟˇ ㄔㄨㄣˊ)

the lips

嘴上無毛，做事不牢(ㄗㄨㄟˇ ㄕㄤˋ ㄨˊ ㄇㄠˊ, ㄗㄨㄛˋ ㄕˋ ㄅㄨˋ ㄌㄠˊ)

Young people cannot be trusted with important tasks because they lack experience.

嘴碎(ㄗㄨㄟˇ ㄙㄨㄟˋ)

talkative; loquacious; garrulous: 他嘴碎。He is garrulous.

嘴嚴(ㄗㄨㄟˇ ㄧㄢˊ)

cautious about speech; capable of keeping secrets

嘴硬(ㄗㄨㄟˇ ㄧㄥˋ)

①to talk toughly ②to refuse to admit a mistake

【嘶】 741 ㄙ sy sī

1. the neighing of a horse: 人喊馬嘶。Men shout and horses neigh.
2. (said of voice) hoarse: 他聲嘶力竭。He shouted himself hoarse and felt exhausted.

嘶啞(ㄙ ㄧㄚˇ)

hoarse-voiced; hoarse

【嗥】 742 ㄏㄠˊ haur háo

to howl; to yelp; the frantic barks or howls of dogs or wolves: 我們聽見遠處狼嗥。We heard wolves howling in the distance.

【嘹】 743 ㄌㄧㄠˊ liau liáo

(said of voice) resonant

嘹喨(ㄌㄧㄠˊ ㄌㄧㄤˋ)

loud and clear; resonant: 她的歌聲嘹喨。Her singing is loud and clear.

【嘻】 744 ㄒㄧ shi xī

1. (in literary text) an interjection of grief or surprise
2. laughing happily

嘻皮笑臉(ㄒㄧ ㄆㄧˊ ㄒㄧㄠˋ ㄌㄧㄢˇ)

laughing in a frolicsome manner; showing a frolicsome expression

嘻嘻(ㄒㄧ ㄒㄧ)

laughing happily

嘻嘻哈哈(ㄒㄧ ㄒㄧ ㄏㄚ ㄏㄚ)

laughing and talking happily

嘻笑(ㄒㄧ ㄒㄧㄠˋ)

to giggle; to titter

【嘸】 745 ㄨˇ wuu wǔ

1. an expletive
2. (in Soochow and Shanghai dialect) same as 無

嘸啥稀奇(ㄨˇ ㄕㄚˊ ㄒㄧ ㄑㄧˊ)

nothing strange; nothing to be proud of

【噎】 746 ㄧㄝ ie yē

1. to be choked with food
2. to choke off

噎住(ㄧㄝ ㄓㄨˋ)

to be choked with food

【嘿】 747 1. ㄏㄟ hei hēi

an interjection: 嘿！快走吧！Hey, hurry up!

【嘿】747 2.（默）ㄇㄛˋ moh mò
1. speechless; silent
2. quiet; still

【噍】748 1.ㄐㄧㄠˋ jiaw jiào
to chew; to munch; to nibble

噍類（ㄐㄧㄠˋ ㄌㄟˋ）
living persons

【噍】748 2.ㄐㄧㄠ jiau jiāo
(said of voice) high and unpleasant

【噍】748 3.ㄐㄧㄡ jiou jiū
(said of birds) chirping

噍噍（ㄐㄧㄡ ㄐㄧㄡ）
(said of birds) chirping

【嘬】749 ㄔㄨㄞˋ chuay chuài （讀音 ㄗㄨㄛ tzuo zuō）
1. to bite
2. to gobble up

十三畫

【噤】750 ㄐㄧㄣˋ jinn jìn
to keep the mouth shut; to shut up

噤若寒蟬（ㄐㄧㄣˋ ㄖㄨㄛˋ ㄏㄢˊ ㄔㄢˊ）
(literally) as silent as a winter cicada—to say or reveal nothing (especially out of fear)

【器】751 ㄑㄧˋ chih qì
1. an instrument; an implement; a utensil; a tool; a piece of apparatus
2. magnanimity
3. talent; ability; capacity: 大器晚成。A great talent takes time to mature.
4. to think highly of (a person)

器皿（ㄑㄧˋ ㄇㄧㄣˇ）
food containers (such as plates, dishes, bowls, etc.); household utensils

器量（ㄑㄧˋ ㄌㄧㄤˋ）
the capacity for magnanimity; tolerance

器官（ㄑㄧˋ ㄍㄨㄢ）
the apparatus; the organs (in animals or plants)

器局（ㄑㄧˋ ㄐㄩˊ）
one's intellectual and moral capacity

器具（ㄑㄧˋ ㄐㄩˋ）
tools; instruments; apparatus; implements; utensils

器械（ㄑㄧˋ ㄒㄧㄝˋ）
a machine; machinery; an apparatus; an appliance

器重（ㄑㄧˋ ㄓㄨㄥˋ）
to have a high opinion of (a person); to think highly of; to regard highly

器識（ㄑㄧˋ ㄕˋ）
one's magnanimity and intellectual outlook

器材（ㄑㄧˋ ㄘㄞˊ）
supplies; implements and materials (for a certain purpose); equipment

器物（ㄑㄧˋ ㄨˋ）
an implement; a tool; an instrument; a utensil

器宇（ㄑㄧˋ ㄩˇ）
one's physical appearance (usually connoting his moral and intellectual capacity)

器宇軒昂（ㄑㄧˋ ㄩˇ ㄒㄩㄢ ㄤˊ）
of dignified bearing

器樂（ㄑㄧˋ ㄩㄝˋ）
instrumental music (as opposed to vocal music)

【噩】752 ㄜˋ eh è
1. startling; awesome; dreadful; alarming
2. grave; serious

噩夢（ㄜˋ ㄇㄥˋ）
a nightmare: 我昨夜做了一個噩夢。I had a nightmare last night.

噩耗（ㄜˋ ㄏㄠˋ）
shocking news (usually news of a person's death)

【噪】753 ㄗㄠˋ tzaw zào
1. to be noisy
2. (said of birds, insects, etc.) to chirp

噪聒（ㄗㄠˋ ㄍㄨㄚ）
noisy; to make loud, confused noise

噪音（ㄗㄠˋ ㄧㄣ）
unpleasant noise; din: 我不喜歡噪音。I don't like noise.

噪音污染（ㄗㄠˋ ㄧㄣ ㄨ ㄖㄢˇ）
noise pollution

【噫】754 ㄧ i yī
an interjection of sorrow or regret (in literary texts); alas

【噬】755 ㄕˋ shyh shì
to bite; to snap at; to gnaw

噬臍何及（ㄕˋ ㄑㄧˊ ㄏㄜˊ ㄐㄧˊ）or 噬臍莫及（ㄕˋ ㄑㄧˊ ㄇㄛˋ ㄐㄧˊ）
(literally) It is too late for a captured musk deer to bite its own navel.—(figuratively) It is too late for one to regret.

【噱】756 1.ㄐㄩㄝˊ jyue jué
loud laughter

【噱】756 2.ㄒㄩㄝ shiue xuē
參看「噱頭」

噱頭（ㄒㄩㄝ ㄊㄡˊ）
(Shanghai dialect) a promotional gimmick; a trick: 這個小丑噱頭眞多。The clown is full of amusing tricks.

【噸】757 ㄉㄨㄣˋ duenn dùn
ton (a unit of weight): 這部卡車運了五噸的煤炭。This truck carries 5 tons of coal.

噸位（ㄉㄨㄣˋ ㄨㄟˋ）
tonnage (of a ship)

【噷】758 ㄏㄇ hm hm̄
(an interjection) H'm!

【噯】759 1.ㄞˋ ay ài
an interjection: 噯，你錯了。Oh! You are mistaken.

【噯】759 2.ㄞˇ ae ǎi
參看「噯氣」

噯氣（ㄞˋ ㄑㄧˋ）
(medicine) belch; eructation

【噹】760 ㄉㄤ dang dāng
a loud, resonant metallic sound

噹啷（ㄉㄤ ㄌㄤ）
clanking sound

【噴】761 1.ㄆㄣ pen pēn
1. to spurt; to gush: 石油從井口噴了出來。Oil gushed from the well.
2. to spray; to sprinkle: 給蔬菜

〔口部〕

噴點水。Sprinkle some waler on the vegetables.
噴門(ㄆㄣ ㄇㄣˊ)
(physiology) cardia
噴飯(ㄆㄣ ㄈㄢˋ)
to spurt food out of the mouth when laughing—(figuratively) to burst out laughing; to split one's sides with laughter
噴嚏(ㄆㄣ ·ㄊㄧ)
sneezing; a sneeze
噴口(ㄆㄣ ㄎㄡˇ)
the crater of a volcano
噴壺(ㄆㄣ ㄏㄨˊ)
a watering can
噴火山(ㄆㄣ ㄏㄨㄛˇ ㄕㄢ)
a volcano
噴漆(ㄆㄣ ㄑㄧ)
to spray paint; to spray lacquer
噴泉(ㄆㄣ ㄑㄩㄢˊ)
a fountain
噴香(ㄆㄣ ㄒㄧㄤ)
fragrant; delicious: 飯菜噴香。The dishes smell delicious.
噴射(ㄆㄣ ㄕㄜˋ)
(said of gas or liquid) to shoot out; to jet
噴射機(ㄆㄣ ㄕㄜˋ ㄐㄧ)or 噴氣機(ㄆㄣ ㄑㄧˋ ㄐㄧ)
a jet airplane
噴水池(ㄆㄣ ㄕㄨㄟˇ ㄔˊ)
a fountain
噴洒(ㄆㄣ ㄙㄚˇ)
to spray; to sprinkle
噴霧器(ㄆㄣ ㄨˋ ㄑㄧˋ)
a spray gun; an atomizer
噴雲吐霧(ㄆㄣ ㄩㄣˊ ㄊㄨˇ ㄨˋ)
to smoke (a pipe, cigarette, etc.)

【噴】 761
2. ㄈㄣˋ fenn fèn
參看「嚏噴」

十四畫

【嚎】 762
ㄏㄠˊ haur háo
to cry loudly; to howl; to wail
嚎啕大哭(ㄏㄠˊ ㄊㄠˊ ㄉㄚˋ ㄎㄨ)
to cry loudly with abandon

【嚅】 763
ㄖㄨˊ ru rú
to talk indistinctly and falteringly
嚅囁(ㄖㄨˊ ㄋㄧㄝˋ)
to falter in one's speech; to mumble in a low voice (as if out of fear)

【嚆】 764
ㄏㄠ hau hāo
to cry; to yell
嚆矢(ㄏㄠ ㄕˇ)
① an arrow flying with a hum ② a harbinger; a prelude; a herald

【嚀】 765
ㄋㄧㄥˊ ning níng
to enjoin; to instruct

【嚇】 766
1. ㄏㄜˋ heh hè
1. to intimidate; to threaten
2. the sound of laughter
嚇嚇(ㄏㄜˋ ㄏㄜˋ)
ha, ha (sound of laughter)
嚇詐(ㄏㄜˋ ㄓㄚˋ)
to take (money, etc.) by threat and deceit
嚇阻(ㄏㄜˋ ㄗㄨˇ)
to stop (someone) by threat

【嚇】 766
2. ㄒㄧㄚˋ shiah xià
to frighten; to startle; to scare; to intimidate: 那種困難嚇不倒我們。Difficulties like that don't scare us.
嚇唬(ㄒㄧㄚˋ ·ㄏㄨ)
to scare; to frighten; to intimidate
嚇人(ㄒㄧㄚˋ ㄖㄣˊ)
① to frighten people ② frightening; terrible; horrible: 那是個嚇人的景象。That was a horrible sight.

【嚏】 767
ㄊㄧˋ tih tì
sneezing; a sneeze
嚏噴(ㄊㄧˋ ·ㄈㄣ)
sneezing; a sneeze

十五畫

【嚕】 768
ㄌㄨ lhu lū
1. verbose; wordy
2. an indistinct speech sound
嚕囌(ㄌㄨ ㄙㄨ)or 嚕哩嚕囌(ㄌㄨ ㄌㄧ ㄌㄨ ㄙㄨ)
to talk incessantly and tediously; verbosity 亦作「囉唆」

十六畫

【嚮】 769
ㄒㄧㄤˋ shianq xiàng
1. to guide; to direct; to lead
2. to lean toward; to be inclined toward
嚮壁虛造(ㄒㄧㄤˋ ㄅㄧˋ ㄒㄩ ㄗㄠˋ)
to fabricate out of nothing: 他的冒險故事是嚮壁虛造的。His account of adventures is fabricated.
嚮導(ㄒㄧㄤˋ ㄉㄠˇ)or(ㄒㄧㄤˋ ㄉㄠˋ)
a guide:嚮導帶領我們逛這個城市。A guide led us around the city.
嚮邇(ㄒㄧㄤˋ ㄦˇ)
to approach
嚮往(ㄒㄧㄤˋ ㄨㄤˇ)
to aspire; to long; to look forward to: 人人嚮往幸福的生活。Everyone looks forward to a happy life.

【嚥】 770
ㄧㄢˋ yann yàn
to swallow: 我們吃東西時要細嚼慢嚥。We must chew carefully and swallow slowly when we eat.
嚥唾沫(ㄧㄢˋ ㄊㄨㄛˋ ·ㄇㄛ)
(literally) to swallow saliva—to have an appetite for something; to crave; to covet
嚥氣(ㄧㄢˋ ㄑㄧˋ)
to breathe one's last; to die

【嚨】 771
ㄌㄨㄥˊ long lóng
the throat

十七畫

【嚴】 772
ㄧㄢˊ yan yán
1. stern; strict; severe; grim; inclement; inexorable; relentless; rigorous; rigid; grave; solemn: 嚴是愛，鬆是害。Strictness helps, and indulgence spoils.
2. reverence
3. tight: 他的嘴很嚴。He is tight-mouthed.
4. father: 家嚴 my father 先嚴 my deceased father
5. a Chinese family name
嚴辦(ㄧㄢˊ ㄅㄢˋ)
to deal with severely; to take a severe disciplinary measure against
嚴密(ㄧㄢˊ ㄇㄧˋ)

rigid; rigorous; strict; exact; accurate; precise; tight; close

嚴明(ㄧㄢˊ ㄇㄧㄥˊ)
(said of discipline) strict and impartial

嚴命(ㄧㄢˊ ㄇㄧㄥˋ)
① a strict order ② an order from one's father

嚴防(ㄧㄢˊ ㄈㄤˊ)
to guard carefully; to remain vigilant; to take strict precautions against: 我們必須嚴防敵人破壞。We must take strict precautions against sabotage by the enemy.

嚴父(ㄧㄢˊ ㄈㄨˋ)
① a stern father ② my father

嚴父慈母(ㄧㄢˊ ㄈㄨˋ ㄘˊ ㄇㄨˇ)
stern father and kind mother—pattern of parental love

嚴冬(ㄧㄢˊ ㄉㄨㄥ)
severe winter; very cold winter

嚴冷(ㄧㄢˊ ㄌㄥˇ)or 嚴寒(ㄧㄢˊ ㄏㄢˊ)
severe cold

嚴厲(ㄧㄢˊ ㄌㄧˋ)
strict; stern; stringent; severe; ruthless

嚴令(ㄧㄢˊ ㄌㄧㄥˋ)
a strict order; to order strictly

嚴格(ㄧㄢˊ ㄍㄜˊ)
strict; stringent; rigid; rigorous: 他們嚴格履行協定條款。They accomplish strictly the terms of the agreement.

嚴苛(ㄧㄢˊ ㄎㄜ)
harsh (administration of law)

嚴酷(ㄧㄢˊ ㄎㄨˋ)
inclement; severe; caustic; ruthless: 嚴酷的評語 caustic remarks

嚴加管束(ㄧㄢˊ ㄐㄧㄚ ㄍㄨㄢˇ ㄕㄨˋ)
to exercise strict discipline over (juniors or subordinates)

嚴謹(ㄧㄢˊ ㄐㄧㄣˇ)
careful; cautious; not given to rashness or perfunctoriness; well-knit: 這篇文章結構嚴謹。The essay is well-knit.

嚴緊(ㄧㄢˊ ㄐㄧㄣˇ)
(said of regulations, requirements, etc.) strict; rigorous; tight: 我們的敵人防守嚴緊。Our enemy guarded carefully.

嚴禁(ㄧㄢˊ ㄐㄧㄣˋ)
to prohibit or forbid strictly: 我們學校嚴禁體罰。Our school strictly forbids corporal punishment.

嚴峻(ㄧㄢˊ ㄐㄩㄣˋ)
stern; severe; rigorous; grim: 嚴峻的態度 a stern (or an uncompromising) attitude

嚴刑拷打(ㄧㄢˊ ㄒㄧㄥˊ ㄎㄠˇ ㄉㄚˇ)
to torture cruelly; to beat up cruelly

嚴刑峻法(ㄧㄢˊ ㄒㄧㄥˊ ㄐㄩㄣˋ ㄈㄚˇ)
severe punishments under strict laws

嚴陣以待(ㄧㄢˊ ㄓㄣˋ ㄧˇ ㄉㄞˋ)
to wait for (an enemy attack) in combat readiness; to be ready in full battle array

嚴整(ㄧㄢˊ ㄓㄥˇ)
well-disciplined; in neat formation: 軍容嚴整。The troops are well-disciplined.

嚴正(ㄧㄢˊ ㄓㄥˋ)
strictly correct or just; rigorous; solemn: 昨天外交部發表一嚴正聲明。The Foreign Ministry issued a solemn statement yesterday.

嚴裝(ㄧㄢˊ ㄓㄨㄤ)
to dress neatly and properly

嚴重(ㄧㄢˊ ㄓㄨㄥˋ)
(said of illness, situation, etc.) serious; severe; grave: 事態嚴重。The situation is grave.

嚴懲(ㄧㄢˊ ㄔㄥˊ)
to punish severely: 我們將嚴懲入侵之敵。We will punish the invaders severely.

嚴師(ㄧㄢˊ ㄕ)
a stern or strict teacher

嚴守中立(ㄧㄢˊ ㄕㄡˇ ㄓㄨㄥ ㄌㄧˋ)
to observe strict neutrality; to remain a neutral strictly

嚴霜(ㄧㄢˊ ㄕㄨㄤ)
severe frost—symbolic of severe temperament

嚴詞(ㄧㄢˊ ㄘˊ)
stern words; strong terms

嚴詞譴責(ㄧㄢˊ ㄘˊ ㄑㄧㄢˇ ㄗㄜˊ)
to denounce in strong terms; to condemn sternly

嚴慈(ㄧㄢˊ ㄘˊ)
father (嚴) and mother (慈)

嚴肅(ㄧㄢˊ ㄙㄨˋ)
serious-looking; serious; solemn; austere: 他的面容嚴肅。He looks serious.

嚴以律己，寬以待人(ㄧㄢˊ ㄧˇ ㄌㄩˋ ㄐㄧˇ, ㄎㄨㄢ ㄧˇ ㄉㄞˋ ㄖㄣˊ)
to be strict with oneself and broad-minded towards others

【嚷】 773 1. ㄖㄤˇ raang rǎng
to shout; to cry; to call out loudly: 別嚷了! Stop shouting.

嚷叫(ㄖㄤˇ ㄐㄧㄠˋ)
to bellow; to howl

【嚷】 773 2. ㄖㄤ rhang rāng
參看「嚷嚷」

嚷嚷(ㄖㄤ ㄖㄤ)
① to shout; to yell: 誰在那兒嚷嚷? Who is shouting there? ② to make widely known: 這件事，你可別嚷嚷。Don't make it widely known.

十八畫

【嚼】 774 ㄐㄩㄝˊ jyue jué (語音 ㄐㄧㄠˊ jyau jiáo)
to chew; to masticate; to munch: 細嚼慢嚥 to chew carefully and swallow slowly

嚼蠟(ㄐㄧㄠˊ ㄌㄚˋ)
as tasteless as chewing wax; dry; uninteresting

嚼舌(ㄐㄧㄠˊ ㄕㄜˊ)or 嚼舌根(ㄐㄧㄠˊ ㄕㄜˊ ㄍㄣ)
① to gossip ② to argue meaninglessly: 沒工夫跟你嚼舌。I've got no time to argue with you.

【囀】 775 ㄓㄨㄢˇ joan zhuǎn
1. to warble; to twitter; to chirp
2. pleasing to the ear

【囁】 776 ㄋㄧㄝˋ nieh niè
to move the mouth (when speaking); to falter in speech

囁嚅(ㄋㄧㄝˋ ㄖㄨˊ)
to speak haltingly

〔口部〕

【囂】777 ㄒㄧㄠ shiau xiāo
1. noise; clamor; hubbub
2. to be haughty or proud
囂風(ㄒㄧㄠ ㄈㄥ)
the restlessness of a society
囂浮(ㄒㄧㄠ ㄈㄨˊ)
① frivolous ② the noisy world
囂張(ㄒㄧㄠ ㄓㄤ)
haughty; bossy; rampant; arrogant; aggressive; to push people around: 囂張一時 to run rampant for a time
囂塵(ㄒㄧㄠ ㄔㄣˊ)
① noise and dust ② the noisy, dusty world

十九畫

【囈】778 ㄧˋ yih yì
to talk in sleep; somniloquy
囈語(ㄧˋ ㄩˇ)
① to talk while asleep; somniloquy: 他常在夢中囈語。He often talks while asleep. ② crazy talk; ravings: 沒人能了解狂人的囈語。Nobody can understand the ravings of a madman.

【囉】779 1. ㄌㄨㄛ lhuo luō
to chatter
囉哩囉唆(ㄌㄨㄛ ㄌㄧ ㄌㄨㄛ ㄙㄨㄛ) or 囉囉唆唆(ㄌㄨㄛ ㄌㄨㄛ ㄙㄨㄛ ㄙㄨㄛ) or 囉唆(ㄌㄨㄛ ㄙㄨㄛ)
vexingly verbose or wordy; long-winded; overelaborate: 他說話太囉唆。He's far too long-winded.

【囉】779 2. ㄌㄨㄛˊ luo luó
1. noisiness
2. a band of outlaws
3. used as a slightly argumentative final particle: 有的看囉! Wait and see. 或 Something is coming up.

【囊】780 ㄋㄤˊ nang náng
1. a bag; a sack; a purse: 行囊 a traveling bag
2. to put in a bag
3. a Chinese family name
囊括(ㄋㄤˊ ㄍㄨㄚ)
to encompass; to include; to embrace; to comprise; to pocket or win all (the medals in a sports meet)
囊括四海(ㄋㄤˊ ㄍㄨㄚ ㄙˋ ㄏㄞˇ)
to bring the whole country under imperial rule
囊空如洗(ㄋㄤˊ ㄎㄨㄥ ㄖㄨˊ ㄒㄧˇ)
to be dead broke; to be penniless
囊中物(ㄋㄤˊ ㄓㄨㄥ ㄨˋ)
(literally) a thing which is already in one's bag—(figuratively) a thing very easy to get
囊螢讀書(ㄋㄤˊ ㄧㄥˊ ㄉㄨˊ ㄕㄨ)
(literally) to study by the light of fireflies gathered in a bag—to study under (financial) difficulties

二十一畫

【囑】781 ㄓㄨˇ juu zhǔ
to ask another to do something; to instruct; to enjoin; to direct; to entrust; to charge
囑咐(ㄓㄨˇ ㄈㄨˋ)
to exhort; to charge (a person) with a task; to instruct or bid (a person to do something): 醫生囑咐他好好休息。The doctor bade him take a good rest.
囑託(ㄓㄨˇ ㄊㄨㄛ)
to entrust (a person with a task); to request (a person to do something): 她囑託我辦這件事。She entrusted me with the task.

囗部
ㄨㄟˊ wei wéi

二畫

【囚】782 ㄑㄧㄡˊ chyou qiú
1. a prisoner; a convict: 死囚 a convict sentenced to death
2. to imprison: 他們把我囚禁起來。They imprisoned me.
囚犯(ㄑㄧㄡˊ ㄈㄢˋ)
a prisoner; a convict; a jailbird
囚房(ㄑㄧㄡˊ ㄈㄤˊ)
a prison; a cell
囚牢(ㄑㄧㄡˊ ㄌㄠˊ)
a prison; a jail: 他們因偷錢被送進囚牢。They were taken (or sent) to prison for stealing money.
囚糧(ㄑㄧㄡˊ ㄌㄧㄤˊ)
prison rations; a prisoner's fare
囚籠(ㄑㄧㄡˊ ㄌㄨㄥˊ)
a wooden cage for confinement of prisoners (used in former times to transfer prisoners from one place to another)
囚禁(ㄑㄧㄡˊ ㄐㄧㄣˋ)
to imprison; to jail; to confine; to detain; to shut up in prison
囚車(ㄑㄧㄡˊ ㄔㄜ)
a prison cart; a police van to transport prisoners
囚首垢面(ㄑㄧㄡˊ ㄕㄡˇ ㄍㄡˋ ㄇㄧㄢˋ)
(said of a person) with unkempt hair and a dirty face

【四】783 ㄙˋ syh sì
1. four; fourth: 他四肢並用爬入洞裏。He crept into the cave on all fours.
2. all around
四胞胎(ㄙˋ ㄅㄠ ㄊㄞ)
quadruplets
四壁(ㄙˋ ㄅㄧˋ)
all the walls of a room: 他家徒四壁。He has nothing but all the walls of his room.—He is very poor.
四壁蕭條(ㄙˋ ㄅㄧˋ ㄒㄧㄠ ㄊㄧㄠˊ)
(literally) Desolation prevails within four walls of the house.—as poor as a church mouse
四表(ㄙˋ ㄅㄧㄠˇ)
all directions; beyond limits of the visible world
四邊(ㄙˋ ㄅㄧㄢ)
all around; four sides
四邊形(ㄙˋ ㄅㄧㄢ ㄒㄧㄥˊ)
a quadrilateral, or tetragon
四不像(ㄙˋ ·ㄅㄨ ㄒㄧㄤˋ)
① name of a wild animal (*Elapurus davidianus*) ② deviant or deviate (from

any accepted norm, standard, etc.); outlandish; monstrous

四平八穩(ㄙˋ ㄆㄧㄥˊ ㄅㄚ ㄨㄣˇ)
completely stable and safe; dependable: 他辦事四平八穩。He is dependable in work.

四面(ㄙˋ ㄇㄧㄢˋ)
four sides; all sides: 我們四面出擊。We hit out in all directions.

四面八方(ㄙˋ ㄇㄧㄢˋ ㄅㄚ ㄈㄤ)
on every side; on all sides; all directions; all quarters; all around: 敵人從四面八方包圍他們。They were surrounded by the enemy on all sides.

四面體(ㄙˋ ㄇㄧㄢˋ ㄊㄧˇ)
a tetrahedron

四面玲瓏(ㄙˋ ㄇㄧㄢˋ ㄌㄧㄥˊ ㄌㄨㄥˊ)
tactful or diplomatic with all sorts of people

四面楚歌(ㄙˋ ㄇㄧㄢˋ ㄔㄨˇ ㄍㄜ)
facing hostility, difficulty, or frustration on all sides

四民(ㄙˋ ㄇㄧㄣˊ)
the four classes of people —scholars, farmers, artisans, and merchants

四分五裂(ㄙˋ ㄈㄣ ㄨˇ ㄌㄧㄝˋ)
to fall to pieces; to be all split up: 入侵部隊內部四分五裂。The ranks of the invading army are all split up.

四方(ㄙˋ ㄈㄤ)
① the four directions (east, west, north, and south) ② every direction; all sides; everywhere: 四方響應。Response came from all sides. ③ a square

四方步(ㄙˋ ㄈㄤ ㄅㄨˋ)
to walk in a pompous manner

四方臉(ㄙˋ ㄈㄤ ㄌㄧㄢˇ)
a square face

四大皆空(ㄙˋ ㄉㄚˋ ㄐㄧㄝ ㄎㄨㄥ)
(Buddhism) all the four elements (earth, water, fire, and air) are absent from the mind so that one is completely indifferent to worldly temptations

四德(ㄙˋ ㄉㄜˊ)
the traditional four fundamentals in girls' education —behavior (婦德), speech (婦言), appearance (婦容), and needlework and cookery (婦功)

四堵(ㄙˋ ㄉㄨˇ)
the four walls

四度空間(ㄙˋ ㄉㄨˋ ㄎㄨㄥ ㄐㄧㄢ)or 四次空間(ㄙˋ ㄘˋ ㄎㄨㄥ ㄐㄧㄢ)
(physics) four dimensional space; the fourth dimension

四通八達(ㄙˋ ㄊㄨㄥ ㄅㄚ ㄉㄚˊ)
(said of a communication network) leading everywhere: 本市公路四通八達。Highways radiate from the city in all directions.

四楞子(ㄙˋ ㄌㄥˊ ·ㄗ)
① to be rude in speech ② a vulgar fellow

四六(ㄙˋ ㄌㄧㄡˋ)
a euphuistic style of parallel sentence structures known especially for pairs of sentences of four and six characters

四鄰(ㄙˋ ㄌㄧㄣˊ)
① the neighboring countries ② neighbors

四鄰八舍(ㄙˋ ㄌㄧㄣˊ ㄅㄚ ㄕㄜˋ)
all the neighbors; all the neighboring households

四兩撥千金(ㄙˋ ㄌㄧㄤˇ ㄅㄛ ㄑㄧㄢ ㄐㄧㄣ)
to accomplish a great task with little effort by clever maneuvers

四顧茫茫(ㄙˋ ㄍㄨˋ ㄇㄤˊ ㄇㄤˊ)
to see nothing but emptiness all around

四國(ㄙˋ ㄍㄨㄛˊ)
Shikoku, an island of Japan

四開(ㄙˋ ㄎㄞ)
quarto

四庫全書(ㄙˋ ㄎㄨˋ ㄑㄩㄢˊ ㄕㄨ)
the *Four Collections of Books; Encyclopedia Sinica; A Complete Library of the Four Treasuries* (i.e. classics, history, philosophy and literature)—compiled during the Ching Dynasty

四合院(ㄙˋ ㄏㄜˊ ㄩㄢˋ)or 四合房(ㄙˋ ㄏㄜˊ ㄈㄤˊ)
a compound with houses around a courtyard

四海
①(ㄙˋ ㄏㄞˇ) the outer limits of the China (supposed to be bound by the sea on all sides in former times)—the world: 四海之內皆兄弟也。All the people of the world are brothers.
②(ㄙˋ ·ㄏㄞ) (in colloquial speech) loyal to one's friends; straightforward

四海爲家(ㄙˋ ㄏㄞˇ ㄨㄟˊ ㄐㄧㄚ)
①(said of emperors) to make the country a big family; to achieve perfect unity within the empire ② to lead a wandering life

四胡(ㄙˋ ㄏㄨˊ)
a four-stringed Chinese musical instrument

四季(ㄙˋ ㄐㄧˋ)
the four seasons: 昆明四季如春。In Kunming it's like spring all the year round.

四季豆(ㄙˋ ㄐㄧˋ ㄉㄡˋ)
string beans; kidney beans

四郊(ㄙˋ ㄐㄧㄠ)
the suburbs of a city; outskirts

四脚朝天(ㄙˋ ㄐㄧㄠˇ ㄔㄠˊ ㄊㄧㄢ)
to fall on one's back

四脚蛇(ㄙˋ ㄐㄧㄠˇ ㄕㄜˊ)
a lizard

四健會(ㄙˋ ㄐㄧㄢˋ ㄏㄨㄟˋ)
the 4-H club (4-H—head, heart, hands and health)

四起(ㄙˋ ㄑㄧˇ)
to rise everywhere; to rise in every direction

四權(ㄙˋ ㄑㄩㄢˊ)
the four rights of the people (election, recall, initiative and referendum) advocated by Dr. Sun Yat-sen

四下(ㄙˋ ㄒㄧㄚˋ)or 四下裏(ㄙˋ ㄒㄧㄚˋ ·ㄌㄧ)
all around; on all sides

四肢(ㄙˋ ㄓ)
the four limbs

四周圍(ㄙˋ ㄓㄡ ㄨㄟˊ)
all around; on all sides; on every side: 房子四周圍都是樹林。Woods lay around the house.

四處(ㄙˋ ㄔㄨˋ)
everywhere; all around; in all directions: 我們四處尋找走失的狗。We looked everywhere for our lost dog.

〔口部〕

四垂or四陲(ㄙˋ ㄔㄨㄟˊ)
the frontiers of a country
四川(ㄙˋ ㄔㄨㄢ)
Szechwan (province)
四重奏(ㄙˋ ㄔㄨㄥˊ ㄗㄡˋ)
(instrumental) quartet: 我很喜歡貝多芬晚期的弦樂四重奏。I like Beethoven's late string quartets very much.
四時(ㄙˋ ㄕˊ)
the four seasons
四史(ㄙˋ ㄕˇ)
The Four Books of History (the *Historical Records*, the *Book of Han*, the *Book of Later Han*, the *Annals of the Three Kingdoms*)
四捨五入(ㄙˋ ㄕㄜˇ ㄨˇ ㄖㄨˋ)
(arithmetic) to count five and higher fractions as units and disregard the rest
四聲(ㄙˋ ㄕㄥ)
①the four tones in ancient Chinese—even, rising, departing and entering tones (平, 上, 去, 入) ② the four tones of Mandarin—first, second, third and fourth tones (陰平, 陽平, 上聲, 去聲)
四書(ㄙˋ ㄕㄨ)
the *Four Books*—the *Great Learning*, the *Doctrine of the Mean*, the *Analects*, and the *Book of Mencius* (大學, 中庸, 論語, 孟子)
四則(ㄙˋ ㄗㄜˊ)
(arithmetic) addition, subtraction, multiplication, and division (加, 減, 乘, 除)
四次方程式(ㄙˋ ㄘˋ ㄈㄤ ㄔㄥˊ ㄕˋ)
a quartic equation, or an equation of the fourth degree
四四方方(ㄙˋ ㄙˋ ㄈㄤ ㄈㄤ)
having the shape of a real square
四散(ㄙˋ ㄙㄢˋ)
to disperse everywhere; to disperse or scatter in all directions: 羣衆看到警察而四散。The crowd dispersed at the sight of the police.
四夷(ㄙˋ ㄧˊ)
the four barbarian tribes on the borders of ancient China
四裔(ㄙˋ ㄧˋ)
all the farthest corners
四野(ㄙˋ ㄧㄝˇ)
all the surrounding wildernesses; a vast expanse of the open ground: 四野寂靜無聲。All is quiet on the vast expanse of the open ground.
四言詩(ㄙˋ ㄧㄢˊ ㄕ)
a type of classical poetry with four characters to a line, popular before the Han Dynasty (206 B.C.-A.D. 220)
四維八德(ㄙˋ ㄨㄟˊ ㄅㄚ ㄉㄜˊ)
the four ethical principles (禮、義、廉、恥) and eight cardinal virtues (忠、孝、仁、愛、信、義、和、平)
四隅(ㄙˋ ㄩˊ)
the four corners
四月(ㄙˋ ㄩㄝˋ)
① April: 四月雨帶來五月花。April showers do bring May flowers. ② the fourth month of the lunar calendar ③ four months

三畫

【回】 784
ㄏㄨㄟˊ hwei huí

1. to return; to go back; to bring back; to turn back
2. to reply; to answer
3. to turn round
4. the number of times: 我來過一回。I have been here once.
5. a kind; a sort: 這完全是兩回事。These are entirely two different kinds of matters.
6. chapters in a novel: 這本小說共一百二十回。This novel has 120 chapters.
7. of Mohammedanism; Moslems

回拜(ㄏㄨㄟˊ ㄅㄞˋ)
to return a visit; to pay a return visit
回報(ㄏㄨㄟˊ ㄅㄠˋ)
①to bring back a report; to return for report ② to repay (a favor or an injury); to reciprocate: 我應回報他的盛情。I must repay him for his hospitality.
回稟(ㄏㄨㄟˊ ㄅㄧㄥˇ)
to report back (to one's superior)
回眸(ㄏㄨㄟˊ ㄇㄡˊ)
(said of a woman) to glance back
回門(ㄏㄨㄟˊ ㄇㄣˊ)
a bride's first visit to her parents' home
回民(ㄏㄨㄟˊ ㄇㄧㄣˊ)
the Mohammedans; the Moslems (Muslems, Muslims)
回訪(ㄏㄨㄟˊ ㄈㄤˇ)
to pay a return visit: 我將回訪閣下。I'll pay a return visit to you.
回府(ㄏㄨㄟˊ ㄈㄨˇ)
to return home
回覆(ㄏㄨㄟˊ ㄈㄨˋ)
to reply; to answer; a reply; an answer: 他回覆說不願做那事。He replied that he would not do that.
回答(ㄏㄨㄟˊ ㄉㄚˊ)
to reply; to answer; to respond; a reply; an answer; a response: 我無法回答那個問題。I couldn't answer the question.
回單(ㄏㄨㄟˊ ㄉㄢ)
a receipt
回電(ㄏㄨㄟˊ ㄉㄧㄢˋ)
①a cable or telegram sent in reply ②to wire back: 請即回電。Wire a reply immediately.
回頭(ㄏㄨㄟˊ ㄊㄡˊ)
①to turn the head around; to turn back ② after a while; later: 回頭再談。We'll talk it over later. ③ to return ④ to repent: 幸好他及早回頭。It was fortunate that he repented before it was too late.
回頭是岸(ㄏㄨㄟˊ ㄊㄡˊ ㄕˋ ㄢˋ)
(literally) Turn the head and there is the shore. —Repent and salvation is at hand. 或 Repentance is salvation.
回條(ㄏㄨㄟˊ ㄊㄧㄠˊ)or 回執(ㄏㄨㄟˊ ㄓˊ)
a brief note in reply; a receipt
回天乏術(ㄏㄨㄟˊ ㄊㄧㄢ ㄈㄚˊ ㄕㄨˋ)
Nothing can be done to revive the dead or to save the dying.
回娘家(ㄏㄨㄟˊ ㄋㄧㄤˊ ㄐㄧㄚ)
(said of a woman) to visit the parental home
回暖(ㄏㄨㄟˊ ·ㄋㄨㄢ)

(said of the weather) to get warm again (after a cold spell)

回來(ㄏㄨㄟˊ ˙ㄌㄞ)
to come back; to return: 他馬上回來。He'll be back in a minute.

回禮(ㄏㄨㄟˊ ㄌㄧˇ)
① to return a salute ② to send a present in return; to present a gift in return

回力球(ㄏㄨㄟˊ ㄌㄧˋ ㄑㄧㄡˊ)
① pelota; jai alai ② the ball used in pelota and jai alai

回祿之災(ㄏㄨㄟˊ ㄌㄨˋ ㄓ ㄗㄞ)
a fire disaster

回籠(ㄏㄨㄟˊ ㄌㄨㄥˊ)
①(said of bank notes, etc.) to return to the bank (which issued the notes) ② to steam again: 把涼包子回回籠。Heat up the cold steamed stuffed buns.

回顧(ㄏㄨㄟˊ ㄍㄨˋ)
to look back; to cast a look behind

回鍋(ㄏㄨㄟˊ ㄍㄨㄛ)
to cook for a second time

回歸(ㄏㄨㄟˊ ㄍㄨㄟ)
① regression ② to regress

回歸線(ㄏㄨㄟˊ ㄍㄨㄟ ㄒㄧㄢˋ)
the tropic: 北回歸線 the tropic of Cancer 南回歸線 the tropic of Capricorn

回歸熱(ㄏㄨㄟˊ ㄍㄨㄟ ㄖㄜˋ)
relapsing fever

回光(ㄏㄨㄟˊ ㄍㄨㄤ)
reflected light

回光返照(ㄏㄨㄟˊ ㄍㄨㄤ ㄈㄢˇ ㄓㄠˋ)
the transient reviving of the dying; a sudden spurt of activity prior to a collapse

回扣(ㄏㄨㄟˊ ㄎㄡˋ)
a commission on sales

回合(ㄏㄨㄟˊ ㄏㄜˊ)
an encounter; a round; a bout

回紇(ㄏㄨㄟˊ ㄏㄜˊ)
the Uigurs

回航(ㄏㄨㄟˊ ㄏㄤˊ)
to sail or fly back

回話(ㄏㄨㄟˊ ㄏㄨㄚˋ)
① to bring back word; to report ② a reply (usually one conveyed by a messenger): 他要我給他帶個回話。He asked me to take him a message by way of reply.

回回
①(ㄏㄨㄟˊ ˙ㄏㄨㄟ) an ancient name for all the Moslem nations
②(ㄏㄨㄟˊ ㄏㄨㄟˊ) every time

回擊(ㄏㄨㄟˊ ㄐㄧˊ)
to fight back; to return fire; to counterattack: 他們拼命回擊。They fought back desperately.

回教(ㄏㄨㄟˊ ㄐㄧㄠˋ)
Mohammedanism; Islam

回教徒(ㄏㄨㄟˊ ㄐㄧㄠˋ ㄊㄨˊ)
a Muslim

回教寺(ㄏㄨㄟˊ ㄐㄧㄠˋ ㄙˋ)
a mosque 亦作「清眞寺」

回敬(ㄏㄨㄟˊ ㄐㄧㄥˋ)
① to return the salute; to give a gift in return ② tit for tat

回絕(ㄏㄨㄟˊ ㄐㄩㄝˊ)
to decline; to refuse: 他一口回絕我的提議。He flatly refused my proposal.

回請(ㄏㄨㄟˊ ㄑㄧㄥˇ)
to return hospitality; to give a return banquet

回去(ㄏㄨㄟˊ ㄑㄩˋ)
① to go back; to return (home or where one came from) ② to return: 請把這錢退回去給他。Please return the money to him.

回心轉意(ㄏㄨㄟˊ ㄒㄧㄣ ㄓㄨㄢˇ ㄧˋ)
① to decide to return from sin to virtue; to repent ② to change one's mind

回信(ㄏㄨㄟˊ ㄒㄧㄣˋ)
① a letter in reply ② to write back ③ a verbal message in a reply; a reply: 我用英文回信給他。I wrote him a reply in English.

回響(ㄏㄨㄟˊ ㄒㄧㄤˇ)
to reverberate; to ring; to echo; to resound; resonance: 雷聲在山谷裏回響。Thunder reverberated in the valley.

回想(ㄏㄨㄟˊ ㄒㄧㄤˇ)
to recollect; to bring back; to recall; to reflect; to look back upon: 這首歌使我回想起小學的生活。The song brought back to my mind our life at the primary school.

回轉(ㄏㄨㄟˊ ㄓㄨㄢˇ)
to turn round

回腸盪氣 or 迴腸盪氣(ㄏㄨㄟˊ ㄔㄤˊ ㄉㄤˋ ㄑㄧˋ)
(said of literary works) very touching; soul-stirring; heartrending

回程(ㄏㄨㄟˊ ㄔㄥˊ)
the return trip

回春(ㄏㄨㄟˊ ㄔㄨㄣ)
① the return of spring: 大地回春。Spring returns to the earth. 或 Spring is here again. ② to bring back to life

回收(ㄏㄨㄟˊ ㄕㄡ)
to retrieve; to recover; to reclaim: 紙回收 the reclamation of paper

回手(ㄏㄨㄟˊ ㄕㄡˇ)
① to fight back; to return a blow for a blow ② to turn round and stretch out one's hand

回升(ㄏㄨㄟˊ ㄕㄥ)
to rise again (after a fall); to pick up: 物價又回升。Prices have risen again.

回生(ㄏㄨㄟˊ ㄕㄥ)
① to bring back to life: 醫生能起死回生嗎? Can the doctor bring the dying back to life? ② to forget through lack of practice; to be out of practice; rusty

回聲(ㄏㄨㄟˊ ㄕㄥ)
an echo; reverberation

回族(ㄏㄨㄟˊ ㄗㄨˊ)
the Moslem population (in China)

回嘴(ㄏㄨㄟˊ ㄗㄨㄟˇ)
to talk back; to retort

回溯(ㄏㄨㄟˊ ㄙㄨˋ)
to recall; to look back upon

回憶(ㄏㄨㄟˊ ㄧˋ) or 回首(ㄏㄨㄟˊ ㄕㄡˇ)
to recollect; to recall; to look back upon; recollection; retrospect: 童年的回憶 the recollections of childhood

回憶錄(ㄏㄨㄟˊ ㄧˋ ㄌㄨˋ)
memoirs; recollections

回郵(ㄏㄨㄟˊ ㄧㄡˊ)
return mail

回音(ㄏㄨㄟˊ ㄧㄣ)
① to echo; an echo; reverberation: 當他唱歌時,山谷發出回音。The valley echoed as he sang. ② a reply; an

answer; a response: 立候回音 hoping for an immediate reply

回味(ㄏㄨㄟˊ ㄨㄟˋ)
to recollect the pleasant flavor of; to ponder over

回文(ㄏㄨㄟˊ ㄨㄣˊ)
the language of the Moslems (in China)

口部

【囟】785 ㄒㄧㄣˋ shinn xìn
the top of the human head; the skull

【因】786 ㄧㄣ in yīn
1. cause; reason: 事出有因。There is good reason for it.
2. for; because of
3. in accordance with; according to; on the basis of; in the light of
4. to follow (a practice, convention, etc.); to carry on

因病(ㄧㄣ ㄅㄧㄥˋ)
due to illness; because of illness: 他因病不能到校。He could not go to school because of illness.

因病下藥(ㄧㄣ ㄅㄧㄥˋ ㄒㄧㄚˋ ㄧㄠˋ)
to apply medicine according to indications

因地制宜(ㄧㄣ ㄉㄧˋ ㄓˋ ㄧˊ)
to take appropriate measures in accordance with local conditions; to take actions that suit local circumstances

因陋就簡(ㄧㄣ ㄌㄡˋ ㄐㄧㄡˋ ㄐㄧㄢˇ)
① to do things in the easy, simple way ② to make do with whatever is available

因革(ㄧㄣ ㄍㄜˊ)
the course of change and development; successive changes; evolution; vicissitudes or history (of a system, institution, etc.) 亦作「沿革」

因果(ㄧㄣ ㄍㄨㄛˇ)
the chain of cause and effect: 前因後果 antecedents and consequences

因果報應(ㄧㄣ ㄍㄨㄛˇ ㄅㄠˋ ㄧㄥˋ)
(Buddhism) the automatic repayment in one's later life of whatever one does; retribution for sin

因果律(ㄧㄣ ㄍㄨㄛˇ ㄌㄩˋ)
the law of causality; the law of causation

因公出差(ㄧㄣ ㄍㄨㄥ ㄔㄨ ㄔㄞ)
to take an official trip; to be absent (from office) on an official errand

因公死亡(ㄧㄣ ㄍㄨㄥ ㄙˇ ㄨㄤˊ)
to die while discharging an official assignment

因禍得福(ㄧㄣ ㄏㄨㄛˋ ㄉㄜˊ ㄈㄨˊ)
to profit from a misfortune

因習(ㄧㄣ ㄒㄧˊ)
to follow routines or conventions without change

因襲(ㄧㄣ ㄒㄧˊ)
to follow conventions and traditions; conventions; conventional; traditional ways

因小失大(ㄧㄣ ㄒㄧㄠˇ ㄕ ㄉㄚˋ)
to lose a big opportunity or large gain because of a trifle consideration; to try to save a little only to lose a lot

因循(ㄧㄣ ㄒㄩㄣˊ)
① to follow (old customs, etc.); to continue in the same old rut ② to procrastinate

因循苟且(ㄧㄣ ㄒㄩㄣˊ ㄍㄡˇ ㄑㄧㄝˇ)
to follow routines without thinking about improvement; to be perfunctory and unimaginative in handling things

因時制宜(ㄧㄣ ㄕˊ ㄓˋ ㄧˊ)
to do what is appropriate according to the circumstances

因勢利導(ㄧㄣ ㄕˋ ㄌㄧˋ ㄉㄠˇ)
to give judicious guidance according to circumstances

因人成事(ㄧㄣ ㄖㄣˊ ㄔㄥˊ ㄕˋ)
to rely on others for success in work; to do something by the help of somebody

因人設事(ㄧㄣ ㄖㄣˊ ㄕㄜˋ ㄕˋ)
to create jobs just to accommodate some people (not because the jobs are indispensable)

因仍舊慣(ㄧㄣ ㄖㄥˊ ㄐㄧㄡˋ ㄍㄨㄢˋ)
to follow the old routines

因子(ㄧㄣ ㄗˇ) or 因數(ㄧㄣ ㄕㄨˋ)
(mathematics) a factor

因此(ㄧㄣ ㄘˇ)
therefore; hence; consequently; thus; for this reason; because of this: 時間已很晚，因此你該去睡覺了。It is very late; hence you must go to bed.

因材施教(ㄧㄣ ㄘㄞˊ ㄕ ㄐㄧㄠˋ)
to teach according to the student's ability or aptitude: 孔子因材施教。Confucius taught disciples in accordance with their aptitude.

因素(ㄧㄣ ㄙㄨˋ)
factors; elements

因案革職(ㄧㄣ ㄢˋ ㄍㄜˊ ㄓˊ)
to get fired because of involvement in a scandal

因而(ㄧㄣ ㄦˊ)
therefore; and so; thereupon: 我病了，因而不能來。I was ill, and therefore could not come.

因噎廢食(ㄧㄣ ㄧㄝ ㄈㄟˋ ㄕˊ)
(literally) to refuse to eat for fear of choking—to refuse making renovations for fear of a little trouble

因應變化(ㄧㄣ ㄧㄥˋ ㄅㄧㄢˋ ㄏㄨㄚˋ)
to change according to the circumstances

因為(ㄧㄣ ㄨㄟˋ)
because; inasmuch as; since; as: 我因為下雨而沒出門。I did not go out because it rained.

因緣(ㄧㄣ ㄩㄢˊ)
(Buddhism) primary and secondary causes; a chance; the chain of cause and effect

四畫

【困】787 ㄎㄨㄣˋ kuenn kùn
1. difficult; hard
2. poor
3. tired; weary; fatigued: 你困了就休息一下吧！Take a rest if you are tired.
4. to trouble; to worry; to harass; to be stranded; to be hard pressed

困乏(ㄎㄨㄣˋ ㄈㄚˊ)
① impoverished ② exhausted; fatigued; weary; tired

困頓(ㄎㄨㄣˋ ㄉㄨㄣˋ)
① tired; exhausted; fatigued ② in financial straits

困難(ㄎㄨㄣˋ ㄋㄢˊ)
difficult; hard; difficulty; hardship; financial diffi-

culties; straitened circumstances: 情況十分困難。Conditions are very difficult.

困難重重(ㄎㄨㄣˋ ㄋㄢˊ ㄔㄨㄥˊ ㄔㄨㄥˊ)
to be beset with difficulties

困苦(ㄎㄨㄣˋ ㄎㄨˇ)
in great distress; suffering hardships; poverty-stricken; (live) in privation: 艱難困苦 difficulties and hardships

困惑(ㄎㄨㄣˋ ㄏㄨㄛˋ)
at a loss; not knowing what to do; perplexed; in perplexity: 他困惑地看着我們。He looked at us in perplexity.

困境(ㄎㄨㄣˋ ㄐㄧㄥˋ)
a difficult position; a predicament; straits: 我們必須擺脫困境。We must extricate ourselves from a difficult position.

困倦(ㄎㄨㄣˋ ㄐㄩㄢˋ)
weary; tired

困窘(ㄎㄨㄣˋ ㄐㄩㄥˇ)
in straitened circumstances; in a difficult position; embarrassment; to embarrass

困窮(ㄎㄨㄣˋ ㄑㄩㄥˊ)
in great financial difficulties; very poor; impoverished; poverty-stricken: 他生活在極度困窮中。He lives in a state of extreme poverty.

困守(ㄎㄨㄣˋ ㄕㄡˇ)
to defend against a siege; to stand a siege

困獸之鬪(ㄎㄨㄣˋ ㄕㄡˋ ㄓ ㄉㄡˋ)
to fight desperately like a cornered wild beast; a desperate fight

困擾(ㄎㄨㄣˋ ㄖㄠˇ)
to perplex; to puzzle; to confuse: 他為一個難題所困擾。He was puzzled by a difficult question.

困厄(ㄎㄨㄣˋ ㄜˋ)
dire straits; distress

困阨(ㄎㄨㄣˋ ㄜˋ)
poverty-stricken

困而學之(ㄎㄨㄣˋ ㄦˊ ㄒㄩㄝˊ ㄓ)
to learn in consequence of frustration

【囤】 788
ㄊㄨㄣˊ twen tún
to store up; to hoard; to stockpile

囤糧(ㄊㄨㄣˊ ㄌㄧㄤˊ)
to store up food for the army

囤貨(ㄊㄨㄣˊ ㄏㄨㄛˋ)
to store up commodities

囤積(ㄊㄨㄣˊ ㄐㄧ)
to hoard commodities for speculation; to corner: 囤積小麥 to corner the wheat market

囤積居奇(ㄊㄨㄣˊ ㄐㄧ ㄐㄩ ㄑㄧˊ)
to store up commodities in the hope of selling them at higher prices later; hoarding and speculation

【囪】 789
ㄘㄨㄥ tsong cōng
a chimney; a flue

【囫】 790
ㄏㄨˊ hwu hú
entire; whole

囫圇(ㄏㄨˊ ㄌㄨㄣˊ)
whole: 囫圇吞下 to swallow a thing whole

囫圇吞棗(ㄏㄨˊ ㄌㄨㄣˊ ㄊㄨㄣ ㄗㄠˇ)
(literally) to swallow a date whole—to accept a fact without understanding or analyzing; to read hastily without thinking

五畫

【囷】 791
ㄐㄩㄣ jiun jūn
a granary

【囹】 792
ㄌㄧㄥˊ ling líng
a prison; a jail

囹圄(ㄌㄧㄥˊ ㄩˇ)
a prison; a jail: 他們因偷錢而身繫囹圄。They were sent to prison for stealing money.

【固】 793
ㄍㄨˋ guh gù
1. stable; firm; sturdy; secure; solid; hard; strong: 這個梯子牢固嗎? Is this ladder secure?
2. obstinate; stubborn; insistent; steadfast: 他像騾子一樣頑固。He is as stubborn as a mule.
3. base; mean; ignorant
4. chronic 參看「固疾」
5. originally; certainly; assuredly; as a matter of course
6. indeed
7. admittedly; no doubt
8. to become solid; to solidify: 果凍冷了就凝固了。Jelly solidifies as it gets cold.
9. to strengthen; to guard; to secure; to consolidate
10. a Chinese family name

固步自封(ㄍㄨˋ ㄅㄨˋ ㄗˋ ㄈㄥ)
參看「故步自封」

固定(ㄍㄨˋ ㄉㄧㄥˋ)
① to fix; to make immovable: 我們把火爐固定在適當的地方。We fixed the stove in place. ② fixed; regular; settled: 他沒有固定的工作和住所。He has no regular work and settled abode.

固定格式(ㄍㄨˋ ㄉㄧㄥˋ ㄍㄜˊ ㄕˋ)
a fixed format

固定匯率(ㄍㄨˋ ㄉㄧㄥˋ ㄏㄨㄟˋ ㄌㄩˋ)
the fixed exchange rate

固定價格(ㄍㄨˋ ㄉㄧㄥˋ ㄐㄧㄚˋ ㄍㄜˊ)
the fixed price

固定成本(ㄍㄨˋ ㄉㄧㄥˋ ㄔㄥˊ ㄅㄣˇ)
fixed cost

固定作用(ㄍㄨˋ ㄉㄧㄥˋ ㄗㄨㄛˋ ㄩㄥˋ)
fixation

固態(ㄍㄨˋ ㄊㄞˋ)
(physics) solid state

固體(ㄍㄨˋ ㄊㄧˇ)
solid (as distinct from liquid or gas)

固陋(ㄍㄨˋ ㄌㄡˋ)
ill-informed; unenlightened; unlearned; ignorant

固疾(ㄍㄨˋ ㄐㄧˊ)
a chronic disease 亦作「痼疾」

固結(ㄍㄨˋ ㄐㄧㄝˊ)
to make or become solid, hard, firm, etc.

固請(ㄍㄨˋ ㄑㄧㄥˇ)
to invite strongly

固執(ㄍㄨˋ ㄓˊ)
obstinate; stubborn; opinionated; persistent

固執己見(ㄍㄨˋ ㄓˊ ㄐㄧˇ ㄐㄧㄢˋ)
to stick to one's opinions

固守(ㄍㄨˋ ㄕㄡˇ)
to defend or guard firmly; to adhere to; to stick to: 別固守老一套的辦法。Don't stick to the old ways.

固守成規(ㄍㄨˋ ㄕㄡˇ ㄔㄥˊ ㄍㄨㄟ)
to stick to old rules

固然(ㄍㄨˋ ㄖㄢˊ)
① of course ② no doubt; true

固若金湯(ㄍㄨˋ ㄖㄨㄛˋ ㄐㄧㄣ ㄊㄤ)
(said of a city, military position, etc.) impregnable

固辭(ㄍㄨˋ ㄘˊ)
to decline firmly

固有(ㄍㄨˋ ㄧㄡˇ)
intrinsic; inherent; innate: 重量是物質的一種固有特性。Weight is an inherent property of matter.

固有文化(ㄍㄨˋ ㄧㄡˇ ㄨㄣˊ ㄏㄨㄚˋ)
traditional culture (of a nation)

六畫

【囿】 794
ㄧㄡˋ yow yòu

1. an enclosure for keeping animals; a menagerie; a garden: 園囿 or 苑囿 a pleasure garden; an enclosure for animals
2. to confine; to enclose

囿於見聞(ㄧㄡˋ ㄩˊ ㄐㄧㄢˋ ㄨㄣˊ)
handicapped by lack of knowledge and experience

囿於成見(ㄧㄡˋ ㄩˊ ㄔㄥˊ ㄐㄧㄢˋ)
bound by prejudice; biased

囿於一隅(ㄧㄡˋ ㄩˊ ㄧˋ ㄩˊ)
confined to a corner; unable to see widely enough

七畫

【圃】 795
ㄆㄨˇ puu pǔ

1. a vegetable garden (or plot); a nursery; an orchard ; a plantation: 苗圃 a seed plot 花圃 a flower nursery
2. a planter; a gardener

【圄】 796
ㄩˇ yeu yǔ

a prison; a jail

八畫

【國】 797
ㄍㄨㄛˊ gwo guó

1. a country; a nation; a kingdom; a state: 全國各地 all over the country 各國 (or 列國) the nations of the world
2. national; governmental
3. Chinese
4. a Chinese family name

國寶(ㄍㄨㄛˊ ㄅㄠˇ)
① a national treasure: 故宮博物院有很多國寶。The National Palace Museum is full of national treasures. ② national currency

國本(ㄍㄨㄛˊ ㄅㄣˇ)
① the foundation of a nation ② an heir apparent to a throne

國幣(ㄍㄨㄛˊ ㄅㄧˋ)
① national currency ② Chinese currency

國賓(ㄍㄨㄛˊ ㄅㄧㄣ)
a state guest; a government guest

國步艱難(ㄍㄨㄛˊ ㄅㄨˋ ㄐㄧㄢ ㄋㄢˊ) or 國步方艱(ㄍㄨㄛˊ ㄅㄨˋ ㄈㄤ ㄐㄧㄢ)
The nation is beset by difficulties. 國步艱難，大家應有此認識。We all must know that our nation is beset by difficulties.

國破家亡(ㄍㄨㄛˊ ㄆㄛˋ ㄐㄧㄚ ㄨㄤˊ)
The country is defeated and the home lost.

國門(ㄍㄨㄛˊ ㄇㄣˊ)
the gateway of a country

國民(ㄍㄨㄛˊ ㄇㄧㄣˊ)
a citizen; the people

國民兵(ㄍㄨㄛˊ ㄇㄧㄣˊ ㄅㄧㄥ)
the militia; a militiaman; a citizen soldier; the national guard (of the United States)

國民平均所得(ㄍㄨㄛˊ ㄇㄧㄣˊ ㄆㄧㄥˊ ㄐㄩㄣ ㄙㄨㄛˇ ㄉㄜˊ)
per capita income

國民福利(ㄍㄨㄛˊ ㄇㄧㄣˊ ㄈㄨˊ ㄌㄧˋ)
national welfare

國民大會代表(ㄍㄨㄛˊ ㄇㄧㄣˊ ㄉㄚˋ ㄏㄨㄟˋ ㄉㄞˋ ㄅㄧㄠˇ) or 國大代表(ㄍㄨㄛˊ ㄉㄚˋ ㄉㄞˋ ㄅㄧㄠˇ)
a member of the National Assembly; a National Assemblyman

國民代表大會(ㄍㄨㄛˊ ㄇㄧㄣˊ ㄉㄞˋ ㄅㄧㄠˇ ㄉㄚˋ ㄏㄨㄟˋ) or 國大(ㄍㄨㄛˊ ㄉㄚˋ)
the National Assembly

國民黨(ㄍㄨㄛˊ ㄇㄧㄣˊ ㄉㄤˇ)
Kuomintang (founded by Dr. Sun Yat-sen); the Nationalist Party

國民革命軍(ㄍㄨㄛˊ ㄇㄧㄣˊ ㄍㄜˊ ㄇㄧㄥˋ ㄐㄩㄣ)
the National Revolutionary Army (of the Kuomintang)

國民教育(ㄍㄨㄛˊ ㄇㄧㄣˊ ㄐㄧㄠˋ ㄩˋ)
compulsory education

國民就業輔導中心(ㄍㄨㄛˊ ㄇㄧㄣˊ ㄐㄧㄡˋ ㄧㄝˋ ㄈㄨˇ ㄉㄠˇ ㄓㄨㄥ ㄒㄧㄣ)
National Employment Service Center

國民性(ㄍㄨㄛˊ ㄇㄧㄣˊ ㄒㄧㄥˋ)
national character

國民學校(ㄍㄨㄛˊ ㄇㄧㄣˊ ㄒㄩㄝˊ ㄒㄧㄠˋ)
a primary school; an elementary school

國民中學(ㄍㄨㄛˊ ㄇㄧㄣˊ ㄓㄨㄥ ㄒㄩㄝˊ)
a junior high school (from the seventh to ninth grade) under the nine-year free education system introduced in China in 1968

國民身分(份)證(ㄍㄨㄛˊ ㄇㄧㄣˊ ㄕㄣ ㄈㄣˋ ㄓㄥˋ)
a citizen's identification card; an ID card

國民生產毛額(ㄍㄨㄛˊ ㄇㄧㄣˊ ㄕㄥ ㄔㄢˇ ㄇㄠˊ ㄜˊ)
gross national product, or GNP

國民所得(ㄍㄨㄛˊ ㄇㄧㄣˊ ㄙㄨㄛˇ ㄉㄜˊ)
national income: 我們的國民所得每年都在增加。Our national income increases every year.

國民外交(ㄍㄨㄛˊ ㄇㄧㄣˊ ㄨㄞˋ ㄐㄧㄠ)
people-to-people diplomacy

國法(ㄍㄨㄛˊ ㄈㄚˇ)
the laws of the land, or the laws of the nation

國法不容(ㄍㄨㄛˊ ㄈㄚˇ ㄅㄨˋ ㄖㄨㄥˊ)
not allowed by laws

國防(ㄍㄨㄛˊ ㄈㄤˊ)
national defense: 國防建設 the building up of national defense

國防部(ㄍㄨㄛˊ ㄈㄤˊ ㄅㄨˋ)
the Ministry of National Defense; the Department of Defense (of the United States)

國父(ㄍㄨㄛˊ ㄈㄨˋ)
① the father of a nation ② Father of the Republic (Dr. Sun Yat-sen): 國父推翻滿清政府。Father of the Republic overthrew the Manchu government.

國定紀念日(ㄍㄨㄛˊ ㄉㄧㄥˋ ㄐㄧˋ ㄋㄧㄢˋ ㄖˋ)
a national commemoration or memorial day

國定假日(ㄍㄨㄛˊ ㄉㄧㄥˋ ㄐㄧㄚˋ ㄖˋ)

a national holiday: 我們上學期有很多國定假日。We had many national holidays last semester.

國都(ㄍㄨㄛˊ ㄉㄨ)
the national capital; the capital

國度(ㄍㄨㄛˊ ㄉㄨˋ)
① institutions of a country ② national expenditure

國泰民安(ㄍㄨㄛˊ ㄊㄞˋ ㄇㄧㄣˊ ㄢ)
The country is prosperous and at peace, and the people live in happiness.

國帑(ㄍㄨㄛˊ ㄊㄤˇ)
national funds

國體(ㄍㄨㄛˊ ㄊㄧˇ)
① the political system of a country ② national prestige

國土(ㄍㄨㄛˊ ㄊㄨˇ)
territory of a nation

國內(ㄍㄨㄛˊ ㄋㄟˋ)
inside the country; domestically or internally; domestic or internal

國內貿易(ㄍㄨㄛˊ ㄋㄟˋ ㄇㄠˋ ㄧˋ)
internal trade; domestic trade

國內電話(ㄍㄨㄛˊ ㄋㄟˋ ㄉㄧㄢˋ ㄏㄨㄚˋ)
domestic telephone

國內新聞(ㄍㄨㄛˊ ㄋㄟˋ ㄒㄧㄣ ㄨㄣˊ)
home news

國內市場(ㄍㄨㄛˊ ㄋㄟˋ ㄕˋ ㄔㄤˇ)
a domestic market

國難(ㄍㄨㄛˊ ㄋㄢˋ)
national crises (or calamities): 國難靡止。There is no end to the national crises.

國難方殷(ㄍㄨㄛˊ ㄋㄢˋ ㄈㄤ ㄧㄣ)
The nation is facing great danger (or in the midst of a crisis). 國難方殷，大家都應努力。We all must work hard because our nation is facing great danger.

國力(ㄍㄨㄛˊ ㄌㄧˋ)
national power (usually connoting resources and potentialities); national strength (or might) : 我們的國力雄厚。We have solid national strength.

國立(ㄍㄨㄛˊ ㄌㄧˋ)
(said of an institution) nationally supported or operated; national: 國立大學 a national university

國曆(ㄍㄨㄛˊ ㄌㄧˋ)
the national (i.e., solar) calendar

國聯(ㄍㄨㄛˊ ㄌㄧㄢˊ)
the League of Nations (short for 國際聯盟)

國歌(ㄍㄨㄛˊ ㄍㄜ)
a national anthem: 學生每天早上都要唱國歌。Students must sing the national anthem every morning.

國故(ㄍㄨㄛˊ ㄍㄨˋ)
① a national misfortune (or tragedy) ② the traditional culture and learning of a nation

國光(ㄍㄨㄛˊ ㄍㄨㄤ)
national glory

國庫(ㄍㄨㄛˊ ㄎㄨˋ)
the national coffers; the national treasury; the national exchequer

國庫券(ㄍㄨㄛˊ ㄎㄨˋ ㄑㄩㄢˋ)
an exchequer bond

國號(ㄍㄨㄛˊ ㄏㄠˋ)
① the name of a dynasty ② the official name of a nation

國花(ㄍㄨㄛˊ ㄏㄨㄚ)
the national flower: 梅花是我們的國花。Plum blossom is our national flower.

國畫(ㄍㄨㄛˊ ㄏㄨㄚˋ)
a Chinese painting: 我買了幾張國畫。I've bought several Chinese paintings.

國貨(ㄍㄨㄛˊ ㄏㄨㄛˋ)
native goods; locally manufactured goods; China-made goods; Chinese goods

國徽(ㄍㄨㄛˊ ㄏㄨㄟ)
the national emblem; the national insignia

國會(ㄍㄨㄛˊ ㄏㄨㄟˋ)
Parliament, the Diet, Congress, etc.

國魂(ㄍㄨㄛˊ ㄏㄨㄣˊ)
national spirit; the soul of a nation; the national genius

國籍(ㄍㄨㄛˊ ㄐㄧˊ)
nationality: 在日內瓦有各種不同國籍的人。There were men of nationalities in Geneva.

國計民生(ㄍㄨㄛˊ ㄐㄧˋ ㄇㄧㄣˊ ㄕㄥ)
the fiscal administration and people's livelihood of a nation

國際(ㄍㄨㄛˊ ㄐㄧˋ)
international: 聯合國是一國際性的組織。The United Nations is an international organization.

國際貿易(ㄍㄨㄛˊ ㄐㄧˋ ㄇㄠˋ ㄧˋ)
international trade; foreign trade

國際法(ㄍㄨㄛˊ ㄐㄧˋ ㄈㄚˇ)
international law

國際法庭(ㄍㄨㄛˊ ㄐㄧˋ ㄈㄚˇ ㄊㄧㄥˊ)
the International Court of Justice (in The Hague, the Netherlands)

國際婦女節(ㄍㄨㄛˊ ㄐㄧˋ ㄈㄨˋ ㄋㄩˇ ㄐㄧㄝˊ)
(internationally observed) Women's Day

國際地位(ㄍㄨㄛˊ ㄐㄧˋ ㄉㄧˋ ㄨㄟˋ)
international status (or standing)

國際電報(ㄍㄨㄛˊ ㄐㄧˋ ㄉㄧㄢˋ ㄅㄠˋ)
the overseas telegram

國際電話(ㄍㄨㄛˊ ㄐㄧˋ ㄉㄧㄢˋ ㄏㄨㄚˋ)
the overseas telephone

國際童軍大露營(ㄍㄨㄛˊ ㄐㄧˋ ㄊㄨㄥˊ ㄐㄩㄣ ㄉㄚˋ ㄌㄨˋ ㄧㄥˊ)
a jamboree

國際勞動節(ㄍㄨㄛˊ ㄐㄧˋ ㄌㄠˊ ㄉㄨㄥˋ ㄐㄧㄝˊ)
(international) Labor Day

國際勞工組織(ㄍㄨㄛˊ ㄐㄧˋ ㄌㄠˊ ㄍㄨㄥ ㄗㄨˇ ㄓ)
International Labor Organization (ILO)

國際聯盟(ㄍㄨㄛˊ ㄐㄧˋ ㄌㄧㄢˊ ㄇㄥˊ)
the League of Nations (1920-1946)

國際關係(ㄍㄨㄛˊ ㄐㄧˋ ㄍㄨㄢ ㄒㄧˋ)
international relations

國際公法(ㄍㄨㄛˊ ㄐㄧˋ ㄍㄨㄥ ㄈㄚˇ)
public international law

國際共管(ㄍㄨㄛˊ ㄐㄧˋ ㄍㄨㄥˋ ㄍㄨㄢˇ)
joint international administration; condominium

國際航道(ㄍㄨㄛˊ ㄐㄧˋ ㄏㄤˊ ㄉㄠˋ)
an international waterway

國際化(ㄍㄨㄛˊ ㄐㄧˋ ㄏㄨㄚˋ)
internationalization

國際換日線(ㄍㄨㄛˊ ㄐㄧˋ ㄏㄨㄢˋ ㄖˋ ㄒㄧㄢˋ)
International Date Line

國際駕駛執照(ㄍㄨㄛˊ ㄐㄧˋ ㄐㄧㄚˋ ㄕˇ ㄓˊ ㄓㄠˋ)
international driving permit license

〔口部〕

國際金融中心(ㄍㄨㄛˊ ㄐㄧˋ ㄐㄧㄣ ㄖㄨㄥˊ ㄓㄨㄥ ㄒㄧㄣ)
the international banking center

國際企業(ㄍㄨㄛˊ ㄐㄧˋ ㄑㄧˋ ㄧㄝˋ)
international enterprises

國際形勢(ㄍㄨㄛˊ ㄐㄧˋ ㄒㄧㄥˊ ㄕˋ)
the international (or world) situation

國際傳眞電報(ㄍㄨㄛˊ ㄐㄧˋ ㄔㄨㄢˊ ㄓㄣ ㄉㄧㄢˋ ㄅㄠˋ)
the overseas facsimile

國際獅子會(ㄍㄨㄛˊ ㄐㄧˋ ㄕ ·ㄗ ㄏㄨㄟˋ)
International Association of Lions' Club

國際商會(ㄍㄨㄛˊ ㄐㄧˋ ㄕㄤ ㄏㄨㄟˋ)
International Chamber of Commerce (ICC)

國際商展(ㄍㄨㄛˊ ㄐㄧˋ ㄕㄤ ㄓㄢˇ)
international trade fair

國際人權公約(ㄍㄨㄛˊ ㄐㄧˋ ㄖㄣˊ ㄑㄩㄢˊ ㄍㄨㄥ ㄩㄝ)
International Covenants on Human Rights

國際組織(ㄍㄨㄛˊ ㄐㄧˋ ㄗㄨˇ ㄓ)
international organizations

國際私法(ㄍㄨㄛˊ ㄐㄧˋ ㄙ ㄈㄚˇ)
private international law

國際奧林匹克委員會(ㄍㄨㄛˊ ㄐㄧˋ ㄠˋ ㄌㄧㄣˊ ㄆㄧˇ ㄎㄜˋ ㄨㄟˇ ㄩㄢˊ ㄏㄨㄟˋ)
International Olympic Committee (IOC)

國際音標(ㄍㄨㄛˊ ㄐㄧˋ ㄧㄣ ㄅㄧㄠ)
the International Phonetic Alphabet (IPA)亦作「萬國音標」

國際文教組織(ㄍㄨㄛˊ ㄐㄧˋ ㄨㄣˊ ㄐㄧㄠˋ ㄗㄨˇ ㄓ)
United Nations Educational, Scientific, and Cultural Organization (UNESCO)

國際語音協會(ㄍㄨㄛˊ ㄐㄧˋ ㄩˇ ㄧㄣ ㄒㄧㄝˊ ㄏㄨㄟˋ)
the International Phonetic Association (IPA)亦作「萬國語音協會」

國家(ㄍㄨㄛˊ ㄐㄧㄚ)
a nation; a country

國家公園(ㄍㄨㄛˊ ㄐㄧㄚ ㄍㄨㄥ ㄩㄢˊ)
a national park

國家科學委員會(ㄍㄨㄛˊ ㄐㄧㄚ ㄎㄜ ㄒㄩㄝˊ ㄨㄟˇ ㄩㄢˊ ㄏㄨㄟˋ)
National Science Council

國家機密(ㄍㄨㄛˊ ㄐㄧㄚ ㄐㄧ ㄇㄧˋ)
state secrets: 每一個國民都要保守國家機密。Every citizen has to keep state secrets.

國家興亡，匹夫有責(ㄍㄨㄛˊ ㄐㄧㄚ ㄒㄧㄥ ㄨㄤˊ, ㄆㄧˇ ㄈㄨ ㄧㄡˇ ㄗㄜˊ)
The rise and fall of a nation is the concern of every citizen.

國家至上(ㄍㄨㄛˊ ㄐㄧㄚ ㄓˋ ㄕㄤˋ)
National interest is above everything else.

國家主義(ㄍㄨㄛˊ ㄐㄧㄚ ㄓㄨˇ ㄧˋ)
nationalism

國家安全會議(ㄍㄨㄛˊ ㄐㄧㄚ ㄢ ㄑㄩㄢˊ ㄏㄨㄟˋ ㄧˋ)
National Security Council

國界(ㄍㄨㄛˊ ㄐㄧㄝˋ)
national boundary

國交(ㄍㄨㄛˊ ㄐㄧㄠ)
diplomatic relations between countries

國將不國，何以家爲(ㄍㄨㄛˊ ㄐㄧㄤ ㄅㄨˋ ㄍㄨㄛˊ, ㄏㄜˊ ㄧˇ ㄐㄧㄚ ㄨㄟˊ)
When the nation is in peril, how can one care about home (or marriage)?

國境(ㄍㄨㄛˊ ㄐㄧㄥˋ)
a border; a national boundary: 難民非法偷越國境。The refugees crossed the border illegally.

國劇(ㄍㄨㄛˊ ㄐㄩˋ)
Peking opera: 你喜歡國劇嗎? Do you like Peking opera?

國君(ㄍㄨㄛˊ ㄐㄩㄣ)
a sovereign; a monarch

國軍(ㄍㄨㄛˊ ㄐㄩㄣ)
the armed forces of the Republic of China

國旗(ㄍㄨㄛˊ ㄑㄧˊ)
the national flag

國情(ㄍㄨㄛˊ ㄑㄧㄥˊ)
the condition of a country; national conditions

國情諮文(ㄍㄨㄛˊ ㄑㄧㄥˊ ㄗ ㄨㄣˊ)
(in the United States) State of the Union message

國慶(ㄍㄨㄛˊ ㄑㄧㄥˋ)or 國慶日(ㄍㄨㄛˊ ㄑㄧㄥˋ ㄖˋ)
the National Day (of a country): 我們的國慶慶祝儀式包括閱兵。Our National Day celebration includes a military parade.

國璽(ㄍㄨㄛˊ ㄒㄧˇ)
① the imperial seal (in old China) ② the official seal of the Central Government

國姓(ㄍㄨㄛˊ ㄒㄧㄥˋ)
the surname of the royal family

國姓爺(ㄍㄨㄛˊ ㄒㄧㄥˋ ㄧㄝˊ)
Koxinga, the name of Cheng Cheng-kung as known to Westerners

國學(ㄍㄨㄛˊ ㄒㄩㄝˊ)
the study of the (Chinese) national classics; the Chinese national literature; Chinese studies

國之四維(ㄍㄨㄛˊ ㄓ ㄙˋ ㄨㄟˊ)
the four cardinal principles of the country

國債(ㄍㄨㄛˊ ㄓㄞˋ)
national debt; public debt

國中(ㄍㄨㄛˊ ㄓㄨㄥ)
short for 國民中學

國恥(ㄍㄨㄛˊ ㄔˇ)
national shame (or humiliation)

國產(ㄍㄨㄛˊ ㄔㄢˇ)
(said of products) native or locally manufactured: 這是一輛國產汽車。This is a locally manufactured car.

國史館(ㄍㄨㄛˊ ㄕˇ ㄍㄨㄢˇ)
Academia Historica; the Bureau of National History

國是(ㄍㄨㄛˊ ㄕˋ)
the affairs of a state; national policies

國事(ㄍㄨㄛˊ ㄕˋ)
national (or state) affairs

國勢(ㄍㄨㄛˊ ㄕˋ)
① national strength ② the condition of a country; the situation in a nation: 國勢不振。The condition of the country is failing.

國手(ㄍㄨㄛˊ ㄕㄡˇ)
(said of athletes, etc.) national representatives, who are the national champions in any lines of activities, especially of sports and games

國殤(ㄍㄨㄛˊ ㄕㄤ)
a martyr to the national cause; a national martyr

國書(ㄍㄨㄛˊ ㄕㄨ)
① credentials (of a diplomat) ②documents exchanged between nations

國術(ㄍㄨㄛˊ ㄕㄨˋ)
Chinese martial arts

國稅(ㄍㄨㄛˊ ㄕㄨㄟˋ)
taxes collected by the national government
國人(ㄍㄨㄛˊ ㄖㄣˊ)
compatriots; people; fellow countrymen
國字(ㄍㄨㄛˊ ㄗˋ)
Chinese characters
國賊(ㄍㄨㄛˊ ㄗㄟˊ)
a traitor of the nation
國葬(ㄍㄨㄛˊ ㄗㄤˋ)
state funeral
國策(ㄍㄨㄛˊ ㄘㄜˋ)
national policies: 我們的國策將永遠不變。We'll never change our national policies.
國粹(ㄍㄨㄛˊ ㄘㄨㄟˋ)
unique cultural features of a nation; national legacies
國色天香(ㄍㄨㄛˊ ㄙㄜˋ ㄊㄧㄢ ㄒㄧㄤ)
the beauty of a woman or peony
國喪(ㄍㄨㄛˊ ㄙㄤ)
national mourning
國醫(ㄍㄨㄛˊ ㄧ)
① a Chinese herb doctor ② Chinese herbal medicine
國有(ㄍㄨㄛˊ ㄧㄡˇ)
state-owned
國有財產局(ㄍㄨㄛˊ ㄧㄡˇ ㄘㄞˊ ㄔㄢˇ ㄐㄩˊ)
The Bureau of National Assets (under the Ministry of Finance)
國宴(ㄍㄨㄛˊ ㄧㄢˋ)
state banquet: 總統以國宴款待國賓。The President treated the state guest with state banquet.
國音(ㄍㄨㄛˊ ㄧㄣ)
the sound system of the Chinese national language; Mandarin pronunciation
國音字母(ㄍㄨㄛˊ ㄧㄣ ㄗˋ ㄇㄨˇ)
the National Phonetic Alphabet (the phonetic alphabet for Mandarin pronunciation)
國營(ㄍㄨㄛˊ ㄧㄥˊ)
state-operated; state-run
國營事業(ㄍㄨㄛˊ ㄧㄥˊ ㄕˋ ㄧㄝˋ)
a state-owned enterprise; state enterprise
國務(ㄍㄨㄛˊ ㄨˋ)
the national affairs; the affairs of a nation
國務卿(ㄍㄨㄛˊ ㄨˋ ㄑㄧㄥ)
Secretary of State (of the U. S. Federal Government)
國務總理(ㄍㄨㄛˊ ㄨˋ ㄗㄨㄥˇ ㄌㄧˇ)
the premier (of the early Chinese Republican Government)
國務院(ㄍㄨㄛˊ ㄨˋ ㄩㄢˋ)
① the Department of State (of the U. S. Federal Government) ② the Cabinet (of the early Chinese Republican Government) ③ State Council (in mainland China)
國外(ㄍㄨㄛˊ ㄨㄞˋ)
outside the country; external; abroad; externally; internationally: 他正在國外求學。He is studying abroad.
國外貿易(ㄍㄨㄛˊ ㄨㄞˋ ㄇㄠˋ ㄧˋ)
foreign trade
國外市場(ㄍㄨㄛˊ ㄨㄞˋ ㄕˋ ㄔㄤˇ)
an overseas (or a foreign) market
國文(ㄍㄨㄛˊ ㄨㄣˊ)
① the written national language ② national language and literature ③ Chinese literature (a course in Chinese schools)
國王(ㄍㄨㄛˊ ㄨㄤˊ)
a king; a monarch
國亡無日(ㄍㄨㄛˊ ㄨㄤˊ ㄨˊ ㄖˋ)
The nation is in extreme peril.
國語(ㄍㄨㄛˊ ㄩˇ)
the national language; Mandarin: 有些外國人很會講國語。Some foreigners can speak Mandarin very well.
國語羅馬字(ㄍㄨㄛˊ ㄩˇ ㄌㄨㄛˊ ㄇㄚˇ ㄗˋ)
Romanized Chinese characters; Gwoyeu Romatzyh
國語文(ㄍㄨㄛˊ ㄩˇ ㄨㄣˊ)
the vernacular style of written Chinese
國語文學(ㄍㄨㄛˊ ㄩˇ ㄨㄣˊ ㄒㄩㄝˊ)
the vernacular literature
國樂(ㄍㄨㄛˊ ㄩㄝˋ)
① Chinese music ② the music officially approved to be played on great ceremonial occasions
國運(ㄍㄨㄛˊ ㄩㄣˋ)
the destiny of the nation: 祝貴國國運昌隆。May the fortunes of your state prosper.

【崙】 798
ㄌㄨㄣˊ luen lún
entire; whole

【圈】 799
1. ㄑㄩㄢ chiuan quān
1. a circle; a ring
2. with a return to the starting point; round: 我們今天早上環湖走了一圈。We walked right round the lake this morning.
3. to circle: 請圈選正確的答案。Please circle the right answers.
4. a circle—a number of persons bound together by having the same interests: 文化圈 literary circles

圈點(ㄑㄩㄢ ㄉㄧㄢˇ)
to mark (a passage) with circles and dots; to punctuate; to mark a good passage with circles
圈套(ㄑㄩㄢ ㄊㄠˋ)
a snare; a trap; a trick: 他落入敵人圈套。He fell into the enemy's trap.
圈內(ㄑㄩㄢ ㄋㄟˋ)
(literally and figuratively) within a circle
圈圈(ㄑㄩㄢ ㄑㄩㄢ)
① to draw circles ② cliques; circles: 別搞小圈圈。Don't form small cliques.
圈子(ㄑㄩㄢ ·ㄗ) or 圈兒(ㄑㄩㄚㄦ)
a circle: 他的生活圈子很小。He moves in a very small circle.
圈外(ㄑㄩㄢ ㄨㄞˋ)
(literally and figuratively) outside a circle

【圈】 799
2. ㄐㄩㄢ jiuan juān
to encircle; to confine

【圈】 799
3. ㄐㄩㄢˋ jiuann juàn
an enclosure or a pen for keeping livestock: 豬圈 a pigpen; a pigsty 牛圈 an enclosure for cows

九畫

【圍】 800
ㄨㄟˊ wei wéi
1. to surround; to enclose; to encircle; to hem in
2. surroundings; environment
3. the circumference of a circle

〔囗部〕

〔口部〕

formed by a person's arms
圍脖兒(ㄨㄟˊ ㄅㄛˊㄦ)or 圍巾(ㄨㄟˊ ㄐㄧㄣ)
a scarf; a muffler
圍標(ㄨㄟˊ ㄅㄧㄠ)
illegal bidding with the government as a victim (worked out by a government employee and a contractor or manufacturer to make sure that the latter gets the contract while the other bidders are willing collaborators)
圍捕(ㄨㄟˊ ㄅㄨˇ)
to arrest (a criminal) by closing in on him from all sides
圍堵政策(ㄨㄟˊ ㄉㄨˇ ㄓㄥˋ ㄘㄜˋ)
a policy of restricting the territorial growth or ideological influence of a hostile nation
圍獵(ㄨㄟˊ ㄌㄧㄝˋ)
to hunt by encircling the game
圍爐(ㄨㄟˊ ㄌㄨˊ)
to sit and chat around the fireplace
圍攻(ㄨㄟˊ ㄍㄨㄥ)
to attack from all sides; to besiege; to beleaguer: 他遭圍攻。He came under attack from all sides. 或 He was caught in a cross fire.
圍困(ㄨㄟˊ ㄎㄨㄣˋ)
to besiege; to beleaguer; to surround; to pin down: 把敵人圍困在少數據點中。Pin down the enemy in a few strongholds.
圍剿(ㄨㄟˊ ㄐㄧㄠˇ)
to attack (bandits or rebels) from all sides; to encircle and suppress
圍棋(ㄨㄟˊ ㄑㄧˊ)
the "encirclement chess," known as *go* in Japan, which was invented by the Chinese at a very early date, played with black and white pieces on a board of 361 crosses
圍牆(ㄨㄟˊ ㄑㄧㄤˊ)
an enclosing wall; a fence
圍裙(ㄨㄟˊ ㄑㄩㄣˊ)
an apron
圍場(ㄨㄟˊ ㄔㄤˊ)
hunting grounds
圍城(ㄨㄟˊ ㄔㄥˊ)
to lay siege to a city; a beleaguered city; a besieged city
圍繞(ㄨㄟˊ ㄖㄠˋ)
to surround; to encircle; to enclose: 一座牆圍繞着這座花園。A wall surrounds the garden.
圍嘴兒(ㄨㄟˊ ㄗㄨㄟˇㄦ)
a bib
圍腰兒(ㄨㄟˊ ㄧㄠㄦ)
(formerly) a girdle

十畫

【園】 801
ㄩㄢˊ yuan yuán
1. a piece of ground used for growing flowers, fruit or vegetables; a garden; a plantation
2. a public garden, park or recreation ground
園圃(ㄩㄢˊ ㄆㄨˇ)
a vegetable garden; an orchard; a plantation
園地(ㄩㄢˊ ㄉㄧˋ)
① a garden ② (in a periodical) a space reserved for publishing articles or letters from readers
園丁(ㄩㄢˊ ㄉㄧㄥ)
a gardener: 我們想雇用一位優秀的園丁。We wish to hire a good gardener.
園林(ㄩㄢˊ ㄌㄧㄣˊ)
a park; a garden
園陵(ㄩㄢˊ ㄌㄧㄥˊ)
an emperor's tomb; a mausoleum
園主(ㄩㄢˊ ㄓㄨˇ)
the owner of a park or garden
園子(ㄩㄢˊ ·ㄗ)
① a garden ② a theater
園藝(ㄩㄢˊ ㄧˋ)
gardening; horticulture; garden husbandry: 他非常愛好園藝。He is very fond of gardening.
園遊會(ㄩㄢˊ ㄧㄡˊ ㄏㄨㄟˋ)
a garden party

【圓】 802
ㄩㄢˊ yuan yuán
1. round; circular; spherical: 它既不圓也不方。It is neither round nor square.
2. complete; to complete; to make plausible; to justify
3. satisfactory; tactful
4. a monetary unit
5. a circle
圓盤(ㄩㄢˊ ㄆㄢˊ)
a disc
圓滿(ㄩㄢˊ ㄇㄢˇ)
① satisfactory; satisfactorily: 對此問題他已圓滿地解決了。The problem has been satisfactorily solved by him. ② rounded out ③ complete
圓夢(ㄩㄢˊ ㄇㄥˋ)
to interpret a dream
圓面積(ㄩㄢˊ ㄇㄧㄢˋ ㄐㄧ)
spherical surface
圓明園(ㄩㄢˊ ㄇㄧㄥˊ ㄩㄢˊ)
the Summer Palace (of the Manchu emperors in Peking)
圓房(ㄩㄢˊ ㄈㄤˊ)
to solemnize a marriage (between one's son and the daughter-in-law brought up in the family when the two reach adulthood)
圓頂(ㄩㄢˊ ㄉㄧㄥˇ)
a round top; a dome: 這座教堂有一漂亮的圓頂。The church has a beautiful dome.
圓通(ㄩㄢˊ ㄊㄨㄥ)
capable of adapting oneself to circumstances; accommodating; flexible: 我們老闆很圓通。Our boss is very accommodating.
圓筒(ㄩㄢˊ ㄊㄨㄥˇ)
a cylinder
圓臉(ㄩㄢˊ ㄌㄧㄢˇ)
a round face
圓顱方趾(ㄩㄢˊ ㄌㄨˊ ㄈㄤ ㄓˇ)
round-skulled and square-footed (referring to man) —all human beings are alike
圓規(ㄩㄢˊ ㄍㄨㄟ)
a pair of compasses (an instrument for making circles)
圓弧(ㄩㄢˊ ㄏㄨˊ)
an arc
圓滑(ㄩㄢˊ ㄏㄨㄚˊ)
tactful; diplomatic; slick and sly
圓環(ㄩㄢˊ ㄏㄨㄢˊ)

a rotary; a traffic circle

圓謊(ㄩㄢˊ ㄏㄨㄤˇ)
to straighten out contradictions in a lie and make it plausible

圓寂(ㄩㄢˊ ㄐㄧˊ)
to die (said of Buddhist monks or nuns); to pass away

圓徑(ㄩㄢˊ ㄐㄧㄥˋ)
a diameter 亦作「直徑」: 圓徑有五公尺。It is five meters in diameter.

圓球(ㄩㄢˊ ㄑㄧㄡˊ)
a ball; a sphere; a globe

圓圈(ㄩㄢˊ ㄑㄩㄢ)
a circle; a ring: 仙子們圍成一圓圈跳舞。The fairies danced in a ring.

圓心(ㄩㄢˊ ㄒㄧㄣ)
the center of a circle

圓形(ㄩㄢˊ ㄒㄧㄥˊ)
round; spherical; circular

圓周(ㄩㄢˊ ㄓㄡ)
the circumference of a circle

圓周率(ㄩㄢˊ ㄓㄡ ㄌㄩˋ)
Ludolphian number (π), ratio of the circumference of a circle to its diameter

圓柱(ㄩㄢˊ ㄓㄨˋ)
a cylinder

圓柱根(ㄩㄢˊ ㄓㄨˋ ㄍㄣ)
a cylindrical root

圓桌(ㄩㄢˊ ㄓㄨㄛ)
a round table

圓桌會議(ㄩㄢˊ ㄓㄨㄛ ㄏㄨㄟˋ ㄧˋ)
a round-table conference or discussion

圓錐(ㄩㄢˊ ㄓㄨㄟ)
(solid geometry) a cone

圓錐根(ㄩㄢˊ ㄓㄨㄟ ㄍㄣ)
a conic root

圓場(ㄩㄢˊ ㄔㄤˇ)
to mediate; to help to effect a compromise: 他是個和事佬喜歡替人打圓場。As a peace-maker, he likes to mediate a dispute of others.

圓唇元音(ㄩㄢˊ ㄔㄨㄣˊ ㄩㄢˊ ㄧㄣ)
(phonetics) a round vowel; a rounded vowel

圓熟(ㄩㄢˊ ㄕㄡˊ)
skillful; skilled; proficient; dexterous

圓潤(ㄩㄢˊ ㄖㄨㄣˋ)
mellow and full: 她天生有一副圓潤的嗓音。She is endowed with a sweet, mellow voice.

圓鑿方枘(ㄩㄢˊ ㄗㄨㄛˋ ㄈㄤ ㄖㄨㄟˋ)
(literally) a square peg in a round hole—a combination of two things incapable of fitting each other

圓舞曲(ㄩㄢˊ ㄨˇ ㄑㄩˇ)
waltz

圓月(ㄩㄢˊ ㄩㄝˋ)
① to drink together in the moonlight on Mid-Autumn Festival (中秋節) ② a full moon

十一畫

【圖】 803 ㄊㄨˊ twu tú

1. a picture; a map; a portrait; a chart; a diagram: 你的書上有很多插圖嗎? Are there many pictures in your book?
2. to seek; to pursue
3. to plan; to scheme; to conspire
4. intention; aim; purpose: 他似乎別有所圖。He seems to have other aims.
5. a Chinese family name

圖飽私囊(ㄊㄨˊ ㄅㄠˇ ㄙ ㄋㄤˊ)
to try to enrich oneself (from public services)

圖報恩德(ㄊㄨˊ ㄅㄠˋ ㄣ ㄉㄜˊ)
to hope or plan to repay kindness or favors

圖表(ㄊㄨˊ ㄅㄧㄠˇ)
charts, diagrams and tables—used in statistics

圖片(ㄊㄨˊ ㄆㄧㄢˋ)
illustrations in separate sheets; pictures; photographs

圖謀(ㄊㄨˊ ㄇㄡˊ)
to plan; to conspire

圖謀不軌(ㄊㄨˊ ㄇㄡˊ ㄅㄨˋ ㄍㄨㄟˇ)
to harbor evil intentions; to make dishonest schemes (particularly referring to revolt, revolution or treason)

圖名(ㄊㄨˊ ㄇㄧㄥˊ)
to pursue fame; for the sake of prestige

圖釘(ㄊㄨˊ ㄉㄧㄥ)
thumbtacks; a drawing pin

圖逃(ㄊㄨˊ ㄊㄠˊ)
to attempt to escape

圖騰(ㄊㄨˊ ㄊㄥˊ)
① a totem ② (in old China) flags embroidered with the patterns of animals representing the various barbarian tribes

圖賴(ㄊㄨˊ ㄌㄞˋ)
to try to deny what one has said or done

圖例(ㄊㄨˊ ㄌㄧˋ)
a brief explanation or key to an illustration, map, etc.

圖利(ㄊㄨˊ ㄌㄧˋ)
to desire to make money or profit; to plan to make money

圖利他人(ㄊㄨˊ ㄌㄧˋ ㄊㄚ ㄖㄣˊ)
(in lawsuits involving government officials) with the intention to profit others

圖畫(ㄊㄨˊ ㄏㄨㄚˋ)
① a drawing; a picture; a painting ② drawing; painting ③ to scheme; to plot; to plan

圖籍(ㄊㄨˊ ㄐㄧˊ)
land charts and census records

圖記(ㄊㄨˊ ㄐㄧˋ)
a seal (of an organization); a stamp

圖解(ㄊㄨˊ ㄐㄧㄝˇ)
diagrams and pictures for teaching purposes; illustrations: 我們老師喜歡用圖解說明。Our teacher likes to explain through diagrams.

圖窮匕見(ㄊㄨˊ ㄑㄩㄥˊ ㄅㄧˇ ㄒㄧㄢˋ)
When the map was unrolled, the dagger was revealed. —The real intention is revealed in the end. 或 The plot is exposed.

圖形(ㄊㄨˊ ㄒㄧㄥˊ)
a sketch; a contour; an outline; a graph; a figure: 幾何圖形 geometric figures

圖章(ㄊㄨˊ ㄓㄤ)
a seal; a chop (usually personal)

圖示(ㄊㄨˊ ㄕˋ)
to indicate by a picture; the picture shows...

圖書(ㄊㄨˊ ㄕㄨ)
maps, charts and books

圖書目錄(ㄊㄨˊ ㄕㄨ ㄇㄨˋ ㄌㄨˋ)
a catalogue of books; a

〔囗部〕

library catalogue

圖書館(ㄊㄨˊ ㄕㄨ ㄍㄨㄢˇ)
a library: 這個圖書館已經開始自動化了。The library has begun to automate.

圖書管理員(ㄊㄨˊ ㄕㄨ ㄍㄨㄢˇ ㄌㄧˇ ㄩㄢˊ)
a librarian

圖書室(ㄊㄨˊ ㄕㄨ ㄕˋ)
a reading room

圖書資料(ㄊㄨˊ ㄕㄨ ㄗ ㄌㄧㄠˋ)
books and reference materials

圖財害命(ㄊㄨˊ ㄘㄞˊ ㄏㄞˋ ㄇㄧㄥˋ)
to murder someone for money

圖案(ㄊㄨˊ ㄢˋ)
①(fine arts) patterns: 我喜歡這壁紙的圖案。I like the pattern of the wallpaper. ②(architecture) designs or drafts

圖樣(ㄊㄨˊ ㄧㄤˋ)
(architecture) a design; a blueprint

【團】 804 ㄊㄨㄢˊ twan tuán

1. a sphere; something shaped like a ball
2. a mass; a lump
3. a group; a party; a mission; an organization; a society
4. (infantry) a regiment, consisting of three battalions of foot soldiers
5. to unite

團拜(ㄊㄨㄢˊ ㄅㄞˋ)
mass greetings (as on New Year's Day); mass congratulations (on auspicious occasions, etc.)

團隊精神(ㄊㄨㄢˊ ㄉㄨㄟˋ ㄐㄧㄥ ㄕㄣˊ)
team spirit

團體(ㄊㄨㄢˊ ㄊㄧˇ)
a group, party or mission; an organization; group (action, etc.)

團體操(ㄊㄨㄢˊ ㄊㄧˇ ㄘㄠ)
callisthenics done by a large group of people with concerted movements under the command of a physical education instructor

團體賽(ㄊㄨㄢˊ ㄊㄧˇ ㄙㄞˋ)
a team competition

團團轉(ㄊㄨㄢˊ ㄊㄨㄢˊ ㄓㄨㄢˋ)
to pace about in an agitated state of mind; to turn round and round

團團圍住(ㄊㄨㄢˊ ㄊㄨㄢˊ ㄨㄟˊ ㄓㄨˋ)
to be completely surrounded (by rows of enemy troops)

團練(ㄊㄨㄢˊ ㄌㄧㄢˋ)
the militia; volunteer home guards

團管區(ㄊㄨㄢˊ ㄍㄨㄢˇ ㄑㄩ)
a regional administration in charge of conscription and mobilization (somewhat like a draft board)

團結(ㄊㄨㄢˊ ㄐㄧㄝˊ)
union; unity; solidarity; to unify; to unite: 團結就是力量。Union is strength.

團聚(ㄊㄨㄢˊ ㄐㄩˋ)
(said of a family, etc.) to meet; to congregate; a meeting; a reunion; a gathering

團契(ㄊㄨㄢˊ ㄑㄧˋ)
fellowship—a Christian association of the youth

團長(ㄊㄨㄢˊ ㄓㄤˇ)
a regiment commander; a commanding officer of a regiment

團扇(ㄊㄨㄢˊ ㄕㄢˋ)
a circular or moon-shaped fan

團坐(ㄊㄨㄢˊ ㄗㄨㄛˋ)
(for many people) to sit around in circle

團員(ㄊㄨㄢˊ ㄩㄢˊ)
a member: 他是合唱團的團員。He is a member of a chorus.

團圓(ㄊㄨㄢˊ ㄩㄢˊ)
a union or reunion (especially of a family): 農曆除夕是全家團圓的日子。Lunar New Year's Eve is the time for family reunion.

土部 ㄊㄨˇ tuu tǔ

【土】 805 ㄊㄨˇ tuu tǔ

1. earth; soil: 大多數植物在沃土中長得最好。Most plants grow best in rich soil.
2. land; territory; domain: 人人守土有責。Everybody is responsible for guarding land from enemy.
3. local; native; indigenous: 他是土生土長的德國人。He is a native German.
4. unrefined; unenlightened
5. rustic; countrified
6. opium
7. an abbreviation for Turkey

土撥鼠(ㄊㄨˇ ㄅㄛ ㄕㄨˇ)
a marmot; a ground hog

土包子(ㄊㄨˇ ㄅㄠ ˙ㄗ)
a rustic or countrified person; a hillbilly; a country bumpkin

土辦法(ㄊㄨˇ ㄅㄢˋ ㄈㄚˇ)
indigenous methods

土崩瓦解(ㄊㄨˇ ㄅㄥ ㄨㄚˇ ㄐㄧㄝˇ)
in total disintegration; in total disorder or confusion

土布(ㄊㄨˇ ㄅㄨˋ)
① cotton cloth or piece goods produced locally ② homewoven or handloomed cloth; homespun cloth

土坯(ㄊㄨˇ ㄆㄧ)
claybricks (as distinct from those treated in a kiln); an unburnt brick

土黴素(ㄊㄨˇ ㄇㄟˊ ㄙㄨˋ)
terramycin; oxytetracycline

土木(ㄊㄨˇ ㄇㄨˋ)or 土木工程(ㄊㄨˇ ㄇㄨˋ ㄍㄨㄥ ㄔㄥˊ)
civil engineering; construction projects: 他們將大興土木。They will go in for large-scale building or construction.

土木工程師(ㄊㄨˇ ㄇㄨˋ ㄍㄨㄥ ㄔㄥˊ ㄕ)
a civil engineer

土法(ㄊㄨˇ ㄈㄚˇ)
an old, local method; a traditional method

土匪(ㄊㄨˇ ㄈㄟˇ)
bandits; brigands: 這鎮為土匪所擾。The town is infested with bandits.

土番(ㄊㄨˇ ㄈㄢ)
uncivilized natives; aborigines

土方(ㄊㄨˇ ㄈㄤ)
① a cubic meter of earth ② a recipe of folk medicine

土房子(ㄊㄨˇ ㄈㄤˊ ˙ㄗ)
a house built with untreated or unburnt bricks

土風舞(ㄊㄨˇ ㄈㄥ ㄨˇ)
folk dance

土伏苓(ㄊㄨˇ ㄈㄨˊ ㄌㄧㄥˊ)
(Chinese herb) China root

土豆(ㄊㄨˇ ㄉㄡˋ)
① peanuts ② potatoes

土地(ㄊㄨˇ ㄉㄧˋ)
① land ② the God of Earth

土地廟(ㄊㄨˇ ㄉㄧˋ ㄇㄧㄠˋ)
the temple of the God of Earth

土地改革(ㄊㄨˇ ㄉㄧˋ ㄍㄞˇ ㄍㄜˊ)or 土改(ㄊㄨˇ ㄍㄞˇ)
land reform; agrarian reform: 新政府實施土地改革。The new government put through land reform.

土地公(ㄊㄨˇ ㄉㄧˋ ㄍㄨㄥ)
the God of Earth 亦作「土地爺」、「土地神」

土地徵收(ㄊㄨˇ ㄉㄧˋ ㄓㄥ ㄕㄡ)
the requisition of private land holdings (for public use)

土地重劃(ㄊㄨˇ ㄉㄧˋ ㄔㄨㄥˊ ㄏㄨㄚˋ)
land consolidation

土地增值稅(ㄊㄨˇ ㄉㄧˋ ㄗㄥ ㄓˊ ㄕㄨㄟˋ)
the land value increment tax; a tax levied on increment of land value

土堆(ㄊㄨˇ ㄉㄨㄟ)or 土墩(ㄊㄨˇ ㄉㄨㄣ)
a mound

土頭土腦(ㄊㄨˇ ㄊㄡˊ ㄊㄨˇ ㄋㄠˇ)
rustic; hillbilly; unsophisticated

土牛木馬(ㄊㄨˇ ㄋㄧㄡˊ ㄇㄨˋ ㄇㄚˇ)
(literally) an earthen ox and a wooden horse—to exist in form only

土牢(ㄊㄨˇ ㄌㄠˊ)
a dungeon

土老兒(ㄊㄨˇ ㄌㄠˇㄦ)
① a rustic old man ② a damned fool

土狼(ㄊㄨˇ ㄌㄤˊ)
a hyena

土瀝青(ㄊㄨˇ ㄌㄧˋ ㄑㄧㄥ)
asphalt

土裏土氣(ㄊㄨˇ ˙ㄌㄧ ㄊㄨˇ ㄑㄧˋ)
rustic; countrified; hillbilly; uncouth; unsophisticated

土鱗魚(ㄊㄨˇ ㄌㄧㄣˊ ㄩˊ)
a mud carp

土高爐(ㄊㄨˇ ㄍㄠ ㄌㄨˊ)
a small-sized homemade blast furnace

土棍(ㄊㄨˇ ㄍㄨㄣˋ)
a local rascal; a local bully; a ruffian

土炕(ㄊㄨˇ ㄎㄤˋ)
a heatable adobe sleeping platform; an adobe *kang*; an earthen bed warmed by a fire underneath (in North China)

土豪劣紳(ㄊㄨˇ ㄏㄠˊ ㄌㄧㄝˋ ㄕㄣ)
local ruffians and the oppressive gentry; evil and powerful elements in a community

土話(ㄊㄨˇ ㄏㄨㄚˋ)
local dialects; patois; indigenous languages

土貨(ㄊㄨˇ ㄏㄨㄛˋ)
local products; local produce

土皇帝(ㄊㄨˇ ㄏㄨㄤˊ ㄉㄧˋ)
a local chieftain; a powerful personage in a community; a local despot; a local tyrant

土階茅茨(ㄊㄨˇ ㄐㄧㄝ ㄇㄠˊ ㄘˊ)
earthen steps and thatched roof

土氣(ㄊㄨˇ ㄑㄧˋ)
rustic; uncouth

土星(ㄊㄨˇ ㄒㄧㄥ)
the planet Saturn

土質(ㄊㄨˇ ㄓˋ)
the condition or nature of the soil

土製(ㄊㄨˇ ㄓˋ)
homemade; crudely manufactured

土著(ㄊㄨˇ ㄓㄨㄛˊ)or(ㄊㄨˇ ㄓㄨˋ)
natives; aborigines

土塚(ㄊㄨˇ ㄓㄨㄥˇ)
a burial mound

土產(ㄊㄨˇ ㄔㄢˇ)
local products

土城(ㄊㄨˇ ㄔㄥˊ)
a city wall made of clay

土生土長(ㄊㄨˇ ㄕㄥ ㄊㄨˇ ㄓㄤˇ)
(said of persons who have never traveled outside their native hearths) to be born and to grow up in the local community

土人(ㄊㄨˇ ㄖㄣˊ)
① the natives (usually referring to uncivilized tribes); aborigines: 土人很親切的接待他。The natives received him kindly. ② a mud doll

土壤(ㄊㄨˇ ㄖㄤˇ)
soil: 大多數植物在肥沃的土壤中長得最好。Most plants grow best in rich soil.

土壤保持(ㄊㄨˇ ㄖㄤˇ ㄅㄠˇ ㄔˊ)
soil conservation

土賊(ㄊㄨˇ ㄗㄟˊ)
bandits

土葬(ㄊㄨˇ ㄗㄤˋ)
a burial in the ground

土司(ㄊㄨˇ ㄙ)
① the chief of a local tribe (especially in the southwestern provinces of China) ② toast: 我吃了兩片烤土司。I ate two slices of toast.

土色(ㄊㄨˇ ㄙㄜˋ)
ashen; pale: 他面如土色。His face turned deadly pale.

土耳其(ㄊㄨˇ ㄦˇ ㄑㄧˊ)
Turkey

土耳其帽(ㄊㄨˇ ㄦˇ ㄑㄧˊ ㄇㄠˋ)
a Turkish cap; a fez

土耳其斯坦(ㄊㄨˇ ㄦˇ ㄑㄧˊ ㄙ ㄊㄢˇ)
Turkistan or Turkestan

土藥(ㄊㄨˇ ㄧㄠˋ)
① native medicine ② domestic opium 參看「洋藥」

土曜日(ㄊㄨˇ ㄧㄠˋ ㄖˋ)
Saturday

土音(ㄊㄨˇ ㄧㄣ)or 土腔(ㄊㄨˇ ㄑㄧㄤ)
local pronunciation; a local accent; a brogue: 他說國語帶有四川土音。He speaks Mandarin with a Szechwan accent.

土語(ㄊㄨˇ ㄩˇ)
local dialects; *patois*

三畫

【在】 806 ㄗㄞˋ tzay zài

1. at; in; on; up to: 你的書在桌子上呢。Your book is on the table.
2. to rest with; to consist in; to depend on: 幸福在於知足。Happiness consists in contentment.
3. to be alive; living; to be present; to exist
4. used to indicate a progressive tense: 她在游泳。She is swimming.

在逃(ㄗㄞˋ ㄊㄠˊ)
(said of a criminal) on the loose or still at large

在堂(ㄗㄞˋ ㄊㄤˊ)
(said of one's parents) still

〔土部〕

alive
在內(ㄗㄞˋ ㄋㄟˋ)
①including; inclusive ②inside
在來米(ㄗㄞˋ ㄌㄞˊ ㄇㄧˇ)
Tsai Lai Rice—a variety of Taiwan paddy
在官言官(ㄗㄞˋ ㄍㄨㄢ ㄧㄢˊ ㄍㄨㄢ)
(literally) When in office, talk like an official.—to speak of one side of a matter only
在公(ㄗㄞˋ ㄍㄨㄥ)
①(to do something) as part of one's duty ②officially; for the sake of the public
在後(ㄗㄞˋ ㄏㄡˋ)
behind; later; as follows
在行(ㄗㄞˋ ㄏㄤˊ)
in the trade; in the know; professional; to be an expert at something: 文學方面我在行。I'm an expert at literature.
在乎(ㄗㄞˋ ㄏㄨ)
①to care; to mind: 有些士兵一天走五十里路毫不在乎。Some soldiers think nothing of marching fifty *li* a day. ②to consist in; to depend on (whether…)
在即(ㄗㄞˋ ㄐㄧˊ)
near at hand; imminent; soon: 入學考試在即。The entrance examination is near at hand.
在家(ㄗㄞˋ ㄐㄧㄚ)
to be at home; to be in: 你媽媽在家嗎? Is your mother in?
在家出家(ㄗㄞˋ ㄐㄧㄚ ㄔㄨ ㄐㄧㄚ)
(said of a layman) to practice abstinence like a Buddhist monk; one who, though retaining family ties, observes all the monastic rules
在家人(ㄗㄞˋ ㄐㄧㄚ ㄖㄣˊ)
a layman (as distinct from a monk)
在假(ㄗㄞˋ ㄐㄧㄚˋ)
on leave
在劫難逃(ㄗㄞˋ ㄐㄧㄝˊ ㄋㄢˊ ㄊㄠˊ)
If one is doomed, one is doomed. 或 There's no escape. 或Nobody can change his fate.
在昔(ㄗㄞˋ ㄒㄧˊ)
once upon a time; formerly; in former times
在下(ㄗㄞˋ ㄒㄧㄚˋ)
my humble self; I; your humble servant
在先(ㄗㄞˋ ㄒㄧㄢ)
①before; at that time; formerly; in the past; beforehand ②in front; ahead
在心(ㄗㄞˋ ㄒㄧㄣ)
to keep in mind; to be attentive; to feel concerned
在學(ㄗㄞˋ ㄒㄩㄝˊ)
to be at school
在職(ㄗㄞˋ ㄓˊ)
to hold a position; on the job; to be at one's post
在職訓練(ㄗㄞˋ ㄓˊ ㄒㄩㄣˋ ㄌㄧㄢˋ)
in-service training
在朝(ㄗㄞˋ ㄔㄠˊ)
(said of officials of cabinet rank in old China) to be a ranking official working near the monarch; to hold office at court
在場(ㄗㄞˋ ㄔㄤˇ)or(ㄗㄞˋ ㄔㄤˊ)
to be present (when an incident or accident occurred); to be on the scene; to be on the spot: 當時他不在場。He wasn't on the scene at the time.
在世(ㄗㄞˋ ㄕˋ)
alive; in this world
在室(ㄗㄞˋ ㄕˋ)
(said of girls) still unmarried
在在(ㄗㄞˋ ㄗㄞˋ)
everywhere
在在皆是(ㄗㄞˋ ㄗㄞˋ ㄐㄧㄝ ㄕˋ)
to be seen everywhere
在座(ㄗㄞˋ ㄗㄨㄛˋ)
to be present (at a gathering): 在座的還有幾位歸國學人。Among those present were a few returned overseas scholars.
在此(ㄗㄞˋ ㄘˇ)
here: 你要的東西在此。Here you are.
在所不免(ㄗㄞˋ ㄙㄨㄛˇ ㄅㄨˋ ㄇㄧㄢˇ)or 在所難免(ㄗㄞˋ ㄙㄨㄛˇ ㄋㄢˊ ㄇㄧㄢˇ)
unavoidable; inevitable; natural
在所不惜(ㄗㄞˋ ㄙㄨㄛˇ ㄅㄨˋ ㄒㄧˊ)
regardless of the cost or sacrifice (The expression is usually preceded by the specific sacrifice one is prepared to make.)
在所不辭(ㄗㄞˋ ㄙㄨㄛˇ ㄅㄨˋ ㄘˊ)
will not refuse under any circumstances; will not hesitate to
在案(ㄗㄞˋ ㄢˋ)
①on record; written in a document (used only in official documents) ②(said of a person) on the police record
在意(ㄗㄞˋ ㄧˋ)
to mind; to care about; to take notice of: 這些小事我是不會在意的。I won't take such trifles to heart.
在押(ㄗㄞˋ ㄧㄚ)
under detention; being imprisoned
在野(ㄗㄞˋ ㄧㄝˇ)
①to be out of power; to hold no official position ②(said of politicians) to be in opposition
在野黨(ㄗㄞˋ ㄧㄝˇ ㄉㄤˇ)
the opposition party or parties
在我(ㄗㄞˋ ㄨㄛˇ)
(It is) up to me
在握(ㄗㄞˋ ㄨㄛˋ)
to be within one's grasp; to be under one's control
在外(ㄗㄞˋ ㄨㄞˋ)
①not including; excluding ②outside
在位(ㄗㄞˋ ㄨㄟˋ)
in power; in the position; on the throne
在望(ㄗㄞˋ ㄨㄤˋ)
①to be visible; to be in view: 輪船隱隱在望。The ship was dimly visible. ②will soon materialize; to be in sight: 和平在望。Peace is now in sight.
在於(ㄗㄞˋ ㄩˊ)
to lie in; to consist in; to be determined by; to depend on: 挽救之道在於教育。The cure lies in education.

【圬】 807
ㄨ u wū
1. a trowel used for plastering
2. to plaster

【圭】 808
ㄍㄨㄟ guei guī
a jade tablet with a square base and a pointed top used

in official ceremonies in ancient China

圭璧(ㄍㄨㄟ ㄅㄧˋ)
①ritual jades worn by feudal lords in ancient China in a formal meeting or audience ②high virtue and integrity of a person

圭臬(ㄍㄨㄟ ㄋㄧㄝˋ)
① ancient timepieces ② a principle for one to look up to: 奉爲圭臬 to look up to as the standard

圭璋(ㄍㄨㄟ ㄓㄤ)
①a valuable jade ②(said of persons) dignity

圭亞那(ㄍㄨㄟ ㄧㄚˇ ㄋㄚˇ)
Guiana

【圯】 809 ㄧˊ yi yí

a bridge

圯上老人(ㄧˊ ㄕㄤˋ ㄌㄠˇ ㄖㄣˊ)
Huang Shih-kung (黃石公)—an old man who was supposed to be a teacher of Chang Liang (張良), a great strategist, who helped Liu Pang (劉邦) establish the Han Dynasty

【地】 810 ㄉㄧˋ dih dì

1. the earth
2. land; soil; ground: 水泥地 concrete floor 耕地 cultivated land
3. a region; a territory; a belt; a place; a locality: 他家地處山區。His house is located in a mountain area.
4. a position; a place; a situation: 我們立於危險之地。We are in a dangerous situation.
5. an adjunct after a word (usually adjective) to form an adverbial phrase: 偷偷地 stealthily 不聲不響地 silently

地保(ㄉㄧˋ ㄅㄠˇ)
a head of a basic community unit, responsible for law and order in the same neighborhood

地板(ㄉㄧˋ ㄅㄢˇ)
woodplanks used for flooring; wood flooring; a floor

地表(ㄉㄧˋ ㄅㄧㄠˇ)
the surface of the earth

地步(ㄉㄧˋ ㄅㄨˋ)
①a situation; a condition: 局勢到了不可收拾的地步。The situation got out of hand. ② extent: 他興奮到不能入睡的地步。He was so excited that he could not get to sleep. ③ room for action

地盤(ㄉㄧˋ ㄆㄢˊ)
①a place or territory occupied by force; a region under one's sphere of influence; a domain ②the crust of the earth ③the foundation of a building or house

地皮(ㄉㄧˋ ㄆㄧˊ)
land for building houses; land-estate; real estate

地痞(ㄉㄧˋ ㄆㄧˇ)
ruffians, rascals, bullies, etc.

地痞流氓(ㄉㄧˋ ㄆㄧˇ ㄌㄧㄡˊ ㄇㄤˊ)
local bullies and loafers

地平線(ㄉㄧˋ ㄆㄧㄥˊ ㄒㄧㄢˋ)
the horizon: 太陽沉到地平線下了。The sun sank below the horizon.

地鋪(ㄉㄧˋ ㄆㄨˋ)
a bed on the floor; a shakedown

地面(ㄉㄧˋ ㄇㄧㄢˋ)
①the surface of the earth ②a region; a territory: 此處已經進入安徽地面。We're now in the Province of Anhwei.

地面衛星站(ㄉㄧˋ ㄇㄧㄢˋ ㄨㄟˋ ㄒㄧㄥ ㄓㄢˋ)
a ground satellite station

地名(ㄉㄧˋ ㄇㄧㄥˊ)
the name of a place

地方(ㄉㄧˋ ㄈㄤ)
①a locality (in contrast with the central government) ②a place ③space; room ④part; respect ⑤ local; locally

地方法院(ㄉㄧˋ ㄈㄤ ㄈㄚˇ ㄩㄢˋ)
a district court: 囚犯被帶到地方法院候審。The prisoner was brought to the district court for trial.

地方分權(ㄉㄧˋ ㄈㄤ ㄈㄣ ㄑㄩㄢˊ)
decentralization; division of powers between local and central governments

地方團體(ㄉㄧˋ ㄈㄤ ㄊㄨㄢˊ ㄊㄧˇ)
local organizations

地方官(ㄉㄧˋ ㄈㄤ ㄍㄨㄢ)
officials of local governments

地方新聞(ㄉㄧˋ ㄈㄤ ㄒㄧㄣ ㄨㄣˊ)
locals; local news: 作爲一個年輕記者，他採訪地方新聞。As a young reporter, he covered the locals.

地方政府(ㄉㄧˋ ㄈㄤ ㄓㄥˋ ㄈㄨˇ)
a local government

地方人士(ㄉㄧˋ ㄈㄤ ㄖㄣˊ ㄕˋ)
distinguished personalities in a locality; local personalities

地方自治(ㄉㄧˋ ㄈㄤ ㄗˋ ㄓˋ)
local self-government

地方色彩(ㄉㄧˋ ㄈㄤ ㄙㄜˋ ㄘㄞˇ)
①local color ②provincialism

地府(ㄉㄧˋ ㄈㄨˇ)
the underworld; Hades

地大物博(ㄉㄧˋ ㄉㄚˋ ㄨˋ ㄅㄛˊ)
vast land and rich natural resources: 中國是個地大物博的國家。China is a big country abounding in natural wealth.

地帶(ㄉㄧˋ ㄉㄞˋ)
a place and its vicinity: 森林地帶 a forest region

地道(ㄉㄧˋ ㄉㄠˋ)
a tunnel

地點(ㄉㄧˋ ㄉㄧㄢˇ)
a site; a location; a place; a spot; a locale: 在這裏建座新公園，地點倒適中。This would be a suitable site for a new park.

地對地飛彈(ㄉㄧˋ ㄉㄨㄟˋ ㄉㄧˋ ㄈㄟ ㄉㄢˋ)
a ground-to-ground missile; a surface-to-surface missile

地對空飛彈(ㄉㄧˋ ㄉㄨㄟˋ ㄎㄨㄥ ㄈㄟ ㄉㄢˋ)
a ground-to-air missile

地段(ㄉㄧˋ ㄉㄨㄢˋ)
the locality of a piece of land (especially referring to the numbered land plots on government file)

地洞(ㄉㄧˋ ㄉㄨㄥˋ)
a hole in the ground; a burrow

地動(ㄉㄧˋ ㄉㄨㄥˋ)
an earthquake

地頭(ㄉㄧˋ ㄊㄡˊ)
a place; a locality: 他地頭熟，聯絡方便。He knows the place well, so he can easily make contact there.

地頭蛇(ㄉㄧˋ ㄊㄡˊ ㄕㄜˊ)

〔土部〕

an influential gangster in a community; a local villain
地攤(ㄉㄧˋ ㄊㄢ)
a stall with goods displaying on the ground for sale: 他在台北擺地攤。He sells articles displayed on sidewalk floor in Taipei.
地毯(ㄉㄧˋ ㄊㄢˇ)
a carpet or rug: 地板上舖着地毯。The floor is covered with a carpet.
地毯轟炸(ㄉㄧˋ ㄊㄢˇ ㄏㄨㄥ ㄓㄚˋ)
carpet bombing
地圖(ㄉㄧˋ ㄊㄨˊ)
a map
地圖判讀(ㄉㄧˋ ㄊㄨˊ ㄆㄢˋ ㄉㄨˊ)
map reading
地雷(ㄉㄧˋ ㄌㄟˊ)
a land mine: 埋地雷 to plant (or lay) mines
地牢(ㄉㄧˋ ㄌㄠˊ)
a dungeon
地老天荒(ㄉㄧˋ ㄌㄠˇ ㄊㄧㄢ ㄏㄨㄤ)
(said of love) to outlast even the heaven and the earth
地理(ㄉㄧˋ ㄌㄧˇ)
① geographical characteristics of a place: 我們熟悉地理民情。We are familiar with the place and its people. ② geography
地理環境(ㄉㄧˋ ㄌㄧˇ ㄏㄨㄢˊ ㄐㄧㄥˋ)
geographical conditions
地理學(ㄉㄧˋ ㄌㄧˇ ㄒㄩㄝˊ)
geography: 我喜歡地理學和歷史學。I like geography and history.
地理位置(ㄉㄧˋ ㄌㄧˇ ㄨㄟˋ ㄓˋ)
a geographical position
地力(ㄉㄧˋ ㄌㄧˋ)
land productivity
地利(ㄉㄧˋ ㄌㄧˋ)
① geographical advantages ② land productivity
地瓜(ㄉㄧˋ ㄍㄨㄚ)
sweet potatoes
地殼(ㄉㄧˋ ㄎㄜˊ)
the crust of the earth
地殼變動(ㄉㄧˋ ㄎㄜˊ ㄅㄧㄢˋ ㄉㄨㄥˋ)
diastrophism
地殼運動(ㄉㄧˋ ㄎㄜˊ ㄩㄣˋ ㄉㄨㄥˋ)
crustal movement
地炕(ㄉㄧˋ ㄎㄤˋ)
a brick bed warmed by a fire underneath (in North China)
地黃(ㄉㄧˋ ㄏㄨㄤˊ)or 地髓(ㄉㄧˋ ㄙㄨㄟˇ)
a foxglove (*Rehmannia glutinosa*)
地基(ㄉㄧˋ ㄐㄧ)
the foundation of a building
地價(ㄉㄧˋ ㄐㄧㄚˋ)
a land price
地價稅(ㄉㄧˋ ㄐㄧㄚˋ ㄕㄨㄟˋ)
land tax
地界(ㄉㄧˋ ㄐㄧㄝˋ)
the border of a piece of land; the borderland
地角天涯(ㄉㄧˋ ㄐㄧㄠˇ ㄊㄧㄢ ㄧㄚˊ)
the farthest end of the earth
地窖(ㄉㄧˋ ㄐㄧㄠˋ)
a cellar; an underground vault: 他把食物貯藏在地窖裡。He stored food in the cellar.
地盡其利(ㄉㄧˋ ㄐㄧㄣˋ ㄑㄧˊ ㄌㄧˋ)
Land should be fully utilized.
地氣(ㄉㄧˋ ㄑㄧˋ)
① a climate ② a subtle essence that supposedly animates the earth
地契(ㄉㄧˋ ㄑㄧˋ)or 地券(ㄉㄧˋ ㄑㄩㄢˋ)
a title deed for landholdings
地球(ㄉㄧˋ ㄑㄧㄡˊ)
the earth; the globe
地球科學(ㄉㄧˋ ㄑㄧㄡˊ ㄎㄜ ㄒㄩㄝˊ)
geoscience
地球儀(ㄉㄧˋ ㄑㄧㄡˊ ㄧˊ)
a terrestrial globe
地球物理學(ㄉㄧˋ ㄑㄧㄡˊ ㄨˋ ㄌㄧˇ ㄒㄩㄝˊ)
geophysics
地錢(ㄉㄧˋ ㄑㄧㄢˊ)
(botany) hepatica
地勤(ㄉㄧˋ ㄑㄧㄣˊ)
(aeronautics) ground service
地區(ㄉㄧˋ ㄑㄩ)
an area; a region; a zone: 熱帶地區最適宜種香蕉。The tropical area is most suitable for growing bananas.
地權(ㄉㄧˋ ㄑㄩㄢˊ)
the right to land; landownership
地峽(ㄉㄧˋ ㄒㄧㄚˊ)
an isthmus
地下(ㄉㄧˋ ㄒㄧㄚˋ)
① underground; subterranean: 礦工們在地下工作。Miners work underground. ② in the grave ③ on the ground
地下道(ㄉㄧˋ ㄒㄧㄚˋ ㄉㄠˋ)
a tunnel; a subway
地下鐵(道)(ㄉㄧˋ ㄒㄧㄚˋ ㄊㄧㄝˇ (ㄉㄠˋ))
an underground railroad; the subway: 我們乘地下鐵到住宅區去。We subwayed uptown.
地下工作(ㄉㄧˋ ㄒㄧㄚˋ ㄍㄨㄥ ㄗㄨㄛˋ)
underground activities; cloak-and-dagger operations: 陰謀者從事地下工作。Plotters work underground.
地下街(ㄉㄧˋ ㄒㄧㄚˋ ㄐㄧㄝ)
an underground center
地下莖(ㄉㄧˋ ㄒㄧㄚˋ ㄐㄧㄥ)
(botany) rhizome; rootstock
地下錢莊(ㄉㄧˋ ㄒㄧㄚˋ ㄑㄧㄢˊ ㄓㄨㄤ)
illegal banks; wildcat banking houses
地下室(ㄉㄧˋ ㄒㄧㄚˋ ㄕˋ)
a basement: 地下室很潮溼。It is rather damp in the basement.
地下商場(ㄉㄧˋ ㄒㄧㄚˋ ㄕㄤ ㄔㄤˇ)or(ㄉㄧˋ ㄒㄧㄚˋ ㄕㄤ ㄔㄤˊ)
a marketplace built below the ground; basement shops
地下水(ㄉㄧˋ ㄒㄧㄚˋ ㄕㄨㄟˇ)
ground water
地下舞廳(ㄉㄧˋ ㄒㄧㄚˋ ㄨˇ ㄊㄧㄥ)
unlicensed cabarets
地心(ㄉㄧˋ ㄒㄧㄣ)
the earth core; the center of the earth
地心吸力(ㄉㄧˋ ㄒㄧㄣ ㄒㄧ ㄌㄧˋ)
gravity; the gravitation of the earth
地形(ㄉㄧˋ ㄒㄧㄥˊ)
topography; terrain: 地形優越 the topographical advantages
地形學(ㄉㄧˋ ㄒㄧㄥˊ ㄒㄩㄝˊ)
geomorphology
地支(ㄉㄧˋ ㄓ)
the twelve Terrestrial Branches used in calculation with the Celestial Stems (天干) to designate years, months, days and hours
地質(ㄉㄧˋ ㄓˊ)
geology
地質學(ㄉㄧˋ ㄓˊ ㄒㄩㄝˊ)
geology
地址(ㄉㄧˋ ㄓˇ)
the address of a place; a location: 他已改變地址。He

has changed his address.

地志 or 地誌(ㄉㄧˋ ㄓˋ)
topography; district history (recording geography and historic sites)

地軸(ㄉㄧˋ ㄓㄡˊ)
the axis of the earth

地震(ㄉㄧˋ ㄓㄣˋ)
earthquakes; seism: 臺灣時遭地震危害。Taiwan often suffers from earthquakes.

地震強度(ㄉㄧˋ ㄓㄣˋ ㄑㄧㄤˊ ㄉㄨˋ)
earthquake intensity

地震區(ㄉㄧˋ ㄓㄣˋ ㄑㄩ)
a seismic area

地震學(ㄉㄧˋ ㄓㄣˋ ㄒㄩㄝˊ)
seismology

地震儀(ㄉㄧˋ ㄓㄣˋ ㄧˊ)
a seismograph or seismometer

地政局(ㄉㄧˋ ㄓㄥˋ ㄐㄩˊ)
the Bureau of Land Administration

地政學(ㄉㄧˋ ㄓㄥˋ ㄒㄩㄝˊ)
geopolitics

地主(ㄉㄧˋ ㄓㄨˇ)
① a host ② a landowner or landlord: 地主極力保護有關土地所有權的利益。The landowners did their best to protect their landowning interests.

地主國(ㄉㄧˋ ㄓㄨˇ ㄍㄨㄛˊ)
the host country

地主之誼(ㄉㄧˋ ㄓㄨˇ ㄓ ㄧˊ)
the friendship or hospitality of a host: 如果你能來，我當盡地主之誼。I'll perform the duties of the host if you can come.

地中海(ㄉㄧˋ ㄓㄨㄥ ㄏㄞˇ)
the Mediterranean Sea

地產(ㄉㄧˋ ㄔㄢˇ)
landed property; real estate: 他做地產生意。He is engaged in real estate business.

地沉(ㄉㄧˋ ㄔㄣˊ)
(geography) ground sinking

地勢(ㄉㄧˋ ㄕˋ)
topography; terrain: 此處地勢險要。The terrain is strategically situated and difficult of access here.

地上權(ㄉㄧˋ ㄕㄤˋ ㄑㄩㄢˊ)
(law) the right to use another's land for building or farming purposes

地熱(ㄉㄧˋ ㄖㄜˋ)
subterranean heat; geothermal energy

地租(ㄉㄧˋ ㄗㄨ)
land rent; the rent of a piece of land

地層(ㄉㄧˋ ㄘㄥˊ)
(geology) a stratum of earth; a single layer of sedimentary rock, representing the deposition of a single geological period

地層學(ㄉㄧˋ ㄘㄥˊ ㄒㄩㄝˊ)
stratigraphy

地位(ㄉㄧˋ ㄨㄟˋ)
the ranking or position (of a person): 政治地位 political position

地域(ㄉㄧˋ ㄩˋ)
① boundaries of a piece of land ② a district; a region

地域觀念(ㄉㄧˋ ㄩˋ ㄍㄨㄢ ㄋㄧㄢˋ)
regionalism

地獄(ㄉㄧˋ ㄩˋ)
hell; Hades; the inferno

地緣政治學(ㄉㄧˋ ㄩㄢˊ ㄓㄥˋ ㄓˋ ㄒㄩㄝˊ)
geopolitics

四畫

【坊】 811 ㄈㄤ fang fāng

1. a community; a subdivision of a city; a neighborhood; a city quarter; a street; a lane
2. a workshop of a trade; a mill: 染坊 a dyer's workshop 磨坊 a flour mill
3. an arch-like memorial building: 貞節牌坊 a chastity arch

坊本(ㄈㄤ ㄅㄣˇ)
a block-printed edition issued by a bookshop

坊間(ㄈㄤ ㄐㄧㄢ)
on the market (especially referring to the bookshops); in the streets; city quarters

坊肆(ㄈㄤ ㄙˋ)
shops

【圾】 812 ㄙㄜ seh sē

garbage; refuse; waste: 把那些垃圾丟掉。Throw the waste away.

【址】 813 ㄓˇ jyy zhǐ

1. land on which to build a house; a location; a site: 校址 a school compound; a campus
2. a foundation

【坂】 814 ㄅㄢˇ baan bǎn

a slope; a hillside 參看「阪」

【均】 815 ㄐㄩㄣ jiun jūn

1. equal; equally; even; level: 他爲勞逸不均而埋怨。He complained of the uneven allocation of work.
2. to be fair
3. all; also; too: 一切相關事宜均已就緒。All things concerned have been completed.
4. a potter's wheel
5. an ancient musical instrument

均平(ㄐㄩㄣ ㄆㄧㄥˊ)
on an average; even

均分(ㄐㄩㄣ ㄈㄣ)
to divide equally; to allot equally

均等(ㄐㄩㄣ ㄉㄥˇ)
equality; equal; impartial; fair: 人的能力並非均等。All men are not equal in ability.

均攤(ㄐㄩㄣ ㄊㄢ)
to share (an obligation, etc.) equally: 他們均攤旅行費用。They shared equally the travel expenses.

均可(ㄐㄩㄣ ㄎㄜˇ)
all can; also can; either will do; all permissible or passable

均衡(ㄐㄩㄣ ㄏㄥˊ)
equality; balance (of power, etc.); equilibrium; balanced; proportionate; harmonious

均權(ㄐㄩㄣ ㄑㄩㄢˊ)
the equality of rights

均權制(ㄐㄩㄣ ㄑㄩㄢˊ ㄓˋ)
a political system envisioned by Dr. Sun Yat-sen which underlines the division of powers between the central and local governments

均質(ㄐㄩㄣ ㄓˊ)
homogenized; homogeneous

均沾 or 均霑(ㄐㄩㄣ ㄓㄢ)
to share the benefits, profits, etc. equally

均勢(ㄐㄩㄣ ㄕˋ)
the balance of power; equilibrium

均一(ㄐㄩㄣ ㄧ)
uniform; equal; homogene-

ous
均匀(ㄐㄩㄣ ㄩㄣˊ)
even (blending, etc.); uniform; well-distributed

〔土部〕

【坍】 816 ㄊㄢ tan tān
sliding of earth (as in a landslide); to fall into ruins; to collapse; to tumble
坍方(ㄊㄢ ㄈㄤ)
a landslide; a landslip; to cave in; to collapse
坍塌(ㄊㄢ ㄊㄚ)
to collapse; to cave in: 大雨使屋頂坍塌。The heavy rain caused the roof to collapse.
坍臺(ㄊㄢ ㄊㄞˊ)
① to expose one's weakness before the public ② to let someone down

【坎】 817 ㄎㄢˇ kaan kǎn
1. a pit; a hole; a depression
2. one of the Eight Diagrams in the *Book of Changes*
3. the sound of percussion
4. a snare; a danger; a crisis
坎培拉(ㄎㄢˇ ㄆㄟˊ ㄌㄚ)
Canberra, the capital of Australia
坎坷(ㄎㄢˇ ㄎㄜˇ)
① unlucky; bad luck ② (said of the road) rough; bumpy; rugged: 這是一條坎坷不平的路。This is a rough and bumpy road.
坎坷一生(ㄎㄢˇ ㄎㄜˇ ㄧˋ ㄕㄥ)
a lifetime of frustrations
坎坑(ㄎㄢˇ ㄎㄥ)
a pit in the ground
坎肩兒(ㄎㄢˇ ㄐㄧㄚㄦ)
a sleeveless jacket or coat
坎穽 or 坎阱(ㄎㄢˇ ㄐㄧㄥˇ)
a snare; a trap

【坐】 818 ㄗㄨㄛˋ tzuoh zuò
1. to sit; a seat: 請坐。Please sit down.
2. to ride (on a bus, train, etc.): 我常坐飛機到日本。I often go to Japan by plane.
3. to kneel
4. to reach; to arrive at
5. (said of a building) to have its back towards
6. to get (profit, etc.) without work
7. to keep on; to persist in
8. (said of a building) to fall back from pressure; to sink: 這堵牆往後坐了。The wall is beginning to give backwards.
9. (said of guns, etc.) to recoil; to kick: 這大砲的後坐力不小。This cannon kicks badly.
10. to be accused for a crime; to be punished 參看「反坐」
11. owing to; because of
坐標(ㄗㄨㄛˋ ㄅㄧㄠ)
(mathematics) coordinates
坐不下(ㄗㄨㄛˋ ˙ㄅㄨ ㄒㄧㄚˋ)
unable to seat oneself—not enough sitting room for the people present
坐不住(ㄗㄨㄛˋ ˙ㄅㄨ ㄓㄨˋ)
can not stay long; can not sit still; restless: 聽說英文不及格，他再也坐不住。When he was told that he failed in English, he could not stay any longer.
坐不穩(ㄗㄨㄛˋ ˙ㄅㄨ ㄨㄣˇ)
① cannot sit steady ② (said of a defective chair) unsteady
坐法(ㄗㄨㄛˋ ㄈㄚˇ)
to be sentenced to imprison for breaking the law
坐大(ㄗㄨㄛˋ ㄉㄚˋ)
to emerge big and strong (usually said of an aggressor who could have been stopped when he was weak)
坐等(ㄗㄨㄛˋ ㄉㄥˇ)
to sit back and wait
坐地(ㄗㄨㄛˋ ㄉㄧˋ)
① to sit on the ground ② to do something on the spot; on the spot
坐地分贓(ㄗㄨㄛˋ ㄉㄧˋ ㄈㄣ ㄗㄤ)
to divide the loot on the spot
坐墊(ㄗㄨㄛˋ ㄉㄧㄢˋ)
a seat cushion: 地板上有好幾個坐墊。There are several cushions on the floor.
坐定(ㄗㄨㄛˋ ㄉㄧㄥˋ)
to be seated
坐牢(ㄗㄨㄛˋ ㄌㄠˊ)
to be jailed or imprisoned; to be shut behind the bars
坐冷板凳(ㄗㄨㄛˋ ㄌㄥˇ ㄅㄢˇ ㄉㄥˋ)
① to hold a position with little or no power ② to be out in the cold
坐力(ㄗㄨㄛˋ ㄌㄧˋ)
the force of recoil
坐立不安(ㄗㄨㄛˋ ㄌㄧˋ ㄅㄨˋ ㄢ)
fidgety; restless; to feel uneasy whether sitting or standing; to fidget: 什麼事令你坐立不安? What's fidgeting you?
坐落(ㄗㄨㄛˋ ㄌㄨㄛˋ)
(said of a house, building, etc.) to be located or situated at: 我們的學校坐落在山脚下。Our school is located at the foot of a hill.
坐骨神經(ㄗㄨㄛˋ ㄍㄨˇ ㄕㄣˊ ㄐㄧㄥ)
the sciatic nerve
坐骨神經痛(ㄗㄨㄛˋ ㄍㄨˇ ㄕㄣˊ ㄐㄧㄥ ㄊㄨㄥˋ)
sciatica
坐觀成敗(ㄗㄨㄛˋ ㄍㄨㄢ ㄔㄥˊ ㄅㄞˋ)
to watch a struggle with detachment; to look on coldly; to be a mere onlooker
坐困(ㄗㄨㄛˋ ㄎㄨㄣˋ)
to be confined; to be walled in: 這些年來他坐困愁城。He has been walled in by his own worries all these years.
坐化(ㄗㄨㄛˋ ㄏㄨㄚˋ)
(said of Buddhist monks) to die remaining seated crosslegged
坐懷不亂(ㄗㄨㄛˋ ㄏㄨㄞˊ ㄅㄨˋ ㄌㄨㄢˋ)
(literally) to retain presence of mind even with a beautiful woman sitting on the lap—to be immune from the temptation of feminine charms
坐騎(ㄗㄨㄛˋ ㄐㄧˋ)
one's horse for riding
坐轎(ㄗㄨㄛˋ ㄐㄧㄠˋ)
to travel by sedan chair
坐井觀天(ㄗㄨㄛˋ ㄐㄧㄥˇ ㄍㄨㄢ ㄊㄧㄢ)
(literally) to look at the sky from the bottom of a well—a very limited view, usually implying shortsightedness, ignorance, shallowness, etc.
坐席(ㄗㄨㄛˋ ㄒㄧˊ)
① to take one's seat at a banquet table ② a seat
坐下(ㄗㄨㄛˋ ㄒㄧㄚˋ)
to sit down 或 Sit down. 請坐下。Sit down, please.

坐享其成(ㄗㄨㄛˋ ㄒㄧㄤˇ ㄑㄧˊ ㄔㄥˊ)
to enjoy the fruit without toil; to enjoy the fruit of toil of others; to reap where one has not sown
坐致(ㄗㄨㄛˋ ㄓˋ)
to make (profit) without working for it
坐鎮(ㄗㄨㄛˋ ㄓㄣˋ)
personally take charge of (an operation or mission) —usually referring to an important official or general
坐莊(ㄗㄨㄛˋ ㄓㄨㄤ)
①(formerly) to be a resident agent for business firms ② to be the banker or dealer in a gambling game
坐吃山空(ㄗㄨㄛˋ ㄔ ㄕㄢ ㄎㄨㄥ)
(literally) Sitting idle, one can consume even a mountain (of food, wealth, etc.). — One cannot live in security without a dependable source of income.
坐車(ㄗㄨㄛˋ ㄔㄜ)
by bus or train: 我每天坐車上學。I go to school by bus every day.
坐禪(ㄗㄨㄛˋ ㄔㄢˊ)
(Buddhism) to sit in deep meditation
坐船(ㄗㄨㄛˋ ㄔㄨㄢˊ)
by boat or ship
坐失良機(ㄗㄨㄛˋ ㄕ ㄌㄧㄤˊ ㄐㄧ)
to let a golden chance slip by
坐視(ㄗㄨㄛˋ ㄕˋ)
to keep hands off; to watch (others suffering or getting licked) without extending a helping hand
坐收漁利(ㄗㄨㄛˋ ㄕㄡ ㄩˊ ㄌㄧˋ)
to reap the spoils of war without lifting a finger; to profit from others' conflict 亦作「坐收漁人之利」
坐山觀虎鬪(ㄗㄨㄛˋ ㄕㄢ ㄍㄨㄢ ㄏㄨˇ ㄉㄡˋ)
(literally) to sit on the top of the mountain to watch the tigers fight—to stand by in safety while others fight, then profit at their expense when both sides are exhausted
坐褥(ㄗㄨㄛˋ ㄖㄨˋ)
a seat cushion
坐蓐(ㄗㄨㄛˋ ㄖㄨˋ)
(said of a woman) in labor
坐罪(ㄗㄨㄛˋ ㄗㄨㄟˋ)
to be punished for crimes committed; to punish or to sentence
坐次(ㄗㄨㄛˋ ㄘˋ)
the order of seats in a meeting or feast
坐以待斃(ㄗㄨㄛˋ ㄧˇ ㄉㄞˋ ㄅㄧˋ)
to do nothing to avert a crisis, peril, etc.; to await one's doom; to resign oneself to death
坐以待旦(ㄗㄨㄛˋ ㄧˇ ㄉㄞˋ ㄉㄢˋ)
to sit and waiting for the morning
坐臥不寧(ㄗㄨㄛˋ ㄨㄛˋ ㄅㄨˋ ㄋㄧㄥˊ)
to feel restless and uneasy; to be on tenterhooks 亦作「坐臥不安」: 他坐臥不寧。He felt restless.
坐位(ㄗㄨㄛˋ ㄨㄟˋ)
a place to sit; a seat: 請留幾個坐位給我們。Please reserve some seats for us.
坐月子(ㄗㄨㄛˋ ㄩㄝˋ ˙ㄗ)
(said of a woman) to be confined; the month after a woman's childbirth

【坑】 819
ㄎㄥ keng kēng

1. a pit; a hole in the ground: 一個蘿蔔一個坑。One radish, one hole.—Everyone has his own task.
2. to bury alive: 焚書坑儒 to burn books and bury scholars alive
3. to entrap

坑騙(ㄎㄥ ㄆㄧㄢˋ)
to cheat by tricks
坑道(ㄎㄥ ㄉㄠˋ)
a tunnel; a pit; an underground passage: 坑道工事 tunnel defenses
坑坑窪窪(ㄎㄥ ㄎㄥ ㄨㄚ ㄨㄚ)
(said of a road surface) full of bumps and holes
坑害(ㄎㄥ ㄏㄞˋ)
to lead into a trap; to entrap
坑殺(ㄎㄥ ㄕㄚ)
to bury alive
坑人(ㄎㄥ ㄖㄣˊ)
to entrap, ensnare or harm someone: 奸商坑人。The profiteers entrapped people.

五畫

【坡】 820
ㄆㄛ po pō

a slope; a bank; a hillside: 陡坡 a steep slope 山坡 a foothill slope
坡地(ㄆㄛ ㄉㄧˋ)
hillside fields; sloping fields; the land on the slopes
坡度(ㄆㄛ ㄉㄨˋ)
the degree of a slope; grade

【坤】 821
ㄎㄨㄣ kuen kūn

1. one of the Eight Diagrams —earth
2. compliance; obedience
3. female; feminine

坤範(ㄎㄨㄣ ㄈㄢˋ) or 坤德(ㄎㄨㄣ ㄉㄜˊ)
① women's virtue ② an exemplary woman
坤伶(ㄎㄨㄣ ㄌㄧㄥˊ) or 坤角兒(ㄎㄨㄣ ㄐㄩㄝˊㄦ)
an actress of Peking opera: 坤伶生活 the life of an actress
坤戲(ㄎㄨㄣ ㄒㄧˋ)
a play with an entirely female cast
坤宅(ㄎㄨㄣ ㄓㄞˊ)
the home of the bride
坤輿(ㄎㄨㄣ ㄩˊ)
another name of the earth

【坦】 822
ㄊㄢˇ taan tǎn

1. wide and smooth; level
2. self-possessed; composed; calm; peaceful
3. frank; straightforward
4. a son-in-law
5. a Chinese family name

坦白(ㄊㄢˇ ㄅㄞˊ)
frank; honest; to tell the truth: 坦白對你說 to be frank with you; frankly speaking
坦腹東牀(ㄊㄢˇ ㄈㄨˋ ㄉㄨㄥ ㄔㄨㄤˊ)
① an ideal son-in-law ② to lie in bed with a bare belly
坦蕩(ㄊㄢˇ ㄉㄤˋ)
① contented and composed; magnanimous ②(said of a road) broad and level
坦途(ㄊㄢˇ ㄊㄨˊ)
a level road; an easy path; a smooth ride (ahead): 爲學之道, 既無捷徑, 亦無坦途。There

is neither shortcut nor easy way to the great achievement in learning.

坦干伊喀(ㄊㄢˇ ㄍㄢ ㄧ ㄎㄚ)
Tanganyika

〔土部〕

坦克車(ㄊㄢˇ ㄎㄜˋ ㄔㄜ)or 坦克(ㄊㄢˇ ㄎㄜˋ)
a tank (an armored vehicle)

坦吉爾(ㄊㄢˇ ㄐㄧˊ ㄦˇ)
Tangier, a seaport in Northwest Africa

坦胸露背(ㄊㄢˇ ㄒㄩㄥ ㄌㄡˋ ㄅㄟˋ)
(said of women wearing plunging neckline dresses) exposing chest and back

坦直(ㄊㄢˇ ㄓˊ)
straightforward

坦率(ㄊㄢˇ ㄕㄨㄞˋ)
frank; straightforward; blunt; bluntly: 他爲人坦率。He is frank and open.

坦然(ㄊㄢˇ ㄖㄢˊ)
self-possessed; calm; peaceful in mind; fearless; fully at ease: 坦然自若 calm and confident

坦桑尼亞(ㄊㄢˇ ㄙㄤ ㄋㄧˊ ㄧㄚˇ)
Tanzania

坦夷(ㄊㄢˇ ㄧˊ)
① level and broad ② peaceful and calm

【坷】 823
ㄎㄜˇ kee kě
1. bad luck; unfortunate
2. rugged, uneven (roads, etc.)

【坼】 824
ㄔㄜˋ cheh chè
1. to crack
2. to chap; to tear; to rip open

【坳】 825
ㄠˋ aw ào
a hollow in the ground; a cavity

坳堂(ㄠˋ ㄊㄤˊ)
a hollow in the ground

【垂】 826
ㄔㄨㄟˊ chwei chuí
1. to hang down; to let fall
2. to hand down; to leave a name in history: 他名垂青史。He left his name in history.
3. nearly; almost; approaching
4. to condescend

垂面(ㄔㄨㄟˊ ㄇㄧㄢˋ)
a perpendicular plane

垂名(ㄔㄨㄟˊ ㄇㄧㄥˊ)
to leave name for future generations

垂暮(ㄔㄨㄟˊ ㄇㄨˋ)
dusk; towards sunset

垂暮之年(ㄔㄨㄟˊ ㄇㄨˋ ㄓ ㄋㄧㄢˊ)
in one's old age

垂髮(ㄔㄨㄟˊ ㄈㄚˇ)or 垂髫(ㄔㄨㄟˊ ㄊㄧㄠˊ)
young children; early childhood

垂釣(ㄔㄨㄟˊ ㄉㄧㄠˋ)
to fish with a hook and line; to go fishing

垂頭(ㄔㄨㄟˊ ㄊㄡˊ)
to hang one's head

垂頭喪氣(ㄔㄨㄟˊ ㄊㄡˊ ㄙㄤˋ ㄑㄧˋ)
to be crestfallen; to be downcast; to be greatly discouraged or disappointed: 他經常垂頭喪氣。He is always downcast in spirit.

垂念(ㄔㄨㄟˊ ㄋㄧㄢˋ)
so gracious as to remember me

垂老(ㄔㄨㄟˊ ㄌㄠˇ)
to be nearly or almost old; (with) one's old age approaching; (in) declining years

垂柳(ㄔㄨㄟˊ ㄌㄧㄡˇ)or 垂楊(ㄔㄨㄟˊ ㄧㄤˊ)
a weeping willow

垂憐(ㄔㄨㄟˊ ㄌㄧㄢˊ)
to have pity on somebody

垂簾聽政(ㄔㄨㄟˊ ㄌㄧㄢˊ ㄊㄧㄥ ㄓㄥˋ)or (ㄔㄨㄟˊ ㄌㄧㄢˊ ㄊㄧㄥˋ ㄓㄥˋ)
(said of an empress dowager) to administer state affairs behind a bamboo screen; to hold court from behind a screen; power-behind-the-throne

垂青(ㄔㄨㄟˊ ㄑㄧㄥ)
to give preferential treatment; to bestow favors: 得蒙垂青，不勝感激。I greatly thank you for the favors you bestowed on me.

垂涎(ㄔㄨㄟˊ ㄒㄧㄢˊ)or 垂涎三尺(ㄔㄨㄟˊ ㄒㄧㄢˊ ㄙㄢ ㄔˇ)or 垂涎欲滴(ㄔㄨㄟˊ ㄒㄧㄢˊ ㄩˋ ㄉㄧ)
to drool; to yearn for; to covet; to crave: 千萬不要垂涎財富和權利。Never covet wealth and power.

垂詢(ㄔㄨㄟˊ ㄒㄩㄣˊ)
to deign to inquire into; to make gracious inquiries

垂直(ㄔㄨㄟˊ ㄓˊ)
perpendicular; vertical

垂直面(ㄔㄨㄟˊ ㄓˊ ㄇㄧㄢˋ)
a vertical plane

垂直距離(ㄔㄨㄟˊ ㄓˊ ㄐㄩˋ ㄌㄧˊ)
a perpendicular distance

垂直線(ㄔㄨㄟˊ ㄓˊ ㄒㄧㄢˋ)
a vertical line

垂成(ㄔㄨㄟˊ ㄔㄥˊ)
drawing close to a successful conclusion; to be approaching success or completion

垂手(ㄔㄨㄟˊ ㄕㄡˇ)
to let the hands hang by the sides: 他垂手站著。He stood with his hands at his sides.

垂手可得(ㄔㄨㄟˊ ㄕㄡˇ ㄎㄜˇ ㄉㄜˊ)
to get it with hands down—easy to obtain or get 參看「唾手可得」

垂死(ㄔㄨㄟˊ ㄙˇ)
at the point of death; dying

垂愛(ㄔㄨㄟˊ ㄞˋ)
to show gracious concern for (me)

垂危(ㄔㄨㄟˊ ㄨㄟˊ)
(said of an illness or situation) to be in imminent danger or in a precarious state

【垃】 827
ㄌㄜˋ leh lè
garbage, refuse and waste

垃圾(ㄌㄜˋ ㄙㄜˋ)
garbage; refuse

垃圾焚化爐(ㄌㄜˋ ㄙㄜˋ ㄈㄣˊ ㄏㄨㄚˋ ㄌㄨˊ)
a refuse incinerator

垃圾堆(ㄌㄜˋ ㄙㄜˋ ㄉㄨㄟ)or 垃圾場(ㄌㄜˋ ㄙㄜˋ ㄔㄤˇ)
a rubbish heap; a garbage heap; a refuse dump

垃圾桶(ㄌㄜˋ ㄙㄜˋ ㄊㄨㄥˇ)
a dustbin

垃圾箱(ㄌㄜˋ ㄙㄜˋ ㄒㄧㄤ)
a garbage container; a garbage can; an ash can

垃圾車(ㄌㄜˋ ㄙㄜˋ ㄔㄜ)
a collection truck

【坪】 828
ㄆㄧㄥˊ pyng píng
1. a level piece of ground: 草坪 a lawn 停機坪 an aircraft park
2. (in Japanese measurement) an area of 6 feet square

六畫

【垠】 829
ㄧㄣˊ yn yín

1. the bank (of a stream)
2. a boundary; a limit: 一望無垠 to extend as far as the eye can see

【垓】 830 ㄍㄞ gai gāi
1. far and remote places; wilds beyond the frontier
2. a boundary; a limit
3. a hundred million

垓下(ㄍㄞ ㄒㄧㄚˋ)
name of a place, southeast of today's Linpi County (靈壁縣) of Anhwei Province (安徽省), where the first emperor of the Han Dynasty beat Hsiang Yü(項羽) in a decisive battle

【垢】 831 ㄍㄡˋ gow gòu
1. dirt; filth; stains: 蓬頭垢面 with disheveled hair and a dirty face
2. shame; disgrace: 含辱忍垢 to endure disgrace and humiliations; (to be forced) to swallow insults
3. (figuratively) evildoers

垢膩(ㄍㄡˋ ㄋㄧˋ) or 垢泥(ㄍㄡˋ ㄋㄧˊ)
dirt and grease on human skin; skin excrement and dirt

垢穢(ㄍㄡˋ ㄏㄨㄟˋ)
dirty

【型】 832 ㄒㄧㄥˊ shyng xíng
1. an earthen mold for casting
2. a model; a pattern; a standard: 我買了一艘船的模型給他。I bought him a model of a ship.
3. a statute; a law
4. a style; a fashion; a type

【垮】 833 ㄎㄨㄚˇ koa kuǎ
1. to topple; to collapse: 這堵牆要垮了。The wall is going to collapse.
2. to wear down
3. to put to rout: 我們決心打垮敵人。We are determined to put the enemy to rout.
4. to fall (out of power)

垮臺(ㄎㄨㄚˇ ㄊㄞˊ)
the fall (of a government, administration, organization, project, person, etc.) ; collapse

七畫

【埋】 834 1.ㄇㄞˊ mai mái
1. to bury: 雪把整個山谷埋起來了。The whole valley is buried in snow.
2. to secrete; to lie in wait

埋沒(ㄇㄞˊ ㄇㄛˋ)
①to conceal from recognition; to bury (one's talents, etc.); to neglect; to stifle: 埋沒人才 to stifle real talents ②to submerge

埋名(ㄇㄞˊ ㄇㄧㄥˊ)
to conceal one's name; to live incognito

埋伏(ㄇㄞˊ ㄈㄨˊ)
an ambush; to ambush; to lie in wait: 他們中了埋伏。They fell into an ambush.

埋頭苦幹(ㄇㄞˊ ㄊㄡˊ ㄎㄨˇ ㄍㄢˋ)
to bury one's head (in studying); to work with all-out effort

埋骨(ㄇㄞˊ ㄍㄨˇ)
①to bury one's remains ②to die: 埋骨沙場 to die on the battlefield

埋葬(ㄇㄞˊ ㄗㄤˋ)
to bury (a corpse)

埋藏(ㄇㄞˊ ㄘㄤˊ)
to hide; to conceal; to bury (a treasure, weapons, etc.)

【埋】 834 2.ㄇㄢˊ man mán
參看「埋怨」

埋怨(ㄇㄢˊ ㄩㄢˋ)
to blame; to grumble; to complain; complaint: 他的話有埋怨之意。There was a note of complaint in what he said.

【城】 835 ㄔㄥˊ cherng chéng
1. a city; a town: 全城的人都知道這事。The whole town knows of it.
2. the walls of a city
3. to surround a city with walls

城北徐公(ㄔㄥˊ ㄅㄟˇ ㄒㄩˊ ㄍㄨㄥ)
a handsome young man

城堡(ㄔㄥˊ ㄅㄠˇ)
a fort; a castle

城邦(ㄔㄥˊ ㄅㄤ)
a city-state

城門(ㄔㄥˊ ㄇㄣˊ)
the gate of a city wall

城門樓(ㄔㄥˊ ㄇㄣˊ ㄌㄡˊ)
battlements of a city wall; towers over city gates; towers over the wall

城門失火，殃及池魚(ㄔㄥˊ ㄇㄣˊ ㄕ ㄏㄨㄛˇ, ㄧㄤ ㄐㄧˊ ㄔˊ ㄩˊ)
to suffer from other's disaster; to be a scapegoat

城府很深(ㄔㄥˊ ㄈㄨˇ ㄏㄣˇ ㄕㄣ)
(said of one's mind) shrewd and deep

城垛(ㄔㄥˊ ㄉㄨㄛˇ)
battlements

城頭(ㄔㄥˊ ㄊㄡˊ)
the top of the city wall

城樓(ㄔㄥˊ ㄌㄡˊ)
a tower on the city wall

城裏人(ㄔㄥˊ ·ㄌㄧ ㄖㄣˊ)
urbanites; townsfolk; city dwellers

城郭(ㄔㄥˊ ㄍㄨㄛ)
the inner and outer city walls

城河(ㄔㄥˊ ㄏㄜˊ) or 城壕(ㄔㄥˊ ㄏㄠˊ)
the moat of a city; the canal around the city wall

城狐社鼠(ㄔㄥˊ ㄏㄨˊ ㄕㄜˋ ㄕㄨˇ)
(literally) foxes in the city walls and rats on the altars —evildoers who have some influential people to fall back upon

城隍廟(ㄔㄥˊ ㄏㄨㄤˊ ㄇㄧㄠˋ)
a temple of the city god

城牆(ㄔㄥˊ ㄑㄧㄤˊ)
the city wall

城區(ㄔㄥˊ ㄑㄩ)
the city proper

城闕(ㄔㄥˊ ㄑㄩㄝˋ)
①the watch towers over city gates ②a palace

城下之盟(ㄔㄥˊ ㄒㄧㄚˋ ㄓ ㄇㄥˊ)
to sign a humiliating treaty after a crushing defeat or when the military situation has become hopeless

城鎮(ㄔㄥˊ ㄓㄣˋ)
cities and towns

城池(ㄔㄥˊ ㄔˊ)
the city wall and moat

城市(ㄔㄥˊ ㄕˋ)
a city or town

城市規劃(ㄔㄥˊ ㄕˋ ㄍㄨㄟ ㄏㄨㄚˋ)
city planning 亦作「都市規劃」

〔土部〕

【埂】 836 ㄍㄥˇ geeng gěng
1. a pit; a cave
2. an irrigation ditch
3. a low bank of earth between fields: 田埂 footpaths between the fields

【埃】 837 ㄞ ai āi
1. fine dust
2. Egypt

埃及(ㄞ ㄐㄧˊ)
Egypt

埃及人(ㄞ ㄐㄧˊ ㄖㄣˊ)
an Egyptian

【埔】 838 ㄆㄨˇ puu pǔ
1. a plain; an arena
2. a port; a mart

八畫

【培】 839 ㄆㄟˊ peir péi
1. to bank up with earth
2. to nourish; to strengthen; to cultivate; to foster: 他正在栽培玫瑰。He is cultivating roses.

培塿(ㄆㄟˊ ㄌㄡˇ)
a small hill

培根(ㄆㄟˊ ㄍㄣ)
① Francis Bacon, 1561-1626, British philosopher ② bacon

培植(ㄆㄟˊ ㄓˊ)
① to plant; to grow (plants); to bank up with earth ② to educate or train; to foster

培養(ㄆㄟˊ ㄧㄤˇ)
① to cultivate by banking up; to grow (plants) ② to raise (kids) ③ to cultivate (one's mind); to educate ④ culture: 培養細菌 the culture of bacteria

培養土(ㄆㄟˊ ㄧㄤˇ ㄊㄨˇ)
specially fertilized earth for pot plants

培養基(ㄆㄟˊ ㄧㄤˇ ㄐㄧ)
a culture medium (for growing bacteria in a laboratory)

培育(ㄆㄟˊ ㄩˋ)
to cultivate and grow; to raise; to breed: 他們努力培育稻米新品種。They try hard to breed new varieties of rice.

【域】 840 ㄩˋ yuh yù
1. a frontier; a boundary
2. a region; a country; an area
3. to live; to stay

域外(ㄩˋ ㄨㄞˋ)
beyond the frontier; a foreign country; outside China

【埠】 841 ㄅㄨˋ buh bù
1. a harbor; a port; a pier: 船在天亮時進埠。The ship entered port at dawn.
2. a mart on the bank of a river or seacoast

埠頭(ㄅㄨˋ ㄊㄡˊ)
a wharf; a port

【埤】 842 1. ㄆㄧˊ pyi pí
1. a low wall; a parapet
2. an increase; increasingly; to add to

埤益(ㄆㄧˊ ㄧˋ)
to increase

【埤】 842 2. ㄅㄟ bei bēi
low-lying

埤汚(ㄅㄟ ㄨ)
(said of one's personality) mean

【執】 843 ㄓˊ jyr zhí
1. to hold; to grasp; to seize
2. to detain; to arrest
3. to maintain or uphold (a principle, etc.); to hold on stubbornly to; to stick to; to persist in: 各執己見。Each stuck to his own view.
4. to shut (gossipers, etc.) up
5. a Chinese family name

執筆(ㄓˊ ㄅㄧˇ)
to write

執鞭(ㄓˊ ㄅㄧㄢ)
to act as a coach driver for someone

執迷不悟(ㄓˊ ㄇㄧˊ ㄅㄨˋ ㄨˋ)
to adhere stubbornly to errors; to hold on to wrong beliefs obstinately

執法(ㄓˊ ㄈㄚˇ)
to enforce (or execute) the law

執法如山(ㄓˊ ㄈㄚˇ ㄖㄨˊ ㄕㄢ)
to uphold the law strictly; to adhere to legal principles without letup or fear (usually referring to law-enforcing officers or judges)

執紼(ㄓˊ ㄈㄨˊ) or 執紼送喪(ㄓˊ ㄈㄨˊ ㄙㄨㄥˋ ㄙㄤ)
to attend a funeral

執弟子禮(ㄓˊ ㄉㄧˋ ㄗˇ ㄌㄧˇ)
to regard oneself as a pupil in dealing with somebody one holds in high esteem

執牛耳(ㄓˊ ㄋㄧㄡˊ ㄦˇ)
to play the leading role; to be in a dominant position

執禮(ㄓˊ ㄌㄧˇ)
to stick to etiquette; to observe the formalities (of weddings, master-pupil relationships, etc.)

執兩用中(ㄓˊ ㄌㄧㄤˇ ㄩㄥˋ ㄓㄨㄥ)
to listen to both sides of opinions and determine from them the course of the Mean

執柯(ㄓˊ ㄎㄜ)
to be a matchmaker

執箕帚(ㄓˊ ㄐㄧ ㄓㄡˇ)
to become someone's wife (a polite expression)

執教(ㄓˊ ㄐㄧㄠˋ)
to be a teacher

執經問難(ㄓˊ ㄐㄧㄥ ㄨㄣˋ ㄋㄢˋ)
to hold the classics and make inquiries

執行(ㄓˊ ㄒㄧㄥˊ)
to execute (an order); to carry out; to implement

執行秘書(ㄓˊ ㄒㄧㄥˊ ㄇㄧˋ ㄕㄨ)
an executive secretary

執行死刑(ㄓˊ ㄒㄧㄥˊ ㄙˇ ㄒㄧㄥˊ)
to carry out a death sentence; to execute a death convict

執行委員(ㄓˊ ㄒㄧㄥˊ ㄨㄟˇ ㄩㄢˊ)
administrative officers; the persons appointed by a ruling party or an assembly to carry out their decisions; the members of an executive committee

執照(ㄓˊ ㄓㄠˋ)
a license; a permit: 你得攜帶駕駛執照。You have to carry your driver's license.

執掌(ㄓˊ ㄓㄤˇ)
to take full charge of; to manage; to superintend; to wield

執政(ㄓˊ ㄓㄥˋ)
to be in power; to hold the

reins of the government
執政黨(ㄓˊ ㄓㄥˋ ㄉㄤˇ)
the party in power; the ruling party
執著(ㄓˊ ㄓㄨㄛˊ)
inflexible; to persist in
執中(ㄓˊ ㄓㄨㄥ)
to follow the middle road; to keep to the golden mean; impartial 亦作「允執厥中」
執事(ㄓˊ ㄕˋ)
① an errand man ② a salutation to the other party in correspondence; Sir; you ③ (Christianity) a church officer; a deacon
執手(ㄓˊ ㄕㄡˇ)
to hold hands
執拗(ㄓˊ ㄠˋ)
persistent; stubbornly recalcitrant
執意(ㄓˊ ㄧˋ)
to stick to one's own view; to hold on stubbornly to one's own ideas; to insist on
執業(ㄓˊ ㄧㄝˋ)
①to engage in a profession or trade ② a vocation or trade
執友(ㄓˊ ㄧㄡˇ)
a bosom friend; friends of the same circle 亦作「摯友」
執言(ㄓˊ ㄧㄢˊ)
to make positive assertions

【基】 844 ㄐㄧ ji jī

1. a foundation; a base: 他們正在興建壩基。They are building the base of a dam.
2. an origin; a basis; a root: 農民是國家的基礎。The farmers form the basis of a nation.
3. on the basis of; according to; on the strength of
4. a group; the base of a chemical compound

基本(ㄐㄧ ㄅㄣˇ)
① a root, foundation or base ② fundamental; basic; elementary ③ basically; on the whole; by and large: 這場音樂會基本上是好的。This concert is good on the whole.
基本單位(ㄐㄧ ㄅㄣˇ ㄉㄢ ㄨㄟˋ)
fundamental units
基本工資(ㄐㄧ ㄅㄣˇ ㄍㄨㄥ ㄗ)
basic wages
基本結構(ㄐㄧ ㄅㄣˇ ㄐㄧㄝˊ ㄍㄡˋ)
primary structure
基本金(ㄐㄧ ㄅㄣˇ ㄐㄧㄣ)or 基金(ㄐㄧ ㄐㄧㄣ)
① a fund; an endowment fund ② subscribed capital
基本知識(ㄐㄧ ㄅㄣˇ ㄓ ㄕˊ)
elementary knowledge
基本原則(ㄐㄧ ㄅㄣˇ ㄩㄢˊ ㄗㄜˊ)
basic principles
基肥(ㄐㄧ ㄈㄟˊ)
main fertilization; fertilizers applied to soil before planting; ground fertilizer
基輔(ㄐㄧ ㄈㄨˇ)
Kiev, a Russian city
基地(ㄐㄧ ㄉㄧˋ)
a base (of operations): 軍事基地 a military base
基調(ㄐㄧ ㄉㄧㄠˋ)
① the central thought; the main theme ② (music) the keynote
基點(ㄐㄧ ㄉㄧㄢˇ)
① the basic point; the starting point; the center: 我們的外交政策要放在獨立的基點上。Our diplomatic policy should rest on the basic point of independency. ② (survey) the base point (BP)
基督(ㄐㄧ ㄉㄨ)
Jesus Christ
基督徒(ㄐㄧ ㄉㄨ ㄊㄨˊ)
a Christian: 這村子裡有很多基督徒。There were a lot of Christians in this village.
基督教(ㄐㄧ ㄉㄨ ㄐㄧㄠˋ)
Christianity (particularly referring to the Protestants)
基督教青年會(ㄐㄧ ㄉㄨ ㄐㄧㄠˋ ㄑㄧㄥ ㄋㄧㄢˊ ㄏㄨㄟˋ)
the Young Men's Christian Association (Y.M.C.A)
基多(ㄐㄧ ㄉㄨㄛ)
Quito, the capital of Ecuador
基尼(ㄐㄧ ㄋㄧˊ)
a guinea, a British monetary unit
基隆(ㄐㄧ ㄌㄨㄥˊ)
Keelung—the northern port city of Taiwan Province
基價(ㄐㄧ ㄐㄧㄚˋ)
a basic price
基金(ㄐㄧ ㄐㄧㄣ)
a reserve fund; a fund for specific use: 許多大學都有作研究用的基金。Many universities have a reserve fund for research.
基金會(ㄐㄧ ㄐㄧㄣ ㄏㄨㄟˋ)
the board of directors of a fund; foundation
基準(ㄐㄧ ㄓㄨㄣˇ)
a pattern; a model; a standard; a rule
基礎(ㄐㄧ ㄔㄨˇ)
① the foundation of a building ② the basis or foundation of an argument, etc.: 他的誠實及工作熱誠是他成功的基礎。His honesty and willingness to work are the foundations of his success.
基礎教育(ㄐㄧ ㄔㄨˇ ㄐㄧㄠˋ ㄩˋ)
elementary education
基石(ㄐㄧ ㄕˊ)
a foundation stone; a cornerstone
基數(ㄐㄧ ㄕㄨˋ)
cardinal numbers (any of the digits from 1 to 9)
基層(ㄐㄧ ㄘㄥˊ)
basic level; a grass-roots unit: 深入基層 to go down to the grass-roots units
基層單位(ㄐㄧ ㄘㄥˊ ㄉㄢ ㄨㄟˋ)
a basic unit; a unit at grass-roots level
基層選舉(ㄐㄧ ㄘㄥˊ ㄒㄩㄢˇ ㄐㄩˇ)
elections at basic level
基層組織(ㄐㄧ ㄘㄥˊ ㄗㄨˇ ㄓ)
① the basic structure or constitution of an organization ② the low-echelon organizations
基業(ㄐㄧ ㄧㄝˋ)
the initial achievements of an empire
基因(ㄐㄧ ㄧㄣ)
a gene: 顯性基因 a dominant gene
基於(ㄐㄧ ㄩˊ)
because of; in view of; on account of: 基於以上理由，我不採納他的意見。In view of the above-mentioned reasons, I didn't take his opinion.

【堂】 845 ㄊㄤˊ tarng táng

1. a hall; an office; a reception

〔土部〕

room: 講堂 a lecture room
2. a meeting place; a court of justice: 公堂 the court
3. a salutation for another's mother
4. an open level place on the hill
5. relatives born of the same grandfather
6. venerable; grave; imposing
7. a set: 一堂瓷器 a set of porcelains
8. a team or a group: 一堂鼓手 a team of drummers

堂伯叔(ㄊㄤˊ ㄅㄛˊ ㄕㄨˊ)
one's father's male first cousins of the same surname

堂堂(ㄊㄤˊ ㄊㄤˊ)
① dignified, venerable (appearances); impressive ② imposing; awe-inspiring; formidable

堂堂大國(ㄊㄤˊ ㄊㄤˊ ㄉㄚˋ ㄍㄨㄛˊ)
a powerful and civilized great country

堂堂正正(ㄊㄤˊ ㄊㄤˊ ㄓㄥˋ ㄓㄥˋ)
dignified and imposing

堂鼓(ㄊㄤˊ ㄍㄨˇ)
a kind of drum used in Peking opera

堂倌(ㄊㄤˊ ㄍㄨㄢ)
a waiter (in restaurants, teahouses, etc.): 堂倌罷工。Waiters of restaurants went on strike.

堂會(ㄊㄤˊ ㄏㄨㄟˋ)
an entertainment party with hired performers held at home on auspicious occasions

堂皇(ㄊㄤˊ ㄏㄨㄤˊ)
① imposing; impressive; grand; stately; magnificent: 他的房子富麗堂皇。His house is beautiful and imposing. ② openly and legally

堂姊妹(ㄊㄤˊ ㄐㄧㄝˇ ㄇㄟˋ)
one's female first cousins on the father's side

堂萱(ㄊㄤˊ ㄒㄩㄢ)
one's mother: 堂萱年邁。My mother is growing old.

堂兄弟(ㄊㄤˊ ㄒㄩㄥ ㄉㄧˋ)
one's male first cousins on the father's side

堂上(ㄊㄤˊ ㄕㄤˋ)
a reference to one's own parents: 堂上健在。Both parents are in good health.

堂子(ㄊㄤˊ ·ㄗ)
a brothel

堂奧(ㄊㄤˊ ㄠˋ)
① the advanced stage of learning, a skill, etc.; profundity of thought or knowledge; depths (of teaching) ② deep, hidden recesses

堂屋(ㄊㄤˊ ㄨ)
the central room (of a one-storey Chinese traditional house consisting of several rooms in a row); the main hall of a building

【堅】 846
ㄐㄧㄢ jian jiān

1. strong and durable: 他有堅決的意志。He has a strong will.
2. solid; firm
3. to dedicate to; to devote to
4. calm; steady; stable; determined
5. close; intimate
6. armor, etc.
7. the strongest position or point of enemy troops: 攻堅 to storm strongholds
8. firmly; steadfastly; resolutely: 堅拒 to refuse firmly
9. a Chinese family name

堅壁清野(ㄐㄧㄢ ㄅㄧˋ ㄑㄧㄥ ㄧㄝˇ)
to fortify the defense works and to leave nothing usable to the invading enemy

堅不吐實(ㄐㄧㄢ ㄅㄨˋ ㄊㄨˇ ㄕˊ)
to refuse to tell the truth; (said of criminal suspects) obstinately refuse to speak up

堅不可摧(ㄐㄧㄢ ㄅㄨˋ ㄎㄜˇ ㄘㄨㄟ)
invulnerable; impregnable

堅定(ㄐㄧㄢ ㄉㄧㄥˋ)
determined; firm of purpose; steadfast; staunch: 堅定的立場 a firm ground

堅定不移(ㄐㄧㄢ ㄉㄧㄥˋ ㄅㄨˋ ㄧˊ)
unwavering; unswerving; unshakable

堅挺(ㄐㄧㄢ ㄊㄧㄥˇ)
(said of business conditions) thriving; flourishing; (said of prices) strong; rising; (said of stock exchange) bullish

堅牢(ㄐㄧㄢ ㄌㄠˊ)
strong; durable; heavily defended (fortresses)

堅固(ㄐㄧㄢ ㄍㄨˋ)
strong; durable; solid; firm; stable: 這房子造得很堅固。This house is very solidly built.

堅果(ㄐㄧㄢ ㄍㄨㄛˇ)
nuts

堅苦卓絕(ㄐㄧㄢ ㄎㄨˇ ㄓㄨㄛˊ ㄐㄩㄝˊ)
to endure all the hardships; firm; determined; showing the greatest fortitude

堅甲利兵(ㄐㄧㄢ ㄐㄧㄚˇ ㄌㄧˋ ㄅㄧㄥ)
(literally) strong armor and crack troops—ready for combat; combat readiness

堅決(ㄐㄧㄢ ㄐㄩㄝˊ)
firmly (opposed to, etc.); determined; resolute; resolutely: 我們堅決支持你。We firmly support you.

堅強(ㄐㄧㄢ ㄑㄧㄤˊ)
① strong; firm; unyielding; staunch: 他父親是一個性格堅強的人。His father is a person of strong character. ② to strengthen

堅信(ㄐㄧㄢ ㄒㄧㄣˋ)
to have absolute faith; to believe firmly

堅貞(ㄐㄧㄢ ㄓㄣ)
chaste; of inflexible virtue

堅持(ㄐㄧㄢ ㄔˊ)or 堅執(ㄐㄧㄢ ㄓˊ)
to insist; to maintain unyieldingly; to persist in: 他堅持他是無辜的。He insisted on his innocence.

堅持到底(ㄐㄧㄢ ㄔˊ ㄉㄠˋ ㄉㄧˇ)
to stick it out; to go through with it: 我們必須堅持到底，不然就要失敗了。We should stick it out, or we will fail.

堅持己見(ㄐㄧㄢ ㄔˊ ㄐㄧˇ ㄐㄧㄢˋ)
to be firm in one's view; to hold on to one's own view

堅稱(ㄐㄧㄢ ㄔㄥ)
to insist on saying; to assert positively

堅實(ㄐㄧㄢ ㄕˊ)
solid; strong; durable; substantial: 這條公路堅實平整。This is a smooth, firmly built highway.

堅守(ㄐㄧㄢ ㄕㄡˇ)
① to firmly stand by (one's promise, principle, etc.): 大家都要堅守崗位。Everybody should stand fast at his post.

② to defend (a place) resolutely

堅忍(ㄐㄧㄢ ㄖㄣˇ)
fortitude; firmness; dedication; determination

堅忍不拔(ㄐㄧㄢ ㄖㄣˇ ㄅㄨˋ ㄅㄚˊ)
invincible; fortitude; determined; unwavering; indomitable; resolute; unmovable

堅韌(ㄐㄧㄢ ㄖㄣˋ)
great strength or durability; superb resilience; fortitude

堅如鐵石(ㄐㄧㄢ ㄖㄨˊ ㄊㄧㄝˇ ㄕˊ)
(said of one's feelings, sentiments, etc.) as hard as iron and stone; flinty (hearts)

堅毅(ㄐㄧㄢ ㄧˋ)
fortitude; determination; dedication

堅硬(ㄐㄧㄢ ㄧㄥˋ)
hard and solid: 石頭是很堅硬的。Stone is very hard.

【堆】 847
ㄉㄨㄟ duei duī

1. to heap up; to pile; to stack: 他的桌上堆滿了書。His desk was piled with books.
2. a heap; a pile; a mass; a crowd: 柴堆 a pile of firewood

堆肥(ㄉㄨㄟ ㄈㄟˊ)
compost—an organic fertilizer

堆疊(ㄉㄨㄟ ㄉㄧㄝˊ)
to pile up to great height

堆垛兒(ㄉㄨㄟ ㄉㄨㄛˇㄦ)
a pile; the things gathered together to form a heap

堆積(ㄉㄨㄟ ㄐㄧ)
to store up; to pile; to amass; to heap up

堆金積玉(ㄉㄨㄟ ㄐㄧㄣ ㄐㄧ ㄩˋ)
a vast fortune with piles of gold and jade

堆砌(ㄉㄨㄟ ㄑㄧˋ)
① to lay (bricks, etc.); to pile up ②(composition) allusions, corny expressions, etc. senselessly heaped together

堆棧(ㄉㄨㄟ ㄓㄢˋ)
a warehouse; a storage; a storehouse

九畫

【報】 848
ㄅㄠˋ baw bào

1. to repay; to recompense; to requite; to respond; to return: 觀衆報以熱烈的掌聲。The audience responded with warm applause.
2. a reward; a retribution
3. to report; to announce; a report: 我明天提出報告。I'll report tomorrow.
4. a newspaper; a periodical; a journal: 畫報 a pictorial 學報 a college journal 你訂什麼報? What newspaper do you take?

報備(ㄅㄠˋ ㄅㄟˋ)
to inform the authorities of what one plans to do (instead of submitting a request for permission)

報表(ㄅㄠˋ ㄅㄧㄠˇ)
forms for reporting statistics, etc.; report forms

報屁股(ㄅㄠˋ ㄆㄧˋ ·ㄍㄨ)
(slang) insignificant spaces on the inside pages of a newspaper where feature articles are printed; supplements of a newspaper

報聘(ㄅㄠˋ ㄆㄧㄣˋ)
to repay a courtesy visit to a friendly nation

報馬(ㄅㄠˋ ㄇㄚˇ)
a courier; a messenger

報名(ㄅㄠˋ ㄇㄧㄥˊ)
to enroll; to enlist; to enter one's name (as in an examination, a competition, etc.)

報明(ㄅㄠˋ ㄇㄧㄥˊ)
to state clearly to the higher authorities

報命(ㄅㄠˋ ㄇㄧㄥˋ)
to report the accomplishment of a mission or an assignment

報幕(ㄅㄠˋ ㄇㄨˋ)
to announce the items on a (theatrical) program

報費(ㄅㄠˋ ㄈㄟˋ)
a newspaper subscription bill

報廢(ㄅㄠˋ ㄈㄟˋ)
① to report (worn-out office equipment, etc.) as unserviceable or useless ② to scrap

報復(ㄅㄠˋ ㄈㄨˋ)
① to avenge; to revenge; to retaliate; vengeance; revenge; retaliation; reprisal: 他向敵人報復。He avenged himself on his enemies. ② to report back (after investigation)

報復關稅(ㄅㄠˋ ㄈㄨˋ ㄍㄨㄢ ㄕㄨㄟˋ)
a retaliatory tariff

報答(ㄅㄠˋ ㄉㄚˊ)
to repay another's kindness: 我如何能報答您的恩惠? How can I ever repay you for your kindness?

報德(ㄅㄠˋ ㄉㄜˊ) or 報恩(ㄅㄠˋ ㄣ)
to repay another's kindness or favors; to show gratitude

報導(ㄅㄠˋ ㄉㄠˇ)
① to report (news); to cover: 記者報導了火災的情況。The reporter covered the fire. ② a news report; a story

報導文學(ㄅㄠˋ ㄉㄠˇ ㄨㄣˊ ㄒㄩㄝˊ)
reportage

報到(ㄅㄠˋ ㄉㄠˋ)
to report one's arrival; to check in; to register: 會員已開始報到。The members have started registering.

報單(ㄅㄠˋ ㄉㄢ)
① an application to pass goods through the customs ② an announcement to friends and relatives of one's success in the civil service examination of former times

報頭(ㄅㄠˋ ㄊㄡˊ)
the masthead of a newspaper

報攤(ㄅㄠˋ ㄊㄢ)
a newsstand; a news stall

報童(ㄅㄠˋ ㄊㄨㄥˊ)
a newspaper delivery boy; a newsboy

報告(ㄅㄠˋ ㄍㄠˋ)
① to report: 他正在報告探險的結果。He's reporting the results of the expedition. ② a report: 氣象報告 a weather report

報告書(ㄅㄠˋ ㄍㄠˋ ㄕㄨ)
a written report

報國(ㄅㄠˋ ㄍㄨㄛˊ)
to devote oneself to the national cause; to dedicate oneself to the service of one's country

報官(ㄅㄠˋ ㄍㄨㄢ)
to notify the local govern-

ment of a crime, an accident, etc.

報關(ㄅㄠˋ ㄍㄨㄢ)
to declare something at the customs; to apply to the customs: 你們有什麼東西要報關嗎? Have you got anything to declare?

報關行(ㄅㄠˋ ㄍㄨㄢ ㄏㄤˊ)
a customs broker; an agency for clearing customs

報館(ㄅㄠˋ ㄍㄨㄢˇ)
a newspaper office

報功(ㄅㄠˋ ㄍㄨㄥ)
to report an achievement or a victory; to claim credit

報考(ㄅㄠˋ ㄎㄠˇ)
to enter one's name in an examination

報刊(ㄅㄠˋ ㄎㄢ)
newspapers and periodicals

報戶口(ㄅㄠˋ ㄏㄨˋ ㄎㄡˇ)
①to apply for a residence permit ②to register: 別忘了給你的新生嬰兒報戶口。Don't forget to register the birth of your baby.

報佳音(ㄅㄠˋ ㄐㄧㄚ ㄧㄣ)
to carol; caroling

報夾(ㄅㄠˋ ㄐㄧㄚˊ)
a newspaper holder or clip

報價(ㄅㄠˋ ㄐㄧㄚˋ)
(economics) ①a quoted price ②to quote

報架(ㄅㄠˋ ㄐㄧㄚˋ)
a newspaper shelf

報捷(ㄅㄠˋ ㄐㄧㄝˊ)
to announce or report a victory or success

報界(ㄅㄠˋ ㄐㄧㄝˋ)
the press; the news circles; the journalistic circles: 此書獲報界之好評。The book was favorably noticed by the press.

報警(ㄅㄠˋ ㄐㄧㄥˇ)
①to report an alarm or emergency ②to report to the police

報喜(ㄅㄠˋ ㄒㄧˇ)
to announce good news (such as a marriage, etc.)

報喜不報憂(ㄅㄠˋ ㄒㄧˇ ㄅㄨˋ ㄅㄠˋ ㄧㄡ)
to report only what is good while concealing what is unpleasant

報系(ㄅㄠˋ ㄒㄧˋ)
a newspaper chain; a syndicate

報銷(ㄅㄠˋ ㄒㄧㄠ)
①to give a statement on one's expenses (especially for one's trip on business); to apply for reimbursement ②to write off: 他剛報銷了一部車。He has just written off a car.

報曉(ㄅㄠˋ ㄒㄧㄠˇ)
(said of cocks' crowing) to announce the arrival of dawn; to herald the break of day

報效(ㄅㄠˋ ㄒㄧㄠˋ)
①to work for; to repay another's kindness by working hard for him ②to give private means for public use

報信(ㄅㄠˋ ㄒㄧㄣˋ)
to report news; to announce; to pass information; to notify

報紙(ㄅㄠˋ ㄓˇ)
① a newspaper: 他為這報紙寫社論。He writes leading articles for the newspaper. ②newsprint

報章(ㄅㄠˋ ㄓㄤ)
①newspapers ②reply letters; return mail

報賬(ㄅㄠˋ ㄓㄤˋ)
to present a bill of expenses (to the employer or the accountant); to render an account

報仇 or 報讎(ㄅㄠˋ ㄔㄡˊ)
to get one's revenge for (an injury, etc.); to avenge (a grievance, etc.): 他立誓要向敵人報仇。He swore to revenge himself on his enemy.

報仇雪恨(ㄅㄠˋ ㄔㄡˊ ㄒㄩㄝˇ ㄏㄣˋ)
to revenge and wipe out a standing grudge (against somebody)

報酬(ㄅㄠˋ ㄔㄡˊ)
①pay; a salary: 不計報酬 not concerned about pay ② remuneration; reward: 讀書所得的報酬不能以金錢衡量。The rewards of study can't always be measured in money. ③to thank; to show gratitude

報失(ㄅㄠˋ ㄕ)
to report the loss of something to the authorities concerned

報時(ㄅㄠˋ ㄕˊ)
to give the correct time

報時台(ㄅㄠˋ ㄕˊ ㄊㄞˊ)
(telephone) the time inquiry service

報社(ㄅㄠˋ ㄕㄜˋ)
a newspaper office: 他在一家報社工作。He works in a newspaper office.

報數(ㄅㄠˋ ㄕㄨˋ)
①(drill) to say aloud the number of each one in a row according to the order of the position where he stands, beginning from the one who stands at the head of the row ②(word of command) Count off!

報稅(ㄅㄠˋ ㄕㄨㄟˋ)
to report tax returns; to declare goods for duties

報人(ㄅㄠˋ ㄖㄣˊ)
a newspaperman; a journalist

報災(ㄅㄠˋ ㄗㄞ)
to report a disaster to the authorities

報載(ㄅㄠˋ ㄗㄞˋ)
according to newspaper reports

報喪(ㄅㄠˋ ㄙㄤ)
to announce a death

報案(ㄅㄠˋ ㄢˋ)
to report a case (such as a theft, missing person, murder, etc.) to the police

報恩(ㄅㄠˋ ㄣ)
to pay a debt of gratitude; to repay another's kindness

報業(ㄅㄠˋ ㄧㄝˋ)
the business of the press

報業公會(ㄅㄠˋ ㄧㄝˋ ㄍㄨㄥ ㄏㄨㄟˋ)
a newspaper association; a press union

報應(ㄅㄠˋ ㄧㄥˋ)
retribution (especially in the Buddhist concept that one inevitably reaps what he sows)

報怨(ㄅㄠˋ ㄩㄢˋ)
to avenge a grievance

【堡】 849 ㄅㄠˇ bao bǎo

1. a walled village; a town
2. a petty military station; a

fort; a fortress
堡壘(ㄅㄠˇ ㄌㄟˇ)
a fortress; a bastion; a stronghold

【堪】 850 ㄎㄢ kan kān
1. to sustain; to bear; to stand: 不堪一擊to be unable to withstand a single blow; to collapse at the first blow
2. fit for; worthy of; adequate for
3. a Chinese family name
堪當重任(ㄎㄢ ㄉㄤ ㄓㄨㄥˋ ㄖㄣˋ)
to be capable of shouldering important tasks; to be able to fill a position of great responsibility
堪察加(ㄎㄢ ㄔㄚˊ ㄐㄧㄚ)
the Kamchatka Peninsula
堪稱佳作(ㄎㄢ ㄔㄥ ㄐㄧㄚ ㄗㄨㄛˋ)
may be rated as an excellent piece of writing or a fine work of art
堪薩斯(ㄎㄢ ㄙㄚˋ ㄙ)
the state of Kansas, U.S.A.
堪虞(ㄎㄢ ㄩˊ)
precarious, distressing, dangerous, etc.
堪輿(ㄎㄢ ㄩˊ)
the science of the influence of a landscape on human destiny; geomancy; the magic art of choosing building or burial sites
堪用(ㄎㄢ ㄩㄥˋ)
good enough for use; usable

【堯】 851 ㄧㄠˊ yau yáo
1. Yao, a legendary sage king in ancient China whose reign is said to have extended from 2357 to 2255 B.C.
2. high; eminent; lofty
3. a Chinese family name
堯天舜日(ㄧㄠˊ ㄊㄧㄢ ㄕㄨㄣˋ ㄖˋ)
an era of blissful peace as in the reigns of Yao and Shun
堯舜(ㄧㄠˊ ㄕㄨㄣˋ)
Yao and Shun, two of the most celebrated sage kings in ancient China

【堰】 852 ㄧㄢˇ yann yàn
a bank of earth; an embankment; a dike; a levee: 在荷蘭境內到處都是堰。There are dikes everywhere in Holland.

【場】 853 ㄔㄤˇ charng cháng (又讀 ㄔㄤˇ chaang chǎng)
1. an area of level ground; an open space
2. an act of a play; an act of an opera
3. the stage: 出場to go on the stage
4. an arena for drill; a playground: 操場an athletic field
5. a farm: 養鴨場a duck farm
6. a site or place for a special purpose, as an examination, a meeting, etc.: 教堂是禮拜的場所。A church is a place of worship.
7. (physics) a field: 電(磁)場an electric (magnetic) field
場圃(ㄔㄤˇ ㄆㄨˇ)
vegetable gardens
場面(ㄔㄤˇ ㄇㄧㄢˋ)or(ㄔㄤˊ ㄇㄧㄢˋ)
① pageantry; a show of wealth, etc.: 他擺出大場面。He made a great show of his wealth. ② a scene; a spectacle: 熱烈友好的場面a scene of warm friendship ③ an appearance; a front: 撐場面to keep up appearances ④ (Chinese opera) the group of accompanying musicians collectively
場地(ㄔㄤˇ ㄉㄧˋ)or(ㄔㄤˊ ㄉㄧˋ)
a playground; a site; a place where a show or game is played, including the space for the audience: 這眞是一個理想的露營場地。This is really an ideal camp site.
場合(ㄔㄤˇ ㄏㄜˊ)or(ㄔㄤˊ ㄏㄜˊ)
an occasion; a situation; a condition: 外交場合 a diplomatic occasion
場場客滿(ㄔㄤˇ ㄔㄤˇ ㄎㄜˋ ㄇㄢˇ)or(ㄔㄤˊ ㄔㄤˊ ㄎㄜˋ ㄇㄢˇ)
a houseful of spectators for every show; a capacity audience for every show
場子(ㄔㄤˇ ·ㄗ)
a place or site where people gather for various purposes
場次(ㄔㄤˇ ㄘˋ)
the number of showings of a film, play, etc.
場所(ㄔㄤˇ ㄙㄨㄛˇ)or(ㄔㄤˊ ㄙㄨㄛˇ)
a location; a place; an arena; a theater; a playground: 投票場所a balloting place 營業場所a place of business
場院(ㄔㄤˇ ㄩㄢˋ)or(ㄔㄤˊ ㄩㄢˋ)
an open yard for sunning newly harvested grains

【堵】 854 ㄉㄨˇ duu dǔ
1. to stop; to block up; to shut off: 把老鼠洞堵死。Stop up the mouseholes.
2. a wall
3. a Chinese family name
堵截(ㄉㄨˇ ㄐㄧㄝˊ)
to stop; to intercept; to block up or cut off an approach to
堵牆(ㄉㄨˇ ㄑㄧㄤˊ)
a wall surrounding a house
堵住(ㄉㄨˇ ㄓㄨˋ)
to block up; to stop: 所有的路都爲大雪所堵住。All the roads were blocked by the heavy snowfall.
堵嘴(ㄉㄨˇ ㄗㄨㄟˇ)
① to stop talking ② to silence others by bribery
堵塞(ㄉㄨˇ ㄙㄜˋ)
to stop up; to block up; a jam: 交通堵塞a traffic jam

十畫

【塊】 855 ㄎㄨㄞˋ kuay kuài
1. a lump (or clod) of earth
2. a lump; a piece; a cube: 把肉切成塊兒。Cut the meat into cubes.
3. a piece of (land, bread, etc.)
4. alone; to be all by oneself
塊頭(ㄎㄨㄞˋ ㄊㄡˊ)
stature; build: 他是個大塊頭。He is a man of large stature.
塊壘(ㄎㄨㄞˋ ㄌㄟˇ)
the dejection one feels at heart
塊根(ㄎㄨㄞˋ ㄍㄣ)
root tubers
塊莖(ㄎㄨㄞˋ ㄐㄧㄥ)
a stem tuber
塊肉餘生記(ㄎㄨㄞˋ ㄖㄡˋ ㄩˊ ㄕㄥ ㄐㄧˋ)

〔土部〕

David Copperfield, by Charles Dickens

【塋】856 ㄧㄥˊ yng yíng
a grave; a tomb
塋墳(ㄧㄥˊ ㄈㄣˊ)or 塋穴(ㄧㄥˊ ㄒㄩㄝˋ)
a grave; a tomb
塋地(ㄧㄥˊ ㄉㄧˋ)or 塋域(ㄧㄥˊ ㄩˋ)
a graveyard; a cemetery

【塌】857 ㄊㄚ ta tā
1. to cave in; to fall in ruins; to collapse: 屋頂塌了。The roof collapsed.
2. to sink; to droop
3. a little house
塌鼻(ㄊㄚ ㄅㄧˊ)
a flat nose; a snub nose
塌臺(ㄊㄚ ㄊㄞˊ)
a business failure; the closing of a shop; a failure; a downfall: 懶惰是他事業塌臺的主要原因。Laziness is the main cause of his downfall in business.
塌下來(ㄊㄚ ㄒㄧㄚˋ ㄌㄞˊ)
to fall down; to cave in; to collapse: 這房子因地震而塌下來。The house collapsed on account of an earthquake.
塌陷(ㄊㄚ ㄒㄧㄢˋ)
to sink; to cave in; to subside: 路基塌陷了。The roadbed has subsided.

【塚】858 (冢) ㄓㄨㄥˇ joong zhǒng
a high tomb; a mound; a grave

【塑】859 ㄙㄨˋ suh sù
1. to mold (in clay, etc.); to sculpt
2. a figure; a model: 這是一尊泥塑。It's a clay figure.
3. plastics
塑膠(ㄙㄨˋ ㄐㄧㄠ)
plastics: 現今塑膠被大量用以代替木材和金屬等。Nowadays plastics are widely used instead of wood, metal, etc.
塑膠布(ㄙㄨˋ ㄐㄧㄠ ㄅㄨˋ)
plastic cloth
塑膠皮(ㄙㄨˋ ㄐㄧㄠ ㄆㄧˊ)
plastic leather
塑膠粉(ㄙㄨˋ ㄐㄧㄠ ㄈㄣˇ)
PVC resins
塑膠袋(ㄙㄨˋ ㄐㄧㄠ ㄉㄞˋ)
plastic bags
塑膠粒(ㄙㄨˋ ㄐㄧㄠ ㄌㄧˋ)
a PVC compound
塑膠花(ㄙㄨˋ ㄐㄧㄠ ㄏㄨㄚ)
plastic flowers
塑膠炸彈(ㄙㄨˋ ㄐㄧㄠ ㄓㄚˋ ㄉㄢˋ)
a plastic bomb
塑像(ㄙㄨˋ ㄒㄧㄤˋ)
① to make an idol, image or statue ② a statue; a plastic figure: 自由女神的塑像是在紐約港內。The Statue of Liberty is in New York Bay.
塑造(ㄙㄨˋ ㄗㄠˋ)
to mold; to make by molding: 我們用黏土塑造成像。We mold statues out of clay.

【塔】860 ㄊㄚˇ taa tǎ
1. a pagoda
2. a tower: 一座白塔立在山頂上。A white tower stands on top of the hill.
3. a lighthouse
塔頂(ㄊㄚˇ ㄉㄧㄥˇ)
the top of a pagoda
塔台(ㄊㄚˇ ㄊㄞˊ)
a control tower
塔里木盆地(ㄊㄚˇ ㄌㄧˇ ㄇㄨˋ ㄆㄣˊ ㄉㄧˋ)
the Tarim Basin
塔虎脫(ㄊㄚˇ ㄏㄨˇ ㄊㄨㄛ)
William Howard Taft, 1857-1930, the 27th president of the United States
塔斯社(ㄊㄚˇ ㄙ ㄕㄜˋ)
Tass, the official Soviet news agency

【塗】861 ㄊㄨˊ twu tú
1. to smear; to apply; to spread (ointment on a wound, etc.): 塗點軟膏 to apply some ointment
2. to scribble; to scrawl
3. to erase; to blot out; to efface; to obliterate; to cross out: 塗掉這個字。Cross out this word.
4. mud; mire
5. same as 途—a way; a road
塗抹(ㄊㄨˊ ㄇㄛˇ)
① to erase; to obliterate ② to scribble; to doodle: 那男孩繼續用鉛筆胡亂塗抹。The boy continued to doodle with a pencil.
塗炭(ㄊㄨˊ ㄊㄢˋ)
mud and coals—(said of people's livelihood) in a distressing plight; in great affliction
塗料(ㄊㄨˊ ㄌㄧㄠˋ)
paint; coating
塗改(ㄊㄨˊ ㄍㄞˇ)
to erase and change the wording of an article, etc.; to alter: 本文件塗改無效。The document is invalid if altered.
塗脂抹粉(ㄊㄨˊ ㄓ ㄇㄛˇ ㄈㄣˇ)
①(literally) to apply rouge and face powder—to doll up ② to whitewash
塗飾(ㄊㄨˊ ㄕˋ)
① to cover with paint, lacquer, etc. ② to daub (plaster, etc.) on a wall; to whitewash
塗鴨(ㄊㄨˊ ㄧㄚ)
① poor calligraphy; to write badly; to scribble ② graffiti

【塘】862 ㄊㄤˊ tarng táng
1. an embankment: a bund; a bank; a dike: 河塘 a river embankment
2. a square pool; a pond; a tank: 魚塘 a fish pond 青蛙跳進池塘。A frog jumped into the pond.

【塞】863 1. ㄙㄜˋ seh sè (語音 ㄙㄞ sai sāi)
1. to block; to stop up; to clog: 樓上的水管塞住了。The water-pipe upstairs is clogged up.
2. to stuff; to squeeze in; to fill
3. a cork or stopper; to cork; to seal
塞門(ㄙㄜˋ ㄇㄣˊ)
① a screen ② a cock
塞責(ㄙㄜˋ ㄗㄜˊ)
to perform one's duties perfunctorily; to dabble in one's work: 別敷衍塞責。Don't perform your duty in a perfunctory manner.
塞滿(ㄙㄞ ㄇㄢˇ)
to stuff full; to fill up
塞住(ㄙㄞ ㄓㄨˋ)
to stop up; to block up: 這條街爲羣衆所塞住。The street was blocked up with crowds.
塞子(ㄙㄞ ·ㄗ)or 塞兒(ㄙㄚㄦ)
a cork; a stopper
塞耳不聞(ㄙㄜˋ ㄦˇ ㄅㄨˋ ㄨㄣˊ)

to turn a deaf ear to

【塞】863
2. ㄙㄞˋ say sài
strategic points along the frontiers: 要塞 a fortress

塞班島(ㄙㄞˋ ㄅㄢ ㄉㄠˇ)
the Saipan Island

塞浦路斯(ㄙㄞˋ ㄆㄨˇ ㄌㄨˋ ㄙ)
Cyprus

塞得港(ㄙㄞˋ ㄉㄜˊ ㄍㄤˇ)
Port Said in Egypt

塞納河(ㄙㄞˋ ㄋㄚˋ ㄏㄜˊ)
the Seine River

塞內加爾(ㄙㄞˋ ㄋㄟˋ ㄐㄧㄚ ㄦˇ)
Senegal

塞爾維亞(ㄙㄞˋ ㄦˇ ㄨㄟˊ ㄧㄚˋ)
Servia or Serbia, a former kingdom on the Balkans

塞外(ㄙㄞˋ ㄨㄞˋ)
beyond the borders; beyond the frontiers (especially northern frontiers of China)

塞翁失馬，焉知非福(ㄙㄞˋ ㄨㄥ ㄕ ㄇㄚˇ，ㄧㄢ ㄓ ㄈㄟ ㄈㄨˊ)
When the old man on the frontier lost his horse, who could have known it was a blessing in disguise?—A loss may turn out to be a gain.

【塡】864
ㄊㄧㄢˊ tyan tián
1. to fill up; to fill in; to stuff: 別塡錯地方。Don't fill in the wrong place.
2. the sound of drumbeats

塡報(ㄊㄧㄢˊ ㄅㄠˋ)
to fill in a form and submit it to the leadership

塡表(ㄊㄧㄢˊ ㄅㄧㄠˇ)
to fill in a blank; to fill out a form

塡補(ㄊㄧㄢˊ ㄅㄨˇ)
to fill (vacancies, etc.); to make up a deficiency; to serve as a filler: 牙醫塡補蛀牙。A dentist fills decayed teeth.

塡平(ㄊㄧㄢˊ ㄆㄧㄥˊ)
to fill up the depressions or holes on the ground

塡發(ㄊㄧㄢˊ ㄈㄚ)
to fill in and issue (as a document, certificate, etc.)

塡房(ㄊㄧㄢˊ ㄈㄤˊ)
a second wife one marries after the death of the first

塡窟窿(ㄊㄧㄢˊ ㄎㄨ ·ㄌㄨㄥ)
① to fill up a hole ② to make up a deficit or deficiency

塡空(ㄊㄧㄢˊ ㄎㄨㄥˋ)
① to fill a vacant position; to fill a vacancy ②參看「塡充①」

塡海(ㄊㄧㄢˊ ㄏㄞˇ)
to reclaim; reclamation

塡寫(ㄊㄧㄢˊ ㄒㄧㄝˇ)
to fill in (a blank, form, etc.): 請在申請表上塡寫你的姓名和學歷。Please fill in your name and educational level on the application form.

塡胸(ㄊㄧㄢˊ ㄒㄩㄥ)
to fill one's breast or heart (with anger, etc.)

塡充(ㄊㄧㄢˊ ㄔㄨㄥ)
①(a form of testing) filling the blanks ② to fill up; to stuff

塡字遊戲(ㄊㄧㄢˊ ㄗˋ ㄧㄡˊ ㄒㄧˋ)
a cross-word puzzle

塡詞(ㄊㄧㄢˊ ㄘˊ)
to compose *tzu* (a variation of old-style Chinese poetry with rigid rules)

塡塞(ㄊㄧㄢˊ ㄙㄜˋ)
to fill with; to stuff with 用沙把這洞口塡塞起來。Fill the hole with sand.

塡鴨(ㄊㄧㄢˊ ㄧㄚ)
① to stuff the duck—a time-honored way of duck feeding by stuffing the ducks to satiation and not letting them to exercise so that their meat will be tender and tasty ② to stuff students with whatever they need to pass an entrance examination to a higher school; to cram

【塢】865
ㄨˋ wuh wù
1. a low wall around a village for defense; an entrenchment; a fortified building; a castle
2. a structure which slants to a lower center on all sides; a depression; a cove; a recess: 船塢 a dock; a dockyard 花塢 a sunken flower bed

十一畫

【墓】866
ㄇㄨˋ muh mù
a grave; a tomb; a mausoleum: 陵墓 an emperor's mausoleum 公墓 a public cemetery

墓碑(ㄇㄨˋ ㄅㄟ) or 墓表(ㄇㄨˋ ㄅㄧㄠˇ)
a tombstone; a gravestone

墓門(ㄇㄨˋ ㄇㄣˊ)
the door of a tomb or grave

墓木已拱(ㄇㄨˋ ㄇㄨˋ ㄧˇ ㄍㄨㄥˇ)
(literally) The saplings around the grave have grown into big trees.— A long time has elapsed since one's death.

墓道(ㄇㄨˋ ㄉㄠˋ)
the path before a grave; the tomb passage

墓地(ㄇㄨˋ ㄉㄧˋ)
the site of a grave or tomb; a cemetery

墓穴(ㄇㄨˋ ㄒㄩㄝˋ)
the vault of a tomb; the cave where the deceased is placed

墓誌銘(ㄇㄨˋ ㄓˋ ㄇㄧㄥˊ)
an epitaph

墓園(ㄇㄨˋ ㄩㄢˊ)
a cemetery ground

【塵】867
ㄔㄣˊ chern chén
1. dust; dirt: 一塵不染 not stained with a particle of dust 他的衣服上佈滿了灰塵。His clothes were covered with dust.
2. trace; trail
3. this world; ways of the world
4. vice; sensual pleasures
5. (Taoism) a lifetime

塵表(ㄔㄣˊ ㄅㄧㄠˇ)
① out-of-the-world; world beyond the material things 亦作「塵外」② excellence; incomparable

塵凡(ㄔㄣˊ ㄈㄢˊ)
this mortal life; ways of the world; this world

塵封(ㄔㄣˊ ㄈㄥ)
to be covered all over by dust—to be laid idle for a long time

塵土(ㄔㄣˊ ㄊㄨˇ)
dust 下雨時塵土變成泥。When it rains, dust turns into mud.

〔土部〕

塵念(ㄔㄣˊ ㄋㄧㄢˋ)
worldly thoughts
塵累(ㄔㄣˊ ㄌㄟˋ)
duties and obligations of the mortal life
塵露(ㄔㄣˊ ㄌㄨˋ)
dust and dew—(figuratively) ①(said of things) insignificant ②(said of human life) transient
塵慮(ㄔㄣˊ ㄌㄩˋ)
worldly worries or desires
塵垢(ㄔㄣˊ ㄍㄡˋ)
dust and dirt
塵囂(ㄔㄣˊ ㄒㄧㄠ)
a place filled with a hubbub and an uproar
塵心(ㄔㄣˊ ㄒㄧㄣ)
worldly desires
塵世(ㄔㄣˊ ㄕˋ)
this mortal life; this world
塵俗(ㄔㄣˊ ㄙㄨˊ)
(Buddhism) this mortal life; this world
塵埃(ㄔㄣˊ ㄞ)
dust; dirt: 如果你沒有每天打掃房間，塵埃將積聚。If you do not sweep your room every day, dust will accumulate.
塵務(ㄔㄣˊ ㄨˋ)
worldly affairs; mundane affairs
塵緣(ㄔㄣˊ ㄩㄢˊ)
worldly passions; mundane desires; love affairs

【塹】 868 ㄑㄧㄢˋ chiann qiàn
1. the moat around a city; a chasm; a trench: 天塹 a natural chasm for defense
2. a pit; a hole or cavity in the ground
塹壕(ㄑㄧㄢˋ ㄏㄠˊ)
moats; trenches

【塾】 869 ㄕㄨˊ shwu shú
1. an anteroom or vestibule
2. a family school; a village school; a private primary school: 家塾 a school at home with a private tutor
塾師(ㄕㄨˊ ㄕ)
the tutor of a family or village school

【境】 870 ㄐㄧㄥˋ jinq jìng
1. a boundary; a frontier; a border: 強盜逃過邊境。The bandits fled across the border.
2. a place; an area
3. a state; a situation; circumstances: 處境困難 to be in a difficult situation
境地(ㄐㄧㄥˋ ㄉㄧˋ)
① territory ② a state; a condition; a position; a situation
境內(ㄐㄧㄥˋ ㄋㄟˋ)
within the border; in the country
境況(ㄐㄧㄥˋ ㄎㄨㄤˋ)
a situation; a condition
境界(ㄐㄧㄥˋ ㄐㄧㄝˋ)
① a boundary ② a situation; a condition ③ a state (of mind); a realm: 理想境界 an ideal state
境遇(ㄐㄧㄥˋ ㄩˋ)
① circumstances; condition ② vicissitudes in one's life; what one has encountered in life
境域(ㄐㄧㄥˋ ㄩˋ)
territory; land within the boundary of a state

【墅】 871 ㄕㄨˋ shuh shù
a villa; a country house: 他在北投有一幢別墅。He has a villa in Peitou.

【墉】 872 ㄩㄥ iong yōng (又讀 ㄩㄥˊ yong yóng)
a fortified wall; a wall
墉垣(ㄩㄥ ㄩㄢˊ)
the city wall

【墊】 873 ㄉㄧㄢˋ diann diàn
1. to advance (money); to pay for another and expect to be paid back
2. a cushion; a pad ; a bed-mat
3. to cushion; to put something under another (to make it level)
4. to sink into
5. to dig
墊被(ㄉㄧㄢˋ ㄅㄟˋ)
a mattress
墊補(ㄉㄧㄢˋ ㄅㄨˇ)
to defray expenses not budgeted
墊平(ㄉㄧㄢˋ ㄆㄧㄥˊ)
to level up 亦作「填平」: 他們想把運動場墊平。They wish to level the playground.
墊付(ㄉㄧㄢˋ ㄈㄨˋ)
to pay for another temporarily
墊款(ㄉㄧㄢˋ ㄎㄨㄢˇ)
① to advance money for another on the understanding that he will return it on a future date ② money thus advanced
墊脚石(ㄉㄧㄢˋ ㄐㄧㄠˇ ㄕˊ)
a steppingstone
墊肩(ㄉㄧㄢˋ ㄐㄧㄢ)
a shoulder pad(or padding)
墊圈(ㄉㄧㄢˋ ㄑㄩㄢ)
(machinery) a washer
墊上運動(ㄉㄧㄢˋ ㄕㄤˋ ㄩㄣˋ ㄉㄨㄥˋ)
gymnastics on mattress
墊子(ㄉㄧㄢˋ ·ㄗ)
cushions; mattresses; mats: 沙發上有好幾個墊子。There are several cushions on the sofa.

十二畫

【墟】 874 ㄒㄩ shiu xū
1. a high mound
2. an ancient town; a ghost town: 廢墟 ruins
3. wild, waste land
4. a periodical marketplace where goods are bartered
5. to ruin; to destroy
墟里(ㄒㄩ ㄌㄧˇ)
a small village
墟市(ㄒㄩ ㄕˋ)
the fair grounds of a village

【墀】 875 ㄔˊ chyr chí
steps leading up to a palace; palace steps

【墜】 876 ㄓㄨㄟˋ juey zhuì
to fall down; to sink; the fall (of a person, a state, etc.): 飛機墜入海中。The plane crashed into the sea.
墜馬(ㄓㄨㄟˋ ㄇㄚˇ)
to fall off a horse
墜地(ㄓㄨㄟˋ ㄉㄧˋ)
① to fall ② failure ③ to come to this world
墜胎(ㄓㄨㄟˋ ㄊㄞ)
abortion; to abort 亦作「墮胎」
墜樓(ㄓㄨㄟˋ ㄌㄡˊ)

to fall from a building; to commit suicide by jumping from a building

墜落(ㄓㄨㄟˋ ㄌㄨㄛˋ)
to fall; to drop

墜毀(ㄓㄨㄟˋ ㄏㄨㄟˇ)
(said of a plane, etc.) to fall and break; to crash: 飛機在山邊墜毀。The airplane crashed on a hillside.

墜緒(ㄓㄨㄟˋ ㄒㄩˋ)
a failing (business, etc.); a hopeless case

墜子(ㄓㄨㄟˋ ·ㄗ)
① earrings; eardrops ② a pendant or pendants attached to a bigger object as ornaments ③a kind of folk song originated in Honan Province and later spread to other northern provinces

【增】 877 ㄗㄥ tzeng zēng
to add to; to increase; to grow; to enlarge: 他的知識與日俱增。His knowledge is steadily on the increase. 他們的友情日增。Their friendship was growing daily.

增補(ㄗㄥ ㄅㄨˇ)
to add to; to supplement; to increase and supplement: 本公司人員略有增補。The staff of our company has been slightly augmented.

增訂(ㄗㄥ ㄉㄧㄥˋ)
(usually said of a book, etc.) to revise and enlarge

增訂本(ㄗㄥ ㄉㄧㄥˋ ㄅㄣˇ)
a revised and enlarged edition: 這是最新增訂本。This is the newest revised and enlarged edition.

增多(ㄗㄥ ㄉㄨㄛ)
to add to; to increase: 他家人口增多。His family increased.

增添(ㄗㄥ ㄊㄧㄢ)
to add to; to supplement: 他的病增添家中的困難。His illness added to the family's troubles.

增添項目(ㄗㄥ ㄊㄧㄢ ㄒㄧㄤˋ ㄇㄨˋ)
an addition item

增光(ㄗㄥ ㄍㄨㄤ)
to glorify; to do credit to; to add to the prestige of: 他爲國增光。He does credit to his country.

增廣(ㄗㄥ ㄍㄨㄤˇ)
to widen (one's knowledge, etc.); to enlarge; to advance: 增廣知識 to widen one's knowledge

增刊(ㄗㄥ ㄎㄢ)
a supplement—as of newspaper, etc.; (said of newspapers, etc.) an enlarged edition on holidays or Sundays

增加(ㄗㄥ ㄐㄧㄚ)
to add to; to increase; increase: 這件事增加我們的困難。This adds to our difficulties.

增加率(ㄗㄥ ㄐㄧㄚ ㄌㄩˋ)
the rate of increase

增價(ㄗㄥ ㄐㄧㄚˋ)
increment

增減(ㄗㄥ ㄐㄧㄢˇ)
increases and decreases; fluctuations

增進(ㄗㄥ ㄐㄧㄣˋ)
to advance; to promote (friendship, etc.); to increase (knowledge, etc.)

增強(ㄗㄥ ㄑㄧㄤˊ)
to strengthen; to heighten; to enhance

增值(ㄗㄥ ㄓˊ)
to increase the value; value increment; appreciation; increment

增值稅(ㄗㄥ ㄓˊ ㄕㄨㄟˋ)
VAT (value-added tax): 土地增值稅 land increment tax

增長(ㄗㄥ ㄓㄤˇ)
increases and advances; a rise; to grow: 我們國家的人口在迅速增長。The population of our country is growing rapidly.

增產(ㄗㄥ ㄔㄢˇ)
to increase production; the increase of production

增刪(ㄗㄥ ㄕㄢ)
(usually said of a script, etc.) to emendate; to revise (a book); to add and to delete

增資(ㄗㄥ ㄗ)
to increase capitalization

增損(ㄗㄥ ㄙㄨㄣˇ)
profits and losses

增益(ㄗㄥ ㄧˋ)
①to increase; to profit; to augment ②(electronics) gain

增援(ㄗㄥ ㄩㄢˊ)
to send reinforcements; to build up troop level

【墨】 878 ㄇㄛˋ moh mò
1. black; dark
2. a black dye
3. a Chinese inkstick; ink
4. calligraphy; handwriting or painting: 遺墨 writing or paintings left by the deceased
5. literate; letters; learning
6. statutes; institutions
7. greedy; covetous; corrupt
8. to tattoo the face—one of the five punishments in ancient China
9. a Chinese family name

墨寶(ㄇㄛˋ ㄅㄠˇ)
treasured calligraphic works

墨斗(ㄇㄛˋ ㄉㄡˇ)
an ink cup used by the carpenter to make markings

墨吏(ㄇㄛˋ ㄌㄧˋ)
corrupt officials

墨綠(ㄇㄛˋ ㄌㄩˋ)
blackish green

墨客(ㄇㄛˋ ㄎㄜˋ)
men of letters 參看「騷人墨客」

墨盒(ㄇㄛˋ ㄏㄜˊ)
a small case containing Chinese ink held by wet cotton; an ink box

墨海(ㄇㄛˋ ㄏㄞˇ)
an ink slab; an inkstone 亦作「硯臺」

墨痕(ㄇㄛˋ ㄏㄣˊ)
ink marks

墨迹(ㄇㄛˋ ㄐㄧ)
the original handwriting of a famous figure; ink marks: 這是孫中山先生的墨迹。This is Dr. Sun Yat-sen's calligraphy.

墨家(ㄇㄛˋ ㄐㄧㄚ)
(Chinese philosophy) the school of Mo Ti(墨翟); the Mohists

墨鏡(ㄇㄛˋ ㄐㄧㄥˋ)
sunglasses

墨西哥(ㄇㄛˋ ㄒㄧ ㄍㄜ)
Mexico

墨西哥人(ㄇㄛˋ ㄒㄧ ㄍㄜ ㄖㄣˊ)

〔土部〕

a Mexican
墨西哥灣(ㄇㄛˋ ㄒㄧ ㄍㄜ ㄨㄢ)
the Gulf of Mexico
墨線(ㄇㄛˋ ㄒㄧㄢˋ)
a thread used by carpenters for marking 亦作「繩墨」
墨刑(ㄇㄛˋ ㄒㄧㄥˊ)
to tattoo the face—an ancient Chinese punishment
墨汁(ㄇㄛˋ ㄓ)or 墨水(ㄇㄛˋ ㄕㄨㄟˇ)
① Chinese dark ink; ink ② letters; learning: 他肚子裏喝了不少墨水。He has read a great many books.
墨竹(ㄇㄛˋ ㄓㄨˊ)
bamboos painted on paper with Chinese ink
墨守成規(ㄇㄛˋ ㄕㄡˇ ㄔㄥˊ ㄍㄨㄟ)
to stick to old rules; conservative: 他墨守成規。He is conservative.
墨子(ㄇㄛˋ ㄗˇ)
Mo Ti (墨翟) or Mocius, one of the great philosophers of the Epoch of Warring States, who preached love without distinction
墨爾缽(ㄇㄛˋ ㄦˇ ㄅㄛ)
Melbourne, an Australian city
墨魚(ㄇㄛˋ ㄩˊ)
the squid; the cuttlefish 亦作「墨斗魚」or「烏賊」

【墩】879 ㄉㄨㄣ duen dūn
1. a mound; a heap
2. a block of stone or wood
3. a cluster

【墮】880 ㄉㄨㄛˋ duoh duò
1. to fall; to sink; to let fall
2. to indulge in evil ways
3. lazy; idle
墮胎(ㄉㄨㄛˋ ㄊㄞ)
abortion; to abort; to have a miscarriage
墮落(ㄉㄨㄛˋ ㄌㄨㄛˋ)
① to indulge in evil ways; to sink in moral standard; to degenerate; degeneracy; 飲酒和賭博使他徹底墮落了。Drinking and gambling sank him completely. ② the fall (of a nation, family, etc.)
墮入(ㄉㄨㄛˋ ㄖㄨˋ)
to sink or lapse into; to land oneself in; to fall into: 那隻熊墮入陷阱裏。The bear fell into the trap.

十三畫

【墳】881 ㄈㄣˊ fern fén
1. a grave; a mound
2. big; large; great
3. the banks of a river
墳墓(ㄈㄣˊ ㄇㄨˋ)
a grave; a tomb
墳地(ㄈㄣˊ ㄉㄧˋ)or 墳場(ㄈㄣˊ ㄔㄤˇ)or (ㄈㄣˊ ㄔㄤˊ)
a place of burial; a cemetery; a graveyard
墳典(ㄈㄣˊ ㄉㄧㄢˇ)
ancient books
墳塋(ㄈㄣˊ ㄧㄥˊ)
① a grave; a tomb ② a graveyard; a cemetery

【壁】882 ㄅㄧˋ bih bì
1. a partition wall; the walls of a room
2. a military breastwork
3. a cliff
壁報(ㄅㄧˋ ㄅㄠˋ)
a wall paper; a wall poster; a wall newspaper
壁燈(ㄅㄧˋ ㄉㄥ)
lamps hung on a screenwall; wall lamps; bracket lamps
壁毯(ㄅㄧˋ ㄊㄢˇ)
tapestry (used to hang on walls)
壁壘分明(ㄅㄧˋ ㄌㄟˇ ㄈㄣ ㄇㄧㄥˊ)
The stands of the opposing camps are distinctively different. —There is no compromise between the contending factions.
壁壘森嚴(ㄅㄧˋ ㄌㄟˇ ㄙㄣ ㄧㄢˊ)
① an unassailable stronghold; strong defense preparations; strongly fortified; closely guarded ② with a clear-cut line of demarcation; a strong sense of partisanship; sharply divided
壁立(ㄅㄧˋ ㄌㄧˋ)
① to stand bolt upright ② poverty-stricken
壁爐(ㄅㄧˋ ㄌㄨˊ)
a fireplace
壁虎(ㄅㄧˋ ㄏㄨˇ)
a house-lizard or gecko
壁虎功(ㄅㄧˋ ㄏㄨˇ ㄍㄨㄥ)
the ability to climb walls without tools
壁畫(ㄅㄧˋ ㄏㄨㄚˋ)
a mural painting; a fresco
壁櫥(ㄅㄧˋ ㄔㄨˊ)
a closet; a wall chest
壁上觀(ㄅㄧˋ ㄕㄤˋ ㄍㄨㄢ)
to watch a fight or struggle without helping either party
壁有耳(ㄅㄧˋ ㄧㄡˇ ㄦˇ)
Beware of eavesdropping!

【墾】883 ㄎㄣˇ keen kěn
to open new land for farming, etc.; to reclaim land: 他開墾過一大片土地。He opened a large piece of land.
墾丁公園(ㄎㄣˇ ㄉㄧㄥ ㄍㄨㄥ ㄩㄢˊ)
Kending Park, Pingtung
墾荒(ㄎㄣˇ ㄏㄨㄤ)
to open up barren land for farming
墾殖(ㄎㄣˇ ㄓˊ)
to reclaim land and cultivate it

【壅】884 ㄩㄥˇ yeong yǒng
(又讀 ㄩㄥ iong yōng)
1. to stop; to block up
2. to bank up the roots of plants
3. to obstruct; to impede (flow, etc.)
壅蔽(ㄩㄥ ㄅㄧˋ)
to conceal; to block up; to cover 亦作「雍閉」
壅隔(ㄩㄥ ㄍㄜˊ)
to block up; to obstruct or stop the flow of (a river, etc.); to dam
壅塞(ㄩㄥ ㄙㄜˋ)
to block up; to obstruct; to impede; to congeal the flow of (a sewerage pipe, etc.): 這條街擠滿群衆壅塞不通。The street was blocked up with crowds.

【壇】885 ㄊㄢˊ tarn tán
1. a platform for sacrificial rites; an altar: 禮堂裏有一個供演講人用的講壇。There is a platform for speakers in the hall.
2. a hall for important meetings and ceremonies in ancient China

十四畫

【壓】 886
ㄧㄚ ia yā

1. to press; to oppress; to pressure: 稅金重壓著他。The taxes pressed him.
2. to control; to quell: 我強壓住心頭怒火。I tried hard to control my anger.
3. to crush
4. (said of enemy troops, etc.) to close in; to press near
5. to hold (a document, etc.) without taking action; to pigeonhole; to shelve
6. a way of making a stroke in Chinese calligraphy
7. to excel; to surpass others (in ability, etc.): 他在考試中壓倒群雄。He excelled all the rest in the examination.

壓寶(ㄧㄚ ㄅㄠˇ)
to place one's stake at a Chinese gambling game in which the odds are three to one; a gambling or guessing game, played with dice under a bowl

壓扁(ㄧㄚ ㄅㄧㄢˇ)
to flatten by pressure: 小盒子給上面的重書壓扁了。The small box was flattened by the pressure of the heavy book on it.

壓不住(ㄧㄚ ·ㄅㄨ ㄓㄨˋ)
to be unable to command or exercise control over a group of people due to lack of prestige, personal ability, etc.

壓迫(ㄧㄚ ㄆㄛˋ)
①to press hard; to oppress; to pressure; to force: 好的統治者不會壓迫貧民。A good ruler will not oppress the poor. ②oppression; pressure: 他們是壓迫下的犧牲者。They are victims of oppression.

壓破(ㄧㄚ ㄆㄛˋ)
to break something by applying pressure; broken by high pressure

壓平(ㄧㄚ ㄆㄧㄥˊ)
to press something so as to make it flat and smooth

壓服(ㄧㄚ ㄈㄨˊ)
to subjugate; to force (a nation, person, etc.) to her knees; to coerce

壓得住(ㄧㄚ ·ㄉㄜ ㄓㄨˋ)
①to have the ability to undertake a task or responsibility ②to keep down (anger, etc.)

壓倒(ㄧㄚ ㄉㄠˇ)
to surpass; to overwhelm; to excel; to win: 困難不能壓倒他們。No difficulty can overwhelm them.

壓倒性勝利(ㄧㄚ ㄉㄠˇ ㄒㄧㄥˋ ㄕㄥˋ ㄌㄧˋ)
an overwhelming victory; a landslide victory

壓隊(ㄧㄚ ㄉㄨㄟˋ)
(literally) to walk behind a team—to supervise, or to oversee

壓臺戲(ㄧㄚ ㄊㄞˊ ㄒㄧˋ)or 壓軸戲(ㄧㄚ ㄓㄡˊ ㄒㄧˋ)
the best act of a show (which usually comes last in a Chinese operatic performance)

壓條(ㄧㄚ ㄊㄧㄠˊ)or 壓枝(ㄧㄚ ㄓ)
(agriculture) layering

壓力(ㄧㄚ ㄌㄧˋ)
①(physics) pressure ②overwhelming force; pressure

壓路機(ㄧㄚ ㄌㄨˋ ㄐㄧ)
a roller (for road-surfacing)

壓根兒(ㄧㄚ ㄍㄜㄦ)
(used in negative assertions) totally; entirely; completely: 他壓根兒不會唱歌。He cannot sing at all.

壓克力(ㄧㄚ ㄎㄜˋ ㄌㄧˋ)
(chemistry) acrylic resin

壓克力玻璃(ㄧㄚ ㄎㄜˋ ㄌㄧˋ ㄅㄛ ·ㄌㄧ)
acrylic-plastic sheets (manufactured in Taiwan under the trademark "Acrypoly")

壓壞(ㄧㄚ ㄏㄨㄞˋ)
damaged by high pressure or a heavy load

壓擠(ㄧㄚ ㄐㄧˇ)
to extrude; extrusion

壓價(ㄧㄚ ㄐㄧㄚˋ)
to force prices down; to demand a lower price

壓緊(ㄧㄚ ㄐㄧㄣˇ)
to make something tight or constrict by applying high pressure; to pack

壓驚(ㄧㄚ ㄐㄧㄥ)
to help someone get over a shock (by entertaining him, etc.); to becalm nerves after a shock

壓境(ㄧㄚ ㄐㄧㄥˋ)
(usually said of enemy troops) to mass on, or approach the border: 敵方大軍壓境。A large enemy force is moving quickly towards the border.

壓卷(ㄧㄚ ㄐㄩㄢˋ)
the composition or writing that excels or surpasses all the others

壓線(ㄧㄚ ㄒㄧㄢˋ)
①(sports) a line ball ②to be kept busy on other's account (like a needlewoman making gold braids for other's wedding dress)

壓制(ㄧㄚ ㄓˋ)
①to suppress (one's anger, etc.); to restrain (usually by force) ②(military) to neutralize (enemy fire by massive bombardment)

壓榨 or 壓搾(ㄧㄚ ㄓㄚˋ)
①to oppress; to extort; oppression; extortion ②to extract (liquids) by applying high pressure

壓寨夫人(ㄧㄚ ㄓㄞˋ ㄈㄨ ㄖㄣˊ)
the wife of a brigand chief; the wife of the leader of bandits

壓軸好戲(ㄧㄚ ㄓㄡˊ ㄏㄠˇ ㄒㄧˋ)
the last but best one of a series of performances

壓住(ㄧㄚ ㄓㄨˋ)
to suppress; to put down by force

壓差(ㄧㄚ ㄔㄚ)
pressure difference

壓車(ㄧㄚ ㄔㄜ)
to go with the truck personally as a supervisor 亦作「押車」

壓舌板(ㄧㄚ ㄕㄜˊ ㄅㄢˇ)
(medicine) a tongue depressor

壓死(ㄧㄚ ㄙˇ)
①to crush to death ②to die after being hit by a car

壓縮(ㄧㄚ ㄙㄨㄛ)
to compress; to condense; to

reduce; to cut down: 棉花壓縮成包。Cotton is compressed into bales.

壓縮性(ㄧㄚ ㄙㄨㄛ ㄒㄧㄥˋ)
compressibility

壓碎(ㄧㄚ ㄙㄨㄟˋ)
to crush to pieces: 他們壓碎石子以製水泥。They make cement by crushing down stone.

壓歲錢(ㄧㄚ ㄙㄨㄟˋ ㄑㄧㄢˊ)
(red paper bags) containing cash distributed to children by elders on lunar New Year's Eve

壓抑(ㄧㄚ ㄧˋ)
to curb; to repress; to suppress (one's emotions, etc.): 操心和憂愁壓抑着她。Care and sorrow oppressed her.

壓韻(ㄧㄚ ㄩㄣˋ)
to rhyme 參看「押韻」

【壎】887 ㄒㄩㄣ shiun xūn
an ancient Chinese wind instrument, made of porcelain and shaped like an egg

壎箎(ㄒㄩㄣ ㄔˊ)
two musical instruments played together harmoniously—signifying the love between brothers

【壑】888 ㄏㄨㄛˋ huoh huò
1. a gully; a channel for water
2. a narrow ravine at the foot of a hill: 林壑之勝 the grandeur of woods and ravines

壑溝(ㄏㄨㄛˋ ㄍㄡ)
a ditch; a narrow strip of water; the moat around a city wall: 死於壑溝 to die in a ditch

【壕】889 ㄏㄠˊ haur háo
1. the ditch around a city wall; a moat
2. a trench; a dugout

壕溝(ㄏㄠˊ ㄍㄡ)
a trench (in warfare); a ditch

十五畫

【壙】890 ㄎㄨㄤˋ kuanq kuàng
1. a vault; a tomb
2. a field; an open (or wild) space
3. to leave vacant or idle

壙穴(ㄎㄨㄤˋ ㄒㄩㄝˋ)
the vault of a tomb

【壘】891 ㄌㄟˇ leei lěi
1. a military wall; a rampart
2. to pile up: 雪愈壘愈高。The snow is piling up.
3. a base (on a baseball diamond): 他在二壘。He is on the second base.
4. a Chinese family name

壘球(ㄌㄟˇ ㄑㄧㄡˊ)
softball: 我喜歡打壘球。I like to play softball.

十六畫

【壟】892 ㄌㄨㄥˇ loong lǒng
1. a grave; a mound of earth
2. a high place in a field

壟斷(ㄌㄨㄥˇ ㄉㄨㄢˋ)
a monopoly; to monopolize; to corner: 他們壟斷了棉花市場。They cornered the cotton market.

【壞】893 ㄏㄨㄞˋ huay huài
1. broken down; decaying; rotten; out of order; useless: 肉類比蔬菜更容易腐壞。Meat decays much easier than vegetables.
2. bad; poor (scores, marks, etc.): 有人說吸煙是一種壞習慣。Some people say that smoking is a bad habit.
3. vicious; mean; evil (persons, etc.)

壞坯子(ㄏㄨㄞˋ ㄆㄟ ·ㄗ)
a bad egg; a lout

壞蛋(ㄏㄨㄞˋ ㄉㄢˋ)
(literally) a rotten egg—a bad fellow; an evil person; a louse; a villain 亦作「壞坯子」

壞東西(ㄏㄨㄞˋ ㄉㄨㄥ ·ㄒㄧ)
a bad person or thing; an evil fellow

壞透(ㄏㄨㄞˋ ㄊㄡˋ)
bad to the bone; rotten to the core; evil to the very marrow: 這個人的品行壞透了。The man's morals are rotten to the core.

壞良心(ㄏㄨㄞˋ ㄌㄧㄤˊ ㄒㄧㄣ)
heartless; a depraved conscience

壞話(ㄏㄨㄞˋ ㄏㄨㄚˋ)
slander: 他根本沒有說他們的壞話。He spoke no ill of them.

壞疽(ㄏㄨㄞˋ ㄐㄩ)
gangrene

壞球(ㄏㄨㄞˋ ㄑㄧㄡˊ)
(baseball) ball

壞血病(ㄏㄨㄞˋ ㄒㄧㄝˇ ㄅㄧㄥˋ)
scurvy; scorbutus

壞心眼兒(ㄏㄨㄞˋ ㄒㄧㄣ ㄧㄚˇㄦ)
malicious; ill-intentioned; devious; devilish

壞主意(ㄏㄨㄞˋ ㄓㄨˇ ㄧˋ)
a wicked or crooked idea; a scheme to trick or trap somebody 亦作「壞念頭」

壞處(ㄏㄨㄞˋ ㄔㄨˋ)
bad points; shortcomings; defects: 從壞處著想，往好處努力。Prepare for the worst; make an effort for the best.

壞事(ㄏㄨㄞˋ ㄕˋ)
① a bad thing; an evil deed
② to ruin something; to make things worse: 鹵莽只會壞事。Overboldness will only make things worse.

壞人(ㄏㄨㄞˋ ㄖㄣˊ)
a bad guy; an evil person

壞死(ㄏㄨㄞˋ ㄙˇ)
a necrosis: 局部壞死 a local necrosis

十七畫

【壤】894 ㄖㄤˇ raang rǎng
1. loose soil
2. earth: 他們倆人的個性有天壤之別。They are vastly different from each other in personality as heaven from earth.
3. a region; a place; a land: 他住在窮鄉僻壤。He lives in a remote and backward region.
4. rich; abundant
5. a Chinese family name

壤土(ㄖㄤˇ ㄊㄨˇ)
loam

壤界(ㄖㄤˇ ㄐㄧㄝˋ)
boundary of a piece of land

二十一畫

【壩】 895 ㄅㄚˋ bah bà

1. an embankment; a dike: 堤壩已築成了。The embankment has been thrown up.
2. a dam: 我們剛完成了一個新的大水壩。We have just completed a new big dam.

壩工(ㄅㄚˋ ㄍㄨㄥ)
dam construction works

士部 ㄕˋ shyh shì

【士】 896 ㄕˋ shyh shì

1. a scholar; a man of learning; a gentleman
2. an official rank in ancient China; an officer
3. a noncommissioned officer
4. a person
5. name of a chessman in Chinese chess
6. a Chinese family name

士飽馬騰(ㄕˋ ㄅㄠˇ ㄇㄚˇ ㄊㄥˊ)
(said of troops) well-fed and highly-motivated

士別三日刮目相看(ㄕˋ ㄅㄧㄝˊ ㄙㄢ ㄖˋ ㄍㄨㄚ ㄇㄨˋ ㄒㄧㄤ ㄎㄢˋ)
(literally) One should make a reappraisal of a scholar after a separation of three days.—A scholar who constantly makes improvement deserves a new appraisal of his achievements every now and then.

士兵(ㄕˋ ㄅㄧㄥ)
soldiers; privates; enlisted men

士敏土(ㄕˋ ㄇㄧㄣˇ ㄊㄨˇ)
cement 亦作「水泥」

士大夫(ㄕˋ ㄉㄚˋ ㄈㄨ)
① a person with official rank; an official ② a general ③ a person of learning; a scholar

士農工商(ㄕˋ ㄋㄨㄥˊ ㄍㄨㄥ ㄕㄤ)
scholars, farmers, workers and merchants—the social castes in ancient China

士林(ㄕˋ ㄌㄧㄣˊ)
the intelligentsia; a scholastic community; literary circles

士官(ㄕˋ ㄍㄨㄢ)
noncommissioned officers

士官長(ㄕˋ ㄍㄨㄢ ㄓㄤˇ)
a master sergeant

士可殺不可辱(ㄕˋ ㄎㄜˇ ㄕㄚ ㄅㄨˋ ㄎㄜˇ ㄖㄨˇ)
A gentleman prefers death to humiliation.

士氣(ㄕˋ ㄑㄧˋ)
① the morale of a fighting force ② the trends and temperaments of scholars in a given era

士紳(ㄕˋ ㄕㄣ)
the gentry

士庶(ㄕˋ ㄕㄨˋ)
the common people

士人(ㄕˋ ㄖㄣˊ)
a scholar; an educated man

士子(ㄕˋ ㄗˇ)
the candidates of the civil service examination in ancient China

士卒(ㄕˋ ㄗㄨˊ)
soldiers; enlisted men; army privates: 戰爭中這隊長總是身先士卒。In war the captain always fought at the head of his men.

士族(ㄕˋ ㄗㄨˊ)
the gentry (in the South and North Dynasties)

士爲知己者死(ㄕˋ ㄨㄟˋ ㄓ ㄐㄧˇ ㄓㄜˇ ㄙˇ)
A gentleman is ready to die for his good friends.

一畫

【壬】 897 ㄖㄣˊ ren rén

1. the ninth of the Ten Celestial Stems
2. artful and crafty
3. great
4. pregnant

壬人(ㄖㄣˊ ㄖㄣˊ)
an artful person; a cunning deceiver

四畫

【壯】 898 ㄓㄨㄤˋ juanq zhuàng

1. big; great
2. strong; robust; vigorous; sturdy: 他是個強壯的小伙子。He is a robust young fellow.
3. portly; stout
4. to strengthen; to make better
5. the prime of one's life
6. another name for the eighth moon of the lunar calendar

壯美(ㄓㄨㄤˋ ㄇㄟˇ)
grandeur and serenity; splendor; sublime

壯大(ㄓㄨㄤˋ ㄉㄚˋ)
① big and strong; vigorous ② to grow in strength; to expand

壯膽(ㄓㄨㄤˋ ㄉㄢˇ)
to strengthen one's courage; to embolden

壯丁(ㄓㄨㄤˋ ㄉㄧㄥ)
① an able-bodied man ② an adult fit for military service

壯圖(ㄓㄨㄤˋ ㄊㄨˊ)
an ambitious attempt; an attempt at something spectacular

壯年(ㄓㄨㄤˋ ㄋㄧㄢˊ)
the prime of one's life

壯麗(ㄓㄨㄤˋ ㄌㄧˋ)
grand and imposing; splendorous

壯烈(ㄓㄨㄤˋ ㄌㄧㄝˋ)
courageous; on a grand and spectacular scale

壯烈犧牲(ㄓㄨㄤˋ ㄌㄧㄝˋ ㄒㄧ ㄕㄥ)
to die as a martyr; to die a hero's death; to die for one's country; to heroically give one's life

壯觀(ㄓㄨㄤˋ ㄍㄨㄢ)
a grand sight; a great sight; a beautiful view; a breathtaking or spectacular view; an impressive sight

壯闊(ㄓㄨㄤˋ ㄎㄨㄛˋ)
vast; grand; magnificent; grandiose

壯健(ㄓㄨㄤˋ ㄐㄧㄢˋ)
healthy and strong

壯舉(ㄓㄨㄤˋ ㄐㄩˇ)
a great achievement; a daring act; a courageous feat; a heroic undertaking: 這是史無前例的壯舉。This is an unprecedented courageous feat.

壯志(ㄓㄨㄤˋ ㄓˋ)

great aspiration; great ambition

壯志凌雲(ㄓㄨㄤˋ ㄓˋ ㄌㄧㄥˊ ㄩㄣˊ)
a soaring ambition or aspiration; with soaring aspirations

壯志未酬(ㄓㄨㄤˋ ㄓˋ ㄨㄟˋ ㄔㄡˊ)
(usually said of a martyr, a hero, etc.) to die before the fulfillment of his ambition or aspiration

壯實(ㄓㄨㄤˋ ·ㄕ)
sturdy; robust: 他是一個壯實的小伙子。He's a sturdy young chap.

壯士(ㄓㄨㄤˋ ㄕˋ)
a brave man; a man of stout heart; a hero; a warrior

壯盛(ㄓㄨㄤˋ ㄕㄥˋ)
strong and prosperous; healthy

壯遊(ㄓㄨㄤˋ ㄧㄡˊ)
① a splendid tour; an exciting trip; a great tour or trip ② to take a long trip for an ambitious project; an ambitious trip—as a trip to space by astronauts

九畫

【壻】 899
(婿) ㄒㄩˋ shiuh xù
1. one's son-in-law
2. one's husband: 他是我的妹壻。He is my younger sister's husband.

【壹】 900
ㄧ i yī
an elaborate form of "一" (one) used mostly in accounting and especially in checks to prevent forgery or alterations

【壺】 901
ㄏㄨˊ hwu hú
1. a pot; a jug; a winevessel
2. any potbellied container with a small opening
3. a Chinese family name

壺中物(ㄏㄨˊ ㄓㄨㄥ ㄨˋ)
wine; liquor; drinks

十畫

【壼】 902
ㄎㄨㄣˇ koen kǔn
a lane, passageway or corridor in a palace

壼範(ㄎㄨㄣˇ ㄈㄢˋ)
a paragon of feminine virtues

十一畫

【壽】 903
ㄕㄡˋ show shòu
1. the life span: 現代醫藥已增加人類的壽命。Modern medicine has increased man's life span.
2. old age; a long life; longevity
3. birthday: 他向張先生祝壽。He congratulated Mr. Chang on his birthday.
4. to die of old age
5. to present another with gold, silk, etc.
6. to toast an elder
7. a Chinese family name

壽比南山(ㄕㄡˋ ㄅㄧˇ ㄋㄢˊ ㄕㄢ)
(a greeting for a person on his birthday) May your life be as lofty as the Southern Mountain Ranges. 或 Many happy returns of the day!

壽屏(ㄕㄡˋ ㄆㄧㄥˊ)
a long vertical scroll inscribed with writings wishing another a long life

壽麵(ㄕㄡˋ ㄇㄧㄢˋ)
long noodles eaten on birthday to symbolize a long life; birthday noodles

壽命(ㄕㄡˋ ㄇㄧㄥˋ)
the life span of a person

壽誕(ㄕㄡˋ ㄉㄢˋ)
a birthday anniversary

壽桃(ㄕㄡˋ ㄊㄠˊ)
longevity peaches—made of flour in the shape of a peach and presented to another on his birthday

壽頭壽腦(ㄕㄡˋ ㄊㄡˊ ㄕㄡˋ ㄋㄠˇ)
stupid-looking

壽堂(ㄕㄡˋ ㄊㄤˊ)
a specially decorated hall where well-wishers come to offer congratulations to a person on his birthday

壽禮(ㄕㄡˋ ㄌㄧˇ)or 壽儀(ㄕㄡˋ ㄧˊ)
birthday gifts or presents

壽聯(ㄕㄡˋ ㄌㄧㄢˊ)
longevity couplets; couplets presented to a person on his birthday wishing him a long life

壽考(ㄕㄡˋ ㄎㄠˇ)
long life

壽器(ㄕㄡˋ ㄑㄧˋ)
a coffin prepared when one is alive

壽險(ㄕㄡˋ ㄒㄧㄢˇ)
life insurance 亦作「人壽保險」

壽星(ㄕㄡˋ ㄒㄧㄥ)
① the host of a birthday feast or party; a reference to a person on his birthday ② the God of Longevity ③ Canopus

壽序(ㄕㄡˋ ㄒㄩˋ)
a writing or literary work wishing another longevity on his birthday

壽終正寢(ㄕㄡˋ ㄓㄨㄥ ㄓㄥˋ ㄑㄧㄣˇ)
to die of old age; to die a natural death (now used in the obituary)

壽冢(ㄕㄡˋ ㄓㄨㄥˇ)
a graveyard laid out before one dies

壽辰(ㄕㄡˋ ㄔㄣˊ)
birthday

壽數(ㄕㄡˋ ㄕㄨˋ)or 壽算(ㄕㄡˋ ㄙㄨㄢˋ)
the allotted life span of a person; a person's destined age

壽材(ㄕㄡˋ ㄘㄞˊ)
① a coffin prepared before one's death ② a coffin

壽衣(ㄕㄡˋ ㄧ)
clothes prepared by a person during his lifetime to assure that he will be properly dressed after his death

夂部
ㄙㄨㄟ suei suī

七畫

【夏】 904
1. ㄒㄧㄚˋ shiah xià
1. summer: 我在一九八五年夏天去美國。I went to America in the summer of 1985.
2. big; spacious
3. a big house; a mansion

4. Cathay, the ancient name of China: 華夏 China; Chinese
5. a dynasty in Chinese history (2205-1782 B.C.): 夏朝, 夏代, 夏室 the Hsia Dynasty
6. a Chinese family name

夏布(ㄒㄧㄚˋ ㄅㄨˋ)
Chinese linen cloth for summer wear

夏天(ㄒㄧㄚˋ ㄊㄧㄢ)
summer; summer days

夏曆(ㄒㄧㄚˋ ㄌㄧˋ)
the traditional Chinese calendar; the lunar calendar

夏令(ㄒㄧㄚˋ ㄌㄧㄥˋ)
summer; summer time

夏令時間(ㄒㄧㄚˋ ㄌㄧㄥˋ ㄕˊ ㄐㄧㄢ)
summer time; daylight saving time

夏令營(ㄒㄧㄚˋ ㄌㄧㄥˋ ㄧㄥˊ)
summer camps; summer camping

夏令衛生(ㄒㄧㄚˋ ㄌㄧㄥˋ ㄨㄟˋ ㄕㄥ)
summer sanitation; public health (measures, etc.) in summer months

夏爐冬扇(ㄒㄧㄚˋ ㄌㄨˊ ㄉㄨㄥ ㄕㄢˋ)
(literally) stoves in summer and fans in winter—(figuratively) to do things the wrong way

夏葛冬裘(ㄒㄧㄚˋ ㄍㄜˊ ㄉㄨㄥ ㄑㄧㄡˊ)
(literally) linens for summer and furs for winter—(figuratively) Right things come at the right time.

夏季(ㄒㄧㄚˋ ㄐㄧˋ)
the summer season: 台灣夏季裏有許多不同的水果。In Taiwan there are many fruits in the summer season.

夏桀(ㄒㄧㄚˋ ㄐㄧㄝˊ)
name of the last emperor of the Hsia Dynasty—a synonym of cruelty and oppression

夏至(ㄒㄧㄚˋ ㄓˋ)
the summer solstice which falls on June 21 or 22 on the Northern Hemisphere

夏至線(ㄒㄧㄚˋ ㄓˋ ㄒㄧㄢˋ)
tropic of Cancer 亦作「北回歸線」

夏裝(ㄒㄧㄚˋ ㄓㄨㄤ)
a summer dress

夏日(ㄒㄧㄚˋ ㄖˋ)
summer days

夏娃(ㄒㄧㄚˋ ㄨㄚ)
(the Bible) Eve

夏威夷(ㄒㄧㄚˋ ㄨㄟ ㄧˊ)
Hawaii

夏禹(ㄒㄧㄚˋ ㄩˇ)
Emperor Yü who started the reign of Hsia—a synonym of virtue and enlightened leadership

【夏】 904
2. ㄐㄧㄚˇ jea jiǎ

參看「夏楚」

夏楚(ㄐㄧㄚˇ ㄔㄨˇ)
a ferule; a rod for punishing pupils

十一畫

【敻】 905
ㄒㄩㄥˋ shionq xiòng

1. to seek
2. preeminent; superior

敻古(ㄒㄩㄥˋ ㄍㄨˇ)
a long, long time ago; in ancient times

敻絕(ㄒㄩㄥˋ ㄐㄩㄝˊ)
peerless; second to none

十八畫

【夔】 906
ㄎㄨㄟˊ kwei kuí

1. (mythology) a one-legged monster
2. name of a court musician in the reign of Emperor Shun (2255 B.C.)
3. name of a feudal state in the Chou Dynasty
4. a Chinese family name

夔龍(ㄎㄨㄟˊ ㄌㄨㄥˊ)
the figures of two animals (夔 and 龍) in ancient bronzes

夔夔(ㄎㄨㄟˊ ㄎㄨㄟˊ)
awe-struck; in fear

夕部
ㄒㄧˋ shih xì

【夕】 907
ㄒㄧˋ shih xì

1. dusk; sunset; evening
2. night: 他在一夕之間成名。He became famous during the night.
3. slant; oblique
4. to meet in the evening
5. a Chinese family name

夕暉(ㄒㄧˋ ㄏㄨㄟ)
slanting rays of the setting sun; brilliance of the sunset

夕照(ㄒㄧˋ ㄓㄠˋ)
the setting sun; its slanting rays; the reflected light of sunset: 滿目青山夕照明。All the verdant mountains are bathed in the glorious setting sun.

夕陽(ㄒㄧˋ ㄧㄤˊ)
the setting sun

二畫

【外】 908
ㄨㄞˋ way wài

1. out; outside: 他在門外等著。He is waiting outside the gates.
2. foreign; alien: 他是個外國學生。He is a foreign student.
3. diplomatic; diplomacy: 他是位外交關係專家。He is an expert in diplomatic relations.
4. besides; in addition
5. a term referring to one's husband 參看「外子」
6. a role in Chinese opera for old men
7. to alienate
8. on wife's or mother's side
9. relatives of one's sisters or daughters

外版書(ㄨㄞˋ ㄅㄢˇ ㄕㄨ)
the books not published by the shop selling them

外幣(ㄨㄞˋ ㄅㄧˋ)
foreign currency

外表(ㄨㄞˋ ㄅㄧㄠˇ)
an outward appearance; an exterior: 他喜歡從外表看人。He likes to judge people by appearances.

外邊(ㄨㄞˋ ㄅㄧㄢ) or 外邊兒(ㄨㄞˋ ㄅㄧㄚㄦ)
① out; outside: 我們到外邊走走。Let's go out for a walk. ② faraway or distant places ③ a border region

外賓(ㄨㄞˋ ㄅㄧㄣ)
foreign visitors; foreign

guests

外部(ㄨㄞˋ ㄅㄨˋ)
the external of anything; outside: 這房子的外部漆成綠色。The house was painted green outside.

〔夕部〕

外埠(ㄨㄞˋ ㄅㄨˋ)
ports or cities outside of one's own

外婆(ㄨㄞˋ ㄆㄛˊ)
one's maternal grandmother

外貌(ㄨㄞˋ ㄇㄠˋ)
an outward appearance; external looks

外貿(ㄨㄞˋ ㄇㄠˋ)
foreign trade; external trade

外貿協會(ㄨㄞˋ ㄇㄠˋ ㄒㄧㄝˊ ㄏㄨㄟˋ)
China External Trade Development Council (CETDC)

外蒙古(ㄨㄞˋ ㄇㄥˊ ㄍㄨˇ)
Outer Mongolia

外面(ㄨㄞˋ ㄇㄧㄢˋ)
① an outward appearance; an exterior; a surface: 那屋子外面是磚砌的。The exterior of the house was of brick. ② outside; out: 車子正在外面等著。The car is waiting outside.

外分泌(ㄨㄞˋ ㄈㄣ ㄇㄧˋ)
exocrine; external secretion

外防禦線(ㄨㄞˋ ㄈㄤˊ ㄩˋ ㄒㄧㄢˋ) or 外圍防禦線(ㄨㄞˋ ㄨㄟˊ ㄈㄤˊ ㄩˋ ㄒㄧㄢˋ)
first-line defense; outer defense lines

外放(ㄨㄞˋ ㄈㄤˋ)
① to send an official in the capital for a provincial post ② to send an official for an overseas assignment

外敷(ㄨㄞˋ ㄈㄨ)
to apply (ointment, etc.)

外帶(ㄨㄞˋ ㄉㄞˋ)
① a tire (cover) ② as well; besides: 這個廠除生產貨車，外帶修理各種車子。Besides producing trucks, this factory repairs various cars as a sideline.

外敵(ㄨㄞˋ ㄉㄧˊ)
a foreign enemy

外地(ㄨㄞˋ ㄉㄧˋ)
parts of the country other than where one is

外調(ㄨㄞˋ ㄉㄧㄠˋ)
to transfer (materials or personnel) to other places

外電(ㄨㄞˋ ㄉㄧㄢˋ)
dispatches from foreign news agencies: 據外電報導，舊金山發生大地震。According to dispatches from foreign news agencies, there was a strong earthquake in San Francisco.

外動詞(ㄨㄞˋ ㄉㄨㄥˋ ㄘˊ)
(grammar) a transitive verb

外太空(ㄨㄞˋ ㄊㄞˋ ㄎㄨㄥ)
outer space

外逃(ㄨㄞˋ ㄊㄠˊ)
① to flee to some other place ② to flee the country

外套(ㄨㄞˋ ㄊㄠˋ)
① an overcoat ② overalls in the Ching Dynasty

外頭(ㄨㄞˋ ˙ㄊㄡ)
outside: 把車子停在外頭。Park your car outside.

外來(ㄨㄞˋ ㄌㄞˊ)
outside; external; foreign: 我們應抵抗外來干涉。We should fight against outside interference.

外來語(ㄨㄞˋ ㄌㄞˊ ㄩˇ)
a term borrowed from a foreign language (such as "kowtow" or "sampan" in English which were borrowed from the Chinese language); foreign terms

外力(ㄨㄞˋ ㄌㄧˋ)
foreign influence; external pressure or influence

外流(ㄨㄞˋ ㄌㄧㄡˊ)
to flow outward; the outflow (of capital, talents, etc.)

外路(ㄨㄞˋ ㄌㄨˋ)
outside; districts, regions, provinces, etc. other than one's own

外路人(ㄨㄞˋ ㄌㄨˋ ㄖㄣˊ)
an outsider; a stranger

外港(ㄨㄞˋ ㄍㄤˇ)
an outport

外國(ㄨㄞˋ ㄍㄨㄛˊ)
a foreign country: 我有很多外國朋友。I have many foreign friends.

外國貨(ㄨㄞˋ ㄍㄨㄛˊ ㄏㄨㄛˋ)
imported goods; commodities of foreign make

外國人(ㄨㄞˋ ㄍㄨㄛˊ ㄖㄣˊ)
a foreigner; an alien: 此城有多少外國人？How many foreigners are there in this town?

外國資本(ㄨㄞˋ ㄍㄨㄛˊ ㄗ ㄅㄣˇ)
foreign capital

外國語(ㄨㄞˋ ㄍㄨㄛˊ ㄩˇ)
a foreign language; a foreign tongue

外觀(ㄨㄞˋ ㄍㄨㄢ)
an outward appearance; external looks: 這建築的外觀很吸引人。The external features of the building are very attractive.

外公(ㄨㄞˋ ㄍㄨㄥ)
one's maternal grandfather

外功(ㄨㄞˋ ㄍㄨㄥ)
(Chinese boxing) training and exercising of one's physical attributes for speed, strength and quick reflex, as opposed to 內功 which involves development of one's internal organs for immense strength and uncanny feats

外科(ㄨㄞˋ ㄎㄜ)
surgery

外科醫生(ㄨㄞˋ ㄎㄜ ㄧ ㄕㄥ) or 外科大夫(ㄨㄞˋ ㄎㄜ ㄉㄞˋ ㄈㄨ)
a surgeon

外殼(ㄨㄞˋ ㄎㄜˊ)
an outer covering; a shell; a case

外客(ㄨㄞˋ ㄎㄜˋ)
guests who are not related to oneself by blood or by marriage

外快(ㄨㄞˋ ㄎㄨㄞˋ)
extra income; perquisites

外號(ㄨㄞˋ ㄏㄠˋ)
a nickname: 他的外號叫「胖仔」。His nickname is "Fatty"

外行(ㄨㄞˋ ㄏㄤˊ)
① a raw hand; a greenhorn; one who knows nothing of the trade; an outsider; a layman: 談到法律，我祇是個外行。Where the law is concerned, I am only a layman. ② inexperienced; unskilled; amateurish

外行話(ㄨㄞˋ ㄏㄤˊ ㄏㄨㄚˋ)
layman's language

外戶(ㄨㄞˋ ㄏㄨˋ)
a door which opens from the outside

外貨(ㄨㄞˋ ㄏㄨㄛˋ)

imported goods; foreign goods
外匯(ㄨㄞˋ ㄏㄨㄟˋ)
foreign exchange
外匯兌換率(ㄨㄞˋ ㄏㄨㄟˋ ㄉㄨㄟˋ ㄏㄨㄢˋ ㄌㄩˋ)
the rate of foreign exchange
外匯管理(ㄨㄞˋ ㄏㄨㄟˋ ㄍㄨㄢˇ ㄌㄧˇ)
foreign exchange control
外匯交易(ㄨㄞˋ ㄏㄨㄟˋ ㄐㄧㄠ ㄧˋ)
foreign exchange transactions
外匯市場(ㄨㄞˋ ㄏㄨㄟˋ ㄕˋ ㄔㄤˇ)
a foreign exchange market
外患(ㄨㄞˋ ㄏㄨㄢˋ)
foreign invasion; foreign aggression; foreign intrusion
外籍(ㄨㄞˋ ㄐㄧˊ)
foreign nationality
外籍人士(ㄨㄞˋ ㄐㄧˊ ㄖㄣˊ ㄕˋ)
foreigners; aliens
外加(ㄨㄞˋ ㄐㄧㄚ)
plus; in addition (to): 你需要錢和時間，外加勤勉努力。You need money and time. In addition, you need diligence.
外家(ㄨㄞˋ ㄐㄧㄚ)
① the parental home of a married woman ② a house to keep "the other woman" ③ a school of Chinese boxing 亦作「少林」
外接圓(ㄨㄞˋ ㄐㄧㄝ ㄩㄢˊ)
(mathematics) a circumscribed circle
外界(ㄨㄞˋ ㄐㄧㄝˋ)
① outsiders; those who are not in the know ② the outside: 夢由內心產生，非來自外界。Dreams come from within, not from the outside. ③ one's environment
外交(ㄨㄞˋ ㄐㄧㄠ)
diplomacy; diplomatic; foreign relations: 這件事須透過外交途徑解決。This event must be settled through diplomatic channels.
外交部(ㄨㄞˋ ㄐㄧㄠ ㄅㄨˋ)
Ministry of Foreign Affairs
外交部長(ㄨㄞˋ ㄐㄧㄠ ㄅㄨˋ ㄓㄤˇ)
Minister of Foreign Affairs
外交團(ㄨㄞˋ ㄐㄧㄠ ㄊㄨㄢˊ)
the diplomatic corps 亦作「使節團」
外交官(ㄨㄞˋ ㄐㄧㄠ ㄍㄨㄢ)
diplomatic officials; diplomats
外交家(ㄨㄞˋ ㄐㄧㄠ ㄐㄧㄚ)
skillful diplomats; experts in diplomacy
外交政策(ㄨㄞˋ ㄐㄧㄠ ㄓㄥˋ ㄘㄜˋ)
foreign policy
外交辭令(ㄨㄞˋ ㄐㄧㄠ ㄘˊ ㄌㄧㄥˋ)
(literally) diplomatic language—tactful remarks; euphemisms; circumlocutions; subterfuges
外角(ㄨㄞˋ ㄐㄧㄠˇ)
(mathematics) exterior angle
外教(ㄨㄞˋ ㄐㄧㄠˋ)
①a term used by the Buddhists to refer to religions other than Buddhism ② amateurish; green; a greenhorn; a novice
外間(ㄨㄞˋ ㄐㄧㄢ)
① the outside ② outsiders; people not in the know
外江人(ㄨㄞˋ ㄐㄧㄤ ㄖㄣˊ)
the southerners' reference to the people along or north of the Yangtze River
外景(ㄨㄞˋ ㄐㄧㄥˇ)
(said of motion picture production) a location; an exterior: 那部電影正在拍外景。The film is on location now.
外戚(ㄨㄞˋ ㄑㄧ)
the power group (usually relatives) of an emperor's mother or wife
外僑(ㄨㄞˋ ㄑㄧㄠˊ)
foreign residents
外欠(ㄨㄞˋ ㄑㄧㄢˋ)
debts not included in a statement
外親(ㄨㄞˋ ㄑㄧㄣ)
blood relatives of the female members of a family
外勤(ㄨㄞˋ ㄑㄧㄣˊ)
a job which involves activities mostly outside an office building, such as that of a news reporter, policeman, etc.; work done outside the office
外強中乾(ㄨㄞˋ ㄑㄧㄤˊ ㄓㄨㄥ ㄍㄢ)
a paper tiger; outwardly strong but inwardly weak
外圈(ㄨㄞˋ ㄑㄩㄢ)
(sports) an outer lane; an outer circle
外銷(ㄨㄞˋ ㄒㄧㄠ)
to export; for export; export: 中國外銷茶及絲到外國。China exported tea and silk to foreign countries.
外縣(ㄨㄞˋ ㄒㄧㄢˋ)
① counties other than one's own ② a provincial capital
外鄉(ㄨㄞˋ ㄒㄧㄤ)
another part of the country; some other place: 他操外鄉口音。He speaks with a nonlocal accent.
外鄉人(ㄨㄞˋ ㄒㄧㄤ ㄖㄣˊ)
strangers; people from other lands
外向(ㄨㄞˋ ㄒㄧㄤˋ)
extrovert; extroversion
外星人(ㄨㄞˋ ㄒㄧㄥ ㄖㄣˊ)
an E. T. (extraterrestrial)
外形(ㄨㄞˋ ㄒㄧㄥˊ)
an appearance; an external form; a contour
外姓(ㄨㄞˋ ㄒㄧㄥˋ)
a family name other than one's own
外痔(ㄨㄞˋ ㄓˋ)
external hemorrhoids
外債(ㄨㄞˋ ㄓㄞˋ)
foreign loans; international loans
外長(ㄨㄞˋ ㄓㄤˇ)
Minister of Foreign Affairs
外傳(ㄨㄞˋ ㄓㄨㄢˋ)
a narrative of events not recorded in history
外重內輕(ㄨㄞˋ ㄓㄨㄥˋ ㄋㄟˋ ㄑㄧㄥ)
a political system under which the central government is weak while the local governments enjoy a large degree of autonomy
外城(ㄨㄞˋ ㄔㄥˊ)
newly-developed communities outside the old city wall
外出(ㄨㄞˋ ㄔㄨ)
to go out; to be out of town; to absent oneself from home or office
外出血(ㄨㄞˋ ㄔㄨ ㄒㄧㄝˇ)
external hemorrhage
外傳(ㄨㄞˋ ㄔㄨㄢˊ)
rumors are circulating...; speculations have it...: 外傳內閣將改組。Rumors have it

〔夕部〕

that there will be a change in the Cabinet.

外史(ㄨㄞˋ ㄕˇ)
①an official in ancient China in charge of the collection of legends and narratives ②histories with a more or less fictitious nature

外室(ㄨㄞˋ ㄕˋ)
a mistress living outside one's own home

外商(ㄨㄞˋ ㄕㄤ)
foreign businessmen

外傷(ㄨㄞˋ ㄕㄤ)
external injuries; bruises; injuries that do not affect internal organs

外甥(ㄨㄞˋ ㄕㄥ)
sister's sons; nephews

外甥女(ㄨㄞˋ ㄕㄥ ㄋㄩˇ)
sister's daughters; nieces

外省(ㄨㄞˋ ㄕㄥˇ)
other provinces

外省人(ㄨㄞˋ ㄕㄥˇ ㄖㄣˊ)
persons from another province

外人(ㄨㄞˋ ㄖㄣˊ)
①outsiders; strangers; the people who do not belong to one's own circle or organization: 此事不足爲外人道。It is not to be mentioned to outsiders. ②foreigners

外資(ㄨㄞˋ ㄗ)
foreign capital

外子(ㄨㄞˋ ㄗˇ)
a reference to one's own husband

外在(ㄨㄞˋ ㄗㄞˋ)
external; extrinsic: 它是外在因素。It's an external factor.

外族(ㄨㄞˋ ㄗㄨˊ)
①families or clans on the maternal side ②foreign or outside clans, tribes or families

外祖(ㄨㄞˋ ㄗㄨˇ)or 外祖父(ㄨㄞˋ ㄗㄨˇ ㄈㄨˋ)or 外公(ㄨㄞˋ ㄍㄨㄥ)
one's maternal grandfather

外祖母(ㄨㄞˋ ㄗㄨˇ ㄇㄨˇ)
one's maternal grandmother

外才(ㄨㄞˋ ㄘㄞˊ)
the talents of an extrovert or mixer

外財(ㄨㄞˋ ㄘㄞˊ)
illegal gains; a windfall; riches acquired accidentally

外宿(ㄨㄞˋ ㄙㄨˋ)
to stay outside (one's own home or dormitory) overnight

外孫(ㄨㄞˋ ㄙㄨㄣ)
sons of one's daughters

外孫女(ㄨㄞˋ ㄙㄨㄣ ㄋㄩˇ)
daughters of one's daughters

外耳(ㄨㄞˋ ㄦˇ)
the external ear

外衣(ㄨㄞˋ ㄧ)
a coat; a jacket; outer clothing; an outer garment

外野(ㄨㄞˋ ㄧㄝˇ)
(baseball) outfield

外野手(ㄨㄞˋ ㄧㄝˇ ㄕㄡˇ)
an outfielder

外延(ㄨㄞˋ ㄧㄢˊ)
①(logic) extension ②(mathematics) exterior extent

外因(ㄨㄞˋ ㄧㄣ)
(philosophy) external cause

外洋(ㄨㄞˋ ㄧㄤˊ)
overseas; abroad

外侮(ㄨㄞˋ ㄨˇ)
foreign aggression; insults or humiliations caused by foreign powers: 我們必須抵禦外侮。We have to resist foreign aggression.

外務(ㄨㄞˋ ㄨˋ)
①foreign affairs ②affairs or work which do not really concern one or which one is not obliged to handle

外務部(ㄨㄞˋ ㄨˋ ㄅㄨˋ)
the Ministry of Foreign Affairs of the late Ching Dynasty

外圍(ㄨㄞˋ ㄨㄟˊ)
anything surrounding the central figure or thing; the perimeter

外圍防禦(ㄨㄞˋ ㄨㄟˊ ㄈㄤˊ ㄩˋ)
perimeter defense; peripheral defense

外圍組織(ㄨㄞˋ ㄨㄟˊ ㄗㄨˇ ㄓ)
peripheral organizations; front organizations

外文(ㄨㄞˋ ㄨㄣˊ)
a foreign language

外語(ㄨㄞˋ ㄩˇ)
a foreign language

外域(ㄨㄞˋ ㄩˋ)
foreign lands

外遇(ㄨㄞˋ ㄩˋ)
to have extramarital affairs

外援(ㄨㄞˋ ㄩㄢˊ)
outside help; foreign aid

外緣(ㄨㄞˋ ㄩㄢˊ)
①the outer rim (of an object) ②desires that come from outside temptations

外圓內方(ㄨㄞˋ ㄩㄢˊ ㄋㄟˋ ㄈㄤ)
smooth and easy-going in manners but highly principled in daily life

外用(ㄨㄞˋ ㄩㄥˋ)
external use; external application

三畫

【多】 909
1. ㄉㄨㄛ duo duō

1. many; much; too much: 他有很多朋友。He has a large number of friends.
2. more than; much more; over: 十比八多二。Ten is two more than eight.
3. much; greatly; highly; very: 病人好多了。The patient is much better now.
4. to praise
5. only
6. a Chinese family name

多胞胎(ㄉㄨㄛ ㄅㄠ ㄊㄞ)
multiple birth

多半(ㄉㄨㄛ ㄅㄢˋ)or 多半兒(ㄉㄨㄛ ㄅㄚˋㄦ)or 多分(ㄉㄨㄛ ㄈㄣˋ)
①most; the greater part: 這支棒球隊的成員多半是學生。Most of the members of this baseball team are students. ②most likely; probably: 天空烏雲密佈，多半要下雨了。The sky is darkly clouded; it will probably rain.

多邊(ㄉㄨㄛ ㄅㄧㄢ)
multilateral

多邊協定(ㄉㄨㄛ ㄅㄧㄢ ㄒㄧㄝˊ ㄉㄧㄥˋ)
a multilateral agreement

多邊形(ㄉㄨㄛ ㄅㄧㄢ ㄒㄧㄥˊ)or 多角形(ㄉㄨㄛ ㄐㄧㄠˇ ㄒㄧㄥˊ)
a polygon

多變(ㄉㄨㄛ ㄅㄧㄢˋ)
changeable; changeful; varied: 你能適應這多變的天氣嗎？Can you be accustomed to the changeable weather?

多病(ㄉㄨㄛ ㄅㄧㄥˋ)
susceptible to diseases; prone to illness; constantly ill

多謀善斷(ㄉㄨㄛ ㄇㄡˊ ㄕㄢˋ ㄉㄨㄢˋ)
resourceful and decisive; sagacious and resolute

多蒙(ㄉㄨㄛ ㄇㄥˊ)
thanks for (your, his, etc. permission, help, etc.)

多面體(ㄉㄨㄛ ㄇㄧㄢˋ ㄊㄧˇ)
a polyhedron

多明尼加(ㄉㄨㄛ ㄇㄧㄥˊ ㄋㄧˊ ㄐㄧㄚ)
the Dominican Republic

多目標(ㄉㄨㄛ ㄇㄨˋ ㄅㄧㄠ)
(said of construction projects) multipurpose

多方面(ㄉㄨㄛ ㄈㄤ ㄇㄧㄢˋ)
many-sided; in many ways: 此書給大家帶來的好處是多方面的。The book has proved useful to us in many ways.

多福多壽(ㄉㄨㄛ ㄈㄨˊ ㄉㄨㄛ ㄕㄡˋ)
happiness and longevity; amply blessed

多大(ㄉㄨㄛ ㄉㄚˋ)
① How big? ② How old? 他的年紀多大? How old is he?

多黨制度(ㄉㄨㄛ ㄉㄤˇ ㄓˋ ㄉㄨˋ)
the multiparty system

多多(ㄉㄨㄛ ㄉㄨㄛ)
a great deal: 請多多幫助這孩子。Please help the child a great deal.

多多少少(ㄉㄨㄛ ㄉㄨㄛ ㄕㄠˇ ㄕㄠˇ)
more or less: 她多多少少有點瘋狂。She is more or less crazy.

多多益善(ㄉㄨㄛ ㄉㄨㄛ ㄧˋ ㄕㄢˋ)
The more, the better.

多端(ㄉㄨㄛ ㄉㄨㄢ)
① many kinds; a great variety: 他作惡多端, 應受嚴懲。He has done many kinds of misdeeds; therefore, he should be punished severely. ② in many ways

多胎孕妊(ㄉㄨㄛ ㄊㄞ ㄩㄣˋ ㄖㄣˋ)
multiple pregnancy

多頭(ㄉㄨㄛ ㄊㄡˊ)
(said of stock exchange) to buy long; taking a long position

多退少補(ㄉㄨㄛ ㄊㄨㄟˋ ㄕㄠˇ ㄅㄨˇ)or 多還少補(ㄉㄨㄛ ㄏㄨㄢˊ ㄕㄠˇ ㄅㄨˇ)
to return the overcharge and demand payment of the shortage, if any (The expression is used when money is paid in advance for a specific use, the cost of which is unknown beforehand.)

多瑙河(ㄉㄨㄛ ㄋㄠˇ ㄏㄜˊ)
the Danube River

多難興邦(ㄉㄨㄛ ㄋㄢˋ ㄒㄧㄥ ㄅㄤ)
Foreign aggressions often awaken a nation from its slumbers and thus help make it strong.

多年不見(ㄉㄨㄛ ㄋㄧㄢˊ ㄅㄨˊ ㄐㄧㄢˋ)
to have not met or seen for many years

多年生植物(ㄉㄨㄛ ㄋㄧㄢˊ ㄕㄥ ㄓˊ ㄨˋ)
perennial plants: 玫瑰是多年生植物。Roses are perennials.

多禮(ㄉㄨㄛ ㄌㄧˇ)
very polite; overcourteous

多倫多(ㄉㄨㄛ ㄌㄨㄣˊ ㄉㄨㄛ)
Toronto, a Canadian city

多氯聯苯(ㄉㄨㄛ ㄌㄩˋ ㄌㄧㄢˊ ㄅㄣˇ)
(chemistry) polychlorinated biphenyl

多哥蘭(ㄉㄨㄛ ㄍㄜ ㄌㄢˊ)
Togoland

多哥共和國(ㄉㄨㄛ ㄍㄜ ㄍㄨㄥˋ ㄏㄜˊ ㄍㄨㄛˊ)
Republic of Togo

多故(ㄉㄨㄛ ㄍㄨˋ)
many troubles or mishaps: 我們國家多故。There are many troubles or crises in our nation.

多寡(ㄉㄨㄛ ㄍㄨㄚˇ)
number; amount: 各省人口多寡不等。The population in every province varies in number.

多寡不拘(ㄉㄨㄛ ㄍㄨㄚˇ ㄅㄨˋ ㄐㄩ)
It doesn't matter how much or how little (you contribute).

多國企業(ㄉㄨㄛ ㄍㄨㄛˊ ㄑㄧˋ ㄧㄝˋ)
multinational enterprises

多管閒事(ㄉㄨㄛ ㄍㄨㄢˇ ㄒㄧㄢˊ ㄕˋ)
to poke one's nose into others' business; to be a busybody: 那個長舌婦總是喜歡多管閒事。The gossip was always poking her nose into other people's business.

多虧(ㄉㄨㄛ ㄎㄨㄟ)
it is fortunate that; we are lucky to; thanks to...: 多虧他給我們帶路。We were lucky to have him leading the way.

多會兒(ㄉㄨㄛ ㄏㄨㄜˇㄦ)
What time...? 或 When...? 或 How much time...? 你要多會兒才能來? When can you come?

多角形(ㄉㄨㄛ ㄐㄧㄠˇ ㄒㄧㄥˊ)or 多邊形(ㄉㄨㄛ ㄅㄧㄢ ㄒㄧㄥˊ)
a polygon; polygonal

多見多聞(ㄉㄨㄛ ㄐㄧㄢˋ ㄉㄨㄛ ㄨㄣˊ)
(literally) to have seen and heard a lot—to have wide experience; sophisticated; well-experienced

多妻制(ㄉㄨㄛ ㄑㄧ ㄓˋ)
polygamy 亦作「一夫多妻」

多歧亡羊(ㄉㄨㄛ ㄑㄧˊ ㄨㄤˊ ㄧㄤˊ)
One will get nowhere if he lacks single-mindedness and perseverance.

多情(ㄉㄨㄛ ㄑㄧㄥˊ)
passionate; emotional; sentimental: 她的美麗即刻打動了他多情的心。Her beauty made an immediate appeal to his passionate temperament.

多謝(ㄉㄨㄛ ㄒㄧㄝˋ)
Many thanks. 或 Thank you very much. 或 Thanks a lot.

多心(ㄉㄨㄛ ㄒㄧㄣ)
① to be very suspicious or oversensitive; distrustful: 他總是對別人多心。He is always distrustful of others. ② tricky; treacherous

多相電流(ㄉㄨㄛ ㄒㄧㄤˋ ㄉㄧㄢˋ ㄌㄧㄡˊ)
(electricity) a polyphase current

多行不義必自斃(ㄉㄨㄛ ㄒㄧㄥˊ ㄅㄨˋ ㄧˋ ㄅㄧˋ ㄗˋ ㄅㄧˋ)
To do evil deeds frequently will bring ruin to the doer.

多種多樣(ㄉㄨㄛ ㄓㄨㄥˇ ㄉㄨㄛ ㄧㄤˋ)
varied; manifold: 它能滿足人們多種多樣的需要。It can meet the manifold needs of the people.

多種經營(ㄉㄨㄛ ㄓㄨㄥˇ ㄐㄧㄥ ㄧㄥˊ)
a diversified undertakings; diversification

多愁善感(ㄉㄨㄛ ㄔㄡˊ ㄕㄢˋ ㄍㄢˇ)
sentimental; emotional and sensitive

多產婦(ㄉㄨㄛ ㄔㄢˇ ㄈㄨˋ)
a multiparous woman

〔夕部〕

〔夕部〕

多產作家(ㄉㄨㄛ ㄔㄢˇ ㄗㄨㄛˋ ㄐㄧㄚ)
a prolific writer
多重人格(ㄉㄨㄛ ㄔㄨㄥˊ ㄖㄣˊ ㄍㄜˊ)
multiple personality
多時(ㄉㄨㄛ ㄕˊ)
a long time: 我們已等候多時。We have waited a long time.
多事(ㄉㄨㄛ ㄕˋ)
officious; interfering; meddling: 我不想多事。I don't wish to interfere in what others do.
多事之秋(ㄉㄨㄛ ㄕˋ ㄓ ㄑㄧㄡ)
time of national crises; troubled times; a year of many troubles; an eventful year
多少(ㄉㄨㄛ ㄕㄠˇ)
① How much? 或 How many? 或 How long? 多少人在屋子裡? How many people are there in the house? ② more or less; somewhat: 我經過此一長途旅行後, 多少有些疲倦了。I am more or less tired after such a long trip.
多神教(ㄉㄨㄛ ㄕㄣˊ ㄐㄧㄠˋ)
polytheism
多數(ㄉㄨㄛ ㄕㄨˋ)
the majority; many: 大多數的人喜愛和平而不要戰爭。The majority of people prefer peace to war.
多子多累(ㄉㄨㄛ ㄗˇ ㄉㄨㄛ ㄌㄟˋ)
The more children one has, the more he toils.
多子多孫(ㄉㄨㄛ ㄗˇ ㄉㄨㄛ ㄙㄨㄣ)
many children and grandchildren (regarded as a blessing among old Chinese)
多災多難(ㄉㄨㄛ ㄗㄞ ㄉㄨㄛ ㄋㄢˋ)
to be plagued by frequent ills; to be dogged by bad luck, misfortune, etc.
多嘴(ㄉㄨㄛ ㄗㄨㄟˇ)
to make statements about things which have nothing to do with oneself; to have a big mouth; to shoot one's mouth off
多此一舉(ㄉㄨㄛ ㄘˇ ㄧˋ ㄐㄩˇ)
a superfluous or unnecessary action, remark, etc.: 何必多此一舉呢? Why take such an unnecessary action?
多次(ㄉㄨㄛ ㄘˋ)
many times; time and again; repeatedly; on many occasions: 這位美國人曾多次訪問中國。This American has visited China many times.
多才多藝(ㄉㄨㄛ ㄘㄞˊ ㄉㄨㄛ ㄧˋ)
versatile; very capable; a master of all trades
多財善賈(ㄉㄨㄛ ㄘㄞˊ ㄕㄢˋ ㄍㄨˇ)
rich and having business acumen
多采多姿 or 多彩多姿(ㄉㄨㄛ ㄘㄞˇ ㄉㄨㄛ ㄗ)
magnificent; colorful; many-faceted
多藏厚亡(ㄉㄨㄛ ㄘㄤˊ ㄏㄡˋ ㄨㄤˊ)
The greater fortune one amasses, the greater loss he will suffer.
多疑(ㄉㄨㄛ ㄧˊ)
suspicious
多義詞(ㄉㄨㄛ ㄧˋ ㄘˊ)
(linguistics) polysemant
多樣化(ㄉㄨㄛ ㄧㄤˋ ㄏㄨㄚˋ)
to diversify; to make varied: 摩天大樓使得天空呈現出多樣化的線條。The skyline is diversified by the skyscrapers.
多聞闕疑(ㄉㄨㄛ ㄨㄣˊ ㄑㄩㄝ ㄧˊ)
Instead of pretending to understand everything, one should listen more to others.
多餘(ㄉㄨㄛ ㄩˊ)
unnecessary; superfluous; superfluity; uncalled-for: 你這話是多餘的。What you say is uncalled-for.
多元論(ㄉㄨㄛ ㄩㄢˊ ㄌㄨㄣˋ)
(philosophy) pluralism
多雲(ㄉㄨㄛ ㄩㄣˊ)
cloudy: 昨天是多雲的天氣。It was cloudy yesterday.

【多】 909
2. ㄉㄨㄛˊ dwo duó
how, what, etc.—in exclamatory statements: 這小孩多聰明啊! How clever the child is!
多麼(ㄉㄨㄛˊ ·ㄇㄜ)
how (good, beautiful, etc.); what: 多麼鮮麗的色彩! What bright colors! 多麼美好的一天! What a lovely day!
多美(ㄉㄨㄛˊ ㄇㄟˇ)
How beautiful! 或 What a beauty! 她長得多美啊! How beautiful she is! 或 What a beauty she is!
多好(ㄉㄨㄛˊ ㄏㄠˇ)
How nice! 或 How wonderful! 或 How good! 她唱得多好啊! How well she sings!

【夙】 910
ㄙㄨˋ suh sù
1. the early morning
2. old or original (desires, etc.)
3. (Buddhism) inborn; inherited 亦作「宿」
夙慧(ㄙㄨˋ ㄏㄨㄟˋ)
to be born intelligent; inborn intelligence
夙駕(ㄙㄨˋ ㄐㄧㄚˋ)
to start a journey early; to set out early
夙昔(ㄙㄨˋ ㄒㄧˊ)
① past times; in the past ② day and night
夙興夜寐(ㄙㄨˋ ㄒㄧㄥ ㄧㄝˋ ㄇㄟˋ)
to rise early and sleep late—very diligent
夙志(ㄙㄨˋ ㄓˋ)
a long-cherished ambition
夙仇(ㄙㄨˋ ㄔㄡˊ)
an old enemy
夙儒(ㄙㄨˋ ㄖㄨˊ)
a learned scholar
夙素 or 宿素(ㄙㄨˋ ㄙㄨˋ)
a long-cherished ambition
夙夜(ㄙㄨˋ ㄧㄝˋ)
day and night
夙夜匪懈(ㄙㄨˋ ㄧㄝˋ ㄈㄟˇ ㄒㄧㄝˋ)
to work diligently day and night
夙緣(ㄙㄨˋ ㄩㄢˊ)
(Buddhism) a relationship forged in the earlier incarnation 亦作「宿緣」
夙怨(ㄙㄨˋ ㄩㄢˋ)
old grudges 亦作「宿怨」
夙願(ㄙㄨˋ ㄩㄢˋ)
an old wish; a long-cherished wish: 這女孩夙願已償。The girl got her long-cherished wish.

五畫

【夜】 911
ㄧㄝˋ yeh yè
1. night; dark; darkness: 夜間我不出門。I don't go out after dark. 冬天晝短夜長。In winter the days are short and the nights long.

2. a night trip; night traveling
夜班(ㄧㄝˋ ㄅㄢ)
night shifts; night work: 大夜班 the graveyard shift 小夜班 the swing shift
夜半(ㄧㄝˋ ㄅㄢˋ)
midnight: 他工作至夜半。He worked until midnight.
夜不閉戶(ㄧㄝˋ ㄅㄨˋ ㄅㄧˋ ㄏㄨˋ)
There's no need to close doors at night. (a description often used to indicate efficient government administration)
夜貓子(ㄧㄝˋ ㄇㄠ ·ㄗ)
① the owl ② a person who enjoys night life
夜盲症(ㄧㄝˋ ㄇㄤˊ ㄓㄥˋ)
night blindness; nyctalopia
夜明珠(ㄧㄝˋ ㄇㄧㄥˊ ㄓㄨ)
a legendary pearl that shines at night
夜幕(ㄧㄝˋ ㄇㄨˋ)
a curtain of night; gathering darkness: 夜幕籠罩着大地。The curtain of darkness covered the earth.
夜大(ㄧㄝˋ ㄉㄚˋ)or 夜間大學(ㄧㄝˋ ㄐㄧㄢ ㄉㄚˋ ㄒㄩㄝˊ)
an evening university
夜度資(ㄧㄝˋ ㄉㄨˋ ㄗ)
the money charged by a prostitute for boudoir favors for a night
夜啼(ㄧㄝˋ ㄊㄧˊ)
the morbid night crying of babies
夜來香(ㄧㄝˋ ㄌㄞˊ ㄒㄧㄤ)
(botany) the tuberose
夜闌人靜(ㄧㄝˋ ㄌㄢˊ ㄖㄣˊ ㄐㄧㄥˋ)or 夜深人靜(ㄧㄝˋ ㄕㄣ ㄖㄣˊ ㄐㄧㄥˋ)
(in) the quiet of the late night; deep in the night; at the dead of night
夜郎自大(ㄧㄝˋ ㄌㄤˊ ㄗˋ ㄉㄚˋ)
the megalomania of the king of Yehlang (who asked the envoy of Han, "Which was bigger, the Han Empire or the tiny state of Yehlang?")—(figuratively) a braggadocio; ignorant and boastful
夜涼如水(ㄧㄝˋ ㄌㄧㄤˊ ㄖㄨˊ ㄕㄨㄟˇ)
the chilling (autumn) night
夜光杯(ㄧㄝˋ ㄍㄨㄤ ㄅㄟ)
a cup made of jade that glows in the night
夜光錶(ㄧㄝˋ ㄍㄨㄤ ㄅㄧㄠˇ)
a watch with luminous markings on the dial
夜工(ㄧㄝˋ ㄍㄨㄥ)
night work; a night job
夜課(ㄧㄝˋ ㄎㄜˋ)
night classes
夜合花(ㄧㄝˋ ㄏㄜˊ ㄏㄨㄚ)
(botany) *Magnolia coco*
夜壺(ㄧㄝˋ ㄏㄨˊ)
a chamber pot 亦作「夜淨兒」
夜間(ㄧㄝˋ ㄐㄧㄢ)or 夜晚(ㄧㄝˋ ㄨㄢˇ)or 夜裏(ㄧㄝˋ ·ㄌㄧ)
the night; nighttime; at night: 那不是個夜間可去的地方。It isn't a place to visit by night.
夜間部(ㄧㄝˋ ㄐㄧㄢ ㄅㄨˋ)
the night department (of a school, college or university)
夜禁(ㄧㄝˋ ㄐㄧㄣˋ)
the night curfew
夜驚(ㄧㄝˋ ㄐㄧㄥ)
nocturnal phobia
夜景(ㄧㄝˋ ㄐㄧㄥˇ)
night scenes (of a locality)
夜靜(ㄧㄝˋ ㄐㄧㄥˋ)
the dead of night; the still of the night
夜勤(ㄧㄝˋ ㄑㄧㄣˊ)
night shift; night work; night duty (especially referring to doctors, policemen, newsmen, etc.)
夜曲(ㄧㄝˋ ㄑㄩˇ)
(music) a nocturne
夜襲(ㄧㄝˋ ㄒㄧˊ)
a night attack or raid; to launch an attack under the cover of night
夜戲(ㄧㄝˋ ㄒㄧˋ)
a night show; an evening performance
夜校(ㄧㄝˋ ㄒㄧㄠˋ)or 夜學(ㄧㄝˋ ㄒㄩㄝˊ)
a night school; an evening school
夜行軍(ㄧㄝˋ ㄒㄧㄥˊ ㄐㄩㄣ)
the night march
夜行人(ㄧㄝˋ ㄒㄧㄥˊ ㄖㄣˊ)
① night travelers ② cavaliers (俠客), thieves, etc. who move about at night
夜叉(ㄧㄝˋ ㄔㄚ)
①(Chinese mythology) a monstrous-looking devil ②(Buddhism) a yaksah (a malevolent spirit)
夜車(ㄧㄝˋ ㄔㄜ)
① a night train ②(figuratively) to study late at night; to burn the midnight oil
夜長夢多(ㄧㄝˋ ㄔㄤˊ ㄇㄥˋ ㄉㄨㄛ)
(literally) The night is long and dreams are many.—There'll be twists and obstacles if a problem or an issue is not settled promptly.
夜場(ㄧㄝˋ ㄔㄤˇ)or(ㄧㄝˋ ㄔㄤˊ)
a night show; an evening show
夜市(ㄧㄝˋ ㄕˋ)
business activities in night hours; markets devoted to nighttime business
夜生活(ㄧㄝˋ ㄕㄥ ㄏㄨㄛˊ)
night life
夜總會(ㄧㄝˋ ㄗㄨㄥˇ ㄏㄨㄟˋ)
a nightclub
夜色(ㄧㄝˋ ㄙㄜˋ)
the dim light of night—moonlight: 他們趁着夜色在花園裏散步。They walked by moonlight in the garden.
夜色蒼茫(ㄧㄝˋ ㄙㄜˋ ㄘㄤ ㄇㄤˊ)
twilight at dusk
夜以繼日(ㄧㄝˋ ㄧˇ ㄐㄧˋ ㄖˋ)
night and day; around the clock; day in and day out: 他夜以繼日地努力工作。He worked hard night and day.
夜夜(ㄧㄝˋ ㄧㄝˋ)
every night; night after night
夜鶯(ㄧㄝˋ ㄧㄥ)
the nightingale
夜未央(ㄧㄝˋ ㄨㄟˋ ㄧㄤ)
It is not dawn yet.
夜晚(ㄧㄝˋ ㄨㄢˇ)
night; in the night: 那是個滿天星斗的夜晚。It was a starry night.

八畫

【夠】 912 (㚇) ㄍㄡˋ gow gou
1. enough; more than enough; too much; sufficient: 座位夠不夠? Are there enough seats? 五個人就很夠了。Five men will be quite enough.

〔夕部〕

〔夕部〕

2. fully; quite: 這地區的天然資源眞夠豐富。The district is quite abundant in natural resources.
夠本(ㄍㄡˋ ㄅㄣˇ)
enough to cover the cost; to be sufficient to cover the cost; enough to break even with the capital invested; to be worth the effort or money
夠不夠(ㄍㄡˋ ㄅㄨˊ ㄍㄡˋ)
Is it enough?
夠朋友(ㄍㄡˋ ㄆㄥˊ ˙ㄧㄡ)
to be such a person whose friendship is worth having; to be true to friends; to be a friend in need
夠忙(ㄍㄡˋ ㄇㄤˊ)
enough work to keep one busy; to have one's hands full
夠面子(ㄍㄡˋ ㄇㄧㄢˋ ˙ㄗ)or 夠體面(ㄍㄡˋ ㄊㄧˇ ˙ㄇㄧㄢ)
(said of concessions made by the other side or receptions accorded by others) enough to preserve one's face—to enjoy enough honor
夠你受的(ㄍㄡˋ ㄋㄧˇ ㄕㄡˋ ˙ㄉㄜ)
enough trouble for you
夠格(ㄍㄡˋ ㄍㄜˊ)
to be qualified; to be up to standard: 他很夠格當教師。He's well qualified to be a teacher.
夠勁兒(ㄍㄡˋ ㄐㄧㄜˋㄦ)
①(said of an onerous task) almost too much to cope with ② strong or hot (in taste, strength, etc.): 這胡椒眞夠勁兒。This pepper is really hot.
夠交情(ㄍㄡˋ ㄐㄧㄠ ˙ㄑㄧㄥ)
the friendship with another person that is deep enough for one to ask a favor of him or to do him a favor
夠瞧的(ㄍㄡˋ ㄑㄧㄠˊ ˙ㄉㄜ)
(colloquial) ridiculous (sights); considerable (burdens); oppressive (heat); chilling (cold); herculean (tasks); impossible (personality); pitiable (conditions): 天氣熱得眞夠瞧的。It's oppressively hot.
夠受(ㄍㄡˋ ㄕㄡˋ)
unbearable; intolerable
夠數(ㄍㄡˋ ㄕㄨˋ)
enough to make up the required number; sufficient in quantity
夠意思(ㄍㄡˋ ㄧˋ ˙ㄙ)
① really something; terrific ② generous; really kind
夠味兒(ㄍㄡˋ ㄨㄜˋㄦ)
enjoyable; pleasant enough; quite satisfactory

十一畫

【夢】913 ㄇㄥˋ menq mèng
1. a dream: 他常做惡夢。He often had bad dreams.
2. to dream; to see visions: 你在做夢吧! You are dreaming (or planning something impossible).
3. wishful thinking; wishful
4. a Chinese family name
夢筆生花(ㄇㄥˋ ㄅㄧˇ ㄕㄥ ㄏㄨㄚ)
(literally) to see one's writing brush blooming in a dream—(figuratively) to be capable of writing felicitously
夢寐(ㄇㄥˋ ㄇㄟˋ)
① the state of sleep and dreaming ② very eagerly ③ visionary; vague
夢寐以求(ㄇㄥˋ ㄇㄟˋ ㄧˇ ㄑㄧㄡˊ)
to crave something so that one even dreams about it; to long for something day and night: 世界和平是人們夢寐以求的事。People are longing for world peace day and night.
夢蘭(ㄇㄥˋ ㄌㄢˊ)
to become pregnant
夢話(ㄇㄥˋ ㄏㄨㄚˋ)
① an absurd and unthinkable speech ② words uttered in one's sleep; somniloquy
夢幻(ㄇㄥˋ ㄏㄨㄢˋ)
illusion; a dream; reverie: 她沈緬於過去的夢幻中。She fell into a reverie about the past.
夢幻泡影(ㄇㄥˋ ㄏㄨㄢˋ ㄆㄠˋ ㄧㄥˇ)
emptiness; nothingness; visionary; illusory
夢魂顚倒(ㄇㄥˋ ㄏㄨㄣˊ ㄉㄧㄢ ㄉㄠˇ)
to be in a trance; bewitched; to fall head over heels (in love)
夢見(ㄇㄥˋ ㄐㄧㄢˋ)
to dream (of meeting someone or seeing something): 他夢見你是個富人。He dreamed that you were a rich man.
夢境(ㄇㄥˋ ㄐㄧㄥˋ)
dreamland; a dream world; a dream: 他覺得好像在夢境裡。He feels as if he were in a dream.
夢鄉(ㄇㄥˋ ㄒㄧㄤ)
asleep; dreamland; sleep; slumber: 他已進入夢鄉了。He has fallen asleep.
夢想(ㄇㄥˋ ㄒㄧㄤˇ)
a daydream; daydreaming; vain hopes; to dream of: 許多人喜歡編織夢想。There are many people who are fond of spinning daydreams.
夢想不到(ㄇㄥˋ ㄒㄧㄤˇ ㄅㄨˋ ㄉㄠˋ)
(said of something very unlikely to happen but actually happened) beyond one's wildest dream
夢熊之喜(ㄇㄥˋ ㄒㄩㄥˊ ㄓ ㄒㄧˇ)
to give birth to a son
夢兆(ㄇㄥˋ ㄓㄠˋ)
a prognostic from a dream
夢中人(ㄇㄥˋ ㄓㄨㄥ ㄖㄣˊ)
a sweetheart
夢遺(ㄇㄥˋ ㄧˊ)
nocturnal emission
夢囈(ㄇㄥˋ ㄧˋ)
① somniloquy ② nonsense
夢遊(ㄇㄥˋ ㄧㄡˊ)
to somnambulate; somnambulation; somnambulism
夢魘(ㄇㄥˋ ㄧㄢˇ)
nightmares; bad dreams

【夤】914 ㄧㄣˊ yn yín
1. to hang on (power, glory, etc.)
2. to respect
3. a remote place
夤夜(ㄧㄣˊ ㄧㄝˋ)
deep in the night
夤緣(ㄧㄣˊ ㄩㄢˊ)
to rise or climb on somebody's coattails

【夥】915 ㄏㄨㄛˇ huoo huǒ
1. many; much; plenty; lots of
2. a partner; a company

3. a waiter; a clerk
4. a crowd
夥伴(ㄏㄨㄛˇ ㄅㄢˋ)
a companion; a partner; a business associate
夥同(ㄏㄨㄛˇ ㄊㄨㄥˊ)
in league with; to gang up with
夥計(ㄏㄨㄛˇ ·ㄐㄧ)
①a waiter; a clerk; an employee in a shop 亦作「伙計」 ②buddy

大部
ㄉㄚˋ dah dà

【大】 916
1. ㄉㄚˋ dah dà
1. big; large: 台北是個大城市。Taipei is a big city.
2. great: 貝多芬是個大音樂家。Beethoven was a great musician.
3. much: 無多大希望。There is not much hope.
4. very; highly; extremely; greatly: 他大爲吃驚。He was greatly surprised.
5. (polite expression) your: 大札 your letter
6. the eldest; senior: 他大我八歲。He is eight years senior to me.
7. full-grown; an adult
8. (referring to date only) before; after: 他大前天來過。He came here two days before yesterday.
9. to make large; to make great
10. a Chinese family name
大壩(ㄉㄚˋ ㄅㄚˋ)
a dam 參看「水壩」
大波斯菊(ㄉㄚˋ ㄅㄛ ㄙ ㄐㄩˊ)
(botany) a cosmos
大伯(ㄉㄚˋ ㄅㄛˊ)
①one's father's elder brother; an uncle 亦作「伯父」 ②an uncle (a polite form of address for an elderly man) 亦作「老伯」
大白
①(ㄉㄚˋ ㄅㄛˊ) ⓐname of a kind of wine-cup ⓑ(said of truth) to come out to the open; to be known by all: 眞相已經大白。The truth has become known to all.
②(ㄉㄚˋ ㄅㄞˊ) whiting
大白菜(ㄉㄚˋ ㄅㄞˊ ㄘㄞˋ)
a Chinese cabbage
大伯子(ㄉㄚˋ ㄅㄞˇ ·ㄗ)
the eldest brother of one's husband
大敗(ㄉㄚˋ ㄅㄞˋ)
①to defeat utterly; to put to rout ②to suffer a severe defeat
大悲(ㄉㄚˋ ㄅㄟ)
(Buddhism) the great deliverance of Buddha from sufferings and afflictions; the great mercy
大寶(ㄉㄚˋ ㄅㄠˇ)
the imperial throne
大班(ㄉㄚˋ ㄅㄢ)
①the manager of a foreign firm in China ②the captain (as of taxi dancers) ③the top class in a kindergarten
大阪(ㄉㄚˋ ㄅㄢˇ)
Osaka, a port city of Japan
大半(ㄉㄚˋ ㄅㄢˋ)
①the larger half; the greater part; for the most part; mostly: 工作完成了大半。The work is mostly done. ②probably; likely: 他大半被交通阻塞困住了。He is probably stuck in a traffic jam.
大本營(ㄉㄚˋ ㄅㄣˇ ㄧㄥˊ)
headquarters
大筆(ㄉㄚˋ ㄅㄧˇ)
①the brush-pen ②your writing; your handwriting
大別(ㄉㄚˋ ㄅㄧㄝˊ)
①a rough distinction; roughly classified ②name of a mountain range in Hupeh Province
大變(ㄉㄚˋ ㄅㄧㄢˋ)
a tragic incident; a big misfortune
大便(ㄉㄚˋ ㄅㄧㄢˋ)
stool; shit; faeces (or feces); excrement; night soil; to empty the bowels; to answer nature's call 參看「大糞」
大便不通(ㄉㄚˋ ㄅㄧㄢˋ ㄅㄨˋ ㄊㄨㄥ)
constipation
大兵(ㄉㄚˋ ㄅㄧㄥ)
①soldiers; foot soldiers ②a big battle
大兵團(ㄉㄚˋ ㄅㄧㄥ ㄊㄨㄢˊ)
large troop formation
大餅(ㄉㄚˋ ㄅㄧㄥˇ)
a kind of large flatbread
大病(ㄉㄚˋ ㄅㄧㄥˋ)
a serious illness or ailment: 他患著大病。He is suffering from a serious illness.
大不列顚(ㄉㄚˋ ㄅㄨˋ ㄌㄧㄝˋ ㄉㄧㄢ)
Great Britain
大不敬(ㄉㄚˋ ㄅㄨˊ ㄐㄧㄥˋ)
①great disrespect (to one's superiors or seniors) ②(in ancient China) a crime—discourtesy to the emperor; lese majesty
大不謂然(ㄉㄚˋ ㄅㄨˊ ㄨㄟˋ ㄖㄢˊ)
to hold an entirely different opinion
大不相同(ㄉㄚˋ ㄅㄨˋ ㄒㄧㄤ ㄊㄨㄥˊ)
entirely or totally different
大不如前(ㄉㄚˋ ㄅㄨˋ ㄖㄨˊ ㄑㄧㄢˊ)
far worse than it was before; to have deteriorated or declined a lot in the interval
大不韙(ㄉㄚˋ ㄅㄨˋ ㄨㄟˇ)
a great error; a heinous crime
大不了(ㄉㄚˋ ·ㄅㄨ ㄌㄧㄠˇ)
①if (the) worst comes to (the) worst; at the worst: 大不了我們也祇損失一萬元。We shall lose at (the) worst only ten thousand dollars. ②serious; frightening: 沒什麼大不了的事情。It's nothing frightening.
大部分(ㄉㄚˋ ㄅㄨˋ ㄈㄣˋ)
a great majority; for the most part; a greater part; mainly: 我班上大部分是女學生。The students in my class are mainly girls.
大牌(ㄉㄚˋ ㄆㄞˊ)
big-name (actors or actresses); (said of movie stars or other performing artists) leading
大砲(ㄉㄚˋ ㄆㄠˋ)
①guns; batteries; howitzers; cannons ②(slang) one who talks big
大鵬(ㄉㄚˋ ㄆㄥˊ)
a roc (a legendary bird)
大批(ㄉㄚˋ ㄆㄧ)

a large batch of; a good deal of; a horde of

大辟(ㄉㄚˋ ㄆㄧˋ)
capital punishment or death sentence (in ancient China)

大媽(ㄉㄚˋ ㄇㄚ)
① father's elder brother's wife; an aunt 亦作「伯母」② an aunt (an affectionate or respectful form of address for an elderly woman)

大麻(ㄉㄚˋ ㄇㄚˊ)
① hemp ② marijuana

大痲瘋(ㄉㄚˋ ㄇㄚˊ ㄈㄥ)
① leprosy ② a leper

大馬(ㄉㄚˋ ㄇㄚˇ)
Malaysia

大馬士革(ㄉㄚˋ ㄇㄚˇ ㄕˋ ㄍㄜˊ)
Damascus, capital of Syria

大麥(ㄉㄚˋ ㄇㄞˋ)
barley

大貓熊(ㄉㄚˋ ㄇㄠ ㄒㄩㄥˊ)
a giant panda

大帽子(ㄉㄚˋ ㄇㄠˋ ˙ㄗ)
①(colloquial) the high and mighty person ② a big hat ③ an unwarranted charge; a political label

大門(ㄉㄚˋ ㄇㄣˊ)
the main entrance; the main door or gate; the door that faces the street

大夢初醒(ㄉㄚˋ ㄇㄥˋ ㄔㄨ ㄒㄧㄥˇ)
the awakening or realization (of past wrongdoings, hopeless pursuits, mistakes, etc.)

大米(ㄉㄚˋ ㄇㄧˇ)
a variety of Chinese rice known to Westerners as "pearl rice"; white rice; rice (as opposed to wheat)

大謬(ㄉㄚˋ ㄇㄧㄡˋ)
a blunder; preposterous; absurd

大謬不然(ㄉㄚˋ ㄇㄧㄡˋ ㄅㄨˋ ㄖㄢˊ)
entirely wrong; greatly mistaken

大名(ㄉㄚˋ ㄇㄧㄥˊ)
① your name (used in formal speech) ② a great name; a reputation ③name of a county in Hopeh Province

大名鼎鼎(ㄉㄚˋ ㄇㄧㄥˊ ㄉㄧㄥˇ ㄉㄧㄥˇ)
the one and only Mr. So-and-so; a big name; very famous; celebrated; well-known: 他是個大名鼎鼎的小說家。He is a celebrated novelist.

大模大樣(ㄉㄚˋ ㄇㄨˊ ㄉㄚˋ ㄧㄤˋ)
① with full composure ② proudly; haughtily; in an open and showy manner; with a swagger

大拇指(ㄉㄚˋ ㄇㄨˇ ㄓˇ)
thumb: 他豎起大拇指叫好。He held up his thumb in approval.

大發雷霆(ㄉㄚˋ ㄈㄚ ㄌㄟˊ ㄊㄧㄥˊ)
to be in a fit of anger or wrath; to be furious; to get into a terrible rage: 他昨晚大發雷霆。He flew (or fell) into a rage last night.

大發雌威(ㄉㄚˋ ㄈㄚ ㄘˊ ㄨㄟ)
①(said of a woman) to get very angry; to blow her top ②(said of a woman athlete) to display great prowess

大法(ㄉㄚˋ ㄈㄚˇ)
the fundamental law; the constitution of a nation

大法官(ㄉㄚˋ ㄈㄚˇ ㄍㄨㄢ)
a grand justice

大法官會議(ㄉㄚˋ ㄈㄚˇ ㄍㄨㄢ ㄏㄨㄟˋ ㄧˋ)
the Council of Grand Justices

大費周章(ㄉㄚˋ ㄈㄟˋ ㄓㄡ ㄓㄤ)
to go into great trouble in doing something; to take great pains

大凡(ㄉㄚˋ ㄈㄢˊ)
generally speaking; in most cases; ordinarily

大糞(ㄉㄚˋ ㄈㄣˋ)
feces or faeces; excrement

大方(ㄉㄚˋ ㄈㄤ)
① generous; liberal ② elegant and composed; natural and poised; easy ③ experts; connoisseurs

大方向(ㄉㄚˋ ㄈㄤ ㄒㄧㄤˋ)
general orientation

大房(ㄉㄚˋ ㄈㄤˊ)
① the family of the eldest son after the old family breaks up ②name of a mountain in Hopeh Province

大放厥辭(ㄉㄚˋ ㄈㄤˋ ㄐㄩㄝˊ ㄘˊ)
to boast or brag wildly; to talk wildly; to talk absurdities or a lot of nonsense

大放異彩(ㄉㄚˋ ㄈㄤˋ ㄧˋ ㄘㄞˇ)
(said of sports performance, etc.) to yield unusually brilliant results

大風(ㄉㄚˋ ㄈㄥ)
a gale; a strong wind

大風大浪(ㄉㄚˋ ㄈㄥ ㄉㄚˋ ㄌㄤˋ)
winds and waves; great storms: 我們的事業是在大風大浪中發展起來的。It is amid great storms that our business made progress.

大婦(ㄉㄚˋ ㄈㄨˋ)
the wife (as distinct from a concubine)

大副(ㄉㄚˋ ㄈㄨˋ)
the first mate (of a ship)

大腹便便(ㄉㄚˋ ㄈㄨˋ ㄆㄧㄢˊ ㄆㄧㄢˊ)
paunchy; potbellied; big-bellied

大腹賈(ㄉㄚˋ ㄈㄨˋ ㄍㄨˇ)
a wealthy but uncultured merchant; a businessman who is only interested in making money

大打出手(ㄉㄚˋ ㄉㄚˇ ㄔㄨ ㄕㄡˇ)
to get into a free-for-all or a brawl

大大(ㄉㄚˋ ㄉㄚˋ)
greatly; enormously: 生產效率大大提高。Productivity has risen greatly.

大大小小(ㄉㄚˋ ˙ㄉㄚ ㄒㄧㄠˇ ㄒㄧㄠˇ)
the big and the small—the whole family

大刀闊斧(ㄉㄚˋ ㄉㄠ ㄎㄨㄛˋ ㄈㄨˇ)
(literally) a big knife and a broad ax—(figuratively) to act decisively and resolutely; to act in a sweeping manner

大刀會(ㄉㄚˋ ㄉㄠ ㄏㄨㄟˋ)
the Society of Big Swords; a quasi-religious secret society in old China

大道(ㄉㄚˋ ㄉㄠˋ)
① a wide road ② the way of virtue and justice

大道理(ㄉㄚˋ ㄉㄠˋ ㄌㄧˇ)
① a persuasive argument; eloquent reasoning; a high-sounding statement ② a major principle; a general principle

大豆(ㄉㄚˋ ㄉㄡˋ)
soybeans

大丹狗(ㄉㄚˋ ㄉㄢ ㄍㄡˇ)
a great Dane

大膽(ㄉㄚˋ ㄉㄢˇ)
bold; boldness; to do things without much forethought

and hesitation: 大膽做它吧! Do it without hesitation.

大敵當前(ㄉㄚˋ ㄉㄧˊ ㄉㄤ ㄑㄧㄢˊ)
a dangerous enemy ahead; confronted with a strong opponent

大抵(ㄉㄚˋ ㄉㄧˇ)
generally speaking; for the most part; on the whole

大地(ㄉㄚˋ ㄉㄧˋ)
① the earth ② the whole territory of a nation

大地主(ㄉㄚˋ ㄉㄧˋ ㄓㄨˇ)
a big landowner or landlord

大地春回(ㄉㄚˋ ㄉㄧˋ ㄔㄨㄣ ㄏㄨㄟˊ)
Spring has returned to the land. 或 Spring is here again. 亦作「大地回春」

大典(ㄉㄚˋ ㄉㄧㄢˇ)
① a grand ceremony ② a collection of great classics

大殿(ㄉㄚˋ ㄉㄧㄢˋ)
① the main hall in a palace ② the main hall of a Buddhist temple

大都(ㄉㄚˋ ㄉㄨ)
most probably; almost; for the most part; generally: 兒童大都喜好遊戲。Children are generally fond of play.

大都市(ㄉㄚˋ ㄉㄨ ㄕˋ)
a large city; a metropolis: 紐約是個繁華的大都市。New York is a busy metropolis.

大度(ㄉㄚˋ ㄉㄨˋ)
magnanimity; generosity; open-mindedness

大肚子(ㄉㄚˋ ㄉㄨˋ ˙ㄗ)
① pregnant ② a big eater ③ a potbelly

大多(ㄉㄚˋ ㄉㄨㄛ)
for the most part; mostly

大多數(ㄉㄚˋ ㄉㄨㄛ ㄕㄨˋ)
a great majority; the majority; a great many: 大多數的人喜愛和平而不要戰爭。The majority of people prefer peace to war.

大憝(ㄉㄚˋ ㄉㄨㄟˋ)
① a principal criminal ② a disgusting fellow

大隊(ㄉㄚˋ ㄉㄨㄟˋ)
①(said of military cadets, militia, or paramilitary units) a battalion ② a group (in air force organization)

大隊人馬(ㄉㄚˋ ㄉㄨㄟˋ ㄖㄣˊ ㄇㄚˇ)
a large number of soldiers and horses; a large detachment of troops

大端(ㄉㄚˋ ㄉㄨㄢ)
main aspects (or features); salient points

大動脈(ㄉㄚˋ ㄉㄨㄥˋ ㄇㄞˋ)or (ㄉㄚˋ ㄉㄨㄥˋ ㄇㄛˋ)
the main artery

大頭針(ㄉㄚˋ ㄊㄡˊ ㄓㄣ)
tacks

大頭菜(ㄉㄚˋ ㄊㄡˊ ㄘㄞˋ)
salted turnips

大提琴(ㄉㄚˋ ㄊㄧˊ ㄑㄧㄣˊ)
a cello

大提琴家(ㄉㄚˋ ㄊㄧˊ ㄑㄧㄣˊ ㄐㄧㄚ)
a cellist

大體(ㄉㄚˋ ㄊㄧˇ)
① generally; on the whole; for the most part; in the main: 我大體上還喜歡。On the whole, I like it. ② the main principle; the main thing: 我們要識大體, 顧全局。We should have the cardinal principles in mind and take the overall situation into account.

大廳(ㄉㄚˋ ㄊㄧㄥ)
a big hall; the main hall; the parlor

大庭廣衆(ㄉㄚˋ ㄊㄧㄥˊ ㄍㄨㄤˇ ㄓㄨㄥˋ)
① public places where the crowd gather ② in public

大腿(ㄉㄚˋ ㄊㄨㄟˇ)
the thigh

大團圓(ㄉㄚˋ ㄊㄨㄢˊ ㄩㄢˊ)
a happy ending; a happy reunion

大同小異(ㄉㄚˋ ㄊㄨㄥˊ ㄒㄧㄠˇ ㄧˋ)
with slight differences only; almost the same; generally similar with differences in detail only; much of a muchness

大同世界(ㄉㄚˋ ㄊㄨㄥˊ ㄕˋ ㄐㄧㄝˋ)
a world where harmony, equality and justice prevail —a political utopia

大統(ㄉㄚˋ ㄊㄨㄥˇ)
① the enterprise of unifying the whole country ② the throne

大腦(ㄉㄚˋ ㄋㄠˇ)
① the cerebrum ② a sarcastic reference to intellectual capacity

大難(ㄉㄚˋ ㄋㄢˋ)
a catastrophe; a disaster; a calamity

大難臨頭(ㄉㄚˋ ㄋㄢˋ ㄌㄧㄣˊ ㄊㄡˊ)
a great calamity just ahead; an imminent catastrophe or disaster; to be faced with great trouble

大逆不道(ㄉㄚˋ ㄋㄧˋ ㄅㄨˋ ㄉㄠˋ)
sedition; treason; traitorous actions; great crimes—as patricide, matricide, or regicide

大年初一(ㄉㄚˋ ㄋㄧㄢˊ ㄔㄨ ㄧ)
the first day of the lunar year; the lunar New Year's Day

大年夜(ㄉㄚˋ ㄋㄧㄢˊ ㄧㄝˋ)
on the night of the lunar New Year's Eve

大娘(ㄉㄚˋ ㄋㄧㄤˊ)
① a reference to father's first wife by children born of a concubine ② a polite salutation for an elderly woman

大牢(ㄉㄚˋ ㄌㄠˊ)
a prison; a jail

大老粗(ㄉㄚˋ ㄌㄠˇ ㄘㄨ)
an uncouth fellow; an uneducated person

大樓(ㄉㄚˋ ㄌㄡˊ)
a multistoried building

大禮(ㄉㄚˋ ㄌㄧˇ)
(in ancient China) the most solemn of ceremonies—including three kneelings and nine kowtows—performed in paying respects to a new master, foster parents, etc.

大禮拜(ㄉㄚˋ ㄌㄧˇ ㄅㄞˋ)
alternate Sunday on which one has a day off; a fortnightly holiday

大禮服(ㄉㄚˋ ㄌㄧˇ ㄈㄨˊ)
formal dress (worn by diplomats or other dignitaries at state functions or on other solemn occasions); ceremonial dress

大禮堂(ㄉㄚˋ ㄌㄧˇ ㄊㄤˊ)
an auditorium

大理石(ㄉㄚˋ ㄌㄧˇ ㄕˊ)
marble: 此碑由大理石刻成。The monument is carved in marble.

大理寺(ㄉㄚˋ ㄌㄧˇ ㄙˋ)

〔大部〕

(in ancient China) the Supreme Court

大理寺卿(ㄉㄚˋ ㄌㄧˇ ㄙˋ ㄑㄧㄥ)
(in ancient China) the president of the Supreme Court

〔大部〕

大力(ㄉㄚˋ ㄌㄧˋ)
energetically; vigorously; with a great effort: 此時我們必須大力發展教育事業。We have to devote our major efforts to developing education now.

大力士(ㄉㄚˋ ㄌㄧˋ ㄕˋ)
a hercules; a man of unusual strength

大麗花(ㄉㄚˋ ㄌㄧˋ ㄏㄨㄚ)
(botany) *Dahlia pinnata*

大連(ㄉㄚˋ ㄌㄧㄢˊ)
Talien—a seaport in Liaoning Province

大殮(ㄉㄚˋ ㄌㄧㄢˋ)
to place the corpse into the coffin; an encoffining ceremony

大量(ㄉㄚˋ ㄌㄧㄤˋ)
① a large quantity; plentiful; abundant; profuse; mass (production, etc.): 今年夏天我們有大量的雨水。We've had great quantities of rain this summer. ② magnanimous; large-minded: 他們是寬宏大量的思想家和政治家。They are large-minded thinkers and statesmen.

大路(ㄉㄚˋ ㄌㄨˋ)
the highroad

大陸(ㄉㄚˋ ㄌㄨˋ)
a continent; the mainland: 歐洲大陸習俗與英國習俗不同。Continental customs differ from those of England.

大陸性氣候(ㄉㄚˋ ㄌㄨˋ ㄒㄧㄥˋ ㄑㄧˋ ㄏㄡˋ)
a continental climate

大露營(ㄉㄚˋ ㄌㄨˋ ㄧㄥˊ)
a jamboree

大亂(ㄉㄚˋ ㄌㄨㄢˋ)
great turmoil; social or political upheaval

大倫(ㄉㄚˋ ㄌㄨㄣˊ)
the important human relations, as parents and children, brothers and sisters, husband and wife, etc.

大略(ㄉㄚˋ ㄌㄩㄝˋ)
① briefly; brief; roughly; generally ②(a man of) great caliber or talent ③ a general outline

大哥(ㄉㄚˋ ㄍㄜ)
① the eldest brother ② elder brother (a polite form of address for a man about one's own age)

大個兒(ㄉㄚˋ ㄍㄜˋㄦ) or 大個子(ㄉㄚˋ ㄍㄜˋ ˙ㄗ)
a big man; a giant; a tall guy

大概(ㄉㄚˋ ㄍㄞˋ)
most probably; for the most part; generally; in general

大幹(ㄉㄚˋ ㄍㄢˋ)
to work energetically; to go all out; to make an all-out effort

大綱(ㄉㄚˋ ㄍㄤ)
an outline; a synopsis; a summary: 請告訴我們他授課的內容大綱。Please give us the outline of his lecture.

大姑娘(ㄉㄚˋ ㄍㄨ ˙ㄋㄧㄤ)
an unmarried young woman; a maiden; a damsel

大姑子(ㄉㄚˋ ㄍㄨ ˙ㄗ)
husband's elder sister; a sister-in-law

大鼓書(ㄉㄚˋ ㄍㄨˇ ㄕㄨ)
(a form of Chinese entertainment) a story told by singing with the accompaniment of drumbeats

大故(ㄉㄚˋ ㄍㄨˋ)
① the death of one's parents ② a big crime

大褂(ㄉㄚˋ ㄍㄨㄚˋ)
the Chinese long gown

大過(ㄉㄚˋ ㄍㄨㄛˋ)
① a big mistake or shortcoming: 他犯了一次大過。He made a serious mistake. ② (said of punishment in school, etc.) a major demerit

大規模(ㄉㄚˋ ㄍㄨㄟ ㄇㄛˊ)
large-scale; on a large scale

大官(ㄉㄚˋ ㄍㄨㄢ)
ranking officials

大觀(ㄉㄚˋ ㄍㄨㄢ)
a grand sight; a magnificent spectacle

大功(ㄉㄚˋ ㄍㄨㄥ)
a great achievement

大功告成(ㄉㄚˋ ㄍㄨㄥ ㄍㄠˋ ㄔㄥˊ)
(said of a big or difficult task) to have finally come to completion; to have been brought to a successful conclusion

大公無私(ㄉㄚˋ ㄍㄨㄥ ㄨˊ ㄙ)
all for the public without selfish considerations; fair and square; impartial: 法律應該一視同仁，大公無私。Law should be uniform and impartial.

大可不必(ㄉㄚˋ ㄎㄜˇ ㄅㄨˋ ㄅㄧˋ)
It's not at all worth it. 或 It's unnecessary.

大可一試(ㄉㄚˋ ㄎㄜˇ ㄧˊ ㄕˋ)
really worth a try

大開眼界(ㄉㄚˋ ㄎㄞ ㄧㄢˇ ㄐㄧㄝˋ)
to see something completely new or very strange; to have a wonderful sight or new experience

大楷(ㄉㄚˋ ㄎㄞˇ)
(Chinese calligraphy) large-sized characters

大考(ㄉㄚˋ ㄎㄠˇ)
the final or terminal examination in school: 她忙於準備大考。She is busily preparing for the final examination.

大塊頭(ㄉㄚˋ ㄎㄨㄞˋ ˙ㄊㄡ)
a tall and bulky fellow; a whale of a man

大快人心(ㄉㄚˋ ㄎㄨㄞˋ ㄖㄣˊ ㄒㄧㄣ)
(usually said of a wrong being righted, justice prevailed, etc.) to give all a lift of the heart; to the immense satisfaction of the people

大合唱(ㄉㄚˋ ㄏㄜˊ ㄔㄤˋ)
a chorus sung by a large choir

大海(ㄉㄚˋ ㄏㄞˇ)
① a widemouthed bowl or wine cup ② the ocean

大海撈針(ㄉㄚˋ ㄏㄞˇ ㄌㄠ ㄓㄣ)
(literally) to fish a needle from the sea—to look for a needle in a haystack

大好(ㄉㄚˋ ㄏㄠˇ)
very good; excellent; golden: 這正是個大好時機。It's a golden opportunity.

大好河山(ㄉㄚˋ ㄏㄠˇ ㄏㄜˊ ㄕㄢ)
beautiful rivers and mountains

大好時光(ㄉㄚˋ ㄏㄠˇ ㄕˊ ㄍㄨㄤ)

the golden years; the prime of one's life
大號(ㄉㄚˋ ㄏㄠˋ)
①large-size ②(music) a tuba; a bass horn
大後方(ㄉㄚˋ ㄏㄡˋ ㄈㄤ)
the rear area
大後天(ㄉㄚˋ ㄏㄡˋ ㄊㄧㄢ)
three days from today; two days after tomorrow
大後年(ㄉㄚˋ ㄏㄡˋ ㄋㄧㄢˊ)
three years from the current year; two years after next
大寒(ㄉㄚˋ ㄏㄢˊ)
(literally) Severe cold, one of the 24 Chinese climatic periods, which falls on January 20 or 21
大喊大叫(ㄉㄚˋ ㄏㄢˇ ㄉㄚˋ ㄐㄧㄠˋ)
① to shout at the top of one's voice: 別對我大喊大叫。Don't shout at me. ② to conduct vigorous propaganda
大漢(ㄉㄚˋ ㄏㄢˋ)
① a tall and strong man; a whale of a man: 他是個彪形大漢。He is a tall and strong fellow. ② the great Han Dynasty
大旱雲霓(ㄉㄚˋ ㄏㄢˋ ㄩㄣˊ ㄋㄧˊ)
(literally) clouds in a serious drought—something yielding high hopes
大亨(ㄉㄚˋ ㄏㄥ)
a big shot; a bigwig; a VIP; a tycoon; a magnate
大戶(ㄉㄚˋ ㄏㄨˋ)
a wealthy and influential family
大戶人家(ㄉㄚˋ ㄏㄨˋ ㄖㄣˊ ㄐㄧㄚ)
a wealthy and influential family; a famous family of long standing
大花臉(ㄉㄚˋ ㄏㄨㄚ ㄌㄧㄢˇ)
(Peking opera) a male role of dignified type
大話(ㄉㄚˋ ㄏㄨㄚˋ)
boasts; bragging; big words; big talks: 他愛說大話。He likes to talk big. 或 He is a boaster.
大火(ㄉㄚˋ ㄏㄨㄛˇ)
a big fire; a conflagration
大夥兒(ㄉㄚˋ ㄏㄨㄛˇㄦ)
① us; we ② a group of people
大禍(ㄉㄚˋ ㄏㄨㄛˋ)
a calamity; a big disaster: 戰爭是可怕的大禍。War is a frightful calamity.
大惑不解(ㄉㄚˋ ㄏㄨㄛˋ ㄅㄨˋ ㄐㄧㄝˇ)
beyond comprehension; incomprehensible; confused
大會(ㄉㄚˋ ㄏㄨㄟˋ)
a rally; a plenary meeting; a convention; a conference: 這是個全體出席的大會。This is a plenary meeting (or session).
大婚(ㄉㄚˋ ㄏㄨㄣ)
the marriage of the emperor
大黃(ㄉㄚˋ ㄏㄨㄤˊ)
(Chinese medicine) rhubarb
大黃蜂(ㄉㄚˋ ㄏㄨㄤˊ ㄈㄥ)
a hornet
大紅(ㄉㄚˋ ㄏㄨㄥˊ)
crimson; deep red; dark red
大紅大綠(ㄉㄚˋ ㄏㄨㄥˊ ㄉㄚˋ ㄌㄩˋ)
gaudy and showy
大吉大利(ㄉㄚˋ ㄐㄧˊ ㄉㄚˋ ㄌㄧˋ)
(literally) unexcelled luck and great prosperity—very smooth going or operation (often used to offer best wishes to a new store, business, etc.)
大計(ㄉㄚˋ ㄐㄧˋ)
① the policy of a state; national plans or programs ② a matter of fundamental importance: 教育乃百年大計。Education is a matter of fundamental importance for generations to come.
大祭司(ㄉㄚˋ ㄐㄧˋ ㄙ)
a high priest
大家(ㄉㄚˋ ㄐㄧㄚ)
① all of us; we ② a rich and influential family of long standing ③ a famous expert; a master: 他是位書法大家。He is a great master of calligraphy.
大家庭(ㄉㄚˋ ㄐㄧㄚ ㄊㄧㄥˊ)
① a big family ② a community
大駕(ㄉㄚˋ ㄐㄧㄚˋ)
① to your gracious presence ② the carriage for a sovereign or emperor
大街小巷(ㄉㄚˋ ㄐㄧㄝ ㄒㄧㄠˇ ㄒㄧㄤˋ)
in every street and alley—all over the city
大捷(ㄉㄚˋ ㄐㄧㄝˊ)
a big victory; a smashing victory
大姊 or 大姐(ㄉㄚˋ ㄐㄧㄝˇ)
the eldest sister
大解(ㄉㄚˋ ㄐㄧㄝˇ)
to empty one's bowels; to go to the stool
大教堂(ㄉㄚˋ ㄐㄧㄠˋ ㄊㄤˊ)
a cathedral
大舅子(ㄉㄚˋ ㄐㄧㄡˋ ˙ㄗ)
one's wife's elder brothers
大襟(ㄉㄚˋ ㄐㄧㄣ)
the right forepart of a Chinese gown
大江(ㄉㄚˋ ㄐㄧㄤ)
①a great river ②the Yangtze River
大將(ㄉㄚˋ ㄐㄧㄤˋ)
① an important general; a capable commander ② a trusted lieutenant; a right-hand man ③ a senior general
大將風度(ㄉㄚˋ ㄐㄧㄤˋ ㄈㄥ ㄉㄨˋ)
the style of a great general or admiral (used as a compliment)
大驚小怪(ㄉㄚˋ ㄐㄧㄥ ㄒㄧㄠˇ ㄍㄨㄞˋ)
to make a fuss; to make much ado about nothing: 不要爲小事情大驚小怪地。Don't make so much fuss about trifles.
大靜脈(ㄉㄚˋ ㄐㄧㄥˋ ㄇㄞˋ) or (ㄉㄚˋ ㄐㄧㄥˋ ㄇㄛˋ)
the vena cava
大局(ㄉㄚˋ ㄐㄩˊ)
① the situation in general: 我們要顧全大局。We have to take the whole situation into account. ② national interests; the fate of a nation
大舉(ㄉㄚˋ ㄐㄩˇ)
① a large-scale (invasion, etc.); to make a decisive move ② a great undertaking
大軍(ㄉㄚˋ ㄐㄩㄣ)
a great concentration of troops; main forces: 大軍隨後就到。The main forces will be here soon.
大氣(ㄉㄚˋ ㄑㄧˋ)
① the atmosphere; atmospheric ② a grand air or deportment ③ heavy breathing ④ magnanimity; openmindedness

〔大部〕

〔大部〕

大氣層(ㄉㄚˋ ㄑㄧˋ ㄘㄥˊ)
the atmospheric boundary layer

大氣壓力(ㄉㄚˋ ㄑㄧˋ ㄧㄚ ㄌㄧˋ)
atmospheric pressure

大器晚成(ㄉㄚˋ ㄑㄧˋ ㄨㄢˇ ㄔㄥˊ)
(literally) A great vessel will be long in completion. — A great man will take time to shape and mature.

大千世界(ㄉㄚˋ ㄑㄧㄢ ㄕˋ ㄐㄧㄝˋ)
①(Buddhism) 1,000,000,000 universes; the boundless universe ②the kaleidoscopic world

大錢(ㄉㄚˋ ㄑㄧㄢˊ)
①real big money ②an old Chinese coin of a low denomination

大前提(ㄉㄚˋ ㄑㄧㄢˊ ㄊㄧˊ)
a major premise; a set principle

大前天(ㄉㄚˋ ㄑㄧㄢˊ ㄊㄧㄢ)
three days ago

大前年(ㄉㄚˋ ㄑㄧㄢˊ ㄋㄧㄢˊ)
the fourth year counted backward, beginning from the current year; three years ago

大秦(ㄉㄚˋ ㄑㄧㄣˊ)
an ancient name for the Roman Empire

大清早(ㄉㄚˋ ㄑㄧㄥ ㄗㄠˇ)
very early in the morning

大情人(ㄉㄚˋ ㄑㄧㄥˊ ㄖㄣˊ)
a Casanova, or ladies' man; a woman's lover

大慶(ㄉㄚˋ ㄑㄧㄥˋ)
①an occasion or event deserving a big celebration ②a national festival or holiday ③birthday (in reference to other's birthday)

大去(ㄉㄚˋ ㄑㄩˋ)
to go away and never to come back—to be dead

大全(ㄉㄚˋ ㄑㄩㄢˊ)
complete works of; a complete collection of; a complete volume on (civil law, etc.)

大權(ㄉㄚˋ ㄑㄩㄢˊ)
the authority or power to reign over a state, or office; great power or authority

大權旁落(ㄉㄚˋ ㄑㄩㄢˊ ㄆㄤˊ ㄌㄨㄛˋ)
Power has fallen into the hands of others. 或to lose one's power to a subordinate while remaining as a figurehead

大權在握(ㄉㄚˋ ㄑㄩㄢˊ ㄗㄞˋ ㄨㄛˋ)
to hold power unchallenged; to assume the reins of government or organization

大溪地(ㄉㄚˋ ㄒㄧ ㄉㄧˋ)
Tahiti

大西洋(ㄉㄚˋ ㄒㄧ ㄧㄤˊ)
the Atlantic Ocean

大喜(ㄉㄚˋ ㄒㄧˇ)
great rejoicing

大喜過望(ㄉㄚˋ ㄒㄧˇ ㄍㄨㄛˋ ㄨㄤˋ)
to be pleased beyond expectations; to be overjoyed

大峽谷(ㄉㄚˋ ㄒㄧㄚˊ ㄍㄨˇ)
the Grand Canyon in the United States

大廈(ㄉㄚˋ ㄒㄧㄚˋ)or(ㄉㄚˋ ㄕㄚˋ)
a big building; a mansion

大寫(ㄉㄚˋ ㄒㄧㄝˇ)
①a capital letter ②the elaborate form of Chinese numerals (used especially in accounting and checks)

大小(ㄉㄚˋ ㄒㄧㄠˇ)
①adults and children ②one's wife and concubine ③sizes (of dresses, shoes, etc.) ④degree of seniority

大小便(ㄉㄚˋ ㄒㄧㄠˇ ㄅㄧㄢˋ)
night soil and urine; the act of discharging such

大小不一(ㄉㄚˋ ㄒㄧㄠˇ ㄅㄨˋ ㄧ)
irregular in size, age, etc.

大小姐(ㄉㄚˋ ㄒㄧㄠˇ ㄐㄧㄝˇ)
①a maiden; a Miss ②a reference to others' elder or eldest daughters

大笑(ㄉㄚˋ ㄒㄧㄠˋ)
to laugh heartily; to roar with laughter: 他們都大笑起來。They all laughed loudly.

大修(ㄉㄚˋ ㄒㄧㄡ)
major repairs; an overhaul

大顯身手(ㄉㄚˋ ㄒㄧㄢˇ ㄕㄣ ㄕㄡˇ)
to display one's skill to the full; to give full play to one's abilities; to give a good account of oneself

大顯神通(ㄉㄚˋ ㄒㄧㄢˇ ㄕㄣˊ ㄊㄨㄥ)
to display one's remarkable skill or abilities to the full

大限(ㄉㄚˋ ㄒㄧㄢˋ)
the time of one's death

大憲章(ㄉㄚˋ ㄒㄧㄢˋ ㄓㄤ)
the Magna Charta, or the Magna Carta, signed by King John of England in 1215

大相逕庭(ㄉㄚˋ ㄒㄧㄤ ㄐㄧㄥˋ ㄊㄧㄥˊ)
totally different; entirely contrary; far apart: 他們的意見和我的大相逕庭。Their view was diametrically opposed to mine.

大興土木(ㄉㄚˋ ㄒㄧㄥ ㄊㄨˇ ㄇㄨˋ)
to start a large-scale building project

大興問罪之師(ㄉㄚˋ ㄒㄧㄥ ㄨㄣˋ ㄗㄨㄟˋ ㄓ ㄕ)
to launch a punitive campaign—to point angrily an accusing finger at someone; to condemn scathingly; to demand an explanation

大刑(ㄉㄚˋ ㄒㄧㄥˊ)
heavy penalties or stiff sentences

大型(ㄉㄚˋ ㄒㄧㄥˊ)
(said of machines, etc.) large-sized; large-scale

大行皇帝(ㄉㄚˋ ㄒㄧㄥˊ ㄏㄨㄤˊ ㄉㄧˋ)
the late emperor

大學(ㄉㄚˋ ㄒㄩㄝˊ)
①a university or college ②*The Great Learning* (one of the *Four Classics*)

大學生(ㄉㄚˋ ㄒㄩㄝˊ ㄕㄥ)
a college or university student; a collegian

大雪(ㄉㄚˋ ㄒㄩㄝˇ)
①a heavy snow ②(literally) Heavy snow—one of the 24 climatic periods in China usually falling on the 7th or 8th of December

大選(ㄉㄚˋ ㄒㄩㄢˇ)
①a presidential election ②general elections for congressmen

大熊座(ㄉㄚˋ ㄒㄩㄥˊ ㄗㄨㄛˋ)
(astronomy) the Ursa Major

大指(ㄉㄚˋ ㄓˇ)
the thumb

大志(ㄉㄚˋ ㄓˋ)
great ambitions; high aims: 他的大志是做一位大政治家。His great ambition is to be a great statesman.

大致(ㄉㄚˋ ㄓˋ)
①generally; for the most

part; as a whole ② more or less; about
大智若愚(ㄉㄚˋ ㄓˋ ㄖㄨㄛˋ ㄩˊ)
The wise man looks dumb (because he never shows off).
大札(ㄉㄚˋ ㄓㄚˊ)
your letter
大展宏圖(ㄉㄚˋ ㄓㄢˇ ㄏㄨㄥˊ ㄊㄨˊ)
to realize one's ambition; to ride on the crest of success
大張撻伐(ㄉㄚˋ ㄓㄤ ㄊㄚˋ ㄈㄚˊ)
to let out a broadside; to attack with full force
大張旗鼓(ㄉㄚˋ ㄓㄤ ㄑㄧˊ ㄍㄨˇ)
① to make a big show; to put up a pageantry ② on a grand scale; in a big way
大丈夫(ㄉㄚˋ ㄓㄤˋ ㄈㄨ)
a real man; a man of fortitude and courage
大主教(ㄉㄚˋ ㄓㄨˇ ㄐㄧㄠˋ)
an archbishop
大著(ㄉㄚˋ ㄓㄨˋ)or 大作(ㄉㄚˋ ㄗㄨㄛˋ)
your work; your script; your book
大專學校(ㄉㄚˋ ㄓㄨㄢ ㄒㄩㄝˊ ㄒㄧㄠˋ)or 大專院校(ㄉㄚˋ ㄓㄨㄢ ㄩㄢˋ ㄒㄧㄠˋ)
colleges and universities
大衆(ㄉㄚˋ ㄓㄨㄥˋ)
the people; the masses; the public
大衆媒介(ㄉㄚˋ ㄓㄨㄥˋ ㄇㄟˊ ㄐㄧㄝˋ)
mass media
大衆化(ㄉㄚˋ ㄓㄨㄥˋ ㄏㄨㄚˋ)
to popularize; popularized; popularization: 我們必須使科學大衆化。We must popularize science.
大衆捷運系統(ㄉㄚˋ ㄓㄨㄥˋ ㄐㄧㄝˊ ㄩㄣˋ ㄒㄧˋ ㄊㄨㄥˇ)
mass rapid transit (MRT)
大衆教育(ㄉㄚˋ ㄓㄨㄥˋ ㄐㄧㄠˋ ㄩˋ)
mass education
大衆消費(ㄉㄚˋ ㄓㄨㄥˋ ㄒㄧㄠ ㄈㄟˋ)
mass consumption
大衆傳播(ㄉㄚˋ ㄓㄨㄥˋ ㄔㄨㄢˊ ㄅㄛˋ)
mass communications
大衆傳播媒體(ㄉㄚˋ ㄓㄨㄥˋ ㄔㄨㄢˊ ㄅㄛˋ ㄇㄟˊ ㄊㄧˇ)
mass (communications) media
大衆文學(ㄉㄚˋ ㄓㄨㄥˋ ㄨㄣˊ ㄒㄩㄝˊ)
popular literature (as newspapers, magazines, novels, short stories, etc.)
大衆娛樂(ㄉㄚˋ ㄓㄨㄥˋ ㄩˊ ㄌㄜˋ)
mass entertainment
大仲馬(ㄉㄚˋ ㄓㄨㄥˋ ㄇㄚˇ)
Alexandre Dumas (*Dumas père*), 1802-70, French dramatist and novelist
大吃大喝(ㄉㄚˋ ㄔ ㄉㄚˋ ㄏㄜ)
to eat and drink extravagantly
大吃一驚(ㄉㄚˋ ㄔ ㄧˋ ㄐㄧㄥ)
to be shocked; to be greatly surprised; to be taken aback: 這消息使我們大吃一驚。The news greatly surprised us.
大澈大悟(ㄉㄚˋ ㄔㄜˋ ㄉㄚˋ ㄨˋ)
(usually said of oneself) a profound and complete realization or understanding ② (theology) the great revelation
大臣(ㄉㄚˋ ㄔㄣˊ)
ranking officials; cabinet ministers
大腸(ㄉㄚˋ ㄔㄤˊ)
the large intestine
大腸桿菌(ㄉㄚˋ ㄔㄤˊ ㄍㄢˇ ㄐㄩㄣˋ)
coliform bacillus
大氅(ㄉㄚˋ ㄔㄤˇ)
an overcoat
大成(ㄉㄚˋ ㄔㄥˊ)
great achievement or accomplishment
大成殿(ㄉㄚˋ ㄔㄥˊ ㄉㄧㄢˋ)
the main hall of the Confucius Temple
大成問題(ㄉㄚˋ ㄔㄥˊ ㄨㄣˋ ㄊㄧˊ)
very questionable; very doubtful; in doubt
大出洋相(ㄉㄚˋ ㄔㄨ ㄧㄤˊ ㄒㄧㄤˋ)
to commit a big blunder in public; to have a major contretemps
大處著墨(ㄉㄚˋ ㄔㄨˋ ㄓㄨㄛˊ ㄇㄛˋ)or 大處落墨(ㄉㄚˋ ㄔㄨˋ ㄌㄨㄛˋ ㄇㄛˋ)
to concentrate on the key points
大處著眼，小處著手(ㄉㄚˋ ㄔㄨˋ ㄓㄨㄛˊ ㄧㄢˇ, ㄒㄧㄠˇ ㄔㄨˋ ㄓㄨㄛˊ ㄕㄡˇ)
to make an overall assessment but to start from details 或 Although beginning a task from the bottom, one mustn't forget the ultimate objective.
大吹大擂(ㄉㄚˋ ㄔㄨㄟ ㄉㄚˋ ㄌㄟˊ)
to brag and blare (about one's success, etc.); to talk big; to give wide publicity; to make a great fanfare; to make a big noise
大醇小疵(ㄉㄚˋ ㄔㄨㄣˊ ㄒㄧㄠˇ ㄘ)
to be sound on the whole though defective in details
大蟲(ㄉㄚˋ ㄔㄨㄥˊ)
a tiger
大師(ㄉㄚˋ ㄕ)
① a master; a maestro ② a reverent title for a Buddhist monk
大師傅(ㄉㄚˋ ㄕ ·ㄈㄨ)
① a head cook; a chef ② a salutation for a Buddhist monk
大失所望(ㄉㄚˋ ㄕ ㄙㄨㄛˇ ㄨㄤˋ)
to be greatly disappointed; to be greatly discouraged
大食(ㄉㄚˋ ㄕˊ)
the Moslem empire built by the Arabs
大使(ㄉㄚˋ ㄕˇ)
an ambassador: 他奉派爲駐美大使。He was appointed ambassador to the United States.
大使館(ㄉㄚˋ ㄕˇ ㄍㄨㄢˇ)
an embassy
大事(ㄉㄚˋ ㄕˋ)
① important events; significant national events; serious matters: 我們要關心國家大事。We have to concern ourselves with the affairs of our country. ② the death of one's parents
大事鋪張(ㄉㄚˋ ㄕˋ ㄆㄨ ㄓㄤ)
to make lavish preparations; to put up a lavish show (especially of a wedding, etc.)
大事化小，小事化無(ㄉㄚˋ ㄕˋ ㄏㄨㄚˋ ㄒㄧㄠˇ, ㄒㄧㄠˇ ㄕˋ ㄏㄨㄚˋ ㄨˊ)
to turn big problems into small problems and small problems into no problem at all
大事記(ㄉㄚˋ ㄕˋ ㄐㄧˋ)
a record of important events; a chronicle
大事宣傳(ㄉㄚˋ ㄕˋ ㄒㄩㄢ ㄔㄨㄢˊ)
to play up; to ballyhoo
大勢所趨(ㄉㄚˋ ㄕˋ ㄙㄨㄛˇ ㄑㄩ)
general trend indicates...; according to the prevailing tendency

〔大部〕

大勢已去(ㄉㄚˋ ㄕˋ ㄧˇ ㄑㄩˋ)
The situation is beyond salvation. 或 The situation is irretrievable, hopeless, etc.

大舌頭(ㄉㄚˋ ㄕㄜˊ ·ㄊㄡ)
(literally) an oversized tongue—unable to speak clearly

大赦(ㄉㄚˋ ㄕㄜˋ)
an amnesty

大少爺(ㄉㄚˋ ㄕㄠˋ ·ㄧㄝ)
① a term used by a servant to address the eldest son of the family ② a dandy; a playboy

大手筆(ㄉㄚˋ ㄕㄡˇ ㄅㄧˇ)
the work or handwriting of a great author or calligrapher

大聲疾呼(ㄉㄚˋ ㄕㄥ ㄐㄧˊ ㄏㄨ)
to urge emphatically; to raise a cry of warning; a clarion call to awaken the public to lurking danger by writings or speeches; to call aloud

大乘(ㄉㄚˋ ㄕㄥˋ)
(Buddhism) the Mahayana or "Great Vehicle" school

大勝(ㄉㄚˋ ㄕㄥˋ)
to win overwhelmingly or decisively; a decisive win; to win a big victory; a major victory

大聖(ㄉㄚˋ ㄕㄥˋ)
an outstanding person; an extraordinary person

大書特書(ㄉㄚˋ ㄕㄨ ㄊㄜˋ ㄕㄨ)
to write repeatedly or elaborately on; to make an issue of something by writing in this manner; to write volumes about—to play up

大暑(ㄉㄚˋ ㄕㄨˇ)
Great heat, one of the 24 Chinese climatic periods, which falls on 23rd or 24th of July

大帥(ㄉㄚˋ ㄕㄨㄞˋ)
① a commander in chief ② a high military officer in the Ching Dynasty

大人(ㄉㄚˋ ㄖㄣˊ)
①(in ancient China) a respectful salutation for one's parents, seniors, etc. ② a grown-up person; an adult; a grown-up

大人物(ㄉㄚˋ ㄖㄣˊ ㄨˋ)
a great personage; a famous or influential person; a VIP; a big shot: 他是個大人物。He is a big shot. 或He is a great personage.

大儒(ㄉㄚˋ ㄖㄨˊ)
a scholar who combines profundity with virtue

大字報(ㄉㄚˋ ㄗˋ ㄅㄠˋ)
a big-character poster

大自然(ㄉㄚˋ ㄗˋ ㄖㄢˊ)
nature; natural phenomena: 人類長期與大自然競爭。Man is engaged in a constant struggle with nature.

大雜燴(ㄉㄚˋ ㄗㄚˊ ㄏㄨㄟˋ)
a hodgepodge

大雜院(ㄉㄚˋ ㄗㄚˊ ㄩㄢˋ)
(in northern China) a big courtyard shared by many families of the low-income class

大作(ㄉㄚˋ ㄗㄨㄛˋ)
① your work; your script; your book, etc. ②(said of violence, etc.) to erupt; to upheave; eruption; upheaval ③(said of music, etc.) to come out in ensemble and rather suddenly

大宗(ㄉㄚˋ ㄗㄨㄥ)
① a large batch; a large amount; lots of ② staple ③ a famous and influential family of long standing

大總統(ㄉㄚˋ ㄗㄨㄥˇ ㄊㄨㄥˇ)
the President—the chief of state of a republic

大慈大悲(ㄉㄚˋ ㄘˊ ㄉㄚˋ ㄅㄟ)
(Buddhism) the great mercy; the great compassion

大才小用(ㄉㄚˋ ㄘㄞˊ ㄒㄧㄠˇ ㄩㄥˋ)
to make little use of great talent; to use talented people for trivial tasks 亦作「大材小用」: 你做這事情是大才小用了。This is a job unworthy of your talents.

大餐(ㄉㄚˋ ㄘㄢ)
① a sumptuous feast or meal ② Western-style foods

大錯特錯(ㄉㄚˋ ㄘㄨㄛˋ ㄊㄜˋ ㄘㄨㄛˋ)
a very serious mistake; to make a gross error; all wet

大錯鑄成(ㄉㄚˋ ㄘㄨㄛˋ ㄓㄨˋ ㄔㄥˊ)
to have committed a big mistake or blunder; to err hopelessly

大葱(ㄉㄚˋ ㄘㄨㄥ)
(botany) the leek

大肆咆哮(ㄉㄚˋ ㄙˋ ㄆㄠˊ ㄒㄧㄠ)
to complain, threaten, etc. loudly; to roar with rage

大嫂(ㄉㄚˋ ㄙㄠˇ)
① one's eldest sister-in-law ② a polite name for women of similar age as oneself

大掃除(ㄉㄚˋ ㄙㄠˇ ㄔㄨˊ)
to make a thorough clean-up (usually before a major festival)

大蘇打(ㄉㄚˋ ㄙㄨ ㄉㄚˇ)
the sodium hyposulfite

大蒜(ㄉㄚˋ ㄙㄨㄢˋ)
garlic

大而化之(ㄉㄚˋ ㄦˊ ㄏㄨㄚˋ ㄓ)
careless; carelessly; perfunctory; perfunctorily; slapdash; slipshod

大而無當(ㄉㄚˋ ㄦˊ ㄨˊ ㄉㄤˋ)
big but useless; large but impractical: 它是個大而無當的計畫。It's an ambitious but impractical plan.

大衣(ㄉㄚˋ ㄧ)
an overcoat

大姨子(ㄉㄚˋ ㄧˊ ·ㄗ)
one's wife's elder sisters

大意(ㄉㄚˋ ㄧˋ)
① the general idea; the gist; a summary ② careless; negligent ③ high ambitions

大意失荆州(ㄉㄚˋ ㄧˋ ㄕ ㄐㄧㄥ ㄓㄡ)
to suffer a major setback due to carelessness

大義滅親(ㄉㄚˋ ㄧˋ ㄇㄧㄝˋ ㄑㄧㄣ)
to uphold justice and righteousness even at the sacrifice of one's blood relations

大義凜然(ㄉㄚˋ ㄧˋ ㄌㄧㄣˇ ㄖㄢˊ)
to maintain the dignity of justice or righteousness

大異其趣(ㄉㄚˋ ㄧˋ ㄑㄧˊ ㄑㄩˋ)
very different; totally different

大牙(ㄉㄚˋ ㄧㄚˊ)
the molar teeth 亦作「臼齒」

大爺
①(ㄉㄚˋ ㄧㄝˊ) ⓐ a rich man ⓑ a term used by a servant to address his master
②(ㄉㄚˋ ·ㄧㄝ) ⓐ an uncle; one's father's elder brother ⓑ

uncle (a respectful form of address for an elderly man)

大業(ㄉㄚˋ ㄧㄝˋ)
a big enterprise

大搖大擺(ㄉㄚˋ ㄧㄠˊ ㄉㄚˋ ㄅㄞˇ)
to swagger; to walk haughtily

大要(ㄉㄚˋ ㄧㄠˋ)
the main points (of a book, article, etc.); a summary; a synopsis; the gist

大有分別(ㄉㄚˋ ㄧㄡˇ ㄈㄣ ㄅㄧㄝˊ)
poles apart or entirely different

大有可觀(ㄉㄚˋ ㄧㄡˇ ㄎㄜˇ ㄍㄨㄢ)
absolutely worth seeing—very considerable

大有可爲(ㄉㄚˋ ㄧㄡˇ ㄎㄜˇ ㄨㄟˊ)
very promising (projects, etc.); very hopeful (situation, etc.); to have bright prospects

大有人在(ㄉㄚˋ ㄧㄡˇ ㄖㄣˊ ㄗㄞˋ)
Such people are by no means rare.

大有文章(ㄉㄚˋ ㄧㄡˇ ㄨㄣˊ ㄓㄤ)
There's something behind all this. 或 There's more to it than meets the eye.

大煙 or 大烟(ㄉㄚˋ ㄧㄢ)
opium

大鹽湖(ㄉㄚˋ ㄧㄢˊ ㄏㄨˊ)
the Great Salt Lake

大言不慚(ㄉㄚˋ ㄧㄢˊ ㄅㄨˋ ㄘㄢˊ)
to boast unabashedly or shamelessly; to talk big

大岩桐(ㄉㄚˋ ㄧㄢˊ ㄊㄨㄥˊ)
(botany) gloxinia

大洋(ㄉㄚˋ ㄧㄤˊ)
① a silver dollar ② an ocean

大洋洲(ㄉㄚˋ ㄧㄤˊ ㄓㄡ)
Oceania; Oceanica

大英博物館(ㄉㄚˋ ㄧㄥ ㄅㄛˊ ㄨˋ ㄍㄨㄢˇ)
the British Museum

大無畏(ㄉㄚˋ ㄨˊ ㄨㄟˋ)
dauntless; fearless; dauntlessness; fearlessness

大我(ㄉㄚˋ ㄨㄛˇ)or(ㄉㄚˋ ㄜˇ)
the big self—the universe, as opposed to the little self—oneself; the public; the state; the nation

大爲(ㄉㄚˋ ㄨㄟˊ)
greatly; significantly; markedly

大爲震怒(ㄉㄚˋ ㄨㄟˊ ㄓㄣˋ ㄋㄨˋ)
to fly into a rage; to become furious; to blow off the top

大文豪(ㄉㄚˋ ㄨㄣˊ ㄏㄠˊ)
a renowned man of letters; a literary giant

大王(ㄉㄚˋ ㄨㄤˊ)
① Your Majesty; Your Highness ② the chief of brigands

大王椰子(ㄉㄚˋ ㄨㄤˊ ㄧㄝˊ ·ㄗ)
the palm tree

大魚大肉(ㄉㄚˋ ㄩˊ ㄉㄚˋ ㄖㄡˋ)
(literally) abundant fish and meat—rich food (implying gluttony)

大禹(ㄉㄚˋ ㄩˇ)
Yü the Great, 2276-2177 B. C., founder of the Hsia Dynasty

大雨傾盆(ㄉㄚˋ ㄩˇ ㄑㄧㄥ ㄆㄣˊ)
a pouring rain; to rain cats and dogs: 現在大雨傾盆。It's raining cats and dogs now.

大約(ㄉㄚˋ ㄩㄝ)
about; around; probably; likely: 現在大約是九點鐘。It's about nine o'clock now.

大月(ㄉㄚˋ ㄩㄝˋ)
① the 31-day months ② the lunar 30-day months

大躍進(ㄉㄚˋ ㄩㄝˋ ㄐㄧㄣˋ)
(Communist terminology) "the great leap forward"

大月氏(ㄉㄚˋ ㄩㄝˋ ㄓ)or(ㄉㄚˋ ㄖㄡˋ ㄓ)
name of an ancient country in southwestern China

大員(ㄉㄚˋ ㄩㄢˊ)
high or ranking officials (usually referring to those of the Central Government)

大元帥(ㄉㄚˋ ㄩㄢˊ ㄕㄨㄞˋ)
a marshal; the commander in chief of the armed forces; a commanding general of a large military force

【大】 916

2. ㄉㄞˋ day dài

參看「大夫」

大夫
①(ㄉㄞˋ ㄈㄨ) (in ancient China) high officials of the state
②(ㄉㄞˋ ·ㄈㄨ) a physician or doctor

一畫

【天】 917

ㄊㄧㄢ tian tiān

1. the sky; the heavens; the vault of heavens; the firmament
2. Nature; God; Heaven: 謝天謝地，你終於來了。Thank God, you've come!
3. nature; natural; not artificial: 這風景具天然美。The scenery has natural beauty.
4. a day: 我每天六點起床。I get up at six every day.
5. seasons; climates; weather: 春天到了。Spring has come.
6. father or husband
7. something indispensable; necessities

天崩地坼(ㄊㄧㄢ ㄅㄥ ㄉㄧˋ ㄔㄜˋ)
deafening sounds—as the falling of heaven and cracking of earth; natural disasters like giant earthquakes and landslides 亦作「天崩地裂」

天邊(ㄊㄧㄢ ㄅㄧㄢ)
the ends of the earth; remotest places

天邊海角(ㄊㄧㄢ ㄅㄧㄢ ㄏㄞˇ ㄐㄧㄠˇ)
the corners of the earth—faraway or distant places

天稟(ㄊㄧㄢ ㄅㄧㄥˇ)
natural endowments; endowed by nature

天不怕地不怕(ㄊㄧㄢ ㄅㄨˋ ㄆㄚˋ ㄉㄧˋ ㄅㄨˋ ㄆㄚˋ)
to fear neither Heaven nor Earth—to fear nothing and no one

天不假年(ㄊㄧㄢ ㄅㄨˋ ㄐㄧㄚˇ ㄋㄧㄢˊ)
(literally) God doesn't give him a life long enough (to accomplish his task, etc.). —usually said of a person who dies on an important job

天棚(ㄊㄧㄢ ㄆㄥˊ)
an awning; a shed; a tent for shading the sun

天平(ㄊㄧㄢ ㄆㄧㄥˊ)or 天秤(ㄊㄧㄢ ㄔㄥˋ)
scales—used in weighing precious stones, gold, etc.

天馬行空(ㄊㄧㄢ ㄇㄚˇ ㄒㄧㄥˊ ㄎㄨㄥ)
(said of calligraphic works or writing) an unrestrained and vigorous style that brims with talent

〔大部〕

天明(ㄊㄧㄢ ㄇㄧㄥˊ)
daybreak; dawn: 他天明即起。He gets up at daybreak.

天命(ㄊㄧㄢ ㄇㄧㄥˋ)
① a heavenly mandate ② fate; destiny ③ one's life span

天罰(ㄊㄧㄢ ㄈㄚˊ)
the punishment meted out by God; God's punishing hands

天翻地覆(ㄊㄧㄢ ㄈㄢ ㄉㄧˋ ㄈㄨˋ)
in total disorder or disarrangement; an extreme upheaval or change; in sheer pandemonium

天分(ㄊㄧㄢ ㄈㄣˋ)
natural endowments; talent; intelligence: 她有音樂天分。She has a talent for music.

天方夜譚(ㄊㄧㄢ ㄈㄤ ㄧㄝˋ ㄊㄢˊ)
The Arabian Nights' Entertainment

天府之國(ㄊㄧㄢ ㄈㄨˇ ㄓ ㄍㄨㄛˊ)
the land of abundance; a country with rich natural resources (usually referring to Szechwan Province)

天父(ㄊㄧㄢ ㄈㄨˋ)
(Christianity) Our Heavenly Father

天賦(ㄊㄧㄢ ㄈㄨˋ)
① inherent and inborn (rights, etc.) ② natural endowments; talent

天賦人權(ㄊㄧㄢ ㄈㄨˋ ㄖㄣˊ ㄑㄩㄢˊ)
inborn human rights; inalienable rights

天大的事(ㄊㄧㄢ ㄉㄚˋ ·ㄉㄜ ㄕˋ)
(literally) matters as big as heavens—important or serious matters; tremendous events

天道(ㄊㄧㄢ ㄉㄠˋ)
① the ways of Heaven; natural law ② weather

天底下(ㄊㄧㄢ ㄉㄧˇ ·ㄒㄧㄚ)
in this world; under the sun; on earth: 天底下沒什麼新奇的事物。There's no new thing under the sun.

天地(ㄊㄧㄢ ㄉㄧˋ)
① heaven and earth—the world; the universe ② a field of activity; scope of operation ③ the upper and lower margins of a scroll ④ a world of difference

天地良心(ㄊㄧㄢ ㄉㄧˋ ㄌㄧㄤˊ ㄒㄧㄣ)
to speak the truth; in fact; from the bottom of my heart; in all fairness or justice

天地間(ㄊㄧㄢ ㄉㄧˋ ㄐㄧㄢ)
in this world; in the universe

天定(ㄊㄧㄢ ㄉㄧㄥˋ)
preordained; predetermined; predestined; fixed by Heaven

天壇(ㄊㄧㄢ ㄊㄢˊ)
the Altar of Heaven in Peking; the Temple of Heaven (in Peking)—where the emperors used to worship

天堂(ㄊㄧㄢ ㄊㄤˊ)
heaven; paradise

天堂地獄(ㄊㄧㄢ ㄊㄤˊ ㄉㄧˋ ㄩˋ)
(literally) heaven and hell — the sharp contrast between happiness and misery

天體(ㄊㄧㄢ ㄊㄧˇ)
heavenly bodies; celestial bodies

天體營(ㄊㄧㄢ ㄊㄧˇ ㄧㄥˊ)
a nudist camp

天天(ㄊㄧㄢ ㄊㄧㄢ)
every day: 他天天讀英文。He studies English every day.

天庭(ㄊㄧㄢ ㄊㄧㄥˊ)
the forehead

天南地北(ㄊㄧㄢ ㄋㄢˊ ㄉㄧˋ ㄅㄟˇ)
① poles apart ② (to chat or talk casually about) every and any subject under the sun; discursive; rambling

天牛(ㄊㄧㄢ ㄋㄧㄡˊ)
(entomology) *Apriona rugicollis,* a variety of destructive beetles; a longicorn

天年(ㄊㄧㄢ ㄋㄧㄢˊ)
① the life span alloted by Heaven; one's natural life span ② fortune in the current year

天怒人怨(ㄊㄧㄢ ㄋㄨˋ ㄖㄣˊ ㄩㄢˋ)
(to incur) the wrath of Heaven and opposition of man (usually referring to outrageous injustice, etc.); widespread indignation and discontent

天籟(ㄊㄧㄢ ㄌㄞˋ)
the sounds of nature (such as those caused by wind, water, insects, etc.)

天藍色(ㄊㄧㄢ ㄌㄢˊ ㄙㄜˋ)
sky blue

天狼星(ㄊㄧㄢ ㄌㄤˊ ㄒㄧㄥ)
the Dog Star

天理(ㄊㄧㄢ ㄌㄧˇ)
natural law; the reason of Heaven

天理循環(ㄊㄧㄢ ㄌㄧˇ ㄒㄩㄣˊ ㄏㄨㄢˊ)
The guilty are always punished and the kind-hearted always rewarded under the law of Heaven. 或The course of nature goes round.

天理昭彰(ㄊㄧㄢ ㄌㄧˇ ㄓㄠ ㄓㄤ)
The law of Heaven always prevails.

天理人情(ㄊㄧㄢ ㄌㄧˇ ㄖㄣˊ ㄑㄧㄥˊ)
(literally) law of nature and feelings of man—reasonable

天良(ㄊㄧㄢ ㄌㄧㄤˊ)
one's conscience

天亮(ㄊㄧㄢ ㄌㄧㄤˋ)
daybreak; daytime: 他們自天亮工作到天黑。They work from dawn till dark.

天靈蓋(ㄊㄧㄢ ·ㄌㄧㄥ ㄍㄞˋ)
the frontal part of the skull; the crown (of the head)

天路歷程(ㄊㄧㄢ ㄌㄨˋ ㄌㄧˋ ㄔㄥˊ)
Pilgrim's Progress, an allegory by John Bunyan

天羅地網(ㄊㄧㄢ ㄌㄨㄛˊ ㄉㄧˋ ㄨㄤˇ)
the dragnet of justice surrounding on all sides; envelopment

天倫之樂(ㄊㄧㄢ ㄌㄨㄣˊ ㄓ ㄌㄜˋ)
family love and joy; family happiness

天各一方(ㄊㄧㄢ ㄍㄜˋ ㄧˋ ㄈㄤ)
to be far apart; to live far apart from each other

天高地厚(ㄊㄧㄢ ㄍㄠ ㄉㄧˋ ㄏㄡˋ)
① the immensity of the universe which is beyond the comprehension of the ignorant ② immensity (of love, kindness, etc.)

天高皇帝遠(ㄊㄧㄢ ㄍㄠ ㄏㄨㄤˊ ㄉㄧˋ ㄩㄢˇ)
(literally) The heaven is high and the emperor is far away.—① It's difficult to get justice. ② One may do whatever one pleases without fear of interference.

天高氣爽(ㄊㄧㄢ ㄍㄠ ㄑㄧˋ ㄕㄨㄤˇ)
(usually said of the crisp air

in autumn) The sky is high and the weather is fine.

天干(ㄊㄧㄢ ㄍㄢ)
the Ten Celestial Stems—used with the Twelve Terrestrial Branches to form a cycle of sixty

天國(ㄊㄧㄢ ㄍㄨㄛˊ)
the Kingdom of Heaven

天工(ㄊㄧㄢ ㄍㄨㄥ)
formed by nature; natural; a work of nature: 巧奪天工。It rivals nature.

天公不作美(ㄊㄧㄢ ㄍㄨㄥ ㄅㄨˊ ㄗㄨㄛˋ ㄇㄟˇ)
(literally) Heaven is not cooperative.— Weather turns foul when some activity requiring fine weather is scheduled to take place.

天空(ㄊㄧㄢ ㄎㄨㄥ)
the sky; the firmament; the void

天河(ㄊㄧㄢ ㄏㄜˊ)
the Milky Way; the Galaxy

天花(ㄊㄧㄢ ㄏㄨㄚ)
(pathology) the smallpox

天花板(ㄊㄧㄢ ㄏㄨㄚ ㄅㄢˇ)
the ceiling (of a room)

天花亂墜(ㄊㄧㄢ ㄏㄨㄚ ㄌㄨㄢˋ ㄓㄨㄟˋ)
exaggerated description (of the attractions of a place, chances of success in a project, etc.)

天火(ㄊㄧㄢ ㄏㄨㄛˇ)
① a fire caused by Heaven, as by lightning ② a fire whose cause can not be ascertained

天昏地暗(ㄊㄧㄢ ㄏㄨㄣ ㄉㄧˋ ㄢˋ)
shrouded by gloom; dark above and below (often referring to the scene in a sandstorm, hurricane attack, etc.)

天荒地老(ㄊㄧㄢ ㄏㄨㄤ ㄉㄧˋ ㄌㄠˇ)
(literally) when the earth and heaven get old—a long, long time (often used by lovers in making vows of eternal love)

天皇(ㄊㄧㄢ ㄏㄨㄤˊ)
① the emperor of Japan; mikado ② the king of heaven

天機(ㄊㄧㄢ ㄐㄧ)
(literally) the secrets of Heaven; the hidden plans of Providence—something inexplicable

天津(ㄊㄧㄢ ㄐㄧㄣ)
Tientsin, a port city in Hopeh Province

天經地義(ㄊㄧㄢ ㄐㄧㄥ ㄉㄧˋ ㄧˋ)
a matter of course; a universal truth: 他認爲這消息是天經地義之事。He took the news as a matter of course.

天井(ㄊㄧㄢ ㄐㄧㄥˇ)
a courtyard; a patio

天氣(ㄊㄧㄢ ㄑㄧˋ)
weather

天氣預報(ㄊㄧㄢ ㄑㄧˋ ㄩˋ ㄅㄠˋ)
a weather forecast

天橋(ㄊㄧㄢ ㄑㄧㄠˊ)
① an overhead bridge or elevated passage; an overline bridge; a platform bridge ② name of an amusement center in Peiping

天譴(ㄊㄧㄢ ㄑㄧㄢˇ)
the wrath of Heaven; God's punishment—fire-and-brimstone

天塹難渡(ㄊㄧㄢ ㄑㄧㄢˋ ㄋㄢˊ ㄉㄨˋ)
The natural barriers (for defense) are insurmountable.

天下(ㄊㄧㄢ ㄒㄧㄚˋ)
① the world: 它是一支天下無敵的軍隊。It was an invincible army in the world. ② (in ancient usage) the whole country of China

天下洶洶(ㄊㄧㄢ ㄒㄧㄚˋ ㄒㄩㄥ ㄒㄩㄥ)
The whole nation is clamoring, tumultuous, or in upheaval.

天下一家(ㄊㄧㄢ ㄒㄧㄚˋ ㄧˋ ㄐㄧㄚ)
All people under the sun are one family. 或 The world is a big family.

天下烏鴉一般黑(ㄊㄧㄢ ㄒㄧㄚˋ ㄨ ㄧㄚ ㄧˋ ㄅㄢ ㄏㄟ)
All crows are black.— Evil people are bad all over the world. 或 In every country dogs bite.

天下爲公(ㄊㄧㄢ ㄒㄧㄚˋ ㄨㄟˊ ㄍㄨㄥ)
The world is for all.

天曉得(ㄊㄧㄢ ㄒㄧㄠˇ ˙ㄉㄜ)
God knows! 或 Heaven knows!

天仙(ㄊㄧㄢ ㄒㄧㄢ)
① a goddess ② a beauty

天仙化人(ㄊㄧㄢ ㄒㄧㄢ ㄏㄨㄚˋ ㄖㄣˊ)
as beautiful as an angel from heaven; a stunning beauty

天險(ㄊㄧㄢ ㄒㄧㄢˇ)
impregnable natural barriers (for defense)

天線(ㄊㄧㄢ ㄒㄧㄢˋ)
an antenna (for radio, TV, etc.)

天香國色(ㄊㄧㄢ ㄒㄧㄤ ㄍㄨㄛˊ ㄙㄜˋ)
a woman of great beauty 亦作「國色天香」

天象(ㄊㄧㄢ ㄒㄧㄤˋ)
celestial phenomena; astronomical phenomena: 他善於觀測天象。He is expert in astronomical observation.

天性(ㄊㄧㄢ ㄒㄧㄥˋ)
natural temperaments; natural quality; a natural disposition: 他是個天性和善慷慨的人。He is by nature a kind, generous fellow.

天旋地轉(ㄊㄧㄢ ㄒㄩㄢˊ ㄉㄧˋ ㄓㄨㄢˇ)
(to feel as if) the heaven and the earth were spinning round; very faint and dizzy

天之驕子(ㄊㄧㄢ ㄓ ㄐㄧㄠ ㄗˇ)
(literally) the apple of God's eye—to be specially favored by Heaven; to be extraordinarily blessed

天職(ㄊㄧㄢ ㄓˊ)
bounden duty; natural duty: 遵守法律是國民的天職。Abiding by the law is a citizen's natural duty.

天眞(ㄊㄧㄢ ㄓㄣ)
naive; naivety; innocent: 他是個天眞無邪的小孩。He's an innocent child.

天眞爛漫(ㄊㄧㄢ ㄓㄣ ㄌㄢˋ ㄇㄢˋ)
innocent and carefree—lovely; honest and without affectation—like a child

天誅地滅(ㄊㄧㄢ ㄓㄨ ㄉㄧˋ ㄇㄧㄝˋ)
to be damned by Heaven and Earth (usually used in swearing)

天竺(ㄊㄧㄢ ㄓㄨˊ)
the ancient name of India

天竺牡丹(ㄊㄧㄢ ㄓㄨˊ ㄇㄨˇ ㄉㄢ)
dahlia 亦作「大理花」

天竺葵(ㄊㄧㄢ ㄓㄨˊ ㄎㄨㄟˊ)
Pelargonium hortorum, geranium

天竺鼠(ㄊㄧㄢ ㄓㄨˊ ㄕㄨˇ)
a guinea pig; a cavy

天主(ㄊㄧㄢ ㄓㄨˇ)
(Christianity) God

天主堂(ㄊㄧㄢ ㄓㄨˇ ㄊㄤˊ)
a Catholic church

天主教(ㄊㄧㄢ ㄓㄨˇ ㄐㄧㄠˋ)
Catholicism; the Roman Catholic Church

天助(ㄊㄧㄢ ㄓㄨˋ)
help from Heaven—unexpected help; an uncanny or very lucky break: 天助自助者。God helps those who help themselves.

天差地遠(ㄊㄧㄢ ㄔㄚ ㄉㄧˋ ㄩㄢˇ)
poles apart; far off the beam

天朝(ㄊㄧㄢ ㄔㄠˊ)
a reference to the Chinese imperial court by Chinese envoys or by barbarians who paid tributes to China

天長地久(ㄊㄧㄢ ㄔㄤˊ ㄉㄧˋ ㄐㄧㄡˇ)
(literally) as old as heaven and earth—a very long time

天成(ㄊㄧㄢ ㄔㄥˊ)
natural; springing from nature

天窗(ㄊㄧㄢ ㄔㄨㄤ)
①a skylight; high windows ②as in 打開天窗說亮話—Let's be quite frank.

天師(ㄊㄧㄢ ㄕ)
the title of the head of the Taoists

天時(ㄊㄧㄢ ㄕˊ)
①weather, or climates ②opportunities of time vouchsafed by Heaven

天使(ㄊㄧㄢ ㄕˇ)
①an angel ②an emissary from the emperor

天山(ㄊㄧㄢ ㄕㄢ)
①Mt. Heaven, also known as the Snow Mountain, in Sinkiang Province ②name of a county in Northeast China

天神(ㄊㄧㄢ ㄕㄣˊ)
gods in heaven; deities

天生(ㄊㄧㄢ ㄕㄥ)
natural; to be born with; congenital; inborn: 鴨子會游泳是天生的。It is natural for ducks to swim.

天生尤物(ㄊㄧㄢ ㄕㄥ ㄧㄡˊ ㄨˋ)
a born siren, sexy kitten, etc.

天書(ㄊㄧㄢ ㄕㄨ)
①(in old China) an imperial order; the emperor's instructions ②(Taoism) a book from Heaven ③a sarcastic reference to a writing difficult to understand or words not easily recognizable

天數(ㄊㄧㄢ ㄕㄨˋ)
a predestined tragedy or disaster

天然(ㄊㄧㄢ ㄖㄢˊ)
natural (as opposed to artificial): 煤與油是天然產物。Coal and oil are natural products.

天然氣(ㄊㄧㄢ ㄖㄢˊ ㄑㄧˋ)
natural gas

天人合一(ㄊㄧㄢ ㄖㄣˊ ㄏㄜˊ ㄧ)
a theory that man is an integral part of nature

天壤之別(ㄊㄧㄢ ㄖㄤˇ ㄓ ㄅㄧㄝˊ)
as far apart as the heaven and earth—vastly different; poles apart

天姿(ㄊㄧㄢ ㄗ)
(a woman's) natural beauty (without the help of make-up)

天資(ㄊㄧㄢ ㄗ)
natural endowments; inborn talent or intellectual capacity

天子(ㄊㄧㄢ ㄗˇ)
(literally) the Son of Heaven—the emperor

天擇(ㄊㄧㄢ ㄗㄜˊ)
the law of natural selection in evolution

天災(ㄊㄧㄢ ㄗㄞ)
a natural disaster; a natural calamity; an act of God: 他們去年遭到天災。They suffered natural disasters last year.

天災人禍(ㄊㄧㄢ ㄗㄞ ㄖㄣˊ ㄏㄨㄛˋ)
natural disasters and man-made calamities; natural disasters and wars

天造地設(ㄊㄧㄢ ㄗㄠˋ ㄉㄧˋ ㄕㄜˋ)
①(said of a couple) matched by Heaven and Earth; a natural match (sometimes, used sarcastically) ②a natural creation; heavenly

天足(ㄊㄧㄢ ㄗㄨˊ)
(women's) natural feet (as distinguished from feet deformed by foot-binding in old China)

天作之合(ㄊㄧㄢ ㄗㄨㄛˋ ㄓ ㄏㄜˊ)
a match by Heaven; a match blessed by God (used in congratulatory messages or greetings to a couple on their wedding)

天縱英明(ㄊㄧㄢ ㄗㄨㄥˋ ㄧㄥ ㄇㄧㄥˊ)
(said of a ruler) born with wisdom and farsightedness

天賜(ㄊㄧㄢ ㄘˋ)
given by Heaven; endowed by Heaven

天才(ㄊㄧㄢ ㄘㄞˊ)
a genius; natural talent: 莎士比亞是個天才。Shakespeare was a genius.

天才兒童(ㄊㄧㄢ ㄘㄞˊ ㄦˊ ㄊㄨㄥˊ)
a child prodigy

天從人願(ㄊㄧㄢ ㄘㄨㄥˊ ㄖㄣˊ ㄩㄢˋ)
(literally) Heaven has complied with man's wishes. —What man hoped to happen has come to pass.

天色(ㄊㄧㄢ ㄙㄜˋ)
the color of the sky; the time of the day as shown by the color of the sky; weather

天鵝(ㄊㄧㄢ ㄜˊ)
a swan

天鵝絨(ㄊㄧㄢ ㄜˊ ㄖㄨㄥˊ)
velvet; velvety

天安門(ㄊㄧㄢ ㄢ ㄇㄣˊ)
Tien An Men (the Gate of Heavenly Peace)

天衣無縫(ㄊㄧㄢ ㄧ ㄨˊ ㄈㄥˋ)
without a trace; perfect (jobs); flawless (lies)

天意(ㄊㄧㄢ ㄧˋ)
the will of Heaven; God's will

天涯海角(ㄊㄧㄢ ㄧㄚˊ ㄏㄞˇ ㄐㄧㄠˇ)
the four corners of the earth; the very ends of the earth—faraway, distant or remote places

天有不測風雲，人有旦夕禍福
(ㄊㄧㄢ ㄧㄡˇ ㄅㄨˋ ㄘㄜˋ ㄈㄥ ㄩㄣˊ, ㄖㄣˊ ㄧㄡˇ ㄉㄢˋ ㄒㄧˋ ㄏㄨㄛˋ ㄈㄨˊ)
Human fortunes are as unpredictable as the weather. 或 In nature there are unexpected storms, while in

life there are unpredictable fortune and misfortune.

天演(ㄊㄧㄢ ㄧㄢˇ)
evolution

天演論(ㄊㄧㄢ ㄧㄢˇ ㄌㄨㄣˋ)
the theory of evolution 亦作「進化論」

天無絕人之路(ㄊㄧㄢ ㄨˊ ㄐㄩㄝˊ ㄖㄣˊ ㄓ ㄌㄨˋ)
God will not close all doors. 或 Heaven will always leave a door open.

天無二日(ㄊㄧㄢ ㄨˊ ㄦˋ ㄖˋ)
(literally) There can not be two suns in the sky.—There cannot be two kings in a country, or two bosses in an office, etc.

天外(ㄊㄧㄢ ㄨㄞˋ)
① unexpected; unexpectedly; a windfall ② far and high

天文(ㄊㄧㄢ ㄨㄣˊ)
heavenly bodies; astronomy

天文地理(ㄊㄧㄢ ㄨㄣˊ ㄉㄧˋ ㄌㄧˇ)
astronomical geography

天文臺(ㄊㄧㄢ ㄨㄣˊ ㄊㄞˊ)
an astronomical observatory; an observatory

天文圖(ㄊㄧㄢ ㄨㄣˊ ㄊㄨˊ)
the star atlas

天文學(ㄊㄧㄢ ㄨㄣˊ ㄒㄩㄝˊ)
astronomy

天文數字(ㄊㄧㄢ ㄨㄣˊ ㄕㄨˋ ㄗˋ)
an astronomical figure; an enormous figure

天文望遠鏡(ㄊㄧㄢ ㄨㄣˊ ㄨㄤˋ ㄩㄢˇ ㄐㄧㄥˋ)
an astronomical telescope

天王星(ㄊㄧㄢ ㄨㄤˊ ㄒㄧㄥ)
the planet Uranus

天網恢恢(ㄊㄧㄢ ㄨㄤˇ ㄏㄨㄟ ㄏㄨㄟ)
The net of Heaven stretches everywhere. —Nobody escapes the judgment of Heaven.

天雨順延(ㄊㄧㄢ ㄩˇ ㄕㄨㄣˋ ㄧㄢˊ)
(said of a ball game, etc.) to be postponed to the following day if it rains on the scheduled date

天淵之別(ㄊㄧㄢ ㄩㄢ ㄓ ㄅㄧㄝˊ)
vastly different; a world of difference

【太】 918 ㄊㄞˋ tay tai

1. very big or large
2. much; too; over; excessively; extremely; very: 天太熱不能工作。It's too hot to work. 再次見到您，實在太高興了。I'm very glad to see you again.
3. a term of respect, used in titles
4. a Chinese family name

太保(ㄊㄞˋ ㄅㄠˇ)
① a very high official in ancient China ② juvenile delinquents

太半(ㄊㄞˋ ㄅㄢˋ)
the greater half 亦作「大半」

太平(ㄊㄞˋ ㄆㄧㄥˊ)
peace; peaceful: 太平無事。All is well. 或 Everything is all right.

太平門(ㄊㄞˋ ㄆㄧㄥˊ ㄇㄣˊ)
(in public buildings, especially in theaters) exits, especially those leading to fire escapes

太平梯(ㄊㄞˋ ㄆㄧㄥˊ ㄊㄧ)
a fire escape; a safety ladder

太平天國(ㄊㄞˋ ㄆㄧㄥˊ ㄊㄧㄢ ㄍㄨㄛˊ)
The Heavenly Kingdom of Peace (1851-1864), founded by Hung Hsiu-chüan (洪秀全) with its capital located in Nanking

太平間(ㄊㄞˋ ㄆㄧㄥˊ ㄐㄧㄢ)
an undertaker's morgue; a mortuary

太平盛世(ㄊㄞˋ ㄆㄧㄥˊ ㄕㄥˋ ㄕˋ)
a reign of peace, order, and prosperity

太平洋(ㄊㄞˋ ㄆㄧㄥˊ ㄧㄤˊ)
the Pacific Ocean

太妹(ㄊㄞˋ ㄇㄟˋ)
a girl delinquent; a wild teenage girl; a tomboy; a bobbysoxer

太廟(ㄊㄞˋ ㄇㄧㄠˋ)
the ancestral shrine of an emperor

太夫人(ㄊㄞˋ ㄈㄨ ㄖㄣˊ)
(in old China) the mother of a nobility; (especially in obituary) mother

太太(ㄊㄞˋ ˙ㄊㄞ)
① a respectful title for women; a madame; Mrs. ② one's wife

太古(ㄊㄞˋ ㄍㄨˇ)
very ancient times; prehistorical times

太公釣魚，願者上鉤(ㄊㄞˋ ㄍㄨㄥ ㄉㄧㄠˋ ㄩˊ, ㄩㄢˋ ㄓㄜˇ ㄕㄤˋ ㄍㄡ)
like Chiang Tai Kung (姜太公) fishing by the Wei River (渭水), the fish willingly rising to his hookless and baitless line—A victim letting himself be caught of his own will.

太空(ㄊㄞˋ ㄎㄨㄥ)
space; the great void: 我們的地球在太空中運行。Our earth moves through space.

太空被(ㄊㄞˋ ㄎㄨㄥ ㄅㄟˋ)
a nylon comforter

太空船(ㄊㄞˋ ㄎㄨㄥ ㄔㄨㄢˊ)
a spacecraft; a spaceship

太空時代(ㄊㄞˋ ㄎㄨㄥ ㄕˊ ㄉㄞˋ)
the space age

太空人(ㄊㄞˋ ㄎㄨㄥ ㄖㄣˊ)
(in U.S.) astronauts; (in U.S.S.R.) cosmonauts

太空總署(ㄊㄞˋ ㄎㄨㄥ ㄗㄨㄥˇ ㄕㄨˇ)
U.S. National Aeronautics and Space Administration (NASA)

太空艙(ㄊㄞˋ ㄎㄨㄥ ㄘㄤ)
a space capsule

太空梭(ㄊㄞˋ ㄎㄨㄥ ㄙㄨㄛ)
a space shuttle; a shuttle

太空衣(ㄊㄞˋ ㄎㄨㄥ ㄧ)
a space suit

太后(ㄊㄞˋ ㄏㄡˋ)
the mother of an emperor, or the empress dowager

太湖(ㄊㄞˋ ㄏㄨˊ)
the Tai Lake lying across Kiangsu and Chekiang provinces

太極圖(ㄊㄞˋ ㄐㄧˊ ㄊㄨˊ)
the diagram of cosmological scheme

太極拳(ㄊㄞˋ ㄐㄧˊ ㄑㄩㄢˊ)
taichichuan, often referred to as "shadowboxing"

太監(ㄊㄞˋ ㄐㄧㄢˋ)
a eunuch

太息(ㄊㄞˋ ㄒㄧˊ)
to sigh; to lament 亦作「嘆息」: 他爲他自己不幸的命運而太息。He sighed over his unhappy fate.

太虛幻境(ㄊㄞˋ ㄒㄩ ㄏㄨㄢˋ ㄐㄧㄥˋ)
an illusory scene; an illusion; a vision

太學(ㄊㄞˋ ㄒㄩㄝˊ)
(in ancient China) an institution of higher learning

established by the state; the Imperial College

太學生(ㄊㄞˋ ㄒㄩㄝˊ ㄕㄥ)
students in an institution of higher learning or the Imperial College

太初(ㄊㄞˋ ㄔㄨ)
the beginning of the world

太師(ㄊㄞˋ ㄕ)
①a very high official in ancient China ②one's teacher's teacher; one's parent's teacher

太師椅(ㄊㄞˋ ㄕ ㄧˇ)
an armchair with a curved back (usually for persons of senior ranks in old China)

太史公(ㄊㄞˋ ㄕˇ ㄍㄨㄥ)
①a title for the greatest Chinese historian, Ssu-Ma Chien (司馬遷), and his father Ssu-Ma Tan (司馬談), also a historian ②the title of the chief court historian

太守(ㄊㄞˋ ㄕㄡˇ)
(in old China) the magistrate of a prefecture

太甚(ㄊㄞˋ ㄕㄣˋ)
too much: 別欺人太甚。Don't push me too much.

太上(ㄊㄞˋ ㄕㄤˋ)
①the uppermost; the topmost ②very ancient times; prehistorical times ③the king or emperor

太上皇(ㄊㄞˋ ㄕㄤˋ ㄏㄨㄤˊ)
①the emperor's father ②(colloquial) a person who exercises supreme powers

太子(ㄊㄞˋ ㄗˇ)
the crown prince

太祖(ㄊㄞˋ ㄗㄨˇ)
①the first emperor of a dynasty ②the earliest ancestor of a clan

太座(ㄊㄞˋ ㄗㄨㄛˋ)
one's wife (a joking expression connoting the dominating position of a wife in the family)

太歲(ㄊㄞˋ ㄙㄨㄟˋ)
①the planet Jupiter ②a powerful and influential figure in a locality

太歲頭上動土(ㄊㄞˋ ㄙㄨㄟˋ ㄊㄡˊ ㄕㄤˋ ㄉㄨㄥˋ ㄊㄨˇ)
to offend or provoke the most powerful

太阿倒持(ㄊㄞˋ ㄜ ㄉㄠˋ ㄔˊ)
to hold the sword by the blade—to yield one's power to another at one's own peril

太醫(ㄊㄞˋ ㄧ)
the emperor's physician; a court physician

太陰(ㄊㄞˋ ㄧㄣ)
①the moon ②lunar

太陽(ㄊㄞˋ ㄧㄤˊ)
the sun: 太陽正照耀著。The sun is shining.

太陽燈(ㄊㄞˋ ㄧㄤˊ ㄉㄥ)
an ultraviolet lamp; a sunlamp

太陽能(ㄊㄞˋ ㄧㄤˊ ㄋㄥˊ)
solar energy

太陽黑點(ㄊㄞˋ ㄧㄤˊ ㄏㄟ ㄉㄧㄢˇ)or 太陽黑子(ㄊㄞˋ ㄧㄤˊ ㄏㄟ ㄗˇ)
sunspots

太陽系(ㄊㄞˋ ㄧㄤˊ ㄒㄧˋ)
the solar system

太陽穴(ㄊㄞˋ ㄧㄤˊ ㄒㄩㄝˊ)
the temples (of a human being)

太陽神(ㄊㄞˋ ㄧㄤˊ ㄕㄣˊ)
Apollo

太陽眼鏡(ㄊㄞˋ ㄧㄤˊ ㄧㄢˇ ㄐㄧㄥˋ)
sunglasses

太原(ㄊㄞˋ ㄩㄢˊ)
Taiyüan—capital of Shansi Province

【夫】 919
1. ㄈㄨ fu fū

1. a man; a male adult: 一夫當關，萬夫莫敵。If one man keeps guard over the pass, ten thousand are unable to get through.
2. those eligible for military service
3. a master
4. a husband

夫婦(ㄈㄨ ㄈㄨˋ)
man and wife; husband and wife; a couple: 夫婦偕老。Husband and wife grow old together.

夫家(ㄈㄨ ㄐㄧㄚ)
the husband's family; the husband's side

夫君(ㄈㄨ ㄐㄩㄣ)
①(in old usage) my husband ②(Tang Dynasty) a friend

夫妻(ㄈㄨ ㄑㄧ)
husband and wife; a couple

夫妻反目(ㄈㄨ ㄑㄧ ㄈㄢˇ ㄇㄨˋ)
the disharmony or discord between husband and wife

夫婿(ㄈㄨ ㄒㄩˋ)
a reference to one's own husband

夫唱婦隨(ㄈㄨ ㄔㄤˋ ㄈㄨˋ ㄙㄨㄟˊ)or 夫婦好合(ㄈㄨ ㄈㄨˋ ㄏㄠˇ ㄏㄜˊ)
(literally) The man sings, and the wife follows.—domestic harmony; harmony between husband and wife

夫人(ㄈㄨ ㄖㄣˊ)
①the wives of feudal lords in ancient China ②the concubines of an emperor ③the wives of high officials ④the legal wife ⑤Lady; Madame; Mrs.

夫子(ㄈㄨ ㄗˇ)
①a title of respect for the elders ②a master ③a reference to one's own husband in old China

夫子自道(ㄈㄨ ㄗˇ ㄗˋ ㄉㄠˋ)
One unconsciously exposes one's own defects while criticizing others.

夫役(ㄈㄨ ㄧˋ)
a servant

【夫】 919
2. ㄈㄨˊ fwu fú

1. a demonstrative pronoun —*that* in most cases
2. a final particle; a particle

【夬】 920
ㄍㄨㄞˋ guay guài

one of the eight diagrams in the *Book of Changes*

【夭】 921
1. ㄧㄠˇ yeau yǎo

1. to die young
2. to suppress; to repress

夭折(ㄧㄠˇ ㄓㄜˊ)
①to die young; an early death ②to come to a premature end: 會議中途夭折。The meeting came to a premature end.

夭壽(ㄧㄠˇ ㄕㄡˋ)
to die young

夭亡(ㄧㄠˇ ㄨㄤˊ)
to die young

【夭】 921
2. ㄧㄠ iau yāo

young; freshlooking; tender

二畫

【失】 922
ㄕ shy shī

1. to let slip; to neglect; to miss: 不要坐失良機。Don't let this opportunity slip.
2. to lose: 他已經失業了。He has lost his job.
3. an omission; a mistake

失敗(ㄕ ㄅㄞˋ)
to fail; a failure; a defeat: 失敗是成功之母。Failure is the mother of success.

失敗主義(ㄕ ㄅㄞˋ ㄓㄨˇ ㄧˋ)
defeatism

失敗主義者(ㄕ ㄅㄞˋ ㄓㄨˇ ㄧˋ ㄓㄜˇ)
a defeatist

失陪(ㄕ ㄆㄟˊ)
Please excuse me for not being able to keep you company for the moment.

失迷(ㄕ ㄇㄧˊ)
to get lost (on the road, etc.) 亦作「迷失」

失眠(ㄕ ㄇㄧㄢˊ)
to suffer from insomnia; insomnia

失面子(ㄕ ㄇㄧㄢˋ ·ㄗ)
to lose face

失民心(ㄕ ㄇㄧㄣˊ ㄒㄧㄣ)
to lose the support of the people

失明(ㄕ ㄇㄧㄥˊ)
to lose one's eyesight; to become blind; blind: 他右眼失明。He is blind in the right eye.

失風(ㄕ ㄈㄥ)
to be caught stealing; to fail in the act of stealing

失盜(ㄕ ㄉㄠˋ)
to be robbed or burglarized

失當(ㄕ ㄉㄤˋ)
improper; improperly; impropriety: 這個案子處理失當。This case was not properly handled.

失地(ㄕ ㄉㄧˋ)
the territory occupied by enemy forces; the territory ceded to the victor; to cede land to the victorious enemy

失掉(ㄕ ㄉㄧㄠˋ)
to lose (a chance, faith, confidence, courage, etc.)

失度(ㄕ ㄉㄨˋ)
excessive; excessively; immoderate; immoderately

失態(ㄕ ㄊㄞˋ)
to misbehave; to conduct oneself ludicrously (after drinking, etc.): 他在宴會中失態。He misbehaved himself in the party.

失調
①(ㄕ ㄊㄧㄠˊ) ⓐ maladjustment; incoordination ⓑ to be careless about one's health, diet, etc.
②(ㄕ ㄉㄧㄠˋ) to be out of tune

失樂園(ㄕ ㄌㄜˋ ㄩㄢˊ)
Paradise Lost: 失樂園是密爾頓的傑作。*Paradise Lost* is Milton's masterpiece.

失禮(ㄕ ㄌㄧˇ)
to commit a breach of etiquette; to be impolite; to be rude; impropriety; misbehavior

失利(ㄕ ㄌㄧˋ)
to suffer a defeat (or setback); to lose

失戀(ㄕ ㄌㄧㄢˋ)
to be jilted; to lose one's love; to get the "Dear John" letter

失靈(ㄕ ㄌㄧㄥˊ)
(said of a machine, instrument, etc.) not to work or not to work properly; to be out of order

失落(ㄕ ㄌㄨㄛˋ)
to lose

失口(ㄕ ㄎㄡˇ)
a slip of the tongue; to say something improper

失款(ㄕ ㄎㄨㄢˇ)
① to lose money ② lost money

失控(ㄕ ㄎㄨㄥˋ)
out of control; runaway

失和(ㄕ ㄏㄜˊ)
to be on bad terms; (said of a couple) to be at loggerheads: 他們失和了。They were on bad terms.

失候(ㄕ ㄏㄡˋ)
①(said of food) to suffer from faulty timing ②(courteous) to be absent and fail to greet somebody when he calls 亦作「失迎」

失怙(ㄕ ㄏㄨˋ)
to lose one's father; to be orphaned: 戰爭使他早年失怙。The war orphaned him at an early age.

失火(ㄕ ㄏㄨㄛˇ)
to catch fire: 昨夜郵局失火。The post office caught fire last night.

失魂落魄(ㄕ ㄏㄨㄣˊ ㄌㄨㄛˋ ㄆㄛˋ)
despondent; listless; despondency; dejection

失計(ㄕ ㄐㄧˋ)
miscalculation; poor scheming or planning

失節(ㄕ ㄐㄧㄝˊ)
①(said of a man) to commit a breach of virtue, especially to surrender to the enemy ②(said of a woman) to commit adultery; to lose chastity

失檢(ㄕ ㄐㄧㄢˇ)
indiscretion; careless in personal conduct or behavior: 他行爲失檢。He committed a grave indiscretion.

失禁(ㄕ ㄐㄧㄣˋ)
incontinence

失敬(ㄕ ㄐㄧㄥˋ)
Excuse me for being disrespectful, or wanting in regard, propriety, etc. (a polite expression in greeting a guest)

失據(ㄕ ㄐㄩˋ)
to lose one's guidance

失覺(ㄕ ㄐㄩㄝˊ)
to fail to perceive; to be negligent

失竊(ㄕ ㄑㄧㄝˋ)
to be stolen; to be visited by a burglar

失去(ㄕ ㄑㄩˋ)
to lose: 不要失去你的自信。Don't lose your confidence.

失效(ㄕ ㄒㄧㄠˋ)
①(law) to lose legal force; to be invalidated; null and void ②(said of medicines, etc.) to lose potency or efficacy (usually owing to a prolonged lapse of time, etc.)

失笑(ㄕ ㄒㄧㄠˋ)
cannot help laughing

失修(ㄕ ㄒㄧㄡ)
wanting in repair or proper maintenance; in a dilapi-

dated state
失陷(ㄕ ㄒㄧㄢˋ)
(said of cities, territory, etc.) to fall to enemy; to be lost to the enemy
失信(ㄕ ㄒㄧㄣˋ)
to break one's word or promise: 他常失信。He always breaks his promise.
失學(ㄕ ㄒㄩㄝˊ)
to lack formal schooling or education; to neglect to learn; not to have learned
失血(ㄕ ㄒㄩㄝˇ)
to lose blood
失之東隅，收之桑榆(ㄕ ㄓ ㄉㄨㄥ ㄩˊ, ㄕㄡ ㄓ ㄙㄤ ㄩˊ)
to suffer a loss in one place but make a gain somewhere else
失之毫釐，差之千里(ㄕ ㄓ ㄏㄠˊ ㄌㄧˊ, ㄔㄚ ㄓ ㄑㄧㄢ ㄌㄧˇ)
A slight mistake will result in a great error in the end.
失之交臂(ㄕ ㄓ ㄐㄧㄠ ㄅㄧˋ)
to miss (a person or chance) at very close range: 機會難得，切勿失之交臂。Don't let slip such a golden opportunity.
失職(ㄕ ㄓˊ)
to be delinquent; dereliction of one's duty; to neglect one's duty
失著(ㄕ ㄓㄠ)
to miscalculate; a miscalculation
失眞(ㄕ ㄓㄣ)
(said of photograph, voice, etc.) to be in disagreement with the actual image or sound; not true to life; to lack fidelity
失政(ㄕ ㄓㄥˋ)
to misrule a nation
失主(ㄕ ㄓㄨˇ)
(law) the owner of lost property or the victim of a robbery, burglary, etc.
失察(ㄕ ㄔㄚˊ)
to be neglectful of one's duty of supervision; to neglect to inquire into
失常(ㄕ ㄔㄤˊ)
off form; to perform below one's normal capacity; odd
失傳(ㄕ ㄔㄨㄢˊ)
lost (arts, skills, etc.); to lose the record of; to lose the tradition of
失寵(ㄕ ㄔㄨㄥˇ)
to fall out of imperial favor; to be in disgrace; to lose one's boss's confidence
失時(ㄕ ㄕˊ)
to miss the opportune moment; to miss the right opportunity
失實(ㄕ ㄕˊ)
inaccurate
失事(ㄕ ㄕˋ)
an accident; to meet with an accident
失恃(ㄕ ㄕˋ)
① to lose one's mother ② to lose somebody or something one used to rely on
失勢(ㄕ ㄕˋ)
to lose one's position, authority, influence, etc.
失手(ㄕ ㄕㄡˇ)
to break something or hurt somebody by accident; to slip
失守(ㄕ ㄕㄡˇ)
① to fail to fulfill one's duty ②(said of a city, territory, etc.) to fall into the hands of the enemy
失閃(ㄕ ㄕㄢˇ)
accident; accidentally
失身(ㄕ ㄕㄣ)
①(said of women) to lose chastity ② to incur danger
失身分 or 失身份(ㄕ ㄕㄣ ˙ㄈㄣ)
(to do something) beneath one's dignity
失神(ㄕ ㄕㄣˊ)
inattentive; absent-minded; careless
失愼(ㄕ ㄕㄣˋ)
① careless; carelessness ② (literary) to cause a fire out of carelessness
失聲(ㄕ ㄕㄥ)
to lose one's voice for crying too much
失足(ㄕ ㄗㄨˊ)
① to slip; to lose one's footing; a slip ② to commit a mistake; to take a wrong step in life
失蹤(ㄕ ㄗㄨㄥ)
missing
失策(ㄕ ㄘㄜˋ)
poor tactic or strategy; bad scheming or planning; a mistake; unwise; inexpedient
失措(ㄕ ㄘㄨㄛˋ)
to lose one's head or presence of mind in fright or panic
失色(ㄕ ㄙㄜˋ)
to lose color; to turn pale; to become pale because of fear or other sudden emotional changes
失散(ㄕ ㄙㄢˋ)
lost and scattered (usually referring to the original script of a book, etc.); to be separated from and lose touch with each other
失速(ㄕ ㄙㄨˋ)
(aviation) to stall
失所(ㄕ ㄙㄨㄛˇ)
to be homeless
失算(ㄕ ㄙㄨㄢˋ)
to miscalculate; a miscalculation
失而復得(ㄕ ㄦˊ ㄈㄨˋ ㄉㄜˊ)
to be lost and found again
失意(ㄕ ㄧˋ)
not doing well; disappointed; very discouraged; frustrated
失業(ㄕ ㄧㄝˋ)
to lose one's job; jobless; unemployed; unemployment
失言(ㄕ ㄧㄢˊ)
to make improper utterances; to say what should not be said; an improper pronouncement, remark, etc.
失迎(ㄕ ㄧㄥˊ)
Excuse me for not having greeted you.
失誤(ㄕ ㄨˋ)
① an error; a slip; an omission ②(golf) duff; (bowling) miss; error; (tennis) fault; (softball & basketball) error
失物(ㄕ ㄨˋ)
lost property
失物招領(ㄕ ㄨˋ ㄓㄠ ㄌㄧㄥˇ)
lost items or articles (found by others) kept for claimants
失望(ㄕ ㄨㄤˋ)
to be disappointed or discouraged; disappointment: 我

〔大部〕

對他甚感失望。I was disappointed in him.

失約(ㄕ ㄩㄝ)
①to break one's promise: 請別失約。Please don't break your promise. ②to break a date or an appointment

【央】 923
ㄧㄤ iang yāng

1. the center; central; middle
2. the finish or conclusion; to finish: 夜未央。The night has not passed off.
3. to request; to entreat

央託(ㄧㄤ ㄊㄨㄛ)
to request (someone) to do something

央告(ㄧㄤ ㄍㄠˋ)
to beg; to beseech

央求(ㄧㄤ ㄑㄧㄡˊ)
to beg; to entreat; to implore; to plead

央請(ㄧㄤ ㄑㄧㄥˇ)
to make a request

【夯】 924
ㄏㄤ hang hāng

1. to raise with force
2. a heavy load; a burden
3. (levee construction) to fill cracks and leaks with earth

三畫

【夷】 925
ㄧˊ yi yí

1. (in ancient China) barbarians in the east
2. foreign tribes or foreigners
3. at ease; peaceful
4. to level; to make level, even or smooth
5. safe
6. to eliminate; to exterminate; to kill; to execute
7. injuries; wounds
8. grades; classes
9. common; usual; ordinary
10. great; big
11. a Chinese family name

夷滅(ㄧˊ ㄇㄧㄝˋ)
to wipe out (a tribe, family, etc.)

夷狄(ㄧˊ ㄉㄧˊ)
the barbarian tribes in the east and north of ancient China

夷戮(ㄧˊ ㄌㄨˋ)
to slaughter

夷九族(ㄧˊ ㄐㄧㄡˇ ㄗㄨˊ)
the execution of nine branches of a family (the most severe punishment in ancient China)

夷爲平地(ㄧˊ ㄨㄟˊ ㄆㄧㄥˊ ㄉㄧˋ)
to level (a town, etc.) with the ground: 大火把建築物夷爲平地。The fire levelled buildings with the ground.

【夸】 926
ㄎㄨㄚ kua kuā

1. big; large
2. lavish; luxurious
3. good-looking; pleasant
4. to brag; to talk big
5. a Chinese family name

夸誕(ㄎㄨㄚ ㄉㄢˋ)
boastful; bragging

四畫

【夾】 927
1. ㄐㄧㄚˊ jya jiá
(又讀 ㄐㄧㄚ jia jiā)

1. to be wedged between; to be sandwiched
2. to squeeze; to press; to occupy both sides of
3. pincers
4. of two or more layers; lined (garments, etc.)
5. a folder to keep sheets of paper, etc.
6. to carry secretly
7. to mix; to mingle

夾子(ㄐㄧㄚ ˙ㄗ)
folders for keeping documents, papers, pictures, etc.; clips

夾被(ㄐㄧㄚˊ ㄅㄟˋ)
a bedcover with a lining

夾板(ㄐㄧㄚˊ ㄅㄢˇ)
①boards for supporting or pressing the sides of anything—as a fractured leg ②plywood

夾縫(ㄐㄧㄚˊ ㄈㄥˋ)
a crack; a narrow opening; a loophole (in the law)

夾帶(ㄐㄧㄚˊ ㄉㄞˋ)
①things brought in secretly such as contraband: 郵寄包裹不能夾帶信件。Don't put letters into a parcel. ②a crib

夾道(ㄐㄧㄚˊ ㄉㄠˋ)
a narrow passageway between two walls or rows of trees, etc.

夾道歡迎(ㄐㄧㄚˊ ㄉㄠˋ ㄏㄨㄢ ㄧㄥˊ)
to line the street to welcome (a state guest, a conquering hero, etc.)

夾攻(ㄐㄧㄚˊ ㄍㄨㄥ) or 夾擊(ㄐㄧㄚˊ ㄐㄧˊ)
to attack from both sides: 我軍被敵人兩面夾攻。Our troops were attacked by the enemies from both sides.

夾七夾八(ㄐㄧㄚˊ ㄑㄧ ㄐㄧㄚˊ ㄅㄚ)
mixed and not pure; mixed up; not clear

夾心(ㄐㄧㄚˊ ㄒㄧㄣ)
with a filling

夾注(ㄐㄧㄚˊ ㄓㄨˋ)
(especially in Chinese classics) explanatory notes immediately following the words or sentences to be explained

夾注號(ㄐㄧㄚˊ ㄓㄨˋ ㄏㄠˋ)
parentheses used to mark off explanatory notes

夾持(ㄐㄧㄚˊ ㄔˊ)
to hold in between

夾書板(ㄐㄧㄚˊ ㄕㄨ ㄅㄢˇ)
a book brace

夾雜(ㄐㄧㄚˊ ㄗㄚˊ)
mixed up

夾層(ㄐㄧㄚˊ ㄘㄥˊ)
a double layer; a secret compartment; a false bottom (of a trunk, etc.)

夾衣(ㄐㄧㄚˊ ㄧ)
lined garments without padding

夾尾巴(ㄐㄧㄚˊ ㄧˇ ㄅㄚ)
(said of dogs) to put the tail between the legs—(figuratively) to act like a coward

【夾】 927
2. ㄐㄧㄚˋ jiah jià

參看「夾竹桃」or「夾生」

夾竹桃(ㄐㄧㄚˋ ㄓㄨˊ ㄊㄠˊ)
an oleander

夾生(ㄐㄧㄚˋ ˙ㄕㄥ)
(usually said of rice) half-cooked; parboiled

五畫

【奄】 928
1. ㄧㄢˇ yean yǎn

1. to cover; to surround
2. suddenly; abruptly; rapidly

3. a Chinese family name
奄忽(ㄧㄢ ㄏㄨ)
suddenly; abruptly; rapidly
奄有(ㄧㄢˇ ㄧㄡˇ)
to put under one's control

〔大部〕

【奄】 928
2. ㄧㄢ ian yān
1. to soak; to bathe; to drown
2. to remain
3. to castrate; a castrated man
奄留(ㄧㄢ ㄌㄧㄡˊ)
to tarry for a long time
奄奄一息(ㄧㄢ ㄧㄢ ㄧˋ ㄒㄧˊ)
dying; barely breathing; at one's last gasp; on the verge of death

【奇】 929
1. ㄑㄧˊ chyi qí
1. strange; uncanny; occult; rare
2. wonderful
3. to feel strange about; to wonder
奇兵(ㄑㄧˊ ㄅㄧㄥ)
(military) to attack by surprise; to ambush; troops used for such a purpose; a surprise attack, etc.
奇謀(ㄑㄧˊ ㄇㄡˊ)
a very clever strategy or trick; an uncanny scheme
奇妙(ㄑㄧˊ ㄇㄧㄠˋ)
wonderful; rare; too good to be true
奇妙莫測(ㄑㄧˊ ㄇㄧㄠˋ ㄇㄛˋ ㄘㄜˋ)
mysterious and inscrutable
奇特(ㄑㄧˊ ㄊㄜˋ)
unique; outstanding; strange
奇談(ㄑㄧˊ ㄊㄢˊ)
a strange story; an unusual story: 我從來沒聽過這種奇談。I've never heard of such a strange story.
奇男子(ㄑㄧˊ ㄋㄢˊ ㄗˇ)
a remarkable man; a man among men
奇女子(ㄑㄧˊ ㄋㄩˇ ㄗˇ)
a remarkable woman
奇怪(ㄑㄧˊ ㄍㄨㄞˋ)
① strange; unusual; odd; surprising: 多奇怪啊! How odd! ② something of unusual or strange sizes or shapes ③ (said of the ways of the world) wonders; kaleidoscopic
奇觀(ㄑㄧˊ ㄍㄨㄢ)
a spectacular or wonderful sight or phenomenon
奇功(ㄑㄧˊ ㄍㄨㄥ)
remarkable achievements; outstanding services
奇花異木(ㄑㄧˊ ㄏㄨㄚ ㄧˋ ㄇㄨˋ)
exotic flowers and unusual trees
奇貨可居(ㄑㄧˊ ㄏㄨㄛˋ ㄎㄜˇ ㄐㄩ)
(literally) rare commodities which can be hoarded for better prices—rare or precious goods
奇蹟(ㄑㄧˊ ㄐㄧ)
miracles; wonders; strange things or happenings
奇技(ㄑㄧˊ ㄐㄧˋ)
an uncanny feat; a stunt; some rare skill
奇景(ㄑㄧˊ ㄐㄧㄥˇ)
wonderful scenes or unusual sights
奇襲(ㄑㄧˊ ㄒㄧˊ)
a surprise attack; to raid; to attack by surprise: 他們決定向敵營奇襲。They decided to attack the enemy's camp by surprise.
奇效(ㄑㄧˊ ㄒㄧㄠˋ)
(said of medicines) with miraculous efficacy
奇形怪狀(ㄑㄧˊ ㄒㄧㄥˊ ㄍㄨㄞˋ ㄓㄨㄤˋ)
of strange, bizarre or grotesque shapes and sizes
奇勛(ㄑㄧˊ ㄒㄩㄣ)
outstanding contribution
奇裝異服(ㄑㄧˊ ㄓㄨㄤ ㄧˋ ㄈㄨˊ)
strange or queer clothing; outlandish dresses
奇恥大辱(ㄑㄧˊ ㄔˇ ㄉㄚˋ ㄖㄨˇ)
① great shame, dishonor or disgrace ② a great insult or humiliation
奇事(ㄑㄧˊ ㄕˋ)
a strange matter; an inexplicable occurrence
奇人(ㄑㄧˊ ㄖㄣˊ)
① a strange or queer person ② a person of unusual ability
奇才(ㄑㄧˊ ㄘㄞˊ)
a rare talent; a genius: 愛因斯坦是個數學奇才。Einstein was a mathematical genius.
奇異(ㄑㄧˊ ㄧˋ)
① strange; unusual; odd; curious ② Chinese translation for GE—General Electric
奇異果(ㄑㄧˊ ㄧˋ ㄍㄨㄛˇ)
kiwi; Chinese gooseberries
奇驗(ㄑㄧˊ ㄧㄢˋ)
①(said of medicines, etc.) unusual efficacy ②(said of fortune-telling, etc.) uncanny accuracy
奇文(ㄑㄧˊ ㄨㄣˊ)
① a remarkable piece of writing ② queer writing
奇聞(ㄑㄧˊ ㄨㄣˊ)
something unheard-of; an electrifying, fantastic story: 這眞是千古奇聞。It is really an unheard-of fantastic story.
奇遇(ㄑㄧˊ ㄩˋ)
an unexpected encounter (usually referring to pleasant encounters)
奇緣(ㄑㄧˊ ㄩㄢˊ)
an unexpected relationship

【奇】 929
2. ㄐㄧ ji jī
odd (numbers): 奇日 on odd days 六十有奇 sixty odd
奇零(ㄐㄧ ㄌㄧㄥˊ)
any number that is not a round figure
奇數(ㄐㄧ ㄕㄨˋ)
an odd number
奇偶(ㄐㄧ ㄡˇ)
odd and even numbers

【奈】 930
ㄋㄞˋ nay nài
1. what; how; but: 其奈我何? What can they do to me?
2. to bear; to endure
奈煩 or 耐煩(ㄋㄞˋ ㄈㄢˊ)
to bear; to endure
奈良(ㄋㄞˋ ㄌㄧㄤˊ)
Nara, ancient Japanese capital
奈何(ㄋㄞˋ ㄏㄜˊ)
① What to do now? 或 What can we do now? 或 What then? 或 Why? ② to cope with; to deal with
奈及利亞(ㄋㄞˋ ㄐㄧˊ ㄌㄧˋ ㄧㄚˋ)
Nigeria

【奉】 931
ㄈㄥˋ fenq fèng
1. to receive with respect
2. an expression of respect
3. to offer; to present
4. to admire; to love and

respect
5. pay; salary
6. to serve; to wait on
7. a Chinese family name
奉派(ㄈㄥˋ ㄆㄞˋ)
to be assigned to do a job or to a post
奉陪(ㄈㄥˋ ㄆㄟˊ)
(a polite expression) to accompany (you); to keep (you) company: 恕不奉陪。I'm sorry to be unable to keep you company.
奉命(ㄈㄥˋ ㄇㄧㄥˋ)or 奉令(ㄈㄥˋ ㄌㄧㄥˋ)
to receive orders from above; (to do something) as ordered
奉天(ㄈㄥˋ ㄊㄧㄢ)
a former name of Mukden, capital of Liaoning Province
奉託(ㄈㄥˋ ㄊㄨㄛ)
May I request you to (forward the letter, etc.)?
奉告(ㄈㄥˋ ㄍㄠˋ)
to let somebody know; to inform: 關於這件事我無可奉告。I have no comment about this matter.
奉公守法(ㄈㄥˋ ㄍㄨㄥ ㄕㄡˇ ㄈㄚˇ)
law-abiding
奉候(ㄈㄥˋ ㄏㄡˋ)
to offer greetings
奉還(ㄈㄥˋ ㄏㄨㄢˊ)
respectfully return with thanks
奉勸(ㄈㄥˋ ㄑㄩㄢˋ)
May I venture to advise you to...?
奉獻(ㄈㄥˋ ㄒㄧㄢˋ)
①to offer (something to a deity, superior, etc.) ②(Christianity) to contribute; contributions to the church
奉行(ㄈㄥˋ ㄒㄧㄥˊ)
to act or perform something as ordered
奉行故事(ㄈㄥˋ ㄒㄧㄥˊ ㄍㄨˋ ㄕˋ)
①to do something perfunctorily ②to follow the old example or traditional practice
奉職(ㄈㄥˋ ㄓˊ)
to work with; to have a job at; to get an appointment: 他奉職於海關。He has a job at the custom house.
奉旨(ㄈㄥˋ ㄓˇ)
on the imperial order
奉召(ㄈㄥˋ ㄓㄠˋ)
to be summoned or recalled by the emperor or chief of a state
奉趙(ㄈㄥˋ ㄓㄠˋ)
to return something with thanks
奉承(ㄈㄥˋ ㄔㄥˊ)
①respectfully receive ②to flatter; to pay court to: 他在奉承你。He is flattering you.
奉上(ㄈㄥˋ ㄕㄤˋ)
May I present...?
奉贈(ㄈㄥˋ ㄗㄥˋ)
with the compliments of...; to present with respect
奉此(ㄈㄥˋ ㄘˇ)
"upon receipt of this..." (a platitude in Chinese documentary writing)
奉祀(ㄈㄥˋ ㄙˋ)
to offer sacrifices (to the dead, etc.)
奉祀官(ㄈㄥˋ ㄙˋ ㄍㄨㄢ)
"a sacrificial official," a government post held from generation to generation by the eldest male descendant of Confucius and four minor sages—Mencius, Tzu-szu, Tseng-tzu and Yen Hui(孟子，子思，曾子，顏回)
奉送(ㄈㄥˋ ㄙㄨㄥˋ)
①to present respectfully ②(shop language) to give away as a gift
奉安(ㄈㄥˋ ㄢ)
(in old China) the burial of the emperor or queen; the burial of the president or founder of a nation
奉養(ㄈㄥˋ ㄧㄤˇ)
to support (one's parents): 子女應該奉養雙親。Children should support their parents.
奉爲典範(ㄈㄥˋ ㄨㄟˊ ㄉㄧㄢˇ ㄈㄢˋ)
to look upon as a model
奉爲圭臬(ㄈㄥˋ ㄨㄟˊ ㄍㄨㄟ ㄋㄧㄝˋ)
to look up to something as a model

六畫

【奔】 932
1.(奔) ㄅㄣ ben bēn
1. to move quickly; to run; to hurry
2. to run for one's life; to flee
3. to elope
奔波(ㄅㄣ ㄅㄛ)
to be on the run; to work very hard; to toil; toil
奔跑(ㄅㄣ ㄆㄠˇ)
to run in a great hurry
奔忙(ㄅㄣ ㄇㄤˊ)
to be on the move constantly; to be in a great hurry; to be busy; to toil
奔命(ㄅㄣ ㄇㄧㄥˋ)
to rush about on errands
奔放(ㄅㄣ ㄈㄤˋ)
①(said of a horse) galloping ②(said of a writing or emotional manifestation) expressive and unrestrained; moving and forceful
奔騰(ㄅㄣ ㄊㄥˊ)
①to gallop ②to surge forward; to roll in surges
奔流(ㄅㄣ ㄌㄧㄡˊ)
a swift flow (of water); a torrent
奔逐(ㄅㄣ ㄓㄨˊ)
①to run after; to chase ②(figuratively) to contest or jockey for position (in politics, etc.)
奔馳(ㄅㄣ ㄔˊ)
to travel quickly; to move fast; to hasten; to run quickly; to speed on: 火車向前奔馳。The train sped on.
奔走(ㄅㄣ ㄗㄡˇ)
①to solicit help (in trying to land a job, get an appointment, etc.) ②to do a job on orders; to run errands: 他替我們所有的鄰居奔走。He ran errands for all our neighbors.
奔竄(ㄅㄣ ㄘㄨㄢˋ)
(usually said of bandits, defeated troops, etc.) to flee; to run in a hurry: 敵人被擊敗後奔竄。The enemy were defeated and fled in disorder.
奔喪(ㄅㄣ ㄙㄤ)
to hasten home upon the death of one's parents

〔大部〕

〔大部〕

【奔】 932
2.(奔) ㄅㄣˋ benn bèn
to go straight forwards; to head for

奔命(ㄅㄣˋ ㄇㄧㄥˋ)
to be in a desperate hurry

【奎】 933
ㄎㄨㄟˊ kwei kuí
1. between the buttocks; the stride made by a man
2. one of the 28 constellations which ancient Chinese astrologers believed to control the literary trends of the world
3. a Chinese family name

奎寧(ㄎㄨㄟˊ ㄋㄧㄥˊ)
quinine: 奎寧是有效的瘧疾預防藥。Quinine is an effectual preventive for malaria.

奎松市(ㄎㄨㄟˊ ㄙㄨㄥ ㄕˋ)
Quezon City, near Manila

【奏】 934
ㄗㄡˋ tzow zòu
1. to report to the throne
2. to play (music or musical instruments): 他們奏國歌。They played the national anthem. 我女兒在彈奏鋼琴。My daughter is playing the piano.
3. to move; to advance

奏本(ㄗㄡˋ ㄅㄣˇ)
a written report or letter to the king or emperor; a memorial

奏明(ㄗㄡˋ ㄇㄧㄥˊ)
to report or explain to the throne; to memorialize to the emperor

奏鳴曲(ㄗㄡˋ ㄇㄧㄥˊ ㄑㄩˇ)
(music) a sonata: 今晚布蘭德爾演奏貝多芬的「月光奏鳴曲」。Tonight Brendel played Beethoven's "Moonlight Sonata".

奏功(ㄗㄡˋ ㄍㄨㄥ)
to have the intended effect; effective; to achieve success: 他那些消除失業的措施奏功了。His measures to cure unemployment have the intended effect.

奏凱(ㄗㄡˋ ㄎㄞˇ)
(literally) to play the song of triumph—to be victorious

奏捷(ㄗㄡˋ ㄐㄧㄝˊ)
(literally) to report the news of victory (to superiors)—to win; to be victorious: 我們的球隊再度奏捷。Our team has won again.

奏效(ㄗㄡˋ ㄒㄧㄠˋ)
effective; efficacious; to have the intended effect

奏摺(ㄗㄡˋ ㄓㄜˊ)
a written report, statement, or letter to the throne; a memorial

奏章(ㄗㄡˋ ㄓㄤ)
a written report or statement to the emperor; a memorial

奏疏(ㄗㄡˋ ㄕㄨ)
a written report or statement to the throne; a memorial

奏議(ㄗㄡˋ ㄧˋ)
a petition to the emperor; a report or statement to the throne; a memorial

奏樂(ㄗㄡˋ ㄩㄝˋ)
to play music (in solemn ceremonies): 他們開始奏樂。They begin to play music.

【奐】 935
ㄏㄨㄢˋ huann huàn
1. leisurely
2. brilliant; colorful; gay; lively
3. excellent; elegant
4. numerous; many
5. a Chinese family name

【契】 936
1. ㄑㄧˋ chih qì
1. a contract; an agreement; a bond: 他與那公司訂一項工作契約。He made a contract with the company for a work.
2. a divining instrument in ancient China
3. to be compatible, harmonious in thought and aspiration
4. to adopt
5. to cut; to carve; to notch

契刀(ㄑㄧˋ ㄉㄠ)
an ancient coin introduced by Wang Mang (王莽) with a round head and a knife-shaped handle

契丹(ㄑㄧˋ ㄉㄢ)
Kitan, a Sinicized ancient country in northern China

契合(ㄑㄧˋ ㄏㄜˊ)
to be in agreement; compatible; harmony: 你所說的與我契合。Your story agrees with mine.

契機(ㄑㄧˋ ㄐㄧ)
①(philosophy) a moment ② a turning point; a critical point of time

契據(ㄑㄧˋ ㄐㄩˋ)
a contract; an agreement; deeds or similar documents

契券(ㄑㄧˋ ㄑㄩㄢˋ)
a written contract or agreement; a bond; a deed

契紙(ㄑㄧˋ ㄓˇ)
a title deed 亦作「所有權狀」

契舟求劍(ㄑㄧˋ ㄓㄡ ㄑㄧㄡˊ ㄐㄧㄢˋ)or (ㄑㄧㄝˋ ㄓㄡ ㄑㄧㄡˊ ㄐㄧㄢˋ)
to carve on a gunwale of a moving boat, marking where a sword was dropped—a foolish undertaking

契友(ㄑㄧˋ ㄧㄡˇ)
an intimate friend; a bosom friend

契文(ㄑㄧˋ ㄨㄣˊ)
① a written agreement ② ancient Chinese characters carved on oracle bones

契約(ㄑㄧˋ ㄩㄝ)
a written contract or agreement

【契】 936
2. ㄑㄧㄝˋ chieh qiè
1. to carve
2. to be separated from

契闊(ㄑㄧㄝˋ ㄎㄨㄛˋ)
to be separated from one another

【奕】 937
ㄧˋ yih yì
1. great; grand; abundant
2. gorgeous; elegant; good-looking
3. worried; unsettled; anxious
4. in good order; in sequence

奕奕(ㄧˋ ㄧˋ)
① grand and graceful; gorgeous ② anxious; unsettled

七畫

【奘】 938
ㄗㄤˋ tzanq zàng
large; stout; thick; powerful

【套】 939
ㄊㄠˋ taw tào
1. a case; an envelope; a wrap-

per; a sheath
2. a trap; a snare; a noose
3. to wear or slip on (a sweater, etc.)
4. to trap or trick a person (into telling the truth)
5. to harness: 他去套牲口。He went and harnessed the livestock.
6. to pattern or model after; a set pattern
7. convention; a formula: "你好嗎?"是一句禮貌的客套話。"How do you do?" is a polite formula.
8. a suit (of clothes); a set (of tableware, etc.)

套杯(ㄊㄠˋ ㄅㄟ)
a set of cups, one inside another

套版(ㄊㄠˋ ㄅㄢˇ)
①(printing) registering ②ancient color woodblock printing

套房(ㄊㄠˋ ㄈㄤˊ)
a suite (of rooms)

套筒(ㄊㄠˋ ㄊㄨㄥˇ)
(machinery) a sleeve

套牢(ㄊㄠˋ ㄌㄠˊ)
lockup; to lock up

套利(ㄊㄠˋ ㄌㄧˋ)
arbitrage; to make a profit (usually by money exchanging)

套管(ㄊㄠˋ ㄍㄨㄢˇ)
(petroleum) a casing pipe

套口供(ㄊㄠˋ ㄎㄡˇ ㄍㄨㄥˋ)
to trap a suspect into admitting his guilt

套褲(ㄊㄠˋ ㄎㄨˋ)
trouser legs worn over one's trousers

套環兒(ㄊㄠˋ ㄏㄨㄚˊㄦ)
①pretzel-like biscuits ②a set of connected rings

套話(ㄊㄠˋ ㄏㄨㄚˋ)or 套語(ㄊㄠˋ ㄩˇ)
①polite, conventional verbal exchanges ②to trap a person into telling the truth

套匯(ㄊㄠˋ ㄏㄨㄟˋ)
illegal remittance of foreign exchange for a profit derived from the discrepancy between official and black market rates of exchange

套間(ㄊㄠˋ ㄐㄧㄢ)
①a small room opening off another ②an apartment; a flat

套曲(ㄊㄠˋ ㄑㄩˇ)
a divertimento 亦作「套數」

套鞋(ㄊㄠˋ ㄒㄧㄝˊ)
overshoes; galoshes

套袖(ㄊㄠˋ ㄒㄧㄡˋ)
an oversleeve

套裝(ㄊㄠˋ ㄓㄨㄤ)
an ensemble

套車(ㄊㄠˋ ㄔㄜ)
to harness an animal to a carriage

套衫(ㄊㄠˋ ㄕㄢ)
a pullover

套色(ㄊㄠˋ ㄙㄜˋ)
(printing) chromatography; color process

套色捲筒機(ㄊㄠˋ ㄙㄜˋ ㄐㄩㄢˇ ㄊㄨㄥˇ ㄐㄧ)
a color rotogravure

套衣(ㄊㄠˋ ㄧ)
an outer garment

套印(ㄊㄠˋ ㄧㄣˋ)
multiple-printing (especially in color printing)

套問(ㄊㄠˋ ㄨㄣˋ)
to find out by asking seemingly unexceptional questions; tactfully sound somebody out

套用(ㄊㄠˋ ㄩㄥˋ)
to apply mechanically; to use indiscriminately: 他喜歡套用成語。He likes to use hackneyed formulas.

【畚】 940
ㄅㄣˇ been běn

a basket or hod for earth

畚斗(ㄅㄣˇ ㄉㄡˇ)
a dustbin

畚箕(ㄅㄣˇ ㄐㄧ)
a hod for collecting household garbage, dust, etc.; a dust basket

【奚】 941
ㄒㄧ shi xī

1. why; how; what; which
2. a servant
3. name of a Tartar tribe in ancient China
4. a Chinese family name

奚落(ㄒㄧ ㄌㄨㄛˋ)
to laugh at; to make a fool of亦作「嘲笑」: 不要奚落她。Don't laugh at her.

奚取(ㄒㄧ ㄑㄩˇ)
What merits or advantages are there?

奚如(ㄒㄧ ㄖㄨˊ)or 奚若(ㄒㄧ ㄖㄨㄛˋ)or 奚似(ㄒㄧ ㄙˋ)
How about it? 或 Why not (do something else)? 或 Would it be better to...?

奚自(ㄒㄧ ㄗˋ)
Wherefrom?

九畫

【奠】 942
ㄉㄧㄢˋ diann diàn

1. to settle; to lay (foundation, etc.)
2. to secure; to consolidate
3. to offer libations

奠邊府(ㄉㄧㄢˋ ㄅㄧㄢ ㄈㄨˇ)
Dienbienphu, in North Vietnam

奠定(ㄉㄧㄢˋ ㄉㄧㄥˋ)
to lay foundation and consolidate it; to settle

奠都(ㄉㄧㄢˋ ㄉㄨ)
to establish a capital

奠基(ㄉㄧㄢˋ ㄐㄧ)
to lay the foundation of a building

奠祭(ㄉㄧㄢˋ ㄐㄧˋ)
the pouring of wine on the ground in sacrifice

奠酒(ㄉㄧㄢˋ ㄐㄧㄡˇ)
a libation of wine

奠儀(ㄉㄧㄢˋ ㄧˊ)or 奠敬(ㄉㄧㄢˋ ㄐㄧㄥˋ)
the money presented to the bereaved family in place of offerings; a money gift for a funeral

【奢】 943
ㄕㄜ she shē

1. extravagant; wasteful; lavish
2. excess; excessive
3. to exaggerate; to brag

奢靡(ㄕㄜ ㄇㄧˇ)
wasteful; lavish spending (of money)

奢華(ㄕㄜ ㄏㄨㄚˊ)
showy; to be indulgent in luxurious and expensive habits

奢想(ㄕㄜ ㄒㄧㄤˇ)
to think wishfully

奢侈(ㄕㄜ ㄔˇ)
luxury; waste; wasteful; prodigal: 他生活於奢侈環境

〔大部〕

中。He lived in luxurious surroundings.

奢侈品(ㄕㄜ ㄔˇ ㄆㄧㄣˇ)
articles of luxury

奢易儉難(ㄕㄜ ㄧˋ ㄐㄧㄢˇ ㄋㄢˊ)
Once one is accustomed to luxury, it is hard for him to live a frugal life.

奢望(ㄕㄜ ㄨㄤˋ)
to entertain hopes beyond one's ability to realize; a wild hope; a fancy; an extravagant wish

奢願(ㄕㄜ ㄩㄢˋ)
to wish for something which one does not deserve; wishful thinking; a wild wish

十畫

【奧】 944
ㄠˋ aw ào

1. mysterious; obscure; profound (learning): 科學家探索宇宙的奧妙。Scientists probed into the mysteries of the universe.
2. a secret cabin or corner of a house or palace
3. Austria

奧秘(ㄠˋ ㄇㄧˋ)
deep, profound and mysterious; subtle; subtlety

奧妙(ㄠˋ ㄇㄧㄠˋ)
① marvels; wonder; mysterious; marvelous; subtle ② the secret of doing something

奧地利(ㄠˋ ㄉㄧˋ ㄌㄧˋ)
Austria 簡稱「奧國」

奧地利人(ㄠˋ ㄉㄧˋ ㄌㄧˋ ㄖㄣˊ)
an Austrian

奧林匹克運動會(ㄠˋ ㄌㄧㄣˊ ㄆㄧˇ ㄎㄜˋ ㄩㄣˋ ㄉㄨㄥˋ ㄏㄨㄟˋ)
the Olympic Games

奧古斯都大帝(ㄠˋ ㄍㄨˇ ㄙ ㄉㄨ ㄉㄚˋ ㄉㄧˋ)
Augustus, 63B.C.-14A.D., the first emperor of Rome

奧克拉荷馬(ㄠˋ ㄎㄜˋ ㄌㄚ ㄏㄜˊ ㄇㄚˇ)
Oklahoma, U.S.A.

奧匈帝國(ㄠˋ ㄒㄩㄥ ㄉㄧˋ ㄍㄨㄛˊ)
Austria-Hungary (1867-1918)

奧旨(ㄠˋ ㄓˇ)
the main theme (of writing, etc.): 這篇短篇小說的奧旨是什麼呢? What is the main theme of this short story?

奧斯曼帝國(ㄠˋ ㄙ ㄇㄢˋ ㄉㄧˋ ㄍㄨㄛˊ)
the Ottoman Empire, founded about 1300 by Osman I 亦作「鄂圖曼帝國」

奧斯陸(ㄠˋ ㄙ ㄌㄨˋ)
Oslo, capital of Norway

奧義(ㄠˋ ㄧˋ)
subtle or hidden meaning; deep and profound meaning

十一畫

【奪】 945
ㄉㄨㄛˊ dwo duó

1. to take by force; to rob: 這場病剝奪了他的體力。This disease had robbed him of his strength.
2. to snatch; to grasp; to carry away (the first prize, etc.)
3. to settle; to decide

奪標(ㄉㄨㄛˊ ㄅㄧㄠ)
to win the first prize—as in a race or contest: 他在賽跑中奪標。He won the first prize in the race.

奪魄(ㄉㄨㄛˊ ㄆㄛˋ)
(literally) to be robbed of one's nerves—terrifying; diabolically monstrous

奪門而出(ㄉㄨㄛˊ ㄇㄣˊ ㄦˊ ㄔㄨ)
to force one's way out; to force a door and rush out

奪目(ㄉㄨㄛˊ ㄇㄨˋ)
(literally) to dazzle the eyes—eye-catching

奪魁(ㄉㄨㄛˊ ㄎㄨㄟˊ)
to win a race or tournament; to emerge at the top in a contest or competitive examination

奪眶而出(ㄉㄨㄛˊ ㄎㄨㄤˋ ㄦˊ ㄔㄨ)
(said of tears) to break out; cannot be kept back: 他感動得眼淚奪眶而出。He was affected so much that his tears started from his eyes.

奪回(ㄉㄨㄛˊ ㄏㄨㄟˊ)
to recapture; to retake; to seize back

奪錦標(ㄉㄨㄛˊ ㄐㄧㄣˇ ㄅㄧㄠ)
to win the first prize—as in a race or game

奪取(ㄉㄨㄛˊ ㄑㄩˇ)
to take by force; to wrest from

奪權(ㄉㄨㄛˊ ㄑㄩㄢˊ)
to seize power; to take over power

奪職(ㄉㄨㄛˊ ㄓˊ)
to be dismissed from office; to deprive (somebody) of office

奪志(ㄉㄨㄛˊ ㄓˋ)
to lose or change one's purpose in life; to change one's belief; to take one's will

奪佔(ㄉㄨㄛˊ ㄓㄢˋ)
to take possession of (something) illegally

奪寵(ㄉㄨㄛˊ ㄔㄨㄥˇ)
to supplant someone in the favor of the emperor; to beat a rival in seeking the favor or confidence of a superior

【獎】 946
ㄐㄧㄤˇ jeang jiǎng

1. to encourage; to exhort
2. to praise; to commend
3. to cite or give a prize or reward (for a merit, etc.)
4. a prize or reward

獎杯(ㄐㄧㄤˇ ㄅㄟ)
a cup (as a prize)

獎牌(ㄐㄧㄤˇ ㄆㄞˊ)
a gold, silver or bronze medal given as an award

獎品(ㄐㄧㄤˇ ㄆㄧㄣˇ)
prizes or rewards

獎勵(ㄐㄧㄤˇ ㄌㄧˋ)
to encourage by rewards

獎金(ㄐㄧㄤˇ ㄐㄧㄣ)
prize money; a bounty; a bonus

獎進(ㄐㄧㄤˇ ㄐㄧㄣˋ)
to encourage to advance further

獎券(ㄐㄧㄤˇ ㄑㄩㄢˋ)
a lottery ticket or raffle ticket: 他賣獎券。He sold lottery tickets.

獎許(ㄐㄧㄤˇ ㄒㄩˇ)
to praise; plaudits; to give encouragement to

獎學金(ㄐㄧㄤˇ ㄒㄩㄝˊ ㄐㄧㄣ)
a scholarship; a fellowship: 他申請一個二千元的獎學金。He applied for a scholarship of two thousand dollars.

獎章(ㄐㄧㄤˇ ㄓㄤ)
a medal: 他獲得獎章的榮譽。He was honored with a medal.

奬狀(ㄐㄧㄤˇ ㄓㄨㄤˋ)
a citation of meritorious services, etc.: 他的老闆以奬狀酬謝他的勞績。His boss rewarded his meritorious services with a citation.

奬懲(ㄐㄧㄤˇ ㄔㄥˊ)
rewards and punishments: 奬懲制度對一個團體是很重要的。The system of rewards and penalties is important to a group.

奬飾(ㄐㄧㄤˇ ㄕˋ)
to praise

奬賞(ㄐㄧㄤˇ ㄕㄤˇ)
① rewards in money, etc. ② to reward

奬掖(ㄐㄧㄤˇ ㄧㄝˋ)
to encourage and help (a young person, the younger generation, etc.)

奬譽(ㄐㄧㄤˇ ㄩˋ)
(said of a superior) to give recognition

十二畫

【奭】 947
1. ㄕˋ shyh shì

1. red
2. a Chinese family name

奭然(ㄕˋ ㄖㄢˊ)
in a free manner; in utter freedom

【奭】 947
2. ㄏㄜˋ heh hè

to be angry

十三畫

【奮】 948
ㄈㄣˋ fenn fèn

1. to rise in force; to arouse; to exert with force
2. (said of a bird) to take wing
3. to advance, promote or invigorate (a cause, etc.)

奮臂(ㄈㄣˋ ㄅㄧˋ)
to raise one's arms and rise; to get up and go

奮臂一呼(ㄈㄣˋ ㄅㄧˋ ㄧˋ ㄏㄨ)
to raise one's hand and issue a rousing call

奮不顧身(ㄈㄣˋ ㄅㄨˊ ㄍㄨˋ ㄕㄣ)
to do something regardless of personal safety: 他奮不顧身救那小孩。He saved the child regardless of his own safety.

奮袂(ㄈㄣˋ ㄇㄟˋ)
to flick one's sleeves (and be ready for action)

奮勉(ㄈㄣˋ ㄇㄧㄢˇ)
to exert with dedication or determination

奮發(ㄈㄣˋ ㄈㄚ)
to rouse oneself; to exert oneself

奮發圖強(ㄈㄣˋ ㄈㄚ ㄊㄨˊ ㄑㄧㄤˊ)
to rejuvenate a nation by dedicated work

奮發有爲(ㄈㄣˋ ㄈㄚ ㄧㄡˇ ㄨㄟˊ)
(often said of a young person) hardworking and promising: 他是個奮發有爲的年輕人。He is a hardworking and promising young man.

奮飛(ㄈㄣˋ ㄈㄟ)
(literally) to spread the wings and fly away—to go far away

奮鬪(ㄈㄣˋ ㄉㄡˋ)
to struggle; to strive; to fight for: 孫中山先生爲革命大業奮鬪終身。Dr. Sun Yat-sen fought all his life for the cause of revolution.

奮力(ㄈㄣˋ ㄌㄧˋ)
to do one's best; to spare no effort

奮激(ㄈㄣˋ ㄐㄧ)
to spur oneself to action

奮擊(ㄈㄣˋ ㄐㄧˊ)
① to strike with force ② to rise up and fight

奮志(ㄈㄣˋ ㄓˋ)
to rise with dedication or determination

奮戰(ㄈㄣˋ ㄓㄢˋ)
to fight bravely

奮勇(ㄈㄣˋ ㄩㄥˇ)
courageously; bravely (especially in fighting enemy troops): 他們奮勇地爲正義而戰。They fought bravely on the side of justice.

女部
ㄋㄩˇ neu nǚ

【女】 949
ㄋㄩˇ neu nǚ

1. a daughter; a girl; a maiden; a lady
2. a woman; a female
3. name of one of the 28 constellations

女伴(ㄋㄩˇ ㄅㄢˋ)
a lady companion; a female companion: 誰是她旅途的女伴? Who are her lady companions on the journey?

女扮男裝(ㄋㄩˇ ㄅㄢˋ ㄋㄢˊ ㄓㄨㄤ)
a woman in a man's clothes; a woman disguising herself as a man

女儐相(ㄋㄩˇ ㄅㄧㄣˋ ㄒㄧㄤˋ)
a bridesmaid

女朋友(ㄋㄩˇ ㄆㄥˊ ㄧㄡˇ)
a girl friend: 昨晚他帶他女朋友去看電影。He took his girl friend to the movies last night.

女僕(ㄋㄩˇ ㄆㄨˊ)
a female servant; a maid

女方(ㄋㄩˇ ㄈㄤ)
on the woman's part (when the other party concerned is a man)

女服務員(ㄋㄩˇ ㄈㄨˊ ㄨˋ ㄩㄢˊ)
① an air hostess; a stewardess ② a waitress

女大不中留(ㄋㄩˇ ㄉㄚˋ ㄅㄨˋ ㄓㄨㄥ ㄌㄧㄡˊ)
A grown daughter cannot be kept unmarried for long.

女大當嫁(ㄋㄩˇ ㄉㄚˋ ㄉㄤ ㄐㄧㄚˋ)
A girl should get married upon reaching womanhood.

女大十八變(ㄋㄩˇ ㄉㄚˋ ㄕˊ ㄅㄚ ㄅㄧㄢˋ)
A girl changes fast in physical appearance from childhood to adulthood.

女德(ㄋㄩˇ ㄉㄜˊ)
① feminine virtues; chastity ② feminine beauty ③ a nun

女低音(ㄋㄩˇ ㄉㄧ ㄧㄣ)
a contralto; an alto

女弟子(ㄋㄩˇ ㄉㄧˋ ㄗˇ)
one's girl student

女童子軍(ㄋㄩˇ ㄊㄨㄥˊ ㄗˇ ㄐㄩㄣ)
girl scouts: 她是女童子軍。She is a girl scout.

女奴(ㄋㄩˇ ㄋㄨˊ)
slave girls

女牢(ㄋㄩˇ ㄌㄠˊ)

〔女部〕

a prison for women criminals; a penitentiary for women

女郎(ㄋㄩˇ ㄌㄤˊ)
a young girl; a young woman; a maiden

女流(ㄋㄩˇ ㄌㄧㄡˊ)
(collectively) women; the weaker sex

女伶(ㄋㄩˇ ㄌㄧㄥˊ)or 女優(ㄋㄩˇ ㄧㄡ)or 女演員(ㄋㄩˇ ㄧㄢˇ ㄩㄢˊ)
an actress: 他妹妹是個名女伶。His sister is a famous actress.

女高音(ㄋㄩˇ ㄍㄠ ㄧㄣ)
a soprano

女管家(ㄋㄩˇ ㄍㄨㄢˇ ㄐㄧㄚ)
a woman head servant; a housekeeper

女工(ㄋㄩˇ ㄍㄨㄥ)
women labor; a girl working in a plant

女紅(ㄋㄩˇ ㄍㄨㄥ)
needlework

女公子(ㄋㄩˇ ㄍㄨㄥ ㄗˇ)
①a polite reference to others' daughters ②the daughter of a feudal prince

女孩(ㄋㄩˇ ㄏㄞˊ)
a girl

女孩兒(ㄋㄩˇ ㄏㄚˊㄦ)
a female child

女皇(ㄋㄩˇ ㄏㄨㄤˊ)
an empress

女角(ㄋㄩˇ ㄐㄧㄠˇ)
an actress; a movie or theatrical role played by a woman

女眷(ㄋㄩˇ ㄐㄩㄢˋ)
the female members of a family

女強人(ㄋㄩˇ ㄑㄧㄤˊ ㄖㄣˊ)
a successful career woman

女青年會(ㄋㄩˇ ㄑㄧㄥ ㄋㄧㄢˊ ㄏㄨㄟˋ)
YWCA—Young Women's Christian Association

女權(ㄋㄩˇ ㄑㄩㄢˊ)
women's rights

女權主義(ㄋㄩˇ ㄑㄩㄢˊ ㄓㄨˇ ㄧˋ)
feminism

女權運動(ㄋㄩˇ ㄑㄩㄢˊ ㄩㄣˋ ㄉㄨㄥˋ)
feminism; a women's liberation movement

女先生(ㄋㄩˇ ㄒㄧㄢ ˙ㄕㄥ)
women teachers

女性(ㄋㄩˇ ㄒㄧㄥˋ)
female; the fair sex

女性荷爾蒙(ㄋㄩˇ ㄒㄧㄥˋ ㄏㄜˊ ㄦˇ ㄇㄥˊ)
female sex hormone

女性化(ㄋㄩˇ ㄒㄧㄥˋ ㄏㄨㄚˋ)
feminization; to feminize

女性中心社會(ㄋㄩˇ ㄒㄧㄥˋ ㄓㄨㄥ ㄒㄧㄣ ㄕㄜˋ ㄏㄨㄟˋ)
matriarchy

女壻 or 女婿(ㄋㄩˇ ㄒㄩˋ)
a son-in-law

女職員(ㄋㄩˇ ㄓˊ ㄩㄢˊ)
a woman employee

女眞(ㄋㄩˇ ㄓㄣ)
Nüchen, or Jurchen, ancestors of the Manchus

女主角(ㄋㄩˇ ㄓㄨˇ ㄐㄧㄠˇ)
a leading lady; a heroine

女主人(ㄋㄩˇ ㄓㄨˇ ㄖㄣˊ)
a hostess

女裝(ㄋㄩˇ ㄓㄨㄤ)
a woman dress

女中丈夫(ㄋㄩˇ ㄓㄨㄥ ㄓㄤˋ ㄈㄨ)or 女中豪傑(ㄋㄩˇ ㄓㄨㄥ ㄏㄠˊ ㄐㄧㄝˊ)
a woman of great capability

女史(ㄋㄩˇ ㄕˇ)
①(formerly) a female official in charge of etiquettes in the palace ② a polite term to address a lady

女士(ㄋㄩˇ ㄕˋ)
Miss...; a lady

女神(ㄋㄩˇ ㄕㄣˊ)
a goddess: 維娜斯是羅馬人所崇拜的女神。Venus was a goddess worshiped by the Roman.

女聲(ㄋㄩˇ ㄕㄥ)
female voice

女生(ㄋㄩˇ ㄕㄥ)
co-eds; girl students

女生宿舍(ㄋㄩˇ ㄕㄥ ㄙㄨˋ ㄕㄜˋ)
a women's dormitory: 她住在女生宿舍。She lived in the women's dormitory.

女生外嚮(ㄋㄩˇ ㄕㄥ ㄨㄞˋ ㄒㄧㄤˋ)
A girl will get married sooner or later and be prone to take the side of her husband (instead of her own family).

女人(ㄋㄩˇ ㄖㄣˊ)
①a woman: 女人善變。Woman changes her mind easily. ② one's wife

女子(ㄋㄩˇ ㄗˇ)
a woman; a girl

女子參政權(ㄋㄩˇ ㄗˇ ㄘㄢ ㄓㄥˋ ㄑㄩㄢˊ)
woman suffrage

女次高音(ㄋㄩˇ ㄘˋ ㄍㄠ ㄧㄣ)or 女中音(ㄋㄩˇ ㄓㄨㄥ ㄧㄣ)
a mezzo-soprano

女厠所(ㄋㄩˇ ㄘㄜˋ ㄙㄨㄛˇ)
a women's lavatory; a ladies' room

女色(ㄋㄩˇ ㄙㄜˋ)
woman's charms

女兒(ㄋㄩˇ ㄦˊ)
① one's daughter ② a girl

女巫(ㄋㄩˇ ㄨ)
a witch 亦作「巫婆」

女爲悅己者容(ㄋㄩˇ ㄨㄟˋ ㄩㄝˋ ㄐㄧˇ ㄓㄜˇ ㄖㄨㄥˊ)
A girl will doll herself up for him who loves her.

女王(ㄋㄩˇ ㄨㄤˊ)
a queen regnant

二畫

【奴】 950
ㄋㄨˊ nu nú

1. a slave; a servant
2. a self-derogatory expression used by a girl to refer to herself in former times
3. a despicable yes-man

奴婢(ㄋㄨˊ ㄅㄧˋ)
slaves; servants

奴僕(ㄋㄨˊ ㄆㄨˊ)
slaves; servants; lackeys

奴隸(ㄋㄨˊ ㄌㄧˋ)
a serf; a slave

奴隸解放(ㄋㄨˊ ㄌㄧˋ ㄐㄧㄝˇ ㄈㄤˋ)
slave emancipation

奴隸制度(ㄋㄨˊ ㄌㄧˋ ㄓˋ ㄉㄨˋ)
slavery: 在某些地方尚有奴隸制度。In certain places slavery is still permitted.

奴隸社會(ㄋㄨˊ ㄌㄧˋ ㄕㄜˋ ㄏㄨㄟˋ)
slave society

奴工(ㄋㄨˊ ㄍㄨㄥ)
slave labor; slave laborers; serfhood

奴工營(ㄋㄨˊ ㄍㄨㄥ ㄧㄥˊ)
a slave labor camp; a concentration camp

奴化(ㄋㄨˊ ㄏㄨㄚˋ)
to enslave; to make a slave of

奴脣婢舌(ㄋㄨˊ ㄔㄨㄣˊ ㄅㄧˋ ㄕㄜˊ)
(said of speech) talkative like a slave or maid

奴家(ㄋㄨˊ ㄐㄧㄚ)

I or me (a self-reference of girls in former times)
奴性(ㄋㄨˊ ㄒㄧㄥˋ)
servility; slavishness; servile attitude
奴才(ㄋㄨˊ ㄘㄞˊ)
①a slave; a serf; a bondman ② a good-for-nothing; a useless fellow; a yes-man ③ used by an official referring to himself when addressing the emperor, especially in the Ching Dynasty
奴役(ㄋㄨˊ ㄧˋ)
to enslave
奴顏婢膝(ㄋㄨˊ ㄧㄢˊ ㄅㄧˋ ㄒㄧ)
servile behavior; fawning; obsequious: 國王喜歡奴顏婢膝的朝臣。The king liked the fawning courtiers.

【奶】951 ㄋㄞˇ nae nǎi
1. the breasts of a woman
2. milk
3. grandma
4. to feed with milk; to breast-feed: 她每天奶孩子。She feeds the baby with milk every day.
5. a term of respect for married women
奶膀子(ㄋㄞˇ ㄆㄤˊ ·ㄗ)
breasts 亦作「奶房」
奶品(ㄋㄞˇ ㄆㄧㄣˇ)
milk products
奶瓶(ㄋㄞˇ ㄆㄧㄥˊ)
a milk bottle: 我找不到奶瓶。I can't find the milk bottle.
奶媽(ㄋㄞˇ ㄇㄚ)or 奶母(ㄋㄞˇ ㄇㄨˇ)
a wet nurse 亦作「乳母」
奶名(ㄋㄞˇ ㄇㄧㄥˊ)
a pet name given to a child by his parents
奶粉(ㄋㄞˇ ㄈㄣˇ)
milk powder
奶頭(ㄋㄞˇ ·ㄊㄡ)
the nipples
奶奶(ㄋㄞˇ ·ㄋㄞ)
①a term of respect for older women ② grandma
奶牛(ㄋㄞˇ ㄋㄧㄡˊ)
a milk cow
奶娘(ㄋㄞˇ ㄋㄧㄤˊ)
a wet nurse
奶酪(ㄋㄞˇ ㄌㄨㄛˋ)
cheese 亦作「乳酪」
奶糕(ㄋㄞˇ ㄍㄠ)
rice pastry used as substitute for milk in feeding babies
奶汁(ㄋㄞˇ ㄓ)
milk (from a woman's breast)
奶罩(ㄋㄞˇ ㄓㄠˋ)
a brassiere or bra
奶茶(ㄋㄞˇ ㄔㄚˊ)
tea with milk
奶水(ㄋㄞˇ ㄕㄨㄟˇ)
milk
奶子(ㄋㄞˇ ·ㄗ)
① the mother's milk ② breasts ③ a wet nurse
奶嘴(ㄋㄞˇ ㄗㄨㄟˇ)
the nipple (of a nursing bottle)
奶油(ㄋㄞˇ ㄧㄡˊ)
butter

三畫

【奸】952 ㄐㄧㄢ jian jiān
1. false
2. selfish
3. disloyal
4. crafty; wicked; villainous; cunning; evil
5. adultery; fornication; licentiousness
6. a traitor; a villain
奸夫(ㄐㄧㄢ ㄈㄨ)
an adulterer
奸婦(ㄐㄧㄢ ㄈㄨˋ)
an adulteress
奸黨(ㄐㄧㄢ ㄉㄤˇ)
a traitorous clique or party
奸佞(ㄐㄧㄢ ㄋㄧㄥˋ)
① cunning and fawning ② a crafty sycophant
奸滑(ㄐㄧㄢ ㄏㄨㄚˊ)
crafty and cunning
奸計(ㄐㄧㄢ ㄐㄧˋ)
a wicked scheme; a cunning trick; a treacherous plot: 他們奸計不得逞。Their wicked scheme failed.
奸細(ㄐㄧㄢ ㄒㄧˋ)
a spy (from the enemy side); a stool pigeon 亦作「間諜」
奸邪(ㄐㄧㄢ ㄒㄧㄝˊ)
① crafty and evil; treacherous ② a crafty and evil person
奸笑(ㄐㄧㄢ ㄒㄧㄠˋ)
a sinister, malicious or villainous smile
奸險(ㄐㄧㄢ ㄒㄧㄢˇ)
crafty, mean and malicious; treacherous
奸雄(ㄐㄧㄢ ㄒㄩㄥˊ)
(usually referring to those in high positions) a very capable but crafty person; a very ambitious scoundrel
奸詐(ㄐㄧㄢ ㄓㄚˋ)
crafty; cunning: 他奸詐如狐狸。He is as cunning as a fox.
奸臣(ㄐㄧㄢ ㄔㄣˊ)
(formerly) a selfish, disloyal and cunning minister; a traitor
奸商(ㄐㄧㄢ ㄕㄤ)
unethical merchants; profiteers
奸人(ㄐㄧㄢ ㄖㄣˊ)
a mean fellow; a villain; a scoundrel
奸賊(ㄐㄧㄢ ㄗㄟˊ)
a scoundrel; a traitor
奸淫(ㄐㄧㄢ ㄧㄣˊ)
① illicit sexual relations; adultery ② lustful; lecherous ③ to rape; to seduce
奸淫擄掠(ㄐㄧㄢ ㄧㄣˊ ㄌㄨˇ ㄌㄩㄝˋ)
to rape and loot

【她】953 ㄊㄚ ta tā
she: 她喜歡古典音樂。She likes classical music.
她們(ㄊㄚ ·ㄇㄣ)
(referring to the feminine) they

【好】954 1. ㄏㄠˇ hao hǎo
1. good; nice; fine; excellent: 這是一本好字典。This is a good dictionary.
2. pleasing (looks, taste, etc.); easy (to deal with, etc.)
3. to finish (dressing, eating, etc.): 他離開之前已把工作做好了。He finished off the work before he left.
4. very; much
5. can; so that: 把這個做完好再開始另外一件。Finish this so that you can start another.
6. All right! 或 Wonderful! 或 Bravo!
7. an exclamatory expression

〔女部〕

8. a friendly meeting
9. fit; suitable; proper

好辦(ㄏㄠˇ ㄅㄢˋ)
easy to manage or arrange: 這件事好辦。The matter can be easily arranged.

好半天(ㄏㄠˇ ㄅㄢˋ ㄊㄧㄢ)
quite a while; a long time

好比(ㄏㄠˇ ㄅㄧˇ)
to be likened to; to be like; to be tantamount to

好不(ㄏㄠˇ ㄅㄨˋ)
very; what; how: 大家見了面,好不歡喜哦! How happy we are to see each other!

好不好(ㄏㄠˇ ·ㄅㄨ ㄏㄠˇ)
① Is it all right? 或 Okay? ② Won't you...?

好不講理(ㄏㄠˇ ·ㄅㄨ ㄐㄧㄤˇ ㄌㄧˇ)
utterly impervious to reasoning or argument

好不容易(ㄏㄠˇ ·ㄅㄨ ㄖㄨㄥˊ ㄧˋ)
① very difficult ② after all the trouble: 他好不容易才擠上了那輛公車。He had a hard time squeezing through the crowd to get on the bus.

好不要臉(ㄏㄠˇ ·ㄅㄨ ㄧㄠˋ ㄌㄧㄢˇ)
brazen; absolutely without shame

好評(ㄏㄠˇ ㄆㄧㄥˊ)
favorable comment; a high opinion: 老師對他頗有好評。The teacher has a rather high opinion of him.

好大(ㄏㄠˇ ㄉㄚˋ)
① How big? ② what a (bad temper, big house, etc.)

好的(ㄏㄠˇ ·ㄉㄜ)
Good! 或 All right. 或 O. K.

好歹(ㄏㄠˇ ㄉㄞˇ)
① emergency; an accident ② by hook or by crook ③ good and bad ④ anyhow; in any case: 好歹試試看。Let's try, anyhow.

好多(ㄏㄠˇ ㄉㄨㄛ)
① How much or many? ② a good deal; so much; so many

好多了(ㄏㄠˇ ㄉㄨㄛ ·ㄌㄜ)
much better: 她已經好多了。She is much better.

好端端(ㄏㄠˇ ㄉㄨㄢ ㄉㄨㄢ)
in perfectly good state or condition; when everything is all right

好天兒(ㄏㄠˇ ㄊㄧㄚㄦ)
a fine day

好聽(ㄏㄠˇ ㄊㄧㄥ)
pleasant to hear: 好聽的話並非人人都愛聽。Not everyone likes sweet words.

好萊塢(ㄏㄠˇ ㄌㄞˊ ㄨ)
Hollywood, California, U.S.A.

好感(ㄏㄠˇ ㄍㄢˇ)
a good opinion; a favorable impression: 我對她有好感。I have a good opinion of her.

好過(ㄏㄠˇ ㄍㄨㄛˋ)
① well-to-do; to be in easy circumstances ② to feel better (after an attack of disease, etc.); to feel fine

好看(ㄏㄠˇ ㄎㄢˋ)
① good-looking; beautiful; nice ② interesting ③ honored; proud ④in an embarrassing situation; on the spot

好合(ㄏㄠˇ ㄏㄜˊ)
(said of couples) to live in perfect union

好好的(ㄏㄠˇ ㄏㄠˇ ·ㄉㄜ)
①(to do something) in earnest or seriously ② perfectly all right

好好先生(ㄏㄠˇ ㄏㄠˇ ㄒㄧㄢ ·ㄕㄥ)
a nice guy who bears no grudge against the world and vice versa; a "soft" fellow who never quarrels with the world; an easy-going person

好好(ㄏㄠˇ ㄏㄠˇ)
① delighted; joyful ② in perfectly good condition; when everything is all right ③ all out; thoroughly ④ carefully; cautiously: 好好地想一想。Think it over carefully.

好漢(ㄏㄠˇ ㄏㄢˋ)
a brave man; a hero: 只有好漢才配得上美人。Only the hero deserves the fair.

好漢不怕出身低(ㄏㄠˇ ㄏㄢˋ ㄅㄨˋ ㄆㄚˋ ㄔㄨ ㄕㄣ ㄉㄧ)
(informal) One's humble origin will not prevent him from achieving success in life.

好漢不吃眼前虧(ㄏㄠˇ ㄏㄢˋ ㄅㄨˋ ㄔ ㄧㄢˇ ㄑㄧㄢˊ ㄎㄨㄟ)
A wise man knows how to avoid being beaten.

好話(ㄏㄠˇ ㄏㄨㄚˋ)
① a good word; a word of praise: 請爲我說句好話。Please put in a good word for me. ② fine words

好極了(ㄏㄠˇ ㄐㄧˊ ·ㄌㄜ)
Excellent! 或 Wonderful! 或 Exquisite! 或 Tops! 他的英文好極了! His English is excellent!

好幾天(ㄏㄠˇ ㄐㄧˇ ㄊㄧㄢ)
quite a few days

好幾個(ㄏㄠˇ ㄐㄧˇ ·ㄍㄜ)
quite a few (people, months, etc.): 昨天有好幾個學生缺席。Quite a few students were absent yesterday.

好傢伙(ㄏㄠˇ ㄐㄧㄚ ·ㄏㄨㄛ)
① The scoundrel! ② Fine thing indeed! ③What a powerful blow!

好久(ㄏㄠˇ ㄐㄧㄡˇ)
① How long? 做這件工作要費好久時間? How long will it take to do the job?② a long time: 我已經等了好久了。I have waited for a long time.

好景不長(ㄏㄠˇ ㄐㄧㄥˇ ㄅㄨˋ ㄔㄤˊ)
The good circumstances don't last long. 或 Good fortune won't last forever.

好球(ㄏㄠˇ ㄑㄧㄡˊ)
Bravo! 或 well played; a good shot

好戲(ㄏㄠˇ ㄒㄧˋ)
① good play ② (sarcastic) great fun: 這回有好戲可看了! We're going to see great fun!

好些(ㄏㄠˇ ㄒㄧㄝ)
① a little better ② many (people, etc.)

好些個(ㄏㄠˇ ㄒㄧㄝ ·ㄍㄜ)
many

好消息(ㄏㄠˇ ㄒㄧㄠ ·ㄒㄧ)
good news: 沒消息便是好消息。No news is good news.

好小子(ㄏㄠˇ ㄒㄧㄠˇ ·ㄗ)
a smart guy; a wise guy

好笑(ㄏㄠˇ ㄒㄧㄠˋ)
laughable; funny; ridiculous: 這個問題有什麼好笑? What is so funny about such a question?

好心(ㄏㄠˇ ㄒㄧㄣ)
well-intentioned; kindness; goodwill; kind-hearted

好像(ㄏㄠˇ ㄒㄧㄤˋ)
to seem; to look like; to resemble very much: 天好像要下雨的樣子。It looks like rain.

好轉(ㄏㄠˇ ㄓㄨㄢˇ)
to take a turn for the better; a favorable turn: 情勢好轉。The situation took a favorable turn.

好吃(ㄏㄠˇ ㄔ)
good to eat; tasty; delicious: 這餐後點心很好吃。The dessert is delicious.

好處(ㄏㄠˇ ·ㄔㄨ)
① good points; advantages ② profit

好使(ㄏㄠˇ ㄕˇ)
① easy to operate; convenient for use ② in order to make

好事(ㄏㄠˇ ㄕˋ)
① good things; wonderful things ② charity; philanthropic acts ③ marriage; wedding ④ a very bad thing (used only in an exclamatory sentence)

好事多磨(ㄏㄠˇ ㄕˋ ㄉㄨㄛ ㄇㄛˊ)
The realization of good things is usually preceded by rough going.

好手(ㄏㄠˇ ㄕㄡˇ)
an adept; an expert; a professional

好受(ㄏㄠˇ ㄕㄡˋ)
pleasant; comfortable; much better

好聲好氣(ㄏㄠˇ ㄕㄥ ㄏㄠˇ ㄑㄧˋ)
in a soft and kindly manner; gently

好說(ㄏㄠˇ ㄕㄨㄛ)
Thanks for your kind word or compliments.

好說歹說(ㄏㄠˇ ㄕㄨㄛ ㄉㄞˇ ㄕㄨㄛ)
to try every possible way to persuade somebody

好說話兒(ㄏㄠˇ ㄕㄨㄛ ㄏㄨㄚˋㄦ)
obliging; good-natured; open to persuasion

好日子(ㄏㄠˇ ㄖˋ ·ㄗ)
① an auspicious day ② a wedding day ③ good days; a happy life: 人人都想要過好日子。Everybody wants to live a happy life.

好人(ㄏㄠˇ ㄖㄣˊ)
① a beauty ② a person of virtue ③ a person who gets along very well with everyone

好人難做(ㄏㄠˇ ㄖㄣˊ ㄋㄢˊ ㄗㄨㄛˋ)
(literally) It's difficult to be a nice guy. — One always gets the blame from somebody no matter how fair and just he is.或 It's difficult to please everybody.

好人好事(ㄏㄠˇ ㄖㄣˊ ㄏㄠˇ ㄕˋ)
good people and exemplary deeds

好人家兒(ㄏㄠˇ ㄖㄣˊ ㄐㄧㄚㄦ)
a good family

好容易(ㄏㄠˇ ㄖㄨㄥˊ ㄧˋ)
with great difficulty; have a hard time (doing something)亦作「好不容易」

好自爲之(ㄏㄠˇ ㄗˋ ㄨㄟˊ ㄓ)
to do one's best (to keep a job, run a business, etc.)

好在(ㄏㄠˇ ㄗㄞˋ)
it's fortunate that; thanks to; fortunately; luckily: 好在他來訪時我在家。Luckily, I was at home when he called.

好死(ㄏㄠˇ ㄙˇ)
to die a natural death (as distinct from an accidental death)

好死不如惡活(ㄏㄠˇ ㄙˇ ㄅㄨˋ ㄖㄨˊ ㄜˋ ㄏㄨㄛˊ)
To live even in adversity is better than to die under the most satisfactory circumstances.

好似(ㄏㄠˇ ㄙˋ)
(it) seems; (it) looks like: 這本書好似很有趣。The book seems quite interesting.

好一個(ㄏㄠˇ ㄧˊ ·ㄍㄜ)
what a: 好一個正人君子! What a just and upright man, indeed!

好意(ㄏㄠˇ ㄧˋ)
to mean well; kindly or benevolently; goodwill; kindness: 謝謝您的好意。Thank you for your kindness.

好意相勸(ㄏㄠˇ ㄧˋ ㄒㄧㄤ ㄑㄩㄢˋ)
to give well-intentioned advice

好意思(ㄏㄠˇ ㄧˋ ·ㄙ)
to have the nerve

好玩(ㄏㄠˇ ㄨㄢˊ)
interesting; full of fun

好望角(ㄏㄠˇ ㄨㄤˋ ㄐㄧㄠˇ)
the Cape of Good Hope, in South Africa

【好】 954
2. ㄏㄠˋ haw hào

1. to love to; to like to; to be fond of
2. to be addicted to
3. what one likes or prefers

好辯(ㄏㄠˋ ㄅㄧㄢˋ)
argumentative; disputatious

好大喜功(ㄏㄠˋ ㄉㄚˋ ㄒㄧˇ ㄍㄨㄥ)
given to vanity; to love to brag and show off

好賭(ㄏㄠˋ ㄉㄨˇ)
fond of gambling

好動(ㄏㄠˋ ㄉㄨㄥˋ)
(said of one's disposition) very active or restless

好高騖遠(ㄏㄠˋ ㄍㄠ ㄨˋ ㄩㄢˇ)
to aim high but care nothing about the fundamental; unrealistic

好客(ㄏㄠˋ ㄎㄜˋ)
to be hospitable: 他是個好客的人。He is a hospitable man.

好靜(ㄏㄠˋ ㄐㄧㄥˋ)
(said of one's disposition) to be fond of tranquility; sedate

好奇(ㄏㄠˋ ㄑㄧˊ)
to be curious; curiosity

好強(ㄏㄠˋ ㄑㄧㄤˊ)
to be eager to do well in everything

好學(ㄏㄠˋ ㄒㄩㄝˊ)
to be fond of studying; to be diligent in the pursuit of knowledge

好戰(ㄏㄠˋ ㄓㄢˋ)
hawkish; warmongering

好整以暇(ㄏㄠˋ ㄓㄥˇ ㄧˇ ㄒㄧㄚˊ)
to remain calm and composed while handling urgent affairs

好吃懶做(ㄏㄠˋ ㄔ ㄌㄢˇ ㄗㄨㄛˋ)
lazy; piggish: 不要這樣好吃懶做。Don't be so lazy.

好事者(ㄏㄠˋ ㄕˋ ㄓㄜˇ)or 好事之徒(ㄏㄠˋ ㄕˋ ㄓ ㄊㄨˊ)
a meddler; a busybody

好尚(ㄏㄠˋ ㄕㄤˋ)
likes; desires; preferences: 你的好尚是什麼? What is your preference?

好生之德(ㄏㄠˋ ㄕㄥ ㄓ ㄉㄜˊ)

〔女部〕

the virtue in sparing animal life; restraint from killing
好生惡死(ㄏㄠˋ ㄕㄥ ㄨˋ ㄙˇ)
to be afraid of death; to cling to life
好勝(ㄏㄠˋ ㄕㄥˋ)
to love to win; to be fond of preeminence; emulative: 他是個好勝的人。He is an emulative person.
好色(ㄏㄠˋ ㄙㄜˋ)
(said of men) to be fond of pleasures of the flesh; lewd; libidinous; lustful
好色不淫(ㄏㄠˋ ㄙㄜˋ ㄅㄨˋ ㄧㄣˊ)
to be fond of beautiful women without being lewd
好逸惡勞(ㄏㄠˋ ㄧˋ ㄨˋ ㄌㄠˊ)
to love ease and hate work; pleasure-seeking
好勇鬥狠(ㄏㄠˋ ㄩㄥˇ ㄉㄡˋ ㄏㄣˇ)
combative; fond of fighting 亦作「好鬥」
好惡(ㄏㄠˋ ㄨˋ)
likes and dislikes
好爲人師(ㄏㄠˋ ㄨㄟˊ ㄖㄣˊ ㄕ)
(literally) to like to be teachers of others—(figuratively) to be fond of giving advice to others despite one's own ignorance
好玩(ㄏㄠˋ ㄨㄢˊ)
pleasure-seeking
好問(ㄏㄠˋ ㄨㄣˋ)
inquisitive; to be fond of asking questions

【妁】955 ㄕㄨㄛˋ shuoh shuò
a matchmaker; a go-between

【如】956 ㄖㄨˊ ru rú
1. like; as: 一日不見，如三秋兮。(詩經・國風・采葛) A day without seeing him/ Is like three seasons.
2. if; supposing: 假如你希望我幫助你，我願幫忙。If you wish, I will help you.
3. as if
4. as good as; equal to: 我不如她。I'm not as good as she is.
5. to follow (advice); to listen to
6. to go to; to arrive at
7. should; ought to
8. on or in (time)

如夢初醒(ㄖㄨˊ ㄇㄥˋ ㄔㄨ ㄒㄧㄥˇ)
(literally) as if awakened from a dream—to come to a sudden realization
如法炮製(ㄖㄨˊ ㄈㄚˇ ㄆㄠˊ ㄓˋ) or 如法泡製(ㄖㄨˊ ㄈㄚˇ ㄆㄠˋ ㄓˋ)
to do things according to an approved routine method; to do something exactly as others have done; to follow suit; to follow the same formula
如飛(ㄖㄨˊ ㄈㄟ)
like flying; quickly; swiftly
如風過耳(ㄖㄨˊ ㄈㄥ ㄍㄨㄛˋ ㄦˇ)
to turn a deaf ear to (exhortations, etc.)
如夫人(ㄖㄨˊ ㄈㄨ ㄖㄣˊ)
a concubine
如墮五里霧中(ㄖㄨˊ ㄉㄨㄛˋ ㄨˇ ㄌㄧˇ ㄨˋ ㄓㄨㄥ)
as if lost in a thick fog; utterly being mystified
如同(ㄖㄨˊ ㄊㄨㄥˊ)
like (a dream,etc.)
如擬(ㄖㄨˊ ㄋㄧˇ)
as suggested (an expression used by a superior in approving a written proposal submitted by a subordinate)
如鳥獸散(ㄖㄨˊ ㄋㄧㄠˇ ㄕㄡˋ ㄙㄢˋ)
to flee helter-skelter
如來(ㄖㄨˊ ㄌㄞˊ)
(Buddhism) one of the designation of Buddha
如雷貫耳(ㄖㄨˊ ㄌㄟˊ ㄍㄨㄢˋ ㄦˇ)
(literally) like thunders roaring in one's ears—(one's famous name) has long been known to people: 久仰大名，如雷貫耳。Your name has long resounded in my ears.
如狼似虎(ㄖㄨˊ ㄌㄤˊ ㄙˋ ㄏㄨˇ)
(literally) like tigers and wolves—(to eat) piggishly; (to treat or loot people) heartlessly and cruelly; (said of appearances) menacing or threatening
如臨大敵(ㄖㄨˊ ㄌㄧㄣˊ ㄉㄚˋ ㄉㄧˊ)
(literally) like confronting a dangerous enemy—very careful or cautious; to take all possible precautions; to make all preparations; to take undue alarm
如鯁在喉(ㄖㄨˊ ㄍㄥˇ ㄗㄞˋ ㄏㄡˊ)
to give vent to one's pent-up feelings
如故(ㄖㄨˊ ㄍㄨˋ)
①(often said of a new acquaintance) like an old friend: 他們一見如故。They felt like old friends at the first meeting. ② as it has always been; as usual 亦作「如舊」
如果(ㄖㄨˊ ㄍㄨㄛˇ)
if; supposing: 如果下雨，我們還是要去嗎? Supposing it rains, shall we still go?
如何(ㄖㄨˊ ㄏㄜˊ)
① How (can we deal with …)? 我如何處理這種事呢? How can I deal with such a case? ② What do you think of it? 或 How about it? ③ What to do now? 或 How is it?
如何是好(ㄖㄨˊ ㄏㄜˊ ㄕˋ ㄏㄠˇ)
What should one do? 或 What is the best way (of doing it)? 她不知如何是好。She doesn't know what she should do.
如虎添翼(ㄖㄨˊ ㄏㄨˇ ㄊㄧㄢ ㄧˋ)
(literally) like adding wings to a tiger—with added strength; greatly strengthened or reinforced
如花似玉(ㄖㄨˊ ㄏㄨㄚ ㄙˋ ㄩˋ)
(literally) like flower and jade—(said of a girl) young, beautiful and pure
如火如荼(ㄖㄨˊ ㄏㄨㄛˇ ㄖㄨˊ ㄊㄨˊ)
(troops) in an imposing array; luxuriant (growth, etc.); like wildfire
如獲至寶(ㄖㄨˊ ㄏㄨㄛˋ ㄓˋ ㄅㄠˇ)
(literally) like acquiring a rare treasure—to get what one has wished or desired for a long time
如飢似渴(ㄖㄨˊ ㄐㄧ ㄙˋ ㄎㄜˇ)
like thirsting or hungering for something eagerly
如膠似漆(ㄖㄨˊ ㄐㄧㄠ ㄙˋ ㄑㄧ)
(literally) like glue and lacquer—very much in love; inseparable
如舊(ㄖㄨˊ ㄐㄧㄡˋ)
as it has always been; as usual
如箭在弦(ㄖㄨˊ ㄐㄧㄢˋ ㄗㄞˋ ㄒㄧㄢˊ)
(literally) as an arrow on the strained cord—ready to

go or start; imminent; no turning back; inevitable

如今(ㄖㄨˊ ㄐㄧㄣ)
now; nowadays

如期(ㄖㄨˊ ㄑㄧˊ)
on time; punctually; at the appointed time; as scheduled; on schedule: 貨物已如期運到。The goods arrived at the appointed time.

如下(ㄖㄨˊ ㄒㄧㄚˋ)
as follows; as below: 其結果如下。The results were as follows.

如新(ㄖㄨˊ ㄒㄧㄣ)
brand as if it were new

如須(ㄖㄨˊ ㄒㄩ)
if (you) want to; if (you) have to: 如須去，你可立即去。If you want to go, you may go at once.

如需(ㄖㄨˊ ㄒㄩ)
if (you) need (any information, etc.)

如兄如弟(ㄖㄨˊ ㄒㄩㄥ ㄖㄨˊ ㄉㄧˋ)
like brothers; a term used by sworn brothers to address each other

如之奈何(ㄖㄨˊ ㄓ ㄋㄞˋ ㄏㄜˊ)
What can I (or we) do about it?

如常(ㄖㄨˊ ㄔㄤˊ)
as usual

如初(ㄖㄨˊ ㄔㄨ)
as always; as it was before

如出一口(ㄖㄨˊ ㄔㄨ ㄧˋ ㄎㄡˇ)
with one voice; unanimously

如出一轍(ㄖㄨˊ ㄔㄨ ㄧˊ ㄔㄜˋ)
(said of events) very similar; almost the same; to be cut from the same cloth

如實(ㄖㄨˊ ㄕˊ)
strictly according to the facts; as things really are; accurately: 他們如實地說明情況。They stated the situation accurately.

如是我聞(ㄖㄨˊ ㄕˋ ㄨㄛˇ ㄨㄣˊ)
① so I heard ②(Buddhism) the beginning clause of Buddha's quotations as recorded by his disciple, Anan

如釋重負(ㄖㄨˊ ㄕˋ ㄓㄨㄥˋ ㄈㄨˋ)
to feel greatly relieved (after discharging a duty)

如手如足(ㄖㄨˊ ㄕㄡˇ ㄖㄨˊ ㄗㄨˊ)
like brothers: 陳先生與李先生兩人如手如足。Mr. Chen and Mr. Lee are like brothers.

如上所述(ㄖㄨˊ ㄕㄤˋ ㄙㄨㄛˇ ㄕㄨˋ)
as stated above; as mentioned above

如數家珍(ㄖㄨˊ ㄕㄨˇ ㄐㄧㄚ ㄓㄣ)
(literally) like counting family treasures—to describe distinctly and in good order; very familiar with one's subject

如數(ㄖㄨˊ ㄕㄨˋ)
(to pay, deliver, etc.) according to the amount agreed upon

如數償還(ㄖㄨˊ ㄕㄨˋ ㄔㄤˊ ㄏㄨㄢˊ)
to pay back in full

如日東升(ㄖㄨˊ ㄖˋ ㄉㄨㄥ ㄕㄥ)
(literally) rising like the sun in the eastern sky — (said of careers, prospects, etc.) beginning to prosper

如日中天(ㄖㄨˊ ㄖˋ ㄓㄨㄥ ㄊㄧㄢ)
(literally) like the sun at the zenith—① to ride on the crest of success ② very influential; very powerful

如入無人之境(ㄖㄨˊ ㄖㄨˋ ㄨˊ ㄖㄣˊ ㄓ ㄐㄧㄥˋ)
(usually said of a victorious army) like walking into a no man's land; to encounter little resistance

如坐針氈(ㄖㄨˊ ㄗㄨㄛˋ ㄓㄣ ㄓㄢ)
(literally) like sitting on a rug of needles—very anxious; uncomfortable; in a state of agitation; to sit on thorns

如醉如癡(ㄖㄨˊ ㄗㄨㄟˋ ㄖㄨˊ ㄔ)
to be drunk with; to fall head over heels in love; to be crazy about

如此(ㄖㄨˊ ㄘˇ)
thus; like this

如此這般(ㄖㄨˊ ㄘˇ ㄓㄜˋ ㄅㄢ)
and so on

如此如此(ㄖㄨˊ ㄘˇ ㄖㄨˊ ㄘˇ)
and so on

如此而已(ㄖㄨˊ ㄘˇ ㄦˊ ㄧˇ)
That is what it all amounts to.

如廁(ㄖㄨˊ ㄘㄜˋ)
to go to the toilet

如喪考妣(ㄖㄨˊ ㄙㄤˋ ㄎㄠˇ ㄅㄧˇ)
(literally) as if to have lost one's parents—very sad; very sorrowful; very worried

如所週知(ㄖㄨˊ ㄙㄨㄛˇ ㄓㄡ ㄓ)
as is well known; as everyone knows: 如所週知，他是一位科學家。As everyone knows, he is a scientist.

如一(ㄖㄨˊ ㄧ)
without change; consistent: 他言行不如一。His actions are not consistent with his words.

如一日(ㄖㄨˊ ㄧ ㄖˋ)
as one day; without any change in a long period; very consistent

如意(ㄖㄨˊ ㄧˋ)
① as one wishes: 祝你萬事如意。May everything turn out as you wish. ②(formerly) a kind of scepter usually made of wood or jade, used as a symbol of Buddha

如意算盤(ㄖㄨˊ ㄧˋ ㄙㄨㄢˋ ㄆㄢˊ)
wishful thinking

如有(ㄖㄨˊ ㄧㄡˇ)
if there be; if anyone has; should it happen that; in case

如影隨形(ㄖㄨˊ ㄧㄥˇ ㄙㄨㄟˊ ㄒㄧㄥˊ)
(said of two persons) to move together always; inseparable; to tag after: 他們倆如影隨形。They two are inseparable.

如晤(ㄖㄨˊ ㄨˋ)
(literally) as face to face —an expression used in letters between brothers, close friends or married couple

如魚得水(ㄖㄨˊ ㄩˊ ㄉㄜˊ ㄕㄨㄟˇ)
(literally) like fish in water —(said of newlyweds, friends, the king and the ministers, etc.) in agreeable circumstances; very satisfied and pleased; to be in one's element

如約(ㄖㄨˊ ㄩㄝ) or 如命(ㄖㄨˊ ㄇㄧㄥˋ)
as agreed upon; according to

如願以償(ㄖㄨˊ ㄩㄢˋ ㄧˇ ㄔㄤˊ)
to have one's wish fulfilled: 最後，他終於如願以償。At last, he has his wish fulfilled.

如怨如慕，如泣如訴(ㄖㄨˊ ㄩㄢˋ ㄖㄨˊ ㄇㄨˋ, ㄖㄨˊ ㄑㄧˋ ㄖㄨˊ ㄙㄨˋ)
(usually said of music) very

pathetic and touching

如雲(ㄖㄨˊ ㄩㄣˊ)
(literally) like gathering clouds—many; plenty or plentiful

【妃】957 ㄈㄟ fei fēi
1. a wife; a spouse
2. the concubine of a king or an emperor
3. the wife or spouse of a crown prince

妃嬪(ㄈㄟ ㄆㄧㄣˊ)
concubines or wives of a king or an emperor

妃子(ㄈㄟ ·ㄗ)
a king's or an emperor's concubine

【妄】958 ㄨㄤˋ wanq wàng
1. absurd; untrue; false
2. ignorant; stupid
3. reckless; rash: 切勿妄加評論。Do not make reckless comments.
4. wild; frantic; frenetic

妄費(ㄨㄤˋ ㄈㄟˋ)
to waste (money, etc.); to lavish; a waste: 眞是妄費精力! What a waste of energy!

妄斷(ㄨㄤˋ ㄉㄨㄢˋ)
to jump to a (or the) conclusion

妄動(ㄨㄤˋ ㄉㄨㄥˋ)
reckless or rash actions; to act recklessly or rashly: 不要輕舉妄動。Don't take any rash action.

妄圖(ㄨㄤˋ ㄊㄨˊ)
to try (or attempt) boldly: 他妄圖游過河流。He attempted boldly to swim across the river.

妄念(ㄨㄤˋ ㄋㄧㄢˋ)
an idea or desire one is not supposed to have; a fancy

妄求(ㄨㄤˋ ㄑㄧㄡˊ)
an absurd pursuit or desire; to wish wildly

妄想(ㄨㄤˋ ㄒㄧㄤˇ)
a daydream; an absurd desire; a fancy; to desire wildly: 那不過是你的妄想。That's only your fancy.

妄人(ㄨㄤˋ ㄖㄣˊ)
a stupid and reckless person; an incorrigible person

妄自菲薄(ㄨㄤˋ ㄗˋ ㄈㄟˇ ㄅㄛˊ)
to underestimate oneself: 別妄自菲薄。Don't underestimate yourself.

妄自尊大(ㄨㄤˋ ㄗˋ ㄗㄨㄣ ㄉㄚˋ)
self-importance; conceited; self-important

妄言(ㄨㄤˋ ㄧㄢˊ)
to speak recklessly or without forethought; a wild talk; a lie; to rant

妄爲(ㄨㄤˋ ㄨㄟˊ)
to act without principle or wildly; untoward behavior; reckless acts

妄語(ㄨㄤˋ ㄩˇ)
a wild talk; a lie: 別信他的妄語。Don't believe his wild talk.

四畫

【妓】959 ㄐㄧˋ jih jì
1. a prostitute; a whore
2. a young woman who sings or dances to amuse her customers, such as 舞妓 (a female dancer), 藝妓 (a geisha)

妓女(ㄐㄧˋ ㄋㄩˇ)
a prostitute; a whore

妓院(ㄐㄧˋ ㄩㄢˋ)
a brothel

【妊】960 ㄖㄣˋ renn rèn
pregnant; to be expecting

妊婦(ㄖㄣˋ ㄈㄨˋ)
a pregnant woman; an expectant mother

妊娠(ㄖㄣˋ ㄕㄣ)
to be pregnant; pregnancy

【妒】961 (妬) ㄉㄨˋ duh dù
jealous; envious; jealousy; envy: 相妒 to be jealous of each other

妒恨(ㄉㄨˋ ㄏㄣˋ)
to be very jealous; bitter jealousy; the hate born of jealousy

妒忌(ㄉㄨˋ ㄐㄧˋ) or 妒嫉(ㄉㄨˋ ㄐㄧˊ)
jealousy; envy: 他妒嫉的理由是什麼? What is the reason of his jealousy?

妒心(ㄉㄨˋ ㄒㄧㄣ)
a jealous mind

妒殺(ㄉㄨˋ ㄕㄚ)
homicide caused by jealousy

【妖】962 ㄧㄠ iau yāo
1. weird; unaccountable; monstrous; supernatural
2. an evil; a monster; a goblin; a phantom; a ghost
3. (usually said of a woman) bewitching; seductive

妖魔鬼怪(ㄧㄠ ㄇㄛˊ ㄍㄨㄟˇ ㄍㄨㄞˋ)
a general term for evil spirits, goblins, devils, demons and monsters

妖媚(ㄧㄠ ㄇㄟˋ)
seductively charming; bewitching: 她給他妖媚的一笑。She gave him a bewitching smile.

妖氛(ㄧㄠ ㄈㄣ) or 妖氣(ㄧㄠ ㄑㄧˋ)
abnormal conditions such as chaos, moral degeneracy, etc.

妖道(ㄧㄠ ㄉㄠˋ)
witchcraft; the black magic

妖孽(ㄧㄠ ㄋㄧㄝˋ)
① unlucky omens ② the monsters who cause great calamities ③ a person like a devil

妖女(ㄧㄠ ㄋㄩˇ)
a fairy enchantress

妖裏妖氣(ㄧㄠ ·ㄌㄧ ㄧㄠ ㄑㄧˋ)
seductive and bewitching

妖蠱(ㄧㄠ ㄍㄨˇ)
(said of a woman) to bewitch a man with seductive charms

妖怪(ㄧㄠ ㄍㄨㄞˋ) or 妖精(ㄧㄠ ㄐㄧㄥ)
① a monster or demon ② a Circe; a siren ③ a spirit transformed from a very old animal, tree, etc.

妖邪(ㄧㄠ ㄒㄧㄝˊ)
weird; strange; wicked; monstrous

妖聲妖氣(ㄧㄠ ㄕㄥ ㄧㄠ ㄑㄧˋ)
(said of a woman) to speak flirtatiously

妖術(ㄧㄠ ㄕㄨˋ)
sorcery; witchcraft: 巫婆施行妖術。The witch practiced witchcraft.

妖嬈(ㄧㄠ ㄖㄠˊ)
flirtatious; bewitching; enchanting; fascinating; charming

妖人(ㄧㄠ ㄖㄣˊ)

an evil enchanter
妖冶(ㄧㄠ ㄧㄝˇ)or 妖艷(ㄧㄠ ㄧㄢˋ)
seductive charms; seductive; bewitchingly pretty; (with) heavy make-up; meretricious
妖言(ㄧㄠ ㄧㄢˊ)
heresies; fallacies; absurd statements
妖言惑衆(ㄧㄠ ㄧㄢˊ ㄏㄨㄛˋ ㄓㄨㄥˋ)
to arouse people with wild talks; to cheat people with sensational speeches; to spread fallacies to deceive people

【妞】 963 ㄋㄧㄡ nhiou niū
a girl; a little girl
妞兒(ㄋㄧㄡㄦ)or 妞妞(ㄋㄧㄡ·ㄋㄧㄡ)
a girl

【妙】 964 ㄇㄧㄠˋ miaw miào
1. wonderful; excellent: 這主意眞妙。That's an wonderful idea.
2. intriguing; very interesting
3. subtle; clever; ingenious: 她回答得很妙。She made a clever answer.
妙不可言(ㄇㄧㄠˋ ㄅㄨˋ ㄎㄜˇ ㄧㄢˊ)
too subtle to be described; ingenious beyond description
妙品(ㄇㄧㄠˋ ㄆㄧㄣˇ)
excellent articles; a masterpiece: 這雕刻品是件妙品。This sculpture is a masterpiece.
妙年(ㄇㄧㄠˋ ㄋㄧㄢˊ)or 妙齡(ㄇㄧㄠˋ ㄌㄧㄥˊ)
young; in one's youth
妙論(ㄇㄧㄠˋ ㄌㄨㄣˋ)
an ingenious comment; a very clever remark: 這眞是妙論。This is really a very clever remark.
妙極了(ㄇㄧㄠˋ ㄐㄧˊ ·ㄌㄜ)
Wonderful! 你的建議妙極了! Your suggestion is wonderful.
妙計(ㄇㄧㄠˋ ㄐㄧˋ)
a subtle scheme; a capital plan; a wonderful idea: 他有妙計。He has a wonderful idea.
妙句(ㄇㄧㄠˋ ㄐㄩˋ)
an exquisite quote: 他引了個妙句。He quoted an exquisite quote.
妙訣(ㄇㄧㄠˋ ㄐㄩㄝˊ)
a clever way; an ingenious method (of doing something, etc.); a knack: 這裡面有妙訣。There's a knack in it.
妙絕古今(ㄇㄧㄠˋ ㄐㄩㄝˊ ㄍㄨˇ ㄐㄧㄣ)
an all-time wonder; unmatched subtlety
妙趣橫生(ㄇㄧㄠˋ ㄑㄩˋ ㄏㄥˊ ㄕㄥ)
full of wit and humor
妙想天開(ㄇㄧㄠˋ ㄒㄧㄤˇ ㄊㄧㄢ ㄎㄞ)
to have fantastic ideas: 他總是妙想天開。He always has some fantastic ideas.
妙手空空(ㄇㄧㄠˋ ㄕㄡˇ ㄎㄨㄥ ㄎㄨㄥ)
① a pickpocket: 當心妙手空空。Beware of pickpockets. ② a crafty but impecunious financier who knows his business; a wheeler-dealer
妙手回春(ㄇㄧㄠˋ ㄕㄡˇ ㄏㄨㄟˊ ㄔㄨㄣ)
the hands that cure—used to praise a good physician
妙人妙事(ㄇㄧㄠˋ ㄖㄣˊ ㄇㄧㄠˋ ㄕˋ)
an interesting person and his amusing episodes
妙哉妙哉(ㄇㄧㄠˋ ㄗㄞ ㄇㄧㄠˋ ㄗㄞ)
Wonderful! Bravo!
妙藥(ㄇㄧㄠˋ ㄧㄠˋ)
an efficacious drug; a wonder drug
妙語(ㄇㄧㄠˋ ㄩˇ)
a wisecrack; an intriguing remark; a witticism
妙語解頤(ㄇㄧㄠˋ ㄩˇ ㄐㄧㄝˇ ㄧˊ)
wisecracks that really tickle
妙語雙關(ㄇㄧㄠˋ ㄩˇ ㄕㄨㄤ ㄍㄨㄢ)
a clever double entendre; an exquisite pun; an ingenious remark which can be interpreted differently and equally appropriate
妙語如珠(ㄇㄧㄠˋ ㄩˇ ㄖㄨˊ ㄓㄨ)
sparkling discourse
妙用(ㄇㄧㄠˋ ㄩㄥˋ)
ingenious uses; (serving unexpected) subtle effects

【妝】 965 ㄓㄨㄤ juang zhuāng
1. to doll up; to adorn oneself; to apply makeup
2. jewels, etc. for adornment
3. to disguise; to pretend
妝扮(ㄓㄨㄤ ㄅㄢˋ)
to doll up
妝點(ㄓㄨㄤ ㄉㄧㄢˇ)
to dress up; to adorn; to apply makeup
妝臺(ㄓㄨㄤ ㄊㄞˊ)
a lady's dressing table
妝樓(ㄓㄨㄤ ㄌㄡˊ)
a lady's private boudoir
妝奩(ㄓㄨㄤ ㄌㄧㄢˊ)
① a lady's dressing case ② the bride's trousseau
妝飾(ㄓㄨㄤ ㄕˋ)
to adorn; to dress up; to deck out; to decorate
妝梳(ㄓㄨㄤ ㄕㄨ)
(said of a woman) to comb and dress one's hair; hairdressing

【妣】 966 ㄅㄧˇ bii bǐ
one's deceased mother

【妤】 967 ㄩˊ yu yú
an official title 參看「婕妤」

【妥】 968 ㄊㄨㄛˇ tuoo tuǒ
1. firm; safe; secure
2. appropriate
3. ready; set; to settle: 這件事情已辦妥了。The matter has been settled.
妥當(ㄊㄨㄛˇ ㄉㄤˋ)
① appropriate or secure ② ready
妥貼 or 妥帖(ㄊㄨㄛˇ ㄊㄧㄝ)
properly (arranged); firmly (placed); satisfactorily (prepared, etc.); fitting
妥協(ㄊㄨㄛˇ ㄒㄧㄝˊ)
① amity ② a compromise; a reconciliation ③ appeasement (in international relations)
妥協份子(ㄊㄨㄛˇ ㄒㄧㄝˊ ㄈㄣˋ ㄗˇ)
an appeaser
妥善(ㄊㄨㄛˇ ㄕㄢˋ)
proper; appropriate; satisfactory (arrangements, etc.)
妥善安排(ㄊㄨㄛˇ ㄕㄢˋ ㄢ ㄆㄞˊ)
to make appropriate arrangements
妥爲照料(ㄊㄨㄛˇ ㄨㄟˊ ㄓㄠˋ ㄌㄧㄠˋ)
to take good care
妥爲安排(ㄊㄨㄛˇ ㄨㄟˊ ㄢ ㄆㄞˊ)
to make proper arrangements: 讓我們事先妥爲安排。Let's make proper arrangements beforehand.

【妨】 969 ㄈㄤˊ farng fáng (又讀 ㄈㄤ fang fāng)
1. to hinder; to impede; to

〔女部〕

obstruct; to interfere with
2. to undermine; to harm; to damage: 試試又何妨? What harm is there in trying?

妨害(ㄈㄤˊ ㄏㄞˋ)
to impair; to be harmful to: 空氣污染妨害健康。Air pollution is harmful to our health.

妨害兵役(ㄈㄤˊ ㄏㄞˋ ㄅㄧㄥ ㄧˋ)
to undermine the draft law of a nation

妨害名譽(ㄈㄤˊ ㄏㄞˋ ㄇㄧㄥˊ ㄩˋ)
to libel; to slander: 那記者被控妨害名譽。The reporter was charged with slandering.

妨害風化(ㄈㄤˊ ㄏㄞˋ ㄈㄥ ㄏㄨㄚˋ)
to undermine public morality (especially referring to pornographic materials)

妨害家庭(ㄈㄤˊ ㄏㄞˋ ㄐㄧㄚ ㄊㄧㄥˊ)
to wreck a family (especially said of adultery)

妨害秩序(ㄈㄤˊ ㄏㄞˋ ㄓˋ ㄒㄩˋ)
an offense against public order

妨害治安(ㄈㄤˊ ㄏㄞˋ ㄓˋ ㄢ)
an offense against public security

妨害自由(ㄈㄤˊ ㄏㄞˋ ㄗˋ ㄧㄡˊ)
an offense against personal freedom

妨礙(ㄈㄤˊ ㄞˋ)
to hinder; to hamper; to impede; to interfere with: 疾病妨礙了他功課上的進步。Illness impeded his progress in study.

妨礙工作(ㄈㄤˊ ㄞˋ ㄍㄨㄥ ㄗㄨㄛˋ)
to hinder one's work

妨礙交通(ㄈㄤˊ ㄞˋ ㄐㄧㄠ ㄊㄨㄥ)
to obstruct traffic flow: 倒下的樹妨礙交通。The fallen trees obstruct traffic flow.

五畫

【妲】 970 ㄉㄚˊ dar dá
the concubine of Chou Hsin who was the last ruler of the Shang Dynasty

妲己(ㄉㄚˊ ㄐㄧˇ)
the concubine of Chou Hsin (紂王辛) who was the last ruler of the Shang Dynasty noted for his cruelty and orgies

【妮】 971 ㄋㄧˊ ni ní
1. a maid
2. a little girl; a little darling

妮婢(ㄋㄧˊ ㄅㄧˋ)
a maidservant

妮子(ㄋㄧˊ ·ㄗ)or 妮兒(ㄋㄧˊㄜㄦ)
a girl

【妯】 972 ㄓㄡˊ jour zhóu
sisters-in-law 參看「妯娌」

妯娌(ㄓㄡˊ ㄌㄧˇ)
sisters-in-law (a reference among the wives of one's husband's brothers)

【妹】 973 ㄇㄟˋ mey mèi
a younger sister

妹妹(ㄇㄟˋ ·ㄇㄟ)or 妹子(ㄇㄟˋ ·ㄗ)
a younger sister

妹夫(ㄇㄟˋ ㄈㄨ)or 妹婿(ㄇㄟˋ ㄒㄩˋ)or 妹丈(ㄇㄟˋ ㄓㄤˋ)
the husband of one's younger sister; a brother-in-law

【妻】 974 1. ㄑㄧ chi qī
one's formal or legal wife

妻黨(ㄑㄧ ㄉㄤˇ)
the members and relatives of wife's family

妻孥(ㄑㄧ ㄋㄨˊ)
one's wife and children

妻女(ㄑㄧ ㄋㄩˇ)
one's wife and daughter(s)

妻離子散(ㄑㄧ ㄌㄧˊ ㄗˇ ㄙㄢˋ)
(literally) wife leaving and children dispersing—The family breaks up. 戰爭使他妻離子散。The war makes his family break up.

妻妾(ㄑㄧ ㄑㄧㄝˋ)
one's wife and concubine(s)

妻室(ㄑㄧ ㄕˋ)
one's formal or legal wife

妻子(ㄑㄧ ㄗˇ)
① one's wife ② one's wife and children

妻兒老小(ㄑㄧ ㄦˊ ㄌㄠˇ ㄒㄧㄠˇ)
a married man's entire family (parents, wife and children)

【妻】 974 2. ㄑㄧˋ chih qì
to marry one's daughter to someone

妻之(ㄑㄧˋ ㄓ)
to get someone marry one's daughter, niece, etc.

【妾】 975 ㄑㄧㄝˋ chieh qiè
1. a concubine
2. (in old China) a polite term used by a woman to refer to herself when speaking to her husband

妾婦(ㄑㄧㄝˋ ㄈㄨˋ)
① a concubine referring to herself ② (derogatory) a common person; an inferior person

【姆】 976 ㄇㄨˇ muu mǔ
1. (in old China) a governess; a woman tutor
2. a matron who looks after small children

姆媽(ㄇㄨˇ ㄇㄚ)
(Shanghai dialect) a term for one's mother

【姊】 977 (姉) ㄐㄧㄝˇ jiee jiě (讀音 ㄗˇ tzyy zǐ)
one's elder sister or sisters

姊兒倆(ㄐㄧㄜˇㄦ ㄌㄧㄚˇ)
the two sisters

姊妹(ㄐㄧㄝˇ ㄇㄟˋ)or(ㄗˇ ㄇㄟˋ)
sisters

姊妹篇(ㄐㄧㄝˇ ㄇㄟˋ ㄆㄧㄢ)or(ㄗˇ ㄇㄟˋ ㄆㄧㄢ)
twin literary products, usually by the same author, which run in the same vein

姊妹花(ㄐㄧㄝˇ ㄇㄟˋ ㄏㄨㄚ)or(ㄗˇ ㄇㄟˋ ㄏㄨㄚ)
beautiful sisters

姊妹校(ㄐㄧㄝˇ ㄇㄟˋ ㄒㄧㄠˋ)
sister universities or schools

姊妹市(ㄐㄧㄝˇ ㄇㄟˋ ㄕˋ)or(ㄗˇ ㄇㄟˋ ㄕˋ)
sister cities

姊們兒(ㄐㄧㄝˇ ·ㄇㄜㄦ)
① sisters old and young ② sisters ③ (colloquial) sisters-in-law or intimate girl friends collectively

姊夫(ㄐㄧㄝˇ ㄈㄨ)or 姊丈(ㄐㄧㄝˇ ㄓㄤˋ)
the husband of one's elder sister

姊姊(ㄐㄧㄝˇ ·ㄐㄧㄝ)
elder sisters

【始】 978 ㄕˇ shyy shǐ
1. the beginning; the start; the

first
2. to start; to begin; to be the first: 火始於廚房。The fire started in the kitchen.
3. only then
4. a Chinese family name

始末(ㄕˇ ㄇㄛˋ)
①from beginning to end—throughout ②the ins and outs (of an incident, story, etc.)

始料未及(ㄕˇ ㄌㄧㄠˋ ㄨㄟˋ ㄐㄧˊ)
unexpected

始亂終棄(ㄕˇ ㄌㄨㄢˋ ㄓㄨㄥ ㄑㄧˋ)
to desert a girl after robbing her of her chastity

始基(ㄕˇ ㄐㄧ)
beginning and foundation

始終(ㄕˇ ㄓㄨㄥ)
from beginning to end; from start to finish; all along; throughout: 比賽始終在友好氣氛中進行。The competition proceeded in a friendly atmosphere from beginning to end.

始終不懈(ㄕˇ ㄓㄨㄥ ㄅㄨˋ ㄒㄧㄝˋ)
untiring perseverance; indefatigable: 他工作始終不懈。He works with indefatigable zeal.

始終不渝(ㄕˇ ㄓㄨㄥ ㄅㄨˋ ㄩˊ)
unswerving; steadfast; steadfastly

始終其事(ㄕˇ ㄓㄨㄥ ㄑㄧˊ ㄕˋ)
to manage something from beginning to end; to dedicate oneself to a job from first to last

始終如一(ㄕˇ ㄓㄨㄥ ㄖㄨˊ ㄧ)
(literally) the same from beginning to end—consistent; unremitting: 他的努力始終如一。His efforts are unremitting.

始創(ㄕˇ ㄔㄨㄤˋ)
to found, initiate, create, or originate: 他們始創一個計劃。They initiated a plan.

始祖(ㄕˇ ㄗㄨˇ)
①the founder ②the first ancestor

始作俑者(ㄕˇ ㄗㄨㄛˋ ㄩㄥˇ ㄓㄜˇ)
the originator (usually of a bad practice, etc.)

始業(ㄕˇ ㄧㄝˋ)
①to establish a business ②A school opens (after a vacation).

始業式(ㄕˇ ㄧㄝˋ ㄕˋ)
the ceremonies marking the beginning of a school year or semester

始願(ㄕˇ ㄩㄢˋ)
①the first wish; the very first ambition ②only then (is one) willing to...

【姍】 979
ㄕㄢ shan shān
1. to ridicule; to laugh at
2. (said of a woman) to walk slowly

姍笑(ㄕㄢ ㄒㄧㄠˋ)
to ridicule 亦作「訕笑」

姍姍來遲(ㄕㄢ ㄕㄢ ㄌㄞˊ ㄔˊ)
to walk or proceed slowly (and keep others waiting); to be late in reaching the destination

【姐】 980
ㄐㄧㄝˇ jiee jiě
1. one's elder sister or sisters
2. a general term for women, usually young

姐妹(ㄐㄧㄝˇ ㄇㄟˋ)
a sister; sisters: 他有姐妹三人。He has three sisters.

姐夫(ㄐㄧㄝˇ ㄈㄨ)or 姐丈(ㄐㄧㄝˇ ㄓㄤˋ)
the husband of one's elder sister; a brother-in-law

姐姐(ㄐㄧㄝˇ ·ㄐㄧㄝ)
one's elder sister

【姑】 981
ㄍㄨ gu gū
1. aunts; the sister of one's father
2. the mother of one's husband
3. the sister of one's husband
4. a general term for unmarried women
5. for the time being; meanwhile; for a while
6. a nun

姑表(ㄍㄨ ㄅㄧㄠˇ)
first cousins when the father of one and the mother of the other are brother and sister

姑婆(ㄍㄨ ㄆㄛˊ)
①the sister of one's grandfather ②the sister of a woman's father-in-law

姑媽(ㄍㄨ ㄇㄚ)or 姑母(ㄍㄨ ㄇㄨˇ)
the sister of one's father; an aunt

姑父 or 姑夫(ㄍㄨ ·ㄈㄨ)or 姑丈(ㄍㄨ ㄓㄤˋ)
the husband of one's father's sister; uncle; a paternal aunt's husband

姑奶奶(ㄍㄨ ㄋㄞˇ ·ㄋㄞ)
the sister of one's paternal grandfather; a grandaunt

姑娘(ㄍㄨ ·ㄋㄧㄤ)
①an unmarried girl; a maiden ②a term used to refer to one's own or another's daughter(s) ③a euphemism for a prostitute

姑姑(ㄍㄨ ·ㄍㄨ)
one's father's sister; an aunt; a paternal aunt

姑且(ㄍㄨ ㄑㄧㄝˇ)
for the time being; in the meantime; to let be

姑且不談(ㄍㄨ ㄑㄧㄝˇ ㄅㄨˋ ㄊㄢˊ)
to leave something aside for the moment

姑息(ㄍㄨ ㄒㄧˊ)
to be indulgent; to be over lenient toward; to be easy with; to spoil (a child); to appease: 我們不應該姑息這些小孩的錯誤。We shouldn't be indulgent towards the children's mistakes.

姑息政策(ㄍㄨ ㄒㄧˊ ㄓㄥˋ ㄘㄜˋ)
a policy of appeasement

姑息養奸(ㄍㄨ ㄒㄧˊ ㄧㄤˇ ㄐㄧㄢ)
To tolerate evil is to encourage evil-doers.

姑置不論(ㄍㄨ ㄓˋ ㄅㄨˋ ㄌㄨㄣˋ)
Let's not talk about (this offense, mistake, etc. which is serious enough).—with the implication that there are other mistakes, offenses, etc. which are even more serious

姑准(ㄍㄨ ㄓㄨㄣˇ)
to permit reluctantly; to permit for the time being: 他姑准我們離開。He permits us to leave for the time being.

姑嫂(ㄍㄨ ㄙㄠˇ)
sisters-in-law (the relationship between a man's sisters and his wife)

姑蘇(ㄍㄨ ㄙㄨ)
Soochow, Kiangsu Province

姑爺(ㄍㄨ ㄧㄝˊ)
a son-in-law

姑爺爺(ㄍㄨ ㄧㄝˊ ·ㄧㄝ)

〔女部〕

the husband of one's father's paternal aunt

姑妄聽之(ㄍㄨ ㄨㄤˋ ㄊㄧㄥ ㄓ)
Let's hear (him) out.—implying the listener's skepticism: 我們暫且姑妄聽之。We may as well hear him out.

姑妄言之(ㄍㄨ ㄨㄤˋ ㄧㄢˊ ㄓ)
Please take my words as a gossip. (a polite and modest expression in making suggestions, etc.)

【姒】 982 ㄙˋ syh sì
1. the wife of one's husband's elder brother
2. (in ancient China) the elder of the twin sisters
3. a Chinese family name

【姓】 983 ㄒㄧㄥˋ shinq xìng
1. surname; one's family name: 他姓楊。He is surnamed Yang.
2. a clan; a family; people

姓名(ㄒㄧㄥˋ ㄇㄧㄥˊ)
the full name of a person

姓氏(ㄒㄧㄥˋ ㄕˋ)
the surname; the family name

【委】 984 1. ㄨㄟˇ woei wěi
1. to depute; to deputize
2. to send; to put in charge of; to commission
3. to give up; to abandon
4. to be frustrated, weakened or tired
5. really; truly; indeed
6. a grievance; a wrong
7. to stoop or lower oneself (in order to avoid an open conflict, etc.)
8. a Chinese family name

委派(ㄨㄟˇ ㄆㄞˋ)
to appoint; to send (one) in charge of; to commission: 他被委派爲本市市長。He was appointed (to be) mayor of the city.

委靡(ㄨㄟˇ ㄇㄧˇ)
listless; dispirited; dejected

委靡不振(ㄨㄟˇ ㄇㄧˇ ㄅㄨˋ ㄓㄣˋ)
dispirited and lethargic; in low spirits; dejected and apathetic

委命(ㄨㄟˇ ㄇㄧㄥˋ)
① to leave oneself to fate; to yield to fate ② to commission; to depute ③ to serve under someone with dedication

委頓(ㄨㄟˇ ㄉㄨㄣˋ)
worn-out; tired down; wearied; broken down

委託 or 委托(ㄨㄟˇ ㄊㄨㄛ)
to commission; to entrust: 他把財產委託他的朋友看管。He entrusted his friend with the property.

委託商行(ㄨㄟˇ ㄊㄨㄛ ㄕㄤ ㄏㄤˊ)
a commission house

委託書(ㄨㄟˇ ㄊㄨㄛ ㄕㄨ)
a power of attorney 亦作「委託狀」

委託人(ㄨㄟˇ ㄊㄨㄛ ㄖㄣˊ)
a client

委託所(ㄨㄟˇ ㄊㄨㄛ ㄙㄨㄛˇ)
a consignment store

委內瑞拉(ㄨㄟˇ ㄋㄟˋ ㄖㄨㄟˋ ㄌㄚ)
Venezuela, in South America

委內瑞拉人(ㄨㄟˇ ㄋㄟˋ ㄖㄨㄟˋ ㄌㄚ ㄖㄣˊ)
a Venezuelan

委過(ㄨㄟˇ ㄍㄨㄛˋ)
to shift blame: 他常委過於人。He often shifts the blame to somebody else.

委咎(ㄨㄟˇ ㄐㄧㄡˋ)
to shift blame to others

委決不下(ㄨㄟˇ ㄐㄩㄝˊ ㄅㄨˋ ㄒㄧㄚˋ)
to be indecisive

委棄(ㄨㄟˇ ㄑㄧˋ)
to give up; to abandon; to discard; to throw away

委屈(ㄨㄟˇ ㄑㄩ)
① a grievance; complaints ② to be frustrated or wronged ③ to take an office, etc. far below one's ability ④ to put someone to inconvenience

委曲(ㄨㄟˇ ㄑㄩ)
① (said of roads, rivers, etc.) winding; tortuous ② the twists of events

委曲求全(ㄨㄟˇ ㄑㄩ ㄑㄧㄡˊ ㄑㄩㄢˊ)
to make great concessions for the purpose of accommodating to a situation

委政(ㄨㄟˇ ㄓㄥˋ)
to deputize a minister to run the government

委實(ㄨㄟˇ ㄕˊ)
really; indeed

委身(ㄨㄟˇ ㄕㄣ)
① to become the wife of... ② to consign oneself to someone or something

委任(ㄨㄟˇ ㄖㄣˋ)
① to appoint; to commission ② the designated appointment rank—the lowest of four major ranks in China's civil service

委任統治(ㄨㄟˇ ㄖㄣˋ ㄊㄨㄥˇ ㄓˋ)
to mandate

委任管理(ㄨㄟˇ ㄖㄣˋ ㄍㄨㄢˇ ㄌㄧˇ)
mandatory administration

委任狀(ㄨㄟˇ ㄖㄣˋ ㄓㄨㄤˋ)
a certificate of appointment or deputation

委罪(ㄨㄟˇ ㄗㄨㄟˋ)
to impute; to blame another (for a mistake committed by oneself)

委瑣(ㄨㄟˇ ㄙㄨㄛˇ)
① petty; trifling; details ② of a wretched appearance ③ being a stickler for forms

委以重任(ㄨㄟˇ ㄧˇ ㄓㄨㄥˋ ㄖㄣˋ)
to entrust someone with an important task

委婉(ㄨㄟˇ ㄨㄢˇ)
soft-spoken or ingratiating; suave and moving (statement, etc.); tactful; unobtrusively

委員(ㄨㄟˇ ㄩㄢˊ)
a member of a committee

委員會(ㄨㄟˇ ㄩㄢˊ ㄏㄨㄟˋ)
a committee; a commission; a council: 委員會今天四點開會。The committee meets today at four.

【委】 984 2. ㄨㄟ uei wēi
參看「委蛇」

委蛇(ㄨㄟ ㄧˊ)
in a carefree manner; descriptive of ease and self-possession

【妳】 985 ㄋㄧˇ nii nǐ
you (the feminine gender)

六畫

【姚】 986 ㄧㄠˊ yau yáo
1. handsome; elegant; good-looking
2. a Chinese family name

【姜】 987 ㄐㄧㄤ jiang jiāng
1. a Chinese family name
2. ginger
姜太公(ㄐㄧㄤ ㄊㄞˋ ㄍㄨㄥ)or 姜子牙(ㄐㄧㄤ ㄗˇ ㄧㄚˊ)
Chiang Tzu-ya, who helped King Wu (武王) found the Chou Dynasty

【姝】 988 ㄕㄨ shu shū
a beautiful girl

【姣】 989 ㄐㄧㄠ jiau jiāo
1. handsome; pretty; beautiful
2. coquettish
姣童(ㄐㄧㄠ ㄊㄨㄥˊ)
a handsome boy
姣好(ㄐㄧㄠ ㄏㄠˇ)
good-looking; pretty; pleasant (looks)

【姤】 990 ㄍㄡˋ gow gòu
1. to pair off; to copulate
2. good; excellent
3. one of the Eight Diagrams in the *Book of Changes*

【姥】 991 ㄌㄠˇ lao lǎo
1. one's maternal grandmother
2. an old woman
姥姥(ㄌㄠˇ ·ㄌㄠ)
① one's maternal grandmother 亦作「外祖母」② a midwife

【姦】 992 ㄐㄧㄢ jian jiān
1. adultery; debauchery; licentiousness
2. to debauch; to ravish; to attack (a woman) sexually
3. a crook
姦夫(ㄐㄧㄢ ㄈㄨ)
① an adulterer ② a man who acts criminally
姦婦(ㄐㄧㄢ ㄈㄨˋ)
an adulteress
姦拐(ㄐㄧㄢ ㄍㄨㄞˇ)
to seduce and abduct (especially a girl)
姦宄(ㄐㄧㄢ ㄍㄨㄟˇ)
thieves and robbers
姦錢(ㄐㄧㄢ ㄑㄧㄢˊ)
(in ancient China) coins produced by unauthorized mints
姦情(ㄐㄧㄢ ㄑㄧㄥˊ)
the circumstances of adultery; the ins and outs of an affair
姦細(ㄐㄧㄢ ㄒㄧˋ)
a spy 亦作「奸細」
姦邪(ㄐㄧㄢ ㄒㄧㄝˊ)
wicked; vicious 亦作「姦回」
姦殺(ㄐㄧㄢ ㄕㄚ)
to kill a woman after sexually molesting her
姦淫(ㄐㄧㄢ ㄧㄣˊ)
fornication; debauchery; adultery; lewdness; to seduce; to rape
姦淫擄掠(ㄐㄧㄢ ㄧㄣˊ ㄌㄨˇ ㄌㄩㄝˋ)
rape and rapine (said of atrocities committed by invading troops)
姦汚(ㄐㄧㄢ ㄨ)
to seduce and rape

【姨】 993 ㄧˊ yi yí
1. the sisters of one's wife
2. the sisters of one's mother
3. a concubine
姨表(ㄧˊ ㄅㄧㄠˇ)
the relatives on one's mother's side
姨表婚(ㄧˊ ㄅㄧㄠˇ ㄏㄨㄣ)
a parallel cousin marriage
姨婆(ㄧˊ ㄆㄛˊ)
a grandaunt
姨媽(ㄧˊ ㄇㄚ)or 姨母(ㄧˊ ㄇㄨˇ)
the married sisters of one's mother
姨妹(ㄧˊ ㄇㄟˋ)
the younger sisters of one's wife
姨父(ㄧˊ ㄈㄨˋ)or 姨丈(ㄧˊ ㄓㄤˋ)or 姨夫(ㄧˊ ·ㄈㄨ)
the husband of a maternal aunt; an uncle
姨太太(ㄧˊ ㄊㄞˋ ·ㄊㄞ)
a concubine
姨娘(ㄧˊ ㄋㄧㄤˊ)
a concubine of one's father
姨姐妹(ㄧˊ ㄐㄧㄝˇ ㄇㄟˋ)or 姨表姐妹(ㄧˊ ㄅㄧㄠˇ ㄐㄧㄝˇ ㄇㄟˋ)
the cousin sisters on one's mother's side
姨兄弟(ㄧˊ ㄒㄩㄥ ㄉㄧˋ)
the male cousins on one's mother's side

【姪】 994 ㄓˊ jyr zhí
1. the children of one's brother —nephews or nieces
2. I; me (when speaking to a family friend of one's father's generation)
姪婦(ㄓˊ ㄈㄨˋ)
the wife of one's nephew
姪女(ㄓˊ ㄋㄩˇ)
a niece—a daughter of one's brother
姪女婿(ㄓˊ ㄋㄩˇ ㄒㄩˋ)or 姪婿(ㄓˊ ㄒㄩˋ)
the husband of one's niece
姪兒(ㄓˊㄦˊ)or 姪子(ㄓˊ ·ㄗ)
nephews—the sons of one's brother
姪兒媳婦(ㄓˊㄦˊ ㄒㄧˊ ㄈㄨˋ)or 姪媳婦(ㄓˊ ㄒㄧˊ ㄈㄨˋ)
the wife of one's nephew

【娙】 995 ㄎㄨㄚ kua kuā
pretty; good-looking; fascinating; elegant

【妍】 996 (姸) ㄧㄢˊ yan yán
1. beautiful; pretty; good-looking; cute; attractive; charming
2. seductive; coquettish
妍麗(ㄧㄢˊ ㄌㄧˋ)
beautiful; attractive; charming; beauty; charms
妍媸 or 妍蚩(ㄧㄢˊ ㄔ)
the beauty and the ugliness

【姹】 997 (奼) ㄔㄚˋ chah chà
1. young (girls)
2. charming; attractive; seductive
3. to boast; to talk big; to lie
姹紫嫣紅 or 奼紫嫣紅(ㄔㄚˋ ㄗˇ ㄧㄢ ㄏㄨㄥˊ)
(said of flowers) beautiful and luxuriant: 花園裡姹紫嫣紅，十分絢麗。With beautiful and luxuriant flowers everywhere, the garden is a blaze of color.

【姻】 998 ㄧㄣ in yīn
1. one's husband's family
2. marriage
3. relations or connections through marriage
姻家(ㄧㄣ ㄐㄧㄚ)
① the families of the married couple ② the elders of such families
姻戚(ㄧㄣ ㄑㄧ)
relatives by marriage
姻親(ㄧㄣ ㄑㄧㄣ)or 姻婭(ㄧㄣ ㄧㄚˋ)

relatives by marriage
姻兄弟(ㄧㄣ ㄒㄩㄥ ㄉㄧˋ)or 姻親兄弟(ㄧㄣ ㄑㄧㄣ ㄒㄩㄥ ㄉㄧˋ)
a cousin-in-law
姻緣(ㄧㄣ ㄩㄢˊ)
the invisible bond that makes a man and a woman husband and wife

〔女部〕

【姿】 999 ㄗ tzy zī
1. the manner; an air; carriage; bearing
2. looks
姿媚(ㄗ ㄇㄟˋ)
elegant and graceful manners
姿貌(ㄗ ㄇㄠˋ)
a woman's looks
姿態(ㄗ ㄊㄞˋ)
① carriage; deportment; bearing: 她姿態優雅。She has a graceful carriage. ② a gesture; a feigned move
姿質 or 資質(ㄗ ㄓˊ)
quality; natural endowments; talent: 她有音樂的姿質。She has a talent for music.
姿勢(ㄗ ㄕˋ)
① carriage; deportment; bearing ② posture; (in photography) a pose: 好的姿勢幫助你保持健康。Good posture helps you to keep well.
姿容(ㄗ ㄖㄨㄥˊ)
(said of a woman) looks —usually implying good looks: 她姿容秀美。She is good-looking.
姿色(ㄗ ㄙㄜˋ)
looks (of a woman); (female) beauty: 她不久就會失去她的姿色。She will soon lose her looks.

【威】 1000 ㄨㄟ uei wēi
1. dignity; majesty
2. authority; might; power
3. awe; awe-inspiring
4. the mother of one's husband
5. a Chinese family name
威逼(ㄨㄟ ㄅㄧ)
to coerce; to intimidate
威逼利誘(ㄨㄟ ㄅㄧ ㄌㄧˋ ㄧㄡˋ)
to threaten and to bribe
威猛(ㄨㄟ ㄇㄥˇ)
domineering
威名(ㄨㄟ ㄇㄧㄥˊ)
prestige; an awe-inspiring reputation: 那件事將有損我們國家的威名。The incident will damage our national prestige.
威風(ㄨㄟ ㄈㄥ)
① power and prestige ② imposing; awe-inspiring; militant bearing
威風凜凜(ㄨㄟ ㄈㄥ ㄌㄧㄣˇ ㄌㄧㄣˇ)
awe-inspiring; imposing
威風掃地(ㄨㄟ ㄈㄥ ㄙㄠˇ ㄉㄧˋ)
to suffer a drastic fall in one's prestige
威服(ㄨㄟ ㄈㄨˊ)
to overawe; to coerce
威尼斯(ㄨㄟ ㄋㄧˊ ㄙ)
Venice, a city in Italy
威力(ㄨㄟ ㄌㄧˋ)
① the force that inspires awe ② military force ③ the destructive force (of a typhoon, earthquake, nuclear device, etc.)
威廉(ㄨㄟ ㄌㄧㄢˊ)
a transliteration of William
威靈頓(ㄨㄟ ㄌㄧㄥˊ ㄉㄨㄣˋ)
① Wellington, capital of New Zealand ② Arthur Wellesley, the Duke of Wellington, 1769-1852
威嚇(ㄨㄟ ㄏㄜˋ)
to awe; to intimidate; to cow
威海衛(ㄨㄟ ㄏㄞˇ ㄨㄟˋ)
Weihaiwei, a naval base on the Shantung Peninsula
威權(ㄨㄟ ㄑㄩㄢˊ)
an authority; power and prestige
威脅(ㄨㄟ ㄒㄧㄝˊ)
to threaten; to intimidate; a threat; intimidation
威信(ㄨㄟ ㄒㄧㄣˋ)
① one's dignity and credit; the prestige built up by keeping good faith: 他威信掃地。His prestige takes a nosedive. ② the name of a county in Yünnan Province
威懾(ㄨㄟ ㄓㄜˊ)
to submit someone to power and threat
威震九州(ㄨㄟ ㄓㄣˋ ㄐㄧㄡˇ ㄓㄡ)
to hold the world in awe; to awe the whole land
威重(ㄨㄟ ㄓㄨㄥˋ)
dignified and awe-inspiring
威勢(ㄨㄟ ㄕˋ)
prestige and influence
威士忌(ㄨㄟ ㄕˋ ㄐㄧˋ)
whisky: 他偶而喝杯威士忌。He takes an occasional whisky.
威斯康辛(ㄨㄟ ㄙ ㄎㄤ ㄒㄧㄣ)
the state of Wisconsin, U.S.A.
威而不猛(ㄨㄟ ㄦˊ ㄅㄨˋ ㄇㄥˇ)
awe-inspiring but kind at heart
威爾遜(ㄨㄟ ㄦˇ ㄒㄩㄣˋ)
(Thomas) Woodrow Wilson, 1856-1924, American President
威爾斯(ㄨㄟ ㄦˇ ㄙ)
Wales, England
威儀(ㄨㄟ ㄧˊ)
majesty; the dignity of demeanor
威嚴(ㄨㄟ ㄧㄢˊ)
① sternness; severity ② an awe-inspiring air
威武(ㄨㄟ ㄨˇ)
an awe-inspiring display of military force, etc.
威武不屈(ㄨㄟ ㄨˇ ㄅㄨˋ ㄑㄩ)
not to be subdued by force; not to bow to the pressure
威武雄壯(ㄨㄟ ㄨˇ ㄒㄩㄥˊ ㄓㄨㄤˋ)
full of power and grandeur
威望(ㄨㄟ ㄨㄤˋ)
prestige; an imposing reputation

【娃】 1001 ㄨㄚˊ wa wá
1. a beautiful woman
2. a baby; a child
3. exquisite; fine
娃子(ㄨㄚˊ ·ㄗ)
①a baby; a child ②a newborn animal ③ a slave (among the minority nationalities in the Liangshan Mountains)
娃娃(ㄨㄚˊ ·ㄨㄚ)
a baby; a young child
娃娃臉(ㄨㄚˊ ·ㄨㄚ ㄌㄧㄢˇ)
a baby face; baby-faced
娃娃車(ㄨㄚˊ ·ㄨㄚ ㄔㄜ)
a baby car; a baby carriage; a baby buggy
娃娃床(ㄨㄚˊ ·ㄨㄚ ㄔㄨㄤˊ)
a crib; a cot
娃娃魚(ㄨㄚˊ ·ㄨㄚ ㄩˊ)
a giant salamander—a

species of fish in Kwangsi and Kweichow that utters cries like a baby

七畫

【娓】1002 ㄨㄟˇ woei wěi
1. complying; subservient
2. beautiful; attractive; pleasant
3. diligent and tireless
娓娓(ㄨㄟˇ ㄨㄟˇ)
(to talk) tirelessly: 她娓娓不倦。She talks tirelessly.
娓娓動聽(ㄨㄟˇ ㄨㄟˇ ㄉㄨㄥˋ ㄊㄧㄥ)
persuasive (accounts, narration, etc.); persuasively: 她說得娓娓動聽。She speaks persuasively.

【娉】1003 ㄆㄧㄥ ping pīng
good-looking; elegant; graceful; charming
娉婷(ㄆㄧㄥ ㄊㄧㄥˊ)
slender and elegant; graceful and charming

【娌】1004 ㄌㄧˇ lii lǐ
sisters-in-law 參看「妯娌」

【姬】1005 ㄐㄧ ji jī
1. a beautiful lady; a charming girl
2. a concubine
3. a Chinese family name
姬妾(ㄐㄧ ㄑㄧㄝˋ)
concubines

【娑】1006 ㄙㄨㄛ suo suō
to dance

【娘】1007 (孃) ㄋㄧㄤˊ niang niáng
1. mother
2. girls or women
娘胎(ㄋㄧㄤˊ ㄊㄞ)
the mother's womb
娘娘(ㄋㄧㄤˊ ˙ㄋㄧㄤ)
① the queen ② a goddess
娘娘腔(ㄋㄧㄤˊ ˙ㄋㄧㄤ ㄑㄧㄤ)
sissy; womanish
娘家(ㄋㄧㄤˊ ㄐㄧㄚ)
one's wife's family
娘舅(ㄋㄧㄤˊ ㄐㄧㄡˋ)
a maternal uncle
娘親(ㄋㄧㄤˊ ㄑㄧㄣ)
one's mother
娘子(ㄋㄧㄤˊ ˙ㄗ)
① a term used for addressing one's wife ② a polite form for addressing a young woman
娘子軍(ㄋㄧㄤˊ ˙ㄗ ㄐㄩㄣ)
① an army made up of women ②(used now figuratively) a team or group of women, as a women's basketball team, etc.
娘兒們(ㄋㄧㄤˊ ㄦ ˙ㄇㄣ)
① women; girls (a derogatory expression) ② mother and child(or children)
娘兒倆(ㄋㄧㄤˊ ㄦ ㄌㄧㄚˇ)
mother and son (or daughter)
娘姨(ㄋㄧㄤˊ ㄧˊ)
(Shanghai dialect) a maidservant; a woman servant (often married)

【娛】1008 ㄩˊ yu yú
to amuse; to give pleasure to; to entertain; amusement; entertainment; pleasure
娛樂(ㄩˊ ㄌㄜˋ)
amusement; entertainment; to amuse; to entertain: 我以收集郵票為娛樂。I find amusement in collecting stamps.
娛樂活動(ㄩˊ ㄌㄜˋ ㄏㄨㄛˊ ㄉㄨㄥˋ)
recreational activities
娛樂場所(ㄩˊ ㄌㄜˋ ㄔㄤˇ ㄙㄨㄛˇ)
entertainment establishments; public places of entertainment
娛樂稅(ㄩˊ ㄌㄜˋ ㄕㄨㄟˋ)
cabaret tax
娛親(ㄩˊ ㄑㄧㄣ)
to please one's parents
娛悅(ㄩˊ ㄩㄝˋ)
① to please somebody ② pleased: 他顯出娛悅的樣子。He looked pleased.

【娜】1009 1. ㄋㄨㄛˇ nuoo nuǒ
tender, slender and graceful

【娜】1009 2. ㄋㄨㄛˊ nuo nuó
the word used in a female name

【娜】1009 3. ㄋㄚˋ nah nà
a word used in the transliteration of a western female name

【娟】1010 ㄐㄩㄢ jiuan juān
pretty; good-looking; graceful; attractive
娟秀(ㄐㄩㄢ ㄒㄧㄡˋ)
good-looking; pretty; cute; beautiful; graceful: 這女孩很娟秀。This girl is beautiful.

【娠】1011 ㄕㄣ shen shēn
pregnant

【娣】1012 ㄉㄧˋ dih dì
the wife of a younger brother of one's husband
娣婦(ㄉㄧˋ ㄈㄨˋ)
the wife of a younger brother of one's husband

【娥】1013 ㄜˊ er é
1. good; beautiful
2. a common name for a girl
3. a Chinese family name
娥眉(ㄜˊ ㄇㄟˊ)
(literally) beautiful eyebrows—a beautiful girl or woman

【娩】1014 1. ㄨㄢˇ woan wǎn
complaisant

【娩】1014 2. ㄇㄧㄢˇ mean miǎn
to give birth to a child
娩痛(ㄇㄧㄢˇ ㄊㄨㄥˋ)
labor pains

八畫

【婆】1015 ㄆㄛˊ por pó
1. an old woman
2. the mother of one's husband
3. one's grandmother
婆婆(ㄆㄛˊ ˙ㄆㄛ)
① the mother of one's husband ② a term of respect for an old lady
婆婆媽媽的(ㄆㄛˊ ˙ㄆㄛ ㄇㄚ ㄇㄚ ˙ㄉㄜ)
① sissy ② over-sentimental; mawkish; maudlin ③ nagging
婆婆家(ㄆㄛˊ ˙ㄆㄛ ㄐㄧㄚ) or 婆家(ㄆㄛˊ ㄐㄧㄚ)
one's husband's family
婆羅門教(ㄆㄛˊ ㄌㄨㄛˊ ㄇㄣˊ ㄐㄧㄠˋ)
Brahmanism
婆羅洲(ㄆㄛˊ ㄌㄨㄛˊ ㄓㄡ)
Island of Borneo

〔女部〕

婆媳(ㄆㄛˊ ㄒㄧˊ)
a woman and her daughter-in-law
婆心(ㄆㄛˊ ㄒㄧㄣ)
a kind and compassionate heart
婆子(ㄆㄛˊ ·ㄗ)
(derogatively) an old woman
婆娑(ㄆㄛˊ ㄙㄨㄛ)
①to make dancing motions ②hovering
婆娑起舞(ㄆㄛˊ ㄙㄨㄛ ㄑㄧˇ ㄨˇ)
to start dancing: 她們婆娑起舞。They start dancing.

【婀】 1016
ㄜ e ē
1. graceful; elegant
2. a Chinese family name
婀娜多姿(ㄜ ㄋㄨㄛˇ ㄉㄨㄛ ㄗ)
graceful; well-poised: 她婀娜多姿。She is very pretty and well-poised.

【娶】 1017
ㄑㄩˇ cheu qŭ
to take a wife
娶親(ㄑㄩˇ ㄑㄧㄣ)or 娶妻(ㄑㄩˇ ㄑㄧ)
(said of a man) to get married; to take a wife
娶媳婦兒(ㄑㄩˇ ㄒㄧˊ ·ㄈㄨㄦ)
①to take a wife ②to get a daughter-in-law

【姘】 1018
(姘) ㄆㄧㄣ pin pin
to make love without a formal wedding; illicit intercourse
姘夫(ㄆㄧㄣ ㄈㄨ)
a man one cohabits with; illegal husband
姘婦(ㄆㄧㄣ ㄈㄨˋ)
a woman one cohabits with out of wedlock; a mistress
姘頭(ㄆㄧㄣ ㄊㄡˊ)
a lover; a paramour
姘居(ㄆㄧㄣ ㄐㄩ)
to live together without a formal wedding; to cohabit

【婁】 1019
1. ㄌㄡˊ lou lóu
1. one of the 28 constellations
2. a Chinese family name

【婁】 1019
2. ㄌㄩˊ liu lǘ
to trail along; to wear

【婁】 1019
3. ㄌㄩˇ leu lǚ
to tether (oxen)

【婉】 1020
ㄨㄢˇ woan wăn
1. amiable; genial; agreeable; pleasant; gently; genially; amicably
2. good-looking; beautiful
婉勸(ㄨㄢˇ ㄑㄩㄢˋ)
to persuade or advise gently; friendly persuasion
婉謝(ㄨㄢˇ ㄒㄧㄝˋ)
to decline (an invitation, a present, etc.) with great gentleness and courtesy: 他婉謝邀請。He declined the invitation with thanks.
婉轉(ㄨㄢˇ ㄓㄨㄢˇ)
(to persuade or state something) mildly, gently, suavely—without hurting another's feelings; tactfully; persuasively
婉商(ㄨㄢˇ ㄕㄤ)
to negotiate or discuss with tact and courtesy
婉順(ㄨㄢˇ ㄕㄨㄣˋ)
complaisant; obliging
婉辭(ㄨㄢˇ ㄘˊ)
①(said of speech) gentle wording; smooth and ingratiating ②to decline with great courtesy
婉言(ㄨㄢˇ ㄧㄢˊ)
soft-spoken; (to advise with) gentle and ingratiating words; to speak tenderly
婉言相勸(ㄨㄢˇ ㄧㄢˊ ㄒㄧㄤ ㄑㄩㄢˋ)
to persuade gently; to plead tactfully
婉約(ㄨㄢˇ ㄩㄝ)
①(said of speech) gentle; smooth and courteous ②(style of poetry) restrained; soft; plaintive

【婕】 1021
ㄐㄧㄝˊ jye jié
the word used in a female name
婕妤(ㄐㄧㄝˊ ㄩˊ)
an official title conferred upon an accomplished imperial concubine during the Han Dynasty

【婚】 1022
ㄏㄨㄣ huen hūn
1. to wed; to marry
2. marriage
婚變(ㄏㄨㄣ ㄅㄧㄢˋ)
a serious marriage trouble such as legal separation or divorce
婚配(ㄏㄨㄣ ㄆㄟˋ)
marriage; to get married
婚禮(ㄏㄨㄣ ㄌㄧˇ)
a wedding ceremony; a wedding
婚齡(ㄏㄨㄣ ㄌㄧㄥˊ)
(legally) marriageable age
婚媾(ㄏㄨㄣ ㄍㄡˋ)
marriage 亦作「婚姻」
婚後(ㄏㄨㄣ ㄏㄡˋ)
after marriage; after wedding
婚假(ㄏㄨㄣ ㄐㄧㄚˋ)
a wedding leave
婚嫁(ㄏㄨㄣ ㄐㄧㄚˋ)
to take a wife or marry a man; to wed; marriage
婚期(ㄏㄨㄣ ㄑㄧˊ)
the date of a wedding
婚前(ㄏㄨㄣ ㄑㄧㄢˊ)
before marriage
婚事(ㄏㄨㄣ ㄕˋ)
marriage
婚生子女(ㄏㄨㄣ ㄕㄥ ㄗˇ ㄋㄩˇ)
the children born in (lawful) wedlock
婚書(ㄏㄨㄣ ㄕㄨ)
a marriage contract or certificate 亦作「結婚證書」
婚喪喜慶(ㄏㄨㄣ ㄙㄤ ㄒㄧˇ ㄑㄧㄥˋ)
marriage, funeral, birth, etc. — important occasions of a family
婚筵(ㄏㄨㄣ ㄧㄢˊ)
a wedding reception; a wedding feast
婚姻(ㄏㄨㄣ ㄧㄣ)
marriage: 她的婚姻很美滿。Her marriage is a very happy one.
婚姻破裂(ㄏㄨㄣ ㄧㄣ ㄆㄛˋ ㄌㄧㄝˋ)
break-down of marriage
婚姻法(ㄏㄨㄣ ㄧㄣ ㄈㄚˇ)
marriage law
婚姻糾紛(ㄏㄨㄣ ㄧㄣ ㄐㄧㄡ ㄈㄣ)
matrimonial dispute
婚姻狀況(ㄏㄨㄣ ㄧㄣ ㄓㄨㄤˋ ㄎㄨㄤˋ)
marital status
婚姻自由(ㄏㄨㄣ ㄧㄣ ㄗˋ ㄧㄡˊ)
freedom of marriage
婚約(ㄏㄨㄣ ㄩㄝ)
a marriage contract; betrothal

【婢】 1023 ㄅㄧˋ bih bì

1. a maidservant; a female slave
2. (in old China) a humble term used by a girl to refer to herself

婢女(ㄅㄧˋ ㄋㄩˇ)
a slave girl; a servant girl; a maidservant

婢學夫人(ㄅㄧˋ ㄒㄩㄝˊ ㄈㄨ ㄖㄣˊ)
(literally) a maidservant trying to imitate the mistress—to mimic awkwardly

婢子(ㄅㄧˋ ㄗˇ)
①a maidservant ②a concubine ③a humble term used by a woman to refer to herself

【婦】 1024 ㄈㄨˋ fuh fù

1. a woman; a female; a matron
2. the wife of one's son
3. a wife
4. a married woman

婦德(ㄈㄨˋ ㄉㄜˊ)
feminine or female virtues—such as chastity, thrift, obedience, etc.

婦道
①(ㄈㄨˋ ㄉㄠˋ) proper rules of female behavior; female virtues, especially chastity
②(ㄈㄨˋ ·ㄉㄠ) womanhood; womenfolk

婦道人家(ㄈㄨˋ ·ㄉㄠ ㄖㄣˊ ㄐㄧㄚ)
(derogatively) womenfolk

婦女(ㄈㄨˋ ㄋㄩˇ)
women; female; womenfolk; womenkind

婦女會(ㄈㄨˋ ㄋㄩˇ ㄏㄨㄟˋ)
a women's association

婦女節(ㄈㄨˋ ㄋㄩˇ ㄐㄧㄝˊ)
Women's Day, on March 8

婦女參政權(ㄈㄨˋ ㄋㄩˇ ㄘㄢ ㄓㄥˋ ㄑㄩㄢˊ) or 婦女投票權(ㄈㄨˋ ㄋㄩˇ ㄊㄡˊ ㄆㄧㄠˋ ㄑㄩㄢˊ)
female suffrage

婦女運動(ㄈㄨˋ ㄋㄩˇ ㄩㄣˋ ㄉㄨㄥˋ)
a women's movement

婦聯會(ㄈㄨˋ ㄌㄧㄢˊ ㄏㄨㄟˋ)
short for 中華婦女聯合會 (Chinese Women's League)

婦科醫生(ㄈㄨˋ ㄎㄜ ㄧ ㄕㄥ)
gynecologist

婦解運動(ㄈㄨˋ ㄐㄧㄝˇ ㄩㄣˋ ㄉㄨㄥˋ)
Women's Liberation; Fem Lib 亦作「女權運動」

婦職(ㄈㄨˋ ㄓˊ)
the duties of a woman or housewife; woman's duty

婦產科(ㄈㄨˋ ㄔㄢˇ ㄎㄜ)
the department of gynecology and obstetrics

婦人(ㄈㄨˋ ㄖㄣˊ)
a woman; a female; a married woman

婦人病(ㄈㄨˋ ㄖㄣˊ ㄅㄧㄥˋ)
women's peculiar diseases

婦人之仁(ㄈㄨˋ ㄖㄣˊ ㄓ ㄖㄣˊ)
womanly kindness

婦孺(ㄈㄨˋ ㄖㄨˊ)
women and children

婦孺皆知(ㄈㄨˋ ㄖㄨˊ ㄐㄧㄝ ㄓ)
(so famous or simple that) it's known even to women and children

婦容(ㄈㄨˋ ㄖㄨㄥˊ)
women's proper deportment and appearance

婦幼(ㄈㄨˋ ㄧㄡˋ)
women and children

婦幼衛生(ㄈㄨˋ ㄧㄡˋ ㄨㄟˋ ㄕㄥ)
hygiene for women and children: 婦幼衛生十分重要。Hygiene for women and children is very important.

【婪】 1025 ㄌㄢˊ lan lán
covetous; greedy; avarice

【娼】 1026 (倡) ㄔㄤ chang chāng
a prostitute; a whore

娼門(ㄔㄤ ㄇㄣˊ)
a house of prostitution

娼婦(ㄔㄤ ㄈㄨˋ)
a whore; a prostitute; a slut; a bitch; a harlot

娼寮(ㄔㄤ ㄌㄧㄠˊ)
a brothel

娼妓(ㄔㄤ ㄐㄧˋ)
a prostitute; a streetwalker

娼家(ㄔㄤ ㄐㄧㄚ)
a brothel keeper

【婭】 1027 ㄧㄚˋ yah yà
a mutual address between one's sons-in-law

【婊】 1028 ㄅㄧㄠˇ beau biǎo
a prostitute

婊子(ㄅㄧㄠˇ ·ㄗ)
a prostitute; a whore

婊子養的(ㄅㄧㄠˇ ·ㄗ ㄧㄤˇ ·ㄉㄜ) or 婊子的兒子(ㄅㄧㄠˇ ·ㄗ ·ㄉㄜ ㄦˊ ·ㄗ) or 婊孫子(ㄅㄧㄠˇ ㄙㄨㄣ ·ㄗ)
You s.o.b.! 或 Bastard!

【娬】 1029 (嫵) ㄨˇ wuu wǔ
attractive; lovely

娬媚(ㄨˇ ㄇㄟˋ)
very attractive or lovely: 她是個娬媚的女孩。She is a very attractive girl.

九畫

【婷】 1030 ㄊㄧㄥˊ tyng tíng
pretty; attractive; graceful

婷婷(ㄊㄧㄥˊ ㄊㄧㄥˊ)
attractive and well poised; graceful

【婺】 1031 ㄨˋ wuh wù
beautiful; charming

【媒】 1032 ㄇㄟˊ mei méi

1. a marriage go-between; a matchmaker
2. a medium

媒婆(ㄇㄟˊ ㄆㄛˊ)
a professional female matchmaker (sometimes used with a slightly derogative connotation)

媒體(ㄇㄟˊ ㄊㄧˇ)
a medium: 報紙和雜誌爲廣告之重要媒體。Newspapers and magazines are important media for advertising.

媒介(ㄇㄟˊ ㄐㄧㄝˋ)
①a go-between ②a medium: 商業電視是一種廣告媒介。Commercial television is a medium for advertising.

媒介體(ㄇㄟˊ ㄐㄧㄝˋ ㄊㄧˇ) or 媒介物(ㄇㄟˊ ㄐㄧㄝˋ ㄨˋ)
a medium: 錢是交易的媒介物。Money is the medium of exchange.

媒妁(ㄇㄟˊ ㄕㄨㄛˋ) or 媒人(ㄇㄟˊ ㄖㄣˊ)
a marriage go-between; a matchmaker

媒妁之言(ㄇㄟˊ ㄕㄨㄛˋ ㄓ ㄧㄢˊ)
(literally) the words of a matchmaker—the marriage arranged by a matchmaker (usually with the consent or approval of one's parents)

〔女部〕

【媚】1033 ㄇㄟˋ mey mèi
1. to fawn on; to flatter
2. to please
3. to love
4. attractive; fascinating; seductive
5. to coax
媚態(ㄇㄟˋ ㄊㄞˋ)
①seductive appearance or gestures of a girl ②fawning manner; obsequiousness
媚世(ㄇㄟˋ ㄕˋ)
to fawn on others; to flatter others
媚人(ㄇㄟˋ ㄖㄣˊ)
attractive, winsome (appearances, or manners); fascinating; enchanting
媚眼(ㄇㄟˋ ㄧㄢˇ)
a soft glance; an ogle: 王小姐向他抛兩三次媚眼。Miss Wang gave him two or three ogles.
媚外(ㄇㄟˋ ㄨㄞˋ)
to fawn on a foreign power; to act obsequiously in dealing with foreigners

【媛】1034 ㄩㄢˋ yuann yuàn
1. a beauty; a beautiful woman
2. (southern dialects) a young lady; a miss

【媧】1035 ㄨㄚ ua wā
the mythical sister and successor of Fu Hsi (伏羲), the legendary emperor (2852-2738 B.C.)

【媖】1036 ㄧㄥ ing yīng
a beautiful woman; beautiful

十畫

【嫁】1037 ㄐㄧㄚˋ jiah jià
1. (said of a woman) to get married; to marry a man
2. to marry off a daughter
3. to impute (blame, a crime, etc.) to another
嫁禍(ㄐㄧㄚˋ ㄏㄨㄛˋ)
to impute blame, a crime, punishment, etc. (to another person)
嫁禍於人(ㄐㄧㄚˋ ㄏㄨㄛˋ ㄩˊ ㄖㄣˊ)
to shift the misfortune onto somebody else; to put the blame on somebody else
嫁鷄隨鷄，嫁狗隨狗(ㄐㄧㄚˋ ㄐㄧ ㄙㄨㄟˊ ㄐㄧ，ㄐㄧㄚˋ ㄍㄡˇ ㄙㄨㄟˊ ㄍㄡˇ)
A woman shares the fate of the man she married, no matter what he is.
嫁接(ㄐㄧㄚˋ ㄐㄧㄝ)
(botany) to graft
嫁娶(ㄐㄧㄚˋ ㄑㄩˇ)
marriage
嫁妝(ㄐㄧㄚˋ ㄓㄨㄤ)
a bride's trousseau; a dowry
嫁人(ㄐㄧㄚˋ ㄖㄣˊ)
(said of women) to marry
嫁怨(ㄐㄧㄚˋ ㄩㄢˋ)
to impute blame or fault to another: 他嫁怨於我。He imputed blame to me.

【嫂】1038 ㄙㄠˇ sao sǎo
the wife of one's elder brother
嫂夫人(ㄙㄠˇ ㄈㄨ ㄖㄣˊ)
(a polite expression to a friend) your wife
嫂子(ㄙㄠˇ ·ㄗ)or 嫂嫂(ㄙㄠˇ ·ㄙㄠ)
the wife of one's elder brother; a sister-in-law

【媳】1039 ㄒㄧˊ shyi xí
a daughter-in-law
媳婦(ㄒㄧˊ ㄈㄨˋ)
①a daughter-in-law: 她是個好媳婦。She is a good daughter-in-law. ②(colloquial) a wife ③a maid-servant

【媵】1040 ㄧㄥˋ yinq yìng
1. to escort ladies to the harem of a newly married wife
2. to present as a gift
媵婢(ㄧㄥˋ ㄅㄧˋ)
a maid who accompanies a bride to her new home

【媸】1041 ㄔ chy chī
ugly

【媼】1042 ㄠˇ ao ǎo
1. an old woman
2. (in old China) a general term for older women
3. the goddess of earth
媼婆(ㄠˇ ㄆㄛˊ)
female examiner of corpses
媼娘(ㄠˇ ㄋㄧㄤˊ)
an old maid

【媽】1043 ㄇㄚ mha mā
1. one's mother
2. a woman servant
媽媽(ㄇㄚ ·ㄇㄚ)
①mama; mother: 她是五個孩子的媽媽。She is a mother of five. ②a woman servant
媽咪(ㄇㄚ ㄇㄧ)
mummy
媽祖(ㄇㄚ ㄗㄨˇ)
Matsu, Goddess of the Sea, worshiped by most fishermen in Fukien and Taiwan provinces: 台灣很多人信媽祖。In Taiwan, many people believe in Matsu.
媽祖廟(ㄇㄚ ㄗㄨˇ ㄇㄧㄠˋ)
a Matsu temple

【媾】1044 ㄍㄡˋ gow gòu
1. to marry; to wed
2. to negotiate peace; amity
3. to couple; to copulate
媾合(ㄍㄡˋ ㄏㄜˊ)
to copulate
媾和(ㄍㄡˋ ㄏㄜˊ)
to negotiate (for) peace; to make peace: 他們終於媾和。They finally negotiated for peace.

【嫉】1045 ㄐㄧˊ jyi jí
1. jealous; envious; jealousy
2. to hate; to detest
嫉妒(ㄐㄧˊ ㄉㄨˋ)
jealous; envy; jealousy
嫉恨(ㄐㄧˊ ㄏㄣˋ)
to envy and hate; to hate out of jealousy: 他嫉恨她。He hates her out of jealousy.
嫉賢害能(ㄐㄧˊ ㄒㄧㄢˊ ㄏㄞˋ ㄋㄥˊ)
to detest the good and to undermine the capable
嫉惡如仇(ㄐㄧˊ ㄜˋ ㄖㄨˊ ㄔㄡˊ)
not to compromise with evil deeds or evil persons; to view good and evil on black-and-white basis: 他嫉惡如仇。He never compromises with evil deeds or evil persons.

【嫌】1046 ㄒㄧㄢˊ shyan xián
1. to detest; to dislike
2. ill will; a grudge: 前嫌盡棄。

All past grudges have been removed.
3. to suspect; suspicion
4. to complain; to reject; to object

嫌忌(ㄒㄧㄢˊ ㄐㄧˋ)
to reject or suspect; to be dissatisfied with what others do

嫌棄(ㄒㄧㄢˊ ㄑㄧˋ)
to reject; to give up in disgust; to abandon (one's wife, or lover); to cold-shoulder

嫌隙(ㄒㄧㄢˊ ㄒㄧˋ)
the suspicion born out of dislike; an old grudge

嫌憎(ㄒㄧㄢˊ ㄗㄥ)
to hate; to dislike

嫌猜(ㄒㄧㄢˊ ㄘㄞ)
dislike and suspicion

嫌疑(ㄒㄧㄢˊ ㄧˊ)
suspicion; to suspect: 他因偷竊嫌疑而被捕。He was arrested on suspicion of theft.

嫌疑犯(ㄒㄧㄢˊ ㄧˊ ㄈㄢˋ)
a suspect (of a crime, etc.)

嫌厭(ㄒㄧㄢˊ ㄧㄢˋ)
to dislike; to loathe

嫌惡(ㄒㄧㄢˊ ·ㄨ)
to loathe

十一畫

【嫠】 1047 ㄌㄧˊ li lí
a widow

嫠婦(ㄌㄧˊ ㄈㄨˋ)
a widow

【嫖】 1048 ㄆㄧㄠˊ pyau piáo
to patronize whorehouses; to visit prostitutes; to go whoring

嫖賭(ㄆㄧㄠˊ ㄉㄨˇ)
to patronize whore houses and gambling houses—to lead a life of debauchery

嫖客(ㄆㄧㄠˊ ㄎㄜˋ)
a patron of brothels

嫖妓(ㄆㄧㄠˊ ㄐㄧˋ)
to visit prostitutes

【嫗】 1049 ㄩˋ yuh yù
an old woman

【嫚】 1050 1. ㄇㄢˋ mann màn
1. to slight; to despise; to insult; to affront
2. haughty; arrogant
3. slowly; negligently

嫚罵(ㄇㄢˋ ㄇㄚˋ)
to slight and insult verbally

【嫚】 1050 2. ㄩㄢ iuan yuān
slender; tender

【嫡】 1051 ㄉㄧˊ dyi dí
1. the legal wife as opposed to a concubine
2. the sons born of the legal wife

嫡派(ㄉㄧˊ ㄆㄞˋ)
the legal or official branch of a family tree—the children born of the legal wife of a man

嫡母(ㄉㄧˊ ㄇㄨˇ)
term used by the children of a concubine to address the legal wife of their father

嫡妻(ㄉㄧˊ ㄑㄧ)
a legal wife

嫡親(ㄉㄧˊ ㄑㄧㄣ)
blood relatives

嫡系(ㄉㄧˊ ㄒㄧˋ)
the legal or official branch of the family tree—the children begotten by the legal wife of a man

嫡出(ㄉㄧˊ ㄔㄨ)
children of the legal wife

嫡傳(ㄉㄧˊ ㄔㄨㄢˊ)
(said of a learning, skill, etc.) handed down directly from the master or his official heir

嫡子(ㄉㄧˊ ㄗˇ)
the sons born of the legal wife of a man

嫡嗣(ㄉㄧˊ ㄙˋ)
the eldest son born of the official wife of a man

【嫣】 1052 ㄧㄢ ian yān
captivating; charming; lovely; fascinating

嫣紅(ㄧㄢ ㄏㄨㄥˊ)
bright red; rich crimson

嫣然一笑(ㄧㄢ ㄖㄢˊ ㄧˊ ㄒㄧㄠˋ)
a captivating smile; to give a winsome smile: 她對他嫣然一笑。She gave him a captivating smile.

【嫦】 1053 ㄔㄤˊ charng cháng
參看「嫦娥」

嫦娥(ㄔㄤˊ ㄜˊ)
(Chinese legend) Chang-o, who ascended the moon after secretly eating her husband's elixir of life

【嫩】 1054 ㄋㄣˋ nenn nèn
1. tender; delicate: 這塊肉很嫩。This meat is very tender. 她的皮膚很嬌嫩。She has very delicate skin.
2. young; immature
3. (of color) light

嫩豆腐(ㄋㄣˋ ㄉㄡˋ ㄈㄨˇ)
tender bean curd

嫩綠(ㄋㄣˋ ㄌㄩˋ)
light green

嫩骨頭(ㄋㄣˋ ㄍㄨˇ ·ㄊㄡ)
① cartilage ②a weak-minded person

嫩寒(ㄋㄣˋ ㄏㄢˊ)
chilly; slightly cold

嫩黃(ㄋㄣˋ ㄏㄨㄤˊ)
light yellow

嫩江(ㄋㄣˋ ㄐㄧㄤ)
Nen River

嫩精(ㄋㄣˋ ㄐㄧㄥ)
a tenderizer: 我們用嫩精使牛肉變軟。We use the tenderizer to tenderize beef.

嫩晴(ㄋㄣˋ ㄑㄧㄥˊ)
fine weather after a long period of rain

嫩枝(ㄋㄣˋ ㄓ)
a sprig

嫩手(ㄋㄣˋ ㄕㄡˇ)
① a raw hand; a new hand ② delicate hands

嫩肉(ㄋㄣˋ ㄖㄡˋ)
tender meat

嫩芽(ㄋㄣˋ ㄧㄚˊ)
a tender shoot

嫩葉(ㄋㄣˋ ㄧㄝˋ)
a young leaf; a tender leaf

十二畫

【嬉】 1055 ㄒㄧ shi xī
to have fun; to sport; to play; to frolic: 業精於勤荒於嬉。The progress of studies comes from hard work and is retarded by frolics.

嬉皮(ㄒㄧ ㄆㄧˊ)
hippies

〔女 部〕

嬉皮笑臉(ㄒㄧ ㄆㄧˊ ㄒㄧㄠˋ ㄌㄧㄢˇ)
grinning cheekily; smiling and grimacing
嬉鬧(ㄒㄧ ㄋㄠˋ)
to romp: 男孩與女孩們彼此嬉鬧。The boys and girls romped together.
嬉戲(ㄒㄧ ㄒㄧˋ)
to frolic; to play; to sport; to have fun; to make merry; to gambol; to romp: 孩子們在海邊嬉戲。Children are sporting on the seashore.
嬉笑(ㄒㄧ ㄒㄧㄠˋ)
to be laughing and playing; a mischievous smile
嬉笑怒罵(ㄒㄧ ㄒㄧㄠˋ ㄋㄨˋ ㄇㄚˋ)
playing, laughing, getting angry and scolding—a stimulating style of writing which makes even merry laughters and angry shoutings delightful reading
嬉遊(ㄒㄧ ㄧㄡˊ)
to play; to sport: 孩子們喜歡嬉遊。Children like to play.

【嫻】 1056
(嫺) ㄒㄧㄢˊ shyan xián
1. refined; gracious
2. skillful; skilled
嫻靜(ㄒㄧㄢˊ ㄐㄧㄥˋ)
quiet and refined (women)
嫻習(ㄒㄧㄢˊ ㄒㄧˊ)
skilled in; adept at: 她嫻習新聞寫作。She is adept at news writing.
嫻熟(ㄒㄧㄢˊ ㄕㄨˊ)
expert; consummate; adept in; skilled in: 他在足球場上表現了嫻熟的技巧。He showed consummate skill at soccer.
嫻雅(ㄒㄧㄢˊ ㄧㄚˇ)
polished; cultured; refined: 她舉止嫻雅。She is refined in manners.
嫻於辭令(ㄒㄧㄢˊ ㄩˊ ㄘˊ ㄌㄧㄥˋ)
skilled in speech; eloquent; to be gifted with a silver tongue: 他是個嫻於辭令的人。He is an eloquent speaker.

【嬋】 1057
ㄔㄢˊ charn chán
graceful; lady-like; attractive; beautiful; pretty
嬋娟(ㄔㄢˊ ㄐㄩㄢ)
① graceful ② the moon; moonlight: 但願人長久，千里共嬋娟。(蘇軾・水調歌頭) Though miles apart, could men but live for ever / Dreaming they shared this moonlight endlessly!

【嬌】 1058
ㄐㄧㄠ jiau jiāo
1. tender; delicate; beautiful; lovely
2. spoiled; pampered; coddled
嬌美(ㄐㄧㄠ ㄇㄟˇ)
beautiful and graceful
嬌媚(ㄐㄧㄠ ㄇㄟˋ)
beautiful; handsome
嬌滴滴(ㄐㄧㄠ ㄉㄧ ㄉㄧ)
charming; fascinatingly beautiful
嬌態(ㄐㄧㄠ ㄊㄞˋ)
delicate and beautiful
嬌童(ㄐㄧㄠ ㄊㄨㄥˊ)
a handsome boy
嬌嫩(ㄐㄧㄠ ㄋㄣˋ)
delicate and soft; tender; fragile
嬌娘(ㄐㄧㄠ ㄋㄧㄤˊ)
a beautiful woman
嬌娜(ㄐㄧㄠ ㄋㄨㄛˊ)
winsome; graceful: 她有嬌娜的姿態。She has a winsome manner.
嬌女(ㄐㄧㄠ ㄋㄩˇ)
a beloved daughter: 她是我的嬌女。She is my beloved daughter.
嬌哥兒(ㄐㄧㄠ ㄍㄜㄦ)
an over-pampered child
嬌貴(ㄐㄧㄠ ㄍㄨㄟˋ)
(said of children) spoiled; coddled
嬌慣(ㄐㄧㄠ ㄍㄨㄢˋ)
to pamper; to coddle; to spoil; to dote: 她嬌慣她的孩子。She pampers her child.
嬌客(ㄐㄧㄠ ㄎㄜˋ)
a son-in-law
嬌喉(ㄐㄧㄠ ㄏㄡˊ)
a pleasing singing voice
嬌憨(ㄐㄧㄠ ㄏㄢ)
lovely and innocent
嬌妻(ㄐㄧㄠ ㄑㄧ)
a beloved wife
嬌氣(ㄐㄧㄠ ㄑㄧˋ)
delicate; not very healthy
嬌小(ㄐㄧㄠ ㄒㄧㄠˇ)
dainty and little: 我的老師個子很嬌小。My teacher is very dainty and little.
嬌小玲瓏(ㄐㄧㄠ ㄒㄧㄠˇ ㄌㄧㄥˊ ㄌㄨㄥˊ)
delicate and refined
嬌羞(ㄐㄧㄠ ㄒㄧㄡ)
bashful; modest and retiring: 她有點兒嬌羞。She is rather bashful.
嬌痴(ㄐㄧㄠ ㄔ)
lovely and innocent; guileless
嬌嗔(ㄐㄧㄠ ㄔㄣ)
(said of women) to get angry
嬌喘(ㄐㄧㄠ ㄔㄨㄢˇ)
(said of women) to gasp for breath for lack of strength
嬌生慣養(ㄐㄧㄠ ㄕㄥ ㄍㄨㄢˋ ㄧㄤˇ)
to grow up in soft surroundings; to live a sheltered life
嬌聲嬌氣的(ㄐㄧㄠ ㄕㄥ ㄐㄧㄠ ㄑㄧˋ ˙ㄉㄜ)
to speak in a seductive tone: 她說話總是嬌聲嬌氣的。She always speaks in a seductive tone.
嬌嬈(ㄐㄧㄠ ㄖㄠˊ)
seductive and charming
嬌柔(ㄐㄧㄠ ㄖㄡˊ)
beautiful and frail
嬌縱(ㄐㄧㄠ ㄗㄨㄥˋ)
to let a child have his own way; to pamper: 他嬌縱他的孩子。He lets his child have his own way.
嬌兒(ㄐㄧㄠ ㄦˊ)
a beloved son
嬌艷(ㄐㄧㄠ ㄧㄢˋ)
beautiful; gorgeous; delicate and charming: 嬌艷的杏花盛開了。The delicate and charming apricot trees are in full blossom.
嬌養慣了(ㄐㄧㄠ ㄧㄤˇ ㄍㄨㄢˋ ˙ㄌㄜ)
accustomed to a soft and pampered life: 她嬌養慣了。She is accustomed to a soft and pampered life.
嬌娃(ㄐㄧㄠ ㄨㄚˊ)
a beauty: 她是個嬌娃。She is a beauty.

十三畫

【嬖】 1059
ㄅㄧˋ bih bì
1. to enjoy the favor of a powerful person (said of people of mean birth)
2. a minion

嬖倖(ㄅㄧˋ ㄒㄧㄥˋ)or 嬖御(ㄅㄧˋ ㄩˋ)
(said of concubines and sycophants) to be favored by the ruler
嬖人(ㄅㄧˋ ㄖㄣˊ)
a favorite of the ruler

【嬗】 1060 ㄕㄢˋ shann shàn
to change; to be replaced

【嬙】 1061 ㄑㄧㄤˊ chyang qiáng
a court lady
嬙媛(ㄑㄧㄤˊ ㄩㄢˊ)
ladies-in-waiting

【嬛】 1062 1. ㄑㄩㄥˊ chyong qióng
lonely; solitary

【嬛】 1062 2. ㄒㄩㄢ shiuan xuān
fickle; frivolous
嬛薄(ㄒㄩㄢ ㄅㄛˊ)
frivolous

【嬡】 1063 ㄞˋ ay ài
the daughter (a complimentary term referring to the daughter of the person one is speaking to)

【嬴】 1064 ㄧㄥˊ yng yíng
1. to win: 他嬴得她的芳心。He won her heart.
2. to have a surplus
3. a Chinese family name
嬴土(ㄧㄥˊ ㄊㄨˇ)
fertile land; fertile soil
嬴秦(ㄧㄥˊ ㄑㄧㄣˊ)
the state of Chin during the Warring States period

【嬝】 1065 (嫋) ㄋㄧㄠˇ neau niǎo
delicate; graceful
嬝嬝(ㄋㄧㄠˇ ㄋㄧㄠˇ)
①(said of a willow) waving gracefully ② (said of a young woman) appealingly slender and delicate ③ (said of smoke, etc.) dying out slowly ④(said of sound) to linger in the air long
嬝娜(ㄋㄧㄠˇ ㄋㄨㄛˋ)
showing womanly beauty; slender and delicate; willowy

十四畫

【嬰】 1066 ㄧㄥ ing yīng
an infant; a baby; a suckling
嬰孩(ㄧㄥ ㄏㄞˊ)or 嬰兒(ㄧㄥ ㄦˊ)
a baby; an infant
嬰兒奶粉(ㄧㄥ ㄦˊ ㄋㄞˇ ㄈㄣˇ)
soft curd milk
嬰兒死亡率(ㄧㄥ ㄦˊ ㄙˇ ㄨㄤˊ ㄌㄩˋ)
the infant mortality rate

【嬲】 1067 ㄋㄧㄠˇ neau niǎo
to dally with; to flirt with

【嬪】 1068 ㄆㄧㄣˊ pyn pín
1. a court lady
2. (said of a woman) to be married to
嬪從(ㄆㄧㄣˊ ㄗㄨㄥˋ)
ladies-in-waiting 亦作「宮女」

十五畫

【嬸】 1069 ㄕㄣˇ sheen shěn
1. an aunt (the wife of one's father's younger brother)
2. a sister-in-law (the wife of one's husband's younger brother)
嬸母(ㄕㄣˇ ㄇㄨˇ)or 嬸娘(ㄕㄣˇ ㄋㄧㄤˊ)or 嬸嬸(ㄕㄣˇ ·ㄕㄣ)
① an aunt (the wife of one's father's younger brother) ② an address for one's aunt

十七畫

【孀】 1070 ㄕㄨㄤ shuang shuāng
a widow
孀婦(ㄕㄨㄤ ㄈㄨˋ)
a widow
孀閨(ㄕㄨㄤ ㄍㄨㄟ)
the chamber of a widow
孀居(ㄕㄨㄤ ㄐㄩ)
to remain in widowhood; to live as a widow: 她孀居數年。She remains in widowhood several years.

【孅】 1071 ㄒㄧㄢ shian xiān
slender; thin; small; fine; delicate
孅介(ㄒㄧㄢ ㄐㄧㄝˋ)
tiny; a small bit
孅手(ㄒㄧㄢ ㄕㄡˇ)
delicate hands (of a woman)
孅弱(ㄒㄧㄢ ㄖㄨㄛˋ)
frail; weak; delicate: 他是個孅弱的孩子。He is a frail child.
孅嗇(ㄒㄧㄢ ㄙㄜˋ)
miserly; stingy

十九畫

【孌】 1072 ㄌㄩㄢˇ leuan lüǎn
1. beautiful; handsome
2. obedient; docile
孌童(ㄌㄩㄢˇ ㄊㄨㄥˊ)
a catamite

子部
ㄗˇ tzyy zǐ

【子】 1073 ㄗˇ tzyy zǐ
1. a child; a son; an offspring: 你的獨生子很受看重。Your only son is highly considered.
2. a seed; an egg: 瓜子 melon seed
3. the first of the twelve Terrestrial Branches (地支)
4. a rank of the nobility equivalent to a viscount
5. a designation used in speaking of or to a man in former times (somewhat similar to 'mister')
子部(ㄗˇ ㄅㄨˋ)
one of the four categories of ancient Chinese books (經、史、子、集)
子民(ㄗˇ ㄇㄧㄣˊ)
the people
子母(ㄗˇ ㄇㄨˇ)
①mother and child ②principal and interest
子母相權(ㄗˇ ㄇㄨˇ ㄒㄧㄤ ㄑㄩㄢˊ)
heavy and light coins circulated side by side in ancient China
子目(ㄗˇ ㄇㄨˋ)
a subdivision (of a division in a code, a book, etc.); a subtitle
子房(ㄗˇ ㄈㄤˊ)
(botany) an ovary

〔子部〕

子代(ㄗˇ ㄉㄞˋ)
a filial generation: 第一子代 the first filial generation
子彈(ㄗˇ ㄉㄢˋ)
a bullet: 子彈差一英吋就擊中他。The bullet missed him by one inch.
子彈箱(ㄗˇ ㄉㄢˋ ㄒㄧㄤ)
a cartridge box
子弟(ㄗˇ ㄉㄧˋ)
① young dependents; children ② those who patronize brothels
子弟兵(ㄗˇ ㄉㄧˋ ㄅㄧㄥ)
an army made up of the sons of the people; our own army
子囊(ㄗˇ ㄋㄤˊ)
(botany) sporangium
子女(ㄗˇ ㄋㄩˇ)
sons and daughters; children (as opposed to parents)
子粒(ㄗˇ ㄌㄧˋ)
seeds; grains; kernels; tiny particles; beans: 子粒飽滿 full grains
子路(ㄗˇ ㄌㄨˋ)
Tzu-lu (a disciple of Confucius)
子規(ㄗˇ ㄍㄨㄟ)
the cuckoo 亦作「杜鵑」
子宮(ㄗˇ ㄍㄨㄥ)
the womb; the uterus
子宮癌(ㄗˇ ㄍㄨㄥ ㄧㄢˊ)
uterine cancer
子宮外孕(ㄗˇ ㄍㄨㄥ ㄨㄞˋ ㄩㄣˋ)
ectopic (or extrauterine) pregnancy
子金(ㄗˇ ㄐㄧㄣ)
interest from principal
子薑(ㄗˇ ㄐㄧㄤ)
young ginger
子句(ㄗˇ ㄐㄩˋ)
(grammar) a clause
子爵(ㄗˇ ㄐㄩㄝˊ)
a viscount
子爵夫人(ㄗˇ ㄐㄩㄝˊ ㄈㄨ ㄖㄣˊ)
a viscountess
子錢(ㄗˇ ㄑㄧㄢˊ)
① money put out at interest ② interest from money lent
子息(ㄗˇ ㄒㄧˊ)
① one's children ② interest (in monetary sense)
子系(ㄗˇ ㄒㄧˋ)
posterity; offspring
子虛(ㄗˇ ㄒㄩ)
① emptiness; nothingness: 聲音化爲子虛。The sound faded into nothingness. ② fiction
子虛烏有(ㄗˇ ㄒㄩ ㄨ ㄧㄡˇ)
pure imagination
子姪 or 子侄(ㄗˇ ㄓˊ)
the generation younger than oneself in the family or clan; one's sons, daughters, nephews and nieces
子時(ㄗˇ ㄕˊ)
the period of the day from 11 p.m. to 1 a.m.
子實(ㄗˇ ㄕˊ)
seeds; grains; kernels; beans
子書(ㄗˇ ㄕㄨ)
ancient Chinese books other than the *Six Classics*
子子孫孫(ㄗˇ ㄗˇ ㄙㄨㄣ ㄙㄨㄣ)
generation after generation of descendants
子思(ㄗˇ ㄙ)
Tzu-szu (Confucius' grandson)
子嗣(ㄗˇ ㄙˋ)
a son; a male offspring: 李先生是他唯一的子嗣。Mr. Li is his only male offspring.
子孫(ㄗˇ ㄙㄨㄣ)
descendants; posterity
子夜(ㄗˇ ㄧㄝˋ)
midnight: 他經常工作到子夜。He usually worked until midnight.
子葉(ㄗˇ ㄧㄝˋ)
a cotyledon
子音(ㄗˇ ㄧㄣ)
a consonant
子午線(ㄗˇ ㄨˇ ㄒㄧㄢˋ)
a meridian 亦作「經線」
子曰(ㄗˇ ㄩㄝ)
Confucius said

【孑】 1074
ㄐㄧㄝˊ jye jié
1. the larvae of mosquitoes
2. solitary; unaccompanied; lonely

孑立(ㄐㄧㄝˊ ㄌㄧˋ)
to stand in isolation; to be alone: 他的房子孑立山邊。His house stands alone on the hillside.
孑孑爲義(ㄐㄧㄝˊ ㄐㄧㄝˊ ㄨㄟˊ ㄧˋ)
petty favors
孑孓(ㄐㄧㄝˊ ㄐㄩㄝˊ)
the larvae of mosquitoes; wigglers
孑然一身(ㄐㄧㄝˊ ㄖㄢˊ ㄧˋ ㄕㄣ)
alone; living without companions: 他至今仍孑然一身。He is still living alone.
孑遺(ㄐㄧㄝˊ ㄧˊ)
the sole survivor

【孓】 1075
ㄐㄩㄝˊ jyue jué
the larvae of mosquitoes

一畫

【孔】 1076
ㄎㄨㄥˇ koong kǒng
1. a hole; an orifice; an opening; an aperture
2. very; exceedingly
3. of or pertaining to Confucius or Confucianism
4. urgent; badly
5. a Chinese family name

孔門(ㄎㄨㄥˇ ㄇㄣˊ)
the Confucianists
孔孟(ㄎㄨㄥˇ ㄇㄥˋ)
Confucius and Mencius: 孔孟乃中國之聖人也。Confucius and Mencius were sages of China.
孔孟之道(ㄎㄨㄥˇ ㄇㄥˋ ㄓ ㄉㄠˋ)
the doctrines of Confucius and Mencius
孔廟(ㄎㄨㄥˇ ㄇㄧㄠˋ)
a Confucian temple: 他們到孔廟去參觀。They went to visit the Confucian temple.
孔明(ㄎㄨㄥˇ ㄇㄧㄥˊ)
another name of 諸葛亮, prime minister of the state of Shu during the Epoch of the Three Kingdoms
孔方兄(ㄎㄨㄥˇ ㄈㄤ ㄒㄩㄥ)
money, or cash (a colloquial expression derived from the fact that a coin is round and has a square hole in the center)
孔夫子(ㄎㄨㄥˇ ㄈㄨ ㄗˇ)
Confucius: 孔夫子被尊稱爲孔聖人。Confucius is called Confucius the Sage.
孔父(ㄎㄨㄥˇ ㄈㄨˋ)
Confucius
孔道(ㄎㄨㄥˇ ㄉㄠˋ)
① a key road ② the Confucian teachings
孔誕(ㄎㄨㄥˇ ㄉㄢˋ)or 孔子誕辰紀念

日(ㄎㄨㄥˇ ㄗˇ ㄉㄢˋ ㄔㄣˊ ㄐㄧˋ ㄋㄧㄢˋ ㄖˋ)
Confucius' Birthday on September 28: 孔子誕辰紀念日是假日。Confucius' Birthday is a holiday.

孔洞(ㄎㄨㄥˇ ㄉㄨㄥˋ)
an opening or a hole

孔老(ㄎㄨㄥˇ ㄌㄠˇ)
Confucius and Lao-tzu

孔林(ㄎㄨㄥˇ ㄌㄧㄣˊ)
the tomb of Confucius in Shangtung

孔急(ㄎㄨㄥˇ ㄐㄧˊ)or 孔殷(ㄎㄨㄥˇ ㄧㄣ)
urgent; urgently; badly

孔教(ㄎㄨㄥˇ ㄐㄧㄠˋ)
Confucianism; the Confucian teachings

孔竅(ㄎㄨㄥˇ ㄑㄧㄠˋ)
said of the eyes, ears, mouth and nose of a human

孔雀(ㄎㄨㄥˇ ㄑㄩㄝˋ)
a peacock: 小孩喜歡孔雀。Children like the peacocks.

孔雀石(ㄎㄨㄥˇ ㄑㄩㄝˋ ㄕˊ)
malachite

孔隙(ㄎㄨㄥˇ ㄒㄧˋ)
a small opening; a hole

孔穴(ㄎㄨㄥˇ ㄒㄩㄝˋ)
a hole; an aperture; an opening

孔聖(ㄎㄨㄥˇ ㄕㄥˋ)
Confucius the Sage

孔子(ㄎㄨㄥˇ ㄗˇ)
Confucius

孔武有力(ㄎㄨㄥˇ ㄨˇ ㄧㄡˇ ㄌㄧˋ)
(said of a man) very strong and brave; herculean: 他是個孔武有力的戰士。He is a herculean warrior.

二畫

【孕】 1077
ㄩㄣˋ yunn yun

to be pregnant; to conceive

孕婦(ㄩㄣˋ ㄈㄨˋ)
a pregnant woman

孕期(ㄩㄣˋ ㄑㄧˊ)
(medicine) pregnancy; gestation

孕育(ㄩㄣˋ ㄩˋ)
to let develop (as in the womb); to nourish; to foster; to nurture; to nurse

三畫

【字】 1078
ㄗˋ tzyh zi

1. a word; a character; a letter; a logograph: 這個字是什麼意思? What does this word mean?
2. to betroth a girl: 她尚待字閨中。She is not betrothed yet.
3. (formerly) a name or style taken at the age of 20, by which one was sometimes called

字碼(ㄗˋ ㄇㄚˇ)
a form of digits used by old-fashioned businessmen to prevent tampering

字模(ㄗˋ ㄇㄛˊ)
(printing) a type matrix

字謎(ㄗˋ ㄇㄧˊ)
a riddle, the answer to which is a single word or character

字面(ㄗˋ ㄇㄧㄢˋ)
words (as found in some text and interpreted literally)

字母(ㄗˋ ㄇㄨˇ)
an alphabet; a letter (of an alphabet): 英文字母有二十六個。There are twenty-six letters in the English alphabet.

字幕(ㄗˋ ㄇㄨˋ)
subtitles (in a motion picture); a transcript of singing lines in Peking opera projected on the screen for the benefit of the audience

字典(ㄗˋ ㄉㄧㄢˇ)
a dictionary; a lexicon; a thesaurus: 字典是他的常伴。A dictionary is his frequent companion.

字體(ㄗˋ ㄊㄧˇ)
(printing) a style of letter or character; a type

字帖(ㄗˋ ㄊㄧㄝˋ)
a copybook

字條(兒)(ㄗˋ ㄊㄧㄠˊ (ㄦ))
a brief note: 他的上司留給他一張字條。His boss left him a brief note.

字裏行間(ㄗˋ ㄌㄧˇ ㄏㄤˊ ㄐㄧㄢ)
between the lines; the overtone (of a piece of writing)

字根(ㄗˋ ㄍㄣ)
(linguistics) a root; a radical

字號(ㄗˋ ㄏㄠˋ)
① a mark made with letters or characters ② the name of a shop or store ③ reputation; fame

字號人物(ㄗˋ ㄏㄠˋ ㄖㄣˊ ㄨˋ)
personages and their reputation

字畫(ㄗˋ ㄏㄨㄚˋ)
① the strokes in a character ② calligraphy and painting

字彙(ㄗˋ ㄏㄨㄟˋ)
① a vocabulary: 他的字彙有限。His vocabulary is limited. ② a glossary

字跡(ㄗˋ ㄐㄧ)
one's handwriting: 她的字跡很難認。Her handwriting was difficult to read.

字跡模糊(ㄗˋ ㄐㄧ ㄇㄛˊ ㄏㄨˊ)
illegible handwriting

字跡工整(ㄗˋ ㄐㄧ ㄍㄨㄥ ㄓㄥˇ)
neat writing

字句(ㄗˋ ㄐㄩˋ)
words and phrases

字據(ㄗˋ ㄐㄩˋ)
a written proof; a receipt; a certificate: 請給我一張此款的字據。Please send me a receipt for the money.

字形(ㄗˋ ㄒㄧㄥˊ)
the form of a (written or printed) character

字紙(ㄗˋ ㄓˇ)
paper with words written or printed upon it

字紙簍兒(ㄗˋ ㄓˇ ㄌㄡˇㄦ)
a wastepaper basket; a wastebasket: 字紙簍兒在那裡呢? Where is the wastebasket?

字斟句酌(ㄗˋ ㄓㄣ ㄐㄩˋ ㄓㄨㄛˊ)
to choose one's words carefully; to weigh every word: 你必須字斟句酌。You must weigh your words.

字首(ㄗˋ ㄕㄡˇ)
a prefix

字書(ㄗˋ ㄕㄨ)
a wordbook; a dictionary

字人(ㄗˋ ㄖㄣˊ)
(said of a girl) to become engaged

字字(ㄗˋ ㄗˋ)
every word

字義(ㄗˋ ㄧˋ)
the definition, connotation, or meaning of a word

〔子部〕

〔子部〕

字眼(ㄗˋ ㄧㄢˇ)
a word; a character: 這個字眼什麼意思? What does this word mean?

字眼兒(ㄗˋ ㄧㄚˇㄦ)
wording; diction; expression

字樣(ㄗˋ ㄧㄤˋ)
① models of Chinese characters ② words and phrases used in a certain context: 在我們的契約裏並無此等字樣。There are no such words and phrases in our contract.

字尾(ㄗˋ ㄨㄟˇ)
a suffix

字源(ㄗˋ ㄩㄢˊ)
the etymology of a word

【存】 1079 ㄘㄨㄣˊ tswen cún

1. to live; to exist; to survive; to remain: 父母俱存。Both parents are still living.
2. to keep; to deposit: 我把錢存入銀行。I keep money in a bank.

存歿(ㄘㄨㄣˊ ㄇㄛˋ)
a question of remaining in existence or not

存歿均感(ㄘㄨㄣˊ ㄇㄛˋ ㄐㄩㄣ ㄍㄢˇ)
Both the dead and the living are grateful.

存放(ㄘㄨㄣˊ ㄈㄤˋ)
to deposit (money); to leave (something somewhere) for safekeeping: 我把行李存放在朋友那裡了。I've left my luggage with a friend of mine.

存放處(ㄘㄨㄣˊ ㄈㄤˋ ㄔㄨˋ)
a depository

存單(ㄘㄨㄣˊ ㄉㄢ)
(accounting) a deposit receipt

存檔(ㄘㄨㄣˊ ㄉㄤˇ)
to keep in the archives; to place on file; to file: 把這些信仔細存檔。File these letters carefully.

存底兒(ㄘㄨㄣˊ ㄉㄧㄜˇㄦ)
to keep the first draft; to keep a file copy

存念(ㄘㄨㄣˊ ㄋㄧㄢˋ)
to have something as a keepsake or as a memento

存欄(ㄘㄨㄣˊ ㄌㄢˊ)
(animal husbandry) the amount of livestock on hand

存糧(ㄘㄨㄣˊ ㄌㄧㄤˊ)
to store up grain

存錄(ㄘㄨㄣˊ ㄌㄨˋ)
to put on record

存根(ㄘㄨㄣˊ ㄍㄣ)
a counterfoil; a stub

存庫(ㄘㄨㄣˊ ㄎㄨˋ)
a treasury; to keep in a vault

存款(ㄘㄨㄣˊ ㄎㄨㄢˇ)
the money put in a bank; a deposit; to make a deposit

存款簿(ㄘㄨㄣˊ ㄎㄨㄢˇ ㄅㄨˋ)
a deposit book

存款單(ㄘㄨㄣˊ ㄎㄨㄢˇ ㄉㄢ)
a deposit slip

存款利息(ㄘㄨㄣˊ ㄎㄨㄢˇ ㄌㄧˋ ㄒㄧˊ)
interest on deposit

存款人(ㄘㄨㄣˊ ㄎㄨㄢˇ ㄖㄣˊ)
a depositor

存候(ㄘㄨㄣˊ ㄏㄡˋ)
to send regards

存戶(ㄘㄨㄣˊ ㄏㄨˋ)
a depositor (of money in a bank, etc.): 存戶要提款。The depositor wants to withdraw his money.

存活(ㄘㄨㄣˊ ㄏㄨㄛˊ)
to survive; to keep alive

存貨(ㄘㄨㄣˊ ㄏㄨㄛˋ)
remaining (still unsold) goods; inventory: 一位店商減價以減少他的存貨。A storekeeper had a sale to reduce his inventory.

存貨表(ㄘㄨㄣˊ ㄏㄨㄛˋ ㄅㄧㄠˇ)
(accounting) a stock sheet

存貨簿(ㄘㄨㄣˊ ㄏㄨㄛˋ ㄅㄨˋ)
(accounting) a stock book

存貨記錄(ㄘㄨㄣˊ ㄏㄨㄛˋ ㄐㄧˋ ㄌㄨˋ)
(accounting) inventory records

存記(ㄘㄨㄣˊ ㄐㄧˋ)
to register for future reference (as an applicant, etc.)

存取(ㄘㄨㄣˊ ㄑㄩˇ)
(computers) access

存息(ㄘㄨㄣˊ ㄒㄧˊ)
the interest from a deposit

存心(ㄘㄨㄣˊ ㄒㄧㄣ)
intentions; intentional; intentionally; on purpose: 他存心傷害她的感情。He hurt her feelings with intention.

存心叵測(ㄘㄨㄣˊ ㄒㄧㄣ ㄆㄛˇ ㄘㄜˋ)
to cherish unscrupulous intentions

存恤(ㄘㄨㄣˊ ㄒㄩˋ)
to give comfort and relief

存續(ㄘㄨㄣˊ ㄒㄩˋ)
to continue to exist; to keep existing

存摺(ㄘㄨㄣˊ ㄓㄜˊ)
a bankbook; a passbook

存查(ㄘㄨㄣˊ ㄔㄚˊ)or 存照(ㄘㄨㄣˊ ㄓㄠˋ)
to keep (a business letter, document, etc.) for future reference; to file (papers)

存車處(ㄘㄨㄣˊ ㄔㄜ ㄔㄨˋ)
a parking lot (for bicycles); a bicycle park 亦作「停車處」

存儲(ㄘㄨㄣˊ ㄔㄨˊ)
to hoard; to store up; to stockpile: 松鼠存儲堅果過冬。A squirrel hoards nuts for the winter.

存儲量(ㄘㄨㄣˊ ㄔㄨˊ ㄌㄧㄤˋ)
(computers) storage capacity; memory capacity

存在(ㄘㄨㄣˊ ㄗㄞˋ)
to exist; to be present; existence: 你相信上帝存在嗎? Do you believe that God exists?

存在主義(ㄘㄨㄣˊ ㄗㄞˋ ㄓㄨˇ ㄧˋ)
existentialism: 沙特提倡存在主義。Sartre popularized existentialism.

存案(ㄘㄨㄣˊ ㄢˋ)
to put (a legal document, etc.) on public record; to file

存而不論(ㄘㄨㄣˊ ㄦˊ ㄅㄨˋ ㄌㄨㄣˋ)
to exclude a problem from consideration though aware of its existence; to ignore

存疑(ㄘㄨㄣˊ ㄧˊ)
① an unanswered question; a remaining doubt ② to leave a doubtful point unquestioned

存有(ㄘㄨㄣˊ ㄧㄡˇ)
being: 我們不知這個世界是何時開始存有的。We do not know when this world came into being.

存慰(ㄘㄨㄣˊ ㄨㄟˋ)
to send a messenger to express sympathy for (a person in mourning, distress, etc.)

存問(ㄘㄨㄣˊ ㄨㄣˋ)
to send a messenger to inquire after (a person)

存亡(ㄘㄨㄣˊ ㄨㄤˊ)
to survive or to perish; to live or to die; life-and-death; survival and downfall

存亡關頭(ㄘㄨㄣˊ ㄨㄤˊ ㄍㄨㄢ ㄊㄡˊ)
at a most critical moment

四畫

【孚】 1080
ㄈㄨˊ fwu fú
1. confidence; trust
2. a Chinese family name

【孛】 1081
ㄅㄟˋ bey bèi
a comet
孛孛(ㄅㄟˋ ㄅㄟˋ)
radiant
孛星(ㄅㄟˋ ㄒㄧㄥ)
a comet 亦作「彗星」

【孜】 1082
ㄗ tzy zī
never weary; unwearied and diligent
孜孜(ㄗ ㄗ)
diligent; industrious
孜孜不倦(ㄗ ㄗ ㄅㄨˋ ㄐㄩㄢˋ)
to work with diligence and without fatigue

【孝】 1083
ㄒㄧㄠˋ shiaw xiào
filial piety; of or having to do with filial piety
孝服(ㄒㄧㄠˋ ㄈㄨˊ)
mourning dress worn by bereaved children
孝婦(ㄒㄧㄠˋ ㄈㄨˋ)
① a filial woman ② a woman in mourning
孝道(ㄒㄧㄠˋ ㄉㄠˋ)
the principle of filial piety
孝悌 or 孝弟(ㄒㄧㄠˋ ㄊㄧˋ)
to be a dutiful son and to be respectful to one's elder brothers
孝男(ㄒㄧㄠˋ ㄋㄢˊ)
a bereaved son (used in an obituary)
孝女(ㄒㄧㄠˋ ㄋㄩˇ)
a bereaved daughter (used in an obituary)
孝廉(ㄒㄧㄠˋ ㄌㄧㄢˊ)
①a term for 舉人 (in Ming and Ching dynasties) ② (Han Dynasty) a person of virtue recommended by a country
孝陵(ㄒㄧㄠˋ ㄌㄧㄥˊ)or 孝陵衛(ㄒㄧㄠˋ ㄌㄧㄥˊ ㄨㄟˋ)
the tomb of Chu Yüan-chang (朱元璋), the founder of the Ming Dynasty, in Nanking
孝經(ㄒㄧㄠˋ ㄐㄧㄥ)
the *Canon of Filial Piety*
孝敬(ㄒㄧㄠˋ ㄐㄧㄥˋ)
① to show filial piety and respect for one's parents: 這些孩子孝敬他們父母。The children treated their parents with filial respect. ② to present one's parents (or superiors) with gifts
孝心(ㄒㄧㄠˋ ㄒㄧㄣ)
filial piety; the love toward parents
孝行(ㄒㄧㄠˋ ㄒㄧㄥˊ)
filial conduct
孝順(ㄒㄧㄠˋ ㄕㄨㄣˋ)
to show filial obedience or devotion for (one's parents)
孝子(ㄒㄧㄠˋ ㄗˇ)
① a devoted child ② a bereaved son
孝子賢孫(ㄒㄧㄠˋ ㄗˇ ㄒㄧㄢˊ ㄙㄨㄣ)
worthy progeny; a true son
孝慈(ㄒㄧㄠˋ ㄘˊ)
filial piety and parental tenderness
孝思(ㄒㄧㄠˋ ㄙ)
the heart of filial piety
孝義(ㄒㄧㄠˋ ㄧˋ)
devotion to one's parents and loyalty to one's friends
孝友(ㄒㄧㄠˋ ㄧㄡˇ)
filial piety and brotherly love

五畫

【孟】 1084
ㄇㄥˋ menq mèng
1. a Chinese family name
2. the eldest of children
3. rude; rough
4. of or having to do with Mencius
5. the first month of a season
孟婆(ㄇㄥˋ ㄆㄛˊ)
the goddess of wind
孟買(ㄇㄥˋ ㄇㄞˇ)
Bombay, India
孟母(ㄇㄥˋ ㄇㄨˇ)
the mother of Mencius
孟母三遷(ㄇㄥˋ ㄇㄨˇ ㄙㄢ ㄑㄧㄢ)
(literally) The mother of Mencius changed her abode three times (to avoid bad influence on her son).—A wise mother would do everything for the healthy growth of her children.
孟德斯鳩(ㄇㄥˋ ㄉㄜˊ ㄙ ㄐㄧㄡ)
Montesquieu (Charles Louis de Secondat, Baron de la Brède et de Montesquieu), 1689-1755, French philosophical writer
孟浪(ㄇㄥˋ ㄌㄤˋ)
rude; rough; rash: 不可孟浪行事。Don't act rashly.
孟浪之言(ㄇㄥˋ ㄌㄤˋ ㄓ ㄧㄢˊ)
reckless talk: 他因孟浪之言而受責。He was scolded for his reckless talk.
孟加拉(ㄇㄥˋ ㄐㄧㄚ ㄌㄚ)
Bengal
孟加拉人(ㄇㄥˋ ㄐㄧㄚ ㄌㄚ ㄖㄣˊ)
Bengalese; Bengali
孟加拉灣(ㄇㄥˋ ㄐㄧㄚ ㄌㄚ ㄨㄢ)
the Bay of Bengal
孟姜女(ㄇㄥˋ ㄐㄧㄤ ㄋㄩˇ)
name of a heroine in Chinese folklore, whose bitter cry over her husband's death at the Great Wall was said to have caused a section of the wall to crumble down
孟春(ㄇㄥˋ ㄔㄨㄣ)
the first month of the spring season
孟什維克(ㄇㄥˋ ㄕˊ ㄨㄟˊ ㄎㄜˋ)
Menshevik
孟子(ㄇㄥˋ ㄗˇ)
Mencius: 孟子是中國的「亞聖」。Mencius is China's "Second Sage".
孟宗竹(ㄇㄥˋ ㄗㄨㄥ ㄓㄨˊ)
famous bamboo south of the Yangtze River
孟月(ㄇㄥˋ ㄩㄝˋ)
the first month of a season (the first, fourth, seventh, and tenth moon)

【季】 1085
ㄐㄧˋ jih jì
1. a season; a quarter of a year
2. the last (month of a season)
3. the youngest (of brothers)
4. a Chinese family name
季票(ㄐㄧˋ ㄆㄧㄠˋ)
a season ticket
季風(ㄐㄧˋ ㄈㄥ)
(meteorology) the monsoon

〔子部〕

亦作「季候風」
季刊(ㄐㄧˋ ㄎㄢ)or 季報(ㄐㄧˋ ㄅㄠˋ)
a quarterly (publication): 紐約客是月刊，不是季刊。*New Yorker* is a monthly, not a quarterly.
季候風(ㄐㄧˋ ㄏㄡˋ ㄈㄥ)
the monsoon, or any other seasonal wind 參看「季風」
季節(ㄐㄧˋ ㄐㄧㄝˊ)
a season: 這是多雨的季節。This is the rainy season.
季節性(ㄐㄧˋ ㄐㄧㄝˊ ㄒㄧㄥˋ)
seasonal: 賣聖誕卡是季節性的生意。The selling of Christmas cards is a seasonal trade.
季軍(ㄐㄧˋ ㄐㄩㄣ)
the second runner-up in a contest; the third prize winner
季常癖(ㄐㄧˋ ㄔㄤˊ ㄆㄧˇ)
henpecked 亦作「懼內症」
季世(ㄐㄧˋ ㄕˋ)
the declining years of a dynasty; a period of decadence
季子(ㄐㄧˋ ㄗˇ)
the youngest son
季月(ㄐㄧˋ ㄩㄝˋ)
the last month of a season (the third, sixth, ninth and twelfth moon)

【孥】1086
ㄋㄨˊ nu nú
one's children

【孤】1087
ㄍㄨ gu gū
1. solitary; lone; lonely; friendless; helpless; unaided
2. fatherless; orphaned: 戰爭使他在早年就變成孤兒。The war orphaned him at an early age.
3. (said of disposition) eccentric
4. negligent in an obligation
孤本(ㄍㄨ ㄅㄣˇ)
the sole copy (of a book) in existence
孤僻(ㄍㄨ ㄆㄧˋ)
(said of a person's disposition) eccentric; idiosyncratic: 他是個孤僻的人。He is an eccentric person.
孤貧(ㄍㄨ ㄆㄧㄣˊ)
lonely and poor
孤墳(ㄍㄨ ㄈㄣˊ)
an isolated grave
孤憤(ㄍㄨ ㄈㄣˋ)
cynical of the world and its way
孤芳自賞(ㄍㄨ ㄈㄤ ㄗˋ ㄕㄤˇ)
to indulge in self-admiration
孤負 or 辜負(ㄍㄨ ㄈㄨˋ)
to fail to live up to; to let down
孤島(ㄍㄨ ㄉㄠˇ)
a solitary island; an isolated island
孤單(ㄍㄨ ㄉㄢ)or 孤另(ㄍㄨ ㄌㄧㄥˋ)
solitary; single; alone; unaccompanied; friendless: 他孤單一人在家。He was alone in the house.
孤獨(ㄍㄨ ㄉㄨˊ)
solitary; friendless; solitude: 愛迪生說:「最好的思想是孤獨中想出來的。」Thomas Alva Edison said: "The best thinking has been done in solitude."
孤特(ㄍㄨ ㄊㄜˋ)
isolated; unaided
孤老(ㄍㄨ ㄌㄠˇ)
① the childless old people ② a woman's paramour ③ the protector of a singsong girl, maid or prostitute
孤陋寡聞(ㄍㄨ ㄌㄡˋ ㄍㄨㄚˇ ㄨㄣˊ)
having seen very little of the world; ignorant
孤立(ㄍㄨ ㄌㄧˋ)
isolation; isolated; unaided: 沒有人能孤立地存在着。No one can live in isolation.
孤立主義(ㄍㄨ ㄌㄧˋ ㄓㄨˇ ㄧˋ)
isolationism
孤零零(ㄍㄨ ㄌㄧㄥˊ ㄌㄧㄥˊ)
lonely; friendless
孤孿(ㄍㄨ ㄌㄨㄢˊ)
a widow; a widower
孤寡(ㄍㄨ ㄍㄨㄚˇ)
① a widow and an orphan ② the humble first-person destination used by the rulers in former times
孤苦伶仃 or 孤苦零丁(ㄍㄨ ㄎㄨˇ ㄌㄧㄥˊ ㄉㄧㄥ)
lonely and helpless; poor and friendless
孤魂(ㄍㄨ ㄏㄨㄣˊ)
① a wandering soul ② one without a family or friends to depend on
孤寂(ㄍㄨ ㄐㄧˊ)
lonely; friendless: 她在陌生人群中甚覺孤寂。She was lonely when among strangers.
孤家寡人(ㄍㄨ ㄐㄧㄚ ㄍㄨㄚˇ ㄖㄣˊ)
alone; a bachelor
孤軍深入(ㄍㄨ ㄐㄩㄣ ㄕㄣ ㄖㄨˋ)
an isolated force penetrating deep into enemy territory
孤掌難鳴(ㄍㄨ ㄓㄤˇ ㄋㄢˊ ㄇㄧㄥˊ)
(literally) A single hand cannot produce clapping sounds. —to be unable to cope with a situation or accomplish something without help
孤證(ㄍㄨ ㄓㄥˋ)
solitary (and therefore dubious) evidence
孤注一擲(ㄍㄨ ㄓㄨˋ ㄧˊ ㄓˋ)
(said of a gambler) to stake all on a single throw of the dice
孤臣孽子(ㄍㄨ ㄔㄣˊ ㄋㄧㄝˋ ㄗˇ)
① a person in disfavor with his ruler and parents ② an unaided person
孤子(ㄍㄨ ㄗˇ)
a male bereaved of his father
孤哀子(ㄍㄨ ㄞ ㄗˇ)
a male bereaved of both his parents
孤傲(ㄍㄨ ㄠˋ)
proud and aloof
孤兒(ㄍㄨ ㄦˊ)
an orphan
孤兒寡婦(ㄍㄨ ㄦˊ ㄍㄨㄚˇ ㄈㄨˋ)
orphans and widows
孤兒院(ㄍㄨ ㄦˊ ㄩㄢˋ)
an orphanage
孤雲野鶴(ㄍㄨ ㄩㄣˊ ㄧㄝˇ ㄏㄜˋ)
descriptive of the carefreeness of a hermit's life (literally like a lone cloud or a wild crane)

六畫

【孩】1088
ㄏㄞˊ hair hái
1. a child; an infant; a baby
2. young; small
孩提(ㄏㄞˊ ㄊㄧˊ)or 孩抱(ㄏㄞˊ ㄅㄠˋ)
a child that still has to be carried in arms; an infant; childhood

孩童(ㄏㄞˊ ㄊㄨㄥˊ)
a child
孩子(ㄏㄞˊ ·ㄗ)or 孩兒(ㄏㄚˊ ㄦ)
a child
孩子氣(ㄏㄞˊ ·ㄗ ㄑㄧˋ)
childish; childishness

七畫

【孫】1089 ㄙㄨㄣ suen sūn
1. a grandchild; a descendant: 曾孫 a great-grandson
2. a Chinese family name
孫女(ㄙㄨㄣ ㄋㄩˇ)
a granddaughter
孫權(ㄙㄨㄣ ㄑㄩㄢˊ)
Sun Chüan, ruler of the state of Wu(吳) during the Epoch of the Three Kingdoms
孫媳(ㄙㄨㄣ ㄒㄧˊ)or 孫媳婦(ㄙㄨㄣ ㄒㄧˊ ㄈㄨˋ)
a granddaughter-in-law; a grandson's wife
孫壻 or 孫婿(ㄙㄨㄣ ㄒㄩˋ)
a grandson-in-law
孫中山(ㄙㄨㄣ ㄓㄨㄥ ㄕㄢ)or 孫逸仙(ㄙㄨㄣ ㄧˋ ㄒㄧㄢ)or 孫文(ㄙㄨㄣ ㄨㄣˊ)
Dr. Sun Yat-sen, father of the Republic of China
孫子(ㄙㄨㄣ ㄗˇ)or 孫武(ㄙㄨㄣ ㄨˇ)
Sun Tzu, a pre-Chin strategist, noted for his book, *The Art of War*
孫子兵法(ㄙㄨㄣ ㄗˇ ㄅㄧㄥ ㄈㄚˇ)
The Art of War by Sun Tzu: 孫子兵法已被譯成英文。*The Art of War* by Sun Tzu was translated into English.
孫子(ㄙㄨㄣ ·ㄗ)or 孫兒(ㄙㄨㄣ ㄦˊ)
① a grandchild ② a grandson

八畫

【孰】1090 ㄕㄨˊ shwu shú
1. (in literary texts) what; which: 是可忍也，孰不可忍也? If he can bear to do this, what may he not bear to do?
2. who; whom
孰是孰非(ㄕㄨˊ ㄕˋ ㄕㄨˊ ㄈㄟ)
Which is right and which is wrong?
孰勝孰負(ㄕㄨˊ ㄕㄥˋ ㄕㄨˊ ㄈㄨˋ)
Who wins and who loses?
孰若(ㄕㄨˊ ㄖㄨㄛˋ)
what is better than; it would be better to

九畫

【孱】1091 ㄔㄢˊ charn chán
weak; feeble; frail
孱夫(ㄔㄢˊ ㄈㄨ)or 孱頭(ㄔㄢˊ ㄊㄡˊ)
a cowardly person; a weakling
孱弱(ㄔㄢˊ ㄖㄨㄛˋ)
feeble; weak; frail: 他是孱弱的老人。He is a feeble old man.

【孳】1092 ㄗ tzy zī
1. to bear or beget in large numbers
2. to work with sustained diligence
孳息(ㄗ ㄒㄧˊ)
① to grow ② interest (from money)
孳生(ㄗ ㄕㄥ)
to grow and multiply: 園中孳生綠草。Green grass grows in the garden.
孳乳(ㄗ ㄖㄨˇ)
to bear or beget abundantly; to grow and multiply
孳孳(ㄗ ㄗ)
working with sustained diligence
孳孳爲利(ㄗ ㄗ ㄨㄟˊ ㄌㄧˋ)
to work hard from morning till night for money
孳孳爲善(ㄗ ㄗ ㄨㄟˊ ㄕㄢˋ)
to persevere in doing good
孳衍(ㄗ ㄧㄢˇ)
to grow in number; to multiply

十一畫

【孵】1093 ㄈㄨ fu fū
1. to hatch (eggs); to incubate
2. to emerge from eggs or spawn
孵卵(ㄈㄨ ㄌㄨㄢˇ)
to hatch eggs; to incubate
孵卵器(ㄈㄨ ㄌㄨㄢˇ ㄑㄧˋ)
an incubator
孵化(ㄈㄨ ㄏㄨㄚˋ)
to emerge from eggs; to spawn

十三畫

【學】1094 ㄒㄩㄝˊ shyue xué (語音 ㄒㄧㄠˊ shyau xiáo)
1. to learn; to study; to imitate: 活到老學到老。It's never too late to learn.
2. of or having to do with learning; academic
學報(ㄒㄩㄝˊ ㄅㄠˋ)
an academic journal; a journal: 他訂了幾份學報。He subscribed some journals.
學步(ㄒㄩㄝˊ ㄅㄨˋ)
(said of a child) to learn to walk
學不像(ㄒㄩㄝˊ ·ㄅㄨ ㄒㄧㄤˋ)or 學不會(ㄒㄩㄝˊ ·ㄅㄨ ㄏㄨㄟˋ)or 學不來(ㄒㄩㄝˊ ·ㄅㄨ ㄌㄞˊ)
to try to imitate or copy in vain
學不厭(ㄒㄩㄝˊ ·ㄅㄨ ㄧㄢˋ)
to learn with indefatigable zeal; tireless in learning
學不完(ㄒㄩㄝˊ ·ㄅㄨ ㄨㄢˊ)
to have an endless amount to learn
學派(ㄒㄩㄝˊ ㄆㄞˋ)
a school (of thought): 他屬於康德學派。He belongs to the Kantian school.
學名(ㄒㄩㄝˊ ㄇㄧㄥˊ)
① the scientific name (of a plant, an animal, etc.) ② a name given to one on beginning school life
學閥(ㄒㄩㄝˊ ㄈㄚˊ)
an academic clique
學費(ㄒㄩㄝˊ ㄈㄟˋ)
tuition
學分(ㄒㄩㄝˊ ㄈㄣ)
units, credits, or semester hours (of course work to meet degree requirements)
學風(ㄒㄩㄝˊ ㄈㄥ)
school discipline; school traditions
學府(ㄒㄩㄝˊ ㄈㄨˇ)
a seat of learning; an insti-

〔子部〕

tute of higher learning: 哈佛大學是著名的學府。Harvard University is a famous institute of higher learning.
學得不錯(ㄒㄩㄝˊ ˙ㄉㄜ ㄅㄨˋ ㄘㄨㄛˋ)or 學得不壞(ㄒㄩㄝˊ ˙ㄉㄜ ㄅㄨˋ ㄏㄨㄞˋ)
to imitate or copy with creditable result
學得像(ㄒㄩㄝˊ ˙ㄉㄜ ㄒㄧㄤˋ)
to imitate or copy with marked skill
學到老，學不了(ㄒㄩㄝˊ ㄉㄠˋ ㄌㄠˇ, ㄒㄩㄝˊ ˙ㄅㄨ ㄌㄧㄠˇ)
Learning is an endless process.
學店(ㄒㄩㄝˊ ㄉㄧㄢˋ)
a school that indulges in making money in total disregard of the students' scholastic progress
學堂(ㄒㄩㄝˊ ㄊㄤˊ)
a school
學徒(ㄒㄩㄝˊ ㄊㄨˊ)
① an apprentice ② a student
學徒制(ㄒㄩㄝˊ ㄊㄨˊ ㄓˋ)
apprenticeship
學童(ㄒㄩㄝˊ ㄊㄨㄥˊ)
school children; primary school students
學年(ㄒㄩㄝˊ ㄋㄧㄢˊ)
an academic year; a school year
學理(ㄒㄩㄝˊ ㄌㄧˇ)
a (scientific) theory
學力(ㄒㄩㄝˊ ㄌㄧˋ)
scholastic ability; scholarship
學歷(ㄒㄩㄝˊ ㄌㄧˋ)
educational background; record of formal schooling
學齡(ㄒㄩㄝˊ ㄌㄧㄥˊ)
school age
學齡前兒童(ㄒㄩㄝˊ ㄌㄧㄥˊ ㄑㄧㄢˊ ㄦˊ ㄊㄨㄥˊ)
preschool children; preschoolers
學齡兒童(ㄒㄩㄝˊ ㄌㄧㄥˊ ㄦˊ ㄊㄨㄥˊ)
school-age children
學館 or 學舘(ㄒㄩㄝˊ ㄍㄨㄢˇ)
a school (usually a small one for private tutoring)
學科(ㄒㄩㄝˊ ㄎㄜ)
a subject; a course (of study or instruction at school): 你最喜歡那一學科? Which course do you like most?
學海(ㄒㄩㄝˊ ㄏㄞˇ)
the sea of learning
學好(ㄒㄩㄝˊ ㄏㄠˇ)
to learn from good examples; to emulate one's betters
學會(ㄒㄩㄝˊ ㄏㄨㄟˋ)
① a learned society; an institute ② to succeed in learning (a skill): 她學會溜冰。She's learned to skate.
學籍(ㄒㄩㄝˊ ㄐㄧˊ)
one's status as a student of a particular school
學級(ㄒㄩㄝˊ ㄐㄧˊ)
grade or form (division of years in a school curriculum)
學界(ㄒㄩㄝˊ ㄐㄧㄝˋ)
the academic circles
學究(ㄒㄩㄝˊ ㄐㄧㄡˋ)
a pedagogue; a pedant; an egghead
學期(ㄒㄩㄝˊ ㄑㄧˊ)
a (school) term; a semester; a quarter: 一年中有兩個學期。There are two semesters in a year.
學前教育(ㄒㄩㄝˊ ㄑㄧㄢˊ ㄐㄧㄠˋ ㄩˋ)
preschool education; infant school education: 他專習學前教育。He majors in preschool education.
學區(ㄒㄩㄝˊ ㄑㄩ)
a school district
學習(ㄒㄩㄝˊ ㄒㄧˊ)
to learn; to study: 你應當學習如何忍耐。You ought to learn how to be patient.
學校(ㄒㄩㄝˊ ㄒㄧㄠˋ)
a school (for education)
學行(ㄒㄩㄝˊ ㄒㄧㄥˋ)
scholastic and moral performance
學制(ㄒㄩㄝˊ ㄓˋ)
an educational system
學者(ㄒㄩㄝˊ ㄓㄜˇ)
a scholar; a learned person
學長(ㄒㄩㄝˊ ㄓㄤˇ)
① one's senior at school ② the head of a department or division (in a college or university under a now obsolete system)
學潮(ㄒㄩㄝˊ ㄔㄠˊ)
a student strike; a campus commotion
學時髦(ㄒㄩㄝˊ ㄕˊ ㄇㄠˊ)
to follow the fashion: 他這樣做是學時髦。He follows the fashion to do this.
學士(ㄒㄩㄝˊ ㄕˋ)
a holder of the bachelor's degree
學士服(ㄒㄩㄝˊ ㄕˋ ㄈㄨˊ)
academicals
學識(ㄒㄩㄝˊ ㄕˋ)
erudition; learning; scholarship; academic attainments: 常識比學識更有價值。Common sense is worth more than learning.
學舌(ㄒㄩㄝˊ ㄕㄜˊ)
to mimic; to parrot
學舍(ㄒㄩㄝˊ ㄕㄜˋ)
a school building
學生(ㄒㄩㄝˊ ㄕㄥ)
a student; a pupil
學生會(ㄒㄩㄝˊ ㄕㄥ ㄏㄨㄟˋ)
a student union; a student association
學生證(ㄒㄩㄝˊ ㄕㄥ ㄓㄥˋ)
a student's identity card
學生時代(ㄒㄩㄝˊ ㄕㄥ ㄕˊ ㄉㄞˋ)
school days
學生自治會(ㄒㄩㄝˊ ㄕㄥ ㄗˋ ㄓˋ ㄏㄨㄟˋ)
a student government
學生運動(ㄒㄩㄝˊ ㄕㄥ ㄩㄣˋ ㄉㄨㄥˋ)
a student movement
學術(ㄒㄩㄝˊ ㄕㄨˋ)
learning; science
學術風氣(ㄒㄩㄝˊ ㄕㄨˋ ㄈㄥ ㄑㄧˋ)
academic atmosphere
學術地位(ㄒㄩㄝˊ ㄕㄨˋ ㄉㄧˋ ㄨㄟˋ)
academic position or standing
學術團體(ㄒㄩㄝˊ ㄕㄨˋ ㄊㄨㄢˊ ㄊㄧˇ)
a learned organization; an academic organization
學術論文(ㄒㄩㄝˊ ㄕㄨˋ ㄌㄨㄣˋ ㄨㄣˊ)
a research paper; a thesis
學術界(ㄒㄩㄝˊ ㄕㄨˋ ㄐㄧㄝˋ)
academic circles
學術自由(ㄒㄩㄝˊ ㄕㄨˋ ㄗˋ ㄧㄡˊ)
academic freedom
學術研究(ㄒㄩㄝˊ ㄕㄨˋ ㄧㄢˊ ㄐㄧㄡˋ)
an academic approach
學術演講(ㄒㄩㄝˊ ㄕㄨˋ ㄧㄢˇ ㄐㄧㄤˇ)
an academic lecture
學說(ㄒㄩㄝˊ ㄕㄨㄛ)
a theory
學然後知不足(ㄒㄩㄝˊ ㄖㄢˊ ㄏㄡˋ ㄓ ㄅㄨˋ ㄗㄨˊ)
One discovers his ignorance

only through learning.

學人(ㄒㄩㄝˊ ㄖㄣˊ)
a scholar

學如逆水行舟(ㄒㄩㄝˊ ㄖㄨˊ ㄋㄧˋ ㄕㄨㄟˇ ㄒㄧㄥˊ ㄓㄡ)
(literally) Learning is like sailing a boat upstream.—either to keep progressing or to be washed backward

學子(ㄒㄩㄝˊ ㄗˇ)
a student

學而不厭(ㄒㄩㄝˊ ㄦˊ ㄅㄨˋ ㄧㄢˋ)
to have an insatiable thirst for knowledge

學而優則仕(ㄒㄩㄝˊ ㄦˊ ㄧㄡ ㄗㄜˊ ㄕˋ)
Excellence in scholarship leads to officialdom.

學以致用(ㄒㄩㄝˊ ㄧˇ ㄓˋ ㄩㄥˋ)
to make use of what one has learned

學藝(ㄒㄩㄝˊ ㄧˋ)
① sciences and arts ② to learn a trade

學業(ㄒㄩㄝˊ ㄧㄝˋ)
school work: 她的學業很重。Her school work is very heavy.

學業成績(ㄒㄩㄝˊ ㄧㄝˋ ㄔㄥˊ ㄐㄧ)
scholastic achievements (or attainments)

學友(ㄒㄩㄝˊ ㄧㄡˇ)
a schoolmate; a fellow student

學有專長(ㄒㄩㄝˊ ㄧㄡˇ ㄓㄨㄢ ㄔㄤˊ)
to have acquired a speciality from study

學樣(ㄒㄩㄝˊ ㄧㄤˋ)
to imitate someone's example

學無止境(ㄒㄩㄝˊ ㄨˊ ㄓˇ ㄐㄧㄥˋ)
There is no limit to knowledge.

學位(ㄒㄩㄝˊ ㄨㄟˋ)
an academic degree

學問(ㄒㄩㄝˊ ㄨㄣˋ)
learning; scholarship; erudition: 他的學問很淵博。The range of his erudition is wide.

學院(ㄒㄩㄝˊ ㄩㄢˋ)
① a college (in a university) ② an academy

十四畫

【孺】 1095 ㄖㄨˊ ru rú
a young child; an infant

孺慕(ㄖㄨˊ ㄇㄨˋ)
to adore someone as a child adores its parents; to love and respect very much

孺子(ㄖㄨˊ ㄗˇ)
a child; a boy: 孺子可教也。That boy is teachable!

十七畫

【孽】 1096 (孼) ㄋㄧㄝˋ nieh niè
1. the son of a concubine
2. a monster
3. sin; evil

孽黨(ㄋㄧㄝˋ ㄉㄤˇ)
the members of a traitorous party, band, etc.

孽障(ㄋㄧㄝˋ ㄓㄤˋ)
①(a term of abuse formerly used by the elders of a family cursing their juniors) an evil creature; vile spawn; wicked children ② (Buddhism) karmic obstruction; retribution for the evil one is supposed to have committed

孽種(ㄋㄧㄝˋ ㄓㄨㄥˇ)
① the seeds of misfortune ② a child born of adultery; a bastard

孽子(ㄋㄧㄝˋ ㄗˇ)
① a son born of a concubine ② a sinner

十九畫

【孿】 1097 ㄌㄩㄢˊ liuan luán
twin

孿生(ㄌㄩㄢˊ ㄕㄥ)or 孿子(ㄌㄩㄢˊ ㄗˇ) or 孿伴兒(ㄌㄩㄢˊ ㄅㄚˋㄦ)
born as twins; to bear twins

宀部
ㄇㄧㄢˊ myan mián

二畫

【宄】 1098 ㄍㄨㄟˇ goei guǐ
a treacherous fellow; a traitor; a thief

【它】 1099 ㄊㄚ ta tā (讀音 ㄊㄨㄛ tuo tuō)
it; that; this: 狗到哪兒去了?它在房裏。Where is the dog? It is in the room.

它們(ㄊㄚ ·ㄇㄣ)
they

【宁】 1100 ㄓㄨˋ juh zhù
1. to store; to save; to stockpile
2. to stand

【宂】 1101 ㄖㄨㄥˇ roong rǒng
1. redundant; superfluous
2. disorderly

宂筆(ㄖㄨㄥˇ ㄅㄧˇ)
① verbosity in writing ② unnecessary strokes in painting

宂費(ㄖㄨㄥˇ ㄈㄟˋ)
unnecessary expenses

宂長(ㄖㄨㄥˇ ㄓㄤˇ)or(ㄖㄨㄥˇ ㄔㄤˊ)or 宂贅(ㄖㄨㄥˇ ㄓㄨㄟˋ)
① redundant; superfluous; supernumerary ② (said of writing) redundant; verbose ③ tediously long

宂雜(ㄖㄨㄥˇ ㄗㄚˊ)
confused; mixed up; disorderly: 他討厭宂雜的房子。He disliked a disorderly room.

宂詞(ㄖㄨㄥˇ ㄘˊ)
superfluous words

宂散(ㄖㄨㄥˇ ㄙㄢˇ)
leisurely; relaxed

宂員(ㄖㄨㄥˇ ㄩㄢˊ)
the superfluous members of a staff or organization; a supernumerary

三畫

【宅】 1102 ㄓㄞˊ jair zhái (讀音 ㄓㄜˋ jeh zhè)
a dwelling; a residence; a house

宅門(ㄓㄞˊ ㄇㄣˊ)
① the gate of an old-style big house ② the family living in such a house

宅第(ㄓㄞˊ ㄉㄧˋ)
a mansion

宅眷(ㄓㄞˊ ㄐㄩㄢˋ)
one's dependents

宅心(ㄓㄞˊ ㄒㄧㄣ)
intention

宅心仁厚(ㄓㄞˊ ㄒㄧㄣ ㄖㄣˊ ㄏㄡˋ)
a benevolent and generous nature

宅神(ㄓㄞˊ ㄕㄣˊ)
household deities; the patron gods of a household

宅子(ㄓㄞˊ ·ㄗ)
a residence; a house: 我的宅子很小。My house is quite small.

宅院(ㄓㄞˊ ㄩㄢˋ)
a house with a courtyard; a house: 他在鄉下有一座宅院。He has a house in the country.

【宇】 1103 ㄩˇ yeu yǔ
1. a house; a roof
2. look; appearance; countenance
3. space

宇內(ㄩˇ ㄋㄟˋ)
in the country; in the world

宇宙(ㄩˇ ㄓㄡˋ)
the universe: 我們的世界只是宇宙的一小部分。Our world is but a small part of the universe.

宇宙爆(ㄩˇ ㄓㄡˋ ㄅㄠˋ)
a cosmic burst

宇宙通訊(ㄩˇ ㄓㄡˋ ㄊㄨㄥ ㄒㄩㄣˋ)
cosmic communication

宇宙論(ㄩˇ ㄓㄡˋ ㄌㄨㄣˋ)
cosmology

宇宙線(ㄩˇ ㄓㄡˋ ㄒㄧㄢˋ)or 宇宙射線(ㄩˇ ㄓㄡˋ ㄕㄜˋ ㄒㄧㄢˋ)
cosmic rays; cosmic radiations

宇宙塵(ㄩˇ ㄓㄡˋ ㄔㄣˊ)
(astronomy) meteoroid

宇宙噪音(ㄩˇ ㄓㄡˋ ㄗㄠˋ ㄧㄣ)
cosmic noise

宇宙速度(ㄩˇ ㄓㄡˋ ㄙㄨˋ ㄉㄨˋ)
cosmic velocity

宇宙醫學(ㄩˇ ㄓㄡˋ ㄧ ㄒㄩㄝˊ)
cosmic or space medicine

宇宙微粒(ㄩˇ ㄓㄡˋ ㄨㄟˊ ㄌㄧˋ)
a cosmic particle

宇宙衛星(ㄩˇ ㄓㄡˋ ㄨㄟˋ ㄒㄧㄥ)
a cosmos satellite

【守】 1104 ㄕㄡˇ shoou shǒu
1. to guard; to protect; to defend; to watch
2. to wait
3. to keep (a secret, etc.)
4. to stick to; to maintain
5. to abide by

守備(ㄕㄡˇ ㄅㄟˋ)
to be on garrison duty; garrison: 守備部隊 garrison force

守門(ㄕㄡˇ ㄇㄣˊ)
to watch the door against burglars

守門員(ㄕㄡˇ ㄇㄣˊ ㄩㄢˊ)
(football) a goalkeeper

守秘密(ㄕㄡˇ ㄇㄧˋ ㄇㄧˋ)
to keep a secret: 這件事你最好守秘密。You had better keep the matter secret.

守法(ㄕㄡˇ ㄈㄚˇ)
to abide by the law

守分(ㄕㄡˇ ㄈㄣˋ)
to be content with one's lot; to stick to what one is suited for

守土(ㄕㄡˇ ㄊㄨˇ)
① to defend the country ② to take care of a locality (as a local official in former times)

守壘員(ㄕㄡˇ ㄌㄟˇ ㄩㄢˊ)
(baseball) a baseman

守靈(ㄕㄡˇ ㄌㄧㄥˊ)
to stand as guards at the bier

守寡(ㄕㄡˇ ㄍㄨㄚˇ)
to remain in widowhood

守口如瓶(ㄕㄡˇ ㄎㄡˇ ㄖㄨˊ ㄆㄧㄥˊ)
to keep one's mouth shut

守候(ㄕㄡˇ ㄏㄡˋ)
to wait; to bide one's time

守護(ㄕㄡˇ ㄏㄨˋ)
to guard; to protect

守紀律(ㄕㄡˇ ㄐㄧˋ ㄌㄩˋ)
to observe the rules; to behave in accordance with the regulations

守節(ㄕㄡˇ ㄐㄧㄝˊ)or 守貞(ㄕㄡˇ ㄓㄣ)
① to remain a widow forever although one is still young ② to stick to principle

守舊(ㄕㄡˇ ㄐㄧㄡˋ)
resistant to advances; sticking to old ways; conservative: 老年人通常比青年人更守舊。Old people are usually more conservative than young people.

守將(ㄕㄡˇ ㄐㄧㄤˋ)
the commanding general in charge of the defense of a city or strategic point

守更(ㄕㄡˇ ㄐㄧㄥ)
to keep watch during the night

守軍(ㄕㄡˇ ㄐㄩㄣ)
defending troops; defenders

守孝(ㄕㄡˇ ㄒㄧㄠˋ)
to be in mourning for one's parent

守信(ㄕㄡˇ ㄒㄧㄣˋ)or 守信用(ㄕㄡˇ ㄒㄧㄣˋ ㄩㄥˋ)
to keep promises; to honor one's words: 人人都應該守信。Everyone should keep his promises.

守職(ㄕㄡˇ ㄓˊ)
to stick to one's duty

守制(ㄕㄡˇ ㄓˋ)
to remain in mourning for one's parent

守正不阿(ㄕㄡˇ ㄓㄥˋ ㄅㄨˋ ㄜ)
to stick to justice or fairness despite pressure

守株待兔(ㄕㄡˇ ㄓㄨ ㄉㄞˋ ㄊㄨˋ)
(originally said of a farmer) to wait by the stump hoping other hares will come by the spot because he once caught a hare there—stupid and unimaginative in doing things

守住(ㄕㄡˇ ㄓㄨˋ)
to hold (a city or position)

守拙(ㄕㄡˇ ㄓㄨㄛˊ)
to be content with one's coarseness; to remain free from ambitions

守中立(ㄕㄡˇ ㄓㄨㄥ ㄌㄧˋ)
to maintain neutrality; to keep away from disputes or conflicts

守車(ㄕㄡˇ ㄔㄜ)
a caboose (of a freight train)

守成(ㄕㄡˇ ㄔㄥˊ)
to keep what one has already accomplished; (usually said of property) to preserve what is handed down by one's ancestors

守成不變(ㄕㄡˇ ㄔㄥˊ ㄅㄨˋ ㄅㄧㄢˋ)
holding to existing custom; reluctant to accept changes: 他唯一的缺點是守成不變。The

only defect he has is that he is reluctant to accept changes.

守城(ㄕㄡˇ ㄔㄥˊ)
to defend a city

守時(ㄕㄡˇ ㄕˊ)
punctual

守身如玉(ㄕㄡˇ ㄕㄣ ㄖㄨˊ ㄩˋ)
to keep one's integrity intact in adversity

守則(ㄕㄡˇ ㄗㄜˊ)
rules; regulations: 工作守則 work regulations

守財奴(ㄕㄡˇ ㄘㄞˊ ㄋㄨˊ)
a miser; a niggard

守喪(ㄕㄡˇ ㄙㄤ)
to remain in mourning for one's parent

守歲(ㄕㄡˇ ㄙㄨㄟˋ)
to see the old year out and the new year in by staying up on the Lunar New Year's Eve

守夜(ㄕㄡˇ ㄧㄝˋ)
to keep night watch

守夜者(ㄕㄡˇ ㄧㄝˋ ㄓㄜˇ)
a watchman

守衛(ㄕㄡˇ ㄨㄟˋ)
to guard; a guard

守望(ㄕㄡˇ ㄨㄤˋ)
to keep watch

守望台(ㄕㄡˇ ㄨㄤˋ ㄊㄞˊ)
a watchtower

守望相助(ㄕㄡˇ ㄨㄤˋ ㄒㄧㄤ ㄓㄨˋ)
(said of neighbors in a community) to help each other in guarding against enemies

守約(ㄕㄡˇ ㄩㄝ)
to keep a promise; to honor a pledge: 你應該守約。You should honor your pledge.

【安】 1105
ㄢ an ān

1. peaceful; quiet; calm; tranquil
2. to quiet; to stabilize; to pacify; to console
3. to put; to place; to arrange
4. to be content with
5. how; why: 安能袖手旁觀? How can one stand by and do nothing?
6. safe; secure; stable
7. a Chinese family name

安邦定國(ㄢ ㄅㄤ ㄉㄧㄥˋ ㄍㄨㄛˊ)
(said of a ruler) to give peace and stability to the country

安步當車(ㄢ ㄅㄨˋ ㄉㄤˋ ㄐㄩ)
① to be content to go on foot instead of riding in a vehicle ② to be content with a simple life

安排(ㄢ ㄆㄞˊ)
arrangements; to arrange; to make arrangements for: 在離開之前，他把業務都安排好了。Before going away, he arranged his business affairs.

安培(ㄢ ㄆㄟˊ)
an ampere

安培計(ㄢ ㄆㄟˊ ㄐㄧˋ)
an ammeter

安貧樂道(ㄢ ㄆㄧㄣˊ ㄌㄜˋ ㄉㄠˋ)
happy to lead a simple, virtuous life: 他安貧樂道。He is happy to lead a simple, virtuous life.

安平古堡(ㄢ ㄆㄧㄥˊ ㄍㄨˇ ㄅㄠˇ)
Fort Zeelandia in Taiwan, built by the Dutch in the 17th century

安眠(ㄢ ㄇㄧㄢˊ)
to sleep peacefully

安眠藥(ㄢ ㄇㄧㄢˊ ㄧㄠˋ)
sleeping pills; hypnotics; soporifics

安民(ㄢ ㄇㄧㄣˊ)
to quiet the people; (after conquering a city) to give peace to the people

安民告示(ㄢ ㄇㄧㄣˊ ㄍㄠˋ ㄕˋ)
a notice to reassure the public

安命(ㄢ ㄇㄧㄥˋ)
content with one's lot; to accept one's lot

安非他命(ㄢ ㄈㄟ ㄊㄚ ㄇㄧㄥˋ)
amphetamine

安分(ㄢ ㄈㄣˋ)
do not go beyond one's bounds; to be law-abiding

安分守己(ㄢ ㄈㄣˋ ㄕㄡˇ ㄐㄧˇ)
content or happy to be what one is; law-abiding: 他們是安分守己的良民。They are law-abiding people.

安放(ㄢ ㄈㄤˋ)
to put in a proper manner; to lay (a keel, etc.)

安撫(ㄢ ㄈㄨˇ) or 安覆(ㄢ ㄈㄨˋ)
to pacify

安富尊榮(ㄢ ㄈㄨˋ ㄗㄨㄣ ㄖㄨㄥˊ)
to enjoy wealth and honor

安打(ㄢ ㄉㄚˇ)
(baseball) a safe hit, a safety hit, or a safety: 那是一支很巧妙的安打。That was a very clever safe hit.

安得(ㄢ ㄉㄜˊ)
How can it be? 或 How could it be?

安道爾(ㄢ ㄉㄠˋ ㄦˇ)
Andorra, a small republic hemmed in by France and Spain

安第斯山脈(ㄢ ㄉㄧˋ ㄙ ㄕㄢ ㄇㄞˋ) or 安廸斯山脈(ㄢ ㄉㄧˊ ㄙ ㄕㄢ ㄇㄛˋ)
the Andes Mountains in South America

安定(ㄢ ㄉㄧㄥˋ)
stable; steadfast; unchanging; to stabilize; stability

安定團結(ㄢ ㄉㄧㄥˋ ㄊㄨㄢˊ ㄐㄧㄝˊ)
stability and unity

安定社會秩序(ㄢ ㄉㄧㄥˋ ㄕㄜˋ ㄏㄨㄟˋ ㄓˋ ㄒㄩˋ)
to maintain social order

安定人心(ㄢ ㄉㄧㄥˋ ㄖㄣˊ ㄒㄧㄣ)
to reassure the public

安頓(ㄢ ㄉㄨㄣˋ)
to put in order; to help settle down; to make proper arrangement (for the family before leaving home for a long period of time)

安東(ㄢ ㄉㄨㄥ)
① Antung Province ② Antung city

安特衛普(ㄢ ㄊㄜˋ ㄨㄟˋ ㄆㄨˇ)
Antwerp, a seaport in northern Belgium

安胎藥(ㄢ ㄊㄞ ㄧㄠˋ)
the medicine given to a pregnant woman to prevent miscarriage

安泰(ㄢ ㄊㄞˋ)
healthy; in good health

安徒生(ㄢ ㄊㄨˊ ㄕㄥ)
Hans Christian Andersen, 1805-1875, Danish writer

安土重遷(ㄢ ㄊㄨˇ ㄓㄨㄥˋ ㄑㄧㄢ)
to be attached to one's native land and unwilling to leave it

安內攘外(ㄢ ㄋㄟˋ ㄖㄤˇ ㄨㄞˋ)
to maintain internal security and to expel foreign invasion

安南(ㄢ ㄋㄢˊ)

Annam
安寧(ㄢ ㄋㄧㄥˊ)
peace; repose; tranquility
安樂(ㄢ ㄌㄜˋ)
comfort: 她在兒女那裏得到安樂。She finds comfort in her children.
安樂國(ㄢ ㄌㄜˋ ㄍㄨㄛˊ)
a Utopia; (Buddhism) Paradise
安樂死(ㄢ ㄌㄜˋ ㄙˇ)
euthanasia
安老院(ㄢ ㄌㄠˇ ㄩㄢˋ)
a home for the old people
安理會(ㄢ ㄌㄧˇ ㄏㄨㄟˋ)or 安全理事會(ㄢ ㄑㄩㄢˊ ㄌㄧˇ ㄕˋ ㄏㄨㄟˋ)
the Security Council (of the United Nations)
安哥拉(ㄢ ㄍㄜ ㄌㄚ)
Angola
安哥拉人(ㄢ ㄍㄜ ㄌㄚ ㄖㄣˊ)
an Angolan
安固 (ㄢ ㄍㄨˋ)
secure
安卡拉(ㄢ ㄎㄚˇ ㄌㄚ)
Ankara, capital of Turkey
安康(ㄢ ㄎㄤ)
in a state of peace and good health: 祝您安康。I wish you the best of health.
安好(ㄢ ㄏㄠˇ)
enjoying peace and good health; well; safe and sound: 全家安好，請勿掛念。You will be pleased to know that everyone in the family is safe and sound.
安徽(ㄢ ㄏㄨㄟ)
Anhwei Province
安魂曲(ㄢ ㄏㄨㄣˊ ㄑㄩˇ)
(music) a requiem
安家(ㄢ ㄐㄧㄚ)
① to insure the welfare of one's family ② to set up a household (by marriage)
安家費(ㄢ ㄐㄧㄚ ㄈㄟˋ)
allowances for the support of dependents (given to draftees or officials assigned to overseas posts)
安家落戶(ㄢ ㄐㄧㄚ ㄌㄨㄛˋ ㄏㄨˋ)
to make one's home in a place; to settle
安靜(ㄢ ㄐㄧㄥˋ)
quiet; tranquil; still; peaceful: 請保持安靜。Keep quiet.
安居樂業(ㄢ ㄐㄩ ㄌㄜˋ ㄧㄝˋ)or 安家樂業(ㄢ ㄐㄧㄚ ㄌㄜˋ ㄧㄝˋ)
(said of people under a good government) to live and work in peace and content
安琪兒(ㄢ ㄑㄧˊ ㄦˊ)
an angel
安慶(ㄢ ㄑㄧㄥˋ)
Anching, capital of Anhwei Province
安全(ㄢ ㄑㄩㄢˊ)
① safe; secure ② safety; security
安全玻璃(ㄢ ㄑㄩㄢˊ ㄅㄛ ·ㄌㄧ)
safety glass
安全瓣(ㄢ ㄑㄩㄢˊ ㄅㄢˋ)
a safety valve
安全別針(ㄢ ㄑㄩㄢˊ ㄅㄧㄝˊ ㄓㄣ)
a safety pin
安全帽(ㄢ ㄑㄩㄢˊ ㄇㄠˋ)
a safety helmet
安全門(ㄢ ㄑㄩㄢˊ ㄇㄣˊ)
an exit
安全閥(ㄢ ㄑㄩㄢˊ ㄈㄚˊ)
a safety valve
安全帶(ㄢ ㄑㄩㄢˊ ㄉㄞˋ)
a safety belt (or strap): 請繫上安全帶。Tie your safety belt, please.
安全島(ㄢ ㄑㄩㄢˊ ㄉㄠˇ)
a traffic island
安全燈(ㄢ ㄑㄩㄢˊ ㄉㄥ)
a miner's lamp; a safety lamp
安全地帶(ㄢ ㄑㄩㄢˊ ㄉㄧˋ ㄉㄞˋ)
a safety zone
安全第一(ㄢ ㄑㄩㄢˊ ㄉㄧˋ ㄧ)
safety first
安全梯(ㄢ ㄑㄩㄢˊ ㄊㄧ)
an emergency staircase
安全剃刀(ㄢ ㄑㄩㄢˊ ㄊㄧˋ ㄉㄠ)
a safety razor
安全理事會(ㄢ ㄑㄩㄢˊ ㄌㄧˇ ㄕˋ ㄏㄨㄟˋ)
the Security Council參看「安理會」
安全感(ㄢ ㄑㄩㄢˊ ㄍㄢˇ)
a sense of security
安全開關(ㄢ ㄑㄩㄢˊ ㄎㄞ ㄍㄨㄢ)
a safety switch
安全火柴(ㄢ ㄑㄩㄢˊ ㄏㄨㄛˇ ㄔㄞˊ)
a safety match
安全期(ㄢ ㄑㄩㄢˊ ㄑㄧˊ)
a safe period
安全期避孕法(ㄢ ㄑㄩㄢˊ ㄑㄧˊ ㄅㄧˋ ㄩㄣˋ ㄈㄚˇ)
rhythm method
安全系統(ㄢ ㄑㄩㄢˊ ㄒㄧˋ ㄊㄨㄥˇ)
the fail-safe system
安全設施(ㄢ ㄑㄩㄢˊ ㄕㄜˋ ㄕ)
safety devices (or equipment, installations)
安全操作(ㄢ ㄑㄩㄢˊ ㄘㄠ ㄗㄨㄛˋ)
safe operation
安全措施(ㄢ ㄑㄩㄢˊ ㄘㄨㄛˋ ㄕ)
safety measures (or precautions)
安全存量(ㄢ ㄑㄩㄢˊ ㄘㄨㄣˊ ㄌㄧㄤˋ)
safety stock
安全因素(ㄢ ㄑㄩㄢˊ ㄧㄣ ㄙㄨˋ)
the factor of security
安息(ㄢ ㄒㄧˊ)
① to rest ② Parthia, an ancient country in W. Asia
安息年(ㄢ ㄒㄧˊ ㄋㄧㄢˊ)
a sabbatical year
安息香(ㄢ ㄒㄧˊ ㄒㄧㄤ)
benzoin
安息日(ㄢ ㄒㄧˊ ㄖˋ)
the Sabbath
安息油(ㄢ ㄒㄧˊ ㄧㄡˊ)
benzol
安歇(ㄢ ㄒㄧㄝ)
to retire for the night; to rest; to sleep
安閒(ㄢ ㄒㄧㄢˊ)
leisure; relaxation
安閒無事(ㄢ ㄒㄧㄢˊ ㄨˊ ㄕˋ)
to have no work or duties
安心(ㄢ ㄒㄧㄣ)
to have peace of mind; to be relieved: 聽到這消息,他就安心了。He was relieved at the news.
安詳(ㄢ ㄒㄧㄤˊ)or 安舒(ㄢ ㄕㄨ)
(said of one's manner) undisturbed; composed
安知非福(ㄢ ㄓ ㄈㄟ ㄈㄨˊ)
Who knows it isn't a blessing in disguise?
安置(ㄢ ㄓˋ)
① to put in a proper place: 請把行李安置好。Please put the luggage in the right place. ② to settle (people in need of employment, refugees, etc.)
安置費(ㄢ ㄓˋ ㄈㄟˋ)
settlement allowances
安枕(ㄢ ㄓㄣˇ)
to sleep in peace
安裝(ㄢ ㄓㄨㄤ)

to install (a device): 電話已經安裝好了。The telephone has been installed.
安插(ㄢ ㄔㄚ)
to plant; to get a position (for a person) in an organization: 老闆在公司裡安插了密探。The boss planted a stool pigeon in the company.
安插親信(ㄢ ㄔㄚ ㄑㄧㄣ ㄒㄧㄣˋ)
to put one's trusted fellows in key positions
安史之亂(ㄢ ㄕˇ ㄓ ㄌㄨㄢˋ)
the rebellion of An Lu-shan (安祿山) and Shih Sze-ming (史思明), 755—763A.D., which shook the foundation of the Tang Dynasty
安適(ㄢ ㄕˋ)
peaceful and comfortable
安身(ㄢ ㄕㄣ)
to find settled place for life; to take shelter
安身立命(ㄢ ㄕㄣ ㄌㄧˋ ㄇㄧㄥˋ)
to enjoy peace and stability both physically and spiritually
安神(ㄢ ㄕㄣˊ)
to calm or quiet down the mind
安睡(ㄢ ㄕㄨㄟˋ)
to sleep undisturbedly; to sleep soundly
安然(ㄢ ㄖㄢˊ)
① safely ② peacefully
安然無恙(ㄢ ㄖㄢˊ ㄨˊ ㄧㄤˋ)
completely uninjured; completely free from trouble; safe and sound
安如磐石(ㄢ ㄖㄨˊ ㄆㄢˊ ㄕˊ)
as solid as a rock: 這城堡安如磐石。The castle is as solid as a rock.
安如泰山(ㄢ ㄖㄨˊ ㄊㄞˋ ㄕㄢ)
(literally) as secure as Mt. Tai—not in the slightest danger
安葬(ㄢ ㄗㄤˋ)
to bury (the dead); to inter: 他昨天安葬。He was buried yesterday.
安坐(ㄢ ㄗㄨㄛˋ)
to sit idly (without making any effort)
安安靜靜(ㄢ ㄢ ㄐㄧㄥˋ ㄐㄧㄥˋ)
peaceful and serene
安安穩穩(ㄢ ㄢ ㄨㄣˇ ㄨㄣˇ)or 安穩(ㄢ ㄨㄣˇ)
secure and stable
安逸(ㄢ ㄧˋ)
ease and comfort
安營(ㄢ ㄧㄥˊ)
(said of troops) to bivouac: 士兵在那兒安營至天明。The soldiers bivouacked there until morning.
安營紮寨(ㄢ ㄧㄥˊ ㄓㄚ ㄓㄞˋ)
to pitch a camp; to camp
安危(ㄢ ㄨㄟˊ)
security and danger
安危與共(ㄢ ㄨㄟˊ ㄩˇ ㄍㄨㄥˋ)
to stick together in security as well as in danger
安慰(ㄢ ㄨㄟˋ)
to console; to comfort; to soothe; to show sympathy for
安穩(ㄢ ㄨㄣˇ)
① smoothly: 船走得很安穩。The boat sailed smoothly. ② peacefully: 他睡得很安穩。He slept peacefully.
安於(ㄢ ㄩˊ)
to be content with; to be satisfied with: 我們安於現狀。We are content with things as they are.

四畫

【宋】 1106 ㄙㄨㄥˋ song sòng
1. the Sung Dynasty (960-1279A.D.); of, or having to do with, the Sung Dynasty
2. a state in the Warring States period
3. a Chinese family name
宋本(ㄙㄨㄥˋ ㄅㄣˇ)
a copy (of a book) printed in the Sung Dynasty
宋體字(ㄙㄨㄥˋ ㄊㄧˇ ㄗˋ)
the form of characters prevalent since the Sung Dynasty now used for a printing type
宋學(ㄙㄨㄥˋ ㄒㄩㄝˊ)
the philosophical theories of the scholars of the Sung Dynasty, especially those of Cheng Yi (程頤), Cheng Hao (程顥) and Chu Hsi (朱熹)
宋朝(ㄙㄨㄥˋ ㄔㄠˊ)
the Sung Dynasty (960-1279 A.D.)
宋史(ㄙㄨㄥˋ ㄕˇ)
the *Annals of the Sung Dynasty* (one of the *Twenty-Four Books of History*)
宋儒(ㄙㄨㄥˋ ㄖㄨˊ)
philosophers of the Sung Dynasty
宋詞(ㄙㄨㄥˋ ㄘˊ)
the poetry of the Sung Dynasty (characterized by lines of irregular length)

【完】 1107 ㄨㄢˊ wan wán
1. to finish; to complete; to bring to a conclusion
2. to run out; to use up
3. whole; complete; perfect; intact: 覆巢之下無完卵。When a bird's nest is overturned, no egg can remain complete.
4. a Chinese family name
完備(ㄨㄢˊ ㄅㄟˋ)
complete with everything; having nothing short
完畢(ㄨㄢˊ ㄅㄧˋ)
finished; completed: 第二期工程已經完畢。The second phase of the project has been completed.
完璧(ㄨㄢˊ ㄅㄧˋ)
① something undamaged or intact ② virginity
完璧歸趙(ㄨㄢˊ ㄅㄧˋ ㄍㄨㄟ ㄓㄠˋ)
to return something intact to its owner
完美(ㄨㄢˊ ㄇㄟˇ)
perfect
完美主義(ㄨㄢˊ ㄇㄟˇ ㄓㄨˇ ㄧˋ)
perfectionism
完滿(ㄨㄢˊ ㄇㄢˇ)
(said of meetings, negotiations, etc.) satisfactory; successful: 這會議完滿結束。The conference came to a satisfactory close.
完膚(ㄨㄢˊ ㄈㄨ)
unhurt skin; unscathed skin
完蛋(ㄨㄢˊ ㄉㄢˋ)
(colloquial) ruined; busted; done for: 我們看到那爆炸時以為他完蛋了。When we saw the explosion, we thought he was done for.
完了(ㄨㄢˊ ˙ㄌㄜ)
① finished; completed; over: 你已將你的工作做完了嗎? Have you finished your

〔宀部〕

〔宀部〕

work? ② hopeless; doomed
完糧(ㄨㄢˊ ㄌㄧㄤˊ)
to pay farm tax
完稿(ㄨㄢˊ ㄍㄠˇ)
to finish a piece of writing; to complete the manuscript
完工(ㄨㄢˊ ㄍㄨㄥ)or 完竣(ㄨㄢˊ ㄐㄩㄣˋ)
(said of work, especially of construction work) finished or completed
完好(ㄨㄢˊ ㄏㄠˇ)
flawless; faultless; perfect; in good condition: 瓷器已到，完好無損。The porcelain has arrived in good condition.
完好無缺(ㄨㄢˊ ㄏㄠˇ ㄨˊ ㄑㄩㄝ)
intact; undamaged
完婚(ㄨㄢˊㄏㄨㄣ)or 完姻(ㄨㄢˊ ㄧㄣ)
to get married
完結(ㄨㄢˊ ㄐㄧㄝˊ)
to come to an end; to end
完聚(ㄨㄢˊ ㄐㄩˋ)
(said of all members of the family) to get together
完清(ㄨㄢˊ ㄑㄧㄥ)
to clear off (accounts)
完全(ㄨㄢˊ ㄑㄩㄢˊ)or 完完全全(ㄨㄢˊ ㄨㄢˊ ㄑㄩㄢˊ ㄑㄩㄢˊ)
complete; entire; perfect; thorough; completely; entirely; fully; totally; thoroughly: 她完全同意我們的意見。She fully agrees with us.
完全獨佔(ㄨㄢˊ ㄑㄩㄢˊ ㄉㄨˊ ㄓㄢˋ)
complete monopoly
完全燃燒(ㄨㄢˊ ㄑㄩㄢˊ ㄖㄢˊ ㄕㄠ)
complete combustion
完全責任(ㄨㄢˊ ㄑㄩㄢˊ ㄗㄜˊ ㄖㄣˋ)
full liability
完整(ㄨㄢˊ ㄓㄥˇ)
complete; whole; undamaged; intact: 許多珍貴的歷史文物完整地保存下來了。Many precious historical relics have been preserved undamaged.
完成(ㄨㄢˊ ㄔㄥˊ)
to accomplish; to complete; to fulfill
完成任務(ㄨㄢˊ ㄔㄥˊ ㄖㄣˋ ㄨˋ)
to complete one's mission; to accomplish a task
完事(ㄨㄢˊ ㄕˋ)
(of an affair) to be over; to finish: 他們工作到深夜才完事。They didn't finish their work until late at night.
完善(ㄨㄢˊ ㄕㄢˋ)
perfect; immaculate; untarnished
完數(ㄨㄢˊ ㄕㄨˋ)
(mathematics) a perfect number
完稅(ㄨㄢˊ ㄕㄨㄟˋ)or 完納(ㄨㄢˊ ㄋㄚˋ)
to pay taxes
完稅憑證(ㄨㄢˊ ㄕㄨㄟˋ ㄆㄧㄥˊ ㄓㄥˋ)
(accounting) duty-paid proof
完稅貨價(ㄨㄢˊ ㄕㄨㄟˋ ㄏㄨㄛˋ ㄐㄧㄚˋ)
(accounting) price duty paid
完人(ㄨㄢˊ ㄖㄣˊ)
a perfect person; a paragon of virtue
完案(ㄨㄢˊ ㄢˋ)
a case closed

【宏】 1108 ㄏㄨㄥˊ horng hóng

1. great; vast; wide; ample
2. a Chinese family name

宏辯(ㄏㄨㄥˊ ㄅㄧㄢˋ)
a well-supported argument: 他的宏辯獲得與會者的讚賞。His well-supported argument wins the applause of the participants.
宏放(ㄏㄨㄥˊ ㄈㄤˋ)
broad-minded and unrestrained
宏富(ㄏㄨㄥˊ ㄈㄨˋ)
rich; abundant
宏達(ㄏㄨㄥˊ ㄉㄚˊ)
learned; intelligent; knowledgeable
宏大(ㄏㄨㄥˊ ㄉㄚˋ)
great; grand; vast; immense
宏都拉斯(ㄏㄨㄥˊ ㄉㄨ ㄌㄚ ㄙ)
Honduras, a republic in NE Central America
宏圖(ㄏㄨㄥˊ ㄊㄨˊ)
an ambitious plan
宏亮(ㄏㄨㄥˊ ㄌㄧㄤˋ)
(said of a voice) loud and clear; sonorous
宏量(ㄏㄨㄥˊ ㄌㄧㄤˋ)
great generosity: 他對窮人之宏量爲人所熟知。His great generosity to the poor is well-known.
宏構(ㄏㄨㄥˊ ㄍㄡˋ)
a majestic building, monument, etc.
宏旨(ㄏㄨㄥˊ ㄓˇ)
the main theme; the leading idea of an article: 愛國乃該文之宏旨。Patriotism is the main theme of the article.
宏儒碩學(ㄏㄨㄥˊ ㄖㄨˊ ㄕㄨㄛˋ ㄒㄩㄝˊ)
a learned person; an erudite person
宏業(ㄏㄨㄥˊ ㄧㄝˋ)
a great achievement
宏揚(ㄏㄨㄥˊ ㄧㄤˊ)
to disseminate
宏偉(ㄏㄨㄥˊ ㄨㄟˇ)
magnificent; grand
宏願(ㄏㄨㄥˊ ㄩㄢˋ)
an ambition; an ambitious plan: 他的宏願是做一個大政治家。His ambition is to be a great statesman.

五畫

【宕】 1109 ㄉㄤˋ danq dàng

1. a quarryman
2. to delay; to procrastinate: 延宕 to procrastinate; to put off 懸宕 to keep unsettled
3. to dissolute

宕戶(ㄉㄤˋ ㄏㄨˋ)
a quarryman

【宓】 1110 ㄇㄧˋ mih mì

1. quiet; silent; still
2. a Chinese family name

【宗】 1111 ㄗㄨㄥ tzong zōng

1. an ancestor; a clan
2. a sect; a religion
3. to believe in
4. a Chinese family name

宗派(ㄗㄨㄥ ㄆㄞˋ)
① branches of a clan or a religion ② schools of philosophy or academic learning
宗派活動(ㄗㄨㄥ ㄆㄞˋ ㄏㄨㄛˊ ㄉㄨㄥˋ)
factional activities
宗派主義(ㄗㄨㄥ ㄆㄞˋ ㄓㄨˇ ㄧˋ)
sectarianism; factionalism
宗派主義者(ㄗㄨㄥ ㄆㄞˋ ㄓㄨˇ ㄧˋ ㄓㄜˇ)
a sectarian; a factionalist
宗廟(ㄗㄨㄥ ㄇㄧㄠˋ)or 宗祧(ㄗㄨㄥ ㄊㄧㄠ)
the ancestral temple (of the ruling family); the imperial ancestral temple
宗法(ㄗㄨㄥ ㄈㄚˇ)
the rules within a clan governing order of succession, marriage, etc.
宗法社會(ㄗㄨㄥ ㄈㄚˇ ㄕㄜˋ ㄏㄨㄟˋ)
a society centered around

clannish rules and practices

宗弟(ㄗㄨㄥ ㄉㄧˋ)
a clansman of one's generation who is younger than oneself

宗老(ㄗㄨㄥ ㄌㄠˇ)
the elders of a clan

宗教(ㄗㄨㄥ ㄐㄧㄠˋ)
religion

宗教派別(ㄗㄨㄥ ㄐㄧㄠˋ ㄆㄞˋ ㄅㄧㄝˊ)
a religious sect

宗教復興(ㄗㄨㄥ ㄐㄧㄠˋ ㄈㄨˋ ㄒㄧㄥ)
religious revival

宗教觀(ㄗㄨㄥ ㄐㄧㄠˋ ㄍㄨㄢ)
religious view of life

宗教界(ㄗㄨㄥ ㄐㄧㄠˋ ㄐㄧㄝˋ)
the religious world

宗教戒律(ㄗㄨㄥ ㄐㄧㄠˋ ㄐㄧㄝˋ ㄌㄩˋ)
religious taboo

宗教教育(ㄗㄨㄥ ㄐㄧㄠˋ ㄐㄧㄠˋ ㄩˋ)
religious education

宗教取向(ㄗㄨㄥ ㄐㄧㄠˋ ㄑㄩˇ ㄒㄧㄤˋ)
religious orientation

宗教信仰(ㄗㄨㄥ ㄐㄧㄠˋ ㄒㄧㄣˋ ㄧㄤˇ)
religious belief

宗教性(ㄗㄨㄥ ㄐㄧㄠˋ ㄒㄧㄥˋ)
religious character

宗教學(ㄗㄨㄥ ㄐㄧㄠˋ ㄒㄩㄝˊ)
the science of religion

宗教制度(ㄗㄨㄥ ㄐㄧㄠˋ ㄓˋ ㄉㄨˋ)
a religious institution

宗教哲學(ㄗㄨㄥ ㄐㄧㄠˋ ㄓㄜˊ ㄒㄩㄝˊ)
philosophy of religion

宗教史(ㄗㄨㄥ ㄐㄧㄠˋ ㄕˇ)
the history of religion

宗教裁判所(ㄗㄨㄥ ㄐㄧㄠˋ ㄘㄞˊ ㄆㄢˋ ㄙㄨㄛˇ)
the Holy Office or tribunal established during the period of Inquisition

宗教儀式(ㄗㄨㄥ ㄐㄧㄠˋ ㄧˊ ㄕˋ)
religious rites; ritual

宗教藝術(ㄗㄨㄥ ㄐㄧㄠˋ ㄧˋ ㄕㄨˋ)
religious art

宗教文化(ㄗㄨㄥ ㄐㄧㄠˋ ㄨㄣˊ ㄏㄨㄚˋ)
religious culture

宗親(ㄗㄨㄥ ㄑㄧㄣ)
① members of the same clan; people of the same ancestry ② brothers by the same mother

宗兄(ㄗㄨㄥ ㄒㄩㄥ)
① a clansman of one's generation who is older than oneself ② a polite designation for a friend with the same surname as oneself

宗枝(ㄗㄨㄥ ㄓ)
a branch of the same clan

宗旨(ㄗㄨㄥ ㄓˇ)
purport; a purpose; an aim; an objective

宗主(ㄗㄨㄥ ㄓㄨˇ)
① a memorial ancestral tablet in ancestral shrine ② the eldest son begotten by one's legal wife 參看「庶子」

宗主國(ㄗㄨㄥ ㄓㄨˇ ㄍㄨㄛˊ)
a suzerain

宗主權(ㄗㄨㄥ ㄓㄨˇ ㄑㄩㄢˊ)
suzerainty; sovereignty; sovereign rights

宗師(ㄗㄨㄥ ㄕ)
one whose virtue and learning command the respect of others

宗室(ㄗㄨㄥ ㄕˋ)
① the imperial family ② the ancestral shrine of a large clan

宗人(ㄗㄨㄥ ㄖㄣˊ)
people of the same clan

宗子(ㄗㄨㄥ ㄗˇ)
the eldest son of one's legal wife

宗族(ㄗㄨㄥ ㄗㄨˊ)or 宗類(ㄗㄨㄥ ㄌㄟˋ)
a clan; a paternal clan

宗祠(ㄗㄨㄥ ㄘˊ)
the ancestral temple or shrine of a clan 亦作「家廟」

宗仰(ㄗㄨㄥ ㄧㄤˇ)
to hold in esteem

【官】 1112 ㄍㄨㄢ guan guān

1. a government official
2. of, or having to do with the government or the state
3. (biology) an organ
4. a Chinese family name

官罷(ㄍㄨㄢ ㄅㄚˋ)
the settlement of people's dispute by official mediation

官報(ㄍㄨㄢ ㄅㄠˋ)
a government journal; an official newspaper; a communiqué

官辦(ㄍㄨㄢ ㄅㄢˋ)
run or operated by the government; government-operated: 這份報紙是官辦的。This newspaper is run by the government.

官逼民反(ㄍㄨㄢ ㄅㄧ ㄇㄧㄣˊ ㄈㄢˇ)
The people are driven to rebellion by tyranny.

官婢(ㄍㄨㄢ ㄅㄧˋ)
the women drafted into lowly service by the government because of offenses

官兵(ㄍㄨㄢ ㄅㄧㄥ)
① officers and men (in the armed forces) ② government troops

官派(ㄍㄨㄢ ㄆㄞˋ)
to be appointed by the government

官賣(ㄍㄨㄢ ㄇㄞˋ)
government monopoly sale

官媒(ㄍㄨㄢ ㄇㄟˊ)
a jail matron

官迷(ㄍㄨㄢ ㄇㄧˊ)
one lured by the splendor of officialdom; an aspirant after government offices

官名(ㄍㄨㄢ ㄇㄧㄥˊ)
the title of a government position

官費(ㄍㄨㄢ ㄈㄟˋ)
the funds from public coffers

官費生(ㄍㄨㄢ ㄈㄟˋ ㄕㄥ)
a government scholarship student

官方(ㄍㄨㄢ ㄈㄤ)
the government (as opposed to private citizens); official (sources, information, etc.)

官方報告(ㄍㄨㄢ ㄈㄤ ㄅㄠˋ ㄍㄠˋ)
an official report

官方統計(ㄍㄨㄢ ㄈㄤ ㄊㄨㄥˇ ㄐㄧˋ)
official statistics

官方消息(ㄍㄨㄢ ㄈㄤ ㄒㄧㄠ ˙ㄒㄧ)
news from government sources

官方組織(ㄍㄨㄢ ㄈㄤ ㄗㄨˇ ㄓ)
official organization

官方人士(ㄍㄨㄢ ㄈㄤ ㄖㄣˊ ㄕˋ)
official quarters

官俸(ㄍㄨㄢ ㄈㄥˋ)
the salary drawn from the government

官府(ㄍㄨㄢ ㄈㄨˇ)
① the local authorities ② a feudal official

官倒(ㄍㄨㄢ ㄉㄠˇ)
(in mainland China) an official or a cadre who abuses his power to line his pocket; an official profiteer

官邸(ㄍㄨㄢ ㄉㄧˇ)
an official residence
官田(ㄍㄨㄢ ㄊㄧㄢˊ)
government-owned farmland
官廳(ㄍㄨㄢ ㄊㄧㄥ)
a government office (or agency)
官能(ㄍㄨㄢ ㄋㄥˊ)
physical faculties (of a human being); body functions
官能心理學(ㄍㄨㄢ ㄋㄥˊ ㄒㄧㄣ ㄌㄧˇ ㄒㄩㄝˊ)
faculty psychology
官能障礙(ㄍㄨㄢ ㄋㄥˊ ㄓㄤˋ ㄞˋ)
functional disorder
官能症(ㄍㄨㄢ ㄋㄥˊ ㄓㄥˋ)
(pathology) functional disease
官吏(ㄍㄨㄢ ㄌㄧˋ)
a government official
官裏(ㄍㄨㄢ ˙ㄌㄧ)
①a government office ②the emperor
官僚(ㄍㄨㄢ ㄌㄧㄠˊ)
bureaucrats
官僚機構(ㄍㄨㄢ ㄌㄧㄠˊ ㄐㄧ ㄍㄡˋ)
a bureaucratic structure
官僚政治(ㄍㄨㄢ ㄌㄧㄠˊ ㄓㄥˋ ㄓˋ)
officialism; bureaucracy
官僚主義者(ㄍㄨㄢ ㄌㄧㄠˊ ㄓㄨˇ ㄧˋ ㄓㄜˇ)
bureaucrat
官僚資本(ㄍㄨㄢ ㄌㄧㄠˊ ㄗ ㄅㄣˇ)
the capital controlled by government officials
官僚作風(ㄍㄨㄢ ㄌㄧㄠˊ ㄗㄨㄛˋ ㄈㄥ)
official red tape; a bureaucratic style of work
官股(ㄍㄨㄢ ㄍㄨˇ)
government-owned stocks (in an enterprise)
官官相護(ㄍㄨㄢ ㄍㄨㄢ ㄒㄧㄤ ㄏㄨˋ)
An official tends to defend another official subjected to criticism. 或 to side with one's associate
官話(ㄍㄨㄢ ㄏㄨㄚˋ)
①the language of officialdom ②Mandarin
官紀(ㄍㄨㄢ ㄐㄧˋ)
the discipline of government officials
官家(ㄍㄨㄢ ㄐㄧㄚ)
①the emperor ②the government authorities
官價(ㄍㄨㄢ ㄐㄧㄚˋ)
an official price (as opposed to a black market price)
官架子(ㄍㄨㄢ ㄐㄧㄚˋ ˙ㄗ)
the airs of an official; bureaucratic airs
官階(ㄍㄨㄢ ㄐㄧㄝ)
the rank (of a military officer or a civil servant)
官眷(ㄍㄨㄢ ㄐㄩㄢˋ)
the dependents of a government official
官軍(ㄍㄨㄢ ㄐㄩㄣ)
government troops
官腔(ㄍㄨㄢ ㄑㄧㄤ)
a bureaucratic tone; official jargon: 打官腔 to stall with official jargon
官銜(ㄍㄨㄢ ㄒㄧㄢˊ)
the formal title (of a government official)
官職(ㄍㄨㄢ ㄓˊ)
a government post or position: 他的官職頗高。His government post is rather high.
官制(ㄍㄨㄢ ㄓˋ)
the system of civil service
官箴(ㄍㄨㄢ ㄓㄣ)
maxims for government officials
官差(ㄍㄨㄢ ㄔㄞ)
①official business ②a government messenger
官娼(ㄍㄨㄢ ㄔㄤ)
a licensed prostitute
官常(ㄍㄨㄢ ㄔㄤˊ)
the duty of government officials
官場(ㄍㄨㄢ ㄔㄤˇ)or 官界(ㄍㄨㄢ ㄐㄧㄝˋ)
officialdom: 他對官場感到厭倦。He is tired of the officialdom.
官場現形記(ㄍㄨㄢ ㄔㄤˇ ㄒㄧㄢˋ ㄒㄧㄥˊ ㄐㄧˋ)
the title of a novel by Li Pao-chia (李寶嘉) of the Ching Dynasty, in which the author made sarcastic descriptions about the practices of officialdom
官事(ㄍㄨㄢ ㄕˋ)
①public affairs ②a lawsuit: 他官事纏身。He was involved in a lawsuit.
官式訪問(ㄍㄨㄢ ㄕˋ ㄈㄤˇ ㄨㄣˋ)
an official visit or call
官紳(ㄍㄨㄢ ㄕㄣ)
officials and the gentry
官聲(ㄍㄨㄢ ㄕㄥ)
(honest, or corrupt) reputation of an official
官商合辦(ㄍㄨㄢ ㄕㄤ ㄏㄜˊ ㄅㄢˋ)or 官私合營(ㄍㄨㄢ ㄙ ㄏㄜˊ ㄧㄥˊ)
jointly run or operated by the government and private citizens: 這個書局是官商合辦的。This bookstore is jointly run by the government and private citizens.
官書(ㄍㄨㄢ ㄕㄨ)
①official documents ②government publications
官署(ㄍㄨㄢ ㄕㄨˇ)
a government agency
官人(ㄍㄨㄢ ㄖㄣˊ)
①a holder of a government office; a government official: 官人把他拿去了。He was arrested by a government official. ②(in ancient China) my husband; your husband
官司(ㄍㄨㄢ ˙ㄙ)
a lawsuit
官衙(ㄍㄨㄢ ㄧㄚˊ)
a government agency
官窰(ㄍㄨㄢ ㄧㄠˊ)
government-operated porcelain kilns of the Sung Dynasty
官癮(ㄍㄨㄢ ㄧㄣˇ)
the obsession to hold a government post: 他官癮很重。He has strong obsession to hold a government post.
官印(ㄍㄨㄢ ㄧㄣˋ)
an official seal of a government agency
官廕(ㄍㄨㄢ ㄧㄣˋ)
government offices conferred upon the offsprings of meritorious officials as a reward
官樣文章(ㄍㄨㄢ ㄧㄤˋ ㄨㄣˊ ㄓㄤ)
(literally) stereotyped writing characteristic of official communications, documents, etc.—something done superficially as a mere formality
官員(ㄍㄨㄢ ㄩㄢˊ)
an official
官運(ㄍㄨㄢ ㄩㄣˋ)
①a person's opportunity of official promotion ②government freight or cargo
官運亨通(ㄍㄨㄢ ㄩㄣˋ ㄏㄥ ㄊㄨㄥ)

to have a successful official career; to advance smoothly in officialdom: 那位市長官運亨通。The mayor has a successful official career.

【宙】 1113 ㄓㄡˋ jow zhòu
infinite time; time without beginning or end; eternity
宙合(ㄓㄡˋ ㄏㄜˊ)
all embracing, or all encompassing

【定】 1114 ㄉㄧㄥˋ dinq dìng
1. to decide; to fix; to settle
2. definite; sure
3. stable
4. to remain

定本(ㄉㄧㄥˋ ㄅㄣˇ)
①a definite foundation or basis ②a finalized version or definite edition (of a book): 四書定本 the definite edition of the *Four Books*
定比定律(ㄉㄧㄥˋ ㄅㄧˇ ㄉㄧㄥˋ ㄌㄩˋ)
the law of definite (or constant) proportions
定聘(ㄉㄧㄥˋ ㄆㄧㄣˋ)
to betroth: 他們已經定聘。They are betrothed.
定評(ㄉㄧㄥˋ ㄆㄧㄥˊ)
a final judgement (as to the worth of a work, a person, etc.)
定名(ㄉㄧㄥˋ ㄇㄧㄥˊ)
to give a name; to christen; to dub
定命(ㄉㄧㄥˋ ㄇㄧㄥˋ) or 定數(ㄉㄧㄥˋ ㄕㄨˋ)
predestination
定命論(ㄉㄧㄥˋ ㄇㄧㄥˋ ㄌㄨㄣˋ)
determinism
定命論者(ㄉㄧㄥˋ ㄇㄧㄥˋ ㄌㄨㄣˋ ㄓㄜˇ)
a determinist
定單(ㄉㄧㄥˋ ㄉㄢ)
an order (for goods)
定點連續攝影機(ㄉㄧㄥˋ ㄉㄧㄢˇ ㄌㄧㄢˊ ㄒㄩˋ ㄕㄜˋ ㄧㄥˇ ㄐㄧ)
a slit camera
定鼎(ㄉㄧㄥˋ ㄉㄧㄥˇ) or 定都(ㄉㄧㄥˋ ㄉㄨ)
to pick a city as capital after uniting the empire
定奪(ㄉㄧㄥˋ ㄉㄨㄛˊ)
to decide; to settle
定理(ㄉㄧㄥˋ ㄌㄧˇ)
(mathematics) a theorem
定力(ㄉㄧㄥˋ ㄌㄧˋ)
(Buddhism) strength of concentration
定例(ㄉㄧㄥˋ ㄌㄧˋ)
an irrevocable or unchangeable rule
定量(ㄉㄧㄥˋ ㄌㄧㄤˋ)
fixed amount; fixed quantity; to fix the amount or quantity
定量配給(ㄉㄧㄥˋ ㄌㄧㄤˋ ㄆㄟˋ ㄐㄧˇ)
rationing
定量分析(ㄉㄧㄥˋ ㄌㄧㄤˋ ㄈㄣ ㄒㄧ)
(chemistry) quantitative analysis
定論(ㄉㄧㄥˋ ㄌㄨㄣˋ)
an accepted argument (not questioned any more)
定率(ㄉㄧㄥˋ ㄌㄩˋ)
a fixed rate; a fixed ratio
定律(ㄉㄧㄥˋ ㄌㄩˋ)
(science) a law
定稿(ㄉㄧㄥˋ ㄍㄠˇ)
①to finalize a manuscript, text, etc. ②a final version or text
定購(ㄉㄧㄥˋ ㄍㄡˋ)
to order (goods, etc.); to place an order for something
定規(ㄉㄧㄥˋ ㄍㄨㄟ)
①an established rule or practice; a set pattern ②to be bent on; to be determined
定冠詞(ㄉㄧㄥˋ ㄍㄨㄢˋ ㄘˊ)
definite article "the"
定貨(ㄉㄧㄥˋ ㄏㄨㄛˋ)
to order goods; to place an order for goods
定貨單(ㄉㄧㄥˋ ㄏㄨㄛˋ ㄉㄢ)
an order form
定婚(ㄉㄧㄥˋ ㄏㄨㄣ)
to be betrothed
定計(ㄉㄧㄥˋ ㄐㄧˋ)
to devise a stratagem
定價(ㄉㄧㄥˋ ㄐㄧㄚˋ)
①to fix a price ②a fixed price; a list price
定見(ㄉㄧㄥˋ ㄐㄧㄢˋ)
a definite opinion; a fixed view
定金(ㄉㄧㄥˋ ㄐㄧㄣ) or 定錢(ㄉㄧㄥˋ ㄑㄧㄢˊ)
down payment; earnest money
定居(ㄉㄧㄥˋ ㄐㄩ)
to settle down
定局(ㄉㄧㄥˋ ㄐㄩˊ)
a foregone conclusion; an irreversible situation
定期(ㄉㄧㄥˋ ㄑㄧˊ)
①periodic; regular ②to fix a time or date (for some activity)
定期保險(ㄉㄧㄥˋ ㄑㄧˊ ㄅㄠˇ ㄒㄧㄢˇ)
term insurance
定期報表(ㄉㄧㄥˋ ㄑㄧˊ ㄅㄠˋ ㄅㄧㄠˇ)
(accounting) periodical statements
定期報告(ㄉㄧㄥˋ ㄑㄧˊ ㄅㄠˋ ㄍㄠˋ)
periodical reports
定期放款(ㄉㄧㄥˋ ㄑㄧˊ ㄈㄤˋ ㄎㄨㄢˇ)
time loans
定期付款(ㄉㄧㄥˋ ㄑㄧˊ ㄈㄨˋ ㄎㄨㄢˇ)
payment on term
定期抵押放款(ㄉㄧㄥˋ ㄑㄧˊ ㄉㄧˇ ㄧㄚ ㄈㄤˋ ㄎㄨㄢˇ)
fixed loans secured
定期刊物(ㄉㄧㄥˋ ㄑㄧˊ ㄎㄢ ㄨˋ)
a periodical (publication)
定期匯票(ㄉㄧㄥˋ ㄑㄧˊ ㄏㄨㄟˋ ㄆㄧㄠˋ)
a dated draft
定期交付(ㄉㄧㄥˋ ㄑㄧˊ ㄐㄧㄠ ㄈㄨˋ)
delivery on term
定期信用放款(ㄉㄧㄥˋ ㄑㄧˊ ㄒㄧㄣˋ ㄩㄥˋ ㄈㄤˋ ㄎㄨㄢˇ)
fixed loans unsecured
定期車票(ㄉㄧㄥˋ ㄑㄧˊ ㄔㄜ ㄆㄧㄠˋ)
a commutation ticket
定期存款(ㄉㄧㄥˋ ㄑㄧˊ ㄘㄨㄣˊ ㄎㄨㄢˇ)
a fixed deposit; a time deposit (T/D)
定期維修(ㄉㄧㄥˋ ㄑㄧˊ ㄨㄟˊ ㄒㄧㄡ)
periodic maintenance
定親(ㄉㄧㄥˋ ㄑㄧㄣ)
to betroth
定情(ㄉㄧㄥˋ ㄑㄧㄥˊ)
①to get married ②to fall in love
定限(ㄉㄧㄥˋ ㄒㄧㄢˋ)
①a fixed limit ②to set a time limit
定心(ㄉㄧㄥˋ ㄒㄧㄣ)
free of worries; confident; composed or calm
定心丸(ㄉㄧㄥˋ ㄒㄧㄣ ㄨㄢˊ)
something capable of setting someone's mind at ease
定向(ㄉㄧㄥˋ ㄒㄧㄤˋ)
to fix the direction; to orientate
定向儀(ㄉㄧㄥˋ ㄒㄧㄤˋ ㄧˊ)

a direction finder

定型(ㄉㄧㄥˋ ㄒㄧㄥˊ)
to finalize the design; already fixed or hardened (as opposed to formative or pliant)

定省(ㄉㄧㄥˋ ㄒㄧㄥˇ)
inquiry after one's own parents in the morning and evening

定性分析(ㄉㄧㄥˋ ㄒㄧㄥˋ ㄈㄣ ㄒㄧ)
(chemistry) qualitative analysis

定製(ㄉㄧㄥˋ ㄓˋ)
to have something made to order

定章(ㄉㄧㄥˋ ㄓㄤ)
fixed regulations or rules

定準(ㄉㄧㄥˋ ㄓㄨㄣˇ)
a fixed standard

定產(ㄉㄧㄥˋ ㄔㄢˇ)
a system of fixed quotas for grain production

定時(ㄉㄧㄥˋ ㄕˊ)
① to set time ② at fixed time

定時電路(ㄉㄧㄥˋ ㄕˊ ㄉㄧㄢˋ ㄌㄨˋ)
timing circuits

定時開關(ㄉㄧㄥˋ ㄕˊ ㄎㄞ ㄍㄨㄢ)
a time switch

定時控制(ㄉㄧㄥˋ ㄕˊ ㄎㄨㄥˋ ㄓˋ)
timing control

定時訊號(ㄉㄧㄥˋ ㄕˊ ㄒㄩㄣˋ ㄏㄠˋ)
timing signals

定時炸彈(ㄉㄧㄥˋ ㄕˊ ㄓㄚˋ ㄉㄢˋ)
a time bomb

定神(ㄉㄧㄥˋ ㄕㄣˊ)
① to compose oneself; to pull oneself together ② to concentrate one's attention

定然(ㄉㄧㄥˋ ㄖㄢˊ)
certainly; definitely

定則(ㄉㄧㄥˋ ㄗㄜˊ)
(science) a rule

定罪(ㄉㄧㄥˋ ㄗㄨㄟˋ)
to declare someone guilty; to convict someone (of a crime)

定做(ㄉㄧㄥˋ ㄗㄨㄛˋ)or 定製(ㄉㄧㄥˋ ㄓˋ)
to be made to order; to custom-tailor; tailor-made: 這件外套是定做的。This coat was made to order.

定額(ㄉㄧㄥˋ ㄜˊ)
a fixed amount or number

定案(ㄉㄧㄥˋ ㄢˋ)
① to decide on a verdict; to reach a conclusion on a case ② a verdict; a final decision

定義(ㄉㄧㄥˋ ㄧˋ)
a definition

定銀(ㄉㄧㄥˋ ㄧㄣˊ)
deposit money

定影劑(ㄉㄧㄥˋ ㄧㄥˇ ㄐㄧˋ)
(photography) a fixer

定位(ㄉㄧㄥˋ ㄨㄟˋ)
① a fixed position; a location; orientation ② to orientate; to position

定員(ㄉㄧㄥˋ ㄩㄢˊ)
a fixed number of staff members

【宛】 1115 ㄨㄢˇ woan wǎn

1. as if; as though
2. crooked; roundabout
3. a Chinese family name

宛轉(ㄨㄢˇ ㄓㄨㄢˇ)
(to persuade, explain, etc.) mildly and indirectly; tactfully

宛然(ㄨㄢˇ ㄖㄢˊ)
as if; as though; like: 這裡山明水秀，宛然江南風景。The scenery here has great charm, as though it were the land south of the Yangtze River.

宛如(ㄨㄢˇ ㄖㄨˊ)or 宛若(ㄨㄢˇ ㄖㄨㄛˋ)
as if; as though; like: 他爬樹宛如一隻貓。He climbed the tree like a cat.

宛若遊龍(ㄨㄢˇ ㄖㄨㄛˋ ㄧㄡˊ ㄌㄨㄥˊ)
(said of a woman's bodily movement) lithesome as a wandering dragon

宛延(ㄨㄢˇ ㄧㄢˊ)
long and winding (roads, lines, etc.); to meander: 一條小溪從山谷中宛延流過。A brook meanders through the valley.

【宜】 1116 ㄧˊ yi yí

1. right; fitting; proper; good
2. should; ought to; had better: 不宜操之過急。You should not act in haste.
3. a matter
4. to fit; to suit; to put in order
5. a Chinese family name

宜男(ㄧˊ ㄋㄢˊ)
(said of a woman) prolific of male children

宜興壺(ㄧˊ ㄒㄧㄥ ㄏㄨˊ)
famous pottery teapots made in Yihsing, Kiangsu

宜室宜家(ㄧˊ ㄕˋ ㄧˊ ㄐㄧㄚ)
to make a harmonious and orderly home (used as a congratulatory message on wedding)

宜然(ㄧˊ ㄖㄢˊ)
suitable

宜人(ㄧˊ ㄖㄣˊ)
pleasant; agreeable; delightful: 此地氣候宜人。The weather here is pleasant.

宜於(ㄧˊ ㄩˊ)
to be suitable for

六畫

【客】 1117 ㄎㄜˋ keh kè

1. a guest
2. a stranger; an alien; a foreigner: 笑問客從何處來。(賀知章·回鄉偶書) "Where do you come from, stranger?" they ask with a giggle.
3. a customer
4. a spectator; an audience
5. foreign; strange; alien
6. an adventurer
7. a Chinese family name

客票(ㄎㄜˋ ㄆㄧㄠˋ)
a free ticket

客滿(ㄎㄜˋ ㄇㄢˇ)
(said of theater tickets, etc.) sold out; a full house

客飯(ㄎㄜˋ ㄈㄢˋ)
meals sold at a fixed price per customer according to the quality of the dishes served

客房(ㄎㄜˋ ㄈㄤˊ)
a guest room

客地(ㄎㄜˋ ㄉㄧˋ)
a strange or an alien land

客店(ㄎㄜˋ ㄉㄧㄢˋ)or 客館(ㄎㄜˋ ㄍㄨㄢˇ)
an inn; a hotel

客隊(ㄎㄜˋ ㄉㄨㄟˋ)
(sports) the visiting team; the guest team: 客隊輸了。The visiting team lost the game.

客套(ㄎㄜˋ ㄊㄠˋ)
civilities; ceremonious greetings or compliments in ad-

dressing one's guest

客堂(ㄎㄜˋ ㄊㄤˊ)
a parlor; a sitting room; a living room; a reception room

客廳(ㄎㄜˋ ㄊㄧㄥ)
a parlor; a living room

客離主安(ㄎㄜˋ ㄌㄧˊ ㄓㄨˇ ㄢ)
The host gets some rest after the guests have left.

客觀(ㄎㄜˋ ㄍㄨㄢ)
objective (as opposed to subjective); not biased: 科學家必須客觀。A scientist must be objective.

客觀批評(ㄎㄜˋ ㄍㄨㄢ ㄆㄧ ㄆㄧㄥˊ)
objective criticism

客觀世界(ㄎㄜˋ ㄍㄨㄢ ㄕˋ ㄐㄧㄝˋ)
the objective world

客觀事物(ㄎㄜˋ ㄍㄨㄢ ㄕˋ ㄨˋ)
objective things (or reality)

客戶(ㄎㄜˋ ㄏㄨˋ)
a client

客貨船(ㄎㄜˋ ㄏㄨㄛˋ ㄔㄨㄢˊ)
a passenger-cargo vessel

客機(ㄎㄜˋ ㄐㄧ)
a passenger plane; an airliner

客家(ㄎㄜˋ ㄐㄧㄚ)
(literally) "guest families" which moved from northern to southern China during periods of invasions by the northern tribes in Chinese history—the Hakka people of South China; the Hakkas

客家話(ㄎㄜˋ ㄐㄧㄚ ㄏㄨㄚˋ)
Hakka

客居異地(ㄎㄜˋ ㄐㄩ ㄧˋ ㄉㄧˋ)
to be a stranger in a strange land

客氣(ㄎㄜˋ ·ㄑㄧ)
sticking to the proprieties; polite; courteous; respectful

客氣話(ㄎㄜˋ ·ㄑㄧ ㄏㄨㄚˋ)
polite remarks

客卿(ㄎㄜˋ ㄑㄧㄥ)
① a foreign-born government official ② one who works for an organization temporarily on guest status

客棧(ㄎㄜˋ ㄓㄢˋ)
an inn

客車(ㄎㄜˋ ㄔㄜ)
a passenger train or bus

客船(ㄎㄜˋ ㄔㄨㄢˊ)
a passenger ship; a liner

客串(ㄎㄜˋ ㄔㄨㄢˋ)
(said of an amateur actor or actress, etc.) to appear onstage for an impromptu performance; to be a guest performer; (said of an established actor or actress) to play unimportant roles for a promotional purpose

客舍(ㄎㄜˋ ㄕㄜˋ)
a hotel 參看「客店」

客商(ㄎㄜˋ ㄕㄤ)
a traveling salesman; a traveling businessman

客人(ㄎㄜˋ ㄖㄣˊ)
a guest

客座教授(ㄎㄜˋ ㄗㄨㄛˋ ㄐㄧㄠˋ ㄕㄡˋ)
a visiting professor

客座指揮(ㄎㄜˋ ㄗㄨㄛˋ ㄓˇ ㄏㄨㄟ)
a guest conductor

客死他鄉(ㄎㄜˋ ㄙˇ ㄊㄚ ㄒㄧㄤ)
to die away from home; to die abroad

客歲(ㄎㄜˋ ㄙㄨㄟˋ)
last year

客位(ㄎㄜˋ ㄨㄟˋ)
the seats reserved for guests

客運(ㄎㄜˋ ㄩㄣˋ)
passenger service, or passenger transportation

客運列車(ㄎㄜˋ ㄩㄣˋ ㄌㄧㄝˋ ㄔㄜ)
a passenger train

【宣】 1118
ㄒㄩㄢ shiuan xuān

1. to announce; to declare
2. to propagate; to circulate
3. a Chinese family name

宣佈 or 宣布(ㄒㄩㄢ ㄅㄨˋ)
to announce

宣佈獨立(ㄒㄩㄢ ㄅㄨˋ ㄉㄨˊ ㄌㄧˋ)
to declare independence

宣佈和約(ㄒㄩㄢ ㄅㄨˋ ㄏㄜˊ ㄩㄝ)
to announce a peace treaty

宣佈戒嚴(ㄒㄩㄢ ㄅㄨˋ ㄐㄧㄝˋ ㄧㄢˊ)
to declare martial law

宣判(ㄒㄩㄢ ㄆㄢˋ)
to announce the verdict: 陪審團宣判「無罪」。The jury announced a verdict of "not guilty."

宣撫(ㄒㄩㄢ ㄈㄨˇ)
to pacify or mollify (the people) by propaganda

宣導(ㄒㄩㄢ ㄉㄠˇ)or(ㄒㄩㄢ ㄉㄠˋ)
to guide (the people) by creating a better understanding

宣讀(ㄒㄩㄢ ㄉㄨˊ)
to read out (a declaration, an announcement, etc.) in public

宣統(ㄒㄩㄢ ㄊㄨㄥˇ)
the reigning title of Henry Pu Yi, the last Manchu emperor of the Ching Dynasty

宣勞
①(ㄒㄩㄢ ㄌㄠˋ) to comfort (people in distress) by an official message
②(ㄒㄩㄢ ㄌㄠˊ) to contribute one's labor, time and energy, etc. to a public cause

宣告(ㄒㄩㄢ ㄍㄠˋ)
to announce; to declare; to pronounce; an announcement; a declaration

宣告破產(ㄒㄩㄢ ㄍㄠˋ ㄆㄛˋ ㄔㄢˇ)
to declare bankruptcy; to go bankrupt

宣告成立(ㄒㄩㄢ ㄍㄠˋ ㄔㄥˊ ㄌㄧˋ)
to proclaim the founding of (a state, organization, etc.)

宣告死亡(ㄒㄩㄢ ㄍㄠˋ ㄙˇ ㄨㄤˊ)
a declaration of death

宣告無效(ㄒㄩㄢ ㄍㄠˋ ㄨˊ ㄒㄧㄠˋ)
to declare something null and void

宣講(ㄒㄩㄢ ㄐㄧㄤˇ)
to preach; to deliver a speech; to orate

宣泄(ㄒㄩㄢ ㄒㄧㄝˋ)
① to reveal, disclose, or divulge (a secret) ② to drain (liquid)

宣泄洪水(ㄒㄩㄢ ㄒㄧㄝˋ ㄏㄨㄥˊ ㄕㄨㄟˇ)
to drain off floodwater

宣紙(ㄒㄩㄢ ㄓˇ)
the fine paper from Hsüancheng (宣城縣) in Anhwei Province, used especially for painting or calligraphic works; rice paper

宣召(ㄒㄩㄢ ㄓㄠˋ)
(said of an emperor) to summon a subject, etc. to an imperial audience

宣戰(ㄒㄩㄢ ㄓㄢˋ)
to declare war; a declaration of war

宣戰書(ㄒㄩㄢ ㄓㄢˋ ㄕㄨ)
a declaration of war

宣稱(ㄒㄩㄢ ㄔㄥ)
to claim; to assert

宣傳(ㄒㄩㄢ ㄔㄨㄢˊ)
to publicize; to promote; (sales) propaganda; (sales) promotion

宣傳品(ㄒㄩㄢ ㄔㄨㄢˊ ㄆㄧㄣˇ)
propaganda material; promotion material

宣傳費(ㄒㄩㄢ ㄔㄨㄢˊ ㄈㄟˋ)
publicity expenses

宣傳電影 (ㄒㄩㄢ ㄔㄨㄢˊ ㄉㄧㄢˋ ㄧㄥˇ)
public relations movies

宣傳隊(ㄒㄩㄢ ㄔㄨㄢˊ ㄉㄨㄟˋ)
a propaganda team

宣傳工具(ㄒㄩㄢ ㄔㄨㄢˊ ㄍㄨㄥ ㄐㄩˋ)
mass media; the instrument of propaganda or publicity

宣傳畫(ㄒㄩㄢ ㄔㄨㄢˊ ㄏㄨㄚˋ)
a picture poster

宣傳機構(ㄒㄩㄢ ㄔㄨㄢˊ ㄐㄧ ㄍㄡˋ)
a propaganda organ

宣傳週(ㄒㄩㄢ ㄔㄨㄢˊ ㄓㄡ)
the publicity week (for publicizing themes such as traffic safety, environmental sanitation, etc.)

宣傳戰(ㄒㄩㄢ ㄔㄨㄢˊ ㄓㄢˋ)
a propaganda war

宣傳車(ㄒㄩㄢ ㄔㄨㄢˊ ㄔㄜ)
a propaganda car

宣傳網(ㄒㄩㄢ ㄔㄨㄢˊ ㄨㄤˇ)
a propagandary network

宣示(ㄒㄩㄢ ㄕˋ)
to make publicly known; to publish

宣誓(ㄒㄩㄢ ㄕˋ)
to take an oath

宣誓就職(ㄒㄩㄢ ㄕˋ ㄐㄧㄡˋ ㄓˊ)
(said of government officials) to be sworn in

宣誓書(ㄒㄩㄢ ㄕˋ ㄕㄨ)
a written oath

宣言(ㄒㄩㄢ ㄧㄢˊ)
a declaration; a manifesto

宣淫(ㄒㄩㄢ ㄧㄣˊ)
to engage in lascivious activities in public

宣揚(ㄒㄩㄢ ㄧㄤˊ)
to publicize and exalt

【室】 1119
ㄕˋ shyh shì

1. a room; an apartment; a home
2. wife

室內(ㄕˋ ㄋㄟˋ)
indoor

室內溜冰場(ㄕˋ ㄋㄟˋ ㄌㄧㄡ ㄅㄧㄥ ㄔㄤˇ)
an indoor skating rink

室內照明(ㄕˋ ㄋㄟˋ ㄓㄠˋ ㄇㄧㄥˊ)
interior illumination

室內裝璜 or 室內裝潢(ㄕˋ ㄋㄟˋ ㄓㄨㄤ ㄏㄨㄤˊ)
interior decoration

室內設計(ㄕˋ ㄋㄟˋ ㄕㄜˋ ㄐㄧˋ)
interior design

室內遊戲(ㄕˋ ㄋㄟˋ ㄧㄡˊ ㄒㄧˋ)
indoor games

室內游泳池(ㄕˋ ㄋㄟˋ ㄧㄡˊ ㄩㄥˇ ㄔˊ)
an indoor swimming pool

室內音樂(ㄕˋ ㄋㄟˋ ㄧㄣ ㄩㄝˋ)or 室內樂(ㄕˋ ㄋㄟˋ ㄩㄝˋ)
chamber music

室內運動(ㄕˋ ㄋㄟˋ ㄩㄣˋ ㄉㄨㄥˋ)
indoor sports

室女(ㄕˋ ㄋㄩˇ)
an unmarried girl; a virgin

室家(ㄕˋ ㄐㄧㄚ)
① a home; a family ② a married couple

室家之樂(ㄕˋ ㄐㄧㄚ ㄓ ㄌㄜˋ)
the connubial bliss

室人(ㄕˋ ㄖㄣˊ)
wife

室如懸磬(ㄕˋ ㄖㄨˊ ㄒㄩㄢˊ ㄑㄧㄥˋ)
(literally) The house is as empty as a hollow musical instrument.—as poor as a church mouse

室外(ㄕˋ ㄨㄞˋ)
outdoor (as opposed to indoor)

室外活動(ㄕˋ ㄨㄞˋ ㄏㄨㄛˊ ㄉㄨㄥˋ)
outdoor activities

室溫(ㄕˋ ㄨㄣ)or 室內溫度(ㄕˋ ㄋㄟˋ ㄨㄣ ㄉㄨˋ)
room temperature

【宥】 1120
ㄧㄡˋ yow yòu

to forgive; to pardon; to be lenient

宥過(ㄧㄡˋ ㄍㄨㄛˋ)
to excuse a mistake

宥恕(ㄧㄡˋ ㄕㄨˋ)
to forgive; to pardon; to excuse

宥罪(ㄧㄡˋ ㄗㄨㄟˋ)
to forgive an offense; to pardon a crime

【宦】 1121
ㄏㄨㄢˋ huann huàn

1. a government official; the government service
2. castrated

宦途(ㄏㄨㄢˋ ㄊㄨˊ)
a career as a government official (with its ups and downs)

宦囊(ㄏㄨㄢˋ ㄋㄤˊ)
savings from a career as a government official

宦官(ㄏㄨㄢˋ ㄍㄨㄢ)
a eunuch 亦作「太監」

宦海(ㄏㄨㄢˋ ㄏㄞˇ)
(archaic expression) officialdom; official circles

宦海浮沉(ㄏㄨㄢˋ ㄏㄞˇ ㄈㄨˊ ㄔㄣˊ)
the ups and downs in officialdom

宦遊(ㄏㄨㄢˋ ㄧㄡˊ)
to leave home and take up government employment

七畫

【宮】 1122
ㄍㄨㄥ gong gōng

1. a palace
2. castration

宮袍(ㄍㄨㄥ ㄆㄠˊ)
court robes

宮門(ㄍㄨㄥ ㄇㄣˊ)
a palace gate

宮燈(ㄍㄨㄥ ㄉㄥ)
a palace lantern (now used for an ornament)

宮殿(ㄍㄨㄥ ㄉㄧㄢˋ)
a palace

宮殿式建築(ㄍㄨㄥ ㄉㄧㄢˋ ㄕˋ ㄐㄧㄢˋ ㄓㄨˊ)
palatial architecture

宮廷(ㄍㄨㄥ ㄊㄧㄥˊ)
the living quarters of a monarch in his palace

宮廷服(ㄍㄨㄥ ㄊㄧㄥˊ ㄈㄨˊ)
court dress

宮廷政變(ㄍㄨㄥ ㄊㄧㄥˊ ㄓㄥˋ ㄅㄧㄢˋ)
a palace coup; a coup

宮廷藝術(ㄍㄨㄥ ㄊㄧㄥˊ ㄧˋ ㄕㄨˋ)
court art

宮廷外交(ㄍㄨㄥ ㄊㄧㄥˊ ㄨㄞˋ ㄐㄧㄠ)
boudoir diplomacy

宮女(ㄍㄨㄥ ㄋㄩˇ)
a court lady; a lady-in-waiting

宮禁(ㄍㄨㄥ ㄐㄧㄣˋ)
① the emperor's living quarters in his palace ② palace

taboos
宮牆(ㄍㄨㄥ ㄑㄧㄤˊ)
①palace walls②the house of one's teacher (a term of respect)
宮闕(ㄍㄨㄥ ㄑㄩㄝˋ)
a palace (as seen from outside)
宮刑(ㄍㄨㄥ ㄒㄧㄥˊ)
castration as a punishment
宮城(ㄍㄨㄥ ㄔㄥˊ)
the imperial capital
宮室(ㄍㄨㄥ ㄕˋ)
①a mansion②wife
宮人(ㄍㄨㄥ ㄖㄣˊ)
①court ladies②(in the Chou Dynasty) the official whose responsibility was to bathe the emperor
宮人草(ㄍㄨㄥ ㄖㄣˊ ㄘㄠˇ)
(botany) an amaryllis
宮娥(ㄍㄨㄥ ㄜˊ)
court ladies; ladies-in-waiting

【宰】 1123 ㄗㄞˇ tzae zǎi
1. to preside; to govern
2. to slaughter; to butcher
3. a Chinese family name
宰輔(ㄗㄞˇ ㄈㄨˇ)or 宰衡(ㄗㄞˇ ㄏㄥˊ)
a premier; a prime minister
宰輔之量(ㄗㄞˇ ㄈㄨˇ ㄓ ㄌㄧㄤˋ)
the capacity to serve as prime minister
宰割(ㄗㄞˇ ㄍㄜ)
①to cut up (meat) ②to partition or dismember (a country) ③to kill; to destroy; to slaughter
宰相(ㄗㄞˇ ㄒㄧㄤˋ)or 宰執(ㄗㄞˇ ㄓˊ)
a prime minister (in former times)
宰相之器(ㄗㄞˇ ㄒㄧㄤˋ ㄓ ㄑㄧˋ)
the potentialities to be a prime minister; the talent for statesmanship
宰殺(ㄗㄞˇ ㄕㄚ)
to slaughter; to butcher; to kill
宰肉(ㄗㄞˇ ㄖㄡˋ)
to cut up meat; to chop meat
宰予(ㄗㄞˇ ㄩˊ)
Tsai Yü, a disciple of Confucius, whose afternoon nap evoked severe admonition from the master

【害】 1124 ㄏㄞˋ hay hài
1. to injure; to hurt; to damage; to destroy
2. to kill
3. damage; injury; harm; detriment
4. a vital point
害病(ㄏㄞˋ ㄅㄧㄥˋ)
to get sick; to fall ill; to be taken ill: 他突然害病了。He was suddenly taken ill.
害怕(ㄏㄞˋ ㄆㄚˋ)
to be afraid of; to be scared of; to fear
害命(ㄏㄞˋ ㄇㄧㄥˋ)
to commit murder
害鳥(ㄏㄞˋ ㄋㄧㄠˇ)
injurious birds; vermin
害羣之馬(ㄏㄞˋ ㄑㄩㄣˊ ㄓ ㄇㄚˇ)
(literally) a horse that troubles the whole herd—a public nuisance; a public enemy; a black sheep: 他是他家的害羣之馬。 He was the black sheep of his family.
害喜(ㄏㄞˋ ㄒㄧˇ)
pregnant
害羞(ㄏㄞˋ ㄒㄧㄡ)
shy; bashful: 她有點害羞。She is rather bashful.
害處(ㄏㄞˋ ㄔㄨˋ)
harm; detriment; disadvantages; shortcomings
害蟲(ㄏㄞˋ ㄔㄨㄥˊ)
injurious or noxious insects
害人(ㄏㄞˋ ㄖㄣˊ)
to harm or injure others; to inflict injury upon others; to involve others in troubles
害人精(ㄏㄞˋ ㄖㄣˊ ㄐㄧㄥ)
a mischief-maker
害死人(ㄏㄞˋ ㄙˇ ㄖㄣˊ)
to bring great trouble to others
害臊(ㄏㄞˋ ㄙㄠˋ)
bashful; shy: 李先生害臊, 不喜歡參加社交集會。Mr. Lee is shy and dislikes parties.

【宴】 1125 ㄧㄢˋ yann yàn
1. to entertain; to feast
2. leisurely; comfort; ease
宴客(ㄧㄢˋ ㄎㄜˋ)
to entertain guests at a banquet
宴會(ㄧㄢˋ ㄏㄨㄟˋ)or 宴席(ㄧㄢˋ ㄒㄧˊ)
a banquet; a dinner party; a feast
宴會廳(ㄧㄢˋ ㄏㄨㄟˋ ㄊㄧㄥ)
a banquet hall
宴集(ㄧㄢˋ ㄐㄧˊ)
to gather together
宴居(ㄧㄢˋ ㄐㄩ)
to lead a leisurely life
宴請(ㄧㄢˋ ㄑㄧㄥˇ)
to entertain (to dinner)
宴饗(ㄧㄢˋ ㄒㄧㄤˇ)
(said of the emperor) to give a great dinner
宴安(ㄧㄢˋ ㄢ)
to live in idle comfort; to feel happy, contented, or relaxed
宴安酖毒(ㄧㄢˋ ㄢ ㄓㄣˋ ㄉㄨˊ)
to live in easy comfort and suffer its poisonous effect
宴爾(ㄧㄢˋ ㄦˇ)or 宴爾新婚(ㄧㄢˋ ㄦˇ ㄒㄧㄣ ㄏㄨㄣ)
the bliss of the newlyweds
宴遊(ㄧㄢˋ ㄧㄡˊ)
a leisurely trip: 他們宴遊杭州。They made a leisurely trip to Hangchow.
宴飲(ㄧㄢˋ ㄧㄣˇ)
to feast; to dine and wine 亦作「燕飲」

【宵】 1126 ㄒㄧㄠ shiau xiāo
night; dark; evening: 通宵 all night; throughout the night
宵禁(ㄒㄧㄠ ㄐㄧㄣˋ)
a curfew (enforced at night for public order): 宵禁業已解除。The curfew has been lifted.
宵小(ㄒㄧㄠ ㄒㄧㄠˇ)
thieves; evildoers: 他們捉到宵小沒有? Have they caught the thieves?
宵行(ㄒㄧㄠ ㄒㄧㄥˊ)
to travel by night
宵征(ㄒㄧㄠ ㄓㄥ)
a journey at night
宵中(ㄒㄧㄠ ㄓㄨㄥ)
midnight
宵人(ㄒㄧㄠ ㄖㄣˊ)
a mean person
宵衣旰食(ㄒㄧㄠ ㄧ ㄍㄢˋ ㄕˊ)
diligent in discharging official duties
宵夜(ㄒㄧㄠ ㄧㄝˋ)
a snack before going to bed;

a midnight snack: 他睡前吃宵夜。He eats a snack before going to bed.

〔宀部〕

【家】 1127 ㄐㄧㄚ jia jiā

1. home; house; household; family; of a household; domestic
2. a specialist (in any branch of art or science): 科學家 a scientist 政治家 a statesman 畫家 a painter

家破人亡(ㄐㄧㄚ ㄆㄛˋ ㄖㄣˊ ㄨㄤˊ)
with one's home in ruins and family members dead or scattered (referring to situations resulting from great disasters)

家貧如洗(ㄐㄧㄚ ㄆㄧㄣˊ ㄖㄨˊ ㄒㄧˇ)
to be in extreme poverty: 他們家貧如洗。They are in extreme poverty.

家僕(ㄐㄧㄚ ㄆㄨˊ) or 家丁(ㄐㄧㄚ ㄉㄧㄥ)
a servant (in a family)

家譜(ㄐㄧㄚ ㄆㄨˇ)
a family pedigree; a family genealogy; a family tree

家門(ㄐㄧㄚ ㄇㄣˊ)
a family (viewed in the light of its social standing)

家廟(ㄐㄧㄚ ㄇㄧㄠˋ)
the ancestral temple or shrine of a family

家母(ㄐㄧㄚ ㄇㄨˇ)
my mother (used in a polite conversation)

家法(ㄐㄧㄚ ㄈㄚˇ)
① the law of the home; domestic discipline; domestic regulations ② the thoughts or teachings of a teacher passed down through generations of followers

家訪(ㄐㄧㄚ ㄈㄤˇ) or 家庭訪問(ㄐㄧㄚ ㄊㄧㄥˊ ㄈㄤˇ ㄨㄣˋ)
a visit to the parents of schoolchildren or young workers

家風(ㄐㄧㄚ ㄈㄥ)
a family tradition; the customs of a family: 「誠實」是我們的家風。"Honesty" is our family tradition.

家父(ㄐㄧㄚ ㄈㄨˋ)
my father (used in a polite conversation)

家道(ㄐㄧㄚ ㄉㄠˋ)
① financial condition of the family; a family livelihood ② principle of homemaking

家道小康(ㄐㄧㄚ ㄉㄠˋ ㄒㄧㄠˇ ㄎㄤ)
to be comfortably off

家道中落(ㄐㄧㄚ ㄉㄠˋ ㄓㄨㄥ ㄌㄨㄛˋ)
to suffer a fall in one's family fortune

家當(ㄐㄧㄚ ㄉㄤˋ)
the belongings of a family; family property

家底(ㄐㄧㄚ ㄉㄧˇ)
the family property accumulated over a long time; resources

家電用品(ㄐㄧㄚ ㄉㄧㄢˋ ㄩㄥˋ ㄆㄧㄣˇ)
home appliances; electric appliances

家天下(ㄐㄧㄚ ㄊㄧㄢ ㄒㄧㄚˋ)
All the world belongs to the ruling house.—monopoly of power by members of a single family

家庭(ㄐㄧㄚ ㄊㄧㄥˊ)
a home; a household: 我們有一個舒適的小家庭。We have a comfortable little home.

家庭背景(ㄐㄧㄚ ㄊㄧㄥˊ ㄅㄟˋ ㄐㄧㄥˇ)
family background

家庭負擔(ㄐㄧㄚ ㄊㄧㄥˊ ㄈㄨˋ ㄉㄢ)
family responsibilities

家庭副業(ㄐㄧㄚ ㄊㄧㄥˊ ㄈㄨˋ ㄧㄝˋ)
household sideline production

家庭地位(ㄐㄧㄚ ㄊㄧㄥˊ ㄉㄧˋ ㄨㄟˋ)
family status

家庭觀念(ㄐㄧㄚ ㄊㄧㄥˊ ㄍㄨㄢ ㄋㄧㄢˋ)
attachment to one's family

家庭工業(ㄐㄧㄚ ㄊㄧㄥˊ ㄍㄨㄥ ㄧㄝˋ)
household industries: 我們並不鼓勵家庭工業。We don't encourage household industries.

家庭計劃(ㄐㄧㄚ ㄊㄧㄥˊ ㄐㄧˋ ㄏㄨㄚˋ)
family planning—birth control

家庭教師(ㄐㄧㄚ ㄊㄧㄥˊ ㄐㄧㄠˋ ㄕ)
a tutor; a private teacher; a governess

家庭教育(ㄐㄧㄚ ㄊㄧㄥˊ ㄐㄧㄠˋ ㄩˋ)
home education; training at home

家庭糾紛(ㄐㄧㄚ ㄊㄧㄥˊ ㄐㄧㄡ ㄈㄣ)
a family quarrel; domestic discord

家庭主婦(ㄐㄧㄚ ㄊㄧㄥˊ ㄓㄨˇ ㄈㄨˋ)
a housewife: 她不善做家庭主婦。She's a bad housewife.

家庭出身(ㄐㄧㄚ ㄊㄧㄥˊ ㄔㄨ ㄕㄣ)
family origin; the class status of one's family

家庭生活(ㄐㄧㄚ ㄊㄧㄥˊ ㄕㄥ ㄏㄨㄛˊ)
home life; family life

家庭作業(ㄐㄧㄚ ㄊㄧㄥˊ ㄗㄨㄛˋ ㄧㄝˋ)
homework

家庭溫暖(ㄐㄧㄚ ㄊㄧㄥˊ ㄨㄣ ㄋㄨㄢˇ)
family love

家徒壁立(ㄐㄧㄚ ㄊㄨˊ ㄅㄧˋ ㄌㄧˋ) or 家徒四壁(ㄐㄧㄚ ㄊㄨˊ ㄙˋ ㄅㄧˋ)
(literally) There stand only the walls of the house. —extremely poor

家僮(ㄐㄧㄚ ㄊㄨㄥˊ)
a young male domestic servant

家奴(ㄐㄧㄚ ㄋㄨˊ)
a domestic servant; a family slave

家累(ㄐㄧㄚ ㄌㄟˋ)
the family as a burden; a family burden

家裏(ㄐㄧㄚ ˙ㄌㄧ)
① a home ② my wife

家規(ㄐㄧㄚ ㄍㄨㄟ)
family rules: 我們家規甚嚴。Our family rules are very strict.

家和萬事興(ㄐㄧㄚ ㄏㄜˊ ㄨㄢˋ ㄕˋ ㄒㄧㄥ)
Harmony in the family is the basis for success in any undertaking.

家伙 or 傢伙(ㄐㄧㄚ ˙ㄏㄨㄛ)
(colloquial) ① furniture; a tool; a utensil; a weapon ② a fellow; a guy

家給人足(ㄐㄧㄚ ㄐㄧˇ ㄖㄣˊ ㄗㄨˊ)
(descriptive of an affluent society) Homes have adequate supplies and people live in contentment.

家計(ㄐㄧㄚ ㄐㄧˋ)
a family livelihood

家祭(ㄐㄧㄚ ㄐㄧˋ)
a funeral service attended by the members of the bereaved family

家家戶戶(ㄐㄧㄚ ㄐㄧㄚ ㄏㄨˋ ㄏㄨˋ)
every family and household: 我們要做到家家戶戶有餘糧。We want to ensure that every household has surplus grain.

家家有本難念的經(ㄐㄧㄚ ㄐㄧㄚ

ㄧㄡˇ ㄅㄣˇ ㄋㄢˊ ㄋㄧㄢˋ ·ㄉㄜ ㄐㄧㄥ
Every family has some sort of trouble. 或 Each family has its own hard nut to crack.
家教(ㄐㄧㄚ ㄐㄧㄠˋ)
① family education ② a private teacher; a tutor
家境(ㄐㄧㄚ ㄐㄧㄥˋ)
the financial condition of a family
家境困難(ㄐㄧㄚ ㄐㄧㄥˋ ㄎㄨㄣˋ ㄋㄢˊ)
with one's family in straitened circumstances
家境好(ㄐㄧㄚ ㄐㄧㄥˋ ㄏㄠˇ)
to come from a well-to-do family
家具 or 家俱(ㄐㄧㄚ ㄐㄩˋ)
furniture
家眷(ㄐㄧㄚ ㄐㄩㄢˋ)
one's family; one's dependents
家雀兒(ㄐㄧㄚ ㄑㄧㄠˇ ㄦ)
a sparrow
家禽(ㄐㄧㄚ ㄑㄧㄣˊ)
domestic fowls; poultry
家慶(ㄐㄧㄚ ㄑㄧㄥˋ)
a happy event of a family
家系(ㄐㄧㄚ ㄒㄧˋ)
lineage
家小(ㄐㄧㄚ ㄒㄧㄠˇ)
my wife and children (used in polite speech)
家信(ㄐㄧㄚ ㄒㄧㄣˋ)or 家書(ㄐㄧㄚ ㄕㄨ)
a letter from home or addressed to a member of the family: 你何時接到家信? When did you receive the letter from home?
家鄉(ㄐㄧㄚ ㄒㄧㄤ)
one's hometown; one's native heath
家鄉話(ㄐㄧㄚ ㄒㄧㄤ ㄏㄨㄚˋ)
the native dialect
家學淵源(ㄐㄧㄚ ㄒㄩㄝˊ ㄩㄢ ㄩㄢˊ)
(from) a family of scholars
家訓(ㄐㄧㄚ ㄒㄩㄣˋ)
family precepts
家兄(ㄐㄧㄚ ㄒㄩㄥ)
my elder brother (used in polite speech)
家宅(ㄐㄧㄚ ㄓㄞˊ)
a family dwelling
家珍(ㄐㄧㄚ ㄓㄣ)
family treasure or heirlooms

家長(ㄐㄧㄚ ㄓㄤˇ)
the head of a family or household
家政(ㄐㄧㄚ ㄓㄥˋ)
① housekeeping ② home economics: 她主修家政。She is a home economics major.
家政學校(ㄐㄧㄚ ㄓㄥˋ ㄒㄩㄝˊ ㄒㄧㄠˋ)
a school of home economics
家主婆(ㄐㄧㄚ ㄓㄨˇ ㄆㄛˊ)
(Soochow dialect) wife
家主公(ㄐㄧㄚ ㄓㄨˇ ㄍㄨㄥ)
(Soochow dialect) husband
家醜(ㄐㄧㄚ ㄔㄡˇ)
a family scandal; the skeleton in the cupboard(or closet)
家醜不可外揚(ㄐㄧㄚ ㄔㄡˇ ㄅㄨˋ ㄎㄜˇ ㄨㄞˋ ㄧㄤˊ)
Domestic scandals should not be publicized. 或 Don't wash your dirty linen in public.
家產(ㄐㄧㄚ ㄔㄢˇ)
family property
家常(ㄐㄧㄚ ㄔㄤˊ)
the daily life of a family; domestic trivia: 他們常一起話家常。They often talk about domestic trivia together.
家常便飯(ㄐㄧㄚ ㄔㄤˊ ㄅㄧㄢˋ ㄈㄢˋ)
① an ordinary plain meal (such as one normally gets at home); potluck ② a common occurrence; routine
家常話(ㄐㄧㄚ ㄔㄤˊ ㄏㄨㄚˋ)
a conversation about domestic routine; an ordinary conversation
家畜(ㄐㄧㄚ ㄔㄨˋ)
livestock; domestic animals
家傳(ㄐㄧㄚ ㄔㄨㄢˊ)
a family heritage; a family trait
家傳秘方(ㄐㄧㄚ ㄔㄨㄢˊ ㄇㄧˋ ㄈㄤ)
a secret recipe handed down in the family 亦作「祖傳秘方」
家世(ㄐㄧㄚ ㄕˋ)
one's descent or origin; one's family background
家室(ㄐㄧㄚ ㄕˋ)
one's dependents
家事(ㄐㄧㄚ ㄕˋ)
household affairs; housekeeping; housework; domestic chores
家聲(ㄐㄧㄚ ㄕㄥ)
family reputation
家書抵萬金(ㄐㄧㄚ ㄕㄨ ㄉㄧˇ ㄨㄢˋ ㄐㄧㄣ)
A letter from home is worth ten thousand pieces of gold.
家塾(ㄐㄧㄚ ㄕㄨˊ)
a family school
家屬(ㄐㄧㄚ ㄕㄨˇ)
one's family or dependents: 她有十位家屬。She has ten dependents.
家人(ㄐㄧㄚ ㄖㄣˊ)
the members of one's family
家賊(ㄐㄧㄚ ㄗㄟˊ)
a thief working from within
家賊難防(ㄐㄧㄚ ㄗㄟˊ ㄋㄢˊ ㄈㄤˊ)
Thieves within a household are hard to guard against. 或 It's difficult to guard against traitors.
家族(ㄐㄧㄚ ㄗㄨˊ)
a family; a clan
家族公司(ㄐㄧㄚ ㄗㄨˊ ㄍㄨㄥ ㄙ)
a family company
家慈(ㄐㄧㄚ ㄘˊ)
my mother (used in polite speech)亦作「家母」
家祠(ㄐㄧㄚ ㄘˊ)
an ancestral temple or shrine
家財(ㄐㄧㄚ ㄘㄞˊ)
family property
家私(ㄐㄧㄚ ㄙ)
family property or wealth
家業(ㄐㄧㄚ ㄧㄝˋ)
family property
家嚴(ㄐㄧㄚ ㄧㄢˊ)
my father (used in polite speech)亦作「家父」
家務(ㄐㄧㄚ ㄨˋ)
domestic chores; household affairs; housework
家喻戶曉(ㄐㄧㄚ ㄩˋ ㄏㄨˋ ㄒㄧㄠˇ)
known to every family and household; well-known; widely known
家園(ㄐㄧㄚ ㄩㄢˊ)
hometown; native heath
家用(ㄐㄧㄚ ㄩㄥˋ)
domestic expenses; family expenses; housekeeping money
家用電腦(ㄐㄧㄚ ㄩㄥˋ ㄉㄧㄢˋ ㄋㄠˇ)
a home computer

【宸】 1128 ㄔㄣˊ chern chén
1. an abode of the emperor

〔宀部〕

〔宀部〕

2. a large mansion
宸遊(ㄔㄣˊ ㄧㄡˊ)
an emperor on tour

【容】 1129
ㄖㄨㄥˊ rong róng
1. a face; an expression; a countenance
2. to contain; to hold
3. to allow; to permit
4. to forgive; to pardon
5. to forbear; forbearance
容不下(ㄖㄨㄥˊ ㄅㄨˋ ㄒㄧㄚˋ)
unable to contain, hold, accommodate or take in
容貌(ㄖㄨㄥˊ ㄇㄠˋ)
looks; a countenance; features: 永遠不要以容貌來取人。Never judge a man by his looks.
容電器(ㄖㄨㄥˊ ㄉㄧㄢˋ ㄑㄧˋ)
a condenser
容圖後報(ㄖㄨㄥˊ ㄊㄨˊ ㄏㄡˋ ㄅㄠˋ)
We (or I) will return your kindness (help, generosity, etc.) at a later date.
容納(ㄖㄨㄥˊ ㄋㄚˋ)
① to contain; to accommodate ② to tolerate; to take in: 他不能容納不同意見。He can't tolerate different opinions.
容量(ㄖㄨㄥˊ ㄌㄧㄤˋ) or 容額(ㄖㄨㄥˊ ㄜˊ)
the capacity (of a container, reservoir, etc.): 這罐的容量有四夸脫。This can has a capacity of four quarts.
容光煥發(ㄖㄨㄥˊ ㄍㄨㄤ ㄏㄨㄢˋ ㄈㄚ)
to have a face radiant with well-being
容或有之(ㄖㄨㄥˊ ㄏㄨㄛˋ ㄧㄡˇ ㄓ)
(The story or claim) may not be a pure fabrication. 或 There might be a grain of truth in it.
容積(ㄖㄨㄥˊ ㄐㄧ)
① floor space ② volume; cubic capacity
容器(ㄖㄨㄥˊ ㄑㄧˋ)
a container
容情(ㄖㄨㄥˊ ㄑㄧㄥˊ)
to be forgiving; to spare; to pardon
容膝(ㄖㄨㄥˊ ㄒㄧ)
(said of room) just big enough for the knees—a very small spot; a tiny nook
容限(ㄖㄨㄥˊ ㄒㄧㄢˋ)
(physics) tolerance; allowance
容許(ㄖㄨㄥˊ ㄒㄩˇ)
to allow; to permit: 如果時間容許, 我會來看你。I will come and see you if time permits.
容受(ㄖㄨㄥˊ ㄕㄡˋ)
① to be able to contain ② to endure; to put up with; to bear
容身(ㄖㄨㄥˊ ㄕㄣ)
to find living space: 無他容身之地。There is no place for him in society.
容恕(ㄖㄨㄥˊ ㄕㄨˋ)
to forgive; to pardon; to excuse
容人(ㄖㄨㄥˊ ㄖㄣˊ)
to be tolerant or magnanimous
容人之過(ㄖㄨㄥˊ ㄖㄣˊ ㄓ ㄍㄨㄛˋ)
to be tolerant of other people's mistakes (wrongdoing, or weaknesses)
容忍(ㄖㄨㄥˊ ㄖㄣˇ)
to endure; to bear; to tolerate; endurance; tolerance; forbearance
容讓(ㄖㄨㄥˊ ㄖㄤˋ)
to make a concession; to yield; to give in: 我不肯容讓一步。I will not yield one step.
容易(ㄖㄨㄥˊ ㄧˋ)
① easy; facile: 來得容易, 去得快。Easy come, easy go. ② apt to; liable to
容顏(ㄖㄨㄥˊ ㄧㄢˊ)
a facial appearance

八畫

【密】 1130
ㄇㄧˋ mih mì
1. dense; tight; thick: 雪下得很密。The snow was falling thick.
2. close; intimate: 他們是親密的朋友。They are intimate friends.
3. secret; confidential; hidden
密報(ㄇㄧˋ ㄅㄠˋ)
to send a secret message (or report); a secret message (or report)
密閉(ㄇㄧˋ ㄅㄧˋ)
airtight; hermetic
密閉管道(ㄇㄧˋ ㄅㄧˋ ㄍㄨㄢˇ ㄉㄠˋ)
a closed conduit
密不透風(ㄇㄧˋ ㄅㄨˋ ㄊㄡˋ ㄈㄥ)
hermetically sealed; tightly shut
密佈 or 密布(ㄇㄧˋ ㄅㄨˋ)
closely or densely spread over; densely covered by (clouds); (with secret agents, guards, etc.) everywhere
密碼(ㄇㄧˋ ㄇㄚˇ)
a secret code
密碼員(ㄇㄧˋ ㄇㄚˇ ㄩㄢˊ)
a cryptographer
密謀(ㄇㄧˋ ㄇㄡˊ)
to plan secretly; to plot; a secret scheme; a plot
密密麻麻(ㄇㄧˋ ㄇㄧˋ ㄇㄚˊ ㄇㄚˊ)
very dense; close and numerous
密訪(ㄇㄧˋ ㄈㄤˇ)
① to pay a secret visit ② to make investigation by traveling incognito
密封(ㄇㄧˋ ㄈㄥ)
to seal tightly or securely
密封容器(ㄇㄧˋ ㄈㄥ ㄖㄨㄥˊ ㄑㄧˋ)
a hermetically sealed chamber
密封文件(ㄇㄧˋ ㄈㄥ ㄨㄣˊ ㄐㄧㄢˋ)
sealed documents
密電(ㄇㄧˋ ㄉㄧㄢˋ)
a confidential telegram; a coded telegram
密度(ㄇㄧˋ ㄉㄨˋ)
density: 水銀的密度比水大得多。Mercury has a much greater density than water.
密談(ㄇㄧˋ ㄊㄢˊ)
to hold a confidential talk or conference; to have a secret or close conversation; to be closeted with; a secret conversation, talk or conference; a tête-à-tête
密探(ㄇㄧˋ ㄊㄢˋ)
a secret detective; a secret agent; a spy: 他僱了一名密探。He hired a secret detective.
密通聲息(ㄇㄧˋ ㄊㄨㄥ ㄕㄥ ㄒㄧ)
to secretly communicate with each other
密令(ㄇㄧˋ ㄌㄧㄥˋ)
a secret or confidential order

密告(ㄇㄧˋ ㄍㄠˋ)
to inform (secretly); to tip off: 他密告他的朋友。He tipped his friend off.
密克羅尼西亞(ㄇㄧˋ ㄎㄜˋ ㄌㄨㄛˊ ㄋㄧˊ ㄒㄧ ㄧㄚˋ)
Micronesia
密函(ㄇㄧˋ ㄏㄢˊ)
a secret letter; a confidential letter
密集(ㄇㄧˋ ㄐㄧˊ)
concentrated; crowded together: 這是一個人口密集的城市。This is a thickly populated city.
密集轟炸(ㄇㄧˋ ㄐㄧˊ ㄏㄨㄥ ㄓㄚˋ)
mass bombing
密集栽植法(ㄇㄧˋ ㄐㄧˊ ㄗㄞ ㄓˊ ㄈㄚˇ)
close planting
密接(ㄇㄧˋ ㄐㄧㄝ)
to adjoin; to be contiguous to: 這兩幢房屋密接在一起。The two houses adjoin.
密件(ㄇㄧˋ ㄐㄧㄢˋ)
confidential or secret documents: 他把密件鎖起來。He locked the confidential documents.
密切(ㄇㄧˋ ㄑㄧㄝˋ)
(said of relations, contact, etc.) close or intimate: 他們必須密切配合。They must act in close coordination.
密切注意(ㄇㄧˋ ㄑㄧㄝˋ ㄓㄨˋ ㄧˋ)
to pay close attention; to watch closely
密西根(ㄇㄧˋ ㄒㄧ ㄍㄣ)
Michigan, U.S.A.
密西西比(ㄇㄧˋ ㄒㄧ ㄒㄧ ㄅㄧˇ)
Mississippi, U.S.A.
密西西比河(ㄇㄧˋ ㄒㄧ ㄒㄧ ㄅㄧˇ ㄏㄜˊ)
the Mississippi River,U.S.A.
密植(ㄇㄧˋ ㄓˊ)
close planting; close sowing
密室(ㄇㄧˋ ㄕˋ)
a secret chamber; a hidden room
密商(ㄇㄧˋ ㄕㄤ)
to hold private counsel; to hold secret talks
密宗(ㄇㄧˋ ㄗㄨㄥ)
(Buddhism) the esoteric doctrine
密蘇里(ㄇㄧˋ ㄙㄨ ㄌㄧˇ)
Missouri, U.S.A.
密爾頓(ㄇㄧˋ ㄦˇ ㄉㄨㄣˋ)
Milton (1608-1674): 失樂園是約翰・密爾頓的傑作。*Paradise Lost* is John Milton's masterpiece.
密醫(ㄇㄧˋ ㄧ)
an unlicensed doctor; a quack
密議(ㄇㄧˋ ㄧˋ)
to hold a secret conference; to be closeted with; a secret conference; a confidential talk
密友(ㄇㄧˋ ㄧㄡˇ)
a close friend; an intimate: 她是我唯一的密友。She is my only close friend.
密網(ㄇㄧˋ ㄨㄤˇ)
a fine net—severe and exacting laws
密約(ㄇㄧˋ ㄩㄝ)
a secret engagement or appointment: 他跟朋友有密約。He has a secret appointment with his friend.
密雲(ㄇㄧˋ ㄩㄣˊ)
dense clouds
密雲不雨(ㄇㄧˋ ㄩㄣˊ ㄅㄨˋ ㄩˇ)
It is extremely cloudy but no rain bursts yet. 或 The storm is still brewing.

【宿】 1131
1. ㄙㄨˋ suh sù
1. to stay overnight; to lodge; to sojourn
2. long-harbored; long-cherished
3. of the former life; inborn; innate; destined
4. veteran; old
5. a Chinese family name

宿命(ㄙㄨˋ ㄇㄧㄥˋ)
predestination
宿命論(ㄙㄨˋ ㄇㄧㄥˋ ㄌㄨㄣˋ)
fatalism
宿頭(ㄙㄨˋ ㄊㄡˊ)
an inn (or a place) to stop at for the night
宿老(ㄙㄨˋ ㄌㄠˇ)
an old man (usually referring to a respectable old man)
宿根(ㄙㄨˋ ㄍㄣ)
①(Buddhism) the root of one's present lot planted in previous existence ②(botany) perennial roots; biennial roots
宿好
①(ㄙㄨˋ ㄏㄠˇ) an old friend
②(ㄙㄨˋ ㄏㄠˋ) a predilection: 他對古典音樂有宿好。He has a predilection for classical music.
宿恨(ㄙㄨˋ ㄏㄣˋ)
an old grudge; an old feud; long-harbored resentment; deep-rooted rancor
宿慧(ㄙㄨˋ ㄏㄨㄟˋ)
innate intelligence
宿疾(ㄙㄨˋ ㄐㄧˊ)
a chronic disease; an old complaint: 咳嗽是他的宿疾。Cough is his chronic disease.
宿將(ㄙㄨˋ ㄐㄧㄤˋ)
a veteran general
宿昔(ㄙㄨˋ ㄒㄧˊ)
① the past; days gone by: 他心中滿懷宿昔之回憶。Memories of the past filled his mind. ② long-standing
宿志(ㄙㄨˋ ㄓˋ)or 宿心(ㄙㄨˋ ㄒㄧㄣ)
a long-cherished ambition or desire; one's heart's desire
宿主(ㄙㄨˋ ㄓㄨˇ)
the host (of parasites)
宿世(ㄙㄨˋ ㄕˋ)
former existence (by the Buddhist concept of life and death as a cycle)
宿舍(ㄙㄨˋ ㄕㄜˋ)
a dormitory; living quarters
宿膳(ㄙㄨˋ ㄕㄢˋ)
board and lodging
宿儒(ㄙㄨˋ ㄖㄨˊ)
a learned scholar
宿賊(ㄙㄨˋ ㄗㄟˊ)
an old experienced thief
宿醉(ㄙㄨˋ ㄗㄨㄟˋ)
hangover: 他宿醉未醒。He hasn't recovered from the hangover.
宿業(ㄙㄨˋ ㄧㄝˋ)
(Buddhism) karma
宿營(ㄙㄨˋ ㄧㄥˊ)
(said of troops) to bivouac for the night
宿緣(ㄙㄨˋ ㄩㄢˊ)
(Buddhism) causation or inheritance from previous existence
宿怨(ㄙㄨˋ ㄩㄢˋ)
an old grudge; long-harbored resentment; an old feud

宿願(ㄙㄨˋ ㄩㄢˋ)
a long-fostered wish; a cherished hope; one's heart's desire: 到巴黎去玩是他的宿願。To take a tour to Paris is his cherished hope.

【宿】 1131
2. ㄒㄧㄡˇ shiow xiǔ
an ancient term for a constellation; an asterism

【宿】 1131
3. ㄒㄧㄡˇ sheou xiǔ
night: 我們談了半宿。We chat till midnight.

宿夕(ㄒㄧㄡˇ ㄒㄧ)
① a single night ② a short period of time

【寂】 1132
ㄐㄧˊ jyi jí
1. the death of a Buddhist monk or nun
2. quiet; still; serene; peaceful; desolate: 萬籟俱寂。All is quiet and still.

寂寞(ㄐㄧˊ ㄇㄛˋ)
lonely; lonesome

寂滅(ㄐㄧˊ ㄇㄧㄝˋ)
(Buddhism) calmness and extinction; nirvana

寂寥(ㄐㄧˊ ㄌㄧㄠˊ)
lonely; still; desolate; deserted: 他在陌生的人羣中甚覺寂寥。He was lonely among strangers.

寂寂(ㄐㄧˊ ㄐㄧˊ)
quiet; still

寂靜(ㄐㄧˊ ㄐㄧㄥˋ)
quiet; still

寂然(ㄐㄧˊ ㄖㄢˊ)
quiet; still; silent: 一切寂然。All is silent.

【寄】 1133
ㄐㄧˋ jih jì
1. to send; to transmit; to mail: 我寄給她一封航空信。I sent her a letter by air mail.
2. to entrust; to consign; to commit; to deposit

寄賣(ㄐㄧˋ ㄇㄞˋ)or 寄售(ㄐㄧˋ ㄕㄡˋ)
to consign (goods, etc.) for sale

寄費(ㄐㄧˋ ㄈㄟˋ)
postage: 一本書的寄費要多少呢? What is the postage for a book?

寄放(ㄐㄧˋ ㄈㄤˋ)or 寄存(ㄐㄧˋ ㄘㄨㄣˊ)
to place or leave (a thing) in (another's) custody; to leave with; to leave in the care of

寄頓(ㄐㄧˋ ㄉㄨㄣˋ)
to place in safekeeping

寄託 or 寄托(ㄐㄧˋ ㄊㄨㄛ)
① to consign or commit (one's soul to God, emotions to writing, etc.) ② to leave with somebody; to entrust to the care of somebody

寄懷(ㄐㄧˋ ㄏㄨㄞˊ)
to express one's feeling (by literary means, etc.) or to consign one's emotions to (writing, etc.)

寄籍(ㄐㄧˋ ㄐㄧˊ)
to have one's home temporarily in another town, country, etc.

寄件人(ㄐㄧˋ ㄐㄧㄢˋ ㄖㄣˊ)
a sender

寄居(ㄐㄧˋ ㄐㄩ)
to live temporarily (with a family, in a place, etc.)

寄情(ㄐㄧˋ ㄑㄧㄥˊ)
to give expression to one's feelings (through writing, etc.)

寄情詩酒(ㄐㄧˋ ㄑㄧㄥˊ ㄕ ㄐㄧㄡˇ)
to abandon oneself to wine and poetry: 李白寄情詩酒。Li Po abandoned himself to wine and poetry.

寄情山水(ㄐㄧˋ ㄑㄧㄥˊ ㄕㄢ ㄕㄨㄟˇ)
to abandon oneself to nature: 吾友寄情山水。My friend abandons himself to nature.

寄銷(ㄐㄧˋ ㄒㄧㄠ)
(accounting) goods-out on a consignment; shipment outward; consignment; consignment-out (outward); consignment sales

寄銷商店(ㄐㄧˋ ㄒㄧㄠ ㄕㄤ ㄉㄧㄢˋ)
a consignment store; a consignment business

寄信(ㄐㄧˋ ㄒㄧㄣˋ)
to send or mail a letter: 我已寄信給他。I have sent him a letter.

寄信人(ㄐㄧˋ ㄒㄧㄣˋ ㄖㄣˊ)
a sender

寄興(ㄐㄧˋ ㄒㄧㄥˋ)
to give vent to one's interest

寄食(ㄐㄧˋ ㄕˊ)
to live with another at his expense; to live by eating at another's table; to be a parasite

寄身(ㄐㄧˋ ㄕㄣ)
to live or sojourn (abroad, etc.) for the time being

寄生(ㄐㄧˋ ㄕㄥ)
parasitism; to be a parasite (on); to be parasitic (on)

寄生動物(ㄐㄧˋ ㄕㄥ ㄉㄨㄥˋ ㄨˋ)
a parasitic animal

寄生昆蟲(ㄐㄧˋ ㄕㄥ ㄎㄨㄣ ㄔㄨㄥˊ)
a parasitic insect

寄生植物(ㄐㄧˋ ㄕㄥ ㄓˊ ㄨˋ)
a parasitic plant

寄生蟲(ㄐㄧˋ ㄕㄥ ㄔㄨㄥˊ)
a parasite

寄人籬下(ㄐㄧˋ ㄖㄣˊ ㄌㄧˊ ㄒㄧㄚˋ)
to live in another's house (either for protection or as a dependent)

寄宿(ㄐㄧˋ ㄙㄨˋ)
to lodge (at another's house); to take up one's lodgings in; to board: 你現在寄宿在何處? Where are you lodging now?

寄宿學校(ㄐㄧˋ ㄙㄨˋ ㄒㄩㄝˊ ㄒㄧㄠˋ)
a boarding school; a residential college

寄宿生(ㄐㄧˋ ㄙㄨˋ ㄕㄥ)
a resident student

寄意(ㄐㄧˋ ㄧˋ)
to send one's regards

寄養(ㄐㄧˋ ㄧㄤˇ)
① to send a child to another family for temporary care ② to depend on others for a living

寄予(ㄐㄧˋ ㄩˇ)
① to place (hope, etc.) on ② to show; to give; to express

寄語(ㄐㄧˋ ㄩˇ)
to send word; to convey a message: 寄語友人報喜訊。Send our dear friends the happy news.

【寅】 1134
ㄧㄣˊ yn yín
1. the third of the twelve Terrestrial Branches (地支)
2. a fellow officer; a colleague
3. a horary sign (for the period from 3 to 5 a.m.)

寅支卯糧(ㄧㄣˊ ㄓ ㄇㄠˇ ㄌㄧㄤˊ)or 寅吃卯糧(ㄧㄣˊ ㄔ ㄇㄠˇ ㄌㄧㄤˊ)
(literally) to have consumed

in the present year the supplies that belong to the next —unable to make both ends meet

寅時(ㄧㄣˊ ㄕˊ)or 寅刻(ㄧㄣˊ ㄎㄜˋ)
the period of the day from 3 a.m. to 5 a.m.

寅月(ㄧㄣˊ ㄩㄝˋ)
the first month of the lunar calendar

【寇】1135 ㄎㄡˋ kow kòu
1. bandits; enemies; robbers
2. to invade; to pillage; to plunder
3. a Chinese family name

寇盜(ㄎㄡˋ ㄉㄠˋ)or 寇匪(ㄎㄡˋ ㄈㄟˇ)
insurgents

寇仇 or 寇讎(ㄎㄡˋ ㄔㄡˊ)
an enemy; a foe

九畫

【富】1136 ㄈㄨˋ fuh fù
1. rich; wealthy; affluent; abundant; plentiful: 他出身於一個富裕的家庭。He comes from a wealthy family.
2. a Chinese family name

富態(ㄈㄨˋ ㄊㄞˋ)
looking gentle and prosperous

富農(ㄈㄨˋ ㄋㄨㄥˊ)
a rich farmer: 他是個富農。He is a rich farmer.

富麗堂皇(ㄈㄨˋ ㄌㄧˋ ㄊㄤˊ ㄏㄨㄤˊ)
majestic; grand; splendid; gorgeous; magnificent; stately: 他住在一所富麗堂皇的房子裡。He lives in a grand house.

富國強兵(ㄈㄨˋ ㄍㄨㄛˊ ㄑㄧㄤˊ ㄅㄧㄥ)
to make one's country rich and to build up its military power

富貴(ㄈㄨˋ ㄍㄨㄟˋ)
wealth and high position

富貴逼人(ㄈㄨˋ ㄍㄨㄟˋ ㄅㄧ ㄖㄣˊ)
① Wealth and honor come to us only of their own accord. ② snobbish

富貴不能淫(ㄈㄨˋ ㄍㄨㄟˋ ㄅㄨˋ ㄋㄥˊ ㄧㄣˊ)
to be impervious to the temptation of wealth and high position; utterly incorruptible

富貴利達(ㄈㄨˋ ㄍㄨㄟˋ ㄌㄧˋ ㄉㄚˊ)
rich and powerful

富貴花(ㄈㄨˋ ㄍㄨㄟˋ ㄏㄨㄚ)
a peony

富豪(ㄈㄨˋ ㄏㄠˊ)
a man of wealth and influence

富戶(ㄈㄨˋ ㄏㄨˋ)
a wealthy family

富家子(ㄈㄨˋ ㄐㄧㄚ ㄗˇ)
children of a wealthy family

富家翁(ㄈㄨˋ ㄐㄧㄚ ㄨㄥ)
a man of wealth; a rich man

富甲天下(ㄈㄨˋ ㄐㄧㄚˇ ㄊㄧㄢ ㄒㄧㄚˋ)
the richest in the world

富強(ㄈㄨˋ ㄑㄧㄤˊ)
(said of a state) wealthy and powerful

富士山(ㄈㄨˋ ㄕˋ ㄕㄢ)
Mt. Fuji, the highest peak in Japan

富商(ㄈㄨˋ ㄕㄤ)
a wealthy merchant

富庶(ㄈㄨˋ ㄕㄨˋ)
(said of land) plentiful and populous

富孀(ㄈㄨˋ ㄕㄨㄤ)
a rich widow

富饒(ㄈㄨˋ ㄖㄠˊ)
plentiful; abundant; rich; plenty; abundance: 這土地礦產富饒。This land is abundant in minerals.

富足(ㄈㄨˋ ㄗㄨˊ)
well-off; well-to-do: 他出身富足之家。He came from a well-to-do family.

富而好禮(ㄈㄨˋ ㄦˊ ㄏㄠˋ ㄌㄧˇ)
wealthy and courteous

富而無驕(ㄈㄨˋ ㄦˊ ㄨˊ ㄐㄧㄠ)
rich but not smug

富爾敦(ㄈㄨˋ ㄦˇ ㄉㄨㄣ)
Robert Fulton, 1765-1815, inventor of the steamboat

富有(ㄈㄨˋ ㄧㄡˇ)
① to abound in; to teem with ② rich; wealthy

富翁(ㄈㄨˋ ㄨㄥ)
a rich man

富於(ㄈㄨˋ ㄩˊ)
rich in (imagination, creative capacity, etc.): 詩人富於想像力。Poets are rich in imagination.

富裕(ㄈㄨˋ ㄩˋ)
rich; wealthy; prosperous

【寐】1137 ㄇㄟˋ mey mèi
a sound sleep; a deep sleep; to doze; to drowse; to sleep

【寒】1138 ㄏㄢˊ harn hán
1. cold; chilly; wintry
2. poor

寒毛(ㄏㄢˊ ・ㄇㄠ)
downy hair (on human body)

寒門(ㄏㄢˊ ㄇㄣˊ)
① a poor family: 他出身寒門。He came from a poor family. ② my poor family (a self-depreciatory expression)

寒風(ㄏㄢˊ ㄈㄥ)
a cold wind: 寒風自北方吹來。A cold wind was blowing from the north.

寒風刺骨(ㄏㄢˊ ㄈㄥ ㄘˋ ㄍㄨˇ)
The cold wind chilled one to the bone.

寒帶(ㄏㄢˊ ㄉㄞˋ)
the Frigid Zone: 阿拉斯加屬於寒帶。Alaska belongs to the Frigid Zone.

寒來暑往(ㄏㄢˊ ㄌㄞˊ ㄕㄨˇ ㄨㄤˇ)
(literally) The cold comes and the heat departs.—a change of seasons; a lapse of time

寒冷(ㄏㄢˊ ㄌㄥˇ)
cold; chilly; chilling: 他怕寒冷。He is afraid of cold.

寒流(ㄏㄢˊ ㄌㄧㄡˊ)
① a cold current; polar currents ② a scholar of little means

寒苦(ㄏㄢˊ ㄎㄨˇ)
poor; in financial straits; destitute

寒劑(ㄏㄢˊ ㄐㄧˋ)
a freezing mixture

寒假(ㄏㄢˊ ㄐㄧㄚˋ)
the winter vacation: 寒假他到日本去。He left for Japan during the winter vacation.

寒賤(ㄏㄢˊ ㄐㄧㄢˋ)
of humble origin

寒噤(ㄏㄢˊ ㄐㄧㄣˋ)
a shudder; a shiver; a tremble: 他打了一個寒噤。A shiver ran over his body.

寒氣(ㄏㄢˊ ㄑㄧˋ)
chilly air; cold air: 寒氣逼人。There is a nip in the air.

寒心(ㄏㄢˊ ㄒㄧㄣ)
to feel the blood running cold; afraid; fearful: 他的無情令人寒心。His ruthlessness makes me afraid.
寒暄(ㄏㄢˊ ㄒㄩㄢ)or 寒溫(ㄏㄢˊ ㄨㄣ)
to talk about the weather (in a conversation); to exchange a few words of greeting with (somebody)
寒顫(ㄏㄢˊ ㄓㄢˋ)
to tremble with cold or fear
寒戰(ㄏㄢˊ ㄓㄢˋ)
a tremble caused by cold; to tremble with cold: 我們因冷而寒戰。We were trembling with cold.
寒窗(ㄏㄢˊ ㄔㄨㄤ)
the financial difficulties of a scholar
寒食(節)(ㄏㄢˊ ㄕˊ (ㄐㄧㄝˊ))
the 105th to 107th day after the winter solstice, a period set aside in memory of Chieh Tsu-tuei (介子推), during which food is supposed to be eaten cold
寒士(ㄏㄢˊ ㄕˋ)
a scholar of little means; a poor scholar: 他是位寒士。He is a poor scholar.
寒舍(ㄏㄢˊ ㄕㄜˋ)
(a self-depreciatory term) my poor house
寒暑表(ㄏㄢˊ ㄕㄨˇ ㄅㄧㄠˇ)
a thermometer
寒傖(ㄏㄢˊ ㄘㄤ)
(colloquial) ① ugly; unsightly ② shabby; disgraceful ③ to ridicule
寒酸(ㄏㄢˊ ㄙㄨㄢ)
① poverty; poverty-stricken condition (especially referring to face-loving intellectuals) ② unpresentable (dress, gifts, etc.)
寒衣(ㄏㄢˊ ㄧ)
winter clothes
寒意(ㄏㄢˊ ㄧˋ)
a nip (or chill) in the air: 初春季節仍有寒意。It's spring but there's still a chill in the air.
寒夜(ㄏㄢˊ ㄧㄝˋ)
a cold night; a chilly night
寒微(ㄏㄢˊ ㄨㄟˊ)
of low station; of humble origin: 他出身寒微。He is a man of humble origin.

【寓】 1139 ㄩˋ yuh yù

1. to live temporarily; to sojourn; to dwell
2. to consign
寓目(ㄩˋ ㄇㄨˋ)
to stare; to gaze; to look closely
寓託(ㄩˋ ㄊㄨㄛ)
to imply (meaning); to show (something) in parables or by indirect means
寓公(ㄩˋ ㄍㄨㄥ)
① a man of wealth living as an exile ②(formerly) a government official residing away from home
寓禁關稅(ㄩˋ ㄐㄧㄣˋ ㄍㄨㄢ ㄕㄨㄟˋ)
prohibitive tariff or duties
寓禁於征(ㄩˋ ㄐㄧㄣˋ ㄩˊ ㄓㄥ)
to try to prohibit a business by taxing it heavily
寓居(ㄩˋ ㄐㄩ)
to make one's home in (a place other than one's native place): 他晚年寓居美國。He made America his home in his old age.
寓所(ㄩˋ ㄙㄨㄛˇ)
one's residence or dwelling
寓意(ㄩˋ ㄧˋ)
a moral (of a fable): 這故事含有多種寓意。There is more than one moral to be drawn from this story.
寓意深刻(ㄩˋ ㄧˋ ㄕㄣ ㄎㄜˋ)
to be pregnant with meaning
寓言(ㄩˋ ㄧㄢˊ)
a fable; an allegory

十畫

【寘】 1140 ㄓˋ jyh zhì

1. to put; to place
2. to discard
3. to make or cause
4. full

十一畫

【寞】 1141 ㄇㄛˋ moh mò

still; silent; quiet; lonely

【察】 1142 ㄔㄚˊ char chá

to examine; to observe; to investigate; to survey; to study; to scrutinize
察辦(ㄔㄚˊ ㄅㄢˋ)
to investigate a case and determine how to handle it
察破(ㄔㄚˊ ㄆㄛˋ)
to see through (a plot, trick, etc.)
察訪(ㄔㄚˊ ㄈㄤˇ)
to investigate by visiting the sources of information
察看(ㄔㄚˊ ㄎㄢˋ)
to observe; to watch
察勘(ㄔㄚˊ ㄎㄢ)
to survey; to examine: 他察勘房間。He examined the room.
察哈爾(ㄔㄚˊ ㄏㄚ ㄦˇ)
Chahar Province
察核(ㄔㄚˊ ㄏㄜˊ)
to investigate a case and then decide what to do
察覺(ㄔㄚˊ ㄐㄩㄝˊ)
to be conscious of; to become aware of; to perceive
察言觀色(ㄔㄚˊ ㄧㄢˊ ㄍㄨㄢ ㄙㄜˋ)
to gather another's frame of mind through his words and expressions

【寧】 1143 ㄋㄧㄥˊ ning níng

1. peace; repose; serenity; tranquility
2. would rather; had rather; would sooner
3. could there be
寧波(ㄋㄧㄥˊ ㄅㄛ)
Ningpo, a city in Chekiang Province
寧波幫(ㄋㄧㄥˊ ㄅㄛ ㄅㄤ)
the merchants from Ningpo (noted for their business acumen)
寧謐(ㄋㄧㄥˊ ㄇㄧˋ)
tranquil
寧非奇事(ㄋㄧㄥˊ ㄈㄟ ㄑㄧˊ ㄕˋ)
Isn't it strange that...?
寧可(ㄋㄧㄥˊ ㄎㄜˇ)or 寧肯(ㄋㄧㄥˊ ㄎㄣˇ)
would rather: 寧可信其有，不可信其無。We'd rather believe it to be true than not.
寧靜(ㄋㄧㄥˊ ㄐㄧㄥˋ)
quiet; tranquil; serene; placid; calm
寧靜以致遠(ㄋㄧㄥˊ ㄐㄧㄥˋ ㄧˇ ㄓˋ ㄩㄢˇ)

to accomplish something lasting by leading quiet life

寧缺毋濫(ㄋㄧㄥˋ ㄑㄩㄝ ㄨˊ ㄌㄢˋ)
It is better to leave a deficiency uncovered than to have it covered without discretion.

寧夏(ㄋㄧㄥˊ ㄒㄧㄚˋ)
Ningxia Province

寧馨兒(ㄋㄧㄥˊ ㄒㄧㄥ ㄦˊ)
a lovely child

寧日(ㄋㄧㄥˊ ㄖˋ)
peaceful days

寧贈外賊，不與家奴(ㄋㄧㄥˋ ㄗㄥˋ ㄨㄞˋ ㄗㄟˊ, ㄅㄨˋ ㄩˇ ㄐㄧㄚ ㄋㄨˊ)
(said of a dictator or warlord) would rather betray the nation in order to keep personal power than introduce democracy

寧死(ㄋㄧㄥˋ ㄙˇ)
would rather die: 他寧死不降。He would rather die than surrender.

寧死不屈(ㄋㄧㄥˋ ㄙˇ ㄅㄨˋ ㄑㄩ)
would rather die than submit (or surrender)

寧爲鷄口，毋爲牛後(ㄋㄧㄥˋ ㄨㄟˊ ㄐㄧ ㄎㄡˇ, ㄨˊ ㄨㄟˊ ㄋㄧㄡˊ ㄏㄡˋ)
would rather have a low but independent position than hold a high position under the control of others

寧爲玉碎，不爲瓦全(ㄋㄧㄥˋ ㄨㄟˊ ㄩˋ ㄙㄨㄟˋ, ㄅㄨˋ ㄨㄟˊ ㄨㄚˇ ㄑㄩㄢˊ)
would rather die for justice than live in disgrace

寧願(ㄋㄧㄥˋ ㄩㄢˋ)
would rather; would sooner

【寡】 1144 ㄍㄨㄚˇ goa guǎ
1. widowed; surviving the spouse
2. lonely; alone; solitary
3. little; few; scant; rare: 失道寡助。An unjust cause finds scant support.

寡不敵衆(ㄍㄨㄚˇ ㄅㄨˋ ㄉㄧˊ ㄓㄨㄥˋ)
to be overwhelmed by sheer number; to be overpowered by the enemy's larger number

寡夫(ㄍㄨㄚˇ ㄈㄨ)
a widower 亦作「鰥夫」

寡婦(ㄍㄨㄚˇ ㄈㄨˋ)
a widow

寡斷(ㄍㄨㄚˇ ㄉㄨㄢˋ)
irresolute; indecisive: 他是個優柔寡斷的領導者。He is an indecisive leader.

寡頭(ㄍㄨㄚˇ ㄊㄡˊ)
an oligarch

寡頭政治(ㄍㄨㄚˇ ㄊㄡˊ ㄓㄥˋ ㄓˋ)
oligarchy

寡陋(ㄍㄨㄚˇ ㄌㄡˋ)
ignorant; having seen little of the world

寡廉鮮恥(ㄍㄨㄚˇ ㄌㄧㄢˊ ㄒㄧㄢˇ ㄔˇ)
shameless; unabashed; having no sense of morality

寡過(ㄍㄨㄚˇ ㄍㄨㄛˋ)
to discipline oneself (so as to commit fewer and fewer mistakes daily)

寡合(ㄍㄨㄚˇ ㄏㄜˊ)
having little intercourse with others

寡歡(ㄍㄨㄚˇ ㄏㄨㄢ)
unhappy: 他獨處時落落寡歡。He was unhappy when alone.

寡見少聞(ㄍㄨㄚˇ ㄐㄧㄢˋ ㄕㄠˇ ㄨㄣˊ)
shallow; poorly informed; ignorance

寡居(ㄍㄨㄚˇ ㄐㄩ)
to live as a widow

寡情(ㄍㄨㄚˇ ㄑㄧㄥˊ)
unfeeling; cold; cold-hearted; heartless

寡人(ㄍㄨㄚˇ ㄖㄣˊ)
(the royal) we

寡恩(ㄍㄨㄚˇ ㄣ)
showing little favor; unkind

寡言(ㄍㄨㄚˇ ㄧㄢˊ)
taciturn; not given to talk: 他是個沈默寡言的人。He is a taciturn man.

寡聞(ㄍㄨㄚˇ ㄨㄣˊ)
having little knowledge: 他因獨處而孤陋寡聞。Living alone, he is ill-informed.

寡慾(ㄍㄨㄚˇ ㄩˋ)
having few desires; ascetic

【寢】 1145 ㄑㄧㄣˇ chiin qǐn
1. to sleep; to rest
2. a tomb
3. a residence
4. stop; end

寢兵(ㄑㄧㄣˇ ㄅㄧㄥ)
to stop wars (or fighting)

寢寐(ㄑㄧㄣˇ ㄇㄟˋ)
to sleep

寢寐難安(ㄑㄧㄣˇ ㄇㄟˋ ㄋㄢˊ ㄢ)
a restless sleep (from worries)

寢陋(ㄑㄧㄣˇ ㄌㄡˋ)
ugly

寢戈(ㄑㄧㄣˇ ㄍㄜ)
(descriptive of combat readiness) to use weapons as pillows

寢饋其中(ㄑㄧㄣˇ ㄎㄨㄟˋ ㄑㄧˊ ㄓㄨㄥ)
completely absorbed (in a subject of study)

寢疾(ㄑㄧㄣˇ ㄐㄧˊ)
to be confined to bed by illness

寢具(ㄑㄧㄣˇ ㄐㄩˋ)
bedding

寢其皮而食其肉(ㄑㄧㄣˇ ㄑㄧˊ ㄆㄧˊ ㄦˊ ㄕˊ ㄑㄧˊ ㄖㄡˋ)
(descriptive of deep hatred) to sleep on his hide and eat his flesh

寢處
①(ㄑㄧㄣˇ ㄔㄨˇ) to sit or to sleep—to rest
②(ㄑㄧㄣˇ ㄔㄨˋ) a sleeping place

寢食不安(ㄑㄧㄣˇ ㄕˊ ㄅㄨˋ ㄢ)
uneasy when eating and sleeping; restless due to deep worries

寢食難忘(ㄑㄧㄣˇ ㄕˊ ㄋㄢˊ ㄨㄤˋ)
constantly in one's mind

寢食俱廢(ㄑㄧㄣˇ ㄕˊ ㄐㄩˋ ㄈㄟˋ)
wanting neither food nor sleep because of deep worries or sorrow

寢室(ㄑㄧㄣˇ ㄕˋ)
a bedroom

【寤】 1146 ㄨˋ wuh wù
to awake from a sound sleep

寤寐(ㄨˋ ㄇㄟˋ)
between sleep and wakefulness

寤夢(ㄨˋ ㄇㄥˋ)
to see something during the day and to dream about it at night

寤生(ㄨˋ ㄕㄥ)
to give birth to a baby while asleep

【寥】 1147 ㄌㄧㄠˊ liau liáo
1. few; not many
2. deserted; desolate; empty

寥寥(ㄌㄧㄠˊ ㄌㄧㄠˊ)
empty; scarce

寥寥無幾(ㄌㄧㄠˊ ㄌㄧㄠˊ ㄨˊ ㄐㄧˇ)
not many; few: 他的朋友寥寥無幾。He has few friends.

寥落(ㄌㄧㄠˊ ㄌㄨㄛˋ)
sparse

寥闊(ㄌㄧㄠˊ ㄎㄨㄛˋ)
expansive; expanse

寥廓(ㄌㄧㄠˊ ㄎㄨㄛˋ)
vast and empty; boundless

寥若晨星(ㄌㄧㄠˊ ㄖㄨㄛˋ ㄔㄣˊ ㄒㄧㄥ)
as few as morning stars

【實】 1148 ㄕˊ shyr shí

1. real; true; actual: 你所說的不確實。What you say is not true.
2. practically: 實際上，這計畫行不通。Practically, the plan did not work well.
3. honest; faithful; sincere
4. concrete; substantial; solid; tangible
5. fact; reality; truth; actuality
6. fruit; seed

實報實銷(ㄕˊ ㄅㄠˋ ㄕˊ ㄒㄧㄠ)
to report expenses honestly; to be reimbursed for what one spends actually

實繁有徒(ㄕˊ ㄈㄢˊ ㄧㄡˇ ㄊㄨˊ)
Many people are involved.

實彈射擊(ㄕˊ ㄉㄢˋ ㄕㄜˋ ㄐㄧˊ)
a live ammunition fire practice

實彈演習(ㄕˊ ㄉㄢˋ ㄧㄢˇ ㄒㄧˊ)
to practice with live ammunition

實地調查(ㄕˊ ㄉㄧˋ ㄉㄧㄠˋ ㄔㄚˊ)
an on-the-spot investigation

實體(ㄕˊ ㄊㄧˇ)
substance (as opposed to form)

實力(ㄕˊ ㄌㄧˋ)
strength (often said of collective strength, including resources and potentialities)

實力相當(ㄕˊ ㄌㄧˋ ㄒㄧㄤ ㄉㄤ)
to match each other in strength; to be well-matched in strength

實利(ㄕˊ ㄌㄧˋ)
practical value; tangible benefits

實例(ㄕˊ ㄌㄧˋ)
a living example; an example

實齡(ㄕˊ ㄌㄧㄥˊ)
age at last birthday

實錄(ㄕˊ ㄌㄨˋ)
a faithful record

實感(ㄕˊ ㄍㄢˇ)
the sensation acquired from an actual experience (not from other media)

實幹(ㄕˊ ㄍㄢˋ)
to take real action

實科(ㄕˊ ㄎㄜ)
practical courses (as opposed to theoretical courses)

實況(ㄕˊ ㄎㄨㄤˋ)
factual conditions; actual conditions; live (broadcasts or telecasts)

實況錄音(ㄕˊ ㄎㄨㄤˋ ㄌㄨˋ ㄧㄣ)
a live recording; an on-the-spot recording

實況轉播(ㄕˊ ㄎㄨㄤˋ ㄓㄨㄢˇ ㄅㄛ)
a live broadcast; a live telecast: 這是實況轉播，不是錄音轉播。It was a live broadcast, not a recording.

實話(ㄕˊ ㄏㄨㄚˋ)
the truth

實話實說(ㄕˊ ㄏㄨㄚˋ ㄕˊ ㄕㄨㄛ)
to tell the truth (without adding or withholding anything)

實惠(ㄕˊ ㄏㄨㄟˋ)
a real benefit; a tangible benefit; beneficial in a tangible way: 我們讓顧客買到經濟實惠的物品。We offer the customers inexpensive but substantial articles.

實績(ㄕˊ ㄐㄧ)
actual results; tangible achievements

實際(ㄕˊ ㄐㄧˋ)
① actual; real; concrete ② practical; realistic: 你這種想法不實際。This idea of yours is unrealistic. ③ reality; practice: 這是個實際和理論相結合的例子。This example is the unity of practice and theory.

實際工資(ㄕˊ ㄐㄧˋ ㄍㄨㄥ ㄗ)
real wages

實際經驗(ㄕˊ ㄐㄧˋ ㄐㄧㄥ ㄧㄢˋ)
practical experience

實際情況(ㄕˊ ㄐㄧˋ ㄑㄧㄥˊ ㄎㄨㄤˋ)
reality; the actual situation

實際收入(ㄕˊ ㄐㄧˋ ㄕㄡ ㄖㄨˋ)
real income

實際人口(ㄕˊ ㄐㄧˋ ㄖㄣˊ ㄎㄡˇ)
actual population

實價(ㄕˊ ㄐㄧㄚˋ)
an honest price; an actual price

實踐(ㄕˊ ㄐㄧㄢˋ)
to practice (a principle); to put in practice: 眞知來自實踐。Genuine knowledge comes from practice.

實踐哲學(ㄕˊ ㄐㄧㄢˋ ㄓㄜˊ ㄒㄩㄝˊ)
practical philosophy

實據(ㄕˊ ㄐㄩˋ)
substantial evidence; substantial proof

實情(ㄕˊ ㄑㄧㄥˊ)
the actual situation; the real picture or real story (of a case)

實缺(ㄕˊ ㄑㄩㄝ)
a vacancy or opening: 內閣裡有實缺。There is a vacancy in the Cabinet.

實權(ㄕˊ ㄑㄩㄢˊ)
real power or authority: 首相有實權。The prime minister has real power.

實習(ㄕˊ ㄒㄧˊ)
(said of students or trainees shortly before or immediately after graduation) to practice what one has been taught

實習工廠(ㄕˊ ㄒㄧˊ ㄍㄨㄥ ㄔㄤˇ)
a factory attached to a school

實習生(ㄕˊ ㄒㄧˊ ㄕㄥ)
a trainee

實習醫生(ㄕˊ ㄒㄧˊ ㄧ ㄕㄥ)
an intern(e)

實效(ㄕˊ ㄒㄧㄠˋ)
real effect; effect

實現(ㄕˊ ㄒㄧㄢˋ)
to realize (a plan, etc.); (said of a dream, etc.) to come true: 這計劃不容易實現。This plan is difficult to realize.

實心(ㄕˊ ㄒㄧㄣ)
① sincere; honest ② in a serious manner ③ solid (as distinct from hollow): 這種車胎是實心的。These tires are solid.

實心眼兒(ㄕˊ ㄒㄧㄣ ㄧㄚˇㄦ)
frank; unfeigned; honest: 這人很實心眼兒。This man is

quite honest.

實像(ㄕˊ ㄒㄧㄤˋ)
(physics) a real image

實行(ㄕˊ ㄒㄧㄥˊ)
to practice (a principle); to carry out; to put into practice

實學(ㄕˊ ㄒㄩㄝˊ)
learning of genuine value

實值(ㄕˊ ㄓˊ)
net value; intrinsic value; real value

實質(ㄕˊ ㄓˊ)
essence; substance

實質所得(ㄕˊ ㄓˊ ㄙㄨㄛˇ ㄉㄜˊ)
real income

實至名歸(ㄕˊ ㄓˋ ㄇㄧㄥˊ ㄍㄨㄟ)
Where there is real ability, there is fame.

實戰(ㄕˊ ㄓㄢˋ)
actual combat

實戰演習(ㄕˊ ㄓㄢˋ ㄧㄢˇ ㄒㄧˊ)
combat exercises with live ammunition

實證(ㄕˊ ㄓㄥˋ)
①(Chinese medicine) a case of a physically strong patient running a high fever or suffering from such disorders as stasis of blood, constipation, etc. ② concrete evidence

實證主義(ㄕˊ ㄓㄥˋ ㄓㄨˇ ㄧˋ)or 實證論(ㄕˊ ㄓㄥˋ ㄌㄨㄣˋ)
(philosophy) positivism

實施(ㄕˊ ㄕ)
to put (regulations, plans, etc.) into effect; to implement: 新的條款已付諸實施。The new provisions have been put into effect.

實事求是(ㄕˊ ㄕˋ ㄑㄧㄡˊ ㄕˋ)
to work conscientiously or seriously; to make conscientious efforts to do things

實收(ㄕˊ ㄕㄡ)
net receipts

實數(ㄕˊ ㄕㄨˋ)
(mathematics) a true number

實字(ㄕˊ ㄗˋ)
a content word (as opposed to a function word or particle)

實在(ㄕˊ ㄗㄞˋ)or 實實在在(ㄕˊ ㄕˊ ㄗㄞˋ ㄗㄞˋ)
① really; truly; certainly; in fact ② real; solid; concrete; tangible ③ well-done: 工作做得很實在。The work is well-done.

實足(ㄕˊ ㄗㄨˊ)
full; solid: 我實足等了三個鐘頭。I waited for three solid hours.

實足年齡(ㄕˊ ㄗㄨˊ ㄋㄧㄢˊ ㄌㄧㄥˊ)
one's full age (as distinct from the age by the Chinese custom of counting the fraction of a year as one full year)

實業(ㄕˊ ㄧㄝˋ)
industry; business

實業家(ㄕˊ ㄧㄝˋ ㄐㄧㄚ)
an industrialist; a businessman; an entrepreneur

實業界(ㄕˊ ㄧㄝˋ ㄐㄧㄝˋ)
industry; the business world or circles; the industrial world or circles: 實業界與政府的意見一致嗎? Does industry agree with the government?

實驗(ㄕˊ ㄧㄢˋ)
to experiment; to test; an experiment; a test: 科學家藉實驗證明理論。Scientists test out theories by experiment.

實驗法(ㄕˊ ㄧㄢˋ ㄈㄚˇ)
the experimental method

實驗劇場(ㄕˊ ㄧㄢˋ ㄐㄩˋ ㄔㄤˇ)
an experimental theater

實驗主義(ㄕˊ ㄧㄢˋ ㄓㄨˇ ㄧˋ)
experimentalism

實驗室(ㄕˊ ㄧㄢˋ ㄕˋ)
a laboratory

實驗員(ㄕˊ ㄧㄢˋ ㄩㄢˊ)
a laboratory technician

實物(ㄕˊ ㄨˋ)
goods or produce (as opposed to money); in kind

實物教學(ㄕˊ ㄨˋ ㄐㄧㄠˋ ㄒㄩㄝˊ)
object teaching

實用(ㄕˊ ㄩㄥˋ)
① practical use ② practical; useful: 那勸告對我很實用。The advice was very useful to me.

實用主義(ㄕˊ ㄩㄥˋ ㄓㄨˇ ㄧˋ)
pragmatism

【寨】 1149 ㄓㄞˋ jay zhài

a stockade

寨主(ㄓㄞˋ ㄓㄨˇ)
a leader (used by bandits in speaking of their leader)

寨子(ㄓㄞˋ ˙ㄗ)
a stockaded village

十二畫

【審】 1150 ㄕㄣˇ sheen shěn

1. to examine; to review; to investigate: 他被警察審問。He was examined by the police.
2. to know; to discern; to appreciate
3. cautious; judicious; careful
4. really; indeed

審判(ㄕㄣˇ ㄆㄢˋ)
① to try (a case or person in a law court) ② a trial: 他因謀殺而受審判。He was on trial for murder.

審判長(ㄕㄣˇ ㄆㄢˋ ㄓㄤˇ)
the chief justice; the presiding judge

審美(ㄕㄣˇ ㄇㄟˇ)
to be esthetic or artistic; to appreciate the beautiful; estheticism; appreciation of the beautiful

審美觀念(ㄕㄣˇ ㄇㄟˇ ㄍㄨㄢ ㄋㄧㄢˋ)
esthetic sense (or notions)

審定(ㄕㄣˇ ㄉㄧㄥˋ)
to authorize (a publication, etc.); to examine and approve: 這建議已由委員會審定。The proposal has been examined and approved by the committee.

審訂(ㄕㄣˇ ㄉㄧㄥˋ)
to examine and revise: 教授們仔細地審訂教材。Professors carefully revise teaching materials.

審度(ㄕㄣˇ ㄉㄨㄛˊ)
to consider the pros and cons; to deliberate

審斷(ㄕㄣˇ ㄉㄨㄢˋ)
to examine and decide; to pass a judgement after an examination

審理(ㄕㄣˇ ㄌㄧˇ)
to try; to hear

審核(ㄕㄣˇ ㄏㄜˊ)
to examine and consider

審計(ㄕㄣˇ ㄐㄧˋ)
an audit; to audit

審計部(ㄕㄣˇ ㄐㄧˋ ㄅㄨˋ)

Ministry of Audit
審查 or 審察(ㄕㄣˇ ㄔㄚˊ)
to examine; to review; to investigate: 審查屬實。The fact was established after investigation.
審處(ㄕㄣˇ ㄔㄨˇ)
①to try and punish: 交由地方法院審處 to hand over to the local court for trial ② to deliberate and decide
審愼(ㄕㄣˇ ㄕㄣˋ)
cautious; careful: 審愼的人不信沒有證據的事。A cautious man doesn't believe things without proof.
審案(ㄕㄣˇ ㄢˋ)
to hold court trial
審議(ㄕㄣˇ ㄧˋ)
① consideration; deliberation; discussion: 這提議正在審議中。The proposal is under discussion. ② the title of a civil post
審議會(ㄕㄣˇ ㄧˋ ㄏㄨㄟˋ)
a deliberative meeting or session
審音(ㄕㄣˇ ㄧㄣ)
to discern or distinguish tones in music or in words
審問(ㄕㄣˇ ㄨㄣˋ)or 審訊(ㄕㄣˇ ㄒㄩㄣˋ)
to hold a hearing (on a legal case); to interrogate a prisoner
審閱(ㄕㄣˇ ㄩㄝˋ)
to examine; to review
審閱稿件(ㄕㄣˇ ㄩㄝˋ ㄍㄠˇ ㄐㄧㄢˋ)
to go over a manuscript

【寫】 1151
1. ㄒㄧㄝˇ shiee xie̊

to write; to sketch; to draw; to represent
寫本(ㄒㄧㄝˇ ㄅㄣˇ)
a handwritten copy (of a book)
寫稿(ㄒㄧㄝˇ ㄍㄠˇ)
to write for (or contribute to) a magazine, etc.
寫照(ㄒㄧㄝˇ ㄓㄠˋ)
an image; a representation; portrayal; a description
寫眞(ㄒㄧㄝˇ ㄓㄣ)
to draw or paint a portrait; to paint or draw a likeness; to portray
寫實(ㄒㄧㄝˇ ㄕˊ)
realistic (as distinct from romantic): 這是一部寫實的小說。This is a realistic novel.
寫實主義(ㄒㄧㄝˇ ㄕˊ ㄓㄨˇ ㄧˋ)
realism
寫生(ㄒㄧㄝˇ ㄕㄥ)
to draw, or paint, from nature; to sketch: 畫家寫生。The artist sketches from nature.
寫生畫(ㄒㄧㄝˇ ㄕㄥ ㄏㄨㄚˋ)
a sketch
寫字(ㄒㄧㄝˇ ㄗˋ)
to practice penmanship or calligraphy; to write
寫字檯(ㄒㄧㄝˇ ㄗˋ ㄊㄞˊ)
a desk
寫字間(ㄒㄧㄝˇ ㄗˋ ㄐㄧㄢ)
an office room
寫字員(ㄒㄧㄝˇ ㄗˋ ㄩㄢˊ)
a scribe; a clerk 亦作「書記」or「抄寫員」
寫作(ㄒㄧㄝˇ ㄗㄨㄛˋ)
writing: 他以寫作爲生。He takes up writing as his career.
寫意(ㄒㄧㄝˇ ㄧˋ)
(said of painting) to make an impressionistic portrayal
寫意畫(ㄒㄧㄝˇ ㄧˋ ㄏㄨㄚˋ)
ideal painting

【寫】 1151
2. ㄒㄧㄝˋ shieh xiè

unrestrained
寫意(兒)(ㄒㄧㄝˋ ㄧˋ(ㄦ))
free and happy

【寬】 1152
ㄎㄨㄢ kuan kuān

1. broad; wide; spacious; vast: 他眼界寬。He has a broad outlook.
2. magnanimous; lenient; tolerant; liberal; forgiving; indulgent
3. to loosen; to widen
4. well-off

寬猛相濟(ㄎㄨㄢ ㄇㄥˇ ㄒㄧㄤ ㄐㄧˋ)
to use a proper mixture of severity and gentleness (in ruling a country, handling one's subordinates, etc.)
寬免(ㄎㄨㄢ ㄇㄧㄢˇ)
to be exempt (from a tax, penalty, etc.)
寬大(ㄎㄨㄢ ㄉㄚˋ)
lenient; magnanimous: 他對孩子們很寬大。He is lenient toward (or to) the children.
寬大爲懷(ㄎㄨㄢ ㄉㄚˋ ㄨㄟˊ ㄏㄨㄞˊ)
magnanimous; forgiving; tolerant; liberal; open-hearted; benignant
寬待(ㄎㄨㄢ ㄉㄞˋ)
to treat generously
寬度(ㄎㄨㄢ ㄉㄨˋ)
width; breadth
寬廣(ㄎㄨㄢ ㄍㄨㄤˇ)
vast; broad; spacious; extensive; wide: 這是一條寬廣的街道。This is a wide street.
寬闊(ㄎㄨㄢ ㄎㄨㄛˋ)
roomy; wide; spacious: 他住在一棟寬闊的公寓裡。He lives in a roomy apartment.
寬厚(ㄎㄨㄢ ㄏㄡˋ)
tolerant and generous
寬宏大量(ㄎㄨㄢ ㄏㄨㄥˊ ㄉㄚˋ ㄌㄧㄤˋ)
magnanimous; open-hearted; broad-minded; benignant
寬假(ㄎㄨㄢ ㄐㄧㄚˇ)
to excuse magnanimously
寬解(ㄎㄨㄢ ㄐㄧㄝˇ)
to ease somebody's anxiety; to ease somebody of his trouble
寬限(ㄎㄨㄢ ㄒㄧㄢˋ)
① to extend a time limit ② a moratorium
寬心(ㄎㄨㄢ ㄒㄧㄣ)
to feel at rest; to set one's mind at ease; to feel free from anxiety
寬窄(ㄎㄨㄢ ㄓㄞˇ)
breadth; width
寬敞(ㄎㄨㄢ ㄔㄤˇ)
spacious; having much room; roomy; commodious: 這是一間寬敞的房子。It is a commodious house.
寬綽(ㄎㄨㄢ ㄔㄨㄛˋ)
① composed; unperturbed; relax; relieved ② with much space or room to spare; spacious ③ well-off
寬弛(ㄎㄨㄢ ㄕˇ)
relaxed; not tense
寬舒(ㄎㄨㄢ ㄕㄨ)
roomy and comfortable
寬恕(ㄎㄨㄢ ㄕㄨˋ)
to forgive; to pardon; forgiveness; pardon
寬容(ㄎㄨㄢ ㄖㄨㄥˊ)
to forgive; to pardon; to excuse; magnanimity; forgiveness; leniency; forbear-

ance; tolerance

寬縱(ㄎㄨㄢ ㄗㄨㄥˋ)
①to impose no restrictions; to be indulgent: 不要這麼寬縱自己。Don't be so self-indulgent. ②breadth and depth

寬鬆(ㄎㄨㄢ ㄙㄨㄥ)
loose and comfortable

寬衣(ㄎㄨㄢ ㄧ)
①a loose garment ②to remove the upper coat (for relaxation): 請寬衣。Do take off your coat.

寬衣解帶(ㄎㄨㄢ ㄧ ㄐㄧㄝˇ ㄉㄞˋ)
to undress

寬銀幕(ㄎㄨㄢ ㄧㄣˊ ㄇㄨˋ)
(movie) Cinerama; wide-screen

寬慰(ㄎㄨㄢ ㄨㄟˋ)
to console; to comfort; to soothe: 他遭遇不幸，我們寬慰他。We comforted him for his misfortune.

寬裕(ㄎㄨㄢ ㄩˋ)
well-to-do; well-off; ample: 時間很寬裕。There's plenty of time yet.

【寮】 1153
ㄌㄧㄠˊ liau liáo

1. a fellow officer or official; a colleague
2. a hut; a cottage

寮國(ㄌㄧㄠˊ ㄍㄨㄛˊ)
Laos

寮國人(ㄌㄧㄠˊ ㄍㄨㄛˊ ㄖㄣˊ)
a Laotian

十三畫

【寰】 1154
ㄏㄨㄢˊ hwan huán

a large domain; a vast space

寰內(ㄏㄨㄢˊ ㄋㄟˋ)
the domain of the empire

寰區(ㄏㄨㄢˊ ㄑㄩ)
all within the country

寰宇(ㄏㄨㄢˊ ㄩˇ)or 寰球(ㄏㄨㄢˊ ㄑㄧㄡˊ)
the world; the earth

十六畫

【寵】 1155
ㄔㄨㄥˇ choong chǒng

1. a concubine
2. to favor; to dote on; to patronize
3. favor or love (especially of the emperor)

寵嬖(ㄔㄨㄥˇ ㄅㄧˋ)
a court favorite

寵壞(ㄔㄨㄥˇ ㄏㄨㄞˋ)
to spoil (a child): 別把孩子寵壞了。Don't spoil the child.

寵姬(ㄔㄨㄥˇ ㄐㄧ)
the emperor's favorite concubine

寵信(ㄔㄨㄥˇ ㄒㄧㄣˋ)
to favor and trust (a subordinate)

寵幸(ㄔㄨㄥˇ ㄒㄧㄥˋ)
to show special favor to a lady or minister

寵辱不驚(ㄔㄨㄥˇ ㄖㄨˋ ㄅㄨˋ ㄐㄧㄥ)
to remain indifferent whether granted favor or subjected to humiliation

寵愛(ㄔㄨㄥˇ ㄞˋ)
to favor or patronize; to dote on: 她寵愛她的孫女。She doted on her granddaughter.

寵兒(ㄔㄨㄥˇ ㄦˊ)
a favored person; a pet; a favorite; a minion

寵遇(ㄔㄨㄥˇ ㄩˋ)
to treat as a favorite

十七畫

【寶】 1156
(寳) ㄅㄠˇ bao bǎo

1. treasure
2. precious; valuable
3. respectable; honorable

寶貝(ㄅㄠˇ ㄅㄟˋ)
①a cherished thing; a jewel ②darling (a term of endearment) ③a kind of cowrie (*Cypraea tigris*) ④a good-for-nothing or queer character: 這人眞是個寶貝！What a fellow!

寶寶(ㄅㄠˇ ·ㄅㄠ)
baby (a term of endearment)

寶刀(ㄅㄠˇ ㄉㄠ)
a treasured sword or dagger

寶刀未老(ㄅㄠˇ ㄉㄠ ㄨㄟˋ ㄌㄠˇ)
old but still vigorous in mind and body

寶島(ㄅㄠˇ ㄉㄠˇ)
a treasure island: 臺灣是個寶島。Taiwan is a treasure island.

寶典(ㄅㄠˇ ㄉㄧㄢˇ)
a valuable book; a treasury of knowledge; a thesaurus: 此書爲知識之寶典。This book is a treasury of knowledge.

寶鼎勳章(ㄅㄠˇ ㄉㄧㄥˇ ㄒㄩㄣ ㄓㄤ)
the Order of Precious Tripod, a Chinese government decoration

寶塔(ㄅㄠˇ ㄊㄚˇ)
a pagoda

寶貴(ㄅㄠˇ ㄍㄨㄟˋ)
valuable; precious: 故宮博物館收藏許多寶貴文物。The National Palace Museum collected and kept many valuable cultural relics.

寶庫(ㄅㄠˇ ㄎㄨˋ)
a treasury; a treasure house: 海洋是礦物和食物的寶庫。The sea is a treasure house of minerals and food.

寶盒(ㄅㄠˇ ㄏㄜˊ)
a jewel box; a box of treasures

寶號(ㄅㄠˇ ㄏㄠˋ)
(an honorific term) your shop, firm or store

寶劍(ㄅㄠˇ ㄐㄧㄢˋ)
a treasured sword

寶眷(ㄅㄠˇ ㄐㄩㄢˋ)
(an honorific term) your family

寶珠(ㄅㄠˇ ㄓㄨ)
a precious jewel

寶刹(ㄅㄠˇ ㄔㄚˋ)
①your temple (an honorific term used in speaking to a monk or nun) ②the pagoda of a temple

寶鈔(ㄅㄠˇ ㄔㄠ)
paper money

寶石(ㄅㄠˇ ㄕˊ)
a precious stone; a gem; a jewel: 她買了許多寶石。She bought many jewels.

寶山(ㄅㄠˇ ㄕㄢ)
a golconda; a source of great wealth

寶山空回(ㄅㄠˇ ㄕㄢ ㄎㄨㄥ ㄏㄨㄟˊ)
to miss a golden chance; to gain nothing from a rare opportunity

寶藏(ㄅㄠˇ ㄗㄤˋ)
a treasury; a treasure house; a collection of treasures

寶座(ㄅㄠˇ ㄗㄨㄛˋ)

the throne
寶物(ㄅㄠˇ ㄨˋ)
a treasure: 那博物館藏有很多寶物。The museum is full of treasures.
寶玉(ㄅㄠˇ ㄩˋ)
a precious stone

〔寸部〕

寸部
ㄘㄨㄣˋ tsuenn cùn

【寸】1157
ㄘㄨㄣˋ tsuenn cùn
1. a measure of length (equal to about 1/10 foot)
2. as small as an inch; small; tiny; little
寸步不離(ㄘㄨㄣˋ ㄅㄨˋ ㄅㄨˋ ㄌㄧˊ)
to tag; to follow closely (without allowing the distance to widen more than an inch)
寸步難移(ㄘㄨㄣˋ ㄅㄨˋ ㄋㄢˊ ㄧˊ)or 寸步難行(ㄘㄨㄣˋ ㄅㄨˋ ㄋㄢˊ ㄒㄧㄥˊ)
hard to walk even an inch; tough going
寸木岑樓(ㄘㄨㄣˋ ㄇㄨˋ ㄘㄣˊ ㄌㄡˊ)
(said of two things in comparison) vastly different in size and weight
寸地(ㄘㄨㄣˋ ㄉㄧˋ)
an inch of land; a tiny piece of land
寸斷(ㄘㄨㄣˋ ㄉㄨㄢˋ)or 寸裂(ㄘㄨㄣˋ ㄌㄧㄝˋ)
(heart) torn to pieces (used to describe extreme grief)
寸鐵(ㄘㄨㄣˋ ㄊㄧㄝˇ)
a dagger (emphasizing its smallness)
寸土必爭(ㄘㄨㄣˋ ㄊㄨˇ ㄅㄧˋ ㄓㄥ)
Even an inch of land has to be fought for.
寸土寸地(ㄘㄨㄣˋ ㄊㄨˇ ㄘㄨㄣˋ ㄉㄧˋ)
a wisp of territory
寸縷無存(ㄘㄨㄣˋ ㄌㄩˇ ㄨˊ ㄘㄨㄣˊ)
There is not even an inch of thread in the house.—descriptive of extreme poverty
寸功(ㄘㄨㄣˋ ㄍㄨㄥ)
a small contribution
寸簡(ㄘㄨㄣˋ ㄐㄧㄢˇ)or 寸札(ㄘㄨㄣˋ ㄓㄚˊ)
a short note: 他留下寸簡。He left me a short note.
寸金難買寸光陰(ㄘㄨㄣˋ ㄐㄧㄣ ㄋㄢˊ ㄇㄞˇ ㄘㄨㄣˋ ㄍㄨㄤ ㄧㄣ)
Money cannot buy time. 或 Time is more precious than gold.
寸進(ㄘㄨㄣˋ ㄐㄧㄣˋ)
① a little progress ② to advance by inches
寸隙難留(ㄘㄨㄣˋ ㄒㄧˋ ㄋㄢˊ ㄌㄧㄡˊ)
It's impossible to stop time passing away.
寸心(ㄘㄨㄣˋ ㄒㄧㄣ)or 寸衷(ㄘㄨㄣˋ ㄓㄨㄥ)
the heart (with emphasis on its smallness and its being the source of sincerity); feelings
寸腸(ㄘㄨㄣˋ ㄔㄤˊ)
innermost feelings
寸長(ㄘㄨㄣˋ ㄔㄤˊ)
modest ability; mediocre ability
寸草不留(ㄘㄨㄣˋ ㄘㄠˇ ㄅㄨˋ ㄌㄧㄡˊ)
to leave not even a blade of grass; to destroy completely (often used as a threat in calling the enemy to surrender)
寸草春暉(ㄘㄨㄣˋ ㄘㄠˇ ㄔㄨㄣ ㄏㄨㄟ)
A mother's love to a child is like spring light to a blade of grass.—One can never fully repay the love and care he has received from his mother no matter how hard he tries to please her.
寸絲不掛(ㄘㄨㄣˋ ㄙ ㄅㄨˋ ㄍㄨㄚˋ)
①to have not even a thread on; to be stark-naked 亦作「一絲不掛」 ②to be completely free from worries or care
寸陰(ㄘㄨㄣˋ ㄧㄣ)
a very short time; a few minutes; a brief moment
寸陰尺璧(ㄘㄨㄣˋ ㄧㄣ ㄔˇ ㄅㄧˋ)
(literally) An inch of time is worth a foot of jade.—Time is more precious than money.
寸陰若歲(ㄘㄨㄣˋ ㄧㄣ ㄖㄨㄛˋ ㄙㄨㄟˋ)
A brief moment seems to last a whole year.—(figuratively) one's longing to see a dear one

三畫

【寺】1158
ㄙˋ syh sì
a temple; a monastery; a shrine; a mosque
寺觀(ㄙˋ ㄍㄨㄢˋ)
Buddhist temples and Taoist temples
寺舍(ㄙˋ ㄕㄜˋ)
a temple building housing monks or nuns
寺人(ㄙˋ ㄖㄣˊ)
eunuchs
寺院(ㄙˋ ㄩㄢˋ)
temples
寺院法(ㄙˋ ㄩㄢˋ ㄈㄚˇ)
canon law

六畫

【封】1159
ㄈㄥ feng fēng
1. a numerary adjunct for letters
2. to install as a feudal lord or a nobleman
3. to seal; to block; to close completely: 山路已被大雪封住。The mountain path is already blocked by the heavy snow.
4. a covering; a wrapper; an envelope
封閉(ㄈㄥ ㄅㄧˋ)
to seal; to close completely: 他封閉漏隙。He sealed a leak.
封閉機場(ㄈㄥ ㄅㄧˋ ㄐㄧ ㄔㄤˊ)
to close an airport
封皮(ㄈㄥ ㄆㄧˊ)
①a covering; a cover; a wrapper ②a sealing tape
封門(ㄈㄥ ㄇㄣˊ)
①to seal a door ②to close a business establishment or an organization (as a form of punishment)
封面(ㄈㄥ ㄇㄧㄢˋ)
the cover (of a book): 這本書需要換新的封面。This book needs a new cover.
封面女郎(ㄈㄥ ㄇㄧㄢˋ ㄋㄩˇ ㄌㄤˊ)
a cover girl; a girl whose photo is used as a magazine cover: 她是個很受歡迎的封面女郎。She is a very popular

cover girl.
封底(ㄈㄥ ㄉㄧˇ)
the back cover
封地(ㄈㄥ ㄉㄧˋ)
a fief; a feud; a manor
封臺(ㄈㄥ ㄊㄞˊ)or 封箱(ㄈㄥ ㄒㄧㄤ)
(said of theater) stopping performance for the period near New Year
封套(ㄈㄥ ㄊㄠˋ)
an envelope; a wrapper
封條(ㄈㄥ ㄊㄧㄠˊ)
a sealing tape
封泥(ㄈㄥ ㄋㄧˊ)
(metallurgy) lute; luting
封蠟(ㄈㄥ ㄌㄚˋ)
sealing wax
封裡(ㄈㄥ ㄌㄧˇ)
① the inside front cover ② the inside back cover
封口(ㄈㄥ ㄎㄡˇ)
① to seal (a letter) ② to block the entrance (to a passage) ③ to heal
封侯(ㄈㄥ ㄏㄡˊ)
to create feudal lords
封建領土(ㄈㄥ ㄐㄧㄢˋ ㄌㄧㄥˇ ㄊㄨˇ)
feudatory
封建割據(ㄈㄥ ㄐㄧㄢˋ ㄍㄜ ㄐㄩˋ)
rule of feudal separationist
封建制度(ㄈㄥ ㄐㄧㄢˋ ㄓˋ ㄉㄨˋ)
feudalism; the feudal system
封建時代(ㄈㄥ ㄐㄧㄢˋ ㄕˊ ㄉㄞˋ)
the feudal age (or times)
封建勢力(ㄈㄥ ㄐㄧㄢˋ ㄕˋ ㄌㄧˋ)
feudalistic influence
封建思想(ㄈㄥ ㄐㄧㄢˋ ㄙ ㄒㄧㄤˇ)
feudalistic ideas; anachronistic thinking
封禁(ㄈㄥ ㄐㄧㄣˋ)
to blockade; to shut up and prevent access 參看「封鎖」
封疆大吏(ㄈㄥ ㄐㄧㄤ ㄉㄚˋ ㄌㄧˋ)
the governor of a border province
封爵(ㄈㄥ ㄐㄩㄝˊ)
to confer a degree of nobility on someone
封殺(ㄈㄥ ㄕㄚ)
(baseball) to shut out; force play
封山(ㄈㄥ ㄕㄢ)
to seal a mountain pass: 昨晚大雪封山。Heavy snow has sealed the mountain passes last night.
封禪(ㄈㄥ ㄕㄢˋ)
the ancient rite of worshipping Heaven and Earth on a mountain with the emperor officiating
封神榜(ㄈㄥ ㄕㄣˊ ㄅㄤˇ)
a classical novel of Chinese gods and heroes
封賞(ㄈㄥ ㄕㄤˇ)
to give tips
封存(ㄈㄥ ㄘㄨㄣˊ)
to seal and put away
封鎖(ㄈㄥ ㄙㄨㄛˇ)
to blockade (a place or region); a blockade: 道路被封鎖。The road was blockaded.
封鎖邊境(ㄈㄥ ㄙㄨㄛˇ ㄅㄧㄢ ㄐㄧㄥˋ)
to close the border
封鎖港口(ㄈㄥ ㄙㄨㄛˇ ㄍㄤˇ ㄎㄡˇ)
to blockade a port
封鎖新聞(ㄈㄥ ㄙㄨㄛˇ ㄒㄧㄣ ㄨㄣˊ)
to suppress news
封邑(ㄈㄥ ㄧˋ)
a manor estate bestowed by a monarch
封印(ㄈㄥ ㄧㄣˋ)
(postal service) a seal
封網(ㄈㄥ ㄨㄤˇ)
(volleyball) to block
封翁(ㄈㄥ ㄨㄥ)or 封君(ㄈㄥ ㄐㄩㄣ)
(in ancient China) a man whose children was high-ranking officials and was thus given a title by the government

七畫

【射】 1160
ㄕㄜˋ sheh shè
(動詞語音 ㄕˊ shyr shí)
(音律名 ㄧˋ yih yì)
(於"僕射"等 ㄧㄝˋ yeh yè)

1. to shoot: 他射下一隻鳥。He shot down a bird.
2. to send out (light, heat, etc.): 太陽射出光與熱。The sun sends out light and heat.
3. archery (listed by Confucius as one of six arts required of a scholar)

射門(ㄕㄜˋ ㄇㄣˊ)
(in soccer, etc.) to shoot or kick the ball toward the goal
射彈(ㄕㄜˋ ㄉㄢˋ)
a projectile
射垛(ㄕㄜˋ ㄉㄨㄛˇ)
a rampart used as a target for practicing shooting arrows
射獵(ㄕㄜˋ ㄌㄧㄝˋ)
hunting: 他很喜歡射獵。He's very fond of hunting.
射擊(ㄕㄜˋ ㄐㄧˊ)
to shoot; shooting
射擊場(ㄕㄜˋ ㄐㄧˊ ㄔㄤˇ)
a shooting range
射擊術(ㄕㄜˋ ㄐㄧˊ ㄕㄨˋ)
marksmanship
射界(ㄕㄜˋ ㄐㄧㄝˋ)
the field of fire
射角(ㄕㄜˋ ㄐㄧㄠˇ)
the angle of fire
射箭(ㄕㄜˋ ㄐㄧㄢˋ)
to shoot an arrow; archery
射精(ㄕㄜˋ ㄐㄧㄥ)
(biology) ejection
射球(ㄕㄜˋ ㄑㄧㄡˊ)
to kick or shoot the ball
射線(ㄕㄜˋ ㄒㄧㄢˋ)
(physics) a ray
射中(ㄕㄜˋ ㄓㄨㄥˋ)
to hit (with a shot) the target; to score a hit
射程(ㄕㄜˋ ㄔㄥˊ)
a range (of the projectile): 他在五哩的射程內射擊。He fires at a range of five miles.
射石飲羽(ㄕㄜˋ ㄕˊ ㄧㄣˇ ㄩˇ)
to have the strong will power that can make an arrow pierce even a stone
射手(ㄕㄜˋ ㄕㄡˇ)
an archer; a shooter; a marksman; a gunner: 他是個好射手。He is a good archer.
射影(ㄕㄜˋ ㄧㄥˇ)
projection

八畫

【專】 1161
ㄓㄨㄢ juan zhuān

1. to concentrate; to focus
2. to monopolize
3. to specialize: 許多學生專攻農業。Many students specialize in agriculture.
4. exclusive; special: 你修的專門學科是什麼? What is your

special study?

專賣(ㄓㄨㄢ ㄇㄞˋ)
a monopoly; the exclusive possession of the trade in some commodity

專賣局(ㄓㄨㄢ ㄇㄞˋ ㄐㄩˊ)
a monopoly bureau

專賣權(ㄓㄨㄢ ㄇㄞˋ ㄑㄩㄢˊ)or 專利權(ㄓㄨㄢ ㄌㄧˋ ㄑㄩㄢˊ)
a patent; a monopoly right

專美(ㄓㄨㄢ ㄇㄟˇ)
to attain distinction alone

專門(ㄓㄨㄢ ㄇㄣˊ)
① a specialty; a special field ② exclusively; specially

專門知識(ㄓㄨㄢ ㄇㄣˊ ㄓ ㄕˋ)
expertise; specialized knowledge

專門人材(ㄓㄨㄢ ㄇㄣˊ ㄖㄣˊ ㄘㄞˊ)
the people with professional skill

專門委員(ㄓㄨㄢ ㄇㄣˊ ㄨㄟˇ ㄩㄢˊ)
a senior specialist in the government

專名(ㄓㄨㄢ ㄇㄧㄥˊ)
a proper name; a proper noun

專訪(ㄓㄨㄢ ㄈㄤˇ)
a report produced by a journalist after having paid a special visit to the person or persons concerned

專電(ㄓㄨㄢ ㄉㄧㄢˋ)
a news dispatch; a special dispatch (or telegram)

專斷(ㄓㄨㄢ ㄉㄨㄢˋ)
to make decisions without consulting others; arbitrary

專題(ㄓㄨㄢ ㄊㄧˊ)
a special subject

專題報導(ㄓㄨㄢ ㄊㄧˊ ㄅㄠˋ ㄉㄠˇ)
a report on a special topic

專題研究(ㄓㄨㄢ ㄊㄧˊ ㄧㄢˊ ㄐㄧㄡˋ)
a monographic study

專題演講(ㄓㄨㄢ ㄊㄧˊ ㄧㄢˇ ㄐㄧㄤˇ)
a lecture on a special topic

專欄(ㄓㄨㄢ ㄌㄢˊ)
a special column (in a newspaper or magazine)

專欄作家(ㄓㄨㄢ ㄌㄢˊ ㄗㄨㄛˋ ㄐㄧㄚ)
a columnist

專利(ㄓㄨㄢ ㄌㄧˋ)
a monopoly; a patent: 他申請到該器具的專利。He got a patent for the gadget.

專利品(ㄓㄨㄢ ㄌㄧˋ ㄆㄧㄣˇ)
a patent; a patent article

專利連鎖店(ㄓㄨㄢ ㄌㄧˋ ㄌㄧㄢˊ ㄙㄨㄛˇ ㄉㄧㄢˋ)
a franchise chain

專利權(ㄓㄨㄢ ㄌㄧˋ ㄑㄩㄢˊ)
a patent; a patent right

專管(ㄓㄨㄢ ㄍㄨㄢˇ)
to take exclusive charge of (a matter)

專攻(ㄓㄨㄢ ㄍㄨㄥ)
to study (a subject) exclusively; to specialize in

專科(ㄓㄨㄢ ㄎㄜ)
a particular course or field of study

專科學校(ㄓㄨㄢ ㄎㄜ ㄒㄩㄝˊ ㄒㄧㄠˋ)
a junior college

專款(ㄓㄨㄢ ㄎㄨㄢˇ)
the fund designated for a specific use

專款專用(ㄓㄨㄢ ㄎㄨㄢˇ ㄓㄨㄢ ㄩㄥˋ)
to earmark a fund for its specified purpose only

專號(ㄓㄨㄢ ㄏㄠˋ)
a special issue (of a periodical)

專函(ㄓㄨㄢ ㄏㄢˊ)
a letter written for a specific purpose

專橫(ㄓㄨㄢ ㄏㄥˊ)
dictatorial; arbitrary; despotic; tyrannical: 我無法忍受他專橫的態度。I can't stand his dictatorial manner.

專橫跋扈(ㄓㄨㄢ ㄏㄥˊ ㄅㄚˊ ㄏㄨˋ)
imperious and despotic

專戶(ㄓㄨㄢ ㄏㄨˋ)
a special bank account

專機(ㄓㄨㄢ ㄐㄧ)
a plane designated for a special use (such as flying a VIP or some valuable goods); a chartered plane

專家(ㄓㄨㄢ ㄐㄧㄚ)
a specialist; an expert

專精(ㄓㄨㄢ ㄐㄧㄥ)
to concentrate one's efforts or energy on

專權(ㄓㄨㄢ ㄑㄩㄢˊ)
to be in full power; to be dictatorial

專修(ㄓㄨㄢ ㄒㄧㄡ)
to study (a subject) exclusively

專修科(ㄓㄨㄢ ㄒㄧㄡ ㄎㄜ)
a two-year program of study in a four-year college that does not lead to a degree and is consequently equivalent to work in a junior (two-year) college

專線(ㄓㄨㄢ ㄒㄧㄢˋ)
① a special railway line ② a special telephone line

專心一志(ㄓㄨㄢ ㄒㄧㄣ ㄧˊ ㄓˋ)
to concentrate or focus one's attention, thoughts, or efforts on

專職(ㄓㄨㄢ ㄓˊ)
① sole duty; specific duty ② full-time

專制(ㄓㄨㄢ ㄓˋ)
tyrannical; despotic; autocratic; dictatorial

專制君主(ㄓㄨㄢ ㄓˋ ㄐㄩㄣ ㄓㄨˇ)
an autocrat

專制政體(ㄓㄨㄢ ㄓˋ ㄓㄥˋ ㄊㄧˇ)or 專制政治(ㄓㄨㄢ ㄓˋ ㄓㄥˋ ㄓˋ)
autocracy

專政(ㄓㄨㄢ ㄓㄥˋ)
dictatorship

專注(ㄓㄨㄢ ㄓㄨˋ)
to concentrate one's attention on; to be absorbed in; to devote one's mind to: 他專注於研究物理學。He devotes his attention to the study of physics.

專著(ㄓㄨㄢ ㄓㄨˋ)
a monograph; a treatise

專車(ㄓㄨㄢ ㄔㄜ)
a train or bus run for a particular purpose

專差(ㄓㄨㄢ ㄔㄞ)
a special messenger (sent exclusively for a particular errand); a specially sent messenger or emissary

專長(ㄓㄨㄢ ㄔㄤˊ)
a special skill; a specialty

專程(ㄓㄨㄢ ㄔㄥˊ)
a special trip

專誠(ㄓㄨㄢ ㄔㄥˊ)
with the exclusive purpose of

專使(ㄓㄨㄢ ㄕˇ)
a special envoy

專擅(ㄓㄨㄢ ㄕㄢˋ)
to act without authorization; to do things without asking for approval

專人(ㄓㄨㄢ ㄖㄣˊ)
a person specially assigned

for a task
專任(ㄓㄨㄢ ㄖㄣˋ)
(of an employee) full time; full-time: 他在那裡專任。He works there full time.
專責(ㄓㄨㄢ ㄗㄜˊ)
a specific responsibility
專才(ㄓㄨㄢ ㄘㄞˊ)
a specialist; a person specially good at something
專案(ㄓㄨㄢ ㄢˋ)
a special case (to be dealt with separately): 這件事應成立專案。This should be made a special case to be dealt with separately.
專一(ㄓㄨㄢ ㄧ)
to concentrate one's attention on; single-minded
專業(ㄓㄨㄢ ㄧㄝˋ)
①a special field of study; a specialized subject; a specialty ② a specialized trade
專業道德(ㄓㄨㄢ ㄧㄝˋ ㄉㄠˋ ㄉㄜˊ)
professional ethics
專業課程(ㄓㄨㄢ ㄧㄝˋ ㄎㄜˋ ㄔㄥˊ)
a specialized course
專業化(ㄓㄨㄢ ㄧㄝˋ ㄏㄨㄚˋ)
specialization
專業精神(ㄓㄨㄢ ㄧㄝˋ ㄐㄧㄥ ㄕㄣˊ)
dedication to a job
專業訓練(ㄓㄨㄢ ㄧㄝˋ ㄒㄩㄣˋ ㄌㄧㄢˋ)
training in a specialty
專業知識(ㄓㄨㄢ ㄧㄝˋ ㄓ ㄕˋ)
professional knowledge
專業人員(ㄓㄨㄢ ㄧㄝˋ ㄖㄣˊ ㄩㄢˊ)
the personnel in a specific field
專有名詞(ㄓㄨㄢ ㄧㄡˇ ㄇㄧㄥˊ ㄘˊ)
a proper noun
專員(ㄓㄨㄢ ㄩㄢˊ)
a specialist in the government; a commissioner (a prefectual official); a senior official
專用(ㄓㄨㄢ ㄩㄥˋ)
to use exclusively; to be used exclusively for
專用電話(ㄓㄨㄢ ㄩㄥˋ ㄉㄧㄢˋ ㄏㄨㄚˋ)
a telephone for special use

【將】 1162
1. ㄐㄧㄤ jiang jiāng
1. (used with a verb expressing future action) going to; about to
2. used with a noun functioning as a direct object
3. to nourish
將來(ㄐㄧㄤ ㄌㄞˊ)
the future; the days to come: 我希望你有一個幸福的將來。I hope you have a happy future before you.
將功補過(ㄐㄧㄤ ㄍㄨㄥ ㄅㄨˇ ㄍㄨㄛˋ)
to make amends for one's faults by good deeds
將功贖罪(ㄐㄧㄤ ㄍㄨㄥ ㄕㄨˊ ㄗㄨㄟˋ)
to atone for mistakes by meritorious service
將計就計(ㄐㄧㄤ ㄐㄧˋ ㄐㄧㄡˋ ㄐㄧˋ)
to adapt one's scheme to that of the opponent; to deal with an opponent by taking advantage of his scheme
將就(ㄐㄧㄤ ㄐㄧㄡˋ)
to make the best of an unsatisfactory situation; to make do with something not good enough; to manage with something unsatisfactory
將近(ㄐㄧㄤ ㄐㄧㄣˋ)
approximately; close to; nearly; almost
將軍(ㄐㄧㄤ ㄐㄩㄣ)
① a general or admiral ② a call to indicate a checkmate (in Chinese chess) ③ to embarrass; to challenge
將信將疑(ㄐㄧㄤ ㄒㄧㄣˋ ㄐㄧㄤ ㄧˊ)
wavering between doubt and belief; half in doubt; skeptical
將錯就錯(ㄐㄧㄤ ㄘㄨㄛˋ ㄐㄧㄡˋ ㄘㄨㄛˋ)
to accept the consequences of a mistake and try to adapt oneself thereto
將要(ㄐㄧㄤ ㄧㄠˋ)
going to or about to (do something); on the point of (doing something): 此機將要起飛。The plane is about to take off.
將養(ㄐㄧㄤ ㄧㄤˇ)or 將息(ㄐㄧㄤ ㄒㄧˊ)
to rest so as to restore one's strength

【將】 1162
2. ㄐㄧㄤˋ jianq jiàng
1. a general; an admiral; a military leader of high rank: 他是一位偉大的將帥。He is a great general.
2. to lead (soldiers)
將兵(ㄐㄧㄤˋ ㄅㄧㄥ)
to command troops
將門(ㄐㄧㄤˋ ㄇㄣˊ)
the family of a high-ranking military officer
將門虎子(ㄐㄧㄤˋ ㄇㄣˊ ㄏㄨˇ ㄗˇ)
a capable young man from a distinguished family
將領(ㄐㄧㄤˋ ㄌㄧㄥˇ)
high-ranking military officers; a general
將令(ㄐㄧㄤˋ ㄌㄧㄥˋ)
the orders given by a commanding general
將官(ㄐㄧㄤˋ ㄍㄨㄢ)
a general officer
將校(ㄐㄧㄤˋ ㄒㄧㄠˋ)
general officers and field officers
將相(ㄐㄧㄤˋ ㄒㄧㄤˋ)
generals and ministers; military and political leaders
將種(ㄐㄧㄤˋ ㄓㄨㄥˇ)
a person born of military forbears
將士(ㄐㄧㄤˋ ㄕˋ)
officers and men
將士用命(ㄐㄧㄤˋ ㄕˋ ㄩㄥˋ ㄇㄧㄥˋ)
(said of troops in combat) Officers and men perform their assigned duties conscientiously.
將帥(ㄐㄧㄤˋ ㄕㄨㄞˋ)
a general
將才(ㄐㄧㄤˋ ㄘㄞˊ)
the talent as a field commander

【尉】 1163
1. ㄨㄟˋ wey wèi
1. a company-grade military officer
2. (in former times) a grade of military official
尉官(ㄨㄟˋ ㄍㄨㄢ)
a military officer above the rank of warrant officer and below that of major; a junior officer

【尉】 1163
2. ㄩˋ yuh yù
as in 尉遲—a double family name

九畫

【尊】 1164
ㄗㄨㄣ tzuen zūn
1. to honor; to respect; to venerate; to revere; to esteem

〔寸部〕

〔寸部〕

2. honored; honorable; noble; esteemed; respectable
尊卑(ㄗㄨㄣ ㄅㄟ)
①seniors and juniors ②superiors and inferiors
尊名(ㄗㄨㄣ ㄇㄧㄥˊ)
(courteously) Your name, Sir?
尊命(ㄗㄨㄣ ㄇㄧㄥˋ)
(courteously) your order
尊夫人(ㄗㄨㄣ ㄈㄨ ㄖㄣˊ)
(courteously) your wife
尊府(ㄗㄨㄣ ㄈㄨˇ)
(courteously) your home
尊大人(ㄗㄨㄣ ㄉㄚˋ ㄖㄣˊ)
(courteously) your father; your esteemed father
尊堂(ㄗㄨㄣ ㄊㄤˊ)
(courteously) your esteemed mother
尊貴(ㄗㄨㄣ ㄍㄨㄟˋ)
noble; honorable; respectable
尊號(ㄗㄨㄣ ㄏㄠˋ)
①titular honors offerred to the king, queen or other members of the royal family ②(courteously) your name
尊駕(ㄗㄨㄣ ㄐㄧㄚˋ)
(courteously) you; your esteemed self
尊教(ㄗㄨㄣ ㄐㄧㄠˋ)
(courteously) your esteemed teaching or instruction
尊見(ㄗㄨㄣ ㄐㄧㄢˋ)
(courteously) your opinion or view; your esteemed opinion: 您對那人尊見如何? What is your opinion of that man?
尊敬(ㄗㄨㄣ ㄐㄧㄥˋ)
to respect; to revere; respect; reverence: 尊敬長者。Show respect to those who are older.
尊君(ㄗㄨㄣ ㄐㄩㄣ)
①(courteously) your esteemed father ②to respect the king
尊前(ㄗㄨㄣ ㄑㄧㄢˊ)
a conventional term placed after the salutation in letters addressed to one's senior
尊親(ㄗㄨㄣ ㄑㄧㄣ)
(courteously) your parents; your esteemed parents
尊顯(ㄗㄨㄣ ㄒㄧㄢˇ)
of high position; noble; honorable; respectable; venerable: 公爵是尊顯之人。A duke is a man of high position.
尊姓大名(ㄗㄨㄣ ㄒㄧㄥˋ ㄉㄚˋ ㄇㄧㄥˊ)
(courteously) your name: 請問尊姓大名? May I know your name?
尊長(ㄗㄨㄣ ㄓㄤˇ)
an older person; an elder; a senior
尊重(ㄗㄨㄣ ㄓㄨㄥˋ)
to venerate; to hold in reverence; to honor; to respect; to esteem; to uphold: 沒有人比我更尊重你的父親。No one esteems your father more than I do.
尊稱(ㄗㄨㄣ ㄔㄥ)
an honorific term; a title of respect; an honorific
尊處(ㄗㄨㄣ ㄔㄨˋ)
(courteously) your abode; your honorable abode
尊崇(ㄗㄨㄣ ㄔㄨㄥˊ)
to revere; to venerate; to hold in reverence; to honor; to esteem: 我們尊崇神聖事物。We revere sacred things.
尊師重道(ㄗㄨㄣ ㄕ ㄓㄨㄥˋ ㄉㄠˋ)
to respect the teacher and his teachings: 人人需尊師重道。Everyone should respect the teacher and his teachings.
尊容(ㄗㄨㄣ ㄖㄨㄥˊ)
①(courteously) your face ②(Buddhism) the venerable face of the Buddha ③(colloquial) that disgusting face of yours (his or hers)
尊榮(ㄗㄨㄣ ㄖㄨㄥˊ)
dignity and honor
尊俎折衝(ㄗㄨㄣ ㄗㄨˇ ㄓㄜˊ ㄔㄨㄥ)
to win a war at the conference table 參看「折衝尊俎」
尊嚴(ㄗㄨㄣ ㄧㄢˊ)
dignity; respectability; honor
尊王攘夷(ㄗㄨㄣ ㄨㄤˊ ㄖㄤˇ ㄧˊ)
to honor the emperor and repel the barbarians (a slogan common in the days before the republic)
尊翁(ㄗㄨㄣ ㄨㄥ)
(courteously) your father

【尋】 1165
1. ㄒㄩㄣˊ shyun xún
1. a measure of length in former times (roughly equivalent to eight feet)
2. to seek; to search
尋寶(ㄒㄩㄣˊ ㄅㄠˇ)
to hunt for treasure; treasure hunt
尋覓(ㄒㄩㄣˊ ㄇㄧˋ)
to search for; to look for; to seek for
尋芳(ㄒㄩㄣˊ ㄈㄤ)
①to go on a picnic for viewing flowers ②to seek carnal pleasure
尋芳客(ㄒㄩㄣˊ ㄈㄤ ㄎㄜˋ)
a patron of brothels
尋訪(ㄒㄩㄣˊ ㄈㄤˇ)
to look for (somebody whose whereabouts is unknown); to try to locate; to make inquiries about
尋短見(ㄒㄩㄣˊ ㄉㄨㄢˇ ㄐㄧㄢˋ)
to end one's own life; to commit suicide: 人不應尋短見。One should not commit suicide.
尋樂(ㄒㄩㄣˊ ㄌㄜˋ) or 尋歡作樂(ㄒㄩㄣˊ ㄏㄨㄢ ㄗㄨㄛˋ ㄌㄜˋ)
to seek amusement; to seek pleasure
尋根問底(ㄒㄩㄣˊ ㄍㄣ ㄨㄣˋ ㄉㄧˇ) or 尋根究底(ㄒㄩㄣˊ ㄍㄣ ㄐㄧㄡˋ ㄉㄧˇ)
to make a thorough investigation; to probe deeply
尋開心(ㄒㄩㄣˊ ㄎㄞ ㄒㄧㄣ)
(dialect) to make fun of; to joke
尋花問柳(ㄒㄩㄣˊ ㄏㄨㄚ ㄨㄣˋ ㄌㄧㄡˇ)
①to enjoy natural beauty in springtime ②to seek carnal pleasure
尋究(ㄒㄩㄣˊ ㄐㄧㄡˋ)
to try insistently to find out (cause, origin)
尋求(ㄒㄩㄣˊ ㄑㄧㄡˊ)
to seek: 大多數人尋求財富。Most men seek wealth.
尋釁(ㄒㄩㄣˊ ㄒㄧㄣˋ)
to pick a quarrel; to provoke
尋找(ㄒㄩㄣˊ ㄓㄠˇ)
to look for; to seek for: 你仍然在尋找工作嗎? Are you still looking for a job?
尋章摘句(ㄒㄩㄣˊ ㄓㄤ ㄓㄞ ㄐㄩˋ)
to labor over the wording in a pointless manner
尋常(ㄒㄩㄣˊ ㄔㄤˊ)
usual; ordinary; common;

commonplace; routine: 給侍者小費是尋常的事。It is usual to tip the waiter.
尋事生非(ㄒㄩㄣˊ ㄕˋ ㄕㄥ ㄈㄟ)
to seek a quarrel; to make trouble
尋人啓事(ㄒㄩㄣˊ ㄖㄣˊ ㄑㄧˇ ㄕˋ)
a notice in a missing person column
尋思(ㄒㄩㄣˊ ㄙ)
to ponder; to consider; to reflect; to meditate: 尋思一下這事該怎麼辦。Think over what to do about it.
尋幽探勝(ㄒㄩㄣˊ ㄧㄡ ㄊㄢˋ ㄕㄥˋ)
to visit scenic spots
尋味(ㄒㄩㄣˊ ㄨㄟˋ)
to relish or enjoy (a literary work): 他這番話耐人尋味。What he has said affords much meaning for enjoying.

【尋】 1165
2. ㄒㄧㄣˊ shyn xín
to beg; to entreat
尋錢的(ㄒㄧㄣˊ ㄑㄧㄢˊ ·ㄉㄜ)
a beggar
尋死覓活(ㄒㄧㄣˊ ㄙˇ ㄇㄧˋ ㄏㄨㄛˊ)
to attempt suicide repeatedly (in order to threaten)

【尋】 1165
3. ㄒㄩㄝˊ shyue xué
to look around
尋摸(ㄒㄩㄝˊ ·ㄇㄛ)
to look around as to seek something

十一畫

【對】 1166
ㄉㄨㄟˋ duey duì
1. right; correct; proper: 說謊是不對的。It's not right to tell lies.
2. parallel; opposing
3. a pair; a couple
4. to check; ascertain
5. to; as to; with regard to
6. to be directed at: 我的話不是針對着你說的。What I said was not directed at you.
對白(ㄉㄨㄟˋ ㄅㄞˊ)
dialogue
對保(ㄉㄨㄟˋ ㄅㄠˇ)
to confirm or verify a guaranty
對半(ㄉㄨㄟˋ ㄅㄢˋ)
a half; one half
對比(ㄉㄨㄟˋ ㄅㄧˇ)
contrast; correlation
對筆跡(ㄉㄨㄟˋ ㄅㄧˇ ㄐㄧ)
to analyze a handwriting (in an effort to ascertain its author)
對邊(ㄉㄨㄟˋ ㄅㄧㄢ)
the opposite side
對簿公庭(ㄉㄨㄟˋ ㄅㄨˋ ㄍㄨㄥ ㄊㄧㄥˊ)
to face or confront each other in court at a trial
對不起(ㄉㄨㄟˋ ·ㄅㄨ ㄑㄧˇ)or 對不住(ㄉㄨㄟˋ ·ㄅㄨ ㄓㄨˋ)
① to let a person down ② I am sorry. 或 I apologize.
對馬海峽(ㄉㄨㄟˋ ㄇㄚˇ ㄏㄞˇ ㄒㄧㄚˊ)
the Tsushima Strait
對罵(ㄉㄨㄟˋ ㄇㄚˋ)
to call each other names
對門(ㄉㄨㄟˋ ㄇㄣˊ)
① the family, or household, right across the front street ②(two buildings) opposite to (each other): 工廠對門是郵局。Opposite to the factory is the post office.
對面(ㄉㄨㄟˋ ㄇㄧㄢˋ)
on the opposite side; right in front: 他家就在我家對面。His house is opposite to mine.
對方(ㄉㄨㄟˋ ㄈㄤ)
the other side; the other party
對付(ㄉㄨㄟˋ ㄈㄨˋ)
to deal with; to cope with
對答(ㄉㄨㄟˋ ㄉㄚˊ)
to answer questions
對答如流(ㄉㄨㄟˋ ㄉㄚˊ ㄖㄨˊ ㄌㄧㄡˊ)
to give answers fluently
對打(ㄉㄨㄟˋ ㄉㄚˇ)
to fight each other; to exchange blows
對得起(ㄉㄨㄟˋ ·ㄉㄜ ㄑㄧˇ)or 對得住(ㄉㄨㄟˋ ·ㄉㄜ ㄓㄨˋ)
not let somebody down; to treat somebody fairly
對待(ㄉㄨㄟˋ ㄉㄞˋ)
to treat (a person kindly, cruelly, etc.): 這公司對待員工一直很好。This firm has always treated its workers well.
對等(ㄉㄨㄟˋ ㄉㄥˇ)
equal
對敵(ㄉㄨㄟˋ ㄉㄧˊ)
opponent; to oppose; to antagonize
對調(ㄉㄨㄟˋ ㄉㄧㄠˋ)
to exchange positions: 我想與你對調工作。I wish to exchange jobs with you.
對頂角(ㄉㄨㄟˋ ㄉㄧㄥˇ ㄐㄧㄠˇ)
(mathematics) vertically opposite angles
對對子(ㄉㄨㄟˋ ㄉㄨㄟˋ ·ㄗ)
to engage in the literary exercise of supplying a sentence that parallels a given one (so as to form an antithesis or couplet)
對臺戲(ㄉㄨㄟˋ ㄊㄞˊ ㄒㄧˋ)
a rival show—(figuratively) competition
對頭
①(ㄉㄨㄟˋ ㄊㄡˊ) right: 這方法對頭。This method is right.
②(ㄉㄨㄟˋ ·ㄊㄡ) an opponent; an adversary; a rival: 他在選舉中擊敗了他的對頭。He defeated his opponent in the election.
對內(ㄉㄨㄟˋ ㄋㄟˋ)
for domestic or internal (consumption, use, etc.)
對牛彈琴(ㄉㄨㄟˋ ㄋㄧㄡˊ ㄊㄢˊ ㄑㄧㄣˊ)
(literally) to play a lute before an ox—to speak to someone about something completely incomprehensible to him; to cast pearls before swine
對壘(ㄉㄨㄟˋ ㄌㄟˇ)
to confront each other; to be encamped face to face: 兩軍對壘。Two armies confronted each other.
對立(ㄉㄨㄟˋ ㄌㄧˋ)
to be opposed to each other; to be in opposition to each other: 求學與工作不應相互對立。Study and work should not be opposed to each other.
對流(ㄉㄨㄟˋ ㄌㄧㄡˊ)
(physics) convection
對聯(ㄉㄨㄟˋ ㄌㄧㄢˊ)
a Chinese couplet (often written and mounted on scrolls to be hung up on the wall)
對路(ㄉㄨㄟˋ ㄌㄨˋ)or 對路子(ㄉㄨㄟˋ ㄌㄨˋ ·ㄗ)
① to satisfy the need: 這些貨到都市正對路。These goods

〔寸部〕

will satisfy the needs of the city. ② to be to one's liking; to suit one

對過兒(ㄉㄨㄟˋ ㄍㄨㄛˋㄦ) or 對過(ㄉㄨㄟˋ ㄍㄨㄛˋ)
① the family, or household, right in front of one's house ② across the way: 他就住在對過兒。He lives just across the way.

〔寸部〕

對光(ㄉㄨㄟˋ ㄍㄨㄤ)
① (said of spectacles) of the right power; ② (cinematography) to focus

對開(ㄉㄨㄟˋ ㄎㄞ)
①(said of buses or trains) to head for each other from two stations along the same road ② folio

對口(ㄉㄨㄟˋ ㄎㄡˇ)
to speak or sing alternately

對口相聲(ㄉㄨㄟˋ ㄎㄡˇ ㄒㄧㄤ ·ㄕㄥ)
the Chinese comic dialogue

對口唱(ㄉㄨㄟˋ ㄎㄡˇ ㄔㄤˋ)
antiphonal singing; dialogue in antiphonal singing

對抗(ㄉㄨㄟˋ ㄎㄤˋ)
to be opposed to each other; to be in opposition to each other; to face each other in opposition

對抗賽(ㄉㄨㄟˋ ㄎㄤˋ ㄙㄞˋ)
a duel meet (between opposing teams from two different cities or countries)

對空射擊(ㄉㄨㄟˋ ㄎㄨㄥ ㄕㄜˋ ㄐㄧˊ)
ground-to-air firing; to fire to the air

對號(ㄉㄨㄟˋ ㄏㄠˋ)
① to check the number ② to fit; to tally ③ a check mark

對號入座(ㄉㄨㄟˋ ㄏㄠˋ ㄖㄨˋ ㄗㄨㄛˋ)
to seat oneself according to the designated number indicated on the ticket

對話(ㄉㄨㄟˋ ㄏㄨㄚˋ)
a dialogue; a conversation

對換(ㄉㄨㄟˋ ㄏㄨㄢˋ)
to exchange; to barter; to swap

對角線(ㄉㄨㄟˋ ㄐㄧㄠˇ ㄒㄧㄢˋ)
(mathematics) a diagonal

對襟(ㄉㄨㄟˋ ㄐㄧㄣ)
the front part of a garment with buttons straight down in the middle

對勁(ㄉㄨㄟˋ ㄐㄧㄣˋ) or 對勁兒(ㄉㄨㄟˋ ㄐㄧㄜˋㄦ)
of the right or agreeable nature; in the right or agreeable condition

對獎(ㄉㄨㄟˋ ㄐㄧㄤˇ)
to check the results of a lottery or raffle to see if one holds the winning ticket

對講機(ㄉㄨㄟˋ ㄐㄧㄤˇ ㄐㄧ)
an interphone; an intercom; an intercommunication system

對局(ㄉㄨㄟˋ ㄐㄩˊ)
to play a game of chess, etc.

對句(ㄉㄨㄟˋ ㄐㄩˋ)
a Chinese couplet or antithesis

對象(ㄉㄨㄟˋ ㄒㄧㄤˋ)
the object (of an action); the subject (of consideration)

對質(ㄉㄨㄟˋ ㄓˋ)
to face each other and exchange questions (in order to find out the truth): 被告與原告對質。The accused was confronted with his accuser.

對峙(ㄉㄨㄟˋ ㄓˋ)
to face each other; to confront each other: 兩軍對峙。The two armies confronted each other.

對折(ㄉㄨㄟˋ ㄓㄜˊ)
a 50% discount: 他們以對折賣舊書。They sold used books at a 50% discount.

對照(ㄉㄨㄟˋ ㄓㄠˋ)
to compare; to contrast; cross reference: 將這些外國貨與本國貨對照一下。Contrast these foreign goods with the domestic product.

對照表(ㄉㄨㄟˋ ㄓㄠˋ ㄅㄧㄠˇ)
a contrastive or comparative table

對仗(ㄉㄨㄟˋ ㄓㄤˋ)
verbal parallelism (in classical Chinese poetry)

對證(ㄉㄨㄟˋ ㄓㄥˋ)
to establish evidence through personal confrontation or signed statement, etc.

對症下藥(ㄉㄨㄟˋ ㄓㄥˋ ㄒㄧㄚˋ ㄧㄠˋ)
(literally) to give the right prescription for an illness —(figuratively) to take the right remedial steps to correct a shortcoming

對酌(ㄉㄨㄟˋ ㄓㄨㄛˊ)
to drink, sitting face to face

對準(ㄉㄨㄟˋ ㄓㄨㄣˇ)
① to adjust (a machine part needing adjustment) to the right or proper position ② to aim at: 這強盜用槍對準他。The bandit aimed at him.

對稱(ㄉㄨㄟˋ ㄔㄣˋ)
symmetry; symmetrical

對唱(ㄉㄨㄟˋ ㄔㄤˋ)
a musical dialogue in antiphonal style; antiphonal singing

對手(ㄉㄨㄟˋ ㄕㄡˇ)
an opponent; an adversary; a match: 我不是他的對手。I am no match for him.

對數(ㄉㄨㄟˋ ㄕㄨˋ)
a logarithm

對數表(ㄉㄨㄟˋ ㄕㄨˋ ㄅㄧㄠˇ)
the logarithmic table

對子(ㄉㄨㄟˋ ·ㄗ) or 對兒(ㄉㄨㄜˋㄦ)
a Chinese couplet or antithesis

對策(ㄉㄨㄟˋ ㄘㄜˋ)
a measure (to deal with a problem, etc.); a countermeasure; a counterplot: 我們必須採取正當的對策,否則將會失敗。We must take the right measure, or we shall fail.

對偶(ㄉㄨㄟˋ ㄡˇ)
① to match; to pair ② verbal parallelism (in poetry)

對岸(ㄉㄨㄟˋ ㄢˋ)
the opposite shore: 他游到對岸。He swam to the opposite shore.

對奕(ㄉㄨㄟˋ ㄧˋ)
to confront each other in a chess game

對應(ㄉㄨㄟˋ ㄧㄥˋ)
corresponding; homologous

對味兒(ㄉㄨㄟˋ ㄨㄜˋㄦ)
① to one's taste ② to seem all right: 你說的話聽起來很對味兒。What you say sounds all right.

對外(ㄉㄨㄟˋ ㄨㄞˋ)
① for foreign or overseas (consumption, use, etc.) ② foreign (policies, etc.) ③ to resist a foreign aggression

對外貿易(ㄉㄨㄟˋ ㄨㄞˋ ㄇㄠˋ ㄧˋ)

foreign trade

對於(ㄉㄨㄟˋ ㄩˊ)
to; as to; in relation to; with regard to: 對於其他，我一無所知。I don't know anything as to the others.

十三畫

【導】 1167 ㄉㄠˋ daw dào (語音 ㄉㄠˇ dao dǎo)
to guide; to lead; to instruct; to conduct; to direct

導播(ㄉㄠˇ ㄅㄛ)
(TV) a director

導彈(ㄉㄠˇ ㄉㄢˋ)
a guided missile

導彈基地(ㄉㄠˇ ㄉㄢˋ ㄐㄧ ㄉㄧˋ)
a missile base

導電(ㄉㄠˇ ㄉㄧㄢˋ)
electric conduction

導電體(ㄉㄠˇ ㄉㄧㄢˋ ㄊㄧˇ) or 導體(ㄉㄠˇ ㄊㄧˇ)
an electric conductor

導尿(ㄉㄠˇ ㄋㄧㄠˋ)
catheterization

導流(ㄉㄠˇ ㄌㄧㄡˊ)
(irrigation) diversion

導論(ㄉㄠˇ ㄌㄨㄣˋ) or 導言(ㄉㄠˇ ㄧㄢˊ)
an introductory remark; an introduction: 他教哲學導論。He taught an introduction to philosophy.

導管(ㄉㄠˇ ㄍㄨㄢˇ)
①(machinery) a conduit; a pipe; a duct ②(biology) a vessel; a duct

導航(ㄉㄠˇ ㄏㄤˊ)
to navigate; navigation

導航系統(ㄉㄠˇ ㄏㄤˊ ㄒㄧˋ ㄊㄨㄥˇ)
a guidance system

導火線(ㄉㄠˇ ㄏㄨㄛˇ ㄒㄧㄢˋ)
① a fuse (for setting off explosives) ② the direct cause (of a development or event)

導火索(ㄉㄠˇ ㄏㄨㄛˇ ㄙㄨㄛˇ)
(military) a (blasting) fuse

導線(ㄉㄠˇ ㄒㄧㄢˋ)
(electricity) a lead; conducting wire

導向飛彈(ㄉㄠˇ ㄒㄧㄤˋ ㄈㄟ ㄉㄢˋ)
guided missiles

導向系統(ㄉㄠˇ ㄒㄧㄤˋ ㄒㄧˋ ㄊㄨㄥˇ)
a guidance system

導致(ㄉㄠˇ ㄓˋ)
to lead to; to cause something to happen: 這將導致無窮的糾紛。This will lead to endless confusion.

導師(ㄉㄠˇ ㄕ)
① a spiritual guide ② a tutor; a teacher charged with the responsibility to provide guidance to a class of students in their conduct or other nonacademic activities

導師制(ㄉㄠˇ ㄕ ㄓˋ)
the tutorial system

導熱(ㄉㄠˇ ㄖㄜˋ)
(physics) heat conduction

導遊(ㄉㄠˇ ㄧㄡˊ)
a tourist guide

導演(ㄉㄠˇ ㄧㄢˇ)
the director (of a dramatic performance)

導引(ㄉㄠˇ ㄧㄣˇ)
Taoist breathing exercises

導源(ㄉㄠˇ ㄩㄢˊ)
①(said of a river) to flow from ② to originate; to come from

小部
ㄒㄧㄠˇ sheau xiǎo

【小】 1168 ㄒㄧㄠˇ sheau xiǎo
1. small; little; tiny
2. minor: 這是小錯。It is a minor fault.
3. young; junior: 他比我小三歲。He is three years junior to me. 或 He is junior to me by three years.
4. humble; mean; lowly
5. light; slight; unimportant; trivial; petty

小把戲(ㄒㄧㄠˇ ㄅㄚˇ ㄒㄧˋ)
a child (in the Wu dialect)

小白臉(ㄒㄧㄠˇ ㄅㄞˊ ㄌㄧㄢˇ)
a handsome young man with effeminate features

小白菜(ㄒㄧㄠˇ ㄅㄞˊ ㄘㄞˋ)
a variety of Chinese cabbage; a pak-choi

小輩(ㄒㄧㄠˇ ㄅㄟˋ)
the members of the younger generation in a family or clan; a junior

小報(ㄒㄧㄠˇ ㄅㄠˋ)
a small newspaper

小班(ㄒㄧㄠˇ ㄅㄢ)
① the lowest of the three grades of kindergarten children ② a first-rate brothel (in Peking)

小半(ㄒㄧㄠˇ ㄅㄢˋ)
the smaller half

小本經營(ㄒㄧㄠˇ ㄅㄣˇ ㄐㄧㄥ ㄧㄥˊ)
(business) to run or operate with a small capital

小本生意(ㄒㄧㄠˇ ㄅㄣˇ ㄕㄥ ㄧˋ)
a small business

小辮兒(ㄒㄧㄠˇ ㄅㄧㄚˋㄦ) or 小辮子(ㄒㄧㄠˇ ㄅㄧㄢˋ ·ㄗ)
a braid: 她把頭髮梳成小辮子。She wears her hair in braids.

小別(ㄒㄧㄠˇ ㄅㄧㄝˊ)
to part for a short while; a brief separation

小別勝新婚(ㄒㄧㄠˇ ㄅㄧㄝˊ ㄕㄥˋ ㄒㄧㄣ ㄏㄨㄣ)
A brief parting is as sweet as a honeymoon.

小癟三(ㄒㄧㄠˇ ㄅㄧㄝˇ ㄙㄢ)
(dialect) a bum; a trash

小標題(ㄒㄧㄠˇ ㄅㄧㄠ ㄊㄧˊ)
a subheading; a subhead

小便(ㄒㄧㄠˇ ㄅㄧㄢˋ) or 小解(ㄒㄧㄠˇ ㄐㄧㄝˇ)
① to urinate; to pass urine; to empty the bladder; to make water ② urine; urination

小步(ㄒㄧㄠˇ ㄅㄨˋ)
to stroll

小部份 or 小部分(ㄒㄧㄠˇ ㄅㄨˋ ㄈㄣˋ)
a small part; a small portion; the minority

小不忍則亂大謀(ㄒㄧㄠˇ ㄅㄨˋ ㄖㄣˇ ㄗㄜˊ ㄌㄨㄢˋ ㄉㄚˋ ㄇㄡˊ)
Lack of forbearance in small matters upsets great plans. 或 He who cannot forbear in small matters spoils great undertakings.

小不點兒(ㄒㄧㄠˇ ·ㄅㄨ ㄉㄧㄚˇㄦ)
a very small or tiny thing or person

小朋友(ㄒㄧㄠˇ ㄆㄥˊ ·ㄧㄡ)
children (a term expressing goodwill): 小朋友是國家未來的主人翁。Children are the

future masters of the nation.
小便宜(ㄒㄧㄠˇ ㄆㄧㄢˊ ·ㄧ)
a small advantage
小品文(ㄒㄧㄠˇ ㄆㄧㄣˇ ㄨㄣˊ)
an essay
小舖子 or 小鋪子(ㄒㄧㄠˇ ㄆㄨˋ ·ㄗ)
a small store: 他開個小舖子。He runs a small store.
小買賣(ㄒㄧㄠˇ ㄇㄞˇ ㄇㄞˋ)
small business
小麥(ㄒㄧㄠˇ ㄇㄞˋ)
wheat: 農夫種小麥。Farmers plant wheat.
小妹(ㄒㄧㄠˇ ㄇㄟˋ)
① a little sister ② a little girl ③a young female servant
小貓(ㄒㄧㄠˇ ㄇㄠ)
a kitten
小貓熊(ㄒㄧㄠˇ ㄇㄠ ㄒㄩㄥˊ)
a lesser panda 亦作「小熊貓」
小滿(ㄒㄧㄠˇ ㄇㄢˇ)
Grain fills—one of a year's 24 solar periods, which falls on May 21 or 22
小門小戶(ㄒㄧㄠˇ ㄇㄣˊ ㄒㄧㄠˇ ㄏㄨˋ)
a poor, humble family
小米(ㄒㄧㄠˇ ㄇㄧˇ)
millet
小民(ㄒㄧㄠˇ ㄇㄧㄣˊ)
a commoner; common people 亦作「老百姓」
小名(ㄒㄧㄠˇ ㄇㄧㄥˊ)
one's childhood name
小拇指(ㄒㄧㄠˇ ㄇㄨˇ ㄓˇ)
one's little finger
小費(ㄒㄧㄠˇ ㄈㄟˋ)
a tip (given to a waiter, porter, etc.)
小販(ㄒㄧㄠˇ ㄈㄢˋ)
stall holders; hawkers; peddlers
小腹(ㄒㄧㄠˇ ㄈㄨˋ)
the lower abdomen
小婦(ㄒㄧㄠˇ ㄈㄨˋ)
① a concubine ② a young woman
小大由之(ㄒㄧㄠˇ ㄉㄚˋ ㄧㄡˊ ㄓ)
to be of either little value or great use
小的
①(ㄒㄧㄠˇ ·ㄉㄜ) the small one: 他要那小的。He wants the small one.
②(ㄒㄧㄠˇ ·ㄉㄧ) (in ancient China) a self reference by servants when speaking to the master
小刀(ㄒㄧㄠˇ ㄉㄠ)
① a small sword ② a pocket knife
小島(ㄒㄧㄠˇ ㄉㄠˇ)
an islet: 我們不知道這小島的名字。We don't know the name of this islet.
小道消息(ㄒㄧㄠˇ ㄉㄠˋ ㄒㄧㄠ ·ㄒㄧ)
hearsay; the grapevine
小旦(ㄒㄧㄠˇ ㄉㄢˋ)
(Chinese opera) a female role
小登科(ㄒㄧㄠˇ ㄉㄥ ㄎㄜ)
(colloquial) to take a wife
小弟(ㄒㄧㄠˇ ㄉㄧˋ)
① a little brother ② a little boy ③ a young male servant
小調(ㄒㄧㄠˇ ㄉㄧㄠˋ)
folk songs; ballads
小店(ㄒㄧㄠˇ ㄉㄧㄢˋ)
① an inn; a lodging house ② a small store ③ my or our store (a self-depreciatory term)
小電影(ㄒㄧㄠˇ ㄉㄧㄢˋ ㄧㄥˇ)
(slang) a porno film; a skin flick
小隊(ㄒㄧㄠˇ ㄉㄨㄟˋ)
a small contingent or detachment
小動作(ㄒㄧㄠˇ ㄉㄨㄥˋ ㄗㄨㄛˋ)
petty action; little tricks
小偷(ㄒㄧㄠˇ ㄊㄡ)
a thief; a burglar
小題大做(ㄒㄧㄠˇ ㄊㄧˊ ㄉㄚˋ ㄗㄨㄛˋ)
to make much of a trifle; a storm in a teacup; to make a mountain out of a molehill: 這未免小題大做。This is making a mountain out of a molehill.
小提琴(ㄒㄧㄠˇ ㄊㄧˊ ㄑㄧㄣˊ)
violin
小蹄子(ㄒㄧㄠˇ ㄊㄧˊ ·ㄗ)
an abusive reference to a maidservant
小天地(ㄒㄧㄠˇ ㄊㄧㄢ ㄉㄧˋ)
small world; limited sphere of activities
小艇(ㄒㄧㄠˇ ㄊㄧㄥˇ)
a small boat; a skiff
小腿(ㄒㄧㄠˇ ㄊㄨㄟˇ)
the calf (of the leg)
小腦(ㄒㄧㄠˇ ㄋㄠˇ)
the cerebellum
小妮子(ㄒㄧㄠˇ ㄋㄧˊ ·ㄗ)
① a girl (expressing endearment) ② a housemaid
小鳥依人(ㄒㄧㄠˇ ㄋㄧㄠˇ ㄧ ㄖㄣˊ)
(said of a child or young girl) lovely and pliant like a little bird
小妞兒(ㄒㄧㄠˇ ㄋㄧㄡㄦ)
a small girl; a young girl
小牛(ㄒㄧㄠˇ ㄋㄧㄡˊ)
a calf
小牛肉(ㄒㄧㄠˇ ㄋㄧㄡˊ ㄖㄡˋ)
veal
小年夜(ㄒㄧㄠˇ ㄋㄧㄢˊ ㄧㄝˋ)
the night before Lunar New Year's Eve
小娘子(ㄒㄧㄠˇ ㄋㄧㄤˊ ·ㄗ)
a young girl
小農(ㄒㄧㄠˇ ㄋㄨㄥˊ)
a farmer with small landholding
小女(ㄒㄧㄠˇ ㄋㄩˇ)
my daughter (a self-depreciatory term)
小喇叭(ㄒㄧㄠˇ ㄌㄚˇ ·ㄅㄚ)
a trumpet
小老婆(ㄒㄧㄠˇ ㄌㄠˇ ·ㄆㄛ)
a concubine
小老頭兒(ㄒㄧㄠˇ ㄌㄠˇ ㄊㄡˊㄦ)
a man who ages prematurely
小嘍囉(ㄒㄧㄠˇ ㄌㄡˊ ·ㄌㄨㄛ)
unimportant followers; lackeys; underlings
小笠原群島(ㄒㄧㄠˇ ㄌㄧˋ ㄩㄢˊ ㄑㄩㄣˊ ㄉㄠˇ)
Bonin Islands or Ogasawara Jima
小綹(ㄒㄧㄠˇ ㄌㄧㄡˇ)or 小李(ㄒㄧㄠˇ ㄌㄧˇ)
a pickpocket
小斂(ㄒㄧㄠˇ ㄌㄧㄢˋ)
to dress up the dead in preparation for the funeral service
小兩口子(ㄒㄧㄠˇ ㄌㄧㄤˇ ㄎㄡˇ ·ㄗ)
a young couple
小路(ㄒㄧㄠˇ ㄌㄨˋ)
a path; a trail: 他們在雪中劃出一條小路。They shovel a path through the snow.
小呂宋(ㄒㄧㄠˇ ㄌㄩˇ ㄙㄨㄥˋ)
Manila
小歌劇(ㄒㄧㄠˇ ㄍㄜ ㄐㄩˋ)
an operetta

小哥兒們(ㄒㄧㄠˇ ㄍㄜㄦ ·ㄇㄣ)
a group of young men

小個子(ㄒㄧㄠˇ ㄍㄜˋ ·ㄗ)
a little chap; a small fellow

小狗(ㄒㄧㄠˇ ㄍㄡˇ)
a young dog; a puppy

小姑(ㄒㄧㄠˇ ㄍㄨ)
one's husband's younger sister

小姑獨處(ㄒㄧㄠˇ ㄍㄨ ㄉㄨˊ ㄔㄨˇ)
to remain a spinster: 她仍然小姑獨處。She remains a spinster.

小姑娘(ㄒㄧㄠˇ ㄍㄨ ·ㄋㄧㄤ)
a missy; a young girl

小褂兒(ㄒㄧㄠˇ ㄍㄨㄚˋㄦ)
a short outer garment

小過(ㄒㄧㄠˇ ㄍㄨㄛˋ)
①a minor mistake ②a minor demerit (recorded for an employee by the employer or for a student by the school authorities)

小鬼(ㄒㄧㄠˇ ㄍㄨㄟˇ)
①the spirits serving the ruler of the lower world ②a mischievous child; an imp

小廣告(ㄒㄧㄠˇ ㄍㄨㄤˇ ㄍㄠˋ)
a classified ad

小工(ㄒㄧㄠˇ ㄍㄨㄥ)
an unskilled laborer

小可(ㄒㄧㄠˇ ㄎㄜˇ)
I, me (a self-depreciatory expression): 小可在此。I am here.

小開(ㄒㄧㄠˇ ㄎㄞ)
(Shanghai dialect) a businessman's son

小楷(ㄒㄧㄠˇ ㄎㄞˇ)
the calligraphy in small characters of the standard type

小考(ㄒㄧㄠˇ ㄎㄠˇ)
a quiz or test conducted for students by the teacher

小口(ㄒㄧㄠˇ ㄎㄡˇ)
an infant as a minor food consumer in the family (as distinct from medium and major consumers)

小口徑(ㄒㄧㄠˇ ㄎㄡˇ ㄐㄧㄥˋ)
(said of gun barrels) small-bore

小看(ㄒㄧㄠˇ ㄎㄢˋ)
to think little of; to make light of; to treat lightly; to slight

小康(ㄒㄧㄠˇ ㄎㄤ)
①(said of a family) well-to-do: 她出身小康之家。She came from a well-to-do family. ②(said of a nation) fairly prosperous and secure

小河(ㄒㄧㄠˇ ㄏㄜˊ)
a rivulet: 小河上有座橋。The rivulet is crossed by a bridge.

小孩(ㄒㄧㄠˇ ㄏㄞˊ)or 小孩子(ㄒㄧㄠˇ ㄏㄞˊ ·ㄗ)or 小孩兒(ㄒㄧㄠˇ ㄏㄚˊㄦ)
a child

小號(ㄒㄧㄠˇ ㄏㄠˋ)
①my or our store (a self-depreciatory term) ②small size (as distinct from medium and large sizes)

小寒(ㄒㄧㄠˇ ㄏㄢˊ)
Little cold—one of the 24 solar periods, into which the year is divided, which falls on January 6 or 7

小戶人家(ㄒㄧㄠˇ ㄏㄨˋ ㄖㄣˊ ㄐㄧㄚ)
a poor, humble family

小花臉(ㄒㄧㄠˇ ㄏㄨㄚ ㄌㄧㄢˇ)
a clown in Chinese opera

小花樣(ㄒㄧㄠˇ ㄏㄨㄚ ㄧㄤˋ)
a little stunt

小划子(ㄒㄧㄠˇ ㄏㄨㄚˊ ·ㄗ)
a small rowing boat

小夥子(ㄒㄧㄠˇ ㄏㄨㄛˇ ·ㄗ)or 小夥兒(ㄒㄧㄠˇ ㄏㄨㄛˇㄦ)
a young fellow

小惠(ㄒㄧㄠˇ ㄏㄨㄟˋ)
small favors

小鷄(ㄒㄧㄠˇ ㄐㄧ)
a chick

小家碧玉(ㄒㄧㄠˇ ㄐㄧㄚ ㄅㄧˋ ㄩˋ)
a daughter of a humble family

小家庭(ㄒㄧㄠˇ ㄐㄧㄚ ㄊㄧㄥˊ)
a small family

小家子(ㄒㄧㄠˇ ㄐㄧㄚ ·ㄗ)
a vulgar, lower-class person

小家子氣(ㄒㄧㄠˇ ㄐㄧㄚ ·ㄗ ㄑㄧˋ)
showing nervous in public, characteristic of people of low birth

小結(ㄒㄧㄠˇ ㄐㄧㄝˊ)
①a brief summary; an interim summary ②to summarize briefly

小節(ㄒㄧㄠˇ ㄐㄧㄝˊ)
①a minor, trivial, or unimportant point; a triviality ②a measure (in music)

小姐(ㄒㄧㄠˇ ㄐㄧㄝˇ)
a young (unmarried) lady

小脚(ㄒㄧㄠˇ ㄐㄧㄠˇ)
the small feet deformed by the practice of foot binding in old China

小轎車(ㄒㄧㄠˇ ㄐㄧㄠˋ ㄔㄜ)
a sedan (car)

小舅子(ㄒㄧㄠˇ ㄐㄧㄡˋ ·ㄗ)
a brother-in-law (one's wife's younger brother)

小襟(ㄒㄧㄠˇ ㄐㄧㄣ)
the inner piece on the right side of a Chinese garment which buttons on the right

小憩(ㄒㄧㄠˇ ㄑㄧˋ)
to rest for a while

小器 or 小氣(ㄒㄧㄠˇ ㄑㄧˋ)
①narrow-minded ②niggardly: 他很小氣。He is niggardly of money.

小氣鬼(ㄒㄧㄠˇ ㄑㄧˋ ㄍㄨㄟˇ)
a niggard

小巧玲瓏(ㄒㄧㄠˇ ㄑㄧㄠˇ ㄌㄧㄥˊ ㄌㄨㄥˊ)
①(said of a woman) small, trim, and lovely; petite ②(said of a decorative item) small and exquisite

小前提(ㄒㄧㄠˇ ㄑㄧㄢˊ ㄊㄧˊ)
the minor premise (of a syllogism)

小圈子(ㄒㄧㄠˇ ㄑㄩㄢ ·ㄗ)
a small circle; an inner circle; a tightly knit clique

小犬(ㄒㄧㄠˇ ㄑㄩㄢˇ)
①a puppy ②(a self-depreciatory term) my son: 小犬明日歸來。My son will come home tomorrow.

小媳婦兒(ㄒㄧㄠˇ ㄒㄧˊ ·ㄈㄨㄦ)
①a little girl engaged to be one's daughter-in-law when grown-up ②a young woman

小寫(ㄒㄧㄠˇ ㄒㄧㄝˇ)
a lowercase letter (of the Roman alphabet)

小心(ㄒㄧㄠˇ ㄒㄧㄣ)
careful; cautious; to pay attention to

小心火燭(ㄒㄧㄠˇ ㄒㄧㄣ ㄏㄨㄛˇ ㄓㄨˊ)
Guard against fire!

小心輕放(ㄒㄧㄠˇ ㄒㄧㄣ ㄑㄧㄥ ㄈㄤˋ)
Handle with care!

小心翼翼(ㄒㄧㄠˇ ㄒㄧㄣ ㄧˋ ㄧˋ)
very timidly; very gingerly; with the greatest circum-

spection: 他小心翼翼地工作。He did his work with great care.

小心眼兒(ㄒㄧㄠˇ ㄒㄧㄣ ㄧㄚˇㄦ)
narrow-minded; extremely sensitive: 她很小心眼兒。She is narrow-minded.

小相公(ㄒㄧㄠˇ ㄒㄧㄤˋ ·ㄍㄨㄥ)
a mah-jong player who, due to oversight, takes in one tile less than the required 13 at the beginning of a game and is thus disqualified to win that particular game

小星(ㄒㄧㄠˇ ㄒㄧㄥ)
a concubine

小型(ㄒㄧㄠˇ ㄒㄧㄥˊ)
small-sized; small; midget; miniature

小型報紙(ㄒㄧㄠˇ ㄒㄧㄥˊ ㄅㄠˋ ㄓˇ)
a tabloid

小型電腦(ㄒㄧㄠˇ ㄒㄧㄥˊ ㄉㄧㄢˋ ㄋㄠˇ)
a minicomputer

小型企業(ㄒㄧㄠˇ ㄒㄧㄥˊ ㄑㄧˋ ㄧㄝˋ)
a small enterprise

小行星(ㄒㄧㄠˇ ㄒㄧㄥˊ ㄒㄧㄥ)
a planetoid; an asteroid

小壻 or 小婿(ㄒㄧㄠˇ ㄒㄩˋ)
① my son-in-law (a self-depreciatory term): 小婿擔任市長職務。My son-in-law served as mayor. ② I or me (when addressing one's own parent-in-law)

小學(ㄒㄧㄠˇ ㄒㄩㄝˊ)
a primary school; an elementary school: 小孩在上中學前先上小學。Children attend primary school before high school.

小學生(ㄒㄧㄠˇ ㄒㄩㄝˊ ㄕㄥ)
a (primary school) pupil; a schoolchild; a schoolboy or schoolgirl

小雪(ㄒㄧㄠˇ ㄒㄩㄝˇ)
① Little snow—one of the twenty-four solar periods, into which the year is divided, falling either on November 22 or 23 ② a light snow

小熊貓(ㄒㄧㄠˇ ㄒㄩㄥˊ ㄇㄠ)
a lesser panda 亦作「小貓熊」

小熊座(ㄒㄧㄠˇ ㄒㄩㄥˊ ㄗㄨㄛˋ)
(astronomy) Ursa Minor

小指(ㄒㄧㄠˇ ㄓˇ)
the little finger

小照(ㄒㄧㄠˇ ㄓㄠˋ)
a portrait

小賬(ㄒㄧㄠˇ ㄓㄤˋ)or 小費(ㄒㄧㄠˇ ㄈㄟˋ)
tips for waiters, etc.

小住(ㄒㄧㄠˇ ㄓㄨˋ)
to live at a place temporarily; to sojourn: 他小住旅館。He sojourns at an inn.

小註(兒)(ㄒㄧㄠˇ ㄓㄨˋ (ㄦ))
footnotes

小酌(ㄒㄧㄠˇ ㄓㄨㄛˊ)or 小飲(ㄒㄧㄠˇ ㄧㄣˇ)
a little drink or a few drinks (of some alcoholic beverage)

小傳(ㄒㄧㄠˇ ㄓㄨㄢˋ)
brief (or short) biography: 他問我如何寫小傳。He asked me how to write a brief (or short) biography.

小篆(ㄒㄧㄠˇ ㄓㄨㄢˋ)
the "small seal," a style of characters much in vogue during the Chin Dynasty shortly before 200 B.C.

小仲馬(ㄒㄧㄠˇ ㄓㄨㄥˋ ㄇㄚˇ)
Dumas fils, the younger Dumas (Alexandre Dumas, 1824-1895, son of Alexandre Dumas, 1802-1870)

小吃(ㄒㄧㄠˇ ㄔ)
① supplementary dishes (usually cold) at a dinner in addition to the regular courses ② a snack

小吃館(ㄒㄧㄠˇ ㄔ ㄍㄨㄢˇ)
a small restaurant; an eatery: 他經營一家小吃館。He runs a small restaurant.

小丑(ㄒㄧㄠˇ ㄔㄡˇ)
a clown: 小孩子喜歡小丑。Children like clowns.

小醜跳梁(ㄒㄧㄠˇ ㄔㄡˇ ㄊㄧㄠˋ ㄌㄧㄤˊ)
petty thieves going on the rampage

小產(ㄒㄧㄠˇ ㄔㄢˇ)
spontaneous abortion; a miscarriage

小腸(ㄒㄧㄠˇ ㄔㄤˊ)
the small intestine

小腸氣(ㄒㄧㄠˇ ㄔㄤˊ ㄑㄧˋ)
hernia 亦作「疝氣」

小成(ㄒㄧㄠˇ ㄔㄥˊ)
small achievement; moderate success

小時(ㄒㄧㄠˇ ㄕˊ)
an hour: 他在那兒停留三小時。He stayed there three hours.

小時了了(ㄒㄧㄠˇ ㄕˊ ㄌㄧㄠˇ ㄌㄧㄠˇ)
very intelligent when young

小時候(ㄒㄧㄠˇ ㄕˊ ·ㄏㄡ)
as a child; in childhood; during one's childhood: 他們從小時候就是好朋友。They are good friends since childhood.

小事(ㄒㄧㄠˇ ㄕˋ)
a trifle; a trivial matter; a triviality

小試(ㄒㄧㄠˇ ㄕˋ)
① to make a casual trial ② the annual prefectural civil service examination in ancient times

小試鋒芒(ㄒㄧㄠˇ ㄕˋ ㄈㄥ ㄇㄤˊ)
to make a casual demonstration of one's capability

小市民(ㄒㄧㄠˇ ㄕˋ ㄇㄧㄣˊ)
the urban petty bourgeois

小舌(ㄒㄧㄠˇ ㄕㄜˊ)
① the uvula ② the ligule

小手小脚(ㄒㄧㄠˇ ㄕㄡˇ ㄒㄧㄠˇ ㄐㄧㄠˇ)
① stingy; miserly; mean ② lacking boldness; timid

小嬸(ㄒㄧㄠˇ ㄕㄣˇ)
a sister-in-law (the wife of one's husband's younger brother)

小聲(ㄒㄧㄠˇ ㄕㄥ)
to lower one's voice; to speak low: 請小聲說話。Speak low, please!

小生(ㄒㄧㄠˇ ㄕㄥ)
the young man's role (especially in Chinese opera)

小生意(ㄒㄧㄠˇ ㄕㄥ ㄧˋ)
small business

小乘(ㄒㄧㄠˇ ㄕㄥˋ)
(Buddhism) the Hinayana (or "Lesser Vehicle") school

小叔(ㄒㄧㄠˇ ㄕㄨˊ)
a brother-in-law (one's husband's younger brother): 她小叔在經商。Her brother-in-law is in business.

小暑(ㄒㄧㄠˇ ㄕㄨˇ)
Slight heat—one of the 24 solar periods, into which the year is divided, falling on July 7 or 8

小樹(ㄒㄧㄠˇ ㄕㄨˋ)
a sapling

小數(ㄒㄧㄠˇ ㄕㄨˋ)

a decimal fraction; a decimal

小數點(ㄒㄧㄠˇ ㄕㄨˇ ㄉㄧㄢˇ)
the decimal point

小說(ㄒㄧㄠˇ ㄕㄨㄛ)
a novel; fiction

小說家(ㄒㄧㄠˇ ㄕㄨㄛ ㄐㄧㄚ)
a novelist

小人(ㄒㄧㄠˇ ㄖㄣˊ)
① a mean person (as opposed to a real gentleman): 他是小人。He is a mean person. ② a self-depreciatory term used by the common people of ancient times in referring to oneself when speaking to government officials or by servants when speaking to the master or mistress

小人國(ㄒㄧㄠˇ ㄖㄣˊ ㄍㄨㄛˊ)
Lilliput; the Land of Pygmies: 小人國是格列佛遊記中的一個國家。Lilliput is a country in *Gulliver's Travels.*

小人兒書(ㄒㄧㄠˇ ㄖㄜˊㄦ ㄕㄨ)
(colloquial) a picture-story book

小資產階級(ㄒㄧㄠˇ ㄗ ㄔㄢˇ ㄐㄧㄝ ㄐㄧˊ)
the petty bourgeoisie: 他們屬於小資產階級。They belong to the bourgeoisie.

小子(ㄒㄧㄠˇ ㄗˇ)
① one's children ② a self-depreciatory term used in referring to oneself ③ young fellow (usually with slight contempt)

小字(ㄒㄧㄠˇ ㄗˋ)
① one's childhood name ② the calligraphy in small characters

小組(ㄒㄧㄠˇ ㄗㄨˇ)
a group formed for a specific purpose

小組討論(ㄒㄧㄠˇ ㄗㄨˇ ㄊㄠˇ ㄌㄨㄣˋ)
a group discussion

小組會議(ㄒㄧㄠˇ ㄗㄨˇ ㄏㄨㄟˋ ㄧˋ)
a sectional conference; a sectional committee; a subcommittee meeting

小册子(ㄒㄧㄠˇ ㄘㄜˋ ˙ㄗ)
a pamphlet or brochure

小才大用(ㄒㄧㄠˇ ㄘㄞˊ ㄉㄚˋ ㄩㄥˋ)
to give great responsibility to a man of common ability

小菜(ㄒㄧㄠˇ ㄘㄞˋ)
plain dishes (as distinct from expensive courses)

小聰明(ㄒㄧㄠˇ ㄘㄨㄥ ˙ㄇㄧㄥ)
clever or smart in a small way: 他的兒子有小聰明。His son is clever in a small way.

小廝(ㄒㄧㄠˇ ㄙ)
a servant (especially a mean one); a subaltern; an underling

小蘇打(ㄒㄧㄠˇ ㄙㄨ ㄉㄚˇ)
sodium bicarbonate

小恩小惠(ㄒㄧㄠˇ ㄣ ㄒㄧㄠˇ ㄏㄨㄟˋ)
petty favors; small favors; economic sops; economic bribes

小兒(ㄒㄧㄠˇ ㄦˊ)
① an infant; a child ② my son (a self-depreciatory term)

小兒痲痺症(ㄒㄧㄠˇ ㄦˊ ㄇㄚˊ ㄅㄧˋ ㄓㄥˋ)
poliomyelitis; polio; infantile paralysis

小兒痲痺疫苗(ㄒㄧㄠˇ ㄦˊ ㄇㄚˊ ㄅㄧˋ ㄧˋ ㄇㄧㄠˊ)
polio vaccine

小兒科(ㄒㄧㄠˇ ㄦˊ ㄎㄜ)
① pediatrics ② (slang) parsimonious

小兒子(ㄒㄧㄠˇ ㄦˊ ˙ㄗ)
the youngest son: 他的小兒子從軍爲國家作戰。His youngest son joined up to fight for the country.

小耳朵(ㄒㄧㄠˇ ㄦˇ ˙ㄉㄨㄛ)
① (slang) DBS (Direct Broadcasting Satellite) 亦作「直播衛星」② a spy

小二(ㄒㄧㄠˇ ㄦˋ)
(formerly) a waiter at a tavern or hotel

小衣(ㄒㄧㄠˇ ㄧ)
a garment covering the lower half of the body; trousers; pants

小姨子(ㄒㄧㄠˇ ㄧˊ ˙ㄗ)
a sister-in-law (one's wife's younger sister)

小意思(ㄒㄧㄠˇ ㄧˋ ˙ㄙ)
① a trifle; a triviality ② a small token of regard (such as a gift)

小鴨(ㄒㄧㄠˇ ㄧㄚ)
a duckling

小丫頭(ㄒㄧㄠˇ ㄧㄚ ˙ㄊㄡ)
① a little girl (expressing contempt or endearment) ② a young housemaid

小亞細亞(ㄒㄧㄠˇ ㄧㄚˇ ㄒㄧ ㄧㄚˇ)
Asia Minor

小夜曲(ㄒㄧㄠˇ ㄧㄝˋ ㄑㄩˇ)
(music) a serenade

小妖精(ㄒㄧㄠˇ ㄧㄠ ㄐㄧㄥ)
a coquettish young girl

小引(ㄒㄧㄠˇ ㄧㄣˇ)
a foreword

小羊(ㄒㄧㄠˇ ㄧㄤˊ)
a lamb: 她像小羊般天眞活潑。She is as innocent as a lamb.

小陽春(ㄒㄧㄠˇ ㄧㄤˊ ㄔㄨㄣ)
balmy weather in the tenth month of the lunar calendar

小巫見大巫(ㄒㄧㄠˇ ㄨ ㄐㄧㄢˋ ㄉㄚˋ ㄨ)
① (literally) a giant in the presence of a supergiant—a man with a little learning in the presence of a great scholar ② no comparison between

小娃娃(ㄒㄧㄠˇ ㄨㄚˊ ˙ㄨㄚ)
a small child: 這小娃娃逗人喜愛。This small child is cute.

小我(ㄒㄧㄠˇ ㄨㄛˇ)
the individual; the ego; the self

小玩藝兒(ㄒㄧㄠˇ ㄨㄢˊ ㄧㄜˋㄦ)
a small toy or plaything

小魚(ㄒㄧㄠˇ ㄩˊ)
a fry

小雨兒(ㄒㄧㄠˇ ㄩㄜˇㄦ)
a light rain; a drizzle: 只不過是一場小雨兒。It's only a drizzle.

小月(ㄒㄧㄠˇ ㄩㄝˋ)
a 30-day month of the Gregorian calendar; a 29-day month of the lunar calendar

一畫

【少】 1169

1. ㄕㄠˇ shao shǎo

1. small or little (in number, quantity, or duration)
2. missing; absent; wanting; lost: 牛群裡少了幾頭牛。A few bulls have been lost from the herd.
3. to do without: 鹽不可少。Salt is something we can not go without.
4. to stop; to quit: 少給我胡

〔小部〕

〔小部〕

謅! Stop talking nonsense!

少不得(ㄕㄠˇ ˙ㄅㄨ ˙ㄉㄜ)
indispensable; not to be dispensed with

少不了(ㄕㄠˇ ˙ㄅㄨ ㄌㄧㄠˇ)
①indispensable; not to be dispensed with; cannot do without ②unlikely to be lost ③unlikely to be small in number or quantity ④to be bound to; to be unavoidable

少不了有你的(ㄕㄠˇ ˙ㄅㄨ ㄌㄧㄠˇ ㄧㄡˇ ㄋㄧˇ ˙ㄉㄜ)
You'll get your share.

少陪(ㄕㄠˇ ㄆㄟˊ)
I'm sorry I can't keep you company any longer.

少待(ㄕㄠˇ ㄉㄞˋ)
to wait for a little while: 請少待片刻。Please wait for a little while.

少停(ㄕㄠˇ ㄊㄧㄥˊ)
①to pause for a little while: 我們少停片刻。Let's pause for a little while. ②Don't pause too often.

少了(ㄕㄠˇ ˙ㄌㄜ)
less than the required or expected amount, quantity, etc.

少了不賣(ㄕㄠˇ ˙ㄌㄜ ㄅㄨˋ ㄇㄞˋ)
not to sell for less

少來(ㄕㄠˇ ㄌㄞˊ)
①to refrain from coming ②to be sparing (in doing something)

少來這一套(ㄕㄠˇ ㄌㄞˊ ㄓㄜˋ ㄧˊ ㄊㄠˋ)
(an expression showing one's displeasure) Let's have no more of this. 或 Let's quit that!

少禮(ㄕㄠˇ ㄌㄧˇ)
I'm sorry for my inadequate regard for propriety. 或 Excuse me for having not shown you enough politeness.

少量(ㄕㄠˇ ㄌㄧㄤˋ)
a small amount (or quantity); a little; a few: 請給我少量的水。Please give me a little water.

少管閒事(ㄕㄠˇ ㄍㄨㄢˇ ㄒㄧㄢˊ ㄕˋ)
Mind your own business.

少刻(ㄕㄠˇ ㄎㄜˋ)
after a little while; a moment later

少候(ㄕㄠˇ ㄏㄡˋ)
Please wait for a little while.

少見(ㄕㄠˇ ㄐㄧㄢˋ)
seldom seen; unique; rare

少見多怪(ㄕㄠˇ ㄐㄧㄢˋ ㄉㄨㄛ ㄍㄨㄞˋ)
to wonder much because one has seen little; to make much ado about nothing; to kick up a fuss: 用不着少見多怪。There's nothing to be surprised at.

少頃(ㄕㄠˇ ㄑㄧㄥˇ)
a little while; a short while; a short time

少許(ㄕㄠˇ ㄒㄩˇ)
a little bit; a little; a sprinkling of

少數(ㄕㄠˇ ㄕㄨˋ)
①a few; a small number (of) ②minority: 少數服從多數。The minority is subordinate to the majority.

少數民族(ㄕㄠˇ ㄕㄨˋ ㄇㄧㄣˊ ㄗㄨˊ)
a minority ethnic group (in a multiracial nation)

少數黨(ㄕㄠˇ ㄕㄨˋ ㄉㄤˇ)
a minority political party

少數人(ㄕㄠˇ ㄕㄨˋ ㄖㄣˊ)
the minority

少說廢話(ㄕㄠˇ ㄕㄨㄛ ㄈㄟˋ ㄏㄨㄚˋ)
Stop talking nonsense! 或 Stop chattering!

少算(ㄕㄠˇ ㄙㄨㄢˋ)
to reduce prices (to an old customer)

少安毋躁(ㄕㄠˇ ㄢ ㄨˊ ㄗㄠˋ)
Be patient! 請少安毋躁! Please be patient!

少有(ㄕㄠˇ ㄧㄡˇ)
rare; scarce

少問(ㄕㄠˇ ㄨㄣˋ)
to refrain from asking

【少】 1169
2. ㄕㄠˋ shaw shào

young; youthful; junior; juvenile

少輩兒(ㄕㄠˋ ㄅㄟˋㄦ)
the younger generation of a family

少白頭(ㄕㄠˋ ㄅㄞˊ ㄊㄡˊ)
①to be prematurely gray ②a youth with graying hair

少不更事(ㄕㄠˋ ㄅㄨˋ ㄍㄥ ㄕˋ)
young and inexperienced: 我們經理少不更事。Our manager is young and inexperienced.

少婦(ㄕㄠˋ ㄈㄨˋ)
a young woman

少東(ㄕㄠˋ ㄉㄨㄥ)
(formerly) the son of the master

少奶奶(ㄕㄠˋ ㄋㄞˇ ˙ㄋㄞ)
the wife of the young lord or master

少年(ㄕㄠˋ ㄋㄧㄢˊ)
①a boy; a juvenile; a youth ②young

少年法庭(ㄕㄠˋ ㄋㄧㄢˊ ㄈㄚˇ ㄊㄧㄥˊ)
a juvenile court

少年犯罪(ㄕㄠˋ ㄋㄧㄢˊ ㄈㄢˋ ㄗㄨㄟˋ)
juvenile delinquency: 少年犯罪問題很嚴重。The problem of juvenile delinquency is very serious.

少年讀物(ㄕㄠˋ ㄋㄧㄢˊ ㄉㄨˊ ㄨˋ)
juvenile books; books for young people

少年老成(ㄕㄠˋ ㄋㄧㄢˊ ㄌㄠˇ ㄔㄥˊ)
young but competent; accomplished though young

少年人(ㄕㄠˋ ㄋㄧㄢˊ ㄖㄣˊ)
a young person; a youth: 他喜歡被少年人包圍。He loved to be surrounded by youths.

少女(ㄕㄠˋ ㄋㄩˇ)
a young girl; a damsel: 我在花園看見幾個漂亮的少女。I saw some pretty young girls in the garden.

少林拳(ㄕㄠˋ ㄌㄧㄣˊ ㄑㄩㄢˊ)
name of a school of boxing started during the Tang Dynasty

少林寺(ㄕㄠˋ ㄌㄧㄣˊ ㄙˋ)
name of a Buddhist monastery famous for its pugilist monks

少將(ㄕㄠˋ ㄐㄧㄤˋ)
major general (in the army, air force and marine corps); rear admiral (in the navy): 那少將升做中將。The major general was promoted lieutenant general.

少校(ㄕㄠˋ ㄒㄧㄠˋ)
major (in the army, air force and marine corps); lieutenant commander (in the navy)

少壯(ㄕㄠˋ ㄓㄨㄤˋ)
young and energetic: 少壯不努力，老大徒傷悲。One who

doesn't work hard in the prime of life would only grieve in the evening of life. 或 Laziness in youth spells regret in old age.

少壯派(ㄕㄠˋ ㄓㄨㄤˋ ㄆㄞˋ)
the stalwarts; a young Turk: 少壯派不肯講和。The stalwarts refuse to negotiate for peace.

少艾(ㄕㄠˋ ㄞˋ)
a young beauty

少爺(ㄕㄠˋ ·ㄧㄝ)
① a young master (of a rich family); a young lord ② your son (an honorific term)

少爺脾氣(ㄕㄠˋ ·ㄧㄝ ㄆㄧˊ ·ㄑㄧ)
to do whatever one pleases

少尉(ㄕㄠˋ ㄨㄟˋ)
second lieutenant (in the army, air force or marine corps); ensign (in the navy)

三畫

【尖】 1170 ㄐㄧㄢ jian jiān

sharp; acute; pointed; keen

尖兵(ㄐㄧㄢ ㄅㄧㄥ)
(military) a point

尖端(ㄐㄧㄢ ㄉㄨㄢ)
a pointed end or head

尖端科學(ㄐㄧㄢ ㄉㄨㄢ ㄎㄜ ㄒㄩㄝˊ)
the frontiers of science

尖利(ㄐㄧㄢ ㄌㄧˋ)
① sharp; keen; cutting: 這是一根尖利的針。This is a sharp needle. ② shrill; piercing: 尖利的汽笛聲 a shrill whistle

尖刻(ㄐㄧㄢ ㄎㄜˋ)
relentless; ruthless; unsympathetic; merciless; exacting; acrimonious: 很少人能忍受他尖刻的話。Few can stand his acrimonious words.

尖銳(ㄐㄧㄢ ㄖㄨㄟˋ)
① sharp—pointed ② penetrating; sharp; keen; incisive ③ shrill; piercing ④ intense; acute; sharp

尖銳化(ㄐㄧㄢ ㄖㄨㄟˋ ㄏㄨㄚˋ)
(said of a situation) to become increasingly acute or grave

尖嘴薄舌(ㄐㄧㄢ ㄗㄨㄟˇ ㄅㄛˊ ㄕㄜˊ)
to have a caustic (or biting) and flippant tongue

尖酸(ㄐㄧㄢ ㄙㄨㄢ)
(said of words, speech, etc.) sarcastic; petty; mean

尖酸刻薄(ㄐㄧㄢ ㄙㄨㄢ ㄎㄜˋ ㄅㄛˊ)
unforgiving; unsympathetic; relentless; ruthless; merciless; pitiless; exacting: 他是個尖酸刻薄的主人。He is an exacting master.

五畫

【尙】 1171 ㄕㄤˋ shanq shàng

1. yet; still: 他的工作尙未完成。He has not finished his work yet.
2. to uphold; to honor; to esteem
3. a Chinese family name

尙比亞(ㄕㄤˋ ㄅㄧˇ ㄧㄚˋ)
Zambia

尙可(ㄕㄤˋ ㄎㄜˇ)
① passable; acceptable: 他的提議尙可。His proposal is acceptable. ② still permissible; still possible

尙佳(ㄕㄤˋ ㄐㄧㄚ)
passable; not too bad: 他的法文尙佳。His French is passable.

尙祈(ㄕㄤˋ ㄑㄧˊ) or 尙希(ㄕㄤˋ ㄒㄧ)
I hope.... 或 I pray....

尙且(ㄕㄤˋ ㄑㄧㄝˇ)
① yet; still ② even

尙西巴(ㄕㄤˋ ㄒㄧ ㄅㄚ)
Zanzibar

尙賢(ㄕㄤˋ ㄒㄧㄢˊ)
the exaltation of the virtuous

尙書(ㄕㄤˋ ㄕㄨ)
① an ancient government post in charge of secretarial duties ② another name for *Book of History* (書經), one of *the Thirteen Classics*

尙友(ㄕㄤˋ ㄧㄡˇ)
to acquaint oneself with people of the past (through reading their books)

尙有可爲(ㄕㄤˋ ㄧㄡˇ ㄎㄜˇ ㄨㄟˊ)
(said of a bad situation) still retrievable

尙無不可(ㄕㄤˋ ㄨˊ ㄅㄨˋ ㄎㄜˇ)
acceptable; passable; permissible

尙武(ㄕㄤˋ ㄨˇ)
militaristic: 斯巴達人尙武。Spartans were militaristic.

尙武精神(ㄕㄤˋ ㄨˇ ㄐㄧㄥ ㄕㄣˊ)
martial spirit: 他是個有尙武精神的青年。He is a youth of martial spirit.

尙勇(ㄕㄤˋ ㄩㄥˇ)
to esteem valor

九畫

【尞】 1172 ㄌㄧㄠˋ liau liào

a Chinese family name

十畫

【尠】 1173 (尟) ㄒㄧㄢˇ shean xiǎn

few; rare 參看「鮮2.」

尢部 ㄨㄤ uang wāng

一畫

【尤】 1174 ㄧㄡˊ you yóu

1. to feel bitter against; to reproach; to blame
2. a mistake; an error
3. especially or particularly
4. outstanding or special
5. a Chinese family name

尤其(ㄧㄡˊ ㄑㄧˊ)
above all; in particular; particularly; especially: 本書的第一章尤其重要。The first chapter of the book is particularly important.

尤甚(ㄧㄡˊ ㄕㄣˋ)
① more than; worse than ② especially so; particularly so

尤人(ㄧㄡˊ ㄖㄣˊ)
to blame others: 他性喜尤人。He likes to blame others.

尤而效之(ㄧㄡˊ ㄦˊ ㄒㄧㄠˋ ㄓ)
to imitate what one knows to be improper

尤有進者(ㄧㄡˊ ㄧㄡˇ ㄐㄧㄣˋ ㄓㄜˇ)
furthermore; in addition: 尤有進者,他下令不得打擾他。

Furthermore, he left orders not to be disturbed.

尤物(ㄧㄡˊ ㄨˋ)
①an uncommon person; a rare personage ② a woman of extraordinary beauty; a rare beauty

四畫

【尨】 1175
1. ㄆㄤˊ parng páng

1. a shaggy dog
2. blended; variegated

尨大(ㄆㄤˊ ㄉㄚˋ)
giant

尨雜(ㄆㄤˊ ㄗㄚˊ)
mixed; variegated

【尨】 1175
2. ㄇㄥˊ meng méng

disorderly; confused

尨茸(ㄇㄥˊ ㄖㄨㄥˊ)
disorderly; confused

【尬】 1176
ㄍㄚˋ gah gà

embarrassed; ill at ease

九畫

【就】 1177
ㄐㄧㄡˋ jiow jiù

1. to receive
2. to undergo
3. to assume
4. to follow
5. to come or go to
6. to suit; to fit; to accommodate oneself to: 我反正有空，就你的時間吧！Make it anytime that suits you; I'm always free.
7. forthwith; right away: 我這就去。I'll be going at once.
8. exactly; precisely: 我就要這隻。This is the one I want.
9. namely
10. even if

就便(ㄐㄧㄡˋ ㄅㄧㄢˋ) or 就手兒(ㄐㄧㄡˋ ㄕㄡˇㄦ)
to do something in the course of doing something else more important (the additional task does not involve too much trouble or divert one's attention from his main work)

就木(ㄐㄧㄡˋ ㄇㄨˋ)
to enter the coffin; about to die

就範(ㄐㄧㄡˋ ㄈㄢˋ)
to come to terms; to give up; to be subdued; to yield: 強盜不肯就範。The robbers refused to yield.

就逮(ㄐㄧㄡˋ ㄉㄞˇ)
to be arrested: 小偷就逮，被送入獄。The thief was arrested and imprisoned.

就得(ㄐㄧㄡˋ ㄉㄟˇ)
must; should (used in connection with suggestion, advice, etc.): 你要病好就得吃藥。If you want to recover, you've got to take drugs.

就道(ㄐㄧㄡˋ ㄉㄠˋ)
to embark on a journey; to start a trip

就地(ㄐㄧㄡˋ ㄉㄧˋ)
on the spot

就地解決(ㄐㄧㄡˋ ㄉㄧˋ ㄐㄧㄝˇ ㄐㄩㄝˊ)
to settle or solve (a problem) right on the spot: 他們就地解決問題。They settled the problem on the spot.

就地取材(ㄐㄧㄡˋ ㄉㄧˋ ㄑㄩˇ ㄘㄞˊ)
①to acquire necessary material locally ②to employ local talents

就地正法(ㄐㄧㄡˋ ㄉㄧˋ ㄓㄥˋ ㄈㄚˇ)
to execute an offender summarily right on the spot (of his offense)

就裏(ㄐㄧㄡˋ ㄌㄧˇ)
the inside story

就教(ㄐㄧㄡˋ ㄐㄧㄠˋ)
to ask for advice

就近(ㄐㄧㄡˋ ㄐㄧㄣˋ)
from the nearest source; at the nearest convenient place

就寢(ㄐㄧㄡˋ ㄑㄧㄣˇ)
to go to bed; to retire for the night

就緒(ㄐㄧㄡˋ ㄒㄩˋ)
(said of preparations) to be complete; to be all set; to take shape; to be in order; ready: 一切都已就緒。Everything is ready (or in order).

就學(ㄐㄧㄡˋ ㄒㄩㄝˊ)
to go to school; to receive schooling

就職(ㄐㄧㄡˋ ㄓˊ)
to be sworn into office; to be sworn in; to be inaugurated; to assume office

就枕(ㄐㄧㄡˋ ㄓㄣˇ)
to go to bed

就正(ㄐㄧㄡˋ ㄓㄥˋ)
to correct oneself by receiving instruction from men of virtue or learning; to submit writings to somebody for comment and correction

就是(ㄐㄧㄡˋ ㄕˋ)
①exactly: 是的，就是如此！Yes, exactly so. ② namely; that is ③even if; even though ④only; but

就是說(ㄐㄧㄡˋ ㄕˋ ㄕㄨㄛ)
that is to say; in other words; namely

就勢(ㄐㄧㄡˋ ㄕˋ)
to take advantage of a situation; to take the opportunity

就事(ㄐㄧㄡˋ ㄕˋ)
①to take up responsibility ②to take account of something

就事論事(ㄐㄧㄡˋ ㄕˋ ㄌㄨㄣˋ ㄕˋ)
to confine the discussion to the matter at issue

就手(ㄐㄧㄡˋ ㄕㄡˇ)
while you're at it

就任(ㄐㄧㄡˋ ㄖㄣˋ)
to take office

就座(ㄐㄧㄡˋ ㄗㄨㄛˋ)
to take one's seat; to be seated: 同學們依次就座。The students took their seats in due order.

就此(ㄐㄧㄡˋ ㄘˇ)
then; thereupon; thereafter

就算(ㄐㄧㄡˋ ㄙㄨㄢˋ)
(colloquial) even if; even though; granted that

就醫(ㄐㄧㄡˋ ㄧ)
to receive or undergo medical treatment: 他已就醫一週。He has undergone medical treatment for one week.

就義(ㄐㄧㄡˋ ㄧˋ)
to become a martyr to a worthy cause or principle

就業(ㄐㄧㄡˋ ㄧㄝˋ)
to get employment; to get a job: 他已就業當教員。He has got a job as a teacher.

就業輔導(ㄐㄧㄡˋ ㄧㄝˋ ㄈㄨˇ ㄉㄠˇ)
placement or appointment service

就要(ㄐㄧㄡˋ ㄧㄠˋ)

to be about to; to be going to; to be on the point of: 飛機就要起飛了。The plane is about to take off.

就養(ㄐㄧㄡˋ ㄧㄤˇ)
①to support one's parents ②to live with one's children as dependents

就位(ㄐㄧㄡˋ ㄨㄟˋ)
to take one's proper or designated position; to take one's seat: 請就位。Take your seat, please.

十四畫

【尷】 1178 ㄍㄢ gan gān
embarrassed; ill at ease

尷尬(ㄍㄢ ㄍㄚˋ)
embarrassing; embarrassed: 不要問令人尷尬的問題。Don't ask embarrassing questions.

尸部 ㄕ shy shī

【尸】 1179 ㄕ shy shī
1. a corpse
2. to preside; to direct

尸體(ㄕ ㄊㄧˇ)
a corpse 參看「屍體」

尸諫(ㄕ ㄐㄧㄢˋ)
to admonish (one's master, lord, etc.) at the cost of one's own life 參看「屍諫」

尸祝代庖(ㄕ ㄓㄨˋ ㄉㄞˋ ㄆㄠˊ)
to perform a duty on behalf of another without authorization

尸首(兒)(ㄕ ㄕㄡˇ (ㄦ))
a corpse 參看「屍體」

尸身(ㄕ ㄕㄣ)
a dead body 參看「屍身」

尸位素餐(ㄕ ㄨㄟˋ ㄙㄨˋ ㄘㄢ)
to neglect the duties of an office while taking the pay; redundant: 這些工人中有很多是尸位素餐。Many of these workers are redundant.

一畫

【尺】 1180 1. ㄔˇ chyy chǐ
1. a unit in Chinese linear measurement, equivalent to ⅓ meter
2. a ruler; a rule

尺璧非寶(ㄔˇ ㄅㄧˋ ㄈㄟ ㄅㄠˇ)
Wealth and treasure is of secondary importance compared with time.

尺布斗粟(ㄔˇ ㄅㄨˋ ㄉㄡˇ ㄙㄨˋ)
brothers quarreling between themselves

尺碼(ㄔˇ ㄇㄚˇ)
①dimensions (of an object) ②measure; size: 你穿多大尺碼的襯衫? What size shirt do you wear?

尺幅千里(ㄔˇ ㄈㄨˊ ㄑㄧㄢ ㄌㄧˇ)
(of a painting) having a thousand miles of contents in a foot of space

尺地(ㄔˇ ㄉㄧˋ)
a very small piece of land

尺地寸土(ㄔˇ ㄉㄧˋ ㄘㄨㄣˋ ㄊㄨˇ)
tiny pieces of land

尺牘(ㄔˇ ㄉㄨˊ)or 尺翰(ㄔˇ ㄏㄢˋ)
letters; correspondence

尺度(ㄔˇ ㄉㄨˋ)
measure; a scale; measurements

尺短寸長(ㄔˇ ㄉㄨㄢˇ ㄘㄨㄣˋ ㄔㄤˊ)or 尺有所短，寸有所長(ㄔˇ ㄧㄡˇ ㄙㄨㄛˇ ㄉㄨㄢˇ，ㄘㄨㄣˋ ㄧㄡˇ ㄙㄨㄛˇ ㄔㄤˊ)
(literally) While there are things for which the foot may be too short, there are things for which the inch can be long enough.—Every person has weak points as well as strong points.

尺土(ㄔˇ ㄊㄨˇ)
a tiny territory

尺土之封(ㄔˇ ㄊㄨˇ ㄓ ㄈㄥ)
a very small fief under the feudalistic system

尺蠖之屈(ㄔˇ ㄏㄨㄛˋ ㄓ ㄑㄩ)
a temporary setback or adversity (used as a consolation to those out of luck)

尺簡(ㄔˇ ㄐㄧㄢˇ)
①slips of bamboo for writing ②a letter; a short note

尺書(ㄔˇ ㄕㄨ)
①letters; correspondence ②books

尺寸(ㄔˇ ㄘㄨㄣˋ)
a small quantity 參看「尺(ㄔ)寸」

尺寸之效(ㄔˇ ㄘㄨㄣˋ ㄓ ㄒㄧㄠˋ)
a modicum of (desired) effect

尺素(ㄔˇ ㄙㄨˋ)
letters; correspondence

【尺】 1180 2. ㄔˊ chyr chí
as in 尺寸—measurements

尺寸(ㄔˊ ˙ㄘㄨㄣ)
measurements; dimensions; size 參看「尺(ㄔˇ)寸」; 這雙鞋子尺寸正好。This shoes is just the right size.

【尺】 1180 3. ㄔㄜˇ chee chě
a note in an old Chinese musical scale: 工尺譜 Chinese musical notes

【尹】 1181 ㄧㄣˇ yiin yǐn
1. to govern; to rule
2. a Chinese family name

二畫

【尻】 1182 ㄎㄠ kau kāo
the sacrum

【尼】 1183 ㄋㄧˊ ni ní
a nun

尼泊爾(ㄋㄧˊ ㄅㄛˊ ㄦˇ)
Nepal

尼泊爾人(ㄋㄧˊ ㄅㄛˊ ㄦˇ ㄖㄣˊ)
a Nepalese

尼布楚(ㄋㄧˊ ㄅㄨˋ ㄔㄨˇ)
Nertchinsk, a city in Siberia

尼父(ㄋㄧˊ ㄈㄨˇ)
Confucius

尼祿(ㄋㄧˊ ㄌㄨˋ)
Nero (A.D. 37-68), Roman emperor

尼羅河(ㄋㄧˊ ㄌㄨㄛˊ ㄏㄜˊ)
the Nile River 或 the Nile

尼龍(ㄋㄧˊ ㄌㄨㄥˊ)
(textile) nylon

尼龍襪(ㄋㄧˊ ㄌㄨㄥˊ ㄨㄚˋ)
nylon socks

尼姑(ㄋㄧˊ ㄍㄨ)
a nun

尼古丁(ㄋㄧˊ ㄍㄨˇ ㄉㄧㄥ)
nicotine

尼加拉大瀑布(ㄋㄧˊ ㄐㄧㄚ ㄌㄚ ㄉㄚˋ ㄆㄨˋ ㄅㄨˋ)
Niagara Falls

尼加拉瓜(ㄋㄧˊ ㄐㄧㄚ ㄌㄚ ㄍㄨㄚ)
Nicaragua
尼日(ㄋㄧˊ ㄖˋ)
Niger (in Africa)
尼日利亞(ㄋㄧˊ ㄖˋ ㄌㄧˋ ㄧㄚˋ)
Nigeria
尼采(ㄋㄧˊ ㄘㄞˇ)
Friedrich Wilhelm Nietzsche (1844—1900), German philosopher
尼斯(ㄋㄧˊ ㄙ)
Nice, a city in France
尼庵(ㄋㄧˊ ㄢ)or 尼姑庵(ㄋㄧˊ ㄍㄨ ㄢ)
a nunnery; a convent

四畫

【尾】 1184 ㄨㄟˇ woei wei

1. the tail; the rear; the stern (of a ship); rear; back
2. last; final
3. remaining
4. a Chinese family name

尾巴(ㄨㄟˇ ·ㄅㄚ)or(ㄧˇ ·ㄅㄚ)
①a tail ② a follower (in a derogatory sense)
尾大不掉(ㄨㄟˇ ㄉㄚˋ ㄅㄨˊ ㄉㄧㄠˋ)
(literally) to have a tail that is too big to wag—to have subordinates too powerful to control
尾端(ㄨㄟˇ ㄉㄨㄢ)
the tail (of something)
尾款(ㄨㄟˇ ㄎㄨㄢˇ)
the remaining sum to be paid upon the completion of a transaction
尾欠(ㄨㄟˇ ㄑㄧㄢˋ)
the balance owing
尾追(ㄨㄟˇ ㄓㄨㄟ)
to chase after: 狗尾追其後。The dog chased after him.
尾聲(ㄨㄟˇ ㄕㄥ)
①(music) a coda ②an epilogue: 序幕和尾聲 a prologue and an epilogue ③an end: 會議已接近尾聲。The meeting is drawing to an end.
尾生之信(ㄨㄟˇ ㄕㄥ ㄓ ㄒㄧㄣˋ)
to stubbornly stick to an appointment when the other party will not show up
尾數(ㄨㄟˇ ㄕㄨˋ)
①an additional number to a whole mentioned in round numbers; an odd sum; odd change ②the balance of an account
尾隨(ㄨㄟˇ ㄙㄨㄟˊ)
to follow close behind; to tail; to shadow: 孩子們尾隨遊行隊伍走了好遠。The kids tailed after the parade for quite a distance.
尾翼(ㄨㄟˇ ㄧˋ)
a tail surface; an empennage
尾牙(ㄨㄟˇ ㄧㄚˊ)
a year-end dinner given by a shop owner to entertain his employees on the 16th day of the twelfth moon, during which an employee would know that he will not be hired for the coming year if the head of a cooked chicken is pointed at his seat

【尿】 1185 ㄋㄧㄠˋ niaw niào

urine; to urinate

尿布(ㄋㄧㄠˋ ㄅㄨˋ)
a diaper; a napkin; a nappy
尿盆(ㄋㄧㄠˋ ㄆㄣˊ)
a chamber pot; a urinal
尿頻(ㄋㄧㄠˋ ㄆㄧㄣˊ)
frequent micturition
尿道(ㄋㄧㄠˋ ㄉㄠˋ)
a urethra; a urinary canal
尿道炎(ㄋㄧㄠˋ ㄉㄠˋ ㄧㄢˊ)
urethritis; the inflammation of the urethra
尿毒症(ㄋㄧㄠˋ ㄉㄨˊ ㄓㄥˋ)
urine poisoning; uremia
尿桶(ㄋㄧㄠˋ ㄊㄨㄥˇ)
a urinal; a urinary; a chamber pot
尿管(ㄋㄧㄠˋ ㄍㄨㄢˇ)
①a urinary canal; a urethra ②a ureter
尿壺(ㄋㄧㄠˋ ㄏㄨˊ)
a urinal; a bedpan; a chamber pot
尿器(ㄋㄧㄠˋ ㄑㄧˋ)
a urinal; a urinary
尿血(ㄋㄧㄠˋ ㄒㄧㄝˇ)
hematuria
尿牀(ㄋㄧㄠˋ ㄔㄨㄤˊ)or 尿炕(ㄋㄧㄠˋ ㄎㄤˋ)
(said of a child) to wet the bed: 小孩尿床。The child wet the bed.
尿失禁(ㄋㄧㄠˋ ㄕ ㄐㄧㄣˋ)
urinary incontinence
尿素(ㄋㄧㄠˋ ㄙㄨˋ)
urea
尿酸(ㄋㄧㄠˋ ㄙㄨㄢ)
uric acid

【局】 1186 ㄐㄩˊ jyu jú

1. an office; a bureau: 氣象局報告每天天氣狀況。The Weather Bureau makes daily reports on weather conditions.
2. a situation; a state of affairs: 政治局勢正在改善中。The political situation is improving.
3. an inning
4. a game

局部(ㄐㄩˊ ㄅㄨˋ)
having to do only with a part; partial; local
局部麻醉(ㄐㄩˊ ㄅㄨˋ ㄇㄚˊ ㄗㄨㄟˋ)
local anesthesia
局部地區(ㄐㄩˊ ㄅㄨˋ ㄉㄧˋ ㄑㄩ)
some areas; parts of an area
局部戰爭(ㄐㄩˊ ㄅㄨˋ ㄓㄢˋ ㄓㄥ)
a local war; a partial war
局騙(ㄐㄩˊ ㄆㄧㄢˋ)
swindling; to cheat; to swindle: 誠實的商人不局騙顧客。Honest merchants do not swindle their customers.
局面(ㄐㄩˊ ㄇㄧㄢˋ)
an aspect; a situation; a state of affairs: 事情出現了嶄新的局面。Things have taken on a new aspect.
局內(ㄐㄩˊ ㄋㄟˋ)or 局內人(ㄐㄩˊ ㄋㄟˋ ㄖㄣˊ)
an insider: 局內人知道那件事。The insiders knew it.
局量(ㄐㄩˊ ㄌㄧㄤˋ)
one's capacity for forgiveness
局限(ㄐㄩˊ ㄒㄧㄢˋ)
to limit; to confine; limited; confined: 他的活動局限於教育界。He confined his activities in educational circles.
局長(ㄐㄩˊ ㄓㄤˇ)
the head or director of a government office or bureau
局勢(ㄐㄩˊ ㄕˋ)
a situation: 目前的國際局勢很危險。The present international situation is dangerous.
局子(ㄐㄩˊ ·ㄗ)
①an office ②a place with-

out the shop front ③ a place for the sale or manufacture of goods ④ the game of chess; a chessboard and chessmen
局促(ㄐㄩˊ ㄘㄨˋ)
① narrow-minded ② nervous; ill at ease ③ narrow; cramped: 這地方太局促，走動不便。This place is too cramped for us to move.
局外人(ㄐㄩˊ ㄨㄞˋ ㄖㄣˊ)
an outsider
局員(ㄐㄩˊ ㄩㄢˊ)
the staff of a bureau

【屁】 1187 ㄆㄧˋ pih pì
1. a fart
2. the hip
屁股(ㄆㄧˋ ·ㄍㄨ)
the hip; the buttocks; the rump; the bottom
屁滾尿流(ㄆㄧˋ ㄍㄨㄣˇ ㄋㄧㄠˋ ㄌㄧㄡˊ)
to be frightened out of one's wits
屁話(ㄆㄧˋ ㄏㄨㄚˋ)
Baloney!
屁精(ㄆㄧˋ ㄐㄧㄥ)
(slang) a catamite

五畫

【居】 1188 ㄐㄩ jiu jū
1. to dwell; to reside; to inhabit; to occupy; an abode; a dwelling: 他居住鄉下。He dwells in the country.
2. to stay put; to be at a standstill: 歲月不居。Time marches on.
3. a Chinese family name
居民(ㄐㄩ ㄇㄧㄣˊ)
residents or inhabitants
居多(ㄐㄩ ㄉㄨㄛ)
to be the majority; mostly: 我們班上南方人居多。Most of the students in our class are southerners.
居停(ㄐㄩ ㄊㄧㄥˊ)
① an employer ② the house of somebody else where one lives temporarily
居里(ㄐㄩ ㄌㄧˇ)
Pierre Curie (1859-1906), French physicist
居里夫人(ㄐㄩ ㄌㄧˇ ㄈㄨ ㄖㄣˊ)
Marie Sklodowska Curie (1867-1934), Polish chemist and physicist in France, wife of Pierre Curie; Madame Curie: 居里夫人是位偉大的科學家。Madame Curie was a great scientist.
居留(ㄐㄩ ㄌㄧㄡˊ)
to reside
居留地(ㄐㄩ ㄌㄧㄡˊ ㄉㄧˋ)
the place of residence (as distinct from the place of birth)
居留權(ㄐㄩ ㄌㄧㄡˊ ㄑㄩㄢˊ)
the right of permanent residence (in a foreign country)
居留證(ㄐㄩ ㄌㄧㄡˊ ㄓㄥˋ)
a residence permit
居高臨下(ㄐㄩ ㄍㄠ ㄌㄧㄣˊ ㄒㄧㄚˋ)
① to overlook; to command a view from a high position ② to enjoy a strategic advantage by holding a high ground overlooking the enemy position
居功(ㄐㄩ ㄍㄨㄥ)
to take credit (for a success, achievement, etc.)
居功自傲(ㄐㄩ ㄍㄨㄥ ㄗˋ ㄠˋ)
to claim credit for oneself and become arrogant
居官(ㄐㄩ ㄍㄨㄢ)
to hold a government office
居官守法(ㄐㄩ ㄍㄨㄢ ㄕㄡˇ ㄈㄚˇ)
to be a law-abiding official
居家(ㄐㄩ ㄐㄧㄚ)
to lead one's life at home; to spend time at home
居間(ㄐㄩ ㄐㄧㄢ)
(to mediate) between two parties
居奇(ㄐㄩ ㄑㄧˊ)
to stockpile goods for sale at higher prices
居心(ㄐㄩ ㄒㄧㄣ)
to harbor (evil) intentions: 歹徒居心何在? What are the hoodlums up to?
居心不良(ㄐㄩ ㄒㄧㄣ ㄅㄨˋ ㄌㄧㄤˊ)
to harbor evil intentions
居心叵測(ㄐㄩ ㄒㄧㄣ ㄆㄛˇ ㄘㄜˋ)
There is no way of telling his (or her) real intentions. 或 to cherish evil designs
居止(ㄐㄩ ㄓˇ)
to stay and live: 此地頗堪居止。It's a nice place to reside in.
居住(ㄐㄩ ㄓㄨˋ)
to reside; to dwell; to inhabit; to live: 他家一直居住在鄉下。His family have always lived in the country.
居中(ㄐㄩ ㄓㄨㄥ)
situated in the middle; in the middle position: 小標題一律居中。Subheads should be placed in the middle of the column.
居中調停(ㄐㄩ ㄓㄨㄥ ㄊㄧㄠˊ ㄊㄧㄥˊ)or 居中斡旋(ㄐㄩ ㄓㄨㄥ ㄨㄛˋ ㄒㄩㄢˊ)
to mediate (between two quarreling parties)
居處
①(ㄐㄩ ㄔㄨˇ)to live (in a place); to occupy (a position)
②(ㄐㄩ ㄔㄨˋ)a residence; a dwelling
居士(ㄐㄩ ㄕˋ)
① a retired scholar; an official out of office ② a secular Buddhist devotee
居室(ㄐㄩ ㄕˋ)
① a room or house for living in ② to cohabit
居首(ㄐㄩ ㄕㄡˇ)
to be at the head; to be in the leading position: 她在全班居首。She is at the head of her class.
居孀(ㄐㄩ ㄕㄨㄤ)
to remain in widowhood
居然(ㄐㄩ ㄖㄢˊ)
incredibly; to my surprise; to my disbelief; to go so far as to
居喪(ㄐㄩ ㄙㄤ)
to be in mourning
居所(ㄐㄩ ㄙㄨㄛˇ)
a residence (usually a temporary one)
居安思危(ㄐㄩ ㄢ ㄙ ㄨㄟˊ)
to think of the time of peril at the time of peace; to be prepared for possible future perils while enjoying peace

【屆】 1189 ㄐㄧㄝˋ jieh jiè
1. a numerary adjunct for periodic terms or events
2. (said of an appointed date) to arrive
3. (said of a term) to expire
屆滿(ㄐㄧㄝˋ ㄇㄢˇ)

(said of a term) to expire: 他的任期行將屆滿。His term of office will soon expire.

屆期(ㄐㄧㄝˋ ㄑㄧˊ)
(said of an appointed time) to arrive

屆時(ㄐㄧㄝˋ ㄕˊ)
at the appointed time (in the future): 屆時請出席。Your presence is requested for the occasion.

【屈】 1190 ㄑㄩ chiu qū

1. to bend; to flex; to bow; to crook
2. to humiliate; to humble; to submit; to subdue: 大丈夫威武不能屈。A great man will not submit to force.
3. wrong; injustice
4. in the wrong
5. to be in an inferior or uncomfortable position: 不要屈居人下。Don't occupy an inferior position.
6. a Chinese family name

屈服(ㄑㄩ ㄈㄨˊ)
to succumb, yield, or submit (to power, a threat, etc.); to give in: 我們絕不向暴力屈服。We should never yield to force.

屈打成招(ㄑㄩ ㄉㄚˇ ㄔㄥˊ ㄓㄠ)
to confess under torture to a crime one hasn't committed

屈駕(ㄑㄩ ㄐㄧㄚˋ)
a conventional phrase used to solicit another's presence on an occasion

屈節(ㄑㄩ ㄐㄧㄝˊ)
to compromise one's integrity; to depart from principle

屈就(ㄑㄩ ㄐㄧㄡˋ)
to accept a job too humble for one's position or ability

屈曲(ㄑㄩ ㄑㄩ)
crooked; winding: 我們沿着屈曲的小溪走去。We went on, following the winding creek.

屈膝(ㄑㄩ ㄒㄧ)
to fall, drop, or go down, on one's knees; to kneel down

屈指可數(ㄑㄩ ㄓˇ ㄎㄜˇ ㄕㄨˇ)
can be counted on one's fingers—very few

屈指一算(ㄑㄩ ㄓˇ ㄧˊ ㄙㄨㄢˋ)
to count on one's fingers

屈折(ㄑㄩ ㄓㄜˊ)
① refraction (of light) ② bent; to bend

屈伸(ㄑㄩ ㄕㄣ)
to move elastically; to be easily bent and stretched; to be flexible; (figuratively) to submit or rise according to circumstances

屈辱(ㄑㄩ ㄖㄨˋ)
humiliation; disgrace; to suffer an insult, humiliation, or disgrace

屈尊(ㄑㄩ ㄗㄨㄣ)
condescension; to condescend

屈從(ㄑㄩ ㄘㄨㄥˊ)
to submit to; to yield to; to give way to

屈原(ㄑㄩ ㄩㄢˊ)
Chü Yüan (343-290 B.C.), a patriotic poet remembered today through the Dragon-Boat Festival on the fifth day of the fifth moon

【屄】 1191 ㄅㄧ bi bī

the vagina

六畫

【屋】 1192 ㄨ u wū

a house; a room; a shelter

屋頂(ㄨ ㄉㄧㄥˇ)
a roof

屋頂花園(ㄨ ㄉㄧㄥˇ ㄏㄨㄚ ㄩㄢˊ)
a roof garden

屋漏偏遭連夜雨(ㄨ ㄌㄡˋ ㄆㄧㄢ ㄗㄠ ㄌㄧㄢˊ ㄧㄝˋ ㄩˇ)
(literally) The rain fell throughout the night with the roof already leaking. ——an added misfortune

屋脊(ㄨ ㄐㄧˇ)
the ridge of a roof

屋主(ㄨ ㄓㄨˇ)
the owner of a house

屋子(ㄨ ˙ㄗ)
a house; a room

屋簷(ㄨ ㄧㄢˊ)
the eaves

屋烏之愛(ㄨ ㄨ ㄓ ㄞˋ)
to extend one's love or affection by association; the love by association

屋宇(ㄨ ㄩˇ)
houses in general

【屍】 1193 ㄕ shy shī

a corpse; a carcass

屍體(ㄕ ㄊㄧˇ)or 屍首(ㄕ ㄕㄡˇ)
a corpse; remains 參看「尸體」

屍骨(ㄕ ㄍㄨˇ)
the skeleton of a corpse 亦作「尸骸」

屍橫遍野(ㄕ ㄏㄥˊ ㄅㄧㄢˋ ㄧㄝˇ)
a field littered with corpses

屍諫(ㄕ ㄐㄧㄢˋ)
to admonish (usually the emperor or a superior) at the cost of one's own life 參看「尸諫」

屍親(ㄕ ㄑㄧㄣ)
the next of kin to a murder victim

屍身(ㄕ ㄕㄣ)
a corpse; a dead body; remains 亦作「屍首」

【屎】 1194 ㄕˇ shyy shǐ

excrement: 屎可用作肥料。Excrement can be used as fertilizer.

屎尿(ㄕˇ ㄋㄧㄠˋ)
excrement and urine; body waste

屎坑(ㄕˇ ㄎㄥ)
a dung pit

七畫

【展】 1195 ㄓㄢˇ jaan zhǎn

1. to open: 景色在我們眼前展開。The view opened out before our eyes.
2. to stretch; to extend: 原野伸展到海邊。The field stretches away to the sea.
3. to unfold; to unroll: 他展開報紙閱讀。He unfolds a newspaper and reads it.
4. to expand; to dilate
5. to prolong
6. to visit

展品(ㄓㄢˇ ㄆㄧㄣˇ)
exhibits; items on display

展墓(ㄓㄢˇ ㄇㄨˋ)
to visit a grave

展覽(ㄓㄢˇ ㄌㄢˇ)
to exhibit; to display; to put on display

展覽會(ㄓㄢˇ ㄌㄢˇ ㄏㄨㄟˋ)

an exhibition or exposition
展開(ㄓㄢˇ ㄎㄞ)
①to spread out; to unfold; to deploy; to dilate ② to start (an activity, task, etc.)
展緩(ㄓㄢˇ ㄏㄨㄢˇ)
①to postpone or put off ② to extend the deadline or time limit
展技(ㄓㄢˇ ㄐㄧˋ)
to demonstrate one's ability or skill to the fullest extent
展卷(ㄓㄢˇ ㄐㄩㄢˋ)
to open a scroll or a book —to apply oneself to study
展期(ㄓㄢˇ ㄑㄧˊ)
①to be postponed; to be put off ② to extend the deadline or time limit
展現(ㄓㄢˇ ㄒㄧㄢˋ)
to present before one's eyes; to develop
展限(ㄓㄢˇ ㄒㄧㄢˋ)
①to extend the deadline or time limit ②(law) to grant a moratorium
展性(ㄓㄢˇ ㄒㄧㄥˋ)
(said of metals) malleability
展轉(ㄓㄢˇ ㄓㄨㄢˇ)
①to turn round and round ② indirectly 亦作「輾轉」
展翅(ㄓㄢˇ ㄔˋ)
to spread the wings; to fly
展出(ㄓㄢˇ ㄔㄨ)
to display or to put on display at an exhibition: 商店均在展出春裝。The stores are displaying new spring clothes.
展示(ㄓㄢˇ ㄕˋ)
to show; to display; to exhibit
展示會(ㄓㄢˇ ㄕˋ ㄏㄨㄟˋ)
an exhibition; a trade show
展望(ㄓㄢˇ ㄨㄤˋ)
to view or survey (physically or mentally, usually in a general, comprehensive way); a general or comprehensive view regarding the prospects of an undertaking, the future development of an event, etc.

【屐】 1196
ㄐㄧ ji jī
wooden shoes; clogs; pattens: 現代人很少穿木屐。Nowadays people scarcely wear clogs.
屐齒(ㄐㄧ ㄔˇ)
the teeth of clogs or pattens

【屑】 1197
ㄒㄧㄝˋ shieh xiè
1. chips; crumbs; bits; odds and ends; trifles
2. to care; to mind
屑意(ㄒㄧㄝˋ ㄧˋ)
to care; to mind

八畫

【屏】 1198
1. ㄆㄧㄥˊ pyng píng
a shield; a screen; to shield; to screen; to guard
屏蔽(ㄆㄧㄥˊ ㄅㄧˋ)
to shield; to protect
屏門(ㄆㄧㄥˊ ㄇㄣˊ)
a door separating the outer and inner courts of an old-style Chinese house
屏幕(ㄆㄧㄥˊ ㄇㄨˋ)
a screen
屏風(ㄆㄧㄥˊ ㄈㄥ)
a screen
屏東(ㄆㄧㄥˊ ㄉㄨㄥ)
Pingtung county in Taiwan
屏障(ㄆㄧㄥˊ ㄓㄤˋ)
a barrier; to shield; to guard; to protect; a protective screen

【屏】 1198
2. ㄅㄧㄥˇ biing bǐng
to reject; to discard; to dismiss; to get rid of; to abandon
屏退(ㄅㄧㄥˇ ㄊㄨㄟˋ)
to order (servants, retainers, etc.) to retire
屏跡 or 屏迹(ㄅㄧㄥˇ ㄐㄧ)
to stay away from; to avoid
屏居(ㄅㄧㄥˇ ㄐㄩ)
to live in retirement; to be out of public life
屏絕(ㄅㄧㄥˇ ㄐㄩㄝˊ)
to stop having contact or intercourse with
屏氣(ㄅㄧㄥˇ ㄑㄧˋ) or 屏息(ㄅㄧㄥˇ ㄒㄧˊ)
to hold one's breath; to bate one's breath: 我們都屏息以聽那聲音再度發生。We all held our breath as we listened for the noise again.
屏棄(ㄅㄧㄥˇ ㄑㄧˋ)
to reject; to discard; to throw away; to abandon
屏斥(ㄅㄧㄥˇ ㄔˋ)
to reproach; to rebuke; to reprove; to accuse
屏除(ㄅㄧㄥˇ ㄔㄨˊ)
to get rid of; to banish; to dismiss; to brush aside: 在讀書時他屏除雜念。While studying, he dismissed distracting thoughts.
屏黜(ㄅㄧㄥˇ ㄔㄨˋ)
to dismiss; to banish

【屜】 1199
(屉) ㄊㄧˋ tih tì
a drawer
屜子(ㄊㄧˋ ·ㄗ)
a drawer

【屙】 1200
ㄜ e ē
to discharge excrement or urine
屙肚(ㄜ ㄉㄨˋ)
diarrhea
屙屎(ㄜ ㄕˇ)
to move the bowels

九畫

【屠】 1201
ㄊㄨˊ twu tú
1. to slaughter; to butcher; to massacre
2. a Chinese family name
屠門大嚼(ㄊㄨˊ ㄇㄣˊ ㄉㄚˋ ㄐㄩㄝˊ)
(literally) to eat meat vicariously in front of a butcher's shop—to enjoy vicariously something which one cannot have
屠販(ㄊㄨˊ ㄈㄢˋ)
butchers and vendors
屠夫(ㄊㄨˊ ㄈㄨ)
a butcher
屠刀(ㄊㄨˊ ㄉㄠ)
a butcher's knife
屠格涅夫(ㄊㄨˊ ㄍㄜˊ ㄋㄧㄝˋ ㄈㄨ)
Ivan Sergeevich Turgenev, 1818-1883, Russian novelist
屠戶(ㄊㄨˊ ㄏㄨˋ)
a butcher
屠城(ㄊㄨˊ ㄔㄥˊ)
to massacre the inhabitants of a captured city; to annihilate a city
屠殺(ㄊㄨˊ ㄕㄚ) or 屠戮(ㄊㄨˊ ㄌㄨˋ)
to massacre; a wholesale slaughter; a massacre

屠燒(ㄊㄨˊ ㄕㄠ)
to kill and to burn on a conquered land

屠宰(ㄊㄨˊ ㄗㄞˇ)
to slaughter (livestock); to butcher

屠宰場(ㄊㄨˊ ㄗㄞˇ ㄔㄤˇ)or(ㄊㄨˊ ㄗㄞˇ ㄔㄤˊ)
a slaughterhouse; an abattoir

屠宰稅(ㄊㄨˊ ㄗㄞˇ ㄕㄨㄟˋ)
slaughter tax (levied on slaughtered animals)

十一畫

【屢】 1202 ㄌㄩˇ leu lǚ
frequently; repeatedly; often; time after time; time and again; again and again: 台灣屢次發生輕微地震。Slight earthquakes frequently happen in Taiwan.

屢敗屢戰(ㄌㄩˇ ㄅㄞˋ ㄌㄩˇ ㄓㄢˋ)
to fight repeatedly in spite of repeated setbacks

屢屢(ㄌㄩˇ ㄌㄩˇ)
frequently; repeatedly; again and again; time and again; time after time

屢見不鮮(ㄌㄩˇ ㄐㄧㄢˋ ㄅㄨˋ ㄒㄧㄢ)
not rare; of ordinary occurrence or common sight; nothing new

屢勸不改(ㄌㄩˇ ㄑㄩㄢˋ ㄅㄨˋ ㄍㄞˇ)
to persist in doing wrong against repeated advice

屢戰屢勝(ㄌㄩˇ ㄓㄢˋ ㄌㄩˇ ㄕㄥˋ)
to fight repeatedly and win every battle

屢試不爽(ㄌㄩˇ ㄕˋ ㄅㄨˋ ㄕㄨㄤˇ)
to have the same result or reaction (usually positive result or reaction) after each try

屢次(ㄌㄩˇ ㄘˋ)
repeatedly; frequently; time and again; again and again; time after time

屢次三番(ㄌㄩˇ ㄘˋ ㄙㄢ ㄈㄢ)
again and again; over and over again; many times

【屣】 1203 ㄒㄧˇ shii xǐ
shoes; sandals: 他視富貴如敝屣。He regards wealth and rank as insignificant as worn-out shoes.

十二畫

【層】 1204 ㄘㄥˊ tserng céng
a layer; a stratum; a story (of a building)

層樓(ㄘㄥˊ ㄌㄡˊ)
a pagoda; a tower; a multistoried building

層巒疊嶂(ㄘㄥˊ ㄌㄨㄢˊ ㄉㄧㄝˊ ㄓㄤˋ)
peaks rising one upon another

層霄(ㄘㄥˊ ㄒㄧㄠ)
the sky; the space above

層狀岩(ㄘㄥˊ ㄓㄨㄤˋ ㄧㄢˊ)
(geology) stratified or bedded rocks

層出不窮(ㄘㄥˊ ㄔㄨ ㄅㄨˋ ㄑㄩㄥˊ)
to be found in layer upon layer without end; to be found in endlessly large numbers; to happen again and again

層次(ㄘㄥˊ ㄘˋ)
①order (of importance or priority)②the arrangement of ideas (in writing or speech)

層雲(ㄘㄥˊ ㄩㄣˊ)
(meteorology) a stratus

【履】 1205 ㄌㄩˇ leu lǚ
1. shoes
2. to step on; to tread on; to walk; to follow: 有些老人步履維艱。Some old people walk with difficulty.

履冰(ㄌㄩˇ ㄅㄧㄥ)
(literally) to walk on ice—cautious; to remain vigilant or alert

履帶(ㄌㄩˇ ㄉㄞˋ)
the track (of a vehicle)

履歷(ㄌㄩˇ ㄌㄧˋ)
one's personal history or background (usually confined to past working experience)

履歷表(ㄌㄩˇ ㄌㄧˋ ㄅㄧㄠˇ)
a biographic sketch (used in applying for a position); curriculum vitae

履舄交錯(ㄌㄩˇ ㄒㄧˋ ㄐㄧㄠ ㄘㄨㄛˋ)
Shoes lie about in disorder. (descriptive of a large number of guests)

履險如夷(ㄌㄩˇ ㄒㄧㄢˇ ㄖㄨˊ ㄧˊ)
to go through danger as if there were no danger at all; to emerge unscathed from danger

履新(ㄌㄩˇ ㄒㄧㄣ)or 履任(ㄌㄩˇ ㄖㄣˋ)
to take or assume one's new office or post

履行(ㄌㄩˇ ㄒㄧㄥˊ)
to fulfill or carry out (a promise, pledge, etc.); to discharge (an obligation, a responsibility, etc.); to perform (a duty); to observe (a treaty): 他應該履行諾言。He should keep his word.

履約(ㄌㄩˇ ㄩㄝ)
to keep or fulfill an agreement; to keep a promise or pledge; to keep an appointment

十四畫

【屨】 1206 ㄐㄩˋ jiuh jù
sandals; shoes made of coarse material

十八畫

【屬】 1207 1. ㄕㄨˇ shuu shǔ
1. a category; a class; a kind
2. to belong to; to be subordinate to; to be governed by

屬地(ㄕㄨˇ ㄉㄧˋ)
a territory; a dependent domain; a colony

屬吏(ㄕㄨˇ ㄌㄧˋ)
subordinate officials

屬僚(ㄕㄨˇ ㄌㄧㄠˊ)
a colleague under one's direction; a subordinate

屬國(ㄕㄨˇ ㄍㄨㄛˊ)
a dependency; a vassal state

屬下(ㄕㄨˇ ㄒㄧㄚˋ)
one's subordinate: 他很信任屬下。He trusts his subordinates very much.

屬性(ㄕㄨˇ ㄒㄧㄥˋ)
an attribute

屬實(ㄕㄨˇ ㄕˊ)
true: 他的口供屬實。His confession was true.

屬望(ㄕㄨˇ ㄨㄤˋ)
(said of a person) popular
屬於(ㄕㄨˇ ㄩˊ)
to belong to: 這商店是屬於我的。This shop belongs to me.
屬員(ㄕㄨˇ ㄩㄢˊ)
a staff member or staffer (of a government agency, etc.)

【屬】 1207
2. ㄓㄨˇ juu zhu
1. to compose (a piece of writing)
2. to instruct; to direct
屬目(ㄓㄨˇ ㄇㄨˋ)
to gaze; to look at eagerly
屬對(ㄓㄨˇ ㄉㄨㄟˋ)
to search for a suitable sentence or poem to match another (a favorite intellectual exercise among the intelligentsia in old Chinese)
屬託(ㄓㄨˇ ㄊㄨㄛ)
to ask or instruct somebody to do something
屬令(ㄓㄨˇ ㄌㄧㄥˋ)
to direct; to instruct
屬草(ㄓㄨˇ ㄘㄠˇ)
to draft (a manuscript, etc.)
屬意(ㄓㄨˇ ㄧˋ)
to have a preference for
屬文(ㄓㄨˇ ㄨㄣˊ)
to compose a piece of writing
屬垣有耳(ㄓㄨˇ ㄩㄢˊ ㄧㄡˇ ㄦˇ)
Beware of eavesdroppers!

屮部
ㄔㄜˋ cheh chè

一畫

【屯】 1208
ㄊㄨㄣˊ twen tún
1. to station (an army)
2. to stockpile
屯兵(ㄊㄨㄣˊ ㄅㄧㄥ)
to station troops
屯田(ㄊㄨㄣˊ ㄊㄧㄢˊ)
to station an army in the countryside and make it engage in farming
屯糧(ㄊㄨㄣˊ ㄌㄧㄤˊ)
to hoard up or stockpile grains
屯墾(ㄊㄨㄣˊ ㄎㄣˇ)
to develop (a region) by means of the militia's labor
屯積(ㄊㄨㄣˊ ㄐㄧ)
to hoard up (goods, food supplies, etc.)
屯聚(ㄊㄨㄣˊ ㄐㄩˋ)
to assemble; to gather together
屯紮(ㄊㄨㄣˊ ㄓㄚ)
to encamp; to be stationed: 軍隊在樹林中屯紮。The troops encamped in the woods.

山部
ㄕㄢ shan shān

【山】 1209
ㄕㄢ shan shān
a mountain; a hill
山撥鼠(ㄕㄢ ㄅㄛ ㄕㄨˇ)
a marmot
山崩(ㄕㄢ ㄅㄥ)
a landslide; a landslip
山崩地裂(ㄕㄢ ㄅㄥ ㄉㄧˋ ㄌㄧㄝˋ)
mountains collapsing and the earth cracking up (descriptive of sound)
山坡(ㄕㄢ ㄆㄛ)
a mountainside; a hillside; a mountain slope
山砲(ㄕㄢ ㄆㄠˋ)
a mountain cannon; artillery pieces used in mountain warfare
山脈(ㄕㄢ ㄇㄞˋ)or(ㄕㄢ ㄇㄛˋ)
a mountain range; mountains
山貓(ㄕㄢ ㄇㄠ)
a wildcat; a lynx
山門(ㄕㄢ ㄇㄣˊ)
a Buddhist monastery or temple
山盟海誓(ㄕㄢ ㄇㄥˊ ㄏㄞˇ ㄕˋ)
a vow between lovers that their mutual love will last as long as the mountain and the sea
山鳴谷應(ㄕㄢ ㄇㄧㄥˊ ㄍㄨˇ ㄧㄥˋ)
the echo in mountains; the mountain echoes
山明水秀(ㄕㄢ ㄇㄧㄥˊ ㄕㄨㄟˇ ㄒㄧㄡˋ)or 山清水秀(ㄕㄢ ㄑㄧㄥ ㄕㄨㄟˇ ㄒㄧㄡˋ)
The mountains are bright and the waters are fair. (descriptive of scenic beauty)
山木自寇(ㄕㄢ ㄇㄨˋ ㄗˋ ㄎㄡˋ)
(literally) The trees in the mountains are felled because timber is useful. — One's ability may be his own ruin.
山峯(ㄕㄢ ㄈㄥ)
a mountaintop
山大王(ㄕㄢ ㄉㄚˋ ㄨㄤˊ)
the leader of a group of outlaws operating from a mountain stronghold
山斗之望(ㄕㄢ ㄉㄡˇ ㄓ ㄨㄤˋ)
(said of one's virtue) respected by all
山地(ㄕㄢ ㄉㄧˋ)
① a mountainous region ② the reservations for the aboriginal people (in the mountainous regions of Taiwan)
山地同胞(ㄕㄢ ㄉㄧˋ ㄊㄨㄥˊ ㄅㄠ)
aboriginal tribes (of the Malayan stock in Taiwan), most of whom live in mountainous regions
山地管制區(ㄕㄢ ㄉㄧˋ ㄍㄨㄢˇ ㄓˋ ㄑㄩ)
the reservations for the aboriginal people
山巔(ㄕㄢ ㄉㄧㄢ)or 山頂(ㄕㄢ ㄉㄧㄥˇ)
a hilltop; a mountaintop; the summit of a mountain
山頂洞人(ㄕㄢ ㄉㄧㄥˇ ㄉㄨㄥˋ ㄖㄣˊ)
(archaeology) Upper Cave Man, a type of primitive man who lived ten to twenty thousand years ago and whose fossil remains were found in 1933 at Choukoutien (周口店) in Hopeh Province
山東(ㄕㄢ ㄉㄨㄥ)
Shantung Province
山東大鼓(ㄕㄢ ㄉㄨㄥ ㄉㄚˋ ㄍㄨˇ)
a style of storytelling to the accompaniment of a drum and two semicircular splices of metals
山洞(ㄕㄢ ㄉㄨㄥˋ)
a cave; a tunnel; a grotto
山頭(ㄕㄢ ㄊㄡˊ)
a mountaintop; a hilltop
山頹木壞(ㄕㄢ ㄊㄨㄟˊ ㄇㄨˋ ㄏㄨㄞˋ)

(figuratively) the death of a sage

山嵐(ㄕㄢ ㄌㄢˊ)
clouds and mists in the mountains

山裏紅(ㄕㄢ ㄌㄧˇ ㄏㄨㄥˊ)
the hill haw

山林(ㄕㄢ ㄌㄧㄣˊ)
① a mountain forest ② the place where a hermit lives

山林地區(ㄕㄢ ㄌㄧㄣˊ ㄉㄧˋ ㄑㄩ)
mountain and forest regions

山林文學(ㄕㄢ ㄌㄧㄣˊ ㄨㄣˊ ㄒㄩㄝˊ)
the literature of recluses (characterized by exclusive interest in nature)

山梁雌雉(ㄕㄢ ㄌㄧㄤˊ ㄘ ㄓˋ)
a hen-pheasant on the hill bridge — (figuratively) a capable man denied the opportunity to use his abilities

山陵(ㄕㄢ ㄌㄧㄥˊ)
① a plateau ② an imperial tomb

山陵崩(ㄕㄢ ㄌㄧㄥˊ ㄅㄥ)
(a euphemism) the death of the emperor or queen

山嶺(ㄕㄢ ㄌㄧㄥˇ)
the mountain range

山路(ㄕㄢ ㄌㄨˋ)
a mountain path

山麓(ㄕㄢ ㄌㄨˋ)
the foot of a mountain

山巒(ㄕㄢ ㄌㄨㄢˊ)
the chain of mountains with pointed peaks

山歌(ㄕㄢ ㄍㄜ)
a mountaineers' song; a kind of folk songs

山高水低(ㄕㄢ ㄍㄠ ㄕㄨㄟˇ ㄉㄧ)
unexpected misfortune, especially referring to death

山高水長(ㄕㄢ ㄍㄠ ㄕㄨㄟˇ ㄔㄤˊ)
(descriptive of the virtues of a great man) to be like lofty mountains and mighty streams

山高水遠(ㄕㄢ ㄍㄠ ㄕㄨㄟˇ ㄩㄢˇ)
(descriptive of a long distance) high mountains and long rivers

山溝(ㄕㄢ ㄍㄡ)
a gully; a ravine; a valley

山岡(ㄕㄢ ㄍㄤ)
a ridge; a mountain ridge

山谷(ㄕㄢ ㄍㄨˇ)
a valley; a dale; a ravine; a gorge; a glen: 台灣有很多風景壯麗的山谷。Many spectacular valleys can be found in Taiwan.

山河(ㄕㄢ ㄏㄜˊ)
mountains and rivers—(figuratively) the territory of a nation

山海關(ㄕㄢ ㄏㄞˇ ㄍㄨㄢ)
Shanhai Pass (at the eastern end of the Great Wall)

山海經(ㄕㄢ ㄏㄞˇ ㄐㄧㄥ)
The Book of Mountains and Seas—the title of a book dealing with geography as known to the ancient Chinese, author unknown

山貨(ㄕㄢ ㄏㄨㄛˋ)
① mountain products (such as haws and chestnuts) ② household utensils made of wood, clay, etc.

山環水抱(ㄕㄢ ㄏㄨㄢˊ ㄕㄨㄟˇ ㄅㄠˋ)
(said of a resort or vacationland) surrounded by mountains and girdled by a river

山洪(ㄕㄢ ㄏㄨㄥˊ)
mountain torrents

山洪暴發(ㄕㄢ ㄏㄨㄥˊ ㄅㄠˋ ㄈㄚ)
A flood is unleashed from the mountains all of a sudden.

山積(ㄕㄢ ㄐㄧ)
so much (or many) as to form a mountain-like heap

山雞(ㄕㄢ ㄐㄧ)
a pheasant

山雞舞鏡(ㄕㄢ ㄐㄧ ㄨˇ ㄐㄧㄥˋ)
(literally) The pheasant dances before a mirror (until it drops dead).—self-appreciation

山脊(ㄕㄢ ㄐㄧˇ)
a mountain ridge; a ridge

山脚(ㄕㄢ ㄐㄧㄠˇ)
the foot of a mountain

山澗(ㄕㄢ ㄐㄧㄢˋ)
mountain creeks

山居(ㄕㄢ ㄐㄩ)
to live away from civilization; to lead the life of a recluse or hermit

山妻(ㄕㄢ ㄑㄧ)
(a self-depreciatory term) my wife

山丘(ㄕㄢ ㄑㄧㄡ)
mountains and hills

山區(ㄕㄢ ㄑㄩ)
a mountain area

山泉(ㄕㄢ ㄑㄩㄢˊ)
a mountain spring

山窮水盡(ㄕㄢ ㄑㄩㄥˊ ㄕㄨㄟˇ ㄐㄧㄣˋ)
to be at the end of the rope; in a desperate situation

山西(ㄕㄢ ㄒㄧ)
Shansi Province

山西梆子(ㄕㄢ ㄒㄧ ㄅㄤ ˙ㄗ)
a style of Chinese opera prevalent in Shansi

山楂(ㄕㄢ ㄓㄚ)
a hawthorn 亦作「山査」

山楂糕(ㄕㄢ ㄓㄚ ㄍㄠ)
a sweetened, reddish jelly-like food made from hawthorn

山寨(ㄕㄢ ㄓㄞˋ)
a mountain fortress (especially one built by bands of bandits)

山珍海錯(ㄕㄢ ㄓㄣ ㄏㄞˇ ㄘㄨㄛˋ) or 山珍海味(ㄕㄢ ㄓㄣ ㄏㄞˇ ㄨㄟˋ)
dainties of all lands and seas; a sumptuous repast

山茱萸(ㄕㄢ ㄓㄨ ㄩˊ)
(botany) a dogwood

山莊(ㄕㄢ ㄓㄨㄤ)
a country house, or villa, built in the mountains

山中(ㄕㄢ ㄓㄨㄥ)
in the mountains

山茶(ㄕㄢ ㄔㄚˊ)
(botany) a camellia

山城(ㄕㄢ ㄔㄥˊ)
a city in the mountains

山川(ㄕㄢ ㄔㄨㄢ)
mountains and rivers

山川修阻(ㄕㄢ ㄔㄨㄢ ㄒㄧㄡ ㄗㄨˇ)
The place is far beyond the mountains and rivers (and therefore requires a long journey to reach).

山重水複(ㄕㄢ ㄔㄨㄥˊ ㄕㄨㄟˇ ㄈㄨˋ)
(said of a place) surrounded by mountain ranges and girdled by winding rivers (and therefore the topography is much complicated)

山神(ㄕㄢ ㄕㄣˊ)
the mountain deity

山水(ㄕㄢ ㄕㄨㄟˇ)

① mountains and rivers ② natural scenery; a landscape
山水畫(ㄕㄢ ㄕㄨㄟˇ ㄏㄨㄚˋ)
a landscape painting
山人(ㄕㄢ ㄖㄣˊ)
a hermit; a recluse
山村(ㄕㄢ ㄘㄨㄣ)
a mountain village
山阿(ㄕㄢ ㄜ)
a bend in a mountain range
山隘(ㄕㄢ ㄞˋ)
a mountain pass
山坳(ㄕㄢ ㄠˋ)
a col
山野(ㄕㄢ ㄧㄝˇ)
mountain villages and the remote wilderness
山崖(ㄕㄢ ㄧㄞˊ)
a cliff
山腰(ㄕㄢ ㄧㄠ) or 山腹(ㄕㄢ ㄈㄨˋ)
the mid-slope of a mountain
山藥(ㄕㄢ ˙ㄧㄠ)
(botany) a yam 亦作「薯蕷」
山陰道上(ㄕㄢ ㄧㄣ ㄉㄠˋ ㄕㄤˋ)
① a sightseeing route with so many scenic wonders that one is constantly kept busy ② a life in which one is constantly kept busy receiving guests
山羊(ㄕㄢ ㄧㄤˊ)
a goat
山陽(ㄕㄢ ㄧㄤˊ)
the southern or sunny side of a mountain
山隝(ㄕㄢ ㄨˋ)
a col
山窩(ㄕㄢ ㄨㄛ)
a place enclosed by mountains
山雨欲來風滿樓(ㄕㄢ ㄩˇ ㄩˋ ㄌㄞˊ ㄈㄥ ㄇㄢˇ ㄌㄡˊ)
The wind sweeping through the tower indicates a rising storm in the mountains. —(figuratively) an omen indicating that something will happen
山芋(ㄕㄢ ㄩˋ)
sweet potatoes
山岳 or 山嶽(ㄕㄢ ㄩㄝˋ)
mountains

三畫

【屹】 1210 ㄧˋ yih yì
(said of a mountain, building, etc.) to rise high; to stand erect or majestical
屹立(ㄧˋ ㄌㄧˋ)
to stand erect; to stand magnificent (like a mountain)
屹然(ㄧˋ ㄖㄢˊ)
firm and erect (like a mountain): 他站在那裡屹然不動。He is standing there firm and erect.

【屺】 1211 ㄑㄧˇ chii qǐ
a bare mountain or hill

四畫

【岔】 1212 ㄔㄚˋ chah chà
1. to branch; to fork; to diverge
2. a branching point; a fork
岔道(ㄔㄚˋ ㄉㄠˋ) or 岔路(ㄔㄚˋ ㄌㄨˋ)
a diverging road
岔開(ㄔㄚˋ ㄎㄞ)
① to branch off; to diverge ② to diverge to (another topic); to change (the subject of conversation) ③ to stagger
岔口(ㄔㄚˋ ㄎㄡˇ)
a fork (in a road): 他們護送他到岔口。They escorted him to a fork in the road.
岔氣(ㄔㄚˋ ㄑㄧˋ)
sudden discomfort in the chest
岔子(ㄔㄚˋ ˙ㄗ) or 岔兒(ㄔㄚˋㄦ)
an accident; a trouble (in the course of an activity): 你放心吧，沒有人會找你岔子。Don't worry; nobody will cause trouble to you.

【岌】 1213 ㄐㄧˊ jyi jí
1. (said of a peak) rising high above others
2. perilous; hazardous
岌岌可危(ㄐㄧˊ ㄐㄧˊ ㄎㄜˇ ㄨㄟˊ)
in a very critical situation; to hang by a thread: 病人的情況岌岌可危。The patient's condition is critical.

【岐】 1214 (歧) ㄑㄧˊ chyi qí
1. Chi, name of a mountain
2. to diverge; to branch
岐黃(ㄑㄧˊ ㄏㄨㄤˊ)
short for 岐伯 and 黃帝, founders of Chinese medicine—(figuratively) the medical profession
岐黃之術(ㄑㄧˊ ㄏㄨㄤˊ ㄓ ㄕㄨˋ)
Chinese herbal medical science
岐山(ㄑㄧˊ ㄕㄢ)
Mt. Chi (There are two: one is in Shansi and the other in Shensi.)

【岑】 1215 ㄘㄣˊ tsern cén
1. a relatively high, pointed hill
2. silent; still; quiet
岑樓(ㄘㄣˊ ㄌㄡˊ)
a mountain-like, lofty and tapering building
岑寂(ㄘㄣˊ ㄐㄧˋ)
quiet; still; silent: 槍聲劃破了夜的岑寂。A shot disturbed the quiet of the night.

五畫

【岡】 1216 (崗) ㄍㄤ gang gāng (又讀 ㄍㄤˇ gaang gǎng)
the ridge (of a hill or mountain)
岡比亞(ㄍㄤ ㄅㄧˇ ㄧㄚˋ)
the Gambia 亦作「甘比亞」
岡比亞人(ㄍㄤ ㄅㄧˇ ㄧㄚˋ ㄖㄣˊ)
a Gambian 亦作「甘比亞人」
岡陵(ㄍㄤ ㄌㄧㄥˊ)
a mound
岡巒起伏(ㄍㄤ ㄌㄨㄢˊ ㄑㄧˇ ㄈㄨˊ)
full of mountain ridges

【岫】 1217 ㄒㄧㄡˋ shiow xiù
1. a cavern; a cave
2. a mountain peak

【岬】 1218 ㄐㄧㄚˇ jea jiǎ
a cape; a promontory; a headland; a point
岬嵑(ㄐㄧㄚˇ ㄐㄧㄝˊ)
continuous
岬角(ㄐㄧㄚˇ ㄐㄧㄠˇ)
a cape; a promontory

【岭】 1219 ㄌㄧㄥˊ ling líng
(said of mountains) waste and remote

〔山部〕

〔山部〕

【岱】 1220 ㄉㄞˋ day dài
Mt. Tai (in Shantung Province, one of the five Sacred Mountains)
岱宗(ㄉㄞˋ ㄗㄨㄥ)or 岱嶽(ㄉㄞˋ ㄩㄝˋ)
Mt. Tai (泰山 in Shantung, one of the five Sacred Mountains)

【岳】 1221 ㄩㄝˋ yueh yuè
1. a great mountain; a high mountain
2. the parents of one's wife
3. a Chinese family name
岳廟(ㄩㄝˋ ㄇㄧㄠˋ)
the shrine dedicated to General Yüeh Fei (岳飛), a hero of the Sung Dynasty
岳母(ㄩㄝˋ ㄇㄨˇ)
① one's mother-in-law (one's wife's mother) ② General Yüeh Fei's mother
岳飛(ㄩㄝˋ ㄈㄟ)
Yüeh Fei (1103-1141), a hero of the Sung Dynasty
岳父(ㄩㄝˋ ㄈㄨˋ)or 岳丈(ㄩㄝˋ ㄓㄤˋ)
one's father-in-law (one's wife's father)
岳家軍(ㄩㄝˋ ㄐㄧㄚ ㄐㄩㄣ)
the invincible troops under the command of Yüeh Fei (岳飛)

【岷】 1222 ㄇㄧㄣˊ min mín
1. the Min River (in Szechwan)
2. Mt. Min (in Szechwan)

【岸】 1223 ㄢˋ ann àn
1. a shore; a bank; a beach; a coast
2. majestic
3. proud
岸巾(ㄢˋ ㄐㄧㄣ)
to wear a head covering in a neglectful manner so as to expose the forehead
岸然(ㄢˋ ㄖㄢˊ)
a solemn and dignified look: 這個老人道貌岸然。The old man looks severe and solemn.

【岩】 1224 ㄧㄢˊ yan yán
1. a large rock
2. a mountain
岩壁(ㄧㄢˊ ㄅㄧˋ)
①(geology) a dyke ② a cliff
岩脈(ㄧㄢˊ ㄇㄞˋ)or(ㄧㄢˊ ㄇㄛˋ)
(geology) a rock vein
岩洞(ㄧㄢˊ ㄉㄨㄥˋ)or 岩穴(ㄧㄢˊ ㄒㄩㄝˋ)
a cavern; a cave; a grotto
岩基(ㄧㄢˊ ㄐㄧ)
(geology) batholith
岩漿(ㄧㄢˊ ㄐㄧㄤ)
(geology) magma; lava
岩牀(ㄧㄢˊ ㄔㄨㄤˊ)
(geology) an intrusive sheet; a lava bed
岩石(ㄧㄢˊ ㄕˊ)
a rock; a crag
岩石學(ㄧㄢˊ ㄕˊ ㄒㄩㄝˊ)
petrology
岩層(ㄧㄢˊ ㄘㄥˊ)
a rock stratum; a rock formation
岩岸(ㄧㄢˊ ㄢˋ)
(geography) a rocky coast
岩鹽(ㄧㄢˊ ㄧㄢˊ)
rock salt

六畫

【峋】 1225 ㄒㄩㄣˊ shyun xún
irregular stretches of mountains

【峒】 1226 1.ㄊㄨㄥˊ torng tóng
Mt. Kungtung—name of a mountain in Kansu Province

【峒】 1226 2.ㄉㄨㄥˋ donq dòng
name of a tribe in Kwangsi and Kweichow
峒蠻(ㄉㄨㄥˋ ㄇㄢˊ)
the Tung tribe (considered as uncivilized)
峒丁(ㄉㄨㄥˋ ㄉㄧㄥ)
the soldiers from the Tung tribe
峒人(ㄉㄨㄥˋ ㄖㄣˊ)
the people of the Tung tribe

【峙】 1227 ㄓˋ jyh zhì
to stand erect like a mountain

七畫

【峨】 1228 ㄜˊ er é
lofty
峨眉(ㄜˊ ㄇㄟˊ)
Mt. Omei (a Buddhist resort in Szechwan)
峨冠博帶(ㄜˊ ㄍㄨㄢ ㄅㄛˊ ㄉㄞˋ)
a high-topped hat and wide waist band (the attire characteristic of an official, or an intellectual, in former times)—(figuratively) the official class; the intellectual class
峨髻(ㄜˊ ㄐㄧˋ)
a large chignon, or knot of hair, worn atop the head
峨然不羣(ㄜˊ ㄖㄢˊ ㄅㄨˋ ㄑㄩㄣˊ)
to stand head and shoulders above others—(figuratively) to excel others far; to be outstanding
峨峨(ㄜˊ ㄜˊ)
with solemn gravity; looking majestic

【峭】 1229 ㄑㄧㄠˋ chiaw qiào
1. steep; precipitous
2. harsh; sharp; stern; unkind; severe
峭拔(ㄑㄧㄠˋ ㄅㄚˊ)
①high and steep ② (said of penmanship or calligraphic style) vigorous: 他的筆鋒峭拔。He has a vigorous style of writing.
峭薄(ㄑㄧㄠˋ ㄅㄛˊ)
strict; unkind; relentless
峭壁(ㄑㄧㄠˋ ㄅㄧˋ)
a precipice; a cliff: 這山的一邊是峭壁。One side of the mountain is a precipitous cliff.
峭厲(ㄑㄧㄠˋ ㄌㄧˋ)
(said of speech, etc.) harsh or sharp
峭刻(ㄑㄧㄠˋ ㄎㄜˋ)
exacting; relentless; unkind; strict
峭急(ㄑㄧㄠˋ ㄐㄧˊ)
impatient; quick-tempered
峭絕(ㄑㄧㄠˋ ㄐㄩㄝˊ)
precipitous; very steep
峭直(ㄑㄧㄠˋ ㄓˊ)
stern; strict

【峯】 1230 ㄈㄥ feng fēng
1. a peak; a summit
2. a hump: 駱駝峯 a camel's hump
峯巒(ㄈㄥ ㄌㄨㄢˊ)

peaks and ridges

【峴】 1231 ㄒㄧㄢˋ shiann xiàn
1. a mountain in Hupeh Province
2. a steep hill
峴港(ㄒㄧㄢˋ ㄍㄤˇ)
Danang, a seaport in central Vietnam

【島】 1232 ㄉㄠˇ dao dǎo
an island; an isle
島民(ㄉㄠˇ ㄇㄧㄣˊ)
an islander
島國(ㄉㄠˇ ㄍㄨㄛˊ)
an island nation
島夷(ㄉㄠˇ ㄧˊ)
savage islanders
島嶼(ㄉㄠˇ ㄩˇ)
islands; islets and islands

【峻】 1233 ㄐㄩㄣˋ jiunn jùn
1. high; lofty
2. steep
3. severe; harsh; rigorous: 她是一位嚴峻的老師。She is a severe teacher.
峻法(ㄐㄩㄣˋ ㄈㄚˇ)
severe, harsh, or rigorous law: 他們贊成嚴刑峻法。They uphold severe punishment and harsh law.
峻嶺(ㄐㄩㄣˋ ㄌㄧㄥˇ)
a lofty range (of mountains)
峻刻(ㄐㄩㄣˋ ㄎㄜˋ)
stern and exacting
峻酷(ㄐㄩㄣˋ ㄎㄨˋ)
severe; relentless; ruthless; merciless
峻急(ㄐㄩㄣˋ ㄐㄧˊ)
intolerant and impatient
峻節(ㄐㄩㄣˋ ㄐㄧㄝˊ)
noble principle
峻拒(ㄐㄩㄣˋ ㄐㄩˋ)
to reject or refuse sternly: 他們峻拒我的要求。They sternly refused me permission.
峻切(ㄐㄩㄣˋ ㄑㄧㄝˋ)
severe and urgent
峻峭(ㄐㄩㄣˋ ㄑㄧㄠˋ)
① high and steep; precipitous ② severe; strict; unkind
峻刑(ㄐㄩㄣˋ ㄒㄧㄥˊ)
severe punishment or penalty

【峽】 1234 ㄒㄧㄚˊ shya xiá
1. a gorge
2. an isthmus
3. straits
峽谷(ㄒㄧㄚˊ ㄍㄨˇ)
(geography) a dale; a gorge; a valley; a canyon
峽灣(ㄒㄧㄚˊ ㄨㄢ)
(geography) a fiord

【峪】 1235 ㄩˋ yuh yù
1. a valley; a ravine
2. Chiayü (嘉峪) in Kansu Province, where the Great Wall terminates

八畫

【崇】 1236 ㄔㄨㄥˊ chorng chóng
1. to honor; to respect; to revere; to adore; to worship; to venerate; to esteem: 她尊崇有學問的人。She always shows respect to those who are learned.
2. high; lofty; noble; dignified; exalted
3. a Chinese family name
崇拜(ㄔㄨㄥˊ ㄅㄞˋ)
to worship; to idolize; to adore; to lionize: 大多數人崇拜英雄。Most people worship heroes.
崇本務實(ㄔㄨㄥˊ ㄅㄣˇ ㄨˋ ㄕˊ)
(said of one's attitude) to do things in a solid manner; practical
崇奉(ㄔㄨㄥˊ ㄈㄥˋ)
to worship
崇論閎議(ㄔㄨㄥˊ ㄌㄨㄣˋ ㄏㄨㄥˊ ㄧˋ)
ringing comments or statements; stirring speeches
崇高(ㄔㄨㄥˊ ㄍㄠ)
lofty; sublime; high
崇敬(ㄔㄨㄥˊ ㄐㄧㄥˋ)
to honor; to revere; to adore; to regard with esteem
崇信(ㄔㄨㄥˊ ㄒㄧㄣˋ)
to worship
崇禎皇帝(ㄔㄨㄥˊ ㄓㄣ ㄏㄨㄤˊ ㄉㄧˋ)
the last emperor of the Ming Dynasty, who reigned during 1628-1644
崇山峻嶺(ㄔㄨㄥˊ ㄕㄢ ㄐㄩㄣˋ ㄌㄧㄥˇ)
lofty and precipitous peaks
崇尚(ㄔㄨㄥˊ ㄕㄤˋ)
① to uphold; to advocate: 他們崇尚勤儉。They advocate industry and thrift. ② fashion; a trend
崇洋(ㄔㄨㄥˊ ㄧㄤˊ)
to admire everything of foreign (especially western) origin

【崎】 1237 1.ㄑㄧ chi qī
rugged; uneven; rough
崎嶇(ㄑㄧ ㄑㄩ)
(said of terrain) uneven; rolling; rough; rugged: 這條小徑崎嶇而多泥。This path is rugged and muddy.

【崎】 1237 2.ㄑㄧˊ chyi qí
the banks of a winding river

【崑】 1238 ㄎㄨㄣ kuen kūn
1. the Kunlun Mountains
2. Kunshan, name of a county and mountain in Kiangsu
崑崙山(ㄎㄨㄣ ㄌㄨㄣˊ ㄕㄢ)
the Kunlun Mountains (between Tibet and Sinkiang extending to Central China, whose highest peak is 25,000 ft.)
崑曲(ㄎㄨㄣ ㄑㄩˇ)
name of a class of tunes originating in Kunshan, Kiangsu 亦作「崑腔」
崑山(ㄎㄨㄣ ㄕㄢ)
① Kunshan—a county in Kiangsu Province ② Mt. Kung—a mountain in Kiangsu Province
崑玉(ㄎㄨㄣ ㄩˋ)
① the jade produced in the Kunlun Mountains ② a polite term used to address the brothers of other people

【崔】 1239 ㄘㄨㄟ tsuei cuī
1. a Chinese family name
2. high and steep
崔嵬(ㄘㄨㄟ ㄨㄟˊ)
① a rocky height or peak ② high; towering
崔巍(ㄘㄨㄟ ㄨㄟˊ)
(said of mountains) lofty and steep

【崖】 1240 ㄧㄞˊ yai yái
1. a cliff; a precipice
2. the brink; the verge

〔山部〕

〔山部〕

3. precipitous; high and steep; forbidding
崖壁(ㄧㄞˊ ㄅㄧˋ)
a precipice
崖略(ㄧㄞˊ ㄌㄩㄝˋ)
an outline
崖谷(ㄧㄞˊ ㄍㄨˇ)
a valley between precipices
崖岸(ㄧㄞˊ ㄢˋ)
haughty
崖鹽(ㄧㄞˊ ㄧㄢˊ)
rock salt 亦作「岩鹽」

【崗】 1241
(岡) ㄍㄤ gang gāng
(又讀 ㄍㄤˇ gaang gǎng)
1. the place where a sentry is posted; a post
2. a position
崗警(ㄍㄤ ㄐㄧㄥˇ)
a policeman who performs his duties at a fixed post
崗哨(ㄍㄤ ㄕㄠˋ)
① a lookout post ② a sentry; a sentinel
崗子(ㄍㄤ ・ㄗ)
① a mound; a hillock ② a ridge
崗位(ㄍㄤˇ ㄨㄟˋ)
one's post; one's duty: 兵士們各堅守戰鬥崗位。The soldiers stood fast at their fighting posts.

【崙】 1242
ㄌㄨㄣˊ luen lún
the Kunlun Mountains

【崛】 1243
ㄐㄩㄝˊ jyue jué
to rise abruptly
崛崎(ㄐㄩㄝˊ ㄑㄧˊ)
steep
崛起(ㄐㄩㄝˊ ㄑㄧˇ)
to rise suddenly

【崢】 1244
ㄓㄥ jeng zhēng
1. lofty
2. outstanding; distinguished
3. steep; perilous; dangerous
4. harsh; severe; rigorous
崢嶸(ㄓㄥ ㄖㄨㄥˊ)
① lofty and steep ②(said of a person) distinguished; outstanding; extraordinary

【崤】 1245
ㄧㄠˊ yau yáo
Mt. Yao, name of a mountain in Honan

【崧】 1246
ㄙㄨㄥ song sōng
1. a high mountain
2. lofty

【崩】 1247
ㄅㄥ beng bēng
1. to collapse; to disintegrate; to fall
2. (said of an emperor) to die
崩塌(ㄅㄥ ㄊㄚ)
to collapse; to crumble: 這房屋因地震而崩塌。The house collapsed on account of an earthquake.
崩坍(ㄅㄥ ㄊㄢ)
to collapse; to crumble; to go to pieces
崩裂(ㄅㄥ ㄌㄧㄝˋ)
to crack up: 炸藥使山石崩裂。The dynamite cracked up the mountain rocks.
崩潰(ㄅㄥ ㄎㄨㄟˋ)
to collapse; to break down; to fall to pieces; to cave in
崩陷(ㄅㄥ ㄒㄧㄢˋ)
to cave in; to fall in; to collapse; to subside; to sink

【崍】 1248
ㄌㄞˊ lai lái
Mt. Lai—name of a mountain in Szechwan

【崌】 1249
ㄐㄩ jiu jū
1. Mount Chü in Szechwan
2. Mt. Chülai (崌崍山) in Szechwan

【崡】 1250
ㄏㄢˊ harn hán
name of a checkpoint during the Chin and Han dynasties, located in what is Honan today

【崦】 1251
ㄧㄢ ian yān
Mt. Yen— name of a mountain in Kansu

九畫

【崴】 1252
ㄨㄟ uei wēi
lofty

【嵑】 1253
ㄐㄧㄝˊ jye jié
lofty (mountains)

【崽】 1254
ㄗㄞˇ tzae zǎi
1. a son
2. a young animal; a whelp
3. as in 西崽—a Chinese servant of a foreigner (a derogatory term)
崽子(ㄗㄞˇ ・ㄗ)
the son of a bitch; s.o.b.

【嵇】 1255
ㄐㄧ ji jī
1. a Chinese family name
2. name of a mountain in Honan
嵇康(ㄐㄧ ㄎㄤ)
Chi Kang, a man of letters of the Wei Dynasty, one of the Seven Wise Men of the Bamboo Grove (竹林七賢)
嵇山(ㄐㄧ ㄕㄢ)
Mt. Chi— name of a mountain in Honan

【嵋】 1256
ㄇㄟˊ mei méi
Mount Omei, a Buddhist resort in Szechwan

【嵌】 1257
ㄑㄧㄢ chian qiān
to inlay; to set in
嵌工(ㄑㄧㄢ ㄍㄨㄥ)
the handicraftsmanship displayed in a piece of jewelry inlaid with gold or stones
嵌金(ㄑㄧㄢ ㄐㄧㄣ)
to inlay with gold
嵌石(ㄑㄧㄢ ㄕˊ)
to inlay with precious stones

【嵐】 1258
ㄌㄢˊ lan lán
mountain vapor; mist
嵐氣(ㄌㄢˊ ㄑㄧˋ)
mountain vapor; mist
嵐影湖光(ㄌㄢˊ ㄧㄥˇ ㄏㄨˊ ㄍㄨㄤ)
the hazy atmosphere of the mountains and the shimmering light of the lake (a description about a scenic spot)

【嵎】 1259
ㄩˊ yu yú
a curved place in the mountains; a corner of a hill

【崿】 1260
ㄜˋ eh è
a cliff; a precipice

十畫

【嵩】 1261
(崧) ㄙㄨㄥ song sōng
1. Mountain Sung, the highest and central peak of the Five

Sacred Mountains, situated in Honan
2. lofty
嵩高(ㄙㄨㄥ ㄍㄠ)or 嵩山(ㄙㄨㄥ ㄕㄢ)
Mt. Sung, the highest and central peak of the Five Sacred Mountains (or Five Peaks), located in Honan
嵩呼(ㄙㄨㄥ ㄏㄨ)
to shout "Long live the Emperor!"
嵩壽(ㄙㄨㄥ ㄕㄡˋ)
longevity; to live as long as Mountain Sung

【嵬】 1262 ㄨㄟ wei wēi
(said of a mountain) high and uneven
嵬然(ㄨㄟ ㄖㄢˊ)
lofty
嵬嵬 or 嵬巍(ㄨㄟ ㄨㄟ)
lofty; towering

【嵊】 1263 ㄕㄥˋ shenq shèng
1. name of a mountain in Chekiang
2. name of a county in Chekiang

【嵯】 1264 ㄘㄨㄛˊ tswo cuó
(said of mountains) high and steep; precipitous
嵯峨(ㄘㄨㄛˊ ㄜˊ)
(said of mountains) high and steep; precipitous

十一畫

【嶇】 1265 ㄑㄩ chiu qū
rugged; uneven; irregular

【嶂】 1266 ㄓㄤˋ janq zhàng
a precipitous mountain

【嶄】 1267 ㄓㄢˇ jaan zhǎn
1. (said of a mountain) high and steep
2. towering (above)
3. novel; new
嶄新(ㄓㄢˇ ㄒㄧㄣ)
brand-new
嶄然(ㄓㄢˇ ㄖㄢˊ)
① completely changed ② (said of a mountain) high and steep

十二畫

【嶙】 1268 ㄌㄧㄣˊ lin lín
(said of mountains) rugged
嶙嶙(ㄌㄧㄣˊ ㄌㄧㄣˊ)
(said of hills) rolling and rugged
嶙峋(ㄌㄧㄣˊ ㄒㄩㄣˊ)
① (said of mountain rocks) rugged; craggy ②(said of a person) upright

【嶒】 1269 ㄘㄥˊ tserng céng
steep; lofty

【嶓】 1270 ㄅㄛ bo bō
name of a mountain in Shensi
嶓冢(ㄅㄛ ㄓㄨㄥˇ)
name of a mountain in Shensi

【嶝】 1271 ㄉㄥˋ denq dèng
a path leading up a mountain

【嶠】 1272 ㄐㄧㄠˋ jiaw jiào
(又讀 ㄑㄧㄠˊ chyau qiáo)
a high pointed mountain

【嶢】 1273 ㄧㄠˊ yau yáo
(said of mountains) high or tall

【嶔】 1274 ㄑㄧㄣ chin qīn
(said of a mountain) lofty
嶔崎磊落(ㄑㄧㄣ ㄑㄧˊ ㄌㄟˇ ㄌㄨㄛˋ)
(said of a person) honest and upright
嶔崟(ㄑㄧㄣ ㄧㄣˊ)
(said of mountains) precipitous

十三畫

【嶧】 1275 ㄧˋ yih yì
peaks rising one upon another

【嶮】 1276 (險) ㄒㄧㄢˇ shean xiǎn
steep; precipitous; lofty

十四畫

【嶸】 1277 ㄖㄨㄥˊ rong róng
(said of mountains) lofty 參看「崢嶸」

【嶺】 1278 ㄌㄧㄥˇ liing lǐng
1. the ridge of a mountain; a mountain range
2. a mountain
嶺表(ㄌㄧㄥˇ ㄅㄧㄠˇ)
the front, or southern side of the Five Ridges (i.e., Kwangtung)
嶺南(ㄌㄧㄥˇ ㄋㄢˊ)
the area south of the Five Ridges (i.e., Kwangtung)

【嶼】 1279 ㄩˇ yeu yǔ
an islet; an island

【嶽】 1280 ㄩㄝˋ yueh yuè
a high mountain
嶽峙(ㄩㄝˋ ㄓˋ)
(said of one's character or bearing) as noble as a lofty peak

十七畫

【巇】 1281 ㄒㄧ shi xī
1. a crack
2. (said of a mountain path) hazardous
巇嶮 or 巇險(ㄒㄧ ㄒㄧㄢˇ)
① steep and difficult to ascend ②(figuratively) full of danger and hardship 亦作「嶮巇」

【巉】 1282 ㄔㄢˊ charn chán
precipitous
巉巖(ㄔㄢˊ ㄧㄢˊ)
a rock; a crag

【巋】 1283 ㄎㄨㄟ kuei kuī
1. grand and secure; stately and lasting
2. rows after rows of small hills
巋然(ㄎㄨㄟ ㄖㄢˊ)
towering; lofty
巋然獨存(ㄎㄨㄟ ㄖㄢˊ ㄉㄨˊ ㄘㄨㄣˊ)
to remain secure majestically while all others have crumbled into decay

十八畫

【巍】 1284 ㄨㄟ wei wēi

towering; lofty; majestic

巍然(ㄨㄟˊ ㄖㄢˊ)
towering; lofty and massive; majestic; imposing

巍然聳立(ㄨㄟˊ ㄖㄢˊ ㄙㄨㄥˇ ㄌㄧˋ)or 巍然矗立(ㄨㄟˊ ㄖㄢˊ ㄔㄨˋ ㄌㄧˋ)
to stand out majestically

巍峨(ㄨㄟˊ ㄜˊ)
towering; lofty; majestic

巍巍(ㄨㄟˊ ㄨㄟˊ)
towering; lofty; majestic; imposing

十九畫

【巒】 1285 ㄌㄨㄢˊ luan luán
a pointed hill

【巔】 1286 ㄉㄧㄢ dian diān
1. a mountain top; a peak; the summit of a mountain
2. a treetop

巔峯(ㄉㄧㄢ ㄈㄥ)
the highest point; a summit; a climax; the zenith; a peak

巔峯狀態(ㄉㄧㄢ ㄈㄥ ㄓㄨㄤˋ ㄊㄞˋ)
(said of athletes, performing artists, etc.) in peak condition

二十畫

【巖】 1287 (岩) ㄧㄢˊ yan yán
1. a rock; a crag
2. a cave

巖洞(ㄧㄢˊ ㄉㄨㄥˋ)
a mountain cave

巖居穴處(ㄧㄢˊ ㄐㄩ ㄒㄩㄝˋ ㄔㄨˇ)
①(said of primitive people) to live in mountain caves ② to live in seclusion or away from civilization as a recluse or hermit

巖穴(ㄧㄢˊ ㄒㄩㄝˋ)
a cave, or cavern

【巘】 1288 ㄧㄢˇ yean yǎn
a peak; a hilltop

巛 部
ㄔㄨㄢ chuan chuān

【川】 1289 ㄔㄨㄢ chuan chuān
1. a river; a stream
2. a flow; a constant flow
3. (cooking) to boil with water
4. Szechwan Province

川北(ㄔㄨㄢ ㄅㄟˇ)
the northern part of Szechwan Province

川貝(ㄔㄨㄢ ㄅㄟˋ)
(Chinese medicine) fritillaria produced in Szechwan Province

川朴(ㄔㄨㄢ ㄆㄛˋ)
(Chinese medicine) *Magnolia obovata*

川東(ㄔㄨㄢ ㄉㄨㄥ)
the eastern part of Szechwan Province

川南(ㄔㄨㄢ ㄋㄢˊ)
the southern part of Szechwan Province

川流不息(ㄔㄨㄢ ㄌㄧㄡˊ ㄅㄨˋ ㄒㄧˊ)
(said of traffic, people, etc.) a constant flow; an incessant flow; continuous

川漢鐵路(ㄔㄨㄢ ㄏㄢˋ ㄊㄧㄝˇ ㄌㄨˋ)
the railway from Chengtu of Szechwan to Hankow of Hupeh

川椒(ㄔㄨㄢ ㄐㄧㄠ)
the pepper produced in Szechwan—used in food seasoning and in Chinese herbal medicine

川薑(ㄔㄨㄢ ㄐㄧㄤ)
the ginger produced in Szechwan—used especially in herbal medicine

川芎(ㄔㄨㄢ ㄑㄩㄥ)
(Chinese medicine) conioselinum

川綢(ㄔㄨㄢ ㄔㄡˊ)
silks from Szechwan

川資(ㄔㄨㄢ ㄗ)
traveling expenses

川澤(ㄔㄨㄢ ㄗㄜˊ)
(literally) rivers and lakes —marshes; swamps

川菜(ㄔㄨㄢ ㄘㄞˋ)
the Szechwan style of cooking or cuisine featuring liberal use of hot pepper and strong seasonings

川鹽(ㄔㄨㄢ ㄧㄢˊ)
the mineral salt produced in Szechwan

三畫

【州】 1290 ㄓㄡ jou zhōu
1. *chou,* an administrative district in ancient China, roughly equivalent to a province today
2. (Chou Dynasty) a region with 2,500 families
3. (in old China) a county
4. a state (in the USA)
5. a place surrounded by water; an islet; a sand bar
6. a Chinese family name

州伯(ㄓㄡ ㄅㄛˊ)
the governor of a *chou* (州)

州判(ㄓㄡ ㄆㄢˋ)
an official rank in ancient China roughly equivalent to a deputy governor

州牧(ㄓㄡ ㄇㄨˋ)
a governor or magistrate in ancient China

州里(ㄓㄡ ㄌㄧˇ)
① an administrative unit in ancient China (州 consists of 2,500 families; 里 consists of 25 families) ② neighborhood

州閭(ㄓㄡ ㄌㄩˊ)
a small village; a hamlet; a neighborhood

州官(ㄓㄡ ㄍㄨㄢ)
①(in ancient China) officials in a *chou* (州) ②(in old China) the magistrate of a *chou* (州)

州官放火(ㄓㄡ ㄍㄨㄢ ㄈㄤˋ ㄏㄨㄛˇ)
(literally) The governor may commit arson with impunity (while the people are not allowed to light their lamps).—(figuratively) Officials in authority are free to indulge in any mischief while interfering in the personal freedom of the people they govern.

州郡(ㄓㄡ ㄐㄩㄣˋ)
an administrative district in ancient China

州縣(ㄓㄡ ㄒㄧㄢˋ)
a county within a *chou* (州)

州治(ㄓㄡ ㄓˋ)
the capital city of a *chou* (州)

州長(ㄓㄡ ㄓㄤˇ)

① the governor of a *chou* (州) ② the governor of a state (in the USA)

州城(ㄓㄡ ㄔㄥˊ)
a town within a *chou*(州)

四畫

【巡】 1291 (廵) ㄒㄩㄣˊ shyun xún

1. to patrol; to inspect; to cruise; to go on circuit: 警察在城裏巡邏。The policemen patrolled the town.
2. a round (of drinks)
3. a policeman; a cop

巡捕(ㄒㄩㄣˊ ㄅㄨˇ)
(formerly) a policeman

巡捕房(ㄒㄩㄣˊ ㄅㄨˇ ㄈㄤˊ)
(formerly) a police station, or police precinct office

巡防(ㄒㄩㄣˊ ㄈㄤˊ)
① a patrolman; a watchman ② to patrol (especially in civil defense)

巡風(ㄒㄩㄣˊ ㄈㄥ)
a guard who keeps a lookout for the police while a criminal act is being committed 參看「把風」

巡撫(ㄒㄩㄣˊ ㄈㄨˇ)
①(in Ming Dynasty) an imperial inspector ② the governor of a province

巡丁(ㄒㄩㄣˊ ㄉㄧㄥ)or 巡役(ㄒㄩㄣˊ ㄧˋ) or 巡差(ㄒㄩㄣˊ ㄔㄞ)
a watchman; a patrolman; a policeman

巡禮(ㄒㄩㄣˊ ㄌㄧˇ)
①a pilgrimage to a holyland ②an inspection or sightseeing tour

巡邏(ㄒㄩㄣˊ ㄌㄨㄛˊ)
to patrol; to make the inspection rounds

巡邏隊(ㄒㄩㄣˊ ㄌㄨㄛˊ ㄉㄨㄟˋ)
a military patrol

巡邏車(ㄒㄩㄣˊ ㄌㄨㄛˊ ㄔㄜ)
a squad car

巡更(ㄒㄩㄣˊ ㄍㄥ)
(said of a watchman) to strike a gong during night patrol

巡官(ㄒㄩㄣˊ ㄍㄨㄢ)
a police inspector

巡航(ㄒㄩㄣˊ ㄏㄤˊ)
to cruise; a cruise

巡迴(ㄒㄩㄣˊ ㄏㄨㄟˊ)
to go the rounds; to tour; to make a circuit of: 馬戲團正在全國各地巡迴演出。The circus is touring the country.

巡迴法庭(ㄒㄩㄣˊ ㄏㄨㄟˊ ㄈㄚˇ ㄊㄧㄥˊ)
a circuit court

巡迴放映隊(ㄒㄩㄣˊ ㄏㄨㄟˊ ㄈㄤˋ ㄧㄥˋ ㄉㄨㄟˋ)
a mobile film projection team

巡迴大使(ㄒㄩㄣˊ ㄏㄨㄟˊ ㄉㄚˋ ㄕˇ)
an ambassador-at-large; a roving ambassador

巡迴圖書館(ㄒㄩㄣˊ ㄏㄨㄟˊ ㄊㄨˊ ㄕㄨ ㄍㄨㄢˇ)
a circulating library

巡迴劇團(ㄒㄩㄣˊ ㄏㄨㄟˊ ㄐㄩˋ ㄊㄨㄢˊ)
an itinerant theatrical troupe

巡迴學校(ㄒㄩㄣˊ ㄏㄨㄟˊ ㄒㄩㄝˊ ㄒㄧㄠˋ)
a circulating school

巡迴審判(ㄒㄩㄣˊ ㄏㄨㄟˊ ㄕㄣˇ ㄆㄢˋ)
(until 1971 in England) assizes

巡檢(ㄒㄩㄣˊ ㄐㄧㄢˇ)
an official in frontier areas vested with the training of the militia and policing authorities in former times

巡警(ㄒㄩㄣˊ ㄐㄧㄥˇ)
① a policeman; a patrolman ② to inspect; to patrol

巡緝(ㄒㄩㄣˊ ㄑㄧˋ)
to patrol to arrest thieves and smugglers

巡行(ㄒㄩㄣˊ ㄒㄧㄥˊ)
to make the rounds of inspection

巡幸(ㄒㄩㄣˊ ㄒㄧㄥˋ)
(said of an emperor) to make an inspection tour

巡查(ㄒㄩㄣˊ ㄔㄚˊ)
to patrol and investigate

巡察(ㄒㄩㄣˊ ㄔㄚˊ)
to make the rounds of inspection

巡視(ㄒㄩㄣˊ ㄕˋ)
(said of ranking officials) to inspect; to make (or be on) an inspection tour

巡哨(ㄒㄩㄣˊ ㄕㄠˋ)or 巡遊(ㄒㄩㄣˊ ㄧㄡˊ)
a military patrol; patrolling

巡守(ㄒㄩㄣˊ ㄕㄡˇ)or 巡狩(ㄒㄩㄣˊ ㄕㄡˋ)
an imperial inspection tour in the country; to make an imperial inspection tour in the country

巡按(ㄒㄩㄣˊ ㄢˋ)
an inspector-general in the Ming Dynasty

巡按使(ㄒㄩㄣˊ ㄢˋ ㄕˇ)or(ㄒㄩㄣˊ ㄢˋ ㄕˋ)
(in early years of the Chinese Republic) the governor of a province

巡弋飛彈(ㄒㄩㄣˊ ㄧˋ ㄈㄟ ㄉㄢˋ)
a cruise missile

巡夜(ㄒㄩㄣˊ ㄧㄝˋ)
to make nightly patrols

巡洋艦(ㄒㄩㄣˊ ㄧㄤˊ ㄐㄧㄢˋ)
a cruiser

巡閱(ㄒㄩㄣˊ ㄩㄝˋ)
to make the rounds of inspection; to inspect

巡閱使(ㄒㄩㄣˊ ㄩㄝˋ ㄕˇ)or(ㄒㄩㄣˊ ㄩㄝˋ ㄕˋ)
a commanding officer or civil administrative chief of a region, usually quite large, in the early days of the Chinese Republic

八畫

【巢】 1292 ㄔㄠˊ chaur cháo

1. living quarters in the trees
2. a bird's nest: 燕子正在簷下築巢。The swallows are making a nest under the eaves.
3. a haunt; a den; a hideout (for bandits, etc.)
4. a Chinese family name

巢父(ㄔㄠˊ ㄈㄨˇ)
a legendary hermit-scholar during the time of Emperor Yao (2356 B.C.), who lived high up in a tree and declined the throne offered by the emperor

巢窟(ㄔㄠˊ ㄎㄨ)or 巢穴(ㄔㄠˊ ㄒㄩㄝˋ)
a den; a lair; a haunt

巢湖(ㄔㄠˊ ㄏㄨˊ)
Chao Lake—name of a lake in Anhwei Province

巢居(ㄔㄠˊ ㄐㄩ)
to live in trees (before the house was introduced)

〔工部〕

工部
ㄍㄨㄥ gong gōng

【工】 1293
ㄍㄨㄥ gong gōng
1. a laborer; a worker
2. a shift; the time used in doing a piece of work
3. work
4. a day's work
5. an engineering or building project
6. a defense work
7. fine; delicate
8. to be skilled in

工本費(ㄍㄨㄥ ㄅㄣˇ ㄈㄟˋ)
the net cost of a product (the cost of raw materials plus labor)
工筆畫(ㄍㄨㄥ ㄅㄧˇ ㄏㄨㄚˋ)
(Chinese painting) very fine, delicate drawings
工兵(ㄍㄨㄥ ㄅㄧㄥ)
(military) ① engineering corps ② a serviceman in the engineering corps
工部(ㄍㄨㄥ ㄅㄨˋ)
(in old China) the Ministry of Public Works
工部侍郎(ㄍㄨㄥ ㄅㄨˋ ㄕˋ ㄌㄤˊ)
(in old China) a Vice Minister of Public Works
工部尙書(ㄍㄨㄥ ㄅㄨˋ ㄕㄤˋ ㄕㄨ)
(in old China) the Minister of Public Works
工棚(ㄍㄨㄥ ㄆㄥˊ)
① a builders' temporary shed ② a work shed
工蜂(ㄍㄨㄥ ㄈㄥ)
a worker or a working bee
工夫(ㄍㄨㄥ ·ㄈㄨ)
① time; leisure: 我沒有工夫和你閒聊。I have no time to chat with you. ② efforts put into a piece of work; labor ③ skill; workmanship; art: 這位魔術師可眞有工夫！The magician's skill is really superb.
工黨(ㄍㄨㄥ ㄉㄤˇ)
① the British Labor Party ② a labor party
工地(ㄍㄨㄥ ㄉㄧˋ)
a building site; a place where an engineering work is under way
工讀(ㄍㄨㄥ ㄉㄨˊ)
to work on a job in order to finance one's study or education
工讀生(ㄍㄨㄥ ㄉㄨˊ ㄕㄥ)
a worker-student; a student who works his way through college
工頭(ㄍㄨㄥ ㄊㄡˊ)
a foreman (of workers)
工農(ㄍㄨㄥ ㄋㄨㄥˊ)
workers and peasants
工力(ㄍㄨㄥ ㄌㄧˋ)
the amount of efforts made; force and skill (especially for calligraphic works and paintings)
工寮(ㄍㄨㄥ ㄌㄧㄠˊ)
a simple hut for workmen at a construction site
工料(ㄍㄨㄥ ㄌㄧㄠˋ)
the cost of labor and materials; labor and raw materials
工棍(ㄍㄨㄥ ㄍㄨㄣˋ)
a labor union official who makes use of his power to promote self-interest instead of the welfare of union members
工科(ㄍㄨㄥ ㄎㄜ)
the engineering department of a college
工會(ㄍㄨㄥ ㄏㄨㄟˋ)
a labor union; a trade union
工價(ㄍㄨㄥ ㄐㄧㄚˋ)
the money paid to a skilled worker (as a goldsmith, jeweler, etc.) for piecework
工匠(ㄍㄨㄥ ㄐㄧㄤˋ)
a skilled worker; a craftsman; an artisan
工具(ㄍㄨㄥ ㄐㄩˋ)
tools; implements: 工匠愛護工具。Artisans take good care of their tools.
工具箱(ㄍㄨㄥ ㄐㄩˋ ㄒㄧㄤ)
a toolbox; a workbox
工具書(ㄍㄨㄥ ㄐㄩˋ ㄕㄨ)
reference books, such as an encyclopedia, dictionary, etc.
工巧(ㄍㄨㄥ ㄑㄧㄠˇ)
① fine and delicate ② a craftsman of unusual artistic skill
工錢(ㄍㄨㄥ ㄑㄧㄢˊ)
pay; wages; the payment for a piece of work
工區(ㄍㄨㄥ ㄑㄩ)
a work area; a work region
工效(ㄍㄨㄥ ㄒㄧㄠˋ)
work efficiency
工學院(ㄍㄨㄥ ㄒㄩㄝˊ ㄩㄢˋ)
a college of engineering
工緻(ㄍㄨㄥ ㄓˋ)
delicate, fine and skillful craftsmanship
工整(ㄍㄨㄥ ㄓㄥˇ)
neat (style, calligraphy, etc.)
工裝(ㄍㄨㄥ ㄓㄨㄤ)
a workman's fatigues; working clothes; overalls
工尺(ㄍㄨㄥ ㄔㄜˇ)
a musical score in old China
工潮(ㄍㄨㄥ ㄔㄠˊ)
labor unrest or agitation; a labor strike; sabotage
工場(ㄍㄨㄥ ㄔㄤˇ)or(ㄍㄨㄥ ㄔㄤˊ)
a workshop; a workplace: 那位工程師監督工場。The engineer supervises the workplace.
工廠(ㄍㄨㄥ ㄔㄤˇ)
a factory; a plant; a workshop
工廠經濟(ㄍㄨㄥ ㄔㄤˇ ㄐㄧㄥ ㄐㄧˋ)
factory economy
工廠制度(ㄍㄨㄥ ㄔㄤˇ ㄓˋ ㄉㄨˋ)
the factory system
工廠自動化(ㄍㄨㄥ ㄔㄤˇ ㄗˋ ㄉㄨㄥˋ ㄏㄨㄚˋ)
factory automation (F. A.)
工程(ㄍㄨㄥ ㄔㄥˊ)
engineering; an engineering or building project—(figuratively) a job or task
工程隊(ㄍㄨㄥ ㄔㄥˊ ㄉㄨㄟˋ)
the public works corps
工程力學(ㄍㄨㄥ ㄔㄥˊ ㄌㄧˋ ㄒㄩㄝˊ)
practical dynamics
工程學(ㄍㄨㄥ ㄔㄥˊ ㄒㄩㄝˊ)
engineering
工程處(ㄍㄨㄥ ㄔㄥˊ ㄔㄨˋ)
the department of engineering; the engineering department of a huge building project
工程師(ㄍㄨㄥ ㄔㄥˊ ㄕ)
an engineer

工程師節(ㄍㄨㄥ ㄔㄥˊ ㄕ ㄐㄧㄝˊ)
Engineer's Day

工時(ㄍㄨㄥ ㄕˊ)
a man-hour

工事(ㄍㄨㄥ ㄕˋ)
① matters pertaining to civil engineering work ② defense works; military fortifications

工商部(ㄍㄨㄥ ㄕㄤ ㄅㄨˋ)
Ministry of Reconstruction and Commerce

工商界(ㄍㄨㄥ ㄕㄤ ㄐㄧㄝˋ)
the industrial and business circles

工商業(ㄍㄨㄥ ㄕㄤ ㄧㄝˋ)
industry and commerce: 他是工商業大亨。He is a magnate in industrial and commercial enterprises.

工人(ㄍㄨㄥ ㄖㄣˊ)
a laborer; a workman

工人階級(ㄍㄨㄥ ㄖㄣˊ ㄐㄧㄝ ㄐㄧˊ)
the working class; labor class

工資(ㄍㄨㄥ ㄗ)
wages

工作(ㄍㄨㄥ ㄗㄨㄛˋ)
① to work ② a piece of work; one's job or duty

工作母機(ㄍㄨㄥ ㄗㄨㄛˋ ㄇㄨˇ ㄐㄧ)
a machine tool

工作分配(ㄍㄨㄥ ㄗㄨㄛˋ ㄈㄣ ㄆㄟˋ)
work allocation

工作服(ㄍㄨㄥ ㄗㄨㄛˋ ㄈㄨˊ)
working clothes

工作大隊(ㄍㄨㄥ ㄗㄨㄛˋ ㄉㄚˋ ㄉㄨㄟˋ)
a team or group of persons dispatched for a special task

工作天(ㄍㄨㄥ ㄗㄨㄛˋ ㄊㄧㄢ)
a man-day: 那項工程需要二十個工作天。That project will take twenty man-days to complete.

工作者(ㄍㄨㄥ ㄗㄨㄛˋ ㄓㄜˇ)
workers: 教育工作者 educational workers 美術工作者 art workers; artists

工作日(ㄍㄨㄥ ㄗㄨㄛˋ ㄖˋ)
a workday: 通常我們一週有六個工作日。Usually we have six workdays per week.

工作人員(ㄍㄨㄥ ㄗㄨㄛˋ ㄖㄣˊ ㄩㄢˊ)
workers; the workers assigned to do a specific task or job

工作物(ㄍㄨㄥ ㄗㄨㄛˋ ㄨˋ)
(law) a product of labor, such as a house, a bridge, etc.

工蟻(ㄍㄨㄥ ㄧˇ)
a worker (ant)

工役(ㄍㄨㄥ ㄧˋ)
a laborer; a worker

工藝(ㄍㄨㄥ ㄧˋ)
technology; a craft: 手工藝 handicrafts

工藝品(ㄍㄨㄥ ㄧˋ ㄆㄧㄣˇ)
handicrafts; handmade products; items made by artisans

工藝設計(ㄍㄨㄥ ㄧˋ ㄕㄜˋ ㄐㄧˋ)
technological design

工業(ㄍㄨㄥ ㄧㄝˋ)
industry; industrial: 輕工業 the light industry 重工業 the heavy industry

工業廢物(ㄍㄨㄥ ㄧㄝˋ ㄈㄟˋ ㄨˋ)
industrial waste

工業垃圾(ㄍㄨㄥ ㄧㄝˋ ㄌㄜˋ ㄙㄜˋ)
industrial refuse

工業革命(ㄍㄨㄥ ㄧㄝˋ ㄍㄜˊ ㄇㄧㄥˋ)
Industrial Revolution: 工業革命發生於十八世紀及十九世紀初期。The Industrial Revolution took place in the 18th and early 19th centuries.

工業國家(ㄍㄨㄥ ㄧㄝˋ ㄍㄨㄛˊ ㄐㄧㄚ)
industrial nations or powers; developed countries

工業公害(ㄍㄨㄥ ㄧㄝˋ ㄍㄨㄥ ㄏㄞˋ)
industrial public nuisances

工業化(ㄍㄨㄥ ㄧㄝˋ ㄏㄨㄚˋ)
industrialization; industrialized: 高度工業化的經濟 highly industrialized economics

工業化學(ㄍㄨㄥ ㄧㄝˋ ㄏㄨㄚˋ ㄒㄩㄝˊ)
industrial chemistry

工業機器人(ㄍㄨㄥ ㄧㄝˋ ㄐㄧ ㄑㄧˋ ㄖㄣˊ)
an industrial robot

工業酒精(ㄍㄨㄥ ㄧㄝˋ ㄐㄧㄡˇ ㄐㄧㄥ)
industrial alcohol

工業區(ㄍㄨㄥ ㄧㄝˋ ㄑㄩ)
an industrial zone; an industrial park 亦作「工業園」

工業學校(ㄍㄨㄥ ㄧㄝˋ ㄒㄩㄝˊ ㄒㄧㄠˋ)
technical schools; industrial schools

工業城市(ㄍㄨㄥ ㄧㄝˋ ㄔㄥˊ ㄕˋ)
an industrial city

工業時代(ㄍㄨㄥ ㄧㄝˋ ㄕˊ ㄉㄞˋ)
an industrial age

工業設計(ㄍㄨㄥ ㄧㄝˋ ㄕㄜˋ ㄐㄧˋ)
industrial design

工業危害(ㄍㄨㄥ ㄧㄝˋ ㄨㄟˊ ㄏㄞˋ)
industrial hazard

工業用電視(ㄍㄨㄥ ㄧㄝˋ ㄩㄥˋ ㄉㄧㄢˋ ㄕˋ)
industrial television (ITV)

工業用具(ㄍㄨㄥ ㄧㄝˋ ㄩㄥˋ ㄐㄩˋ)
equipment and tools used in industries

工業用水(ㄍㄨㄥ ㄧㄝˋ ㄩㄥˋ ㄕㄨㄟˇ)
industrial water

工友(ㄍㄨㄥ ㄧㄡˇ)
an office boy; an office errand man

工務局(ㄍㄨㄥ ㄨˋ ㄐㄩˊ)
the (municipal) bureau of public works

工穩(ㄍㄨㄥ ㄨㄣˇ)
(usually said of literary works, calligraphy, wording of documents, etc.) neat and proper; flawless

工於心計(ㄍㄨㄥ ㄩˊ ㄒㄧㄣ ㄐㄧˋ)
scheming; crafty

工欲善其事，必先利其器(ㄍㄨㄥ ㄩˋ ㄕㄢˋ ㄑㄧˊ ㄕˋ，ㄅㄧˋ ㄒㄧㄢ ㄌㄧˋ ㄑㄧˊ ㄑㄧˋ)
Good tools are prerequisite to the successful execution of a job.

二畫

【左】 1294 ㄗㄨㄛˇ tzuoo zuǒ

1. the left side
2. the east side: 江左 the east side of the river 山左 the east side of the mountain
3. improper
4. supporting (documents, evidence, etc.); to assist
5. to be demoted; to descend
6. inconvenience; inconvenient
7. erroneous; mistaken
8. unduly stubborn
9. a Chinese family name
10. to disobey; to disregard

左臂(ㄗㄨㄛˇ ㄅㄟˋ)
the left arm

左邊(ㄗㄨㄛˇ ㄅㄧㄢ) or 左邊兒(ㄗㄨㄛˇ ㄅㄧㄚㄦ) or 左面(ㄗㄨㄛˇ ㄇㄧㄢˋ)
the left side; the left-hand side: 來，坐到我的左邊。Come and sit on my left.

左鞭右打(ㄗㄨㄛˇ ㄅㄧㄢ ㄧㄡˋ ㄉㄚˇ)
to make deceiving moves;

pretending to strike in one direction but actually delivering the blow in another direction

左不過(ㄗㄨㄛˇ ·ㄅㄨ ㄍㄨㄛˋ)
certainly; must be; can't be otherwise

左派(ㄗㄨㄛˇ ㄆㄞˋ)
①a radical; a leftist ②a leftist faction: 政黨的左派 the left faction of the party

左脾氣(ㄗㄨㄛˇ ㄆㄧˊ ·ㄑㄧ)
a stubbornly peevish temper

左撇子(ㄗㄨㄛˇ ㄆㄧㄝ ·ㄗ)
a left-handed person; a southpaw; a portsider

左方(ㄗㄨㄛˇ ㄈㄤ)
on the left; to the left

左輔右弼(ㄗㄨㄛˇ ㄈㄨˇ ㄧㄡˋ ㄅㄧˋ)
the emperor's top ministers

左道旁門(ㄗㄨㄛˇ ㄉㄠˋ ㄆㄤˊ ㄇㄣˊ)
①heresy ②unlawful and tricky ways; evil ways

左袒(ㄗㄨㄛˇ ㄊㄢˇ)
to be biased; to favor one side

左提右挈(ㄗㄨㄛˇ ㄊㄧˊ ㄧㄡˋ ㄑㄧㄝˋ)
to give mutual help or assistance

左圖右史(ㄗㄨㄛˇ ㄊㄨˊ ㄧㄡˋ ㄕˇ)
a large private collection of books; an impressive personal library

左鄰右舍(ㄗㄨㄛˇ ㄌㄧㄣˊ ㄧㄡˋ ㄕㄜˋ)
neighbors

左輪鎗(ㄗㄨㄛˇ ㄌㄨㄣˊ ㄑㄧㄤ)
a revolver; a six-shooter

左改右改(ㄗㄨㄛˇ ㄍㄞˇ ㄧㄡˋ ㄍㄞˇ)
to make changes over and over again

左顧右盼(ㄗㄨㄛˇ ㄍㄨˋ ㄧㄡˋ ㄆㄢˋ)
①to look left and right—inattentive; lack of concentration ②flirtatious ③to cheat in the examination

左近(ㄗㄨㄛˇ ㄐㄧㄣˋ)
in the neighborhood; in the vicinity: 左近有銀行嗎? Is there a bank in the vicinity?

左遷(ㄗㄨㄛˇ ㄑㄧㄢ)or 左黜(ㄗㄨㄛˇ ㄔㄨˋ)or 左除(ㄗㄨㄛˇ ㄔㄨˊ)
to be demoted

左傾(ㄗㄨㄛˇ ㄑㄧㄥ)
left-leaning: 社會黨員是左傾的。The socialists are left-leaning.

左券(ㄗㄨㄛˇ ㄑㄩㄢˋ)
a winning hand; full confidence in (winning)

左舷(ㄗㄨㄛˇ ㄒㄧㄢˊ)
the port (of a ship)

左心室(ㄗㄨㄛˇ ㄒㄧㄣ ㄕˋ)
the left ventricle

左心耳(ㄗㄨㄛˇ ㄒㄧㄣ ㄦˇ)or 左心房(ㄗㄨㄛˇ ㄒㄧㄣ ㄈㄤˊ)
the left auricle

左行(ㄗㄨㄛˇ ㄒㄧㄥˊ)
①(said of writing) from left to right—Western written languages ②to keep to the left

左性子(ㄗㄨㄛˇ ㄒㄧㄥˋ ·ㄗ)
a peevish or very stubborn temper; cantankerous

左支右絀(ㄗㄨㄛˇ ㄓ ㄧㄡˋ ㄔㄨˋ)
not have enough money to cover the expenses; hard-pressed for money; in financial straits; to be in straitened circumstances

左證(ㄗㄨㄛˇ ㄓㄥˋ)
supporting evidence (of one's statement, etc.) 亦作「佐證」

左轉(ㄗㄨㄛˇ ㄓㄨㄢˇ)
to turn left

左傳(ㄗㄨㄛˇ ㄓㄨㄢˋ)or 左氏傳(ㄗㄨㄛˇ ㄕˋ ㄓㄨㄢˋ)
Spring and Autumn with Commentary by Tso Chiu-ming — a commentary on *the Spring and Autumn Annals* (春秋), authored by Tso Chiu-ming(左丘明)of the Chou Dynasty

左丞相(ㄗㄨㄛˇ ㄔㄥˊ ㄒㄧㄤˋ)
an old official rank, roughly equivalent to vice premiership

左史(ㄗㄨㄛˇ ㄕˇ)
an official historian

左手(ㄗㄨㄛˇ ㄕㄡˇ)
①the left hand ②the left-hand side

左首(ㄗㄨㄛˇ ㄕㄡˇ)
the left side

左書(ㄗㄨㄛˇ ㄕㄨ)
①(Chinese calligraphy) the "clerical" style ②characters written by one's left hand

左衽 or 左袵(ㄗㄨㄛˇ ㄖㄣˋ)
①to wear the clothes of a barbarian ②the barbarian clothes buttoning on the left side

左宗棠(ㄗㄨㄛˇ ㄗㄨㄥ ㄊㄤˊ)
Tso Chung-tang, one of the major figures in the suppression of the Taiping Rebellion

左側(ㄗㄨㄛˇ ㄘㄜˋ)
on the left side

左思右想(ㄗㄨㄛˇ ㄙ ㄧㄡˋ ㄒㄧㄤˇ)
to think over and over; to ponder; to muse

左嗓子(ㄗㄨㄛˇ ㄙㄤˇ ·ㄗ)
a high-pitched and unpleasant voice; a voice which is high but not refined

左翼(ㄗㄨㄛˇ ㄧˋ)
① (politics) the left wing or leftist ②(ball games) the left wing ③(military operations) the left flank

左右(ㄗㄨㄛˇ ㄧㄡˋ)
①left and right—nearby; by one's side; at hand: 她的小孩子常在她左右。Her children are always by her side. ②servants; aides ③a term of respect placed after the name when addressing another (usually in correspondence) ④to influence or sway; to be influenced or swayed

左右逢源(ㄗㄨㄛˇ ㄧㄡˋ ㄈㄥˊ ㄩㄢˊ)
to get help from all sides; to have everything going one's way

左右袒(ㄗㄨㄛˇ ㄧㄡˋ ㄊㄢˇ)
to take sides; to be unneutral; to be biased

左右開弓(ㄗㄨㄛˇ ㄧㄡˋ ㄎㄞ ㄍㄨㄥ)
to slap someone's face with both hands

左右手(ㄗㄨㄛˇ ㄧㄡˋ ㄕㄡˇ)
①left and right hands ②able assistants; top aides

左右翼(ㄗㄨㄛˇ ㄧㄡˋ ㄧˋ)
the left and right wings or flanks

左右爲難(ㄗㄨㄛˇ ㄧㄡˋ ㄨㄟˊ ㄋㄢˊ)
to know not which side to turn to—to be indecisive; to be in a dilemma

左驗(ㄗㄨㄛˇ ㄧㄢˋ)
a witness

左擁右抱(ㄗㄨㄛˇ ㄩㄥˇ ㄧㄡˋ ㄅㄠˋ)
(literally) to have a woman

in each arm—(figuratively) to have two or more concubines; to have several mistresses at the same time

【巧】 1295 ㄑㄧㄠˇ cheau qiǎo

1. clever; witty
2. ingenious; artful; skillful
3. a clever feat; a stunt
4. pretty; cute
5. coincidence; coincidental; coincidentally; opportune

巧辯(ㄑㄧㄠˇ ㄅㄧㄢˋ)
a plausible argument; an ingenious argument

巧不可階(ㄑㄧㄠˇ ㄅㄨˋ ㄎㄜˇ ㄐㄧㄝ)
unmatched in ingenuity

巧妙(ㄑㄧㄠˇ ㄇㄧㄠˋ)
ingenuity; ingenious; skillful; clever: 巧妙的戰術 ingenious tactics 巧妙的回答 a clever answer

巧妙手段(ㄑㄧㄠˇ ㄇㄧㄠˋ ㄕㄡˇ ㄉㄨㄢˋ)
an ingenious or clever move

巧婦難爲無米之炊(ㄑㄧㄠˇ ㄈㄨˋ ㄋㄢˊ ㄨㄟˊ ㄨˊ ㄇㄧˇ ㄓ ㄔㄨㄟ)
(literally) Even the cleverest woman cannot prepare a meal without rice.—(figuratively) Nobody can accomplish anything without the necessary means.

巧得很(ㄑㄧㄠˇ ˙ㄉㄜ ㄏㄣˇ)
quite by coincidence; as luck would have it; fortunately

巧當兒(ㄑㄧㄠˇ ㄉㄤˋㄦ)
①(at) the opportune moment ②coincidence

巧奪天工(ㄑㄧㄠˇ ㄉㄨㄛˊ ㄊㄧㄢ ㄍㄨㄥ)
(often referring to a work of art) ingenuity that rivals the work of God

巧立名目(ㄑㄧㄠˇ ㄌㄧˋ ㄇㄧㄥˊ ㄇㄨˋ)
to fabricate various excuses; to invent all sorts of names

巧固球(ㄑㄧㄠˇ ㄍㄨˋ ㄑㄧㄡˊ)
tchouk ball

巧克力糖(ㄑㄧㄠˇ ㄎㄜˋ ㄌㄧˋ ㄊㄤˊ)
chocolate

巧合(ㄑㄧㄠˇ ㄏㄜˊ)
a coincidence

巧極了(ㄑㄧㄠˇ ㄐㄧˊ ˙ㄌㄜ)
quite by coincidence; extremely coincidental; extremely fortunate

巧計(ㄑㄧㄠˇ ㄐㄧˋ)
an ingenious scheme; a very clever device; a capital plan

巧妻常伴拙夫眠(ㄑㄧㄠˇ ㄑㄧ ㄔㄤˊ ㄅㄢˋ ㄓㄨㄛˊ ㄈㄨ ㄇㄧㄢˊ)
Smart girls usually have dumb men for husbands.

巧取豪奪(ㄑㄧㄠˇ ㄑㄩˇ ㄏㄠˊ ㄉㄨㄛˊ)
to rob others by hook or by crook

巧笑(ㄑㄧㄠˇ ㄒㄧㄠˋ)
(said of women) an artful smile; to smile artfully

巧詐(ㄑㄧㄠˇ ㄓㄚˋ)
artful; tricky; ingenious fraud: 他是一個巧詐的政客。He is a tricky politician.

巧事(ㄑㄧㄠˇ ㄕˋ)
a coincidence

巧舌如簧(ㄑㄧㄠˇ ㄕㄜˊ ㄖㄨˊ ㄏㄨㄤˊ)
a very plausible tongue

巧手(ㄑㄧㄠˇ ㄕㄡˇ)
a skillful person; a dab: 她是網球巧手。she's a dab at tennis.

巧言令色(ㄑㄧㄠˇ ㄧㄢˊ ㄌㄧㄥˋ ㄙㄜˋ)
sweet words and insinuating manners (which are seldom associated with virtue)

巧遇(ㄑㄧㄠˇ ㄩˋ)
a chance encounter

【巨】 1296 (鉅) ㄐㄩˋ jiuh jù

1. great; big: 我們聽見一聲巨響。We heard a great noise.
2. very
3. a Chinese family name

巨擘(ㄐㄩˋ ㄅㄛˋ)
①the thumb ②an outstanding person; the foremost figure (in a field); a magnate: 他是建築業的巨擘。He is a magnate in the construction business.

巨富(ㄐㄩˋ ㄈㄨˋ)
a multimillionaire; a person of immense wealth

巨大(ㄐㄩˋ ㄉㄚˋ)
giant (size); mammoth; gargantuan; gigantic

巨盜(ㄐㄩˋ ㄉㄠˋ)
a notorious bandit; a monstrous villain or robber

巨蠹(ㄐㄩˋ ㄉㄨˋ)
an influential criminal; Public Enemy No. One

巨頭(ㄐㄩˋ ㄊㄡˊ)
a national leader; a big chief

巨頭會議(ㄐㄩˋ ㄊㄡˊ ㄏㄨㄟˋ ㄧˋ)
a summit conference; a meeting of chiefs

巨流(ㄐㄩˋ ㄌㄧㄡˊ)
a mighty current: 許多小溪滙成一股巨流。Many brooks converge into a mighty current.

巨量(ㄐㄩˋ ㄌㄧㄤˋ)
a tremendous amount; a great deal

巨輪(ㄐㄩˋ ㄌㄨㄣˊ)
①a large wheel ②a large ship

巨構(ㄐㄩˋ ㄍㄡˋ)
(of literature, etc.) a great work; (of a movie, etc.) a colossal production

巨賈(ㄐㄩˋ ㄍㄨˇ)
a business tycoon; a business magnate

巨工(ㄐㄩˋ ㄍㄨㄥ)
a gigantic task; a mammoth project

巨款(ㄐㄩˋ ㄎㄨㄢˇ)
a huge sum of money

巨猾(ㄐㄩˋ ㄏㄨㄚˊ)
a notorious swindler; a very evil person

巨奸(ㄐㄩˋ ㄐㄧㄢ)
a big swindler; a person of many evils; a big crook

巨艦(ㄐㄩˋ ㄐㄧㄢˋ)
a large warship

巨匠(ㄐㄩˋ ㄐㄧㄤˋ)
a maestro; a master; an expert; a leading figure (in the literary, painting, etc. world)

巨細(ㄐㄩˋ ㄒㄧˋ)
(the) big and (the) small

巨細靡遺(ㄐㄩˋ ㄒㄧˋ ㄇㄧˇ ㄧˊ)
not to leave out any detail; not to leave out anything, big or small

巨星(ㄐㄩˋ ㄒㄧㄥ)
①(astronomy) a giant star ②a giant

巨型(ㄐㄩˋ ㄒㄧㄥˊ)
a large model (of cars, etc.)

巨著(ㄐㄩˋ ㄓㄨˋ)
a great book; a monumental literary work

巨室(ㄐㄩˋ ㄕˋ)
①a powerful or influential family ②a big house or palace

巨人(ㄐㄩˋ ㄖㄣˊ)
a giant: 他是這個時代的巨人。He is a giant of the present era.

巨子(ㄐㄩˋ ㄗˇ)
① a business tycoon ② a master; a maestro

巨額(ㄐㄩˋ ㄜˊ)
a great deal of; a tremendous amount of; a huge sum of: 建大廈要花一筆巨額的錢。Building a mansion takes a great amount of money.

巨案(ㄐㄩˋ ㄢˋ)
a sensational case

巨毋霸 or 巨無霸(ㄐㄩˋ ㄨˊ ㄅㄚˋ)
① name of a giant during the time of Wang Mang (王莽) ② (figuratively) a giant

巨萬(ㄐㄩˋ ㄨㄢˋ)
an immense amount (of money, wealth, etc.)

四畫

【巫】1297
ㄨ wu wū
(語音 ㄨ u wū)

1. a wizard or witch
2. witchcraft; sorcery
3. a Chinese family name

巫婆(ㄨ ㄆㄛˊ)
a witch

巫蠱(ㄨ ㄍㄨˇ)
the art of casting a spell over somebody

巫覡(ㄨ ㄒㄧˊ)
witches and wizards; (collectively) sorcerers

巫峽(ㄨ ㄒㄧㄚˊ)
Wu Gorge—one of the three gorges of the upper Yangtze River

巫祝(ㄨ ㄓㄨˋ)
a witch or a wizard

巫師(ㄨ ㄕ)
a sorcerer; a wizard

巫山(ㄨ ㄕㄢ)
①Mountain Wu, in the east of Szechwan ② name of a county in Szechwan

巫山雲雨(ㄨ ㄕㄢ ㄩㄣˊ ㄩˇ)
a rendezvous between two lovers—coitus

巫術(ㄨ ㄕㄨˋ)
sorcery; black magic; witchery

巫醫(ㄨ ㄧ)
a witch doctor

七畫

【差】1298
1. ㄔㄚ cha chā

1. errors; mistakes: 未犯差錯的人，亦未能成一事。One who never made a mistake never made anything.
2. difference; discrepancy: 這沒有什麼差別。It makes no difference.
3. (mathematics) difference: 七與十五之差爲八。The difference between seven and fifteen is eight.

差別(ㄔㄚ ㄅㄧㄝˊ)
discrepancy; difference; distinction

差別關稅(ㄔㄚ ㄅㄧㄝˊ ㄍㄨㄢ ㄕㄨㄟˋ)
differential duties

差可(ㄔㄚ ㄎㄜˇ)
barely passable

差號(ㄔㄚ ㄏㄠˋ)
the "～" sign to show the difference between two figures

差價(ㄔㄚ ㄐㄧㄚˋ)
price differences: 季節差價 seasonal price differences

差距(ㄔㄚ ㄐㄩˋ)
gap; disparity; difference: 你的意見和我的差距很大。There is a wide gap between your opinion and mine.

差強人意(ㄔㄚ ㄑㄧㄤˊ ㄖㄣˊ ㄧˋ)
barely satisfactory; barely passable

差遲 or 差池(ㄔㄚ ㄔˊ)
① accidents ② errors; miscalculations; mistakes

差數(ㄔㄚ ㄕㄨˋ)
(mathematics) difference

差錯(ㄔㄚ ㄘㄨㄛˋ)
① errors; mistakes; miscalculations ② accidents

差額(ㄔㄚ ㄜˊ)
the difference between two amounts or figures

差以毫釐，謬以千里(ㄔㄚ ㄧˇ ㄏㄠˊ ㄌㄧˊ, ㄇㄧㄡˋ ㄧˇ ㄑㄧㄢ ㄌㄧˇ)
A slight error in the beginning results in a big mistake in the end. 亦作「差之毫釐，失之千里」

差異(ㄔㄚ ㄧˋ)
① discrepancy; difference; variance; variation ② to differ

差誤(ㄔㄚ ㄨˋ)
errors; blunders; miscalculations

【差】1298
2. ㄔㄚˋ chah chà

1. to differ
2. wrong: 此言差矣。You are wrong there.
3. to want; to fall short of: 距約定的時間還差半小時。It wants half an hour to the appointed time.
4. not up to standard; poor: 他的記憶力很差。He has a poor memory.

差不多(ㄔㄚˋ ·ㄅㄨ ㄉㄨㄛ)
① with little difference; almost the same ② almost; nearly; approximately ③ just about enough

差得多(ㄔㄚˋ ·ㄉㄜ ㄉㄨㄛ)
① very different; much difference; poles apart ② far below (the required sum, standard, criterion, etc.)

差點兒(ㄔㄚˋ ㄉㄧㄚˇㄦ)
① almost; nearly: 這盤棋他差點兒贏了。He almost won the chess game. ② with a slight difference; nearly the same ③ not good enough

差勁(ㄔㄚˋ ㄐㄧㄣˋ)
disappointing; poor (work, records, etc.): 她本學期的成績很差勁。She made a poor record this term.

【差】1298
3. ㄔㄞ chai chāi

1. a messenger; an errand man: 這青年担任一家公司的信差。This young man serves as a messenger in a company.
2. to dispatch; to send (a person)
3. one's duty or job; one's official business or assignment
4. an errand: 他被派出差。He was sent on an errand.

差派(ㄔㄞ ㄆㄞˋ)
to dispatch or appoint (a person to do a job, etc.)

差遣(ㄔㄞ ㄑㄧㄢˇ)or 差使(ㄔㄞ ㄕˇ)
to dispatch or send (a person on an errand, etc.): 他差遣她去買麵包。He dispatched her to buy bread.

差事(ㄔㄞ ㄕˋ)
a job

差人(ㄔㄞ ㄖㄣˊ)or 差役(ㄔㄞ ㄧˋ)or 差使(ㄔㄞ ㄕˇ)
the servants of an official; an official messenger

【差】 1298 4. ㄘ tsy cī
uneven; irregular

差等(ㄘ ㄉㄥˇ)
classification; classes

己部
ㄐㄧˇ jii jǐ

【己】 1299 ㄐㄧˇ jii jǐ
1. self; one's own; oneself: 人不應該專爲自己而活。One should not live for oneself alone.
2. the sixth of the ten Celestial Stems (天干)

己方(ㄐㄧˇ ㄈㄤ)
one's own side

己飢己溺(ㄐㄧˇ ㄐㄧ ㄐㄧˇ ㄋㄧˋ)
(literally) to feel responsible for the hungry and the drowning of the people —(said of a person in authority) to feel responsible for the welfare of the people

己身(ㄐㄧˇ ㄕㄣ)
oneself; one's own person

己任(ㄐㄧˇ ㄖㄣˋ)
one's duty, responsibility or obligation

己所不欲，勿施於人(ㄐㄧˇ ㄙㄨㄛˇ ㄅㄨˋ ㄩˋ, ㄨˋ ㄕ ㄩˊ ㄖㄣˊ)
Do not do to others what you don't want to be done to you.

【已】 1300 ㄧˇ yii yǐ
1. to cease; to stop
2. to come to an end; to finish; to complete
3. already: 郵差已經來了。The postman has been here already.
4. used to indicate the past
5. excessive; very; much
6. a final particle to add emphasis: 相信你祇是開玩笑而已。I believe you only joke about this.

已滿(ㄧˇ ㄇㄢˇ)
① already full; already filled up ②(said of a time limit) already expired: 他的任期已滿。His term of office has expired.

已定(ㄧˇ ㄉㄧㄥˋ)
already settled; already fixed; to have come to a final arrangement: 諸事已定。All affairs are already settled.

已故(ㄧˇ ㄍㄨˋ)
already dead; the deceased; the late...: 已故的主席定下這條規則。The late chairman set up this rule.

已過(ㄧˇ ㄍㄨㄛˋ)
already past; to have passed already

已開發國家(ㄧˇ ㄎㄞ ㄈㄚ ㄍㄨㄛˊ ㄐㄧㄚ)
a developed country

已還(ㄧˇ ㄏㄨㄢˊ)
already repaid; already returned

已極(ㄧˇ ㄐㄧˊ)
the utmost; the extreme limit: 目前的情況危險已極。The present situation is in the utmost danger.

已久(ㄧˇ ㄐㄧㄡˇ)
(for) a long time already

已經(ㄧˇ ㄐㄧㄥ)
already; some time ago: 這點已經說過了。This has been dealt with already.

已決(ㄧˇ ㄐㄩㄝˊ)
to have already decided

已去(ㄧˇ ㄑㄩˋ)
already gone

已知數(ㄧˇ ㄓ ㄕㄨˋ)
(mathematics) a known number, or known quantity

已甚(ㄧˇ ㄕㄣˋ)
excessive; quite enough; to go to extremes

已然(ㄧˇ ㄖㄢˊ)
to be already so; to have already become a fact

已足(ㄧˇ ㄗㄨˊ)
already sufficient: 我們的旅費已足。Our traveling expenses are already sufficient.

已死(ㄧˇ ㄙˇ)
already dead: 她已死多年。She has been dead for many years.

已而(ㄧˇ ㄦˊ)
①to give up one's vain pursuit ② then; afterward

已矣(ㄧˇ ㄧˇ)
an expression to indicate total disappointment or desperation

已完(ㄧˇ ㄨㄢˊ)
① already finished or completed; to bring to completion ② already hopeless

已往(ㄧˇ ㄨㄤˇ)
before; in the past

【巳】 1301 ㄙˋ syh sì
1. the sixth of the twelve Terrestrial Branches (地支)
2. 9 to 11 a.m.
3. a Chinese family name

巳時(ㄙˋ ㄕˊ)or 巳牌(ㄙˋ ㄆㄞˊ)
the period of the day from 9 a.m. to 11 a.m.

一畫

【巴】 1302 ㄅㄚ ba bā
1. name of an ancient state which occupied today's eastern Szechwan
2. a crust formed as a result of heat or dryness
3. to expect; to hope for anxiously
4. used with parts of human body (such as hands, cheeks, chin, etc.)
5. a final particle implying closeness or adhesion
6. to be close to: 前不巴村，後不巴店 to be close neither to a village ahead nor to an inn behind—in a desolate place
7. (physics) a bar: 毫巴 a millibar
8. a Chinese family name

巴巴(ㄅㄚ ㄅㄚ)
① an expression indicating anxiousness or urgency ② especially ③(used for the sound) of slapping

〔己部〕

巴貝多(ㄅㄚ ㄅㄟˋ ㄉㄨㄛ)
Barbados
巴比倫(ㄅㄚ ㄅㄧˇ ㄌㄨㄣˊ)
Babylon
巴比合金(ㄅㄚ ㄅㄧˇ ㄏㄜˊ ㄐㄧㄣ)
babbitt; Babbitt metal
巴不得(ㄅㄚ ·ㄅㄨ ·ㄉㄜ)
an expression indicating expectancy—can't wait to...; would that; to be only too anxious (to do something)
巴布亞新幾內亞(ㄅㄚ ㄅㄨˋ ㄧㄚˇ ㄒㄧㄣ ㄐㄧˇ ㄋㄟˋ ㄧㄚˇ)
Papua New Guinea
巴答(ㄅㄚ ㄉㄚ)
the sound of a slap, a stroke, or an object falling
巴達維亞(ㄅㄚ ㄉㄚˊ ㄨㄟˊ ㄧㄚˇ)
Batavia, or Jakarta, capital of Indonesia
巴得(ㄅㄚ ㄉㄜˊ)
an expression indicating expectancy—Would it.... 或 May....
巴到(ㄅㄚ ㄉㄠˋ)
to have waited patiently or anxiously until
巴豆(ㄅㄚ ㄉㄡˋ)
(botany) a croton
巴頭探腦(ㄅㄚ ㄊㄡˊ ㄊㄢˋ ㄋㄠˇ)
to stretch one's head in search or prying
巴拿馬(ㄅㄚ ㄋㄚˊ ㄇㄚˇ)
Panama
巴拿馬運河(ㄅㄚ ㄋㄚˊ ㄇㄚˇ ㄩㄣˋ ㄏㄜˊ)
the Panama Canal
巴拉圭(ㄅㄚ ㄌㄚ ㄍㄨㄟ)
Paraguay
巴拉松(ㄅㄚ ㄌㄚ ㄙㄨㄥ)
parathion
巴勒斯坦(ㄅㄚ ㄌㄜˋ ㄙ ㄊㄢˇ)
Palestine
巴攬(ㄅㄚ ㄌㄢˇ)
something to hold on to; a principle to hold on to
巴黎(ㄅㄚ ㄌㄧˊ)
Paris
巴黎和會(ㄅㄚ ㄌㄧˊ ㄏㄜˊ ㄏㄨㄟˋ)
the Paris Peace Conference (held at Versailles), which led to the signing of a peace treaty (1919) between the Allies and Germany following World War I
巴里島(ㄅㄚ ㄌㄧˇ ㄉㄠˇ)
Bali Island
巴林(ㄅㄚ ㄌㄧㄣˊ)
Bahrain
巴格達(ㄅㄚ ㄍㄜˊ ㄉㄚˊ)
Bagdad or Baghdad, capital of Iraq
巴高枝兒(ㄅㄚ ㄍㄠ ㄓㄜㄦ)
(literally) to stretch with effort for a higher branch—to try hard to advance one's social position by any means within one's command
巴高望上(ㄅㄚ ㄍㄠ ㄨㄤˋ ㄕㄤˋ)
to seek advancement or promotion
巴庫(ㄅㄚ ㄎㄨˋ)
Baku, a city in Russia
巴哈(ㄅㄚ ㄏㄚ)
Johann Sebastian Bach (1685-1750), German musician and composer
巴哈馬群島(ㄅㄚ ㄏㄚ ㄇㄚˇ ㄑㄩㄣˊ ㄉㄠˇ)
the Bahamas
巴基斯坦(ㄅㄚ ㄐㄧ ㄙ ㄊㄢˇ)
Pakistan
巴基斯坦人(ㄅㄚ ㄐㄧ ㄙ ㄊㄢˇ ㄖㄣˊ)
a Pakistani; the Pakistanis
巴結(ㄅㄚ ·ㄐㄧㄝ)
① to curry favor; to toady; to flatter; to try hard to please ② to exert oneself for advancement; to manage to come by
巴西(ㄅㄚ ㄒㄧ)
Brazil
巴峽(ㄅㄚ ㄒㄧㄚˊ)
Pa Gorge—one of the three gorges of the upper Yangtze River
巴想(ㄅㄚ ㄒㄧㄤˇ)
to hope or await anxiously
巴掌(ㄅㄚ ·ㄓㄤ)
① the palm of the hand ② a slap
巴士(ㄅㄚ ㄕˋ)
a bus
巴士底獄(ㄅㄚ ㄕˋ ㄉㄧˇ ㄩˋ)
the Bastille
巴士海峽(ㄅㄚ ㄕˋ ㄏㄞˇ ㄒㄧㄚˊ)
the Bashi Channel
巴蛇(ㄅㄚ ㄕㄜˊ)
a big snake; a serpent
巴蜀(ㄅㄚ ㄕㄨˇ)
two ancient states in modern Szechwan
巴斯脫(ㄅㄚ ㄙ ㄊㄨㄛ)
Louis Pasteur, 1822-1895, French chemist
巴斯噶(ㄅㄚ ㄙ ㄍㄚˊ)
Blaise Pascal, 1623-1662, French scientist
巴塞隆納(ㄅㄚ ㄙㄞ ㄌㄨㄥˊ ㄋㄚˋ)
Barcelona, a seaport in Northeast Spain
巴爾幹半島(ㄅㄚ ㄦˇ ㄍㄢˋ ㄅㄢˋ ㄉㄠˇ)
the Balkan Peninsula
巴爾札克(ㄅㄚ ㄦˇ ㄓㄚˊ ㄎㄜˋ)
Honoré de Balzac (1799-1850), French novelist
巴顏喀喇山(ㄅㄚ ㄧㄢˊ ㄎㄚ ㄌㄚˇ ㄕㄢ)
Bayan Kara Shan where the Yangtze River and the Yellow River begin
巴望(ㄅㄚ ㄨㄤˋ)
to hope for anxiously

六畫

【巷】 1303
ㄒㄧㄤˋ shiang xiàng
a lane; an alley
巷陌(ㄒㄧㄤˋ ㄇㄛˋ)
(collectively) streets and lanes
巷道(ㄒㄧㄤˋ ㄉㄠˋ)
①(mining) a tunnel ② an alley; a lane; a back street
巷口(ㄒㄧㄤˋ ㄎㄡˇ)
either end of a lane; an entrance to a lane
巷戰(ㄒㄧㄤˋ ㄓㄢˋ)
street-fighting
巷子(ㄒㄧㄤˋ ·ㄗ)
a lane; an alley
巷議(ㄒㄧㄤˋ ㄧˋ)
local rumors or gossips; the comments among the men in the street
巷尾(ㄒㄧㄤˋ ㄨㄟˇ)
the end of a lane or alley

九畫

【巽】 1304
ㄒㄩㄣˋ shiunn xùn
1. subservient; submissive; mild; bland
2. the 5th of the Eight Diagrams
3. a Chinese family name
巽他羣島(ㄒㄩㄣˋ ㄊㄚ ㄑㄩㄣˊ ㄉㄠˇ)
the Sunda Islands including Sumatra, Java, Bali, Lom-

bok, Sumbawa and Flores

巾部
ㄐㄧㄣ jin jīn

【巾】 1305
ㄐㄧㄣ jin jīn

1. a napkin, kerchief or towel: 她丟了手巾。She lost her handkerchief.
2. a headgear; articles for dressing the hair

巾帕(ㄐㄧㄣ ㄆㄚˋ)
①a napkin or kerchief ② a headwrapper

巾幗(ㄐㄧㄣ ㄍㄨㄛˊ)
①female; woman; womankind ② articles for decorating a woman's head such as headwrappers, hairpins, etc.

巾幗鬚眉(ㄐㄧㄣ ㄍㄨㄛˊ ㄒㄩ ㄇㄟˊ)
(literally) a man among women—a woman who acts and talks like a man courageously, straightforwardly, frankly, etc.

巾幗英雄(ㄐㄧㄣ ㄍㄨㄛˊ ㄧㄥ ㄒㄩㄥˊ)
a heroine

巾櫛(ㄐㄧㄣ ㄐㄧㄝˊ)
(literally) towel and comb—lowly service a woman renders to a man

巾箱(ㄐㄧㄣ ㄒㄧㄤ)
a small box for keeping napkins or kerchiefs

巾箱本(ㄐㄧㄣ ㄒㄧㄤ ㄅㄣˇ)
a pocket-size book; the condensed version of a book

巾幘(ㄐㄧㄣ ㄗㄜˊ)
a headwrapper; a hairdressing article of linen, silk, etc.

二畫

【市】 1306
ㄕˋ shyh shì

1. a marketplace; a market; a place for bartering goods
2. a city
3. to buy or sell
4. a Chinese family name

市舶司(ㄕˋ ㄅㄛˊ ㄙ)
an office (in old China) located at seaports functioning like today's customs

市面(ㄕˋ ㄇㄧㄢˋ)or 市面兒(ㄕˋ ㄇㄧㄚˋㄦ)
①business situations; market conditions: 台北市面繁榮。Business in Taipei is flourishing. ② the world of the rich; the sights and splendors in big cities

市民(ㄕˋ ㄇㄧㄣˊ)
the residents of a city; citizens

市民文化(ㄕˋ ㄇㄧㄣˊ ㄨㄣˊ ㄏㄨㄚˋ)
civic culture

市畝(ㄕˋ ㄇㄨˇ)
a unit in Chinese measurement roughly 6,000 square feet in area

市道小人(ㄕˋ ㄉㄠˋ ㄒㄧㄠˇ ㄖㄣˊ)
a small-time trader (who counts only the pennies)

市內(ㄕˋ ㄋㄟˋ)
in the city

市里(ㄕˋ ㄌㄧˇ)
a unit of length equivalent to 500 meters

市立(ㄕˋ ㄌㄧˋ)
established with city government funds; operated by, or under the jurisdiction of a city government; municipal

市棍(ㄕˋ ㄍㄨㄣˋ)
a city shark; a rascal of a city or marketplace

市公所(ㄕˋ ㄍㄨㄥ ㄙㄨㄛˇ)
a city or town office

市儈(ㄕˋ ㄎㄨㄞˋ)
①a broker ②a crafty businessman: 市儈祇顧賺錢。A crafty businessman knows only how to make money.

市儈氣(ㄕˋ ㄎㄨㄞˋ ㄑㄧˋ)
vulgar and greedy (persons)

市虎(ㄕˋ ㄏㄨˇ)
①automobiles (which maim or kill people like tigers on the loose) ② If repeated often, a lie is accepted as a truth.

市集(ㄕˋ ㄐㄧˊ)
a gathering held regularly at intervals for trading or bartering purposes; a market

市價(ㄕˋ ㄐㄧㄚˋ)
market prices; the current price (of a commodity): 這種貨品的市價是多少? What is the market price of this product?

市郊(ㄕˋ ㄐㄧㄠ)
the suburbs or outskirts of a city; suburbia: 在夏天他們遷居市郊。They moved to the suburbs in summer.

市斤(ㄕˋ ㄐㄧㄣ)
a catty (equaling to 500 grams or half a kilogram)

市井之徒(ㄕˋ ㄐㄧㄥˇ ㄓ ㄊㄨˊ)
vulgar people who place money before anything else in life

市井無賴(ㄕˋ ㄐㄧㄥˇ ㄨˊ ㄌㄞˋ)
the scoundrels of the marketplace

市區(ㄕˋ ㄑㄩ)
①the area within the city limits ②the downtown area: 市區的公車交通極為便利。Bus service in the downtown area is excellent.

市制(ㄕˋ ㄓˋ)or 市用制(ㄕˋ ㄩㄥˋ ㄓˋ)
a supplementary system in Chinese measurement

市鎮(ㄕˋ ㄓㄣˋ)
small towns; towns

市鎮公所(ㄕˋ ㄓㄣˋ ㄍㄨㄥ ㄙㄨㄛˇ)
a town office

市長(ㄕˋ ㄓㄤˇ)
the mayor of a city: 他是這城市的市長。He is the mayor of the city.

市政(ㄕˋ ㄓㄥˋ)
municipal administration

市政府(ㄕˋ ㄓㄥˋ ㄈㄨˇ)
a city government

市尺(ㄕˋ ㄔˇ)
a unit of Chinese measurement equivalent to ⅓ of a meter

市朝(ㄕˋ ㄔㄠˊ)
a public place or square (in a city)

市廛(ㄕˋ ㄔㄢˊ)
①a business district ② stores in a market or street

市場(ㄕˋ ㄔㄤˇ)or(ㄕˋ ㄔㄤˊ)
(domestic or world) market; a marketplace: 市場正欣欣向榮。The market is flourishing.

市場調查(ㄕˋ ㄔㄤˇ ㄉㄧㄠˋ ㄔㄚˊ)
a market survey

市場價格(ㄕˋ ㄔㄤˇ ㄐㄧㄚˋ ㄍㄜˊ)

the market price

市聲(ㄕˋ ㄕㄥ)
(literally) the voices of the marketplace—hawkings and hagglings

市容(ㄕˋ ㄖㄨㄥˊ)
the appearance of a city (including buildings, roads, environmental sanitation, etc.)

市肆(ㄕˋ ㄙˋ)
shops and stores in a market

市恩(ㄕˋ ㄣ)
to distribute favors with a view to gaining popularity

市議會(ㄕˋ ㄧˋ ㄏㄨㄟˋ)
a city council

市隱(ㄕˋ ㄧㄣˇ)
a hermit in a city

【布】 1307 ㄅㄨˋ buh bù

1. cloth; textiles
2. to declare, announce or proclaim
3. to display; to distribute or disseminate; to spread out
4. a Chinese family name

布帛(ㄅㄨˋ ㄅㄛˊ)
(collectively) cloth or textiles

布被之譏(ㄅㄨˋ ㄅㄟˋ ㄓ ㄐㄧ)
pretending to be humble or thrifty

布匹 or 布疋(ㄅㄨˋ ㄆㄧˇ)
piece goods; dry goods

布票(ㄅㄨˋ ㄆㄧㄠˋ)
a cloth coupon

布幕(ㄅㄨˋ ㄇㄨˋ)
the curtain of a stage

布防(ㄅㄨˋ ㄈㄤˊ)
to deploy troops in anticipation of an enemy attack; to organize the defence

布達佩斯(ㄅㄨˋ ㄉㄚˊ ㄆㄟˋ ㄙ)
Budapest, capital of Hungary

布達拉寺(ㄅㄨˋ ㄉㄚˊ ㄌㄚ ㄙˋ)
Potala, palace of the Dalai Lama at Lhasa

布袋(ㄅㄨˋ ㄉㄞˋ)
a sack made of cloth; a calico sack (for grains, etc.)

布袋蓮(ㄅㄨˋ ㄉㄞˋ ㄌㄧㄢˊ)
a water hyacinth

布袋戲(ㄅㄨˋ ㄉㄞˋ ㄒㄧˋ)
a kind of puppet show typical in southeast China featuring figures of tiny sacks topped with painted heads manipulated with hands and fingers

布袋裝(ㄅㄨˋ ㄉㄞˋ ㄓㄨㄤ)
the sack dress

布道(ㄅㄨˋ ㄉㄠˋ)
(religion) to preach the Gospel; to evangelize

布店(ㄅㄨˋ ㄉㄧㄢˋ)
a drapery store

布丁(ㄅㄨˋ ㄉㄧㄥ)
a pudding

布頭(ㄅㄨˋ ㄊㄡˊ)
odd bits of cloth

布農(ㄅㄨˋ ㄋㄨㄥˊ)
the Bunu tribe among the aborigines in Taiwan

布拉格(ㄅㄨˋ ㄌㄚ ㄍㄜˊ)
Prague, the capital of Czechoslovakia

布雷(ㄅㄨˋ ㄌㄟˊ)
to lay mines; to mine

布簾(ㄅㄨˋ ㄌㄧㄢˊ)
a door curtain made of cloth

布魯塞爾(ㄅㄨˋ ㄌㄨˇ ㄙㄞˋ ㄦˇ)
Brussels, capital of Belgium

布隆迪(ㄅㄨˋ ㄌㄨㄥˊ ㄉㄧˊ)
Burundi 亦作「蒲隆地」

布告(ㄅㄨˋ ㄍㄠˋ)
① a public notice: 他在張貼布告。He is pasting up a notice. ② to make a public announcement

布告欄(ㄅㄨˋ ㄍㄠˋ ㄌㄢˊ)
a notice board; a bulletin board

布穀(ㄅㄨˋ ㄍㄨˇ)
① a cuckoo ② to sow seeds of grain

布穀鳥(ㄅㄨˋ ㄍㄨˇ ㄋㄧㄠˇ)
a cuckoo

布鼓雷門(ㄅㄨˋ ㄍㄨˇ ㄌㄟˊ ㄇㄣˊ)
to show off one's limited knowledge in the presence of a learned man; to make oneself a laughingstock

布褐(ㄅㄨˋ ㄏㄜˊ)
① unbleached cotton clothes ② commoners

布景(ㄅㄨˋ ㄐㄧㄥˇ)
(in motion picture production or stage shows) sets; a setting 亦作「佈景」

布局(ㄅㄨˋ ㄐㄩˊ)
① overall arrangement; layout; distribution: 台北新市區的布局尚可。The layout of new urban districts in Taipei is acceptable. ② the composition (of a picture, a piece of writing, etc.) ③ the position (of pieces on a chessboard)

布置(ㄅㄨˋ ㄓˋ)
to fix up; to decorate: 他們正在布置會場。They are fixing up a place for a meeting.

布政使(ㄅㄨˋ ㄓㄥˋ ㄕˇ) or (ㄅㄨˋ ㄓㄥˋ ㄕˋ)
(Ching Dynasty) a provincial official in charge of civil and financial administration

布施(ㄅㄨˋ ㄕ)
(Buddhism) almsgiving; donation: 不要懇求別人布施。Don't beg others for alms.

布商(ㄅㄨˋ ㄕㄤ)
dry goods dealers; clothiers

布爾喬亞(ㄅㄨˋ ㄦˇ ㄑㄧㄠˊ ㄧㄚˇ)
the bourgeois 亦作「中產階級」

布爾希維克(ㄅㄨˋ ㄦˇ ㄒㄧ ㄨㄟˊ ㄎㄜˋ)
Bolshevik, a member of the Russian Communist Party

布衣(ㄅㄨˋ ㄧ)
① dresses made of common cloth ② commoners

布衣之交(ㄅㄨˋ ㄧ ㄓ ㄐㄧㄠ)
a friend one made when one was a commoner or in humble circumstances

布宜諾斯艾利斯(ㄅㄨˋ ㄧˊ ㄋㄨㄛˋ ㄙ ㄞˋ ㄌㄧˋ ㄙ)
Buenos Aires, capital of Argentina

三畫

【帆】 1308 1.(帆) ㄈㄢ farn fán

1. a sail (of a boat): 我們的船將所有的帆都張開了。Our ship had all sail spread.
2. a boat

帆篷(ㄈㄢ ㄆㄥˊ)
a sail

帆檣(ㄈㄢ ㄑㄧㄤˊ)
the mast of a ship

帆柱(ㄈㄢ ㄓㄨˋ)
a mast

帆船(ㄈㄢ ㄔㄨㄢˊ)
a sailboat

帆影(ㄈㄢˊ ㄧㄥˇ)
(literally) the shadows of sails—boats in water

【帆】 1308
2. (帆) ㄈㄢ fan fān
canvas; sailcloth: 船起滿帆疾駛。The ship flew all its canvas.

帆布(ㄈㄢ ㄅㄨˋ)
canvas

帆布鞋(ㄈㄢ ㄅㄨˋ ㄒㄧㄝˊ)
canvas shoes

四畫

【希】 1309
ㄒㄧ shi xī
1. rare; strange; precious: 那博物館中藏有很多希世之寶。The museum is full of rare treasures.
2. to hope; to expect; to wish; to desire; to long: 我希望明天不會下雨。I hope it will not rain tomorrow.
3. to come to a stop gradually
4. to become silent
5. very; much
6. a Chinese family name

希伯來人(ㄒㄧ ㄅㄛˊ ㄌㄞˊ ㄖㄣˊ)
Hebrew (the race)

希伯來文(ㄒㄧ ㄅㄛˊ ㄌㄞˊ ㄨㄣˊ)
Hebrew (the language)

希慕(ㄒㄧ ㄇㄨˋ)
to long for; to be desirous of: 這位女伶希慕成名。This actress longs for fame.

希特勒(ㄒㄧ ㄊㄜˋ ㄌㄜˋ)
Adolf Hitler (1889-1945), German dictator

希圖(ㄒㄧ ㄊㄨˊ)
to hope and scheme for

希臘(ㄒㄧ ㄌㄚˋ)
Greece; Greek

希臘教會(ㄒㄧ ㄌㄚˋ ㄐㄧㄠˋ ㄏㄨㄟˋ)or 希臘正教(ㄒㄧ ㄌㄚˋ ㄓㄥˋ ㄐㄧㄠˋ)
Greek Orthodox Church, or Orthodox Eastern Church

希臘主義(ㄒㄧ ㄌㄚˋ ㄓㄨˇ ㄧˋ)
Grecism; Hellenism

希臘人(ㄒㄧ ㄌㄚˋ ㄖㄣˊ)
a Greek

希臘字母(ㄒㄧ ㄌㄚˋ ㄗˋ ㄇㄨˇ)
the Greek alphabet

希臘文化(ㄒㄧ ㄌㄚˋ ㄨㄣˊ ㄏㄨㄚˋ)
Greek culture

希罕(ㄒㄧ ㄏㄢˇ)
① rare; uncommon ② to care; to value; to hold preciously

希冀(ㄒㄧ ㄐㄧˋ)
to desire; to wish for: 我們都希冀獲得快樂和健康。We all desire happiness and health.

希奇(ㄒㄧ ㄑㄧˊ)
① strange; rare; uncommon ② to value; to attach importance to; to appreciate

希企(ㄒㄧ ㄑㄧˋ)or 希求(ㄒㄧ ㄑㄧㄡˊ)
to hope for; to hope to

希寵(ㄒㄧ ㄔㄨㄥˇ)
to curry favor (especially from a superior)

希世之珍(ㄒㄧ ㄕˋ ㄓ ㄓㄣ)
a very rare treasure; an invaluable gem; a timeless treasure

希榮(ㄒㄧ ㄖㄨㄥˊ)
to aspire for the glory of high office

希有(ㄒㄧ ㄧㄡˇ)
very rare

希有之事(ㄒㄧ ㄧㄡˇ ㄓ ㄕˋ)
a rarity; an uncommon occurrence

希微(ㄒㄧ ㄨㄟˊ)
extremely little (amount); very little

希望(ㄒㄧ ㄨㄤˋ)
a hope; a wish; expectations; to hope; to wish; to desire; to look forward to: 希望全落空了。All hope is gone.

五畫

【帔】 1310
ㄆㄟˋ pey pèi
a cape (usually worn by a woman)

【帑】 1311
ㄊㄤˇ taang tǎng
1. a treasury
2. public funds or money

帑藏(ㄊㄤˇ ㄗㄤˋ)
a treasury

【帕】 1312
ㄆㄚˋ pah pà
1. a turban
2. to wrap and bind
3. a handkerchief
4. a veil
5. a curtain made of cloth

帕米爾(ㄆㄚˋ ㄇㄧˇ ㄦˇ)
the Pamirs, known as the "roof of the world"

帕頭(ㄆㄚˋ ㄊㄡˊ)
a turban; a headdress

帕子(ㄆㄚˋ ·ㄗ)
a kerchief used for carrying a package

【帖】 1313
1. ㄊㄧㄝ tie tiē
1. submissive or obedient
2. proper

帖伏 or 帖服(ㄊㄧㄝ ㄈㄨˊ)
submissive and subservient

帖耳(ㄊㄧㄝ ㄦˇ)
(literally) to droop one's ears like a dog—submissive

【帖】 1313
2. ㄊㄧㄝˇ tiee tiě
1. an invitation card: 市長發出宴客請帖。The mayor sent out invitation cards to a dinner party.
2. a label; a placard; a document
3. a copybook (of calligraphy)
4. a medical prescription

帖子(ㄊㄧㄝˇ ·ㄗ)or 帖兒(ㄊㄧㄝˇㄦ)
① an invitation card or letter ② a money order

【帖】 1313
3. ㄊㄧㄝˋ tieh tiè
1. to write on silk
2. to engrave characters of famous calligraphers on stone
3. test papers (in the dynasties of Tang, Sung and Yüan)

帖木兒(ㄊㄧㄝˋ ㄇㄨˋ ㄦˊ)
Timur, a Mongolian conqueror who founded the Timur Empire, 1369-1502, in the greater part of the Middle East and parts of India

帖括(ㄊㄧㄝˋ ㄍㄨㄚ)
(formerly) a style of formal writing adopted by candidates during civil service examinations

【帗】 1314
ㄈㄨˊ fwu fú
(in ancient China) a multicolored prop used in dancing rituals

【帘】 1315
ㄌㄧㄢˊ lian lián
1. a flag sign of a winehouse or tavern
2. a door or window screen

〔巾部〕

帘子(ㄌㄧㄢˊ ·ㄗ)or 帘兒(ㄌㄧㄚˊㄦ)
a screen for a door or a window

【帙】 1316
ㄓˋ jyh zhì
a book wrapper or casing: 書桌上有一帙公文。There is a casing of documents on the desk.

【帚】 1317
ㄓㄡˇ jou zhǒu
a broom; a besom

帚星(ㄓㄡˇ ㄒㄧㄥ)
① a comet ② a jinx

【帛】 1318
ㄅㄛˊ bor bó
1. (collectively) silk fabrics
2. a Chinese family name

帛帶(ㄅㄛˊ ㄉㄞˋ)
a silk waist band worn by officials or wealthy men in old China

帛書(ㄅㄛˊ ㄕㄨ)
a letter, a book or a document written on silk (before paper was invented)

六畫

【帥】 1319
ㄕㄨㄞˋ shuay shuài
(又讀 ㄕㄨㄛˋ shuoh shuò)
1. the commanding general; commander-in-chief: 誰是陸軍統帥? Who's the commanding general of the army?
2. to command; to lead
3. to follow or comply (with instruction or orders)
4. (slang) dashing; smart-looking: 他長得眞帥。He is very smart-looking.
5. a Chinese family name

帥領(ㄕㄨㄞˋ ㄌㄧㄥˇ)
to command: 誰帥領陸軍? Who commands the army?

帥令(ㄕㄨㄞˋ ㄌㄧㄥˋ)
the orders of the commander-in-chief

帥旗(ㄕㄨㄞˋ ㄑㄧˊ)
the flag of the commander-in-chief

帥字旗(ㄕㄨㄞˋ ㄗˋ ㄑㄧˊ)
a flag on which the character "帥" is embroidered; the flag of the commander-in-chief

帥印(ㄕㄨㄞˋ ㄧㄣˋ)
the seal of the commander-in-chief

【帝】 1320
ㄉㄧˋ dih dì
1. the emperor; a ruler
2. a god; a deified being
3. Heaven (as a divine being)
4. imperial

帝都(ㄉㄧˋ ㄉㄨ)
the imperial capital

帝庭(ㄉㄧˋ ㄊㄧㄥˊ)
the Heavenly court

帝國(ㄉㄧˋ ㄍㄨㄛˊ)
an empire; a monarchy

帝國大學(ㄉㄧˋ ㄍㄨㄛˊ ㄉㄚˋ ㄒㄩㄝˊ)
Imperial University (of Tokyo)

帝國主義(ㄉㄧˋ ㄍㄨㄛˊ ㄓㄨˇ ㄧˋ)
imperialism

帝嚳(ㄉㄧˋ ㄎㄨˋ)
name of an ancient emperor (accession, c. 2435 B.C.)

帝號(ㄉㄧˋ ㄏㄠˋ)
the appellation of an emperor

帝畿(ㄉㄧˋ ㄐㄧ)
the imperial capital and its environs

帝京(ㄉㄧˋ ㄐㄧㄥ)
the imperial capital

帝居(ㄉㄧˋ ㄐㄩ)
the imperial capital 參看「帝畿」

帝闕(ㄉㄧˋ ㄑㄩㄝˋ)
the gate of the emperor's palace

帝鄉(ㄉㄧˋ ㄒㄧㄤ)
① the hometown of the emperor ② the palace of the King of Heaven; heavenly abodes

帝制(ㄉㄧˋ ㄓˋ)
the institutions of an empire; monarchy

帝雉(ㄉㄧˋ ㄓˋ)
(fowl) a mikado pheasant

帝摯(ㄉㄧˋ ㄓˋ)
name of an ancient emperor (accession, c. 2365 B.C.)

帝室(ㄉㄧˋ ㄕˋ)
the royal family

帝舜(ㄉㄧˋ ㄕㄨㄣˋ)
Emperor Shun (accession, c. 2255 B.C.), one of China's sage kings

帝祚(ㄉㄧˋ ㄗㄨㄛˋ)
the imperial throne

帝俄(ㄉㄧˋ ㄜˊ)
tsarist Russia

帝業(ㄉㄧˋ ㄧㄝˋ)
the reign of an emperor; an empire

帝堯(ㄉㄧˋ ㄧㄠˊ)
Emperor Yao (accession, c. 2356 B.C.), one of China's sage kings

帝位(ㄉㄧˋ ㄨㄟˋ)
the emperor's throne

帝王(ㄉㄧˋ ㄨㄤˊ)
the emperor; the king; the throne

七畫

【帨】 1321
ㄕㄨㄟˋ shuey shuì
a kerchief; a handkerchief

【師】 1322
ㄕ shy shī
1. a division in the Chinese army
2. an army
3. a model; an example
4. a master; a teacher; a tutor
5. to teach
6. to pattern or model after another
7. a specialist (especially of medicine, painting, music, divining, etc.)
8. a local administrative chief
9. a Chinese family name

師保萬民(ㄕ ㄅㄠˇ ㄨㄢˋ ㄇㄧㄣˊ)
to act as teacher and guardian of the myriad people

師表(ㄕ ㄅㄧㄠˇ)
a paragon or model worthy of emulation: 她不愧是爲人師表。She is worthy of the name of teacher.

師部(ㄕ ㄅㄨˋ)
a division headquarters

師妹(ㄕ ㄇㄟˋ)
① a younger female fellow student under the same master or teacher ② a polite salutation for the teacher's daughter younger than oneself

師門(ㄕ ㄇㄣˊ)
a school or sect founded by a master

師母(ㄕ ㄇㄨˇ)or 師娘(ㄕ ㄋㄧㄤˊ)
①the wife of one's tutor, teacher or master ②a polite reference to the wife of one's senior
師法(ㄕ ㄈㄚˇ)
①to pattern after; to imitate; to emulate ②methods taught by one's teacher
師範(ㄕ ㄈㄢˋ)
①worthy of being patterned after ②a master, tutor or teacher ③to imitate; to emulate ④short for normal schools
師範大學(ㄕ ㄈㄢˋ ㄉㄚˋ ㄒㄩㄝˊ)
a normal university: 師範大學的目的是培訓師資。A normal university aims at training teachers.
師範教育(ㄕ ㄈㄢˋ ㄐㄧㄠˋ ㄩˋ)
normal education
師範學校(ㄕ ㄈㄢˋ ㄒㄩㄝˊ ㄒㄧㄠˋ)
a normal school
師範學院(ㄕ ㄈㄢˋ ㄒㄩㄝˊ ㄩㄢˋ)
a normal (or teachers) college
師範專科學校(ㄕ ㄈㄢˋ ㄓㄨㄢ ㄎㄜ ㄒㄩㄝˊ ㄒㄧㄠˋ)
a junior teachers college
師範生(ㄕ ㄈㄢˋ ㄕㄥ)
the students of a normal school or university
師傅(ㄕ ㄈㄨˋ)
①(collectively) teachers; masters; tutors ②the tutors of a king or an emperor ③a polite term of address for an artisan as a carpenter, cook, etc.
師父(ㄕ ·ㄈㄨ)
①tutors; masters; teachers ②a respectful term of address for monks, nuns, etc.
師道(ㄕ ㄉㄠˋ)
the teacher's status and teachings: 我們應當尊崇師道。We should respect the teacher's status and teachings.
師弟(ㄕ ㄉㄧˋ)
①a younger male fellow student or apprentice under the same tutor ②a polite salutation for the teacher's son younger than oneself
師徒(ㄕ ㄊㄨˊ)
the master and his student(s) or apprentice(s)
師團(ㄕ ㄊㄨㄢˊ)
(in Japanese military system) a division of approximately 10,000 men which can be expanded to 20,000 in wartime
師老無功(ㄕ ㄌㄠˇ ㄨˊ ㄍㄨㄥ)
troops fighting for a long time without success; bogged down in a war
師旅(ㄕ ㄌㄩˇ)
divisions and brigades—troops in general
師姑(ㄕ ㄍㄨ)
a polite salutation for a Buddhist nun
師古(ㄕ ㄍㄨˇ)
to pattern after the ancient or old (ways, methods, etc.)
師姊(ㄕ ㄐㄧㄝˇ)
①an elder female fellow student under the same master or teacher ②a polite salutation for the teacher's daughter elder than oneself
師其故智(ㄕ ㄑㄧˊ ㄍㄨˋ ㄓˋ)
to copy an old plan or method
師心自用(ㄕ ㄒㄧㄣ ㄗˋ ㄩㄥˋ)
conceited; opinionated: 他這個人師心自用。He is an opinionated person.
師兄(ㄕ ㄒㄩㄥ)
①an elder male fellow student under the same master or tutor ②a polite salutation for the teacher's son elder than oneself
師直爲壯(ㄕ ㄓˊ ㄨㄟˊ ㄓㄨㄤˋ)
The morale of troops will be high if they fight for a just cause.
師長(ㄕ ㄓㄤˇ)
①one's teachers; faculty members ②a division commander
師丈(ㄕ ㄓㄤˋ)
the husband of one's teacher
師承(ㄕ ㄔㄥˊ)
to have learned under (especially referring to a particular school of learning)
師出無名(ㄕ ㄔㄨ ㄨˊ ㄇㄧㄥˊ)
to fight a war without a just cause
師事(ㄕ ㄕˋ)
to serve and respect (another) as one's teacher
師生(ㄕ ㄕㄥ)
teachers and students
師資(ㄕ ㄗ)
①the qualifications of a teacher ②teachers
師恩如海(ㄕ ㄣ ㄖㄨˊ ㄏㄞˇ)
The bequeathal of a good teacher is as deep as the sea. 或 The benefits one gets from his teacher are immeasurable.
師爺(ㄕ ㄧㄝˊ)
①one's teacher's father ②one's teacher's teacher ③(in ancient China) a confidential secretary who knows all the tricks of officialdom and the loopholes of the law
師友(ㄕ ㄧㄡˇ)
①a friend from whom one can seek advice②(in ancient China) an official post in charge of the princes' education
師嚴道尊(ㄕ ㄧㄢˊ ㄉㄠˋ ㄗㄨㄣ)
The teacher is strict in teaching; therefore, what he teaches will be respected.

【席】 1323 ㄒㄧˊ shyi xí
1. a mat
2. a feast
3. a seat; to take a seat
4. to rely on
5. (rarely) a sail
6. a Chinese family name

席不暇暖(ㄒㄧˊ ㄅㄨˋ ㄒㄧㄚˊ ㄋㄨㄢˇ)
(literally) cannot sit long enough to warm the seat—very busy
席夢思牀(ㄒㄧˊ ㄇㄥˋ ㄙ ㄔㄨㄤˊ)
a Simmons bed
席豐履厚(ㄒㄧˊ ㄈㄥ ㄌㄩˇ ㄏㄡˋ)
(usually said of large inherited wealth) very well-to-do
席地而坐(ㄒㄧˊ ㄉㄧˋ ㄦˊ ㄗㄨㄛˋ)
to sit on the ground
席卷 or 席捲(ㄒㄧˊ ㄐㄩㄢˇ)
①to roll up like a mat—to take away everything ②to sweep across
席卷天下 or 席捲天下(ㄒㄧˊ ㄐㄩㄢˇ ㄊㄧㄢ ㄒㄧㄚˋ)

〔巾部〕

(literally) to roll the world up like a mat—to take all of it; to conquer the world

席捲而去(ㄒㄧˊ ㄐㄩㄢˇ ㄦˊ ㄑㄩˋ)
to leave nothing behind; to take everything away

席珍待聘(ㄒㄧˊ ㄓㄣ ㄉㄞˋ ㄆㄧㄣˋ)
a man of capability awaiting employment

席上(ㄒㄧˊ ㄕㄤˋ)
①scholars; the learned ② on the dining table

席上之珍(ㄒㄧˊ ㄕㄤˋ ㄓ ㄓㄣ)
(literally) the dainties for a feast—the virtues of a person

席次(ㄒㄧˊ ㄘˋ)
the order of seats; seating arrangement

席位(ㄒㄧˊ ㄨㄟˋ)
a seat (at a conference, in a legislative assembly, etc.)

八畫

【帳】 1324 ㄓㄤˋ janq zhàng

1. a canopy above the bed
2. a tent
3. a curtain or screen; a mosquito net
4. a scroll (sent as a gift for a wedding, birthday party, funeral, etc.)
5. same as 賬

帳簿(ㄓㄤˋ ㄅㄨˋ)
an account book; books of accounts 亦作「賬簿」

帳棚(ㄓㄤˋ ㄆㄥˊ)
a tent

帳篷(ㄓㄤˋ ㄆㄥˊ)
a tent; a mat-shed

帳幔(ㄓㄤˋ ㄇㄢˋ)
a tent

帳目(ㄓㄤˋ ㄇㄨˋ)
accounts; itemized bills 亦作「賬目」

帳幕(ㄓㄤˋ ㄇㄨˋ)
a tent 參看「帳棚」

帳房(ㄓㄤˋ ㄈㄤˊ)
①a cashier; a bursar ②a cashier's office 亦作「賬房」

帳單(ㄓㄤˋ ㄉㄢ)
a bill; a check 亦作「賬單」

帳頂(ㄓㄤˋ ㄉㄧㄥˇ)
the top of a mosquito net

帳簾(ㄓㄤˋ ㄌㄧㄢˊ)
screens or curtains for doors or windows

帳鉤(ㄓㄤˋ ㄍㄡ)
hooks for holding open a mosquito net; curtain-hooks

帳款(ㄓㄤˋ ㄎㄨㄢˇ)
funds on account; credit

帳戶(ㄓㄤˋ ㄏㄨˋ)
a bank account: 我想在銀行開立帳戶。I want to open an account in this bank.

帳戶名稱(ㄓㄤˋ ㄏㄨˋ ㄇㄧㄥˊ ㄔㄥ)
name of an account; title of an account

帳子(ㄓㄤˋ ˙ㄗ)
a mosquito net

帳簷(ㄓㄤˋ ㄧㄢˊ)
the flaps along the edge of a tent roof

帳務(ㄓㄤˋ ㄨˋ)
accounts in general 亦作「賬務」

【帶】 1325 ㄉㄞˋ day dài

1. a girdle; a sash; a belt; a band; a ribbon; a string; a tie
2. to wear (a smile, sword, etc.)
3. to bear; to take or bring along: 請帶這封信給他。Please bring this letter to him.
4. to lead (the way, troops, etc.); to head (an army, etc.)
5. a climatic zone: 臺灣位在亞熱帶。Taiwan is in the subtropical zone.

帶兵(ㄉㄞˋ ㄅㄧㄥ)
①to lead troops ②to carry arms

帶兵官(ㄉㄞˋ ㄅㄧㄥ ㄍㄨㄢ)
an officer who has a field command (as distinct from a staff officer doing office work)

帶病工作(ㄉㄞˋ ㄅㄧㄥˋ ㄍㄨㄥ ㄗㄨㄛˋ)
to keep on working in spite of one's illness: 她帶病繼續工作。She went on working in spite of her illness.

帶髮修行(ㄉㄞˋ ㄈㄚˇ ㄒㄧㄡ ㄒㄧㄥˊ)
to submit to Buddhist discipline while still wearing one's hair (A Buddhist monk or nun is supposed to have his or her head shaved.)

帶分數(ㄉㄞˋ ㄈㄣ ㄕㄨˋ)
(mathematics) a mixed fraction

帶電(ㄉㄞˋ ㄉㄧㄢˋ)
electrification

帶電體(ㄉㄞˋ ㄉㄧㄢˋ ㄊㄧˇ)
an electrified body

帶隊(ㄉㄞˋ ㄉㄨㄟˋ)
①to lead a group ②the leader of a group, party or mission

帶動(ㄉㄞˋ ㄉㄨㄥˋ)
to drive; to spur on; to bring along: 這機器是由蒸汽所帶動的。This machinery is driven by steam.

帶頭(ㄉㄞˋ ㄊㄡˊ)
to pioneer; to initiate; to lead; to do trailblazing work

帶頭作用(ㄉㄞˋ ㄊㄡˊ ㄗㄨㄛˋ ㄩㄥˋ)
the example set by someone in pioneering work

帶徒弟(ㄉㄞˋ ㄊㄨˊ ㄉㄧˋ)
to train apprentices

帶牛佩犢(ㄉㄞˋ ㄋㄧㄡˊ ㄆㄟˋ ㄉㄨˊ)
to take to farming after discarding the arms

帶來(ㄉㄞˋ ˙ㄌㄞ)
to bring here

帶累(ㄉㄞˋ ㄌㄟˋ)
to compromise oneself; to get others involved in (trouble, etc.)

帶厲山河(ㄉㄞˋ ㄌㄧˋ ㄕㄢ ㄏㄜˊ)
(a congratulatory greeting to a feudal lord on his inauguration) May the land bestowed on you remain forever in your family!

帶領(ㄉㄞˋ ㄌㄧㄥˇ)
to lead (an army, a party, etc.): 這探險隊係由我叔父帶領。The expedition was led by my uncle.

帶路(ㄉㄞˋ ㄌㄨˋ) or 帶道(ㄉㄞˋ ㄉㄠˋ)
to lead the way

帶壞(ㄉㄞˋ ㄏㄨㄞˋ)
to lead astray: 這小孩被不良的同伴帶壞了。The boy was led astray by bad companions.

帶回(ㄉㄞˋ ㄏㄨㄟˊ)
to bring back: 士兵們帶回十個俘虜。The soldiers came back bringing ten prisoners with them.

帶甲(ㄉㄞˋ ㄐㄧㄚˇ)

armored (fighters or soldiers)

帶勁(ㄉㄞˋ ㄐㄧㄣˋ)
①energetic; forceful: 他做事可眞帶勁。He works energetically. ②interesting; exciting; wonderful; terrific: 這場網球比賽眞帶勁。This tennis tournament is really terrific.

帶菌者(ㄉㄞˋ ㄐㄩㄣˋ ㄓㄜˇ)
(medicine) a carrier

帶球走(ㄉㄞˋ ㄑㄧㄡˊ ㄗㄡˇ)
(basketball) traveling; running with the ball

帶去(ㄉㄞˋ ˙ㄑㄩ)
to bring away; to take along: 你不能把這些報紙帶去。You cannot bring away these newspapers with you.

帶小數(ㄉㄞˋ ㄒㄧㄠˇ ㄕㄨˋ)
a whole number with a decimal

帶孝(ㄉㄞˋ ㄒㄧㄠˋ)
to wear mourning

帶笑(ㄉㄞˋ ㄒㄧㄠˋ)
smilingly; wearing a smile

帶羞(ㄉㄞˋ ㄒㄧㄡ)
to look shy or bashful

帶信(ㄉㄞˋ ㄒㄧㄣˋ)or 帶信兒(ㄉㄞˋ ㄒㄧㄜˋㄦ)
to take or bring a message; to bear a message

帶徵(ㄉㄞˋ ㄓㄥ)
a system of taxation in which the government can postpone levying taxes for famine, flood, etc. but people must pay a portion of the postponed taxes in each of the following years

帶手兒(ㄉㄞˋ ㄕㄡˇㄦ)
to do something at one's convenience

帶傷(ㄉㄞˋ ㄕㄤ)
to get wounded or injured

帶上(ㄉㄞˋ ˙ㄕㄤ)
①to present to you ②to bring out (the prisoner, etc.) ③to send or attach as incidental; in addition to

帶子(ㄉㄞˋ ˙ㄗ)
a piece of string; a ribbon; laces (of shoes, boots, etc.)

帶彩(ㄉㄞˋ ㄘㄞˇ)
(Peking opera) to play the act of bleeding from wound or injury

帶魚(ㄉㄞˋ ㄩˊ)
ribbonfish; hairtail

【帷】 1326
ㄨㄟˊ wei wéi

a curtain; a screen; a tent

帷薄不修(ㄨㄟˊ ㄅㄛˊ ㄅㄨˋ ㄒㄧㄡ)
(literally) The curtains are not fixed.—lewdness or debauchery of the females of one's family

帷幔(ㄨㄟˊ ㄇㄢˋ)
screens; cloth partitions

帷幕(ㄨㄟˊ ㄇㄨˋ)
①a tent ②參看「帷幄」

帷房(ㄨㄟˊ ㄈㄤˊ)
(literally) a curtained room—a woman's bedchamber

帷蓋(ㄨㄟˊ ㄍㄞˋ)
(literally) the curtain and cover of a cart—a repayment for services rendered

帷幄(ㄨㄟˊ ㄨㄛˋ)
a military tent 亦作「帷幕」: 司令官運籌帷幄。The commander devises strategies within the command tent.

【常】 1327
ㄔㄤˊ charng cháng

1. common; ordinary; normal: 這個字常用嗎? Is this word in common use?
2. long; lasting; permanent (jobs, etc.); eternal: 人生無常。Nothing is permanent in life.
3. often; frequent; frequently; regular; regularly: 她常去看電影。She goes to the movies quite often.
4. ordinarily; usually; on ordinary occasions
5. a rule; a principle
6. a Chinese family name

常備兵(ㄔㄤˊ ㄅㄟˋ ㄅㄧㄥ)
regulars (as distinct from reservists)

常備軍(ㄔㄤˊ ㄅㄟˋ ㄐㄩㄣ)
the standing army

常步走(ㄔㄤˊ ㄅㄨˋ ㄗㄡˇ)
(military drill) to march in measured steps but in a less rigid manner than goose step

常法(ㄔㄤˊ ㄈㄚˇ)
a law, practice, or principle that lasts

常服(ㄔㄤˊ ㄈㄨˊ)
ordinary or everyday clothes (as distinguished from formal dress)

常典(ㄔㄤˊ ㄉㄧㄢˇ)
usual rites; regular ceremony

常度(ㄔㄤˊ ㄉㄨˋ)
①a normal manner ②ordinary rules

常態(ㄔㄤˊ ㄊㄞˋ)
a normal carriage or manner; a normal state

常談(ㄔㄤˊ ㄊㄢˊ)
commonplace talks or remarks; platitudes

常年(ㄔㄤˊ ㄋㄧㄢˊ)
throughout the year; all the year round

常年費(ㄔㄤˊ ㄋㄧㄢˊ ㄈㄟˋ)
regular annual fees

常年大會(ㄔㄤˊ ㄋㄧㄢˊ ㄉㄚˋ ㄏㄨㄟˋ)
annual meetings or conventions

常禮(ㄔㄤˊ ㄌㄧˇ)
common or everyday courtesy

常禮服(ㄔㄤˊ ㄌㄧˇ ㄈㄨˊ)
ordinary formal clothes as distinguished from full formal dress

常理(ㄔㄤˊ ㄌㄧˇ)
convention; general consent

常例(ㄔㄤˊ ㄌㄧˋ)
regular order or procedures; usual or common practices; an ordinary way

常綠植物(ㄔㄤˊ ㄌㄩˋ ㄓˊ ㄨˋ)
an evergreen plant

常綠樹(ㄔㄤˊ ㄌㄩˋ ㄕㄨˋ)
evergreen trees: 松、柏和針樅是常綠樹。The pine, cedar and spruce are evergreen trees.

常規(ㄔㄤˊ ㄍㄨㄟ)
ordinary rules or practices

常軌(ㄔㄤˊ ㄍㄨㄟˇ)
the ordinary course of events

常客(ㄔㄤˊ ㄎㄜˋ)
a frequent guest; a frequenter (of bars, theaters, etc.)

常會(ㄔㄤˊ ㄏㄨㄟˋ)
①regular meetings or conventions ②to be apt to; to happen often

常久(ㄔㄤˊ ㄐㄧㄡˇ)
for a long time: 你常久沒來

了。You have not been here for a long time.
常見(ㄔㄤˊ ㄐㄧㄢˋ)
to see or to be seen frequently: 我們常見他去公園。We often see him go to the park.
常青(ㄔㄤˊ ㄑㄧㄥ)or 常綠(ㄔㄤˊ ㄌㄩˋ)
evergreen
常情(ㄔㄤˊ ㄑㄧㄥˊ)
man's natural action or reaction under certain circumstances
常去(ㄔㄤˊ ㄑㄩˋ)
to go often: 在夏天他常去游泳。In summer he often goes swimming.
常州(ㄔㄤˊ ㄓㄡ)
Changchow, a city in Kiangsu along the Shanghai-Nanking Railway
常住(ㄔㄤˊ ㄓㄨˋ)
①(Buddhism) changeless; permanent ②a permanent lodger—a monk or a nun ③ a Buddhist ritual apparatus ④a temple
常駐(ㄔㄤˊ ㄓㄨˋ)
①standing (members, etc.) ②(said of a taxcollector, policeman, etc.) to be stationed (at a school, factory, locality, etc.) ③ durable (beauty, charm or youthfulness)
常產(ㄔㄤˊ ㄔㄢˇ)
immovable property; real estate
常常(ㄔㄤˊ ㄔㄤˊ)
often; frequently: 她常常讀書到深夜。She often studies deep into the night.
常川(ㄔㄤˊ ㄔㄨㄢ)
incessantly; constantly; regularly
常春藤(ㄔㄤˊ ㄔㄨㄣ ㄊㄥˊ)
ivy; bindwood
常事(ㄔㄤˊ ㄕˋ)
①an oft-repeated incident or event; routine ②a commonplace happening
常識(ㄔㄤˊ ㄕˋ)
①general knowledge (as distinct from expertise) ② common sense ③a subject in primary school curricula which includes the ABCs of natural and social sciences
常設(ㄔㄤˊ ㄕㄜˋ)
standing; permanent
常勝軍(ㄔㄤˊ ㄕㄥˋ ㄐㄩㄣ)
①the "Ever Triumphant Army", a term referring to the rifle troops which quelled the Taiping Rebellion in the Ching Dynasty ② an invincible army
常數(ㄔㄤˊ ㄕㄨˋ)
(mathematics) a constant
常人(ㄔㄤˊ ㄖㄣˊ)
ordinary people; an ordinary man; a normal person
常任(ㄔㄤˊ ㄖㄣˋ)
standing (members of a committee, government organ, etc.)
常有(ㄔㄤˊ ㄧㄡˇ)
usually; often; more often than not
常言(ㄔㄤˊ ㄧㄢˊ)
a popular saying; a proverb: 常言道:「健康勝於財富。」As the saying goes, "Health is above wealth."
常務委員(ㄔㄤˊ ㄨˋ ㄨㄟˇ ㄩㄢˊ)or 常委(ㄔㄤˊ ㄨㄟˇ)
the standing members of a committee
常溫(ㄔㄤˊ ㄨㄣ)
①normal atmospheric temperature (between 15° and 25°C) ②homoiothermy
常用(ㄔㄤˊ ㄩㄥˋ)
to use often; used often

九畫

【幅】 1328
ㄈㄨˊ fwu fú
1. the breadth of cloth or paper; a width (of cloth)
2. a border
3. a numerary adjunct for pictures, scrolls, etc.: 她畫了一幅母親的肖像。She painted a portrait of her mother.
幅度(ㄈㄨˊ ㄉㄨˋ)
①(said of stocks, commodity prices, etc.) the rate of rise or fall ②a range; an extent
幅寬(ㄈㄨˊ ㄎㄨㄢ)
the breadth (of a piece of cloth, etc.)
幅員(ㄈㄨˊ ㄩㄢˊ)
(literally) breadth and circumference—the territory (of a country)
幅員遼闊(ㄈㄨˊ ㄩㄢˊ ㄌㄧㄠˊ ㄎㄨㄛˋ)
(said of a country) very large: 中國是幅員遼闊的國家。China is a country with a vast territory.

【帽】 1329
ㄇㄠˋ maw mào
1. a hat; a headwear
2. a cap (of a fountain pen, screw, etc.)
帽襻(ㄇㄠˋ ㄆㄢˋ)
a hatband
帽鋪(ㄇㄠˋ ㄆㄨˋ)or 帽店(ㄇㄠˋ ㄉㄧㄢˋ)
a hat shop
帽帶(ㄇㄠˋ ㄉㄞˋ)
hat strings
帽花(ㄇㄠˋ ㄏㄨㄚ)
ornaments at the front of a hat (usually of jewels, etc.)
帽徽(ㄇㄠˋ ㄏㄨㄟ)
insignia on a cap
帽架(ㄇㄠˋ ㄐㄧㄚˋ)
a hatrack or stand; a hat tree
帽匠(ㄇㄠˋ ㄐㄧㄤˋ)
a hatter
帽針(ㄇㄠˋ ㄓㄣ)
a hatpin
帽章(ㄇㄠˋ ㄓㄤ)
a hat badge; a badge for a cap
帽舌(ㄇㄠˋ ㄕㄜˊ)
a visor
帽商(ㄇㄠˋ ㄕㄤ)
a milliner; a hatter
帽子(ㄇㄠˋ ·ㄗ)
①a hat; a headgear; a cap ② a label; a brand; a tag
帽簷(ㄇㄠˋ ㄧㄢˊ)
the brim of a hat
帽纓(ㄇㄠˋ ㄧㄥ)
a hat ribbon to hold the hat

【幀】 1330
ㄓㄥˋ jenq zhèng
1. a numerary adjunct (for paintings, pictures, photos, etc.)
2. one of a pair—as of scrolls

【幃】 1331
ㄨㄟˊ wei wéi
1. a curtain
2. a perfume bag
幃幄 or 帷幄(ㄨㄟˊ ㄨㄛˋ)

a military tent

【幄】 1332 ㄨㄛˋ woh wò
a big tent: 士兵常居於帷幄中。Soldiers usually live in big tents.

十畫

【幌】 1333 ㄏㄨㄤˇ hoang huǎng
a curtain; a cloth screen; a strip of cloth

幌子(ㄏㄨㄤˇ ·ㄗ)
①a flag-sign for a wine-shop or a store ②a front (especially a gaudy front) ③something to dazzle or cheat another with, as boasts or swashbuckling ways; a facade

十一畫

【幔】 1334 ㄇㄢˋ mann màn
1. a curtain; a screen
2. a tent

幔亭(ㄇㄢˋ ㄊㄧㄥˊ)
a tent pavilion

幔帳(ㄇㄢˋ ㄓㄤˋ)
a curtain; a screen; a canopy

幔室(ㄇㄢˋ ㄕˋ)
a tent chamber

幔子(ㄇㄢˋ ·ㄗ)
a curtain; a cloth screen

【幕】 1335 ㄇㄨˋ muh mù
1. a screen; a curtain
2. a tent
3. an advisor; staffs; private secretaries
4. an act: 那是一齣三幕五景的話劇。It is a play in three acts and five scenes.
5. to cover

幕賓(ㄇㄨˋ ㄅㄧㄣ)or 幕友(ㄇㄨˋ ㄧㄡˇ) or 幕客(ㄇㄨˋ ㄎㄜˋ)
staffs

幕府(ㄇㄨˋ ㄈㄨˇ)
① the office of the commanding officer ② a secretary or secretaries in such an office ③(in Japan) shogunate (government by a shogun or shoguns)

幕天席地(ㄇㄨˋ ㄊㄧㄢ ㄒㄧˊ ㄉㄧˋ)
(literally) to have the sky for canopy and the earth for mat—ambitious and broad-minded

幕僚(ㄇㄨˋ ㄌㄧㄠˊ)
staffs; secretaries; advisors

幕後(ㄇㄨˋ ㄏㄡˋ)
behind the scenes; backstage

幕後交易(ㄇㄨˋ ㄏㄡˋ ㄐㄧㄠ ㄧˋ)
behind-the-scenes deals

幕後新聞(ㄇㄨˋ ㄏㄡˋ ㄒㄧㄣ ㄨㄣˊ)
behind-the-scenes news; inside story

幕後人物(ㄇㄨˋ ㄏㄡˋ ㄖㄣˊ ㄨˋ)
behind-the-scenes personalities; string-pullers

幕後操縱(ㄇㄨˋ ㄏㄡˋ ㄘㄠ ㄗㄨㄥˋ)
to pull strings behind the scenes

幕燕(ㄇㄨˋ ㄧㄢˋ)
(literally) swallows that nest in a tent—being unaware of one's precarious situation

【幗】 1336 ㄍㄨㄛˊ gwo guó
a woman's headdress

【幘】 1337 ㄗㄜˊ tzer zé
a turban; a headdress

【幛】 1338 ㄓㄤˋ janq zhàng
a scroll of silk or cloth mounted or embroidered with appropriate wording sent as a gift for a wedding, funeral, etc.

幛子(ㄓㄤˋ ·ㄗ)
same as 幛

十二畫

【幟】 1339 ㄓˋ jyh zhì
1. a flag; a pennant; a pennon
2. a mark; a sign

【幞】 1340 ㄆㄨˊ pwu pú
a turban; a headdress; a scarf

幞頭(ㄆㄨˊ ㄊㄡˊ)
a turban; a headdress; a scarf

【幡】 1341 ㄈㄢ fan fān
1. a flag; a pennant; a pennon; a streamer
2. sudden; suddenly: 那浪子幡然改途。That vagabond suddenly repents and changes his course.

幡兒(ㄈㄚㄦ)
a streamer-like object held by the sons of the deceased at a funeral

幡信(ㄈㄢ ㄒㄧㄣˋ)
(in ancient China) a flag marked with the title of a high official

幡幟(ㄈㄢ ㄓˋ)
flags; pennants; streamers

幡幢(ㄈㄢ ㄔㄨㄤˊ)
flags; pennants; streamers; pendant streamers of silk hung before a shrine

幡然(ㄈㄢ ㄖㄢˊ)
suddenly; to come to a sudden realization

【幢】 1342 ㄔㄨㄤˊ chwang chuáng
1. a curtain for a carriage
2. a numerary adjunct for buildings of more than one story
3. flags, pennants, streamers, etc.
4. flickering; waving

幢隊(ㄔㄨㄤˊ ㄉㄨㄟˋ)
a squad of soldiers holding pennants to lead marching troops

幢節(ㄔㄨㄤˊ ㄐㄧㄝˊ)
a kind of tally broken in two pieces to prove the identity of the holders

幢幢(ㄔㄨㄤˊ ㄔㄨㄤˊ)
wavering; flapping in the wind: 屋子裏人影幢幢。The shadows of people are moving about in the house.

【幣】 1343 ㄅㄧˋ bih bì
1. currency; money; a legal tender: 外幣 foreign currency 紙幣 paper currency
2. a present; an offering

幣帛(ㄅㄧˋ ㄅㄛˊ)
gifts (in money and silks)

幣貢(ㄅㄧˋ ㄍㄨㄥˋ)
(in ancient China) tributes offered by the feudal princes

幣值(ㄅㄧˋ ㄓˊ)
the purchasing power of a currency

幣制(ㄅㄧˋ ㄓˋ)
a currency system

幣制改革(ㄅㄧˋ ㄓˋ ㄍㄞˇ ㄍㄜˊ)
currency reform

〔干部〕

幣制局(ㄅㄧˋ ㄓˋ ㄐㄩˊ)
a government agency in charge of the minting of coins, issuance of banknotes and other related matters in the early republican years

十四畫

【幬】 1344
1. ㄔㄡˊ chour chóu
a curtain; a canopy

【幬】 1344
2. ㄉㄠˋ daw dào
to cover

【幫】 1345
(帮) ㄅㄤ bang bāng
1. to help; to assist: 我幫他找到他的手錶。I helped him (to) find his watch.
2. a gang; a group; a class; a fleet
3. the sides of a shoe or gutter

幫辦(ㄅㄤ ㄅㄢˋ)
①to assist in managing ② the deputy director of a department under a cabinet ministry ③an assistant manager

幫派(ㄅㄤ ㄆㄞˋ)
a faction

幫浦(ㄅㄤ ㄆㄨˇ)
a pump

幫忙(ㄅㄤ ㄇㄤˊ)
help; assistance; to help or assist

幫倒忙(ㄅㄤ ㄉㄠˋ ㄇㄤˊ)
to cause trouble while trying to help

幫工(ㄅㄤ ㄍㄨㄥ)
an assistant of a skilled worker

幫夥(ㄅㄤ ㄏㄨㄛˇ)
assistants in a shop

幫會(ㄅㄤ ㄏㄨㄟˋ)
① secret societies ② an underworld gang

幫錢(ㄅㄤ ㄑㄧㄢˊ)
to help with money

幫腔(ㄅㄤ ㄑㄧㄤ)
①to give verbal support to a person (usually one of higher position) ②to follow another in singing

幫閒(ㄅㄤ ㄒㄧㄢˊ)
parasitism; to be a parasite

幫兇(ㄅㄤ ㄒㄩㄥ)
an accomplice in a crime or a condemnable act

幫助(ㄅㄤ ㄓㄨˋ)
to help; to assist; help or assistance: 他幫助我學日文。He helped me to learn Japanese.

幫襯(ㄅㄤ ㄔㄣˋ)
help; aid; assistance

幫手(ㄅㄤ ㄕㄡˇ)
a helper; an assistant; a helpmate: 你是我的有力幫手。You were a great helper to me.

幫嘴(ㄅㄤ ㄗㄨㄟˇ)
to help in an altercation; to speak for another

【幪】 1346
ㄇㄥˊ meng méng
a cover; a screen; to cover

幪幪(ㄇㄥˊ ㄇㄥˊ)
lush or luxuriant (growth of vegetation)

十五畫

【幮】 1347
ㄔㄨˊ chwu chú
a bed-screen or mosquito net that looks like a small cabinet

干部
ㄍㄢ gan gān

【干】 1348
ㄍㄢ gan gān
1. to offend; to oppose; to invade
2. to jam (radiobroadcasts, etc.); to interfere; to intervene
3. to concern; to involve
4. to seek; to beseech
5. the bank (of a river, etc.)
6. a shield
7. (how) many or much; a group
8. a stem; the Celestial Stems
9. a Chinese family name

干貝(ㄍㄢ ㄅㄟˋ)
a dried scallop

干冒(ㄍㄢ ㄇㄠˋ)
to transgress; to offend intentionally

干名采譽(ㄍㄢ ㄇㄧㄥˊ ㄘㄞˇ ㄩˋ)
to seek publicity

干犯(ㄍㄢ ㄈㄢˋ)
①to offend ②to invade

干黷 or 干瀆(ㄍㄢ ㄉㄨˊ)
(a polite expression) to offend by beseeching

干撓(ㄍㄢ ㄋㄠˊ)
①to interfere; to harass: 請不要干撓我的工作。Please don't interfere with my work. ②(said of radiobroadcasts) to jam

干你屁事(ㄍㄢ ㄋㄧˇ ㄆㄧˋ ㄕˋ)
(abusive) None of your business. 或 What has that got to do with you?!

干連(ㄍㄢ ㄌㄧㄢˊ)
to involve; to implicate; involvement; implication

干祿(ㄍㄢ ㄌㄨˋ)
①to seek an official post ② official emolument

干戈(ㄍㄢ ㄍㄜ)
(literally) shields and spears —warfare; armed conflicts

干戈相見(ㄍㄢ ㄍㄜ ㄒㄧㄤ ㄐㄧㄢˋ)
to declare war on each other

干戈擾擾(ㄍㄢ ㄍㄜ ㄖㄠˇ ㄖㄠˇ)
incessant wars and the resultant unrest

干己(ㄍㄢ ㄐㄧˇ)
to concern oneself

干進(ㄍㄢ ㄐㄧㄣˋ)
to seek official promotion or a higher office in the government

干將(ㄍㄢ ㄐㄧㄤ)
name of a famous sword, made by a master ironsmith of that name in the Epoch of Spring and Autumn

干求(ㄍㄢ ㄑㄧㄡˊ)
to request; to beseech; to importune

干卿底事(ㄍㄢ ㄑㄧㄥ ㄉㄧˇ ㄕˋ)
What has that got to do with you? 或 None of your business!

干係(ㄍㄢ ㄒㄧˋ)
involvement; concern; implication

干休(ㄍㄢ ㄒㄧㄡ)
to give up; to bring to an end

干支(ㄍㄢ ㄓ)

the system of Celestial Stems and Terrestrial Branches which makes the 60-year cycle

干政(ㄍㄢ ㄓㄥˋ)
to interfere in politics

干證(ㄍㄢ ㄓㄥˋ)
the witnesses involved in a lawsuit

干城(ㄍㄢ ㄔㄥˊ)
defenders; protectors; champions

干城之選(ㄍㄢ ㄔㄥˊ ㄓ ㄒㄩㄢˇ)
a capable general who can be trusted with the defense of the nation

干時(ㄍㄢ ㄕˊ)
to suit the occasion; to seek to keep up with the times

干世(ㄍㄢ ㄕˋ)
to seek to conform with the world

干涉(ㄍㄢ ㄕㄜˋ)
to interfere; interference; intervention

干擾(ㄍㄢ ㄖㄠˇ) or 干撓(ㄍㄢ ㄋㄠˊ)
① to disturb; to interfere ② (physics) interference; to jam

干謁(ㄍㄢ ㄧㄝˋ)
to seek an audience with someone in power, hoping for a position

干預 or 干與(ㄍㄢ ㄩˋ)
to intervene; to interfere; intervention

干譽(ㄍㄢ ㄩˋ)
to seek for higher reputation

干雲蔽日(ㄍㄢ ㄩㄣˊ ㄅㄧˋ ㄖˋ)
(said of tall and luxuriant trees) towering into the clouds and covering up the sun

二畫

【平】 1349
ㄆㄧㄥˊ pyng píng

1. level; even: 桌面不平。The table is not level.
2. equal; equity; equality
3. peaceful; amity
4. to conquer; to quell (a revolt); to calm down
5. to control; to regulate
6. (said of prices) to go back to normal after sharp rises: 最近物價平落。Recently prices have dropped to normal.
7. (sports) to make the same score; to tie; to draw; a draw: 這場棒球賽最後打平了。The baseball game ended in a draw.
8. to pacify; to bring peace to: 治國平天下 to rule a country and unify the world in peace
9. short for Peiping: 她喜愛平劇。She is fond of Peiping opera.
10. a Chinese family name

平白(ㄆㄧㄥˊ ㄅㄞˊ) or 平白無故(ㄆㄧㄥˊ ㄅㄞˊ ㄨˊ ㄍㄨˋ)
without reason or cause; without provocation: 他平白挨一頓罵。He got a scolding without reason.

平輩(ㄆㄧㄥˊ ㄅㄟˋ)
of the same generation

平版(ㄆㄧㄥˊ ㄅㄢˇ)
(printing) a lithographic plate

平板(ㄆㄧㄥˊ ㄅㄢˇ)
dull and stereotyped; flat

平板玻璃(ㄆㄧㄥˊ ㄅㄢˇ ㄅㄛ ·ㄌㄧ)
plate glass

平步青雲(ㄆㄧㄥˊ ㄅㄨˋ ㄑㄧㄥ ㄩㄣˊ)
(said of a career or social position) a meteoric rise

平平(ㄆㄧㄥˊ ㄆㄧㄥˊ)
average; common; usual; ordinary; so-so

平平安安(ㄆㄧㄥˊ ㄆㄧㄥˊ ㄢ ㄢ)
peaceful(ly); without any accident: 我們希望你平平安安的回家。We hope you return home peacefully.

平平穩穩(ㄆㄧㄥˊ ㄆㄧㄥˊ ㄨㄣˇ ㄨㄣˇ)
sure and steady; peaceful and without mishaps

平鋪直敍(ㄆㄧㄥˊ ㄆㄨ ㄓˊ ㄒㄩˋ)
factual description; straight reporting; (said of a narration) without turns or twists

平脈(ㄆㄧㄥˊ ㄇㄞˋ) or (ㄆㄧㄥˊ ㄇㄛˋ)
(medicine) a normal pulse; the pulse of a healthy person

平面(ㄆㄧㄥˊ ㄇㄧㄢˋ)
a plane, or plane surface

平面圖(ㄆㄧㄥˊ ㄇㄧㄢˋ ㄊㄨˊ)
a plane (of a building or machine)

平面幾何(ㄆㄧㄥˊ ㄇㄧㄢˋ ㄐㄧˇ ㄏㄜˊ)
plane geometry

平面鏡(ㄆㄧㄥˊ ㄇㄧㄢˋ ㄐㄧㄥˋ)
a plane mirror

平面三角(ㄆㄧㄥˊ ㄇㄧㄢˋ ㄙㄢ ㄐㄧㄠˇ)
plane trigonometry

平民(ㄆㄧㄥˊ ㄇㄧㄣˊ)
a commoner; a civilian

平民教育(ㄆㄧㄥˊ ㄇㄧㄣˊ ㄐㄧㄠˋ ㄩˋ)
education of the masses; adult education 亦作「民衆教育」

平民政治(ㄆㄧㄥˊ ㄇㄧㄣˊ ㄓㄥˋ ㄓˋ)
popular government; democracy

平明(ㄆㄧㄥˊ ㄇㄧㄥˊ)
at dawn or daybreak: 他平明即起。He gets up at daybreak.

平反(ㄆㄧㄥˊ ㄈㄢˇ)
to reverse or redress a miscarriage of justice

平凡(ㄆㄧㄥˊ ㄈㄢˊ)
common; ordinary; usual; not outstanding or remarkable

平分(ㄆㄧㄥˊ ㄈㄣ)
to divide into equal shares; to divide equally

平分秋色(ㄆㄧㄥˊ ㄈㄣ ㄑㄧㄡ ㄙㄜˋ)
(said of two sides) to share (top honors, fame, etc.); to equal each other in (achievements, scores, etc.)

平方(ㄆㄧㄥˊ ㄈㄤ)
(mathematics) a square

平方根(ㄆㄧㄥˊ ㄈㄤ ㄍㄣ)
a square root

平房(ㄆㄧㄥˊ ㄈㄤˊ)
a one-storied house; a bungalow

平服(ㄆㄧㄥˊ ㄈㄨˊ)
to stabilize; stable; steadfast

平復(ㄆㄧㄥˊ ㄈㄨˋ)
①(said of situations, social order, etc.) to return to normal; to calm down; to subside ② to recover from an illness, etc.

平旦(ㄆㄧㄥˊ ㄉㄢˋ)
dawn; daybreak

平淡(ㄆㄧㄥˊ ㄉㄢˋ)
ordinary; commonplace; insipid; nothing particular or remarkable: 那是一個平淡的故事。That is an insipid story.

平淡無奇(ㄆㄧㄥˊ ㄉㄢˋ ㄨˊ ㄑㄧˊ)

〔干部〕

nothing extraordinary or remarkable; insipid or dull

平淡無味(ㄆㄧㄥˊ ㄉㄢˋ ㄨˊ ㄨㄟˋ)
insipid; without flavor; tasteless

平等(ㄆㄧㄥˊ ㄉㄥˇ)
①equality; equal ②name of a county in Honan Province

平等待遇(ㄆㄧㄥˊ ㄉㄥˇ ㄉㄞˋ ㄩˋ)
equal treatment

平等互利(ㄆㄧㄥˊ ㄉㄥˇ ㄏㄨˋ ㄌㄧˋ)
equality and mutual benefit

平糴(ㄆㄧㄥˊ ㄉㄧˊ)
In ancient China, the government bought grain during bumper harvests in order to sell it at a low price in the time of scarcity.

平底船(ㄆㄧㄥˊ ㄉㄧˇ ㄔㄨㄢˊ)
a flat-bottom boat

平地(ㄆㄧㄥˊ ㄉㄧˋ)
① the plain; a piece of level ground ② suddenly

平地風波(ㄆㄧㄥˊ ㄉㄧˋ ㄈㄥ ㄅㄛ)
an unexpected turn of event; troubles that arise all of a sudden

平地登天(ㄆㄧㄥˊ ㄉㄧˋ ㄉㄥ ㄊㄧㄢ)
a sudden rise (to fame, success, etc.): 求學問不能希望平地登天。In the pursuit of knowledge, one cannot expect a sudden rise.

平地一聲雷(ㄆㄧㄥˊ ㄉㄧˋ ㄧˋ ㄕㄥ ㄌㄟˊ)
(literally) a bolt from the blue—a sudden shot to fame

平定(ㄆㄧㄥˊ ㄉㄧㄥˋ)
①(often said of situations, etc.) settled: 這裡情勢已平定下來。The situation here is settled. ②to quell (rebellions, etc.)

平臺(ㄆㄧㄥˊ ㄊㄞˊ)
① a flat-top building ② a stadium-like building ③ balcony, open porch or portico

平頭(ㄆㄧㄥˊ ㄊㄡˊ)
① block—having no indentation in addresses, headings, etc. ② a crew cut; closely cropped hair: 他留着平頭。He has closely cropped hair. ③ common; ordinary

平頭正臉(ㄆㄧㄥˊ ㄊㄡˊ ㄓㄥˋ ㄌㄧㄢˇ)
a neat appearance (of a person)

平坦(ㄆㄧㄥˊ ㄊㄢˇ)
level, even and smooth (roads, going, etc.): 這條公路的路面寬濶平坦。This highway has a broad and smooth surface.

平糶(ㄆㄧㄥˊ ㄊㄧㄠˋ)
In ancient China, the government sold grain at a low price in the time of scarcity, when the market price was high.

平添(ㄆㄧㄥˊ ㄊㄧㄢ)
to add or acquire something unexpectedly

平年(ㄆㄧㄥˊ ㄋㄧㄢˊ)
an ordinary year (as distinct from a leap year)

平列(ㄆㄧㄥˊ ㄌㄧㄝˋ)
of equal rank

平林(ㄆㄧㄥˊ ㄌㄧㄣˊ)
wood groves on level ground

平亂(ㄆㄧㄥˊ ㄌㄨㄢˋ)
to suppress a rebellion or revolt

平光(ㄆㄧㄥˊ ㄍㄨㄤ)
(said of eyeglasses) ordinary lenses which are neither concave nor convex

平康(ㄆㄧㄥˊ ㄎㄤ)
a brothel

平曠(ㄆㄧㄥˊ ㄎㄨㄤˋ)
open and flat (fields, land, etc.)

平空(ㄆㄧㄥˊ ㄎㄨㄥ)
to occur without any reason or cause; to fabricate or invent

平和(ㄆㄧㄥˊ ㄏㄜˊ)
① mildly; mild: 他的性情平和。He is of a mild disposition. ② name of a county in Fukien Province

平漢鐵路(ㄆㄧㄥˊ ㄏㄢˋ ㄊㄧㄝˇ ㄌㄨˋ)
the Peiping-Hankow Railway

平衡(ㄆㄧㄥˊ ㄏㄥˊ)
equilibrium; balance; (muscular) coordination

平衡力(ㄆㄧㄥˊ ㄏㄥˊ ㄌㄧˋ)
equilibrant

平衡稅(ㄆㄧㄥˊ ㄏㄥˊ ㄕㄨㄟˋ)
(international trade) countervailing duties

平滑(ㄆㄧㄥˊ ㄏㄨㄚˊ)
even and smooth

平話 or 評話(ㄆㄧㄥˊ ㄏㄨㄚˋ)
storytelling (using the style of language of the professional storytellers in Sung Dynasty somewhere between the spoken and the written languages)

平緩(ㄆㄧㄥˊ ㄏㄨㄢˇ)
① gently: 這條河水流平緩。The river flows gently. ② mild; gentle: 他說話語調平緩。He speaks in a mild tone.

平假名(ㄆㄧㄥˊ ㄐㄧㄚˇ ㄇㄧㄥˊ)
a form of Japanese phonetic signs which are often used in place of the Chinese characters

平價(ㄆㄧㄥˊ ㄐㄧㄚˋ)
① a fair price: 他以平價出售了他的房子。He has sold his house at a fair price. ② to lower prices

平交道(ㄆㄧㄥˊ ㄐㄧㄠ ㄉㄠˋ)
a level crossing; the intersection between a railroad and a roadway

平肩(ㄆㄧㄥˊ ㄐㄧㄢ)
① shoulder-to-shoulder ② of equal footing or rank

平津(ㄆㄧㄥˊ ㄐㄧㄣ)
Peiping and Tientsin; the Peiping and Tientsin area

平靖(ㄆㄧㄥˊ ㄐㄧㄥˋ)
peace and order; settled

平靜(ㄆㄧㄥˊ ㄐㄧㄥˋ)
quiet; calm: 沒有風，一切都是平靜的。There was no wind and everything was calm.

平居(ㄆㄧㄥˊ ㄐㄩ)
(literally) on usual days—ordinarily

平局(ㄆㄧㄥˊ ㄐㄩˊ)
a draw; a tie: 這場網球比賽最後打成平局。The tennis game finally ended in a draw.

平劇(ㄆㄧㄥˊ ㄐㄩˋ)
Peiping opera; Peking opera; Chinese opera

平均(ㄆㄧㄥˊ ㄐㄩㄣ)
the average; even (distribution, etc.)

平均地權(ㄆㄧㄥˊ ㄐㄩㄣ ㄉㄧˋ ㄑㄩㄢˊ)
the equalization of land rights (envisaged by Dr. Sun Yat-sen, with a three-fold measure—the purchase of private land at the values declared, the levy of land

tax at the land value assessed and the government takeover of increment of land value)

平均年齡(ㄆㄧㄥˊ ㄐㄩㄣ ㄋㄧㄢˊ ㄌㄧㄥˊ)
composite life

平均利潤(ㄆㄧㄥˊ ㄐㄩㄣ ㄌㄧˋ ㄖㄨㄣˋ)
the average of profit

平均計算(ㄆㄧㄥˊ ㄐㄩㄣ ㄐㄧˋ ㄙㄨㄢˋ)
a general average; on the average

平均價(ㄆㄧㄥˊ ㄐㄩㄣ ㄐㄧㄚˋ)
average price

平均成本(ㄆㄧㄥˊ ㄐㄩㄣ ㄔㄥˊ ㄅㄣˇ)
average cost

平均壽命(ㄆㄧㄥˊ ㄐㄩㄣ ㄕㄡˋ ㄇㄧㄥˋ)
mean life

平均數(ㄆㄧㄥˊ ㄐㄩㄣ ㄕㄨˋ)
a mean; an average

平均速度(ㄆㄧㄥˊ ㄐㄩㄣ ㄙㄨˋ ㄉㄨˋ)
average speed; mean velocity

平均溫度(ㄆㄧㄥˊ ㄐㄩㄣ ㄨㄣ ㄉㄨˋ)
the mean temperature

平起平坐(ㄆㄧㄥˊ ㄑㄧˇ ㄆㄧㄥˊ ㄗㄨㄛˋ)
① to treat another as one's equal ② to show no deference

平情而論(ㄆㄧㄥˊ ㄑㄧㄥˊ ㄦˊ ㄌㄨㄣˋ)
objectively speaking

平權(ㄆㄧㄥˊ ㄑㄩㄢˊ)
equal rights

平昔(ㄆㄧㄥˊ ㄒㄧˊ)
in the past; in the past days

平息(ㄆㄧㄥˊ ㄒㄧˊ)
(said of an uprising or waves, etc.) to come to an end; to subside; to cause to stop; to quell: 海嘯平息了。The tidal waves subsided.

平心靜氣(ㄆㄧㄥˊ ㄒㄧㄣ ㄐㄧㄥˋ ㄑㄧˋ)
to be calm and fair (in resolving a dispute, etc.); to think calmly in detachment

平心而論(ㄆㄧㄥˊ ㄒㄧㄣ ㄦˊ ㄌㄨㄣˋ)
to discuss something fairly; to be fair: 平心而論, 他是個勤勉的學生。To be fair to him, he is a diligent student.

平信(ㄆㄧㄥˊ ㄒㄧㄣˋ)
ordinary mail: 她寄了一封平信給他。She sent a letter to him by ordinary mail.

平行(ㄆㄧㄥˊ ㄒㄧㄥˊ)
① parallel: 這條街和那條街平行。This street is parallel to that one. ② of equal rank; on the same footing

平行線(ㄆㄧㄥˊ ㄒㄧㄥˊ ㄒㄧㄢˋ)
parallel lines

平行四邊形(ㄆㄧㄥˊ ㄒㄧㄥˊ ㄙˋ ㄅㄧㄢ ㄒㄧㄥˊ)
a parallelogram

平直(ㄆㄧㄥˊ ㄓˊ)
fair and frank

平治(ㄆㄧㄥˊ ㄓˋ)
peace; tranquillity and good order

平展(ㄆㄧㄥˊ ㄓㄢˇ)
(said of land, plain, etc.) open and flat

平章(ㄆㄧㄥˊ ㄓㄤ)
① to make comments (on literary works) ② an official post in ancient China

平整(ㄆㄧㄥˊ ㄓㄥˇ)
① to level: 他們平整了一塊土地。They leveled a plot of land. ② neat; smooth

平正(ㄆㄧㄥˊ ㄓㄥˋ)
fair and just; without trickery or chicanery

平裝本(ㄆㄧㄥˊ ㄓㄨㄤ ㄅㄣˇ)
paperback (books); a paperbound edition

平常(ㄆㄧㄥˊ ㄔㄤˊ)
① normal; natural ② usual; as usual ③ ordinary; common; so-so: 這種現象很平常。This sort of thing is quite a common occurrence. ④ usually; ordinarily: 她平常於星期六晚上出去。She usually goes out on Saturday nights.

平常心(ㄆㄧㄥˊ ㄔㄤˊ ㄒㄧㄣ)
the absence of excitement, overanxiety, expectation, etc.; composure; calmness

平時(ㄆㄧㄥˊ ㄕˊ)
ordinarily; in normal times; in time of peace: 他平時在十點鐘睡覺。Ordinarily he goes to bed at ten o'clock.

平時不燒香，臨時抱佛脚(ㄆㄧㄥˊ ㄕˊ ㄅㄨˋ ㄕㄠ ㄒㄧㄤ, ㄌㄧㄣˊ ㄕˊ ㄅㄠˋ ㄈㄛˊ ㄐㄧㄠˇ)
(literally) One embraced the feet of Buddha in supplication but neglected burning incense to him when one did not need his help.— Last-minute efforts are useless if no preparatory work has been done beforehand.

平視(ㄆㄧㄥˊ ㄕˋ)
to look at something with the line of sight parallel to the ground

平射砲(ㄆㄧㄥˊ ㄕㄜˋ ㄆㄠˋ)
a cannon which fires along a flat trajectory (as distinct from a howitzer)

平手(ㄆㄧㄥˊ ㄕㄡˇ)
(in a competition, etc.) to draw; to tie another; to come out with even scores as one's opponent: 這些隊賽成平手。The teams drew.

平身(ㄆㄧㄥˊ ㄕㄣ)
Stand up. 或At ease. (the emperor's command to his minister after the latter had kowtowed to him)

平上去入(ㄆㄧㄥˊ ㄕㄤˇ ㄑㄩˋ ㄖㄨˋ)
level tone, falling-rising tone, falling tone, and entering tone—the four tones in classical Chinese phonetics

平生(ㄆㄧㄥˊ ㄕㄥ)
in all one's life; throughout one's life: 這是他平生的志願。This is his lifelong wish.

平聲(ㄆㄧㄥˊ ㄕㄥ)
level tone—the first tone in classical Chinese phonetics

平順(ㄆㄧㄥˊ ㄕㄨㄣˋ)
① smooth and orderly ② the name of a county in Shansi Province

平日(ㄆㄧㄥˊ ㄖˋ)
on usual days; ordinarily; on usual occasions: 她平日喜歡運動。Ordinarily she likes sports.

平壤(ㄆㄧㄥˊ ㄖㄤˇ)
Pyongyang, capital of Communist North Korea

平仄(ㄆㄧㄥˊ ㄗㄜˋ)
level and oblique tones—the four tones in classical Chinese phonetics (the first tone belongs to 平 while the remaining three tones belong to 仄)

平色(ㄆㄧㄥˊ ㄙㄜˋ)
the weight (or contents) and quality of silver

平素(ㄆㄧㄥˊ ㄙㄨˋ)
usually; ordinarily: 這女孩平

〔干部〕

〔干部〕

素不愛說話。This girl is usually very quiet.
平綏鐵路(ㄆㄧㄥˊ ㄙㄨㄟ ㄊㄧㄝˇ ㄌㄨˋ)
the Peiping-Kweisui Railway
平安(ㄆㄧㄥˊ ㄢ)
safe and sound; free from danger; peace: 全家平安。The whole family is safe and sound.
平安醮(ㄆㄧㄥˊ ㄢ ㄐㄧㄠˋ)
a religious service held in an area after an epidemic
平安無事(ㄆㄧㄥˊ ㄢ ㄨˊ ㄕˋ)
All is well. 或 safe and without any mishaps; safe and sound; in good order
平一宇內(ㄆㄧㄥˊ ㄧ ㄩˇ ㄋㄟˋ)
the unification of a nation after quelling rebellions
平議(ㄆㄧㄥˊ ㄧˋ)
a fair and just discussion; a fair commentary that takes care of both sides of an argument
平易近人(ㄆㄧㄥˊ ㄧˋ ㄐㄧㄣˋ ㄖㄣˊ)
(said of one's personality) easy to approach; easy to get along with: 我的鄰居們都平易近人。My neighbors are easy to get along with.
平野(ㄆㄧㄥˊ ㄧㄝˇ)
an open field
平穩(ㄆㄧㄥˊ ㄨㄣˇ)
steady and smooth (bus rides, driving, etc.); stable: 這次飛行很平穩。The flight was smooth.
平原(ㄆㄧㄥˊ ㄩㄢˊ)
a plain; a steppe
平原君(ㄆㄧㄥˊ ㄩㄢˊ ㄐㄩㄣ)
a famous official of Chao (趙) in the Epoch of Warring States, who had many protégés with various talents
平允(ㄆㄧㄥˊ ㄩㄣˇ)
fair and proper; just and appropriate
平庸(ㄆㄧㄥˊ ㄩㄥ)
commonplace; dull (persons, etc.); without talent: 這學生資質平庸，但很努力。Though without talent, this student works hard.

三畫

【年】 1350
ㄋㄧㄢˊ nian nián
1. a year: 我到此地恰恰一年了。It is just a year since I arrived here.
2. one's age: 他們的年齡是四歲、七歲、九歲。Their ages are 4, 7 and 9.
3. a Chinese family name
年伯(ㄋㄧㄢˊ ㄅㄛˊ)
a term used to address the 同年 of one's father 參看「同年②」
年輩(ㄋㄧㄢˊ ㄅㄟˋ)
age and generation
年表(ㄋㄧㄢˊ ㄅㄧㄠˇ)
a chronicle
年譜(ㄋㄧㄢˊ ㄆㄨˇ)
a biography arranged in chronological order
年邁(ㄋㄧㄢˊ ㄇㄞˋ) or 年老(ㄋㄧㄢˊ ㄌㄠˇ)
to get old; aged
年貌(ㄋㄧㄢˊ ㄇㄠˋ)
the age and appearance of a person (recorded for identification before the invention of photography)
年飯(ㄋㄧㄢˊ ㄈㄢˋ) or 年夜飯(ㄋㄧㄢˊ ㄧㄝˋ ㄈㄢˋ)
the dinner for the whole family on the eve of the Lunar New Year
年分 or 年份(ㄋㄧㄢˊ ·ㄈㄣ)
age; time; a particular year: 這件古董的年分比那件久。This piece of antique is older than that one.
年方二八(ㄋㄧㄢˊ ㄈㄤ ㄦˋ ㄅㄚ)
(said of girls) only 16 years of age
年俸(ㄋㄧㄢˊ ㄈㄥˋ) or 年薪(ㄋㄧㄢˊ ㄒㄧㄣ)
an annual salary; annual pay
年富力強(ㄋㄧㄢˊ ㄈㄨˋ ㄌㄧˋ ㄑㄧㄤˊ)
the prime of one's life: 青年時期年富力強。Youthhood is the prime of one's life.
年代(ㄋㄧㄢˊ ㄉㄞˋ)
① an age, era, generation, etc. ② years in a decade
年底(ㄋㄧㄢˊ ㄉㄧˇ)
the end of a year
年度(ㄋㄧㄢˊ ㄉㄨˋ)
a year fixed arbitrarily for convenience, a better administrative purpose, etc., as a fiscal year, a school year, etc.
年度計畫(ㄋㄧㄢˊ ㄉㄨˋ ㄐㄧˋ ㄏㄨㄚˋ)
an annual plan
年度決算(ㄋㄧㄢˊ ㄉㄨˋ ㄐㄩㄝˊ ㄙㄨㄢˋ)
(accounting) annual closing
年度總報告(ㄋㄧㄢˊ ㄉㄨˋ ㄗㄨㄥˇ ㄅㄠˋ ㄍㄠˋ)
general annual reports
年頭(ㄋㄧㄢˊ ㄊㄡˊ)
① times: 年頭好。Times are good. ② the beginning of a year ③ a year ④ a harvest: 今年年頭眞好。This year's harvest is rich indeed.
年頭年尾(ㄋㄧㄢˊ ㄊㄡˊ ㄋㄧㄢˊ ㄨㄟˇ)
the beginning and the end of a year
年內(ㄋㄧㄢˊ ㄋㄟˋ)
within the year: 他將在年內回來。He will be back within the year.
年年(ㄋㄧㄢˊ ㄋㄧㄢˊ)
every year; year after year
年來(ㄋㄧㄢˊ ㄌㄞˊ)
① in recent years ② during the year past
年禮(ㄋㄧㄢˊ ㄌㄧˇ)
New Year's presents
年利(ㄋㄧㄢˊ ㄌㄧˋ) or 年息(ㄋㄧㄢˊ ㄒㄧˊ)
annual interest (rate)
年例(ㄋㄧㄢˊ ㄌㄧˋ)
customs or routines handed down year after year
年曆(ㄋㄧㄢˊ ㄌㄧˋ)
a calendar with the whole year printed on one sheet
年力就衰(ㄋㄧㄢˊ ㄌㄧˋ ㄐㄧㄡˋ ㄕㄨㄞ)
aging and feeble
年齡(ㄋㄧㄢˊ ㄌㄧㄥˊ)
age: 他們同年齡。They are of the same age.
年齡結構(ㄋㄧㄢˊ ㄌㄧㄥˊ ㄐㄧㄝˊ ㄍㄡˋ)
age structure
年輪(ㄋㄧㄢˊ ㄌㄨㄣˊ)
annual rings (indicating the age of a tree)
年糕(ㄋㄧㄢˊ ㄍㄠ)
New Year's cake; glutinous rice cake eaten during the Lunar New Year's holidays
年高德劭(ㄋㄧㄢˊ ㄍㄠ ㄉㄜˊ ㄕㄠˋ)
advanced in years and virtue
年庚八字(ㄋㄧㄢˊ ㄍㄥ ㄅㄚ ㄗˋ)
the hour, day, month and

year of a person's birth—used by fortunetellers to tell a person's fortune or whether a couple are well-matched

年羹堯(ㄋㄧㄢˊ ㄍㄥ ㄧㄠˊ)
Nien Keng-yao, a general in the early Ching Dynasty

年穀(ㄋㄧㄢˊ ㄍㄨˇ)
an annual harvest or crop; the total amount of grain harvested in a year

年關(ㄋㄧㄢˊ ㄍㄨㄢ)
(literally) the crisis of a year — the end of a year when all accounts and debts must be settled: 年關近了。The end of the year is coming near.

年光荏苒(ㄋㄧㄢˊ ㄍㄨㄤ ㄖㄣˇ ㄖㄢˇ)
(said of time) to elapse gradually and imperceptibly

年功(ㄋㄧㄢˊ ㄍㄨㄥ)
the merits one earns during his years of service—a reference used in consideration of promotion or granting of pension, etc.

年號(ㄋㄧㄢˊ ㄏㄠˋ)
the title of an emperor's reign

年華(ㄋㄧㄢˊ ㄏㄨㄚˊ)
time; years; age: 李小姐年華雙十。Miss Lee is twenty years of age.

年華虛度(ㄋㄧㄢˊ ㄏㄨㄚˊ ㄒㄩ ㄉㄨˋ)
to have spent one's best years without any achievements; to have wasted the best years of one's life

年畫兒(ㄋㄧㄢˊ ㄏㄨㄚˋㄦ)
drawings or pictures sold at Lunar New Year, usually on the subject of good luck

年貨(ㄋㄧㄢˊ ㄏㄨㄛˋ)
food items and other consumer goods that a household must keep in store for the Lunar New Year's holidays when shops are closed

年會(ㄋㄧㄢˊ ㄏㄨㄟˋ)
an annual meeting or convention: 這家公司在下週一舉行年會。This company will hold an annual meeting next Monday.

年級(ㄋㄧㄢˊ ㄐㄧˊ)
(in school) a grade: 美國的小學有八個年級。An elementary school in America has eight grades.

年紀(ㄋㄧㄢˊ ㄐㄧˋ)
years; age: 她的年紀多大? How (many years) old is she?

年假(ㄋㄧㄢˊ ㄐㄧㄚˋ)
New Year's holidays or vacation

年節(ㄋㄧㄢˊ ㄐㄧㄝˊ)
the three major festivals of the year—the Dragon Boat, the Mid-Autumn and the Lunar New Year festivals

年久失修(ㄋㄧㄢˊ ㄐㄧㄡˇ ㄕ ㄒㄧㄡ)
in a dilapidated condition; worn down by the years without repair

年間(ㄋㄧㄢˊ ㄐㄧㄢ)
a certain period of time, such as the reign of an emperor, etc.

年鑑(ㄋㄧㄢˊ ㄐㄧㄢˋ)
an almanac; a yearbook

年金(ㄋㄧㄢˊ ㄐㄧㄣ)
an annuity

年近歲迫(ㄋㄧㄢˊ ㄐㄧㄣˋ ㄙㄨㄟˋ ㄆㄛˋ)
The Lunar New Year is approaching fast.

年景(ㄋㄧㄢˊ ㄐㄧㄥˇ)
① New Year's scenes ② a harvest

年前(ㄋㄧㄢˊ ㄑㄧㄢˊ)
before the turn of the year

年歉(ㄋㄧㄢˊ ㄑㄧㄢˋ)
a year of poor harvest

年輕(ㄋㄧㄢˊ ㄑㄧㄥ)
young; youthful; youth

年輕貌美(ㄋㄧㄢˊ ㄑㄧㄥ ㄇㄠˋ ㄇㄟˇ)
young and pretty

年禧(ㄋㄧㄢˊ ㄒㄧ)
New Year's greetings

年下(ㄋㄧㄢˊ ·ㄒㄧㄚ)
during the New Year's holidays

年限(ㄋㄧㄢˊ ㄒㄧㄢˋ)
the number of years set as a time limit within which a job must be completed; a service life

年兄(ㄋㄧㄢˊ ㄒㄩㄥ)
(in old China) a mutual reference among those who passed the same imperial civil service examination

年紙(ㄋㄧㄢˊ ㄓˇ)
paper items made for the New Year Festival—door couplets, paper horses, etc.

年長(ㄋㄧㄢˊ ㄓㄤˇ)
old or aged; older: 我較他年長。I am older than he.

年終(ㄋㄧㄢˊ ㄓㄨㄥ)
the close or end of the year

年終考績(ㄋㄧㄢˊ ㄓㄨㄥ ㄎㄠˇ ㄐㄧ)
the grading of an employee's performance at the end of the year

年齒(ㄋㄧㄢˊ ㄔˇ)
the age of a person

年成(ㄋㄧㄢˊ ·ㄔㄥ)
the harvests of the year

年初(ㄋㄧㄢˊ ㄔㄨ)
the beginning of the year: 去年年初我曾見過他。I saw him at the beginning of last year.

年事(ㄋㄧㄢˊ ㄕˋ)
the age of a person

年少(ㄋㄧㄢˊ ㄕㄠˋ)
young

年壽(ㄋㄧㄢˊ ㄕㄡˋ)
the age of a person; the length of a person's life span

年深日久(ㄋㄧㄢˊ ㄕㄣ ㄖˋ ㄐㄧㄡˇ)
after a long lapse of time; as the years go by

年賞(ㄋㄧㄢˊ ㄕㄤˇ)
a year-end award; a year-end bonus

年入(ㄋㄧㄢˊ ㄖㄨˋ)
annual income

年資(ㄋㄧㄢˊ ㄗ)
① the years one spends in an endeavor or job ② seniority

年租(ㄋㄧㄢˊ ㄗㄨ)
an annual rental (of a piece of land, a house, etc.)

年祚(ㄋㄧㄢˊ ㄗㄨㄛˋ)
one's life span

年菜(ㄋㄧㄢˊ ㄘㄞˋ)
food and dishes prepared for the Lunar New Year

年歲(ㄋㄧㄢˊ ㄙㄨㄟˋ)
① the age of a person ② years; an age ③ harvests

年誼(ㄋㄧㄢˊ ㄧˊ)
the friendship among those who passed the same impe-

rial civil service examination in old China
年夜(ㄋㄧㄢˊ ㄧㄝˋ)
New Year's Eve: 每年年夜我們都有家庭團圓。We have a family reunion every New Year's Eve.
年幼無知(ㄋㄧㄢˊ ㄧㄡˋ ㄨˊ ㄓ)
ignorance for being young of age (often used in court verdict or petition pleading leniency for a young offender)
年湮代遠(ㄋㄧㄢˊ ㄧㄣ ㄉㄞˋ ㄩㄢˇ)
① time immemorial ② oblivion resulting from the passing of the years
年尾(ㄋㄧㄢˊ ㄨㄟˇ)
the end of the year
年逾不惑(ㄋㄧㄢˊ ㄩˊ ㄅㄨˋ ㄏㄨㄛˋ)
to have passed 40: 我們的老師已年逾不惑。Our teacher has passed the age of forty.
年月(ㄋㄧㄢˊ ㄩㄝˋ)
① times; an age ② the exact time when a given event occurred

〔干部〕

五畫

【并】 1351 1.(併) ㄅㄧㄥˋ binq bìng
1. on a level with; even; equal
2. and; also; or; at the same time; together with 參看「並」
并日而食(ㄅㄧㄥˋ ㄖˋ ㄦˊ ㄕˊ)
to eat on alternate days—to live a poor life

【并】 1351 2.ㄅㄧㄥ bing bīng
Pingchou, one of the ancient Chinese administrative divisions, consisting of parts of today's Hopeh, Shansi, etc.
并州快剪(ㄅㄧㄥ ㄓㄡ ㄎㄨㄞˋ ㄐㄧㄢˇ)
scissors made in Pingchou—famous for sharp blades (now used figuratively to depict a person with a quick and witty tongue or crisp writing)

【幸】 1352 ㄒㄧㄥˋ shinq xìng
1. well-being and happiness: 他們都有幸福愉快之感。They all have a sense of well-being and happiness.
2. fortunately; luckily; thanks to: 我們幸而及時趕到那裏。We fortunately got there in time.
3. to feel happy about; to favor
4. an imperial tour or progress
5. a Chinese family name
幸免於難(ㄒㄧㄥˋ ㄇㄧㄢˇ ㄩˊ ㄋㄢˋ)
to have a narrow escape from (death, etc.); to have luckily survived an accident or incident
幸福(ㄒㄧㄥˋ ㄈㄨˊ)
happiness and well-being; bliss
幸福主義(ㄒㄧㄥˋ ㄈㄨˊ ㄓㄨˇ ㄧˋ)
eudemonism
幸得(ㄒㄧㄥˋ ㄉㄜˊ)
fortunately; thanks to
幸虧(ㄒㄧㄥˋ ㄎㄨㄟ)or 幸好(ㄒㄧㄥˋ ㄏㄠˇ)or 幸喜(ㄒㄧㄥˋ ㄒㄧˇ)
luckily; fortunately; thanks to
幸臣(ㄒㄧㄥˋ ㄔㄣˊ)
a favorite courtier
幸事(ㄒㄧㄥˋ ㄕˋ)
① something that happened out of sheer luck ② something pleasant
幸甚(ㄒㄧㄥˋ ㄕㄣˋ)
① very much hoped for ② very much blessed
幸災樂禍(ㄒㄧㄥˋ ㄗㄞ ㄌㄜˋ ㄏㄨㄛˋ)
to rejoice in the calamity of others; to take pleasure in others' misfortune; to gloat over others' misfortune
幸蘇涸轍(ㄒㄧㄥˋ ㄙㄨ ㄏㄜˊ ㄔㄜˋ)
(literally) to pump water into a dried pond to save the fish—to give financial help to those in need
幸而(ㄒㄧㄥˋ ㄦˊ)
luckily; fortunately; thanks to
幸有(ㄒㄧㄥˋ ㄧㄡˇ)
to be fortunate to have
幸勿推卻(ㄒㄧㄥˋ ㄨˋ ㄊㄨㄟ ㄑㄩㄝˋ)
(We're) hopeful that you won't refuse or reject; please do not refuse (our offer, request, etc.)
幸未(ㄒㄧㄥˋ ㄨㄟˋ)
Fortunately, it's not....
幸運(ㄒㄧㄥˋ ㄩㄣˋ)
① good fortune; good luck ② lucky
幸運之神(ㄒㄧㄥˋ ㄩㄣˋ ㄓ ㄕㄣˊ)
Lady Luck; the goddess of fortune
幸運兒(ㄒㄧㄥˋ ㄩㄣˋ ㄦˊ)
a person who always gets good breaks; a lucky guy

十畫

【幹】 1353 ㄍㄢˋ gann gàn
1. the trunk (of a tree or of a human body): 樹幹支持着樹枝。The trunk supports the branches.
2. the main part of anything
3. capabilities; talents; capable; skillful: 他是一位能幹的教員。He is a capable instructor.
4. to do; to attend to business; to manage: 這件事沒甚麼好幹的。This matter is not worth doing.
5. (slang) to kill
幹部(ㄍㄢˋ ㄅㄨˋ)
a cadre; a hardcore member of any organization
幹不來(ㄍㄢˋ ·ㄅㄨ ㄌㄞˊ)
cannot be done; cannot be managed
幹不了(ㄍㄢˋ ·ㄅㄨ ㄌㄧㄠˇ)
cannot be done or managed (because of incompetence)
幹不幹(ㄍㄢˋ ·ㄅㄨ ㄍㄢˋ)
Will you do it?
幹不出(ㄍㄢˋ ·ㄅㄨ ㄔㄨ)
cannot do (such a cruel or unethical thing)
幹麼(ㄍㄢˋ ㄇㄚˊ)
① Why? 或 Why (are you) doing this? 他幹麼不走? Why didn't he leave? ② What (do you do)? 你在幹麼? What are you doing?
幹得來(ㄍㄢˋ ·ㄉㄜ ㄌㄞˊ)
can be done or managed
幹得了(ㄍㄢˋ ·ㄉㄜ ㄌㄧㄠˇ)
can be done or managed (denoting competence)
幹的好事(ㄍㄢˋ ·ㄉㄜ ㄏㄠˇ ㄕˋ)
① See what you have done! ② How did you dare do such a thing!?
幹得出(ㄍㄢˋ ·ㄉㄜ ㄔㄨ)
capable of, or not above doing (a sordid or mean

act)

幹道(ㄍㄢˋ ㄉㄠˋ)or 幹線(ㄍㄢˋ ㄒㄧㄢˋ) or 幹路(ㄍㄢˋ ㄌㄨˋ)
a trunk line; a main line

幹掉(ㄍㄢˋ ㄉㄧㄠˋ)
to kill or eliminate (a person)

幹頭兒(ㄍㄢˋ ㄊㄡˊㄦ)
worth the effort: 那事沒什麼幹頭兒。That is not worth the effort.

幹吏(ㄍㄢˋ ㄌㄧˋ)
a capable official

幹練(ㄍㄢˋ ㄌㄧㄢˋ)
capable and experienced: 李先生是一個幹練的人。Mr. Lee is a capable and experienced person.

幹略(ㄍㄢˋ ㄌㄩㄝˋ)
capable and full of ideas

幹活兒(ㄍㄢˋ ㄏㄨㄛˊㄦ)
to work; to do a job: 幹活兒去吧! Let's get to work.

幹勁兒(ㄍㄢˋ ㄐㄧㄣˋㄦ)
enthusiasm; eagerness in doing things; drive; vigor

幹器(ㄍㄢˋ ㄑㄧˋ)
capability

幹事(ㄍㄢˋ ㄕˋ)
①to manage business or affairs; to do a job ②a clerk; a member of an executive committee

幹甚麼(ㄍㄢˋ ㄕㄜˊ ·ㄇㄜ)
① What are you doing? ② What do you want? ③ Why (do you…)? 你幹甚麼不走? Why don't you leave?

幹才(ㄍㄢˋ ㄘㄞˊ)
①a very capable person; a person gifted with managing talent ②capability

幹員(ㄍㄢˋ ㄩㄢˊ)
a very capable officer or official

幺部
ㄧㄠ iau yāo

【幺】 1354
(么) ㄧㄠ iau yāo

1. tiny; small; insignificant
2. the youngest son or daughter of a family: 他是我們的幺弟。He is our youngest brother.
3. one on dice; one
4. lone; alone
5. a Chinese family name

幺麼(ㄧㄠ ㄇㄛˊ)
tiny; diminutive; minute

幺麼小醜(ㄧㄠ ㄇㄛˊ ㄒㄧㄠˇ ㄔㄡˇ)
a petty skunk; a despicable wretch

幺妹(ㄧㄠ ㄇㄟˋ)
the youngest sister

幺豚(ㄧㄠ ㄊㄨㄣˊ)
a little pig

幺小(ㄧㄠ ㄒㄧㄠˇ)
diminutive; puny; minute

幺兒(ㄧㄠ ㄦˊ)
the youngest son

幺二三(ㄧㄠ ㄦˋ ㄙㄢ)
one, two, three—the lowest combination in dice

一畫

【幻】 1355
ㄏㄨㄢˋ huann huàn

1. illusion; hallucination; magic; fantasy: 別把幻想當作現實。Don't regard illusions as reality.
2. illusory; unreal; deceptive; changeable

幻夢(ㄏㄨㄢˋ ㄇㄥˋ)
a daydream; a fantasy; a fantasm: 她生活在幻夢的世界中。She lives in a world of fantasy.

幻滅(ㄏㄨㄢˋ ㄇㄧㄝˋ)
disillusionment

幻燈(ㄏㄨㄢˋ ㄉㄥ)
a magic lantern

幻燈片(ㄏㄨㄢˋ ㄉㄥ ㄆㄧㄢˋ)
a slide

幻燈機(ㄏㄨㄢˋ ㄉㄥ ㄐㄧ)
a slide projector

幻化(ㄏㄨㄢˋ ㄏㄨㄚˋ)
①magical change; metamorphosis ②death

幻景(ㄏㄨㄢˋ ㄐㄧㄥˇ)
a mirage; fata morgana

幻境(ㄏㄨㄢˋ ㄐㄧㄥˋ)
①a dreamland ②(said of a Buddhist concept) the illusory world of the mortals

幻覺(ㄏㄨㄢˋ ㄐㄩㄝˊ)
hallucination; illusion; a fantasy; a fantasm; a phantasm

幻想(ㄏㄨㄢˋ ㄒㄧㄤˇ)
to daydream; to be lost in reverie; a daydream; reverie; a fantasy; illusion; a vision: 她沈湎於舊日的幻想中。She fell into a reverie about the past.

幻想曲(ㄏㄨㄢˋ ㄒㄧㄤˇ ㄑㄩˇ)
a fantasia or fantasy (a form of musical composition)

幻象(ㄏㄨㄢˋ ㄒㄧㄤˋ)
a mental image; a vision; an illusion; a phantasm or fantasm

幻塵(ㄏㄨㄢˋ ㄔㄣˊ)
(said of a Buddhist concept) the illusory world of the mortals 亦作「幻境②」

幻世(ㄏㄨㄢˋ ㄕˋ)
(said of a Buddhist concept) the illusory world of the mortals 亦作「幻塵」

幻術(ㄏㄨㄢˋ ㄕㄨˋ)
magic; sorcery; theurgy; thaumaturgy

幻影(ㄏㄨㄢˋ ㄧㄥˇ)
an unreal and visionary image

二畫

【幼】 1356
ㄧㄡˋ yow yòu

1. young; delicate; tender; immature
2. to take care of the young

幼苗(ㄧㄡˋ ㄇㄧㄠˊ)
a tender seedling

幼發拉底河(ㄧㄡˋ ㄈㄚ ㄌㄚ ㄉㄧˇ ㄏㄜˊ)
the Euphrates (River)

幼童(ㄧㄡˋ ㄊㄨㄥˊ)
a young child

幼童軍(ㄧㄡˋ ㄊㄨㄥˊ ㄐㄩㄣ)
a cub scout

幼嫩(ㄧㄡˋ ㄋㄣˋ)
young and tender; delicate

幼年(ㄧㄡˋ ㄋㄧㄢˊ)
childhood: 他們從幼年開始即爲好友。They are good friends since childhood.

幼女(ㄧㄡˋ ㄋㄩˇ)
a young girl

幼女童軍(ㄧㄡˋ ㄋㄩˇ ㄊㄨㄥˊ ㄐㄩㄣ)
a brownie

幼根(ㄧㄡˋ ㄍㄣ)
(botany) a radicle

〔幺部〕

幼小(ㄧㄡˋ ㄒㄧㄠˇ)
young and small

幼稚 or 幼穉(ㄧㄡˋ ㄓˋ)
immature; naive; unsophisticated

幼稚可笑(ㄧㄡˋ ㄓˋ ㄎㄜˇ ㄒㄧㄠˋ)
ridiculously childish

幼稚教育(ㄧㄡˋ ㄓˋ ㄐㄧㄠˋ ㄩˋ)
preschool education

幼稚園(ㄧㄡˋ ㄓˋ ㄩㄢˊ)
a kindergarten

幼主(ㄧㄡˋ ㄓㄨˇ)
a youthful monarch; a monarch who is crowned in childhood

幼蟲(ㄧㄡˋ ㄔㄨㄥˊ)
a larva: 蝌蚪是青蛙的幼蟲。The tadpole is the larva of the frog.

幼弱(ㄧㄡˋ ㄖㄨㄛˋ)
young and delicate

幼子(ㄧㄡˋ ㄗˇ)
a young son

幼兒(ㄧㄡˋ ㄦˊ)
an infant; a baby

幼兒期(ㄧㄡˋ ㄦˊ ㄑㄧˊ)
infancy

幼芽(ㄧㄡˋ ㄧㄚˊ)
young buds; plumules: 樹木在生長幼芽。The trees are unfolding their buds.

六畫

【幽】 1357
ㄧㄡ iou yōu

1. dark; gloomy; obscure
2. lonely; solitary; secluded
3. quiet; tranquil
4. deep; profound
5. hidden; secret
6. to imprison; to confine

幽閉(ㄧㄡ ㄅㄧˋ)
①to keep in confinement; to confine ②formerly, to sterilize a woman (as punishment)

幽閉恐懼症(ㄧㄡ ㄅㄧˋ ㄎㄨㄥˇ ㄐㄩˋ ㄓㄥˋ)
claustrophobia

幽默(ㄧㄡ ㄇㄛˋ)
humorous; humor

幽默文學(ㄧㄡ ㄇㄛˋ ㄨㄣˊ ㄒㄩㄝˊ)
humorous literature

幽美(ㄧㄡ ㄇㄟˇ)
pathetically beautiful; showing melancholy beauty

幽門(ㄧㄡ ㄇㄣˊ)
(anatomy) the pylorus

幽眇(ㄧㄡ ㄇㄧㄠˇ)
①distant; remote ②exquisite and delicate

幽冥(ㄧㄡ ㄇㄧㄥˊ)
①dark; gloomy; somber; obscure ②(Buddhism) hell; the lower world

幽明異路(ㄧㄡ ㄇㄧㄥˊ ㄧˋ ㄌㄨˋ)
The dead and the living do not mix.

幽憤(ㄧㄡ ㄈㄣˋ)
the sulks; resentment; to be sulky; to sulk; to resent

幽房(ㄧㄡ ㄈㄤˊ)
a secluded inner room

幽浮(ㄧㄡ ㄈㄨˊ)
UFO (unidentified flying object)

幽獨(ㄧㄡ ㄉㄨˊ)
solitary; lonely

幽蘭(ㄧㄡ ㄌㄢˊ)
(botany) an orchid

幽流(ㄧㄡ ㄌㄧㄡˊ)
subterranean flow of water

幽囹(ㄧㄡ ㄌㄧㄥˊ)
to keep in confinement; to confine

幽靈(ㄧㄡ ㄌㄧㄥˊ)
the disembodied spirit of a dead person; a ghost: 你喜歡幽靈故事嗎? Do you like ghost stories?

幽谷(ㄧㄡ ㄍㄨˇ)
a deep valley

幽會(ㄧㄡ ㄏㄨㄟˋ)
a tryst, or secret meeting (between a couple in love)

幽婚(ㄧㄡ ㄏㄨㄣ)
the marriage between a living person and a dead person

幽魂(ㄧㄡ ㄏㄨㄣˊ)
the spirit of a dead person; a ghost

幽界(ㄧㄡ ㄐㄧㄝˋ)
the lower world; Hades

幽禁(ㄧㄡ ㄐㄧㄣˋ)
to confine; to imprison

幽靜(ㄧㄡ ㄐㄧㄥˋ)
tranquil; placid; serene

幽居(ㄧㄡ ㄐㄩ)
to live in retirement; to live away from society

幽棲(ㄧㄡ ㄑㄧ)
to live away from society

幽期(ㄧㄡ ㄑㄧˊ)
①contemplated time for retirement ②an appointment for a secret meeting (especially between a couple in love)亦作「幽會」

幽囚(ㄧㄡ ㄑㄧㄡˊ)
to confine; to imprison; to shut up 亦作「幽禁」

幽情(ㄧㄡ ㄑㄧㄥˊ)
a pensive mood; the musing state of mind

幽閑(ㄧㄡ ㄒㄧㄢˊ)
①(said of a woman) gentle and graceful ②leisurely and carefree

幽香(ㄧㄡ ㄒㄧㄤ)
a delicate, faint fragrance

幽深(ㄧㄡ ㄕㄣ)
deep and dark

幽人(ㄧㄡ ㄖㄣˊ)
a recluse; a hermit

幽壤(ㄧㄡ ㄖㄤˇ)
the lower world; Hades

幽思(ㄧㄡ ㄙ)
sober musing; melancholy contemplation

幽邃(ㄧㄡ ㄙㄨㄟˋ)
profound; unfathomable

幽暗(ㄧㄡ ㄢˋ)
dim; gloomy

幽雅(ㄧㄡ ㄧㄚˇ)
chaste and elegant

幽咽(ㄧㄡ ㄧㄝˋ)
the sobs, or murmurs, of flowing water: 山間有幽咽的泉水。There are murmuring springs in the mountain areas.

幽幽(ㄧㄡ ㄧㄡ)
①deep; profound; unfathomable ②dim

幽微(ㄧㄡ ㄨㄟˊ)
(said of sound, smell, etc.) obscure; weak

幽怨(ㄧㄡ ㄩㄢˋ)
hidden bitterness (of a lady frustrated in love)

九畫

【幾】 1358
1. ㄐㄧˇ jii jǐ

1. how many; how much
2. a few; several; some: 我已經讀過好幾遍了。I have read it several times.

3. which; when

幾番風雨(ㄐㄧˇ ㄈㄢ ㄈㄥ ㄩˇ)
(the devastation of) a few storms and gusts

幾分(ㄐㄧˇ ㄈㄣ)
a bit; somewhat; rather: 他有幾分醉意。He is a bit tipsy.

幾分姿色(ㄐㄧˇ ㄈㄣ ㄗ ㄙㄜˋ)
rather charming looks (of a woman)

幾度(ㄐㄧˇ ㄉㄨˋ)
① several times ② how many times ③ how many degrees ④ several degrees

幾多(ㄐㄧˇ ㄉㄨㄛ)
how many; how much

幾天(ㄐㄧˇ ㄊㄧㄢ)
① several days: 過幾天我便回來。I'll be back in several days. ② how many days

幾年(ㄐㄧˇ ㄋㄧㄢˊ)
①several years ②how many years

幾何(ㄐㄧˇ ㄏㄜˊ)
① how much ② geometry

幾何畫(ㄐㄧˇ ㄏㄜˊ ㄏㄨㄚˋ)
a geometric pattern

幾何級數(ㄐㄧˇ ㄏㄜˊ ㄐㄧˊ ㄕㄨˋ)
a geometric progression

幾何學(ㄐㄧˇ ㄏㄜˊ ㄒㄩㄝˊ)
geometry

幾回(ㄐㄧˇ ㄏㄨㄟˊ)or 幾次(ㄐㄧˇ ㄘˋ)
① several times; on several occasions: 我曾見過他幾回。I have met him on several occasions. ② how many times

幾許(ㄐㄧˇ ㄒㄩˇ)
how many; how much: 不知幾許。No one can tell how much.

幾十(ㄐㄧˇ ㄕˊ)
①(a few or several) dozens of; (a few or several) scores of ② how many tens

幾時(ㄐㄧˇ ㄕˊ)
what time; when: 你幾時能來? When can you come?

幾曾(ㄐㄧˇ ㄘㄥˊ)
Was it ever so? 或 Has it ever happened?

幾兒(ㄐㄧㄜˇㄦ)
what time; what day; when

幾樣(ㄐㄧˇ ㄧㄤˋ)
① several kinds; several sorts; a few kinds; a few sorts: 她買了幾樣甜點。She bought several kinds of desserts. ② how many kinds; how many sorts

【幾】 1358 2. ㄐㄧ ji jī

1. small; minute; tiny; slight
2. nearly; almost: 這兩者相去幾希。The two are very nearly the same.
3. an omen; a portent

幾殆(ㄐㄧ ㄉㄞˋ)
in great danger

幾納樹(ㄐㄧ ㄋㄚˋ ㄕㄨˋ)
(botany) the cinchona

幾納霜(ㄐㄧ ㄋㄚˋ ㄕㄨㄤ)
(medicine) quinine 亦作「金雞納霜」

幾內亞(ㄐㄧ ㄋㄟˋ ㄧㄚˋ)
Guinea

幾乎(ㄐㄧ ㄏㄨ)
almost; nearly: 幾乎沒有一個人相信這消息。Almost no one believed the news.

幾幾乎(ㄐㄧ ㄐㄧ ㄏㄨ)
almost; nearly 參看「幾乎」

幾希(ㄐㄧ ㄒㄧ)
(said of the degree of difference) slight; little; not much

幾兆(ㄐㄧ ㄓㄠˋ)
an omen; a portent; an augury

幾事(ㄐㄧ ㄕˋ)
details

幾微(ㄐㄧ ㄨㄟˊ)
an omen; a portent; an augury: 他能洞察幾微。He can know much from the omens.

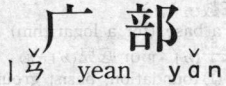

广部
ㄧㄢˇ yean yǎn

二畫

【庀】 1359 ㄆㄧˇ pii pǐ

to prepare; to provide; to arrange

三畫

【庄】 1360 (莊) ㄓㄨㄤ juang zhuāng

1. a farmhouse
2. a marketplace
3. a banker (in gambling games)
4. a cottage

四畫

【庇】 1361 ㄅㄧˋ bih bì

to hide; to conceal; to harbor; to protect

庇短(ㄅㄧˋ ㄉㄨㄢˇ)
to conceal (or shield) a defect

庇護(ㄅㄧˋ ㄏㄨˋ)
① to give protection to; to harbor ② asylum; refuge: 他將尋求政治庇護。He will seek political asylum. ③ Chinese transliteration for Pius

庇護所(ㄅㄧˋ ㄏㄨˋ ㄙㄨㄛˇ)
a sanctuary or asylum

庇祐(ㄅㄧˋ ㄧㄡˋ)
(said of a god) to give divine assistance to a mortal

庇蔭(ㄅㄧˋ ㄧㄣˋ)
to shelter; to harbor

【庋】 1362 ㄐㄧˇ jii jǐ

1. a cupboard; a closet
2. to put into a cupboard or closet; to put into the proper place; to put away; to store up

庋置(ㄐㄧˇ ㄓˋ)
to put into the proper place; to put away

庋藏(ㄐㄧˇ ㄘㄤˊ)
to put away for safekeeping

【序】 1363 ㄒㄩˋ shiuh xù

1. a preface; a foreword; an introduction
2. the sequence of things; order: 井然有序 in perfect order

序跋(ㄒㄩˋ ㄅㄚˊ)
the style or composition of prefaces and postscripts

序幕(ㄒㄩˋ ㄇㄨˋ)
the prologue; the prelude; the curtain raiser

序列(ㄒㄩˋ ㄌㄧㄝˋ)
a rank; order

序論(ㄒㄩˋ ㄌㄨㄣˋ)
an introduction (in a piece of writing)

序曲(ㄒㄩˋ ㄑㄩˇ)
a prelude

序齒(ㄒㄩˋ ㄔˇ)
the order of seniority (in age)

序數(ㄒㄩˋ ㄕㄨˋ)
an ordinal number

序次(ㄒㄩˋ ㄘˋ)
the sequence of things; order

序言(ㄒㄩˋ ㄧㄢˊ)or 序文(ㄒㄩˋ ㄨㄣˊ)
a preface; a foreword

五畫

【底】 1364 ㄉㄧˇ dii dǐ

① underside; base; bottom; basis; foundation ② the end; the last part

底版(ㄉㄧˇ ㄅㄢˇ)
a photographic plate; a negative

底本(ㄉㄧˇ ㄅㄣˇ)
①(said of a book) the master copy; the original manuscript copy ② capital (in business)

底邊(ㄉㄧˇ ㄅㄧㄢ)
the base (of a triangle, etc.)

底牌(ㄉㄧˇ ㄆㄞˊ)
cards in one's hand: 亮底牌 to show the cards in one's hand—to show one's last power or strength

底盤(ㄉㄧˇ ㄆㄢˊ)
a chassis (of an automobile, a car, a radio, etc.)

底片(ㄉㄧˇ ㄆㄧㄢˋ)
(photography) a negative

底面(ㄉㄧˇ ㄇㄧㄢˋ)
the base (of a cone, etc.)

底定(ㄉㄧˇ ㄉㄧㄥˋ)
① to establish peace in a region after an insurgence is put down ② to settle, still (disturbed waters)

底特律(ㄉㄧˇ ㄊㄜˋ ㄌㄩˋ)
Detroit, in Michigan

底裏(ㄉㄧˇ ㄌㄧˇ)
the invisible side; the inside

底格里斯河(ㄉㄧˇ ㄍㄜˊ ㄌㄧˇ ㄙ ㄏㄜˊ)
the Tigris (River)

底稿(ㄉㄧˇ ㄍㄠˇ)
a manuscript; MS. or ms.

底極(ㄉㄧˇ ㄐㄧˊ)
the ultimate point; extremity

底架(ㄉㄧˇ ㄐㄧㄚˋ)
a chassis (of an automobile, a car, a radio, etc.)

底價(ㄉㄧˇ ㄐㄧㄚˋ)
the floor or minimum price

底角(ㄉㄧˇ ㄐㄧㄠˇ)
a base angle (of a triangle, etc.)

底漆(ㄉㄧˇ ㄑㄧ)
priming (of paint); primer 亦作「底層漆」

底缺(ㄉㄧˇ ㄑㄩㄝ)
an authorized vacancy or opening (for personnel) in a government agency

底細(ㄉㄧˇ ㄒㄧˋ)
① the unapparent details (of a matter); ins and outs ② the unknown background (of a person)

底下
①(ㄉㄧˇ ˙ㄒㄧㄚ) the underside; the downward position
②(ㄉㄧˇ ㄒㄧㄚˋ) mean; depraved

底下人(ㄉㄧˇ ˙ㄒㄧㄚ ㄖㄣˊ)
servants; underlings

底線(ㄉㄧˇ ㄒㄧㄢˋ)
the base line; the bottom line

底薪(ㄉㄧˇ ㄒㄧㄣ)
base pay

底止(ㄉㄧˇ ㄓˇ)
an end; termination; a limit: 他的忍耐已達底止。He was at the end of his patience.

底滯(ㄉㄧˇ ㄓˋ)
to clog; to obstruct; to hamper; to hinder

底數(ㄉㄧˇ ㄕㄨˋ)
a base (for a logarithm)

底子(ㄉㄧˇ ˙ㄗ)or 底兒(ㄉㄧㄜˇㄦ)
① foundation; basis; groundwork: 他的作文底子好。He has a good basis in composition. ② a manuscript; a rough draft or sketch ③ a shoe sole

底座(ㄉㄧˇ ㄗㄨㄛˋ)
a support; a base; a stand; a pedestal

底册(ㄉㄧˇ ㄘㄜˋ)
the original copy (in bound form)

底層(ㄉㄧˇ ㄘㄥˊ)
① the bottom layer ② the ground floor

底樣(ㄉㄧˇ ㄧㄤˋ)
the original pattern (to be copied); a sample; a pattern

底蘊(ㄉㄧˇ ㄩㄣˋ)
the reality beneath the surface; inside information; the inner secret

【庖】 1365 ㄆㄠˊ paur páo

the kitchen; the cuisine

庖代(ㄆㄠˊ ㄉㄞˋ)
to act for another

庖丁(ㄆㄠˊ ㄉㄧㄥ)
a cook; a cook named Ding

庖犧(ㄆㄠˊ ㄒㄧ)or 伏羲(ㄈㄨˊ ㄒㄧ)
Fu-hsi, a legendary emperor of ancient China

庖廚(ㄆㄠˊ ㄔㄨˊ)
a kitchen

【店】 1366 ㄉㄧㄢˋ diann diàn

1. a commercial establishment; a shop; a store: 他的父親開一家小店鋪。His father keeps a small shop.
2. an inn; a hotel: 他住在此店中。He is stopping in this inn.

店鋪(ㄉㄧㄢˋ ㄆㄨˋ)
a store; a shop

店面(ㄉㄧㄢˋ ㄇㄧㄢˋ)
a shop front

店底(ㄉㄧㄢˋ ㄉㄧˇ)
the stock in trade

店東(ㄉㄧㄢˋ ㄉㄨㄥ)
a proprietor (of a store)

店檯(ㄉㄧㄢˋ ㄊㄞˊ)
a shop counter

店客(ㄉㄧㄢˋ ㄎㄜˋ)
a customer

店夥(ㄉㄧㄢˋ ㄏㄨㄛˇ)
a shop clerk

店家(ㄉㄧㄢˋ ㄐㄧㄚ)
a manager (of an inn, shop, etc.): 店家對顧客慇勤招待。The manager of the shop serves the customer enthusiastically.

店錢(ㄉㄧㄢˋ ㄑㄧㄢˊ)
inn expenses; the cost of lodging; a hotel bill

店小二(ㄉㄧㄢˋ ㄒㄧㄠˇ ㄦˋ)
a waiter (in an inn or tavern)

店主(ㄉㄧㄢˋ ㄓㄨˇ)
a proprietor (of a store or shop)亦作「店東」
店肆(ㄉㄧㄢˋ ㄙˋ)
a shop; a store; a firm
店務(ㄉㄧㄢˋ ㄨˋ)
routine work in a store or shop
店員(ㄉㄧㄢˋ ㄩㄢˊ)
a shop clerk; a shopman; a salesman or saleswoman: 他是那百貨公司的店員。He is a clerk of that department store.

【庚】 1367
ㄍㄥ geng gēng
1. the seventh of the Ten Celestial Stems (天干)
2. the age (of a person): 請問貴庚? May I know your age?
庚帖(ㄍㄥ ㄊㄧㄝˇ)
a card containing the horoscopes of a betrothed couple
庚子賠款(ㄍㄥ ㄗˇ ㄆㄟˊ ㄎㄨㄢˇ)
the indemnities for the Boxer Uprising; Boxer Indemnity
庚子之役(ㄍㄥ ㄗˇ ㄓ ㄧˋ)
the Boxer Uprising or Rebellion (against foreign aggressors in 1900, as a result of which, China was forced to make economic and territorial concessions)

【府】 1368
ㄈㄨˇ fuu fŭ
1. a mansion
2. a government agency; a government office
3. an administrative district in former times; a prefecture
4. your home
5. a treasury; archives
府邸(ㄈㄨˇ ㄉㄧˇ)
a mansion
府第(ㄈㄨˇ ㄉㄧˋ)
a mansion 亦作「府邸」
府帑(ㄈㄨˇ ㄊㄤˇ)
the money in the treasury
府庫(ㄈㄨˇ ㄎㄨˋ)
a treasury for public funds
府君(ㄈㄨˇ ㄐㄩㄣ)
①(formerly) the magistrate of a prefecture ②a reference to one's ancestors
府學(ㄈㄨˇ ㄒㄩㄝˊ)
a prefectural school (in former times)
府治(ㄈㄨˇ ㄓˋ)
the seat of a prefectural government during the Ming and Ching dynasties
府綢(ㄈㄨˇ ㄔㄡˊ)
a kind of stiff silk fabric produced in Shantung Province; poplin; pongee
府試(ㄈㄨˇ ㄕˋ)
a prefectural examination under the former system of civil service examinations
府上(ㄈㄨˇ ·ㄕㄤ)
① your native place ② your home ③ your family

六畫

【度】 1369
1. ㄉㄨˋ duh dù
1. an instrument for measuring length
2. a kilowatt-hour
3. a unit of measurement for angles, temperature, etc.; a degree: 直角爲九十度。A right angle is an angle of 90 degrees.
4. (number of) times: 他曾數度前往巴黎。He has been to Paris several times.
5. a system: 該公司制度健全。This company has a sound system.
6. a manner; bearing: 這青年風度翩翩。This youth has a charming manner.
7. to pass: 他將在何處度暑假? Where will he pass the summer holidays?
8. consideration; careful thought: 我把生死置之度外。I have given no thought to personal safety.
度命(ㄉㄨˋ ㄇㄧㄥˋ)
to make a living
度牒(ㄉㄨˋ ㄉㄧㄝˊ)
the certificate issued to a Buddhist monk or nun at the time of ordainment
度量(ㄉㄨˋ ㄌㄧㄤˋ)
① an instrument for measuring ② the capacity for forgiveness; the degree of magnanimity
度量衡(ㄉㄨˋ ㄌㄧㄤˋ ㄏㄥˊ)
weights and measures
度假(ㄉㄨˋ ㄐㄧㄚˋ)
to spend one's holidays (or vacation); to go vacationing
度曲(ㄉㄨˋ ㄑㄩˇ)
① to sing in accordance with the score ② to compose tunes
度支(ㄉㄨˋ ㄓ)
an official in charge of the nation's finance
度世(ㄉㄨˋ ㄕˋ)
to transcend the worldly life (as a Buddhist way of salvation)
度數(ㄉㄨˋ ㄕㄨˋ)
a reading (of a barometer, thermometer, water meter, etc.)
度日(ㄉㄨˋ ㄖˋ)
to make a living (usually said of poorly-paid jobs)
度日如年(ㄉㄨˋ ㄖˋ ㄖㄨˊ ㄋㄧㄢˊ)
to pass days as if they were years (because of deep anxiety, worries, or misery)
度外(ㄉㄨˋ ㄨㄞˋ)
outside one's consideration
度越(ㄉㄨˋ ㄩㄝˋ)
to transcend; to surpass; to exceed

【度】 1369
2. ㄉㄨㄛˋ duoh duò
to consider; to measure; to infer
度德量力(ㄉㄨㄛˋ ㄉㄜˊ ㄌㄧㄤˋ ㄌㄧˋ)
to act with due consideration of one's own abilities

【庠】 1370
ㄒㄧㄤˊ shyang xiáng
a school during the Chou Dynasty
庠序(ㄒㄧㄤˊ ㄒㄩˋ)
schools
庠生(ㄒㄧㄤˊ ㄕㄥ)
a student of a prefectural or county school in former times

【庥】 1371
ㄒㄧㄡ shiou xiū
to shelter; to protect

七畫

【座】 1372
ㄗㄨㄛˋ tzuoh zuò
a seat; a stand: 請入座。Please take your seat.
座標 or 坐標(ㄗㄨㄛˋ ㄅㄧㄠ)

(mathematics) coordinates
座談(ㄗㄨㄛˋ ㄊㄢˊ)
to have an informal discussion
座談會(ㄗㄨㄛˋ ㄊㄢˊ ㄏㄨㄟˋ)
a discussion meeting; a symposium; a panel discussion
座落(ㄗㄨㄛˋ ㄌㄨㄛˋ)
to be situated or located at; a site or locality 亦作「坐落」
座前(ㄗㄨㄛˋ ㄑㄧㄢˊ)
a conventional phrase placed after the salutation in a letter addressed to one's senior
座像(ㄗㄨㄛˋ ㄒㄧㄤˋ)
a seated portrait or statue
座上客(ㄗㄨㄛˋ ㄕㄤˋ ㄎㄜˋ)
a guest of honor
座次(ㄗㄨㄛˋ ㄘˋ)
seating order
座兒(ㄗㄨㄛˋㄦ)
a seat
座右銘(ㄗㄨㄛˋ ㄧㄡˋ ㄇㄧㄥˊ)
a motto:「天助自助」是一句很好的座右銘。"God helps those who help themselves" is a good motto.
座無虛席(ㄗㄨㄛˋ ㄨˊ ㄒㄩ ㄒㄧˊ)
There is standing room only.
座位(ㄗㄨㄛˋ ㄨㄟˋ)
a seat

【庫】 1373 ㄎㄨˋ kuh kù

1. a storeroom; a storehouse; a warehouse; a granary: 我們的貨物已經入庫。Our goods are already in the granary.
2. a treasury: 海洋是礦物和食物的寶庫。The sea is a treasury of minerals and food.

庫兵(ㄎㄨˋ ㄅㄧㄥ)
the troops guarding the national treasury (in the Ching Dynasty)
庫部(ㄎㄨˋ ㄅㄨˋ)
(in ancient China) a department under the Defense Ministry, in charge of arms and supplies
庫平(ㄎㄨˋ ㄆㄧㄥˊ)
(in ancient China) a scale used by the national treasury as a standard in taxation
庫房(ㄎㄨˋ ㄈㄤˊ)
a storeroom; a storehouse; a warehouse
庫倫(ㄎㄨˋ ㄌㄨㄣˊ)
Kulun, or Ulan Bator, or Ulan Bator Khoto, in Mongolia
庫券(ㄎㄨˋ ㄑㄩㄢˋ)
government reserve notes (as distinct from banknotes issued by a commercial bank); treasury notes
庫收(ㄎㄨˋ ㄕㄡ)
the receipts of the treasury
庫容(ㄎㄨˋ ㄖㄨㄥˊ)
storage capacity
庫藏(ㄎㄨˋ ㄗㄤˋ)
the contents of a storeroom
庫存(ㄎㄨˋ ㄘㄨㄣˊ)
a stock; reserve: 這家公司有大量庫存貨物。This company has a large stock of commodities.
庫頁島(ㄎㄨˋ ㄧㄝˋ ㄉㄠˇ)
Sakhalin
庫銀(ㄎㄨˋ ㄧㄣˊ)
the silver money minted by the government

【庭】 1374 ㄊㄧㄥˊ tyng tíng

1. a hall
2. a yard
3. the imperial court
4. a court of justice: 這件案子將在庭外和解。The case will be settled out of court.

庭決(ㄊㄧㄥˊ ㄐㄩㄝˊ)
to hand down a sentence summarily
庭訓(ㄊㄧㄥˊ ㄒㄩㄣˋ)
exhortation or admonition from one's father
庭長(ㄊㄧㄥˊ ㄓㄤˇ)
a chief justice; a presiding judge; the president of a law court
庭中(ㄊㄧㄥˊ ㄓㄨㄥ)
in the yard
庭除(ㄊㄧㄥˊ ㄔㄨˊ)
the ground before the steps leading to the hall of a house
庭舍(ㄊㄧㄥˊ ㄕㄜˋ)
a house
庭上(ㄊㄧㄥˊ ㄕㄤˋ)
① in court (of justice) ② at (imperial) court
庭議(ㄊㄧㄥˊ ㄧˋ)
a court meeting
庭闈(ㄊㄧㄥˊ ㄨㄟˊ)
① parents' abode ② parents
庭園(ㄊㄧㄥˊ ㄩㄢˊ)
a garden
庭院(ㄊㄧㄥˊ ㄩㄢˋ)
a courtyard; a garden

八畫

【庵】 1375 ㄢ an ān

1. a hut; a cottage
2. a nunnery

庵堂(ㄢ ㄊㄤˊ)
a nunnery; a convent
庵主(ㄢ ㄓㄨˇ)
the superior (of a convent or nunnery)
庵寺(ㄢ ㄙˋ)
① a nunnery ② a temple

【庶】 1376 ㄕㄨˋ shuh shù

1. born of a concubine
2. numerous; various; populous
3. general; common
4. the common people; the commoners
5. almost; nearly

庶民(ㄕㄨˋ ㄇㄧㄣˊ) or 庶衆(ㄕㄨˋ ㄓㄨㄥˋ) or 庶人(ㄕㄨˋ ㄖㄣˊ)
the common people; the commoners; the multitude; the populace; the masses
庶母(ㄕㄨˋ ㄇㄨˇ)
one's father's concubine
庶婦(ㄕㄨˋ ㄈㄨˋ)
the wives of a concubine's children
庶孽(ㄕㄨˋ ㄋㄧㄝˋ)
the son of a concubine
庶女(ㄕㄨˋ ㄋㄩˇ)
a commoner's daughter
庶類(ㄕㄨˋ ㄌㄟˋ)
a multitude of things or beings
庶黎(ㄕㄨˋ ㄌㄧˊ)
the common people; the multitude; the masses
庶官(ㄕㄨˋ ㄍㄨㄢ)
officials of all ranks
庶乎(ㄕㄨˋ ㄏㄨ)
① almost; nearly ② probably; maybe
庶幾(ㄕㄨˋ ㄐㄧ)
① almost; nearly ② probably; maybe ③ the capable

and the virtuous
庶吉士(ㄕㄨˋ ㄐㄧˊ ㄕˋ)
one of the official titles conferred on those who have passed the annual civil service examination with high grades during the Ming and Ching dynasties
庶羞(ㄕㄨˋ ㄒㄧㄡ)
the various kinds of delicacies
庶長(ㄕㄨˋ ㄓㄤˇ)
①the eldest son of a concubine ② an official title during the Chin and Han dynasties
庶政(ㄕㄨˋ ㄓㄥˋ)
the numerous affairs of the state
庶出(ㄕㄨˋ ㄔㄨ)
the offspring of a concubine
庶事(ㄕㄨˋ ㄕˋ)
general affairs
庶子(ㄕㄨˋ ㄗˇ)
① the son of a concubine ② an ancient official title
庶孫(ㄕㄨˋ ㄙㄨㄣ)
the grandson of a concubine
庶務(ㄕㄨˋ ㄨˋ)
general affairs
庶務員(ㄕㄨˋ ㄨˋ ㄩㄢˊ)
a general affairs clerk

【康】 1377
ㄎㄤ kang kāng
1. healthy: 孩子們看來很健康。The children look very healthy.
2. peaceful
3. abundant
4. level, even and smooth (road, etc.)
5. a Chinese family name
康復(ㄎㄤ ㄈㄨˋ)
recovery (from illness): 祝你早日康復。I wish you a speedy recovery.
康德(ㄎㄤ ㄉㄜˊ)
Immanuel Kant (1724-1804), German philosopher
康定(ㄎㄤ ㄉㄧㄥˋ)
Kangting, capital of Sikang Province
康泰(ㄎㄤ ㄊㄞˋ)
healthy and free from trouble
康涅狄克(ㄎㄤ ㄋㄧㄝˋ ㄉㄧˊ ㄎㄜˋ)
the state of Connecticut, U.S.A.
康年(ㄎㄤ ㄋㄧㄢˊ)
an abundant year; a plentiful year
康寧(ㄎㄤ ㄋㄧㄥˊ)
healthy and undisturbed
康樂(ㄎㄤ ㄌㄜˋ)
①(wholesome) recreation ② peace and happiness: 敬祝康樂。I wish you peace and happiness.
康健(ㄎㄤ ㄐㄧㄢˋ)
in good health; healthy
康強(ㄎㄤ ㄑㄧㄤˊ)
healthy and strong
康衢(ㄎㄤ ㄑㄩˊ)
a level and easy highway
康熙字典(ㄎㄤ ㄒㄧ ㄗˋ ㄉㄧㄢˇ)
Kang Hsi Tzu Tien (a 42-volume dictionary compiled during the reign of Kang Hsi in the Ching Dynasty)
康莊大道(ㄎㄤ ㄓㄨㄤ ㄉㄚˋ ㄉㄠˋ)
a level and easy thoroughfare leading to many places
康有為(ㄎㄤ ㄧㄡˇ ㄨㄟˊ)
Kang Yu-wei, a scholar who advocated political reform during the reign of Emperor Kwang Hsü (光緒) of the Ching Dynasty

【庸】 1378
ㄩㄥ iong yōng
(又讀 ㄩㄥˊ yong yóng)
1. mediocre; common
2. stupid
3. a hired laborer
4. to require; need
5. to reward
6. an interrogative (as how, etc.)
庸民(ㄩㄥ ㄇㄧㄣˊ)
the common people; the masses
庸夫愚婦(ㄩㄥ ㄈㄨ ㄩˊ ㄈㄨˋ)
simple, ignorant people
庸碌(ㄩㄥ ㄌㄨˋ)or 庸庸碌碌(ㄩㄥ ㄩㄥ ㄌㄨˋ ㄌㄨˋ)
mediocre; common
庸詎(ㄩㄥ ㄐㄩˋ)or 庸孰(ㄩㄥ ㄕㄨˊ)
an interrogative in formal text—how; is it not
庸行(ㄩㄥ ㄒㄧㄥˊ)
a regular course of action
庸虛(ㄩㄥ ㄒㄩ)
mediocre and incapable (usually said of oneself in self-depreciation)
庸中佼佼(ㄩㄥ ㄓㄨㄥ ㄐㄧㄠˇ ㄐㄧㄠˇ)
a giant among many dwarfs —outstanding
庸豎(ㄩㄥ ㄕㄨˋ)
a mediocre person
庸人(ㄩㄥ ㄖㄣˊ)
a mediocre person
庸人自擾(ㄩㄥ ㄖㄣˊ ㄗˋ ㄖㄠˇ)
(literally) Stupid people create trouble for themselves.
庸才(ㄩㄥ ㄘㄞˊ)
a man of mediocre ability
庸俗(ㄩㄥ ㄙㄨˊ)
vulgar; unrefined
庸闇(ㄩㄥ ㄢˋ)
stupidity; ignorance; ignorant
庸醫(ㄩㄥ ㄧ)
① a quack doctor; a quack; a charlatan ② a term used to scold a doctor who makes mistakes in treatment
庸醫殺人(ㄩㄥ ㄧ ㄕㄚ ㄖㄣˊ)
homicide by quackery
庸言庸行(ㄩㄥ ㄧㄢˊ ㄩㄥ ㄒㄧㄥˊ)
commonplace words and deeds

【庹】 1379
ㄊㄨㄛˇ tuoo tuǒ
the distance between one's two middle fingertips when one outstretches one's arms

九畫

【庾】 1380
ㄩˇ yeu yǔ
1. an enclosed place for storing grain
2. a unit of an ancient measure of capacity, equivalent to 16 decaliters
3. a Chinese family name
庾信(ㄩˇ ㄒㄧㄣˋ)
Yü Hsin (513-581 A.D.), a man of letters in the Epoch of Division Between North and South

【廁】 1381
1. ㄘㄜˋ tseh cè
a toilet, lavatory or latrine
廁所(ㄘㄜˋ ㄙㄨㄛˇ)
a water closet; a toilet; a lavatory; a rest room; a latrine; a men's room; a

〔广部〕

〔广部〕

women's room

【厠】 1381
2. ㄘ tsyh cì
to mingle with; to be a member of
厠身社會(ㄘ ㄕㄣ ㄕㄜˋ ㄏㄨㄟˋ)
to be a member of society
厠足其間(ㄘ ㄗㄨˊ ㄑㄧˊ ㄐㄧㄢ)
to participate in; to be directly concerned

【厠】 1381
3. ㄙˋ syh sì
used only in 茅厠—a latrine, lavatory, etc.

【廂】 1382
ㄒㄧㄤ shiang xiāng
1. the wing (of a building); a side room
2. a box in the theater
3. the vicinity or outskirts of a city
廂兵(ㄒㄧㄤ ㄅㄧㄥ) or 廂軍(ㄒㄧㄤ ㄐㄩㄣ)
the garrison troops of the Tang and Sung dynasties
廂房(ㄒㄧㄤ ㄈㄤˊ) or 廂屋(ㄒㄧㄤ ㄨ)
a side room

十畫

【廈】 1383
ㄒㄧㄚˋ shiah xià
(語音 ㄕㄚˋ shah shà)
a tall building; an edifice
廈門(ㄒㄧㄚˋ ㄇㄣˊ)
Amoy, a port city in Fukien Province

【廉】 1384
ㄌㄧㄢˊ lian lián
1. incorrupt; incorruptible; honest; upright
2. inexpensive; cheap
3. to examine; to inspect
4. a Chinese family name
廉白(ㄌㄧㄢˊ ㄅㄛˊ)
immaculate
廉頗(ㄌㄧㄢˊ ㄆㄛ)
Lien Po, a general of the state of Chao during the Warring States period
廉明(ㄌㄧㄢˊ ㄇㄧㄥˊ)
(said of officials) incorruptible and intelligent; clean-handed and clearheaded
廉俸(ㄌㄧㄢˊ ㄈㄥˋ)
extra allowances paid to government officials in addition to regular salaries during the Ching Dynasty
廉得其情(ㄌㄧㄢˊ ㄉㄜˊ ㄑㄧˊ ㄑㄧㄥˊ)
to learn the truth after investigation
廉吏(ㄌㄧㄢˊ ㄌㄧˋ)
an incorrupt official
廉價(ㄌㄧㄢˊ ㄐㄧㄚˋ)
a low price
廉價品(ㄌㄧㄢˊ ㄐㄧㄚˋ ㄆㄧㄣˇ) or 廉價貨物(ㄌㄧㄢˊ ㄐㄧㄚˋ ㄏㄨㄛˋ ㄨˋ)
cheap goods; a bargain
廉節(ㄌㄧㄢˊ ㄐㄧㄝˊ)
frugal; thrifty
廉潔(ㄌㄧㄢˊ ㄐㄧㄝˊ)
incorrupt; incorruptible; honest; disinterestedness and purity
廉介(ㄌㄧㄢˊ ㄐㄧㄝˋ)
incorrupt and uncompromising
廉直(ㄌㄧㄢˊ ㄓˊ)
honest and upright
廉恥(ㄌㄧㄢˊ ㄔˇ)
the integrity of character and a sense of honor
廉察(ㄌㄧㄢˊ ㄔㄚˊ)
to inspect; to investigate; to examine
廉士(ㄌㄧㄢˊ ㄕˋ)
a man of principle: 廉吏必爲廉士。An incorrupt official must be a man of principle.
廉售(ㄌㄧㄢˊ ㄕㄡˋ)
to sell at a low price
廉讓(ㄌㄧㄢˊ ㄖㄤˋ)
to sell (property) at a low price: 他廉讓他的車子。He sold his car at a low price.
廉隅(ㄌㄧㄢˊ ㄩˊ)
punctilious; scrupulous
廉遠堂高(ㄌㄧㄢˊ ㄩㄢˇ ㄊㄤˊ ㄍㄠ)
(said of a monarch) dignified

【廊】 1385
ㄌㄤˊ lang láng
a portico; a corridor; a hallway: 她站在走廊上。She stood in the corridor.
廊廟(ㄌㄤˊ ㄇㄧㄠˋ)
the court (of a monarch)
廊廟器(ㄌㄤˊ ㄇㄧㄠˋ ㄑㄧˋ)
capacity for administering the affairs of state
廊廟之志(ㄌㄤˊ ㄇㄧㄠˋ ㄓ ㄓˋ)
political aspiration or ambition
廊房(ㄌㄤˊ ㄈㄤˊ)
houses built by the government near the city towers in Peiping and leased to the people during the Ming Dynasty
廊下(ㄌㄤˊ ㄒㄧㄚˋ)
a corridor; a portico; a hallway
廊子(ㄌㄤˊ ·ㄗ)
a corridor; a portico; a hallway
廊腰(ㄌㄤˊ ㄧㄠ)
the corner of a corridor
廊簷(ㄌㄤˊ ㄧㄢˊ)
a portico

【廋】 1386
ㄙㄡ sou sōu
1. to conceal; to hide
2. to search
廋疏(ㄙㄡ ㄕㄨ)
to search
廋辭(ㄙㄡ ㄘˊ)
a riddle; a puzzle; an enigma
廋語(ㄙㄡ ㄩˇ)
a riddle; a puzzle; an enigma

十一畫

【廄】 1387
ㄐㄧㄡˋ jiow jiù
a stable
廄肥(ㄐㄧㄡˋ ㄈㄟˊ)
the animal refuse used as fertilizer
廄卒(ㄐㄧㄡˋ ㄗㄨˊ)
a groom

【廖】 1388
ㄌㄧㄠˋ liaw liào
a Chinese family name

【廑】 1389
ㄐㄧㄣˇ jiin jǐn
1. a hut; a cottage
2. eager
廑念(ㄐㄧㄣˇ ㄋㄧㄢˋ)
eager attention or concern
廑注(ㄐㄧㄣˇ ㄓㄨˋ)
eager attention or concern

【廓】 1390
ㄎㄨㄛˋ kuoh kuò
1. open; wide
2. empty
廓土(ㄎㄨㄛˋ ㄊㄨˇ)
an open ground
廓落(ㄎㄨㄛˋ ㄌㄨㄛˋ)
wide; open

廓清(ㄎㄨㄛˋ ㄑㄧㄥ)
to liquidate; to clean up; to wipe out

廓然(ㄎㄨㄛˋ ㄖㄢˊ)
① spacious ② vast; boundless ③ unprejudiced; unbiased

廓爾喀(ㄎㄨㄛˋ ㄦˇ ㄎㄚˇ)
① the Gurkha people of Nepal ② old name of Nepal

【蔭】 1391 ㄧㄣˋ yinn yìn

to shelter; to harbor; to protect

蔭庇(ㄧㄣˋ ㄅㄧˋ)
to protect; to shelter; to harbor; protection; shelter

蔭監(ㄧㄣˋ ㄐㄧㄢˋ)
(Ching Dynasty) the system in which the offspring of distinguished officials admitted to the Imperial Academy in recognition of the latter's contribution

蔭生(ㄧㄣˋ ㄕㄥ)
(Ching Dynasty) the offspring of distinguished officials admitted to the Imperial Academy in recognition of the latter's contribution

十二畫

【廚】 1392 ㄔㄨˊ chwu chú

1. a kitchen; a cookroom
2. a closet; a chest; a wardrobe; a cupboard

廚房(ㄔㄨˊ ㄈㄤˊ)
a kitchen

廚夫(ㄔㄨˊ ㄈㄨ)or 廚子(ㄔㄨˊ ˙ㄗ)
a chef; a cook

廚娘(ㄔㄨˊ ㄋㄧㄤˊ)
a female cook; a kitchenmaid

廚櫃(ㄔㄨˊ ㄍㄨㄟˋ)
a closet; a chest; a cupboard

廚具(ㄔㄨˊ ㄐㄩˋ)
kitchen utensils

廚師傅(ㄔㄨˊ ㄕ ˙ㄈㄨ)or 廚司務(ㄔㄨˊ ㄙ ㄨˋ)
a chef; a cook

【廛】 1393 ㄔㄢˊ charn chán

1. living space for one family in ancient times
2. a store; a shop

廛肆(ㄔㄢˊ ㄙˋ)
a store; a shop

【廝】 1394 ㄙ sy sī

1. a servant; a person who performs mean labor
2. a fellow; a guy
3. each other; together

廝伴(ㄙ ㄅㄢˋ)
to keep (a person) company

廝併(ㄙ ㄅㄧㄥˋ)
to fight desperately

廝打(ㄙ ㄉㄚˇ)
to have a mêlée; to fight

廝徒(ㄙ ㄊㄨˊ)or 廝僕(ㄙ ㄆㄨˊ)or 廝隸(ㄙ ㄌㄧˋ)or 廝役(ㄙ ㄧˋ)or 廝養(ㄙ ㄧㄤˇ)
the servants performing mean duties

廝鬧(ㄙ ㄋㄠˋ)
to have a spree

廝濫(ㄙ ㄌㄢˋ)
meanness; baseness

廝共(ㄙ ㄍㄨㄥˋ)
in company with each other; together

廝會(ㄙ ㄏㄨㄟˋ)
to meet each other

廝混(ㄙ ㄏㄨㄣˋ)
① to mix with each other; to mingle ② to fool around together ③ to make trouble

廝見(ㄙ ㄐㄧㄢˋ)
to see each other

廝下(ㄙ ㄒㄧㄚˋ)
a mean or lowly position

廝纏(ㄙ ㄔㄢˊ)
to tangle with each other

廝殺(ㄙ ㄕㄚ)
to slaughter one another (as in a battle); to fight at close quarters (with weapons)

廝舍(ㄙ ㄕㄜˋ)
the living quarters of people who perform mean labor

廝守(ㄙ ㄕㄡˇ)
to wait upon each other; to take care of each other

廝認(ㄙ ㄖㄣˋ)
to recognize each other

【廟】 1395 ㄇㄧㄠˋ miaw miào

a temple; a shrine: 廟是奉祀神的地方。A temple is a building used for offering sacrifices to a god or gods.

廟堂(ㄇㄧㄠˋ ㄊㄤˊ)
① the ancestral temple of the royal family ② the court (of a monarch)

廟堂文學(ㄇㄧㄠˋ ㄊㄤˊ ㄨㄣˊ ㄒㄩㄝˊ)
court literature

廟廊(ㄇㄧㄠˋ ㄌㄤˊ)
the imperial court

廟略(ㄇㄧㄠˋ ㄌㄩㄝˋ)or 廟算(ㄇㄧㄠˋ ㄙㄨㄢˋ)
decision made at court (of the monarch)

廟號(ㄇㄧㄠˋ ㄏㄠˋ)
the posthumous title of an emperor

廟會(ㄇㄧㄠˋ ㄏㄨㄟˋ)
a fair held at the site of a temple when the faithful converge to worship the deity: 他們去趕廟會了。They went to the temple fair.

廟諱(ㄇㄧㄠˋ ㄏㄨㄟˋ)
name of a deceased emperor

廟寢(ㄇㄧㄠˋ ㄑㄧㄣˇ)
the imperial ancestral temple

廟主(ㄇㄧㄠˋ ㄓㄨˇ)
the head priest of a temple

廟祝(ㄇㄧㄠˋ ㄓㄨˋ)
a person whose duty is to keep incense burning at a temple; a temple attendant

廟策(ㄇㄧㄠˋ ㄘㄜˋ)
the planning made at the imperial court

廟議(ㄇㄧㄠˋ ㄧˋ)
deliberation at (imperial) court

廟宇(ㄇㄧㄠˋ ㄩˇ)
a temple; a shrine

【廠】 1396 ㄔㄤˇ chaang chǎng

a factory; a plant; a workshop

廠棚(ㄔㄤˇ ㄆㄥˊ)
a crude plant or factory building

廠房(ㄔㄤˇ ㄈㄤˊ)
a factory building

廠房設計(ㄔㄤˇ ㄈㄤˊ ㄕㄜˋ ㄐㄧˋ)
a plant designing

廠條(ㄔㄤˇ ㄊㄧㄠˊ)
the silver ingots minted by the government mint in the early republican days, each worth 1,000 silver coins; gold ingots

〔广部〕

廠址(ㄔㄤˇ ㄓˇ)
a factory address; a factory site or location

廠長(ㄔㄤˇ ㄓㄤˇ)
a factory manager; a plant superintendent

廠主(ㄔㄤˇ ㄓㄨˇ)
a factory owner; a mill owner

廠場設備(ㄔㄤˇ ㄔㄤˇ ㄕㄜˋ ㄅㄟˋ)
plant equipment

廠商(ㄔㄤˇ ㄕㄤ)
manufacturers

廠營(ㄔㄤˇ ㄧㄥˊ)
the temporary barracks for troops

【廡】 1397 ㄨˇ wuu wǔ

1. small rooms around a main building
2. (said of vegetation) dense or luxuriant

【廢】 1398 ㄈㄟˋ fey fèi

1. to give up; to abandon; to discontinue; to abolish: 做事不要半途而廢。Don't give up halfway in doing anything.
2. to reject: 不以人廢言。Do not reject an opinion because of the speaker.
3. useless; disused: 我家門前有一口廢井。In front of my house there is a disused well.
4. disabled

廢票(ㄈㄟˋ ㄆㄧㄠˋ)
①an invalidated ballot ②a used ticket

廢品(ㄈㄟˋ ㄆㄧㄣˇ)
①a waste product ②scrap; waste

廢品回收(ㄈㄟˋ ㄆㄧㄣˇ ㄏㄨㄟˊ ㄕㄡ)
waste recovery

廢帝(ㄈㄟˋ ㄉㄧˋ)
a dethroned emperor

廢掉(ㄈㄟˋ ㄉㄧㄠˋ)
to abolish; to abrogate

廢鐵(ㄈㄟˋ ㄊㄧㄝˇ)
scrap iron

廢料(ㄈㄟˋ ㄌㄧㄠˋ)
useless materials; scrap materials; waste materials 參看「廢品」

廢后(ㄈㄟˋ ㄏㄡˋ)
a dethroned queen; a queen divorced by the monarch; an ex-empress or ex-queen

廢話(ㄈㄟˋ ㄏㄨㄚˋ)
a superfluous statement; a meaningless remark; rubbish; nonsense: 少廢話! No more nonsense!

廢疾(ㄈㄟˋ ㄐㄧˊ)
①an incapacitating disease; an incurable disease ②a disabled person

廢氣(ㄈㄟˋ ㄑㄧˋ)
waste gas; exhaust

廢棄(ㄈㄟˋ ㄑㄧˋ)
to abandon as useless; to scrap; to discard

廢寢忘餐(ㄈㄟˋ ㄑㄧㄣˇ ㄨㄤˋ ㄘㄢ)
so absorbed (in a pursuit) as to neglect sleep and meals

廢墟(ㄈㄟˋ ㄒㄩ)
ruins (of a city, castle, etc.)

廢學(ㄈㄟˋ ㄒㄩㄝˊ)
to discontinue one's education

廢止(ㄈㄟˋ ㄓˇ)
to abolish; to cancel; to abrogate; to annul; to repeal; to rescind; to discontinue

廢紙(ㄈㄟˋ ㄓˇ)
wastepaper; a scrap of paper

廢置不用(ㄈㄟˋ ㄓˋ ㄅㄨˋ ㄩㄥˋ)
to shelve or put aside as useless

廢除(ㄈㄟˋ ㄔㄨˊ)
to abolish; to cancel; to annul; to abrogate; to repeal; to rescind; to discontinue: 不平等條約應該被廢除。All unequal treaties should be abrogated.

廢弛(ㄈㄟˋ ㄕˇ)or(ㄈㄟˋ ㄔˊ)
to neglect

廢水(ㄈㄟˋ ㄕㄨㄟˇ)
waste water; liquid waste

廢水處理(ㄈㄟˋ ㄕㄨㄟˇ ㄔㄨˇ ㄌㄧˇ)
waste water treatment

廢人(ㄈㄟˋ ㄖㄣˊ)
a disabled person

廢業(ㄈㄟˋ ㄧㄝˋ)
to give up a business; to neglect one's work

廢物(ㄈㄟˋ ㄨˋ)
①waste material; rubbish; scrap; ②a good-for-nothing

廢物利用(ㄈㄟˋ ㄨˋ ㄌㄧˋ ㄩㄥˋ)
the utilization of waste material

【廣】 1399 ㄍㄨㄤˇ goang guǎng

1. wide; broad; spacious; extensive
2. to stretch; to extend
3. Kwangtung or Kwangsi

廣播(ㄍㄨㄤˇ ㄅㄛ)or(ㄍㄨㄤˇ ㄅㄛˋ)
①to broadcast; to telecast ②a broadcast

廣播電臺(ㄍㄨㄤˇ ㄅㄛ ㄉㄧㄢˋ ㄊㄞˊ)
a broadcasting station; a radio station

廣播公司(ㄍㄨㄤˇ ㄅㄛ ㄍㄨㄥ ㄙ)
a broadcasting company

廣播節(ㄍㄨㄤˇ ㄅㄛ ㄐㄧㄝˊ)
Broadcasting Day (falling on March 26 annually)

廣播節目(ㄍㄨㄤˇ ㄅㄛ ㄐㄧㄝˊ ㄇㄨˋ)
①a radio program; a broadcast: 你喜歡那一項廣播節目? What is your favorite radio program? ②a television program; a telecast

廣播劇(ㄍㄨㄤˇ ㄅㄛ ㄐㄩˋ)
a radio drama; a radio play

廣播網(ㄍㄨㄤˇ ㄅㄛ ㄨㄤˇ)
a broadcasting network

廣播員(ㄍㄨㄤˇ ㄅㄛ ㄩㄢˊ)
a radio announcer; a broadcaster

廣博(ㄍㄨㄤˇ ㄅㄛˊ)
wide; extensive: 他對這主題有廣博的知識。His knowledge of this subject is extensive.

廣被(ㄍㄨㄤˇ ㄅㄟˋ)
far-reaching (love or benefit)

廣漠(ㄍㄨㄤˇ ㄇㄛˋ)
boundless; vast

廣袤(ㄍㄨㄤˇ ㄇㄠˋ)
length and breadth (of a land); area

廣泛(ㄍㄨㄤˇ ㄈㄢˋ)
extensive; comprehensive; widespread

廣方言館(ㄍㄨㄤˇ ㄈㄤ ㄧㄢˊ ㄍㄨㄢˇ)
a school for training translators, set up in Shanghai by Li Hung-chang (李鴻章) during the Ching Dynasty

廣大(ㄍㄨㄤˇ ㄉㄚˋ)
vast

廣大無邊(ㄍㄨㄤˇ ㄉㄚˋ ㄨˊ ㄅㄧㄢ)
boundless: 廣大無邊的海洋 a boundless ocean

廣島(ㄍㄨㄤˇ ㄉㄠˇ)
Hiroshima, Japan
廣度(ㄍㄨㄤˇ ㄉㄨˋ)
scope; range
廣東(ㄍㄨㄤˇ ㄉㄨㄥ)
Kwangtung Province
廣庭(ㄍㄨㄤˇ ㄊㄧㄥˊ)
① a large yard or garden ② a public place
廣土衆民(ㄍㄨㄤˇ ㄊㄨˇ ㄓㄨㄥˋ ㄇㄧㄣˊ)
(said of a country) having a large territory and a large population
廣內(ㄍㄨㄤˇ ㄋㄟˋ)
the royal library in the Han Dynasty
廣陵散(ㄍㄨㄤˇ ㄌㄧㄥˊ ㄙㄢˇ)
(originally) name of a piece of Chinese harp music—any ancient learning or skill that has not been handed down to posterity; a lost art
廣告(ㄍㄨㄤˇ ㄍㄠˋ)
advertisement
廣告部(ㄍㄨㄤˇ ㄍㄠˋ ㄅㄨˋ)
the advertising department (of a commercial firm)
廣告牌(ㄍㄨㄤˇ ㄍㄠˋ ㄆㄞˊ)
a billboard
廣告片(ㄍㄨㄤˇ ㄍㄠˋ ㄆㄧㄢˋ)
an advertising film
廣告費(ㄍㄨㄤˇ ㄍㄠˋ ㄈㄟˋ)
advertising rates
廣告欄(ㄍㄨㄤˇ ㄍㄠˋ ㄌㄢˊ)
the ad column (in a newspaper)
廣告公司(ㄍㄨㄤˇ ㄍㄠˋ ㄍㄨㄥ ㄙ)
an advertising agency
廣告客戶(ㄍㄨㄤˇ ㄍㄠˋ ㄎㄜˋ ㄏㄨˋ)
an advertiser
廣告業(ㄍㄨㄤˇ ㄍㄠˋ ㄧㄝˋ)
advertising
廣開才路(ㄍㄨㄤˇ ㄎㄞ ㄘㄞˊ ㄌㄨˋ)
to open all avenues for people of talent
廣開言路(ㄍㄨㄤˇ ㄎㄞ ㄧㄢˊ ㄌㄨˋ)
to encourage freedom of speech: 民主的政府廣開言路。A democratic government encourages freedom of speech.
廣闊(ㄍㄨㄤˇ ㄎㄨㄛˋ)
wide; extensive; vast; spacious; broad: 河在愈近海處愈廣闊。The river grows broader as it nears the sea.
廣寒宮(ㄍㄨㄤˇ ㄏㄢˊ ㄍㄨㄥ)
a mythological palace on the moon
廣貨(ㄍㄨㄤˇ ㄏㄨㄛˋ)
a Kwangtung product
廣結善緣(ㄍㄨㄤˇ ㄐㄧㄝˊ ㄕㄢˋ ㄩㄢˊ)
to make friends all around
廣交(ㄍㄨㄤˇ ㄐㄧㄠ)
to make friends extensively; to have a large number of friends: 他廣交朋友。He has a large number of friends.
廣角鏡頭(ㄍㄨㄤˇ ㄐㄧㄠˇ ㄐㄧㄥˋ ㄊㄡˊ)
a wide-angle lens
廣九鐵路(ㄍㄨㄤˇ ㄐㄧㄡˇ ㄊㄧㄝˇ ㄌㄨˋ)
the Canton-Kowloon Railway
廣錢通神(ㄍㄨㄤˇ ㄑㄧㄢˊ ㄊㄨㄥ ㄕㄣˊ)
Money is all-powerful.
廣西(ㄍㄨㄤˇ ㄒㄧ)
Kwangsi Province
廣廈萬間(ㄍㄨㄤˇ ㄒㄧㄚˋ ㄨㄢˋ ㄐㄧㄢ)
(literally) ten thousand spacious buildings to house the homeless—the help that benefits large numbers of people
廣行善事(ㄍㄨㄤˇ ㄒㄧㄥˊ ㄕㄢˋ ㄕˋ)
to perform good deeds extensively; to be philanthropic
廣州(ㄍㄨㄤˇ ㄓㄡ)
Canton, or Kwangchow, capital of Kwangtung Province
廣州灣(ㄍㄨㄤˇ ㄓㄡ ㄨㄢ)
Kwangchow Bay (the southwestern coast of Kwangtung Province)
廣衆(ㄍㄨㄤˇ ㄓㄨㄥˋ)
the multitude of people
廣長舌(ㄍㄨㄤˇ ㄔㄤˊ ㄕㄜˊ)
eloquence
廣場(ㄍㄨㄤˇ ㄔㄤˇ)or(ㄍㄨㄤˇ ㄔㄤˊ)
a square (in a city); a plaza: 他們聆聽廣場上樂隊的演奏。They are listening to the band playing in the square.
廣瘡(ㄍㄨㄤˇ ㄔㄨㄤ)
syphilis
廣嗣(ㄍㄨㄤˇ ㄙˋ)
to have many children
廣而言之(ㄍㄨㄤˇ ㄦˊ ㄧㄢˊ ㄓ)
generally speaking; in a general sense
廣益(ㄍㄨㄤˇ ㄧˋ)
to solicit good advice
廣義(ㄍㄨㄤˇ ㄧˋ)
the wider sense (of a term); the broad definition
廣韻(ㄍㄨㄤˇ ㄩㄣˋ)
Kwang Yun, a riming dictionary, authorized during the Sung Dynasty

十三畫

【廨】 1400 ㄒㄧㄝˋ shieh xiè
a public office; a government building
廨宇(ㄒㄧㄝˋ ㄩˇ)
a government office building

【廩】 1401 ㄌㄧㄣˇ liin lǐn
1. a granary
2. to supply (foodstuffs)
3. to stockpile
廩餼(ㄌㄧㄣˇ ㄒㄧˋ)
government-supplied foodstuffs
廩食(ㄌㄧㄣˇ ㄕˊ)
government-supplied foodstuffs
廩膳(ㄌㄧㄣˇ ㄕㄢˋ)
government-supplied meals
廩生(ㄌㄧㄣˇ ㄕㄥ)
the scholars who lived on government grants during the Ming and Ching dynasties
廩人(ㄌㄧㄣˇ ㄖㄣˊ)
an official in charge of government granaries
廩倉(ㄌㄧㄣˇ ㄘㄤ)
a public granary
廩粟(ㄌㄧㄣˇ ㄙㄨˋ)
government-supplied millet

十六畫

【廬】 1402 ㄌㄨˊ lu lú
1. a thatched cottage
2. Mt. Lu (in Kiangsi)
廬墓(ㄌㄨˊ ㄇㄨˋ)
① to mourn for one's deceased parent by dwelling in a hut built by the grave; to tend the grave ② the grave and hut for those tending it
廬帳(ㄌㄨˊ ㄓㄤˋ)
a tent used as a dwelling
廬舍(ㄌㄨˊ ㄕㄜˋ)

〔廴部〕

a cottage; a hut: 沿着湖邊有幾幢廬舍。Along the bank of the lake there are a few huts.
廬山(ㄌㄨˊ ㄕㄢ)
Mt. Lu, a famous summer resort (in Kiangsi)
廬山眞面目(ㄌㄨˊ ㄕㄢ ㄓㄣ ㄇㄧㄢˋ ㄇㄨˋ)
(literally) the real appearance of Mt. Lu (which is often shrouded in fog)—the real appearance (of a thing or person in disguise)

【龐】 1403 ㄆㄤˊ parng páng
1. disorderly; confused; numerous and jumbled
2. huge; enormous
3. a face
4. a Chinese family name
龐貝(ㄆㄤˊ ㄅㄟˋ)
Pompeii, an ancient city in SW Italy, near Naples
龐培(ㄆㄤˊ ㄆㄟˊ)
Gnaeus Pompeius Magnus, 106-48 B.C., Roman general
龐眉皓髮(ㄆㄤˊ ㄇㄟˊ ㄏㄠˋ ㄈㄚˇ)
bushy brows and white hair (of an aged man)
龐大(ㄆㄤˊ ㄉㄚˋ)
immense; huge; enormous
龐然大物(ㄆㄤˊ ㄖㄢˊ ㄉㄚˋ ㄨˋ)
① a huge object ② a mammoth animal
龐雜(ㄆㄤˊ ㄗㄚˊ)
disorderly; confused
龐錯(ㄆㄤˊ ㄘㄨㄛˋ)
disorderly; confused

十八畫

【廱】 1404 ㄩㄥ iong yōng
1. harmonious
2. an imperial university or academy
廱廱(ㄩㄥ ㄩㄥ)
(said of sound) harmonious

二十二畫

【廳】 1405 ㄊㄧㄥ ting tīng
1. a central or main room of a house
2. a hall
3. a government agency
廳房(ㄊㄧㄥ ㄈㄤˊ)
a central room open to a number of other rooms; a hall
廳堂(ㄊㄧㄥ ㄊㄤˊ)
the central room of a house; a hall
廳長(ㄊㄧㄥ ㄓㄤˇ)
the director of a department under a provincial government
廳事(ㄊㄧㄥ ㄕˋ)
an office 亦作「聽事」

廴部
ㄧㄣˇ yiin yǐn

四畫

【延】 1406 ㄧㄢˊ yan yán
1. to extend; to spread; to lengthen
2. to delay; to defer; to postpone: 這會議將延後。The meeting will be postponed.
3. to prolong
4. to invite
5. to procrastinate: 他以各種藉口拖延歸期。He procrastinated his return on various pretexts.
延聘(ㄧㄢˊ ㄆㄧㄣˋ)
to invite the service of
延蔓(ㄧㄢˊ ㄇㄢˋ)
to spread like a vine
延宕(ㄧㄢˊ ㄉㄤˋ)
to procrastinate; slow in taking action
延眺(ㄧㄢˊ ㄊㄧㄠˋ)
to crane the neck to look
延納(ㄧㄢˊ ㄋㄚˋ)
to employ (talents)
延年益壽(ㄧㄢˊ ㄋㄧㄢˊ ㄧˋ ㄕㄡˋ)
to lengthen one's life
延攬(ㄧㄢˊ ㄌㄢˇ)
to recruit the service of (talented men)
延擱(ㄧㄢˊ ㄍㄜ)
①to procrastinate ② to neglect
延會(ㄧㄢˊ ㄏㄨㄟˋ)
to put off a meeting
延緩(ㄧㄢˊ ㄏㄨㄢˇ)
to postpone; to put off; to defer
延接(ㄧㄢˊ ㄐㄧㄝ)
to receive (guests)
延見(ㄧㄢˊ ㄐㄧㄢˋ)
to grant an interview with someone; to give an audience to someone: 經理延見了他。The manager gave him an interview.
延頸擧踵(ㄧㄢˊ ㄐㄧㄥˇ ㄐㄩˇ ㄓㄨㄥˇ)or
延頸企足(ㄧㄢˊ ㄐㄧㄥˇ ㄑㄧˋ ㄗㄨˊ)or
延企(ㄧㄢˊ ㄑㄧˋ)
(literally) with a craned neck and on tiptoe—to expect or look forward anxiously
延期(ㄧㄢˊ ㄑㄧˊ)
① to be postponed; to be put off: 這會議延期到下禮拜。The meeting has been put off until next week. ② to extend: 我希望我的簽證能延期。I hope that my visa can be extended.
延請(ㄧㄢˊ ㄑㄧㄥˇ)
to invite (talented people to provide assistance); to extend an invitation to
延釐(ㄧㄢˊ ㄒㄧ)
a term written on the wall facing the gate, used for inviting luck
延性(ㄧㄢˊ ㄒㄧㄥˋ)or 延展性(ㄧㄢˊ ㄓㄢˇ ㄒㄧㄥˋ)
(physics) ductility
延續(ㄧㄢˊ ㄒㄩˋ)
to continue; to be continued: 不能讓這種情況延續下去。This situation must not be allowed to continue.
延遲(ㄧㄢˊ ㄔˊ)
to delay; to be delayed
延長(ㄧㄢˊ ㄔㄤˊ)
to lengthen; to extend; to prolong: 會議將延長四天。The conference will be prolonged for four more days.
延長記號(ㄧㄢˊ ㄔㄤˊ ㄐㄧˋ ㄏㄠˋ)
(music) a pause
延長線(ㄧㄢˊ ㄔㄤˊ ㄒㄧㄢˋ)
an extension line; an extension
延時炸彈(ㄧㄢˊ ㄕˊ ㄓㄚˋ ㄉㄢˋ)
a delayed-action bomb
延燒(ㄧㄢˊ ㄕㄠ)

(said of fire) to spread

延壽(ㄧㄢˊ ㄕㄡˋ)
to prolong one's life

延伸(ㄧㄢˊ ㄕㄣ)
to extend; to stretch; to elongate: 這條公路一直延伸到海邊。This highway stretches right to the coast.

延入(ㄧㄢˊ ㄖㄨˋ)
to invite to enter

延髓(ㄧㄢˊ ㄙㄨㄟˇ) or 延腦(ㄧㄢˊ ㄋㄠˇ)
medulla oblongata; the afterbrain

延安(ㄧㄢˊ ㄢ)
Yenan, a county in Shensi Province

延誤(ㄧㄢˊ ㄨˋ)
to fail because of procrastination

延譽(ㄧㄢˊ ㄩˋ)
to make someone's good name widely known

【廷】 1407 ㄊㄧㄥˊ tyng tíng
the imperial court; the court

廷對(ㄊㄧㄥˊ ㄉㄨㄟˋ)
to respond to the emperor's queries at court

廷魁(ㄊㄧㄥˊ ㄎㄨㄟˊ)
the top successful candidate in the imperial examination

廷杖(ㄊㄧㄥˊ ㄓㄤˋ)
to beat a courtier with cane at court in the presence of other courtiers; caning a courtier at court in the presence of other courtiers as a punishment

廷爭(ㄊㄧㄥˊ ㄓㄥ)
to debate at court in the emperor's presence

廷試(ㄊㄧㄥˊ ㄕˋ)
the imperial examination (the last step in the periodic civil service examinations in former times)

廷議(ㄊㄧㄥˊ ㄧˋ)
a discussion at imperial court; a court discussion; a court meeting

六畫

【建】 1408 ㄐㄧㄢˋ jiann jiàn
1. to establish; to build; to construct: 我們必須重建家園。We have to rebuild our homeland.
2. to bring up; to propose; to suggest: 他建議更改計畫。He proposed a change of plan.

建白(ㄐㄧㄢˋ ㄅㄛˊ)
to state one's opinion on public affairs

建坪(ㄐㄧㄢˋ ㄆㄧㄥˊ)
the floor space of a building in *ping* (equivalent to 36 square feet)

建黨(ㄐㄧㄢˋ ㄉㄤˇ)
to found a political party

建都(ㄐㄧㄢˋ ㄉㄨ)
to select a city as the capital (of the empire)

建立(ㄐㄧㄢˋ ㄌㄧˋ)
to establish; to set up; to build; to found

建國(ㄐㄧㄢˋ ㄍㄨㄛˊ)
① to found (or to establish) a state ② to build up a country

建國方略(ㄐㄧㄢˋ ㄍㄨㄛˊ ㄈㄤ ㄌㄩㄝˋ)
Plans for National Reconstruction, by Dr. Sun Yat-sen

建國大綱(ㄐㄧㄢˋ ㄍㄨㄛˊ ㄉㄚˋ ㄍㄤ)
Fundamentals of National Reconstruction, by Dr. Sun Yat-sen

建功立業(ㄐㄧㄢˋ ㄍㄨㄥ ㄌㄧˋ ㄧㄝˋ)
to make a great contribution and accomplish great tasks

建基(ㄐㄧㄢˋ ㄐㄧ)
to lay the foundations

建交(ㄐㄧㄢˋ ㄐㄧㄠ)
to establish diplomatic relations

建教合作(ㄐㄧㄢˋ ㄐㄧㄠˋ ㄏㄜˊ ㄗㄨㄛˋ)
cooperation between a school or university and a business establishment or factory whereby the students get practical experience by working for the latter while the latter get free manpower or research contracts

建艦(ㄐㄧㄢˋ ㄐㄧㄢˋ)
to build a warship

建軍(ㄐㄧㄢˋ ㄐㄩㄣ)
to build a fighting force

建制(ㄐㄧㄢˋ ㄓˋ)
organization of a government agency or military unit

建築(ㄐㄧㄢˋ ㄓㄨˊ)
① to build; to construct ② a building or structure

建築學(ㄐㄧㄢˋ ㄓㄨˊ ㄒㄩㄝˊ)
architecture

建築師(ㄐㄧㄢˋ ㄓㄨˊ ㄕ)
an architect

建築物(ㄐㄧㄢˋ ㄓㄨˊ ㄨˋ)
a building; a structure: 這是一幢優美的建築物。This is a fine building.

建朝(ㄐㄧㄢˋ ㄔㄠˊ)
to found a dynasty

建設(ㄐㄧㄢˋ ㄕㄜˋ)
to construct; to build; construction: 他們正在努力建設他們的家鄉。They are trying hard to construct their hometown.

建設廳(ㄐㄧㄢˋ ㄕㄜˋ ㄊㄧㄥ)
Department of Reconstruction (of a provincial government)

建設性的(ㄐㄧㄢˋ ㄕㄜˋ ㄒㄧㄥˋ ˙ㄉㄜ)
constructive: 我們需要建設性的批評。We need constructive criticism.

建樹(ㄐㄧㄢˋ ㄕㄨˋ)
an achievement; contribution

建造(ㄐㄧㄢˋ ㄗㄠˋ)
to build; to construct; to frame: 他們正在建造房屋。They are building a house.

建安七子(ㄐㄧㄢˋ ㄢ ㄑㄧ ㄗˇ)
the seven leading writers during the Chien An Period at the end of the Han Dynasty—孔融、陳琳、王粲、徐幹、阮瑀、應瑒、劉楨

建安文學(ㄐㄧㄢˋ ㄢ ㄨㄣˊ ㄒㄩㄝˊ)
literature of the Chien An Period, noted both for excellence and abundance

建議(ㄐㄧㄢˋ ㄧˋ)
to propose; to suggest; proposal; suggestion: 我們建議休會。We propose that the meeting be adjourned.

建議案(ㄐㄧㄢˋ ㄧˋ ㄢˋ)
a (parliamentary) motion; a proposal: 這項建議案已在會議中通過了。The motion was adopted at the meeting.

〔廾部〕

廾部
ㄍㄨㄥˇ goong gǒng

一畫

【廿】 1409
ㄋㄧㄢˋ niann niàn
twenty
廿四史(ㄋㄧㄢˋ ㄙˋ ㄕˇ)
the *Twenty-Four Books of History*, or the *Twenty-Four Dynastic Histories* (up to the Ming Dynasty, authorized during the Ching Dynasty)

二畫

【弁】 1410
ㄅㄧㄢˋ biann biàn
1. a conical cap worn on ceremonious occasions in ancient times
2. in the Ching Dynasty low-ranking military officers
3. a Chinese family name
弁髦(ㄅㄧㄢˋ ㄇㄠˊ)
① useless things ② to slight; to underestimate; to despise
弁冕(ㄅㄧㄢˋ ㄇㄧㄢˇ)
an ancient cap worn on ceremonious occasions
弁目(ㄅㄧㄢˋ ㄇㄨˋ)
a squad leader (in the infantry units of the Ching Dynasty)
弁絰(ㄅㄧㄢˋ ㄉㄧㄝˊ)
a patch of coarse linen worn on the mourning cap during a funeral service
弁言(ㄅㄧㄢˋ ㄧㄢˊ)
a preface; a foreword; an introductory remark

四畫

【弄】 1411
ㄋㄨㄥˋ nonq nòng
(讀音 ㄌㄨㄥˋ lonq lòng)
1. to play with; to sport with: 孩子們喜歡玩弄泥沙。Children like to play with sand.
2. to make fun of; to mock
3. to handle; to do; to perform: 你要把事情弄好。You should do a good job.
弄筆(ㄋㄨㄥˋ ㄅㄧˇ)
to distort facts or exaggerate in writing
弄兵(ㄋㄨㄥˋ ㄅㄧㄥ)
to start a war or a rebellion recklessly
弄飯(ㄋㄨㄥˋ ㄈㄢˋ)
to prepare a meal
弄通(ㄋㄨㄥˋ ㄊㄨㄥ)
to get a good grasp of
弄鬼(ㄋㄨㄥˋ ㄍㄨㄟˇ)
to hatch plots; to play tricks behind the scenes
弄口(ㄋㄨㄥˋ ㄎㄡˇ)
to sow discord by making false statements
弄好(ㄋㄨㄥˋ ㄏㄠˇ)
① to get or put into (good) shape ② to finish doing something ③ to do well
弄糊塗(ㄋㄨㄥˋ ㄏㄨˊ ㄊㄨˊ)
to puzzle; to confuse
弄壞(ㄋㄨㄥˋ ㄏㄨㄞˋ)
to bungle; to spoil: 他把事情弄壞了。He bungled the job.
弄假成眞(ㄋㄨㄥˋ ㄐㄧㄚˇ ㄔㄥˊ ㄓㄣ)
to turn simulation into reality unintentionally
弄僵(ㄋㄨㄥˋ ㄐㄧㄤ)
to bring to a deadlock
弄巧成拙(ㄋㄨㄥˋ ㄑㄧㄠˇ ㄔㄥˊ ㄓㄨㄛˊ)
to bungle an ingenious scheme; to suffer a setback in trying to take advantage of a situation
弄錢(ㄋㄨㄥˋ ㄑㄧㄢˊ)
to raise money
弄淸(ㄋㄨㄥˋ ㄑㄧㄥ)
to make clear; to clarify; to gain a clear idea of; to understand fully: 我們必須弄淸事實。We have to understand the facts fully.
弄權(ㄋㄨㄥˋ ㄑㄩㄢˊ)
to abuse one's power
弄小(ㄋㄨㄥˋ ㄒㄧㄠˇ)
to keep a concubine
弄璋(ㄋㄨㄥˋ ㄓㄤ)
to give birth to a son
弄潮兒(ㄋㄨㄥˋ ㄔㄠˊ ㄦˊ)
① a seaman ② a beach swimmer
弄臣(ㄋㄨㄥˋ ㄔㄣˊ)
an emperor's minion; a court jester
弄出事來(ㄋㄨㄥˋ ㄔㄨ ㄕˋ ·ㄌㄞ)
to get into trouble as a result of doing something
弄蛇(ㄋㄨㄥˋ ㄕㄜˊ)
to handle snakes
弄姿(ㄋㄨㄥˋ ㄗ)
(said of women) to assume a charming pose; to act coquettishly
弄糟(ㄋㄨㄥˋ ㄗㄠ)
to make a mess of; to mess up; to bungle; to spoil
弄髒(ㄋㄨㄥˋ ㄗㄤ)
to stain; to soil; to pollute; to smudge; to smear
弄嘴弄舌(ㄋㄨㄥˋ ㄗㄨㄟˇ ㄋㄨㄥˋ ㄕㄜˊ)
to talk idly
弄錯(ㄋㄨㄥˋ ㄘㄨㄛˋ)
to make a mistake; to commit an error: 你弄錯了時間。You made a mistake about the time.
弄死(ㄋㄨㄥˋ ㄙˇ)
to kill; to do away with
弄孫(ㄋㄨㄥˋ ㄙㄨㄣ)
to amuse oneself by playing with grandchildren
弄瓦(ㄋㄨㄥˋ ㄨㄚˇ)
to give birth to a daughter
弄月(ㄋㄨㄥˋ ㄩㄝˋ)
to enjoy the moonlight; to admire the moon

六畫

【弇】 1412
ㄧㄢˇ yean yǎn
1. a narrow-necked container
2. to cover
3. profound

【弈】 1413
ㄧˋ yih yì
the "go" game
弈徒(ㄧˋ ㄊㄨˊ)
a "go" player; a "go" fan
弈具(ㄧˋ ㄐㄩˋ)
the black and white stones and the chessboard for the "go" game
弈棋(ㄧˋ ㄑㄧˊ)
the "go" game
弈聖(ㄧˋ ㄕㄥˋ)
a "go" wizard, usually referring to Huang Lung-shih (黃龍士) during the reign of

Kang Hsi in the Ching Dynasty

十二畫

【弊】1414 ㄅㄧˋ bih bì
1. bad; undesirable
2. dishonesty; fraud
3. exhausted; tired; worn-out
4. disadvantages; harm: 這樣做有利有弊。There are both advantages and disadvantages to work in such a way.

弊病(ㄅㄧˋ ㄅㄧㄥˋ)or 弊竇(ㄅㄧˋ ㄉㄡˋ) or 弊端(ㄅㄧˋ ㄉㄨㄢ)
corrupt practices; drawbacks: 每件事都有其弊病。Everything has its drawback.

弊害(ㄅㄧˋ ㄏㄞˋ)
harm; damage: 那樣做並無弊害。There is no harm in doing that.

弊壞(ㄅㄧˋ ㄏㄨㄞˋ)
worn and damaged

弊車羸馬(ㄅㄧˋ ㄐㄩ ㄌㄟˊ ㄇㄚˇ)
(descriptive of incorruptible officials) a decrepit cart drawn by a lean horse

弊絕風清(ㄅㄧˋ ㄐㄩㄝˊ ㄈㄥ ㄑㄧㄥ)
姬茵(said of a clean government) absolutely free from corruption

弊帚自珍(ㄅㄧˋ ㄓㄡˇ ㄗˋ ㄓㄣ)or 弊帚千金(ㄅㄧˋ ㄓㄡˇ ㄑㄧㄢ ㄐㄧㄣ)
One loves some thing of little value simply because it is his own.

弊政(ㄅㄧˋ ㄓㄥˋ)
misrule; maladministration

弋部
ㄧˋ yih yì

【弋】1415 ㄧˋ yih yì
1. to catch; to take
2. to shoot with arrow and bow

弋獵(ㄧˋ ㄌㄧㄝˋ)
to hunt

弋獲(ㄧˋ ㄏㄨㄛˋ)
to catch (game in hunting, a thief, etc.)

弋取(ㄧˋ ㄑㄩˇ)
to catch

弋陽腔(ㄧˋ ㄧㄤˊ ㄑㄧㄤ)
a singing style in Chinese opera 亦作「高腔」

三畫

【式】1416 ㄕˋ shyh shì
1. fashion; style; form; a mode: 她穿着最新款式的外衣。She wears a coat of the latest style.
2. a pattern; a type; a model; an example
3. a system: 這是教授英語的一種良好方式。This is a good system of teaching English.
4. a ceremony

式子(ㄕˋ ·ㄗ)
(mathematics) a formula or equation

式樣(ㄕˋ ㄧㄤˋ)
a type; a model; a mode; a style

式微(ㄕˋ ㄨㄟˊ)
the decline (of a nation, a dynasty, a family, etc.)

十畫

【弒】1417 ㄕˋ shyh shì
to kill or murder one's superior, senior, etc.

弒母(ㄕˋ ㄇㄨˇ)
matricide; to commit matricide

弒父(ㄕˋ ㄈㄨˋ)
patricide; to commit patricide

弒逆者(ㄕˋ ㄋㄧˋ ㄓㄜˇ)
one who commits patricide or regicide

弒君(ㄕˋ ㄐㄩㄣ)
regicide; to commit regicide

弒兄(ㄕˋ ㄒㄩㄥ)
fratricide (murder of one's own elder brother)

弓部
ㄍㄨㄥ gong gōng

【弓】1418 ㄍㄨㄥ gong gōng
1. a bow: 小提琴是用弓拉奏的。A violin is played with a bow.
2. bent; arching; arched: 彩虹在天上成弓形。A bright rainbow arched above.
3. a measure of length (equal to five Chinese feet)

弓背(ㄍㄨㄥ ㄅㄟˋ)
to bend the back like a bow; a back arched like a bow

弓袋(ㄍㄨㄥ ㄉㄞˋ)
a bow case 參看「弓韃」

弓弩手(ㄍㄨㄥ ㄋㄨˇ ㄕㄡˇ)or 弓箭手(ㄍㄨㄥ ㄐㄧㄢˋ ㄕㄡˇ)or 弓手(ㄍㄨㄥ ㄕㄡˇ)
an archer: 他是一個優良的弓箭手。He is a good archer.

弓韃(ㄍㄨㄥ ㄐㄧㄢ)
a bow case

弓箭(ㄍㄨㄥ ㄐㄧㄢˋ)or 弓矢(ㄍㄨㄥ ㄕˇ)
bow and arrow

弓匠(ㄍㄨㄥ ㄐㄧㄤˋ)
a bowyer

弓鞋(ㄍㄨㄥ ㄒㄧㄝˊ)
the shoes with upturned end worn by women with bound feet in former times

弓弦(ㄍㄨㄥ ㄒㄧㄢˊ)
a bowstring: 他的情緒緊張得有如弓弦。His nerves are as taut as a bowstring.

弓形(ㄍㄨㄥ ㄒㄧㄥˊ)
(mathematics) a segment of a circle

弓人(ㄍㄨㄥ ㄖㄣˊ)
an ancient official whose duty was to make bows

弓腰(ㄍㄨㄥ ㄧㄠ)
to curve one's body backward like an arch

弓影(ㄍㄨㄥ ㄧㄥˇ)or 弓蛇(ㄍㄨㄥ ㄕㄜˊ)
(literally) the reflection of a bow in a wine cup mistaken for a snake—a false alarm

一畫

〔弋・弓部〕

〔弓部〕

【引】 1419 ㄧㄣˇ yiin yǐn

1. to pull; to attract: 拋磚引玉 to cast a brick to attract jade; to throw out a minnow to catch a whale
2. to guide: 盲人有時由狗引路。A blind man is sometimes guided by a dog.
3. to introduce
4. to quote: 傳教士引用聖經。The minister quoted from the Bible.
5. to retire
6. a unit of length (=33 ⅓ metres)
7. to cause; to make

引避(ㄧㄣˇ ㄅㄧˋ)
①to yield one's place ②to avoid

引滿(ㄧㄣˇ ㄇㄢˇ)
①to draw a bow to the full ②to fill the cup to the brim

引發(ㄧㄣˇ ㄈㄚ)
(chemistry) initiation

引風吹火(ㄧㄣˇ ㄈㄥ ㄔㄨㄟ ㄏㄨㄛˇ)
①to fan the flame ②to excite or stir up trouble

引得(ㄧㄣˇ ㄉㄜˊ)
an index (a transliteration of the English word)

引導(ㄧㄣˇ ㄉㄠˇ)or(ㄧㄣˇ ㄉㄠˋ)
to guide; to lead

引逗(ㄧㄣˇ ㄉㄡˋ)
to entice

引渡(ㄧㄣˇ ㄉㄨˋ)
to extradite; extradition

引對(ㄧㄣˇ ㄉㄨㄟˋ)
to summon for an imperial court interview

引慝(ㄧㄣˇ ㄊㄜˋ)
to assume blame

引退(ㄧㄣˇ ㄊㄨㄟˋ)
to retire; to resign: 他已從校刊編輯的職務引退。He has resigned from the editorship of the school paper.

引狼入室(ㄧㄣˇ ㄌㄤˊ ㄖㄨˋ ㄕˋ)
(literally) to usher the wolf into the house—to bring in a troublemaker

引力(ㄧㄣˇ ㄌㄧˋ)
attracting force; attraction; gravitation: 萬有引力 universal gravitation

引領(ㄧㄣˇ ㄌㄧㄥˇ)
to stretch the neck in order to have a better look

引領而望(ㄧㄣˇ ㄌㄧㄥˇ ㄦˊ ㄨㄤˋ)
to long for; to expect eagerly

引路(ㄧㄣˇ ㄌㄨˋ)
to lead the way

引港(ㄧㄣˇ ㄍㄤˇ)
to act as a pilot in a harbor

引弓(ㄧㄣˇ ㄍㄨㄥ)
to draw the bow

引號(ㄧㄣˇ ㄏㄠˋ)
a quotation mark; a quote

引航(ㄧㄣˇ ㄏㄤˊ)
pilotage

引吭高歌(ㄧㄣˇ ㄏㄤˊ ㄍㄠ ㄍㄜ)
to sing aloud

引火(ㄧㄣˇ ㄏㄨㄛˇ)
to ignite; to light; to kindle a fire: 他們擦火柴引火。They kindled a fire by scratching a match.

引火焚身(ㄧㄣˇ ㄏㄨㄛˇ ㄈㄣˊ ㄕㄣ)
to get oneself into trouble

引火點(ㄧㄣˇ ㄏㄨㄛˇ ㄉㄧㄢˇ)
the ignition point; the flashing point

引接(ㄧㄣˇ ㄐㄧㄝ)
to receive (guests)

引咎(ㄧㄣˇ ㄐㄧㄡˋ)
to take the blame on oneself: 他對這事件引咎。He takes the blame on himself in this matter.

引咎辭職(ㄧㄣˇ ㄐㄧㄡˋ ㄘˊ ㄓˊ)
to resign from office as a gesture to show self-reproach

引見(ㄧㄣˇ ㄐㄧㄢˋ)
to present a person to the emperor, a high official, etc.

引薦(ㄧㄣˇ ㄐㄧㄢˋ)
to recommend

引進(ㄧㄣˇ ㄐㄧㄣˋ)
①to recommend ②to introduce from elsewhere: 我們必須引進新的技術與裝備。We have to import new technology and equipment.

引經據典(ㄧㄣˇ ㄐㄧㄥ ㄐㄩˋ ㄉㄧㄢˇ)
①to quote from classics ②pedantic

引頸(ㄧㄣˇ ㄐㄧㄥˇ)
to crane one's neck to look forward

引頸就戮(ㄧㄣˇ ㄐㄧㄥˇ ㄐㄧㄡˋ ㄌㄨˋ)
to stretch the neck to be beheaded

引決(ㄧㄣˇ ㄐㄩㄝˊ)
to commit suicide

引起(ㄧㄣˇ ㄑㄧˇ)
to cause; to give rise to; to trigger: 切勿引起公憤。Never arouse public indignation.

引擎(ㄧㄣˇ ㄑㄧㄥˊ)
an engine: 他發動了汽車的引擎。He started the engine of his car.

引嫌(ㄧㄣˇ ㄒㄧㄢˊ)
to step away from a delicate case in order to avoid others' suspicion

引線(ㄧㄣˇ ㄒㄧㄢˋ)
①a sewing needle ②a go-between ③a fuse

引信(ㄧㄣˇ ㄒㄧㄣˋ)
a fuse

引證(ㄧㄣˇ ㄓㄥˋ)
to cite supporting facts, proofs, or evidence

引錐刺股(ㄧㄣˇ ㄓㄨㄟ ㄘˋ ㄍㄨˇ)
(literally) to prick one's own thigh with a drill to keep oneself from falling asleep—to goad oneself to hard work

引出(ㄧㄣˇ ㄔㄨ)
to draw forth; to lead: 我們的討論可引出正確的結論。Our discussion can draw a correct conclusion.

引伸 or 引申(ㄧㄣˇ ㄕㄣ)
to extend in meaning; to expound

引商刻羽(ㄧㄣˇ ㄕㄤ ㄎㄜˋ ㄩˇ)
highbrow music

引書爲證(ㄧㄣˇ ㄕㄨ ㄨㄟˊ ㄓㄥˋ)
to cite proofs from books

引水(ㄧㄣˇ ㄕㄨㄟˇ)
①to pilot a ship into a harbor ②to draw water ③(irrigation) diversion

引水工程(ㄧㄣˇ ㄕㄨㄟˇ ㄍㄨㄥ ㄔㄥˊ)
diversion works

引水人(ㄧㄣˇ ㄕㄨㄟˇ ㄖㄣˊ)
a harbor pilot 亦作「領航員」

引水隧道(ㄧㄣˇ ㄕㄨㄟˇ ㄙㄨㄟˋ ㄉㄠˋ)
a diversion tunnel

引稅(ㄧㄣˇ ㄕㄨㄟˋ)
salt tax 亦作「鹽稅」

引人注目(ㄧㄣˇ ㄖㄣˊ ㄓㄨˋ ㄇㄨˋ)
noticeable; conspicuous

引人入勝(ㄧㄣˇ ㄖㄣˊ ㄖㄨˋ ㄕㄥˋ)
①to lead one into wonderland ②(of books) absorbing
引入(ㄧㄣˇ ㄖㄨˋ)
to lead into; to draw into
引入歧途(ㄧㄣˇ ㄖㄨˋ ㄑㄧˊ ㄊㄨˊ)
to lead (somebody) astray: 別把小孩們引入歧途。Don't lead the children astray.
引子(ㄧㄣˇ ·ㄗ)
①a prologue; a prelude; a preface; an introduction ②a supplementary dose (in Chinese herb medicine)
引以爲戒(ㄧㄣˇ ㄧˇ ㄨㄟˊ ㄐㄧㄝˋ)
to learn a lesson (from a previous error)
引藥(ㄧㄣˇ ㄧㄠˋ)
a supplementary dose (in Chinese medicine) which leads the principal drug to the seat of the disease
引誘(ㄧㄣˇ ㄧㄡˋ)
to induce; to lure; to attract; to entice; to tempt; to seduce
引言(ㄧㄣˇ ㄧㄢˊ)
a preface; a foreword
引文(ㄧㄣˇ ㄨㄣˊ)
a quoted passage; a quotation
引用(ㄧㄣˇ ㄩㄥˋ)
to quote: 讓我引用莎士比亞的話給你。Let me quote you the words of Shakespeare.

【弔】 1420
(吊) ㄉㄧㄠˋ diaw diào
1. to condole; to console
2. to mourn
3. to hang; to suspend; suspended
弔膀子(ㄉㄧㄠˋ ㄅㄤˇ ·ㄗ)
to lure the other sex by casting coquettish glances, making indecent remarks, etc.
弔臂(ㄉㄧㄠˋ ㄅㄧˋ)
the arm of a crane
弔民伐罪(ㄉㄧㄠˋ ㄇㄧㄣˊ ㄈㄚˊ ㄗㄨㄟˋ)
to console the people by punishing the wicked (often used by revolutionaries as a slogan in overthrowing the monarch)
弔帶(ㄉㄧㄠˋ ㄉㄞˋ)
suspenders; garters
弔燈(ㄉㄧㄠˋ ㄉㄥ)
a low-hanging ceiling lamp, such as a chandelier
弔桶(ㄉㄧㄠˋ ㄊㄨㄥˇ)
a well bucket
弔鉤(ㄉㄧㄠˋ ㄍㄡ)
(machinery) a hook
弔桿(ㄉㄧㄠˋ ㄍㄢ)
a suspended pole
弔古(ㄉㄧㄠˋ ㄍㄨˇ)
to think of the ancients or ancient events
弔詭(ㄉㄧㄠˋ ㄍㄨㄟˇ)
bizarre
弔客(ㄉㄧㄠˋ ㄎㄜˋ)
one who attends a funeral service as a friend of the deceased or of the bereaved family
弔環(ㄉㄧㄠˋ ㄏㄨㄢˊ)
(gymnastics) flying rings
弔祭(ㄉㄧㄠˋ ㄐㄧˋ)
to mourn over (somebody's death)
弔架(ㄉㄧㄠˋ ㄐㄧㄚˋ)
a suspended frame or stand
弔起(ㄉㄧㄠˋ ㄑㄧˇ)
①to hang ②to lift by crane
弔橋(ㄉㄧㄠˋ ㄑㄧㄠˊ)
①a suspension bridge ②a drawbridge over the moat
弔銷(ㄉㄧㄠˋ ㄒㄧㄠ)
to revoke; to withdraw: 政府弔銷他的護照。The government withdrew his passport.
弔孝(ㄉㄧㄠˋ ㄒㄧㄠˋ)
to condole with a bereaved son
弔鐘花(ㄉㄧㄠˋ ㄓㄨㄥ ㄏㄨㄚ)
a bellflower 亦作「風鈴草」
弔車(ㄉㄧㄠˋ ㄔㄜ)
①a wrecker (a truck crane) ②a cable car
弔牀(ㄉㄧㄠˋ ㄔㄨㄤˊ)
a hammock: 他在花園中的弔床上小睡。He takes a nap in a hammock in his garden.
弔扇(ㄉㄧㄠˋ ㄕㄢˋ)
a ceiling fan
弔死(ㄉㄧㄠˋ ㄙˇ)
to hang (a criminal); to die by hanging
弔死鬼(ㄉㄧㄠˋ ㄙˇ ㄍㄨㄟˇ)
the ghost of one who has committed suicide by hanging
弔喪(ㄉㄧㄠˋ ㄙㄤ)
to attend a memorial service; to condole
弔嗓子(ㄉㄧㄠˋ ㄙㄤˇ ·ㄗ)
(Chinese opera) to sing aloud off stage as a vocal training and practice
弔索(ㄉㄧㄠˋ ㄙㄨㄛˇ)
a sling: 鋼絲弔索 a wire sling 繩弔索 a rope sling
弔兒郎當(ㄉㄧㄠˋ ㄦ ㄌㄤˊ ㄉㄤ)
to act or behave irreverently; to do things perfunctorily; to regard nothing as serious
弔唁(ㄉㄧㄠˋ ㄧㄢˋ)
to mourn in sympathy; to condole
弔唁函電(ㄉㄧㄠˋ ㄧㄢˋ ㄏㄢˊ ㄉㄧㄢˋ)
messages of condolence
弔影(ㄉㄧㄠˋ ㄧㄥˇ)
(literally) to have sympathetic communication with no one but one's own shadow——to be completely alone
弔慰(ㄉㄧㄠˋ ㄨㄟˋ)
to condole with
弔胃口(ㄉㄧㄠˋ ㄨㄟˋ ㄎㄡˇ)
to tantalize
弔文(ㄉㄧㄠˋ ㄨㄣˊ)
a message of condolence; words of condolence; a funeral oration; a memorial address

二畫

【弗】 1421
ㄈㄨˊ fwu fú
not
弗蘭克林(ㄈㄨˊ ㄌㄢˊ ㄎㄜˋ ㄌㄧㄣˊ)
Benjamin Franklin, 1706-1790, American statesman and philosopher
弗克(ㄈㄨˊ ㄎㄜˋ)
unable
弗齒(ㄈㄨˊ ㄔˇ)
not held in esteem
弗成(ㄈㄨˊ ㄔㄥˊ)
not satisfactory; not good
弗如(ㄈㄨˊ ㄖㄨˊ)
not as good as; not equal to; worse than: 他對那位學者自愧弗如。He felt ashamed that he is not as good as that scholar.
弗豫(ㄈㄨˊ ㄩˋ)

〔弓部〕

not well; not in good health

【弘】 1422 ㄏㄨㄥˊ horng hóng
1. great; magnanimous; capacious
2. to enlarge; to broaden
弘大(ㄏㄨㄥˊ ㄉㄚˋ)
great; immense
弘量(ㄏㄨㄥˊ ㄌㄧㄤˋ)
magnanimous; liberal; generous; large capacity for forgiveness; magnanimity
弘毅(ㄏㄨㄥˊ ㄧˋ)
having a broad and strong mind
弘揚(ㄏㄨㄥˊ ㄧㄤˊ)
to propagate; to promote; to develop: 他的志願是弘揚文化。His ambition is to promote and develop the culture.
弘遠(ㄏㄨㄥˊ ㄩㄢˇ)
far and wide
弘願(ㄏㄨㄥˊ ㄩㄢˋ)
great ambition

三畫

【弛】 1423 ㄕˇ shyy shǐ (又讀 ㄔˊ chyr chí)
to unstring; to relax; to neglect: 不要鬆弛警戒。Don't relax your vigilance.
弛廢(ㄕˇ ㄈㄟˋ)
to neglect; negligence
弛緩(ㄕˇ ㄏㄨㄢˇ)
to relax
弛禁(ㄕˇ ㄐㄧㄣˋ)
to rescind a prohibition; to lift or remove a restriction
弛張(ㄕˇ ㄓㄤ)
tension and relaxation

四畫

【弟】 1424 1. ㄉㄧˋ dih dì
1. a younger brother
2. a junior
弟妹(ㄉㄧˋ ㄇㄟˋ)
younger brothers and sisters
弟婦(ㄉㄧˋ ㄈㄨˋ) or 弟媳(ㄉㄧˋ ㄒㄧˊ)
a sister-in-law (younger brother's wife)
弟弟(ㄉㄧˋ ·ㄉㄧ)
a younger brother
弟兄(ㄉㄧˋ ㄒㄩㄥ)
① brothers: 我們是親弟兄。We are blood brothers. ② soldiers
弟子(ㄉㄧˋ ㄗˇ)
① a disciple; a pupil; a student ② a youngster; a youth

【弟】 1424 2. (悌) ㄊㄧˋ tih tì
to show brotherly love

五畫

【弦】 1425 ㄒㄧㄢˊ shyan xián
1. strings (of bows, musical instruments, etc.): 一條弦斷了。One of the strings broke.
2. the chord of an arc
3. the first or last quarter of a lunar month
弦歌(ㄒㄧㄢˊ ㄍㄜ)
① to sing with stringed accompaniment ② the means of education
弦歌不輟(ㄒㄧㄢˊ ㄍㄜ ㄅㄨˋ ㄔㄨㄛˋ)
The schooling goes on without interruption.
弦琴(ㄒㄧㄢˊ ㄑㄧㄣˊ)
a stringed instrument with a number of strings
弦線(ㄒㄧㄢˊ ㄒㄧㄢˋ)
strings (of a musical instrument)
弦柱(ㄒㄧㄢˊ ㄓㄨˋ)
the neck (of a stringed instrument)
弦索(ㄒㄧㄢˊ ㄙㄨㄛˇ)
the strings of instruments
弦誦(ㄒㄧㄢˊ ㄙㄨㄥˋ)
to chant (music or passages from classics)
弦音(ㄒㄧㄢˊ ㄧㄣ)
the music (from a stringed instrument)
弦外之音(ㄒㄧㄢˊ ㄨㄞˋ ㄓ ㄧㄣ)
overtones; implied meaning; connotations: 他的話有弦外之音。There are overtones in his remarks.
弦月(ㄒㄧㄢˊ ㄩㄝˋ)
a crescent moon
弦樂隊(ㄒㄧㄢˊ ㄩㄝˋ ㄉㄨㄟˋ)
a string orchestra (or band)
弦樂器(ㄒㄧㄢˊ ㄩㄝˋ ㄑㄧˋ)
a stringed instrument

【弧】 1426 ㄏㄨˊ hwu hú
1. a wooden bow
2. a segment of a circle
弧度(ㄏㄨˊ ㄉㄨˋ)
circular measure
弧光燈(ㄏㄨˊ ㄍㄨㄤ ㄉㄥ)
an arc light; an arc lamp
弧角(ㄏㄨˊ ㄐㄧㄠˇ)
a spherical angle
弧形(ㄏㄨˊ ㄒㄧㄥˊ)
an arc; a curve
弧矢形(ㄏㄨˊ ㄕˇ ㄒㄧㄥˊ)
a segment of a circle

【弨】 1427 ㄔㄠ chau chāo
a bow

【弩】 1428 ㄋㄨˇ nuu nǔ
a crossbow
弩砲(ㄋㄨˇ ㄆㄠˋ)
a sling shot; a catapult
弩末(ㄋㄨˇ ㄇㄛˋ)
powerless because of exhaustion; weakened; exhausted; spent
弩弓(ㄋㄨˇ ㄍㄨㄥ)
a crossbow
弩箭離弦(ㄋㄨˇ ㄐㄧㄢˋ ㄌㄧˊ ㄒㄧㄢˊ)
as fast as the arrow flies off the string
弩張劍拔(ㄋㄨˇ ㄓㄤ ㄐㄧㄢˋ ㄅㄚˊ)
(literally) with bows drawn and swords unsheathed—War is likely to start at any moment.
弩手(ㄋㄨˇ ㄕㄡˇ)
an archer; a crossbowman 亦作「射手」: 他是國內最佳的弩手。He is the best archer in our country.
弩牙(ㄋㄨˇ ㄧㄚˊ)
the trigger of a crossbow

六畫

【弭】 1429 ㄇㄧˇ mii mǐ
1. to stop; to end: 那位將軍出兵弭亂。The general led the army to stop the rebellion.
2. the ends of a bow
弭謗(ㄇㄧˇ ㄅㄤˋ)
to stop slanders
弭兵(ㄇㄧˇ ㄅㄧㄥ)
to stop war; to have a truce; to cease hostilities
弭亂(ㄇㄧˇ ㄌㄨㄢˋ)
to stop disturbance of a

civil war
弭患(ㄇㄧˇ ㄏㄨㄢˋ)
to eliminate trouble
弭轍(ㄇㄧˇ ㄔㄜˋ)
to travel very fast
弭災(ㄇㄧˇ ㄗㄞ)
to end disaster

【弮】 1430
ㄑㄩㄢ chiuan quān
a bowstring

七畫

【弰】 1431
ㄕㄠ shau shāo
the ends of a bow

【弱】 1432
ㄖㄨㄛˋ ruoh ruò
1. weak; fragile; feeble; tender; delicate; infirm: 他病後覺得很虛弱。He felt very weak after illness.
2. inferior: 她的能力並不比別人弱。She's not inferior to others in capability.
3. young
4. a little less than: 三分之一弱 a little less than one-third
弱不好弄(ㄖㄨㄛˋ ㄅㄨˋ ㄏㄠˋ ㄌㄨㄥˋ)
not fond of playing in childhood
弱不禁風(ㄖㄨㄛˋ ㄅㄨˋ ㄐㄧㄣ ㄈㄥ)
so weak as to have inadequate strength to withstand the wind
弱不勝衣(ㄖㄨㄛˋ ㄅㄨˋ ㄕㄥ ㄧ)
(said of a woman) so fragile as to lack even the strength to bear the weight of clothing
弱風(ㄖㄨㄛˋ ㄈㄥ)
southeast wind
弱弟(ㄖㄨㄛˋ ㄉㄧˋ)
a young brother
弱點(ㄖㄨㄛˋ ㄉㄧㄢˇ)
a weak point; a weakness
弱女(ㄖㄨㄛˋ ㄋㄩˇ)
a young girl
弱柳(ㄖㄨㄛˋ ㄌㄧㄡˇ)
①a pliant willow tree ②a prostitute
弱國(ㄖㄨㄛˋ ㄍㄨㄛˊ)
a weak nation
弱冠(ㄖㄨㄛˋ ㄍㄨㄢˋ)
a twenty-year-old man (who has just undergone the capping ceremony); a youth
弱息(ㄖㄨㄛˋ ㄒㄧˊ)
my child
弱小(ㄖㄨㄛˋ ㄒㄧㄠˇ)
small and weak
弱小民族(ㄖㄨㄛˋ ㄒㄧㄠˇ ㄇㄧㄣˊ ㄗㄨˊ)
a small nation
弱質(ㄖㄨㄛˋ ㄓˊ)
feeble constitution; infirm
弱者(ㄖㄨㄛˋ ㄓㄜˇ)
the weak and the timid
弱視(ㄖㄨㄛˋ ㄕˋ)
amblyopia
弱勢團體(ㄖㄨㄛˋ ㄕˋ ㄊㄨㄢˊ ㄊㄧˇ)
an underprivileged group; a social group that has little or no influence in public affairs
弱水三千(ㄖㄨㄛˋ ㄕㄨㄟˇ ㄙㄢ ㄑㄧㄢ)
the river Jo (also known as 張掖河) with a supposed course of 3000 *li*
弱肉強食(ㄖㄨㄛˋ ㄖㄡˋ ㄑㄧㄤˊ ㄕˊ)
the stronger preying upon the weaker; the weak falling victim to the strong—the law of the jungle
弱卒(ㄖㄨㄛˋ ㄗㄨˊ)
weak soldiers; soldiers having no fighting capability: 弱卒會在戰爭中被淘汰。Weak soldiers will be eliminated in the war.
弱歲(ㄖㄨㄛˋ ㄙㄨㄟˋ)
a youth

八畫

【張】 1433
ㄓㄤ jang zhāng
1. to open; to stretch; to extend: 張開你的手。Open your hands.
2. to display
3. a sheet (of paper); a leaf (of a book): 請拿一張紙給我。Bring me a sheet of paper, please.
4. a Chinese family name
張伯倫(ㄓㄤ ㄅㄛˊ ㄌㄨㄣˊ)
Arthur Neville Chamberlain, 1869-1940, British prime minister
張本(ㄓㄤ ㄅㄣˇ)
①advance preparations or arrangements ②(in writing or storytelling) an advance hint of what to follow
張目(ㄓㄤ ㄇㄨˋ)
①to help publicize an unworthy cause ②to open one's eyes wide
張飛(ㄓㄤ ㄈㄟ)
Chang Fei, a general of the state of Shu (蜀) during the period of the Three Kingdoms
張大其辭(ㄓㄤ ㄉㄚˋ ㄑㄧˊ ㄘˊ)
to make exaggerated statements
張道陵(ㄓㄤ ㄉㄠˋ ㄌㄧㄥˊ)
Chang Tao-lin, a Taoist in the Han Dynasty, named as the first head priest of the Taoist sect 五斗米教
張燈結彩(ㄓㄤ ㄉㄥ ㄐㄧㄝˊ ㄘㄞˇ)
decorated with lanterns and colored hangings (for a joyous occasion)
張貼(ㄓㄤ ㄊㄧㄝ)
to paste up (labels, posters, etc.): 此處禁止張貼。Post no bills here.
張天師(ㄓㄤ ㄊㄧㄢ ㄕ)
the title of the head priest of the Taoist sect created during the Later Han Dynasty, conferred on the descendants of Chang Taolin (張道陵), and abolished in the republican time
張力(ㄓㄤ ㄌㄧˋ)
tensile strength; tension
張力計(ㄓㄤ ㄌㄧˋ ㄐㄧˋ)
(physics) a tensimeter
張良(ㄓㄤ ㄌㄧㄤˊ)
Chang Liang, the tactician who helped Liu Pang (劉邦) found the Han Dynasty
張羅(ㄓㄤ ㄌㄨㄛˊ)
①to raise funds ②to set a snare for birds ③to serve guests ④to take care of; to get busy about
張掛(ㄓㄤ ㄍㄨㄚˋ)
to hang up
張冠李戴(ㄓㄤ ㄍㄨㄢ ㄌㄧˇ ㄉㄞˋ)
(literally) Chang's hat on Li's head—wrong attribution; a mistake in identification; misappropriation
張開(ㄓㄤ ㄎㄞ)
to stretch open; to open
張口結舌(ㄓㄤ ㄎㄡˇ ㄐㄧㄝˊ ㄕㄜˊ)
agape and tongue-tied: 所有

的孩子們對他的大膽都吃驚得張口結舌。All the children were agape and tongue-tied at his daring.

張狂(ㄓㄤ ㄎㄨㄤˊ)
to abandon oneself to pleasure; to dissipate without inhibition

張皇失措 or 張惶失措(ㄓㄤ ㄏㄨㄤˊ ㄕ ㄘㄨㄛˋ)
to lose composure; panicky

張家口(ㄓㄤ ㄐㄧㄚ ㄎㄡˇ)
Kalgan, or Changchiakou (in Inner Mongolia)

張家長，李家短(ㄓㄤ ㄐㄧㄚ ㄔㄤˊ, ㄌㄧˇ ㄐㄧㄚ ㄉㄨㄢˇ)
(literally) The Changs are long and the Lis are short. —typical subject matter of a gossip

張騫(ㄓㄤ ㄑㄧㄢ)
Chang Chien, a soldier of fortune of the Han Dynasty, whose exploits helped China pacify the tribes to the west

張獻忠(ㄓㄤ ㄒㄧㄢˋ ㄓㄨㄥ)
Chang Hsien-chung, one of the rebels who contributed to the fall of the Ming Dynasty

張巡(ㄓㄤ ㄒㄩㄣˊ)
Chang Hsun (709-757), a hero who died in the rebellion of An Lu-shan (安祿山) during the Tang Dynasty

張之洞(ㄓㄤ ㄓ ㄉㄨㄥˋ)
Chang Chih-tung, a war minister and governor of several provinces in the Ching Dynasty, who advocated modernization of China during the late 19th century

張敞畫眉(ㄓㄤ ㄔㄤˇ ㄏㄨㄚˋ ㄇㄟˊ)
marital bliss (張敞 an able and straightforward official of the Han Dynasty, chiefly known for his painting his wife's eyebrows)

張弛(ㄓㄤ ㄕˇ)
tension and relaxation; fast and loose

張設(ㄓㄤ ㄕㄜˋ)
to set up curtains, decorations, etc. for a ceremony

張手(ㄓㄤ ㄕㄡˇ)
to open one's hands

張作霖(ㄓㄤ ㄗㄨㄛˋ ㄌㄧㄣˊ)
Chang Tso-lin, a warlord in Manchuria in the 1920's

張嘴(ㄓㄤ ㄗㄨㄟˇ)
① to open the mouth ② to ask for a loan or a favor

張三李四(ㄓㄤ ㄙㄢ ㄌㄧˇ ㄙˋ)
anybody; (every) Tom, Dick, and Harry

張儀(ㄓㄤ ㄧˊ)
Chang Yi, a strategist during the Warring States Epoch, who advocated alliance with the state of Chin

張牙舞爪(ㄓㄤ ㄧㄚˊ ㄨˇ ㄓㄠˇ)
(said of wild beasts) to frighten people by showing the fangs and flourishing the paws

張揚(ㄓㄤ ㄧㄤˊ)
to publicize; to make widely known (usually said of a scandal, secret, etc.): 這事還未決定，不可張揚開來。This matter is not yet decided; don't make it widely known.

張望(ㄓㄤ ㄨㄤˋ)
to look around; to look about

1434

【強】 1. (強、彊) ㄑㄧㄤˊ chyang qiáng

1. strong; powerful; vigorous: 他比他的弟弟強壯。He is stronger than his younger brother.
2. better: 勝利強於失敗。It is better to win than to lose.
3. violent: 那次地震很強烈。The earthquake was very violent.

強暴(ㄑㄧㄤˊ ㄅㄠˋ)
① violent; fierce; ferocious; atrocious ② rape

強迫進食(ㄑㄧㄤˊ ㄆㄛˋ ㄐㄧㄣˋ ㄕˊ)
to force-feed; force-feeding

強風(ㄑㄧㄤˊ ㄈㄥ)
(meteorology) strong breeze

強打者(ㄑㄧㄤˊ ㄉㄚˇ ㄓㄜˇ)
a slugger

強大(ㄑㄧㄤˊ ㄉㄚˋ)
powerful and strong

強得多(ㄑㄧㄤˊ ˙ㄉㄜ ㄉㄨㄛ)
① much better than ② much stronger than

強盜(ㄑㄧㄤˊ ㄉㄠˋ)
a robber; a bandit

強敵(ㄑㄧㄤˊ ㄉㄧˊ)
a formidable foe or enemy; a powerful foe or enemy

強調(ㄑㄧㄤˊ ㄉㄧㄠˋ)
to emphasize; to stress

強度(ㄑㄧㄤˊ ㄉㄨˋ)
intensity (of light, magnetic force, etc.)

強挺(ㄑㄧㄤˊ ㄊㄧㄥˇ)
unyielding; indomitable

強弩之末(ㄑㄧㄤˊ ㄋㄨˇ ㄓ ㄇㄛˋ)
(literally) at the end of an arrow's flight—weakened; spent; exhausted; powerless

強力膠(ㄑㄧㄤˊ ㄌㄧˋ ㄐㄧㄠ)
glue

強烈(ㄑㄧㄤˊ ㄌㄧㄝˋ)
violent; strong; intense; severe; acute; keen: 他有強烈的政治信仰。He has intense political convictions.

強梁(ㄑㄧㄤˊ ㄌㄧㄤˊ)
a bully; a ruffian

強幹(ㄑㄧㄤˊ ㄍㄢˋ)
competent; capable; able

強梗(ㄑㄧㄤˊ ㄍㄥˇ)
to obstruct like a bully

強固(ㄑㄧㄤˊ ㄍㄨˋ)
strong; solid

強國(ㄑㄧㄤˊ ㄍㄨㄛˊ)
a powerful country; a power

強攻(ㄑㄧㄤˊ ㄍㄨㄥ)
to take by storm; to storm

強悍(ㄑㄧㄤˊ ㄏㄢˋ)
fierce; truculent

強橫(ㄑㄧㄤˊ ㄏㄥˊ)
high-handed; tyrannical; despotic; dictatorial

強化(ㄑㄧㄤˊ ㄏㄨㄚˋ)
to strengthen; to intensify; to consolidate

強記(ㄑㄧㄤˊ ㄐㄧˋ)
having a good memory; strong in memory

強加(ㄑㄧㄤˊ ㄐㄧㄚ)
to impose; to force: 不要把你的觀點強加於別人。Don't force your viewpoint on others.

強姦(ㄑㄧㄤˊ ㄐㄧㄢ)
to rape; to violate; to assault or attack sexually

強健(ㄑㄧㄤˊ ㄐㄧㄢˋ)
strong and healthy: 她雖然年老但很強健。Though she is old, she remains very strong and healthy.

強諫(ㄑㄧㄤˊ ㄐㄧㄢˋ)
to admonish vigorously
強將手下無弱兵(ㄑㄧㄤˊ ㄐㄧㄤˋ ㄕㄡˇ ㄒㄧㄚˋ ㄨˊ ㄖㄨㄛˋ ㄅㄧㄥ)
There are no weak troops under a strong general.
強勁(ㄑㄧㄤˊ ㄐㄧㄥˋ)
powerful; forceful; strong: 沿岸有強勁的海風。Along the coast there was a strong wind blowing from the sea.
強權(ㄑㄧㄤˊ ㄑㄩㄢˊ)
brute force; might
強權即公理(ㄑㄧㄤˊ ㄑㄩㄢˊ ㄐㄧˊ ㄍㄨㄥ ㄌㄧˇ)
Might is right.
強心劑(ㄑㄧㄤˊ ㄒㄧㄣ ㄐㄧˋ)
a heart stimulant
強心針(ㄑㄧㄤˊ ㄒㄧㄣ ㄓㄣ)
a cardinala ampoule
強行(ㄑㄧㄤˊ ㄒㄧㄥˊ)
to force: 那名醉漢強行闖入別人的屋子。That drunkard forced his way into another person's house.
強震(ㄑㄧㄤˊ ㄓㄣˋ)
(geology) a strong shock
強壯(ㄑㄧㄤˊ ㄓㄨㄤˋ)
strong; vigorous; virile; robust; energetic
強壯劑(ㄑㄧㄤˊ ㄓㄨㄤˋ ㄐㄧˋ)
a tonic; an invigorant
強中自有強中手(ㄑㄧㄤˊ ㄓㄨㄥ ㄗˋ ㄧㄡˇ ㄑㄧㄤˊ ㄓㄨㄥ ㄕㄡˇ)
No matter how strong you are, there's always someone stronger.
強身(ㄑㄧㄤˊ ㄕㄣ)
to strengthen the body; to be conducive to health
強盛(ㄑㄧㄤˊ ㄕㄥˋ)
(said of a nation, dynasty, etc.) strong and prosperous: 和平使國家強盛。Peace makes a nation strong and prosperous.
強人(ㄑㄧㄤˊ ㄖㄣˊ)
① robbers; highwaymen ② a powerful person; a strongman
強人政治(ㄑㄧㄤˊ ㄖㄣˊ ㄓㄥˋ ㄓˋ)
government under a powerful ruler
強韌(ㄑㄧㄤˊ ㄖㄣˋ)
strong; tough; tenacious; resilient
強似(ㄑㄧㄤˇ ㄙˋ)
to be better than; to be superior to
強硬(ㄑㄧㄤˊ ㄧㄥˋ)
① hard; strong; tough; stiff: 措詞強硬的聲明 a strongly worded statement ② defiant; truculent

【強】 1434 2. (強、彊) ㄑㄧㄤˇ cheang qiǎng

1. to force
2. to make an effort; to strive: 他強作鎮靜。He made an effort to appear composed.

強逼(ㄑㄧㄤˇ ㄅㄧ) or 強迫(ㄑㄧㄤˇ ㄆㄛˋ)
to force (one to do something); to make (one take some action) by force or coercion: 我強迫他作此事。I forced him to do this.
強辯(ㄑㄧㄤˇ ㄅㄧㄢˋ)
to obstinately stick to false reasoning or a lame excuse
強迫教育(ㄑㄧㄤˇ ㄆㄛˋ ㄐㄧㄠˋ ㄩˋ)
compulsory or mandatory education
強迫降落(ㄑㄧㄤˇ ㄆㄛˋ ㄐㄧㄤˋ ㄌㄨㄛˋ)
a forced landing
強迫遷移(ㄑㄧㄤˇ ㄆㄛˋ ㄑㄧㄢ ㄧˊ)
forced migration
強派(ㄑㄧㄤˇ ㄆㄞˋ)
to force one to contribute or buy something
強買強賣(ㄑㄧㄤˇ ㄇㄞˇ ㄑㄧㄤˇ ㄇㄞˋ)
to buy or sell under coercion
強聒不舍(ㄑㄧㄤˇ ㄍㄨㄚ ㄅㄨˋ ㄕㄜˇ)
to preach tirelessly
強記(ㄑㄧㄤˇ ㄐㄧˋ)
to force oneself to memorize
強借(ㄑㄧㄤˇ ㄐㄧㄝˋ)
to borrow forcibly
強求(ㄑㄧㄤˇ ㄑㄧㄡˊ)
to demand; to extort; to exact; to impose
強取(ㄑㄧㄤˇ ㄑㄩˇ)
to take by force: 他強取了我的筆。He took my pen by force.
強制(ㄑㄧㄤˇ ㄓˋ)
forcible; compulsory; to compel; to force
強制執行(ㄑㄧㄤˇ ㄓˋ ㄓˊ ㄒㄧㄥˊ)
to execute forcibly; forcible execution
強制處分(ㄑㄧㄤˇ ㄓˋ ㄔㄨˇ ㄈㄣˋ)
to subject to a forcible measure
強佔(ㄑㄧㄤˇ ㄓㄢˋ)
to occupy forcibly; to take (property, one's wife, etc.) by force
強使(ㄑㄧㄤˇ ㄕˇ)
to force; to compel: 他強使別人服從。He compelled obedience.
強人所難(ㄑㄧㄤˇ ㄖㄣˊ ㄙㄨㄛˇ ㄋㄢˊ)
to impose a difficult task on someone; to force someone to do something against his will
強詞奪理(ㄑㄧㄤˇ ㄘˊ ㄉㄨㄛˊ ㄌㄧˇ)
to argue irrationally
強顏歡笑(ㄑㄧㄤˇ ㄧㄢˊ ㄏㄨㄢ ㄒㄧㄠˋ)
to force a smile; to assume a joyous mood reluctantly

【強】 1434 3. (強、彊) ㄐㄧㄤˋ jianq jiàng

inflexible; obstinate; stubborn: 他像騾子般的倔強。He is as stubborn as a mule.

強脾氣(ㄐㄧㄤˋ ㄆㄧˊ ˙ㄑㄧ)
an obstinate disposition

九畫

【弼】 1435 ㄅㄧˋ bih bì

1. a device for regulating bows; a bow regulator
2. to correct
3. to assist; to aid: 國王有良臣輔弼。The king has good ministers to assist him.

弼教(ㄅㄧˋ ㄐㄧㄠˋ)
to assist in education

十畫

【彀】 1436 ㄍㄡˋ gow gòu

1. to draw a bow to the full
2. a trap; a snare
3. sufficient: 她有足彀的東西了。She has quite sufficient.

十二畫

【彈】 1437 1. ㄉㄢˋ dann dàn

a pellet; a bullet; a bomb: 他被流彈擊中。He was hit by a stray bullet.

彈片(ㄉㄢˋ ㄆㄧㄢˋ)
a shell fragment; shrapnel
彈道(ㄉㄢˋ ㄉㄠˋ)
a trajectory
彈道飛彈(ㄉㄢˋ ㄉㄠˋ ㄈㄟ ㄉㄢˋ)
a ballistic missile
彈道學(ㄉㄢˋ ㄉㄠˋ ㄒㄩㄝˊ)
ballistics
彈頭(ㄉㄢˋ ㄊㄡˊ)
a projectile nose; a warhead
彈膛(ㄉㄢˋ ㄊㄤˊ)
a chamber
彈弓(ㄉㄢˋ ㄍㄨㄥ)
a slingshot; a catapult
彈殼(ㄉㄢˋ ㄎㄜˊ)
an empty cartridge case
彈痕(ㄉㄢˋ ㄏㄣˊ)
a bullet mark
彈夾(ㄉㄢˋ ㄐㄧㄚˊ)
a magazine (of an automatic firearm)
彈盡援絕(ㄉㄢˋ ㄐㄧㄣˋ ㄩㄢˊ ㄐㄩㄝˊ)
The ammunition is gone, and reinforcements are nowhere in sight.
彈匣(ㄉㄢˋ ㄒㄧㄚˊ)
(military) a magazine
彈著點(ㄉㄢˋ ㄓㄨㄛˊ ㄉㄧㄢˇ)
the point of impact
彈子(戲)(ㄉㄢˋ ˙ㄗ (ㄒㄧˋ))
billiards; marbles
彈子房(ㄉㄢˋ ˙ㄗ ㄈㄤˊ)
a billiard room; a billiard saloon; a poolroom
彈子檯(ㄉㄢˋ ˙ㄗ ㄊㄞˊ)
a billiard table
彈藥(ㄉㄢˋ ㄧㄠˋ)
ammunition
彈藥庫(ㄉㄢˋ ㄧㄠˋ ㄎㄨˋ)
an ammunition depot; a magazine
彈丸(ㄉㄢˋ ㄨㄢˊ)
a pellet
彈丸小國(ㄉㄢˋ ㄨㄢˊ ㄒㄧㄠˇ ㄍㄨㄛˊ)
a tiny country
彈丸之地(ㄉㄢˋ ㄨㄢˊ ㄓ ㄉㄧˋ)
a very small piece of land
彈雨(ㄉㄢˋ ㄩˇ)
a hail of bullets

【彈】 1437
2. ㄊㄢˊ tarn tán

1. to rebound
2. to play (a stringed instrument sounded by snapping action): 她正在彈鋼琴。She is playing the piano.
3. to impeach: 法官被彈劾受賄。The judge was impeached for taking a bribe.

彈墨線(ㄊㄢˊ ㄇㄛˋ ㄒㄧㄢˋ)
to strike a line with an inky string (as a carpenter does)
彈腿(ㄊㄢˊ ㄊㄨㄟˇ)
a leg action in Chinese boxing
彈力(ㄊㄢˊ ㄌㄧˋ)
elasticity; elastic force
彈冠(ㄊㄢˊ ㄍㄨㄢ)
to flip one's cap (so as to remove dust in preparation for an official career)
彈冠相慶(ㄊㄢˊ ㄍㄨㄢ ㄒㄧㄤ ㄑㄧㄥˋ)
(said of people) to rejoice over the downfall of the guilty or the rise of the virtuous and capable
彈劾(ㄊㄢˊ ㄏㄜˊ)
to impeach
彈劾權(ㄊㄢˊ ㄏㄜˊ ㄑㄩㄢˊ)
the power to impeach; impeachment power
彈簧(ㄊㄢˊ ㄏㄨㄤˊ)
a spring (for absorbing shock, etc.)
彈簧刀(ㄊㄢˊ ㄏㄨㄤˊ ㄉㄠ)
a switchblade
彈簧墊(ㄊㄢˊ ㄏㄨㄤˊ ㄉㄧㄢˋ)
a trampoline
彈簧秤(ㄊㄢˊ ㄏㄨㄤˊ ㄔㄥˋ)
a spring balance
彈琴(ㄊㄢˊ ㄑㄧㄣˊ)
to play (stringed instruments); to play the piano or an organ
彈性(ㄊㄢˊ ㄒㄧㄥˋ)
elasticity; resilience: 橡皮有很大的彈性。Rubber has great elasticity.
彈性疲乏(ㄊㄢˊ ㄒㄧㄥˋ ㄆㄧˊ ㄈㄚˊ)
elastic fatigue
彈性橡皮(ㄊㄢˊ ㄒㄧㄥˋ ㄒㄧㄤˋ ㄆㄧˊ)
India rubber; caoutchouc
彈指之間(ㄊㄢˊ ㄓˇ ㄓ ㄐㄧㄢ)
in a snap of the fingers —(figuratively) a very brief space of time
彈唱(ㄊㄢˊ ㄔㄤˋ)
to sing and play (the piano, guitar, etc.) at the same time
彈奏(ㄊㄢˊ ㄗㄡˋ)
to play (a stringed musical instrument)
彈詞(ㄊㄢˊ ㄘˊ)
stories put into rhyme for chanting with accompaniment of musical instruments
彈壓(ㄊㄢˊ ㄧㄚ)
to put down or suppress (a riot, uprising, etc.)

【彆】 1438
ㄅㄧㄝˋ bieh biè

awkward
彆扭(ㄅㄧㄝˋ ㄋㄧㄡˇ)
① awkward; refractory; uncomfortable; difficult: 那個人眞彆扭。That chap is really refractory. ② an awkward situation
彆氣(ㄅㄧㄝˋ ㄑㄧˋ)
silently resentful

十四畫

【彌】 1439
ㄇㄧˊ mi mí

1. to fill; to complete: 煙彌漫了那房間。Smoke filled the room.
2. more

彌補(ㄇㄧˊ ㄅㄨˇ)
to stop or fill up (a gap); to make up for or offset (a loss, shortcoming, etc.); to supplement
彌滿(ㄇㄧˊ ㄇㄢˇ)
to be full
彌漫(ㄇㄧˊ ㄇㄢˋ)
to be present all over; to fill the air: 煙霧彌漫 heavy with smoke; smoke-laden
彌封(ㄇㄧˊ ㄈㄥ)
to seal the examinee's name on an examination paper
彌縫(ㄇㄧˊ ㄈㄥˊ)
① to fill cracks ② to cover up mistakes
彌天大謊(ㄇㄧˊ ㄊㄧㄢ ㄉㄚˋ ㄏㄨㄤˇ)
a monstrous lie
彌天大罪(ㄇㄧˊ ㄊㄧㄢ ㄉㄚˋ ㄗㄨㄟˋ)
a great crime (so great as to fill the universe)
彌陀(ㄇㄧˊ ㄊㄨㄛˊ)
Amida; Amitabha
彌年(ㄇㄧˊ ㄋㄧㄢˊ)
the completion of one whole year
彌勒(ㄇㄧˊ ㄌㄜˋ)
Maitreya, the Buddhist Messiah or next Buddha, whose potbellied statue at a Bud-

dhist temple always carries a ear-to-ear grin
彌留(ㄇㄧˊ ㄌㄧㄡˊ)
on the point of death from a serious disease
彌合(ㄇㄧˊ ㄏㄜˊ)
to close; to bridge
彌撒(ㄇㄧˊ ㄙㄚ)
(Catholic) a Mass
彌賽亞(ㄇㄧˊ ㄙㄞˋ ㄧㄚˇ)
the Messiah
彌望(ㄇㄧˊ ㄨㄤˋ)
as far as the eye can see
彌月(ㄇㄧˊ ㄩㄝˋ)
the completion of the first month after birth of a child

十九畫

【彎】 1440 ㄨㄢ uan wān
to bend; to curve: 他把一鐵線彎成圓圈。He bends a wire into a loop.
彎路(ㄨㄢ ㄌㄨˋ)
① a crooked road; a tortuous path ② a roundabout way; a detour: 開車時少走彎路。When you are driving, you should avoid detours.
彎弓(ㄨㄢ ㄍㄨㄥ)
① a drawn bow ② ready to shoot the arrow ③ an arch
彎接管(ㄨㄢ ㄐㄧㄝ ㄍㄨㄢˇ)
a bend (to connect two pipes)
彎曲(ㄨㄢ ㄑㄩ)
bent; curved: 這是一張彎曲的弓。This is a bent bow.
彎子(ㄨㄢ ·ㄗ)or 彎兒(ㄨㄚㄦ)
a curve; a bend
彎腰曲背(ㄨㄢ ㄧㄠ ㄑㄩ ㄅㄟˋ)
(said of a standing posture) not straight or erect
彎彎曲曲(ㄨㄢ ㄨㄢ ㄑㄩ ㄑㄩ)
having many bends or curves; winding; twisting; snaky: 這條小河彎彎曲曲。This stream has many bends.

彐部 ㄐㄧˋ jih jì

五畫

【彔】 1441 ㄌㄨˋ luh lù
1. to carve wood
2. an abbreviated form of 祿
彔彔(ㄌㄨˋ ㄌㄨˋ)
very distinct or clear

六畫

【彖】 1442 ㄊㄨㄢˋ tuann tuàn
1. a chapter of generalization on divination in the *Book of Changes*; a work expounding the *Book of Changes*
2. a hog; a hedgehog; a porcupine
彖辭(ㄊㄨㄢˋ ㄘˊ)
a chapter of generalization on divination in the *Book of Changes*, which was supposedly authored by King Wen (文王) of the Chou Dynasty

八畫

【彗】 1443 ㄏㄨㄟˋ huey huì
1. a broom
2. a comet
3. to expose to sunlight
彗星(ㄏㄨㄟˋ ㄒㄧㄥ)
a comet
彗掃(ㄏㄨㄟˋ ㄙㄠˇ)
to sweep with a broom
彗雲(ㄏㄨㄟˋ ㄩㄣˊ)
clouds that look like dust swept by a broom

九畫

【彘】 1444 ㄓˋ jyh zhì
a hog; a pig; a swine
彘肩(ㄓˋ ㄐㄧㄢ)
the shoulder of a hog

十畫

【彙】 1445 ㄏㄨㄟˋ huey huì
1. a category; a class; a series
2. to categorize; to classify
3. to collect (materials, data, etc.)
彙報(ㄏㄨㄟˋ ㄅㄠˋ)
to collect (all information) and report; to make a collective report
彙編(ㄏㄨㄟˋ ㄅㄧㄢ)
to edit (assembled reports, data, etc.)
彙刊(ㄏㄨㄟˋ ㄎㄢ)
a collection of articles of similar nature; a publication of articles by an organization
彙核(ㄏㄨㄟˋ ㄏㄜˊ)
to examine collectively
彙集(ㄏㄨㄟˋ ㄐㄧˊ)
to collect (materials, data, etc.)
彙解(ㄏㄨㄟˋ ㄐㄧㄝˇ)
a collection of opinions, for expounding a book, etc.
彙注(ㄏㄨㄟˋ ㄓㄨˋ)
a collection of footnotes, remarks, etc., for expounding a book, etc.
彙纂(ㄏㄨㄟˋ ㄗㄨㄢˇ)
to classify; to categorize; to edit
彙册(ㄏㄨㄟˋ ㄘㄜˋ)
to collect, categorize and arrange (materials, data, reports, etc.) into a volume for review, inspection, etc.
彙萃(ㄏㄨㄟˋ ㄘㄨㄟˋ)
to collect (materials, data, reports, etc.)

十五畫

【彝】 1446 (彛) ㄧˊ yi yí
1. a vessel for wine; a goblet
2. laws or regulations
3. normal nature
4. regular; constant
5. the vessels or items used in ceremonies at temples, etc., such as bells, tripods, chalices, etc.
彝器(ㄧˊ ㄑㄧˋ)
the vessels or items used in ceremonies at temples, etc.
彝憲(ㄧˊ ㄒㄧㄢˋ)
laws; regulations; rules
彝訓(ㄧˊ ㄒㄩㄣˋ)
regular exhortations

彡 部
ㄕㄢ shan shān

四畫

【彤】 1447 ㄊㄨㄥˊ torng tóng

1. red; vermilion
2. name of an ancient state

彤管(ㄊㄨㄥˊ ㄍㄨㄢˇ)
(literally) a red tube—a red-tube writing brush, used in ancient China by lady historians

彤弓(ㄊㄨㄥˊ ㄍㄨㄥ)
a crimson bow 參看「彤矢」

彤矢(ㄊㄨㄥˊ ㄕˇ)
a crimson arrow, which was bestowed with the crimson bow to noblemen of merits by emperors in ancient China

彤史(ㄊㄨㄥˊ ㄕˇ)
court-appointed lady historians during the Tang and Ming dynasties

彤闈(ㄊㄨㄥˊ ㄨㄟˊ)
an imperial palace

彤雲(ㄊㄨㄥˊ ㄩㄣˊ)
red clouds

【形】 1448 (形) ㄒㄧㄥˊ shyng xíng

1. a form; a shape; an appearance; a figure: 她的外形修長而優雅。She has a tall graceful form.
2. a complexion
3. a terrain; a contour
4. expression; description; to describe: 這風景美得難以形容。The scenery was beautiful beyond description.
5. in comparison
6. to show; to manifest

形便(ㄒㄧㄥˊ ㄅㄧㄢˋ)
advantages offered by terrain

形貌(ㄒㄧㄥˊ ㄇㄠˋ)
the appearance of a person; a countenance

形單影隻(ㄒㄧㄥˊ ㄉㄢ ㄧㄥˇ ㄓ)
only me and my shadow—to be all alone

形態(ㄒㄧㄥˊ ㄊㄞˋ)
an appearance; a form; a state

形態學(ㄒㄧㄥˊ ㄊㄞˋ ㄒㄩㄝˊ)
morphology

形體(ㄒㄧㄥˊ ㄊㄧˇ)
the human body which has a form or shape (as contrasted to the spirit which is invisible)

形同虛設(ㄒㄧㄥˊ ㄊㄨㄥˊ ㄒㄩ ㄕㄜˋ)
to exist in name only

形格勢禁(ㄒㄧㄥˊ ㄍㄜˊ ㄕˋ ㄐㄧㄣˋ)
unable to act freely; to have one's hands tied

形骸(ㄒㄧㄥˊ ㄏㄞˊ)
one's body or skeleton

形穢(ㄒㄧㄥˊ ㄏㄨㄟˋ)
a vulgar appearance

形跡 or 形迹(ㄒㄧㄥˊ ㄐㄧ)
① one's appearance and manner ② one's behavior or conduct

形跡可疑(ㄒㄧㄥˊ ㄐㄧ ㄎㄜˇ ㄧˊ)
behavior or a manner that arouses suspicion

形解(ㄒㄧㄥˊ ㄐㄧㄝˇ)
postmortem; dismemberment of a body

形銷骨立(ㄒㄧㄥˊ ㄒㄧㄠ ㄍㄨˇ ㄌㄧˋ)
thin and bony; emaciated

形相(ㄒㄧㄥˊ ㄒㄧㄤˋ)
① a form; an appearance: 他有高尚的形相。He is a man of noble appearance. ② to look somebody up and down

形象(ㄒㄧㄥˊ ㄒㄧㄤˋ)
① a form; an appearance; the physical description of a person; an image ②(fine arts) form as contrasted to substance

形形色色(ㄒㄧㄥˊ ㄒㄧㄥˊ ㄙㄜˋ ㄙㄜˋ)
of all shapes and colors; a great variety and diversity: 這家商店有形形色色的玩具。This shop has a variety of toys.

形質(ㄒㄧㄥˊ ㄓˊ)
form and substance

形制(ㄒㄧㄥˊ ㄓˋ)
①the design of a manufactured object ② to command a situation by holding a strategic position

形狀(ㄒㄧㄥˊ ㄓㄨㄤˋ)
the appearance, form or shape of a thing

形成(ㄒㄧㄥˊ ㄔㄥˊ)
formation; to form; to take shape; to produce as a result: 熱使水形成水蒸氣。Heat causes the formation of steam from water.

形成組織(ㄒㄧㄥˊ ㄔㄥˊ ㄗㄨˇ ㄓ)
(botany) cambium

形式(ㄒㄧㄥˊ ㄕˋ)
① form; outward appearance; shape ② formality; for appearance's sake ③ style

形式邏輯(ㄒㄧㄥˊ ㄕˋ ㄌㄨㄛˊ ㄐㄧˊ)
formalistic logic; formal science

形式主義(ㄒㄧㄥˊ ㄕˋ ㄓㄨˇ ㄧˋ)
formalism

形式上(ㄒㄧㄥˊ ㄕˋ ·ㄕㄤ)
nominally; for formality's sake

形勢(ㄒㄧㄥˊ ㄕˋ)
① a situation; condition ② a terrain or contour: 這地區形勢險要。This district is a strategically important terrain.

形聲(ㄒㄧㄥˊ ㄕㄥ)
determinative-phonetics—one of the six groups into which the Chinese characters are classified (This group of characters is formed by a radical—the determinative—and a phonetic, with the former element indicating the category within which the meaning of the word is to be sought while the latter indicating the pronunciation.)

形勝之地(ㄒㄧㄥˊ ㄕㄥˋ ㄓ ㄉㄧˋ)
① an advantageous terrain; vantage ground ② a scenic spot

形如槁木(ㄒㄧㄥˊ ㄖㄨˊ ㄍㄠˇ ㄇㄨˋ)
as lean as a rake; thin and emaciated

形容(ㄒㄧㄥˊ ㄖㄨㄥˊ)
① to describe ② appearance; form; shape

形容枯槁(ㄒㄧㄥˊ ㄖㄨㄥˊ ㄎㄨ ㄍㄠˇ)
a thin, bony, or emaciated appearance

形容盡致(ㄒㄧㄥˊ ㄖㄨㄥˊ ㄐㄧㄣˋ ㄓˋ)

an accurate and detailed description

形容詞(ㄒㄧㄥˊ ㄖㄨㄥˊ ㄘˊ)
an adjective

形蹤(ㄒㄧㄥˊ ㄗㄨㄥ)
① the traces or tracks of a person; the whereabouts of a person ② the behavior or conduct of a person

形蹤不定(ㄒㄧㄥˊ ㄗㄨㄥ ㄅㄨˋ ㄉㄧㄥˋ)
to have no fixed residence; to wander here and there unpredictably

形蹤詭秘(ㄒㄧㄥˊ ㄗㄨㄥ ㄍㄨㄟˇ ㄇㄧˋ)
(said of a person) of dubious background, or of many secrets and of doubtful character; secretive movements

形似(ㄒㄧㄥˊ ㄙˋ)
to resemble; to look like; shaped like

形色倉皇(ㄒㄧㄥˊ ㄙㄜˋ ㄘㄤ ㄏㄨㄤˊ)
to look anxious and tense; to appear in a big hurry—as a fugitive

形而下學(ㄒㄧㄥˊ ㄦˊ ㄒㄧㄚˋ ㄒㄩㄝˊ)
concrete science

形而上學(ㄒㄧㄥˊ ㄦˊ ㄕㄤˋ ㄒㄩㄝˊ)
metaphysics

形影不離(ㄒㄧㄥˊ ㄧㄥˇ ㄅㄨˋ ㄌㄧˊ)
(usually said of lovers and devoted couples) inseparable, like a person and his shadow

形影相弔(ㄒㄧㄥˊ ㄧㄥˇ ㄒㄧㄤ ㄉㄧㄠˋ)
(literally) body and shadow comforting each other—solitary; lonely

形影相隨(ㄒㄧㄥˊ ㄧㄥˇ ㄒㄧㄤ ㄙㄨㄟˊ)
to follow somebody like his shadow—inseparable; very intimate

六畫

【彥】 1449 ㄧㄢˋ yann yàn

a man of ability and virtue; an erudite scholar

彥會(ㄧㄢˋ ㄏㄨㄟˋ)
a gathering of distinguished personalities

彥士(ㄧㄢˋ ㄕˋ)
a refined and accomplished scholar

七畫

【彧】 1450 ㄩˋ yuh yù

refined, learned and accomplished; abundant

八畫

【彫】 1451 (雕) ㄉㄧㄠ diau diāo

1. to tattoo; to carve; to paint; to engrave
2. to wither; emaciated: 花彫謝了。 The flowers withered.
3. to adorn or decorate

彫勵(ㄉㄧㄠ ㄌㄧˋ)
to decorate or hide (one's defects, etc.); to beautify

彫弓(ㄉㄧㄠ ㄍㄨㄥ)
an ornamental bow

彫牆(ㄉㄧㄠ ㄑㄧㄤˊ)
a wall decorated with a painting or drawing

彫喪(ㄉㄧㄠ ㄙㄤˋ)
to look depressed or dejected

【彩】 1452 ㄘㄞˇ tsae cǎi

1. colors; variegated colors
2. makeup in various Chinese operas
3. special feats or stunts in Chinese operas
4. ornamental; brilliant; gay
5. stakes in a gambling game; prize money

彩筆(ㄘㄞˇ ㄅㄧˇ)
① the pen that produces masterpieces ② color crayons

彩排(ㄘㄞˇ ㄆㄞˊ)
a dress rehearsal: 這些演員們今天有一場彩排。The actors have a dress rehearsal today.

彩票(ㄘㄞˇ ㄆㄧㄠˋ)
a lottery ticket; a raffle ticket: 他以賣彩票爲生。He makes a living by selling lottery tickets.

彩屏(ㄘㄞˇ ㄆㄧㄥˊ)
ornamental screens; multicolored screens

彩鳳隨鴉(ㄘㄞˇ ㄈㄥˋ ㄙㄨㄟˊ ㄧㄚ)
(literally) a beautiful phoenix mated to a crow—a perfect woman married to a worthless man

彩帶(ㄘㄞˇ ㄉㄞˋ)
a colored ribbon (or streamer)

彩旦(ㄘㄞˇ ㄉㄢˋ)
(Chinese opera) the clown who plays the role of a female, usually of the vicious type

彩蛋(ㄘㄞˇ ㄉㄢˋ)
(arts and crafts) a painted eggshell; a painting on an eggshell

彩陶文化(ㄘㄞˇ ㄊㄠˊ ㄨㄣˊ ㄏㄨㄚˋ)
(archaeology) Painted-Pottery Culture

彩頭(ㄘㄞˇ ㄊㄡˊ)
good luck; lucky

彩禮(ㄘㄞˇ ㄌㄧˇ)
the presents for the bride's family

彩繪(ㄘㄞˇ ㄏㄨㄟˋ)
a colored drawing or pattern

彩虹(ㄘㄞˇ ㄏㄨㄥˊ)
a rainbow

彩轎(ㄘㄞˇ ㄐㄧㄠˋ)
a bridal sedan chair

彩氣(ㄘㄞˇ ㄑㄧˋ)
good luck or fortune

彩球(ㄘㄞˇ ㄑㄧㄡˊ)
① a ball-shaped bundle of colored silk ribbons for decoration ② the corona around the sun during an eclipse

彩錢(ㄘㄞˇ ㄑㄧㄢˊ)
(Chinese opera) money given to an actor who plays the act of being wounded

彩霞(ㄘㄞˇ ㄒㄧㄚˊ)
rosy clouds in the morning or evening

彩車(ㄘㄞˇ ㄔㄜ)
a float (in a parade)

彩綢(ㄘㄞˇ ㄔㄡˊ)
silk of various colors

彩飾(ㄘㄞˇ ㄕˋ)
to adorn; to ornament; ornaments; adornments

彩色(ㄘㄞˇ ㄙㄜˋ)
color (film, pictures, photography, etc.)

彩色版(ㄘㄞˇ ㄙㄜˋ ㄅㄢˇ)
chromolithograph printing

彩色電視(ㄘㄞˇ ㄙㄜˋ ㄉㄧㄢˋ ㄕˋ)
color television

彩色軟片(ㄘㄞˇ ㄙㄜˋ ㄖㄨㄢˇ ㄆㄧㄢˋ)
color film

彩色印刷(ㄘㄞˇ ㄙㄜˋ ㄧㄣˋ ㄕㄨㄚ)
chromolithograph; color lithography

彩葉芋(ㄘㄞˇ ㄧㄝˋ ㄩˋ)
galadium

彩釉(ㄘㄞˇ ㄧㄡˋ)
color ceramic glaze

彩雲(ㄘㄞˇ ㄩㄣˊ)
clouds of many hues: 天空佈滿了彩雲。There are clouds of many hues in the sky.

彩暈(ㄘㄞˇ ㄩㄣˋ)
halos of many colors

【彬】 1453
ㄅㄧㄣ bin bīn

1. intelligent, refined and gentle: 他是一個文質彬彬的人。He is an intelligent and refined gentleman.
2. a Chinese family name

彬彬(ㄅㄧㄣ ㄅㄧㄣ)
refined, gentle and elegant

彬彬君子(ㄅㄧㄣ ㄅㄧㄣ ㄐㄩㄣ ㄗˇ)
a refined gentleman

彬彬有禮(ㄅㄧㄣ ㄅㄧㄣ ㄧㄡˇ ㄌㄧˇ)
refined and courteous; suave

彬蔚(ㄅㄧㄣ ㄨㄟˋ)
extremely erudite and refined

【彪】 1454
ㄅㄧㄠ biau biāo

1. a tiger cub
2. stripes or streaks on the skin of a tiger
3. tall and big; shining and brilliant; outstanding
4. a Chinese family name

彪炳(ㄅㄧㄠ ㄅㄧㄥˇ)
brilliant and shining; splendid (achievements, examples, etc.)

彪煥(ㄅㄧㄠ ㄏㄨㄢˋ)
brilliant and shining; outstanding and elegant

彪休(ㄅㄧㄠ ㄒㄧㄡ)
angry; wrathful

彪形(ㄅㄧㄠ ㄒㄧㄥˊ)
tall and big

彪形大漢(ㄅㄧㄠ ㄒㄧㄥˊ ㄉㄚˋ ㄏㄢˋ)
a whale of a man

九畫

【彭】 1455
ㄆㄥˊ perng péng

1. a Chinese family name
2. big
3. longevity
4. proud

彭彭(ㄆㄥˊ ㄆㄥˊ)
① to be numerous ② descriptive of a team of horses advancing without stopping

彭公案(ㄆㄥˊ ㄍㄨㄥ ㄢˋ)
a famous Chinese novel (a forerunner of modern detective stories), authored by 貪夢道人 of the Ching Dynasty

彭亨(ㄆㄥˊ ㄏㄥ)
① potbellied ② proud and smug

彭殤(ㄆㄥˊ ㄕㄤ)
longevity and early death

彭祖(ㄆㄥˊ ㄗㄨˇ)
name of a legendary official in the reign of Emperor Yao (2356 B.C.), who was said to have lived 800 years

十一畫

【彰】 1456
ㄓㄤ jang zhāng

1. ornamental; colorful
2. evident; obvious; clear
3. to manifest; to make known; to display

彰明(ㄓㄤ ㄇㄧㄥˊ)
① to manifest; to clarify; to expound ② name of a county in Szechwan

彰明較著(ㄓㄤ ㄇㄧㄥˊ ㄐㄧㄠˋ ㄓㄨˋ)
extremely obvious and ostensible

彰化(ㄓㄤ ㄏㄨㄚˋ)
Changhua, a county in central Taiwan

彰顯(ㄓㄤ ㄒㄧㄢˇ)
to manifest; to show forth; obvious

彰彰(ㄓㄤ ㄓㄤ)
famous; well-known; evident: 她的德行彰彰在人耳目。Her virtues are evident to everybody.

彰善癉惡(ㄓㄤ ㄕㄢˋ ㄉㄢˋ ㄜˋ)
to publicize and encourage the good and detest the evil

彰往察來(ㄓㄤ ㄨㄤˇ ㄔㄚˊ ㄌㄞˊ)
to evidence the past and scrutinize the future

十二畫

【影】 1457
ㄧㄥˇ yiing yǐng

1. a shadow; an image; a reflection
2. a trace; a vague impression: 我早就忘得沒影兒。I haven't the vaguest impression of it.
3. to copy and imitate
4. to hide; to conceal
5. a sundial

影本(ㄧㄥˇ ㄅㄣˇ)
a facsimile edition; a rubbing

影壁(ㄧㄥˇ ㄅㄧˋ)
a protecting wall immediately inside or outside the front door of a house

影片(ㄧㄥˇ ㄆㄧㄢˋ)
a motion picture; movies; the film of a motion picture

影評(ㄧㄥˇ ㄆㄧㄥˊ)
brief comments on motion pictures; film criticism or evaluation

影評人(ㄧㄥˇ ㄆㄧㄥˊ ㄖㄣˊ)
a movie critic

影迷(ㄧㄥˇ ㄇㄧˊ)
a movie fan: 這位電影明星有很多影迷。This movie star has a great number of fans.

影碟片(ㄧㄥˇ ㄉㄧㄝˊ ㄆㄧㄢˋ)
a videodisk

影碟機(ㄧㄥˇ ㄉㄧㄝˊ ㄐㄧ)
a videodisk player

影壇(ㄧㄥˇ ㄊㄢˊ)
the movie circles; moviedom

影集(ㄧㄥˇ ㄐㄧˊ)
a miniseries (or a mini series)

影劇界(ㄧㄥˇ ㄐㄩˋ ㄐㄧㄝˋ)
the entertainment world; movie and drama circles

影戲(ㄧㄥˇ ㄒㄧˋ)
① a motion picture ② a kind of shadowgraph performance

影響(ㄧㄥˇ ㄒㄧㄤˇ)
influence; impact; effect; to affect; to influence

影像(ㄧㄥˇ ㄒㄧㄤˋ)
an image; a portrait: 她看見鏡中她的影像。She saw her image in the mirror.

影星(ㄧㄥˇ ㄒㄧㄥ)
a movie star
影展(ㄧㄥˇ ㄓㄢˇ)
a photographic exhibition; a film festival
影鈔(ㄧㄥˇ ㄔㄠ)
to make a true-to-life copy (of old books of great value, etc.)
影事(ㄧㄥˇ ㄕˋ)
(Buddhism) a theory that everything in this world is made up of shadows and visions which will vanish in no time
影射(ㄧㄥˇ ㄕㄜˋ)
① to counterfeit (trademarks, etc.); to delude; to humbug ② to hint by suggestive remarks or association
影子(ㄧㄥˇ ·ㄗ)or 影兒(ㄧㄥˇㄦ)
① a shadow ② (figuratively) a trace; a sign; a vague impression
影子內閣(ㄧㄥˇ ·ㄗ ㄋㄟˋ ㄍㄜˊ)
a shadow cabinet
影從(ㄧㄥˇ ㄘㄨㄥˊ)
to follow like a shadow
影印(ㄧㄥˇ ㄧㄣˋ)
① photogravure ② xerography; to xerox
影印本(ㄧㄥˇ ㄧㄣˋ ㄅㄣˇ)
a photolithographic edition; a photostatic copy
影印中心(ㄧㄥˇ ㄧㄣˋ ㄓㄨㄥ ㄒㄧㄣ)
a copy center
影影綽綽(ㄧㄥˇ ㄧㄥˇ ㄔㄨㄛˋ ㄔㄨㄛˋ)
shadowy; vague outlines (of somebody, etc.)
影院(ㄧㄥˇ ㄩㄢˋ)
a movie theater

彳部
ㄔˋ chyh chì

【彳】 1458
ㄔˋ chyh chì
1. short steps or paces
2. a step taken with the left foot
3. a phonetic sign for "ch"
彳亍(ㄔˋ ㄔㄨˋ)
to walk (with left and right feet)

四畫

【彷】 1459
1. ㄆㄤˊ parng páng
hesitating; unsettled
彷徨(ㄆㄤˊ ㄏㄨㄤˊ)
to hesitate; undecided: 他曾在歧路彷徨過。He hesitated at the crossroads.
彷徉(ㄆㄤˊ ㄧㄤˊ)
① unsettled; doubtful ② to roam about

【彷】 1459
2. ㄈㄤˇ faang fǎng
like; similar to; to resemble: 它們的形狀相彷彿。They resemble each other in shape.
彷彿(ㄈㄤˇ ㄈㄨˊ)
① to seem; as if ② to be more or less the same; to be alike

【役】 1460
ㄧˋ yih yì
1. military service
2. to guard the frontier
3. to dispatch
4. to employ as a servant
5. to serve; a servant
6. to do; to undertake
役夫(ㄧˋ ㄈㄨ)
a laborer; a servant
役男(ㄧˋ ㄋㄢˊ)
the male citizens between 18 and 45 who are eligible for military service
役齡(ㄧˋ ㄌㄧㄥˊ)
enlistment age
役志(ㄧˋ ㄓˋ)
to bring one's will into submission
役種(ㄧˋ ㄓㄨㄥˇ)
the classification of military service status such as militia, reserve, standing, etc.
役使(ㄧˋ ㄕˇ)
to employ as a servant; to make (someone) work
役使動物(ㄧˋ ㄕˇ ㄉㄨㄥˋ ㄨˋ)
beasts of burden; draft animals
役屬(ㄧˋ ㄕㄨˇ)
to control; to master
役人(ㄧˋ ㄖㄣˊ)
① (in old China) underlings in a magistrate's office; an attendant ② to order other people to do work; to be served by others
役卒(ㄧˋ ㄗㄨˊ)
lictors; runners
役於人(ㄧˋ ㄩˊ ㄖㄣˊ)
to serve others
役於外物(ㄧˋ ㄩˊ ㄨㄞˋ ㄨˋ)
to crave for worldly goods; to be a slave to material comfort

五畫

【彼】 1461
ㄅㄧˇ bii bǐ
1. that; those: 彼書遠較此書爲佳。That book is much better than this one.
2. the other; another: 他們彼此感情融洽。They are friendly to one another.
3. there: 我將迅速到達彼處。I shall soon be there.
彼輩(ㄅㄧˇ ㄅㄟˋ)
those people; that gang
彼方(ㄅㄧˇ ㄈㄤ)
the other party; the other side
彼得大帝(ㄅㄧˇ ㄉㄜˊ ㄉㄚˋ ㄉㄧˋ)
Peter the Great (1672-1725), Russian emperor
彼等(ㄅㄧˇ ㄉㄥˇ)
those people
彼此(ㄅㄧˇ ㄘˇ)
you and me; both parties; that and this; each other: 他們每天彼此見面。They saw each other every day.
彼此彼此(ㄅㄧˇ ㄘˇ ㄅㄧˇ ㄘˇ)
We are alike. 或 We are in similar position.或 The feeling is mutual.
彼此之間(ㄅㄧˇ ㄘˇ ㄓ ㄐㄧㄢ)
between you, between them; between you and me; between two persons or parties
彼蒼(ㄅㄧˇ ㄘㄤ)
the heavens
彼岸(ㄅㄧˇ ㄢˋ)
① the other side (of the river, ocean, etc.) ② (Buddhism) paradise
彼一時此一時(ㄅㄧˇ ㄧˋ ㄕˊ ㄘˇ ㄧˋ ㄕˊ)
Time makes all the differ-

〔彳部〕

ence. 或 Different times call for different actions.

【往】 1462
1. ㄨㄤˇ woang wǎng

1. to go toward; to depart; to be bound for: 這車開往基隆。The train is bound for Keelung.
2. formerly; past; bygone; gone: 既往不咎。Let bygones be bygones.

往返(ㄨㄤˇ ㄈㄢˇ)
to come and go; to arrive and depart; to make a round trip; to and fro: 往返要多少時間? How long does it take to go there and back?

往復(ㄨㄤˇ ㄈㄨˋ)
① continuous ② comings and goings between friends, etc.

往年(ㄨㄤˇ ㄋㄧㄢˊ)
in the years past; in bygone years

往來(ㄨㄤˇ ㄌㄞˊ)
① to go and return ② personal contact between two persons or parties, etc.: 他們倆往來密切。The two of them are in close contact.

往來銀行(ㄨㄤˇ ㄌㄞˊ ㄧㄣˊ ㄏㄤˊ)
a bank with whom the credits opened

往來無阻(ㄨㄤˇ ㄌㄞˊ ㄨˊ ㄗㄨˇ)
freedom of movements; coming and going without hindrance

往古來今(ㄨㄤˇ ㄍㄨˇ ㄌㄞˊ ㄐㄧㄣ)
from ancient time until now; since time immemorial

往後(ㄨㄤˇ ㄏㄡˋ)
① backward; going back ② hereafter; in the future; from now on: 往後我們要更加用功。From now on we'll study more diligently.

往還(ㄨㄤˇ ㄏㄨㄢˊ)
① coming and going ② contact between two people or parties: 他們兩家常有往還。Their two families always keep in contact with each other.

往教(ㄨㄤˇ ㄐㄧㄠˋ)
to ask the teacher to come to the pupil's place to teach (an act considered disrespectful to the teacher)

往昔(ㄨㄤˇ ㄒㄧˊ)
in the past; in ancient times: 我們不知道他往昔的生活情形。We know nothing of his life in the past.

往哲(ㄨㄤˇ ㄓㄜˊ)
ancient saints and sages

往者已矣(ㄨㄤˇ ㄓㄜˇ ㄧˇ ㄧˇ)
What's gone is gone.

往常(ㄨㄤˇ ㄔㄤˊ)
usually; heretofore; in the past; used to

往時(ㄨㄤˇ ㄕˊ)
formerly; in the past

往事(ㄨㄤˇ ㄕˋ)
things that have come to pass

往事休提(ㄨㄤˇ ㄕˋ ㄒㄧㄡ ㄊㄧˊ)
Let bygones be bygones.

往聖(ㄨㄤˇ ㄕㄥˋ)
ancient sages

往日(ㄨㄤˇ ㄖˋ)
in the olden days; in the past; in bygone days

往往(ㄨㄤˇ ㄨㄤˇ)
usually; often; frequently; more often than not: 他禮拜天往往待在家裏。He usually stays at home on Sundays.

往往如此(ㄨㄤˇ ㄨㄤˇ ㄖㄨˊ ㄘˇ)
It happens frequently that...; usually like that

【往】 1462
2. ㄨㄤˋ wanq wàng

an adverb indicating time or direction: 水往低處流。Water naturally flows downhill.

往好處想(ㄨㄤˋ ㄏㄠˇ ㄔㄨˋ ㄒㄧㄤˇ)
to think of the better possibilities of a situation, etc.

往後走(ㄨㄤˋ ㄏㄡˋ ㄗㄡˇ)
to turn back and proceed

往壞處想(ㄨㄤˋ ㄏㄨㄞˋ ㄔㄨˋ ㄒㄧㄤˇ)
to think of the unfavorable possibilities of a situation, etc.

往前看(ㄨㄤˋ ㄑㄧㄢˊ ㄎㄢˋ)
to look forward

往下說(ㄨㄤˋ ㄒㄧㄚˋ ㄕㄨㄛ)
to talk on或 Go ahead. 或 Please continue.

往上跑(ㄨㄤˋ ㄕㄤˋ ㄆㄠˇ)
to run up; to go uphill

往左拐(ㄨㄤˋ ㄗㄨㄛˇ ㄍㄨㄞˇ)
to turn left: 這條路是往左拐的。The road is turning off to the left.

往右轉(ㄨㄤˋ ㄧㄡˋ ㄓㄨㄢˇ)
to turn right

【征】 1463
ㄓㄥ jeng zhēng

1. to journey far away
2. to attack; to reduce to submission; to conquer; to tame
3. to levy taxes; to collect taxes
4. to take; to snatch
5. a Chinese family name

征旆(ㄓㄥ ㄆㄟˋ)
(in old China) military standards for troops marching to war

征馬(ㄓㄥ ㄇㄚˇ)
① a war horse; a charger ② a traveler's horse

征伐(ㄓㄥ ㄈㄚˊ)
to battle; to be on the warpath; a punitive military action

征帆(ㄓㄥ ㄈㄢˊ)
the boat that makes long voyages

征夫(ㄓㄥ ㄈㄨ)or 征人(ㄓㄥ ㄖㄣˊ)
① a traveler who has journeyed far ② a warrior or soldier

征服(ㄓㄥ ㄈㄨˊ)
to conquer; conquest: 他們用武力征服了敵人。They conquered the enemy by force of arms.

征服者(ㄓㄥ ㄈㄨˊ ㄓㄜˇ)
a conqueror

征服自然(ㄓㄥ ㄈㄨˊ ㄗˋ ㄖㄢˊ)
to conquer nature; the conquest of nature: 科學家企圖征服自然。Scientists attempt to conquer nature.

征討(ㄓㄥ ㄊㄠˇ)
to quell (an uprising, rebellion, etc.); to subjugate

征途(ㄓㄥ ㄊㄨˊ)
the journey of a traveler; a traveler's progress

征斂(ㄓㄥ ㄌㄧㄢˋ)
to levy and collect taxes

征客(ㄓㄥ ㄎㄜˋ)
the person who has journeyed a long way; a traveler

征戰(ㄓㄥ ㄓㄢˋ)
to fight in battle

征塵(ㄓㄥ ㄔㄣˊ)
the dust on the route by which a traveler comes from

afar; the dust on the traveler's clothing
征收(ㄓㄥ ㄕㄡ)
to levy and collect (taxes); to impose: 政府每年征收稅金。The government levies and collects taxes every year.
征屬(ㄓㄥ ㄕㄨˇ)
dependents of conscripts; dependents of servicemen fighting at the front
征戍(ㄓㄥ ㄕㄨˋ)
to garrison on the frontiers
征衣(ㄓㄥ ㄧ)
① traveling clothes ② warrior's costume

【徂】 1464
ㄘㄨˊ tswu cú
1. to go to; to go ahead; to advance
2. the preposition "to"
3. to die
4. past
徂落(ㄘㄨˊ ㄌㄨㄛˋ)
to pass away; to die
徂謝(ㄘㄨˊ ㄒㄧㄝˋ)
① to wither; to fade ② to die
徂暑(ㄘㄨˊ ㄕㄨˇ)
the hottest days of summer
徂歲(ㄘㄨˊ ㄙㄨㄟˋ)
the past year; last year

【彿】 1465
ㄈㄨˊ fwu fú
like; similar to; as if

六畫

【待】 1466
1. ㄉㄞˋ day dài
1. to treat; to entertain: 這位老師待人誠懇。This teacher treats people sincerely.
2. to await; to wait for
3. need
4. until
5. a Chinese family name
待辦(ㄉㄞˋ ㄅㄢˋ)
yet to be taken care of
待斃(ㄉㄞˋ ㄅㄧˋ)
to await death; to be a sitting duck
待哺(ㄉㄞˋ ㄅㄨˇ)
to wait for feeding (as babies)
待補(ㄉㄞˋ ㄅㄨˇ)
① (said of an alternate candidate, etc.) to await a vacancy for him to fill ② a pending further supplement, or addition
待聘(ㄉㄞˋ ㄆㄧㄣˋ)
to wait for employment
待命(ㄉㄞˋ ㄇㄧㄥˋ)
to await orders
待發(ㄉㄞˋ ㄈㄚ)
ready to depart: 他們整裝待發。They have packed up and are ready to depart.
待得(ㄉㄞˋ ㄉㄜˊ)
to wait for; to wait until (one gets old, etc.)
待旦(ㄉㄞˋ ㄉㄢˋ)
to wait for the morning (usually said of soldiers on night watch, or people working hard through the night)
待敵(ㄉㄞˋ ㄉㄧˊ)
to wait for the enemy; to lie in ambush
待漏(ㄉㄞˋ ㄌㄡˋ)
(said of courtiers) to wait for the emperor to appear at court at an early hour in the morning
待理不理(ㄉㄞˋ ㄌㄧˇ ㄅㄨˋ ㄌㄧˇ)
a lukewarm reception; to give the cold shoulder to another
待領(ㄉㄞˋ ㄌㄧㄥˇ)
(said of money, articles) to wait for a claimant
待客(ㄉㄞˋ ㄎㄜˋ)
to receive guests; to entertain guests
待考(ㄉㄞˋ ㄎㄠˇ)
(said of a report, theory, statement, etc.) remaining to be confirmed or substantiated
待機(ㄉㄞˋ ㄐㄧ)
to await the opportune moment (for action)
待價而沽(ㄉㄞˋ ㄐㄧㄚˋ ㄦˊ ㄍㄨ)
to wait for the right (favorable) price to sell
待見(ㄉㄞˋ ㄐㄧㄢˋ)
① to like; to be fond of ② to wait to be received (by the host, etc.)
待舉(ㄉㄞˋ ㄐㄩˇ)
to be ready for action
待宵草(ㄉㄞˋ ㄒㄧㄠ ㄘㄠˇ)
an evening primrose
待續(ㄉㄞˋ ㄒㄩˋ)
to be continued
待制(ㄉㄞˋ ㄓˋ)
(in ancient China) an advisor; a staff officer
待詔(ㄉㄞˋ ㄓㄠˋ)
① an official rank in the Ming and Ching dynasties ② a barber ③ a shop clerk
待茶(ㄉㄞˋ ㄔㄚˊ)
to entertain guests with tea
待查(ㄉㄞˋ ㄔㄚˊ)
yet to be investigated: 此事是否屬實待查。Whether it is true or not is yet to be investigated.
待時(ㄉㄞˋ ㄕˊ)
to bide one's time
待人接物(ㄉㄞˋ ㄖㄣˊ ㄐㄧㄝ ㄨˋ)or 待物(ㄉㄞˋ ㄨˋ)
the way one treats people: 她待人接物和藹可親。She treats people kindly.
待如己出(ㄉㄞˋ ㄖㄨˊ ㄐㄧˇ ㄔㄨ)
to treat a child as if he were one's own
待字閨中(ㄉㄞˋ ㄗˋ ㄍㄨㄟ ㄓㄨㄥ)
(said of a young woman) not betrothed yet
待罪(ㄉㄞˋ ㄗㄨㄟˋ)
① to wait for punishment ② (in old China) a term referring to oneself when addressing a superior
待業(ㄉㄞˋ ㄧㄝˋ)
(in mainland China) out of employment
待要(ㄉㄞˋ ㄧㄠˋ)
to be about to
待遇(ㄉㄞˋ ㄩˋ)
① pay, salary, or remuneration ② the manner of treating people
待月西廂(ㄉㄞˋ ㄩㄝˋ ㄒㄧ ㄒㄧㄤ)
(literally) to wait under the moon at the West Chamber —to wait for one's lover in the night; to have a nocturnal rendezvous with one's lover

【待】 1466
2. ㄉㄞ dai dāi
1. to stay: 他在台北待了三週。He stayed in Taipei for three weeks.
2. later
待不住(ㄉㄞ ·ㄅㄨ ㄓㄨˋ)
can't or won't stay long

〔彳部〕

彳部

待到(ㄉㄞ ㄉㄠˋ)
to wait until
待了半天(ㄉㄞ ˙ㄌㄜ ㄅㄢˋ ㄊㄧㄢ)
to have stayed for a long while
待兩天(ㄉㄞ ㄌㄧㄤˇ ㄊㄧㄢ)
to wait for a few days; two days later; to have stayed for a few days
待一會兒(ㄉㄞ ㄧˋ ㄏㄨㄜˇㄦ)
moments later; just a little while
待在家裏(ㄉㄞ ㄗㄞˋ ㄐㄧㄚ ˙ㄌㄧ)
to stay at home; to stay in

【徇】 1467 1. (殉) ㄒㄩㄣˋ shiunn xùn
1. to show; to display
2. to issue orders in the army
3. to follow; to comply with
4. quick
5. to die for a cause
徇難(ㄒㄩㄣˋ ㄋㄢˋ)
to die for a just cause or for one's country
徇行(ㄒㄩㄣˋ ㄒㄧㄥˊ)
to make rounds of inspection
徇首(ㄒㄩㄣˋ ㄕㄡˇ)
to show the head (of a decapitated offender) to people, troops, etc. to warn against repetition of the offense
徇義(ㄒㄩㄣˋ ㄧˋ)
to follow the cause of righteousness even at the expense of one's life; to die a martyr's death

【徇】 1467 2. ㄒㄩㄣˊ shyun xún
1. pervading
2. to profit
徇情(ㄒㄩㄣˊ ㄑㄧㄥˊ)
favoritism; to let personal feelings influence one's decision
徇私(ㄒㄩㄣˊ ㄙ)
to profit oneself; favoritism; nepotism
徇私舞弊(ㄒㄩㄣˊ ㄙ ㄨˇ ㄅㄧˋ)
to play favoritism and commit irregularities

【很】 1468 ㄏㄣˇ heen hěn
1. very; quite: 你的話很有道理。What you said was very reasonable.
2. fierce; cruel; truculent
3. disobedient; intractable; quarrelsome
4. dispute; quarrel

【徉】 1469 ㄧㄤˊ yang yáng
1. to stray; to roam: 他常在林間徜徉。He often roams about the forest.
2. hesitating; unsettled

【徊】 1470 ㄏㄨㄞˊ hwai huái (又讀 ㄏㄨㄟˊ hwei huí)
1. hesitating; irresolute; indecisive
2. to move to and fro; to walk around

【律】 1471 ㄌㄩˋ liuh lǜ
1. a law; a rule; a regulation; a statute
2. to bind by law; to control or restrain; to discipline
3. a series of standard bamboo tuning pitch pipes used in ancient music
4. a form in Chinese poetry—a stanza of eight lines
律賦(ㄌㄩˋ ㄈㄨˋ)
a form of literary style, called *fu* (賦), with couplets of an identical number of characters neatly paired off word for word
律度(ㄌㄩˋ ㄉㄨˋ)
laws and institutions
律例(ㄌㄩˋ ㄌㄧˋ)
laws or statutes and precedents
律令(ㄌㄩˋ ㄌㄧㄥˋ)
① laws and regulations; orders given according to law ② a Taoist incantation
律呂(ㄌㄩˋ ㄌㄩˇ)
a series of 12 standard bamboo tuning pitch pipes used in ancient Chinese music
律己(ㄌㄩˋ ㄐㄧˇ)
to discipline oneself; self-restraint; to be strict with oneself: 律己以嚴，待人以寬。One should be strict with oneself but liberal toward others.
律詩(ㄌㄩˋ ㄕ)
a poem of eight lines with five or seven characters each and with certain rules about rhymes, tones, and antitheses, popular since the Tang Dynasty
律師(ㄌㄩˋ ㄕ)
① a lawyer; a barrister ② a polite expression for Buddhist monks
律師公會(ㄌㄩˋ ㄕ ㄍㄨㄥ ㄏㄨㄟˋ)
a bar association
律師事務所(ㄌㄩˋ ㄕ ㄕˋ ㄨˋ ㄙㄨㄛˇ)
a lawyer's office

【後】 1472 ㄏㄡˋ how hòu
1. behind; at the back of
2. afterwards; to come after
3. descendants; posterity
4. an auxiliary to indicate "then" or "afterwards"
5. a Chinese family name
後輩(ㄏㄡˋ ㄅㄟˋ)
① juniors; inferiors ② descendants; posterity
後備軍(ㄏㄡˋ ㄅㄟˋ ㄐㄩㄣ)
reserve forces
後備軍人(ㄏㄡˋ ㄅㄟˋ ㄐㄩㄣ ㄖㄣˊ)
military reservists
後半部(ㄏㄡˋ ㄅㄢˋ ㄅㄨˋ)
the latter portion of a book or movie
後半天(ㄏㄡˋ ㄅㄢˋ ㄊㄧㄢ)
the latter half of a day
後半晌兒(ㄏㄡˋ ㄅㄢˋ ㄕㄤˇㄦ)
the late afternoon or evening
後半生(ㄏㄡˋ ㄅㄢˋ ㄕㄥ)
the latter half of one's life
後半夜(ㄏㄡˋ ㄅㄢˋ ㄧㄝˋ)
after midnight; in the wee hours
後邊兒(ㄏㄡˋ ㄅㄧㄚㄦ)
behind; at the back of
後補(ㄏㄡˋ ㄅㄨˇ)
① to make amends ② to replenish
後部(ㄏㄡˋ ㄅㄨˋ)
behind; the back of
後排(ㄏㄡˋ ㄆㄞˊ)
a back row: 後排座位 back row seats
後門(ㄏㄡˋ ㄇㄣˊ)
① the back door; the rear gate (of a city wall) ② backdoor influence: 走後門 to get something done through pull
後面(ㄏㄡˋ ˙ㄇㄧㄢ)
① behind; at the back: 這房子後面有一花園。There is a

garden at the back of the house. ② afterwards; what is to follow: 這個問題我後面還要講。I'll come back to this question later.

後命(ㄏㄡˋ ㄇㄧㄥˋ)
further orders or instructions

後母(ㄏㄡˋ ㄇㄨˇ)
one's stepmother 亦作「繼母」

後方(ㄏㄡˋ ㄈㄤ)
the rear (as contrasted to the war front)

後方勤務(ㄏㄡˋ ㄈㄤ ㄑㄧㄣˊ ㄨˋ)
logistics

後房(ㄏㄡˋ ㄈㄤˊ)
① the living quarters for one's concubines ② the rear rooms of a house

後夫(ㄏㄡˋ ㄈㄨ)
one's second husband (after the divorce or death of the first)

後福(ㄏㄡˋ ㄈㄨˊ)
the blessings to follow; the good days to come (in a person's life); luck in one's later life

後代(ㄏㄡˋ ㄉㄞˋ)
descendants or posterity; future generations: 他們是孔子的後代。They are the descendants of Confucius.

後凋(ㄏㄡˋ ㄉㄧㄠ)
(literally) the last (among plants) to wither—the perseverance of a person in his virtuous ways

後殿(ㄏㄡˋ ㄉㄧㄢˋ)
the rear court rooms in a palace

後段(ㄏㄡˋ ㄉㄨㄢˋ)
① the latter part of a piece of writing or a musical composition, etc. ② the back rows in a theater, etc.

後盾(ㄏㄡˋ ㄉㄨㄣˋ)
a support or supporter; a prop to lean back; a backing

後臺(ㄏㄡˋ ㄊㄞˊ)
① a backstage ② (usually in politics) one's backing or backers; good connections: 他的後臺很硬。He has very strong backing.

後臺老板(ㄏㄡˋ ㄊㄞˊ ㄌㄠˇ ㄅㄢˇ)
(powerful and influential) backers; the string-puller behind the scenes; backstage bosses

後頭骨(ㄏㄡˋ ㄊㄡˊ ㄍㄨˇ)
(anatomy) the parietal bone

後頭(ㄏㄡˋ ˙ㄊㄡ)
① behind; at the back of (a person) ② in the future; days to come

後唐(ㄏㄡˋ ㄊㄤˊ)
the Posterior Tang Dynasty (923-936 A.D.)

後膛鎗(ㄏㄡˋ ㄊㄤˊ ㄑㄧㄤ)
a breechloading gun; a rifle; a breechloader

後天(ㄏㄡˋ ㄊㄧㄢ)
① the day after tomorrow: 我後天將去學校。I will go to school the day after tomorrow. ② acquired; postnatal

後天性免疫不全症候群(ㄏㄡˋ ㄊㄧㄢ ㄒㄧㄥˋ ㄇㄧㄢˇ ㄧˋ ㄅㄨˋ ㄑㄩㄢˊ ㄓㄥˋ ㄏㄡˋ ㄑㄩㄣˊ)
AIDS (Acquired Immune Deficiency Syndrome) 亦作「愛滋病」

後庭(ㄏㄡˋ ㄊㄧㄥˊ)
imperial harems or seraglios

後圖(ㄏㄡˋ ㄊㄨˊ)
to plan later; future planning

後腿兒(ㄏㄡˋ ㄊㄨㄟˇㄦ)
the hind legs of an animal

後退(ㄏㄡˋ ㄊㄨㄟˋ)
to retreat; to withdraw; retreat; withdrawal

後腦(ㄏㄡˋ ㄋㄠˇ)
the hindbrain, consisting of the cerebellum and medulla oblongata

後腦杓子(ㄏㄡˋ ㄋㄠˇ ㄕㄠˊ ˙ㄗ)
the back side of one's head

後年(ㄏㄡˋ ㄋㄧㄢˊ)
the year after next

後娘(ㄏㄡˋ ㄋㄧㄤˊ)
one's stepmother

後來(ㄏㄡˋ ㄌㄞˊ)
① then; afterwards: 後來的情況怎麼樣? What happened afterwards? ② latecomers; to come afterward

後來居上(ㄏㄡˋ ㄌㄞˊ ㄐㄩ ㄕㄤˋ)
The latecomer (or newcomer) ends up in front. 他因年輕力壯, 所以後來居上。As he was young and energetic, he ended up in front.

後力不繼(ㄏㄡˋ ㄌㄧˋ ㄅㄨˋ ㄐㄧˋ)
to lack the strength to continue

後梁(ㄏㄡˋ ㄌㄧㄤˊ)
① the Posterior Liang Dynasty (907-923 A.D.) ② the Later Liang Dynasty (555-587 A.D.)

後路(ㄏㄡˋ ㄌㄨˋ)
① the rear of an army; the route of retreat ② room for a manoeuver; a road for retreat: 聰明人預先留下後路。A wise man leaves room for a manoeuver.

後感(ㄏㄡˋ ㄍㄢˇ)
① an afterthought; a reflection after an event; feelings incurred after an event has taken place ② a review

後跟(ㄏㄡˋ ㄍㄣ)or 後跟兒(ㄏㄡˋ ㄍㄜㄦ)
the heel

後顧(ㄏㄡˋ ㄍㄨˋ)
① to look back (to the past): 後顧不如前瞻。It is better to look ahead into the future than to look back to the past. ② to think of the future; to plan for the future

後顧之憂(ㄏㄡˋ ㄍㄨˋ ㄓ ㄧㄡ)
the worries behind; trouble back at home—as the wife and children left behind by a fighting man on the front

後果(ㄏㄡˋ ㄍㄨㄛˇ)
consequences

後宮(ㄏㄡˋ ㄍㄨㄥ)
① the inner courts of the ancient Chinese emperor; imperial harems or seraglios ② the concubines of a monarch

後漢(ㄏㄡˋ ㄏㄢˋ)
① the Later Han Dynasty, also known as Eastern Han (25-220 A.D.) ② the Posterior Han Dynasty (947-950 A.D.) during the Epoch of the Five Dynasties

後漢書(ㄏㄡˋ ㄏㄢˋ ㄕㄨ)
The History of Later Han, a 120-volume work, compiled and authored by Fan Yeh (范曄) of the Sung Dynasty

後花園(ㄏㄡˋ ㄏㄨㄚ ㄩㄢˊ)
a backyard; a garden at the back of a house

〔彳部〕

後悔(ㄏㄡˋ ㄏㄨㄟˇ)
to regret; to repent; remorse: 我毫不後悔。I have no regrets.
後悔不已(ㄏㄡˋ ㄏㄨㄟˇ ㄅㄨˋ ㄧˇ)
to be overcome with regret
後悔無及(ㄏㄡˋ ㄏㄨㄟˇ ㄨˊ ㄐㄧˊ)or 後悔莫及(ㄏㄡˋ ㄏㄨㄟˇ ㄇㄛˋ ㄐㄧˊ)
It will be too late to regret. 或 It's useless crying over spilled milk.
後會有期(ㄏㄡˋ ㄏㄨㄟˋ ㄧㄡˇ ㄑㄧˊ)
See you again. 曲終人散,後會有期。The meeting is over; see you again.
後患(ㄏㄡˋ ㄏㄨㄢˋ)
the lurking dangers which will become manifest afterward (usually said of a vanquished enemy permitted to retain potentials for a comeback)
後患無窮(ㄏㄡˋ ㄏㄨㄢˋ ㄨˊ ㄑㄩㄥˊ)
an endless flow of disastrous aftermath (because no preventive measures are taken)
後脊梁(ㄏㄡˋ ㄐㄧˇ ㄌㄧㄤˊ)
the spinal column; the spine; the backbone
後記(ㄏㄡˋ ㄐㄧˋ)
a postscript
後繼無人(ㄏㄡˋ ㄐㄧˋ ㄨˊ ㄖㄣˊ)
There is no successor (capable of continuing the task).
後甲板(ㄏㄡˋ ㄐㄧㄚˇ ㄅㄢˇ)
the quarterdeck of a ship
後街(ㄏㄡˋ ㄐㄧㄝ)
the back street; the street at the back of one's house
後脚(ㄏㄡˋ ㄐㄧㄠˇ)
① the rear foot (in walking) ② immediately after (used with 前脚)
後勁
①(ㄏㄡˋ ㄐㄧㄣˋ) ⓐ (said of liquor, etc.) aftereffects ⓑ staying power (of a person, horse, etc.); the strength one reserves for a final thrust ②(ㄏㄡˋ ㄐㄧㄥˋ) crack troops in the rear
後進(ㄏㄡˋ ㄐㄧㄣˋ)
juniors; the rising generation
後晉(ㄏㄡˋ ㄐㄧㄣˋ)
the Posterior Tsin Dynasty (936-946 A.D.), a reign during the Epoch of the Five Dynasties
後妻(ㄏㄡˋ ㄑㄧ)
one's second wife (after the divorce or death of the first)
後期(ㄏㄡˋ ㄑㄧˊ)
① to be behind schedule; to take place after the time fixed ② the latter part of an era
後起之秀(ㄏㄡˋ ㄑㄧˇ ㄓ ㄒㄧㄡˋ)
a standout among the rising generation; a remarkable young person
後勤(ㄏㄡˋ ㄑㄧㄣˊ)
logistic service in the rear
後驅(ㄏㄡˋ ㄑㄩ)
a rear guard
後效(ㄏㄡˋ ㄒㄧㄠˋ)
future performance
後先輝映(ㄏㄡˋ ㄒㄧㄢ ㄏㄨㄟ ㄧㄥˋ)
(said of masterpieces, shining personalities, etc. of different generations) to add brilliance or greatness to each other
後現代主義(ㄏㄡˋ ㄒㄧㄢˋ ㄉㄞˋ ㄓㄨˇ ㄧˋ)
postmodernism
後序 or 後敍(ㄏㄡˋ ㄒㄩˋ)
an epilogue
後續部隊(ㄏㄡˋ ㄒㄩˋ ㄅㄨˋ ㄉㄨㄟˋ)
follow-up units
後學(ㄏㄡˋ ㄒㄩㄝˊ)
① students of the younger generation ② a polite expression referring to oneself when addressing an elder, superior, etc.
後知後覺(ㄏㄡˋ ㄓ ㄏㄡˋ ㄐㄩㄝˊ)
to know afterwards
後肢(ㄏㄡˋ ㄓ)
hind legs
後者(ㄏㄡˋ ㄓㄜˇ)
the latter (as opposed to the former)
後周(ㄏㄡˋ ㄓㄡ)
① the Posterior Chou Dynasty (951-960 A.D.) ② the Later Chou Dynasty (557-588 A.D.), also known as the Northern Chou
後主(ㄏㄡˋ ㄓㄨˇ)
the last emperor of a dynasty
後車(ㄏㄡˋ ㄔㄜ)
the carriage(s) occupied by one's entourage
後塵(ㄏㄡˋ ㄔㄣˊ)
(literally) dust kicked up by someone walking in front—(to follow in another's) footsteps
後世(ㄏㄡˋ ㄕˋ)
descendants; future generations; posterity: 我們爲後世的利益而種樹。We plant trees for the benefit of posterity.
後市(ㄏㄡˋ ㄕˋ)
the afternoon market
後事(ㄏㄡˋ ㄕˋ)
① matters calling for immediate attention after a person's death—as funerals, etc. ② (usually used at the end of a chapter in old novels) what happened afterwards (would be told in the next chapter)
後視鏡(ㄏㄡˋ ㄕˋ ㄐㄧㄥˋ)
a rearview (or rear-vision) mirror
後手(ㄏㄡˋ ㄕㄡˇ)
① preparations made to meet contingencies ② (in chess) a passive or defensive move
後身(ㄏㄡˋ ㄕㄣ)
① one's next or future life; the next incarnation ② the back of a dress or garment
後生可畏(ㄏㄡˋ ㄕㄥ ㄎㄜˇ ㄨㄟˋ)
The young hold potentials for greatness. 或 There is no limit to the youngsters' promise.
後生小子(ㄏㄡˋ ㄕㄥ ㄒㄧㄠˇ ㄗˇ)
young greenhorns; naive youths
後述(ㄏㄡˋ ㄕㄨˋ)
as follows; as stated below
後燃器(ㄏㄡˋ ㄖㄢˊ ㄑㄧˋ)
an afterburner
後人(ㄏㄡˋ ㄖㄣˊ)
① people of future generations; one's descendants or posterity ② to be behind others (in doing good things, charity work, etc.)
後任(ㄏㄡˋ ㄖㄣˋ)
the successor to an office after the incumbent quits
後奏曲(ㄏㄡˋ ㄗㄡˋ ㄑㄩˇ)
(music) an epilogue; a postlude

後坐力(ㄏㄡˋ ㄗㄨㄛˋ ㄌㄧˋ)
recoil

後此(ㄏㄡˋ ㄘˇ)
after this

後死(ㄏㄡˋ ㄙˇ)
a survivor

後嗣(ㄏㄡˋ ㄙˋ)
descendants; posterity

後遺症(ㄏㄡˋ ㄧˊ ㄓㄥˋ)
(pathology) sequela; after-effect

後裔(ㄏㄡˋ ㄧˋ)
descendants

後尾兒(ㄏㄡˋ ㄧㄜˇㄦ)
① the end ② after; behind

後腰(ㄏㄡˋ ㄧㄠ)
the back of one's waist

後言(ㄏㄡˋ ㄧㄢˊ)
① gossips or slanders behind one's back ② an account of happenings which occurred later than the event being told

後影兒(ㄏㄡˋ ㄧㄥˇㄦ)
the outline of someone's back

後五代(ㄏㄡˋ ㄨˇ ㄉㄞˋ)
a period of 53 years between A.D. 907 and 960, during which five dynastic changes (梁, 唐, 晉, 漢, 周) took place before the reunification of China under the Sung Dynasty founded by the House of Chao

後魏(ㄏㄡˋ ㄨㄟˋ)
the Later Wei Dynasty (386-534 A.D.)

後衛(ㄏㄡˋ ㄨㄟˋ)
① the rear guard (in military operations) ② the fullback (in football); the guard (in basketball)

後衛陣地(ㄏㄡˋ ㄨㄟˋ ㄓㄣˋ ㄉㄧˋ)
the position of the rear guard which provides cover for the withdrawal of the main force

後援(ㄏㄡˋ ㄩㄢˊ)
reinforcement from the rear; support: 後援部隊已到達前線。The supporting troops have reached the front.

後院(ㄏㄡˋ ㄩㄢˋ)
a backyard: 他到後院去整修籬笆。He went out into the backyard to fix the fence.

七畫

【徐】 1473 ㄒㄩˊ shyu xú

1. slow; calm; composed; gently: 早晨清風徐來。A refreshing breeze is blowing gently in the morning.
2. Hsü—a state in ancient China occupying part of today's Anhwei Province
3. a Chinese family name

徐步(ㄒㄩˊ ㄅㄨˋ)
to walk slowly; to walk in a leisurely manner

徐圖發展(ㄒㄩˊ ㄊㄨˊ ㄈㄚ ㄓㄢˇ)
gradually plan for future development, expansion, etc.

徐娘半老(ㄒㄩˊ ㄋㄧㄤˊ ㄅㄢˋ ㄌㄠˇ)
(originally) Lady Hsü, a concubine of Emperor Yüan of the Liang Dynasty, who carried on amorous affairs even when she was getting old — a flirtatious middle-aged woman who still retains traces of her erstwhile beauty

徐光啓(ㄒㄩˊ ㄍㄨㄤ ㄑㄧˇ)
Hsü Kuang-chi (1562-1633), a high official in the Ming Dynasty, who was famed for his translation of Western books dealing with astronomy and geometry

徐緩(ㄒㄩˊ ㄏㄨㄢˇ)
slowly; unhurriedly: 她徐緩地走進房間。She walked slowly into the room.

徐徐(ㄒㄩˊ ㄒㄩˊ)
① steady; calm; relaxed and dignified ② slow; slowly: 國旗徐徐升起。The national flag slowly went up the pole.

徐徐而來(ㄒㄩˊ ㄒㄩˊ ㄦˊ ㄌㄞˊ)
to come with relaxed and dignified steps: 那老人徐徐而來。The old man came with relaxed and dignified steps.

徐州(ㄒㄩˊ ㄓㄡ)
① Hsüchow, a city in Kiangsu Province, famous for its strategic position ② one of the nine ancient Chinese political divisions

【徑】 1474 ㄐㄧㄥˋ jinq jìng

1. a narrow path; a byway; a shortcut: 求學無捷徑。There is no shortcut to knowledge.
2. a diameter
3. to decide and proceed (to do something, etc.) without getting orders, etc.; direct; straight: 你可徑行辦理。You may deal with the matter straightaway.
4. already—implying a sense of surprise

徑庭(ㄐㄧㄥˋ ㄊㄧㄥˊ)
quite different; poles apart: 他們對此議論大相徑庭。They are poles apart on this argument.

徑路(ㄐㄧㄥˋ ㄌㄨˋ)
a byway; a narrow path

徑情(ㄐㄧㄥˋ ㄑㄧㄥˊ)
at will; unrestrained

徑行(ㄐㄧㄥˋ ㄒㄧㄥˊ)
to proceed on (a task, etc.) or make (a decision, etc.) at one's own discretion or without authorization

徑直(ㄐㄧㄥˋ ㄓˊ)
straight; directly; straightaway: 飛機將徑直飛往洛杉磯。The plane will fly nonstop to Los Angeles.

徑尺(ㄐㄧㄥˋ ㄔˇ)
a caliber ruler

徑自(ㄐㄧㄥˋ ㄗˋ)
without leave; without consulting anyone: 他悶聲不吭地徑自走了。He left abruptly without saying a word.

徑寸(ㄐㄧㄥˋ ㄘㄨㄣˋ)
a circle or sphere with a diameter of one inch

徑賽(ㄐㄧㄥˋ ㄙㄞˋ)
(sports) track events

徑一周三(ㄐㄧㄥˋ ㄧ ㄓㄡ ㄙㄢ)
The ratio between the diameter and the circumference is roughly 1 : 3 according to an ancient Chinese calculation.

徑踰(ㄐㄧㄥˋ ㄩˊ)
to proceed on other than regular course; to trespass

【徒】 1475 ㄊㄨˊ twu tú

1. disciples; followers; pupils; apprentices

2. a crowd; a gang; a group of people
3. to go on foot: 徒步旅行比坐車要花費較長的時間。It takes longer to travel on foot than by car.
4. a punishment
5. only; merely; in vain: 不徒無益，反而有害。It is not only useless but harmful.
6. empty, as empty-handed; barehanded: 男孩們徒手爭鬥。These boys were fighting with bare hands.
7. foot soldiers; infantry

徒搏(ㄊㄨˊ ㄅㄛˊ)
hand-to-hand combat

徒兵(ㄊㄨˊ ㄅㄧㄥ)
foot soldiers; infantry

徒步(ㄊㄨˊ ㄅㄨˋ)
to go on foot

徒法不行(ㄊㄨˊ ㄈㄚˇ ㄅㄨˋ ㄒㄧㄥˊ)
Good laws without enforcement are useless.

徒費口舌(ㄊㄨˊ ㄈㄟˋ ㄎㄡˇ ㄕㄜˊ)
(literally) to use one's tongue in vain—to waste one's breath (in persuading another, etc.)

徒黨(ㄊㄨˊ ㄉㄤˇ)
a clique; a faction; a band; followers (used derogatively)

徒弟(ㄊㄨˊ ㄉㄧˋ)
an apprentice; a disciple; a pupil

徒讀父書(ㄊㄨˊ ㄉㄨˊ ㄈㄨˋ ㄕㄨ)
unable to profit from what one has read

徒託空言(ㄊㄨˊ ㄊㄨㄛ ㄎㄨㄥ ㄧㄢˊ)
to boast; to jaw but do nothing; to render lip service

徒勞(ㄊㄨˊ ㄌㄠˊ)
futile effort; fruitless labor: 他徒勞往返。He made a futile round trip. 或 He hurried to and fro for nothing.

徒勞無功(ㄊㄨˊ ㄌㄠˊ ㄨˊ ㄍㄨㄥ)
to labor in vain; to work without achieving anything; to avail (someone) nothing

徒隸(ㄊㄨˊ ㄌㄧˋ)
a prisoner undergoing labor service as a form of punishment

徒歌(ㄊㄨˊ ㄍㄜ)
to sing without accompaniment of any musical instrument

徒呼負負(ㄊㄨˊ ㄏㄨ ㄈㄨˋ ㄈㄨˋ)
to exclaim in disappointment for having achieved nothing

徒騎(ㄊㄨˊ ㄐㄧˋ)
foot and horse; infantry and cavalry

徒裼(ㄊㄨˊ ㄒㄧˊ)
barefooted and barebreasted

徒跣(ㄊㄨˊ ㄒㄧㄢˇ)
to move on one's bare feet

徒行(ㄊㄨˊ ㄒㄧㄥˊ)
to go on foot; to walk; to hike

徒刑(ㄊㄨˊ ㄒㄧㄥˊ)
a prison term; imprisonment

徒衆(ㄊㄨˊ ㄓㄨㄥˋ)
a gang; a crowd; a group of followers

徒師(ㄊㄨˊ ㄕ)
foot soldiers; infantry

徒涉(ㄊㄨˊ ㄕㄜˋ)
to wade across (a stream, etc.)

徒首(ㄊㄨˊ ㄕㄡˇ)
bareheaded (after the helmet is lost in battle)

徒手(ㄊㄨˊ ㄕㄡˇ)
empty-handed; barehanded; unarmed

徒手體操(ㄊㄨˊ ㄕㄡˇ ㄊㄧˇ ㄘㄠ)
calisthenics

徒手致富(ㄊㄨˊ ㄕㄡˇ ㄓˋ ㄈㄨˋ)
to start out empty-handed and become rich later; from rags to riches

徒善(ㄊㄨˊ ㄕㄢˋ)
① a well-intentioned plan which is not feasible ② kind-hearted but taking no action

徒屬(ㄊㄨˊ ㄕㄨˇ)
followers; disciples

徒然(ㄊㄨˊ ㄖㄢˊ)
in vain; useless; meaningless; ineffectual

徒子徒孫(ㄊㄨˊ ㄗˇ ㄊㄨˊ ㄙㄨㄣ)
(mostly used comically or abusively) followers

徒增(ㄊㄨˊ ㄗㄥ)
to increase (cost, trouble, age, etc.) without gaining advantage of any kind

徒卒(ㄊㄨˊ ㄗㄨˊ)
foot soldiers; infantry

徒坐(ㄊㄨˊ ㄗㄨㄛˋ)
to sit in leisure; to sit without doing anything

徒爾(ㄊㄨˊ ㄦˇ)
only to ... (without serving a useful purpose)

徒擁虛名(ㄊㄨˊ ㄩㄥˇ ㄒㄩ ㄇㄧㄥˊ)
to have an undeserved reputation; a reputation not backed by facts

八畫

【得】 1476
1. ㄉㄜˊ der dé

1. to get; to obtain; to acquire; to gain; to attain; to effect; to win: 今天的富裕生活得來不易。The rich life we have today was not easily won.
2. complacent
3. agreement; harmony
4. can; may; to be able to
5. All right! 或 That's enough! 得，就這麼辦。All right! Just go ahead.

得罷且罷(ㄉㄜˊ ㄅㄚˋ ㄑㄧㄝˇ ㄅㄚˋ)
It's better to forget about it.

得標(ㄉㄜˊ ㄅㄧㄠ)
(in an open tender) to win the contract; to be awarded the contract

得便(ㄉㄜˊ ㄅㄧㄢˋ)
at (your) convenience

得病(ㄉㄜˊ ㄅㄧㄥˋ)
to get sick or ill; to fall sick

得不到(ㄉㄜˊ ·ㄅㄨ ㄉㄠˋ) or 得不着(ㄉㄜˊ ·ㄅㄨ ㄓㄠˊ)
cannot get

得不償失(ㄉㄜˊ ㄅㄨˋ ㄔㄤˊ ㄕ)
(literally) What one gains cannot offset the losses. —not worth the effort

得票(ㄉㄜˊ ㄆㄧㄠˋ)
to gain votes; the votes one obtained in an election

得民(ㄉㄜˊ ㄇㄧㄣˊ)
to get popular support; to win the people's heart

得法(ㄉㄜˊ ㄈㄚˇ)
to do something in the right way: 他解釋得不甚得法。He did not explain in the right way.

得非(ㄉㄜˊ ㄈㄟ)
Can it be...?

得分(ㄉㄜˊ ㄈㄣ)

to score; a score (in sports competitions, contests, etc.)
得得(ㄉㄜˊ ㄉㄜˊ)
①(descriptive of walking) leisurely ② specially; on purpose
得到(ㄉㄜˊ ㄉㄠˋ)
to succeed in getting or obtaining
得道(ㄉㄜˊ ㄉㄠˋ)
to attain perfection in Taoism or Buddhism; to enter Nirvana; to attain enlightment
得道多助(ㄉㄜˊ ㄉㄠˋ ㄉㄨㄛ ㄓㄨˋ)
Those who uphold justice shall not be alone.
得當(ㄉㄜˊ ㄉㄤˋ)
proper; appropriate (ways, measures, arrangements, etc.)
得體(ㄉㄜˊ ㄊㄧˇ)
proper (deportment, behavior, conduct, etc.)
得天獨厚(ㄉㄜˊ ㄊㄧㄢ ㄉㄨˊ ㄏㄡˋ)
(said of a land rich in natural resources or a gifted person) to be particularly favored by nature; to be endowed by nature
得天下(ㄉㄜˊ ㄊㄧㄢ ㄒㄧㄚˋ)
to unite the country and ascend the throne
得年(ㄉㄜˊ ㄋㄧㄢˊ)
to die at an age below 60: 李君得年五十有八。Mr. Lee died at the age of 58.
得了(ㄉㄜˊ ˙ㄌㄜ)
① Stop it! 或 Hold it! 或 Well! ② finished; completed
得力(ㄉㄜˊ ㄌㄧˋ)
① capable (assistants, etc.); competent; very useful ② thanks to ③ to benefit from; to get help from; to profit from
得隴望蜀(ㄉㄜˊ ㄌㄨㄥˇ ㄨㄤˋ ㄕㄨˇ)
greedy; avarice; cupidity; to have insatiable desires
得過且過(ㄉㄜˊ ㄍㄨㄛˋ ㄑㄧㄝˇ ㄍㄨㄛˋ)
to harbor no ambition of achievement; easygoing; to make do; to be satisfied with whatever lot one has; resigned; to muddle on or along; to drift along
得空兒(ㄉㄜˊ ㄎㄨㄥˋㄦ)
to have spare time or leisure; in (one's) spare time; at leisure
得計(ㄉㄜˊ ㄐㄧˋ)
to have a winning hand; to succeed
得濟(ㄉㄜˊ ㄐㄧˋ)
①(said of an old person) to get financial support from one's offspring ②(said of a plan, scheme, arrangement, etc.) useful; satisfactory
得救(ㄉㄜˊ ㄐㄧㄡˋ)
(especially in Christianity) to obtain salvation; to be saved
得間(ㄉㄜˊ ㄐㄧㄢˋ)
to get a chance to start doing something
得勁(ㄉㄜˊ ㄐㄧㄣˋ)
① easy and comfortable going ② fit for use; handy
得獎(ㄉㄜˊ ㄐㄧㄤˇ)
to win (or be awarded) a prize: 得獎人 a prizewinner 得獎單位 a prizewinning unit
得君(ㄉㄜˊ ㄐㄩㄣ)
to win imperial favor or confidence
得其所哉(ㄉㄜˊ ㄑㄧˊ ㄙㄨㄛˇ ㄗㄞ)
to be in one's element (like fish in water); in a very satisfactory position or circumstance; very much satisfied
得竅(ㄉㄜˊ ㄑㄧㄠˋ)
to get the knack of (doing something, etc.)
得悉(ㄉㄜˊ ㄒㄧ)
(usually used in correspondence, etc.) to have learned that...; to hear of
得暇(ㄉㄜˊ ㄒㄧㄚˊ)or(ㄉㄜˊ ㄒㄧㄚˋ)
to get spare time or leisure; to have the leisure or time to (undertake a task, etc.); in one's spare time; at leisure
得匣還珠(ㄉㄜˊ ㄒㄧㄚˊ ㄏㄨㄢˊ ㄓㄨ)
to place emphasis on the wrong thing; misdirected attention
得閒(ㄉㄜˊ ㄒㄧㄢˊ)
to get leisure or find leisure for; (usually used in letters) at (your) leisure
得新厭舊(ㄉㄜˊ ㄒㄧㄣ ㄧㄢˋ ㄐㄧㄡˋ)
to disdain the old when one gets the new—(figuratively) to favor a concubine and treat the legal wife with disdain
得心應手(ㄉㄜˊ ㄒㄧㄣ ㄧㄥˋ ㄕㄡˇ)
(literally) The hand moves as the mind wishes.—very smooth operation or going; to show facility
得幸(ㄉㄜˊ ㄒㄧㄥˋ)
to have won the favor of the throne
得知(ㄉㄜˊ ㄓ)
to have learned; to have become acquainted with
得職(ㄉㄜˊ ㄓˊ)
① to get an official post ② to hold one's occupation in content
得志(ㄉㄜˊ ㄓˋ)
to have one's ambition fulfilled; to be successful in one's career: 他少年得志。He enjoys success when young.
得中(ㄉㄜˊ ㄓㄨㄥˋ)
to pass the imperial examination
得逞(ㄉㄜˊ ㄔㄥˇ)
to succeed
得寵(ㄉㄜˊ ㄔㄨㄥˇ)
to be favored; to win the favor of (used in connection with concubines, courtiers, etc.)
得失(ㄉㄜˊ ㄕ)
gain and loss; success and failure; merits and faults (of a plan, measure, etc.); advantages and disadvantages
得失榮枯(ㄉㄜˊ ㄕ ㄖㄨㄥˊ ㄎㄨ)
gain and loss; ups and downs—the vicissitudes of life
得失參半(ㄉㄜˊ ㄕ ㄘㄢ ㄅㄢˋ)
to have both merits and demerits, advantages and disadvantages, or gain and loss, etc.
得時(ㄉㄜˊ ㄕˊ)
to be in luck; riding with Lady Luck
得實(ㄉㄜˊ ㄕˊ)
to find out the truth from a prisoner
得勢(ㄉㄜˊ ㄕˋ)
to be in a powerful position; to become influential; to be

〔彳部〕

at the helm; to have the advantage of
得手(ㄉㄜˊ ㄕㄡˇ)
to succeed (in performing a task, usually a criminal act)
得神(ㄉㄜˊ ㄕㄣˊ)
lifelike; vivid (impersonation, etc.)
得勝(ㄉㄜˊ ㄕㄥˋ)
to win; to triumph over an enemy or opponent
得數(ㄉㄜˊ ㄕㄨˋ)
the solution of a problem in arithmetic
得人(ㄉㄜˊ ㄖㄣˊ)
to have got the right man (for a job)
得人心(ㄉㄜˊ ㄖㄣˊ ㄒㄧㄣ)
to be popular; to have won the favor of the people
得子(ㄉㄜˊ ㄗˇ)
to get a son; to give birth to a boy
得罪(ㄉㄜˊ ㄗㄨㄟˋ)
① to offend: 我們不怕得罪人。We are not afraid of giving offence. ② to violate the law
得策(ㄉㄜˊ ㄘㄜˋ)
the best policy; advisability
得寸進尺(ㄉㄜˊ ㄘㄨㄣˋ ㄐㄧㄣˋ ㄔˇ)
The more one gets, the more one wants. 或 Small concessions lead to greater demands.
得色(ㄉㄜˊ ㄙㄜˋ)
an air of complacency; smug
得所(ㄉㄜˊ ㄙㄨㄛˇ)
to be rightly placed; to be in an ideal position or place
得一望二(ㄉㄜˊ ㄧ ㄨㄤˋ ㄦˋ)
to have an insatiable desire to acquire more
得宜(ㄉㄜˊ ㄧˊ)
proper; appropriate; suitable
得以(ㄉㄜˊ ㄧˇ)
to be able to
得益(ㄉㄜˊ ㄧˋ)
to benefit from
得意(ㄉㄜˊ ㄧˋ)
to be complacent; to be very satisfied; (said of a person in business or politics) very successful
得意揚揚(ㄉㄜˊ ㄧˋ ㄧㄤˊ ㄧㄤˊ)
an air of complacency; an appearance of extreme satisfaction; proudly
得意忘形(ㄉㄜˊ ㄧˋ ㄨㄤˋ ㄒㄧㄥˊ)
to have one's head turned by success; to be too complacent to watch one's manners; to be carried away by one's success; to get dizzy with success
得意忘言(ㄉㄜˊ ㄧˋ ㄨㄤˋ ㄧㄢˊ)
a tacit understanding; an understanding without words; a meeting of minds
得一枝棲(ㄉㄜˊ ㄧˋ ㄓ ㄑㄧ)
to get a job (not a very good one) after a long period of unemployment
得未曾有(ㄉㄜˊ ㄨㄟˋ ㄘㄥˊ ㄧㄡˇ)
to have never happened
得魚忘筌(ㄉㄜˊ ㄩˊ ㄨㄤˋ ㄑㄩㄢˊ)
(literally) to get the fish but forget the fish trap—ungrateful
得用(ㄉㄜˊ ㄩㄥˋ)
to be suitable for use; to be useful

【得】 1476 2. ㄉㄟˇ deei děi
1. must; should; ought to
2. to need; to take
得負責任(ㄉㄟˇ ㄈㄨˋ ㄗㄜˊ ㄖㄣˋ)
should be responsible for; must shoulder the responsibility
得用功(ㄉㄟˇ ㄩㄥˋ ㄍㄨㄥ)
must be more studious; should put in more time studying

【得】 1476 3. ˙ㄉㄜ ·de de
an adverbial expletive: 那辦得到。That can be done. 我冷得發抖。I trembled with cold.

【徘】 1477 ㄆㄞˊ pair pái
1. hesitating; irresolute; indecisive
2. to walk to and fro; to move around; to linger around; to pace up and down
徘徊(ㄆㄞˊ ㄏㄨㄞˊ)
① to linger; to walk to and fro; to move around without purpose ② hesitating; irresolute ③ to fluctuate
徘徊流連(ㄆㄞˊ ㄏㄨㄞˊ ㄌㄧㄡˊ ㄌㄧㄢˊ)
to walk to and fro hesitatingly with reluctance to leave
徘徊觀望(ㄆㄞˊ ㄏㄨㄞˊ ㄍㄨㄢ ㄨㄤˋ)
to take an observer's seat; to see but cannot make up one's mind; to wait and see; to wait for the dust to settle
徘徊歧途(ㄆㄞˊ ㄏㄨㄞˊ ㄑㄧˊ ㄊㄨˊ)
to linger around the wrong (or evil) path; to hesitate at the crossroads

【徜】 1478 ㄔㄤˊ charng cháng
going to and fro; lingering; loitering
徜徉(ㄔㄤˊ ㄧㄤˊ)
lingering or loitering

【徙】 1479 ㄒㄧˇ shii xǐ
1. to move one's abode; to migrate; to shift
2. to be exiled
徙邊(ㄒㄧˇ ㄅㄧㄢ)
to move or banish prisoners to the border areas
徙貫(ㄒㄧˇ ㄍㄨㄢˋ)
to move one's residence to another place
徙居(ㄒㄧˇ ㄐㄩ)
to change one's residence; to move; to migrate
徙宅忘妻(ㄒㄧˇ ㄓㄞˊ ㄨㄤˋ ㄑㄧ)
(said of one's absurdity or preposterousness) to move one's living place but forget (to take along) one's wife
徙善(ㄒㄧˇ ㄕㄢˋ)
to change for the better; to reform
徙任(ㄒㄧˇ ㄖㄣˋ)
to be transferred to another post
徙移(ㄒㄧˇ ㄧˊ)
to move; (said of birds, fish, etc.) to migrate: 有些鳥類隨季節徙移。Some birds migrate.
徙倚(ㄒㄧˇ ㄧˇ)
irresolution; indecision; to linger in hesitation
徙義(ㄒㄧˇ ㄧˋ)
to change one's course toward what is right

【從】 1480 1. (从) ㄘㄨㄥˊ tsorng cóng
1. from; by; whence; through: 我們從國外買來這些貨物。We get these goods from foreign countries.
2. to undertake; to manage; to

dedicate oneself to; to attend to; to engage in: 他從事多項冒險事業。He engages in risky undertakings.
3. to follow; to yield to; to listen to; to comply with; to obey: 我們應當遵從醫生的要求。We should comply with the doctor's request.
4. a follower; an attendant

從便(ㄘㄨㄥˊ ㄅㄧㄢˋ)
whenever convenient

從不(ㄘㄨㄥˊ ㄅㄨˋ)
never; to have never (done a thing): 他上學從不遲到。He has never been late for school.

從旁(ㄘㄨㄥˊ ㄆㄤˊ)
(to help, to encourage, etc.) from the side: 你可從旁觀看。You may see it from the side.

從風(ㄘㄨㄥˊ ㄈㄥ)
to follow the trend; to submit (to a powerful nation) quickly; to comply with a leader's call, etc.

從豐(ㄘㄨㄥˊ ㄈㄥ)or 從優(ㄘㄨㄥˊ ㄧㄡ)
liberally (as of payment); (to pay) according to a higher scale

從頭至尾(ㄘㄨㄥˊ ㄊㄡˊ ㄓˋ ㄨㄟˇ)
from beginning to end; throughout: 這本旅遊的書從頭至尾都很有趣。The book of travels was interesting from beginning to end.

從天而降(ㄘㄨㄥˊ ㄊㄧㄢ ㄦˊ ㄐㄧㄤˋ)
(literally) to descend from heaven—very unexpectedly

從來(ㄘㄨㄥˊ ㄌㄞˊ)
from the beginning (used only in a negative expression)

從流(ㄘㄨㄥˊ ㄌㄧㄡˊ)
to yield to one's environment; to follow the prevailing fashion

從良(ㄘㄨㄥˊ ㄌㄧㄤˊ)
(said of a prostitute) to get married, or to become a decent woman again; to come back to normal civic life

從龍(ㄘㄨㄥˊ ㄌㄨㄥˊ)
(literally) to follow the dragon—to follow the new emperor and start a new reign

從略(ㄘㄨㄥˊ ㄌㄩㄝˋ)
to forgo (mentioning it since it's of no consequence); to omit: 此處原文從略。The text is omitted here.

從公(ㄘㄨㄥˊ ㄍㄨㄥ)
to manage or dedicate to official affairs

從寬(ㄘㄨㄥˊ ㄎㄨㄢ)
to be lenient (usually said of meting out punishment)

從緩(ㄘㄨㄥˊ ㄏㄨㄢˇ)
to bide one's time; to postpone; to put off

從簡(ㄘㄨㄥˊ ㄐㄧㄢˇ)
(said of ceremonies) to be simple; to forgo pageantry

從諫如流(ㄘㄨㄥˊ ㄐㄧㄢˋ ㄖㄨˊ ㄌㄧㄡˊ)
to listen to or follow good advice as water flows downward

從今以後(ㄘㄨㄥˊ ㄐㄧㄣ ㄧˇ ㄏㄡˋ)
from now on; from this day on

從井救人(ㄘㄨㄥˊ ㄐㄧㄥˇ ㄐㄧㄡˋ ㄖㄣˊ)
to risk one's life or to compromise one's own interest without doing others any good

從軍(ㄘㄨㄥˊ ㄐㄩㄣ)
to enlist oneself in military service; to become a soldier

從其所好(ㄘㄨㄥˊ ㄑㄧˊ ㄙㄨㄛˇ ㄏㄠˋ)
to cater to one's wishes

從前(ㄘㄨㄥˊ ㄑㄧㄢˊ)
once upon a time; a long time ago; some time ago; formerly; in the past; before: 我從前看過那部影片。I've seen that film before.

從輕發落(ㄘㄨㄥˊ ㄑㄧㄥ ㄈㄚ ㄌㄨㄛˋ)
to use leniency in meting out punishment

從權(ㄘㄨㄥˊ ㄑㄩㄢˊ)
to be flexible; to handle something without rigid application of rules

從小(ㄘㄨㄥˊ ㄒㄧㄠˇ)
from one's childhood; since one was very young: 他們從小即爲好友。They are good friends since childhood.

從新做人(ㄘㄨㄥˊ ㄒㄧㄣ ㄗㄨㄛˋ ㄖㄣˊ)
(said of a criminal, etc.) to start one's life anew

從心所欲(ㄘㄨㄥˊ ㄒㄧㄣ ㄙㄨㄛˇ ㄩˋ)
to do as one wishes (connoting an absence of opposition or objection); as one pleases: 他從心所欲。He does as he pleases.

從征(ㄘㄨㄥˊ ㄓㄥ)
on active military service

從政(ㄘㄨㄥˊ ㄓㄥˋ)
to enter politics; to become a government official

從政黨員(ㄘㄨㄥˊ ㄓㄥˋ ㄉㄤˇ ㄩㄢˊ)
a member of a political party who holds a government post

從中(ㄘㄨㄥˊ ㄓㄨㄥ)
① in the process (of doing something): 有人從中漁利。Someone profits from it. ② from the inside (of something) ③ in the middle

從衆(ㄘㄨㄥˊ ㄓㄨㄥˋ)
to follow the others; to comply with public opinion; to do as others do

從長計議(ㄘㄨㄥˊ ㄔㄤˊ ㄐㄧˋ ㄧˋ)
to take time to make careful deliberations

從事(ㄘㄨㄥˊ ㄕˋ)
to be engaged in (a task); to devote oneself to (a career, task, job, etc.)

從善如登(ㄘㄨㄥˊ ㄕㄢˋ ㄖㄨˊ ㄉㄥ)
To follow what is right is like walking uphill (or climbing a hill).

從善如流(ㄘㄨㄥˊ ㄕㄢˋ ㄖㄨˊ ㄌㄧㄡˊ)
to forge ahead in doing what is right

從屬(ㄘㄨㄥˊ ㄕㄨˇ)
subordinate

從人(ㄘㄨㄥˊ ㄖㄣˊ)
entourage; attendants; servants

從戎(ㄘㄨㄥˊ ㄖㄨㄥˊ)
to join the armed service; to enlist in the armed service

從早到晚(ㄘㄨㄥˊ ㄗㄠˇ ㄉㄠˋ ㄨㄢˇ)
from morning till night

從此以後(ㄘㄨㄥˊ ㄘˇ ㄧˇ ㄏㄡˋ)
from now on; from this moment on; henceforth

從俗(ㄘㄨㄥˊ ㄙㄨˊ)
to follow local customs; to follow traditions; to conform to conventions

從速辦理(ㄘㄨㄥˊ ㄙㄨˋ ㄅㄢˋ ㄌㄧˇ)
to expedite the execution

(of an official instruction, etc.); to do something with dispatch

從而(ㄘㄨㄥˊ ㄦˊ)
and thereupon; thus; as a result; then; so then

從一而終(ㄘㄨㄥˊ ㄧ ㄦˊ ㄓㄨㄥ)
to be faithful to one husband all her life (even after she is divorced or in widowhood)

從嚴(ㄘㄨㄥˊ ㄧㄢˊ)
severely; strictly

從違(ㄘㄨㄥˊ ㄨㄟˊ)
to follow or object (an order, etc.); to obey or reject

從未(ㄘㄨㄥˊ ㄨㄟˋ)
to have never (happened, etc.)

【從】 1480
2. (从) ㄗㄨㄥˋ tzonq zòng

1. entourage; an attendant; a servant: 牧師是上帝之僕從。A priest is a servant of God.
2. secondary; the relation other than one's direct blood relatives
3. an accessory: 他是這謀殺案的從犯。He is an accessory to the murder.
4. vice or deputy

從伯(ㄗㄨㄥˋ ㄅㄛˊ)
one's father's paternal male cousins who are older than him

從妹(ㄗㄨㄥˋ ㄇㄟˋ)
a younger female cousin

從母(ㄗㄨㄥˋ ㄇㄨˇ)
maternal aunts; one's mother's sisters

從犯(ㄗㄨㄥˋ ㄈㄢˋ)
an accessory

從父(ㄗㄨㄥˋ ㄈㄨˋ)
one's father's brothers; paternal uncles

從弟(ㄗㄨㄥˋ ㄉㄧˋ)
sons of one's paternal uncles, who are younger than oneself; male cousins

從女(ㄗㄨㄥˋ ㄋㄩˇ)
a niece

從吏(ㄗㄨㄥˋ ㄌㄧˋ)
a subordinate to an official

從官(ㄗㄨㄥˋ ㄍㄨㄢ)
an official aide; an official whose duties are to attend to the personal affairs of the chief

從刑(ㄗㄨㄥˋ ㄒㄧㄥˊ)
accessory punishment—as deprivation of rights, confiscation of property, etc.

從兄(ㄗㄨㄥˋ ㄒㄩㄥ)
sons of one's paternal uncles, who are older than oneself; male cousins

從者(ㄗㄨㄥˋ ㄓㄜˇ)
attendants; servants

從叔(ㄗㄨㄥˋ ㄕㄨˊ)
one's father's paternal male cousins who are younger than him

從子(ㄗㄨㄥˋ ㄗˇ)
a nephew

從孫(ㄗㄨㄥˋ ㄙㄨㄣ)
grandsons of one's brothers

【從】 1480
3. ㄘㄨㄥ tsong cōng

1. lax; easy
2. plentiful; abundant
3. to urge; to persuade strongly

從容(ㄘㄨㄥ ㄖㄨㄥˊ)
①unhurried; naturally; calm; composed; unflinchingly ② plentiful; plenty of

從容不迫(ㄘㄨㄥ ㄖㄨㄥˊ ㄅㄨˋ ㄆㄛˋ)
in an unhurried or leisurely manner

【從】 1480
4. (縱) ㄗㄨㄥ tzong zōng

from north to south

從橫 or 從衡(ㄗㄨㄥ ㄏㄥˊ)
vertical and horizontal: 合從連橫 the opposite theories of the vertical alliance of six states against Chin (秦) and the horizontal alliance of the states with Chin (秦) during the Warring States Period

【徠】 1481
ㄌㄞˊ lai lái

the ancient version of 來—to come; to induce (customers) to come; to solicit (customers or business); to encourage (customers) to come to buy

【御】 1482
ㄩˋ yuh yù

1. to drive a chariot or carriage
2. a driver; an attendant
3. to resist; to keep out
4. to control; to manage; to superintend; to tame (a shrew); to harness
5. imperial
6. to wait on; to set before, as food; to offer or present to
7. a Chinese family name

御寶(ㄩˋ ㄅㄠˇ)
the imperial seal; the seal of the emperor

御筆(ㄩˋ ㄅㄧˇ)
the handwriting or painting of the emperor

御批(ㄩˋ ㄆㄧ)
the comments made by an emperor

御風(ㄩˋ ㄈㄥ)
to fly; to ride the winds

御夫有術(ㄩˋ ㄈㄨ ㄧㄡˇ ㄕㄨˋ)
very skilful in keeping one's husband on leash or under harness

御女(ㄩˋ ㄋㄩˇ)
① court women; court ladies ② to have sexual intercourse with a woman

御覽(ㄩˋ ㄌㄢˇ)
① to have been read by the emperor ② books provided for the emperor's reading

御林軍(ㄩˋ ㄌㄧㄣˊ ㄐㄩㄣ)
imperial guards; troops assigned for the protection of the emperor

御溝(ㄩˋ ㄍㄡ)
a ditch which flows through the imperial garden

御河(ㄩˋ ㄏㄜˊ)
① a river used exclusively by the emperor ② a small stream running through the Forbidden City ③ name of a river in Shansi (山西)

御花園(ㄩˋ ㄏㄨㄚ ㄩㄢˊ)
an imperial garden; the emperor's garden

御駕(ㄩˋ ㄐㄧㄚˋ)
① the imperial carriage ② the emperor

御駕親征(ㄩˋ ㄐㄧㄚˋ ㄑㄧㄣ ㄓㄥ)
The emperor personally led his soldiers in a military operation.

御街(ㄩˋ ㄐㄧㄝ)
the streets in the capital
御妻(ㄩˋ ㄑㄧ)
to control one's wife
御前(ㄩˋ ㄑㄧㄢˊ)
in the presence of the emperor
御前會議(ㄩˋ ㄑㄧㄢˊ ㄏㄨㄟˋ ㄧˋ)
a conference in which the emperor takes part
御前試(ㄩˋ ㄑㄧㄢˊ ㄕˋ)
the Imperial Examination in old China for selecting high officials with the emperor's officiating
御旨(ㄩˋ ㄓˇ)
an imperial decree
御製(ㄩˋ ㄓˋ)
① poems and writings authored by the emperor ② vessels produced in the imperial kiln
御札(ㄩˋ ㄓㄚˊ)
instructions or orders issued by the emperor
御者(ㄩˋ ㄓㄜˇ)
① the driver of a carriage or chariot ② an attendant
御仗(ㄩˋ ㄓㄤˋ)
the imperial guard
御師(ㄩˋ ㄕ)
a court physician; the emperor's physician
御食(ㄩˋ ㄕˊ)
① the food for the emperor ② to attend on the senior at the table
御史(ㄩˋ ㄕˇ)
an official rank in ancient China with varied duties in the various dynasties, the prominent ones being those of censoring and impeachment; a censor
御史大夫(ㄩˋ ㄕˇ ㄉㄚˋ ㄈㄨ)
an imperial censor, whose duty is to censure and impeach the officials
御膳(ㄩˋ ㄕㄢˋ)
the imperial cuisine
御膳房(ㄩˋ ㄕㄢˋ ㄈㄤˊ)
the imperial kitchen
御書(ㄩˋ ㄕㄨ)
① books offered to the emperor for reading ② writings authored by the emperor
御人(ㄩˋ ㄖㄣˊ)
① a driver ② a maid ③ a woman ④ to control others
御容(ㄩˋ ㄖㄨㄥˊ)
a portrait of the emperor
御賜(ㄩˋ ㄙˋ)
bestowed by the emperor
御醫(ㄩˋ ㄧ)
the emperor's physician
御宴(ㄩˋ ㄧㄢˋ)
a royal feast
御宇(ㄩˋ ㄩˇ)
the reign of an emperor over the nation
御苑(ㄩˋ ㄩㄢˋ)
an imperial park
御用(ㄩˋ ㄩㄥˋ)
(said of articles, etc.) used by the emperor; for the use of the emperor

九畫

1483
【徧】 ㄅㄧㄢˋ biann biàn (語音 ㄆㄧㄢˋ piann piàn)

1. everywhere; all over: 他遊徧天下。He has traveled all over the world.
2. the whole (world, etc.)

徧佈 or 徧布(ㄅㄧㄢˋ ㄅㄨˋ)
all over; everywhere
徧地(ㄅㄧㄢˋ ㄉㄧˋ)
everywhere; all places
徧體鱗傷(ㄅㄧㄢˋ ㄊㄧˇ ㄌㄧㄣˊ ㄕㄤ)
to suffer injuries all over one's body; the whole body covered with wounds
徧歷(ㄅㄧㄢˋ ㄌㄧˋ)
①to have experienced (every hardship, danger, etc.) ② to have traveled or reached (all corners of the world, all places, etc.)
徧告(ㄅㄧㄢˋ ㄍㄠˋ)
to inform all people or everybody; to pass the word around
徧觀(ㄅㄧㄢˋ ㄍㄨㄢ)
to see them all; to have observed everything
徧及(ㄅㄧㄢˋ ㄐㄧˊ)
all over; to have reached everywhere
徧照(ㄅㄧㄢˋ ㄓㄠˋ)
to shine upon all, as the sun
徧身(ㄅㄧㄢˋ ㄕㄣ)
all over one's body; the whole body
徧搜(ㄅㄧㄢˋ ㄙㄡ)
to search everywhere

1484
【徨】 ㄏㄨㄤˊ hwang huáng

1. agitated; alarmed
2. irresolute

徨徨(ㄏㄨㄤˊ ㄏㄨㄤˊ)
alarmed and anxious; agitated and indecisive

1485
【復】 ㄈㄨˋ fuh fù

1. to return; to come back
2. to answer; to reply
3. to repeat; again; repeatedly
4. to recover; a recovery: 祝早日康復。Best wishes for a quick recovery.
5. to return to a normal or original state
6. a Chinese family name

復辟(ㄈㄨˋ ㄅㄧˋ)
①(said of a monarch) to return to the throne after being deposed ② the restoration of monarchy (after revolution ushers in a republican government)
復命(ㄈㄨˋ ㄇㄧㄥˋ)
to report to a superior or elder after completing an assigned mission
復發(ㄈㄨˋ ㄈㄚ)
(said of illness) a relapse; to relapse
復返(ㄈㄨˋ ㄈㄢˇ)
to return
復旦(ㄈㄨˋ ㄉㄢˋ)
the dawning of light after darkness
復電(ㄈㄨˋ ㄉㄧㄢˋ)
a cable reply; to cable a reply: 我復電慶賀她。I cabled congratulations to her.
復古(ㄈㄨˋ ㄍㄨˇ)
to revive old customs, traditions, etc.
復工(ㄈㄨˋ ㄍㄨㄥ)
(said of workers on strike, etc.) to go back to work; (said of a plant after work stoppage) to start operations again
復課(ㄈㄨˋ ㄎㄜˋ)
to resume classes
復刊(ㄈㄨˋ ㄎㄢ)

〔彳部〕

to resume publication
復合(ㄈㄨˋ ㄏㄜˊ)
to reunite
復核(ㄈㄨˋ ㄏㄜˊ)
to reexamine; to review
復函(ㄈㄨˋ ㄏㄢˊ)
①to write a letter in reply ②a letter in reply
復活(ㄈㄨˋ ㄏㄨㄛˊ)
resurrection; to revive
復活節(ㄈㄨˋ ㄏㄨㄛˊ ㄐㄧㄝˊ)
the Easter holiday
復籍(ㄈㄨˋ ㄐㄧˊ)
to regain one's nationality
復交(ㄈㄨˋ ㄐㄧㄠ)
to reestablish diplomatic relations; to resume friendship
復舊(ㄈㄨˋ ㄐㄧㄡˋ)
to return to the original condition
復健(ㄈㄨˋ ㄐㄧㄢˋ)
rehabilitation
復健中心(ㄈㄨˋ ㄐㄧㄢˋ ㄓㄨㄥ ㄒㄧㄣ)
a rehabilitation center
復權(ㄈㄨˋ ㄑㄩㄢˊ)
to restore one's lost right
復習(ㄈㄨˋ ㄒㄧˊ)
to review lessons learned 亦作「複習」
復校(ㄈㄨˋ ㄒㄧㄠˋ)
to reactivate a school; reactivation of a school
復現(ㄈㄨˋ ㄒㄧㄢˋ)
to reappear; reappearance
復新(ㄈㄨˋ ㄒㄧㄣ)
to make new; to make (something) look new
復興(ㄈㄨˋ ㄒㄧㄥ)
a revival; a return to prosperity renaissance; to revive; to restore (a nation's power and glory)
復行視事(ㄈㄨˋ ㄒㄧㄥˊ ㄕˋ ㄕˋ)
to resume office after stepping down from a public post
復醒(ㄈㄨˋ ㄒㄧㄥˇ)
to wake up again
復姓(ㄈㄨˋ ㄒㄧㄥˋ)
to resume the original family name
復學(ㄈㄨˋ ㄒㄩㄝˊ)
to go back to school (after a prolonged absence for health or other reasons); to resume one's interrupted studies
復職(ㄈㄨˋ ㄓˊ)
to reinstate an official to his former position; reinstatement
復診(ㄈㄨˋ ㄓㄣˇ)
visits to a doctor, hospital, etc. after the first visit for the treatment of the same disease
復政(ㄈㄨˋ ㄓㄥˋ)
(said of a monarch) to regain power
復轉(ㄈㄨˋ ㄓㄨㄢˇ)
to repay; to return
復熾(ㄈㄨˋ ㄔˋ)
to flare up again; to become rampant again
復查(ㄈㄨˋ ㄔㄚˊ)
to check; to reexamine
復仇 or 復讎(ㄈㄨˋ ㄔㄡˊ)
① to take one's revenge; to avenge ② a reprisal; revenge; vengeance
復出(ㄈㄨˋ ㄔㄨ)
to come out of retirement again; to come out again
復審(ㄈㄨˋ ㄕㄣˇ)
①to reexamine ② (law) to review a case
復生(ㄈㄨˋ ㄕㄥ)
to become alive again
復任(ㄈㄨˋ ㄖㄣˋ)
to return to one's former office; to take up a position one held formerly
復次(ㄈㄨˋ ㄘˋ)
to repeat over and over—in detail (used mostly in Buddhist Scriptures)
復甦 or 復穌 or 復蘇(ㄈㄨˋ ㄙㄨ)
(said of vegetation) to come to life again; to revive; recovery: 花在水中復甦。Flowers revive in water.
復議(ㄈㄨˋ ㄧˋ)
to discuss a proposal or project which had been rejected or discarded previously
復業(ㄈㄨˋ ㄧㄝˋ)
to resume or return to business again
復位(ㄈㄨˋ ㄨㄟˋ)
to be restored to the throne
復元(ㄈㄨˋ ㄩㄢˊ)
(said of a patient, store, etc.) to have recovered; to be as good as new
復原(ㄈㄨˋ ㄩㄢˊ)
to return to the original state or condition; to restore
復員(ㄈㄨˋ ㄩㄢˊ)
to demobilize; demobilization
復員令(ㄈㄨˋ ㄩㄢˊ ㄌㄧㄥˋ)
demobilization orders

【循】 1486 ㄒㄩㄣˊ shyun xún

1. to follow; to comply with
2. to postpone; to procrastinate
3. in orderly fashion
4. (obsolete) to touch
5. to inspect

循便(ㄒㄩㄣˊ ㄅㄧㄢˋ)
to take advantage of expediency; to be guided by expediency in performing tasks, etc.
循名責實(ㄒㄩㄣˊ ㄇㄧㄥˊ ㄗㄜˊ ㄕˊ)
①to do things in a pragmatic manner ②to do rather than preach; to stress results instead of rhetoric ③ to expect the reality to correspond to the name
循分(ㄒㄩㄣˊ ㄈㄣˋ)
to act according to one's duty; to fulfill one's obligations
循理(ㄒㄩㄣˊ ㄌㄧˇ)
in accordance with reason, rules, or common practices: 他未循理行事。He did not act in accordance with reason.
循吏(ㄒㄩㄣˊ ㄌㄧˋ)
a square and benevolent official
循例(ㄒㄩㄣˊ ㄌㄧˋ)
in accordance with precedents, common practices, or former examples; according to rules
循良(ㄒㄩㄣˊ ㄌㄧㄤˊ)
(usually said of officials) properly discharge duties with meritorious records
循規蹈矩(ㄒㄩㄣˊ ㄍㄨㄟ ㄉㄠˇ ㄐㄩˇ)
to observe all rules and regulations; to toe the line in all sincerity; law-abiding; to obey the rules and regulations
循環(ㄒㄩㄣˊ ㄏㄨㄢˊ)
to move in a cycle; to come

round in order; to circulate; circulation

循環法(ㄒㄩㄣˊ ㄏㄨㄢˊ ㄈㄚˇ)
a method of teaching in which the teaching materials become progressively complicated as the grades go up although the subjects taught remain the same

循環器(ㄒㄩㄣˊ ㄏㄨㄢˊ ㄑㄧˋ)
organs of circulation

循環系統(ㄒㄩㄣˊ ㄏㄨㄢˊ ㄒㄧˋ ㄊㄨㄥˇ)
the circulatory system

循環小數(ㄒㄩㄣˊ ㄏㄨㄢˊ ㄒㄧㄠˇ ㄕㄨˋ)
recurring decimals

循環賽(ㄒㄩㄣˊ ㄏㄨㄢˊ ㄙㄞˋ)
a round robin

循階(ㄒㄩㄣˊ ㄐㄧㄝ)
to advance step by step; to get promoted in good order, according to one's seniority, merits, service records, etc.

循序(ㄒㄩㄣˊ ㄒㄩˋ)
to follow in proper sequence; to proceed in good order, or step by step

循序漸進(ㄒㄩㄣˊ ㄒㄩˋ ㄐㄧㄢˋ ㄐㄧㄣˋ)
to follow in proper sequence and make gradual progress; to follow in order and advance step by step; to proceed in an orderly way and step by step

循循善誘(ㄒㄩㄣˊ ㄒㄩㄣˊ ㄕㄢˋ ㄧㄡˋ)
(said of a good teacher, etc.) to lead students gradually and patiently on the right path (of learning, etc.)

循資(ㄒㄩㄣˊ ㄗ)
to get promotion according to seniority

循俗(ㄒㄩㄣˊ ㄙㄨˊ)
to follow customs and traditions

十畫

【徬】 1487
ㄆㄤˊ parng páng
anxious, agitated and indecisive

徬徨(ㄆㄤˊ ㄏㄨㄤˊ)
to be anxious, agitated and not knowing what to do

【徭】 1488
ㄧㄠˊ yau yáo
compulsory labor service; conscript labor

徭賦(ㄧㄠˊ ㄈㄨˋ)
compulsory labor and land tax

徭糧(ㄧㄠˊ ㄌㄧㄤˊ)
food provisions for forced laborers

徭戍(ㄧㄠˊ ㄕㄨˋ)
compulsory service on the frontier

徭役(ㄧㄠˊ ㄧˋ)
compulsory labor service; corvée

【徯】 1489
ㄒㄧ shi xī
1. to wait for; to expect
2. a narrow path; a shortcut

徯待(ㄒㄧ ㄉㄞˋ)
to expect; to look forward to

徯徑(ㄒㄧ ㄐㄧㄥˋ)
a narrow path; a shortcut; a snap course: 求學無徯徑。There is no shortcut to knowledge.

【微】 1490
ㄨㄟ wei wēi
(又讀 ㄨㄟ uei wēi)
1. small; minute; diminutive; trifling; little; slight: 相差甚微。The difference is slight.
2. low; mean; humble: 他出身微賤。He is a man of mean birth.
3. a polite expression for "I, my, me"
4. weak; sickly; feeble: 她以微弱的聲音說話。She spoke in a weak voice.
5. subtle
6. obscure
7. hidden; concealed
8. to spy
9. if not; but for
10. a Chinese family name

微波(ㄨㄟ ㄅㄛ)
microwaves

微波爐(ㄨㄟ ㄅㄛ ㄌㄨˊ)
a microwave oven

微薄(ㄨㄟ ㄅㄛˊ)
low; mean; trifling; thin; little

微辯(ㄨㄟ ㄅㄧㄢˋ)
to hint by sarcastic remarks

微不足道(ㄨㄟ ㄅㄨˋ ㄗㄨˊ ㄉㄠˋ)
(literally) too small to be worth mentioning—too trifling to be of any consequence; insignificant

微茫(ㄨㄟ ㄇㄤˊ)
obscure; unclear; uncertain

微眇(ㄨㄟ ㄇㄧㄠˇ)
small; trifling; very slight

微妙(ㄨㄟ ㄇㄧㄠˋ)
subtle (positions); delicate (relations); obscure and mysterious (meanings, etc.): 現在國際情勢甚為微妙。The international situation is very delicate at present.

微分學(ㄨㄟ ㄈㄣ ㄒㄩㄝˊ)
differential calculus

微風(ㄨㄟ ㄈㄥ)
a breeze

微服出遊(ㄨㄟ ㄈㄨˊ ㄔㄨ ㄧㄡˊ)
to make a tour in mufti; to make a tour in disguise

微電腦(ㄨㄟ ㄉㄧㄢˋ ㄋㄠˇ)
a microcomputer

微調(ㄨㄟ ㄊㄧㄠˊ)
fine tuning; trimming

微粒子(ㄨㄟ ㄌㄧˋ ㄗˇ)
① corpuscles or particles ② *Nosema bombycis*

微量(ㄨㄟ ㄌㄧㄤˋ)
trace; micro

微觀(ㄨㄟ ㄍㄨㄢ)
microscopic

微管現象(ㄨㄟ ㄍㄨㄢˇ ㄒㄧㄢˋ ㄒㄧㄤˋ) or 微管引力(ㄨㄟ ㄍㄨㄢˇ ㄧㄣˇ ㄌㄧˋ)
capillary phenomena, or capillarity

微乎其微(ㄨㄟ ㄏㄨ ㄑㄧˊ ㄨㄟ)
extremely trifling or minute; an iota; very little: 他一個人的力量是微乎其微的。On his own he can do very little.

微積分(ㄨㄟ ㄐㄧ ㄈㄣ)
calculus

微賤(ㄨㄟ ㄐㄧㄢˋ)
low and mean; inferior; humble

微晶(ㄨㄟ ㄐㄧㄥ)
microlite

微情(ㄨㄟ ㄑㄧㄥˊ)
a subtle affair; a delicate affair

微息(ㄨㄟ ㄒㄧˊ)
weak and feeble

微細(ㄨㄟ ㄒㄧˋ)
very small; minute

微血管(ㄨㄟ ㄒㄧㄝˇ ㄍㄨㄢˇ)
(anatomy) capillaries

微小(ㄨㄟ ㄒㄧㄠˇ)

①diminutive; very small; minute ②very low (voices, sounds, etc.)
微笑(ㄨㄟ ㄒㄧㄠˋ)
to smile; a smile: 她露出奇怪的微笑。She smiled a strange smile.
微嫌(ㄨㄟ ㄒㄧㄢˊ)
slight animosity: 他們之間存有微嫌。There exist slight animosities between them.
微行(ㄨㄟ ㄒㄧㄥˊ)
①to go out in mufti or disguise; to travel incognito ②a narrow path
微醺(ㄨㄟ ㄒㄩㄣ)
slightly drunk
微旨(ㄨㄟ ㄓˇ)
a deep or abstruse meaning or idea
微震(ㄨㄟ ㄓㄣˋ)
an earthquake of low intensity; microseism; a slight shock: 昨夜有微震。A slight shock occurred last night.
微衷(ㄨㄟ ㄓㄨㄥ)
my true feelings, or innermost sentiments (used in polite conversation or correspondence, particularly with superiors)
微忱(ㄨㄟ ㄔㄣˊ)
a slight token of my regard
微塵(ㄨㄟ ㄔㄣˊ)
①fine dust ②(Buddhism) very minute
微時(ㄨㄟ ㄕˊ)
when one was poor and low
微傷(ㄨㄟ ㄕㄤ)
slightly injured
微生蟲(ㄨㄟ ㄕㄥ ㄔㄨㄥˊ)
microbes; bacteria; germs
微生物(ㄨㄟ ㄕㄥ ㄨˋ)
microbes; microorganisms
微生物學(ㄨㄟ ㄕㄥ ㄨˋ ㄒㄩㄝˊ)
microbiology
微弱(ㄨㄟ ㄖㄨㄛˋ)
weak or feeble (voices, strength, etc.): 她以微弱的聲音歌唱。She sang in a feeble voice.
微子(ㄨㄟ ㄗˇ)
①an adopted son ②name of the stepbrother of Emperor Chou of the Shang Dynasty
微罪不舉(ㄨㄟ ㄗㄨㄟˋ ㄅㄨˋ ㄐㄩˇ)
to forgive minor offenses
微辭 or 微詞(ㄨㄟ ㄘˊ)
a hint or circumlocution (to point out another's mistake, fault, etc.); veiled criticism
微意(ㄨㄟ ㄧˋ)
a token of sincerity, gratitude, etc. (an expression used in presenting someone with a gift)
微言大義(ㄨㄟ ㄧㄢˊ ㄉㄚˋ ㄧˋ)
to expound the "great way" with subtle and profound language; sublime words with deep meaning
微驗(ㄨㄟ ㄧㄢˋ)
to spy on another; to secretly observe another's intention, etc.
微恙(ㄨㄟ ㄧㄤˋ)
a slight indisposition
微微(ㄨㄟ ㄨㄟ)
small; minute; diminutive
微微的(ㄨㄟ ·ㄨㄟ ·ㄉㄜ)
slightly; gently
微雨(ㄨㄟ ㄩˇ)
a light rain; a drizzle

十二畫

【徵】 1491
1. ㄓㄥ jeng zhēng

1. to summon
2. to levy or raise (taxes): 政府向人民徵稅。The government levied taxes on people.
3. to call to arms
4. to ask; to inquire
5. to request; to seek for
6. to prove; to evidence
7. signs: 病人已有好轉的徵候。The patient has shown signs of a turn for the better.
8. a Chinese family name

徵辟(ㄓㄥ ㄅㄧˋ)
to use or draft commoners as officials; to appoint commoners to public offices
徵兵(ㄓㄥ ㄅㄧㄥ)
to draft able-bodied male citizens for military service
徵兵制(ㄓㄥ ㄅㄧㄥ ㄓˋ)
the conscription system (as distinct from the volunteer system)
徵聘(ㄓㄥ ㄆㄧㄣˋ)
to solicit a competent person for a vacancy
徵募(ㄓㄥ ㄇㄨˋ)
to enlist and hire
徵發(ㄓㄥ ㄈㄚ)
to requisition supplies and labor service from the people for public use
徵答(ㄓㄥ ㄉㄚˊ)
to solicit answers to questions or problems
徵調(ㄓㄥ ㄉㄧㄠˋ)
to issue orders to conscript men and make military deployment
徵歌(ㄓㄥ ㄍㄜ)
to summon singers or musicians to perform
徵歌選色(ㄓㄥ ㄍㄜ ㄒㄩㄢˇ ㄙㄜˋ)
to pursue sensory pleasure
徵候(ㄓㄥ ㄏㄡˋ)
symptoms, signs, or indications
徵候群(ㄓㄥ ㄏㄡˋ ㄑㄩㄣˊ)
a symptom group 亦作「併合症狀」or「綜合病徵」
徵集(ㄓㄥ ㄐㄧˊ)
to collect or requisition; to levy: 戰時徵集隊伍。Troops are levied in time of war.
徵求(ㄓㄥ ㄑㄧㄡˊ)
to seek; to solicit (answers, etc.); to want (an office clerk, etc.)
徵求會員(ㄓㄥ ㄑㄧㄡˊ ㄏㄨㄟˋ ㄩㄢˊ)
to recruit or enlist members; to canvass for members
徵求意見(ㄓㄥ ㄑㄧㄡˊ ㄧˋ ㄐㄧㄢˋ)
to ask for opinions; to solicit others' views; to seek the opinion of: 我們徵求專家對教學的意見。We ask for experts' opinions on teaching.
徵信錄(ㄓㄥ ㄒㄧㄣˋ ㄌㄨˋ)
a financial report or statement of income and expenditure of a foundation, charity organization, etc.
徵信所(ㄓㄥ ㄒㄧㄣˋ ㄙㄨㄛˇ)
a credit information office
徵象(ㄓㄥ ㄒㄧㄤˋ)
a symptom; indication; a sign
徵詢(ㄓㄥ ㄒㄩㄣˊ)
to solicit opinions, consent, etc.
徵召(ㄓㄥ ㄓㄠˋ)
to draft the capable and vir-

tuous for public service
徵兆(ㄓㄥ ㄓㄠˋ)
a symptom; an omen; symptomatic
徵逐(ㄓㄥ ㄓㄨˊ)
exchanges of visits, etc. between friends
徵詩(ㄓㄥ ㄕ)
to ask another for a poem
徵實(ㄓㄥ ㄕˊ)
to verify; verification
徵收(ㄓㄥ ㄕㄡ)
to collect (taxes, duty, etc.); to levy and collect
徵稅(ㄓㄥ ㄕㄨㄟˋ)
to levy and collect taxes: 政府為了國家的消費而徵稅。The government levies taxes for national expenses.
徵驗(ㄓㄥ ㄧㄢˋ)
to verify; verification; to examine whether the results have come up to expectations
徵引(ㄓㄥ ㄧㄣˇ)
①to recommend a person (for a job, a new position, etc.) ②to evidence; to prove
徵文(ㄓㄥ ㄨㄣˊ)
to solicit writings publicly (as in a contest, etc.)
徵用(ㄓㄥ ㄩㄥˋ)
to requisition; requisition; to conscript; to take over for use; to commandeer

【徵】 1491
2. ㄓˇ jyy zhǐ
one of the five musical notes in Chinese scale

【徹】 1492
ㄔㄜˋ cheh chè
1. penetrating; discerning
2. to remove
3. a tax in tithe
4. to manage; to cultivate (farms)
5. to destroy
6. to deprive; to take away
徹底(ㄔㄜˋ ㄉㄧˇ)
①(said of a stream, etc.) to be able to see the bottom ②to get to the bottom of; thorough; exhaustive
徹底澄清(ㄔㄜˋ ㄉㄧˇ ㄔㄥˊ ㄑㄧㄥ)
to clarify a matter thoroughly; to make a thorough investigation of (a case, etc.): 他發表聲明徹底澄清此情勢。He issued a statement to clarify the situation thoroughly.
徹頭徹尾(ㄔㄜˋ ㄊㄡˊ ㄔㄜˋ ㄨㄟˇ)
thoroughly; thorough; (to understand something, etc.) from beginning to end; through and through
徹骨(ㄔㄜˋ ㄍㄨˇ)
penetrating the bone; to the bone: 寒風徹骨。The bitter wind chills one to the bone.
徹上徹下(ㄔㄜˋ ㄕㄤˋ ㄔㄜˋ ㄒㄧㄚˋ)
from top to bottom; thoroughly; up and down everywhere
徹夜(ㄔㄜˋ ㄧㄝˋ)
all through the night; from dusk to dawn; all night: 他徹夜不眠。He lay awake all night.
徹悟(ㄔㄜˋ ㄨˋ)
to understand thoroughly

【德】 1493
ㄉㄜˊ der dé
1. morality; decency; virtues
2. favor; kindness
3. behavior; conduct
4. to feel grateful
5. Germany; German
德薄能鮮(ㄉㄜˊ ㄅㄛˊ ㄋㄥˊ ㄒㄧㄢˇ)
(a self-derogatory expression used in polite exchanges) I'm lacking in both virtues and abilities.
德便(ㄉㄜˊ ㄅㄧㄢˋ)
convenience; proper and convenient
德配(ㄉㄜˊ ㄆㄟˋ)
(a polite expression) a virtuous wife
德配天地(ㄉㄜˊ ㄆㄟˋ ㄊㄧㄢ ㄉㄧˋ)
a paragon of virtue; very virtuous
德謨克拉西(ㄉㄜˊ ㄇㄛˊ ㄎㄜˋ ㄌㄚ ㄒㄧ)
a transliteration of "democracy"
德門(ㄉㄜˊ ㄇㄣˊ)
a family of high moral standing
德拉瓦(ㄉㄜˊ ㄌㄚ ㄨㄚˇ)
the state of Delaware, U.S.A.
德高望重(ㄉㄜˊ ㄍㄠ ㄨㄤˋ ㄓㄨㄥˋ)
(said of a person) of virtue and prestige; of good moral standing and reputation; to enjoy high prestige and command universal respect
德國(ㄉㄜˊ ㄍㄨㄛˊ)
Germany
德國痲疹(ㄉㄜˊ ㄍㄨㄛˊ ㄇㄚˊ ㄓㄣˇ)
German measles
德克薩斯(ㄉㄜˊ ㄎㄜˋ ㄙㄚˋ ㄙ)or 德州(ㄉㄜˊ ㄓㄡ)
the state of Texas, U.S.A.
德黑蘭(ㄉㄜˊ ㄏㄜ ㄌㄢˊ)
Teheran, the capital of Iran
德行(ㄉㄜˊ ㄒㄧㄥˋ)
①morality and conduct: 他的德行永遠令人欽佩。His morality and conduct are always admirable. ②(colloquial) manners or appearances; mannerisms
德政(ㄉㄜˊ ㄓㄥˋ)
benevolent administration or government
德澤(ㄉㄜˊ ㄗㄜˊ)
the kindness and charity extended to the people
德才兼備(ㄉㄜˊ ㄘㄞˊ ㄐㄧㄢ ㄅㄟˋ)
to have both ability and virtue
德操(ㄉㄜˊ ㄘㄠ)
morality and conduct; virtuous behavior
德意志(ㄉㄜˊ ㄧˋ ㄓˋ)
Deutschland; Germany
德音(ㄉㄜˊ ㄧㄣ)
①virtuous utterances ②(I'm eagerly awaiting) your kind reply ③excellent fame
德文(ㄉㄜˊ ㄨㄣˊ)
the German language; German: 我不會講德文。I cannot speak German.
德望(ㄉㄜˊ ㄨㄤˋ)
virtuous conduct and high prestige: 他德望兼具。He is a man of virtuous conduct and high prestige.
德育(ㄉㄜˊ ㄩˋ)
moral education; ethical training: 德育是一件重要的事情。Moral education is an important thing.

十三畫

【徼】 1494
1. ㄐㄧㄠˋ jiaw jiào
1. frontiers or boundaries
2. to take an inspection trip

〔彳部〕

徼外(ㄐㄧㄠˇ ㄨㄞˋ)
beyond the frontiers; land out of borders

【徼】 1494
2. (僥) ㄐㄧㄠˇ jeau jiǎo

to be lucky; fortunate

徼幸(ㄐㄧㄠˇ ㄒㄧㄥˋ)
lucky; (said of happy events) beyond one's expectations

【徼】 1494
3. ㄧㄠ iau yāo

1. to pray for
2. to shade; to hide

徼福(ㄧㄠ ㄈㄨˊ)
to pray for blessings

十四畫

【徽】 1495
ㄏㄨㄟ huei huī

1. good and beautiful; honorable
2. stops on a lute
3. a streamer, flag, pennant, etc.; a flag-sign
4. an emblem; a badge; insignia
5. Anhwei or Huichow

徽墨(ㄏㄨㄟ ㄇㄛˋ)
the inkstick produced at Huichow of Anhwei Province, considered the best of its kind

徽號(ㄏㄨㄟ ㄏㄠˋ)
① a flag with an emblem ② a high-sounding title

徽州(ㄏㄨㄟ ㄓㄡ)
Huichow, a district in Anhwei Province, famous for producing inksticks

徽章(ㄏㄨㄟ ㄓㄤ)
a badge

徽宗(ㄏㄨㄟ ㄗㄨㄥ)
Emperor Hui Tsung of the Sung Dynasty, whose reign extended from 1101 to 1125 A.D., noted for his accomplishments as an artist

心 部
ㄒㄧㄣ shin xīn

【心】 1496
ㄒㄧㄣ shin xīn

1. the heart
2. the mind
3. conscience; moral nature
4. intention; idea; ambition; design
5. the core; the middle, center or inside
6. one of the 28 constellations

心搏(ㄒㄧㄣ ㄅㄛˊ)
(physiology) heartbeat

心版(ㄒㄧㄣ ㄅㄢˇ)
the mind

心病(ㄒㄧㄣ ㄅㄧㄥˋ)
① mental disorder; the illness caused by deep worries ② worries which one cannot share with another

心不在焉(ㄒㄧㄣ ㄅㄨˋ ㄗㄞˋ ㄧㄢ)
absent-minded; absence of mind: 他上課總是心不在焉。He is always absent-minded in classes.

心不由主(ㄒㄧㄣ ㄅㄨˋ ㄧㄡˊ ㄓㄨˇ)
cannot control one's mind or emotion; cannot help but...

心平氣和(ㄒㄧㄣ ㄆㄧㄥˊ ㄑㄧˋ ㄏㄜˊ)
① to be perfectly calm; calmly: 我們心平氣和地討論問題。We discussed the question calmly. ② to be very fair, without involving one's personal feelings

心滿意足(ㄒㄧㄣ ㄇㄢˇ ㄧˋ ㄗㄨˊ)
to be fully contented; complacent

心迷(ㄒㄧㄣ ㄇㄧˊ)
to be confused of mind; to be puzzled

心明如鏡(ㄒㄧㄣ ㄇㄧㄥˊ ㄖㄨˊ ㄐㄧㄥˋ)
(literally) The mind is as clear as a mirror.—devoid of personal emotions, feelings or sense of gain and loss

心明眼亮(ㄒㄧㄣ ㄇㄧㄥˊ ㄧㄢˇ ㄌㄧㄤˋ)
(to talk) without hiding anything; to lay all one's cards on the table; to be frank

心目中(ㄒㄧㄣ ㄇㄨˋ ㄓㄨㄥ)
① in one's heart or mind; in one's mental view ② in one's memory: 他仍活在我們的心目中。He still lives in our memories.

心慕手追(ㄒㄧㄣ ㄇㄨˋ ㄕㄡˇ ㄓㄨㄟ)
(literally) What one's heart admires the hands follow.—trying one's best to emulate someone whom he admires

心法(ㄒㄧㄣ ㄈㄚˇ)
①(Buddhism) teaching without scriptures—through persuasion and a meeting of minds ②(a way of teaching) by sharing the tutor's thoughts with his pupils

心非(ㄒㄧㄣ ㄈㄟ)
The mind disagrees (with what the lips utter). 他一向口是心非。His mind always disagrees with what he says.

心扉(ㄒㄧㄣ ㄈㄟ)
(figuratively) the door of one's heart

心煩(ㄒㄧㄣ ㄈㄢˊ)
piqued; annoyed; fretful

心煩意亂(ㄒㄧㄣ ㄈㄢˊ ㄧˋ ㄌㄨㄢˋ)
fretful and confused; to be upset

心房(ㄒㄧㄣ ㄈㄤˊ)
①(anatomy) auricles ② the seat of one's inmost thoughts and secret feelings; soul; mind

心房擴大(ㄒㄧㄣ ㄈㄤˊ ㄎㄨㄛˋ ㄉㄚˋ)
dilation of heart

心浮(ㄒㄧㄣ ㄈㄨˊ)
frivolous; restless; impatient; flighty

心浮氣躁(ㄒㄧㄣ ㄈㄨˊ ㄑㄧˋ ㄗㄠˋ)
to be unsettled and short-tempered; to be restless and fretful

心服(ㄒㄧㄣ ㄈㄨˊ)
to have one's heart won; to submit, admire, etc. sincerely and willingly

心服口服(ㄒㄧㄣ ㄈㄨˊ ㄎㄡˇ ㄈㄨˊ)
to admit somebody's superiority, etc. with sincerity; fully convinced

心腹(ㄒㄧㄣ ㄈㄨˋ)
① faith; loyalty ②(military) a region of great strategic importance ③ a confidant; a trusted subordinate

心腹話(ㄒㄧㄣ ㄈㄨˋ ㄏㄨㄚˋ)
a confidential talk: 他向我說心腹話。He told me something in strict confidence.

心腹之患(ㄒㄧㄣ ㄈㄨˋ ㄓ ㄏㄨㄢˋ)
the threat from within (the organization, nation, etc.); serious hidden trouble or danger; a festering wound: 貪污腐化是該國的心腹之患。Corruption in that country is a festering wound.

心腹事(ㄒㄧㄣ ㄈㄨˋ ㄕˋ)
one's innermost secrets

心得(ㄒㄧㄣ ㄉㄜˊ)
what one gains from intense study, meditation or long practice

心到(ㄒㄧㄣ ㄉㄠˋ)
the sincerity of one's heart (as distinct from the formality or mere show of piety)

心膽俱裂(ㄒㄧㄣ ㄉㄢˇ ㄐㄩˋ ㄌㄧㄝˋ)
to be frightened out of one's wits; to be terror-stricken

心蕩神馳(ㄒㄧㄣ ㄉㄤˋ ㄕㄣˊ ㄔˊ)
to be infatuated (with a stunning beauty, etc.); to lose control of one's mind and will; to fall head over heels for

心地(ㄒㄧㄣ ㄉㄧˋ)
conscience; intentions; the true nature of a person; a person's mind; character; moral nature: 她是個心地單純的女孩。She is a simple-minded girl.

心地光明(ㄒㄧㄣ ㄉㄧˋ ㄍㄨㄤ ㄇㄧㄥˊ)
clear conscience; upright

心地善良(ㄒㄧㄣ ㄉㄧˋ ㄕㄢˋ ㄌㄧㄤˊ)
good-natured; kind-hearted

心電圖(ㄒㄧㄣ ㄉㄧㄢˋ ㄊㄨˊ)
an electrocardiogram

心電感應(ㄒㄧㄣ ㄉㄧㄢˋ ㄍㄢˇ ㄧㄥˋ)
telepathy

心毒手辣(ㄒㄧㄣ ㄉㄨˊ ㄕㄡˇ ㄌㄚˋ)
callous and cruel; cold-blooded; merciless at heart and in deeds

心多(ㄒㄧㄣ ㄉㄨㄛ)
over-suspicious

心動(ㄒㄧㄣ ㄉㄨㄥˋ)
① palpitation or fluttering of the heart ② to become interested in something (usually as a result of persuasion)

心態(ㄒㄧㄣ ㄊㄞˋ)
mentality

心頭(ㄒㄧㄣ ㄊㄡˊ)
① the heart; the mind; intentions ② the hearts of animals

心頭火起(ㄒㄧㄣ ㄊㄡˊ ㄏㄨㄛˇ ㄑㄧˇ)
to be angry; to be infuriated

心頭肉(ㄒㄧㄣ ㄊㄡˊ ㄖㄡˋ)
the apple of one's eye; something or someone dear to the heart

心投意合(ㄒㄧㄣ ㄊㄡˊ ㄧˋ ㄏㄜˊ)
(usually said of intimate friends or lovers, etc.) to be in perfect agreement; to be in rapport: 他與女朋友心投意合。He is in rapport with his girlfriend.

心疼(ㄒㄧㄣ ㄊㄥˊ)
①(literally) heartache; the heart bleeds (over financial loss, the suffering of a beloved one, etc.): 我爲她心疼。My heart bleeds for her. ② to love dearly

心跳(ㄒㄧㄣ ㄊㄧㄠˋ)
① heartbeat ② palpitation of the heart caused by fear or anxiety

心跳口跳(ㄒㄧㄣ ㄊㄧㄠˋ ㄎㄡˇ ㄊㄧㄠˋ)
to be in an extreme hurry which causes confusion and trepidation

心田(ㄒㄧㄣ ㄊㄧㄢˊ)
① one's heart: 我將你的恩惠記在心田。I have your best favor at heart. ② one's disposition or intentions

心痛(ㄒㄧㄣ ㄊㄨㄥˋ)
to feel the pangs of heart

心勞日拙(ㄒㄧㄣ ㄌㄠˊ ㄖˋ ㄓㄨㄛˊ)
to make laborious pretensions without contributing anything; to make tiring and useless pretensions

心理(ㄒㄧㄣ ㄌㄧˇ)
① mentality; psychology ② thought and ideas ③ mental; psychogenic

心理病態(ㄒㄧㄣ ㄌㄧˇ ㄅㄧㄥˋ ㄊㄞˋ)
a morbid state of mind; mental abnormality

心理分析(ㄒㄧㄣ ㄌㄧˇ ㄈㄣ ㄒㄧ)
psychoanalysis

心理輔導(ㄒㄧㄣ ㄌㄧˇ ㄈㄨˇ ㄉㄠˇ)
psychological counseling

心理健康(ㄒㄧㄣ ㄌㄧˇ ㄐㄧㄢˋ ㄎㄤ)
mental health

心理建設(ㄒㄧㄣ ㄌㄧˇ ㄐㄧㄢˋ ㄕㄜˋ)
psychological fortification; mental readjustment

心理現象(ㄒㄧㄣ ㄌㄧˇ ㄒㄧㄢˋ ㄒㄧㄤˋ)
mental phenomena

心理學(ㄒㄧㄣ ㄌㄧˇ ㄒㄩㄝˊ)
psychology; mental management

心理戰(ㄒㄧㄣ ㄌㄧˇ ㄓㄢˋ)
psychological warfare, or psywar

心理作用(ㄒㄧㄣ ㄌㄧˇ ㄗㄨㄛˋ ㄩㄥˋ)
imaginary perception; mental reaction

心理測驗(ㄒㄧㄣ ㄌㄧˇ ㄘㄜˋ ㄧㄢˋ)
a mental test

心理因素(ㄒㄧㄣ ㄌㄧˇ ㄧㄣ ㄙㄨˋ)
a psychological factor

心理衛生(ㄒㄧㄣ ㄌㄧˇ ㄨㄟˋ ㄕㄥ)
mental hygiene

心力(ㄒㄧㄣ ㄌㄧˋ)
the exercise of one's mental capabilities; mental power; the vigor of the mind

心力交瘁(ㄒㄧㄣ ㄌㄧˋ ㄐㄧㄠ ㄘㄨㄟˋ)
to feel exhausted both mentally and physically

心裏(ㄒㄧㄣ ˙ㄌㄧ)
① the region of the human body around the chest ② in one's heart; in one's mind; mentally

心裏話(ㄒㄧㄣ ˙ㄌㄧ ㄏㄨㄚˋ)
one's innermost thoughts and feelings: 他說出群衆的心裏話。He gave voice to the innermost feelings of the crowd.

心裏有數(ㄒㄧㄣ ˙ㄌㄧ ㄧㄡˇ ㄕㄨˋ)
aware of something without speaking out

心連心(ㄒㄧㄣ ㄌㄧㄢˊ ㄒㄧㄣ)
heart linked to heart: 父母與子女心連心。The hearts of parents and their children are linked to each other.

心靈(ㄒㄧㄣ ㄌㄧㄥˊ)
mind; spirit; spiritual; mental

心靈手巧(ㄒㄧㄣ ㄌㄧㄥˊ ㄕㄡˇ ㄑㄧㄠˇ)
The mind is clever as the hands are nimble. 或 clever and deft: 她心靈手巧。She is clever and deft.

心領(ㄒㄧㄣ ㄌㄧㄥˇ)
① to understand without verbal exchange ② to appreciate (the offer of service or

a gift while declining it): 你的好意我心領了。I appreciate your kindness but must decline your offer.

心領神會(ㄒ丨ㄣ ㄌ丨ㄥˇ ㄕㄣˊ ㄏㄨㄟˋ)
to know or understand without being told

心亂(ㄒ丨ㄣ ㄌㄨㄢˋ)
confused and perturbed

心亂如麻(ㄒ丨ㄣ ㄌㄨㄢˋ ㄖㄨˊ ㄇㄚˊ)
extremely confused and disturbed; to have one's mind as confused as a tangled skein

心律(ㄒ丨ㄣ ㄌㄩˋ)
(medicine) the rhythm of the heart

心略(ㄒ丨ㄣ ㄌㄩㄝˋ)
scheming; schemes; artful

心高氣傲(ㄒ丨ㄣ ㄍㄠ ㄑ丨ˋ ㄠˋ)
proud and arrogant

心肝(ㄒ丨ㄣ ㄍㄢ)
① a darling; a honey; a sweetheart ② conscience

心甘情願(ㄒ丨ㄣ ㄍㄢ ㄑ丨ㄥˊ ㄩㄢˋ)
to be totally willing; willingly

心廣體胖(ㄒ丨ㄣ ㄍㄨㄤˇ ㄊ丨ˇ ㄆㄢˊ)
A clear conscience (or absence of worries) contributes to physical well-being. 或 fit and happy: 他心廣體胖。He feels fit and happy.

心開(ㄒ丨ㄣ ㄎㄞ)
to have one's mind opened; to be tremendously benefited intellectually

心口(ㄒ丨ㄣ ㄎㄡˇ)
① the region of the human body between the ribs; the bosom ② one's utterance and what he really thinks

心口如一(ㄒ丨ㄣ ㄎㄡˇ ㄖㄨˊ 丨)
(literally) The mouth agrees with the mind.—to speak one's mind frankly; to say what one thinks; to be frank and unreserved; to practice what one preaches

心坎(ㄒ丨ㄣ ㄎㄢˇ) or 心坎兒(ㄒ丨ㄣ ㄎㄚˇㄦ)
① the heart's chord ② dear to the heart; bosom ③ the center of the heart; the bottom of one's heart

心肯(ㄒ丨ㄣ ㄎㄣˇ)
an acceptance in the heart; inner approval or assent

心虧(ㄒ丨ㄣ ㄎㄨㄟ)
a guilty conscience

心寬(ㄒ丨ㄣ ㄎㄨㄢ)
open-minded; carefree; optimistic; feeling at peace with the world

心曠神怡(ㄒ丨ㄣ ㄎㄨㄤˋ ㄕㄣˊ 丨ˊ)
to feel way above par; the spiritual uplift which one often experiences when he enjoys the beauty of nature; to feel on top of the world

心孔(ㄒ丨ㄣ ㄎㄨㄥˇ)
intellectual capacity

心寒膽怯(ㄒ丨ㄣ ㄏㄢˊ ㄉㄢˇ ㄑ丨ㄝˋ)
shuddering and fearful; extreme apprehension; trepidation

心狠(ㄒ丨ㄣ ㄏㄣˇ)
heartless; hardhearted; flinty; unfeeling; callous

心花怒放(ㄒ丨ㄣ ㄏㄨㄚ ㄋㄨˋ ㄈㄤˋ)
to be brimming with joy; to feel exuberantly happy; to be elated: 他因成功而心花怒放。He is highly elated over the success.

心火(ㄒ丨ㄣ ㄏㄨㄛˇ)
①(Chinese medicine) the "inner temperature" of a patient ②(literally) the fire of the heart—the fidgets ③ one of the 28 constellations

心懷(ㄒ丨ㄣ ㄏㄨㄞˊ)
to entertain; to cherish; to harbor: 他心懷叵測。He cherishes evil designs.

心灰意懶(ㄒ丨ㄣ ㄏㄨㄟ 丨ˋ ㄌㄢˇ)
to be downcast and disappointed; extremely discouraged; to be disheartened: 不要因一次失敗而心灰意懶。Don't be disheartened by a single failure.

心灰意冷(ㄒ丨ㄣ ㄏㄨㄟ 丨ˋ ㄌㄥˇ)
pessimistic and dejected due to repeated failures and frustrations; to feel discouraged and hopeless

心回意轉(ㄒ丨ㄣ ㄏㄨㄟˊ 丨ˋ ㄓㄨㄢˇ)
to change one's mind; to give up one's old (evil) ways; to repent; to start a new life

心慌(ㄒ丨ㄣ ㄏㄨㄤ)
to be greatly shaken and perturbed; panicky

心慌意亂(ㄒ丨ㄣ ㄏㄨㄤ 丨ˋ ㄌㄨㄢˋ)
to lose one's wits totally; to be shaken and perturbed; extremely nervous: 面臨危機別心慌意亂。Don't lose your wits in the face of a crisis.

心肌(ㄒ丨ㄣ ㄐ丨)
(anatomy) cardiac muscle; myocardium

心機(ㄒ丨ㄣ ㄐ丨)
schemes, devices or designs; craftiness

心跡 or 心迹(ㄒ丨ㄣ ㄐ丨)
real intentions; innermost feelings

心疾(ㄒ丨ㄣ ㄐ丨ˊ)
① illness caused by deep worries ② a mental ailment

心急(ㄒ丨ㄣ ㄐ丨ˊ)
impatient: 不要如此心急! Don't be so impatient!

心急腿慢(ㄒ丨ㄣ ㄐ丨ˊ ㄊㄨㄟˇ ㄇㄢˋ)
the more impatient the slower the movement

心計(ㄒ丨ㄣ ㄐ丨ˋ)
devices, schemes or designs of the mind; scheming; calculating: 這商人工於心計。The businessman is adept at scheming.

心悸(ㄒ丨ㄣ ㄐ丨ˋ)
palpitation of the heart—a symptom of psychoneurosis

心交(ㄒ丨ㄣ ㄐ丨ㄠ)
a close or intimate friend

心焦(ㄒ丨ㄣ ㄐ丨ㄠ)
anxious; impatient; very eager; worried; vexed: 他們對她的延遲漸感心焦。They became anxious at her delay.

心堅石穿(ㄒ丨ㄣ ㄐ丨ㄢ ㄕˊ ㄔㄨㄢ)
With a strong will power, nothing is impossible.

心匠(ㄒ丨ㄣ ㄐ丨ㄤˋ)
a welding of ideas into plans

心旌(ㄒ丨ㄣ ㄐ丨ㄥ)
wavering; an unsettled state of mind

心經(ㄒ丨ㄣ ㄐ丨ㄥ)
the Buddhist sutra of the heart of prajna

心驚膽戰(ㄒ丨ㄣ ㄐ丨ㄥ ㄉㄢˇ ㄓㄢˋ)
shuddering and terrified; to tremble with fear; to shake with fear: 這景象使他心驚膽

戰。The sight makes him shake with fear.

心驚肉跳(ㄒㄧㄣ ㄐㄧㄥ ㄖㄡˋ ㄊㄧㄠˋ)
trembling with fear; to make one's flesh creep; trepidation

心境(ㄒㄧㄣ ㄐㄧㄥˋ)
a mood; a humor: 她心境非常愉快。She is in a very happy mood.

心鏡(ㄒㄧㄣ ㄐㄧㄥˋ)
(literally) the mirror of the heart—the cleanliness of one's mind

心淨 or 心靜(ㄒㄧㄣ ㄐㄧㄥˋ)
a mind free of worries and cares; calm

心淨地自涼(ㄒㄧㄣ ㄐㄧㄥˋ ㄉㄧˋ ㄗˋ ㄌㄧㄤˊ)
When the mind is free of worries and cares, one will feel cooler (in hot weather).

心期(ㄒㄧㄣ ㄑㄧˊ)
① what one secretly aspires ② mutual approval or admiration

心契(ㄒㄧㄣ ㄑㄧˋ)
①(literally) a meeting of minds—a bosom friend; a very close friend ② teamwork

心怯(ㄒㄧㄣ ㄑㄧㄝˋ)
timid; timorous; shy

心竅(ㄒㄧㄣ ㄑㄧㄠˋ)
the pores of one's mind—the source of one's intellectual capacity; the capacity for clear thinking; the intellect 亦作「心孔」: 他財迷心竅。He was obsessed by a lust for gold.

心情(ㄒㄧㄣ ㄑㄧㄥˊ)
a mood; the frame (or state) of one's mind

心曲(ㄒㄧㄣ ㄑㄩ)
(literally) ① the innermost being; the corner of one's heart; the hidden feelings; the mind ② something weighing on one's mind; one's secret concern

心細(ㄒㄧㄣ ㄒㄧˋ)
cautious; careful; carefulness: 他膽大心細。He is both courageous and cautious.

心邪形穢(ㄒㄧㄣ ㄒㄧㄝˊ ㄒㄧㄥˊ ㄏㄨㄟˋ)
When the mind is filthy, the appearance will not look any better.

心弦(ㄒㄧㄣ ㄒㄧㄢˊ)
the heart's cord; heartstrings: 她的歌聲動人心弦。Her singing played upon our heartstrings.

心險(ㄒㄧㄣ ㄒㄧㄢˇ)
crafty and evil-minded

心心念念(ㄒㄧㄣ ㄒㄧㄣ ㄋㄧㄢˋ ㄋㄧㄢˋ)
to remember always; to keep in mind always

心心相印(ㄒㄧㄣ ㄒㄧㄣ ㄒㄧㄤ ㄧㄣˋ)
a complete meeting of minds; in complete rapport; all of one mind: 我倆心心相印。Both of us are all of one mind.

心香(ㄒㄧㄣ ㄒㄧㄤ)
sincerity; devotion; piety

心想(ㄒㄧㄣ ㄒㄧㄤˇ)
to think; to expect; to figure

心性(ㄒㄧㄣ ㄒㄧㄥˋ)
temperament; tempers; constitution of the mind

心虛(ㄒㄧㄣ ㄒㄩ)
apprehension caused by one's feeling of guilt; a guilty conscience: 他做賊心虛。He had a guilty conscience.

心許(ㄒㄧㄣ ㄒㄩˇ)
a tacit acceptance or approval; acclaim without words

心許目成(ㄒㄧㄣ ㄒㄩˇ ㄇㄨˋ ㄔㄥˊ)
to convey love by exchanging longing glances

心緒(ㄒㄧㄣ ㄒㄩˋ)
a mood; the state of mind: 他心緒不寧。He is in a disturbed state of mind.

心血(ㄒㄧㄣ ㄒㄩㄝˋ)
energy; painstaking care (or efforts): 我們在這計畫上費盡心血。We expended all our energies on this project.

心血來潮(ㄒㄧㄣ ㄒㄩㄝˋ ㄌㄞˊ ㄔㄠˊ)
to hit upon a sudden idea; to have a brainstorm; in an impulsive moment; a whim: 他心血來潮已忘乎所以。He forgot himself in an impulsive moment.

心懸兩地(ㄒㄧㄣ ㄒㄩㄢˊ ㄌㄧㄤˇ ㄉㄧˋ)
(literally) a mind concerned with two places—divided attention; to have worries at two places at the same time

心胸(ㄒㄧㄣ ㄒㄩㄥ)
① will; ambition ② capacity for tolerance; breadth of mind: 我們心胸開闊。We are broad-minded.

心織筆耕(ㄒㄧㄣ ㄓ ㄅㄧˇ ㄍㄥ)
(said of a writing career) The pen labors on the ideas of the mind.

心直口快(ㄒㄧㄣ ㄓˊ ㄎㄡˇ ㄎㄨㄞˋ)
honest and outspoken: 年輕人心直口快。The young man is honest and outspoken.

心志(ㄒㄧㄣ ㄓˋ)
will power; fortitude: 心志可以克服習慣。Will power can conquer habit.

心智(ㄒㄧㄣ ㄓˋ)
mentality; the abilities and powers of the mind

心折(ㄒㄧㄣ ㄓㄜˊ)
to have one's heart won; to admire without reservations

心窄(ㄒㄧㄣ ㄓㄞˇ)
narrow-minded

心照不宣(ㄒㄧㄣ ㄓㄠˋ ㄅㄨˋ ㄒㄩㄢ)
a tacit understanding or agreement: 我們心照不宣。We have a tacit understanding.

心證(ㄒㄧㄣ ㄓㄥˋ)
① (Buddhism) the accord between mind and truth ② (law) to pass a judgment according to the judge's conviction after listening to the arguments of both parties

心中(ㄒㄧㄣ ㄓㄨㄥ)
in one's heart or mind

心中有數(ㄒㄧㄣ ㄓㄨㄥ ㄧㄡˇ ㄕㄨˋ)
to have a pretty good idea of; to know fairly well; to know at heart: 我對工作進行情況心中有數。I have a pretty clear idea of how the work is progressing.

心潮(ㄒㄧㄣ ㄔㄠˊ)
emotions which churn inside like the flow and ebb of the tide; surging thoughts and emotions: 他感到心潮澎湃。He felt an upsurge of emotion.

心腸(ㄒㄧㄣ ㄔㄤˊ)
① heart: 他是一個心腸仁慈的人。He is a man with a kind heart. ② affections; sympathies ③ conscience ④ a natural bent of the mind

〔心部〕

心傳(ㄒㄧㄣ ㄔㄨㄢˊ)
①to teach ②the secret of teaching

心室(ㄒㄧㄣ ㄕˋ)
ventricles

心事(ㄒㄧㄣ ㄕˋ)
①secrets in one's mind ②something weighing on one's mind: 她最近有些心事煩擾她。She's had something weighing on her mind recently.

心手相應(ㄒㄧㄣ ㄕㄡˇ ㄒㄧㄤ ㄧㄥˋ)
(usually said of calligraphy or writing) As the mind wills, the hand responds.

心善(ㄒㄧㄣ ㄕㄢˋ)
kind-hearted; a kind heart

心神(ㄒㄧㄣ ㄕㄣˊ)
①a mood; the state of mind ②attention

心神不定(ㄒㄧㄣ ㄕㄣˊ ㄅㄨˋ ㄉㄧㄥˋ)
a restless or unstable mood; a confused state of mind; to have no peace of mind; to be distracted

心神不安(ㄒㄧㄣ ㄕㄣˊ ㄅㄨˋ ㄢ)
to feel uneasy or perturbed

心上(ㄒㄧㄣ ㄕㄤˋ)
in one's mind; in one's heart

心上人(ㄒㄧㄣ ㄕㄤˋ ㄖㄣˊ)
a sweetheart; a lover

心聲(ㄒㄧㄣ ㄕㄥ)
①spoken language ②the heart's desire; intentions; thoughts

心術(ㄒㄧㄣ ㄕㄨˋ)
designs; schemes; intentions: 他的心術不正。He harbors evil intentions.

心如刀割(ㄒㄧㄣ ㄖㄨˊ ㄉㄠ ㄍㄜ)
(literally) a heart being cut by a knife—heartbroken; heart-stricken; to stab somebody to the heart

心如止水(ㄒㄧㄣ ㄖㄨˊ ㄓˇ ㄕㄨㄟˇ)
(literally) The heart is like still water.—a mind without worries, cares, ambitions or worldly desires

心如死灰(ㄒㄧㄣ ㄖㄨˊ ㄙˇ ㄏㄨㄟ)
One's heart is like dead ashes.

心軟(ㄒㄧㄣ ㄖㄨㄢˇ)
soft-hearted; kind-hearted; tender-hearted

心臟(ㄒㄧㄣ ㄗㄤˋ)
the heart (as an organ)

心臟病(ㄒㄧㄣ ㄗㄤˋ ㄅㄧㄥˋ)
heart disease

心臟病發作(ㄒㄧㄣ ㄗㄤˋ ㄅㄧㄥˋ ㄈㄚ ㄗㄨㄛˋ)
a heart attack

心臟痙攣(ㄒㄧㄣ ㄗㄤˋ ㄐㄧㄥˋ ㄌㄨㄢˊ)
stenocardia

心臟移植(ㄒㄧㄣ ㄗㄤˋ ㄧˊ ㄓˊ)
heart transplantation

心臟炎(ㄒㄧㄣ ㄗㄤˋ ㄧㄢˊ)
carditis

心醉(ㄒㄧㄣ ㄗㄨㄟˋ)
①to admire without reserve ②to be captivated or held spellbound; to be in ecstasies over; to be charmed; to be fascinated: 他對音樂心醉神迷。He was in ecstasies over music.

心慈面軟(ㄒㄧㄣ ㄘˊ ㄇㄧㄢˋ ㄖㄨㄢˇ)
tender-hearted and unable to turn down others' requests

心裁(ㄒㄧㄣ ㄘㄞˊ)
(usually said of objects of art or handicrafts) design; style

心粗(ㄒㄧㄣ ㄘㄨ)
thoughtless; careless: 心粗的孩子常犯錯誤。Thoughtless boys often make blunders.

心存魏闕(ㄒㄧㄣ ㄘㄨㄣˊ ㄨㄟˋ ㄑㄩㄝˋ)
undying loyalty to one's own country while living on a strange land

心思(ㄒㄧㄣ ㄙ)
①ideas; thoughts; intelligence ②intentions ③a state of mind; a mood: 我沒有心思去看電影。I was not in the mood to see a movie.

心死(ㄒㄧㄣ ㄙˇ)
heartless; abandoned; in a state of stupor

心碎(ㄒㄧㄣ ㄙㄨㄟˋ)
heartbreak; heartbroken: 她的死令他心碎。Her death left him broken-hearted.

心酸(ㄒㄧㄣ ㄙㄨㄢ)
heartsick; heartsore; grief-stricken; to sadden; to feel sad

心算(ㄒㄧㄣ ㄙㄨㄢˋ)
mental arithmetic

心愛(ㄒㄧㄣ ㄞˋ)
to be extremely fond of; (things or persons) dear to one's heart

心安(ㄒㄧㄣ ㄢ)
heartsease; peace of mind; calmness of emotion; carefree

心安理得(ㄒㄧㄣ ㄢ ㄌㄧˇ ㄉㄜˊ)
to have achieved a perfect peace of mind; to feel no qualm; to feel at ease and justified

心耳(ㄒㄧㄣ ㄦˇ)
(anatomy) the auricles

心儀(ㄒㄧㄣ ㄧˊ)
admiration in one's mind for another; to look upon someone as a model due to admiration: 我心儀其人。I admired that person.

心意(ㄒㄧㄣ ㄧˋ)
①ideas; intentions; opinions; decisions: 我們不了解他的心意。We don't understand his intention. ②regard: 這禮物是我們大家的一點心意。This gift is a token of our regard.

心藥(ㄒㄧㄣ ㄧㄠˋ)
(literally) the medicine for the heart—anything which removes one's worries and anxieties, or satisfies one's secret longings or desires

心有餘悸(ㄒㄧㄣ ㄧㄡˇ ㄩˊ ㄐㄧˋ)
one's heart still fluttering with fear; to have a lingering fear

心有餘而力不足(ㄒㄧㄣ ㄧㄡˇ ㄩˊ ㄦˊ ㄌㄧˋ ㄅㄨˋ ㄗㄨˊ)
ability or resources at one's command inadequate to achieve what is desired, or to do what one wishes: 我們感到心有餘而力不足。We feel unable to do what we want very much to do.

心眼(兒)(ㄒㄧㄣ ㄧㄢˇ(ㄦ))
①one's intention; conscience ②mind (especially used in "a narrow mind" or "narrow-minded"); over-attention to details ③cleverness or wits

心癢(ㄒㄧㄣ ㄧㄤˇ)
an itching heart—an intense desire (to make a try, etc.)

心漾(ㄒㄧㄣ ㄧㄤˋ)
one's heart aroused by desires (usually carnal)

心營目注(ㄒㄧㄣ ㄧㄥˊ ㄇㄨˋ ㄓㄨˋ)

to watch closely while making plans at heart
心影(ㄒㄧㄣ ㄧㄥˇ)
impression; mental image
心無旁騖(ㄒㄧㄣ ㄨˊ ㄆㄤˊ ㄨˋ)
single-minded; without distraction
心無二用(ㄒㄧㄣ ㄨˊ ㄦˋ ㄩㄥˋ)
One's attention cannot be divided by two undertakings simultaneously. 或 To succeed in an undertaking, one needs single-mindedness or concentration.
心窩(ㄒㄧㄣ ㄨㄛ)
① in one's heart ② the region between the ribs
心爲之動(ㄒㄧㄣ ㄨㄟˊ ㄓ ㄉㄨㄥˋ)
to be tempted
心悅誠服(ㄒㄧㄣ ㄩㄝˋ ㄔㄥˊ ㄈㄨˊ)
to concede or submit willingly; to be completely convinced: 他對你的批評心悅誠服。He conceded willingly your criticism.
心猿意馬(ㄒㄧㄣ ㄩㄢˊ ㄧˋ ㄇㄚˇ)
① cannot make up one's mind; indecision ② restless and whimsical; fanciful and fickle; capricious
心願(ㄒㄧㄣ ㄩㄢˋ)
① a wish (usually a long-cherished one); aspiration; a dream ② a promise to a god

一畫

【必】 1497
ㄅㄧˋ bih bì
1. most certainly; must; necessarily
2. an emphatic particle
必敗(ㄅㄧˋ ㄅㄞˋ)
will certainly be defeated; will certainly fail: 驕兵必敗。An army puffed up with pride will certainly be defeated.
必備條件(ㄅㄧˋ ㄅㄟˋ ㄊㄧㄠˊ ㄐㄧㄢˋ)
the requisitions (for)
必必剝剝(ㄅㄧˋ ㄅㄧˋ ㄅㄛ ㄅㄛ)
"pi pi po po"—the crackling sounds of a burning log, etc.
必不可免(ㄅㄧˋ ㄅㄨˋ ㄎㄜˇ ㄇㄧㄢˇ)
unavoidable; inevitable
必不可少(ㄅㄧˋ ㄅㄨˋ ㄎㄜˇ ㄕㄠˇ)
absolutely necessary
必非(ㄅㄧˋ ㄈㄟ)
certainly not
必得
①(ㄅㄧˋ ㄉㄟˇ) must; to have to: 我必得立刻去做這件事。I must do it at once.
②(ㄅㄧˋ ㄉㄜˊ) determined to possess something; to have to obtain something by every possible means
必定(ㄅㄧˋ ㄉㄧㄥˋ)
most certainly; must; to be sure to
必讀(ㄅㄧˋ ㄉㄨˊ)
a must for reading
必恭必敬(ㄅㄧˋ ㄍㄨㄥ ㄅㄧˋ ㄐㄧㄥˋ)
displaying full courtesy; showing great politeness; showing great respect
必修科(ㄅㄧˋ ㄒㄧㄡ ㄎㄜ)
a required course in the college curriculum; an obligatory course
必需(ㄅㄧˋ ㄒㄩ)
what is essential or indispensable; necessary incidentals or outlays: 食物與空氣是生命所必需的。Food and air are indispensable to life.
必須(ㄅㄧˋ ㄒㄩ)
must; to have to: 人必須吃東西才能活。Man must eat to live.
必需品(ㄅㄧˋ ㄒㄩ ㄆㄧㄣˇ)
daily necessities; consumer goods; necessaries; necessary wants; requisites
必傳之作(ㄅㄧˋ ㄔㄨㄢˊ ㄓ ㄗㄨㄛˋ)
(literally) a work that will certainly go down to posterity—a masterpiece
必勝(ㄅㄧˋ ㄕㄥˋ)
will most certainly win; cannot fail or be defeated
必然(ㄅㄧˋ ㄖㄢˊ)
to have to be (like this); inevitable
必然之勢(ㄅㄧˋ ㄖㄢˊ ㄓ ㄕˋ)
a natural trend; a certainty
必死(ㄅㄧˋ ㄙˇ)
will certainly die or get killed
必死之心(ㄅㄧˋ ㄙˇ ㄓ ㄒㄧㄣ)
with one's back to the wall; determination arising from a desperate situation
必要(ㄅㄧˋ ㄧㄠˋ)
necessary; necessity; need; requisite: 沒有必要再討論了。There's no need to discuss it any more.
必要條件(ㄅㄧˋ ㄧㄠˋ ㄊㄧㄠˊ ㄐㄧㄢˋ)
a necessary condition

二畫

【忉】 1498
ㄉㄠ dau dāo
grieved; distressed
忉怛(ㄉㄠ ㄉㄚˊ)
grieved; distressed; sad; worried
忉忉(ㄉㄠ ㄉㄠ)
distressed; worried

三畫

【忌】 1499
ㄐㄧˋ jih jì
1. jealous; to envy: 他妒忌的理由是什麼? What is the reason for his jealousy?
2. to fear; a fear (usually superstitious)
3. to shun
4. to prohibit or proscribe (usually for superstitious purposes); taboo: 百無禁忌。Nothing is taboo.
5. death anniversaries of one's parents or grandparents
忌憚(ㄐㄧˋ ㄉㄢˋ)
fears that keep a person from committing irregularities; to dread; dread; scruple
忌賭(ㄐㄧˋ ㄉㄨˇ)
to quit gambling
忌妒(ㄐㄧˋ ㄉㄨˋ)
to be jealous of; envy
忌刻(ㄐㄧˋ ㄎㄜˋ)
jealous and acrid
忌口(ㄐㄧˋ ㄎㄡˇ) or 忌嘴(ㄐㄧˋ ㄗㄨㄟˇ)
to be on a diet (because of ailment, etc.); to avoid certain foods
忌恨(ㄐㄧˋ ㄏㄣˋ) or 忌心(ㄐㄧˋ ㄒㄧㄣ)
jealousy; to envy and hate
忌諱(ㄐㄧˋ ㄏㄨㄟˋ)
① things which one does not like others to do or say; things which one avoids saying or doing; a taboo ② to avoid as taboo ③ to avoid

as harmful ④ vinegar

忌酒(ㄐㄧˋ ㄐㄧㄡˇ)or 戒酒(ㄐㄧㄝˋ ㄐㄧㄡˇ)
to quit drinking; to give up alcohol; to abstain from wine

忌妻(ㄐㄧˋ ㄑㄧ)
a jealous wife

忌辰(ㄐㄧˋ ㄔㄣˊ)or 忌日(ㄐㄧˋ ㄖˋ)
death anniversaries of one's parents, etc.; (in ancient China) the death anniversary of the emperor or empress of the reigning dynasty

忌煙(ㄐㄧˋ ㄧㄢ)
to quit smoking 亦作「戒煙」: 他已忌煙。He has quit smoking.

【忍】 1500 ㄖㄣˇ reen rěn

1. to endure; to bear; to tolerate; to put up with; to suffer; to stand: 我再也不能忍耐那噪音。I couldn't put up with the noise any longer.
2. merciless; truculence
3. to forbear; to repress

忍不住(ㄖㄣˇ ˙ㄅㄨ ㄓㄨˋ)
①cannot stand it any more; unable to resist ②can not help (laughing, etc.)

忍冬(ㄖㄣˇ ㄉㄨㄥ)
(botany) honeysuckle

忍涕(ㄖㄣˇ ㄊㄧˋ)
to hold back one's tears

忍痛(ㄖㄣˇ ㄊㄨㄥˋ)
to bear or suffer pain with dignity (to give up or sell something) reluctantly: 我們忍痛割愛。We parted reluctantly with what we treasured.

忍耐(ㄖㄣˇ ㄋㄞˋ)
patience; forbearance; to persevere; patient

忍淚(ㄖㄣˇ ㄌㄟˋ)
to hold back one's tears

忍垢(ㄖㄣˇ ㄍㄡˋ)
to live in shame or disgrace

忍飢挨餓(ㄖㄣˇ ㄐㄧ ㄞˊ ㄜˋ)
to suffer hunger

忍俊不禁(ㄖㄣˇ ㄐㄩㄣˋ ㄅㄨˋ ㄐㄧㄣ)
cannot help smiling or laughing; cannot repress one's smile

忍氣吞聲(ㄖㄣˇ ㄑㄧˋ ㄊㄨㄣ ㄕ...)
to restrain one's temper and say nothing; to keep quiet and swallow the insults

忍笑(ㄖㄣˇ ㄒㄧㄠˋ)
to hold back laughter; to stifle a laugh

忍心(ㄖㄣˇ ㄒㄧㄣ)
unfeeling; merciless; hardhearted; to steel one's heart; to have the heart to

忍心害理(ㄖㄣˇ ㄒㄧㄣ ㄏㄞˋ ㄌㄧˇ)
to do a cruel thing or commit a crime in cold blood

忍性(ㄖㄣˇ ㄒㄧㄥˋ)
to forcibly restrain one's temper

忍住(ㄖㄣˇ ㄓㄨˋ)
to restrain or hold back the manifestation of feelings by the force of will: 她不能忍住她的好奇心。She could not restrain her curiosity.

忍受(ㄖㄣˇ ㄕㄡˋ)
to endure; to bear; to suffer; to stand: 我們忍受艱難困苦。We endured hardships.

忍讓(ㄖㄣˇ ㄖㄤˋ)
to forbear; to be forbearing and conciliatory

忍辱(ㄖㄣˇ ㄖㄨˋ)
to bear disgrace and insults while discharging one's duties conscientiously

忍辱負重(ㄖㄣˇ ㄖㄨˋ ㄈㄨˋ ㄓㄨㄥˋ)
to endure or suffer all disgrace and insults in order to accomplish a task

忍死(ㄖㄣˇ ㄙˇ)
to live when one would rather die (for the sake of a noble cause, etc.)

忍尤含垢(ㄖㄣˇ ㄧㄡˊ ㄏㄢˊ ㄍㄡˋ)
to be able to endure all disgrace and hardships; to swallow insults

忍無可忍(ㄖㄣˇ ㄨˊ ㄎㄜˇ ㄖㄣˇ)
beyond one's endurance; to have one's patience or forbearance tested too far; can not stand (insults or provocation) any longer; to come to the end of one's patience

【忒】 1501 1. ㄊㄜ te tē
a word descriptive of sound

【忒】 1501 2. ㄊㄜˋ teh tè
1. excessive; too; very: 坡忒陡。The slope is very steep.
2. to change
3. to err

忒殺(ㄊㄜˋ ㄕㄚ)or 忒煞(ㄊㄜˋ ㄕㄚˋ)
excessive; too much

忒甚(ㄊㄜˋ ㄕㄣˋ)
much; too much

【忐】 1502 ㄊㄢˇ taan tǎn

1. timid; apprehensive
2. indecisive; vacillating

忐忑(ㄊㄢˇ ㄊㄜˋ)
① indecisive; vacillating ② apprehensive ③ a fidget; to fidget ④ honesty

【忑】 1503 ㄊㄜˋ teh tè

1. nervous; apprehensive
2. indecisive

【志】 1504 ㄓˋ jyh zhì

1. to make up one's mind to pursue some object; to be bent on doing something
2. will; purpose; determination: 有志者事竟成。Where there's a will, there's a way.
3. an ideal; a desire; ambition; interest; wish: 他有志於此。He takes a deep interest in this.
4. annals; records

志不在此(ㄓˋ ㄅㄨˊ ㄗㄞˋ ㄘˇ)
to have an ambition for things beyond what is presently available or obtainable

志大才疏(ㄓˋ ㄉㄚˋ ㄘㄞˊ ㄕㄨ)
to have high aspirations but little ability

志得意滿(ㄓˋ ㄉㄜˊ ㄧˋ ㄇㄢˇ)
fully satisfied or contented; complacent

志同道合(ㄓˋ ㄊㄨㄥˊ ㄉㄠˋ ㄏㄜˊ)
(said of a group of people) to share the same ambition and purpose; of one mind: 我們志同道合。We share the same ambition and purpose.

志略(ㄓˋ ㄌㄩㄝˋ)
① ambition and talent ② to record the general outline ③ a sketch; a synopsis; annals

志怪(ㄓˋ ㄍㄨㄞˋ)
to record the weird, occult and mysterious; a collection of such

志節(ㄓˋ ㄐㄧㄝˊ)
one's ambition and moral fortitude

志氣(ㄓˋ ㄑㄧˋ)
ambition; will; the determination and courage to get ahead

志趣(ㄓˋ ㄑㄩˋ)
purpose and interest; inclination; a bent: 他的志趣是音樂。He has a bent for music.

志趣相投(ㄓˋ ㄑㄩˋ ㄒㄧㄤ ㄊㄡˊ)
(friends) of similar purpose and interest

志向(ㄓˋ ㄒㄧㄤˋ)
purpose; ambition; aspiration: 我們應有遠大的志向。We should have lofty aspirations.

志行(ㄓˋ ㄒㄧㄥˋ)
purpose and behavior; principle and conduct

志學(ㄓˋ ㄒㄩㄝˊ)
to dedicate oneself to the pursuit of learning

志士(ㄓˋ ㄕˋ)
① a man of purpose and virtue ② a man of high ambitions

志士仁人(ㄓˋ ㄕˋ ㄖㄣˊ ㄖㄣˊ)
people of purpose and virtues; people with lofty ideals

志書(ㄓˋ ㄕㄨ)
a record of geographical names, people, products, customs, relics, histories, etc. of various localities

志在必得(ㄓˋ ㄗㄞˋ ㄅㄧˋ ㄉㄜˊ)
to get it at any cost; determined to have

志在千里(ㄓˋ ㄗㄞˋ ㄑㄧㄢ ㄌㄧˇ)
cherishing a great ambition

志操(ㄓˋ ㄘㄠ)
ambition and moral fortitude

志願(ㄓˋ ㄩㄢˋ)
① to volunteer; voluntary; free choice ② aspiration; ambition; an ideal: 他的志願是做一個大政治家。His ambition is to be a great statesman.

志願兵(ㄓˋ ㄩㄢˋ ㄅㄧㄥ)
volunteers

志願軍(ㄓˋ ㄩㄢˋ ㄐㄩㄣ)
an army made up of volunteers

志願書(ㄓˋ ㄩㄢˋ ㄕㄨ)
a pledge in writing; an application form

【忘】 1505

1. ㄨㄤˋ wanq wàng

1. to forget: 別忘了給我打電話。Don't forget to phone me. 飲水不忘掘井人。When we drink the water, think of those who dug the well.
2. to omit; to miss (a line, etc.)
3. to neglect; to overlook

忘本(ㄨㄤˋ ㄅㄣˇ)
① ungrateful; to bite the hand that feeds one ② to forget one's past suffering

忘不了(ㄨㄤˋ ˙ㄅㄨ ㄌㄧㄠˇ)
will not or cannot forget

忘掉(ㄨㄤˋ ㄉㄧㄠˋ)
to forget; to let slip from one's mind: 你們應該把這件不愉快的事忘掉。You should forget the unpleasantness.

忘年交(ㄨㄤˋ ㄋㄧㄢˊ ㄐㄧㄠ)
a friendship in which the difference in age between the friends is forgotten

忘了(ㄨㄤˋ ˙ㄌㄜ)
to forget; to have forgotten; to be oblivious of: 我忘了你將要來此。I forgot (that) you were coming.

忘懷(ㄨㄤˋ ㄏㄨㄞˊ)
unmindful; to forget; forgetful; to dismiss from one's mind: 他們忘懷得失。They are unmindful of their gains and losses.

忘機(ㄨㄤˋ ㄐㄧ)
without a single scheme or design in one's mind; to be at peace with the world; a carefree state of mind

忘記(ㄨㄤˋ ㄐㄧˋ)
① to fail to remember; to forget; to have forgotten; oblivescence: 我忘記帶我的樂譜。I forgot to bring my music-book. ② to neglect: 我們不能忘記自己的責任。We must not neglect our duties.

忘舊(ㄨㄤˋ ㄐㄧㄡˋ)
to forget the old (friends, folks, etc.); snobbish

忘其所以(ㄨㄤˋ ㄑㄧˊ ㄙㄨㄛˇ ㄧˇ)
to be carried away; to be beside oneself with enthusiasm, joy, etc.

忘情(ㄨㄤˋ ㄑㄧㄥˊ)
to be unmindful of all emotions and the ups and downs of life; to be unmoved

忘卻(ㄨㄤˋ ㄑㄩㄝˋ)
to forget: 有些事情是難忘卻的。Some things are hard to forget.

忘形(ㄨㄤˋ ㄒㄧㄥˊ)
to get carried away; to be beside oneself with joy, etc.: 你忘形了！You are beside yourself with joy!

忘形之交(ㄨㄤˋ ㄒㄧㄥˊ ㄓ ㄐㄧㄠ)
a friendship in which all rules of good manners or etiquette can be ignored

忘性(ㄨㄤˋ ㄒㄧㄥˋ)
absent-mindedness; forgetfulness

忘食(ㄨㄤˋ ㄕˊ)
so busy or concentrated as to forget mealtime: 他發奮忘食。He was roused to such diligence as to forget his meals.

忘身忘家(ㄨㄤˋ ㄕㄣ ㄨㄤˋ ㄐㄧㄚ)
(literally) to forget one's family and oneself—complete dedication

忘餐(ㄨㄤˋ ㄘㄢ)
(literally) to forget one's meals—dedication; devotion; deep absorption

忘恩負義(ㄨㄤˋ ㄣ ㄈㄨˋ ㄧˋ)
ungrateful; to be forgetful of all favors one has been given

忘憂(ㄨㄤˋ ㄧㄡ)
to forget cares and worries

忘憂草(ㄨㄤˋ ㄧㄡ ㄘㄠˇ)
day lily—*Hemerocallis fulva*

忘我(ㄨㄤˋ ㄨㄛˇ)
oblivious of self-existence; selfless: 他忘我地工作。He worked selflessly.

【忘】 1505

2. 讀音 ㄨㄤˊ wang wáng

忘八(ㄨㄤˊ ˙ㄅㄚ)
① a tortoise ② a cuckold 參看「王八」

【忙】 1506

ㄇㄤˊ mang máng

1. busy; short of time; fully occupied: 你在忙什麼？What are you busy at? 他忙於準備考試。He is busy in preparing for the examination.
2. hurried; in haste; to make

haste; hurry: 不要忙，時間還多着哩。Don't hurry. There's plenty of time.

忙不迭(ㄇㄤˊ ˙ㄅㄨ ㄉㄧㄝˊ)
to hasten to do something; to do something with eagerness; to do something with alacrity

忙不過來(ㄇㄤˊ ˙ㄅㄨ ㄍㄨㄛˋ ㄌㄞˊ)
to have more work than one can handle properly; very busy

忙迫(ㄇㄤˊ ㄆㄛˋ)
pressed with work

忙忙碌碌(ㄇㄤˊ ㄇㄤˊ ㄌㄨˋ ㄌㄨˋ)or 忙碌(ㄇㄤˊ ㄌㄨˋ)
① busy; fully occupied ② hurriedly; in great haste

忙得不可開交(ㄇㄤˊ ˙ㄉㄜ ㄅㄨˋ ㄎㄜˇ ㄎㄞ ㄐㄧㄠ)
as busy as one can possibly be; to have one's hands full (of work)

忙得很(ㄇㄤˊ ˙ㄉㄜ ㄏㄣˇ)
very busy

忙裏偷閒(ㄇㄤˊ ˙ㄌㄧ ㄊㄡ ㄒㄧㄢˊ)
to steal a moment of leisure under the pressure of heavy workload: 我常忙裏偷閒。I often steal a moment of leisure in the midst of pressing affairs.

忙亂(ㄇㄤˊ ㄌㄨㄢˋ)
busy and flurried; to be in a rush and a muddle

忙工(ㄇㄤˊ ㄍㄨㄥ)
a hired temporary farm hand during the sowing or harvest seasons

忙中有錯(ㄇㄤˊ ㄓㄨㄥ ㄧㄡˇ ㄘㄨㄛˋ)
Haste makes waste. 或 Errors are likely to occur in haste.

忙甚麼(ㄇㄤˊ ㄕㄜˊ ˙ㄇㄜ)
What (are you) busy about? 或 Why the rush?

忙人(ㄇㄤˊ ㄖㄣˊ)
a busy person

忙於(ㄇㄤˊ ㄩˊ)
busy doing something

忙月(ㄇㄤˊ ㄩㄝˋ)
(originally) the busy months in farming (120 days after the approach of summer); the busy months in every trade

【忖】 1507 ㄘㄨㄣˇ tsoen cǔn
to surmise; to consider; to presume; to suppose

忖度(ㄘㄨㄣˇ ㄉㄨㄛˋ)or 忖摸(ㄘㄨㄣˇ ˙ㄇㄛ)
to suppose; to consider; to gauge what's on another's mind; to presume; to surmise: 我們忖度這遲延是由某種意外所致。We surmised that the delay was caused by some accident.

忖量(ㄘㄨㄣˇ ㄌㄧㄤˊ)
① to consider; to reflect ② to suppose; to gauge what's on another's mind; to conjecture

忖思(ㄘㄨㄣˇ ㄙ)
to imagine 亦作「忖想」

四畫

【忡】 1508 ㄔㄨㄥ chong chōng
worried; anxious; uneasy; sad

忡怔(ㄔㄨㄥ ㄓㄥ)
feeling anxious and unsettled

忡忡(ㄔㄨㄥ ㄔㄨㄥ)
worried and sad; laden with anxiety: 他憂心忡忡。He felt laden with anxiety.

【忤】 1509 ㄨˇ wuu wǔ
1. recalcitrant; stubbornly defiant; disobedient; uncongenial: 我與人無忤。I am not uncongenial to anyone else.
2. a blunder; a mistake; wrong

忤逆(ㄨˇ ㄋㄧˋ)
① recalcitrant; stubborn defiance ② disobedient to one's parents (a crime in former times)

忤視(ㄨˇ ㄕˋ)
to look at with a jaundiced eye; to look defiantly at

忤耳(ㄨˇ ㄦˇ)
(said of words, utterances, etc.) to grate on the ear

忤物(ㄨˇ ㄨˋ)
to disagree with others; to be at odds with others; can not get along with people

【快】 1510 ㄎㄨㄞˋ kuay kuài
1. quickly; fast; hasty; soon; prompt; rapid: 他做得很快。He did it quickly. 她進步很快。She has made rapid progress.
2. nearly; near: 暑假快到了。The summer vacation is drawing near.
3. to hurry up; to make haste: 快上車吧！Hurry up and get on the bus!
4. quick-witted; ingenious: 你腦子快。You're quick-witted.
5. sharp (blades, etc.); keen
6. pleasant; happy; to make happy; pleasurable: 他心中不快。He feels unhappy.
7. (in old China) as in 捕快—the criminal police; a constable; a sheriff deputy
8. honest; straightforward

快報(ㄎㄨㄞˋ ㄅㄠˋ)
a dispatch; a bulletin

快班(ㄎㄨㄞˋ ㄅㄢ)
a jailor; a policeman 亦作「馬快」

快板(ㄎㄨㄞˋ ㄅㄢˇ)or 快板兒(ㄎㄨㄞˋ ㄅㄚˇㄦ)
(Chinese opera) quick tempo

快步(ㄎㄨㄞˋ ㄅㄨˋ)
(military) a half step; a trot

快跑(ㄎㄨㄞˋ ㄆㄠˇ)
to run fast; Go quick! On the double!

快馬加鞭(ㄎㄨㄞˋ ㄇㄚˇ ㄐㄧㄚ ㄅㄧㄢ)
(literally) to use the whip on a fast horse—to proceed as quickly as possible; posthaste

快慢(ㄎㄨㄞˋ ㄇㄢˋ)
speed

快門(ㄎㄨㄞˋ ㄇㄣˊ)
a camera shutter

快刀斬亂麻(ㄎㄨㄞˋ ㄉㄠ ㄓㄢˇ ㄌㄨㄢˋ ㄇㄚˊ)
(literally) to chop a bunch of tangled hemp with a sharp knife—to straighten up a complicated or messy situation by taking drastic steps and with dispatch; to cut the Gordian knot

快當(ㄎㄨㄞˋ ˙ㄉㄤ)
quickly; with expedition; prompt; quick: 她是個既細心又快當的祕書。She is a careful and prompt secretary.

快遞(ㄎㄨㄞˋ ㄉㄧˋ)

express delivery; special delivery

快點兒(ㄎㄨㄞˋ ㄉㄧㄢˇㄦ)
Make it snappy. 或 Be quick!

快電(ㄎㄨㄞˋ ㄉㄧㄢˋ)
an urgent cable

快讀(ㄎㄨㄞˋ ㄉㄨˊ)
fast reading; speed-reading

快艇(ㄎㄨㄞˋ ㄊㄧㄥˇ)
a speedboat; a motorboat

快樂(ㄎㄨㄞˋ ㄌㄜˋ)or 快活(ㄎㄨㄞˋ ˙ㄏㄨㄛ)
happy; joy; joyful; cheerful: 他因升遷而顯得快樂。He showed joy at being promoted.

快樂主義(ㄎㄨㄞˋ ㄌㄜˋ ㄓㄨˇ ㄧˋ)
hedonism

快來(ㄎㄨㄞˋ ㄌㄞˊ)
Come quick! 或 to come or arrive very soon

快覽(ㄎㄨㄞˋ ㄌㄢˇ)
a collection of categorized daily information for reference; a directory

快乾(ㄎㄨㄞˋ ㄍㄢ)
quick-drying

快感(ㄎㄨㄞˋ ㄍㄢˇ)
a pleasant feeling

快幹(ㄎㄨㄞˋ ㄍㄢˋ)
Do it promptly! 或 to do quickly

快鍋(ㄎㄨㄞˋ ㄍㄨㄛ)
a digester; a pressure cooker

快攻(ㄎㄨㄞˋ ㄍㄨㄥ)
a quick attack (in ball games)

快快兒的(ㄎㄨㄞˋ ㄎㄨㄞˋㄦ ˙ㄉㄜ)
quickly; promptly

快捷(ㄎㄨㄞˋ ㄐㄧㄝˊ)
speedy; fast; nimble

快些(ㄎㄨㄞˋ ˙ㄒㄧㄝ)
Hurry! 或faster than; quicker than: 快些! 你要遲到了。Hurry up! You'll be late.

快心(ㄎㄨㄞˋ ㄒㄧㄣ)
to be pleased; to feel happy

快信(ㄎㄨㄞˋ ㄒㄧㄣˋ)
an express letter

快壻 or 快婿(ㄎㄨㄞˋ ㄒㄩˋ)
an intelligent and promising son-in-law; an attractive son-in-law

快照(ㄎㄨㄞˋ ㄓㄠˋ)
a snapshot

快車(ㄎㄨㄞˋ ㄔㄜ)
an express train: 我沒趕上這班快車。I missed the express train.

快車道(ㄎㄨㄞˋ ㄔㄜ ㄉㄠˋ)
a fast-traffic lane on a street; a speedway

快事(ㄎㄨㄞˋ ㄕˋ)
happenings that make the heart throb with joy; something done with overwhelming public approval; a delightful experience

快適(ㄎㄨㄞˋ ㄕˋ)
happy and contented; pleased and satisfied: 他顯出快適的樣子。He looked pleased and satisfied.

快手快脚(ㄎㄨㄞˋ ㄕㄡˇ ㄎㄨㄞˋ ㄐㄧㄠˇ)
(literally) nimble of hands and fast of feet—to do things quickly; to perform a task with expedition

快書(ㄎㄨㄞˋ ㄕㄨ)
quick patter (rhythmic storytelling accompanied by bamboo or copper clappers)

快說(ㄎㄨㄞˋ ㄕㄨㄛ)
Speak up! 或 Be quick! 或 Speak quickly. 儘量快說。Speak as quick as you can.

快人快事(ㄎㄨㄞˋ ㄖㄣˊ ㄎㄨㄞˋ ㄕˋ)
a heroic deed performed by a straightforward person

快人快語(ㄎㄨㄞˋ ㄖㄣˊ ㄎㄨㄞˋ ㄩˇ)
the straight talk of a straightforward person

快哉(ㄎㄨㄞˋ ㄗㄞ)
How pleasant!

快走(ㄎㄨㄞˋ ㄗㄡˇ)
Hurry, let's go. 或 Beat it!

快嘴快舌(ㄎㄨㄞˋ ㄗㄨㄟˇ ㄎㄨㄞˋ ㄕㄜˊ)
quick of tongue; prone to talk rashly

快餐(ㄎㄨㄞˋ ㄘㄢ)
a simple meal consisting of a couple of dishes which are served promptly in small restaurants; a quick meal; a snack

快速(ㄎㄨㄞˋ ㄙㄨˋ)
fast; quick; prompt: 不要說得這樣快速。Don't speak so fast.

快意(ㄎㄨㄞˋ ㄧˋ)
pleasing; satisfying

快郵代電(ㄎㄨㄞˋ ㄧㄡˊ ㄉㄞˋ ㄉㄧㄢˋ)or 代電(ㄉㄞˋ ㄉㄧㄢˋ)
official correspondence between government agencies having no direct superior-subordinate relationship

快我朶頤(ㄎㄨㄞˋ ㄨㄛˇ ㄉㄨㄛˇ ㄧˊ)
to please my palate (the expression is often seen on the walls of Chinese restaurants as a sort of ad boasting the chef's skill)

快慰(ㄎㄨㄞˋ ㄨㄟˋ)
happy; satisfying; to be pleased

快完(ㄎㄨㄞˋ ㄨㄢˊ)
nearly completed or finished; almost set

【忮】 1511 ㄓˋ jyh zhì
jealous; jealousy; to dislike

忮求(ㄓˋ ㄑㄧㄡˊ)
jealous and greedy

忮心(ㄓˋ ㄒㄧㄣ)
jealousy

【忭】 1512 ㄅㄧㄢˋ biann biàn
overjoyed; pleased; delighted: 聽到你的成功我大爲忻忭。I was overjoyed at your success.

忭賀(ㄅㄧㄢˋ ㄏㄜˋ)
to congratulate with joy; to celebrate

忭懽(ㄅㄧㄢˋ ㄏㄨㄢ)
pleased and delighted

忭頌(ㄅㄧㄢˋ ㄙㄨㄥˋ)
to be pleased to offer best wishes

忭躍(ㄅㄧㄢˋ ㄩㄝˋ)
great joy; tremendous pleasure; to leap with joy: 他舞興忭躍。He danced for great joy.

【忱】 1513 ㄔㄣˊ chern chén
1. sincere; sincerity
2. to rely on

忱悃(ㄔㄣˊ ㄎㄨㄣˇ)
genuine feelings; sincere sentiments

忱辭(ㄔㄣˊ ㄘˊ)
words uttered in all sincerity; words from the bottom of one's heart

【忸】 1514 ㄋㄧㄡˇ neou niǔ
(讀音 ㄋㄩˋ niuh nǜ)
1. to be accustomed to; to be

〔心部〕

inclined to (evils, etc.)
2. bashful; ashamed

忸怩(ㄋㄧㄡˇ ㄋㄧˊ)
blush; ashamed; bashful; coyly

忸怕(ㄋㄧㄡˇ ㄕˋ)
to be accustomed to

【忻】 1515
(欣) ㄒㄧㄣ shin xīn
happy; joy; delight

忻忭(ㄒㄧㄣ ㄅㄧㄢˋ)
great joy; overjoyed

【忪】 1516
1. ㄓㄨㄥ jong zhōng
1. agitated
2. frightened

【忪】 1516
2. ㄙㄨㄥ song sōng
參看「惺忪」

【忠】 1517
ㄓㄨㄥ jong zhōng
1. faithful; loyal; sincere; patriotic; constant; loyalty; sincerity: 他忠於國家。He is loyal to his country.
2. devoted; honest (advice, etc.)

忠烈(ㄓㄨㄥ ㄌㄧㄝˋ)
to be loyal till death; patriotism; martyrdom

忠烈祠(ㄓㄨㄥ ㄌㄧㄝˋ ㄘˊ)
a martyrs' shrine

忠良(ㄓㄨㄥ ㄌㄧㄤˊ)
① faithful and honest ② virtuous persons

忠告(ㄓㄨㄥ ㄍㄠˋ)or(ㄓㄨㄥ ㄍㄨˋ)
honest or sincere advice; sincere counsel

忠肝義膽(ㄓㄨㄥ ㄍㄢ ㄧˋ ㄉㄢˇ)
having good faith, virtue and patriotism

忠告善道(ㄓㄨㄥ ㄍㄨˋ ㄕㄢˋ ㄉㄠˋ)
to offer advice with sincerity and tact

忠厚(ㄓㄨㄥ ㄏㄡˋ)
honest and tolerant; kind and big-hearted

忠君愛國(ㄓㄨㄥ ㄐㄩㄣ ㄞˋ ㄍㄨㄛˊ)
patriotic and loyal to the throne

忠孝兩全(ㄓㄨㄥ ㄒㄧㄠˋ ㄌㄧㄤˇ ㄑㄩㄢˊ)
both loyal to one's country and filial to one's parents; to be perfect both as a national hero and as a dutiful son

忠心(ㄓㄨㄥ ㄒㄧㄣ)
loyalty; faithfulness; sincerity

忠心耿耿(ㄓㄨㄥ ㄒㄧㄣ ㄍㄥˇ ㄍㄥˇ)
loyal, faithful and true: 他們是忠心耿耿的愛國者。They are loyal and constant patriots.

忠信(ㄓㄨㄥ ㄒㄧㄣˋ)
faithful and honest

忠直(ㄓㄨㄥ ㄓˊ)
straightforward; faithful and upright

忠貞(ㄓㄨㄥ ㄓㄣ)
loyal (subjects, etc.); patriotic (citizens, elements, etc.); faithful and true: 他忠貞不渝。He is unswerving in his loyalty.

忠貞不貳(ㄓㄨㄥ ㄓㄣ ㄅㄨˋ ㄦˋ)
the loyalty that can stand all tests and trials

忠臣不事二主(ㄓㄨㄥ ㄔㄣˊ ㄅㄨˋ ㄕˋ ㄦˋ ㄓㄨˇ)
A loyal subject (or official) never serves two kings (or masters).

忠誠(ㄓㄨㄥ ㄔㄥˊ)
loyal; faithful; staunch

忠實(ㄓㄨㄥ ㄕˊ)
① loyal and faithful: 他很忠實地守信約。He kept his promise faithfully. ② reliable or truthful (reports, etc.)

忠恕(ㄓㄨㄥ ㄕㄨˋ)
magnanimity—a summation of Confucian teaching: "to be true to one's principles and benevolent in their application towards others"

忠義(ㄓㄨㄥ ㄧˋ)
① faithful and virtuous ② people of loyalty and virtue

忠言(ㄓㄨㄥ ㄧㄢˊ)
sincere advice

忠言逆耳(ㄓㄨㄥ ㄧㄢˊ ㄋㄧˋ ㄦˇ)
Honest advice is often grating on the ear. 或 Truth seldom sounds pleasant.

忠於國家(ㄓㄨㄥ ㄩˊ ㄍㄨㄛˊ ㄐㄧㄚ)
to be faithful to one's fatherland

忠勇(ㄓㄨㄥ ㄩㄥˇ)
loyal and courageous

【念】 1518
ㄋㄧㄢˋ niann niàn
1. to think of; to miss; to remember (someone): 他們老念着你。They miss you very much.
2. to read out aloud; to chant; to intone; to mumble: 把它念給我聽。Read it to me.
3. to study; to attend school: 他念過中學。He attended middle school.
4. twenty
5. a Chinese family name

念白(ㄋㄧㄢˋ ㄅㄞˊ)
the spoken part in Chinese opera

念佛(ㄋㄧㄢˋ ㄈㄛˊ)
to call out Buddha's name aloud as an expression of devotion; to call out "Amitabha" aloud to show devotion; to pray to Buddha

念法(ㄋㄧㄢˋ ㄈㄚˇ)
① pronunciation ② a method of studying

念叨(ㄋㄧㄢˋ ·ㄉㄠ)
① to mention in what one says; to be always talking about; to remember ② to nag; to be garrulous ③ to talk over

念頭(ㄋㄧㄢˋ ·ㄊㄡ)
an idea; a thought; intention: 不知她有什麼念頭。I don't know what her intentions are.

念念不忘(ㄋㄧㄢˋ ㄋㄧㄢˋ ㄅㄨˋ ㄨㄤˋ)
lasting memory of; to have (somebody or something) always in one's mind; to bear in mind constantly

念念有詞(ㄋㄧㄢˋ ㄋㄧㄢˋ ㄧㄡˇ ㄘˊ)
to mumble; to mutter: 那老人口中念念有詞。The old man was mumbling (away) to himself.

念舊(ㄋㄧㄢˋ ㄐㄧㄡˋ)
to remember old friends; to cherish old friendship: 他非常念舊。He cherishes old friendship very much.

念經(ㄋㄧㄢˋ ㄐㄧㄥ)
to chant or intone (Buddhist) scriptures

念咒(ㄋㄧㄢˋ ㄓㄡˋ)
to chant or intone charms

念珠(ㄋㄧㄢˋ ㄓㄨ)
a Buddhist rosary (with 108 beads)

念熟(ㄋㄧㄢˋ ㄕㄡˊ)or(ㄋㄧㄢˋ ㄕㄨˊ)

to learn by heart; to read over and over until one can memorize what is being read

念書(ㄋㄧㄢˋ ㄕㄨ)
①to read a book aloud ②to study ③to receive an education

念茲在茲(ㄋㄧㄢˋ ㄗ ㄗㄞˋ ㄗ)
to bear in mind always; to have (somebody or something) constantly in one's mind

念誦(ㄋㄧㄢˋ ·ㄙㄨㄥ)
①to recite; to intone; to read out ②to remember (somebody) in speaking to another

【忽】 1519 ㄏㄨ hu hū

1. suddenly; abruptly; unexpectedly: 我忽發奇想。I suddenly hit upon a wild idea.
2. to disregard; to be careless or indifferent; to neglect
3. to forget
4. one millionth of a tael
5. a Chinese family name

忽必烈(ㄏㄨ ㄅㄧˋ ㄌㄧㄝˋ)
Kublai, the fifth emperor of the Yüan (Mongol) Dynasty, who reigned from 1260 to 1294

忽明忽滅(ㄏㄨ ㄇㄧㄥˊ ㄏㄨ ㄇㄧㄝˋ)
flickering; appearing and disappearing, as a distant star, a blinking light, etc.

忽發奇想(ㄏㄨ ㄈㄚ ㄑㄧˊ ㄒㄧㄤˇ)
to suddenly hit upon a wild idea; to suddenly harbor a dream; to suddenly come upon a strange notion

忽地(ㄏㄨ ㄉㄧˋ)
suddenly; abruptly; unexpectedly

忽冷忽熱(ㄏㄨ ㄌㄥˇ ㄏㄨ ㄖㄜˋ)
① now hot, now cold — abrupt changes of temperature ②sudden changes in one's affection, attitude, enthusiasm, etc.

忽略(ㄏㄨ ㄌㄩㄝˋ)
to overlook; to neglect; an oversight

忽忽(ㄏㄨ ㄏㄨ)
①fast; quickly ②restless; dejected; to look lost or absent-minded: 他忽忽若有所失。He looks absent-minded.

忽忽不樂(ㄏㄨ ㄏㄨ ㄅㄨˋ ㄌㄜˋ)
to be discouraged and unhappy

忽忽一年(ㄏㄨ ㄏㄨ ㄧˋ ㄋㄧㄢˊ)
another year slipping away imperceptibly 或 Suddenly, another year has come to an end.

忽見(ㄏㄨ ㄐㄧㄢˋ)
to see suddenly; to behold all of a sudden

忽起忽落(ㄏㄨ ㄑㄧˇ ㄏㄨ ㄌㄨㄛˋ)
①sudden rise and sudden fall, as a flying object or a darting bird ②the erratic fluctuation of market prices, etc. ③sudden changes (of mood); now…, now…

忽親(ㄏㄨ ㄑㄧㄣ)
(said of men) to get married while in mourning for parents

忽視(ㄏㄨ ㄕˋ)
to disregard; to overlook; to neglect; to treat with indifference; to give a cold shoulder: 我們不應忽視我們的弱點。We should not overlook our weaknesses.

忽哨(ㄏㄨ ㄕㄠˋ)
to whistle; a whistle (usually used as a signal to start a collective action by a band of people, as bandits, etc.)

忽然(ㄏㄨ ㄖㄢˊ)or 忽然間(ㄏㄨ ㄖㄢˊ ㄐㄧㄢ)
suddenly; unexpectedly

忽作忽止(ㄏㄨ ㄗㄨㄛˋ ㄏㄨ ㄓˇ)
by fits and starts

忽而(ㄏㄨ ㄦˊ)
suddenly; unexpectedly; now …, now…: 她忽而哭, 忽而笑。She cried and laughed unexpectedly.

忽有感觸(ㄏㄨ ㄧㄡˇ ㄍㄢˇ ㄔㄨˋ)
to be seized by a sudden feeling; to be unexpectedly moved or touched

忽微(ㄏㄨ ㄨㄟˊ)
an extremely fine particle; something of infinitesimal quantity or weight

忽聞(ㄏㄨ ㄨㄣˊ)
to hear suddenly; to learn of something unexpectedly

【忿】 1520 ㄈㄣˋ fenn fèn

1. anger; indignation; fury: 他的餘忿未平。His anger has not yet appeased.
2. complaining; hatred; a grudge

忿懣(ㄈㄣˋ ㄇㄣˋ)
anger; a grudge; animus; indignation: 他對我有忿懣。He bears me a grudge.

忿悶(ㄈㄣˋ ㄇㄣˋ)
angry and complaining; bitter

忿忿不平(ㄈㄣˋ ㄈㄣˋ ㄅㄨˋ ㄆㄧㄥˊ)
resentful and complaining; bitter; indignant and disturbed

忿怒(ㄈㄣˋ ㄋㄨˋ)
indignation; wrath; fury; angry; furious; indignant

忿戾(ㄈㄣˋ ㄌㄧˋ)
angry and perverseness

忿厲粗暴(ㄈㄣˋ ㄌㄧˋ ㄘㄨ ㄅㄠˋ)
angry, fierce and rough

忿恨(ㄈㄣˋ ㄏㄣˋ)
wrath; fury; indignation; animosity; resentment; angry; hateful

忿火(ㄈㄣˋ ㄏㄨㄛˇ)
the flames of anger; fury or furies

忿恚(ㄈㄣˋ ㄏㄨㄟˋ)
hate and anger

忿懥(ㄈㄣˋ ㄓˋ)
anger; wrath; fury

忿爭(ㄈㄣˋ ㄓㄥ)
to argue or fight in anger; to wrangle; wrangling

忿躁(ㄈㄣˋ ㄗㄠˋ)
irascible

忿言(ㄈㄣˋ ㄧㄢˊ)
angry words or utterances

忿怨(ㄈㄣˋ ㄩㄢˋ)
to harbor a grudge; animus: 他對我忿怨。He has a grudge against me.

【忞】 1521 ㄇㄧㄣˊ min mín

to strive for improvement or progress

【忝】 1522 ㄊㄧㄢˇ tean tiǎn

1. ashamed; to disgrace: 他有忝家族聲名。He disgraced his family's name.
2. a depreciatory expression

referring to oneself
3. to be unworthy of the honor

忝不知恥(ㄊㄧㄢˇ ㄅㄨˋ ㄓ ㄔˇ)or 忝不知羞(ㄊㄧㄢˇ ㄅㄨˋ ㄓ ㄒㄧㄡ)
shameless; brazen-faced

忝附蔦蘿(ㄊㄧㄢˇ ㄈㄨˋ ㄋㄧㄠˇ ㄌㄨㄛˊ)
I'm honored to be related to you (by marriage).

忝列門牆(ㄊㄧㄢˇ ㄌㄧㄝˋ ㄇㄣˊ ㄑㄧㄤˊ)
to have served and learned under a master; to have the honor to be accepted as your disciple 或 I've learned under you.

忝居(ㄊㄧㄢˇ ㄐㄩ)
(a self-depreciatory expression) I've shamefully occupied (a position which I don't deserve).

忝眷(ㄊㄧㄢˇ ㄐㄩㄢˋ)
a self-reference used by the father of a bride or groom at the wedding

忝竊(ㄊㄧㄢˇ ㄑㄧㄝˋ)
(a self-depreciatory expression) to usurp

忝任(ㄊㄧㄢˇ ㄖㄣˋ)
to have served (in an office); I have served as…

忝辱家門(ㄊㄧㄢˇ ㄖㄨˇ ㄐㄧㄚ ㄇㄣˊ)
to disgrace one's family

忝爲知己(ㄊㄧㄢˇ ㄨㄟˊ ㄓ ㄐㄧˇ)
As an intimate friend of yours, I…; (I'm sure you'll forgive me) since we have been good friends

〔心部〕

五畫

【怍】 1523 ㄗㄨㄛˋ tzuoh zuò
1. shame
2. to change color; to blush

怍色(ㄗㄨㄛˋ ㄙㄜˋ)
ashamed; to blush; to color

怍意(ㄗㄨㄛˋ ㄧˋ)
to feel ashamed; to be ashamed

【怏】 1524 ㄧㄤˋ yanq yàng
discontented; disheartened; dispirited

怏然(ㄧㄤˋ ㄖㄢˊ)
unhappy; discontent

怏悒(ㄧㄤˋ ㄧˋ)
discontent; melancholy; sad

怏怏(ㄧㄤˋ ㄧㄤˋ)
discontented; dispirited; sad

怏鬱(ㄧㄤˋ ㄩˋ)
the depression of feelings; pensiveness; gloom; melancholy

【怖】 1525 ㄅㄨˋ buh bù
1. terrified; frightened
2. to frighten; to threaten

怖慄(ㄅㄨˋ ㄌㄧˋ)
trembling with fear

怖駭(ㄅㄨˋ ㄏㄞˋ)
frightened; scared; alarmed

怖禍(ㄅㄨˋ ㄏㄨㄛˋ)
a terrifying danger or calamity

怖懼(ㄅㄨˋ ㄐㄩˋ)
a scare; fear; dread: 懷疑和焦慮變成怖懼。Doubt and anxiety changed into dread.

怖懾(ㄅㄨˋ ㄓㄜˊ)
scared and faint-hearted

怖畏(ㄅㄨˋ ㄨㄟˋ)
to dread; to be scared; to be afraid

【怕】 1526 ㄆㄚˋ pah pà
1. to fear; to dread; afraid; scared or frightened; apprehensive: 此次地震你駭怕嗎? Were you frightened by the earthquake?
2. maybe; perhaps; I am afraid ...; I suppose.... 我怕無法幫助你。I am afraid I can't help you.
3. a Chinese family name

怕不怕(ㄆㄚˋ ·ㄅㄨ ㄆㄚˋ)
Are you afraid? 或 Are you scared?

怕得罪人(ㄆㄚˋ ㄉㄜˊ ㄗㄨㄟˋ ㄖㄣˊ)
afraid of offending others (by speaking frankly, etc.)

怕得很(ㄆㄚˋ ·ㄉㄜ ㄏㄣˇ)
very much scared; in great fear

怕的是(ㄆㄚˋ ·ㄉㄜ ㄕˋ)
What I am afraid of is that....

怕他不來(ㄆㄚˋ ㄊㄚ ㄅㄨˋ ㄌㄞˊ)
① afraid that he won't come ② He will come, because he has to!

怕他不成(ㄆㄚˋ ㄊㄚ ㄅㄨˋ ㄔㄥˊ)
(an expression of defiance) What? We are afraid of him!

怕他什麼(ㄆㄚˋ ㄊㄚ ㄕㄜˊ ·ㄇㄜ)
① What is there to be afraid of him? ② Don't be afraid of him!

怕老婆(ㄆㄚˋ ㄌㄠˇ ·ㄆㄛ)or 怕太太(ㄆㄚˋ ㄊㄞˋ ·ㄊㄞ)
henpecked

怕冷(ㄆㄚˋ ㄌㄥˇ)
to dread cold (weather, etc.); to dislike the cold

怕前怕後(ㄆㄚˋ ㄑㄧㄢˊ ㄆㄚˋ ㄏㄡˋ)
timid and apprehensive of everything

怕羞(ㄆㄚˋ ㄒㄧㄡ)
shy; bashful: 她有點怕羞。She is rather bashful.

怕甚麼(ㄆㄚˋ ㄕㄜˊ ·ㄇㄜ)
(an expression of encouragement) What is there to be afraid of? 或 What are you afraid of?

怕事(ㄆㄚˋ ㄕˋ)
to be timid and overcautious: 他膽小怕事。He was timid and overcautious.

怕是(ㄆㄚˋ ·ㄕ)
(I'm) afraid that…; maybe; perhaps (referring to some unpleasant fact or consequence)

怕生(ㄆㄚˋ ㄕㄥ)
(said of a child) to be shy with strangers

怕熱(ㄆㄚˋ ㄖㄜˋ)
to dislike heat; to feel discomfortable in hot weather

怕人(ㄆㄚˋ ㄖㄣˊ)
① terrifying; frightening; horrible ②(said of wild beasts and birds) to shun human beings

怕死(ㄆㄚˋ ㄙˇ)
afraid of death; very nervous and scared

怕臊(ㄆㄚˋ ㄙㄠˋ)
shy; bashful

怕癢(ㄆㄚˋ ㄧㄤˇ)
to be afraid of tickling

【怙】 1527 ㄏㄨˋ huh hù
1. to rely on; to presume on
2. one's father; things or persons that one relies on: 他自幼失怙。He has had nobody to rely on since childhood.

怙富(ㄏㄨˋ ㄈㄨˋ)
to presume on one's wealth

怙過(ㄏㄨˋ ㄍㄨㄛˋ)
showing no regret for one's faults or errors; showing no repentance for one's wrongdoings
怙終不改(ㄏㄨˋ ㄓㄨㄥ ㄅㄨˋ ㄍㄞˇ)
to persist in one's (wrongful) ways: 頑抗的學生怙終不改。The recalcitrant students persist in their ways.
怙寵(ㄏㄨˋ ㄔㄨㄥˇ)
to be proud and arrogant for having won the favor of a powerful or influential person
怙恃(ㄏㄨˋ ㄕˋ)
① those one relies on (as troops, gangsters, an influential person, etc.) ② one's parents—father(怙) and mother(恃)
怙勢(ㄏㄨˋ ㄕˋ)
to presume on one's power, position or influence
怙惡不悛(ㄏㄨˋ ㄜˋ ㄅㄨˋ ㄑㄩㄢ)
incorrigible (criminals); obdurate and irreclaimable; to be steeped in evil and refuse to repent
怙惡淩人(ㄏㄨˋ ㄜˋ ㄌㄧㄥˊ ㄖㄣˊ)
to intimidate and oppress others
怙依(ㄏㄨˋ ㄧ)
things or persons that one relies on

【怛】 1528
ㄉㄚˊ dar dá
1. grieved; distressed
2. surprised; shocked; alarmed
3. (obsolete) striving and toiling
怛怛(ㄉㄚˊ ㄉㄚˊ)
toiling; grieved
怛化(ㄉㄚˊ ㄏㄨㄚˋ)
①(said of mankind) dead; to die; to pass away ② the process of change—(figuratively) a dying person
怛傷(ㄉㄚˊ ㄕㄤ)
distressed; grieved

【怦】 1529
ㄆㄥ peng pēng
eager; anxious; impulsive
怦怦(ㄆㄥ ㄆㄥ)
① eager and anxious (to do something) ② faithful and upright ③ with quick beating; pit-a-pat: 我的心怦怦地跳。My heart went pit-a-pat.
怦然(ㄆㄥ ㄖㄢˊ)
with a sudden shock; palpitating (with excitement): 她怦然心動。She was palpitating with excitement.

【怡】 1530
ㄧˊ yi yí
1. harmony; on good terms
2. pleasure; joy; jubilation
3. a Chinese family name
怡蕩(ㄧˊ ㄉㄤˋ)
to find pleasure in wanton ways
怡樂(ㄧˊ ㄌㄜˋ)
pleasures
怡和(ㄧˊ ㄏㄜˊ)
delightful harmony; on very pleasant terms (with each other)
怡情養性(ㄧˊ ㄑㄧㄥˊ ㄧㄤˇ ㄒㄧㄥˋ)
(said of things or environs) to contribute to one's peace of mind or inner tranquility
怡情悅性(ㄧˊ ㄑㄧㄥˊ ㄩㄝˋ ㄒㄧㄥˋ)
to please one's mind and delight one's spirit
怡神(ㄧˊ ㄕㄣˊ)
to inspire peace and harmony in one's mind
怡聲(ㄧˊ ㄕㄥ)
a soft and tender voice that is pleasing
怡然(ㄧˊ ㄖㄢˊ)
pleasant and contented; satisfied and happy
怡然自得(ㄧˊ ㄖㄢˊ ㄗˋ ㄉㄜˊ)
happy and contented; to have found one's inner peace
怡色(ㄧˊ ㄙㄜˋ)
a pleasant look; to look pleased or cheerful
怡怡(ㄧˊ ㄧˊ)
harmony; harmonious—as brothers
怡顏(ㄧˊ ㄧㄢˊ)
a pleasant look; smiling
怡養(ㄧˊ ㄧㄤˇ)
to enjoy good health and live a happy life
怡悅(ㄧˊ ㄩㄝˋ)
to find joy in; to take delight in

【性】 1531
ㄒㄧㄥˋ shinq xìng
1. nature; natural property; disposition; temper
2. a quality or property
3. sex
性暴(ㄒㄧㄥˋ ㄅㄠˋ)
hot-tempered; irascible
性本善(ㄒㄧㄥˋ ㄅㄣˇ ㄕㄢˋ)or 性善(ㄒㄧㄥˋ ㄕㄢˋ)
the theory of Mencius that men are born good
性別(ㄒㄧㄥˋ ㄅㄧㄝˊ)
the sex of a person—male or female
性別檢查(ㄒㄧㄥˋ ㄅㄧㄝˊ ㄐㄧㄢˇ ㄔㄚˊ)
a sex check
性變態(ㄒㄧㄥˋ ㄅㄧㄢˋ ㄊㄞˋ)
sex perversion
性病(ㄒㄧㄥˋ ㄅㄧㄥˋ)
venereal diseases—VD
性病醫院(ㄒㄧㄥˋ ㄅㄧㄥˋ ㄧ ㄩㄢˋ)
a VD hospital
性癖(ㄒㄧㄥˋ ㄆㄧˇ)
idiosyncrasy; one's hobbies, peculiar likes and dislikes, etc.
性命(ㄒㄧㄥˋ ㄇㄧㄥˋ)
a person's life: 醫生救了他的性命。The doctor saved his life.
性命干連(ㄒㄧㄥˋ ㄇㄧㄥˋ ㄍㄢ ㄌㄧㄢˊ)
It's a serious matter involving a person's life.
性命交關(ㄒㄧㄥˋ ㄇㄧㄥˋ ㄐㄧㄠ ㄍㄨㄢ)
a matter of life and death
性發(ㄒㄧㄥˋ ㄈㄚ)
tempers flaring; to get mad
性犯罪(ㄒㄧㄥˋ ㄈㄢˋ ㄗㄨㄟˋ)
sexual offence
性分(ㄒㄧㄥˋ ㄈㄣˋ)
the natural property, disposition and endowments of a person
性地(ㄒㄧㄥˋ ㄉㄧˋ)
one's natural qualities of mind and character 亦作「心地」
性能(ㄒㄧㄥˋ ㄋㄥˊ)
① natural ability ② qualities and capabilities of machinery
性冷感症(ㄒㄧㄥˋ ㄌㄥˇ ㄍㄢˇ ㄓㄥˋ)
frigidity
性烈(ㄒㄧㄥˋ ㄌㄧㄝˋ)
fierce tempered; fiery tempered; a fiery disposition
性靈(ㄒㄧㄥˋ ㄌㄧㄥˊ)
natural disposition and intelligence

〔心部〕

〔心部〕

性格(ㄒㄧㄥˋ ㄍㄜˊ)
disposition; personality; character: 他的性格開朗。He has a bright and cheerful disposition.
性格分析(ㄒㄧㄥˋ ㄍㄜˊ ㄈㄣ ㄒㄧ)
(sociology) character analysis
性感(ㄒㄧㄥˋ ㄍㄢˇ)
sex appeal; sexy
性感明星(ㄒㄧㄥˋ ㄍㄢˇ ㄇㄧㄥˊ ㄒㄧㄥ)
(in motion pictures) sex sirens; sex-pots; sexy stars
性荷爾蒙(ㄒㄧㄥˋ ㄏㄜˊ ㄦˇ ㄇㄥˊ)
(physiology) sex hormone
性急(ㄒㄧㄥˋ ㄐㄧˊ)
impetuous; impulsive; impatient: 這個人性急得很。This man is very impatient.
性交(ㄒㄧㄥˋ ㄐㄧㄠ)
sexual intercourse
性教育(ㄒㄧㄥˋ ㄐㄧㄠˋ ㄩˋ)
sex education
性靜情逸(ㄒㄧㄥˋ ㄐㄧㄥˋ ㄑㄧㄥˊ ㄧˋ)
a quiet and easy disposition
性器(ㄒㄧㄥˋ ㄑㄧˋ)or 性器官(ㄒㄧㄥˋ ㄑㄧˋ ㄍㄨㄢ)
sexual organs; genitals; reproductive organs
性情(ㄒㄧㄥˋ ·ㄑㄧㄥ)
disposition; temperament: 她的性情溫柔。She has a gentle disposition.
性細胞(ㄒㄧㄥˋ ㄒㄧˋ ㄅㄠ)
germ cell
性向(ㄒㄧㄥˋ ㄒㄧㄤˋ)
disposition
性向測驗(ㄒㄧㄥˋ ㄒㄧㄤˋ ㄘㄜˋ ㄧㄢˋ)
aptitude test
性行爲(ㄒㄧㄥˋ ㄒㄧㄥˊ ㄨㄟˊ)
sexual behavior
性知識(ㄒㄧㄥˋ ㄓ ㄕˋ)
sex knowledge; information regarding human sexual behaviors, organs, etc.
性質(ㄒㄧㄥˋ ㄓˊ)
property; characteristics; nature: 我們應弄清產品的性質。We should ascertain the property of the product.
性週期(ㄒㄧㄥˋ ㄓㄡ ㄑㄧˊ)
sexual cycle
性眞(ㄒㄧㄥˋ ㄓㄣ)
(Buddhism) the real self; the natural quality or property of a person

性徵(ㄒㄧㄥˋ ㄓㄥ)
(biology) sexual character
性子(ㄒㄧㄥˋ ·ㄗ)
① a temper; a disposition: 她在使性子。She got into a temper. ② strength; potency
性色(ㄒㄧㄥˋ ㄙㄜˋ)
colors indicative of different sexes of animals, especially insects
性騷擾(ㄒㄧㄥˋ ㄙㄠ ㄖㄠˇ)
sexual harassment
性惡(ㄒㄧㄥˋ ㄜˋ)
the theory advocated by Hsün Tzu (荀子) that men are born evil
性愛(ㄒㄧㄥˋ ㄞˋ)
sexual love
性無能(ㄒㄧㄥˋ ㄨˊ ㄋㄥˊ)
impotence; impotent
性慾(ㄒㄧㄥˋ ㄩˋ)
sexual desire or urge
性慾衝動(ㄒㄧㄥˋ ㄩˋ ㄔㄨㄥ ㄉㄨㄥˋ)
sexual impulse

【怩】 1532
ㄋㄧˊ ni ní

1. shy and bashful; coyly: 她忸怩作態。She behaves coyly.
2. to blush; to look embarrassed

【怫】 1533
1. ㄈㄨˊ fwu fú

depressed and discontented
怫鬱(ㄈㄨˊ ㄩˋ)
depressed and discontented

【怫】 1533
2. ㄈㄟˋ fey fei

angry; annoyed; indignant
怫恚(ㄈㄟˋ ㄏㄨㄟˋ)
angry; indignant
怫然作色(ㄈㄟˋ ㄖㄢˊ ㄗㄨㄛˋ ㄙㄜˋ)
to color with anger; to get mad

【怯】 1534
ㄑㄧㄝˋ chieh qiè
(語音 ㄑㄩㄝˋ chiueh què)

1. lacking in courage; cowardly: 她是一個膽怯的人。She is a coward.
2. nervous; socially timid; fright; fear; afraid
怯夫(ㄑㄧㄝˋ ㄈㄨ)
a coward
怯頭怯腦(ㄑㄧㄝˋ ㄊㄡˊ ㄑㄧㄝˋ ㄋㄠˇ)
(usually used by city people to ridicule country folks) nervous and clumsy, timid and unsophisticated
怯懦(ㄑㄧㄝˋ ㄋㄨㄛˋ)
cowardice
怯官(ㄑㄧㄝˋ ㄍㄨㄢ)
official fright—a fear of meeting government officials or policemen
怯懼(ㄑㄧㄝˋ ㄐㄩˋ)
to fear; to be nervous out of fear
怯陣(ㄑㄧㄝˋ ㄓㄣˋ)
① to feel nervous when going into battle ② to have stage fright
怯症(ㄑㄧㄝˋ ㄓㄥˋ)
① impotent; impotency ② the fear and nervousness caused by poor health
怯場(ㄑㄧㄝˋ ㄔㄤˊ)or(ㄑㄧㄝˋ ㄔㄤˇ)
stage fright: 大多數的新手都怯場。Most of the tyros have stage fright.
怯上(ㄑㄧㄝˋ ㄕㄤˋ)
superior fright—a fear of facing one's superiors
怯生(ㄑㄧㄝˋ ㄕㄥ)
(dialect) shy with strangers
怯弱(ㄑㄧㄝˋ ㄖㄨㄛˋ)
timid, weak and cowardly; cowardice
怯疑(ㄑㄧㄝˋ ㄧˊ)
timid and vacillating

【怪】 1535
ㄍㄨㄞˋ guay guài

1. strange; queer; monstrous; odd; peculiar: 你說怪不怪? Isn't this strange? 多麼奇怪! How strange!
2. to be surprised at: 那有什麼可怪的? Is that anything to be surprised at?
3. a ghost; a goblin; an apparition; a monster; an evil spirit
4. uncanny; weird: 他們被一聲奇怪的尖叫所驚醒。They were awakened by a weird shriek.
5. rather; very (interesting, tired, etc.): 這行李怪沉的。The baggage is rather heavy.
6. to blame: 不能怪你們。You are not to blame. 或 It's not your fault.
怪病(ㄍㄨㄞˋ ㄅㄧㄥˋ)
a strange or rare disease or ailment; an ailment that can

not be diagnosed

怪不得(ㄍㄨㄞˋ ·ㄅㄨ ·ㄉㄜ)
①No wonder! 或it explains why... ② cannot put the blame on: 這事怪不得他。We cannot put the blame on him.

怪癖(ㄍㄨㄞˋ ㄆㄧˇ)
strange hobbies; eccentric behavior; eccentricities

怪僻(ㄍㄨㄞˋ ㄆㄧˋ)
peculiar; eccentric; queer

怪模怪樣(ㄍㄨㄞˋ ·ㄇㄨ ㄍㄨㄞˋ ㄧㄤˋ)
queer appearance and manner; acting in a strange manner (usually said of beatniks or hippies)

怪誕不經(ㄍㄨㄞˋ ㄉㄢˋ ㄅㄨˋ ㄐㄧㄥ)
weird, wild, uncanny, or absurd (stories, accounts, etc.)

怪道(ㄍㄨㄞˋ ㄉㄠˋ)
no wonder that...; small wonder that...: 怪道他沒來。No wonder (that) he did not come.

怪特(ㄍㄨㄞˋ ㄊㄜˋ)
strange and peculiar; extraordinary

怪態(ㄍㄨㄞˋ ㄊㄞˋ)
affected and disgusting manners; revolting mannerisms

怪談(ㄍㄨㄞˋ ㄊㄢˊ)
weird talks; accounts of something uncanny

怪力亂神(ㄍㄨㄞˋ ㄌㄧˋ ㄌㄨㄢˋ ㄕㄣˊ)
extraordinary things, feats of strength, disorder, and spiritual beings (which Confucius avoided touching in his conversations)

怪裡怪氣(ㄍㄨㄞˋ ·ㄌㄧ ㄍㄨㄞˋ ㄑㄧˋ)
eccentric; strange; queer

怪論(ㄍㄨㄞˋ ㄌㄨㄣˋ)
absurd talks; wild talks; strange statements

怪可憐的(ㄍㄨㄞˋ ㄎㄜˇ ㄌㄧㄢˊ ·ㄉㄜ)
very pitiable

怪傑(ㄍㄨㄞˋ ㄐㄧㄝˊ)
an extraordinary person; an outstanding person; a man among men

怪笑(ㄍㄨㄞˋ ㄒㄧㄠˋ)
to laugh without cause; a laugh that grates on the ear; sardonic laughter

怪現象(ㄍㄨㄞˋ ㄒㄧㄢˋ ㄒㄧㄤˋ)
strange phenomena (of a society, nature, etc.)

怪石(ㄍㄨㄞˋ ㄕˊ)
rocks of grotesque shapes

怪石嶙峋(ㄍㄨㄞˋ ㄕˊ ㄌㄧㄣˊ ㄒㄩㄣˊ)
weird-looking rocks presenting a sight of rugged beauty

怪事(ㄍㄨㄞˋ ㄕˋ)
How strange! 或 strange happenings or things: 怪事年年有。Wonders will never cease.

怪手(ㄍㄨㄞˋ ㄕㄡˇ)
an excavator

怪獸(ㄍㄨㄞˋ ㄕㄡˋ)
a rare animal (especially a large-sized one); a legendary animal

怪聲怪氣(ㄍㄨㄞˋ ㄕㄥ ㄍㄨㄞˋ ㄑㄧˋ)
to speak in an unpleasant falsetto: 他說話怪聲怪氣。He spoke in an unpleasant falsetto.

怪人(ㄍㄨㄞˋ ㄖㄣˊ)
a peculiar person

怪哉(ㄍㄨㄞˋ ㄗㄞ)
Strange! 或 How strange! 或 What a strange thing!

怪異(ㄍㄨㄞˋ ㄧˋ)
strange; wild (talks, account, etc.); weird; uncanny

怪物(ㄍㄨㄞˋ ·ㄨ)
① a monster; a strange creature ② an eccentric fellow: 他是一個怪物。He is an eccentric fellow.

怪偉(ㄍㄨㄞˋ ㄨㄟˇ)
great and grotesque (in size and shape)

【怳】 1536
(恍) ㄏㄨㄤˇ hoang huǎng

1. despondent; dejected
2. wild; mad; flurried

怳惚(ㄏㄨㄤˇ ㄏㄨ)
① a state of daze, stupor or trance ② (descriptive of something) vague

【怔】 1537
ㄓㄥ jeng zhēng

terrified; stunned; scared

怔忪(ㄓㄥ ㄓㄨㄥ)
scared and nervous; fearful; frightened

怔忡(ㄓㄥ ㄔㄨㄥ)
(Chinese medicine) a disease resembling neurosis with such common symptoms as palpitation of the heart, melancholia and aptness to get tired; severe palpitation

怔營(ㄓㄥ ㄧㄥˊ)
scared and nervous

【怜】 1538
1. (伶) ㄌㄧㄥˊ ling líng

(often said of a child, young girl, etc.) agile, nimble, or bright; cute and pleasing

怜悧 or 伶俐(ㄌㄧㄥˊ ㄌㄧˋ)
agile; nimble; bright and pleasing; cute: 她十分伶俐。She has a nimble mind.

怜牙悧齒(ㄌㄧㄥˊ ㄧㄚˊ ㄌㄧˋ ㄔˇ)
to have the gift of the gab; to have a glib tongue

【怜】 1538
2. ㄌㄧㄢˊ lian lián

an abbreviated form of 憐—to pity; pity

【怓】 1539
ㄋㄠˊ nau náo

confusion; confused; wild

怓怓(ㄋㄠˊ ㄋㄠˊ)
to be prone to talk ceaselessly and unintelligently; to babble

【怗】 1540
ㄊㄧㄝ tie tiē

1. observant; submissive; subservient; compliant
2. peaceful; quiet

怗服(ㄊㄧㄝ ㄈㄨˊ)
submissive; compliant; resigned

怗靜(ㄊㄧㄝ ㄐㄧㄥˋ)
peaceful and quiet

【怵】 1541
ㄔㄨˋ chuh chù

1. scared; afraid; timorous; frightened
2. to entice; to induce

怵迫之徒(ㄔㄨˋ ㄆㄛˋ ㄓ ㄊㄨˊ)
a person who is tempted and coerced; a person under duress

怵目驚心(ㄔㄨˋ ㄇㄨˋ ㄐㄧㄥ ㄒㄧㄣ)
frightening; shocking

怵惕(ㄔㄨˋ ㄊㄧˋ)
scared and cautious; fear; fearful and conscious

怵場(ㄔㄨˋ ㄔㄤˊ)or(ㄔㄨˋ ㄔㄤˇ)
stage fright; the fear of facing a large crowd

怵然(ㄔㄨˋ ㄖㄢˊ)
scared; to look frightened

【怎】 1542
1. ㄗㄣˇ tzeen zěn
why; how; what: 事情是怎樣發生的呢? How did it happen? 她怎不早說呀? Why didn't she say so earlier?
怎的 or 怎地(ㄗㄣˇ ・ㄉㄜ)
how; in what way; what
怎奈(ㄗㄣˇ ㄋㄞˋ)
but alas; except that; unfortunately: 怎奈我那時不在家。Unfortunately, I was not at home then.
怎能(ㄗㄣˇ ㄋㄥˊ)
how can (he do this to me?) 或 how could (you...?)
怎敢(ㄗㄣˇ ㄍㄢˇ)
How can one dare? 或 don't dare: 我怎敢和他談話。I don't dare to speak to him.
怎見得(ㄗㄣˇ ㄐㄧㄢˋ ・ㄉㄜ)
How? 或 Why? 或 How come?
怎生(ㄗㄣˇ ㄕㄥ)
How? 或 In what way?
怎樣(ㄗㄣˇ ㄧㄤˋ)
How? 或 In what way? 這件事你怎樣解釋? How do you explain it?
怎樣好(ㄗㄣˇ ・ㄧㄤ ㄏㄠˇ)
Which is the better way? 或 What (can we, I, etc.) do now?

【怎】 1542
2. ㄗㄜˇ tzee ze
Why? 或 How? 或 What?
怎麼(ㄗㄜˇ ・ㄇㄜ) or 怎麼着(ㄗㄜˇ ・ㄇㄜ ・ㄓㄜ) or 怎麼樣(ㄗㄜˇ ・ㄇㄜ ㄧㄤˋ) or 怎樣(ㄗㄣˇ ㄧㄤˋ)
Why? 或 How? 或 What? 這是怎麼回事? What's all this about? 坐公車去怎麼樣? How about going by bus?
怎麼辦(ㄗㄜˇ ・ㄇㄜ ㄅㄢˋ)
How (or what) to do now? 或 What should (I, etc.) do?
怎麼得了(ㄗㄜˇ ・ㄇㄜ ㄉㄜˊ ㄌㄧㄠˇ)
There is no telling the serious consequences.
怎麼搞的(ㄗㄜˇ ・ㄇㄜ ㄍㄠˇ ・ㄉㄜ)
How did it happen? 或 How did you mess it up? 或 Look at what you've done!
怎麼好(ㄗㄜˇ ・ㄇㄜ ㄏㄠˇ)
Which is better? 或 don't know what to do now: 我不知怎麼好。I don't know what to do.
怎麼會(ㄗㄜˇ ・ㄇㄜ ㄏㄨㄟˋ)
How could this be possible? 或 How could it be like this? 或 How could it happen?
怎麼行(ㄗㄜˇ ・ㄇㄜ ㄒㄧㄥˊ)
How could it be possible? (with the implied answer "It's impossible.")
怎麼着(ㄗㄜˇ ・ㄇㄜ ・ㄓㄜ)
① what about ② whatever happens
怎麼成(ㄗㄜˇ ・ㄇㄜ ㄔㄥˊ)
How could this be done? 或 How could this be possible? (with the implied answer "It's impossible." 或 "It can not be done.")
怎麼說(ㄗㄜˇ ・ㄇㄜ ㄕㄨㄛ)
What do you say? 或 What (did he, etc.) say?

【怒】 1543
ㄋㄨˋ nuh nù
1. temper; anger; rage; angry; furious: 他惱羞成怒。He lost his temper from embarrassment. 他勃然大怒。He flew into a rage.
2. to put forth with vigor (as plants, etc.); to sprout; to spring up
3. forceful and vigorous
怒臂(ㄋㄨˋ ㄅㄧˋ)
to raise one's arms in anger
怒不可遏(ㄋㄨˋ ㄅㄨˋ ㄎㄜˇ ㄜˋ)
(literally) The anger cannot be suppressed.—furious; to be beside oneself with anger: 他怒不可遏。He was beside himself with anger.
怒馬(ㄋㄨˋ ㄇㄚˇ)
a sturdy and powerful horse
怒罵(ㄋㄨˋ ㄇㄚˋ)
to curse in rage
怒目切齒(ㄋㄨˋ ㄇㄨˋ ㄑㄧㄝˋ ㄔˇ)
(literally) to cast an angry look while grinding one's teeth—intense hatred or fury
怒目相視(ㄋㄨˋ ㄇㄨˋ ㄒㄧㄤ ㄕˋ)
to look black at each other; to look daggers at each other: 他們怒目相視。They looked daggers at each other.
怒目而視(ㄋㄨˋ ㄇㄨˋ ㄦˊ ㄕˋ)
to look at angrily
怒髮衝冠(ㄋㄨˋ ㄈㄚˇ ㄔㄨㄥ ㄍㄨㄢ)
(literally) so angry that the hair stands up and tips off the hat—intense anger; to bristle with anger
怒放(ㄋㄨˋ ㄈㄤˋ)
① in full bloom: 玫瑰花怒放。The roses are in full bloom. ②(figuratively) wild with joy: 她心花怒放。She was wild with joy.
怒濤(ㄋㄨˋ ㄊㄠ)
furious billows; roaring waves; turbulent waters
怒猊渴驥(ㄋㄨˋ ㄋㄧˊ ㄎㄜˇ ㄐㄧˋ)
(said of Chinese calligraphy) forceful and vigorous (style)
怒號(ㄋㄨˋ ㄏㄠˊ)
(said of winds) howling; roaring : 狂風怒號。A violent wind is howling.
怒吼(ㄋㄨˋ ㄏㄡˇ)
to roar; roars; stentorian calls (also used figuratively)
怒恨(ㄋㄨˋ ㄏㄣˋ)
raging animosity or hatred; full of anger and spite
怒火(ㄋㄨˋ ㄏㄨㄛˇ)
flames of fury; fury: 他滿腔怒火。He was filled with fury.
怒轟轟 or 怒哄哄 or 怒烘烘(ㄋㄨˋ ㄏㄨㄥ ㄏㄨㄥ)
roaring fury; very angry; furiously
怒江(ㄋㄨˋ ㄐㄧㄤ)
the Salween River
怒氣(ㄋㄨˋ ㄑㄧˋ)
anger; wrath; rage; fury
怒氣填胸(ㄋㄨˋ ㄑㄧˋ ㄊㄧㄢˊ ㄒㄩㄥ)
(literally) a breast filled with anger—brimming with fury
怒氣沖沖(ㄋㄨˋ ㄑㄧˋ ㄔㄨㄥ ㄔㄨㄥ)
furious; angry; in a great rage: 他怒氣沖沖。He was in a great rage.
怒叱(ㄋㄨˋ ㄔˋ)
to shout in rage; angry shouts
怒潮(ㄋㄨˋ ㄔㄠˊ)
an angry tide; an overwhelming aspiration
怒視(ㄋㄨˋ ㄕˋ)
an angry look; to look at someone angrily
怒容滿面(ㄋㄨˋ ㄖㄨㄥˊ ㄇㄢˇ ㄇㄧㄢˋ)

flushed with rage; to look furious: 他怒容滿面。His face was flushed with rage.

怒色(ㄋㄨˋ ㄙㄜˋ)
an angry air or look: 他面帶怒色。He wore an angry look.

怒惡(ㄋㄨˋ ㄜˋ)
wrath and spite

怒意(ㄋㄨˋ ㄧˋ)
anger; wrath; (an action, utterance, expression, etc.) indicative of anger

【思】 1544
ㄙ sy si

1. to think; to contemplate; to consider: 你應該三思而後行。You should think twice before doing that.
2. memory; remembrance; to remember; to recall; to think of
3. to mourn; to grieve
4. to admire
5. to pine for
6. a final particle to sound off an expression

思辨(ㄙ ㄅㄧㄢˋ)
① speculation; to speculate ②(usually sarcastically) armchair thinking ③ to analyze mentally

思辨哲學(ㄙ ㄅㄧㄢˋ ㄓㄜˊ ㄒㄩㄝˊ)
speculative philosophy

思不出位(ㄙ ㄅㄨˋ ㄔㄨ ㄨㄟˋ)
(literally) not to think of things outside one's position —without ambition; do not entertain high aspirations

思慕(ㄙ ㄇㄨˋ)
① to admire (a girl, etc.) ② to remember (old days, etc.)

思凡(ㄙ ㄈㄢˊ)
(said of monks, nuns, angels, etc.) to think of worldly pleasures

思婦(ㄙ ㄈㄨˋ)
① a woman who bosoms sad thoughts or memories ② the name of a legendary bird

思念(ㄙ ㄋㄧㄢˋ)
to remember (old days, friends, etc.); to recall

思戀(ㄙ ㄌㄧㄢˋ)
to cherish the memory of

思量(ㄙ ㄌㄧㄤˊ)
to think; to consider; to turn over; to contemplate; consideration; contemplation: 一個人應愼重思量後再決定。One must consider the matter well before deciding.

思路(ㄙ ㄌㄨˋ)
(literally) the paths or ramifications of one's thought —the clarity of thinking, or the lack of it (usually said of writing): 他打斷我的思路。He interrupted my train of thought.

思慮(ㄙ ㄌㄩˋ)
consideration; contemplation; to think carefully; to turn over and over in the mind

思過(ㄙ ㄍㄨㄛˋ)
to ponder or ruminate upon one's faults; to repent

思過半矣(ㄙ ㄍㄨㄛˋ ㄅㄢˋ ㄧˇ)
(literally) to have thought more than half—to have already understood or realized a lot

思歸鳥(ㄙ ㄍㄨㄟ ㄋㄧㄠˇ)
the goatsucker亦作「子規」or「蚊母鳥」

思考(ㄙ ㄎㄠˇ)
to ponder; to contemplate; to think; rumination; contemplation: 人是能思考的動物。Man is a thinking animal.

思考力(ㄙ ㄎㄠˇ ㄌㄧˋ)
the power to think, analyze and speculate

思舊(ㄙ ㄐㄧㄡˋ)
to remember old times, friends, etc.

思齊(ㄙ ㄑㄧˊ)
to wish to equal (a sage, etc.); to want to emulate: 見賢思齊 to see the virtuous and think of equaling or emulating them

思前想後(ㄙ ㄑㄧㄢˊ ㄒㄧㄤˇ ㄏㄡˋ)
to ponder over (a matter, problem, situation, etc.)

思親(ㄙ ㄑㄧㄣ)
to think of one's relatives, especially parents

思鄉(ㄙ ㄒㄧㄤ)or 思家(ㄙ ㄐㄧㄚ)
to think of one's home; homesick

思鄉病(ㄙ ㄒㄧㄤ ㄅㄧㄥˋ)
homesickness; nostalgia

思想(ㄙ ㄒㄧㄤˇ)
① to think of; to remember; to recall ② thought; ideas; mentality; ideological inclination; ideology

思想落伍(ㄙ ㄒㄧㄤˇ ㄌㄨㄛˋ ㄨˇ)
old-fashioned in thinking; outdated ideas

思想家(ㄙ ㄒㄧㄤˇ ㄐㄧㄚ)
a thinker

思想戰(ㄙ ㄒㄧㄤˇ ㄓㄢˋ)
ideological warfare; the battle over people's minds

思想自由(ㄙ ㄒㄧㄤˇ ㄗˋ ㄧㄡˊ)
freedom of thought

思想幼稚(ㄙ ㄒㄧㄤˇ ㄧㄡˋ ㄓˋ)
childish thinking; naive

思省(ㄙ ㄒㄧㄥˇ)
① to think of ② to inspect

思緒(ㄙ ㄒㄩˋ)
a train of thought; the paths of one's thought; myriad ramifications of one's thought: 他思緒紛亂。He was in a confused state of mind.

思致(ㄙ ㄓˋ)
the power of thinking

思潮(ㄙ ㄔㄠˊ)
① the prevailing trend of thought; popular ideas: 民主政治是一種國際思潮。Democracy is an international trend. ② the changing tides of one's thought: 他的思潮起伏不定。His disquieting thoughts surged in his mind.

思春(ㄙ ㄔㄨㄣ)
(usually said of girls) to pine for the opposite sex

思深慮遠(ㄙ ㄕㄣ ㄌㄩˋ ㄩㄢˇ)or 思深憂遠(ㄙ ㄕㄣ ㄧㄡ ㄩㄢˇ)
to think deep and far ahead

思惹情牽(ㄙ ㄖㄜˇ ㄑㄧㄥˊ ㄑㄧㄢ)
to be a prisoner of love; to admire (a girl, etc.) deeply

思如泉湧(ㄙ ㄖㄨˊ ㄑㄩㄢˊ ㄩㄥˇ)
(literally) ideas coming like a swelling spring—brimming with ideas and thoughts

思存(ㄙ ㄘㄨㄣˊ)
to show concern or interest; to favor in heart (a choice, candidate, etc.)

思忖(ㄙ ㄘㄨㄣˇ)
to think; to consider; to ponder; to contemplate: 我們思忖了許多事情。We pondered many things.

〔心部〕

思索(ㄙ ㄙㄨㄛˇ)
(literally) to search one's mind for an answer—to study; to ponder over: 我用心思索了一夜。I did some hard thinking all night.

思憶(ㄙ ㄧˋ)
to think of and remember (old times, friends, etc.); to recall; to cherish the memory of

思議(ㄙ ㄧˋ)
thinkable; imaginable

思維 or 思惟(ㄙ ㄨㄟˊ)
thought; thinking; pondering over

【怠】 1545 ㄉㄞˋ day dài

1. idle; remiss; lax; negligent
2. to treat coldly

怠慢(ㄉㄞˋ ㄇㄢˋ)
① to neglect a visitor or guest (often used as a polite expression): 不要怠慢了來客。See that none of the visitors are neglected. ② lax and crude; idle and remiss

怠廢(ㄉㄞˋ ㄈㄟˋ)
idle

怠惰(ㄉㄞˋ ㄉㄨㄛˋ)
idle and lazy

怠工(ㄉㄞˋ ㄍㄨㄥ)or 怠業(ㄉㄞˋ ㄧㄝˋ)
① a slowdown ② to goof off

怠忽(ㄉㄞˋ ㄏㄨ)
to be remiss; to neglect: 他怠忽職守。He was remiss in his duties.

怠緩(ㄉㄞˋ ㄏㄨㄢˇ)
idle and lax; procrastinating

怠荒(ㄉㄞˋ ㄏㄨㄤ)
to idle and waste (time, etc.)

怠倦(ㄉㄞˋ ㄐㄩㄢˋ)
tired of work; lax and tired

怠情養性(ㄉㄞˋ ㄑㄧㄥˊ ㄧㄤˇ ㄒㄧㄥˋ)
to renounce aggressiveness and practice relaxation

怠息(ㄉㄞˋ ㄒㄧˊ)
to idle and rest

怠隙(ㄉㄞˋ ㄒㄧˋ)
an opportunity—as when the enemy relaxes his vigilance; an opportune moment for one to take advantage of

怠散(ㄉㄞˋ ㄙㄢˋ)
remiss, lax and negligent

【急】 1546 ㄐㄧˊ jyi jí

1. quick; quickly; with expedition: 他急急開門。He quickly opened the door.
2. urgent; hurried; hasty: 她急忙走了。She left in a hurry.
3. anxious; very eager; worried

急巴巴(ㄐㄧˊ ㄅㄚ ㄅㄚ)
very anxious; very anxiously

急奔(ㄐㄧˊ ㄅㄣ)or 急步(ㄐㄧˊ ㄅㄨˋ)
to walk hurriedly

急變(ㄐㄧˊ ㄅㄧㄢˋ)
a quick turn of events; an emergency; a crisis; a presto chango

急病(ㄐㄧˊ ㄅㄧㄥˋ)
a sudden illness; an emergency medical case

急不可待(ㄐㄧˊ ㄅㄨˋ ㄎㄜˇ ㄉㄞˋ)
so urgent that there is no time for waiting; extremely anxious

急不暇擇(ㄐㄧˊ ㄅㄨˋ ㄒㄧㄚˊ ㄗㄜˊ)
too urgent to make a wise or careful choice

急迫(ㄐㄧˊ ㄆㄛˋ)
urgent; pressing: 這件事很急迫。The matter is pressing.

急拍(ㄐㄧˊ ㄆㄞ)
(music) allegro or presto

急脈緩受(ㄐㄧˊ ㄇㄛˋ ㄏㄨㄢˇ ㄕㄡˋ)
to counter fierce and sudden thrust with slow but steady measures

急忙(ㄐㄧˊ ㄇㄤˊ)
urgently; hastily; hurriedly; quickly; in a hurry

急風暴雨(ㄐㄧˊ ㄈㄥ ㄅㄠˋ ㄩˇ)
a violent storm; a hurricane; a tempest

急電(ㄐㄧˊ ㄉㄧㄢˋ)
①an urgent cable ②to call urgently: 我們急電回答。We urgently cabled in reply.

急圖(ㄐㄧˊ ㄊㄨˊ)
① urgent business or tasks ② to make quick plans (to cope with a crisis, an emergency, etc.); to counter quickly

急湍(ㄐㄧˊ ㄊㄨㄢ)
a swift flow of water; angry torrents

急難(ㄐㄧˊ ㄋㄢˋ)
① a critical time; a crisis; an emergency; a disaster ② to offer help in an emergency

急淚(ㄐㄧˊ ㄌㄟˋ)
sudden tears

急來抱佛脚(ㄐㄧˊ ㄌㄞˊ ㄅㄠˋ ㄈㄛˊ ㄐㄧㄠˇ)
to seek help in time of emergency (implying lack of preparation when one has plenty of time)

急流(ㄐㄧˊ ㄌㄧㄡˊ)
swift currents; rapids

急流勇退(ㄐㄧˊ ㄌㄧㄡˊ ㄩㄥˇ ㄊㄨㄟˋ)
to retire when one has ridden the crest of success

急公好義(ㄐㄧˊ ㄍㄨㄥ ㄏㄠˋ ㄧˋ)
to be enthusiastic about charity work; zealous for public welfare or interests: 那老人急公好義。The old man was zealous for the public welfare.

急功近利(ㄐㄧˊ ㄍㄨㄥ ㄐㄧㄣˋ ㄌㄧˋ)
so eager to be successful that one sees only the immediate advantages: 他急功近利。He was eager for quick success and instant benefit.

急客(ㄐㄧˊ ㄎㄜˋ)
an unexpected visitor; a self-invited guest

急口令(ㄐㄧˊ ㄎㄡˇ ㄌㄧㄥˋ)
a tongue twister 亦作「繞口令」

急壞(ㄐㄧˊ ㄏㄨㄞˋ)
to feel extremely worried but helpless; anxious but powerless

急激(ㄐㄧˊ ㄐㄧ)
radical; vehement

急急忙忙(ㄐㄧˊ ·ㄐㄧ ㄇㄤˊ ㄇㄤˊ)
in great haste; in a great hurry

急救(ㄐㄧˊ ㄐㄧㄡˋ)
first-aid; first aid: 我們買了些急救藥品。We bought a lot of first-aid medicine

急救法(ㄐㄧˊ ㄐㄧㄡˋ ㄈㄚˇ)
first-aid methods or techniques

急救方(ㄐㄧˊ ㄐㄧㄡˋ ㄈㄤ)
a prescription for an emergency case

急救箱(ㄐㄧˋ ㄐㄧㄡˋ ㄒㄧㄤ)
a first-aid kit

急就(ㄐㄧˊ ㄐㄧㄡˋ)

hurriedly made, composed, etc.; improvised; to complete rapidly

急就章(ㄐㄧˊ ㄐㄧㄡˋ ㄓㄤ)
hurriedly composed writing; an article written or a task performed under tremendous pressure of time or at short notice; an improvisation

急件(ㄐㄧˊ ㄐㄧㄢˋ)
an urgent document; a dispatch

急進(ㄐㄧˊ ㄐㄧㄣˋ)
to forge ahead vigorously

急進份子(ㄐㄧˊ ㄐㄧㄣˋ ㄈㄣˋ ㄗˇ)
a radical

急進派(ㄐㄧˊ ㄐㄧㄣˋ ㄆㄞˋ)
a radical or an extremist faction

急進主義(ㄐㄧˊ ㄐㄧㄣˋ ㄓㄨˇ ㄧˋ)
radicalism; extremism

急降(ㄐㄧˊ ㄐㄧㄤˋ)
to dive sharply; to drop sharply

急驚風(ㄐㄧˊ ㄐㄧㄥ ㄈㄥ)
(Chinese medicine) a disease among children, especially of infants, symptomized by involuntary, incessant twitchings of the limbs and tightly shut mouth; infantile eclampsia; acute infantile convulsions; sudden onset of infantile convulsion

急驚風偏遇慢郎中(ㄐㄧˊ ㄐㄧㄥ ㄈㄥ ㄆㄧㄢ ㄩˋ ㄇㄢˋ ㄌㄤˊ ㄓㄨㄥ)
① One is impatient while the other takes it easy. ② One sees no need to hurry while something requires one's immediate attention.

急景凋年(ㄐㄧˊ ㄐㄧㄥˇ ㄉㄧㄠ ㄋㄧㄢˊ)
Time slips away fast, and the year is approaching its end.

急遽(ㄐㄧˊ ㄐㄩˋ)
quick (falls, rises, advances, etc.); urgent; hasty: 急遽的變化 a rapid change

急起直追(ㄐㄧˊ ㄑㄧˇ ㄓˊ ㄓㄨㄟ)
to rise and make a hot chase; to make amends as quickly as possible; to try to catch up in great haste

急切(ㄐㄧˊ ㄑㄧㄝˋ)
① urgent; eager; anxiously (awaiting, etc.) ② in a hurry; in haste

急先鋒(ㄐㄧˊ ㄒㄧㄢ ㄈㄥ)
① a brave vanguard ② a most aggressive, daring henchman

急相(ㄐㄧˊ ㄒㄧㄤˋ)
an anxious expression or manner

急行(ㄐㄧˊ ㄒㄧㄥˊ)
① to walk hurriedly ② to start doing something immediately

急行軍(ㄐㄧˊ ㄒㄧㄥˊ ㄐㄩㄣ)
a forced march; a rapid march

急性(ㄐㄧˊ ㄒㄧㄥˋ)
(medicine) an acute case

急性闌尾炎(ㄐㄧˊ ㄒㄧㄥˋ ㄌㄢˊ ㄨㄟˇ ㄧㄢˊ)
acute appendicitis 亦作「急性盲腸炎」

急性子(ㄐㄧˊ ㄒㄧㄥˋ ˙ㄗ)
quick-tempered; prone to do things quickly; rash; impatient; impetuous 亦作「急性兒」

急性胃炎(ㄐㄧˊ ㄒㄧㄥˋ ㄨㄟˋ ㄧㄢˊ)
acute gastritis

急需(ㄐㄧˊ ㄒㄩ)
to need urgently: 我急需幫助。I was in need of immediate help.

急智(ㄐㄧˊ ㄓˋ)
quick-witted; a calm and quickly responsive mind, especially in a crisis; a mind capable of making quick and intelligent decisions, especially in time of crisis or danger; wit

急診(ㄐㄧˊ ㄓㄣˇ)
(medicine) an emergency case; emergency treatment

急症(ㄐㄧˊ ㄓㄥˋ)
(medicine) an emergency case

急轉直下(ㄐㄧˊ ㄓㄨㄢˇ ㄓˊ ㄒㄧㄚˋ)
a quick and decisive turn of events for the worse; rapid deterioration of a situation; to take a sudden turn and then develop rapidly

急轉彎(ㄐㄧˊ ㄓㄨㄢˇ ㄨㄢ)
① to make a sharp turn ② a hairpin turn

急中生智(ㄐㄧˊ ㄓㄨㄥ ㄕㄥ ㄓˋ)
suddenly hit upon a way out of a predicament; driven by circumstances to find a way out; a bright idea that hits one in an emergency

急事(ㄐㄧˊ ㄕˋ)
an urgent matter

急煞(ㄐㄧˊ ㄕㄚˋ)
to be very worried or anxious but powerless to do anything about it

急煞車(ㄐㄧˊ ㄕㄚˋ ㄔㄜ)
① to brake a car abruptly; to brake a car to a screeching stop: 他來個急煞車。He braked his car abruptly. ② to bring to a halt

急甚麼(ㄐㄧˊ ㄕㄜˊ ˙ㄇㄜ)
What's the hurry? 或 No need to hurry. (There is plenty of time.)

急如星火(ㄐㄧˊ ㄖㄨˊ ㄒㄧㄥ ㄏㄨㄛˇ)
(literally) as urgent as sparks that may start a conflagration—extremely urgent: 災民需用醫藥急如星火。Medical aid must be sent to the victims posthaste.

急則生變(ㄐㄧˊ ㄗㄜˊ ㄕㄥ ㄅㄧㄢˋ)
Hastiness upsets carefully laid out plans. 或 Rashness spoils chances of success.

急躁(ㄐㄧˊ ㄗㄠˋ)
rash and impatient; peevish; impetuous; irritable

急促(ㄐㄧˊ ㄘㄨˋ)
① urgently; hastily; hurriedly ②(said of time) short: 時間很急促，我們必須對那件事下決心。Time is running short. We must make up our mind about it.

急色鬼(ㄐㄧˊ ㄙㄜˋ ㄍㄨㄟˇ)or 急色兒(ㄐㄧˊ ㄙㄜˋ ㄦˊ)
a prurient male in constant heat; a woman-grabber

急速(ㄐㄧˊ ㄙㄨˋ)
hurriedly; hastily: 事情急速變化。The matter changed quickly

急務(ㄐㄧˊ ㄨˋ)
pressing and urgent business: 我有急務在身。I have some urgent task on hand.

急彎(ㄐㄧˊ ㄨㄢ)
a sharp turn: 車子拐了個急彎。The car made a sharp turn.

急於(ㄐㄧˊ ㄩˊ)

〔心部〕

to be in a hurry or anxious to (finish the task, conclude the war, etc.); eager: 他急於完成任務。He is eager to fulfill a task.

〔心部〕

急雨(ㄐㄧˊ ㄩˇ)
a heavy downpour; a driving rain

急用(ㄐㄧˊ ㄩㄥˋ)
(for) urgent use or need: 我們應節約儲蓄，以備急用。We should practice economy and save money against a rainy day.

【怨】 1547
ㄩㄢˋ yuann yuàn

1. ill will; hatred; enmity; animus; resentment; to resent: 他怨恨批評。He resents criticism.
2. to complain; to blame (others); to impute: 她總是在抱怨。She is always complaining.

怨不得(ㄩㄢˋ ·ㄅㄨ ·ㄉㄜ)
no wonder; cannot blame

怨命(ㄩㄢˋ ㄇㄧㄥˋ)
to blame one's fate (for all misfortunes encountered)

怨誹(ㄩㄢˋ ㄈㄟˇ)
blames or curses; to blame; to murmur against

怨忿(ㄩㄢˋ ㄈㄣˋ)
animus; bitterness; a grudge; ill will

怨毒(ㄩㄢˋ ㄉㄨˊ)
malice; hatred; venom; enmity

怨懟(ㄩㄢˋ ㄉㄨㄟˋ)
ill will; hatred; a grudge

怨歎(ㄩㄢˋ ㄊㄢˋ)
to sigh with bitterness

怨天尤人(ㄩㄢˋ ㄊㄧㄢ ㄧㄡˊ ㄖㄣˊ)
(literally) to murmur against Heaven and blame others (for one's misfortune)—(figuratively) to impute all faults and wrongs to others; to be neurotically dissatisfied: 他不怨天尤人。He didn't blame God or man.

怨女(ㄩㄢˋ ㄋㄩˇ)
an old maid or spinster

怨女曠夫(ㄩㄢˋ ㄋㄩˇ ㄎㄨㄤˋ ㄈㄨ)
unmarried women and men (who could be easily persuaded to marry to mutual satisfaction)

怨骨(ㄩㄢˋ ㄍㄨˇ)
those who died with grudges or complaints

怨鬼(ㄩㄢˋ ㄍㄨㄟˇ)
the ghost of a wronged man—as a man executed by mistake, etc.

怨恨(ㄩㄢˋ ㄏㄣˋ)
ill will; enmity; animus; grudges: 他對我有怨恨。He bears me a grudge

怨結(ㄩㄢˋ ㄐㄧㄝˊ)
a pent-up hatred or grudge

怨氣(ㄩㄢˋ ㄑㄧˋ)
spite; resentment; complaints; strong dissatisfaction: 我一肚子怨氣。I was full of complaints.

怨仇(ㄩㄢˋ ㄔㄡˊ)
an old enemy

怨聲載道(ㄩㄢˋ ㄕㄥ ㄗㄞˋ ㄉㄠˋ)
(said of bad administration, etc.) Complaints can be heard everywhere. 或 Cries of discontent rise all round.

怨入骨髓(ㄩㄢˋ ㄖㄨˋ ㄍㄨˇ ㄙㄨㄟˇ)
to hate to the very marrow

怨咨(ㄩㄢˋ ㄗ)
to repine; to grumble

怨色(ㄩㄢˋ ㄙㄜˋ)
a resentful look

怨艾(ㄩㄢˋ ㄞˋ)
(literally) resentment; a grudge

怨偶 or 怨耦(ㄩㄢˋ ㄡˇ)
a couple who love each other no more; an unharmonious couple; a couple at loggerheads

怨尤(ㄩㄢˋ ㄧㄡˊ)
spite; complaining; a grudge; a grumble; bitterness

怨言(ㄩㄢˋ ㄧㄢˊ)
complaints; spiteful remarks; grumbles: 他從未發過一句怨言。He has never uttered a word of complaint.

怨望(ㄩㄢˋ ㄨㄤˋ)
ill will; hatred; animus

【怹】 1548
ㄊㄢ tan tān

a polite version of 他

【怱】 1549
(悤、匆) ㄘㄨㄥ tsong cōng

hasty; hastily; hurriedly

怱忙(ㄘㄨㄥ ㄇㄤˊ)
haste; in haste; hastily; hurriedly: 我怱忙作出決定。I made a hasty decision.

怱促(ㄘㄨㄥ ㄘㄨˋ) or 怱遽(ㄘㄨㄥ ㄐㄩˋ)
haste; hastily: 他怱促離去。He left in haste.

怱怱(ㄘㄨㄥ ㄘㄨㄥ)
hurriedly; suddenly and imperceptibly (said of the passage of time): 他怱怱吃了一餐飯。He took a hurried meal.

六畫

【恂】 1550
ㄒㄩㄣˊ shyun xún

1. to trust; to have faith in
2. sincere
3. suddenly
4. afraid; scared

恂達(ㄒㄩㄣˊ ㄉㄚˊ)
intelligent

恂慄(ㄒㄩㄣˊ ㄌㄧˋ)
scared; severe-looking; awe-inspiring

恂恂(ㄒㄩㄣˊ ㄒㄩㄣˊ)
① faithfully; trustingly; simple and sincere ② courteously

恂直(ㄒㄩㄣˊ ㄓˊ)
frank and sincere

恂實(ㄒㄩㄣˊ ㄕˊ)
sincerely honest

恂然(ㄒㄩㄣˊ ㄖㄢˊ)
sincerely

【恆】 1551
(恒) ㄏㄥˊ herng héng

1. constant; regular; persevering: 我們讀書要持之以恆。We persevere in our studies.
2. lasting; continual; continually
3. a Chinese family name

恆民(ㄏㄥˊ ㄇㄧㄣˊ)
common people; ordinary people

恆風(ㄏㄥˊ ㄈㄥ)
a permanent wind

恆等(ㄏㄥˊ ㄉㄥˇ)
(mathematics) identically equal; identical

恆例(ㄏㄥˊ ㄌㄧˋ)
common practices

恆河(ㄏㄥˊ ㄏㄜˊ)
the Ganges River, in north-

ern India
恆河沙數(ㄏㄥˊ ㄏㄜˊ ㄕㄚ ㄕㄨˋ)
(literally) the sands of the Ganges; too many to be counted—innumerable; countless
恆久(ㄏㄥˊ ㄐㄧㄡˇ)
constancy; constant; lasting; forever; enduring
恆情(ㄏㄥˊ ㄑㄧㄥˊ)
general propensities; common practices
恆心(ㄏㄥˊ ㄒㄧㄣ)
perseverance: 我們要是沒有恆心可學不好。Unless we persevere with a subject, we can't hope to master it.
恆星(ㄏㄥˊ ㄒㄧㄥ)
fixed stars
恆星年(ㄏㄥˊ ㄒㄧㄥ ㄋㄧㄢˊ)
a sidereal year
恆星系(ㄏㄥˊ ㄒㄧㄥ ㄒㄧˋ)
a stellar system; a galaxy
恆星時(ㄏㄥˊ ㄒㄧㄥ ㄕˊ)
sidereal time
恆星日(ㄏㄥˊ ㄒㄧㄥ ㄖˋ)
a sidereal day
恆星月(ㄏㄥˊ ㄒㄧㄥ ㄩㄝˋ)
a sidereal month
恆齒(ㄏㄥˊ ㄔˇ)
(anatomy) permanent teeth
恆產(ㄏㄥˊ ㄔㄢˇ)
immovable property—real estate
恆常(ㄏㄥˊ ㄔㄤˊ)
① permanent; enduring; constant ② regular; common (practices, etc.)
恆春(ㄏㄥˊ ㄔㄨㄣ)
Hengchun, a town on the southernmost end of Taiwan
恆山(ㄏㄥˊ ㄕㄢ)
Mountain Heng, also known as the Northern Mountain, located between Hopeh and Shansi Provinces
恒言(ㄏㄥˊ ㄧㄢˊ)
a common saying; a proverb
恆溫器(ㄏㄥˊ ㄨㄣ ㄑㄧˋ)
a thermostat
恆溫層(ㄏㄥˊ ㄨㄣ ㄘㄥˊ)
a stratum of invariable temperature; the stratosphere

【恃】 1552 ㄕˋ shyh shì

to rely on; to depend on; to presume upon: 他有恃無恐。He feels secure in the knowledge that he has strong backing.
恃刁(ㄕˋ ㄉㄧㄠ)or 恃橫(ㄕˋ ㄏㄥˋ)
to rely on crooked ways and violence
恃力(ㄕˋ ㄌㄧˋ)or 恃強(ㄕˋ ㄑㄧㄤˊ)
to rely on one's power; to rely on force
恃論平允(ㄕˋ ㄌㄨㄣˋ ㄆㄧㄥˊ ㄩㄣˇ)
to pass a fair opinion
恃貴(ㄕˋ ㄍㄨㄟˋ)
to presume on one's high position or blue blood
恃強凌弱(ㄕˋ ㄑㄧㄤˊ ㄌㄧㄥˊ ㄖㄨㄛˋ)
to use one's strength (or power) to bully the weak: 他恃強凌弱。He uses his strength to bully the weak.
恃衆(ㄕˋ ㄓㄨㄥˋ)
to presume on numbers; to take advantage of superiority in numbers (to commit an act of violence)
恃寵(ㄕˋ ㄔㄨㄥˇ)
to presume on being a favorite (of a high-placed personality): 他恃寵而驕。His haughtiness relies on his master's (or superior's) love and indulgence.
恃勢(ㄕˋ ㄕˋ)
to presume on one's position or influence
恃才傲物(ㄕˋ ㄘㄞˊ ㄠˋ ㄨˋ)
to be arrogant because of one's talents or ability: 他恃才傲物。He is inordinately proud of his ability.
恃愛(ㄕˋ ㄞˋ)
(usually used in polite correspondence) to presume on your kindness and affection

【恌】 1553 ㄊㄧㄠ tiau tiāo

1. flippant; playful; sportive; frivolous

【恓】 1554 ㄒㄧ shi xī

frightened and worried
恓惶(ㄒㄧ ㄏㄨㄤˊ)
frightened and worried; vexed

【恍】 1555 ㄏㄨㄤˇ hoang huǎng

1. absent-minded; unconscious
2. all of a sudden; suddenly
3. seem; as if
恍惚(ㄏㄨㄤˇ ㄏㄨ)or 恍恍惚惚(ㄏㄨㄤˇ ㄏㄨㄤˇ ㄏㄨ ㄏㄨ)
①in a trance; absent-minded; unconscious: 他精神恍惚。He was in a trance. ②dimly; faintly
恍然大悟(ㄏㄨㄤˇ ㄖㄢˊ ㄉㄚˋ ㄨˋ)
to come to understand suddenly
恍然若失(ㄏㄨㄤˇ ㄖㄢˊ ㄖㄨㄛˋ ㄕ)
to feel as if one had lost his bearings
恍如隔世(ㄏㄨㄤˇ ㄖㄨˊ ㄍㄜˊ ㄕˋ)
so different that it is as if a generation had passed
恍如一場大夢(ㄏㄨㄤˇ ㄖㄨˊ ㄧˋ ㄔㄤˇ ㄉㄚˋ ㄇㄥˋ)
It seems as if it were a dream.
恍若(ㄏㄨㄤˇ ㄖㄨㄛˋ)or 恍如(ㄏㄨㄤˇ ㄖㄨˊ)
as if; as though; rather like

【恟】 1556 ㄒㄩㄥ shiong xiōng

1. afraid; frightened
2. noisy
恟懼(ㄒㄩㄥ ㄐㄩˋ)
afraid; frightened
恟恟(ㄒㄩㄥ ㄒㄩㄥ)
tumultuous

【恢】 1557 ㄏㄨㄟ huei huī

1. great; immense; enormous; vast; extensive
2. to recover; to restore; to regain: 他很快地恢復健康。He regained his health quickly.
恢復(ㄏㄨㄟ ㄈㄨˋ)
to restore; to regain; to recover: 恢復知覺 to recover consciousness
恢復健康(ㄏㄨㄟ ㄈㄨˋ ㄐㄧㄢˋ ㄎㄤ)
to restore one's health; to recover from illness
恢復青春(ㄏㄨㄟ ㄈㄨˋ ㄑㄧㄥ ㄔㄨㄣ)
to be rejuvenated; to regain youth
恢復秩序(ㄏㄨㄟ ㄈㄨˋ ㄓˋ ㄒㄩˋ)
to restore order
恢復自由(ㄏㄨㄟ ㄈㄨˋ ㄗˋ ㄧㄡˊ)
to regain freedom; restoration of freedom
恢復元氣(ㄏㄨㄟ ㄈㄨˋ ㄩㄢˊ ㄑㄧˋ)
to recover energy or strength (after a calamity, illness, etc.)
恢復原狀(ㄏㄨㄟ ㄈㄨˋ ㄩㄢˊ ㄓㄨㄤˋ)
to restore the original condi-

tion; to be restored to the original condition

恢誕(ㄏㄨㄟ ㄉㄢˋ)
exaggerated

恢廓(ㄏㄨㄟ ㄎㄨㄛˋ)
broad-minded

恢恢(ㄏㄨㄟ ㄏㄨㄟ)
spacious; extensive; vast: 天網恢恢，疏而不漏。Nobody escapes the judgement of Heaven.

恢恢有餘(ㄏㄨㄟ ㄏㄨㄟ ㄧㄡˇ ㄩˊ)
to have plenty of space; very spacious; very roomy

恢宏 or 恢弘(ㄏㄨㄟ ㄏㄨㄥˊ)
extensive; broad; magnanimous

恢張(ㄏㄨㄟ ㄓㄤ)
to extend

恢偉(ㄏㄨㄟ ㄨㄟˇ)
great

【恨】 1558 ㄏㄣˋ henn hèn

1. to resent; to hate; hatred; hate: 她懷恨在心。She nursed hatred in her heart.
2. to regret

恨不相逢未嫁時(ㄏㄣˋ ㄅㄨˋ ㄒㄧㄤ ㄈㄥˊ ㄨㄟˋ ㄐㄧㄚˋ ㄕˊ)
to regret meeting one's lover only after marriage (to another man)

恨不得(ㄏㄣˋ ˙ㄅㄨ ˙ㄉㄜ)
to wish that one could (do something which is not proper to do); to itch to: 我恨不得馬上投入戰場。I itched to plunge into the battlefield.

恨不能(ㄏㄣˋ ˙ㄅㄨ ㄋㄥˊ)
to wish that one could (do something impossible or beyond one's means to do)

恨透了(ㄏㄣˋ ㄊㄡˋ ˙ㄌㄜ)
to hate to the utmost degree; to detest

恨鐵不成鋼(ㄏㄣˋ ㄊㄧㄝˇ ㄅㄨˋ ㄔㄥˊ ㄍㄤ)
to be exasperated at a son's failure to make good

恨海(ㄏㄣˋ ㄏㄞˇ)
deep hatred

恨事(ㄏㄣˋ ㄕˋ)
a regrettable thing; something lamented; a matter for regret

恨人(ㄏㄣˋ ㄖㄣˊ)
①a misanthrope or misanthropist ②a sentimental person ③a frustrated man given to regrets

恨入骨髓(ㄏㄣˋ ㄖㄨˋ ㄍㄨˇ ㄙㄨㄟˇ)
to hate to the marrow; to hate with one's soul

恨晚(ㄏㄣˋ ㄨㄢˇ)
to regret that something happened too late 參看「相見恨晚」

恨惡(ㄏㄣˋ ㄨˋ)
to loathe

【恤】 1559 (卹) ㄒㄩˋ shiuh xù

1. to relieve; to help
2. to sympathize; to be considerate: 我甚體恤他。I understand and sympathize with him.

恤病(ㄒㄩˋ ㄅㄧㄥˋ)
to show sympathy for the sick

恤貧(ㄒㄩˋ ㄆㄧㄣˊ)
to give relief to the poor

恤民(ㄒㄩˋ ㄇㄧㄣˊ)
to be mindful of the people's hardships

恤老(ㄒㄩˋ ㄌㄠˇ)
to relieve the aged

恤嫠(ㄒㄩˋ ㄌㄧˊ)
to relieve widows

恤孤(ㄒㄩˋ ㄍㄨ)
to relieve orphans

恤金(ㄒㄩˋ ㄐㄧㄣ)
relief payment; compensation

恤刑(ㄒㄩˋ ㄒㄧㄥˊ)
very careful in meting out punishment

恤政(ㄒㄩˋ ㄓㄥˋ)
benevolent government

恤然(ㄒㄩˋ ㄖㄢˊ)
startled; astonished

恤養金(ㄒㄩˋ ㄧㄤˇ ㄐㄧㄣ)
a pension

【恪】 1560 ㄎㄜˋ keh kè (又讀 ㄑㄩㄝˋ chiueh què)

respectful; reverent; to respect; respectfully

恪勤(ㄎㄜˋ ㄑㄧㄣˊ)
cautious and industrious

恪守(ㄎㄜˋ ㄕㄡˇ)
to observe (rules) strictly; scrupulously abide by (a treaty, promise, etc.); carefully obey (laws, orders, tradition)

恪慎(ㄎㄜˋ ㄕㄣˋ)
respectful and cautious; careful; reverent

恪遵(ㄎㄜˋ ㄗㄨㄣ)
to obey or follow (orders, rules, etc.) with respect

【恫】 1561 1. ㄊㄨㄥ tong tōng

pain

恫瘝 or 恫矜(ㄊㄨㄥ ㄍㄨㄢ)
hardship; illness

恫瘝在抱(ㄊㄨㄥ ㄍㄨㄢ ㄗㄞˋ ㄅㄠˋ)
to show intimate concern over the people's hardships

【恫】 1561 2. ㄉㄨㄥˋ donq dòng

to threaten, intimidate, or scare loudly

恫嚇(ㄉㄨㄥˋ ㄏㄜˋ)
to threaten; to intimidate; to scare

恫喝(ㄉㄨㄥˋ ㄏㄜˋ)
to threaten, intimidate, or scare loudly; to browbeat; to bully

恫疑虛喝(ㄉㄨㄥˋ ㄧˊ ㄒㄩ ㄏㄜˋ)
to threaten loudly; to bully; to browbeat

【恇】 1562 ㄎㄨㄤ kuang kuāng

afraid; timid; timorous; fearful

恇懼(ㄎㄨㄤ ㄐㄩˋ)
afraid; fearful; timorous

恇怯(ㄎㄨㄤ ㄑㄧㄝˋ)
timid

【恬】 1563 ㄊㄧㄢˊ tyan tián

quiet; peaceful; undisturbed

恬波(ㄊㄧㄢˊ ㄅㄛ)
calm waters

恬不知恥(ㄊㄧㄢˊ ㄅㄨˋ ㄓ ㄔˇ)
brazen-faced; to be totally devoid of sense of shame; not feel ashamed; to have no sense of shame; to be shameless: 他恬不知恥。He has no sense of shame.

恬不爲怪(ㄊㄧㄢˊ ㄅㄨˋ ㄨㄟˊ ㄍㄨㄞˋ)
not surprised at all

恬謐(ㄊㄧㄢˊ ㄇㄧˋ)
tranquil; peaceful; quiet

恬澹 or 恬淡(ㄊㄧㄢˊ ㄉㄢˋ)
indifferent to worldly gain; contented: 他過恬淡生活。He

leads a tranquil life without worldly desires.
恬退(ㄊㄧㄢˊ ㄊㄨㄟˋ)
contented and reserved; uninterested in wealth and glory
恬和(ㄊㄧㄢˊ ㄏㄜˊ)
quiet and gentle
恬靜(ㄊㄧㄢˊ ㄐㄧㄥˋ)
undisturbed; having peace of mind; tranquil
恬然(ㄊㄧㄢˊ ㄖㄢˊ)
easygoing; undisturbed; unhurried; unperturbed; calm; nonchalant: 我處之恬然。I remain undisturbed.
恬逸(ㄊㄧㄢˊ ㄧˋ)
free from worry or disturbance; peaceful and leisurely

【恰】 1564 ㄑㄧㄚˋ chiah qià
proper; appropriate; suitable
恰待(ㄑㄧㄚˋ ㄉㄞˋ)
just on the point of (doing something)
恰到好處(ㄑㄧㄚˋ ㄉㄠˋ ㄏㄠˇ ㄔㄨˋ)
neither too much nor too little; just right: 此事恰到好處。The matter is just right.
恰當(ㄑㄧㄚˋ ㄉㄤˋ)
appropriate; fitting; apt; apposite: 作禮貌上的拜訪是恰當的。It is fitting to make courtesy calls.
恰好(ㄑㄧㄚˋ ㄏㄠˇ)
①just; exactly: 那恰好是我所要的。That's exactly what I want. ②by coincidence
恰恰(ㄑㄧㄚˋ ㄑㄧㄚˋ)
①by coincidence ②the chirping of birds ③just; exactly: 它恰恰相反。It is just the opposite. 或 It is exactly the reverse.
恰巧(ㄑㄧㄚˋ ㄑㄧㄠˇ)
coinciding luckily; by coincidence; by chance; as chance would have it: 昨天恰巧他也在那裡。He happened to be there yesterday, too.
恰值(ㄑㄧㄚˋ ㄓˊ)
just at the time of
恰正(ㄑㄧㄚˋ ㄓㄥˋ)
just when
恰如(ㄑㄧㄚˋ ㄖㄨˊ)or 恰似(ㄑㄧㄚˋ ㄙˋ)
just like; just as if; just as though
恰如其分(ㄑㄧㄚˋ ㄖㄨˊ ㄑㄧˊ ㄈㄣˋ)
just suited or becoming to one's importance; appropriate
恰遇(ㄑㄧㄚˋ ㄩˋ)
to chance upon

【恊】 1565 ㄒㄧㄝˊ shye xié
1. to intimidate
2. fearful and timid
3. same as 協

【恁】 1566 ㄖㄣˋ renn rèn
1. this; such; so; that
2. how; what: 他恁的大膽! How bold he is!
恁般(ㄖㄣˋ ㄅㄢ)
to such an extent
恁麼(ㄖㄣˋ ·ㄇㄜ)
①in this way; like this ②what; which
恁的(ㄖㄣˋ ㄉㄧˋ)
①in this way; to such an extent ②why; how 參看「恁地」
恁地(ㄖㄣˋ ㄉㄧˋ)
①in this way; to such an extent ②how; why: 恁地道他們不是人? Why do you say that they are brutes?
恁時(ㄖㄣˋ ㄕˊ)
when that happens; then
恁時節(ㄖㄣˋ ㄕˊ ㄐㄧㄝˊ)
when that time comes; at that time

【恐】 1567 ㄎㄨㄥˇ koong kǒng
1. to fear; to dread
2. I am afraid.... 消息恐不可靠。I am afraid the news is not reliable.
恐怖(ㄎㄨㄥˇ ㄅㄨˋ)
terror; horror; fear
恐怖病(ㄎㄨㄥˇ ㄅㄨˋ ㄅㄧㄥˋ)
phobia
恐怖分子(ㄎㄨㄥˇ ㄅㄨˋ ㄈㄣˋ ㄗˇ)
terrorists
恐怖主義(ㄎㄨㄥˇ ㄅㄨˋ ㄓㄨˇ ㄧˋ)
terrorism
恐怖時代(ㄎㄨㄥˇ ㄅㄨˋ ㄕˊ ㄉㄞˋ)
①an age of terror ②the Reign of Terror
恐怕(ㄎㄨㄥˇ ㄆㄚˋ)
(with reference to an unpleasant fact) probably; perhaps; I think; maybe 或 I am afraid that.... 我恐怕不能來。I am afraid that I cannot come.
恐龍(ㄎㄨㄥˇ ㄌㄨㄥˊ)
a dinosaur
恐嚇 or 恐喝(ㄎㄨㄥˇ ㄏㄜˋ)
to intimidate; to scare; to threaten; to menace; to blackmail
恐嚇罪(ㄎㄨㄥˇ ㄏㄜˋ ㄗㄨㄟˋ)
an offense of blackmail or intimidation
恐慌(ㄎㄨㄥˇ ㄏㄨㄤ)
①panic; panicky ②(economic) depression or crises
恐懼(ㄎㄨㄥˇ ㄐㄩˋ)
fear; dread; fright
恐其(ㄎㄨㄥˇ ㄑㄧˊ)
possibly or probably (with reference to a fearful fact)

【恕】 1568 ㄕㄨˋ shuh shù
1. to forgive; to excuse: 我們寬恕他。We forgave him.
2. Excuse me. 恕難從命。I regret that I cannot comply with your wishes.
3. benevolence
恕不奉陪(ㄕㄨˋ ㄅㄨˋ ㄈㄥˋ ㄆㄟˊ)
I am sorry but I cannot keep you company. 或 Excuse my inability to keep you company.
恕不一一(ㄕㄨˋ ㄅㄨˋ ㄧ ㄧ)
I am sorry I cannot go into details. (a phrase common in correspondence)
恕不遠送(ㄕㄨˋ ㄅㄨˋ ㄩㄢˇ ㄙㄨㄥˋ)
I am sorry I cannot escort you farther. 或 Excuse my inability to escort you farther.
恕道(ㄕㄨˋ ㄉㄠˋ)
the principle of forgiveness; magnanimity; the principle of reciprocity
恕過(ㄕㄨˋ ㄍㄨㄛˋ)
to pardon the mistake; to forgive a fault
恕罪(ㄕㄨˋ ㄗㄨㄟˋ)
to forgive a fault; to pardon an offense; to forgive a sin: 請恕罪。Please forgive my fault.
恕邀(ㄕㄨˋ ㄧㄠ)
Excuse my, or our, informality in requesting your presence. (a conventional phrase

〔心部〕

on an invitation card)
恕宥(ㄕㄨˋ ㄧㄡˋ)
to forgive; to excuse

【恚】 1569
ㄏㄨㄟˋ huey huì
to rage; to anger: 他既愧且恚。He was shamed and angered.
恚憤(ㄏㄨㄟˋ ㄈㄣˋ)
to be enraged; to be indignant
恚怒(ㄏㄨㄟˋ ㄋㄨˋ)
to be enraged; to be indignant; to be furious
恚恨(ㄏㄨㄟˋ ㄏㄣˋ)
to hate vehemently
恚怨(ㄏㄨㄟˋ ㄩㄢˋ)
to resent bitterly

【恝】 1570
ㄐㄧㄚˊ jya jiá
indifferent; unworried; unconcerned
恝置(ㄐㄧㄚˊ ㄓˋ)
to disregard; to neglect; to ignore

【恙】 1571
ㄧㄤˋ yanq yàng
1. disease: 我偶感微恙。I felt slightly indisposed.
2. worry
恙蟲(ㄧㄤˋ ㄔㄨㄥˊ)
a chigger or jigger; a redbug

【恣】 1572
1. ㄗˋ tzyh zì
to throw off restraint; to dissipate; to debauch
恣情(ㄗˋ ㄑㄧㄥˊ)
to abandon oneself to passion; to give rein to passion
恣行無忌(ㄗˋ ㄒㄧㄥˊ ㄨˊ ㄐㄧˋ)
to throw off all restraint; to act without the least regard for accepted rules or standards
恣性(ㄗˋ ㄒㄧㄥˋ)
unrestrained behavior
恣縱(ㄗˋ ㄗㄨㄥˋ)
① having no regard for rules; heedless of restraint ② licentious; morally unrestrained; dissolute; libertine
恣肆(ㄗˋ ㄙˋ)
licentious; willful; heedless of restraint
恣意(ㄗˋ ㄧˋ)
unscrupulous; unbridled; willful
恣意妄爲(ㄗˋ ㄧˋ ㄨㄤˋ ㄨㄟˊ)
to act willfully; to act as one pleases; to act without regard for any authority; to behave unscrupulously

【恣】 1572
2. ㄘ tsy cī
參看「恣睢」
恣睢(ㄘ ㄙㄨㄟ)
① carefree; unbridled ② extremely conceited

【恩】 1573
ㄣ en ēn
favor; grace; gratitude; kindness; benevolence; mercy; charity: 我向他報恩。I paid a debt of gratitude to him.
恩俸(ㄣ ㄈㄥˋ)
a pension
恩撫金(ㄣ ㄈㄨˇ ㄐㄧㄣ)
the pensions given to the families of those who were killed in action
恩德(ㄣ ㄉㄜˊ)
benevolence; benignity; charity; generosity; kindness; bounty; favor; grace
恩德在民(ㄣ ㄉㄜˊ ㄗㄞˋ ㄇㄧㄣˊ)
(said of government officials) with benevolence felt by the people
恩典(ㄣ ㄉㄧㄢˇ)
①(in old China) an imperial favor ② a favor
恩同再造(ㄣ ㄊㄨㄥˊ ㄗㄞˋ ㄗㄠˋ)
unusual favor or help rendered to someone in bad luck, which enables him to stand on his own feet again
恩禮(ㄣ ㄌㄧˇ)
gifts and kindness; gracious courtesy
恩禮有加(ㄣ ㄌㄧˇ ㄧㄡˇ ㄐㄧㄚ)
(said of persons in high position) to shower someone with favors and courtesy
恩格爾(ㄣ ㄍㄜˊ ㄦˇ)
Friedrich Engels, 1820-1895, German socialist
恩公(ㄣ ㄍㄨㄥ)
a benefactor
恩科(ㄣ ㄎㄜ)
civil service examinations held on auspicious occasions of the nation such as an imperial wedding, coronation, etc. (as distinct from regular civil service examinations which were held between fixed intervals)
恩化(ㄣ ㄏㄨㄚˋ)
to reform, influence, or convert (people) by benevolence
恩惠(ㄣ ㄏㄨㄟˋ)
a kind act; kindness; charity; bounty
恩給(ㄣ ㄐㄧˇ)
a pension
恩舊(ㄣ ㄐㄧㄡˋ)
the friends bound by ties lasting through generations
恩將仇報(ㄣ ㄐㄧㄤ ㄔㄡˊ ㄅㄠˋ)
to return evil for good; ungrateful; to return kindness with hatred; to requite kindness with enmity
恩眷(ㄣ ㄐㄩㄢˋ)
imperial favor
恩情(ㄣ ㄑㄧㄥˊ)
loving-kindness; devotion (between friends, teacher and student, husband and wife, etc.); kindness and affection: 父母的恩情說不完。We can never say enough about our parents' devotion for us.
恩幸(ㄣ ㄒㄧㄥˋ)
imperial favor
恩詔(ㄣ ㄓㄠˋ)
an edict proclaiming an imperial act of grace
恩准(ㄣ ㄓㄨㄣˇ)
to grant graciously
恩仇分明(ㄣ ㄔㄡˊ ㄈㄣ ㄇㄧㄥˊ)
to make a clear distinction between kindnesses and wrongs done by others
恩寵(ㄣ ㄔㄨㄥˇ)
the emperor's affection or favor
恩師(ㄣ ㄕ)
a teacher to whom one is greatly indebted; one's beloved or respected teacher
恩赦(ㄣ ㄕㄜˋ)
gracious pardon; amnesty
恩深義重(ㄣ ㄕㄣ ㄧˋ ㄓㄨㄥˋ)
The spiritual debt is deep and great.
恩賞(ㄣ ㄕㄤˇ)
the emperor's reward
恩人(ㄣ ㄖㄣˊ) or 恩主(ㄣ ㄓㄨˇ)
a benefactor; a benefactress

恩榮(ㄣ ㄖㄨㄥˊ)
honor granted by the emperor
恩榮宴(ㄣ ㄖㄨㄥˊ ㄧㄢˋ)
an imperial banquet in honor of those who have lately passed the Imperial Examination
恩澤(ㄣ ㄗㄜˊ)
the pervading benevolence (of the ruler)
恩賜(ㄣ ㄙˋ)
①a gift of grace from the emperor ②to bestow (favors)
恩愛(ㄣ ㄞˋ)
(said of a married couple) mutual affection; loving; love between husband and wife
恩愛夫妻(ㄣ ㄞˋ ㄈㄨ ㄑㄧ)
loving husband and wife; a devoted couple; an affectionate couple
恩義(ㄣ ㄧˋ)
spiritual debt; gratitude
恩廕(ㄣ ㄧㄣˋ)
the conferment of an official rank on a minister's son as a special favor
恩威並用(ㄣ ㄨㄟ ㄅㄧㄥˋ ㄩㄥˋ)
to make proper use of both kindness and sternness in dealing with subordinates, subjugated people, etc.; to apply the carrot and stick judiciously
恩遇(ㄣ ㄩˋ)
①to treat someone with grace or kindness ②special recognition of the ruler or the superior
恩怨(ㄣ ㄩㄢˋ)
①gratitude and grudges ②resentment; grievance: 我不計較個人恩怨。I don't allow myself to be swayed by personal resentment.

【恧】 1574
ㄋㄩˋ niuh nǜ
ashamed
恧縮(ㄋㄩˋ ㄙㄨㄛ)
to recoil on account of shame

【息】 1575
ㄒㄧˊ shyi xí
1. a breath
2. news; tidings
3. to stop; to end: 風止雨息。The wind has ceased and the rain stopped.
4. interest (on money): 我們請求無息貸款。We asked for an interest-free loan.
5. a son
6. to rest: 我們按時作息。We work and rest according to the timetable.
息謗(ㄒㄧˊ ㄅㄤˋ)
to silence slanders
息兵(ㄒㄧˊ ㄅㄧㄥ)or 息戰(ㄒㄧˊ ㄓㄢˋ)
to stop fighting; to end hostilities
息婦 or 媳婦(ㄒㄧˊ ㄈㄨˋ)
①a daughter-in-law ②wife
息燈 or 熄燈(ㄒㄧˊ ㄉㄥ)
to put out the light; to turn off the light
息念頭(ㄒㄧˊ ㄋㄧㄢˋ ·ㄊㄡ)
to give up the idea
息怒(ㄒㄧˊ ㄋㄨˋ)
to let one's anger cool off: 請息怒。Please let your anger cool off. 或 Please calm your anger.
息干戈(ㄒㄧˊ ㄍㄢ ㄍㄜ)
to end hostilities; to stop fighting: 兩國互息干戈。Two nations ended hostilities.
息款(ㄒㄧˊ ㄎㄨㄢˇ)or 息金(ㄒㄧˊ ㄐㄧㄣ) or 息錢(ㄒㄧˊ ㄑㄧㄢˊ)
interest (on money)
息火 or 熄火(ㄒㄧˊ ㄏㄨㄛˇ)
to put out a fire
息跡(ㄒㄧˊ ㄐㄧ)or 息影(ㄒㄧˊ ㄧㄥˇ)
to live in retirement
息交絕遊(ㄒㄧˊ ㄐㄧㄠ ㄐㄩㄝˊ ㄧㄡˊ)
to break off intercourse with the world; to go into seclusion
息肩(ㄒㄧˊ ㄐㄧㄢ)
to put down one's burden; to be relieved of a responsibility
息息相關(ㄒㄧˊ ㄒㄧˊ ㄒㄧㄤ ㄍㄨㄢ)
related as closely as each breath is to the next; to be closely bound up
息心(ㄒㄧˊ ㄒㄧㄣ)
to set one's heart at rest
息燭 or 熄燭(ㄒㄧˊ ㄓㄨˊ)
to blow out the candle
息事(ㄒㄧˊ ㄕˋ)
to settle a matter
息事寧人(ㄒㄧˊ ㄕˋ ㄋㄧㄥˊ ㄖㄣˊ)
to settle disputes and bring about peace: 我們應息事寧人。We should settle our disputes and bring about peace among us.
息災延命(ㄒㄧˊ ㄗㄞ ㄧㄢˊ ㄇㄧㄥˋ)
to end disasters and prolong lives
息訟(ㄒㄧˊ ㄙㄨㄥˋ)
to terminate a lawsuit
息業(ㄒㄧˊ ㄧㄝˋ)
to stop one's trade or business

【恭】 1576
ㄍㄨㄥ gong gōng
respectful; reverent; deferential: 他對年齡較大的人總是恭敬。He is always respectful to older people.
恭奉(ㄍㄨㄥ ㄈㄥˋ)
to accept with respect
恭讀(ㄍㄨㄥ ㄉㄨˊ)
to read respectfully
恭賀(ㄍㄨㄥ ㄏㄜˋ)
I, or we, congratulate you upon; to congratulate; congratulation: 請接受我的恭賀。Please accept my congratulations.
恭賀新禧(ㄍㄨㄥ ㄏㄜˋ ㄒㄧㄣ ㄒㄧ)
Best wishes for a Happy New Year. 或 Happy New Year.
恭候(ㄍㄨㄥ ㄏㄡˋ)
to await respectfully
恭謹(ㄍㄨㄥ ㄐㄧㄣˇ)
respectfully serious
恭敬(ㄍㄨㄥ ㄐㄧㄥˋ)or 恭恭敬敬 (ㄍㄨㄥ ㄍㄨㄥ ㄐㄧㄥˋ ㄐㄧㄥˋ)
respectful; reverent; deferential (also used adverbially): 我們恭恭敬敬地向老師學習。We learned respectfully from our teachers.
恭敬不如從命(ㄍㄨㄥ ㄐㄧㄥˋ ㄅㄨˋ ㄖㄨˊ ㄘㄨㄥˊ ㄇㄧㄥˋ)
Obedience is a better way of showing respect than outward reverence.
恭謙(ㄍㄨㄥ ㄑㄧㄢ)
respect and modesty
恭請(ㄍㄨㄥ ㄑㄧㄥˇ)
to invite respectfully; to invite with respect
恭喜(ㄍㄨㄥ ㄒㄧˇ)
①Congratulations! ②to work: 你在那裡恭喜? Where are you

〔心部〕

〔心部〕

working?
恭喜發財(ㄍㄨㄥ ㄒㄧˇ ㄈㄚ ㄘㄞˊ)
(a familiar Lunar New Year's greeting) Congratulations and be prosperous.
恭祝(ㄍㄨㄥ ㄓㄨˋ)
I, or we, congratulate you upon
恭順(ㄍㄨㄥ ㄕㄨㄣˋ)
obedient; docile; submissive; allegiance
恭謁(ㄍㄨㄥ ㄧㄝˋ)
to pay a call with respect
恭迎(ㄍㄨㄥ ㄧㄥˊ)
to welcome respectfully
恭維 or 恭惟(ㄍㄨㄥ ㄨㄟˊ)
to pay compliments; to praise; to flatter: 他們非常恭維他。They paid him a high compliment.

【恥】 1577
(耻) ㄔˇ chyy chǐ
shame; disgrace; humiliation; to feel ashamed: 他恥爲人師。He is ashamed to be called a teacher.
恥骨(ㄔˇ ㄍㄨˇ)
(anatomy) the pubic bone; a pubis
恥笑(ㄔˇ ㄒㄧㄠˋ)
to laugh at; to ridicule; to sneer at; to mock; to scoff at
恥辱(ㄔˇ ㄖㄨˇ)
shame; disgrace; humiliation
恥與爲伍(ㄔˇ ㄩˇ ㄨㄟˊ ㄨˇ)
to feel ashamed to be in (their, his) company

【恉】 1578
ㄓˇ jyy zhǐ
same as 旨—purport; meaning; intention

七畫

【悃】 1579
ㄎㄨㄣˇ koen kǔn
honest; sincere
悃愊無華(ㄎㄨㄣˇ ㄅㄧˋ ㄨˊ ㄏㄨㄚˊ)
honest and simple
悃款(ㄎㄨㄣˇ ㄎㄨㄢˇ)
① single-minded ② sincere
悃誠(ㄎㄨㄣˇ ㄔㄥˊ)
sincere

【悁】 1580
1. ㄐㄩㄢˋ jiuann juàn
impatient; irritable
悁急(ㄐㄩㄢˋ ㄐㄧˊ)
impatient; irritable; anxious; fretful; restless

【悁】 1580
2. ㄐㄩㄢ jiuan juān
indignant; angry
悁忿(ㄐㄩㄢ ㄈㄣˋ)
angry; enraged; indignant
悁悁(ㄐㄩㄢ ㄐㄩㄢ)
① sad; unhappy; worried; fretting ② angry; irritable

【悄】 1581
ㄑㄧㄠˇ cheau qiǎo
quiet
悄悄地(ㄑㄧㄠˇ ㄑㄧㄠˇ ·ㄉㄜ)
stealthily; secretly; in a clandestine way; quietly: 我悄悄地走過去。I walked over quietly.
悄聲(ㄑㄧㄠˇ ㄕㄥ)
quietly; in a low voice
悄然(ㄑㄧㄠˇ ㄖㄢˊ)
① quietly: 他悄然離去。He left quietly. ② sorrowfully: 她悄然淚下。She shed tears sorrowfully.
悄語(ㄑㄧㄠˇ ㄩˇ)
to talk in a low voice; to speak softly; to whisper

【悅】 1582
ㄩㄝˋ yueh yuè
to delight; to gratify; to please; contented; pleased; gratified; happy; happily; glad; gladly: 他取悅於人。He tried to please others.
悅目(ㄩㄝˋ ㄇㄨˋ)
pleasant to the eye; having a pleasant appearance
悅服(ㄩㄝˋ ㄈㄨˊ)
to concede or submit willingly
悅口(ㄩㄝˋ ㄎㄡˇ)
tasty; savory; palatable
悅心(ㄩㄝˋ ㄒㄧㄣ)
to gladden; to cheer
悅人(ㄩㄝˋ ㄖㄣˊ)
pleasant; pleasing; delightful
悅澤(ㄩㄝˋ ㄗㄜˊ)
pleasantly bright; gorgeous
悅從(ㄩㄝˋ ㄘㄨㄥˊ)
to follow or submit willingly
悅色(ㄩㄝˋ ㄙㄜˋ)
a happy look or expression
悅耳(ㄩㄝˋ ㄦˇ)
pleasant to the ear; musical: 她的歌聲悅耳。Her singing is pleasant.
悅意(ㄩㄝˋ ㄧˋ)
① pleasantness; agreeableness ② an expression of happiness
悅豫(ㄩㄝˋ ㄩˋ)
delighted; pleased; happy

【悌】 1583
ㄊㄧˋ tih tì
to show brotherly love; love and respect for one's elder brother
悌睦(ㄊㄧˋ ㄇㄨˋ)
to live at peace as brothers
悌友(ㄊㄧˋ ㄧㄡˇ)
to be kind to friends; to show brotherly love for friends

【悔】 1584
ㄏㄨㄟˇ hoei huǐ
to regret; to repent; remorse
悔不當初(ㄏㄨㄟˇ ㄅㄨˋ ㄉㄤ ㄔㄨ)
to regret a previous mistake
悔改(ㄏㄨㄟˇ ㄍㄞˇ)
to repent of (a sin); to be repentant of; to repent and mend one's ways
悔過(ㄏㄨㄟˇ ㄍㄨㄛˋ)
to show penitence; to be penitent; to be repentant: 他悔過自新。He repented and turned over a new leaf.
悔過書(ㄏㄨㄟˇ ㄍㄨㄛˋ ㄕㄨ)
a written statement of repentance pledging not to commit the same offense again (a form of punishment)
悔恨(ㄏㄨㄟˇ ㄏㄣˋ)
to feel remorse for; to regret; remorse
悔禍(ㄏㄨㄟˇ ㄏㄨㄛˋ)
to wish the disaster would not be repeated
悔氣(ㄏㄨㄟˇ ㄑㄧˋ)
bad luck
悔心(ㄏㄨㄟˇ ㄒㄧㄣ)
penitence
悔之已晚(ㄏㄨㄟˇ ㄓ ㄧˇ ㄨㄢˇ)
It is too late to repent or regret.
悔之晚矣(ㄏㄨㄟˇ ㄓ ㄨㄢˇ ㄧˇ)
It will be too late to regret. (often used in warning or

dissuading somebody from doing something)
悔罪(ㄏㄨㄟˇ ㄗㄨㄟˋ)
to repent of a sin; to show repentance; to show penitence
悔尤(ㄏㄨㄟˇ ㄧㄡˊ)
a cause for self-reproach
悔悟(ㄏㄨㄟˇ ㄨˋ)
to awake from sin; to repent: 他悔悟他的罪過。He repented of his sin.

【悒】 1585 ㄧˋ yih yì
troubled in the mind; unhappy
悒悶(ㄧˋ ㄇㄣˋ)
depressed; low-spirited
悒憤(ㄧˋ ㄈㄣˋ)
unhappy with anger; to resent
悒悒(ㄧˋ ㄧˋ)
sad; grieved; worried; depressed; unhappy: 他悒悒不樂。He felt depressed.
悒快(ㄧˋ ㄧㄤˋ)
sad; grieved; unhappy; dejected; depressed
悒鬱(ㄧˋ ㄩˋ)
melancholy; disconsolate; unhappy

【悍】 1586 ㄏㄢˋ hann hàn
1. violent; fierce; cruel
2. brave; audacious: 他短小精悍。He is short but brave.
3. stubborn
悍婦(ㄏㄢˋ ㄈㄨˋ)
a shrew; a virago; a termagant
悍戾(ㄏㄢˋ ㄌㄧˋ)
cruel; atrocious
悍梗(ㄏㄢˋ ㄍㄥˇ)
stubbornly defiant; recalcitrant
悍將(ㄏㄢˋ ㄐㄧㄤˋ)
① a brave general ② a recalcitrant general
悍妻(ㄏㄢˋ ㄑㄧ)
a shrewish wife
悍戇(ㄏㄢˋ ㄓㄨㄤˋ)
fierce and simple-minded
悍室(ㄏㄢˋ ㄕˋ)
a shrewish wife
悍然(ㄏㄢˋ ㄖㄢˊ)
outrageously; rudely; unreasonably
悍然不顧(ㄏㄢˋ ㄖㄢˊ ㄅㄨˋ ㄍㄨˋ)
to ignore (advice) stubbornly
悍藥(ㄏㄢˋ ㄧㄠˋ)
a violent medicine; a drastic remedy

【悚】 1587 ㄙㄨㄥˇ soong sǒng
fearful; terrified; frightened
悚惕(ㄙㄨㄥˇ ㄊㄧˋ)
fearful
悚慄(ㄙㄨㄥˇ ㄌㄧˋ)or 悚惶(ㄙㄨㄥˇ ㄏㄨㄤˊ)or 悚懼(ㄙㄨㄥˇ ㄐㄩˋ)
to tremble with fear; frightened; terrified
悚然(ㄙㄨㄥˇ ㄖㄢˊ)
in terror; terror-stricken: 毛骨悚然 to be in terror with one's hair standing on end

【悛】 1588 ㄑㄩㄢ chiuan quān
to repent; to reform: 他怙惡不悛。He was incorrigible and refused to repent.
悛改(ㄑㄩㄢ ㄍㄞˇ)
to reform oneself; to repent of one's sin
悛懌(ㄑㄩㄢ ㄧˋ)
to reform oneself; to repent of one's sin

【悖】 1589 ㄅㄟˋ bey bèi
to go against; to go counter to; to revolt against; contrary to
悖叛(ㄅㄟˋ ㄆㄢˋ)
to revolt; to rebel
悖謾(ㄅㄟˋ ㄇㄢˋ)
arrogantly impolite; disrespectful; to show irreverence
悖謬(ㄅㄟˋ ㄇㄧㄡˋ)
absurd; irrational; unreasonable; preposterous
悖德(ㄅㄟˋ ㄉㄜˊ)
to be immoral
悖逆(ㄅㄟˋ ㄋㄧˋ)
to revolt; to rebel: 他悖逆不道。He revolted against established values.
悖理(ㄅㄟˋ ㄌㄧˇ)
absurd; unreasonable; irrational; contrary to reason
悖禮(ㄅㄟˋ ㄌㄧˇ)
uncivil; impolite; contrary to etiquette: 他的行爲悖禮。His behavior was uncivil.
悖戾(ㄅㄟˋ ㄌㄧˋ)
to deviate from accepted rules or standards; to be perverse
悖亂(ㄅㄟˋ ㄌㄨㄢˋ)
revolt; rebellion; sedition
悖棄(ㄅㄟˋ ㄑㄧˋ)
to turn away from something in revolt
悖入悖出(ㄅㄟˋ ㄖㄨˋ ㄅㄟˋ ㄔㄨ)
Things ill-gotten are ill-spent. 或 Evil begets evil.

【悟】 1590 ㄨˋ wuh wù
to become aware of; to realize; to awake to; to comprehend
悟道(ㄨˋ ㄉㄠˋ)
(Buddhism) to awake to Truth
悟空(ㄨˋ ㄎㄨㄥ)
①(Buddhism) to awake to the nihility of life ② name of a fictitious monkey with supernatural powers
悟性(ㄨˋ ㄒㄧㄥˋ)
the capacity for understanding; understanding; the power of understanding; the power of insight
悟禪(ㄨˋ ㄔㄢˊ)
to come to understand the principle of Zen (禪)

【悝】 1591 1. ㄌㄧˇ lii lǐ
sad; grieved; worried

【悝】 1591 2. ㄎㄨㄟ kuei kuī
to ridicule

【悠】 1592 ㄧㄡ iou yōu
1. far; long; vast; extensive
2. sad; pensive; meditative
3. gentle; slow; soft
4. to swing
悠邈(ㄧㄡ ㄇㄧㄠˇ)
far or distant (in space or time)
悠緬(ㄧㄡ ㄇㄧㄢˇ)
far or distant (in space or time)
悠忽(ㄧㄡ ㄏㄨ)
to idle away the time; lazy and idle
悠久(ㄧㄡ ㄐㄧㄡˇ)or 悠長(ㄧㄡ ㄔㄤˊ)
long in time
悠閒(ㄧㄡ ㄒㄧㄢˊ)

〔心部〕

leisurely; unrestrained; unhurried: 他悠閒地工作。He worked leisurely.

悠著(ㄧㄡ ·ㄓㄜ)
①to refrain from excesses ②(dialect) to take things easy

悠然(ㄧㄡ ㄖㄢˊ)
unhurriedly; in a leisurely manner; naturally

悠哉悠哉(ㄧㄡ ㄗㄞ ㄧㄡ ㄗㄞ)
①anxiously ②free from restraint; carefree

悠悠(ㄧㄡ ㄧㄡ)
①leisurely; unhurried; slow: 他悠悠自得。He was leisurely and content. ②far or vast (in space or time) ③meditative; pensive; sad ④long; distant; remote

悠悠蕩蕩(ㄧㄡ ㄧㄡ ㄉㄤˋ ㄉㄤˋ)
drifting gently

悠悠忽忽(ㄧㄡ ㄧㄡ ㄏㄨ ㄏㄨ)
①spending time idly ②to be in a trance

悠悠蒼天(ㄧㄡ ㄧㄡ ㄘㄤ ㄊㄧㄢ)
O thou vast and azure Heaven!

悠揚(ㄧㄡ ㄧㄤˊ)
①flowing gently sometimes high, sometimes low (as sound); melodious ②extending far (as scenery)

悠颺(ㄧㄡ ㄧㄤˊ)
(said of wind) rising gently

悠遠(ㄧㄡ ㄩㄢˇ)
distant; far (in time or space): 他聆聽那些悠遠的往事。He listened to those events of the distant past.

【悉】 1593
ㄒㄧ shi xī

1. to know
2. all; whole; total; entire: 此悉爲我所有。This was all taken by me.

悉力(ㄒㄧ ㄌㄧˋ)
with all one's strength; with might and main

悉皆(ㄒㄧ ㄐㄧㄝ)
altogether; entirely; without exception

悉心(ㄒㄧ ㄒㄧㄣ)
with one's whole heart; with concentrated effort; to take the utmost care

悉數(ㄒㄧ ㄕㄨˋ)
all; the entire sum (of money): 我們將悉數奉還。We will return all that has been borrowed.

悉索敝賦(ㄒㄧ ㄙㄨㄛˇ ㄅㄧˋ ㄈㄨˋ)
to mobilize all military forces for a punitive war

【患】 1594
ㄏㄨㄢˋ huann huàn

1. suffering; adversity; disaster; peril: 我們應當防患於未然。We ought to take preventive measures of disaster.
2. trouble; worry: 何患之有。There is no need to worry.
3. to be troubled by; to be worried about

患病(ㄏㄨㄢˋ ㄅㄧㄥˋ)
to get sick; to fall ill

患部(ㄏㄨㄢˋ ㄅㄨˋ)
(said of wounds or skin diseases) the infected part

患得患失(ㄏㄨㄢˋ ㄉㄜˊ ㄏㄨㄢˋ ㄕ)
to worry about worldly gain and loss: 他患得患失的。He was swayed by considerations of gain and loss.

患難(ㄏㄨㄢˋ ㄋㄢˋ)
suffering; distress; adversity; trouble: 他是一個可以共患難的人。He is a man who can be trusted in times of trouble.

患難之交(ㄏㄨㄢˋ ㄋㄢˋ ㄓ ㄐㄧㄠ)
the friendship cemented in adversity

患寡患貧(ㄏㄨㄢˋ ㄍㄨㄚˇ ㄏㄨㄢˋ ㄆㄧㄣˊ)
to be concerned over the nation's dwindling population and increasing poverty

患苦(ㄏㄨㄢˋ ㄎㄨˇ)
distress; adversity; suffering

患者(ㄏㄨㄢˋ ㄓㄜˇ)
a patient (at a hospital): 那醫生有許多位患者。The doctor has a large number of patients.

患處(ㄏㄨㄢˋ ㄔㄨˋ)
the infected part; the wounded part

【悤】 1595
(匆) ㄘㄨㄥ tsong cōng

excited; hurried; agitated

悤忙(ㄘㄨㄥ ㄇㄤˊ)or 悤卒(ㄘㄨㄥ ㄘㄨˋ) or 悤遽(ㄘㄨㄥ ㄐㄩˋ)
hurried; hasty; flurried

悤悤(ㄘㄨㄥ ㄘㄨㄥ)
①hurriedly; hastily; in haste ②obviously; apparently

【您】 1596
ㄋㄧㄣˊ nin nín

a deferential form of "你"

八畫

【悱】 1597
ㄈㄟˇ feei fěi

1. inarticulate; unable to give vent to one's emotion; unable to explain one's self; to be at a loss for words
2. sorrowful

悱憤(ㄈㄟˇ ㄈㄣˋ)
sadness kept to oneself; peeved; infuriated; vexed

悱惻(ㄈㄟˇ ㄘㄜˋ)
affected by sorrow; sad at heart; sorrowful 參看「纏綿悱惻」

【悵】 1598
ㄔㄤˋ chanq chàng

disappointed; frustrated; dissatisfied; sorry

悵恨(ㄔㄤˋ ㄏㄣˋ)
bitterness from disappointment

悵悵(ㄔㄤˋ ㄔㄤˋ)
unhappy because of disappointment

悵然(ㄔㄤˋ ㄖㄢˊ)
disappointed: 我悵然若失。I felt disappointed.

悵惋(ㄔㄤˋ ㄨㄢˋ)
to regret (the failure of a hope) sorrowfully

悵惘(ㄔㄤˋ ㄨㄤˇ)
depressed; in low spirits; distracted

悵望(ㄔㄤˋ ㄨㄤˋ)
to long pensively or wistfully

【悸】 1599
ㄐㄧˋ jih jì

1. palpitation of the heart
2. fear: 我心有餘悸。I had a lingering fear.

悸動(ㄐㄧˋ ㄉㄨㄥˋ)
to palpitate with terror

【悻】 1600
ㄒㄧㄥˋ shinq xìng

angry; indignant; enraged

悻悻然(ㄒㄧㄥˋ ㄒㄧㄥˋ ㄖㄢˊ)or 悻悻(ㄒㄧㄥˋ ㄒㄧㄥˋ)
angry; enraged; huffish; anger; huff: 他悻悻而去。He

went away angry.
悻直(ㄒㄧㄥˋ ㄓˊ)
blunt; bluff; brusque

【悴】 1601
ㄘㄨㄟˋ tsuey cuì
1. haggard; worn-out; tired out: 他滿面憔悴之容。He has a haggard face.
2. worried; sad
悴薄(ㄘㄨㄟˋ ㄅㄛˊ)
weakened; enfeebled; impoverished
悴賤(ㄘㄨㄟˋ ㄐㄧㄢˋ)
needy and lowly
悴族(ㄘㄨㄟˋ ㄗㄨˊ)
a family or clan that has seen better days

【悼】 1602
ㄉㄠˋ daw dào
to mourn (for or over); to lament; to regret; to grieve: 我們哀悼死者。We mourned for the dead.
悼痛(ㄉㄠˋ ㄊㄨㄥˋ)
to mourn in anguish
悼念(ㄉㄠˋ ㄋㄧㄢˋ)
to mourn; to grieve over
悼歌(ㄉㄠˋ ㄍㄜ)
a funeral hymn; a dirge
悼惜(ㄉㄠˋ ㄒㄧˊ)
to deplore or lament (one's death): 他悼惜摯友。He deplored the loss of his dear friend.
悼傷(ㄉㄠˋ ㄕㄤ)
to remember (the deceased) with sorrow
悼詞(ㄉㄠˋ ㄘˊ)
a memorial speech
悼亡(ㄉㄠˋ ㄨㄤˊ)
to be bereaved of one's wife

【悾】 1603
ㄎㄨㄥ kong kōng
sincere; candid
悾悾(ㄎㄨㄥ ㄎㄨㄥ)
①sincere; candid ②simple-minded

【悽】 1604
ㄑㄧ chi qī
1. grieved; sorrowful; afflicted
2. tragic; pathetic; pitiful; grievous
悽涼(ㄑㄧ ㄌㄧㄤˊ)
dreary; desolate: 戰爭帶來滿目悽涼。The war brought desolation all round.
悽苦(ㄑㄧ ㄎㄨˇ)
suffering tragically
悽惶(ㄑㄧ ㄏㄨㄤˊ)
①sorrowful and apprehensive ②in a hurry
悽戚(ㄑㄧ ㄑㄧ)
tragically unhappy
悽悽(ㄑㄧ ㄑㄧ)
pathetic; pitiful; grievous
悽悽惶惶(ㄑㄧ ㄑㄧ ㄏㄨㄤˊ ㄏㄨㄤˊ)
hurriedly; hastily
悽切(ㄑㄧ ㄑㄧㄝˋ)
pathetic; pitiful; saddening; grievous
悽楚(ㄑㄧ ㄔㄨˇ)
pathetic; pitiful; saddening; grievous: 那是一種悽楚的景象。It is a pitiful sight.
悽愴(ㄑㄧ ㄔㄨㄤˋ)
①pathetic; pitiful; saddening ②cold; dreary; desolate
悽傷(ㄑㄧ ㄕㄤ)
sad; sorrowful
悽然(ㄑㄧ ㄖㄢˊ)
sad; sorrowful: 他悽然淚下。He shed tears in sadness.
悽惻(ㄑㄧ ㄘㄜˋ)
sad; sorrowful
悽慘(ㄑㄧ ㄘㄢˇ)
tragic; heartrending
悽婉(ㄑㄧ ㄨㄢˇ)
pathetic or pitiful (said especially of sounds); plaintive
悽惘(ㄑㄧ ㄨㄤˇ)
sad and dejected

【惆】 1605
ㄔㄡˊ chour chóu
1. regretful; rueful; disconsolate; melancholy
2. disappointed; frustrated
惆悵(ㄔㄡˊ ㄔㄤˋ)
rueful; regretful; to be saddened
惆然(ㄔㄡˊ ㄖㄢˊ)
regretful; wistful; disappointed; downcast; heavy-hearted
惆惋(ㄔㄡˊ ㄨㄢˇ)
regretful; wistful

【情】 1606
ㄑㄧㄥˊ chyng qíng
1. feelings; emotions; sentiments: 天理人情 law of nature and feelings of a man
2. fact; detail; situation; condition
3. love; affection; passion: 父母親情深似海。Parents' affection for their children is as deep as the ocean.
4. nature; reason
情報(ㄑㄧㄥˊ ㄅㄠˋ)
information; intelligence reports: 這陌生人刺探情報。The stranger pried for information.
情報司(ㄑㄧㄥˊ ㄅㄠˋ ㄙ)
Department of Information, Ministry of Foreign Affairs
情報網(ㄑㄧㄥˊ ㄅㄠˋ ㄨㄤˇ)
an intelligent network
情報員(ㄑㄧㄥˊ ㄅㄠˋ ㄩㄢˊ)
a secret agent; an intelligence agent
情弊(ㄑㄧㄥˊ ㄅㄧˋ)
dishonest practices; irregularities
情不自禁(ㄑㄧㄥˊ ㄅㄨˋ ㄗˋ ㄐㄧㄣˋ)
to be seized with an impulse; to feel an irresistible impulse
情貌(ㄑㄧㄥˊ ㄇㄠˋ)
internal and external reverence or loyalty
情面(ㄑㄧㄥˊ ·ㄇㄧㄢ)
①friendship; regard for others ②face (self-respect, good name, reputation); feelings; sensibilities: 請給我留情面。Please spare my feelings.
情面難卻(ㄑㄧㄥˊ ㄇㄧㄢˋ ㄋㄢˊ ㄑㄩㄝˋ)
hard to refuse or decline for the sake of friendship or face
情分(ㄑㄧㄥˊ ·ㄈㄣ)
①friendship ②good intentions; good will; solicitude
情夫(ㄑㄧㄥˊ ㄈㄨ)
the paramour of a married woman
情婦(ㄑㄧㄥˊ ㄈㄨˋ)
a mistress; the other woman
情竇初開(ㄑㄧㄥˊ ㄉㄡˋ ㄔㄨ ㄎㄞ)
(said of girls) to reach puberty; the time when a girl becomes sex-conscious; first awaking of love
情敵(ㄑㄧㄥˊ ㄉㄧˊ)
a rival in a love affair
情調(ㄑㄧㄥˊ ㄉㄧㄠˋ)
①a mood; taste; an atmosphere ②(psychology) affective feeling tone
情態(ㄑㄧㄥˊ ㄊㄞˋ)
①a situation; a condition ②

〔心部〕

demeanor; spirit; a mood

情投意合(ㄑㄧㄥˊ ㄊㄡˊ ㄧˋ ㄏㄜˊ)
to be congenial; to agree in tastes and temperament: 我們倆情投意合。We both found each other congenial.

情天恨海(ㄑㄧㄥˊ ㄊㄧㄢ ㄏㄣˋ ㄏㄞˇ)
the deep love or regret between men and women

情同手足(ㄑㄧㄥˊ ㄊㄨㄥˊ ㄕㄡˇ ㄗㄨˊ)
to be attached to each other like brothers; with brotherly love for each other

情濃(ㄑㄧㄥˊ ㄋㄨㄥˊ)
strong affection

情累(ㄑㄧㄥˊ ㄌㄟˋ)
the burden of love

情郎(ㄑㄧㄥˊ ㄌㄤˊ)
a girl's lover

情理(ㄑㄧㄥˊ ㄌㄧˇ)
reason; common sense

情理難容(ㄑㄧㄥˊ ㄌㄧˇ ㄋㄢˊ ㄖㄨㄥˊ)
contrary to reason or common sense; preposterous; absurd

情侶(ㄑㄧㄥˊ ㄌㄩˇ)
lovers

情歌(ㄑㄧㄥˊ ㄍㄜ)
a love song

情甘(ㄑㄧㄥˊ ㄍㄢ)
willing; voluntary: 我情甘等待。I am willing to wait.

情感(ㄑㄧㄥˊ ㄍㄢˇ)
emotions; feelings; frame of mind; affection; sentiments; friendship between two persons

情感衝動(ㄑㄧㄥˊ ㄍㄢˇ ㄔㄨㄥ ㄉㄨㄥˋ)
an emotional impulse; an outburst of emotion

情況(ㄑㄧㄥˊ ㄎㄨㄤˋ)
① a situation; state of affairs; circumstances: 他們的情況如何? How do matters stand with them? ② military situation

情況不明(ㄑㄧㄥˊ ㄎㄨㄤˋ ㄅㄨˋ ㄇㄧㄥˊ)
the situation unknown

情海(ㄑㄧㄥˊ ㄏㄞˇ)
deep love; the vast, tumultuous sea of love between men and women

情好(ㄑㄧㄥˊ ㄏㄠˇ)
an attachment; friendship

情話(ㄑㄧㄥˊ ㄏㄨㄚˋ)
① whispers of love; sweet nothings; lovers' prattle ② intimate talks or words; hearty talks

情話綿綿(ㄑㄧㄥˊ ㄏㄨㄚˋ ㄇㄧㄢˊ ㄇㄧㄢˊ)
occupied with endless whispers of love

情火(ㄑㄧㄥˊ ㄏㄨㄛˇ) or 情焰(ㄑㄧㄥˊ ㄧㄢˋ)
the flames of love

情懷(ㄑㄧㄥˊ ㄏㄨㄞˊ)
a mood; feelings

情急智生(ㄑㄧㄥˊ ㄐㄧˊ ㄓˋ ㄕㄥ)
Good ideas come in time of crisis.

情節(ㄑㄧㄥˊ ㄐㄧㄝˊ)
① a plot (of a play, novel, etc.) ② details (of an affair or event); circumstances

情景(ㄑㄧㄥˊ ㄐㄧㄥˇ)
a scene; a sight: 有一場感人的情景。There is a moving sight.

情境(ㄑㄧㄥˊ ㄐㄧㄥˋ)
circumstances; a situation

情趣(ㄑㄧㄥˊ ㄑㄩˋ)
① quiet appeal to the emotions; sentiment; interest: 這首詩寫得很有情趣。This poem is full of interest. ② temperament and interest: 他們情趣相投。They are temperamentally compatible.

情見乎辭(ㄑㄧㄥˊ ㄒㄧㄢˋ ㄏㄨ ㄘˊ)
The feeling or sincerity is alive in the words.

情性(ㄑㄧㄥˊ ㄒㄧㄥˋ)
temperament — the real nature or character

情形(ㄑㄧㄥˊ ·ㄒㄧㄥ)
a situation; circumstances; state of affairs; conditions

情緒(ㄑㄧㄥˊ ㄒㄩˋ)
① emotions; feelings; spirits; a mood: 他們情緒低落。They are in low spirits. ② depression; the sulks

情知(ㄑㄧㄥˊ ㄓ)
to know for sure (said of something going on secretly or before it takes place)

情致(ㄑㄧㄥˊ ㄓˋ)
effect on the emotions; appeal

情致纏綿(ㄑㄧㄥˊ ㄓˋ ㄔㄢˊ ㄇㄧㄢˊ)
(said of a poem, story, etc.) to have a delicate lasting effect on the emotions

情至義盡(ㄑㄧㄥˊ ㄓˋ ㄧˋ ㄐㄧㄣˋ)
with entire sincerity

情狀(ㄑㄧㄥˊ ㄓㄨㄤˋ)
a situation: 他發現自己處於危險的情狀。He found himself in a dangerous situation.

情場(ㄑㄧㄥˊ ㄔㄤˊ)
the arena of love

情場老手(ㄑㄧㄥˊ ㄔㄤˊ ㄌㄠˇ ㄕㄡˇ)
a skirt chaser

情場失意(ㄑㄧㄥˊ ㄔㄤˊ ㄕ ㄧˋ)
frustrated in love; jilted: 他最近在情場失意。Recently he was frustrated in love.

情腸(ㄑㄧㄥˊ ㄔㄤˊ)
a loving heart

情長紙短(ㄑㄧㄥˊ ㄔㄤˊ ㄓˇ ㄉㄨㄢˇ)
(a cliché in correspondence) The paper is too short to contain what I have to say.

情詩(ㄑㄧㄥˊ ㄕ)
amatory poems; love poems

情實(ㄑㄧㄥˊ ㄕˊ)
① facts of an affair or case ② The crime has been confirmed.

情史(ㄑㄧㄥˊ ㄕˇ)
a love story

情事(ㄑㄧㄥˊ ㄕˋ)
the facts

情勢(ㄑㄧㄥˊ ㄕˋ)
a situation; the state of affairs: 情勢危急。This situation is dangerous.

情殺(ㄑㄧㄥˊ ㄕㄚ)
murder caused by love entanglement

情深似海(ㄑㄧㄥˊ ㄕㄣ ㄙˋ ㄏㄞˇ)
(usually said of parental love) Love is as deep as the sea.

情商(ㄑㄧㄥˊ ㄕㄤ)
to ask for a favor as a friend

情書(ㄑㄧㄥˊ ㄕㄨ)
a love letter; a billet-doux

情人(ㄑㄧㄥˊ ㄖㄣˊ)
a paramour, sweetheart or lover

情人節(ㄑㄧㄥˊ ㄖㄣˊ ㄐㄧㄝˊ)
St. Valentine's Day

情人眼裏出西施(ㄑㄧㄥˊ ㄖㄣˊ ㄧㄢˇ ㄌㄧˇ ㄔㄨ ㄒㄧ ㄕ)
Love makes one blind to all imperfections. 或 Beauty is in the eye of the beholder.

情操(ㄑㄧㄥˊ ㄘㄠ)
①sentiment (connoting high-brow and complicated sentiment) ②noble thoughts and feelings
情絲不斷(ㄑㄧㄥˊ ㄙ ㄅㄨˋ ㄉㄨㄢˋ)
The ties of love remain unbroken.
情死(ㄑㄧㄥˊ ㄙˇ)
martyrdom to love; to commit suicide for the sake of love
情愫 or 情素(ㄑㄧㄥˊ ㄙㄨˋ)
innermost feelings
情愛(ㄑㄧㄥˊ ㄞˋ)
love (between men and women)
情誼 or 情義(ㄑㄧㄥˊ ㄧˋ)
friendly relations; friendship; amity
情意(ㄑㄧㄥˊ ㄧˋ)
feeling; sentiment; affection
情意綿綿(ㄑㄧㄥˊ ㄧˋ ㄇㄧㄢˊ ㄇㄧㄢˊ)
long-lasting love expressing itself in a subdued but sweet form
情由(ㄑㄧㄥˊ ㄧㄡˊ)
reason; cause
情有可原(ㄑㄧㄥˊ ㄧㄡˇ ㄎㄜˇ ㄩㄢˊ)
pardonable; excusable; under extenuating circumstances
情有所鍾(ㄑㄧㄥˊ ㄧㄡˇ ㄙㄨㄛˇ ㄓㄨㄥ)
to have already had a lover in one's heart
情文並茂(ㄑㄧㄥˊ ㄨㄣˊ ㄅㄧㄥˋ ㄇㄠˋ)
(said of a composition) rich in feelings and eloquent in expression
情網(ㄑㄧㄥˊ ㄨㄤˇ)
the cobweb of love; the snare of love: 她陷入情網。She fell into the cobweb of love.
情慾 or 情欲(ㄑㄧㄥˊ ㄩˋ)
passion; sensual or carnal desire; lust; eroticism
情願(ㄑㄧㄥˊ ㄩㄢˋ)
①to be willing ②would rather

【惇】 1607 ㄉㄨㄣ duen dūn
sincere; kind; generous
惇惇(ㄉㄨㄣ ㄉㄨㄣ)
kind; generous; sincere
惇惠(ㄉㄨㄣ ㄏㄨㄟˋ)
benign; benignant
惇誨(ㄉㄨㄣ ㄏㄨㄟˋ)
to teach kindly

【惋】 1608 ㄨㄢˋ wann wàn
1. to regret
2. to be alarmed
惋歎(ㄨㄢˋ ㄊㄢˋ)
to regret; to deplore
惋慟(ㄨㄢˋ ㄊㄨㄥˋ)
to deplore; to lament
惋惜(ㄨㄢˋ ㄒㄧˊ)
to feel sorry for (a loss, etc.); to regret
惋傷(ㄨㄢˋ ㄕㄤ)
to regret sorrowfully
惋愕(ㄨㄢˋ ㄜˋ)
to be alarmed; to be astonished

【惕】 1609 ㄊㄧˋ tih tì
1. cautious; careful; prudent; watchout; to be on the alert
2. afraid
3. anxious
惕惕(ㄊㄧˋ ㄊㄧˋ)
apprehensive; fearful
惕厲(ㄊㄧˋ ㄌㄧˋ)
to exercise caution and discipline
惕息(ㄊㄧˋ ㄒㄧˊ)
to pant from fear or anxiety

【惓】 1610 ㄑㄩㄢˊ chyuan quán
sincere; candid
惓惓(ㄑㄩㄢˊ ㄑㄩㄢˊ)
sincere; candid
惓惓於懷(ㄑㄩㄢˊ ㄑㄩㄢˊ ㄩˊ ㄏㄨㄞˊ)
to remember something or somebody at heart constantly

【惘】 1611 ㄨㄤˇ woang wǎng
dejected; frustrated; discouraged
惘然(ㄨㄤˇ ㄖㄢˊ)
in a daze; at a loss; stupefied

【惚】 1612 ㄏㄨ hu hū
absent-minded; entranced

【惙】 1613 ㄔㄨㄛˋ chuoh chuò
melancholy; doleful; mournful; gloomy
惙怛(ㄔㄨㄛˋ ㄉㄚˊ)
mournful; doleful; rueful
惙惙(ㄔㄨㄛˋ ㄔㄨㄛˋ)
melancholy; gloomy

【惛】 1614 ㄏㄨㄣ huen hūn
1. confused
2. senile
惛憊(ㄏㄨㄣ ㄅㄟˋ)
muddleheaded
惛眊(ㄏㄨㄣ ㄇㄠˋ)
senile; senility
惛懵(ㄏㄨㄣ ㄇㄥˊ)
dim-eyed
惛惛(ㄏㄨㄣ ㄏㄨㄣ)
①confused in mind ②absorbed; carried away; entranced

【惝】 1615 ㄊㄤˇ taang tǎng (又讀 ㄔㄤˇ chaang chǎng)
dispirited; disheartened; discouraged
惝怳(ㄊㄤˇ ㄏㄨㄤˇ)
dispirited; dejected; disheartened; despondent; discouraged
惝怳無定(ㄊㄤˇ ㄏㄨㄤˇ ㄨˊ ㄉㄧㄥˋ)
dispirited and distracted
惝然(ㄊㄤˇ ㄖㄢˊ)
crestfallen; dispirited; discouraged; disheartened; dejected

【惦】 1616 ㄉㄧㄢˋ diann diàn
to remember; to bear in mind; to miss; to be concerned about; to keep thinking about
惦念(ㄉㄧㄢˋ ㄋㄧㄢˋ)
to worry about; to feel or regret the absence or loss of; to miss (a friend or beloved one): 一切均好請勿惦念。Everything is fine. Don't worry about me.
惦懷(ㄉㄧㄢˋ ㄏㄨㄞˊ)
to remember nostalgically; to be nostalgic about
惦記(ㄉㄧㄢˋ ㄐㄧˋ) or 惦掛(ㄉㄧㄢˋ ㄍㄨㄚˋ)
to keep thinking about; to feel concern about someone far away

【惜】 1617 ㄒㄧˊ shyi xí
1. to pity; to sympathize; to regret; to feel sorry for somebody: 我爲他感到惋惜。I felt sorry for him.
2. to value highly; to have a

〔心部〕

high opinion of (something); to show love or fondness for
3. to spare; to grudge

惜別(ㄒㄧˊ ㄅㄧㄝˊ)
reluctant to part company; to say good-bye

惜墨如金(ㄒㄧˊ ㄇㄛˋ ㄖㄨˊ ㄐㄧㄣ)
(said of a calligrapher or a painter) to grudge ink as if it were gold—reluctant to write or paint

惜福(ㄒㄧˊ ㄈㄨˊ)
to refrain from leading an excessively comfortable life; to make sparing use of one's wealth

惜老憐貧(ㄒㄧˊ ㄌㄠˇ ㄌㄧㄢˊ ㄆㄧㄣˊ)
to pity the aged and the poor

惜力(ㄒㄧˊ ㄌㄧˋ)
to contribute one's labor very reluctantly; to be sparing of one's energy

惜乎(ㄒㄧˊ ㄏㄨ)
It is a pity that.... 或 What a pity!

惜指失掌(ㄒㄧˊ ㄓˇ ㄕ ㄓㄤˇ)
(literally) to lose the hand in trying to save the fingers—to be penny-wise and pound-foolish

惜字紙(ㄒㄧˊ ㄗˋ ㄓˇ)
to treat written or printed paper with respect

惜寸陰(ㄒㄧˊ ㄘㄨㄣˋ ㄧㄣ) or 惜分陰(ㄒㄧˊ ㄈㄣ ㄧㄣ)
to be careful not to waste even a moment; to harness one's time

惜玉憐香(ㄒㄧˊ ㄩˋ ㄌㄧㄢˊ ㄒㄧㄤ)
to be tender to the fair sex; to be tender toward pretty girls

【惟】 1618
(唯) ㄨㄟˊ wei wéi

1. to think; to meditate
2. only; alone
3. but; however

惟妙惟肖(ㄨㄟˊ ㄇㄧㄠˋ ㄨㄟˊ ㄒㄧㄠˋ)
so skillfully imitated as to be indistinguishable from the original

惟命是聽(ㄨㄟˊ ㄇㄧㄥˋ ㄕˋ ㄊㄧㄥ) or 惟命是從(ㄨㄟˊ ㄇㄧㄥˋ ㄕˋ ㄘㄨㄥˊ)
always do as one is told; to be slavishly obedient

惟獨(ㄨㄟˊ ㄉㄨˊ)
only; alone: 別人都回家了，惟獨我還在工作。Only I kept on working when all the others had gone home.

惟利是圖(ㄨㄟˊ ㄌㄧˋ ㄕˋ ㄊㄨˊ)
interested only in material gain

惟恐(ㄨㄟˊ ㄎㄨㄥˇ)
for fear that; lest; afraid of nothing but; The only fear is that...: 他努力讀書惟恐落後。He strives to study for fear that he should fall behind.

惟恐天下不亂(ㄨㄟˊ ㄎㄨㄥˇ ㄊㄧㄢ ㄒㄧㄚˋ ㄅㄨˋ ㄌㄨㄢˋ)
to be displeased to see the prospect of peace in the world; anxious to see trouble

惟心(ㄨㄟˊ ㄒㄧㄣ)
spiritualistic

惟心論(ㄨㄟˊ ㄒㄧㄣ ㄌㄨㄣˋ)
spiritualism; idealism

惟一(ㄨㄟˊ ㄧ)
the only one; the only thing of its kind

惟有(ㄨㄟˊ ㄧㄡˇ)
only

惟物(ㄨㄟˊ ㄨˋ)
materialistic

惟物論(ㄨㄟˊ ㄨˋ ㄌㄨㄣˋ)
materialism

惟物史觀(ㄨㄟˊ ㄨˋ ㄕˇ ㄍㄨㄢ)
materialistic view of history; historical materialism

惟我獨尊(ㄨㄟˊ ㄨㄛˇ ㄉㄨˊ ㄗㄨㄣ)
(literally) No one is noble but me.—egoistic; arrogant

惟我論(ㄨㄟˊ ㄨㄛˇ ㄌㄨㄣˋ)
solipsism; egoism

【悶】 1619
1. ㄇㄣˋ menn mèn

melancholy; depressed; bored; in low spirits

悶悶不樂(ㄇㄣˋ ˙ㄇㄣ ㄅㄨˋ ㄌㄜˋ)
sulky; unhappy; depressed: 他悶悶不樂。He felt depressed and unhappy.

悶得慌(ㄇㄣˋ ˙ㄉㄜ ˙ㄏㄨㄤ) or 悶得很(ㄇㄣˋ ˙ㄉㄜ ㄏㄣˇ)
bored; to feel restless (because there is nothing interesting to occupy one's time)

悶雷(ㄇㄣˋ ㄌㄟˊ)
① a thunderbolt; a thunderclap ② an unpleasant surprise; shock

悶葫蘆(ㄇㄣˋ ㄏㄨˊ ˙ㄌㄨ)
something difficult to understand; a riddle or puzzle

悶酒(ㄇㄣˋ ㄐㄧㄡˇ)
alcoholic drinks for drowning one's cares, sorrows, etc. (usually said of drinking alone)

悶氣(ㄇㄣˋ ㄑㄧˋ)
the sulks; pent-up sorrow or resentment: 他在生悶氣。He was sulky. 或 He was in the sulks.

悶香(ㄇㄣˋ ㄒㄧㄤ)
incense with a choking smell

悶沈沈(ㄇㄣˋ ㄔㄣˊ ㄔㄣˊ)
depressed; heavy-hearted; melancholy

悶躁(ㄇㄣˋ ㄗㄠˋ)
melancholy and irritable

【悶】 1619
2. ㄇㄣ mhen mēn

1. (said of weather, rooms, etc.) oppressive or suffocating; stuffy
2. (said of a sound) muffled
3. to shut oneself or somebody indoors
4. to cover the tea pot for a while when one makes tea with boiling water

悶得慌(ㄇㄣ ˙ㄉㄜ ˙ㄏㄨㄤ) or 悶得很(ㄇㄣ ˙ㄉㄜ ㄏㄣˇ)
very stuffy

悶頭兒(ㄇㄣ ㄊㄡˊㄦ)
(to do something) diligently but quietly; silently

悶氣(ㄇㄣ ㄑㄧˋ)
oppressive air (due to poor ventilation)

悶着(ㄇㄣ ˙ㄓㄜ)
① to refrain from speaking out ② stewing or being stewed

悶聲不響(ㄇㄣ ㄕㄥ ㄅㄨˋ ㄒㄧㄤˇ)
to keep one's mouth shut; to remain quiet; to remain silent

悶熱(ㄇㄣ ㄖㄜˋ)
sticky; oppressive; humid; sultry; sweltering

悶死(ㄇㄣ ㄙˇ)
to die of suffocation; to die of asphyxiation; to be suffocated

【怒】1620 ㄋㄧˋ nih nì
pensive; worried

【惑】1621 ㄏㄨㄛˋ huoh huò
1. to confuse; to perplex; to delude; to beguile; to mislead; to misguide; to puzzle: 他大惑不解。He was greatly puzzled.
2. to doubt; to suspect

惑溺(ㄏㄨㄛˋ ㄋㄧˋ)
to indulge in

惑弄(ㄏㄨㄛˋ ㄋㄨㄥˋ)
to delude; to befool; to beguile

惑亂(ㄏㄨㄛˋ ㄌㄨㄢˋ)
to delude or confuse

惑志(ㄏㄨㄛˋ ㄓˋ)
suspicion; doubt

惑衆(ㄏㄨㄛˋ ㄓㄨㄥˋ)
to mislead; to delude or confuse the people: 他們造謠惑衆。They fabricated rumors to mislead people.

惑術(ㄏㄨㄛˋ ㄕㄨˋ)
deceitful tricks; guile; ruses

【悲】1622 ㄅㄟ bei bēi
1. sad; sorrowful; mournful; woeful; rueful; doleful
2. to lament; to deplore; to mourn; to pity; to sympathize

悲悲切切(ㄅㄟ ㄅㄟ ㄑㄧㄝˋ ㄑㄧㄝˋ)
full of grief

悲不自勝(ㄅㄟ ㄅㄨˋ ㄗˋ ㄕㄥ)
to abandon oneself to grief; unable to restrain one's grief; to be overcome with grief

悲憫(ㄅㄟ ㄇㄧㄣˇ)
to pity; to have sympathy for; to have compassion for

悲鳴(ㄅㄟ ㄇㄧㄥˊ)
to cry mournfully; to bemoan

悲憤(ㄅㄟ ㄈㄣˋ)
①to lament and resent (an injustice) ②grief and indignation: 他悲憤塡膺。He is filled with grief and indignation.

悲風(ㄅㄟ ㄈㄥ)
the baleful sound of wind; a moaning wind

悲夫(ㄅㄟ ㄈㄨˊ)
Alas! 或What a pity! 或How sad it is!

悲悼(ㄅㄟ ㄉㄠˋ)
to mourn (for or over)

悲調(ㄅㄟ ㄉㄧㄠˋ)
a mournful tune

悲歎(ㄅㄟ ㄊㄢˋ)
to lament; to deplore; to sigh over

悲啼(ㄅㄟ ㄊㄧˊ)
to cry mournfully

悲天憫人(ㄅㄟ ㄊㄧㄢ ㄇㄧㄣˇ ㄖㄣˊ)
to be concerned over the destiny of mankind; the feeling for the universal compassion and cosmic pity; to bemoan the state of the universe and to pity the fate of mankind

悲痛(ㄅㄟ ㄊㄨㄥˋ)
grieved; deep sorrow; painfully sad: 我們感到深切的悲痛。We are deeply grieved.

悲慟(ㄅㄟ ㄊㄨㄥˋ)
to weep loudly for sorrow

悲憐(ㄅㄟ ㄌㄧㄢˊ)
to take pity on (a person)

悲涼(ㄅㄟ ㄌㄧㄤˊ)
sad and dreary; somber; dismal

悲歌(ㄅㄟ ㄍㄜ)
a song of lament; an elegy

悲觀(ㄅㄟ ㄍㄨㄢ)
pessimistic

悲觀主義(ㄅㄟ ㄍㄨㄢ ㄓㄨˇ ㄧˋ)
pessimism

悲懷(ㄅㄟ ㄏㄨㄞˊ)
sad feelings; a sorrowful mood

悲歡離合(ㄅㄟ ㄏㄨㄢ ㄌㄧˊ ㄏㄜˊ)
the sorrow of parting and the joy of union in life; weal and woe, parting and meeting—the vicissitudes of life

悲笳(ㄅㄟ ㄐㄧㄚ)
a mournful tune from a military flageolet

悲劇(ㄅㄟ ㄐㄩˋ)
a tragedy: 哈姆雷特是一齣悲劇。*Hamlet* is a tragedy.

悲戚(ㄅㄟ ㄑㄧ)
rueful; doleful; mournful

悲泣(ㄅㄟ ㄑㄧˋ)
to sob, or weep, sorrowfully

悲切(ㄅㄟ ㄑㄧㄝˋ)
mournful

悲秋(ㄅㄟ ㄑㄧㄡ)
to feel sad with the coming of autumn

悲喜交集(ㄅㄟ ㄒㄧˇ ㄐㄧㄠ ㄐㄧˊ)
intermingling of sorrow and joy; mixed feelings of grief and joy

悲喜劇(ㄅㄟ ㄒㄧˇ ㄐㄩˋ)
a tragicomedy

悲壯(ㄅㄟ ㄓㄨㄤˋ)
tragically heroic; heroically tragic

悲愁(ㄅㄟ ㄔㄡˊ)
melancholy; sad; grievous; pensive

悲傷(ㄅㄟ ㄕㄤ)
sad; sorrowful

悲聲(ㄅㄟ ㄕㄥ)
plaintive cries; sad voice

悲哉(ㄅㄟ ㄗㄞ)
Alas! 或 How sad it is! 或 How lamentable! 或 What a pity!

悲惻(ㄅㄟ ㄘㄜˋ)
sad; sorrowful; woeful

悲慘(ㄅㄟ ㄘㄢˇ)
tragic; tragical; pathetic; miserable

悲從中來(ㄅㄟ ㄘㄨㄥˊ ㄓㄨㄥ ㄌㄞˊ)
to feel sadness welling up

悲酸(ㄅㄟ ㄙㄨㄢ)
sad and bitter

悲哀(ㄅㄟ ㄞ)
mournful; woeful

【惠】1623 ㄏㄨㄟˋ huey huì
1. to benefit; benefit; to profit; profit; to favor; a favor
2. kind; benevolent; gracious
3. gentle and yielding

惠風(ㄏㄨㄟˋ ㄈㄥ)
a gentle wind; a breeze

惠特曼(ㄏㄨㄟˋ ㄊㄜˋ ㄇㄢˋ)
Walt Whitman, 1819-1892, American poet

惠臨(ㄏㄨㄟˋ ㄌㄧㄣˊ)
(honorific expression) to favor with one's presence: 敬請惠臨。Your presence is requested.

惠顧(ㄏㄨㄟˋ ㄍㄨˋ)
①to be my customer; to patronize (my business establishment) ②your kindness, favor or patronage

惠鑒(ㄏㄨㄟˋ ㄐㄧㄢˋ)
for your gracious perusal (a conventional phrase placed after the salutation in a letter)

惠恤(ㄏㄨㄟˋ ㄒㄩˋ)
to give relief to (the poor or victims of a disaster)

惠政(ㄏㄨㄟˋ ㄓㄥˋ)
benevolent rule or administration

惠示(ㄏㄨㄟˋ ㄕˋ)
(honorific expression) to condescend to show or instruct

惠聲(ㄏㄨㄟˋ ㄕㄥ)
the prestige of humanitarian rule

惠然肯來(ㄏㄨㄟˋ ㄖㄢˊ ㄎㄣˇ ㄌㄞˊ)
to be so kind as to come; to honor me with your presence

惠澤(ㄏㄨㄟˋ ㄗㄜˊ)
kindness; benevolence; favor

惠存(ㄏㄨㄟˋ ㄘㄨㄣˊ)
to be so kind as to keep (my gift); to condescend to accept; to keep as a souvenir: 敬請惠存。Please keep (this photograph, book, etc. as a souvenir).

惠賜(ㄏㄨㄟˋ ㄙˋ)
to be kind enough to give (me something); to bestow graciously

惠而不費(ㄏㄨㄟˋ ㄦˊ ㄅㄨˋ ㄈㄟˋ)
kindness that costs one nothing; a kind act which does not cost much

惠音(ㄏㄨㄟˋ ㄧㄣ)
your esteemed letter; your kind letter

【惡】 1624
1. ㄜˋ eh è

1. bad; evil; wicked; vice; wickedness: 他無惡不作。He stops at nothing in doing evil.
2. fierce; ferocious

惡霸(ㄜˋ ㄅㄚˋ)
a powerful bully; a local bandit leader; a local tyrant; a local despot

惡報(ㄜˋ ㄅㄠˋ)
deserved punishment for evil done; retribution; evil recompense

惡病(ㄜˋ ㄅㄧㄥˋ)
①a malignant disease; disgusting disease ②a euphemism for venereal diseases

惡癖(ㄜˋ ㄆㄧˇ)
a bad habit

惡罵(ㄜˋ ㄇㄚˋ)
abuse; vilification; vicious abuse

惡魔(ㄜˋ ㄇㄛˊ) or 惡鬼(ㄜˋ ㄍㄨㄟˇ)
an evil spirit; a demon; a fiend; the devil; Satan

惡眉惡眼(ㄜˋ ㄇㄟˊ ㄜˋ ㄧㄢˇ)
a fierce or ferocious look

惡夢(ㄜˋ ㄇㄥˋ)
a nightmare: 我昨夜做了個惡夢。I had a nightmare last night.

惡名(ㄜˋ ㄇㄧㄥˊ)
a bad reputation; ill fame; a bad name; infamy; notoriety

惡模惡樣(ㄜˋ ㄇㄨˊ ㄜˋ ㄧㄤˋ)
a fierce or ferocious appearance

惡木(ㄜˋ ㄇㄨˋ)
wood of inferior quality

惡風(ㄜˋ ㄈㄥ)
a bad custom; evil ways

惡德(ㄜˋ ㄉㄜˊ)
vice; corruption; immorality

惡毒(ㄜˋ ㄉㄨˊ)
venomous; malicious; vicious: 他們惡毒地攻擊我們。They viciously attack us.

惡徒(ㄜˋ ㄊㄨˊ)
a scoundrel; a rascal; a villain; a rogue; a knave

惡逆(ㄜˋ ㄋㄧˋ)
(old criminal law) a crime as beating or killing one's parents

惡念(ㄜˋ ㄋㄧㄢˋ)
evil intentions

惡辣(ㄜˋ ㄌㄚˋ)
villainous; knavish

惡例(ㄜˋ ㄌㄧˋ)
a bad precedent; a bad example

惡劣(ㄜˋ ㄌㄧㄝˋ)
①of very poor quality, very inferior ②rude; revolting; distasteful ③vile; satanic

惡劣環境(ㄜˋ ㄌㄧㄝˋ ㄏㄨㄢˊ ㄐㄧㄥˋ)
adverse circumstances

惡劣氣候(ㄜˋ ㄌㄧㄝˋ ㄑㄧˋ ㄏㄡˋ)
vile weather

惡劣行徑(ㄜˋ ㄌㄧㄝˋ ㄒㄧㄥˊ ㄐㄧㄥˋ)
disgusting conduct

惡劣手段(ㄜˋ ㄌㄧㄝˋ ㄕㄡˇ ㄉㄨㄢˋ)
mean tricks

惡劣作風(ㄜˋ ㄌㄧㄝˋ ㄗㄨㄛˋ ㄈㄥ)
abominable behavior

惡感(ㄜˋ ㄍㄢˇ)
unfriendly feeling; ill will; enmity; dislike; hate; malice

惡果(ㄜˋ ㄍㄨㄛˇ)
undesirable consequences; disastrous effect; evil results of evildoing

惡鬼(ㄜˋ ㄍㄨㄟˇ)
a bad spirit; a fiend; a demon

惡貫滿盈(ㄜˋ ㄍㄨㄢˋ ㄇㄢˇ ㄧㄥˊ)
to reach the limit of crimes (tolerated by Heaven); to come to the end of a criminal career

惡棍(ㄜˋ ㄍㄨㄣˋ)
a villain; a rascal; a scoundrel; a hoodlum; a hooligan; a ruffian

惡客(ㄜˋ ㄎㄜˋ)
an ill-meaning guest

惡口(ㄜˋ ㄎㄡˇ)
an abusive tongue; bad language: 他惡口傷人。He uses bad language to insult people.

惡耗(ㄜˋ ㄏㄠˋ)
news of death or disaster

惡漢(ㄜˋ ㄏㄢˋ)
a rascal; a scoundrel; a villain; a knave; a ruffian

惡狠狠(ㄜˋ ㄏㄣˇ ㄏㄣˇ)
ferocious

惡化(ㄜˋ ㄏㄨㄚˋ)
to get worse; to deteriorate; to degenerate; to worsen; to be aggravated; to go from bad to worse: 雙方關係不斷惡化。The relations between the both sides have steadily deteriorated.

惡疾(ㄜˋ ㄐㄧˊ)
a malignant disease

惡計(ㄜˋ ㄐㄧˋ)
a vicious scheme; a cruel design; an evil plan

惡氣(ㄜˋ ㄑㄧˋ)
noxious air; offensive gas

惡錢(ㄜˋ ㄑㄧㄢˊ)
counterfeit coin

惡犬(ㄜˋ ㄑㄩㄢˇ)
a fierce dog

惡習(ㄜˋ ㄒㄧˊ)
a bad habit: 他染上惡習。He contracted a bad habit.

惡戲(ㄜˋ ㄒㄧˋ)

a practical joke; mischief
惡相(ㄜˋ ㄒㄧㄤˋ)
a fierce or ferocious look
惡行(ㄜˋ ㄒㄧㄥˋ)
an evil deed; a wicked act; a misdeed; evildoing; evil conduct; vice
惡性(ㄜˋ ㄒㄧㄥˋ)
malignant; virulent; vicious; unsound
惡性補習(ㄜˋ ㄒㄧㄥˋ ㄅㄨˇ ㄒㄧˊ)
unhealthy cram sessions (at schools)
惡性倒閉(ㄜˋ ㄒㄧㄥˋ ㄉㄠˇ ㄅㄧˋ)
fraudulent insolvency; fraudulent closedown
惡性循環(ㄜˋ ㄒㄧㄥˋ ㄒㄩㄣˊ ㄏㄨㄢˊ)
a vicious circle
惡性腫瘤(ㄜˋ ㄒㄧㄥˋ ㄓㄨㄥˇ ㄌㄧㄡˊ)
a malignant tumor
惡戰(ㄜˋ ㄓㄢˋ)
hard fighting
惡濁(ㄜˋ ㄓㄨㄛˊ)
foul; filthy; dirty
惡臭(ㄜˋ ㄔㄡˋ)
an offensive odor; a bad smell; an unpleasant smell; a stink; a stench
惡瘡(ㄜˋ ㄔㄨㄤ)
a foul ulcer
惡食(ㄜˋ ㄕˊ)
bad food; poor food; coarse food
惡勢力(ㄜˋ ㄕˋ ㄌㄧˋ)
vicious power; pressure groups; evil force
惡事傳千里(ㄜˋ ㄕˋ ㄔㄨㄢˊ ㄑㄧㄢ ㄌㄧˇ)
An evil deed will become known a thousand miles off. 或 Scandal travels fast.
惡少(ㄜˋ ㄕㄠˋ)
a young hoodlum; a hooligan; a juvenile delinquent
惡訕(ㄜˋ ㄕㄢˋ)
to slander; to libel
惡聲(ㄜˋ ㄕㄥ)
① abusive language ② an inauspicious sound
惡人(ㄜˋ ㄖㄣˊ)
a bad man; a wicked person; a scoundrel; a villain
惡作劇(ㄜˋ ㄗㄨㄛˋ ㄐㄩˋ)
mischief; a practical joke
惡俗(ㄜˋ ㄙㄨˊ)
a bad custom or practice
惡歲(ㄜˋ ㄙㄨㄟˋ)
a bad year; a year of poor harvest
惡衣惡食(ㄜˋ ㄧ ㄜˋ ㄕˊ)
① to be clothed poorly and eat poorly ② poor clothing and poor food
惡意(ㄜˋ ㄧˋ)
① malicious; spiteful ② malice; evil intentions; sinister motives
惡有惡報(ㄜˋ ㄧㄡˇ ㄜˋ ㄅㄠˋ)
Evil will be recompensed with evil.
惡言(ㄜˋ ㄧㄢˊ)
abusing language; abusive language: 勿口出惡言。Don't use abusing language.
惡因(ㄜˋ ㄧㄣ)
the cause of evil or disaster
惡語(ㄜˋ ㄩˇ)
bad language; abusive language
惡語中傷(ㄜˋ ㄩˇ ㄓㄨㄥˋ ㄕㄤ)
viciously slander; to calumniate
惡運(ㄜˋ ㄩㄣˋ)
bad luck; ill luck

【惡】 1624
2. ㄜˇ ee ě
to disgust; to sicken; to scorn
惡心(ㄜˇ ·ㄒㄧㄣ)
① nauseated; disgusted: 我感到惡心。I felt nauseated. ② disgusting; disgust; sickening

【惡】 1624
3. ㄨˋ wuh wù
to hate; to detest; to dislike; to abhor; to loathe
惡嫌(ㄨˋ ㄒㄧㄢˊ)
to hate; to detest; to abhor; to loathe
惡惡(ㄨˋ ㄜˋ)
to hate evil

【惡】 1624
4. ㄨ u wū
1. how; where
2. O; oh; ah

九畫

【惰】 1625
ㄉㄨㄛˋ duoh duò
lazy; idle; indolent: 懶惰爲萬惡之源。Idleness is the parent of all vice.
惰民(ㄉㄨㄛˋ ㄇㄧㄣˊ)
a caste of people in Chekiang-Kiangsu area formerly barred from officialdom and believed to be descendants of prisoners under the Sung Dynasty
惰力(ㄉㄨㄛˋ ㄌㄧˋ)
inertia; momentum
惰懈(ㄉㄨㄛˋ ㄒㄧㄝˋ)
to be negligent or neglectful
惰性(ㄉㄨㄛˋ ㄒㄧㄥˋ)
inertia; sloth; laziness

【惱】 1626
ㄋㄠˇ nao nǎo
1. to anger; to exasperate; to annoy; to irritate; to vex; to trouble
2. angered; offended; vexed; annoyed
惱巴巴(ㄋㄠˇ ㄅㄚ ㄅㄚ)
angry; cross; annoyed
惱悶(ㄋㄠˇ ㄇㄣˋ)
troubled in the mind; grieved and sad
惱犯(ㄋㄠˇ ㄈㄢˋ)
to anger; to annoy; to enrage; to infuriate
惱忿忿地(ㄋㄠˇ ㄈㄣˋ ㄈㄣˋ ·ㄉㄜ)
indignantly; angrily
惱怒(ㄋㄠˇ ㄋㄨˋ)
① angry; indignant; irritated ② anger; indignation; rage
惱了(ㄋㄠˇ ·ㄌㄜ)
angered; enraged; infuriated; offended
惱亂(ㄋㄠˇ ㄌㄨㄢˋ)
to disturb to trouble
惱恨(ㄋㄠˇ ㄏㄣˋ)
to be angry at; to be offended by; to be vexed at; to resent
惱火(ㄋㄠˇ ㄏㄨㄛˇ)
to become irritated; annoyed; to see red
惱氣(ㄋㄠˇ ㄑㄧˋ)
anger; rage; indignation; irritation
惱羞成怒(ㄋㄠˇ ㄒㄧㄡ ㄔㄥˊ ㄋㄨˋ)
to be moved to anger by the feeling of shame; to fly into a rage from shame
惱心(ㄋㄠˇ ㄒㄧㄣ)
irritated state of mind
惱人(ㄋㄠˇ ㄖㄣˊ)
to disturb peace of mind; irritating
惱人春色(ㄋㄠˇ ㄖㄣˊ ㄔㄨㄣ ㄙㄜˋ)

suffering from love in spring

惱意(ㄋㄠˇ ㄧˋ)
the feeling of anger

【惴】 1627
ㄓㄨㄟˋ juey zhuì
worried; afraid; anxious; apprehensive

惴慄(ㄓㄨㄟˋ ㄌㄧˋ)
to tremble with fear; to shudder

惴恐(ㄓㄨㄟˋ ㄎㄨㄥˇ)
to fear; to dread

惴懼(ㄓㄨㄟˋ ㄐㄩˋ)
anxious and worried; in fear and trembling

惴惴(ㄓㄨㄟˋ ㄓㄨㄟˋ)
timorous; afraid; fearful; apprehensive; to feel uneasy or apprehensive

【惵】 1628
ㄉㄧㄝˊ dye dié
afraid; fearful; terrified

惵惵(ㄉㄧㄝˊ ㄉㄧㄝˊ)
terrified; fearful; timorous; afraid

惵息(ㄉㄧㄝˊ ㄒㄧˊ)
holding breath from fear

【惲】 1629
ㄩㄣˋ yunn yùn
1. to plan; to consider; to deliberate
2. a Chinese family name

惲謀(ㄩㄣˋ ㄇㄡˊ)
to scheme; to plan

惲議(ㄩㄣˋ ㄧˋ)
to discuss; to deliberate

【惶】 1630
ㄏㄨㄤˊ hwang huáng
1. afraid; fearful; apprehensive
2. anxious; uneasy
3. flurried; hurried

惶恐(ㄏㄨㄤˊ ㄎㄨㄥˇ)
apprehensive; fearful; afraid

惶汗(ㄏㄨㄤˊ ㄏㄢˋ)
to perspire from fear or apprehension

惶惑(ㄏㄨㄤˊ ㄏㄨㄛˋ)
anxious and perplexed; uneasy and confused; suspicious and fearful

惶惶(ㄏㄨㄤˊ ㄏㄨㄤˊ)
① anxious; uneasy; apprehensive; perturbed; in a state of anxiety ② hurried; hasty

惶遽(ㄏㄨㄤˊ ㄐㄩˋ)
to lose one's head; to lose self-possession; scared: 他的神色惶遽。He looked scared.

惶擾(ㄏㄨㄤˊ ㄖㄠˇ)
to agitate; to perturb

【愒】 1631
ㄎㄞˋ kay kài
to idle away (time)

愒時(ㄎㄞˋ ㄕˊ)
to idle away the time

愒日(ㄎㄞˋ ㄖˋ)
to idle away the days

【愐】 1632
ㄇㄧㄢˇ mean miǎn
1. to remember; to give thought to
2. shy

愐倎(ㄇㄧㄢˇ ·ㄊㄧㄢ)
bashful; shy; modest: 她有點愐倎。She is rather bashful.

愐懷(ㄇㄧㄢˇ ㄏㄨㄞˊ)
to think of; to remember

【愕】 1633
ㄜˋ eh è
startled; astonished; amazed

愕顧(ㄜˋ ㄍㄨˋ)
to look in amazement

愕視(ㄜˋ ㄕˋ)
to stare in amazement

愕然(ㄜˋ ㄖㄢˊ)
astonished; flabbergasted; dumbfounded; stunned: 他愕然四顧。He looked around in astonishment.

愕愕(ㄜˋ ㄜˋ)
startled; astonished; amazed; stunned; astounded

【愣】 1634
ㄌㄥˋ lenq lèng
1. dumbfounded; agape with horror; stupefied
2. reckless; irresponsible; rash; rude
3. outspoken

愣頭愣腦(ㄌㄥˋ ·ㄊㄡ ㄌㄥˋ ㄋㄠˇ)
① rash; reckless ② stupid-looking; stupid; in a stupor

愣頭磕腦(ㄌㄥˋ ·ㄊㄡ ㄎㄜ ㄋㄠˇ)
① stupid ② rash

愣小子(ㄌㄥˋ ㄒㄧㄠˇ ·ㄗ)
a little fool; a rash young fellow; a young hothead

愣住了(ㄌㄥˋ ㄓㄨˋ ·ㄌㄜ)
to become speechless or stunned because of astonishment, an unexpected question, etc.; to be taken aback

愣葱(ㄌㄥˋ ㄘㄨㄥ)
a rash fellow

【惸】 1635
ㄑㄩㄥˊ chyong qióng
1. worried; distressed
2. brotherless; friendless

惸獨(ㄑㄩㄥˊ ㄉㄨˊ)
brotherless and childless; helpless and lonely; friendless

惸嫠(ㄑㄩㄥˊ ㄌㄧˊ)
a friendless widow

惸惸(ㄑㄩㄥˊ ㄑㄩㄥˊ)
worried; distressed; anxious

【惺】 1636
1. ㄒㄧㄥ shing xīng
1. clever; intelligent; wise
2. wavering; indecisive

惺惺(ㄒㄧㄥ ㄒㄧㄥ)
① intelligent; clever ② wakeful; alert 參看「假惺惺」

惺惺惜惺惺(ㄒㄧㄥ ㄒㄧㄥ ㄒㄧˊ ㄒㄧㄥ ㄒㄧㄥ)
Clever people like clever people. 或 The wise people appreciate one another.

惺惺作態(ㄒㄧㄥ ㄒㄧㄥ ㄗㄨㄛˋ ㄊㄞˋ)
to be affected; to simulate (friendship, innocence, etc.)

惺忪(ㄒㄧㄥ ㄙㄨㄥ)
① wavering; indecisive ② (said of eyes) not yet fully open on waking up: 她睡眼惺忪。She has a drowsy look.

惺憁(ㄒㄧㄥ ㄙㄨㄥ)
① intelligent; wise ② a man of intelligence

【惺】 1636
2. ㄒㄧㄥˇ shiing xǐng
to become aware of; to awake from ignorance

惺悟(ㄒㄧㄥˇ ㄨˋ)
to awake to (the truth); to realize

【愀】 1637
ㄑㄧㄠˇ cheau qiǎo
1. anxious-looking
2. to show a sudden change of expression

愀愴(ㄑㄧㄠˇ ㄔㄨㄤˋ)
rueful; doleful; sad; sorrowful

愀然(ㄑㄧㄠˇ ㄖㄢˊ)
① showing a sudden change of expression; turning pale or red suddenly ② anxious; sorrowful

【惻】 1638 ㄘㄜˋ tseh cè
to feel anguish
惻怛(ㄘㄜˋ ㄉㄚˊ)
sad and worried
惻愴(ㄘㄜˋ ㄔㄨㄤˋ)
sad; mournful; grieved
惻然(ㄘㄜˋ ㄖㄢˊ)
sadly; sorrowfully
惻惻(ㄘㄜˋ ㄘㄜˋ)
in anguish; sad; sorrowful
惻隱之心(ㄘㄜˋ ㄧㄣˇ ㄓ ㄒㄧㄣ)
natural compassion; innate mercy; a sense of pity; the sense of mercy

【愎】 1639 ㄅㄧˋ bih bì
perverse; self-willed; obstinate; stubborn
愎諫(ㄅㄧˋ ㄐㄧㄢˋ)
deaf to remonstrances

【愉】 1640 ㄩˊ yu yú
happy; contented; pleased: 他面有不愉之色。He wore an unhappy expression.
愉樂(ㄩˊ ㄌㄜˋ)
pleasant and joyful
愉快(ㄩˊ ㄎㄨㄞˋ)
cheerful; happy; pleased; delighted: 她心情愉快。She was in a cheerful frame of mind.
愉色(ㄩˊ ㄙㄜˋ)
a pleased look; a cheerful expression
愉逸(ㄩˊ ㄧˋ)
happy and leisurely
愉悅(ㄩˊ ㄩㄝˋ)
joyful; glad; happy

【愔】 1641 ㄧㄣ in yīn
peaceful; composed; serene
愔愔(ㄧㄣ ㄧㄣ)
peaceful; composed; serene

【愊】 1642 ㄅㄧˋ bih bì
1. sincere; honest
2. melancholy; depressed

【愜】 1643 ㄑㄧㄝˋ chieh qiè
cheerful; satisfied; contented
愜當(ㄑㄧㄝˋ ㄉㄤˋ)
proper; appropriate: 這是愜當之論。This is a proper remark.
愜懷(ㄑㄧㄝˋ ㄏㄨㄞˊ)
satisfied; contented
愜情(ㄑㄧㄝˋ ㄑㄧㄥˊ)
satisfied; contented
愜心(ㄑㄧㄝˋ ㄒㄧㄣ)
satisfied; contented
愜意(ㄑㄧㄝˋ ㄧˋ)
satisfied; contented: 結果令人愜意。The result was satisfactory.

【想】 1644 ㄒㄧㄤˇ sheang xiǎng
1. to think; to consider; to suppose: 讓我想一想。Let me think it over.
2. to hope; to expect
3. to plan
4. to remember with longing; to miss
5. to want; would like to: 他也想試一試。He'd also like to have a try.
想必(ㄒㄧㄤˇ ㄅㄧˋ)or 想必是(ㄒㄧㄤˇ ㄅㄧˋ ㄕˋ)
presumably; probably; most likely: 這事想必他知道。He most probably knows this.
想不到(ㄒㄧㄤˇ ˙ㄅㄨ ㄉㄠˋ)
to one's surprise; unexpectedly: 那眞是想不到的事! That is something quite unexpected!
想不通(ㄒㄧㄤˇ ˙ㄅㄨ ㄊㄨㄥ)
can't figure it out; incomprehensible; beyond comprehension
想不開(ㄒㄧㄤˇ ˙ㄅㄨ ㄎㄞ)
unable to take a resigned attitude; to take some misfortune too seriously; to take things too hard: 你們太想不開。You take things too hard.
想不起來(ㄒㄧㄤˇ ˙ㄅㄨ ㄑㄧˇ ㄌㄞˊ)
unable to call to mind; can not remember
想法子(ㄒㄧㄤˇ ㄈㄚˊ ˙ㄗ)
to devise means; to think of a scheme
想法(ㄒㄧㄤˇ ㄈㄚˇ)
the way of looking at something; an idea; an opinion; a view: 這想法不錯。This is a good idea.
想得到(ㄒㄧㄤˇ ˙ㄉㄜ ㄉㄠˋ)
to think; to imagine; to expect
想得開(ㄒㄧㄤˇ ˙ㄉㄜ ㄎㄞ)
not to take to heart; to take philosophically; to try to look on the bright side of things
想得要命(ㄒㄧㄤˇ ˙ㄉㄜ ㄧㄠˋ ㄇㄧㄥˋ)
to want to do or get something very badly
想到(ㄒㄧㄤˇ ㄉㄠˋ)
to think of; to remember; to hit upon (an idea): 我忽然想到一件重要的事情。I suddenly think of something important.
想當然(ㄒㄧㄤˇ ㄉㄤ ㄖㄢˊ)
as may be taken for granted; presumably; to assume something as a matter of course
想頭(ㄒㄧㄤˇ ˙ㄊㄡ)
① a notion; thought; an idea: 他有個想頭。He's got an idea. ② expectation; hope: 沒什麼想頭了。There's no hope now. ③ thinking
想通(ㄒㄧㄤˇ ㄊㄨㄥ)
to straighten out one's thinking; to become convinced: 你要是仍無法想通,可以問問其他人。Ask the others if you're still not convinced.
想念(ㄒㄧㄤˇ ㄋㄧㄢˋ)
to give thought to (a person); to miss (something or someone): 我們都很想念你。We all miss you very much.
想來(ㄒㄧㄤˇ ㄌㄞˊ)
in my conjecture; in my guess; it may be assumed that; presumably; to suppose; to think of: 想來眞是後悔。When I come to think of it, I really feel sorry.
想來想去(ㄒㄧㄤˇ ㄌㄞˊ ㄒㄧㄤˇ ㄑㄩˋ)
to turn (a matter) over and over in one's mind; to ponder
想開了(ㄒㄧㄤˇ ㄎㄞ ˙ㄌㄜ)
to have succeeded in getting over a loss or misfortune; to stop worrying: 我們想開了。We stop worrying now.
想家(ㄒㄧㄤˇ ㄐㄧㄚ)
homesick; nostalgic
想見(ㄒㄧㄤˇ ㄐㄧㄢˋ)
to infer; to gather; to imagine; to visualize: 我想見其爲人。I imagine what he was

〔心部〕

like.
想起(ㄒㄧㄤˇ ㄑㄧˇ)
to think of; to remember; to occur
想想看(ㄒㄧㄤˇ ㄒㄧㄤˇ ㄎㄢˋ)
to think about it
想像(ㄒㄧㄤˇ ㄒㄧㄤˋ)
to imagine; to fancy: 她想像自己是詩人。She imagines herself to be a poet.
想像力(ㄒㄧㄤˇ ㄒㄧㄤˋ ㄌㄧˋ)
imagination; imaginative power or faculty: 他有很強的想像力。He has a very strong imagination.
想著(ㄒㄧㄤˇ ˙ㄓㄜ)
to keep in mind
想入非非(ㄒㄧㄤˇ ㄖㄨˋ ㄈㄟ ㄈㄟ)
to let one's imagination run wild; to indulge in wishful thinking; to build castles in the air
想死(ㄒㄧㄤˇ ㄙˇ)
① to long for death; to get tired of life ② to long very much for; dying for
想一想(ㄒㄧㄤˇ ˙ㄧ ˙ㄒㄧㄤ)
to pause to think
想要(ㄒㄧㄤˇ ㄧㄠˋ)
to want to; to feel like: 我想要回家。I want to go home.
想望(ㄒㄧㄤˇ ㄨㄤˋ)
① to hope; to expect; to desire; to long for ② to admire

【惹】 1645
ㄖㄜˇ ree rě

to provoke; to rouse; to induce; to attract; to cause; to bring upon oneself; to offend; to incur: 我可沒惹她呀! I did nothing to provoke her.
惹不起(ㄖㄜˇ ˙ㄅㄨ ㄑㄧˇ)
① not daring to provoke or offend ② too powerful or vicious to be provoked or offended
惹麻煩(ㄖㄜˇ ㄇㄚˊ ㄈㄢˊ)
to excite trouble; to invite trouble
惹得(ㄖㄜˇ ㄉㄜˊ)
to have provoked or aroused; to have been provoked or aroused
惹得起(ㄖㄜˇ ˙ㄉㄜ ㄑㄧˇ)
to dare to provoke
惹亂子(ㄖㄜˇ ㄌㄨㄢˋ ˙ㄗ)
to bring trouble
惹火燒身(ㄖㄜˇ ㄏㄨㄛˇ ㄕㄠ ㄕㄣ)
to bring trouble upon oneself; to ask for trouble
惹禍(ㄖㄜˇ ㄏㄨㄛˋ)
to bring disaster or misfortune; to stir up trouble; to bring calamity on oneself: 這都是他惹的禍。It was he who stirred up the trouble.
惹起(ㄖㄜˇ ㄑㄧˇ)
to incite; to provoke; to incur
惹氣(ㄖㄜˇ ㄑㄧˋ)
to provoke one to anger; to incur wrath
惹嫌(ㄖㄜˇ ㄒㄧㄢˊ)
to incur hatred; to provoke dislike
惹事(ㄖㄜˇ ㄕˋ)
to create trouble
惹是非(ㄖㄜˇ ㄕˋ ㄈㄟ)or 惹是生非(ㄖㄜˇ ㄕˋ ㄕㄥ ㄈㄟ)
to incur unnecessary trouble; to stir up ill will; to provoke a dispute; to stir up trouble
惹人討厭(ㄖㄜˇ ㄖㄣˊ ㄊㄠˇ ㄧㄢˋ)
to make a nuisance of oneself
惹人注目(ㄖㄜˇ ㄖㄣˊ ㄓㄨˋ ㄇㄨˋ)
to attract attention (particularly undesirable attention)
惹草拈花(ㄖㄜˇ ㄘㄠˇ ㄋㄧㄢˊ ㄏㄨㄚ)
(said of men) to have one love affair after another; to have promiscuous relations with women
惹厭(ㄖㄜˇ ㄧㄢˋ)
to incur dislike

【愁】 1646
ㄔㄡˊ chour chóu

1. sad; distressed; worried; unhappy; melancholy
2. depressing; saddening; gloomy
3. to worry about; to be anxious about
4. sorrow; woe

愁眉(ㄔㄡˊ ㄇㄟˊ)
knitted brows; a distressed look
愁眉不展(ㄔㄡˊ ㄇㄟˊ ㄅㄨˋ ㄓㄢˇ)
to wear a sad or distressed expression
愁眉苦臉(ㄔㄡˊ ㄇㄟˊ ㄎㄨˇ ㄌㄧㄢˇ)
a sad or worried look; a distressed expression
愁悶(ㄔㄡˊ ㄇㄣˋ)
unhappy; distressed; distressful; worried; to feel gloomy
愁歎(ㄔㄡˊ ㄊㄢˋ)
to give sighs of distress
愁苦(ㄔㄡˊ ㄎㄨˇ)
distress; misery
愁海(ㄔㄡˊ ㄏㄞˇ)
a very great amount of worries; a sea of worries
愁懷(ㄔㄡˊ ㄏㄨㄞˊ)
sad feelings; sadness
愁緒(ㄔㄡˊ ㄒㄩˋ)
a sad mood; a gloomy mood
愁吃愁穿(ㄔㄡˊ ㄔ ㄔㄡˊ ㄔㄨㄢ)
to have to worry about food and clothing; to suffer from poverty
愁腸(ㄔㄡˊ ㄔㄤˊ)
a tangled feeling of grief
愁腸百結(ㄔㄡˊ ㄔㄤˊ ㄅㄞˇ ㄐㄧㄝˊ)
It is as if the worries were tied in knots to one another.
愁腸寸斷(ㄔㄡˊ ㄔㄤˊ ㄘㄨㄣˋ ㄉㄨㄢˋ)
The sorrow is so deep that it seems to have cut the bowels to pieces.
愁城(ㄔㄡˊ ㄔㄥˊ)
the realm of sorrow
愁容滿面(ㄔㄡˊ ㄖㄨㄥˊ ㄇㄢˇ ㄇㄧㄢˋ)
to wear a sad look; to look distressed: 他愁容滿面。He looked distressed.
愁滋味(ㄔㄡˊ ㄗ ㄨㄟˋ)
the taste of sorrow: 少年不識愁滋味。The taste of sorrow was unknown to a youth.
愁坐(ㄔㄡˊ ㄗㄨㄛˋ)
to sit quietly in sorrow or distress
愁思(ㄔㄡˊ ㄙ)
sorrowful thoughts
愁意(ㄔㄡˊ ㄧˋ)
an expression of sorrow; a touch of sorrow
愁顏(ㄔㄡˊ ㄧㄢˊ)
a distressed or sad look
愁霧(ㄔㄡˊ ㄨˋ)
a depressing fog or mist (often used figuratively)
愁雲(ㄔㄡˊ ㄩㄣˊ)
depressing clouds; heavy clouds (often used figuratively)

【愍】 1647
ㄇㄧㄣˇ miin mǐn
to pity; to commiserate
愍憐(ㄇㄧㄣˇ ㄌㄧㄢˊ)
to pity (for)
愍恤(ㄇㄧㄣˇ ㄒㄩˋ)
to feel pity; to show kindness (toward people)

【愆】 1648
ㄑㄧㄢ chian qiān
1. a fault; a mistake; a misdemeanor
2. to lose
3. a malignant disease
愆過(ㄑㄧㄢ ㄍㄨㄛˋ)
a fault; a mistake
愆期(ㄑㄧㄢ ㄑㄧˊ)
to fail to meet a deadline; to be behind time; to fall behind schedule; to pass the appointed time
愆滯(ㄑㄧㄢ ㄓˋ)
behind time or schedule
愆尤(ㄑㄧㄢ ㄧㄡˊ)or 愆爽(ㄑㄧㄢ ㄕㄨㄤˇ)
a fault; an offense; a mistake

【愈】 1649
ㄩˋ yuh yù
1. to recover (from illness); to heal 亦作「瘉」: 他病愈。He recovers from an illness.
2. to a greater degree; even more
愈多愈好(ㄩˋ ㄉㄨㄛ ㄩˋ ㄏㄠˇ)
The more, the better.
愈合(ㄩˋ ㄏㄜˊ)
(medicine) to heal 亦作「瘉合」
愈加(ㄩˋ ㄐㄧㄚ)
increasingly; more and more
愈甚(ㄩˋ ㄕㄣˋ)
intenser; to become intense
愈益(ㄩˋ ㄧˋ)
increasingly; more and more
愈愈(ㄩˋ ㄩˋ)
to wax more and more; to become greater

【意】 1650
ㄧˋ yih yì
1. a thought; an idea; sentiments
2. intention; inclination
3. expectations
4. meaning: 詞不達意。The words fail to express the meaning.
5. a hint; suggestion: 天氣頗有秋意。The weather makes us feel that autumn has set in.
意表(ㄧˋ ㄅㄧㄠˇ)
expectations: 此事出人意表。The matter is beyond our expectations.
意馬心猿(ㄧˋ ㄇㄚˇ ㄒㄧㄣ ㄩㄢˊ)
indecisive; wavering
意大利(ㄧˋ ㄉㄚˋ ㄌㄧˋ)
Italy
意大利人(ㄧˋ ㄉㄚˋ ㄌㄧˋ ㄖㄣˊ)
an Italian
意到筆隨(ㄧˋ ㄉㄠˋ ㄅㄧˇ ㄙㄨㄟˊ)
(literally) The pen follows where the mind reaches.—to write with ease
意態(ㄧˋ ㄊㄞˋ)
an air; bearing; a manner; an appearance
意圖(ㄧˋ ㄊㄨˊ)
intention; intent; design; to intend to do something
意念(ㄧˋ ㄋㄧㄢˋ)
an idea
意懶心灰(ㄧˋ ㄌㄢˇ ㄒㄧㄣ ㄏㄨㄟ)
greatly discouraged
意裏意思(ㄧˋ ˙ㄌㄧ ㄧˋ ㄙ)
to speak hesitatingly and indistinctly
意料(ㄧˋ ㄌㄧㄠˋ)
expectations: 這結果出乎意料。The result was unexpected.
意會(ㄧˋ ㄏㄨㄟˋ)
to sense; to perceive spontaneously (not through explanations): 只可意會,不可言傳。It can be sensed, but not explained in words.
意見(ㄧˋ ㄐㄧㄢˋ)
① an opinion; a suggestion; a view; an idea; a proposal: 我們交換意見。We exchanged ideas. ② objection; different opinions; complaint: 他們對你意見很多。They have a lot of complaints about you.
意見簿(ㄧˋ ㄐㄧㄢˋ ㄅㄨˋ)
a visitors' book
意見溝通(ㄧˋ ㄐㄧㄢˋ ㄍㄡ ㄊㄨㄥ)
communication
意見箱(ㄧˋ ㄐㄧㄢˋ ㄒㄧㄤ)
a suggestion box
意見書(ㄧˋ ㄐㄧㄢˋ ㄕㄨ)
written opinions; proposals submitted in written form
意匠(ㄧˋ ㄐㄧㄤˋ)
① creativity; ingenuity ② novel design; artistic conception
意匠慘淡(ㄧˋ ㄐㄧㄤˋ ㄘㄢˇ ㄉㄢˋ)
an ingenious composition and color scheme (said of painting)
意境(ㄧˋ ㄐㄧㄥˋ)
a frame of mind; a mood; conception
意氣(ㄧˋ ㄑㄧˋ)
spirits; heart; emotion
意氣風發(ㄧˋ ㄑㄧˋ ㄈㄥ ㄈㄚ)
high-spirited and vigorous
意氣沮喪(ㄧˋ ㄑㄧˋ ㄐㄩˇ ㄙㄤˋ)
in low spirits; crestfallen; dispirited; disheartened; depressed
意氣相投(ㄧˋ ㄑㄧˋ ㄒㄧㄤ ㄊㄡˊ)
congenial; to share the same aspirations and have the same temperament: 他們意氣相投。They are alike in temperament.
意氣之爭(ㄧˋ ㄑㄧˋ ㄓ ㄓㄥ)
to quarrel over a matter of emotion (rather than reason)
意氣衝天(ㄧˋ ㄑㄧˋ ㄔㄨㄥ ㄊㄧㄢ)
high-spirited
意氣自得(ㄧˋ ㄑㄧˋ ㄗˋ ㄉㄜˊ)or 意氣自如(ㄧˋ ㄑㄧˋ ㄗˋ ㄖㄨˊ)or 意氣自若(ㄧˋ ㄑㄧˋ ㄗˋ ㄖㄨㄛˋ)
easy and dignified
意氣揚揚(ㄧˋ ㄑㄧˋ ㄧㄤˊ ㄧㄤˊ)
triumphant; in high spirits; elated
意氣用事(ㄧˋ ㄑㄧˋ ㄩㄥˋ ㄕˋ)
to act on impulse; to be influenced by sentiments or emotions (rather than the mind) in handling things: 他們意氣用事。They acted on impulse.
意趣(ㄧˋ ㄑㄩˋ)
intent; implication
意下(ㄧˋ ㄒㄧㄚˋ)
① in one's heart or mind ② an opinion; an idea
意下如何(ㄧˋ ㄒㄧㄚˋ ㄖㄨˊ ㄏㄜˊ)
How about it? 或 What do you think?
意想不到(ㄧˋ ㄒㄧㄤˇ ㄅㄨˋ ㄉㄠˋ)
unexpected; unexpectedly; beyond expectation; never thought of
意向(ㄧˋ ㄒㄧㄤˋ)

〔心部〕

intentions; inclinations: 敵軍意向不明。The enemy's inclinations are not clear.

意象(ㄧˋ ㄒㄧㄤˋ)
an image; imagery; an idea; a concept

意興(ㄧˋ ㄒㄧㄥˋ)
interest; enthusiasm: 意興索然 to have not the least interest

意興闌珊(ㄧˋ ㄒㄧㄥˋ ㄌㄢˊ ㄕㄢ)
to feel dispirited

意緒(ㄧˋ ㄒㄩˋ)
① threads of thoughts ② a mood; a state of mind

意旨(ㄧˋ ㄓˇ)
intent; intention; meaning; wish; will

意志(ㄧˋ ㄓˋ)
volition; will; will power: 我們鍛煉意志。We discipline our will power.

意志消沉(ㄧˋ ㄓˋ ㄒㄧㄠ ㄔㄣˊ)
pessimistic; depressed; dejected; low-spirited; despondent

意轉心回(ㄧˋ ㄓㄨㄢˇ ㄒㄧㄣ ㄏㄨㄟˊ)
to change one's mind

意中(ㄧˋ ㄓㄨㄥ)
expected; anticipated

意中人(ㄧˋ ㄓㄨㄥ ㄖㄣˊ)
the man, or lady, of one's heart; the person with whom one is in love; the person one is in love with; the person of one's heart

意識(ㄧˋ ㄕˋ)
consciousness

意識到(ㄧˋ ㄕˋ ㄉㄠˋ)
to be conscious of; to realize: 他意識到自己的責任重大。He was conscious of his great responsibilities.

意識流(ㄧˋ ㄕˋ ㄌㄧㄡˊ)
(psychology) stream of consciousness

意識形態(ㄧˋ ㄕˋ ㄒㄧㄥˊ ㄊㄞˋ)
ideology

意在筆先(ㄧˋ ㄗㄞˋ ㄅㄧˇ ㄒㄧㄢ)or 意在筆前(ㄧˋ ㄗㄞˋ ㄅㄧˇ ㄑㄧㄢˊ)
The idea seems to run ahead of the brush. (said of painting or calligraphy)

意在言外(ㄧˋ ㄗㄞˋ ㄧㄢˊ ㄨㄞˋ)
The real meaning is not expressed but implied.

意思(ㄧˋ ˙ㄙ)
① meaning: 他不明白我的意思。He doesn't understand what I mean. ② intention; wish; desire: 你是不是有意思跟我妹妹見面? Do you wish to meet my sister? ③ interest; interesting; fun: 打籃球很有意思。Basketball is a lot of fun.

意思意思(ㄧˋ ˙ㄙ ㄧˋ ˙ㄙ)
to serve as a token

意色(ㄧˋ ㄙㄜˋ)
mental condition and facial expression

意義(ㄧˋ ㄧˋ)
meaning; significance: 我不懂他話中的意義。I could not understand the significance of his words.

意譯(ㄧˋ ㄧˋ)
free translation; paraphrase

意有未盡(ㄧˋ ㄧㄡˇ ㄨㄟˋ ㄐㄧㄣˋ)
to wish to continue doing something one has done for a long time

意淫(ㄧˋ ㄧㄣˊ)
to get satisfaction by imagining a sexual act; mental adultery

意外(ㄧˋ ㄨㄞˋ)
① unexpected; unforeseen; accidental; surprising ② a surprise; an accident: 我有一項出你意外的消息奉告。I have a surprise for you.

意外保險(ㄧˋ ㄨㄞˋ ㄅㄠˇ ㄒㄧㄢˇ)
accident insurance

意外風波(ㄧˋ ㄨㄞˋ ㄈㄥ ㄅㄛ)
unforeseen trouble

意外事件(ㄧˋ ㄨㄞˋ ㄕˋ ㄐㄧㄢˋ)
an accident

意味(ㄧˋ ㄨㄟˋ)
① an impression; a touch; a flavor ② to portend

意味着(ㄧˋ ㄨㄟˋ ˙ㄓㄜ)
to signify; to mean

意味深長(ㄧˋ ㄨㄟˋ ㄕㄣ ㄔㄤˊ)
profound in meaning; meaningful: 他帶著意味深長的微笑。He wore a meaningful smile.

意欲(ㄧˋ ㄩˋ)
volition; desire; to want to do something

意願(ㄧˋ ㄩㄢˋ)
inclination; wish; volition

【愚】 1651 ㄩˊ yu yú

1. stupid; foolish; silly; unwise; unintelligent
2. to fool; to cheat; to deceive
3. (courteous self-reference) I; me

愚笨(ㄩˊ ㄅㄣˋ)
stupid; foolish

愚不可及(ㄩˊ ㄅㄨˋ ㄎㄜˇ ㄐㄧˊ)
most foolish: 他愚不可及。He couldn't be more foolish.

愚昧(ㄩˊ ㄇㄟˋ)
benighted; stupid; ignorant: 他愚昧無知。He is a benighted man.

愚蒙(ㄩˊ ㄇㄥˊ)
ignorant; stupid

愚民(ㄩˊ ㄇㄧㄣˊ)
① the ignorant masses ② to prevent people from knowing the truth; to keep people in ignorance

愚民政策(ㄩˊ ㄇㄧㄣˊ ㄓㄥˋ ㄘㄜˋ)
the policy to keep the people in ignorance under a dictatorship; obscurantism; the policy to misguide and cheat people

愚夫愚婦(ㄩˊ ㄈㄨ ㄩˊ ㄈㄨˋ)
① the masses ② the ignorant multitude; the uneducated public

愚呆(ㄩˊ ㄉㄞ)
blockheaded; dull; slow to learn; unintelligent

愚弟(ㄩˊ ㄉㄧˋ)
a self-depreciatory reference to oneself in addressing a colleague of similar age (usually used in correspondence)

愚鈍(ㄩˊ ㄉㄨㄣˋ)
(in mind) dull; dull-witted; stupid

愚懦(ㄩˊ ㄋㄨㄛˋ)
stupid and cowardly

愚弄(ㄩˊ ㄋㄨㄥˋ)
to make a fool of somebody

愚陋(ㄩˊ ㄌㄡˋ)
stupid and vulgar

愚魯(ㄩˊ ㄌㄨˇ)
stupid; dull

愚公移山(ㄩˊ ㄍㄨㄥ ㄧˊ ㄕㄢ)
A determined effort can move a mountain. 或 Where there is a will, there is a

way.
愚見(ㄩˊ ㄐㄧㄢˋ)
(self-depreciatory term) my humble opinion
愚孝(ㄩˊ ㄒㄧㄠˋ)
blind devotion to one's parents
愚兄(ㄩˊ ㄒㄩㄥ)
a self-depreciatory reference to oneself when addressing a colleague or friend less advanced in age (usually used in correspondence)
愚直(ㄩˊ ㄓˊ)or 愚戇(ㄩˊ ㄓㄨㄤˋ)
stupidly honest
愚者千慮，必有一得(ㄩˊ ㄓㄜˇ ㄑㄧㄢ ㄌㄩˋ, ㄅㄧˋ ㄧㄡˇ ㄧˋ ㄉㄜˊ)
Even a fool may hits on a good idea.
愚者一得(ㄩˊ ㄓㄜˇ ㄧˋ ㄉㄜˊ)
a lucky hit by a fool (an expression often used to show one's modesty when praised for some clever act); a fluke
愚拙(ㄩˊ ㄓㄨㄛˊ)
stupid and clumsy
愚忠(ㄩˊ ㄓㄨㄥ)
blind devotion to one's lord
愚蠢(ㄩˊ ㄔㄨㄣˇ)
stupid; dull
愚人(ㄩˊ ㄖㄣˊ)
a fool; a simpleton
愚人節(ㄩˊ ㄖㄣˊ ㄐㄧㄝˊ)
All Fools' Day
愚騃(ㄩˊ ㄞˊ)
ignorant and stupid
愚而好自用(ㄩˊ ㄦˊ ㄏㄠˋ ㄗˋ ㄩㄥˋ)
stupid but willful
愚意(ㄩˊ ㄧˋ)
my humble opinion
愚頑(ㄩˊ ㄨㄢˊ)
stupid and obstinate
愚妄(ㄩˊ ㄨㄤˋ)
stupid and rash; ignorant but self-important; stupid but conceited

【感】 1652
ㄍㄢˇ gaan gǎn
1. to find; to feel; to sense; to perceive; to respond to: 我感到我自己錯了。I sensed that I myself was wrong.
2. to affect, move, or touch
3. feeling; sensation; emotion
4. to be grateful
感佩(ㄍㄢˇ ㄆㄟˋ)
to show one's appreciation for the help received
感冒(ㄍㄢˇ ㄇㄠˋ)
① a cold ② to catch a cold
感銘(ㄍㄢˇ ㄇㄧㄥˊ)
very grateful; to always remember a favor one has received
感慕(ㄍㄢˇ ㄇㄨˋ)
to feel gratitude and adoration for; to thank and adore
感憤(ㄍㄢˇ ㄈㄣˋ)
to be indignant
感奮(ㄍㄢˇ ㄈㄣˋ)
to be moved to action
感奮激厲(ㄍㄢˇ ㄈㄣˋ ㄐㄧ ㄌㄧˋ)
encouragement and stimulation
感德(ㄍㄢˇ ㄉㄜˊ)
to be grateful for a kindness
感戴(ㄍㄢˇ ㄉㄞˋ)
to feel gratitude and respect for
感到(ㄍㄢˇ ㄉㄠˋ)
to feel; to sense
感電(ㄍㄢˇ ㄉㄧㄢˋ)
electric induction; electrification
感動(ㄍㄢˇ ㄉㄨㄥˋ)
(mentally) to move, affect, or touch: 她的演說令人感動得流淚。Her speech moved people to tears.
感歎(ㄍㄢˇ ㄊㄢˋ)
to exclaim
感歎號(ㄍㄢˇ ㄊㄢˋ ㄏㄠˋ)
the exclamation mark; the exclamation point
感同身受(ㄍㄢˇ ㄊㄨㄥˊ ㄕㄣ ㄕㄡˋ)
to feel deeply moved by a kindness (shown to somebody else) as if one were actually the object thereof (an expression used often in letters asking favors on behalf of someone else)
感念(ㄍㄢˇ ㄋㄧㄢˋ)
to remember with gratitude
感念五中(ㄍㄢˇ ㄋㄧㄢˋ ㄨˇ ㄓㄨㄥ)
to feel deep gratitude
感官(ㄍㄢˇ ㄍㄨㄢ)
① the senses ② a sensory organ
感光(ㄍㄢˇ ㄍㄨㄤ)
to be exposed to light
感光劑(ㄍㄢˇ ㄍㄨㄤ ㄐㄧˋ)
sensitizer
感光紙(ㄍㄢˇ ㄍㄨㄤ ㄓˇ)
sensitized or sensitive paper
感慨(ㄍㄢˇ ㄎㄞˇ)
emotional excitement; regrets; painful recollections: 他感慨萬千。He was filled with regrets.
感慨系之(ㄍㄢˇ ㄎㄞˇ ㄒㄧˋ ㄓ)
to feel deeply touched about something
感喟(ㄍㄢˇ ㄎㄨㄟˋ)
to feel moved and sigh
感愧交集(ㄍㄢˇ ㄎㄨㄟˋ ㄐㄧㄠ ㄐㄧˊ)
moved and ashamed simultaneously
感荷(ㄍㄢˇ ㄏㄜˋ)
gratitude
感化(ㄍㄢˇ ㄏㄨㄚˋ)
to reform (a person); to influence (a person) by personal examples of moral uprightness: 我們想要感化犯人。We try to reform the prisoners.
感化教育(ㄍㄢˇ ㄏㄨㄚˋ ㄐㄧㄠˋ ㄩˋ)
reformatory education (for juvenile delinquents)
感化院(ㄍㄢˇ ㄏㄨㄚˋ ㄩㄢˋ)
a reformatory
感懷(ㄍㄢˇ ㄏㄨㄞˊ)
① stirred or aroused emotions (often used in titles of old-style poems) ② to recall with emotion
感激(ㄍㄢˇ ㄐㄧ)
① to feel grateful: 他對你的一切幫助甚表感激。He felt grateful for all you did. ② to be moved, touched, or affected
感激涕零(ㄍㄢˇ ㄐㄧ ㄊㄧˋ ㄌㄧㄥˊ)
moved to tears (by kindness, generosity, etc.)
感舊(ㄍㄢˇ ㄐㄧㄡˋ)
① to remember the deceased with emotion ② to remember the bygone days with emotion
感覺(ㄍㄢˇ ㄐㄩㄝˊ)
① sense; perception; feeling; sensation: 我對顏色有敏銳的感覺。I have a keen perception of color. ② to feel; to sense; to become aware of: 你感覺怎麼樣? How do you feel now?

〔心部〕

感覺器官(ㄍㄢˇ ㄐㄩㄝˊ ㄑ丨ˋ ㄍㄨㄢ)
sensory organs
感覺神經(ㄍㄢˇ ㄐㄩㄝˊ ㄕㄣˊ ㄐ丨ㄥ)
sensory nerves
感情(ㄍㄢˇ ㄑ丨ㄥˊ)
feelings; affection; emotions; devotion (between friends, relatives, etc.): 他是個凡事訴諸感情而少用理智的人。He is a man who feels but seldom thinks.
感情破裂(ㄍㄢˇ ㄑ丨ㄥˊ ㄆㄛˋ ㄌ丨ㄝˋ)
(said of friends, married couples, etc.) to fall out
感情主義(ㄍㄢˇ ㄑ丨ㄥˊ ㄓㄨˇ 丨ˋ)
emotionalism
感情衝動(ㄍㄢˇ ㄑ丨ㄥˊ ㄔㄨㄥ ㄉㄨㄥˋ)
an impulse (to do something); impulsiveness; to act on momentary impulse
感情作用(ㄍㄢˇ ㄑ丨ㄥˊ ㄗㄨㄛˋ ㄩㄥˋ)
action of the emotions
感情用事(ㄍㄢˇ ㄑ丨ㄥˊ ㄩㄥˋ ㄕˋ)
to appeal to emotions; to give free rein to emotions; swayed by one's feelings
感謝(ㄍㄢˇ ㄒ丨ㄝˋ)
to thank; gratitude: 我表示衷心的感謝。I express heartfelt thanks.
感想(ㄍㄢˇ ㄒ丨ㄤˇ)
mental reaction; an impression; an opinion: 請你談談你對這電視節目的感想。Please tell us your impressions of the T.V. program.
感性(ㄍㄢˇ ㄒ丨ㄥˋ)
perceptual
感性文化(ㄍㄢˇ ㄒ丨ㄥˋ ㄨㄣˊ ㄏㄨㄚˋ)
sensate culture
感召(ㄍㄢˇ ㄓㄠˋ)
the inspiration (to do a noble or brave deed) given by religious teachings, great leaders, etc.
感觸(ㄍㄢˇ ㄔㄨˋ)
effect on the mind; feeling; mental reaction: 他很感觸地說:「我老了!」He said with deep feeling,"I'm old!"
感受(ㄍㄢˇ ㄕㄡˋ)
to perceive; to feel; to be affected by: 我們感受到我們的拜訪不受歡迎。We perceived that our visit were unwelcome.
感傷(ㄍㄢˇ ㄕㄤ)
sentimental; sentimentality: 這是一個感傷的故事。This is a sentimental story.
感傷主義(ㄍㄢˇ ㄕㄤ ㄓㄨˇ 丨ˋ)
sentimentalism
感染(ㄍㄢˇ ㄖㄢˇ)
to be infected with; to tinge; to affect; to contract (a disease): 作家的激情感染了每個讀者。The author's passion affected all his readers.
感恩(ㄍㄢˇ ㄣ)
to be grateful; to feel thankful
感恩圖報(ㄍㄢˇ ㄣ ㄊㄨˊ ㄅㄠˋ)
to feel grateful for a kind act and plan to repay it
感恩節(ㄍㄢˇ ㄣ ㄐ丨ㄝˊ)
Thanksgiving Day
感應(ㄍㄢˇ 丨ㄥˋ)
① to feel and respond ② (physics) induction
感應電(ㄍㄢˇ 丨ㄥˋ ㄉ丨ㄢˋ)
induced electricity
感應器(ㄍㄢˇ 丨ㄥˋ ㄑ丨ˋ)
an induction machine
感應圈(ㄍㄢˇ 丨ㄥˋ ㄑㄩㄢ)
an induction coil
感悟(ㄍㄢˇ ㄨˋ)
to realize; to become aware of

【愛】 1653 ㄞˋ ay ài

1. to love; to like; to be fond of; to be kind to: 我愛上她了。I've fallen in love with her.
2. love; affection; kindness; benevolence; likes: 他極愛冒險。He has a strong love of adventure.
3. to be apt to: 她愛發脾氣。She is apt to lose her temper.

愛不忍釋(ㄞˋ ㄅㄨˋ ㄖㄣˇ ㄕˋ)or 愛不釋手(ㄞˋ ㄅㄨˋ ㄕˋ ㄕㄡˇ)
loving something too much to part with it; to fondle admiringly
愛漂亮(ㄞˋ ㄆ丨ㄠˋ ·ㄌ丨ㄤ)
to like to look pretty or attractive
愛莫能助(ㄞˋ ㄇㄛˋ ㄋㄥˊ ㄓㄨˋ)
desirous but unable to help; willing to help but unable to do so
愛默生(ㄞˋ ㄇㄛˋ ㄕㄥ)
Ralph Waldo Emerson, 1803-1882, American poet and philosopher
愛美(ㄞˋ ㄇㄟˇ)
① to love beauty ② to be fond of making up
愛美觀念(ㄞˋ ㄇㄟˇ ㄍㄨㄢ ㄋ丨ㄢˋ)
esthetic sense
愛面子(ㄞˋ ㄇ丨ㄢˋ ·ㄗ)
to be concerned about face-saving; to be sensitive about one's reputation
愛民如子(ㄞˋ ㄇ丨ㄣˊ ㄖㄨˊ ㄗˇ)
(said of a ruler or an official) to love the subjects as if they were his own children
愛慕(ㄞˋ ㄇㄨˋ)
to adore; adoration: 我們相互愛慕。We adore each other.
愛撫(ㄞˋ ㄈㄨˇ)
to show tender care for; to caress
愛達荷(ㄞˋ ㄉㄚˊ ㄏㄜˊ)
the state of Idaho, U. S. A.
愛德華(ㄞˋ ㄉㄜˊ ㄏㄨㄚˊ)
a transliteration of Edward
愛的結晶(ㄞˋ ·ㄉㄜ ㄐ丨ㄝˊ ㄐ丨ㄥ)
(literally) the crystallization of love—the child of a couple in love
愛戴(ㄞˋ ㄉㄞˋ)
to love and support (a political leader, etc.); to enjoy popular support
愛迪生(ㄞˋ ㄉ丨ˊ ㄕㄥ)
Thomas Alva Edison, 1847-1931, American inventor
愛丁堡(ㄞˋ ㄉ丨ㄥ ㄅㄠˇ)
Edinburgh, Scotland
愛他主義(ㄞˋ ㄊㄚ ㄓㄨˇ 丨ˋ)
altruism
愛女(ㄞˋ ㄋㄩˇ)
a beloved daughter; a favorite daughter
愛理不理的(ㄞˋ ㄌ丨ˇ ㄅㄨˋ ㄌ丨ˇ ·ㄉㄜ)
①(listening to another person) in an unenthusiastic manner, or with little interest ② cold and indifferent: 她老是一副愛理不理的樣子。She always looked cold and indifferent.
愛憐(ㄞˋ ㄌ丨ㄢˊ)
to show love or fondness for
愛戀(ㄞˋ ㄌ丨ㄢˋ)
to be in love with; to feel

deeply attached to
愛顧(ㄞˋ ㄍㄨˋ)
①to take loving care of ②(customers') kind patronization of a store
愛國(ㄞˋ ㄍㄨㄛˊ)
patriotic
愛國公債(ㄞˋ ㄍㄨㄛˊ ㄍㄨㄥ ㄓㄞˋ)
government bonds
愛國心(ㄞˋ ㄍㄨㄛˊ ㄒㄧㄣ)
patriotism
愛國主義(ㄞˋ ㄍㄨㄛˊ ㄓㄨˇ ㄧˋ)
patriotism
愛國運動(ㄞˋ ㄍㄨㄛˊ ㄩㄣˋ ㄉㄨㄥˋ)
a patriotic movement
愛克司光(ㄞˋ ㄎㄜˋ ㄙ ㄍㄨㄤ)
X ray; Roentgen rays
愛克司光照相(ㄞˋ ㄎㄜˋ ㄙ ㄍㄨㄤ ㄓㄠˋ ㄒㄧㄤˋ)
a roentgenogram
愛河永浴(ㄞˋ ㄏㄜˊ ㄩㄥˇ ㄩˋ)
to bathe forever in the river of love (a conventional phrase in congratulatory messages on the occasion of a wedding)
愛好(ㄞˋ ㄏㄠˋ)
to be interested in, or to love (sport, art, etc.): 我們愛好和平。We love peace. 或 We are peace-loving.
愛好者(ㄞˋ ㄏㄠˋ ㄓㄜˇ)
a lover (of art, sports, etc.); an amateur; an enthusiast; a fan: 音樂愛好者 a music-lover
愛護(ㄞˋ ㄏㄨˋ)
to give kind protection to; to take kind care of
愛火(ㄞˋ ㄏㄨㄛˇ)or 愛欿(ㄞˋ ㄧㄢˋ)
(Buddhism) passion; sexual drive
愛妾(ㄞˋ ㄑㄧㄝˋ)
a beloved concubine
愛琴海(ㄞˋ ㄑㄧㄣˊ ㄏㄞˇ)
Aegean Sea, an arm of the Mediterranean Sea between Greece and Turkey
愛卿(ㄞˋ ㄑㄧㄥ)
my darling (a form of address found in older novels); my beloved wife
愛情(ㄞˋ ㄑㄧㄥˊ)
love (between man and woman)
愛情不專(ㄞˋ ㄑㄧㄥˊ ㄅㄨˋ ㄓㄨㄢ)
changeable or unstable in love; fickle
愛情專一(ㄞˋ ㄑㄧㄥˊ ㄓㄨㄢ ㄧ)
steadfast in love
愛犬(ㄞˋ ㄑㄩㄢˇ)
a beloved dog
愛羣(ㄞˋ ㄑㄩㄣˊ)
①to love company; gregarious ②to love the multitude
愛惜(ㄞˋ ㄒㄧˊ)
①to prize; to cherish; to value: 我們愛惜我們團體的榮譽。We cherish the good name of our group. ②stingy; niggardly; miserly
愛心(ㄞˋ ㄒㄧㄣ)
compassion; kindness
愛新覺羅(ㄞˋ ㄒㄧㄣ ㄐㄩㄝˊ ㄌㄨㄛˊ)
Aisin Gioro, the family name of the Manchu rulers during the Ching Dynasty
愛虛榮(ㄞˋ ㄒㄩ ㄖㄨㄥˊ)
vainglorious
愛寵(ㄞˋ ㄔㄨㄥˇ)
①to love (one lower in position); to favor: 他獲得他雙親的愛寵。He won his parents' favor. ②one's beloved person
愛沙尼亞(ㄞˋ ㄕㄚ ㄋㄧˊ ㄧㄚˇ)
Estonia
愛神(ㄞˋ ㄕㄣˊ)
Cupid
愛人(ㄞˋ ㄖㄣˊ)
①a sweetheart; a lover ②to love others
愛人如己(ㄞˋ ㄖㄣˊ ㄖㄨˊ ㄐㄧˇ)
to love others as one loves oneself
愛滋病毒(ㄞˋ ㄗ ㄅㄧㄥˋ ㄉㄨˊ)
AIDS virus
愛子(ㄞˋ ㄗˇ)
a beloved son; a favorite son
愛憎(ㄞˋ ㄗㄥ)
love and hate: 他愛憎分明。He is clear about what to love and what to hate.
愛才若命(ㄞˋ ㄘㄞˊ ㄖㄨㄛˋ ㄇㄧㄥˋ)or 愛才若渴(ㄞˋ ㄘㄞˊ ㄖㄨㄛˋ ㄎㄜˇ)
very fond of talented people
愛財若命(ㄞˋ ㄘㄞˊ ㄖㄨㄛˋ ㄇㄧㄥˋ)
to love wealth as much as life; very stingy; miserly
愛斯基摩(ㄞˋ ㄙ ㄐㄧ ㄇㄛˊ)
the Eskimos
愛死症(ㄞˋ ㄙˇ ㄓㄥˋ)or 愛死病(ㄞˋ ㄙˇ ㄅㄧㄥˋ)or 愛滋病(ㄞˋ ㄗ ㄅㄧㄥˋ)
AIDS (acquired immune deficiency syndrome)
愛阿華(ㄞˋ ㄚ ㄏㄨㄚˊ)
the state of Iowa, U. S. A.
愛爾蘭(ㄞˋ ㄦˇ ㄌㄢˊ)
Ireland
愛爾蘭人(ㄞˋ ㄦˇ ㄌㄢˊ ㄖㄣˊ)
an Irish
愛因斯坦(ㄞˋ ㄧㄣ ㄙ ㄊㄢˇ)
Albert Einstein, 1879-1955, Jewish physicist and mathematician known for his theory of relativity
愛屋及烏(ㄞˋ ㄨ ㄐㄧˊ ㄨ)
(literally) When one loves a house, one tends to love even the crows perching on it.—to extend love to someone who is close or dear to one's direct object of love 或 Love me, love my dog.
愛物(ㄞˋ ㄨˋ)
①a cherished object ②to love all creatures
愛用(ㄞˋ ㄩㄥˋ)
to love to use; to prefer to use

十畫

【愧】1654 (媿) ㄎㄨㄟˋ kuey kuì
ashamed; shameful; abashed; conscience-stricken; to have something on one's conscience: 我問心無愧。I have a clear conscience.
愧不敢當(ㄎㄨㄟˋ ㄅㄨˋ ㄍㄢˇ ㄉㄤ)
(an expression used to show humbleness and politeness) ashamed to accept (an honor); do not deserve (a gift, compliment, etc.)
愧服(ㄎㄨㄟˋ ㄈㄨˊ)
to admire (another) with a feeling of shame about one's own inferiority
愧天怍人(ㄎㄨㄟˋ ㄊㄧㄢ ㄗㄨㄛˋ ㄖㄣˊ)
to feel shame before Heaven and fellow human beings
愧難見人(ㄎㄨㄟˋ ㄋㄢˊ ㄐㄧㄢˋ ㄖㄣˊ)
ashamed to be seen in public
愧赧(ㄎㄨㄟˋ ㄋㄢˇ)
to redden from shame
愧恧(ㄎㄨㄟˋ ㄋㄩˋ)

〔心部〕

to feel shame; ashamed
愧汗(ㄎㄨㄟˋ ㄏㄢˋ)
perspiration of shame
愧恨(ㄎㄨㄟˋ ㄏㄣˋ)
remorseful; to feel mortification as well as resentment: 我內心深自愧恨。I feel bitterly remorseful.
愧悔(ㄎㄨㄟˋ ㄏㄨㄟˇ)
to feel mortified and regretful
愧疚(ㄎㄨㄟˋ ㄐㄧㄡˋ)
to feel the discomfort of shame; to feel a sense of guilt; to suffer a guilty conscience
愧心(ㄎㄨㄟˋ ㄒㄧㄣ)
a feeling of shame: 他感到愧心。He feels ashamed at heart.
愧煞(ㄎㄨㄟˋ ㄕㄚˋ)
to feel very much ashamed
愧怍(ㄎㄨㄟˋ ㄗㄨㄛˋ)
to feel shame; ashamed
愧色(ㄎㄨㄟˋ ㄙㄜˋ)
an expression of shame: 他毫無愧色。He looks unashamed.
愧無以報(ㄎㄨㄟˋ ㄨˊ ㄧˇ ㄅㄠˋ)
ashamed of one's inability to repay a favor

【愴】 1655 ㄔㄨㄤˋ chuanq chuàng
broken-hearted; sad; sorrowful
愴恨(ㄔㄨㄤˋ ㄌㄧㄤˋ)
sad; sorrowful
愴怳(ㄔㄨㄤˋ ㄏㄨㄤˇ)
disheartened; depressed; discouraged
愴愴(ㄔㄨㄤˋ ㄔㄨㄤˋ)
in anguish of sorrow; broken-hearted; anguished
愴然(ㄔㄨㄤˋ ㄖㄢˊ)
broken-hearted; sick at heart; in anguish of sorrow: 她愴然淚下。She burst into sorrowful tears.
愴惻(ㄔㄨㄤˋ ㄘㄜˋ)
sad; grieved; sorrowful

【愫】 1656 ㄙㄨˋ suh sù
sincerity; honesty

【慍】 1657 ㄩㄣˋ yunn yùn
angry; indignant; displeased; irritated; vexed: 他面有慍色。He looked irritated.
慍懟(ㄩㄣˋ ㄉㄨㄟˋ)
to resent
慍怒(ㄩㄣˋ ㄋㄨˋ)
angry; irritated; displeased; chagrin
慍恨(ㄩㄣˋ ㄏㄣˋ)
indignation; resentment; rancor
慍恚(ㄩㄣˋ ㄏㄨㄟˋ)
to feel resentment; rancorous
慍容(ㄩㄣˋ ㄖㄨㄥˊ)
a displeased look; an angry appearance; a face of resentment
慍色(ㄩㄣˋ ㄙㄜˋ)
a displeased look; an angry appearance

【愷】 1658 (凱) ㄎㄞˇ kae kǎi
joyful; good; kind; gentle
愷悌(ㄎㄞˇ ㄊㄧˋ)
happy and easygoing; friendly; amiable
愷歌 or 凱歌(ㄎㄞˇ ㄍㄜ)
the song of triumph
愷切(ㄎㄞˇ ㄑㄧㄝˋ)
gently and sincerely
愷撒(ㄎㄞˇ ㄙㄚ)
Julius Caesar, 100-44 B.C., Roman general, statesman, and historian
愷樂(ㄎㄞˇ ㄩㄝˋ)
the tune or music in celebration of victory

【愾】 1659 ㄎㄞˋ kay kài
enmity; hatred; anger; wrath: 我們同仇敵愾。We share a bitter hatred of the enemy.
愾憤(ㄎㄞˋ ㄈㄣˋ)
angry; to show wrath

【慄】 1660 ㄌㄧˋ lih lì
to shudder; to tremble
慄慄(ㄌㄧˋ ㄌㄧˋ)
① timorous; fearful; terrified; frightful ② cold; chilly
慄冽(ㄌㄧˋ ㄌㄧㄝˋ)
piercingly cold; bone-chilling; chilly
慄斯(ㄌㄧˋ ㄙ)
to act in an obsequious manner in order to please somebody

【愼】 1661 ㄕㄣˋ shenn shèn
cautious; careful; scrupulous; prudent
愼默(ㄕㄣˋ ㄇㄛˋ)
cautious and reticent
愼密(ㄕㄣˋ ㄇㄧˋ)
meticulous
愼獨(ㄕㄣˋ ㄉㄨˊ)
to exercise caution about one's personal life; to be cautious when one is alone
愼刑(ㄕㄣˋ ㄒㄧㄥˊ)
to mete out penalties very carefully
愼終追遠(ㄕㄣˋ ㄓㄨㄥ ㄓㄨㄟ ㄩㄢˇ)
thoroughgoing about the funeral rites for parents and the worship of ancestors
愼重(ㄕㄣˋ ㄓㄨㄥˋ)
cautious; careful; prudent; discreet: 處理這個問題必須愼重。The problem has to be handled with great care.
愼重其事(ㄕㄣˋ ㄓㄨㄥˋ ㄑㄧˊ ㄕˋ)
to take careful precautions; to do something in a serious manner
愼始(ㄕㄣˋ ㄕˇ)
careful or cautious about the beginning (of an activity)
愼思明辨(ㄕㄣˋ ㄙ ㄇㄧㄥˊ ㄅㄧㄢˋ)
to think carefully and clearly
愼言愼行(ㄕㄣˋ ㄧㄢˊ ㄕㄣˋ ㄒㄧㄥˊ)
to exercise caution in speech and conduct: 我勸告他愼言愼行。I advised him to exercise caution in speech and conduct.
愼微(ㄕㄣˋ ㄨㄟˊ)
careful about minute details

【慊】 1662 1. ㄑㄧㄢˋ chiann qiàn
to resent
慊慊(ㄑㄧㄢˋ ㄑㄧㄢˋ)
resentful and discontented

【慊】 1662 2. ㄑㄧㄝˋ chieh qiè
contented; gratified; pleased; satisfied

【慌】 1663 ㄏㄨㄤ huang huāng
to lose self-possession; to lose one's head; panic; confused: 我心慌意亂。I lose my

head totally.
慌忙(ㄏㄨㄤ ㄇㄤˊ)
hurried and flustered; hurry-scurry; in a great rush: 我們慌忙趕到現場。We went to the spot in a great rush.
慌了神兒(ㄏㄨㄤ ·ㄌㄜ ㄕㄜˊㄦ)
to lose one's head; to lose self-possession
慌亂(ㄏㄨㄤ ㄌㄨㄢˋ)
in a hurry and confusion
慌張(ㄏㄨㄤ ㄓㄤ)or 慌慌張張(ㄏㄨㄤ ·ㄏㄨㄤ ㄓㄤ ㄓㄤ)or 慌裏慌張(ㄏㄨㄤ ·ㄌㄧ ㄏㄨㄤ ㄓㄤ)
lacking self-possession; nervous and confused; flustered

【慆】 1664 ㄊㄠ tau tāo
1. fleeting
2. for an extended period; long
3. delighted; happy
4. suspicious; doubtful
5. to cover up; to hide
慆慆(ㄊㄠ ㄊㄠ)
for an extended period; long
慆淫(ㄊㄠ ㄧㄣˊ)
excessive neglect (of duties, serious pursuits, etc.); to live a licentious life

【慉】 1665 ㄒㄩˋ shiuh xù
to bring up; to raise
慉結(ㄒㄩˋ ㄐㄧㄝˊ)
melancholy; depressed

【慈】 1666 ㄘˊ tsyr cí
1. kind; benevolent; benignant; charitable; merciful; loving; fond: 父慈子孝。The father is loving and his son is filial.
2. of one's mother; maternal
慈悲(ㄘˊ ㄅㄟ)
benevolence; pity; mercy; clemency
慈眉善目(ㄘˊ ㄇㄟˊ ㄕㄢˋ ㄇㄨˋ)
a benign face; a benignant look
慈命(ㄘˊ ㄇㄧㄥˋ)
the commands of one's mother; one's mother's command
慈母(ㄘˊ ㄇㄨˇ)
① a loving mother; a fond mother; a kind mother ② a reference to one's father's concubine who raised one as if one were her own child
慈母敗子(ㄘˊ ㄇㄨˇ ㄅㄞˋ ㄗˇ)
A fond mother spoils the son.
慈父(ㄘˊ ㄈㄨˋ)
an affectionate father; a kind father
慈姑
①(ㄘˊ ㄍㄨ) a kind mother-in-law; one's husband's mother ②(ㄘˊ ·ㄍㄨ) (botany) arrowhead 亦作「茨菰」
慈和(ㄘˊ ㄏㄜˊ)
friendly and kind to each other or one another
慈航普渡(ㄘˊ ㄏㄤˊ ㄆㄨˇ ㄉㄨˋ)
(literally) The "barge of mercy" ferries all the miserable people to the world of bliss.—(Buddhism) the salvation through charity to others (particularly referring to the Goddess of Mercy or *Avalokitesvara Bodhisattva*)
慈誨(ㄘˊ ㄏㄨㄟˋ)
the teachings of one's mother; maternal instructions
慈禧太后(ㄘˊ ㄒㄧˇ ㄊㄞˋ ㄏㄡˋ)
Empress Dowager Tzu Hsi, 1835-1908, who dominated the Manchu court for 47 years toward the end of the Ching Dynasty
慈祥(ㄘˊ ㄒㄧㄤˊ)
(said of elderly persons) benevolent; kind; benign; benignant
慈訓(ㄘˊ ㄒㄩㄣˋ)
the teachings of one's mother
慈善(ㄘˊ ㄕㄢˋ)
benevolence; charity; philanthropy; humanitarianism
慈善機構(ㄘˊ ㄕㄢˋ ㄐㄧ ㄍㄡˋ)
a charity organization
慈善家(ㄘˊ ㄕㄢˋ ㄐㄧㄚ)
a philanthropist; a man of charity
慈善事業(ㄘˊ ㄕㄢˋ ㄕˋ ㄧㄝˋ)
a charitable enterprise; a philanthropic undertaking
慈愛(ㄘˊ ㄞˋ)
(said of elderly persons) benevolence; affection; love; kindness: 我母親對我非常慈愛。My mother's love for me was very great.
慈幼(ㄘˊ ㄧㄡˋ)
to love the young
慈顏(ㄘˊ ㄧㄢˊ)
① your kindly face (a term of respectful address to elders or parents) ② the face of one's mother
慈烏反哺(ㄘˊ ㄨ ㄈㄢˇ ㄅㄨˇ)
(literally) the feeding of its mother by a crow—filial piety
慈幃 or 慈闈(ㄘˊ ㄨㄟˊ)
a reference to one's mother
慈雲(ㄘˊ ㄩㄣˊ)
(Buddhism) the Buddha heart—immeasurable kindness and mercy

【慂】 1667 ㄩㄥˇ yeong yǒng
to persuade; to urge

【態】 1668 ㄊㄞˋ tay tài
1. an attitude; a position
2. a manner; carriage; bearing; deportment
3. a situation; a condition; circumstances
4. (physics) state of matter
態度(ㄊㄞˋ ㄉㄨˋ)
① an attitude; a position: 我們必須採取堅定的態度。We must take a firm attitude. ② a manner: 我喜歡他坦率的態度。I like his frank manner.
態度和平(ㄊㄞˋ ㄉㄨˋ ㄏㄜˊ ㄆㄧㄥˊ)
friendly; a peaceful attitude
態度好(ㄊㄞˋ ㄉㄨˋ ㄏㄠˇ)
well-mannered; courteous; well-behaved; elegant
態度壞(ㄊㄞˋ ㄉㄨˋ ㄏㄨㄞˋ)
ill-mannered; impolite; discourteous; impertinent
態度嫺雅(ㄊㄞˋ ㄉㄨˋ ㄒㄧㄢˊ ㄧㄚˇ)
to have refined manners
態勢(ㄊㄞˋ ㄕˋ)
①(military) a situation ② a posture

【慇】 1669 ㄧㄣ in yīn
1. mournful; sorrowful
2. regardful; respectful
慇懃(ㄧㄣ ㄑㄧㄣˊ)
polite; courteous; civil; attentions; attentive: 他向他的老板獻慇懃。He was attentive to his boss.
慇憂(ㄧㄣ ㄧㄡ)

〔心部〕

deep grief; distress; sorrow
慇慇(ㄧㄣ ㄧㄣ)
mournful; sorrowful; sad; melancholy

〔心部〕

【慁】1670 (慁) ㄏㄨㄣˋ huenn hùn
1. to disturb; to distress; to upset
2. to disgrace
3. to worry

【愬】1671 (訴) ㄙㄨˋ suh sù
1. to tell; to complain
2. scared, frightened

【愿】1672 ㄩㄢˋ yuann yuàn
sincere; honest; faithful; virtuous

十一畫

【慘】1673 ㄘㄢˇ tsaan cǎn
1. sorrowful; sad; miserable; tragic: 他慘遭不幸。He died a tragic death.
2. cruel; merciless; brutal
3. dark; gloomy; dull
4. disastrously
慘白(ㄘㄢˇ ㄅㄞˊ)
dreadfully pale; pale
慘敗(ㄘㄢˇ ㄅㄞˋ)
to suffer a crushing or ignominious defeat; crushing defeat
慘變(ㄘㄢˇ ㄅㄧㄢˋ)
a tragic change; a tragedy
慘不忍睹(ㄘㄢˇ ㄅㄨˋ ㄖㄣˇ ㄉㄨˇ)
so tragic that one cannot bear to look at it
慘怛(ㄘㄢˇ ㄉㄚˊ)
heavy-hearted; sad; grieved
慘澹 or 慘淡(ㄘㄢˇ ㄉㄢˋ)
①lacking brightness; dull; gloomy; dismal; dim: 天色慘淡。It was dismal weather. ②laborious; arduous; with strenuous effort
慘澹經營 or 慘淡經營(ㄘㄢˇ ㄉㄢˋ ㄐㄧㄥ ㄧㄥˊ)
to manage with great pains; to build up a business from scratch; to keep an enterprise going by painstaking effort; to take great pains to carry on one's work under difficult circumstances
慘痛(ㄘㄢˇ ㄊㄨㄥˋ)
bitter; very painful; agonizing: 我們獲得慘痛的教訓。We learned a bitter lesson.
慘虐(ㄘㄢˇ ㄋㄩㄝˋ)
extreme cruelty
慘慄(ㄘㄢˇ ㄌㄧˋ)
bitterly cold
慘烈(ㄘㄢˇ ㄌㄧㄝˋ)
(said of weather, etc.) very severe
慘綠少年(ㄘㄢˇ ㄌㄩˋ ㄕㄠˋ ㄋㄧㄢˊ)
(literally) a young man in dark green—a handsome young man
慘酷(ㄘㄢˇ ㄎㄨˋ)
cruel and sadistic; ruthless; merciless; pitiless
慘禍(ㄘㄢˇ ㄏㄨㄛˋ)
a terrible disaster; a frightful calamity
慘急(ㄘㄢˇ ㄐㄧˊ)
to enforce the law in a harsh manner
慘叫(ㄘㄢˇ ㄐㄧㄠˋ)
to give a bloodcurdling scream or shriek
慘劇(ㄘㄢˇ ㄐㄩˋ)
a tragic event; a tragedy; a calamity
慘絕人寰(ㄘㄢˇ ㄐㄩㄝˊ ㄖㄣˊ ㄏㄨㄢˊ)
a rare tragedy on earth; bloodcurdling (atrocities)
慘切(ㄘㄢˇ ㄑㄧㄝˋ)
tragic; heartbreaking; sad; pathetic
慘兮兮的(ㄘㄢˇ ㄒㄧ ㄒㄧ ·ㄉㄜ)
sad-looking
慘相(ㄘㄢˇ ㄒㄧㄤˋ)
a woebegone look; a crestfallen look; a pitiable condition
慘狀(ㄘㄢˇ ㄓㄨㄤˋ)
a tragic sight; a sad sight; a miserable condition; a pitiful sight
慘重(ㄘㄢˇ ㄓㄨㄥˋ)
heavy; grievous; disastrous
慘愴(ㄘㄢˇ ㄔㄨㄤˋ)
anguished; grieved
慘殺(ㄘㄢˇ ㄕㄚ)
to kill by cruel or violent means; to slaughter
慘然(ㄘㄢˇ ㄖㄢˊ)
sad; saddened; grieved
慘遭橫禍(ㄘㄢˇ ㄗㄠ ㄏㄥˋ ㄏㄨㄛˋ)
to meet a tragic accident
慘惻(ㄘㄢˇ ㄘㄜˋ)
anguished; grieved
慘死(ㄘㄢˇ ㄙˇ)
to meet a violent or tragic death
慘案(ㄘㄢˇ ㄢˋ)
a cruel murder case; a case of cold-blooded massacre
慘無天日(ㄘㄢˇ ㄨˊ ㄊㄧㄢ ㄖˋ)
(said of the life under a tyrannical government) so dark, or full of suffering, that it is as if the sun were not in the sky
慘無人道(ㄘㄢˇ ㄨˊ ㄖㄣˊ ㄉㄠˋ)
inhuman; inhumane; brutal; cold-blooded; very cruel
慘獄(ㄘㄢˇ ㄩˋ)
a case that involves a mass execution

【慢】1674 ㄇㄢˋ mann màn
1. slow; sluggish: 這條河流得很慢。The stream is very sluggish.
2. negligent
3. haughty; rude; disrespectful; arrogant; supercilious
4. to postpone; to defer: 且慢! Hold on a moment. 或 Just a moment!
慢板(ㄇㄢˋ ㄅㄢˇ)
①(Peking opera) a slow movement or passage ②(music) adagio
慢步(ㄇㄢˋ ㄅㄨˋ)
to walk slowly; to slow-poke
慢跑(ㄇㄢˋ ㄆㄠˇ)
to jog; jogging
慢慢(ㄇㄢˋ ㄇㄢˋ)or 慢慢兒(ㄇㄢˋ ㄇㄚㄦ)
①leisurely; slowly; unhurriedly; to take one's time ②by and by; gradually; little by little
慢慢來(ㄇㄢˋ ·ㄇㄢ ㄌㄞˊ)or 慢來(ㄇㄢˋ ㄌㄞˊ)
①Don't rush! Take your time. ②to come or occur slowly or gradually
慢打法器(ㄇㄢˋ ㄉㄚˇ ㄈㄚˇ ㄑㄧˋ)
(literally) to refrain from beating the gong for Buddhist services—to refrain from giving publicity to something

慢待(ㄇㄢˋ ㄉㄞˋ)
(often used in a polite conversation) to treat (a guest) rudely or discourteously; to treat haughtily or discourteously
慢到(ㄇㄢˋ ㄉㄠˋ)
to arrive late
慢點兒(ㄇㄢˋ ㄉㄧㄚˇㄦ)
Be slower! 或 to slow down a bit: 告訴司機開慢點兒。Tell the driver to go slower.
慢調(ㄇㄢˋ ㄉㄧㄠˋ)
a slow movement (in music)
慢動作(ㄇㄢˋ ㄉㄨㄥˋ ㄗㄨㄛˋ)
slow motion
慢騰騰(ㄇㄢˋ ·ㄊㄥ ·ㄊㄥ)
at a leisurely pace; unhurriedly; sluggishly
慢條斯理(ㄇㄢˋ ㄊㄧㄠˊ ㄙ ㄌㄧˇ)
unhurried; unhurriedly; without haste; leisurely; very slowly and imperturbably: 她說話做事總是慢條斯理的。She always speaks slowly and acts unhurriedly.
慢呑呑(ㄇㄢˋ ㄊㄨㄣ ㄊㄨㄣ)
irritatingly slow; exasperatingly slow: 他們慢呑呑地來回於河上。They slow-poked up and down the river.
慢工出巧匠(ㄇㄢˋ ㄍㄨㄥ ㄔㄨ ㄑㄧㄠˇ ㄐㄧㄤˋ) or 慢工出細活(ㄇㄢˋ ㄍㄨㄥ ㄔㄨ ㄒㄧˋ ㄏㄨㄛˊ)
Fine products come from slow work. 或 Slow work means careful work. 參看「欲速不達」
慢客(ㄇㄢˋ ㄎㄜˋ)
to treat a guest impolitely or rudely; to give a cold reception to a guest
慢火(ㄇㄢˋ ㄏㄨㄛˇ)
a slow fire (in cooking)
慢驚風(ㄇㄢˋ ㄐㄧㄥ ㄈㄥ)
(pathology) eclampsia
慢鏡頭(ㄇㄢˋ ㄐㄧㄥˋ ㄊㄡˊ)
slow motion in the movies
慢些(ㄇㄢˋ ·ㄒㄧㄝ)
slower than; to slow down a bit; not so fast
慢行(ㄇㄢˋ ㄒㄧㄥˊ)
to walk slowly: 經過村莊時慢行。Go slow through the village.
慢性病(ㄇㄢˋ ㄒㄧㄥˋ ㄅㄧㄥˋ)
a chronic disease
慢性子(ㄇㄢˋ ㄒㄧㄥˋ ·ㄗ)
① a sluggish disposition; a phlegmatic disposition ② a slowpoke; a slow coach ③ not active in doing things
慢著(ㄇㄢˋ ·ㄓㄜ)
Go slow! 或 Wait a minute!
慢車(ㄇㄢˋ ㄔㄜ)
a way train; a stopping train; a local train; a slow train
慢車道(ㄇㄢˋ ㄔㄜ ㄉㄠˋ)
slow-traffic lanes
慢世(ㄇㄢˋ ㄕˋ)
to disregard social conventions and common practices; cynical
慢手慢脚(ㄇㄢˋ ㄕㄡˇ ㄇㄢˋ ㄐㄧㄠˇ)
slow in doing things; slow-moving; sluggish
慢說(ㄇㄢˋ ㄕㄨㄛ)
① to speak slowly ② not to speak now ③ let alone; to say nothing of
慢走(ㄇㄢˋ ㄗㄡˇ)
① Don't go yet! 或 Halt! 或 Wait a minute! ② (polite formula) Good-bye! 或 Take care.
慢藏誨盜(ㄇㄢˋ ㄘㄤˊ ㄏㄨㄟˋ ㄉㄠˋ)
Slackness in putting things away is tantamount to teaching others to steal. 或 To be careless of jewels is to invite thieves.
慢悠悠地(ㄇㄢˋ ㄧㄡ ㄧㄡ ·ㄉㄜ)
unhurriedly; without haste; in a leisurely manner

【慣】 1675 ㄍㄨㄢˋ guann guàn

1. habitual; customary; usual; accustomed
2. to spoil (a child)
3. to be accustomed to; to be used to

慣例(ㄍㄨㄢˋ ㄌㄧˋ)
usual practice; established practice; custom
慣壞(ㄍㄨㄢˋ ㄏㄨㄞˋ)
to spoil (a child): 別把孫子慣壞了。Don't spoil the grandson.
慣技(ㄍㄨㄢˋ ㄐㄧˋ)
a customary trick; the usual gimmick
慣竊(ㄍㄨㄢˋ ㄑㄧㄝˋ)
a habitual thief; an incorrigible thief
慣行犯(ㄍㄨㄢˋ ㄒㄧㄥˊ ㄈㄢˋ)
a habitual criminal; a confirmed criminal; a hardened offender
慣性(ㄍㄨㄢˋ ㄒㄧㄥˋ)
(physics) inertia: 慣性使火車滑過了車站。Inertia carried the train past the station.
慣常(ㄍㄨㄢˋ ㄔㄤˊ)
customary; usual
慣賊(ㄍㄨㄢˋ ㄗㄟˊ)
a habitual thief
慣養(ㄍㄨㄢˋ ㄧㄤˇ)
to let (a child) grow up in comfort; to spoil: 他嬌生慣養的。He was brought up by indulgent parents.
慣於(ㄍㄨㄢˋ ㄩˊ)
accustomed to; used to
慣用(ㄍㄨㄢˋ ㄩㄥˋ)
in common use; commonly used
慣用伎倆(ㄍㄨㄢˋ ㄩㄥˋ ㄐㄧˋ ㄌㄧㄤˇ)
customary tactics; old tricks
慣用手法(ㄍㄨㄢˋ ㄩㄥˋ ㄕㄡˇ ㄈㄚˇ)
a habitual practice

【慥】 1676 ㄗㄠˋ tzaw zào (又讀 ㄘㄠˋ tsaw cào)

sincere; kindhearted
慥慥(ㄗㄠˋ ㄗㄠˋ)
sincere and honest; earnestly; wholeheartedly

【慟】 1677 ㄊㄨㄥˋ tonq tòng

extreme grief
慟哭(ㄊㄨㄥˋ ㄎㄨ)
to weep bitterly

【慨】 1678 ㄎㄞˇ kae kǎi (又讀 ㄎㄞˋ kay kài)

1. to sigh emotionally
2. generous; magnanimous

慨憤(ㄎㄞˇ ㄈㄣˋ)
indignant; angry
慨歎(ㄎㄞˇ ㄊㄢˋ)
to deplore or lament with sighs
慨諾(ㄎㄞˇ ㄋㄨㄛˋ) or 慨允(ㄎㄞˇ ㄩㄣˇ)
to consent generously or readily
慨恨(ㄎㄞˇ ㄏㄣˋ)
indignant; angry
慨乎言之(ㄎㄞˇ ㄏㄨ ㄧㄢˊ ㄓ)
to say it with a sigh (in-

dicating the speaker's nostalgia, sense of regret or loss, etc.)

慨想(ㄎㄞˇ ㄒㄧㄤˇ)
to think of or remember with emotion

慨然(ㄎㄞˇ ㄖㄢˊ)
① to sigh with deep feelings ② generous; kind; magnanimous

1679
【慷】 ㄎㄤ kang kāng (又讀 ㄎㄤˇ kaang kǎng)
1. ardent; impassioned
2. generous; liberal; magnanimous; unselfish

慷他人之慨(ㄎㄤ ㄊㄚ ㄖㄣˊ ㄓ ㄎㄞˇ)
to show generosity or unselfishness by another's wealth; to be generous at the expense of others

慷慨(ㄎㄤ ㄎㄞˇ)
① generous; unselfish; liberal ② (usually said of a hero) vehement; fervent; ardent

慷慨悲憤(ㄎㄤ ㄎㄞˇ ㄅㄟ ㄈㄣˋ)
impassioned by lamentation and indignation

慷慨悲歌(ㄎㄤ ㄎㄞˇ ㄅㄟ ㄍㄜ)
to chant in a heroic but mournful tone

慷慨激昂(ㄎㄤ ㄎㄞˇ ㄐㄧ ㄤˊ)
(said of speech or conduct) impassioned; arousing

慷慨解囊(ㄎㄤ ㄎㄞˇ ㄐㄧㄝˇ ㄋㄤˊ)
to make generous contributions (of funds)

慷慨就義(ㄎㄤ ㄎㄞˇ ㄐㄧㄡˋ ㄧˋ)
to sacrifice one's life heroically for a cause, belief, or principle

慷慨成仁(ㄎㄤ ㄎㄞˇ ㄔㄥˊ ㄖㄣˊ) or 慷慨捐軀(ㄎㄤ ㄎㄞˇ ㄐㄩㄢ ㄑㄩ)
to sacrifice one's life heroically for justice; to die heroically in battle

1680
【慳】 ㄑㄧㄢ chian qiān
1. stingy; niggardly; parsimonious; close
2. deficient

慳囊(ㄑㄧㄢ ㄋㄤˊ)
(literally) a moneybag which is closed after money is put in—(figuratively) a miser; a niggard

慳吝(ㄑㄧㄢ ㄌㄧㄣˋ)
stingy; niggardly; miserly

1681
【慵】 ㄩㄥ iong yōng (又讀 ㄩㄥˊ yong yóng)
indolent; lazy; idle

慵惰(ㄩㄥ ㄉㄨㄛˋ) or 慵懶(ㄩㄥ ㄌㄢˇ)
lazy; indolent; idle; inactive

慵困(ㄩㄥ ㄎㄨㄣˋ)
tired and indolent

1682
【慴】 ㄓㄜˊ jer zhé
fearful; terrified; frightened

慴伏(ㄓㄜˊ ㄈㄨˊ)
to submit out of fear

1683
【慪】 ㄡˋ ow òu
1. same as 嘔—to irritate; to exasperate
2. to be stingy about something

慪氣(ㄡˋ ㄑㄧˋ)
to become exasperated; to be difficult and sulky

慪人(ㄡˋ ㄖㄣˊ)
exasperating; disgusting

1684
【憀】 ㄌㄧㄠˊ liau liáo
1. to rely; to depend
2. disappointed; sad; forlorn
3. clear; easy to understand
4. for the time being

憀亮(ㄌㄧㄠˊ ㄌㄧㄤˋ)
loud and clear

1685
【慝】 ㄊㄜˋ teh tè
an evil idea; evil; vice; iniquity

1686
【愨】 ㄑㄩㄝˋ chiueh què
honest; prudent

1687
【慫】 ㄙㄨㄥˇ soong sǒng
to instigate; to incite

慫動(ㄙㄨㄥˇ ㄉㄨㄥˋ)
to instigate; to incite

慫慂 or 慫恿(ㄙㄨㄥˇ ㄩㄥˇ)
to instigate; to incite; to egg on

1688
【慚】 (慙) ㄘㄢˊ tsarn cán
ashamed; mortified; humiliated: 他大言不慚。He was shamelessly boastful.

慚鳧企鶴(ㄘㄢˊ ㄈㄨˊ ㄑㄧˋ ㄏㄜˋ)
ashamed of one's inadequacy while envying another's competence

慚德(ㄘㄢˊ ㄉㄜˊ)
ashamed of being defective in morality

慚赧(ㄘㄢˊ ㄋㄢˇ)
to redden from shame

慚恧(ㄘㄢˊ ㄋㄩˋ)
to feel shame; ashamed

慚愧(ㄘㄢˊ ㄎㄨㄟˋ)
ashamed

慚恨(ㄘㄢˊ ㄏㄣˋ)
mortified; humiliated; to feel hurt

慚惶(ㄘㄢˊ ㄏㄨㄤˊ)
ashamed and bewildered; embarrassed

慚沮(ㄘㄢˊ ㄐㄩˇ)
ashamed and depressed

慚怍(ㄘㄢˊ ㄗㄨㄛˋ)
to feel ashamed; to feel shame

慚色(ㄘㄢˊ ㄙㄜˋ)
a shamefaced look

慚悚(ㄘㄢˊ ㄙㄨㄥˇ)
affected with shame and fear

1689
【慧】 ㄏㄨㄟˋ huey huì
intelligent; bright; wise

慧門法海(ㄏㄨㄟˋ ㄇㄣˊ ㄈㄚˇ ㄏㄞˇ)
(literally) the gate of intelligence and the sea of truth—the Buddhistic faith

慧目(ㄏㄨㄟˋ ㄇㄨˋ)
(Buddhism) discerning eyes

慧能(ㄏㄨㄟˋ ㄋㄥˊ)
Hui Neng, a noted Buddhist monk in the Tang Dynasty, the sixth patriarch of the Zen (禪) sect

慧力(ㄏㄨㄟˋ ㄌㄧˋ)
(Buddhism) the power of intelligence

慧根(ㄏㄨㄟˋ ㄍㄣ)
(Buddhism) the root of wisdom that can lead one to truth

慧光(ㄏㄨㄟˋ ㄍㄨㄤ)
(Buddhism) the wisdom which, like the light, pierces darkness

慧劍(ㄏㄨㄟˋ ㄐㄧㄢˋ)
(Buddhism) the sword of wisdom which cuts away illusion

慧劍斬情絲(ㄏㄨㄟˋ ㄐㄧㄢˋ ㄓㄢˇ ㄑㄧㄥˊ ㄙ)

to cut the thread of carnal love with the sword of wisdom
慧黠(ㄏㄨㄟˋ ㄒㄧㄚˊ)
(literary language) clever and artful; shrewd; astute
慧心(ㄏㄨㄟˋ ㄒㄧㄣ)
(Buddhism) a bright mind; a clear, alert mind; intelligence; the enlightened mind
慧星(ㄏㄨㄟˋ ㄒㄧㄥ)
a comet
慧性(ㄏㄨㄟˋ ㄒㄧㄥˋ)
intelligence
慧中(ㄏㄨㄟˋ ㄓㄨㄥ)
intelligent inside (usually used together with the expression "beautiful outside" in describing a woman)
慧日(ㄏㄨㄟˋ ㄖˋ)
the wisdom of Buddha
慧眼(ㄏㄨㄟˋ ㄧㄢˇ)
① discerning eyes; insight; one's penetrating insight ② (Buddhism) the eye of religious insight
慧眼識英雄(ㄏㄨㄟˋ ㄧㄢˇ ㄕˋ ㄧㄥ ㄒㄩㄥˊ)
Discerning eyes can tell greatness from mediocrity.

【慰】 1690
ㄨㄟˋ wey wèi

to console; to comfort; to soothe; to assuage; to relieve: 鄰居們安慰這個受傷孩子的母親。Neighbors comforted the mother of the wounded child.
慰勞(ㄨㄟˋ ㄌㄠˊ)
to entertain and cheer (sometimes by means of material gifts)
慰留(ㄨㄟˋ ㄌㄧㄡˊ)
to try to retain (a person intending to resign) in office
慰解(ㄨㄟˋ ㄐㄧㄝˇ)
to console by relieving one's pain or depression
慰藉(ㄨㄟˋ ㄐㄧㄝˋ)
to console; to comfort; to soothe; to give solace
慰情勝無(ㄨㄟˋ ㄑㄧㄥˊ ㄕㄥˋ ㄨˊ)
Though it gives nothing but a little comfort, it is better than nothing.
慰存(ㄨㄟˋ ㄘㄨㄣˊ)
to show sympathy; to comfort
慰安(ㄨㄟˋ ㄢ)
to soothe; to comfort
慰唁(ㄨㄟˋ ㄧㄢˋ)
to condole with (the bereaved)
慰問(ㄨㄟˋ ㄨㄣˋ)
to show sympathy by making inquiries; to express sympathy and solicitude: 請向他們轉達我眞誠的慰問。Please convey to them my sincere solicitude.
慰問團(ㄨㄟˋ ㄨㄣˋ ㄊㄨㄢˊ)
a group sent to convey greetings and appreciation
慰問金(ㄨㄟˋ ㄨㄣˋ ㄐㄧㄣ)
money sent to express one's gratitude or sympathy

【慼】 1691
(慽) ㄑㄧ chi qi

1. mournful; woeful
2. ashamed
慼貌(ㄑㄧ ㄇㄠˋ)
an appearance of sorrow
慼慼(ㄑㄧ ㄑㄧ)
sorrowful; sad; rueful
慼容(ㄑㄧ ㄖㄨㄥˊ)
a sad look; a sorrowful expression
慼憂(ㄑㄧ ㄧㄡ)
sad and depressed

【慾】 1692
ㄩˋ yuh yù

desire; appetite; passion; lust; greed: 她食慾不振。She is suffering from lack of appetite.
慾念(ㄩˋ ㄋㄧㄢˋ)
desire; a longing; a craving
慾令智昏(ㄩˋ ㄌㄧㄥˋ ㄓˋ ㄏㄨㄣ)
Greed can benumb reason.
慾海無邊(ㄩˋ ㄏㄞˇ ㄨˊ ㄅㄧㄢ)
Greed knows no bounds.
慾火(ㄩˋ ㄏㄨㄛˇ)
passion; the fire of lust
慾火焚身(ㄩˋ ㄏㄨㄛˇ ㄈㄣˊ ㄕㄣ)
The fire of lust is so hot that it consumes the body.
慾壑難塡(ㄩˋ ㄏㄨㄛˋ ㄋㄢˊ ㄊㄧㄢˊ)
The gulf of greed is hard to fill. 或 Greed is hard to satisfy.
慾障(ㄩˋ ㄓㄤˋ)
(Buddhism) desire as a barrier to salvation
慾望(ㄩˋ ㄨㄤˋ)
desire; a longing; aspirations; a craving; an urge: 他有做電影明星的慾望。He has an urge to become a cinema star.

【慕】 1693
ㄇㄨˋ muh mù

1. to yearn for; to long for
2. to adore; to admire: 我仰慕你已久。I have long looked up to you with admiration.
慕名(ㄇㄨˋ ㄇㄧㄥˊ)
① eager for fame ② to admire another's reputation
慕名而來(ㄇㄨˋ ㄇㄧㄥˊ ㄦˊ ㄌㄞˊ)
① to be attracted to a place by its reputation as a scenic spot, etc. ② to visit a stranger far away because of his or her reputation as a hero, great beauty, etc.
慕尼黑(ㄇㄨˋ ㄋㄧˊ ㄏㄟ)
① Munich, Germany ② (figuratively) international appeasement
慕化(ㄇㄨˋ ㄏㄨㄚˋ)
(said of barbarians) to be drawn and assimilated by civilization
慕效(ㄇㄨˋ ㄒㄧㄠˋ)
to imitate in admiration
慕勢(ㄇㄨˋ ㄕˋ)
to try to cling to one in power
慕容(ㄇㄨˋ ㄖㄨㄥˊ)
a family name of the Hsien-pei (鮮卑) tribe, which founded three of the sixteen small states in China during the Tsin (晉) Dynasty
慕義(ㄇㄨˋ ㄧˋ)
to admire righteousness; to emulate a good action
慕悅(ㄇㄨˋ ㄩㄝˋ)
mutual liking

【憂】 1694
ㄧㄡ iou you

1. sad; pensive; mournful; grieved
2. anxiety: 她無憂無慮。She is free from anxieties.
3. to worry about; concerned about; anxious; apprehensive
憂悶(ㄧㄡ ㄇㄣˋ)
to suffer mental agonies; worried; grieved; depressed; low-spirited
憂憤(ㄧㄡ ㄈㄣˋ)
grieved and indignant

憂天憫人(ㄧㄡ ㄊㄧㄢ ㄇㄧㄣˇ ㄖㄣˊ)
to worry about the destiny of mankind

憂樂相共(ㄧㄡ ㄌㄜˋ ㄒㄧㄤ ㄍㄨㄥˋ)
to share worries and blessings

憂勞成疾(ㄧㄡ ㄌㄠˊ ㄔㄥˊ ㄐㄧˊ)
to lose one's health because of care

憂慮(ㄧㄡ ㄌㄩˋ)
worried; anxious; apprehensive; to worry; worries; anxiety: 我甚感憂慮。I felt extremely anxious.

憂國憂民(ㄧㄡ ㄍㄨㄛˊ ㄧㄡ ㄇㄧㄣˊ)
to be concerned about the fate of the nation

憂患(ㄧㄡ ㄏㄨㄢˋ)
suffering; hardship; misery; distress; trouble; worry: 他飽經憂患。He has gone through a good deal of hardship.

憂患餘生(ㄧㄡ ㄏㄨㄢˋ ㄩˊ ㄕㄥ)
to survive countless worries and distresses

憂煎(ㄧㄡ ㄐㄧㄢ)
in agonies of worry

憂懼(ㄧㄡ ㄐㄩˋ)
anxious and fearful; worried and apprehensive

憂懼萬狀(ㄧㄡ ㄐㄩˋ ㄨㄢˋ ㄓㄨㄤˋ)
extremely anxious and fearful

憂戚(ㄧㄡ ㄑㄧ)
sad and worried

憂心(ㄧㄡ ㄒㄧㄣ)
a sad heart

憂心忡忡(ㄧㄡ ㄒㄧㄣ ㄔㄨㄥ ㄔㄨㄥ)
care-ridden; to have a heart loaded with worry

憂心如焚(ㄧㄡ ㄒㄧㄣ ㄖㄨˊ ㄈㄣˊ)
very anxious; deeply worried

憂形於色(ㄧㄡ ㄒㄧㄥˊ ㄩˊ ㄙㄜˋ)
to wear a sad or worried expression

憂愁(ㄧㄡ ㄔㄡˊ)
melancholy; grief; grievous; mournful; sad

憂傷(ㄧㄡ ㄕㄤ)
worried and grieved

憂容(ㄧㄡ ㄖㄨㄥˊ)or 憂色(ㄧㄡ ㄙㄜˋ)
a sad or worried look

憂思(ㄧㄡ ㄙ)
pensive

憂悒(ㄧㄡ ㄧˋ)
melancholy; depressed; cheerless; dispirited; dejected

憂鬱(ㄧㄡ ㄩˋ)
melancholy; depressed; dejected; cheerless; despondent: 他非常憂鬱地走開。He went away in great dejection.

憂鬱症(ㄧㄡ ㄩˋ ㄓㄥˋ)
melancholia; hypochondria

【慮】 1695 ㄌㄩˋ liuh lǜ

1. to consider; to take into account: 一個人應慎重考慮後，才做決定。One must consider the matter well before deciding.
2. to worry about; anxious about: 此事不足爲慮。This matter gives no cause for anxiety.

慮患(ㄌㄩˋ ㄏㄨㄢˋ)
apprehensive of trouble

慮及(ㄌㄩˋ ㄐㄧˊ)
to have anticipated; to have taken into account: 他早慮及會有麻煩。He had anticipated trouble.

慮事(ㄌㄩˋ ㄕˋ)
①to make plans for a matter ②to have misgivings about a matter

慮遠(ㄌㄩˋ ㄩㄢˇ)
to think far ahead; to plan for the distant future

【慶】 1696 ㄑㄧㄥˋ chinq qìng

1. festivity; blessing; felicity; joy
2. to celebrate; to congratulate; to rejoice

慶弔(ㄑㄧㄥˋ ㄉㄧㄠˋ)
congratulations on happy occasions and condolences on bereavements

慶典(ㄑㄧㄥˋ ㄉㄧㄢˇ)
national festivities and celebration ceremonies

慶功論賞(ㄑㄧㄥˋ ㄍㄨㄥ ㄌㄨㄣˊ ㄕㄤˇ)
to confer honors according to merits in service while celebrating a success or victory

慶功宴(ㄑㄧㄥˋ ㄍㄨㄥ ㄧㄢˋ)
a dinner party in celebration of triumph; a celebration party

慶賀(ㄑㄧㄥˋ ㄏㄜˋ)
to celebrate; to rejoice over; to offer congratulations: 他的成功值得慶賀。His success deserves congratulation.

慶幸(ㄑㄧㄥˋ ㄒㄧㄥˋ)
to congratulate or rejoice oneself

慶祝(ㄑㄧㄥˋ ㄓㄨˋ)
to celebrate; celebration: 他們慶祝豐收。They celebrated a bumper harvest.

慶壽(ㄑㄧㄥˋ ㄕㄡˋ)
to celebrate the birthday (of an old person)

慶賞(ㄑㄧㄥˋ ㄕㄤˇ)
to celebrate and reward

慶生會(ㄑㄧㄥˋ ㄕㄥ ㄏㄨㄟˋ)
a birthday party

十二畫

【憍】 1697 ㄐㄧㄠ jiau jiāo

self-conceited; arrogant

【憐】 1698 ㄌㄧㄢˊ lian lián

1. to sympathize; to pity; to commiserate: 同病相憐。Fellow sufferers have mutual sympathy.
2. to feel tender regard for
3. touching

憐貧(ㄌㄧㄢˊ ㄆㄧㄣˊ)
to pity or commiserate the poor

憐憫 or 憐閔 or 憐愍(ㄌㄧㄢˊ ㄇㄧㄣˇ)
to pity; to take compassion on; to commiserate

憐惜(ㄌㄧㄢˊ ㄒㄧˊ)
to feel tender regard for: 我們憐惜孩子。We feel tender regard for our children.

憐下(ㄌㄧㄢˊ ㄒㄧㄚˋ)
to have tender regard for one's subordinates; kind to one's inferiors

憐香惜玉(ㄌㄧㄢˊ ㄒㄧㄤ ㄒㄧˊ ㄩˋ)
to have a tender heart for the fair sex

憐恤(ㄌㄧㄢˊ ㄒㄩˋ)
to help or relieve out of compassion: 我們憐恤那些無助的孤兒。We help those helpless orphans out of compassion.

憐才(ㄌㄧㄢˊ ㄘㄞˊ)

to have sympathy for talented persons
憐愛(ㄌㄧㄢˊ ㄞˋ)
to have tender regard for; to feel pity and love for

【憎】 1699
ㄗㄥ tzeng zēng
to hate; to loathe; to abhor; to abominate; to detest: 他愛憎分明。He is clear about what to love and what to hate.
憎妒(ㄗㄥ ㄉㄨˋ)
to bear a jealous hatred for
憎恨(ㄗㄥ ㄏㄣˋ)
to hate; to hold a grudge against
憎嫉(ㄗㄥ ㄐㄧˊ)
to feel a jealous hatred for
憎嫌(ㄗㄥ ㄒㄧㄢˊ)
to hate; to dislike
憎惡
①(ㄗㄥ ㄨˋ)to hate; to loathe; to abominate; to detest; to abhor
②(ㄗㄥ ㄜˋ)to hate evil
憎怨(ㄗㄥ ㄩㄢˋ)
to bear a grudge against; to feel bitterness for

【憔】 1700
ㄑㄧㄠˊ chyau qiáo
emaciated; haggard; worn
憔慮(ㄑㄧㄠˊ ㄌㄩˋ)
impatient and anxious
憔悴(ㄑㄧㄠˊ ㄘㄨㄟˋ)
① to have a worn look; to look haggard ② to suffer distress, worries, etc. ③(said of plants) withered

【憚】 1701
ㄉㄢˋ dann dàn
to fear; to shirk; to dread
憚煩(ㄉㄢˋ ㄈㄢˊ)
afraid of trouble; to dislike taking trouble
憚服(ㄉㄢˋ ㄈㄨˊ)
to submit from awe
憚勞(ㄉㄢˋ ㄌㄠˊ)
to avoid trouble; to shrink from toils
憚改(ㄉㄢˋ ㄍㄞˇ)
reluctant to correct for fear of difficulty or trouble; afraid to reform: 過則勿憚改。 Don't be afraid to correct errors.

【憧】 1702
ㄔㄨㄥ chong chōng
1. indecisive; irresolute
2. to yearn; to aspire
憧憬(ㄔㄨㄥ ㄐㄧㄥˇ)
to imagine something or a place with yearning or longing
憧憧(ㄔㄨㄥ ㄔㄨㄥ)
indecisive; irresolute

【憬】 1703
ㄐㄧㄥˇ jiing jǐng
to realize; to come to understand; to awake
憬然(ㄐㄧㄥˇ ㄖㄢˊ)
aware; knowing
憬悟(ㄐㄧㄥˇ ㄨˋ)
to become aware of; to realize; to come to understand; to come to see the truth: 我憬悟了。I came to see the truth.

【憒】 1704
ㄎㄨㄟˋ kuey kuì
muddleheaded; confused in one's mind
憒眊(ㄎㄨㄟˋ ㄇㄠˋ)
muddleheaded; dull-witted
憒亂(ㄎㄨㄟˋ ㄌㄨㄢˋ)
confused in one's mind; at a loss; dazed
憒憒(ㄎㄨㄟˋ ㄎㄨㄟˋ)
confused; muddleheaded

【憫】 1705
ㄇㄧㄣˇ miin mǐn
1. to pity; to commiserate; to feel concerned over: 其情可憫。His case deserves sympathy.
2. to sorrow;to grieve
憫惜(ㄇㄧㄣˇ ㄒㄧ)
to pity; to have compassion on
憫恤(ㄇㄧㄣˇ ㄒㄩˋ)
to pity and help
憫惻(ㄇㄧㄣˇ ㄘㄜˋ)
to pity

【憮】 1706
ㄨˇ wuu wǔ
regretful; disappointed
憮然(ㄨˇ ㄖㄢˊ)
regretfully; disappointedly: 他憮然興嘆。He gave a sigh of disappointment.

【憭】 1707
1.ㄌㄧㄠˊ liau liáo
severe; inclement
憭慄(ㄌㄧㄠˊ ㄌㄧˋ)
cold; inclement; severe; dreary; dismal

【憭】 1707
2. ㄌㄧㄠˇ leau liǎo
clear; intelligible

【憦】 1708
ㄌㄠˋ law lào
to regret; to feel remorse

【憯】 1709
(慘) ㄘㄢˇ tsaan cǎn
sad; sorrowful; grieved

【憑】 1710
ㄆㄧㄥˊ pyng píng
1. to rely upon
2. to lean on
3. to be based on; to go by; to base on; to take as a basis
4. a basis; proof; evidence: 口說無憑。Oral agreement can not serve as evidence.
5. no matter (what, how, etc.)
憑本事(ㄆㄧㄥˊ ㄅㄣˇ ·ㄕ)
by virtue of sheer competence or talent (as distinct from pure luck or chance)
憑票(ㄆㄧㄥˊ ㄆㄧㄠˋ)
by showing tickets
憑票入座(ㄆㄧㄥˊ ㄆㄧㄠˋ ㄖㄨˋ ㄗㄨㄛˋ)
to gain admission by showing tickets; admission by ticket
憑單(ㄆㄧㄥˊ ㄉㄢ)
a certificate; a receipt
憑弔(ㄆㄧㄥˊ ㄉㄧㄠˋ)
① to pay homage to (the deceased) ② to contemplate (a ruin, relics, etc.) with emotion
憑眺(ㄆㄧㄥˊ ㄊㄧㄠˋ)
to look far from an eminence
憑欄(ㄆㄧㄥˊ ㄌㄢˊ)
to lean upon a balustrade or a railing
憑良心(ㄆㄧㄥˊ ㄌㄧㄤˊ ㄒㄧㄣ)
as one's conscience dictates
憑口說(ㄆㄧㄥˊ ㄎㄡˇ ㄕㄨㄛ)
to make an unfounded assertion; mere talk
憑空(ㄆㄧㄥˊ ㄎㄨㄥ)
without substantial support or proof; without foundation or good reason
憑几(ㄆㄧㄥˊ ㄐㄧ)
to lean on a desk
憑藉(ㄆㄧㄥˊ ㄐㄧㄝˋ)
①by means of; on the

〔心部〕

strength of ② to rely on: 我憑藉自己的力量。I relied on my own strength. ③ something on which one relies
憑據(ㄆㄧㄥˊ ㄐㄩˋ)
a basis (for belief or supposition); grounds; reasons; proof; evidence
憑信(ㄆㄧㄥˊ ㄒㄧㄣˋ)
to rely upon, or accept, as well-founded
憑虛公子(ㄆㄧㄥˊ ㄒㄩ ㄍㄨㄥ ㄗˇ)
(literally) a nonexistent gentleman—existing in name only
憑虛御風(ㄆㄧㄥˊ ㄒㄩ ㄩˋ ㄈㄥ)
to ride winds; to sail about in the void
憑摺(ㄆㄧㄥˊ ㄓㄜˊ)
a passbook
憑照(ㄆㄧㄥˊ ㄓㄠˋ)
certificates and licenses
憑仗(ㄆㄧㄥˊ ㄓㄤˋ)
to rely upon; to depend upon; by dint of
憑證(ㄆㄧㄥˊ ㄓㄥˋ)
a voucher; proof; evidence
憑準(ㄆㄧㄥˊ ㄓㄨㄣˇ)
a standard; a criterion
憑中(ㄆㄧㄥˊ ㄓㄨㄥ)
① in the presence of a witness ② a witness to a legal document
憑恃(ㄆㄧㄥˊ ㄕˋ)
to rely upon; to depend upon; to lean upon
憑軾結轍(ㄆㄧㄥˊ ㄕˋ ㄐㄧㄝˊ ㄔㄜˋ)
to travel fast on a chariot or cart
憑甚麼(ㄆㄧㄥˊ ㄕㄜˊ ·ㄇㄜ)
on what basis; why; on what ground: 你憑什麼說這話? What is your basis for saying so?
憑依(ㄆㄧㄥˊ ㄧ)
to rely upon; to depend upon; to be based on; to lean upon

【憋】 1711 ㄅㄧㄝ bie bie
1. to suppress inner feelings with efforts: 我憋了一肚子火。I was filled with pent-up anger.
2. to feel oppressed: 教室裡太悶,憋得人透不過氣來。The classroom was so stuffy; I could hardly breathe.
憋不住(ㄅㄧㄝ ·ㄅㄨ ㄓㄨˋ)
cannot suppress (feelings, emotions, etc.); cannot help (speaking out something)
憋悶(ㄅㄧㄝ ㄇㄣˋ)
melancholy; depressed
憋得慌(ㄅㄧㄝ ·ㄉㄜ ·ㄏㄨㄤ)
to feel oppressed: 我心裡憋得慌。I feel very much oppressed.
憋扭(ㄅㄧㄝ ·ㄋㄧㄡ)
① to be of contrary opinion ②(said of performance, writing, etc.) clumsy; not smooth
憋氣(ㄅㄧㄝ ㄑㄧˋ)
① to suffer breathing obstruction ② to suppress resentment, grudge, etc.

【憊】 1712 ㄅㄟˋ bey bèi
tired; exhausted; weary
憊累(ㄅㄟˋ ㄌㄟˋ)
tired; weary; exhausted
憊懶(ㄅㄟˋ ㄌㄢˇ)
tired and indolent
憊倦(ㄅㄟˋ ㄐㄩㄢˋ)
tired; exhausted; weary; fatigued: 我太憊倦了以致於站不住。I am too tired to stand.
憊色(ㄅㄟˋ ㄙㄜˋ)
a tired look; an expression of fatigue: 她面有憊色。She had a tired look.

【憩】 1713 (憇) ㄑㄧˋ chih qì
to rest; to repose
憩息(ㄑㄧˋ ㄒㄧˊ) or 憩歇(ㄑㄧˋ ㄒㄧㄝ)
to pause for rest; to rest; to take a rest

【憙】 1714 ㄒㄧˇ shii xǐ
happy; glad; delighted; pleased; joyful

【憝】 1715 ㄉㄨㄟˋ duey duì
1. wicked or vicious persons
2. to hate

【憖】 1716 ㄧㄣˋ yinn yìn
1. willing
2. cautious

【憨】 1717 ㄏㄢ han hān
1. silly; stupid; foolish
2. naive; straightforward
憨態(ㄏㄢ ㄊㄞˋ)
① naive; straightforward: 她憨態可掬。She is charmingly naive. ② a silly appearance
憨頭憨腦(ㄏㄢ ㄊㄡˊ ㄏㄢ ㄋㄠˇ)
stupid; silly; idiotic
憨厚(ㄏㄢ ㄏㄡˋ)
simple and honest
憨寢(ㄏㄢ ㄑㄧㄣˇ)
to sleep soundly
憨笑(ㄏㄢ ㄒㄧㄠˋ)
to giggle; to titter; to smile foolishly
憨直(ㄏㄢ ㄓˊ)
honest and straightforward
憨癡(ㄏㄢ ㄔ)
idiotic; silly; stupid
憨子(ㄏㄢ ·ㄗ)
a nincompoop; an idiot

【憲】 1718 ㄒㄧㄢˋ shiann xiàn
1. law; a code; a statute; an ordinance; a constitution
2. intelligent
3. a reference to superiors
憲兵(ㄒㄧㄢˋ ㄅㄧㄥ)
military police; gendarmes: 憲兵奉命維持治安。The military police were ordered to keep public security.
憲法(ㄒㄧㄢˋ ㄈㄚˇ)
constitution (of a national government): 美國有成文的憲法。The United States has a written constitution.
憲法條文(ㄒㄧㄢˋ ㄈㄚˇ ㄊㄧㄠˊ ㄨㄣˊ)
constitutional provisions
憲法草案(ㄒㄧㄢˋ ㄈㄚˇ ㄘㄠˇ ㄢˋ)
a draft constitution
憲典(ㄒㄧㄢˋ ㄉㄧㄢˇ)
a body of laws; a code
憲台(ㄒㄧㄢˋ ㄊㄞˊ)
Your Excellency (a salutation for one's superior)
憲天(ㄒㄧㄢˋ ㄊㄧㄢ)
the highest authorities
憲令(ㄒㄧㄢˋ ㄌㄧㄥˋ)
laws and ordinances
憲綱(ㄒㄧㄢˋ ㄍㄤ)
legal provisions
憲章(ㄒㄧㄢˋ ㄓㄤ)
a charter
憲政(ㄒㄧㄢˋ ㄓㄥˋ)
constitutional government; constitutional rule
憲政時期(ㄒㄧㄢˋ ㄓㄥˋ ㄕˊ ㄑㄧˊ)
the Constitutional Period

〔心部〕

(the final of the three stages of the political growth of the Republic of China envisaged by Dr. Sun Yat-sen)

憲則(ㄒㄧㄢˋ ㄗㄜˊ)
laws and institutions

十三畫

【憤】 1719 ㄈㄣˋ fenn fèn
to resent; indignant; indignation; angry: 別引起公憤。Don't rouse public indignation.

憤不欲生(ㄈㄣˋ ㄅㄨˋ ㄩˋ ㄕㄥ)
to tire of life at the extremity of indignation

憤懣(ㄈㄣˋ ㄇㄣˋ)
① indignant; resentful ② depressed and discontented

憤憤不平(ㄈㄣˋ ㄈㄣˋ ㄅㄨˋ ㄆㄧㄥˊ)
resentful or indignant because of injustice

憤怒(ㄈㄣˋ ㄋㄨˋ)
anger; wrath; indignation; rage: 他甚憤怒。He was in a rage.

憤慨(ㄈㄣˋ ㄎㄞˇ)
anger (especially at injustice); indignation: 他表示憤慨。He expressed his indignation.

憤恨(ㄈㄣˋ ㄏㄣˋ)
resentment; bitterness; rancor: 他心中對你並無憤恨。He has no rancor at heart against you.

憤激(ㄈㄣˋ ㄐㄧ)
vehemence; excitement; fury

憤切(ㄈㄣˋ ㄑㄧㄝˋ)
to grind the teeth with anger

憤世嫉俗(ㄈㄣˋ ㄕˋ ㄐㄧˊ ㄙㄨˊ)or 憤嫉(ㄈㄣˋ ㄐㄧˊ)
resentful of the world; misanthropic; cynical

憤然(ㄈㄣˋ ㄖㄢˊ)
angrily: 她憤然離去。She left angrily.

憤惋(ㄈㄣˋ ㄨㄢˇ)
resentful and regretful

【憶】 1720 ㄧˋ yih yì
to remember; to bear in mind; to recall; to recollect

憶念(ㄧˋ ㄋㄧㄢˋ)
nostalgic memory; recollection

憶苦思甜(ㄧˋ ㄎㄨˇ ㄙ ㄊㄧㄢˊ)
to recall one's past misfortune and think over one's present happiness

憶及(ㄧˋ ㄐㄧˊ)
to call to mind; to remember; to recollect

憶舊(ㄧˋ ㄐㄧㄡˋ)
to recall the bygone days with nostalgia; to recollect the past

憶起(ㄧˋ ㄑㄧˇ)
to call to mind; to remember; to recall: 他憶起童年時代的日子。He recollected his childhood days.

憶昔(ㄧˋ ㄒㄧˊ)
to recall the bygone days with nostalgia; to recollect the past

【憾】 1721 ㄏㄢˋ hann hàn
regret; remorse; dissatisfaction

憾恨(ㄏㄢˋ ㄏㄣˋ)
chagrin

憾事(ㄏㄢˋ ㄕˋ)
a regrettable thing; a matter for regret

憾怨(ㄏㄢˋ ㄩㄢˋ)
chagrin

【憺】 1722 ㄉㄢˋ dann dàn
1. content and stable
2. to fear

憺然(ㄉㄢˋ ㄖㄢˊ)
content; satisfied

【懂】 1723 ㄉㄨㄥˇ doong dǒng
to understand; to comprehend; to know: 我不懂英語。I don't know English.

懂不懂(ㄉㄨㄥˇ ˙ㄅㄨ ㄉㄨㄥˇ)
Do you understand?

懂得(ㄉㄨㄥˇ ˙ㄉㄜ)
to understand; to comprehend; to know: 他什麼也不懂得。He knows nothing.

懂道理(ㄉㄨㄥˇ ㄉㄠˋ ㄌㄧˇ)
to be reasonable; to be considerate

懂情理(ㄉㄨㄥˇ ㄑㄧㄥˊ ㄌㄧˇ)
reasonable and understanding

懂事(ㄉㄨㄥˇ ㄕˋ)
(said of the young) familiar with human affairs; sensible: 她是一個懂事的孩子。She is a sensible child.

懂人情(ㄉㄨㄥˇ ㄖㄣˊ ㄑㄧㄥˊ)
to understand human nature; to understand how to behave

懂人意(ㄉㄨㄥˇ ㄖㄣˊ ㄧˋ)
to understand the ideas of man

【懆】 1724 ㄘㄠˇ tsao cǎo
anxious; uneasy; apprehensive

懆懆(ㄘㄠˇ ㄘㄠˇ)
uneasy; anxious; apprehensive

【懈】 1725 ㄒㄧㄝˋ shieh xiè
negligent; remiss; relaxed; inattentive: 我們要努力不懈。We must strive without cease.

懈慢(ㄒㄧㄝˋ ㄇㄢˋ)
neglectful; negligent

懈怠(ㄒㄧㄝˋ ㄉㄞˋ)
to neglect; to goldbrick; slack; negligent; to slack; to relax: 工作不可懈怠。Don't get slack at your work.

懈弛(ㄒㄧㄝˋ ㄔˊ)
to relax

懈意(ㄒㄧㄝˋ ㄧˋ)
indolence; inactivity

【懊】 1726 ㄠˋ aw ào
to regret; to resent; regretful; remorseful; resentful: 做過的事已經做過了，懊悔無益。What is done is done and regret is of no use.

懊悶(ㄠˋ ㄇㄣˋ)
to eat one's heart out; to pine away

懊惱(ㄠˋ ㄋㄠˇ)
to feel remorseful and angry; upset

懊恨(ㄠˋ ㄏㄣˋ)
resentful

懊悔(ㄠˋ ㄏㄨㄟˇ)
to regret; regretful; remorseful: 我懊悔不該錯怪了他。I regretted having blamed him unjustly.

懊喪(ㄠˋ ㄙㄤˋ)
depressed; dejected; despondent: 她為什麼神情如此懊喪?

〔心部〕

Why is she looking so dejected?

【懍】 1727 ㄌㄧㄣˇ liin lǐn
1. filled with awe; awe-struck
2. inspiring awe; awful

懍慄(ㄌㄧㄣˇ ㄌㄧˋ)
trembling with awe; fearful

懍懍(ㄌㄧㄣˇ ㄌㄧㄣˇ)
① awe-struck; awe-stricken ② inspiring awe; dignified

懍然(ㄌㄧㄣˇ ㄖㄢˊ)
① awe-struck; awe-stricken; filled with awe ② inspiring fear

【懌】 1728 ㄧˋ yih yì
delighted; pleased; happy; glad

懌悅(ㄧˋ ㄩㄝˋ)
delighted; pleased; happy; glad

【應】 1729 1. ㄧㄥ ing yīng
should; ought to; need: 你應該趁熱把咖啡喝掉。You should drink your coffee while it is hot.

應辦(ㄧㄥ ㄅㄢˋ)
(said of tasks, business, etc.) that should be handled

應否(ㄧㄥ ㄈㄡˇ)
should or should not

應付費用(ㄧㄥ ㄈㄨˋ ㄈㄟˋ ㄩㄥˋ)
expenses payable

應付利息(ㄧㄥ ㄈㄨˋ ㄌㄧˋ ㄒㄧˊ)
interest payable

應付借款(ㄧㄥ ㄈㄨˋ ㄐㄧㄝˋ ㄎㄨㄢˇ)
loans payable

應付項目(ㄧㄥ ㄈㄨˋ ㄒㄧㄤˋ ㄇㄨˋ)
payables

應付帳款(ㄧㄥ ㄈㄨˋ ㄓㄤˋ ㄎㄨㄢˇ)
accounts payable

應負之責(ㄧㄥ ㄈㄨˋ ㄓ ㄗㄜˊ)
inescapable responsibility

應得(ㄧㄥ ㄉㄜˊ)
that one deserves to receive; deserved; due: 你罪有應得。You deserve your punishment.

應當(ㄧㄥ ㄉㄤ)
duty-bound; should; ought to: 咱們是同學，應當互相幫助。As classmates we ought to help each other.

應該(ㄧㄥ ㄍㄞ)
ought to; should: 他不應該作那種事情。He should not do things like that. 兒童應該服從他們的父母。Children should obey their parents.

應計工資(ㄧㄥ ㄐㄧˋ ㄍㄨㄥ ㄗ)
accrued wages

應計薪工(ㄧㄥ ㄐㄧˋ ㄒㄧㄣ ㄍㄨㄥ)
accrued payroll

應計項目(ㄧㄥ ㄐㄧˋ ㄒㄧㄤˋ ㄇㄨˋ)
accrued items

應屆畢業生(ㄧㄥ ㄐㄧㄝˋ ㄅㄧˋ ㄧㄝˋ ㄕㄥ)
graduating students or pupils; this year's graduates

應興應革(ㄧㄥ ㄒㄧㄥ ㄧㄥ ㄍㄜˊ)
what should be started and what should be abolished; necessary innovation and abolishment

應行事項(ㄧㄥ ㄒㄧㄥˊ ㄕˋ ㄒㄧㄤˋ)
things that should be done

應須(ㄧㄥ ㄒㄩ)
should; ought to; duty-bound

應收票據(ㄧㄥ ㄕㄡ ㄆㄧㄠˋ ㄐㄩˋ)
(accounting) bills receivable; notes receivable

應收利息(ㄧㄥ ㄕㄡ ㄌㄧˋ ㄒㄧˊ)
interest accrued

應收股利(ㄧㄥ ㄕㄡ ㄍㄨˇ ㄌㄧˋ)
(accounting) dividends receivable

應收項目(ㄧㄥ ㄕㄡ ㄒㄧㄤˋ ㄇㄨˋ)
(accounting) receivables

應收帳款(ㄧㄥ ㄕㄡ ㄓㄤˋ ㄎㄨㄢˇ)
(accounting) account receivable

應有(ㄧㄥ ㄧㄡˇ)
due; proper; deserved: 他做出應有的貢獻。He made a due contribution.

應有盡有(ㄧㄥ ㄧㄡˇ ㄐㄧㄣˋ ㄧㄡˇ)
Everything that has to be available is available. 或 Nothing is wanting.

【應】 1729 2. ㄧㄥˋ yinq yìng
1. to respond to; to answer; to echo; to react to: 我喊他，他不應。I called him, but he didn't answer.
2. to comply with; to grant: 菩薩是有求必應。Buddha grants whatever is requested.
3. to deal with; to cope with: 這事是你接下來的，由你應付吧。You're the one who took on the job, so you deal with it.
4. to assent to
5. a Chinese family name

應變(ㄧㄥˋ ㄅㄧㄢˋ)
①to adapt oneself to changes ②to prepare oneself for change ③(physics) strain

應變措施(ㄧㄥˋ ㄅㄧㄢˋ ㄘㄨㄛˋ ㄕ)
an emergency measure

應聘(ㄧㄥˋ ㄆㄧㄣˋ)
to accept an offer of employment

應卯(ㄧㄥˋ ㄇㄠˇ)
(said of officials in former times) to answer the morning roll call

應門(ㄧㄥˋ ㄇㄣˊ)
① to keep the gate; to be a gatekeeper ② to answer the door: 我應門。I answered the door.

應募(ㄧㄥˋ ㄇㄨˋ)
① to subscribe (to shares) ② to answer a draft call: 他兒子應募入伍。His son responded to a call for recruits.

應付(ㄧㄥˋ ㄈㄨˋ)
①to deal with; to cope with; to handle: 他應付自如。He handles a situation with ease. ② to do something perfunctorily: 他採取應付的態度。He took a perfunctory attitude. ③ to make do with: 我這些長靴，今年冬天還可以應付過去。I'll make do with these boots for this winter.

應答(ㄧㄥˋ ㄉㄚˊ)
to reply; to answer: 我應答如流。I reply readily and fluently.

應電荷(ㄧㄥˋ ㄉㄧㄢˋ ㄏㄜˊ)
(physics) induced charge

應對(ㄧㄥˋ ㄉㄨㄟˋ)
① to answer questions ② repartee: 他擅長應對。He is accomplished in repartee.

應對如流(ㄧㄥˋ ㄉㄨㄟˋ ㄖㄨˊ ㄌㄧㄡˊ)
to answer questions fluently

應天順人(ㄧㄥˋ ㄊㄧㄢ ㄕㄨㄣˋ ㄖㄣˊ)
(said of monarchs) in harmony with Heaven and men

應諾(ㄧㄥˋ ㄋㄨㄛˋ)
to assent; to consent; to promise; to undertake: 他應諾五點鐘到這裡來。He undertook to be here at five

o'clock.
應力(ㄧㄥˋ ㄌㄧˋ)
(physics) stress: 正應力 direct stress 內應力 internal stress
應考(ㄧㄥˋ ㄎㄠˇ)or 應試(ㄧㄥˋ ㄕˋ)
to participate in an examination; to sit for an examination: 去年應考的人很多。Many sat for the examination last year.
應機立斷(ㄧㄥˋ ㄐㄧ ㄌㄧˋ ㄉㄨㄢˋ)
to make quick decisions when an opportunity offers itself: 老板要應機立斷。The boss must make quick decisions as situation demands.
應急(ㄧㄥˋ ㄐㄧˊ)
to meet an emergency; for use in time of emergency
應急措施(ㄧㄥˋ ㄐㄧˊ ㄘㄨㄛˋ ㄕ)
an emergency measure
應接(ㄧㄥˋ ㄐㄧㄝ)
to receive (visitors or customers)
應接不暇(ㄧㄥˋ ㄐㄧㄝ ㄅㄨˋ ㄒㄧㄚˊ)
too busy to make proper response to
應景詩(ㄧㄥˋ ㄐㄧㄥˇ ㄕ)
occasional verses
應景兒(ㄧㄥˋ ㄐㄧㄥˇㄦ)
to do something appropriate on the occasion
應舉(ㄧㄥˋ ㄐㄩˇ)
to become a candidate in the imperial civil service examination
應許(ㄧㄥˋ ㄒㄩˇ)
to assent; to promise: 他們應許援助。They promised help.
應選(ㄧㄥˋ ㄒㄩㄢˇ)
to be a candidate in an election; to run for an elective post
應詔(ㄧㄥˋ ㄓㄠˋ)
to respond to an imperial decree
應召(ㄧㄥˋ ㄓㄠˋ)
to respond to a call or summons
應召女郎(ㄧㄥˋ ㄓㄠˋ ㄋㄩˇ ㄌㄤˊ)
a call girl
應召站(ㄧㄥˋ ㄓㄠˋ ㄓㄢˋ)
a call girl center
應召入伍(ㄧㄥˋ ㄓㄠˋ ㄖㄨˋ ㄨˇ)
to be drafted (for military service)

應戰(ㄧㄥˋ ㄓㄢˋ)
to accept a challenge; to meet the enemy on the battlefield: 我們沉着應戰。We met the attack calmly.
應診(ㄧㄥˋ ㄓㄣˇ)
(said of a doctor) to see patients
應徵(ㄧㄥˋ ㄓㄥ)
① to respond to a want ad ② to be recruited: 他應徵入伍。He was recruited into the army.
應徵稿件(ㄧㄥˋ ㄓㄥ ㄍㄠˇ ㄐㄧㄢˋ)
contributions to a magazine, etc. at the editor's public invitation
應酬(ㄧㄥˋ ㄔㄡˊ)
① social appointments ② to treat with courtesy: 我們應酬幾句。We exchange a few polite words.
應承(ㄧㄥˋ ㄔㄥˊ)
① to assent; to consent: 這件事她一口應承下來了。She agreed to do it without hesitation. ② to pledge
應時(ㄧㄥˋ ㄕˊ)
① to adapt oneself to the times ② to meet the current requirements; seasonable: 葡萄正應時。Grapes are in season. ③ at the appointed time ④ at once; immediately
應時水果(ㄧㄥˋ ㄕˊ ㄕㄨㄟˇ ㄍㄨㄛˇ)
the fruits of the season
應時貨品(ㄧㄥˋ ㄕˊ ㄏㄨㄛˋ ㄆㄧㄣˇ)
seasonable merchandise
應市(ㄧㄥˋ ㄕˋ)
to go on the market; to be put on the market; to be offered for sale
應試(ㄧㄥˋ ㄕˋ)
to take examinations; to sit for examinations
應手(ㄧㄥˋ ㄕㄡˇ)
smoothly; without a hitch
應聲(ㄧㄥˋ ㄕㄥ)
① an echo ② to happen right at the sound of something
應聲蟲(ㄧㄥˋ ㄕㄥ ㄔㄨㄥˊ)
a yes-man; a servile sycophant
應聲而倒(ㄧㄥˋ ㄕㄥ ㄦˊ ㄉㄠˇ)
to fall as soon as the bang (of the gun) was heard

應邀(ㄧㄥˋ ㄧㄠ)
at somebody's invitation; on invitation
應驗(ㄧㄥˋ ㄧㄢˋ)
(said of prophecies, expectations, etc.) to come true, or to be fulfilled: 她的話應驗了。What she said has come true.
應毋庸議(ㄧㄥˋ ㄨˊ ㄩㄥ ㄧˋ)
The matter should not be considered. (a cliché to say "no" to a request or suggestion in official correspondence)
應援(ㄧㄥˋ ㄩㄢˊ)
to render assistance at another's request
應允(ㄧㄥˋ ㄩㄣˇ)
to assent; to consent; an assent: 他們獲得我的應允。They had my assent.
應運而生(ㄧㄥˋ ㄩㄣˋ ㄦˊ ㄕㄥ)
to come with the tide of fashion; to rise because of a demand, opportunity, etc.; to arise at the historic moment
應用(ㄧㄥˋ ㄩㄥˋ)
① to utilize; to make use of ② for practical application; applied: 我們把理論應用於實踐。We apply theory to practice.
應用品(ㄧㄥˋ ㄩㄥˋ ㄆㄧㄣˇ)
necessities; consumer goods
應用科學(ㄧㄥˋ ㄩㄥˋ ㄎㄜ ㄒㄩㄝˊ)
applied science: 他決定研究應用科學。He decided to study applied science.
應用心理學(ㄧㄥˋ ㄩㄥˋ ㄒㄧㄣ ㄌㄧˇ ㄒㄩㄝˊ)
applied psychology
應用數學(ㄧㄥˋ ㄩㄥˋ ㄕㄨˋ ㄒㄩㄝˊ)
applied mathematics
應用文(ㄧㄥˋ ㄩㄥˋ ㄨㄣˊ)
business writing; practical writing

【懃】 1730
ㄑㄧㄣˊ chyn qín
cordial; hearty
懃懃懇懇(ㄑㄧㄣˊ ㄑㄧㄣˊ ㄎㄣˇ ㄎㄣˇ)
cordial and sincere

【懇】 1731
ㄎㄣˇ keen kěn
cordial; sincere; earnest: 他說話很誠懇。He is sincere in his statement.

〔心部〕

懇談(ㄎㄣˇ ㄊㄢˊ)
to have a sincere talk; to talk in a sincere manner
懇託(ㄎㄣˇ ㄊㄨㄛ)
to make a sincere request; to ask or request earnestly
懇留(ㄎㄣˇ ㄌㄧㄡˊ)
to make a sincere or earnest attempt to make a person stay
懇諫(ㄎㄣˇ ㄐㄧㄢˋ)
to admonish with sincerity; to admonish earnestly
懇乞(ㄎㄣˇ ㄑㄧˇ)
to entreat
懇切(ㄎㄣˇ ㄑㄧㄝˋ)
very sincere; earnest: 他的言詞懇切。He spoke in an earnest tone.
懇求(ㄎㄣˇ ㄑㄧㄡˊ)
to entreat; to beseech; to implore; to plead: 他懇求我幫忙。He entreats a favor of me.
懇親會(ㄎㄣˇ ㄑㄧㄣ ㄏㄨㄟˋ)
PTA (parent-teacher association or meeting)
懇請(ㄎㄣˇ ㄑㄧㄥˇ)
to ask earnestly; to implore; to entreat; to beseech; to plead: 懇請協助。Your assistance is earnestly requested.
懇摯(ㄎㄣˇ ㄓˋ)
sincere; earnest; eager: 他的情意懇摯。He showed his sincere feelings.
懇准(ㄎㄣˇ ㄓㄨㄣˇ)
to beg your kind permission
懇商(ㄎㄣˇ ㄕㄤ)
to ask for a favor earnestly; to seek consent sincerely
懇辭(ㄎㄣˇ ㄘˊ)
to decline (an offer) earnestly

【懋】 1732
ㄇㄠˋ maw mào
1. grand; majestic; great
2. trade
3. to encourage
懋典(ㄇㄠˋ ㄉㄧㄢˇ)
a grand occasion
懋功(ㄇㄠˋ ㄍㄨㄥ)
great achievements
懋績(ㄇㄠˋ ㄐㄧ)
great achievements or contribution
懋遷(ㄇㄠˋ ㄑㄧㄢ)
trade; commerce
懋勳(ㄇㄠˋ ㄒㄩㄣ)
great exploits or contribution
懋賞(ㄇㄠˋ ㄕㄤˇ)
to reward in order to encourage

十四畫

【懥】 1733
ㄓˋ jyh zhì
enraged; indignant; angry; resentful

【懦】 1734
ㄋㄨㄛˋ nuoh nuò
timid; cowardly; weak: 那個人怯懦如兎。That fellow is as timid as a rabbit.
懦夫(ㄋㄨㄛˋ ㄈㄨ)
a coward: 他是懦夫。He is a coward.
懦鈍(ㄋㄨㄛˋ ㄉㄨㄣˋ)
weak and dull
懦怯(ㄋㄨㄛˋ ㄑㄧㄝˋ)
coward; timid
懦弱(ㄋㄨㄛˋ ㄖㄨㄛˋ)
weak; cowardly

【懕】 1735
(懨) ㄧㄢ ian yān
1. sickly; in poor health
2. peaceful; tranquil
懕懕(ㄧㄢ ㄧㄢ)
① sickly; in poor health ② peaceful; content

【懣】 1736
ㄇㄣˋ menn mèn
resentful; sullen; sulky

【懟】 1737
ㄉㄨㄟˋ duey duì
to resent; to hate; rancor: 他心中對你並無怨懟。He has no rancor at heart against you.

十五畫

【懲】 1738
ㄔㄥˊ cherng chéng
(又讀 ㄔㄥˇ cheeng chěng)
1. to punish; to chastise; to reprimand; to reprove; to warn
2. to stop
懲辦(ㄔㄥˊ ㄅㄢˋ)
to take disciplinary action against
懲罰(ㄔㄥˊ ㄈㄚˊ)
to punish; to chastise; to penalize; a penalty: 他受到一次嚴厲的懲罰。He paid a severe penalty.
懲忿窒欲(ㄔㄥˊ ㄈㄣˋ ㄓˋ ㄩˋ)
to curb one's temper and desire
懲戒(ㄔㄥˊ ㄐㄧㄝˋ)
to reprimand; to discipline; to punish
懲戒處分(ㄔㄥˊ ㄐㄧㄝˋ ㄔㄨˇ ㄈㄣˋ)
disciplinary action (against government officials) ranging from reprimand to dismissal
懲前毖後(ㄔㄥˊ ㄑㄧㄢˊ ㄅㄧˋ ㄏㄡˋ)or 懲毖(ㄔㄥˊ ㄅㄧˋ)
to act cautiously in consequence of the penalty received for a previous offense
懲治(ㄔㄥˊ ㄓˋ)
to remedy by punishment
懲處(ㄔㄥˊ ㄔㄨˇ)
to penalize; to punish: 他依法懲處犯人。He punished the criminals in accordance with the law.
懲惡勸善(ㄔㄥˊ ㄜˋ ㄑㄩㄢˋ ㄕㄢˋ)
to punish wickedness and encourage virtue
懲一警百(ㄔㄥˊ ㄧ ㄐㄧㄥˇ ㄅㄞˇ)
to punish one person as a warning to a hundred others
懲役(ㄔㄥˊ ㄧˋ)
hard labor as a form of punishment

十六畫

【懷】 1739
ㄏㄨㄞˊ hwai huái
1. bosom; breast
2. to hold; to harbor: 他不懷好意。He harbored evil designs.
3. to think of; to recollect
4. to conceive (a child): 她懷了孩子。She became pregnant.
5. mind: 他的胸懷坦白。He is frank and open-minded.
6. as in 開懷暢飲(to drink to one's heart's content)
7. a Chinese family name
懷寶遯世(ㄏㄨㄞˊ ㄅㄠˇ ㄉㄨㄣˋ ㄕˋ)
to possess great talent but to live as a recluse
懷抱(ㄏㄨㄞˊ ㄅㄠˋ)
① an embrace; a hug; to

embrace; to hug ② the ideas one entertains; ambition ③ to cherish: 我們懷抱遠大的理想。We cherish lofty ideals.
懷璧其罪(ㄏㄨㄞˊ ㄅㄧˋ ㄑㄧˊ ㄗㄨㄟˋ)
(literally) The precious stone lands its innocent possessor in jail.—An innocent man gets into trouble because of his wealth.
懷錶(ㄏㄨㄞˊ ㄅㄧㄠˇ)
a pocket watch
懷服(ㄏㄨㄞˊ ㄈㄨˊ)
to yield; to submit; to give in
懷胎(ㄏㄨㄞˊ ㄊㄞ) or 懷孕(ㄏㄨㄞˊ ㄩㄣˋ) or 懷妊(ㄏㄨㄞˊ ㄖㄣˋ)
to become pregnant; to conceive: 她懷孕五個月了。She is five months pregnant.
懷土(ㄏㄨㄞˊ ㄊㄨˇ)
homesick; to yearn for home
懷念(ㄏㄨㄞˊ ㄋㄧㄢˋ)
to have a sweet memory of; to remember with longing or nostalgia; to think of; to long for; to miss: 我懷念遠方的友人。I thought of an absent friend who was far away.
懷祿(ㄏㄨㄞˊ ㄌㄨˋ)
to yearn for a high official position
懷古(ㄏㄨㄞˊ ㄍㄨˇ)
to look back upon the past; to think of the past with emotion
懷鬼胎(ㄏㄨㄞˊ ㄍㄨㄟˇ ㄊㄞ)
to harbor an evil scheme; to conceive mischief
懷恨(ㄏㄨㄞˊ ㄏㄣˋ) or 懷仇(ㄏㄨㄞˊ ㄔㄡˊ)
to bear a grudge; to nurse hatred; to harbor resentment
懷舊(ㄏㄨㄞˊ ㄐㄧㄡˋ)
① to recollect the good old days; to think of the bygone days with yearning; to yearn for the past ② to think of old friends
懷瑾握瑜(ㄏㄨㄞˊ ㄐㄧㄣˇ ㄨㄛˋ ㄩˊ)
(literally) to hold gems in one's bosom and grasp jades in one's hand—to be in possession of learning and virtue
懷奇(ㄏㄨㄞˊ ㄑㄧˊ)
to possess a rare talent or ability
懷鉛提槧(ㄏㄨㄞˊ ㄑㄧㄢ ㄊㄧˊ ㄑㄧㄢˋ)
to have writing instruments constantly with oneself; to be ready to write down anything encountered
懷邪(ㄏㄨㄞˊ ㄒㄧㄝˊ)
to harbor evil
懷挾(ㄏㄨㄞˊ ㄒㄧㄝˊ)
to secretly carry notes or books into an examination room
懷鄉(ㄏㄨㄞˊ ㄒㄧㄤ)
homesick
懷想(ㄏㄨㄞˊ ㄒㄧㄤˇ)
to think of with yearning; to remember with fondness; to yearn for
懷中(ㄏㄨㄞˊ ㄓㄨㄥ)
① in the arms ② in the mind
懷春(ㄏㄨㄞˊ ㄔㄨㄣ)
(usually said of young girls) to begin to think of love, or become sexually awakened
懷柔(ㄏㄨㄞˊ ㄖㄡˊ)
to conciliate; to appease; to pacify
懷柔政策(ㄏㄨㄞˊ ㄖㄡˊ ㄓㄥˋ ㄘㄜˋ)
conciliationism; a conciliatory policy (adopted by a powerful country in dealing with a weak nation or subjugated people)
懷才不遇(ㄏㄨㄞˊ ㄘㄞˊ ㄅㄨˋ ㄩˋ)
to have talent but no opportunity to use it
懷藏(ㄏㄨㄞˊ ㄘㄤˊ)
to conceal (weapons, jewels, etc.)
懷俄明(ㄏㄨㄞˊ ㄜˊ ㄇㄧㄥˊ)
the state of Wyoming, U.S.A.
懷貳(ㄏㄨㄞˊ ㄦˋ)
to harbor a treasonous intention, idea, or design
懷疑(ㄏㄨㄞˊ ㄧˊ)
to doubt; to suspect; to question; suspicious; doubt: 我懷疑這故事的眞實性。I doubt the truth of this story.
懷憂(ㄏㄨㄞˊ ㄧㄡ)
to be concerned or worried

【懶】 1740 ㄌㄢˇ laan lǎn

lazy; indolent; idle; inactive; listless; reluctant; disinclined: 他是一個懶人。He's a lazy fellow.
懶得(ㄌㄢˇ ˙ㄉㄜ)
not to feel like (doing something); not disposed or too tired to do anything; not to be in the mood to; to be disinclined to 亦作「懶待」: 我懶得出去。I don't feel like going out.
懶得動(ㄌㄢˇ ˙ㄉㄜ ㄉㄨㄥˋ)
lethargic; disinclined to move
懶得要命(ㄌㄢˇ ˙ㄉㄜ ㄧㄠˋ ㄇㄧㄥˋ)
very lazy
懶怠(ㄌㄢˇ ㄉㄞˋ) or 懶惰(ㄌㄢˇ ㄉㄨㄛˋ)
lazy; idle; indolent; slothful; inactive: 不要這樣懶惰。Don't be so lazy.
懶惰成性(ㄌㄢˇ ㄉㄨㄛˋ ㄔㄥˊ ㄒㄧㄥˋ)
to be habitually lazy; to have laziness as one's second nature
懶骨頭(ㄌㄢˇ ㄍㄨˇ ˙ㄊㄡ)
lazybones; a lazy person
懶慣了(ㄌㄢˇ ㄍㄨㄢˋ ˙ㄌㄜ)
accustomed to being lazy
懶漢(ㄌㄢˇ ㄏㄢˋ)
a lazy fellow
懶蟲(ㄌㄢˇ ㄔㄨㄥˊ)
(abusive) a lazy person; lazybones
懶散(ㄌㄢˇ ㄙㄢˇ)
indolent; inactive; sluggish: 不要這樣懶散，振作起來。Do not be so sluggish. Pull yourself together.
懶洋洋(ㄌㄢˇ ㄧㄤˊ ˙ㄧㄤ)
indolent; sluggish
懶於(ㄌㄢˇ ㄩˊ)
too lazy to do something; not enthusiastic about something: 他懶於做功課。He is too lazy to do his homework.

【懵】 1741 1. (懞) ㄇㄥˊ meng méng

ignorant
懵懵無知(ㄇㄥˊ ㄇㄥˊ ㄨˊ ㄓ)
quite ignorant
懵然(ㄇㄥˊ ㄖㄢˊ)
ignorant

【懵】 1741 2. ㄇㄥˇ meeng měng

muddleheaded; confused
懵懂(ㄇㄥˇ ㄉㄨㄥˇ)
①to have a confused mind;

muddleheaded ② dull-witted; ignorant

【懸】 1742 ㄒㄩㄢ shyuan xuán

1. to hang or be hanged or hung; to suspend or be suspended
2. to be in suspension; to be in suspense; unsettled; unsolved: 這筆賬懸了數年了。This account has remained unsettled for many years.
3. unfounded; without a basis; unsupported
4. far apart
5. to be concerned for

懸瀑(ㄒㄩㄢˊ ㄆㄨˋ)
a cascade; a waterfall

懸門(ㄒㄩㄢˊ ㄇㄣˊ)
a suspended gate which could be dropped

懸法(ㄒㄩㄢˊ ㄈㄚˇ)
to display written laws on some hangings

懸浮(ㄒㄩㄢˊ ㄈㄨˊ)
(physics) suspension

懸膽(ㄒㄩㄢˊ ㄉㄢˇ)
a drooping nose like a suspended gall

懸燈結綵(ㄒㄩㄢˊ ㄉㄥ ㄐㄧㄝˊ ㄘㄞˇ)
to celebrate an occasion by hanging lanterns and festoons

懸擬(ㄒㄩㄢˊ ㄋㄧˇ)
to make conjectures

懸念(ㄒㄩㄢˊ ㄋㄧㄢˋ)
worry and concern for a friend or close family member far away: 他突然失踪使我們大爲懸念。His sudden disappearance causes us considerable concern.

懸梁自盡(ㄒㄩㄢˊ ㄌㄧㄤˊ ㄗˋ ㄐㄧㄣˋ)
to hang oneself; to commit suicide by hanging

懸隔(ㄒㄩㄢˊ ㄍㄜˊ)
① remote; inaccessible ② to be separated by a great distance

懸鈎子(ㄒㄩㄢˊ ㄍㄡ ㄗˇ)
blackberry 亦作「山莓」

懸谷(ㄒㄩㄢˊ ㄍㄨˇ)
(geography) hanging valley

懸掛(ㄒㄩㄢˊ ㄍㄨㄚˋ)
to hang (decorations); to suspend: 此畫懸掛在牆上。The picture was hanging on the wall.

懸空(ㄒㄩㄢˊ ㄎㄨㄥ)
to be suspended (or hung) in the air

懸河(ㄒㄩㄢˊ ㄏㄜˊ)
① to pour continually ② to speak eloquently or glibly: 她口若懸河地表達自己的意思。She expressed herself in a flow of words.

懸衡(ㄒㄩㄢˊ ㄏㄥˊ)
to show (laws, etc.) as a public standard

懸壺濟世(ㄒㄩㄢˊ ㄏㄨˊ ㄐㄧˋ ㄕˋ)
to practice medicine or pharmacy

懸記(ㄒㄩㄢˊ ㄐㄧˋ)
prophecy; a prediction; forecast

懸絕(ㄒㄩㄢˊ ㄐㄩㄝˊ)
completely different

懸旗(ㄒㄩㄢˊ ㄑㄧˊ)
to hoist a flag; to hang a flag

懸缺(ㄒㄩㄢˊ ㄑㄩㄝ)
an unfilled vacancy or opening (in a government agency): 我們公司尚有懸缺。There is an unfilled vacancy in our company.

懸心(ㄒㄩㄢˊ ㄒㄧㄣ)
concerned about someone or something

懸心吊胆(ㄒㄩㄢˊ ㄒㄧㄣ ㄉㄧㄠˋ ㄉㄢˇ)
on tenterhooks; to be filled with anxiety or fear

懸想(ㄒㄩㄢˊ ㄒㄧㄤˇ)
to speculate; to conjecture; to imagine

懸虛(ㄒㄩㄢˊ ㄒㄩ)
hard to believe; unbelievable; incredible

懸針(ㄒㄩㄢˊ ㄓㄣ)
① a tadpole ② the hanging-needle stroke, an upright stroke in calligraphy seen in the character for ten (十)

懸腸掛肚(ㄒㄩㄢˊ ㄔㄤˊ ㄍㄨㄚˋ ㄉㄨˋ)
to harbor deep concern for something, as if it were suspended on one's bowels

懸揣(ㄒㄩㄢˊ ㄔㄨㄞˇ)
to speculate or conjecture

懸首(ㄒㄩㄢˊ ㄕㄡˇ)
to hang the head of a decapitated criminal in the market or over the city gate

懸賞(ㄒㄩㄢˊ ㄕㄤˇ)
to offer a prize, or reward (for the capture of a criminal, etc.): 警方懸賞緝拿該逃犯。The police offered a reward for the capture of the runaway criminal.

懸殊(ㄒㄩㄢˊ ㄕㄨ)
to differ by a wide margin; very different; a great disparity; a wide gap: 那個國家貧富懸殊。There is a wide gap between the rich and the poor in that country.

懸在空中(ㄒㄩㄢˊ ㄗㄞˋ ㄎㄨㄥ ㄓㄨㄥ)
to suspend or be suspended in midair

懸索橋(ㄒㄩㄢˊ ㄙㄨㄛˇ ㄑㄧㄠˊ)
a suspension bridge 亦作「吊橋」

懸案(ㄒㄩㄢˊ ㄢˋ)
an unsettled case; an outstanding issue (between nations)

懸而未決(ㄒㄩㄢˊ ㄦˊ ㄨㄟˋ ㄐㄩㄝˊ)
suspense; in suspense: 歷經數日，事情仍是懸而未決。For some days matters hung in suspense.

懸疑(ㄒㄩㄢˊ ㄧˊ)
suspense

懸崖(ㄒㄩㄢˊ ㄧㄞˊ)
a precipice

懸崖勒馬(ㄒㄩㄢˊ ㄧㄞˊ ㄌㄜˋ ㄇㄚˇ)
(literally) to rein in the horse at the edge of a precipice—to stop just before committing a serious blunder; to stop before it is too late

懸崖峭壁(ㄒㄩㄢˊ ㄧㄞˊ ㄑㄧㄠˋ ㄅㄧˋ)
overhanging precipices and steep cliffs

懸腕(ㄒㄩㄢˊ ㄨㄢˋ) or 懸肘(ㄒㄩㄢˊ ㄓㄡˇ)
to keep the arm off the desk (when writing characters in order to gain forcefulness in the strokes)

懸望(ㄒㄩㄢˊ ㄨㄤˋ)
to hope with misgivings

十七畫

【懺】 1743 ㄔㄢˋ chann chàn

to confess one's sin; to repent

懺禮(ㄔㄢˋ ㄌㄧˇ)
a ritual for penance; a ceremony of penitence

懺悔(ㄔㄢˋ ㄏㄨㄟˇ)
to repent of one's sin; to feel or show repentance: 他懺悔自己的罪過。He repented of his sin.

懺悔錄(ㄔㄢˋ ㄏㄨㄟˇ ㄌㄨˋ)
confessions

懺悔自新(ㄔㄢˋ ㄏㄨㄟˇ ㄗˋ ㄒㄧㄣ)
to repent and turn over a new leaf

十八畫

【懼】 1744 ㄐㄩˋ jiuh jù

1. to fear; to dread; to be afraid of; in fear of: 人們恐懼生病。People dread falling ill (or to fall ill).
2. to frighten

懼怕(ㄐㄩˋ ㄆㄚˋ)
to fear; to dread; to be afraid of

懼內(ㄐㄩˋ ㄋㄟˋ)
henpecked

懼高症(ㄐㄩˋ ㄍㄠ ㄓㄥˋ)
acrophobia

懼怯(ㄐㄩˋ ㄑㄩㄝˋ)
timid; afraid

懼者不來(ㄐㄩˋ ㄓㄜˇ ㄅㄨˋ ㄌㄞˊ)
He who has come is no coward. 亦作「來者不懼」

懼水症(ㄐㄩˋ ㄕㄨㄟˇ ㄓㄥˋ)
hydrophobia 亦作「恐水症」

懼色(ㄐㄩˋ ㄙㄜˋ)
a look of fear

【懾】 1745 ㄓㄜˊ jer zhé

fearful; awe-struck: 他懾於淫威之下。He is terrorized by tyrannical methods.

懾服(ㄓㄜˊ ㄈㄨˊ)
to yield from fear; to submit because of fear

懾慴(ㄓㄜˊ ㄓㄜˊ)
to lose one's courage in fear

【懿】 1746 (懿) ㄧˋ yih yì

1. virtuous; fine; good; exemplary
2. having to do with womanly virtue; modest; chaste

懿範(ㄧˋ ㄈㄢˋ)
a fine example or model of womanly virtue; exemplary character

懿德(ㄧˋ ㄉㄜˊ)
① fine virtue ② woman's worthy or meritorious character

懿戚(ㄧˋ ㄑㄧ)
the emperor's relatives by marriage

懿親(ㄧˋ ㄑㄧㄣ)
close relatives

懿行(ㄧˋ ㄒㄧㄥˋ)
① a virtuous deed ② women's virtuous conduct

懿旨(ㄧˋ ㄓˇ)
a decree by the empress; a command or wish of the empress or empress dowager

懿言(ㄧˋ ㄧㄢˊ)
fine words

懿望(ㄧˋ ㄨㄤˋ)
good reputation

【懽】 1747 (歡) ㄏㄨㄢ huan huān

happy; glad; joyous

十九畫

【戀】 1748 ㄌㄧㄢˋ liann liàn

1. to love (one of the other sex); to be in love: 他們在戀愛中。They are in love with each other.
2. to feel a persistent attachment (for a thing)

戀母情結(ㄌㄧㄢˋ ㄇㄨˇ ㄑㄧㄥˊ ㄐㄧㄝˊ)
Oedipus complex

戀慕(ㄌㄧㄢˋ ㄇㄨˋ)
to have a tender feeling towards; to lose one's heart to; to pine for; to love at a distance or silently

戀父情結(ㄌㄧㄢˋ ㄈㄨˋ ㄑㄧㄥˊ ㄐㄧㄝˊ)
Electra complex

戀戀不捨(ㄌㄧㄢˋ ㄌㄧㄢˋ ㄅㄨˋ ㄕㄜˇ)
to feel a persistent attachment (for a thing or a person); to feel reluctant to part company with (a person or thing)

戀歌(ㄌㄧㄢˋ ㄍㄜ)
a love song

戀家(ㄌㄧㄢˋ ㄐㄧㄚ)
to be reluctant to leave home; to prefer to stay at home; to long for home; to be reluctant to be away from home

戀舊(ㄌㄧㄢˋ ㄐㄧㄡˋ)
① to yearn for the past; to long for the good old days ② to yearn for old friends, or for a place one visited before

戀奸情熱(ㄌㄧㄢˋ ㄐㄧㄢ ㄑㄧㄥˊ ㄖㄜˋ)
to have an illicit and passionate love affair

戀情(ㄌㄧㄢˋ ㄑㄧㄥˊ)
love between man and woman

戀棧(ㄌㄧㄢˋ ㄓㄢˋ)
reluctant to give up a position (particularly a public post) one is holding; to cling to an official post when one should leave

戀主(ㄌㄧㄢˋ ㄓㄨˇ)
to feel an attachment for one's master

戀人(ㄌㄧㄢˋ ㄖㄣˊ)
a sweetheart; a lover

戀愛(ㄌㄧㄢˋ ㄞˋ)
tender passions; a romantic attachment

二十畫

【戄】 1749 ㄐㄩㄝˊ jyue jué

1. respectful
2. awe-struck

戄然(ㄐㄩㄝˊ ㄖㄢˊ)
awe-struck; surprisingly

二十四畫

【戇】 1750 ㄓㄨㄤˋ juanq zhuàng

simple-minded

戇直(ㄓㄨㄤˋ ㄓˊ)
simple and upright; simple and honest; blunt and tactless: 他爲人戇直。He is simple and honest.

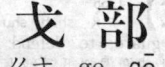

戈部
ㄍㄜ ge gē

【戈】 1751 ㄍㄜ ge gē

〔戈部〕

1. a spear; a lance; a javelin
2. a Chinese family name
戈比(ㄍㄜ ㄅㄧˇ)
(a coin of the U.S.S.R.) kopek, kopeck, or copeck
戈壁(ㄍㄜ ㄅㄧˋ)
Mongolian for "desert"
戈壁大沙漠(ㄍㄜ ㄅㄧˋ ㄉㄚˋ ㄕㄚ ㄇㄛˋ)
the Gobi Desert
戈矛(ㄍㄜ ㄇㄠˊ)
spears and lances: 戰士們攜帶戈矛。The warriors carried spears and lances.
戈登(ㄍㄜ ㄉㄥ)
Charles George Gordon, 1833-1885, a British general who helped put down the Taiping Rebellion
戈戟(ㄍㄜ ㄐㄧˇ)
spears; lances

一畫

【戊】 1752
ㄨˋ wuh wù
the fifth of the Ten Celestial Stems
戊戌政變(ㄨˋ ㄒㄩ ㄓㄥˋ ㄅㄧㄢˋ)
the Coup of Wu Hsü Year (1898), in which Kang Yuwei (康有爲) and other progressives tried in vain to introduce political reforms in China
戊夜(ㄨˋ ㄧㄝˋ)
the predawn hours

【戉】 1753
ㄩㄝˋ yueh yuè
a large ax 亦作「鉞」

二畫

【戌】 1754
ㄒㄩ shiu xū
the eleventh of the Twelve Terrestrial Branches
戌時(ㄒㄩ ㄕˊ)
7-9 p.m.
戌月(ㄒㄩ ㄩㄝˋ)
the ninth month of the lunar year

【戍】 1755
ㄕㄨˋ shuh shù
to guard; to defend: 英勇戰士戍衛邊疆抵禦敵人。The brave soldiers defended the frontier regions against enemies.
戍邊(ㄕㄨˋ ㄅㄧㄢ)
to guard the border or the frontier; to garrison the frontier
戍樓(ㄕㄨˋ ㄌㄡˊ)
a garrison watchtower
戍鼓(ㄕㄨˋ ㄍㄨˇ)
the drums of garrison troops
戍守(ㄕㄨˋ ㄕㄡˇ)or 戍衛(ㄕㄨˋ ㄨㄟˋ)
to be stationed as garrison troops at (a fortified place, the border, etc.); to set up the frontier garrison: 軍隊被派在邊區戍守。The troops were stationed at the border.
戍人(ㄕㄨˋ ㄖㄣˊ)or 戍卒(ㄕㄨˋ ㄗㄨˊ)
garrison soldiers; a frontier guard
戍役(ㄕㄨˋ ㄧˋ)
garrison duty or military service as a punishment in former times

【戎】 1756
ㄖㄨㄥˊ rong róng
1. war; fighting
2. arms; the apparatus of war
3. military affairs; army: 許多青年投筆從戎。Many young people cast aside the pen to join the army.
4. barbarians to the west
5. great
6. you
7. to help
戎馬(ㄖㄨㄥˊ ㄇㄚˇ)
war-horses; army horses
戎馬倥傯(ㄖㄨㄥˊ ㄇㄚˇ ㄎㄨㄥˇ ㄗㄨㄥˇ)
to lead a hectic life with war horses; to have a hectic military career (usually said of ranking commanders)
戎馬之間(ㄖㄨㄥˊ ㄇㄚˇ ㄓ ㄐㄧㄢ)
among war-horses; on the fighting line
戎馬生涯(ㄖㄨㄥˊ ㄇㄚˇ ㄕㄥ ㄧㄚˊ)
an army life; a military career
戎幕(ㄖㄨㄥˊ ㄇㄨˋ)
a military camp
戎服(ㄖㄨㄥˊ ㄈㄨˊ)
military dress
戎狄(ㄖㄨㄥˊ ㄉㄧˊ)
barbarians to the west and the north of ancient China
戎旅(ㄖㄨㄥˊ ㄌㄩˇ)
the army
戎略(ㄖㄨㄥˊ ㄌㄩㄝˋ)
war plans; strategy
戎行(ㄖㄨㄥˊ ㄏㄤˊ)
the army; the armed forces; the ranks
戎機(ㄖㄨㄥˊ ㄐㄧ)
military secrets (or strategy)
戎車(ㄖㄨㄥˊ ㄐㄩ)
a war vehicle; a chariot
戎器(ㄖㄨㄥˊ ㄑㄧˋ)
arms; weapons
戎裝(ㄖㄨㄥˊ ㄓㄨㄤ)or 戎衣(ㄖㄨㄥˊ ㄧ)
military dress; military uniform
戎事(ㄖㄨㄥˊ ㄕˋ)
military affairs
戎首(ㄖㄨㄥˊ ㄕㄡˇ)
the one who starts a war; the top war criminal
戎衣(ㄖㄨㄥˊ ㄧ)
armor
戎伍(ㄖㄨㄥˊ ㄨˇ)
the ranks; the army; the armed forces

三畫

【成】 1757
ㄔㄥˊ cherng chéng
1. completed; accomplished; finished; fixed; settled; to accomplish; to succeed; to complete: 他完成了他的工作。He completed his work.
2. to achieve
3. to become: 他已成爲很著名的人。He has become quite a famous man.
4. acceptable; all right: 成!我在十點時和你見面。All right, I'll meet you at ten.
5. able; capable
6. one tenth
7. a Chinese family name
成敗(ㄔㄥˊ ㄅㄞˋ)
success or failure: 成敗全憑此舉。Success or failure depends on this one action.
成敗利鈍(ㄔㄥˊ ㄅㄞˋ ㄌㄧˋ ㄉㄨㄣˋ)
successes and failures; advantages and disadvantages: 成敗利鈍尙難逆料。Whether it will be successful or not is still difficult to predict.
成本(ㄔㄥˊ ㄅㄣˇ)
(commerce) cost
成本分析(ㄔㄥˊ ㄅㄣˇ ㄈㄣ ㄒㄧ)

cost analysis

成本會計(ㄔㄥˊ ㄅㄣˇ ㄎㄨㄞˋ ㄐㄧˋ)
cost accounting

成本計算(ㄔㄥˊ ㄅㄣˇ ㄐㄧˋ ㄙㄨㄢˋ)
(accounting) costing; cost-finding

成本價格(ㄔㄥˊ ㄅㄣˇ ㄐㄧㄚˋ ㄍㄜˊ)
(accounting) the cost price

成病(ㄔㄥˊ ㄅㄧㄥˋ)
to fall ill; to become sick

成不了氣候(ㄔㄥˊ ㄅㄨˋ ㄌㄧㄠˇ ㄑㄧˋ ㄏㄡˋ)
(informal) unable to become formidable

成批(ㄔㄥˊ ㄆㄧ)
group by group; in batches

成品(ㄔㄥˊ ㄆㄧㄣˇ)
finished products

成眠(ㄔㄥˊ ㄇㄧㄢˊ)
(literary language) to fall asleep; to go to sleep: 他整夜不能成眠。He couldn't fall asleep all night.

成名(ㄔㄥˊ ㄇㄧㄥˊ)
to achieve fame; to become famous

成命(ㄔㄥˊ ㄇㄧㄥˋ)
① already issued orders ② the determinate appointment

成法(ㄔㄥˊ ㄈㄚˇ)
① promulgated laws; existing laws ② to become a law

成佛(ㄔㄥˊ ㄈㄛˊ)
to become a Buddha

成分(ㄔㄥˊ ㄈㄣˋ)
① an ingredient; a component; composition ② a factor ③ personal background

成方兒(ㄔㄥˊ ㄈㄤㄦ)
patent medicine; apothecary's formulas; physician's prescriptions

成風(ㄔㄥˊ ㄈㄥ)
to become a common practice; to become the order of the day: 時下勤儉成風。Diligence and frugality are now the order of the day.

成服(ㄔㄥˊ ㄈㄨˊ)
to put on mourning dress after the remains of the deceased is laid in the coffin for funeral service

成副兒(ㄔㄥˊ ㄈㄨˋㄦ)
to form an acceptable set (said of pieces or cards held in one's hand in mah-jong or a card game)

成丁(ㄔㄥˊ ㄉㄧㄥ)
(said of a male) to come of age

成都(ㄔㄥˊ ㄉㄨ)
Chengtu, capital city of Szechwan Province

成堆(ㄔㄥˊ ㄉㄨㄟ)
to pile up; to make into a pile; to be in heaps: 我的家庭作業成堆未做。My homework has piled up.

成對(ㄔㄥˊ ㄉㄨㄟˋ)
to match; to form a pair

成套(ㄔㄥˊ ㄊㄠˋ)
① to form a complete set: 這些器具是成套的。These instruments form a complete set. ② a whole set

成湯(ㄔㄥˊ ㄊㄤ)
Prince Tang, who overthrew the tyrant Chieh of Hsia (夏桀) and established the Shang Dynasty in 1766 B.C.

成天(ㄔㄥˊ ㄊㄧㄢ)
all day long; the whole day: 他成天無所事事。He has been doing nothing all day long.

成年(ㄔㄥˊ ㄋㄧㄢˊ)
① to come of age; to reach adulthood: 他三個月後就成年了。He will reach adulthood in three months. ② adult: 他是成年人。He is an adult. ③ the whole year long; through out the whole year

成年累月(ㄔㄥˊ ㄋㄧㄢˊ ㄌㄟˇ ㄩㄝˋ)
year after year and month after month; year in, year out

成年期(ㄔㄥˊ ㄋㄧㄢˊ ㄑㄧˊ)
adulthood

成了(ㄔㄥˊ ˙ㄌㄜ)
acceptable; all right; okay; O.K.; enough; accomplished

成禮(ㄔㄥˊ ㄌㄧˇ)
to complete the ceremonies; to solemnize

成立(ㄔㄥˊ ㄌㄧˋ)
① to establish; to found; to come into existence; to set up: 他最近成立一家新店舖。He has set up a new store recently. ② (said of a relation, theory, etc.) to hold good or to be recognized as irrefutable; to hold water

成立大會(ㄔㄥˊ ㄌㄧˋ ㄉㄚˋ ㄏㄨㄟˋ)
the inaugural meeting (of an organization): 他們開過成立大會。They held an inaugural meeting.

成例(ㄔㄥˊ ㄌㄧˋ)
an established precedent

成殮(ㄔㄥˊ ㄌㄧㄢˋ)
to have the deceased properly dressed and put into coffin

成個兒(ㄔㄥˊ ㄍㄜˋㄦ)
① to grow to a good size ② to be in the proper form ③ the whole piece

成果(ㄔㄥˊ ㄍㄨㄛˇ)
results achieved; achievements; the fruits (of efforts): 他的成功是努力工作的成果。His success was the result of hard work.

成規(ㄔㄥˊ ㄍㄨㄟ)
an established practice, rule or regulation; a rut: 別墨守成規。Don't stick to conventions.

成功(ㄔㄥˊ ㄍㄨㄥ)
① to complete one's work ② success: 他終於獲得成功。He finally achieved success.

成何體統(ㄔㄥˊ ㄏㄜˊ ㄊㄧˇ ㄊㄨㄥˇ)
What a scandal!

成歡(ㄔㄥˊ ㄏㄨㄢ)
① to enjoy oneself to one's heart's content ② to have sexual relation

成婚(ㄔㄥˊ ㄏㄨㄣ)
to get married

成績(ㄔㄥˊ ㄐㄧ)
records established or set; results; a showing

成績單(ㄔㄥˊ ㄐㄧ ㄉㄢ)
a report card; a transcript of a student's scholastic record in school

成吉思汗(ㄔㄥˊ ㄐㄧˊ ㄙ ㄏㄢˋ)
Genghis Khan or Jenghiz Khan, 1162-1227, Mongolian conqueror

成家(ㄔㄥˊ ㄐㄧㄚ)
(said of men reaching adulthood) to have a family; to get married

成家立業(ㄔㄥˊ ㄐㄧㄚ ㄌㄧˋ ㄧㄝˋ)
(said of men reaching adulthood) to get married and start a career

成交(ㄔㄥˊ ㄐㄧㄠ)

〔戈部〕

to get accepted by both parties, or to go through a business deal; the consummation of a business transaction; to strike (or close) a bargain: 我們終於和他成交了。We finally closed a bargain with him.

成就(ㄔㄥˊ ㄐㄧㄡˋ)
an achievement; an accomplishment: 實現這個計畫眞是件偉大的成就。It was a great accomplishment to carry out the plan.

成就感(ㄔㄥˊ ㄐㄧㄡˋ ㄍㄢˇ)
a sense of fulfillment; the feeling of having accomplished something important

成姦(ㄔㄥˊ ㄐㄧㄢ)
to have illicit sexual relations

成見(ㄔㄥˊ ㄐㄧㄢˋ)
a prejudice; a preconception; a bias: 他對此計畫有成見。He has a bias towards (or against) the plan.

成精作怪(ㄔㄥˊ ㄐㄧㄥ ㄗㄨㄛˋ ㄍㄨㄞˋ)
(said of animals or plants in the mind of the superstitious) to turn into a mischievous spirit

成局(ㄔㄥˊ ㄐㄩˊ)
① an irrevocable situation ② to become fixed or irrevocable

成器(ㄔㄥˊ ㄑㄧˋ)
to become a useful person

成千累萬(ㄔㄥˊ ㄑㄧㄢ ㄌㄟˇ ㄨㄢˋ)or 成千成萬(ㄔㄥˊ ㄑㄧㄢ ㄔㄥˊ ㄨㄢˋ)
hundreds upon thousands; tens of thousands; countless; numerous

成親(ㄔㄥˊ ㄑㄧㄣ)
to get married

成擒(ㄔㄥˊ ㄑㄧㄣˊ)
to get captured

成全(ㄔㄥˊ ㄑㄩㄢˊ)
to help (others) accomplish something

成羣(ㄔㄥˊ ㄑㄩㄣˊ)
in groups; in large numbers; in hordes; swarms: 成羣的牛羊 herds of cattle and sheep

成羣打夥(ㄔㄥˊ ㄑㄩㄣˊ ㄉㄚˇ ㄏㄨㄛˇ)
to band together; to gather in groups; to form into groups

成羣結隊(ㄔㄥˊ ㄑㄩㄣˊ ㄐㄧㄝˊ ㄉㄨㄟˋ)
to band together; to gather in groups; in crowds (or throngs)

成效(ㄔㄥˊ ㄒㄧㄠˋ)
result; effect; efficacy; effectiveness: 這藥對那種病無成效。The medicine has no efficacy in that disease.

成效卓著(ㄔㄥˊ ㄒㄧㄠˋ ㄓㄨㄛˊ ㄓㄨˋ)
The achievement is outstanding.

成憲(ㄔㄥˊ ㄒㄧㄢˋ)
existing laws

成心(ㄔㄥˊ ㄒㄧㄣ)
① intentionally; on purpose; with deliberate intent: 他成心跟我們作對。He purposely antagonized us. ② a preconceived notion

成行(ㄔㄥˊ ㄒㄧㄥˊ)
to embark on a journey

成形(ㄔㄥˊ ㄒㄧㄥˊ)
to take shape: 我們的新圖書館計畫開始成形了。Our plans of a new library are beginning to take shape.

成性(ㄔㄥˊ ㄒㄧㄥˋ)
to become habitual; to become second nature: 這個傢伙偷竊成性。Stealing has become that villain's second nature.

成長(ㄔㄥˊ ㄓㄤˇ)
to grow up; growth: 她成長得多麼快啊! How quickly she is growing!

成竹在胸(ㄔㄥˊ ㄓㄨˊ ㄗㄞˋ ㄒㄩㄥ)
to know what one is doing; to have already made careful planning for what one is doing 亦作「胸有成竹」

成仇(ㄔㄥˊ ㄔㄡˊ)
to become enemies; to be at feud with

成蟲(ㄔㄥˊ ㄔㄨㄥˊ)
(zoology) an imago

成事(ㄔㄥˊ ㄕˋ)
① bygones ② to succeed in doing something ③ things done

成事不足，敗事有餘(ㄔㄥˊ ㄕˋ ㄅㄨˋ ㄗㄨˊ, ㄅㄞˋ ㄕˋ ㄧㄡˇ ㄩˊ)
(literally) to have a capacity not enough for success yet more than enough for disaster—apt to bungle; to be unable to accomplish anything but liable to spoil things

成事在天(ㄔㄥˊ ㄕˋ ㄗㄞˋ ㄊㄧㄢ)
(Man proposes but) God disposes. 或 Heaven makes the final decision as to how things shall end up.

成熟(ㄔㄥˊ ㄕㄡˊ)or(ㄔㄥˊ ㄕㄨˊ)
to mature; to ripen: 葡萄成熟了。The grapes are ripe.

成數(ㄔㄥˊ ㄕㄨˋ)
① whole numbers ② percentage

成說(ㄔㄥˊ ㄕㄨㄛ)
① an accepted theory or formulation ② to pledge one's word

成雙(ㄔㄥˊ ㄕㄨㄤ)
to form a pair; to match

成日(ㄔㄥˊ ㄖˋ)
the whole day; all day: 他成日遊手好閒無所事事。He has been loitering about and doing nothing all day.

成人(ㄔㄥˊ ㄖㄣˊ)
an adult; a grownup

成人教育(ㄔㄥˊ ㄖㄣˊ ㄐㄧㄠˋ ㄩˋ)
adult education

成人之美(ㄔㄥˊ ㄖㄣˊ ㄓ ㄇㄟˇ)
to help fulfill another's cherished hopes; to assist others in achieving an objective

成仁取義(ㄔㄥˊ ㄖㄣˊ ㄑㄩˇ ㄧˋ)
to die to preserve one's principle intact; to be a martyr to one's principle

成則王侯，敗則賊(ㄔㄥˊ ㄗㄜˊ ㄨㄤˊ ㄏㄡˊ, ㄅㄞˋ ㄗㄜˊ ㄗㄜˊ)
(literally) The victors are declared kings and marquises, while the vanquished are branded thieves and traitors.—Might is right.

成災(ㄔㄥˊ ㄗㄞ)
to cause disaster: 豪雨成災。The downpour caused a disastrous flood.

成總兒(ㄔㄥˊ ㄗㄨㄥˇ ㄦ)
① to put together a round sum ② in whole batches

成材(ㄔㄥˊ ㄘㄞˊ)
to become a useful person

成色(ㄔㄥˊ ㄙㄜˋ)
① the percentage of pure metal in an alloy ② worthy stuff; quality: 我們看成色定價

錢。We fix the prices according to the quality.

成俗(ㄔㄥˊ ㄙㄨˊ)

①an established social custom ②to become a social custom

成訟(ㄔㄥˊ ㄙㄨㄥˋ)

to become a legal case well; to take a matter into court

成誦(ㄔㄥˊ ㄙㄨㄥˋ)

to have learned a passage so well as to be able to recite it

成案(ㄔㄥˊ ㄢˋ)

a legal precedent

成衣(ㄔㄥˊ ㄧ)

ready-made clothes; garments: 那是件成衣。It's a ready-made suit.

成衣鋪(ㄔㄥˊ ㄧ ㄆㄨˋ)

a tailor shop

成議(ㄔㄥˊ ㄧˋ)

an already adopted resolution or agreement; to come to an agreement

成窰(ㄔㄥˊ ㄧㄠˊ)

name of a kiln in the Ming Dynasty, which produced the finest porcelain ware of the period

成藥(ㄔㄥˊ ㄧㄠˋ)

patent medicine; medicine already prepared by a pharmacy

成因(ㄔㄥˊ ㄧㄣ)

the cause of formation; a contributing factor

成樣(ㄔㄥˊ ㄧㄤˋ)

an established model (of manufactured goods); to perpetuate as a model

成爲(ㄔㄥˊ ㄨㄟˊ)

to become; to turn into: 她已經成爲一個出色的作家。She's become an excellent writer.

成爲泡影(ㄔㄥˊ ㄨㄟˊ ㄆㄠˋ ㄧㄥˇ)

to end in naught; to come to nothing: 他的計劃已成爲泡影。His plan has come to nothing.

成文(ㄔㄥˊ ㄨㄣˊ)

①existing writings: 不可抄襲成文。Don't copy existing writings. ②presentable 亦作「成樣兒」

成文法(ㄔㄥˊ ㄨㄣˊ ㄈㄚˇ)

written or statute law; a statute; lex scripta

成問題(ㄔㄥˊ ㄨㄣˋ ㄊㄧˊ)

to be a problem; to be open to question, doubt, or objection

成語(ㄔㄥˊ ㄩˇ)

an idiom; a phrase

成員(ㄔㄥˊ ㄩㄢˊ)

a member: 他是這小組的成員。He is a member of the group.

【戒】 1758 ㄐㄧㄝˋ jieh jiè

1. to warn; to admonish; to caution
2. to abstain from; to refrain from; to give up
3. to guard against; to avoid
4. a commandment; Buddhist monastic discipline

戒備(ㄐㄧㄝˋ ㄅㄟˋ)

on guard (against enemy attacks, natural disasters, etc.); on the alert

戒備森嚴(ㄐㄧㄝˋ ㄅㄟˋ ㄙㄣ ㄧㄢˊ)

to be heavily guarded

戒不掉(ㄐㄧㄝˋ ·ㄅㄨ ㄉㄧㄠˋ)

to try in vain to abstain (from a bad habit)

戒刀(ㄐㄧㄝˋ ㄉㄠ)

the knife of interdiction (used by Buddhists)

戒牒(ㄐㄧㄝˋ ㄉㄧㄝˊ)

the certificate of the Buddhist vow

戒掉(ㄐㄧㄝˋ ㄉㄧㄠˋ)

to abstain or give up (a bad habit)

戒定慧(ㄐㄧㄝˋ ㄉㄧㄥˋ ㄏㄨㄟˋ)

(Buddhism) discipline, meditation, wisdom—Discipline wards off bodily evil, meditation calms mental disturbance, and wisdom gets rid of delusion and proves truth.

戒賭(ㄐㄧㄝˋ ㄉㄨˇ)

to abstain from gambling; to give up gambling: 這賭徒決心戒賭了。The gambler determined to give up gambling.

戒壇(ㄐㄧㄝˋ ㄊㄢˊ)

a place for taking the Buddhist vow

戒條(ㄐㄧㄝˋ ㄊㄧㄠˊ) or 戒律(ㄐㄧㄝˋ ㄌㄩˋ)

commandments; don'ts; (Buddhism) the rules

戒塗 or 戒途(ㄐㄧㄝˋ ㄊㄨˊ)

to prepare for a trip

戒臘(ㄐㄧㄝˋ ㄌㄚˋ)

the number of years a Buddhist monk has been ordained

戒葷(ㄐㄧㄝˋ ㄏㄨㄣ)

to go on a vegetarian diet

戒酒(ㄐㄧㄝˋ ㄐㄧㄡˇ)

to abstain from alcohol: 醫生囑他戒酒。The doctor ordered him to abstain from wine.

戒懼(ㄐㄧㄝˋ ㄐㄩˋ)

to be afraid and watchful

戒絕(ㄐㄧㄝˋ ㄐㄩㄝˊ)

to get rid of (a bad habit, drug addiction, etc.) completely

戒心(ㄐㄧㄝˋ ㄒㄧㄣ)

watchfulness; vigilance; on one's guard; wariness

戒指(ㄐㄧㄝˋ ㄓˇ)

a ring (on a finger)

戒尺(ㄐㄧㄝˋ ㄔˇ)

a ferule; a teacher's ruler for beating pupils

戒除(ㄐㄧㄝˋ ㄔㄨˊ)

to abstain from; to give up: 他戒除了一項惡習。He gave up a bad habit.

戒奢崇儉(ㄐㄧㄝˋ ㄕㄜ ㄔㄨㄥˊ ㄐㄧㄢˇ)

to refrain from luxury and uphold frugality

戒色(ㄐㄧㄝˋ ㄙㄜˋ) or 戒淫(ㄐㄧㄝˋ ㄧㄣˊ)

to abstain from carnal pleasure

戒煙(ㄐㄧㄝˋ ㄧㄢ)

to give up smoking; to abstain from smoking; to refrain from smoking: 他已戒煙了。He has given up smoking.

戒嚴(ㄐㄧㄝˋ ㄧㄢˊ)

to proclaim martial law; to impose a curfew

戒嚴令(ㄐㄧㄝˋ ㄧㄢˊ ㄌㄧㄥˋ)

martial law

戒嚴時期(ㄐㄧㄝˋ ㄧㄢˊ ㄕˊ ㄑㄧˊ)

the period during which martial law is in force

【我】 1759 ㄨㄛˇ woo woˇ (讀音 ㄜˇ ee eˇ)

1. I; me; my
2. we; our; us: 我軍爲自由而戰。Our army battled for freedom.
3. self: 我敬重他忘我的獻身精

〔戈部〕

〔戈部〕

神。I admire his selfless devotion.
我輩(ㄨㄛˇ ㄅㄟˋ)
we; us
我慢(ㄨㄛˇ ㄇㄢˋ)
(Buddhism) egotism; exalting self and depreciating others; self-intoxication
我們(ㄨㄛˇ ˙ㄇㄣ) or 我等(ㄨㄛˇ ㄉㄥˇ) or 我曹(ㄨㄛˇ ㄘㄠˊ)
we; us
我們的(ㄨㄛˇ ˙ㄇㄣ ˙ㄉㄜ)
our; ours
我方(ㄨㄛˇ ㄈㄤ)
our side; we
我國(ㄨㄛˇ ㄍㄨㄛˊ)
our country
我家(ㄨㄛˇ ㄐㄧㄚ)
my home; my house
我見猶憐(ㄨㄛˇ ㄐㄧㄢˋ ㄧㄡˊ ㄌㄧㄢˊ)
Even I, a woman, cannot help loving her upon seeing her. (The statement is attributed to the wife of Huan Wen (桓溫) when she saw the concubine he had taken. The expression is now used by both sexes to describe a very beautiful woman.)
我軍(ㄨㄛˇ ㄐㄩㄣ)
our troops; our military forces; our army
我行我素(ㄨㄛˇ ㄒㄧㄥˊ ㄨㄛˇ ㄙㄨˋ)
to act according to one's will regardless of others' opinions; to stick to one's old way of doing things
我執(ㄨㄛˇ ㄓˊ)
(Buddhism) *atma-graha*; holding to the concept of the ego
我儕(ㄨㄛˇ ㄔㄞˊ)
we; us
我朝(ㄨㄛˇ ㄔㄠˊ)
our dynasty
我人(ㄨㄛˇ ㄖㄣˊ)
we; us
我自己(ㄨㄛˇ ㄗˋ ㄐㄧˇ)
I myself
我武維揚(ㄨㄛˇ ㄨˇ ㄨㄟˊ ㄧㄤˊ)
Our national influence has been spreading. 或 My military prowess is displayed.

四畫

【或】 1760 ㄏㄨㄛˋ huoh huò
1. a certain; some
2. perhaps; probably; maybe: 他明晨或可抵達。He may arrive tomorrow morning.
3. or: 你可離去或留下。You can go or stay.
或明或暗(ㄏㄨㄛˋ ㄇㄧㄥˊ ㄏㄨㄛˋ ㄢˋ)
either overt or covert
或大或小(ㄏㄨㄛˋ ㄉㄚˋ ㄏㄨㄛˋ ㄒㄧㄠˇ)
either large or small; big or little; irregular in size
或多或少(ㄏㄨㄛˋ ㄉㄨㄛ ㄏㄨㄛˋ ㄕㄠˇ)
more or less
或體(ㄏㄨㄛˋ ㄊㄧˇ)
an alternative style of Chinese characters
或來或往(ㄏㄨㄛˋ ㄌㄞˊ ㄏㄨㄛˋ ㄨㄤˇ)
either coming or going; back and forth; to and fro
或可(ㄏㄨㄛˋ ㄎㄜˇ)
may be possible; probably can: 我或可儘早前來。I will come as soon as I possibly can.
或許(ㄏㄨㄛˋ ㄒㄩˇ)
perhaps; probably; maybe: 或許我能做此事。Probably I can do it.
或者(ㄏㄨㄛˋ ㄓㄜˇ)
or; perhaps: 請把這本書交給張先生或者李先生。Please give this book to either Mr. Chang or Mr. Lee.
或是(ㄏㄨㄛˋ ㄕˋ)
① perhaps: 或是如此。Perhaps so. ② or: 它是黑的或是白的? Is it black or white?
或然率(ㄏㄨㄛˋ ㄖㄢˊ ㄌㄩˋ) or 或然性(ㄏㄨㄛˋ ㄖㄢˊ ㄒㄧㄥˋ)
(mathematics) probability
或人(ㄏㄨㄛˋ ㄖㄣˊ)
someone
或早或晚(ㄏㄨㄛˋ ㄗㄠˇ ㄏㄨㄛˋ ㄨㄢˇ)
sooner or later 亦作「或遲或早」
或此或彼(ㄏㄨㄛˋ ㄘˇ ㄏㄨㄛˋ ㄅㄧˇ)
either this or that; here and there; hither and thither
或謂(ㄏㄨㄛˋ ㄨㄟˋ) or 或曰(ㄏㄨㄛˋ ㄩㄝ) or 或云(ㄏㄨㄛˋ ㄩㄣˊ)
some people say that...
或問(ㄏㄨㄛˋ ㄨㄣˋ)
someone may ask

【戕】 1761 ㄑㄧㄤˊ chyang qiáng
1. to slay; to kill; to destroy: 自戕 to commit suicide; to kill oneself
2. to be injurious
戕害(ㄑㄧㄤˊ ㄏㄞˋ)
to slay
戕賊(ㄑㄧㄤˊ ㄗㄟˊ)
to injure; to destroy; to ruin; to do violence to

【戔】 1762 ㄐㄧㄢ jian jiān
small; little; tiny
戔戔(ㄐㄧㄢ ㄐㄧㄢ)
tiny; small
戔戔之數(ㄐㄧㄢ ㄐㄧㄢ ㄓ ㄕㄨˋ)
an insignificant amount (of money)

七畫

【戚】 1763 ㄑㄧ chi qī
1. relatives by marriage: 皇親國戚 relatives of an emperor
2. sad; mournful; woeful; sorrow; woe: 我們休戚相關。We share joys and sorrows.
3. a battle-ax
4. a Chinese family name
戚里(ㄑㄧ ㄌㄧˇ)
an exclusive village for imperial relatives by marriage
戚繼光(ㄑㄧ ㄐㄧˋ ㄍㄨㄤ)
Chi Chi-kuang, a general of the Ming Dynasty, credited with repelling the invasion of Japanese pirates
戚舊(ㄑㄧ ㄐㄧㄡˋ)
relatives and old friends: 戚舊星散。Relatives and old friends scattered like stars.
戚戚(ㄑㄧ ㄑㄧ)
① woeful; mournful ② moved; affected; touched
戚然(ㄑㄧ ㄖㄢˊ)
melancholy; distressed; depressed; dejected: 戚然動容 to change countenance for being distressed
戚容(ㄑㄧ ㄖㄨㄥˊ)
a sad look; a sorrowful expression
戚誼(ㄑㄧ ㄧˊ)
the ties between relatives

【戛】 1764 (戞) ㄐㄧㄚˊ jya jiá
1. a lance
2. natural principles
3. to tap; to strike
戛戛(ㄐㄧㄚˊ ㄐㄧㄚˊ)
difficult
戛戛獨造(ㄐㄧㄚˊ ㄐㄧㄚˊ ㄉㄨˊ ㄗㄠˋ)
to go one's unique and independent way; creative; original; out of the common run
戛戛乎其難哉(ㄐㄧㄚˊ ㄐㄧㄚˊ ㄏㄨ ㄑㄧˊ ㄋㄢˊ ㄗㄞ)
How unmanageably difficult it is! 或 How formidable or impossible the task is!
戛然長鳴(ㄐㄧㄚˊ ㄖㄢˊ ㄔㄤˊ ㄇㄧㄥˊ)
long and loud cries
戛然而止(ㄐㄧㄚˊ ㄖㄢˊ ㄦˊ ㄓˇ)
(said of a sound) to stop abruptly

八畫

【戟】 1765 (戦) ㄐㄧˇ jii jǐ
a two-pronged spear or lance; a halberd
戟門(ㄐㄧˇ ㄇㄣˊ)
the door of a noble family
戟手(ㄐㄧˇ ㄕㄡˇ)or 戟指(ㄐㄧˇ ㄓˇ)
to point at another and scold him

九畫

【戡】 1766 ㄎㄢ kan kān
1. to subdue; to suppress; to put down
2. to kill; to slay
戡定(ㄎㄢ ㄉㄧㄥˋ)
to put down or suppress (a rebellion); to subdue (barbarian tribes)
戡亂(ㄎㄢ ㄌㄨㄢˋ)
to suppress a rebellion: 他戡亂有功。He was meritorious for suppressing a rebellion.
戡夷(ㄎㄢ ㄧˊ)
to subdue barbarian tribes

【戢】 1767 ㄐㄧˊ jyi jí
1. to put away or store up
2. to fold; to cease; to restrain: 戢怒 to restrain one's anger; to become placated
戢暴鋤強(ㄐㄧˊ ㄅㄠˋ ㄔㄨˊ ㄑㄧㄤˊ)
to run down the tyrants
戢兵(ㄐㄧˊ ㄅㄧㄥ)
to cease hostilities
戢鱗(ㄐㄧˊ ㄌㄧㄣˊ)
to await opportunity in seclusion
戢翼(ㄐㄧˊ ㄧˋ)
①(said of a bird) to fold the wings: 戢翼而棲 to fold the wings and roost ② (figuratively) to retire
戢影(ㄐㄧˊ ㄧㄥˇ)
to retire (from active life)

【戥】 1768 ㄉㄥˇ deeng děng
a small steelyard for weighing gold, jewels, etc.
戥盤(ㄉㄥˇ ㄆㄢˊ)
the weighing scale of a small steelyard
戥盒(ㄉㄥˇ ㄏㄜˊ)
a case for keeping a small steelyard
戥星(ㄉㄥˇ ㄒㄧㄥ)
the sliding weight of a small steelyard
戥秤(ㄉㄥˇ ㄔㄥˋ)or 戥子(ㄉㄥˇ ·ㄗ)
a small steelyard for weighing gold, jewels, etc.

十畫

【戩】 1769 ㄐㄧㄢˇ jean jiǎn
1. to exterminate
2. blessing
3. full; complete; entirely

【截】 1770 ㄐㄧㄝˊ jye jié
1. to cut; to section; to truncate: 截成兩段 to cut in two
2. a slice; a division; a section; a segment; a chunk
3. to detain; to withhold
4. to keep; to set in order
5. to stop; to close; to end; to intercept
截面(ㄐㄧㄝˊ ㄇㄧㄢˋ)
a section (of a solid body cut straight through): 橫截面 a cross section
截斷(ㄐㄧㄝˊ ㄉㄨㄢˋ)
to disrupt; to interrupt; to cut off: 我們截斷了敵人的後路。We cut off the enemy's retreat.
截斷交通(ㄐㄧㄝˊ ㄉㄨㄢˋ ㄐㄧㄠ ㄊㄨㄥ)
to disrupt communication
截留(ㄐㄧㄝˊ ㄌㄧㄡˊ)
to withhold goods that ought to be issued or delivered
截稿(ㄐㄧㄝˊ ㄍㄠˇ)
the deadline for the editor of a newspaper to send the last news copy to the composition room
截開(ㄐㄧㄝˊ ㄎㄞ)
to cut apart
截獲(ㄐㄧㄝˊ ㄏㄨㄛˋ)
to capture by interception
截擊(ㄐㄧㄝˊ ㄐㄧˊ)
to intercept (a marching army, a convoy, etc.)
截角(ㄐㄧㄝˊ ㄐㄧㄠˇ)
to cut off or tear off a corner (of an envelope, a ticket, etc.); to truncate; truncated
截句(ㄐㄧㄝˊ ㄐㄩˋ)
a poem of 4 lines, with 5 or 7 characters in each line, and the third line blank 亦作「絕句」
截去一段(ㄐㄧㄝˊ ㄑㄩˋ ㄧˊ ㄉㄨㄢˋ)
to cut off a portion
截線(ㄐㄧㄝˊ ㄒㄧㄢˋ)
(mathematics) a transversal
截肢(ㄐㄧㄝˊ ㄓ)
amputation
截止(ㄐㄧㄝˊ ㄓˇ)
to close (application, registration, etc.) upon reaching the deadline; to come to an end: 報名登記已經截止了。The registration has come to an end.
截趾適履(ㄐㄧㄝˊ ㄓˇ ㄕˋ ㄌㄩˇ)
(literally) to trim the foot to suit the shoe—to do something very foolishly or in an impractical manner 亦作「削足適履」
截至(ㄐㄧㄝˊ ㄓˋ)
by (a specified time); up to
截住(ㄐㄧㄝˊ ㄓㄨˋ)
to stop; to interrupt; to obstruct; to hinder; to intercept: 他說到這裏突然截住。He suddenly stopped short at this point.
截長補短(ㄐㄧㄝˊ ㄔㄤˊ ㄅㄨˇ ㄉㄨㄢˇ)
(literally) to cut what is too long to supplement what is

〔戈部〕

too short—to even up scarcity and superabundance
截然(ㄐㄧㄝˊ ㄖㄢˊ)
distinctly; markedly; sharply; completely; entirely: 這兩兄弟的性格截然不同。The two brothers were completely different in personality.
截人歸路(ㄐㄧㄝˊ ㄖㄣˊ ㄍㄨㄟ ㄌㄨˋ)
to cut someone's route of retreat
截兒(ㄐㄧㄝˊㄦ)
a slice; a section; a division; a part

【戧】1771
1. ㄑㄧㄤ chiang qiāng
1. to be broken off; to clash
2. against; in an opposite direction

【戧】1771
2. ㄑㄧㄤˋ chianq qiàng
to support; to prop up; to shore up
戧金(ㄑㄧㄤˋ ㄐㄧㄣ)
gold jewelries; to sprinkle gold (on furniture, etc.)
戧柱(ㄑㄧㄤˋ ㄓㄨˋ)
a side support (for a falling house, etc.)
戧銀(ㄑㄧㄤˋ ㄧㄣˊ)
silver jewelries

十一畫

【戮】1772
ㄌㄨˋ luh lù
1. to slay; to massacre; to slaughter
2. to unite or join
戮民(ㄌㄨˋ ㄇㄧㄣˊ)
people who are serving their terms of imprisonment
戮力(ㄌㄨˋ ㄌㄧˋ)
to join forces; to cooperate; to join hands
戮力同心(ㄌㄨˋ ㄌㄧˋ ㄊㄨㄥˊ ㄒㄧㄣ)
to join forces and work for a common cause
戮誅(ㄌㄨˋ ㄓㄨ) or 戮殺(ㄌㄨˋ ㄕㄚ)
to slay
戮屍(ㄌㄨˋ ㄕ)
to chop up a corpse (for punishment)
戮尸梟示(ㄌㄨˋ ㄕ ㄒㄧㄠ ㄕˋ)
to execute a criminal and exhibit his head as a warning to potential lawbreakers

十二畫

【戰】1773
ㄓㄢˋ jann zhàn
1. war; warfare; fighting; battle
2. to contest; to fight; to contend: 他們爲了維護獨立而戰。They were fighting to preserve their independence.
3. to shudder; to shiver; to tremble: 他冷得打(寒)戰。He shivered with cold.
4. a Chinese family name
戰敗(ㄓㄢˋ ㄅㄞˋ)
to suffer (a) defeat; to be defeated
戰敗國(ㄓㄢˋ ㄅㄞˋ ㄍㄨㄛˊ)
a defeated nation; the vanquished country
戰備(ㄓㄢˋ ㄅㄟˋ)
war preparations; combat readiness: 我們應加強戰備。We should step up combat readiness.
戰報(ㄓㄢˋ ㄅㄠˋ)
war bulletins; the reports from the battle front
戰袍(ㄓㄢˋ ㄆㄠˊ)
battle dress (in former times); combat uniform
戰馬(ㄓㄢˋ ㄇㄚˇ)
a war-horse; a battle steed
戰歿(ㄓㄢˋ ㄇㄛˋ)
to die in battle; to be killed in action
戰法(ㄓㄢˋ ㄈㄚˇ)
tactics
戰犯(ㄓㄢˋ ㄈㄢˋ)
a war criminal
戰俘(ㄓㄢˋ ㄈㄨˊ)
prisoners of war
戰抖(ㄓㄢˋ ㄉㄡˇ)
to shudder; to shiver; to tremble 亦作「顫抖」
戰鬥(ㄓㄢˋ ㄉㄡˋ)
①to fight; to combat; to engage in a battle: 我們在戰鬥中把敵人打敗了。We defeated the enemy in the battle. ②action (in military sense): 兵士們在戰鬥。The soldiers are in action.
戰鬥力(ㄓㄢˋ ㄉㄡˋ ㄌㄧˋ)
fighting capability; combat strength
戰鬥轟炸機(ㄓㄢˋ ㄉㄡˋ ㄏㄨㄥ ㄓㄚˋ ㄐㄧ)
a fighter-bomber
戰鬥機(ㄓㄢˋ ㄉㄡˋ ㄐㄧ)
a fighter plane; a fighter
戰鬥艦(ㄓㄢˋ ㄉㄡˋ ㄐㄧㄢˋ)
a battleship
戰鬥巡洋艦(ㄓㄢˋ ㄉㄡˋ ㄒㄩㄣˊ ㄧㄤˊ ㄐㄧㄢˋ)
a battle cruiser
戰鬥任務(ㄓㄢˋ ㄉㄡˋ ㄖㄣˋ ㄨˋ)
a combat mission
戰鬥演習(ㄓㄢˋ ㄉㄡˋ ㄧㄢˇ ㄒㄧˊ)
military maneuvers or exercises; a war game
戰鬥員(ㄓㄢˋ ㄉㄡˋ ㄩㄢˊ)
a combatant
戰地(ㄓㄢˋ ㄉㄧˋ)
a battlefield
戰地記者(ㄓㄢˋ ㄉㄧˋ ㄐㄧˋ ㄓㄜˇ)
a war correspondent (for mass communication media)
戰地政務(ㄓㄢˋ ㄉㄧˋ ㄓㄥˋ ㄨˋ)
the civil administration in a war zone or theater of war
戰慄(ㄓㄢˋ ㄌㄧˋ)
to shiver; to shudder; to tremble: 他嚇得全身戰慄。He trembled all over with fear.
戰利品(ㄓㄢˋ ㄌㄧˋ ㄆㄧㄣˇ)
a war trophy; a trophy; booty; a prize; spoils of war; spoils; loot
戰亂(ㄓㄢˋ ㄌㄨㄢˋ)
chaos and social upheavals brought about by war
戰略(ㄓㄢˋ ㄌㄩㄝˋ)
strategy
戰略核子武器(ㄓㄢˋ ㄌㄩㄝˋ ㄏㄜˊ ㄗˇ ㄨˇ ㄑㄧˋ)
strategic nuclear weapons
戰略轟炸機(ㄓㄢˋ ㄌㄩㄝˋ ㄏㄨㄥ ㄓㄚˋ ㄐㄧ)
a strategic bomber; a long-range bomber
戰略計劃(ㄓㄢˋ ㄌㄩㄝˋ ㄐㄧˋ ㄏㄨㄚˋ)
a strategic plan
戰鼓(ㄓㄢˋ ㄍㄨˇ)
battle drums
戰國七雄(ㄓㄢˋ ㄍㄨㄛˊ ㄑㄧ ㄒㄩㄥˊ)
the seven states (秦、楚、齊、韓、趙、魏、燕) in the Epoch of Warring States 參看「戰國時代」
戰國時代(ㄓㄢˋ ㄍㄨㄛˊ ㄕˊ ㄉㄞˋ)
the Epoch of Warring States (403-221B.C.) during which

seven states (秦、楚、齊、韓、趙、魏、燕) contended for hegemony until Chin (秦) emerged victorious to become the unchallenged ruler of the empire under the First Emperor (始皇帝)

戰國策(ㄓㄢˋ ㄍㄨㄛˊ ㄘㄜˋ)
Record of the Warring States, compiled in the Former Han Dynasty

戰果(ㄓㄢˋ ㄍㄨㄛˇ)
military achievements; war results: 他們取得輝煌的戰果。They achieved splendid results on the battlefield.

戰功(ㄓㄢˋ ㄍㄨㄥ) or 戰庸(ㄓㄢˋ ㄩㄥ)
military exploits; distinguished services in war

戰況(ㄓㄢˋ ㄎㄨㄤˋ)
the war situation; the progress of a battle: 目前戰況不明。The war situation is unknown to us.

戰壕(ㄓㄢˋ ㄏㄠˊ)
a trench

戰後(ㄓㄢˋ ㄏㄡˋ)
postwar; after the war: 戰後問題 postwar problems

戰火(ㄓㄢˋ ㄏㄨㄛˇ)
flames of war

戰禍(ㄓㄢˋ ㄏㄨㄛˋ)
the calamities (or disasters) of war

戰績(ㄓㄢˋ ㄐㄧ)
military successes (or exploits, feats); battle achievements

戰績輝煌(ㄓㄢˋ ㄐㄧ ㄏㄨㄟ ㄏㄨㄤˊ)
brilliant combat performances; extraordinary battle achievements

戰機(ㄓㄢˋ ㄐㄧ)
① an opportunity for combat: 他們喪失了致勝的戰機。They missed the opportunity to win a battle. ② a fighter

戰艦(ㄓㄢˋ ㄐㄧㄢˋ)
a warship; a battleship

戰局(ㄓㄢˋ ㄐㄩˊ)
the war situation; the tide of the war

戰前(ㄓㄢˋ ㄑㄧㄢˊ)
prewar; before the war

戰區(ㄓㄢˋ ㄑㄩ)
a theater of war; a war zone or area

戰線(ㄓㄢˋ ㄒㄧㄢˋ)
a battle line; a battle front; the action front

戰戰兢兢(ㄓㄢˋ ㄓㄢˋ ㄐㄧㄥ ㄐㄧㄥ)
trembling with fear; very cautious; with fear and trepidation

戰陣(ㄓㄢˋ ㄓㄣˋ)
the deployment of troops; order of battle

戰爭(ㄓㄢˋ ㄓㄥ)
war

戰爭保險(ㄓㄢˋ ㄓㄥ ㄅㄠˇ ㄒㄧㄢˇ)
war risk insurance

戰爭販子(ㄓㄢˋ ㄓㄥ ㄈㄢˋ ˙ㄗ)
a warmonger

戰爭狀態(ㄓㄢˋ ㄓㄥ ㄓㄨㄤˋ ㄊㄞˋ)
a state of war; a state of hostilities

戰爭與和平(ㄓㄢˋ ㄓㄥ ㄩˇ ㄏㄜˊ ㄆㄧㄥˊ)
① war and peace ② *War and Peace,* by Leo Tolstoy (1828-1910)

戰車(ㄓㄢˋ ㄔㄜ)
① a tank (an armored vehicle) ② a chariot

戰場(ㄓㄢˋ ㄔㄤˇ) or (ㄓㄢˋ ㄔㄤˊ)
a battlefield; a war field; a battleground

戰船(ㄓㄢˋ ㄔㄨㄢˊ)
a war vessel; a man-of-war; a warship

戰時(ㄓㄢˋ ㄕˊ)
wartime

戰時國際公法(ㄓㄢˋ ㄕˊ ㄍㄨㄛˊ ㄐㄧˋ ㄍㄨㄥ ㄈㄚˇ)
wartime international law

戰史(ㄓㄢˋ ㄕˇ)
war history; military history

戰士(ㄓㄢˋ ㄕˋ)
a warrior; a fighting man; an enlisted man: 他曾是位英勇的戰士。He was a brave warrior.

戰事(ㄓㄢˋ ㄕˋ)
war; hostilities; fighting; clashes: 戰事已停止了嗎? Has the fighting stopped yet?

戰守(ㄓㄢˋ ㄕㄡˇ)
offense and defense

戰勝(ㄓㄢˋ ㄕㄥˋ)
to conquer; to win a victory; to emerge victorious; to be victorious; to be the victor: 他戰勝了對手。He was victorious over his rival.

戰勝國(ㄓㄢˋ ㄕㄥˋ ㄍㄨㄛˊ)
a victorious nation

戰勝攻取(ㄓㄢˋ ㄕㄥˋ ㄍㄨㄥ ㄑㄩˇ)
to triumph in every battle and succeed in every invasion

戰書(ㄓㄢˋ ㄕㄨ)
a written declaration of war

戰術(ㄓㄢˋ ㄕㄨˋ)
tactics; the art of war

戰術轟炸機(ㄓㄢˋ ㄕㄨˋ ㄏㄨㄥ ㄓㄚˋ ㄐㄧ)
a tactical bomber; a short-range bomber

戰死(ㄓㄢˋ ㄙˇ)
to die in battle; to be killed in action: 他戰死在沙場。He died on the battlefield.

戰役(ㄓㄢˋ ㄧˋ)
a (military) campaign; a battle: 諾曼第登陸是一場英勇的戰役。The Normandy landing was a daring battle.

戰友(ㄓㄢˋ ㄧㄡˇ)
a comrade in arms

戰無不勝，攻無不克(ㄓㄢˋ ㄨˊ ㄅㄨˊ ㄕㄥˋ, ㄍㄨㄥ ㄨˊ ㄅㄨˊ ㄎㄜˋ)
to triumph in every battle and succeed in every invasion; to go undefeated

戰雲瀰漫(ㄓㄢˋ ㄩㄣˊ ㄇㄧˊ ㄇㄢˋ)
The clouds of war hang low. 或 War is imminent.

十三畫

【戲】 1774
1. (戲) ㄒㄧˋ shih xì

1. to play; to toy; to sport: 小羊在田裡嬉戲。Lambs sport in the fields.
2. to jest; to have fun; to make fun
3. a drama; a play; a show: 我們去看戲吧! Let's go to the play.
4. a game

戲班(ㄒㄧˋ ㄅㄢ)
a dramatic troupe

戲本子(ㄒㄧˋ ㄅㄣˇ ˙ㄗ)
a script (of a play); a text for a play or an opera

戲票(ㄒㄧˋ ㄆㄧㄠˋ)
an admission ticket for a play

戲碼(ㄒㄧˋ ㄇㄚˇ)

a repertoire (particularly that of Peking opera)
戲迷(ㄒㄧˋ ㄇㄧˊ)
a drama fan
戲目(ㄒㄧˋ ㄇㄨˋ)
a theatrical program
戲法(兒)(ㄒㄧˋ ㄈㄚˇ(ㄦ))
jugglery; a trick; sleight of hand; magic
戲單子(ㄒㄧˋ ㄉㄢ ·ㄗ)
the program of a play; a playbill
戲臺(ㄒㄧˋ ㄊㄞˊ)
a stage (for plays)
戲弄(ㄒㄧˋ ㄋㄨㄥˋ)or 戲耍(ㄒㄧˋ ㄕㄨㄚˇ)
to play a trick on; to tease
戲謔(ㄒㄧˋ ㄋㄩㄝˋ)
a joke; a witticism; a pleasantry; a jest; fun
戲館子(ㄒㄧˋ ㄍㄨㄢˇ ·ㄗ)
a playhouse; a theater
戲考(ㄒㄧˋ ㄎㄠˇ)
A Collection of Plays
戲具(ㄒㄧˋ ㄐㄩˋ)
theatrical appurtenances; stage properties 亦作「道具」
戲劇(ㄒㄧˋ ㄐㄩˋ)
drama; the theater; a play: 他是研究戲劇的人。He is a student of drama.
戲劇團(ㄒㄧˋ ㄐㄩˋ ㄊㄨㄢˊ)
a dramatic troupe
戲劇化(ㄒㄧˋ ㄐㄩˋ ㄏㄨㄚˋ)
to dramatize; dramatic; to playact; theatrical: 戲劇化的悲哀表現 a theatrical display of grief
戲劇家(ㄒㄧˋ ㄐㄩˋ ㄐㄧㄚ)
a playwright; a dramatist
戲劇節(ㄒㄧˋ ㄐㄩˋ ㄐㄧㄝˊ)
Drama Day (falling on February 15)
戲劇界(ㄒㄧˋ ㄐㄩˋ ㄐㄧㄝˋ)
the dramatic circles; the theatrical circles
戲曲(ㄒㄧˋ ㄑㄩˇ)
a drama; a play; a theatrical composition; a traditional opera: 地方戲曲 local operas
戲嬉(ㄒㄧˋ ㄒㄧ)
to play; merrymaking
戲箱(ㄒㄧˋ ㄒㄧㄤ)
boxes for keeping theatrical properties and garments
戲照(ㄒㄧˋ ㄓㄠˋ)
a photo of a person in stage costume
戲裝(ㄒㄧˋ ㄓㄨㄤ)
theatrical (or stage) costume
戲水(ㄒㄧˋ ㄕㄨㄟˇ)
to play with water; to play in water
戲子(ㄒㄧˋ ㄗˇ)
a dramatic player; an actor or actress (a derogatory reference to show biz personalities who used to occupy the lowest social stratum in ancient China)
戲詞(ㄒㄧˋ ㄘˊ)
the words of an actor's part; an actor's lines 亦作「臺詞」
戲言(ㄒㄧˋ ㄧㄢˊ)
a joke; a witticism; a jest: 戲言中常含眞理。Many a true word is spoken in jest.
戲文(ㄒㄧˋ ㄨㄣˊ)
theatrical writing; drama
戲園子(ㄒㄧˋ ㄩㄢˊ ·ㄗ)or 戲場(ㄒㄧˋ ㄔㄤˇ)or(ㄒㄧˋ ㄔㄤˊ)or 戲樓(ㄒㄧˋ ㄌㄡˊ)
a playhouse; a theater
戲院(ㄒㄧˋ ㄩㄢˋ)
a theater; a movie house

【戲】 1774
2. ㄏㄨ hu hū
alas; oh; o; ah

十四畫

【戴】 1775
ㄉㄞˋ day dài
1. to wear on the head, the nose, the ear, or the hand; to put on
2. to support; to sustain; to bear
3. a Chinese family name
4. to respect; to honor: 我們十分愛戴他。We love and respect him very much.
戴不上(ㄉㄞˋ ·ㄅㄨ ㄕㄤˋ)
incapable of wearing (or being worn) on the head
戴盆望天(ㄉㄞˋ ㄆㄣˊ ㄨㄤˋ ㄊㄧㄢ)
(literally) to try to view the sky with a tray on the head —to take an action contrary to one's objective
戴帽子(ㄉㄞˋ ㄇㄠˋ ·ㄗ)
① to wear a hat or a cap ② (said of a business broker) to demand payment in addition to what is due ③ to falsely accuse someone of a crime (usually political in nature)
戴綠頭巾(ㄉㄞˋ ㄌㄩˋ ㄊㄡˊ ㄐㄧㄣ)
to be a cuckold 亦作「戴綠帽」
戴高帽(ㄉㄞˋ ㄍㄠ ㄇㄠˋ)
to receive a flattery or compliment; to flatter
戴孝(ㄉㄞˋ ㄒㄧㄠˋ)
to go into mourning (for a parent, relative, etc.); to be in mourning: 他爲母親戴孝。He is in mourning for his mother.
戴星(ㄉㄞˋ ㄒㄧㄥ)
to leave home at dawn and return in the evening 參看「戴月披星」
戴罪立功(ㄉㄞˋ ㄗㄨㄟˋ ㄌㄧˋ ㄍㄨㄥ)
to atone for a mistake or failure by meritorious services; to redeem oneself by good services
戴眼鏡(ㄉㄞˋ ㄧㄢˇ ㄐㄧㄥˋ)
to wear glasses or spectacles
戴月披星(ㄉㄞˋ ㄩㄝˋ ㄆㄧ ㄒㄧㄥ)
to be outdoors when there are the moon and the stars in the sky; to travel, work, or play outdoors at night
戴圓履方(ㄉㄞˋ ㄩㄢˊ ㄌㄩˇ ㄈㄤ)
to stand between Heaven and Earth

【戳】 1776
ㄔㄨㄛ chuo chuō
1. to jab; to poke; to pierce: 他在今天的報紙上戳一個洞。He poked a hole in today's newspaper.
2. a chop; a stamp; a seal: 橡皮戳 a rubber stamp
戳記(ㄔㄨㄛ ㄐㄧˋ)
a stamp; a seal; a business stamp
戳穿(ㄔㄨㄛ ㄔㄨㄢ)
to puncture; to lay bare; to expose; to uncover: 我們戳穿了他的謊言和詭辯。We laid bare his lies and sophistry.
戳子(ㄔㄨㄛ ·ㄗ)or 戳兒(ㄔㄨㄛㄦ)
a stamp; a seal; a chop: 他在文件上蓋戳子。He put a seal on the document.
戳印(ㄔㄨㄛ ㄧㄣˋ)
to stamp; a stamp

戶部
ㄏㄨˋ huh hù

【戶】1777 ㄏㄨˋ huh hù
1. a door: 戶外很冷。It is rather cold out of doors.
2. a household; a family: 他的名字家喻戶曉。His name became a household word.
3. a Chinese family name

戶部(ㄏㄨˋ ㄅㄨˋ)
(in ancient times) Ministry of Finance

戶頭(ㄏㄨˋ ㄊㄡˊ)or 戶名(ㄏㄨˋ ㄇㄧㄥˊ)
① a depositor (in banking); a bank account: 他在銀行開戶頭。He opened an account in the bank. ② the family head; the householder

戶庭(ㄏㄨˋ ㄊㄧㄥˊ)
the entrance hall (of a house)

戶內(ㄏㄨˋ ㄋㄟˋ)
indoor; indoors

戶內運動(ㄏㄨˋ ㄋㄟˋ ㄩㄣˋ ㄉㄨㄥˋ)
indoor games

戶口(ㄏㄨˋ ㄎㄡˇ)
households; registered permanent residence

戶口普查(ㄏㄨˋ ㄎㄡˇ ㄆㄨˇ ㄔㄚˊ)
census taking; a census

戶口米(ㄏㄨˋ ㄎㄡˇ ㄇㄧˇ)
rice rationed for family consumption; rationed rice

戶口名簿(ㄏㄨˋ ㄎㄡˇ ㄇㄧㄥˊ ㄅㄨˋ)
a household identification book

戶口謄本(ㄏㄨˋ ㄎㄡˇ ㄊㄥˊ ㄅㄣˇ)or 戶口抄本(ㄏㄨˋ ㄎㄡˇ ㄔㄠ ㄅㄣˇ)
a transcript of one's household register; a census register; a family register

戶戶(ㄏㄨˋ ㄏㄨˋ)
every household

戶籍(ㄏㄨˋ ㄐㄧˊ)
a domicile; household registration

戶籍簿(ㄏㄨˋ ㄐㄧˊ ㄅㄨˋ)
a domiciliary register

戶籍法(ㄏㄨˋ ㄐㄧˊ ㄈㄚˇ)
census law; household registration law

戶限(ㄏㄨˋ ㄒㄧㄢˋ)
a threshold; a doorsill

戶限爲穿(ㄏㄨˋ ㄒㄧㄢˋ ㄨㄟˊ ㄔㄨㄢ)
There are so many visitors that the doorsill has worn through under their feet.

戶長(ㄏㄨˋ ㄓㄤˇ)
the household head; the family head

戶政(ㄏㄨˋ ㄓㄥˋ)
the administration with regard to residents and residence

戶樞(ㄏㄨˋ ㄕㄨ)
a door pivot; a door hinge; a door axis

戶樞不蠹(ㄏㄨˋ ㄕㄨ ㄅㄨˋ ㄉㄨˋ)
(literally) The door pivot will not become worm-eaten. —Human faculties should be constantly used to prevent them from getting rusty.

戶稅(ㄏㄨˋ ㄕㄨㄟˋ)
household tax: 你繳納多少戶稅? How much household tax do you pay?

戶牖(ㄏㄨˋ ㄧㄡˇ)
① doors and windows ② (academic or philosophic) schools or sects

戶外(ㄏㄨˋ ㄨㄞˋ)
outdoor: 你喜歡戶外活動嗎? Do you like outdoor activities?

戶外運動(ㄏㄨˋ ㄨㄞˋ ㄩㄣˋ ㄉㄨㄥˋ)
outdoor games

一畫

【戹】1778 (厄) ㄜˋ eh è
narrow; strait; straits; difficult

四畫

【戾】1779 ㄌㄧˋ lih lì
1. perverse; recalcitrant; irregular; abnormal
2. atrocity; atrocious; violence; violent
3. to come to ; up to

戾氣(ㄌㄧˋ ㄑㄧˋ)
perversity; disharmony; irregularity

戾愆(ㄌㄧˋ ㄑㄧㄢ)
sin; crime; guilt

【戽】1780 ㄏㄨˋ huh hù
a pail; a bucket

戽斗(ㄏㄨˋ ㄉㄡˇ)
a device operated by manual labor to draw water for irrigation of the farms

戽水(ㄏㄨˋ ㄕㄨㄟˇ)
to draw water for farm irrigation by the above device

【房】1781 ㄈㄤˊ farng fáng
1. a house; a building: 他的房子在沿街第三家。His house is three doors down the street.
2. a room; a chamber: 他們正在佈置新房。They are arranging their bridal chamber.
3. a compartmentalized structure
4. a wife; a concubine
5. a Chinese family name

房門(ㄈㄤˊ ㄇㄣˊ)
a door to a room

房地產(ㄈㄤˊ ㄉㄧˋ ㄔㄢˇ)
real estates

房地產經紀人(ㄈㄤˊ ㄉㄧˋ ㄔㄢˇ ㄐㄧㄥ ㄐㄧˋ ㄖㄣˊ)
a realtor

房頂(ㄈㄤˊ ㄉㄧㄥˇ)
the roof of a house 亦作「屋頂」

房東(ㄈㄤˊ ㄉㄨㄥ)
the landlord or landlady (of a house)

房東太太(ㄈㄤˊ ㄉㄨㄥ ㄊㄞˋ ·ㄊㄞ)
a landlady

房柁(ㄈㄤˊ ㄊㄨㄛˊ)
a ridgepole; a ridgepiece

房檁(ㄈㄤˊ ㄌㄧㄣˇ)
a house beam 亦作「房梁」

房梁(ㄈㄤˊ ㄌㄧㄤˊ)
a house beam

房客(ㄈㄤˊ ㄎㄜˋ)
the tenant (of a house); a guest (at a hotel, etc.)

房脊(ㄈㄤˊ ㄐㄧˇ)
the ridge of the roof

房間(ㄈㄤˊ ㄐㄧㄢ)
a room; a chamber: 這所房屋有多少房間? How many rooms are there in this house?

房捐(ㄈㄤˊ ㄐㄩㄢ)
house tax 亦作「房屋稅」

房契(ㄈㄤˊ ㄑㄧˋ)
a house ownership certificate
房錢(ㄈㄤˊ ㄑㄧㄢˊ)
house rentals 參看「房租」
房玄齡(ㄈㄤˊ ㄒㄩㄢˊ ㄌㄧㄥˊ)
Fang Hsüan-ling, 578-648, a statesman who helped Emperor Tai Tsung of the Tang Dynasty to bring about one of the most prosperous eras in Chinese history
房主(ㄈㄤˊ ㄓㄨˇ)
a house proprietor or owner
房中術(ㄈㄤˊ ㄓㄨㄥ ㄕㄨˋ)
the art of lovemaking
房產(ㄈㄤˊ ㄔㄢˇ)
property in the form of a house or houses
房事(ㄈㄤˊ ㄕˋ)
sexual activity; lovemaking
房舍(ㄈㄤˊ ㄕㄜˋ)
a house
房子(ㄈㄤˊ ·ㄗ)
a house; a building
房租(ㄈㄤˊ ㄗㄨ)
a house rental
房簷(ㄈㄤˊ ㄧㄢˊ)
eaves
房屋(ㄈㄤˊ ㄨ)
a house; a building
房屋稅(ㄈㄤˊ ㄨ ㄕㄨㄟˋ)
the building tax

【所】 1782 ㄙㄨㄛˇ suoo suǒ

1. a place; a location; a position: 這就是意外事件發生的所在地。This is the place where the accident happened.
2. a building; an office: 他在律師事務所做事。He works in a lawyer's office.
3. that which

所費不貲(ㄙㄨㄛˇ ㄈㄟˋ ㄅㄨˋ ㄗ)
to have spent a fortune; to incur a considerable or great expense
所答非所問(ㄙㄨㄛˇ ㄉㄚˊ ㄈㄟ ㄙㄨㄛˇ ㄨㄣˋ)
to give an irrelevant answer
所得(ㄙㄨㄛˇ ㄉㄜˊ)
① income ② what one gets or receives: 所得不償所失。What one gets cannot make up for what one loses.
所得稅(ㄙㄨㄛˇ ㄉㄜˊ ㄕㄨㄟˋ)
income tax
所到之處(ㄙㄨㄛˇ ㄉㄠˋ ㄓ ㄔㄨˋ)
wherever one goes
所天(ㄙㄨㄛˇ ㄊㄧㄢ)
① one's sovereign ② one's father ③ one's husband
所羅門(ㄙㄨㄛˇ ㄌㄨㄛˊ ㄇㄣˊ)
Solomon, 993-953 B.C., king of Israel (son of David)
所感(ㄙㄨㄛˇ ㄍㄢˇ)
one's impression about something
所好(ㄙㄨㄛˇ ㄏㄠˋ)
one's hobbies or likes: 我對他的所好與所惡一無所知。I know nothing of his likes and dislikes.
所懷(ㄙㄨㄛˇ ㄏㄨㄞˊ)
the ideas in one's mind; thoughts
所歡(ㄙㄨㄛˇ ㄏㄨㄢ)
a sweetheart; a lover
所見所聞(ㄙㄨㄛˇ ㄐㄧㄢˋ ㄙㄨㄛˇ ㄨㄣˊ)
what one has seen and heard
所期(ㄙㄨㄛˇ ㄑㄧˊ)
one's expectations from someone or something
所欽(ㄙㄨㄛˇ ㄑㄧㄣ)
① a respected friend ② a brother
所向披靡(ㄙㄨㄛˇ ㄒㄧㄤˋ ㄆㄧ ㄇㄧˇ)
(said of an invincible army) victorious wherever it goes
所向無敵(ㄙㄨㄛˇ ㄒㄧㄤˋ ㄨˊ ㄉㄧˊ)
to encounter no significant opponent on the way; undefeatable; invincible
所需(ㄙㄨㄛˇ ㄒㄩ)
needs or requirements (in doing something): 耐心是教學所需的要件。Patience is a requirement in teaching.
所學(ㄙㄨㄛˇ ㄒㄩㄝˊ)
one's specialty; what one has majored in
所知(ㄙㄨㄛˇ ㄓ)
① what one knows ② an acquaintance
所致(ㄙㄨㄛˇ ㄓˋ)
as a result of; to result from: 這損害由火災所致。The damage resulted from the fire.
所長
①(ㄙㄨㄛˇ ㄓㄤˇ) the head or director of an office
②(ㄙㄨㄛˇ ㄔㄤˊ) one's specialty; what one excels in
所識(ㄙㄨㄛˇ ㄕˋ)
acquaintances: 他所識甚多。He has a large circle of acquaintances.
所事(ㄙㄨㄛˇ ㄕˋ)
everything
所事非人(ㄙㄨㄛˇ ㄕˋ ㄈㄟ ㄖㄣˊ)
① to serve under the wrong leader ② to have married a bad man
所生(ㄙㄨㄛˇ ㄕㄥ)
parents
所屬(ㄙㄨㄛˇ ㄕㄨˇ)
① subordinates; subordinate agencies ② the authority to which an agency belongs
所自(ㄙㄨㄛˇ ㄗˋ) or 所從(ㄙㄨㄛˇ ㄘㄨㄥˊ)
cause; origin; source
所載(ㄙㄨㄛˇ ㄗㄞˇ)
what is printed, published or reported in a publication
所在(ㄙㄨㄛˇ ㄗㄞˋ)
① where one dwells ② a place; a location; a position: 這就是肇事的所在。This is the place where the accident happened.
所在地(ㄙㄨㄛˇ ㄗㄞˋ ㄉㄧˋ)
the place where an institution or organization is located; a seat: 大學是求學研究的所在地。A university is a seat of learning.
所作所爲(ㄙㄨㄛˇ ㄗㄨㄛˋ ㄙㄨㄛˇ ㄨㄟˊ)
actions; behavior; conduct; what one does and how he behaves
所藏(ㄙㄨㄛˇ ㄘㄤˊ)
one's collection (of rare books, masterpieces, etc.)
所司(ㄙㄨㄛˇ ㄙ)
what a person or an agency is in charge of; a function
所思(ㄙㄨㄛˇ ㄙ)
① one's thoughts: 他看起來若有所思。He looked as if he were absorbed in thought. ② the person one is in love with
所以(ㄙㄨㄛˇ ㄧˇ)
therefore; so; consequently: 我病了，所以不能來。I was ill, and therefore could not come.
所以然(ㄙㄨㄛˇ ㄧˇ ㄖㄢˊ)

reason; cause: 我們只知其然却不知其所以然。We only know it is so, but do not know (the reason) why it is so.

所由(ㄙㄨㄛˇ ㄧㄡˊ)
①a cause ②a local magistrate

所有(ㄙㄨㄛˇ ㄧㄡˇ)
①what one owns; belongings; possessions ②to own: 這房子爲誰所有? Who owns this house? ③all; every: 我把所有的錢都給了他。I gave him all the money I had.

所有權(ㄙㄨㄛˇ ㄧㄡˇ ㄑㄩㄢˊ)
ownership; proprietary rights

所有權狀(ㄙㄨㄛˇ ㄧㄡˇ ㄑㄩㄢˊ ㄓㄨㄤˋ)
an ownership certificate

所有者(ㄙㄨㄛˇ ㄧㄡˇ ㄓㄜˇ)
an owner; a proprietor: 他是該旅館的所有者。He is the proprietor of the hotel.

所有人(ㄙㄨㄛˇ ㄧㄡˇ ㄖㄣˊ)
an owner; a proprietor: 他將錶歸還所有人。He returned the watch to the owner.

所有物(ㄙㄨㄛˇ ㄧㄡˇ ㄨˋ)
belongings; possessions

所爲何來(ㄙㄨㄛˇ ㄨㄟˋ ㄏㄜˊ ㄌㄞˊ)
What for? 或 What are you here for?

所謂(ㄙㄨㄛˇ ㄨㄟˋ)
①so-called: 他是個所謂的君子。He is a so-called gentleman. ②what is called

所餘(ㄙㄨㄛˇ ㄩˊ)
what remains; what is left; a remnant; leftovers: 你可把所餘全都拿去。You may have all those that remain.

所願(ㄙㄨㄛˇ ㄩㄢˋ)
one's wishes: 這女孩之所願已實現。The girl has got her wish.

五畫

【扁】 1783
1. ㄅㄧㄢˇ bean biǎn

1. flat: 這箱子被壓扁了。The box was crushed flat.
2. a tablet
3. an ancient surname

扁柏(ㄅㄧㄢˇ ㄅㄞˇ)
Japanese cypress

扁平(ㄅㄧㄢˇ ㄆㄧㄥˊ)
thin and flat

扁豆(ㄅㄧㄢˇ ㄉㄡˋ)
lentil

扁擔(ㄅㄧㄢˇ ˙ㄉㄢ)
a flat carrying pole or shouldering pole

扁蹋鼻(ㄅㄧㄢˇ ㄊㄚˋ ㄅㄧˊ)
a snub nose

扁桃腺(ㄅㄧㄢˇ ㄊㄠˊ ㄒㄧㄢˋ)
the tonsils

扁桃腺腫大(ㄅㄧㄢˇ ㄊㄠˊ ㄒㄧㄢˋ ㄓㄨㄥˇ ㄉㄚˋ)
hypertrophy of tonsils

扁桃腺炎(ㄅㄧㄢˇ ㄊㄠˊ ㄒㄧㄢˋ ㄧㄢˊ)
tonsillitis; quinsy

扁球面(ㄅㄧㄢˇ ㄑㄧㄡˊ ㄇㄧㄢˋ)
(mathematics) an oblate spheroid

扁鵲(ㄅㄧㄢˇ ㄑㄩㄝˋ)
Pien Chüeh, a famed physician of the Epoch of Warring States

扁食(ㄅㄧㄢˇ ㄕˊ)
dumpling or ravioli

扁額(ㄅㄧㄢˇ ㄜˊ)
a large plaque hanging over a door or in the living room 亦作「匾額」

【扁】 1783
2. ㄆㄧㄢ pian piān

small

扁舟(ㄆㄧㄢ ㄓㄡ)
a small boat; a skiff

【扃】 1784
1. ㄐㄩㄥ jiong jiōng

a bolt; to bolt (doors); to shut a door

扃門(ㄐㄩㄥ ㄇㄣˊ)
to bolt the doors

扃門謝客(ㄐㄩㄥ ㄇㄣˊ ㄒㄧㄝˋ ㄎㄜˋ)
to shut the door and decline visitors

扃關(ㄐㄩㄥ ㄍㄨㄢ)
a bolt or bar (for doors)

扃鍵(ㄐㄩㄥ ㄐㄧㄢˋ)
①to lock ②a door bolt

【扃】 1784
2. ㄐㄩㄥˇ jeong jiǒng

perceiving; discerning

扃扃(ㄐㄩㄥˇ ㄐㄩㄥˇ)
perceiving; discerning; discriminating

六畫

【扆】 1785
ㄧˇ yii yǐ

a screen decorated with a design in hatchets placed behind the emperor in the imperial audience chamber

【扇】 1786
1. ㄕㄢˋ shann shàn

1. a fan
2. a numerary auxiliary for door or gate leaves: 他打破了一扇窗戶。He broke a window.

扇骨子(ㄕㄢˋ ㄍㄨˇ ˙ㄗ)
the framework of a fan; the ribs of a fan

扇形(ㄕㄢˋ ㄒㄧㄥˊ)
fan-shaped; a sector (of a circle)

扇墜兒(ㄕㄢˋ ㄓㄨㄟˋㄦ)
a pendant attached to a fan

扇子(ㄕㄢˋ ˙ㄗ)
a fan

扇舞(ㄕㄢˋ ㄨˇ)
fan dance

【扇】 1786
2. (搧) ㄕㄢ shan shān

to fan; to instigate; to incite

扇風(ㄕㄢ ㄈㄥ)
to fan the air

扇風點火(ㄕㄢ ㄈㄥ ㄉㄧㄢˇ ㄏㄨㄛˇ)
to fan a fire—to inflame and agitate people; to stir up trouble or chaos

扇動(ㄕㄢ ㄉㄨㄥˋ)
to incite; to instigate: 他扇動兩家吵架。He instigated a quarrel between the two families.

扇惑(ㄕㄢ ㄏㄨㄛˋ)
to instigate and mislead; to agitate; to lead astray by incitement: 他的謊言扇惑了我。His lies misled me.

扇枕溫被(ㄕㄢ ㄓㄣˇ ㄨㄣ ㄅㄟˋ)
to cool the pillow and warm the bedding (for one's parents); to be a model of filial piety 亦作「扇枕溫席」

扇揚(ㄕㄢ ㄧㄤˊ)
to glorify; to uphold; to exalt; to spread out: 這消息很快就扇揚開了。The news soon spread out.

〔手部〕

七畫

【扈】 1787
ㄏㄨˋ huh hù
1. to follow as escort or retinue
2. insolent; impertinent
3. a Chinese family name

扈蹕(ㄏㄨˋ ㄅㄧˋ)
to escort the emperor in travel

扈輦(ㄏㄨˋ ㄋㄧㄢˇ) or 扈駕(ㄏㄨˋ ㄐㄧㄚˋ)
to escort the emperor in travel

扈從(ㄏㄨˋ ㄗㄨㄥˋ)
the escort or retinue of the emperor when he travels

八畫

【扉】 1788
ㄈㄟ fei fēi
a door leaf

扉葉 or 扉頁(ㄈㄟ ㄧㄝˋ)
a flyleaf; a title page

手部
ㄕㄡˇ shoou shǒu

【手】 1789
ㄕㄡˇ shoou shǒu
1. hand; of the hand; having to do with the hand: 他們手牽手地走開了。They walked away hand in hand. 那是件手編的毛衣。It is a hand- knitted woolen sweater.
2. to have in one's hand; to hold: 他陷入敵人手中。He fell into the enemy's hands.
3. a skilled person; a person
4. action
5. personally

手把(ㄕㄡˇ ㄅㄚˇ)
a handle

手搏(ㄕㄡˇ ㄅㄛˊ)
to fight with bare hands

手拜(ㄕㄡˇ ㄅㄞˋ)
to worship or pay homage by kowtowing

手背(ㄕㄡˇ ㄅㄟˋ)
① the back of the hand ② (gambling) having bad luck

手背朝下(ㄕㄡˇ ㄅㄟˋ ㄔㄠˊ ㄒㄧㄚˋ)
to hold out one's hand with the open palm—to beg for money or help

手臂(ㄕㄡˇ ㄅㄟˋ)or(ㄕㄡˇ ㄅㄧˋ)
the arm from the wrist up

手版 or 手板(ㄕㄡˇ ㄅㄢˇ)or 手本(ㄕㄡˇ ㄅㄣˇ)
① (in former times) an official calling card presented when requesting an interview with one's superior ② (Ching Dynasty) a memo presented by a successful candidate in a formal visit to the examiner

手板子(ㄕㄡˇ ㄅㄢˇ ·ㄗ)
a ferule

手筆(ㄕㄡˇ ㄅㄧˇ)
① a literary work or handwriting (by a famed person): 那藝術家的作品表現出名家手筆。The artist's work showed a master's hand. ② the courage of spending money on a grand scale: 他自小手筆就闊。He has been liberal with money since his childhood.

手錶(ㄕㄡˇ ㄅㄧㄠˇ)
a wrist watch

手邊(ㄕㄡˇ ㄅㄧㄢ)
at hand; handy: 他寫作時總放本字典在手邊。When he writes, he always keeps a dictionary at hand.

手不釋卷(ㄕㄡˇ ㄅㄨˋ ㄕˋ ㄐㄩㄢˋ)
to hold a book in hand all the time; to be studying constantly; to read avariciously

手不停揮(ㄕㄡˇ ㄅㄨˋ ㄊㄧㄥˊ ㄏㄨㄟ)
to write without rest; to be assiduously engaged in writing

手不老實(ㄕㄡˇ ㄅㄨˋ ㄌㄠˇ ·ㄕ)
light-fingered; given to pilfering; thievish

手不穩(ㄕㄡˇ ㄅㄨˋ ㄨㄣˇ)
light-fingered; thievish

手帕(ㄕㄡˇ ㄆㄚˋ)
a handkerchief

手模(ㄕㄡˇ ㄇㄛˊ)
an impression of the thumb in place of a signature; a fingerprint

手慢(ㄕㄡˇ ㄇㄢˋ)
slow in action; slow-moving

手忙脚亂(ㄕㄡˇ ㄇㄤˊ ㄐㄧㄠˇ ㄌㄨㄢˋ)
to be in a flurry; to be flustered; to be very busy: 他一陣手忙脚亂。He is all in a fluster.

手面闊綽(ㄕㄡˇ ㄇㄧㄢˋ ㄎㄨㄛˋ ㄔㄨㄛˋ)
extravagantly generous or liberal; lavish

手民(ㄕㄡˇ ㄇㄧㄣˊ)
① an engraver of printing blocks; a compositor ② a carpenter

手民誤植(ㄕㄡˇ ㄇㄧㄣˊ ㄨˋ ㄓˊ)
a typographic mistake or error; a misprint

手法(ㄕㄡˇ ㄈㄚˇ)
workmanship; artistry; skill; technique

手風琴(ㄕㄡˇ ㄈㄥ ㄑㄧㄣˊ)
an accordion

手縫
①(ㄕㄡˇ ㄈㄥˊ) ⓐ to tailor or make dress personally ⓑ to sew by hand
②(ㄕㄡˇ ㄈㄥˋ) the spaces between the fingers

手到病除(ㄕㄡˇ ㄉㄠˋ ㄅㄧㄥˋ ㄔㄨˊ)
to cure a patient by a mere touch

手到擒來(ㄕㄡˇ ㄉㄠˋ ㄑㄧㄣˊ ㄌㄞˊ)
to capture an enemy easily

手底下(ㄕㄡˇ ㄉㄧˇ ·ㄒㄧㄚ)
① one's subordinates: 他從不信任手底下。He never trusts his subordinates. ② ways of doing things

手電筒(ㄕㄡˇ ㄉㄧㄢˋ ㄊㄨㄥˇ)
a flashlight; an electric torch

手段(ㄕㄡˇ ㄉㄨㄢˋ)
① the means (as opposed to the end) ② a devious way of dealing with people

手動機器(ㄕㄡˇ ㄉㄨㄥˋ ㄐㄧ ㄑㄧˋ)
a hand-operated machine; a manually operated machine

手套(ㄕㄡˇ ㄊㄠˋ)
gloves; gauntlets; mittens: 他昨天買了一副手套。He bought a pair of gloves yesterday.

手頭(ㄕㄡˇ ㄊㄡˊ)
① on hand; at hand; in hand: 我手頭還有些錢。I still have some money in hand. ② financial conditions 參看「手頭緊」or「手頭鬆」③ personal experience

手頭好(ㄕㄡˇ ㄊㄡˊ ㄏㄠˇ)
dexterous; deft
手頭緊(ㄕㄡˇ ㄊㄡˊ ㄐㄧㄣˇ)
① short of cash (or money) ② closefisted
手頭巧(ㄕㄡˇ ㄊㄡˊ ㄑㄧㄠˇ)
skillful in the use of the hands; dexterous; deft
手頭字(ㄕㄡˇ ㄊㄡˊ ㄗˋ)
words in everyday use; everyday words
手頭鬆(ㄕㄡˇ ㄊㄡˊ ㄙㄨㄥ)or 手頭寬(ㄕㄡˇ ㄊㄡˊ ㄎㄨㄢ)
liberal in spending; to be quite well off at the moment; to be in easy circumstances
手談(ㄕㄡˇ ㄊㄢˊ)
to play a "go" game
手提(ㄕㄡˇ ㄊㄧˊ)
portable; to carry with a hand: 他有一台手提打字機。He has a portable typewriter.
手提袋(ㄕㄡˇ ㄊㄧˊ ㄉㄞˋ)
a valise; a Boston bag; a handbag
手提箱(ㄕㄡˇ ㄊㄧˊ ㄒㄧㄤ)
a portmanteau; an attaché case; a suitcase
手推車(ㄕㄡˇ ㄊㄨㄟ ㄔㄜ)or 手車(ㄕㄡˇ ㄔㄜ)
a handcart; a wheelbarrow
手拿(ㄕㄡˇ ㄋㄚˊ)
to hold in hand; to take by hand
手拉手(ㄕㄡˇ ㄌㄚ ㄕㄡˇ)
hand in hand
手辣(ㄕㄡˇ ㄌㄚˋ)
ruthless: 那是一種心狠手辣的行爲。That was an act of savage, ruthless ferocity.
手泐(ㄕㄡˇ ㄌㄜˋ)
① a personally handwritten article ② a personal letter 亦作「手書」
手榴彈(ㄕㄡˇ ㄌㄧㄡˊ ㄉㄢˋ)
a hand grenade
手令(ㄕㄡˇ ㄌㄧㄥˋ)
a personally handwritten order (by a man at the top)
手爐(ㄕㄡˇ ㄌㄨˊ)
a portable charcoal stove (used as a hand warmer)
手稿(ㄕㄡˇ ㄍㄠˇ)
manuscript
手骨(ㄕㄡˇ ㄍㄨˇ)
bones of the human forelimbs
手工(ㄕㄡˇ ㄍㄨㄥ)
① handwork; handiwork ② by hand: 這是手工做的嗎? Was this made by hand?
手工藝(ㄕㄡˇ ㄍㄨㄥ ㄧˋ)
handicrafts; handiwork
手工藝品(ㄕㄡˇ ㄍㄨㄥ ㄧˋ ㄆㄧㄣˇ)
handicraft articles; fancy works
手工業(ㄕㄡˇ ㄍㄨㄥ ㄧㄝˋ)
a manual trade
手銬(ㄕㄡˇ ㄎㄠˋ)
handcuffs: 犯人都帶上手銬。The prisoners were all put on handcuffs.
手快(ㄕㄡˇ ㄎㄨㄞˋ)
quick in action; nimble: 他眼明手快。He's sharp of sight and quick of hand.
手翰(ㄕㄡˇ ㄏㄢˋ)
a personally handwritten letter
手虎口(ㄕㄡˇ ㄏㄨˇ ㄎㄡˇ)
the space between the thumb and the index finger
手滑(ㄕㄡˇ ㄏㄨㄚˊ)
to do something at will
手揮目送(ㄕㄡˇ ㄏㄨㄟ ㄇㄨˋ ㄙㄨㄥˋ)
conveyance of a double meaning
手迹(ㄕㄡˇ ㄐㄧ)
one's handwriting (or painting)
手機關鎗(ㄕㄡˇ ㄐㄧ ㄍㄨㄢ ㄑㄧㄤ)
a Lewis machine gun; a Lewis gun; a Lewis automatic rifle; a Thompson submachine gun; a Tommy gun
手急眼快(ㄕㄡˇ ㄐㄧˊ ㄧㄢˇ ㄎㄨㄞˋ)
moving or acting quickly; nimble; to be quick of eye and deft of hand
手技(ㄕㄡˇ ㄐㄧˋ)
① manual skill ② jugglery; sleight of hand
手脚(ㄕㄡˇ ㄐㄧㄠˇ)
① hand and foot ② motion; action ③ tricks; juggles: 我懷疑有人從中動過手脚。I suspect that someone must have juggled things.
手脚不乾淨(ㄕㄡˇ ㄐㄧㄠˇ ㄅㄨˋ ㄍㄢ ㄐㄧㄥˋ)
(slang) to be in the habit of stealing
手脚利落(ㄕㄡˇ ㄐㄧㄠˇ ㄌㄧˋ ㄌㄨㄛˋ)
nimble; agile
手簡(ㄕㄡˇ ㄐㄧㄢˇ)
a letter
手巾(ㄕㄡˇ ㄐㄧㄣ)
a towel
手緊(ㄕㄡˇ ㄐㄧㄣˇ)
① short of cash ② thrifty; reluctant to spend money
手絹兒(ㄕㄡˇ ㄐㄩㄢˋㄦ)
a handkerchief
手卷(ㄕㄡˇ ㄐㄩㄢˇ)
a scroll
手啓(ㄕㄡˇ ㄑㄧˇ)
handwritten by (a conventional phrase for ending a letter)
手氣(ㄕㄡˇ ㄑㄧˋ)
(gambling) luck
手巧(ㄕㄡˇ ㄑㄧㄠˇ)
dexterous; skillful
手球(ㄕㄡˇ ㄑㄧㄡˊ)
(sports) handball
手鎗(ㄕㄡˇ ㄑㄧㄤ)
a pistol; a revolver; a gun
手輕(ㄕㄡˇ ㄑㄧㄥ)
light-handed
手下(ㄕㄡˇ ㄒㄧㄚˋ)
① subordinates ② under the leadership of: 我們在他手下工作。We work under him.
手下敗將(ㄕㄡˇ ㄒㄧㄚˋ ㄅㄞˋ ㄐㄧㄤˋ)
one who has suffered defeat at (my, your, etc.) hands
手下留情(ㄕㄡˇ ㄒㄧㄚˋ ㄌㄧㄡˊ ㄑㄧㄥˊ)
to show leniency or mercy
手心(ㄕㄡˇ ㄒㄧㄣ)
the center of the palm—(figuratively) control
手相(ㄕㄡˇ ㄒㄧㄤˋ)
the lines of the palm by which fortunetellers tell one's fortune: 看手相 to read one's palm
手相家(ㄕㄡˇ ㄒㄧㄤˋ ㄐㄧㄚ)
a palmist
手相術(ㄕㄡˇ ㄒㄧㄤˋ ㄕㄨˋ)
palmistry
手續(ㄕㄡˇ ㄒㄩˋ)
procedures; red tape; formalities
手續費(ㄕㄡˇ ㄒㄩˋ ㄈㄟˋ)
service charges
手植(ㄕㄡˇ ㄓˊ)
(said of a tree) personally planted (by a dignitary, etc.)
手指頭(ㄕㄡˇ ㄓˊ ·ㄊㄡ)

〔手部〕

〔手部〕

① fingertips ② fingers

手指(ㄕㄡˇ ㄓˇ)
① a finger ② to point at something with the index finger: 他手指著什麼? What is he pointing at?

手紙(ㄕㄡˇ ㄓˇ)
toilet paper

手札(ㄕㄡˇ ㄓㄚˊ)
a personally handwritten letter

手摺(ㄕㄡˇ ㄓㄜˊ)
① (in former times) paper for making appeals to a superior official ② an account book (of a merchant)

手詔(ㄕㄡˇ ㄓㄠˋ)
a personally handwritten imperial decree or edict

手掌(ㄕㄡˇ ㄓㄤˇ)
the palm (of the hand)

手杖(ㄕㄡˇ ㄓㄤˋ)
a cane; a walking stick

手鐲(ㄕㄡˇ ㄓㄨㄛˊ)
a bracelet

手重(ㄕㄡˇ ㄓㄨㄥˋ)
heavy-handed; with too much force

手車(ㄕㄡˇ ㄔㄜ)
a wheelbarrow; a pushcart; a handcart 參看「手推車」

手抄(ㄕㄡˇ ㄔㄠ)
to copy by hand; to make a handwritten copy

手抄本(ㄕㄡˇ ㄔㄠ ㄅㄣˇ)
a hand-copied book; a handwritten copy

手示(ㄕㄡˇ ㄕˋ)
personally handwritten instructions or directions

手勢(ㄕㄡˇ ㄕˋ)
a gesture; a sign; to sign: 他做友善的手勢。He made a friendly gesture.

手煞車(ㄕㄡˇ ㄕㄚˋ ㄔㄜ)
a hand brake

手上(ㄕㄡˇ ·ㄕㄤ)
in one's hands

手書(ㄕㄡˇ ㄕㄨ)
a personally handwritten message or article; a personal letter

手術(ㄕㄡˇ ㄕㄨˋ)
a surgical operation; surgery

手術刀(ㄕㄡˇ ㄕㄨˋ ㄉㄠ)
a scalpel

手術台(ㄕㄡˇ ㄕㄨˋ ㄊㄞˊ)
an operation table

手術室(ㄕㄡˇ ㄕㄨˋ ㄕˋ)
an operation room

手刃(ㄕㄡˇ ㄖㄣˋ)
to kill someone personally with a sword

手軟(ㄕㄡˇ ㄖㄨㄢˇ)
to hesitate to inflict punishment from pity; the pity toward an intended victim

手澤(ㄕㄡˇ ㄗㄜˊ)
personal implements and handwritings left behind by one's immediate ancestors

手足(ㄕㄡˇ ㄗㄨˊ)
brothers

手足情深(ㄕㄡˇ ㄗㄨˊ ㄑㄧㄥˊ ㄕㄣ)
The love between brothers is deep. 或 Blood is thicker than water.

手足之情(ㄕㄡˇ ㄗㄨˊ ㄓ ㄑㄧㄥˊ)
brotherly affection

手足重繭(ㄕㄡˇ ㄗㄨˊ ㄔㄨㄥˊ ㄐㄧㄢˇ)
with hands and feet covered with thick calluses as a result of hard work

手足無措(ㄕㄡˇ ㄗㄨˊ ㄨˊ ㄘㄨㄛˋ)
to be at a loss what to do

手刺(ㄕㄡˇ ㄘˋ)
a visiting card (of an official)

手册(ㄕㄡˇ ㄘㄜˋ)
a handbook; a manual: 英文文法手册 a handbook of English grammar

手策(ㄕㄡˇ ㄘㄜˋ)
the means (as opposed to the end)

手肅(ㄕㄡˇ ㄙㄨˋ)
personally handwritten by (a conventional phrase at the end of a letter)

手鬆(ㄕㄡˇ ㄙㄨㄥ)
spending money freely or lavishly; spendthrift; liberal; generous; freehanded; openhanded

手兒(ㄕㄡˇㄦ)
① the hand ② skill; workmanship; craft ③ a trick; means ④ handiwork

手藝(ㄕㄡˇ ㄧˋ)
handicraft; skill to enable one to earn a living; a trade

手藝人(ㄕㄡˇ ㄧˋ ㄖㄣˊ)
a craftsman; an artisan

手眼快(ㄕㄡˇ ㄧㄢˇ ㄎㄨㄞˋ)
quick in action; nimble

手淫(ㄕㄡˇ ㄧㄣˊ)
masturbation; self-abuse

手印(ㄕㄡˇ ㄧㄣˋ)
an impression of the thumb as a signature

手癢(ㄕㄡˇ ㄧㄤˇ)
① an itch on one's hands ② to have an itch to do something

手無縛鷄之力(ㄕㄡˇ ㄨˊ ㄈㄨˊ ㄐㄧ ㄓ ㄌㄧˋ)
to lack the strength to truss up a chicken

手無寸鐵(ㄕㄡˇ ㄨˊ ㄘㄨㄣˋ ㄊㄧㄝˇ)
(literally) to carry not even an inch of iron—totally unarmed

手舞足蹈(ㄕㄡˇ ㄨˇ ㄗㄨˊ ㄉㄠˋ)
to wave the arms and stamp the feet for joy; to caper beyond oneself with joy

手腕(ㄕㄡˇ ㄨㄢˋ)
① the wrist ② ability; tricks; skill; tact: 外交手腕 diplomacy; diplomatic skill

手腕子(ㄕㄡˇ ㄨㄢˋ ·ㄗ)
the wrist

手紋(ㄕㄡˇ ㄨㄣˊ)
the lines on the palm

手語(ㄕㄡˇ ㄩˇ)
① dactylology; sign language ② to play string instruments

手諭(ㄕㄡˇ ㄩˋ)
a personally written order

【才】1790
ㄘㄞˊ tsair cái

1. natural abilities; a gift; talent; a mental faculty: 她有音樂的天才。She is a talent for music.
2. a gifted person; a talented person; a brilliant man; a talent: 她是位才藝出衆的演員。She is a talented performer.
3. people of a certain type: 奴才 a flunky; a flunkey
4. certainly; indeed: 我才不怕他呢! I'm certainly not afraid of him.
5. just; just now: 節目才剛開始。The program has just started.

才筆(ㄘㄞˊ ㄅㄧˇ)

a literary talent
才貌(ㄘㄞˊ ㄇㄠˋ)
talent and appearance
才貌雙全(ㄘㄞˊ ㄇㄠˋ ㄕㄨㄤ ㄑㄩㄢˊ)
(said of women) talented and good-looking; impressive both in talent and appearance; brilliant and pretty
才名(ㄘㄞˊ ㄇㄧㄥˊ)
a reputation for talent or brilliance
才分(ㄘㄞˊ ㄈㄣˋ)
natural abilities, gifts or talent; brilliance of mind
才大心細(ㄘㄞˊ ㄉㄚˋ ㄒㄧㄣ ㄒㄧˋ)
to have a great talent and an attentive mind; gifted and careful
才德全備(ㄘㄞˊ ㄉㄜˊ ㄑㄩㄢˊ ㄅㄟˋ)or 才德兼備(ㄘㄞˊ ㄉㄜˊ ㄐㄧㄢ ㄅㄟˋ)
to have both talent and virtue; talented and virtuous
才童(ㄘㄞˊ ㄊㄨㄥˊ)
a talented child; a whiz kid; a child prodigy
才難(ㄘㄞˊ ㄋㄢˊ)
Talents are hard to find. 或 Really able men are difficult to come by.
才能(ㄘㄞˊ ㄋㄥˊ)or 才力(ㄘㄞˊ ㄌㄧˋ)
talent; abilities; a gift: 他是位極有才能的人。He is a man of great talent.
才女(ㄘㄞˊ ㄋㄩˇ)
a talented woman: 她是位才女。She is a talented woman.
才郎(ㄘㄞˊ ㄌㄤˊ)
my talented husband
才略(ㄘㄞˊ ㄌㄩㄝˋ)
talent for scheming
才高意廣(ㄘㄞˊ ㄍㄠ ㄧˋ ㄍㄨㄤˇ)
to have a brilliant mind and a broad vision
才幹(ㄘㄞˊ ㄍㄢˋ)
talent or ability to get things done; competence: 他具有做將軍的才幹。He had great ability as a general.
才華(ㄘㄞˊ ㄏㄨㄚˊ)
brilliance (of mind); a gift; talent
才華出衆(ㄘㄞˊ ㄏㄨㄚˊ ㄔㄨ ㄓㄨㄥˋ)
of uncommon brilliance: 王先生才華出衆。Mr. Wang is a person of uncommon brilliance.
才兼文武(ㄘㄞˊ ㄐㄧㄢ ㄨㄣˊ ㄨˇ)
talented both mentally and physically; having both military and literary gifts
才盡(ㄘㄞˊ ㄐㄧㄣˋ)
to have exhausted one's talent
才具(ㄘㄞˊ ㄐㄩˋ)
natural capacity or abilities
才氣(ㄘㄞˊ ㄑㄧˋ)
talent; brilliance; keen intelligence
才氣洋溢(ㄘㄞˊ ㄑㄧˋ ㄧㄤˊ ㄧˋ)
a brilliant mind; brilliant intelligence
才情(ㄘㄞˊ ㄑㄧㄥˊ)
brilliant expression of emotions (in a writing)
才學(ㄘㄞˊ ㄒㄩㄝˊ)
intelligence and scholarship
才智(ㄘㄞˊ ㄓˋ)
intelligence; brilliance; wisdom and ability
才儲八斗(ㄘㄞˊ ㄔㄨˇ ㄅㄚ ㄉㄡˇ)
exceedingly talented or brilliant 亦作「才高八斗」
才士(ㄘㄞˊ ㄕˋ)
a man of ability or talent; a brilliant man
才識(ㄘㄞˊ ㄕˋ)
ability and insight: 他才識過人。He is gifted with talent and insight far beyond the average person.
才疏學淺(ㄘㄞˊ ㄕㄨ ㄒㄩㄝˊ ㄑㄧㄢˇ)
untalented and unlearned; to have little talent and less learning (a polite expression referring to oneself)
才人(ㄘㄞˊ ㄖㄣˊ)
①a talented person; a man of talent; a brilliant man ② a rank of ladies-in-waiting during the Tsin, Tang and Sung dynasties
才子(ㄘㄞˊ ㄗˇ)
a talented person; a man of talent; a brilliant man; a genius
才子佳人(ㄘㄞˊ ㄗˇ ㄐㄧㄚ ㄖㄣˊ)
marriage between the brilliant man and the beautiful woman; an ideal couple; gifted scholars and beautiful ladies
才子書(ㄘㄞˊ ㄗˇ ㄕㄨ)
(literally) books by brilliant writers—specifically referring to 莊子、離騷、史記、杜詩、水滸傳、西廂記
才思(ㄘㄞˊ ㄙ)
brilliant thoughts (as reflected in a writing)
才思敏捷(ㄘㄞˊ ㄙ ㄇㄧㄣˇ ㄐㄧㄝˊ)
to have an agile imagination
才藝卓絕(ㄘㄞˊ ㄧˋ ㄓㄨㄛˊ ㄐㄩㄝˊ)
to stand out in talent and skill
才媛(ㄘㄞˊ ㄩㄢˋ)
a talented woman; a gifted maiden

一畫

【扎】 1791
1. ㄓㄚ ja zhā
to pierce; to prick: 他的手指上扎了一根刺。He pricked his finger on a thorn.
扎蓬棵(ㄓㄚ ㄆㄥˊ ㄎㄜ)
uncombed hair 亦稱「蓬髮」
扎猛子(ㄓㄚ ㄇㄥˇ ˙ㄗ)
to plunge headlong into the water
扎根(ㄓㄚ ㄍㄣ)
to take root
扎花兒(ㄓㄚ ㄏㄨㄚㄦ)
to embroider a design
扎心(ㄓㄚ ㄒㄧㄣ)
heartbreaking
扎針(ㄓㄚ ㄓㄣ)
to perform an acupuncture; to acupuncture; to have acupuncture treatment
扎實(ㄓㄚ ˙ㄕ)
solid; firm: 他的事業很扎實。He had a solid business.
扎手(ㄓㄚ ㄕㄡˇ)
①to prick the hand: 小心扎手。Mind you don't prick your hands. ②difficult to handle; thorny: 他這個人可眞扎手。He is really difficult to handle.
扎手舞脚(ㄓㄚ ㄕㄡˇ ㄨˇ ㄐㄧㄠˇ)
to make exaggerated gestures
扎耳朵(ㄓㄚ ㄦˇ ˙ㄉㄨㄛ)
unpleasant to the ear; to grate
扎耳朵眼兒(ㄓㄚ ㄦˇ ˙ㄉㄨㄛ ㄧㄚˇㄦ)
to pierce the earlobe in order to wear an earring
扎眼(ㄓㄚ ㄧㄢˇ)

①dazzling; offending to the eye; loud; garish: 陽光太扎眼了。The sunshine is too dazzling. ②offensively conspicuous

〔手部〕

【扎】 1791
2. ㄓㄚˊ jar zhá
to struggle; to strive
扎掙(ㄓㄚˊ ·ㄓㄥ)
to struggle; to strive 亦作「掙扎」
扎掙不住(ㄓㄚˊ ·ㄓㄥ ㄅㄨˋ ㄓㄨˋ)
to struggle or strive in vain; cannot keep up or maintain
扎營(ㄓㄚˊ ㄧㄥˊ)
to pitch a tent; to encamp

二畫

【扑】 1792
ㄆㄨ pu pū
to beat; to strike
扑罰(ㄆㄨ ㄈㄚˊ)
flogging or whipping as a punishment; a scourge
扑撻(ㄆㄨ ㄊㄚˋ)
to whip; to lash; to flog
扑擊(ㄆㄨ ㄐㄧˊ)
to hit; to strike
扑作教刑(ㄆㄨ ㄗㄨㄛˋ ㄐㄧㄠˋ ㄒㄧㄥˊ)
to use the rod to teach and punish

【扒】 1793
1. ㄅㄚ ba bā
1. to claw; to strip
2. to rake: 扒土 to rake earth
3. to climb; to scale
扒皮(ㄅㄚ ㄆㄧˊ)
to peel off the skin
扒得高跌得重(ㄅㄚ ·ㄉㄜ ㄍㄠ ㄉㄧㄝ ·ㄉㄜ ㄓㄨㄥˋ)
The higher one climbs, the harder he falls.
扒住(ㄅㄚ ㄓㄨˋ)
to hold on to; to cling to

【扒】 1793
2. ㄆㄚˊ par pá
1. to gather up; to rake up: 她把落葉扒在一起。She raked the fallen leaves together.
2. to stew; to braise
3. to scratch; to claw
扒灰(ㄆㄚˊ ㄏㄨㄟ)
(literally) to scoop up ashes —to commit incest with a daughter-in-law
扒竊(ㄆㄚˊ ㄑㄧㄝˋ)
to pick pockets and steal; pickpockets and burglars: 我被扒竊了。I had my pocket picked.
扒手(ㄆㄚˊ ㄕㄡˇ)
a pickpocket: 當心扒手! Beware of pickpockets!
扒山虎(ㄆㄚˊ ㄕㄢ ㄏㄨˇ)
①a sedan chair for transportation in mountains ②a kind of ivy

【打】 1794
1. ㄉㄚˇ daa dǎ
1. to strike; to beat
2. to attack; to fight: 他們打了一場硬仗。They fought a hard battle.
3. to smash: 盤子打破在地上。The dish smashed on the floor.
4. to make, do, get, fetch, play, buy, etc. (depending on the object):我們來打網球吧。Let's play tennis.
5. from; to; toward: 你打那兒來? Where did you come from?
打靶(ㄉㄚˇ ㄅㄚˇ)
target practice
打靶場(ㄉㄚˇ ㄅㄚˇ ㄔㄤˇ)
a target range; a shooting gallery
打把式(ㄉㄚˇ ㄅㄚˇ ㄕˋ)
to demonstrate pugilistic skills
打擺子(ㄉㄚˇ ㄅㄞˇ ·ㄗ)
malaria; to suffer from malaria
打敗(ㄉㄚˇ ㄅㄞˋ)
①to defeat; to beat; to worst ②to suffer a defeat; to be defeated
打敗仗(ㄉㄚˇ ㄅㄞˋ ㄓㄤˋ)
to suffer a defeat; to be defeated in battle
打包(ㄉㄚˇ ㄅㄠ)
①to pack ②the bundle carried on the back by a traveling Buddhist monk
打包票(ㄉㄚˇ ㄅㄠ ㄆㄧㄠˋ)
to vouch for; to guarantee: 我敢打包票,禮物一定準時送到。I guarantee that the gifts will be delivered on time.
打飽嗝兒(ㄉㄚˇ ㄅㄠˇ ㄍㄜˊㄦ)
to belch after a solid meal
打抱不平(ㄉㄚˇ ㄅㄠˋ ㄅㄨˋ ㄆㄧㄥˊ)
to help the victims of injustice; to try to redress an injustice to the weak; to come out against the powerful on behalf of the downtrodden
打扮(ㄉㄚˇ ㄅㄢˋ)
①(said of a woman, an actor or actress) to make up ②to dress up; dressed like; to dress: 孩子們打扮得像春天的花朵一樣。The dressed children looked like spring flowers.
打邊鼓(ㄉㄚˇ ㄅㄧㄢ ㄍㄨˇ)
to incite; to instigate; to drum up
打辮子(ㄉㄚˇ ㄅㄧㄢˋ ·ㄗ)
to wear a pigtail, or a pair of pigtails; to knit a pigtail
打補靪(ㄉㄚˇ ㄅㄨˇ ·ㄉㄧㄥ)
to put a patch (on a shoe sole, a garment, etc.)
打不破(ㄉㄚˇ ·ㄅㄨ ㄆㄛˋ)
①unbreakable: 這是隻打不破的碗。It's an unbreakable bowl. ②to try in vain to break
打不得(ㄉㄚˇ ·ㄅㄨ ㄉㄜˊ)
cannot be beaten with impunity; cannot beat and get away with it
打不倒(ㄉㄚˇ ·ㄅㄨ ㄉㄠˇ)
①unconquerable; that cannot be knocked down ②to try in vain to knock down
打不到(ㄉㄚˇ ·ㄅㄨ ㄉㄠˋ)
①to try in vain to hit ②that cannot be hit
打不過(ㄉㄚˇ ·ㄅㄨ ㄍㄨㄛˋ)
to be no fighting match for
打不開(ㄉㄚˇ ·ㄅㄨ ㄎㄞ)
①that cannot be opened: 門打不開。The door cannot be opened. ②to try in vain to open
打不還手(ㄉㄚˇ ·ㄅㄨ ㄏㄨㄢˊ ㄕㄡˇ)
not to strike back when attacked
打不死(ㄉㄚˇ ·ㄅㄨ ㄙˇ)
①still alive after a hard beating ②to try in vain to beat to death
打不碎(ㄉㄚˇ ·ㄅㄨ ㄙㄨㄟˋ)
①that cannot be broken to pieces; unbreakable: 那是張打不碎的唱片。It's an unbreakable record. ②to try in vain to break to pieces
打破(ㄉㄚˇ ㄆㄛˋ)
to smash to pieces; to break: 玻璃窗被打破了。The window-

pane is broken.
打破紀錄(ㄉㄚˇ ㄆㄛˋ ㄐㄧˋ ㄌㄨˋ)
to break the record; to set a new record; to rewrite the record
打破前例(ㄉㄚˇ ㄆㄛˋ ㄑㄧㄢˊ ㄌㄧˋ)
to depart from precedents
打破砂鍋問到底(ㄉㄚˇ ㄆㄛˋ ㄕㄚ ㄍㄨㄛ ㄨㄣˋ ㄉㄠˋ ㄉㄧˇ)
to interrogate persistently; to fire one question after another; to raise an endless stream of questions (a pun on 問 and 璺)
打拍子(ㄉㄚˇ ㄆㄞ ˙ㄗ)
to beat time (for a singer, dancer, etc.)
打牌(ㄉㄚˇ ㄆㄞˊ)
to play a card game, mah-jong, etc.: 他喜歡打牌。He likes to play cards.
打砲(ㄉㄚˇ ㄆㄠˋ)
① to fire shells; to fire artillery pieces ② (slang) to visit a brothel
打屁股(ㄉㄚˇ ㄆㄧˋ ˙ㄍㄨ)
spanking; to flog the buttocks as a form of punishment: 他打這頑皮小孩的屁股。He spanked the naughty child.
打票(ㄉㄚˇ ㄆㄧㄠˋ)
to buy tickets
打鋪蓋(ㄉㄚˇ ㄆㄨ ˙ㄍㄞ)
to set up a bed
打撲克(ㄉㄚˇ ㄆㄨ ㄎㄜˋ)
to play poker
打麻將(ㄉㄚˇ ㄇㄚˊ ㄐㄧㄤˋ)
to play mah-jong
打馬虎眼(ㄉㄚˇ ㄇㄚˇ ˙ㄏㄨ ㄧㄢˇ)
to exploit other's carelessness; to pretend to be ignorant of something in order to gloss it over; to act dumb
打罵(ㄉㄚˇ ㄇㄚˋ)
to beat and scold; maltreatment (to a child, orphan, etc.)
打磨(ㄉㄚˇ ˙ㄇㄛ)
to polish; to burnish
打麥(ㄉㄚˇ ㄇㄞˋ)
to thresh wheat or barley
打毛線衣(ㄉㄚˇ ㄇㄠˊ ㄒㄧㄢˋ ㄧ)
to knit a woolen sweater
打門(ㄉㄚˇ ㄇㄣˊ)
to knock at a door
打悶棍(ㄉㄚˇ ㄇㄣˋ ㄍㄨㄣˋ)
to rob a victim after beating him unconscious with a club
打鳴兒(ㄉㄚˇ ㄇㄧㄥˊㄦ)
(said of a rooster) to crow
打明兒起(ㄉㄚˇ ㄇㄧㄥˊㄦ ㄑㄧˇ)
to begin from tomorrow: 打明兒起，要更努力用功啦。You have to study harder from tomorrow on.
打發(ㄉㄚˇ ˙ㄈㄚ)
① to dispatch; to send away: 他把客人打發走了。He sent the guests away. ② to fire; to dismiss: 老板將那位員工打發走了。The boss dismissed the worker from his job. ③ to spend (time)
打翻(ㄉㄚˇ ㄈㄢ)
to overturn; to tip over; to knock over: 誰把瓶子打翻了? Who knocked that bottle over?
打分數(ㄉㄚˇ ㄈㄣ ㄕㄨˋ)
to grade (students' papers); to grade (a performance): 老師在試卷上打分數。The teacher graded the papers.
打粉底(ㄉㄚˇ ㄈㄣˇ ㄉㄧˇ)
to apply grease paint in makeup
打打鬧鬧(ㄉㄚˇ ˙ㄉㄚ ㄋㄠˋ ㄋㄠˋ)
to fight in jest or for fun; boisterous
打打談談(ㄉㄚˇ ˙ㄉㄚ ㄊㄢˊ ㄊㄢˊ)
to fight and talk alternately (without reaching a real settlement); to fight, then talk, then fight again, and then talk again
打得好(ㄉㄚˇ ˙ㄉㄜ ㄏㄠˇ)
① to deserve the beating or spanking ② an excellent performance (said of ball players, knitting women, etc.)
打得火熱(ㄉㄚˇ ˙ㄉㄜ ㄏㄨㄛˇ ㄖㄜˋ)
① to be in the middle of a white-hot battle ② to be passionately in love with each other
打倒(ㄉㄚˇ ㄉㄠˇ)
to knock down; to overthrow; (slogans) down with...: 他打倒他的敵人。He knocked his enemy down.
打稻(ㄉㄚˇ ㄉㄠˋ)
to thrash rice
打鬥(ㄉㄚˇ ㄉㄡˋ)
a fight; a skirmish; to fight
打蛋(ㄉㄚˇ ㄉㄢˋ)
to beat, stir or whip eggs
打蛋機(ㄉㄚˇ ㄉㄢˋ ㄐㄧ)
an egg beater
打彈子(ㄉㄚˇ ㄉㄢˋ ˙ㄗ)
to play billiards
打燈籠(ㄉㄚˇ ㄉㄥ ㄌㄨㄥˊ)
to hold a lighted lantern (when traveling by night)
打底(ㄉㄚˇ ㄉㄧˇ)
(textile and dyeing) bottoming
打底稿(ㄉㄚˇ ㄉㄧˇ ㄍㄠˇ)
to prepare a draft
打底子(ㄉㄚˇ ㄉㄧˇ ˙ㄗ)
① to sketch (a plan, picture, etc.) ② to lay a foundation
打地鋪(ㄉㄚˇ ㄉㄧˋ ˙ㄆㄨ)
to make a bed on the floor or the ground
打疊(ㄉㄚˇ ㄉㄧㄝˊ)
① to pile up one atop the other ② to arrange
打掉(ㄉㄚˇ ㄉㄧㄠˋ)
to destroy; to knock out; to wipe out: 他們把那棟建築物打掉。They destroyed the building.
打點(ㄉㄚˇ ㄉㄧㄢˇ)
① to examine and put in order; to pack up (luggage): 你的東西打點好沒有? Have you packed (up) your things? ② to bribe
打點滴(ㄉㄚˇ ㄉㄧㄢˇ ㄉㄧ)
to administer intravenous drip
打電報(ㄉㄚˇ ㄉㄧㄢˋ ㄅㄠˋ)
to send a telegram or cable; to telegraph a message; to telegraph; to cable a message
打電話(ㄉㄚˇ ㄉㄧㄢˋ ㄏㄨㄚˋ)
to make a telephone call; to telephone a message; to telephone
打賭(ㄉㄚˇ ㄉㄨˇ)
to make a bet; to wager; to bet: 我打賭她今晚準會來。I bet she'll come tonight.
打哆嗦(ㄉㄚˇ ㄉㄨㄛ ˙ㄙㄨㄛ)
to tremble; to shiver (especially in cold weather): 她冷得直打哆嗦。She shivered with cold.
打盹兒(ㄉㄚˇ ㄉㄨㄣˇㄦ)
to doze; to take a nap: 他在

〔手部〕

〔手部〕

椅子上打盹。He napped in the chair.
打對臺(ㄉㄚˇ ㄉㄨㄟˋ ㄊㄞˊ)
to compete in business
打斷(ㄉㄚˇ ㄉㄨㄢˋ)
① to break ② to interrupt; to cut short; to punctuate
打斷念頭(ㄉㄚˇ ㄉㄨㄢˋ ㄋㄧㄢˋ ·ㄊㄡ)
to give up an idea
打斷說話(ㄉㄚˇ ㄉㄨㄢˋ ㄕㄨㄛ ㄏㄨㄚˋ)
to interrupt a person while he is speaking
打動(ㄉㄚˇ ㄉㄨㄥˋ)
to move (a person mentally); to make someone interested in something; to succeed in persuading someone to do something: 他的話深深地打動了我的心。I was deeply moved by his words.
打胎(ㄉㄚˇ ㄊㄞ)
to have an abortion on purpose
打頭陣(ㄉㄚˇ ㄊㄡˊ ㄓㄣˋ)
to lead the attack; to be at the foremost front in an attack
打頭兒(ㄉㄚˇ ㄊㄡˊㄦ)
from the beginning; from the start: 咱們再打頭兒來好嗎? Let's do it from the start, shall we?
打探(ㄉㄚˇ ㄊㄢˋ)
to find out
打探子(ㄉㄚˇ ㄊㄢˋ ·ㄗ)
to dispatch spies or detectives
打嚏噴(ㄉㄚˇ ㄊㄧˋ ·ㄈㄣ)or 打噴嚏(ㄉㄚˇ ㄆㄣ ㄊㄧˋ)
to sneeze; to make a sneeze
打鐵的(ㄉㄚˇ ㄊㄧㄝ ·ㄉㄜ)
a blacksmith
打鐵趁熱(ㄉㄚˇ ㄊㄧㄝ ㄔㄣˋ ㄖㄜˋ)
Strike while the iron is hot. 或 To do a job while the favorable condition exists.
打聽(ㄉㄚˇ ·ㄊㄧㄥ)
to inquire; to find out through inquiries; to make inquiries: 他設法打聽那件事。He tries to make inquiries about that thing.
打退(ㄉㄚˇ ㄊㄨㄟˋ)
to beat back (or off); to repulse: 他們打退敵人的進攻。They repulsed an enemy attack.
打退堂鼓(ㄉㄚˇ ㄊㄨㄟˋ ㄊㄤˊ ㄍㄨˇ)
to give up a pursuit without attaining the goal; to give up halfway; to back out: 我們不能遇到困難就打退堂鼓了。We can't back out the moment we run up against a little difficulty.
打通(ㄉㄚˇ ㄊㄨㄥ)
to open a connecting road; to establish a connection; to remove the block in a passage; to get through
打通關(ㄉㄚˇ ㄊㄨㄥ ㄍㄨㄢ)
to take on everyone else at the table in turn in the finger-guessing game while drinking
打鬧(ㄉㄚˇ ㄋㄠˋ)
to quarrel and fight noisily
打蠟(ㄉㄚˇ ㄌㄚˋ)
to rub, or treat with wax; to wax
打來回(ㄉㄚˇ ㄌㄞˊ ㄏㄨㄟˊ)
to make a round trip; to make a return trip
打雷(ㄉㄚˇ ㄌㄟˊ)
to thunder
打擂臺(ㄉㄚˇ ㄌㄟˋ ㄊㄞˊ)
(said of Chinese pugilists) to join a contest in feats of prowess on stage
打撈(ㄉㄚˇ ㄌㄠ)
to salvage sunken ships; to drag sunken things out of water: 我們打撈到一具屍體。We retrieved a corpse from the water.
打冷戰(ㄉㄚˇ ㄌㄥˇ ㄓㄢˋ)
① to shudder ② to fight a cold war
打獵(ㄉㄚˇ ㄌㄧㄝˋ)
to go hunting; to go on a hunting expedition: 他很喜歡打獵。He's very fond of hunting.
打量(ㄉㄚˇ ㄌㄧㄤˋ)
① to size up; to look someone up and down: 她上下打量著那個陌生人。She looked the stranger up and down. ② to think; to suppose; to conjecture
打領帶(ㄉㄚˇ ㄌㄧㄥˇ ㄉㄞˋ)
to tie a necktie
打落門牙和血吞(ㄉㄚˇ ㄌㄨㄛˋ ㄇㄣˊ ㄧㄚˊ ㄏㄨㄛˋ ㄒㄩㄝˋ ㄊㄨㄣ)
to suffer great loss or pain with fortitude
打落水狗(ㄉㄚˇ ㄌㄨㄛˋ ㄕㄨㄟˇ ㄍㄡˇ)
(literally) to beat a drowning dog—to attack someone already down in his luck
打歌(ㄉㄚˇ ㄍㄜ)
to promote a new song by singing it frequently in public appearance
打嗝兒(ㄉㄚˇ ㄍㄜˊㄦ)
to hiccough; to hiccup; to have the hiccups
打個照面(ㄉㄚˇ ·ㄍㄜ ㄓㄠˋ ㄇㄧㄢˋ)
to meet face to face
打個照會(ㄉㄚˇ ·ㄍㄜ ㄓㄠˋ ㄏㄨㄟˋ)
to let someone know; to give someone a notice
打高空(ㄉㄚˇ ㄍㄠ ㄎㄨㄥ)
to make grandiose but impractical plans; to talk persuasively without substance; to embellish narrative or rumors
打狗看主人(ㄉㄚˇ ㄍㄡˇ ㄎㄢˋ ㄓㄨˇ ㄖㄣˊ)
(literally) to consider who its master is before beating a dog—to use discretion as to the possibility of reprisal when bullying people with powerful connections
打狗欺主(ㄉㄚˇ ㄍㄡˇ ㄑㄧ ㄓㄨˇ)
(literally) To beat a dog is to insult its master.—To humiliate the protected is to humiliate the protector.
打箍(ㄉㄚˇ ㄍㄨ)
to hoop; to put a hoop around something
打鼓(ㄉㄚˇ ㄍㄨˇ)
① to beat a drum ② to feel uncertain or nervous: 他的心裏直在打鼓。He felt extremely nervous.
打穀(ㄉㄚˇ ㄍㄨˇ)
to thresh grain
打滾兒(ㄉㄚˇ ㄍㄨㄣˇㄦ)
to roll about
打官話(ㄉㄚˇ ㄍㄨㄢ ㄏㄨㄚˋ)
to talk in the formal language of officialdom
打官腔(ㄉㄚˇ ㄍㄨㄢ ㄑㄧㄤ)
bureaucratic jargon
打官司(ㄉㄚˇ ㄍㄨㄢ ·ㄙ)
to have a lawsuit; to go to law: 我要和你打官司。I'll go to law with you.

打光棍(ㄉㄚˇ ㄍㄨㄤ ㄍㄨㄣˋ)
(said of a man) to remain a bachelor; to stay a single man

打工(ㄉㄚˇ ㄍㄨㄥ)
to do odd jobs as distinct from a regular employment

打躬(ㄉㄚˇ ㄍㄨㄥ)
to make a deep bow

打拱作揖(ㄉㄚˇ ㄍㄨㄥˇ ㄗㄨㄛˋ ㄧ)or 打躬作揖(ㄉㄚˇ ㄍㄨㄥ ㄗㄨㄛˋ ㄧ)
to salute with folded hands again and again; to fold the hands and make deep bows—to beg humbly

打卡(ㄉㄚˇ ㄎㄚˇ)
to record the time of one's presence or departure by punching a time clock

打卡機(ㄉㄚˇ ㄎㄚˇ ㄐㄧ)
a key punch machine

打卡鐘(ㄉㄚˇ ㄎㄚˇ ㄓㄨㄥ)
a time clock

打瞌睡(ㄉㄚˇ ㄎㄜ ㄕㄨㄟˋ)
to doze: 他看書時打瞌睡。He dozed over a book.

打開(ㄉㄚˇ ㄎㄞ)
① to open: 請把門打開。Please open the door. ② to turn on: 請打開收音機。Turn on the radio, please.

打開天窗說亮話(ㄉㄚˇ ㄎㄞ ㄊㄧㄢ ㄔㄨㄤ ㄕㄨㄛ ㄌㄧㄤˋ ㄏㄨㄚˋ)
to speak frankly; frankly speaking 或 Let's not mince matters.

打開僵局(ㄉㄚˇ ㄎㄞ ㄐㄧㄤ ㄐㄩˊ)
to break the impasse; to find the solution to a problem; to get out of a difficult situation: 我們終於打開僵局了。We finally found the solution to the problem.

打開眼界(ㄉㄚˇ ㄎㄞ ㄧㄢˇ ㄐㄧㄝˋ)
to widen one's horizons

打坑(ㄉㄚˇ ㄎㄥ)
to dig or excavate a pit

打垮(ㄉㄚˇ ㄎㄨㄚˇ)
to strike down; to defeat; to beat

打孔(ㄉㄚˇ ㄎㄨㄥˇ)
to drill a hole; to punch a hole; to perforate

打孔機(ㄉㄚˇ ㄎㄨㄥˇ ㄐㄧ)
a perforator; a puncher

打哈哈(ㄉㄚˇ ㄏㄚ ·ㄏㄚ)
① to roar with laughter ② to have fun; to frolic; to make merry: 快別拿他打哈哈。Don't make fun of him. ③ to talk irrelevantly in an apparent effort to avoid touching the real issue

打哈欠(ㄉㄚˇ ㄏㄚ ·ㄑㄧㄢ)or 打哈息(ㄉㄚˇ ㄏㄚ ·ㄒㄧ)
to yawn

打鼾(ㄉㄚˇ ㄏㄢ)
to snore

打寒噤(ㄉㄚˇ ㄏㄢˊ ㄐㄧㄣˋ)
to tremble or shudder because of cold

打呼嚕(ㄉㄚˇ ㄏㄨ ·ㄌㄨ)
to snore

打火機(ㄉㄚˇ ㄏㄨㄛˇ ㄐㄧ)
a (cigarette) lighter

打火石(ㄉㄚˇ ㄏㄨㄛˇ ㄕˊ)
a flint

打火印(ㄉㄚˇ ㄏㄨㄛˇ ㄧㄣˋ)or 打烙印(ㄉㄚˇ ㄌㄠˋ ㄧㄣˋ)
to brand (cattle)

打諢(ㄉㄚˇ ㄏㄨㄣˋ)
to crack jokes; to joke; to jest; to mock in fun

打基礎(ㄉㄚˇ ㄐㄧ ㄔㄨˇ)
to do spadework; to lay the foundations; to prepare oneself for bigger tasks ahead

打擊(ㄉㄚˇ ㄐㄧˊ)
to deal a blow upon; to give a blow to; to strike a blow against: 打擊不良風氣，人人有責。It's everyone's duty to strike a blow against unhealthy tendencies.

打擊率(ㄉㄚˇ ㄐㄧˊ ㄌㄩˋ)
a batting average

打擊手(ㄉㄚˇ ㄐㄧˊ ㄕㄡˇ)
a batter

打擊樂器(ㄉㄚˇ ㄐㄧˊ ㄩㄝˋ ㄑㄧˋ)
a percussion instrument

打家劫舍(ㄉㄚˇ ㄐㄧㄚ ㄐㄧㄝˊ ㄕㄜˋ)
to raid homes and plunder houses; to rob

打架(ㄉㄚˇ ㄐㄧㄚˋ)
to have a brawl, a blow, a row or a fight: 他們吵嘴後就打起架來。After words they came to blows.

打劫(ㄉㄚˇ ㄐㄧㄝˊ)
to commit robbery or pillage; to plunder; to loot

打結子(ㄉㄚˇ ㄐㄧㄝˊ ·ㄗ)
to tie a knot; to make a knot

打交道(ㄉㄚˇ ㄐㄧㄠ ㄉㄠˋ)
to have intercourse; to associate with; to have dealings with: 他和各式各樣的朋友打交道。He associated with all kinds of people.

打攪(ㄉㄚˇ ㄐㄧㄠˇ)
to bother; to disturb; to trouble: 不要打攪他。Don't disturb him.

打醮(ㄉㄚˇ ㄐㄧㄠˋ)
to hold services for pacifying ghosts (usually on the Ghost Festival, on the 15th day of the seventh moon)

打酒(ㄉㄚˇ ㄐㄧㄡˇ)
to buy wine or liquor (by quantity, not by bottles)

打尖(ㄉㄚˇ ㄐㄧㄢ)
to make a brief stopover; to lodge temporarily

打緊(ㄉㄚˇ ㄐㄧㄣˇ)
serious; important: 不打緊。It does not matter. 或 It is of no importance.

打更(ㄉㄚˇ ㄐㄧㄥ)
to beat the night watches

打旗語(ㄉㄚˇ ㄑㄧˊ ㄩˇ)
to signal with a flag; to use semaphore

打起精神(ㄉㄚˇ ㄑㄧˇ ㄐㄧㄥ ㄕㄣˊ)
to cheer up; to pluck up spirits; to keep one's chin up

打氣(ㄉㄚˇ ㄑㄧˋ)
① to fill a tire, balloon, etc. with air or gas; to inflate ② (figuratively) to invigorate or encourage; to pep up

打氣筒(ㄉㄚˇ ㄑㄧˋ ㄊㄨㄥˇ)
an air pump

打橋牌(ㄉㄚˇ ㄑㄧㄠˊ ㄆㄞˊ)
to play a bridge game

打秋風(ㄉㄚˇ ㄑㄧㄡ ㄈㄥ)or 打抽豐(ㄉㄚˇ ㄔㄡ ㄈㄥ)
to seek gratuitous financial help

打鞦韆(ㄉㄚˇ ㄑㄧㄡ ㄑㄧㄢ)
to sit in a swing; to swing

打球(ㄉㄚˇ ㄑㄧㄡˊ)
to play a ball game

打千(ㄉㄚˇ ㄑㄧㄢ)
to salute by falling on one knee

打搶(ㄉㄚˇ ㄑㄧㄤˇ)

〔手部〕

〔手部〕

to loot; to rob by force

打情罵俏(ㄉㄚˇ ㄑㄧㄥˊ ㄇㄚˋ ㄑㄧㄠˋ)
to tease one's lover by showing false displeasure

打趣(ㄉㄚˇ ㄑㄩˋ)
to make fun of another; to tease; to poke fun

打圈子(ㄉㄚˇ ㄑㄩㄢ·ㄗ)
①to circle: 風箏在空中打圈子。The kite circled in the sky. ②(figuratively) to bog down: 不要在瑣事上打圈子。Don't get bogged down in trifles.

打拳(ㄉㄚˇ ㄑㄩㄢˊ)
to practice boxing

打群架(ㄉㄚˇ ㄑㄩㄣˊ ㄐㄧㄚˋ)
to engage in a gang fight

打消(ㄉㄚˇ ㄒㄧㄠ)
to give up (an intention, etc.): 他打消了創業的念頭。He gave up the idea of starting a business.

打小報告(ㄉㄚˇ ㄒㄧㄠˇ ㄅㄠˋ ㄍㄠˋ)
to inform secretly on a colleague, etc.

打小算盤(ㄉㄚˇ ㄒㄧㄠˇ ㄙㄨㄢˋ ㄆㄢˊ)
to show petty shrewdness

打先鋒(ㄉㄚˇ ㄒㄧㄢ ㄈㄥ)
to fight in the van; to be a pioneer

打信號(ㄉㄚˇ ㄒㄧㄣˋ ㄏㄠˋ)
to signal; to communicate by signals

打響(ㄉㄚˇ ㄒㄧㄤˇ)
①to start shooting; to begin to exchange fire ② to win initial success

打雪仗(ㄉㄚˇ ㄒㄩㄝˇ ㄓㄤˋ)
to have a snowball fight

打知名度(ㄉㄚˇ ㄓ ㄇㄧㄥˊ ㄉㄨˋ)
to seek publicity

打摺(ㄉㄚˇ ㄓㄜˊ)
to fold

打折扣(ㄉㄚˇ ㄓㄜˊ ㄎㄡˋ)
①to allow a discount; at a discount: 這家商店打折扣出售商品。This shop sells goods at a discount. ② to detract (from some desirable quality)

打招呼(ㄉㄚˇ ㄓㄠ ·ㄏㄨ)
①to say hello; to greet a person: 他說聲「早安」向朋友打招呼。He greeted a friend by saying "Good morning." ② to use one's influence in other's behalf

打照面(ㄉㄚˇ ㄓㄠˋ ㄇㄧㄢˋ)
to meet face to face; to have an encounter with someone

打戰 or 打顫(ㄉㄚˇ ㄓㄢˋ) or 打冷顫(ㄉㄚˇ ㄌㄥˇ ㄓㄢˋ)
to shudder: 她一看到蛇便直打顫。She shuddered at the sight of a snake.

打針(ㄉㄚˇ ㄓㄣ)
to give or receive an injection; to give or receive a shot

打仗(ㄉㄚˇ ㄓㄤˋ)
to engage in a battle; to fight; to wage war: 他們準備好去打仗。They were ready to fight in the war.

打主意(ㄉㄚˇ ㄓㄨˇ ㄧˋ)
①to devise a course of action; to decide what to do ② to scheme for something to which one has no claim; to try to obtain ③to try to win the affection of a young woman

打住(ㄉㄚˇ ㄓㄨˋ)
Hold! 或 Stop it! 或 Halt!

打轉兒(ㄉㄚˇ ㄓㄨㄢˋㄦ)
①to move in a circle; to spin; to revolve: 陀螺在地上打轉兒。The top was spinning on the ground. ②to go round

打樁(ㄉㄚˇ ㄓㄨㄤ)
to hammer in piles or stakes; to impale; piling

打樁機(ㄉㄚˇ ㄓㄨㄤ ㄐㄧ)
a pile driver; a pile engine

打腫臉充胖子(ㄉㄚˇ ㄓㄨㄥˇ ㄌㄧㄢˇ ㄔㄨㄥ ㄆㄤˋ ·ㄗ)
(literally) to feign obesity by slapping one's own face until it becomes swollen—(figuratively) to try to satisfy one's own vanity at any cost

打中(ㄉㄚˇ ㄓㄨㄥˋ)
to hit the mark

打中要害(ㄉㄚˇ ㄓㄨㄥˋ ㄧㄠˋ ㄏㄞˋ)
to hit the vital spot

打赤膊(ㄉㄚˇ ㄔˋ ㄅㄛˊ)
to bare the upper body

打赤脚(ㄉㄚˇ ㄔˋ ㄐㄧㄠˇ)
to go barefoot (barefooted)

打喳喳(ㄉㄚˇ ㄔㄚ ·ㄔㄚ)
to whisper; to speak very softly and low

打茶圍(ㄉㄚˇ ㄔㄚˊ ㄨㄟˊ)
to hold a merrymaking tea party at a brothel

打岔(ㄉㄚˇ ㄔㄚˋ)
to interrupt another's speech; to break into a conversation: 當別人談話時，打岔是不禮貌的。It is not polite to interrupt when someone is talking.

打柴(ㄉㄚˇ ㄔㄞˊ)
to collect firewood

打吵子(ㄉㄚˇ ㄔㄠˇ ·ㄗ)
to be noisy; to brawl

打成平手(ㄉㄚˇ ㄔㄥˊ ㄆㄧㄥˊ ㄕㄡˇ)
to fight to a standoff; to fight to a draw: 這球賽結果打成平手。The game ended in a draw.

打成一片(ㄉㄚˇ ㄔㄥˊ ㄧˊ ㄆㄧㄢˋ)
to combine into a whole; to be united so as to form a single body

打蟲(ㄉㄚˇ ㄔㄨㄥˊ)
to get rid of intestinal parasites by means of drugs

打手巾把子(ㄉㄚˇ ㄕㄡˇ ㄐㄧㄣ ㄅㄚˇ ·ㄗ)
(said of waiters or waitresses) to hand out hot towels on a train, at a theater, etc.

打手心(ㄉㄚˇ ㄕㄡˇ ㄒㄧㄣ)
to beat the palm (of a child as a punishment)

打手銃(ㄉㄚˇ ㄕㄡˇ ㄔㄨㄥˋ)
(slang) masturbation

打手勢(ㄉㄚˇ ㄕㄡˇ ㄕˋ)
to gesticulate: 他沒有說話，只打手勢要我跟他走。He did not speak, but with a gesture told me to follow him.

打手印(ㄉㄚˇ ㄕㄡˇ ㄧㄣˋ)
to make an impression of the hand as a signature

打手(ㄉㄚˇ ·ㄕㄡ)
thugs hired by men of wealth or power; bouncers

打閃(ㄉㄚˇ ㄕㄢˇ)
(said of lightning) to flash

打傷(ㄉㄚˇ ㄕㄤ)
to wound or injure by beating

打勝仗(ㄉㄚˇ ㄕㄥˋ ㄓㄤˋ)
to be victorious; to win a war

打水(ㄉㄚˇ ㄕㄨㄟˇ)

to draw water (from a well, a spring, etc.)
打水漂兒(ㄉㄚˇ ㄕㄨㄟˇ ㄆㄧㄠ ㄦ)
to make ducks and drakes
打擾(ㄉㄚˇ ㄖㄠˇ)
to disturb; to bother; to trouble: 我很抱歉打擾你。I am sorry to disturb you.
打如意算盤(ㄉㄚˇ ㄖㄨˊ ㄧˋ ㄙㄨㄢˋ ·ㄆㄢ)
to expect things to turn out as one wishes
打入(ㄉㄚˇ ㄖㄨˋ)
①to work one's way into (a secret organization, a tight-knit group, etc.) ② to enter by attacking ③ to throw into; to banish… to
打入冷宮(ㄉㄚˇ ㄖㄨˋ ㄌㄥˇ ㄍㄨㄥ)
to put (the queen or an imperial concubine) under confinement (after she has lost the emperor's favor)
打字(ㄉㄚˇ ㄗˋ)
to do typing work; to typewrite; to type
打字機(ㄉㄚˇ ㄗˋ ㄐㄧ)
a typewriter
打字員(ㄉㄚˇ ㄗˋ ㄩㄢˊ)
a typist
打雜兒(ㄉㄚˇ ㄗㄚˊ ㄦ)
to drudge; to do a handyman's work; to do odds and ends
打坐(ㄉㄚˇ ㄗㄨㄛˋ)
(said of a Buddhist) to sit in meditation
打嘴巴(ㄉㄚˇ ㄗㄨㄟˇ ·ㄅㄚ)
to slap someone on the face or cheek
打草稿(ㄉㄚˇ ㄘㄠˇ ㄍㄠˇ)
to prepare a draft
打草驚蛇(ㄉㄚˇ ㄘㄠˇ ㄐㄧㄥ ㄕㄜˊ)
(literally) to beat the grass and startle the snakes—to cause undesired agitation; to alert unintentionally a criminal in hiding as a result of clumsy police moves
打從(ㄉㄚˇ ㄘㄨㄥˊ)
from; since
打死(ㄉㄚˇ ㄙˇ)
to beat to death; to shoot to death
打掃(ㄉㄚˇ ㄙㄠˇ)
to clean (a room, house, etc.): 她在打掃房間。She is cleaning up her room.
打傘(ㄉㄚˇ ㄙㄢˇ)
to use an umbrella
打散(ㄉㄚˇ ㄙㄢˋ)
to break up; to scatter: 那聲巨響把鳥群打散了。The loud noise scattered the birds.
打碎(ㄉㄚˇ ㄙㄨㄟˋ)
to smash to pieces; to break to pieces: 誰把那瓶子打碎了? Who broke that bottle to pieces?
打算(ㄉㄚˇ ㄙㄨㄢˋ)
① to plan; to intend; to prepare: 我打算當工程師。I intend to become an engineer. ② a plan; intention: 你有打算到那裡去嗎? Have you any intention of going there?
打算盤(ㄉㄚˇ ㄙㄨㄢˋ ·ㄆㄢ)
① to use an abacus; to work an abacus ② to plan; to reckon ③ calculating; shrewd
打暗號(ㄉㄚˇ ㄢˋ ㄏㄠˋ)
to give a prearranged signal; to hint; to give a cue
打耳光(ㄉㄚˇ ㄦˇ ㄍㄨㄤ)
to slap somebody in the face; to box a person's ears; to give someone a box on the ear
打牙祭(ㄉㄚˇ ㄧㄚˊ ㄐㄧˋ)
to have a rare sumptuous meal; to have something special to eat
打噎(ㄉㄚˇ ㄧㄝ)
to belch; to hiccup
打野雞(ㄉㄚˇ ㄧㄝˇ ㄐㄧ)
to visit a brothel
打野外(ㄉㄚˇ ㄧㄝˇ ㄨㄞˋ)
to receive field training in combat techniques
打藥(ㄉㄚˇ ㄧㄠˋ)
a laxative; a cathartic; a purgative
打游擊(ㄉㄚˇ ㄧㄡˊ ㄐㄧˊ)
①to engage in guerrilla warfare ②(humorously) to use, borrow or take another's belongings without permission; to board or lodge at one place after another without payment
打油詩(ㄉㄚˇ ㄧㄡˊ ㄕ)
doggerel; ragged verse
打眼(ㄉㄚˇ ㄧㄢˇ)
①to drill a hole; to punch a hole; to perforate ② to pay more than a thing is worth
打印(ㄉㄚˇ ㄧㄣˋ)
to affix a stamp to something
打印子(ㄉㄚˇ ㄧㄣˋ ·ㄗ)
a high-interest loan paid back in installments, each of which is certified by placing a chop when it is paid
打烊(ㄉㄚˇ ㄧㄤˊ)
to close the store for the night: 這家店昨天晚上九點打烊。The store closed at 9 last night.
打樣(ㄉㄚˇ ㄧㄤˋ)
①to draw a design; to prepare drawings (for a building, a machine, etc.)②(printing) to make a proof; to print a galley proof
打魚(ㄉㄚˇ ㄩˊ)
to catch fish with nets
打樂器(ㄉㄚˇ ㄩㄝˋ ㄑㄧˋ)
(said of an orchestra) percussion instruments
打圓場(ㄉㄚˇ ㄩㄢˊ ㄔㄤˇ)
to mediate a dispute; to smooth things over

【打】 1794
2. ㄉㄚˊ dar dá
a dozen: 他買了一打原子筆。He bought a dozen ball pens.

【扔】 1795
ㄖㄥ rheng reng
1. to throw; to hurl: 把那本書扔給我。Throw me that book.
2. to abandon; to discard
扔掉(ㄖㄥ ㄉㄧㄠˋ)
to throw away; to cast away: 不要扔掉那些雜誌。Don't throw away those magazines.
扔過去(ㄖㄥ ㄍㄨㄛˋ ·ㄑㄩ)
to throw or hurl over (to the other side)
扔開(ㄖㄥ ㄎㄞ)
to dismiss from consideration
扔棄(ㄖㄥ ㄑㄧˋ)
to throw away; to discard; to get rid of
扔下(ㄖㄥ ·ㄒㄧㄚ)
to throw down; to leave behind; to put aside: 她扔下手邊的工作,逛街去了。She put

〔手部〕

aside her work and went shopping.

三畫

手部

【扞】 1796 ㄏㄢˋ hann hàn
1. to resist; to oppose; to obstruct
2. to defend; to guard; to withstand

扞蔽(ㄏㄢˋ ㄅㄧˋ)
a protective barrier

扞格(ㄏㄢˋ ㄍㄜˊ)
to conflict; incompatible

扞格不入(ㄏㄢˋ ㄍㄜˊ ㄅㄨˋ ㄖㄨˋ)
incompatible; to disagree; to contradict; to conflict; do not mesh: 他所說的話與事實扞格不入。His statement contradicts with the facts.

扞拒(ㄏㄢˋ ㄐㄩˋ)
to withstand; to resist; to oppose: 她的父母扞拒這門親事。Her parents are opposed to the match.

扞衛(ㄏㄢˋ ㄨㄟˋ)
to defend; to guard: 軍人的職責是扞衛國家。The duty of a soldier is to defend his country.

扞禦(ㄏㄢˋ ㄩˋ)
to guard against; to keep back

【扣】 1797 ㄎㄡˋ kow kòu
1. to tap; to strike; to rap; to pull
2. to fasten; to button; to buckle
3. to detain; to confine
4. to deduct
5. a button; a hook; a buckle
6. to impound; to withhold
7. to cover on top

扣扳機(ㄎㄡˋ ㄅㄢ ㄐㄧ)
to pull the trigger

扣槃捫燭(ㄎㄡˋ ㄆㄢˊ ㄇㄣˊ ㄓㄨˊ)
to understand a fact superficially or erroneously (as a certain blind man did when, mistaking the sun for a sound and sunlight for a shape, he tried to know what they were like by tapping a tray and feeling a candle which, he had been told, resembled the sun and sunlight respectively)

扣馬而諫(ㄎㄡˋ ㄇㄚˇ ㄦˊ ㄐㄧㄢˋ)
(literally) to stop the horse and admonish the rider—to admonish a person just before he makes a reckless move

扣帽子(ㄎㄡˋ ㄇㄠˋ ˙ㄗ)
to put a label on someone

扣門(ㄎㄡˋ ㄇㄣˊ)
to knock at a door: 誰在扣門? Who is knocking at the door?

扣抵(ㄎㄡˋ ㄉㄧˇ)
to withhold money or goods from a debtor as payment of his debt

扣牢(ㄎㄡˋ ㄌㄠˊ)
to tie securely

扣籃(ㄎㄡˋ ㄌㄢˊ)
(basketball) to dunk; dunking

扣留(ㄎㄡˋ ㄌㄧㄡˊ)
① to keep in custody; to detain; to confine: 警察扣留那人以便進一步偵訊。The police detained that man to make further inquiries. ② to suspend; to impound: 警察扣留他的行車執照。The policeman suspended his driving license.

扣繳額(ㄎㄡˋ ㄐㄧㄠˇ ㄜˊ)
a deductible amount (as distinct from a taxable amount); a tax write-off

扣減(ㄎㄡˋ ㄐㄧㄢˇ)
to deduct

扣緊(ㄎㄡˋ ㄐㄧㄣˇ)
to button tightly; to fasten tightly

扣起來(ㄎㄡˋ ㄑㄧˇ ˙ㄌㄞ)
① to button up (one's coat, etc.) ② to take (a person) into custody

扣薪(ㄎㄡˋ ㄒㄧㄣ)
to deduct a certain amount from an employee's pay (as a punishment, or compensation for damaged public property, etc.)

扣住(ㄎㄡˋ ㄓㄨˋ)
held or fastened (by a button, hook, etc.); to hook

扣除(ㄎㄡˋ ㄔㄨˊ)
to deduct: 會計員從他的薪水中扣除稅金。The accountant deducted taxes from his salary.

扣肉(ㄎㄡˋ ㄖㄡˋ)
a Chinese dish of richly seasoned steamed pork

扣人心絃(ㄎㄡˋ ㄖㄣˊ ㄒㄧㄣ ㄒㄧㄢˊ)
(said of music, writing, etc.) very touching

扣子(ㄎㄡˋ ˙ㄗ)
a button; a buckle; a hook

扣押(ㄎㄡˋ ㄧㄚ)
to detain; to confine; to keep in custody; to seize: 如果你不還債,你的財產將被扣押。If you don't pay your debt, your property will be seized.

扣壓(ㄎㄡˋ ㄧㄚ)
to withhold; to pigeonhole: 扣壓公文 to withhold a public document

扣問(ㄎㄡˋ ㄨㄣˋ)
to stop and ask

【扛】 1798 ㄎㄤˊ karng káng
to lift (especially when only a single person is involved); to shoulder: 每位軍人都扛著槍。Each soldier shoulders a gun.

扛夫(ㄎㄤˊ ㄈㄨ)
a porter; a worker employed to carry loads on his shoulders

扛鼎(ㄎㄤˊ ㄉㄧㄥˇ)
to lift a tripod (as a feat of strength)

扛在肩上(ㄎㄤˊ ㄗㄞˋ ㄐㄧㄢ ˙ㄕㄤ)
to carry on the shoulder; to shoulder

【托】 1799 ㄊㄨㄛ tuo tuō
1. to hold, or lift, on the palm: 他用手托住頭。He held his head in his hands.
2. to entrust; to charge; to consign; to rely; to ask: 我把這封信交托給你。I entrust this letter to you.
3. a tray; a pad

托跋氏(ㄊㄨㄛ ㄅㄚˊ ㄕˋ)
the House of Toba, the ruling family of the Northern Wei Dynasty (386-534 A.D.)

托鉢(ㄊㄨㄛ ㄅㄛ)
(Buddhism) to beg for alms

托病(ㄊㄨㄛ ㄅㄧㄥˋ)
on the pretext of sickness; to use sickness as an excuse:

他托病不見客。He refused to see visitors on the pretext of sickness.

托盤(ㄊㄨㄛ ㄆㄢˊ)
a tray

托墨(ㄊㄨㄛ ㄇㄛˋ)
(said of writing paper) properly absorbent of ink

托夢(ㄊㄨㄛ ㄇㄥˋ)
(said of a spirit or deity) to convey a message to a mortal through his dream

托名(ㄊㄨㄛ ㄇㄧㄥˊ)
to do something in the name of someone else

托福(ㄊㄨㄛ ㄈㄨˊ)
Thanks. (used in reply to others' congratulations on a success, a narrow escape, etc.)

托福測驗(ㄊㄨㄛ ㄈㄨˊ ㄘㄜˋ ㄧㄢˋ)
Test of English as a Foreign Language (TOEFL)

托付(ㄊㄨㄛ ㄈㄨˋ)
to entrust; to charge; to consign: 他把財產托付給他的朋友看管。He entrusted his friend with the property.

托辣斯(ㄊㄨㄛ ㄌㄚˋ ㄙ)
a trust (a combination of corporations under a board of trustees)

托賴(ㄊㄨㄛ ㄌㄞˋ)
to rely upon, or be indebted to (a phrase usually used to show one's modesty)

托領(ㄊㄨㄛ ㄌㄧㄥˇ)
the base of the collar (on a garment)

托洛斯基(ㄊㄨㄛ ㄌㄨㄛˋ ㄙ ㄐㄧ)
Leon Trotsky (or Trotski), 1879-1940, Russian Communist leader murdered on the order of Stalin

托孤(ㄊㄨㄛ ㄍㄨ)
to entrust to another's care the children one is about to leave behind as orphans

托故(ㄊㄨㄛ ㄍㄨˋ)
to rely on a pretext; to use an excuse: 她托故不來。She failed to come on some pretext.

托管(ㄊㄨㄛ ㄍㄨㄢˇ)
trusteeship; mandate

托管地(ㄊㄨㄛ ㄍㄨㄢˇ ㄉㄧˋ)
a trust territory

托身(ㄊㄨㄛ ㄕㄣ)
to have a place to live in or work in

托人情(ㄊㄨㄛ ㄖㄣˊ ㄑㄧㄥˊ)
to ask an influential person to help arrange something; to gain one's end through pull

托子(ㄊㄨㄛ ˙ㄗ) or 托兒(ㄊㄨㄛㄦ)
① a pad (underneath an object) ② a tray; a salver ③ a base; a support

托足(ㄊㄨㄛ ㄗㄨˊ)
to have a foothold; to have a place to live in

托辭(ㄊㄨㄛ ㄘˊ)
① to put forth a false reason or motive; to make excuses ② a pretext; an excuse

托兒所(ㄊㄨㄛ ㄦˊ ㄙㄨㄛˇ)
a nursery school

托爾斯泰(ㄊㄨㄛ ㄦˇ ㄙ ㄊㄞˋ)
Leo (or Lev) Nikolaevich Tolstoy, 1828-1910, Russian writer

托運(ㄊㄨㄛ ㄩㄣˋ)
to consign for shipment; to check

托運人(ㄊㄨㄛ ㄩㄣˋ ㄖㄣˊ)
a consignor

托運物(ㄊㄨㄛ ㄩㄣˋ ㄨˋ)
a consignment

【扦】 1800
ㄑㄧㄢ chian qiān

1. to pierce; to penetrate; to pick
2. a pick: 牙扦 a toothpick

扦脚(ㄑㄧㄢ ㄐㄧㄠˇ)
to trim toenails; pedicure

扦手(ㄑㄧㄢ ㄕㄡˇ)
a customs examiner or searcher

【扠】 1801
ㄔㄚ cha chā

a harpoon

扠腰(ㄔㄚ ㄧㄠ)
akimbo: 他兩手扠腰而立。He stood with arms akimbo.

四畫

【扭】 1802
ㄋㄧㄡˇ neou niǔ

1. to wrench; to twist; to turn; to wring: 他扭到足踝。He turned his ankle.
2. to seize; to grasp: 他將小偷扭送警方。He seized the thief and handed him over to the police.

扭打(ㄋㄧㄡˇ ㄉㄚˇ)
to have a grapple or to grapple with somebody

扭搭扭搭(ㄋㄧㄡˇ ˙ㄉㄚ ㄋㄧㄡˇ ˙ㄉㄚ)
turning or swiveling from side to side

扭斷(ㄋㄧㄡˇ ㄉㄨㄢˋ)
to dislocate (the bones) by twisting or wrenching; to twist and break (something)

扭揑(ㄋㄧㄡˇ ㄋㄧㄝ)
① to twist the waist from side to side when walking (as a woman does); to mince ② to do things in an unmanly way

扭扭揑揑(ㄋㄧㄡˇ ㄋㄧㄡˇ ㄋㄧㄝ ㄋㄧㄝ)
① twisting the waist from side to side (like a woman); mincingly ② unmanly in handling business; to be affectively bashful

扭扭舞(ㄋㄧㄡˇ ㄋㄧㄡˇ ㄨˇ)
the twist

扭了脖子(ㄋㄧㄡˇ ˙ㄌㄜ ㄅㄛˊ ˙ㄗ)
to have sprained the neck

扭力(ㄋㄧㄡˇ ㄌㄧˋ)
(physics) torsion

扭乾(ㄋㄧㄡˇ ㄍㄢ)
to wring (a towel, clothes, etc.) dry

扭筋(ㄋㄧㄡˇ ㄐㄧㄣ)
a sprain

扭曲(ㄋㄧㄡˇ ㄑㄩ)
to twist: 他的面容因痛苦而扭曲。His face was twisted with pain.

扭曲作直(ㄋㄧㄡˇ ㄑㄩ ㄗㄨㄛˋ ㄓˊ)
to distort the fact

扭轉(ㄋㄧㄡˇ ㄓㄨㄢˇ)
① to wring; to wrench; to twist ② to turn (the tide of a war or contest) for the better ③ to turn round

扭轉乾坤(ㄋㄧㄡˇ ㄓㄨㄢˇ ㄑㄧㄢˊ ㄎㄨㄣ)
to retrieve a hopeless situation; to tip the scale when a situation appears hopeless

扭傷(ㄋㄧㄡˇ ㄕㄤ)
a sprain; a wrench; to wrench: 他扭傷手腕了。He sprained his wrist.

扭送(ㄋㄧㄡˇ ㄙㄨㄥˋ)

to seize and hand over (to the authorities)
扭毆(ㄋㄧㄡˇ ㄡ)
to have a grapple or to grapple with somebody
扭一扭(ㄋㄧㄡˇ ·ㄧ ·ㄋㄧㄡ)
to give a twist
扭腰(ㄋㄧㄡˇ ㄧㄠ)
①to twist the hip or the waist ②to sprain one's back

【扮】 1803 ㄅㄢˋ bann bàn
to dress up; to disguise; to play
扮鬼臉(ㄅㄢˋ ㄍㄨㄟˇ ㄌㄧㄢˇ)
to make faces
扮戲(ㄅㄢˋ ㄒㄧˋ)
to perform on stage; to play a role in a play
扮相(ㄅㄢˋ ㄒㄧㄤˋ)
the stage appearance or makeup (of an actor or actress)
扮裝(ㄅㄢˋ ㄓㄨㄤ)
to disguise; to make up
扮作(ㄅㄢˋ ㄗㄨㄛˋ)
to dress up as; to disguise as: 那警察扮作一個商人。The policeman disguised himself as a merchant.
扮演(ㄅㄢˋ ㄧㄢˇ)
to play or act (a part or role): 他扮演哈姆雷特。He played Hamlet.

【扶】 1804 ㄈㄨˊ fwu fú
1. to support; to prop up; to aid; to help; to shield; to shelter; to harbor; to protect: 請扶這位老人進來。Help this old man in, please.
2. to lean upon
扶病(ㄈㄨˊ ㄅㄧㄥˋ)or 扶疾(ㄈㄨˊ ㄐㄧˊ)
to brave sickness; to work while in ill health: 他扶病出席。He was present in spite of illness.
扶不起的阿斗(ㄈㄨˊ ㄅㄨˋ ㄑㄧˇ ·ㄉㄜ ㄚ ㄉㄡˇ)
one who is so incompetent that no amount of help can make him successful
扶梯(ㄈㄨˊ ㄊㄧ)
a flight of stairs with a handrail or balustrade; a staircase
扶老攜幼(ㄈㄨˊ ㄌㄠˇ ㄒㄧ ㄧㄡˋ)
①to help the aged along and lead the young by the hand ②to go or appear with one's whole family regardless of age
扶靈(ㄈㄨˊ ㄌㄧㄥˊ)or 扶柩(ㄈㄨˊ ㄐㄧㄡˋ) or 扶櫬(ㄈㄨˊ ㄔㄣˋ)
to escort a casket or coffin; to serve as a pallbearer
扶鸞(ㄈㄨˊ ㄌㄨㄢˊ)or 扶乩(ㄈㄨˊ ㄐㄧ) or 扶箕(ㄈㄨˊ ㄐㄧ)
a form of planchette; the superstitious practice of providing a sand table on which an invoked spirit is supposed to spell out a message
扶輪社(ㄈㄨˊ ㄌㄨㄣˊ ㄕㄜˋ)
Rotary Club
扶植(ㄈㄨˊ ㄓˊ)
to help grow or develop; to patronize a junior employee
扶著(ㄈㄨˊ ·ㄓㄜ)
to support or prop: 他被扶著回家。He was supported home.
扶杖(ㄈㄨˊ ㄓㄤˋ)or 扶笻(ㄈㄨˊ ㄑㄩㄥˊ)
to lean on a staff or stick
扶正(ㄈㄨˊ ㄓㄥˋ)
to give a concubine the status of a legitimate wife
扶助(ㄈㄨˊ ㄓㄨˋ)
to aid; to help; to assist; to support: 我們應扶助老弱。We should help the old and the weak.
扶持(ㄈㄨˊ ㄔˊ)or 扶挾(ㄈㄨˊ ㄒㄧㄝˊ)
to back up; to support: 隊友們扶持著那受傷的球員。Teammates supported the injured player.
扶手(ㄈㄨˊ ·ㄕㄡ)
a handrail (of a staircase) or any support to be held by the hand
扶疏(ㄈㄨˊ ㄕㄨ)
(said of a plant) branching out with a thick foliage; luxuriant; lush: 枝葉扶疏。The branches and leaves are luxuriant.
扶桑(ㄈㄨˊ ㄙㄤ)
①(botany) hibiscus ②where the sun rises ③(archaic or poetic) Japan
扶蘇(ㄈㄨˊ ㄙㄨ)
the elder son of the First Emperor of Chin (秦始皇帝), who was murdered immediately after his father's death
扶翼(ㄈㄨˊ ㄧˋ)
to support; to shelter; to protect
扶掖(ㄈㄨˊ ㄧㄝˋ)
to shelter; to protect; to support; to harbor
扶搖直上(ㄈㄨˊ ㄧㄠˊ ㄓˊ ㄕㄤˋ)
①to rise (in a career) very fast as if to be lifted by a cyclone; to be promoted quickly ②(said of prices, etc.) to rise rapidly; to skyrocket: 物價扶搖直上。The prices are skyrocketing.
扶養(ㄈㄨˊ ㄧㄤˇ)
to provide with means of livelihood; to provide subsistence or sustenance for; to support
扶危定傾(ㄈㄨˊ ㄨㄟˊ ㄉㄧㄥˋ ㄑㄧㄥ)
to deliver the country from distress
扶危濟困(ㄈㄨˊ ㄨㄟˊ ㄐㄧˋ ㄎㄨㄣˋ)
to help those in danger and relieve those in distress
扶揄(ㄈㄨˊ ㄩˊ)
to raise high; to uphold

【扯】 1805 ㄔㄜˇ chee chě
1. to tear
2. to pull; to drag; to haul; to strain
3. to lump
4. to talk nonsense; to lie; to prevaricate; to digress
扯不動(ㄔㄜˇ ·ㄅㄨ ㄉㄨㄥˋ)
cannot tear or be torn
扯破(ㄔㄜˇ ㄆㄛˋ)or 扯碎(ㄔㄜˇ ㄙㄨㄟˋ)
to tear to pieces or shreds: 我扯破了衣服。I've torn my coat.
扯篷拉縴(ㄔㄜˇ ㄆㄥˊ ㄌㄚ ㄑㄧㄢˋ)
(literally) to hoist the sail and pull the towline—①to render assistance ②to make double effort
扯票(ㄔㄜˇ ㄆㄧㄠˋ)
①to kill the hostage held for ransom ②to destroy (a ballot, ticket, etc.)
扯倒(ㄔㄜˇ ㄉㄠˇ)
to give up a plan or pursuit
扯淡(ㄔㄜˇ ㄉㄢˋ)
to talk nonsense: 不要扯淡

了！Don't talk nonsense!

扯脫(ㄔㄜˇ ㄊㄨㄛ)
to break loose

扯拉(ㄔㄜˇ ㄌㄚ)
①to make baseless reference to another person in a nonsensical talk ②to pull about 亦作「拉扯」

扯開嗓子(ㄔㄜˇ ㄎㄞ ㄙㄤˇ ·ㄗ)
to shout at the top of one's voice; to strain the vocal cords by shouting

扯後腿(ㄔㄜˇ ㄏㄡˋ ㄊㄨㄟˇ)
to hinder someone from action

扯謊(ㄔㄜˇ ㄏㄨㄤˇ)
to tell a lie; to lie: 不要扯謊啦！Don't lie to me!

扯旗(ㄔㄜˇ ㄑㄧˊ)
to raise or hoist a flag (so as to display it)

扯著脖子(ㄔㄜˇ ·ㄓㄜ ㄅㄛˊ ·ㄗ)
to strain the neck in shouting

扯住(ㄔㄜˇ ㄓㄨˋ)
to grasp firmly

扯臊(ㄔㄜˇ ㄙㄠˋ)
to talk nonsense shamelessly

【扳】 1806
ㄅㄢ ban bān

1. to pull
2. to count (on one's fingers)

扳倒(ㄅㄢ ㄉㄠˇ)
to pull down

扳開(ㄅㄢ ㄎㄞ)
to pull open

扳機(ㄅㄢ ㄐㄧ)
a trigger

扳轉(ㄅㄢ ㄓㄨㄢˇ)
①to turn around (an object) ②to tip the scale; to turn the tide

扳手(ㄅㄢ ㄕㄡˇ)
①a spanner; a wrench ②a lever (on a machine)

【扱】 1807
1. ㄒㄧ shi xī

1. to gather; to collect
2. to kneel and bow with both hands touching the ground or the floor

扱地(ㄒㄧ ㄉㄧˋ)
to kneel and bow with both hands touching the ground

扱引高賢(ㄒㄧ ㄧㄣˇ ㄍㄠ ㄒㄧㄢˊ)
to gather men of wisdom

【扱】 1807
2. ㄔㄚ cha chā

to insert

扱衽(ㄔㄚ ㄖㄣˋ)
to tuck the skirts of a garment into the girdle

【批】 1808
ㄆㄧ pi pī

1. to comment; to judge; to criticize: 他批評時事。He commented on current events.
2. a whole batch (of things or people); a large quantity or number; wholesale: 他大批地發出申請函。He sent out application letters wholesale.
3. to slap

批八字兒(ㄆㄧ ㄅㄚˊ ㄗㄜˋㄦ)
to tell fortune from the year, month, day and hour of one's birth; to make an astrologer's comment

批駁(ㄆㄧ ㄅㄛˊ)
to turn down (an appeal or request) or reverse (a decision by a subordinate), usually by writing on the paper carrying the message; to reject (an official request); to refute: 主任批駁了她的建議。The director rejected her suggestion.

批辦(ㄆㄧ ㄅㄢˋ)
to handle (business) by writing instructions on the paper carrying messages

批判(ㄆㄧ ㄆㄢˋ)or 批斷(ㄆㄧ ㄉㄨㄢˋ)
to appraise; to judge

批評(ㄆㄧ ㄆㄧㄥˊ)
to criticize; criticism; comment: 他對這問題未作批評。He made no comment on the subject.

批評家(ㄆㄧ ㄆㄧㄥˊ ㄐㄧㄚ)
a critic: 他是位文學批評家。He's a literary critic.

批發(ㄆㄧ ㄈㄚ)
wholesale: 以批發售出的日用品 a commodity sold by wholesale

批發價(ㄆㄧ ㄈㄚ ㄐㄧㄚˋ)
a wholesale price

批發商(ㄆㄧ ㄈㄚ ㄕㄤ)
a wholesale dealer; a wholesaler; a wholesale merchant

批覆(ㄆㄧ ㄈㄨˋ)or 批答(ㄆㄧ ㄉㄚˊ)
to reply (to a message from a subordinate), usually by writing on the paper carrying the message

批鬥(ㄆㄧ ㄉㄡˋ)
to criticize and denounce someone

批點(ㄆㄧ ㄉㄧㄢˇ)
to punctuate and annotate (a text)

批逆鱗(ㄆㄧ ㄋㄧˋ ㄌㄧㄣˊ)
to offend the emperor or a powerful person

批令(ㄆㄧ ㄌㄧㄥˋ)
instructions (usually given in reply to inquiries)

批改(ㄆㄧ ㄍㄞˇ)
to correct (students' papers)

批購(ㄆㄧ ㄍㄡˋ)
to buy wholesale: 我們批購貨物。We buy goods wholesale.

批亢擣虛(ㄆㄧ ㄎㄤˋ ㄉㄠˇ ㄒㄩ)
to attack vital and unguarded points of an enemy

批回(ㄆㄧ ㄏㄨㄟˊ)
to reply (to a message from a subordinate), usually by writing on the paper carrying the message

批紅判白(ㄆㄧ ㄏㄨㄥˊ ㄆㄢˋ ㄅㄛˊ)
to graft plants of various colors in order to produce new varieties

批頰(ㄆㄧ ㄐㄧㄚˊ)or 批面(ㄆㄧ ㄇㄧㄢˋ)
to slap one in the face; to box one's ear

批郤導窾(ㄆㄧ ㄒㄧˋ ㄉㄠˇ ㄎㄨㄢˇ)
to manage or handle business properly

批行(ㄆㄧ ㄒㄧㄥˊ)
to endorse a proposal submitted by a subordinate in written form

批正(ㄆㄧ ㄓㄥˋ)or 批削(ㄆㄧ ㄒㄩㄝˋ)
to improve (a copy written by another)

批註(ㄆㄧ ㄓㄨˋ)
to write commentaries; to annotate with comments; annotations and commentaries: 有些人一面讀書一面做批註。Some people annotate as they read.

批准(ㄆㄧ ㄓㄨㄣˇ)
to give official approval or permission for; to approve; to ratify; ratification: 這條約已被批准。The treaty has

〔手部〕

been ratified.

批示(ㄆㄧ ㄕˋ)
to instruct or direct (usually by writing on the paper carrying a message from a subordinate)

批首(ㄆㄧ ㄕㄡˇ)
(in annual civil service examinations of former times) the head of the successful candidates

批語(ㄆㄧ ㄩˇ)
comments; a commentary (usually referring to a teacher's comments written at the end of a student's composition)

批諭(ㄆㄧ ㄩˋ)
imperial rescripts or directions

批閱(ㄆㄧ ㄩㄝˋ)
to read (a message from a subordinate) and write down comments or instructions

批月抹風(ㄆㄧ ㄩㄝˋ ㄇㄛˇ ㄈㄥ)
(said of a poet) to sing in praise of the beauty of nature

【找】 1809
ㄓㄠˇ jao zhǎo

1. to seek; to look for; to search for; to find: 其理由不難找到。The reason is not far to seek.
2. to return (change): 這是找給你的錢。Here's your change.

找徧 or 找遍(ㄓㄠˇ ㄅㄧㄢˋ)
to have searched or looked everywhere

找補(ㄓㄠˇ ·ㄅㄨ)
to pay or return what is owed (either by the buyer or by the seller); to make up a deficiency

找不著(ㄓㄠˇ ·ㄅㄨ ㄓㄠˊ) or 找不到(ㄓㄠˇ ·ㄅㄨ ㄉㄠˋ)
to search or look in vain

找麻煩(ㄓㄠˇ ㄇㄚˊ ·ㄈㄢ)
① to ask for trouble; to ask for it ② to pick on somebody; to find fault ③ to give somebody trouble

找門路(ㄓㄠˇ ㄇㄣˊ ㄌㄨˋ)
to look for employment by seeking help from the right connections

找面子(ㄓㄠˇ ㄇㄧㄢˋ ·ㄗ)
to try to recover lost face or honor; to try to save face

找到了(ㄓㄠˇ ㄉㄠˋ ·ㄌㄜ) or 找著了(ㄓㄠˇ ㄓㄠˊ ·ㄌㄜ)
to have succeeded in finding

找對頭(ㄓㄠˇ ㄉㄨㄟˋ ·ㄊㄡ)
to look for the real adversary

找對象(ㄓㄠˇ ㄉㄨㄟˋ ㄒㄧㄤˋ)
to look for a partner in marriage

找換(ㄓㄠˇ ㄏㄨㄢˋ)
to give change for money of larger denominations

找齊(ㄓㄠˇ ㄑㄧˊ)
① to make equal; to even up ② to make up a deficiency

找錢(ㄓㄠˇ ㄑㄧㄢˊ)
to give change

找尋(ㄓㄠˇ ㄒㄩㄣˊ)
to search for; to look for: 他正在找尋他的弟弟。He's looking for his younger brother.

找碴兒(ㄓㄠˇ ㄔㄚˊㄦ) or 找錯兒(ㄓㄠˇ ㄘㄨㄛˋㄦ)
to look for excuse or occasion for a quarrel or fight; to pick (up) quarrels

找事(ㄓㄠˇ ㄕˋ)
① to look for jobs; to seek employment: 他整天忙著找事。He spent all day looking for a job. ② to look for trouble

找人(ㄓㄠˇ ㄖㄣˊ)
to look for someone: 我在找人。I'm looking for someone.

找死(ㄓㄠˇ ㄙˇ)
to invite death; to seek death

【抃】 1810
ㄅㄧㄢˋ biann biàn

to clap hands; to cheer

抃掌(ㄅㄧㄢˋ ㄓㄤˇ) or 抃手(ㄅㄧㄢˋ ㄕㄡˇ)
to clap hands; to applaud

抃舞(ㄅㄧㄢˋ ㄨˇ)
to cheer and dance; to make merry; to dance for joy

抃悅(ㄅㄧㄢˋ ㄩㄝˋ)
to clap hands for joy; to cheer

抃踊(ㄅㄧㄢˋ ㄩㄥˇ)
to cheer and dance

【技】 1811
ㄐㄧˋ jih jì

skill; ingenuity; dexterity; special ability; tricks

技不如人(ㄐㄧˋ ㄅㄨˋ ㄖㄨˊ ㄖㄣˊ)
to be inferior to others in skills

技能(ㄐㄧˋ ㄋㄥˊ)
skill; technical ability

技工(ㄐㄧˋ ㄍㄨㄥ)
a skilled worker

技擊(ㄐㄧˋ ㄐㄧˊ)
martial arts

技巧(ㄐㄧˋ ㄑㄧㄠˇ)
ingenuity; dexterity; adroitness; skill: 技巧必經由練習獲得。Technique must be gained by practice.

技正(ㄐㄧˋ ㄓㄥˋ)
the title of a senior specialist (an official rank in some organizations)

技師(ㄐㄧˋ ㄕ)
an engineer or a technician

技士(ㄐㄧˋ ㄕˋ)
the title of a specialist (an official rank below 技正 in some organizations)

技術(ㄐㄧˋ ㄕㄨˋ)
techniques; technology; skill: 修理鐘需要技術。It takes skill to repair a clock.

技術犯規(ㄐㄧˋ ㄕㄨˋ ㄈㄢˋ ㄍㄨㄟ)
a technical foul

技術高超(ㄐㄧˋ ㄕㄨˋ ㄍㄠ ㄔㄠ)
in possession of superb skills or superb techniques

技術官僚(ㄐㄧˋ ㄕㄨˋ ㄍㄨㄢ ㄌㄧㄠˊ)
a technocrat

技術工人(ㄐㄧˋ ㄕㄨˋ ㄍㄨㄥ ㄖㄣˊ)
a skilled worker

技術性(ㄐㄧˋ ㄕㄨˋ ㄒㄧㄥˋ)
technical; of a technical nature: 這是技術性的工作。This is a technical job.

技術學校(ㄐㄧˋ ㄕㄨˋ ㄒㄩㄝˊ ㄒㄧㄠˋ)
a technical school

技術指導(ㄐㄧˋ ㄕㄨˋ ㄓˇ ㄉㄠˇ)
① technological guidance; technical guidance ② a technical adviser

技術水準(ㄐㄧˋ ㄕㄨˋ ㄕㄨㄟˇ ㄓㄨㄣˇ)
technological standards

技術(人)員(ㄐㄧˋ ㄕㄨˋ (ㄖㄣˊ) ㄩㄢˊ)
technical personnel; technicians

技佐(ㄐㄧˋ ㄗㄨㄛˇ)
the title of a junior specialist (an official rank below 技士 in some organiza-

tions)

技藝(ㄐㄧˋ ㄧˋ)
skill; art; craft

技癢(ㄐㄧˋ ㄧㄤˇ)
anxious or itching to demonstrate some skill; to itch for a chance to display one's skill

【抄】 1812 ㄔㄠ chau chāo

1. to copy; to transcribe; transcription; to plagiarize: 這是抄寫之誤。It's a mistake in transcription.
2. to confiscate
3. to seize; to take: 他抄起一把鐵鍬就幹起活來了。He took up a spade and plunged into the job.

抄本(ㄔㄠ ㄅㄣˇ)
a handwritten copy; a transcript

抄附(ㄔㄠ ㄈㄨˋ)
to append a copy of...

抄道(ㄔㄠ ㄉㄠˋ)
to take a shortcut; (colloquial) a shortcut

抄賭(ㄔㄠ ㄉㄨˇ)
to search a place for gamblers

抄謄(ㄔㄠ ㄊㄥˊ)
to transcribe; to make a copy of; to make a transcript of

抄拿(ㄔㄠ ㄋㄚˊ)
to seize; to grab

抄錄(ㄔㄠ ㄌㄨˋ)or 抄寫(ㄔㄠ ㄒㄧㄝˇ)or 抄繕(ㄔㄠ ㄕㄢˋ)
to copy by hand; to make a copy of

抄掠(ㄔㄠ ㄌㄩㄝˋ)
to plagiarize

抄稿(ㄔㄠ ㄍㄠˇ)
to make a neat copy (of a draft)

抄後路(ㄔㄠ ㄏㄡˋ ㄌㄨˋ)
to outflank the enemy and attack them from the rear

抄獲(ㄔㄠ ㄏㄨㄛˋ)
to discover by searching; to ferret out

抄集(ㄔㄠ ㄐㄧˊ)
to collect by copying

抄家(ㄔㄠ ㄐㄧㄚ)or 抄沒(ㄔㄠ ㄇㄛˋ)
to confiscate the property of an offender

抄家滅門(ㄔㄠ ㄐㄧㄚ ㄇㄧㄝˋ ㄇㄣˊ)
to confiscate the property and exterminate the family (of an offender)

抄近路(ㄔㄠ ㄐㄧㄣˋ ㄌㄨˋ)
to take a shortcut; to cut corners: 他抄近路去。He took a shortcut.

抄襲(ㄔㄠ ㄒㄧˊ)
①to plagiarize; to copy off: 他常抄襲別人文字。He often plagiarized. ②to attack the flank of

抄下來(ㄔㄠ ㄒㄧㄚˋ ·ㄌㄞ)
to take down (words from the blackboard, a book, etc.)

抄呈(ㄔㄠ ㄔㄥˊ)
to submit a copy of...

抄手(ㄔㄠ ㄕㄡˇ)
①a copyist ②(Szechwan dialect) same as 餛飩

抄書(ㄔㄠ ㄕㄨ)
to plagiarize a book (in school composition, etc.)

抄錯(ㄔㄠ ㄘㄨㄛˋ)
to make inadvertent mistakes in copying or plagiarizing

抄送(ㄔㄠ ㄙㄨㄥˋ)
to send a copy of...; to make a copy for

【抉】 1813 ㄐㄩㄝˊ jyue jué

1. to choose; to pick; to select
2. to gouge; to dig

抉目(ㄐㄩㄝˊ ㄇㄨˋ)
to gouge out an eye or eyes

抉剔(ㄐㄩㄝˊ ㄊㄧ)
to pick out; to choose; to select

抉弦(ㄐㄩㄝˊ ㄒㄧㄢˊ)
to draw a bow

抉摘(ㄐㄩㄝˊ ㄓㄞ)
to choose; to select; to pick out

抉拾(ㄐㄩㄝˊ ㄕˊ)
devices used by archers to facilitate efforts to draw a bow

抉首(ㄐㄩㄝˊ ㄕㄡˇ)
to decapitate; to behead

抉擇(ㄐㄩㄝˊ ㄗㄜˊ)
choice; to choose

【抆】 1814 ㄨㄣˋ wenn wèn

to wipe

抆淚(ㄨㄣˋ ㄌㄟˋ)
to wipe one's tears away

抆拭(ㄨㄣˋ ㄕˋ)
to wipe away

【抒】 1815 ㄕㄨ shu shū

1. to give expression to; to express: 讓我們各抒己見吧。Let's freely express our own views.
2. to relieve; to ease; to lighten; to unburden: 他對我抒發他的隱衷(心事)。He unburdened himself of his feelings to me.

抒發(ㄕㄨ ㄈㄚ)
to express; to voice; to give expression to: 這首歌抒發了他的愛國熱情。The song expresses his patriotic fervor.

抒難 or 紓難(ㄕㄨ ㄋㄢˋ)
to relieve, ease, or lighten distress

抒念(ㄕㄨ ㄋㄧㄢˋ)
to be relieved of thoughts or emotions burdening one's mind

抒懷(ㄕㄨ ㄏㄨㄞˊ)
to relieve the heart of emotions

抒情(ㄕㄨ ㄑㄧㄥˊ)
to express one's feelings

抒情詩(ㄕㄨ ㄑㄧㄥˊ ㄕ)
a lyric; a lyric poem; lyric poetry

抒情文(ㄕㄨ ㄑㄧㄥˊ ㄨㄣˊ)
lyrical writing

抒寫(ㄕㄨ ㄒㄧㄝˇ)
to express; to describe

抒意(ㄕㄨ ㄧˋ)
to express one's ideas

【抓】 1816 ㄓㄨㄚ jua zhuā

1. to scratch: 貓抓了我。The cat scratched me.
2. to grasp; to seize; to take; to snatch; to make a snatch at; to clutch; to catch: 他抓住我的手，熱誠地與我握手。He caught my hand and shook it heartily.
3. to arrest: 警察抓住這小偷並送進獄中。The police arrested the thief and put him in prison.

抓辮子(ㄓㄨㄚ ㄅㄧㄢˋ ·ㄗ)
to seize on someone's mistake; to capitalize on someone's vulnerable spot

抓不起來(ㄓㄨㄚ ·ㄅㄨ ㄑㄧˇ ·ㄌㄞ)

〔手部〕

〔手部〕

incapable of taking, or being taken, by clutching or grasping
抓破(ㄓㄨㄚ ㄆㄛˋ)
to injure skin by scratching; to damage tissue by scratching
抓破臉(ㄓㄨㄚ ㄆㄛˋ ㄌㄧㄢˇ)
① to hurt the face by scratching ② to break off friendly relations ③(said of a flower) white with red spots
抓賭(ㄓㄨㄚ ㄉㄨˇ)
(said of the police or other law enforcement agencies) to raid unlicensed gambling houses; to break up a gambling party
抓頭(ㄓㄨㄚ ㄊㄡˊ)
to scratch the head (often indicating puzzlement)
抓功夫兒(ㄓㄨㄚ ㄍㄨㄥ ·ㄈㄨㄦ)
to find leisure out of a busy life; to steal time for idling
抓空(ㄓㄨㄚ ㄎㄨㄥˋ)
to use leisure moments
抓會(ㄓㄨㄚ ㄏㄨㄟˋ)
to bid for a loan from a private monetary cooperative in competition with other members
抓尖兒(ㄓㄨㄚ ㄐㄧㄚㄦ)
to come off first; to get the best portion
抓鬮兒(ㄓㄨㄚ ㄐㄧㄡㄦ)
to draw lots
抓緊(ㄓㄨㄚ ㄐㄧㄣˇ)
to grasp firmly; to pay close attention to; to hold...tight; to seize: 我們要抓緊好時機。Let's seize a good opportunity.
抓局(ㄓㄨㄚ ㄐㄩˊ)
to raid a gambling den
抓舉(ㄓㄨㄚ ㄐㄩˇ)
(weightlifting) a snatch
抓取(ㄓㄨㄚ ㄑㄩˇ)
to take by grasping
抓權(ㄓㄨㄚˇ ㄑㄩㄢˊ)
to grab power
抓瞎(ㄓㄨㄚ ㄒㄧㄚ)
to lose one's head; to lose composure
抓住(ㄓㄨㄚ ㄓㄨˋ)
① to grasp; to grip; to clutch: 他抓住一根繩子。He grasped a rope. ② to keep from going away; to hold ③ to grip somebody's attention
抓壯丁(ㄓㄨㄚ ㄓㄨㄤˋ ㄉㄧㄥ)
to impress young men into military service
抓碴兒(ㄓㄨㄚ ㄔㄚˊㄦ)
to seek excuses for quarrels; to pick (up) quarrels
抓差(ㄓㄨㄚ ㄔㄞ)
to draft someone for a particular task; to force someone into service
抓人(ㄓㄨㄚ ㄖㄣˊ)
① to dragoon people (for military service, slavery, etc.) ② to arrest
抓賊(ㄓㄨㄚ ㄗㄟˊ)
to catch a thief
抓彩(ㄓㄨㄚ ㄘㄞˇ)
to draw lots for a lottery; to raffle
抓耳撓腮(ㄓㄨㄚ ㄦˇ ㄋㄠˊ ㄙㄞ)
① to tweak one's ears and scratch one's cheeks ② impatient; uneasy ③ flurried; agitated ④ depressed; anguished
抓一把(ㄓㄨㄚ ㄧˋ ㄅㄚˇ)
to take a handful
抓藥(ㄓㄨㄚ ㄧㄠˋ)
to buy (Chinese herbal) medicine according to a doctor's prescription
抓癢(ㄓㄨㄚ ㄧㄤˇ)
to scratch an itchy part

【抔】 1817
ㄆㄡˊ pour póu
to scoop up with both hands
抔土(ㄆㄡˊ ㄊㄨˇ)
① a double handful of earth ② a grave
抔土未乾(ㄆㄡˊ ㄊㄨˇ ㄨㄟˋ ㄍㄢ)
(literally) The grave is still fresh.—It is not long since his, or her, death.
抔錢濟貧(ㄆㄡˊ ㄑㄧㄢˊ ㄐㄧˋ ㄆㄧㄣˊ)
(literally) to give money in double handfuls to relieve the poor—to give generously to help the poor
抔飲(ㄆㄡˊ ㄧㄣˇ)
to drink out of the hands

【把】 1818
1. ㄅㄚˇ baa bǎ
1. a handle; a hold
2. to take: 他把著小孩的手教他怎麼做。He took his child by the hand and taught him how to do it.
3. to hold: 她在給孩子把尿。She is holding her baby out to let it urinate.
4. to guard; to watch over; to keep under surveillance
5. a bundle; a grasp; a handful: 一把泥土 a handful of clay
6. around; about; approximately; more or less: 我花了個把月。It took me about a month.
7. sworn
8. (now rarely) to give
9. (colloquial) used before a direct object, followed by a transitive verb: 他把故事講完了。He finished telling the story.
把臂(ㄅㄚˇ ㄅㄧˋ)
(literally) arm in arm—very intimate: 他們是把臂之交。They are intimate friends.
把柄(ㄅㄚˇ ㄅㄧㄥˇ)or 把鼻(ㄅㄚˇ ㄅㄧˊ)
a hold (on somebody); an utterance that yields a bargaining advantage to the other party; a handle
把袂(ㄅㄚˇ ㄇㄟˋ)
(said of two persons) to catch hold of each other's sleeves — (figuratively) to be very friendly to each other
把門(ㄅㄚˇ ㄇㄣˊ)
to stand watch at a door or gate; to guard a door
把風(ㄅㄚˇ ㄈㄥ)
a person posted as a lookout, especially, in a robbery or other criminal acts
把舵(ㄅㄚˇ ㄉㄨㄛˋ)
① to steer the rudder ② a helmsman
把頭(ㄅㄚˇ ㄊㄡˊ)
a labor contractor
把尿(ㄅㄚˇ ㄋㄧㄠˋ)
to help a small child urinate by holding his legs apart
把來(ㄅㄚˇ ㄌㄞˊ)
to use something to blame, threaten, cheat, please, etc.
把牢(ㄅㄚˇ ㄌㄠˊ)
strong; dependable
把攬(ㄅㄚˇ ·ㄌㄢ)
to use undue influence to

monopolize (a piece of business, etc.); to arrange to do a catchall job

把關(ㄅㄚˇ ㄍㄨㄢ)
①to guard a pass ②to check on

把口兒(ㄅㄚˇ ㄎㄡˇㄦ)
exactly at the intersection of roads; right at the road corner

把家(ㄅㄚˇ ㄐㄧㄚ)
to guard family belongings jealously

把酒(ㄅㄚˇ ㄐㄧㄡˇ)
to hold a wineglass—to drink

把卷(ㄅㄚˇ ㄐㄩㄢˋ)
to hold a book in one's hand; to read

把戲(ㄅㄚˇ ㄒㄧˋ)
①acrobatic performances as juggling, etc.: 他用球耍把戲。He juggled with balls. ②a trick or scheme: 他愛耍鬼把戲。He likes to play dirty tricks. ③a child; a toddler

把兄弟(ㄅㄚˇ ㄒㄩㄥ ㄉㄧˋ)
sworn brothers: 他們是把兄弟。They are sworn brothers.

把盞(ㄅㄚˇ ㄓㄢˇ)
to hold winecups; to drink

把捉(ㄅㄚˇ ㄓㄨㄛ)
①to grasp ②to assess: 把捉不定。It's difficult to assess.

把持(ㄅㄚˇ ㄔˊ)
to monopolize; to dominate or control: 他想把持一切。He wants to monopolize everything.

把持不定(ㄅㄚˇ ㄔˊ ㄅㄨˋ ㄉㄧㄥˋ)
vacillating; undecided

把勢(ㄅㄚˇ ㄕˋ)
vain gestures

把式(ㄅㄚˇ ˙ㄕ)
①movements in Chinese boxing ②a skilled laborer ③a skill

把守(ㄅㄚˇ ㄕㄡˇ)
to watch over; to guard or defend (a city, etc.): 他們英勇地把守城門。They bravely guarded the city gate.

把手(ㄅㄚˇ ㄕㄡˇ)
①to hold hands: 他們把手言歡。They hold hands and converse cheerfully. ②a handle: 我們握着把手提桶。We carry a bucket by the handle.

把子(ㄅㄚˇ ˙ㄗ)
①a group of (bandits, soldiers, etc.) ②a group of sworn brothers ③a posture held by a warrior in Chinese opera; poise

把總(ㄅㄚˇ ㄗㄨㄥˇ)
(formerly) a company grade officer

把兒(ㄅㄚˇㄦ)
a bundle; a grasp; a handful

把晤(ㄅㄚˇ ㄨˋ)
to meet; to see each other

把握(ㄅㄚˇ ㄨㄛˋ)
①something one holds in hand ②confident; sure; to have absolute confidence ③to have a firm grasp of the situation: 我們應把握時機。We should seize the opportunity.

把玩(ㄅㄚˇ ㄨㄢˊ)
to keep at hand for appreciation; to fondle

把穩(ㄅㄚˇ ㄨㄣˇ)
firm; stable; steady; dependable; trustworthy

【把】 1818 2. ㄅㄚˋ bah bà

a handle

把子(ㄅㄚˋ ˙ㄗ)
a handle

把兒(ㄅㄚˋㄦ) or 把手(ㄅㄚˋ ㄕㄡˇ)
a handle: 槍把兒 a rifle butt

把兒鏡子(ㄅㄚˋㄦ ㄐㄧㄥˋ ˙ㄗ)
a mirror with a handle

【投】 1819 ㄊㄡˊ tour tóu

1. to throw; to pitch; to toss: 他向我們投石。He threw a stone at us.
2. to present as a gift
3. to lodge; to stay: 你現在投宿在何處? Where are you lodging now?
4. to head (west, etc.)
5. agreeable; congenial; harmonious; to fit in with; to cater to
6. to join; to submit to: 他已經投軍了。He has already joined the army.
7. to project; to cast: 樹投影於草地上。The tree projects a shadow on the grass.
8. to deliver (mail, etc.); to send (letters, scripts, etc.)

投保(ㄊㄡˊ ㄅㄠˇ)
to take out an insurance policy

投保人(ㄊㄡˊ ㄅㄠˇ ㄖㄣˊ)
a policyholder

投報(ㄊㄡˊ ㄅㄠˋ)
to give and return love tokens, etc.

投奔(ㄊㄡˊ ㄅㄣ)
①to flee (to freedom): 他們投奔自由了。They escaped to freedom. ②to seek employment or protection from somebody

投筆從戎(ㄊㄡˊ ㄅㄧˇ ㄘㄨㄥˊ ㄖㄨㄥˊ)
to throw away one's pen and get into a military uniform; (said of a student or intellectual) to join the army voluntarily

投標(ㄊㄡˊ ㄅㄧㄠ)
to bid in a public tender

投鞭斷流(ㄊㄡˊ ㄅㄧㄢ ㄉㄨㄢˋ ㄌㄧㄡˊ)
a quotation from Fu Chien (苻堅): "If each of my mounted troops throws in his whip, the flow of the river will be stopped." (used boastfully by an invading army to intimidate the defenders)

投票(ㄊㄡˊ ㄆㄧㄠˋ)
to cast a vote; to ballot; a vote; poll: 我投票給張先生。I gave my vote to Mr. Chang.

投票表決(ㄊㄡˊ ㄆㄧㄠˋ ㄅㄧㄠˇ ㄐㄩㄝˊ)
to decide by voting

投票法(ㄊㄡˊ ㄆㄧㄠˋ ㄈㄚˇ)
laws and regulations governing balloting

投票權(ㄊㄡˊ ㄆㄧㄠˋ ㄑㄩㄢˊ)
the ballot; the right to vote

投票箱(ㄊㄡˊ ㄆㄧㄠˋ ㄒㄧㄤ) or 投票匭(ㄊㄡˊ ㄆㄧㄠˋ ㄍㄨㄟˇ)
a ballotbox

投票選舉(ㄊㄡˊ ㄆㄧㄠˋ ㄒㄩㄢˇ ㄐㄩˇ)
to elect by ballot; elections

投票人(ㄊㄡˊ ㄆㄧㄠˋ ㄖㄣˊ)
a voter

投票所(ㄊㄡˊ ㄆㄧㄠˋ ㄙㄨㄛˇ)
a polling place; a place where voters cast their ballots; polls

投袂而起(ㄊㄡˊ ㄇㄟˋ ㄦˊ ㄑㄧˇ)
(literally) to throw up one's sleeves and rise—to rise up suddenly (indicating deter-

mination or indignation)

投門路(ㄊㄡˊ ㄇㄣˊ ˙ㄌㄨ)
to seek a job by looking for the right connections

投明(ㄊㄡˊ ㄇㄧㄥˊ)
(literally) to head oneself in the direction of light—to shift one's allegiance to the cause of justice and righteousness

投命(ㄊㄡˊ ㄇㄧㄥˋ)
to die for (a cause, etc.); to give one's life to

投暮(ㄊㄡˊ ㄇㄨˋ)
to get dark; dusk

投分(ㄊㄡˊ ㄈㄣˋ)
to have a meeting of minds; on very friendly terms

投放(ㄊㄡˊ ㄈㄤˋ)
① to throw in ② to put (money) into circulation; to put (goods) on the market

投附(ㄊㄡˊ ㄈㄨˋ)
to offer one's services to (a leader, cause, etc.)

投彈(ㄊㄡˊ ㄉㄢˋ)
① to drop a bomb ② to throw a hand grenade

投敵(ㄊㄡˊ ㄉㄧˊ)
to defect (or desert) to the enemy

投遞(ㄊㄡˊ ㄉㄧˋ)
to send or deliver (letters, etc.); delivery

投店(ㄊㄡˊ ㄉㄧㄢˋ)
to seek lodging in a tavern; to put up at an inn

投胎(ㄊㄡˊ ㄊㄞ)
to get into the cycle of reincarnation

投桃報李(ㄊㄡˊ ㄊㄠˊ ㄅㄠˋ ㄌㄧˇ)
to return a favor with a favor

投體(ㄊㄡˊ ㄊㄧˇ)
to worship; to kowtow; to admire tremendously

投托(ㄊㄡˊ ㄊㄨㄛ)
to place in the care of another

投籃(ㄊㄡˊ ㄌㄢˊ)
(basketball) to shoot; to try for the basket: 他跳起投籃。He jumped and shot.

投戈(ㄊㄡˊ ㄍㄜ)
(literally) to throw away weapons—to effect a ceasefire or truce

投戈講藝(ㄊㄡˊ ㄍㄜ ㄐㄧㄤˇ ㄧˋ)
(literally) to lay aside weapons (for a while) so as to pursue learning—Even in war, one should not forget about learning.

投稿(ㄊㄡˊ ㄍㄠˇ)
a contributed article; to contribute an article; to submit a piece of writing for publication

投稿者(ㄊㄡˊ ㄍㄠˇ ㄓㄜˇ)
one who contributes articles (especially unsolicited) for publication by a newspaper or magazine

投竿(ㄊㄡˊ ㄍㄢ)
to fish with a hook and line

投考(ㄊㄡˊ ㄎㄠˇ)
to take an entrance examination of a school; to go in for an examination

投靠(ㄊㄡˊ ㄎㄠˋ)
to go and seek refuge with somebody; to join and serve (a new leader, master, etc.); to seek the patronage of the high and mighty

投河(ㄊㄡˊ ㄏㄜˊ)
to commit suicide by throwing oneself into the river; to drown oneself

投合(ㄊㄡˊ ㄏㄜˊ)
to see eye to eye; in rapport; to agree with; to cater to

投壺(ㄊㄡˊ ㄏㄨˊ)
(in ancient China) a game during a feast in which the winner was decided by the number of arrows thrown into a distant pot

投火(ㄊㄡˊ ㄏㄨㄛˇ)
to jump into the fire; to commit suicide in this manner; to throw into the fire

投懷送抱(ㄊㄡˊ ㄏㄨㄞˊ ㄙㄨㄥˋ ㄅㄠˋ)
(said of a woman) overtly aggressive in love affairs; acting like a man-chaser

投繯(ㄊㄡˊ ㄏㄨㄢˊ)
to commit suicide by hanging

投荒(ㄊㄡˊ ㄏㄨㄤ)
to head for or flee to distant places

投機(ㄊㄡˊ ㄐㄧ)
① to speculate; speculation (as in stocks, houses, lands, etc.): 他投機股票買賣。He speculated in stocks. ② to see eye to eye; the meeting of minds; agreeable; congenial: 他們談得很投機。They talked very congenially.

投機分子(ㄊㄡˊ ㄐㄧ ㄈㄣˋ ㄗˇ)
an opportunist; a speculator; a soldier of fortune: 他是個投機分子。He is an opportunist.

投機取巧(ㄊㄡˊ ㄐㄧ ㄑㄩˇ ㄑㄧㄠˇ)
to speculate and take advantage of an opportunity; to use every trick in shortcuts and finesse; to cut corners; the ways of an opportunist

投機事業(ㄊㄡˊ ㄐㄧ ㄕˋ ㄧㄝˋ)
speculative business

投寄(ㄊㄡˊ ㄐㄧˋ)
to send a letter to: 我已投寄給他好幾封信。I have sent him several letters.

投交(ㄊㄡˊ ㄐㄧㄠ)
friendly intercourse; friendship

投進去(ㄊㄡˊ ㄐㄧㄣˋ ㄑㄩˋ)
to throw in (or into)

投井(ㄊㄡˊ ㄐㄧㄥˇ)
to drown oneself in a well

投井下石(ㄊㄡˊ ㄐㄧㄥˇ ㄒㄧㄚˋ ㄕˊ)
to attack someone who has already fallen from power; to kick a man when he is down

投軍(ㄊㄡˊ ㄐㄩㄣ)
to enlist oneself; to join the army; to become a serviceman: 今年許多學生投軍了。Many students enlisted in the army this year.

投其所好(ㄊㄡˊ ㄑㄧˊ ㄙㄨㄛˇ ㄏㄠˋ)
to cater to another's pleasure; to please someone by doing what he wishes to be done without being told; to suit one's fancy

投契(ㄊㄡˊ ㄑㄧˋ)
meeting of minds (between friends); to get along well; to be congenial: 他們相處得很投契。They get along well together.

投棄(ㄊㄡˊ ㄑㄧˋ)
to abandon or give up (sinful ways, old methods, etc.)

投親(ㄊㄡˊ ㄑㄧㄣ)
(said of an orphan, etc.) to go and live with one's relatives; to seek refuge with one's relatives

投下(ㄊㄡˊ ㄒㄧㄚˋ)
① to throw down; to drop ② to invest (capital): 他在書籍上投下大筆金錢。He invested large sums in books.

投效(ㄊㄡˊ ㄒㄧㄠˋ)
to offer one's services to

投閒置散(ㄊㄡˊ ㄒㄧㄢˊ ㄓˋ ㄙㄢˋ)
to stay idle; to occupy an insignificant position (especially said of people of talent)

投降(ㄊㄡˊ ㄒㄧㄤˊ)
to surrender; surrender; to capitulate: 我們決不向敵人投降。We shall never surrender to the enemy.

投擲(ㄊㄡˊ ㄓˊ)
to throw (a discus, etc.); to throw away: 他使勁地投擲標槍。He threw the javelin vigorously.

投止 or 投趾(ㄊㄡˊ ㄓˇ)
to stay at or with

投炸彈(ㄊㄡˊ ㄓㄚˋ ㄉㄢˋ)
to drop bombs from a plane; to throw bombs

投杼之疑(ㄊㄡˊ ㄓㄨˋ ㄓ ㄧˊ)
When slanderers are many, a lie will become believable. 或 A lie, if repeated often enough, becomes a truth to the listener.

投誠(ㄊㄡˊ ㄔㄥˊ)
(said of enemy troops, bandits, etc.) to voluntarily surrender to the government forces; to return to allegiance

投師(ㄊㄡˊ ㄕ)
to seek instruction from a master

投石打狗(ㄊㄡˊ ㄕˊ ㄉㄚˇ ㄍㄡˇ)
to throw a stone at a dog

投石問路(ㄊㄡˊ ㄕˊ ㄨㄣˋ ㄌㄨˋ)
(said of burglars) to throw a stone into a house to find out if the occupants are awake

投射(ㄊㄡˊ ㄕㄜˋ)
① to project; to shoot: 金色的陽光投射到平靜的湖面上。The sun cast its golden rays on the calm lake. ② to harvest profit from speculation

投射點(ㄊㄡˊ ㄕㄜˋ ㄉㄧㄢˇ)
(physics) an incident point

投射角(ㄊㄡˊ ㄕㄜˋ ㄐㄧㄠˇ)
(physics) an angle of incidence

投射器(ㄊㄡˊ ㄕㄜˋ ㄑㄧˋ)
a projector

投射線(ㄊㄡˊ ㄕㄜˋ ㄒㄧㄢˋ)
(physics) an incident ray

投射物(ㄊㄡˊ ㄕㄜˋ ㄨˋ)
a projectile

投首(ㄊㄡˊ ㄕㄡˇ)
① to confess to a criminal act ② to give oneself up to the authorities

投手(ㄊㄡˊ ㄕㄡˇ)
(baseball) a pitcher

投身(ㄊㄡˊ ㄕㄣ)
① to give oneself to (the revolutionary cause, a military career, etc.); to throw oneself into ② to find employment or shelter

投生(ㄊㄡˊ ㄕㄥ)
to get reincarnated

投書(ㄊㄡˊ ㄕㄨ)or 投函(ㄊㄡˊ ㄏㄢˊ)
to send a letter to (a newspaper editor, etc.)

投鼠忌器(ㄊㄡˊ ㄕㄨˇ ㄐㄧˋ ㄑㄧˋ)
a quotation from Chia Yi (賈誼), "afraid to kill the rat for fear of damaging the vase in which it's hiding"—① One is afraid to impeach a corrupt official for fear of incriminating the emperor. ② to have scruples in doing something; to fear the repercussions of a certain action

投水(ㄊㄡˊ ㄕㄨㄟˇ)
① to jump into the water ② to commit suicide in this manner

投稅(ㄊㄡˊ ㄕㄨㄟˋ)
to pay taxes

投入(ㄊㄡˊ ㄖㄨˋ)
① to throw in: 他投入戰鬥之中。He threw himself into the battle. ② to join (the army, revolutionaries, etc.): 他已投入民主黨。He has joined himself to the Democratic Party.

投入資本(ㄊㄡˊ ㄖㄨˋ ㄗ ㄅㄣˇ)
invested capital; vested proprietorship (capital)

投資(ㄊㄡˊ ㄗ)
to invest; investment: 他把錢投資在股票上。He invested his money in stocks.

投資公司(ㄊㄡˊ ㄗ ㄍㄨㄥ ㄙ)
an investment company

投資市場(ㄊㄡˊ ㄗ ㄕˋ ㄔㄤˇ)
an investment market

投子(ㄊㄡˊ ˙ㄗ)
dice 亦作「骰子」: 他賭投子輸得一文不名。He diced away all his money.

投簪(ㄊㄡˊ ㄗㄢ)
to give up one's official position

投刺(ㄊㄡˊ ㄘˋ)
① to present one's visiting card; to pay a call on ② to retire from public life

投死(ㄊㄡˊ ㄙˇ)
to be faithful till one breathes his last

投宿(ㄊㄡˊ ㄙㄨˋ)
to stay or check in (at a hotel, etc.) for the night; to put up for the night

投梭(ㄊㄡˊ ㄙㄨㄛ)
① to put up strong resistance against a rapist; to reject harshly when being seduced ② fast and agile

投案(ㄊㄡˊ ㄢˋ)
to appear before court in answer to summons; to surrender oneself to justice or the police: 他已向警方投案。He has surrendered himself to the police.

投郵(ㄊㄡˊ ㄧㄡˊ)
to mail; to send a letter or package by mail

投影(ㄊㄡˊ ㄧㄥˇ)
①(mathematics) projection ②(art) cast shadow ③ to project: 樹投影於草上。The tree projects a shadow on the grass.

投影畫(ㄊㄡˊ ㄧㄥˇ ㄏㄨㄚˋ)or 投影圖(ㄊㄡˊ ㄧㄥˇ ㄊㄨˊ)
a projective drawing

投網(ㄊㄡˊ ㄨㄤˇ)
(literally) to get caught by the net—(usually said of a criminal at large) to get

〔手部〕

caught; to get trapped or snared
投獄(ㄊㄡˊ ㄩˋ)
to jail; to imprison
投緣(ㄊㄡˊ ㄩㄢˊ)
to be on intimate terms at once; to have a meeting of minds

【抗】 1820 ㄎㄤˋ kanq kàng
1. to resist; to oppose: 他們抵抗攻擊。They resisted the attack.
2. to reject; to refute; to rebuke; to defy
3. high and virtuous
4. to raise; to set up
5. to hide; to conceal; to screen; to secrete
6. a Chinese family name
抗暴(ㄎㄤˋ ㄅㄠˋ)
to oppose tyranny
抗辯(ㄎㄤˋ ㄅㄧㄢˋ)
to speak out in one's own defense; to refute; to rebut or retort
抗病(ㄎㄤˋ ㄅㄧㄥˋ)
(agriculture) disease-resistant
抗捕(ㄎㄤˋ ㄅㄨˇ)
to resist arrest
抗邁(ㄎㄤˋ ㄇㄞˋ)
elegant and outstanding; smart and remarkable
抗命(ㄎㄤˋ ㄇㄧㄥˋ)
to disobey orders
抗敵(ㄎㄤˋ ㄉㄧˊ)
① to resist or fight enemy troops ② to treat as equals; to equal or match: 她的聰明伶俐可以與他抗敵。She equals him in cleverness.
抗毒素(ㄎㄤˋ ㄉㄨˊ ㄙㄨˋ)
an antitoxin
抗體(ㄎㄤˋ ㄊㄧˇ)
an antibody
抗禮(ㄎㄤˋ ㄌㄧˇ)
to equal; to treat each other as equals without regard to etiquette or formalities
抗力(ㄎㄤˋ ㄌㄧˋ)
(physics) resistance or resistance strength
抗糧(ㄎㄤˋ ㄌㄧㄤˊ)
to refuse to pay farm tax in kind
抗論(ㄎㄤˋ ㄌㄨㄣˋ)
① a straightforward statement ② to retort; to argue against
抗告(ㄎㄤˋ ㄍㄠˋ)
(law) interlocutory appeal
抗旱(ㄎㄤˋ ㄏㄢˋ)
drought-resistant; drought-resistance: 這種植物能抗旱。This plant is drought-resistant.
抗衡(ㄎㄤˋ ㄏㄥˊ)
to contend; to compete; to match: 在辯論上無人可以與他抗衡。No one can match him in argument.
抗節不附(ㄎㄤˋ ㄐㄧㄝˊ ㄅㄨˋ ㄈㄨˋ)
to uphold one's high principles without submitting to threats, bribery, etc.
抗拒(ㄎㄤˋ ㄐㄩˋ)
to resist; to oppose
抗心希古(ㄎㄤˋ ㄒㄧㄣ ㄒㄧ ㄍㄨˇ)
a heart of gold that rivals those of the ancients
抗行
①(ㄎㄤˋ ㄒㄧㄥˋ) virtuous conduct or behavior
②(ㄎㄤˋ ㄒㄧㄥˊ) to match each other; to be able to rival with
抗直(ㄎㄤˋ ㄓˊ)
straightforward and upright
抗志不屈(ㄎㄤˋ ㄓˋ ㄅㄨˋ ㄑㄩ)
to adhere to high purposes and not to submit to threats, etc.
抗戰(ㄎㄤˋ ㄓㄢˋ)
① a war of resistance; to fight the invading army ② the War of Resistance against Japan (1937-1945)
抗戰到底(ㄎㄤˋ ㄓㄢˋ ㄉㄠˋ ㄉㄧˇ)
to fight an invading enemy to the last man
抗戰時期(ㄎㄤˋ ㄓㄢˋ ㄕˊ ㄑㄧˊ)
the period of the War of Resistance (especially the one against the Japanese 1937-1945)
抗震(ㄎㄤˋ ㄓㄣˋ)
anti-seismic
抗爭(ㄎㄤˋ ㄓㄥ)
to contend; to oppose; to resist
抗塵走俗(ㄎㄤˋ ㄔㄣˊ ㄗㄡˇ ㄙㄨˊ)
to be on constant run for worldly pursuit
抗傳(ㄎㄤˋ ㄔㄨㄢˊ)
to refuse to answer a court summons
抗手(ㄎㄤˋ ㄕㄡˇ)
to raise one's hand (as a salute)
抗聲(ㄎㄤˋ ㄕㄥ)
to raise one's voice
抗生素(ㄎㄤˋ ㄕㄥ ㄙㄨˋ)
antibiotics
抗疏(ㄎㄤˋ ㄕㄨ)
a straight and frank report to the emperor
抗水性(ㄎㄤˋ ㄕㄨㄟˇ ㄒㄧㄥˋ)
water-resistance; a water-resisting property
抗稅(ㄎㄤˋ ㄕㄨㄟˋ)
to refuse to pay taxes
抗日戰爭(ㄎㄤˋ ㄖˋ ㄓㄢˋ ㄓㄥ)
the War of Resistance Against Japanese Aggression; the Sino-Japanese War (1937-1945)
抗熱(ㄎㄤˋ ㄖㄜˋ)
heat-resistant
抗熱板(ㄎㄤˋ ㄖㄜˋ ㄅㄢˇ)
the heat shield
抗熱材料(ㄎㄤˋ ㄖㄜˋ ㄘㄞˊ ㄌㄧㄠˋ)
heat-resistant material
抗議(ㄎㄤˋ ㄧˋ)
to protest; a protest; to raise one's voice against: 他對判決提出抗議。He made a protest against the verdict.
抗議書(ㄎㄤˋ ㄧˋ ㄕㄨ)
a form of protest; a written protest
抗議遊行(ㄎㄤˋ ㄧˋ ㄧㄡˊ ㄒㄧㄥˊ)
a protest march
抗藥性(ㄎㄤˋ ㄧㄠˋ ㄒㄧㄥˋ)
resistance to the action of a drug
抗顏(ㄎㄤˋ ㄧㄢˊ)
to be calm and fearless in face of threats, etc.
抗氧化劑(ㄎㄤˋ ㄧㄤˇ ㄏㄨㄚˋ ㄐㄧˋ)
antioxidant
抗違(ㄎㄤˋ ㄨㄟˊ)
to oppose; to disobey (orders, etc.): 你曾抗違父母之命嗎? Did you ever disobey your parents?
抗原(ㄎㄤˋ ㄩㄢˊ)
(medicine) an antigen

【抖】 1821 ㄉㄡˇ doou dǒu

1. to shiver; to tremble: 他的聲音因憤怒而顫抖。His voice trembled with anger.
2. to shake; to jerk: 她把衣服上的雪抖掉。She shook the snow off her clothes.
3. to rouse
4. (colloquial) to make good; to become well-to-do

抖翻(ㄉㄡˇ ·ㄈㄢ)
to turn up; to expose; to dig up old stories to discredit somebody: 他抖翻了他們的秘密。He exposed their secrets.

抖動(ㄉㄡˇ ㄉㄨㄥˋ)
to shake; to tremble; to vibrate: 樹葉在風中抖動。The leaves tremble in the wind.

抖摟(ㄉㄡˇ ·ㄌㄡ)
①to exhaust one's means; to waste; to squander ②to expose another's secrets ③ to catch cold ④to shake off

抖攬(ㄉㄡˇ ㄌㄢˇ)
to solicit 亦作「兜攬」

抖亂(ㄉㄡˇ ㄌㄨㄢˋ)
a shallow, gaudy, small-time louse (usually young)

抖起來了(ㄉㄡˇ ㄑㄧˇ ㄌㄞˊ ·ㄌㄜ)
to become ostensibly successful and prosperous; to make good

抖出來(ㄉㄡˇ ㄔㄨ ·ㄌㄞ)
to spill out

抖擻精神(ㄉㄡˇ ㄙㄡˇ ㄐㄧㄥ ㄕㄣˊ)
to pull oneself together or to muster one's energies (for an important task ahead)

抖威風(ㄉㄡˇ ㄨㄟ ㄈㄥ)
to throw one's weight around

【折】 1822
1. ㄓㄜˊ jer zhé

1. to break; to snap 別把樹枝折斷了。Don't break the branches.
2. to bend; to humble; to bow: 悲哀挫折了他的銳氣。Sorrow has bowed his spirit.
3. to decide a course; to judge
4. to sell, barter or exchange: 她將英鎊折換成美元。She exchanged pounds for dollars.
5. a discount in the price
6. to fold: 他把紙對折，然後放到一邊。He folded the paper in half and put it away.
7. to tear into halves; to destroy
8. to submit to; to be willing
9. a Chinese family name

折半(ㄓㄜˊ ㄅㄢˋ)
to reduce by half; to reduce to half; to sell at half price: 本書按原價折半出售。This book sells at half price.

折變(ㄓㄜˊ ㄅㄧㄢˋ)
①to substitute one thing for another of equal value or price ②to auction one's property to repay debts

折磨(ㄓㄜˊ ㄇㄛˊ)
to submit to an ordeal; trials and afflictions; grillings; torment: 她受牙痛的折磨。She suffered torment from an aching tooth.

折賣(ㄓㄜˊ ㄇㄞˋ)
to sell or auction one's property (to repay debts, etc.)

折服(ㄓㄜˊ ㄈㄨˊ)
①to acknowledge the superiority of others ②to submit; to bring into submission: 他不肯折服。He would not submit.

折福(ㄓㄜˊ ㄈㄨˊ)
to reduce blessings in one's later life because of excessive easy living (sometimes used as a polite expression in response to great favors bestowed upon oneself)

折抵(ㄓㄜˊ ㄉㄧˇ)
to set off against

折疊(ㄓㄜˊ ㄉㄧㄝˊ)
to fold: 請把報紙折疊好。Fold up the newspaper,please.

折疊床(ㄓㄜˊ ㄉㄧㄝˊ ㄔㄨㄤˊ)
a folding bed

折疊椅(ㄓㄜˊ ㄉㄧㄝˊ ㄧˇ)
a folding chair

折兌(ㄓㄜˊ ㄉㄨㄟˋ)
to exchange (gold or silver) for money; to convert

折斷(ㄓㄜˊ ㄉㄨㄢˋ)
to snap; to break: 槳啪噠一聲折斷了。The oar broke with a snap.

折頭(ㄓㄜˊ ·ㄊㄡ)
a discount rate

折柳(ㄓㄜˊ ㄌㄧㄡˇ)
(literally) to break a willow branch—to send off a friend

折桂(ㄓㄜˊ ㄍㄨㄟˋ)
to pass the imperial civil service examination, particularly one held in autumn

折光(ㄓㄜˊ ㄍㄨㄤ)
refracted light; to refract light

折肱(ㄓㄜˊ ㄍㄨㄥ)
experienced

折扣(ㄓㄜˊ ㄎㄡˋ)
abatement; a discount in the price; a discount rate; a rebate: 那是打過折扣的價錢。That is the discounted price.

折扣率(ㄓㄜˊ ㄎㄡˋ ㄌㄩˋ)
the discount rate

折合(ㄓㄜˊ ㄏㄜˊ)
(said of two currencies, etc.) equivalent to

折回(ㄓㄜˊ ㄏㄨㄟˊ)
to turn back (half way): 難民到邊界時被折回。The refugees were turned back at the frontier.

折戟(ㄓㄜˊ ㄐㄧˇ)
to break the spear—as a token of peace or truce

折價(ㄓㄜˊ ㄐㄧㄚˋ)
(said of an article used in repaying a debt, etc.) equivalent to

折節(ㄓㄜˊ ㄐㄧㄝˊ)
①to act obsequiously ②to change the habit or way of living

折節讀書(ㄓㄜˊ ㄐㄧㄝˊ ㄉㄨˊ ㄕㄨ)
to take a sudden liking to studying

折交(ㄓㄜˊ ㄐㄧㄠ)
to pay proportionately

折舊(ㄓㄜˊ ㄐㄧㄡˋ)
depreciation (especially said of machinery in use)

折舊率(ㄓㄜˊ ㄐㄧㄡˋ ㄌㄩˋ)
the depreciation rate

折箭爲盟(ㄓㄜˊ ㄐㄧㄢˋ ㄨㄟˊ ㄇㄥˊ)
to break an arrow as a vow or pledge to keep one's promise

折劵(ㄓㄜˊ ㄑㄩㄢˋ)
to destroy a debtor's IOU—to renounce the right of asking for repayment; to destroy a deed without asking for money

折現(ㄓㄜˊ ㄒㄧㄢˋ)
to convert into cash

折線(ㄓㄜˊ ㄒㄧㄢˋ)
(mathematics) a broken line

〔手部〕

折枝(ㄓㄜˊ ㄓ)
①to massage ②to snap a twig ③a style of flower painting with one or two stems minus the root

折賬 or 折帳(ㄓㄜˊ ㄓㄤˋ)
to repay a creditor in kind

折中 or 折衷(ㄓㄜˊ ㄓㄨㄥ)
to compromise; a compromise: 這是個折中的辦法。It's a compromise.

折衝(ㄓㄜˊ ㄔㄨㄥ)
to ward off the enemy; to repulse the enemy

折衝尊俎(ㄓㄜˊ ㄔㄨㄥ ㄗㄨㄣ ㄗㄨˇ)
(literally) to fight off the enemy over cups of wine—to subdue an enemy by diplomacy; to win a war at the conference table

折煞 or 折殺(ㄓㄜˊ ·ㄕㄚ)
to break one's luck

折射(ㄓㄜˊ ㄕㄜˋ)
refraction; to refract: 水可使光折射。Water refracts light.

折射角(ㄓㄜˊ ㄕㄜˋ ㄐㄧㄠˇ)
a refraction angle; an angle of refraction

折射線(ㄓㄜˊ ㄕㄜˋ ㄒㄧㄢˋ)
a refractor ray

折壽(ㄓㄜˊ ㄕㄡˋ)
(said of excessive happiness, blessings, etc.) that will cut one's natural allotment of life expectancy

折扇(ㄓㄜˊ ㄕㄢˋ)
a folding fan 亦作「摺扇」

折入(ㄓㄜˊ ㄖㄨˋ)
①to turn into another street ②capital recovered after suffering losses in business

折辱(ㄓㄜˊ ㄖㄨˋ)
to humiliate; to insult

折子(ㄓㄜˊ ·ㄗ)
a folding notebook

折足覆餗(ㄓㄜˊ ㄗㄨˊ ㄈㄨˋ ㄙㄨˋ)
not equal to the task

折算(ㄓㄜˊ ㄙㄨㄢˋ)
calculated at; equivalent to (said of the value of property, possessions, etc.)

折損(ㄓㄜˊ ㄙㄨㄣˇ)
to damage; damage (in property, reputation, etc.): 因火災使得那房子受到相當的折損。The fire did considerable damage to the building.

折頁(ㄓㄜˊ ㄧㄝˋ)
(printing) folding

折腰(ㄓㄜˊ ㄧㄠ)
to bow; to humble oneself

折獄(ㄓㄜˊ ㄩˋ)
to decide a lawsuit

【折】 1822
2. ㄕㄜˊ sher shé

1. to lose money; to fail in business
2. to break; to snap: 釣魚竿折了。The fishing pole broke.

折本(ㄕㄜˊ ㄅㄣˇ)
to lose money; to get into the red: 那是折本生意。That's a losing business.

折了(ㄕㄜˊ ·ㄌㄜ)
broken

折耗(ㄕㄜˊ ㄏㄠˋ)
to lose money

【折】 1822
3. ㄓㄜ je zhē

1. to turn upside down; to fall head over heels; to somersault; a somersault: 他折了個跟斗。He turned a somersault.
2. to pour all out

折騰(ㄓㄜ ·ㄊㄥ)
①to turn upside down ②to squander; to waste; to spend (money) extravagantly; to exhaust all reserves ③to toss about

折跟頭(ㄓㄜ ㄍㄣ ·ㄊㄡ)
to somersault; to fall head over heels

【抑】 1823
ㄧˋ yih yì

1. to press down; to repress: 他的創作天才被壓抑太久了。His creative talents had been repressed for too long.
2. to restrain; to force to (do, perform, etc.): 你不可抑制他們的自由。You must not restrain them of their liberty.
3. to bend or lower (one's head)
4. or; or if; still; else; either; then
5. but; an opening particle of an expression
6. an exclamatory, roughly equivalent to "oh," or "alas"
7. to stop

抑勒(ㄧˋ ㄌㄜˋ)
to repress and restrain (one's anger, etc.)

抑且(ㄧˋ ㄑㄧㄝˇ) or 抑或(ㄧˋ ㄏㄨㄛˋ)
besides; moreover; or

抑強扶弱(ㄧˋ ㄑㄧㄤˊ ㄈㄨˊ ㄖㄨㄛˋ)
to restrain the strong and help the weak; to curb the violent and assist the weak

抑止(ㄧˋ ㄓˇ)
to restrain; to check; to stop; to suppress: 老師抑止孩子們惡作劇。The teacher restrained children from doing mischief.

抑制(ㄧˋ ㄓˋ)
to repress; to restrain; to control: 她不能抑制她的好奇心。She could not restrain her curiosity.

抑首(ㄧˋ ㄕㄡˇ)
to bend or lower one's head

抑挫(ㄧˋ ㄘㄨㄛˋ)
to curb

抑塞(ㄧˋ ㄙㄜˋ)
①to give no chance to; to reject ②despondency; dejection

抑遏(ㄧˋ ㄜˋ)
to curb; to restrain; to suppress; to coerce: 她無法抑遏住她的憤怒。She could not restrain her anger.

抑壓(ㄧˋ ㄧㄚ)
to coerce; to curb; to restrain

抑揚(ㄧˋ ㄧㄤˊ)
①rising and falling in cadence ②the flow of sentiments in a writing ③to praise and to censure ④the rise and fall (of one's career, etc.)

抑揚頓挫(ㄧˋ ㄧㄤˊ ㄉㄨㄣˋ ㄘㄨㄛˋ)
melodious; rich in melody; cadence; modulation in tone

抑鬱(ㄧˋ ㄩˋ)
despondency; sad and melancholy: 他對自己的健康不佳感到抑鬱不安。He was despondent about his poor health.

【扼】 1824
(扼) ㄜˋ eh è

1. to repress; to restrain; to control
2. to clutch; to grasp; to grip
3. to hold and defend (a city, etc.)

扼喉撫背(ㄜˋ ㄏㄡˊ ㄈㄨˇ ㄅㄟˋ)
to hold the best strategic positions (which will render the enemy helpless)
扼吭(ㄜˋ ㄏㄤˊ)
to choke; to throttle
扼虎(ㄜˋ ㄏㄨˇ)
to choke a tiger to death —very powerful; with enormous strength
扼據(ㄜˋ ㄐㄩˋ)
to occupy and hold (key positions, etc.)
扼險(ㄜˋ ㄒㄧㄢˇ)
to hold the most strategic position (in military operations)
扼制(ㄜˋ ㄓˋ)
to repress; to keep under control by force
扼殺(ㄜˋ ㄕㄚ)
to strangle; to smother; to throttle
扼守(ㄜˋ ㄕㄡˇ)
to hold and defend (a strategic position): 我軍勇敢地扼守堡壘。Our soldiers held the fort bravely.
扼阻要塞(ㄜˋ ㄗㄨˇ ㄧㄠˋ ㄙㄞˋ)
(military) a stronghold which will jeopardize military operations of the enemy
扼死(ㄜˋ ㄙˇ)
to strangle; to throttle
扼要(ㄜˋ ㄧㄠˋ)
①to hold a strategic position ②main points of a statement or article; in summary: 請扼要說明。Please tell us the key points.
扼腕(ㄜˋ ㄨㄢˋ)
(literally) to seize one's wrist — ① disappointment; regret ② anger ③ excitement

【承】1825 ㄔㄥˊ cherng chéng

1. to receive; to inherit; to succeed (another in a task, etc.): 他沒有兒子繼承他。He had no son to succeed him.
2. to undertake; to make it one's responsibility
3. by (order of)
4. to continue; to carry on, as a theme
5. to hold; to contain; to support; to bear: 我無法再承受他的無禮。I can support his insolence no longer.
6. to confess: 他坦承自己不懂。He confessed (that) he did not understand it.
7. obliged; with thanks: 承您幫助，十分感激。We are very much obliged to you for your help.
8. to please; to flatter: 他在奉承你。He is flattering you.

承包(ㄔㄥˊ ㄅㄠ)
to undertake to do a job; to undertake a construction job under contract; to contract
承包商(ㄔㄥˊ ㄅㄠ ㄕㄤ)
a contractor
承保(ㄔㄥˊ ㄅㄠˇ)
to accept insurance; to act as a guarantor
承辦(ㄔㄥˊ ㄅㄢˋ)
to handle (a case); to be responsible for (a task); to undertake: 該律師免費承辦那宗案件。The lawyer undertook that case without a fee.
承辦人員(ㄔㄥˊ ㄅㄢˋ ㄖㄣˊ ㄩㄢˊ)
officials concerned (in a task); officials in charge of a specific task
承敝 or 承弊(ㄔㄥˊ ㄅㄧˋ)
in the wake of a declining period
承平(ㄔㄥˊ ㄆㄧㄥˊ)
successive peaceful reigns
承蒙(ㄔㄥˊ ㄇㄥˊ)
to be obliged to; much indebted to...: 承蒙您的好意，心裏非常感激。I am greatly indebted to you for your kindness.
承命(ㄔㄥˊ ㄇㄧㄥˋ)
to accept instructions
承乏(ㄔㄥˊ ㄈㄚˊ)
a conventional expression used by an incumbent referring to himself
承奉(ㄔㄥˊ ㄈㄥˋ)
by order of; in compliance with an order: 軍隊承奉指揮官的命令前進。The army advanced by order of the commander.
承擔(ㄔㄥˊ ㄉㄢ) or 承當(ㄔㄥˊ ㄉㄤ)
to shoulder or to take (the responsibility, task, etc.): 我對這行動承擔全責。I take full responsibility for this action.
承兌(ㄔㄥˊ ㄉㄨㄟˋ)
to accept; acceptance
承祧(ㄔㄥˊ ㄊㄧㄠ)
to adopt as an heir
承諾(ㄔㄥˊ ㄋㄨㄛˋ)
a promise; to promise; to agree to; to undertake: 我不能作承諾。I can not promise.
承攬(ㄔㄥˊ ㄌㄢˇ)
to take full charge or responsibility (usually under contract); to manage or undertake a task, project, etc.
承露盤(ㄔㄥˊ ㄌㄨˋ ㄆㄢˊ)
a plate for collecting dewdrops which Chinese emperors used to pray to gods
承購(ㄔㄥˊ ㄍㄡˋ)
to act as a purchasing agent
承管(ㄔㄥˊ ㄍㄨㄢˇ)
to take full charge and responsibility (of)
承歡(ㄔㄥˊ ㄏㄨㄢ)
①to please parents ②to cater to (superiors)
承歡膝下(ㄔㄥˊ ㄏㄨㄢ ㄒㄧ ㄒㄧㄚˋ)
to please one's parents by living with them
承繼(ㄔㄥˊ ㄐㄧˋ)
①to inherit ②to continue an unfinished task left by a predecessor
承繼權(ㄔㄥˊ ㄐㄧˋ ㄑㄩㄢˊ)
the right of inheritance
承繼人(ㄔㄥˊ ㄐㄧˋ ㄖㄣˊ)
an heir or heiress
承接(ㄔㄥˊ ㄐㄧㄝ)
to receive and carry on; to continue; to succeed to
承教(ㄔㄥˊ ㄐㄧㄠˋ)
much obliged for your instructions, advice, etc.
承情(ㄔㄥˊ ㄑㄧㄥˊ)
much obliged for your kindness
承襲(ㄔㄥˊ ㄒㄧˊ)
to inherit (a title, etc.): 他承襲了父親的爵位。He inherited his father's title.
承銷(ㄔㄥˊ ㄒㄧㄠ)
consignment-in (or inward); goods-in on consignments; shipment inward
承銷人(ㄔㄥˊ ㄒㄧㄠ ㄖㄣˊ)
a consignee

〔手部〕

承先啓後(ㄔㄥˊ ㄒㄧㄢ ㄑㄧˇ ㄏㄡˋ)
to be heir to ancient sages and the teacher of posterity (usually said of a person of profound learning)

承轉(ㄔㄥˊ ㄓㄨㄢˇ)
to forward (a document to the next level above or below)

承重(ㄔㄥˊ ㄓㄨㄥˋ)
bearing; load-bearing

承重孫(ㄔㄥˊ ㄔㄨㄥˊ ㄙㄨㄣ)
eldest grandson whose deceased father was heir to the grandparents—a term referring to oneself in the death announcement of either of one's grandparents

承寵(ㄔㄥˊ ㄔㄨㄥˇ)
Thank you for your kindness and favors.

承受(ㄔㄥˊ ㄕㄡˋ)
to take; to receive; to accept; to bear: 他承受不了那喧鬧聲。 He can't bear the noise.

承上啓下(ㄔㄥˊ ㄕㄤˋ ㄑㄧˇ ㄒㄧㄚˋ)
to carry on; to continue (a statement, an account, etc.); to pass on (learning, etc.)

承認(ㄔㄥˊ ㄖㄣˋ)
① to confess; to admit: 他承認偷了錢。He confessed to having stolen money. ② to recognize (a nation, a new regime, etc): 他們承認他是合法繼承人。They recognized him as the lawful heir.

承載(ㄔㄥˊ ㄗㄞˋ)
to bear the weight of

承造(ㄔㄥˊ ㄗㄠˋ)
to manufacture or build something for someone else

承租(ㄔㄥˊ ㄗㄨ)
to rent

承恩(ㄔㄥˊ ㄣ)
to receive grace (from the emperor, etc.)

承顏(ㄔㄥˊ ㄧㄢˊ)
① to be pleased to meet ② to carry favor by fawning

承問(ㄔㄥˊ ㄨㄣˋ)
Thank you for inquiring.

承望(ㄔㄥˊ ㄨㄤˋ)
to think of; to expect

承允(ㄔㄥˊ ㄩㄣˇ)
to agree; to promise

承運(ㄔㄥˊ ㄩㄣˋ)
(said of the throne) to be ordained by Heaven; to have received the heavenly mandate

五畫

【抱】 1826 ㄅㄠˋ baw bào

1. to embrace; to enfold; to hold in the arms: 他擁抱著她。He embraced her in his arms.
2. to harbor; to cherish; to bosom
3. to adopt
4. aspirations; ambition: 她的抱負是成爲一位醫生。Her ambition is to become a doctor.
5. a Chinese family name

抱悲觀(ㄅㄠˋ ㄅㄟ ㄍㄨㄢ)
to feel pessimistic; to be pessimistic

抱病(ㄅㄠˋ ㄅㄧㄥˋ)or 抱恙(ㄅㄠˋ ㄧㄤˋ)
indisposed; sick or ill: 她抱病工作。She went on working in spite of ill health.

抱不平(ㄅㄠˋ ㄅㄨˋ ㄆㄧㄥˊ)
indignant at injustice; to feel the injustice done to another and wish to help: 他替她打抱不平。He defended her against an injustice.

抱樸(ㄅㄠˋ ㄆㄨˊ)
to harbor no ambitions and be content with what one already has; free from passions and desires

抱璞(ㄅㄠˋ ㄆㄨˊ)
to possess talent which is not recognized

抱佛脚(ㄅㄠˋ ㄈㄛˊ ㄐㄧㄠˇ)
(literally) to clasp Buddha's feet—a last-minute rush

抱負(ㄅㄠˋ ㄈㄨˋ)
aspirations; ambition

抱負不凡(ㄅㄠˋ ㄈㄨˋ ㄅㄨˋ ㄈㄢˊ)
to entertain high aspirations; very ambitious

抱定決心(ㄅㄠˋ ㄉㄧㄥˋ ㄐㄩㄝˊ ㄒㄧㄣ)
determined; to hold on to one's determination

抱獨身主義(ㄅㄠˋ ㄉㄨˊ ㄕㄣ ㄓㄨˇ ㄧˋ)
to decide to live as a bachelor or spinster

抱頭痛哭(ㄅㄠˋ ㄊㄡˊ ㄊㄨㄥˋ ㄎㄨ)
to bury one's head in one's arms and cry bitterly

抱頭鼠竄(ㄅㄠˋ ㄊㄡˊ ㄕㄨˇ ㄘㄨㄢˋ)
to flee ignominiously; to run helter-skelter

抱樂觀(ㄅㄠˋ ㄌㄜˋ ㄍㄨㄢ)
to feel optimistic; to be optimistic

抱關擊柝(ㄅㄠˋ ㄍㄨㄢ ㄐㄧˊ ㄊㄨㄛˋ)
(literally) doorkeepers and night watchmen—humblest government employees

抱愧(ㄅㄠˋ ㄎㄨㄟˋ)
to feel ashamed

抱空窩(ㄅㄠˋ ㄎㄨㄥ ㄨㄛ)
(literally) to guard an empty nest—to cherish no ambitions; unsuccessful but resigned

抱憾(ㄅㄠˋ ㄏㄢˋ)
to deplore; to regret; to be sorry about

抱恨終身(ㄅㄠˋ ㄏㄣˋ ㄓㄨㄥ ㄕㄣ)or 抱恨終天(ㄅㄠˋ ㄏㄣˋ ㄓㄨㄥ ㄊㄧㄢ)
to feel remorse for the rest of one's life; to regret something to the end of one's days

抱節君(ㄅㄠˋ ㄐㄧㄝˊ ㄐㄩㄣ)
bamboo

抱緊(ㄅㄠˋ ㄐㄧㄣˇ)
to hold tightly in one's arms

抱歉(ㄅㄠˋ ㄑㄧㄢˋ)
to feel sorry about; to regret: 抱歉給你添麻煩。I am sorry to trouble you.

抱屈(ㄅㄠˋ ㄑㄩ)
to bear a grudge; to harbor resentment

抱屈含寃(ㄅㄠˋ ㄑㄩ ㄏㄢˊ ㄩㄢ)
to be wronged and aggrieved; to bear a deep grudge

抱薪救火(ㄅㄠˋ ㄒㄧㄣ ㄐㄧㄡˋ ㄏㄨㄛˇ)
to add fuel to the fire—to make the situation even worse

抱着(ㄅㄠˋ ˙ㄓㄜ)
to hold in one's arms; to embrace

抱住(ㄅㄠˋ ㄓㄨˋ)
to hold in one's arms; to hold on to

抱柱(ㄅㄠˋ ㄓㄨˋ)
to keep one's promise faithfully

抱罪(ㄅㄠˋ ㄗㄨㄟˋ)

to be conscious of guilt; to be ashamed

抱殘守缺(ㄅㄠˋ ㄘㄢˊ ㄕㄡˇ ㄑㄩㄝ)
(literally) to cherish broken and worn-out things—extremely conservative; sticking to old ways

抱粗腿(ㄅㄠˋ ㄘㄨ ㄊㄨㄟˇ)
to have strong support or backing of an influential person

抱一(ㄅㄠˋ ㄧ)
to stick to one principle

抱腰(ㄅㄠˋ ㄧㄠ)
to assist; to help; to lend support to

抱養(ㄅㄠˋ ㄧㄤˇ)
to adopt and raise: 他們抱養那小孩爲後嗣。They adopted the child as their heir.

抱窩(ㄅㄠˋ ㄨㄛ) or 抱蛋(ㄅㄠˋ ㄉㄢˋ)
(said of hens, etc.) to hatch eggs; to brood

抱甕灌園(ㄅㄠˋ ㄨㄥˋ ㄍㄨㄢˋ ㄩㄢˊ)
(literally) to water the vegetable garden with an urn in one's arms—to do things in an unimaginative or inefficient way; to make a lot of efforts but get poor result

抱怨(ㄅㄠˋ ㄩㄢˋ)
to complain; to grumble; to blame (another)

【抨】 1827
ㄆㄥ peng pēng

to impeach; to censure; to attack or to assail by words

抨劾(ㄆㄥ ㄏㄜˊ) or 抨彈(ㄆㄥ ㄊㄢˊ)
to impeach; to censure

抨擊(ㄆㄥ ㄐㄧˊ)
to attack or assail by words; to criticize; to lash

【披】 1828
ㄆㄧ pi pī
(又讀 ㄆㄟ pei pēi)

1. to open (a book, scroll, etc.); to unroll
2. to spread out; to disperse
3. to thumb through or read casually
4. to throw on (a garment, etc.); to wear untidily

披麻帶孝(ㄆㄧ ㄇㄚˊ ㄉㄞˋ ㄒㄧㄠˋ)
to put on mourning apparel (especially said of sons or daughters of the deceased)

披靡(ㄆㄧ ㄇㄧˇ)
①(said of grass, etc.) blown about by the wind ②(said of an army) beaten and scattered; routed; to put to rout; to flee

披髮(ㄆㄧ ㄈㄚˇ)
disheveled hair

披風(ㄆㄧ ㄈㄥ)
a cape

披拂(ㄆㄧ ㄈㄨˊ)
windblown

披讀(ㄆㄧ ㄉㄨˊ)
to read; to open and read

披頭(ㄆㄧ ㄊㄡˊ)
the Beatles—a British vocal group popular in the mid-1960's

披頭散髮(ㄆㄧ ㄊㄡˊ ㄙㄢˋ ㄈㄚˇ)
disheveled hair (often referring to an untidy woman); with hair in disarray

披覽(ㄆㄧ ㄌㄢˇ)
to peruse; to open and read: 他披覽群書。He perused books of all sorts.

披離(ㄆㄧ ㄌㄧˊ)
blown about, as leaves; scattered

披瀝(ㄆㄧ ㄌㄧˋ) or 披肝瀝膽(ㄆㄧ ㄍㄢ ㄌㄧˋ ㄉㄢˇ)
to open one's heart and talk; to have a heart-to-heart talk; to talk without reserve; to be perfectly frank

披露(ㄆㄧ ㄌㄨˋ)
to reveal; to make known; to publish

披露心曲(ㄆㄧ ㄌㄨˋ ㄒㄧㄣ ㄑㄩ)
to tell one's innermost thoughts

披掛(ㄆㄧ ㄍㄨㄚˋ)
to wear full battle dress; to saddle up

披掛上陣(ㄆㄧ ㄍㄨㄚˋ ㄕㄤˋ ㄓㄣˋ)
to wear full battle dress and go into battle

披豁(ㄆㄧ ㄏㄨㄛˋ)
to open one's heart in perfect frankness; to talk without reserve

披懷(ㄆㄧ ㄏㄨㄞˊ)
to be very frank; to open one's heart; to harbor no secret

披紅(ㄆㄧ ㄏㄨㄥˊ)
to drape a person with red silk—to congratulate or celebrate his success, exploits, etc.

披枷帶鎖(ㄆㄧ ㄐㄧㄚ ㄉㄞˋ ㄙㄨㄛˇ)
(said of criminals) manacled and cangued

披甲(ㄆㄧ ㄐㄧㄚˇ)
to wear armor

披肩(ㄆㄧ ㄐㄧㄢ)
a shawl

披堅執銳(ㄆㄧ ㄐㄧㄢ ㄓˊ ㄖㄨㄟˋ)
to wear armor and hold weapons—in full combat-readiness

披襟(ㄆㄧ ㄐㄧㄣ)
①to open the front of one's garment ②to be honest and sincere

披荊斬棘(ㄆㄧ ㄐㄧㄥ ㄓㄢˇ ㄐㄧˊ)
①to cultivate land as a pioneer ②to travel through thick bushes and dense jungles ③to fight an uphill battle: 他披荊斬棘以獲成功。He fought an uphill battle to win success.

披卷(ㄆㄧ ㄐㄩㄢˋ)
to open a volume and read

披心(ㄆㄧ ㄒㄧㄣ)
①to open and show one's heart—perfectly honest and sincere ②extremely attentive and careful

披星戴月(ㄆㄧ ㄒㄧㄥ ㄉㄞˋ ㄩㄝˋ)
①to travel by night: 他披星戴月趕回家。He went home by night.②to toil night and day

披猖揚厲(ㄆㄧ ㄔㄤ ㄧㄤˊ ㄌㄧˋ)
(said of gangsters) to treat law and order with contempt

披沙揀金(ㄆㄧ ㄕㄚ ㄐㄧㄢˇ ㄐㄧㄣ)
(literally) to spread the sand and pick the gold—to be extremely careful in making selection; to get essentials from a large mass of material

披緇(ㄆㄧ ㄗ)
to become a monk or nun

披散著頭(ㄆㄧ ㄙㄢˋ ˙ㄓㄜ ㄊㄡˊ)
with disheveled hair

披索(ㄆㄧ ㄙㄨㄛˇ)
(monetary) peso

披衣(ㄆㄧ ㄧ)
to throw on clothes: 她披衣而起。She threw on a gown

and rose.

披翫(ㄆㄧ ㄨㄢˋ)
to read and appreciate

披閱(ㄆㄧ ㄩㄝˋ)
to read

披雲霧見青天(ㄆㄧ ㄩㄣˊ ㄨˋ ㄐㄧㄢˋ ㄑㄧㄥ ㄊㄧㄢ)
(literally) to open the clouds and see the blue skies—to see the truth after the dust settles

【抵】 1829 ㄉㄧˇ dii dǐ

1. to resist; to oppose: 他們勇敢地抵抗敵人。They resisted the enemy bravely.
2. to prop; to sustain
3. to offset; to balance: 收支相抵。The accounts are balanced.
4. to substitute; to give as an equivalent
5. to offer as collateral
6. to arrive at; to reach (a place): 我們已平安抵達。We have arrived safely.
7. to go against; to offend against (the law and regulations)

抵埠(ㄉㄧˇ ㄅㄨˋ)
to reach port; to arrive in port

抵不住(ㄉㄧˇ ·ㄅㄨ ㄓㄨˋ)
① unable to resist or hold out ②(said of a collateral) inadequate or insufficient

抵冒(ㄉㄧˇ ㄇㄠˋ)
to offend

抵命(ㄉㄧˇ ㄇㄧㄥˋ)
a life for a life

抵法(ㄉㄧˇ ㄈㄚˇ)
to be punished by law

抵達(ㄉㄧˇ ㄉㄚˊ)
to arrive at or reach (a place)

抵擋(ㄉㄧˇ ㄉㄤˇ)
to resist; to sustain; to ward off: 他們抵擋敵人的攻擊。They ward off the enemy's attack.

抵當(ㄉㄧˇ ㄉㄤˋ)
to offer as a collateral; to give as an equivalent

抵敵(ㄉㄧˇ ㄉㄧˊ)
to resist the enemy

抵賴(ㄉㄧˇ ㄌㄞˋ)
to deny mistakes or crimes one has committed, or to renege a promise one has given: 你的過錯是不容抵賴的。Your fault cannot be denied.

抵扣(ㄉㄧˇ ㄎㄡˋ)
to deduct from

抵抗(ㄉㄧˇ ㄎㄤˋ)
to resist; to oppose; to fight against (an enemy, etc.); to withstand; to hold out against; resistance: 他們正在抵抗敵人的攻擊。They are withstanding the enemy's attack.

抵抗力(ㄉㄧˇ ㄎㄤˋ ㄌㄧˋ)
the force or power of resistance

抵抗器(ㄉㄧˇ ㄎㄤˋ ㄑㄧˋ)
(electricity) a rheostat 亦作「變阻器」

抵抗圈(ㄉㄧˇ ㄎㄤˋ ㄑㄩㄢ)
(electricity) a resistance coil

抵抗性(ㄉㄧˇ ㄎㄤˋ ㄒㄧㄥˋ)
resistibility

抵換(ㄉㄧˇ ㄏㄨㄢˋ)
to substitute (one thing for another)

抵借(ㄉㄧˇ ㄐㄧㄝˋ)
to pledge against a loan

抵瑕蹈隙(ㄉㄧˇ ㄒㄧㄚˊ ㄉㄠˇ ㄒㄧˋ)
to exploit the shortcomings of another

抵銷(ㄉㄧˇ ㄒㄧㄠ)
to offset; to counteract; to neutralize; to nullify

抵銷關稅(ㄉㄧˇ ㄒㄧㄠ ㄍㄨㄢ ㄕㄨㄟˋ)
countervailing duties

抵制(ㄉㄧˇ ㄓˋ)
① to resist ② to boycott: 他們抵制日貨。They boycotted Japanese goods.

抵制外貨(ㄉㄧˇ ㄓˋ ㄨㄞˋ ㄏㄨㄛˋ)
to boycott foreign goods

抵債(ㄉㄧˇ ㄓㄞˋ)
to pay a debt with goods or by labor

抵掌而談(ㄉㄧˇ ㄓㄤˇ ㄦˊ ㄊㄢˊ)
to talk pleasantly or intimately; to have a pleasant conversation

抵賬 or 抵帳(ㄉㄧˇ ㄓㄤˋ)
to repay a debt with goods or articles of equivalent value

抵住(ㄉㄧˇ ㄓㄨˋ)
to resist; to hold out

抵償(ㄉㄧˇ ㄔㄤˊ)
to compensate; to atone for: 沒有什麼可以抵償一個人健康的損失。Nothing can compensate for the loss of one's health.

抵觸(ㄉㄧˇ ㄔㄨˋ)
in contravention of (the law or regulations); to contravene: 這是與法律相抵觸的舉動。It is an act in contravention of the law.

抵充(ㄉㄧˇ ㄔㄨㄥ)
to use something as a substitute

抵數(ㄉㄧˇ ㄕㄨˋ)
to balance an account

抵足而眠(ㄉㄧˇ ㄗㄨˊ ㄦˊ ㄇㄧㄢˊ)
(said of very good friends) to share the same bed

抵罪(ㄉㄧˇ ㄗㄨㄟˋ)
to mete out appropriate punishment for a crime committed

抵死(ㄉㄧˇ ㄙˇ)
① to persist; to insist; persistently: 我們抵死不降。We persistently refuse to surrender. ② excessive

抵押(ㄉㄧˇ ㄧㄚ)
to mortgage; to collateralize

抵押品(ㄉㄧˇ ㄧㄚ ㄆㄧㄣˇ)
collateral; security; pledges: 她拿他的錶當抵押品。She held his watch as a pledge.

抵押權(ㄉㄧˇ ㄧㄚ ㄑㄩㄢˊ)
(law) the right of the creditor to receive payment on priority basis upon the selling of the property offered him as security by the debtor; mortgage

抵押書(ㄉㄧˇ ㄧㄚ ㄕㄨ)
a letter of hypothecation

抵押人(ㄉㄧˇ ㄧㄚ ㄖㄣˊ)
a mortgagor

抵牾(ㄉㄧˇ ㄨˇ)
to conflict with; to go against

抵禦(ㄉㄧˇ ㄩˋ)
to resist; to withstand

抵禦外侮(ㄉㄧˇ ㄩˋ ㄨㄞˋ ㄨˇ)
to resist foreign aggression

【抹】 1830 1. ㄇㄛˇ moo mǒ

1. to wipe; to rub; to mop
2. to smear; to apply to: 他雙手抹上油。He smeared his

hands with grease.
3. to obliterate; to blot out: 好幾個字都被塗抹掉了。Several words have been blotted out.

抹脖子(ㄇㄛˇ ㄅㄛˊ ˙ㄗ)or 抹頸(ㄇㄛˇ ㄐㄧㄥˇ)
to commit suicide by slicing one's throat

抹布(ㄇㄛˇ ㄅㄨˋ)
a dish cloth; a mopper; a cleaning rag

抹片(ㄇㄛˇ ㄆㄧㄢˋ)
a smear (a small quantity of something spread thinly on a slide for microscopic examination)

抹了良心(ㄇㄛˇ ˙ㄌㄜ ㄌㄧㄤˊ ㄒㄧㄣ)
to blot out all the moral sense; unconscionable; devoid of conscience

抹淚(ㄇㄛˇ ㄌㄟˋ)
to wipe away one's tears

抹乾(ㄇㄛˇ ㄍㄢ)
to wipe dry

抹乾淨(ㄇㄛˇ ㄍㄢ ㄐㄧㄥˋ)
to wipe clean

抹黑(ㄇㄛˇ ㄏㄟ)
(informal) to blacken someone's name; to throw mud at; to bring shame on; to discredit; mudslinging 亦作「中傷」

抹去(ㄇㄛˇ ㄑㄩˋ)or 抹掉(ㄇㄛˇ ㄉㄧㄠˋ)
to wipe out; to obliterate; to blot out; to cross out; to erase: 這男孩抹去了所有鉛筆的筆跡。The boy erased all pencil marks.

抹稀泥(ㄇㄛˇ ㄒㄧ ㄋㄧˊ)
to calm an angry person with soft and gentle words

抹下臉來(ㄇㄛˇ ㄒㄧㄚˋ ㄌㄧㄢˇ ㄌㄞˊ)
to show anger or displeasure suddenly

抹香鯨(ㄇㄛˇ ㄒㄧㄤ ㄐㄧㄥ)
sperm whale, so named on account of the ambergris (龍涎香)

抹桌子(ㄇㄛˇ ㄓㄨㄛ ˙ㄗ)
to wipe a table

抹殺(ㄇㄛˇ ㄕㄚ)or 抹煞(ㄇㄛˇ ㄕㄚ)
purposely fail to mention (one's merits, achievements, etc.); to withhold recognition for; do not give credit to: 他們抹殺了某些事實。They purposely failed to mention certain facts.

抹子(ㄇㄛˇ ˙ㄗ)
a trowel for plastering; a mason's spade for applying mortar

抹一鼻子灰(ㄇㄛˇ ㄧˋ ㄅㄧˊ ˙ㄗ ㄏㄨㄟ)
to get rebuffed when trying to please; to get an awkward rebuff; to suffer a snub

【抹】 1830
2. ㄇㄛˋ moh mò

1. to plaster: 他在抹牆。He's plastering a wall.
2. a tight undergarment
3. to turn: 他們剛抹過轉角。They just turned the corner of the road.

抹灰(ㄇㄛˋ ㄏㄨㄟ)
(construction) plastering

抹胸(ㄇㄛˋ ㄒㄩㄥ)
a tight undergarment for women worn across the breasts; a stomacher

抹額(ㄇㄛˋ ㄜˊ)
a sort of scarf worn across the forehead; a kind of turban

【抽】 1831
ㄔㄡ chou chōu

1. to draw out; to pull out or open; to take out: 他從書架上抽出一本書。He took a book out of his bookshelf.
2. to sprout; to put forth shoots; to bud: 樹在春天開始抽出嫩芽。Trees begin to bud in the spring.
3. to rid; to take away
4. to whip; to lash: 他正在抽陀螺。He is whipping a top.
5. to smoke (cigarettes, etc.): 他抽煙斗。He was smoking a pipe.
6. to shrink: 這件襯衫一洗就抽。This shirt shrinks in the wash.

抽鼻兒(ㄔㄡ ㄅㄧㄜˊㄦ)
to take a deep breath by the nose so as to halt it from running for a while in a bad cold

抽風(ㄔㄡ ㄈㄥ)
(medicine) convulsions

抽風機(ㄔㄡ ㄈㄥ ㄐㄧ)
an exhaust fan

抽搭(ㄔㄡ ㄉㄚ)
the sound of irregular and heavy breathing after a good cry; to sob in the wake of a bitter cry

抽打(ㄔㄡ ㄉㄚˇ)
to lash; to whip: 他用鞭子抽打馬背。He lashed his horse across the back with a whip.

抽刀(ㄔㄡ ㄉㄠ)
to draw a knife or blade

抽調(ㄔㄡ ㄉㄧㄠˋ)
to transfer (personnel or material)

抽丁(ㄔㄡ ㄉㄧㄥ)
to draft able-bodied men for military service; to press-gang

抽動(ㄔㄡ ㄉㄨㄥˋ)
to twitch; a spasm; a spasmodic jerk: 這小孩抽動著嘴像是要哭。The child's mouth twitched as if she were about to cry.

抽頭聚賭(ㄔㄡ ㄊㄡˊ ㄐㄩˋ ㄉㄨˇ)
to operate an unlicensed gambling joint

抽頭兒(ㄔㄡ ㄊㄡˊㄦ)
(said of a gambling house, etc.) to collect from the gamblers a certain percentage of their wins

抽屜(ㄔㄡ ˙ㄊㄧ)
a drawer: 他封住抽屜，使人無法打開。He sealed up a drawer so that it couldn't be opened.

抽工夫兒(ㄔㄡ ㄍㄨㄥ ˙ㄈㄨㄦ)
to spare some time; at one's spare time; to find time (for a task, etc.): 他抽不出工夫兒做那件事。He is unable to find time to do it.

抽考(ㄔㄡ ㄎㄠˇ)
① to select at random a few students from a class for a test ② an unannounced quiz or test

抽空兒(ㄔㄡ ㄎㄨㄥˋㄦ)or 抽閒(ㄔㄡ ㄒㄧㄢˊ)
to find time (to do something); at one's spare time: 出國之前請抽空去探望她。Try and find time to visit her before going abroad.

抽換(ㄔㄡ ㄏㄨㄢˋ)
① to change by rotation as of railroad ties or parts of machinery ② to change the contents of a package with-

out destroying the wrapping
抽筋(ㄔㄡ ㄐㄧㄣ)
to be seized by spasms or cramps: 他的腿抽筋了。He had a cramp in the leg.
抽筋拔骨(ㄔㄡ ㄐㄧㄣ ㄅㄚˊ ㄍㄨˇ)
very reluctantly; with great difficulty
抽獎(ㄔㄡ ㄐㄧㄤˇ)
to draw a lottery or raffle: 抽獎機 a lottery wheel
抽泣(ㄔㄡ ㄑㄧˋ)
to sob: 她抽泣著述說她的悲慘故事。She sobbed out her sad story.
抽球(ㄔㄡ ㄑㄧㄡˊ)
(sports) to drive
抽籤(ㄔㄡ ㄑㄧㄢ)
to draw (or cast) lots: 我們抽籤決定誰當隊長。We draw lots to decide who should be captain.
抽取(ㄔㄡ ㄑㄩˇ)
① to charge or collect a certain percentage of a sum ② to take at random from a batch of samples, etc.
抽薪止沸(ㄔㄡ ㄒㄧㄣ ㄓˇ ㄈㄟˋ)
(literally) to stop the boiling by taking out the fire —to stop or prevent trouble by removing the cause
抽象(ㄔㄡ ㄒㄧㄤˋ)
abstract (as opposed to concrete): 請勿如此抽象地談問題。Please don't speak in such abstract terms.
抽象名詞(ㄔㄡ ㄒㄧㄤˋ ㄇㄧㄥˊ ㄘˊ)
abstract nouns
抽象概念(ㄔㄡ ㄒㄧㄤˋ ㄍㄞˋ ㄋㄧㄢˋ)
abstract concepts or ideas
抽象畫(ㄔㄡ ㄒㄧㄤˋ ㄏㄨㄚˋ)
abstract painting
抽選(ㄔㄡ ㄒㄩㄢˇ)
to select from a lot
抽壯丁(ㄔㄡ ㄓㄨㄤˋ ㄉㄧㄥ)
to draft able-bodied men for military service; to press-gang
抽查(ㄔㄡ ㄔㄚˊ)
to investigate, survey or test a part of a group
抽出(ㄔㄡ ㄔㄨ)
to draw out; to pull out; to take out: 他把手從口袋抽出。He drew his hand from his pocket.
抽紗(ㄔㄡ ㄕㄚ)
drawnwork
抽身(ㄔㄡ ㄕㄣ)
to get away (while one is fully occupied): 希望於下星期一開始我能抽身去度一星期的假。I hope to get away next Monday for a week.
抽水(ㄔㄡ ㄕㄨㄟˇ)
to pump water: 他們從河裏抽水。They pumped water from the river.
抽水馬桶(ㄔㄡ ㄕㄨㄟˇ ㄇㄚˇ ㄊㄨㄥˇ)
a flush toilet
抽水機(ㄔㄡ ㄕㄨㄟˇ ㄐㄧ)
a water pump: 村裏的抽水機供應全村的用水。A village pump is one that supplies the whole village with water.
抽稅(ㄔㄡ ㄕㄨㄟˋ)
to levy taxes
抽簪(ㄔㄡ ㄗㄢ)
(literally) to pull out the pins of one's official cap—to renounce one's office
抽絲(ㄔㄡ ㄙ)
① to reel silk ② to do things slowly
抽絲剝繭(ㄔㄡ ㄙ ㄅㄛ ㄐㄧㄢˇ)
to make a painstaking investigation or examination
抽穗(ㄔㄡ ㄙㄨㄟˋ)
heading; earing: 玉蜀黍正在抽穗。The corn is in the ear.
抽鴉片(ㄔㄡ ㄧㄚ ㄆㄧㄢˋ)
to smoke opium
抽芽(ㄔㄡ ㄧㄚˊ)
to sprout; to put forth shoots; to bud
抽噎(ㄔㄡ ㄧㄝ)
to sob; sobs; spasms of muscles around the throat, as during or after a cry
抽油煙機(ㄔㄡ ㄧㄡˊ ㄧㄢ ㄐㄧ)
a suction fan installed above a kitchen range to remove oily smoke from the kitchen
抽烟 or 抽煙(ㄔㄡ ㄧㄢ)
to smoke (a pipe, cigars, cigarets, etc.): 這部車內不可抽煙。You must not smoke in this carriage.
抽印(ㄔㄡ ㄧㄣˋ)
to offprint: 抽印本 an offprint
抽樣(ㄔㄡ ㄧㄤˋ)
a sample; sampling
抽樣調查(ㄔㄡ ㄧㄤˋ ㄉㄧㄠˋ ㄔㄚˊ)
sampling

【押】 1832 ㄧㄚ ia yā

1. to mortgage; to pawn; to pledge; to obtain loans against securities: 他以車子作押。He left his car as security.
2. to detain or imprison (temporarily): 看押 to keep under detention
3. to escort: 他們把小偷押到警所去。They escorted the thief to the police station.
4. a signature: 畫押 to mark (a document) in lieu of signature (for the illiterate); to sign

押寶(ㄧㄚ ㄅㄠˇ)
a gambling game, played with dice under a bowl
押票(ㄧㄚ ㄆㄧㄠˋ)
a warrant for arrest
押封(ㄧㄚ ㄈㄥ)
to seal and attach (property)
押當(ㄧㄚ ㄉㄤˋ)
① to pawn: 我押當了手錶。I pawned my watch. ② a pawnshop
押定(ㄧㄚ ㄉㄧㄥˋ)
to sign an agreement
押頭(ㄧㄚ ·ㄊㄡ)
collateral; goods offered as security
押款(ㄧㄚ ㄎㄨㄢˇ)
to obtain loans against security; to mortgage
押貨(ㄧㄚ ㄏㄨㄛˋ)
① to mortgage goods ② to escort a shipment of goods from one place to another
押匯(ㄧㄚ ㄏㄨㄟˋ)
documentary draft negotiation
押解(ㄧㄚ ㄐㄧㄝˋ)
to transfer or deport (suspects, prisoners, goods, etc.) from one place to another under escort or guard: 這個間諜被押解出境。The spy was deported under escort.
押金(ㄧㄚ ㄐㄧㄣ)
a cash pledge; a deposit
押陣(ㄧㄚ ㄓㄣˋ)
(formerly) crack troops, etc.

which were supposed to secure the whole position in a battle

押賬 or 押帳(ㄧㄚ ㄓㄤˋ)
goods, etc. offered as security for a loan

押租(ㄧㄚ ㄗㄨ)
key money advanced by the lodger as a guarantee of his compliance with the terms of the renting agreement; a rent deposit; deposit money

押歲錢(ㄧㄚ ㄙㄨㄟˋ ㄑㄧㄢˊ)
money given to children by elders on the Lunar New Year's Eve

押送(ㄧㄚ ㄙㄨㄥˋ)
to send (goods or criminals) to another place under escort or guard

押尾(ㄧㄚ ㄨㄟˇ) or 押字(ㄧㄚ ㄗˋ)
to sign one's name at the end of a legal document

押運(ㄧㄚ ㄩㄣˋ)
to supervise and escort the transportation of goods, etc.

押韻(ㄧㄚ ㄩㄣˋ)
to rhyme: 使一字與另一字押韻 to rhyme one word with another

【拄】 1833 ㄓㄨˇ juu zhǔ

1. a post; a prop
2. to lean on (a stick, etc.): 他拄著拐杖走路。He walked with (the help of) a stick.
3. to ridicule; to make sarcastic remarks

拄笏看山(ㄓㄨˇ ㄏㄨˋ ㄎㄢˋ ㄕㄢ)
to have a deep liking for natural charms even when occupying a high position; to retain refined taste despite the corruptive influence of officialdom

拄杖(ㄓㄨˇ ㄓㄤˋ) or 拄拐(ㄓㄨˇ ㄍㄨㄞˇ) or 拄棍(ㄓㄨˇ ㄍㄨㄣˋ)
a crutch, staff or stick: 他們拄杖而行。They went on crutches.

【拂】 1834 1. ㄈㄨˊ fwu fú

1. to brush; to shake; to whisk: 她拂去桌子上的碎屑。She whisked the crumbs from the table.
2. to dust; a duster: 請小心拂拭。Please dust carefully.
3. to oppose; to disobey: 他不忍拂其雙親意。He does not have the heart to disobey his parents' wishes.
4. to expel; to drive away

拂面(ㄈㄨˊ ㄇㄧㄢˋ)
(said of breezes, leaves, etc.) to brush or caress the face lightly or gently: 春風拂面。The spring wind caresses the cheeks.

拂拂(ㄈㄨˊ ㄈㄨˊ)
the soft blowing of breezes

拂逆(ㄈㄨˊ ㄋㄧˋ) or 拂戾(ㄈㄨˊ ㄌㄧˋ)
① disagreeable ② disastrous

拂慮(ㄈㄨˊ ㄌㄩˋ)
to drive away cares and worries; to be carefree

拂曉(ㄈㄨˊ ㄒㄧㄠˇ) or 拂曙(ㄈㄨˊ ㄕㄨˇ)
daybreak; dawn

拂袖(ㄈㄨˊ ㄒㄧㄡˋ)
to shake one's sleeve—an expression of displeasure or anger

拂袖而去(ㄈㄨˊ ㄒㄧㄡˋ ㄦˊ ㄑㄩˋ)
to leave in displeasure or anger

拂晨(ㄈㄨˊ ㄔㄣˊ)
daybreak; dawn

拂塵(ㄈㄨˊ ㄔㄣˊ)
① to shake off dust; to whisk the dust off ② a duster made of long animal hairs

拂除(ㄈㄨˊ ㄔㄨˊ)
to wipe off; to brush off (dust, etc.): 我不能將這塊泥土拂除。I can't brush the dirt off.

拂拭(ㄈㄨˊ ㄕˋ)
to wipe and clean (a piece of furniture, etc.): 將桌子拂拭乾淨。Wipe the table clean.

拂暑(ㄈㄨˊ ㄕㄨˇ)
to expel the heat (of summer)

拂人性(ㄈㄨˊ ㄖㄣˊ ㄒㄧㄥˋ)
to go against human nature

拂耳(ㄈㄨˊ ㄦˇ)
(said of words, etc.) that grate on the ear

拂衣(ㄈㄨˊ ㄧ)
① to tidy up one's dress upon leaving ② to resign and retire

拂意(ㄈㄨˊ ㄧˋ)
to run counter to one's ideas; to feel thwarted

【拂】 1834 2. (弼) ㄅㄧˋ bih bì

1. to aid; to assist
2. to make correct or right

拂士(ㄅㄧˋ ㄕˋ)
a wise counselor; a straightforward adviser

【拇】 1835 ㄇㄨˇ muu mǔ

1. the thumb
2. the big toe

拇指(ㄇㄨˇ ㄓˇ)
the thumb

拇趾(ㄇㄨˇ ㄓˇ)
the big toe

拇戰(ㄇㄨˇ ㄓㄢˋ)
a finger guessing game (played at drinking parties)

拇印(ㄇㄨˇ ㄧㄣˋ)
a thumbprint—used in lieu of a chop in an agreement, etc.

【拈】 1836 ㄋㄧㄢ nian niān

1. to take or hold with fingers; to pick up: 那些書是信手拈來的。Those books were picked up at random.
2. to draw (lots)

拈筆(ㄋㄧㄢ ㄅㄧˇ)
to take a pen; to pick up a pen to write; to write

拈掇(ㄋㄧㄢ ㄉㄨㄛˊ)
to point out; to refer to

拈題(ㄋㄧㄢ ㄊㄧˊ)
to select a topic or theme for a piece of writing

拈弄(ㄋㄧㄢ ㄋㄨㄥˋ)
to finger and play; to fondle: 這女孩在拈弄着洋娃娃。The girl is fondling her doll.

拈花惹草(ㄋㄧㄢ ㄏㄨㄚ ㄖㄜˇ ㄘㄠˇ)
to fool around with women; to play Casanova; lewd and prurient; to have many love affairs

拈花微笑(ㄋㄧㄢ ㄏㄨㄚ ㄨㄟˊ ㄒㄧㄠˋ)
to gain a thorough understanding of esoteric Buddhist teachings

拈鬮(ㄋㄧㄢ ㄐㄧㄡ)
to draw lots

拈香(ㄋㄧㄢ ㄒㄧㄤ)
to offer incense; to burn joss sticks: 她去廟裡拈香。She went to the temple to offer incense.

拈鬚(ㄋㄧㄢ ㄒㄩ)

〔手部〕

to finger one's beard; to stroke one's beard

拈酸(ㄋㄧㄢ ㄙㄨㄢ) or 拈酸吃醋(ㄋㄧㄢ ㄙㄨㄢ ㄔ ㄘㄨˋ)
to be jealous

1837
【拆】 ㄔㄞ chai chāi (讀音 ㄔㄜˋ cheh chè)

1. to split; to break; to rip open: 他拆開一封信。He ripped open a letter.
2. to take down; to tear down (a house, etc.); to destroy; to dismantle; to take apart: 他把機器拆了。He took the machine apart.
3. to analyze; to scrutinize

拆字(ㄔㄜˋ ㄗˋ)
to take apart characters and recombine them for fortune-telling 亦作「測字」

拆字格(ㄔㄜˋ ㄗˋ ㄍㄜˊ)
a kind of poem-writing by dissecting and combining characters in a poem

拆白(ㄔㄞ ㄅㄞˊ)
to swindle

拆白黨(ㄔㄞ ㄅㄞˊ ㄉㄤˇ)
swindlers

拆房屋(ㄔㄞ ㄈㄤˊ ㄨ)
to tear or pull down a house

拆封(ㄔㄞ ㄈㄥ)
to break up a seal; to open a sealed envelope

拆東牆補西壁(ㄔㄞ ㄉㄨㄥ ㄑㄧㄤˊ ㄅㄨˇ ㄒㄧ ㄅㄧˋ)
(literally) to mend the west wall by tearing down the east wall—to try very hard to make ends meet

拆臺(ㄔㄞ ㄊㄞˊ)
(literally) to pull down the stage—to split up; to pull away a prop; to render an organization, operation, measure, etc. ineffective; to obstruct; to counteract: 別拆我的臺。Don't undermine what I am doing.

拆爛汚(ㄔㄞ ㄌㄢˋ ㄨ)
① to do a slipshod piece of work with damaging result; to do slovenly work; to be irresponsible ② to fail to keep a promise or an appointment

拆股(ㄔㄞ ㄍㄨˇ)
to dissolve a partnership

拆開(ㄔㄞ ㄎㄞ)
to take apart; to dismantle (a machine, etc.); to pull apart; to part from each other; to open (a package, letter, etc.); to separate

拆夥(ㄔㄞ ㄏㄨㄛˇ)
to break up partnership; to part company

拆壞(ㄔㄞ ㄏㄨㄞˋ)
to damage; to destroy

拆毀(ㄔㄞ ㄏㄨㄟˇ)
to damage; to destroy; to demolish

拆息(ㄔㄞ ㄒㄧˊ)
short-term interest

拆洗(ㄔㄞ ㄒㄧˇ)
to unpick (a cover, bedspread, etc.) and wash; to take apart (a machine, etc.) for cleaning

拆卸(ㄔㄞ ㄒㄧㄝˋ)
to take apart a large cargo (usually a large piece of machinery, etc.) for unloading purposes; to dismantle

拆線(ㄔㄞ ㄒㄧㄢˋ)
(medicine) to take out stitches

拆信(ㄔㄞ ㄒㄧㄣˋ)
to open a letter

拆除(ㄔㄞ ㄔㄨˊ)
to dismantle and get rid of; to pull down (an old house); to remove; to demolish: 工人們拆除了那建築物。The workers pulled the building down.

拆穿(ㄔㄞ ㄔㄨㄢ)
to expose (a secret, scheme, etc.); to see through (a mystery, secret arrangement, etc.): 他拆穿了他們的陰謀。He exposed their plot.

拆穿西洋鏡(ㄔㄞ ㄔㄨㄢ ㄒㄧ ㄧㄤˊ ㄐㄧㄥˋ)
to expose a secret arrangement, device, scheme, etc.

拆船(ㄔㄞ ㄔㄨㄢˊ)
to break up or scrap a ship; shipbreaking

拆散(ㄔㄞ ㄙㄢˋ)
to break up or split apart (a family, a married couple, etc.); to dismantle

拆散鴛鴦(ㄔㄞ ㄙㄢˋ ㄩㄢ ㄧㄤ)
(said of some happenings or incidents) to separate lovers or break up a married couple

拆閱(ㄔㄞ ㄩㄝˋ)
to open (a letter, document, etc.) and read

1838
【拉】 1. ㄌㄚ lha lā

1. to pull; to drag; to hold; to seize; to draw: 把你的椅子拉近桌子。Draw your chair nearer to the table.
2. to discharge (especially stool, urine, etc.)
3. to lengthen; to elongate: 薄暮時影子拉得長長的。The shadows lengthened at dusk.
4. to play: 他在早晨拉提琴。He plays the violin in the morning.

拉巴脫(ㄌㄚ ㄅㄚ ㄊㄨㄛ)
Rabat, capital of Morocco

拉巴拉他(ㄌㄚ ㄅㄚ ㄌㄚ ㄊㄚ)
① La Plata, a seaport in eastern Argentina ② Río de la Plata, capital of Buenos Aires Province

拉巴斯(ㄌㄚ ㄅㄚ ㄙ)
① La Paz, former capital of Bolivia in South America ② La Paz, a seaport of Mexico, on the Gulf of California

拉拔(ㄌㄚ ·ㄅㄚ)
to help (a protégé) advance

拉不斷扯不斷(ㄌㄚ ·ㄅㄨ ㄉㄨㄢˋ ㄔㄜˇ ·ㄅㄨ ·ㄉㄨㄢ)
long, drawn-out nagging; loquacious; talkative

拉不動(ㄌㄚ ·ㄅㄨ ㄉㄨㄥˋ)
unable to make it move by pulling

拉不開(ㄌㄚ ·ㄅㄨ ㄎㄞ)
cannot pull it open (as a drawer, window, etc.)

拉不下臉來(ㄌㄚ ·ㄅㄨ ㄒㄧㄚˋ ㄌㄧㄢˇ ·ㄌㄞ)
cannot do something for fear of hurting another person's feelings

拉不出來(ㄌㄚ ·ㄅㄨ ㄔㄨ ·ㄌㄞ)
① cannot pull out ② constipated

拉篷(ㄌㄚ ㄆㄥˊ)
to haul up the sail; to set sail

拉皮條(ㄌㄚ ㄆㄧˊ ㄊㄧㄠˊ)

to act as a procurer; to act as a pimp
拉票(ㄌㄚ ㄆㄧㄠˋ)
to solicit votes; to canvass
拉平(ㄌㄚ ㄆㄧㄥˊ)
to even up; to end up in a draw; to draw: 兩隊的比分拉平。The game ended in a draw.
拉買賣(ㄌㄚ ㄇㄞˇ ·ㄇㄞ)
to act as a broker; to solicit business
拉麵 or 拉麪(ㄌㄚ ㄇㄧㄢˋ)
noodles made by pulling the dough instead of cutting it by knife
拉斐爾(ㄌㄚ ㄈㄟˇ ㄦˇ)
Sanzio Raphael, 1483-1520, Italian painter
拉夫(ㄌㄚ ㄈㄨ)
to impress civilians for military service or as coolies in war
拉倒(ㄌㄚ ㄉㄠˇ)
①Never mind. 或 Let's forget it. 這件事我看還是拉倒吧! Let's forget it! ② to pull down
拉丁(ㄌㄚ ㄉㄧㄥ)
Latin
拉丁美洲(ㄌㄚ ㄉㄧㄥ ㄇㄟˇ ㄓㄡ)
Latin America
拉丁化(ㄌㄚ ㄉㄧㄥ ㄏㄨㄚˋ)
Latinized
拉丁教會(ㄌㄚ ㄉㄧㄥ ㄐㄧㄠˋ ㄏㄨㄟˋ)
the Latin Church
拉丁文(ㄌㄚ ㄉㄧㄥ ㄨㄣˊ)
Latin (language)
拉肚子(ㄌㄚ ㄉㄨˋ ·ㄗ)
to suffer from diarrhea; to have loose bowels
拉替身兒(ㄌㄚ ㄊㄧˋ ·ㄕㄜㄦ)
①(in Chinese folklore) The ghost of a person who died because of injustice has to cause the death of another person in order to achieve his own reincarnation. ② to look for someone to be the scapegoat for oneself
拉脫維亞(ㄌㄚ ㄊㄨㄛ ㄨㄟˊ ㄧㄚˇ)
Latvia
拉尿(ㄌㄚ ㄋㄧㄠˋ)
to urinate
拉弄(ㄌㄚ ·ㄋㄨㄥ)
① to pull apart ② wear and tear

拉拉扯扯(ㄌㄚ ㄌㄚ ㄔㄜˇ ㄔㄜˇ)
① to pull and drag a person, asking him to do something against his will ② to digress (in speaking)
拉拉雜雜(ㄌㄚ ㄌㄚ ㄗㄚˊ ㄗㄚˊ)or 拉雜(ㄌㄚ ㄗㄚˊ)
(said of writing, narration, etc.) not well organized and without a central theme
拉力(ㄌㄚ ㄌㄧˋ)
(physics) pulling force
拉力試驗(ㄌㄚ ㄌㄧˋ ㄕˋ ㄧㄢˋ)
(machinery) a pull test; a tension test
拉鍊(ㄌㄚ ㄌㄧㄢˋ)
a zipper; a zip fastener
拉攏(ㄌㄚ ·ㄌㄨㄥ)
① to befriend another person with a view to winning him over; to draw someone over to one's side; to draw persons with different views together: 不要受敵人拉攏。Don't get roped in by the enemy. ② to make two persons or parties become friends
拉哥斯(ㄌㄚ ㄍㄜ ㄙ)
Lagos, capital of Nigeria
拉過來(ㄌㄚ ㄍㄨㄛˋ ·ㄌㄞ)
to drag here
拉關係(ㄌㄚ ㄍㄨㄢ ·ㄒㄧ)
to seek special favor or help from somebody by elaborating on one's relationship (usually remote and indirect) with him; to try to cement ties or establish connections with an ulterior motive
拉廣告(ㄌㄚ ㄍㄨㄤˇ ㄍㄠˋ)
to solicit advertisements from business firms
拉弓(ㄌㄚ ㄍㄨㄥ)
to draw a bow
拉客(ㄌㄚ ㄎㄜˋ)
(said of a prostitute, etc.) to solicit patrons forcibly
拉開(ㄌㄚ ·ㄎㄞ)
① to pull apart (two persons fighting); to pull open (wrapping paper, drawers, etc.); to draw aside: 把門拉開。Pull the door open. ② to increase the distance between: 兩隊比分已拉開了。The gap between the scores has widened.
拉後腿(ㄌㄚ ㄏㄡˋ ㄊㄨㄟˇ)
to hold someone back; to be a drag on someone
拉胡琴兒(ㄌㄚ ㄏㄨˊ ·ㄑㄧㄜㄦ)
to play the Chinese violin (a two-string instrument)
拉壞了(ㄌㄚ ㄏㄨㄞˋ ·ㄌㄜ)
①damaged because of pulling ② weakened by diarrhea
拉回(ㄌㄚ ㄏㄨㄟˊ)
to pull back
拉家帶口(ㄌㄚ ㄐㄧㄚ ㄉㄞˋ ㄎㄡˇ)
to have a family burden
拉架(ㄌㄚ ㄐㄧㄚˋ)
to mediate in a street fight; to stop a brawl by separating the disputants
拉交情(ㄌㄚ ㄐㄧㄠ ㄑㄧㄥˊ)
to show friendship to someone (usually with a selfish motive or having an ax to grind); to try to seek the friendship of influential persons
拉角(ㄌㄚ ㄐㄧㄠˇ)
to hire employees, actors, actresses, etc. from a rivaling company by offering them high pay, high positions or other incentives
拉緊(ㄌㄚ ㄐㄧㄣˇ)
① to draw or pull tight ② to hang on firmly
拉近(ㄌㄚ ㄐㄧㄣˋ)
to draw close or near
拉鋸(ㄌㄚ ㄐㄩˋ)
① to cut with a saw ② to be locked in a seesaw struggle
拉鋸戰(ㄌㄚ ㄐㄩˋ ㄓㄢˋ)
a seesaw battle; stalemate
拉起(ㄌㄚ ㄑㄧˇ)
to pull up; to draw back
拉縴(ㄌㄚ ㄑㄧㄢˋ)
① to tow a boat against the current in a swift stream from the bank ② to act as a go-between
拉稀(ㄌㄚ ㄒㄧ)
to suffer from diarrhea; to have loose bowels
拉下臉來(ㄌㄚ ㄒㄧㄚˋ ㄌㄧㄢˇ ·ㄌㄞ)
to make a long face; to look mean
拉下水(ㄌㄚ ㄒㄧㄚˋ ㄕㄨㄟˇ)
to drag someone into the

mire; to make an accomplice of someone; to corrupt someone

拉賬(ㄌㄚ ㄓㄤˋ)
to run into debt

拉主顧(ㄌㄚ ㄓㄨˇ ˙ㄍㄨ)
to attract or solicit customers

拉住(ㄌㄚ ㄓㄨˋ)
to hold on firmly: 我們過街時要拉住我的手。Hold on to my hand tightly while we cross the street.

拉持(ㄌㄚ ˙ㄔ)
(dialect) to bring someone up

拉車(ㄌㄚ ㄔㄜ)
to pull or haul a cart (or ricksha)

拉車的(ㄌㄚ ㄔㄜ ˙ㄉㄜ)
a ricksha puller

拉扯(ㄌㄚ ㄔㄜˇ)
①to pull and drag ②to implicate or involve ③to talk a lot outside of one's topic; to indulge in aimless talks

拉長(ㄌㄚ ㄔㄤˊ)
①to prolong (business, voice, etc.) ②to draw

拉出去(ㄌㄚ ㄔㄨ ˙ㄑㄩ)
to pull out; to drag out

拉屎(ㄌㄚ ㄕˇ)
to go to stool; to empty the bowels; to move one's bowels

拉舌頭(ㄌㄚ ㄕㄜˊ ˙ㄊㄡ)
to gossip; to slander

拉手(ㄌㄚ ㄕㄡˇ)
①to hold another's hands ②to pull by the hand ③to join hands; to work together ④a knob

拉手兒(ㄌㄚ ㄕㄡˇㄦ)
①to hold hands; to shake hands ②to collaborate in a scheme, conspiracy, etc.

拉伸(ㄌㄚ ㄕㄣ)
(textile) drawing; stretch

拉上補下(ㄌㄚ ㄕㄤˋ ㄅㄨˇ ㄒㄧㄚˋ)
to even things up

拉生意(ㄌㄚ ㄕㄥ ˙ㄧ)
to solicit business; to tout

拉雜(ㄌㄚ ㄗㄚˊ)
①rambling; jumbled; ill-organized: 那篇文章寫得太拉雜。That article is very badly organized. ②(said of a room, etc.) untidy; confused

拉絲(ㄌㄚ ㄙ)
①(metallurgy) wiredrawing: 拉絲機a wiredrawing machine ②(said of action) to hesitate ③(said of speech) long-winded

拉斯維加斯(ㄌㄚ ㄙ ㄨㄟˊ ㄐㄧㄚ ㄙ)
Las Vegas, a gambling resort in New Mexico, U.S.A.

拉撒(ㄌㄚ ㄙㄚ)or 拉颯(ㄌㄚ ㄙㄚˋ)
refuse; garbage 亦作「垃圾」

拉薩(ㄌㄚ ㄙㄚˋ)
Lhasa, capital of Tibet

拉曳(ㄌㄚ ㄧˋ)
to pull; to drag

拉洋片(ㄌㄚ ㄧㄤˊ ㄆㄧㄢ)
①a show of still pictures (through a magnifying glass, the viewer looks at pictures which are changed at regular intervals by pulling a rope) ②to talk big

拉網(ㄌㄚ ㄨㄤˇ)
to pull a net

拉運(ㄌㄚ ㄩㄣˋ)
to pull a cart; to transport

【拉】 1838
2. ㄌㄚˊ la lá

參看「拉遢」

拉遢(ㄌㄚˊ ˙ㄊㄚ)
dirty; untidy

【拊】 1839
ㄈㄨˇ fuu fǔ

1. to touch with hand lightly or tenderly; to pat
2. to indulge
3. to slap; to tap
4. the handle of a vessel or utensil

拊背扼喉(ㄈㄨˇ ㄅㄟˋ ㄜˋ ㄏㄡˊ)
to occupy a strategic or advantageous position

拊髀(ㄈㄨˇ ㄅㄧˋ)
to slap one's own buttocks in excitement or despair

拊髀興歎(ㄈㄨˇ ㄅㄧˋ ㄒㄧㄥ ㄊㄢˋ)
to lament one's own inability to resume work

拊心(ㄈㄨˇ ㄒㄧㄣ)or 拊膺(ㄈㄨˇ ㄧㄥ)
to slap one's chest—an expression of distress or indignation

拊循(ㄈㄨˇ ㄒㄩㄣˊ)
to comfort; to soothe

拊掌(ㄈㄨˇ ㄓㄤˇ)or 拊手(ㄈㄨˇ ㄕㄡˇ)
to clap hands: 他們拊掌大笑。They clapped hands and laughed.

【拋】 1840
(抛) ㄆㄠ pau pāo

1. to throw; to cast; to hurl: 他把球拋給我。He threw the ball to me.
2. to abandon; to reject; to give up; to throw away
3. to cast aside; to leave behind

拋盤(ㄆㄠ ㄆㄢˊ)
(stock market) to buy or sell futures

拋撇(ㄆㄠ ㄆㄧㄝ)
to abandon; to throw away

拋錨(ㄆㄠ ㄇㄠˊ)
①to cast anchor ②(said of a car) to develop engine trouble and become stuck midway; to break down

拋頭露面(ㄆㄠ ㄊㄡˊ ㄌㄨˋ ㄇㄧㄢˋ)
(said of women in old China) to go out and be seen in public; to hold a job which involves a lot of exposure to the public (considered unbecoming to a decent woman)

拋體運動(ㄆㄠ ㄊㄧˇ ㄩㄣˋ ㄉㄨㄥˋ)
projectile movement

拋戈棄甲(ㄆㄠ ㄍㄜ ㄑㄧˋ ㄐㄧㄚˇ)
to throw away weapons and armor—to be routed

拋空(ㄆㄠ ㄎㄨㄥ)
(stock market) to sell short

拋荒(ㄆㄠ ㄏㄨㄤ)
to lay idle; to become rusty because of lack of practice

拋棄(ㄆㄠ ㄑㄧˋ)or 拋捨(ㄆㄠ ㄕㄜˇ)
to abandon; to throw away; to give up: 我們決不拋棄眞正的朋友。We shall never give up our true friends.

拋繡球(ㄆㄠ ㄒㄧㄡˋ ㄑㄧㄡˊ)or 拋綵球(ㄆㄠ ㄘㄞˇ ㄑㄧㄡˊ)
to throw an embroidered ball—to choose a husband

拋擲(ㄆㄠ ㄓˋ)
①to cast; to throw; to hurl: 獵人向一野獸拋擲標槍。The hunter hurled a spear at a wild animal. ②to throw away; to abandon

拋磚引玉(ㄆㄠ ㄓㄨㄢ ㄧㄣˇ ㄩˋ)
(literally) to throw a brick

and to get a piece of jade in return—a polite term in requesting an exchange of literary works or in making a donation to a worthy cause in the hope others may follow suit

拋出(ㄆㄠ ㄔㄨ)
①to throw out; to cast away ②(especially in the stock market) to sell short; to sell

拋射(ㄆㄠ ㄕㄜˋ)
to project

拋售(ㄆㄠ ㄕㄡˋ)
to dump large stocks of merchandise in the market in order to force down prices and relieve shortage of supply

拋梭(ㄆㄠ ㄙㄨㄛ)
to throw the shuttle

拋物線(ㄆㄠ ㄨˋ ㄒㄧㄢˋ)
a parabola

【拌】 1841
1. ㄅㄢˋ bann bàn
to mix: 你會拌沙拉嗎? Can you mix salad?

拌麵(ㄅㄢˋ ㄇㄧㄢˋ)
noodles served with soy sauce, sesame butter, etc.

拌和(ㄅㄢˋ ㄏㄨㄛˋ)
to mix properly; to blend: 油和水不能拌和在一起。Oil and water do not blend.

拌和車(ㄅㄢˋ ㄏㄨㄛˋ ㄔㄜ)
a truck mixer 亦作「混凝土拌和車」

拌嘴(ㄅㄢˋ ㄗㄨㄟˇ)
to wrangle; to quarrel; to bicker

拌勻(ㄅㄢˋ ㄩㄣˊ)
to mix evenly or properly

【拌】 1841
2. ㄆㄢˋ pann pàn
to throw away; to abandon

拌命(ㄆㄢˋ ㄇㄧㄥˋ)
to risk one's life

拌石(ㄆㄢˋ ㄕˊ)
to throw a stone

【拐】 1842
ㄍㄨㄞˇ goai guǎi
1. to kidnap; to abduct: 這孩子昨天被拐走了。The child was abducted yesterday.
2. to turn or change direction (in walking, driving, etc.): 路在此處拐向北邊。The road turns to the north here.
3. to swindle
4. same as 柺—a staff for an old person; a cane

拐脖兒(ㄍㄨㄞˇ ㄅㄛˊㄦ)
an elbow (of a stovepipe)

拐騙(ㄍㄨㄞˇ ㄆㄧㄢˋ)or 拐誘(ㄍㄨㄞˇ ㄧㄡˋ)
①to abduct; to kidnap ②to swindle

拐賣(ㄍㄨㄞˇ ㄇㄞˋ)
to abduct or kidnap and sell; to engage in white slavery

拐販(ㄍㄨㄞˇ ㄈㄢˋ)
to deal in white slavery

拐帶(ㄍㄨㄞˇ ㄉㄞˋ)
to abduct; to kidnap

拐逃(ㄍㄨㄞˇ ㄊㄠˊ)
to abscond with money or valuables, or both

拐過去(ㄍㄨㄞˇ ㄍㄨㄛˋ ·ㄑㄩ)
to make a turn; to turn the corner

拐孩子(ㄍㄨㄞˇ ㄏㄞˊ ·ㄗ)
to kidnap a child

拐回來(ㄍㄨㄞˇ ㄏㄨㄟˊ ·ㄌㄞ)
①to turn back ②to take back things in confusion illegally (as in a busy store, etc.); to filch ③to give something to another and then take it back

拐角(兒)(ㄍㄨㄞˇ ㄐㄧㄠˇ (ㄦ))
①to turn the corner ②at the corner: 這房屋在大街的拐角上。The building is located at the corner of the main street.

拐肘(ㄍㄨㄞˇ ㄓㄡˇ)
the elbow

拐杖(ㄍㄨㄞˇ ㄓㄤˋ)
a staff; a stick; crutches: 他拿著拐杖走路。He walks with the help of a stick.

拐子(ㄍㄨㄞˇ ·ㄗ)
a kidnapper; a swindler; an abductor

拐子馬(ㄍㄨㄞˇ ·ㄗ ㄇㄚˇ)
(Sung Dynasty) a tactical horse-formation used by a famous barbarian general, Chin Wu-chu (金兀朮), who linked three horses together in a row in mounting a charge on the battlefield

拐彎兒(ㄍㄨㄞˇ ㄨㄢㄦ)
①to turn the corner: 拐彎兒時要慢行。Slow down when turning a corner. ②at the corner: 請在大街拐彎兒處與我碰面。Meet me at the corner of the street.

拐彎抹角兒(ㄍㄨㄞˇ ㄨㄢ ㄇㄛˋ ㄐㄧㄠˇㄦ)
①to proceed along a zigzag road ②a roundabout way of talking; circumlocution; to beat around the bush: 說話要直截了當，不要拐彎抹角兒。Get to the point. Don't beat about the bush.

【拑】 1843
ㄑㄧㄢˊ chyan qián
to hold; to grasp

拑釘子(ㄑㄧㄢˊ ㄉㄧㄥ ·ㄗ)
to pull out a nail

拑口(ㄑㄧㄢˊ ㄎㄡˇ)
to hold the tongue

拑住他(ㄑㄧㄢˊ ㄓㄨˋ ㄊㄚ)
Hold him tight!

【拍】 1844
ㄆㄞ pai pāi
(讀音 ㄆㄛ poh pò)
1. to strike with the hand; to slap; to clap; to pat; to swat: 他拍著她的肩膀。He clapped her on the shoulder.
2. the time or beat of a piece of music: 這首歌是幾拍的? What time is the song in?
3. to fawn; to flatter: 他是在拍你的馬屁。He is flattering you.

拍巴掌(ㄆㄞ ㄅㄚ ·ㄓㄤ)or 拍掌(ㄆㄞ ㄓㄤˇ)
to clap hands

拍板(ㄆㄞ ㄅㄢˇ)
①to beat time ②castanets

拍髀(ㄆㄞ ㄅㄧˋ)
①to pat the thigh ②a sword worn at one's waist

拍片(ㄆㄞ ㄆㄧㄢˋ)
to shoot a film

拍馬屁(ㄆㄞ ㄇㄚˇ ㄆㄧˋ)or 拍馬(ㄆㄞ ㄇㄚˇ)
to flatter; to soft-soap; to claw (or curry) favor

拍賣(ㄆㄞ ㄇㄞˋ)
to auction off; an auction

拍賣者(ㄆㄞ ㄇㄞˋ ㄓㄜˇ)
an auctioneer

拍門(ㄆㄞ ㄇㄣˊ)
to knock or strike at the

door

拍打(ㄆㄞ ˙ㄉㄚ)
to pat; to slap or tap lightly: 他拍打身上的雪。He patted the snow off his clothes.

拍電(ㄆㄞ ㄉㄧㄢˋ)or 拍發電報(ㄆㄞ ㄈㄚ ㄉㄧㄢˋ ㄅㄠˋ)
to cable; to send a telegram

拍電影(ㄆㄞ ㄉㄧㄢˋ ㄧㄥˇ)
to shoot a film; to photograph with a movie camera

拍擊(ㄆㄞ ㄐㄧˊ)
to strike; to slap: 他以手拍擊膝蓋。He struck his knee with his hand.

拍肩膀(ㄆㄞ ㄐㄧㄢ ㄅㄤˇ)
to pat on the shoulder

拍球(ㄆㄞ ㄑㄧㄡˊ)
to bounce a ball; to pat a ball

拍胸脯(ㄆㄞ ㄒㄩㄥ ㄆㄨˊ)
to pat one's chest (to show confidence, defiance, acceptance of a challenge or responsibility, etc.)

拍紙簿(ㄆㄞ ㄓˇ ㄅㄨˋ)
a writing pad

拍照(ㄆㄞ ㄓㄠˋ)
to take a picture or photo: 我們把它拍照下來。Let's take a picture of it.

拍桌子(ㄆㄞ ㄓㄨㄛ ˙ㄗ)
to pound the table—a gesture of anger, surprise or admiration

拍攝(ㄆㄞ ㄕㄜˋ)
to take (a picture); to shoot: 他在拍攝一張照片。He is taking a photo.

拍手(ㄆㄞ ㄕㄡˇ)
to clap hands

拍手喝采(ㄆㄞ ㄕㄡˇ ㄏㄜˋ ㄘㄞˇ)
to clap hands and shout "Bravo!"

拍子(ㄆㄞ ˙ㄗ)
①(music) time; rhythm; a beat: 打拍子 to beat time ② a fly swatter ③a bat; a racket: 網球拍子 a tennis racket

拍子記號(ㄆㄞ ˙ㄗ ㄐㄧˋ ㄏㄠˋ)
(music) a time signature 亦作「拍號」

拍蒼蠅(ㄆㄞ ㄘㄤ ㄧㄥˊ)
to swat a fly

拍案(ㄆㄞ ㄢˋ)
to pound the table—a gesture of anger or surprise

拍案叫絕(ㄆㄞ ㄢˋ ㄐㄧㄠˋ ㄐㄩㄝˊ)
to show extreme surprise or admiration by pounding the table

拍案驚奇(ㄆㄞ ㄢˋ ㄐㄧㄥ ㄑㄧˊ)
name of a collection of short stories edited in the Ming Dynasty

拍外景(ㄆㄞ ㄨㄞˋ ㄐㄧㄥˇ)
(cinema) to be on location

【拎】 1845
ㄌㄧㄥ lhing ling

to haul; to take; to carry; to lift: 她拎著菜籃上市場。She carried a basket in her hand to the market.

拎他一把(ㄌㄧㄥ ㄊㄚ ㄧˋ ㄅㄚˇ)
to lend him a helping hand 或 Give him a hand.

拎起一桶水(ㄌㄧㄥ ㄑㄧˇ ㄧˋ ㄊㄨㄥˇ ㄕㄨㄟˇ)
to haul a bucket of water; to draw a bucket of water

【拒】 1846
ㄐㄩˋ jiuh jiù

1. to defend; to ward off; to resist: 他們擋拒敵人的攻擊。They warded off the enemy's attack.
2. to refuse; to reject: 他拒絕同我一起去。He refused to go with me.

拒捕(ㄐㄩˋ ㄅㄨˇ)
to resist arrest; to resist being arrested

拒馬(ㄐㄩˋ ㄇㄚˇ)
an abatis

拒付(ㄐㄩˋ ㄈㄨˋ)
to refuse to pay; to dishonor (a check)

拒敵(ㄐㄩˋ ㄉㄧˊ)
to resist the enemy; to keep the enemy at bay; to ward off or defend against the enemy

拒繳(ㄐㄩˋ ㄐㄧㄠˇ)
to refuse to pay (taxes or money one is obliged to pay)

拒諫飾非(ㄐㄩˋ ㄐㄧㄢˋ ㄕˋ ㄈㄟ)
to refuse to listen to counsels and cover up one's faults

拒絕(ㄐㄩˋ ㄐㄩㄝˊ)or 拒卻(ㄐㄩˋ ㄑㄩㄝˋ)
to refuse; to reject; to turn down; a refusal: 他拒絕我的幫助。He refused my offer of help.

拒絕來往(ㄐㄩˋ ㄐㄩㄝˊ ㄌㄞˊ ㄨㄤˇ)
to sever communications, intercourse or relations

拒絕往來戶(ㄐㄩˋ ㄐㄩㄝˊ ㄨㄤˇ ㄌㄞˊ ㄏㄨˋ)
a client with very poor credit standing and thus denied the banking service; a dishonored account

拒性(ㄐㄩˋ ㄒㄧㄥˋ)
(physics) impenetrability

拒守(ㄐㄩˋ ㄕㄡˇ)
to guard; to defend (a position, territory, etc.)

拒霜(ㄐㄩˋ ㄕㄨㄤ)
(botany) a hibiscus 亦作「芙蓉」

拒人於千里之外(ㄐㄩˋ ㄖㄣˊ ㄩˊ ㄑㄧㄢ ㄌㄧˇ ㄓ ㄨㄞˋ)
(literally) to keep people a thousand miles away — extremely indifferent and cool

【拓】 1847
1. ㄊㄨㄛˋ tuoh tuò

1. to expand; to aggrandize; to open up (new frontiers, etc.); to develop: 我們應開拓邊遠地區。We should open up the frontier regions.
2. to push with hands

拓拔(ㄊㄨㄛˋ ㄅㄚˊ)
the Toba family which founded the Northern Wei Dynasty in the 4th century

拓邊(ㄊㄨㄛˋ ㄅㄧㄢ)or 拓境(ㄊㄨㄛˋ ㄐㄧㄥˋ)
to open up borderlands; to open up new frontiers

拓地(ㄊㄨㄛˋ ㄉㄧˋ)or 拓土(ㄊㄨㄛˋ ㄊㄨˇ)
to expand the territory (of a nation); territorial expansion

拓提(ㄊㄨㄛˋ ㄊㄧˊ)
a temple or monastery

拓落(ㄊㄨㄛˋ ㄌㄨㄛˋ)
① mortified and alone ② spacious

拓荒(ㄊㄨㄛˋ ㄏㄨㄤ)
to open up virgin soil; to reclaim a barren tract of land

拓殖(ㄊㄨㄛˋ ㄓˊ)
to open up new land for settlement

拓展(ㄊㄨㄛˋ ㄓㄢˇ)

to expand (business, etc.); to realize (great ambitions, etc.); to expand and develop: 他正努力拓展業務。He is trying to expand his business.

【拓】 1847
2. (搨) ㄊㄚˋ tah tà
to copy characters from an ancient tablet or tomb by rubbing over a paper placed on its surface; to make rubbings of inscriptions: 這幅碑帖拓得甚好。This rubbing of inscription is well made.

拓本(ㄊㄚˋ ㄅㄣˇ)
a stone rubbing, especially of the ancient inscription; a book of rubbing

【拔】 1848
ㄅㄚˊ bar bá
1. to pull out; to uproot: 風將一些樹連根拔起。The wind uprooted some trees.
2. to promote (another to a higher position, etc.): 拔擢俊才 to select and promote the talents
3. to stand out; outstanding; remarkable
4. to attack and take (a city); to capture
5. as in 海拔—elevation; above sea level: 海拔五千英尺 5,000 feet above sea level

拔本塞原(ㄅㄚˊ ㄅㄣˇ ㄙㄜˋ ㄩㄢˊ)
to despise the source; to abandon the origin

拔步(ㄅㄚˊ ㄅㄨˋ)or 拔脚(ㄅㄚˊ ㄐㄧㄠˇ)
to walk with big and quick strides; to take to one's heels

拔不出腿來(ㄅㄚˊ ·ㄅㄨ ㄔㄨ ㄊㄨㄟˇ ㄌㄞˊ)
cannot get away (from something); cannot get rid of (something); can not get off from pressing duties

拔毛(ㄅㄚˊ ㄇㄠˊ)
to pluck out hairs

拔茅連茹 (ㄅㄚˊ ㄇㄠˊ ㄌㄧㄢˊ ㄖㄨˊ)
(originally) from the *Book of Changes:* "The good will attract people of their own kind."—(figuratively) Once a capable man is recruited by the emperor for a high office, his talented friends will flock to the imperial court without being invited.

拔苗助長(ㄅㄚˊ ㄇㄧㄠˊ ㄓㄨˋ ㄓㄤˇ)
to try to help the seedlings grow by pulling them upward—(figuratively) to spoil things by excessive enthusiasm 亦作「揠苗助長」

拔得頭籌(ㄅㄚˊ ㄉㄜˊ ㄊㄡˊ ㄔㄡˊ)
to become the first to do something

拔刀相助(ㄅㄚˊ ㄉㄠ ㄒㄧㄤ ㄓㄨˋ)
to help another (usually a stranger) for the sake of justice

拔地擎天(ㄅㄚˊ ㄉㄧˋ ㄑㄧㄥˊ ㄊㄧㄢ)
remarkable and outstanding (heroes, etc.)

拔釘鎚(ㄅㄚˊ ㄉㄧㄥ ㄔㄨㄟˊ)
a claw hammer

拔都(ㄅㄚˊ ㄉㄨ)
①(Mongolian) bravery; courage ②name of a general in the Yüan (Mongol) Dynasty

拔腿(ㄅㄚˊ ㄊㄨㄟˇ)
to take to one's heels

拔根(ㄅㄚˊ ㄍㄣ)
to uproot

拔罐子(ㄅㄚˊ ㄍㄨㄢˋ ·ㄗ)
(Chinese medicine) cupping

拔貢(ㄅㄚˊ ㄍㄨㄥˋ)
(Ching Dynasty) outstanding young scholars selected to the capital for a civil service examination once every 12 years with the top ones kept for government assignments

拔河(ㄅㄚˊ ㄏㄜˊ)
a tug of war

拔虎鬚(ㄅㄚˊ ㄏㄨˇ ㄒㄩ)
(literally) to pluck the tiger's hair—too rash or ignorant to realize the danger of offending a powerful personage

拔尖兒(ㄅㄚˊ ㄐㄧㄚㄦ)
top-notch; to come off first; to get the best position 亦作「抓尖兒」: 他的成績是拔尖兒的。He's a top-notch student.

拔劍(ㄅㄚˊ ㄐㄧㄢˋ)
to draw a sword; to whip out a sword

拔薦(ㄅㄚˊ ㄐㄧㄢˋ)
to recommend for a post

拔取(ㄅㄚˊ ㄑㄩˇ)
to take or capture (a city, etc.)

拔去眼中釘(ㄅㄚˊ ㄑㄩˋ ㄧㄢˇ ㄓㄨㄥ ㄉㄧㄥ)
(literally) to pull out the sting in one's eye—(figuratively) to remove a person one hates most

拔羣(ㄅㄚˊ ㄑㄩㄣˊ)or 拔萃(ㄅㄚˊ ㄘㄨㄟˋ)
(said of persons) to stand out; outstanding: 他表現得出類拔萃。He stands out among his fellows.

拔薤(ㄅㄚˊ ㄒㄧㄝˋ)
to eliminate bullies

拔幟易幟(ㄅㄚˊ ㄓˋ ㄧˋ ㄓˋ)
to occupy the enemy camp or position; to triumph by force of arms

拔著短籌(ㄅㄚˊ ·ㄓㄜ ㄉㄨㄢˇ ㄔㄡˊ)
to die young

拔寨(ㄅㄚˊ ㄓㄞˋ)or 拔營(ㄅㄚˊ ㄧㄥˊ)
to break up a camp

拔擢(ㄅㄚˊ ㄓㄨㄛˊ)
to promote; to raise: 拔擢某人爲經理 to raise a man to manager

拔城(ㄅㄚˊ ㄔㄥˊ)
to take or capture a city

拔出來(ㄅㄚˊ ㄔㄨ ·ㄌㄞ)
to pull out; to draw out; to extract

拔除(ㄅㄚˊ ㄔㄨˊ)
to uproot; to eradicate; to remove; to pluck; to wipe out: 他拔除園中野草。He is plucking up weeds from the garden.

拔十得五(ㄅㄚˊ ㄕˊ ㄉㄜˊ ㄨˇ)
to get only half of what one asked for

拔舌地獄(ㄅㄚˊ ㄕㄜˊ ㄉㄧˋ ㄩˋ)
(Buddhism) the hell where the tongue is pulled out, as a punishment for an oral sin

拔身(ㄅㄚˊ ㄕㄣ)
to get away (from pressing duties); to escape

拔樹尋根(ㄅㄚˊ ㄕㄨˋ ㄒㄩㄣˊ ㄍㄣ)
to go to the very source of something

拔草(ㄅㄚˊ ㄘㄠˇ)
to weed: 他們正在園裡拔草。They are weeding the garden.

拔俗(ㄅㄚˊ ㄙㄨˊ)
to rise far above the com-

〔手部〕

mon lot; outstanding and unique

拔牙(ㄅㄚˊ ㄧㄚˊ)
to extract a tooth

拔尤(ㄅㄚˊ ㄧㄡˊ)
to promote men of outstanding ability

拔營(ㄅㄚˊ ㄧㄥˊ)
to pull up stakes and roll up tents (at the end of a camporee, bivouac, etc.); to strike camp

【拗】 1849
1. ㄠˇ ao ǎo

to bend or twist so as to break

拗折(ㄠˇ ㄓㄜˊ) or 拗斷(ㄠˇ ㄉㄨㄢˋ)
to break by twisting

【拗】 1849
2. ㄠˋ aw ào
(又讀 ㄧㄠˋ yaw yào)
(語音 ㄋㄧㄡˋ niow niù)

1. obstinate; stubborn; unmanageable; recalcitrant
2. hard to pronounce; awkward-sounding

拗不過(ㄋㄧㄡˋ ·ㄅㄨ ㄍㄨㄛˋ)
to be unable to dissuade; to fail to talk someone out of doing something

拗性(ㄋㄧㄡˋ ㄒㄧㄥˋ)
obstinacy; stubbornness; recalcitrance 亦作「執拗」

拗彆(ㄠˋ ·ㄅㄧㄝ)
recalcitrant; stubbornly defiant; obstinate

拗體詩(ㄠˋ ㄊㄧˇ ㄕ)
poems that do not conform to the rule of conventional versification

拗強(ㄠˋ ㄐㄧㄤˋ)
obstinate and pigheaded; recalcitrant

拗相公(ㄠˋ ㄒㄧㄤˋ ·ㄍㄨㄥ)
"The Obstinate Lord", a sobriquet given to Wang An-shih (王安石)

拗口(ㄧㄠˋ ㄎㄡˇ)
to twist the tongue; tongue-twisting

拗口令(ㄧㄠˋ ㄎㄡˇ ㄌㄧㄥˋ)
a tongue twister 亦作「繞口令」

【拗】 1849
3. ㄩˋ yuh yù

to restrain; to repress; to curb; to suppress

【拖】 1850
(拕) ㄊㄨㄛ tuo tuō

1. to drag along, after or out: 他拖着我陪他去看電影。He dragged me along with him to a movie.
2. to procrastinate; to drag out; to delay: 時候已晚，不要拖了。It's getting late; don't delay.
3. to involve; to implicate

拖把(ㄊㄨㄛ ·ㄅㄚ)
a mop

拖帶(ㄊㄨㄛ ㄉㄞˋ)
①to drag along ② to involve; to implicate (a whole family, etc.)

拖刀計(ㄊㄨㄛ ㄉㄠ ㄐㄧˋ)
a delaying tactic

拖宕(ㄊㄨㄛ ㄉㄤˋ)
to procrastinate; to delay

拖沓(ㄊㄨㄛ ㄊㄚˋ)
to do things in a muddled manner; confused, indecisive and sloppy

拖泥帶水(ㄊㄨㄛ ㄋㄧˊ ㄉㄞˋ ㄕㄨㄟˇ)
(literally) to drag through mud and water—confused, sloppy and muddled (style of writing or acting); not snappy or clean-cut; unable to make a decision

拖拉(ㄊㄨㄛ ㄌㄚ)
①dilatory: 他辦事總是拖拉。He is always dilatory in doing things. ② to put off: 他工作從不拖拉。He never puts off his work.

拖累(ㄊㄨㄛ ㄌㄟˋ)
①to involve or implicate; to suffer because of another's fault ② a drag; a burden: 子女過多對父母是個拖累。Too many children are a burden to their parents.

拖露(ㄊㄨㄛ ㄌㄡˋ)
to hang down

拖輪(ㄊㄨㄛ ㄌㄨㄣˊ)
a tugboat; a tug; a towboat

拖垮(ㄊㄨㄛ ㄎㄨㄚˇ)
to be worn down; to be bled white or weakened

拖後腿(ㄊㄨㄛ ㄏㄡˋ ㄊㄨㄟˇ)
to hold back or hinder; to obstruct

拖家帶眷(ㄊㄨㄛ ㄐㄧㄚ ㄉㄞˋ ㄐㄩㄢˋ)
to have a family burden

拖欠(ㄊㄨㄛ ㄑㄧㄢˋ)
to owe and delay payment for a long time; arrears

拖鞋(ㄊㄨㄛ ㄒㄧㄝˊ)
slippers: 他買了一雙新拖鞋。He bought a new pair of slippers.

拖車(ㄊㄨㄛ ㄔㄜ)
a trailer

拖長(ㄊㄨㄛ ㄔㄤˊ)
① to lengthen ② to drag on (or out): 他以長篇演講拖長了開會時間。He dragged out a meeting with long speeches.

拖船(ㄊㄨㄛ ㄔㄨㄢˊ)
a tugboat

拖牀(ㄊㄨㄛ ㄔㄨㄤˊ)
to procrastinate in getting up; reluctant to get up

拖屍(ㄊㄨㄛ ㄕ)
to "toss"—a joke played upon new students in English and American colleges and schools

拖時間(ㄊㄨㄛ ㄕˊ ㄐㄧㄢ)
to stall for time; to delay

拖人下水(ㄊㄨㄛ ㄖㄣˊ ㄒㄧㄚˋ ㄕㄨㄟˇ)
to implicate another intentionally; to involve others in an illegal or unethical undertaking

拖曳(ㄊㄨㄛ ㄧˋ)
to drag; to pull; to tow: 這貨車容易拖曳。The wagon draws easily. 那遊艇是用拖船拖曳。The barge was tugged by a tugboat.

拖曳機(ㄊㄨㄛ ㄧˋ ㄐㄧ)
a tractor

拖油瓶(ㄊㄨㄛ ㄧㄡˊ ㄆㄧㄥˊ)
a woman's children by previous marriage

拖延(ㄊㄨㄛ ㄧㄢˊ)
to procrastinate; to delay; to postpone; to drag on: 他拖延歸期。He procrastinated his return.

拖網(ㄊㄨㄛ ㄨㄤˇ)
a trawl; a dragnet; a trawl net

【拙】 1851
ㄓㄨㄛˊ jwo zhuó

1. stupid; crude; poor (works, etc.); slow and clumsy: 他拙於言詞。He is clumsy in expressing himself.

2. a conventional term referring to oneself
拙笨(ㄓㄨㄛˊ ㄅㄣˋ)
stupid; clumsy: 他是個拙笨的工人。He is a clumsy workman.
拙筆(ㄓㄨㄛˊ ㄅㄧˇ)
my poor writing; my clumsy pen (used in polite conversation)
拙夫(ㄓㄨㄛˊ ㄈㄨ)
a clumsy husband; my clumsy husband (used in polite conversation)
拙劣(ㄓㄨㄛˊ ㄌㄧㄝˋ)
clumsy and inferior: 他們賣手工拙劣的貨品。They sell goods of inferior workmanship.
拙稿(ㄓㄨㄛˊ ㄍㄠˇ)
my poor manuscript, article, or writing (used in polite conversation)
拙工(ㄓㄨㄛˊ ㄍㄨㄥ)
a poor craftsman; an incompetent worker
拙宦(ㄓㄨㄛˊ ㄏㄨㄢˋ)
an official who does not know how to exert his influence to make extra money
拙計(ㄓㄨㄛˊ ㄐㄧˋ)
a foolish scheme; my stupid plan (used in polite conversation)
拙見(ㄓㄨㄛˊ ㄐㄧㄢˋ)
my humble idea or view (used in polite conversation): 依拙見，他不日可癒。In my opinion, he will recover soon.
拙荆(ㄓㄨㄛˊ ㄐㄧㄥ)or 拙妻(ㄓㄨㄛˊ ㄑㄧ)
my stupid wife (used in polite conversation)
拙性(ㄓㄨㄛˊ ㄒㄧㄥˋ)
stupidity; slow-witted; clumsy
拙著(ㄓㄨㄛˊ ㄓㄨˋ)or 拙作(ㄓㄨㄛˊ ㄗㄨㄛˋ)
my (poor) writing; my clumsy work (used in polite conversation)
拙實(ㄓㄨㄛˊ ㄕˊ)
raw and sturdy; big and strong; solidly built
拙嘴笨腮(ㄓㄨㄛˊ ㄗㄨㄟˇ ㄅㄣˋ ㄙㄞ)or 拙嘴笨舌(ㄓㄨㄛˊ ㄗㄨㄟˇ ㄅㄣˋ ㄕㄜˊ)
slow of tongue and clumsy in utterance

【拘】 1852
ㄐㄩ jiu jū
1. to apprehend; to detain; to arrest
2. inflexible; to adhere rigidly to (conventions, etc.)
3. confined; restricted; not free; restrained: 他是無拘無束的。He was unrestrained.
拘捕(ㄐㄩ ㄅㄨˇ)
to detain or arrest (a suspect); to take in: 他因偷竊而被拘捕。He was arrested for theft.
拘票(ㄐㄩ ㄆㄧㄠˋ)
a warrant for arrest
拘縻(ㄐㄩ ㄇㄧˊ)
to feel restricted; to have one's hands tied; straitjacketed
拘提(ㄐㄩ ㄊㄧ)
(law) to summon a defendant by forcible means for a court trial
拘拿(ㄐㄩ ㄋㄚˊ)
to arrest: 警察正要拘拿那個兇手。The police are going to arrest the murderer.
拘泥(ㄐㄩ ㄋㄧˋ)or 拘板(ㄐㄩ ㄅㄢˇ)
to be tied down by conventions; to adhere to laws and rules, etc.; to the very letter; to go strictly by the book
拘泥不通(ㄐㄩ ㄋㄧˋ ㄅㄨˋ ㄊㄨㄥ)
slow-witted, stubborn and stupid
拘泥小節(ㄐㄩ ㄋㄧˋ ㄒㄧㄠˇ ㄐㄧㄝˊ)
to be tied down by trifles or petty conventions; to be punctilious
拘女(ㄐㄩ ㄋㄩˇ)
girls who were employed by the imperial household and were not allowed to marry
拘禮(ㄐㄩ ㄌㄧˇ)
strict adherence to social etiquette
拘留(ㄐㄩ ㄌㄧㄡˊ)or 拘繫(ㄐㄩ ㄒㄧˋ)
to detain; detention: 他已遭拘留。He is under arrest.
拘留所(ㄐㄩ ㄌㄧㄡˊ ㄙㄨㄛˇ)
a detention house to keep criminal suspects pending a court decision
拘攣(ㄐㄩ ㄌㄩㄢˊ)
① involuntary twitchings of the limbs; cramps; spasms ② restrained and restricted
拘忌(ㄐㄩ ㄐㄧˋ)
to be restricted by cares and worries; restrained by superstitions
拘介(ㄐㄩ ㄐㄧㄝˋ)
(said of the conduct of a person) clean and virtuous
拘檢(ㄐㄩ ㄐㄧㄢˇ)
restricted and restrained
拘謹(ㄐㄩ ㄐㄧㄣˇ)
restrained and cautious—implying social timidity
拘禁(ㄐㄩ ㄐㄧㄣˋ)or 拘押(ㄐㄩ ㄧㄚ) or 拘管(ㄐㄩ ㄍㄨㄢˇ)
to detain; to imprison: 警察將他拘押在派出所裏。The police held him at the station house.
拘拘(ㄐㄩ ㄐㄩ)
① sticking to forms; formalistic ② hunchbacked
拘拘縮縮(ㄐㄩ ·ㄐㄩ ㄙㄨㄛ ㄙㄨㄛ)
restricted and shrinking; shy and timid; uneasy and awkward (manner)
拘囚(ㄐㄩ ㄑㄧㄡˊ)
to imprison; to put behind bars
拘牽(ㄐㄩ ㄑㄧㄢ)
to restrict; to restrain
拘墟(ㄐㄩ ㄒㄩ)
provincial; shortsighted and narrow-minded
拘執(ㄐㄩ ㄓˊ)
① to detain or imprison ② to be tied down by conventions
拘住(ㄐㄩ ㄓㄨˋ)
to seize; to restrain
拘守(ㄐㄩ ㄕㄡˇ)
holding fast to (conventions, traditions, etc.)
拘束(ㄐㄩ ㄕㄨˋ)
① to tie (someone) down; to restrain; restrained ② timid and awkward; not feeling at home
拘儒(ㄐㄩ ㄖㄨˊ)
a narrow-minded scholar; a pedant
拘役(ㄐㄩ ㄧˋ)
(law) forced labor service under detention imposed on an offender for not more

〔手部〕

than 60 days
拘押(ㄐㄩ ㄧㄚ)
to take into custody; to put under arrest
拘文(ㄐㄩ ㄨㄣˊ)
adherence to the letter of rules, etc.

〔手部〕

【拚】 1853 ㄆㄢˋ pann pàn

1. to go all out; to try very hard to: 他拚命做生意。He goes all out to do his business.
2. at the risk of; to disregard
3. to reject; to abandon; to discard

拚命(ㄆㄢˋ ㄇㄧㄥˋ)or 拚死(ㄆㄢˋ ㄙˇ)
to go all out (for a cause) even at the risk of one's life; to risk one's life: 他拚命去拯救他人。He risked his life to save another.
拚棄(ㄆㄢˋ ㄑㄧˋ)or 拚除(ㄆㄢˋ ㄔㄨˊ), or 拚去(ㄆㄢˋ ㄑㄩˋ)
to reject; to abandon
拚財(ㄆㄢˋ ㄘㄞˊ)
to make rash speculations

【抿】 1854 ㄇㄧㄣˇ miin mǐn

1. to smooth (hair); to stroke; to caress
2. to purse up (lips); to contract; to tuck: 她抿着嘴唇。She pursed up her lips.
3. to sip; a sip: 她抿一口茶。She sipped her tea.

抿頭(ㄇㄧㄣˇ ㄊㄡˊ)
(especially said of women) to smooth one's hair
抿子(ㄇㄧㄣˇ ·ㄗ)
a small brush for smoothing the hair; a small hairbrush
抿嘴笑(ㄇㄧㄣˇ ㄗㄨㄟˇ ㄒㄧㄠˋ)
to smile with mouth closed; to pucker in smile: 她抿着嘴笑。She smiled with closed lips.

【招】 1855 ㄓㄠ jau zhāo

1. to beckon with one's hand; to summon: 招之即來，揮之即去 to be at one's beck and call
2. to raise (an army, capital, etc.); to recruit
3. to confess; to admit: 他不打自招。He confessed without being pressed.
4. a poster; a notice; a signboard
5. to cause; to effect; to incite; to incur; to invite: 這樣的談論會招來非議。Such talk will invite criticism.
6. to entice; to induce: 她在招生意。She is inducing customers.
7. to welcome; to receive
8. to infect; to be infectious
9. (now rarely) a target; a bull's-eye
10. a move; a trick; a device: 這一招可眞厲害。This was a beautiful move.
11. a Chinese family name

招標(ㄓㄠ ㄅㄧㄠ)
to invite to a tender (or bids, or public bidding); invitation to bid at a tender
招兵(ㄓㄠ ㄅㄧㄥ)
to recruit soldiers; to raise troops
招兵買馬(ㄓㄠ ㄅㄧㄥ ㄇㄞˇ ㄇㄚˇ)
to raise an army (usually in preparation for an insurrection); to prepare for war; to expand a fighting force
招兵聚將(ㄓㄠ ㄅㄧㄥ ㄐㄩˋ ㄐㄧㄤˋ)
to summon troops
招牌(ㄓㄠ ㄆㄞˊ)
① the signboard of a store or any other business concern ② the reputation of a large business firm or a quality product
招盤(ㄓㄠ ㄆㄢˊ)
(said of a shop) to solicit a buyer who will take over the whole business
招聘(ㄓㄠ ㄆㄧㄣˋ)
to advertise for office vacancies: 他們招聘技術工人。They advertised for skilled workers.
招門納壻(ㄓㄠ ㄇㄣˊ ㄋㄚˋ ㄒㄩˋ)
(a Chinese custom) to take a husband (Children thus born will bear the wife's family name.)
招募(ㄓㄠ ㄇㄨˋ)
① to enlist troops (usually mercenaries) ② to solicit (investment, capital, etc.)
招風(ㄓㄠ ㄈㄥ)
to catch the wind—(figuratively) to attract too much attention and invite trouble
招風耳(ㄓㄠ ㄈㄥ ㄦˇ)
protruding ears
招蜂引蝶(ㄓㄠ ㄈㄥ ㄧㄣˇ ㄉㄧㄝˊ)
(said of a woman) to act like a habitual flirt; to make passes to men without discrimination
招福(ㄓㄠ ㄈㄨˊ)
to welcome and invite blessings
招撫(ㄓㄠ ㄈㄨˇ)
to call to surrender; to pacify
招撫使(ㄓㄠ ㄈㄨˇ ㄕˋ)or(ㄓㄠ ㄈㄨˇ ㄕˇ)
formerly, High Commissioner for Pacification
招附(ㄓㄠ ㄈㄨˋ)
to call the enemy to join one's own side
招待(ㄓㄠ ㄉㄞˋ)
① to receive; to welcome; to serve; to entertain: 他招待他的朋友吃飯。He entertained his friends at dinner. ② reception: 謝謝您的熱誠招待。Thank you for your kind hospitality. ③ a receptionist
招待會(ㄓㄠ ㄉㄞˋ ㄏㄨㄟˋ)
a reception
招待券(ㄓㄠ ㄉㄞˋ ㄑㄩㄢˋ)
a free ticket; a complimentary ticket
招待室(ㄓㄠ ㄉㄞˋ ㄕˋ)
a reception room
招待所(ㄓㄠ ㄉㄞˋ ㄙㄨㄛˇ)
a guest house; a hostel
招待員(ㄓㄠ ㄉㄞˋ ㄩㄢˊ)
a receptionist; a touring guide; a steward; an usher; one appointed to receive visitors
招瞪(ㄓㄠ ㄉㄥˋ)
(literally) to invite a stare—to incur resentment or disgust
招討(ㄓㄠ ㄊㄠˇ)
to call for surrender and quell rebellion
招討使(ㄓㄠ ㄊㄠˇ ㄕˋ)or(ㄓㄠ ㄊㄠˇ ㄕˇ)
an officer responsible for calling for surrender and quelling uprisings
招提(ㄓㄠ ㄊㄧˊ)
(Sanskrit) a temple
招貼(ㄓㄠ ㄊㄧㄝ)
① posters; notices; placards

②to placard

招女壻(ㄓㄠ ㄋㄩˇ ㄒㄩˋ)
(said of a family without a male heir) to marry the daughter to a man who will live with her family and bear her family name亦作「招贅」

招徠(ㄓㄠ ㄌㄞˊ)
to induce customers to purchase; to solicit customers; to canvass: 推銷員走遍全城招徠顧主訂貨。Salesmen canvassed the whole city for subscriptions.

招攬(ㄓㄠ ㄌㄢˇ)
①to collect; to gather together ②(commerce) to canvass; to solicit customers

招攬訟事(ㄓㄠ ㄌㄢˇ ㄙㄨㄥˋ ㄕˋ)
to incite or instigate litigations for personal gain

招冷(ㄓㄠ ㄌㄥˇ)
to catch cold

招領(ㄓㄠ ㄌㄧㄥˇ)
to advertise for the claimant or legal owner of a lost article; a public request to call for lost-and-found

招股(ㄓㄠ ㄍㄨˇ)
to solicit shareholders; to call for capital

招供(ㄓㄠ ㄍㄨㄥˋ)
①to confess (to a crime, etc.) ②a confession (by a criminal)

招考(ㄓㄠ ㄎㄠˇ)
to advertise for employees or students through competitive examinations

招呼(ㄓㄠ ㄏㄨ)
①to beckon; to call; to accost: 他向我打招呼。He beckoned (to) me. ②to receive; to take care of: 請招呼一下老年人。Please take care of old people. ③to engage in a fight ④to watch out; to take care; to mind

招呼站(ㄓㄠ ㄏㄨ ㄓㄢˋ)
a designated bus or taxi stop

招花惹草(ㄓㄠ ㄏㄨㄚ ㄖㄜˇ ㄘㄠˇ)
(usually said of a man) lascivious; to play Don Juan or Casanova亦作「拈花惹草」

招禍(ㄓㄠ ㄏㄨㄛˋ)
to invite troubles; to invite disasters

招麾(ㄓㄠ ㄏㄨㄟ)
to command

招魂(ㄓㄠ ㄏㄨㄣˊ)
(an ancient rite) to call home the soul of the dead

招集(ㄓㄠ ㄐㄧˊ)
to gather together

招嫉(ㄓㄠ ㄐㄧˊ)
to invite jealousy; to bring upon oneself envy or jealousy

招架(ㄓㄠ ㄐㄧㄚˋ)
to resist; to defend; to ward off blows; to hold one's own

招架不住(ㄓㄠ ㄐㄧㄚˋ ㄅㄨˋ ㄓㄨˋ)
to be unable to hold on or unable to hold off; to be no match (for someone)

招咎(ㄓㄠ ㄐㄧㄡˋ)
to invite troubles

招親(ㄓㄠ ㄑㄧㄣ)
to take a husband; to get married at the bride's home

招權納賄(ㄓㄠ ㄑㄩㄢˊ ㄋㄚˋ ㄏㄨㄟˋ)
(said of government officials) to abuse one's powers and take bribes

招笑兒(ㄓㄠ ㄒㄧㄠˋㄦ)
to incite laughter; hilarious; funny; to incur ridicule; to be laughable (or funny)

招賢(ㄓㄠ ㄒㄧㄢˊ)
(said of a ruler) to solicit the service of the virtuous and capable

招賢館(ㄓㄠ ㄒㄧㄢˊ ㄍㄨㄢˇ)
a reception center for the accommodation of those answering the ruler's call for public service

招降(ㄓㄠ ㄒㄧㄤˊ)
to call for surrender (of the enemy, etc.)

招致(ㄓㄠ ㄓˋ)
to bring about; to incur; to result in; to invite; to induce: 此信招致許多問題。This letter invited many problems.

招展(ㄓㄠ ㄓㄢˇ)
(said of a banner, etc.) to sway; to flutter; to wave

招承(ㄓㄠ ㄔㄥˊ)
to confess; a confession

招式(ㄓㄠ ㄕˋ)
a stance or posture in Chinese martial art

招收(ㄓㄠ ㄕㄡ)
to advertise for students, apprentices, etc.

招手兒(ㄓㄠ ㄕㄡˇㄦ)
to beckon with the hand; to wave a hand: 他向我們招手致意。He waved his greetings to us.

招商局(ㄓㄠ ㄕㄤ ㄐㄩˊ)
The China Merchants' Steam Navigation Company, a steamship company established in the late 19th century and nationalized in 1927 under the Ministry of Communications

招生(ㄓㄠ ㄕㄥ)
to advertise for students; to enrol students

招生簡章(ㄓㄠ ㄕㄥ ㄐㄧㄢˇ ㄓㄤ)
a brochure listing the essential points a student needs to know before taking the entrance examination of a school, which is sent upon request

招生委員會(ㄓㄠ ㄕㄥ ㄨㄟˇ ㄩㄢˊ ㄏㄨㄟˋ)
a commission set up by a school for handling admission of students

招數(ㄓㄠ ㄕㄨˋ)
①a scheme; a trick; a device ②one move in Chinese martial arts

招惹(ㄓㄠ ㄖㄜˇ)
to incur; to bring upon oneself; to cause (trouble, etc.); to provoke: 疏忽招惹禍事。Carelessness invites accidents.

招認(ㄓㄠ ㄖㄣˋ)
①confession ②to confess (to a certain crime, etc.)

招災(ㄓㄠ ㄗㄞ)or招非(ㄓㄠ ㄈㄟ)
to invite disasters; to bring disasters upon oneself

招災惹禍(ㄓㄠ ㄗㄞ ㄖㄜˇ ㄏㄨㄛˋ)
to court disasters; to invite troubles

招租(ㄓㄠ ㄗㄨ)
(said of a house) for rent; to advertise for tenants

招罪(ㄓㄠ ㄗㄨㄟˋ)
①(said of excesses, etc.) to invite curses from Heaven

〔手部〕

〔手部〕

②to bring something bad upon oneself

招財進寶(ㄓㄠ ㄘㄞˊ ㄐㄧㄣˋ ㄅㄠˇ)
to bring in wealth and riches (a self-congratulatory idiom written on a piece of red paper put up in a store to bring good luck)

招安(ㄓㄠ ㄢ)
to grant amnesty and enlistment to bandits, etc.

招兒(ㄓㄠㄦ)
①a trick or strike in Chinese martial arts ②(now also used figuratively) a trick; a scheme ③a poster; a signboard

招邀 or 招要(ㄓㄠ ㄧㄠ)
to invite; to request somebody to come

招搖(ㄓㄠ ㄧㄠˊ)
to swagger with full pomp; to attract undue publicity; to act ostentatiously

招搖過市(ㄓㄠ ㄧㄠˊ ㄍㄨㄛˋ ㄕˋ)
to swagger around town; to swagger down the streets

招搖撞騙(ㄓㄠ ㄧㄠˊ ㄓㄨㄤˋ ㄆㄧㄢˋ)
to swindle or cheat by posing as a VIP or claiming to be related to a VIP

招延(ㄓㄠ ㄧㄢˊ)
to recruit (the capable and virtuous)

招引(ㄓㄠ ㄧㄣˇ)
to invite (troubles, etc.); to incur; to cause; to attract; to induce: 亮光招引飛蛾。Bright lights attract moths.

招隱(ㄓㄠ ㄧㄣˇ)
①to recruit people in retirement for government service ②to invite or persuade to rusticate or live in anonymity in an out-of-the-way place

招物議(ㄓㄠ ㄨˋ ㄧˋ)
to incur criticisms: 他的話已招物議。What he said has incurred criticisms.

招怨(ㄓㄠ ㄩㄢˋ)
to incur animosity or grudges; to inspire hatred

招怨樹敵(ㄓㄠ ㄩㄢˋ ㄕㄨˋ ㄉㄧˊ)
to inspire animosity and make enemy

【拜】 1856 ㄅㄞˋ bay bài

1. to do obeisance; to salute; to pay respects to
2. to appoint (as a government official); an appointment
3. to visit; to pay a visit to; to call on or at: 他拜訪一位朋友。He made a call on a friend of his.
4. a Chinese family name

拜把子(ㄅㄞˋ ㄅㄚˇ ·ㄗ)
to become sworn brothers by going through the ritual of making vows of eternal friendship

拜拜(ㄅㄞˋ ·ㄅㄞ)
①to bring hands together and take a bow—as women and children did in old China ②a worshipping festival in Taiwan

拜別(ㄅㄞˋ ㄅㄧㄝˊ)
to say good-bye or farewell; to take leave

拜表(ㄅㄞˋ ㄅㄧㄠˇ)
to present a report, petition, etc. to the emperor; to memorialize the emperor

拜門(ㄅㄞˋ ㄇㄣˊ)
①to call on another and offer thanks ②to become a pupil or apprentice to a master

拜盟(ㄅㄞˋ ㄇㄥˊ)
to become sworn brothers

拜廟(ㄅㄞˋ ㄇㄧㄠˋ)
to worship at a temple

拜命(ㄅㄞˋ ㄇㄧㄥˋ)
①to receive an order ②to express thanks for an assignment

拜墓(ㄅㄞˋ ㄇㄨˋ) or 拜墳(ㄅㄞˋ ㄈㄣˊ)
to worship at the tomb

拜佛(ㄅㄞˋ ㄈㄛˊ)
to worship Buddha

拜訪(ㄅㄞˋ ㄈㄤˇ)
to pay a visit; to visit; to call on: 我明天要到他家拜訪。I shall call at his house tomorrow.

拜服(ㄅㄞˋ ㄈㄨˊ)
to admire (another's erudition, courage, moral strength, etc.); to be won heart and soul

拜覆(ㄅㄞˋ ㄈㄨˋ)
a term of respect in a replying letter

拜禱(ㄅㄞˋ ㄉㄠˇ)
to pray

拜倒(ㄅㄞˋ ㄉㄠˇ)
to prostrate oneself; to fall on one's knees; to grovel

拜倒石榴裙下(ㄅㄞˋ ㄉㄠˇ ㄕˊ ·ㄌㄧㄡ ㄑㄩㄣˊ ㄒㄧㄚˋ)
to fall head over heels for a woman

拜墊(ㄅㄞˋ ㄉㄧㄢˋ)
a cushion for the kneeling rite

拜讀(ㄅㄞˋ ㄉㄨˊ)
(a polite expression) to read with respect: 來函已拜讀。I've read your letter.

拜堂(ㄅㄞˋ ㄊㄤˊ)
(in old China) the wedding ceremony in which the bride and her bridegroom underwent the kneeling rituals in the ceremonial hall

拜帖(ㄅㄞˋ ㄊㄧㄝˇ)
a visiting card

拜天地(ㄅㄞˋ ㄊㄧㄢ ㄉㄧˋ)
(in old China) the wedding ceremony in which the bride and bridegroom must kowtow to Heaven and Earth

拜託(ㄅㄞˋ ㄊㄨㄛ)
a polite expression in asking another to do something for oneself

拜年(ㄅㄞˋ ㄋㄧㄢˊ)
to call on another and offer New Year's greetings

拜老師(ㄅㄞˋ ㄌㄠˇ ㄕ) or 拜師(ㄅㄞˋ ㄕ)
to become a pupil or apprentice to a master in a solemn ceremony

拜禮(ㄅㄞˋ ㄌㄧˇ) or 拜見禮(ㄅㄞˋ ㄐㄧㄢˋ ㄌㄧˇ)
gifts that one gives to those who pay respects to oneself

拜領(ㄅㄞˋ ㄌㄧㄥˇ)
to accept with thanks

拜跪(ㄅㄞˋ ㄍㄨㄟˋ)
to kneel and kowtow—the most respectful form of salute to an elder or a superior

拜官(ㄅㄞˋ ㄍㄨㄢ)
to be appointed to a public office

拜客(ㄅㄞˋ ㄎㄜˋ)

to visit; to call on
拜懇(ㄅㄞˋ ㄎㄣˇ)
to beg humbly; to implore; to request
拜賀(ㄅㄞˋ ㄏㄜˋ)
to congratulate; to offer congratulations
拜候(ㄅㄞˋ ㄏㄡˋ)
to visit; to call on
拜火教(ㄅㄞˋ ㄏㄨㄛˇ ㄐㄧㄠˋ)
Zoroastrianism 亦作「祆教」
拜會(ㄅㄞˋ ㄏㄨㄟˋ) or 拜望(ㄅㄞˋ ㄨㄤˋ)
to visit; to call on
拜嘉(ㄅㄞˋ ㄐㄧㄚ)
to receive with pleasure your favor, gifts, advice, etc.
拜節(ㄅㄞˋ ㄐㄧㄝˊ)
to offer greetings on festivals; to pay respects on festivals
拜教(ㄅㄞˋ ㄐㄧㄠˋ)
to submit to another's exhortations
拜見(ㄅㄞˋ ㄐㄧㄢˋ)
to visit, or call on (an elder or superior)
拜金主義(ㄅㄞˋ ㄐㄧㄣ ㄓㄨˇ ㄧˋ)
mammonism
拜金主義者(ㄅㄞˋ ㄐㄧㄣ ㄓㄨˇ ㄧˋ ㄓㄜˇ)
a mammonist
拜爵(ㄅㄞˋ ㄐㄩㄝˊ)
to be knighted
拜匣(ㄅㄞˋ ㄒㄧㄚˊ)
a wooden box in which a visitor places his calling card, gift, etc.
拜謝(ㄅㄞˋ ㄒㄧㄝˋ)
to express one's thanks
拜相(ㄅㄞˋ ㄒㄧㄤˋ)
to be appointed prime minister
拜占庭(ㄅㄞˋ ㄓㄢˋ ㄊㄧㄥˊ)
Byzantium, the ancient name of Istanbul, Turkey; Byzantine
拜占庭帝國(ㄅㄞˋ ㄓㄢˋ ㄊㄧㄥˊ ㄉㄧˋ ㄍㄨㄛˊ)
the Byzantine Empire (395-1453)
拜手(ㄅㄞˋ ㄕㄡˇ)
an old form of obeisance by placing the hands palms down on the ground and then placing the head on the hands
拜壽(ㄅㄞˋ ㄕㄡˋ)
to congratulate one on his birthday; to come to offer birthday greetings
拜神(ㄅㄞˋ ㄕㄣˊ)
to worship gods
拜疏(ㄅㄞˋ ㄕㄨˋ)
to present reports, petitions, etc. to the emperor; to memorialize the emperor
拜在門下(ㄅㄞˋ ㄗㄞˋ ㄇㄣˊ ㄒㄧㄚˋ)
to become a pupil or apprentice to someone
拜祖(ㄅㄞˋ ㄗㄨˇ)
ancestor worship
拜辭(ㄅㄞˋ ㄘˊ)
to take leave; to say good-bye: 她依依不捨地跟他拜辭。She took an affectionate leave of him.
拜掃(ㄅㄞˋ ㄙㄠˇ)
to pay respects or worship at the tomb (of one's ancestors, etc.)
拜偶像(ㄅㄞˋ ㄡˇ ㄒㄧㄤˋ)
idol-worshipping
拜謁(ㄅㄞˋ ㄧㄝˋ)
to pay a courtesy call; to wait on (or upon); to pay one's respects to somebody: 我拿著一封介紹信去拜謁他。I waited upon him with a letter of introduction.
拜印(ㄅㄞˋ ㄧㄣˋ)
to be appointed to a public office
拜物教(ㄅㄞˋ ㄨˋ ㄐㄧㄠˋ)
fetishism, or fetichism
拜違(ㄅㄞˋ ㄨㄟˊ)
to say good-bye

六畫

【拭】 1857 ㄕˋ shyh shì
1. to wipe; to rub (eyes, etc.): 將污跡拭去。Wipe out the stain.
2. to dust; to clean: 她拭去椅子上的灰塵。She dusted the chairs.

拭目以待(ㄕˋ ㄇㄨˋ ㄧˇ ㄉㄞˋ)
to wipe or rub the eyes and take a good look at what is going to happen—to wait for the result anxiously (or to wait and see)
拭拂(ㄕˋ ㄈㄨˊ)
to wipe, dust and clean
拭淚(ㄕˋ ㄌㄟˋ)
to wipe tears
拭淨(ㄕˋ ㄐㄧㄥˋ)
to wipe and clean

【拮】 1858 ㄐㄧㄝˊ jye jié
laboring hard; occupied

拮据(ㄐㄧㄝˊ ㄐㄩ)
① troubles or difficulties ② in financial straits ③ to seize and grasp with the claws

【拯】 1859 ㄓㄥˇ jeeng zhěng
1. to save; to deliver
2. to raise; to lift up

拯民於水火之中(ㄓㄥˇ ㄇㄧㄣˊ ㄩˊ ㄕㄨㄟˇ ㄏㄨㄛˇ ㄓ ㄓㄨㄥ)
to deliver the people from extreme sufferings
拯焚救溺(ㄓㄥˇ ㄈㄣˊ ㄐㄧㄡˋ ㄋㄧˋ)
(literally) to save people from fire and drowning—to deliver the people from extreme misery
拯救(ㄓㄥˇ ㄐㄧㄡˋ)
① deliverance ② to save; to rescue; to deliver: 把我們從邪惡中拯救出來吧! Deliver us from evil!
拯恤(ㄓㄥˇ ㄒㄩˋ)
to save and help (the refugees, the poor, etc.)

【括】 1860 ㄎㄨㄛˋ kuoh kuò (又讀 ㄍㄨㄚ gua guā)
1. to include; to embrace; to enclose; to sum up; to comprise: 總括言之，她是一個可愛的女孩。To sum up, she is a nice girl.
2. to seek; to search for; to ransack: 土匪搜括了鎮上的糧食。The bandits ransacked the town of food.
3. to come; to arrive
4. to bound; to tie
5. to restrain

括號(ㄎㄨㄛˋ ㄏㄠˋ)
(mathematics) the sign of aggregation
括弧(ㄎㄨㄛˋ ㄏㄨˊ)
parentheses; braces; brackets —( ) ; { } ; 〔 〕
括線(ㄎㄨㄛˋ ㄒㄧㄢˋ)
a vinculum—a straight line over figures

〔手部〕

括約肌(ㄎㄨㄛˋ ㄩㄝ ㄐㄧ)
(anatomy) a constrictor; a sphincter

【拱】 1861 ㄍㄨㄥˇ goong gǒng
1. to fold hands before the breast when making a bow; to salute
2. to encircle with the hands
3. to surround: 衆星拱月。A myriad of stars surround the moon.
4. (architecture) arched (doors, windows, etc.)
5. to raise up (in the middle); to hump up; to arch: 新出的芽兒把土都拱起來了。The young shoots have raised up the soil.

拱把(ㄍㄨㄥˇ ㄅㄚˇ)
the circumference of something which is the same as the circle formed by two hands

拱壩(ㄍㄨㄥˇ ㄅㄚˋ)
an arch dam

拱北(ㄍㄨㄥˇ ㄅㄟˇ) or 拱辰(ㄍㄨㄥˇ ㄔㄣˊ)
All the border tribes pay homage to the country, like stars encircling Polaris.

拱抱(ㄍㄨㄥˇ ㄅㄠˋ)
to encircle with two arms; to surround: 絕壁拱抱著小海灣。The cove was surrounded by cliffs.

拱璧(ㄍㄨㄥˇ ㄅㄧˋ)
a large piece of jade

拱別(ㄍㄨㄥˇ ㄅㄧㄝˊ)
to bid farewell by holding one's hands together in an up-and-down motion

拱默(ㄍㄨㄥˇ ㄇㄛˋ)
to salute in silence

拱門(ㄍㄨㄥˇ ㄇㄣˊ)
an arched door or doorway

拱木(ㄍㄨㄥˇ ㄇㄨˋ)
a large tree whose trunk can be encircled only with two arms

拱道(ㄍㄨㄥˇ ㄉㄠˋ)
an archway

拱頂(ㄍㄨㄥˇ ㄉㄧㄥˇ)
a dome; a vault

拱廊(ㄍㄨㄥˇ ㄌㄤˊ)
a cloister

拱立(ㄍㄨㄥˇ ㄌㄧˋ)
to stand in a reverent posture

拱肩縮背(ㄍㄨㄥˇ ㄐㄧㄢ ㄙㄨㄛ ㄅㄟˋ)
to shrink one's shoulders and bow one's back—as in cold weather, or an expression of obsequiousness

拱橋(ㄍㄨㄥˇ ㄑㄧㄠˊ)
an arch bridge

拱手(ㄍㄨㄥˇ ㄕㄡˇ)
to fold one's hands in a bow (usually in greeting or saying farewell)

拱手讓人(ㄍㄨㄥˇ ㄕㄡˇ ㄖㄤˋ ㄖㄣˊ)
to give up something to others without putting up a fight

拱瓦(ㄍㄨㄥˇ ㄨㄚˇ)
curved tiles which are slightly raised in the middle

拱衛(ㄍㄨㄥˇ ㄨㄟˋ)
to guard; to stand in circular positions and defend

【拴】 1862 ㄕㄨㄢ shuan shuān
1. to tie up; to fasten: 請將馬拴在樹上。Tie the horse to the tree, please.
2. to drive a wedge between two parties

拴兒(ㄕㄨㄚㄦ)
① a wooden peg for joining two objects together ② a cork

拴不住心(ㄕㄨㄢ ·ㄅㄨ ㄓㄨˋ ㄒㄧㄣ)
①(said of a woman) unable to hold a man's heart ② unable to keep one's mind fixed

拴馬(ㄕㄨㄢ ㄇㄚˇ)
to tie up a horse

拴馬樁(ㄕㄨㄢ ㄇㄚˇ ㄓㄨㄤ)
a post for fastening a horse

拴縛(ㄕㄨㄢ ㄈㄨˊ)
to tie up (with a rope or chain, etc.): 他們將他的雙手拴縛起來。They tied his hands together.

拴扣兒(ㄕㄨㄢ ㄎㄡˋㄦ)
① to make a knot ② to alienate two parties; to drive a wedge between two persons

拴捆(ㄕㄨㄢ ㄎㄨㄣˇ)
to bind; to tie up

拴著(ㄕㄨㄢ ·ㄓㄜ)
tied up; fastened

拴住(ㄕㄨㄢ ㄓㄨˋ)
① to hold (one's attention, heart, etc.) ② to tie up; to make fast: 把船拴住。Make the boat fast.

拴上(ㄕㄨㄢ ·ㄕㄤ)
to fasten (the door, window, etc.): 他把門拴上了。He fastened the door.

拴繩子(ㄕㄨㄢ ㄕㄥˊ ·ㄗ)
to tie or fasten with a rope

拴束(ㄕㄨㄢ ㄕㄨˋ)
① to pack (one's baggage, etc.); to tie up ② to restrain (one's heart)

拴娃娃(ㄕㄨㄢ ㄨㄚˊ ·ㄨㄚ)
(an old Chinese superstition) to tie a string around a clay baby at a temple or take it home, hoping to beget a child

【拶】 1863 ㄗㄢˇ tzaan zǎn (又讀 ㄗㄚˊ tzar zá)
a torture device in old China consisting of several contractible wooden sticks, in between which the fingers of a suspect were placed and pressed to extort confessions

拶指(ㄗㄢˇ ㄓˇ)
to press the fingers with the device described above

拶子(ㄗㄢˇ ·ㄗ)
an old Chinese torture device 參看「拶」

【拾】 1864 1. ㄕˊ shyr shí
1. to pick up; to collect
2. to put away: 請把你的書收拾整齊。Please put your books away.
3. a formal form of the figure "ten" used to prevent fraud in a document or check
4. an armlet used by archers

拾得(ㄕˊ ㄉㄜˊ)
to find; to pick up

拾得者(ㄕˊ ㄉㄜˊ ㄓㄜˇ)
the founder; one who picks up something lost by another person

拾掇(ㄕˊ ㄉㄨㄛˊ) or (ㄕˊ ·ㄉㄨㄛ)
① to tidy up; to arrange in order ②(colloquial) to punish; to discipline ③ to repair; to fix

拾漏子(ㄕˊ ㄌㄡˋ ·ㄗ) or 拾漏兒(ㄕˊ

ㄌㄡˋㄦ)
to take advantage of a loophole, etc.

拾零(ㄕˊ ㄌㄧㄥˊ)
①to collect bits (which others have discarded) ②a collection of interesting tidbits or anecdotes, etc.

拾荒(ㄕˊ ㄏㄨㄤ)
to glean and collect scraps (to eke out an existence)

拾芥(ㄕˊ ㄐㄧㄝˋ)
just for the picking or taking—very easily gotten

拾金不昧(ㄕˊ ㄐㄧㄣ ㄅㄨˋ ㄇㄟˋ)
to pick up a piece of lost gold and return it to the owner

拾起(ㄕˊ ˙ㄑㄧ)
to pick up

拾取(ㄕˊ ㄑㄩˇ)or 拾摭(ㄕˊ ㄓˊ)
to collect; to pick up

拾人涕唾(ㄕˊ ㄖㄣˊ ㄊㄧˋ ㄊㄨㄛˋ)
to repeat what others have said or written; to plagiarize; to practice me-tooism

拾人牙慧(ㄕˊ ㄖㄣˊ ㄧㄚˊ ㄏㄨㄟˋ)
to pick up what others have said or written and take it as one's own idea—to plagiarize 亦作「拾人唾餘」

拾翠踏青(ㄕˊ ㄘㄨㄟˋ ㄊㄚˋ ㄑㄧㄥ)
to go to scenic spots; to enjoy natural charms

拾穗(ㄕˊ ㄙㄨㄟˋ)
to glean

拾穗人(ㄕˊ ㄙㄨㄟˋ ㄖㄣˊ)
the gleaner

拾遺(ㄕˊ ㄧˊ)
①to pick up what others have lost and keep it as one's own: 路不拾遺。No one pockets anything found on the road. ②a collection of anecdotes which have not been recorded by other historians ③an official post in the Tang Dynasty with the responsibility of counseling on the conduct of the emperor

【拾】 1864
2. ㄕㄜˋ sheh shè

to go up; to ascend

拾級而上(ㄕㄜˋ ㄐㄧˊ ㄦˊ ㄕㄤˋ)or 拾級而登(ㄕㄜˋ ㄐㄧˊ ㄦˊ ㄉㄥ)
to ascend by stairs; to go up by a flight of steps; to mount up a flight of steps

【拾】 1864
3. ㄕ shy shī

拾翻(ㄕ ˙ㄈㄢ)
to turn upside down

【持】 1865
ㄔˊ chyr chí

1. to hold; to grasp: 他手中持著一本書。He is holding a book in his hands.
2. to maintain; to support; to keep; to uphold: 要小心保持你的名譽。Be careful to maintain your reputation.
3. to manage; to preside
4. a tie or stalemate

持筆(ㄔˊ ㄅㄧˇ)
to hold the pen—to write

持票人(ㄔˊ ㄆㄧㄠˋ ㄖㄣˊ)
a check holder; the bearer of a check or bill

持平(ㄔˊ ㄆㄧㄥˊ)
fair and unbiased

持滿(ㄔˊ ㄇㄢˇ)
①brimming and in danger of spilling out (implying over-confidence, complacency, etc.) ②to draw a bowfully and be ready to shoot

持法(ㄔˊ ㄈㄚˇ)
to maintain or enforce law or discipline

持法森嚴(ㄔˊ ㄈㄚˇ ㄙㄣ ㄧㄢˊ)
to administer sharp justice

持服(ㄔˊ ㄈㄨˊ)
three years of mourning for one's parents

持刀(ㄔˊ ㄉㄠ)
to hold a knife

持橐簪筆(ㄔˊ ㄊㄨㄛˊ ㄗㄢ ㄅㄧˇ)
to serve as a counselor or adviser

持兩端(ㄔˊ ㄌㄧㄤˇ ㄉㄨㄢ)
hesitating as to which of two opposing groups to support

持祿(ㄔˊ ㄌㄨˋ)
to hold an office without achieving anything

持論(ㄔˊ ㄌㄨㄣˋ)
to present an argument; to put a case; to express a view

持論公允(ㄔˊ ㄌㄨㄣˋ ㄍㄨㄥ ㄩㄣˇ)
to hold an unbiased view; to make impartial comments or statements

持衡(ㄔˊ ㄏㄥˊ)
①to observe and measure the capability of a person ②to weigh the advantages and disadvantages

持戟(ㄔˊ ㄐㄧˇ)
①a soldier ②an aide

持家(ㄔˊ ㄐㄧㄚ)
①to run one's home; to manage the household ②to keep the family estates

持節(ㄔˊ ㄐㄧㄝˊ)
to serve as a diplomatic envoy

持戒(ㄔˊ ㄐㄧㄝˋ)
(said of a Buddhist monk or nun) to observe the commandments

持械搶刼(ㄔˊ ㄐㄧㄝˋ ㄑㄧㄤˇ ㄐㄧㄝˊ)
armed robbery; to commit robbery with firearms

持久(ㄔˊ ㄐㄧㄡˇ)
to hold out; to last for a long time; lasting; durable: 我們必須建立持久的和平。We must make a durable peace.

持久戰(ㄔˊ ㄐㄧㄡˇ ㄓㄢˋ)
a military strategy adopted by the weaker of the belligerents to avoid decisive battles so that the war will become protracted and the other side worn down by attrition; a long-drawn-out war; a war of attrition

持槍(ㄔˊ ㄑㄧㄤ)
①to hold a gun ②(military) to port arms

持續(ㄔˊ ㄒㄩˋ)
①continuous; incessant; uninterrupted: 雨已經持續下了一禮拜了。We've had a week of incessant rain. ②to hold; to go on: 天氣持續暖和。The weather held warm.

持之以恆(ㄔˊ ㄓ ㄧˇ ㄏㄥˊ)
to persevere: 他讀書持之以恆。He persevered in his studies.

持之有故(ㄔˊ ㄓ ㄧㄡˇ ㄍㄨˋ)
a view or opinion which finds its source in ancient sayings; a well-founded view or opinion

持齋(ㄔˊ ㄓㄞ)
(said of Buddhists) to stick

〔手部〕

to a vegetarian diet

持正(ㄔˊ ㄓㄥˋ)
fair and just; to uphold justice and propriety

持重(ㄔˊ ㄓㄨㄥˋ)
① to observe rules of justice and propriety ② to act cautiously and carefully: 他老成持重。He acts cautiously and carefully. ③ dignified

持身(ㄔˊ ㄕㄣ)
to conduct oneself (properly)

持身涉世(ㄔˊ ㄕㄣ ㄕㄜˋ ㄕˋ)
to exercise proper restraints in dealing with the world

持勝(ㄔˊ ㄕㄥˋ)
to maintain one's superiority or advantage

持贈(ㄔˊ ㄗㄥˋ)
to carry and present to; to present (a gift) to

持喪(ㄔˊ ㄙㄤ)
to be in mourning

持異議(ㄔˊ ㄧˋ ㄧˋ)
to maintain a different or opposite view: 他們各持異議。They are divided in their opinions.

持有(ㄔˊ ㄧㄡˇ)
to hold: 他持有美國護照。He holds an American passport.

持養(ㄔˊ ㄧㄤˇ)
① to preserve (one's energy, vitality, etc.) by sticking to a regimen ② to comply with or respect (one's idea, view, etc.)

持盈保泰(ㄔˊ ㄧㄥˊ ㄅㄠˇ ㄊㄞˋ)
(said of the high and mighty) to remain modest and humble and thus to be rewarded with security on his position; to maintain good luck by restraint

持危扶傾(ㄔˊ ㄨㄟ ㄈㄨˊ ㄑㄧㄥ)
to act as a champion of justice; to uphold justice; to come to the aid of the weak and the unfortunate

【按】 1866
ㄢˋ ann àn

1. to place the hand on; to press, control, etc. with one's hand: 按鈕使鈴響。Press the button to ring the bell.
2. to examine
3. to stop; to halt; to repress; to leave aside: 他按不住心頭怒火。He is unable to repress his anger.
4. to impeach; to censure
5. according to; in (good order); as: 我將按你的建議去做。I'll do as you advise.
6. to follow (a map, river, etc.)
7. a note; a comment: 編者按 the editor's note (or comment)

按兵不動(ㄢˋ ㄅㄧㄥ ㄅㄨˋ ㄉㄨㄥˋ)
① to refuse to send troops to relieve friendly forces in distress; to keep back army from battle ② to bide one's time; to take no action; to remain motionless

按部就班(ㄢˋ ㄅㄨˋ ㄐㄧㄡˋ ㄅㄢ)
(to do things) in good order or according to logical order 或 First things first. 訛作「按步就班」

按轡(ㄢˋ ㄆㄟˋ)
to rein in the horse (to keep it from galloping)

按摩(ㄢˋ ㄇㄛˊ)
① massage ② to massage

按摩女(ㄢˋ ㄇㄛˊ ㄋㄩˇ)
a masseuse

按摩師(ㄢˋ ㄇㄛˊ ㄕ)
a masseur

按脈(ㄢˋ ㄇㄛˋ)
(said of a Chinese herb doctor) to feel the patient's pulse; to take the pulse

按名次(ㄢˋ ㄇㄧㄥˊ ㄘˋ)
according to the order of names listed on a roster

按法嚴懲(ㄢˋ ㄈㄚˇ ㄧㄢˊ ㄔㄥˊ)
to mete out severe punishment according to law

按討(ㄢˋ ㄊㄠˇ)
to investigate a rebellion and put it down; to quell an uprising

按圖索驥(ㄢˋ ㄊㄨˊ ㄙㄨㄛˇ ㄐㄧˋ)
① (literally) to find a horse according to a drawing —using a hackneyed method; lacking originality, initiative or imagination in doing a job; to try to locate something by following up a clue ② to use something as a starting point for further exploration or study

按捺(ㄢˋ ㄋㄚˋ)
to restrain, repress or hold back (one's anger, etc.): 他按捺不住激動的心情。He was unable to hold back his excitement.

按鈕(ㄢˋ ㄋㄧㄡˇ)
① a push button ② to push the button

按年(ㄢˋ ㄋㄧㄢˊ)
yearly; annually

按理(ㄢˋ ㄌㄧˇ)
according to common practice or simple reasoning; normally

按例(ㄢˋ ㄌㄧˋ)
according to precedents

按鈴(ㄢˋ ㄌㄧㄥˊ)
to press the button of a buzzer; to ring the bell

按劍(ㄢˋ ㄐㄧㄢˋ)
to place one's hand on one's sword; to grasp one's sword

按期(ㄢˋ ㄑㄧˊ)
according to the dates, periods, etc. agreed upon or specified; on time; on schedule: 這份雜誌將按期出版。The magazine will come out on time.

按下不表(ㄢˋ ㄒㄧㄚˋ ㄅㄨˋ ㄅㄧㄠˇ)
(literally) Let's suspend the narration for a while (and talk about....)—(in old novels) Let's now turn to....

按下去(ㄢˋ ㄒㄧㄚˋ ˙ㄑㄩ)
to press down

按序(ㄢˋ ㄒㄩˋ)
according to the order of sequence; in (regular) sequence

按址(ㄢˋ ㄓˇ)
(to find a place) according to the address

按著(ㄢˋ ˙ㄓㄜ)
① according to ② to repress or restrain (one's anger, etc.)

按照(ㄢˋ ㄓㄠˋ)
according to; in accordance with; in conformity with: 他未按照命令行事。He did not act in accordance with the orders.

按住(ㄢˋ ㄓㄨˋ)
to repress or restrain; to press down and not to let go

按察(ㄢˋ ㄔㄚˊ)
to investigate; to examine

按察使(ㄢˋ ㄔㄚˊ ㄕˇ)or(ㄢˋ ㄔㄚˊ ㄕˋ)
a provincial official in old China roughly equivalent to today's chief prosecutor of a high court

按成兒(ㄢˋ ㄔㄥˊㄦ)
according to the percentage; proportionately

按時(ㄢˋ ㄕˊ)
① according to the time specified or agreed upon ② on time: 他昨晚按時抵達。He arrived on time last night. ③ regularly

按手(ㄢˋ ㄕㄡˇ)
(Christianity) to place the hand on the head of the ordained in an ordination ceremony

按數(ㄢˋ ㄕㄨˋ)or 按額(ㄢˋ ㄜˊ)
according to the number; proportionately

按說(ㄢˋ ㄕㄨㄛ)
according to common sense, common practice, etc.; ordinarily; normally: 按說這時該下雨了。Ordinarily it should be raining at this time of the year.

按日(ㄢˋ ㄖˋ)
daily; every day

按次(ㄢˋ ㄘˋ)
according to order

按壓(ㄢˋ ㄧㄚ)
(said of bureaucracy) to shelve an official business without justification

按問(ㄢˋ ㄨㄣˋ)
to investigate, examine and question

按語(ㄢˋ ㄩˇ)
according to (investigation, surveys, references, data, etc.)

按月(ㄢˋ ㄩㄝˋ)
monthly; by the month: 他按月來此一次。He comes here monthly.

【指】 1867
1. ㄓˇ jyy zhǐ

1. the finger: 她用手指指我。She was pointing her finger at me.
2. to point; to direct: 他指出了我的錯誤。He pointed out my mistake.
3. to indicate; to refer to; to mean
4. the number of people
5. intentions
6. the main theme
7. to hope
8. to depend on: 我們就指望這點錢度日。We depended on this money for expenses.

指標(ㄓˇ ㄅㄧㄠ)
① (mathematics) characteristic ② an index sign; a target: 他們完成計畫的指標。They attained the targets set in the plan.

指不勝屈(ㄓˇ ㄅㄨˋ ㄕㄥ ㄑㄩ)
too many to be counted; countless

指派(ㄓˇ ㄆㄞˋ)
to appoint; to assign: 他們指派了一位新秘書。They appointed a new secretary.

指摹 or 指模(ㄓˇ ㄇㄛˊ)
a fingerprint

指迷(ㄓˇ ㄇㄧˊ)
to direct another out of a maze; to show or indicate the way; to give advice or guidance

指明(ㄓˇ ㄇㄧㄥˊ)
to indicate clearly; to point out; to single out: 把你喜歡的那些指明給我看。Point me out the ones you would like.

指名(ㄓˇ ㄇㄧㄥˊ)
to mention by name; to single out by name

指名道姓(ㄓˇ ㄇㄧㄥˊ ㄉㄠˋ ㄒㄧㄥˋ)
to mention someone's name; to name names

指法(ㄓˇ ㄈㄚˇ)
① fingering ② a book or manual explaining how fingers are used or applied in a certain kind of work or art, such as playing string instruments, typing, etc.

指腹爲婚(ㄓˇ ㄈㄨˋ ㄨㄟˊ ㄏㄨㄣ)
(in old China) a prenatal betrothal

指導(ㄓˇ ㄉㄠˇ)or(ㄓˇ ㄉㄠˋ)
① direction or guidance: 我的課業需要些指導。I need some guidance with my studies. ② to instruct; to direct; to guide; to supervise: 老師指導學生的課業。The teacher directs the work of his students.

指導委員會(ㄓˇ ㄉㄠˇ ㄨㄟˇ ㄩㄢˊ ㄏㄨㄟˋ)
a steering committee

指導員(ㄓˇ ㄉㄠˇ ㄩㄢˊ)or(ㄓˇ ㄉㄠˋ ㄩㄢˊ)
a supervisor

指點(ㄓˇ ㄉㄧㄢˇ)
to give directions or pointers; to teach; to advise; to instruct: 教練耐心地指點他的球員。The coach patiently instructs his players.

指頂花(ㄓˇ ㄉㄧㄥˇ ㄏㄨㄚ)
a foxglove

指定(ㄓˇ ㄉㄧㄥˋ)
① to appoint; to assign: 指定開會的時間爲八點。The time appointed for the meeting was eight o'clock. ② to indicate clearly and with certainty: 我指定這幢房子給我的兒子。I mean this house for my son. ③ to allot; to set aside (a sum of money for a certain purpose, etc.)

指東話西(ㄓˇ ㄉㄨㄥ ㄏㄨㄚˋ ㄒㄧ)
(literally) to point to the east and talk the west—irrelevant; to mislead with talk; to talk nonsense; to try to avoid the main theme by talking about something else 亦作「指東說西」

指天畫地(ㄓˇ ㄊㄧㄢ ㄏㄨㄚˋ ㄉㄧˋ)
① to talk straight and frankly ② to talk wildly; to behave without regard to decorum

指天誓日(ㄓˇ ㄊㄧㄢ ㄕˋ ㄖˋ)
to swear by Heaven and the sun—to swear by all the gods

指禿說瞎(ㄓˇ ㄊㄨ ㄕㄨㄛ ㄒㄧㄚ)
(literally) to point to the bald and talk of the blind—to talk circuitously

指南(ㄓˇ ㄋㄢˊ)
to indicate a definite direction; a directory; a guidebook; a primer

指南針(ㄓˇ ㄋㄢˊ ㄓㄣ)
a compass

指南車(ㄓˇ ㄋㄢˊ ㄔㄜ)
a chariot which showed correct directions, said to have been invented by the legendary Huangti(黃帝)

〔手部〕

〔手部〕

指令(ㄓˇ ㄌㄧㄥˋ)
a directive; an order; instructions from a higher office: 他發出一連串的指令。He issued a stream of directives.

指路碑(ㄓˇ ㄌㄨˋ ㄅㄟ)
roadside tablets showing direction

指路標(ㄓˇ ㄌㄨˋ ㄅㄧㄠ)
a signpost; a finger post; a guidepost 亦作「指路牌」

指鹿爲馬(ㄓˇ ㄌㄨˋ ㄨㄟˊ ㄇㄚˇ)
(literally) to call a stag a horse—to confound right and wrong

指骨(ㄓˇ ㄍㄨˇ)
phalanges of fingers

指顧間(ㄓˇ ㄍㄨˋ ㄐㄧㄢ)
in a short while

指顧間事(ㄓˇ ㄍㄨˋ ㄐㄧㄢ ㄕˋ)
in no time at all; to happen very soon; in a matter of moments

指歸(ㄓˇ ㄍㄨㄟ)
a concourse where all points meet; a main theme or tenet

指靠(ㄓˇ ㄎㄠˋ)
to depend on (for one's livelihood); to look to (for help); to count on: 這件事我們就指靠你了。We'll depend on you for this.

指控(ㄓˇ ㄎㄨㄥˋ)
to accuse; to charge ; accusation; a charge: 他們指控他受賄。They accused him of taking bribes.

指痕(ㄓˇ ㄏㄣˊ)
fingermarks; marks made by fingernails

指畫(ㄓˇ ㄏㄨㄚˋ)
① finger painting; to paint by using finger paints ② a finger painting

指揮 or 指麾(ㄓˇ ㄏㄨㄟ)
to conduct or direct (an orchestra, etc.); to command (an army, etc.): 這兒誰負責指揮? Who commands here?

指揮棒(ㄓˇ ㄏㄨㄟ ㄅㄤˋ)
the baton (for a conductor)

指揮部(ㄓˇ ㄏㄨㄟ ㄅㄨˋ)
the command post; headquarters

指揮刀(ㄓˇ ㄏㄨㄟ ㄉㄠ)
the saber of a commanding officer

指揮官(ㄓˇ ㄏㄨㄟ ㄍㄨㄢ)
the commanding officer; the commander

指揮若定(ㄓˇ ㄏㄨㄟ ㄖㄨㄛˋ ㄉㄧㄥˋ)
to retain full composure even in command of a big operation (especially said of those given a major assignment for the first time); to direct (work, etc.) with perfect ease; to give highly competent leadership

指環(ㄓˇ ㄏㄨㄢˊ)
a ring: 他送她一個指環。He presented her a ring.

指婚(ㄓˇ ㄏㄨㄣ)
(Ching Dynasty) marriages of members of the royal family with their mates picked by the emperor

指鷄罵狗(ㄓˇ ㄐㄧ ㄇㄚˋ ㄍㄡˇ)
(literally) to point at a chicken and revile the dog—to scold indirectly or in circumlocution

指教(ㄓˇ ㄐㄧㄠˋ)
① direction and guidance ② (a polite expression) your advice or counsel: 請你多多指教。Kindly give us your advice.

指向(ㄓˇ ㄒㄧㄤˋ)
to point to; to direct to: 指標牌指向北邊。The signboard points north.

指指點點(ㄓˇ ·ㄓ ㄉㄧㄢˇ ㄉㄧㄢˇ)
① gesticulating ② to point; to point out; to indicate

指摘(ㄓˇ ㄓㄜˊ)
to point out the faults of another; to blame; to criticize

指針(ㄓˇ ㄓㄣ)
① a guide; a manual ② an index; an indication needle in a measuring instrument

指掌(ㄓˇ ㄓㄤˇ)
① pointing at one's palm: 易如指掌 to be as easy as pointing at one's palm ② fingers and palms: 瞭如指掌 to be as clear as one were looking at one's own fingers and palms

指正(ㄓˇ ㄓㄥˋ)
① to correct ② (a polite expression) to present herewith for your correction: 請惠予指正。Please oblige me with your valuable comments.

指證(ㄓˇ ㄓㄥˋ)
to produce evidence (in court, etc.); to prove

指斥(ㄓˇ ㄔˋ)
to refute; to rebuke; to accuse: 他嚴厲指斥她的疏忽。He rebuked her strongly for her negligence.

指使(ㄓˇ ㄕˇ)
to hire or entice another to do a task for oneself; to instigate or incite behind the scenes: 不要受別人指使。Don't act at the instigation of others.

指事(ㄓˇ ㄕˋ)
"pointing to situations", or "indirect symbols"—one of six categories under which Chinese characters are roughly grouped, which is formed by various kinds of substitutions, such as making parts stand for wholes, attributes for things, effects for causes, instruments for activities, gestures for actions, etc. in a metaphorical way

指示(ㄓˇ ㄕˋ)
① instruction; indication ② to direct; to instruct; to show; to indicate: 你能指示我去郵局的方向嗎? Can you direct me to the post office?

指示代名詞(ㄓˇ ㄕˋ ㄉㄞˋ ㄇㄧㄥˊ ㄘˊ)
demonstrative pronouns

指示劑(ㄓˇ ㄕˋ ㄐㄧˋ)
(chemistry) an indicator

指示器(ㄓˇ ㄕˋ ㄑㄧˋ)
an indicator

指示形容詞(ㄓˇ ㄕˋ ㄒㄧㄥˊ ㄖㄨㄥˊ ㄘˊ)
demonstrative adjectives

指手畫脚(ㄓˇ ㄕㄡˇ ㄏㄨㄚˋ ㄐㄧㄠˇ)
to gesticulate profusely

指書(ㄓˇ ㄕㄨ)
to write with one's finger instead of a pen

指數(ㄓˇ ㄕㄨˋ)
index; exponent; index number

指日(ㄓˇ ㄖˋ)
in a matter of days; in a few days

指日高陞(ㄓˇ ㄖˋ ㄍㄠ ㄕㄥ)
to get promoted soon (a well-wishing expression)

指日可下(ㄓˇ ㄖˋ ㄎㄜˇ ㄒㄧㄚˋ)
to capture (an enemy-held city, strategic position, etc.) very soon

指日可待(ㄓˇ ㄖˋ ㄎㄜˇ ㄉㄞˋ)
can be expected very shortly or soon: 我們的勝利是指日可待的。Our victory can be expected very shortly.

指認(ㄓˇ ㄖㄣˋ)
to identify (a suspect, a lost item, etc.) from a group

指責(ㄓˇ ㄗㄜˊ)
to accuse; to censure; to charge; to disparage: 他受到輿論的指責。He was subjected to the censure of public opinion.

指桑罵槐(ㄓˇ ㄙㄤ ㄇㄚˋ ㄏㄨㄞˊ)
(literally) to point to the mulberry and revile the locust tree—to scold somebody indirectly

指要(ㄓˇ ㄧㄠˋ)
the theme; the essential points

指引(ㄓˇ ㄧㄣˇ)
to direct; to guide; guidance: 我在他的指引之下完成了論文。I wrote my dissertation under his guidance.

指紋(ㄓˇ ㄨㄣˊ)or 指印(ㄓˇ ㄧㄣˋ)
a fingerprint; a dactylogram

指紋學(ㄓˇ ㄨㄣˊ ㄒㄩㄝˊ)
dactylography

指望(ㄓˇ ㄨㄤˋ)
to hope for; to expect; expectations; to look forward to: 我們都指望最好的一面。We're hoping for the best.

【指】 1867 2. ㄓˊ jyr zhí

指頭(ㄓˊ ·ㄊㄡ)
fingers

指頭畫(ㄓˊ ·ㄊㄡ ㄏㄨㄚˋ)
paintings with fingers; finger painting

指頭尖兒(ㄓˊ ·ㄊㄡ ㄐㄧㄚㄦ)
the tip of the finger; a fingertip

【指】 1867 3. ㄓ jy zhī

指甲(ㄓ ·ㄐㄧㄚ)
a fingernail

指甲刀(ㄓ ·ㄐㄧㄚ ㄉㄠ)
nailclippers

指甲蓋兒(ㄓ ·ㄐㄧㄚ ㄍㄚˋㄦ)
a fingernail

指甲心兒(ㄓ ·ㄐㄧㄚ ㄒㄧㄜㄦ)
where the fingernail joins the flesh

指甲草(ㄓ ·ㄐㄧㄚ ㄘㄠˇ)
balsamine

指甲油(ㄓ ·ㄐㄧㄚ ㄧㄡˊ)
fingernail polish

【挑】 1868 1. ㄊㄧㄠ tiau tiāo

1. to carry things with a pole on one's shoulder; to shoulder: 他挑起生產的重擔。He shouldered heavy loads in production.
2. to select; to choose; to pick: 挑最好的。Pick the best one.
3. to pick by pitchfork

挑不動(ㄊㄧㄠ ·ㄅㄨ ㄉㄨㄥˋ)or 挑不起(ㄊㄧㄠ ·ㄅㄨ ㄑㄧˇ)
too heavy to carry

挑肥揀瘦(ㄊㄧㄠ ㄈㄟˊ ㄐㄧㄢˇ ㄕㄡˋ)
to be very particular in one's selection (of a mate or things); to be fastidious

挑夫(ㄊㄧㄠ ㄈㄨ)
a coolie; a bearer; a porter

挑大梁(ㄊㄧㄠ ㄉㄚˋ ㄌㄧㄤˊ)
to play the leading role; to shoulder the main responsibility

挑擔(ㄊㄧㄠ ㄉㄢˋ)
to carry a load with a carrying pole

挑剔(ㄊㄧㄠ ·ㄊㄧ)
① to be very particular in making selection; to be over-punctilious in making a choice: 他對食物很挑剔。He is particular about his food. ② to find fault with somebody or something; to nitpick

挑開(ㄊㄧㄠ ㄎㄞ)
to brush aside with a poker or stick

挑好的(ㄊㄧㄠ ㄏㄠˇ ·ㄉㄜ)
to choose or select the better ones; to pick the good ones

挑花(ㄊㄧㄠ ㄏㄨㄚ)
to embroider; a kind of embroidery

挑揀(ㄊㄧㄠ ㄐㄧㄢˇ)
to pick; to select or choose

挑精選肥(ㄊㄧㄠ ㄐㄧㄥ ㄒㄩㄢˇ ㄈㄟˊ)
to pick the best; to be very choosy

挑取(ㄊㄧㄠ ㄑㄩˇ)
to pick; to choose; to select

挑選(ㄊㄧㄠ ㄒㄩㄢˇ)
to select; to choose; to pick; to take one's pick of: 他挑選了一套新衣服。He picked out a new suit.

挑飭(ㄊㄧㄠ ㄔˋ)
to make punctilious demands; to pick on another; to find fault

挑水的(ㄊㄧㄠ ㄕㄨㄟˇ ·ㄉㄜ)
a water bearer

挑字眼兒(ㄊㄧㄠ ㄗˋ ㄧㄚˇㄦ)
to pick on someone for negligible faults or flaws

挑子(ㄊㄧㄠ ·ㄗ)or 挑兒(ㄊㄧㄠㄦ)
loads, things, stock-in-trade, etc. carried by means of a carrying pole

挑刺兒(ㄊㄧㄠ ㄘㄜˋㄦ)
to find fault; to be captious

挑錯(ㄊㄧㄠ ㄘㄨㄛˋ)
to find fault; to pick flaws

挑三揀四(ㄊㄧㄠ ㄙㄢ ㄐㄧㄢˇ ㄙˋ)
to pick and choose; to be choosy: 購物的顧客越來越喜歡挑三揀四。The shopping public is getting more choosy.

挑么挑六(ㄊㄧㄠ ㄧㄠ ㄊㄧㄠ ㄌㄧㄡˋ)
to indulge in faultfinding; to pick flaws

挑眼(ㄊㄧㄠ ㄧㄢˇ)or 挑眼兒(ㄊㄧㄠ ㄧㄚˇㄦ)
to pick flaws; to find fault; to be fastidious (about formalities, etc.)

挑挖(ㄊㄧㄠ ㄨㄚ)
to dredge; to clear (a waterway, etc.)

挑運費(ㄊㄧㄠ ㄩㄣˋ ㄈㄟˋ)
porterage

【挑】 1868 2. ㄊㄧㄠˇ teau tiǎo

1. to stir; to provoke; to arouse
2. to dally; to make a pass at; to seduce

挑撥(ㄊㄧㄠˇ ㄅㄛ)
to provoke or arouse; to

〔手部〕

instigate; to cause disputes; to cause the alienation; to sow discord: 她在朋友之間挑撥是非。She causes the alienation between friends by spreading rumors.

挑撥離間(ㄊㄧㄠˇ ㄅㄛ ㄌㄧˊ ㄐㄧㄢˋ)
to stir up ill will or bad feelings; to sow discord

挑逗 or 挑鬥(ㄊㄧㄠˇ ㄉㄡˋ)
to seduce; to arouse amorous desires

挑燈(ㄊㄧㄠˇ ㄉㄥ)
to stir the wick of a lamp so that it will put forth more light

挑燈夜戰(ㄊㄧㄠˇ ㄉㄥ ㄧㄝˋ ㄓㄢˋ)
to continue working by lamplight

挑動(ㄊㄧㄠˇ ㄉㄨㄥˋ)
① to arouse; to seduce ② to instigate; to incite

挑弄(ㄊㄧㄠˇ ㄋㄨㄥˋ)
to tease; to play a joke on

挑弄是非(ㄊㄧㄠˇ ㄋㄨㄥˋ ㄕˋ ㄈㄟ)
to arouse ill will between two parties; to stir up one side against the other

挑起(ㄊㄧㄠˇ ㄑㄧˇ)
to provoke; to stir up; to instigate

挑情(ㄊㄧㄠˇ ㄑㄧㄥˊ)
to make amorous advances; to arouse one of the other sex in love making 參看「調情」

挑戲(ㄊㄧㄠˇ ㄒㄧˋ)
to make a pass at a woman with amorous intentions 亦作「調戲」

挑釁(ㄊㄧㄠˇ ㄒㄧㄣˋ)
to provoke

挑戰(ㄊㄧㄠˇ ㄓㄢˋ)
to challenge to a duel; a challenge; to provoke or pick up a fight

挑戰行爲(ㄊㄧㄠˇ ㄓㄢˋ ㄒㄧㄥˊ ㄨㄟˊ)
provocative actions

挑戰書(ㄊㄧㄠˇ ㄓㄢˋ ㄕㄨ)
a cartel; a written challenge

挑事(ㄊㄧㄠˇ ㄕˋ)
to stir up trouble; to sow discord

挑唆(ㄊㄧㄠˇ ㄙㄨㄛ)
to stir up something with mischievous intentions; to alienate people by arousing ill will among them: 別在背後挑唆。Don't stir up trouble behind the scenes.

【挑】 1868
3. ㄊㄠ tau tāo
light and frivolous

挑達(ㄊㄠ ㄊㄚˋ)
to walk to and fro in a free manner

【拽】 1869
1. ㄓㄨㄞ juai zhuāi
to fling; to hurl

【拽】 1869
2. ㄓㄨㄞˋ juay zhuài
to pull; to drag; to catch: 他一把拽住它不放。He caught hold of it and would not let it go.

【拽】 1869
3. ㄧㄝˋ yeh yè (又讀 ㄧˋ yih yì)
1. to trail; to drag after: 她的衣服在地上拖拽著。Her dress trailed on the ground.
2. to pull or drag

【挖】 1870
ㄨㄚ ua wā
1. to scoop out; to dig out: 他們在挖防空洞。They were digging an air-raid shelter.
2. to engrave with a knife; to cut or gouge

挖補(ㄨㄚ ㄅㄨˇ)
① to gouge and mend (a surfaced road, etc.) ② cutting and mending (of writings, etc.)

挖煤(ㄨㄚ ㄇㄟˊ)
to mine for coal

挖墊(ㄨㄚ ㄉㄧㄢˋ)
a kind of needle work in old China done by cutting off various forms on a piece of cloth and mounting them on another piece of cloth of different color so as to make a picture or design

挖洞(ㄨㄚ ㄉㄨㄥˋ)or挖窟窿(ㄨㄚ ㄎㄨ ·ㄌㄨㄥ)
to make a hole or cave; to dig out a hole; to scoop (out) a hole

挖泥(ㄨㄚ ㄋㄧˊ)
to dredge (up) mud

挖泥機(ㄨㄚ ㄋㄧˊ ㄐㄧ)
a dredger

挖泥船(ㄨㄚ ㄋㄧˊ ㄔㄨㄢˊ)
a suction dredger (a boat)

挖改(ㄨㄚ ㄍㄞˇ)
(said of a piece of writing, etc.) to cut and make changes

挖根(ㄨㄚ ㄍㄣ)
to uproot

挖苦(ㄨㄚ ㄎㄨˇ)
① to ridicule; to make sarcastic remarks ② a dig: 這是挖苦他的。This was a dig at him.

挖空(ㄨㄚ ㄎㄨㄥ)
to hollow

挖空心思(ㄨㄚ ㄎㄨㄥ ㄒㄧㄣ ㄙ)
to cudgel (or rack) one's brains: 他挖空心思找適當的辭句。He dredged into himself for words.

挖角(ㄨㄚ ㄐㄧㄠˇ)
to lure away the employees of another company or organization by making attractive offers

挖井(ㄨㄚ ㄐㄧㄥˇ)
to dig a well

挖掘(ㄨㄚ ㄐㄩㄝˊ)
to dig; to excavate; to unearth: 他在挖掘地下寶藏。He's unearthing buried treasure.

挖掘機(ㄨㄚ ㄐㄩㄝˊ ㄐㄧ)
an excavator; a navvy 亦作「挖土機」or「怪手」

挖牆脚(ㄨㄚ ㄑㄧㄤˊ ㄐㄧㄠˇ)
to undermine the foundation

挖塚(ㄨㄚ ㄓㄨㄥˇ)
to dig a grave; grave-digging

挖出來(ㄨㄚ ㄔㄨ ·ㄌㄞ)
to dig out; to gouge out; to excavate

挖肉補瘡(ㄨㄚ ㄖㄡˋ ㄅㄨˇ ㄔㄨㄤ)
(literally) to cut a piece of flesh to mend a wound—to make up for a deficit by raising loans

挖耳朵(ㄨㄚ ㄦˇ ·ㄉㄨㄛ)
to pick ears

挖眼睛(ㄨㄚ ㄧㄢˇ ·ㄐㄧㄥ)
to gouge out eyes

【拷】 1871
ㄎㄠˇ kao kǎo
to flog, whip, torture, etc. (in order to get a confession, etc.)

拷貝(ㄎㄠˇ ㄅㄟˋ)
a copy

拷打(ㄎㄠˇ ㄉㄚˇ)

to flog or whip; to torture: 土匪將他嚴刑拷打。The bandit subjected him to severe torture.
拷問(ㄎㄠˇ ㄨㄣˋ)or 拷訊(ㄎㄠˇ ㄒㄩㄣˋ)
to extort information, confessions, etc. by means of torture: 他受拷問。He is subjected to torture.

【挓】1872 ㄓㄚ ja zhā
參看「挓挱」
挓挱(ㄓㄚ ·ㄕㄚ)
widespread; open 亦作「扎煞」

【拳】1873 ㄑㄩㄢˊ chyuan quán
1. a fist: 我給了他一拳。I gave him a blow with the fist.
2. sparring feats; various forms of boxing: 他們彼此拳鬥。They boxed with each other.
3. strength
拳棒(ㄑㄩㄢˊ ㄅㄤˋ)
fighting feats
拳匪(ㄑㄩㄢˊ ㄈㄟˇ)
(contemptuous) the Boxers of the late 19th century, whose slogan was "supporting the Ching Dynasty and wiping out the foreign devils"
拳打(ㄑㄩㄢˊ ㄉㄚˇ)or 拳毆(ㄑㄩㄢˊ ㄡ)
to strike with fists
拳打脚踢(ㄑㄩㄢˊ ㄉㄚˇ ㄐㄧㄠˇ ㄊㄧ)
to cuff and kick; to beat up; to strike and kick
拳頭(ㄑㄩㄢˊ ·ㄊㄡ)
a fist: 他用拳頭打我。He struck me with his fist.
拳來脚去(ㄑㄩㄢˊ ㄌㄞˊ ㄐㄧㄠˇ ㄑㄩˋ)
to give tit for tat; to exchange blows
拳擊(ㄑㄩㄢˊ ㄐㄧˊ)
boxing; the boxing art; to strike with fist: 你喜歡拳擊嗎? Do you like boxing?
拳擊手(ㄑㄩㄢˊ ㄐㄧˊ ㄕㄡˇ)
a boxer; a pugilist
拳擊手套(ㄑㄩㄢˊ ㄐㄧˊ ㄕㄡˇ ㄊㄠˋ)
boxing gloves
拳脚(ㄑㄩㄢˊ ㄐㄧㄠˇ)
Chinese boxing (which uses both the fists and the feet)
拳脚交加(ㄑㄩㄢˊ ㄐㄧㄠˇ ㄐㄧㄠ ㄐㄧㄚ) or 拳足交加(ㄑㄩㄢˊ ㄗㄨˊ ㄐㄧㄠ ㄐㄧㄚ)
to beat up with fists and kicks; a violent beating
拳跼 or 拳局(ㄑㄩㄢˊ ㄐㄩˊ)
to be confined or restrained to a small place
拳曲(ㄑㄩㄢˊ ㄑㄩ)
① to bend oneself as a fist ② to be gnarled and twisted
拳拳服膺(ㄑㄩㄢˊ ㄑㄩㄢˊ ㄈㄨˊ ㄧㄥ)
to adhere to faithfully; to have a sincere belief in
拳師(ㄑㄩㄢˊ ㄕ)
an expert in the art of boxing; a boxing master; a boxer: 他是一個好拳師。He is a good boxer.
拳師狗(ㄑㄩㄢˊ ㄕ ㄍㄡˇ)
a boxer (dog)
拳術(ㄑㄩㄢˊ ㄕㄨˋ)or 拳法(ㄑㄩㄢˊ ㄈㄚˇ)
the boxing art; the pugilistic art
拳賽(ㄑㄩㄢˊ ㄙㄞˋ)
a boxing match
拳握(ㄑㄩㄢˊ ㄨㄛˋ)
to hold in the fist
拳王(ㄑㄩㄢˊ ㄨㄤˊ)
a boxing champion
拳勇(ㄑㄩㄢˊ ㄩㄥˇ)
a tough and powerful boxer; a good boxer

【拿】1874 (挐) ㄋㄚˊ na ná
1. to hold in one's hand; to grasp; to take: 誰拿了我的筆? Who has taken my pen?
2. to arrest; to apprehend; to capture: 將他拿下! Arrest him!
3. to use; to employ (a method, device, etc.)
4. with; in: 請拿事實來證明。Please prove with facts.
5. (now rarely) to be confined or restrained
拿班做勢(ㄋㄚˊ ㄅㄢ ㄗㄨㄛˋ ㄕˋ)
to act affectedly; affectations 亦作「裝腔作勢」
拿拌(ㄋㄚˊ ㄅㄢˋ)
to embarrass or make it difficult for another intentionally
拿不定主意(ㄋㄚˊ ㄅㄨˋ ㄉㄧㄥˋ ㄓㄨˇ ㄧˋ)
cannot make up one's mind: 他永遠拿不定主意。He would never make up his mind.
拿不動(ㄋㄚˊ ·ㄅㄨ ㄉㄨㄥˋ)
cannot take or hold it—too heavy
拿不了(ㄋㄚˊ ·ㄅㄨ ㄌㄧㄠˇ)
① cannot take or hold it —too heavy ② cannot take them all—too many
拿不起來(ㄋㄚˊ ·ㄅㄨ ㄑㄧˇ ·ㄌㄞ)
①cannot raise it—too heavy ② cannot control
拿不著(ㄋㄚˊ ·ㄅㄨ ㄓㄠˊ)
① can't reach it—too far out ② cannot get (the first prize, award, etc.)
拿不住(ㄋㄚˊ ·ㄅㄨ ㄓㄨˋ)
① cannot be grasped—too slippery; cannot keep in possession ② cannot hold it —too heavy ③ cannot seize or arrest ④ cannot control
拿不出手(ㄋㄚˊ ·ㄅㄨ ㄔㄨ ㄕㄡˇ)
not be presentable
拿不穩(ㄋㄚˊ ·ㄅㄨ ㄨㄣˇ)
cannot hold it steadily; unable to get a firm grasp; cannot be sure
拿破崙(ㄋㄚˊ ㄆㄛˋ ㄌㄨㄣˊ)
Napoleon Bonaparte (1769-1821), a famous French military strategist and emperor
拿大頂(ㄋㄚˊ ㄉㄚˋ ㄉㄧㄥˇ)
to stand on one's hands
拿得動(ㄋㄚˊ ·ㄉㄜ ㄉㄨㄥˋ)
able to hold or take it—not too heavy
拿得了(ㄋㄚˊ ·ㄉㄜ ㄌㄧㄠˇ)
able to take or hold them —not too many
拿得起(ㄋㄚˊ ·ㄉㄜ ㄑㄧˇ)
able to afford it
拿得起，放得下(ㄋㄚˊ ·ㄉㄜ ㄑㄧˇ, ㄈㄤˋ ·ㄉㄜ ㄒㄧㄚˋ)
able to advance or retreat, to attack or withdraw, etc. as the occasion demands; flexible; adaptable
拿得起來(ㄋㄚˊ ·ㄉㄜ ㄑㄧˇ ·ㄌㄞ)
① able to afford it ② able to raise it—not too heavy ③ (a person) of decision and determination ④(said of a person) competent
拿得住(ㄋㄚˊ ·ㄉㄜ ㄓㄨˋ)
① able to hold it steadily ② able to have a firm grasp on ③ able to restrain (a prisoner, etc.)
拿刀動杖(ㄋㄚˊ ㄉㄠ ㄉㄨㄥˋ ㄓㄤˋ)
to use force
拿定方針(ㄋㄚˊ ㄉㄧㄥˋ ㄈㄤ ㄓㄣ)

〔手部〕

〔手部〕

to decide on a way, measure, or policy without backing down
拿定主意(ㄋㄚˊ ㄉㄧㄥˋ ㄓㄨˇ ㄧˋ)
to make up one's mind; to be determined: 她拿定主意了。Her mind is made up.
拿捏(ㄋㄚˊ ·ㄋㄧㄝ)
① deliberately make things difficult for others ② to pretend to observe rules of propriety
拿過來(ㄋㄚˊ ㄍㄨㄛˋ ·ㄌㄞ) or 拿來(ㄋㄚˊ ·ㄌㄞ)
Bring it here. 或 Take it here.
拿開(ㄋㄚˊ ·ㄎㄞ)
Take it away! 或 to take away
拿獲(ㄋㄚˊ ㄏㄨㄛˋ)
to apprehend or arrest (a criminal)
拿架子(ㄋㄚˊ ㄐㄧㄚˋ ·ㄗ)
to play the VIP; to put on airs; haughty; arrogant
拿究(ㄋㄚˊ ㄐㄧㄡˋ)
to arrest and prosecute
拿緝(ㄋㄚˊ ㄑㄧˋ)
to search and arrest
拿去(ㄋㄚˊ ·ㄑㄩ)
Take it away. 或 to take away
拿主意(ㄋㄚˊ ㄓㄨˇ ·ㄧ)
to make a decision; to make up one's mind; to decide
拿住(ㄋㄚˊ ㄓㄨˋ)
① to apprehend; to put under arrest or custody ② to hold firmly
拿出(ㄋㄚˊ ㄔㄨ)
to take out; to produce: 他拿出一本書。He took a book out.
拿手(ㄋㄚˊ ㄕㄡˇ)
to be particularly good or dexterous at; one's special skill or ability: 我對剪紙很拿手。I am good at making paper-cuts.
拿手好戲(ㄋㄚˊ ㄕㄡˇ ㄏㄠˇ ㄒㄧˋ)
one's specialty; a part in which one feels particularly at home or competent; what one most excels in
拿人(ㄋㄚˊ ㄖㄣˊ)
to arrest a criminal
拿三搬四(ㄋㄚˊ ㄙㄢ ㄅㄢ ㄙˋ)
to resist orders and disobey instructions
拿送(ㄋㄚˊ ㄙㄨㄥˋ)
to arrest and turn over to court
拿穩(ㄋㄚˊ ㄨㄣˇ)
① to hold steadily ② to predict with confidence: 這件事他們拿穩嗎? Are they sure of it?
拿問(ㄋㄚˊ ㄨㄣˋ)
to detain for questioning

【挈】 1875 ㄑㄧㄝˋ chieh qiè

1. to lead: 挈出紅塵 to lead a person away from the mundane world
2. to rise above; to raise

挈領(ㄑㄧㄝˋ ㄌㄧㄥˇ)
to present the main points; to make a summary or a synopsis
挈眷(ㄑㄧㄝˋ ㄐㄩㄢˋ)
to travel with one's dependents

七畫

【挨】 1876 ㄞ ai āi (又讀 ㄞˊ air ái)

1. (to stay) near, next to, close to; to lean to: 他挨著窗子坐著。He is sitting by the window.
2. to suffer (from cold, hunger, etc.): 他在挨餓。He is suffering from hunger.
3. to wait; to delay; to put off: 我們再挨三天。Let's wait another three days.
4. according to order; in good order: 還沒挨到她吧? It isn't her turn yet, is it?
5. (now rarely) to rub; to scratch

挨罵(ㄞ ㄇㄚˋ)
to be blamed; to take the blame; to suffer revilement; to be scolded
挨磨(ㄞ ㄇㄛˊ)
to delay; to procrastinate
挨門兒(ㄞ ㄇㄜˊㄦ)
from door to door
挨門挨戶(ㄞ ㄇㄣˊ ㄞ ㄏㄨˋ)
to go from door to door: 他挨門挨戶給他們禮物。He went from door to door to give them presents.
挨佛勒斯峰(ㄞ ㄈㄛˊ ㄌㄜˋ ㄙ ㄈㄥ)
Mount Everest
挨打(ㄞ ㄉㄚˇ)
to come under attack; to suffer a beating; to deserve a beating: 這小孩應該挨打。The child deserves a beating.
挨推(ㄞ ㄊㄨㄟ)
to delay, procrastinate and shirk (one's responsibility, etc.)
挨冷受凍(ㄞ ㄌㄥˇ ㄕㄡˋ ㄉㄨㄥˋ)
to suffer from cold
挨個兒(ㄞ ㄍㄜˋㄦ)
one by one; in turn: 我們挨個兒上車吧。Let's get on the bus one by one.
挨靠(ㄞ ㄎㄠˋ)
① to lean on; to depend on; to rely on ② to be near to
挨擠(ㄞ ㄐㄧˇ)
to be pushed here and there in a large crowd
挨肩擦膀(ㄞ ㄐㄧㄢ ㄘㄚ ㄅㄤˇ)
to rub shoulders; to be near and intimate 亦作「挨肩兒」
挨近(ㄞ ㄐㄧㄣˋ)
near to; to be close to: 他家挨近火車站。His house is close to the railway station.
挨牆靠壁兒(ㄞ ㄑㄧㄤˊ ㄎㄠˋ ㄅㄧˋㄦ)
(literally) to lean on the wall—to place things in a safe place so that they won't get kicked over
挨著(ㄞ ·ㄓㄜ)
① next to: 他挨著她坐。He sits next to her. ② one by one: 他們一個挨著一個過去。They passed one by one.
挨著大樹有柴燒(ㄞ ·ㄓㄜ ㄉㄚˋ ㄕㄨˋ ㄧㄡˇ ㄔㄞˊ ㄕㄠ)
(literally) When you live close to big trees, there'll be enough firewood.—One's livelihood or career is assured if he has powerful friends.
挨揍(ㄞ ㄗㄡˋ)
to take a beating
挨次(ㄞ ㄘˋ)
in order; according to order; one after another: 乘客們挨次上車。The passengers got on the bus one after another.
挨餓(ㄞ ㄜˋ)

to suffer from hunger or starvation
挨挨蹭蹭(ㄞ ㄞ ㄘㄥˋ ㄘㄥˋ)
very crowded

【挪】 1877
ㄋㄨㄛˊ nuo nuó
to move; to shift; to transfer: 請把椅子挪到那兒。Move the chair over there, please.
挪不動(ㄋㄨㄛˊ ·ㄅㄨ ㄉㄨㄥˋ)
cannot move it
挪不開(ㄋㄨㄛˊ ·ㄅㄨ ㄎㄞ)
cannot move away
挪墊(ㄋㄨㄛˊ ㄉㄧㄢˋ)
to borrow from public fund for private use
挪東補西(ㄋㄨㄛˊ ㄉㄨㄥ ㄅㄨˇ ㄒㄧ)
to make up deficiency at one place by drawing upon the surplus at another
挪動(ㄋㄨㄛˊ ㄉㄨㄥˋ)
to move
挪款(ㄋㄨㄛˊ ㄎㄨㄢˇ)
to transfer money or an account
挪借(ㄋㄨㄛˊ ㄐㄧㄝˋ)
to borrow from the public funds; to get a short-term loan
挪移(ㄋㄨㄛˊ ㄧˊ)
① to move ② to borrow from the public funds
挪威(ㄋㄨㄛˊ ㄨㄟ)
Norway
挪威人(ㄋㄨㄛˊ ㄨㄟ ㄖㄣˊ)
a Norwegian
挪用(ㄋㄨㄛˊ ㄩㄥˋ)
to use money for a purpose not originally intended; to embezzle; to misappropriate
挪用公款(ㄋㄨㄛˊ ㄩㄥˋ ㄍㄨㄥ ㄎㄨㄢˇ)
to embezzle public money; misappropriation of public funds

【挱】 1878
1.ㄙㄨㄛ suo suō
to touch; to feel with hands

【挱】 1878
2.ㄕㄚ sha shā
widespread; open

【挫】 1879
ㄘㄨㄛˋ tsuoh cuò
1. to defeat; to frustrate: 他想做那件事而遭受挫折。He was frustrated in an attempt to do it.
2. to damp: 沒什麼東西可以使他興致挫減。Nothing could damp his spirits.
3. to humiliate; to treat harshly
挫敗(ㄘㄨㄛˋ ㄅㄞˋ)
a setback; a defeat; failure
挫磨(ㄘㄨㄛˋ ㄇㄛˊ)
to ill-use; to ill-treat; ill-treatment
挫敵(ㄘㄨㄛˋ ㄉㄧˊ)
to defeat the enemy; to give the enemy a bloody nose
挫折(ㄘㄨㄛˋ ㄓㄜˊ)
① a setback; defeat; failure: 他屢遭挫折。He often suffered setbacks. ② to frustrate
挫辱(ㄘㄨㄛˋ ㄖㄨˋ)
to humiliate; to put to shame
挫銳(ㄘㄨㄛˋ ㄖㄨㄟˋ)
to damp the morale (of the enemy); to demoralize

【振】 1880
1. ㄓㄣˋ jenn zhèn
1. to arouse to action; to raise; to rise: 他的精神振奮起來。His spirits rose.
2. to pull up; to save; to relieve: 振作起精神,正視人生。Pull yourself together and face up to life.
3. to shake; to flap as wings: 大將軍威振天下。The great general's power shook the world.
4. to restore order
振筆直書(ㄓㄣˋ ㄅㄧˇ ㄓˊ ㄕㄨ)
to write rapidly; to wield the pen furiously
振臂(ㄓㄣˋ ㄅㄧˋ)
to raise one's arm
振臂一呼(ㄓㄣˋ ㄅㄧˋ ㄧˋ ㄏㄨ)
to raise one's arm and issue a clarion call; to arouse to action
振兵(ㄓㄣˋ ㄅㄧㄥ)
to rally the troops
振怖(ㄓㄣˋ ㄅㄨˋ)
to alarm
振靡(ㄓㄣˋ ㄇㄧˇ)
to awaken the weak and enervated
振奮(ㄓㄣˋ ㄈㄣˋ)
① to arouse to action; to arouse; to stimulate; to excite ② heartening; encouraging; exciting
振幅(ㄓㄣˋ ㄈㄨˊ)
(physics) amplitude
振盪(ㄓㄣˋ ㄉㄤˋ)
①(physics) vibration ②(electricity) oscillation
振動(ㄓㄣˋ ㄉㄨㄥˋ)
(physics) vibration; to vibrate: 火車經過時房屋在振動。The house vibrates when a train passes.
振鈴(ㄓㄣˋ ㄌㄧㄥˊ)
to ring a bell
振聾發聵(ㄓㄣˋ ㄌㄨㄥˊ ㄈㄚ ㄍㄨㄟˋ)
(said of ringing statements) to awaken the laggard and to arouse the phlegmatic
振旅(ㄓㄣˋ ㄌㄩˇ)
the neat formation of a triumphant army; the orderly return of a victorious army
振古(ㄓㄣˋ ㄍㄨˇ)
from ancient times
振翮(ㄓㄣˋ ㄏㄜˊ) or 振翼(ㄓㄣˋ ㄧˋ)
to spread the wings; to flap; ready to take off: 鳥正振翼飛翔。The bird is flapping its wings.
振起(ㄓㄣˋ ㄑㄧˇ)
to stir up; to get aroused; to rise and meet a challenge: 你應該振起精神來。You should put forth fresh energy.
振興(ㄓㄣˋ ㄒㄧㄥ)
to promote or develop (industrial endeavor, etc.); to prosper
振振有詞(ㄓㄣˋ ㄓㄣˋ ㄧㄡˇ ㄘˊ)
to talk fluently and loudly (as if one has all the reasons on his side); never short of words in defending oneself against a charge, criticism, etc.
振翅(ㄓㄣˋ ㄔˋ)
to flap (wings); to flutter: 鳥在樹林中振翅(鼓翼)。The birds fluttered in the trees.
振刷(ㄓㄣˋ ㄕㄨㄚ)
to rise; to arouse (oneself)
振作(ㄓㄣˋ ㄗㄨㄛˋ)
to arouse (oneself); to bestir (oneself); to brace up: 喂!振作起精神來。Come, bestir yourself! 或 Brace up!
振衣(ㄓㄣˋ ㄧ)
to shake one's clothing
振纓(ㄓㄣˋ ㄧㄥ)

to rise to officialdom; to become an official
振威(ㄓㄣˋ ㄨㄟ)
to inspire awe; to extend one's imposing prestige

〔手部〕

【振】 1880
2. ㄓㄣ jen zhēn
benevolent and generous
振振(ㄓㄣ ㄓㄣ)
benevolent and generous; noble

【挼】 1881
ㄋㄨㄛˊ nuo nuó
(讀音ㄖㄨㄛˊ ruo ruó)
1. to rub; to stroke
2. to crumple (paper into a ball, etc.)
挼搓(ㄖㄨㄛˊ ㄘㄨㄛ)
to crumple

【挹】 1882
ㄧˋ yih yì
1. to decant liquids, especially wine
2. to retreat
挹彼注此(ㄧˋ ㄅㄧˇ ㄓㄨˋ ㄘˇ)
(literally) to pour from one vessel to another—to make up the deficiency of one by drawing upon the surplus of another
挹掬(ㄧˋ ㄐㄩˊ)
to scoop up water with hands
挹注(ㄧˋ ㄓㄨˋ)
to supplement; to draw from one to make up the deficits in another
挹酌(ㄧˋ ㄓㄨㄛˊ)
to pour out wine

【挽】 1883
ㄨㄢˇ woan wǎn
1. to draw (a bow, etc.); to pull: 他挽著弓。He drew a bow.
2. to restore
3. to seize
4. to roll up (sleeves, etc.): 他們挽起袖子。They rolled up their sleeves.
挽留(ㄨㄢˇ ㄌㄧㄡˊ)
to request to stay; to urge to stay
挽弓當挽強(ㄨㄢˇ ㄍㄨㄥ ㄉㄤ ㄨㄢˇ ㄑㄧㄤˊ)
(literally) If you want to draw a bow, take the most powerful. —to try the toughest so as to get the most far-reaching result
挽回(ㄨㄢˇ ㄏㄨㄟˊ)
to try with effort to turn back an adverse tide; to retrieve; to redeem: 他挽回了名譽。He redeemed his honor.
挽回大局(ㄨㄢˇ ㄏㄨㄟˊ ㄉㄚˋ ㄐㄩˊ)
to save the general situation from worsening; to restore the general situation
挽髻(ㄨㄢˇ ㄐㄧˋ)
to tie the hair into a knot
挽救(ㄨㄢˇ ㄐㄧㄡˋ)
to save (a situation, a failing concern, etc.): 醫生挽救了病人的生命。The doctor saved the patient's life.
挽袖(ㄨㄢˇ ㄒㄧㄡˋ)
to roll up sleeves
挽住(ㄨㄢˇ ㄓㄨˋ)
to hold back; to hold another (from going away, etc.)
挽車(ㄨㄢˇ ㄔㄜ)
to pull a cart
挽手(ㄨㄢˇ ㄕㄡˇ)
to hold hands; arm in arm; hand in hand: 他們挽手離去。They walked away hand in hand.
挽引(ㄨㄢˇ ㄧㄣˇ)
to pull with force

【挺】 1884
ㄊㄧㄥˇ tiing tǐng
1. to stand straight (or upright); to square; to straighten; rigid: 他挺起胸膛。He squared his shoulders.
2. to pull up
3. unyielding; unbending; tough
4. outstanding; remarkable; eminent; prominent
5. to thrust forward (as one's breast)
6. to sustain; to endure; to pull through; to stand; to hold out: 她挺得住嗎? Can she stand it?
7. very; pretty
8. the number of machine guns: 一百多挺機槍 over one hundred machine guns
挺拔(ㄊㄧㄥˇ ㄅㄚˊ)
independent, outstanding and eminent
挺不住(ㄊㄧㄥˇ ·ㄅㄨ ㄓㄨˋ)
cannot stand it; cannot take it any more—too heavy, difficult, etc: 她挺不住這種寒冷了。She cannot stand this cold any longer.
挺挺(ㄊㄧㄥˇ ㄊㄧㄥˇ)
straightforward; unyielding or unbending; stiff: 他直挺挺地躺着。He lied stiff.
挺立(ㄊㄧㄥˇ ㄌㄧˋ)
to stand upright; to stand erect; to stand up straight
挺好(ㄊㄧㄥˇ ㄏㄠˇ)
very good; quite good: 那個主意挺好。That idea is very good.
挺節(ㄊㄧㄥˇ ㄐㄧㄝˊ)
to hold fast to one's principle; virtuous
挺緊(ㄊㄧㄥˇ ㄐㄧㄣˇ)
to pull tight; very tight
挺進(ㄊㄧㄥˇ ㄐㄧㄣˋ)
(said of troops) to drive on boldly; to push forward
挺進隊(ㄊㄧㄥˇ ㄐㄧㄣˋ ㄉㄨㄟˋ) or 挺進軍(ㄊㄧㄥˇ ㄐㄧㄣˋ ㄐㄩㄣ)
tough vanguard units
挺舉(ㄊㄧㄥˇ ㄐㄩˇ)
(weightlifting) clean and jerk
挺秀(ㄊㄧㄥˇ ㄒㄧㄡˋ)
(looking) elegant and prominent
挺胸(ㄊㄧㄥˇ ㄒㄩㄥ)
to thrust out one's chest
挺直(ㄊㄧㄥˇ ㄓˊ)
straight and upright; erect: 他挺直身子站著。He stood erect.
挺屍(ㄊㄧㄥˇ ㄕ)
a stiff corpse—(now comically) to sleep in this manner
挺身(ㄊㄧㄥˇ ㄕㄣ)
to straighten one's back
挺身而出(ㄊㄧㄥˇ ㄕㄣ ㄦˊ ㄔㄨ)
to thrust oneself out to face a challenge; to stand up and volunteer to help
挺升(ㄊㄧㄥˇ ㄕㄥ)
(said of prices) to rise steeply
挺然不羣(ㄊㄧㄥˇ ㄖㄢˊ ㄅㄨˋ ㄑㄩㄣˊ)
towering above others; outstanding; to be distinguished from others
挺而走險(ㄊㄧㄥˇ ㄦˊ ㄗㄡˇ ㄒㄧㄢˇ)
① to risk danger in desperation; to make a reckless

move ②to be forced to break the law 亦作「鋌而走險」

挺硬(ㄊㄧㄥˇ ㄧㄥˋ)
very hard; stiff and stubborn; unyielding and tough

【捃】 1885
ㄐㄩㄣˋ jiunn jùn
to pick up; to gather; to collect

捃華(ㄐㄩㄣˋ ㄏㄨㄚˊ)
to gather the most important or significant points or parts; a collection of such; to select the most essential points

捃摭(ㄐㄩㄣˋ ㄓˊ)
to collect (samples, specimens, etc.)

捃拾(ㄐㄩㄣˋ ㄕˊ)
to collect; to gather; to pick up

【捆】 1886
ㄎㄨㄣˇ koen kǔn
1. to bind; to tie up: 他在捆包裹。He is tying up his parcel.
2. a bundle: 一捆乾草 a bundle of hay

捆綁(ㄎㄨㄣˇ ㄅㄤˇ)
to bind: 他們把他的手脚捆綁起來。They bound him hand and foot.

捆縛(ㄎㄨㄣˇ ㄈㄨˋ)
to bind; to tie up; bound

捆起來(ㄎㄨㄣˇ ㄑㄧˇ ·ㄌㄞ)
to tie up (a prisoner, etc.): 我會把你的東西用手帕捆起來。I'll tie up your things in a handkerchief.

捆住(ㄎㄨㄣˇ ㄓㄨˋ)
to tie up; to bind up

捆上(ㄎㄨㄣˇ ·ㄕㄤ)
to bind up

捆子(ㄎㄨㄣˇ ·ㄗ) or 捆兒(ㄎㄨㄜˇㄦ)
a bundle

捆鎖(ㄎㄨㄣˇ ㄙㄨㄛˇ)
to chain or fetter; anything that serves as such

捆押(ㄎㄨㄣˇ ㄧㄚ)
to put under restraint; to tie up and escort (a criminal)

【捋】 1887
1. ㄌㄜˋ leh lè
to pluck; to gather in the fingers

捋虎鬚(ㄌㄜˋ ㄏㄨˇ ㄒㄩ)
(literally) to pluck the tiger's whiskers—to offend the powerful

【捋】 1887
2. ㄌㄩˇ leu lǚ
to stroke (one's beard, etc.); to smooth out with fingers: 他把紙捋平。He smoothed out a piece of paper.

捋鬍鬚(ㄌㄩˇ ㄏㄨˊ ㄒㄩ)
to stroke one's beard

【捋】 1887
3. ㄌㄨㄛ lhuo luō
1. to rub one's palm along (something long)
2. to squeeze with hands

捋奶(ㄌㄨㄛ ㄋㄞˇ)
to milk (a cow, goat, etc.)

捋胳膊(ㄌㄨㄛ ㄍㄜ ·ㄅㄛ)
to pull up one's sleeves and show the arms

捋汗(ㄌㄨㄛ ㄏㄢˋ)
to be very much embarrassed

【捉】 1888
ㄓㄨㄛ juo zhuō
1. to seize; to grasp; to catch; to hold: 他捉住小偷不放。He seized hold of the thief and would not let him go.
2. to apprehend; to arrest: 他們在捕捉竊賊。They were apprehending a thief.

捉摸不定(ㄓㄨㄛ ㄇㄛ ㄅㄨˋ ㄉㄧㄥˋ)
unfathomable; unpredictable; difficult to ascertain; elusive: 那個意思叫我捉摸不定。The meaning is elusive to me.

捉脈(ㄓㄨㄛ ㄇㄛˋ)
(said of Chinese herb doctors) to feel the patient's pulse

捉迷藏(ㄓㄨㄛ ㄇㄧˊ ㄘㄤˊ)
①to play hide-and-seek; hide-and-seek ②to beat about the bush

捉刀(ㄓㄨㄛ ㄉㄠ)
to ghostwrite; to have something written by a ghostwriter

捉拿(ㄓㄨㄛ ㄋㄚˊ) or 捉搦(ㄓㄨㄛ ㄋㄨㄛˋ)
to apprehend; to arrest: 警方捉拿逃犯。The police arrested an escaped prisoner.

捉弄(ㄓㄨㄛ ㄌㄨㄥˋ)
to play a joke (or trick) on (somebody); to make fun of; to harass

捉虎容易放虎難(ㄓㄨㄛ ㄏㄨˇ ㄖㄨㄥˊ ㄧˋ ㄈㄤˋ ㄏㄨˇ ㄋㄢˊ)
(literally) It's easier to catch a tiger than to set it free.—It's easier to start something than to conclude it satisfactorily.

捉姦(ㄓㄨㄛ ㄐㄧㄢ)
to catch a person in the act of adultery (usually by the wronged husband or wife)

捉襟見肘(ㄓㄨㄛ ㄐㄧㄣ ㄐㄧㄢˋ ㄓㄡˇ)
hard-pressed for money; in financial straits

捉狹(ㄓㄨㄛ ㄒㄧㄚˊ)
mischievous

捉狹鬼(ㄓㄨㄛ ㄒㄧㄚˊ ㄍㄨㄟˇ)
one who likes to play jokes; a mischievous fellow

捉住(ㄓㄨㄛ ㄓㄨˋ)
to catch; to seize

捉賊(ㄓㄨㄛ ㄗㄟˊ)
to catch thieves: 作賊喊著捉賊。The thief was crying, "Stop the thief!"

捉妖(ㄓㄨㄛ ㄧㄠ)
(Taoism) to catch the evil spirit; to exorcise

【挾】 1889
ㄒㄧㄝˊ shye xié
(又讀 ㄒㄧㄚˊ shya xiá)
1. to clasp or hold under the arm: 他挾著一個書包。He carried a satchel under the arm.
2. to embrace; to bosom
3. to presume upon (one's influence, advantage, etc.)
4. to extort; to blackmail; to hold (a crown prince, etc.) as a hostage

挾帶
①(ㄒㄧㄝˊ ㄉㄞˋ)to carry under arms
②(ㄐㄧㄚˊ ㄉㄞˋ)ⓐ to smuggle ⓑ things smuggled (into a country or an examination room, etc.)

挾泰山以超北海(ㄒㄧㄝˊ ㄊㄞˋ ㄕㄢ ㄧˇ ㄔㄠ ㄅㄟˇ ㄏㄞˇ)
(literally) to clasp Mt. Tai under the arm and cross the North Sea—an impossible task

挾天子以令諸侯(ㄒㄧㄝˊ ㄊㄧㄢ ㄗˇ ㄧˇ ㄌㄧㄥˋ ㄓㄨ ㄏㄡˊ)

to usurp power by holding the emperor as a hostage and acting in his name

挾貴(ㄒㄧㄝˊ ㄍㄨㄟˋ)
to presume upon one's blue blood or high position

挾貴自重(ㄒㄧㄝˊ ㄍㄨㄟˋ ㄗˋ ㄓㄨㄥˋ)
to be proud of one's high position

挾恨(ㄒㄧㄝˊ ㄏㄣˋ)or 挾仇(ㄒㄧㄝˊ ㄔㄡˊ) or 挾怨(ㄒㄧㄝˊ ㄩㄢˋ)
to bear a grudge

挾嫌(ㄒㄧㄝˊ ㄒㄧㄢˊ)
to bear a grudge; to harbor resentment

挾制(ㄒㄧㄝˊ ㄓˋ)
to force someone into submission by taking advantage of his weaknesses or threatening to expose his secrets

挾持(ㄒㄧㄝˊ ㄔˊ)
①to grasp someone on both sides by the arms ②to hold someone under duress

挾勢(ㄒㄧㄝˊ ㄕˋ)
to presume upon one's influence or high position

【捍】 1890 ㄏㄢˋ hann hàn
to defend; to guard; to ward off: 他們捍衛這城以禦敵。They defended the city against the enemy.

捍海塘(ㄏㄢˋ ㄏㄞˇ ㄊㄤˊ)
①name of a dike built in the first decades of the 10th century by Chien Liu (錢鏐) at today's Hangchow ②name of a dike along the sea coast of Kiangsu and Chekiang built during the Tang Dynasty

捍衛(ㄏㄢˋ ㄨㄟˋ)
to defend (a nation's territory, etc.); to protect: 捍衛國家是軍人的責任。The duty of a soldier is to defend his country.

捍禦(ㄏㄢˋ ㄩˋ)
to ward off; to guard against

【捌】 1891 ㄅㄚ ba bā
1. an elaborate form of eight (八)—used in checks or accounts to prevent fraud
2. to pull apart; to break 亦作「扒」

【捕】 1892 ㄅㄨˇ buu bǔ
1. to arrest; to apprehend; to catch; to seize: 他已被捕。He is under arrest. 或 He is arrested.
2. (formerly) a policeman

捕票(ㄅㄨˇ ㄆㄧㄠˋ)
a warrant for arrest; an arrest warrant

捕房(ㄅㄨˇ ㄈㄤˊ)
(formerly) a police station or precinct in the foreign settlements or concessions

捕風捉影(ㄅㄨˇ ㄈㄥ ㄓㄨㄛ ㄧㄥˇ)
(literally) to chase the wind and catch the shadow—talks that are not substantiated by any evidence or proof

捕頭(ㄅㄨˇ ㄊㄡˊ)
(formerly) a head constable

捕拿(ㄅㄨˇ ㄋㄚˊ)
to arrest; to apprehend; to capture; to catch

捕撈(ㄅㄨˇ ㄌㄠ)
to fish for (aquatic animals and plants); to catch: 他們在捕撈龍蝦。They're catching lobsters.

捕撈能力(ㄅㄨˇ ㄌㄠ ㄋㄥˊ ㄌㄧˋ)
fishing capacity

捕快(ㄅㄨˇ ㄎㄨㄞˋ)
(formerly) constables or policemen

捕獲(ㄅㄨˇ ㄏㄨㄛˋ)
to arrest; to catch; to capture: 有五名敵人被捕獲。Five of the enemy were captured.

捕鯨船(ㄅㄨˇ ㄐㄧㄥ ㄔㄨㄢˊ)
a whaleboat; a whaleship; a whaler

捕捉(ㄅㄨˇ ㄓㄨㄛ)
to chase or hunt down; to seize; to arrest; to capture: 他在捕捉昆蟲。He was catching insects.

捕蟲燈(ㄅㄨˇ ㄔㄨㄥˊ ㄉㄥ)
a lamp installed on farms to catch insects in night hours

捕蟲葉(ㄅㄨˇ ㄔㄨㄥˊ ㄧㄝˋ)
an insect-catching leaf

捕蟲網(ㄅㄨˇ ㄔㄨㄥˊ ㄨㄤˇ)
an insect-catching net

捕食(ㄅㄨˇ ㄕˊ)
to catch and feed on; to prey on: 猫捕食老鼠。Cats prey upon mice.

捕殺(ㄅㄨˇ ㄕㄚ)
to catch and kill (wild or unlicensed dogs, etc.)

捕手(ㄅㄨˇ ㄕㄡˇ)
(baseball) a catcher: 他是位好捕手。He is a good catcher.

捕鼠器(ㄅㄨˇ ㄕㄨˇ ㄑㄧˋ)
a mousetrap

捕役(ㄅㄨˇ ㄧˋ)or 捕差(ㄅㄨˇ ㄔㄞ)
(formerly) constables or policemen

捕蠅器(ㄅㄨˇ ㄧㄥˊ ㄑㄧˋ)
a flytrap

捕蠅紙(ㄅㄨˇ ㄧㄥˊ ㄓˇ)
a flypaper

捕蠅草(ㄅㄨˇ ㄧㄥˊ ㄘㄠˇ)
a flycatcher; a flytrap

捕魚(ㄅㄨˇ ㄩˊ)
to catch fish; to fish: 他們在海上捕魚。They fished on the sea.

【捐】 1893 ㄐㄩㄢ jiuan juān
1. tax; duty; charge; dues: 稅捐 taxes and surtaxes
2. to donate; to contribute; to subscribe: 他捐了一大筆錢給那所孤兒院。He donated a large sum of money to that orphanage.
3. to buy or purchase (an official rank)
4. to give up (one's life for a cause, etc.)
5. to remove

捐背(ㄐㄩㄢ ㄅㄟˋ)
to desert; to walk out on somebody

捐命(ㄐㄩㄢ ㄇㄧㄥˋ)
to die

捐納(ㄐㄩㄢ ㄋㄚˋ)
to buy a government appointment with grain or money

捐官(ㄐㄩㄢ ㄍㄨㄢ)
to purchase an official rank or a title (especially in the Ching Dynasty)

捐款(ㄐㄩㄢ ㄎㄨㄢˇ)
①to donate money ②donations

捐款收入(ㄐㄩㄢ ㄎㄨㄢˇ ㄕㄡ ㄖㄨˋ)
contribution receipts

捐棄(ㄐㄩㄢ ㄑㄧˋ)
to renounce; to reject; to relinquish; to give up

捐棄成見(ㄐㄩㄢ ㄑㄧˋ ㄔㄥˊ ㄐㄧㄢˋ)

to cast away all prejudices; to divest prejudices from one's mind

捐錢(ㄐㄩㄢ ㄑㄧㄢˊ)

to donate money; donations

捐軀(ㄐㄩㄢ ㄑㄩ)

to die for one's country or duty

捐軀赴義(ㄐㄩㄢ ㄑㄩ ㄈㄨˋ ㄧˋ)

to die for the cause of justice and righteousness

捐血(ㄐㄩㄢ ㄒㄧㄝˇ)

①to donate blood ②blood donation

捐獻(ㄐㄩㄢ ㄒㄧㄢˋ)

to contribute; contributions; donations: 請惠予捐獻。Contributions are requested.

捐助(ㄐㄩㄢ ㄓㄨˋ)

to contribute; to donate (to help the poor, relief work, etc.): 他們經常捐助紅十字會。They often contributed to the Red Cross.

捐輸(ㄐㄩㄢ ㄕㄨ)

to donate; to contribute; to make financial contributions to the government

捐稅(ㄐㄩㄢ ㄕㄨㄟˋ)

taxes and surcharges

捐貲 or 捐資(ㄐㄩㄢ ㄗ)

to donate one's property

捐贈(ㄐㄩㄢ ㄗㄥˋ)

①(said of a newspaper, radio or TV station, etc.) to allot free space, time, services, etc. for a worthy cause ②to donate or contribute: 林先生把這批藏書捐贈給我們學校。Mr. Lin has donated this library to our school.

捐册(ㄐㄩㄢ ㄘㄜˋ) or 捐簿(ㄐㄩㄢ ㄅㄨˋ)

a book recording names of the donators and the amounts donated

【捎】 1894
1. ㄕㄠ shau shāo

1. to carry; to take or bring along at one's convenience: 請捎個口信給他。Please take a message to him.
2. to brush over lightly
3. to wipe out

捎帶(ㄕㄠ ㄉㄞˋ)

to carry; to take along at one's convenience

【捎】 1894
2. ㄕㄠˋ shaw shào

1. (said of colors, etc.) to fade; to discolor
2. to sprinkle water
3. to watch secretly; to spy on; to glance at

捎色(ㄕㄠˋ ㄙㄜˋ)

to discolor; to fade

【捏】 1895
(揑) ㄋㄧㄝ nhie niē

1. to knead; to pinch; to squeeze or press with fingers: 麵包師正在捏揉麵團。The baker was kneading dough.
2. to mold (mud, etc.): 他用黏土捏成一座半身雕塑像。He molded clay into a bust.
3. to fabricate; to trump up; to make up

捏報(ㄋㄧㄝ ㄅㄠˋ) or 捏告(ㄋㄧㄝ ㄍㄠˋ)

to present a false report or charge; to fabricate a report or charge; to fake a report

捏弄(ㄋㄧㄝ ㄋㄨㄥˋ)

①to fabricate; to trump up ②to bring together (two people, a couple, etc.)

捏控(ㄋㄧㄝ ㄎㄨㄥˋ) or 捏稱(ㄋㄧㄝ ㄔㄥ)

to fabricate a charge or an accusation

捏合(ㄋㄧㄝ ㄏㄜˊ)

to bring a couple together; to try to make a pair get into a union

捏陷(ㄋㄧㄝ ㄒㄧㄢˋ)

to incriminate another by fabricated charges

捏著(ㄋㄧㄝ ˙ㄓㄜ)

to squeeze or hold with fingers

捏著鼻子(ㄋㄧㄝ ˙ㄓㄜ ㄅㄧˊ ˙ㄗ)

①to hold one's nose (as a protection against obnoxious odors) ②to get ready for an unpleasant experience ahead

捏手捏脚(ㄋㄧㄝ ㄕㄡˇ ㄋㄧㄝ ㄐㄧㄠˇ)

stealthily; to move around lightly; to pussyfoot

捏神捏鬼(ㄋㄧㄝ ㄕㄣˊ ㄋㄧㄝ ㄍㄨㄟˇ)

to do or negotiate stealthily

捏造(ㄋㄧㄝ ㄗㄠˋ)

to fabricate (evidence, etc.); to trump up (charges, etc.); to fake; to make up: 他們捏造口實。They trumped up an excuse.

捏造罪名(ㄋㄧㄝ ㄗㄠˋ ㄗㄨㄟˋ ㄇㄧㄥˊ)

to fabricate an accusation

捏造謠言(ㄋㄧㄝ ㄗㄠˋ ㄧㄠˊ ㄧㄢˊ)

to fabricate and spread rumors; to invent slanders: 他捏造謠言。He fabricated a story.

捏詞(ㄋㄧㄝ ㄘˊ)

lies; slanders

捏塑(ㄋㄧㄝ ㄙㄨˋ)

to mold (mud) into a statue, etc.: 我們用黏土捏塑出塑像。We mold statues out of clay.

捏酸(ㄋㄧㄝ ㄙㄨㄢ)

to feign gentleness and erudition; to pretend to be a scholar

捏一把汗(ㄋㄧㄝ ㄧˋ ㄅㄚˇ ㄏㄢˋ)

to break out into cold perspiration (before, during or immediately after a very dangerous situation, narrow escape, etc.); to be breathless with anxiety; to be seized with fear or deep concern

【挶】 1896
ㄐㄩˊ jyu jú

a receptacle for earth

八畫

【捨】 1897
(舍) ㄕㄜˇ shee shě

1. to reject; to give up; to abandon; to relinquish; to renounce; to part with; to forsake; to let go: 捨棄所有的爛蘋果。Reject all spotted apples.
2. to give alms; to give to charity: 施捨給窮人 to give alms to the poor

捨本逐末(ㄕㄜˇ ㄅㄣˇ ㄓㄨˊ ㄇㄛˋ)

to concentrate on details but forget the main purpose or objective; to attend to trifles to the extent of neglecting essentials

捨不得(ㄕㄜˇ ㄅㄨˋ ˙ㄉㄜ) or 捨不了(ㄕㄜˇ ˙ㄅㄨ ㄌㄧㄠˇ)

reluctant to give up, let go, etc. (because of emotional attachment or high value of the object to be given up); to hate to part with: 她捨不

〔手部〕

得亂花一分錢。She hates to waste a single cent.
捨命(ㄕㄜˇ ㄇㄧㄥˋ)
in disregard of one's safety or life; to give up one's life; to risk one's life
捨得(ㄕㄜˇ ˙ㄉㄜ)
to be willing to part with (a person, thing, etc.); not to grudge: 他很捨得付出你所要的價錢。He is quite willing to pay the price you asked.
捨短取長(ㄕㄜˇ ㄉㄨㄢˇ ㄑㄩˇ ㄔㄤˊ)
to disregard shortcomings and adopt good points
捨己從人(ㄕㄜˇ ㄐㄧˇ ㄘㄨㄥˊ ㄖㄣˊ)
to give up one's views and follow those of another person
捨己爲人(ㄕㄜˇ ㄐㄧˇ ㄨㄟˋ ㄖㄣˊ)
to give up one's own interests for the sake of others
捨近求遠(ㄕㄜˇ ㄐㄧㄣˋ ㄑㄧㄡˊ ㄩㄢˇ)
to reject what is near at hand and seek for what is far away 亦作「捨近取遠」
捨棄(ㄕㄜˇ ㄑㄧˋ)
to give up or renounce; to abandon; to relinquish: 我永遠不捨棄我的朋友。I would never abandon my friends.
捨身(ㄕㄜˇ ㄕㄣ)
to give up one's life (for a cause, principle, etc.): 他捨身救了那男孩。He gave his life to rescue the boy.
捨生取義(ㄕㄜˇ ㄕㄥ ㄑㄩˇ ㄧˋ)
to give up one's life for righteousness; to sacrifice oneself for righteousness; to prefer honor to life; to lay down one's life for a just cause
捨死忘生(ㄕㄜˇ ㄙˇ ㄨㄤˋ ㄕㄥ)
to disregard one's safety or life—full devotion or dedication

【捧】 1898 ㄆㄥˇ peeng pěng

1. to hold something in both hands; to scoop up something with one's hands: 他雙手捧著一些蘋果。He held some apples in his hands.
2. to boost; to flatter; to treat as a VIP: 她把他捧得太高了。She praised him too highly.
3. to support, cheer or render assistance by one's presence

捧腹(ㄆㄥˇ ㄈㄨˋ)or 捧腹大笑(ㄆㄥˇ ㄈㄨˋ ㄉㄚˋ ㄒㄧㄠˋ)or 捧腹絕倒(ㄆㄥˇ ㄈㄨˋ ㄐㄩㄝˊ ㄉㄠˇ)
to hold one's sides with laughter: 他的笑話令我們捧腹。His joke made us burst out laughing.
捧讀(ㄆㄥˇ ㄉㄨˊ)
to have the privilege of reading your (book, letter, etc.); to read carefully 亦作「捧誦」
捧角兒(ㄆㄥˇ ㄐㄩㄝˊㄦ)
to cheer one's favorite actor or actress with constant presence, applause, cash reward, gifts, etc.
捧心(ㄆㄥˇ ㄒㄧㄣ)
(said of homely women) to ape the mannerism of a beautiful woman
捧著雞毛當令箭(ㄆㄥˇ ˙ㄓㄜ ㄐㄧ ㄇㄠˊ ㄉㄤ ㄌㄧㄥˋ ㄐㄧㄢˋ)
to make a fuss about a casual remark of the boss
捧住(ㄆㄥˇ ㄓㄨˋ)
to hold firmly and securely
捧臭脚(ㄆㄥˇ ㄔㄡˋ ㄐㄧㄠˇ)
(literally) to hold with respect an odorous foot — to act obsequiously
捧場(ㄆㄥˇ ㄔㄤˇ)or(ㄆㄥˇ ㄔㄤˊ)
to render support or assistance, by one's presence, endorsement, etc.
捧上天(ㄆㄥˇ ㄕㄤˋ ㄊㄧㄢ)
to overpraise someone: 他們把他捧上天。They praised him to the skies.
捧日(ㄆㄥˇ ㄖˋ)
to support (a king, leader, etc.)

【捩】 1899 ㄌㄧㄝˋ lieh liè

1. to twist with hands
2. to rip or tear apart

【捭】 1900 ㄅㄞˇ bae bǎi

1. to open; to spread out
2. to strike with both hands

捭闔縱橫(ㄅㄞˇ ㄏㄜˊ ㄗㄨㄥˋ ㄏㄥˊ)
suave and ingenious persuasion 亦作「縱橫捭闔」

【捫】 1901 ㄇㄣˊ men mén

1. to feel or touch with hands; to hold
2. to search (in one's pocket, etc.)

捫心自問(ㄇㄣˊ ㄒㄧㄣ ㄗˋ ㄨㄣˋ)
to examine oneself; introspection
捫心無愧(ㄇㄣˊ ㄒㄧㄣ ㄨˊ ㄎㄨㄟˋ)
to examine oneself and find nothing to be ashamed of
捫蝨而談(ㄇㄣˊ ㄕ ㄦˊ ㄊㄢˊ)
to talk freely without being awed in the presence of the high and mighty
捫舌(ㄇㄣˊ ㄕㄜˊ)
to hold the tongue with fingers so that one cannot talk; to hold one's tongue

【据】 1902 1. ㄐㄩ jiu jū

as in 拮据—stiff joints in the hand, used most often to describe financial stringency or short of money

【据】 1902 2. ㄐㄩˋ jiuh jù

1. same as 據—according to
2. same as 倨—arrogant; haughty

【捱】 1903 ㄞˊ air ái

1. to suffer; to endure
2. to procrastinate; to put off
3. to rub (shoulders)
4. to draw near; to come close to

捱不住(ㄞˊ ˙ㄅㄨ ㄓㄨˋ)
cannot endure any more
捱過(ㄞˊ ㄍㄨㄛˋ)
to weather, or to survive (a crisis, an ordeal, etc.): 這船平安捱過風暴。The ship weathered the storm.
捱苦(ㄞˊ ㄎㄨˇ)
to endure hardships
捱肩擦背(ㄞˊ ㄐㄧㄢ ㄘㄚ ㄅㄟˋ)
to rub shoulders and backs in a large crowd
捱一會(ㄞˊ ㄧˋ ㄏㄨㄟˋ)
to delay a moment; to endure a moment

【抻】 1904 ㄔㄣ chen chēn

1. to stretch; to lengthen (as in making noodles, etc.)
2. to drag out; to draw out: 把它抻出來。Draw it out.

抻麵(ㄔㄣ ㄇㄧㄢˋ)
to make noodles by length-

ening dough

捵練(ㄔㄣ ㄌㄧㄢˋ)

to embarrass someone by making him solve a difficult problem or answer a tough question

捵長(ㄔㄣ ㄔㄤˊ)

to lengthen

【捺】 1905 ㄋㄚˋ nah nà

1. to press hard with hands; to press down
2. a downstroke slanting toward the right in Chinese calligraphy
3. to repress; to restrain: 他無法按捺住他的好奇心。He could not restrain his curiosity.
4. to stitch

捺擱(ㄋㄚˋ ㄍㄜ)

to delay something intentionally

捺印(ㄋㄚˋ ㄧㄣˋ)

① to press one's thumbprint on a document, etc., in place of a signature or chop ② a seal or chop

【捽】 1906 ㄗㄨˊ tzwu zú (語音 ㄗㄨㄛˊ tzwo zuó)

1. to hold with hands; to seize; to grasp
2. to pull up
3. to go against; to contradict; to be in conflict with

捽頸(ㄗㄨˊ ㄐㄧㄥˇ)

to seize by the throat

捽住頭髮(ㄗㄨˊ ·ㄓㄨ ㄊㄡˊ ·ㄈㄚ)

to grasp by the hair 亦作「捽髮」

【捲】 1907 ㄐㄩㄢˇ jeuan juǎn

1. to roll up; a roll: 她把毛線捲成球。She rolled the wool into a ball.
2. to curl (hair, etc.); curly (hair): 她的頭髮捲成一束。Her hair curled into a lock.
3. to sweep off: 一個巨浪把獨木舟捲走了。A huge wave swept the canoe away.

捲伴兒(ㄐㄩㄢˇ ㄅㄢˋㄦ)

to abduct a woman

捲包兒(ㄐㄩㄢˇ ㄅㄠㄦ)

to clear up everything and escape; to abscond with money and property

捲盤(ㄐㄩㄢˇ ㄆㄢˊ)

a reel

捲鋪蓋(ㄐㄩㄢˇ ㄆㄨ ·ㄍㄞ)

(literally) to roll up one's bedclothes—to quit a job for good

捲髮(ㄐㄩㄢˇ ㄈㄚˇ)

① to curl hair (at a hairdresser's, etc.); to keep the hair in curl ② curly hair

捲地皮(ㄐㄩㄢˇ ㄉㄧˋ ㄆㄧˊ)

(said of public officials) to practice graft and corruption

捲逃(ㄐㄩㄢˇ ㄊㄠˊ)

(especially said of a married woman or an employee) to clear up everything and run away; to abscond

捲土重來(ㄐㄩㄢˇ ㄊㄨˇ ㄔㄨㄥˊ ㄌㄞˊ)

to stage a comeback; resurgence

捲筒(ㄐㄩㄢˇ ㄊㄨㄥˇ)

a reel

捲筒機(ㄐㄩㄢˇ ㄊㄨㄥˇ ㄐㄧ)

a rotary printing machine; a web press 亦作「捲筒印刷機」

捲筒紙(ㄐㄩㄢˇ ㄊㄨㄥˇ ㄓˇ)

a web

捲簾(ㄐㄩㄢˇ ㄌㄧㄢˊ)

to roll up a screen or curtain

捲甲(ㄐㄩㄢˇ ㄐㄧㄚˇ)

to gather the armors—to stop fighting

捲起(ㄐㄩㄢˇ ㄑㄧˇ)

① to roll up (sleeves, screens, etc.): 他捲起了袖子。He rolled up his sleeves. ② to cause (an incident, trouble) ③ to sweep off

捲席(ㄐㄩㄢˇ ㄒㄧˊ)

to roll up the mat—to go away; to travel

捲袖(ㄐㄩㄢˇ ㄒㄧㄡˋ)

to roll up the sleeves; to curl up one's sleeves

捲心菜(ㄐㄩㄢˇ ㄒㄧㄣ ㄘㄞˋ)

a cabbage 亦作「甘藍」

捲尺(ㄐㄩㄢˇ ㄔˇ)

a tape measure or tapeline

捲舌音(ㄐㄩㄢˇ ㄕㄜˊ ㄧㄣ)

the pronunciation of a Chinese character which requires the tongue to roll up

捲繞(ㄐㄩㄢˇ ㄖㄠˋ)

to wind

捲入(ㄐㄩㄢˇ ㄖㄨˋ)

to be drawn into; to be involved in; to become embroiled in: 他捲入一場糾紛。He was involved in a dispute.

捲入漩渦(ㄐㄩㄢˇ ㄖㄨˋ ㄒㄩㄢˊ ㄨㄛ)

to be drawn into a whirlpool—to get involved in a conflict, trouble, etc.

捲子(ㄐㄩㄢˇ ·ㄗ)or 捲兒(ㄐㄩㄚˇㄦ)

rolls; small cakes of bread

捲烟(ㄐㄩㄢˇ ㄧㄢ)

cigarettes

捲雲(ㄐㄩㄢˇ ㄩㄣˊ)

(meteorology) cirrus

【捻】 1908 1. ㄋㄧㄢˇ nean niǎn

1. to nip with fingers
2. the "Nien Bandits"
3. to twist: 這條繩是由許多線捻成的。This rope is twisted from many threads.
4. to follow up
5. something made by twisting: 紙捻兒 a twist of paper

捻匪(ㄋㄧㄢˇ ㄈㄟˇ)

the "Nien Bandits", who collaborated with the Taiping rebels (太平軍) during the mid-nineteenth century 亦作「捻子」

捻燈(ㄋㄧㄢˇ ㄉㄥ)

to turn up the wick of a lamp

捻子(ㄋㄧㄢˇ ·ㄗ)or 捻兒(ㄋㄧㄚˇㄦ)

① something twisted into the shape of a piece of thread ② the "Nien Bandits"

【捻】 1908 2. ㄋㄧㄝ nhie niē

to pinch or knead with the fingers

捻花(ㄋㄧㄝ ㄏㄨㄚ)

to pluck flowers

捻手捻脚(ㄋㄧㄝ ㄕㄡˇ ㄋㄧㄝ ㄐㄧㄠˇ)

stealthily or clandestinely; to pussyfoot

【捷】 1909 (㨗) ㄐㄧㄝ jye jié

1. to win; to triumph; the prizes of a victory: 我軍首戰告捷。Our army won the first battle.
2. swift; quick; rapid; agile; fast; alert: 他是個工作敏捷的

〔手部〕

〔手部〕

人。He is a rapid worker.
3. a Chinese family name
捷報(ㄐㄧㄝˊ ㄅㄠˋ)
a report of success in an examination; a war bulletin announcing a victory: 捷報頻頻傳來。Reports of victory keep pouring in.
捷克人(ㄐㄧㄝˊ ㄎㄜˋ ㄖㄣˊ)
a Czechoslovak; a Czechoslovakian
捷克斯拉夫(ㄐㄧㄝˊ ㄎㄜˋ ㄙ ㄌㄚ ㄈㄨ) or 捷克(ㄐㄧㄝˊ ㄎㄜˋ)
Czechoslovakia
捷口(ㄐㄧㄝˊ ㄎㄡˇ)
a sharp tongue; swift in verbal response
捷徑(ㄐㄧㄝˊ ㄐㄧㄥˋ)
a shortcut; a snap course: 求學無捷徑。There is no shortcut to knowledge.
捷黠(ㄐㄧㄝˊ ㄒㄧㄚˊ)
shrewd; cunning; crafty
捷書(ㄐㄧㄝˊ ㄕㄨ)
a report of victory
捷足先得(ㄐㄧㄝˊ ㄗㄨˊ ㄒㄧㄢ ㄉㄜˊ) or 捷足先登(ㄐㄧㄝˊ ㄗㄨˊ ㄒㄧㄢ ㄉㄥ)
The first prize will go to the nimblest. 或 The early bird catches the worm. 或 to beat others to a goal or an objective: 他們捷足先登，把最好的工作搶走了。They grabbed the best work before the others had a chance to.
捷速(ㄐㄧㄝˊ ㄙㄨˋ)
rapidly; quickly
捷運(ㄐㄧㄝˊ ㄩㄣˋ)
rapid transit
捷運系統(ㄐㄧㄝˊ ㄩㄣˋ ㄒㄧˋ ㄊㄨㄥˇ)
a system for rapid transit

【掂】 1910
ㄉㄧㄢ dian diān

to estimate the weight of something by weighing it with hands: 請掂掂這有多重。Weigh this in your hand, please.
掂對(ㄉㄧㄢ ㄉㄨㄟˋ)
to weigh and consider (situations, alternatives, etc.)
掂斤播兩(ㄉㄧㄢ ㄐㄧㄣ ㄅㄛˋ ㄌㄧㄤˇ)
to concentrate on details; to make a fuss over trifles
掂算(ㄉㄧㄢ ㄙㄨㄢˋ)
to consider; to ponder; to estimate; to weigh

【掀】 1911
ㄒㄧㄢ shian xiān

1. to lift with the hands; to raise: 進房前請掀門簾。Lift the door curtain before you enter the room.
2. to stir; to stir up; to cause; to rise; to expose; to reveal: 我不喜歡掀人罪狀。I don't like to expose others' crime.
掀被(ㄒㄧㄢ ㄅㄟˋ)
to throw off a coverlet
掀不動(ㄒㄧㄢ ˙ㄅㄨ ㄉㄨㄥˋ)
unable to move it or lift it
掀不開(ㄒㄧㄢ ˙ㄅㄨ ㄎㄞ)
cannot lift (a lid, a cover, etc.)
掀房頂(ㄒㄧㄢ ㄈㄤˊ ㄉㄧㄥˇ)
to lift the roof off a house
掀風播浪(ㄒㄧㄢ ㄈㄥ ㄅㄛˋ ㄌㄤˋ)
to stir up a turmoil or an upheaval; to cause unrest; to stir up trouble 亦作「興風作浪」
掀動(ㄒㄧㄢ ㄉㄨㄥˋ)
to raise; to stir up; to instigate; to lift
掀騰(ㄒㄧㄢ ㄊㄥˊ)
to stir; to overturn
掀天(ㄒㄧㄢ ㄊㄧㄢ)
①(said of a billow) to rise to the sky: 海浪掀天。Waves rise to the sky. ②(said of sound, noise, etc.) to reach the heaven
掀天揭地(ㄒㄧㄢ ㄊㄧㄢ ㄐㄧㄝ ㄉㄧˋ) or 掀天動地(ㄒㄧㄢ ㄊㄧㄢ ㄉㄨㄥˋ ㄉㄧˋ)
(said of an extraordinary achievement, ability, etc.) to stir the heavens and shake the earth; overwhelming (force)
掀天事業(ㄒㄧㄢ ㄊㄧㄢ ㄕˋ ㄧㄝˋ)
an awe-inspiring achievement or endeavor
掀簾子(ㄒㄧㄢ ㄌㄧㄢˊ ˙ㄗ)
to pull aside a screen or curtain
掀開(ㄒㄧㄢ ㄎㄞ)
to cause; to open; to uncover or unveil (a secret, etc.); to expose: 他們掀開了他的陰謀。They exposed his plot.
掀起(ㄒㄧㄢ ㄑㄧˇ)
to stir up (a movement, etc.); to surge: 大海掀起了巨浪。Large waves surged on the sea.
掀腫(ㄒㄧㄢ ㄓㄨㄥˇ)
a swelling
掀唇(ㄒㄧㄢ ㄔㄨㄣˊ)
to open the mouth; to speak
掀髯(ㄒㄧㄢ ㄖㄢˊ)
the rising of the beard when laughing or smiling
掀舞(ㄒㄧㄢ ㄨˇ)
(said of waves) churning and pounding

【掃】 1912
1. (埽) ㄙㄠˇ sao sǎo

1. to sweep with a broom; to clear away; to clean
2. to wipe out; to weed out; to exterminate; to mop up
3. sweepingly; totally
4. to paint (the eyebrows, etc.)
5. to pass over to examine; to sweep: 他向教室掃了一眼。He swept his eyes over the classroom.
掃平(ㄙㄠˇ ㄆㄧㄥˊ) or 掃清(ㄙㄠˇ ㄑㄧㄥ)
to put down; to crush; to suppress; to quell an uprising, etc.
掃眉(ㄙㄠˇ ㄇㄟˊ)
to paint eyebrows
掃眉才子(ㄙㄠˇ ㄇㄟˊ ㄘㄞˊ ㄗˇ)
a female scholar
掃描(ㄙㄠˇ ㄇㄧㄠˊ)
(electricity) scanning
掃墓(ㄙㄠˇ ㄇㄨˋ) or 掃墳(ㄙㄠˇ ㄈㄣˊ)
(literally) to sweep the tomb—to pay respects to one's ancestor at his grave
掃房(ㄙㄠˇ ㄈㄤˊ) or 掃舍(ㄙㄠˇ ㄕㄜˋ)
to sweep a house—in preparation for the new year, etc.
掃蕩(ㄙㄠˇ ㄉㄤˋ)
to make a clean sweep of (enemy troops, rebels, etc.); a mop-up operation
掃地(ㄙㄠˇ ㄉㄧˋ)
① to sweep the floor ②(said of reputation) to soil: 他威信掃地。He is shorn of his prestige.
掃地出門(ㄙㄠˇ ㄉㄧˋ ㄔㄨ ㄇㄣˊ)
to force a family to leave their home without taking anything with them (as the Chinese Communists did to landlords and wealthy families in the mainland China)

掃斷(ㄙㄠˇ ㄉㄨㄢˋ)
totally eliminated

掃榻(ㄙㄠˇ ㄊㄚˋ)
to sweep the mat—to welcome a visitor

掃榻以待(ㄙㄠˇ ㄊㄚˋ ㄧˇ ㄉㄞˋ)
to tidy the bedding and await (your) coming; to welcome (your) visit

掃堂腿(ㄙㄠˇ ㄊㄤˊ ㄊㄨㄟˇ)
(Chinese boxing) a feat in which the boxer squats with one leg extended while managing a quick spin to fell his adversary

掃田刮地(ㄙㄠˇ ㄊㄧㄢˊ ㄍㄨㄚ ㄉㄧˋ)
to engage in manual labor; to toil; to do menial work

掃雷艇(ㄙㄠˇ ㄌㄟˊ ㄊㄧㄥˇ)or 掃雷艦(ㄙㄠˇ ㄌㄟˊ ㄐㄧㄢˋ)
a minesweeper

掃臉(ㄙㄠˇ ㄌㄧㄢˇ)
to lose face

掃乾淨(ㄙㄠˇ ㄍㄢ ㄐㄧㄥˋ)
to sweep clean: 在冬天，街上的雪必須掃乾淨。In winter, the streets have to be cleared of snow.

掃黑(ㄙㄠˇ ㄏㄟ)
to crack down on crime

掃黃(ㄙㄠˇ ㄏㄨㄤˊ)
to crack down on pornography

掃興(ㄙㄠˇ ㄒㄧㄥˋ)
① to throw cold water on; to spoil pleasure ② to feel disappointed or discouraged: 眞掃興！How disappointing!

掃塵(ㄙㄠˇ ㄔㄣˊ)
① to sweep clean ② to quell rebellions

掃除(ㄙㄠˇ ㄔㄨˊ)
① to sweep up; to clean ② to eliminate (bad habits, undesirable elements, rebels, etc.); to wipe out; to remove: 讓我們掃除一切疑惑。Let's remove all doubts.

掃除天地(ㄙㄠˇ ㄔㄨˊ ㄊㄧㄢ ㄉㄧˋ)
to rid the world of bad elements; to bring peace and justice to the world

掃除文盲(ㄙㄠˇ ㄔㄨˊ ㄨㄣˊ ㄇㄤˊ)
to eliminate illiteracy

掃射(ㄙㄠˇ ㄕㄜˋ)
① to strafe (with machine-gun fire) ② to look around: 他用目光掃射房間一遍。His glance swept around the room.

掃數(ㄙㄠˇ ㄕㄨˋ)
totally; completely

【掃】 1912
2. (掃) ㄙㄠˋ saw sào

a broom

掃帚(ㄙㄠˋ ·ㄓㄡ)or 掃把(ㄙㄠˋ ㄅㄚˇ)
a broom: 沒掃帚我無法打掃。I can't sweep without a broom.

掃帚星(ㄙㄠˋ ·ㄓㄡ ㄒㄧㄥ)
①(astronomy) a comet ② any person who brings bad luck; a jinx

【授】 1913
ㄕㄡˋ show shòu

1. to give; to hand over to; to confer (a degree, prize, etc.)
2. to teach; to tutor: 函授 to teach by correspondence
3. to give up (one's life, etc.)

授兵(ㄕㄡˋ ㄅㄧㄥ)
(in ancient China) to hand over arms to soldiers at the outbreak of war

授命(ㄕㄡˋ ㄇㄧㄥˋ)
to sacrifice one's life; to give up one's life

授粉(ㄕㄡˋ ㄈㄣˇ)
(botany) to pollinate; pollination

授田(ㄕㄡˋ ㄊㄧㄢˊ)
to allot public land to a person for the farming purpose

授徒(ㄕㄡˋ ㄊㄨˊ)
to teach students or pupils

授課(ㄕㄡˋ ㄎㄜˋ)
to teach; to tutor: 他每週必須授課十小時。He has to teach ten hours every week.

授記(ㄕㄡˋ ㄐㄧˋ)
(Buddhism) to prophesy; prophecy

授戒(ㄕㄡˋ ㄐㄧㄝˋ)
to give rules for a monk or nun to observe in the initiation ceremony

授獎(ㄕㄡˋ ㄐㄧㄤˇ)
to award a prize

授精(ㄕㄡˋ ㄐㄧㄥ)
to inseminate; insemination: 人工授精 artificial insemination

授爵(ㄕㄡˋ ㄐㄩㄝˊ)
to elevate to the peerage

授旗(ㄕㄡˋ ㄑㄧˊ)
to give the national flag to a sports team leaving for competitions abroad, etc.

授槍(ㄕㄡˋ ㄑㄧㄤ)
to issue rifles to new recruits

授權(ㄕㄡˋ ㄑㄩㄢˊ)
① to authorize; to delegate powers ② to license

授勳(ㄕㄡˋ ㄒㄩㄣ)
to confer orders; to award a decoration

授職(ㄕㄡˋ ㄓˊ)
to confer a rank; to give an official job to

授時(ㄕㄡˋ ㄕˊ)
(in ancient China) to teach people the knowledge of calendar to insure timely cultivation of the land

授室(ㄕㄡˋ ㄕˋ)
to accept a daughter-in-law in a formal ceremony

授首(ㄕㄡˋ ㄕㄡˇ)
to get killed; to be beheaded

授受(ㄕㄡˋ ㄕㄡˋ)
to give and receive; to give and accept; to grant and receive: 公務人員不得私相授受。Public servants should not give and accept privately.

授受不親(ㄕㄡˋ ㄕㄡˋ ㄅㄨˋ ㄑㄧㄣ)
(formerly) no physical contact between a man and a woman except man and wife

授人以柄(ㄕㄡˋ ㄖㄣˊ ㄧˇ ㄅㄧㄥˇ)
to give others something to talk about oneself; to offer another a hold on oneself

授餐(ㄕㄡˋ ㄘㄢ)
to give someone food

授意(ㄕㄡˋ ㄧˋ)
to intimate; to inspire; to make someone do something by giving a hint or suggestion

授業(ㄕㄡˋ ㄧㄝˋ)
to teach; to tutor

授與(ㄕㄡˋ ㄩˇ)
to confer; to give

【掇】 1914
ㄉㄨㄛˊ dwo duó

1. to collect; to gather
2. to plagiarize; to pirate

3. to select; to pluck
掇弄(ㄉㄨㄛˊ ㄋㄨㄥˋ)
①to stir up (conflicts, etc.) ②to handle a matter; to deal with something
掇拾(ㄉㄨㄛˊ ㄕˊ)
to collect; to select
掇採(ㄉㄨㄛˊ ㄘㄞˇ)
to gather; to select; to pluck

【掄】 1915
1. ㄌㄨㄣˊ luen lún
to select; to choose
掄魁(ㄌㄨㄣˊ ㄎㄨㄟˊ)
to head the list of successful candidates in the imperial civil service examination
掄選(ㄌㄨㄣˊ ㄒㄩㄢˇ)or 掄擇(ㄌㄨㄣˊ ㄗㄜˊ)
to select (competent persons, adequate materials, etc.)
掄才(ㄌㄨㄣˊ ㄘㄞˊ)
to select men of ability
掄元(ㄌㄨㄣˊ ㄩㄢˊ)
to come out first in examinations

【掄】 1915
2. ㄌㄨㄣ lhuen lūn
1. to turn or spin with hands or arms; to swing
2. to brandish; to wave
3. to squander
掄刀(ㄌㄨㄣ ㄉㄠ)
to swing a knife (at somebody)
掄棍(ㄌㄨㄣ ㄍㄨㄣˋ)
to swing a stick
掄拳(ㄌㄨㄣ ㄑㄩㄢˊ)
to swing a fist

【掎】 1916
ㄐㄧˇ jii jǐ
to draw aside; to drag; to pull
掎角(ㄐㄧˇ ㄐㄧㄠˇ)
(literally) to seize the horns and tie up the feet—to defeat (the enemy)
掎摭(ㄐㄧˇ ㄓˊ)
①to find fault with ②to gather

【掏】 1917
ㄊㄠ tau tāo
1. to take out; to pull out: 他從口袋裏掏出鑰匙。He took a key out of his pocket.
2. to dig; to scoop out: 他在牆上掏個洞。He dug a hole in the wall.
3. to steal from somebody's pocket: 她的錢被扒手掏走了。She had her money stolen by a pickpocket.
掏摸(ㄊㄠ ㄇㄛ)
①to search and feel (in the pocket, etc.) ②to steal ③to be given (money, etc.) after begging, etc.
掏溝(ㄊㄠ ㄍㄡ)
to dredge a gutter or ditch
掏井(ㄊㄠ ㄐㄧㄥˇ)
to dredge a well
掏錢(ㄊㄠ ㄑㄧㄢˊ)
to take out money; to spend money
掏出來(ㄊㄠ ㄔㄨ ·ㄌㄞ)
to pull out or draw out
掏耳朵(ㄊㄠ ㄦˇ ·ㄉㄨㄛ)
to pick or clean ears
掏腰包(ㄊㄠ ㄧㄠ ㄅㄠ)
(colloquial) to spend one's own money; to shell out

【掐】 1918
ㄑㄧㄚ chia qiā
1. to dig the nail into
2. to cut with fingernails; to nip; to pinch; to give a pinch
3. to hold; to grasp; to clutch; to gather with the hand
掐斷(ㄑㄧㄚ ㄉㄨㄢˋ)
to break; to nip
掐頭去尾(ㄑㄧㄚ ㄊㄡˊ ㄑㄩˋ ㄨㄟˇ)
to do away with unnecessary parts or details at both ends: 引用報紙的話你不能掐頭去尾。If you quote passages from newspapers, you should quote them in full.
掐喉嚨(ㄑㄧㄚ ㄏㄡˊ ㄌㄨㄥˊ)
to seize by the throat; to choke
掐花兒(ㄑㄧㄚ ㄏㄨㄚㄦ)
to pluck flowers with fingernails
掐尖兒(ㄑㄧㄚ ㄐㄧㄚㄦ)
①to cut off branches of plants so as to hasten growth ②to practice irregularities, etc. in a deal in order to get profits, kickbacks, etc.
掐指一算(ㄑㄧㄚ ㄓˇ ㄧˊ ㄙㄨㄢˋ)or 掐算(ㄑㄧㄚ ㄙㄨㄢˋ)
to count; to calculate
掐住(ㄑㄧㄚ ㄓㄨˋ)
to seize; to grasp; to hold: 在恐懼中她掐住他的臂。In fright she seized his arm.
掐死(ㄑㄧㄚ ㄙˇ)
to choke to death by strangling with hands

【掊】 1919
1. ㄆㄡˇ poou pǒu
to strike; to cut; to cudgel; to break; to attack
掊斗折衡(ㄆㄡˇ ㄉㄡˇ ㄓㄜˊ ㄏㄥˊ)
to break the measure and destroy the scales so as to prevent wrangling (a political philosophy advocated by 莊子)
掊擊(ㄆㄡˇ ㄐㄧˊ)
to strike; to break

【掊】 1919
2. ㄆㄡˊ pour póu
to exact; to collect (taxes)
掊克(ㄆㄡˊ ㄎㄜˋ)or 掊斂(ㄆㄡˊ ㄌㄧㄢˋ)
to exact high taxes from people; to levy heavy taxes from people

【掉】 1920
ㄉㄧㄠˋ diaw diào
1. to turn: 請把椅子掉過來。Please turn the chair round.
2. to fall; to drop; to shed: 她掉下幾滴眼淚。She shed a few tears.
3. to lose; to be missing: 我掉了手錶。I've lost my watch.
4. to fall behind; to lag behind
5. to change; to substitute
6. to move; to shake; to wag
7. used as an adverbial particle after verbs expressing conditions of fulfillment: 吃掉 to eat off 擦掉 to wipe off
掉背臉(ㄉㄧㄠˋ ㄅㄟˋ ㄌㄧㄢˇ)
to turn one's face
掉包兒(ㄉㄧㄠˋ ㄅㄠㄦ)
to substitute in secret an object with something else identical in appearance but different in quality or contents; to substitute stealthily one thing for another
掉臂不顧(ㄉㄧㄠˋ ㄅㄧˋ ㄅㄨˋ ㄍㄨˋ)or 掉臂而去(ㄉㄧㄠˋ ㄅㄧˋ ㄦˊ ㄑㄩˋ)
to walk out on (somebody)
掉皮(ㄉㄧㄠˋ ㄆㄧˊ)
to peel off
掉隊(ㄉㄧㄠˋ ㄉㄨㄟˋ)
to drop out; to fall behind
掉動(ㄉㄧㄠˋ ㄉㄨㄥˋ)

〔手部〕

①to move; to stir ②to change; to exchange
掉胎(ㄉㄧㄠˋ ㄊㄞ)
to abort; abortion; to miscarry; a miscarriage
掉頭(ㄉㄧㄠˋ ㄊㄡˊ)
①to turn one's head (and walk away) ②to shake one's head ③to turn back; to turn round; to turn about ④to get killed; to get beheaded
掉頭就走(ㄉㄧㄠˋ ㄊㄡˊ ㄐㄧㄡˋ ㄗㄡˇ)or 掉頭不顧(ㄉㄧㄠˋ ㄊㄡˊ ㄅㄨˋ ㄍㄨˋ)
to turn one's head and walk away; to turn away and leave
掉腦袋(ㄉㄧㄠˋ ㄋㄠˇ ·ㄉㄞ)
to get beheaded
掉淚(ㄉㄧㄠˋ ㄌㄟˋ)
to come to tears; tears falling
掉過來(ㄉㄧㄠˋ ㄍㄨㄛˋ ·ㄌㄞ)
①to turn around ②on the other hand
掉花槍(ㄉㄧㄠˋ ㄏㄨㄚ ㄑㄧㄤ)
to play tricks; to divert another's attention by words or action (in order to gain time, etc.)
掉換(ㄉㄧㄠˋ ㄏㄨㄢˋ)
to change; to exchange; to invert; to substitute: 我們掉換一下座位吧! Let's change seats.
掉魂(ㄉㄧㄠˋ ㄏㄨㄣˊ)
to lose one's wits; terrified; very scared
掉價(ㄉㄧㄠˋ ㄐㄧㄚˋ)
to fall the price
掉下來(ㄉㄧㄠˋ ㄒㄧㄚˋ ·ㄌㄞ)
to fall down
掉轉(ㄉㄧㄠˋ ㄓㄨㄢˇ)
to turn back; to turn round
掉舌(ㄉㄧㄠˋ ㄕㄜˊ)
①eloquent; to speak eloquently and persuasively ②to chatter ③to stir up ill will between others by loose gossip
掉書袋(ㄉㄧㄠˋ ㄕㄨ ㄉㄞˋ)
excessive fondness of making literary quotations and historical allusions; to parade learning
掉色(ㄉㄧㄠˋ ㄙㄜˋ)or 掉色兒(ㄉㄧㄠˋ ㄕㄞˇㄦ)
to discolor; to fade: 這種質料不掉色。This material won't fade.
掉以輕心(ㄉㄧㄠˋ ㄧˇ ㄑㄧㄥ ㄒㄧㄣ)
to lower one's guard; to treat something lightly
掉尾(ㄉㄧㄠˋ ㄨㄟˇ)
to wag the tail

【排】 1921
ㄆㄞˊ pair pái
1. a row; a line; a rank
2. to arrange; to put in order; to fall in line: 把椅子排好。Put the chairs in order.
3. (military) a platoon
4. to clear out; to drain away; to discharge: 水不久就會排出去了。The water will soon drain away.
5. to reject; to expel; to exclude
6. to rehearse
7. a raft: 竹排 a bamboo raft
8. to push
排八卦(ㄆㄞˊ ㄅㄚ ㄍㄨㄚˋ)
to arrange the Eight Diagrams
排班(ㄆㄞˊ ㄅㄢ)
①to fall in line (according to order, ranks, etc.) ②to arrange turns of work
排版(ㄆㄞˊ ㄅㄢˇ)
(printing) to set type ; composing; typesetting
排筆(ㄆㄞˊ ㄅㄧˇ)
a row of brushes (used by house painters)
排比(ㄆㄞˊ ㄅㄧˇ)
①to arrange in order ②(linguistics) parallelism
排便(ㄆㄞˊ ㄅㄧㄢˋ)
defecation; the evacuation of the bowels; a bowel movement
排排坐(ㄆㄞˊ ㄆㄞˊ ㄗㄨㄛˋ)
to sit in rows
排砲(ㄆㄞˊ ㄆㄠˋ)
(military) a volley of artillery fire; a salvo; a broadside
排門兒(ㄆㄞˊ ㄇㄜˊㄦ)
from door to door; door-to-door
排悶(ㄆㄞˊ ㄇㄣˋ)
to kill time; to dispel boredom: 你如何排悶? How did you kill time?
排名(ㄆㄞˊ ㄇㄧㄥˊ)
to list names according to the order of seniority or position
排檔(ㄆㄞˊ ㄉㄤˇ)
a gear (in an automobile engine)
排隊(ㄆㄞˊ ㄉㄨㄟˋ)
to fall in line or formation; to line up; to stand in a queue: 請排隊上車。Please queue up for a bus.
排他性(ㄆㄞˊ ㄊㄚ ㄒㄧㄥˋ)
exclusiveness; impenetrability
排闥直入(ㄆㄞˊ ㄊㄚˋ ㄓˊ ㄖㄨˋ)
to push the door open and walk straight into a house; to barge in; to walk straight in without knocking
排頭(ㄆㄞˊ ·ㄊㄡ)
to stand first in the line; a file leader
排難解紛(ㄆㄞˊ ㄋㄢˋ ㄐㄧㄝˇ ㄈㄣ)
to mediate disputes; to offer good offices to the parties in dispute
排尿(ㄆㄞˊ ㄋㄧㄠˋ)
to urinate; to micturate
排列(ㄆㄞˊ ㄌㄧㄝˋ)
①to arrange in series, rows, etc.: 請將我書架上的書排列好。Please arrange my books on the shelf in order. ②(mathematics) permutation or arrangement
排練(ㄆㄞˊ ㄌㄧㄢˋ)
to rehearse for a show; rehearsal: 這齣戲需要多排練。This play will need a lot of rehearsal.
排卵(ㄆㄞˊ ㄌㄨㄢˇ)
(biology) to ovulate
排律(ㄆㄞˊ ㄌㄩˋ)
a verse form, made up of an indefinite number of rhymed couplets with five or seven characters in each line
排骨(ㄆㄞˊ ·ㄍㄨ)
①ribs of animals; spareribs ②(slang) a skinny person
排課(ㄆㄞˊ ㄎㄜˋ)
to work out a teaching schedule (at a school)
排開(ㄆㄞˊ ㄎㄞ)
to spread out
排行(ㄆㄞˊ ㄏㄤˊ)
one's seniority among

〔手部〕

brothers and sisters: 他排行老大。He's the first child of the family.
排華(ㄆㄞˊ ㄏㄨㄚˊ)
anti-Chinese
排擠(ㄆㄞˊ ㄐㄧˇ)
① to expel somebody out of an inner circle or clique, etc. ② to push aside; to elbow out: 他們互相排擠。They try to squeeze the others out.
排解(ㄆㄞˊ ㄐㄧㄝˇ)
to resolve (disputes); to mediate; to make peace; to reconcile
排解糾紛(ㄆㄞˊ ㄐㄧㄝˇ ㄐㄧㄡ ㄈㄣ)
to mediate a quarrel; to reconcile a dispute
排氣管(ㄆㄞˊ ㄑㄧˋ ㄍㄨㄢˇ)
an exhaust pipe
排球(ㄆㄞˊ ㄑㄧㄡˊ)
volleyball
排遣(ㄆㄞˊ ㄑㄧㄢˇ)
(said of a disappointed person) to find comfort in; to divert oneself from loneliness
排戲(ㄆㄞˊ ㄒㄧˋ)
to rehearse for a show
排泄(ㄆㄞˊ ㄒㄧㄝˋ)
to excrete; to discharge; excretion
排泄器(ㄆㄞˊ ㄒㄧㄝˋ ㄑㄧˋ)or 排泄器官(ㄆㄞˊ ㄒㄧㄝˋ ㄑㄧˋ ㄍㄨㄢ)
excretory organs
排泄物(ㄆㄞˊ ㄒㄧㄝˋ ㄨˋ)
excreta; excrement
排簫(ㄆㄞˊ ㄒㄧㄠ)
a kind of ancient musical instrument consisting of a cluster of bamboo pipes ranging from 16 to 20 in number
排陣(ㄆㄞˊ ㄓㄣˋ)
to deploy troops: 軍隊排陣備戰。The army is arranged for battle.
排長(ㄆㄞˊ ㄓㄤˇ)
a platoon leader
排斥(ㄆㄞˊ ㄔˋ)
to expel; to repel; to discriminate against
排場(ㄆㄞˊ ㄔㄤˊ)or(ㄆㄞˊ ㄔㄤˇ)
① ostentation and extravagance: 他喜歡講排場。He goes in for ostentation and extravagance. ② a person's social position
排除(ㄆㄞˊ ㄔㄨˊ)
to get rid of; to remove; to eliminate: 我們必須排除任何可能導致意外的因素。We have to eliminate any possible causes of accidents.
排除障礙(ㄆㄞˊ ㄔㄨˊ ㄓㄤˋ ㄞˋ)
to remove an obstacle
排除異己(ㄆㄞˊ ㄔㄨˊ ㄧˋ ㄐㄧˇ)or 排斥異己(ㄆㄞˊ ㄔˋ ㄧˋ ㄐㄧˇ)
to get rid of those who hold a view different from one's own or who do not conform to one's ideas; to eliminate those not belonging to one's clique, etc.; to expel "outsiders"
排除萬難(ㄆㄞˊ ㄔㄨˊ ㄨㄢˋ ㄋㄢˊ)
to overcome all difficulties
排沙揀金 or 排沙簡金(ㄆㄞˊ ㄕㄚ ㄐㄧㄢˇ ㄐㄧㄣ)
① to sift sand for gold ② to be expert at selecting (the right person or thing) for a job, etc.
排山倒海(ㄆㄞˊ ㄕㄢ ㄉㄠˇ ㄏㄞˇ)
overwhelming or sweeping
排水(ㄆㄞˊ ㄕㄨㄟˇ)
to drain water; drainage
排水量(ㄆㄞˊ ㄕㄨㄟˇ ㄌㄧㄤˋ)
① the volume of water displacement ② displacement (of a ship)
排水溝(ㄆㄞˊ ㄕㄨㄟˇ ㄍㄡ)
a discharge ditch; a drainage ditch
排水溝渠(ㄆㄞˊ ㄕㄨㄟˇ ㄍㄡ ㄑㄩˊ)
escape canals
排水管(ㄆㄞˊ ㄕㄨㄟˇ ㄍㄨㄢˇ)
a drainpipe
排水工程(ㄆㄞˊ ㄕㄨㄟˇ ㄍㄨㄥ ㄔㄥˊ)
drainage works
排水口(ㄆㄞˊ ㄕㄨㄟˇ ㄎㄡˇ)
a drainage outlet
排水系統(ㄆㄞˊ ㄕㄨㄟˇ ㄒㄧˋ ㄊㄨㄥˇ)
a drainage system
排字(ㄆㄞˊ ㄗˋ)
① to set types; typesetting; composition ② to form words or figures with colored cardboards held in the hands of persons seated or standing in rows
排字房(ㄆㄞˊ ㄗˋ ㄈㄤˊ)
a composition room (in a printing shop)
排字機(ㄆㄞˊ ㄗˋ ㄐㄧ)
a linotype
排演(ㄆㄞˊ ㄧㄢˇ)
to rehearse for a show: 他們正在排演一齣歌劇。They are rehearsing an opera.
排印(ㄆㄞˊ ㄧㄣˋ)
to set type and print; typesetting and printing
排外(ㄆㄞˊ ㄨㄞˋ)
antiforeign; chauvinistic; ultranationalistic: 他是個盲目排外的人。He had blind opposition to everything foreign.
排外主義(ㄆㄞˊ ㄨㄞˋ ㄓㄨˇ ㄧˋ)
exclusivism
排灣(ㄆㄞˊ ㄨㄢ)
the Paiwans, an aboriginal tribe in Taiwan

【掘】 1922
ㄐㄩㄝˊ jyue jué
to dig; to excavate; to make a hole or cave
掘地(ㄐㄩㄝˊ ㄉㄧˋ)
to dig the earth
掘洞(ㄐㄩㄝˊ ㄉㄨㄥˋ)
to dig a hole; to make a hole or cave
掘土機(ㄐㄩㄝˊ ㄊㄨˇ ㄐㄧ)
an excavator 亦作「挖土機」
掘開(ㄐㄩㄝˊ ㄎㄞ)
to dig (a closed cave, etc.)
掘坑(ㄐㄩㄝˊ ㄎㄥ)
to dig or make a pit
掘壕(ㄐㄩㄝˊ ㄏㄠˊ)
to entrench; to dig in
掘金(ㄐㄩㄝˊ ㄐㄧㄣ)
to dig for gold; gold digging: 礦工們在掘金。The miners were digging for gold.
掘金者(ㄐㄩㄝˊ ㄐㄧㄣ ㄓㄜˇ)
①a gold digger ②an opportunist or adventurist
掘強 or 倔強(ㄐㄩㄝˊ ㄐㄧㄤˋ)
intransigent; stubborn; obstinate
掘井(ㄐㄩㄝˊ ㄐㄧㄥˇ)
to dig a well
掘塚(ㄐㄩㄝˊ ㄓㄨㄥˇ)
to prepare a tomb; to dig a grave
掘穿(ㄐㄩㄝˊ ㄔㄨㄢ)
to dig through
掘鑿(ㄐㄩㄝˊ ㄗㄠˊ)
excavation
掘藏(ㄐㄩㄝˊ ㄗㄤˋ)

〔手部〕

to sack a tomb for its hidden treasure
掘足類(ㄐㄩㄝˊ ㄗㄨˊ ㄌㄟˋ)
(zoology) scaphopoda

1923
【掖】 1. ㄧˋ yih yì (語音 ㄧㄝˋ yeh yè)
1. to support another; to extend a helping hand; to promote
2. armpits
3. side; by the side
4. side apartments in the palace

掖門(ㄧˋ ㄇㄣˊ)
a small side door of the palace
掖庭(ㄧˋ ㄊㄧㄥˊ)
side apartments or quarters of a palace
掖垣(ㄧˋ ㄩㄢˊ)
sidewalls of a palace

1923
【掖】 2. ㄧㄝ ie yē
1. to conceal; to tuck away; to hide
2. to fold; to roll up (part of one's clothing)

掖掖蓋蓋(ㄧㄝ・ㄧㄝ ㄍㄞˋ ㄍㄞˋ)
stealthily; clandestinely

1924
【拼】 (拚) ㄆㄧㄣ pin pīn
1. to join together; to incorporate; to put together; to make a whole
2. to spell (a word)
3. to risk

拼版(ㄆㄧㄣ ㄅㄢˇ)
(printing) a makeup
拼盤(ㄆㄧㄣ ㄆㄢˊ)
assorted cold dishes; *hors d'oeuvres*
拼命(ㄆㄧㄣ ㄇㄧㄥˋ)
① to risk one's life ② exerting the utmost strength; with all one's might: 他拼命讀書。He studies very hard.
拼法(ㄆㄧㄣ ㄈㄚˇ)
spelling
拼到底(ㄆㄧㄣ ㄉㄠˋ ㄉㄧˇ)
to fight to the bitter end
拼湊(ㄆㄧㄣ ㄘㄡˋ)
① to put bits together to make a whole ② (machinery) to cannibalize ③ to raise money here and there
拼死(ㄆㄧㄣ ㄙˇ)
to risk one's life; to fight desperately
拼音(ㄆㄧㄣ ㄧㄣ)
to spell phonetically; to pronounce a word by enunciating the phonetic signs
拼音字母(ㄆㄧㄣ ㄧㄣ ㄗˋ ㄇㄨˇ)
the phonetic alphabet

1925
【掙】 1. ㄓㄥ jeng zhēng
1. to make efforts; to strive
2. to get free from

掙脫(ㄓㄥ ㄊㄨㄛ)
to break away with force; to shake off
掙開(ㄓㄥ ㄎㄞ)
to get free with effort
掙扎(ㄓㄥ ㄓㄚˊ)
to struggle; a struggle; to strive

1925
【掙】 2. ㄓㄥˋ jenq zhèng
1. to struggle (for one's life, etc.)
2. to earn (money, etc.)

掙命(ㄓㄥˋ ㄇㄧㄥˋ)
to fight or struggle for one's life
掙飯吃(ㄓㄥˋ ㄈㄢˋ ㄔ)
to earn a living
掙家立業(ㄓㄥˋ ㄐㄧㄚ ㄌㄧˋ ㄧㄝˋ)
to establish a home and make achievements
掙錢(ㄓㄥˋ ㄑㄧㄢˊ)
to earn money

1926
【掞】 ㄕㄢˋ shann shàn
easy; smooth; suave; comfortable

掞張(ㄕㄢˋ ㄓㄤ)
suave but exaggerating (in one's statement, etc.); smooth but untruthful
掞藻(ㄕㄢˋ ㄗㄠˇ)
the smooth, flowery literary style

1927
【掠】 ㄌㄩㄝˋ liueh lüè
1. to take by force; to rob; to plunder; to pillage
2. to brush; to pass lightly on the side; to sweep past; to skim over: 輕風掠面。A gentle breeze brushed my face.
3. to whip; to flog
4. a long stroke to the left in Chinese calligraphy

掠美(ㄌㄩㄝˋ ㄇㄟˇ)
to take credit for what has been done by somebody else
掠地(ㄌㄩㄝˋ ㄉㄧˋ)
(said of troops) to conquer land; to seize land; to plunder the land conquered
掠奪(ㄌㄩㄝˋ ㄉㄨㄛˊ)
to seize or rob by force; to plunder; to pillage
掠過(ㄌㄩㄝˋ ㄍㄨㄛˋ)
to skim over; to flicker across: 我母親的嘴角上掠過一絲微笑。A faint smile flickered across my mother's lips.
掠取(ㄌㄩㄝˋ ㄑㄩˇ)
to take by force; to rob
掠食(ㄌㄩㄝˋ ㄕˊ)
to hunt for food
掠影浮光(ㄌㄩㄝˋ ㄧㄥˇ ㄈㄨˊ ㄍㄨㄤ)
superficial

1928
【掛】 (挂) ㄍㄨㄚˋ guah guà
1. to hang up; to suspend: 夜空中掛着一輪明月。A bright moon hung in the night sky.
2. to ring off: 他已經把電話掛斷了。He's hung up.
3. to worry; to think of; anxious: 他非常掛念他母親的病。He's much worried about his mother's illness.
4. with one's name registered or listed; recorded; to register: 我要掛牙科。I want to register for dental surgery.
5. to hitch; to get caught: 她的毛衣給釘子掛住了。Her sweater got caught on a nail.

掛不下(ㄍㄨㄚˋ ・ㄅㄨ ㄒㄧㄚˋ)
There's no room to hang it.
掛不住(ㄍㄨㄚˋ ・ㄅㄨ ㄓㄨˋ)
① cannot be hung securely ② to feel ashamed
掛牌(ㄍㄨㄚˋ ㄆㄞˊ)
① to go into practice (said of lawyers, doctors, etc.) ② (said of banks) to hang out a bulletin board listing the current exchange rates
掛麵(ㄍㄨㄚˋ ㄇㄧㄢˋ)
thin, string-like dried noodles; vermicelli
掛名(ㄍㄨㄚˋ ㄇㄧㄥˊ)
in name only; nominally; titular: 他是掛名的總經理。He is the general manager only in

name.

掛單(ㄍㄨㄚˋ ㄉㄢ)or 掛錫(ㄍㄨㄚˋ ㄒㄧ)
(said of a traveling Buddhist monk) to lodge in a temple for the night

掛燈(ㄍㄨㄚˋ ㄉㄥ)
a low-hanging ceiling lamp

掛頭牌(ㄍㄨㄚˋ ㄊㄡˊ ㄆㄞˊ)
to play the leading role (especially in show business)

掛圖(ㄍㄨㄚˋ ㄊㄨˊ)
a wall chart or map

掛念(ㄍㄨㄚˋ ㄋㄧㄢˋ)or 掛懷(ㄍㄨㄚˋ ㄏㄨㄞˊ)or 掛心(ㄍㄨㄚˋ ㄒㄧㄣ)
to think of; to be anxious about; to worry about; to be on one's mind: 我如晚回, 請勿掛念。Don't be anxious if I am late.

掛累(ㄍㄨㄚˋ ㄌㄟˋ)
to involve (another) in

掛零(ㄍㄨㄚˋ ㄌㄧㄥˊ)
odd (as, 50-odd); more than

掛慮(ㄍㄨㄚˋ ㄌㄩˋ)
to be worried or anxious about

掛鉤(ㄍㄨㄚˋ ㄍㄡ)
① a hook for hanging clothes, etc. (usually nailed to the wall) ②(said of railway cars) the coupling links ③ to establish contact with

掛冠(ㄍㄨㄚˋ ㄍㄨㄢ)
(literally) to hang up one's official cap—to quit or resign: 他掛冠而去。He resigned and went home.

掛號(ㄍㄨㄚˋ ㄏㄠˋ)
① registered (mail, etc.); to register a mail: 請把此信掛號。Please register this letter. ② to register (at the outpatient department of a hospital): 請排隊掛號。Please line up to register.

掛號信(ㄍㄨㄚˋ ㄏㄠˋ ㄒㄧㄣˋ)
a registered letter

掛號處(ㄍㄨㄚˋ ㄏㄠˋ ㄔㄨˋ)
a register office (of a hospital)

掛紅(ㄍㄨㄚˋ ㄏㄨㄥˊ)
① to hang red silk for congratulations on the opening of a new shop ② a sign of repentance by the perpetrator of an offense by hanging a piece of red silk or cloth at the door of his victim

掛劍(ㄍㄨㄚˋ ㄐㄧㄢˋ)
to hang the precious sword on its admirer's grave—a last gift to show one's memory of the deceased

掛欠(ㄍㄨㄚˋ ㄑㄧㄢˋ)or 掛賬(ㄍㄨㄚˋ ㄓㄤˋ)
(to buy) on credit; to owe

掛孝(ㄍㄨㄚˋ ㄒㄧㄠˋ)
to wear mourning

掛鐘(ㄍㄨㄚˋ ㄓㄨㄥ)
a wall clock

掛齒(ㄍㄨㄚˋ ㄔˇ)
to mention: 這點小事, 何足掛齒。Such a trifling thing is not worth mentioning.

掛車(ㄍㄨㄚˋ ㄔㄜ)
(said of a locomotive) to hook up with the train

掛失(ㄍㄨㄚˋ ㄕ)
to report the loss (of a check, etc.) to the bank to prevent the bearer from cashing it

掛上(ㄍㄨㄚˋ ·ㄕㄤ)
① to hang up ② to enter into the book (of one's debts, etc.)

掛帥(ㄍㄨㄚˋ ㄕㄨㄞˋ)
①to be appointed commander-in-chief; to assume command; to assume leadership ② to dominate; to be the most important

掛彩(ㄍㄨㄚˋ ㄘㄞˇ)
① to hang colored silk in celebration of happy occasions ② to get wounded in action; (now comically) to get injured in a brawl or fight, etc.

掛礙(ㄍㄨㄚˋ ㄞˋ)
to meet many obstacles and obstructions

掛一漏萬(ㄍㄨㄚˋ ㄧ ㄌㄡˋ ㄨㄢˋ)or 掛漏(ㄍㄨㄚˋ ㄌㄡˋ)
(literally) to list one item while missing 10,000 others —totally incomplete or inadequate (a polite expression often used by an editor or compiler in the preface of a book)

掛衣鉤(ㄍㄨㄚˋ ㄧ ㄍㄡ)
a clothes hook

掛意(ㄍㄨㄚˋ ㄧˋ)
to mind: 不管你做什麼我都不掛意。I don't mind what you do.

掛羊頭賣狗肉(ㄍㄨㄚˋ ㄧㄤˊ ㄊㄡˊ ㄇㄞˋ ㄍㄡˇ ㄖㄡˋ)
(literally) to sell dog meat while hanging a sheep's head outside the shop as advertisement—to cheat

【採】 1929 ㄘㄞˇ tsae cǎi

1. to pluck (flowers, etc.); to gather; to collect; to extract; to pick: 請爲我採一些花。Please gather me some flowers.
2. to select; to adopt: 經理採用他的意見。The manager adopted his idea.
3. (now rarely) to drag
4. (now rarely) to beckon; to take notice of

採辦(ㄘㄞˇ ㄅㄢˋ)
to purchase; to procure

採買(ㄘㄞˇ ㄇㄞˇ)or 採購(ㄘㄞˇ ㄍㄡˋ)
to pick and buy; to purchase; procurement

採煤(ㄘㄞˇ ㄇㄟˊ)
coal mining; coal cutting

採伐(ㄘㄞˇ ㄈㄚˊ)
to fell (trees); to open up (a mine)

採訪(ㄘㄞˇ ㄈㄤˇ)
to cover (a news item or story); to interview

採訪部(ㄘㄞˇ ㄈㄤˇ ㄅㄨˋ)
the city desk

採訪記者(ㄘㄞˇ ㄈㄤˇ ㄐㄧˋ ㄓㄜˇ)
a news reporter

採訪新聞(ㄘㄞˇ ㄈㄤˇ ㄒㄧㄣ ㄨㄣˊ)
to cover a news item

採訪主任(ㄘㄞˇ ㄈㄤˇ ㄓㄨˇ ㄖㄣˋ)
a city editor

採風(ㄘㄞˇ ㄈㄥ)
to collect folk songs

採風問俗(ㄘㄞˇ ㄈㄥ ㄨㄣˋ ㄙㄨˊ)
to learn local practices and customs

採納(ㄘㄞˇ ㄋㄚˋ)
to accept or adopt (an idea, opinion, proposal, etc.): 他不肯採納我的建議。He won't accept my proposal.

採納良言(ㄘㄞˇ ㄋㄚˋ ㄌㄧㄤˊ ㄧㄢˊ)
to accept good counsel

採蓮(ㄘㄞˇ ㄌㄧㄢˊ)

to pick the cupules of lotus
採錄(ㄘㄞˇ ㄌㄨˋ)
to collect and record
採購(ㄘㄞˇ ㄍㄡˋ)
to make purchases for an organization; to purchase
採購團(ㄘㄞˇ ㄍㄡˋ ㄊㄨㄢˊ)
a purchase mission
採光(ㄘㄞˇ ㄍㄨㄤ)
① lighting ② to pick or pluck until none is left
採鑛(ㄘㄞˇ ㄎㄨㄤˋ)
to mine (for minerals): 露天採鑛 opencut mining
採花(ㄘㄞˇ ㄏㄨㄚ)
① to pluck flowers ②(said of bandits, etc.) to force into a house in the night and commit rape
採花賊(ㄘㄞˇ ㄏㄨㄚ ㄗㄟˊ)
a rapist
採集(ㄘㄞˇ ㄐㄧˊ)
to gather (samples, etc.); to collect (materials, etc.): 他喜歡採集標本。He likes to collect specimens.
採擷(ㄘㄞˇ ㄐㄧㄝˊ)
to quote from; to take selections (from a book, article, etc.)
採取(ㄘㄞˇ ㄑㄩˇ)
to take or adopt (an attitude, a measure, etc.)
採取主動(ㄘㄞˇ ㄑㄩˇ ㄓㄨˇ ㄉㄨㄥˋ)
to take the initiative
採薪(ㄘㄞˇ ㄒㄧㄣ)
to gather firewood
採薪之憂(ㄘㄞˇ ㄒㄧㄣ ㄓ ㄧㄡ)
ill or sick; illness or sickness
採信(ㄘㄞˇ ㄒㄧㄣˋ)
to believe; to accept as true: 那個人講的話不足採信。We cannot believe what that man says.
採選(ㄘㄞˇ ㄒㄩㄢˇ)
to select; to pick (for use or purchase)
採摘(ㄘㄞˇ ㄓㄜˊ)
① to select and pick (tea leaves, etc.) ② to quote from; to translate in part or select from (a book, article, etc.)
採珠(ㄘㄞˇ ㄓㄨ)
to dive for pearls
採茶(ㄘㄞˇ ㄔㄚˊ)
to pick tea leaves
採場(ㄘㄞˇ ㄔㄤˇ)or 採礦場(ㄘㄞˇ ㄎㄨㄤˋ ㄔㄤˇ)
(mining) a stope
採石場(ㄘㄞˇ ㄕˊ ㄔㄤˇ)or(ㄘㄞˇ ㄕˊ ㄔㄤˊ)
(mining) a stone pit; a quarry
採生折割(ㄘㄞˇ ㄕㄥ ㄓㄜˊ ㄍㄜ)
a witchcraft that resembled voodoo
採擇(ㄘㄞˇ ㄗㄜˊ)
to pick or select: 他提出幾種辦法供你採擇。He has proposed several measures for you to choose from.
採桑(ㄘㄞˇ ㄙㄤ)
to gather mulberry leaves
採藥(ㄘㄞˇ ㄧㄠˋ)
① to gather herbs of medicinal value ② to become a hermit
採油(ㄘㄞˇ ㄧㄡˊ)
(petroleum) oil extraction; oil recovery
採用(ㄘㄞˇ ㄩㄥˋ)
to adopt (a suggestion, new technique, etc.)

【探】 1930
1. ㄊㄢˋ tann tàn
1. to find; to search; to locate; to prospect; to feel (in a pocket or bag)
2. to watch; to spy; a spy; a detective; to investigate; a secret agent
3. to try; to venture; to tempt
4. to stick out: 行車時不要探身車窗外。Don't stick out of the window while the train is in motion.
5. to explore
6. to visit; to inquire about: 他常常在假日探親訪友。He often visits his relatives and friends on holidays.

探病(ㄊㄢˋ ㄅㄧㄥˋ)
to visit the sick
探馬(ㄊㄢˋ ㄇㄚˇ)
a mounted scout
探明(ㄊㄢˋ ㄇㄧㄥˊ)
to find out by inquiry; to prove
探訪(ㄊㄢˋ ㄈㄤˇ)
① to investigate; to make inquiries; to seek out by inquiry or search: 探訪民間傳奇 to seek out the folklore ② to pay a visit to; to visit
探討(ㄊㄢˋ ㄊㄠˇ)
to investigate; to study; to explore (possibilities, etc.); to approach (a problem, etc.); to discuss (causes or effects, etc.)
探頭探腦(ㄊㄢˋ ㄊㄡˊ ㄊㄢˋ ㄋㄠˇ)
to act stealthily
探聽(ㄊㄢˋ ㄊㄧㄥ)
to investigate secretly; to spy; to pry into; to try to find out: 不要探聽人家的私事。Don't pry into other people's private affairs.
探聽虛實(ㄊㄢˋ ㄊㄧㄥ ㄒㄩ ㄕˊ)
to try to find out about an opponent or adversary; to try to ascertain the strength of the enemy
探囊取物(ㄊㄢˋ ㄋㄤˊ ㄑㄩˇ ㄨˋ)
as easy as taking things out of one's own pocket
探驪得珠(ㄊㄢˋ ㄌㄧˊ ㄉㄜˊ ㄓㄨ)
(said of a writing) to the point; relevant or pertinent
探戈(ㄊㄢˋ ㄍㄜ)
(dancing) tango
探口氣(ㄊㄢˋ ㄎㄡˇ ·ㄑㄧ)
to sound out another person's views (by making seemingly irrelevant remarks or indirect references)
探勘(ㄊㄢˋ ㄎㄢ)
to prospect: 在一地區探勘銀鑛 to prospect a region for silver
探礦(ㄊㄢˋ ㄎㄨㄤˋ)
to prospect mineral deposits
探空火箭(ㄊㄢˋ ㄎㄨㄥ ㄏㄨㄛˇ ㄐㄧㄢˋ)
a sounding rocket
探花(ㄊㄢˋ ㄏㄨㄚ)
(formerly) one who finished third in the imperial examination
探騎(ㄊㄢˋ ㄐㄧˋ)
a mounted spy or scout
探究(ㄊㄢˋ ㄐㄧㄡˋ)
to investigate; to probe: 科學家探究自然現象。Scientists investigate natural phenomena.
探監(ㄊㄢˋ ㄐㄧㄢ)
to visit a prisoner
探求(ㄊㄢˋ ㄑㄧㄡˊ)
to seek; to search for; to study; to find out; to look

〔手部〕

〔手部〕

into
探親(ㄊㄢˋ ㄑㄧㄣ)
to visit one's relatives
探取(ㄊㄢˋ ㄑㄩˇ)
to draw money in advance
探悉(ㄊㄢˋ ㄒㄧ)
to learn after investigating, spying, or obtaining information from some (usually indirect) sources: 他從有關當局探悉此事。He learned the matter from the authorities concerned.
探險(ㄊㄢˋ ㄒㄧㄢˇ)
to undertake an exploratory trip; exploration: 他到北極地區探險。He went to explore the Arctic regions.
探險隊(ㄊㄢˋ ㄒㄧㄢˇ ㄉㄨㄟˋ)
an expedition team; an exploration party
探險家(ㄊㄢˋ ㄒㄧㄢˇ ㄐㄧㄚ)
an explorer
探信(ㄊㄢˋ ㄒㄧㄣˋ)or 探詢(ㄊㄢˋ ㄒㄩㄣˊ)
to make inquiries
探照燈(ㄊㄢˋ ㄓㄠˋ ㄉㄥ)
a searchlight
探春(ㄊㄢˋ ㄔㄨㄣ)
a spring outing; an excursion to the countryside in early spring
探視(ㄊㄢˋ ㄕˋ)
to visit (a patient , etc.): 醫生探視他的病人。A doctor visits his patients.
探身子(ㄊㄢˋ ㄕㄣ ·ㄗ)
to bend forward (for a better look)
探子(ㄊㄢˋ ·ㄗ)
a scout; a spy; a detective
探測(ㄊㄢˋ ㄘㄜˋ)
to survey; to sound; to probe: 他們將探測基隆港口的水深。They will sound the entrance to the harbor of Keelung.
探喪(ㄊㄢˋ ㄙㄤ)
to condole with someone on his bereavement
探索(ㄊㄢˋ ㄙㄨㄛˇ)
to probe; to search for; to look into; to seek; to find out; to study; to explore: 他喜歡探索宇宙的奧秘。He likes to explore the secrets of the universe.
探案(ㄊㄢˋ ㄢˋ)
detective stories; adventures of a detective
探幽尋勝(ㄊㄢˋ ㄧㄡ ㄒㄩㄣˊ ㄕㄥˋ)
to visit scenic spots: 很多人喜歡在春天探幽尋勝。Many people like to visit scenic spots in spring.
探友(ㄊㄢˋ ㄧㄡˇ)
to visit friends
探問(ㄊㄢˋ ㄨㄣˋ)
to inquire about or after
探望(ㄊㄢˋ ㄨㄤˋ)
① to visit: 他們回國探望親友。They returned to their home country to visit relatives and friends. ② to look about
探原 or 探源(ㄊㄢˋ ㄩㄢˊ)
to make an exhaustive investigation or study in order to find out the root cause or source of something

【探】 1930
2. ㄊㄢ tan tān

to try; to tempt; to test
探湯(ㄊㄢ ㄊㄤ)
(literally) to test boiling water with one's hand and get scalded—(figuratively) A burnt child dreads the fire.

【控】 1931
ㄎㄨㄥˋ konq kòng

1. to accuse; to charge; to sue: 司機被控超速。The driver is charged with speeding.
2. to control; control: 遙控 remote control
3. to draw (a bow)
4. (now rarely) to throw; to hit

控馬(ㄎㄨㄥˋ ㄇㄚˇ)
to rein in a horse
控告(ㄎㄨㄥˋ ㄍㄠˋ)
to sue somebody in court; to accuse
控弦(ㄎㄨㄥˋ ㄒㄧㄢˊ)
to draw a bow
控制(ㄎㄨㄥˋ ㄓˋ)
to control; control; to dominate: 飛機如失去控制，必定撞毀。If an airplane is out of control, it will certainly be smashed.
控詞(ㄎㄨㄥˋ ㄘˊ)
a charge; a complaint
控訴(ㄎㄨㄥˋ ㄙㄨˋ)
① to appeal to a higher court ② to accuse before an authority
控訴狀(ㄎㄨㄥˋ ㄙㄨˋ ㄓㄨㄤˋ)
a written appeal
控訴人(ㄎㄨㄥˋ ㄙㄨˋ ㄖㄣˊ)
the appellant

【接】 1932
ㄐㄧㄝ jie jiē

1. to receive; to accept; to take with the hand: 我昨天接到你的來信。I received your letter yesterday.
2. to welcome; to meet: 我會到車站接你。I'll go to the station to meet you.
3. to join; to connect: 起來發問的人一個接著一個。People got up to ask questions one after another.
4. to graft
5. to come close to; to make contact with
6. to succeed to

接駁(ㄐㄧㄝ ㄅㄛˊ)
to ferry train passengers by bus across a gap between two sections of a railroad
接班(ㄐㄧㄝ ㄅㄢ)
to relieve another in work
接辦(ㄐㄧㄝ ㄅㄢˋ)
to succeed another in managing a task; to carry on the work left unfinished by another
接棒(ㄐㄧㄝ ㄅㄤˋ)
(originally) to receive the stick or pin from the preceding runner in a relay race—(figuratively) to continue the work left unfinished by a leading scholar, thinker, etc.
接不住(ㄐㄧㄝ ·ㄅㄨ ㄓㄨˋ)
cannot catch it—the object being too fast or out of the way, etc.
接不上(ㄐㄧㄝ ·ㄅㄨ ·ㄕㄤ)
① cannot be connected ② disruption in continuity
接片機(ㄐㄧㄝ ㄆㄧㄢˋ ㄐㄧ)
a splicer
接木法(ㄐㄧㄝ ㄇㄨˋ ㄈㄚˇ)
(botany) graft method
接防(ㄐㄧㄝ ㄈㄤˊ)
(said of military troops) to relieve friendly forces from their duties by taking over their assignment
接防部隊(ㄐㄧㄝ ㄈㄤˊ ㄅㄨˋ ㄉㄨㄟˋ)

a relieving unit
接風(ㄐㄧㄝ ㄈㄥ)
a welcome party in honor of a distinguished visitor or someone who returns after a long period of absence from home
接風酒(ㄐㄧㄝ ㄈㄥ ㄐㄧㄡˇ)
a welcome feast 參看「接風」
接待(ㄐㄧㄝ ㄉㄞˋ)
to receive (a guest); reception: 受到親切接待 to be accorded a cordial reception
接待單位(ㄐㄧㄝ ㄉㄞˋ ㄉㄢ ㄨㄟˋ)
a host organization
接待室(ㄐㄧㄝ ㄉㄞˋ ㄕˋ)
a reception room
接待人員(ㄐㄧㄝ ㄉㄞˋ ㄖㄣˊ ㄩㄢˊ)
reception personnel
接待外賓(ㄐㄧㄝ ㄉㄞˋ ㄨㄞˋ ㄅㄧㄣ)
to receive foreign guests
接待員(ㄐㄧㄝ ㄉㄞˋ ㄩㄢˊ)
a receptionist
接到(ㄐㄧㄝ ㄉㄠˋ)
to receive
接地線(ㄐㄧㄝ ㄉㄧˋ ㄒㄧㄢˋ)
(electricity) a ground wire; an earth lead
接頭(ㄐㄧㄝ ㄊㄡˊ)
① to have a firm grasp of the situation so that one can manage a matter by oneself; to know ② to get in touch with; to make contact with (the responsible person) ③ a joint
接替(ㄐㄧㄝ ㄊㄧˋ)
to relieve; to succeed (a predecessor); to take over; to substitute for
接通(ㄐㄧㄝ ㄊㄨㄥ)
to put through: 請幫我接通經理。Please put me through to the Manager.
接納(ㄐㄧㄝ ㄋㄚˋ)
to accept (a proposal, advice, etc.)
接力(ㄐㄧㄝ ㄌㄧˋ)
a relay: 八百公尺接力 a 800-meter relay
接力棒(ㄐㄧㄝ ㄌㄧˋ ㄅㄤˋ)
a relay baton
接力賽跑(ㄐㄧㄝ ㄌㄧˋ ㄙㄞˋ ㄆㄠˇ)
a relay race
接連(ㄐㄧㄝ ㄌㄧㄢˊ)
repeatedly; continuously; to continue; on end; one after another
接連不斷(ㄐㄧㄝ ㄌㄧㄢˊ ㄅㄨˊ ㄉㄨㄢˋ)
continuously; incessantly; in succession
接骨(ㄐㄧㄝ ㄍㄨˇ)
to unite a fractured bone; to set broken bones
接骨眼兒(ㄐㄧㄝ ·ㄍㄨ ㄧㄚˇㄦ)
the critical moment; the right time; an opportune moment 亦作「節骨眼兒」
接過來(ㄐㄧㄝ ㄍㄨㄛˋ ·ㄌㄞ)
to receive; to take over
接管(ㄐㄧㄝ ㄍㄨㄢˇ)
to take over (the management of)
接客(ㄐㄧㄝ ㄎㄜˋ)
①(said of a hotel, etc.) to receive lodgers or guests ② (said of prostitutes) to receive patrons in boudoirs
接合(ㄐㄧㄝ ㄏㄜˊ)
to connect; to assemble
接合面(ㄐㄧㄝ ㄏㄜˊ ㄇㄧㄢˋ)
(mineralogy) a composition face or plane
接濟(ㄐㄧㄝ ㄐㄧˋ)
to give financial or material assistance to
接駕(ㄐㄧㄝ ㄐㄧㄚˋ)
(originally) to welcome or receive the king; (figuratively) to welcome or receive someone
接界(ㄐㄧㄝ ㄐㄧㄝˋ)or 接境(ㄐㄧㄝ ㄐㄧㄥˋ)
to border on; to share a common border; adjacent
接交(ㄐㄧㄝ ㄐㄧㄠ)
to make friends with
接角(ㄐㄧㄝ ㄐㄧㄠˇ)
an adjacent angle
接見(ㄐㄧㄝ ㄐㄧㄢˋ)
to grant an audience to; to receive (a visitor, etc.): 總統每年都要接見許多外賓。The President has to receive many foreign guests every year.
接近(ㄐㄧㄝ ㄐㄧㄣˋ)
to draw near; to come close; to approach; near to; approaching: 我們的科技正接近國際水平。Our technology is approaching the international level.
接頸交臂(ㄐㄧㄝ ㄐㄧㄥˇ ㄐㄧㄠ ㄅㄧˋ)
to neck; to be very intimate with; to make love with
接球(ㄐㄧㄝ ㄑㄧㄡˊ)
to catch the ball; to return a served ball
接戲(ㄐㄧㄝ ㄒㄧˋ)
(said of an actor or actress) to sign a contract for a role in a new movie
接洽(ㄐㄧㄝ ㄒㄧㄚˊ)
to contact, discuss or negotiate; to take up a matter with; to arrange (business, etc.) with; to consult with: 我將同有關部門接洽。I will take up the matter with the department concerned.
接線(ㄐㄧㄝ ㄒㄧㄢˋ)
① to connect (telephone) lines; to make a telephone connection ② to wire
接線生(ㄐㄧㄝ ㄒㄧㄢˋ ㄕㄥ)
a switchboard operator
接續(ㄐㄧㄝ ㄒㄩˋ)
continuously; to continue; to connect
接續香烟(ㄐㄧㄝ ㄒㄩˋ ㄒㄧㄤ ㄧㄢ)
to continue the family line
接續詞(ㄐㄧㄝ ㄒㄩˋ ㄘˊ)
a conjunction 亦作「連接詞」
接枝(ㄐㄧㄝ ㄓ)
(botany) to graft; a graft
接著(ㄐㄧㄝ ·ㄓㄜ)
① then; shortly afterwards; thereupon: 春天先來,接着就是夏天。First comes spring, then summer. ② to follow; to add: 你先走,我接着就來。You go first and I'll follow. ③ to catch: 給你一個梨,接着! Here's a pear for you. Catch!
接戰(ㄐㄧㄝ ㄓㄢˋ)
to meet in battle
接住(ㄐㄧㄝ ㄓㄨˋ)
to catch (a flying object): 你能接住他的球嗎? Can you catch his ball?
接篆(ㄐㄧㄝ ㄓㄨㄢˋ)or 接印(ㄐㄧㄝ ㄧㄣˋ)
to take over the seal of office—to take over a public post
接踵(ㄐㄧㄝ ㄓㄨㄥˇ)
one on the heels of another—to come in close succes-

〔手部〕

〔手部〕

sion

接踵而至(ㄐㄧㄝ ㄓㄨㄥˇ ㄦˊ ㄓˋ)
to come in quick succession; to follow at the heels of

接觸(ㄐㄧㄝ ㄔㄨˋ)
①(said of nations) to wage war against each other ②to make contact with; to come in contact with; contact: 促進兩國文化的接觸 to promote cultural contacts between two countries

接觸不良(ㄐㄧㄝ ㄔㄨˋ ㄅㄨˋ ㄌㄧㄤˊ)
loose or poor contact

接觸劑(ㄐㄧㄝ ㄔㄨˋ ㄐㄧˋ)
a catalyst

接充(ㄐㄧㄝ ㄔㄨㄥ)
to replace (someone)

接事(ㄐㄧㄝ ㄕˋ)
to take over an office or official duties: 新校長昨天接事。The new chancellor took over yesterday.

接煞(ㄐㄧㄝ ㄕㄚˋ)
(folklore) to receive the soul of the deceased within 10 to 18 days after his death

接收(ㄐㄧㄝ ㄕㄡ)
to take over; to receive

接收天線(ㄐㄧㄝ ㄕㄡ ㄊㄧㄢ ㄒㄧㄢˋ)
a receiving antenna

接收儀式(ㄐㄧㄝ ㄕㄡ ㄧˊ ㄕˋ)
a takeover ceremony

接手(ㄐㄧㄝ ㄕㄡˇ)
①to carry on the task of the predecessor: 他將接手他父親的事業。He will carry on his father's business. ②assistants or aides

接受(ㄐㄧㄝ ㄕㄡˋ)
to accept (an invitation, an assignment, etc.); to take: 你最好接受我的意見。You had better take my advice.

接受教訓(ㄐㄧㄝ ㄕㄡˋ ㄐㄧㄠˋ ㄒㄩㄣˋ)
to learn a lesson

接上帶下(ㄐㄧㄝ ㄕㄤˋ ㄉㄞˋ ㄒㄧㄚˋ)
to link what precedes with what follows

接生(ㄐㄧㄝ ㄕㄥ)
to assist in childbirth; to practice midwifery

接生婆(ㄐㄧㄝ ㄕㄥ ㄆㄛˊ)
a midwife 亦作「助產士」

接任(ㄐㄧㄝ ㄖㄣˋ)
to take over an office; to succeed: 他的職務已由他人接任。His job has been taken over by another.

接壤(ㄐㄧㄝ ㄖㄤˇ)
adjoining boundary; adjacency; adjacent to; contiguous to

接壤地區(ㄐㄧㄝ ㄖㄤˇ ㄉㄧˋ ㄑㄩ)
contiguous areas

接財神(ㄐㄧㄝ ㄘㄞˊ ㄕㄣˊ)
to welcome back the "God of Wealth" (a Chinese custom during the Lunar New Year)

接送(ㄐㄧㄝ ㄙㄨㄥˋ)
①to receive and send off (guests or visitors) ②transportation to and from a certain place

接二連三(ㄐㄧㄝ ㄦˋ ㄌㄧㄢˊ ㄙㄢ)
one after another; continuously; repeatedly: 他們接二連三地跑來。They came running one after another.

接引(ㄐㄧㄝ ㄧㄣˇ)
to guide; to receive

接應(ㄐㄧㄝ ㄧㄥˋ)
to stand ready for assistance; to come to somebody's aid; to coordinate with; to supply: 誰來接應我? Who will come to my aid?

接物待人(ㄐㄧㄝ ㄨˋ ㄉㄞˋ ㄖㄣˊ)
to attend a matter and to receive a person

接尾詞(ㄐㄧㄝ ㄨㄟˇ ㄘˊ)or **接尾語**(ㄐㄧㄝ ㄨㄟˇ ㄩˇ)
a suffix

接吻(ㄐㄧㄝ ㄨㄣˇ)
to kiss; a kiss

接吻魚(ㄐㄧㄝ ㄨㄣˇ ㄩˊ)
kissing gourami

【推】 1933 ㄊㄨㄟ tuei tuī

1. to push; to shove: 他把門推開。He pushed the door open.
2. to look into; to find out; to ponder; to infer; to deduce
3. to shirk; to shift (responsibility, etc.); to refuse: 別想把責任推給我。Don't try to shift the responsibility onto me.
4. to elect; to recommend; to praise; to esteem: 我們推他擔任主席。We elect him as chairman.
5. to move along; to change in succession (as seasons)
6. to extend; to enlarge

推波助瀾(ㄊㄨㄟ ㄅㄛ ㄓㄨˋ ㄌㄢˊ)
to add fuel to the fire; to egg on; to instigate; to incite

推背圖(ㄊㄨㄟ ㄅㄟˋ ㄊㄨˊ)
a book of prophecy, allegedly written by Li Chun-feng (李淳風) and Yüan Tien-kang (袁天綱) of the Tang Dynasty

推鉋(ㄊㄨㄟ ㄅㄠˋ)
a plane (for leveling wood)

推本溯源(ㄊㄨㄟ ㄅㄣˇ ㄙㄨˋ ㄩㄢˊ)
to go into the source of a matter; to trace the origins

推病(ㄊㄨㄟ ㄅㄧㄥˋ)
to feign sickness; to excuse oneself on the pretext of illness: 他推病不上學。He feigned that he was sick and did not go to school.

推不開(ㄊㄨㄟ ˙ㄅㄨ ㄎㄞ)
unable to push away; unable to get out of (an involvement, etc.); unable to shirk (responsibility, etc.)

推不出(ㄊㄨㄟ ˙ㄅㄨ ㄔㄨ)
①unable to decline ②unable to push out

推牌九(ㄊㄨㄟ ㄆㄞˊ ㄐㄧㄡˇ)
to play a gambling game of *pai chiu* (a kind of domino)

推派代表(ㄊㄨㄟ ㄆㄞˋ ㄉㄞˋ ㄅㄧㄠˇ)
to elect representatives (to present a petition, to a negotiation, etc.)

推磨(ㄊㄨㄟ ㄇㄛˋ)
to turn a mill manually

推翻(ㄊㄨㄟ ㄈㄢ)
①to overthrow (a government, etc.); to topple ②to stultify (a theory, principle, etc.); to repudiate (an agreement); to cancel: 他們推翻原定計畫。They cancel their original plan.

推戴(ㄊㄨㄟ ㄉㄞˋ)
to support (a leader, etc.)

推倒(ㄊㄨㄟ ㄉㄠˇ)
①to overturn; to topple ②to shove: 他把她推倒在地。He shoved her to the ground.

推擋(ㄊㄨㄟ ㄉㄤˇ)
(table tennis) half volley

推宕(ㄊㄨㄟ ㄉㄤˋ)or **推延**(ㄊㄨㄟ ㄧㄢˊ)
to delay; to procrastinate

推定(ㄊㄨㄟ ㄉㄧㄥˋ)
to infer; to deduce

推度(ㄊㄨㄟ ㄉㄨㄛˋ)
to infer; to conclude; to speculate
推斷(ㄊㄨㄟ ㄉㄨㄢˋ)
to infer; to predict by means of inference; inference
推動(ㄊㄨㄟ ㄉㄨㄥˋ)
to push (a sales project, etc.); to lend impetus to (a movement, etc.); to propel; to expedite
推頭(ㄊㄨㄟ ㄊㄡˊ)
to cut hair with clippers
推土機(ㄊㄨㄟ ㄊㄨˇ ㄐㄧ)
a bulldozer
推託(ㄊㄨㄟ ㄊㄨㄛ)
to make excuses; to shirk; to plead: 推託責任 to evade or shift responsibility
推拏 or 推拿(ㄊㄨㄟ ㄋㄚˊ)
①to massage ② to fix a dislocated bone by massage
推來推去(ㄊㄨㄟ ㄌㄞˊ ㄊㄨㄟ ㄑㄩˋ)
①to pass the buck ② (to refuse to accept a present, assignment, etc.) by pushing it back and forth
推類(ㄊㄨㄟ ㄌㄟˋ)
to reason by analogy
推理(ㄊㄨㄟ ㄌㄧˇ)
to reason (out); reasoning; to infer
推理小說(ㄊㄨㄟ ㄌㄧˇ ㄒㄧㄠˇ ㄕㄨㄛ)
detective stories
推論(ㄊㄨㄟ ㄌㄨㄣˋ)
①inference; to infer: 人類曾用各種方法作觀察及推論。Men have observed and inferred in all sorts of ways. ② (mathematics) corollary
推聾裝啞(ㄊㄨㄟ ㄌㄨㄥˊ ㄓㄨㄤ ㄧㄚˇ)
to pretend to be deaf and mute—to avoid getting involved in something by pretending ignorance
推乾淨兒(ㄊㄨㄟ ㄍㄢ ㄐㄧㄥˋㄦ)
to shirk all one's responsibilities; to pass the buck
推轂(ㄊㄨㄟ ㄍㄨˇ)
①to recommend (men of abilities) ② to help people achieve something
推故(ㄊㄨㄟ ㄍㄨˋ)
to make excuses: 他推故不來。He excused himself from coming.
推廣(ㄊㄨㄟ ㄍㄨㄤˇ)
to propagate; to extend; to popularize; to spread: 推廣國語 to popularize Mandarin
推廣教育(ㄊㄨㄟ ㄍㄨㄤˇ ㄐㄧㄠˋ ㄩˋ)
extension education
推開(ㄊㄨㄟ ㄎㄞ)
①to push away ②to get away from (social activities, etc.)
推己及人(ㄊㄨㄟ ㄐㄧˇ ㄐㄧˊ ㄖㄣˊ)
to put oneself in another's position; to be considerate
推究(ㄊㄨㄟ ㄐㄧㄡˋ)
to study; to reason out; to investigate
推薦(ㄊㄨㄟ ㄐㄧㄢˋ)
to recommend (somebody for a job, etc.): 他們推薦我擔任這項工作。They recommended me for the job.
推薦書(ㄊㄨㄟ ㄐㄧㄢˋ ㄕㄨ)or 推薦信(ㄊㄨㄟ ㄐㄧㄢˋ ㄒㄧㄣˋ)
a letter of recommendation: 請寫給我一封推薦信。Please write me a recommendation.
推襟送抱(ㄊㄨㄟ ㄐㄧㄣ ㄙㄨㄥˋ ㄅㄠˋ)
to be sincere in dealing with others
推進(ㄊㄨㄟ ㄐㄧㄣˋ)
to push forward; to move ahead; to advance
推進機(ㄊㄨㄟ ㄐㄧㄣˋ ㄐㄧ)or 推進器(ㄊㄨㄟ ㄐㄧㄣˋ ㄑㄧˋ)
the propeller (of a ship, plane, etc.)
推獎(ㄊㄨㄟ ㄐㄧㄤˇ)
to praise
推舉(ㄊㄨㄟ ㄐㄩˇ)
①to elect (to an office, etc.); to recommend for a post ②(weightlifting) to press
推敲(ㄊㄨㄟ ㄑㄧㄠ)
①to weigh or consider words in writing ②to investigate or examine carefully
推敲詞句(ㄊㄨㄟ ㄑㄧㄠ ㄘˊ ㄐㄩˋ)
to weigh one's words
推求(ㄊㄨㄟ ㄑㄧㄡˊ)
to ascertain; to analyze and study (for a solution, an answer, etc.)
推遷(ㄊㄨㄟ ㄑㄧㄢ)
to make excuses and delay; to procrastinate
推鉛球(ㄊㄨㄟ ㄑㄧㄢ ㄑㄧㄡˊ)
(track and field) ①shot put ②to throw or put the shot
推卻(ㄊㄨㄟ ㄑㄩㄝˋ)
to decline (an invitation, offer, etc.): 我推卻他的聚餐邀約。I declined his invitation to dinner.
推卸(ㄊㄨㄟ ㄒㄧㄝˋ)
to be irresponsible; to shirk (responsibility): 他因爲推卸工作而失去職業。He lost his job because he shirked his work.
推卸責任(ㄊㄨㄟ ㄒㄧㄝˋ ㄗㄜˊ ㄖㄣˋ)
to shirk one's responsibility
推銷(ㄊㄨㄟ ㄒㄧㄠ)
to promote sales; to sell
推銷員(ㄊㄨㄟ ㄒㄧㄠ ㄩㄢˊ)
a salesman or saleswoman
推心置腹(ㄊㄨㄟ ㄒㄧㄣ ㄓˋ ㄈㄨˋ)
to treat others with the utmost sincerity; to put every trust in
推想(ㄊㄨㄟ ㄒㄧㄤˇ)
to infer; to deduce
推行(ㄊㄨㄟ ㄒㄧㄥˊ)
to promote (a cause, movement, etc.); to implement (a policy)
推許(ㄊㄨㄟ ㄒㄩˇ)
to praise; to approve (a performance): 教練對球隊的良好表現備加推許。The coach praised the team for its fine playing.
推選(ㄊㄨㄟ ㄒㄩㄢˇ)
to elect
推重(ㄊㄨㄟ ㄓㄨㄥˋ)
to hold in high esteem; to admire; admiration: 他是大家所推重的人。He is the admiration of everyone.
推陳出新(ㄊㄨㄟ ㄔㄣˊ ㄔㄨ ㄒㄧㄣ)
to find new ways of doing things from old theories; to find something new in what is old
推誠(ㄊㄨㄟ ㄔㄥˊ)
to place confidence in; to act in sincerity
推誠相見(ㄊㄨㄟ ㄔㄥˊ ㄒㄧㄤ ㄐㄧㄢˋ)
to deal with or treat somebody with sincerity
推出(ㄊㄨㄟ ㄔㄨ)
①to push out ② to present (a picture, a show, etc.)
推崇(ㄊㄨㄟ ㄔㄨㄥˊ)

to hold in high esteem; to respect; to praise highly: 他們對這位科學家推崇備至。They have the greatest esteem for the scientist.

推食解衣(ㄊㄨㄟ ㄕˊ ㄐㄧㄝˇ ㄧ)
to do anything one possibly can to help (as a friend in need)

推事(ㄊㄨㄟ ㄕˋ)
(court) a judge

推讓(ㄊㄨㄟ ㄖㄤˋ)
to yield to someone as a token of deference to the other party; to decline (a position, favor, etc. out of modesty)

推讓之風(ㄊㄨㄟ ㄖㄤˋ ㄓ ㄈㄥ)
the practice of yielding or showing deference

推子(ㄊㄨㄟ ˙ㄗ)
a hair clipper

推燥居溼(ㄊㄨㄟ ㄗㄠˋ ㄐㄩ ㄕ)
to give the best to the young

推尊(ㄊㄨㄟ ㄗㄨㄣ)
to admire and respect

推辭(ㄊㄨㄟ ㄘˊ)
to decline (an offer, invitation, etc.); to reject

推測(ㄊㄨㄟ ㄘㄜˋ)
① to infer; to deduce; to predict; to conjecture: 我推測他會贏。I predict that he will win. ② conjecture: 謠言引起很多推測。The rumor raised much conjecture.

推三阻四(ㄊㄨㄟ ㄙㄢ ㄗㄨˇ ㄙˋ)
to make numerous excuses; to decline with all sorts of excuses

推算(ㄊㄨㄟ ㄙㄨㄢˋ)
to calculate; calculation; to reckon

推恩(ㄊㄨㄟ ㄣ)
to extend benevolence to others (especially said of a ruler)

推移(ㄊㄨㄟ ㄧˊ)
① changes; vicissitudes ② to follow others ③ to transpose

推壓(ㄊㄨㄟ ㄧㄚ)
(said of bureaucrats in handling official business) to delay and procrastinate

推延(ㄊㄨㄟ ㄧㄢˊ)
to delay; to procrastinate; to put off

推諉(ㄊㄨㄟ ㄨㄟˇ)
to shirk (responsibility, etc.); to make excuses: 他們都有推諉之詞。They all had excuses to offer.

推輓 or 推挽(ㄊㄨㄟ ㄨㄢˇ)
①(literally) to push and pull—to recommend a young man for a job ②(electricity) push-pull

推問(ㄊㄨㄟ ㄨㄣˋ)
to examine and investigate; to interrogate (in court)

推原(ㄊㄨㄟ ㄩㄢˊ)
to trace the cause (of an incident, etc.)

【措】 1934
ㄘㄨㄛˋ tsuoh cuò

1. to place
2. to collect; to arrange; to manage; to handle
3. to abandon; to renounce
4. to make preparation for an undertaking; to make plans

措大(ㄘㄨㄛˋ ㄉㄚˋ)
① a scholar; a pedant ② a penniless fellow 亦作「窮措大」

措置(ㄘㄨㄛˋ ㄓˋ)
to execute; to arrange; to manage

措置失當(ㄘㄨㄛˋ ㄓˋ ㄕ ㄉㄤˋ)
to mismanage; mismanagement

措施(ㄘㄨㄛˋ ㄕ)
a (political, financial, etc.) measure; a step

措手不及(ㄘㄨㄛˋ ㄕㄡˇ ㄅㄨˋ ㄐㄧˊ)
to be caught unawares or unprepared; to be taken by surprise: 我們打他個措手不及。Let's make a surprise attack on them.

措辭(ㄘㄨㄛˋ ㄘˊ)
wording (of a letter, diplomatic note, etc.); diction

措意(ㄘㄨㄛˋ ㄧˋ)
to pay attention to; to mind

【掩】 1935
ㄧㄢˇ yean yǎn

1. to cover; to hide; to conceal; to cover up: 他敏於掩飾他的無知。He was clever at covering up his ignorance.
2. to shut; to close: 不要關門，讓它半掩著。Don't close the door, let it half shut.
3. to mount a surprise attack; to take or catch by surprise

掩鼻而過(ㄧㄢˇ ㄅㄧˊ ㄦˊ ㄍㄨㄛˋ)
to cover the nose and hurry away (from a stench)

掩蔽(ㄧㄢˇ ㄅㄧˋ)
to cover; to conceal; to take cover; to shelter; cover: 黑夜掩蔽了他的惡行。The night covered his evil deed.

掩不住(ㄧㄢˇ ˙ㄅㄨ ㄓㄨˋ)
unable to cover or hide; can not shut out

掩埋(ㄧㄢˇ ㄇㄞˊ)
to bury: 海盜將財寶掩埋在土裡。Pirates buried treasure in the ground.

掩門(ㄧㄢˇ ㄇㄣˊ)
to close the door; to shut the door

掩面而泣(ㄧㄢˇ ㄇㄧㄢˋ ㄦˊ ㄑㄧˋ)
to cover one's face and weep

掩目捕雀(ㄧㄢˇ ㄇㄨˋ ㄅㄨˇ ㄑㄩㄝˋ)
(literally) to cover the eyes and try to catch the bird—to fool oneself; self-deception

掩體(ㄧㄢˇ ㄊㄧˇ)
a rampart or emplacement (for a crew-served weapon); a bunker

掩蓋(ㄧㄢˇ ㄍㄞˋ)
to cover up; to conceal: 他企圖掩蓋事實。He tried to cover up (or conceal) the facts.

掩口(ㄧㄢˇ ㄎㄡˇ)
to cover one's mouth with one's hand

掩口而笑(ㄧㄢˇ ㄎㄡˇ ㄦˊ ㄒㄧㄠˋ)
to laugh in secret; to hide one's smile

掩護(ㄧㄢˇ ㄏㄨˋ)
① to cover (friendly troops on a special assignment) ② camouflage; to camouflage

掩懷(ㄧㄢˇ ㄏㄨㄞˊ)
to throw on a garment without buttoning up

掩卷(ㄧㄢˇ ㄐㄩㄢˋ)
to close books; to stop reading: 掩卷而睡 to close the book and fall asleep

掩旗息鼓(ㄧㄢˇ ㄑㄧˊ ㄒㄧˊ ㄍㄨˇ)
to stop clamoring; to stay quiet; to keep silent 亦作「偃旗息鼓」

掩泣(ㄧㄢˇ ㄑㄧˋ)
to cover one's face and

weep; to weep silently
掩襲(ㄧㄢˇ ㄒㄧˊ)
to mount a surprise attack
掩飾(ㄧㄢˇ ㄕˋ)
to cover; to conceal; to paper over; to gloss over: 不要嘗試掩飾錯誤。Don't try to gloss over your mistakes.
掩殺(ㄧㄢˇ ㄕㄚ)
to attack by surprise
掩上(ㄧㄢˇ ·ㄕㄤ)
to shut (the door, window, etc.)
掩人耳目(ㄧㄢˇ ㄖㄣˊ ㄦˇ ㄇㄨˋ)
to deceive others; to hoodwink people
掩藏(ㄧㄢˇ ㄘㄤˊ)
to hide; to conceal
掩耳不聞(ㄧㄢˇ ㄦˇ ㄅㄨˋ ㄨㄣˊ)
to turn a deaf ear: 他對我的一切解釋掩耳不聞。He was deaf to all my excuses.
掩耳盜鈴(ㄧㄢˇ ㄦˇ ㄉㄠˋ ㄌㄧㄥˊ)
(literally) to cover one's ears when he steals a bell—to deceive oneself
掩映(ㄧㄢˇ ㄧㄥˋ)
① the mingling, or contrast, of light and shadow (usually said of enchanting scenery) ② to set off (one another): 紅瓦綠竹相掩映。The red tiles and green bamboos set each other off.

【掮】 1936
ㄑㄧㄢˊ chyan qián
to bear a load on the shoulder
掮客(ㄑㄧㄢˊ ㄎㄜˋ)
a broker: 他是個政治掮客。He is a political broker.

【掬】 1937
ㄐㄩˊ jyu jú
1. to hold in both hands
2. (classifier) a double handful of
掬水(ㄐㄩˊ ㄕㄨㄟˇ)
to scoop up water with the hands

【捶】 1938
ㄔㄨㄟˊ chwei chuí
1. to beat; to thrash; to pound
2. a stick for beating: 鼓捶 a drumstick
捶平(ㄔㄨㄟˊ ㄆㄧㄥˊ)
to flatten by pounding
捶扑(ㄔㄨㄟˊ ㄆㄨ)
to beat up a criminal
捶打(ㄔㄨㄟˊ ㄉㄚˇ)
to beat; to thump: 他捶打桌子。He thumped the table.
捶鍊(ㄔㄨㄟˊ ㄌㄧㄢˋ)
to submit to strict disciplinary training
捶鼓(ㄔㄨㄟˊ ㄍㄨˇ)
to beat a drum 亦作「搥鼓」
捶胸頓足(ㄔㄨㄟˊ ㄒㄩㄥ ㄉㄨㄣˋ ㄗㄨˊ)
to beat one's breast and stamp one's feet—in deep grief
捶楚(ㄔㄨㄟˊ ㄔㄨˇ)
(an ancient form of punishment) flogging

【掫】 1939
ㄗㄡ tzou zōu
to be on the night watch

【掌】 1940
ㄓㄤˇ jaang zhǎng
1. the palm of the hand; the sole of the foot; paws of an animal
2. to slap with one's hand; to smack
3. to have charge of; to supervise; to control
4. to stand; to bear
5. a Chinese family name
掌兵權(ㄓㄤˇ ㄅㄧㄥ ㄑㄩㄢˊ)
to wield military power; to command the armed forces
掌燈(ㄓㄤˇ ㄉㄥ)
to light the lantern or lamp (at nightfall)
掌舵(ㄓㄤˇ ㄉㄨㄛˋ)
① to steer a ship; the steersman; the helmsman ② the man in charge
掌理(ㄓㄤˇ ㄌㄧˇ)
to supervise, manage or take charge of: 他掌理一家大百貨公司的業務。He manages the business of a large department store.
掌骨(ㄓㄤˇ ㄍㄨˇ)
the metacarpal bones
掌故(ㄓㄤˇ ㄍㄨˋ)
① historical anecdotes or records; national legends ② national institutions
掌櫃(ㄓㄤˇ ㄍㄨㄟˋ)
a shopkeeper
掌櫃的(ㄓㄤˇ ㄍㄨㄟˋ ·ㄉㄜ)
① a manager; a shopkeeper; a superintendent ② a reference to one's husband ③ a respectful term of address
掌管(ㄓㄤˇ ㄍㄨㄢˇ)
to take charge of; to supervise; to manage: 他掌管這裏的一切。He takes care of everything here.
掌頰(ㄓㄤˇ ㄐㄧㄚˊ)
to slap someone's face
掌權(ㄓㄤˇ ㄑㄩㄢˊ)
to be in power or authority
掌心(ㄓㄤˇ ㄒㄧㄣ)
the center of the palm
掌政(ㄓㄤˇ ㄓㄥˋ)
to head a government
掌狀脈(ㄓㄤˇ ㄓㄨㄤˋ ㄇㄛˋ)
palmate veins
掌中戲(ㄓㄤˇ ㄓㄨㄥ ㄒㄧˋ)
a kind of puppet show in Taiwan
掌上明珠(ㄓㄤˇ ㄕㄤˋ ㄇㄧㄥˊ ㄓㄨ) or 掌珠(ㄓㄤˇ ㄓㄨ)
a beloved daughter; the apple of one's eye
掌聲(ㄓㄤˇ ㄕㄥ)
clapping; applause: 他博得熱烈的掌聲。He received warm applause.
掌聲如雷(ㄓㄤˇ ㄕㄥ ㄖㄨˊ ㄌㄟˊ)
thunderous applause
掌印(ㄓㄤˇ ㄧㄣˋ)
to have charge of the official seal—the man in charge
掌握(ㄓㄤˇ ㄨㄛˋ)
①in one's grasp; within one's power; at the mercy of: 他們正在我們的掌握中。They're at our mercy now. ② to control; to take into one's own hands ③ to master; to have a good command of: 掌握現代科學知識 to master modern scientific knowledge
掌紋(ㄓㄤˇ ㄨㄣˊ)
hand lines (in palmistry)

【掣】 1941
ㄔㄜˋ cheh chè
1. to pull; to drag; to draw
2. to hinder
3. to snatch away
掣電(ㄔㄜˋ ㄉㄧㄢˋ)
in the twinkle of an eye; as fast as lightning
掣後腿(ㄔㄜˋ ㄏㄡˋ ㄊㄨㄟˇ)
(literally) to pull the leg from behind—to hinder
掣肘(ㄔㄜˋ ㄓㄡˇ)
to impede another from

〔手部〕

doing work; a handicap
掣收據(ㄔㄜˋ ㄕㄡ ㄐㄩˋ)
to make or take a receipt
掣曳(ㄔㄜˋ ㄧˋ)
to pull

【掰】 1942
ㄅㄞ bai bāi
to pull apart with hands
掰開(ㄅㄞ ·ㄎㄞ)
to pull apart with hands
掰交情(ㄅㄞ ㄐㄧㄠ ·ㄑㄧㄥ)
to break friendship; to sever relations

【掔】 1943
(牽) ㄑㄧㄢ chian qiān
1. thick; firm; substantial
2. to drag along; to pull
3. to lead

九畫

【揀】 1944
ㄐㄧㄢˇ jean jiǎn
1. to select; to choose; to pick: 謹慎揀擇你的朋友。Choose your friends carefully.
2. to pick up (something another has left behind, etc.)
揀別(ㄐㄧㄢˇ ㄅㄧㄝˊ)
to distinguish; to tell one thing from another: 揀別是非 to distinguish between right and wrong
揀破爛的(ㄐㄧㄢˇ ㄆㄛˋ ㄌㄢˋ ·ㄉㄜ)
a ragpicker; a ragman
揀佛燒香(ㄐㄧㄢˇ ㄈㄛˊ ㄕㄠ ㄒㄧㄤ)
(literally) to offer incense to the right deity—to curry favor with the right person
揀肥挑瘦(ㄐㄧㄢˇ ㄈㄟˊ ㄊㄧㄠ ㄕㄡˋ)
to be very particular or choosy
揀到便宜(ㄐㄧㄢˇ ㄉㄠˋ ㄆㄧㄢˊ ·ㄧ)
to get the better (of a bargain, etc.)
揀選(ㄐㄧㄢˇ ㄒㄩㄢˇ)
to choose; to select; to pick
揀柴(ㄐㄧㄢˇ ㄔㄞˊ)
to gather firewood
揀擇(ㄐㄧㄢˇ ㄗㄜˊ)
to select; to choose

【揄】 1945
ㄩˊ yu yú
1. to draw out; to scoop out (grain from a mortar)
2. to praise; to show the merits of
3. to hang
揄袂(ㄩˊ ㄇㄟˋ)
to walk with hands swinging in one's sleeves
揄揚(ㄩˊ ㄧㄤˊ)
to praise; to recommend: 揄揚友人 to recommend one's friend

【揆】 1946
ㄎㄨㄟˊ kwei kuí
1. to survey and weigh; to consider; to investigate; to estimate
2. a premier; a prime minister
3. important affairs; events
4. principles; reasons
揆度(ㄎㄨㄟˊ ㄉㄨㄛˊ)
to investigate and consider; to observe and estimate
揆情度理(ㄎㄨㄟˊ ㄑㄧㄥˊ ㄉㄨㄛˊ ㄌㄧˇ)
measured or weighed by reason and common practice
揆席(ㄎㄨㄟˊ ㄒㄧˊ)
a prime minister or premier
揆測(ㄎㄨㄟˊ ㄘㄜˋ)
to calculate or guess; to estimate

【掾】 1947
ㄩㄢˋ yuann yuàn
a general term referring to public officials in ancient China
掾史(ㄩㄢˋ ㄕˇ)
secretaries in ancient Chinese public offices
掾屬(ㄩㄢˋ ㄕㄨˇ)
aides and subordinates of an official
掾佐(ㄩㄢˋ ㄗㄨㄛˇ)
assistants or subordinates of an official

【揉】 1948
ㄖㄡˊ rou róu
1. to rub; to knead: 她用雙手揉眼睛。She rubbed her eyes with her hands.
2. to crumple by hand: 他把信揉成一團。He crumpled up the letter into a ball.
3. to massage
4. to subdue; to make smooth or peaceful
5. mixed-up; confused
揉輪(ㄖㄡˊ ㄌㄨㄣˊ)
to bend trees to make wheels
揉合(ㄖㄡˊ ㄏㄜˊ)
to combine; to blend; to merge; to incorporate: 他的論文揉合了理論與實際。His thesis combines theory with practice.
揉雜(ㄖㄡˊ ㄗㄚˊ)
mixed-up
揉搓(ㄖㄡˊ ㄘㄨㄛ)
① to rub; to massage ② to tease or play jokes on
揉碎(ㄖㄡˊ ㄙㄨㄟˋ)
to crumble to pieces: 小女孩將麵包揉碎。The little girl crumbled her bread.
揉眼睛(ㄖㄡˊ ㄧㄢˇ ·ㄐㄧㄥ)
to rub eyes

【描】 1949
ㄇㄧㄠˊ miau miáo
1. to trace; to draw; to sketch; to retouch: 這張照片應予修描。The photograph should be retouched.
2. to describe; to depict
描摹(ㄇㄧㄠˊ ㄇㄛˊ)
to imitate (an old painting, etc.); to copy
描摹盡致(ㄇㄧㄠˊ ㄇㄛˊ ㄐㄧㄣˋ ㄓˋ)
to imitate or describe (a person's manner, etc.) to the very last detail
描圖(ㄇㄧㄠˊ ㄊㄨˊ)
tracing
描花(ㄇㄧㄠˊ ㄏㄨㄚ)
to make a flower design
描畫(ㄇㄧㄠˊ ㄏㄨㄚˋ)
to draw; to paint; to depict; to describe: 此景之美非筆墨所能描畫。Words can't describe the beauty of the scene.
描繪(ㄇㄧㄠˊ ㄏㄨㄟˋ)
to paint; to sketch; to depict; to describe
描紅(ㄇㄧㄠˊ ㄏㄨㄥˊ)
(said of children) to learn to write by tracing in black ink over the characters printed in red
描金(ㄇㄧㄠˊ ㄐㄧㄣ)
to paint in gold (usually on lacquerware, etc.); to gild
描寫(ㄇㄧㄠˊ ㄒㄧㄝˇ)
to describe; to depict; to portray; description
描出(ㄇㄧㄠˊ ㄔㄨ)
to portray; to depict vividly
描述(ㄇㄧㄠˊ ㄕㄨˋ)
to describe
描字(ㄇㄧㄠˊ ㄗˋ)
to trace writing; to paint

characters

【揍】 1950 ㄗㄡˋ tzow zòu

1. to beat; to slug (somebody); to hit hard: 揍他一頓。Beat him up.
2. to break (a glass, etc.); to smash

揍人(ㄗㄡˋ ㄖㄣˊ)
to slug a person

揍一頓(ㄗㄡˋ ㄧˊ ㄉㄨㄣˋ)
to give a sound beating; to beat

【提】 1951 1. ㄊㄧˊ tyi tí

1. to lift by hand; to pull up; to raise; to arouse; to carry: 他手裏提着書包。He carried a satchel in his hand.
2. to cause to rise or happen
3. to mention; to bring forward; to suggest; to propose (a motion, etc.): 我提議早些動身。I propose to start early.
4. to obtain; to make delivery; to draw out
5. to manage; to control
6. a rising stroke (in Chinese calligraphy)
7. a Chinese family name

提拔(ㄊㄧˊ ㄅㄚˊ)
to promote (a person); to elevate; to give (somebody) a pull: 提拔英才 to elevate a talent

提包(ㄊㄧˊ ㄅㄠ)
a handbag; a bag; a valise

提筆(ㄊㄧˊ ㄅㄧˇ)
to lift one's pen—to write

提不起來(ㄊㄧˊ ·ㄅㄨ ㄑㄧˇ ㄌㄞˊ)
① unable to lift ② to have sunk too deep for rescue (said of a dissipated person)

提不起精神(ㄊㄧˊ ·ㄅㄨ ㄑㄧˇ ㄐㄧㄥ ㄕㄣˊ)
unable to pull oneself together (for a task ahead, etc.); to feel tired and spiritless

提票(ㄊㄧˊ ㄆㄧㄠˋ)
a summons which orders a person to appear in court

提名(ㄊㄧˊ ㄇㄧㄥˊ)
to nominate; nomination: 他被提名為候選人。He was nominated for election.

提防(ㄊㄧˊ ㄈㄤˊ)
to be cautious or watchful; to be on the alert; to guard against

提袋(ㄊㄧˊ ㄉㄞˋ)
a handbag

提到(ㄊㄧˊ ㄉㄠˋ)
① to mention: 他提到一本有用的書。He mentioned a useful book. ② to have summoned (prisoners) to court

提單(ㄊㄧˊ ㄉㄢ)
a bill of lading (B/L) 參看「提貨單」

提燈會(ㄊㄧˊ ㄉㄥ ㄏㄨㄟˋ)
a lantern parade or procession

提調(ㄊㄧˊ ㄉㄧㄠˋ)
an official post in ancient China equivalent to a subordinate executive or business manager of an office

提督(ㄊㄧˊ ㄉㄨ)
(in ancient China) a provincial commander in chief

提臺(ㄊㄧˊ ㄊㄞˊ)
(in ancient China) a polite term of address for a provincial commander in chief

提頭兒(ㄊㄧˊ ·ㄊㄡㄦ)
something worth mentioning

提條件(ㄊㄧˊ ㄊㄧㄠˊ ㄐㄧㄢˋ)
to specify the terms (of a deal)

提桶(ㄊㄧˊ ㄊㄨㄥˇ)
a pail

提籃(ㄊㄧˊ ㄌㄢˊ)
a handbasket

提鍊(ㄊㄧˊ ㄌㄧㄢˋ)
to refine (crude oil, etc.); to extract: 從礦砂中提鍊金屬 to extract metal from ore

提梁(ㄊㄧˊ ㄌㄧㄤˊ)
the handles of handbags, baskets, vessels, etc.

提高(ㄊㄧˊ ㄍㄠ)
to lift (morale, etc.); to raise (prices, etc.); to heighten (vigilance, etc.); to put to a higher position; to enhance; to increase; to improve: 提高嗓子 to raise one's voice

提高警覺(ㄊㄧˊ ㄍㄠ ㄐㄧㄥˇ ㄐㄩㄝˊ)
to be on the ball;to heighten one's vigilance; to keep a watchful eye on

提綱(ㄊㄧˊ ㄍㄤ)
an outline: 他熬夜寫演講提綱。He sat up late making the outline for the speech.

提綱挈領(ㄊㄧˊ ㄍㄤ ㄑㄧㄝˋ ㄌㄧㄥˇ)
to mention the main points; to bring out the essentials: 我將提綱挈領地談一談。I'll just touch briefly on the essentials.

提供(ㄊㄧˊ ㄍㄨㄥ)
① to offer (proposals, opinions, etc.); to provide (assistance, etc.): 提供貸款 to offer a loan ② to sponsor (a TV or radio program, etc.)

提款(ㄊㄧˊ ㄎㄨㄢˇ)
to draw money from a bank

提壺(ㄊㄧˊ ㄏㄨˊ)
① to take a wine vessel (to buy wine) ② the name of a bird

提貨(ㄊㄧˊ ㄏㄨㄛˋ)
to make delivery of goods or cargo; to pick up goods: 我們將到港口提貨。We'll pick up the goods at the port.

提貨單(ㄊㄧˊ ㄏㄨㄛˋ ㄉㄢ)
a bill of lading (B/L)

提及(ㄊㄧˊ ㄐㄧˊ)
to mention

提交(ㄊㄧˊ ㄐㄧㄠ)
① to hand over to the custody of ② to submit to another body for discussion

提舉(ㄊㄧˊ ㄐㄩˇ)
to promote someone

提起(ㄊㄧˊ ㄑㄧˇ)
① to lift up; to arouse (oneself to action, etc.) ② to mention; to speak of: 他每天都提起你。He spoke of (or mentioned) you every day.

提起公訴(ㄊㄧˊ ㄑㄧˇ ㄍㄨㄥ ㄙㄨˋ)
to indict; to arraign; to accuse

提起精神(ㄊㄧˊ ㄑㄧˇ ㄐㄧㄥ ㄕㄣˊ)
to cheer up; to raise one's spirit; to brace oneself up

提挈(ㄊㄧˊ ㄑㄧㄝˋ)
① to help; assistance; recommendation for a job ② to carry

提挈同黨(ㄊㄧˊ ㄑㄧㄝˋ ㄊㄨㄥˊ ㄉㄤˇ)
to recommend party members

提前(ㄊㄧˊ ㄑㄧㄢˊ)
① to give precedence or priority to ② (to complete a

task, etc.) ahead of schedule; to advance to an earlier date: 會議日期提前了。The date of the meeting has been moved up.

提前考試(ㄊㄧˊ ㄑㄧㄢˊ ㄎㄠˇ ㄕˋ)
to take an examination ahead of schedule

提親(ㄊㄧˊ ㄑㄧㄣ)
a matchmaking; to talk about the marriage of a young man or woman

提琴(ㄊㄧˊ ㄑㄧㄣˊ)
a violin

提請(ㄊㄧˊ ㄑㄧㄥˇ)
to make a proposal and request for discussion or approval; to submit something (for approval, etc.)

提取(ㄊㄧˊ ㄑㄩˇ)
①to draw (deposits from the bank) ②to pick up; to make delivery of goods (from a warehouse, etc.) ③to extract; to abstract; to recover

提攜(ㄊㄧˊ ㄒㄧ)or(ㄊㄧˊ ㄒㄧㄝ)
help; assistance; to help; to aid

提心弔膽(ㄊㄧˊ ㄒㄧㄣ ㄉㄧㄠˋ ㄉㄢˇ)
to be scared; cautious and anxious; in constant fear; jittery

提箱(ㄊㄧˊ ㄒㄧㄤ)
a suitcase

提醒(ㄊㄧˊ ㄒㄧㄥˇ)
to remind; to call attention to: 請你提醒我回覆那封信。Please remind me to answer that letter.

提訊(ㄊㄧˊ ㄒㄩㄣˋ)
to arraign 參看「提審」

提倡(ㄊㄧˊ ㄔㄤˋ)
to promote (a cause, etc.); to advocate; to encourage; to recommend; recommendation: 勤儉建國的觀念值得提倡。The idea of building our country through diligence and thrift deserves recommendation.

提倡新說(ㄊㄧˊ ㄔㄤˋ ㄒㄧㄣ ㄕㄨㄛ)
to set forth a new doctrine

提成(ㄊㄧˊ ㄔㄥˊ)
to take a certain percentage of a sum; to deduct a percentage (from a sum of money)

提出(ㄊㄧˊ ㄔㄨ)
to raise (a question, etc.); to propose (a bill, motion, etc.); to put forth; to lodge; to put forward: 請提出建議。Please put forward your proposal.

提示(ㄊㄧˊ ㄕˋ)
①to hint; a hint ②(teaching) presentation (of new ideas as related to what a pupil already knows); to brief ③(drama) to prompt; to give a cue: 如果我忘了台詞，請給我提示一下。Prompt me if I forget my lines.

提示機宜(ㄊㄧˊ ㄕˋ ㄐㄧ ㄧˊ)
to indicate a policy

提手躡脚(ㄊㄧˊ ㄕㄡˇ ㄋㄧㄝˋ ㄐㄧㄠˇ)
to walk on tiptoe

提神(ㄊㄧˊ ㄕㄣˊ)
①to be cautious or vigilant; to watch out ②to arouse; to stimulate; to elate; to refresh: 你喝杯茶或咖啡提神吧! Refresh yourself with a cup of tea or coffee.

提審(ㄊㄧˊ ㄕㄣˇ)
to bring forward for trial

提升(ㄊㄧˊ ㄕㄥ)
to promote (an officer, etc.); to elevate: 提升他當總經理。Promote him to be general manager.

提早(ㄊㄧˊ ㄗㄠˇ)
to advance to an earlier hour or date; ahead of schedule; in advance: 請提早通知一聲。Please notify in advance.

提訴(ㄊㄧˊ ㄙㄨˋ)
to prosecute; a prosecution

提案(ㄊㄧˊ ㄢˋ)
a motion; a proposal; a draft resolution

提案人(ㄊㄧˊ ㄢˋ ㄖㄣˊ)
one who makes a motion or proposal

提議(ㄊㄧˊ ㄧˋ)
to propose; to put forth suggestions; a proposal, suggestion, motion, etc.: 他的提議被否決了。His proposal was rejected.

提議人(ㄊㄧˊ ㄧˋ ㄖㄣˊ)
one who makes a proposal or suggestion

提掖(ㄊㄧˊ ㄧㄝˋ)
to recommend for promotion; to lead and support (a person); to give assistance and help: 他們經常提掖後輩。They often lead and support the juniors.

提要(ㄊㄧˊ ㄧㄠˋ)
①to bring forth the main points ②the main points; a synopsis; a resume; a summary: 你能告訴我本課內容提要嗎? Could you tell me the capsule summary of the lesson?

提腕(ㄊㄧˊ ㄨㄢˋ)
(calligraphy) to write without the wrist touching the desk

【提】 1951
2. ㄉㄧ di dī
to hold or take in hand

提溜(ㄉㄧ ·ㄌㄧㄡ)
to hold or take in hand

提溜著心(ㄉㄧ ·ㄌㄧㄡ ·ㄓㄜ ㄒㄧㄣ)
to be anxious, worried and nervous

【揕】 1952
ㄓㄣˋ jenn zhèn
to strike; to stab; to thrust

【揖】 1953
ㄧ i yī
1. to bow with hands folding in front
2. to yield politely; to defer to

揖拜(ㄧ ㄅㄞˋ)
to make a bow with the hands folding in front (usually during greeting or parting)

揖別(ㄧ ㄅㄧㄝˊ)
to bid adieu

揖客(ㄧ ㄎㄜˋ)
to greet a guest; to salute a visitor by folding hands in front

揖謝(ㄧ ㄒㄧㄝˋ)
to bow in thanks

揖讓(ㄧ ㄖㄤˋ)
①courtesy between the host and his guests ②to abdicate; to give up a position for a better man

揖讓再三(ㄧ ㄖㄤˋ ㄗㄞˋ ㄙㄢ)
to bow complaisantly and give way again and again 亦作「再三揖讓」

【插】 1954
(揷) ㄔㄚ cha chā
1. to insert; to put in; to stick into: 他把双手插在口袋裏。He put his hands in his pockets.
2. to interpose; to get a word in edgeways
3. to plant
4. to take part in

插播廣告(ㄔㄚ ㄅㄛ ㄍㄨㄤˇ ㄍㄠˋ)
a spot announcement

插播新聞(ㄔㄚ ㄅㄛ ㄒㄧㄣ ㄨㄣˊ)
spot news

插班(ㄔㄚ ㄅㄢ)
to place a student from another school according to his grade; to enter another school according to one's grade

插班生(ㄔㄚ ㄅㄢ ㄕㄥ)
a student who enters another school according to his grade

插屏(ㄔㄚ ㄆㄧㄥˊ)
① a miniature screen for ornamental purpose ②framed paintings or calligraphy hanging on the wall

插隊(ㄔㄚ ㄉㄨㄟˋ)
to cut in; to push in

插頭(ㄔㄚ ·ㄊㄡ)
a plug: 三(脚)插頭 a three-pin plug

插天(ㄔㄚ ㄊㄧㄢ)
(said of high peaks) to soar into the sky

插圖(ㄔㄚ ㄊㄨˊ)
illustrations or plates (in a book, magazine, etc.): 這本書有幾幅彩色插圖。The book has several color plates.

插柳成蔭(ㄔㄚ ㄌㄧㄡˇ ㄔㄥˊ ㄧㄣˋ)
to do something which brings results easily

插關兒(ㄔㄚ ·ㄍㄨㄚㄦ)
a kind of door bolt

插科打諢(ㄔㄚ ㄎㄜ ㄉㄚˇ ㄏㄨㄣˋ)
(said of clowns in a show) to ad-lib; buffooneries; jesting

插花(ㄔㄚ ㄏㄨㄚ)
① to arrange flowers; flower arrangement ②(in old China) the top candidates of the imperial examinations who wore flowers to show distinction

插話(ㄔㄚ ㄏㄨㄚˋ)or 插言(ㄔㄚ ㄧㄢˊ)
① to break into a conversation ② an irrelevant episode; digression

插畫(ㄔㄚ ㄏㄨㄚˋ)
illustrations (in a book, magazine, etc.) 參看「插圖」

插架(ㄔㄚ ㄐㄧㄚˋ)
a bamboo shelf suspended on the wall

插脚(ㄔㄚ ㄐㄧㄠˇ)or 插足(ㄔㄚ ㄗㄨˊ)
to have a foothold in (an organization, activity, etc.); to participate in; to gain a place

插句(ㄔㄚ ㄐㄩˋ)
a parenthesis 亦作「插入語」

插曲(ㄔㄚ ㄑㄩˇ)
① a musical interlude ② songs and tunes used in motion picture dubbing ③ an episode

插圈弄套(ㄔㄚ ㄑㄩㄢ ㄋㄨㄥˋ ㄊㄠˋ)or 插圖弄計(ㄔㄚ ㄊㄨˊ ㄋㄨㄥˋ ㄐㄧˋ)
to trap or snare others with tricks

插敍(ㄔㄚ ㄒㄩˋ)
narration interspersed with flashbacks

插枝(ㄔㄚ ㄓ)
(botany) a cutting; to plant by sticking branches in soil

插燭(ㄔㄚ ㄓㄨˊ)
to put a candle onto a candlestick

插翅難飛(ㄔㄚ ㄔˋ ㄋㄢˊ ㄈㄟ)
(literally) Even if you were given wings, you couldn't fly away.—completely surrounded

插手(ㄔㄚ ㄕㄡˇ)
to take part in; to meddle: 他插手別人的事情。He meddles in other people's affairs.

插身(ㄔㄚ ㄕㄣ)or 插足(ㄔㄚ ㄗㄨˊ)
to take part in; to join in; to edge in; to involve in: 這裏很難插身。It's difficult to take part in here.

插入(ㄔㄚ ㄖㄨˋ)
to stick into; to insert; to plug in: 他把硬幣插入投幣口。He inserted a coin into the slot.

插座(ㄔㄚ ㄗㄨㄛˋ)
a receptacle; a socket; an outlet

插嘴(ㄔㄚ ㄗㄨㄟˇ)or 插口(ㄔㄚ ㄎㄡˇ)
to interrupt a narration, conversation, etc.; to put a word in; to chip in: 他無法插嘴。He could not get a word in edgeways.

插草標(ㄔㄚ ㄘㄠˇ ㄅㄧㄠ)
(an old custom) to put up a wisp of straw to indicate that an item is for sale

插秧(ㄔㄚ ㄧㄤ)
to transplant rice seedlings

【揚】 1955
ㄧㄤˊ yang yáng
1. to raise: 他揚起左手。He raised his left hand.
2. (said of flames) blazing
3. to wave; to flutter
4. to praise; to acclaim: 人人讚揚他是個偉大的演員。Everybody acclaimed him as a great actor.
5. to display; to expose; to make evident; to make known
6. high or raised (voice, cry, etc.)
7. to scatter; to spread: 消息很快就傳揚整個城市。The news quickly spread all over town.
8. to stir; to get excited
9. a Chinese family name

揚波(ㄧㄤˊ ㄅㄛ)
the swelling of waves

揚鑣(ㄧㄤˊ ㄅㄧㄠ)
to raise the bridle—to part from a friend

揚鞭(ㄧㄤˊ ㄅㄧㄢ)
to raise the whip—to leave

揚眉吐氣(ㄧㄤˊ ㄇㄟˊ ㄊㄨˇ ㄑㄧˋ)
to feel proud and elated after one suddenly comes to fame, wealth or good luck

揚名(ㄧㄤˊ ㄇㄧㄥˊ)
to become famous: 他以一個鋼琴家而揚名。He was famous as a pianist.

揚名天下(ㄧㄤˊ ㄇㄧㄥˊ ㄊㄧㄢ ㄒㄧㄚˋ)
to be known throughout the land; to have one's name spread far and wide; to become world-famous

揚帆(ㄧㄤˊ ㄈㄢˊ)
to set sail

揚湯止沸(ㄧㄤˊ ㄊㄤ ㄓˇ ㄈㄟˋ)
(literally) to try to stop water from boiling by stirring it (without removing the fire underneath the pot)

〔手部〕

〔手部〕

—①a stupid way of solving a problem ②to provide temporary relief to the suffering people
揚花(ㄧㄤˊ ㄏㄨㄚ)
flowering (of cereal crops)
揚棄(ㄧㄤˊ ㄑㄧˋ)
① to discard; to renounce: 我們不可揚棄老朋友。We should not discard our old friends. ② (philosophy) to sublate
揚琴(ㄧㄤˊ ㄑㄧㄣˊ)
a dulcimer
揚清激濁(ㄧㄤˊ ㄑㄧㄥ ㄐㄧ ㄓㄨㄛˊ)
to publicize the good deeds of good people in the hope that others will emulate them
揚雄(ㄧㄤˊ ㄒㄩㄥˊ)
Yang Hsiung (53 B.C.—18 A.D.), alias 子雲, a scholar-writer in the Han Dynasty
揚州(ㄧㄤˊ ㄓㄡ)
①Yangchow, one of nine administrative divisions in ancient China ②Yangchow, a city on the northern shore of the lower Yangtze River
揚州八怪(ㄧㄤˊ ㄓㄡ ㄅㄚ ㄍㄨㄞˋ)
the eight artists of Yangchow in the Ching Dynasty, famous for their eccentricities and originality (金農、羅聘、鄭燮、李方膺、汪士愼、高翔、黃愼、李鱓)
揚塵(ㄧㄤˊ ㄔㄣˊ)
to raise dust
揚長而去(ㄧㄤˊ ㄔㄤˊ ㄦˊ ㄑㄩˋ)
to stride away without looking back; to take leave rudely; to hold one's head proudly high while walking away with big strides; to stalk off; to swagger off
揚善(ㄧㄤˊ ㄕㄢˋ)
to spread or make known others' good deeds
揚聲(ㄧㄤˊ ㄕㄥ)
①to raise one's voice ②to boast prestige
揚子江(ㄧㄤˊ ㄗˇ ㄐㄧㄤ)
the Yangtze River
揚言(ㄧㄤˊ ㄧㄢˊ)
to spread words; to pass the word that; to exaggerate; to declare in public: 他揚言要報復。He spread words to retaliate.
揚揚(ㄧㄤˊ ㄧㄤˊ)
triumphantly; complacently
揚揚自得(ㄧㄤˊ ㄧㄤˊ ㄗˋ ㄉㄜˊ)
to be very pleased with oneself; to be complacent
揚揚得意(ㄧㄤˊ ㄧㄤˊ ㄉㄜˊ ㄧˋ)
to be smug and complacent
揚威(ㄧㄤˊ ㄨㄟ)
to show one's great authority, superiority, power, etc. to attain eminence (in a certain field, etc.)

【揜】 1956
(掩) ㄧㄢˇ yean yǎn
1. to rob; to take by force
2. to cover up; to conceal
3. to shut

【揠】 1957
ㄧㄚˋ yah yà
to pull up or out
揠苗助長(ㄧㄚˋ ㄇㄧㄠˊ ㄓㄨˋ ㄓㄤˇ)
(literally) to pull up the seedling hoping to make it grow faster—a stupid and self-defeating effort; to spoil things by excessive enthusiasm

【換】 1958
ㄏㄨㄢˋ huann huàn
to exchange; to change; to alter; to substitute: 請你幫我換十元的零錢好嗎? Can you change a ten-dollar bill for me?
換班(ㄏㄨㄢˋ ㄅㄢ)
(said of factory workers) to change a shift; to relieve (guard, or sentry duties)
換邊(ㄏㄨㄢˋ ㄅㄧㄢ)
(sports) to change sides
換毛(ㄏㄨㄢˋ ㄇㄠˊ)or 換羽(ㄏㄨㄢˋ ㄩˇ)
to molt: 小鳥正在換毛。The bird's feathers are molting.
換擋(ㄏㄨㄢˋ ㄉㄤˇ)
to shift gears
換調(ㄏㄨㄢˋ ㄉㄧㄠˋ)
transition 亦作「調換」
換湯不換藥(ㄏㄨㄢˋ ㄊㄤ ㄅㄨˋ ㄏㄨㄢˋ ㄧㄠˋ)
a change in form but not in content
換替(ㄏㄨㄢˋ ㄊㄧˋ)
①by turns; alternately: 他們通常換替著開車。They usually drive by turns. ②to replace 亦作「替換」
換帖(ㄏㄨㄢˋ ㄊㄧㄝˇ)
to exchange cards containing all personal details and thus become sworn brothers
換流機(ㄏㄨㄢˋ ㄌㄧㄡˊ ㄐㄧ)or 換頻機(ㄏㄨㄢˋ ㄆㄧㄣˊ ㄐㄧ)
an inverted converter; an inverted frequency converter
換崗(ㄏㄨㄢˋ ㄍㄤˇ)
to relieve a guard or sentry; the changing of the guards: 中午會有人來換崗。You will be relieved at noon.
換骨(ㄏㄨㄢˋ ㄍㄨˇ)
①(Taoism) to change mortal into immortal bones ②to effect basic or fundamental change
換貨(ㄏㄨㄢˋ ㄏㄨㄛˋ)
to exchange goods; to barter
換換口味(ㄏㄨㄢˋ ˙ㄏㄨㄢ ㄎㄡˇ ˙ㄨㄟ)
to have a change in diet, environment, etc.
換季(ㄏㄨㄢˋ ㄐㄧˋ)
①the change of seasons ②to change clothing or uniforms according to the season
換氣(ㄏㄨㄢˋ ㄑㄧˋ)
to breathe; to take breath (in swimming): 我將頭伸出水面換氣。I got my head above the water to take breath.
換錢(ㄏㄨㄢˋ ㄑㄧㄢˊ)
①to change money (into small change) ②to convert one currency to another ③to barter goods for money
換取(ㄏㄨㄢˋ ㄑㄩˇ)
to change; to exchange
換血(ㄏㄨㄢˋ ㄒㄧㄝˇ)
blood exchange transfusion
換新(ㄏㄨㄢˋ ㄒㄧㄣ)
to change something for a new one
換主(ㄏㄨㄢˋ ㄓㄨˇ)
to change the owner; to change ownership
換車(ㄏㄨㄢˋ ㄔㄜ)
to change buses, trains, etc.: 我們必須在台中換車。We have to change trains at Taichung.
換上(ㄏㄨㄢˋ ˙ㄕㄤ)
to make changes; to substitute

換人(ㄏㄨㄢˋ ㄖㄣˊ)
substitution (of players)
換算(ㄏㄨㄢˋ ㄙㄨㄢˋ)
to convert (one system of measurement into another)
換算表(ㄏㄨㄢˋ ㄙㄨㄢˋ ㄅㄧㄠˇ)
a conversion table
換衣(ㄏㄨㄢˋ ㄧ)or 換衣服(ㄏㄨㄢˋ ㄧ ·ㄈㄨ)
to change a dress
換牙(ㄏㄨㄢˋ ㄧㄚˊ)
(said of a child) to grow permanent teeth
換藥(ㄏㄨㄢˋ ㄧㄠˋ)
①to change a medical prescription ②to change a fresh dressing for a wound
換言之(ㄏㄨㄢˋ ㄧㄢˊ ㄓ)or 換句話說(ㄏㄨㄢˋ ㄐㄩˋ ㄏㄨㄚˋ ㄕㄨㄛ)
in other words: 換句話說，她不會來。In other words, she will not come.
換樣兒(ㄏㄨㄢˋ ㄧㄤˋㄦ)
to change in appearance; to change fashion
換文(ㄏㄨㄢˋ ㄨㄣˊ)
an exchange of diplomatic notes
換約(ㄏㄨㄢˋ ㄩㄝ)
to exchange the instruments of ratification of a treaty
換韻(ㄏㄨㄢˋ ㄩㄣˋ)
to shift to another rhyme

【握】 1959 ㄨㄛˋ woh wò

1. to hold fast; to grasp; to grip: 她因害怕而握住我的手。She gripped my hand in fear.
2. a handful
握筆(ㄨㄛˋ ㄅㄧˇ)
to hold a pen
握臂(ㄨㄛˋ ㄅㄧˋ)
to grasp the arm (of an old friend)—to meet an old friend
握別(ㄨㄛˋ ㄅㄧㄝˊ)
to part; to shake hands at parting; to say good-bye: 握別以來，已逾三月。It is more than three months since we parted.
握髮(ㄨㄛˋ ㄈㄚˇ)
(said of a leader) to be anxious to meet men of ability
握符(ㄨㄛˋ ㄈㄨˊ)
to be in command (of an army, etc.)
握力(ㄨㄛˋ ㄌㄧˋ)
the power of gripping; a grip
握力計(ㄨㄛˋ ㄌㄧˋ ㄐㄧˋ)
a hand dynamometer
握管(ㄨㄛˋ ㄍㄨㄢˇ)
to hold a pen—to write or paint
握翰(ㄨㄛˋ ㄏㄢˋ)
to hold a pen—to write or paint 參看「握筆」or「握管」
握緊(ㄨㄛˋ ㄐㄧㄣˇ)
to hold fast; to grasp firmly
握卷(ㄨㄛˋ ㄐㄩㄢˋ)
to hold a book—to read
握權(ㄨㄛˋ ㄑㄩㄢˊ)
to be in power or authority; to be in command; to hold the reins (of government, etc.)
握拳(ㄨㄛˋ ㄑㄩㄢˊ)
to make a fist; to clench one's fist
握拳透爪(ㄨㄛˋ ㄑㄩㄢˊ ㄊㄡˋ ㄓㄠˇ)
to harbor a deep hatred for
握手(ㄨㄛˋ ㄕㄡˇ)
to shake hands: 這兩人握手。The two men shook hands.
握手言歡(ㄨㄛˋ ㄕㄡˇ ㄧㄢˊ ㄏㄨㄢ)
to hold hands and converse cheerfully

【揣】 1960 ㄔㄨㄞˇ choai chuǎi

1. to measure; to weigh; to estimate; to calculate; to reckon
2. to try; to probe (for possibilities); to put out a feeler
揣摩(ㄔㄨㄞˇ ㄇㄛˊ)
①to study; to learn; to ponder; to examine ②to assume; to speculate; to guess
揣度(ㄔㄨㄞˇ ㄉㄨㄛˋ)
to speculate; to conjecture; to appraise; to make an intelligent guess
揣練(ㄔㄨㄞˇ ㄌㄧㄢˋ)
to study and imitate (a good author, etc.)
揣骨(ㄔㄨㄞˇ ㄍㄨˇ)
a branch of physiognomy in which a fortuneteller feels the bones (especially facial) of a person to tell his or her fortune
揣想(ㄔㄨㄞˇ ㄒㄧㄤˇ)
to imagine; to conjecture; to make an intelligent guess
揣測(ㄔㄨㄞˇ ㄘㄜˋ)
to conjecture; to fathom; to speculate; to make an intelligent guess
揣測之詞(ㄔㄨㄞˇ ㄘㄜˋ ㄓ ㄘˊ)
a mere speculation or conjecture

【揩】 1961 ㄎㄞ kai kāi

to wipe; to scrub; to rub; to dust; to clean
揩背(ㄎㄞ ㄅㄟˋ)
to scrub a customer's back for a fee at an old-fashioned public bath
揩面(ㄎㄞ ㄇㄧㄢˋ)
to wipe the face
揩乾淨(ㄎㄞ ㄍㄢ ·ㄐㄧㄥ)
to wipe clean: 把地板揩乾淨。Wipe the floor clean.
揩油(ㄎㄞ ㄧㄡˊ)or(ㄎㄚ ㄧㄡˊ)
①to make some (usually small) outside gains not included in a deal; to report a purchase at a blown-up price (so that one gets the difference) ②(said of a male) to caress or touch a woman without her knowledge or when she is unable or it is inconvenient for her to offer resistance
揩眼淚(ㄎㄞ ㄧㄢˇ ㄌㄟˋ)
to wipe away tears

【揪】 1962 (揫) ㄐㄧㄡ jiou jiū

1. to clutch; to grasp with one's hand; to grab; to hold fast; to seize
2. to pull; to drag: 把他從床上揪起來。Drag him from his bed.
3. to pick on
揪辮子(ㄐㄧㄡ ㄅㄧㄢˋ ·ㄗ)
to seize somebody's queue—to seize upon somebody's mistakes or shortcomings
揪扭(ㄐㄧㄡ ㄋㄧㄡˇ)
to seize by hand; to grapple
揪心(ㄐㄧㄡ ㄒㄧㄣ)
①anxious; nervous; worried ②heartrending; agonizing; gnawing
揪心錢(ㄐㄧㄡ ㄒㄧㄣ ㄑㄧㄢˊ)
(said of a miser) money

〔手部〕

〔手部〕

spent with a bleeding heart

揪住(ㄐㄧㄡ ·ㄓㄨ)
to seize or grasp (somebody) with force

揪出(ㄐㄧㄡ ㄔㄨ)
to uncover; to ferret out

揪耳朵(ㄐㄧㄡ ㄦˇ ·ㄉㄨㄛ)
to hold (another) by the ear; to seize another's ear

【揮】 1963 ㄏㄨㄟ huei huī

1. to wield (a sword, pen, etc.); to move; to shake; to wave; to brandish; to make a light or rapid stroke
2. to conduct; to direct (troop movements, a concert, a course of action, etc.)
3. to wipe away (sweat, tears, etc.)
4. to scatter; to sprinkle
5. to squander (money, etc.)
6. to swing (fists)

揮鞭(ㄏㄨㄟ ㄅㄧㄢ)
to wave a whip; to swish a whip

揮兵(ㄏㄨㄟ ㄅㄧㄥ)
to march troops to war

揮發(ㄏㄨㄟ ㄈㄚ)
to volatilize; volatilization; to evaporate

揮發油(ㄏㄨㄟ ㄈㄚ ㄧㄡˊ)
gasoline, naphtha, or other volatile oils; benzine

揮刀(ㄏㄨㄟ ㄉㄠ)
to wield a sword; to brandish a sword

揮動(ㄏㄨㄟ ㄉㄨㄥˋ)
to wield (a sword, etc.); to swing (fists, etc.)

揮淚(ㄏㄨㄟ ㄌㄟˋ)
to shed tears

揮戈(ㄏㄨㄟ ㄍㄜ)
① to brandish one's weapons ② to lead troops to battle

揮毫(ㄏㄨㄟ ㄏㄠˊ)
(said of calligraphers) to wield the writing brush—to write

揮翰(ㄏㄨㄟ ㄏㄢˋ)
to write

揮汗成雨(ㄏㄨㄟ ㄏㄢˋ ㄔㄥˊ ㄩˇ)
① drops of perspiration falling down like a shower ② a considerable amount of people; a squeeze of people

揮霍(ㄏㄨㄟ ㄏㄨㄛˋ)
to spend freely; to squander

揮霍無度(ㄏㄨㄟ ㄏㄨㄛˋ ㄨˊ ㄉㄨˋ)
to squander money

揮劍(ㄏㄨㄟ ㄐㄧㄢˋ)
to brandish a sword; to whip out a sword

揮金如土(ㄏㄨㄟ ㄐㄧㄣ ㄖㄨˊ ㄊㄨˇ)
to squander money like dirt

揮軍(ㄏㄨㄟ ㄐㄩㄣ)
to march troops to war: 那位將軍揮軍上陣。The general marched his troops to war.

揮拳(ㄏㄨㄟ ㄑㄩㄢˊ)
to swing fists—to strike somebody

揮麈(ㄏㄨㄟ ㄓㄨˇ)or 揮犀(ㄏㄨㄟ ㄒㄧ)
to wave a long-haired duster—to engage in a leisurely conversation on unworldly subjects

揮手(ㄏㄨㄟ ㄕㄡˇ)
to wave one's hand (in greeting or bidding farewell): 他向我揮手致意。He waved greetings to me.

揮觴(ㄏㄨㄟ ㄕㄤ)
to raise a cup—to drink

揮灑(ㄏㄨㄟ ㄙㄚˇ)
to write or paint freely

揮舞(ㄏㄨㄟ ㄨˇ)
to wave; to wield; to brandish

【揭】 1964 ㄐㄧㄝ jie jiē

1. to lift up or off; to raise high
2. to unveil, uncover or unearth; to expose; to tear off; to take off: 把盒蓋揭開。Take that cover off this box.
3. to announce; to publicize
4. a Chinese family name

揭榜(ㄐㄧㄝ ㄅㄤˇ)
to publish or make public a list of successful candidates; to announce the results of an examination

揭破(ㄐㄧㄝ ㄆㄛˋ)
to expose or uncover (a secret, conspiracy, etc.)

揭幕(ㄐㄧㄝ ㄇㄨˋ)
to raise or lift the curtain (of a meeting, exhibition, etc.); to unveil—to inaugurate

揭幕禮(ㄐㄧㄝ ㄇㄨˋ ㄌㄧˇ)
an opening ceremony: 新戲院舉行揭幕禮。The new theater held an unveiling ceremony.

揭發(ㄐㄧㄝ ㄈㄚ)
to expose (a plot, scandal, etc.)

揭封(ㄐㄧㄝ ㄈㄥ)
to tear off the seal

揭底(ㄐㄧㄝ ㄉㄧˇ)
to reveal the inside story

揭短(ㄐㄧㄝ ㄉㄨㄢˇ)
to expose the blemishes (or faults) of others

揭貼(ㄐㄧㄝ ㄊㄧㄝ)or 揭帖(ㄐㄧㄝ ㄊㄧㄝˇ)
① libelous posters, pamphlets, or anonymous letters ② to put up a poster, bulletin, etc.

揭露(ㄐㄧㄝ ㄌㄨˋ)
to uncover or expose (another's secret, etc.); to unmask: 警方揭露了罪犯的陰謀。The police exposed the criminal's plot.

揭蓋兒(ㄐㄧㄝ ㄍㄚˋㄦ)
(literally) to lift up the lid—to uncover or unveil (the inside story)

揭竿而起(ㄐㄧㄝ ㄍㄢ ㄦˊ ㄑㄧˇ)
to raise the standard of revolt with poles—to start a revolution or an uprising 亦作「揭竿起義」

揭開(ㄐㄧㄝ ㄎㄞ)
① to pull apart or separate ② to uncover; to unmask; to reveal: 天文學揭開了宇宙的奧秘。Astronomy reveals the secrets of the universe.

揭曉(ㄐㄧㄝ ㄒㄧㄠˇ)
to make public; to publish; to announce

揭櫫(ㄐㄧㄝ ㄓㄨ)
to announce (goals, objectives, etc. of a movement, cause, etc.); to proclaim; to publish

揭穿(ㄐㄧㄝ ㄔㄨㄢ)
to expose (a conspiracy, trick, etc.); to belie; to lay bare: 我們要揭穿這個僞君子的陰謀。We want to expose this hypocrite's conspiracy.

揭瘡疤(ㄐㄧㄝ ㄔㄨㄤ ㄅㄚ)
to reopen old wounds (in order to put someone to shame)

揭示(ㄐㄧㄝ ㄕˋ)
①to make public; to put up a public notice; to announce ②to reveal; to bring to light ③(figuratively) to delineate (the inner world of the characters in a novel)
揭示板(ㄐㄧㄝ ㄕˋ ㄅㄢˇ)
a bulletin board
揭人陰私(ㄐㄧㄝ ㄖㄣˊ ㄧㄣ ㄙ)
to expose another person's secrets

【援】 1965 ㄩㄢˊ yuan yuán
1. to lead
2. to take hold of; to pull by hand
3. to aid; to help; to reinforce; to rescue: 我們必須增援前線之部隊。We must reinforce the troops at the front.
4. to invoke (a law, precedent, etc.): 有例可援。There's a precedent to invoke.
援筆(ㄩㄢˊ ㄅㄧˇ)
to take up a pen to write
援兵(ㄩㄢˊ ㄅㄧㄥ)
reinforcements
援例(ㄩㄢˊ ㄌㄧˋ)or 援以爲例(ㄩㄢˊ ㄧˇ ㄨㄟˊ ㄌㄧˋ)
to follow a precedent; to invoke a precedent: 他溜了出去，我也援例行事。He sneaked out, and I followed suit.
援救(ㄩㄢˊ ㄐㄧㄡˋ)
to rescue; to come to the aid of
援據(ㄩㄢˊ ㄐㄩˋ)
to adduce or cite as proof
援軍(ㄩㄢˊ ㄐㄩㄣ)
(military) reinforcements; relief troops
援照(ㄩㄢˊ ㄓㄠˋ)
according to; to adduce; to cite (as an example, reason, etc.)
援助(ㄩㄢˊ ㄓㄨˋ)
to aid; aid; to help: 紅十字會援助水災難民。The Red Cross aids flood victims.
援手(ㄩㄢˊ ㄕㄡˇ)
①to extend a helping hand ②a helper
援案(ㄩㄢˊ ㄢˋ)
to quote a precedent; in accordance with a precedent
援引(ㄩㄢˊ ㄧㄣˇ)
to cite (a precedent) as proof, etc.
援用(ㄩㄢˊ ㄩㄥˋ)
to invoke or quote (a precedent, provisions of laws, etc.)

【揲】 1966 ㄕㄜˊ sher shé
to sort out divining stalks

【揸】 1967 ㄓㄚ ja zhā
to pick up with fingers; to grasp by hand

【揶】 1968 ㄧㄝˊ ye yé
to jeer at; to ridicule; to play a joke on
揶揄(ㄧㄝˊ ㄩˊ)
to ridicule; to jeer at; to play a joke on; to tease; to taunt; teases: 不要揶揄別人的錯誤或不幸。Do not jeer at the mistakes or misfortunes of others.

【揝】 1969 1.(攥) ㄗㄨㄢˋ tzuann zuàn
to hold or seize with the hand; to grip; to clench; to grasp

【揝】 1969 2.(攢) ㄗㄢˇ tzaan zǎn
to save (money); to hoard
揝錢(ㄗㄢˇ ㄑㄧㄢˊ)
to save money; to save up

【揹】 1970 (背) ㄅㄟ bei bēi
to carry on the back; to shoulder (a load, responsibility, etc.)
揹包袱(ㄅㄟ ㄅㄠ ·ㄈㄨ)
①to carry a fardel on the back; to carry a burden ②to have a weight on one's mind; to take on a mental burden: 你不要因此揹包袱。Don't let it weigh on your mind.
揹黑鍋(ㄅㄟ ㄏㄟ ㄍㄨㄛ)
to be made the scapegoat for somebody; to take blame for someone: 他替他的兄弟揹黑鍋。He takes blame for his brother.

【揎】 1971 ㄒㄩㄢ shiuan xuān
1. to pull up the sleeves and show the arms
2. to fight with bare hands
揎拳擄袖(ㄒㄩㄢ ㄑㄩㄢˊ ㄌㄨˇ ㄒㄧㄡˋ)
to pull up the sleeves—to get ready to work or fight

十畫

【搉】 1972 ㄑㄩㄝˋ chiueh què
1. to knock; to strike
2. to discuss; to negotiate; to consult
搉商(ㄑㄩㄝˋ ㄕㄤ)
to consult; to discuss; consultation; discussion 亦作「商搉」

【搊】 1973 ㄔㄡ chou chōu
1. to pluck stringed instruments with fingers
2. to tighten
3. to hold and support

【搋】 1974 ㄔㄨㄞ chuai chuāi
1. to conceal something in the bosom
2. to knead (dough); to rub
搋麪(ㄔㄨㄞ ㄇㄧㄢˋ)
to knead dough
搋手兒(ㄔㄨㄞ ㄕㄡˇㄦ)
to put each hand in the other sleeve (in order to keep both hands warm)
搋在懷裏(ㄔㄨㄞ ㄗㄞˋ ㄏㄨㄞˊ ·ㄌㄧ)
to carry or hold in the bosom

【損】 1975 ㄙㄨㄣˇ soen sǔn
1. to detract; to damage; to injure; to destroy; harm; damage: 吸煙對你有損無益。Smoking does you more harm than good.
2. to lose; loss
3. to reduce; to decrease
4. weak; emaciated
5. to ridicule; to jeer at
6. wicked and mean; cruel: 這話眞損透了。It is really mean to say so.
7. (Chinese medicine) long-term emaciation
損德(ㄙㄨㄣˇ ㄉㄜˊ)
to cause damage to one's virtue (for too many wrong-doings)
損到家(ㄙㄨㄣˇ ㄉㄠˋ ㄐㄧㄚ)
①to reduce (prices) to cost level ②(said of utterances, actions) very mean; cruel

〔手部〕

〔手部〕

and heartless

損年(ㄙㄨㄣˇ ㄋㄧㄢˊ)
to shorten one's life span; to die young

損害(ㄙㄨㄣˇ ㄏㄞˋ)
to impair; to cause damage or loss; to injure; damages or losses: 抽菸會損害健康。Smoking will impair one's health.

損害賠償(ㄙㄨㄣˇ ㄏㄞˋ ㄆㄟˊ ㄔㄤˊ)
schadenersatz; indemnity; compensation

損耗(ㄙㄨㄣˇ ㄏㄠˋ)
to deplete; to exhaust (supply); to weaken (strength); loss

損壞(ㄙㄨㄣˇ ㄏㄨㄞˋ)
to damage; damage; spoilage: 損壞公物要賠償。One should pay for public property he damaged.

損失(ㄙㄨㄣˇ ㄕ)
losses; casualties: 四十鎊的損失對我而言是很大的。A loss of ₤40 is great to me.

損失不貲(ㄙㄨㄣˇ ㄕ ㄅㄨˋ ㄗ)
to suffer no small amount of damage

損失總數(ㄙㄨㄣˇ ㄕ ㄗㄨㄥˇ ㄕㄨˋ)
total loss

損壽(ㄙㄨㄣˇ ㄕㄡˋ)
to shorten one's life (because of overindulgence, etc.)

損傷(ㄙㄨㄣˇ ㄕㄤ)
losses; casualties; to hurt (another's feelings, etc.)

損傷元氣(ㄙㄨㄣˇ ㄕㄤ ㄩㄢˊ ㄑㄧˋ)
to suffer tremendous loss in strength or resources

損人(ㄙㄨㄣˇ ㄖㄣˊ)
① to ridicule others; to make caustic remarks; to injure another with mean words: 他老是愛損人。He always delights in making caustic remarks. ② to cause material damage to others

損人利己(ㄙㄨㄣˇ ㄖㄣˊ ㄌㄧˋ ㄐㄧˇ)
to profit oneself at the expense of others

損益(ㄙㄨㄣˇ ㄧˋ)
profit and loss; increase and decrease: 損益相抵。The gains offset the losses.

損益表(ㄙㄨㄣˇ ㄧˋ ㄅㄧㄠˇ)
a statement of profit and loss; an income statement

損友(ㄙㄨㄣˇ ㄧㄡˇ)
an injurious friend; bad company

損陰壞德(ㄙㄨㄣˇ ㄧㄣ ㄏㄨㄞˋ ㄉㄜˊ)or 損陰騭(ㄙㄨㄣˇ ㄧㄣ ㄓˋ)
to indulge in evildoings; to harm by underhand means

【搆】 1976 ㄍㄡˋ gow gòu

1. to pull; to drag
2. to reach
3. to implicate
4. to make (war, peace, etc.); to bring (a disaster, a grudge, etc.); to incur (animosity, etc.)
5. to compose

搆不著(ㄍㄡˋ ·ㄅㄨ ㄓㄠˊ)
unable to reach it

搆兵(ㄍㄡˋ ㄅㄧㄥ)
to be at war or on the warpath: 這兩個國家爲了爭覇權而搆兵。The two states were on the warpath for supremacy.

搆和(ㄍㄡˋ ㄏㄜˊ)
to make or negotiate for peace

搆禍(ㄍㄡˋ ㄏㄨㄛˋ)
to bring disaster upon oneself; to incur misfortune

搆陷(ㄍㄡˋ ㄒㄧㄢˋ)
to set a trap to incriminate someone; to frame up a charge against someone

搆訟(ㄍㄡˋ ㄙㄨㄥˋ)
to go to law; to enter a lawsuit: 他們已搆訟多年。They had proceeded in a lawsuit for years.

搆怨(ㄍㄡˋ ㄩㄢˋ)
to incur an animosity or a grudge

【搏】 1977 ㄅㄛˊ bor bó

1. to pounce on (or at); to spring upon
2. to grasp; to catch; to arrest; to seize
3. to strike; to box; to engage in a hand-to-hand combat

搏髀(ㄅㄛˊ ㄅㄧˋ)
to keep the beat (of a song, tune, etc.) by slapping one's hip

搏鬭(ㄅㄛˊ ㄉㄡˋ)
to battle; to wrestle; to fight; to struggle: 他們與暴風雨搏鬭。They battled against the storm.

搏虎(ㄅㄛˊ ㄏㄨˇ)
to fight a tiger with one's bare hands

搏擊(ㄅㄛˊ ㄐㄧˊ)
to strike; to fight with hands

搏香弄粉(ㄅㄛˊ ㄒㄧㄤ ㄋㄨㄥˋ ㄈㄣˇ)
to doll up oneself; to apply a lot of make-up

搏戰(ㄅㄛˊ ㄓㄢˋ)
to combat; to box; to engage in hand-to-hand combat 參看「搏鬭」

搏殺(ㄅㄛˊ ㄕㄚ)
to fight and kill

搏手(ㄅㄛˊ ㄕㄡˇ)
at the end of one's wits

搏影(ㄅㄛˊ ㄧㄥˇ)
to fight the shadow (descriptive of a regular army fighting an elusive guerrilla force)

【搔】 1978 ㄙㄠ sau sāo

1. to scratch lightly
2. to irritate; to annoy

搔背(ㄙㄠ ㄅㄟˋ)
to scratch the back

搔爬(ㄙㄠ ㄆㄚˊ)
to scratch lightly

搔動(ㄙㄠ ㄉㄨㄥˋ)
disturbance; commotion; to become restless 亦作「騷動」

搔頭(ㄙㄠ ㄊㄡˊ)or 搔首(ㄙㄠ ㄕㄡˇ)
to scratch one's head (in perplexity, etc.); to rub gently

搔頭摸耳(ㄙㄠ ㄊㄡˊ ㄇㄛ ㄦˇ)
hesitating; undecided

搔虎頭弄虎鬚(ㄙㄠ ㄏㄨˇ ㄊㄡˊ ㄋㄨㄥˋ ㄏㄨˇ ㄒㄩ)
to offend the mighty and powerful

搔著癢處(ㄙㄠ ·ㄓㄠ ㄧㄤˇ ㄔㄨˋ)
① to touch somebody to the quick ② to say something exactly to the point: 你的話正好搔著癢處。What you said was just to the point.

搔首弄姿(ㄙㄠ ㄕㄡˇ ㄋㄨㄥˋ ㄗ)
(said of women) to act coquettishly to attract men's attention; to flirt

搔首踟躕(ㄙㄠ ㄕㄡˇ ㄔˊ ㄔㄨˊ)
to be at a loss as to what to do; to be in perplexity; to

hesitate; to be undecided
搔擾(ㄙㄠ ㄖㄠˇ)
to annoy; to harass; to cause disturbances 亦作「騷擾」
搔癢(ㄙㄠ 丨ㄤˇ)
to scratch the itching place

【搾】 1979 ㄓㄚˋ jah zhà
to press (for juice or oil); to extract; to squeeze; to wring: 貪官搾取人民的金錢。Corrupt officials squeeze people's money by pressure.
搾甘蔗(ㄓㄚˋ ㄍㄢ ㄓㄜˋ)
to press sugar cane (for juice)
搾果機(ㄓㄚˋ ㄍㄨㄛˇ ㄐ丨)or 搾汁機(ㄓㄚˋ ㄓ ㄐ丨)
a juicer
搾果汁(ㄓㄚˋ ㄍㄨㄛˇ ㄓ)
to press or squeeze fruit for juice
搾取(ㄓㄚˋ ㄑㄩˇ)
① to extract; to press for juice or oil ② to extort; to exploit; to rob
搾菜(ㄓㄚˋ ㄘㄞˋ)
a kind of salted vegetable root; the hot pickled mustard tuber
搾油(ㄓㄚˋ 丨ㄡˊ)
to press (soybeans, peanuts, etc.) for oil; to extract oil

【搓】 1980 ㄘㄨㄛ tsuo cuō
1. to rub hands; to rub between the hands
2. to scrub
3. to twist (a thread, etc.) between the hands
搓板(ㄘㄨㄛ ㄅㄢˇ)
a washboard
搓麻將(ㄘㄨㄛ ㄇㄚˊ ㄐ丨ㄤˋ)
to play mah-jong
搓麻繩(ㄘㄨㄛ ㄇㄚˊ ㄕㄥˊ)
to make cord by twisting hemp fibers between the palms
搓弄(ㄘㄨㄛ ㄋㄨㄥˋ)
to rub
搓線(ㄘㄨㄛ ㄒ丨ㄢˋ)
to twist a thread between the hands
搓手(ㄘㄨㄛ ㄕㄡˇ)
to rub one's hands together
搓手頓脚(ㄘㄨㄛ ㄕㄡˇ ㄉㄨㄣˋ ㄐ丨ㄠˇ)
to wring one's hands and stamp one's feet—to be anxious and impatient
搓繩子(ㄘㄨㄛ ㄕㄥˊ ·ㄗ)
to make a rope by twisting the strands together
搓揉(ㄔㄨㄛ ㄖㄡˊ)
to rub; to massage (a swelling, sore spot, etc.): 護士搓揉我扭傷的背。The nurse rubbed my lame back.
搓澡(ㄘㄨㄛ ㄗㄠˇ)
to scrub and wash —a special service in a Chinese bath-house
搓作一團(ㄘㄨㄛ ㄗㄨㄛˋ 丨 ㄊㄨㄢˊ)
to roll or crumble (a sheet of paper, etc.) into a ball
搓碎(ㄘㄨㄛ ㄙㄨㄟˋ)
to rub into powder or bits
搓衣裳(ㄘㄨㄛ 丨 ·ㄕㄤ)
to clean garments by rubbing

【搽】 1981 ㄔㄚˊ char chá
to rub on (ointment, etc.); to smear; to anoint; to paint
搽粉(ㄔㄚˊ ㄈㄣˇ)
to powder (the face, etc.): 她在鼻子上搽粉。She powdered her nose.
搽脂抹粉(ㄔㄚˊ ㄓ ㄇㄛˇ ㄈㄣˇ)
to apply powder and rouge; to doll up
搽藥(ㄔㄚˊ 丨ㄠˋ)
to rub on some external medicine, ointment, etc.

【搗】 1982 ㄉㄠˇ dao dǎo
1. to thresh (grains); to hull or unhusk
2. to beat; to pound
3. to drive; to attack
4. to sabotage
搗米(ㄉㄠˇ ㄇ丨ˇ)
to hull rice with a pestle and a mortar
搗蛋(ㄉㄠˇ ㄉㄢˋ)
to make trouble; to be mischievous; to cause a disturbance; to sabotage; to raise hell; heckling: 他是個調皮搗蛋的男孩。He is a mischievous boy.
搗爛(ㄉㄠˇ ㄌㄢˋ)
to pound something until it becomes pulp
搗亂(ㄉㄠˇ ㄌㄨㄢˋ)
to cause disturbance; to sabotage; to make trouble: 我正忙，你別搗亂。I am busy. Do not disturb me.
搗亂份子(ㄉㄠˇ ㄌㄨㄢˋ ㄈㄣˋ ㄗˇ)
troublemakers; the "bad elements"; saboteurs
搗鬼(ㄉㄠˇ ㄍㄨㄟˇ)
to play tricks; to gossip and cause trouble; to sow discord
搗毀(ㄉㄠˇ ㄏㄨㄟˇ)
to smash; to sabotage; to damage or destroy: 我軍已搗毀敵人基地。Our army had destroyed the enemy base.
搗碎(ㄉㄠˇ ㄙㄨㄟˋ)
to pound to pieces
搗藥(ㄉㄠˇ 丨ㄠˋ)
to pound medicine in a mortar

【搖】 1983 丨ㄠˊ yau yáo
1. to wag; to shake; to wave; to rock: 使用前搖一搖。Shake before using.
2. (said of one's confidence, determination, etc.) to sway, wobble, shake: 他的信心未爲旁人的話所動搖。His determination was not shaken by anything people said.
3. to scull; to row (a boat, etc.): 你會搖船嗎? Can you row a boat?
4. to agitate; to incite; to annoy
搖擺(丨ㄠˊ ㄅㄞˇ)
to swing to and fro; to oscillate; oscillation; to vacillate; vacillation: 樹枝在風中搖擺。The branches of the trees swayed in the wind.
搖筆即來(丨ㄠˊ ㄅ丨ˇ ㄐ丨ˊ ㄌㄞˊ)
(said of a writer) to be brimming with ideas; to be gifted with the ability of writing quickly
搖盪(丨ㄠˊ ㄉㄤˋ)
to sway; to swing; to wobble; unstable (situations, etc.)
搖動(丨ㄠˊ ㄉㄨㄥˋ)
to shake; to rock; to wave; to sway: 服藥前先搖動瓶子。Shake the bottle before taking the medicine.
搖頭(丨ㄠˊ ㄊㄡˊ)or 搖首(丨ㄠˊ ㄕㄡˇ)

〔手部〕

to shake one's head—in disapproval or out of sympathy

搖頭擺尾(ㄧㄠˊ ㄊㄡˊ ㄅㄞˇ ㄨㄟˇ)
(literally) to shake the head and wag the tail (like a dog hoping to please the master)—to act obsequiously; to assume an air of complacency

搖頭晃腦(ㄧㄠˊ ㄊㄡˊ ㄏㄨㄤˋ ㄋㄠˇ)
the funny manner of a half-witted scholar in reading a book—to look pleased with oneself; to assume an air of self-approbation or self-conceit

搖來搖去(ㄧㄠˊ ㄌㄞˊ ㄧㄠˊ ㄑㄩˋ)
① to swagger along ② to swing to and fro

搖籃(ㄧㄠˊ ㄌㄢˊ) or 搖籃兒(ㄧㄠˊ ㄌㄚˊㄦ)
a cradle—(figuratively) the place of origin: 黃河是中國古代文化的搖籃。The Yellow River was the cradle of ancient Chinese culture.

搖籃曲(ㄧㄠˊ ㄌㄢˊ ㄑㄩˇ)
a cradle song; a lullaby; a nursery song

搖鈴(ㄧㄠˊ ㄌㄧㄥˊ)
to ring the bell

搖鈴兒的(ㄧㄠˊ ㄌㄧㄥˊㄦ ˙ㄉㄜ)
a peddler who announces his presence by ringing a handbell

搖滾樂(ㄧㄠˊ ㄍㄨㄣˇ ㄩㄝˋ)
rock'n'roll; rock music 亦作「搖擺樂」。

搖鼓兒(ㄧㄠˊ ㄍㄨˇㄦ)
a small drum with a handle and two suspending beads, one on each side, which beat the drum when the handle is twisted

搖撼(ㄧㄠˊ ㄏㄢˋ)
to shake violently

搖會(ㄧㄠˊ ㄏㄨㄟˋ)
to throw the dice to determine who should get the loan at the periodic meeting of a small loan association

搖晃(ㄧㄠˊ ˙ㄏㄨㄤ)
to shake (a bottle, etc.); to swing to and fro; shaky; unsteady

搖旗吶喊(ㄧㄠˊ ㄑㄧˊ ㄋㄚˋ ㄏㄢˇ)
(literally) to wave flags and shout—to cheer or encourage

搖錢樹(ㄧㄠˊ ㄑㄧㄢˊ ㄕㄨˋ)
(literally) a money tree—a hen that lays golden eggs; anything or anyone one depends on as a steady dollar-earner

搖船(ㄧㄠˊ ㄔㄨㄢˊ)
to row a boat

搖脣鼓舌(ㄧㄠˊ ㄔㄨㄣˊ ㄍㄨˇ ㄕㄜˊ)
to instigate by talking; to persuade someone (to do evil things) by sweet talk

搖手(ㄧㄠˊ ㄕㄡˇ)
to wave one's hand (to indicate disapproval, admonition, etc.)

搖身一變(ㄧㄠˊ ㄕㄣ ㄧˊ ㄅㄧㄢˋ)
①(often said of an upstart, turncoat, etc.) to transform into another person all of a sudden ②(in fairy tales) to change to another form in the twinkle of the eye

搖椅(ㄧㄠˊ ㄧˇ)
a rocking chair; a swinging chair

搖曳(ㄧㄠˊ ㄧˋ)
① wavering gently; shaking: 樹在風中搖曳。The trees were shaking in the wind. ②(said of light) flickering: 燭光在微風中搖曳。The candlelight flickered in the breeze. ③(said of a girl's hips) to sway enticingly

搖搖擺擺(ㄧㄠˊ ㄧㄠˊ ㄅㄞˇ ㄅㄞˇ)
to swagger; to swing

搖搖晃晃(ㄧㄠˊ ㄧㄠˊ ㄏㄨㄤˋ ㄏㄨㄤˋ)
faltering; tottering; shaky

搖搖欲跌(ㄧㄠˊ ㄧㄠˊ ㄩˋ ㄉㄧㄝˊ)
tottering; shaky (economy, regimes, etc.)

搖搖欲墜(ㄧㄠˊ ㄧㄠˊ ㄩˋ ㄓㄨㄟˋ)
shaky; wobbling; on the verge of collapse; very unstable (regimes, authority, etc.): 這棟建築物搖搖欲墜。The building is shaky.

搖尾乞憐(ㄧㄠˊ ㄨㄟˇ ㄑㄧˇ ㄌㄧㄢˊ)
(literally) to wag the tail and court favor—to fawn and be obsequious: 小狗向牠的主人搖尾乞憐。The puppy was fawning on its master.

【搢】 1984
ㄐㄧㄣˋ jinn jìn

1. to stick into
2. to shake

搢笏(ㄐㄧㄣˋ ㄏㄨˋ)
to stick the official tablet into the girdle

搢紳(ㄐㄧㄣˋ ㄕㄣ)
the gentry; the official class; the officialdom

【搘】 1985
ㄓ jy zhī

to support; to prop up

搘拄(ㄓ ㄓㄨˇ)
a prop; a support

【搥】 1986
ㄔㄨㄟˊ chwei chuí

to pound; to beat; to strike with a stick or fist: 誰在用拳搥門? Who is pounding (on) the door with fists?

搥背(ㄔㄨㄟˊ ㄅㄟˋ)
to massage the back by pounding with fists

搥打(ㄔㄨㄟˊ ㄉㄚˇ)
to pound with fists; to beat

搥檯拍凳(ㄔㄨㄟˊ ㄊㄞˊ ㄆㄞ ㄉㄥˋ)
(literally) to pound the table and slap the chair—in great rage

搥鼓(ㄔㄨㄟˊ ㄍㄨˇ)
to beat a drum

搥胸頓足(ㄔㄨㄟˊ ㄒㄩㄥ ㄉㄨㄣˋ ㄗㄨˊ)
to beat the breast and stamp the feet—in deep grief

搥腰(ㄔㄨㄟˊ ㄧㄠ)
to massage the waist by light pounding

【搜】 1987
ㄙㄡ sou sōu

1. to search; to seek
2. to inquire into; to investigate

搜捕(ㄙㄡ ㄅㄨˇ)
to hunt for (a fugitive); to search and arrest: 警察在樹林搜捕逃犯。The police hunted the woods for a fugitive.

搜票(ㄙㄡ ㄆㄧㄠˋ)
a search warrant

搜討(ㄙㄡ ㄊㄠˇ)
to study carefully; to scrutinize and investigate

搜剔(ㄙㄡ ㄊㄧ)
select; choosy; faultfinding; to pick; to weed out (textual errors)

搜拿(ㄙㄡ ㄋㄚˊ)
to hunt for (a fugitive)

搜羅(ㄙㄡ ㄌㄨㄛˊ)

①to seek and invite (men of ability, specialists, etc.) ②to collect (rare stamps, antiques, etc.) ③to scratch the bottom (for money, materials, etc.)

搜購(ㄙㄡ ㄍㄡˋ)
to collect or select for purchase

搜根剔齒(ㄙㄡ ㄍㄣ ㄊㄧ ㄔˇ)
to be very choosy; very particular about one's choice

搜括(ㄙㄡ ㄍㄨㄚ)
①to search ②to extort; to loot; to plunder

搜看(ㄙㄡ ㄎㄢˋ)or 搜閱(ㄙㄡ ㄩㄝˋ)
to search (a room, or building)

搜集(ㄙㄡ ㄐㄧˊ)
to seek and gather; to collect (rare stamps, books, data, evidence against a suspect, etc.): 他喜歡搜集昆蟲標本。He likes to collect insect specimens.

搜救(ㄙㄡ ㄐㄧㄡˋ)
to search for and rescue

搜檢(ㄙㄡ ㄐㄧㄢˇ)
to search and investigate

搜緝(ㄙㄡ ㄑㄧˋ)
to search for (a criminal, etc.); to hunt down (an escaped prisoner, etc.)

搜求(ㄙㄡ ㄑㄧㄡˊ)
to seek; to find; to look for

搜尋(ㄙㄡ ㄒㄩㄣˊ)
to search for; to seek and find

搜尋時間(ㄙㄡ ㄒㄩㄣˊ ㄕˊ ㄐㄧㄢ)
(computers) search time

搜章摘句(ㄙㄡ ㄓㄤ ㄓㄞ ㄐㄩˋ)
to search for chapters and pick sentences

搜查(ㄙㄡ ㄔㄚˊ)
to search (a house, a person, etc.)

搜出來(ㄙㄡ ㄔㄨ ·ㄌㄞ)
to search out; to find; to recover (stolen goods, evidence of crime, etc.)

搜身(ㄙㄡ ㄕㄣ)
to frisk

搜索(ㄙㄡ ㄙㄨㄛˇ)
to search; to reconnoiter

搜索枯腸(ㄙㄡ ㄙㄨㄛˇ ㄎㄨ ㄔㄤˊ)
to cudgel (or rack) one's brains (for new ideas, etc.)

搜索前進(ㄙㄡ ㄙㄨㄛˇ ㄑㄧㄢˊ ㄐㄧㄣˋ)
to advance and reconnoiter

搜索狀(ㄙㄡ ㄙㄨㄛˇ ㄓㄨㄤˋ)
a search warrant

【搭】 1988
ㄉㄚ da dā

1. to attach to; to join together; to add to: 張弓搭箭 to attach an arrow to the bow
2. to hang over: 把衣服搭在竹竿上。Hang the laundry on the bamboo pole.
3. to raise; to build (a shed, etc.); to put up; to pitch (a tent, etc.): 他們正在搭帳篷。They are pitching a tent.
4. to travel by; to take (a passage on a bus, train, boat, etc.): 他搭便車到車站。He hitched a ride to the station.
5. to help; to rescue
6. a short garment
7. a cover; to cover

搭把手(ㄉㄚ ㄅㄚˇ ㄕㄡˇ)
to give a helping hand: 您願意搭把手兒，幫我一下嗎? Will you give me a hand?

搭伴兒(ㄉㄚ ㄅㄚˋㄦ)
to keep company; to go together

搭幫(ㄉㄚ ㄅㄤ)
(to travel, etc.) in company or together

搭配(ㄉㄚ ㄆㄟˋ)
①to match (colors, etc.) ②to select (items as a present to a person, or dishes for a feast, etc.) ③to mate; to arrange in pairs or groups ④(said of words) to go together: 這兩個片語搭配不當。These two phrases do not go together.

搭棚(ㄉㄚ ㄆㄥˊ)
to put up a shed or a makeshift shelter

搭姘頭(ㄉㄚ ㄆㄧㄣ ·ㄊㄡ)
to cohabit with somebody without being married

搭擋(ㄉㄚ ·ㄉㄤ)
a partner; to cooperate; to work together: 我們倆是老搭擋。We two are old partners.

搭談(ㄉㄚ ㄊㄢˊ)
to talk to; to have conversation with

搭客(ㄉㄚ ㄎㄜˋ)
①the passengers (of a bus, train, boat, plane, etc.) ②to take passengers

搭話(ㄉㄚ ㄏㄨㄚˋ)
to strike up a conversation with somebody

搭伙(ㄉㄚ ㄏㄨㄛˇ)
to eat regularly in (a mess, etc.)

搭夥(ㄉㄚ ㄏㄨㄛˇ)
to go into partnership; to join

搭機(ㄉㄚ ㄐㄧ)
to board an airplane

搭架子(ㄉㄚ ㄐㄧㄚˋ ·ㄗ)
①to put up a scaffold ②to put on airs; to look down a social nose upon

搭街坊(ㄉㄚ ㄐㄧㄝ ·ㄈㄤ)
to be neighbors

搭截題(ㄉㄚ ㄐㄧㄝˊ ㄊㄧˊ)
(in the Ching Dynasty civil service examinations) the designated composition title that consists of a combination of disconnected quotations from the classics, often ridiculous or meaningless, for the purpose of preventing speculation in advance on the part of the participants

搭脚(ㄉㄚ ㄐㄧㄠˇ)
to get a foothold

搭救(ㄉㄚ ㄐㄧㄡˋ)
to rescue; to help; to go to the rescue of: 警察從盜匪手裏搭救一人。The police rescued a man from bandits.

搭箭(ㄉㄚ ㄐㄧㄢˋ)
to get ready to shoot an arrow

搭橋(ㄉㄚ ㄑㄧㄠˊ)
to build a bridge: 工程師在河上搭橋。The engineers built a bridge over the river.

搭腔(ㄉㄚ ㄑㄧㄤ)
①to answer; to respond ②to talk to each other

搭線(ㄉㄚ ㄒㄧㄢˋ)
①to make contact ②to act as a go-between or matchmaker

搭住(ㄉㄚ ㄓㄨˋ)
to take up one's lodgings

搭車(ㄉㄚ ㄔㄜ)

〔手部〕

to take a car, bus or train: 我們搭(火)車到那裏去。We took a train to go there.

搭乘(ㄉㄚ ㄔㄥˊ)
to travel by (air, ship, bus, etc.): 我搭乘火車上班。I go to work by train.

搭船(ㄉㄚ ㄔㄨㄢˊ)
to board a ship

搭訕(ㄉㄚ ㄕㄢˋ)
to converse heedlessly or absent-mindedly

搭上(ㄉㄚ ·ㄕㄤ)
①to take (a bus, ship, plane, etc.): 你昨天搭上公車了嗎? Did you take the bus yesterday? ②to add to ③to make contact or liaison with

搭載(ㄉㄚ ㄗㄞˋ)
to carry (passengers): 這輛公車可搭載五十名乘客。The bus will carry fifty passengers.

1989
【搶】 1. ㄑ丨ㄤˇ cheang qiǎng

1. to take by force; to snatch; to rob; to loot: 他把信搶了過去。He snatched away the letter.
2. to do something in haste, as in an emergency; to rush
3. to oppose
4. to try to beat others in a performance; to vie for; to scramble for a ball, position, etc: 搶球 to scramble for the ball

搶白(ㄑ丨ㄤˇ ㄅㄞˊ)
to reprimand or to refute someone to his face: 我被他搶白了一頓。I was refuted by him rudely.

搶跑(ㄑ丨ㄤˇ ㄆㄠˇ) or 搶走(ㄑ丨ㄤˇ ㄗㄡˇ)
to take away by force

搶渡(ㄑ丨ㄤˇ ㄉㄨˋ)
to cross (a river) speedily

搶奪(ㄑ丨ㄤˇ ㄉㄨㄛˊ) or 搶掠(ㄑ丨ㄤˇ ㄌㄩㄝˋ)
to rob; to loot; to plunder; robbery; looting: 士兵們搶掠屠殺了三天。The soldiers looted and massacred for three days.

搶灘(ㄑ丨ㄤˇ ㄊㄢ)
to make a beach landing in face of enemy resistance; to make a forced beach landing

搶購(ㄑ丨ㄤˇ ㄍㄡˋ)
to try to beat others in making purchases (as in time of war, etc.); a shopping rush; panic buying

搶光(ㄑ丨ㄤˇ ㄍㄨㄤ)
to take away by force everything that is movable

搶婚(ㄑ丨ㄤˇ ㄏㄨㄣ)
to carry away a woman and marry her by force

搶劫(ㄑ丨ㄤˇ ㄐ丨ㄝˊ)
to rob; robbery; to take by force

搶劫一空(ㄑ丨ㄤˇ ㄐ丨ㄝˊ 丨ˋ ㄎㄨㄥ)
to loot or rob to the last pin

搶救(ㄑ丨ㄤˇ ㄐ丨ㄡˋ)
to make emergency rescue; to take urgent steps to save (precious articles, etc. from destruction): 醫生搶救病人。The doctors gave emergency treatment to the patient.

搶鏡頭(ㄑ丨ㄤˇ ㄐ丨ㄥˋ ㄊㄡˊ)
①to steal the show; to outshine others ②(said of cameramen) to fight for a vantage point in taking news pictures

搶親(ㄑ丨ㄤˇ ㄑ丨ㄣ)
to take a woman for marriage by force

搶修(ㄑ丨ㄤˇ ㄒ丨ㄡ)
to race against time in making a repair job: 工人搶修河堤。The workers rushed to repair dykes.

搶先(ㄑ丨ㄤˇ ㄒ丨ㄢ)
to rush ahead; to try to be the first; to try to beat others in performing something

搶出風頭(ㄑ丨ㄤˇ ㄔㄨ ㄈㄥ ㄊㄡˊ)
to try to outshine others

搶收(ㄑ丨ㄤˇ ㄕㄡ)
to rush in the harvest; to get the harvest in quickly

搶手貨(ㄑ丨ㄤˇ ㄕㄡˇ ㄏㄨㄛˋ)
a commodity in great demand

搶上風(ㄑ丨ㄤˇ ㄕㄤˋ ㄈㄥ)
to jockey for (an advantageous) position

搶嘴(ㄑ丨ㄤˇ ㄗㄨㄟˇ)
①to try to beat others in being the first to talk ②argumentative; assertive

搶案(ㄑ丨ㄤˇ ㄢˋ)
(law) a case of robbery

搶運(ㄑ丨ㄤˇ ㄩㄣˋ)
to rush delivery (of goods); to race against time in sending out or transporting (materials, cargoes, etc.)

1989
【搶】 2. ㄑ丨ㄤ chiang qiāng

1. head (winds); adverse
2. to strike; to hit; to knock

搶風(ㄑ丨ㄤ ㄈㄥ)
head winds

1990
【搦】 ㄋㄨㄛˋ nuoh nuò

1. to hold; to seize
2. to challenge
3. to incite
4. to suppress; to restrain

搦管(ㄋㄨㄛˋ ㄍㄨㄢˇ)
to hold a pen—to write

搦戰(ㄋㄨㄛˋ ㄓㄢˋ)
to challenge to battle

1991
【搧】 (扇) ㄕㄢ shan shān

1. to fan
2. to stir up; to incite
3. to slap on the face

搧風(ㄕㄢ ㄈㄥ)
to fan

搧動(ㄕㄢ ㄉㄨㄥˋ)
to stir up; to incite; to agitate

搧火(ㄕㄢ ㄏㄨㄛˇ)
to fan a fire

搧扇(ㄕㄢ ㄕㄢˋ)
to fan with a fan

搧耳光(ㄕㄢ ㄦˇ ㄍㄨㄤ)
to box the ear

1992
【搨】 (拓) ㄊㄚˋ tah tà

1. to take a rubbing of an inscription on stone, etc.
2. to make an exact copy with paper and a writing brush

搨碑(ㄊㄚˋ ㄅㄟ)
to take a rubbing of an inscription on a stone tablet

搨本(ㄊㄚˋ ㄅㄣˇ) or 搨片(ㄊㄚˋ ㄆ丨ㄢˋ)
a rubbing from a stone tablet or bronze vessel

1993
【搬】 ㄅㄢ ban bān

1. to move; to transport: 他們搬到鄉下了。They moved to

the country.
2. to present
搬東西(ㄅㄢ ㄉㄨㄥ ·ㄒㄧ)
to move things
搬動(ㄅㄢ ㄉㄨㄥˋ)
to move; to shift: 不要搬動我桌上的東西。Don't move the things on my table.
搬弄(ㄅㄢ ㄋㄨㄥˋ)
①to move something about ②to fiddle with ③to show off; to display
搬弄是非(ㄅㄢ ㄋㄨㄥˋ ㄕˋ ㄈㄟ)
to stir up or incite trouble between people; to say bad things about one person in the presence of another; to sow discord
搬來搬去(ㄅㄢ ㄌㄞˊ ㄅㄢ ㄑㄩˋ)
to carry or move here and there
搬家(ㄅㄢ ㄐㄧㄚ)
to move from one dwelling to another; to change one's residence: 我們下個月搬家。We're moving next month.
搬救兵(ㄅㄢ ㄐㄧㄡˋ ㄅㄧㄥ)
to call in reinforcements; to ask for help
搬磚砸脚(ㄅㄢ ㄓㄨㄢ ㄗㄚˊ ㄐㄧㄠˇ)
to hurt oneself by one's own doing; to boomerang
搬移(ㄅㄢ ㄧˊ)or 搬遷(ㄅㄢ ㄑㄧㄢ)
to move
搬運(ㄅㄢ ㄩㄣˋ)
to move; to transport; to carry
搬運費(ㄅㄢ ㄩㄣˋ ㄈㄟˋ)
carriage; freight: 這筆搬運費我付不起。The freight was more than I could pay.
搬運公司(ㄅㄢ ㄩㄣˋ ㄍㄨㄥ ㄙ)
a moving company, or a transportation company

【搪】 1994 ㄊㄤˊ tarng táng
1. to ward off; to keep out: 這棚子搪不住風雨。The shed cannot keep out wind and rain.
2. to parry
搪不過去(ㄊㄤˊ ·ㄅㄨ ㄍㄨㄛˋ ·ㄑㄩ)
unable to parry
搪突(ㄊㄤˊ ㄊㄨˊ)
abrupt; rude 參看「唐突」; 她說這話太搪突了。It's rude of her to say so.
搪饑(ㄊㄤˊ ㄐㄧ)
to ward off hunger by eating whatever is available
搪賬(ㄊㄤˊ ㄓㄤˋ)
to evade paying of debts 亦作「搪帳」
搪差使(ㄊㄤˊ ㄔㄞ ·ㄕ)or 搪差事(ㄊㄤˊ ㄔㄞ ㄕˋ)
to do something for appearance's sake; to perform a task perfunctorily; to goldbrick
搪瓷(ㄊㄤˊ ㄘˊ)
enamel
搪塞(ㄊㄤˊ ㄙㄜˋ)
to parry something; to stall somebody off; to perform a task perfunctorily or for form's sake: 搪塞他幾句。Stall him off with a vague answer.

【搐】 1995 ㄔㄨˋ chuh chù
spasm; cramp; convulsions; to shake involuntarily; to twitch

【搯】 1996 (掏) ㄊㄠ tau tāo
to pull out; to take out (money, cigarettes, etc.): 他搯出槍來。He took out a gun.

【摁】 1997 ㄣˋ enn èn
1. to press (a doorbell, etc.)
2. to delay or hold
摁電鈴(ㄣˋ ㄉㄧㄢˋ ㄌㄧㄥˊ)
to press an electric bell

【搵】 1998 ㄨㄣˋ wenn wèn
1. to wipe off (tears) 參看「抆淚」: 搵英雄淚 to wipe off a hero's tears
2. to press with fingers

【搠】 1999 ㄕㄨㄛˋ shuoh shuò
1. to thrust (at one's enemy)
2. to smear; to daub

【摀】 2000 ㄨˇ wuu wǔ
1. to cover; to conceal; to hide
2. to put into an airtight container (in cooking)
摀不住(ㄨˇ ·ㄅㄨ ㄓㄨˋ)
cannot be covered or concealed: 這種事情是摀不住的。Such things cannot be covered.
摀蓋(ㄨˇ ㄍㄞˋ)
①to cover up; to hide (the truth); to keep secret ②to disguise; to masquerade
摀起來(ㄨˇ ㄑㄧˇ ·ㄌㄞ)
①to imprison ②(cooking) to put food in airtight container (for steaming, etc.)
摀著耳朵(ㄨˇ ·ㄓㄜ ㄦˇ ·ㄉㄨㄛ)
to cover one's ears
摀上眼睛(ㄨˇ ㄕㄤˋ ㄧㄢˇ ㄐㄧㄥ)
to cover up one's eyes
摀摀蓋蓋(ㄨˇ ·ㄨ ㄍㄞˋ ㄍㄞˋ)
secretive; hiding and concealing

【搌】 2001 ㄓㄢˇ jaan zhǎn
1. to bind
2. to wipe; to mop
搌布(ㄓㄢˇ ㄅㄨˋ)
a mopping cloth; a dishcloth: 用搌布將玻璃擦乾淨。Clean the glass with a mopping cloth.

【搴】 2002 ㄑㄧㄢ chian qiān
to pull or pluck up
搴旗斬將(ㄑㄧㄢ ㄑㄧˊ ㄓㄢˇ ㄐㄧㄤˋ)or 搴旗取將(ㄑㄧㄢ ㄑㄧˊ ㄑㄩˇ ㄐㄧㄤˋ)
(literally) to pull up the enemy flag and kill the opposing general—to defeat the enemy decisively

【搞】 2003 ㄍㄠˇ gao gǎo
1. to stir up; to cause trouble; to make a mess of; to mix up: 你把事情搞糟了。You have made a mess of things.
2. to do; to carry on; to be engaged in: 他是搞建築的。He is engaged in building.
3. to get; to secure: 幫我們搞點吃的來。Go and get us something to eat.
4. to set up; to start; to organize: 我們打算在學校搞個合唱團。We are planning to set up a chorus in our school.
搞把戲(ㄍㄠˇ ㄅㄚˇ ㄒㄧˋ)
to play tricks
搞鬼(ㄍㄠˇ ㄍㄨㄟˇ)
(said of a person) to cause trouble or pull legs in secret
搞垮(ㄍㄠˇ ㄎㄨㄚˇ)
to overthrow; to cause to fail
搞好(ㄍㄠˇ ㄏㄠˇ)
to make a good job of; to do well

〔手部〕

搞花樣(ㄍㄠˇ ㄏㄨㄚ ㄧㄤˋ)
to play tricks; to cheat; to deceive

搞七搞八(ㄍㄠˇ ㄑㄧ ㄍㄠˇ ㄅㄚ)
to annoy; to cause mischief; to cause delay by doing a lot of useless things

搞錢(ㄍㄠˇ ㄑㄧㄢˊ)
to make money (by illegal means)

搞清楚(ㄍㄠˇ ㄑㄧㄥ ·ㄔㄨ)
to make clear; to clarify (a matter, etc.)

搞政治(ㄍㄠˇ ㄓㄥˋ ㄓˋ)
to play politics

搞運動(ㄍㄠˇ ㄩㄣˋ ㄉㄨㄥˋ)
to carry on a movement (or campaign)

十一畫

【摘】 2004 ㄓㄞ jai zhāi (讀音 ㄓㄜˊ jer zhé)

1. to take off (one's hat, etc.); to pluck; to pick
2. to choose; to select
3. to jot down (notes)
4. to expose; to unveil (a conspiracy, etc.)

摘發(ㄓㄜˊ ㄈㄚ)
to make charges (of crimes)

摘奸發伏(ㄓㄜˊ ㄐㄧㄢ ㄈㄚ ㄈㄨˊ)
to expose or reveal conspiracies and secrets

摘帽子(ㄓㄞ ㄇㄠˋ ·ㄗ)
to take off one's hat

摘東補西(ㄓㄞ ㄉㄨㄥ ㄅㄨˇ ㄒㄧ)
(literally) to pluck from the east to repair the west—to try very hard to make both ends meet

摘錄(ㄓㄞ ㄌㄨˋ)
an excerpt; to make an extract of a report, article, document, etc.

摘花(ㄓㄞ ㄏㄨㄚ)
to pluck flowers

摘記(ㄓㄞ ㄐㄧˋ)
notes or observations (by an author); to jot down: 我摘記了要點。I jotted down the important points.

摘句(ㄓㄞ ㄐㄩˋ)
quotations; quotes; to make quotations: 這本書包括一些無名作者的摘句。The book contained quotations from obscure authors.

摘取(ㄓㄞ ㄑㄩˇ)
to select; to pick; to take

摘下(ㄓㄞ ㄒㄧㄚˋ)
to pick off (flowers, etc.); to take off: 他把眼鏡摘下來。He takes off his glasses.

摘除(ㄓㄞ ㄔㄨˊ)
to excise

摘要(ㄓㄞ ㄧㄠˋ)
① to summarize; to make an epitome ② an epitome; an abstract

摘由(ㄓㄜˊ ㄧㄡˊ)
to excerpt the most important points (of an official document for filing purpose); excerpts (of an official document)

【摑】 2005 ㄍㄨㄛˊ gwo guó

to slap another on his face; to smack; to box: 她摑了她兒子耳光。She boxed her son on his ear.

【摜】 2006 ㄍㄨㄢˋ guann guàn

1. to throw to the ground
2. to be accustomed or used to

摜砲(ㄍㄨㄢˋ ㄆㄠˋ)
a type of firecracker which explodes when thrown to the ground with force

摜交(ㄍㄨㄢˋ ㄐㄧㄠ)
to wrestle; wrestling

摜出(ㄍㄨㄢˋ ㄔㄨ)
to throw off

摜紗帽(ㄍㄨㄢˋ ㄕㄚ ㄇㄠˋ)
to resign a government post in anger; to quit one's job

【摟】 2007 1. ㄌㄡˊ lou lóu

to drag; to pull; to drag away

【摟】 2007 2. ㄌㄡ lhou lōu

1. to hold up; to tuck up: 她摟起衣裳裝花。She held up the lower part of her long gown to put flowers.
2. to squeeze or extort (money, etc.)
3. to gather up; to collect; to rake together: 一位老婦人正在摟柴火。An old woman is raking up twigs and dead leaves (for fuel).

摟攬(ㄌㄡ ㄌㄢˇ)
to monopolize (a project, business, etc.); to contract to do certain services

摟錢(ㄌㄡ ㄑㄧㄢˊ)
to exact money (often said of dishonest officials, etc.)

摟算(ㄌㄡ ㄙㄨㄢˋ)
to calculate; to audit; to check an account

摟衣裳(ㄌㄡ ㄧ ·ㄕㄤ)
to hold up the lower part of one's gown

【摟】 2007 3. ㄌㄡˇ loou lǒu

to hold in the arms; to embrace; to hug

摟抱(ㄌㄡˇ ㄅㄠˋ)
to hold in the arms; to embrace

摟著(ㄌㄡˇ ·ㄓㄜ)
to embrace; to press to one's chest: 母親摟著女兒。The mother embraced her daughter.

摟住(ㄌㄡˇ ㄓㄨˋ)
to hold in the arms; to embrace

【摒】 2008 ㄅㄧㄥˋ binq bìng

1. to get rid of; to expel; to remove; to dismiss; to brush aside
2. to arrange in order

摒擋(ㄅㄧㄥˋ ㄉㄤˋ)
to arrange in order; to pack up for traveling: 摒擋一切 to get everything ready

摒絕(ㄅㄧㄥˋ ㄐㄩㄝˊ)
to cut loose entirely

摒棄(ㄅㄧㄥˋ ㄑㄧˋ)
to abandon; to get rid of: 我永遠不會摒棄我的朋友。I would never abandon my friends.

摒除(ㄅㄧㄥˋ ㄔㄨˊ)
to get rid of; to remove (bad habits, evil thoughts, etc.): 他已摒除一切壞習慣。He has got rid of all his bad habits.

【摛】 2009 ㄔ chy chī

1. (said of fame, news, etc.) to spread
2. to brandish (a pen)
3. to be known widely

擒翰(ㄑㄧㄣˊ ㄏㄢˋ)
to write a composition; to brandish a pen
擒藻(ㄑㄧㄣˊ ㄗㄠˇ) or 擒詞(ㄑㄧㄣˊ ㄘˊ)
to write in a flowery style; to use poetic diction; to weave an ornate passage

【摔】 2010
ㄕㄨㄞ shuai shuāi
1. to throw to the ground; to fling; to break: 我把腿摔斷了。I had a fall and broke my leg.
2. to get rid of; to shake off (a tail, etc.)
3. to fall down; to tumble; to lose one's balance: 他從馬背上摔下。He fell off his horse.
摔破(ㄕㄨㄞ ㄆㄛˋ)
①to suffer bruises or injuries in a fall ②to break something by dashing it on the ground; to become broken after falling to the ground
摔牌(ㄕㄨㄞ ㄆㄞˊ)
(literally) to dash one's reputation to the ground—to smear one's reputation
摔倒(ㄕㄨㄞ ㄉㄠˇ)
①(said of a person) to fall down ②(in wrestling, etc.) to fell the opponent or to throw the opponent to the ground
摔掉(ㄕㄨㄞ ˙ㄉㄧㄠ)
①to throw away; to dash down; to cast off: 不要把舊書摔掉。Don't throw away used books. ②to shake off (a tail, annoying companion, etc.)
摔跟頭(ㄕㄨㄞ ㄍㄣ ˙ㄊㄡ)
①to fall flat②to fail ignominiously in an endeavor; to blunder
摔跤(ㄕㄨㄞ ㄐㄧㄠ)
to fall down; to suffer a fall: 他因摔跤而受傷。He was hurt by a fall.
摔角(ㄕㄨㄞ ㄐㄧㄠˇ)
to wrestle; wrestling
摔折(ㄕㄨㄞ ㄓㄜˊ)
to break (a bone, stick, etc.) after falling to the ground
摔傷(ㄕㄨㄞ ㄕㄤ)
to get hurt in a fall: 他滑雪時摔傷了。He got hurt in a fall when he was skiing.
摔死(ㄕㄨㄞ ㄙˇ)
to fall to death; to be dashed to death
摔碎(ㄕㄨㄞ ㄙㄨㄟˋ)
to break into pieces after falling or being dashed to the ground; to shatter; to smash: 我倒茶時，不小心摔碎一個杯子。I shattered a cup when I tried to have a cup of tea.

【摭】 2011
ㄓˊ jyr zhí
to pick up from the ground; to take up; to collect
摭取(ㄓˊ ㄑㄩˇ)
①to pick up; to take; to collect ②to plagiarize
摭拾(ㄓˊ ㄕˊ)
to pick; to collect (samples, gossip, phrases)
摭拾遺文(ㄓˊ ㄕˊ ㄧˊ ㄨㄣˊ)
to make random quotes from obsolete writings
摭採(ㄓˊ ㄘㄞˇ)
to collect

【摧】 2012
ㄘㄨㄟ tsuei cuī
1. to break; to smash; to destroy; to injure; to harm: 我們的軍隊無堅不摧。Our army is capable of destroying any stronghold.
2. to damp
3. to cause to cease; to extinguish
4. to be sad and sorrowful; to grieve
摧敗(ㄘㄨㄟ ㄅㄞˋ)
①to beat the enemy ②to grieve
摧鋒陷陣(ㄘㄨㄟ ㄈㄥ ㄒㄧㄢˋ ㄓㄣˋ)
to mow down enemy troops and take their position
摧頹(ㄘㄨㄟ ㄊㄨㄟˊ)
①dilapidated; in ruins ②to idle about
摧枯拉朽(ㄘㄨㄟ ㄎㄨ ㄌㄚ ㄒㄧㄡˇ)
(literally) to destroy or pull apart something already in a state of ruin or decay—easily accomplished
摧壞(ㄘㄨㄟ ㄏㄨㄞˋ)
to destroy
摧毀(ㄘㄨㄟ ㄏㄨㄟˇ)
to destroy (enemy positions, heavy weapons, etc.)
摧堅折銳(ㄘㄨㄟ ㄐㄧㄢ ㄓㄜˊ ㄖㄨㄟˋ)
to defeat the enemy's crack troops and break their main force
摧陷(ㄘㄨㄟ ㄒㄧㄢˋ)
to smash enemy resistance and take their position
摧陷廓清(ㄘㄨㄟ ㄒㄧㄢˋ ㄎㄨㄛˋ ㄑㄧㄥ)
to defeat and completely wipe out (the forces of evil, etc.)
摧折(ㄘㄨㄟ ㄓㄜˊ)
to break; to destroy; to smash
摧殘(ㄘㄨㄟ ㄘㄢˊ)
①to destroy; to ruin: 切勿摧殘你的健康。Never ruin your health. ②to humiliate

【摶】 2013
ㄊㄨㄢˊ twan tuán
1. to roll round with the hand; to knead
2. to rely on
3. to take or follow (a trail, etc.)
摶飯(ㄊㄨㄢˊ ㄈㄢˋ)
to roll rice balls
摶風(ㄊㄨㄢˊ ㄈㄥ)
(literally) to ride on the wind—to rise very quickly
摶土作人(ㄊㄨㄢˊ ㄊㄨˇ ㄗㄨㄛˋ ㄖㄣˊ)
to mold the mud and create man (according to the Chinese version of Genesis, man was created in this manner by Nü Wa (女媧), the mythical sister and successor of Fu-hsi (伏羲))
摶沙(ㄊㄨㄢˊ ㄕㄚ)
(literally) a ball of sand—lacking cohesion and unity of purpose

【摳】 2014
ㄎㄡ kou kōu
1. to raise
2. to grope for
3. to inquire into; to delve into
4. to dig with fingers (or something pointed): 他在地上摳個洞。He dug a hole in the ground.
5. to be stingy
摳破(ㄎㄡ ㄆㄛˋ)
to damage or injure by scratching
摳破臉(ㄎㄡ ㄆㄛˋ ㄌㄧㄢˇ)
(to take action, measures, etc.) in disregard of the

〔手部〕

"face" of the other party
摳門兒(ㄎㄡ ㄇㄜˊㄦ)
stingy; miserly; niggardly
摳得緊(ㄎㄡ ·ㄉㄜ ㄐ丨ㄣˇ)
to be very stingy
摳字眼兒(ㄎㄡ ㄗˋ 丨ㄚˇㄦ)
to pay too much attention to the different meanings of words; to find fault with diction

〔手部〕

【摎】 2015
ㄐ丨ㄡ jiou jiū
entwined—as branches of a tree

【摺】 2016
ㄓㄜˊ jer zhé
1. to fold (paper, etc.); to plait
2. a folder; a folded brochure
3. curved and winding
4. to pull and break
摺門(ㄓㄜˊ ㄇㄣˊ)
folding doors
摺刀(ㄓㄜˊ ㄉㄠ)
a folding knife; a pocket knife
摺疊(ㄓㄜˊ ㄉ丨ㄝˊ)
to fold up (clothing, etc.); to plait together: 把信摺疊好放入信封。Fold the letter and put it in an envelope.
摺痕(ㄓㄜˊ ㄏㄣˊ)
a crease; a fold; a line made by folding
摺角(ㄓㄜˊ ㄐ丨ㄠˇ)
to make a dog-ear; to dog-ear
摺裙(ㄓㄜˊ ㄑㄩㄣˊ)
a plaited skirt 亦作「百摺裙」: 她喜歡穿摺裙。She likes to wear plaited skirts.
摺紙工(ㄓㄜˊ ㄓˇ ㄍㄨㄥ)
(in primary school) paper folding as a kind of manual training
摺尺(ㄓㄜˊ ㄔˇ)
a folding ruler
摺床(ㄓㄜˊ ㄔㄨㄤˊ)
a folding bed
摺扇(ㄓㄜˊ ㄕㄢˋ)or 摺疊扇(ㄓㄜˊ ㄉ丨ㄝˊ ㄕㄢˋ)
a folding fan
摺子(ㄓㄜˊ ·ㄗ)
a piece of paper folded into pages
摺奏(ㄓㄜˊ ㄗㄡˋ)
a memorial submitted to the emperor 亦作「奏摺」

【摸】 2017
ㄇㄛ mho mō
(又讀 ㄇㄠ mhau māo)
1. to feel or touch lightly with fingers; to caress
2. to grope: 我們摸索著走過黑暗的街道。We groped our way through the dark streets.
3. to try to find out; to feel out: 我摸透了這裡的情況。I have found out the situation here.
4. to seek after; to try to get at
摸不清(ㄇㄛ ·ㄅㄨ ㄑ丨ㄥ)
do not understand; not quite sure
摸不著邊兒(ㄇㄛ ·ㄅㄨ ㄓㄠˊ ㄅ丨ㄚㄦ)
(literally) unable to touch the edge—cannot understand at all
摸不著門兒(ㄇㄛ ·ㄅㄨ ㄓㄠˊ ㄇㄜˊㄦ)
(literally) cannot find the door—do not have the slightest idea; do not understand at all; cannot find the proper approach
摸不著頭腦(ㄇㄛ ·ㄅㄨ ㄓㄠˊ ㄊㄡˊ ㄋㄠˇ)
to be at a loss; cannot make head or tail of it: 我當時摸不著頭腦，不知如何說好。I was then at a loss for words.
摸摸(ㄇㄛ ·ㄇㄛ)
to feel; to touch: 讓我摸摸看。Let me have a feel.
摸骨相(ㄇㄛ ㄍㄨˇ ㄒ丨ㄤˋ)
a kind of physiognomy practiced by blind fortunetellers who tell the fortune of clients by feeling their bones, especially facial bones
摸黑兒(ㄇㄛ ㄏㄜㄦ)
to do something in the dark: 他常常摸黑兒趕路。He often gropes his way on dark nights.
摸瞎(ㄇㄛ ㄒ丨ㄚ)
to move around in the dark
摸彩(ㄇㄛ ㄘㄞˇ)
to draw lots to determine the prize winners in a raffle or lottery
摸索(ㄇㄛ ㄙㄨㄛˇ)
① to feel about; to feel (in one's pocket, etc.); to grope (in the dark, the meaning of, etc.): 我們在黑暗的走廊上摸索着走。We groped our way along the dark corridor. ② to do things slowly
摸魚(ㄇㄛ ㄩˊ)or 摸灰(ㄇㄛ ㄏㄨㄟ)
to idle; to loaf on a job

【摽】 2018
1. ㄅ丨ㄠ biau biāo
1. to motion (somebody) to go out
2. to strike
3. high; lofty
4. sometimes used in place of 標—to glorify, etc.
5. the razor of a sword
6. to throw away; to give up; to abandon
摽牌(ㄅ丨ㄠ ㄆㄞˊ)
a rattan shield (used in ancient warfare)
摽末(ㄅ丨ㄠ ㄇㄛˋ)
the edge of a sword

【摽】 2018
2. ㄆ丨ㄠˇ peau piǎo
1. to fall; falling
2. to lock together: 這兩個男孩摽着胳膊走。These two boys walk locked arm in arm.
摽梅(ㄆ丨ㄠˇ ㄇㄟˊ)
the fruit of a plum tree that are ripe and about to fall—(said of girls) marriageable age

【摶】 2019
(扦) ㄑ丨ㄢ chian qiān
1. to stick into
2. a rod with a sharp point used by a tidewaiter to examine goods; anything of the similar shape
3. to trim feet (a special Chinese bathhouse service)

【摴】 2020
ㄕㄨ shu shū
1. comfortable; easy
2. an ancient Chinese gambling game roughly resembling today's dice game
摴蒲(ㄕㄨ ㄆㄨˊ)
an ancient Chinese gambling game roughly resembling today's dice game

【摷】 2021
ㄌ丨ㄠˋ liaw liào
1. to put down; to lay down
2. to leave behind
摷跤(ㄌ丨ㄠˋ ㄐ丨ㄠ)
a form of wrestling
摷下(ㄌ丨ㄠˋ ·ㄒ丨ㄚ)

①to put down; to lay down ②to leave behind: 母親死了，撂下二個小孩。The mother died, leaving two children behind.

撂手(ㄌㄧㄠˋ ㄕㄡˇ)
to pocket one's hands; to have nothing to do with it; to give up: 你不應該撂手不管。You should not wash your hands of the matter.

【摩】2022 ㄇㄛ mo mó

1. to chafe; to scour; to rub; to scrape: 峻嶺摩天。The high mountains seem to scrape the sky.
2. friction
3. to feel with the hand
4. (now rarely) to work and encourage each other (especially in study)
5. to learn from long and constant study

摩門教(ㄇㄛˊ ㄇㄣˊ ㄐㄧㄠˋ)
Mormon Church, or Church of Jesus Christ of Latter-day Saints

摩登(ㄇㄛˊ ㄉㄥ)
modern; fashionable: 她穿上一襲摩登的服裝。She is in a fashionable dress.

摩登女郎(ㄇㄛˊ ㄉㄥ ㄋㄩˇ ㄌㄤˊ)
a modern girl

摩頂(ㄇㄛˊ ㄉㄧㄥˇ)
the ordainment of a Buddhist monk

摩頂放踵(ㄇㄛˊ ㄉㄧㄥˇ ㄈㄤˋ ㄓㄨㄥˇ)
to scrape one's whole body from crown to heel—(figuratively) to dedicate oneself completely to the welfare of mankind

摩天大樓(ㄇㄛˊ ㄊㄧㄢ ㄉㄚˋ ㄌㄡˊ)or 摩天樓(ㄇㄛˊ ㄊㄧㄢ ㄌㄡˊ)
skyscrapers

摩托(ㄇㄛˊ ㄊㄨㄛ)
a motor

摩托卡(ㄇㄛˊ ㄊㄨㄛ ㄎㄚˇ)
a motorcar, or automobile

摩托化(ㄇㄛˊ ㄊㄨㄛ ㄏㄨㄚˋ)
motorization

摩托車(ㄇㄛˊ ㄊㄨㄛ ㄔㄜ)
a motorcycle: 他昨天買了一輛嶄新的摩托車。He bought a brand-new motorcycle yesterday.

摩納哥(ㄇㄛˊ ㄋㄚˋ ㄍㄜ)
Monaco

摩尼教(ㄇㄛˊ ㄋㄧˊ ㄐㄧㄠˋ)
Manicheism

摩羯宮(ㄇㄛˊ ㄐㄧㄝˊ ㄍㄨㄥ)or 摩羯座(ㄇㄛˊ ㄐㄧㄝˊ ㄗㄨㄛˋ)
(astronomy) Capricornus

摩肩接踵(ㄇㄛˊ ㄐㄧㄢ ㄐㄧㄝ ㄓㄨㄥˇ)
to rub shoulders and follow one another in close succession—as in a crowd; to jostle one another in a crowd

摩拳擦掌(ㄇㄛˊ ㄑㄩㄢˊ ㄘㄚ ㄓㄤˇ)
①to get ready for a fight ②to be eager to start on a task

摩西(ㄇㄛˊ ㄒㄧ)
Moses, the Hebrew prophet who led the Israelites out of Egypt and delivered the Law during their years of wandering in the wilderness

摩擦(ㄇㄛˊ ㄘㄚ)
①to chafe; to scour ②friction; conflict and disagreement

摩擦力(ㄇㄛˊ ㄘㄚ ㄌㄧˋ)
frictional force

摩擦聲(ㄇㄛˊ ㄘㄚ ㄕㄥ)
(phonetics) fricatives

摩擦生熱(ㄇㄛˊ ㄘㄚ ㄕㄥ ㄖㄜˋ)
Friction generates heat.

摩抄 or 摩挲
①(ㄇㄛˊ ㄙㄨㄛ) to caress, touch, rub, etc. with the hand ②(ㄇㄚ ˙ㄙㄚ) to smooth out creases with the hand

摩爾人(ㄇㄛˊ ㄦˇ ㄖㄣˊ)
the Moors

【摹】2023 ㄇㄛˊ mo mó

1. to copy; to make an exact copy
2. to model or pattern after; to imitate

摹本(ㄇㄛˊ ㄅㄣˇ)
①an exact copy of the original; a facsimile ②(now rarely) a kind of embroidered satin

摹仿(ㄇㄛˊ ㄈㄤˇ)
to copy; to model or pattern after; to imitate; to ape 亦作「模仿」

摹擬(ㄇㄛˊ ㄋㄧˇ)
to model or pattern after; to simulate

摹臨(ㄇㄛˊ ㄌㄧㄣˊ)
(art and calligraphy) to copy or imitate the works of ancient masters 亦作「臨摹」

摹古(ㄇㄛˊ ㄍㄨˇ)
to model or pattern after ancient (styles, customs, etc.)

摹刻(ㄇㄛˊ ㄎㄜˋ)
①to carve a replica ②a carved reproduction of an inscription

摹寫(ㄇㄛˊ ㄒㄧㄝˇ)
①to trace the original (writing, calligraphy, etc.) ②to describe; to depict

摹印(ㄇㄛˊ ㄧㄣˋ)
one of the eight calligraphic styles in the Chin Dynasty, usually used in today's seals

【摯】2024 ㄓˋ jyh jhì

1. sincere; cordial
2. a Chinese family name

摯友(ㄓˋ ㄧㄡˇ)
a bosom friend: 他是我的摯友。He is my bosom (or intimate) friend.

【揅】2025 (研) ㄧㄢˊ yan yán

1. to grind; to powder
2. to study thoroughly

揅經(ㄧㄢˊ ㄐㄧㄥ)
to study the classics

十二畫

【撅】2026 ㄐㄩㄝ jiue juē

1. to break; to snap: 他把樹枝撅成兩段。He broke the twig in two.
2. to stick up; to protrude

撅豎小人(ㄐㄩㄝ ㄕㄨˋ ㄒㄧㄠˇ ㄖㄣˊ)
a mean fellow

撅嘴(ㄐㄩㄝ ㄗㄨㄟˇ)
to protrude the lips (in displeasure); to pout 亦作「噘嘴」

【撐】2027 (撑) ㄔㄥ cheng chēng

1. to prop; to support: 她用兩手撐着下巴。She held her chin in her hands.
2. to stretch tight; to burst: 他撐病了。He is sick with bursting pressure.
3. to pole or punt (a raft or a

〔手部〕

boat)
4. to maintain; to keep up; to go on with
5. to open

撐不住(ㄔㄥ ˙ㄅㄨ ㄓㄨˋ)
too weak to prop up or support

撐破(ㄔㄥ ㄆㄛˋ)
to burst: 群衆把門撐破了。The crowd burst open the door.

撐得慌(ㄔㄥ ˙ㄉㄜ ˙ㄏㄨㄤ)
having an excessively full stomach

撐得住(ㄔㄥ ˙ㄉㄜ ㄓㄨˋ)
strong enough to prop up or support: 木橋的力量撐得住一列火車嗎? Is a wooden bridge strong enough to support a railway train?

撐天柱地(ㄔㄥ ㄊㄧㄢ ㄓㄨˋ ㄉㄧˋ)
(literally) to support the heaven and pillar the earth—to assume an important responsibility in the nation

撐竿跳(ㄔㄥ ㄍㄢ ㄊㄧㄠˋ)
the pole vault

撐開(ㄔㄥ ㄎㄞ)
to prop open: 請你把麻袋撐開。Please hold open the gunny bag.

撐拒(ㄔㄥ ㄐㄩˋ)
to resist desperately

撐起(來)(ㄔㄥ ㄑㄧˇ (˙ㄌㄞ))
to prop up

撐住(ㄔㄥ ㄓㄨˋ)
to prop with a pole; to prop from under

撐持(ㄔㄥ ㄔˊ)
to prop up; to shore up; to sustain: 他們努力著撐持局面。They tried hard to shore up a shaky situation.

撐腸拄腹(ㄔㄥ ㄔㄤˊ ㄓㄨˇ ㄈㄨˋ)
to fill the stomach

撐場面(ㄔㄥ ㄔㄤˇ ㄇㄧㄢˋ)or(ㄔㄥ ㄔㄤˊ ㄇㄧㄢˋ)
to maintain an outward show of prosperity; to keep up appearances

撐船(ㄔㄥ ㄔㄨㄢˊ)or 撐舟(ㄔㄥ ㄓㄡ)
to pole (or punt) a boat

撐傘(ㄔㄥ ㄙㄢˇ)
to prop open an umbrella

撐腰(ㄔㄥ ㄧㄠ)
to support, or to give backing to someone; to stand by someone

[手部]

【撈】 2028
ㄌㄠ lhau lāo
(讀音 ㄌㄠˊ lau láo)

1. to pull or drag out of the water
2. to fish up; to get by improper means: 他喜歡混水撈魚。He is fond of fishing in troubled waters.

撈本兒(ㄌㄠ ㄅㄜˇㄦ)
①to win back money (lost in gambling) ②to recover invested capital

撈摸(ㄌㄠ ㄇㄛ)
to search underwater for; to feel about in water

撈起(ㄌㄠ ㄑㄧˇ)
to recover from water, the riverbed, the sea bottom, etc.

撈取(ㄌㄠ ㄑㄩˇ)
to fish for; to gain

撈屍(ㄌㄠ ㄕ)
to recover the body of a drowned person

撈一票(ㄌㄠ ㄧˋ ㄆㄧㄠˋ)
to make money, legally or otherwise: 走, 咱們也撈一票去。Go, let's make money at it, too.

撈一把(ㄌㄠ ㄧˋ ㄅㄚˇ)
to reap some profit; to profiteer

撈魚(ㄌㄠ ㄩˊ)
to catch fish by a net, a bucket, etc.

撈什子(ㄌㄠˊ ㄕㄜˊ ˙ㄗ)
a disgusting thing; an eyesore

【撒】 2029
1. ㄙㄚ sa sā

1. to relax; to ease
2. to loosen; to unleash
3. to exhibit; to display; to show

撒潑(ㄙㄚ ㄆㄛ)
to behave rudely; to be in a tantrum; to be unreasonable and make a scene: 她又在撒潑了。She is in one of her tantrums again.

撒潑打滾(ㄙㄚ ㄆㄛ ㄉㄚˇ ㄍㄨㄣˇ)
to fly into a tantrum (as a peevish child)

撒馬(ㄙㄚ ㄇㄚˇ)
to give free rein to a horse

撒糞(ㄙㄚ ㄈㄣˋ)
①to defecate; to empty the bowels ②to talk rubbish

撒放(ㄙㄚ ㄈㄤˋ)
to release; to unleash

撒瘋撒癡(ㄙㄚ ㄈㄥ ㄙㄚ ㄔ)
headlong; reckless

撒旦(ㄙㄚ ㄉㄢˋ)
Satan

撒地尼亞(ㄙㄚ ㄉㄧˋ ㄋㄧˊ ㄧㄚˋ)
Sardinia 亦作「薩丁尼亞」

撒腿(ㄙㄚ ㄊㄨㄟˇ)or撒鴨子(ㄙㄚ ㄧㄚ ˙ㄗ)
to take to one's heels; to run

撒溺 or 撒尿(ㄙㄚ ㄋㄧㄠˋ)
to urinate; to pass urine; to piss; to pee

撒賴(ㄙㄚ ㄌㄞˋ)
to behave like a rascal; to show villainy; to make a scene; to act shamelessly

撒科打諢(ㄙㄚ ㄎㄜ ㄉㄚˇ ㄏㄨㄣˋ)
to introduce comic remarks in dialogue

撒開(ㄙㄚ ㄎㄞ)
①to get away ②to part ③to release; to let go

撒哈拉沙漠(ㄙㄚ ㄏㄚ ㄌㄚ ㄕㄚ ㄇㄛˋ)
the Sahara Desert

撒歡兒(ㄙㄚ ㄏㄨㄚㄦ)
to gambol; to frolic; to romp about (as a cat)

撒謊(ㄙㄚ ㄏㄨㄤˇ)
to tell a lie; to lie: 不要對我撒謊。Don't lie to me.

撒嬌(ㄙㄚ ㄐㄧㄠ)
①to show pettishness, as a spoilt child ②(said of a woman) to pretend to be angry or displeased

撒脚(ㄙㄚ ㄐㄧㄠˇ)
to take to one's heels

撒酒風兒(ㄙㄚ ㄐㄧㄡˇ ㄈㄥㄦ)
to show drunkenness

撒氣(ㄙㄚ ㄑㄧˋ)
①to vent anger: 你別拿我撒氣嘛。Don't vent your anger on me. ②to let air out (from a ball, tire, etc.): 前輪撒氣了。The front tire is flat.

撒線(ㄙㄚ ㄒㄧㄢˋ)
to let out the string (of a kite)

撒手(ㄙㄚ ㄕㄡˇ)
①to relax the hold or grasp ②to neglect a responsibility: 這件事你不能撒手不管。You cannot neglect the

responsibility of the business.
撒手鐧(ㄙㄚ ㄕㄡˇ ㄐㄧㄢˋ)
an unexpected thrust with the mace—(figuratively) the climaxing act; one's specialty
撒手西歸(ㄙㄚ ㄕㄡˇ ㄒㄧ ㄍㄨㄟ)
to die
撒手塵寰(ㄙㄚ ㄕㄡˇ ㄔㄣˊ ㄏㄨㄢˊ)
to pass away
撒嘴(ㄙㄚ ㄗㄨㄟˇ)
to relax the bite
撒村(ㄙㄚ ㄘㄨㄣ)
to use vulgar or profane language; to curse; to swear
撒野(ㄙㄚ ㄧㄝˇ)
to act boorishly; to act wildly; to behave atrociously
撒網(ㄙㄚ ㄨㄤˇ)
① to cast a net; to spread a net ② to invite relatives and friends on an occasion with the intention of collecting presents

【撒】 2029
2. ㄙㄚˇ saa sǎ
to scatter; to sprinkle; to disperse; to spread; to spill: 她在食物上撒鹽。She sprinkled food with salt.
撒播(ㄙㄚˇ ㄅㄛ)
① broadcast sowing ② to sow
撒豆成兵(ㄙㄚˇ ㄉㄡˋ ㄔㄥˊ ㄅㄧㄥ)
(literally) to turn sprinkled beans into soldiers—to work miracles
撒種(ㄙㄚˇ ㄓㄨㄥˇ)
to sow seeds: 如何撒種，如何收穫。As a man sows, so shall he reap.
撒施(ㄙㄚˇ ㄕ)
to spread fertilizer over fields; to broadcast (fertilizer)
撒水(ㄙㄚˇ ㄕㄨㄟˇ)
to sprinkle or spray water
撒水車(ㄙㄚˇ ㄕㄨㄟˇ ㄔㄜ)
a truck sprayer; a street sprinkler: 撒水車在街上撒水。A truck sprayer sprinkles the street with water.
撒散(ㄙㄚˇ ㄙㄢˋ)
to spread; to scatter about; to strew; to sprinkle: 秋葉撒散在草地上。Autumn leaves strewed the lawn.
撒鹽(ㄙㄚˇ ㄧㄢˊ)
① to sprinkle salt ② to snow

【撤】 2030
ㄔㄜˋ cheh chè
to remove; to withdraw; to take back; to take away; to evacuate
撤保(ㄔㄜˋ ㄅㄠˇ)
to withdraw a guaranty
撤辦(ㄔㄜˋ ㄅㄢˋ)
to fire a delinquent official and subject him to disciplinary action
撤兵(ㄔㄜˋ ㄅㄧㄥ)
to withdraw troops: 敵人不得不自邊境撤兵。The enemy had to withdraw from the border.
撤廢(ㄔㄜˋ ㄈㄟˋ)
to abolish; to rescind; to revoke
撤防(ㄔㄜˋ ㄈㄤˊ)
to withdraw a garrison; to withdraw from a defended position
撤退(ㄔㄜˋ ㄊㄨㄟˋ)
(said of troops) to move back or withdraw: 軍隊撤退。The troops withdrew.
撤離(ㄔㄜˋ ㄌㄧˊ)
(said of troops) to move away or withdraw; to evacuate: 軍隊撤離碉堡。The soldiers evacuated the fort.
撤簾(ㄔㄜˋ ㄌㄧㄢˊ)
(said of an empress dowager) to turn over the reign of government to the young monarch when he comes of age
撤回(ㄔㄜˋ ㄏㄨㄟˊ)
to take back or withdraw: 原告已撤回起訴。The plaintiff has withdrawn charges.
撤去(ㄔㄜˋ ㄑㄩˋ)or 撤走(ㄔㄜˋ ㄗㄡˇ)
to remove; to withdraw; to pull out
撤席(ㄔㄜˋ ㄒㄧˊ)
to remove a dinner table (after a feast is over)
撤銷(ㄔㄜˋ ㄒㄧㄠ)
to abolish; to do away with
撤職(ㄔㄜˋ ㄓˊ)
to remove from office: 那位警官必須撤職。That police officer must be removed from his position.
撤差(ㄔㄜˋ ㄔㄞ)
to dismiss from a position; to fire: 你再遲到就要被撤差了。If you're late again, you will be dismissed (from your job).
撤懲(ㄔㄜˋ ㄔㄥˊ)
to remove from office and subject to disciplinary action
撤出(ㄔㄜˋ ㄔㄨ)
(said of troops) to withdraw or pull out
撤除(ㄔㄜˋ ㄔㄨˊ)
to abolish; to do away with; to remove; to dismantle
撤守(ㄔㄜˋ ㄕㄡˇ)
(said of a garrison) to withdraw or move back
撤任(ㄔㄜˋ ㄖㄣˋ)
to remove from office

【撥】 2031
ㄅㄛ bo bō
1. to dispel; to remove
2. to move; to transfer
3. to poke
4. to distribute; to issue
5. to set aside; to set apart; to appropriate; to allocate: 撥幾個房間給新生。Set aside a few rooms for the new students.
撥付(ㄅㄛ ㄈㄨˋ)
to make payment; to appropriate
撥電話號碼(ㄅㄛ ㄉㄧㄢˋ ㄏㄨㄚˋ ㄏㄠˋ ㄇㄚˇ)
to dial a telephone number
撥動(ㄅㄛ ㄉㄨㄥˋ)
① to move (the minute hand, etc.) by finger ② to turn (a switch)
撥剌(ㄅㄛ ㄌㄚˋ)
① the sound of fish jumping out of water or a sound similar to that ② not in the proper position ③ to draw the bow
撥浪鼓(ㄅㄛ ㄌㄤˋ ㄍㄨˇ)
a kind of rattle for children; a rattle drum
撥亂反正(ㄅㄛ ㄌㄨㄢˋ ㄈㄢˇ ㄓㄥˋ)
to put down rebellions and restore order; to bring order out of chaos

撥弄(ㄅㄛ ㄌㄨㄥˋ)
①to toy with ②to move to and fro; to pluck(a stringed instrument); to fiddle with: 這個小女孩正在撥弄琴弦。The little girl is plucking the strings of a fiddle. ③to stir up (disputes)

撥弄是非(ㄅㄛ ㄌㄨㄥˋ ㄕˋ ㄈㄟ)
to stir up (disputes): 撥弄是非的人終將自取其辱。Those who like to stir up disputes will finally invite humiliation.

撥給(ㄅㄛ ㄍㄟˇ)
to appropriate (supplies, funds, etc.): 前房撥給你的朋友用。The front room is appropriated to your friend.

撥開(ㄅㄛ ㄎㄞ)
to push aside

撥款(ㄅㄛ ㄎㄨㄢˇ)
to issue or appropriate funds; an appropriation: 已撥款一千萬爲建築新校舍之用。Ten million dollars has been appropriated for the new school buildings.

撥火棍(ㄅㄛ ㄏㄨㄛˇ ㄍㄨㄣˋ)
a poker (for stirring fire)

撥交(ㄅㄛ ㄐㄧㄠ)
to issue (supplies) to; to appropriate (funds) to

撥正(ㄅㄛ ㄓㄥˋ)
to set correct

撥準(ㄅㄛ ㄓㄨㄣˇ)
to set (a clock) correct

撥充(ㄅㄛ ㄔㄨㄥ)
to appropriate something for (a specific use)

撥冗(ㄅㄛ ㄖㄨㄥˇ)
to set aside a little time (for a special purpose) out of a tight schedule

撥雲見日(ㄅㄛ ㄩㄣˊ ㄐㄧㄢˋ ㄖˋ)
(literally) to dispel the clouds and see the sun—to give up sin in favor of virtue

撥用(ㄅㄛ ㄩㄥˋ)
to set apart for a specific use; to appropriate

【撳】 2032
ㄑㄧㄣˋ chinn qìn

to press with the hand

撳鈕戰爭(ㄑㄧㄣˋ ㄋㄧㄡˇ ㄓㄢˋ ㄓㄥ)
push-button warfare

撳鈴(ㄑㄧㄣˋ ㄌㄧㄥˊ)
to push a bell

撳壓(ㄑㄧㄣˋ ㄧㄚ)
to press down; to push down

【撏】 2033
ㄒㄩㄣˊ shyun xún

to take; to pick; to pluck

撏撦 or 撏扯(ㄒㄩㄣˊ ㄔㄜˇ)
to pick here and there

【撇】 2034
1. ㄆㄧㄝ pie piē

1. to cast away; to throw away; to abandon; to neglect: 他撇下妻兒。He abandoned his wife and children.
2. to skim

撇掉(ㄆㄧㄝ ㄉㄧㄠˋ)
to throw away; to cast away; to discard; to abandon: 不要把舊書撇掉。Don't throw away used books.

撇開(ㄆㄧㄝ ㄎㄞ)
to dismiss or exclude (from discussion or consideration); to set aside: 我們撇開這個問題不談。We'll dismiss this issue and not talk about it.

撇棄(ㄆㄧㄝ ㄑㄧˋ)
to cast away; to abandon; to give up; to discard

撇清(ㄆㄧㄝ ㄑㄧㄥ)
to pretend innocence

撇下不管(ㄆㄧㄝ ㄒㄧㄚˋ ㄅㄨˋ ㄍㄨㄢˇ)
① to disregard (one's responsibility): 工作暫且撇下不管。The work is disregarded temporarily. ② to desert (wife, children, etc.): 你不能將妻兒撇下不管。You should not desert your wife and children.

【撇】 2034
2. ㄆㄧㄝˇ piee piě

1. (calligraphy) a stroke made in the lower left direction
2. to purse the mouth (in contempt or to resist an impulse to cry)

撇蘭(ㄆㄧㄝˇ ㄌㄢˊ)
to raise money (for a drinking party, etc.) by drawing lots

撇嘴(ㄆㄧㄝˇ ㄗㄨㄟˇ)
to purse the mouth (in contempt, or to resist an impulse to cry)

【撓】 2035
ㄋㄠˊ nau náo

1. to bend; to daunt; to subjugate; to yield; to submit to superior force
2. to hinder; to obstruct: 罷工阻撓了工廠作業。A strike obstructed the work of the factory.
3. to scratch; to rub

撓敗(ㄋㄠˊ ㄅㄞˋ)or 撓北(ㄋㄠˊ ㄅㄟˋ)
to suffer defeat

撓頭(ㄋㄠˊ ㄊㄡˊ)
to scratch one's head (when one faces a difficult problem)—(figuratively) difficult to tackle; knotty; full of difficulty: 這可是撓頭的事。This is a knotty problem.

撓鉤(ㄋㄠˊ ㄍㄡ)
①a hook with a long handle used in fire fighting ②name of an ancient weapon

撓屈(ㄋㄠˊ ㄑㄩ)
to yield; to submit; to give way

撓性(ㄋㄠˊ ㄒㄧㄥˋ)
pliant; flexibility

撓折(ㄋㄠˊ ㄓㄜˊ)
to bend and break

撓癢癢(ㄋㄠˊ ㄧㄤˇ ˙ㄧㄤ)
to scratch an itchy part

【撙】 2036
ㄗㄨㄣˇ tzoen zǔn

1. to comply with
2. to economize; to save: 她每個月都撙下一些錢。She saved some money every month.

撙節(ㄗㄨㄣˇ ㄐㄧㄝˊ)
①to follow rule and order; to restrain; to exercise self-restraint ②to economize

撙節開支(ㄗㄨㄣˇ ㄐㄧㄝˊ ㄎㄞ ㄓ)
to economize expenses; to retrench

撙省(ㄗㄨㄣˇ ㄕㄥˇ)
to economize: 我們必須撙省燈光和燃料。We must economize on light and fuel.

【撚】 2037
ㄋㄧㄢˇ nean niǎn

to twist with fingers; to toy with

撚虎鬚(ㄋㄧㄢˇ ㄏㄨˇ ㄒㄩ)
to twist a tiger's whiskers—recklessly bold

撚錢(ㄋㄧㄢˇ ㄑㄧㄢˊ)
to spin a coin (for amusement, etc.)

撚香(ㄋㄧㄢˇ ㄒㄧㄤ)
to burn joss sticks in worship
撚鬚(ㄋㄧㄢˇ ㄒㄩ)
to toy with or stroke one's beard
撚指間(ㄋㄧㄢˇ ㄓˇ ㄐㄧㄢ)
at the snap of one's fingers—in an instant; in a jiffy
撚酸(ㄋㄧㄢˇ ㄙㄨㄢ)
to be jealous

【撕】 2038 ㄙ sy sī
to tear; to rip: 他將那封信撕得粉碎。He tore the letter into tiny pieces.
撕破(ㄙ ㄆㄛˋ)
to tear; to rip: 紙很容易撕破。Paper tears easily.
撕票(ㄙ ㄆㄧㄠˋ)
to kill a hostage
撕打(ㄙ ㄉㄚˇ)
to beat up; to maul
撕掉(ㄙ ㄉㄧㄠˋ)
to tear up; to tear off: 誰撕掉佈告? Who has torn the notice down from the notice board?
撕爛(ㄙ ㄌㄢˋ)
to tear to shreds; to rip to pieces
撕開(ㄙ ㄎㄞ)
to tear open; to rip open: 他撕開信封。He tore the envelope open.
撕毀(ㄙ ㄏㄨㄟˇ)
to destroy by tearing; to tear; to rip
撕去(ㄙ ㄑㄩˋ)or 撕走(ㄙ ㄗㄡˇ)
to tear off; to tear away
撕下(來)(ㄙ ㄒㄧㄚˋ (·ㄌㄞ))
to tear off (a leaf from a book, calendar, etc.): 撕下他的假面具。Tear off his mask.
撕碎(ㄙ ㄙㄨㄟˋ)
to tear or rip to pieces: 他將窗帘撕碎。He ripped the curtains to pieces.

【撞】 2039 ㄓㄨㄤˋ juanq zhuàng
1. to bump; to run into; to collide; to dash
2. to meet by chance
撞壁(ㄓㄨㄤˋ ㄅㄧˋ)
to be up against a blank wall—to be faced with difficulties
撞破(ㄓㄨㄤˋ ㄆㄛˋ)
①to hurt or damage by bumping ②to surprise somebody in an illegal act or awkward situation
撞騙(ㄓㄨㄤˋ ㄆㄧㄢˋ)
to swindle: 誠實的人不會撞騙。An honest man does not swindle.
撞大運(ㄓㄨㄤˋ ㄉㄚˋ ㄩㄣˋ)
to try one's luck
撞倒(ㄓㄨㄤˋ ㄉㄠˇ)
to knock down by bumping: 牆被卡車撞倒了。The wall was knocked down by a truck.
撞個滿懷(ㄓㄨㄤˋ ·ㄍㄜ ㄇㄢˇ ㄏㄨㄞˊ)
to bump into somebody
撞鬼(ㄓㄨㄤˋ ㄍㄨㄟˇ)
①to encounter a ghost ②to run around in distraction
撞開(ㄓㄨㄤˋ ㄎㄞ)
to knock away by bumping; to burst open
撞壞(ㄓㄨㄤˋ ㄏㄨㄞˋ)
to damage by bumping: 一輛公車撞壞了他的汽車。A bus ran into his car and damaged it.
撞擊(ㄓㄨㄤˋ ㄐㄧˊ)
to ram; to dash; to strike: 波浪撞擊岩石。The waves dashed on the rocks.
撞見(ㄓㄨㄤˋ ㄐㄧㄢˋ)
to meet unexpectedly; to run into; to bump into
撞球(ㄓㄨㄤˋ ㄑㄧㄡˊ)
①billiards ②billiard balls
撞球場(ㄓㄨㄤˋ ㄑㄧㄡˊ ㄔㄤˇ)or(ㄓㄨㄤˋ ㄑㄧㄡˊ ㄔㄤˊ)
a billiard room; a billiard saloon; a billiard parlor; a poolroom
撞針(ㄓㄨㄤˋ ㄓㄣ)
the firing pin (in a firearm)
撞傷(ㄓㄨㄤˋ ㄕㄤ)
to injure by bumping (as in car accidents)
撞入(ㄓㄨㄤˋ ㄖㄨˋ)or 撞進(ㄓㄨㄤˋ ㄐㄧㄣˋ)
to thrust into; to burst into: 他撞入房間。He burst into the room.
撞死(ㄓㄨㄤˋ ㄙˇ)
to kill by bumping (as in car accidents)

【撟】 2040 1.(矯) ㄐㄧㄠˇ jeau jiǎo
to put right; to set right
撟捷(ㄐㄧㄠˇ ㄐㄧㄝˊ)
nimble; agile 亦作「矯捷」

【撟】 2040 2. ㄐㄧㄠˋ jiaw jiào
to raise; to lift up
撟舌(ㄐㄧㄠˋ ㄕㄜˊ)
to raise the tongue in a futile effort to speak; to become speechless (as a result of extreme fear or surprise); tongue-tied

【撦】 2041 (扯) ㄔㄜˇ chee chě
to tear
撦破(ㄔㄜˇ ㄆㄛˋ)
to tear open 亦作「扯破」

【撫】 2042 ㄈㄨˇ fuu fǔ
1. to stroke; to touch
2. to soothe; to comfort; to console; to relieve
3. to bring up; to rear; to nurture; to foster
撫髀興歎(ㄈㄨˇ ㄅㄧˋ ㄒㄧㄥ ㄊㄢˋ)
to sigh in disappointment (said of one living in retirement but still burning with ambition)
撫摸(ㄈㄨˇ ㄇㄛ)or 撫摩(ㄈㄨˇ ㄇㄛˊ)
to pass one's hand over; to feel; to stroke
撫臺(ㄈㄨˇ ㄊㄞˊ)
a provincial governor (during the Ching Dynasty)
撫弄(ㄈㄨˇ ㄋㄨㄥˋ)
to stroke; to fondle
撫孤(ㄈㄨˇ ㄍㄨ)
to bring up orphans
撫棺痛哭(ㄈㄨˇ ㄍㄨㄢ ㄊㄨㄥˋ ㄎㄨ)
to mourn loudly over a coffin
撫躬自問(ㄈㄨˇ ㄍㄨㄥ ㄗˋ ㄨㄣˋ)
to perform self-examination
撫劍(ㄈㄨˇ ㄐㄧㄢˋ)
①to place the left hand on the sword one wears ②to hold a sword
撫今追昔(ㄈㄨˇ ㄐㄧㄣ ㄓㄨㄟ ㄒㄧˊ)
to contemplate the present and recall the past with emotion
撫軍(ㄈㄨˇ ㄐㄩㄣ)
①a provincial governor

〔手部〕

(during the Ching Dynasty) ②a military title in ancient China
撫琴(ㄈㄨˇ ㄑㄧㄣˊ)
to strum a stringed instrument
撫卹(ㄈㄨˇ ㄒㄩˋ)
to relieve; to comfort and compensate a bereaved family
撫卹金(ㄈㄨˇ ㄒㄩˋ ㄐㄧㄣ)
a pension: 他靠撫卹金過日子。He lives on a pension.
撫掌(ㄈㄨˇ ㄓㄤˇ)
to clap hands (to show happiness)
撫順(ㄈㄨˇ ㄕㄨㄣˋ)
Fushun (a city in Liaoning Province)
撫字(ㄈㄨˇ ㄗˋ)
①to love children ②(said of government officials in old China) to treat the people kindly
撫存(ㄈㄨˇ ㄘㄨㄣˊ)
to comfort and relieve
撫綏(ㄈㄨˇ ㄙㄨㄟ)
to soothe the people
撫愛(ㄈㄨˇ ㄞˋ)
to caress; to fondle
撫養(ㄈㄨˇ ㄧㄤˇ)
to bring up; to rear; to nurture: 是他祖母把他撫養大的。It was his grandmother that brought him up.
撫慰(ㄈㄨˇ ㄨㄟˋ)
to soothe; to comfort; to console: 母親用手撫慰孩子。The child was caressed by his mother with her hand.
撫育(ㄈㄨˇ ㄩˋ)
to bring up; to rear: 她獨力撫育子女。She reared her children alone.

〔手部〕

【播】 2043
ㄅㄛ boh bō
(語音 ㄅㄛˋ bo bò)
1. to sow; to seed: 尙不到播種的時候。It's not yet time to sow.
2. to spread; to propagate: 這消息很快傳播開了。The news soon spread.
3. to move
4. to cast away; to abandon
播報(ㄅㄛˋ ㄅㄠˋ)
to broadcast
播放(ㄅㄛˋ ㄈㄤˋ)
to broadcast (news, etc.) on the air: 這家電台正在播放晚間新聞。The station is broadcasting the evening news.
播蕩(ㄅㄛˋ ㄉㄤˋ)
to live in vagrancy; to be homeless
播弄(ㄅㄛˋ ㄋㄨㄥˋ)
①to stir up disputes on purpose ②to make a mess (of something)
播棄(ㄅㄛˋ ㄑㄧˋ)
to throw away; to cast away; to abandon; to discard
播遷(ㄅㄛˋ ㄑㄧㄢ)
to live a wandering life
播種(ㄅㄛˋ ㄓㄨㄥˇ)
to sow seed; to sow; to seed
播種機(ㄅㄛˋ ㄓㄨㄥˇ ㄐㄧ)
a sowing machine; a seeder; a drill (for row seeding)
播散(ㄅㄛˋ ㄙㄢˋ)
to disseminate
播送(ㄅㄛˋ ㄙㄨㄥˋ)
to broadcast (messages, programs, etc.); to transmit by radio
播音(ㄅㄛˋ ㄧㄣ)
to make broadcasts; to transmit; transmission
播音員(ㄅㄛˋ ㄧㄣ ㄩㄢˊ)
a broadcaster; an announcer
播揚(ㄅㄛˋ ㄧㄤˊ)
to propagate and uphold

【撩】 2044
1. ㄌㄧㄠˊ liau liáo
1. to provoke; to excite; to stir up; to tease; to tantalize
2. disorderly; confused
撩撥(ㄌㄧㄠˊ ㄅㄛ)
to provoke; to entice
撩蜂剔蠍(ㄌㄧㄠˊ ㄈㄥ ㄊㄧ ㄒㄧㄝ)
(literally) to provoke the bees and vex the scorpions—to provoke a wicked being and bring trouble upon oneself
撩逗(ㄌㄧㄠˊ ㄉㄡˋ)
to provoke; to entice
撩動肝火(ㄌㄧㄠˊ ㄉㄨㄥˋ ㄍㄢ ㄏㄨㄛˇ)
to stir up anger
撩慄(ㄌㄧㄠˊ ㄌㄧˋ)
dreary; dismal 亦作「憭慄」
撩亂(ㄌㄧㄠˊ ㄌㄨㄢˋ)
confused; disorderly
撩情(ㄌㄧㄠˊ ㄑㄧㄥˊ)
to flirt
撩人(ㄌㄧㄠˊ ㄖㄣˊ)
to make one excited

【撩】 2044
2. ㄌㄧㄠ lhiau liāo
1. to raise; to hold up
2. to sprinkle
撩起(ㄌㄧㄠ ㄑㄧˇ)
to raise or lift up (a curtain, screen, etc.)
撩水(ㄌㄧㄠ ㄕㄨㄟˇ)
to scoop water with the hands to sprinkle it
撩衣(ㄌㄧㄠ ㄧ)
to hold up the lower part of a garment

【撬】 2045
1. ㄑㄧㄠˋ chiaw qiào
to pry; to prize
撬不動(ㄑㄧㄠˋ ·ㄅㄨ ㄉㄨㄥˋ)
incapable of prying or being pried
撬不開(ㄑㄧㄠˋ ·ㄅㄨ ㄎㄞ)
incapable of prying open or being pried open
撬門(ㄑㄧㄠˋ ㄇㄣˊ)
to pry a door open
撬開(ㄑㄧㄠˋ ㄎㄞ)
to open by prying
撬孔(ㄑㄧㄠˋ ㄎㄨㄥˇ)
to make a hole by prying

【撬】 2045
2. ㄑㄧㄠ chiau qiāo
to raise; to lift

【撲】 2046
ㄆㄨ pu pū
1. to beat; to strike; to pound
2. to dash; to smash
3. to throw oneself on; to spring at
4. to flap; to flutter
撲鼻(ㄆㄨ ㄅㄧˊ)
to come suddenly into one's nostrils (as a strong smell): 香氣撲鼻。A sweet smell greeted us.
撲撲(ㄆㄨ ㄆㄨ)
throbs (of the heart, etc.); to throb: 他的心因興奮而撲撲地跳。His heart was throbbing with excitement.
撲滿(ㄆㄨ ㄇㄢˇ)
a savings box; a piggy bank
撲滅(ㄆㄨ ㄇㄧㄝˋ)
to exterminate (vermins); to extinguish (a fire)

撲面(ㄆㄨ ㄇㄧㄢˋ)
to brush the face (as a gust of wind): 和風撲面而來。The light breeze brushes my face.
撲罰(ㄆㄨ ㄈㄚˊ)
flogging; corporal punishment
撲粉(ㄆㄨ ㄈㄣˇ)
① to powder (one's face) ② talcum powder; face powder
撲打(ㄆㄨ ㄉㄚˇ)
to beat; to pat; to swat
撲的(ㄆㄨ ˙ㄉㄜ)
① used for the sound ② suddenly
撲燈蛾(ㄆㄨ ㄉㄥ ㄜˊ)
a night butterfly
撲地(ㄆㄨ ㄉㄧˋ)
① all over the ground ② to lie on the ground ③ the sound of an object dropping into the water, etc. ④ suddenly
撲跌(ㄆㄨ ㄉㄧㄝˊ)
bumping and falling (in wrestling, etc.)
撲騰(ㄆㄨ ˙ㄊㄥ)
① the sound of jumping; a thump ② to dance awkwardly ③ to be extravagant in spending ④ to make a big splash
撲通(ㄆㄨ ㄊㄨㄥ)
a plop; a splash; a thump
撲漉(ㄆㄨ ㄌㄨˋ)
whiz; the sound of a bird flapping its wings
撲落(ㄆㄨ ㄌㄨㄛˋ)
scattered about
撲過來(ㄆㄨ ㄍㄨㄛˋ ˙ㄌㄞ)
to come in a dash
撲克(ㄆㄨ ˙ㄎㄜ)
poker (a gambling game)
撲克牌(ㄆㄨ ˙ㄎㄜ ㄆㄞˊ)
playing cards
撲空(ㄆㄨ ㄎㄨㄥ)
① to fail to meet a person one intended to meet ② to do a thing in vain
撲救(ㄆㄨ ㄐㄧㄡˋ)
to fight (a fire)
撲哧(ㄆㄨ ㄔ)
① a chuckle ② a splash
撲食(ㄆㄨ ㄕˊ)
to seize for prey
撲殺(ㄆㄨ ㄕㄚ)
to kill
撲朔迷離(ㄆㄨ ㄕㄨㄛˋ ㄇㄧˊ ㄌㄧˊ)
①(said of a person) to look both like a man and a woman ② vague or ambiguous; complicated and confusing
撲簌簌(ㄆㄨ ㄙㄨˋ ㄙㄨˋ)
① dropping; trickling down ② rolling
撲兒(ㄆㄨㄦ)
a powder puff 亦作「粉撲兒」

【撰】2047
ㄓㄨㄢˋ juann zhuàn
to write; to compose: 他常常爲報紙撰稿。He often writes articles for newspapers.
撰擬(ㄓㄨㄢˋ ㄋㄧˇ)
to draw up or compose (a document)
撰錄(ㄓㄨㄢˋ ㄌㄨˋ)
to make a selection
撰稿(ㄓㄨㄢˋ ㄍㄠˇ)
to prepare manuscripts; to write
撰稿人(ㄓㄨㄢˋ ㄍㄠˇ ㄖㄣˊ)
a copywriter; a writer
撰寫(ㄓㄨㄢˋ ㄒㄧㄝˇ)
to write or compose (usually light works)
撰著(ㄓㄨㄢˋ ㄓㄨˋ)
to write or author (usually imposing works)
撰述(ㄓㄨㄢˋ ㄕㄨˋ)
to write an account of (facts, happenings, etc.); to narrate
撰文(ㄓㄨㄢˋ ㄨㄣˊ)
to compose; to write

【撮】2048
1. ㄘㄨㄛ tsuo cuō
(又讀 ㄘㄨㄛˋ tsuoh cuò)
1. to take with fingers
2. to gather
3. to extract; to summarize
4. a pinch of: 一小撮鹽 a pinch of salt
撮土(ㄘㄨㄛ ㄊㄨˇ)
① to take earth with fingers ② a pinch of earth
撮牛奶(ㄘㄨㄛ ㄋㄧㄡˊ ㄋㄞˇ)
to milk a cow
撮弄(ㄘㄨㄛ ㄋㄨㄥˋ)
① to juggle ② to instigate; to incite ③ to make fun of; to kid; to make a fool of
撮口呼(ㄘㄨㄛ ㄎㄡˇ ㄏㄨ) or (ㄘㄨㄛˇ ㄎㄡˇ ㄏㄨ)
(traditional Chinese phonetics) rhymes containing a rounded front vowel as in 魚(yü)、圓(yüan)、虛(hsü), etc.
撮合(ㄘㄨㄛ ㄏㄜˊ)
to bring (two persons or parties) together; to make a match
撮合山(ㄘㄨㄛ ㄏㄜˊ ㄕㄢ)
a matchmaker
撮箕(ㄘㄨㄛ ㄐㄧ)
a dustpan
撮壤(ㄘㄨㄛ ㄖㄤˇ)
a pinch of soil
撮要(ㄘㄨㄛ ㄧㄠˋ)
to select what is important; to make extracts; a synopsis; an abstract; an extract
撮影(ㄘㄨㄛ ㄧㄥˇ)
photography

【撮】2048
2. ㄗㄨㄛˇ tzuoo zuǒ
a tuft (of hair, grass, etc.)
撮子(ㄗㄨㄛˇ ˙ㄗ)
a tuft (of hair)

【撝】2049
ㄏㄨㄟ huei huī
1. to wave; to brandish
2. modest; humble
撝謙(ㄏㄨㄟ ㄑㄧㄢ)
modest; humble
撝損(ㄏㄨㄟ ㄙㄨㄣˇ)
to humble 亦作「撝遜」
撝挹(ㄏㄨㄟ ㄧˋ)
to be extremely modest or polite

【撣】2050
(揮) ㄉㄢˇ daan dǎn
1. to dust; to brush lightly; to whisk
2. a duster
撣灰(ㄉㄢˇ ㄏㄨㄟ)
to brush off dust; to dust: 請更加小心地撣灰。Please dust more carefully.
撣子(ㄉㄢˇ ˙ㄗ)
a duster: 鷄毛撣子 a feather duster

十三畫

【撻】2051
ㄊㄚˋ tah tà
to strike; to chastise; to flog;

〔手部〕

〔手部〕

to whip

撻伐(ㄊㄚˋ ㄈㄚˊ)
to send troops to punish; to launch a punitive expedition: 大張撻伐 to declare war on a country to punish its iniquities

撻罰(ㄊㄚˋ ㄈㄚˊ)
flogging; corporal punishment; to flog

撻市(ㄊㄚˋ ㄕˋ)
to disgrace somebody in public

撻辱(ㄊㄚˋ ㄖㄨˋ)
to beat and disgrace

【撼】 2052 ㄏㄢˋ hann hàn
to shake; to rock; to jolt; to joggle

撼頓(ㄏㄢˋ ㄉㄨㄣˋ)
to shake; to stagger; to totter

撼動(ㄏㄢˋ ㄉㄨㄥˋ)
to shake; to rock

撼天動地(ㄏㄢˋ ㄊㄧㄢ ㄉㄨㄥˋ ㄉㄧˋ)
to shake both the heaven and the earth—to cause a great sensation

撼落(ㄏㄢˋ ㄌㄨㄛˋ)
to shake and drop; to shake down

撼山岳，泣鬼神(ㄏㄢˋ ㄕㄢ ㄩㄝˋ，ㄑㄧˋ ㄍㄨㄟˇ ㄕㄣˊ)
so moving or affecting as to shake the mountains and wring tears from the spirits

撼樹(ㄏㄢˋ ㄕㄨˋ)
to shake a tree

撼搖(ㄏㄢˋ ㄧㄠˊ)
to shake; to rock; to jolt; to joggle

【撾】 2053 ㄓㄨㄚ jua zhuā
to beat; to strike

撾鼓(ㄓㄨㄚ ㄍㄨˇ)
to beat a drum

【擂】 2054 1. ㄌㄟˊ lei léi
1. to grind; to pestle
2. to beat; to hit: 我擂了他一下。I give him a punch.

擂鉢(ㄌㄟˊ ㄅㄛ)
a mortar (for grinding)

擂鼓(ㄌㄟˊ ㄍㄨˇ)
to beat a drum

擂鼓篩鑼(ㄌㄟˊ ㄍㄨˇ ㄕㄞ ㄌㄨㄛˊ)
to beat the drum and strike the gong—to have fanfare

【擂】 2054 2. ㄌㄟˋ ley lèi
see「擂臺」

擂臺(ㄌㄟˋ ㄊㄞˊ)
a platform for contests in martial arts; a ring (for martial contests); an arena

【擄】 2055 ㄌㄨˇ luu lǔ (又讀 ㄌㄨㄛˇ luoo luǒ)
to capture; to take captive

擄掠(ㄌㄨˇ ㄌㄩㄝˋ)
to plunder; to rob; to pillage

擄獲(ㄌㄨˇ ㄏㄨㄛˋ)
to capture; to take captive

擄劫(ㄌㄨˇ ㄐㄧㄝˊ)
to plunder; to rob

擄人勒贖(ㄌㄨˇ ㄖㄣˊ ㄌㄜˋ ㄕㄨˊ)
to kidnap a person for ransom

【擁】 2056 ㄩㄥˇ yeong yǒng (又讀 ㄩㄥ iong yōng)
1. to hug; to embrace; to hold
2. to have; to possess
3. to crowd; to throng; to swarm
4. to follow; to support

擁被而臥(ㄩㄥˇ ㄅㄟˋ ㄦˊ ㄨㄛˋ)
to lie down and cover oneself with a quilt

擁抱(ㄩㄥˇ ㄅㄠˋ)
to embrace; to hug; to hold in one's arms: 他熱烈地擁抱她。He held her to him in a warm embrace.

擁鼻(ㄩㄥˇ ㄅㄧˊ)
to hold one's nose

擁兵自重(ㄩㄥˇ ㄅㄧㄥ ㄗˋ ㄓㄨㄥˋ)
(said of warlords) to maintain an army and defy orders from the central government

擁兵自衛(ㄩㄥˇ ㄅㄧㄥ ㄗˋ ㄨㄟˋ)
to maintain an army for personal safety

擁戴(ㄩㄥˇ ㄉㄞˋ)
to support a leader or ruler; support

擁立(ㄩㄥˇ ㄌㄧˋ)
to set up a ruler or leader and declare allegiance to him

擁爐賞雪(ㄩㄥˇ ㄌㄨˊ ㄕㄤˇ ㄒㄩㄝˇ)
to enjoy the view of snow by the fireplace (a typical idle enjoyment of the old Chinese intelligentsia)

擁護(ㄩㄥˇ ㄏㄨˋ)
to advocate; to endorse; to support; to back

擁擠(ㄩㄥˇ ㄐㄧˇ)
crowded; packed: 假日時車輛特別擁擠。The vehicles are especially crowded on holiday.

擁擠不堪(ㄩㄥˇ ㄐㄧˇ ㄅㄨˋ ㄎㄢ)
intolerably crowded: 這個房間擁擠不堪。The room was intolerably crowded.

擁經問疾(ㄩㄥˇ ㄐㄧㄥ ㄨㄣˋ ㄐㄧˊ)
(said of a person in power) to treat a former teacher with respect

擁衾(ㄩㄥˇ ㄑㄧㄣ)
to go to bed

擁腫(ㄩㄥˇ ㄓㄨㄥˇ)
①(said of rock) rugged or gnarled ②morbidly swollen; unusually corpulent ③stupid and ignorant 亦作「臃腫」

擁上來(ㄩㄥˇ ㄕㄤˋ ·ㄌㄞ)
to come in a swarm

擁上心來(ㄩㄥˇ ㄕㄤˋ ㄒㄧㄣ ·ㄌㄞ)
(said of memories, emotions, etc.) to well up

擁書(ㄩㄥˇ ㄕㄨ)
to possess a large collection of books

擁入(ㄩㄥˇ ㄖㄨˋ)
to crowd into

擁塞(ㄩㄥˇ ㄙㄜˋ)
to clog or be clogged; to block up or be blocked up; a jam

擁遏(ㄩㄥˇ ㄜˋ)
to obstruct; to block

擁有(ㄩㄥˇ ㄧㄡˇ)
to have; to possess; to own: 中國擁有豐富的礦藏。China has rich mineral resources.

【擅】 2057 ㄕㄢˋ shann shàn
1. unauthorized; unilateral; arbitrary
2. to monopolize; to take exclusive possession
3. to be good at; to be expert in

擅便(ㄕㄢˋ ㄅㄧㄢˋ)
to consult one's own conve-

nience only

擅兵(ㄕㄢˋ ㄅㄧㄥ)
to maintain an army without authorization

擅美(ㄕㄢˋ ㄇㄟˇ)
to get all (the) credit: 我不敢擅美。I dare not claim all credit to myself.

擅命(ㄕㄢˋ ㄇㄧㄥˋ)
to defy restrictions or orders; to arrogate power to oneself

擅離職守(ㄕㄢˋ ㄌㄧˊ ㄓˊ ㄕㄡˇ)
to be absent without leave; to leave one's post without permission

擅利(ㄕㄢˋ ㄌㄧˋ)
to enjoy monopoly

擅改(ㄕㄢˋ ㄍㄞˇ)
to change or revise without authorization: 請不要擅改我的稿子。Please do not change or revise my manuscript.

擅國(ㄕㄢˋ ㄍㄨㄛˊ)
to assume the reins of government; to usurp the powers of the throne

擅取(ㄕㄢˋ ㄑㄩˇ)
to take without authorization (or permission)

擅權(ㄕㄢˋ ㄑㄩㄢˊ)
to assume dictatorial powers

擅長(ㄕㄢˋ ㄔㄤˊ)
to excel in; to be good at: 他擅長數學。He excels in mathematics.

擅場(ㄕㄢˋ ㄔㄤˇ)or(ㄕㄢˋ ㄔㄤˊ)
to dominate the scene

擅自(ㄕㄢˋ ㄗˋ)
to do something without authorization

擅自作主(ㄕㄢˋ ㄗˋ ㄗㄨㄛˋ ㄓㄨˇ)
to take an unauthorized action; to make a decision without authorization

擅作主張(ㄕㄢˋ ㄗㄨㄛˋ ㄓㄨˇ ㄓㄤ)
to make an unilateral or arbitrary decision

擅作威福(ㄕㄢˋ ㄗㄨㄛˋ ㄨㄟ ㄈㄨˊ)
to punish or reward according to one's whim

擅違(ㄕㄢˋ ㄨㄟˊ)
to disobey; to violate (regulations)

擅用(ㄕㄢˋ ㄩㄥˋ)
to use without permission

【操】 2058
ㄘㄠ tsau cāo

1. to handle; to manage
2. to hold; to grasp
3. to exercise; to drill
4. to speak
5. a Chinese family name

操法(ㄘㄠ ㄈㄚˇ)
method or procedure of military drill, physical exercises, etc.

操刀(ㄘㄠ ㄉㄠ)
to hold a knife or sword

操刀必割(ㄘㄠ ㄉㄠ ㄅㄧˋ ㄍㄜ)
to be sure to take advantage of a chance when it comes

操刀傷錦(ㄘㄠ ㄉㄠ ㄕㄤ ㄐㄧㄣˇ)
to do something beyond one's capability and end in failure

操典(ㄘㄠ ㄉㄧㄢˇ)
a drill manual; drill regulations

操勞(ㄘㄠ ㄌㄠˊ)
① to be under the weight of cares; to be loaded with cares; to work hard ② to take care; to look after

操勞過度(ㄘㄠ ㄌㄠˊ ㄍㄨㄛˋ ㄉㄨˋ)
to be excessively loaded with cares; to overwork (or strain) oneself; to burn the candle at both ends: 他因操勞過度而生病。He got ill by (or through) overwork.

操練(ㄘㄠ ㄌㄧㄢˋ)
to drill (in the military sense); to practice

操戈(ㄘㄠ ㄍㄜ)
to take up arms: 同室操戈 an internecine fight

操觚(ㄘㄠ ㄍㄨ)
① to engage in writing ② to practice a profession or craft

操奇計贏(ㄘㄠ ㄑㄧˊ ㄐㄧˋ ㄧㄥˊ)
(said of businessmen) shrewd and canny

操切(ㄘㄠ ㄑㄧㄝˋ)
hasty; eager; rash

操琴(ㄘㄠ ㄑㄧㄣˊ)
to accompany a singer with a fiddle, etc. (especially in Chinese opera)

操槍(ㄘㄠ ㄑㄧㄤ)
rifle drill: 學生們到兵營操槍。The students went to the barracks for rifle drill.

操權(ㄘㄠ ㄑㄩㄢˊ)
to wield power

操券(ㄘㄠ ㄑㄩㄢˋ)
to be sure of success

操心(ㄘㄠ ㄒㄧㄣ)
① to worry about; to trouble about; to take pains: 請不要操心。Please don't worry about it. ② to rack one's brains

操行(ㄘㄠ ㄒㄧㄥˋ)
conduct (in the moral sense); behavior or conduct of a student

操之過急(ㄘㄠ ㄓ ㄍㄨㄛˋ ㄐㄧˊ)
to be too eager for success

操舟(ㄘㄠ ㄓㄡ)
to steer a boat

操持(ㄘㄠ ㄔˊ)
to manage; to handle: 她終日操持家務。She managed household affairs all day long.

操場(ㄘㄠ ㄔㄤˇ)or(ㄘㄠ ㄔㄤˊ)
an athletic ground; a drill ground; a playground: 他們在操場上玩足球。They are playing football in the playground.

操手(ㄘㄠ ㄕㄡˇ)
(said of boxers) to spar as a practice

操守(ㄘㄠ ㄕㄡˇ)
discretion in conduct; attention to moral principles; moral fortitude; integrity

操神(ㄘㄠ ㄕㄣˊ)
to worry; to tax the mind or energy

操作(ㄘㄠ ㄗㄨㄛˋ)
to manipulate or operate (a machine); operation: 操作方法 the method of operation

操縱(ㄘㄠ ㄗㄨㄥˋ)
to manage, control, manipulate or operate (activities, machines, people, etc.)

操演(ㄘㄠ ㄧㄢˇ)
to drill; to exercise

【擔】 2059
1. (担) ㄉㄢ dan dān

to shoulder; to take upon oneself; to undertake; to suffer; to endure

擔保(ㄉㄢ ㄅㄠˇ)
to guarantee; to pledge; a

guaranty or guarantee; a pledge: 你能拿出什麼做擔保? What guarantee can you offer?
擔保人(ㄉㄢ ㄅㄠˇ ㄖㄣˊ)
a guarantor (or guarantee)
擔不是(ㄉㄢ ㄅㄨˊ ㄕˋ)
to bear the blame; to take the blame
擔不起(ㄉㄢ ·ㄅㄨ ㄑㄧˇ)
incapable of shouldering (a responsibility); do not dare to assume a responsibility
擔風險(ㄉㄢ ㄈㄥ ㄒㄧㄢˇ)
to run a risk
擔負(ㄉㄢ ㄈㄨˋ)
① a burden; responsibility ②to assume a responsibility; to undertake; to shoulder; to bear: 他不願擔負責任。He was not willing to shoulder responsibility.
擔待(ㄉㄢ ㄉㄞˋ)
to be lenient; to be magnanimous
擔戴(ㄉㄢ ㄉㄞˋ)
to assume responsibility for; to take upon oneself
擔當(ㄉㄢ ㄉㄤ)
to take (responsibility) upon oneself, or undertake (a task): 我懷疑他能否擔當重任。I wonder if he can take on heavy responsibilities.
擔擱(ㄉㄢ ㄍㄜ)
to delay; delay: 疾病擔擱了他學業的進步。Illness delayed his progress of study.
擔荷(ㄉㄢ ㄏㄜˋ)
to shoulder a burden; to assume a responsibility
擔架(ㄉㄢ ㄐㄧㄚˋ)
a stretcher (for carrying the sick and injured)
擔架兵(ㄉㄢ ㄐㄧㄚˋ ㄅㄧㄥ)
a stretcher-bearer
擔驚受怕(ㄉㄢ ㄐㄧㄥ ㄕㄡˋ ㄆㄚˋ)
to remain in a state of apprehension; to feel alarmed; to be in a state of anxiety
擔險(ㄉㄢ ㄒㄧㄢˇ)
to run a risk
擔心(ㄉㄢ ㄒㄧㄣ)
to worry; to feel anxious: 每週寫信給你母親, 免得她擔心。Write to your mother every week lest she might feel anxious.
擔承(ㄉㄢ ㄔㄥˊ)
to undertake, or assume the responsibility for (a task): 爲了家計, 他擔承額外工作。For the sake of the family's livelihood, he takes on extra work.
擔水(ㄉㄢ ㄕㄨㄟˇ)
to carry water with a carrying pole
擔任(ㄉㄢ ㄖㄣˋ)
to take charge of (a task); to work in the capacity of; to hold the post of
擔錯(ㄉㄢ ㄘㄨㄛˋ)
to take the blame for others
擔憂(ㄉㄢ ㄧㄡ)
to be anxious; to be apprehensive; to worry: 不用爲她的安全擔憂。Don't be anxious about her safety.

【擔】 2059
2. ㄉㄢˋ dann dàn

1. a load; a burden: 一擔菜(米) a load of vegetables (rice)
2. as in 扁擔—a carrying pole
3. a unit of weight or capacity
擔擔麵(ㄉㄢˋ ㄉㄢˋ ㄇㄧㄢˋ)
cooked noodles with liberal use of seasoning—a specialty in Szechwan cookery
擔子(ㄉㄢˋ ·ㄗ)
a load or burden upon the shoulder or the back

【擇】 2060
ㄗㄜˊ tzer zé
(又讀 ㄓㄞˊ jair zhái)

to select; to choose; to pick out: 二者任擇其一。Choose either of the two.
擇配(ㄗㄜˊ ㄆㄟˋ)
to choose a spouse
擇木(ㄗㄜˊ ㄇㄨˋ)
(literally) to choose a perch—to choose a master: 良禽擇木而棲。Good birds select trees on which they roost.
擇肥而噬(ㄗㄜˊ ㄈㄟˊ ㄦˊ ㄕˋ)
(literally) to select the fat ones and eat them—to select the rich for extortion
擇地(ㄗㄜˊ ㄉㄧˋ)
to choose a site (for a conference, building, etc.)
擇對(ㄗㄜˊ ㄉㄨㄟˋ)
to select a spouse or a mate
擇鄰(ㄗㄜˊ ㄌㄧㄣˊ)
to select neighbors
擇吉(ㄗㄜˊ ㄐㄧˊ)
to select an auspicious day (for a wedding, the opening of a store, etc.)
擇吉開張(ㄗㄜˊ ㄐㄧˊ ㄎㄞ ㄓㄤ)
to choose an auspicious day to start a business
擇交(ㄗㄜˊ ㄐㄧㄠ)
to select friends
擇期(ㄗㄜˊ ㄑㄧˊ)
to select a good time or day (for an undertaking, a wedding, etc.)
擇親(ㄗㄜˊ ㄑㄧㄣ)
to make marriage arrangements for one's children
擇婿(ㄗㄜˊ ㄒㄩˋ)
to choose a good husband for one's daughter
擇選(ㄗㄜˊ ㄒㄩㄢˇ)
to select; to choose 亦作「選擇」
擇食(ㄗㄜˊ ㄕˊ)
to select one's food: 飢不擇食。When one is starving, all food is delicious to him.
擇善固執(ㄗㄜˊ ㄕㄢˋ ㄍㄨˋ ㄓˊ)
to choose what is good and stick to it
擇善而從(ㄗㄜˊ ㄕㄢˋ ㄦˊ ㄘㄨㄥˊ)
to choose what is good and follow it
擇日(ㄗㄜˊ ㄖˋ)
to choose a good day (for an undertaking or ceremony)
擇人而事(ㄗㄜˊ ㄖㄣˊ ㄦˊ ㄕˋ)
① to choose the virtuous to serve ② to find the right man to marry
擇偶(ㄗㄜˊ ㄡˇ)
to select a spouse or a mate
擇業(ㄗㄜˊ ㄧㄝˋ)
to choose an occupation
擇友(ㄗㄜˊ ㄧㄡˇ)
to choose friends 參看「擇交」

【擋】 2061
1. ㄉㄤˋ danq dàng

used in the combination of 摒擋—to arrange in order; to pack up for traveling

【擋】 2061
2. ㄉㄤˇ daang dǎng

1. to obstruct; to impede; to stop; to resist; to ward off;

to block; to get in the way of: 防波堤無法擋住海浪的力量。The sea wall cannot resist the force of the waves.
2. a fender; a blind
3. a gear: 前進(後退)擋 forward (reverse) gear 低速擋 low (bottom) gear

擋不住(ㄉㄤˇ ˙ㄅㄨ ㄓㄨˋ)
incapable of blocking, hindering, impeding, stopping or shutting out

擋風(ㄉㄤˇ ㄈㄥ)
to keep the wind away; to keep off the wind

擋風玻璃(ㄉㄤˇ ㄈㄥ ㄅㄛ ˙ㄌㄧ)
a windshield

擋頭陣(ㄉㄤˇ ㄊㄡˊ ㄓㄣˋ)
to fight as a vanguard

擋土牆(ㄉㄤˇ ㄊㄨˇ ㄑㄧㄤˊ)
(construction) a retaining wall

擋泥板(ㄉㄤˇ ㄋㄧˊ ㄅㄢˇ)
a mudguard, or a fender

擋路(ㄉㄤˇ ㄌㄨˋ)
to be in the way; to obstruct traffic: 落石擋路。The roads were obstructed by falls of rock.

擋橫兒(ㄉㄤˇ ㄏㄥˊㄦ)
to guard someone from violence

擋駕(ㄉㄤˇ ㄐㄧㄚˋ)
to decline to receive visitors; to stop visitors from entering a place or calling on somebody

擋箭牌(ㄉㄤˇ ㄐㄧㄢˋ ㄆㄞˊ)
①a shield ②(figuratively) anyone or anything which is used as a protective shield; an excuse; a pretext

擋住(ㄉㄤˇ ㄓㄨˋ)
to block; to impede; to hinder; to obstruct: 濃霧擋住了司機的視線。The thick mist obstructed the driver's view.

擋眼(ㄉㄤˇ ㄧㄢˇ)
to obstruct one's view

擋雨(ㄉㄤˇ ㄩˇ)
to keep off the rain; to shelter one from the rain: 她撐著傘擋雨。She held an umbrella to shelter herself from the rain.

【擒】 2062
ㄑㄧㄣˊ chyn qín
to arrest; to capture; to seize: 罪犯已就擒。The criminal has submitted to arrest.

擒捕(ㄑㄧㄣˊ ㄅㄨˇ)
to arrest; to capture

擒拿(ㄑㄧㄣˊ ㄋㄚˊ)
to arrest; to capture

擒拿法(ㄑㄧㄣˊ ㄋㄚˊ ㄈㄚˇ)or 擒拿術(ㄑㄧㄣˊ ㄋㄚˊ ㄕㄨˋ)
arrest technique

擒獲(ㄑㄧㄣˊ ㄏㄨㄛˋ)
to arrest; to capture

擒斬(ㄑㄧㄣˊ ㄓㄢˇ)
to capture and behead

擒住(ㄑㄧㄣˊ ㄓㄨˋ)
to succeed in capturing

擒捉(ㄑㄧㄣˊ ㄓㄨㄛ)
to arrest; to capture

擒賊先擒王(ㄑㄧㄣˊ ㄗㄟˊ ㄒㄧㄢ ㄑㄧㄣˊ ㄨㄤˊ)
(literally) If you want to capture a group of bandits, capture the ringleader first. —to assign priority properly; to stress what should be done first

擒縱(ㄑㄧㄣˊ ㄗㄨㄥˋ)
arresting and releasing; alternate measures of severity and mercy

【據】 2063
(据) ㄐㄩˋ jiuh jù
1. according to; on the basis of; on the grounds of
2. to depend on
3. to occupy; to take possession of; to seize
4. proof; evidence
5. a Chinese family name

據報(ㄐㄩˋ ㄅㄠˋ)or 據報導(ㄐㄩˋ ㄅㄠˋ ㄉㄠˇ)
according to reports

據點(ㄐㄩˋ ㄉㄧㄢˇ)
a base (for operations or activities); a fortified point; a stronghole

據理力爭(ㄐㄩˋ ㄌㄧˇ ㄌㄧˋ ㄓㄥ)
to argue vigorously on the basis of sound reason or justice

據情(ㄐㄩˋ ㄑㄧㄥˊ)
according to circumstances

據悉(ㄐㄩˋ ㄒㄧ)
It is reported that....

據險(ㄐㄩˋ ㄒㄧㄢˇ)
to hold strategic positions

據稱(ㄐㄩˋ ㄔㄥ)
according to reports, claims, or assertions

據傳(ㄐㄩˋ ㄔㄨㄢˊ)
a story is going around that; the story goes that; rumour has it that; it is rumoured that

據實(ㄐㄩˋ ㄕˊ)
according to the fact

據守(ㄐㄩˋ ㄕㄡˇ)
to hold a position against attack; to make a stand; to stand one's ground

據說(ㄐㄩˋ ㄕㄨㄛ)
It is said that.... 或 according to hearsay

據此(ㄐㄩˋ ㄘˇ)
(a conventional phrase in official correspondence) on these grounds

據有(ㄐㄩˋ ㄧㄡˇ)
to take possession of; to appropriate

據我看(來)(ㄐㄩˋ ㄨㄛˇ ㄎㄢˋ (ㄌㄞˊ))
as I see it; in my opinion: 據我看來，你錯了。In my opinion, you're wrong.

據我所知(ㄐㄩˋ ㄨㄛˇ ㄙㄨㄛˇ ㄓ)
as far as I know

據爲己有(ㄐㄩˋ ㄨㄟˊ ㄐㄧˇ ㄧㄡˇ)
to take possession (of what does not belong to oneself)

據云(ㄐㄩˋ ㄩㄣˊ)
according to report; it is said that…

【擗】 2064
ㄆㄧˋ pih pì
to beat the breast

擗踊(ㄆㄧˋ ㄩㄥˇ)
to beat the breast and stamp the feet in great grief

【擀】 2065
ㄍㄢˇ gaan gǎn
1. to stretch out with a rolling pin: 擀餃子皮 to roll out dumpling wrappers
2. to polish; to shine

擀麪(ㄍㄢˇ ㄇㄧㄢˋ)
to roll dough

擀麪杖(ㄍㄢˇ ㄇㄧㄢˋ ㄓㄤˋ)
a rolling pin

【擐】 2066
ㄏㄨㄢˋ huann huàn
to put on; to wear

擐甲執兵(ㄏㄨㄢˋ ㄐㄧㄚˇ ㄓˊ ㄅㄧㄥ)

to put on one's armor and take up arms

【撿】 2067 ㄐㄧㄢˇ jean jiǎn

to pick up; to collect; to gather: 我昨天撿到一個錢包。I picked up a purse yesterday.

撿破爛(ㄐㄧㄢˇ ㄆㄛˋ ㄌㄢˋ)
to collect scrap

撿破爛的(ㄐㄧㄢˇ ㄆㄛˋ ㄌㄢˋ ·ㄉㄜ)
a rag picker; a junk collector

撿起來(ㄐㄧㄢˇ ㄑㄧˇ ·ㄌㄞ)
to pick up (from the ground or floor): 將地上的紙片撿起來。Pick up the scraps of paper on the floor.

撿柴(ㄐㄧㄢˇ ㄔㄞˊ)
to collect firewood

【擓】 2068 ㄎㄨㄞˇ koai kuǎi

1. to scratch (lightly)
2. to carry on the arm

擓破(ㄎㄨㄞˇ ㄆㄛˋ)
to break by scratching

擓籃子(ㄎㄨㄞˇ ㄌㄢˊ ·ㄗ)
to carry a basket on the arm

擓癢癢兒(ㄎㄨㄞˇ ㄧㄤˇ ·ㄧㄤㄦ)
to scratch an itchy spot

【擊】 2069 ㄐㄧˊ jyi jí

to beat; to strike; to attack; to hit; to bump into: 聲東擊西 to make a feint attack on the east but strike on the west

擊敗(ㄐㄧˊ ㄅㄞˋ)
to defeat; to beat; to conquer: 被擊敗的敵人很快就投降了。The beaten enemy soon surrendered.

擊斃(ㄐㄧˊ ㄅㄧˋ)
to beat to death; to shoot to death

擊破(ㄐㄧˊ ㄆㄛˋ)
to smash or defeat (an enemy force); to crush (enemy defense): 各個擊破 to destroy one by one

擊缶(ㄐㄧˊ ㄈㄡˇ)
to beat time with a percussion instrument made of clay

擊倒(ㄐㄧˊ ㄉㄠˇ)
to knock down; to floor

擊柝(ㄐㄧˊ ㄊㄨㄛˋ)
to beat the watches

擊退(ㄐㄧˊ ㄊㄨㄟˋ)
to beat back; to drive back; to repel; to repulse: 敵人慘遭擊退。The enemy was badly beaten back.

擊落(ㄐㄧˊ ㄌㄨㄛˋ)
to shoot down (aircraft); to down: 他們擊落一些鴨子。They shot down several ducks.

擊鼓鳴冤(ㄐㄧˊ ㄍㄨˇ ㄇㄧㄥˊ ㄩㄢ)
(in old China) to beat the drum at the magistrate's door to bring a grievance to his attention

擊潰(ㄐㄧˊ ㄎㄨㄟˋ)
① to knock to pieces ② to defeat; to rout (the enemy troops)

擊毀(ㄐㄧˊ ㄏㄨㄟˇ)
to smash; to wreck; to shatter; to destroy

擊楫中流(ㄐㄧˊ ㄐㄧˊ ㄓㄨㄥ ㄌㄧㄡˊ)
to vow to annihilate the rebels—referring to Tsu Ti (祖逖), a general who made such a vow while crossing a river

擊節稱賞(ㄐㄧˊ ㄐㄧㄝˊ ㄔㄥ ㄕㄤˇ)
to applaud; to admire greatly; to show appreciation (of a poem or a piece of music) by beating time

擊劍(ㄐㄧˊ ㄐㄧㄢˋ)
fencing: 我哥哥是擊劍教師。My elder brother is a fencing master.

擊球(ㄐㄧˊ ㄑㄧㄡˊ)
(baseball) batting

擊掌(ㄐㄧˊ ㄓㄤˇ)
to clap hands

擊筑(ㄐㄧˊ ㄓㄨˊ)
to strike a stringed instrument which resembles 箏 but is played with a bamboo rod

擊沉(ㄐㄧˊ ㄔㄣˊ)
to sink (vessels by bombarding, bombing, or torpedoing)

擊傷(ㄐㄧˊ ㄕㄤ)
to wound (with bullets); to damage (a vessel, airplane, tank, etc.) by shelling, bombing, etc.

擊賞(ㄐㄧˊ ㄕㄤˇ)
to show appreciation by clapping hands

擊壤(ㄐㄧˊ ㄖㄤˇ)
(literally) to play pushpin—to live in peace and comfort

擊刺(ㄐㄧˊ ㄘˋ)
to stab: 他由背後擊刺敵人。He stabbed his enemy in the back.

擊碎(ㄐㄧˊ ㄙㄨㄟˋ)
to knock to pieces; to smash to pieces: 石頭擊碎窗戶。The rock smashed the window.

【擎】 2070 ㄑㄧㄥˊ chyng qíng

to lift; to support; to prop up: 衆擎易舉。It is much easier for many people to lift a load.

擎天柱(ㄑㄧㄥˊ ㄊㄧㄢ ㄓㄨˋ)
a mythological pillar supporting the heaven—a person who is the mainstay of a nation or a family

擎天神(ㄑㄧㄥˊ ㄊㄧㄢ ㄕㄣˊ)
Atlas (a Titan, son of Iapetus)

擎起(ㄑㄧㄥˊ ㄑㄧˇ)
to lift up

擎手(ㄑㄧㄥˊ ㄕㄡˇ)
to raise one's hands—to stop doing a thing

【擘】 2071 ㄅㄛˋ boh bò

1. the thumb
2. an outstanding person; an authority in a certain field
3. to split; to tear apart; to break: 擘紙 to tear paper

擘裂(ㄅㄛˋ ㄌㄧㄝˋ)
to hew apart; to rend apart; to cleave; to split

擘窠(ㄅㄛˋ ㄎㄜ)
the technique of writing characters of gigantic size

擘開(ㄅㄛˋ ㄎㄞ)
to open (hard-rinded fruit); to break open; to break off

擘箜篌(ㄅㄛˋ ㄎㄨㄥ ㄏㄡˊ)
name of an ancient musical instrument

擘畫(ㄅㄛˋ ㄏㄨㄚˋ)
to plan; to scheme; to make arrangements for: 此事尙待擘畫。This has yet to be planned.

擘肌分理(ㄅㄛˋ ㄐㄧ ㄈㄣ ㄌㄧˇ)
to make a very detailed

analysis
擘張(ㄅㄛˋ ㄓㄤ)
to draw (a bow)

十四畫

【擠】 2072 ㄐㄧˇ jii jǐ
1. to push; to jostle: 別擠。Do not push. 或 Stop pushing.
2. to wring; to squeeze; to twist; to press: 把水擠掉 to squeeze the water out; to wring out water
3. to crowd; to throng; to cram; to pack: 不要統統擠在一塊。Don't all crowd together.

擠不動(ㄐㄧˇ ·ㄅㄨ ㄉㄨㄥˋ)
unable to budge because of crowdedness
擠眉弄眼(ㄐㄧˇ ㄇㄟˊ ㄋㄨㄥˋ ㄧㄢˇ)
to make eyes; to wink
擠滿(ㄐㄧˇ ㄇㄢˇ)
to pack (a place, car, etc.) to capacity: 這房間擠滿了客人。The room was crowded with guests.
擠兌(ㄐㄧˇ ㄉㄨㄟˋ)
a run on a bank
擠奶(ㄐㄧˇ ㄋㄞˇ) or 擠乳(ㄐㄧˇ ㄖㄨˇ)
to draw or press milk; to milk a cow
擠來擠去(ㄐㄧˇ ㄌㄞˊ ㄐㄧˇ ㄑㄩˋ)
to push about; to jostle
擠咕眼兒(ㄐㄧˇ ·ㄍㄨ ㄧㄚˇㄦ)
to wink
擠擠插插(ㄐㄧˇ ·ㄐㄧ ㄔㄚ ㄔㄚ)
crowded
擠進擠出(ㄐㄧˇ ㄐㄧㄣˋ ㄐㄧˇ ㄔㄨ)
to squeeze in and out (of a crowded place)
擠陷(ㄐㄧˇ ㄒㄧㄢˋ)
to do harm intentionally
擠上去(ㄐㄧˇ ㄕㄤˋ ·ㄑㄩ)
to force oneself up (onto a crowded bus, etc.)
擠抑(ㄐㄧˇ ㄧˋ) or 擠軋(ㄐㄧˇ ㄧㄚˋ)
to keep another down or out
擠壓(ㄐㄧˇ ㄧㄚ)
extruding
擠牙膏(ㄐㄧˇ ㄧㄚˊ ㄍㄠ)
to squeeze toothpaste from the tube

【擡】 2073 (抬) ㄊㄞˊ tair tái
to lift; to raise; to carry: 他擡起右手。He raised his right hand.

擡不動(ㄊㄞˊ ·ㄅㄨ ㄉㄨㄥˋ)
incapable of lifting or being lifted
擡頭(ㄊㄞˊ ㄊㄡˊ)
① to raise one's head ② (said of the price) an upsurge; (said of fortune) a turn for the better ③ a bank's salutation for a client
擡頭挺胸(ㄊㄞˊ ㄊㄡˊ ㄊㄧㄥˇ ㄒㄩㄥ)
(literally) chin up and chest out—full of confidence or pride
擡頭見喜(ㄊㄞˊ ㄊㄡˊ ㄐㄧㄢˋ ㄒㄧˇ)
to raise one's head and see bliss (a self-congratulatory expression written on a slip of red paper pasted up at a prominent place in a house to greet the Chinese Lunar New Year)
擡高身價(ㄊㄞˊ ㄍㄠ ㄕㄣ ㄐㄧㄚˋ)
to raise oneself in others' esteem (by means of stratagems instead of real accomplishments)
擡高物價(ㄊㄞˊ ㄍㄠ ㄨˋ ㄐㄧㄚˋ)
to raise commodity prices; to effect a price hike
擡槓(ㄊㄞˊ ㄍㄤˋ)
to argue for the sake of arguing; to wrangle; to quarrel; to bicker: 他們倆已擡槓好幾個小時了。Those two have been bickering for hours.
擡轎的(ㄊㄞˊ ㄐㄧㄠˋ ·ㄉㄜ)
① a sedan-chair bearer ② supporters; followers
擡轎子(ㄊㄞˊ ㄐㄧㄠˋ ·ㄗ)
① to carry a sedan chair ② to gang up in cheating someone in gambling ③ to support or help someone
擡舉(ㄊㄞˊ ㄐㄩˇ)
to do a good turn or favor; a good turn or favor
擡手動脚(ㄊㄞˊ ㄕㄡˇ ㄉㄨㄥˋ ㄐㄧㄠˇ)
personal behavior or bearing; manner

【擢】 2074 ㄓㄨㄛˊ jwo zhuó
1. to take out; to pull out; to extract; to pick out; to select
2. to promote; to raise (in rank)

擢髮難數(ㄓㄨㄛˊ ㄈㄚˇ ㄋㄢˊ ㄕㄨˇ)
① guilty of faults as innumerable as one's hair ② to be too numerous to count
擢第(ㄓㄨㄛˊ ㄉㄧˋ)
to get chosen by passing an examination
擢秀(ㄓㄨㄛˊ ㄒㄧㄡˋ)
①(said of vegetation) luxuriant ②(said of a person) talented, or gifted
擢升 or 擢昇(ㄓㄨㄛˊ ㄕㄥ)
to promote (an official, etc.); to advance (to a higher position or rank)
擢引(ㄓㄨㄛˊ ㄧㄣˇ)
to pick and promote (promising employees or subordinates)
擢用(ㄓㄨㄛˊ ㄩㄥˋ)
to pick and promote (promising employees or subordinates)

【擣】 2075 (搗) ㄉㄠˇ dao dǎo
1. to pound; to beat
2. to attack
3. to harass; to disturb

擣米(ㄉㄠˇ ㄇㄧˇ)
to hull rice in a mortar
擣爛(ㄉㄠˇ ㄌㄢˋ)
to pound into a pulp
擣練(ㄉㄠˇ ㄌㄧㄢˋ)
to mix or knead by pounding
擣亂(ㄉㄠˇ ㄌㄨㄢˋ)
to make trouble
擣鬼(ㄉㄠˇ ㄍㄨㄟˇ)
to do mischief
擣虛(ㄉㄠˇ ㄒㄩ)
to launch a surprise attack
擣衣(ㄉㄠˇ ㄧ)
to wash clothes by pounding them with a wooden pounder
擣藥(ㄉㄠˇ ㄧㄠˋ)
to mix drugs by pounding in a mortar

【擬】 2076 ㄋㄧˇ nii nǐ
1. to plan; to intend; to decide; to determine
2. to draft; to draw up; to design
3. to imitate

擬辦(ㄋㄧˇ ㄅㄢˋ)
to intend to execute or man-

〔手部〕

age (a cliché in official documents)
擬定(ㄋㄧˇ ㄉㄧㄥˋ)
to draw up or map out (a plan); to draft
擬態(ㄋㄧˇ ㄊㄞˋ)
mimicry (of insects); imitation
擬妥(ㄋㄧˇ ㄊㄨㄛˇ)
to have drawn up (a plan, a draft, etc.)
擬稿(ㄋㄧˇ ㄍㄠˇ)
to prepare manuscripts or write copies (for publication)
擬古(ㄋㄧˇ ㄍㄨˇ)
to imitate classical models
擬規畫圓(ㄋㄧˇ ㄍㄨㄟ ㄏㄨㄚˋ ㄩㄢˊ)
(literally) to draw circles with a compass— to stick to convention unimaginatively
擬就(ㄋㄧˇ ㄐㄧㄡˋ)
to have completed formulation or preparation (of a plan, a draft, etc.)
擬具(ㄋㄧˇ ㄐㄩˋ)
to draw up (a proposal, a plan, etc.)
擬請(ㄋㄧˇ ㄑㄧㄥˇ)
to intend to ask or request
擬人法(ㄋㄧˇ ㄖㄣˊ ㄈㄚˇ)
(rhetoric) personification 亦作「擬人化」
擬作(ㄋㄧˇ ㄗㄨㄛˋ)
an imitation
擬議(ㄋㄧˇ ㄧˋ)
① a tentative decision reached after discussion ② a proposal for deliberation: 他的擬議不會被採用的。His recommendations won't be adopted.

【擯】 2077
ㄅㄧㄣˋ binn bìn

1. to expel; to reject; to oust; to get rid of; to discard
2. same as 儐—an usher

擯落(ㄅㄧㄣˋ ㄌㄨㄛˋ)
to suffer rejection and downfall
擯介(ㄅㄧㄣˋ ㄐㄧㄝˋ)
a person serving to bridge the gap between the host and the guest
擯棄(ㄅㄧㄣˋ ㄑㄧˋ)
to cast away; to set aside; to discard; to desert
擯相(ㄅㄧㄣˋ ㄒㄧㄤˋ)
① the master of ceremonies ② the best man or bridesmaid 亦作「儐相」: 誰當你的女擯相? Who will be your bridesmaid?
擯斥(ㄅㄧㄣˋ ㄔˋ)
to reject; to expel; to repudiate: 他們將他擯斥於圈外。They expelled him from their circle.
擯除(ㄅㄧㄣˋ ㄔㄨˊ)
to expel; to oust; to eliminate; to dispense with
擯黜(ㄅㄧㄣˋ ㄔㄨˋ)
to banish; to exile

【擦】 2078
ㄘㄚ tsa cā

1. to wipe; to mop; to scrub; to polish
2. to spread on; to put on
3. to rub; to graze; to scratch
4. to brush; to shaved

擦玻璃(ㄘㄚ ㄅㄛ ·ㄌㄧ)
to wipe glass; to wipe window panes
擦布(ㄘㄚ ㄅㄨˋ)
wiping rags
擦皮鞋(ㄘㄚ ㄆㄧˊ ㄒㄧㄝˊ)
to shine shoes
擦抹(ㄘㄚ ㄇㄛˇ)
to wipe
擦地板(ㄘㄚ ㄉㄧˋ ㄅㄢˇ)
to scrub the floor; to mop the floor
擦銅油(ㄘㄚ ㄊㄨㄥˊ ㄧㄡˊ)
brass polish
擦臉(ㄘㄚ ㄌㄧㄢˇ)
to wipe one's face
擦亮(ㄘㄚ ㄌㄧㄤˋ)
to shine (shoes, utensils, etc.): 好好擦亮靴子。Put a good shine on the boots.
擦亮眼睛(ㄘㄚ ㄌㄧㄤˋ ㄧㄢˇ ㄐㄧㄥ)
① to remove the scales from one's eyes ② to be watchful
擦乾(ㄘㄚ ㄍㄢ)
to swab up; to wipe dry
擦乾淨(ㄘㄚ ㄍㄢ ·ㄐㄧㄥ)
to wipe clean; to clean by wiping: 將濺出的牛奶擦乾淨。Wipe up the spilt milk.
擦黑兒(ㄘㄚ ㄏㄜㄦ)
approaching evening; dusk
擦汗(ㄘㄚ ㄏㄢˋ)
to wipe off sweat or perspiration: 運動之後要記得擦汗。Remember to wipe off sweat after exercise.
擦槍(ㄘㄚ ㄑㄧㄤ)
to swab rifles
擦去(ㄘㄚ ·ㄑㄩ)
to wipe off: 他擦去臉上的汗。He wiped the sweat from his face.
擦洗(ㄘㄚ ㄒㄧˇ)
to scrub: 這地板需要好好擦洗一番。The floor needs a good scrub.
擦鞋童(ㄘㄚ ㄒㄧㄝˊ ㄊㄨㄥˊ)
a shoeshine boy; a shoeblack
擦鞋油(ㄘㄚ ㄒㄧㄝˊ ㄧㄡˊ)
shoe polish
擦車(ㄘㄚ ㄔㄜ)
to wax a car, bicycle, etc.
擦拭(ㄘㄚ ㄕˋ)
to clean; to cleanse
擦身而過(ㄘㄚ ㄕㄣ ㄦˊ ㄍㄨㄛˋ)or 擦肩而過(ㄘㄚ ㄐㄧㄢ ㄦˊ ㄍㄨㄛˋ)
to pass each other so close that they almost rub each other; to brush past somebody
擦傷(ㄘㄚ ㄕㄤ)
a scratch; to suffer a scratch: 他擦傷了膝蓋。He rubbed the skin off his knee.
擦子(ㄘㄚ ·ㄗ)
a rubber; an eraser
擦擦(ㄘㄚ ㄘㄚ)
the sound of footsteps
擦油(ㄘㄚ ㄧㄡˊ)
to coat with oil; to apply pomade; to oil; to varnish or grease

【擱】 2079
ㄍㄜ ge gē

1. to lay; to leave; to put: 他把手擱在口袋中。He put his hands in his pockets.
2. to file: 把這些信件仔細擱起來。File these letters carefully.
3. to delay; to put aside

擱筆(ㄍㄜ ㄅㄧˇ)
to lay down the pen—to stop writing: 我已擱筆十年了。I've stopped writing for ten years.
擱不下(ㄍㄜ ·ㄅㄨ ㄒㄧㄚˋ)
unable to lay down or aside (work); unable to forget: 她擱不下那些瑣事。She is unable to forget those trifles.

擱不住(ㄍㄜ ˙ㄅㄨ ㄓㄨˋ)
①not fit to be kept long ② cannot stand
擱得下(ㄍㄜ ˙ㄉㄜ ㄒㄧㄚˋ)
capable of putting down or aside: 我怎麼擱得下這麼重要的事呢? How can I put aside such an important matter?
擱得住(ㄍㄜ ˙ㄉㄜ ㄓㄨˋ)
fit to be kept long
擱起(ㄍㄜ ˙ㄑㄧ)
to delay; to hold up
擱淺(ㄍㄜ ㄑㄧㄢˇ)
①to be held up by some obstacle; to run aground; to get stranded: 船擱淺了。The ship got stranded (or ran aground). ②(said of negotiations) to come to a deadlock: 會議完全擱淺了。The meeting has totally come to a deadlock.
擱下(ㄍㄜ ˙ㄒㄧㄚ)
to put aside or lay down (work): 他把工作擱下了。He put aside his work.
擱置(ㄍㄜ ㄓˋ)
to shelve or pigeonhole (a plan, proposal, etc.): 我們擱置了一項動議。We have shelved a motion.

【擭】2080 ㄏㄨㄛˋ huoh huò
1. a trap; a snare
2. to catch; to seize

【擤】2081 ㄒㄧㄥˇ shiing xǐng
to blow (the nose)
擤鼻涕(ㄒㄧㄥˇ ㄅㄧˊ ㄊㄧˋ)or 擤鼻子(ㄒㄧㄥˇ ㄅㄧˊ ˙ㄗ)
to blow the nose

【擰】2082 1. ㄋㄧㄥˊ ning níng
to twist; to pinch; to wring: 把溼毛巾擰乾。Wring out the wet towel.
擰眉瞪眼(ㄋㄧㄥˊ ㄇㄟˊ ㄉㄥˋ ㄧㄢˇ)
to look angry
擰眉立目(ㄋㄧㄥˊ ㄇㄟˊ ㄌㄧˋ ㄇㄨˋ)
to look angry

【擰】2082 2. ㄋㄧㄥˇ niing nǐng
1. to wrench; to twist; to screw: 請把瓶蓋擰開。Screw (or Twist) the cap off the bottle, please.
2. wrong; mistaken
3. to differ; to disagree
擰了(ㄋㄧㄥˇ ˙ㄌㄜ)
to fail: 我們的計畫全擰了。All our plans failed.
擰開(ㄋㄧㄥˇ ㄎㄞ)
to wrench apart: 他擰開門鎖。He wrenched the locked door open.

【擰】2082 3. ㄋㄧㄥˋ ninq nìng
determined; dogged; stubborn
擰性(ㄋㄧㄥˋ ˙ㄒㄧㄥ)
doggedness; stubbornness
擰種(ㄋㄧㄥˋ ㄓㄨㄥˇ)
a stubborn fellow

【擪】2083 ㄧㄝˋ yeh yè
to press with a finger

十五畫

【擲】2084 ㄓˊ jyr zhí
to throw; to cast
擲標槍(ㄓˊ ㄅㄧㄠ ㄑㄧㄤ)
(sports) ① javelin throw ② to throw the javelin
擲瓶(ㄓˊ ㄆㄧㄥˊ)
to throw the bottle (in launching a ship)
擲彈筒(ㄓˊ ㄉㄢˋ ㄊㄨㄥˇ)
a grenade launcher
擲地(ㄓˊ ㄉㄧˋ)
to throw to the ground
擲地金聲(ㄓˊ ㄉㄧˋ ㄐㄧㄣ ㄕㄥ)or 擲地有聲(ㄓˊ ㄉㄧˋ ㄧㄡˇ ㄕㄥ)
(said of literary works) extremely elegant and valuable: 他的文章眞是擲地有聲。His articles are indeed extremely valuable.
擲鐵餅(ㄓˊ ㄊㄧㄝˇ ㄅㄧㄥˇ)
(sports) discus throw
擲鐵球(ㄓˊ ㄊㄧㄝˇ ㄑㄧㄡˊ)or 擲鉛球(ㄓˊ ㄑㄧㄢ ㄑㄧㄡˊ)
(sports) shot put
擲還(ㄓˊ ㄏㄨㄢˊ)
to return (something) to me 或 Please return (something) to me.
擲交(ㄓˊ ㄐㄧㄠ)
to hand over; please hand... to me
擲下(ㄓˊ ㄒㄧㄚˋ)
please hand…to me
擲骰子 or 擲色子(ㄓˊ ㄕㄞˇ ˙ㄗ)
to cast dice; to throw dice
擲梭(ㄓˊ ㄙㄨㄛ)
(said of time) to pass as quickly as a shuttle

【擷】2085 ㄒㄧㄝˊ shye xié (又讀 ㄐㄧㄝˊ jye jié)
to pick; to collect; to gather
擷芳(ㄒㄧㄝˊ ㄈㄤ)
to pick flowers
擷取精華(ㄒㄧㄝˊ ㄑㄩˇ ㄐㄧㄥ ㄏㄨㄚˊ)
to pick the best
擷采(ㄒㄧㄝˊ ㄘㄞˇ)
to cull; to pick; to gather

【擴】2086 ㄎㄨㄛˋ kuoh kuò
to enlarge; to magnify; to expand; to extend
擴大(ㄎㄨㄛˋ ㄉㄚˋ)
①to enlarge; to expand; to magnify; to widen; to broaden: 擴大眼界 to widen one's outlook; to broaden one's horizons ②to swell; to distend; to dilate
擴建(ㄎㄨㄛˋ ㄐㄧㄢˋ)
to extend (a factory, mine, etc.)
擴軍(ㄎㄨㄛˋ ㄐㄩㄣ)
a military buildup; armament expansion; to enlarge military forces
擴展(ㄎㄨㄛˋ ㄓㄢˇ)
to stretch; to expand; to extend; to spread: 日本的貿易很快地擴展至世界各地。Japanese trade expanded rapidly in all parts of the world.
擴張(ㄎㄨㄛˋ ㄓㄤ)
①to stretch; to extend; to spread; to expand ②to dilate; dilation: 血管擴張 blood vessel dilation
擴充(ㄎㄨㄛˋ ㄔㄨㄥ)
to expand; to enlarge; expansion; extension
擴散(ㄎㄨㄛˋ ㄙㄢˋ)
① (physics) to diffuse; diffusion ②to scatter about
擴音器(ㄎㄨㄛˋ ㄧㄣ ㄑㄧˋ)
a megaphone; a microphone

【擺】2087 ㄅㄞˇ bae bǎi
1. to arrange; to display; to place; to put: 把這本書擺到架子上。Put the book on the shelf.
2. to wave; to swing; to oscil-

late; to wag: 這隻狗的尾巴來回地擺動著。The dog's tail waves to and fro.
3. a pendulum
4. to assume; to put on

擺撥(ㄅㄞˇ ㄅㄛ)
to dismiss from attention; to put aside

擺佈(ㄅㄞˇ ㄅㄨˋ)
①to manage or handle (a person): 我絕不任人擺佈。I'll never allow myself to be ordered about. ②to arrange

擺不開(ㄅㄞˇ ˙ㄅㄨ ㄎㄞ) or 擺不下(ㄅㄞˇ ˙ㄅㄨ ㄒㄧㄚˋ)
① There is no room to place it. ② The business in hand cannot be shaken off.

擺平(ㄅㄞˇ ㄆㄧㄥˊ)
①(slang) to make satisfied ②to put down something securely

擺譜兒(ㄅㄞˇ ㄆㄨˇㄦ)
to take pains to show off; to try to appear rich and elegant

擺門面(ㄅㄞˇ ㄇㄣˊ ㄇㄧㄢˋ) or 擺場面(ㄅㄞˇ ㄔㄤˇ ㄇㄧㄢˋ)
to keep up appearances

擺飯(ㄅㄞˇ ㄈㄢˋ)
to lay the table for a meal

擺渡(ㄅㄞˇ ˙ㄉㄨ)
to cross a river on a ferry; to ferry

擺動(ㄅㄞˇ ㄉㄨㄥˋ)
to sway; to flicker; to swing; to oscillate

擺動角(ㄅㄞˇ ㄉㄨㄥˋ ㄐㄧㄠˇ)
an angle of oscillation

擺攤兒(ㄅㄞˇ ㄊㄚㄦ)
to set up a (vending) stand

擺頭(ㄅㄞˇ ㄊㄡˊ)
to shake one's head (to show disapproval)

擺脫(ㄅㄞˇ ㄊㄨㄛ)
to free oneself from; to cast off; to get away from; to shake off (a tailer)

擺弄(ㄅㄞˇ ㄋㄨㄥˋ)
①to toy with; to play with ②to make fun of; to trick

擺擂臺(ㄅㄞˇ ㄌㄟˋ ㄊㄞˊ)
to give an open challenge

擺列(ㄅㄞˇ ㄌㄧㄝˋ)
to display in neat rows; to place in order

擺龍門陣(ㄅㄞˇ ㄌㄨㄥˊ ㄇㄣˊ ㄓㄣˋ)
to get together and gossip; to make leisurely conversation

擺供(ㄅㄞˇ ㄍㄨㄥˋ)
to offer sacrifices

擺開(ㄅㄞˇ ㄎㄞ)
to arrange; to place for display

擺闊(ㄅㄞˇ ㄎㄨㄛˋ)
to show off one's wealth

擺空架子(ㄅㄞˇ ㄎㄨㄥ ㄐㄧㄚˋ ˙ㄗ)
to affect superiority

擺好(ㄅㄞˇ ㄏㄠˇ)
to place or set properly

擺架子(ㄅㄞˇ ㄐㄧㄚˋ ˙ㄗ)
to be arrogant; to be snobbish; to put on airs

擺酒(席)(ㄅㄞˇ ㄐㄧㄡˇ (ㄒㄧˊ))
to give a banquet

擺局(ㄅㄞˇ ㄐㄩˊ)
to arrange a ruse

擺齊(ㄅㄞˇ ㄑㄧˊ)
to place in neat order: 把架子上的東西全擺齊。Place everything on the shelf in neat order.

擺下(ㄅㄞˇ ˙ㄒㄧㄚ)
①to put down ②to arrange

擺針(ㄅㄞˇ ㄓㄣ)
an oscillating needle (on a meter, etc.)

擺陣(ㄅㄞˇ ㄓㄣˋ)
to deploy troops

擺桌子(ㄅㄞˇ ㄓㄨㄛ ˙ㄗ)
to set the table

擺出(來)(ㄅㄞˇ ㄔㄨ (˙ㄌㄞ))
①to take out for display ②to assume; to put on: 他擺出一副無辜的樣子。He assumed a look of innocence.

擺錘(ㄅㄞˇ ㄔㄨㄟˊ)
a pendulum

擺時(ㄅㄞˇ ㄕˊ)
the period of oscillation

擺設(ㄅㄞˇ ㄕㄜˋ)
to furnish and decorate (a room): 屋裏擺設得很好。The house is well furnished.

擺設兒(ㄅㄞˇ ㄕㄜˋㄦ)
articles for interior decoration: 這間屋子有很多小擺設兒。There are a lot of knickknacks in this room.

擺手(ㄅㄞˇ ㄕㄡˇ)
to swing one's arms: 他擺手向我告別。He waved goodbye to me.

擺上(ㄅㄞˇ ˙ㄕㄤ)
to put up (for display)

擺子(ㄅㄞˇ ˙ㄗ)
malaria 亦作「瘧疾」

擺夷(ㄅㄞˇ ㄧˊ)
a small ethnic group living in Szechwan and Yünnan

擺樣子(ㄅㄞˇ ㄧㄤˋ ˙ㄗ)
to put on for appearance's sake

擺烏龍(ㄅㄞˇ ㄨ ㄌㄨㄥˊ)
to talk irresponsibly; to speak with exaggeration

擺尾(ㄅㄞˇ ㄨㄟˇ)
to wag the tail

【擾】 2088 ㄖㄠˇ rao rǎo

1. to disturb; to agitate; to harass; to trouble
2. to trespass on somebody's hospitality: 叨擾,叨擾。Thank you for your hospitality.
3. disorder

擾民(ㄖㄠˇ ㄇㄧㄣˊ)
to harass the people (by tyrannical policies, etc.)

擾動(ㄖㄠˇ ㄉㄨㄥˋ)
to disturb; to agitate

擾亂(ㄖㄠˇ ㄌㄨㄢˋ)
to disturb; to agitate; to harass (enemy troops); to create confusion: 別擾亂我的視線。Don't interfere with my view.

擾亂治安(ㄖㄠˇ ㄌㄨㄢˋ ㄓˋ ㄢ)
to disturb peace and order

擾害(ㄖㄠˇ ㄏㄞˋ)
to harass and injure

擾攘(ㄖㄠˇ ㄖㄤˇ)
disturbance; tumult; hustle and bustle

【擿】 2089 ㄊㄧˋ tih tì

1. to instigate; to incite
2. to expose

擿伏(ㄊㄧˋ ㄈㄨˊ)
to bring a secret to light; to expose evil

擿問(ㄊㄧˋ ㄨㄣˋ)
to interrogate

【擻】 2090 ㄙㄡˇ soou sǒu

to shake; to quake; to tremble; to flutter

擻抖抖(ㄙㄡˇ ㄉㄡˇ ㄉㄡˇ)

trembling; shivering

【攄】2091 ㄕㄨ shu shū
to make known; to vent

攄憤(ㄕㄨ ㄈㄣˋ)
to vent one's indignation

攄懷(ㄕㄨ ㄏㄨㄞˊ)
to give vent to one's emotion

攄陳(ㄕㄨ ㄔㄣˊ)
to present (a proposal, an opinion, etc.)

攄誠(ㄕㄨ ㄔㄥˊ)
to be frank

攄意(ㄕㄨ ㄧˋ)
to give expression to one's feelings

【攆】2092 ㄋㄧㄢˇ nean niǎn
1. to expel; to oust; to drive
2. to catch up

攆不開(ㄋㄧㄢˇ ·ㄅㄨ ㄎㄞ)
to try in vain to drive (a person) away; impossible to drive (a person) away

攆跑了(ㄋㄧㄢˇ ㄆㄠˇ ·ㄌㄜ)
to have driven (someone) away

攆逐(ㄋㄧㄢˇ ㄓㄨˊ)
to drive (someone) away; to throw (someone) out; to expel; to oust

攆出去(ㄋㄧㄢˇ ㄔㄨ ·ㄑㄩ)
to throw (someone) out; to drive away: 你不該把他攆出去的。You shouldn't have thrown him out.

攆走(ㄋㄧㄢˇ ㄗㄡˇ)
to drive (someone) away; to dismiss: 他攆走一個做事愛拖延的工人。He dismissed a dilatory worker.

【攀】2093 ㄆㄢ pan pān
1. to hold to; to climb; to hang on; to clamber
2. to involve

攀附(ㄆㄢ ㄈㄨˋ)
to hang on or to attach oneself to (power, glory, etc.)

攀登(ㄆㄢ ㄉㄥ)
to climb; to scale

攀談(ㄆㄢ ㄊㄢˊ)
to strike up a conversation; to drag another into conversation: 他們用英語攀談。They struck up a conversation in English.

攀留(ㄆㄢ ㄌㄧㄡˊ)
to detain (a guest)

攀連(ㄆㄢ ㄌㄧㄢˊ)
to involve; to implicate

攀戀(ㄆㄢ ㄌㄧㄢˋ)
to regret the resignation of (a popular superior, official, etc.)

攀鱗(ㄆㄢ ㄌㄧㄣˊ)
to ride on the coattails of a brilliant master

攀龍附鳳(ㄆㄢ ㄌㄨㄥˊ ㄈㄨˋ ㄈㄥˋ)
(literally) to hang on a dragon and stick to a phoenix—to establish oneself by riding on the coattails of a brilliant master; to put oneself under the patronage of a bigwig

攀龍附驥(ㄆㄢ ㄌㄨㄥˊ ㄈㄨˋ ㄐㄧˋ)
(literally) to ride on a dragon and a steed—to try to achieve success by riding on the coattails of a brilliant master

攀桂(ㄆㄢ ㄍㄨㄟˋ)
(in old China) to pass the civil service examination

攀供(ㄆㄢ ㄍㄨㄥ)
to offer a false testimony to implicate someone

攀花折柳(ㄆㄢ ㄏㄨㄚ ㄓㄜˊ ㄌㄧㄡˇ)
(literally) to injure flowers and willows—to lead a life of debauchery

攀親(ㄆㄢ ㄑㄧㄣ)
① to seek marriage ② to remind others (particularly the influential and wealthy) of the relationship one has with them

攀親道故(ㄆㄢ ㄑㄧㄣ ㄉㄠˋ ㄍㄨˋ)
to claim the ties of blood or friendship

攀折(ㄆㄢ ㄓㄜˊ)
to injure (a plant) by picking or breaking

攀扯(ㄆㄢ ㄔㄜˇ)
to drag into an affair; to implicate: 他被攀扯於一件罪案中。He is implicated in a crime.

攀纏(ㄆㄢ ㄔㄢˊ)
to hang on persistently; to keep annoying by inappropriate talks or requests

攀鞍上馬(ㄆㄢ ㄢ ㄕㄤˋ ㄇㄚˇ)
to mount a horse

攀援(ㄆㄢ ㄩㄢˊ)
to hang on an influential person

攀緣(ㄆㄢ ㄩㄢˊ)
①(Buddhism) to be affected by one's environment ② to climb; to clamber

攀緣莖(ㄆㄢ ㄩㄢˊ ㄐㄧㄥ)
(botany) clinging stem

攀轅扣馬(ㄆㄢ ㄩㄢˊ ㄎㄡˋ ㄇㄚˇ)
(said of people in old China) to try to stop the departure of a popular official by stopping his carriage from leaving

攀轅臥轍(ㄆㄢ ㄩㄢˊ ㄨㄛˋ ㄔㄜˋ)
(said of people in old China) to try to stop the departure of a popular official by grasping the shafts of his carriage and lying down in the wheel ruts

十六畫

【攏】2094 1. ㄌㄨㄥˇ loong lǒng
1. to gather; to collect; to tie: 把乾草攏住。Tie the hay in a bundle.
2. to lean
3. to come alongside; to approach; to reach
4. to add up; to sum up
5. to comb (hair)

攏頭(ㄌㄨㄥˇ ㄊㄡˊ)
to comb hair

攏共(ㄌㄨㄥˇ ㄍㄨㄥˋ)
altogether; in total

攏總(ㄌㄨㄥˇ ㄗㄨㄥˇ)
altogether; in total

攏岸(ㄌㄨㄥˇ ㄢˋ)
(said of a ship) to approach the shore

【攏】2094 2. ㄌㄨㄥˊ long lóng
a special fingering in playing the lute

十七畫

【攔】2095 ㄌㄢˊ lan lán
to impede; to obstruct; to hinder; to block; to bar; to hold back

〔手部〕

攔不住(ㄌㄢˊ ·ㄅㄨ ㄓㄨˋ)
incapable of impeding or being impeded; cannot stop or be stopped

攔擋(ㄌㄢˊ ㄉㄤˇ)
to impede; to obstruct; to hinder; to block: 球員想攔擋他的對手。The player tried to block his opponent.

攔路(ㄌㄢˊ ㄌㄨˋ)or 攔道(ㄌㄢˊ ㄉㄠˋ)
to block the way: 攔路搶劫 to waylay; to hold up

攔河壩(ㄌㄢˊ ㄏㄜˊ ㄅㄚˋ)
a dam (across a river)

攔擊(ㄌㄢˊ ㄐㄧˊ)
to intercept and attack; to volley

攔街虎(ㄌㄢˊ ㄐㄧㄝ ㄏㄨˇ)
a street robber

攔劫(ㄌㄢˊ ㄐㄧㄝˊ)
to intercept and rob

攔截(ㄌㄢˊ ㄐㄧㄝˊ)
to intercept; to attack or stop on the way

攔住(ㄌㄢˊ ·ㄓㄨˋ)
to obstruct; to block; to hinder; to stop

攔車(ㄌㄢˊ ㄔㄜ)
to interrupt the course of a vehicle; to stop a vehicle

攔沙壩(ㄌㄢˊ ㄕㄚ ㄅㄚˋ)
a check dam

攔水閘(ㄌㄢˊ ㄕㄨㄟˇ ㄓㄚˊ)
a dam lock; a dam gate

攔阻(ㄌㄢˊ ㄗㄨˇ)
to impede; to obstruct; to hinder; to block; to stop: 倒下的樹木攔阻道路。The fallen trees obstruct the road.

攔腰(ㄌㄢˊ ㄧㄠ)
①by the waist: 他把我攔腰抱住。He held me by the waist. ② to cut across in the middle

【攖】 2096
ㄧㄥ ing yīng
1. to offend; to irritate
2. to disturb; to stir up

攖其鋒(ㄧㄥ ㄑㄧˊ ㄈㄥ)
to blunt the thrust (of an attacking force)

攖人心(ㄧㄥ ㄖㄣˊ ㄒㄧㄣ)
to disturb peace of mind

【攘】 2097
1. ㄖㄤˇ raang rǎng
confused; disorderly

攘攘(ㄖㄤˇ ㄖㄤˇ)
in a state of confusion: 街上人潮熙熙攘攘。Streams of people busily come and go on the street.

【攘】 2097
2. ㄖㄤˊ rang ráng
1. to take by force
2. to eliminate; to repel; to resist
3. to shake

攘辟(ㄖㄤˊ ㄅㄧˋ)
to stand off; to make way

攘臂(ㄖㄤˊ ㄅㄧˋ)
to bare one's hands—to rise to action with a determined shake of the arms

攘臂高呼(ㄖㄤˊ ㄅㄧˋ ㄍㄠ ㄏㄨ)
to raise one's hands and shout

攘袂(ㄖㄤˊ ㄇㄟˋ)
to push up one's sleeves and bare one's arms—to rise to action with a determined shake of the arms

攘奪(ㄖㄤˊ ㄉㄨㄛˊ)
to take by force

攘詬(ㄖㄤˊ ㄍㄡˋ)
to clear oneself of a dishonor; to cleanse oneself of dishonor

攘竊(ㄖㄤˊ ㄑㄧㄝˋ)
to steal; to pilfer; to filch

攘袖(ㄖㄤˊ ㄒㄧㄡˋ)
to roll up sleeves

攘場(ㄖㄤˊ ㄔㄤˊ)or(ㄖㄤˊ ㄔㄤˊ)
to spread harvested grain over an area

攘除(ㄖㄤˊ ㄔㄨˊ)
to rid; to eliminate; to dispel

攘善(ㄖㄤˊ ㄕㄢˋ)
to appropriate other's credit or honor to be his own

攘災(ㄖㄤˊ ㄗㄞ)
to ward off calamities; to avoid disaster

攘夷(ㄖㄤˊ ㄧˊ)
to repel the barbarians

【攙】 2098
ㄔㄢ chan chān
1. to lead (a person) by the hand; to support or assist somebody while standing or walking
2. to mix; to blend

攙扶(ㄔㄢ ㄈㄨˊ)
to lead (a person) by the hand

攙合(ㄔㄢ ㄏㄜˊ)or 攙和(ㄔㄢ ㄏㄜˊ)
to mix; to blend; to mingle

攙話接舌(ㄔㄢ ㄏㄨㄚˋ ㄐㄧㄝ ㄕㄜˊ)
to slander others

攙夥(ㄔㄢ ㄏㄨㄛˇ)
to mix up; to jumble together

攙假(ㄔㄢ ㄐㄧㄚˇ)
to add impurities; to adulterate: 攙假的食物有害健康。Adulterated food is bad for the health.

攙起(ㄔㄢ ㄑㄧˇ)
to help someone stand up by giving him a hand

攙親(ㄔㄢ ㄑㄧㄣ)
to help the bride out of her sedan chair (a rite performed usually by a relatively well-to-do matron among her new relatives)

攙雜(ㄔㄢ ㄗㄚˊ)
to make impure; to add imitation goods or inferior products to a shipment of merchandise in violation of business ethics: 別把糖和鹽攙雜在一起。Don't mix up the sugar with the salt.

攙嘴(ㄔㄢ ㄗㄨㄟˇ)
to interrupt

十八畫

【攛】 2099
ㄘㄨㄢ tsuan cuān
1. to throw; to fling
2. to urge; to persuade
3. to do in a hurry

攛掇(ㄘㄨㄢ ·ㄉㄨㄛ)
to urge; to persuade; to induce; to egg on: 他們攛掇我們一同去。They urged us to go with them.

攛弄(ㄘㄨㄢ ·ㄋㄨㄥ)
to urge; to persuade; to induce

【攜】 2100
(攜、携、擕) ㄒㄧㄝˊ shye xié
(讀音 ㄒㄧ shi xī)
1. to take; to carry
2. to help; to lead

攜抱(ㄒㄧㄝˊ ㄅㄠˋ)
to carry in one's arms

攜帶(ㄒㄧㄝˊ ㄉㄞˋ)
to carry with oneself; to

take along
攜同(ㄒㄧㄝˊ ㄊㄨㄥˊ)
to bring along
攜眷(ㄒㄧㄝˊ ㄐㄩㄢˋ)
to take one's family along: 如果我出國讀書，我想攜眷同行。If I study abroad, I want to travel with my family.
攜手(ㄒㄧㄝˊ ㄕㄡˇ)
① to hold each other's hand: 讓我們攜手同進。Let's join hands and advance together. ② to cooperate
攜貳(ㄒㄧㄝˊ ㄦˋ)
to cherish treachery
攜幼(ㄒㄧㄝˊ ㄧㄡˋ)
to take one's young children along

【攝】 2101 ㄕㄜˋ sheh she
1. to take in; to absorb; to attract
2. to take a photograph (or a shot) of
3. to regulate
4. to represent
攝理(ㄕㄜˋ ㄌㄧˇ)
to manage in place of another; to hold (an office) in an acting capacity
攝力(ㄕㄜˋ ㄌㄧˋ)
(physics) attraction
攝錄放映機(ㄕㄜˋ ㄌㄨˋ ㄈㄤˋ ㄧㄥˋ ㄐㄧ)
(television) a camcorder
攝護腺(ㄕㄜˋ ㄏㄨˋ ㄒㄧㄢˋ)
the prostate; the prostate gland
攝魂(ㄕㄜˋ ㄏㄨㄣˊ)
to summon souls of the dead
攝魂奪魄(ㄕㄜˋ ㄏㄨㄣˊ ㄉㄨㄛˊ ㄆㄛˋ)
to hold spellbound; spellbinding
攝取(ㄕㄜˋ ㄑㄩˇ)
① to take in; to absorb; to assimilate ② to take a photograph of; to shoot
攝行(ㄕㄜˋ ㄒㄧㄥˊ)
to act for another
攝製(ㄕㄜˋ ㄓˋ)
(said of a movie or documentary) produced by; to produce
攝政(ㄕㄜˋ ㄓㄥˋ) or 攝主(ㄕㄜˋ ㄓㄨˇ)
to serve as regent; the Prince Regent
攝政王(ㄕㄜˋ ㄓㄥˋ ㄨㄤˊ)
the Prince Regent
攝篆(ㄕㄜˋ ㄓㄨㄢˋ)
to act as a deputy
攝持(ㄕㄜˋ ㄔˊ)
to take proper care of one's life
攝氏寒暑表(ㄕㄜˋ ㄕˋ ㄏㄢˊ ㄕㄨˇ ㄅㄧㄠˇ) or 攝氏溫度計(ㄕㄜˋ ㄕˋ ㄨㄣ ㄉㄨˋ ㄐㄧˋ)
a centigrade thermometer; a Celsius thermometer
攝生(ㄕㄜˋ ㄕㄥ)
to pay attention to health; to keep fit; hygiene: 你應該學習攝生之道。You should learn how to keep fit.
攝影(ㄕㄜˋ ㄧㄥˇ)
photography; to take a photograph of: 我們畢業時攝影留念。We took a souvenir photograph at graduation.
攝影棚(ㄕㄜˋ ㄧㄥˇ ㄆㄥˊ)
a sound stage; a (movie) studio
攝影機(ㄕㄜˋ ㄧㄥˇ ㄐㄧ)
a camera
攝位(ㄕㄜˋ ㄨㄟˋ)
to assume the throne in place of the legitimate ruler
攝衛(ㄕㄜˋ ㄨㄟˋ)
to take care of one's health

十九畫

【攢】 2102 1. ㄗㄢˇ tzaan zǎn
to hoard; to save; to accumulate
攢錢(ㄗㄢˇ ㄑㄧㄢˊ)
to hoard money: 這對夫婦正攢錢買別墅。The couple are saving money to buy a villa.

【攢】 2102 2. ㄘㄨㄢˊ tswan cuán
to bring together; to gather; to assemble; to collect
攢盤兒(ㄘㄨㄢˊ ㄆㄚˊㄦ)
a sundry dish
攢眉蹙額(ㄘㄨㄢˊ ㄇㄟˊ ㄘㄨˋ ㄜˊ)
to knit the brows: 她攢眉蹙額，似乎感到不快。She knitted her brows and looked displeased.
攢蹄(ㄘㄨㄢˊ ㄊㄧˊ)
(said of horses) to gallop
攢盒(ㄘㄨㄢˊ ㄏㄜˊ)
a container for holding various foods simultaneously
攢聚(ㄘㄨㄢˊ ㄐㄩˋ)
to huddle together; to crowd together: 孩子們攢聚在一起取暖。The children huddled together for warmth.
攢錢(ㄘㄨㄢˊ ㄑㄧㄢˊ)
to put money together (for some purpose)
攢簇(ㄘㄨㄢˊ ㄘㄨˋ)
to crowd together
攢毆(ㄘㄨㄢˊ ㄡ)
to gather together and beat (a person)

【攤】 2103 ㄊㄢ tan tān
1. to spread; to open: 把棉被攤開曬一曬。Spread the quilt to dry in the sun.
2. to divide equally; to apportion: 分攤責任 to distribute responsibility
3. a booth; a stand; a stall: 水果攤 a fruit stall
4. a collection of liquid; a pool of (water, mud, blood, etc.): 我的車子陷入一攤泥中。My car stuck in a pool of mud of the road.
攤牌(ㄊㄢ ㄆㄞˊ)
a showdown; to have a showdown
攤派(ㄊㄢ ㄆㄞˋ)
to apportion
攤販(ㄊㄢ ㄈㄢˋ)
a vender or stallkeeper; a seller on the sidewalk
攤開(ㄊㄢ ㄎㄞ)
to spread out; to unfold
攤款(ㄊㄢ ㄎㄨㄢˇ) or 攤錢(ㄊㄢ ㄑㄧㄢˊ)
to share the burden of a payment: 每人攤款一百元。Each will share one hundred dollars.
攤還(ㄊㄢ ㄏㄨㄢˊ)
to repay in installments; to amortize
攤認(ㄊㄢ ㄖㄣˋ)
① to share (a financial burden) ② to subscribe (to charitable projects, funds, etc.)
攤子(ㄊㄢ ·ㄗ) or 攤兒(ㄊㄚㄦ)
a stand; a booth; a stall
攤位(ㄊㄢ ㄨㄟˋ)
a stall or booth (especially a fixed one in a market)

〔手部〕

【攞】 2104 ㄌㄨㄛ lhuo luō
to tuck; to pull
攞起衣服(ㄌㄨㄛ ·ㄑㄧ ㄧ ·ㄈㄨ)
to tuck up the skirt of a garment

【攧】 2105 ㄉㄧㄢ dian diān
to stumble; to fall

【攣】 2106 ㄌㄩㄢˊ liuan luán
1. tangled; entwined
2. crooked
3. contraction: 痙攣 spasm; convulsions
攣其手足(ㄌㄩㄢˊ ㄑㄧˊ ㄕㄡˇ ㄗㄨˊ)
hands and feet crooked
攣弱(ㄌㄩㄢˊ ㄖㄨㄛˋ)
crooked and weak
攣縮(ㄌㄩㄢˊ ㄙㄨㄛ)
a spasm; a twitch; contraction
攣腕(ㄌㄩㄢˊ ㄨㄢˋ)
a sort of arthropathy

二十畫

【攩】 2107 ㄉㄤˇ daang dǎng
1. to impede; to obstruct; to hinder; to block 亦作「擋」
2. a party; a faction; a clique; an association 亦作「黨」

【攪】 2108 1. ㄐㄧㄠˇ jeau jiǎo
1. to stir; to mix
2. to agitate; to disturb; to annoy
攪拌(ㄐㄧㄠˇ ㄅㄢˋ)
to stir or churn; to mix: 你無法將油與水攪拌在一塊兒。You can't mix oil with water.
攪拌器(ㄐㄧㄠˇ ㄅㄢˋ ㄑㄧˋ)
a mixer; an agitator
攪動(ㄐㄧㄠˇ ㄉㄨㄥˋ)
to mix; to churn; to stir: 船的推進器攪動水產生泡沫。The ship's propeller churned the waves to foam.
攪亂(ㄐㄧㄠˇ ㄌㄨㄢˋ)
to disturb; to ruffle; to disarrange
攪和(ㄐㄧㄠˇ ·ㄏㄜ)
① to mix evenly by stirring; to mingle ② to mix up; to confuse: 別把這兩碼事攪和在一起。Don't mix up these two different matters.
攪混(ㄐㄧㄠˇ ·ㄏㄨㄣ)
to mix by stirring; to blend; to mingle
攪局(ㄐㄧㄠˇ ㄐㄩˊ)
to spoil; to disturb
攪擾(ㄐㄧㄠˇ ㄖㄠˇ)
to disturb; to stir
攪勻(ㄐㄧㄠˇ ㄩㄣˊ)
to make even by stirring; to mix

【攪】 2108 2. (搞) ㄍㄠˇ gao gǎo
to do; to manage; to handle: 胡攪 to make a mess of
攪鬼(ㄍㄠˇ ㄍㄨㄟˇ)
to play underhand tricks

【攫】 2109 ㄐㄩㄝˊ jyue jué
to seize; to take hold of; to snatch; to catch
攫搏(ㄐㄩㄝˊ ㄅㄛˊ)
to snatch with the claw or the paw
攫奪(ㄐㄩㄝˊ ㄉㄨㄛˊ)
to seize; to snatch; to grab
攫拏(ㄐㄩㄝˊ ㄋㄚˊ)
to scramble for
攫取(ㄐㄩㄝˊ ㄑㄩˇ)
to take by force; to seize

【攥】 2110 (揝) ㄗㄨㄢˋ tzuann zuàn
to grasp; to grip; to clutch: 他一把攥住我的手。He caught hold of my hand.

二十一畫

【攬】 2111 (擥) ㄌㄢˇ laan lǎn
1. to be in full possession of: 總攬權綱 to hold the reins of government; to get hold of the power in the state
2. to take into one's arms: 她把兒子攬在懷裏。She clasped her son to her bosom.
3. to make a selective collection of
4. to take on; to undertake
5. to grasp; to monopolize: 包攬 to monopolize; to undertake the whole thing
6. to round up: 延攬人才 to round up talents
攬筆(ㄌㄢˇ ㄅㄧˇ)
to take the pen—to write
攬轡(ㄌㄢˇ ㄆㄟˋ)
to hold the reins
攬轡澄清(ㄌㄢˇ ㄆㄟˋ ㄔㄥˊ ㄑㄧㄥ)
to aspire to bring perfect order to the nation when one enters upon a political career
攬貨(ㄌㄢˇ ㄏㄨㄛˋ)
to monopolize the distribution or delivery of certain goods
攬鏡自照(ㄌㄢˇ ㄐㄧㄥˋ ㄗˋ ㄓㄠˋ)
to hold a mirror to watch one's own reflection
攬取(ㄌㄢˇ ㄑㄩˇ)
to get hold of
攬權(ㄌㄢˇ ㄑㄩㄢˊ)
to grasp full authority; to arrogate power to oneself
攬勝(ㄌㄢˇ ㄕㄥˋ)
to enjoy scenery; to see scenic sights

二十二畫

【攮】 2112 ㄋㄤˇ naang nǎng
to thrust; to stab: 他的手臂被攮了一刀。He was stabbed in the arm.
攮子(ㄋㄤˇ ·ㄗ)
a dagger or bodkin

支部
ㄓ jy zhī

【支】 2113 ㄓ jy zhī
1. to pay; to disburse; to defray
2. to support; to sustain; to bear
3. to prop up; to put up
4. to prick up; to raise: 她支着耳朵聽。She pricked up her ears.
5. to send away; to put somebody off: 她把推銷員給支走了。She sent the salesman away.
6. a branch; a subdivision; an offshoot: 我們住在一家郵政支局附近。We lived near a branch post office.

7. a term for indicating amount or number: 一支蠟燭 one candle 一支筆 one pen
8. (textile) count: 六十支紗 60-count yarn
9. as in 地支, the Terrestrial Branches used in calculation with the Celestial Stems (天干)

支撥(ㄓ ㄅㄛ)
to make (funds) available

支部(ㄓ ㄅㄨˋ)
① branch headquarters (of a political party) ② the radical (支)

支派(ㄓ ㄆㄞˋ)
① a subdivision; a branch (of a school of thought) ② to order; to send; to appoint

支配(ㄓ ㄆㄟˋ)
① to control; to dominate: 人受環境的支配。Man is governed by circumstances. ② to manage; to administer; to allocate; to arrange: 他善於支配自己的金錢。He is good at budgeting his money.

支票(ㄓ ㄆㄧㄠˋ)
a cheque or check: 空頭支票 a bad (or rubber) check 旅行支票 a traveler's check

支票簿(ㄓ ㄆㄧㄠˋ ㄅㄨˋ)
a checkbook

支脈(ㄓ ㄇㄞˋ)
a branch (of a mountain range); an offshoot: 這座山是天山的支脈。The mountain is an offshoot of the Tienshan Mountains.

支費(ㄓ ㄈㄟˋ)
expenses; payment

支付(ㄓ ㄈㄨˋ)
to pay (what is owed); to defray

支付憑單(ㄓ ㄈㄨˋ ㄆㄧㄥˊ ㄉㄢ)
(accounting) payment vouchers

支點(ㄓ ㄉㄧㄢˇ)
a point of support; a fulcrum

支店(ㄓ ㄉㄧㄢˋ)
a branch store: 我們在這個城市有許多支店。We have many branch stores in the city.

支隊(ㄓ ㄉㄨㄟˋ)
a military detachment or contingent: 游擊支隊 a guerrilla detachment

支那(ㄓ ㄋㄚˋ)
China (a term used in the Buddhist scriptures and formerly used by the Japanese)

支那通(ㄓ ㄋㄚˋ ㄊㄨㄥ)
a China expert or Sinologue (a term formerly used by the Japanese)

支那語(ㄓ ㄋㄚˋ ㄩˇ)
the Chinese language (a term formerly used by the Japanese)

支孽(ㄓ ㄋㄧㄝˋ) or 支庶(ㄓ ㄕㄨˋ)
the son of a concubine

支離(ㄓ ㄌㄧˊ)
① to disintegrate; to disunite ② incoherent; disjointed; fragmented; broken

支離破碎(ㄓ ㄌㄧˊ ㄆㄛˋ ㄙㄨㄟˋ)
completely disintegrated; torn to pieces; fragmented: 我只能聽到他們支離破碎的談話。I could hear only fragments of their conversation.

支流(ㄓ ㄌㄧㄡˊ)
① a tributary (of a river): 漢水是揚子江的支流之一。The Han River is one of the tributaries of the Yangtze River. ② minor aspects; nonessentials

支領(ㄓ ㄌㄧㄥˇ)
to draw money

支路(ㄓ ㄌㄨˋ)
a branch way

支根(ㄓ ㄍㄣ)
(botany) a lateral root

支款(ㄓ ㄎㄨㄢˇ)
to withdraw money

支行(ㄓ ㄏㄤˊ)
a subbranch (of a bank)

支架(ㄓ ㄐㄧㄚˋ)
a support; a stand; a trestle

支節(ㄓ ㄐㄧㄝˊ)
a joint (of bones, etc.)

支解(ㄓ ㄐㄧㄝˇ)
to dismember

支氣管(ㄓ ㄑㄧˋ ㄍㄨㄢˇ)
bronchi

支氣管氣喘(ㄓ ㄑㄧˋ ㄍㄨㄢˇ ㄑㄧˋ ㄔㄨㄢˇ)
bronchial asthma

支氣管炎(ㄓ ㄑㄧˋ ㄍㄨㄢˇ ㄧㄢˊ)
bronchitis

支取(ㄓ ㄑㄩˇ)
to draw (money): 我想到銀行支取一筆款子。I want to go to the bank and draw some money.

支線(ㄓ ㄒㄧㄢˋ)
a branch line; a feeder (line): 鐵路(公路)支線 a feeder railway (highway)

支柱(ㄓ ㄓㄨˋ)
a prop; a support; a stay

支持(ㄓ ㄔˊ)
to support; to sustain; to bear; support; backing

支持不住(ㄓ ㄔˊ ㄅㄨˋ ㄓㄨˋ)
unable to keep up efforts; unable to hold out: 我凍得支持不住了。 I am so cold that I cannot bear any longer.

支撐(ㄓ ㄔㄥ)
to prop up; to support; to sustain

支撐危局(ㄓ ㄔㄥ ㄨㄟˊ ㄐㄩˊ)
to play a leading role during a national crisis

支出(ㄓ ㄔㄨ)
expense; expenditure; outlay; disbursement; to spend; to expend

支絀(ㄓ ㄔㄨˋ)
short of money; hard up; needy

支使(ㄓ ㄕˇ)
① to engage the services or labor of; to order about ② to send away

支子(ㄓ ㄗˇ)
the son of a concubine

支移(ㄓ ㄧˊ)
to make up a deficit by drawing upon the surplus

支頤(ㄓ ㄧˊ)
to support the chin with the hand

支應(ㄓ ㄧㄥˋ)
① to take charge of cash receipts and payments ② to look after; to attend to; to take care of; to deal with

支吾(ㄓ ˙ㄨ)
①to speak haltingly; to falter; to hem and haw: 她支吾地說了一個藉口。She faltered out an excuse. ② to deal with (a person) just for the occasion

支吾其詞(ㄓ ˙ㄨ ㄑㄧˊ ㄘˊ)
to speak haltingly or ambiguously (with a view to hid-

〔支部〕

〔攴部〕

ing the truth); to hem and haw; to speak evasively

支援(ㄓ ㄩㄢˊ)
to aid; to support; to assist; to help

支援部隊(ㄓ ㄩㄢˊ ㄅㄨˋ ㄉㄨㄟˋ)
a support unit

支用(ㄓ ㄩㄥˋ)
to disburse

八畫

【攲】 2114 ㄑㄧ chi qī
to incline; to lean; to slant

攲倒(ㄑㄧ ㄉㄠˇ)
to slant and fall

攲傾(ㄑㄧ ㄑㄧㄥ)
to slant; to incline

攲斜(ㄑㄧ ㄒㄧㄝˊ)
to slant; to incline; to lurch

攲側(ㄑㄧ ㄘㄜˋ)
to incline; to lean; to lurch

攲臥(ㄑㄧ ㄨㄛˋ)
to lie in a reclined position

攲危(ㄑㄧ ㄨㄟˊ)
tottering

攴部
ㄆㄨ pu pū

二畫

【收】 2115 ㄕㄡ shou shōu
1. to draw together; to gather; to collect
2. to contain: 這本字典收字一萬五千。The dictionary contains 15,000 entries.
3. to receive; to accept; to take: 她收到他的禮物，但未接受。She received a gift from him, but did not accept it.
4. to end; to come to a close
5. to retrieve; to take back; to put away

收報機(ㄕㄡ ㄅㄠˋ ㄐㄧ)
a telegraph receiver

收編(ㄕㄡ ㄅㄧㄢ)
to reorganize and incorporate (rebel troops, bandits, etc.) into government forces

收兵(ㄕㄡ ㄅㄧㄥ)
to recall troops; to end hostilities; to call off a battle

收捕(ㄕㄡ ㄅㄨˇ)
to arrest

收不回來(ㄕㄡ ·ㄅㄨ ㄏㄨㄟˊ ·ㄌㄞ)
impossible to get back, regain, or recover

收不住脚(ㄕㄡ ·ㄅㄨ ㄓㄨˋ ㄐㄧㄠˇ)
① unable to put an end to a pursuit ② unable to come to a quick stop (such as during a foot race)

收盤(ㄕㄡ ㄆㄢˊ)
the closing quotation (of a stock or commodity) for the day

收票員(ㄕㄡ ㄆㄧㄠˋ ㄩㄢˊ)
a ticket collector

收沒(ㄕㄡ ㄇㄛˋ)
to confiscate 亦作「沒收」

收埋(ㄕㄡ ㄇㄞˊ)
to collect and bury (dead bodies)

收買(ㄕㄡ ㄇㄞˇ)
① to bribe: 他們用貴重的禮物收買他。They bribed him with costly presents. ② to buy up ③ to win (support, people's hearts, etc. by less than honorable means): 議員想收買人心。The legislator tried to win popular support.

收發(ㄕㄡ ㄈㄚ)
① to receive and send out (official papers, documents, etc.) ② an office clerk who takes care of the receiving and sending out of official correspondence

收發報機(ㄕㄡ ㄈㄚ ㄅㄠˋ ㄐㄧ)
a transmitter-receiver; a transceiver

收發室(ㄕㄡ ㄈㄚ ㄕˋ)
an office through which official correspondence of an organization is received or sent out

收費(ㄕㄡ ㄈㄟˋ)
to collect fees; to charge

收費站(ㄕㄡ ㄈㄟˋ ㄓㄢˋ)
a toll station

收服(ㄕㄡ ㄈㄨˊ)
to subdue and win the allegiance of (someone)

收復(ㄕㄡ ㄈㄨˋ)
to recover (lost territory): 將軍已收復失陷的城鎮。The general has recovered a conquered town.

收復河山(ㄕㄡ ㄈㄨˋ ㄏㄜˊ ㄕㄢ)
to recover lost territory

收到(ㄕㄡ ㄉㄠˋ)
to receive; to obtain; to achieve: 我這個月收到很多請帖。I have received many invitations this month.

收攤(ㄕㄡ ㄊㄢ)
to pack up the stall or booth (after a day's business is over)

收條(ㄕㄡ ㄊㄧㄠˊ)
(informal) a receipt 亦作「收據」

收聽(ㄕㄡ ㄊㄧㄥ)
to tune in ; to listen to (the radio): 我每天早上都收聽你的節目。I listen to your program every morning.

收納(ㄕㄡ ㄋㄚˋ)
to accept

收孥(ㄕㄡ ㄋㄨˊ)
to try an offender's family along with him

收淚(ㄕㄡ ㄌㄟˋ)
to stop crying

收攬(ㄕㄡ ㄌㄢˇ)
① to collect extensively ② to win (the people's hearts)

收禮(ㄕㄡ ㄌㄧˇ)
to accept a present or gift

收留(ㄕㄡ ㄌㄧㄡˊ)
to give shelter to; to take somebody in

收殮(ㄕㄡ ㄌㄧㄢˋ)
to prepare a corpse for burial

收斂(ㄕㄡ ㄌㄧㄢˋ)
① to collect (taxes, grains, etc.) ② to draw together; to contract ③ to weaken or disappear ④ to pull in one's horns; to become less flagrant in behavior

收斂劑(ㄕㄡ ㄌㄧㄢˋ ㄐㄧˋ)
(medicine) astringents

收錄(ㄕㄡ ㄌㄨˋ)
① to employ; to enter; to enroll; to recruit ② to include (in a list, etc.): 這篇文章已收錄在我編的讀本裏。The article is included in the reader I edited. ③ to

record: 我從不收錄新聞廣播。I never make a recording of the news broadcast.

收羅(ㄕㄡ ㄌㄨㄛˊ)
①to collect; to gather ②to enlist

收羅人才(ㄕㄡ ㄌㄨㄛˊ ㄖㄣˊ ㄘㄞˊ)
to recruit qualified personnel

收攏(ㄕㄡ ㄌㄨㄥˇ)
to draw something in

收割(ㄕㄡ ㄍㄜ)or 收刈(ㄕㄡ ㄧˋ)
to reap; to harvest

收割機(ㄕㄡ ㄍㄜ ㄐㄧ)
a reaping machine; a harvester

收購(ㄕㄡ ㄍㄡˋ)
to buy up; to purchase: 他收購他們所有的玩具。He bought up all the toys they had.

收歸國有(ㄕㄡ ㄍㄨㄟ ㄍㄨㄛˊ ㄧㄡˇ)
to nationalize (enterprises)

收工(ㄕㄡ ㄍㄨㄥ)
to end the day's work; to knock off: 該收工了。It's time to knock off.

收口(兒)(ㄕㄡ ㄎㄡˇ (ㄦ))
the closure of a wound (as a result of healing)

收看(ㄕㄡ ㄎㄢˋ)
to watch (television)

收款人(ㄕㄡ ㄎㄨㄢˇ ㄖㄣˊ)
a recipient (of remittance); a payee

收款員(ㄕㄡ ㄎㄨㄢˇ ㄩㄢˊ)
a receiving teller

收貨(ㄕㄡ ㄏㄨㄛˋ)
to receive delivered goods

收貨人(ㄕㄡ ㄏㄨㄛˋ ㄖㄣˊ)
a consignee 亦作「受貨人」

收穫(ㄕㄡ ㄏㄨㄛˋ)
①harvest; fruit (of efforts); gains ②to reap; to reward: 這是一次很有收穫的旅行。This is a most rewarding trip.

收回(ㄕㄡ ㄏㄨㄟˊ)
to recover; to recall; to retrieve; to recoup; repossession: 他收回發出的文件。He recalled the documents which had been issued.

收回成命(ㄕㄡ ㄏㄨㄟˊ ㄔㄥˊ ㄇㄧㄥˋ)
to withdraw an order; to revoke a command

收賄(ㄕㄡ ㄏㄨㄟˋ)
to accept bribes; bribery: 公務員收賄是重罪。Bribery of a public official is a felony.

收集(ㄕㄡ ㄐㄧˊ)
collection; to collect; to gather: 這些畫的收集花費了他畢生之力。The collection of these paintings took him a lifetime.

收繳(ㄕㄡ ㄐㄧㄠˇ)
to take over; to capture

收監(ㄕㄡ ㄐㄧㄢ)
to imprison; to commit to jail; to take into custody

收件人(ㄕㄡ ㄐㄧㄢˋ ㄖㄣˊ)
an addressee; a consignee

收驚(ㄕㄡ ㄐㄧㄥ)
to quiet the soul of a terrified child by a charm; to stop a child's crying by charms

收據(ㄕㄡ ㄐㄩˋ)
a receipt: 請給我此款的收據。Please send me a receipt for the money.

收齊(ㄕㄡ ㄑㄧˊ)
to get into a collection everything that must go therein

收起(ㄕㄡ ㄑㄧˇ)
to pack up; to cut out; to stop: 你還是收起你的空談泛論吧。You'd better stop this worthless talk.

收訖(ㄕㄡ ㄑㄧˋ)
received

收錢(ㄕㄡ ㄑㄧㄢˊ)
to collect payments

收繫(ㄕㄡ ㄒㄧˋ)
to keep in confinement

收下(ㄕㄡ ·ㄒㄧㄚ)
to accept; to receive: 他收下了朋友的禮物。He accepted a present from his friend.

收效(ㄕㄡ ㄒㄧㄠˋ)
to get the desired result or effect; to prove effective

收心(ㄕㄡ ㄒㄧㄣ)
to bring the mind back from distraction; to concentrate attention

收支(ㄕㄡ ㄓ)
income and expenditure; revenue and expenditure; earnings and expenses; receipts and disbursements

收支表(ㄕㄡ ㄓ ㄅㄧㄠˇ)
the accounts of receipts and payments; the statement of income and expenditure; the statement of receipts and disbursements

收支平衡(ㄕㄡ ㄓ ㄆㄧㄥˊ ㄏㄥˊ)
The accounts are balanced. 或 Income and expenditure are balanced.

收支員(ㄕㄡ ㄓ ㄩㄢˊ)
a cashier

收執(ㄕㄡ ㄓˊ)
①to receive and keep (a receipt, etc.) ②a receipt

收債(ㄕㄡ ㄓㄞˋ)
to collect debts

收帳 or 收賬(ㄕㄡ ㄓㄤˋ)
to collect payments of bills

收帳人(ㄕㄡ ㄓㄤˋ ㄖㄣˊ)
a collector; a bill collector

收場(ㄕㄡ ㄔㄤˇ)or(ㄕㄡ ㄔㄤˊ)
①the end of an affair or a story; conclusion; denouement; ending: 這小說有圓滿的收場。This novel had a happy ending. ②to wind up; to end up: 他做事總是草草收場。He winds up everything hastily.

收成(ㄕㄡ ㄔㄥˊ)
harvest: 去年收成不好。We had poor harvests last year.

收拾(ㄕㄡ ·ㄕ)
①to put (things) in order; to clear away; to tidy: 你現在可以收拾碗筷了。You can clear the table now. ②to manage ③to torture; to punish: 他們早晚要收拾那個壞蛋。They will punish the rascal one of these days.

收拾停當(ㄕㄡ ·ㄕ ㄊㄧㄥˊ ㄉㄤˋ)
to put in good order

收拾殘局(ㄕㄡ ·ㄕ ㄘㄢˊ ㄐㄩˊ)
to clear up a messy situation

收受(ㄕㄡ ㄕㄡˋ)
to receive; to accept

收生婆(ㄕㄡ ㄕㄥ ㄆㄛˊ)
a midwife

收束(ㄕㄡ ㄕㄨˋ)
①to bring together; to collect ②to bring to a close; to wind up: 寫到這裡，我的信也該收束了。It's time for me to wind up my letter.

收稅(ㄕㄡ ㄕㄨㄟˋ)
to collect taxes: 政府的歲入

〔攴部〕

靠收稅。The government obtains revenue from taxes.

收稅單(ㄕㄡ ㄕㄨㄟˋ ㄉㄢ)
a tax form

收入(ㄕㄡ ㄖㄨˋ)
①to take in; to include ② income; earnings; revenue; receipts: 低收入家庭需要政府幫忙。Low-income families need government help.

收入表(ㄕㄡ ㄖㄨˋ ㄅㄧㄠˇ)
the account of receipts; an income statement

收容(ㄕㄡ ㄖㄨㄥˊ)
to give shelter to; to accommodate

收容所(ㄕㄡ ㄖㄨㄥˊ ㄙㄨㄛˇ)
a camp, temporary home or reception center (for refugees); an asylum

收贓(ㄕㄡ ㄗㄤ)
to receive stolen property

收租(ㄕㄡ ㄗㄨ)
to collect rents or rentals

收藏(ㄕㄡ ㄘㄤˊ)
to collect and keep

收藏家(ㄕㄡ ㄘㄤˊ ㄐㄧㄚ)
a collector: 他是古董收藏家。He is an antique collector.

收存(ㄕㄡ ㄘㄨㄣˊ)
to receive for keeps; to receive for custody

收縮(ㄕㄡ ㄙㄨㄛ)
①to shrink; to contract; to deflate: 這種布下水後會收縮。This kind of cloth shrinks in the wash. ②systole

收縮壓(ㄕㄡ ㄙㄨㄛ ㄧㄚ)
systolic pressure

收益(ㄕㄡ ㄧˋ)
to get benefit; to benefit; to profit; earnings; returns; income

收益稅(ㄕㄡ ㄧˋ ㄕㄨㄟˋ)
revenue tax

收押(ㄕㄡ ㄧㄚ)
to take (a criminal suspect) into custody; to detain

收音機(ㄕㄡ ㄧㄣ ㄐㄧ)
a radio receiving set; a radio

收銀機(ㄕㄡ ㄧㄣˊ ㄐㄧ)
a cash register

收養(ㄕㄡ ㄧㄤˇ)
to adopt (a child); (child) adoption

收尾(ㄕㄡ ㄨㄟˇ)
①to come to a conclusion; to wind up ②a concluding passage, movement, etc.

三畫

【攸】 2116
ㄧㄡ iou yōu

1. far; distant
2. fast; fleeting
3. same as 所 — the place where
4. to concern
5. a Chinese family name

攸關(ㄧㄡ ㄍㄨㄢ)
to concern (reputation, life, etc.); a matter of (reputation, life and death, etc.)

攸然(ㄧㄡ ㄖㄢˊ)
joyfully; leisurely

攸攸(ㄧㄡ ㄧㄡ)
①far; distant ②deep

【改】 2117
ㄍㄞˇ gae gǎi

1. to change; to transform; to convert; to alter; to modify
2. to correct
3. to revise
4. to switch over to: 今年大部分農民改種蔬菜。Most of the farmers switch over to growing vegetables this year.

改版(ㄍㄞˇ ㄅㄢˇ)
to make a revision (of a book); to change the format (of a newspaper)

改編(ㄍㄞˇ ㄅㄧㄢ)
①to make a revision (of a book) ②to reorganize (a military unit, etc.) ③(said of a movie, stage play, etc.) adapted from or based on (a book, novel, etc.): 這部電影是由小說改編的。The movie was adapted from a novel.

改變(ㄍㄞˇ ㄅㄧㄢˋ)
to change; to alter; to modify; to transform; to convert

改變主意(ㄍㄞˇ ㄅㄧㄢˋ ㄓㄨˇ ㄧˋ)
to change one's mind

改不了(ㄍㄞˇ ·ㄅㄨ ㄌㄧㄠˇ)
cannot change; cannot be changed 亦作「改不過來」: 人性是改不了的。Human nature cannot be changed.

改判(ㄍㄞˇ ㄆㄢˋ)
to change a sentence (meted out by a lower court); to amend a judgement; to commute

改脾氣(ㄍㄞˇ ㄆㄧˊ ·ㄑㄧ)
to change one's disposition

改名換姓(ㄍㄞˇ ㄇㄧㄥˊ ㄏㄨㄢˋ ㄒㄧㄥˋ)
to change one's whole name

改道(ㄍㄞˇ ㄉㄠˋ)
①to change the course (of a river): 黃河曾多次改道。The Yellow River has changed its course many times. ②to change one's route

改掉(ㄍㄞˇ ㄉㄧㄠˋ)
to give up; to drop

改訂(ㄍㄞˇ ㄉㄧㄥˋ)
①to revise (a book); to reformulate ②to choose a new date (for a scheduled event)

改動(ㄍㄞˇ ㄉㄨㄥˋ)
to change; to modify: 我在文字上做少許改動。I made a few changes in wording.

改頭換面(ㄍㄞˇ ㄊㄡˊ ㄏㄨㄢˋ ㄇㄧㄢˋ)
to change only the appearance; to change the outward look without changing the substance

改天(ㄍㄞˇ ㄊㄧㄢ)
some other day

改途 or 改塗(ㄍㄞˇ ㄊㄨˊ)
to take a new road; to use a new approach or method

改圖(ㄍㄞˇ ㄊㄨˊ)
to change the plan

改土歸流(ㄍㄞˇ ㄊㄨˇ ㄍㄨㄟ ㄌㄧㄡˊ)
to replace hereditary local chieftains with nonhereditary appointees from the central government (a practice adopted during the Ming and Ching dynasties in dealing with the southwestern aboriginal tribes)

改良(ㄍㄞˇ ㄌㄧㄤˊ)
to ameliorate; to improve; to better

改良主義(ㄍㄞˇ ㄌㄧㄤˊ ㄓㄨˇ ㄧˋ)
reformism

改良種(ㄍㄞˇ ㄌㄧㄤˊ ㄓㄨㄥˇ)
the improved variety or species (created by cross-breeding)

改革(ㄍㄞˇ ㄍㄜˊ)
to reform; a reform: 新政府

實施多項必要改革。The new government put through many needed reforms.
改過(ㄍㄞˇ ㄍㄨㄛˋ)
to mend one's ways; to correct one's mistakes
改過遷善(ㄍㄞˇ ㄍㄨㄛˋ ㄑㄧㄢ ㄕㄢˋ)
to repent and be good
改過自新(ㄍㄞˇ ㄍㄨㄛˋ ㄗˋ ㄒㄧㄣ)
to turn over a new leaf; to correct one's errors and make a fresh start; to reform
改觀(ㄍㄞˇ ㄍㄨㄢ)
to assume a new look; to change the appearance of
改口(ㄍㄞˇ ㄎㄡˇ)or 改嘴(ㄍㄞˇ ㄗㄨㄟˇ)
to say something different from what one is expected to say or has been saying; to eat one's words; to correct oneself
改行(ㄍㄞˇ ㄏㄤˊ)
to change one's trade, profession or career
改悔(ㄍㄞˇ ㄏㄨㄟˇ)
to repent 亦作「悔改」: 那傢伙毫無改悔之意。That guy shows not the least sign of repentance.
改換(ㄍㄞˇ ㄏㄨㄢˋ)
to replace; to change: 他已改換一套新的做法。He has changed over to new ways.
改嫁(ㄍㄞˇ ㄐㄧㄚˋ)or 改醮(ㄍㄞˇ ㄐㄧㄠˋ)
(said of a woman) to remarry
改節(ㄍㄞˇ ㄐㄧㄝˊ)
to change one's principles; to turn renegade; to switch loyalty (to a new ruler)
改建(ㄍㄞˇ ㄐㄧㄢˋ)
to remodel; to rebuild: 他去年改建老房子。He remodeled an old house last year.
改進(ㄍㄞˇ ㄐㄧㄣˋ)
to improve; to better: 尙有改進餘地。There is room for improvement.
改期(ㄍㄞˇ ㄑㄧˊ)
to postpone a scheduled event: 期中考已改期。The midterm examination has been postponed.
改邪歸正(ㄍㄞˇ ㄒㄧㄝˊ ㄍㄨㄟ ㄓㄥˋ)
to give up evil and return to virtue; to turn over a new leaf
改寫(ㄍㄞˇ ㄒㄧㄝˇ)
to rewrite; to adapt: 這個故事是爲電影而改寫的。The story was adapted for the movies.
改弦更張(ㄍㄞˇ ㄒㄧㄢˊ ㄍㄥ ㄓㄤ)
to start a thorough reform; to make a complete change; to make a fresh start
改弦易轍(ㄍㄞˇ ㄒㄧㄢˊ ㄧˋ ㄓㄜˊ)
to change rules and systems; to effect a thorough reform; to change one's course; to strike out on a new path
改憲(ㄍㄞˇ ㄒㄧㄢˋ)
to amend the constitution
改削(ㄍㄞˇ ㄒㄩㄝ)
to correct errors and delete superfluities (in a draft)
改選(ㄍㄞˇ ㄒㄩㄢˇ)
to hold a new election; to reelect: 班長每年改選一次。A new class leader is elected every year.
改制(ㄍㄞˇ ㄓˋ)
to change a system
改轍(ㄍㄞˇ ㄓㄜˊ)
(literally) to get the vehicle out of the old ruts—to take a new course
改正(ㄍㄞˇ ㄓㄥˋ)
to correct; to rectify; to reform; to amend
改鑄(ㄍㄞˇ ㄓㄨˋ)
to recast; to mint again
改錐(ㄍㄞˇ ㄓㄨㄟ)
a screwdriver
改裝(ㄍㄞˇ ㄓㄨㄤ)
① to change dress ② to convert (a machine, vehicle, etc.) for a new use; to refit; to reequip
改朝換代(ㄍㄞˇ ㄔㄠˊ ㄏㄨㄢˋ ㄉㄞˋ)
the change of regime
改常(ㄍㄞˇ ㄔㄤˊ)
to change the usual attitude
改善(ㄍㄞˇ ㄕㄢˋ)
to improve; to ameliorate; improvement: 這些國家間的關係已略有改善。The relations among these countries have shown some improvement.
改日(ㄍㄞˇ ㄖˋ)
some other time; later on
改造(ㄍㄞˇ ㄗㄠˋ)
to remodel; to remold; to rebuild; to convert; to reconstruct; to reform: 要對一個人思想改造是不容易的。It's not easy to remold one's ideology.
改葬(ㄍㄞˇ ㄗㄤˋ)
to reinter
改組(ㄍㄞˇ ㄗㄨˇ)
to reshuffle (an organization); to reorganize
改作文(ㄍㄞˇ ㄗㄨㄛˋ ㄨㄣˊ)
to correct compositions (for students)
改次(ㄍㄞˇ ㄘˋ)
some other time; on some other occasion
改錯(ㄍㄞˇ ㄘㄨㄛˋ)
to correct mistakes
改竄(ㄍㄞˇ ㄘㄨㄢˋ)
to emend
改歲(ㄍㄞˇ ㄙㄨㄟˋ)
to enter a new year; to begin a new year
改惡從善(ㄍㄞˇ ㄜˋ ㄘㄨㄥˊ ㄕㄢˋ)
to turn over a new leaf; to improve one's behavior
改易(ㄍㄞˇ ㄧˋ)
to change; to transform
改樣(ㄍㄞˇ ㄧㄤˋ)or 改式(ㄍㄞˇ ㄕˋ)
to alter the style of
改物(ㄍㄞˇ ㄨˋ)
to change systems and institutions (of previous reigns)
改元(ㄍㄞˇ ㄩㄢˊ)
to change the reigning title (after a new emperor ascends the throne); to change the title of a reign

【攻】 2118
ㄍㄨㄥ gong gōng

1. to attack; to raid; to assault
2. to accuse; to charge; to assail; to criticize; to rebuke
3. to work at; to apply oneself to; to study

攻拔(ㄍㄨㄥ ㄅㄚˊ)
to storm and capture
攻砭(ㄍㄨㄥ ㄅㄧㄢ)
to acupuncture
攻破(ㄍㄨㄥ ㄆㄛˋ)
to attack and conquer; to make a breakthrough; to breach
攻伐(ㄍㄨㄥ ㄈㄚˊ)or(ㄍㄨㄥ ㄈㄚ)
to send troops against (bandits, rebels, etc.)
攻防(ㄍㄨㄥ ㄈㄤˊ)

〔支 部〕

〔攴 部〕

offense and defense

攻打(ㄍㄨㄥ ㄉㄚˇ)
to attack; to raid; to invade

攻讀(ㄍㄨㄥ ㄉㄨˊ)or 攻書(ㄍㄨㄥ ㄕㄨ)
to apply oneself diligently to study: 他正在攻讀博士學位。He is working for a doctorate.

攻克(ㄍㄨㄥ ㄎㄜˋ)
to attack and conquer; to take

攻乎異端(ㄍㄨㄥ ㄏㄨ ㄧˋ ㄉㄨㄢ)
to apply oneself to heretical doctrines or thoughts

攻擊(ㄍㄨㄥ ㄐㄧˊ)
①to attack; to assault; to launch an offensive ②to accuse; to charge (or attack verbally); to vilify

攻擊點(ㄍㄨㄥ ㄐㄧˊ ㄉㄧㄢˇ)
the point of attack

攻擊出發線(ㄍㄨㄥ ㄐㄧˊ ㄔㄨ ㄈㄚ ㄒㄧㄢˋ)
(military) the line of departure

攻訐(ㄍㄨㄥ ㄐㄧㄝˊ)
to accuse; to charge; to rake up somebody's past and attack him; to censure; to flay

攻堅(ㄍㄨㄥ ㄐㄧㄢ)
to attack the enemy's strongest fortifications; to assault fortified positions; to storm strongholds

攻進(ㄍㄨㄥ ㄐㄧㄣˋ)
to breach enemy defense and enter (a position, city, etc.)

攻其無備(ㄍㄨㄥ ㄑㄧˊ ㄨˊ ㄅㄟˋ)
to attack when the enemy is unprepared; to take somebody by surprise

攻取(ㄍㄨㄥ ㄑㄩˇ)
to attack and capture

攻下(ㄍㄨㄥ ㄒㄧㄚˋ)
①to succeed in capturing (a city, a fort, etc.) by attack ②to overcome

攻陷(ㄍㄨㄥ ㄒㄧㄢˋ)
to succeed in capturing (a city, a fort, etc.) by attack

攻心(ㄍㄨㄥ ㄒㄧㄣ)
to launch a psychological offense

攻心爲上(ㄍㄨㄥ ㄒㄧㄣ ㄨㄟˊ ㄕㄤˋ)
Psychological offense is the best of tactics.

攻佔(ㄍㄨㄥ ㄓㄢˋ)
to attack and occupy: 敵人攻佔我們的堡壘。The enemy occupied our fort.

攻城砲(ㄍㄨㄥ ㄔㄥˊ ㄆㄠˋ)
a siege gun

攻城略地(ㄍㄨㄥ ㄔㄥˊ ㄌㄩㄝˋ ㄉㄧˋ)
to attack cities and invade territories

攻勢(ㄍㄨㄥ ㄕˋ)
the offensive: 軍隊採取攻勢。The army took the offensive.

攻殺(ㄍㄨㄥ ㄕㄚ)
to attack and massacre

攻守(ㄍㄨㄥ ㄕㄡˇ)
offense and defense

攻守同盟(ㄍㄨㄥ ㄕㄡˇ ㄊㄨㄥˊ ㄇㄥˊ)
an alliance for offense and defense; a military alliance for mutual defense

攻人之短(ㄍㄨㄥ ㄖㄣˊ ㄓ ㄉㄨㄢˇ)
to criticize the faults of others

攻錯(ㄍㄨㄥ ㄘㄨㄛˋ)or 攻玉(ㄍㄨㄥ ㄩˋ)
to mend one's own faults by observing the virtues of others

攻無不克(ㄍㄨㄥ ㄨˊ ㄅㄨˋ ㄎㄜˋ)
all-conquering; invincible

四畫

【放】 2119 ㄈㄤˋ fanq fàng

1. to let go; to release; to free; to liberate; to loosen; to relax: 她不放我走。She won't let me go.
2. to put; to place
3. to put in; to add: 菜裏多放點鹽。Put a bit more salt in the dish.
4. to dissipate; to debauch; to indulge

放爆竹(ㄈㄤˋ ㄅㄠˋ ㄓㄨˊ)
to set off firecrackers

放榜(ㄈㄤˋ ㄅㄤˇ)
to announce or publish the result of a competitive examination

放不下心(ㄈㄤˋ ·ㄅㄨ ㄒㄧㄚˋ ㄒㄧㄣ)
cannot stop worrying

放不下手(ㄈㄤˋ ·ㄅㄨ ㄒㄧㄚˋ ㄕㄡˇ)
cannot stop doing something

放砲(ㄈㄤˋ ㄆㄠˋ)
①to fire an artillery piece; blasting ②to shoot off one's mouth

放盤(ㄈㄤˋ ㄆㄢˊ)
(stock) the opening quotation 參看「開盤」

放屁(ㄈㄤˋ ㄆㄧˋ)
①to let out gas; to break wind ② Nonsense! 或 Shit! What a crap! 別放屁。Don't talk nonsense.

放馬後砲(ㄈㄤˋ ㄇㄚˇ ㄏㄡˋ ㄆㄠˋ)
to criticize or make comments on something after it is already over; to second-guess

放免(ㄈㄤˋ ㄇㄧㄢˇ)
to acquit (a suspect)

放牧(ㄈㄤˋ ㄇㄨˋ)
to put out to pasture; to graze; to herd

放牧地(ㄈㄤˋ ㄇㄨˋ ㄉㄧˋ)
a pasture

放風箏(ㄈㄤˋ ㄈㄥ ㄓㄥ)
to fly a kite

放大(ㄈㄤˋ ㄉㄚˋ)
to magnify; to enlarge; to amplify: 我想把這照片放大。I want to have the photograph enlarged.

放大鏡(ㄈㄤˋ ㄉㄚˋ ㄐㄧㄥˋ)
a magnifying glass

放膽(ㄈㄤˋ ㄉㄢˇ)
to get bold; to act boldly and with confidence

放誕(ㄈㄤˋ ㄉㄢˋ)
rash or reckless(in conduct or speech)

放蕩(ㄈㄤˋ ㄉㄤˋ)
dissolute; debauched; dissipated; unconventional: 他的行爲總是放蕩不羈。His behavior is always unconventional and unbridled.

放刁(ㄈㄤˋ ㄉㄧㄠ)
to show villainy; to act in a rascally manner 亦作「要無賴」

放電(ㄈㄤˋ ㄉㄧㄢˋ)
electric discharge

放毒(ㄈㄤˋ ㄉㄨˊ)
to put poison in food, water, etc.; to poison

放牛(ㄈㄤˋ ㄋㄧㄡˊ)
to graze cattle; to pasture cattle

放浪(ㄈㄤˋ ㄌㄤˋ)
to debauch; to dissipate

放浪形骸(ㄈㄤˋ ㄌㄤˋ ㄒㄧㄥˊ ㄏㄞˊ)
to abandon oneself to Bohemianism
放冷箭(ㄈㄤˋ ㄌㄥˇ ㄐㄧㄢˋ)
to injure others secretly
放利(ㄈㄤˋ ㄌㄧˋ)
to lend money for interest
放糧(ㄈㄤˋ ㄌㄧㄤˊ)
to distribute relief grains in a disaster-stricken area
放量(ㄈㄤˋ ㄌㄧㄤˋ)
(to drink) to full capacity
放領(ㄈㄤˋ ㄌㄧㄥˇ)
to lease (public land)
放龍入海(ㄈㄤˋ ㄌㄨㄥˊ ㄖㄨˋ ㄏㄞˇ)
(literally) to release a dragon into the sea—to give a man the chance to make the best of his abilities
放歌(ㄈㄤˋ ㄍㄜ)
to sing with uninhibited loudness
放高利貸(ㄈㄤˋ ㄍㄠ ㄌㄧˋ ㄉㄞˋ)
to lend money at high interest; to practice usury
放過(ㄈㄤˋ ㄍㄨㄛˋ)
to let go; to let slip away; to overlook
放光(ㄈㄤˋ ㄍㄨㄤ)
to emit light; to shine; to gleam; to glisten; to glitter
放工(ㄈㄤˋ ㄍㄨㄥ)
① to close work (for lunch, for the night, etc.); to quit work; to knock off ② to give workers a holiday
放開(ㄈㄤˋ ㄎㄞ)
to relax or loosen (a grasp, etc.); to let go
放寬(ㄈㄤˋ ㄎㄨㄢ)
to ease or relax (restrictions, etc.); to liberalize
放寬期限(ㄈㄤˋ ㄎㄨㄢ ㄑㄧˊ ㄒㄧㄢˋ)
to extend a time limit
放款(ㄈㄤˋ ㄎㄨㄢˇ)
a loan; loaning; to loan
放空氣(ㄈㄤˋ ㄎㄨㄥ ㄑㄧˋ)
to put out feelers; to send out trial balloons; to create an impression: 他放空氣說他要辭職。He created the impression that he would resign.
放虎歸山(ㄈㄤˋ ㄏㄨˇ ㄍㄨㄟ ㄕㄢ)
to let a tiger back to mountains—to sow the seeds of calamity 亦作「縱虎歸山」

放花(ㄈㄤˋ ㄏㄨㄚ)or 放花炮(ㄈㄤˋ ㄏㄨㄚ ㄆㄠˋ)
to set off fireworks
放火(ㄈㄤˋ ㄏㄨㄛˇ)
to set fire; to commit arson
放懷(ㄈㄤˋ ㄏㄨㄞˊ)
① to be uninhibited; to one's heart's content ② to be free from anxiety; to stop worrying
放假(ㄈㄤˋ ㄐㄧㄚˋ)
to have or give a holiday or vacation
放棄(ㄈㄤˋ ㄑㄧˋ)
① to give up; to abandon; to renounce; to discard; to relinquish ②(law) to waive; waiver
放槍(ㄈㄤˋ ㄑㄧㄤ)
to fire a gun
放晴(ㄈㄤˋ ㄑㄧㄥˊ)
(said of the weather) to clear up: 天一放晴，我們就攻擊。We'll attack as soon as it clears up.
放下(ㄈㄤˋ ·ㄒㄧㄚ)
to put down; to lay down: 我無法放下手頭的工作。I cannot put aside the work on hand.
放下屠刀(ㄈㄤˋ ㄒㄧㄚˋ ㄊㄨˊ ㄉㄠ)
(literally) to lay down the butcher knife—to repent and reform
放下屠刀，立地成佛(ㄈㄤˋ ㄒㄧㄚˋ ㄊㄨˊ ㄉㄠ, ㄌㄧˋ ㄉㄧˋ ㄔㄥˊ ㄈㄛˊ)
A butcher becomes a Buddha the moment he drops his cleaver.—A wrongdoer may become a man of virtue once he does good.
放心(ㄈㄤˋ ㄒㄧㄣ)
to stop worrying; to be free from anxiety; to rest assured
放心不下(ㄈㄤˋ ㄒㄧㄣ ㄅㄨˋ ㄒㄧㄚˋ)
to be kept in suspense
放響砲(ㄈㄤˋ ㄒㄧㄤˇ ㄆㄠˋ)
to set off firecrackers
放行(ㄈㄤˋ ㄒㄧㄥˊ)
to let go; to let pass: 請放行。Please let us pass.
放學(ㄈㄤˋ ㄒㄩㄝˊ)
to return home from school at the end of the day's classes: 學校下午四時半放學。The school closes at 4:30 p.m.

放置(ㄈㄤˋ ㄓˋ)
to place; to put down
放債(ㄈㄤˋ ㄓㄞˋ)
to make loans; to extend loans; to lend money for interest
放粥(ㄈㄤˋ ㄓㄡ)
to distribute free meals for the starving; to operate a soup kitchen
放賑(ㄈㄤˋ ㄓㄣˋ)
to distribute relief materials to the poor; to give alms
放賬(ㄈㄤˋ ㄓㄤˋ)
to make loans
放諸四海而皆準(ㄈㄤˋ ㄓㄨ ㄙˋ ㄏㄞˇ ㄦˊ ㄐㄧㄝ ㄓㄨㄣˇ)or 放之四海而皆準(ㄈㄤˋ ㄓ ㄙˋ ㄏㄞˇ ㄦˊ ㄐㄧㄝ ㄓㄨㄣˇ)
(said of a principle, theory, etc.) to be applicable everywhere
放逐(ㄈㄤˋ ㄓㄨˊ)
to exile; to banish
放長線釣大魚(ㄈㄤˋ ㄔㄤˊ ㄒㄧㄢˋ ㄉㄧㄠˋ ㄉㄚˋ ㄩˊ)
(literally) To catch a big fish, one must cast a long line.—to make a bigger investment with a view to gaining a bigger reward
放唱片(ㄈㄤˋ ㄔㄤˋ ㄆㄧㄢˋ)
to play a phonograph
放出(ㄈㄤˋ ㄔㄨ)
to give forth; to send out; to emit: 太陽放出光和熱。The sun emits light and heat.
放黜(ㄈㄤˋ ㄔㄨˋ)
to exile; to banish
放銃(ㄈㄤˋ ㄔㄨㄥˋ)
(mah-jong game) to release a tile that enables any one of the other three players to complete his winning pattern
放射(ㄈㄤˋ ㄕㄜˋ)
to emit; to radiate; to send out; to emanate
放射線(ㄈㄤˋ ㄕㄜˋ ㄒㄧㄢˋ)
radioactive rays
放射性(ㄈㄤˋ ㄕㄜˋ ㄒㄧㄥˋ)
radioactivity
放射性同位素(ㄈㄤˋ ㄕㄜˋ ㄒㄧㄥˋ ㄊㄨㄥˊ ㄨㄟˋ ㄙㄨˋ)
a radioisotope
放哨(ㄈㄤˋ ㄕㄠˋ)
to go on patrol duty; to

〔攴部〕

stand sentry; to stand guard
放手(ㄈㄤˋ ㄕㄡˇ)
①to loosen the grasp or hold; to let go: 抓緊,不要放手。Hold it tight and don't let go. ②to give up ③to have a free hand
放手去做(ㄈㄤˋ ㄕㄡˇ ㄑㄩˋ ㄗㄨㄛˋ)
to act without considering consequences or difficulties
放生(ㄈㄤˋ ㄕㄥ)
to free or release a captured animal (out of pity)
放生池(ㄈㄤˋ ㄕㄥ ㄔˊ)
a pond where fishes are released
放聲大哭(ㄈㄤˋ ㄕㄥ ㄉㄚˋ ㄎㄨ)
to cry loudly
放水(ㄈㄤˋ ㄕㄨㄟˇ)
①to let water out; to draw off ②to let the other side win (a game, contest, etc.) purposely; to throw a game
放熱(ㄈㄤˋ ㄖㄜˋ)
exothermic
放任(ㄈㄤˋ ㄖㄣˋ)
to leave alone; to let (a person) do as he pleases; to let (a matter) take its own course
放任政策(ㄈㄤˋ ㄖㄣˋ ㄓㄥˋ ㄘㄜˋ)or 放任主義(ㄈㄤˋ ㄖㄣˋ ㄓㄨˇ ㄧˋ)
laissez faire or laisser faire
放恣(ㄈㄤˋ ㄗˋ)
to disregard all restrictions; to be licentious
放在心裏(ㄈㄤˋ ㄗㄞˋ ㄒㄧㄣ ˙ㄌㄧ)
to keep in mind; to bear in mind
放走(ㄈㄤˋ ㄗㄡˇ)
to release; to set free; to let go: 你照我的話做,我就放她走。Do as I tell you, and I'll set her free.
放縱(ㄈㄤˋ ㄗㄨㄥˋ)
①to debauch; to dissipate; to indulge ②to break rules of conduct
放肆(ㄈㄤˋ ㄙˋ)
to take liberties; unruly; unbridled: 他的行為很放肆。His behavior is unbridled.
放散(ㄈㄤˋ ㄙㄢˋ)
(said of smoke, scent, etc.) to diffuse; to spread
放鬆(ㄈㄤˋ ㄙㄨㄥ)
to relax; to ease; to loosen; to slacken
放送(ㄈㄤˋ ㄙㄨㄥˋ)
to broadcast; to send out (over a loudspeaker, etc.)
放言高論(ㄈㄤˋ ㄧㄢˊ ㄍㄠ ㄌㄨㄣˋ)
to speak or write in an outspoken manner; high-flown talk
放閻王賬(ㄈㄤˋ ㄧㄢˊ ㄨㄤˊ ㄓㄤˋ)
to practice usury
放眼(ㄈㄤˋ ㄧㄢˇ)
to take a broad view; to scan widely
放燄口(ㄈㄤˋ ㄧㄢˋ ㄎㄡˇ)
a Buddhist ritual wherein the monks chant sutra for the dead and give food to hungry ghosts
放焰火(ㄈㄤˋ ㄧㄢˋ ㄏㄨㄛˇ)
to set off fireworks
放洋(ㄈㄤˋ ㄧㄤˊ)
①to spend some time abroad ②(said of a ship) to put out to sea
放養(ㄈㄤˋ ㄧㄤˇ)
to put (fish, etc.) in a suitable place to breed: 水池裏放養了許多種魚。Various kinds of fish are being bred in the pond.
放映(ㄈㄤˋ ㄧㄥˋ)
to project (on the screen); to show: 環球電影院今晚放映什麼片子? What will show at Universal Cinema this evening?
放映機(ㄈㄤˋ ㄧㄥˋ ㄐㄧ)
a projector
放映室(ㄈㄤˋ ㄧㄥˋ ㄕˋ)
a projection room
放穩重些(ㄈㄤˋ ㄨㄣˇ ㄓㄨㄥˋ ˙ㄒㄧㄝ)
Be gentlemanlike!

【攽】 2120
ㄅㄧㄣ bin bīn
1. to divide
2. to reduce

五畫

【政】 2121
ㄓㄥˋ jenq zhèng
1. government
2. administration; management
3. politics; political affairs
政變(ㄓㄥˋ ㄅㄧㄢˋ)
a coup d'état; a coup: 有些謀叛者試圖要發動政變。Some conspirators tried to stage a coup d'état.
政柄(ㄓㄥˋ ㄅㄧㄥˇ)
reins of government
政府(ㄓㄥˋ ㄈㄨˇ)
a government
政府機關(ㄓㄥˋ ㄈㄨˇ ㄐㄧ ㄍㄨㄢ)
a government agency; a government organization
政黨(ㄓㄥˋ ㄉㄤˇ)
a political party
政黨政治(ㄓㄥˋ ㄉㄤˇ ㄓㄥˋ ㄓˋ)
a form of democracy wherein the majority party forms the cabinet with the opposition acting as watchdog
政敵(ㄓㄥˋ ㄉㄧˊ)
a political rival; a political enemy
政體(ㄓㄥˋ ㄊㄧˇ)
the form of government; a political system; a polity
政通人和(ㄓㄥˋ ㄊㄨㄥ ㄖㄣˊ ㄏㄜˊ)
The government functions well, and the people enjoy peace.
政令(ㄓㄥˋ ㄌㄧㄥˋ)
a government order (or decree)
政論(ㄓㄥˋ ㄌㄨㄣˋ)
articles, statements or comments about politics
政論家(ㄓㄥˋ ㄌㄨㄣˋ ㄐㄧㄚ)
a political commentator; a publicist
政略(ㄓㄥˋ ㄌㄩㄝˋ)
a government policy
政綱(ㄓㄥˋ ㄍㄤ)
the platform (of a political party)
政綱不振(ㄓㄥˋ ㄍㄤ ㄅㄨˋ ㄓㄣˋ)
The political platform does not rouse.
政工(ㄓㄥˋ ㄍㄨㄥ)
(military) political work
政工幹校(ㄓㄥˋ ㄍㄨㄥ ㄍㄢˋ ㄒㄧㄠˋ)
Political Staff College (operated by the Ministry of National Defense)
政工人員(ㄓㄥˋ ㄍㄨㄥ ㄖㄣˊ ㄩㄢˊ)
(military) political staff officers
政躬康泰(ㄓㄥˋ ㄍㄨㄥ ㄎㄤ ㄊㄞˋ)
(an expression used in addressing a high government official) May you be healthy and strong.

政客(ㄓㄥˋ ㄎㄜˋ)
a politician who places personal gain above public interests: 他不過是個小政客。He is only a petty politician.
政況(ㄓㄥˋ ㄎㄨㄤˋ)
political situations
政績(ㄓㄥˋ ㄐㄧ)
administrative achievements (of a government, ruler, or magistrate)
政績斐然(ㄓㄥˋ ㄐㄧ ㄈㄟˇ ㄖㄢˊ)
One's achievement in politics is distinguished.
政界(ㄓㄥˋ ㄐㄧㄝˋ)
political circles; officialdom; the political arena: 他在一九八六年退出政界。He withdrew from political circles in 1986.
政教(ㄓㄥˋ ㄐㄧㄠˋ)
the state and the church
政教分離(ㄓㄥˋ ㄐㄧㄠˋ ㄈㄣ ㄌㄧˊ)
the separation of the church from the state
政教合一(ㄓㄥˋ ㄐㄧㄠˋ ㄏㄜˊ ㄧ)
the unification of the state and the church
政見(ㄓㄥˋ ㄐㄧㄢˋ)
political views; politics; platform
政局(ㄓㄥˋ ㄐㄩˊ)
the political situation or scene
政權(ㄓㄥˋ ㄑㄩㄢˊ)
reins of government; regime; political power
政修年豐(ㄓㄥˋ ㄒㄧㄡ ㄋㄧㄢˊ ㄈㄥ)
The people enjoy good government and good crops.
政制(ㄓㄥˋ ㄓˋ)
a political system; a government hierarchy
政治(ㄓㄥˋ ㄓˋ)
① politics; political affairs ② government administration
政治庇護(ㄓㄥˋ ㄓˋ ㄅㄧˋ ㄏㄨˋ)
political asylum
政治犯(ㄓㄥˋ ㄓˋ ㄈㄢˋ)
a political offender; a political prisoner; a political criminal
政治地理(ㄓㄥˋ ㄓˋ ㄉㄧˋ ㄌㄧˇ)
political geography
政治活動(ㄓㄥˋ ㄓˋ ㄏㄨㄛˊ ㄉㄨㄥˋ)
political activities
政治家(ㄓㄥˋ ㄓˋ ㄐㄧㄚ)
a statesman
政治局(ㄓㄥˋ ㄓˋ ㄐㄩˊ)
Political Bureau; Politburo (of Communist parties)
政治學(ㄓㄥˋ ㄓˋ ㄒㄩㄝˊ)
political science; politics
政治史(ㄓㄥˋ ㄓˋ ㄕˇ)
political history
政治生涯(ㄓㄥˋ ㄓˋ ㄕㄥ ㄧㄚˊ)
one's political life
政爭(ㄓㄥˋ ㄓㄥ)
political strife
政潮(ㄓㄥˋ ㄔㄠˊ)
a political upheaval or crisis
政事(ㄓㄥˋ ㄕˋ)
affairs of the government; the principles and business of government
政聲(ㄓㄥˋ ㄕㄥ)
one's reputation as a statesman or magistrate; reputation of an official
政策(ㄓㄥˋ ㄘㄜˋ)
a policy
政要(ㄓㄥˋ ㄧㄠˋ)
government VIPs; ranking officials of the government or political parties; high-ranking government officials
政務(ㄓㄥˋ ㄨˋ)
affairs of the government
政務官(ㄓㄥˋ ㄨˋ ㄍㄨㄢ)
high-ranking government officials in charge of administrative affairs (as distinct from 事務官, who are executive officers)
政務委員(ㄓㄥˋ ㄨˋ ㄨㄟˇ ㄩㄢˊ)
a minister without portfolio

【故】 2122 ㄍㄨˋ guh gù

1. former; past; earlier; previous; old; antique; ancient
2. intentional; willful; on purpose; knowingly: 他明知故犯。He committed the offense willfully.
3. cause; reason: 他不知何故失踪。The reason for his disappearance remains unknown.
4. to die: 王先生昨晚病故。Mr. Wang died of illness last night.
5. an incident; an event; a matter; a happening
6. consequently; hence; therefore
7. a friend; an acquaintance: 他跟我非親非故。He is neither my relative nor my friend.

故步自封(ㄍㄨˋ ㄅㄨˋ ㄗˋ ㄈㄥ)
to confine oneself to the old method or traditional way; very conservative 訛作「固步自封」
故犯(ㄍㄨˋ ㄈㄢˋ)
to offend knowingly or willfully: 我不會原諒明知故犯的人。I'll not forgive those who offend knowingly.
故夫(ㄍㄨˋ ㄈㄨ)
(my) late husband
故道(ㄍㄨˋ ㄉㄠˋ)
① the old road; the old way ② the old method
故蹈前轍(ㄍㄨˋ ㄉㄠˋ ㄑㄧㄢˊ ㄔㄜˋ)
to continue to tread on the former ruts
故地(ㄍㄨˋ ㄉㄧˋ)
an old haunt
故都(ㄍㄨˋ ㄉㄨ)
a former capital
故態(ㄍㄨˋ ㄊㄞˋ)
① one's former attitude ② one's usual attitude
故態復萌(ㄍㄨˋ ㄊㄞˋ ㄈㄨˋ ㄇㄥˊ)
The old (bad) attitude is back.
故土(ㄍㄨˋ ㄊㄨˇ)
one's homeland; one's native land
故土難移(ㄍㄨˋ ㄊㄨˇ ㄋㄢˊ ㄧˊ)
It is hard to leave one's homeland.
故弄玄虛(ㄍㄨˋ ㄋㄨㄥˋ ㄒㄩㄢˊ ㄒㄩ)
to puzzle people intentionally; to mystify deliberately
故老(ㄍㄨˋ ㄌㄠˇ)
respectable old people
故里(ㄍㄨˋ ㄌㄧˇ)
one's home village; one's hometown; one's native heath
故吏(ㄍㄨˋ ㄌㄧˋ)
a former subordinate
故國(ㄍㄨˋ ㄍㄨㄛˊ)
① one's fatherland; one's mother country ② an old country ③ one's hometown
故國喬木(ㄍㄨˋ ㄍㄨㄛˊ ㄑㄧㄠˊ ㄇㄨˋ)
(figuratively) an ancient and famous family
故國之思(ㄍㄨˋ ㄍㄨㄛˊ ㄓ ㄙ)

〔攴部〕

nostalgic memories of one's mother country

故宮(ㄍㄨˋ ㄍㄨㄥ)
a former palace

故宮博物院(ㄍㄨˋ ㄍㄨㄥ ㄅㄛˊ ㄨˋ ㄩㄢˋ)
National Palace Museum (housing China's art treasures)

故伎(ㄍㄨˋ ㄐㄧˋ)
a stock trick; old tactics: 他再次重施故伎。He played the same old trick again.

故家(ㄍㄨˋ ㄐㄧㄚ)
a family with illustrious ancestors

故交(ㄍㄨˋ ㄐㄧㄠ)or 故知(ㄍㄨˋ ㄓ)or 故友(ㄍㄨˋ ㄧㄡˇ)
an old friend

故舊(ㄍㄨˋ ㄐㄧㄡˋ)
old friends

故劍之思(ㄍㄨˋ ㄐㄧㄢˋ ㄓ ㄙ)
to remember a former wife with tender feelings

故居(ㄍㄨˋ ㄐㄩ)
one's former residence

故去(ㄍㄨˋ ㄑㄩˋ)
to die; to pass away: 他的一位朋友在上個月故去。One of his friends passed away last month.

故鄉(ㄍㄨˋ ㄒㄧㄤ)
one's native place, land, or province; one's hometown or village; one's homeland; one's birthplace

故墟(ㄍㄨˋ ㄒㄩ)
historic remains; ruins

故址(ㄍㄨˋ ㄓˇ)
an ancient landmark; a historic spot; a place of historic interest

故紙堆(ㄍㄨˋ ㄓˇ ㄉㄨㄟ)
old books (used in a derogatory sense)

故智(ㄍㄨˋ ㄓˋ)
an old scheme; a repeatedly used trick

故障(ㄍㄨˋ ㄓㄤˋ)
a bug or breakdown (of a machine); a stoppage; trouble: 我車子的引擎發生了故障。My car had engine trouble.

故主(ㄍㄨˋ ㄓㄨˇ)
the late king or master; the former king or master

故轍(ㄍㄨˋ ㄔㄜˋ)
(literally) an old rut—an old method or system

故常(ㄍㄨˋ ㄔㄤˊ)
constant

故城(ㄍㄨˋ ㄔㄥˊ)
an old city

故失(ㄍㄨˋ ㄕ)
an improper verdict; miscarriage of justice

故實(ㄍㄨˋ ㄕˊ)
a past fact; an incident in former times

故事(ㄍㄨˋ ˙ㄕ)
a story; a narrative; a tale: 請你講個故事給我們聽。Please tell us a story.

故殺(ㄍㄨˋ ㄕㄚ)
premeditated murder

故書(ㄍㄨˋ ㄕㄨ)
an antique book

故人(ㄍㄨˋ ㄖㄣˊ)
① an old friend ② one's former wife

故入故出(ㄍㄨˋ ㄖㄨˋ ㄍㄨˋ ㄔㄨ)
(law) to mete out penalties not commensurate with the offenses committed

故入人罪(ㄍㄨˋ ㄖㄨˋ ㄖㄣˊ ㄗㄨㄟˋ)
to accuse someone of a crime falsely

故作不知(ㄍㄨˋ ㄗㄨㄛˋ ㄅㄨˋ ㄓ)
to play dumb; to pretend ignorance

故縱(ㄍㄨˋ ㄗㄨㄥˋ)
to go beyond restrictions intentionally

故此(ㄍㄨˋ ㄘˇ)
on this account; for this reason; therefore

故所(ㄍㄨˋ ㄙㄨㄛˇ)
an old place

故而(ㄍㄨˋ ㄦˊ)or 故爾(ㄍㄨˋ ㄦˇ)
therefore; on this account; for this reason

故意(ㄍㄨˋ ㄧˋ)
intentional; on purpose; willfully; deliberately; intentionally; purposely

故吾(ㄍㄨˋ ㄨˊ)or 故我(ㄍㄨˋ ㄨㄛˇ)
my former self

故違(ㄍㄨˋ ㄨㄟˊ)
to disobey; to violate knowingly

故宇(ㄍㄨˋ ㄩˇ)
one's former residence

故園(ㄍㄨˋ ㄩㄢˊ)
one's hometown and the countryside around it

六畫

2123
【效】 (効) ㄒㄧㄠˋ shiaw xiào

1. to imitate; to mimic; to follow
2. effect; effectiveness; efficacy
3. to devote
4. to offer

效顰(ㄒㄧㄠˋ ㄆㄧㄣˊ)
to blindly imitate with ludicrous effect

效命(ㄒㄧㄠˋ ㄇㄧㄥˋ)
① to obey orders ② to pursue an end at the cost of one's life

效法(ㄒㄧㄠˋ ㄈㄚˇ)
to take as a model; to imitate

效能(ㄒㄧㄠˋ ㄋㄥˊ)
effect

效勞(ㄒㄧㄠˋ ㄌㄠˊ)
to render service; to work for

效力(ㄒㄧㄠˋ ㄌㄧˋ)
① effect; efficacy: 這殺蟲劑很有效力。The insecticide is efficacious. ② to render service: 我願爲國效力。I will serve my country.

效率(ㄒㄧㄠˋ ㄌㄩˋ)
efficiency

效果(ㄒㄧㄠˋ ㄍㄨㄛˇ)
effect; result: 懲罰似乎對他沒什麼效果。Punishment does not seem to have much effect on him.

效忠(ㄒㄧㄠˋ ㄓㄨㄥ)
to be loyal to; to pledge allegiance to; allegiance

效誠(ㄒㄧㄠˋ ㄔㄥˊ)
to be faithful; to be sincere

效死(ㄒㄧㄠˋ ㄙˇ)
to render service at the cost of one's life

效益(ㄒㄧㄠˋ ㄧˋ)
beneficial result; benefit

效尤(ㄒㄧㄠˋ ㄧㄡˊ)
to imitate vice knowingly

效驗(ㄒㄧㄠˋ ㄧㄢˋ)
actual proof of efficacy; desired effect

效應(ㄒㄧㄠˋ ㄧㄥˋ)
(physics) effect

效用(ㄒㄧㄠˋ ㄩㄥˋ)
usefulness; use; utility
效用遞減律(ㄒㄧㄠˋ ㄩㄥˋ ㄉㄧˋ ㄐㄧㄢˇ ㄌㄩˋ)
the law of diminishing returns
效用說(ㄒㄧㄠˋ ㄩㄥˋ ㄕㄨㄛ)
utility theory

【敉】 2124 ㄇㄧˇ mii mǐ
to stabilize; to quiet; to pacify; to soothe
敉平(ㄇㄧˇ ㄆㄧㄥˊ)
to succeed in putting down a revolt or rebellion; to subjugate
敉寧(ㄇㄧˇ ㄋㄧㄥˊ)
to give peace; to pacify

七畫

【敍】 2125 (敘、叙) ㄒㄩˋ shiuh xù
1. to tell; to narrate; to describe; to express
2. to talk about; to chat: 若得閒請來一敍。Please come over for a chat if you are free.
3. to arrange in order
4. to rate or evaluate (as a basis for reward, appointment, etc.); to assess
敍別(ㄒㄩˋ ㄅㄧㄝˊ)
to get together for talk before a separation; to say good-bye to each other; to have a farewell talk
敍談(ㄒㄩˋ ㄊㄢˊ)
to get together and chat; to chitchat
敍利亞(ㄒㄩˋ ㄌㄧˋ ㄧㄚˇ)
Syria
敍錄(ㄒㄩˋ ㄌㄨˋ)
commentaries
敍功(ㄒㄩˋ ㄍㄨㄥ)
to rate and reward merits or contributions
敍功行賞(ㄒㄩˋ ㄍㄨㄥ ㄒㄧㄥˊ ㄕㄤˇ)
to go over the records and decide on awards
敍寒溫(ㄒㄩˋ ㄏㄢˊ ㄨㄣ)or 敍寒暄(ㄒㄩˋ ㄏㄢˊ ㄒㄩㄢ)
to make mutual inquiries after a long separation
敍家常(ㄒㄩˋ ㄐㄧㄚ ㄔㄤˊ)
to talk about daily life
敍舊(ㄒㄩˋ ㄐㄧㄡˋ)
to talk about the old days
敍情(ㄒㄩˋ ㄑㄧㄥˊ)
to bare one's heart (in conversation, writing, etc.)
敍勳(ㄒㄩˋ ㄒㄩㄣ)
to rate and reward merits or contributions
敍傳(ㄒㄩˋ ㄓㄨㄢˋ)
to write a preface for a book
敍事詩(ㄒㄩˋ ㄕˋ ㄕ)
a narrative poem
敍事文(ㄒㄩˋ ㄕˋ ㄨㄣˊ)
a narration
敍述(ㄒㄩˋ ㄕㄨˋ)
to narrate; to recount; to relate
敍說(ㄒㄩˋ ㄕㄨㄛ)
to tell; to narrate
敍言(ㄒㄩˋ ㄧㄢˊ)or 敍文(ㄒㄩˋ ㄨㄣˊ)
a preface; a foreword 亦作「序言」or「序文」
敍用(ㄒㄩˋ ㄩㄥˋ)
to employ (as government officials); to appoint

【教】 2126 1. ㄐㄧㄠˋ jiaw jiào
1. a religion: 他不信基督教。He does not believe in the Christian religion.
2. an order; a directive
3. to educate
4. to incite; to urge; to bid; to instigate
5. to instruct; instruction(s); to advise; advice: 請不吝賜教。Please advise me graciously.
6. to have; to make; to let: 誰教你進那屋子的? Who let you into the building?
教本(ㄐㄧㄠˋ ㄅㄣˇ)
a textbook
教鞭(ㄐㄧㄠˋ ㄅㄧㄢ)
① a pointer or rod (used by a teacher) ② a teaching career
教不倦(ㄐㄧㄠˋ ˙ㄅㄨ ㄐㄩㄢˋ)
diligent or untiring in teaching
教派(ㄐㄧㄠˋ ㄆㄞˋ)
religious sects or denominations
教門(ㄐㄧㄠˋ ㄇㄣˊ)
① the door to Buddhism ② Islam
教名(ㄐㄧㄠˋ ㄇㄧㄥˊ)
one's Christian name or forename
教母(ㄐㄧㄠˋ ㄇㄨˇ)
godmother
教法(ㄐㄧㄠˋ ㄈㄚˇ)
teaching methods; pedagogy
教坊(ㄐㄧㄠˋ ㄈㄤ)
an institution for the training of musicians and songstresses (in former times)
教父(ㄐㄧㄠˋ ㄈㄨˋ)
godfather
教導(ㄐㄧㄠˋ ㄉㄠˇ)or(ㄐㄧㄠˋ ㄉㄠˋ)
① to teach and guide; to instruct ② guidance
教導主任(ㄐㄧㄠˋ ㄉㄠˇ ㄓㄨˇ ㄖㄣˋ)or(ㄐㄧㄠˋ ㄉㄠˋ ㄓㄨˇ ㄖㄣˋ)
the head teacher or assistant principal (in a primary school)
教導有方(ㄐㄧㄠˋ ㄉㄠˇ ㄧㄡˇ ㄈㄤ)or(ㄐㄧㄠˋ ㄉㄠˋ ㄧㄡˇ ㄈㄤ)
skillful in teaching and providing guidance (The expression is often used in citations for outstanding teachers and schools.)
教督(ㄐㄧㄠˋ ㄉㄨ)
to teach and supervise
教頭(ㄐㄧㄠˋ ㄊㄡˊ)
the head instructor (of martial arts); chief trainer
教堂(ㄐㄧㄠˋ ㄊㄤˊ)
a church; a mosque; a cathedral; a chapel; a tabernacle; a temple; a shrine
教條(ㄐㄧㄠˋ ㄊㄧㄠˊ)
a doctrine; a dogma; a creed; a tenet
教條主義(ㄐㄧㄠˋ ㄊㄧㄠˊ ㄓㄨˇ ㄧˋ)
doctrinairism; dogmatism
教廷(ㄐㄧㄠˋ ㄊㄧㄥˊ)
the Holy See; the Vatican
教廷大使(ㄐㄧㄠˋ ㄊㄧㄥˊ ㄉㄚˋ ㄕˇ)
an apostolic nuncio
教廷公使(ㄐㄧㄠˋ ㄊㄧㄥˊ ㄍㄨㄥ ㄕˇ)
an apostolic internuncio
教徒(ㄐㄧㄠˋ ㄊㄨˊ)
a (religious) believer or follower
教猱升木(ㄐㄧㄠˋ ㄋㄠˊ ㄕㄥ ㄇㄨˋ)
(literally) to teach monkeys to climb a tree—to encourage wicked people to do wicked things

〔攴部〕

教練(ㄐㄧㄠˋ ㄌㄧㄢˋ)
①a coach (of athletes); an instructor ②to train; to drill; to coach

教練機(ㄐㄧㄠˋ ㄌㄧㄢˋ ㄐㄧ)
a trainer

教練車(ㄐㄧㄠˋ ㄌㄧㄢˋ ㄔㄜ)
a learner-driven vehicle

教令(ㄐㄧㄠˋ ㄌㄧㄥˋ)
① the commands, or orders, of a ruler (as distinct from the law) ②a religious decree or proclamation

教規(ㄐㄧㄠˋ ㄍㄨㄟ)
rules of a religion; canons

教官(ㄐㄧㄠˋ ㄍㄨㄢ)
a military instructor; a drillmaster

教科書(ㄐㄧㄠˋ ㄎㄜ ㄕㄨ)
the textbook

教化(ㄐㄧㄠˋ ㄏㄨㄚˋ)
① culture ② to bring enlightenment to the people by education; to civilize the masses by education

教會(ㄐㄧㄠˋ ㄏㄨㄟˋ)
the church: 天主教會 the Catholic Church

教會學校(ㄐㄧㄠˋ ㄏㄨㄟˋ ㄒㄩㄝˊ ㄒㄧㄠˋ)
a missionary school; a church school

教誨(ㄐㄧㄠˋ ㄏㄨㄟˋ)
to teach and admonish; teachings and admonitions

教皇(ㄐㄧㄠˋ ㄏㄨㄤˊ)
the Pope; the Pontiff

教誡(ㄐㄧㄠˋ ㄐㄧㄝˋ)
prohibitions of a religion or religious sect

教具(ㄐㄧㄠˋ ㄐㄩˋ)
teaching aids (such as charts, samples, etc.)

教區(ㄐㄧㄠˋ ㄑㄩ)
a diocese; a parish

教習(ㄐㄧㄠˋ ㄒㄧˊ)
to teach; to instruct

教學(ㄐㄧㄠˋ ㄒㄩㄝˊ)
① instruction; teaching ② to teach and to learn; teaching and learning

教學法(ㄐㄧㄠˋ ㄒㄩㄝˊ ㄈㄚˇ)
pedagogy; teaching methods
參看「教授法」

教學相長(ㄐㄧㄠˋ ㄒㄩㄝˊ ㄒㄧㄤ ㄓㄤˇ)
The teacher and the student can profit from each other.

教訓(ㄐㄧㄠˋ ㄒㄩㄣˋ)or(ㄐㄧㄠˋ ·ㄒㄩㄣ)
①a moral; a lesson: 那件車禍給了他一個教訓。The car accident taught him a lesson. ②to admonish; admonitions; teachings; a scolding: 我狠狠地教訓他一頓。I gave him a good scolding.

教訓詩(ㄐㄧㄠˋ ㄒㄩㄣˋ ㄕ)
didactic poetry

教職(ㄐㄧㄠˋ ㄓˊ)
the occupation of teaching: 他擔任教職已四十年。He has been teaching for forty years.

教職員(ㄐㄧㄠˋ ㄓˊ ㄩㄢˊ)
the teaching and administrative staff of a school

教戰(ㄐㄧㄠˋ ㄓㄢˋ)
to teach martial arts

教長(ㄐㄧㄠˋ ㄓㄤˇ)
a mullah or mulla; an imam

教主(ㄐㄧㄠˋ ㄓㄨˇ)
the founder of a religion; a religious leader

教場(ㄐㄧㄠˋ ㄔㄤˇ)or(ㄐㄧㄠˋ ㄔㄤˊ)
a military drill ground

教師(ㄐㄧㄠˋ ㄕ)
a teacher; a school teacher; a pedagogue: 經驗是最好的教師。Experience is the best teacher.

教師節(ㄐㄧㄠˋ ㄕ ㄐㄧㄝˊ)
Teacher's Day (falling on September 28 and corresponding to Confucius' birthday)

教士(ㄐㄧㄠˋ ㄕˋ)
an evangelist; a preacher; a missionary; a priest; a clergyman

教室(ㄐㄧㄠˋ ㄕˋ)
a classroom: 你的教室裏有多少桌子? How many desks are there in your classroom?

教社(ㄐㄧㄠˋ ㄕㄜˋ)
(Catholicism) an order

教授(ㄐㄧㄠˋ ㄕㄡˋ)
a professor: 他是心理學副教授。He is an associate professor of psychology.

教授法(ㄐㄧㄠˋ ㄕㄡˋ ㄈㄚˇ)or **教學法**(ㄐㄧㄠˋ ㄒㄩㄝˊ ㄈㄚˇ)
teaching methods; the method of instruction; pedagogy

教授得法(ㄐㄧㄠˋ ㄕㄡˋ ㄉㄜˊ ㄈㄚˇ)
to have tact in teaching

教澤(ㄐㄧㄠˋ ㄗㄜˊ)
cultural influence

教宗(ㄐㄧㄠˋ ㄗㄨㄥ)
the Pope; the Pontiff

教材(ㄐㄧㄠˋ ㄘㄞˊ)
teaching materials

教唆(ㄐㄧㄠˋ ㄙㄨㄛ)
to instigate; to incite; to abet; to suborn: 她教唆他做蠢事。She abetted him in his folly.

教唆犯(ㄐㄧㄠˋ ㄙㄨㄛ ㄈㄢˋ)
an abettor

教唆罪(ㄐㄧㄠˋ ㄙㄨㄛ ㄗㄨㄟˋ)
the offense of instigation or subornation; the guilt of instigation

教案(ㄐㄧㄠˋ ㄢˋ)
a teaching plan (prepared by a teacher before class time)

教益(ㄐㄧㄠˋ ㄧˋ)
a useful lesson; enlightenment

教義(ㄐㄧㄠˋ ㄧˋ)
the doctrine of a religion; a creed

教友(ㄐㄧㄠˋ ㄧㄡˇ)
a fellow believer (of a religion); a member of a church

教友派(ㄐㄧㄠˋ ㄧㄡˇ ㄆㄞˋ)or **教友會**(ㄐㄧㄠˋ ㄧㄡˇ ㄏㄨㄟˋ)
Society of Friends, founded in 1650 by George Fox in England (also called Quakers)

教養(ㄐㄧㄠˋ ㄧㄤˇ)
to bring up; to rear; upbringing: 他很有教養。He was well brought up.

教務(ㄐㄧㄠˋ ㄨˋ)
instructional affairs (as distinct from administrative affairs in a school)

教務長(ㄐㄧㄠˋ ㄨˋ ㄓㄤˇ)
the dean of studies (of a college or university)

教務主任(ㄐㄧㄠˋ ㄨˋ ㄓㄨˇ ㄖㄣˋ)
the dean of studies (of a primary or secondary school)

教務處(ㄐㄧㄠˋ ㄨˋ ㄔㄨˋ)
the office of the dean of studies

教諭(ㄐㄧㄠˋ ㄩˋ)
an official instructor (in a public school in former times)

教育(ㄐㄧㄠˋ ㄩˋ)
①to educate ②education
教育部(ㄐㄧㄠˋ ㄩˋ ㄅㄨˋ)
Ministry of Education
教育部長(ㄐㄧㄠˋ ㄩˋ ㄅㄨˋ ㄓㄤˇ)
a minister of education; an education minister
教育費(ㄐㄧㄠˋ ㄩˋ ㄈㄟˋ)
the cost of education; an education bill
教育方針(ㄐㄧㄠˋ ㄩˋ ㄈㄤ ㄓㄣ)
a policy for education; an educational policy
教育廳(ㄐㄧㄠˋ ㄩˋ ㄊㄧㄥ)
Department of Education (under a provincial government)
教育廳長(ㄐㄧㄠˋ ㄩˋ ㄊㄧㄥ ㄓㄤˇ)
the commissioner of education or education commissioner (under a provincial government)
教育科(ㄐㄧㄠˋ ㄩˋ ㄎㄜ)
an education section (under a county or city government)
教育科長(ㄐㄧㄠˋ ㄩˋ ㄎㄜ ㄓㄤˇ)
the chief of the education section (under a city or county government)
教育會(ㄐㄧㄠˋ ㄩˋ ㄏㄨㄟˋ)
an educational association
教育基金(ㄐㄧㄠˋ ㄩˋ ㄐㄧ ㄐㄧㄣ)
educational funds
教育基金會(ㄐㄧㄠˋ ㄩˋ ㄐㄧ ㄐㄧㄣ ㄏㄨㄟˋ)
an educational foundation
教育家(ㄐㄧㄠˋ ㄩˋ ㄐㄧㄚ)
an educator or educationist
教育界(ㄐㄧㄠˋ ㄩˋ ㄐㄧㄝˋ)
educational circles
教育局(ㄐㄧㄠˋ ㄩˋ ㄐㄩˊ)
the bureau of education (under a special municipal government)
教育局長(ㄐㄧㄠˋ ㄩˋ ㄐㄩˊ ㄓㄤˇ)
the director of the bureau of education (under a special municipal government)
教育系(ㄐㄧㄠˋ ㄩˋ ㄒㄧˋ)
the department of education (in a university)
教育心理學(ㄐㄧㄠˋ ㄩˋ ㄒㄧㄣ ㄌㄧˇ ㄒㄩㄝˊ)
educational psychology
教育行政(ㄐㄧㄠˋ ㄩˋ ㄒㄧㄥˊ ㄓㄥˋ)
educational administration
教育學(ㄐㄧㄠˋ ㄩˋ ㄒㄩㄝˊ)
pedagogy; pedagogics
教育制度(ㄐㄧㄠˋ ㄩˋ ㄓˋ ㄉㄨˋ)
the educational system
教育程度(ㄐㄧㄠˋ ㄩˋ ㄔㄥˊ ㄉㄨˋ)
the level of education; educational attainment
教育總長(ㄐㄧㄠˋ ㄩˋ ㄗㄨㄥˇ ㄓㄤˇ)
Director-General of Education (a title used in the early republican years which was equivalent to the Education Minister)
教員(ㄐㄧㄠˋ ㄩㄢˊ)
a member of the teaching profession; a teacher
教員休息室(ㄐㄧㄠˋ ㄩㄢˊ ㄒㄧㄡ ㄒㄧˊ ㄕˋ)
a staff room; a common room

【教】 2126
2. ㄐㄧㄠ jiau jiāo
to teach; to guide: 他教我們做實驗。He taught us how to conduct experiments.
教法(ㄐㄧㄠ ㄈㄚˇ)
teaching methods
教給(ㄐㄧㄠ ㄍㄟˇ)
to impart (knowledge or skill) to someone
教壞(ㄐㄧㄠ ㄏㄨㄞˋ)
to misguide; to lead astray
教書(ㄐㄧㄠ ㄕㄨ)
to teach (usually for a living): 我哥哥在小學教書。My brother teaches in a primary school.
教書匠(ㄐㄧㄠ ㄕㄨ ㄐㄧㄤˋ)
a teacher (used in a derogatory sense): 我當了十年的教書匠。I have been a teacher for ten years.

【敏】 2127
ㄇㄧㄣˇ miin mǐn
1. quick; agile; speedy; clever; smart; nimble; sensitive: 這孩子很聰敏。The child is very clever.
2. diligent; industrious; earnest; eager
敏力(ㄇㄧㄣˇ ㄌㄧˋ)
to apply oneself diligently
敏感(ㄇㄧㄣˇ ㄍㄢˇ)
① sensitive; susceptible ② (medicine) allergic
敏慧(ㄇㄧㄣˇ ㄏㄨㄟˋ)
clever; sharp-witted; keen; quick in understanding
敏捷(ㄇㄧㄣˇ ㄐㄧㄝˊ)
agile; adroit; quick; nimble: 他的頭腦敏捷。He is quick in mind.
敏求(ㄇㄧㄣˇ ㄑㄧㄡˊ)
to pursue diligently or earnestly
敏銳(ㄇㄧㄣˇ ㄖㄨㄟˋ)
keen; sharp; sharp-witted; acute: 他的目光敏銳。He has sharp eyes.
敏而好古(ㄇㄧㄣˇ ㄦˊ ㄏㄠˋ ㄍㄨˇ)
to imitate the ancients diligently
敏悟(ㄇㄧㄣˇ ㄨˋ)
quick to understand: 他學習語言的敏悟力很強。He is quick at learning languages.
敏於事而慎於言(ㄇㄧㄣˇ ㄩˊ ㄕˋ ㄦˊ ㄕㄣˋ ㄩˊ ㄧㄢˊ)
speedy as a worker and cautious as a speaker; quick in work and cautious in speech

【救】 2128
ㄐㄧㄡˋ jiow jiù
to save; to relieve; to rescue; to deliver; to aid; to help
救兵(ㄐㄧㄡˋ ㄅㄧㄥ)
relieving troops; reinforcements
救兵如救火(ㄐㄧㄡˋ ㄅㄧㄥ ㄖㄨˊ ㄐㄧㄡˋ ㄏㄨㄛˇ)
The urgency to despatch relieving troops or reinforcements is similar to that of firefighting—the sooner the better.
救民(ㄐㄧㄡˋ ㄇㄧㄣˊ)
to save the people
救命(ㄐㄧㄡˋ ㄇㄧㄥˋ)
①to save one's life ②Help!
救命恩人(ㄐㄧㄡˋ ㄇㄧㄥˋ ㄣ ㄖㄣˊ)
the savior of one's life
救溺(ㄐㄧㄡˋ ㄋㄧˋ)
to save the life of a drowning person
救國(ㄐㄧㄡˋ ㄍㄨㄛˊ)
to save one's country
救國救民(ㄐㄧㄡˋ ㄍㄨㄛˊ ㄐㄧㄡˋ ㄇㄧㄣˊ)
to save the country and people from an impending danger
救苦救難(ㄐㄧㄡˋ ㄎㄨˇ ㄐㄧㄡˋ ㄋㄢˋ)
to relieve the suffering and the distressed
救護(ㄐㄧㄡˋ ㄏㄨˋ)

〔攴部〕

to relieve and nurse (the wounded, etc.); to rescue
救護法(ㄐㄧㄡˋ ㄏㄨˋ ㄈㄚˇ)
techniques of first aid
救護站(ㄐㄧㄡˋ ㄏㄨˋ ㄓㄢˋ)
an aid station
救護車(ㄐㄧㄡˋ ㄏㄨˋ ㄔㄜ)
an ambulance (a vehicle for carrying people who are ill, wounded in war or hurt in accidents)
救活(ㄐㄧㄡˋ ㄏㄨㄛˊ)
to resuscitate; to revive
救火(ㄐㄧㄡˋ ㄏㄨㄛˇ)
① to fight a fire; to try to extinguish a fire ② fire-fighting
救火隊(ㄐㄧㄡˋ ㄏㄨㄛˇ ㄉㄨㄟˋ)
a fire brigade
救火機(ㄐㄧㄡˋ ㄏㄨㄛˇ ㄐㄧ)
a fire extinguisher
救火車(ㄐㄧㄡˋ ㄏㄨㄛˇ ㄔㄜ)
a fire engine
救火揚沸(ㄐㄧㄡˋ ㄏㄨㄛˇ ㄧㄤˊ ㄈㄟˋ)
(literally) to try to stop water boiling by stirring it instead of removing the fire underneath—to try to solve a problem without removing the root cause
救火員(ㄐㄧㄡˋ ㄏㄨㄛˇ ㄩㄢˊ)
a fireman
救飢(ㄐㄧㄡˋ ㄐㄧ)
to relieve the starving
救急(ㄐㄧㄡˋ ㄐㄧˊ)
① to give help in emergency; to help meet an urgent need ② to apply first aid
救急不救窮(ㄐㄧㄡˋ ㄐㄧˊ ㄅㄨˋ ㄐㄧㄡˋ ㄑㄩㄥˊ)
One may give financial aid to others in an emergency but should not do so if they are perennially in need of money.
救濟(ㄐㄧㄡˋ ㄐㄧˋ)
to relieve (the suffering, the poor, etc.); to succor
救濟金(ㄐㄧㄡˋ ㄐㄧˋ ㄐㄧㄣ)
relief funds
救濟權(ㄐㄧㄡˋ ㄐㄧˋ ㄑㄩㄢˊ)
(law) secondary right
救濟院(ㄐㄧㄡˋ ㄐㄧˋ ㄩㄢˋ)
an institution for the poor; a poorhouse; a workhouse
救駕(ㄐㄧㄡˋ ㄐㄧㄚˋ)
to come to the rescue of the emperor; to come to the aid of the monarch
救窮(ㄐㄧㄡˋ ㄑㄩㄥˊ)
to relieve the poor
救星(ㄐㄧㄡˋ ㄒㄧㄥ)
a savior
救治(ㄐㄧㄡˋ ㄓˋ)
to treat and cure (the sick); to remedy: 這種藥可救治你的頭痛。This medicine will cure your headache.
救主(ㄐㄧㄡˋ ㄓㄨˇ)
the Savior; the Messiah
救助(ㄐㄧㄡˋ ㄓㄨˋ)
to relieve or help (persons)
救時(ㄐㄧㄡˋ ㄕˊ)
to save the age (from degeneration)
救世(ㄐㄧㄡˋ ㄕˋ)
to save mankind; to save the world
救世軍(ㄐㄧㄡˋ ㄕˋ ㄐㄩㄣ)
the Salvation Army
救世主(ㄐㄧㄡˋ ㄕˋ ㄓㄨˇ)
① the Savior; the Messiah ② *Messiah*, an oratorio (1742) by George Frideric Handel
救生(ㄐㄧㄡˋ ㄕㄥ)
① to save the dying; to save one's life ② lifesaving
救生帶(ㄐㄧㄡˋ ㄕㄥ ㄉㄞˋ)
a life belt
救生艇(ㄐㄧㄡˋ ㄕㄥ ㄊㄧㄥˇ)
a lifeboat
救生圈(ㄐㄧㄡˋ ㄕㄥ ㄑㄩㄢ)
a life ring; a life buoy
救生船(ㄐㄧㄡˋ ㄕㄥ ㄔㄨㄢˊ)
a lifeboat
救生衣(ㄐㄧㄡˋ ㄕㄥ ㄧ)
a life jacket
救生員(ㄐㄧㄡˋ ㄕㄥ ㄩㄢˊ)
a lifeguard; a lifesaver
救人一命，勝造七級浮屠(ㄐㄧㄡˋ ㄖㄣˊ ㄧˊ ㄇㄧㄥˋ, ㄕㄥˋ ㄗㄠˋ ㄑㄧ ㄐㄧˊ ㄈㄨˊ ㄊㄨˊ)
Better save one life than build a seven-story pagoda.
救災(ㄐㄧㄡˋ ㄗㄞ)
to relieve victims of a disaster
救藥(ㄐㄧㄡˋ ㄧㄠˋ)
to remedy; to cure—to save the situation; to rectify abuses; to redress
救亡圖存(ㄐㄧㄡˋ ㄨㄤˊ ㄊㄨˊ ㄘㄨㄣˊ)
to save one's country so that it may survive
救援(ㄐㄧㄡˋ ㄩㄢˊ)
to help or aid (the distressed)
救援投手(ㄐㄧㄡˋ ㄩㄢˊ ㄊㄡˊ ㄕㄡˇ)
(baseball) a relief pitcher

【敕】 2129 (勅) ㄔˋ chyh chì

1. an imperial order or decree
2. cautious
3. to warn; to caution

敕命(ㄔˋ ㄇㄧㄥˋ)
an imperial order to confer a title or rank on an official
敕封(ㄔˋ ㄈㄥ)
the imperial appointment or bestowal of titles of nobility
敕牒(ㄔˋ ㄉㄧㄝˊ)
an imperial order
敕勒(ㄔˋ ㄌㄜˋ)
one of the ethnic tribes in the west
敕令(ㄔˋ ㄌㄧㄥˋ)
a rescript
敕授(ㄔˋ ㄕㄡˋ)
the imperial appointment or bestowal of titles of nobility
敕身(ㄔˋ ㄕㄣ)
to discipline oneself; to be prudent in conduct
敕書(ㄔˋ ㄕㄨ)
an imperial letter
敕葬(ㄔˋ ㄗㄤˋ)
to bury with a funeral organized by an imperial order
敕贈(ㄔˋ ㄗㄥˋ)
the imperial appointment or bestowal of titles of nobility

【敖】 2130 1. ㄠˊ aur áo

leisurely; idle
敖民(ㄠˊ ㄇㄧㄣˊ)
loafers; idlers
敖得薩(ㄠˊ ㄉㄜˊ ㄙㄚˋ)
Odessa, a Russian port city
敖盪(ㄠˊ ㄉㄤˋ)
to loaf about; to frisk or play about; to idle away one's time
敖戲(ㄠˊ ㄒㄧˋ)
to play; to frolic
敖敖(ㄠˊ ㄠˊ)
tall; long
敖遊(ㄠˊ ㄧㄡˊ)

to travel or wander idly

【敖】2130 2.(傲) ㄠˋ aw ào

1. proud; haughty
2. to make fun of

敖弄(ㄠˋ ㄌㄨㄥˋ)
to make fun of; to poke fun at

【敗】2131 ㄅㄞˋ bay bài

1. to defeat or be defeated; to thwart or be thwarted; to go down; to fail; to lose
2. to decline; to decay; to wither
3. to spoil or be spoiled; to corrupt or be corrupted

敗北(ㄅㄞˋ ㄅㄟˇ)
to suffer defeat; a defeat; to lose a battle

敗筆(ㄅㄞˋ ㄅㄧˇ)
① a worn-out writing brush; a spoiled pen ② poor calligraphy; a flaw in the making of a stroke — a faulty expression in writing

敗門風(ㄅㄞˋ ㄇㄣˊ ㄈㄥ)
to tarnish the good name of one's family; to disgrace one's family

敗盟(ㄅㄞˋ ㄇㄥˊ)
to break a covenant

敗名(ㄅㄞˋ ㄇㄧㄥˊ)
to tarnish one's reputation; to disgrace oneself

敗德(ㄅㄞˋ ㄉㄜˊ)
evil conduct; licentious behaviors

敗敵(ㄅㄞˋ ㄉㄧˊ)
to crush the enemy; to defeat the enemy

敗退(ㄅㄞˋ ㄊㄨㄟˋ)
to retreat after defeat

敗類(ㄅㄞˋ ㄌㄟˋ)
① to ruin or corrupt one's fellows ② corrupt people; the dregs of society; the scum of a community; a degenerate

敗柳殘花(ㄅㄞˋ ㄌㄧㄡˇ ㄘㄢˊ ㄏㄨㄚ)
prostitutes; immoral women

敗露(ㄅㄞˋ ㄌㄨˋ)
(said of a crime, plot, etc.) to fail and be exposed

敗落(ㄅㄞˋ ㄌㄨㄛˋ)
to fall into a decline; to go down: 這部電影反映人性的敗落。The movie reflects the decline of human nature.

敗火(ㄅㄞˋ ㄏㄨㄛˇ)
to alleviate fever; to relieve inflammation or internal heat

敗壞(ㄅㄞˋ ㄏㄨㄞˋ)
to corrupt or be corrupted; to ruin or be ruined: 賭博敗壞社會風氣。Gambling corrupts the morals of society.

敗壞門楣(ㄅㄞˋ ㄏㄨㄞˋ ㄇㄣˊ ㄇㄟˊ)
to disgrace one's family

敗績(ㄅㄞˋ ㄐㄧ)
a defeat

敗家子(ㄅㄞˋ ㄐㄧㄚ ㄗˇ)or 敗子(ㄅㄞˋ ㄗˇ)
a prodigal; a spendthrift; a wastrel

敗將(ㄅㄞˋ ㄐㄧㄤˋ)
① a defeated enemy general ② one who is defeated in a contest: 他是我的手下敗將。He is the one who has suffered defeat at my hands.

敗軍(ㄅㄞˋ ㄐㄩㄣ)
a defeated army

敗軍之將不足言勇(ㄅㄞˋ ㄐㄩㄣ ㄓ ㄐㄧㄤˋ ㄅㄨˋ ㄗㄨˊ ㄧㄢˊ ㄩㄥˇ)
The general of a defeated army is in no position to claim bravery.

敗血(ㄅㄞˋ ㄒㄧㄝˇ)or(ㄅㄞˋ ㄒㄩㄝˋ)
poisonous blood

敗血病(ㄅㄞˋ ㄒㄧㄝˇ ㄅㄧㄥˋ)or 敗血症(ㄅㄞˋ ㄒㄧㄝˇ ㄓㄥˋ)
septicemia

敗血膿毒症(ㄅㄞˋ ㄒㄧㄝˇ ㄋㄨㄥˊ ㄉㄨˊ ㄓㄥˋ)or(ㄅㄞˋ ㄒㄩㄝˋ ㄋㄨㄥˊ ㄉㄨˊ ㄓㄥˋ)
septicopyemia

敗興而歸(ㄅㄞˋ ㄒㄧㄥˋ ㄦˊ ㄍㄨㄟ)
to come back disappointed: 我乘興而去，敗興而歸。I went with great enthusiasm and came back disappointed.

敗絮(ㄅㄞˋ ㄒㄩˋ)
waste cotton—a dry and useless thing

敗陣(ㄅㄞˋ ㄓㄣˋ)
a defeat

敗仗(ㄅㄞˋ ㄓㄤˋ)
a defeat

敗事(ㄅㄞˋ ㄕˋ)
to spoil or bungle a matter

敗肉(ㄅㄞˋ ㄖㄡˋ)
spoiled meat

敗走(ㄅㄞˋ ㄗㄡˇ)
to flee after defeat

敗挫(ㄅㄞˋ ㄘㄨㄛˋ)
to defeat; to frustrate; to thwart

敗訴(ㄅㄞˋ ㄙㄨˋ)
to lose a lawsuit: 他因敗訴而破產。Losing the lawsuit bankrupted him.

敗葉(ㄅㄞˋ ㄧㄝˋ)
shriveled leaves; fallen leaves

敗亡(ㄅㄞˋ ㄨㄤˊ)
to be defeated and overthrown

【敔】2132 ㄩˇ yeu yǔ

an ancient musical instrument

八畫

【敝】2133 ㄅㄧˋ bih bì

1. worn-out; broken; tattered
2. exhausted; tired
3. (a self-depreciatory term) my, or our: 歡迎蒞臨敝公司。Welcome to our firm.

敝店(ㄅㄧˋ ㄉㄧㄢˋ)
my humble store: 敝店供應各種參考書。My humble store offers all kinds of reference books.

敝屨(ㄅㄧˋ ㄐㄩˋ)
worn-out shoes

敝國(ㄅㄧˋ ㄍㄨㄛˊ)
(a self-depreciatory term) my or our country

敝屣(ㄅㄧˋ ㄒㄧˇ)
worn-out shoes—useless things

敝校(ㄅㄧˋ ㄒㄧㄠˋ)
(a self-depreciatory term) my or our school: 敝校創立於一九四八年。Our school was founded in 1948.

敝鄉(ㄅㄧˋ ㄒㄧㄤ)
(a self-depreciatory term) my or our hometown or village

敝姓(ㄅㄧˋ ㄒㄧㄥˋ)
(a self-depreciatory term) my family name

敝帚千金(ㄅㄧˋ ㄓㄡˇ ㄑㄧㄢ ㄐㄧㄣ)
(literally) My worn-out broom is worth a thousand crowns.—Everyone values

things of his own.
敝帚自珍(ㄅㄧˋ ㄓㄡˇ ㄗˋ ㄓㄣ)
(literally) My worn-out broom is a treasure to me. —Everyone values things of his own.
敝處(ㄅㄧˋ ㄔㄨˋ)
(a self-depreciatory term) my place
敝舍(ㄅㄧˋ ㄕㄜˋ)
(a self-depreciatory term) my house: 請駕臨敝舍一敍。Please come to my house and have a talk.
敝衣惡食(ㄅㄧˋ ㄧ ㄜˋ ㄕˊ)
meanly clothed and poorly fed — having a very low standard of living
敝邑(ㄅㄧˋ ㄧˋ)
(a self-depreciatory term) my kingdom
敝友(ㄅㄧˋ ㄧㄡˇ)
(a self-depreciatory term) my friend
敝寓(ㄅㄧˋ ㄩˋ)
(a self-depreciatory term) my residence

〔攴部〕

【敞】2134 ㄔㄤˇ chaang chǎng
1. open; uncovered
2. spacious; broad
敞篷(兒)車(ㄔㄤˇ ㄆㄥˊ(ㄦ) ㄔㄜ)
an open coach; an open car
敞地兒(ㄔㄤˇ ㄉㄧˋ ㄦ)
open ground; unsheltered ground
敞廳(ㄔㄤˇ ㄊㄧㄥ)
a spacious hall; a large hall
敞亮(ㄔㄤˇ ·ㄌㄧㄤ)
spacious and light: 你的房子很敞亮。Your house is light and spacious.
敞開(ㄔㄤˇ ㄎㄞ)
to open; to unfold: 請把門敞開。Open the door wide, please.
敞快(ㄔㄤˇ ·ㄎㄨㄞ)
straightforward and broad-minded
敞胸露懷(ㄔㄤˇ ㄒㄩㄥ ㄌㄡˋ ㄏㄨㄞˊ)or 敞胸(ㄔㄤˇ ㄒㄩㄥ)or 敞着懷(ㄔㄤˇ ·ㄓㄜ ㄏㄨㄞˊ)
to bare the breast; décolleté
敞著(ㄔㄤˇ ·ㄓㄜ)
open
敞車(ㄔㄤˇ ㄔㄜ)
an open carriage; an open wagon; an open freight car

【敠】2135 ㄉㄨㄛˊ dwo duó
1. to weigh (a thing) in the hand
2. to weigh and consider (a matter)

【敢】2136 ㄍㄢˇ gaan gǎn
1. to dare: 我不敢去。I dare not go.
2. to have the confidence to; to be sure; to be certain
3. bold; courageous; daring
4. to make bold; to venture
敢當(ㄍㄢˇ ㄉㄤ)
to dare to accept (a compliment, responsibility, etc.)
敢怒而不敢言(ㄍㄢˇ ㄋㄨˋ ㄦˊ ㄅㄨˋ ㄍㄢˇ ㄧㄢˊ)
angry but not daring to speak out; to choke with silent fury; to suppress one's rage
敢請(ㄍㄢˇ ㄑㄧㄥˇ)
I venture to request....
敢情(ㄍㄢˇ ·ㄑㄧㄥ)
① naturally; of course; as might be expected ② at the start; originally ③ perhaps; maybe
敢是(ㄍㄢˇ ㄕˋ)
perhaps; maybe
敢作敢當(ㄍㄢˇ ㄗㄨㄛˋ ㄍㄢˇ ㄉㄤ)
to have the courage to accept the consequences of one's doing; to shoulder responsibility bravely
敢作敢爲(ㄍㄢˇ ㄗㄨㄛˋ ㄍㄢˇ ㄨㄟˊ)
to have the courage to do what one believes should be done
敢死(ㄍㄢˇ ㄙˇ)
to dare to die; to defy death
敢死隊(ㄍㄢˇ ㄙˇ ㄉㄨㄟˋ)
a suicide squad; a death band; a dare-to-die corps; a commando unit given a very dangerous mission
敢言(ㄍㄢˇ ㄧㄢˊ)
courageous enough to express one's beliefs
敢問(ㄍㄢˇ ㄨㄣˋ)
I venture to ask....
敢於(ㄍㄢˇ ㄩˊ)
to dare to; to be bold in; to have the courage to

【散】2137 1. ㄙㄢˋ sann sàn
1. to scatter; to disperse: 烏雲散了。Dark clouds dispersed.
2. to end; to be over; to stop: 戲散了。The play has ended.
3. to disseminate; to give out
散播(ㄙㄢˋ ㄅㄛˋ)
to disseminate; to spread: 不要散播謠言。Don't spread rumors.
散佈 or 散布(ㄙㄢˋ ㄅㄨˋ)
① to scatter; to sprinkle; to strew ② to spread; to disseminate: 她喜歡散布流言蜚語。She likes to spread slanderous rumors.
散步(ㄙㄢˋ ㄅㄨˋ)
to take a walk, a stroll, or a ramble: 我們在鄉間散步很開心。We had a pleasant walk in the country.
散漫(ㄙㄢˋ ㄇㄢˋ)
incompact; loose; disorganized
散悶(ㄙㄢˋ ㄇㄣˋ)
to dissipate care or worries; to kill time
散發(ㄙㄢˋ ㄈㄚ)
① to send out; to emit: 這朵花散發著香味。The flower is sending forth a sweet smell. ② to distribute; to issue; to give out
散髮(ㄙㄢˋ ㄈㄚˇ)
disheveled hair; unkempt hair
散隊(ㄙㄢˋ ㄉㄨㄟˋ)
to break up a formation
散攤子(ㄙㄢˋ ㄊㄢ ·ㄗ)
(said of a group) to break up
散落(ㄙㄢˋ ㄌㄨㄛˋ)
to fall here and there; to be strewn or scattered
散亂(ㄙㄢˋ ㄌㄨㄢˋ)
confused; in disorder
散館(ㄙㄢˋ ㄍㄨㄢˇ)
(said of students of private schools in former times) to end the day's sessions
散光(ㄙㄢˋ ㄍㄨㄤ)or(ㄙㄢˇ ㄍㄨㄤ)
astigmatism; astigmatic
散光眼鏡(ㄙㄢˋ ㄍㄨㄤ ㄧㄢˇ ㄐㄧㄥˋ)or(ㄙㄢˇ ㄍㄨㄤ ㄧㄢˇ ㄐㄧㄥˋ)
astigmatic lenses
散工(ㄙㄢˋ ㄍㄨㄥ)

to leave the factory after the day's work is over
散開(ㄙㄢˋ ㄎㄞ)
to disperse; to scatter
散花(ㄙㄢˋ ㄏㄨㄚ)
to strew flowers as offering; to display textile flowers in a Buddhist ceremony
散夥(ㄙㄢˋ ㄏㄨㄛˇ)
(said of a group) to break up; to dissolve; to disband
散會(ㄙㄢˋ ㄏㄨㄟˋ)
to dissolve a meeting; (said of a meeting) to be over: 主席宣布散會。The chairman declared the meeting over.
散見(ㄙㄢˋ ㄐㄧㄢˋ)
to be seen at scattered places (especially in books)
散心(ㄙㄢˋ ㄒㄧㄣ)
to have some recreation; to drive away one's cares; to relieve boredom
散場(ㄙㄢˋ ㄔㄤˇ)
(said of a show, a meeting, etc.) to be over
散失(ㄙㄢˋ ㄕ)
to get scattered and lost; missing
散熱(ㄙㄢˋ ㄖㄜˋ)
to dissipate heat
散熱器(ㄙㄢˋ ㄖㄜˋ ㄑㄧˋ)
a radiator
散財(ㄙㄢˋ ㄘㄞˊ)
to give away money generously for charitable projects

【散】 2137
2. ㄙㄢˇ saan sǎn
1. loose; loosened
2. idle; leisurely
3. powdered medicine
散兵(ㄙㄢˇ ㄅㄧㄥ)
① soldiers in combat formation; skirmishers ② stragglers
散兵坑(ㄙㄢˇ ㄅㄧㄥ ㄎㄥ)
(military) a foxhole
散兵線(ㄙㄢˇ ㄅㄧㄥ ㄒㄧㄢˋ)
(military) an open skirmish line
散兵遊勇(ㄙㄢˇ ㄅㄧㄥ ㄧㄡˊ ㄩㄥˇ)
straggling troops
散木(ㄙㄢˇ ㄇㄨˋ)
odd pieces of wood; useless timber
散夫(ㄙㄢˇ ㄈㄨ)
an unskilled worker
散彈(ㄙㄢˇ ㄉㄢˋ)
a grapeshot; a pellet
散淡(ㄙㄢˇ ㄉㄢˋ)
to lead an idle life; to relax
散蕩(ㄙㄢˇ ㄉㄤˋ)
to play idly; to loaf about
散官(ㄙㄢˇ ㄍㄨㄢ)
one who holds a sinecure post in a government agency
散逛(ㄙㄢˇ ・ㄍㄨㄤ)
to loaf about
散工(ㄙㄢˇ ㄍㄨㄥ)
odd jobs: 他靠做散工生活。He makes a living by doing odd jobs.
散記(ㄙㄢˇ ㄐㄧˋ)
random notes
散居(ㄙㄢˇ ㄐㄩ)
to live in scattered places: 游擊隊員散居在山區。The guerrillas lived scattered in the mountains.
散曲(ㄙㄢˇ ㄑㄩˇ)
(Chinese opera) a piece with neither action nor dialogue; a type of verse popular in the Yüan Dynasty, with tonal patterns modeled on tunes drawn from folk music
散職(ㄙㄢˇ ㄓˊ)
a featherbedding or sinecure post
散帙(ㄙㄢˇ ㄓˋ)
to open a book
散裝(ㄙㄢˇ ㄓㄨㄤ)
loose; not in a package; bulk; in bulk
散沙(ㄙㄢˇ ㄕㄚ)
loose sand—(figuratively) lack of the spirit of cooperation
散人(ㄙㄢˇ ㄖㄣˊ)
an idle man; a person not harnessed with duties
散儒(ㄙㄢˇ ㄖㄨˊ)or 散才(ㄙㄢˇ ㄘㄞˊ)
a scholar who disdains social conventions
散文(ㄙㄢˇ ㄨㄣˊ)
prose: 這故事是用散文寫的。The story is in prose.
散文詩(ㄙㄢˇ ㄨㄣˊ ㄕ)
a prose poem

【敦】 2138
1. ㄉㄨㄣ duen dūn
1. honest; sincere; candid
2. to deepen or strengthen (relations, etc.)
3. to urge; to press
敦品力學(ㄉㄨㄣ ㄆㄧㄣˇ ㄌㄧˋ ㄒㄩㄝˊ)
upright in character and diligent in the pursuit of knowledge
敦聘(ㄉㄨㄣ ㄆㄧㄣˋ)
to cordially invite (to render some service)
敦樸(ㄉㄨㄣ ㄆㄨˊ)
honest; sincere; upright
敦勉(ㄉㄨㄣ ㄇㄧㄢˇ)
honest and diligent
敦睦(ㄉㄨㄣ ㄇㄨˋ)
to have cordial and friendly ties; to promote friendly relations
敦敦實實(ㄉㄨㄣ ・ㄉㄨㄣ ㄕˊ ㄕˊ)
honest; cordial; upright; sincere
敦倫(ㄉㄨㄣ ㄌㄨㄣˊ)
① sexual act between husband and wife ② to strengthen moral ties between humans
敦厚(ㄉㄨㄣ ㄏㄡˋ)or 敦篤(ㄉㄨㄣ ㄉㄨˇ)
honest; sincere
敦煌(ㄉㄨㄣ ㄏㄨㄤˊ)
Tunhwang, Kansu Province
敦煌石室(ㄉㄨㄣ ㄏㄨㄤˊ ㄕˊ ㄕˋ)or 敦煌石窟(ㄉㄨㄣ ㄏㄨㄤˊ ㄕˊ ㄎㄨ)
the Caves of Tunhwang, a treasure house of Buddhist scriptures, paintings and statues
敦親睦族(ㄉㄨㄣ ㄑㄧㄣ ㄇㄨˋ ㄗㄨˊ)
to strengthen the relations among kinsfolk and among different clans
敦請(ㄉㄨㄣ ㄑㄧㄥˇ)
to extend a cordial invitation to; to invite cordially
敦促(ㄉㄨㄣ ㄘㄨˋ)
to urge or press earnestly: 父親敦促我早日起程。Father urged me to start on my journey early.

【敦】 2138
2. ㄉㄨㄟˋ duey duì
a sort of container

九畫

【敬】 2139
ㄐㄧㄥˋ jinq jìng
1. to respect; to revere; to honor; to esteem; respect; respectfully: 我很尊敬她。I

〔攴部〕

have great respect for her.
2. to present; to offer
3. a Chinese family name

敬稟者(ㄐㄧㄥˋ ㄅㄧㄥˇ ㄓㄜˇ)
a conventional phrase referring to oneself used at the beginning of a letter addressed to an elder or superior

敬陪末座(ㄐㄧㄥˋ ㄆㄟˊ ㄇㄛˋ ㄗㄨㄛˋ)
to sit below the salt; to sit at an inconspicuous seat

敬佩(ㄐㄧㄥˋ ㄆㄟˋ)
to admire; to respect; to esteem; to think highly of: 我們敬佩那女孩的勇氣。We admired the girl for her courage.

敬慕(ㄐㄧㄥˋ ㄇㄨˋ)
to respect and admire

敬奉(ㄐㄧㄥˋ ㄈㄥˋ)
① to receive respectfully ② to present (or offer) respectfully

敬服(ㄐㄧㄥˋ ㄈㄨˊ)
to respect, esteem or admire unreservedly

敬覆者(ㄐㄧㄥˋ ㄈㄨˋ ㄓㄜˇ)
a conventional phrase referring to oneself at the beginning of a letter in reply

敬老(ㄐㄧㄥˋ ㄌㄠˇ)
to respect the old

敬老尊賢(ㄐㄧㄥˋ ㄌㄠˇ ㄗㄨㄣ ㄒㄧㄢˊ)
to revere the aged and honor the wise

敬禮(ㄐㄧㄥˋ ㄌㄧˇ)
to salute; to extend one's greetings

敬領(ㄐㄧㄥˋ ㄌㄧㄥˇ)
to accept with respect

敬告(ㄐㄧㄥˋ ㄍㄠˋ)
to tell respectfully

敬鬼神而遠之(ㄐㄧㄥˋ ㄍㄨㄟˇ ㄕㄣˊ ㄦˊ ㄩㄢˇ ㄓ)or(ㄐㄧㄥˋ ㄍㄨㄟˇ ㄕㄣˊ ㄦˊ ㄩㄢˋ ㄓ)
to keep at a respectable distance; to avoid someone (or something) as if he (or it) were plague

敬賀(ㄐㄧㄥˋ ㄏㄜˋ)
to congratulate with respect

敬候(ㄐㄧㄥˋ ㄏㄡˋ)
① to inquire after respectfully ② to await respectfully

敬酒(ㄐㄧㄥˋ ㄐㄧㄡˇ)
to drink a toast; to toast: 我們向新娘新郎敬酒。We drank a toast to the bride and bridegroom.

敬酒不吃吃罰酒(ㄐㄧㄥˋ ㄐㄧㄡˇ ㄅㄨˋ ㄔ ㄔ ㄈㄚˊ ㄐㄧㄡˇ)
to refuse a toast only to drink a penalty—(figuratively) to yield to somebody's pressure after first turning down his request; to be constrained to do what one at first refused

敬謹(ㄐㄧㄥˋ ㄐㄧㄣˇ)
respectfully; deferentially

敬軍(ㄐㄧㄥˋ ㄐㄩㄣ)
to honor the armed forces

敬啓(ㄐㄧㄥˋ ㄑㄧˇ)
to state with respect (a conventional phrase in correspondence)

敬啓者(ㄐㄧㄥˋ ㄑㄧˇ ㄓㄜˇ)
a conventional phrase referring to the letter writer placed at the beginning of the letter

敬虔(ㄐㄧㄥˋ ㄑㄧㄢˊ)
pious; devout

敬請(ㄐㄧㄥˋ ㄑㄧㄥˇ)
to invite respectfully

敬請指教(ㄐㄧㄥˋ ㄑㄧㄥˇ ㄓˇ ㄐㄧㄠˋ)
I humbly request your advice.

敬惜字紙(ㄐㄧㄥˋ ㄒㄧˊ ㄗˋ ㄓˇ)
to cherish paper bearing written or printed words

敬謝(ㄐㄧㄥˋ ㄒㄧㄝˋ)
to thank respectfully

敬謝不敏(ㄐㄧㄥˋ ㄒㄧㄝˋ ㄅㄨˋ ㄇㄧㄣˇ)
to decline a request politely

敬獻(ㄐㄧㄥˋ ㄒㄧㄢˋ)
to offer (a present) to a superior or an elder

敬香(ㄐㄧㄥˋ ㄒㄧㄤ)
to offer incense (to ancestors or deities)

敬祝(ㄐㄧㄥˋ ㄓㄨˋ)
to wish respectfully (a conventional phrase used at the end of a letter)

敬重(ㄐㄧㄥˋ ㄓㄨㄥˋ)
to respect; to esteem; to revere; to have high regard for

敬茶(ㄐㄧㄥˋ ㄔㄚˊ)
to serve tea to guests

敬陳(ㄐㄧㄥˋ ㄔㄣˊ)
to state respectfully

敬稱(ㄐㄧㄥˋ ㄔㄥ)
an honorific appellation; an honorific

敬呈(ㄐㄧㄥˋ ㄔㄥˊ)
to present with respect

敬師(ㄐㄧㄥˋ ㄕ)
to respect teachers: 學生應該敬師。Students should respect teachers.

敬事(ㄐㄧㄥˋ ㄕˋ)
to handle business with respectful attention

敬神(ㄐㄧㄥˋ ㄕㄣˊ)
to revere the gods: 有些原始社會的人非常敬神。Some primitive societies pay great reverence to gods.

敬贈(ㄐㄧㄥˋ ㄗㄥˋ)
to present respectfully

敬遵(ㄐㄧㄥˋ ㄗㄨㄣ)
to obey respectfully

敬頌(ㄐㄧㄥˋ ㄙㄨㄥˋ)
(a conventional phrase used at the end of a letter) to wish with respect

敬愛(ㄐㄧㄥˋ ㄞˋ)
to respect and love: 他是我們敬愛的教授。He is our esteemed and beloved professor.

敬而遠之(ㄐㄧㄥˋ ㄦˊ ㄩㄢˇ ㄓ)or(ㄐㄧㄥˋ ㄦˊ ㄩㄢˋ ㄓ)
to keep a person or a thing at a respectful distance; to keep a person or a thing at arm's length 參看「敬鬼神而遠之」

敬意(ㄐㄧㄥˋ ㄧˋ)
respects; regards: 我要向你表示由衷的敬意。I want to extend my heartfelt respects to you.

敬業樂羣(ㄐㄧㄥˋ ㄧㄝˋ ㄧㄠˋ ㄑㄩㄣˊ)
to respect work and enjoy company

敬煙(ㄐㄧㄥˋ ㄧㄢ)
to offer cigarettes

敬仰(ㄐㄧㄥˋ ㄧㄤˇ)
to admire; to esteem; to respect

敬畏(ㄐㄧㄥˋ ㄨㄟˋ)
to hold in awe; to stand in awe of; to revere; to venerate

十畫

【敲】 2140
ㄑㄧㄠ chiau qiāo

1. to rap; to strike; to tap; to beat; to knock
2. as in 敲扑—a truncheon
3. to extort; to blackmail; to overcharge

敲梆(ㄑㄧㄠ ㄅㄤ)or 敲更(ㄑㄧㄠ ㄍㄥ)
to beat the watches; to sound night watch with a clapper

敲邊鼓(ㄑㄧㄠ ㄅㄧㄢ ㄍㄨˇ)
to speak for someone in order to help him

敲破(ㄑㄧㄠ ㄆㄛˋ)
to smash; to shatter

敲枰(ㄑㄧㄠ ㄆㄧㄥˊ)
to play a "go" game

敲門(ㄑㄧㄠ ㄇㄣˊ)
to knock at (or on) the door: 你聽到敲門聲嗎? Did you hear someone knock?

敲門磚(ㄑㄧㄠ ㄇㄣˊ ㄓㄨㄢ)
(literally) a brickbat used to knock at a door and thrown away after the door is open—learning used merely as a means for achieving success; a steppingstone to success

敲木魚(ㄑㄧㄠ ㄇㄨˋ ㄩˊ)
to beat the wooden drum (when chanting a Buddhist sutra)

敲打(ㄑㄧㄠ ㄉㄚˇ)
to tap; to rap; to knock; to beat

敲鑼(ㄑㄧㄠ ㄌㄨㄛˊ)
to beat a gong

敲鼓(ㄑㄧㄠ ㄍㄨˇ)
to beat drums

敲骨吸髓(ㄑㄧㄠ ㄍㄨˇ ㄒㄧ ㄙㄨㄟˇ)
(literally) to crush the bone and suck the marrow—① to read an article carefully in order to profit thereby ② cruel, bloodsucking exploitation; to suck the lifeblood

敲擊(ㄑㄧㄠ ㄐㄧˊ)
to beat; to knock

敲經念佛(ㄑㄧㄠ ㄐㄧㄥ ㄋㄧㄢˋ ㄈㄛˊ)
to beat time and chant a prayer

敲起警鐘(ㄑㄧㄠ ㄑㄧˇ ㄐㄧㄥˇ ㄓㄨㄥ)
to sound the alarm bell

敲敲打打(ㄑㄧㄠ ·ㄑㄧㄠ ㄉㄚˇ ㄉㄚˇ)
to beat drums, gongs, etc. continually

敲詐(ㄑㄧㄠ ㄓㄚˋ)
to blackmail; to extort; to racketeer

敲竹槓(ㄑㄧㄠ ㄓㄨˊ ㄍㄤˋ)
to squeeze a person for money; to extort money; to fleece; to sponge a person

敲鐘(ㄑㄧㄠ ㄓㄨㄥ)
to toll a bell

敲詩(ㄑㄧㄠ ㄕ)
a riddle in verse form

敲碎(ㄑㄧㄠ ㄙㄨㄟˋ)
to knock or beat to pieces

十一畫

【敵】 2141
ㄉㄧˊ dyi dí

1. an enemy; a foe; a rival: 他是我的情敵。He is my rival in love.
2. to oppose; to resist
3. to match; to rival; to equal: 在這方面無人能與他匹敵。No one could rival him in this respect.

敵兵(ㄉㄧˊ ㄅㄧㄥ)
an enemy soldier; the hostile troops

敵不住(ㄉㄧˊ ·ㄅㄨ ㄓㄨˋ)or 敵不過(ㄉㄧˊ ·ㄅㄨ ㄍㄨㄛˋ)
to be no match for

敵黨(ㄉㄧˊ ㄉㄤˇ)
a hostile group or party

敵對(ㄉㄧˊ ㄉㄨㄟˋ)
to turn against; to be hostile to; to oppose: 愛與恨是敵對的。Love is opposed to hate.

敵對行爲(ㄉㄧˊ ㄉㄨㄟˋ ㄒㄧㄥˊ ㄨㄟˊ)
a hostile act

敵體(ㄉㄧˊ ㄊㄧˇ)
equal standing or status

敵國(ㄉㄧˊ ㄍㄨㄛˊ)
① a hostile country; a hostile power ② a foreign country equal to one's own in terms of strength ③(said of personal wealth) capable of matching the national treasury

敵愾(ㄉㄧˊ ㄎㄞˋ)
enmity; hostility; hatred toward the enemy

敵愾同仇(ㄉㄧˊ ㄎㄞˋ ㄊㄨㄥˊ ㄔㄡˊ)
to hate a common enemy and fight against him together

敵寇(ㄉㄧˊ ㄎㄡˋ)
an enemy

敵後(ㄉㄧˊ ㄏㄡˋ)
behind enemy lines; the enemy's rear area: 報人員深入敵後。The agents penetrated into the enemy's rear area.

敵機(ㄉㄧˊ ㄐㄧ)
an enemy plane; a hostile plane

敵騎(ㄉㄧˊ ㄐㄧˋ)
enemy cavalry units

敵艦(ㄉㄧˊ ㄐㄧㄢˋ)
an enemy warship; a hostile ship: 我們的飛機轟炸敵艦。Our planes bombed the enemy's ship.

敵軍(ㄉㄧˊ ㄐㄩㄣ)
enemy troops; hostile forces: 敵軍被迫撤退。The enemy were forced to retreat.

敵前登陸(ㄉㄧˊ ㄑㄧㄢˊ ㄉㄥ ㄌㄨˋ)
to make a landing in face of enemy resistance

敵情(ㄉㄧˊ ㄑㄧㄥˊ)
the enemy's situation: 他派出飛機偵察敵情。He sent planes to make a reconnaissance of the enemy's situation.

敵住(ㄉㄧˊ ㄓㄨˋ)
to hold the enemy at bay

敵衆我寡(ㄉㄧˊ ㄓㄨㄥˋ ㄨㄛˇ ㄍㄨㄚˇ)
We are outnumbered by the enemy.

敵屍遍野(ㄉㄧˊ ㄕ ㄅㄧㄢˋ ㄧㄝˇ)
The battlefield is littered with killed enemy soldiers.

敵視(ㄉㄧˊ ㄕˋ)
to regard with hostility

敵勢(ㄉㄧˊ ㄕˋ)
the strength (or morale) of the enemy

敵手(ㄉㄧˊ ㄕㄡˇ)
an opponent, a match, a rival, an antagonist, an adversary, or an enemy of equal strength: 我看你不是他的敵手。I think you are no match for him.

敵人(ㄉㄧˊ ㄖㄣˊ)
an enemy; a foe: 疾病是人類的敵人。Disease is an enemy of mankind.

敵意(ㄉㄧˊ ㄧˋ)

〔攴部〕

enmity; hostility; antagonism: 他們懷着敵意的面孔顯示他不受歡迎。Their hostile looks showed that he was unwelcome.

敵營(ㄉㄧˊ ㄧㄥˊ)
an enemy camp: 我機成功地突襲敵營。Our planes made a raid upon the enemy camp successfully.

【敷】2142 ㄈㄨ fu fū
1. to apply or spread over (a surface); to paint
2. to suffice; to be enough
3. to state; to explain; to expound

敷粉(ㄈㄨ ㄈㄣˇ)
to powder: 她在鼻子上敷粉。She powdered her nose.

敷化(ㄈㄨ ㄏㄨㄚˋ)
to teach and convert (heathens or barbarians)

敷教(ㄈㄨ ㄐㄧㄠˋ)
to spread a religion or a culture

敷政(ㄈㄨ ㄓㄥˋ)
to execute administration

敷陳(ㄈㄨ ㄔㄣˊ)
to state in detail

敷陳其事(ㄈㄨ ㄔㄣˊ ㄑㄧˊ ㄕˋ)
to set forth the fact

敷設(ㄈㄨ ㄕㄜˋ)
to install; to arrange; to lay; to fix: 工人正忙着敷設鐵軌。The workers are busy laying a railway track.

敷榮(ㄈㄨ ㄖㄨㄥˊ)
to blossom; to sprout

敷藥(ㄈㄨ ㄧㄠˋ)
to salve; to apply a salve

敷衍(ㄈㄨ ㄧㄢˇ)
① to act in a perfunctory manner: 他辦事認眞，從不敷衍。He is very conscientious and never does his work perfunctorily. ② to deal with a person insincerely: 那女孩敷衍的答了幾句就走了。The girl made a few casual answers and left.

敷衍了事(ㄈㄨ ㄧㄢˇ ㄌㄧㄠˇ ㄕˋ)
to carry out a task in a perfunctory manner

敷衍塞責(ㄈㄨ ㄧㄢˇ ㄙㄜˋ ㄗㄜˊ)
to discharge a responsibility in a perfunctory manner

敷文(ㄈㄨ ㄨㄣˊ)
to write literary compositions

【數】2143 1. ㄕㄨˋ shuh shù
1. number; quantity; sum; amount: 圖書館遺失的書籍爲數衆多。The number of books missing from the library is large.
2. (mathematics) numbers: 複名數 compound numbers
3. several; a few
4. a plan; an idea: 她心中有數。She has a good idea of how things stand.
5. fate; destiny: 凡事皆有定數。Everything is destined.
6. art

數倍(ㄕㄨˋ ㄅㄟˋ)
several times; manifold

數碼(兒)(ㄕㄨˋ ㄇㄚˇ(ㄦ))
① number; amount ② a numeral: 阿拉伯數碼 Arabic numerals

數目(ㄕㄨˋ ㄇㄨˋ)
number; sum

數目字(ㄕㄨˋ ㄇㄨˋ ㄗˋ)
numerals; numbers; digits

數滴(ㄕㄨˋ ㄉㄧ)
several drops; a few drops

數天(ㄕㄨˋ ㄊㄧㄢ)
several days; a few days: 他每隔數天來看我們。He came to see us every few days.

數年(ㄕㄨˋ ㄋㄧㄢˊ)
several years; a few years: 我學英文已有數年。I have studied English for several years.

數年如一日(ㄕㄨˋ ㄋㄧㄢˊ ㄖㄨˊ ㄧˊ ㄖˋ)
with perseverance and consistency

數量(ㄕㄨˋ ㄌㄧㄤˋ)
quantity; amount: 只有數量方面的差別。There is only quantitative difference.

數口之家(ㄕㄨˋ ㄎㄡˇ ㄓ ㄐㄧㄚ)
a family of several members; a small family

數盡(ㄕㄨˋ ㄐㄧㄣˋ)
running out of life; days numbered

數據(ㄕㄨˋ ㄐㄩˋ)
data: 這些數據已列於諸表中。These data are listed in tables.

數學(ㄕㄨˋ ㄒㄩㄝˊ)
mathematics

數學家(ㄕㄨˋ ㄒㄩㄝˊ ㄐㄧㄚ)
a mathematician

數值(ㄕㄨˋ ㄓˊ)
numerical value

數日(ㄕㄨˋ ㄖˋ)
several days; a few days: 我要在那裏停留數日。I'm going to stay there for a few days.

數字(ㄕㄨˋ ㄗˋ)
① a numeral; a figure; a digit: 那個是天文數字。It's an astronomical figure. ② quantity: 不要只追求數字。Don't just go after quantity.

數罪併罰(ㄕㄨˋ ㄗㄨㄟˋ ㄅㄧㄥˋ ㄈㄚˊ)
combined punishment for several offences

數次(ㄕㄨˋ ㄘˋ)
several times; a few times: 我已經這樣說過數次了。I have said so several times.

數額(ㄕㄨˋ ㄜˊ)
amount; sum: 我做的還不足規定數額。What I have done falls short of the amount required.

數兒(ㄕㄨˋㄦ)
① numbers ② plans; calculations; reckonings

數以萬計(ㄕㄨˋ ㄧˇ ㄨㄢˋ ㄐㄧˋ)
by tens of thousands; numerous

數易寒暑(ㄕㄨˋ ㄧˋ ㄏㄢˊ ㄕㄨˇ)
to go through many changes of seasons

數位(ㄕㄨˋ ㄨㄟˋ)
digital

數月(ㄕㄨˋ ㄩㄝˋ)
several months; a few months: 我們已數月未見。We haven't seen each other for several months.

【數】2143 2. ㄕㄨˇ shuu shǔ
1. to count; to enumerate
2. to count (as best, etc.); to be reckoned as exceptionally (good, bad, etc.): 這裏數我最小。I am the youngest here.

數不過來(ㄕㄨˇ ·ㄅㄨ ㄍㄨㄛˋ ㄌㄞˊ)
too many to be counted; innumerable; countless

數不清(ㄕㄨˇ ·ㄅㄨ ㄑㄧㄥ)
innumerable; countless: 太多

了，我數不清。There were so many that I couldn't keep count of them.

數米而炊(ㄕㄨˇ ㄇㄧˇ ㄦˊ ㄔㄨㄟ)
(literally) to count the grains of rice before cooking it—to be contemptibly parsimonious or overcareful

數得著(ㄕㄨˇ ·ㄉㄜ ㄓㄠˊ)
can be accounted among (the best, most notorious, etc.): 他是班上數得着的好學生。He is one of the outstanding students in the class.

數典忘祖(ㄕㄨˇ ㄉㄧㄢˇ ㄨㄤˋ ㄗㄨˇ)
(literally) to enumerate past records but ignore one's ancestry—to forget one's origin; ungrateful

數來寶(ㄕㄨˇ ㄌㄞˊ ㄅㄠˇ)
a beggar that begs by beating time and chanting rhymed words in flattery

數落(ㄕㄨˇ ·ㄌㄨㄛ)
to scold somebody by enumerating his wrongdoings; to blame; to reprove: 老師把她數落一頓。The teacher gave her a good scolding.

數黑論黃(ㄕㄨˇ ㄏㄟ ㄌㄨㄣˋ ㄏㄨㄤˊ)
to talk wildly; to make unfounded or exaggerated statements

數錢(ㄕㄨˇ ㄑㄧㄢˊ)
to count money: 這守財奴每晚都在數錢。The miser counted his money every night.

數數兒(ㄕㄨˇ ㄕㄨˋㄦ)
to name numbers; to count

數數看(ㄕㄨˇ ·ㄕㄨ ㄎㄢˋ)
to count and see (how many there are): 數數看班上有多少學生。Count and see how many students there are in the class.

數說(ㄕㄨˇ ㄕㄨㄛ)
① to accuse; to reproach ② to enumerate

數一數二(ㄕㄨˇ ㄧ ㄕㄨˇ ㄦˋ)
either the best or second only to the best; one of the best: 他是本國數一數二的翻譯高手。He is one of the best translators in this country.

數一數(ㄕㄨˇ ·ㄧ ㄕㄨˇ)
to count

數往知來(ㄕㄨˇ ㄨㄤˇ ㄓ ㄌㄞˊ)
to deduce what is likely to happen in the future by reviewing what has taken place in the past

【數】 2143
3. ㄕㄨㄛˋ shuoh shuò
often; frequently

數見不鮮(ㄕㄨㄛˋ ㄐㄧㄢˋ ㄅㄨˋ ㄒㄧㄢ)
not uncommon; found not infrequently; nothing new: 這種事情數見不鮮。Such occurrences are not uncommon.

數數(ㄕㄨㄛˋ ㄕㄨㄛˋ)
frequently; often

數四(ㄕㄨㄛˋ ㄙˋ)
over and over again; repeatedly

【敺】 2144
1. (驅) ㄑㄩ chiu qū
to drive away; to expel

【敺】 2144
2. (毆) ㄡ ou ōu
to beat; to assault physically

十二畫

【整】 2145
ㄓㄥˇ jeeng zhěng

1. orderly; systematic; neat; tidy: 椅子一排排的很整齊。The chairs are in orderly rows.
2. sharp: 現在是七點整。It's seven o'clock sharp.
3. whole; complete; entire; intact: 請整句唸出來。Read the whole sentence, please.
4. to tidy; to set in order; to adjust; to arrange; to repair; to make ready

整備(ㄓㄥˇ ㄅㄟˋ)
to make ready

整編(ㄓㄥˇ ㄅㄧㄢ)
to reorganize troops: 軍隊明年要整編。The army will be reorganized next year.

整旆(ㄓㄥˇ ㄆㄟˋ)
to set out; to begin a journey

整批(ㄓㄥˇ ㄆㄧ)
batch

整風運動(ㄓㄥˇ ㄈㄥ ㄩㄣˋ ㄉㄨㄥˋ)
rectification movement

整黨(ㄓㄥˇ ㄉㄤˇ)
to consolidate a party organization

整隊(ㄓㄥˇ ㄉㄨㄟˋ)
①(said of troops, etc.) to form neat lines; to file ② the whole unit, band, column, etc.

整頓(ㄓㄥˇ ㄉㄨㄣˋ)
to put in order, or to put to right a poorly managed organization, firm, etc.: 他們的棒球隊需要好好整頓一下。Their baseball team needs a good shake-up.

整套(ㄓㄥˇ ㄊㄠˋ)
the whole set: 整套設備都是嶄新的。The complete set of equipment is brand-new.

整體(ㄓㄥˇ ㄊㄧˇ)
the whole

整體規劃(ㄓㄥˇ ㄊㄧˇ ㄍㄨㄟ ㄏㄨㄚˋ)
corporate planning

整天(ㄓㄥˇ ㄊㄧㄢ)
the whole day; all day long

整年(ㄓㄥˇ ㄋㄧㄢˊ)
the whole year; all the year round; throughout the year

整理(ㄓㄥˇ ㄌㄧˇ)
to arrange; to put in order; to adjust; to regulate; to straighten up: 我把自己的房間整理好。I put my room in order.

整列(ㄓㄥˇ ㄌㄧㄝˋ)
①(said of a group of people) to form neat lines ② the whole row or column

整流器(ㄓㄥˇ ㄌㄧㄡˊ ㄑㄧˋ)
(physics) ① a rectifier ② a commutator

整個(兒)(ㄓㄥˇ ㄍㄜˋ(ㄦ))
wholly; entirely; whole; entire: 整個教室響起熱烈的掌聲。The whole classroom resounded with warm applause.

整塊(ㄓㄥˇ ㄎㄨㄞˋ)
the whole piece: 他把整塊蛋糕吃掉了。He has eaten the whole cake.

整合(ㄓㄥˇ ㄏㄜˊ)
(geology) conformity

整行(ㄓㄥˇ ㄏㄤˊ)
the whole line

整潔(ㄓㄥˇ ㄐㄧㄝˊ)
neat and clean: 她將房間收拾得很整潔。She kept her room clean and tidy.

整舊如新(ㄓㄥˇ ㄐㄧㄡˋ ㄖㄨˊ ㄒㄧㄣ)
to repair something and make it brand-new

整軍經武(ㄓㄥˇ ㄐㄩㄣ ㄐㄧㄥ ㄨˇ)

to strengthen armaments; to beef up national defense
整齊(ㄓㄥˇ ㄑㄧˊ)
①neat; orderly; tidy; well-arranged ②even; well-balanced
整齊花(ㄓㄥˇ ㄑㄧˊ ㄏㄨㄚ)
(botany) regular flower
整齊劃一(ㄓㄥˇ ㄑㄧˊ ㄏㄨㄚˋ ㄧ)
neat and uniform
整修(ㄓㄥˇ ㄒㄧㄡ)
to rebuild; to renovate; recondition; to touch up
整形(ㄓㄥˇ ㄒㄧㄥˊ)
orthopedics
整形手術(ㄓㄥˇ ㄒㄧㄥˊ ㄕㄡˇ ㄕㄨˋ)
plastic operation
整治(ㄓㄥˇ ㄓˋ)
①to set in order; to adjust and repair; to fix ②to dredge (a river): 市政府計畫整治河道。The municipal government plans to dredge waterways. ③to punish: 這男孩得整治一下。The boy needs to be punished.
整裝(ㄓㄥˇ ㄓㄨㄤ)
to dress up
整裝待發(ㄓㄥˇ ㄓㄨㄤ ㄉㄞˋ ㄈㄚ)
(usually said of troops on an expedition) to pack up and be ready to go
整莊(ㄓㄥˇ ˙ㄓㄨㄤ)
whole; intact; entire
整飭(ㄓㄥˇ ㄔˋ)
①orderly; systematic ②to set to order; to subject to orderly control
整除(ㄓㄥˇ ㄔㄨˊ)
to be divided with no remainder; to divide exactly
整數(ㄓㄥˇ ㄕㄨˋ)
a whole number; an integer; an integral number; a round number; a round sum
整日(ㄓㄥˇ ㄖˋ)or 整日價(ㄓㄥˇ ㄖˋ ˙ㄍㄚ)
the whole day; all day long
整日整夜(ㄓㄥˇ ㄖˋ ㄓㄥˇ ㄧㄝˋ)
whole day and night
整人(ㄓㄥˇ ㄖㄣˊ)
(slang) to give someone a hard time; to fix somebody
整容(ㄓㄥˇ ㄖㄨㄥˊ)
①to improve one's looks by plastic surgery ②to tidy one's appearance (by shaving, a haircut, etc.); face-lifting
整容醫生(ㄓㄥˇ ㄖㄨㄥˊ ㄧ ㄕㄥ)
a plastic surgeon
整存零付(ㄓㄥˇ ㄘㄨㄣˊ ㄌㄧㄥˊ ㄈㄨˋ)
to deposit a whole sum and withdraw the interest in monthly installments
整存整付(ㄓㄥˇ ㄘㄨㄣˊ ㄓㄥˇ ㄈㄨˋ)
to deposit a sum and withdraw the principal and interest in a lump sum at the expiration of the deposit period
整肅(ㄓㄥˇ ㄙㄨˋ)
①strict; rigid; stern ②to purge (a government or political leader) ③to rectify
整衣(ㄓㄥˇ ㄧ)
to adjust one's clothes
整夜(ㄓㄥˇ ㄧㄝˋ)
all night; the whole night; throughout the night: 我們整夜看守。We watched all night.

十三畫

【斁】 2146 1. ㄧˋ yih yì
to dislike; to be tired; to be weary of

【斁】 2146 2. ㄉㄨˋ duh dù
to corrupt; to spoil

【斂】 2147 ㄌㄧㄢˋ liann liàn
1. to draw together; to contract
2. to hold back; to restrain
3. to collect; to gather
斂步(ㄌㄧㄢˋ ㄅㄨˋ)
to slow down one's steps—to hesitate to advance further
斂法(ㄌㄧㄢˋ ㄈㄚˇ)
tax law
斂迹 or 斂跡(ㄌㄧㄢˋ ㄐㄧ)
to abstain from vice; (said of undesirable elements) to be subdued
斂局(ㄌㄧㄢˋ ㄐㄩˊ)
to gather people together for gambling
斂錢(ㄌㄧㄢˋ ㄑㄧㄢˊ)
to collect money illegally or immorally
斂手(ㄌㄧㄢˋ ㄕㄡˇ)
to refrain or abstain from doing something
斂然(ㄌㄧㄢˋ ㄖㄢˊ)
gathered; assembled
斂衽(ㄌㄧㄢˋ ㄖㄣˋ)
to pull the lapels of one's garment together respectfully in saluting
斂容(ㄌㄧㄢˋ ㄖㄨㄥˊ)
to assume a serious expression; to put on a sober face
斂足(ㄌㄧㄢˋ ㄗㄨˊ)
to slow down one's steps—to hesitate to advance further
斂財(ㄌㄧㄢˋ ㄘㄞˊ)
to collect wealth illegally or immorally
斂翼(ㄌㄧㄢˋ ㄧˋ)
to fold the wings—to flinch
斂怨(ㄌㄧㄢˋ ㄩㄢˋ)
to accumulate hatred

十四畫

【斃】 2148 ㄅㄧˋ bih bì
1. to come to a bad end; decline; destruction
2. to fall; to prostrate
3. dead; to come to the end of life
4. (colloquial) to kill or execute by shooting; to shoot
斃命(ㄅㄧˋ ㄇㄧㄥˋ)
to meet violent death; to get killed
斃敵(ㄅㄧˋ ㄉㄧˊ)
to kill enemy troops (usually followed by the number of enemy soldiers killed)

十六畫

【斆】 2149 ㄒㄧㄠˋ shiaw xiào
1. to teach
2. to be awakened; to realize

文部
ㄨㄣˊ wen wén

【文】 2150 1. ㄨㄣˊ wen wén
1. a composition; an article: 他寫了一篇談交通的文章。He

〔文部〕

wrote an article on traffic.
2. language: 他會說英文。He can speak the English language.
3. literature; culture; education
4. elegant; cultured; polished; suave; civil; polite; urbane; mild
5. civilian or civil (as opposed to military): 文職 civilian posts
6. a former monetary unit
7. as in 一文不名 (to own nothing): 他一文不名。He owns nothing.
8. a Chinese family name

文筆(ㄨㄣˊ ㄅㄧˇ)
the pen; literary talent: 文筆勝於刀劍。The pen is mightier than the sword.

文柄(ㄨㄣˊ ㄅㄧㄥˇ)
the duties of a chief secretary in handling the correspondence for a government agency or high official

文不對題(ㄨㄣˊ ˙ㄅㄨ ㄉㄨㄟˋ ㄊㄧˊ)
The content of the writing is inconsistent with the title. 你說的都是文不對題的話。All you are saying is beside the mark.

文不加點(ㄨㄣˊ ˙ㄅㄨ ㄐㄧㄚ ㄉㄧㄢˇ)
to write with facility

文憑(ㄨㄣˊ ㄆㄧㄥˊ)
a diploma: 她拿到工程文憑。She has got a diploma in engineering.

文墨(ㄨㄣˊ ㄇㄛˋ)
① writing as an occupation ② writing ③ cultured; elegant

文墨人兒(ㄨㄣˊ ㄇㄛˋ ㄖㄜˊㄦ)
an intellectual; a scholarly person

文貌(ㄨㄣˊ ㄇㄠˋ)
courtesy; politeness; civility

文盲(ㄨㄣˊ ㄇㄤˊ)
an illiterate: 政府努力掃除文盲。The government tried hard to wipe out illiteracy.

文廟(ㄨㄣˊ ㄇㄧㄠˋ)
a Confucian temple

文面(ㄨㄣˊ ㄇㄧㄢˋ)
to tattoo the face (as punishment)

文名(ㄨㄣˊ ㄇㄧㄥˊ)
literary fame: 他熱衷追求文名。He is eager to pursue literary fame.

文明(ㄨㄣˊ ㄇㄧㄥˊ)
civilized; civilization: 中國是文明古國。China is a country with an ancient civilization.

文明結婚(ㄨㄣˊ ㄇㄧㄥˊ ㄐㄧㄝˊ ㄏㄨㄣ)
a Western-style wedding

文明戲(ㄨㄣˊ ㄇㄧㄥˊ ㄒㄧˋ)
a crude stage play

文法(ㄨㄣˊ ㄈㄚˇ)
grammar: 我發現德文文法很難。I find German grammar very difficult.

文房(ㄨㄣˊ ㄈㄤˊ)
a study; a library

文房四寶(ㄨㄣˊ ㄈㄤˊ ㄙˋ ㄅㄠˇ)
the four treasures in the study—the writing brush, the ink stick, the writing paper and the inkstone

文風(ㄨㄣˊ ㄈㄥ)
① literary style ② popular interest in learning

文風不動(ㄨㄣˊ ㄈㄥ ㄅㄨˋ ㄉㄨㄥˋ)
① calm; quiet; not given to excitement ② no change from origin

文德(ㄨㄣˊ ㄉㄜˊ)
the refining influence of learning and art

文旦(ㄨㄣˊ ㄉㄢˋ)
a shaddock; a pomelo

文定(ㄨㄣˊ ㄉㄧㄥˋ)
to become betrothed; a betrothal

文牘(ㄨㄣˊ ㄉㄨˊ)
① business correspondence; documents ② a secretary

文壇(ㄨㄣˊ ㄊㄢˊ)
the literary circles, world, or arena

文壇耆宿(ㄨㄣˊ ㄊㄢˊ ㄑㄧˊ ㄙㄨˋ)
an elder scholar commanding wide respect in the literary world

文體(ㄨㄣˊ ㄊㄧˇ)
literary style: 兒童讀物應有明晰流暢的文體。Books for children should have a clear, easy style.

文天祥(ㄨㄣˊ ㄊㄧㄢ ㄒㄧㄤˊ)
Wen Tien-hsiang, 1236–1283, last prime minister of the Sung Dynasty, who was executed by the Mongols after a three-year imprisonment

文鳥(ㄨㄣˊ ㄋㄧㄠˇ)
the Java sparrow (*Padda oryzivora*)

文理(ㄨㄣˊ ㄌㄧˇ)
the reasoning and arrangement of a literary composition; the sequence of thought; literary form and literary ideas

文例(ㄨㄣˊ ㄌㄧˋ)
illustrative articles or passages

文林(ㄨㄣˊ ㄌㄧㄣˊ)
a writers' resort

文稿(ㄨㄣˊ ㄍㄠˇ)
a manuscript

文告(ㄨㄣˊ ㄍㄠˋ)
a public notice; an announcement in writing; a manifesto; a message from the president issued on an important occasion

文過其實(ㄨㄣˊ ㄍㄨㄛˋ ㄑㄧˊ ㄕˊ)
(said of a writing) beautiful in words but poor in contents

文官(ㄨㄣˊ ㄍㄨㄢ)
a civil servant

文官考試(ㄨㄣˊ ㄍㄨㄢ ㄎㄠˇ ㄕˋ)
a civil service examination

文科(ㄨㄣˊ ㄎㄜ)
the liberal arts

文庫(ㄨㄣˊ ㄎㄨˋ)
a collection of literary works; a library

文豪(ㄨㄣˊ ㄏㄠˊ)
a literary lion; a great writer

文翰(ㄨㄣˊ ㄏㄢˋ)
① literary writings ② a pheasant-like bird

文虎(ㄨㄣˊ ㄏㄨˇ)
lantern riddles, or lantern puzzles

文化(ㄨㄣˊ ㄏㄨㄚˋ)
culture; civilization: 中國文化注重道德。Chinese culture emphasizes morality.

文化復興(ㄨㄣˊ ㄏㄨㄚˋ ㄈㄨˋ ㄒㄧㄥ)
cultural revitalization

文化大革命(ㄨㄣˊ ㄏㄨㄚˋ ㄉㄚˋ ㄍㄜˊ ㄇㄧㄥˋ)
the Great Cultural Revolution

文化流氓(ㄨㄣˊ ㄏㄨㄚˋ ㄌㄧㄡˊ ㄇㄤˊ)
a cultural villain

文化界(ㄨㄣˊ ㄏㄨㄚˋ ㄐㄧㄝˋ)
參看「文化圈」
文化交流(ㄨㄣˊ ㄏㄨㄚˋ ㄐㄧㄠ ㄌㄧㄡˊ)
cultural exchange
文化圈(ㄨㄣˊ ㄏㄨㄚˋ ㄑㄩㄢ)
the intellectual or literary circles
文化史(ㄨㄣˊ ㄏㄨㄚˋ ㄕˇ)
cultural history
文化事業(ㄨㄣˊ ㄏㄨㄚˋ ㄕˋ ㄧㄝˋ)
cultural enterprises
文化水準(ㄨㄣˊ ㄏㄨㄚˋ ㄕㄨㄟˇ ㄓㄨㄣˇ)
the cultural standing or level
文化人(ㄨㄣˊ ㄏㄨㄚˋ ㄖㄣˊ)
cultured people
文火(ㄨㄣˊ ㄏㄨㄛˇ)
a slow fire (in cooking)
文會(ㄨㄣˊ ㄏㄨㄟˋ)
a literary society
文集(ㄨㄣˊ ㄐㄧˊ)
a collection of prose works
文籍(ㄨㄣˊ ㄐㄧˊ)
books
文教(ㄨㄣˊ ㄐㄧㄠˋ)
culture and education
文件(ㄨㄣˊ ㄐㄧㄢˋ)
documents; legal papers: 他的一些重要文件被竊了。Some of his important papers were stolen.
文景之治(ㄨㄣˊ ㄐㄧㄥˇ ㄓ ㄓˋ)
the enlightened administration during the reign of Emperors Wen and Ching (179-143 B.C.) of the Han Dynasty
文靜(ㄨㄣˊ ㄐㄧㄥˋ)
gracefully quiet: 她是一位個性文靜的女人。She's a woman of gracefully quiet character.
文具(ㄨㄣˊ ㄐㄩˋ)
writing tools; stationery
文卷(ㄨㄣˊ ㄐㄩㄢˋ)
documents; papers: 我們已將這些文卷歸檔了。We have placed the documents on our files.
文君新寡(ㄨㄣˊ ㄐㄩㄣ ㄒㄧㄣ ㄍㄨㄚˇ)
a newly widowed woman
文起八代之衰(ㄨㄣˊ ㄑㄧˇ ㄅㄚ ㄉㄞˋ ㄓ ㄕㄨㄞ)
(literally) spearheading a literary resurgence after a decline during the eight dynasties—the Eastern Han (東漢), Wei (魏), Tsin (晉), Sung (宋), Chi (齊), Liang (梁), Chen (陳) and Sui (隋) Dynasties—which preceded the Tang Dynasty—a eulogy for Han Yü (韓愈), a great writer of the Tang period
文契(ㄨㄣˊ ㄑㄧˋ)
legal papers concerning business or property transactions
文氣(ㄨㄣˊ ㄑㄧˋ)
the emotional impact or spirit of a writing
文情並茂(ㄨㄣˊ ㄑㄧㄥˊ ㄅㄧㄥˋ ㄇㄠˋ)
Both the language and the content are excellent.
文曲星(ㄨㄣˊ ㄑㄩ ㄒㄧㄥ)
name of a constellation that sheds particular influence on literary geniuses
文戲(ㄨㄣˊ ㄒㄧˋ)
(Chinese opera) a play without war scenes
文獻(ㄨㄣˊ ㄒㄧㄢˋ)
records; documents; literature (in science)
文心雕龍(ㄨㄣˊ ㄒㄧㄣ ㄉㄧㄠ ㄌㄨㄥˊ)
The Literary Mind and Carving of Dragons, a treatise in literary criticism by Liu Hsieh (劉勰), a fifth century writer
文學(ㄨㄣˊ ㄒㄩㄝˊ)
literature; letters and scholarship
文學批評(ㄨㄣˊ ㄒㄩㄝˊ ㄆㄧ ㄆㄧㄥˊ)
literary criticism
文學革命(ㄨㄣˊ ㄒㄩㄝˊ ㄍㄜˊ ㄇㄧㄥˋ)
a literary revolution
文學家(ㄨㄣˊ ㄒㄩㄝˊ ㄐㄧㄚ)
a man of letters; a literary man; a litterateur
文學界(ㄨㄣˊ ㄒㄩㄝˊ ㄐㄧㄝˋ)
the literary world, circles, or arena
文學史(ㄨㄣˊ ㄒㄩㄝˊ ㄕˇ)
literary history; the history of literature
文學士(ㄨㄣˊ ㄒㄩㄝˊ ㄕˋ)
Bachelor of Arts (B.A.)
文學作品(ㄨㄣˊ ㄒㄩㄝˊ ㄗㄨㄛˋ ㄆㄧㄣˇ)
literary works
文學研究會(ㄨㄣˊ ㄒㄩㄝˊ ㄧㄢˊ ㄐㄧㄡˋ ㄏㄨㄟˋ)
a literary society
文學院(ㄨㄣˊ ㄒㄩㄝˊ ㄩㄢˋ)
a college of liberal arts
文選(ㄨㄣˊ ㄒㄩㄢˇ)
① a selection of literary works; an anthology ② the title of a 60-volume work edited by Hsiao Tung (蕭統), prince of the Liang Dynasty 亦作「昭明文選」
文選爛，秀才半(ㄨㄣˊ ㄒㄩㄢˇ ㄌㄢˋ, ㄒㄧㄡˋ ㄘㄞˊ ㄅㄢˋ)
Extensive reading makes one a scholar.
文職(ㄨㄣˊ ㄓˊ)
a civil post (as distinct from a military post)
文質彬彬(ㄨㄣˊ ㄓˋ ㄅㄧㄣ ㄅㄧㄣ)
fine both in accomplishments and in nature; elegant and refined in manner
文治(ㄨㄣˊ ㄓˋ)
civil administration
文治武功(ㄨㄣˊ ㄓˋ ㄨˇ ㄍㄨㄥ)
political and military achievements
文摘(ㄨㄣˊ ㄓㄞ)
an abstract; a digest
文縐縐(ㄨㄣˊ ㄓㄡ ㄓㄡ)or(ㄨㄣˊ ㄓㄡˋ ㄓㄡˋ)
showing affected elegance; pedantic
文章(ㄨㄣˊ ㄓㄤ)
an article; a composition
文章憎命(ㄨㄣˊ ㄓㄤ ㄗㄥ ㄇㄧㄥˋ)
Literary talents are generally ill-starred in their lives.
文竹(ㄨㄣˊ ㄓㄨˊ)
(botany) asparagus fern
文抄公(ㄨㄣˊ ㄔㄠ ㄍㄨㄥ)
a plagiarist
文丑(ㄨㄣˊ ㄔㄡˇ)
(Chinese opera) a clown that does not perform acrobatics or fighting
文場(ㄨㄣˊ ㄔㄤˇ)or(ㄨㄣˊ ㄔㄤˊ)
① an examination hall (for the civil service examination in former times) ② music accompanying singing and slow-motion acting as opposed to that accompanying fighting scenes in Chinese opera ③ the literary arena
文石(ㄨㄣˊ ㄕˊ)
① stones with streaks or mottles ② agate 亦作「瑪瑙」
文史(ㄨㄣˊ ㄕˇ)

the literature and history; humanities
文士(ㄨㄣˊ ㄕˋ)
a man of letters
文身(ㄨㄣˊ ㄕㄣ)
to tattoo the body
文書(ㄨㄣˊ ㄕㄨ)
① documents; records; archives ② an archivist; an office clerk
文殊(ㄨㄣˊ ㄕㄨ)
Manjusri, a Buddhist Bodhisattva, considered as an idealization of wisdom
文人(ㄨㄣˊ ㄖㄣˊ)
① a man of letters ② a man with a civilian background (as opposed to one with a military background)
文人畫(ㄨㄣˊ ㄖㄣˊ ㄏㄨㄚˋ)
a school of painting done by amateur literati
文人相輕(ㄨㄣˊ ㄖㄣˊ ㄒㄧㄤ ㄑㄧㄥ)
Men of letters tend to despise one another.
文人無行(ㄨㄣˊ ㄖㄣˊ ㄨˊ ㄒㄧㄥˊ)
Men of letters are normally Bohemians.
文弱(ㄨㄣˊ ㄖㄨㄛˋ)
effeminate; not soldierly: 他因缺少運動故看來文弱。He looks effeminate for want of exercise.
文弱書生(ㄨㄣˊ ㄖㄨㄛˋ ㄕㄨ ㄕㄥ)
an effeminate scholar
文字(ㄨㄣˊ ㄗˋ)
①a letter; a character; written language ② writing
文字交(ㄨㄣˊ ㄗˋ ㄐㄧㄠ)
friendship cemented by literature
文字學(ㄨㄣˊ ㄗˋ ㄒㄩㄝˊ)
etymology
文字處理機(ㄨㄣˊ ㄗˋ ㄔㄨˇ ㄌㄧˇ ㄐㄧ)
a word processor
文字獄(ㄨㄣˊ ㄗˋ ㄩˋ)
literary persecution
文責自負(ㄨㄣˊ ㄗㄜˊ ㄗˋ ㄈㄨˋ)
The writer is responsible for the consequences of this article. (a footnote for contributed articles published by a newspaper or magazine)
文藻(ㄨㄣˊ ㄗㄠˇ)
language or phraseology (of a poem, etc.)
文辭(ㄨㄣˊ ㄘˊ)
diction; phraseology; language
文才(ㄨㄣˊ ㄘㄞˊ)
literary talent; literary gift: 這位青年作家很有文才。This young writer has great literary talent.
文采(ㄨㄣˊ ㄘㄞˇ)
① elegant appearances ② beautiful or gorgeous color
文從字順(ㄨㄣˊ ㄘㄨㄥˊ ㄗˋ ㄕㄨㄣˋ)
The language is idiomatic and the wording is apposite.
文思(ㄨㄣˊ ㄙ)
thoughts expressed in writing: 他的文思明晰流暢。His thoughts expressed in writing are lucid and smooth.
文案(ㄨㄣˊ ㄢˋ)
① a business communication which requires some action ② a secretary; a clerk
文以載道(ㄨㄣˊ ㄧˇ ㄗㄞˋ ㄉㄠˋ)
Writings are for conveying truth.
文義(ㄨㄣˊ ㄧˋ)
the meaning of a written article, passage, or sentence
文藝(ㄨㄣˊ ㄧˋ)
literature (as one of the fine arts); belles-lettres
文藝批評(ㄨㄣˊ ㄧˋ ㄆㄧ ㄆㄧㄥˊ)
literary criticism
文藝復興(ㄨㄣˊ ㄧˋ ㄈㄨˋ ㄒㄧㄥ)
the Renaissance
文藝節(ㄨㄣˊ ㄧˋ ㄐㄧㄝˊ)
Literature Day (falling on May 4)
文藝界(ㄨㄣˊ ㄧˋ ㄐㄧㄝˋ)
the literary circles
文藝政策(ㄨㄣˊ ㄧˋ ㄓㄥˋ ㄘㄜˋ)
a set of guiding rules laid down by the government for literary workers
文藝思潮(ㄨㄣˊ ㄧˋ ㄙ ㄔㄠˊ)
the trend of literary thoughts
文雅(ㄨㄣˊ ㄧㄚˇ)
graceful; refined; polished
文妖(ㄨㄣˊ ㄧㄠ)
a literary sorcerer
文鰩魚(ㄨㄣˊ ㄧㄠˊ ㄩˊ)
a flying fish (*Cypselurus agoo*)亦作「飛魚」or「文魚」
文言(ㄨㄣˊ ㄧㄢˊ)or 文言文(ㄨㄣˊ ㄧㄢˊ ㄨㄣˊ)
the literary language used in old China which is vastly different from the modern language; classical Chinese
文無定法(ㄨㄣˊ ㄨˊ ㄉㄧㄥˋ ㄈㄚˇ)
There are no hard and fast rules one can follow in order to write well.
文武(ㄨㄣˊ ㄨˇ)
① polite letters and martial arts ② civil and military; for peace or for war
文武百官(ㄨㄣˊ ㄨˇ ㄅㄞˇ ㄍㄨㄢ)or 文武官員(ㄨㄣˊ ㄨˇ ㄍㄨㄢ ㄩㄢˊ)
all the civil and military officials
文武全才(ㄨㄣˊ ㄨˇ ㄑㄩㄢˊ ㄘㄞˊ)or 文武雙全(ㄨㄣˊ ㄨˇ ㄕㄨㄤ ㄑㄩㄢˊ)
a master of both the pen and the sword; to be well versed in both polite letters and martial arts
文武場(ㄨㄣˊ ㄨˇ ㄔㄤˇ)
musicians performing on a Peking Opera stage
文物(ㄨㄣˊ ㄨˋ)
the products of a culture; cultural artifacts
文物制度(ㄨㄣˊ ㄨˋ ㄓˋ ㄉㄨˋ)
cultural products and social institutions
文王(ㄨㄣˊ ㄨㄤˊ)
King Wen, who paved the way for the founding of the Chou Dynasty (1111—256 B.C.) by his son, King Wu
文苑(ㄨㄣˊ ㄩㄢˋ)
a writers' gathering place
文運(ㄨㄣˊ ㄩㄣˋ)
the vicissitudes of literature

【文】 2150
2. ㄨㄣˋ wenn wèn
to cover up; to conceal; to gloss over
文過(ㄨㄣˋ ㄍㄨㄛˋ)
to cover up one's fault
文過飾非(ㄨㄣˋ ㄍㄨㄛˋ ㄕˋ ㄈㄟ)
to cover up one's fault by clever use of words in writing
文飾(ㄨㄣˋ ㄕˋ)
to deceive by an impressive appearance

八畫

【斌】2151 ㄅㄧㄣ bin bīn
equally fine in external accomplishments and internal qualities

【斐】2152 ㄈㄟˇ feei fěi
1. elegant; beautiful
2. a Chinese family name

斐斐(ㄈㄟˇ ㄈㄟˇ)
(said of writing) elegant; beautiful

斐濟(ㄈㄟˇ ㄐㄧˋ)
Fiji

斐然(ㄈㄟˇ ㄖㄢˊ)
(said of results, achievements, etc.) striking; brilliant; excellent; very satisfactory

斐然成章(ㄈㄟˇ ㄖㄢˊ ㄔㄥˊ ㄓㄤ)
(said of a literary piece) to show striking literary merit; beautifully composed

【斑】2153 ㄅㄢ ban bān
1. speckles; spots; mottles
2. mottled; variegated; motley: 這小丑穿着顏色斑駁的外衣。The jester wears a motley coat.

斑白(ㄅㄢ ㄅㄛˊ)
(said of hair) gray: 他的頭髮已變成斑白了。His hair has turned gray.

斑駁(ㄅㄢ ㄅㄛˊ)
motley (in color)

斑斑(ㄅㄢ ㄅㄢ)
mottled; spotted

斑斑點點(ㄅㄢ ·ㄅㄢ ㄉㄧㄢˇ ㄉㄧㄢˇ)
mottled; speckled; spotted

斑鬢(ㄅㄢ ㄅㄧㄣˋ)
gray hair at the temples; graying temples

斑馬(ㄅㄢ ㄇㄚˇ)
a zebra

斑馬線(ㄅㄢ ㄇㄚˇ ㄒㄧㄢˋ)
a pedestrian crossing (marked with stripes like those of a zebra); a zebra crossing

斑點(ㄅㄢ ㄉㄧㄢˇ)
specks; spots; mottles: 這水果有很多的斑點。This fruit is badly specked.

斑斕(ㄅㄢ ㄌㄢˊ)
gorgeous; resplendent

斑鳩(ㄅㄢ ㄐㄧㄡ)
the ringdove; the wood pigeon; the cushat

斑晶(ㄅㄢ ㄐㄧㄥ)
phenocryst

斑疹(ㄅㄢ ㄓㄣˇ)
maculae

斑疹傷寒(ㄅㄢ ㄓㄣˇ ㄕㄤ ㄏㄢˊ)
typhus

斑竹(ㄅㄢ ㄓㄨˊ)
(botany) mottled bamboo

斑衣(ㄅㄢ ㄧ)
colorful dress (especially referring to children's wear)

斑紋(ㄅㄢ ㄨㄣˊ)
stripes; striped: 斑馬身上有斑紋。Zebras are striped.

九畫

【斒】2154 ㄅㄢ ban bān
1. variegated; motley
2. gorgeous; resplendent

斒斕(ㄅㄢ ㄌㄢˊ)
①(said of writing) resplendent; gorgeous ②variegated color; multicolored

十七畫

【斕】2155 ㄌㄢˊ lan lán
multicolored

斗部
ㄉㄡˇ doou dǒu

【斗】2156 ㄉㄡˇ doou dǒu
1. Chinese peck (a unite of dry measure for grain)
2. a large container for wine
3. one of the 28 constellations

斗杓(ㄉㄡˇ ㄅㄧㄠ)or 斗柄(ㄉㄡˇ ㄅㄧㄥˇ)
(astronomy) the handle of the Big Dipper

斗篷(ㄉㄡˇ ·ㄆㄥ)
a mantle; a cape

斗方名士(ㄉㄡˇ ㄈㄤ ㄇㄧㄥˊ ㄕˋ)
a pretender to refinement and elegance

斗膽(ㄉㄡˇ ㄉㄢˇ)
great intrepidity or boldness; to make bold: 你敢跟老板頂撞,眞是斗膽。It was bold of you to contradict your boss.

斗南(ㄉㄡˇ ㄋㄢˊ)
a prime minister

斗南一人(ㄉㄡˇ ㄋㄢˊ ㄧ ㄖㄣˊ)
(literally) the only one south of the Big Dipper —one who knows no equal under the sun

斗牛(ㄉㄡˇ ㄋㄧㄡˊ)
the Big Dipper and Altair

斗笠(ㄉㄡˇ ㄌㄧˋ)
a broad-brimmed rain hat (usually worn by farmers)

斗量(ㄉㄡˇ ㄌㄧㄤˊ)
to measure with a peck

斗箕(ㄉㄡˇ ·ㄐㄧ)or 斗記(ㄉㄡˇ ㄐㄧˋ)
a fingerprint (especially of the thumb)

斗酒百篇(ㄉㄡˇ ㄐㄧㄡˇ ㄅㄞˇ ㄆㄧㄢ)
great capacity for drinking and poetry (taken from a line of 杜甫:「李白斗酒詩百篇」)

斗酒隻鷄(ㄉㄡˇ ㄐㄧㄡˇ ㄓ ㄐㄧ)
some wine and a chicken —offerings to the spirit of the dead

斗帳(ㄉㄡˇ ㄓㄤˋ)
a small tent

斗轉參橫(ㄉㄡˇ ㄓㄨㄢˇ ㄕㄣ ㄏㄥˊ)
(literally) The Big Dipper has turned so that its handle is pointing horizontally. —Day is breaking.

斗食(ㄉㄡˇ ㄕˊ)
a petty official (receiving a peck of grain as pay)

斗室(ㄉㄡˇ ㄕˋ)
a little room; a small room: 他整天待在斗室之中。He stayed in a small room all day.

斗筲之人(ㄉㄡˇ ㄕㄠ ㄓ ㄖㄣˊ)
shallow common men (Confucius' description of officials of his times)

斗粟尺布(ㄉㄡˇ ㄙㄨˋ ㄔˇ ㄅㄨˋ)
brothers at loggerheads

六畫

【料】2157 ㄌㄧㄠˋ liaw liào
1. to conjecture; to reckon; to estimate

2. to infer; to anticipate; to foresee
3. to consider; to calculate
4. to manage; to handle; to care
5. material; stuff: 原料 raw material 燃料 fuel
6. makings; stuff: 他是讀書的料。He has got the makings of a scholar.

料到(ㄌㄧㄠˋ ㄉㄠˋ)
to foresee; to expect: 我沒料到她會遲到。I didn't expect her to be late.

料度(ㄌㄧㄠˋ ㄉㄨㄛˋ)
① to estimate; to reckon ② to infer

料理(ㄌㄧㄠˋ ㄌㄧˇ)
① to manage; to arrange; to take care of; to attend to; to dispose of: 我們能自己料理生活。We can take care of ourselves now. ② a Japanese dish; Japanese cooking

料估(ㄌㄧㄠˋ ㄍㄨ)
to estimate; to conjecture; to calculate

料峭(ㄌㄧㄠˋ ㄑㄧㄠˋ)
cold; chilly

料想(ㄌㄧㄠˋ ㄒㄧㄤˇ)
to reckon; to imagine; to expect; to presume; to suppose; to guess; to conjecture: 我料想不出那人究竟是誰。I can't imagine who that man can be. 我料想他很快就會回來。I presume that he will be back very soon. 他料想老板一定會批准他的請求。He fully expected that the boss would grant his request.

料中(ㄌㄧㄠˋ ㄓㄨㄥˋ)
to guess correctly

料事如神(ㄌㄧㄠˋ ㄕˋ ㄖㄨˊ ㄕㄣˊ)
to foresee with divine accuracy

料子(ㄌㄧㄠˋ ·ㄗ) or 料兒(ㄌㄧㄠˋ ㄦ)
cloth; fabric; material

料算(ㄌㄧㄠˋ ㄙㄨㄢˋ)
to reckon; to estimate

七畫

【斛】 2158 ㄏㄨˊ hwu hú
a dry measure 10 or 5 times that of 斗

【斜】 2159 ㄒㄧㄝˊ shye xié
inclined; sloping; slanting; leaning; oblique; diagonal

斜邊(ㄒㄧㄝˊ ㄅㄧㄢ)
①(mathematics) the leg (of a triangle); the hypotenuse, or hypothenuse (of a right-angled triangle) ② (machinery) a bevel edge

斜坡(ㄒㄧㄝˊ ㄆㄛ)
a slope: 士兵們爬上了一個陡峭的斜坡。The soldiers climbed a steep slope.

斜面(ㄒㄧㄝˊ ㄇㄧㄢˋ)
①(mathematics) an inclined plane ② (machinery) an oblique plane; a bevel (face)

斜風細雨(ㄒㄧㄝˊ ㄈㄥ ㄒㄧˋ ㄩˇ)
light wind and drizzling rain

斜度(ㄒㄧㄝˊ ㄉㄨˋ)
gradient; the degree of inclination

斜對面(ㄒㄧㄝˊ ㄉㄨㄟˋ ㄇㄧㄢˋ) or 斜對過兒(ㄒㄧㄝˊ ㄉㄨㄟˋ ㄍㄨㄛˋㄦ)
diagonally opposite

斜躺(ㄒㄧㄝˊ ㄊㄤˇ)
to recline

斜體字(ㄒㄧㄝˊ ㄊㄧˇ ㄗˋ)
(printing) italics

斜睨(ㄒㄧㄝˊ ㄋㄧˋ)
to look askance—to look down upon; to despise

斜高(ㄒㄧㄝˊ ㄍㄠ)
(mathematics) a slant height

斜暉(ㄒㄧㄝˊ ㄏㄨㄟ)
the slanting beams of the setting sun

斜角(ㄒㄧㄝˊ ㄐㄧㄠˇ)
①(mathematics) an oblique angle ② (machinery) a bevel angle

斜線(ㄒㄧㄝˊ ㄒㄧㄢˋ)
an oblique line

斜照(ㄒㄧㄝˊ ㄓㄠˋ)
① to shine obliquely ② the setting sun

斜視(ㄒㄧㄝˊ ㄕˋ)
① strabismus; squint ② to look askance; to cast a sidelong glance

斜視矯正手術(ㄒㄧㄝˊ ㄕˋ ㄐㄧㄠˇ ㄓㄥˋ ㄕㄡˇ ㄕㄨˋ)
strabotomy

斜眼(ㄒㄧㄝˊ ㄧㄢˇ)
①(medicine) strabismus ② squint-eye or cross-eye ③ a squint-eyed or cross-eyed person

斜陽(ㄒㄧㄝˊ ㄧㄤˊ)
the declining sun; the setting sun: 斜陽將盡。The setting sun is fading away.

斜紋布(ㄒㄧㄝˊ ㄨㄣˊ ㄅㄨˋ)
(textile) twill; drill

八畫

【斝】 2160 ㄐㄧㄚˇ jea jiǎ
(archeology) a jade wine cup

九畫

【斟】 2161 ㄓㄣ jen zhēn
1. to fill a cup with (tea or wine); to pour (a beverage) into a cup: 請給我斟一杯酒。Please pour me a glass of wine.
2. to consider: 我們會將此事詳予斟議。We will carefully consider this matter.

斟滿(ㄓㄣ ㄇㄢˇ)
to fill a cup or glass to the brim

斟酒(ㄓㄣ ㄐㄧㄡˇ)
to pour wine or liquor into a cup or glass

斟酌(ㄓㄣ ㄓㄨㄛˊ)
① to fill a cup, or glass, with wine or liquor ② to consider; consideration

斟茶(ㄓㄣ ㄔㄚˊ)
to fill a cup or glass with tea: 主人斟茶待客。The host fills a cup with tea to entertain his guest.

斟愖(ㄓㄣ ㄔㄣˊ)
to hesitate; hesitating

十畫

【斡】 2162 ㄨㄛˋ woh wò
to revolve; to turn; to rotate

斡旋(ㄨㄛˋ ㄒㄩㄢˊ)
to mediate; to use one's good offices or influence (in settling a dispute); mediation

斡轉(ㄨㄛˋ ㄓㄨㄢˇ)

〔斗部〕

〔斤部〕

to revolve; to rotate
斡運(ㄨㄛˋ ㄩㄣˋ)
to move in a circle

【斠】 2163 ㄐㄧㄠˋ jiaw jiào
a leveling stick (used for measuring the volume of grain, etc.)

斤 部
ㄐㄧㄣ jin jīn

【斤】 2164 ㄐㄧㄣ jin jīn
1. catty (a unit of weight): 她買了十斤米。She bought ten catties of rice.
2. an ax
3. discerning; keen in observation
斤兩(ㄐㄧㄣ ㄌㄧㄤˇ)
weight: 主任說的話很有斤兩。What the chief said carried a lot of weight.
斤斤較量(ㄐㄧㄣ ㄐㄧㄣ ㄐㄧㄠˋ ㄌㄧㄤˋ) or 斤斤計較(ㄐㄧㄣ ㄐㄧㄣ ㄐㄧˋ ㄐㄧㄠˋ)
to be particular about every point, detail, or trifle; to be calculating: 他斤斤較量個人得失。He is preoccupied with his personal gains and losses.
斤斤其明(ㄐㄧㄣ ㄐㄧㄣ ㄑㄧˊ ㄇㄧㄥˊ)
discerning; keen in observation; penetrating: 此人斤斤其明。This person is keen in observation.

一畫

【斥】 2165 ㄔˋ chyh chì
1. to accuse; to blame; to reproach; to reprove; to censure
2. to expel; to drive off; to banish; to eject: 他們將敵人斥逐出城。They expel the enemy from the town.
3. to survey; to observe; to reconnoiter
斥罷(ㄔˋ ㄅㄚˋ)
to dismiss (from office)
斥罵 or 叱罵(ㄔˋ ㄇㄚˋ)
to condemn; to upbraid; to denounce; to scold
斥退(ㄔˋ ㄊㄨㄟˋ)
to repel; to expel; to eject; to dismiss angrily
斥力(ㄔˋ ㄌㄧˋ)
(physics) repulsion
斥革(ㄔˋ ㄍㄜˊ)
to dismiss or remove (from office)
斥喝(ㄔˋ ㄏㄜˋ)
to scold
斥候(ㄔˋ ㄏㄡˋ)
① to reconnoiter; to patrol ② patrols
斥逐(ㄔˋ ㄓㄨˊ)
to expel; to repel; to banish; to eject
斥資(ㄔˋ ㄗ)
to contribute money
斥責 or 叱責(ㄔˋ ㄗㄜˊ)
to reprimand; to rebuke; to reprove; to reproach; to censure; to denounce

四畫

【斧】 2166 ㄈㄨˇ fuu fǔ
1. a hatchet; an ax
2. to chop; to cut
3. to trim: 請斧正拙作。Please trim and correct my work.
斧柯(ㄈㄨˇ ㄎㄜ) or 斧柄(ㄈㄨˇ ㄅㄧㄥˇ)
(literally) the handle of a hatchet—the reins of government
斧削(ㄈㄨˇ ㄒㄩㄝ)
(literally) to pare off with a hatchet—to correct (a composition) freely
斧鑕 or 斧質(ㄈㄨˇ ㄓˋ)
beheading by means of an ax
斧正 or 斧政(ㄈㄨˇ ㄓㄥˋ)
to correct (a composition) freely 參看「斧削」
斧石(ㄈㄨˇ ㄕˊ)
(mineral) axinite
斧子(ㄈㄨˇ ·ㄗ) or 斧頭(ㄈㄨˇ ·ㄊㄡ) or 斧斤(ㄈㄨˇ ㄐㄧㄣ)
an ax (axe); a hatchet
斧藻(ㄈㄨˇ ㄗㄠˇ)
to embellish; to decorate
斧鑿痕(ㄈㄨˇ ㄗㄨㄛˊ ㄏㄣˊ)
(literally) marks of the hatchet and the chisel —traces of laborious correction in a literary piece
斧鉞(ㄈㄨˇ ㄩㄝˋ)
the executioner's ax—(figuratively) capital punishment

五畫

【斫】 2167 ㄓㄨㄛˊ jwo zhuó
to chop or cut (wood)
斫木(ㄓㄨㄛˊ ㄇㄨˋ)
to chop or cut wood
斫斷(ㄓㄨㄛˊ ㄉㄨㄢˋ)
to chop off; to cut off; to sever by cutting or chopping
斫頭(ㄓㄨㄛˊ ㄊㄡˊ)
to behead; to decapitate
斫斬(ㄓㄨㄛˊ ㄓㄢˇ)
to chop; to cut; to hew
斫殺(ㄓㄨㄛˊ ㄕㄚ)
to kill with a hatchet, an ax, etc.

七畫

【斬】 2168 ㄓㄢˇ jaan zhǎn
1. to cut
2. to kill; to behead
斬伐(ㄓㄢˇ ㄈㄚˊ) or (ㄓㄢˇ ㄈㄚ)
① to conquer; to subjugate ② to execute; to behead ③ to fell (trees); to prune
斬釘截鐵(ㄓㄢˇ ㄉㄧㄥ ㄐㄧㄝˊ ㄊㄧㄝˇ)
to speak, or act, with determination and courage
斬斷情絲(ㄓㄢˇ ㄉㄨㄢˋ ㄑㄧㄥˊ ㄙ)
to cut off the threads of love
斬頭去尾(ㄓㄢˇ ㄊㄡˊ ㄑㄩˋ ㄨㄟˇ)
to make incomplete or short by omitting the foremost and hindmost parts
斬馘(ㄓㄢˇ ㄍㄨㄛˊ)
to behead; to decapitate
斬獲(ㄓㄢˇ ㄏㄨㄛˋ)
to cause enemy troops heavy casualties and material loss; to score a victory on the battlefield
斬將搴旗(ㄓㄢˇ ㄐㄧㄤˋ ㄑㄧㄢ ㄑㄧˊ)
to behead enemy generals and capture their flags (descriptive of bravery and prowess in battle)
斬決(ㄓㄢˇ ㄐㄩㄝˊ)

to carry out an execution by beheading the criminal

斬新 or 嶄新(ㄓㄢˇ ㄒㄧㄣ)
brand-new

斬首(ㄓㄢˇ ㄕㄡˇ)
to guillotine; to behead

斬首示衆(ㄓㄢˇ ㄕㄡˇ ㄕˋ ㄓㄨㄥˋ)
to behead a criminal and exhibit the severed head to the public as a warning to would-be offenders

斬草除根(ㄓㄢˇ ㄘㄠˇ ㄔㄨˊ ㄍㄣ)
(literally) to remove weed by rooting it out—to eliminate the cause of trouble completely

斬衰(ㄓㄢˇ ㄘㄨㄟ)
the mourning worn for one's parents or husband (the coarsest sack cloth with fringes unhemmed)

斬刈(ㄓㄢˇ ㄧˋ)
to mow down

斬妖(ㄓㄢˇ ㄧㄠ)
to exorcise evil spirits

八畫

【斮】 2169 ㄓㄨㄛˊ jwo zhuó

to cut; to pare

斮脛(ㄓㄨㄛˊ ㄐㄧㄥˋ)
to cut off one's legs as punishment

斮趾(ㄓㄨㄛˊ ㄓˇ)
to cut off one's toes as punishment

斮足(ㄓㄨㄛˊ ㄗㄨˊ)
to cut off one's feet as punishment

【斯】 2170 ㄙ sy sī

1. this; these; such; here
2. a connecting particle—then; thus
3. to tear; to rip; to cut away

斯巴達(ㄙ ㄅㄚ ㄉㄚˊ)
Sparta

斯磨(ㄙ ㄇㄛˊ)
to grind

斯摩稜斯克(ㄙ ㄇㄛˊ ㄌㄥˊ ㄙ ㄎㄜˋ)
Smolensk, a Russian city

斯芬克士(ㄙ ㄈㄣ ㄎㄜˋ ㄕˋ)
(Greek mythology) the Sphinx

斯德哥爾摩(ㄙ ㄉㄜˊ ㄍㄜ ㄦˇ ㄇㄛˊ)
Stockholm, capital of Sweden

斯多噶學派(ㄙ ㄉㄨㄛ ㄍㄜˇ ㄒㄩㄝˊ ㄆㄞˋ)
the Stoics; the Stoic School

斯拉夫(ㄙ ㄌㄚ ㄈㄨ)
Slav

斯里蘭卡(ㄙ ㄌㄧˇ ㄌㄢˊ ㄎㄚˇ)
Sri Lanka

斯堪的那維亞(ㄙ ㄎㄢ ㄉㄧˊ ㄋㄚˋ ㄨㄟˊ ㄧㄚˇ)
Scandinavia

斯須之間(ㄙ ㄒㄩ ㄓ ㄐㄧㄢ)
in an instant

斯時(ㄙ ㄕˊ)
this time; such a time

斯世(ㄙ ㄕˋ)
this worldly life: 他覺得斯世恍如幻夢。He feels that this worldly life is like a dream.

斯事(ㄙ ㄕˋ)
this matter

斯人而有斯疾(ㄙ ㄖㄣˊ ㄦˊ ㄧㄡˇ ㄙ ㄐㄧˊ)
That such a man should have such a sickness!—It is a pity that such a good man should contract such a disease!

斯斯文文(ㄙ ·ㄙ ㄨㄣˊ ㄨㄣˊ)or 斯文(ㄙ ·ㄨㄣ)
cultured; refined; elegant; gentle: 他談話斯文。His language is refined.

斯文敗類(ㄙ ㄨㄣˊ ㄅㄞˋ ㄌㄟˋ)
polished scoundrels; ruffians in scholars' gowns

斯文人(ㄙ ㄨㄣˊ ㄖㄣˊ)
a polished person; cultured people

斯文掃地(ㄙ ㄨㄣˊ ㄙㄠˇ ㄉㄧˋ)
the decadence of the intellectuals

九畫

【新】 2171 ㄒㄧㄣ shin xīn

1. new; fresh; novel
2. beginning; starting
3. modern; recent
4. the prefix "neo"
5. the Hsin Dynasty (8-22 A.D.)

新版(ㄒㄧㄣ ㄅㄢˇ)
the new edition (of a book): 這本書最近有新版。The new edition of this book has been published recently.

新編(ㄒㄧㄣ ㄅㄧㄢ)
① newly compiled; a new version ② newly organized

新兵(ㄒㄧㄣ ㄅㄧㄥ)
recruits

新派(ㄒㄧㄣ ㄆㄞˋ)
the new school; the modern school

新片預告(ㄒㄧㄣ ㄆㄧㄢˋ ㄩˋ ㄍㄠˋ)
a notice announcing films to be shown

新馬(ㄒㄧㄣ ㄇㄚˇ)
Singapore and Malaysia 亦作「星馬」

新墨西哥(ㄒㄧㄣ ㄇㄛˋ ㄒㄧ ㄍㄜ)
the state of New Mexico, U.S.A.

新莽(ㄒㄧㄣ ㄇㄤˇ)
Wang Mang (王莽), 45B.C.-23A.D., who founded the short-lived Hsin Dynasty (8-22A.D.) after usurping the throne from the house of Liu of the Han Dynasty

新米(ㄒㄧㄣ ㄇㄧˇ)
fresh rice; newly-harvested rice

新苗(ㄒㄧㄣ ㄇㄧㄠˊ)or 新芽(ㄒㄧㄣ ㄧㄚˊ)
young shoots; young sprouts

新民(ㄒㄧㄣ ㄇㄧㄣˊ)
to improve the people; to introduce new life to the people

新名詞(ㄒㄧㄣ ㄇㄧㄥˊ ㄘˊ)
new terms; new terminology

新發明(ㄒㄧㄣ ㄈㄚ ㄇㄧㄥˊ)
a new invention

新法(ㄒㄧㄣ ㄈㄚˇ)
① a new method; a new technique ② new laws (particularly referring to the political renovation introduced by Wang An-shih (王安石) of the Sung Dynasty)

新房(ㄒㄧㄣ ㄈㄤˊ)
① a bridal chamber ② a new house

新婦(ㄒㄧㄣ ㄈㄨˋ)
a bride

新大陸(ㄒㄧㄣ ㄉㄚˋ ㄌㄨˋ)
the New World; the Western Hemisphere

新德里(ㄒㄧㄣ ㄉㄜˊ ㄌㄧˇ)
New Delhi, capital of India

新到(ㄒㄧㄣ ㄉㄠˋ)
having just arrived

新臺幣(ㄒㄧㄣ ㄊㄞˊ ㄅㄧˋ)
New Taiwan Dollar (NT$)

〔斤部〕

新唐書(ㄒㄧㄣ ㄊㄤˊ ㄕㄨ)
the *New History of Tang* (one of the *Twenty-Four Histories*), by Ou-Yang Hsiu (歐陽修), Sung Chi (宋祁), etc.

新體詩(ㄒㄧㄣ ㄊㄧˇ ㄕ)or 新詩(ㄒㄧㄣ ㄕ)
modern poetry, or *pai hua* poetry (in Chinese literature)

新年(ㄒㄧㄣ ㄋㄧㄢˊ)
New Year: 敬祝新年快樂。I wish you a happy New Year.

新娘(ㄒㄧㄣ ㄋㄧㄤˊ)or 新娘子(ㄒㄧㄣ ㄋㄧㄤˊ ·ㄗ)or 新嫁娘(ㄒㄧㄣ ㄐㄧㄚˋ ㄋㄧㄤˊ)
a bride

新來(ㄒㄧㄣ ㄌㄞˊ)
having just come or arrived: 他們是新來的旅客。They are the tourists who have just arrived.

新來乍到(ㄒㄧㄣ ㄌㄞˊ ㄓㄚˋ ㄉㄠˋ)
being a newcomer

新郎(ㄒㄧㄣ ㄌㄤˊ)
a bridegroom

新浪漫主義(ㄒㄧㄣ ㄌㄤˋ ㄇㄢˋ ㄓㄨˇ ㄧˋ)
neoromanticism

新曆(ㄒㄧㄣ ㄌㄧˋ)
the solar calendar; the Gregorian calendar

新綠(ㄒㄧㄣ ㄌㄩˋ)
fresh verdure; fresh foliage

新古典主義(ㄒㄧㄣ ㄍㄨˇ ㄉㄧㄢˇ ㄓㄨˇ ㄧˋ)
neoclassicism

新鬼(ㄒㄧㄣ ㄍㄨㄟˇ)
the spirit of the newly deceased

新貴(ㄒㄧㄣ ㄍㄨㄟˋ)
a newly appointed official; a new VIP

新官上任三把火(ㄒㄧㄣ ㄍㄨㄢ ㄕㄤˋ ㄖㄣˋ ㄙㄢ ㄅㄚˇ ㄏㄨㄛˇ)
A newly inaugurated official tends to be very strict with his subordinates or enthusiastic about his job at the beginning (and is likely to relax as time goes by). 或 A new broom sweeps clean.

新宮(ㄒㄧㄣ ㄍㄨㄥ)
a newly built palace

新喀里多尼亞(ㄒㄧㄣ ㄎㄚˋ ㄌㄧˇ ㄉㄨㄛ ㄋㄧˊ ㄧㄚˋ)
New Caledonia

新科(ㄒㄧㄣ ㄎㄜ)
having just passed the civil service examination (in old China)

新開(ㄒㄧㄣ ㄎㄞ)
newly opened

新刊(ㄒㄧㄣ ㄎㄢ)
newly published

新罕布夏(ㄒㄧㄣ ㄏㄢˇ ㄅㄨˋ ㄒㄧㄚˋ)
the state of New Hampshire, U.S.A.

新歡(ㄒㄧㄣ ㄏㄨㄢ)
a new sweetheart or lover

新婚(ㄒㄧㄣ ㄏㄨㄣ)
newly married

新婚夫婦(ㄒㄧㄣ ㄏㄨㄣ ㄈㄨ ㄈㄨˋ)
newlyweds

新婚旅行(ㄒㄧㄣ ㄏㄨㄣ ㄌㄩˇ ㄒㄧㄥˊ)
a honeymoon tour

新幾內亞(ㄒㄧㄣ ㄐㄧ ㄋㄟˋ ㄧㄚˋ)
New Guinea

新紀錄(ㄒㄧㄣ ㄐㄧˋ ㄌㄨˋ)
a new record

新紀元(ㄒㄧㄣ ㄐㄧˋ ㄩㄢˊ)
a new era: 現在是進步的新紀元。It is a new era of progress.

新加坡(ㄒㄧㄣ ㄐㄧㄚ ㄆㄛ)
Singapore

新家庭(ㄒㄧㄣ ㄐㄧㄚ ㄊㄧㄥˊ)
the home of a newly married couple

新交(ㄒㄧㄣ ㄐㄧㄠ)
a new friend

新教(ㄒㄧㄣ ㄐㄧㄠˋ)
Protestantism

新舊交替(ㄒㄧㄣ ㄐㄧㄡˋ ㄐㄧㄠ ㄊㄧˋ)
the transition from the old to the new

新舊兒(ㄒㄧㄣ ㄐㄧㄡˋㄦ)
the degree of oldness

新金山(ㄒㄧㄣ ㄐㄧㄣ ㄕㄢ)
Melbourne, Australia

新近(ㄒㄧㄣ ㄐㄧㄣˋ)
recently; newly; lately: 這位詩人新近寫了不少詩。The poet has written quite a number of poems lately.

新進(人員)(ㄒㄧㄣ ㄐㄧㄣˋ (ㄖㄣˊ ㄩㄢˊ))
① new employees of an organization ② a novice

新疆(ㄒㄧㄣ ㄐㄧㄤ)
Sinkiang or Chinese Turkestan

新居(ㄒㄧㄣ ㄐㄩ)
a new residence

新局面(ㄒㄧㄣ ㄐㄩˊ ㄇㄧㄢˋ)
a new situation

新句(ㄒㄧㄣ ㄐㄩˋ)
an original expression (in poetry)

新劇(ㄒㄧㄣ ㄐㄩˋ)
Western-style drama (as opposed to traditional Chinese drama or opera)

新軍(ㄒㄧㄣ ㄐㄩㄣ)
① the Western-style army organized toward the end of the Ching Dynasty ② a newly organized army

新奇(ㄒㄧㄣ ㄑㄧˊ)
novel; new

新氣象(ㄒㄧㄣ ㄑㄧˋ ㄒㄧㄤˋ)
a pervasive new spirit; a prevailing new atmosphere

新青年(ㄒㄧㄣ ㄑㄧㄥ ㄋㄧㄢˊ)
a youth with new thoughts

新晴(ㄒㄧㄣ ㄑㄧㄥˊ)
(said of the sky) having just cleared up

新曲(ㄒㄧㄣ ㄑㄩˇ)
a new song; a new musical composition; a new tune: 她以新曲娛客。She delighted her guests with her new song.

新禧(ㄒㄧㄣ ㄒㄧ)or(ㄒㄧㄣ ㄒㄧˇ)
Happy New Year!

新西蘭(ㄒㄧㄣ ㄒㄧ ㄌㄢˊ)
New Zealand 亦作「紐西蘭」

新消息(ㄒㄧㄣ ㄒㄧㄠ ·ㄒㄧ)
the latest news; the latest information

新秀(ㄒㄧㄣ ㄒㄧㄡˋ)
a person who has begun to distinguish himself in a given field

新鮮(ㄒㄧㄣ ·ㄒㄧㄢ)
① fresh ② new; novel; original

新星(ㄒㄧㄣ ㄒㄧㄥ)
① (astronomy) a nova; a new star ② a new cinemactor or cinemactress

新興(ㄒㄧㄣ ㄒㄧㄥ)
newly risen; rising; new and developing; burgeoning

新型(ㄒㄧㄣ ㄒㄧㄥˊ)
a new type; a new pattern

新學(ㄒㄧㄣ ㄒㄩㄝˊ)
① a young science or discipline ② newly learned

新學制(ㄒㄧㄣ ㄒㄩㄝˊ ㄓˋ)
a new educational system
新選(ㄒㄧㄣ ㄒㄩㄢˇ)
newly elected: 他是新選的主席。He is the newly elected president.
新知(ㄒㄧㄣ ㄓ)
① new friends ② new knowledge; new learning
新制(ㄒㄧㄣ ㄓˋ)
a new system
新政(ㄒㄧㄣ ㄓㄥˋ)
renovated government administration; the New Deal
新竹(ㄒㄧㄣ ㄓㄨˊ)
Hsinchu, Taiwan Province
新著(ㄒㄧㄣ ㄓㄨˋ)
a new work (by a writer): 一本論現代藝術的新著正在銷售中。A new book on modern art is now on sale.
新妝(ㄒㄧㄣ ㄓㄨㄤ)
① the look of a woman immediately after make-up ② a new fashion in dressing
新裝(ㄒㄧㄣ ㄓㄨㄤ)
① a new dress ② newly installed
新潮派(ㄒㄧㄣ ㄔㄠˊ ㄆㄞˋ)
an avant-garde school
新潮流(ㄒㄧㄣ ㄔㄠˊ ㄌㄧㄡˊ)
a new trend
新愁(ㄒㄧㄣ ㄔㄡˊ)
fresh sorrows
新仇舊恨(ㄒㄧㄣ ㄔㄡˊ ㄐㄧㄡˋ ㄏㄣˋ)
new hatred piled on old
新陳代謝(ㄒㄧㄣ ㄔㄣˊ ㄉㄞˋ ㄒㄧㄝˋ)
①(biology) metabolism ② the new superseding the old; the replacement of the old with the new
新出土(ㄒㄧㄣ ㄔㄨ ㄊㄨˇ)
newly dug out or unearthed
新出爐(ㄒㄧㄣ ㄔㄨ ㄌㄨˊ)
① freshly baked ② newly produced or manufactured
新出手(ㄒㄧㄣ ㄔㄨ ㄕㄡˇ)
having just entered upon a career
新春(ㄒㄧㄣ ㄔㄨㄣ)
① the early spring ② the Lunar New Year
新創(ㄒㄧㄣ ㄔㄨㄤˋ)
newly devised; newly started; newly founded
新詩(ㄒㄧㄣ ㄕ)
free verse written in the vernacular 亦作「新體詩」
新石器時代(ㄒㄧㄣ ㄕˊ ㄑㄧˋ ㄕˊ ㄉㄞˋ)
the Neolithic Age
新時代(ㄒㄧㄣ ㄕˊ ㄉㄞˋ)
a new era: 新時代有新任務。A new era has a new task.
新式(ㄒㄧㄣ ㄕˋ)
of a new style; of a new model; modern: 她的服裝是新式的。Her dress is of a new style.
新世界(ㄒㄧㄣ ㄕˋ ㄐㄧㄝˋ)
the New World; the Western Hemisphere
新設(ㄒㄧㄣ ㄕㄜˋ)
newly established; newly inaugurated; newly activated
新手(ㄒㄧㄣ ㄕㄡˇ)
a new hand (at a job); a greenhorn; a novice
新生(ㄒㄧㄣ ㄕㄥ)
① newborn ② a new student ③ a new life; rebirth; regeneration
新生代(ㄒㄧㄣ ㄕㄥ ㄉㄞˋ)
the Cenozoic or Cainozoic Era
新生地(ㄒㄧㄣ ㄕㄥ ㄉㄧˋ)
reclaimed land; tidal land
新生活運動(ㄒㄧㄣ ㄕㄥ ㄏㄨㄛˊ ㄩㄣˋ ㄉㄨㄥˋ)
the New Life Movement (to modernize and discipline daily life, initiated by President Chiang Kai-shek in 1934)
新生界(ㄒㄧㄣ ㄕㄥ ㄐㄧㄝˋ)
the Cenozoic or Cainozoic group
新書(ㄒㄧㄣ ㄕㄨ)
a new book
新人(ㄒㄧㄣ ㄖㄣˊ)
① new employees; new talent; new appointees; new figures; new hands ② a bride ③ a new love ④ a man with modern thoughts
新人房(ㄒㄧㄣ ㄖㄣˊ ㄈㄤˊ)
a room of a newly married couple
新人生觀(ㄒㄧㄣ ㄖㄣˊ ㄕㄥ ㄍㄨㄢ)
a new outlook on life; a new view of life
新人物(ㄒㄧㄣ ㄖㄣˊ ㄨˋ)
a man with modern ideas
新任(ㄒㄧㄣ ㄖㄣˋ)
newly appointed; newly sworn-in
新澤西州(ㄒㄧㄣ ㄗㄜˊ ㄒㄧ ㄓㄡ)
the state of New Jersey, U.S.A.
新造(ㄒㄧㄣ ㄗㄠˋ)
newly-built; newly manufactured: 這種汽車是在德國新造的。This automobile is newly manufactured in Germany.
新村(ㄒㄧㄣ ㄘㄨㄣ)
a new residential quarter; a new housing development
新思想(ㄒㄧㄣ ㄙ ㄒㄧㄤˇ)
modern thinking; modern thoughts
新歲(ㄒㄧㄣ ㄙㄨㄟˋ)
the beginning of a new year
新藝綜合體(ㄒㄧㄣ ㄧˋ ㄗㄨㄥ ㄏㄜˊ ㄊㄧˇ)
(movie) CinemaScope 亦作「超視綜合體」
新印象派(ㄒㄧㄣ ㄧㄣˋ ㄒㄧㄤˋ ㄆㄞˋ)
neo-impressionism
新英格蘭(ㄒㄧㄣ ㄧㄥ ㄍㄜˊ ㄌㄢˊ)
New England
新穎(ㄒㄧㄣ ㄧㄥˇ)
novel; new; original: 這篇論文的題材新穎。The subject of this treatise is original.
新五代史(ㄒㄧㄣ ㄨˇ ㄉㄞˋ ㄕˇ)
the *New History of the Five Dynasties* (one of the *Twenty-Four Histories*), by Ou-Yang Hsiu (歐陽修)
新文化(ㄒㄧㄣ ㄨㄣˊ ㄏㄨㄚˋ)
modern culture, or culture oriented to modern science and new development in the humanities
新文化運動(ㄒㄧㄣ ㄨㄣˊ ㄏㄨㄚˋ ㄩㄣˋ ㄉㄨㄥˋ)
the New Culture Movement (around the time of the May 4th Movement in 1919)
新文學(ㄒㄧㄣ ㄨㄣˊ ㄒㄩㄝˊ)
new literature, or vernacular literature, after the May 4th Movement in 1919
新文字(ㄒㄧㄣ ㄨㄣˊ ㄗˋ)
Romanized or Latinized Chinese characters
新文藝(ㄒㄧㄣ ㄨㄣˊ ㄧˋ)
new literature, or vernacular literature
新聞(ㄒㄧㄣ ㄨㄣˊ)
news

〔斤部〕

新聞媒體(ㄒㄧㄣ ㄨㄣˊ ㄇㄟˊ ㄊㄧˇ)
news media
新聞通訊社(ㄒㄧㄣ ㄨㄣˊ ㄊㄨㄥ ㄒㄩㄣˋ ㄕㄜˋ)
a news agency
新聞稿(ㄒㄧㄣ ㄨㄣˊ ㄍㄠˇ)
a press release
新聞官(ㄒㄧㄣ ㄨㄣˊ ㄍㄨㄢ)
an information officer
新聞廣播(ㄒㄧㄣ ㄨㄣˊ ㄍㄨㄤˇ ㄅㄛ)
a news broadcast; a newscast
新聞公報(ㄒㄧㄣ ㄨㄣˊ ㄍㄨㄥ ㄅㄠˋ)
a press communiqué
新聞記者(ㄒㄧㄣ ㄨㄣˊ ㄐㄧˋ ㄓㄜˇ)
a journalist; a reporter; a correspondent
新聞界(ㄒㄧㄣ ㄨㄣˊ ㄐㄧㄝˋ)
the circle of journalists; the press circle
新聞檢查(ㄒㄧㄣ ㄨㄣˊ ㄐㄧㄢˇ ㄔㄚˊ)
press censorship
新聞學(ㄒㄧㄣ ㄨㄣˊ ㄒㄩㄝˊ)
journalism
新聞紙(ㄒㄧㄣ ㄨㄣˊ ㄓˇ)
newspapers and news magazines
新聞處(ㄒㄧㄣ ㄨㄣˊ ㄔㄨˋ)
the information service
新聞人物(ㄒㄧㄣ ㄨㄣˊ ㄖㄣˊ ㄨˋ)
people in the news
新聞自由(ㄒㄧㄣ ㄨㄣˊ ㄗˋ ㄧㄡˊ)
freedom of the press
新聞文學(ㄒㄧㄣ ㄨㄣˊ ㄨㄣˊ ㄒㄩㄝˊ)
journalistic literature
新約全書(ㄒㄧㄣ ㄩㄝ ㄑㄩㄢˊ ㄕㄨ)
the New Testament
新月(ㄒㄧㄣ ㄩㄝˋ)
①(astronomy) a new moon ②a crescent moon; a crescent
新元史(ㄒㄧㄣ ㄩㄢˊ ㄕˇ)
the *New History of Yüan* (one of the *Twenty-Five Histories*), by Ko Shao-min(柯劭忞)

十畫

【斲】 2172 (斵) ㄓㄨㄛˊ jwo zhuó

to chop; to hew
斲雕爲樸(ㄓㄨㄛˊ ㄉㄧㄠ ㄨㄟˊ ㄆㄨˊ)
to do away with vanity and adopt unadorned simplicity
斲輪老手(ㄓㄨㄛˊ ㄌㄨㄣˊ ㄌㄠˇ ㄕㄡˇ)
an expert wheelwright—(figuratively) an old hand; an experienced man
斲喪(ㄓㄨㄛˊ ㄙㄤˋ)
①to chop down completely ②to waste one's vitality by dissipation

十四畫

【斷】 2173 ㄉㄨㄢˋ duann duàn

1. to cut apart; to sever
2. to give up; to abstain from
3. to judge; to decide; to conclude: 聰明人當機立斷。A wise man decides promptly and opportunely.
4. to break; broken: 我打斷他們的談話。I broke off their conversation.
5. absolutely; decidedly; certainly: 這個故事斷不可信。This story is absolutely incredible.

斷編殘簡(ㄉㄨㄢˋ ㄅㄧㄢ ㄘㄢˊ ㄐㄧㄢˇ)
fragmentary works (of a writer)亦作「斷簡殘編」
斷片(ㄉㄨㄢˋ ㄆㄧㄢˋ)
①fragments; *disjecta membra* ②disruption of a movie show caused by the mechanical trouble of the projector
斷命(ㄉㄨㄢˋ ㄇㄧㄥˋ)
to die
斷髮文身(ㄉㄨㄢˋ ㄈㄚˇ ㄨㄣˊ ㄕㄣ)
(literally) to cut the hair and tattoo the body—to have barbarous customs
斷代(ㄉㄨㄢˋ ㄉㄞˋ)
a division of history into periods
斷電(ㄉㄨㄢˋ ㄉㄧㄢˋ)
power failure; a blackout
斷定(ㄉㄨㄢˋ ㄉㄧㄥˋ)
to determine; to conclude; to decide
斷斷不可(ㄉㄨㄢˋ ㄉㄨㄢˋ ㄅㄨˋ ㄎㄜˇ)
absolutely impermissible: 斷斷不可在此吸煙。Smoking is absolutely impermissible here.
斷斷續續(ㄉㄨㄢˋ ㄉㄨㄢˋ ㄒㄩˋ ㄒㄩˋ)
intermittent; off and on; broken: 自中午後,就一直斷斷續續地下雨。It has been raining on and off since noon.
斷頭臺(ㄉㄨㄢˋ ㄊㄡˊ ㄊㄞˊ)
a guillotine
斷頭將軍(ㄉㄨㄢˋ ㄊㄡˊ ㄐㄧㄤ ㄐㄩㄣ)
one who would rather die than surrender
斷屠(ㄉㄨㄢˋ ㄊㄨˊ)
to prohibit the butchering of animals on certain occasions
斷奶(ㄉㄨㄢˋ ㄋㄞˇ)or 斷乳(ㄉㄨㄢˋ ㄖㄨˇ)
to wean or be weaned
斷難相允(ㄉㄨㄢˋ ㄋㄢˊ ㄒㄧㄤ ㄩㄣˇ)
It is absolutely hard for one to consent....
斷爛朝報(ㄉㄨㄢˋ ㄌㄢˋ ㄔㄠˊ ㄅㄠˋ)
a worthless record or historical document
斷糧(ㄉㄨㄢˋ ㄌㄧㄤˊ)
to run out of food supply
斷路(ㄉㄨㄢˋ ㄌㄨˋ)
①to break off friendly relations ②to cut off a road for a retreat
斷根(ㄉㄨㄢˋ ㄍㄣ)
to be cured completely (as a disease or addiction)
斷港絕潢(ㄉㄨㄢˋ ㄍㄤˇ ㄐㄩㄝˊ ㄏㄨㄤˊ)
to reach a dead end
斷口(ㄉㄨㄢˋ ㄎㄡˇ)
(geology) a fracture
斷鶴續鳧(ㄉㄨㄢˋ ㄏㄜˋ ㄒㄩˋ ㄈㄨˊ)
(literally) to try to shorten the leg of a crane and lengthen that of an owl—to go against reason
斷後(ㄉㄨㄢˋ ㄏㄡˋ)
①to cover a retreat ②to have no offspring
斷乎(ㄉㄨㄢˋ ㄏㄨ)
absolutely; decidedly; positively
斷魂(ㄉㄨㄢˋ ㄏㄨㄣˊ)
①to be entranced; to be enraptured ②overpowered by grief
斷機教子(ㄉㄨㄢˋ ㄐㄧ ㄐㄧㄠˋ ㄗˇ)or 斷織(ㄉㄨㄢˋ ㄓ)
to break the loom to show one's child that the learning effort should not be interrupted
斷交(ㄉㄨㄢˋ ㄐㄧㄠ)
①to break off relations with someone ②to sever diplomatic relations
斷酒(ㄉㄨㄢˋ ㄐㄧㄡˇ)
①to abstain from alcohol ②

to prohibit the manufacture, transportation, and sale of alcoholic beverages

斷見(ㄉㄨㄢˋ ㄐㄧㄢˋ)
(Buddhism) the view that life ends with death

斷井頹垣(ㄉㄨㄢˋ ㄐㄧㄥˇ ㄊㄨㄟˊ ㄩㄢˊ)
(literally) The wells are dry and the fences are dilapidated.—completely deserted and in ruins

斷句(ㄉㄨㄢˋ ㄐㄩˋ)
①to punctuate the unpunctuated ancient writings when one reads them ②to punctuate

斷絕(ㄉㄨㄢˋ ㄐㄩㄝˊ)
to break off (relations); to sever

斷絕邦交(ㄉㄨㄢˋ ㄐㄩㄝˊ ㄅㄤ ㄐㄧㄠ)
to sever diplomatic ties

斷絕來往(ㄉㄨㄢˋ ㄐㄩㄝˊ ㄌㄞˊ ㄨㄤˇ)
to break off friendly relations

斷絕關係(ㄉㄨㄢˋ ㄐㄩㄝˊ ㄍㄨㄢ ·ㄒㄧ)
to sever relations; to disown (a prodigal son)

斷七(ㄉㄨㄢˋ ㄑㄧ)
the Buddhist service on each seventh day within 49 days after one's death

斷氣(ㄉㄨㄢˋ ㄑㄧˋ)
①to breathe one's last ②cut off the gas

斷虀畫粥(ㄉㄨㄢˋ ㄐㄧ ㄏㄨㄚˋ ㄓㄡ)
to eat sparingly because of poverty

斷袖之癖(ㄉㄨㄢˋ ㄒㄧㄡˋ ㄓ ㄆㄧˇ)
male homosexuality

斷絃(ㄉㄨㄢˋ ㄒㄧㄢˊ)
to be bereaved of one's wife

斷線(ㄉㄨㄢˋ ㄒㄧㄢˋ)
disconnection; line rupture

斷線風箏(ㄉㄨㄢˋ ㄒㄧㄢˋ ㄈㄥ ㄓㄥ)
①a blown off kite ②a thing or person that, once away, is not heard of any more: 她有如斷線風箏一般無影無踪。She is not heard of any more, like a blown off kite.

斷續(ㄉㄨㄢˋ ㄒㄩˋ)
off and on; intermittent

斷章取義(ㄉㄨㄢˋ ㄓㄤ ㄑㄩˇ ㄧˋ)
to interpret a thing out of context

斷種(ㄉㄨㄢˋ ㄓㄨㄥˇ)
to end a family line; to have no heir

斷腸(ㄉㄨㄢˋ ㄔㄤˊ)
to break the heart; heartbroken

斷除(ㄉㄨㄢˋ ㄔㄨˊ)
to remove (obstacles, bad habits, etc.)

斷炊(ㄉㄨㄢˋ ㄔㄨㄟ)
to be so impoverished as to have to stop cooking meals

斷食(ㄉㄨㄢˋ ㄕˊ)
to starve to death voluntarily

斷水(ㄉㄨㄢˋ ㄕㄨㄟˇ)
stoppage of water supply; out of water supply; to cut off water supply

斷然(ㄉㄨㄢˋ ㄖㄢˊ)
①absolutely; definitely; positively; decidedly ②resolute; drastic

斷層(ㄉㄨㄢˋ ㄘㄥˊ)
(geology) a fault

斷送(ㄉㄨㄢˋ ㄙㄨㄥˋ)
to lose for good: 她的錯誤使她斷送了名譽。Her fault has made her lose her reputation for good.

斷案(ㄉㄨㄢˋ ㄢˋ)
①to close a legal case ②(logic) a conclusion

斷疑(ㄉㄨㄢˋ ㄧˊ)
to resolve doubts

斷崖絕壁(ㄉㄨㄢˋ ㄧㄞˊ ㄐㄩㄝˊ ㄅㄧˋ)
broken ridges and steep cliffs

斷言(ㄉㄨㄢˋ ㄧㄢˊ)
to be absolutely sure; to say with certainty: 他的朋友們斷言他是無罪的。His friends said with certainty that he was innocent.

斷無此理(ㄉㄨㄢˋ ㄨˊ ㄘˇ ㄌㄧˇ)
It is absolutely against reason. 或 It is definitely illogical.

斷語(ㄉㄨㄢˋ ㄩˇ)
judgment; a verdict; a conclusion: 愼重一點，不要遽下斷語。Be careful not to jump to conclusions.

斷獄(ㄉㄨㄢˋ ㄩˋ)
to close a trial by announcing the verdict

斷垣殘壁(ㄉㄨㄢˋ ㄩㄢˊ ㄘㄢˊ ㄅㄧˋ)
the broken fences and walls—descriptive of a desolate scene

方部
ㄈㄤ fang fāng

〔方部〕

【方】 2174
ㄈㄤ fang fāng

1.square; rectangular
2.honest; morally upright: 他爲人方正。He is an honest person.
3.a region; an area; a place
4.a prescription; a recipe
5.a direction
6.occultism
7.just now; just then; just: 她年方十八。She is just eighteen years old.
8.(mathematics) power
9.(classifier) short for square meter or cubic meter
10.side; party: 友誼是雙方面的事。Friendship is a two-sided affair.
11.a method; a way
12.an aspect
13.one side
14.a Chinese family name

方苞(ㄈㄤ ㄅㄠ)
Fang Pao, 1668-1749, a classical writer and originator of a school of writing known as 桐城派

方便(ㄈㄤ ㄅㄧㄢˋ)
①convenient; handy; a convenient method ②to give somebody a break; to do somebody a favor ③(colloquial) to go to the lavatory

方便之門(ㄈㄤ ㄅㄧㄢˋ ㄓ ㄇㄣˊ)
a favor or break for somebody

方步(ㄈㄤ ㄅㄨˋ)
a square pace

方袍(ㄈㄤ ㄆㄠˊ)
a Buddhist monk or priest

方帽(ㄈㄤ ㄇㄠˋ)
square caps worn by college graduates

方面(ㄈㄤ ㄇㄧㄢˋ)
①a direction; a quarter; a district; a sphere; a field: 這家公司有許多方面需要改革。Reforms in many directions

are needed in this company. ②(in this or that) respect; (on the one, or other) hand; (on this or that) topic, subject, etc.

方面大耳(ㄈㄤ ㄇㄧㄢˋ ㄉㄚˋ ㄦˇ)
a square face with large ears (regarded by fortune-tellers as a look of good fortune)

方命(ㄈㄤ ㄇㄧㄥˋ)
to disobey an order

方法(ㄈㄤ ㄈㄚˇ)
a method; a way; a means: 有任何方法到達那裏嗎? Is (Are) there any means of getting there?

方法論(ㄈㄤ ㄈㄚˇ ㄌㄨㄣˋ)
methodology

方底圓蓋(ㄈㄤ ㄉㄧˇ ㄩㄢˊ ㄍㄞˋ)
A square peg cannot fit a round hole.—incompatible

方糖(ㄈㄤ ㄊㄤˊ)
cube sugar; sugar cubes

方內(ㄈㄤ ㄋㄟˋ)
within the boundaries of the country

方里(ㄈㄤ ㄌㄧˇ)
a square *li* (250,000 square meters)

方哩(ㄈㄤ ㄌㄧˇ)
a square mile

方領矩步(ㄈㄤ ㄌㄧㄥˇ ㄐㄩˇ ㄅㄨˋ)
dressed in scholarly clothes and showing refined manners

方略(ㄈㄤ ㄌㄩㄝˋ)
a general plan

方格(ㄈㄤ ㄍㄜˊ)
a square (in a checkerboard pattern)

方格紙(ㄈㄤ ㄍㄜˊ ㄓˇ)
graph paper

方根(ㄈㄤ ㄍㄣ) or 方程根(ㄈㄤ ㄔㄥˊ ㄍㄣ)
(mathematics) a root

方括號(ㄈㄤ ㄍㄨㄚ ㄏㄠˋ)
square brackets ([ ])

方國(ㄈㄤ ㄍㄨㄛˊ)
feudal princes who pay allegiance to a common sovereign

方軌(ㄈㄤ ㄍㄨㄟˇ)
(said of two carriages) to go abreast

方塊字(ㄈㄤ ㄎㄨㄞˋ ㄗˋ)
①Chinese characters written on square pieces of paper, used to teach a child to read ②square print

方技(ㄈㄤ ㄐㄧˋ)
(in ancient China) occultism, divination, medical practice, etc.

方劑(ㄈㄤ ㄐㄧˋ)
a medical prescription

方家(ㄈㄤ ㄐㄧㄚ)
a famous master or expert

方駕(ㄈㄤ ㄐㄧㄚˋ)
①(said of two carriages) to go abreast ②(said of two persons) evenly matched; equal in ability

方解石(ㄈㄤ ㄐㄧㄝˇ ㄕˊ)
calcite

方今(ㄈㄤ ㄐㄧㄣ)
now; at present; currently

方巾(ㄈㄤ ㄐㄧㄣ)
a kind of hood worn by intellectuals during the Ming Dynasty

方且(ㄈㄤ ㄑㄧㄝˇ)
even; still

方鉛礦(ㄈㄤ ㄑㄧㄢ ㄎㄨㄤˋ)
galena

方孝孺(ㄈㄤ ㄒㄧㄠˋ ㄖㄨˊ)
Fang Hsiao-ju, an upright scholar of the early Ming Dynasty, who was killed on the order of the third Ming emperor (明成祖)

方向(ㄈㄤ ㄒㄧㄤˋ)
orientation; a direction; a course: 他朝著公園的方向走去。He went off in the direction of the park.

方向盤(ㄈㄤ ㄒㄧㄤˋ ㄆㄢˊ)
a steering wheel

方向舵(ㄈㄤ ㄒㄧㄤˋ ㄉㄨㄛˋ)
a side rudder

方興未艾(ㄈㄤ ㄒㄧㄥ ㄨㄟˋ ㄞˋ)
to be still growing; to be still making progress; to be in the ascendant: 這項社會革新運動方興未艾。The social reform movement is still growing.

方形(ㄈㄤ ㄒㄧㄥˊ)
a rectangle

方知(ㄈㄤ ㄓ)
to know for the first time

方趾圓顱(ㄈㄤ ㄓˇ ㄩㄢˊ ㄌㄨˊ)
(literally) a creature with rectangular feet and a round head—a human being

方志(ㄈㄤ ㄓˋ)
a geographic account

方舟(ㄈㄤ ㄓㄡ)
①(said of two ships) to sail abreast ② an ark

方針(ㄈㄤ ㄓㄣ)
a principle; a policy; a course of action

方鎮(ㄈㄤ ㄓㄣˋ)
a magistrate with military power (in former times)

方丈
①(ㄈㄤ ㄓㄤˋ) a square *chang* (a little more than 100 square feet)
②(ㄈㄤ ˙ㄓㄤ) the head priest of a Buddhist temple

方正(ㄈㄤ ㄓㄥˋ)
(said of one's conduct) irreproachable: 他是一位方正的法學專家。He is an irreproachable jurist.

方桌(ㄈㄤ ㄓㄨㄛ)
a rectangular table

方尺(ㄈㄤ ㄔˇ)
a square *chih* (a little larger than a square foot)

方城之戰(ㄈㄤ ㄔㄥˊ ㄓ ㄓㄢˋ)
mah-jong game

方程式(ㄈㄤ ㄔㄥˊ ㄕˋ)
an equation

方始(ㄈㄤ ㄕˇ)
to have just begun

方士(ㄈㄤ ㄕˋ)
an occultist; an alchemist

方式(ㄈㄤ ㄕˋ)
a mode; a manner; a way

方生未死(ㄈㄤ ㄕㄥ ㄨㄟˋ ㄙˇ)
The new order has been born, but the old establishment is not yet completely dead.

方術(ㄈㄤ ㄕㄨˋ)
①(in old China) occultism, divination, or medical practice ② doctrines and policies

方枘圓鑿(ㄈㄤ ㄖㄨㄟˋ ㄩㄢˊ ㄗㄨㄛˋ)
A square peg cannot fit a round hole.—incompatible

方字(ㄈㄤ ㄗˋ)
characters written or printed on square pieces of paper for use in teaching children to read

方子(ㄈㄤ ˙ㄗ)

a medical prescription
方策(ㄈㄤ ㄘㄜˋ)
strategy; a plan
方才 or 方纔(ㄈㄤ ㄘㄞˊ)
just now; just a moment ago: 你的妹妹方才還在這兒。Your younger sister was here just a moment ago.
方寸(ㄈㄤ ㄘㄨㄣˋ)
①a square *tsun* (a little larger than a square inch) ② the heart
方寸不亂(ㄈㄤ ㄘㄨㄣˋ ㄅㄨˋ ㄌㄨㄢˋ)
to remain calm; to maintain composure
方寸地(ㄈㄤ ㄘㄨㄣˋ ㄉㄧˋ)
the heart
方寸無主(ㄈㄤ ㄘㄨㄣˋ ㄨˊ ㄓㄨˇ)
bewildered; confused; dismayed
方俗(ㄈㄤ ㄙㄨˊ)
local customs
方案(ㄈㄤ ㄢˋ)
a plan; a project; a design; a scheme; a program
方以類聚(ㄈㄤ ㄧˇ ㄌㄟˋ ㄐㄩˋ)
Only people of similar character and disposition can become good friends.
方裔(ㄈㄤ ㄧˋ)
the frontier region
方言(ㄈㄤ ㄧㄢˊ)
a dialect
方言字典(ㄈㄤ ㄧㄢˊ ㄗˋ ㄉㄧㄢˇ)
a dialect dictionary
方音(ㄈㄤ ㄧㄣ)
a regional accent in pronunciation
方外(ㄈㄤ ㄨㄞˋ)
beyond this world
方外之人(ㄈㄤ ㄨㄞˋ ㄓ ㄖㄣˊ)
Buddhist or Taoist priests
方位(ㄈㄤ ㄨㄟˋ)
the points of the compass; a direction; a bearing
方位角(ㄈㄤ ㄨㄟˋ ㄐㄧㄠˇ)
(surveying) azimuth, the angle measured clockwise from the south or north
方輿(ㄈㄤ ㄩˊ)
the earth
方隅(ㄈㄤ ㄩˊ)
boundaries
方圓 or 方員(ㄈㄤ ㄩㄢˊ)
① neighborhood ② squares and circles

四畫

【於】 2175
1. ㄩˊ yu yú
1. in; on; at; by; from
2. than; then; to; with reference to
3. compared with: 他的英文優於她。Her English cannot compare with his.
4. a Chinese family name
於理甚當(ㄩˊ ㄌㄧˇ ㄕㄣˋ ㄉㄤˋ)
appropriate; proper; reasonable; justified
於後(ㄩˊ ㄏㄡˋ)
afterwards; as follows
於己無損(ㄩˊ ㄐㄧˇ ㄨˊ ㄙㄨㄣˇ)
It doesn't hurt oneself (but may do a lot of good to others).
於今(ㄩˊ ㄐㄧㄣ)
now; at present
於下(ㄩˊ ㄒㄧㄚˋ)
as follows; below
於心何忍(ㄩˊ ㄒㄧㄣ ㄏㄜˊ ㄖㄣˇ)
Where's your conscience? 或 How could one stand such (callousness without offering help)?
於是(ㄩˊ ㄕˋ)
then; so; thus; thereafter; thereupon: 於是我們判定他錯了。Thus we decided that he was wrong.
於是乎(ㄩˊ ㄕˋ ㄏㄨ)
then; thereupon; so; in this way; thus
於是焉(ㄩˊ ㄕˋ ㄧㄢ)
thereupon
於事無補(ㄩˊ ㄕˋ ㄨˊ ㄅㄨˇ)
It doesn't help the situation. 或 It does nothing good.
於左(ㄩˊ ㄗㄨㄛˇ)
① on the left ② as follows
於此(ㄩˊ ㄘˇ)
here; in this place
於斯(ㄩˊ ㄙ)
in this place; here
於右(ㄩˊ ㄧㄡˋ)
① on the right ② as above
於焉(ㄩˊ ㄧㄢ)
① then; thereupon ② here

【於】 2175
2. ㄨ u wū
an interjection roughly equivalent to hurrah, bravo, alas, etc.
於穆(ㄨ ㄇㄨˋ)
Bravo!
於乎 or 於戲(ㄨ ㄏㄨ)
Ah!
於皇(ㄨ ㄏㄨㄤˊ)
Wonderful!
於鑠(ㄨ ㄕㄨㄛˋ)
Hurray!
於邑(ㄨ ㄧˋ)
alas (showing anxiety or sorrow)

五畫

【施】 2176
ㄕ shy shī
1. to act; to do; to make
2. to bestow; to grant; to give (alms, etc.)
3. to apply
4. a Chinese family name
施肥(ㄕ ㄈㄟˊ)
to apply fertilizers
施粉(ㄕ ㄈㄣˇ)
to apply face powder; to powder one's face
施放(ㄕ ㄈㄤˋ)
to discharge; to fire
施耐庵(ㄕ ㄋㄞˋ ㄢ)
Shih Nai-an (c.1290-c.1365), author of *All Men Are Brothers* (水滸傳)
施禮(ㄕ ㄌㄧˇ)
to make a bow; to curtsy; to salute: 賓主互相施禮。The host and the guest saluted each other.
施工(ㄕ ㄍㄨㄥ)
to start construction or building
施工中(ㄕ ㄍㄨㄥ ㄓㄨㄥ)
under construction; abuilding: 這座橋樑正施工中。The bridge is under construction.
施加(ㄕ ㄐㄧㄚ)
to exert; to bring to bear on
施教(ㄕ ㄐㄧㄠˋ)
to teach; to educate; to instruct
施救(ㄕ ㄐㄧㄡˋ)
to rescue and resuscitate
施洗(ㄕ ㄒㄧˇ)
to baptize
施洗約翰(ㄕ ㄒㄧˇ ㄩㄝ ㄏㄢˋ)
John the Baptist
施行(ㄕ ㄒㄧㄥˊ)

①(law) to come into force; to enforce; enforcement; to put into operation; to act; to execute ② to perform

施行細則(ㄕ ㄒㄧㄥˊ ㄒㄧˋ ㄗㄜˊ)
bylaws; detailed regulations governing the implementation of a statute

施脂粉(ㄕ ㄓ ㄈㄣˇ)
to apply cosmetics

施齋(ㄕ ㄓㄞ)
to give food to a Buddhist monk or nun

施粥(ㄕ ㄓㄡ)
to offer relief to the poor by operating a soup kitchen

施展(ㄕ ㄓㄢˇ)
to display (one's feat, talent, skill, etc.); to give free play to: 他常施展他的本領。He often gives full play to his talent.

施賑(ㄕ ㄓㄣˋ)
to give to the poor

施政(ㄕ ㄓㄥˋ)
(government) to administer; to govern; to execute government orders

施政報告(ㄕ ㄓㄥˋ ㄅㄠˋ ㄍㄠˋ)
an administrative report (delivered by a head of state, province, etc. to the legislature, assembly, etc.)

施主(ㄕ ㄓㄨˇ)
one who contributes to the Buddhist faith; a term of address used by monks or nuns referring to a believer in Buddhism

施逞(ㄕ ㄔㄥˇ)
to display or exhibit (one's feat, talent, etc.)

施施(ㄕ ㄕ)
complacently; leisurely

施食(ㄕ ㄕˊ)
① to feed the poor; to give relief to the poor by feeding them ②(Buddhism) to offer food to monks or spirits of those starved to death

施捨(ㄕ ㄕㄜˇ)
to give to charity

施人慎勿念(ㄕ ㄖㄣˊ ㄕㄣˋ ㄨˋ ㄋㄧㄢˋ)
Don't try to remember the good turns one has done to others.

施恩(ㄕ ㄣ)
to give favors to others

施醫(ㄕ ㄧ)
to give free medical service

施藥(ㄕ ㄧㄠˋ)
to dispense medicine free of charge

施威(ㄕ ㄨㄟ)
① to impress with force ②(said of gods) to show anger or power

施為(ㄕ ㄨㄟˊ)
action; behavior; conduct

施與(ㄕ ㄩˇ)
to give to the poor; to give to charity

施用(ㄕ ㄩㄥˋ)
to use; to employ

【斿】 2177
ㄧㄡˊ you yóu

1. to swim
2. to rove about freely
3. ornaments hanging down from banners

六畫

【旁】 2178
1. (㫄) ㄆㄤˊ parng páng

1. side (branches, doors, ways, etc.); the side
2. by the side of; nearby
3. other; else

旁礴(ㄆㄤˊ ㄅㄛˊ)
all-embracing; overwhelming

旁白(ㄆㄤˊ ㄅㄞˊ)
(drama) aside

旁邊(ㄆㄤˊ ㄅㄧㄢ)or 旁邊兒(ㄆㄤˊ ㄅㄧㄚㄦ)
① the side; by the side of ② nearby; in the vicinity of

旁門(ㄆㄤˊ ㄇㄣˊ)
a side door

旁門左道(ㄆㄤˊ ㄇㄣˊ ㄗㄨㄛˇ ㄉㄠˋ)
heresy; unorthodox ways

旁聽(ㄆㄤˊ ㄊㄧㄥ)
to sit at a meeting or class in the capacity as an observer, guest, auditor, etc.

旁聽席(ㄆㄤˊ ㄊㄧㄥ ㄒㄧˊ)
seats reserved for visitors or observers at a meeting or court proceeding; gallery seats

旁聽生(ㄆㄤˊ ㄊㄧㄥ ㄕㄥ)
an auditor (at a class)

旁孽(ㄆㄤˊ ㄋㄧㄝˋ)
a son borne by one's concubine

旁觀(ㄆㄤˊ ㄍㄨㄢ)
to look on; to watch from the sidelines

旁觀者(ㄆㄤˊ ㄍㄨㄢ ㄓㄜˇ)
an onlooker; a bystander; a spectator

旁觀者清(ㄆㄤˊ ㄍㄨㄢ ㄓㄜˇ ㄑㄧㄥ)
The onlooker is clearheaded (because he can see what's going on with detachment). 或 The onlooker sees most of the game.

旁及(ㄆㄤˊ ㄐㄧˊ)
to touch on (something else) incidentally; to take up (along with something more important): 他專攻文學，旁及藝術。He majors in literature, but also takes an interest in art.

旁妻(ㄆㄤˊ ㄑㄧ)
a concubine

旁切圓(ㄆㄤˊ ㄑㄧㄝ ㄩㄢˊ)
(geometry) an escribed circle

旁敲側擊(ㄆㄤˊ ㄑㄧㄠ ㄘㄜˋ ㄐㄧˊ)
to ask seemingly irrelevant questions or speak aimlessly with a hidden purpose; to teach or enlighten by indirect approach; to make oblique references

旁求(ㄆㄤˊ ㄑㄧㄡˊ)
to solicit (men of abilities, etc.) from all sides; to search everywhere 亦作「遍求」

旁系(ㄆㄤˊ ㄒㄧˋ)
a lateral family line (as distinct from the direct lineage) 參看「旁支」

旁行(ㄆㄤˊ ㄒㄧㄥˊ)
① to travel far and wide ② a written language that goes from left to right, as English, French, etc.

旁行斜上(ㄆㄤˊ ㄒㄧㄥˊ ㄒㄧㄝˊ ㄕㄤˋ)
Occidental languages

旁訓(ㄆㄤˊ ㄒㄩㄣˋ)
footnotes of scriptures or classics

旁支(ㄆㄤˊ ㄓ)
a collateral branch (of a family)

旁枝(ㄆㄤˊ ㄓ)
a side branch

旁徵曲引(ㄆㄤˊ ㄓㄥ ㄑㄩ ㄧㄣˇ)
to quote widely or extensively

旁證(ㄆㄤˊ ㄓㄥˋ)
circumstantial evidence; indirect evidence; collateral evidence

旁注 or 旁註(ㄆㄤˊ ㄓㄨˋ)
annotations; footnotes; notes

旁岔兒(ㄆㄤˊ ㄔㄚˋㄦ)
an interruption; an outgrowth or offshoot (usually undesirable)

旁出(ㄆㄤˊ ㄔㄨ)
an offshoot; children born of a concubine

旁生(ㄆㄤˊ ㄕㄥ)
①(Buddhism) domestic animals ②to occur from beside

旁人(ㄆㄤˊ ㄖㄣˊ)
① bystanders; onlookers; outsiders ② the others: 我必須和旁人商量。I must consult with the others.

旁若無人(ㄆㄤˊ ㄖㄨㄛˋ ㄨˊ ㄖㄣˊ)
to act as if there weren't any bystanders; with full composure (connoting over-confidence or arrogance)

旁坐(ㄆㄤˊ ㄗㄨㄛˋ)
(in ancient China) to involve one's relatives in a criminal offense

旁壓力(ㄆㄤˊ ㄧㄚ ㄌㄧˋ)
(physics) lateral pressure

【旁】 2178
2. ㄅㄤˋ bang bàng

參看「旁午」

旁午(ㄅㄤˋ ㄨˇ)
① busy; complicated ② criss-cross

【旂】 2179
ㄑㄧˊ chyi qí

a flag or streamer attached with small bells; a flag

【旃】 2180
ㄓㄢ jan zhān

1. a flag or banner with a bent staff
2. an auxiliary particle used like 之 or 焉 to give force to the verb
3. woolen fabrics
4. a Chinese family name

【旆】 2181
ㄆㄟˋ pey pèi

a general name for flags, banners, streamers, pennons, etc.

旆旆(ㄆㄟˋ ㄆㄟˋ)
①(descriptive of flags) flying in the wind ②(said of plants) growing luxuriantly

【旄】 2182
1. ㄇㄠˊ mau máo

a kind of ancient flag with the oxtails set up at the top of its staff

旄車(ㄇㄠˊ ㄐㄩ)
an ancient war chariot

【旄】 2182
2.(耄) ㄇㄠˋ maw mào

old

旄倪(ㄇㄠˋ ㄋㄧˊ)
old and young

【旅】 2183
ㄌㄩˇ leu lǚ

1. to travel; to lodge: 她每年夏季在歐洲旅行。She travels in Europe every summer.
2. a traveler; a passenger; a lodger
3. a multitude; people
4. disciples; pupils; followers; subordinates
5. order; sequence; to arrange
6. (military) a brigade; troops
7. (now rarely) a sacrifice to the mountains
8. to proceed together; to do things together

旅伴(ㄌㄩˇ ㄅㄢˋ)
a traveling companion

旅費(ㄌㄩˇ ㄈㄟˋ)
traveling expenses

旅店(ㄌㄩˇ ㄉㄧㄢˋ)
a tavern; an inn

旅途(ㄌㄩˇ ㄊㄨˊ)
the route by which one travels from one place to another; on one's way (to a destination); during one's trip

旅力(ㄌㄩˇ ㄌㄧˋ)
① the common effort of all ② one's muscular strength

旅館(ㄌㄩˇ ㄍㄨㄢˇ)
a hotel; a hostel; an inn

旅客(ㄌㄩˇ ㄎㄜˋ)
a traveler; a passenger; a lodger

旅進旅退(ㄌㄩˇ ㄐㄧㄣˋ ㄌㄩˇ ㄊㄨㄟˋ)
(literally) to advance and retreat together with others —having no opinion of one's own

旅居(ㄌㄩˇ ㄐㄩ)
to stay in a place for a while; temporary lodging

旅行(ㄌㄩˇ ㄒㄧㄥˊ)
to travel; to go in a group from one place to another; travels

旅行袋(ㄌㄩˇ ㄒㄧㄥˊ ㄉㄞˋ)
a traveling bag

旅行團(ㄌㄩˇ ㄒㄧㄥˊ ㄊㄨㄢˊ)
a traveling party; a tourist group: 這個旅行團正在作環島旅行。This tourist group is going round the island.

旅行支票(ㄌㄩˇ ㄒㄧㄥˊ ㄓ ㄆㄧㄠˋ)
a traveler's check

旅行指南(ㄌㄩˇ ㄒㄧㄥˊ ㄓˇ ㄋㄢˊ)
a guidebook

旅行車(ㄌㄩˇ ㄒㄧㄥˊ ㄔㄜ)
a station wagon

旅行社(ㄌㄩˇ ㄒㄧㄥˊ ㄕㄜˋ)
a travel agency; a travel bureau

旅長(ㄌㄩˇ ㄓㄤˇ)
the commanding officer of a brigade

旅程(ㄌㄩˇ ㄔㄥˊ)
the route a traveler takes from one place to another; during one's trip; on one's way; a journey

旅食(ㄌㄩˇ ㄕˊ)
① to stay at one place as a visitor ② mess for a large group of people

旅社(ㄌㄩˇ ㄕㄜˋ)
a hotel; a hostel; an inn

旅生(ㄌㄩˇ ㄕㄥ)
(said of wild plants) to grow spontaneously

旅順(ㄌㄩˇ ㄕㄨㄣˋ)
Port Arthur (Lüshun), in Liaoning Province

旅人(ㄌㄩˇ ㄖㄣˊ)
① a traveler ② one who lives away from home

旅次(ㄌㄩˇ ㄘˋ)
① the place where a tourist, traveler or visitor takes up his lodgings ② during one's trip or tour

旅次行軍(ㄌㄩˇ ㄘˋ ㄒㄧㄥˊ ㄐㄩㄣ)
(said of troops) to march without taking security measures

旅遊(ㄌㄩˇ ㄧㄡˊ)

a tour; tourism: 他們徒步旅遊本島。They made a walking tour of this island.
旅思(ㄌㄩˇ ㄙ)
a traveler's thoughts

〔方部〕

七畫

2184
【旋】 1. ㄒㄩㄢˊ shyuan xuán

1. to return; to turn back: 我們的部隊已凱旋。Our troops have returned in triumph.
2. to revolve; to circle; to spin; to move in an orbit:一隻鷹在空中盤旋。A hawk is circling in the sky.
3. a very short while; a moment; soon: 全部門票旋即售罄。All tickets were soon sold out.
4. to urinate

旋得旋失(ㄒㄩㄢˊ ㄉㄜˊ ㄒㄩㄢˊ ㄕ)
to gain and lose within a short while, as playing the stocks
旋里(ㄒㄩㄢˊ ㄌㄧˇ)or旋鄉(ㄒㄩㄢˊ ㄒㄧㄤ)
to return to one's hometown
旋螺(ㄒㄩㄢˊ ㄌㄨㄛˊ)
①a screw ② a variety of the mollusk family with a univalve shell
旋律(ㄒㄩㄢˊ ㄌㄩˋ)
melody: 這首歌的旋律哀怨。This song has a doleful melody.
旋即(ㄒㄩㄢˊ ㄐㄧˊ)
forthwith; immediately afterwards
旋乾轉坤(ㄒㄩㄢˊ ㄑㄧㄢˊ ㄓㄨㄢˇ ㄎㄨㄣ)
(literally) to turn heaven into earth and vice versa —immense power to reverse a situation 亦作「旋轉乾坤」
旋轉(ㄒㄩㄢˊ ㄓㄨㄢˇ)
to turn round and round; to revolve; to gyrate; to rotate; to spin: 輪子繞軸旋轉。A wheel revolves round its axis.
旋轉門(ㄒㄩㄢˊ ㄓㄨㄢˇ ㄇㄣˊ)
a revolving door
旋踵(ㄒㄩㄢˊ ㄓㄨㄥˇ)
a very short time: 他旋踵間便把薪金花完了。He spent his salary in a very short time.
旋繞(ㄒㄩㄢˊ ㄖㄠˋ)
to revolve around; to move in an orbit; to orbit
旋窰(ㄒㄩㄢˊ ㄧㄠˊ)
a rotary kiln
旋渦(ㄒㄩㄢˊ ㄨㄛ)
① a whirlpool ② a turbulent and difficult situation 亦作「漩渦」
旋淵(ㄒㄩㄢˊ ㄩㄢ)
an abyss

2184
【旋】 2. ㄒㄩㄢˋ shiuann xuàn

1. to whirl; a whirl
2. at the time; at the last moment
3. to heat wine

旋風(ㄒㄩㄢˋ ㄈㄥ)
a whirlwind; a cyclone

2185
【旌】 ㄐㄧㄥ jing jīng

1. a kind of flag, banner, standard, etc. ornamented with feathers: 旌旗臨風招展。Flags are waving in the breeze.
2. to cite (one's merits, virtues, etc.); to make manifest: 政府每年旌表善人。The government cites the virtuous people every year.

旌表(ㄐㄧㄥ ㄅㄧㄠˇ)
the honor conferred upon the virtuous and capable (by the emperor, etc.); to confer such an honor
旌門(ㄐㄧㄥ ㄇㄣˊ)
a family cited by the government for community service or exemplary virtue, whose door is made distinct from others by a plaque bearing the citation
旌銘(ㄐㄧㄥ ㄇㄧㄥˊ)
(during the burial ceremony) a flag indicating the death of a person, usually one known for his distinguished service
旌節(ㄐㄧㄥ ㄐㄧㄝˊ)
① a flag and staff held by a high official in the Tang Dynasty ② a decorated staff used by ancient emissaries as credentials
旌旗(ㄐㄧㄥ ㄑㄧˊ)
a general name for flags and banners
旌旗蔽空(ㄐㄧㄥ ㄑㄧˊ ㄅㄧˋ ㄎㄨㄥ)or 旌旗蔽日(ㄐㄧㄥ ㄑㄧˊ ㄅㄧˋ ㄖˋ)
(literally) There are so many flags that they cover the whole sky (or darken the sun).—a very large army
旌旗所指(ㄐㄧㄥ ㄑㄧˊ ㄙㄨㄛˇ ㄓˇ)
wherever the army goes (the enemy is crushed)
旌卹(ㄐㄧㄥ ㄒㄩˋ)
rewards given to the family of the deceased in recognition of his meritorious service; posthumous rewards for distinguished service

2186
【旎】 ㄋㄧˇ nii nǐ

1. romantic; tender; charming 參看「旖旎」
2. the fluttering of flags

2187
【族】 ㄗㄨˊ tzwu zú

1. a tribe; a clan; a family; relatives
2. a race (of people)
3. a class or group of things with common features: 水族 aquatic animals

族伯(ㄗㄨˊ ㄅㄛˊ)
older fellow clansmen of one's father's generation
族譜(ㄗㄨˊ ㄆㄨˇ)
the pedigree of a clan: 他們詳細審查他的族譜和背景。They scrutinized his pedigree and background.
族母(ㄗㄨˊ ㄇㄨˇ)
the wife of one's father's cousin
族父(ㄗㄨˊ ㄈㄨˋ)
one's father's male third cousins of the same surname
族弟(ㄗㄨˊ ㄉㄧˋ)
paternal male third cousins younger than oneself
族類(ㄗㄨˊ ㄌㄟˋ)
of the same clan or race
族居(ㄗㄨˊ ㄐㄩ)
to live together as a clan
族群(ㄗㄨˊ ㄑㄩㄣˊ)
an ethnic group
族姓(ㄗㄨˊ ㄒㄧㄥˋ)
① family names in a clan ② family standing and background
族兄(ㄗㄨˊ ㄒㄩㄥ)
paternal male third cousins older than oneself

族長(ㄗㄨˊ ㄓㄤˇ)
the oldest of the highest generation in a clan; the chief of a clan
族誅(ㄗㄨˊ ㄓㄨ)
to execute all of one's relatives for his personal offense or crime
族叔(ㄗㄨˊ ㄕㄨˊ)
fellow clansmen of one's father's generation but younger than one's father
族人(ㄗㄨˊ ㄖㄣˊ)
fellow clansmen
族葬(ㄗㄨˊ ㄗㄤˋ)
to be buried with the other deceased members of the same clan
族望(ㄗㄨˊ ㄨㄤˋ)
a famous or prestigious clan

八畫

【旐】2188
ㄓㄠˋ jaw zhào
(in the ancient times) a flag with tortoises and snakes emblazoned on it

九畫

【旒】2189
ㄌㄧㄡˊ liou liú
1. a silk string used to hold a piece of jade hung on ancient ceremonial caps
2. a colored streamer hung on a flag

十畫

【旗】2190
ㄑㄧˊ chyi qí
1. a flag; a pennant; a banner; a streamer
2. a sign; an insignia; an emblem
3. an administrative division of Mongolia (蒙古) and Tsinghai (青海)
4. the Manchus
旗袍(ㄑㄧˊ ㄆㄠˊ)
chi-pao, an all-purpose long gown worn by women in modern China (introduced by the Manchus)
旗杆 or 旗竿(ㄑㄧˊ ㄍㄢ)
a flagstaff; a flagpole; a flag post
旗鼓(ㄑㄧˊ ㄍㄨˇ)
(military) the flags and the drums—instruments of giving orders
旗鼓相當(ㄑㄧˊ ㄍㄨˇ ㄒㄧㄤ ㄉㄤ)
of approximately equal strength, ability, etc.: 他們旗鼓相當，所以比賽十分激烈。They were well-matched, so that the game was hotly contested.
旗開得勝(ㄑㄧˊ ㄎㄞ ㄉㄜˊ ㄕㄥˋ)
to win in the first battle, game or match; to win speedy success
旗號(ㄑㄧˊ ㄏㄠˋ)
an army signal; a flag
旗艦(ㄑㄧˊ ㄐㄧㄢˋ)
a flagship
旗槍(ㄑㄧˊ ㄑㄧㄤ)
① banners and spears ② a kind of green tea
旗幟(ㄑㄧˊ ㄓˋ)
flags, pennants, streamers, etc.
旗手(ㄑㄧˊ ㄕㄡˇ)
a flagman
旗人(ㄑㄧˊ ㄖㄣˊ)
a Mongol, Manchu or Chinese who was a member of any one of the twenty-four banners during the Ching Dynasty (The term is used now to refer to the Manchus exclusively.)
旗子(ㄑㄧˊ ·ㄗ)
a flag
旗魚(ㄑㄧˊ ㄩˊ)
spearfish (*Xiphias gladius*)
旗語(ㄑㄧˊ ㄩˇ)
flag-signals

【旖】2191
ㄧˇ yii yǐ
1. romantic; tender
2. charming; lovely; attractive; graceful
3. the fluttering of flags
旖旎(ㄧˇ ㄋㄧˇ)
①(said of flags) fluttering ② (said of scenery) enchanting
旖旎風光(ㄧˇ ㄋㄧˇ ㄈㄥ ㄍㄨㄤ)
a romantic or charming sight

十四畫

【旛】2192
ㄈㄢ fan fān
1. a general name of flags or streamers
2. a silk (usually rectangular) pennant for hanging

十五畫

【旝】2193
ㄎㄨㄞˋ kuay kuài
1. a flag used by a general
2. a coach used in ancient warfare for shooting stones

十六畫

【旟】2194
ㄩˊ yu yú
1. a military flag or standard; a flag with falcons emblazoned on it
2. (said of flags) fluttering

无部
ㄨˊ wu wú

【无】2195
ㄨˊ wu wú
the ancient form of 無—not; no; negative; without
无妄(ㄨˊ ㄨㄤˋ)
a diagram in the *Book of Changes* (易經) indicating truth and honesty
无妄之災(ㄨˊ ㄨㄤˋ ㄓ ㄗㄞ)
an unexpected trouble or bad break; a disaster brought on not by oneself

一畫

【旡】2196
ㄐㄧˋ jih jì
to choke in eating

七畫

【既】2197
(旣) ㄐㄧˋ jih jì
1. since; as; now that; inasmuch as: 你既然問我，我就告訴你。Since you ask, I will tell you.

2. already: 他的成功已是既成的事實。His success is already an accomplished fact.
3. all
4. to finish
5. a Chinese family name

既明且哲(ㄐㄧˋ ㄇㄧㄥˊ ㄑㄧㄝˇ ㄓㄜˊ)
both intelligent and wise

既得利益(ㄐㄧˋ ㄉㄜˊ ㄌㄧˋ ㄧˋ)
vested interests

既得權(ㄐㄧˋ ㄉㄜˊ ㄑㄩㄢˊ)
vested rights

既定(ㄐㄧˋ ㄉㄧㄥˋ)
① already decided or fixed: 那是我們的既定目標。It is our fixed goal. ② (said of a rebellion, etc.) already quelled

既來之則安之(ㄐㄧˋ ㄌㄞˊ ㄓ ㄗㄜˊ ㄢ ㄓ)
Since we (or you) are already here, let's make ourselves (or yourself) at home.

既成事實(ㄐㄧˋ ㄔㄥˊ ㄕˋ ㄕˊ)
de facto; a fact already accomplished; a *fait accompli*; an accomplished fact

既是(ㄐㄧˋ ㄕˋ)or 既然(ㄐㄧˋ ㄖㄢˊ)
since (it is so, etc.); this being the case

既然如此(ㄐㄧˋ ㄖㄢˊ ㄖㄨˊ ㄘˇ)
this being the case; since it is so: 既然如此，讓我們重新考慮這件事。Since it is so, let us reconsider this matter.

既遂犯(ㄐㄧˋ ㄙㄨㄟˋ ㄈㄢˋ)
a criminal who has accomplished his criminal act

既而(ㄐㄧˋ ㄦˊ)
then; not long afterwards; later; subsequently

既往不咎(ㄐㄧˋ ㄨㄤˇ ㄅㄨˋ ㄐㄧㄡˋ)
Let bygones be bygones. 或 No postmortems. 或 to forgive somebody's past misdeeds

既望(ㄐㄧˋ ㄨㄤˋ)
the 16th day of every month (in the lunar calendar)

日部
ㄖˋ ryh rì

【日】 2198
ㄖˋ ryh rì

1. the sun
2. a day
3. daily; every day
4. Japan; Japanese
5. time: 往日 the past times 夏日 summertime
6. day; daytime

日薄西山(ㄖˋ ㄅㄛˊ ㄒㄧ ㄕㄢ)
(literally) The sun is near the west mountain.—declining rapidly; old age; approaching one's grave

日報(ㄖˋ ㄅㄠˋ)
a daily newspaper (especially the morning paper)

日班(ㄖˋ ㄅㄢ)
the day shift (in factories, etc.): 最近他輪值日班。He has been on the day shift recently.

日斑(ㄖˋ ㄅㄢ)
(astronomy) sunspot 亦作「太陽黑子」

日本(ㄖˋ ㄅㄣˇ)
Japan: 他去過日本三次。He has been to Japan three times.

日本海(ㄖˋ ㄅㄣˇ ㄏㄞˇ)
the Japan Sea

日晡(ㄖˋ ㄅㄨ)
dusk; sundown; sunset

日不暇給(ㄖˋ ㄅㄨˋ ㄒㄧㄚˊ ㄐㄧˇ)
too many things to do in a day; very busy; to wish there were 36 hours in a day

日迫(ㄖˋ ㄆㄛˋ)
to get closer day by day 或 Time is running out.

日偏蝕(ㄖˋ ㄆㄧㄢ ㄕˊ)
(astronomy) the partial eclipse of the sun

日平西(ㄖˋ ㄆㄧㄥˊ ㄒㄧ)
dusk; sundown

日沒(ㄖˋ ㄇㄛˋ)
sunset

日沒沉西(ㄖˋ ㄇㄛˋ ㄔㄣˊ ㄒㄧ)
sundown; sunset; dusk

日冕(ㄖˋ ㄇㄧㄢˇ)
(astronomy) corona, a faintly luminous envelope outside of the sun's chromosphere

日暮途窮(ㄖˋ ㄇㄨˋ ㄊㄨˊ ㄑㄩㄥˊ)
at the end of one's rope; at one's wits' end; in a desperate position

日暮途遠(ㄖˋ ㄇㄨˋ ㄊㄨˊ ㄩㄢˇ)
in a desperate position; having no one to turn to

日復一日(ㄖˋ ㄈㄨˋ ㄧˊ ㄖˋ)
day after day; day in and day out

日德蘭半島(ㄖˋ ㄉㄜˊ ㄌㄢˊ ㄅㄢˋ ㄉㄠˇ)
Jutland

日頭(ㄖˋ ˙ㄊㄡ)
① the sun ② daytime

日圖三餐，夜圖一宿(ㄖˋ ㄊㄨˊ ㄙㄢ ㄘㄢ, ㄧㄝˋ ㄊㄨˊ ㄧˋ ㄙㄨˇ)
The people have no other ambition than food in their stomachs and a roof over their heads.

日內(ㄖˋ ㄋㄟˋ)
in a few days

日內瓦(ㄖˋ ㄋㄟˋ ㄨㄚˇ)
Geneva, Switzerland

日來(ㄖˋ ㄌㄞˊ)
in recent days; the last few days

日理萬機(ㄖˋ ㄌㄧˇ ㄨㄢˋ ㄐㄧ)
(literally) to manage 10,000 things in a day—very busy (said of rulers or prime ministers running the affairs of the state)

日利(ㄖˋ ㄌㄧˋ)or 日息(ㄖˋ ㄒㄧˊ)
daily interest (rate)

日曆(ㄖˋ ㄌㄧˋ)
a calendar

日裏(ㄖˋ ˙ㄌㄧ)or 日間(ㄖˋ ㄐㄧㄢ)
in the daytime; at daytime

日落風生(ㄖˋ ㄌㄨㄛˋ ㄈㄥ ㄕㄥ)
Gentle breezes come with the sunset. (an expression to describe a natural scene at dusk)

日輪(ㄖˋ ㄌㄨㄣˊ)
① the sun disc ② a Japanese merchantman

日晷(ㄖˋ ㄍㄨㄟˇ)or 日表(ㄖˋ ㄅㄧㄠˇ)
a sundial

日光(ㄖˋ ㄍㄨㄤ)
① sunshine; the light of the sun ② Nikko, a mountain resort in Japan

日光燈(ㄖˋ ㄍㄨㄤ ㄉㄥ)
a fluorescent lamp

日光能(ㄖˋ ㄍㄨㄤ ㄋㄥˊ)
solar energy

日光療法(ㄖˋ ㄍㄨㄤ ㄌㄧㄠˊ ㄈㄚˇ)
heliotherapy

日光節約時間(ㄖˋ ㄍㄨㄤ ㄐㄧㄝˊ ㄩㄝ

ㄕ ㄐㄧㄢ)
daylight saving time

日光浴(ㄖˋ ㄍㄨㄤ ㄩˋ)
sunbath

日光浴室(ㄖˋ ㄍㄨㄤ ㄩˋ ㄕˋ)
a solarium

日工(ㄖˋ ㄍㄨㄥ)
① daywork ② day labor ③ a day laborer

日課(ㄖˋ ㄎㄜˋ)
daily courses (of study); a daily curriculum

日刊(ㄖˋ ㄎㄢ)
a daily publication, newspaper, etc.

日虧(ㄖˋ ㄎㄨㄟ)
(business) daily losses

日後(ㄖˋ ㄏㄡˋ)
in the days to come; in future

日貨(ㄖˋ ㄏㄨㄛˋ)
Japanese goods

日暉(ㄖˋ ㄏㄨㄟ)
the rays of the sun

日環蝕(ㄖˋ ㄏㄨㄢˊ ㄕˊ)
an annular eclipse of the sun

日機(ㄖˋ ㄐㄧ)
Japanese airplanes

日積月累(ㄖˋ ㄐㄧ ㄩㄝˋ ㄌㄟˇ)
day after day and month after month; gradual accumulation over a long time

日給(ㄖˋ ㄐㄧˇ)
daily wages

日計(ㄖˋ ㄐㄧˋ)
to calculate by the day

日計不足，歲計有餘(ㄖˋ ㄐㄧˋ ㄅㄨˋ ㄗㄨˊ, ㄙㄨㄟˋ ㄐㄧˋ ㄧㄡˇ ㄩˊ)
Time and patience beget success.

日記(ㄖˋ ㄐㄧˋ)
a diary

日記本(ㄖˋ ㄐㄧˋ ㄅㄣˇ)
a diary book; a notebook (registering one's daily engagements or appointments)

日記帳(ㄖˋ ㄐㄧˋ ㄓㄤˋ)
(accounting) daily account; day-by-day account

日久天長(ㄖˋ ㄐㄧㄡˇ ㄊㄧㄢ ㄔㄤˊ)
for a long, long time; for keeps

日久見人心(ㄖˋ ㄐㄧㄡˇ ㄐㄧㄢˋ ㄖㄣˊ ㄒㄧㄣ)
Time reveals a person's heart.

日久情生(ㄖˋ ㄐㄧㄡˇ ㄑㄧㄥˊ ㄕㄥ)
Having been together for a long time, people come to have a tender feeling for each other.

日久厭生(ㄖˋ ㄐㄧㄡˇ ㄧㄢˋ ㄕㄥ)
Familiarity begets contempt.

日久玩生(ㄖˋ ㄐㄧㄡˇ ㄨㄢˊ ㄕㄥ)
Discipline tends to get lax as time goes by.

日就月將(ㄖˋ ㄐㄧㄡˋ ㄩㄝˋ ㄐㄧㄤ)
to progress or improve with the day

日間(ㄖˋ ㄐㄧㄢ)
at daytime; in the daytime: 我在日間不能睡覺。I cannot sleep in the daytime.

日見 or 日漸(ㄖˋ ㄐㄧㄢˋ)
with each passing day; day by day: 病人的健康日見好轉。The patient is getting better day by day.

日艦(ㄖˋ ㄐㄧㄢˋ)
a Japanese warship

日進(ㄖˋ ㄐㄧㄣˋ)
to improve or increase with each passing day; constant improvement

日居月諸(ㄖˋ ㄐㄩ ㄩㄝˋ ㄓㄨ)
① the sun and the moon ② the elapsing of time

日軍(ㄖˋ ㄐㄩㄣ)
Japanese troops

日期(ㄖˋ ㄑㄧ)or(ㄖˋ ㄑㄧˊ)
date

日僑(ㄖˋ ㄑㄧㄠˊ)
Japanese residents in a foreign country

日前(ㄖˋ ㄑㄧㄢˊ)
a few days ago; recently: 日前我們曾見面。We met a few days ago.

日趨(ㄖˋ ㄑㄩ)
with each passing day; gradually; day by day

日趨下流(ㄖˋ ㄑㄩ ㄒㄧㄚˋ ㄌㄧㄡˊ)
to sink lower and lower with each passing day; to get meaner and more depraved with the day

日全蝕(ㄖˋ ㄑㄩㄢˊ ㄕˊ)
a total eclipse of the sun

日息(ㄖˋ ㄒㄧˊ)
interest per diem

日夕(ㄖˋ ㄒㄧˋ)
day and night: 他日夕工作不停。He worked day and night without stopping.

日戲(ㄖˋ ㄒㄧˋ)
a matinee

日校(ㄖˋ ㄒㄧㄠˋ)
a day school

日新(ㄖˋ ㄒㄧㄣ)or日新又新(ㄖˋ ㄒㄧㄣ ㄧㄡˋ ㄒㄧㄣ)
daily renewal or modernization; constant progress

日新月異(ㄖˋ ㄒㄧㄣ ㄩㄝˋ ㄧˋ)
continuous improvement; ever newer

日薪(ㄖˋ ㄒㄧㄣ)
day wages

日行一善(ㄖˋ ㄒㄧㄥˊ ㄧˊ ㄕㄢˋ)
to do one good deed a day

日省月試(ㄖˋ ㄒㄧㄥˇ ㄩㄝˋ ㄕˋ)
to watch with a critical eye over a long period of time (to see if something or someone is really good)

日削月朘(ㄖˋ ㄒㄩㄝ ㄩㄝˋ ㄐㄩㄢ)
(said of corrupt officials) to exploit the people

日誌(ㄖˋ ㄓˋ)
a daily record

日照(ㄖˋ ㄓㄠˋ)
① sunshine ② an umbrella

日中(ㄖˋ ㄓㄨㄥ)
① high noon ② the equinox

日中則昃(ㄖˋ ㄓㄨㄥ ㄗㄜˊ ㄗㄜˋ)
to decline after reaching the zenith

日中爲市(ㄖˋ ㄓㄨㄥ ㄨㄟˊ ㄕˋ)
①(in ancient China) to barter goods at a market at noontime ② (in modern usage) to do business during the daytime

日常(ㄖˋ ㄔㄤˊ)
daily; usually; ordinarily; common

日常生活(ㄖˋ ㄔㄤˊ ㄕㄥ ㄏㄨㄛˊ)
daily life: 健康的人過愉快的日常生活。Healthy people lead a happy daily life.

日長一線(ㄖˋ ㄔㄤˊ ㄧˊ ㄒㄧㄢˋ)
Daytime gradually lengthens after the winter solstice.

日場(ㄖˋ ㄔㄤˇ)or(ㄖˋ ㄔㄤˊ)
(said of shows, concerts, etc.) the morning or the afternoon show; a matinee

日程(ㄖˋ ㄔㄥˊ)

①an itinerary ②the agenda on a specific day (of a conference)

日出(ㄖˋ ㄔㄨ)
sunrise: 日出時天氣變得較暖。It becomes warmer at sunrise.

日出而作(ㄖˋ ㄔㄨ ㄦˊ ㄗㄨㄛˋ)
to start work at daybreak (and retire at sunset): 農夫們日出而作，日入而息。Farmers start work at daybreak and retire at sunset.

日戳(ㄖˋ ㄔㄨㄛ)
①a date stamp; a dater ②a datemark

日蝕 or 日食(ㄖˋ ㄕˊ)
(astronomy) solar eclipse

日食萬錢(ㄖˋ ㄕˊ ㄨㄢˋ ㄑㄧㄢˊ)
to spend money lavishly; to live in extreme luxury

日射病(ㄖˋ ㄕㄜˋ ㄅㄧㄥˋ)
sunstroke

日曬雨淋(ㄖˋ ㄕㄞˋ ㄩˇ ㄌㄧㄣˊ)
to be exposed to the inclemency of the elements

日甚一日(ㄖˋ ㄕㄣˋ ㄧˊ ㄖˋ)
getting more serious, painful, etc. day after day; to get worse with each passing day; to increase in intensity constantly

日上三竿(ㄖˋ ㄕㄤˋ ㄙㄢ ㄍㄢ)
rather late in the morning—about 9 a.m. (often used to describe someone who gets up late)

日升月恆(ㄖˋ ㄕㄥ ㄩㄝˋ ㄏㄥˊ)
ever increasing, growing or rising; ever prosperous

日日(ㄖˋ ㄖˋ)
every day; daily: 他日日運動。He does exercise every day.

日日新(ㄖˋ ㄖˋ ㄒㄧㄣ)
daily renovation, reformation or change

日入而息(ㄖˋ ㄖㄨˋ ㄦˊ ㄒㄧˊ)
(to start work at daybreak and) to retire at sunset

日子(ㄖˋ ˙ㄗ)
①time; duration ②life; living: 這些難民過著悲慘的日子。The refugees led a miserable life. ③a day; a date

日昨(ㄖˋ ㄗㄨㄛˊ)
yesterday

日坐愁城(ㄖˋ ㄗㄨㄛˋ ㄔㄡˊ ㄔㄥˊ)
to be in deep worry every day; to be deeply worried every day

日俄戰爭(ㄖˋ ㄜˋ ㄓㄢˋ ㄓㄥ)
the Russo-Japanese War, 1904-1905

日耳曼(ㄖˋ ㄦˇ ㄇㄢˋ)
the Germans

日以繼夜(ㄖˋ ㄧˇ ㄐㄧˋ ㄧㄝˋ)
day and night; continuously or incessantly

日益(ㄖˋ ㄧˋ)
increasingly; day by day

日夜(ㄖˋ ㄧㄝˋ)
day and night

日曜日(ㄖˋ ㄧㄠˋ ㄖˋ)
Sunday

日有進步(ㄖˋ ㄧㄡˇ ㄐㄧㄣˋ ㄅㄨˋ)
to show improvements or progress day by day; progressing constantly

日有起色(ㄖˋ ㄧㄡˇ ㄑㄧˇ ㄙㄜˋ)
improving with each passing day; turning for the better steadily

日有所思，夜有所夢(ㄖˋ ㄧㄡˇ ㄙㄨㄛˇ ㄙ, ㄧㄝˋ ㄧㄡˇ ㄙㄨㄛˇ ㄇㄥˋ)
One dreams at night what one thinks in the day.

日影(ㄖˋ ㄧㄥˇ)
shadows caused by the sun

日文(ㄖˋ ㄨㄣˊ)
the Japanese language: 他對日文有興趣。He is much interested in Japanese.

日語(ㄖˋ ㄩˇ)
the Japanese (spoken) language

日月(ㄖˋ ㄩㄝˋ)
①the sun and the moon ②time ③life; living; livelihood ④saints and sages ⑤emperor and empress

日月潭(ㄖˋ ㄩㄝˋ ㄊㄢˊ)
Sun Moon Lake, a resort in central Taiwan

日月經天(ㄖˋ ㄩㄝˋ ㄐㄧㄥ ㄊㄧㄢ)
eternal and self-evident, like the sun and the moon in the sky

日月重光(ㄖˋ ㄩㄝˋ ㄔㄨㄥˊ ㄍㄨㄤ)
(literally) The sun and the moon shine again. (used figuratively to describe a joyful event such as the downfall of a despot, liberation from enemy occupation, etc.)

日月如梭(ㄖˋ ㄩㄝˋ ㄖㄨˊ ㄙㄨㄛ)
(literally) The sun and the moon pass over the sky as fast as a weaver's shuttle. —How fast time flies! 或 *Tempus fugit!*

日月無光(ㄖˋ ㄩㄝˋ ㄨˊ ㄍㄨㄤ)
(literally) The sun and the moon are dimmed. (often used to mean darkness in a figurative sense to describe life under tyranny, foreign occupation, etc.)

日暈(ㄖˋ ㄩㄣˋ)
the halo of the sun; coronas

日用品(ㄖˋ ㄩㄥˋ ㄆㄧㄣˇ)or 日用必需品(ㄖˋ ㄩㄥˋ ㄅㄧˋ ㄒㄩ ㄆㄧㄣˇ)
daily necessities; consumer goods

一畫

【旦】 2199 ㄉㄢˋ dann dàn

1. daybreak; dawn
2. day; morning
3. a female role in Chinese opera

旦不保夕(ㄉㄢˋ ㄅㄨˋ ㄅㄠˇ ㄒㄧˋ)
not knowing how the day will end; in imminent danger; precarious

旦暮(ㄉㄢˋ ㄇㄨˋ)
①morning and evening ②in a brief span of time

旦旦(ㄉㄢˋ ㄉㄢˋ)
①every day; daily ②sincerely

旦角 or 旦脚(ㄉㄢˋ ㄐㄩㄝˊ)
a female role in Chinese opera

旦夕之間(ㄉㄢˋ ㄒㄧˋ ㄓ ㄐㄧㄢ)
within a single day; between morning and evening—a very short time

旦日(ㄉㄢˋ ㄖˋ)
①tomorrow ②dawn

二畫

【旨】 2200 ㄓˇ jyy zhǐ

1. a purpose; will; intention; objective
2. an imperial decree
3. good; excellent; beautiful
4. tasty; pleasant to the palate;

delicious
旨甘(ㄓˇ ㄍㄢ)
delicacies; dainties
旨歸(ㄓˇ ㄍㄨㄟ)
① principle ② objective
旨酒(ㄓˇ ㄐㄧㄡˇ)
good wine
旨趣(ㄓˇ ㄑㄩˋ)
purposes and intentions; objectives and interest
旨哉斯言(ㄓˇ ㄗㄞ ㄙ ㄧㄢˊ)
What an admirable statement (or remark)!
旨在(ㄓˇ ㄗㄞˋ)
with the intention of; aiming at; designed to
旨意(ㄓˇ ㄧˋ)
① will; intention ② an imperial decree; God's will

【早】 2201
ㄗㄠˇ tzao zǎo

1. early; earlier; soon; beforehand; previous; premature; in advance
2. morning
3. ago; before
4. Good morning!

早班(ㄗㄠˇ ㄅㄢ)
the morning shift
早半天兒(ㄗㄠˇ ˙ㄅㄢ ㄊㄧㄚㄦ) or 早半晌兒(ㄗㄠˇ ˙ㄅㄢ ㄕㄤㄦ)
morning; before noon
早眠早起(ㄗㄠˇ ㄇㄧㄢˊ ㄗㄠˇ ㄑㄧˇ)
to keep good hours; to go to bed early and get up early the next morning (recommended as a healthy habit)
早飯(ㄗㄠˇ ㄈㄢˋ)
breakfast: 早飯已準備好了。Breakfast is ready.
早到(ㄗㄠˇ ㄉㄠˋ)
to arrive early; to arrive ahead of time
早稻(ㄗㄠˇ ㄉㄠˋ)
paddies that ripen early
早稻田大學(ㄗㄠˇ ㄉㄠˋ ㄊㄧㄢˊ ㄉㄚˋ ㄒㄩㄝˊ)
Waseda University, Japan
早點(ㄗㄠˇ ㄉㄧㄢˇ)
breakfast 參看「早飯」
早點兒(ㄗㄠˇ ㄉㄧㄚˇㄦ)
earlier; sooner: 請早點兒來。Please come earlier.
早退(ㄗㄠˇ ㄊㄨㄟˋ)
to retire from office or factory earlier than others
早年(ㄗㄠˇ ㄋㄧㄢˊ)
years ago; in bygone years; many years ago
早慧(ㄗㄠˇ ㄏㄨㄟˋ)
clever in one's childhood; an early bloomer; precocious
早婚(ㄗㄠˇ ㄏㄨㄣ)
early marriage; to marry young
早計(ㄗㄠˇ ㄐㄧˋ)
early planning
早就(ㄗㄠˇ ㄐㄧㄡˋ)
to have already...: 他早就回家了。He had already returned home.
早期(ㄗㄠˇ ㄑㄧˊ)
the early stage; the early phase: 這些小說是他的早期作品。These novels are his early works.
早起
①(ㄗㄠˇ ㄑㄧˇ) to get up early; early to rise
②(ㄗㄠˇ ˙ㄑㄧ) early in the morning
早些箇(ㄗㄠˇ ㄒㄧㄝ ˙ㄍㄜ) or 早些兒(ㄗㄠˇ ㄒㄧㄜㄦ)
sooner; earlier
早先(ㄗㄠˇ ㄒㄧㄢ)
some time ago; before
早知如此(ㄗㄠˇ ㄓ ㄖㄨˊ ㄘˇ)
If it had been known that things would turn out this way....
早占勿藥(ㄗㄠˇ ㄓㄢ ㄨˋ ㄧㄠˋ)
(said of a sick person) to have gotten well early; to get well very soon
早車(ㄗㄠˇ ㄔㄜ)
the morning train
早朝(ㄗㄠˇ ㄔㄠˊ)
(said of an emperor) to attend the imperial court session in the early morning
早潮(ㄗㄠˇ ㄔㄠˊ)
morning tides
早產(ㄗㄠˇ ㄔㄢˇ)
premature birth
早晨(ㄗㄠˇ ˙ㄔㄣ)
morning; dawn; daybreak; early morning
早場(ㄗㄠˇ ㄔㄤˇ)
a morning show (at a cinema, theater, etc.)
早出晚歸(ㄗㄠˇ ㄔㄨ ㄨㄢˇ ㄍㄨㄟ)
(often said of a busy person, etc.) to go out early and return late
早春(ㄗㄠˇ ㄔㄨㄣ)
① early spring ② early spring tea
早市(ㄗㄠˇ ㄕˋ)
a morning market
早世(ㄗㄠˇ ㄕˋ) or 早夭(ㄗㄠˇ ㄧㄠ)
to die very young
早熟(ㄗㄠˇ ㄕㄡˊ) or (ㄗㄠˇ ㄕㄨˊ)
①(said of plants, etc.) to ripen early ②(said of a person) to reach puberty early ③ precocious
早上(ㄗㄠˇ ㄕㄤˋ)
early in the morning
早衰(ㄗㄠˇ ㄕㄨㄞ)
(medicine) premature senility (or decrepitude)
早睡(ㄗㄠˇ ㄕㄨㄟˋ)
to sleep early
早日(ㄗㄠˇ ㄖˋ)
at an earlier date; soon: 祝你早日恢復健康。I hope you'll get well soon.
早則(ㄗㄠˇ ㄗㄜˊ)
① fortunately ② already
早操(ㄗㄠˇ ㄘㄠ)
morning calisthenics; exercises before the first class in school
早餐(ㄗㄠˇ ㄘㄢ)
breakfast
早歲(ㄗㄠˇ ㄙㄨㄟˋ)
in one's youth
早安(ㄗㄠˇ ㄢ)
Good morning!
早已(ㄗㄠˇ ㄧˇ)
to have already...: 客人早已離去。The guests had already left.
早晚(ㄗㄠˇ ㄨㄢˇ)
① morning and evening ② sooner or later

【旬】 2202
ㄒㄩㄣˊ shyun xún

1. a period of ten days
2. a period of ten years (usually used to indicate a person's age)
3. widespread; throughout
4. to tour; to inspect 亦作「巡」

旬年(ㄒㄩㄣˊ ㄋㄧㄢˊ)
① a full year ② ten years
旬刊(ㄒㄩㄣˊ ㄎㄢ)
a ten-day periodical; a magazine issued once every ten

days
旬休(ㄒㄩㄣ ㄒㄧㄡ)
(originated in the Tang Dynasty) one day of rest in ten for government officials
旬朔(ㄒㄩㄣ ㄕㄨㄛˋ)
ten days or one month
旬日(ㄒㄩㄣˊ ㄖˋ)
ten days
旬歲(ㄒㄩㄣˊ ㄙㄨㄟˋ)
a whole year
旬月(ㄒㄩㄣˊ ㄩㄝˋ)
① a whole month ② ten months

【旭】 2203 ㄒㄩˋ shiuh xù
1. brightness or radiance of daybreak
2. the rising sun
3. proud, smug or complacent
旭旭(ㄒㄩˋ ㄒㄩˋ)
① proud, smug or complacent ② uproarious ③ description of the rising sun
旭日(ㄒㄩˋ ㄖˋ)
the rising sun
旭日初升(ㄒㄩˋ ㄖˋ ㄔㄨ ㄕㄥ)
early in the morning 或 The sun is rising.

【旮】 2204 ㄍㄚ ga gā
a corner
旮旯子(ㄍㄚ ㄌㄚˊ ·ㄗ)or 旮旯兒(ㄍㄚ ㄌㄚˊㄦ)
a nook; a corner

【旯】 2205 ㄌㄚˊ la lá
a corner

三畫

【旰】 2206 ㄍㄢˋ gann gàn
evening; late
旰旰(ㄍㄢˋ ㄍㄢˋ)
blossoming and robust; luxuriant
旰食(ㄍㄢˋ ㄕˊ)
a late meal—too busy
旰食宵衣(ㄍㄢˋ ㄕˊ ㄒㄧㄠ ㄧ)
(literally) to eat late and get up early—too busy

【旱】 2207 ㄏㄢˋ hann hàn
1. drought; dry
2. (by) land route (as opposed to waterway)
旱魃(ㄏㄢˋ ㄅㄚˊ)
the demon of drought
旱稻(ㄏㄢˋ ㄉㄠˋ)
upland rice; dry rice
旱地(ㄏㄢˋ ㄉㄧˋ)
nonirrigated farmland; dry land
旱天(ㄏㄢˋ ㄊㄧㄢ)
dry days; dry weather; a drought
旱田(ㄏㄢˋ ㄊㄧㄢˊ)
dry farmland; uplands
旱年(ㄏㄢˋ ㄋㄧㄢˊ)
a year of drought
旱潦(ㄏㄢˋ ㄌㄠˋ)
droughts and floods
旱路(ㄏㄢˋ ㄌㄨˋ)or 旱道(ㄏㄢˋ ㄉㄠˋ)
a land route; an overland route
旱海(ㄏㄢˋ ㄏㄞˇ)
a desert
旱荒(ㄏㄢˋ ㄏㄨㄤ)
famine brought about by drought
旱季(ㄏㄢˋ ㄐㄧˋ)
a dry season
旱象(ㄏㄢˋ ㄒㄧㄤˋ)
the signs of drought
旱災(ㄏㄢˋ ㄗㄞ)
a drought: 幾年前印度曾有嚴重的旱災。India was afflicted with a severe drought a few years ago.
旱煙(ㄏㄢˋ ㄧㄢ)
tobacco smoked in an ordinary pipe (as contrasted with 水煙 smoked in a water pipe)

四畫

【旺】 2208 ㄨㄤˋ wanq wàng
1. prosperous; to prosper; to flourish
2. vigorous; prolific; productive
3. (said of light, fires, etc.) brilliant; bright or brightly
旺地(ㄨㄤˋ ㄉㄧˋ)
a good land; a prosperous place
旺季(ㄨㄤˋ ㄐㄧˋ)
(said of business) a boom season; a busy season: 目前的旺季能維持多久? How long can the present boom season last?
旺盛(ㄨㄤˋ ㄕㄥˋ)
① prosperous; prolific; productive; vigorous: 那位老人仍然精力旺盛。The old man is still vigorous. ②high (morale)
旺月(ㄨㄤˋ ㄩㄝˋ)
a busy or boom month; the best month of the year in sales and income
旺運(ㄨㄤˋ ㄩㄣˋ)
good fortune; good luck

【旻】 2209 ㄇㄧㄣˊ min mín
autumn
旻天(ㄇㄧㄣˊ ㄊㄧㄢ)
① autumn ② the heavens
旻序(ㄇㄧㄣˊ ㄒㄩˋ)
autumn festivals

【昂】 2210 ㄤˊ arng áng
1. to raise
2. lofty and proud; bold and not easily bent; straightforward
3. high
4. expensive; costly
昂貴(ㄤˊ ㄍㄨㄟˋ)
expensive; costly: 這部車子非常昂貴。This car is very expensive.
昂首(ㄤˊ ㄕㄡˇ)or 昂頭(ㄤˊ ㄊㄡˊ)
to raise one's head high
昂首闊步(ㄤˊ ㄕㄡˇ ㄎㄨㄛˋ ㄅㄨˋ)
to stride forward with one's chin up; to stride proudly ahead
昂然(ㄤˊ ㄖㄢˊ)
proud and bold; haughtily
昂藏(ㄤˊ ㄘㄤˊ)
tall and elegant; dignified
昂藏六尺之軀(ㄤˊ ㄘㄤˊ ㄌㄧㄡˋ ㄔˇ ㄓ ㄑㄩ)
a man (connoting pride, dignity, etc.)
昂昂(ㄤˊ ㄤˊ)
proud and outstanding
昂揚(ㄤˊ ㄧㄤˊ)
high-spirited

【昃】 2211 ㄗㄜˋ tzeh zè
after noon; afternoon; the sun on the western side of the sky

【昆】 2212 ㄎㄨㄣ kuen kūn
1. an elder brother
2. descendants; posterity
3. multitudes

4. together; in unison
昆布(ㄎㄨㄣ ㄅㄨˋ)
kelp (*Laminaria japonica*)亦作「海帶」
昆明(ㄎㄨㄣ ㄇㄧㄥˊ)
Kunming, capital of Yunnan Province
昆明湖(ㄎㄨㄣ ㄇㄧㄥˊ ㄏㄨˊ)
the Kunming Lake 亦作「滇池」or「昆明池」
昆明池(ㄎㄨㄣ ㄇㄧㄥˊ ㄔˊ)
①the Tien Lake(滇池) ②a man-made lake in Shensi Province, dug by order of Emperor Wu of the Han Dynasty
昆侖 or 崑崙(ㄎㄨㄣ ㄌㄨㄣˊ)
the Kunlun Mountains between Tibet and Sinkiang
昆季(ㄎㄨㄣ ㄐㄧˋ)
brothers (the elder and younger brothers)
昆曲(ㄎㄨㄣ ㄑㄩˇ)
① Kun opera ② melodies for Kun opera
昆仲(ㄎㄨㄣ ㄓㄨㄥˋ)or 昆弟(ㄎㄨㄣ ㄉㄧˋ)
brothers
昆蟲(ㄎㄨㄣ ㄔㄨㄥˊ)
insects
昆蟲學(ㄎㄨㄣ ㄔㄨㄥˊ ㄒㄩㄝˊ)
entomology
昆蟲學家(ㄎㄨㄣ ㄔㄨㄥˊ ㄒㄩㄝˊ ㄐㄧㄚ)
an entomologist
昆玉(ㄎㄨㄣ ㄩˋ)
(a polite expression) your brothers

【昇】2213 ㄕㄥ sheng shēng
1. to ascend
2. peace; peaceful
3. a Chinese family name
昇平(ㄕㄥ ㄆㄧㄥˊ)
time of peace
昇天(ㄕㄥ ㄊㄧㄢ)
①(Taoism) to ascend to heaven after becoming immortal ②(Christianity) the Ascension
昇格(ㄕㄥ ㄍㄜˊ)
to elevate status; elevation of status
昇汞(ㄕㄥ ㄍㄨㄥˇ)or(ㄕㄥ ㄏㄨㄥˋ)
(chemistry) corrosive sublimate; mercuric chloride ($HgCl_2$)
昇華(ㄕㄥ ㄏㄨㄚˊ)
①(chemistry) to sublime; sublimation ②the rising of things to a higher level; sublimation; distillation: 藝術是現實生活的昇華。Art is the distillation of real life.
昇級(ㄕㄥ ㄐㄧˊ)
to promote; to advance to the higher class
昇降(ㄕㄥ ㄐㄧㄤˋ)
promotion and demotion
昇降機(ㄕㄥ ㄐㄧㄤˋ ㄐㄧ)
an elevator

【昉】2214 ㄈㄤˇ faang fǎng
1. dawn; daybreak
2. beginning

【昊】2215 ㄏㄠˋ haw hào
1. summer time
2. the sky; the heavens
昊天(ㄏㄠˋ ㄊㄧㄢ)
①summer time; the summer season ②the sky; the heavens
昊天上帝(ㄏㄠˋ ㄊㄧㄢ ㄕㄤˋ ㄉㄧˋ)
The Reigning Sovereign in the Heavens
昊天罔極(ㄏㄠˋ ㄊㄧㄢ ㄨㄤˇ ㄐㄧˊ)
(said of parental love) as vast as the boundless heavens

【昌】2216 ㄔㄤ chang chāng
1. proper; good; straight (talk)
2. prosperous; robust; vigorous; to make prosperous; to glorify
3. light; brightness
4. a Chinese family name
昌明(ㄔㄤ ㄇㄧㄥˊ)
①to expound and elaborate ②flourishing; advanced; developing: 現代科學昌明。Science is flourishing at the present time. ③glorious; bright ④name of a kind of tea produced in Szechwan (四川)
昌大(ㄔㄤ ㄉㄚˋ)
to increase in greatness; to make prosperous
昌時(ㄔㄤ ㄕˊ)or 昌期(ㄔㄤ ㄑㄧˊ)
an era of peace and justice
昌盛(ㄔㄤ ㄕㄥˋ)
①powerful; prosperous; abundant: 我們的生意越來越昌盛。Our business becomes more and more prosperous. ②glory
昌辭(ㄔㄤ ㄘˊ)
beautiful expressions (in writing)
昌言(ㄔㄤ ㄧㄢˊ)
①proper words or comments ②straight talk

【明】2217 ㄇㄧㄥˊ ming míng
1. light; bright; brilliant
2. clear; understandable; to clarify; to understand; obvious; evident
3. intelligent; clever
4. eyesight; the seeing faculty
5. day; daybreak; dawn
6. to state; to show; to assert
7. next (day or year)
8. the Ming Dynasty (1368-1644 A. D.)
9. honest; aboveboard
10. a Chinese family name
明擺著(ㄇㄧㄥˊ ㄅㄞˇ ·ㄓㄜ)
to be clear and evident; obviously
明白(ㄇㄧㄥˊ ·ㄅㄞ)
①to understand; to know (a trick, secret, etc.) ②clever and bright; smart ③clear and evident; obvious
明白了當(ㄇㄧㄥˊ ·ㄅㄞ ㄌㄧㄠˇ ㄉㄤˋ)
clear-cut; straightforward; distinct
明白人(ㄇㄧㄥˊ ·ㄅㄞ ㄖㄣˊ)
a reasonable person; a considerate person
明版(ㄇㄧㄥˊ ㄅㄢˇ)
①a printing plate engraved in the Ming Dynasty 亦作「明板」②a Ming Dynasty edition
明辨是非(ㄇㄧㄥˊ ㄅㄧㄢˋ ㄕˋ ㄈㄟ)
to know distinctly what is right and what is wrong; to make a clear distinction between right and wrong
明碼(ㄇㄧㄥˊ ㄇㄚˇ)
①plain code; the ordinary telegraph code ②a listed price
明媒正娶(ㄇㄧㄥˊ ㄇㄟˊ ㄓㄥˋ ㄑㄩˇ)
a formal wedding or marriage
明媚(ㄇㄧㄥˊ ㄇㄟˋ)
fair and enchanting, or bright and charming (scenery, especially referring to

〔日部〕

springtime): 春日風光明媚。In spring days the landscape is bright and beautiful.

明眸皓齒(ㄇㄧㄥˊ ㄇㄡˊ ㄏㄠˋ ㄔˇ)
(said of a beautiful woman) with bright eyes and sparkling teeth

明眸善睞(ㄇㄧㄥˊ ㄇㄡˊ ㄕㄢˋ ㄌㄞˋ)
the enticing glances of a beauty

明滅(ㄇㄧㄥˊ ㄇㄧㄝˋ)
sometimes in view and sometimes hidden; visible and vanishing (as stars in a cloudy night or fishing lights at sea)

明明(ㄇㄧㄥˊ ㄇㄧㄥˊ)
obviously; plainly; undoubtedly: 這明明是他的錯嘛! This is obviously his fault.

明明白白(ㄇㄧㄥˊ ·ㄇㄧㄥ ㄅㄞˊ ㄅㄞˊ)
clear; clearly; obviously; evidently

明目張膽(ㄇㄧㄥˊ ㄇㄨˋ ㄓㄤ ㄉㄢˇ)
(to do some shameful or unlawful acts) openly or shamelessly; without caring about any onlookers; brazenly

明妃(ㄇㄧㄥˊ ㄈㄟ)
alias Wang Chao-chün (王昭君), a lady at the court of the early Han Dynasty who later married a chieftain of the Huns in the performance of a matrimonial diplomacy

明礬(ㄇㄧㄥˊ ㄈㄢˊ)
alum

明礬石(ㄇㄧㄥˊ ㄈㄢˊ ㄕˊ)
alumite or alunite

明分(ㄇㄧㄥˊ ㄈㄣˋ)
an obvious duty or obligation

明達(ㄇㄧㄥˊ ㄉㄚˊ)
intelligent and broad-minded

明德(ㄇㄧㄥˊ ㄉㄜˊ)
the highest virtue; illustrious virtue

明代(ㄇㄧㄥˊ ㄉㄞˋ)
the Ming Dynasty

明燈(ㄇㄧㄥˊ ㄉㄥ)
a bright lamp; a beacon

明斷(ㄇㄧㄥˊ ㄉㄨㄢˋ)
a fair and intelligent judgment; an unbiased and wise decision

明太祖(ㄇㄧㄥˊ ㄊㄞˋ ㄗㄨˇ)
Chu Yüan-chang (朱元璋), the founding emperor of the Ming Dynasty (1328-1398 A. D.)

明堂(ㄇㄧㄥˊ ㄊㄤˊ)
① a hall where solemn ceremonies were held in ancient China ② (a geomantic term) the place where water gathers before a grave

明天(ㄇㄧㄥˊ ㄊㄧㄢ)
tomorrow

明駝(ㄇㄧㄥˊ ㄊㄨㄛˊ)
a camel

明尼蘇達(ㄇㄧㄥˊ ㄋㄧˊ ㄙㄨ ㄉㄚˊ)
Minnesota, U. S. A.

明年(ㄇㄧㄥˊ ·ㄋㄧㄢ)
next year; the coming year

明來暗往(ㄇㄧㄥˊ ㄌㄞˊ ㄢˋ ㄨㄤˇ)
to have overt and covert contacts with somebody

明朗(ㄇㄧㄥˊ ㄌㄤˇ)
① open-minded; straightforward ② to become clear; to clarify: 風雨後,天色變明朗了。After the storm, the sky became clear.

明理(ㄇㄧㄥˊ ㄌㄧˇ)
understanding; reasonable

明麗(ㄇㄧㄥˊ ㄌㄧˋ)
bright and beautiful: 她喜歡明麗的秋色。She likes the bright and beautiful autumn scene.

明瞭(ㄇㄧㄥˊ ㄌㄧㄠˇ)
① to understand; to get a clear idea (of something): 有些人不能明瞭現代文學。Some people can't understand modern literature. ② clear and evident

明亮(ㄇㄧㄥˊ ㄌㄧㄤˋ)
bright (eyes, etc.); well-illuminated (rooms, etc.)

明令(ㄇㄧㄥˊ ㄌㄧㄥˋ)
a written order; a government order or decree

明溝(ㄇㄧㄥˊ ㄍㄡ)
an open ditch or gutter

明火執仗(ㄇㄧㄥˊ ㄏㄨㄛˇ ㄓˊ ㄓㄤˋ)
armed robbery committed openly

明慧(ㄇㄧㄥˊ ㄏㄨㄟˋ)
intelligent or bright

明晃晃(ㄇㄧㄥˊ ·ㄏㄨㄤ ·ㄏㄨㄤ)
bright and shining

明鑑(ㄇㄧㄥˊ ㄐㄧㄢˋ)
① a clear mirror: 戲劇是人生的明鑑。Drama is the clear mirror of life. ② (your) superb intelligence; (your) penetrating judgment

明經(ㄇㄧㄥˊ ㄐㄧㄥ)
① a person well versed in Chinese classics ② a title for winners in the imperial examinations in the Ching Dynasty

明淨(ㄇㄧㄥˊ ㄐㄧㄥˋ)
bright and clean; clear and bright

明鏡高懸(ㄇㄧㄥˊ ㄐㄧㄥˋ ㄍㄠ ㄒㄩㄢˊ)
(literally) a clear mirror hung on high—perspicuousness or transcending intelligence in judgment

明鏡兒(ㄇㄧㄥˊ ㄐㄧㄥˋㄦ)
clear-minded; perspicuous

明器(ㄇㄧㄥˊ ㄑㄧˋ)
vessels, etc. that are buried with the deceased

明棄暗取(ㄇㄧㄥˊ ㄑㄧˋ ㄢˋ ㄑㄩˇ)
to discard openly but take secretly

明槍暗箭(ㄇㄧㄥˊ ㄑㄧㄤ ㄢˋ ㄐㄧㄢˋ)
overt and covert attack

明槍易躲, 暗箭難防(ㄇㄧㄥˊ ㄑㄧㄤ ㄧˋ ㄉㄨㄛˇ, ㄢˋ ㄐㄧㄢˋ ㄋㄢˊ ㄈㄤˊ)
It's easy to dodge an open attack but difficult to escape from a clandestine one.

明搶(ㄇㄧㄥˊ ㄑㄧㄤˇ)
open robbery

明確(ㄇㄧㄥˊ ㄑㄩㄝˋ)
clear and definite; unequivocal (statement, terms, etc.): 我們要求一個明確的答覆。We demand a clear and definite answer.

明晰(ㄇㄧㄥˊ ㄒㄧ)
clear and lucid: 教師給予我們明晰的解釋。The teacher gave us a clear and lucid explanation.

明蝦(ㄇㄧㄥˊ ㄒㄧㄚ)
a prawn

明曉得(ㄇㄧㄥˊ ㄒㄧㄠˇ ·ㄉㄜ)
knowingly; knowing the consequences of doing something; well aware; with the full knowledge that

明效(ㄇㄧㄥˊ ㄒㄧㄠˋ)
obvious results; telling effects

明修棧道，暗度陳倉(ㄇㄧㄥˊ ㄒㄧㄡ ㄓㄢˋ ㄉㄠˋ, ㄢˋ ㄉㄨˋ ㄔㄣˊ ㄘㄤ)
to feign action in one place and to make the real move in another

明顯(ㄇㄧㄥˊ ㄒㄧㄢˇ)
evident; obvious; clear; distinct: 這很明顯是他缺席的藉口。This is evidently a pretext for his absence.

明心迹(ㄇㄧㄥˊ ㄒㄧㄣ ㄐㄧ)
to tell what's in one's mind; to get (one's purpose, intention, etc.) off one's chest

明心見性(ㄇㄧㄥˊ ㄒㄧㄣ ㄐㄧㄢˋ ㄒㄧㄥˋ)
to enlighten the mind and realize the Buddha-nature immanent in all beings

明信片(ㄇㄧㄥˊ ㄒㄧㄣˋ ㄆㄧㄢˋ)
a postcard; a postal card

明星(ㄇㄧㄥˊ ㄒㄧㄥ)
① a bright star ② a movie star ③ Venus

明知(ㄇㄧㄥˊ ㄓ)
to know perfectly well; to be fully aware

明知故犯(ㄇㄧㄥˊ ㄓ ㄍㄨˋ ㄈㄢˋ)
to commit a crime, mistake, etc. intentionally; to run a risk, etc. even though one knows what's in store for him

明知故問(ㄇㄧㄥˊ ㄓ ㄍㄨˋ ㄨㄣˋ)
to ask about something one already knows

明志(ㄇㄧㄥˊ ㄓˋ)
to state one's own views, attitude, ambition, etc: 這位詩人寫這首詩以明志。The poet wrote this poem to state his ambition.

明智(ㄇㄧㄥˊ ㄓˋ)
sensible; sagacious; wise

明智之舉(ㄇㄧㄥˊ ㄓˋ ㄓ ㄐㄩˇ)
a wise move; an intelligent or sensible act

明治天皇(ㄇㄧㄥˊ ㄓˋ ㄊㄧㄢ ㄏㄨㄤˊ)
Emperor Mutsuhito of Japan whose reign, Meiji, extended from 1867 to 1912

明治維新(ㄇㄧㄥˊ ㄓˋ ㄨㄟˊ ㄒㄧㄣ)
the Meiji restoration, which marked the beginning of Japan's modernization

明哲(ㄇㄧㄥˊ ㄓㄜˊ)
a wise and virtuous person

明哲保身(ㄇㄧㄥˊ ㄓㄜˊ ㄅㄠˇ ㄕㄣ)
(often said of people living under tyranny) A wise person who knows what's best for himself can safeguard his personal security. 或 to be worldly wise and play safe

明徵(ㄇㄧㄥˊ ㄓㄥ)
evident signs: 烏雲是天雨的明徵嗎? Are dark clouds the evident signs of rain?

明爭暗鬪(ㄇㄧㄥˊ ㄓㄥ ㄢˋ ㄉㄡˋ)
to fight overtly and covertly (often said of intramural fights)

明證(ㄇㄧㄥˊ ㄓㄥˋ)
irrefutable proof or evidence

明正典刑(ㄇㄧㄥˊ ㄓㄥˋ ㄉㄧㄢˇ ㄒㄧㄥˊ)
to execute (a criminal) openly

明珠(ㄇㄧㄥˊ ㄓㄨ)
① a glossy pearl ② a person of rare ability ③ a beloved daughter: 她是父母的掌上明珠。She is her parents' beloved daughter.

明珠彈雀(ㄇㄧㄥˊ ㄓㄨ ㄊㄢˊ ㄑㄩㄝˋ)
(literally) to kill a bird with a valuable pearl—to attain an insignificant goal by costly means

明珠出老蚌(ㄇㄧㄥˊ ㄓㄨ ㄔㄨ ㄌㄠˇ ㄅㄤˋ)
an old couple blessed with the birth of a child

明珠入抱(ㄇㄧㄥˊ ㄓㄨ ㄖㄨˋ ㄅㄠˋ)
an expression for congratulating a friend on the birth of a daughter

明珠暗投(ㄇㄧㄥˊ ㄓㄨ ㄢˋ ㄊㄡˊ)
① to have talent but cannot find the right employment ② to take a job that's well below one's ability ③ a good person joining a gang of villains

明主(ㄇㄧㄥˊ ㄓㄨˇ)
an enlightened ruler

明恥教戰(ㄇㄧㄥˊ ㄔˇ ㄐㄧㄠˋ ㄓㄢˋ)
to teach people ways of war to defend national honor; to train people for recovery of a lost territory

明察(ㄇㄧㄥˊ ㄔㄚˊ)
to be sharp and perspicacious; not to be fooled or taken in

明察秋毫(ㄇㄧㄥˊ ㄔㄚˊ ㄑㄧㄡ ㄏㄠˊ)
able to examine the tiniest things (as the tip of a hair)—sharp discerning intelligence

明査暗訪(ㄇㄧㄥˊ ㄔㄚˊ ㄢˋ ㄈㄤˇ)
to investigate openly and secretly

明澈(ㄇㄧㄥˊ ㄔㄜˋ)
bright and limpid; transparent

明澈如鏡(ㄇㄧㄥˊ ㄔㄜˋ ㄖㄨˊ ㄐㄧㄥˋ)
to be like a mirror: 湖水明澈如鏡。The lake is like a mirror.

明朝(ㄇㄧㄥˊ ㄔㄠˊ)
the Ming Dynasty (1368-1644 A.D.)

明成祖(ㄇㄧㄥˊ ㄔㄥˊ ㄗㄨˇ)
Chu Ti (朱棣), 1359-1424 A.D., the third emperor of the Ming Dynasty, who usurped the throne from his nephew

明窗淨几(ㄇㄧㄥˊ ㄔㄨㄤ ㄐㄧㄥˋ ㄐㄧ)
a neat and well-lighted house or room

明史(ㄇㄧㄥˊ ㄕˇ)
the *History of the Ming Dynasty,* authored by Chang Ting-yü (張廷玉) and others of the Ching Dynasty under the imperial order, containing some 336 volumes

明示(ㄇㄧㄥˊ ㄕˋ)
clear indication; to express clearly

明室(ㄇㄧㄥˊ ㄕˋ)
① a well-lighted room ② the Ming Dynasty

明升暗降(ㄇㄧㄥˊ ㄕㄥ ㄢˋ ㄐㄧㄤˋ)
a promotion in appearance but a demotion in fact; to kick upstairs

明說(ㄇㄧㄥˊ ㄕㄨㄛ)
to speak frankly; to speak up

明日(ㄇㄧㄥˊ ㄖˋ)or 明兒(ㄇㄧㄥˊㄦ)
① tomorrow ② one of these days; some day

明日黃花(ㄇㄧㄥˊ ㄖˋ ㄏㄨㄤˊ ㄏㄨㄚ)
① outmoded; obsolete; out of fashion: 這種款式已成明日黃花。This fashion has already become outmoded. ② what has already taken place

明人不做暗事(ㄇㄧㄥˊ ㄖㄣˊ ㄅㄨˋ ㄗㄨㄛˋ

〔日部〕

ㄢˋ ㄕˋ)
An honest man does not engage in clandestine dealings.

明若觀火(ㄇㄧㄥˊ ㄖㄨㄛˋ ㄍㄨㄢ ㄏㄨㄛˇ)
as obvious as a glowing fire

明暗(ㄇㄧㄥˊ ㄢˋ)
brightness and darkness

明言(ㄇㄧㄥˊ ㄧㄢˊ)
to state clearly; to speak out

明眼人(ㄇㄧㄥˊ ㄧㄢˇ ㄖㄣˊ)
a man of clear mind and high intelligence

明瓦(ㄇㄧㄥˊ ㄨㄚˇ)
transparent tiles

明文規定(ㄇㄧㄥˊ ㄨㄣˊ ㄍㄨㄟ ㄉㄧㄥˋ)
in black and white; clearly stipulated in regulations, laws, contracts, agreements, etc.

明王(ㄇㄧㄥˊ ㄨㄤˊ)
① an enlightened ruler ② (Buddhism) the rajas, mingwang or fierce spirits

日部

【昏】 2218
ㄏㄨㄣ huen hūn

1. dusk; dark
2. confused; muddled; mixed-up; demented
3. unclear of sight; dizzy
4. (now rarely) same as婚—to marry
5. a Chinese family name

昏憊(ㄏㄨㄣ ㄅㄟˋ)
dog-tired

昏昧(ㄏㄨㄣ ㄇㄟˋ)or 昏愚(ㄏㄨㄣ ㄩˊ)
stupid; stupidity

昏迷(ㄏㄨㄣ ㄇㄧˊ)
in a coma; unconscious; delirious; stupor

昏明(ㄏㄨㄣ ㄇㄧㄥˊ)
day and night

昏倒(ㄏㄨㄣ ㄉㄠˇ)
to faint; to swoon: 她一看見血便昏倒。She swoons at the sight of blood.

昏定晨省(ㄏㄨㄣ ㄉㄧㄥˋ ㄔㄣˊ ㄒㄧㄥˇ)
to inquire after one's parents in the morning and evening—duties of a filial son; to visit or care for one's parents day and night

昏頭昏腦(ㄏㄨㄣ ㄊㄡˊ ㄏㄨㄣ ㄋㄠˇ)
to feel dizzy, confused, and mixed-up

昏天黑地(ㄏㄨㄣ ㄊㄧㄢ ㄏㄟ ㄉㄧˋ)
① very dark (as before a storm) ② stupid or ignorant ③ dizzy

昏亂(ㄏㄨㄣ ㄌㄨㄢˋ)
stupid and confused; muddled and delirious

昏聵(ㄏㄨㄣ ㄎㄨㄟˋ)
(literally) to be poor of vision and hard of hearing —muddled, confused and stupid

昏黑(ㄏㄨㄣ ㄏㄟ)
dark

昏花(ㄏㄨㄣ ㄏㄨㄚ)
poor of vision; dim-sighted; indistinct vision: 老眼昏花 dim-sighted from old age

昏昏(ㄏㄨㄣ ㄏㄨㄣ)
slumberous

昏昏沉沉(ㄏㄨㄣ ㄏㄨㄣ ㄔㄣˊ ㄔㄣˊ)
dizzy and sleepy; slumberous

昏昏欲睡(ㄏㄨㄣ ㄏㄨㄣ ㄩˋ ㄕㄨㄟˋ)
drowsy; sleepy: 今天下午我昏昏欲睡。I was sleepy this afternoon.

昏黃(ㄏㄨㄣ ㄏㄨㄤˊ)
twilight; dim: 他在昏黃的燈光下看書。He read by a dim light.

昏厥(ㄏㄨㄣ ㄐㄩㄝˊ)
to faint; to swoon: 她突然昏厥過去。All of a sudden she fainted away.

昏君(ㄏㄨㄣ ㄐㄩㄣ)
a muddle-headed monarch

昏曉(ㄏㄨㄣ ㄒㄧㄠˇ)
morning and evening

昏眩(ㄏㄨㄣ ㄒㄩㄢˋ)
dizzy; faint; giddy

昏睡(ㄏㄨㄣ ㄕㄨㄟˋ)
deep slumber; lethargic sleep

昏暗(ㄏㄨㄣ ㄢˋ)
dim; dusky

昏暈(ㄏㄨㄣ ㄩㄣ)
dizzy

昏庸(ㄏㄨㄣ ㄩㄥ)or 昏愚(ㄏㄨㄣ ㄩˊ)
stupid; imbecile; muddle-headed

【易】 2219
ㄧˋ yih yì

1. to exchange; to barter
2. to change (places, jobs, owners, etc.)
3. easy
4. amiable; lenient
5. the *Book of Changes*
6. a Chinese family name

易北河(ㄧˋ ㄅㄟˇ ㄏㄜˊ)
the Elbe River in Europe

易卜生(ㄧˋ ㄅㄨˇ ㄕㄥ)
Henrik Ibsen, 1828-1906, Norwegian playwright and poet

易名(ㄧˋ ㄇㄧㄥˊ)
① to change one's names ② to give a posthumous title to a person

易發難制(ㄧˋ ㄈㄚ ㄋㄢˊ ㄓˋ)
It's easier to start something than to stop it.

易放難收(ㄧˋ ㄈㄤˋ ㄋㄢˊ ㄕㄡ)
It's easier to indulge in an expensive habit than to get rid of it.

易得者易失(ㄧˋ ㄉㄜˊ ㄓㄜˇ ㄧˋ ㄕ)
Easy get, easy lose. 或 Easy come, easy go.

易地皆然(ㄧˋ ㄉㄧˋ ㄐㄧㄝ ㄖㄢˊ)
(said of a universal practice, principle, etc.) It's the same everywhere.

易地而處(ㄧˋ ㄉㄧˋ ㄦˊ ㄔㄨˇ)
to look at a matter from the other fellow's viewpoint

易怒(ㄧˋ ㄋㄨˋ)
prone to anger; irascible

易開罐(ㄧˋ ㄎㄞ ㄍㄨㄢˋ)
a ring-pull can

易經(ㄧˋ ㄐㄧㄥ)
the *Book of Changes*

易曉(ㄧˋ ㄒㄧㄠˇ)
clear and intelligible; easy to understand: 他的解釋明白易曉。His explanation is clear and intelligible.

易行(ㄧˋ ㄒㄧㄥˊ)
easy to practice; easy to do: 這計畫簡便易行。This project is simple and easy to do.

易姓(ㄧˋ ㄒㄧㄥˋ)
① to change one's family name ② (in old China) to change dynasties

易學難精(ㄧˋ ㄒㄩㄝˊ ㄋㄢˊ ㄐㄧㄥ)
easy to learn but difficult to master: 英語易學難精。English is easy to learn but difficult to master.

易幟(ㄧˋ ㄓˋ)
(said of a city or strategic point) to change hands

易主(ㄧˋ ㄓㄨˇ)
to change owners or masters

易轍(ㄧˋ ㄔㄜˋ)
to renovate; to make a dras-

tic change
易手(ㄧˋ ㄕㄡˇ)
to change hands
易水(ㄧˋ ㄕㄨㄟˇ)
the I River in Hopeh Province
易水歌(ㄧˋ ㄕㄨㄟˇ ㄍㄜ)
the *Song of the I River* (when Ching Ko (荆軻) was sent to Chin (秦) to assassinate its tyrant, Shih-huang (始皇), he was sent off with the *Song of the I River*, which reads: "The winds heave as the I River turns cold. The hero goes away and return he will not.")
易燃物(ㄧˋ ㄖㄢˊ ㄨˋ)
combustibles; inflammables
易人(ㄧˋ ㄖㄣˊ)
to change a person (for a job)
易如反掌(ㄧˋ ㄖㄨˊ ㄈㄢˇ ㄓㄤˇ)
as easy as turning over the palm of one's hand: 解答這個問題易如反掌。To answer this question is as easy as turning over the palm of one's hand.
易子而食(ㄧˋ ㄗˇ ㄦˊ ㄕˊ)
(said of people during severe famines) to exchange children for eating
易俗(ㄧˋ ㄙㄨˊ)
to change practices or customs; to reform customs or practices
易易(ㄧˋ ㄧˋ)
very easy
易牙(ㄧˋ ㄧㄚˊ)
I Yah, a famous culinary artist in the Epoch of Spring and Autumn
易言之(ㄧˋ ㄧㄢˊ ㄓ)
in other words
易位(ㄧˋ ㄨㄟˋ)
①to change places or positions; to transpose ② to dethrone
易於進行(ㄧˋ ㄩˊ ㄐㄧㄣˋ ㄒㄧㄥˊ)
easy to proceed; easy to manage: 這項計畫易於進行。The plan is easy to proceed.
易與(ㄧˋ ㄩˇ)
(said of a person) easy to cope with; easy to get along with

【昔】2220
ㄒㄧˊ shyi xí
1. bygone; of old; formerly; ancient
2. a night; an evening
3. the end
昔年(ㄒㄧˊ ㄋㄧㄢˊ)
bygone years; past years; former years
昔酒(ㄒㄧˊ ㄐㄧㄡˇ)
old wine; vintage wine
昔昔(ㄒㄧˊ ㄒㄧˊ)
every night 亦作「夕夕」
昔賢(ㄒㄧˊ ㄒㄧㄢˊ)
ancient sages
昔者(ㄒㄧˊ ㄓㄜˇ)
in former times; in ancient times; before; formerly
昔時(ㄒㄧˊ ㄕˊ)
in former times; in the olden days
昔日(ㄒㄧˊ ㄖˋ)
in the olden days; in former days(or times)
昔人(ㄒㄧˊ ㄖㄣˊ)
the ancient people
昔歲(ㄒㄧˊ ㄙㄨㄟˋ)
last year

【昕】2221
ㄒㄧㄣ shin xīn
daybreak; dawn
昕夕從公(ㄒㄧㄣ ㄒㄧˋ ㄘㄨㄥˊ ㄍㄨㄥ)
to devote oneself to official duties day and night

【昀】2222
ㄩㄣˊ yun yún
1. daybreak; sunrise; dawn
2. sunshine

五畫

【星】2223
ㄒㄧㄥ shing xīng
1. any heavenly body that shines; stars, planets, satellites, etc.
2. a spark or sparks
3. droplets; small particles of anything; very tiny
4. name of one of the 28 constellations
5. a movie star
6. by night; nocturnal
7. an ancient percussion musical instrument consisting of two or more brass-cup-like pieces played by hitting them against one another
8. a Chinese family name
星奔(ㄒㄧㄥ ㄅㄣ)
to travel, run away or escape by night
星卜(ㄒㄧㄥ ㄅㄨˇ)
astrology and divination
星眸(ㄒㄧㄥ ㄇㄡˊ)
starry eyes; bright eyes
星芒狀(ㄒㄧㄥ ㄇㄤˊ ㄓㄨㄤˋ)
resembling a star-polygon
星命(ㄒㄧㄥ ㄇㄧㄥˋ)
astrology
星發(ㄒㄧㄥ ㄈㄚ)
to start out by night
星斗(ㄒㄧㄥ ㄉㄡˇ)
stars; heavenly bodies
星等(ㄒㄧㄥ ㄉㄥˇ)
(astronomy) visual magnitude; apparent magnitude
星探(ㄒㄧㄥ ㄊㄢˋ)
a talent scout in the movie industry
星條旗(ㄒㄧㄥ ㄊㄧㄠˊ ㄑㄧˊ)
Stars and Stripes—the national flag of the United States
星團(ㄒㄧㄥ ㄊㄨㄢˊ)
(astronomy) a constellation; a cluster
星離雨散(ㄒㄧㄥ ㄌㄧˊ ㄩˇ ㄙㄢˋ)
to separate and disperse rapidly
星曆(ㄒㄧㄥ ㄌㄧˋ)
the sidereal calendar
星列(ㄒㄧㄥ ㄌㄧㄝˋ)
arrayed like stars
星流(ㄒㄧㄥ ㄌㄧㄡˊ)
to act quickly—like a comet
星羅棋布(ㄒㄧㄥ ㄌㄨㄛˊ ㄑㄧˊ ㄅㄨˋ)
numerous and arrayed like stars in heaven or pieces on a chessboard (usually said of archipelagos, etc.)
星光(ㄒㄧㄥ ㄍㄨㄤ)
starlight: 她在星光閃閃的夜晚外出散步。She went out for a walk on a starlight night.
星光燦爛(ㄒㄧㄥ ㄍㄨㄤ ㄘㄢˋ ㄌㄢˋ)
a star-studded gathering
星河(ㄒㄧㄥ ㄏㄜˊ)
(astronomy) the Milky Way
星號(ㄒㄧㄥ ㄏㄠˋ)
an asterisk(☆)
星漢(ㄒㄧㄥ ㄏㄢˋ)
the stars; the Milky Way
星火(ㄒㄧㄥ ㄏㄨㄛˇ)

①a very urgent matter ②a spark; a small fire

星迴(ㄒㄧㄥ ㄏㄨㄟˊ)
(literally) when the stars return to their old positions —A year has elapsed.

〔日部〕

星際旅行(ㄒㄧㄥ ㄐㄧˋ ㄌㄩˇ ㄒㄧㄥˊ)
interstellar travel; space travel: 這部電影描寫星際旅行。This movie describes space travel.

星家(ㄒㄧㄥ ㄐㄧㄚ)
an astrologist

星加坡(ㄒㄧㄥ ㄐㄧㄚ ㄆㄛ)
Singapore 亦作「新加坡」or「星洲」or「星島」

星期(ㄒㄧㄥ ㄑㄧˊ)
week: 她將於一個星期後到達。She will arrive here in a week.

星期六(ㄒㄧㄥ ㄑㄧˊ ㄌㄧㄡˋ)
Saturday: 星期六是一週的第七天。Saturday is the seventh day of the week.

星期日(ㄒㄧㄥ ㄑㄧˊ ㄖˋ)or 星期天(ㄒㄧㄥ ㄑㄧˊ ㄊㄧㄢ)
Sunday

星期四(ㄒㄧㄥ ㄑㄧˊ ㄙˋ)
Thursday

星期三(ㄒㄧㄥ ㄑㄧˊ ㄙㄢ)
Wednesday

星期二(ㄒㄧㄥ ㄑㄧˊ ㄦˋ)
Tuesday

星期一(ㄒㄧㄥ ㄑㄧˊ ㄧ)
Monday

星期五(ㄒㄧㄥ ㄑㄧˊ ㄨˇ)
Friday

星球(ㄒㄧㄥ ㄑㄧㄡˊ)
planets; stars: 地球是一個星球。The Earth is a planet.

星羣(ㄒㄧㄥ ㄑㄩㄣˊ)
a group of stars; a constellation

星系(ㄒㄧㄥ ㄒㄧˋ)
(astronomy) a galaxy: 星系團 a cluster of galaxies

星宿
①(ㄒㄧㄥ ㄒㄧㄡˋ) planets or stars in heaven; constellations: 十二星宿 the twelve constellations
②(ㄒㄧㄥ ˙ㄙㄨ) a person who is considered an incarnation of a star

星宿海(ㄒㄧㄥ ㄒㄧㄡˋ ㄏㄞˇ)
name of a place in Chinghai, formerly believed to be the source of the Yellow River, the second largest river in China

星象(ㄒㄧㄥ ㄒㄧㄤˋ)
to divine according to the brightness, dimness, etc. of stars—astrology

星象學(ㄒㄧㄥ ㄒㄧㄤˋ ㄒㄩㄝˊ)
astrometry 亦作「天體測定學」or「測天學」

星星
①(ㄒㄧㄥ ㄒㄧㄥ) spots, specks; a hint of grey (in the hair, etc.): 昨晚天空晴朗，一星星雲彩也沒有。Last night the sky was clear and bright without a speck of cloud.
②(ㄒㄧㄥ ˙ㄒㄧㄥ) stars, planets and satellites

星星點點(ㄒㄧㄥ ㄒㄧㄥ ㄉㄧㄢˇ ㄉㄧㄢˇ)
droplets and particles; tiny and small amounts; bit by bit; a bit

星星之火可以燎原(ㄒㄧㄥ ㄒㄧㄥ ㄓ ㄏㄨㄛˇ ㄎㄜˇ ㄧˇ ㄌㄧㄠˊ ㄩㄢˊ)
(literally) A spark may cause a conflagration. —Small things may cause big trouble.

星形(ㄒㄧㄥ ㄒㄧㄥˊ)
a star-polygon

星占學(ㄒㄧㄥ ㄓㄢ ㄒㄩㄝˊ)
astrology 亦作「占星學」or「星學」

星馳(ㄒㄧㄥ ㄔˊ)
to travel very fast like a shooting star

星辰(ㄒㄧㄥ ㄔㄣˊ)
stars; heavenly bodies

星士(ㄒㄧㄥ ㄕˋ)
an astrologist

星霜(ㄒㄧㄥ ㄕㄨㄤ)
①a whole year ②time (in terms of years)

星子(ㄒㄧㄥ ˙ㄗ)or 星兒(ㄒㄧㄥㄦ)
tiny bits, droplets or particles

星座(ㄒㄧㄥ ㄗㄨㄛˋ)
(astronomy) a constellation; a star and its satellites

星散(ㄒㄧㄥ ㄙㄢˋ)
to scatter and spread like stars

星移斗轉(ㄒㄧㄥ ㄧˊ ㄉㄡˇ ㄓㄨㄢˇ)
①A night has passed. ②the movements of the stars—the flight of time

星翳(ㄒㄧㄥ ㄧˋ)
white spots on the cornea

星夜(ㄒㄧㄥ ㄧㄝˋ)
①night; a starlit night ②(to travel, escape, etc.) by night; by starlight

星夜奔馳(ㄒㄧㄥ ㄧㄝˋ ㄅㄣ ㄔˊ)
to travel urgently by night

星月交輝(ㄒㄧㄥ ㄩㄝˋ ㄐㄧㄠ ㄏㄨㄟ)
(literally) The moon and the stars vie for brilliance. —any gathering or congregation of famous or august personalities

星雲(ㄒㄧㄥ ㄩㄣˊ)
(astronomy) a nebula

星殞(ㄒㄧㄥ ㄩㄣˇ)
①the falling of meteoroid to the earth ②the death of a movie star or important personality

【映】 2224
ㄧㄥˋ yinq yìng

1. to mirror; to reflect; a reflection
2. to project (slides, pictures, etc.)
3. to shine; shining; to blind; blinding (glare, light, etc.)

映帶(ㄧㄥˋ ㄉㄞˋ)
(said of a beautiful natural scene) mountains, lakes, trees, flowers, etc. in their perspective that merge together to form an enchanting sight

映奪(ㄧㄥˋ ㄉㄨㄛˊ)
to dazzle or catch (the eyes)

映象(ㄧㄥˋ ㄒㄧㄤˋ)
image

映雪讀書(ㄧㄥˋ ㄒㄩㄝˇ ㄉㄨˊ ㄕㄨ)
to study by the glare of snow (said of Sun Kang (孫康), a poor scholar of the Tsin Dynasty)

映照(ㄧㄥˋ ㄓㄠˋ)
to shine and reflect; to combine to make a pretty scene; bright and shining

映襯(ㄧㄥˋ ㄔㄣˋ)
to set off

映山紅(ㄧㄥˋ ㄕㄢ ㄏㄨㄥˊ)
azaleas 亦作「杜鵑花」

映日(ㄧㄥˋ ㄖˋ)
bright sunlight

映眼(ㄧㄥˋ ㄧㄢˇ)

dazzling; glaring

映演(ㄧㄥˇ ㄧㄢˇ)
to project (a film or slide on the screen)

【春】 2225
ㄔㄨㄣ chuen chūn
1. spring, the first of the four seasons
2. sensuality; lustful; lewd; pornographic
3. alive; vitality; living: 枯木逢春。A withered tree comes to life again.
4. joyful
5. youth: 她善於保養她的青春。She keeps her youth well.
6. wine (especially in the Tang Dynasty)

春榜(ㄔㄨㄣ ㄅㄤˇ)
the announcement of successful candidates for the national civil service examination (進士) in ancient China, which usually took place in spring

春冰(ㄔㄨㄣ ㄅㄧㄥ)
(literally) spring ice—thin ice, implying a dangerous situation

春餅(ㄔㄨㄣ ㄅㄧㄥˇ)
thin pancake (usually eaten in spring festivals)

春忙(ㄔㄨㄣ ㄇㄤˊ)
the planting season

春夢(ㄔㄨㄣ ㄇㄥˋ)
(literally) a spring dream—something that is illusory and transient

春夢無痕(ㄔㄨㄣ ㄇㄥˋ ㄨˊ ㄏㄣˊ)
(literally) the traceless dream of spring—something that vanishes without leaving a trace

春分(ㄔㄨㄣ ㄈㄣ)
the vernal equinox, about March 21

春方(ㄔㄨㄣ ㄈㄤ)
aphrodisiacs; drugs that stimulate sexual desires

春風(ㄔㄨㄣ ㄈㄥ)
① spring breezes ② good education ③ sexual intercourse ④ favor; grace ⑤ happy smiles

春風滿面(ㄔㄨㄣ ㄈㄥ ㄇㄢˇ ㄇㄧㄢˋ)
to smile broadly; a cheerful look

春風風人(ㄔㄨㄣ ㄈㄥ ㄈㄥˋ ㄖㄣˊ)
grace that has spread to all; benefits that are enjoyed by people far and wide

春風得意(ㄔㄨㄣ ㄈㄥ ㄉㄜˊ ㄧˋ)
to attain a high official rank; to ride on the crest of success

春風化雨(ㄔㄨㄣ ㄈㄥ ㄏㄨㄚˋ ㄩˇ)
education of the young; salutary influence of education

春風一度(ㄔㄨㄣ ㄈㄥ ㄧˊ ㄉㄨˋ)
sexual intercourse

春臺(ㄔㄨㄣ ㄊㄞˊ)
① peaceful and prosperous time ② (in ancient China) the Department of Rites ③ a dining table

春條兒(ㄔㄨㄣ ㄊㄧㄠˊㄦ)
lucky sayings or words written on red paper hung or pasted at the doorway of a newly opened store, etc. 參看「春聯」

春天(ㄔㄨㄣ ㄊㄧㄢ)
spring; springtime

春牛(ㄔㄨㄣ ㄋㄧㄡˊ)
(an old Chinese custom) the Spring Ox made of clay to usher in spring

春暖花開(ㄔㄨㄣ ㄋㄨㄢˇ ㄏㄨㄚ ㄎㄞ)
During the warmth of spring all the flowers bloom.

春女(ㄔㄨㄣ ㄋㄩˇ)
young girls who entertain romantic thoughts

春雷(ㄔㄨㄣ ㄌㄟˊ)
spring thunder (which is believed to awaken the wildlife from hibernation)

春蘭秋菊(ㄔㄨㄣ ㄌㄢˊ ㄑㄧㄡ ㄐㄩˊ)
(literally) spring orchids and autumn chrysanthemums—① things grown or done at the right time ② Everything has its own proud days.

春聯(ㄔㄨㄣ ㄌㄧㄢˊ)
New Year's couplets written on strips of red paper and pasted on doors (usually containing words of luck)

春霖(ㄔㄨㄣ ㄌㄧㄣˊ)
spring rains; spring showers: 春霖有利於耕種。Spring rains benefit farming.

春露秋霜(ㄔㄨㄣ ㄌㄨˋ ㄑㄧㄡ ㄕㄨㄤ)
① grace and severity ② the flight of time

春羅(ㄔㄨㄣ ㄌㄨㄛˊ)
a variety of silk goods

春耕(ㄔㄨㄣ ㄍㄥ)
spring cultivation: 農夫們忙於春耕。The farmers were busy with spring cultivation.

春官(ㄔㄨㄣ ㄍㄨㄢ)
(in the Chou Dynasty) the official in charge of rites

春光(ㄔㄨㄣ ㄍㄨㄤ)
① spring scenes (natural charms in spring) ② lustful scenes—as a sexual act

春光明媚(ㄔㄨㄣ ㄍㄨㄤ ㄇㄧㄥˊ ㄇㄟˋ)
a sunlit and enchanting scene of spring

春光洩漏(ㄔㄨㄣ ㄍㄨㄤ ㄒㄧㄝˋ ㄌㄡˋ)
An illicit affair became known.

春宮(ㄔㄨㄣ ㄍㄨㄥ)
① pornographic pictures, drawings, etc. ② living quarters of the crown prince

春宮圖(ㄔㄨㄣ ㄍㄨㄥ ㄊㄨˊ) or 春畫(ㄔㄨㄣ ㄏㄨㄚˋ)
pornographic drawings

春困秋乏(ㄔㄨㄣ ㄎㄨㄣˋ ㄑㄧㄡ ㄈㄚˊ)
One feels dizziness in spring and fatigue in autumn.

春寒料峭(ㄔㄨㄣ ㄏㄢˊ ㄌㄧㄠˋ ㄑㄧㄠˋ)
the chill of early spring

春華(ㄔㄨㄣ ㄏㄨㄚ)
flowers in spring—youthhood 亦作「春花」

春華秋實(ㄔㄨㄣ ㄏㄨㄚ ㄑㄧㄡ ㄕˊ)
(literally) spring flowers and autumn fruits—showy appearance and virtuous substance

春花秋月(ㄔㄨㄣ ㄏㄨㄚ ㄑㄧㄡ ㄩㄝˋ)
(literally) the spring flowers and the autumn moon—① the best things at the best time ② flight of time

春暉(ㄔㄨㄣ ㄏㄨㄟ)
the light of the spring sun—parental love and care

春回大地(ㄔㄨㄣ ㄏㄨㄟˊ ㄉㄚˋ ㄉㄧˋ)
Spring returns to the good earth.

春紅(ㄔㄨㄣ ㄏㄨㄥˊ)
the flowers of spring

春季(ㄔㄨㄣ ㄐㄧˋ)
spring

春祭(ㄔㄨㄣ ㄐㄧˋ)

〔日部〕

〔日部〕

spring sacrifices; rites for ancestor-worshipping in spring

春假(ㄔㄨㄣ ㄐㄧㄚˇ)
spring holidays; the spring vacation

春節(ㄔㄨㄣ ㄐㄧㄝˊ)
the Lunar New Year Festival; the Lunar New Year's holidays

春酒(ㄔㄨㄣ ㄐㄧㄡˇ)
feasts during the Lunar New Year's holidays

春景(ㄔㄨㄣ ㄐㄧㄥˇ)
the beautiful scenes of spring

春捲(ㄔㄨㄣ ㄐㄩㄢˇ)
spring rolls (meat and vegetables rolled with thin cakes eaten as a snack)

春期(ㄔㄨㄣ ㄑㄧˊ)
puberty

春祈秋報(ㄔㄨㄣ ㄑㄧˊ ㄑㄧㄡ ㄅㄠˋ)
(in the *Book of Rites*) to pray (for rain) in spring and offer thanks (for crops) in fall

春氣(ㄔㄨㄣ ㄑㄧˋ)
warmth given by the spring sun—that stimulates growth and ardor of youth

春秋(ㄔㄨㄣ ㄑㄧㄡ)
① a year; a full round of the seasons ② spring and autumn ③ age ④ annals of any state during the period of Warring States ⑤ *Spring and Autumn Annals*—a history by Confucius, based on the annals of the state of Lu (722-481B.C.) ⑥ annals; history

春秋筆削(ㄔㄨㄣ ㄑㄧㄡ ㄅㄧˇ ㄒㄩㄝ)
(said of a chronicle writer) to be keen, honest and strict in observing and judging things or people

春秋鼎盛(ㄔㄨㄣ ㄑㄧㄡ ㄉㄧㄥˇ ㄕㄥˋ)
in the prime of one's life

春秋時代(ㄔㄨㄣ ㄑㄧㄡ ㄕˊ ㄉㄞˋ)
the Epoch of Spring and Autumn, approximately from 770 to 403 B. C.

春情(ㄔㄨㄣ ㄑㄧㄥˊ)
sexual desire; the longing for the opposite sex

春情發動期(ㄔㄨㄣ ㄑㄧㄥˊ ㄈㄚ ㄉㄨㄥˋ ㄑㄧˊ)
puberty

春禊(ㄔㄨㄣ ㄒㄧˋ)
(in ancient China) a gathering by the waterside in lunar March, where people tried to wash away their bad luck

春宵(ㄔㄨㄣ ㄒㄧㄠ)
① spring nights ② night rendezvous between lovers; a wedding night

春宵苦短(ㄔㄨㄣ ㄒㄧㄠ ㄎㄨˇ ㄉㄨㄢˇ)
The night of rendezvous is always too short (to the lovers). 或 The wedding night is always too short (to the newlyweds).

春宵一刻值千金(ㄔㄨㄣ ㄒㄧㄠ ㄧˊ ㄎㄜˋ ㄓˊ ㄑㄧㄢ ㄐㄧㄣ)
One minute in a night of rendezvous is worth a thousand pieces of gold. 或 Every minute of the wedding night is precious.

春曉(ㄔㄨㄣ ㄒㄧㄠˇ)
morning in spring

春心(ㄔㄨㄣ ㄒㄧㄣ)
lustful thoughts; spring desire

春心蕩漾(ㄔㄨㄣ ㄒㄧㄣ ㄉㄤˋ ㄧㄤˋ)
the surging of lustful desire

春汛(ㄔㄨㄣ ㄒㄩㄣˋ)
the spring flood (especially referring to the spring inundation of the Yellow River)

春裝(ㄔㄨㄣ ㄓㄨㄤ)
spring clothes; the spring fashion

春愁秋思(ㄔㄨㄣ ㄔㄡˊ ㄑㄧㄡ ㄙ)
spring longings and autumn thoughts

春試(ㄔㄨㄣ ㄕˋ)or 春闈(ㄔㄨㄣ ㄨㄟˊ)
(in ancient China) the national civil service examination which usually took place in spring

春事(ㄔㄨㄣ ㄕˋ)
spring planting

春申君(ㄔㄨㄣ ㄕㄣ ㄐㄩㄣ)
a title of Prime Minister Huang Hsieh (黃歇) of Chu during the period of Warring States

春聲(ㄔㄨㄣ ㄕㄥ)
the chirping of birds and gurgling of streams heard in spring

春色(ㄔㄨㄣ ㄙㄜˋ)
① spring scenery ② a joyful appearance or expression ③ sensual or carnal scenes

春色惱人(ㄔㄨㄣ ㄙㄜˋ ㄋㄠˇ ㄖㄣˊ)
The scenes of spring are really distracting.

春筍(ㄔㄨㄣ ㄙㄨㄣˇ)
young woman's fingers (likened to the delicate, tender and slender spring bamboo shoots)

春意(ㄔㄨㄣ ㄧˋ)
① spring in the air; high spirits in spring ② thoughts of love

春藥(ㄔㄨㄣ ㄧㄠˋ)
aphrodisiac; drugs that induce sexual desire

春遊(ㄔㄨㄣ ㄧㄡˊ)
spring outings

春鶯(ㄔㄨㄣ ㄧㄥ)
the mango-bird; the Chinese oriole

春雨(ㄔㄨㄣ ㄩˇ)
spring rains or showers

【昧】 2226 ㄇㄟˋ mey mèi

1. obscure; dark
2. to hide; to pocket
3. to ignore (one's conscience, etc.)
4. blind; ignorant
5. to faint; fainting

昧昧(ㄇㄟˋ ㄇㄟˋ)
① dark; obscure ② stupid; ignorant ③ (now rarely) deep and profound

昧瞀(ㄇㄟˋ ㄇㄡˋ)or(ㄇㄟˋ ㄇㄠˋ)
stupid and ignorant

昧旦(ㄇㄟˋ ㄉㄢˋ)
dawn; daybreak

昧良心(ㄇㄟˋ ㄌㄧㄤˊ ㄒㄧㄣ)
to ignore one's conscience; to do evil against one's conscience: 我們決不昧着良心。We'll never do evil against our conscience.

昧起來(ㄇㄟˋ ˙ㄑㄧ ˙ㄌㄞ)
to hide another person's things

昧下(ㄇㄟˋ ㄒㄧㄚˋ)
to hide another person's things

昧心(ㄇㄟˋ ㄒㄧㄣ)
to ignore one's conscience

昧心錢(ㄇㄟˋ ㄒㄧㄣ ㄑㄧㄢˊ)
money obtained by dishonest or evil means

昧視(ㄇㄟˋ ㄕˋ)
to watch or inspect in secret

昧爽(ㄇㄟˋ ㄕㄨㄤˇ)
dawn; daybreak 亦作「昧旦」

昧死(ㄇㄟˋ ㄙˇ)
(an expression found in memorials to the emperors of the Chin and Han dynasties) to deserve death for daring to speak to Your Majesty this way

昧於事理(ㄇㄟˋ ㄩˊ ㄕˋ ㄌㄧˇ)
to be ignorant of good reason, judgment, common practice, etc.

【昨】 2227
ㄗㄨㄛˊ tzwo zuó
yesterday; lately; past

昨非(ㄗㄨㄛˊ ㄈㄟ)
past mistakes

昨天(ㄗㄨㄛˊ ㄊㄧㄢ)or 昨日(ㄗㄨㄛˊ ㄖˋ) or 昨兒(ㄗㄨㄛˊㄦ)or 昨兒個(ㄗㄨㄛˊㄦ ·ㄍㄜ)
yesterday: 昨天我很忙。I was very busy yesterday.

昨朝(ㄗㄨㄛˊ ㄓㄠ)
yesterday morning: 昨朝下大雨。It rained hard yesterday morning.

昨死今生(ㄗㄨㄛˊ ㄙˇ ㄐㄧㄣ ㄕㄥ)
(literally) to be dead yesterday and alive today—to be reborn; to lead a new life from now on

昨晚(ㄗㄨㄛˊ ㄨㄢˇ)or 昨兒晚上(ㄗㄨㄛˊㄦ ㄨㄢˇ ·ㄕㄤ)or 昨夜(ㄗㄨㄛˊ ㄧㄝˋ)
last night

【昭】 2228
ㄓㄠ jau zhāo
1. bright; brightness; luminous
2. prominent; eminent; evident; obvious
3. to make open; to show; to display: 他們對我昭示厚誼。They showed me great kindness.
4. a Chinese family name

昭明(ㄓㄠ ㄇㄧㄥˊ)
① evident; clear ② to become bright ②(now rarely) a comet

昭明太子(ㄓㄠ ㄇㄧㄥˊ ㄊㄞˋ ㄗˇ)
Hsiao Tung (蕭統), the eldest son of Emperor Wu of the Liang Dynasty (502-556 A.D.)

昭明文選(ㄓㄠ ㄇㄧㄥˊ ㄨㄣˊ ㄒㄩㄢˇ)
the title of a collection of Chinese literary works edited by Hsiao Tung of the Liang Dynasty

昭穆(ㄓㄠ ㄇㄨˋ)
(in ancient rites) a system of arranging emperors' temples

昭代(ㄓㄠ ㄉㄞˋ)
an enlightened age or reign; (in ancient China) our dynasty or my dynasty

昭告(ㄓㄠ ㄍㄠˋ)
to declare or announce to the public; to make known publicly

昭君(ㄓㄠ ㄐㄩㄣ)
Wang Chiang (王嬙), a lady of the Han court, who was later married to a chieftain of a northern tribe in the performance of matrimonial diplomacy

昭顯(ㄓㄠ ㄒㄧㄢˇ)
prominent; eminent; evident; famous

昭信中外(ㄓㄠ ㄒㄧㄣˋ ㄓㄨㄥ ㄨㄞˋ)
to inspire confidence and faith within and without the nation

昭雪(ㄓㄠ ㄒㄩㄝˇ)
to redress (a miscarriage of justice); to rehabilitate

昭昭(ㄓㄠ ㄓㄠ)
clear and evident; known to all

昭彰(ㄓㄠ ㄓㄤ)
prominent; eminent; obvious; evident: 他的罪惡昭彰。He has committed obvious crimes.

昭著(ㄓㄠ ㄓㄨˋ)
famous; eminent: 他是一位昭著的學者。He is an eminent scholar.

昭灼(ㄓㄠ ㄓㄨㄛˊ)
bright; shining; dazzling

昭示(ㄓㄠ ㄕˋ)
to decree, declare, etc. officially; announcement, declaration, notice, proclamation, etc.

昭然(ㄓㄠ ㄖㄢˊ)
clear and obvious; evident

昭然若揭(ㄓㄠ ㄖㄢˊ ㄖㄨㄛˋ ㄐㄧㄝ)
very obvious; all too clear: 他的野心昭然若揭。His ambition is very obvious.

昭如日星(ㄓㄠ ㄖㄨˊ ㄖˋ ㄒㄧㄥ)
as evident and obvious as the sun and the stars

昭容(ㄓㄠ ㄖㄨㄥˊ)
① lady officials in ancient court ② a musical style in the Han Dynasty

昭蘇(ㄓㄠ ㄙㄨ)
to wake up; to come to (from a coma, etc.)

昭儀(ㄓㄠ ㄧˊ)
an official rank for ladies in the imperial palace

昭耀(ㄓㄠ ㄧㄠˋ)
bright and brilliant; shining

昭陽宮(ㄓㄠ ㄧㄤˊ ㄍㄨㄥ)
name of a palace in the Han Dynasty

【是】 2229
ㄕˋ shyh shì
1. yes; right; positive (as contrasted to negative)
2. the verb to be (for all persons and numbers): 他是我的朋友。He is my friend.
3. this, that, or which: 是日天氣晴朗。It was fine this day.
4. a Chinese family name

是必(ㄕˋ ㄅㄧˋ)
must be; surely; certainly: 他是必疲倦了。He must be tired.

是不是(ㄕˋ ·ㄅㄨ ㄕˋ)
Is it true or not? 或Are you ...? 或Is he...? 他是不是在這裏? Is he here?

是非(ㄕˋ ㄈㄟ)
①right or wrong; right and wrong; yes and no ②gossip; scandal: 她太喜歡說是非。She is too fond of gossip. ③ discord

是非顛倒(ㄕˋ ㄈㄟ ㄉㄧㄢ ㄉㄠˇ)
to confound right and wrong

是非題(ㄕˋ ㄈㄟ ㄊㄧˊ)
a true-or-false problem

是非曲直(ㄕˋ ㄈㄟ ㄑㄩ ㄓˊ)
right and wrong, proper and improper; right and wrong, reasonable and absurd

是非之地(ㄕˋ ㄈㄟ ㄓ ㄉㄧˋ)
a place where one is apt to

〔日部〕

〔日部〕

get into trouble
是非之心(ㄕˋ ㄈㄟ ㄓ ㄒㄧㄣ)
the instinct to tell right from wrong; one's conscience; the feeling of approving and disapproving
是非人(ㄕˋ ㄈㄟ ㄖㄣˊ)
one who stirs up strife or misunderstanding
是非自有公論(ㄕˋ ㄈㄟ ㄗˋ ㄧㄡˇ ㄍㄨㄥ ㄌㄨㄣˋ)
Public opinion is the best judge of who's right and who's wrong. 或 There's always an unbiased view on the right or wrong of a matter.
是否(ㄕˋ ㄈㄡˇ)
Is it...? 或 Are you...? 或 Is he...? 或 whether or not; yes or no: 他是否正在建造一所房子? Is he building a house?
是否有當(ㄕˋ ㄈㄡˇ ㄧㄡˇ ㄉㄤˋ)
whether this is proper (I am eagerly awaiting your instruction.)
是的(ㄕˋ ·ㄉㄜ)
yes; right; correct; affirmative 或 That's it.
是古非今(ㄕˋ ㄍㄨˇ ㄈㄟ ㄐㄧㄣ)
to consider anything old (to be) good and reject everything that is modern
是故(ㄕˋ ㄍㄨˋ)
therefore: 她生病了，是故未能來。She was ill, and therefore could not come.
是可忍孰不可忍(ㄕˋ ㄎㄜˇ ㄖㄣˇ ㄕㄨˊ ㄅㄨˋ ㄎㄜˇ ㄖㄣˇ)
If this can be endured, what else can not?
是何道理(ㄕˋ ㄏㄜˊ ㄉㄠˋ ㄌㄧˇ)
Why? 或 For what reason? 他遲到是何道理? Why was he late?
是何居心(ㄕˋ ㄏㄜˊ ㄐㄩ ㄒㄧㄣ)
What evil intention is this! 或 How mean you are!
是幸(ㄕˋ ㄒㄧㄥˋ)
It would be fortunate indeed if you...; for which (the nation, the people, etc.) will be thankful; for which I'll be much obliged
是正(ㄕˋ ㄓㄥˋ)
to check and correct
是是非非(ㄕˋ ㄕˋ ㄈㄟ ㄈㄟ)
gossip(s); scandal(s)
是日(ㄕˋ ㄖˋ)
that day; this day
是啊(ㄕˋ ·ㄖㄚ)
Yeah! Oh, yes!
是所至禱(ㄕˋ ㄙㄨㄛˇ ㄓˋ ㄉㄠˇ)
for which I sincerely pray; for which I'm truly obliged (an expression often used in letters)
是以(ㄕˋ ㄧˇ)
therefore; hence
是耶非耶(ㄕˋ ㄧㄝˊ ㄈㄟ ㄧㄝˊ)
Is it true or not? 或 Yes or no?
是樣兒(ㄕˋ ㄧㄤˋㄦ)
to look good; becoming; fashionable
是味兒(ㄕˋ ㄨㄟˋㄦ)
delicious; tasteful
是爲(ㄕˋ ㄨㄟˊ)
it is; this is
是爲至要(ㄕˋ ㄨㄟˊ ㄓˋ ㄧㄠˋ)
which is very important (a conventional phrase in letters addressed to one's children or people of lower position)

【昱】 2230 ㄩˋ yuh yù
1. sunshine; light; brightness; shining; dazzling
2. tomorrow
昱昱(ㄩˋ ㄩˋ)
dazzling

【昴】 2231 ㄇㄠˇ mao mǎo
name of a star, one of the 28 constellations
昴星(ㄇㄠˇ ㄒㄧㄥ)
the Pleiades

【昶】 2232 ㄔㄤˇ chaang chǎng
1. a long day
2. comfortable and easy

【昫】 2233 ㄒㄩˇ sheu xǔ
the warmth of the rising sun
昫嫗 or 昫育(ㄒㄩˇ ㄩˋ)
to caress—as sunshine

【昳】 2234 1. ㄉㄧㄝˊ dye dié
the setting sun

【昳】 2234 2. ㄧˋ yih yì
bright
昳麗(ㄧˋ ㄌㄧˋ)
radiantly beautiful

【昝】 2235 ㄗㄢˇ tzaan zǎn
a Chinese family name

【昪】 2236 ㄅㄧㄢˋ biann biàn
1. happy; joyful; pleasing
2. sunshine
3. light; brightness; bright

【昺】 2237 (昞) ㄅㄧㄥˇ biing bǐng
bright; glorious; brilliant; radiant

【昜】 2238 (陽) ㄧㄤˊ yang yáng
bright; glorious

六畫

【晏】 2239 ㄧㄢˋ yann yàn
1. clear (sky, sea, water, etc.)
2. late
3. peaceful; quiet
4. a Chinese family name
晏寂(ㄧㄢˋ ㄐㄧˊ)
very quiet and silent
晏駕(ㄧㄢˋ ㄐㄧㄚˋ)
the death of an emperor
晏起(ㄧㄢˋ ㄑㄧˇ)
to get up late
晏寢(ㄧㄢˋ ㄑㄧㄣˇ)
to sit up late
晏朝(ㄧㄢˋ ㄔㄠˊ)
the evening session of the imperial court
晏然(ㄧㄢˋ ㄖㄢˊ)
peaceful and easy; quiet and comfortable: 這位老者晏然自得。This old gentleman looks peaceful and easy.
晏如(ㄧㄢˋ ㄖㄨˊ)
peaceful and easy
晏子(ㄧㄢˋ ㄗˇ)
Yen Ying (晏嬰), prime minister of Chi (齊) in the reign of Ching Kung (景公) during the Epoch of Spring and Autumn, famous for personal integrity and hard work
晏子春秋(ㄧㄢˋ ㄗˇ ㄔㄨㄣ ㄑㄧㄡ)
a collection of episodes of Yen Ying by an unknown author
晏晏(ㄧㄢˋ ㄧㄢˋ)
mild and tender

【時】 2240 (旹) ㄕˊ shyr shí

1. a season
2. an era; an epoch; an age; a period
3. time; fixed time
4. hours
5. often; frequently
6. fashionable
7. proper and adequate
8. opportune (moments); opportunity
9. timely; seasonable
10. now...now...; sometimes... sometimes...
11. a Chinese family name

時輩(ㄕˊ ㄅㄟˋ)
capable persons of the time

時弊(ㄕˊ ㄅㄧˋ)
current failings; present-day errors; ills of the time

時變(ㄕˊ ㄅㄧㄢˋ)
① the development of national or international events ② a change of seasons

時病(ㄕˊ ㄅㄧㄥˋ)
① the malady of the age ② (Chinese medicine) seasonal ailments

時不再來(ㄕˊ ㄅㄨˋ ㄗㄞˋ ㄌㄞˊ)
Such opportunity will not present itself again.

時不可失(ㄕˊ ㄅㄨˋ ㄎㄜˇ ㄕ)
Now or never! 或 Don't lose the opportune moment or opportunity.

時不我與(ㄕˊ ㄅㄨˋ ㄨㄛˇ ㄩˇ)
Time and tide wait for no one.

時不常兒(ㄕˊ ˙ㄅㄨ ㄔㄤˊ ㄦˊ)
often; frequently: 這事時不常兒發生。It happens frequently.

時牌(ㄕˊ ㄆㄞˊ)
(in ancient China) ivory boards on which time of the day was announced

時派(ㄕˊ ㄆㄞˋ)or 時道(ㄕˊ ㄉㄠˋ)
fashionable (dress, behavior, conduct, etc.)

時評(ㄕˊ ㄆㄧㄥˊ)
news commentaries; comments on current events

時髦(ㄕˊ ㄇㄠˊ)
fashionable; modern; up-to-date: 她戴着一頂時髦的帽子。She wears a fashionable hat.

時命(ㄕˊ ㄇㄧㄥˋ)
① one's fate, fortune or luck ②current government orders

時分(ㄕˊ ㄈㄣˋ)
① seasons; periods ② time

時風(ㄕˊ ㄈㄥ)
timely winds

時代(ㄕˊ ㄉㄞˋ)
an era; an epoch; a period; an age; times

時代病(ㄕˊ ㄉㄞˋ ㄅㄧㄥˋ)
diseases of the modern times — anxiety, neurosis, suspicion, etc.

時代精神(ㄕˊ ㄉㄞˋ ㄐㄧㄥ ㄕㄣˊ)
① the spirit or aspiration of a certain period or age ② aggressive spirit

時代青年(ㄕˊ ㄉㄞˋ ㄑㄧㄥ ㄋㄧㄢˊ)
the modern youth (connoting progressiveness in outlook)

時代雜誌(ㄕˊ ㄉㄞˋ ㄗㄚˊ ㄓˋ)
Time magazine

時代錯誤(ㄕˊ ㄉㄞˋ ㄘㄨㄛˋ ㄨˋ)
anachronism

時代思潮(ㄕˊ ㄉㄞˋ ㄙ ㄔㄠˊ)
the current trend of thoughts: 現在的時代思潮是民主與科學。The current trend of thoughts is democracy and science.

時態(ㄕˊ ㄊㄞˋ)
(grammar) tense

時鳥(ㄕˊ ㄋㄧㄠˇ)
migrating birds; birds of the season 亦作「候鳥」

時來運轉(ㄕˊ ㄌㄞˊ ㄩㄣˋ ㄓㄨㄢˇ)
to get a break (after a long period of bad luck)

時令(ㄕˊ ㄌㄧㄥˋ)
time of year; seasons

時論(ㄕˊ ㄌㄨㄣˋ)
public opinion of the time

時過境遷(ㄕˊ ㄍㄨㄛˋ ㄐㄧㄥˋ ㄑㄧㄢ)
Things have changed with the passage of time.

時光(ㄕˊ ㄍㄨㄤ)
time: 時光會證明誰是對的。Time will show who is right.

時刻(ㄕˊ ㄎㄜˋ)
① time; hour ② always; constantly; continually

時刻表(ㄕˊ ㄎㄜˋ ㄅㄧㄠˇ)
a timetable; a schedule

時候(ㄕˊ ㄏㄡˋ)
time; hour; moment; juncture: 現在是什麼時候了? What time is it?

時貨(ㄕˊ ㄏㄨㄛˋ)
seasonable commodities

時會(ㄕˊ ㄏㄨㄟˋ)
① good luck; opportunity; the opportune moment ② (now rarely) to meet frequently

時諱(ㄕˊ ㄏㄨㄟˋ)
things or words, etc. to be avoided in conversations during a certain period of time

時機(ㄕˊ ㄐㄧ)
the opportune moment; opportunity

時機成熟(ㄕˊ ㄐㄧ ㄔㄥˊ ㄕㄡˊ)
(literally) The opportunity is ripe.—The right time has come. 或 The opportune moment is here.

時疾(ㄕˊ ㄐㄧˊ)
(Chinese medicine) seasonal ailments or diseases

時忌(ㄕˊ ㄐㄧˋ)
things, words, ideas, etc. to be avoided in conversations during certain times

時價(ㄕˊ ㄐㄧㄚˋ)
current prices; prevailing prices; (in a menu) according to the cost of the time when the dish is served

時節
①(ㄕˊ ㄐㄧㄝˊ)ⓐ occasion ⓑ a period of the year; season ②(ㄕˊ˙ㄐㄧㄝ)ⓐ time ⓑ a period of the year

時艱(ㄕˊ ㄐㄧㄢ)
perils of the time; difficult times or critical national situations

時間(ㄕˊ ㄐㄧㄢ)
①time; the hour: 時間即金錢。Time is money. ②time—as opposed to space

時間表(ㄕˊ ㄐㄧㄢ ㄅㄧㄠˇ)
a timetable; a schedule

時間性(ㄕˊ ㄐㄧㄢ ㄒㄧㄥˋ)
the time factor: 新聞報導有時間性。News reports must be timely.

時禁(ㄕˊ ㄐㄧㄣˋ)
current prohibitions

時景(ㄕˊ ㄐㄧㄥˇ)

scenery at the time or of the season
時局(ㄕˊ ㄐㄩˊ)
the national situation; the state of national affairs; the world situation
時局平靖(ㄕˊ ㄐㄩˊ ㄆㄧㄥˊ ㄐㄧㄥˋ)
in time of peace; a peaceful situation
時期(ㄕˊ ㄑㄧˊ)
① times; a period; an age; an era ② duration
時氣
①(ㄕˊ ㄑㄧˋ) ⓐa climate ⓑan epidemic
②(ㄕˊ ˙ㄑㄧ)luck of the moment
時下(ㄕˊ ㄒㄧㄚˋ)
nowadays; in these days: 時下人們旅行都坐汽車了。Nowadays people travel in automobiles.
時效(ㄕˊ ㄒㄧㄠˋ)
(law) prescription; the duration of validity
時鮮(ㄕˊ ㄒㄧㄢ)
seasonable delicacies
時賢(ㄕˊ ㄒㄧㄢˊ)
contemporary men of ability and integrity
時限(ㄕˊ ㄒㄧㄢˋ)
a time limit; a deadline: 這張信用狀是有時限的。This letter of credit has a time limit.
時興(ㄕˊ ㄒㄧㄥ)
fashionable or seasonable; in vogue; popular; prevailing; faddish
時行(ㄕˊ ㄒㄧㄥˊ)
① fashionable or prevailing in a certain period of time; faddish ② (now rarely) to wait for the opportune moment to take action
時序(ㄕˊ ㄒㄩˋ)
seasons; times
時序易遷(ㄕˊ ㄒㄩˋ ㄧˋ ㄑㄧㄢ)
The seasons change.
時雪(ㄕˊ ㄒㄩㄝˇ)
a timely snow
時值(ㄕˊ ㄓˊ)
①the time being...; the time coinciding with... 或 It happened at a time when... ② the going price
時至今日(ㄕˊ ㄓˋ ㄐㄧㄣ ㄖˋ)
at this late hour; up to now
時針(ㄕˊ ㄓㄣ)
the hour hand of a clock or watch
時政(ㄕˊ ㄓㄥˋ)
① to take certain measures in government administration as the time demands ② government orders and regulations at the time
時症(ㄕˊ ㄓㄥˋ)
(Chinese medicine) ailments or diseases caused by abnormal weather conditions; an epidemic
時裝(ㄕˊ ㄓㄨㄤ)
① dresses in style or vogue; latest fashion; fashionable dresses ②(in show biz) modern dresses (as contrasted to ancient costumes)
時裝展覽(ㄕˊ ㄓㄨㄤ ㄓㄢˇ ㄌㄢˇ)
a fashion show
時中(ㄕˊ ㄓㄨㄥ)
propriety; proper and exact; impeccable; impeccability
時鐘(ㄕˊ ㄓㄨㄥ)
a clock
時差(ㄕˊ ㄔㄚ)
①(astronomy) the equation of time ② the time difference of two places located on different longitudes or time zones
時辰(ㄕˊ ˙ㄔㄣ)
① the 12 divisions of a day named after the 12 Terrestrial Branches: 子, 丑, 寅, 卯, 辰, 巳, 午, 未, 申, 酉, 戌, 亥 ② the time for...; an opportunity: 這時辰起程正好。It is the right time for us to go.
時常(ㄕˊ ㄔㄤˊ)
often; usually; frequently: 她時常想起往事。She often recalls the past.
時時(ㄕˊ ㄕˊ)
often; frequently; continually: 這種事時時發生。Things like this happen frequently.
時時刻刻(ㄕˊ ㄕˊ ㄎㄜˋ ㄎㄜˋ)
continuously; constantly; always
時…時…(ㄕˊ…ㄕˊ…)
off and on; intermittent; now ... now...
時食(ㄕˊ ㄕˊ)
seasonable delicacies
時式(ㄕˊ ㄕˋ)
the modern style; the modern fashion
時事(ㄕˊ ㄕˋ)
the current state of affairs; current events
時事評論(ㄕˊ ㄕˋ ㄆㄧㄥˊ ㄌㄨㄣˋ)
criticisms on current events
時勢(ㄕˊ ㄕˋ)
the trend of times; the time and circumstances
時勢使然(ㄕˊ ㄕˋ ㄕˇ ㄖㄢˊ)
It's the natural outcome of the time and circumstances.
時勢造英雄(ㄕˊ ㄕˋ ㄗㄠˋ ㄧㄥ ㄒㄩㄥˊ)
A hero is nothing but a product of his time. 或 There would be no heroes if the time and circumstances do not give them the opportunity to distinguish themselves.
時尚(ㄕˊ ㄕㄤˋ)or 時好(ㄕˊ ㄏㄠˇ)
a fad; current fashion or style
時衰(ㄕˊ ㄕㄨㄞ)
the decline of luck, fortune, etc.
時日(ㄕˊ ㄖˋ)
① time ② an auspicious time ③ this day
時日變更線(ㄕˊ ㄖˋ ㄅㄧㄢˋ ㄍㄥ ㄒㄧㄢˋ)
the international date line 亦作「國際換日線」
時人(ㄕˊ ㄖㄣˊ)
contemporaries
時而(ㄕˊ ㄦˊ)
from time to time; sometimes
時而後言(ㄕˊ ㄦˊ ㄏㄡˋ ㄧㄢˊ)
to wait for the right moment to talk
時宜(ㄕˊ ㄧˊ)
what is considered proper at the time
時疫(ㄕˊ ㄧˋ)
an epidemic
時彥(ㄕˊ ㄧㄢˋ)
contemporary men of ability and integrity
時諺(ㄕˊ ㄧㄢˋ)
mottos or proverbs in a certain period of time
時樣(ㄕˊ ㄧㄤˋ)
the vogue, style or fashion at the time

時務(ㄕˊ ㄨˋ)
①circumstances of the time: 他不識時務。He shows no understanding of the times. ② farm work calling for one's attention at the moment
時文(ㄕˊ ㄨㄣˊ)
a peculiar style of writing adopted by candidates during the civil service examinations of the Ching Dynasty known as the "eight-legged" writing (八股文)
時望(ㄕˊ ㄨㄤˋ)
① celebrities of the time ② popular fame; popular support: 這位詩人深負時望。This poet enjoys popular fame.
時雨(ㄕˊ ㄩˇ)
① timely rains ② culture and education
時遇(ㄕˊ ㄩˋ)
favors one receives; a good break one gets; one's luck
時遇不濟(ㄕˊ ㄩˋ ㄅㄨˋ ㄐㄧˋ)
to be out of luck: 每個人都會有時遇不濟的時候。Everyone would be out of luck sometimes.
時運亨通(ㄕˊ ㄩㄣˋ ㄏㄥ ㄊㄨㄥ)
to be lucky; to hit the jackpot: 他近來時運亨通。He has been lucky and prosperous recently.

【晉】 2241 (晋) ㄐㄧㄣˋ jinn jìn
1. to advance; to increase; to flourish
2. Tsin (a state during the Epoch of Spring and Autumn, occupying parts of today's Shansi and Hopeh Provinces)
3. another name for Shansi Province
4. the Tsin Dynasty (265-420 A. D.)
5. a Chinese family name
晉封(ㄐㄧㄣˋ ㄈㄥ)
(Ching Dynasty) to bestow honors on the parents, grandparents, great-grandparents and wife of one who had rendered meritorious services to the state
晉國(ㄐㄧㄣˋ ㄍㄨㄛˊ)
the state of Tsin during the Epoch of Spring and Autumn 參看「晉 2.」
晉級(ㄐㄧㄣˋ ㄐㄧˊ)
promotion; to promote
晉接(ㄐㄧㄣˋ ㄐㄧㄝ)
to receive (visitors, etc.); to welcome
晉見(ㄐㄧㄣˋ ㄐㄧㄢˋ)
to call on (a superior); to have an audience with
晉京(ㄐㄧㄣˋ ㄐㄧㄥ)
to proceed to the national capital
晉爵(ㄐㄧㄣˋ ㄐㄩㄝˊ)
to rise in (feudal or noble) rank
晉朝(ㄐㄧㄣˋ ㄔㄠˊ)
the Tsin Dynasty (265-420 A. D.)
晉授(ㄐㄧㄣˋ ㄕㄡˋ)
(Ching Dynasty) to confer further honors on
晉升(ㄐㄧㄣˋ ㄕㄥ)
to rise in rank; to promote; to increase
晉書(ㄐㄧㄣˋ ㄕㄨ)
The History of the Tsin Dynasty, a 130-volume work compiled by 21 historians during the Tang Dynasty
晉謁(ㄐㄧㄣˋ ㄧㄝˋ)
to visit or call on (a superior or leader)
晉武帝(ㄐㄧㄣˋ ㄨˇ ㄉㄧˋ)
Ssu-Ma Yen (司馬炎), 236-290 A.D., the founding emperor of the Tsin Dynasty
晉文公(ㄐㄧㄣˋ ㄨㄣˊ ㄍㄨㄥ)
Wen Kung, a ruler of the state of Tsin in the Epoch of Spring and Autumn
晉約秦盟(ㄐㄧㄣˋ ㄩㄝ ㄑㄧㄣˊ ㄇㄥˊ)
to enter into a matrimonial contract 參看「秦晉之好」

【晃】 2242 1. ㄏㄨㄤˇ hoang huǎng
1. brightness
2. dazzling; glaring
3. a flash; to flash past; to appear and disappear very quickly
晃朗(ㄏㄨㄤˇ ㄌㄤˇ)
bright and brilliant
晃晃(ㄏㄨㄤˇ ㄏㄨㄤˇ)
dazzling (usually used to describe light reflected from polished metals)
晃曜 or 晃耀(ㄏㄨㄤˇ ㄧㄠˋ)
radiant

【晃】 2242 2. ㄏㄨㄤˋ huanq huàng
to rock; to sway; to shake
晃蕩(ㄏㄨㄤˋ ㄉㄤˋ)
to sway; to oscillate; to shake: 旗子在風中不停地晃蕩。The flag kept swaying in the wind.
晃動(ㄏㄨㄤˋ ㄉㄨㄥˋ)
to rock; to sway: 這船有點晃動。The boat rocks a bit.
晃晃悠悠(ㄏㄨㄤˋ ·ㄏㄨㄤ ㄧㄡ ㄧㄡ)
to stagger; to wobble; swaying; unstable
晃搖(ㄏㄨㄤˋ ·ㄧㄠ)
to sway; swaying; to shake; oscillating
晃漾(ㄏㄨㄤˋ ㄧㄤˋ)
to sway; swaying

【晁】 2243 ㄔㄠˊ chaur cháo
1. an ancient form of 朝
2. a Chinese family name

【晌】 2244 ㄕㄤˇ shaang shǎng
1. high noon
2. a certain duration or interval of time
3. (Northeast China dialect) a day's work
晌飯(ㄕㄤˇ ㄈㄢˋ)
(dialect) a midday meal; lunch
晌午(ㄕㄤˇ ·ㄏㄨㄛ)
(colloquial) high noon; midday

七畫

【晟】 2245 ㄕㄥˋ shenq shèng (又讀 ㄔㄥˊ cherng chéng)
the brightness of the sun; light; splendor

【晚】 2246 ㄨㄢˇ woan wǎn
1. sunset; evening; night: 明晚以前我不會回來。I shan't be back before tomorrow night.
2. late: 晚做總比不做好。Better late than never.
3. drawing toward the end
4. younger; junior
晚輩(ㄨㄢˇ ㄅㄟˋ)

the younger generation; one's juniors
晚報(ㄨㄢˇ ㄅㄠˋ)
an evening paper; an afternoon paper
晚班(ㄨㄢˇ ㄅㄢ)
the night shift
晚半天兒(ㄨㄢˇ ·ㄅㄢ ㄊㄧㄚㄦ)
late afternoon
晚半晌兒(ㄨㄢˇ ·ㄅㄢ ㄕㄤˇㄦ)
dusk; the twilight hour
晚明小品(ㄨㄢˇ ㄇㄧㄥˊ ㄒㄧㄠˇ ㄆㄧㄣˇ)
essays of the late Ming Dynasty
晚飯(ㄨㄢˇ ㄈㄢˋ)or 晚餐(ㄨㄢˇ ㄘㄢ)
dinner; supper
晚福(ㄨㄢˇ ㄈㄨˊ)
good fortune that comes late in one's life; happiness in one's closing years; old age bliss
晚達(ㄨㄢˇ ㄉㄚˊ)
to attain officialdom or get rich and well-to-do in the latter part of one's life
晚禱(ㄨㄢˇ ㄉㄠˇ)
evening prayers; vespers
晚到(ㄨㄢˇ ㄉㄠˋ)
to arrive late
晚稻(ㄨㄢˇ ㄉㄠˋ)or 晚禾(ㄨㄢˇ ㄏㄜˊ)
a late crop of rice; the second rice crop of a year
晚唐(ㄨㄢˇ ㄊㄤˊ)
the late Tang Dynasty (often mentioned in connection with poetry)
晚年(ㄨㄢˇ ㄋㄧㄢˊ)
old age; one's later (or remaining) years
晚娘(ㄨㄢˇ ㄋㄧㄤˊ)
a stepmother
晚娘面孔(ㄨㄢˇ ㄋㄧㄤˊ ㄇㄧㄢˋ ㄎㄨㄥˇ)
(literally) a stepmother's face—an unsmiling face; a sullen look
晚了(ㄨㄢˇ ·ㄌㄜ)
It's getting late. 或 It's too late.
晚來(ㄨㄢˇ ㄌㄞˊ)
to come late
晚禮服(ㄨㄢˇ ㄌㄧˇ ㄈㄨˊ)
formal evening dress
晚會(ㄨㄢˇ ㄏㄨㄟˋ)
a night party; an evening gathering or meeting
晚婚(ㄨㄢˇ ㄏㄨㄣ)
late marriage; to marry late in one's life: 他晚婚。He married late in his life.
晚節(ㄨㄢˇ ㄐㄧㄝˊ)
① one's integrity in his closing years ② old age; one's closing years ③ closing years of a dynasty
晚間(ㄨㄢˇ ㄐㄧㄢ)
evening; night; nocturnal: 他習慣於晚間讀書。He is used to studying at night.
晚近(ㄨㄢˇ ㄐㄧㄣˋ)
lately; recently; modern
晚進(ㄨㄢˇ ㄐㄧㄣˋ)
a newcomer; a junior
晚景(ㄨㄢˇ ㄐㄧㄥˇ)
① scenes at sunset ② circumstances in one's old age
晚期(ㄨㄢˇ ㄑㄧˊ)
the later period
晚起(ㄨㄢˇ ㄑㄧˇ)
to rise or get up late
晚秋(ㄨㄢˇ ㄑㄧㄡ)
late autumn
晚霞(ㄨㄢˇ ㄒㄧㄚˊ)
rosy clouds just before sunset; sunset clouds
晚香玉(ㄨㄢˇ ㄒㄧㄤ ㄩˋ)
(botany) white lily, or tuberose (*Polianthes tuberosa*)
晚學(ㄨㄢˇ ㄒㄩㄝˊ)or 晚學生(ㄨㄢˇ ㄒㄩㄝˊ ·ㄕㄥ)
your pupil (a polite term referring to oneself when addressing a senior)
晚照(ㄨㄢˇ ㄓㄠˋ)
the shining of the setting sun
晚莊稼(ㄨㄢˇ ㄓㄨㄤ ·ㄐㄧㄚ)
a late harvest; a late crop
晚車(ㄨㄢˇ ㄔㄜ)
a night train or bus: 我沒趕上往台中的晚車。I missed the night train for Taichung.
晚場(ㄨㄢˇ ㄔㄤˇ)
an evening show; an evening performance
晚食當肉(ㄨㄢˇ ㄕˊ ㄉㄤˋ ㄖㄡˋ)
Eating late is as good as enjoying meat.
晚世(ㄨㄢˇ ㄕˋ)
modern times; recent years
晚熟(ㄨㄢˇ ㄕㄡˊ)
①(said of plants) to ripen late ②(said of a person) to mature late; a late bloomer
晚上(ㄨㄢˇ ·ㄕㄤ)
in the evening or night: 秋天晚上很涼爽。It is cool in the autumn evening.
晚生(ㄨㄢˇ ㄕㄥ)
a humble term referring to oneself when addressing a senior or superior
晚歲(ㄨㄢˇ ㄙㄨㄟˋ)
①in recent years; lately ② a late harvest ③ old age; one's later years
晚安(ㄨㄢˇ ㄢ)
Good evening! 或 Good night!
晚宴(ㄨㄢˇ ㄧㄢˋ)
a dinner party
晚豔(ㄨㄢˇ ㄧㄢˋ)
①chrysanthemum ②flowers that blossom late
晚運(ㄨㄢˇ ㄩㄣˋ)
one's lot during old age

【晝】 2247
ㄓㄡˋ jow zhòu
1. day; daytime; daylight
2. a Chinese family name
晝盲(ㄓㄡˋ ㄇㄤˊ)
(medicine) hemeralopia
晝分(ㄓㄡˋ ㄈㄣ)
high noon
晝伏夜行(ㄓㄡˋ ㄈㄨˊ ㄧㄝˋ ㄒㄧㄥˊ)
to lie low in daytime and act at night
晝短圈(ㄓㄡˋ ㄉㄨㄢˇ ㄑㄩㄢ)
the Tropic of Capricorn 亦作「南回歸線」
晝晦(ㄓㄡˋ ㄏㄨㄟˋ)
dim sunshine (as in a cloudy day, etc.)
晝寢(ㄓㄡˋ ㄑㄧㄣˇ)
to take a nap; a siesta; to be asleep during the day
晝長圈(ㄓㄡˋ ㄔㄤˊ ㄑㄩㄢ)
the Tropic of Cancer 亦作「北回歸線」
晝日(ㄓㄡˋ ㄖˋ)
a day; daytime
晝夜(ㄓㄡˋ ㄧㄝˋ)
day and night; round the clock: 他們晝夜警戒。They were on a round-the-clock alert.
晝夜不息(ㄓㄡˋ ㄧㄝˋ ㄅㄨˋ ㄒㄧˊ)
(to work, etc.) day and night without rest or stop
晝夜平分(ㄓㄡˋ ㄧㄝˋ ㄆㄧㄥˊ ㄈㄣ)
the equinox

晝夜平分線(ㄓㄡˋ ㄧㄝˋ ㄆㄧㄥˊ ㄈㄣ ㄒㄧㄢˋ) the equinoctial line 亦作「赤道」

【晞】 2248 ㄒㄧ shi xī
1. to dry in the sun; dry
2. sunshine at daybreak
晞髮(ㄒㄧ ㄈㄚˇ) to loosen the hair in order to dry it

【晡】 2249 ㄅㄨ bu bū
afternoon
晡時(ㄅㄨ ㄕˊ) late afternoon (about 4 p.m.)

【晤】 2250 ㄨˋ wuh wù
1. to meet; to see face to face
2. enlightened; wise
晤面(ㄨˋ ㄇㄧㄢˋ) to meet; to see each other
晤對(ㄨˋ ㄉㄨㄟˋ) to meet face to face
晤談(ㄨˋ ㄊㄢˊ) to meet and talk; to converse; to discuss face to face
晤歌(ㄨˋ ㄍㄜ) to sing face to face
晤商(ㄨˋ ㄕㄤ) a face-to-face negotiation; to discuss in an interview
晤言(ㄨˋ ㄧㄢˊ) or 晤語(ㄨˋ ㄩˇ) to meet and talk

【晦】 2251 ㄏㄨㄟˋ huey huì
1. the last day of every month in the lunar calendar
2. night; evening; dark
3. obscure; indistinguishable
4. unlucky; bad luck
晦盲(ㄏㄨㄟˋ ㄇㄤˊ) to see nothing because of darkness
晦蒙(ㄏㄨㄟˋ ㄇㄥˊ) dark, obscure, or gloomy (used figuratively to describe the chaos of troubled times)
晦明(ㄏㄨㄟˋ ㄇㄧㄥˊ) night and day
晦冥(ㄏㄨㄟˋ ㄇㄧㄥˊ) dark and gloomy
晦匿(ㄏㄨㄟˋ ㄋㄧˋ) to retire into obscurity
晦迹(ㄏㄨㄟˋ ㄐㄧ) to retire into obscurity
晦氣(ㄏㄨㄟˋ ㄑㄧˋ) unlucky; bad luck; to encounter rough going
晦氣星(ㄏㄨㄟˋ ㄑㄧˋ ㄒㄧㄥ) the deity that metes out bad luck to a person; a star of ill luck
晦顯(ㄏㄨㄟˋ ㄒㄧㄢˇ) obscure and obvious; obscurity and manifestation
晦朔(ㄏㄨㄟˋ ㄕㄨㄛˋ) the last and first days of a lunar month
晦暗(ㄏㄨㄟˋ ㄢˋ) dark; gloomy
晦往明來(ㄏㄨㄟˋ ㄨㄤˇ ㄇㄧㄥˊ ㄌㄞˊ) as day follows night and night follows day

【晧】 2252 ㄏㄠˋ haw hào
1. daybreak
2. bright and brilliant

【晨】 2253 ㄔㄣˊ chern chén
1. morning; daybreak
2. (said of a cock) to announce the arrival of morning; to crow at dawn
晨風(ㄔㄣˊ ㄈㄥ) ① morning breezes: 我們享受自山上吹來的晨風。We are enjoying the morning breeze that comes from the mountain. ② name of a bird of the hawk family
晨光(ㄔㄣˊ ㄍㄨㄤ) daylight; daybreak; the dimness before dawn
晨昏(ㄔㄣˊ ㄏㄨㄣ) or 晨夕(ㄔㄣˊ ㄒㄧ) morning and evening
晨昏顛倒(ㄔㄣˊ ㄏㄨㄣ ㄉㄧㄢ ㄉㄠˇ) to mistake morning for evening and evening for morning—confused
晨昏定省(ㄔㄣˊ ㄏㄨㄣ ㄉㄧㄥˋ ㄒㄧㄥˇ) to pay respects to one's elders—especially to one's parents—in the morning (when they get up) and in the evening (when they retire)
晨雞(ㄔㄣˊ ㄐㄧ) the crowing of cocks at daybreak
晨間(ㄔㄣˊ ㄐㄧㄢ) in the morning: 很多人在晨間慢跑。Many people jog in the morning.
晨曦(ㄔㄣˊ ㄒㄧ) morning light; daybreak
晨星(ㄔㄣˊ ㄒㄧㄥ) ① morning stars ② things that are scarce and rare
晨鐘暮鼓(ㄔㄣˊ ㄓㄨㄥ ㄇㄨˋ ㄍㄨˇ) (literally) the bell in the morning and the drum in the evening—bells and drums used in Buddhist temples in announcing time and arousing people to renewed faith 亦作「暮鼓晨鐘」
晨炊(ㄔㄣˊ ㄔㄨㄟ) morning cooking; breakfast
晨操(ㄔㄣˊ ㄘㄠ) morning exercise; morning calisthenics: 晨操有益於健康。Morning exercises are good for the health.

八畫

【晬】 2254 ㄗㄨㄟˋ tzuey zuì
1. the first birth anniversary of a child
2. anniversary
晬盤(ㄗㄨㄟˋ ㄆㄢˊ) a tray holding various articles taken before a child on the first anniversary of his birth to see which of the articles he grasps as a test to determine the career he is likely to follow in the future

【普】 2255 ㄆㄨˇ puu pǔ
1. universal; widespread; general; everywhere; all: 電視提供了普遍性的娛樂。Television provides universal entertainment.
2. Prussia
3. a Chinese family name
普偏 or 普遍(ㄆㄨˇ ㄅㄧㄢˋ) universal; general; widespread; everywhere; common: 運動受到普遍的喜愛。There is a general interest in sports.
普偏性 or 普遍性(ㄆㄨˇ ㄅㄧㄢˋ ㄒㄧㄥˋ) universality
普法戰爭(ㄆㄨˇ ㄈㄚˇ ㄓㄢˋ ㄓㄥ) the Franco-Prussian War in 1870-1871 A. D.
普汎(ㄆㄨˇ ㄈㄢˋ)

〔日部〕

general; widespread; universal

普渡(ㄆㄨˇ ㄉㄨˋ)
(Buddhism) to save all with mercy

普渡衆生(ㄆㄨˇ ㄉㄨˋ ㄓㄨㄥˋ ㄕㄥ)
(Buddhism) to deliver or save all beings: 佛教的宗旨在普渡衆生。The purpose of Buddhism is to deliver all beings.

普天同慶(ㄆㄨˇ ㄊㄧㄢ ㄊㄨㄥˊ ㄑㄧㄥˋ)
The whole world joins in the rejoicing, celebration or congratulations.

普天之下(ㄆㄨˇ ㄊㄧㄢ ㄓ ㄒㄧㄚˋ)
all under the heavens; all over the world

普天率土(ㄆㄨˇ ㄊㄧㄢ ㄕㄨㄞˋ ㄊㄨˇ)
the whole world

普陀山(ㄆㄨˇ ㄊㄨㄛˊ ㄕㄢ)
Mount Puto at Tinghai County (定海) of Chekiang Province, the site of one of the biggest Buddhist temples in China

普通(ㄆㄨˇ ㄊㄨㄥ)
ordinary; common; plain; average: 冬天裡感冒是很普通的。Colds are common in winter.

普通名詞(ㄆㄨˇ ㄊㄨㄥ ㄇㄧㄥˊ ㄘˊ)
common nouns

普通法(ㄆㄨˇ ㄊㄨㄥ ㄈㄚˇ)
common law

普通考試(ㄆㄨˇ ㄊㄨㄥ ㄎㄠˇ ㄕˋ)
the junior-grade civil service examination (in modern China)

普通會計(ㄆㄨˇ ㄊㄨㄥ ㄎㄨㄞˋ ㄐㄧˋ)
general accounting

普通話(ㄆㄨˇ ㄊㄨㄥ ㄏㄨㄚˋ)
the common dialect of the Chinese language; Mandarin

普通教育(ㄆㄨˇ ㄊㄨㄥ ㄐㄧㄠˋ ㄩˋ)
elementary education: 每個人都應當接受普通教育。Everyone should receive elementary education.

普通心理學(ㄆㄨˇ ㄊㄨㄥ ㄒㄧㄣ ㄌㄧˇ ㄒㄩㄝˊ)
general psychology

普通支票(ㄆㄨˇ ㄊㄨㄥ ㄓ ㄆㄧㄠˋ)
an open check

普林斯頓(ㄆㄨˇ ㄌㄧㄣˊ ㄙ ㄉㄨㄣˋ)
① Princeton, in New Jersey
② Princeton University

普魯士(ㄆㄨˇ ㄌㄨˇ ㄕˋ)
Prussia

普羅文學(ㄆㄨˇ ㄌㄨㄛˊ ㄨㄣˊ ㄒㄩㄝˊ)
proletarian literature

普告天下(ㄆㄨˇ ㄍㄠˋ ㄊㄧㄢ ㄒㄧㄚˋ)
to announce to the world; to make publicly known

普及(ㄆㄨˇ ㄐㄧˊ)
① universal; available to all ② to popularize; to disseminate

普及本(ㄆㄨˇ ㄐㄧˊ ㄅㄣˇ)
a cheap edition; a paperback edition

普及教育(ㄆㄨˇ ㄐㄧˊ ㄐㄧㄠˋ ㄩˋ)
universal education; compulsory or mandatory education

普降甘霖(ㄆㄨˇ ㄐㄧㄤˋ ㄍㄢ ㄌㄧㄣˊ)
timely rain for all drought areas

普希金(ㄆㄨˇ ㄒㄧ ㄐㄧㄣ)
Alexander Pushkin, 1799-1837, Russian poet

普選(ㄆㄨˇ ㄒㄩㄢˇ)
universal suffrage; general elections

普照(ㄆㄨˇ ㄓㄠˋ)
(said of sunshine, God's grace, etc.) to shine upon all: 陽光普照大地。The sun shines every corner of the land.

普查(ㄆㄨˇ ㄔㄚˊ)
a general survey

普施(ㄆㄨˇ ㄕ)
to give contributions to charity in every direction

普洱茶(ㄆㄨˇ ㄦˇ ㄔㄚˊ)
tea brick produced at 普洱 in Yunnan Province

【景】 2256

1. ㄐㄧㄥˇ jiing jǐng

1. scenery; views: 我很喜歡山景。I enjoy mountain scenery very much.
2. prospects; circumstances; situations: 好景不常。The good circumstances don't last long.
3. (in motion pictures, stage shows, etc.) settings; background scenes: 休息時間換景。The scenes are changed during the intervals.
4. big and strong
5. great
6. high
7. bright and luminous
8. to admire; to respect: 我們都景仰誠實的人。We all respect honest persons.
9. a Chinese family name

景命(ㄐㄧㄥˇ ㄇㄧㄥˋ)
the ruling power of the emperor (In ancient China, the emperor claimed that his ruling power was from Heaven.)

景慕(ㄐㄧㄥˇ ㄇㄨˋ)
to admire and respect: 他的聰明爲人所景慕。His cleverness is much admired and respected.

景福(ㄐㄧㄥˇ ㄈㄨˊ)
① great blessings; big happiness ② name of a reign in the Tang Dynasty (892-893A.D.)

景德鎭(ㄐㄧㄥˇ ㄉㄜˊ ㄓㄣˋ)
Ching Te Chen — a city in Kiangsi Province famous for its porcelains

景泰藍(ㄐㄧㄥˇ ㄊㄞˋ ㄌㄢˊ)
cloisonné, or Peiping enamel

景觀(ㄐㄧㄥˇ ㄍㄨㄢ)
(geography) landscape: 這地區的自然景觀很美妙。The natural landscape in this district is wonderful.

景況(ㄐㄧㄥˇ ㄎㄨㄤˋ)
(personal or general) circumstances, situations, conditions, etc.: 他的健康景況達到最佳地步。He is at the top of his condition.

景教(ㄐㄧㄥˇ ㄐㄧㄠˋ)
Nestorianism, a sect of Christianity, in the Tang Dynasty

景氣(ㄐㄧㄥˇ ㄑㄧˋ)
(economics) prosperity; booming: 和平帶來景氣。Peace brings prosperity.

景象(ㄐㄧㄥˇ ㄒㄧㄤˋ)
appearances; conditions; outlooks; scenes; sights

景星(ㄐㄧㄥˇ ㄒㄧㄥ)
auspicious stars

景星勳章(ㄐㄧㄥˇ ㄒㄧㄥ ㄒㄩㄣ ㄓㄤ)
the Order of Brilliant Star (one of the Chinese government decorations)

景行(ㄐㄧㄥˇ ㄒㄧㄥˋ)

high virtues
景致 or 景緻(ㄐㄧㄥˇ ㄓˋ)
scenery; scenes; views; pleasing views; a vista
景狀(ㄐㄧㄥˇ ㄓㄨㄤˋ)
appearances; conditions; circumstances
景色(ㄐㄧㄥˇ ㄙㄜˋ)
scenery; views; scenes; landscapes: 此山景色如畫。This mountain scenery is picturesque.
景兒(ㄐㄧㄥˇㄦ)
appearances; conditions; circumstances
景仰(ㄐㄧㄥˇ ㄧㄤˇ)
to admire and respect; to hold in deep respect; to look up to
景物(ㄐㄧㄥˇ ㄨˋ)
scenery; landscapes: 景物宜人 delightful scenery
景遇(ㄐㄧㄥˇ ㄩˋ)
(literally) circumstances; one's lot: 他目前的景遇相當不錯。His present circumstances are rather good.
景雲(ㄐㄧㄥˇ ㄩㄣˊ)
① bright clouds of many colors ② name of a reign (710-711) in the Tang Dynasty

【景】 2256
2. (影) ㄧㄥˇ yiing yǐng
shadow; reflection; image
景附(ㄧㄥˇ ㄈㄨˋ)
to follow closely
景從(ㄧㄥˇ ㄘㄨㄥˊ)
to follow (a great master, leader, etc.) like a shadow; popular support or following 亦作「影從」
景印(ㄧㄥˇ ㄧㄣˋ)
to print with photolithographic plates; a photolithographic copy or edition

【晰】 2257
ㄒㄧ shi xī
clear; clearly; distinct: 她的口齒清晰。Her speech is distinct.

【晳】 2258
ㄒㄧ shi xī
1. (said of one's skin) fair; white: 她的皮膚白晳晳。Her skin is very white.
2. to discriminate; to distinguish or differentiate

【晴】 2259
ㄑㄧㄥˊ chyng qíng
1. (said of the weather) fine; fair; bright; clear; not raining
2. when the rain stops
晴天(ㄑㄧㄥˊ ㄊㄧㄢ)
a fine day; a cloudless day: 明天會是晴天嗎? Will it be a fine day tomorrow?
晴天霹靂(ㄑㄧㄥˊ ㄊㄧㄢ ㄆㄧ ㄌㄧˋ)
a bolt from the blue 亦作「青天霹靂」
晴朗(ㄑㄧㄥˊ ㄌㄤˇ)
(said of the sky) fine and cloudless
晴空(ㄑㄧㄥˊ ㄎㄨㄥ)
a clear sky; a cloudless sky
晴空萬里(ㄑㄧㄥˊ ㄎㄨㄥ ㄨㄢˋ ㄌㄧˇ)
The clear sky stretches thousands of miles.—a clear and boundless sky
晴和(ㄑㄧㄥˊ ㄏㄜˊ)
fine and balmy (weather)
晴雨表(ㄑㄧㄥˊ ㄩˇ ㄅㄧㄠˇ) or 晴雨計(ㄑㄧㄥˊ ㄩˇ ㄐㄧˋ)
a barometer
晴雨無阻(ㄑㄧㄥˊ ㄩˇ ㄨˊ ㄗㄨˇ)
rain or shine

【晶】 2260
ㄐㄧㄥ jing jīng
1. crystal
2. bright; clear; brilliant; radiant; glittering
晶體(ㄐㄧㄥ ㄊㄧˇ)
(radio) crystal
晶婚紀念(ㄐㄧㄥ ㄏㄨㄣ ㄐㄧˋ ㄋㄧㄢˋ)
the crystal (the 15th) wedding anniversary
晶晶(ㄐㄧㄥ ㄐㄧㄥ)
bright and brilliant
晶質(ㄐㄧㄥ ㄓˊ)
crystalloid
晶質岩(ㄐㄧㄥ ㄓˊ ㄧㄢˊ)
crystalline rocks
晶狀體(ㄐㄧㄥ ㄓㄨㄤˋ ㄊㄧˇ)
(anatomy) crystalline lens, a doubly convex, transparent body in the eye
晶簇(ㄐㄧㄥ ㄘㄨˋ)
crystal druse
晶熒(ㄐㄧㄥ ㄧㄥˊ)
radiant; brilliant; shining
晶瑩(ㄐㄧㄥ ㄧㄥˊ)
sparkling: 荷葉上有晶瑩的露珠。There are sparkling dewdrops on the leaves of the lotus.

【晷】 2261
ㄍㄨㄟˇ goei guǐ
1. shadows caused by the sun
2. a sundial
3. time
晷刻(ㄍㄨㄟˇ ㄎㄜˋ)
① time ② a short time
晷儀(ㄍㄨㄟˇ ㄧˊ)
a sundial
晷影(ㄍㄨㄟˇ ㄧㄥˇ)
shadows

【智】 2262
ㄓˋ jyh zhì
1. talented; capable; intelligent; clever; wise; wisdom; knowledge; wit: 這人足智多謀。This person is wise and resourceful.
2. prudence
3. a Chinese family name
智謀(ㄓˋ ㄇㄡˊ)
cleverness; tactics; strategy; resourcefulness: 這些智謀將對他有所幫助。These tactics will help him.
智多星(ㄓˋ ㄉㄨㄛ ㄒㄧㄥ)
① a nickname for Wu Yung (吳用), the resourceful strategist in the *All Men Are Brothers* (水滸傳) ② a resourceful person; a mastermind
智囊(ㄓˋ ㄋㄤˊ)
a wise person; a wise advisor
智囊團(ㄓˋ ㄋㄤˊ ㄊㄨㄢˊ)
a brain trust; a think tank
智能(ㄓˋ ㄋㄥˊ)
intelligence and capability; knowledge and ability
智能不足(ㄓˋ ㄋㄥˊ ㄅㄨˋ ㄗㄨˊ)
mental retardation
智力(ㄓˋ ㄌㄧˋ)
intelligence: 他是一個缺乏智力的男孩。He is a boy who shows very little intelligence.
智力年齡(ㄓˋ ㄌㄧˋ ㄋㄧㄢˊ ㄌㄧㄥˊ)
mental age
智力商數(ㄓˋ ㄌㄧˋ ㄕㄤ ㄕㄨˋ) or 智商(ㄓˋ ㄕㄤ)
intelligence quotient (I.Q.)
智力測驗(ㄓˋ ㄌㄧˋ ㄘㄜˋ ㄧㄢˋ)
an intelligence test; an IQ test
智利(ㄓˋ ㄌㄧˋ)

Chile, or Chili
智利硝石(ㄓˋ ㄌㄧˋ ㄒㄧㄠ ㄕˊ)
Chile saltpeter
智慮(ㄓˋ ㄌㄩˋ)
wisdom: 他的爲人智慮深沉。He is a man of profound wisdom.
智略(ㄓˋ ㄌㄩㄝˋ)
intelligence and tact
智過萬人(ㄓˋ ㄍㄨㄛˋ ㄨㄢˋ ㄖㄣˊ)
(One's) intelligence is greater than that of 10,000 men put together.—extremely intelligent
智慧(ㄓˋ ㄏㄨㄟˋ)
wisdom; intelligence
智慧劍(ㄓˋ ㄏㄨㄟˋ ㄐㄧㄢˋ)
the power of making decisions which takes courage to make
智慧財產權(ㄓˋ ㄏㄨㄟˋ ㄘㄞˊ ㄔㄢˇ ㄑㄩㄢˊ)
intellectual property rights
智器(ㄓˋ ㄑㄧˋ)
talent
智巧(ㄓˋ ㄑㄧㄠˇ)
brains and tact: 他們沒有智巧。They have no brains and tact.
智取(ㄓˋ ㄑㄩˇ)
to triumph by means of strategy or tactics
智者 or 知者(ㄓˋ ㄓㄜˇ)
a wise man
智者千慮，必有一失(ㄓˋ ㄓㄜˇ ㄑㄧㄢ ㄌㄩˋ, ㄅㄧˋ ㄧㄡˇ ㄧˋ ㄕ)
(literally) No matter how hard an intelligent person thinks, he's going to miss something. 或 No one is infallible.
智齒(ㄓˋ ㄔˇ)
wisdom teeth
智識(ㄓˋ ㄕˋ)or 知識(ㄓ ㄕˋ)
knowledge: 智識即是力量。Knowledge is power.
智識份子(ㄓˋ ㄕˋ ㄈㄣˋ ㄗˇ)or 知識份子(ㄓ ㄕˋ ㄈㄣˋ ㄗˇ)
intellectuals; educated people; the intelligentsia
智識階級(ㄓˋ ㄕˋ ㄐㄧㄝ ㄐㄧˊ)or 知識階級(ㄓ ㄕˋ ㄐㄧㄝ ㄐㄧˊ)
the intelligentsia
智術(ㄓˋ ㄕㄨˋ)
trickery; stratagem
智仁勇(ㄓˋ ㄖㄣˊ ㄩㄥˇ)
wisdom, kindness and courage—motto of the Chinese boy scouts
智愚(ㄓˋ ㄩˊ)
the intelligent and the ignorant; the wise and the foolish
智育(ㄓˋ ㄩˋ)
education that aims at cultivating one's intelligence; mental training; intellectual education
智圓行方(ㄓˋ ㄩㄢˊ ㄒㄧㄥˊ ㄈㄤ)
round in knowledge but square in behavior—to be quick-witted in mind and never casual in one's behavior
智勇兼備(ㄓˋ ㄩㄥˇ ㄐㄧㄢ ㄅㄟˋ)or 智勇雙全(ㄓˋ ㄩㄥˇ ㄕㄨㄤ ㄑㄩㄢˊ)
combining the qualities of intelligence and bravery; both intelligent and brave; both prudent and courageous

【晾】 2263

ㄌㄧㄤˋ liang liàng

1. to dry in the air; to air; to hang in the wind to dry
2. to dry in the sun

晾乾(ㄌㄧㄤˋ ㄍㄢ)
to dry in the air; to hang in the wind to dry
晾開(ㄌㄧㄤˋ ㄎㄞ)
to spread out to dry
晾衣服(ㄌㄧㄤˋ ㄧ ·ㄈㄨ)
to hang clothes in the wind to dry; to dry clothes on laundry lines; to air clothes
晾一晾(ㄌㄧㄤˋ · ㄧ ㄌㄧㄤˋ)
to dry in the air

九畫

【暄】 2264

ㄒㄩㄢ shiuan xuān

1. comfortable and genial (climates); warm
2. (dialect) fluffy

暄風(ㄒㄩㄢ ㄈㄥ)
spring breeze
暄暖(ㄒㄩㄢ ㄋㄨㄢˇ)
warm and comfortable: 天氣漸漸暄暖了。It is getting warm and comfortable.
暄涼(ㄒㄩㄢ ㄌㄧㄤˊ)
greetings to one another
暄妍(ㄒㄩㄢ ㄧㄢˊ)
warm weather and captivating scenery (in spring)

【暇】 2265

ㄒㄧㄚˊ shiah xià
(又讀 ㄒㄧㄚˊ shya xiá)

leisure; free time; spare time

暇晷(ㄒㄧㄚˋ ㄍㄨㄟˇ)
leisure; spare time
暇時(ㄒㄧㄚˋ ㄕˊ)
leisure; spare time
暇日(ㄒㄧㄚˋ ㄖˋ)
free days; leisure; spare time: 他們在暇日時常爬山。They often go mountaineering in their free days.
暇逸(ㄒㄧㄚˋ ㄧˋ)
relaxation; to relax; to idle
暇豫(ㄒㄧㄚˋ ㄩˋ)
leisurely; relaxed; relaxation

【暉】 2266

ㄏㄨㄟ huei huī

1. the sunshine; the light of the sun
2. bright; radiant

暉暉(ㄏㄨㄟ ㄏㄨㄟ)
(said of the sky) clear and bright
暉夜(ㄏㄨㄟ ㄧㄝˋ)
a firefly
暉映(ㄏㄨㄟ ㄧㄥˋ)
bright and brilliant

【暈】 2267

1. ㄩㄣ iun yūn

1. to faint; to swoon
2. giddy and dizzy
3. (usually used sarcastically) to do things without a purpose

暈倒(ㄩㄣ ㄉㄠˇ)
to faint and fall; to swoon: 她一看見血便暈倒了。She swoons at the sight of blood.
暈頭(ㄩㄣ ·ㄊㄡ)
①(sarcastically) a bloody fool; a blockhead; an imbecile ② to feel dizzy
暈頭巴腦(ㄩㄣ ·ㄊㄡ ㄅㄚ ㄋㄠˇ)
to feel dizzy and giddy
暈頭轉向(ㄩㄣ ·ㄊㄡ ㄓㄨㄢˇ ㄒㄧㄤˋ)
① to feel dizzy and giddy ② so confused that one doesn't know what to do, say, etc.: 這門科目眞難，把我搞得暈頭轉向。This course is really difficult; it has got me confused.

暈過去(ㄩㄣ ˙ㄍㄨㄛ ˙ㄑㄩ)
to pass out; to faint
暈厥(ㄩㄣ ㄐㄩㄝˊ)
(medicine) syncope; a faint; to faint: 他因飢餓而暈厥。He fainted from hunger.

【暈】 2267
2. ㄩㄣˋ yunn yùn
1. (meteorology) a halo; vapors; a mist
2. dazzled; to feel faint or dizzy
暈飛機(ㄩㄣˋ ㄈㄟ ㄐㄧ)
airsick
暈氣(ㄩㄣˋ ㄑㄧˋ)
fog, mist or vapor that reflects the colors of the sun
暈車(ㄩㄣˋ ㄔㄜ)
to be bussick, trainsick or carsick
暈船(ㄩㄣˋ ㄔㄨㄢˊ)
to be seasick: 她容易暈船。She is liable to be seasick.

【暑】 2268
ㄕㄨˇ shuu shǔ
1. hot; heat; the heat of summer
2. mid-summer; summer
暑伏(ㄕㄨˇ ㄈㄨˊ)
the hottest spell of summer; dog days
暑天(ㄕㄨˇ ㄊㄧㄢ)
hot days; summertime
暑假(ㄕㄨˇ ㄐㄧㄚˋ)
summer vacation: 他們在海濱度暑假。They spent their summer vacation at the seashore.
暑期(ㄕㄨˇ ㄑㄧˊ)
① summer ② the summer vacation
暑期班(ㄕㄨˇ ㄑㄧˊ ㄅㄢ)
a summer class or school
暑期學校(ㄕㄨˇ ㄑㄧˊ ㄒㄩㄝˊ ㄒㄧㄠˋ)
a summer school
暑氣(ㄕㄨˇ ㄑㄧˋ)
the heat of summer; the scorching heat
暑氣迫人(ㄕㄨˇ ㄑㄧˋ ㄆㄛˋ ㄖㄣˊ)
The summer heat is very oppressive.
暑熱(ㄕㄨˇ ㄖㄜˋ)
the scorching heat; the heat of summer
暑熱天(ㄕㄨˇ ㄖㄜˋ ㄊㄧㄢ) or 暑天(ㄕㄨˇ ㄊㄧㄢ)
hot summer days; hot weather; dog days
暑溽(ㄕㄨˇ ㄖㄨˋ)
hot and steamy; hot and humid
暑歲(ㄕㄨˇ ㄙㄨㄟˋ)
a year of heat and drought
暑暍(ㄕㄨˇ ㄧㄝˋ)
sunstroke
暑月(ㄕㄨˇ ㄩㄝˋ)
summer months

【暗】 2269
ㄢˋ ann àn
1. dim; dark; obscure: 天色漸漸暗了。It's getting dark.
2. stupid; ignorant: 他不是愚暗，祇是懶。He's not stupid, merely lazy.
3. secret; clandestine; stealthy
4. hidden (meanings, drainage systems, rocks, etc.): 他的話另有暗義。His words had a hidden meaning.
暗盤(ㄢˋ ㄆㄢˊ)
a price or quotation which is kept from public knowledge but made known to selected few
暗碼(ㄢˋ ㄇㄚˇ)
① a secret code ② secret signs used by a store to indicate the actual value of a commodity—which is not known to outsiders
暗昧(ㄢˋ ㄇㄟˋ)
① stupid and ignorant: 這孩子心智暗昧。This boy is mentally stupid. ② stealthy or clandestine ③ obscure (due to the lapse of time)
暗門子(ㄢˋ ㄇㄣˊ ˙ㄗ) or 暗娼(ㄢˋ ㄔㄤ)
unlicensed prostitutes
暗面描寫(ㄢˋ ㄇㄧㄢˋ ㄇㄧㄠˊ ㄒㄧㄝˇ)
a realistic description of the seamy side of life
暗房(ㄢˋ ㄈㄤˊ)
① (photography) a darkroom ② (now rarely) a room in which a woman gives birth to a child
暗訪(ㄢˋ ㄈㄤˇ)
to make secret inquiries; to investigate in secret; a secret investigation
暗淡 or 暗澹(ㄢˋ ㄉㄢˋ)
① (said of colors, etc.) faded, dull and not fresh ② (said of business, future prospects, etc.) dim; dismal
暗鬭(ㄢˋ ㄉㄡˋ)
a secret struggle, jockeying for power, favor, etc.
暗地搗鬼(ㄢˋ ㄉㄧˋ ㄉㄠˇ ㄍㄨㄟˇ)
to make trouble secretly
暗地裏(ㄢˋ ㄉㄧˋ ˙ㄌㄧ)
secretly; clandestinely; stealthily; on the sly
暗度陳倉(ㄢˋ ㄉㄨˋ ㄔㄣˊ ㄘㄤ)
secret rendezvous between lovers; illicit affairs; adultery
暗探(ㄢˋ ㄊㄢˋ)
① a plainclothes man; a detective; a spy: 他雇用一名私人暗探。He hired a private detective. ② to spy; to investigate in secret
暗樓子(ㄢˋ ㄌㄡˊ ˙ㄗ)
a hidden attic or garret
暗裏(ㄢˋ ㄌㄧˇ)
secretly; inwardly; in one's heart: 他暗裏幫助他們。He helped them secretly.
暗裏算計(ㄢˋ ㄌㄧˇ ㄙㄨㄢˋ ㄐㄧˋ)
to calculate in one's mind; to make calculations in secret
暗流(ㄢˋ ㄌㄧㄡˊ)
a subterranean flow; an undercurrent
暗溝(ㄢˋ ㄍㄡ)
a sewer; an underground or covered drain
暗合(ㄢˋ ㄏㄜˊ)
an unintentional meeting of minds or agreement; agreement without prior consultation
暗害(ㄢˋ ㄏㄞˋ)
to injure another secretly; to assassinate or murder
暗號(ㄢˋ ㄏㄠˋ)
a secret mark, sign, signal or password
暗含著(ㄢˋ ㄏㄢˊ ˙ㄓㄜ)
to speak with an overtone; to convey meaning in between the lines; to insinuate; to imply
暗花兒(ㄢˋ ㄏㄨㄚㄦ)
indistinct grains, stripes, etc. of wood, porcelain, etc.
暗火(ㄢˋ ㄏㄨㄛˇ)
a dying fire
暗疾(ㄢˋ ㄐㄧˊ)
ailments or diseases which

〔日部〕

are hidden from view—as piles, V. D., etc. 亦作「隱疾」

暗計(ㄢˋ ㄐㄧˋ)
①to calculate or count in one's heart ②a secret design or trick; a conspiracy

暗記(ㄢˋ ㄐㄧˋ)
①to memorize; to bear in mind ②a secret sign 參看「暗號」

暗礁(ㄢˋ ㄐㄧㄠ)
①a submerged (or hidden) reef: 那艘船撞到暗礁沉沒。The ship was wrecked on the hidden reef. ②an unseen obstacle

暗九(ㄢˋ ㄐㄧㄡˇ)
(said of one's age) a multiple of nine which begins from 18 and ends at 81

暗箭(ㄢˋ ㄐㄧㄢˋ)
(literally) a secret arrow —secret activities designed to hurt somebody

暗箭傷人(ㄢˋ ㄐㄧㄢˋ ㄕㄤ ㄖㄣˊ)
to hurt another by clandestine means; to stab somebody in the back: 暗箭傷人是不道德的行爲。It is immoral conduct to hurt others by clandestine means.

暗泣(ㄢˋ ㄑㄧˋ)
to weep behind others' backs; to weep without uttering sound

暗器(ㄢˋ ㄑㄧˋ)
(in old Chinese fighting art) hidden weapons, usually a projectile

暗喜(ㄢˋ ㄒㄧˇ)
to feel happy or delighted secretly

暗笑(ㄢˋ ㄒㄧㄠˋ)
to laugh in one's heart; to laugh behind another's back; to laugh up one's sleeve

暗香(ㄢˋ ㄒㄧㄤ)
aroma or fragrance which is not strong but very persistent

暗香疏影(ㄢˋ ㄒㄧㄤ ㄕㄨ ㄧㄥˇ)
a descriptive phrase for Chinese plum flowers (梅花)

暗箱(ㄢˋ ㄒㄧㄤ)
a camera obscura

暗想(ㄢˋ ㄒㄧㄤˇ)
to muse; to ponder; to turn over in one's mind: 她把問題再暗想一次。She mused the question once more.

暗轉(ㄢˋ ㄓㄨㄢˇ)
①to get a transfer or promotion in secret ②(drama) a dark change

暗中(ㄢˋ ㄓㄨㄥ)
①secretly; in secret; on the sly; surreptitiously; stealthily; clandestinely; privately: 我暗中得知此事。I was told about the matter in secret. ②(to do something) in the dark or without light

暗中摸索(ㄢˋ ㄓㄨㄥ ㄇㄛ ㄙㄨㄛˇ)
to grope in the dark: 他在暗中摸索着找門柄。He groped for the doorhandle in the dark.

暗嘲(ㄢˋ ㄔㄠˊ)
to laugh in secret; to ridicule; to be sarcastic: 醫生常在戲劇裏被暗嘲。Doctors are often ridiculed in the plays.

暗潮(ㄢˋ ㄔㄠˊ)
①an undercurrent; a hidden current of water beneath the surface ②an undercurrent; a behind-the-scenes maneuver, conflict, struggle, etc.

暗娼(ㄢˋ ㄔㄤ)
unlicensed prostitutes

暗場(ㄢˋ ㄔㄤˇ)or(ㄢˋ ㄔㄤˊ)
details in a play which are not acted out but revealed in narration, dialogues, etc.

暗處(ㄢˋ ㄔㄨˋ)
①a dark place; an obscure corner ②a secret place

暗示(ㄢˋ ㄕˋ)
①to hint; to suggest; to drop a hint: 我曾暗示他不夠謹愼。I hinted at his imprudence. ②a hint; an insinuation; a suggestion: 他們似乎沒有懂我的暗示。They don't seem to take my hint.

暗室(ㄢˋ ㄕˋ)
①a dark, obscure or out-of-the-way place ②a dark room for detaining rebellious prisoners ③a darkroom for developing photographs

暗事(ㄢˋ ㄕˋ)
clandestine actions or illicit conduct

暗殺(ㄢˋ ㄕㄚ)
assassination; to assassinate

暗殺黨(ㄢˋ ㄕㄚ ㄉㄤˇ)
a gang of assassins

暗射(ㄢˋ ㄕㄜˋ)
to insinuate

暗傷(ㄢˋ ㄕㄤ)
①an internal injury of human body ②invisible damage of an object

暗自(ㄢˋ ㄗˋ)
inwardly; to oneself; secretly: 他暗自慶幸。He considered himself lucky secretly.

暗操賤業(ㄢˋ ㄘㄠ ㄐㄧㄢˋ ㄧㄝˋ)
to engage in unlicensed prostitution

暗藏(ㄢˋ ㄘㄤˊ)
to hide; to conceal

暗藏春色(ㄢˋ ㄘㄤˊ ㄔㄨㄣ ㄙㄜˋ)
(said of a building which usually looks respectable) to have hidden corners, cabins, etc. for amorous purposes

暗色(ㄢˋ ㄙㄜˋ)
dark colors; deep colors; cold colors

暗算(ㄢˋ ㄙㄨㄢˋ)
a secret plot; to plot in secret; to plot against

暗筍(ㄢˋ ㄙㄨㄣˇ)
bamboo shoots which are still beneath the surface of the ground

暗送秋波(ㄢˋ ㄙㄨㄥˋ ㄑㄧㄡ ㄅㄛ)
①to convey love by stealing a look at the other party ②to establish secret contact with the enemy camp, opposing faction, etc.

暗暗(ㄢˋ ㄢˋ)
①obscure ②secret

暗無天日(ㄢˋ ㄨˊ ㄊㄧㄢ ㄖˋ)
①(said of a place, room, etc.) very dark ②(said of a nation, locality, etc.) where the jungle law reigns; lawlessness; total absence of justice

暗喻(ㄢˋ ㄩˋ)
a concealed analogy; a metaphor

2270
【暖】 (煖) ㄋㄨㄢˇ noǎn nuǎn

warm, genial (weather): 天氣一天比一天暖和了。It is get-

ting warmer day by day.
暖房(ㄋㄨㄢˇ ㄈㄤˊ)
①a housewarming party sponsored by friends and relatives on the eve of one's wedding or moving in ②a hothouse; a greenhouse
暖流(ㄋㄨㄢˇ ㄌㄧㄡˊ)
①(geography) warm ocean currents ②(meteorology) warm air currents
暖爐(ㄋㄨㄢˇ ㄌㄨˊ)
a stove for keeping a room warm in winter; a brazier
暖鍋(ㄋㄨㄢˇ ㄍㄨㄛ)
a tin, brass or pottery vessel in which food is kept steaming hot with a slow fire burning underneath; a chafing pot
暖炕(ㄋㄨㄢˇ ㄎㄤˋ)
(in North China) to warm the clay (or brick) bed by keeping a small fire under it throughout the night; such a clay (or brick) bed
暖壺(ㄋㄨㄢˇ ㄏㄨˊ)
①a thermos bottle ②a vessel wrapped in cotton, etc. for keeping tea warm
暖烘烘(ㄋㄨㄢˇ ㄏㄨㄥ ㄏㄨㄥ)
very warm
暖和(ㄋㄨㄢˇ ·ㄏㄨㄛ)
①warm: 她坐在暖和的陽光中。She sat in the warm sunshine. ②to warm up
暖轎(ㄋㄨㄢˇ ㄐㄧㄠˋ)
a sedan chair with drapes around to protect the rider from cold
暖氣(ㄋㄨㄢˇ ㄑㄧˋ)
warm vapor; (in air-conditioning) warm air
暖氣爐(ㄋㄨㄢˇ ㄑㄧˋ ㄌㄨˊ)
a gas heater
暖氣管(ㄋㄨㄢˇ ㄑㄧˋ ㄍㄨㄢˇ)
a heating pipe
暖氣裝置(ㄋㄨㄢˇ ㄑㄧˋ ㄓㄨㄤ ㄓˋ) or 暖氣設備(ㄋㄨㄢˇ ㄑㄧˋ ㄕㄜˋ ㄅㄟˋ)
central heating installation; a heater
暖手(ㄋㄨㄢˇ ㄕㄡˇ)
to warm the hands: 他在冬天打字前先暖手。In winter he warms his hands before typing.
暖壽(ㄋㄨㄢˇ ㄕㄡˋ)
a feast or party taking place on the eve of one's birthday
暖水瓶(ㄋㄨㄢˇ ㄕㄨㄟˇ ㄆㄧㄥˊ)
a thermos bottle
暖熱(ㄋㄨㄢˇ ㄖㄜˋ)
very warm
暖融融(ㄋㄨㄢˇ ㄖㄨㄥˊ ㄖㄨㄥˊ)
warm, cozy and comfortable
暖翠(ㄋㄨㄢˇ ㄘㄨㄟˋ)
the verdant hills in the warm spring
暖色(ㄋㄨㄢˇ ㄙㄜˋ)
warm colors: 紅、黃、橙三色被稱爲暖色。Red, yellow and orange are called warm colors.
暖酥(ㄋㄨㄢˇ ㄙㄨ)
a girl's breasts (which are warm and soft)
暖耳(ㄋㄨㄢˇ ㄦˇ)
earmuffs

【暌】 2271
ㄎㄨㄟ kwei kuí
1. in opposition
2. to separate; to part
暌合(ㄎㄨㄟˊ ㄏㄜˊ)
to meet and to part; union and separation
暌索(ㄎㄨㄟˊ ㄙㄨㄛˇ)
to get separated from each other
暌違(ㄎㄨㄟˊ ㄨㄟˊ)
(said of friends) separated; parted; separation: 我們已暌違數載。It's years since we parted.

十畫

【暝】 2272
1. ㄇㄧㄥˊ ming míng
obscure; dark: 天色將暝。It is getting dark.
暝曚(ㄇㄧㄥˊ ㄇㄥˊ)
obscure: 霧使景色暝曚不淸。Mist made the view obscure.

【暝】 2272
2. ㄇㄧㄥˋ minq mìng
night

【暢】 2273
ㄔㄤˋ chanq chàng
1. smoothly; fluently
2. easily accessible
3. with gusto; to one's heart's content
4. long; expanding
5. luxuriant; luxuriance
6. (to state or elaborate) freely; without restraint; clear
7. very
8. a Chinese family name
暢茂(ㄔㄤˋ ㄇㄠˋ)
luxuriant; prosperous; flourishing
暢達(ㄔㄤˋ ㄉㄚˊ)
clearly and smoothly: 譯文暢達。The translation reads clearly and smoothly.
暢談(ㄔㄤˋ ㄊㄢˊ)
to talk to one's heart's content
暢通(ㄔㄤˋ ㄊㄨㄥ)
unimpeded; unblocked: 前面的公路暢通無阻。The highway is unimpeded ahead.
暢流(ㄔㄤˋ ㄌㄧㄡˊ)
flowing freely
暢快(ㄔㄤˋ ㄎㄨㄞˋ)
cheerful and exuberant; spiritually elevated
暢懷(ㄔㄤˋ ㄏㄨㄞˊ)
comfortable and joyful; to one's heart's content
暢銷(ㄔㄤˋ ㄒㄧㄠ)
a booming sale; to sell well; to sell briskly
暢銷書(ㄔㄤˋ ㄒㄧㄠ ㄕㄨ)
a best seller
暢行無阻(ㄔㄤˋ ㄒㄧㄥˊ ㄨˊ ㄗㄨˇ)
to meet no obstacle wherever one goes; to pass unimpeded
暢敍(ㄔㄤˋ ㄒㄩˋ)
to converse joyfully; to talk to one's heart's content: 他們暢敍離情。They conversed joyfully about the days during their separation.
暢暢(ㄔㄤˋ ㄔㄤˋ)
joyful and peaceful
暢然(ㄔㄤˋ ㄖㄢˊ)
joyfully
暢所欲言(ㄔㄤˋ ㄙㄨㄛˇ ㄩˋ ㄧㄢˊ)
to get something off one's chest; to talk to one's heart's content; to assert without any restraint; to speak one's mind freely
暢所欲爲(ㄔㄤˋ ㄙㄨㄛˇ ㄩˋ ㄨㄟˊ)
to do whatever one likes
暢遂(ㄔㄤˋ ㄙㄨㄟˋ)
luxuriant (growth of plants, etc.); flourishing
暢遊(ㄔㄤˋ ㄧㄡˊ)
to enjoy a sightseeing tour:

〔日部〕

那些旅客們暢遊名勝古蹟。The tourists enjoyed a trip to places of historic interest.

暢飲(ㄔㄤˋ ㄧㄣˇ)
to drink to one's heart's content: 他們通宵暢飲。They drank to their hearts' content all night.

暢旺(ㄔㄤˋ ㄨㄤˋ)
flourishing or prosperous; booming

暢鬱(ㄔㄤˋ ㄩˋ)
(said of plants) flourishing and prospering

暢月(ㄔㄤˋ ㄩㄝˋ)
the eleventh moon of the lunar year

十一畫

【暮】 2274 ㄇㄨˋ muh mù
1. sunset; evening; dusk
2. closing (years); ending; late: 歲聿其暮。The year is drawing to its ending.

暮年(ㄇㄨˋ ㄋㄧㄢˊ)
closing years of one's life; old age; declining years

暮齡(ㄇㄨˋ ㄌㄧㄥˊ)
closing years of one's life; aged: 他已屆暮齡。He is aged.

暮鼓晨鐘(ㄇㄨˋ ㄍㄨˇ ㄔㄣˊ ㄓㄨㄥ)
①(literally) evening drums and morning bells—used in Buddhist temples to tell time ② ringing statements or remarks which arouse the public from degeneracy or warn against lurking danger, etc.

暮景(ㄇㄨˋ ㄐㄧㄥˇ)
one's circumstances (especially, financial) during his closing years

暮氣(ㄇㄨˋ ㄑㄧˋ)
lifelessness; despondence and emaciation; gloom; dejection

暮氣沉沉(ㄇㄨˋ ㄑㄧˋ ㄔㄣˊ ㄔㄣˊ)
①(said of a person) despondent and dejected; a defeatist attitude; gloomy; indolent; lethargy ② (said of atmosphere) dead and dull; gloomy; lethargy

暮秋(ㄇㄨˋ ㄑㄧㄡ)
late autumn

暮齒(ㄇㄨˋ ㄔˇ)
late in one's life; one's closing years; aged

暮春(ㄇㄨˋ ㄔㄨㄣ)
late spring

暮世(ㄇㄨˋ ㄕˋ)
recently; the world nowadays

暮生兒(ㄇㄨˋ ㄕㄥ ㄦˊ)
a posthumous child

暮色(ㄇㄨˋ ㄙㄜˋ)
dusk; twilight; the gloaming

暮色朦朧(ㄇㄨˋ ㄙㄜˋ ㄇㄥˊ ㄌㄨㄥˊ)
glimmering twilight

暮歲(ㄇㄨˋ ㄙㄨㄟˋ)
①the end of the year ② closing years of one's life; twilight of one's life

暮靄(ㄇㄨˋ ㄞˇ)
the evening mists: 暮靄籠罩着田野。The evening mists were hovering over the field.

【暫】 2275 ㄓㄢˋ jann zhàn (讀音 ㄗㄢˋ tzann zàn)
1. temporarily; for a short time; not lasting
2. suddenly; abruptly

暫別(ㄓㄢˋ ㄅㄧㄝˊ)
a short separation; to part for a short time

暫定(ㄓㄢˋ ㄉㄧㄥˋ)
①(said of time) tentatively set on, at, etc.: 學習期限暫定一年。The term of study is tentatively set on one year. ②(said of a number, price, place, etc.) tentatively fix at

暫停(ㄓㄢˋ ㄊㄧㄥˊ)
①to stop, halt or suspend temporarily: 會議暫停了。The meeting has been suspended temporarily. ②a time-out

暫留(ㄓㄢˋ ㄌㄧㄡˊ)
to stay for a short time

暫候(ㄓㄢˋ ㄏㄡˋ)
to wait for a short time

暫緩(ㄓㄢˋ ㄏㄨㄢˇ)
to hold for a while; to postpone or delay for a while; to put off; to defer: 我們最好暫緩作出決定。We had better put off (or defer) making a decision.

暫濟燃眉(ㄓㄢˋ ㄐㄧˋ ㄖㄢˊ ㄇㄟˊ)
to temporarily relieve an emergency or an urgent need (often used in asking for a short-term loan)

暫借(ㄓㄢˋ ㄐㄧㄝˋ)
to borrow for a short time: 我可以暫借你的鋼筆嗎? May I borrow your pen for a short time?

暫且(ㄓㄢˋ ㄑㄧㄝˇ)
for the time being: 會議暫且告一段落吧。Let's stop the meeting for the time being.

暫缺(ㄓㄢˋ ㄑㄩㄝ)
①(said of a post) to be left vacant for the time being ② (said of a commodity) to run short of stock at the moment

暫歇(ㄓㄢˋ ㄒㄧㄝ)
to rest for a while; to stay for a short time

暫行(ㄓㄢˋ ㄒㄧㄥˊ)
temporary; for the time being; provisional

暫行法(ㄓㄢˋ ㄒㄧㄥˊ ㄈㄚˇ)
provisional laws; temporary laws

暫住(ㄓㄢˋ ㄓㄨˋ)
to stay for a while; to lodge temporarily at...

暫齒(ㄓㄢˋ ㄔˇ)
temporary teeth or milk teeth 亦作「乳齒」

暫時(ㄓㄢˋ ㄕˊ)
for the time being; temporarily: 那雜誌暫時停刊。The magazine temporarily suspended publication.

暫延(ㄓㄢˋ ㄧㄢˊ)
to postpone tentatively to...; to adjourn temporarily

【暴】 2276 1. ㄅㄠˋ baw bào
1. cruel; savage; fierce; atrocious; violent: 他對待犯人非常殘暴。He is very cruel to the prisoners.
2. sudden
3. short-tempered; hot-tempered: 他的脾氣暴躁。He has a hot (or quick) temper.

暴斃(ㄅㄠˋ ㄅㄧˋ)
to meet a sudden death

暴病(ㄅㄠˋ ㄅㄧㄥˋ)
a sudden illness; to fall ill suddenly: 他突發暴病。He fell ill suddenly.

暴脾氣(ㄅㄠˋ ㄆㄧˊ ·ㄑㄧ)
a hot temper

暴民(ㄅㄠˋ ㄇㄧㄣˊ)
mobs or mobsters: 暴民圍聚法庭。Mobs collected round the court.
暴發(ㄅㄠˋ ㄈㄚ)
①a violent eruption; a sudden flareup ②to break out; to erupt ③to become rich or to attain a high position all of a sudden
暴發戶(ㄅㄠˋ ㄈㄚ ㄏㄨˋ)
an upstart; a parvenu; *nouveau riche*
暴風(ㄅㄠˋ ㄈㄥ)or 暴風雨(ㄅㄠˋ ㄈㄥ ㄩˇ)
a storm; a tempest: 這場暴風雨造成很重的損害。The storm did a lot of harm.
暴風半徑(ㄅㄠˋ ㄈㄥ ㄅㄢˋ ㄐㄧㄥˋ)
the radius of a typhoon or hurricane
暴風雪(ㄅㄠˋ ㄈㄥ ㄒㄩㄝˇ)
a snowstorm; a blizzard
暴富(ㄅㄠˋ ㄈㄨˋ)
sudden wealth
暴跌(ㄅㄠˋ ㄉㄧㄝ)
(said of prices) to nose-dive; to drop sharply; to slump: 本公司上個月的銷售量暴跌。Sales slumped badly in our company last month.
暴動(ㄅㄠˋ ㄉㄨㄥˋ)
a riot; a rebellion; an insurrection
暴投(ㄅㄠˋ ㄊㄡˊ)
(baseball) a wild pitch
暴跳如雷(ㄅㄠˋ ㄊㄧㄠˋ ㄖㄨˊ ㄌㄟˊ)
to be infuriated; to be enraged; furious; stamping and roaring with anger
暴殄天物(ㄅㄠˋ ㄊㄧㄢˇ ㄊㄧㄢ ㄨˋ)
to waste gifts of God; a reckless waste of grains, etc.
暴徒(ㄅㄠˋ ㄊㄨˊ)
a rioter; a ruffian; a thug; a mobster; a mob; a gangster
暴怒(ㄅㄠˋ ㄋㄨˋ)
furious; mad; to blow one's top; a rage
暴虐(ㄅㄠˋ ㄋㄩㄝˋ)
cruel; tyrannical; despotic; brutal; atrocious
暴雷(ㄅㄠˋ ㄌㄟˊ)
a sudden clap of thunder
暴力(ㄅㄠˋ ㄌㄧˋ)
violence; brute force; naked force
暴利(ㄅㄠˋ ㄌㄧˋ)
sudden huge profits
暴戾(ㄅㄠˋ ㄌㄧˋ)
despotic and tyrannical; cruel and fierce
暴戾恣睢(ㄅㄠˋ ㄌㄧˋ ㄘˋ ㄙㄨㄟ)
tyrannical; despotic; cruel
暴烈(ㄅㄠˋ ㄌㄧㄝˋ)
violent; fierce; wild
暴斂(ㄅㄠˋ ㄌㄧㄢˋ)
to extort; to collect illegitimate wealth
暴亂(ㄅㄠˋ ㄌㄨㄢˋ)
a riot; a rebellion; a revolt
暴掠(ㄅㄠˋ ㄌㄩㄝˋ)
to plunder; to pillage: 敵人把所發現之財物均暴掠而去。The enemy plundered all the goods they found.
暴貴者(ㄅㄠˋ ㄍㄨㄟˋ ㄓㄜˇ)
a parvenu; an upstart
暴客(ㄅㄠˋ ㄎㄜˋ)
a robber
暴橫(ㄅㄠˋ ㄏㄥˋ)
tyrannical; despotic; atrocious; cruel
暴忽(ㄅㄠˋ ㄏㄨ)
evanescent; transient
暴虎馮河(ㄅㄠˋ ㄏㄨˇ ㄆㄧㄥˊ ㄏㄜˊ)
(literally) to try to fight a tiger with bare hands and cross a river without a boat—intrepid but foolish; foolhardy
暴桀(ㄅㄠˋ ㄐㄧㄝˊ)
disobedient; recalcitrant; defiant
暴君(ㄅㄠˋ ㄐㄩㄣ)
a tyrant; a despot: 暴君殘虐無度。The tyrant rioted in cruelty.
暴棄(ㄅㄠˋ ㄑㄧˋ)
to despair
暴行(ㄅㄠˋ ㄒㄧㄥˊ)
savage acts; violence; atrocities
暴性子(ㄅㄠˋ ㄒㄧㄥˋ ·ㄗ)
a hot temper: 他是一個暴性子的人。He is a hot-tempered man.
暴漲(ㄅㄠˋ ㄓㄤˇ)
(said of a water level or a commodity price) to rise sharply or quickly; to skyrocket: 河水暴漲。The river sharply rose.
暴政(ㄅㄠˋ ㄓㄥˋ)
tyrannical rule; the tyranny of the government
暴躁(ㄅㄠˋ ㄗㄠˋ)
irritable; fretful; irascible; choleric
暴卒(ㄅㄠˋ ㄗㄨˊ)
to die of a sudden illness; to die a violent death
暴飲暴食(ㄅㄠˋ ㄧㄣˇ ㄅㄠˋ ㄕˊ)
to eat and drink excessively
暴雨(ㄅㄠˋ ㄩˇ)
torrential rain; a squall: 此地六月間常有暴雨。We often have torrential rain here in June.

【暴】 2276
2.(曝) ㄆㄨˋ puh pù
to expose
暴面(ㄆㄨˋ ㄇㄧㄢˋ)
to make an appearance; to appear
暴露(ㄆㄨˋ ㄌㄨˋ)
to expose or be exposed; exposure: 他的陰謀已暴露無遺。His plot has been thoroughly exposed.
暴露狂(ㄆㄨˋ ㄌㄨˋ ㄎㄨㄤˊ)
(psychiatry) ①exhibitionism ②an exhibitionist
暴骨(ㄆㄨˋ ㄍㄨˇ)
to expose one's bones to the elements; to die in the wilds
暴光(ㄆㄨˋ ㄍㄨㄤ)
(photography) exposure
暴章(ㄆㄨˋ ㄓㄤ)
to show
暴著(ㄆㄨˋ ㄓㄨˋ)
conspicuous; striking
暴師(ㄆㄨˋ ㄕ)
to station troops in the wilds
暴曬(ㄆㄨˋ ㄕㄞˋ)
to expose to sunshine: 別暴曬陽光太久。Don't expose yourself to sunshine too long.
暴顋龍門(ㄆㄨˋ ㄙㄞ ㄌㄨㄥˊ ㄇㄣˊ)
(formerly) to flunk the civil service examination

【暵】 2277
ㄏㄢˋ hann hàn
to expose to sunshine; to dry; to be scorched up; withered; wizened
暵暵(ㄏㄢˋ ㄏㄢˋ)
exposed to scorching sun-

〔日部〕

shine

【暱】 2278 (昵) ㄋㄧˋ nih nì

intimate; close: 她與他很親暱。She is on intimate terms with him.

暱交(ㄋㄧˋ ㄐㄧㄠ)
close friendship

暱就(ㄋㄧˋ ㄐㄧㄡˋ)
to draw near to

暱嫌(ㄋㄧˋ ㄒㄧㄢˊ)
a personal grudge

暱愛(ㄋㄧˋ ㄞˋ)
love or affection (between opposite sexes) 亦作「昵愛」

暱友(ㄋㄧˋ ㄧㄡˇ)
a close friend: 他們是暱友。They are close friends.

〔日部〕

十二畫

【暹】 2279 ㄒㄧㄢ shian xiān

(said of the sun) to rise

暹羅(ㄒㄧㄢ ㄌㄨㄛˊ)
Siam, old name of Thailand

【曇】 2280 ㄊㄢˊ tarn tán

clouds: 山巔隱在雲曇中。The summit of the mountain is lost in the clouds.

曇曇(ㄊㄢˊ ㄊㄢˊ)
cloudy; overcast

曇花(ㄊㄢˊ ㄏㄨㄚ)
the epiphyllum; an orchid cactus

曇花一現(ㄊㄢˊ ㄏㄨㄚ ㄧˊ ㄒㄧㄢˋ)
(said of glory, favorable situation, etc.) to appear and then quickly disappear; to last for a very brief period of time like the epiphyllum blooming at night; short-lived; a flash in the pan

【暨】 2281 ㄐㄧˋ jih jì

1. and
2. to reach; to attain; to overtake
3. up to; till

暨南大學(ㄐㄧˋ ㄋㄢˊ ㄉㄚˋ ㄒㄩㄝˊ)
National Chinan University

暨今(ㄐㄧˋ ㄐㄧㄣ)
up to the present; till now 亦作「至今」

【曆】 2282 ㄌㄧˋ lih lì

1. a calendar
2. an era; an age
3. to calculate; to count

曆本(ㄌㄧˋ ㄅㄣˇ)
a calendar (as a table or register)

曆法(ㄌㄧˋ ㄈㄚˇ)
a calendar (as a system)

曆象(ㄌㄧˋ ㄒㄧㄤˋ)
to calculate the movements of the heavenly bodies

曆書(ㄌㄧˋ ㄕㄨ)
an almanac

曆數(ㄌㄧˋ ㄕㄨˋ)
① Heaven's will; the determinate appointment of Heaven; fate ② farming seasons

【曄】 2283 ㄧㄝˋ yeh yè

1. bright; radiant
2. prosperous; thriving

曄然(ㄧㄝˋ ㄖㄢˊ)
prosperous; thriving

曄曄(ㄧㄝˋ ㄧㄝˋ)
prosperous; thriving

【曈】 2284 ㄊㄨㄥˊ torng tóng

twilight before sunrise

曈曨(ㄊㄨㄥˊ ㄌㄨㄥˊ)
twilight before sunrise

【曉】 2285 ㄒㄧㄠˇ sheau xiǎo

1. daybreak; dawn: 天將破曉。It is now toward daybreak.
2. to tell; to explain: 他被曉示立即出發。He was told to start at once.
3. to know; to understand: 他知曉實情。He knows the truth.

曉譬(ㄒㄧㄠˇ ㄆㄧˋ)
to explain with examples

曉風殘月(ㄒㄧㄠˇ ㄈㄥ ㄘㄢˊ ㄩㄝˋ)
(literally) the morning breeze and the lingering moon—nature at daybreak

曉得(ㄒㄧㄠˇ ˙ㄉㄜ)
to know; to be aware of: 天曉得! God knows!

曉霞(ㄒㄧㄠˇ ㄒㄧㄚˊ)
rosy clouds at daybreak

曉行夜宿(ㄒㄧㄠˇ ㄒㄧㄥˊ ㄧㄝˋ ㄙㄨˋ)
to start early and stop late during a journey

曉暢(ㄒㄧㄠˇ ㄔㄤˋ)
(said of writing) clear and fluent: 這篇文章以曉暢的文體寫成。This article is written in a clear and fluent style.

曉示(ㄒㄧㄠˇ ㄕˋ)
to tell explicitly; to explain; to notify

曉事(ㄒㄧㄠˇ ㄕˋ)
(said of a person) understanding and experienced

曉色(ㄒㄧㄠˇ ㄙㄜˋ)
the scene in the early morning

曉以大義(ㄒㄧㄠˇ ㄧˇ ㄉㄚˋ ㄧˋ)
(to persuade someone to follow the right path) by telling him what is right

曉悟(ㄒㄧㄠˇ ㄨˋ)
to understand; to realize

曉諭(ㄒㄧㄠˇ ㄩˋ)
to explain; to tell; to give explicit instructions

【曀】 2286 ㄧˋ yih yì

dim; obscure; cloudy

【曌】 2287 ㄓㄠˋ jaw zhào

same as 照, coined by 武則天 and used as her name

【暾】 2288 ㄊㄨㄣ tuen tūn

sunrise

暾暾(ㄊㄨㄣ ㄊㄨㄣ)
bright; glowing; blazing

十三畫

【曖】 2289 ㄞˋ ay ài

1. dim; indistinct
2. ambiguous; vague

曖昧(ㄞˋ ㄇㄟˋ)
① ambiguous; equivocal; obscure; vague: 他的態度曖昧。He assumes an ambiguous attitude. ② a secret impropriety

曖昧行爲(ㄞˋ ㄇㄟˋ ㄒㄧㄥˊ ㄨㄟˊ)
scandals (especially illicit affairs)

曖曖(ㄞˋ ㄞˋ)
dim; obscure; dark

【曏】 2290 ㄒㄧㄤˋ shianq xiàng

1. a period of time
2. once upon a time

曏者(ㄒㄧㄤˋ ㄓㄜˇ)
once upon a time

十四畫

【曙】 2291 ㄕㄨˋ shuh shù
dawn; daybreak
曙光(ㄕㄨˋ ㄍㄨㄤ)
the first light of morning; light at dawn
曙後星孤(ㄕㄨˋ ㄏㄡˋ ㄒㄧㄥ ㄍㄨ)
an orphaned girl
曙日(ㄕㄨˋ ㄖˋ)
in the morning
曙色(ㄕㄨˋ ㄙㄜˋ)
light at daybreak; the light of early dawn; the gray of the morning

【曚】 2292 ㄇㄥˊ meng méng
dim; obscure
曚曨(ㄇㄥˊ ㄌㄨㄥˊ)
dim; obscure: 雲遮月曚曨。The moon was obscured by clouds. 亦作「朦朧」

【曜】 2293 ㄧㄠˋ yaw yào (又讀 ㄩㄝˋ yueh yuè)
1. daylight; sunshine
2. to shine; to glisten
曜靈(ㄧㄠˋ ㄌㄧㄥˊ)
the sun

【曛】 2294 ㄒㄩㄣ shiun xūn
1. twilight; dusk
2. the dim glow of the setting sun
曛黑(ㄒㄩㄣ ㄏㄟ)
dusky
曛黃(ㄒㄩㄣ ㄏㄨㄤˊ)
sunset; dusk

十五畫

【曠】 2295 ㄎㄨㄤˋ kuanq kuàng
1. open; wide; broad; empty; vast; spacious; unoccupied
2. free from worries and petty ideas
3. to neglect; neglect
曠費(ㄎㄨㄤˋ ㄈㄟˋ)
to waste
曠廢(ㄎㄨㄤˋ ㄈㄟˋ)
to neglect: 勿曠廢你的工作和職守。Don't neglect your work and duty.
曠放(ㄎㄨㄤˋ ㄈㄤˋ)
free and composed
曠夫(ㄎㄨㄤˋ ㄈㄨ)
an unmarried man of marriageable age
曠達(ㄎㄨㄤˋ ㄉㄚˊ)
unrestrained; free; broad-minded: 他是一位曠達的學者。He is a broad-minded scholar.
曠代(ㄎㄨㄤˋ ㄉㄞˋ)
unequaled by one's contemporaries: 她是曠代佳人。She is a beauty unequaled by her contemporaries.
曠蕩(ㄎㄨㄤˋ ㄉㄤˋ)
①(said of space) boundless; endless ②unrestrained; free
曠土(ㄎㄨㄤˋ ㄊㄨˇ)
a wilderness; a wasteland
曠古未有(ㄎㄨㄤˋ ㄍㄨˇ ㄨㄟˋ ㄧㄡˇ)
unprecedented in history
曠官(ㄎㄨㄤˋ ㄍㄨㄢ)
a negligent official
曠工(ㄎㄨㄤˋ ㄍㄨㄥ)
to neglect work
曠課(ㄎㄨㄤˋ ㄎㄜˋ)
to be absent from class without leave; to cut school; to play truant; to truant
曠久(ㄎㄨㄤˋ ㄐㄧㄡˇ)
lasting; long
曠學(ㄎㄨㄤˋ ㄒㄩㄝˊ)
to neglect one's studies; to play truant
曠職(ㄎㄨㄤˋ ㄓˊ)
①to be absent from the office without leave ②to neglect official duties
曠世(ㄎㄨㄤˋ ㄕˋ)
unequaled by one's contemporaries
曠世之才(ㄎㄨㄤˋ ㄕˋ ㄓ ㄘㄞˊ)
a man of brilliance unequaled by his contemporaries
曠日持久(ㄎㄨㄤˋ ㄖˋ ㄔˊ ㄐㄧㄡˇ)
to maintain a situation for a long time to no avail; long-drawn-out; protracted
曠逸(ㄎㄨㄤˋ ㄧˋ)
unrestrained
曠野(ㄎㄨㄤˋ ㄧㄝˇ)
wild plains; a prairie; the open fields
曠原(ㄎㄨㄤˋ ㄩㄢˊ)
wild plains; a wilderness; a prairie; the open fields

【曝】 2296 ㄆㄨˋ puh pù
to expose to sunlight; to sun
曝背(ㄆㄨˋ ㄅㄟˋ)
to turn the back to the sun and enjoy its warmth
曝露(ㄆㄨˋ ㄌㄨˋ)
to expose oneself to the weather 亦作「暴露」
曝光(ㄆㄨˋ ㄍㄨㄤ)
(photography) exposure
曝獻(ㄆㄨˋ ㄒㄧㄢˋ)
to offer a humble but sincere gift or service
曝曬(ㄆㄨˋ ㄕㄞˋ)
to expose to sunlight; to sun
曝書(ㄆㄨˋ ㄕㄨ)
to sun books

十六畫

【曦】 2297 ㄒㄧ shi xī
sunshine; sunlight
曦光(ㄒㄧ ㄍㄨㄤ)
sunshine; sunlight

【曨】 2298 (朧) ㄌㄨㄥˊ long lóng
1. vague; dim: 對於往事她僅有曚曨的記憶。She has only a dim recollection of the past.
2. bright

十七畫

【曩】 2299 ㄋㄤˇ naang nǎng
past; former
曩昔(ㄋㄤˇ ㄒㄧˊ)
in the past; in former times
曩者(ㄋㄤˇ ㄓㄜˇ)
in the past; in former times
曩時(ㄋㄤˇ ㄕˊ)
in former times; in the past
曩日(ㄋㄤˇ ㄖˋ)
bygone days

十九畫

【曬】 2300 (晒) ㄕㄞˋ shay shài
to expose to sunlight; to dry in the sun
曬不透(ㄕㄞˋ ·ㄅㄨ ㄊㄡˋ)
impervious to sunshine

〔日部〕

曬棚(ㄕㄞˋ ㄆㄥˊ)
a drying stand or rack
曬臺(ㄕㄞˋ ㄊㄞˊ)
a terrace where the laundry is dried in the sun
曬太陽(ㄕㄞˋ ㄊㄞˋ •ㄧㄤ)
to be exposed to the sun; to bask in the sun
曬圖(ㄕㄞˋ ㄊㄨˊ)
to make a blueprint; a blueprint 亦作「曬藍圖」
曬暖兒(ㄕㄞˋ ㄋㄨㄚˇㄦ)
to bask in the sun
曬乾(ㄕㄞˋ ㄍㄢ)
to dry in the sun
曬黑(ㄕㄞˋ ㄏㄟ)
(said of skin) darkened by overexposure to the sun
曬場(ㄕㄞˋ ㄔㄤˊ)or(ㄕㄞˋ ㄔㄤˇ)
a drying yard
曬鹽(ㄕㄞˋ ㄧㄢˊ)
to sun seawater to obtain salt

曰部
ㄩㄝ iue yuē

【曰】 2301
ㄩㄝ iue yuē
1. (an archaic usage) to say
2. to call; to name

二畫

【曲】 2302
1. ㄑㄩ chiu qū
1. bent; crooked; twisted; winding
2. little known; obscure
3. wrong; unjustifiable

曲筆(ㄑㄩ ㄅㄧˇ)
to distort facts in writing
曲庇(ㄑㄩ ㄅㄧˋ)
to conceal (another's mistake) by distortion of facts
曲阜(ㄑㄩ ㄈㄨˋ)
Chüfu, Shantung Province, where Confucius was born
曲度(ㄑㄩ ㄉㄨˋ)
(mathematics) curvature
曲突徙薪(ㄑㄩ ㄊㄨˊ ㄒㄧˇ ㄒㄧㄣ)
(literally) to bend the chimney and remove the fuel—to take precautions before it is too late
曲撓(ㄑㄩ ㄋㄠˊ)
unjust accusation; unfair blame
曲欄(ㄑㄩ ㄌㄢˊ)
a winding balustrade
曲裏拐彎兒(ㄑㄩ •ㄌㄧ ㄍㄨㄞˇ ㄨㄚㄦ)
winding; labyrinthine; zigzag; tortuous
曲流(ㄑㄩ ㄌㄧㄡˊ)
(geography) a meander
曲棍球(ㄑㄩ ㄍㄨㄣˋ ㄑㄧㄡˊ)
① hockey ② a hockey ball
曲肱而枕之(ㄑㄩ ㄍㄨㄥ ㄦˊ ㄓㄣˋ ㄓ)
(literally) to use one's bent arm as a pillow—to be poor but content
曲拱(ㄑㄩ ㄍㄨㄥˇ)
arched
曲解(ㄑㄩ ㄐㄧㄝˇ)
to misconstrue; to misinterpret; to twist; to distort: 這話意思很明確，你無法曲解。These remarks are so clear that you can't distort them.
曲徑(ㄑㄩ ㄐㄧㄥˋ)
a winding path
曲徑通幽(ㄑㄩ ㄐㄧㄥˋ ㄊㄨㄥ ㄧㄡ)
a winding path leading to a secluded place
曲全(ㄑㄩ ㄑㄩㄢˊ)
to suppress one's own feelings for the sake of greater interests
曲線(ㄑㄩ ㄒㄧㄢˋ)
(mathematics) curved line; curve
曲線板(ㄑㄩ ㄒㄧㄢˋ ㄅㄢˇ)
a curved ruler
曲線美(ㄑㄩ ㄒㄧㄢˋ ㄇㄟˇ)
① linear beauty ② (said of a woman) curvaceous, or curvacious; shapely
曲直(ㄑㄩ ㄓˊ)
right and wrong: 你眞是曲直不分。You really cannot distinguish between right and wrong.
曲折(ㄑㄩ ㄓㄜˊ)
① bends; turns; curves; turns and twists; tortuous: 那條路有許多曲折之處。The road is full of turns and twists. ② complications of an affair; complicated
曲折有致(ㄑㄩ ㄓㄜˊ ㄧㄡˇ ㄓˋ)
(said of a speech or literary work) delightfully complicated
曲折語(ㄑㄩ ㄓㄜˊ ㄩˇ)
inflective language 亦作「屈折語」
曲尺(ㄑㄩ ㄔˇ)
a (carpenter's) square
曲成(ㄑㄩ ㄔㄥˊ)
to fulfill somehow or other; to accomplish by hook or by crook
曲士(ㄑㄩ ㄕˋ)
an obscure person; a cramped scholar
曲室(ㄑㄩ ㄕˋ)
a secret chamber
曲射(ㄑㄩ ㄕㄜˋ)
(military) curved fire
曲射砲(ㄑㄩ ㄕㄜˋ ㄆㄠˋ)
(military) a howitzer; a curve-fire gun
曲蟮(ㄑㄩ ㄕㄢˋ)
an earthworm
曲說(ㄑㄩ ㄕㄨㄛ)
a biased statement
曲從(ㄑㄩ ㄘㄨㄥˊ)
to obey or yield reluctantly: 他曲從她的決定。He reluctantly obeyed her decision.
曲意(ㄑㄩ ㄧˋ)
to make a special concession to achieve others' goals
曲意逢迎(ㄑㄩ ㄧˋ ㄈㄥˊ ㄧㄥˊ)
to try in every way to flatter someone; to ingratiate oneself with someone

【曲】 2302
2. ㄑㄩˇ cheu qŭ
1. a type of verse for singing, which emerged in the Southern Sung (南宋) and Kin (金) dynasties and became popular in the Yüan Dynasty
2. a piece of music; a song: 她當衆高歌一曲。She cheerfully sang a song in public.

曲本(ㄑㄩˇ ㄅㄣˇ)
a music book
曲牌(ㄑㄩˇ ㄆㄞˊ)
names of various music tunes
曲譜(ㄑㄩˇ ㄆㄨˇ)
title of a 14-book collection of music compiled during the Ching Dynasty
曲調(ㄑㄩˇ ㄉㄧㄠˋ)

tunes; melodies

曲高和寡(ㄑㄩˇ ㄍㄠ ㄏㄜˋ ㄍㄨㄚˇ)
(literally) Highbrow music can be appreciated by only a few people.— caviare to the general 或 The profounder a theory is, the fewer its supporters are. 或 The more virtuous a person is, the fewer friends he has.

曲終人散(ㄑㄩˇ ㄓㄨㄥ ㄖㄣˊ ㄙㄢˋ)
The music is over and the people are gone.—the sadness one feels after a fanfare

曲終奏雅(ㄑㄩˇ ㄓㄨㄥ ㄗㄡˋ ㄧㄚˇ)
(said of a writing, speech, or performance) a brilliant conclusion

曲子(ㄑㄩˇ ˙ㄗ)or 曲兒(ㄑㄩㄜˇㄦ)
a number; a song; a tune; a melody: 他以口哨吹流行的曲子。He whistles a popular tune.

【曳】 2303
ㄧˋ yih yì
(語音 ㄧㄝˋ yeh yè)

to haul; to tug; to drag; to trail

曳白(ㄧˋ ㄅㄞˊ)
(in an examination) to pass over a blank page without writing anything on it through inadvertence

曳光彈(ㄧˋ ㄍㄨㄤ ㄉㄢˋ)
(military) a tracer bullet

曳裾王門(ㄧˋ ㄐㄩ ㄨㄤˊ ㄇㄣˊ)
to live as a protégé of a feudal lord

曳杖(ㄧˋ ㄓㄤˋ)
to walk with a cane

曳踵(ㄧˋ ㄓㄨㄥˇ)or 曳足(ㄧˋ ㄗㄨˊ)
to drag one's feet

曳引機(ㄧˋ ㄧㄣˇ ㄐㄧ)
a tractor

曳尾塗中(ㄧˋ ㄨㄟˇ ㄊㄨˊ ㄓㄨㄥ)
(literally) to wag the tail in the mire—to live in seclusion; to lead an obscure life

三畫

【更】 2304
1. ㄍㄥ geng gēng

1. the watches of the night (formerly the night was divided into five periods and each covered two hours)
2. a night watchman
3. to change; to alter; to shift
4. to experience: 他少不更事。He is young and inexperienced.
5. to alternate: 日夜彼此更替。Day and night alternate with each other.

更僕難數(ㄍㄥ ㄆㄨˊ ㄋㄢˊ ㄕㄨˇ)
too many to enumerate

更名(ㄍㄥ ㄇㄧㄥˊ)
to change one's name

更番(ㄍㄥ ㄈㄢ)
to work by turns; to take turns: 讓我們更番做這件事。Let us take turns at doing it.

更夫(ㄍㄥ ㄈㄨ)or 更卒(ㄍㄥ ㄗㄨˊ)
a night watchman

更賦(ㄍㄥ ㄈㄨˋ)
(in ancient China) the tax paid to the government in lieu of frontier service

更代(ㄍㄥ ㄉㄞˋ)
to take turns; to work by turns

更迭(ㄍㄥ ㄉㄧㄝˊ)
to make a change; to alternate: 雨天與晴天交替更迭。Wet days alternate with fine days.

更訂(ㄍㄥ ㄉㄧㄥˋ)
to revise: 那本字典需要更訂。That dictionary needs to be revised.

更端(ㄍㄥ ㄉㄨㄢ)
to have a new complication

更動(ㄍㄥ ㄉㄨㄥˋ)
to shift; to switch; to change: 人事更動 personnel changes

更替(ㄍㄥ ㄊㄧˋ)
to alternate; to take turns

更年期(ㄍㄥ ㄋㄧㄢˊ ㄑㄧˊ)
(physiology) the menopause

更樓(ㄍㄥ ㄌㄡˊ)
a watchtower

更漏(ㄍㄥ ㄌㄡˋ)
an hourglass; a sandglass

更改(ㄍㄥ ㄍㄞˇ)
to change (over); to alter; to modify: 我們的決定是不能更改的。Our decision is unalterable.

更鼓(ㄍㄥ ㄍㄨˇ)
a night watchman's drum

更換(ㄍㄥ ㄏㄨㄢˋ)or 更易(ㄍㄥ ㄧˋ)
to change; to replace; to alter

更休(ㄍㄥ ㄒㄧㄡ)
to rest by turns

更新(ㄍㄥ ㄒㄧㄣ)
to renew; to renovate: 萬象更新。All things change from old to new.

更行(ㄍㄥ ㄒㄧㄥˊ)
(said of a woman) to remarry

更姓(ㄍㄥ ㄒㄧㄥˋ)
to change one's surname; to change one's family name

更張(ㄍㄥ ㄓㄤ)
to change; to alter

更正(ㄍㄥ ㄓㄥˋ)
to correct; to put right; correction

更始(ㄍㄥ ㄕˇ)
to renovate; to renew

更事(ㄍㄥ ㄕˋ)
experienced in affairs of the world

更深人靜(ㄍㄥ ㄕㄣ ㄖㄣˊ ㄐㄧㄥˋ)
The night is late and people are quiet. 或 Deep is the night and all is quiet.

更戍(ㄍㄥ ㄕㄨˋ)
to shift garrison forces

更次(ㄍㄥ ㄘˋ)
①(formerly) the watches of the night ② the time of a night watch

更衣(ㄍㄥ ㄧ)
① to change clothes ② to go to toilet

更衣室(ㄍㄥ ㄧ ㄕˋ)
a changeroom; a dressing room; a locker room; a toilet

更易(ㄍㄥ ㄧˋ)
to alter; to change

【更】 2304
2. ㄍㄥˋ genq gèng

more; further; to a greater degree

更妙(ㄍㄥˋ ㄇㄧㄠˋ)
still better; more interesting

更多(ㄍㄥˋ ㄉㄨㄛ)
more; still more

更好(ㄍㄥˋ ㄏㄠˇ)
better 或 So much the better.

更壞(ㄍㄥˋ ㄏㄨㄞˋ)

〔曰部〕

worse; even worse; worse still
更加(ㄍㄥˋ ㄐㄧㄚ)
even more
更兼(ㄍㄥˋ ㄐㄧㄢ)
in addition; furthermore; besides
更少(ㄍㄥˋ ㄕㄠˇ)
still less
更生(ㄍㄥˋ ㄕㄥ)
to start life anew; to have a new life; to regenerate; to revive: 他在病後獲得更生。After his illness he started his life anew.
更勝一籌(ㄍㄥˋ ㄕㄥˋ ㄧˊ ㄔㄡˊ)
even better
更有甚者(ㄍㄥˋ ㄧㄡˇ ㄕㄣˋ ㄓㄜˇ)
what is more

五畫

【曷】 2305 ㄏㄜˊ her hé
1. what
2. why not
3. how
曷故(ㄏㄜˊ ㄍㄨˋ)
why; what for
曷興乎來(ㄏㄜˊ ㄒㄧㄥ ㄏㄨ ㄌㄞˊ)
Why not come and do it?
曷若(ㄏㄜˊ ㄖㄨㄛˋ)
Wouldn't it be better to...?

六畫

【書】 2306 ㄕㄨ shu shū
1. writings; a book: 她正忙於寫一本書。She is engaged in writing a book.
2. to write: 請在紙的兩面書寫。Please write on both sides of the paper.
3. a letter: 家書抵萬金。A letter from home is worth ten thousand pieces of gold.
4. a document; a certificate
5. the style of the calligraphy; script: 楷書 standard script of handwriting
書包(ㄕㄨ ㄅㄠ)
a satchel; a schoolbag
書報(ㄕㄨ ㄅㄠˋ)
books and newspapers
書本(ㄕㄨ ㄅㄣˇ)or 書本兒(ㄕㄨ ㄅㄜˇㄦ)
a book
書不盡言(ㄕㄨ ㄅㄨˋ ㄐㄧㄣˋ ㄧㄢˊ)
(a sentence often used at the end of a letter) Written words are a poor vehicle of thoughts. 或 I have more to say than what is contained in this letter.
書皮(ㄕㄨ ㄆㄧˊ)
the binding of a book; book covers; a book jacket
書癖(ㄕㄨ ㄆㄧˇ)
bibliomania
書評(ㄕㄨ ㄆㄧㄥˊ)
a book review
書鋪(ㄕㄨ ㄆㄨˋ)
a bookstore
書眉(ㄕㄨ ㄇㄟˊ)
the upper margin of a book page
書面(ㄕㄨ ㄇㄧㄢˋ)
written form of communication
書面答覆(ㄕㄨ ㄇㄧㄢˋ ㄉㄚˊ ㄈㄨˋ)
a written reply; an answer in writing
書名(ㄕㄨ ㄇㄧㄥˊ)
the title of a book: 這本書的書名很奇特。The title of this book is unique.
書名號(ㄕㄨ ㄇㄧㄥˊ ㄏㄠˋ)
the "book title" mark (a punctuation mark in present-day written Chinese, consisting of a wavy line placed usually to the left of the title)
書目(ㄕㄨ ㄇㄨˋ)
a book catalogue: 參考書目 a booklist; a title catalogue
書法(ㄕㄨ ㄈㄚˇ)
calligraphy
書坊(ㄕㄨ ㄈㄤ)
a bookstore
書房(ㄕㄨ ㄈㄤˊ)
① a study: 你在她書房裏可以找到她。You will find her in her study. ②(in former times) a small private school
書獃子 or 書呆子(ㄕㄨ ㄉㄞ ˙ㄗ)or 書癡(ㄕㄨ ㄔ)
a studious idiot; a pedant; a bookworm
書丹(ㄕㄨ ㄉㄢ)
to write an epitaph
書單(ㄕㄨ ㄉㄢ)
a booklist
書店(ㄕㄨ ㄉㄧㄢˋ)
a bookstore
書牘(ㄕㄨ ㄉㄨˊ)
letters; correspondence
書蠹(ㄕㄨ ㄉㄨˋ)
a bookworm
書套(ㄕㄨ ㄊㄠˋ)
a book jacket; a slipcase
書攤(ㄕㄨ ㄊㄢ)or 書攤兒(ㄕㄨ ㄊㄚㄦ)or 書攤子(ㄕㄨ ㄊㄢ ˙ㄗ)
a bookstand; a bookstall
書體(ㄕㄨ ㄊㄧˇ)
calligraphic style
書僮(ㄕㄨ ㄊㄨㄥˊ)
(in former times) a boy attendant at school or in one's study
書奴(ㄕㄨ ㄋㄨˊ)
(calligraphy) a slavish imitator
書樓(ㄕㄨ ㄌㄡˊ)
a library
書林(ㄕㄨ ㄌㄧㄣˊ)
a treasury of books
書簏(ㄕㄨ ㄌㄨˋ)
a learned and yet useless person
書槅子(ㄕㄨ ㄍㄜˊ ˙ㄗ)
a bookshelf
書賈(ㄕㄨ ㄍㄨˇ)
a book dealer; a bookseller
書歸正傳(ㄕㄨ ㄍㄨㄟ ㄓㄥˋ ㄓㄨㄢˋ)
Let us come back to our main story. (a phrase often used by storytellers)
書櫃(ㄕㄨ ㄍㄨㄟˋ)
a bookcase
書館(ㄕㄨ ㄍㄨㄢˇ)
①(in former times) a private school ② a bookstore
書館兒(ㄕㄨ ㄍㄨㄚˇㄦ)
a public gathering place where storytellers entertain the audience
書客(ㄕㄨ ㄎㄜˋ)
a bookseller
書口(ㄕㄨ ㄎㄡˇ)
the outer margin of a book page (where the book title and page number are printed)
書刊(ㄕㄨ ㄎㄢ)
books and magazines: 現今的書刊銷路很大。Nowadays books and magazines have a large circulation.

書庫(ㄕㄨ ㄎㄨˋ)
the stock room of a library
書儈(ㄕㄨ ㄎㄨㄞˋ)
a book dealer
書空咄咄(ㄕㄨ ㄎㄨㄥ ㄉㄨㄛˋ ㄉㄨㄛˋ)
(literally) to write in the air, "How strange! How strange!"—to be out of one's senses (from disappointment, etc.); in great disillusion
書後(ㄕㄨ ㄏㄡˋ)
a book review attached to a literary work, written either by the author himself or someone else
書函(ㄕㄨ ㄏㄢˊ)
a letter; correspondence
書翰(ㄕㄨ ㄏㄢˋ)
a letter; correspondence
書畫(ㄕㄨ ㄏㄨㄚˋ)
works of calligraphy and painting
書畫同源(ㄕㄨ ㄏㄨㄚˋ ㄊㄨㄥˊ ㄩㄢˊ)
Calligraphy and painting are of the same origin. (being both the products of the writing brush)—a concept among Chinese literati in former times
書畫家(ㄕㄨ ㄏㄨㄚˋ ㄐㄧㄚ)
a master in calligraphy and painting
書籍(ㄕㄨ ㄐㄧˊ)
books
書脊(ㄕㄨ ㄐㄧˇ)
the spine (of a book)
書記(ㄕㄨ ㄐㄧˋ)
a clerk
書記官(ㄕㄨ ㄐㄧˋ ㄍㄨㄢ)
a clerk of a law court
書記長(ㄕㄨ ㄐㄧˋ ㄓㄤˇ)
a secretary-general; a chief clerk
書家(ㄕㄨ ㄐㄧㄚ) or 書法家(ㄕㄨ ㄈㄚˇ ㄐㄧㄚ)
a calligraphic master; a calligrapher
書夾(ㄕㄨ ㄐㄧㄚˊ)
bookends
書架(ㄕㄨ ㄐㄧㄚˋ)
a bookshelf; a bookrack
書價(ㄕㄨ ㄐㄧㄚˋ)
book prices: 書價似乎不貴。Book prices seem reasonable.
書柬 or 書簡(ㄕㄨ ㄐㄧㄢˇ)
letters
書經(ㄕㄨ ㄐㄧㄥ)
the *Book of History* (one of the *Five Classics*)
書局(ㄕㄨ ㄐㄩˊ)
a bookstore
書卷(ㄕㄨ ㄐㄩㄢˋ)
books and scrolls
書卷氣(ㄕㄨ ㄐㄩㄢˋ ㄑㄧˋ)
bookishness; a savor of books or learning (always used in a laudatory sense)
書契(ㄕㄨ ㄑㄧˋ)
a certificate (of ownership, etc.); a deed
書篋(ㄕㄨ ㄑㄧㄝˋ)
a bookcase
書簽(ㄕㄨ ㄑㄧㄢ)
① a book label pasted on the cover ② a bookmark 亦作「書籤」
書寫(ㄕㄨ ㄒㄧㄝˇ)
to write
書信(ㄕㄨ ㄒㄧㄣˋ)
letters; correspondence
書香(ㄕㄨ ㄒㄧㄤ)
the "fragrance of books"—the general environment favorable to scholars
書香門第(ㄕㄨ ㄒㄧㄤ ㄇㄣˊ ㄉㄧˋ)
a literary family
書帙(ㄕㄨ ㄓˋ)
a book jacket
書札(ㄕㄨ ㄓㄚˊ)
letters
書齋(ㄕㄨ ㄓㄞ)
a study
書桌(ㄕㄨ ㄓㄨㄛ)
a desk; a writing desk: 她正在書桌上寫字。She is writing at her desk.
書種(ㄕㄨ ㄓㄨㄥˇ)
people given to learning
書場(ㄕㄨ ㄔㄤˇ) or (ㄕㄨ ㄔㄤˊ)
a house where stories are told
書城(ㄕㄨ ㄔㄥˊ)
a place or building in which there are a number of bookstores
書櫥(ㄕㄨ ㄔㄨˊ)
a bookcase
書生(ㄕㄨ ㄕㄥ)
a student; a scholar; a bookish person
書生本色(ㄕㄨ ㄕㄥ ㄅㄣˇ ㄙㄜˋ)
essential characteristics of a scholar (especially commendable characteristics)
書生之見(ㄕㄨ ㄕㄥ ㄓ ㄐㄧㄢˋ)
the impractical view of a bookish person; a pedantic view
書聖(ㄕㄨ ㄕㄥˋ)
a calligraphic prodigy
書册(ㄕㄨ ㄘㄜˋ)
a book (as distinct from a scroll)
書肆(ㄕㄨ ㄙˋ)
a bookstore
書案(ㄕㄨ ㄢˋ)
a desk
書衣(ㄕㄨ ㄧ)
a book jacket
書頁(ㄕㄨ ㄧㄝˋ)
a page
書業(ㄕㄨ ㄧㄝˋ)
① writing as an occupation ② book business
書院(ㄕㄨ ㄩㄢˋ)
①(in former times) a school ② a euphemism for a "brothel" in certain parts of China

七畫

【曹】 2307
ㄘㄠˊ tsaur cáo
1. a plural particle: 爾曹 all of you; you
2. a Chinese family name
曹丕(ㄘㄠˊ ㄆㄧ)
Tsao Pi (187-226), poet and founder of the Wei Dynasty, son of Tsao Tsao (曹操)
曹達灰(ㄘㄠˊ ㄉㄚˊ ㄏㄨㄟ)
soda ash 亦作「蘇打灰」
曹大家(ㄘㄠˊ ㄉㄚˋ ㄍㄨ)
Pan Chao (班昭), a historian who lived in the lst century A.D., younger sister of Pan Ku(班固)
曹雪芹(ㄘㄠˊ ㄒㄩㄝˇ ㄑㄧㄣˊ)
Tsao Hsüeh-chin, also known as Tsao Chan (曹霑) (1719-1764), author of *The Dream of the Red Chamber* (紅樓夢)
曹植(ㄘㄠˊ ㄓˊ)
Tsao Chih(192-232), also known as Tsao Tze-chien (曹子建), poet and younger

〔日部〕

〔日部〕

brother of Tsao Pi (曹丕)
曹長石(ㄘㄠˊ ㄔㄤˊ ㄕˊ)
albite
曹操(ㄘㄠˊ ㄘㄠ)
Tsao Tsao (155-220), father of Tsao Pi (曹丕) and Tsao Chih (曹植), skilled in strategy and versed in literature
曹魏(ㄘㄠˊ ㄨㄟˋ)
the Wei Dynasty (220-265) of the Tsao family, as distinct from the Northern Wei Dynasty (386-534) of the Toba family

2308
【曼】 ㄇㄢˋ mann màn (又讀 ㄨㄢˋ wann wàn)
1. delicately beautiful; graceful: 輕歌曼舞 soft music and graceful dances
2. long; vast; prolonged; long-drawn-out
3. a Chinese family name
曼曼(ㄇㄢˋ ㄇㄢˋ)
long and distant
曼妙(ㄇㄢˋ ㄇㄧㄠˋ)
(said of dancing) lithe and graceful: 她的舞姿曼妙。Her dance is lithe and graceful.
曼陀林(ㄇㄢˋ ㄊㄨㄛˊ ㄌㄧㄣˊ)
(music) a mandolin
曼麗(ㄇㄢˋ ㄌㄧˋ)
delicately beautiful
曼谷(ㄇㄢˋ ㄍㄨˇ)
Bangkok, the capital of Thailand
曼徹斯特(ㄇㄢˋ ㄔㄜˋ ㄙ ㄊㄜˋ)
Manchester, an industrial city in England
曼壽(ㄇㄢˋ ㄕㄡˋ)
longevity
曼聲(ㄇㄢˋ ㄕㄥ)
to vocalize in a prolonged tone
曼澤(ㄇㄢˋ ㄗㄜˊ)
gorgeous; resplendent
曼辭(ㄇㄢˋ ㄘˊ)
(in writing) ornate language
曼延(ㄇㄢˋ ㄧㄢˊ)
to continue or extend endlessly

八畫

2309
【曾】 1. ㄗㄥ tzeng zēng
1. older or younger by three generations
2. a Chinese family name
曾母投杼(ㄗㄥ ㄇㄨˇ ㄊㄡˊ ㄓㄨˋ)
Persistent rumors against someone can shake the strongest confidence in him.
曾國藩(ㄗㄥ ㄍㄨㄛˊ ㄈㄢˊ)
Tseng Kuo-fan, 1811-1872, who helped the Manchus put down the Taiping Rebellion
曾參(ㄗㄥ ㄕㄣ) or 曾子(ㄗㄥ ㄗˇ)
Tseng Shen, a disciple of Confucius
曾祖母(ㄗㄥ ㄗㄨˇ ㄇㄨˇ)
one's great-grandmother
曾祖父(ㄗㄥ ㄗㄨˇ ㄈㄨˋ)
one's great-grandfather
曾孫(ㄗㄥ ㄙㄨㄣ)
one's great-grandchild; one's great-grandchildren
曾孫女(ㄗㄥ ㄙㄨㄣ ㄋㄩˇ)
one's great-granddaughter

2309
【曾】 2. ㄘㄥˊ tserng céng
ever; once: 數年前我曾見過他一面。I met him once a few years ago.
曾幾何時(ㄘㄥˊ ㄐㄧˇ ㄏㄜˊ ㄕˊ)
only a short time ago; before long (an expression used in connection with drastic changes)
曾經(ㄘㄥˊ ㄐㄧㄥ)
to have had the experience of; to have already: 曾經有人看見她。Somebody has already seen her.
曾經滄海(ㄘㄥˊ ㄐㄧㄥ ㄘㄤ ㄏㄞˇ)
to have experienced great things

2310
【替】 ㄊㄧˋ tih tì
1. to take the place of; to replace; to substitute
2. to decay; to decline
3. to neglect
4. for; on behalf of: 別替他担心。Don't worry about him.
替代(ㄊㄧˋ ㄉㄞˋ)
to substitute
替代物(ㄊㄧˋ ㄉㄞˋ ㄨˋ)
a substitute: 石油可製出橡膠的替代物。Substitutes for rubber can be made from petroleum.
替頭兒(ㄊㄧˋ ·ㄊㄡㄦ)
(superstition) a substitute sought among the living by a haunting ghost
替工(ㄊㄧˋ ㄍㄨㄥ)
a substitute worker
替壞(ㄊㄧˋ ㄏㄨㄞˋ)
to decay; to deteriorate; to decline
替換(ㄊㄧˋ ·ㄏㄨㄢ)
to replace; to substitute: 有甚麼東西能替換母愛嗎? Can anything replace a mother's love?
替懈(ㄊㄧˋ ㄒㄧㄝˋ)
to neglect
替手(ㄊㄧˋ ㄕㄡˇ)
a substitute or alternate (worker, contestant, etc.); an understudy; a standby
替身(ㄊㄧˋ ㄕㄣ)
a double; an understudy
替身演員(ㄊㄧˋ ㄕㄣ ㄧㄢˇ ㄩㄢˊ)
a stunt man
替人(ㄊㄧˋ ㄖㄣˊ)
a substitute (for another person)
替死鬼(ㄊㄧˋ ㄙˇ ㄍㄨㄟˇ)
a scapegoat

2311
【最】 ㄗㄨㄟˋ tzuey zuì
extreme; superlative
最大(ㄗㄨㄟˋ ㄉㄚˋ)
the biggest; the largest; the greatest; the maximum
最大公約數(ㄗㄨㄟˋ ㄉㄚˋ ㄍㄨㄥ ㄩㄝ ㄕㄨˋ)
(mathematics) the greatest common divisor
最低(ㄗㄨㄟˋ ㄉㄧ)
the lowest; the minimum; the least: 我們已將費用減至最低。We have reduced our expenses to the minimum.
最低工資(ㄗㄨㄟˋ ㄉㄧ ㄍㄨㄥ ㄗ)
the minimum wage
最低限度(ㄗㄨㄟˋ ㄉㄧ ㄒㄧㄢˋ ㄉㄨˋ)
① the lowest limit ② at least
最多(ㄗㄨㄟˋ ㄉㄨㄛ)
the most; at most: 錢最多的人不一定永遠是最快樂的人。Those who have the most money are not always the happiest.
最短(ㄗㄨㄟˋ ㄉㄨㄢˇ)
the shortest
最高(ㄗㄨㄟˋ ㄍㄠ)
the highest; the superlative;

the supreme; the paramount; the topmost; the uppermost; the maximum

最高法院(ㄗㄨㄟˋ ㄍㄠ ㄈㄚˇ ㄩㄢˋ)
the Supreme Court

最高峯(ㄗㄨㄟˋ ㄍㄠ ㄈㄥ)
the summit; the climax

最高當局(ㄗㄨㄟˋ ㄍㄠ ㄉㄤ ㄐㄩˊ)
the highest authorities

最高統帥(ㄗㄨㄟˋ ㄍㄠ ㄊㄨㄥˇ ㄕㄨㄞˋ)
the supreme commander; the commander in chief of the armed forces

最高公因數(ㄗㄨㄟˋ ㄍㄠ ㄍㄨㄥ ㄧㄣ ㄕㄨˋ)
(mathematics) the highest or greatest common factor

最高級(ㄗㄨㄟˋ ㄍㄠ ㄐㄧˊ)
① the highest; the summit ② (linguistics) the superlative degree

最高權力(ㄗㄨㄟˋ ㄍㄠ ㄑㄩㄢˊ ㄌㄧˋ)
the supreme power

最高學府(ㄗㄨㄟˋ ㄍㄠ ㄒㄩㄝˊ ㄈㄨˇ)
the highest seat of learning

最高潮(ㄗㄨㄟˋ ㄍㄠ ㄔㄠˊ)
the climax; the culmination: 夏天的炎熱已達最高潮。The heat of summer has reached its climax.

最好(ㄗㄨㄟˋ ㄏㄠˇ)
① the best: 這是我所讀過最好的書。This is the best book I have ever read. ② had better: 你最好現在就走。You had better go now.

最後(ㄗㄨㄟˋ ㄏㄡˋ)
last; the last; the ultimate; the final: 他是最後到達的人。He was the last man to arrive.

最後通牒(ㄗㄨㄟˋ ㄏㄡˋ ㄊㄨㄥ ㄉㄧㄝˊ)
an ultimatum

最後審判(ㄗㄨㄟˋ ㄏㄡˋ ㄕㄣˇ ㄆㄢˋ)
the Last Judgment

最後勝利(ㄗㄨㄟˋ ㄏㄡˋ ㄕㄥˋ ㄌㄧˋ)
the final victory

最後一滴(ㄗㄨㄟˋ ㄏㄡˋ ㄧˊ ㄉㄧ)
the last drop

最後一人(ㄗㄨㄟˋ ㄏㄡˋ ㄧˊ ㄖㄣˊ)
the last man: 他是發言的最後一人。He was the last man to speak.

最後五分鐘(ㄗㄨㄟˋ ㄏㄡˋ ㄨˇ ㄈㄣ ㄓㄨㄥ)
the last five minutes; the last minutes which may spell the success or failure of an undertaking; the crucial moment

最壞(ㄗㄨㄟˋ ㄏㄨㄞˋ)
the worst; the meanest; the most vicious

最惠國(ㄗㄨㄟˋ ㄏㄨㄟˋ ㄍㄨㄛˊ)
the most favored nation

最惠國條款(ㄗㄨㄟˋ ㄏㄨㄟˋ ㄍㄨㄛˊ ㄊㄧㄠˊ ㄎㄨㄢˇ)
a most-favored-nation clause

最佳(ㄗㄨㄟˋ ㄐㄧㄚ) or 最優(ㄗㄨㄟˋ ㄧㄡ)
the best; the superlative

最近(ㄗㄨㄟˋ ㄐㄧㄣˋ)
① the nearest; the closest; the proximate: 我們從最近的路線來的。We came by the nearest route. ② recently; recent; lately: 我最近在街上碰見了他。Recently I met him on the street.

最敬禮(ㄗㄨㄟˋ ㄐㄧㄥˋ ㄌㄧˇ)
the most respectful salutation; the deepest homage

最小(ㄗㄨㄟˋ ㄒㄧㄠˇ)
the least; the smallest; the minimum

最小公倍數(ㄗㄨㄟˋ ㄒㄧㄠˇ ㄍㄨㄥ ㄅㄟˋ ㄕㄨˋ)
(mathematics) the least common multiple; the lowest common multiple

最小公分母(ㄗㄨㄟˋ ㄒㄧㄠˇ ㄍㄨㄥ ㄈㄣ ㄇㄨˇ)
(mathematics) the least common denominator

最先(ㄗㄨㄟˋ ㄒㄧㄢ)
① the first; the earliest; the foremost ② at first; in the beginning

最新(ㄗㄨㄟˋ ㄒㄧㄣ)
the newest; the latest

最新發明(ㄗㄨㄟˋ ㄒㄧㄣ ㄈㄚ ㄇㄧㄥˊ)
the latest invention

最新樣式(ㄗㄨㄟˋ ㄒㄧㄣ ㄧㄤˋ ㄕˋ)
the latest style

最終(ㄗㄨㄟˋ ㄓㄨㄥ)
the final; the last; the ultimate

最長(ㄗㄨㄟˋ ㄔㄤˊ)
the longest

最初(ㄗㄨㄟˋ ㄔㄨ)
① the first; the earliest ② at first; in the beginning

最少(ㄗㄨㄟˋ ㄕㄠˇ)
the least; the minimum

最上乘(ㄗㄨㄟˋ ㄕㄤˋ ㄕㄥˋ)
first-rate; top-notch; the best

最矮(ㄗㄨㄟˋ ㄞˇ)
(said of stature) the shortest; (said of houses) the lowest

九畫

【會】 2312
1. ㄏㄨㄟˋ huey huì

1. to meet: 明天我將和他相會。I will meet him tomorrow.
2. to assemble; to gather; to converge
3. a meeting; a convention; a conference: 俱樂部召開一次會議。The club held a meeting.
4. an association; a society
5. a private banking cooperative
6. to be able to: 他會彈鋼琴。He is able to play the piano.
7. to understand; to comprehend; to realize
8. shall; will
9. a chief city; a capital: 省會 the provincial capital

會不會(ㄏㄨㄟˋ ·ㄅㄨ ㄏㄨㄟˋ)
① Is it likely that...? ② Can (you, he, etc.) do...or not?

會盟(ㄏㄨㄟˋ ㄇㄥˊ)
(said of feudal lords) to meet for concluding treaties

會面(ㄏㄨㄟˋ ㄇㄧㄢˋ)
to meet face to face: 我們約定了星期三和她會面。We have an appointment to meet her on Wednesday.

會費(ㄏㄨㄟˋ ㄈㄟˋ)
membership fees; dues

會典(ㄏㄨㄟˋ ㄉㄧㄢˇ)
a record of laws and systems of a dynasty

會頭(ㄏㄨㄟˋ ㄊㄡˊ)
one who initiates a private banking cooperative and who receives the first payments from other members

會談(ㄏㄨㄟˋ ㄊㄢˊ)
talks: 我們已舉行了許多次會談。 We've had many talks.

會通(ㄏㄨㄟˋ ㄊㄨㄥ)
to understand; to master

會同(ㄏㄨㄟˋ ㄊㄨㄥˊ)
together with

會舘 or 會館(ㄏㄨㄟˋ ㄍㄨㄢˇ)
① a union building ② a club house for residents from the

same province or county

會客(ㄏㄨㄟˋ ㄎㄜˋ)
to receive callers (or visitors)

會客時間(ㄏㄨㄟˋ ㄎㄜˋ ㄕˊ ㄐㄧㄢ)
the time for receiving visitors; visiting hours

會客室(ㄏㄨㄟˋ ㄎㄜˋ ㄕˋ)
a reception room

會考(ㄏㄨㄟˋ ㄎㄠˇ)
a general examination for students from various schools

會合(ㄏㄨㄟˋ ㄏㄜˊ)
to assemble; to gather; to meet; to converge; to join: 我們必須再會合討論此事。We must meet again to discuss it.

會合點(ㄏㄨㄟˋ ㄏㄜˊ ㄉㄧㄢˇ)
① a point of convergence ② (military) a meeting point

會話(ㄏㄨㄟˋ ㄏㄨㄚˋ)
a conversation; a chat; a talk; a dialogue

會集(ㄏㄨㄟˋ ㄐㄧˊ)
to assemble; to gather together

會籍(ㄏㄨㄟˋ ㄐㄧˊ)
membership (of an association)

會見(ㄏㄨㄟˋ ㄐㄧㄢˋ)
to meet (a person): 我在一個宴會上會見一個老朋友。I met with an old friend at a dinner party.

會聚(ㄏㄨㄟˋ ㄐㄩˋ)
to assemble; to flock together

會聚透鏡(ㄏㄨㄟˋ ㄐㄩˋ ㄊㄡˋ ㄐㄧㄥˋ)
convergent lenses

會聚鏡(ㄏㄨㄟˋ ㄐㄩˋ ㄐㄧㄥˋ)
a convergent mirror

會期(ㄏㄨㄟˋ ㄑㄧˊ)
① the time of a meeting ② the duration of a meeting

會齊(ㄏㄨㄟˋ ㄑㄧˊ)
to be all present at a gathering

會錢(ㄏㄨㄟˋ ㄑㄧㄢˊ)
regular payments made by members of a private banking cooperative

會銜(ㄏㄨㄟˋ ㄒㄧㄢˊ)
jointly sign an official document (other than a treaty, agreement, etc.)

會心(ㄏㄨㄟˋ ㄒㄧㄣ)
to come to an understanding without explanation; meeting of minds

會心的微笑(ㄏㄨㄟˋ ㄒㄧㄣ ˙ㄉㄜ ㄨㄟ ㄒㄧㄠˋ)
an insinuative smile; an understanding smile

會址(ㄏㄨㄟˋ ㄓˇ)
the address of an association or organization

會戰(ㄏㄨㄟˋ ㄓㄢˋ)
a major battle

會診(ㄏㄨㄟˋ ㄓㄣˇ)
(medicine) the consultation of doctors; (group) consultation

會章(ㄏㄨㄟˋ ㄓㄤ)
the charter of an association or organization

會長(ㄏㄨㄟˋ ㄓㄤˇ)
the president of an association or organization

會賬 or **會帳**(ㄏㄨㄟˋ ㄓㄤˋ)
to buy one's friend a meal or a drink

會鈔(ㄏㄨㄟˋ ㄔㄠ)
to buy one's friend a meal or a drink

會場(ㄏㄨㄟˋ ㄔㄤˊ)or(ㄏㄨㄟˋ ㄔㄤˇ)
the place of a meeting; the site of a conference; a conference (or assembly) hall

會師(ㄏㄨㄟˋ ㄕ)
a rendezvous of friendly forces; to join forces

會試(ㄏㄨㄟˋ ㄕˋ)
(in old China) a general examination (for successful candidates from all over the country) held at the Ministry of Education prior to the imperial examination

會社(ㄏㄨㄟˋ ㄕㄜˋ)
① a company in Japan ② an association

會審(ㄏㄨㄟˋ ㄕㄣˇ)
to review or try jointly: 經過會審，這人被判決有罪。The man was tried jointly and found guilty.

會商(ㄏㄨㄟˋ ㄕㄤ)
to negotiate; to confer; to consult: 他們會商一項貸款。They negotiated a loan.

會說(ㄏㄨㄟˋ ㄕㄨㄛ)
able to talk persuasively or eloquently

會水(ㄏㄨㄟˋ ㄕㄨㄟˇ)
able to swim

會葬(ㄏㄨㄟˋ ㄗㄤˋ)
a mass burial

會餐(ㄏㄨㄟˋ ㄘㄢ)
to dine together; to have a dinner party

會萃(ㄏㄨㄟˋ ㄘㄨㄟˋ)
to converge

會所(ㄏㄨㄟˋ ㄙㄨㄛˇ)
the office of an association or organization

會意(ㄏㄨㄟˋ ㄧˋ)
① to understand the meaning; to take a hint ② "meeting of ideas", or associative compounds, one of six categories under which Chinese characters are grouped (The meaning of a character under this category is suggested by its significant combination of two or more pictographs.)

會議(ㄏㄨㄟˋ ㄧˋ)
a conference; a meeting: 許多國際會議曾在日內瓦舉行。Many international conferences have been held in Geneva.

會議記錄(ㄏㄨㄟˋ ㄧˋ ㄐㄧˋ ㄌㄨˋ)
minutes

會要(ㄏㄨㄟˋ ㄧㄠˋ)
a record of social backgrounds of a dynasty

會友(ㄏㄨㄟˋ ㄧㄡˇ)
① a fellow member of an association or organization ② to meet a friend

會晤(ㄏㄨㄟˋ ㄨˋ)
to meet: 兩國外交官定期會晤。The diplomats of two countries meet regularly.

會務(ㄏㄨㄟˋ ㄨˋ)
the business of a meeting, conference, convention, association, etc.

會元(ㄏㄨㄟˋ ㄩㄢˊ)
the head of the successful candidates in civil service examinations in former times

會員(ㄏㄨㄟˋ ㄩㄢˊ)
a member of an association, society, etc.

會員大會(ㄏㄨㄟˋ ㄩㄢˊ ㄉㄚˋ ㄏㄨㄟˋ)

a general assembly

會員國(ㄏㄨㄟˋ ㄩㄢˊ ㄍㄨㄛˊ)
a member nation (or state)

【會】 2312
2. ㄏㄨㄟˇ hoei huǐ
a brief period of time; a moment

會子(ㄏㄨㄟˇ・ㄗ)or 會兒(ㄏㄨㄜˇㄦ)
a moment: 請稍等一會兒! Just a moment!

【會】 2312
3. ㄎㄨㄞˋ kuay kuài
to add; to compute

會計(ㄎㄨㄞˋ ㄐㄧˋ)
①accounting ②an accountant; a treasurer: 他在一家百貨公司當會計。He works in a department store as an accountant.

會計部(ㄎㄨㄞˋ ㄐㄧˋ ㄅㄨˋ)
an accounting department

會計年度(ㄎㄨㄞˋ ㄐㄧˋ ㄋㄧㄢˊ ㄉㄨˋ)
a fiscal year (as distinct from a calendar year)

會計學(ㄎㄨㄞˋ ㄐㄧˋ ㄒㄩㄝˊ)
accounting: 他主修會計學。He majored in accounting.

會計主任(ㄎㄨㄞˋ ㄐㄧˋ ㄓㄨˇ ㄖㄣˋ)
an accountant general; a chief accountant

會計處(ㄎㄨㄞˋ ㄐㄧˋ ㄔㄨˋ)
an accounting section or department; a comptroller's office

會計師(ㄎㄨㄞˋ ㄐㄧˋ ㄕ)
C.A.(a chartered accountant); C.P.A.(a certified public accountant)

會計室(ㄎㄨㄞˋ ㄐㄧˋ ㄕˋ)
an accountant's office

會計人員(ㄎㄨㄞˋ ㄐㄧˋ ㄖㄣˊ ㄩㄢˊ)
accounting personnel

【會】 2312
4. ㄍㄨㄟˋ guey guì

會稽(ㄍㄨㄟˋ ㄐㄧ)
Kueichi, Chekiang Province

十畫

【朅】 2313
ㄑㄧㄝˋ chieh qiè
to depart; to go; to leave

月部
ㄩㄝˋ yueh yuè

【月】 2314
ㄩㄝˋ yueh yuè
1. the moon
2. the month

月白(ㄩㄝˋ ㄅㄞˊ)
bluish white; pale blue

月白風清(ㄩㄝˋ ㄅㄞˊ ㄈㄥ ㄑㄧㄥ)
(descriptive of nocturnal beauty) The moon is pale and the breeze is refreshing.

月報(ㄩㄝˋ ㄅㄠˋ)
① a monthly report ② a monthly journal

月半(ㄩㄝˋ ㄅㄢˋ)
the 15th day of a month

月表(ㄩㄝˋ ㄅㄧㄠˇ)
a monthly chronology

月餅(ㄩㄝˋ ㄅㄧㄥˇ)
a moon cake: 中國人在中秋節吃月餅。The Chinese eat moon cakes during the Mid-Autumn Festival.

月票(ㄩㄝˋ ㄆㄧㄠˋ)
a monthly ticket

月杪(ㄩㄝˋ ㄇㄧㄠˇ)
the end of a month

月明星稀(ㄩㄝˋ ㄇㄧㄥˊ ㄒㄧㄥ ㄒㄧ)
(descriptive of nocturnal beauty) The moon is bright and the stars are few.

月分(ㄩㄝˋ ㄈㄣˋ)
the month; monthly

月分牌兒(ㄩㄝˋ ㄈㄣˋ ㄆㄚˊㄦ)
a calendar

月俸(ㄩㄝˋ ㄈㄥˋ)
a monthly salary: 你的月俸若干? What is your monthly salary?

月大(ㄩㄝˋ ㄉㄚˋ)
a 30-day month of the lunar calendar; a 31-day month of the Gregorian calendar

月底(ㄩㄝˋ ㄉㄧˇ)
the end of a month

月臺(ㄩㄝˋ ㄊㄞˊ)
a platform (at a railway station): 在火車站,鐵軌旁有一座月臺。There is a platform beside the track at the railway station.

月臺票(ㄩㄝˋ ㄊㄞˊ ㄆㄧㄠˋ)
a platform ticket

月老(ㄩㄝˋ ㄌㄠˇ)
a matchmaker

月曆(ㄩㄝˋ ㄌㄧˋ)
①a calendar, each page of which is a table of the days of a month (as distinct from one of which each page shows a day) ②(in ancient China) a record of government orders to be announced every month

月裏嫦娥(ㄩㄝˋ ・ㄌㄧ ㄔㄤˊ ㄜˊ)
a legendary fairy of the moon—a beauty

月亮(ㄩㄝˋ ・ㄌㄧㄤ)
the moon: 那晚沒有月亮。It was a night with no moon visible in the sky.

月令(ㄩㄝˋ ㄌㄧㄥˋ)
a chapter of the *Book of Rites* (禮記)

月桂(ㄩㄝˋ ㄍㄨㄟˋ)
a laurel (*Laurus nobilis*)

月光(ㄩㄝˋ ㄍㄨㄤ)
moonlight: 他們坐在皎潔的月光下。They sat in the bright moonlight.

月宮(ㄩㄝˋ ㄍㄨㄥ)
a legendary palace on the moon

月刊(ㄩㄝˋ ㄎㄢ)
a monthly publication; a monthly: 這雜誌是月刊。It is a monthly magazine.

月華(ㄩㄝˋ ㄏㄨㄚˊ)
①brightness of the moon ②(astronomy) the halo around the moon; the lunar corona

月季票(ㄩㄝˋ ㄐㄧˋ ㄆㄧㄠˋ)
a season ticket: 他買了一張火車的月季票。He bought a railway season ticket.

月季花(ㄩㄝˋ ㄐㄧˋ ㄏㄨㄚ)
a rose (*Rosa chinensis*)

月經(ㄩㄝˋ ㄐㄧㄥ)or 月信(ㄩㄝˋ ㄒㄧㄣˋ) or 月事(ㄩㄝˋ ㄕˋ)
menses; periods; monthlies

月經布(ㄩㄝˋ ㄐㄧㄥ ㄅㄨˋ) or 月經帶(ㄩㄝˋ ㄐㄧㄥ ㄉㄞˋ)
a hygienic band; a sanitary napkin; a sanitary belt

月經不調(ㄩㄝˋ ㄐㄧㄥ ㄅㄨˋ ㄊㄧㄠˊ)
irregular menses; menoxenia

月經停止(ㄩㄝˋ ㄐㄧㄥ ㄊㄧㄥˊ ㄓˇ)
menopause; cessation of menses

月經過多(ㄩㄝˋ ㄐㄧㄥ ㄍㄨㄛˋ ㄉㄨㄛ)
menorrhagia; the excessive menstruation

月經過少(ㄩㄝˋ ㄐㄧㄥ ㄍㄨㄛˋ ㄕㄠˇ)
hypomenorrhea

月經周期(ㄩㄝˋ ㄐㄧㄥ ㄓㄡ ㄑㄧˊ)
menstrual cycles

月球(ㄩㄝˋ ㄑㄧㄡˊ)
the moon: 月球繞地球運行。The moon revolves round the earth.

月琴(ㄩㄝˋ ㄑㄧㄣˊ)
a four-stringed musical instrument

月息(ㄩㄝˋ ㄒㄧˊ)or 月利(ㄩㄝˋ ㄌㄧˋ)
monthly interest; monthly interest rate

月下(ㄩㄝˋ ㄒㄧㄚˋ)
under the moon: 他們在月下散步。They walked under the moon.

月下老人(ㄩㄝˋ ㄒㄧㄚˋ ㄌㄠˇ ㄖㄣˊ)
a matchmaker

月小(ㄩㄝˋ ㄒㄧㄠˇ)
a 29-day month of the lunar calendar; a 30-day month of the Gregorian calendar

月薪(ㄩㄝˋ ㄒㄧㄣ)
a monthly salary

月支(ㄩㄝˋ ㄓ)
① monthly expenses ② to draw (a certain amount) every month ③ same as 月氏 (see below)

月氏(ㄩㄝˋ ㄓ)
name of a nomadic people who used to live in Central Asia

月終(ㄩㄝˋ ㄓㄨㄥ)or 月尾(ㄩㄝˋ ㄨㄟˇ) or 月底(ㄩㄝˋ ㄉㄧˇ)
the end of a month: 我們於月底到歐洲去。We will leave for Europe at the end of the month.

月初(ㄩㄝˋ ㄔㄨ)or 月頭(ㄩㄝˋ ㄊㄡˊ)
the beginning of a month

月蝕 or 月食(ㄩㄝˋ ㄕˊ)
(astronomy) a lunar eclipse

月朔(ㄩㄝˋ ㄕㄨㄛˋ)
the first day of each moon

月子(ㄩㄝˋ ·ㄗ)
the month of confinement after giving birth to a child

月色(ㄩㄝˋ ㄙㄜˋ)
moonlight: 美麗的湖水在燦爛的月色下閃爍如水晶。In the brilliant moonlight the beautiful lake sparkles like crystals.

月牙兒 or 月芽兒(ㄩㄝˋ ㄧㄚˊㄦ)
the new moon or crescent moon

月夜(ㄩㄝˋ ㄧㄝˋ)
a moonlight night; a moonlit night

月曜日(ㄩㄝˋ ㄧㄠˋ ㄖˋ)
Monday

月望(ㄩㄝˋ ㄨㄤˋ)
the 15th day of each moon

月餘(ㄩㄝˋ ㄩˊ)
more than a month

月月紅(ㄩㄝˋ ㄩㄝˋ ㄏㄨㄥˊ)
American beauty (a flower)

月圓則虧(ㄩㄝˋ ㄩㄢˊ ㄗㄜˊ ㄎㄨㄟ)
(literally) The moon begins to wane the moment it becomes full.—Decline inevitably follows culmination.

月暈(ㄩㄝˋ ㄩㄣˋ)
the halo of the moon; the lunar aureole

二畫

【有】 2315
1. ㄧㄡˇ yeou yŏu
to have; to be present; to exist; there is

有把握(ㄧㄡˇ ㄅㄚˇ ㄨㄛˋ)
confident of success

有背景(ㄧㄡˇ ㄅㄟˋ ㄐㄧㄥˇ)
to have powerful connections

有備無患(ㄧㄡˇ ㄅㄟˋ ㄨˊ ㄏㄨㄢˋ)
There is no danger when there is preparedness.

有板有眼(ㄧㄡˇ ㄅㄢˇ ㄧㄡˇ ㄧㄢˇ)
①(said of singing performances) rhythmical; adhering to the exact rhythm ②(said of speech) the articulate ③(said of conduct) systematic

有辦法(ㄧㄡˇ ㄅㄢˋ ㄈㄚˇ)
① to have a way to solve some problem; to know how to do something ② to be resourceful

有本領(ㄧㄡˇ ㄅㄣˇ ㄌㄧㄥˇ)
capable; talented; resourceful: 他是一個有本領的音樂家。He is a talented musician.

有鼻子有眼兒(ㄧㄡˇ ㄅㄧˊ ·ㄗ ㄧㄡˇ ㄧㄚˇㄦ)
① lifelike; with every detail vividly described ② plausible; convincing

有邊兒(ㄧㄡˇ ㄅㄧㄚㄦ)
to begin to take shape; likely to succeed

有病(ㄧㄡˇ ㄅㄧㄥˋ)
sick; ill; feeling unwell: 我恐怕他可能有病了。I'm afraid he may have fallen ill.

有不是(ㄧㄡˇ ㄅㄨˊ ·ㄕ)
to have done wrong: 你們兩人都有不是。Both of you have done wrong.

有盼兒(ㄧㄡˇ ㄆㄚˋㄦ)
hopeful; promising

有憑有據(ㄧㄡˇ ㄆㄧㄥˊ ㄧㄡˇ ㄐㄩˋ)
well-founded: 這控告有憑有據。The accusation is well-founded.

有門兒(ㄧㄡˇ ㄇㄜˊㄦ)
①(said of works by beginners, etc.) to show qualities measuring up to certain standards; to get the hang of ② likely to be realized or to come true; to be hopeful (of success)

有眉目(ㄧㄡˇ ㄇㄟˊ ㄇㄨˋ)
to begin to take shape; about to materialize

有毛病(ㄧㄡˇ ㄇㄠˊ ·ㄅㄧㄥ)
① sick; ill ② something wrong; out of order: 這車有毛病。Something is wrong with the car.

有面子(ㄧㄡˇ ㄇㄧㄢˋ ·ㄗ)
to have one's face or honor preserved; to have one's vanity satisfied

有名(ㄧㄡˇ ㄇㄧㄥˊ)
famous; renowned; noted; well-known; illustrious; distinguished: 李白是一位有名的中國詩人。Li Po was a noted Chinese poet.

有名堂(ㄧㄡˇ ㄇㄧㄥˊ ㄊㄤˊ)
(colloquial) to be promising; to show encouraging signs

有名有姓(ㄧㄡˇ ㄇㄧㄥˊ ㄧㄡˇ ㄒㄧㄥˋ)
a person who really exists (as distinct from a fictitious character)

有名無實(ㄧㄡˇ ㄇㄧㄥˊ ㄨˊ ㄕˊ)
to exist only in name

有名望(ㄧㄡˇ ㄇㄧㄥˊ ㄨㄤˋ)
famous; renowned; noted; distinguished; prestigious

有命(ㄧㄡˇ ㄇㄧㄥˋ)
to be alive

有目共睹(ㄧㄡˇ ㄇㄨˋ ㄍㄨㄥˋ ㄉㄨˇ)
known to everyone with eyes open; to be obvious to all

有份兒 or 有分兒(ㄧㄡˇ ㄈㄜˋㄦ)
to have a share; to have taken a part in; to participate in

有飯大家喫(ㄧㄡˇ ㄈㄢˋ ㄉㄚˋ ㄐㄧㄚ ㄔ)
to let everyone have a finger in the pie

有分寸(ㄧㄡˇ ㄈㄣ ㄘㄨㄣˋ)
having a sense of propriety; knowing how far to go and when to stop

有夫之婦(ㄧㄡˇ ㄈㄨ ㄓ ㄈㄨˋ)
a married woman

有福同享，有禍同當(ㄧㄡˇ ㄈㄨˊ ㄊㄨㄥˊ ㄒㄧㄤˇ, ㄧㄡˇ ㄏㄨㄛˋ ㄊㄨㄥˊ ㄉㄤ)
to share bliss and misfortune together

有福氣(ㄧㄡˇ ㄈㄨˊ ˙ㄑㄧ)
to be blessed or favored by fortune: 他很有福氣，有一個好兒子。He was fortunate enough to have a good son.

有得(ㄧㄡˇ ㄉㄜˊ)
① to have learned or acquired something ② in store

有德(ㄧㄡˇ ㄉㄜˊ)
virtuous; righteous: 他是個有德的人。He is a man of virtue.

有的(ㄧㄡˇ ˙ㄉㄜ)
① some: 有的人喜歡運動，有的人不喜歡。 Some people like sports, and others do not. ② Yes, there is.... 或 Yes, I have....

有的是(ㄧㄡˇ ˙ㄉㄜ ㄕˋ)
to be found everywhere; to have plenty of: 他有的是時間。He has all the time in the world.

有待(ㄧㄡˇ ㄉㄞˋ)
① to wait until ② to require or need (improvement, investigation, etc.)

有道(ㄧㄡˇ ㄉㄠˋ)
① learned and virtuous ② reasonable; right; lawful ③ Good government prevails.

有道理(ㄧㄡˇ ㄉㄠˋ ㄌㄧˇ)
reasonable; plausible; convincing

有膽量(ㄧㄡˇ ㄉㄢˇ ㄌㄧㄤˋ)
to have the courage or guts

有敵無我(ㄧㄡˇ ㄉㄧˊ ㄨˊ ㄨㄛˇ)
If the enemy triumphs, there will be no place for us.

有底(ㄧㄡˇ ㄉㄧˇ)
to know the true character of a matter

有點兒(ㄧㄡˇ ㄉㄧㄚˇㄦ)
some; a little; somewhat; sort of: 我對此工作有點兒厭倦了。I am somewhat tired of this work.

有毒(ㄧㄡˇ ㄉㄨˊ)
poisonous; venomous

有頭緒(ㄧㄡˇ ㄊㄡˊ ㄒㄩˋ)
to be near solution or success; to have found the clue

有頭兒(ㄧㄡˇ ㄊㄡˊㄦ)
to begin to show promise of success

有頭有臉兒(ㄧㄡˇ ㄊㄡˊ ㄧㄡˇ ㄌㄧㄚˇㄦ)
① honored; respected ② presentable

有頭有尾(ㄧㄡˇ ㄊㄡˊ ㄧㄡˇ ㄨㄟˇ)
complete; finished; to do a job from beginning to end: 這是一個有頭有尾的故事嗎? Is this a complete story?

有頭無尾(ㄧㄡˇ ㄊㄡˊ ㄨˊ ㄨㄟˇ)
to leave a job incomplete or unfinished; to quit doing something halfway

有蹄類(ㄧㄡˇ ㄊㄧˊ ㄌㄟˋ)
(zoology) the Ungulata

有條不紊(ㄧㄡˇ ㄊㄧㄠˊ ㄅㄨˋ ㄨㄣˋ)
methodical; systematic; orderly: 他的頭腦有條不紊。He has an orderly mind.

有條件的(ㄧㄡˇ ㄊㄧㄠˊ ㄐㄧㄢˋ ˙ㄉㄜ)
conditional; with conditions attached: 這提議是有條件的。The offer is conditional.

有條有理(ㄧㄡˇ ㄊㄧㄠˊ ㄧㄡˇ ㄌㄧˇ)
logical; orderly; systematic

有天沒日(ㄧㄡˇ ㄊㄧㄢ ㄇㄟˊ ㄖˋ)
(said of remarks) outrageous; heinous; flagrant

有天無日(ㄧㄡˇ ㄊㄧㄢ ㄨˊ ㄖˋ)
devoid of justice

有托而逃(ㄧㄡˇ ㄊㄨㄛ ㄦˊ ㄊㄠˊ)
to shirk responsibility under an excuse

有你沒我(ㄧㄡˇ ㄋㄧˇ ㄇㄟˊ ㄨㄛˇ)
You and I cannot coexist.—We are sworn enemies.

有你的(ㄧㄡˇ ㄋㄧˇ ˙ㄉㄜ)
① Excellent! 或 Very good! (used in praising another's performance) ② You'll have your share.

有年(ㄧㄡˇ ㄋㄧㄢˊ)
① to have been in existence for years ② a year of bumper crops; a year of plenty

有了(ㄧㄡˇ ˙ㄌㄜ)
① to have obtained what was wanted: 他有了些錢。He has got some money. ② to have found the answer or solution 或 I've got it. ③ to become pregnant: 他的太太有(喜)了。His wife is pregnant.

有來頭(ㄧㄡˇ ㄌㄞˊ ˙ㄊㄡ)
(colloquial) not the ordinary kind; of some special importance or distinction

有來有去的(ㄧㄡˇ ㄌㄞˊ ㄧㄡˇ ㄑㄩˋ ˙ㄉㄜ)
(said of an article, a statement, a speech, etc.) to sound reasonable, convincing, etc.

有來有往(ㄧㄡˇ ㄌㄞˊ ㄧㄡˇ ㄨㄤˇ)
(said of exchanging gifts or rendering help to others) reciprocal

有賴(ㄧㄡˇ ㄌㄞˋ)
to depend on; to rest on

有勞(ㄧㄡˇ ㄌㄠˊ)
(a conventional phrase used in thanking for or soliciting another's assistance) to have troubled (you) 或 Please do me a favor by....

有落兒(ㄧㄡˇ ㄌㄠˋㄦ)
to have found a means of support or a way to make a living

有禮(ㄧㄡˇ ㄌㄧˇ)
polite; courteous; civil; well-mannered: 那個有禮的孩子把座位讓給我。That polite boy gave me his seat.

有理(ㄧㄡˇ ㄌㄧˇ)
① reasonable; logical: 他說的有理。What he says is quite reasonable. ② justified; to

〔月部〕

have justice on one's side ③ (mathematics) rational

有理無情(ㄧㄡˇ ㄌㄧˇ ㄨˊ ㄑㄧㄥˊ)
①to disregard personal feelings ② reluctantly; unwillingly

有利(ㄧㄡˇ ㄌㄧˋ)
profitable; advantageous; beneficial; favorable; helpful; conducive

有利必有弊(ㄧㄡˇ ㄌㄧˋ ㄅㄧˋ ㄧㄡˇ ㄅㄧˋ)
Advantages are inevitably accompanied by disadvantages.

有利可圖(ㄧㄡˇ ㄌㄧˋ ㄎㄜˇ ㄊㄨˊ)
(said of material profit) profitable: 這一樁買賣大家都有利可圖。This deal is profitable to all of us.

有力者(ㄧㄡˇ ㄌㄧˋ ㄓㄜˇ)
a powerful person: 他在這區域是一個有力者。He is a powerful person in this neighborhood.

有例在先(ㄧㄡˇ ㄌㄧˋ ㄗㄞˋ ㄒㄧㄢ)
There are precedents for that.

有臉(ㄧㄡˇ ㄌㄧㄢˇ)
①respectable; honorable; proud: 她雖貧窮,卻是個有臉的人物。She is poor but respectable. ② favored; loved

有兩下子(ㄧㄡˇ ㄌㄧㄤˇ ㄒㄧㄚˋ ˙ㄗ)
to have a real skill; to know one's stuff

有感(ㄧㄡˇ ㄍㄢˇ)
a comment on something (usually used as a suffix of a title of a literary composition)

有感地震(ㄧㄡˇ ㄍㄢˇ ㄉㄧˋ ㄓㄣˋ)
an earthquake that is strong enough to be felt without a seismograph

有感而發(ㄧㄡˇ ㄍㄢˇ ㄦˊ ㄈㄚ)
to make a comment out of personal feeling

有骨頭(ㄧㄡˇ ㄍㄨˇ ˙ㄊㄡ)
manly; indomitable

有骨氣(ㄧㄡˇ ㄍㄨˇ ㄑㄧˋ)
adhering to moral principles; to have integrity

有過之無不及(ㄧㄡˇ ㄍㄨㄛˋ ㄓ ㄨˊ ㄅㄨˋ ㄐㄧˊ)
to go even farther than

有鬼(ㄧㄡˇ ㄍㄨㄟˇ)
There's something fishy.

有關(ㄧㄡˇ ㄍㄨㄢ)
to have something to do with; to concern

有關方面(ㄧㄡˇ ㄍㄨㄢ ㄈㄤ ㄇㄧㄢˋ)
the parties concerned; interested parties

有瓜葛(ㄧㄡˇ ㄍㄨㄚ ˙ㄍㄜ)
①to have relations ②to have complications

有乖母教(ㄧㄡˇ ㄍㄨㄞ ㄇㄨˇ ㄐㄧㄠˋ)
(said of an independent-minded girl) to act against her mother's teachings about old virtues of women

有光紙(ㄧㄡˇ ㄍㄨㄤ ㄓˇ)
paper with a glossy surface; glazed paper

有功(ㄧㄡˇ ㄍㄨㄥ)
to have provided great services; to make contributions to

有口難言(ㄧㄡˇ ㄎㄡˇ ㄋㄢˊ ㄧㄢˊ)
unable to speak for self-defense or self-justification under certain circumstances

有口皆碑(ㄧㄡˇ ㄎㄡˇ ㄐㄧㄝ ㄅㄟ)
praised by all

有口無心(ㄧㄡˇ ㄎㄡˇ ㄨˊ ㄒㄧㄣ)
to say what one does not mean; to be sharp-tongued but not malicious

有虧職守(ㄧㄡˇ ㄎㄨㄟ ㄓˊ ㄕㄡˇ)
guilty of dereliction of duty; to have neglected one's responsibility or duty

有空(ㄧㄡˇ ㄎㄨㄥˋ)
to have time (for doing something)

有何不可(ㄧㄡˇ ㄏㄜˊ ㄅㄨˋ ㄎㄜˇ)
Why not? 或 What's wrong with this or that?

有何爲證(ㄧㄡˇ ㄏㄜˊ ㄨㄟˊ ㄓㄥˋ)
Can you prove it?

有害(ㄧㄡˇ ㄏㄞˋ)
harmful; detrimental: 酗酒對健康有害。To indulge in excessive drinking is harmful to health.

有害無益(ㄧㄡˇ ㄏㄞˋ ㄨˊ ㄧˋ)
not helpful but harmful

有後(ㄧㄡˇ ㄏㄡˋ)
to have offspring (particularly male children)

有行無市(ㄧㄡˇ ㄏㄤˊ ㄨˊ ㄕˋ)
(said of the stock market, etc.) to have only quotations but no actual trading

有恆(ㄧㄡˇ ㄏㄥˊ)
persistent; persevering; tenacious

有機體(ㄧㄡˇ ㄐㄧ ㄊㄧˇ)
an organism

有機可乘(ㄧㄡˇ ㄐㄧ ㄎㄜˇ ㄔㄥˊ)
to have loopholes to exploit

有機化合物(ㄧㄡˇ ㄐㄧ ㄏㄨㄚˋ ㄏㄜˊ ㄨˋ)
an organic compound

有機化學(ㄧㄡˇ ㄐㄧ ㄏㄨㄚˋ ㄒㄩㄝˊ)
organic chemistry

有給職(ㄧㄡˇ ㄐㄧˇ ㄓˊ)
a paid post

有計畫(ㄧㄡˇ ㄐㄧˋ ㄏㄨㄚˋ)
in a planned way; according to plan

有加利樹(ㄧㄡˇ ㄐㄧㄚ ㄌㄧˋ ㄕㄨˋ)
a eucalyptus

有加無已(ㄧㄡˇ ㄐㄧㄚ ㄨˊ ㄧˇ)
to become worse or more serious: 這病人的病勢有加無已。The patient is worse than ever.

有價證券(ㄧㄡˇ ㄐㄧㄚˋ ㄓㄥˋ ㄑㄩㄢˋ)
securities; negotiable or marketable securities

有脚書櫥(ㄧㄡˇ ㄐㄧㄠˇ ㄕㄨ ㄔㄨˊ)
a walking encyclopedia

有教無類(ㄧㄡˇ ㄐㄧㄠˋ ㄨˊ ㄌㄟˋ)
to provide education for all people without discrimination:孔子有教無類。Confucius provided education for all people without discrimination.

有救(ㄧㄡˇ ㄐㄧㄡˋ)
capable of being saved; still hopeful

有舊(ㄧㄡˇ ㄐㄧㄡˋ)
to have had friendship in the past: 她與他們有舊。She has had friendship with them in the past.

有間(ㄧㄡˇ ㄐㄧㄢˋ)
①to be disloyal ②for a moment; for a little while

有見識(ㄧㄡˇ ㄐㄧㄢˋ ㄕˊ)
farsighted; to have an analytical mind

有鑒於此(ㄧㄡˇ ㄐㄧㄢˋ ㄩˊ ㄘˇ)
in view of this; because of this

有勁(ㄧㄡˇ ㄐㄧㄣˋ)
①strong; potent: 他已六十多歲, 可是還非常有勁。He is well over sixty, but is still

going strong. ② interesting; amusing ③ full of zest or gusto
有講究(ㄧㄡˇ ㄐㄧㄤˇ ˙ㄐㄧㄡ)
① exacting; requiring particular skill ② to stick to formalities
有經驗(ㄧㄡˇ ㄐㄧㄥ ㄧㄢˋ)
experienced; to have had the experience of: 這位教授對教學有經驗。This professor is experienced in teaching.
有其父必有其子(ㄧㄡˇ ㄑㄧˊ ㄈㄨˋ ㄅㄧˋ ㄧㄡˇ ㄑㄧˊ ㄗˇ)
Like father, like son.
有期徒刑(ㄧㄡˇ ㄑㄧˊ ㄊㄨˊ ㄒㄧㄥˊ)
(law) imprisonment for a definite term (as opposed to life imprisonment)
有起色(ㄧㄡˇ ㄑㄧˇ ㄙㄜˋ)
to show signs of a rise, improvement, etc.: 他的生意日有起色。His business shows signs of improvement every day.
有氣(ㄧㄡˇ ㄑㄧˋ)
angry; furious; indignant
有氣兒(ㄧㄡˇ ㄑㄧˋㄦ)
① still alive; still breathing ② angry; furious; indignant
有氣無力(ㄧㄡˇ ㄑㄧˋ ㄨˊ ㄌㄧˋ)
Breath is present but vigor is absent.—descriptive of a very feeble voice, half-hearted performance, etc.
有求必應(ㄧㄡˇ ㄑㄧㄡˊ ㄅㄧˋ ㄧㄥˋ)
unable to say no to seekers of help; to respond to every plea
有錢(ㄧㄡˇ ㄑㄧㄢˊ)
rich; wealthy; well-to-do; well-off
有錢能使鬼推磨(ㄧㄡˇ ㄑㄧㄢˊ ㄋㄥˊ ㄕˇ ㄍㄨㄟˇ ㄊㄨㄟ ㄇㄛˋ)
(literally) Money can make the ghost work the mill. —Money can work miracles. 或 Money makes the mare go.
有情(ㄧㄡˇ ㄑㄧㄥˊ)
① affected by love; to have a tender feeling for one of the opposite sex ② (Buddhism) any creature
有情人終成眷屬(ㄧㄡˇ ㄑㄧㄥˊ ㄖㄣˊ ㄓㄨㄥ ㄔㄥˊ ㄐㄩㄢˋ ㄕㄨˇ)
The lovers finally got married.
有頃(ㄧㄡˇ ㄑㄧㄥˇ)
for a moment; for a little while
有請(ㄧㄡˇ ㄑㄧㄥˇ)
So-and-so requests the pleasure of seeing you.
有趣(ㄧㄡˇ ㄑㄩˋ)
interesting; fascinating; amusing: 這個故事很有趣。This story is very interesting.
有窮(ㄧㄡˇ ㄑㄩㄥˊ)
to have an end; to have a limit; to be exhaustible
有喜(ㄧㄡˇ ㄒㄧˇ)
pregnant
有隙(ㄧㄡˇ ㄒㄧˋ)
to harbor a grudge
有隙可乘(ㄧㄡˇ ㄒㄧˋ ㄎㄜˇ ㄔㄥˊ)
There is a flaw or chance for attack.
有夏(ㄧㄡˇ ㄒㄧㄚˋ)
China
有些(ㄧㄡˇ ㄒㄧㄝ)
① some; a few ② somewhat
有血有肉(ㄧㄡˇ ㄒㄧㄝˇ ㄧㄡˇ ㄖㄡˋ)
(said of descriptions in literary works, etc.) true to life; lifelike; vivid
有效(ㄧㄡˇ ㄒㄧㄠˋ)
effective; effectual; valid: 這項合同在五年內有效。This contract shall be valid for five years.
有閑階級(ㄧㄡˇ ㄒㄧㄢˊ ㄐㄧㄝ ㄐㄧˊ)
the leisure class
有限(ㄧㄡˇ ㄒㄧㄢˋ)
limited; restricted; finite
有限公司(ㄧㄡˇ ㄒㄧㄢˋ ㄍㄨㄥ ㄙ)
a limited company; a limited-liability company
有限責任(ㄧㄡˇ ㄒㄧㄢˋ ㄗㄜˊ ㄖㄣˋ)
limited liability
有線(ㄧㄡˇ ㄒㄧㄢˋ)
wired; equipped with wires
有線電(ㄧㄡˇ ㄒㄧㄢˋ ㄉㄧㄢˋ)
telegraph
有心(ㄧㄡˇ ㄒㄧㄣ)
to have an intention; to intend; to have a mind to; to set one's mind on
有心胸(ㄧㄡˇ ㄒㄧㄣ ㄒㄩㄥ)
ambitious; independent-minded; to have eyesight aiming high and far
有心人(ㄧㄡˇ ㄒㄧㄣ ㄖㄣˊ)
① thinking people; feeling people ② a person who has a mind to do something useful
有心眼兒(ㄧㄡˇ ㄒㄧㄣ ㄧㄚˇㄦ)
shrewd; vigilant: 他是一個有心眼兒的商人。He is a shrewd businessman.
有形(ㄧㄡˇ ㄒㄧㄥˊ)
visible; tangible; concrete
有性生殖(ㄧㄡˇ ㄒㄧㄥˋ ㄕㄥ ㄓˊ)
sexual reproduction; gamogenesis; syngamy
有鬚眉氣(ㄧㄡˇ ㄒㄩ ㄇㄟˊ ㄑㄧˋ)
(said of women) to have manly qualities: 這位國會女議員有鬚眉氣。This congresswoman has manly qualities.
有學問(ㄧㄡˇ ㄒㄩㄝˊ ㄨㄣˋ)
learned; erudite: 他的朋友都是有學問的。His friends are all learned.
有志竟成(ㄧㄡˇ ㄓˋ ㄐㄧㄥˋ ㄔㄥˊ)
Where there is a will there is a way. 亦作「有志者事竟成」
有志之士(ㄧㄡˇ ㄓˋ ㄓ ㄕˋ)
a man of high ambitions; a man with lofty ideals; a man of noble aspirations
有志一同(ㄧㄡˇ ㄓˋ ㄧˋ ㄊㄨㄥˊ)
to be of the same mind
有治人無治法(ㄧㄡˇ ㄓˋ ㄖㄣˊ ㄨˊ ㄓˋ ㄈㄚˇ)
Good laws without capable law enforcers are useless.
有朝一日(ㄧㄡˇ ㄓㄠ ㄧˊ ㄖˋ)
some day in the future
有助於(ㄧㄡˇ ㄓㄨˋ ㄩˊ)
to be conducive to; to conduce to: 新鮮空氣有助於健康。Fresh air is conducive to health.
有著落(ㄧㄡˇ ㄓㄨㄛˊ ㄌㄨㄛˋ)
to have found reliable (financial) support
有準兒(ㄧㄡˇ ㄓㄨㄣˇㄦ)
① aimed at a target ② confident of success ③ determined; resolute
有種(ㄧㄡˇ ㄓㄨㄥˇ)
to have guts
有翅難展(ㄧㄡˇ ㄔˋ ㄋㄢˊ ㄓㄢˇ)
unable to make use of one's ability
有巢氏(ㄧㄡˇ ㄔㄠˊ ㄕˋ)
name of a legendary Chinese ruler who taught the people

〔月部〕

to build tree houses for protection against wild beasts

有產階級(ㄧㄡˇ ㄔㄢˇ ㄐㄧㄝ ㄐㄧˊ)
the propertied class; the owner class; the wealthy class; the bourgeoisie

有成(ㄧㄡˇ ㄔㄥˊ)
to have achieved success

有出入(ㄧㄡˇ ㄔㄨ ㄖㄨˋ)
to have discrepancy; to disagree; to be inconsistent

有失體統(ㄧㄡˇ ㄕ ㄊㄧˇ ㄊㄨㄥˇ)
very disgraceful

有失身份(ㄧㄡˇ ㄕ ㄕㄣ ㄈㄣˋ)
to be beneath one's dignity

有時(ㄧㄡˇ ㄕˊ)
sometimes; occasionally; now and then: 祖父母有時會來看我們。My grandparents occasionally visit us.

有史以來(ㄧㄡˇ ㄕˇ ㄧˇ ㄌㄞˊ)
since the dawn of history

有始有終(ㄧㄡˇ ㄕˇ ㄧㄡˇ ㄓㄨㄥ)
to carry out an undertaking from start to finish—not to give up halfway

有始無終(ㄧㄡˇ ㄕˇ ㄨˊ ㄓㄨㄥ)
to give up halfway; to leave an undertaking unfinished

有事(ㄧㄡˇ ㄕˋ)
① to be occupied; to be busy; to have business: 你今晚有事嗎? Have you any business on this evening? ② to meet with an accident; to get into trouble; if something happens

有室(ㄧㄡˇ ㄕˋ)
to have a home; to have a wife

有識之士(ㄧㄡˇ ㄕˋ ㄓ ㄕˋ)
knowledgeable people; farsighted people; thinking people; a man of insight

有勢力(ㄧㄡˇ ㄕˋ ㄌㄧˋ)
powerful; influential

有恃無恐(ㄧㄡˇ ㄕˋ ㄨˊ ㄎㄨㄥˇ)
There is no fear when one has something to fall back upon.

有守(ㄧㄡˇ ㄕㄡˇ)
to adhere to principles; to have moral fortitude

有守有爲(ㄧㄡˇ ㄕㄡˇ ㄧㄡˇ ㄨㄟˊ)
to uphold principles; to act according to principles

有身(ㄧㄡˇ ㄕㄣ)
pregnant; pregnancy

有神(ㄧㄡˇ ㄕㄣˊ)
① to show mental liveliness; spirited; full of spirit ② miraculous

有神論(ㄧㄡˇ ㄕㄣˊ ㄌㄨㄣˋ)
theism

有傷風化(ㄧㄡˇ ㄕㄤ ㄈㄥ ㄏㄨㄚˋ)
harmful to public morals

有傷大雅(ㄧㄡˇ ㄕㄤ ㄉㄚˋ ㄧㄚˇ)
to constitute a breach of decorum

有傷和氣(ㄧㄡˇ ㄕㄤ ㄏㄜˊ ㄑㄧˋ)
harmful to *esprit de corps*; detrimental to friendship: 爭吵有傷和氣。Quarrels are detrimental to friendship.

有賞有罰(ㄧㄡˇ ㄕㄤˇ ㄧㄡˇ ㄈㄚˊ)
to mete out punishments or rewards as the case demands

有聲電影(ㄧㄡˇ ㄕㄥ ㄉㄧㄢˋ ㄧㄥˇ)
a talking picture; a talkie; a sound film

有聲有色(ㄧㄡˇ ㄕㄥ ㄧㄡˇ ㄙㄜˋ)
(said of a description or performance) vivid; impressive:那是一場有聲有色的演講。It was an impressive speech.

有生之年(ㄧㄡˇ ㄕㄥ ㄓ ㄋㄧㄢˊ)
for the rest of one's life

有生以來(ㄧㄡˇ ㄕㄥ ㄧˇ ㄌㄞˊ)
since one's birth

有數(ㄧㄡˇ ㄕㄨˋ)
① governed by principle ② arranged by fate ③ confident; to know what one is doing

有數兒(ㄧㄡˇ ㄕㄨˋㄦ)
① rare ② confident; to know what one is doing ③ to know how many; to know the exact number

有說有笑(ㄧㄡˇ ㄕㄨㄛ ㄧㄡˇ ㄒㄧㄠˋ)
to talk and laugh; cheerful; lively

有染(ㄧㄡˇ ㄖㄢˇ)
to have an affair with

有人(ㄧㄡˇ ㄖㄣˊ)
① some people; somebody; someone; anyone: 家裏有人嗎? Is there anyone at home? ② There is somebody there. 或There are some people inside.

有人家兒(ㄧㄡˇ ㄖㄣˊ ㄐㄧㄚㄦ)
(said of a girl) already betrothed

有人緣兒(ㄧㄡˇ ㄖㄣˊ ㄩㄚˊㄦ)
(said of people) likable; popular

有如(ㄧㄡˇ ㄖㄨˊ)
just like; as if; as though

有則改之，無則加勉(ㄧㄡˇ ㄗㄜˊ ㄍㄞˇ ㄓ, ㄨˊ ㄗㄜˊ ㄐㄧㄚ ㄇㄧㄢˇ)
to correct the mistakes, if any, and to keep the good record if none has been committed

有增無減(ㄧㄡˇ ㄗㄥ ㄨˊ ㄐㄧㄢˇ)
① to increase steadily ② to get steadily worse or serious

有作爲(ㄧㄡˇ ㄗㄨㄛˋ ㄨㄟˊ)
capable of outstanding achievements

有嘴無心(ㄧㄡˇ ㄗㄨㄟˇ ㄨˊ ㄒㄧㄣ)
to say what one does not mean 參看「有口無心」

有罪(ㄧㄡˇ ㄗㄨㄟˋ)
guilty; sinful

有此一說(ㄧㄡˇ ㄘˇ ㄧˋ ㄕㄨㄛ)
There has been such a report, theory, etc.

有才(ㄧㄡˇ ㄘㄞˊ)
gifted; talented

有才之士(ㄧㄡˇ ㄘㄞˊ ㄓ ㄕˋ)
a man of talent

有才無命(ㄧㄡˇ ㄘㄞˊ ㄨˊ ㄇㄧㄥˋ)
(said of a person) gifted but out of luck—The result is failure.

有司(ㄧㄡˇ ㄙ)
an official

有色人種(ㄧㄡˇ ㄙㄜˋ ㄖㄣˊ ㄓㄨㄥˇ)
colored races

有素(ㄧㄡˇ ㄙㄨˋ)
(said of friendship, training, etc.) to have a solid foundation

有所不知(ㄧㄡˇ ㄙㄨㄛˇ ㄅㄨˋ ㄓ)
to be unaware of something

有所不爲(ㄧㄡˇ ㄙㄨㄛˇ ㄅㄨˋ ㄨㄟˊ)
There are certain things that a man of principle will not stoop to.

有礙(ㄧㄡˇ ㄞˋ)
detrimental; harmful: 抽煙有礙健康。Smoking is detrimental to health.

有礙觀瞻(ㄧㄡˇ ㄞˋ ㄍㄨㄢ ㄓㄢ)
to leave a very bad impression to the beholder; to be an eyesore

有案可查(ㄧㄡˇ ㄢˋ ㄎㄜˇ ㄔㄚˊ)

to be a matter of record; to be on record
有一次(ㄧㄡˇ ㄧˊ ㄘˋ)
on one occasion; once
有一天(ㄧㄡˇ ㄧˋ ㄊㄧㄢ)
one day; someday
有一手兒(ㄧㄡˇ ㄧˋ ㄕㄡˇㄦ)
to have remarkable skill
有益(ㄧㄡˇ ㄧˋ)
profitable; beneficial; useful
有益處(ㄧㄡˇ ㄧˋ ㄔㄨˋ)or(ㄧㄡˇ ㄧˊ ·ㄔㄨ)
advantageous; beneficial; profitable; useful; conducive; helpful: 這字典對年輕學生很有益處。This dictionary is very useful for (or to) young students.
有意(ㄧㄡˇ ㄧˋ)
① to intend; purposeful; intentional: 我有意於次日離去。I intended to leave the next day. ② to show interest; to be interested; to be inclined to: 你有意出去散步嗎? Do you feel inclined for a walk?
有意見(ㄧㄡˇ ㄧˋ ㄐㄧㄢˋ)
to have something to say; to have reservations
有意識(ㄧㄡˇ ㄧˋ ㄕˋ)
conscious
有意思(ㄧㄡˇ ㄧˋ ·ㄙ)
interesting; exciting; enjoyable; amusing: 他是一個很有意思的人。He's a most interesting man.
有意義的(ㄧㄡˇ ㄧˋ ㄧˋ ·ㄉㄜ)
meaningful; significant
有意無意之間(ㄧㄡˇ ㄧˋ ㄨˊ ㄧˋ ㄓ ㄐㄧㄢ)
between consciousness and unconsciousness; consciously or unconsciously
有要沒緊(ㄧㄡˇ ㄧㄠˋ ㄇㄟˊ ㄐㄧㄣˇ)
important but not urgent
有言在先(ㄧㄡˇ ㄧㄢˊ ㄗㄞˋ ㄒㄧㄢ)
to have agreed before; to have said previously; to have made the promise beforehand; to forewarn
有眼不識泰山(ㄧㄡˇ ㄧㄢˇ ㄅㄨˋ ㄕˋ ㄊㄞˋ ㄕㄢ)
to fail to recognize a great person
有眼無珠(ㄧㄡˇ ㄧㄢˇ ㄨˊ ㄓㄨ)
(literally) to have eyes without eyeballs—to lack discerning power

有因(ㄧㄡˇ ㄧㄣ)
There is a reason for it. 這錯誤事出有因。There is a reason for this mistake.
有癮(ㄧㄡˇ ㄧㄣˇ)
to be addicted to; to have formed a habit
有氧舞蹈(ㄧㄡˇ ㄧㄤˇ ㄨˇ ㄉㄠˇ)
aerobic dancing
有無相通(ㄧㄡˇ ㄨˊ ㄒㄧㄤ ㄊㄨㄥ)
to render financial assistance among good friends
有我無敵(ㄧㄡˇ ㄨㄛˇ ㄨˊ ㄉㄧˊ)
If we are to survive, the enemy must be vanquished.
有味兒(ㄧㄡˇ ㄨㄟˋㄦ)
① tasty; delicious: 這道餐後點心很有味兒。This dessert is delicious. ② (said of artistic works, dramatic performances, etc.) delightful ③ to stink
有外遇(ㄧㄡˇ ㄨㄞˋ ㄩˋ)
(said of a married person) to have an extramarital affair
有爲(ㄧㄡˇ ㄨㄟˊ)
capable of great achievements
有聞必錄(ㄧㄡˇ ㄨㄣˊ ㄅㄧˋ ㄌㄨˋ)
to record everything one has heard
有問必答(ㄧㄡˇ ㄨㄣˋ ㄅㄧˋ ㄉㄚˊ)
to answer all questions asked
有問題(ㄧㄡˇ ㄨㄣˋ ㄊㄧˊ)
questionable; doubtful; unreliable: 我的去留尙有問題。It is doubtful whether I shall go or stay.
有望(ㄧㄡˇ ㄨㄤˋ)
hopeful; promising
有餘(ㄧㄡˇ ㄩˊ)
① to have enough and to spare ② odd
有緣(ㄧㄡˇ ㄩㄢˊ)
linked by ties of fate
有孕(ㄧㄡˇ ㄩㄣˋ)
pregnant
有勇無謀(ㄧㄡˇ ㄩㄥˇ ㄨˊ ㄇㄡˊ)
to be foolhardy
有用(ㄧㄡˇ ㄩㄥˋ)
useful; practical; beneficial: 他想做社會上有用的人。He wants to be a useful member of society.

【有】 2315
2. ㄧㄡˋ yow yòu
same as 又—again

四畫

【朋】 2316
ㄆㄥˊ perng péng
1. a friend; a companion: 我們是很要好的朋友。We are great friends.
2. a group; a clique
朋比爲奸(ㄆㄥˊ ㄅㄧˇ ㄨㄟˊ ㄐㄧㄢ)
to clique together for insidious purposes; to gang up for evil doings
朋分(ㄆㄥˊ ㄈㄣ)
to share (profits) with each other or one another
朋黨(ㄆㄥˊ ㄉㄤˇ)
a faction; a clique
朋儔(ㄆㄥˊ ㄔㄡˊ)
a companion; a friend
朋從(ㄆㄥˊ ㄘㄨㄥˊ)
to stick together as a result of congenial tastes
朋友(ㄆㄥˊ ㄧㄡˇ)
a friend: 他是我的朋友。He is a friend of mine.

【服】 2317
1. ㄈㄨˊ fwu fú
1. clothes; dress; garments; costume
2. mourning
3. to wear (clothes)
4. to obey; to be convinced; to yield; to concede; to admit
5. to serve
6. to take (medicine)
7. to be accustomed to; to be acclimated to
服兵役(ㄈㄨˊ ㄅㄧㄥ ㄧˋ)
to undergo military service
服滿(ㄈㄨˊ ㄇㄢˇ)
① to complete (a period of mourning or prescribed tour of service) ② to serve up (a prison term)
服法(ㄈㄨˊ ㄈㄚˇ)
instructions about how to take medicine
服服帖帖(ㄈㄨˊ ·ㄈㄨ ㄊㄧㄝ ㄊㄧㄝ)or 服帖(ㄈㄨˊ ㄊㄧㄝ)
obedient; docile: 我的孩子都很服帖。My boys are very obedient.
服毒(ㄈㄨˊ ㄉㄨˊ)
to take poison

〔月部〕

服勞役(ㄈㄨˊ ㄌㄠˊ ㄧˋ)
to undergo labor service (usually as a form of punishment)
服具(ㄈㄨˊ ㄐㄩˋ)
articles for use in funeral
服氣(ㄈㄨˊ ㄑㄧˋ)
① to practice Taoist breath control ② to yield or submit willingly
服勤(ㄈㄨˊ ㄑㄧㄣˊ)
to work hard; to toil; to be on duty
服刑(ㄈㄨˊ ㄒㄧㄥˊ)
to serve a prison term
服制(ㄈㄨˊ ㄓˋ)
rules of mourning according to relationship with the deceased
服裝(ㄈㄨˊ ㄓㄨㄤ)
costumes; dress; clothes
服裝表演(ㄈㄨˊ ㄓㄨㄤ ㄅㄧㄠˇ ㄧㄢˇ)
a fashion show
服裝設計(ㄈㄨˊ ㄓㄨㄤ ㄕㄜˋ ㄐㄧˋ)
dress designing
服食(ㄈㄨˊ ㄕˊ)
① to take Taoist pills ② to take food
服式(ㄈㄨˊ ㄕˋ)
the style of dress; costume
服飾(ㄈㄨˊ ㄕˋ)
costume and accessories
服侍(ㄈㄨˊ ˙ㄕ)
to wait upon; to attend on
服輸(ㄈㄨˊ ㄕㄨ)
to concede defeat
服水土(ㄈㄨˊ ㄕㄨㄟˇ ㄊㄨˇ)
① to acclimatize; to adapt oneself to the natural environment of a strange land ②(biology) adaptation
服軟(ㄈㄨˊ ㄖㄨㄢˇ)
to yield to the soft approach
服罪(ㄈㄨˊ ㄗㄨㄟˋ)
to admit one's crime
服從(ㄈㄨˊ ㄘㄨㄥˊ)
to obey; to follow; to submit to; obedience
服色(ㄈㄨˊ ㄙㄜˋ)
① the color of clothes ② colorful clothes
服喪(ㄈㄨˊ ㄙㄤ)
to remain in mourning
服餌(ㄈㄨˊ ㄦˇ)
to take Taoist pills
服役(ㄈㄨˊ ㄧˋ)
① to undergo hard labor ② to undergo military service: 他被徵召服役。He was called up for military service.
服妖(ㄈㄨˊ ㄧㄠ)
① monstrous dress; outrageous clothes ② to subjugate evil spirits
服藥(ㄈㄨˊ ㄧㄠˋ)
to take medicine
服膺(ㄈㄨˊ ㄧㄥ)
to keep (a teaching, principle, etc.) in mind and stick to (it)
服硬(ㄈㄨˊ ㄧㄥˋ)
to yield to force
服務(ㄈㄨˊ ㄨˋ)
① to render service; service ② to work as an employee: 他在一家銀行服務。He works in a bank.
服務臺(ㄈㄨˊ ㄨˋ ㄊㄞˊ)
a service desk
服務中心(ㄈㄨˊ ㄨˋ ㄓㄨㄥ ㄒㄧㄣ)
a service center
服務業(ㄈㄨˊ ㄨˋ ㄧㄝˋ)
service industry
服務員(ㄈㄨˊ ㄨˋ ㄩㄢˊ)
an attendant; a steward
服用(ㄈㄨˊ ㄩㄥˋ)
① to take (medicine, etc.): 他服用了幾片阿斯匹靈。He took down some aspirin tablets. ② clothes and tools

【服】 2317
2. ㄈㄨˋ fuh fù
(Chinese medicine) a dose: 一服藥 a dose of medicine

五畫

【朏】 2318
ㄈㄟˇ feei fěi
the light of a crescent moon

六畫

【朔】 2319
ㄕㄨㄛˋ shuoh shuò
1. to begin
2. north
3. the first day of the month of the lunar calendar
朔邊(ㄕㄨㄛˋ ㄅㄧㄢ)
the northern frontier
朔馬(ㄕㄨㄛˋ ㄇㄚˇ)
horses of northern breeds
朔漠(ㄕㄨㄛˋ ㄇㄛˋ)
the northern deserts
朔方(ㄕㄨㄛˋ ㄈㄤ)
dreary land in the north
朔風(ㄕㄨㄛˋ ㄈㄥ)
a biting north wind
朔氣(ㄕㄨㄛˋ ㄑㄧˋ)
① the 24 solar periods of the year ② cold air
朔雪(ㄕㄨㄛˋ ㄒㄩㄝˇ)
the heavy snow in the north
朔日(ㄕㄨㄛˋ ㄖˋ)
the first day of each month of the lunar calendar
朔牖(ㄕㄨㄛˋ ㄧㄡˇ)
a northern window
朔望(ㄕㄨㄛˋ ㄨㄤˋ)
the first and the 15th days of the lunar month
朔月(ㄕㄨㄛˋ ㄩㄝˋ)
the first day of the lunar month

【朕】 2320
ㄓㄣˋ jenn zhèn
1. the royal "we" (used exclusively by the emperor or king to mean "I")
2. omens; auguries; portents; signs
朕兆(ㄓㄣˋ ㄓㄠˋ)
omens; portents; auguries; signs: 無有朕兆可尋。There are no signs for us to read.

【朓】 2321
ㄊㄧㄠˋ tiaw tiào
at the end of a lunar month when the moon is setting in the west

七畫

【朗】 2322
ㄌㄤˇ laang lǎng
1. bright; clear: 晴朗的天空無雲。A clear sky is free from clouds.
2. resonant; sonorously; sonorous
朗讀(ㄌㄤˇ ㄉㄨˊ)
to read aloud: 請朗讀這個故事。Please read the story aloud.
朗朗(ㄌㄤˇ ㄌㄤˇ)
① bright; clear ② resonant; sonorant; sonorous
朗照(ㄌㄤˇ ㄓㄠˋ)
to shine brightly: 今晨陽光朗

照。This morning the sun shone brightly.

朗誦(ㄌㄤˇ ㄙㄨㄥˋ)
to recite aloud

朗月(ㄌㄤˇ ㄩㄝˋ)
a bright moon: 一對情侶在朗月下散步。A pair of lovers walked under the bright moon.

朗詠(ㄌㄤˇ ㄩㄥˇ)
to chant (verses)

【望】 2323 ㄨㄤˋ wanq wàng

1. to view; to watch; to gaze into the distance
2. to hope; to expect
3. the 15th day of each month of the lunar calendar
4. reputation; prestige
5. to call on; to visit

望八(ㄨㄤˋ ㄅㄚ)
expecting the 80th birthday very soon

望巴巴(ㄨㄤˋ ㄅㄚ ㄅㄚ)
anxious; apprehensive: 他望巴巴會見你。He was anxious to meet you.

望不見(ㄨㄤˋ ˙ㄅㄨ ㄐㄧㄢˋ)or 望不到(ㄨㄤˋ ˙ㄅㄨ ㄉㄠˋ)
incapable of seeing or being seen

望梅止渴(ㄨㄤˋ ㄇㄟˊ ㄓˇ ㄎㄜˇ)
(literally) to quench one's thirst by watching plums—to have imaginary satisfaction; to console oneself with false hopes

望門投止(ㄨㄤˋ ㄇㄣˊ ㄊㄡˊ ㄓˇ)
to stop for the night at any house one happens to come across

望門寡(ㄨㄤˋ ㄇㄣˊ ㄍㄨㄚˇ)
a woman bereaved of her fiancé

望彌撒(ㄨㄤˋ ㄇㄧˊ ㄙㄚ)
to go to Mass; to attend a Mass

望風披靡(ㄨㄤˋ ㄈㄥ ㄆㄧ ㄇㄧˇ)
to flee helter-skelter at the mere sight of the oncoming force

望風撲影(ㄨㄤˋ ㄈㄥ ㄆㄨ ㄧㄥˇ)
to search without any clue; to give a wild-goose chase; to launch a witch hunt

望風逃竄(ㄨㄤˋ ㄈㄥ ㄊㄠˊ ㄘㄨㄢˋ)or 望風而逃(ㄨㄤˋ ㄈㄥ ㄦˊ ㄊㄠˊ)
to flee upon hearing the news (that a powerful enemy is approaching)

望帝(ㄨㄤˋ ㄉㄧˋ)
a cuckoo 亦作「杜鵑」

望衡對宇(ㄨㄤˋ ㄏㄥˊ ㄉㄨㄟˋ ㄩˇ)
to live near each other

望見(ㄨㄤˋ ㄐㄧㄢˋ)
to have seen; to see: 我望見有甚麼東西在動。I saw something move.

望氣(ㄨㄤˋ ㄑㄧˋ)
to read the future from the clouds (an ancient form of divination)

望秋先零(ㄨㄤˋ ㄑㄧㄡ ㄒㄧㄢ ㄌㄧㄥˊ)
to show the feebleness of old age while still young

望重士林(ㄨㄤˋ ㄓㄨㄥˋ ㄕˋ ㄌㄧㄣˊ)
to enjoy high prestige among scholars; to command respect in the academic circle

望塵莫及(ㄨㄤˋ ㄔㄣˊ ㄇㄛˋ ㄐㄧˊ)
to gaze at another's fast progress; to be left far behind; unable to compare with another's accomplishment, etc.

望穿秋水(ㄨㄤˋ ㄔㄨㄢ ㄑㄧㄡ ㄕㄨㄟˇ)
to gaze with eager expectation (until the eyes are bored through); to aspire earnestly

望日(ㄨㄤˋ ㄖˋ)
the 15th day of every lunar month

望子成龍(ㄨㄤˋ ㄗˇ ㄔㄥˊ ㄌㄨㄥˊ)
to hope one's children will have a bright future

望族(ㄨㄤˋ ㄗㄨˊ)
a respected family in a community; a family of renown

望色(ㄨㄤˋ ㄙㄜˋ)
to diagnose a disease from the patient's appearance

望歲(ㄨㄤˋ ㄙㄨㄟˋ)
to pray or hope for a bumper crop

望而卻步(ㄨㄤˋ ㄦˊ ㄑㄩㄝˋ ㄅㄨˋ)
to hesitate to approach upon seeing a difficult or dangerous situation

望而生畏(ㄨㄤˋ ㄦˊ ㄕㄥ ㄨㄟˋ)
to be awe-stricken by merely looking at it

望眼欲穿(ㄨㄤˋ ㄧㄢˇ ㄩˋ ㄔㄨㄢ)
to aspire earnestly

望洋興歎(ㄨㄤˋ ㄧㄤˊ ㄒㄧㄥ ㄊㄢˋ)
to feel powerless and frustrated in the face of a great task

望文生義(ㄨㄤˋ ㄨㄣˊ ㄕㄥ ㄧˋ)
to misconstrue the meaning of a word or phrase prima facie; to interpret without real understanding

望聞問切(ㄨㄤˋ ㄨㄣˊ ㄨㄣˋ ㄑㄧㄝˋ)
(Chinese medicine) the four essential steps a doctor takes to diagnose a disease: to observe the symptoms, to listen to the patient's description of his ailment, to ask the patient relevant questions, and to feel the patient's pulse

望月(ㄨㄤˋ ㄩㄝˋ)
the full moon 參看「滿月①」

望遠鏡(ㄨㄤˋ ㄩㄢˇ ㄐㄧㄥˋ)
a telescope: 天文望遠鏡 an astronomical telescope

八畫

【朝】 2324 1. ㄓㄠ jau zhāo

1. morning
2. a day

朝不保夕(ㄓㄠ ㄅㄨˋ ㄅㄠˇ ㄒㄧˋ)
(literally) One is uncertain in the morning whether one will be safe in the evening. —precarious; in constant fear; jittery

朝不謀夕(ㄓㄠ ㄅㄨˋ ㄇㄡˊ ㄒㄧˋ)
to fail to plan even for the immediate future

朝暮人(ㄓㄠ ㄇㄨˋ ㄖㄣˊ)
a person destined to die soon

朝發夕至(ㄓㄠ ㄈㄚ ㄒㄧˋ ㄓˋ)
Road condition is so good or the distance so short that one can reach one's destination in the evening if one starts out in the morning.

朝暾(ㄓㄠ ㄊㄨㄣ)
the morning sun

朝令夕改(ㄓㄠ ㄌㄧㄥˋ ㄒㄧˋ ㄍㄞˇ)
(literally) to issue an order in the morning and change it in the evening—to change rules very frequently; to make unforeseen changes in

policy

朝露(ㄓㄠ ㄌㄨˋ)
morning dew—a symbol of transience: 人生如朝露。Human life is as evanescent as the morning dew.

朝會(ㄓㄠ ㄏㄨㄟˋ)
a morning rally (in schools)

朝菌(ㄓㄠ ㄐㄩㄣˋ)
ephemeral fungus; morning mushrooms

朝氣(ㄓㄠ ㄑㄧˋ)
fresh spirit; exuberance and aggressiveness: 工作要有朝氣。Put a little more fresh spirit into your work.

朝氣蓬勃(ㄓㄠ ㄑㄧˋ ㄆㄥˊ ㄅㄛˊ)
full of youthful spirit; full of vigor and vitality

朝乾夕惕(ㄓㄠ ㄑㄧㄢˊ ㄒㄧˋ ㄊㄧˋ)
diligent and alert from morning till night

朝秦暮楚(ㄓㄠ ㄑㄧㄣˊ ㄇㄨˋ ㄔㄨˇ)
(literally) to support Chin in the morning and Chu in the evening—to be fickle or capricious

朝曦(ㄓㄠ ㄒㄧ)
the morning sun

朝夕(ㄓㄠ ㄒㄧˋ)
①day and night; always; constantly: 他們朝夕相處。They were together from morning to night. ②a very brief period of time

朝旭(ㄓㄠ ㄒㄩˋ)
the morning sun

朝朝暮暮(ㄓㄠ ㄓㄠ ㄇㄨˋ ㄇㄨˋ)
every day; always; day and night

朝生暮死(ㄓㄠ ㄕㄥ ㄇㄨˋ ㄙˇ)
(said of life) transient; ephemeral

朝思暮想(ㄓㄠ ㄙ ㄇㄨˋ ㄒㄧㄤˇ)
to yearn day and night

朝三暮四(ㄓㄠ ㄙㄢ ㄇㄨˋ ㄙˋ)
to be inconsistent; to be fickle or changeable; to chop about

朝陽(ㄓㄠ ㄧㄤˊ)
the morning sun

朝陽鳴鳳(ㄓㄠ ㄧㄤˊ ㄇㄧㄥˊ ㄈㄥˋ)
outspoken admonitions

朝聞道，夕死可矣(ㄓㄠ ㄨㄣˊ ㄉㄠˋ, ㄒㄧˋ ㄙˇ ㄎㄜˇ ㄧˇ)
If a man in the morning hear the right way, he may die in the evening without regret. —Truth is so valuable that one is willing to die soon after learning it.

朝饔夕飧(ㄓㄠ ㄩㄥ ㄒㄧˋ ㄙㄨㄣ)
to do nothing but eat and drink

【朝】 2324 2. ㄔㄠˊ chaur cháo

1. an imperial court
2. a dynasty
3. to go to imperial court
4. to face

朝拜(ㄔㄠˊ ㄅㄞˋ)
①to worship; to pay respects to (a sovereign) ②to pilgrimage

朝報(ㄔㄠˊ ㄅㄠˋ)
(in old China) a government bulletin

朝班(ㄔㄠˊ ㄅㄢ)or 朝列(ㄔㄠˊ ㄌㄧㄝˋ)
the assemblage of courtiers at the imperial court

朝柄(ㄔㄠˊ ㄅㄧㄥˇ)
the power of a sovereign

朝聘(ㄔㄠˊ ㄆㄧㄣˋ)
official intercourse among feudal princes during the Epoch of Warring States

朝帽(ㄔㄠˊ ㄇㄠˋ)
the cap worn in audience with the monarch

朝服(ㄔㄠˊ ㄈㄨˊ)
court robes; formal dress worn in audience with the monarch

朝代(ㄔㄠˊ ㄉㄞˋ)
a dynasty

朝天(ㄔㄠˊ ㄊㄧㄢ)
①to be presented at court; to go to court ②to face upward

朝廷(ㄔㄠˊ ㄊㄧㄥˊ)
the court (of a sovereign); an imperial court: 那是朝廷的意旨。It was the wish of the court.

朝綱(ㄔㄠˊ ㄍㄤ)
①rules of an imperial court ②the imperial court

朝貴(ㄔㄠˊ ㄍㄨㄟˋ)
powerful courtiers

朝貢(ㄔㄠˊ ㄍㄨㄥˋ)
to present tribute to the sovereign

朝考(ㄔㄠˊ ㄎㄠˇ)
the final court examination (under the former civil service examination system)

朝後(ㄔㄠˊ ㄏㄡˋ)
to face backward

朝見(ㄔㄠˊ ㄐㄧㄢˋ)
to be received in audience by a sovereign

朝覲(ㄔㄠˊ ㄐㄧㄣˋ)
to be received in audience by a sovereign

朝前(ㄔㄠˊ ㄑㄧㄢˊ)
to face forward

朝鮮(ㄔㄠˊ ㄒㄧㄢ)
an old name of Korea

朝鮮半島(ㄔㄠˊ ㄒㄧㄢ ㄅㄢˋ ㄉㄠˇ)
the Korean Peninsula

朝獻(ㄔㄠˊ ㄒㄧㄢˋ)
to offer a gift to the throne on the occasion of an audience

朝章(ㄔㄠˊ ㄓㄤ)
rules of an imperial court

朝政(ㄔㄠˊ ㄓㄥˋ)
the affairs of the state: 朝政紊亂。The affairs of the state were in disorder.

朝珠(ㄔㄠˊ ㄓㄨ)
a string of 108 beads made of coral, amber, etc. worn by officials of the Ching Dynasty

朝臣(ㄔㄠˊ ㄔㄣˊ)
(collectively) the court

朝山(ㄔㄠˊ ㄕㄢ)or 朝聖(ㄔㄠˊ ㄕㄥˋ)
to go on a pilgrimage: 他們前往聖地朝聖。They went on a pilgrimage to a sacred place.

朝聖團(ㄔㄠˊ ㄕㄥˋ ㄊㄨㄢˊ)
a pilgrimage mission; a hadji (or haji) mission

朝衣朝冠(ㄔㄠˊ ㄧ ㄔㄠˊ ㄍㄨㄢ)
dressed up for audience with the emperor

朝儀(ㄔㄠˊ ㄧˊ)
the proprieties for audience with the emperor

朝議(ㄔㄠˊ ㄧˋ)
a civil official post in the Ching Dynasty

朝野(ㄔㄠˊ ㄧㄝˇ)
the government and the people

朝隱(ㄔㄠˊ ㄧㄣˇ)
a very unobtrusive or self-effacing courtier

朝陽(ㄔㄠˊ ㄧㄤˊ)
①the eastern slope of a mountain ② with a sunny, usually southern, aspect: 這房屋朝陽。The house has a southern aspect.
朝望(ㄔㄠˊ ㄨㄤˋ)
respected courtiers

【期】2325 1. ㄑㄧˊ chyi qí (又讀 ㄑㄧ chi qī)
1. periods; times: 法國大革命時期 the period of the French Revolution
2. a designated time; a time limit: 這計畫必須在指定期限內實行。The project must be carried out within the designated time.
3. to expect; to hope; to wait: 勝利可期。Victory may be expected.
期票(ㄑㄧˊ ㄆㄧㄠˋ)
a time draft; a promissory note: 這是一張五百元的期票。This is a promissory note for $500.
期末考試(ㄑㄧˊ ㄇㄛˋ ㄎㄠˇ ㄕˋ) or 期考(ㄑㄧˊ ㄎㄠˇ) or 期終考試(ㄑㄧˊ ㄓㄨㄥ ㄎㄠˇ ㄕˋ)
the terminal examination; the final examination of a school term; the final 亦作「學期考試」: 他期末考試及格了。He passed the final examination.
期滿(ㄑㄧˊ ㄇㄢˇ)
The term (or period) has expired. 他的假期於星期二期滿。His vacation expires on Tuesday.
期待(ㄑㄧˊ ㄉㄞˋ)
to expect; to hope
期刊(ㄑㄧˊ ㄎㄢ)
a periodical publication; a periodical
期貨(ㄑㄧˊ ㄏㄨㄛˋ)
(economics) futures; goods to be delivered at a specified time; the future delivery
期會(ㄑㄧˊ ㄏㄨㄟˋ)
to meet at a time fixed in advance
期間(ㄑㄧˊ ㄐㄧㄢ)
a period; a term: 有很長的期間我們沒有他的消息。There were long periods when we had no news of him.
期期(ㄑㄧˊ ㄑㄧˊ) or 期期艾艾(ㄑㄧˊ ㄑㄧˊ ㄞˋ ㄞˋ)
stammering: 他期期艾艾地向她道謝。He stammered his thanks to her.
期限(ㄑㄧˊ ㄒㄧㄢˋ)
a time limit; a deadline
期許(ㄑㄧˊ ㄒㄩˇ)
to expect to; expectation: 我們對你期許甚殷。We have great expectations of you.
期中報告(ㄑㄧˊ ㄓㄨㄥ ㄅㄠˋ ㄍㄠˋ)
(accounting) an interim report
期中考試(ㄑㄧˊ ㄓㄨㄥ ㄎㄠˇ ㄕˋ)
a midterm examination
期成(ㄑㄧˊ ㄔㄥˊ)
to hope for success
期日(ㄑㄧˊ ㄖˋ)
the date fixed for some purpose
期頤(ㄑㄧˊ ㄧˊ)
a 100-year-old person; a centenarian
期望(ㄑㄧˊ ㄨㄤˋ)
to expect; to hope: 我們都期望最好的一面。We're hoping for the best.
期約(ㄑㄧˊ ㄩㄝ)
to agree on a time for the delivery of a bribe

【期】2325 2. (朞) ㄐㄧ ji jī
one year
期服(ㄐㄧ ㄈㄨˊ)
one-year mourning (observed for one's grandparents, father's brothers, etc.)
期年(ㄐㄧ ㄋㄧㄢˊ)
the first anniversary; a complete year
期月(ㄐㄧ ㄩㄝˋ)
① one year ② one month

十畫

【朢】2326 ㄨㄤˋ wanq wàng
the original form of 望—the 15th day of each month of the lunar calendar

十二畫

【朣】2327 ㄊㄨㄥˊ torng tóng
the rising moon
朣朧(ㄊㄨㄥˊ ㄌㄨㄥˊ)
the appearance of the moon beginning to increase in brightness

十四畫

【朦】2328 ㄇㄥˊ meng méng
1. the state of the moon just before setting
2. dim; vague; hazy
3. to deceive; to swindle
朦朧(ㄇㄥˊ ㄌㄨㄥˊ)
①the appearance of the moon just before setting ② dim; vague; hazy; drowsy: 他醉眼朦朧。His eyes were drowsy from drink.

十六畫

【朧】2329 ㄌㄨㄥˊ long lóng
the moon's brightness
朧明(ㄌㄨㄥˊ ㄇㄧㄥˊ)
the moon's brightness
朧朣(ㄌㄨㄥˊ ㄊㄨㄥˊ)
the sound of a drum
朧朧(ㄌㄨㄥˊ ㄌㄨㄥˊ)
the brightness of the moon

木部 ㄇㄨˋ muh mù

【木】2330 ㄇㄨˋ muh mù
1. a tree
2. wood; timber; lumber
3. made of wood; wooden
4. simple; honest
5. senseless; benumbed; dull: 她的手凍麻木了。Her hands were benumbed by cold.
6. a coffin
木板(ㄇㄨˋ ㄅㄢˇ)
planks; boards
木版(ㄇㄨˋ ㄅㄢˇ)
a wood engraving; a woodcut
木本(ㄇㄨˋ ㄅㄣˇ)
woody (plants)
木本水源(ㄇㄨˋ ㄅㄣˇ ㄕㄨㄟˇ ㄩㄢˊ)
(literally) A tree has its root, and a stream has its

〔木部〕

source.—Everything has an origin.

木筆(ㄇㄨˋ ㄅㄧˇ)
(botany) a lily magnolia 亦作「辛夷」

木簰 or 木排(ㄇㄨˋ ㄆㄞˊ) or 木筏(ㄇㄨˋ ㄈㄚˊ)
a wooden raft

木片(ㄇㄨˋ ㄆㄧㄢˋ)
a wood chip

木馬(ㄇㄨˋ ㄇㄚˇ)
(gymnastics) a horse

木棉(ㄇㄨˋ ㄇㄧㄢˊ)
silk cotton

木芙蓉(ㄇㄨˋ ㄈㄨˊ ㄖㄨㄥˊ)
(botany) *Hibiscus mutabilis*

木雕泥塑(ㄇㄨˋ ㄉㄧㄠ ㄋㄧˊ ㄙㄨˋ)
(literally) carved from wood and molded from clay—very stupid

木蠹(ㄇㄨˋ ㄉㄨˋ)
Cossus ligniperda

木鐸(ㄇㄨˋ ㄉㄨㄛˊ)
① a bell with a wooden clapper ② a teacher

木鐸警鐘(ㄇㄨˋ ㄉㄨㄛˊ ㄐㄧㄥˇ ㄓㄨㄥ)
statements that arouse the public from apathy or complacency

木頭(ㄇㄨˋ ·ㄊㄡ)
① wood; timber ② a stupid fellow

木頭人兒(ㄇㄨˋ ·ㄊㄡ ㄖㄜˊㄦ)
a stupid fellow; an idiot

木炭(ㄇㄨˋ ㄊㄢˋ)
charcoal: 在火中多放些木炭。Put some more charcoal on the fire.

木炭畫(ㄇㄨˋ ㄊㄢˋ ㄏㄨㄚˋ)
a charcoal drawing; a fusain

木訥(ㄇㄨˋ ㄋㄜˋ)
honest and slow-witted; lacking the ability to talk well

木乃伊(ㄇㄨˋ ㄋㄞˇ ㄧ)
a mummy

木牛流馬(ㄇㄨˋ ㄋㄧㄡˊ ㄌㄧㄡˊ ㄇㄚˇ)
a legendary mechanical device for hauling war supplies, said to be invented by Chu-Ko Liang (諸葛亮) during the Epoch of the Three Kingdoms

木臘(ㄇㄨˋ ㄌㄚˋ)
wood wax

木蘭(ㄇㄨˋ ㄌㄢˊ)
① a deciduous magnolia (*Magnolia obovata*) ② Hua Mu-lan (花木蘭) (circa 500 A.D.), a heroine who joined the military service in place of her sick father for 12 years without betraying her real identity

木梨(ㄇㄨˋ ㄌㄧˊ)
a tough pear

木料(ㄇㄨˋ ㄌㄧㄠˋ)
wooden material; wood; lumber: 桌子通常是木料做的。Tables are usually made of wood.

木瘤(ㄇㄨˋ ㄌㄧㄡˊ)
a gnarl

木蓮(ㄇㄨˋ ㄌㄧㄢˊ)
a magnolia

木瓜(ㄇㄨˋ ㄍㄨㄚ)
① a papaya (fruit) ② a papaya (tree) 亦作「木瓜樹」

木棍(ㄇㄨˋ ㄍㄨㄣˋ) or 木棒(ㄇㄨˋ ㄅㄤˋ)
a wooden club: 他以木棒擊球。He hit the ball with his wooden club.

木工(ㄇㄨˋ ㄍㄨㄥ)
① a carpenter; a woodworker ② carpentry

木工場(ㄇㄨˋ ㄍㄨㄥ ㄔㄤˇ)
a woodworking plant or shop

木刻(ㄇㄨˋ ㄎㄜˋ)
wood engraving; a woodcut

木化石(ㄇㄨˋ ㄏㄨㄚˋ ㄕˊ)
wood opal

木屐(ㄇㄨˋ ㄐㄧ)
clogs; pattens

木鷄(ㄇㄨˋ ㄐㄧ)
① a simpleton ② a woodcock

木簡(ㄇㄨˋ ㄐㄧㄢˇ)
a wooden tablet (used as writing paper in ancient times)

木槿(ㄇㄨˋ ㄐㄧㄣˇ)
a hibiscus; a China rose

木漿(ㄇㄨˋ ㄐㄧㄤ)
(papermaking) wood pulp

木匠(ㄇㄨˋ ㄐㄧㄤˋ)
a carpenter; a woodworker

木強 or 木彊(ㄇㄨˋ ㄐㄧㄤˋ)
stiff; inexorable; uncompromising; inflexible

木精(ㄇㄨˋ ㄐㄧㄥ)
wood spirit; wood alcohol 亦作「甲醇」

木器(ㄇㄨˋ ㄑㄧˋ)
wooden articles; wooden furniture

木器店(ㄇㄨˋ ㄑㄧˋ ㄉㄧㄢˋ)
a wooden article store; a wooden furniture store

木琴(ㄇㄨˋ ㄑㄧㄣˊ)
(music) a xylophone

木樨 or 木犀(ㄇㄨˋ ㄒㄧ)
(botany) *Osmanthus fragrans*

木屑竹頭(ㄇㄨˋ ㄒㄧㄝˋ ㄓㄨˊ ㄊㄡˊ)
odds and ends that may prove useful someday

木杴(ㄇㄨˋ ㄒㄧㄢ)
a wooden winnowing spade; a wooden shovel

木箱(ㄇㄨˋ ㄒㄧㄤ)
a wooden box; a wooden trunk: 他把書籍裝在木箱中。He packed the books in a wooden box.

木星(ㄇㄨˋ ㄒㄧㄥ)
the planet Jupiter

木札(ㄇㄨˋ ㄓㄚˊ)
a wooden tag

木柵(ㄇㄨˋ ㄓㄚˋ)
a stockade

木主(ㄇㄨˋ ㄓㄨˇ)
sacred wooden tablets (at temples, chapels, etc.)

木樁(ㄇㄨˋ ㄓㄨㄤ)
a wooden post or pile

木柴(ㄇㄨˋ ㄔㄞˊ)
firewood

木廠(ㄇㄨˋ ㄔㄤˇ)
a timber mill

木槌(ㄇㄨˋ ㄔㄨㄟˊ)
a gavel; a wooden hammer

木蝨(ㄇㄨˋ ㄕ)
a wood louse

木石(ㄇㄨˋ ㄕˊ)
a lifeless thing; a senseless being

木石心腸(ㄇㄨˋ ㄕˊ ㄒㄧㄣ ㄔㄤˊ)
flinty-hearted; unfeeling

木舌(ㄇㄨˋ ㄕㄜˊ)
reticent; silent

木梳(ㄇㄨˋ ㄕㄨ)
a wooden comb

木栓(ㄇㄨˋ ㄕㄨㄢ)
a cork

木然(ㄇㄨˋ ㄖㄢˊ)
stupefied

木人(ㄇㄨˋ ㄖㄣˊ)
a dull fellow; a simpleton

木人石心(ㄇㄨˋ ㄖㄣˊ ㄕˊ ㄒㄧㄣ)
pitiless; unfeeling; heartless
木作(ㄇㄨˋ ㄗㄨㄛˋ)
①a carpenter's shop ② a carpenter
木材(ㄇㄨˋ ㄘㄞˊ)
lumber; timber: 這桌子是木材製的。This table is made of timber.
木材行(ㄇㄨˋ ㄘㄞˊ ㄏㄤˊ)
a lumber company
木醋(ㄇㄨˋ ㄘㄨˋ)
wood vinegar
木塞(ㄇㄨˋ ㄙㄞ)
a cork
木索(ㄇㄨˋ ㄙㄨㄛˇ)
an instrument of torture (for squeezing hands or feet)
木燧(ㄇㄨˋ ㄙㄨㄟˋ)
wood for producing fire by friction
木偶(ㄇㄨˋ ㄡˇ)
a puppet
木偶戲(ㄇㄨˋ ㄡˇ ㄒㄧˋ)
a puppet show: 她喜歡看木偶戲。She is fond of the puppet show.
木耳(ㄇㄨˋ ㄦˇ)
edible fungus from trees (*Auricularia auricula*)
木已成舟(ㄇㄨˋ ㄧˇ ㄔㄥˊ ㄓㄡ)
(literally) The timber has been turned into a boat already.—It is irrevocable.或 It is an accomplished fact.
木曜日(ㄇㄨˋ ㄧㄠˋ ㄖˋ)
Thursday
木屋(ㄇㄨˋ ㄨ)
a log cabin: 他們住在一間木屋裏。They lived in a log cabin.
木碗(ㄇㄨˋ ㄨㄢˇ)
a wooden bowl
木魚(ㄇㄨˋ ㄩˊ)
a skull-shaped wooden drum, which a Buddhist monk or nun beats while chanting
木鳶(ㄇㄨˋ ㄩㄢ)
a wooden kite (a legendary flying machine)
木俑(ㄇㄨˋ ㄩㄥˇ)
a wooden image or figure to be buried with the deceased

一畫

【未】2331 ㄨㄟˋ wey wèi
1. not yet: 這工作尚未做完。The work is not yet finished.
2. not: 我未曾見過他。I have not seen him.
3. the eighth of the Twelve Terrestrial Branches
4. 1:00-3:00 p.m.
5. a Chinese family name
未必(ㄨㄟˋ ㄅㄧˋ)
not always; not necessarily: 那未必如此。It is not necessarily so.
未必盡然(ㄨㄟˋ ㄅㄧˋ ㄐㄧㄣˋ ㄖㄢˊ)
not always so; not necessarily so
未便(ㄨㄟˋ ㄅㄧㄢˋ)
not convenient; improper; inadvisable; not in a position to
未卜先知(ㄨㄟˋ ㄅㄨˇ ㄒㄧㄢ ㄓ)
to foresee accurately
未萌(ㄨㄟˋ ㄇㄥˊ)
yet to bud; yet to come into existence or develop
未免(ㄨㄟˋ ㄇㄧㄢˇ)
① It must be admitted that... ② necessarily; unavoidably
未付(ㄨㄟˋ ㄈㄨˋ)
unpaid; outstanding (debts, accounts, etc.): 他未付的帳加起來一共有七百元。His unpaid bills amounted to $700.
未到貨(ㄨㄟˋ ㄉㄠˋ ㄏㄨㄛˋ)
goods afloat
未定(ㄨㄟˋ ㄉㄧㄥˋ)
uncertain; unfixed; undefined: 他的行期未定。The date of his departure is uncertain.
未定之天(ㄨㄟˋ ㄉㄧㄥˋ ㄓ ㄊㄧㄢ)
uncertainty
未定草(ㄨㄟˋ ㄉㄧㄥˋ ㄘㄠˇ)or 未定稿(ㄨㄟˋ ㄉㄧㄥˋ ㄍㄠˇ)
a preliminary draft
未妥(ㄨㄟˋ ㄊㄨㄛˇ)
yet to be brought to a proper state; not proper: 那樣做未妥。It isn't proper to act like that.
未能(ㄨㄟˋ ㄋㄥˊ)
to fail to; cannot: 他們未能了解我的意思。They failed to see what I meant.
未能免俗(ㄨㄟˋ ㄋㄥˊ ㄇㄧㄢˇ ㄙㄨˊ)
incapable of being exempted from usual custom; unable to avoid following conventional practices
未來(ㄨㄟˋ ㄌㄞˊ)
future; in the future: 我們的未來似難預測。Our future seems very uncertain.
未來派(ㄨㄟˋ ㄌㄞˊ ㄆㄞˋ)
futurists; futurism
未老先衰(ㄨㄟˋ ㄌㄠˇ ㄒㄧㄢ ㄕㄨㄞ)
to become senile before one's time
未了(ㄨㄟˋ ㄌㄧㄠˇ)
unsettled; unfixed; unfinished: 這問題仍然未了。The problem is still unsettled.
未了公案(ㄨㄟˋ ㄌㄧㄠˇ ㄍㄨㄥ ㄢˋ)
an unsettled problem
未了緣(ㄨㄟˋ ㄌㄧㄠˇ ㄩㄢˊ)or 未了因(ㄨㄟˋ ㄌㄧㄠˇ ㄧㄣ)
(Buddhism) ties carried over from the previous life
未敢苟同(ㄨㄟˋ ㄍㄢˇ ㄍㄡˇ ㄊㄨㄥˊ)
(literary language) to beg to differ; cannot agree: 請你原諒，你的意見，我未敢苟同。I beg your pardon! I cannot agree with you.
未冠(ㄨㄟˋ ㄍㄨㄢˋ)
prior to the capping ceremony which takes place when a young man is 20 years old
未可(ㄨㄟˋ ㄎㄜˇ)
cannot: 此案未可定奪。This case cannot be decided.
未可厚非(ㄨㄟˋ ㄎㄜˇ ㄏㄡˋ ㄈㄟ)
shouldn't be blamed too much for that—no serious mistake committed
未可知(ㄨㄟˋ ㄎㄜˇ ㄓ)
uncertain: 他們抵達的日期尚未可知。The date of their arrival is uncertain.
未開發(ㄨㄟˋ ㄎㄞ ㄈㄚ)
(said of land, resources, etc.) undeveloped; uncultivated
未開化的(ㄨㄟˋ ㄎㄞ ㄏㄨㄚˋ ·ㄉㄜ)
① uncivilized ② underdeveloped
未婚(ㄨㄟˋ ㄏㄨㄣ)
unmarried; single
未婚夫(ㄨㄟˋ ㄏㄨㄣ ㄈㄨ)

〔木部〕

〔木部〕

one's fiancé

未婚男子(ㄨㄟˋ ㄏㄨㄣ ㄋㄢˊ ㄗˇ)
a bachelor

未婚妻(ㄨㄟˋ ㄏㄨㄣ ㄑㄧ)
one's fiancée

未遑(ㄨㄟˋ ㄏㄨㄤˊ)
busy; occupied; too busy to; too occupied to

未及(ㄨㄟˋ ㄐㄧˊ)
unable to make it in time; not enough time left to do it

未幾(ㄨㄟˋ ㄐㄧˇ)
① soon afterwards: 未幾，他曾向我解釋。Soon afterwards he explained it to me. ② not many

未見(ㄨㄟˋ ㄐㄧㄢˋ)
to have not seen; not yet seen: 我未見過人被絞死。I've never seen a man hanged.

未盡事宜(ㄨㄟˋ ㄐㄧㄣˋ ㄕˋ ㄧˊ)
unfinished matters; unsettled affairs

未經(ㄨㄟˋ ㄐㄧㄥ)
to have not yet (gone through)

未竟之志(ㄨㄟˋ ㄐㄧㄥˋ ㄓ ㄓˋ)
an unfulfilled ambition: 做個偉大的政治家是他的未竟之志。To be a great statesman is his unfulfilled ambition.

未決(ㄨㄟˋ ㄐㄩㄝˊ)
undecided; uncertain; unsettled: 那仍是個未決的問題。It was still an undecided question.

未悉(ㄨㄟˋ ㄒㄧ)
① not knowing; unfamiliar ② unknown

未詳(ㄨㄟˋ ㄒㄧㄤˊ)
not knowing or known in detail

未知鹿死誰手(ㄨㄟˋ ㄓ ㄌㄨˋ ㄙˇ ㄕㄟˊ ㄕㄡˇ)
unable to predict who will be the winner

未知數(ㄨㄟˋ ㄓ ㄕㄨˋ)
①(mathematics) an unknown number ② unknown; uncertain

未之有焉(ㄨㄟˋ ㄓ ㄧㄡˇ ㄧㄢ)
impossible; could not happen; never heard of: 如此意外事件似乎未之有焉。Such an accident seems impossible.

未嘗(ㄨㄟˋ ㄔㄤˊ)
①(to be used before another negative expression to form a positive statement) not necessarily ② never: 我生平未嘗聽說或見過這樣的東西。Never in my life have I heard or seen such a thing.

未嘗不可(ㄨㄟˋ ㄔㄤˊ ㄅㄨˋ ㄎㄜˇ)
It is not necessarily impermissible or impossible.

未成品(ㄨㄟˋ ㄔㄥˊ ㄆㄧㄣˇ)
unfinished work

未成年(ㄨㄟˋ ㄔㄥˊ ㄋㄧㄢˊ)or 未成人(ㄨㄟˋ ㄔㄥˊ ㄖㄣˊ)
not yet come of age; minor

未成熟(ㄨㄟˋ ㄔㄥˊ ㄕㄨˊ)
unripe; immature: 她是一個未成熟的女郎。She is an immature girl.

未時(ㄨㄟˋ ㄕˊ)
the period of the day from 1 p.m. to 3 p.m.

未始(ㄨㄟˋ ㄕˇ)
not necessarily (used before another negative expression to form a positive statement)

未然(ㄨㄟˋ ㄖㄢˊ)
before it happens: 我們應防患未然。We should prevent trouble before it happens.

未入流(ㄨㄟˋ ㄖㄨˋ ㄌㄧㄡˊ)
① government employees of the lowest rank during the Ming and Ching Dynasties ② any skill that is below the accepted standard

未若(ㄨㄟˋ ㄖㄨㄛˋ)
not as good as; can not be compared with: 我的英文未若他。My English is not as good as his.

未曾(ㄨㄟˋ ㄘㄥˊ)
never before: 我未曾到過那裏。Never before have I been there.

未曾有(ㄨㄟˋ ㄘㄥˊ ㄧㄡˇ)
to have not happened before; unprecedented: 這是歷史上未曾有的奇蹟。This is a miracle unprecedented in history.

未遂(ㄨㄟˋ ㄙㄨㄟˋ)
attempted without success

未遂犯(ㄨㄟˋ ㄙㄨㄟˋ ㄈㄢˋ)
a convict guilty of an attempted offense

未有(ㄨㄟˋ ㄧㄡˇ)
to have never had; to have never been; can never be: 我對那件事從未有過懷疑。I have never had any doubts whatever of that.

未央(ㄨㄟˋ ㄧㄤ)
① not yet halfway through ② not exhausted

未央宮(ㄨㄟˋ ㄧㄤ ㄍㄨㄥ)
name of a palace built in the Han Dynasty

未完(ㄨㄟˋ ㄨㄢˊ)
unfinished; not completed

未亡人(ㄨㄟˋ ㄨㄤˊ ㄖㄣˊ)
a widow: 在戰爭中許多婦女成爲未亡人。A great many women became widows in the war.

未雨綢繆(ㄨㄟˋ ㄩˇ ㄔㄡˊ ㄇㄡˊ)
to take precautions before it is too late; to take protective measures in advance

未月(ㄨㄟˋ ㄩㄝˋ)
the sixth month of the lunar calendar

【末】 2332 ㄇㄛˋ moh mò

1. last; final
2. late; recent
3. trivial; unimportant; insignificant
4. the end; the tip
5. the four limbs

末班(ㄇㄛˋ ㄅㄢ)
① petty officials ② the last scheduled bus, train, ship, or airplane in a day

末末了兒(ㄇㄛˋ ㄇㄛˋ ㄌㄧㄠˇㄦ)
the last portion; the end

末民(ㄇㄛˋ ㄇㄧㄣˊ)
the humblest people — laborers and traders

末代(ㄇㄛˋ ㄉㄞˋ)
the last reign (of a dynasty)

末代孫(ㄇㄛˋ ㄉㄞˋ ㄙㄨㄣ)
late descendants

末奈何 or 沒奈何(ㄇㄛˋ ㄋㄞˋ ㄏㄜˊ)
Nothing can be done about it. 或 There is no way out.

末年(ㄇㄛˋ ㄋㄧㄢˊ)
the declining years of one's life, a dynasty, etc.

末了(ㄇㄛˋ ㄌㄧㄠˇ)or 末了兒(ㄇㄛˋ ㄌㄧㄠˇㄦ)
the end; the last part; last; in the end; finally

末流(ㄇㄛˋ ㄌㄧㄡˊ)

① later adherents (to a school of thought, religious sect, etc.) ② decadent customs or conventions of troubled times
末路(ㄇㄛˋ ㄌㄨˋ)
a miserable end
末路窮途(ㄇㄛˋ ㄌㄨˋ ㄑㄩㄥˊ ㄊㄨˊ)
a miserable end which one is driven to; to face a stone wall; to reach the end of the rope; to be at one's wits' end: 他到了末路窮途。He arrived at a miserable end.
末官(ㄇㄛˋ ㄍㄨㄢ)
a petty official; a low official
末光(ㄇㄛˋ ㄍㄨㄤ)
lingering light; dim light
末後(ㄇㄛˋ ㄏㄡˋ)
the end; the final part
末技(ㄇㄛˋ ㄐㄧˋ)
a trivial skill; an insignificant stunt
末季(ㄇㄛˋ ㄐㄧˋ)
the last part of a period
末節(ㄇㄛˋ ㄐㄧㄝˊ)
minor details
末席(ㄇㄛˋ ㄒㄧˊ)
the least prominent seat: 他坐在末席。He took the lowest seat at table.
末行(ㄇㄛˋ ㄒㄧㄥˊ)
minor details
末學(ㄇㄛˋ ㄒㄩㄝˊ)
① superficial learning; insignificant learning ② a polite self-reference
末學膚受(ㄇㄛˋ ㄒㄩㄝˊ ㄈㄨ ㄕㄡˋ)
to have acquired only skin-deep learning or superficial scholarship
末學後進(ㄇㄛˋ ㄒㄩㄝˊ ㄏㄡˋ ㄐㄧㄣˋ)
(a polite term referring to oneself) a younger student with superficial learning
末著(ㄇㄛˋ ㄓㄠ)
the last stratagem
末世(ㄇㄛˋ ㄕˋ)
the last years (of a dynasty)
末梢(ㄇㄛˋ ㄕㄠ)
the tip; the end
末梢神經(ㄇㄛˋ ㄕㄠ ㄕㄣˊ ㄐㄧㄥ)
the peripheral nervous system
末日(ㄇㄛˋ ㄖˋ)
① the last day; the end; doom ② (Christianity) Doomsday; Judgment Day; the Day of Judgment
末造(ㄇㄛˋ ㄗㄠˋ)
the last days of a dynasty; the decaying period
末座(ㄇㄛˋ ㄗㄨㄛˋ)
the least prominent seat 參看「敬陪末座」
末次(ㄇㄛˋ ㄘˋ)
the last time
末俗(ㄇㄛˋ ㄙㄨˊ)
decadent customs and practices during a period of decline
末議(ㄇㄛˋ ㄧˋ)
trivial argument; unimportant discussion
末藝(ㄇㄛˋ ㄧˋ)
an insignificant skill; a small skill
末業(ㄇㄛˋ ㄧㄝˋ) or 末作(ㄇㄛˋ ㄗㄨㄛˋ)
(in ancient China) commerce and industry which were regarded as secondary occupations; traditionally lower professions
末葉(ㄇㄛˋ ㄧㄝˋ)
① posterity; descendants ② the last part of a dynasty ③ the latter part of a century
末尾(ㄇㄛˋ ㄨㄟˇ)
the end: 他忘記在信的末尾簽字。He's forgotten to sign his name at the end of the letter.

【本】 2333 ㄅㄣˇ been běn

1. the root of a plant
2. the root; the origin; the source; the basis; the foundation
3. original
4. a book; a copy
5. capital (in business)
6. our; this; the present
7. according to; based on
8. the beginning; the starting point

本班(ㄅㄣˇ ㄅㄢ)
this (or our) class, squad, team, section, etc.: 他是本班第一名。He is (at the) top of this class.
本部(ㄅㄣˇ ㄅㄨˋ)
① headquarters; the head office ② this ministry; our ministry
本埠(ㄅㄣˇ ㄅㄨˋ)
this city; the local area
本票(ㄅㄣˇ ㄆㄧㄠˋ)
a cashier's check; a banker's check; a bank check
本末(ㄅㄣˇ ㄇㄛˋ)
① the beginning and the end ② the whole story: 告訴我這故事的本末。Tell me the whole story.
本末倒置(ㄅㄣˇ ㄇㄛˋ ㄉㄠˋ ㄓˋ)
to mistake the means for the end; to put the cart before the horse; to attend to the superficials and neglect the essentials
本名(ㄅㄣˇ ㄇㄧㄥˊ)
one's formal name (as distinct from pen names, nicknames or other aliases)
本命年(ㄅㄣˇ ㄇㄧㄥˋ ㄋㄧㄢˊ)
one's year of birth considered in relation to the Twelve Terrestrial Branches
本分(ㄅㄣˇ ㄈㄣˋ)
one's part; one's role; one's duty
本俸(ㄅㄣˇ ㄈㄥˋ) or 本薪(ㄅㄣˇ ㄒㄧㄣ)
the basic salary (exclusive of various additional allowances)
本夫(ㄅㄣˇ ㄈㄨ)
one's legitimate husband
本大利寬(ㄅㄣˇ ㄉㄚˋ ㄌㄧˋ ㄎㄨㄢ)
A large capital will yield a large profit.
本當(ㄅㄣˇ ㄉㄤ)
should have, or ought to have: 你本當在昨天就告訴我。You ought to have told me yesterday.
本黨(ㄅㄣˇ ㄉㄤˇ)
our party; this party
本地(ㄅㄣˇ ㄉㄧˋ)
the local area
本地風光(ㄅㄣˇ ㄉㄧˋ ㄈㄥ ㄍㄨㄤ)
local scenery
本地貨(ㄅㄣˇ ㄉㄧˋ ㄏㄨㄛˋ)
local goods; locally manufactured products; locally grown goods
本地人(ㄅㄣˇ ㄉㄧˋ ㄖㄣˊ)
a native: 我父親是本地人。My father is a native of this place.
本地郵件(ㄅㄣˇ ㄉㄧˋ ㄧㄡˊ ㄐㄧㄢˋ)

mail addressed to recipients within a city or community

本隊(ㄅㄣˇ ㄉㄨㄟˋ)
this (or our) detachment, unit, group, etc.

本題(ㄅㄣˇ ㄊㄧˊ)
the main subject; the point at issue; the main issue; the main question; the major theme

本體(ㄅㄣˇ ㄊㄧˇ)
a thing in itself; substance

本體論(ㄅㄣˇ ㄊㄧˇ ㄌㄨㄣˋ)
ontology

本土(ㄅㄣˇ ㄊㄨˇ)
the mainland; a country proper

本土文化(ㄅㄣˇ ㄊㄨˇ ㄨㄣˊ ㄏㄨㄚˋ)
indigenous culture

本能(ㄅㄣˇ ㄋㄥˊ)
instinct

本年(ㄅㄣˇ ㄋㄧㄢˊ)
this year; the present year; the current year

本來(ㄅㄣˇ ㄌㄞˊ)
① from the beginning; originally ② of course; it goes without saying

本來面目(ㄅㄣˇ ㄌㄞˊ ㄇㄧㄢˋ ㄇㄨˋ)
true looks; true colors; true features

本壘(ㄅㄣˇ ㄌㄟˇ)
(baseball) home base

本利(ㄅㄣˇ ㄌㄧˋ)
principal and interest

本領(ㄅㄣˇ ㄌㄧㄥˇ)
ability; skill; talent

本論(ㄅㄣˇ ㄌㄨㄣˋ)
① the main contention ② the main body of an expository writing

本該(ㄅㄣˇ ㄍㄞ)
ought to have; should have

本國(ㄅㄣˇ ㄍㄨㄛˊ)
one's home country; one's mother country

本國人(ㄅㄣˇ ㄍㄨㄛˊ ㄖㄣˊ)
a fellow countryman; a compatriot

本科(ㄅㄣˇ ㄎㄜ)
a main course (as distinct from preparatory courses)

本號(ㄅㄣˇ ㄏㄠˋ)
our store or company

本行(ㄅㄣˇ ㄏㄤˊ)
① one's trade; one's specialty: 建築是我的本行。Architecture is my speciality. ② this bank; our bank

本籍(ㄅㄣˇ ㄐㄧˊ)
one's original domicile; one's permanent home address: 他的本籍是紐約。His original domicile is New York.

本紀(ㄅㄣˇ ㄐㄧˋ)
biographic sketches of emperors

本家(ㄅㄣˇ ㄐㄧㄚ)
① the original home ② a reference to somebody having the same family name as one's own

本家兒(ㄅㄣˇ ㄐㄧㄚㄦ)
of one's own family

本屆(ㄅㄣˇ ㄐㄧㄝˋ)
current; this year's: 本屆畢業生都是女生。This year's graduates are all girls.

本金(ㄅㄣˇ ㄐㄧㄣ)
principal as distinct from interest

本軍(ㄅㄣˇ ㄐㄩㄣ)
this army; our army

本期(ㄅㄣˇ ㄑㄧˊ)
① this term; the current season ② the present class (of students or cadets)

本錢(ㄅㄣˇ ㄑㄧㄢˊ)
capital (in business)

本息(ㄅㄣˇ ㄒㄧˊ)
principal and interest

本校(ㄅㄣˇ ㄒㄧㄠˋ)
our (or this) school

本縣(ㄅㄣˇ ㄒㄧㄢˋ)
our (or this) county, prefecture, etc.

本心(ㄅㄣˇ ㄒㄧㄣ)
one's conscience

本鄉(ㄅㄣˇ ㄒㄧㄤ)
our (or this) village

本鄉本土(ㄅㄣˇ ㄒㄧㄤ ㄅㄣˇ ㄊㄨˇ)
one's homeland: 他的父親死於本鄉本土。His father died in his homeland.

本相(ㄅㄣˇ ㄒㄧㄤˋ)
the real look

本刑(ㄅㄣˇ ㄒㄧㄥˊ)
the standard penalty for a specific offense, to which the judge refers in meting out additional or reduced punishment

本性(ㄅㄣˇ ㄒㄧㄥˋ)
the real nature

本性難移(ㄅㄣˇ ㄒㄧㄥˋ ㄋㄢˊ ㄧˊ)
One's nature cannot be altered. 或 The leopard can't change its spots.

本質(ㄅㄣˇ ㄓˊ)
essential qualities; essential characteristics; essence; the intrinsic nature

本職(ㄅㄣˇ ㄓˊ)
one's job (or duty): 我做好本職工作。I did my own job well.

本旨(ㄅㄣˇ ㄓˇ)
the real intention; the real meaning

本着(ㄅㄣˇ ˙ㄓㄜ)
in line with; in conformity with; in the light of; in accordance with

本宅(ㄅㄣˇ ㄓㄞˊ)
one's own residence

本週(ㄅㄣˇ ㄓㄡ)
this week

本州(ㄅㄣˇ ㄓㄡ)
Honshu, one of the principal islands of Japan

本朝(ㄅㄣˇ ㄔㄠˊ)
the present dynasty; our dynasty

本初子午線(ㄅㄣˇ ㄔㄨ ㄗˇ ㄨˇ ㄒㄧㄢˋ)
the prime meridian

本師(ㄅㄣˇ ㄕ)
① one's teacher ② this division; our division

本市(ㄅㄣˇ ㄕˋ)
this city; our city: 我住在本市。I live in this city.

本事
①(ㄅㄣˇ ㄕˋ) a story (or a plot) of a play, movie, etc.
②(ㄅㄣˇ ˙ㄕ) ability; skill; talent: 他是個有本事的人。He is a man of ability.

本身(ㄅㄣˇ ㄕㄣ)
oneself; personally; itself; in itself; per se

本生燈(ㄅㄣˇ ㄕㄥ ㄉㄥ)
a Bunsen burner

本省(ㄅㄣˇ ㄕㄥˇ)
this province; our province

本省人(ㄅㄣˇ ㄕㄥˇ ㄖㄣˊ)
a native of this province

本日(ㄅㄣˇ ㄖˋ)
today

本人(ㄅㄣˇ ㄖㄣˊ)

①I; me ②himself; herself; yourself ③personally
本字(ㄅㄣˇ ㄗˋ)
the standard form of a character (as distinct from the corrupted form or simplified form of the character)
本子(ㄅㄣˇ ·ㄗ)or 本兒(ㄅㄜˇㄦ)
a book; a notebook
本草綱目(ㄅㄣˇ ㄘㄠˇ ㄍㄤ ㄇㄨˋ)
Compendium of Materia Medica, a pharmaceutical work by Li Shih-chen (李時珍) in the Ming Dynasty (1386-1644), which lists all the animals, vegetables and other objects believed to contain medicinal properties in traditional Chinese medicine
本色(ㄅㄣˇ ㄙㄜˋ)
①the original color ②the real look; the true qualities or characteristics
本訴(ㄅㄣˇ ㄙㄨˋ)
the lawsuit filed by the original plaintiff after the defendant files a countersuit
本素(ㄅㄣˇ ㄙㄨˋ)
the original element
本案(ㄅㄣˇ ㄢˋ)
the case under consideration; the present case; this case: 本案是一個特例。This case is a special one.
本意(ㄅㄣˇ ㄧˋ)
the original intention
本義(ㄅㄣˇ ㄧˋ)
the original meaning; the real meaning
本業(ㄅㄣˇ ㄧㄝˋ)
①(in ancient China) farming which was considered the most important sector of the economy ②one's own occupation: 他更換了本業。He changed his own occupation.
本因坊(ㄅㄣˇ ㄧㄣ ㄈㄤ)
Honinbo, one of the most coveted titles among professional *go* players in Japan
本銀(ㄅㄣˇ ㄧㄣˊ)
capital (in business)
本應(ㄅㄣˇ ㄧㄥ)
should have; ought to have: 你本應更加注意的。You should have been more careful.
本務(ㄅㄣˇ ㄨˋ)
one's real duty: 保衛國家是軍人的本務。To defend the country is soldiers' real duty.
本位(ㄅㄣˇ ㄨㄟˋ)
a standard; a basis
本位貨幣(ㄅㄣˇ ㄨㄟˋ ㄏㄨㄛˋ ㄅㄧˋ)
standard money
本文(ㄅㄣˇ ㄨㄣˊ)
the main body of a writing
本月(ㄅㄣˇ ㄩㄝˋ)
this month
本源(ㄅㄣˇ ㄩㄢˊ)
the ultimate source
本願(ㄅㄣˇ ㄩㄢˋ)
one's real wish; long-cherished desire: 致富並非我的本願。To become rich is not my long-cherished desire.

【札】 2334 ㄓㄚˊ jar zhá

1. (in ancient China) a thin wooden tablet for writing
2. correspondence; a letter
3. (in ancient China) documents or instructions to a subordinate
4. (now rarely) to die before one comes of age

札幌(ㄓㄚˊ ㄏㄨㄤˇ)
Sapporo, a city in Japan
札記(ㄓㄚˊ ㄐㄧˋ)
a notebook in which one records his comments on the book he is reading
札子(ㄓㄚˊ ·ㄗ)
a document sent by a superior

【朮】 2335 ㄓㄨˊ jwu zhú

Podophyllum versipelle, a plant with violet, green or red flowers and white roots, used in herbal medicine
朮酒(ㄓㄨˊ ㄐㄧㄡˇ)
wine in which the plant 朮 has been soaked; medicinal wine

二畫

【朱】 2336 ㄓㄨ ju zhū

1. red; vermilion
2. a Chinese family name

朱筆(ㄓㄨ ㄅㄧˇ)
a writing brush dipped in red ink (originally used by an emperor in signing decrees, now often used by school teachers to correct students' papers)
朱批(ㄓㄨ ㄆㄧ)
writing comments or remarks in red with a brush
朱墨本(ㄓㄨ ㄇㄛˋ ㄅㄣˇ)
editions printed during the Wan Li reign of the Ming Dynasty with dark characters and running commentaries or footnotes in red
朱墨爛然(ㄓㄨ ㄇㄛˋ ㄌㄢˋ ㄖㄢˊ)
with profuse comments written in red
朱買臣(ㄓㄨ ㄇㄞˇ ㄔㄣˊ)
Chu Mai-chen, a ranking official of the Han Dynasty, who refused to retake his wife who deserted him while he was poor
朱門(ㄓㄨ ㄇㄣˊ)
rich and influential families
朱門酒肉臭(ㄓㄨ ㄇㄣˊ ㄐㄧㄡˇ ㄖㄡˋ ㄔㄡˋ)
behind the red gate wine overflows and meat rots—The rich are excessively wealthy (while the poor suffer stark poverty).
朱邸(ㄓㄨ ㄉㄧˇ)
residence of a king or nobleman
朱樓(ㄓㄨ ㄌㄡˊ)
houses of the wealthy and influential
朱理安(ㄓㄨ ㄌㄧˇ ㄢ)
Julian or Julianus Flavius Claudius, 331-363, Roman emperor
朱理安曆(ㄓㄨ ㄌㄧˇ ㄢ ㄌㄧˋ)
the Julian calendar
朱梁(ㄓㄨ ㄌㄧㄤˊ)
the Liang Dynasty (907-923), founded by Chu Wen (朱溫)
朱輪華轂(ㄓㄨ ㄌㄨㄣˊ ㄏㄨㄚˊ ㄍㄨˇ)
red and ornate carriages used by noblemen in ancient times
朱古力(ㄓㄨ ㄍㄨˇ ㄌㄧˋ)
chocolate 亦作「巧克力」
朱黃(ㄓㄨ ㄏㄨㄤˊ)
red and yellow, the two colors used in proofreading
朱紅(ㄓㄨ ㄏㄨㄥˊ)

〔木部〕

bright red; vermilion
朱槿(ㄓㄨ ㄐㄧㄣˇ)
(botany) Chinese hibiscus 亦作「扶桑」、「大紅花」
朱漆(ㄓㄨ ㄑㄧ)
red paint; red lacquer
朱熹(ㄓㄨ ㄒㄧ)
Chu Hsi, alias 元晦 or 晦庵 (1130-1200 A.D.), a great scholar of the Sung Dynasty, famous for his commentary on the Confucian classics which has been considered a standard exposition
朱軒(ㄓㄨ ㄒㄩㄢ)
a carriage used by high officials in old China
朱陳婚姻(ㄓㄨ ㄔㄣˊ ㄏㄨㄣ ㄧㄣ)or 朱陳結好(ㄓㄨ ㄔㄣˊ ㄐㄧㄝˊ ㄏㄠˇ)
a good matrimonial match; the two parties of a marriage
朱脣皓齒(ㄓㄨ ㄔㄨㄣˊ ㄏㄠˋ ㄔˇ)
(literally) red lips and sparkling teeth—a very beautiful girl
朱砂 or 硃砂(ㄓㄨ ㄕㄚ)
cinnabar
朱儒 or 侏儒(ㄓㄨ ㄖㄨˊ)
a dwarf; a pygmy or pigmy
朱衣(ㄓㄨ ㄧ)
the red robe worn by the emperor during summer
朱顏(ㄓㄨ ㄧㄢˊ)
① the beautiful face of a young lady ② the beautiful face of a youth
朱顏鶴髮(ㄓㄨ ㄧㄢˊ ㄏㄜˋ ㄈㄚˇ)
The hair is snow-white but the face is that of a young person.
朱殷(ㄓㄨ ㄧㄣ)
dark-red
朱溫(ㄓㄨ ㄨㄣ)
Chu Wen, alias 朱全忠, Emperor Tai Tsu(太祖), the founder of the Liang Dynasty
朱愚(ㄓㄨ ㄩˊ)
stupid; ignorant
朱元璋(ㄓㄨ ㄩㄢˊ ㄓㄤ)
Chu Yüan-chang, the founding emperor of the Ming Dynasty, who reigned from 1368 to 1399

【朴】 2337
1. ㄆㄛ poh po

saltpeter
朴硝(ㄆㄛ ㄒㄧㄠ)
(Chinese medicine) saltpeter
朴資茅斯(ㄆㄛ ㄗ ㄇㄠˊ ㄙ)
① Portsmouth, an English naval base in Southampton ② Portsmouth, a naval base in New Hampshire, U.S.A.
朴資茅斯條約(ㄆㄛ ㄗ ㄇㄠˊ ㄙ ㄊㄧㄠˊ ㄩㄝ)
The Treaty of Portsmouth, signed between Russia and Japan in 1905, at Portsmouth, New Hampshire, U.S.A.

【朴】 2337
2. (樸) ㄆㄨˊ pwu pú
1. (said of clothing, manner, etc.) plain; simple
2. a kind of oak (*Quercus dentata*)
朴茂(ㄆㄨˊ ㄇㄠˋ)
sincere and honest
朴鈍(ㄆㄨˊ ㄉㄨㄣˋ)
(said of a knife or other old weapons) blunt
朴陋(ㄆㄨˊ ㄌㄡˋ)
things in their original state—without any artificial decoration, chiseling, etc.
朴忠(ㄆㄨˊ ㄓㄨㄥ)
honest, loyal or faithful
朴樹(ㄆㄨˊ ㄕㄨˋ)
the hackberry

【朽】 2338
ㄒㄧㄡˇ sheou xiǔ
1. to rot; to decay; rotten; decayed: 這房子已腐朽。The house is in decay.
2. old and useless: 他老朽得不能走了。He is so old and useless that he can't walk.
朽敗(ㄒㄧㄡˇ ㄅㄞˋ)
decayed and rotten
朽邁(ㄒㄧㄡˇ ㄇㄞˋ)
(said of a person) old and useless; senile
朽木(ㄒㄧㄡˇ ㄇㄨˋ)
① rotten wood; decayed trees ② a hopeless person; a good-for-nothing
朽木不可雕(ㄒㄧㄡˇ ㄇㄨˋ ㄅㄨˋ ㄎㄜˇ ㄉㄧㄠ)
(literally) Decayed wood cannot be carved. —A congenital defeatist cannot be taught to succeed. 或 You can't teach old dogs new tricks.

朽木糞土(ㄒㄧㄡˇ ㄇㄨˋ ㄈㄣˋ ㄊㄨˇ)
decayed wood and filthy soil—a hopeless person
朽腐(ㄒㄧㄡˇ ㄈㄨˇ)
rotten; rotting
朽蠹(ㄒㄧㄡˇ ㄉㄨˋ)
① decayed and bitten by worms, etc. ② to over-hoard grains so that they rot
朽爛(ㄒㄧㄡˇ ㄌㄢˋ)
decayed and rotten
朽骨(ㄒㄧㄡˇ ㄍㄨˇ)
decaying bones
朽壞(ㄒㄧㄡˇ ㄏㄨㄞˋ)
to decay; to rot; decayed; rotten; rot: 開始朽壞了。Rot has set in.
朽穢(ㄒㄧㄡˇ ㄏㄨㄟˋ)
rotten and filthy
朽壤(ㄒㄧㄡˇ ㄖㄤˇ)
filthy earth—something that grows nothing

【朵】 2339
(朶) ㄉㄨㄛˇ duoo duǒ
1. a flower; a cluster of flowers; a bud
2. a lobe of the ear
朵朵(ㄉㄨㄛˇ ㄉㄨㄛˇ)
every (flower)
朵翰(ㄉㄨㄛˇ ㄏㄢˋ)or 朵雲(ㄉㄨㄛˇ ㄩㄣˊ)
your esteemed letter
朵頤(ㄉㄨㄛˇ ㄧˊ)
the movement of the jaw in eating—the palate

三畫

【李】 2340
ㄌㄧˇ lii lǐ
1. plums
2. (now rare) a judge; a justice
3. a Chinese family name
李白(ㄌㄧˇ ㄅㄞˊ (ㄅㄛˊ))or 李太白(ㄌㄧˇ ㄊㄞˋ ㄅㄞˊ (ㄅㄛˊ))
Li Po (701-762), one of the greatest Chinese poets in the Tang Dynasty
李代桃僵(ㄌㄧˇ ㄉㄞˋ ㄊㄠˊ ㄐㄧㄤ)
to substitute this for that
李唐(ㄌㄧˇ ㄊㄤˊ)
① the Tang Dynasty—so called because the founding emperor of the dynasty was named Li Yüan (李淵) ② name of a famous landscape painter in the Sung Dynasty
李後主(ㄌㄧˇ ㄏㄡˋ ㄓㄨˇ)or 李煜

(ㄌㄧˇ ㄩˇ)
Li Yü (937-978), the last monarch of the Southern Tang Dynasty, noted for his literary genius and was also blamed for indirectly encouraging the practice of foot-binding among Chinese women

李鴻章(ㄌㄧˇ ㄏㄨㄥˊ ㄓㄤ)
Li Hung-chang (1823-1901), a prime minister in the late Ching Dynasty

李清照(ㄌㄧˇ ㄑㄧㄥ ㄓㄠˋ)
Li Ching-chao (1081-1151?), a famous woman poet of the Sung Dynasty

李下不整冠(ㄌㄧˇ ㄒㄧㄚˋ ㄅㄨˋ ㄓㄥˇ ㄍㄨㄢ)
(literally) Do not adjust your hat under a plum tree. —One should avoid circumstances in which one is likely to be suspected of dishonest practices.

李下之嫌(ㄌㄧˇ ㄒㄧㄚˋ ㄓ ㄒㄧㄢˊ)
a position that invites suspicion; to be found in a suspicious position 亦作「瓜田李下」

李樹(ㄌㄧˇ ㄕㄨˋ)
the plum tree

李子(ㄌㄧˇ ·ㄗ)
plums

李斯(ㄌㄧˇ ㄙ)
Li Ssu, a prime minister during the reign of Chin Shih Huang (秦始皇)

李耳(ㄌㄧˇ ㄦˇ)
another name of Lao-tzu (老子), a philosopher of Confucius' time

【杉】 2341 ㄕㄢ shan shān

the various species of fir and pine; a China fir

杉木(ㄕㄢ ㄇㄨˋ)
fir wood

杉杆子(ㄕㄢ ㄍㄢ ·ㄗ)or 杉篙(ㄕㄢ ㄍㄠ)
straight and slender fir timber for building scaffolds and makeshift shelters

【杈】 2342 1. ㄔㄚ cha chā

1. the branches of a tree
2. a pitchfork; a fishfork; a wooden fork; a hayfork
3. any fork-like object
4. a kind of weapon in ancient China

杈枒(ㄔㄚ ㄧㄚˊ)
a forked branch

【杈】 2342 2. ㄔㄚˋ chah chà

杈子(ㄔㄚˋ ㄗˇ)or杈兒(ㄔㄚˋㄦ)
a cheval-de-frise; chevaux-de-frise

【杌】 2343 ㄨˋ wuh wù

1. a tree without a branch; the stump of a tree
2. a square stool
3. worried and anxious

杌凳(ㄨˋ ㄉㄥˋ)
a square stool

杌隉(ㄨˋ ㄋㄧㄝˋ)
worried and anxious; unquiet; uneasy

杌子(ㄨˋ ·ㄗ)
a stool or bench

【杏】 2344 ㄒㄧㄥˋ shinq xìng

1. an apricot
2. almonds—apricot kernels
3. apricot flowers

杏脯(ㄒㄧㄥˋ ㄈㄨˇ)
dried or preserved apricot meat

杏壇(ㄒㄧㄥˋ ㄊㄢˊ)
(originally) the site where Confucius taught his disciples—(in a broad sense) the teaching profession

杏臉(ㄒㄧㄥˋ ㄌㄧㄢˇ)
an almond-shaped face—the beautiful face of a woman

杏林(ㄒㄧㄥˋ ㄌㄧㄣˊ)
a term used in praising a good and kind physician or referring to the medical profession in general

杏酪(ㄒㄧㄥˋ ㄌㄨㄛˋ)
almond milk; a drink made from almonds

杏乾兒(ㄒㄧㄥˋ ㄍㄚㄦ)
dried apricot meat

杏核兒(ㄒㄧㄥˋ ㄏㄜˊㄦ)or(ㄒㄧㄥˋ ㄏㄨˊㄦ)
almonds

杏花(ㄒㄧㄥˋ ㄏㄨㄚ)
apricot blossoms

杏花村(ㄒㄧㄥˋ ㄏㄨㄚ ㄘㄨㄣ)
scenery of springtime in the country where apricot blossoms grow profusely (often used in Chinese poems)

杏花雨(ㄒㄧㄥˋ ㄏㄨㄚ ㄩˇ)
the rain that usually comes in the wake of the apricot blossom season

杏黃色(ㄒㄧㄥˋ ㄏㄨㄤˊ ㄙㄜˋ)
a bright-yellow color like the apricot's, deeper than that of the orange; apricot yellow

杏實(ㄒㄧㄥˋ ㄕˊ)
the apricot fruit

杏樹(ㄒㄧㄥˋ ㄕㄨˋ)
the apricot tree

杏仁兒(ㄒㄧㄥˋ ㄖㄣˊㄦ)
almonds; apricot kernels

杏仁兒粉(ㄒㄧㄥˋ ㄖㄣˊㄦ ㄈㄣˇ)
almond powder; ground almonds

杏仁兒茶(ㄒㄧㄥˋ ㄖㄣˊㄦ ㄔㄚˊ)
almond flavored tea (with ricesoup, sugar and almond powder as chief ingredients)

杏子(ㄒㄧㄥˋ ㄗˇ)or 杏兒(ㄒㄧㄥˋㄦ)
the apricot fruit

杏靨(ㄒㄧㄥˋ ㄧㄝˋ)
① apricot blossoms ② the beauty of a girl ③ a beautiful oval face

杏眼(ㄒㄧㄥˋ ㄧㄢˇ)
apricot-like eyes — a woman's large eyes

杏眼桃腮(ㄒㄧㄥˋ ㄧㄢˇ ㄊㄠˊ ㄙㄞ)
large eyes and rosy cheeks (of a beauty)

杏眼圓睜(ㄒㄧㄥˋ ㄧㄢˇ ㄩㄢˊ ㄓㄥ)
the angry look of a woman: 她杏眼圓睜。She has an angry look.

杏月(ㄒㄧㄥˋ ㄩㄝˋ)
the second month of the lunar calendar

【杓】 2345 1. ㄅㄧㄠ biau biāo

name of a constellation—the handle of the Dipper

【杓】 2345 2. (勺) ㄕㄠˊ shaur sháo

a receptacle or container, as a cup, ladle, spoon, etc.; the handle of such

杓子(ㄕㄠˊ ·ㄗ)
a wooden ladle

【材】 2346 ㄘㄞˊ tsair cái

1. materials—especially timber

〔木部〕

—for building houses, furniture, etc.
2. material in its broadest sense: 他就地取材。He obtained material from local sources.
3. properties of a substance
4. ability; aptitude: 他因材施敎。He taught students in accordance with their aptitude.
5. a coffin

材木(ㄘㄞˊ ㄇㄨˋ)
timber—for building, etc.

材能 or 才能(ㄘㄞˊ ㄋㄥˊ)
ability; capability

材吏(ㄘㄞˊ ㄌㄧˋ)
an able or capable official

材料(ㄘㄞˊ ㄌㄧㄠˋ)
① materials—for all building purposes; raw materials ② materials (such as data, statistics, figure, information for writing an article, story, novel, etc.) ③ ingredients of a preparation (of food, medicine, etc.) ④ makings; stuff: 他不是演戲的材料。He hasn't the makings of an actor.

材幹(ㄘㄞˊ ㄍㄢˋ)
① gifts; talent; ability: 他的材幹過人。His ability surpasses that of all others. ② timber

材器(ㄘㄞˊ ㄑㄧˋ)
① ability; capability; caliber (of a person) ② timber good for building purposes

材士(ㄘㄞˊ ㄕˋ)
men of ability

材人(ㄘㄞˊ ㄖㄣˊ)
① men of ability ② (in ancient China) a female court official 亦作「才人」

材藝(ㄘㄞˊ ㄧˋ)
ability and art: 他材藝兼備。He is perfect in both ability and art.

材武(ㄘㄞˊ ㄨˇ)
①(with) both ability and courage ② military ability: 他的材武出名。He is distinguished for military ability.

【村】 2347
(邨) ㄘㄨㄣ tsuen cūn

1. a village; the countryside; a hamlet
2. vulgar; coarse
3. naive ; simple-minded
4. (now rarely) to embarrass
5. (now rarely) to scold

村夫(ㄘㄨㄣ ㄈㄨ)
① a villager ② a vulgar and naive person

村夫子(ㄘㄨㄣ ㄈㄨ ㄗˇ)
a village scholar; a pedant

村夫俗子(ㄘㄨㄣ ㄈㄨ ㄙㄨˊ ㄗˇ)
an uneducated person; an illiterate

村夫野老(ㄘㄨㄣ ㄈㄨ ㄧㄝˇ ㄌㄠˇ)
villagers and aged rustics

村婦(ㄘㄨㄣ ㄈㄨˋ)
a village woman; a country woman; a vulgar woman

村女(ㄘㄨㄣ ㄋㄩˇ)
a country girl; farmers' daughters 參看「村姑」

村落(ㄘㄨㄣ ㄌㄨㄛˋ)
a village; a hamlet: 該村落荒涼。The village is desolate.

村姑(ㄘㄨㄣ ㄍㄨ)
village girls; farmers' daughters

村話(ㄘㄨㄣ ㄏㄨㄚˋ)
(literally) rustic talk—vulgar talk; filthy language

村居(ㄘㄨㄣ ㄐㄩ)
to live in the country; to rusticate

村氣(ㄘㄨㄣ ㄑㄧˋ)
vulgarity of the countryside

村墟(ㄘㄨㄣ ㄒㄩ)
a village market; a village marketplace

村學堂(ㄘㄨㄣ ㄒㄩㄝˊ ㄊㄤˊ)
(in old China) a village school

村學究(ㄘㄨㄣ ㄒㄩㄝˊ ㄐㄧㄡˋ)
a village scholar; a pedant

村鎭(ㄘㄨㄣ ㄓㄣˋ)
villages and small towns

村長(ㄘㄨㄣ ㄓㄤˇ)
the village chief

村莊(ㄘㄨㄣ ㄓㄨㄤ)
a village; a farmstead

村塾(ㄘㄨㄣ ㄕㄨˊ)
(in old China) a village school

村人(ㄘㄨㄣ ㄖㄣˊ)
villagers

村子(ㄘㄨㄣ ·ㄗ)
a village; a hamlet

村俗(ㄘㄨㄣ ㄙㄨˊ)
village customs or traditions

【杖】 2348
ㄓㄤˋ janq zhàng

1. a stick; a staff; a cane
2. (an old punishment) to beat with a cane; flogging with a stick
3. (now rarely) a mourning staff
4. to presume on (one's connections, influence, etc.)

杖頭錢(ㄓㄤˋ ㄊㄡˊ ㄑㄧㄢˊ)
wine-money (so called because the money was usually fastened on the top of a cane or staff in old China)

杖藜(ㄓㄤˋ ㄌㄧˊ)
a staff of chenopodium; to use such a staff to help an old person in walking, etc.

杖履(ㄓㄤˋ ㄌㄩˇ)
a respectful term of address for the elders

杖期(ㄓㄤˋ ㄐㄧ)
one-year mourning after the death of one's wife or father's concubine

杖期生(ㄓㄤˋ ㄐㄧ ㄕㄥ)
a reference to the husband in an obituary announcing the death of his wife (used only when the husband's parents are dead)

杖擊(ㄓㄤˋ ㄐㄧˊ)
to hit or beat with a cane

杖刑(ㄓㄤˋ ㄒㄧㄥˊ)
(in old China) the punishment by caning

杖者(ㄓㄤˋ ㄓㄜˇ)
elders—who hold canes or staffs

杖著 or 仗著(ㄓㄤˋ ·ㄓㄜ)
to rely on; to presume on

杖勢 or 仗勢(ㄓㄤˋ ㄕˋ)
to presume on one's position, connections, influence, etc.

杖責(ㄓㄤˋ ㄗㄜˊ)
to punish by caning; to flagellate; to cane

杖策(ㄓㄤˋ ㄘㄜˋ)
to hold a whip in the hand

杖義執言 or 仗義執言(ㄓㄤˋ ㄧˋ ㄓˊ ㄧㄢˊ)
to speak out courageously for what is right

【杜】 2349
ㄉㄨˋ duh dù

1. to plug (a hole, leak, etc.); to stop; to prevent; to put an end to something
2. to shut out; to restrict; to impede
3. the russet pear (*Pyrus betulaefolia*)
4. to fabricate; to practice forgery
5. a Chinese family name

杜弊(ㄉㄨˋ ㄅㄧˋ)
to prevent corrupt practices; to stop or put an end to illegal practices

杜門(ㄉㄨˋ ㄇㄣˊ)
① to close one's door (and shut out visitors) ② to stay in the house

杜門卻掃(ㄉㄨˋ ㄇㄣˊ ㄑㄩㄝˋ ㄙㄠˇ)
to shut one's door to the outside world

杜門謝客(ㄉㄨˋ ㄇㄣˊ ㄒㄧㄝˋ ㄎㄜˋ)
to shut out visitors; to refuse to see visitors; to close one's door to visitors

杜牧(ㄉㄨˋ ㄇㄨˋ)
Tu Mu (803-852), a famous poet of the Tang Dynasty

杜甫(ㄉㄨˋ ㄈㄨˇ)
Tu Fu (712-770), one of the greatest poets of China in the Tang Dynasty

杜魯門(ㄉㄨˋ ㄌㄨˇ ㄇㄣˊ)
Harry S. Truman (1884-1972), 33rd U.S. President

杜口(ㄉㄨˋ ㄎㄡˇ)
to shut one's mouth and say nothing

杜康(ㄉㄨˋ ㄎㄤ)
① Tu Kang, a man good at brewing wine in the Chou Dynasty ② another name of wine

杜諫(ㄉㄨˋ ㄐㄧㄢˋ)
to persuade or advise (a superior, the emperor, etc.) to stop (a bad practice, etc.)

杜漸防微(ㄉㄨˋ ㄐㄧㄢˋ ㄈㄤˊ ㄨㄟˊ)
to nip (a bad practice, etc.) in the bud

杜絕(ㄉㄨˋ ㄐㄩㄝˊ)
① to stop (a bad practice, etc.) for good; to eradicate ② to cut off (relations with) ③ irrevocable (contracts, title deeds, etc.)

杜絕後患(ㄉㄨˋ ㄐㄩㄝˊ ㄏㄡˋ ㄏㄨㄢˋ)
to prevent and eliminate possible harmful consequences

杜鵑(ㄉㄨˋ ㄐㄩㄢ)
a cuckoo 亦作「子規」

杜鵑花(ㄉㄨˋ ㄐㄩㄢ ㄏㄨㄚ)
azaleas

杜撰(ㄉㄨˋ ㄓㄨㄢˋ)
to fabricate (a story, etc.); to trump up; to make up: 她講的是眞有其事，不是杜撰的。What she said is true, not made up.

杜松(ㄉㄨˋ ㄙㄨㄥ)
a needle juniper (*Juniperus rigida*)

杜松子酒(ㄉㄨˋ ㄙㄨㄥ ㄗˇ ㄐㄧㄡˇ)
gin

【杞】 2350 ㄑㄧˇ chii chǐ

1. a species of willow
2. a medlar
3. Chi, name of a state in the Chou Dynasty in today's Honan Province
4. a Chinese family name

杞柳(ㄑㄧˇ ㄌㄧㄡˇ)
a kind of willow

杞人憂天(ㄑㄧˇ ㄖㄣˊ ㄧㄡ ㄊㄧㄢ)
The man of Chi worried that the sky might fall down.— A man entertains imaginary or groundless fears.

杞梓(ㄑㄧˇ ㄗˇ)
fine wood—good for carving; good timber

【束】 2351 ㄕㄨˋ shuh shù

1. to bind
2. a bunch; a bundle
3. to control; to restrain; restraint
4. a Chinese family name

束帛(ㄕㄨˋ ㄅㄛˊ)
a bundle of silk—a betrothal present from the groom's side in ancient China

束馬懸車(ㄕㄨˋ ㄇㄚˇ ㄒㄩㄢˊ ㄔㄜ)
(said of roads) very rugged

束髮(ㄕㄨˋ ㄈㄚˇ)
to reach boyhood—teens or teenage

束縛(ㄕㄨˋ ㄈㄨˊ)
restraint; restrictions; bondage; to restrain; to bind up

束縛電荷(ㄕㄨˋ ㄈㄨˊ ㄉㄧㄢˋ ㄏㄜˊ)
(electricity) a bound charge

束躬(ㄕㄨˋ ㄍㄨㄥ)
to restrain oneself; to control oneself; self-restraint

束脩(ㄕㄨˋ ㄒㄧㄡ)
(literally) ten pieces of dried meat—tuition; the charge or fee given to a private tutor for instruction or teaching

束胸(ㄕㄨˋ ㄒㄩㄥ)
(said of a woman in old China) to bind the breasts tightly with a piece of cloth (because flat-chested women were considered beautiful in those days)

束之高閣(ㄕㄨˋ ㄓ ㄍㄠ ㄍㄜˊ)
(literally) to place (something) high in the attic—to shelve it and forget about it; to lay aside and neglect; to pigeonhole

束裝(ㄕㄨˋ ㄓㄨㄤ)
to pack up

束裝就道(ㄕㄨˋ ㄓㄨㄤ ㄐㄧㄡˋ ㄉㄠˋ)
to pack up for a journey

束手(ㄕㄨˋ ㄕㄡˇ)
to have one's hands tied—no way out; powerless; at the end of the rope: 群醫束手。The doctors can do nothing to help.

束手待斃(ㄕㄨˋ ㄕㄡˇ ㄉㄞˋ ㄅㄧˋ)
(literally) to wait for one's death with hands tied—to be a sitting duck

束手就擒(ㄕㄨˋ ㄕㄡˇ ㄐㄧㄡˋ ㄑㄧㄣˊ)
to put up no fight and allow oneself to be caught

束手無策(ㄕㄨˋ ㄕㄡˇ ㄨˊ ㄘㄜˋ)
no way out; powerless; at the end of the rope

束身(ㄕㄨˋ ㄕㄣ)
self-control; to restrain oneself

束腰(ㄕㄨˋ ㄧㄠ)
① a waist band or belt ② to tighten one's waist with a band so that it appears slender; to girdle the waist

【杠】 2352 ㄍㄤ gang gāng

1. a flag pole
2. a bridge

【杆】 2353 ㄍㄢ gan gān

1. a wooden pole; the shaft of

a spear
2. rod, a unit of measurement which equals to 5.5 yards
3. a wooden fence; a balustrade; a railing

杆子(ㄍㄢ ·ㄗ)or 杆兒(ㄍㄚㄦ)
①a pole; a rod ②a gang of bandits

杆子頭(ㄍㄢ ·ㄗ ㄊㄡˊ)
the ringleader of a gang

【杙】2354 ㄧˋ yih yì
a tiny wooden post; a boundary mark or fence

四畫

【杪】2355 ㄇㄧㄠˇ meau miǎo
1. the tip of a small branch
2. the end (of a period)

杪末(ㄇㄧㄠˇ ㄇㄛˋ)
the endpoint; the tip

杪杪(ㄇㄧㄠˇ ㄇㄧㄠˇ)
very tiny

杪冬(ㄇㄧㄠˇ ㄉㄨㄥ)
the end of the winter (other seasons are spoken of in a similar manner)

杪小 or 渺小(ㄇㄧㄠˇ ㄒㄧㄠˇ)
tiny

【杭】2356 ㄏㄤˊ harng háng
1. Hangchow
2. same as 航 —to sail; to cross a stream; to navigate
3. a Chinese family name

杭州(ㄏㄤˊ ㄓㄡ)
Hangchow, capital city of Chekiang Province

杭州灣(ㄏㄤˊ ㄓㄡ ㄨㄢ)
the Gulf of Hangchow at the estuary of the Chientang River (錢塘江)

杭綢(ㄏㄤˊ ㄔㄡˊ)
silk from Hangchow (considered the best)

【杯】2357 ㄅㄟ bei bēi
a cup; a tumbler; a glass; a goblet

杯盤狼藉(ㄅㄟ ㄆㄢˊ ㄌㄤˊ ㄐㄧˊ)
(literally) Empty glasses and plates are scattered all over. —The feast is over.

杯葛(ㄅㄟ ㄍㄜˊ)
① a boycott ② to boycott: 他們企圖杯葛他。They tried to boycott him.

杯弓蛇影(ㄅㄟ ㄍㄨㄥ ㄕㄜˊ ㄧㄥˇ)
(literally) to mistake the shadow of a bow in one's cup for a snake—a false alarm; extremely suspicious

杯酒釋兵權(ㄅㄟ ㄐㄧㄡˇ ㄕˋ ㄅㄧㄥ ㄑㄩㄢˊ)
a stratagem used by Chao Kuang-yin (趙匡胤), founder of the Sung Dynasty (960—1279), who persuaded his generals to give up their troops during a grand feast

杯中物(ㄅㄟ ㄓㄨㄥ ㄨˋ)
(literally) the thing in the cup—wine; alcoholic drinks

杯水車薪(ㄅㄟ ㄕㄨㄟˇ ㄐㄩ ㄒㄧㄣ)
(literally) to use a cup of water to put out a cartload of burning firewood—too inadequate and useless; an utterly inadequate measure

杯子(ㄅㄟ ·ㄗ)
a cup; a tumbler; a glass

【杲】2358 ㄍㄠˇ gao gǎo
1. bright—as the shining sun
2. high

杲杲(ㄍㄠˇ ㄍㄠˇ)
bright and scintillating

【杳】2359 ㄧㄠˇ yeau yǎo
1. deep and expansive
2. quiet; silent

杳眇(ㄧㄠˇ ㄇㄧㄠˇ)
distant and indistinguishable

杳冥(ㄧㄠˇ ㄇㄧㄥˊ)
deep, dark and obscure

杳然(ㄧㄠˇ ㄖㄢˊ)
quiet and silent; lonely

杳如黃鶴(ㄧㄠˇ ㄖㄨˊ ㄏㄨㄤˊ ㄏㄜˋ)
to disappear like the yellow crane—nowhere to be found; to disappear without leaving a trace

杳杳無踪(ㄧㄠˇ ㄧㄠˇ ㄨˊ ㄗㄨㄥ)
gone without leaving a trace

杳無音信(ㄧㄠˇ ㄨˊ ㄧㄣ ㄒㄧㄣˋ)
without any news of someone for a long time

【東】2360 ㄉㄨㄥ dong dōng
1. the east; eastern
2. to travel eastward
3. the host; the master; the owner
4. a Chinese family name

東北(ㄉㄨㄥ ㄅㄟˇ)
① northeast ② Manchuria

東半球(ㄉㄨㄥ ㄅㄢˋ ㄑㄧㄡˊ)
the Eastern Hemisphere

東奔西走(ㄉㄨㄥ ㄅㄣ ㄒㄧ ㄗㄡˇ)
to run about busily; to work hard for something which involves lots of leg work

東邊(ㄉㄨㄥ ㄅㄧㄢ)
the east side; on the east

東跑西顛(ㄉㄨㄥ ㄆㄠˇ ㄒㄧ ㄉㄧㄢ)
to run about busily; to work hard for something which involves lots of leg work

東拼西湊(ㄉㄨㄥ ㄆㄧㄣ ㄒㄧ ㄘㄡˋ)
to scrape (money, etc.) for a purchase, project, etc.; topatch up from bits

東普魯士(ㄉㄨㄥ ㄆㄨˇ ㄌㄨˇ ㄕˋ)
East Prussia

東門(ㄉㄨㄥ ㄇㄣˊ)
the east gate (of a city wall)

東非(ㄉㄨㄥ ㄈㄟ)
Eastern Africa

東方(ㄉㄨㄥ ㄈㄤ)
① the east ② Oriental ③ a Chinese family name

東方發白(ㄉㄨㄥ ㄈㄤ ㄈㄚ ㄅㄞˊ)
(literally) The eastern sky is turning fish-belly gray. —daybreak: 他東方發白即起。He gets up at daybreak.

東方大港(ㄉㄨㄥ ㄈㄤ ㄉㄚˋ ㄍㄤˇ)
a projected harbor proposed by Dr. Sun Yat-sen, which is to be located on the eastern China coast

東方正教(ㄉㄨㄥ ㄈㄤ ㄓㄥˋ ㄐㄧㄠˋ)
the Greek Orthodox Church

東方文化(ㄉㄨㄥ ㄈㄤ ㄨㄣˊ ㄏㄨㄚˋ)
Oriental culture

東風(ㄉㄨㄥ ㄈㄥ)
an east wind

東風吹馬耳(ㄉㄨㄥ ㄈㄥ ㄔㄨㄟ ㄇㄚˇ ㄦˇ)
to turn a deaf ear to; to pay no attention to; indifferent and aloof; to go in one ear and out the other

東扶西倒(ㄉㄨㄥ ㄈㄨˊ ㄒㄧ ㄉㄠˇ)
(literally) to brace up one while the others tumble down—It's difficult to educate people or to cultivate plants.

東德(ㄉㄨㄥ ㄉㄜˊ)

〔木部〕

East Germany 參看「西德」
東倒西歪(ㄉㄨㄥ ㄉㄠˇ ㄒㄧ ㄨㄞ)
①(said of drunkards) to walk unsteadily ②(said of a scene, room, village, etc.) dilapidated
東道主(ㄉㄨㄥ ㄉㄠˋ ㄓㄨˇ)
the host at a dinner party: 他眞是個善於款待客人的東道主。He is such a good host.
東都(ㄉㄨㄥ ㄉㄨ)
(in ancient China) Loyang (洛陽), the eastern capital
東渡(ㄉㄨㄥ ㄉㄨˋ)
to take a sea-voyage eastward (especially referring to a trip to Japan)
東坦(ㄉㄨㄥ ㄊㄢˇ)
one's son-in-law
東塗西抹(ㄉㄨㄥ ㄊㄨˊ ㄒㄧ ㄇㄛˇ)
① (said of small children) to smear here and there ② (a polite term referring to oneself) to practice calligraphy; to write at random or without much thought
東土(ㄉㄨㄥ ㄊㄨˇ)
land in the east—Japan
東南(ㄉㄨㄥ ㄋㄢˊ)
southeast
東南西北(ㄉㄨㄥ ㄋㄢˊ ㄒㄧ ㄅㄟˇ)
(literally) east, south, west and north—all directions
東南亞(ㄉㄨㄥ ㄋㄢˊ ㄧㄚˇ)
Southeast Asia
東南亞公約組織(ㄉㄨㄥ ㄋㄢˊ ㄧㄚˇ ㄍㄨㄥ ㄩㄝ ㄗㄨˇ ㄓ)
Southeast Asia Treaty Organization (SEATO)
東挪西借(ㄉㄨㄥ ㄋㄨㄛˊ ㄒㄧ ㄐㄧㄝˋ)
to borrow all around; to scrape up money (for a purchase, etc.)
東拉西扯(ㄉㄨㄥ ㄌㄚ ㄒㄧ ㄔㄜˇ)
to talk aimlessly or without much thought; to ramble
東鱗西爪(ㄉㄨㄥ ㄌㄧㄣˊ ㄒㄧ ㄓㄠˇ)
odds and ends; a bit here and a bit there; fragmentary
東零西亂(ㄉㄨㄥ ㄌㄧㄥˊ ㄒㄧ ㄌㄨㄢˋ)
in complete disarray or disorder
東羅馬帝國(ㄉㄨㄥ ㄌㄨㄛˊ ㄇㄚˇ ㄉㄧˋ ㄍㄨㄛˊ)
the Eastern Roman Empire
東拐西騙(ㄉㄨㄥ ㄍㄨㄞˇ ㄒㄧ ㄆㄧㄢˋ)
to swindle on all sides
東宮(ㄉㄨㄥ ㄍㄨㄥ)
① the palace in which the crown prince lives ② the crown prince ③ a Chinese family name
東海(ㄉㄨㄥ ㄏㄞˇ)
the East China Sea
東海揚塵(ㄉㄨㄥ ㄏㄞˇ ㄧㄤˊ ㄔㄣˊ)
(literally) Dust rises from the East China Sea.—unpredictability of world affairs
東漢(ㄉㄨㄥ ㄏㄢˋ)
the Eastern Han (25-220 A.D.), also known as the Later Han which began after Emperor Kuang Wu (光武帝) moved its capital to Loyang, Honan, and ended during the reign of Emperor Hsien (獻帝)
東胡(ㄉㄨㄥ ㄏㄨˊ)
ancient name of the Tungusic tribes
東加王國(ㄉㄨㄥ ㄐㄧㄚ ㄨㄤˊ ㄍㄨㄛˊ)
the Kingdom of Tonga
東家(ㄉㄨㄥ ˙ㄐㄧㄚ)
① the owner of a house where one stays; the host ② the owner of a company or shop
東交民巷(ㄉㄨㄥ ㄐㄧㄠ ㄇㄧㄣˊ ㄒㄧㄤˋ)
(formerly) the Legation Quarter in Peking
東漸(ㄉㄨㄥ ㄐㄧㄢ)
(usually said of Western civilization, etc.) to gradually spread to the east
東晉(ㄉㄨㄥ ㄐㄧㄣˋ)
the Eastern Tsin Dynasty (317-420)
東進(ㄉㄨㄥ ㄐㄧㄣˋ)
to advance eastward: 大軍東進。The great army advanced eastward.
東江(ㄉㄨㄥ ㄐㄧㄤ)
the East River, a tributary of the Pearl River (珠江)
東經(ㄉㄨㄥ ㄐㄧㄥ)
longitude east of Greenwich
東京(ㄉㄨㄥ ㄐㄧㄥ)
① Tokyo ② (in the Han Dynasty) Loyang ③ (in the Sung Dynasty) Kaifeng
東京灣(ㄉㄨㄥ ㄐㄧㄥ ㄨㄢ)
the Gulf of Tongking
東君(ㄉㄨㄥ ㄐㄩㄣ)
① the god of spring ② the sun god
東西
①(ㄉㄨㄥ ㄒㄧ) ⓐ east and west ⓑ from east to west
②(ㄉㄨㄥ ˙ㄒㄧ) ⓐ things; objects; matters: 她愛吃甜的東西。She is too fond of sweet things. ⓑ a contemptible fellow: 他眞不是東西! What a despicable creature he is!
東周(ㄉㄨㄥ ㄓㄡ)
the Eastern Chou Dynasty (770-256 B.C.)
東張西望(ㄉㄨㄥ ㄓㄤ ㄒㄧ ㄨㄤˋ)
to look around; to gaze around; to look about furtively: 不要東張西望的。Stop gazing around.
東廠(ㄉㄨㄥ ㄔㄤˇ)
a secret police setup run by eunuchs during the Ming Dynasty
東窗事發(ㄉㄨㄥ ㄔㄨㄤ ㄕˋ ㄈㄚ)
(said of a conspiracy, secret plot, clandestine plan, etc.) to be exposed or bared; to come to light 或 The game is up.
東牀坦腹(ㄉㄨㄥ ㄔㄨㄤˊ ㄊㄢˇ ㄈㄨˋ)
an ideal son-in-law
東床快婿(ㄉㄨㄥ ㄔㄨㄤˊ ㄎㄨㄞˋ ㄒㄩˋ)
a son-in-law
東施效顰 or 東施效矉(ㄉㄨㄥ ㄕ ㄒㄧㄠˋ ㄆㄧㄣˊ)
an ugly woman Tung Shih (東施) tried awkwardly to imitate the famous beauty Hsi Shih (西施) knitting her brows, and thus made herself even more awkward and nauseating—to imitate awkwardly
東食西宿(ㄉㄨㄥ ㄕˊ ㄒㄧ ㄙㄨˋ)
to go wherever profit is—very greedy
東沙羣島(ㄉㄨㄥ ㄕㄚ ㄑㄩㄣˊ ㄉㄠˇ)
the Pratas Islands (Tungsha Chuntao)
東山再起(ㄉㄨㄥ ㄕㄢ ㄗㄞˋ ㄑㄧˇ)
(said of a retired person, etc.) to take up official duties again; to return to officialdom; to be reinstated; to stage a comeback: 他準備東山再起。He was prepared to stage a comeback.

〔木部〕

〔木部〕

東人(ㄉㄨㄥ ㄖㄣˊ)
an employer; a master
東三省(ㄉㄨㄥ ㄙㄢ ㄕㄥˇ)
the Three Northeastern Provinces, in Manchuria —Heilungkiang (黑龍江), Kirin (吉林) and Liaoning (遼寧), the three provinces were redivided into nine provinces after World War II
東歐(ㄉㄨㄥ ㄡ)
Eastern Europe
東一句，西一句(ㄉㄨㄥ ㄧˊ ㄐㄩˋ, ㄒㄧ ㄧˊ ㄐㄩˋ)
① to converse completely without sequence or order; to talk incoherently ② utterances from all sides which amount to nothing; everybody talking at once
東亞(ㄉㄨㄥ ㄧㄚˋ)
East Asia
東印度公司(ㄉㄨㄥ ㄧㄣˋ ㄉㄨˋ ㄍㄨㄥ ㄙ)
East India Company
東印度羣島(ㄉㄨㄥ ㄧㄣˋ ㄉㄨˋ ㄑㄩㄣˊ ㄉㄠˇ)
the East Indies
東洋(ㄉㄨㄥ ㄧㄤˊ)
Japan
東洋車(ㄉㄨㄥ ㄧㄤˊ ㄔㄜ)
a rickshaw
東洋參(ㄉㄨㄥ ㄧㄤˊ ㄕㄣ)
a variety of ginseng grown in Japan
東洋水仙(ㄉㄨㄥ ㄧㄤˊ ㄕㄨㄟˇ ㄒㄧㄢ)
daffodils; narcissuses
東瀛(ㄉㄨㄥ ㄧㄥˊ)
Japan
東魏(ㄉㄨㄥ ㄨㄟˋ)
the Eastern Wei (534-550)
東嶽(ㄉㄨㄥ ㄩㄝˋ)
another name of Mountain Tai (泰山) in Shantung Province, one of the Five Sacred Mountains in China

【杵】 2361 ㄔㄨˇ chuu chǔ

1. a pestle; a baton used to pound the laundry: 鐵杵磨成針。An iron pestle can be ground into a needle.
2. to poke: 我用手指頭杵了他一下。I gave him a poke with a finger.

杵歌(ㄔㄨˇ ㄍㄜ)
a tune sung by the Taiwan aborigines while they are pounding grains in a mortar with a pestle
杵臼關節(ㄔㄨˇ ㄐㄧㄡˋ ㄍㄨㄢ ㄐㄧㄝˊ)
(physiology) ball-and-socket joints; enarthroses
杵臼之交(ㄔㄨˇ ㄐㄧㄡˋ ㄓ ㄐㄧㄠ)
true friendship which disregards discrepancy in wealth, influence, fame, etc.

【枇】 2362 ㄆㄧˊ pyi pí

loquats
枇杷門巷(ㄆㄧˊ ㄆㄚˊ ㄇㄣˊ ㄒㄧㄤˋ)
brothels; red-light districts
枇杷(ㄆㄧˊ ·ㄆㄚ)
loquats
枇杷露(ㄆㄧˊ ·ㄆㄚ ㄌㄨˋ)
diluted loquat extract (used as a medicine)
枇杷膏(ㄆㄧˊ ·ㄆㄚ ㄍㄠ)
condensed loquat extract (used as a medicine)

【杷】 2363 ·ㄆㄚ ·pa pa

loquats

【杼】 2364 ㄓㄨˋ juh zhù

the shuttle of a loom
杼柚(ㄓㄨˋ ㄓㄡˊ)
looms

【板】 2365 ㄅㄢˇ baan bǎn

1. a board; a plank
2. a plate (of tin, aluminum, etc.); a slab
3. printing blocks
4. rigid; stern; straight; stiff

板板六十四(ㄅㄢˇ ㄅㄢˇ ㄌㄧㄡˋ ㄕˊ ㄙˋ)
rigid; inflexible; to stick to rules strictly
板本(ㄅㄢˇ ㄅㄣˇ)
books printed from wooden blocks
板本學(ㄅㄢˇ ㄅㄣˇ ㄒㄩㄝˊ)
textual study; a course of study to determine which books were printed in which age, dynasty, etc.
板壁(ㄅㄢˇ ㄅㄧˋ)
boards partitioning a house, room, etc.; wooden walls
板門店(ㄅㄢˇ ㄇㄣˊ ㄉㄧㄢˋ)
Panmunjom in Korea
板斧(ㄅㄢˇ ㄈㄨˇ)
a hatchet
板蕩(ㄅㄢˇ ㄉㄤˋ)
a world of disorder; a time of turmoil or upheavals; social confusion and chaos
板蕩識忠臣(ㄅㄢˇ ㄉㄤˋ ㄕˋ ㄓㄨㄥ ㄔㄣˊ)
The true and faithful can be easily spotted in time of trouble.
板凳(ㄅㄢˇ ㄉㄥˋ)
a wooden stool
板鈦礦(ㄅㄢˇ ㄊㄞˋ ㄎㄨㄤˋ)
brookite
板栗(ㄅㄢˇ ㄌㄧˋ)
chestnuts
板畫(ㄅㄢˇ ㄏㄨㄚˋ)
a woodcut
板起面孔(ㄅㄢˇ ·ㄑㄧ ㄇㄧㄢˋ ㄎㄨㄥˇ)
to make a long face
板橋(ㄅㄢˇ ㄑㄧㄠˊ)
① a bridge built of wooden planks ② a city in Taipei Hsien, Taiwan
板球(ㄅㄢˇ ㄑㄧㄡˊ)
(sports) cricket: 板球流行於英國。Cricket is popular in England.
板滯(ㄅㄢˇ ㄓˋ)
stiff and rigid; pedantic
板著臉(ㄅㄢˇ ·ㄓㄜ ㄌㄧㄢˇ)
to pull a long face; to keep a straight face
板車(ㄅㄢˇ ㄔㄜ)
a kind of hand-pulled cart for transporting heavy objects
板上釘釘(ㄅㄢˇ ㄕㄤˋ ㄉㄧㄥˋ ㄉㄧㄥ)
immovable; determined; decided
板書(ㄅㄢˇ ㄕㄨ)
writing on the blackboard
板子(ㄅㄢˇ ·ㄗ)
① a flat bamboo, etc. for beating criminals in old China; a rod for disciplining children; a flogging board ② a printing block
板擦兒(ㄅㄢˇ ㄘㄚㄦ)
a wiper or an eraser (for a blackboard, etc.); a brush for applying whitewash
板鴨(ㄅㄢˇ ㄧㄚ)
a salted duck pressed and stretched like a plate (a specialty in Nanking)
板眼(ㄅㄢˇ ㄧㄢˇ)
① the rest and beat of music ② to be methodical in one's work; the orderly way of performing a task

【松】2366
ㄙㄨㄥ song sōng
1. pines; firs
2. a Chinese family name
松柏(ㄙㄨㄥ ㄅㄛˊ)
①the pine and the cypress
②the conifers
松柏後凋(ㄙㄨㄥ ㄅㄛˊ ㄏㄡˋ ㄉㄧㄠ)
(literally) The leaves of pines and cypresses are always the last to fall. —Honesty and virtue will last.
松柏節操(ㄙㄨㄥ ㄅㄛˊ ㄐㄧㄝˊ ㄘㄠ)
honest and virtuous conduct; fortitude; lofty character: 他是具有松柏節操的人。He is a man of lofty character.
松柏長青(ㄙㄨㄥ ㄅㄛˊ ㄔㄤˊ ㄑㄧㄥ)or 松柏長春(ㄙㄨㄥ ㄅㄛˊ ㄔㄤˊ ㄔㄨㄣ)
(a congratulatory expression on someone's birthday) May you live long and remain strong like the evergreen pine and cypress!
松木(ㄙㄨㄥ ㄇㄨˋ)
pine-wood boards or planks, etc. (for building purposes)
松風水月(ㄙㄨㄥ ㄈㄥ ㄕㄨㄟˇ ㄩㄝˋ)
(literally) the soughing of pines and the reflection of the moon on the water—the soothing surroundings of nature
松濤(ㄙㄨㄥ ㄊㄠˊ)
the soughing of the wind in the pines which sounds like roaring waves
松林(ㄙㄨㄥ ㄌㄧㄣˊ)
a pinery
松果(ㄙㄨㄥ ㄍㄨㄛˇ)
a strobile
松鶴遐齡(ㄙㄨㄥ ㄏㄜˋ ㄒㄧㄚˊ ㄌㄧㄥˊ)
longevity
松花(ㄙㄨㄥ ㄏㄨㄚ)
a preserved egg
松花江(ㄙㄨㄥ ㄏㄨㄚ ㄐㄧㄤ)
the Sungari River
松花兒(ㄙㄨㄥ ㄏㄨㄚㄦ)
the fruit of a species of cypress
松節油(ㄙㄨㄥ ㄐㄧㄝˊ ㄧㄡˊ)
turpentine: 松節油是用來稀釋油漆的。Turpentine was used to mix with paints.
松江(ㄙㄨㄥ ㄐㄧㄤ)
Sungkiang, a province in Manchuria
松楸(ㄙㄨㄥ ㄑㄧㄡ)
(originally) trees planted at a tomb or grave—(figuratively) a tomb or grave
松毬(ㄙㄨㄥ ㄑㄧㄡˊ)
a pine cone
松香(ㄙㄨㄥ ㄒㄧㄤ)or 松膠(ㄙㄨㄥ ㄐㄧㄠ)or 松脂(ㄙㄨㄥ ㄓ)
rosin; colophony
松香油(ㄙㄨㄥ ㄒㄧㄤ ㄧㄡˊ)or 松脂油(ㄙㄨㄥ ㄓ ㄧㄡˊ)
retinol; rosin oil
松蕈(ㄙㄨㄥ ㄒㄩㄣˋ)or 松菌(ㄙㄨㄥ ㄐㄩㄣˋ)or 松茸(ㄙㄨㄥ ㄖㄨㄥˊ)
pine mushrooms
松針(ㄙㄨㄥ ㄓㄣ)
pine needles
松竹梅(ㄙㄨㄥ ㄓㄨˊ ㄇㄟˊ)
the pine, the bamboo and the flowering plum—the three companions in the cold of the year
松鼠(ㄙㄨㄥ ㄕㄨˇ)
the squirrel: 這座公園以松鼠多而著名。This park is well-known for its squirrels.
松樹(ㄙㄨㄥ ㄕㄨˋ)
a pine
松仁(ㄙㄨㄥ ㄖㄣˊ)or 松仁兒(ㄙㄨㄥ ㄖㄜˊㄦ)
the kernels in the pine cone
松子(ㄙㄨㄥ ㄗˇ)
pine nuts; pine seeds

【枏】2367
(楠) ㄋㄢˊ nan nán
Machilus nanmu, a variety of evergreen tree, commonly known as cedar, with elliptical leaves, light green blossoms and dark, purplish fruit, even-grained, yellowish, fine wood, used for furniture or coffins which can last for hundreds of years
枏木 or 楠木(ㄋㄢˊ ㄇㄨˋ)
nanmu (*Phoebe nanmu*)

【枉】2368
ㄨㄤˇ woang wǎng
1. to waste; useless; in vain
2. crooked
3. to wrong; to do or suffer wrong; aggrieved; oppression
4. (in polite language) to request another to deign or condescend to
枉法(ㄨㄤˇ ㄈㄚˇ)
to abuse law; to twist law to suit one's own purpose; to pervert the law: 一位重要的官員貪贓枉法。An important official took bribes and perverted the law.
枉費(ㄨㄤˇ ㄈㄟˋ)
to waste; to try in vain; to be of no avail: 你是在枉費唇舌。You are wasting your breath.
枉費工夫(ㄨㄤˇ ㄈㄟˋ ㄍㄨㄥ ·ㄈㄨ)
to waste time and energy; to spend time and work in vain
枉費心機(ㄨㄤˇ ㄈㄟˋ ㄒㄧㄣ ㄐㄧ)
to scheme, plan or cudgel one's brains to no purpose or in vain; to get nowhere despite the trouble taken: 他枉費心機。He racked his brains in vain.
枉道事人(ㄨㄤˇ ㄉㄠˋ ㄕˋ ㄖㄣˊ)
to distort the truth in order to please others
枉斷(ㄨㄤˇ ㄉㄨㄢˋ)
to abuse law by distorting it; to decide unfairly
枉顧(ㄨㄤˇ ㄍㄨˋ)
You have deigned to call on me.
枉己正人(ㄨㄤˇ ㄐㄧˇ ㄓㄥˋ ㄖㄣˊ)
a crook trying to tell others how to be a gentleman; a dishonest person telling others to behave
枉駕(ㄨㄤˇ ㄐㄧㄚˋ)
I'm honored by your visit.
枉曲(ㄨㄤˇ ㄑㄩ)
bent; crooked; warped
枉尺直尋(ㄨㄤˇ ㄔˇ ㄓˊ ㄒㄩㄣˊ)
to compromise on minor points so as to gain on the major issue; to bend in small places and straight in total
枉然(ㄨㄤˇ ㄖㄢˊ)
useless; to no purpose; in vain; futile: 我的一切工作均歸枉然。All my work was in vain.
枉攘(ㄨㄤˇ ㄖㄤˇ)
tumultuous; disorderly
枉死(ㄨㄤˇ ㄙˇ)
to die through injustice; death as a result of injustice; to be wronged and

[木部]

driven to death

枉死鬼(ㄨㄤˇ ㄙˇ ㄍㄨㄟˇ)
the spirit of one who died through injustice

【枌】 2369
ㄈㄣˊ fern fén
a variety of elm with small seeds and white bark

枌榆(ㄈㄣˊ ㄩˊ)
①a kind of elm ②(originally) the native place of the founding emperor of the Han Dynasty—one's native place or hometown

【枋】 2370
ㄈㄤ fang fāng
sandalwood

【析】 2371
ㄒㄧ shi xī
1. to split; to rip or break apart; to divide; to separate
2. to interpret; to explain; to analyze
3. a Chinese family name

析骨(ㄒㄧ ㄍㄨˇ)or 析骸(ㄒㄧ ㄏㄞˊ)
to break apart a skeleton

析居(ㄒㄧ ㄐㄩ)
(said of brothers) to live under different roofs — to divide family property

析產(ㄒㄧ ㄔㄢˇ)
to divide family property; to split the inheritance (among children of the deceased)

析出(ㄒㄧ ㄔㄨ)
(chemistry) to separate out

析爨(ㄒㄧ ㄘㄨㄢˋ)or 析煙(ㄒㄧ ㄧㄢ)
(said of brothers) to divide family property and live under different roofs

析疑(ㄒㄧ ㄧˊ)
to explain a doubt; to clarify a doubt

析義(ㄒㄧ ㄧˋ)
interpretation and elaboration of the meaning of something

【枒】 2372
ㄧㄚˊ ya yá
1. the felloe of a wheel
2. disorderly growth of twigs

枒杈(ㄧㄚˊ ㄔㄚˋ)
crotches; disorderly growth of twigs

【枕】 2373
1. ㄓㄣˇ jeen zhěn
a pillow

枕伴(ㄓㄣˇ ㄅㄢˋ)
a pillow-companion—a bed fellow

枕邊人(ㄓㄣˇ ㄅㄧㄢ ㄖㄣˊ)
wife (who shares the same pillow with her husband)

枕邊言(ㄓㄣˇ ㄅㄧㄢ ㄧㄢˊ)
pillow talk—private talks between husband and wife

枕畔(ㄓㄣˇ ㄆㄢˋ)
beside the pillow

枕木(ㄓㄣˇ ㄇㄨˋ)
railroad ties; railway sleepers: 枕木支墊兩條火車軌道。Sleepers support two railway tracks.

枕簟(ㄓㄣˇ ㄉㄧㄢˋ)
the pillow and mat—bedding

枕套(ㄓㄣˇ ㄊㄠˋ)
a pillowcase; a pillowslip

枕頭(ㄓㄣˇ ·ㄊㄡ)
a pillow: 枕頭是睡覺時用來墊頭的。A pillow is used to support one's head in bed.

枕冷衾寒(ㄓㄣˇ ㄌㄥˇ ㄑㄧㄣ ㄏㄢˊ)
the pillow is cold and the bed, chilly—after the departure or death of one's spouse

枕骨(ㄓㄣˇ ㄍㄨˇ)
the occiput; the occipital bone

枕巾(ㄓㄣˇ ㄐㄧㄣ)
a towel used to cover a pillow; a pillow cover

枕席(ㄓㄣˇ ㄒㄧˊ)
①the pillow and the mat—bedding ②a mat used to cover a pillow; a pillow mat

枕席難安(ㄓㄣˇ ㄒㄧˊ ㄋㄢˊ ㄢ)
cannot sleep—very worried and anxious

枕席之間(ㄓㄣˇ ㄒㄧˊ ㄓ ㄐㄧㄢ)
while in bed

枕中書(ㄓㄣˇ ㄓㄨㄥ ㄕㄨ)
①a Taoist account of immortals authored by Ko Hung (葛洪) of the Tsin Dynasty ②secret alchemistic formulas (hidden in one's pillow to prevent leakage)

【枕】 2373
2. ㄓㄣˋ jenn zhèn
to use something as a pillow; to pillow

枕戈待旦(ㄓㄣˋ ㄍㄜ ㄉㄞˋ ㄉㄢˋ)
(literally) to use the spear as a pillow and wait for the morning—to be on the alert; ever-prepared for emergency; to maintain combat readiness

枕塊(ㄓㄣˋ ㄎㄨㄞˋ)
(literally) to pillow on a clod of earth—mourning for one's parents

枕藉(ㄓㄣˋ ㄐㄧㄝˋ)
to lie in complete disarray or to lie about on each other

枕經籍史(ㄓㄣˋ ㄐㄧㄥ ㄐㄧˊ ㄕˇ)or 枕經籍書(ㄓㄣˋ ㄐㄧㄥ ㄐㄧˊ ㄕㄨ)
to be excessively fond of ancient books

枕石漱流(ㄓㄣˋ ㄕˊ ㄕㄨˋ ㄌㄧㄡˊ)
to pillow one's head on rocks and rinse one's mouth in streams—to retire from the world

【枘】 2374
ㄖㄨㄟˋ ruey ruì
a wooden handle

枘鑿(ㄖㄨㄟˋ ㄗㄨㄛˋ)
(literally) a square handle and a round socket—not fitting; incompatible; cannot see eye to eye

【林】 2375
ㄌㄧㄣˊ lin lín
1. a forest; a grove; a copse
2. a collection of books, works, literary extracts, etc.
3. circles; many; numerous; a great body of (capable persons, etc.): 他聞名於藝林。He was famous in the art circles.
4. a Chinese family name

林薄(ㄌㄧㄣˊ ㄅㄛˊ)
a dense growth of trees and undergrowth; a jungle

林班(ㄌㄧㄣˊ ㄅㄢ)
(forestry) forest divisions; forest lots; forest compartments

林表(ㄌㄧㄣˊ ㄅㄧㄠˇ)
the edge of a forest

林逋(ㄌㄧㄣˊ ㄅㄨ)
Lin Pu, 967-1028, a hermit poet of the Sung Dynasty 參看「梅妻鶴子」

林莽(ㄌㄧㄣˊ ㄇㄤˇ)
trees and undergrowth; the jungle

林杪(ㄌㄧㄣˊ ㄇㄧㄠˇ)
the edge of a forest

林木(ㄌㄧㄣˊ ㄇㄨˋ)

a forest; woods
林帶(ㄌㄧㄣˊ ㄉㄞˋ)
a forest belt
林立(ㄌㄧㄣˊ ㄌㄧˋ)
(literally) to stand up like a forest—a great many; a forest of (stacks, derricks, etc.): 基隆港內檣桅林立。There is a forest of masts in the Keelung harbor.
林林總總(ㄌㄧㄣˊ ㄌㄧㄣˊ ㄗㄨㄥˇ ㄗㄨㄥˇ)
numerous; multitudinous; in great abundance
林肯(ㄌㄧㄣˊ ㄎㄣˇ)
Abraham Lincoln (1809-1865), the 16th U.S. President
林壑(ㄌㄧㄣˊ ㄏㄨㄛˋ)
the tranquility of trees and valleys
林間學校(ㄌㄧㄣˊ ㄐㄧㄢ ㄒㄩㄝˊ ㄒㄧㄠˋ)
an open-air school, often located in a forest, copse, etc.
林區(ㄌㄧㄣˊ ㄑㄩ)
a forest zone; a forest region; a forest
林泉(ㄌㄧㄣˊ ㄑㄩㄢˊ)
(literally) the forest and the spring—a secluded place; an ideal spot for retirement
林泉之士(ㄌㄧㄣˊ ㄑㄩㄢˊ ㄓ ㄕˋ)
a recluse
林下(ㄌㄧㄣˊ ㄒㄧㄚˋ)
(literary) retirement
林相改良(ㄌㄧㄣˊ ㄒㄧㄤˋ ㄍㄞˇ ㄌㄧㄤˊ)
forest conversion
林產(ㄌㄧㄣˊ ㄔㄢˇ)
products of the forest; timber
林場(ㄌㄧㄣˊ ㄔㄤˇ)or(ㄌㄧㄣˊ ㄔㄤˊ)
① wooded land; a forest ② a logging station
林紓(ㄌㄧㄣˊ ㄕㄨ)or 林琴南(ㄌㄧㄣˊ ㄑㄧㄣˊ ㄋㄢˊ)
Lin Shu, 1852-1924, a writer of classic prose and translator of Western fictions
林子(ㄌㄧㄣˊ ·ㄗ)
a grove; a clump of trees; a forest
林則徐(ㄌㄧㄣˊ ㄗㄜˊ ㄒㄩˊ)
Lin Tse-hsü, 1785-1850, whose ban on British opium import into China led to the Opium War
林藪(ㄌㄧㄣˊ ㄙㄡˇ)
a grove; rich growth of trees; woods and jungle: 我們在林藪間散步很開心。We had a pleasant walk in the rich growth of trees.
林森(ㄌㄧㄣˊ ㄙㄣ)
Lin Sen, 1868-1943, chairman of the National Government of China during 1932-1943
林業(ㄌㄧㄣˊ ㄧㄝˋ)
the forestry industry
林蔭(ㄌㄧㄣˊ ㄧㄣˋ)
the shade under trees
林蔭大道(ㄌㄧㄣˊ ㄧㄣˋ ㄉㄚˋ ㄉㄠˋ)
an avenue; a boulevard: 我們行駛在環繞市區的林蔭大道上。We motored around the city on the boulevard.
林園(ㄌㄧㄣˊ ㄩㄢˊ)
wooded land; a park of trees and vegetation

【枝】 2376

1. ㄓ jy zhi
1. the branches of a tree; a branch
2. limbs
3. to branch off

枝蔓(ㄓ ㄇㄢˋ)
branches and knots—complications; complexities; confused
枝頭(ㄓ ㄊㄡˊ)
on the branch
枝條(ㄓ ㄊㄧㄠˊ)
a twig
枝幹(ㄓ ㄍㄢˋ)
the trunk and the branches: 樹根支撐着枝幹。The root supports the trunk and the branches.
枝根(ㄓ ㄍㄣ)
ramose roots
枝節(ㄓ ㄐㄧㄝˊ)
①branches and knots—minor matters: 這是枝節問題。This is a minor problem. ②complications; obstacles; unexpected difficulties: 不要橫生枝節。Don't raise unexpected difficulties.
枝解 or 支解(ㄓ ㄐㄧㄝˇ)
(an ancient punishment or torture) amputation of a criminal's limbs
枝棲(ㄓ ㄑㄧ)
a roof over one's head; a place to live or make a living
枝枝節節(ㄓ ㄓ ㄐㄧㄝˊ ㄐㄧㄝˊ)
complications; complexities; diversities; minor issues: 不要太注意那些枝枝節節的問題。Don't pay too much attention to those minor issues.
枝梢(ㄓ ㄕㄠ)
the tapering part of a branch; the tip of a branch
枝子(ㄓ ·ㄗ)or 枝兒(ㄓㄜㄦ)
a branch; a bough
枝辭(ㄓ ㄘˊ)or 枝辭蔓語(ㄓ ㄘˊ ㄇㄢˋ ㄩˇ)
incoherent speeches; unintelligible expressions
枝粗葉茂(ㄓ ㄘㄨ ㄧㄝˋ ㄇㄠˋ)
(literally) The branches are thick and the leaves are many.—sturdy and vigorous; virile and prolific
枝椏(ㄓ ㄧㄚ)
branches; twigs 亦作「枝丫」
枝葉(ㄓ ㄧㄝˋ)
① children; offspring ② complications and diversities ③ branches and leaves
枝葉扶疏(ㄓ ㄧㄝˋ ㄈㄨˊ ㄕㄨ)
(said of trees) luxuriant

【枝】 2376

2. ㄑㄧˊ chyi qí
參看「枝指」
枝指(ㄑㄧˊ ㄓˇ)
an additional finger; a forked finger

【果】 2377

ㄍㄨㄛˇ guoo guǒ
1. the fruit of a plant: 他不大吃水果。He does not eat much fruit.
2. effect (in cause and effect); result; fruit; a consequence
3. surely; really; truly; exactly
4. to stuff; to fill
5. to succeed
6. a Chinese family name

果報(ㄍㄨㄛˇ ㄅㄠˋ)
(Buddhism) One reaps what he planted in his previous life. — the retribution for good or evil deeds
果不出所料(ㄍㄨㄛˇ ·ㄅㄨ ㄔㄨ ㄙㄨㄛˇ ㄌㄧㄠˋ)
as expected; as anticipated

〔木部〕

〔木部〕

果盤(ㄍㄨㄛˇ ㄆㄢˊ)
a fruit tray
果皮(ㄍㄨㄛˇ ㄆㄧˊ)
peel; the skin of a fruit; the pericarp or outer covering of the seed; peelings
果皮箱(ㄍㄨㄛˇ ㄆㄧˊ ㄒㄧㄤ)
a garbage can or box for peelings, candy wrappings, etc.
果品(ㄍㄨㄛˇ ㄆㄧㄣˇ)
fruits
果木(ㄍㄨㄛˇ ㄇㄨˋ)
a tree that bears edible fruit; fruit trees 亦作「果樹」
果脯(ㄍㄨㄛˇ ㄈㄨˇ)
dried or preserved fruit
果腹(ㄍㄨㄛˇ ㄈㄨˋ)
to fill one's stomach (usually with poor food); to feed on
果碟兒(ㄍㄨㄛˇ ㄉㄧㄝˊㄦ)or 果碟子(ㄍㄨㄛˇ ㄉㄧㄝˊ ·ㄗ)
a small plate to hold fruit in a feast
果斷(ㄍㄨㄛˇ ㄉㄨㄢˋ)
decision with courage; (said of a person) of determination; resolute: 她辦事果斷。She handled affairs in a decisive manner.
果糖(ㄍㄨㄛˇ ㄊㄤˊ)
fructose, or fruit sugar; levulose
果嶺(ㄍㄨㄛˇ ㄌㄧㄥˇ)
(golf) green
果乾(ㄍㄨㄛˇ ㄍㄢ)
dehydrated fruit
果敢(ㄍㄨㄛˇ ㄍㄢˇ)
having the determination and courage to do something
果梗(ㄍㄨㄛˇ ㄍㄥˇ)
a fruit stem
果盒(ㄍㄨㄛˇ ㄏㄜˊ)
a deep tray of various shapes with matching cover for fruit and candies to be presented to guests
果核(ㄍㄨㄛˇ ㄏㄜˊ)
a kernel; a fruit stone; a pit
果決(ㄍㄨㄛˇ ㄐㄩㄝˊ)
daring and determined: 你必須果決實行你的計劃。You must carry out your plan with determination.
果心(ㄍㄨㄛˇ ㄒㄧㄣ)
the core (of an apple, etc.)
果汁(ㄍㄨㄛˇ ㄓ)
fruit juice: 他早餐喝一杯果汁。He drank a glass of fruit juice at breakfast.
果汁機(ㄍㄨㄛˇ ㄓ ㄐㄧ)
① a juicer 亦作「搾汁機」② a blender 亦作「攪和器」
果渣(ㄍㄨㄛˇ ㄓㄚ)
marc
果眞(ㄍㄨㄛˇ ㄓㄣ)
really; if really
果實(ㄍㄨㄛˇ ㄕˊ)
fruit: 這蘋果樹果實累累。The apple tree has fruit growing in close clusters.
果肉(ㄍㄨㄛˇ ㄖㄡˋ)
pulp
果然(ㄍㄨㄛˇ ㄖㄢˊ)
① exactly as one expected ② a kind of long-tailed monkey ③ having eaten enough
果然如此(ㄍㄨㄛˇ ㄖㄢˊ ㄖㄨˊ ㄘˇ)
① It happened exactly as expected. ② if really: 果然如此，你就可放心了。If this is really true, it'll take a load off your mind.
果仁(ㄍㄨㄛˇ ㄖㄣˊ)
the meat of a nut or in a fruit stone; a kernel
果如所料(ㄍㄨㄛˇ ㄖㄨˊ ㄙㄨㄛˇ ㄌㄧㄠˋ)
It happened exactly as predicted. 或 Just as one expects.
果若(ㄍㄨㄛˇ ㄖㄨㄛˋ)
if really
果子(ㄍㄨㄛˇ ·ㄗ)
fruit: 蘋果、橙子和香蕉是果子。Apples, oranges, and bananas are fruit.
果子狸(ㄍㄨㄛˇ ·ㄗ ㄌㄧˊ)
a masked (or gem-faced) civet
果子露(ㄍㄨㄛˇ ·ㄗ ㄌㄨˋ)
concentrated fruit syrup
果子乾兒(ㄍㄨㄛˇ ·ㄗ ㄍㄚㄦ)
sweetened and dried fruit boiled until thickened, to be served cool
果子醬(ㄍㄨㄛˇ ·ㄗ ㄐㄧㄤˋ)
fruit jam
果子鹽(ㄍㄨㄛˇ ·ㄗ ㄧㄢˊ)
fruit salt
果酸(ㄍㄨㄛˇ ㄙㄨㄢ)
(chemistry) tartaric acid
果阿(ㄍㄨㄛˇ ㄚˋ)
Goa, a territory of Portugal on the SW coast of India before 1962
果兒(ㄍㄨㄛˇㄦ)
① fruit of small size ② eggs
果爾(ㄍㄨㄛˇ ㄦˇ)
① if really so ② as expected or predicted
果毅(ㄍㄨㄛˇ ㄧˋ)
determination and fortitude
果蠅(ㄍㄨㄛˇ ㄧㄥˊ)
a fruit fly
果園兒(ㄍㄨㄛˇ ㄩㄚˊㄦ)or 果園子(ㄍㄨㄛˇ ㄩㄢˊ ·ㄗ)
an orchard: 這些蘋果是由附近的果園兒生產的。These apples come from an orchard near here.

【枚】 2378 ㄇㄟˊ mei méi

1. the stalk; the trunk as opposed to branches
2. a numerary auxiliary (used in connection with coins, fruits, stamps, bombs, etc.): 她買了五枚梅子。She bought five plums.
3. a gag for troops marching at night when silence means a lot
4. a Chinese family name

枚舉(ㄇㄟˊ ㄐㄩˇ)
to enumerate; to recount one by one

【杰】 2379 (傑) ㄐㄧㄝˊ jye jié

a hero; an outstanding person

五畫

【枯】 2380 ㄎㄨ ku kū

1. withered; dry: 他的想像力好像已經枯竭了。His imagination seems to have dried up.
2. dried wood
3. ill health; emaciated

枯木發榮(ㄎㄨ ㄇㄨˋ ㄈㄚ ㄖㄨㄥˊ)
(literally) A withered old tree suddenly puts forth new sprouts.—good fortune that comes late in one's life or after a long spell of bad luck
枯木逢春(ㄎㄨ ㄇㄨˋ ㄈㄥˊ ㄔㄨㄣ)

Spring comes to the withered tree.—to get a new lease of life; good fortune that comes after a long spell of bad luck

枯槁(ㄎㄨ ㄍㄠˇ)
①(said of a person's appearance) pale, dry and emaciated; haggard: 他的形容枯槁。He looks haggard. ②withered and dry

枯乾(ㄎㄨ ㄍㄢ)
dry (branches, or fruit)

枯骨(ㄎㄨ ㄍㄨˇ)
dry bones—bones or skeleton of a person dead for a long time

枯涸(ㄎㄨ ㄏㄜˊ)
(usually said of wells, rivers, etc.) dry or waterless: 水源枯涸了。The fountainhead has dried up.

枯候(ㄎㄨ ㄏㄡˋ)
to wait interminably

枯黃(ㄎㄨ ㄏㄨㄤˊ)
withered and yellow: 蘋果樹葉逐漸枯黃了。The leaves of apple trees are beginning to turn yellow.

枯寂(ㄎㄨ ㄐㄧˊ)
lonesome; lonely

枯瘠(ㄎㄨ ㄐㄧˊ)
withered, dry and lean

枯竭(ㄎㄨ ㄐㄧㄝˊ)
(said of source of supply) exhausted; dried up: 我們的財源枯竭了。Our financial resources were exhausted.

枯井(ㄎㄨ ㄐㄧㄥˇ)
a dried-up well; a dry well

枯窘(ㄎㄨ ㄐㄩㄥˇ)
dry and embarrassed—poverty-stricken

枯朽(ㄎㄨ ㄒㄧㄡˇ)
dry and decayed; rotten: 一棵蘋果樹枯朽了。An apple tree was dry and decayed.

枯禪(ㄎㄨ ㄔㄢˊ)
(Buddhism) to sit in meditation

枯腸(ㄎㄨ ㄔㄤˊ)
(literally) an impoverished mind

枯瘦(ㄎㄨ ㄕㄡˋ)
withered and thin

枯樹生花(ㄎㄨ ㄕㄨˋ ㄕㄥ ㄏㄨㄚ)
(literally) A withered tree suddenly blossoms.—to hit the jackpot after a long spell of bad luck

枯榮(ㄎㄨ ㄖㄨㄥˊ)
ups and downs (of one's life); rise and fall (of a nation)

枯燥(ㄎㄨ ㄗㄠˋ)
① dry ② uninteresting; dull

枯燥無味(ㄎㄨ ㄗㄠˋ ㄨˊ ㄨㄟˋ)
dry and tasteless—uninteresting; monotonous

枯坐(ㄎㄨ ㄗㄨㄛˋ)
to sit there all by oneself doing nothing

枯死(ㄎㄨ ㄙˇ)
to wither; to dry up and die: 許多樹都枯死了。Many trees dried up.

枯索(ㄎㄨ ㄙㄨㄛˇ)
withered and lifeless

枯葉(ㄎㄨ ㄧㄝˋ)
dried leaves: 秋天枯葉脫落。The dried leaves fall in autumn.

枯萎(ㄎㄨ ㄨㄟ)
withered: 炎熱的太陽使草都枯萎了。The hot sun withered up the grass.

枯魚(ㄎㄨ ㄩˊ)
dried fish

【枳】 2381 ㄓˇ jyy zhǐ

1. a trifoliate orange
2. a variety of orange with a very thick skin

枳殼(ㄓˇ ㄎㄜˊ)
the large ripe fruit of a variety of orange which is used in herbal medicine

枳棘(ㄓˇ ㄐㄧˊ)
thorns; thorny; plants with many thorns

枳實(ㄓˇ ㄕˊ)
the small green fruit of a variety of orange with thick skin which is used in herbal medicine

【柺】 2382 ㄍㄨㄞˇ goai guǎi

a staff for an old person; a cane: 他依憑柺杖。He leaned on his staff.

柺棒(ㄍㄨㄞˇ ㄅㄤˋ)
a cane; an old person's staff

柺棍(ㄍㄨㄞˇ ㄍㄨㄣˋ)
an old person's staff; a cane

柺杖(ㄍㄨㄞˇ ㄓㄤˋ)
an old person's staff; a cane

【枵】 2383 ㄒㄧㄠ shiau xiāo

empty

枵腹從公(ㄒㄧㄠ ㄈㄨˋ ㄘㄨㄥˊ ㄍㄨㄥ)
to do one's duty even with an empty stomach

【枲】 2384 ㄒㄧˇ shii xǐ

the male nettle-hemp

【架】 2385 ㄐㄧㄚˋ jiah jià

1. a prop; a stand; a rack; a frame
2. to prop up; to set up; to support
3. a framework or scaffold
4. to frame up (a charge, etc.); to fabricate
5. to lay something on
6. a quarrel

架不住(ㄐㄧㄚˋ ·ㄅㄨ ㄓㄨˋ)
① cannot support or sustain the weight ② cannot endure any more; cannot stand (the pressure); cannot stand up again ③ to be no match for

架票(ㄐㄧㄚˋ ㄆㄧㄠˋ)
to kidnap

架得住(ㄐㄧㄚˋ ·ㄉㄜ ㄓㄨˋ)
① able to support it; can sustain the weight: 這個輕書架，能架得住這些書嗎? Can this light shelf sustain all these books? ② able to endure it

架空(ㄐㄧㄚˋ ㄎㄨㄥ)
① to make up; to invent (a story) ② built on stilts ③ impracticable; unpractical ④ to take away one's power by subtle means

架起(ㄐㄧㄚˋ ㄑㄧˇ)
① to set up; to prop up; to support ② to put on a rack

架橋(ㄐㄧㄚˋ ㄑㄧㄠˊ)
to build a bridge

架式(ㄐㄧㄚˋ ㄕˋ)
a style; a manner; a pose; a stance: 這兩個男孩擺出打鬥的架式相互威脅。The two boys took fighting poses to threaten each other.

架勢(ㄐㄧㄚˋ ㄕˋ)
(colloquial) a posture; a stance; a manner

架設(ㄐㄧㄚˋ ㄕㄜˋ)

to build over something; to erect (above the ground or water level, as on stilts or posts)

架子(ㄐㄧㄚˋ ˙ㄗ)or 架兒(ㄐㄧㄚˋㄦ)
①a rack; a stand; a frame; a scaffold ②a skeleton; an outline

架子大(ㄐㄧㄚˋ ˙ㄗ ㄉㄚˋ)
putting on airs of self-importance; a haughty manner: 他架子大。He has a haughty manner.

架走(ㄐㄧㄚˋ ㄗㄡˇ)
to take or carry a person away by force; to kidnap: 我們把她強行架走。We carried her away by force.

架次(ㄐㄧㄚˋ ㄘˋ)
(said of planes on a bombing mission, etc.) a sortie

架訟(ㄐㄧㄚˋ ㄙㄨㄥˋ)
to persuade another to file charges in court or start a lawsuit

【枷】 2386 ㄐㄧㄚ jia jiā
a cangue; a pillory—worn by prisoners in former times: 他應受枷刑。He deserves to be put in the pillory.

枷鎖(ㄐㄧㄚ ㄙㄨㄛˇ)
①the cangue and lock ②(figuratively) bondage; shackles: 他擺脫了精神枷鎖。He was free from spiritual shackles.

【柿】 2387 ㄕˋ shyh shì
the persimmon

柿餅(ㄕˋ ㄅㄧㄥˇ)
flattened and dried persimmon

柿箱(ㄕˋ ㄒㄧㄤ)
boxes or cases made of persimmon wood

柿子(ㄕˋ ˙ㄗ)
the persimmon fruit: 柿子熟了。The persimmon fruit became red.

【枸】 2388 1. ㄍㄡˇ goou gǒu
a medlar

枸杞(ㄍㄡˇ ㄑㄧˇ)
Lycium chinense, a Chinese wolfberry

【枸】 2388 2. ㄍㄡ gou gōu

枸橘(ㄍㄡ ㄐㄩˊ)
a large acid orange

【枸】 2388 3. ㄐㄩˇ jeu jǔ

枸櫞(ㄐㄩˇ ㄩㄢˊ)
citrus medica, a citron

【枹】 2389 ㄈㄨ fu fū (又讀 ㄈㄨˊ fwu fú)
a drumstick

枹鼓(ㄈㄨ ㄍㄨˇ)
①a drum beaten on the battlefield to boast morale ②a drum beaten to warn the invasion of bandits in the Han Dynasty

【柒】 2390 ㄑㄧ chi qī
another form of 七 (seven), used in writing checks, etc. to prevent fraud

【枻】 2391 ㄧˋ yih yì
1. a rowing sweep
2. an instrument for correcting a bow

【柎】 2392 ㄈㄨ fu fū
the calyx of a flower

【柄】 2393 ㄅㄧㄥˇ biing bǐng (又讀 ㄅㄧㄥˋ binq bìng)
1. the handle of something
2. authority; power
3. to operate; to handle; to control
4. a handle: 刀柄the handle of a knife

柄國(ㄅㄧㄥˇ ㄍㄨㄛˊ)
to reign over a state; to hold the political power in a nation

柄臣(ㄅㄧㄥˇ ㄔㄣˊ)
a minister with full authority; a powerful minister

柄用(ㄅㄧㄥˇ ㄩㄥˋ)
to be held in esteem by the monarch and given authority

【柏】 2394 讀音 ㄅㄛˊ bor bó (語音 ㄅㄞˇ bae bǎi)
1. a cypress
2. a Chinese family name

柏府(ㄅㄛˊ ㄈㄨˇ)
the imperial censorate

柏臺(ㄅㄛˊ ㄊㄞˊ)
the imperial censorate

柏拉圖(ㄅㄛˊ ㄌㄚ ㄊㄨˊ)
Plato, 427-347 B.C., Greek philosopher

柏林(ㄅㄛˊ ㄌㄧㄣˊ)
Berlin, Germany

柏梁體(ㄅㄛˊ ㄌㄧㄤˊ ㄊㄧˇ)
a form of poetry in the Han Dynasty, originated by Emperor Wu, accentuating rhymes

柏樹(ㄅㄛˊ ㄕㄨˋ)
the cypress

柏油(ㄅㄛˊ ㄧㄡˊ)or(ㄅㄞˇ ㄧㄡˊ)
asphalt: 他們這裡有好的柏油路。They have good asphalt roads here.

【某】 2395 ㄇㄡˇ moou mǒu
1. a certain person or thing
2. formerly used in place of "I": 某不敢同意。I cannot agree.

某某(ㄇㄡˇ ㄇㄡˇ)
so-and-so; a certain person

某年(ㄇㄡˇ ㄋㄧㄢˊ)
a certain year

某家(ㄇㄡˇ ㄐㄧㄚ)
a certain family; a certain household: 我知道某家。I know of a certain family.

某甲(ㄇㄡˇ ㄐㄧㄚˇ)
a certain person; a Mr. So-and-so—one whose name is unknown, unimportant, or better not to be mentioned; a pronoun referring to any third party

某些(ㄇㄡˇ ㄒㄧㄝ)
certain (things, people, etc.)

某種(ㄇㄡˇ ㄓㄨㄥˇ)
certain (reasons, results, etc.)

某處(ㄇㄡˇ ㄔㄨˋ)
a certain place; somewhere: 他住在某處。He lived in a certain place.

某時(ㄇㄡˇ ㄕˊ)or 某時候(ㄇㄡˇ ㄕˊ ˙ㄏㄡ)
a certain time; sometime: 此事發生在上月某時。It happened sometime last month.

某數(ㄇㄡˇ ㄕㄨˋ)
a certain number or figure

某日(ㄇㄡˇ ㄖˋ)
a certain day

某人(ㄇㄡˇ ㄖㄣˊ)

①a certain person—referring to someone whose name is not mentioned for one reason or another ②a pronoun used in place of one's own name

某月(ㄇㄡˇ ㄩㄝˋ)
a certain month

【染】 2396 ㄖㄢˇ raan rǎn
1. to dye: 她把頭髮染成紅色。she dyed her hair red.
2. to soil; to pollute: 這房間一塵不染。This room was not soiled by a speck of dust.
3. to get infected; to catch a disease; infectious: 他染上了痢疾。He has caught dysentery.
4. to have an affair with
5. (in Chinese painting and calligraphy) to make strokes

染病(ㄖㄢˇ ㄅㄧㄥˋ)
to get infected; to catch a disease; to fall ill

染布(ㄖㄢˇ ㄅㄨˋ)
to dye cloth

染髮(ㄖㄢˇ ㄈㄚˇ)
to dye hair

染坊(ㄖㄢˇ ㄈㄤˊ)
a dyeing mill

染毒(ㄖㄢˇ ㄉㄨˊ)
①to be infected with venereal disease ②to use narcotics

染料(ㄖㄢˇ ㄌㄧㄠˋ)
dyestuff; dye

染缸(ㄖㄢˇ ㄍㄤ)
a dyeing tub, usually of a large size

染工(ㄖㄢˇ ㄍㄨㄥ)
a dyer

染翰(ㄖㄢˇ ㄏㄢˋ)
to soak a writing brush with ink

染化(ㄖㄢˇ ㄏㄨㄚˋ)
to educate; to exert good influence on

染疾(ㄖㄢˇ ㄐㄧˊ)
to contract a disease; to fall ill: 我怕他可能染疾了。I am afraid he may have fallen ill.

染指甲(ㄖㄢˇ ㄓˇ ·ㄐㄧㄚ)
to paint fingernails

染指(ㄖㄢˇ ㄓˇ)
to have a "cut" in illegal profit; to encroach on

染指書(ㄖㄢˇ ㄓˇ ㄕㄨ)
finger-writing (in Chinese calligraphy)

染色(ㄖㄢˇ ㄙㄜˋ)
to dye

染色體(ㄖㄢˇ ㄙㄜˋ ㄊㄧˇ)
(genetics) a chromosome

染惡習(ㄖㄢˇ ㄜˋ ㄒㄧˊ)
to take on bad habits, practices, etc.: 有些人容易染惡習。Some people easily take on bad habits.

染污(ㄖㄢˇ ㄨ)
to stain; to smear; to make dirty; to contaminate

【柔】 2397 ㄖㄡˊ rou róu
1. soft and tender
2. amiable; pliant; yielding; submissive; gentle; supple
3. the new grass budding in spring

柔媚(ㄖㄡˊ ㄇㄟˋ)
amiable, pliant and yielding

柔道(ㄖㄡˊ ㄉㄠˋ)
judo

柔荑(ㄖㄡˊ ㄊㄧˊ)
the young cogongrass—(figuratively) the soft and white fingers of a woman

柔嫩(ㄖㄡˊ ㄋㄣˋ)
soft and tender

柔能克剛(ㄖㄡˊ ㄋㄥˊ ㄎㄜˋ ㄍㄤ)
(literally) The soft will conquer the hard.—Soft and subtle approach can disarm a man of hot temper.

柔和(ㄖㄡˊ ㄏㄜˊ)
soft; gentle; amiable; tender; supple

柔翰(ㄖㄡˊ ㄏㄢˋ)
the Chinese writing brush

柔化(ㄖㄡˊ ㄏㄨㄚˋ)
to soften; to tend to become weak and lax; to melt

柔情(ㄖㄡˊ ㄑㄧㄥˊ)
soft and sentimental; tender thoughts or affection; the tender feelings of a lover

柔情似水(ㄖㄡˊ ㄑㄧㄥˊ ㄙˋ ㄕㄨㄟˇ)
tender and soft as water

柔性(ㄖㄡˊ ㄒㄧㄥˋ)
pliancy; femininity; gentleness; softness; flexibility

柔腸寸斷(ㄖㄡˊ ㄔㄤˊ ㄘㄨㄣˋ ㄉㄨㄢˋ)
brokenhearted

柔聲(ㄖㄡˊ ㄕㄥ)
a soft voice

柔順(ㄖㄡˊ ㄕㄨㄣˋ)
gentle and yielding

柔日(ㄖㄡˊ ㄖˋ)
the days that bear the even-numbered signs of the Celestial Stems (天干) —as 乙丁己辛癸

柔韌(ㄖㄡˊ ㄖㄣˋ)
pliable yet tough—as silk, leather, etc.

柔茹剛吐(ㄖㄡˊ ㄖㄨˊ ㄍㄤ ㄊㄨˇ)
to oppress the weak and fear the strong

柔弱(ㄖㄡˊ ㄖㄨㄛˋ)
weak (physique); soft and meek; low and gentle (voice, etc.); feminine

柔軟(ㄖㄡˊ ㄖㄨㄢˇ)
soft; yielding; lithe

柔軟體操(ㄖㄡˊ ㄖㄨㄢˇ ㄊㄧˇ ㄘㄠ)
calisthenics

柔魚(ㄖㄡˊ ㄩˊ)
Ommastrephes pacificus, a kind of boneless fish pale in color with light-brown dots and a triangular tail, a favorite food for people on the South China coast

柔遠(ㄖㄡˊ ㄩㄢˇ)
to apply gentleness in the policy toward frontier people (in order to win their hearts)

【柑】 2398 ㄍㄢ gan gān
a mandarin orange

柑橘(ㄍㄢ ㄐㄩˊ)
①oranges and tangerines ②citruses

柑子(ㄍㄢ ·ㄗ)
a mandarin orange: 他喝了一杯柑子汁。He drank a glass of mandarin orange juice.

【柳】 2399 ㄌㄧㄡˇ leou liǔ
1. a willow tree: 柳樹生長在河邊。Willows grew beside the stream.
2. name of one of the 28 Constellations
3. (figuratively) a singsong house; the red-light district: 紳士不逛花街柳巷。The gentlemen avoid wandering in red-light district.
4. a tumor; a swelling; a lump

〔木部〕

5. a Chinese family name
柳眉(ㄌㄧㄡˇ ㄇㄟˊ)
the eyebrows of a beautiful woman—like leaves of the willow
柳眉倒豎(ㄌㄧㄡˇ ㄇㄟˊ ㄉㄠˋ ㄕㄨˋ)
(said of a girl) to look angry; to raise eyebrows in anger
柳眉杏眼(ㄌㄧㄡˇ ㄇㄟˊ ㄒㄧㄥˋ ㄧㄢˇ)
graceful eyebrows and large eyes
柳體(ㄌㄧㄡˇ ㄊㄧˇ)or 柳字(ㄌㄧㄡˇ ㄗˋ)
name of a calligraphic style created by Liu Kung-chüan (柳公權) of the Tang Dynasty
柳條(ㄌㄧㄡˇ ㄊㄧㄠˊ)
① a withy; an osier; a willow branch ② withy-like grain, patterns, etc.
柳條籃(ㄌㄧㄡˇ ㄊㄧㄠˊ ㄌㄢˊ)
an osier basket; a willow basket
柳公權(ㄌㄧㄡˇ ㄍㄨㄥ ㄑㄩㄢˊ)
Liu Kung-chüan, A. D. 778-865, a famous calligrapher in the Tang Dynasty
柳花(ㄌㄧㄡˇ ㄏㄨㄚ)
the willow blossom
柳下惠(ㄌㄧㄡˇ ㄒㄧㄚˋ ㄏㄨㄟˋ)
another name of Chan Chin (展禽), a virtuous scholar of the Epoch of Spring and Autumn, whose name has become a synonym for fortitude against the temptation of women
柳線(ㄌㄧㄡˇ ㄒㄧㄢˋ)
long withies; willow branches
柳巷花街(ㄌㄧㄡˇ ㄒㄧㄤˋ ㄏㄨㄚ ㄐㄧㄝ)
streets and lanes where brothels abound; the red-light district 亦作「花街柳巷」
柳絮(ㄌㄧㄡˇ ㄒㄩˋ)
willow catkins
柳枝(ㄌㄧㄡˇ ㄓ)
a withy; a willow branch
柳橙(ㄌㄧㄡˇ ㄔㄥˊ)
an orange
柳杉(ㄌㄧㄡˇ ㄕㄢ)
(botany) cryptomeria
柳宗元(ㄌㄧㄡˇ ㄗㄨㄥ ㄩㄢˊ)
Liu Tzung-yüan, 773-819, one of the eight greatest prose writers of the Tang and Sung Dynasties

柳絲(ㄌㄧㄡˇ ㄙ)
fine willow branches
柳暗花明(ㄌㄧㄡˇ ㄢˋ ㄏㄨㄚ ㄇㄧㄥˊ)
dense willow trees and bright flowers—an enchanting sight in springtime
柳暗花明又一村(ㄌㄧㄡˇ ㄢˋ ㄏㄨㄚ ㄇㄧㄥˊ ㄧㄡˋ ㄧˋ ㄘㄨㄣ)
Every cloud has a silver lining.
柳芽兒(ㄌㄧㄡˇ ㄧㄚˊㄦ)
willow buds or sprouts
柳葉兒(ㄌㄧㄡˇ ㄧㄝˋㄦ)
① willow leaves ② a kind of food made of flour dough shaped like willow leaves
柳腰(ㄌㄧㄡˇ ㄧㄠ)
a willowy waist; a slender waist: 柳腰娉婷。A lady who has a willowy waist is elegant and graceful.
柳陰(ㄌㄧㄡˇ ㄧㄣ)
shade of willow trees
柳永(ㄌㄧㄡˇ ㄩㄥˇ)
Liu Yung, died circa A. D. 1045, the most popular writer of lyrical songs (詞) of the Sung Dynasty

【柘】 2400 ㄓㄜˋ jeh zhè

1. *Cudrania tricuspidata,* a thorny tree about 15 feet high whose leaves can be used in place of mulberry leaves in feeding silkworms and whose bark contains a yellow dye
2. sugarcane
柘彈(ㄓㄜˋ ㄉㄢˋ)
a slingshot made of the tree
柘榴(ㄓㄜˋ ㄌㄧㄡˊ)
the pomegranate
柘黃(ㄓㄜˋ ㄏㄨㄤˊ)
a yellow dye made from the bark of the tree
柘蠶(ㄓㄜˋ ㄘㄢˊ)
silkworms fed on the leaves of the tree
柘絲(ㄓㄜˋ ㄙ)
silk from worms fed on these leaves

【柙】 2401 ㄒㄧㄚˊ shya xiá

1. a cage or a pen for wild beasts, especially the fierce ones
2. a scabbard; a case for a sword

【柚】 2402 ㄧㄡˋ yow yòu

1. a pumelo or pomelo; a shaddock
2. a teak; a teak tree
柚木(ㄧㄡˋ ㄇㄨˋ)
① a teak; a teak tree ② teak; teakwood
柚子(ㄧㄡˋ ·ㄗ)
a pumelo or pomelo; a shaddock

【柜】 2403 ㄐㄩˇ jeu jǔ

1. a tree of the willow family
2. same as 欅, a very large tree whose beautiful fine-grained wood is good for making furniture, etc.
柜柳(ㄐㄩˇ ㄌㄧㄡˇ)
① a tree of the willow family ② same as above「柜2.」

【柞】 2404 ㄗㄨㄛˋ tzuoh zuò

Xylosma congesta, an evergreen thorny tree with small leaves, fine and sturdy wood; an oak
柞綢(ㄗㄨㄛˋ ㄔㄡˊ)
a tussah silk fabric
柞蠶(ㄗㄨㄛˋ ㄘㄢˊ)
tussah silkworms
柞蠶絲(ㄗㄨㄛˋ ㄘㄢˊ ㄙ)
tussah silk

【柝】 2405 ㄊㄨㄛˋ tuoh tuò

a watchman's rattle; a watchman's clapper; a knocker

【柢】 2406 ㄉㄧˇ dii dǐ

the root; the foundation; the base

【柩】 2407 ㄐㄧㄡˋ jiow jiù

a coffin with a corpse in it
柩車(ㄐㄧㄡˋ ㄔㄜ)
a hearse

【柯】 2408 ㄎㄜ ke kē

1. *Pasania cuspidata,* a tall evergreen tree
2. the handle of an ax
3. the stalk or the trunk of a plant
4. a Chinese family name
柯達(ㄎㄜ ㄉㄚˊ)
Kodak, a brand name

柯駕(ㄎㄜ ㄐㄧㄚˋ)
a respectful reference to the marriage go-between
柯維納(ㄎㄜ ㄨㄟˊ ㄋㄚˋ)
Montecorvino, A.D. 1247-1328, an Italian priest who went to China as a missionary in A. D. 1289, and later translated the *New Testament* into Chinese

【柱】 2409
ㄓㄨˋ juh zhù
1. a pillar; a post: 門廊的屋頂由磚柱支撐。The roof of the porch was supported by brick pillars.
2. a cylinder
3. to support
4. to stab; to pierce
柱面(ㄓㄨˋ ㄇㄧㄢˋ)
(mathematics) a cylindrical surface
柱頂(ㄓㄨˋ ㄉㄧㄥˇ)
(architecture) the uppermost portion of a column or pillar; a capital
柱頭(ㄓㄨˋ ㄊㄡˊ)
(botany) a stigma
柱廊(ㄓㄨˋ ㄌㄤˊ)
a colonnade
柱下史(ㄓㄨˋ ㄒㄧㄚˋ ㄕˇ)or 柱史(ㄓㄨˋ ㄕˇ)
an official rank originated in the Chin Dynasty, similar to that of an imperial censor
柱臣(ㄓㄨˋ ㄔㄣˊ)
the important ministers of a nation
柱石(ㄓㄨˋ ㄕˊ)
the pillars of a nation; the key ministers of a nation: 三軍是國家的柱石。The armed forces are the pillars of a nation.
柱石岩(ㄓㄨˋ ㄕˊ ㄧㄢˊ)
the basalt (of a column)
柱子(ㄓㄨˋ ·ㄗ)
a pillar; a post

【柬】 2410
ㄐㄧㄢˇ jean jiǎn
1. a letter; an invitation or visiting card
2. to select; to pick
柬埔寨(ㄐㄧㄢˇ ㄆㄨˇ ㄓㄞˋ)
Cambodia
柬帖(ㄐㄧㄢˇ ㄊㄧㄝˇ)
① an invitation card ② (in old China) a red visiting card
柬請(ㄐㄧㄢˇ ㄑㄧㄥˇ)
to invite by letter or by invitation card
柬邀(ㄐㄧㄢˇ ㄧㄠ)
to invite by letter or by invitation card

【查】 2411
1. ㄔㄚˊ char chá
1. to investigate; to check; to seek out; to look into: 讓我們把這件事查個水落石出。Let's get to the bottom of the matter.
2. (used at the beginning of the official correspondence) It appears....或 It seems....或 It is known....或 It is found that....
3. a wooden raft
查辦(ㄔㄚˊ ㄅㄢˋ)
to investigate into the irregularities (of an official or employee) and mete out due punishment: 我們將他撤職查辦。We dismiss him and have him prosecuted.
查不出來(ㄔㄚˊ ·ㄅㄨ ㄔㄨ ·ㄌㄞ)
cannot find out (a fact); cannot check out (a figure)
查票(ㄔㄚˊ ㄆㄧㄠˋ)
to examine or check tickets
查明(ㄔㄚˊ ㄇㄧㄥˊ)
to investigate and clarify; to examine to the last detail; to find out: 他已查明事實眞相。He has found out the truth.
查房間(ㄔㄚˊ ㄈㄤˊ ㄐㄧㄢ)
① (said of the police) to check hotel guests at their rooms ② (said of doctors) to make the rounds of the wards: 醫生通常在上午查房間。The doctors usually make the rounds of the wards in the morning.
查訪(ㄔㄚˊ ㄈㄤˇ)
to go around and make inquiries; to investigate
查封(ㄔㄚˊ ㄈㄥ)
the execution of a court order by which all property of a debtor would be placed under legal custody until further action
查德(ㄔㄚˊ ㄉㄜˊ)
Chad
查點(ㄔㄚˊ ㄉㄧㄢˇ)
to check (the number of prisoners, students, a list of goods, etc.)
查對(ㄔㄚˊ ㄉㄨㄟˋ)
to check or examine one by one; to verify: 你查對一下這些數目字好嗎? Will you check these figures?
查理(ㄔㄚˊ ㄌㄧˇ)
a transliteration of Charles
查理曼大帝(ㄔㄚˊ ㄌㄧˇ ㄇㄢˋ ㄉㄚˋ ㄉㄧˋ)
Charlemagne the Great, A. D. 742-814
查理斯敦(ㄔㄚˊ ㄌㄧˇ ㄙ ㄉㄨㄣ)
① Charleston, capital of West Virginia, U.S.A. ② a seaport in South Carolina, U.S.A.
查考(ㄔㄚˊ ㄎㄠˇ)
to investigate; to examine; to ponder; to ascertain: 我想查考這所學校的建校日期。I wish to ascertain the date of the establishment of this school.
查看(ㄔㄚˊ ㄎㄢˋ)
to examine; to investigate; to look into (a matter): 市長查看災情。The mayor looked into the extent of the disaster.
查勘(ㄔㄚˊ ㄎㄢ)
to survey and examine; to investigate: 警方查勘犯罪的現場。The police surveyed the scene of the crime.
查庫(ㄔㄚˊ ㄎㄨˋ)
to inspect the treasury; the inspection of the treasury
查核(ㄔㄚˊ ㄏㄜˊ)
to check and examine; to investigate
查號台(ㄔㄚˊ ㄏㄠˋ ㄊㄞˊ)
directory information
查戶口(ㄔㄚˊ ㄏㄨˋ ㄎㄡˇ)
(said of the police or census officials) to make checks from house to house: 警察每年查戶口。The policemen check on household occupants every year.
查獲(ㄔㄚˊ ㄏㄨㄛˋ)
to hunt down and seize; to ferret out; to track down: 警察查獲逃犯。The policemen

〔木部〕

tracked down a fugitive criminal.

查究(ㄔㄚˊ ㄐㄧㄡˋ)

to search into (a matter); to seek out (the cause, etc. of something): 政府查究責任。The government found out who should be held responsible. 警方查究辦理。The policemen investigate and act accordingly.

查禁(ㄔㄚˊ ㄐㄧㄣˋ)

to prohibit or ban after investigation (usually said of pornographic books, immoral shows, gambling, etc.): 警察查禁這本書。The policeman banned this book.

查經(ㄔㄚˊ ㄐㄧㄥ)

to study the Bible; Bible study

查卷(ㄔㄚˊ ㄐㄩㄢˋ)

①to check examination papers already graded to see if there is any mistake in grading ②to look into official files to find something for reference

查訖(ㄔㄚˊ ㄑㄧˋ)

checked

查勤(ㄔㄚˊ ㄑㄧㄣˊ)

to make the rounds and check officers, etc. to see if they are doing their duties during office hours

查清(ㄔㄚˊ ㄑㄧㄥ)

to investigate thoroughly; to clarify: 偵探已查清他的來歷。The detective has found out his background.

查詢(ㄔㄚˊ ㄒㄩㄣˊ)

to inquire about; to inquire: 我向他查詢她的事。I inquired of him about her.

查照(ㄔㄚˊ ㄓㄠˋ)

(a documentary usage) to have learned (from your letter, etc.); to look into and act accordingly: 請查照辦理。Please consider and act accordingly.

查賬 or 查帳(ㄔㄚˊ ㄓㄤˋ)

to audit (accounts); an audit: 每年一次的查賬在十二月舉行。The yearly audit takes place each December.

查賬員 or 查帳員(ㄔㄚˊ ㄓㄤˋ ㄩㄢˊ)

an auditor

查證(ㄔㄚˊ ㄓㄥˋ)

to investigate and verify; to check

查抄(ㄔㄚˊ ㄔㄠ)

(in old China) to search out the property of a criminal (usually a corrupt official) and confiscate it: 法院查抄犯人財產。The court made an inventory of a criminal's possessions and confiscated them.

查出(ㄔㄚˊ ㄔㄨ)

to find out; to discover

查鋪(ㄔㄚˊ ㄆㄨˋ)

(military) to check the beds at night; a bed check

查哨(ㄔㄚˊ ㄕㄠˋ)

(military) to tour the guard posts to see if the sentries are doing their jobs; to go the rounds of guard posts; to inspect the sentries

查收(ㄔㄚˊ ㄕㄡ)

to check the goods delivered and take them over 或 Please find....

查稅(ㄔㄚˊ ㄕㄨㄟˋ)

tax inspection

查字典(ㄔㄚˊ ㄗˋ ㄉㄧㄢˇ)

to consult a dictionary; to look it up in a dictionary: 我查字典。I looked up a word in the dictionary.

查案(ㄔㄚˊ ㄢˋ)

to investigate into a case

查夜(ㄔㄚˊ ㄧㄝˋ)

(the police usage) to make the rounds within the beat; to go the rounds at night; night patrol

查驗(ㄔㄚˊ ㄧㄢˋ)

to investigate; to examine; to inspect: 移民官員查驗護照。The immigration officer examined passports.

查無實據(ㄔㄚˊ ㄨˊ ㄕˊ ㄐㄩˋ)

(a cliché in official correspondence) It has been found that the report (or accusation) is not substantiated by facts. 或 Investigation reveals no evidence.

查問(ㄔㄚˊ ㄨㄣˋ) or 查訊(ㄔㄚˊ ㄒㄩㄣˋ)

to make inquiry; to look into; to investigate; to interrogate: 法官查問犯人。The judge interrogated a prisoner.

查閱(ㄔㄚˊ ㄩㄝˋ)

to consult (a book, etc.); to study (the Bible, etc.)

【查】 2411
2. ㄓㄚ ja zha

a Chinese family name

【柰】 2412
ㄋㄞˋ nay nài

1. an apple tree
2. how
3. Then what?
4. sometimes used with a negative—(no) way out of a dilemma
5. to bear; to endure

柰何(ㄋㄞˋ ㄏㄜˊ)

①no way out; what other alternative (when there isn't any) ②to punish; to deal with; to injure 亦作「奈何」

柰花(ㄋㄞˋ ㄏㄨㄚ)

apple blossoms

柰園(ㄋㄞˋ ㄩㄢˊ) or 柰苑(ㄋㄞˋ ㄩㄢˋ)

a Buddhist temple

【柴】 2413
ㄔㄞˊ chair chái

1. firewood; brushwood; faggots
2. thin; emaciated
3. (now rarely) a fence
4. a Chinese family name

柴門(ㄔㄞˊ ㄇㄣˊ)

①a door of brushwood—a poor family ②to shut one's door to all visitors

柴米(ㄔㄞˊ ㄇㄧˇ)

fuel and rice—the household needs

柴米夫妻(ㄔㄞˊ ㄇㄧˇ ㄈㄨ ㄑㄧ)

a couple who live from hand to mouth; a pair who got married for financial reasons

柴米油鹽(ㄔㄞˊ ㄇㄧˇ ㄧㄡˊ ㄧㄢˊ)

daily necessities; everyday goods

柴扉(ㄔㄞˊ ㄈㄟ)

a door of brushwood—a poor family

柴可夫(ㄔㄞˊ ㄎㄜˇ ㄈㄨ)

Anton Pavlovich Chekhov, 1860-1904, Russian writer

柴可夫斯基(ㄔㄞˊ ㄎㄜˇ ㄈㄨ ㄙ ㄐㄧ)

Peter Ilich Tchaikovsky, 1840—1893, Russian composer

柴行(ㄔㄞˊ ㄏㄤˊ)

a shop where faggots or firewood is sold

柴胡(ㄔㄞˊ ㄏㄨˊ)
Bupleurum falcatum, a plant about two to four inches tall with yellow flowers whose roots are used in herbal medicine

柴火(ㄔㄞˊ ㄏㄨㄛˇ)or 柴薪(ㄔㄞˊ ㄒㄧㄣ)
firewood; fuel

柴荆(ㄔㄞˊ ㄐㄧㄥ)
to live in the country; to rusticate

柴車(ㄔㄞˊ ㄔㄜ)
a crude carriage

柴窰(ㄔㄞˊ ㄧㄠˊ)
name of a famous pottery kiln built in Honan during the Epoch of the Five Dynasties

柴油(ㄔㄞˊ ㄧㄡˊ)
diesel oil

【柷】 2414 ㄓㄨˋ juh zhù
an ancient instrument made of wood which is played at the start of an orchestra

【柮】 2415 ㄉㄨㄛˋ duoh duò
firewood

【柵】 2416 ㄓㄚˋ jah zhà
a fence of bamboos or wood; a palisade; a railing of posts; window-bars

柵門(ㄓㄚˋ ㄇㄣˊ)
a door in a palisade

柵欄兒(ㄓㄚˋ ·ㄌㄚㄦ)
a fence; a palisade; a railing: 他們住家四周有柵欄兒。They have a fence around their house.

柵極電路(ㄓㄚˋ ㄐㄧˊ ㄉㄧㄢˋ ㄌㄨˋ)
(electricity) a grid circuit

【柶】 2417 ㄙˋ syh sì
a dagger-shaped ritual vessel in ancient China, made of horn

【柁】 2418 1.(舵) ㄉㄨㄛˋ duoh duò
the rudder or helm of a ship; a rudder

【柁】 2418 2. ㄊㄨㄛˊ two tuó
large tie beams; girders

【枰】 2419 ㄆㄧㄥˊ pyng píng
1. a chessboard
2. a chess game

【枱】 2420 ㄊㄞˊ tair tái
1. same as 檯—a desk or table
2. an ancient unit of measurement

枱球(ㄊㄞˊ ㄑㄧㄡˊ)
table tennis

六畫

【栓】 2421 ㄕㄨㄢ shuan shuān
1. a wooden pin; a peg
2. a bolt; a plug: 門栓 a door bolt
3. a stopper; a cork

栓子(ㄕㄨㄢ ㄗˇ)
(medicine) an embolus

【栻】 2422 ㄕˋ shyh shì
1. name of a kind of tree
2. a wooden object used in divination

【栖】 2423 (棲) ㄑㄧ chi qī (又讀 ㄒㄧ shi xī)
1. (said of birds) to roost; to perch
2. to settle; to live; to stay

栖遑(ㄑㄧ ㄏㄨㄤˊ)
uneasy and anxious

栖栖皇皇(ㄑㄧ ㄑㄧ ㄏㄨㄤˊ ㄏㄨㄤˊ)
vexed; rushing about

栖栖然(ㄑㄧ ㄑㄧ ㄖㄢˊ)
bustling and excited

【栝】 2424 ㄍㄨㄚ gua guā
1. same as 檜—a Chinese juniper
2. the pointed end of an arrow

【栩】 2425 ㄒㄩˇ sheu xǔ
1. a species of oak
2. glad; pleased

栩栩(ㄒㄩˇ ㄒㄩˇ)
vivid; lively

栩栩然(ㄒㄩˇ ㄒㄩˇ ㄖㄢˊ)
very glad and pleased

栩栩如生(ㄒㄩˇ ㄒㄩˇ ㄖㄨˊ ㄕㄥ)
(said of a portrait, etc.) true to life; lifelike; to the life: 舅父的畫像畫得栩栩如生。The portrait is my uncle to the life.

【栗】 2426 ㄌㄧˋ lih lì
1. a chestnut tree
2. strong and tough; firm; durable
3. respectful; fearful; awe-inspiring
4. to tremble: 他不寒而栗。He trembled with fear.
5. dignified; majestic
6. a Chinese family name

栗苞(ㄌㄧˋ ·ㄅㄠ)
a chestnut burr

栗木(ㄌㄧˋ ㄇㄨˋ)
chestnut

栗犢(ㄌㄧˋ ㄉㄨˊ)
a calf (whose horns are as large as chestnuts)

栗碌(ㄌㄧˋ ㄌㄨˋ)
busy; pressing official duties

栗黃(ㄌㄧˋ ㄏㄨㄤˊ)
chestnuts

栗鼠(ㄌㄧˋ ㄕㄨˇ)
a squirrel

栗子(ㄌㄧˋ ·ㄗ)
chestnuts

栗色(ㄌㄧˋ ㄙㄜˋ)
chestnut color; maroon

栗尾(ㄌㄧˋ ㄨㄟˇ)
a Chinese writing brush

【株】 2427 ㄓㄨ ju zhū
1. a tree; a numerary auxiliary for counting trees or similar things
2. roots that grow above the ground

株蔓(ㄓㄨ ㄇㄢˋ)
to involve people, relatives, etc. in a crime

株連(ㄓㄨ ㄌㄧㄢˊ)
to involve others in a crime one committed (especially in ancient China when the friends or relatives of a person who committed treason could get such incrimination); to implicate

株戮(ㄓㄨ ㄌㄨˋ)
to be executed for a crime committed by one's relatives or friends

株幹(ㄓㄨ ㄍㄢˋ)
the trunk of a tree

株守(ㄓㄨ ㄕㄡˇ)
to take no action but wish that something would come

one's way

【核】 2428 ㄏㄜˊ her hé

1. a kernel; a fruit stone; a walnut; a pit
2. to investigate; to examine; to verify; to study; to check
3. a nucleus; nuclear
4. a hard lump

核爆(ㄏㄜˊ ㄅㄠˋ)
nuclear blast; a nuclear explosion

核辦(ㄏㄜˊ ㄅㄢˋ)
to study and examine (a case, etc.) and act accordingly; to consider and carry out accordingly

核膜(ㄏㄜˊ ㄇㄛˊ)
the membrane enclosing the nucleus of a cell

核反應(ㄏㄜˊ ㄈㄢˇ ㄧㄥˋ)
nuclear reaction

核分裂(ㄏㄜˊ ㄈㄣ ㄌㄧㄝˋ)or 核子分裂(ㄏㄜˊ ㄗˇ ㄈㄣ ㄌㄧㄝˋ)
nuclear fission

核輻射(ㄏㄜˊ ㄈㄨˊ ㄕㄜˋ)
nuclear radiation

核覆(ㄏㄜˊ ㄈㄨˋ)
to make a reply after thorough investigation

核彈頭(ㄏㄜˊ ㄉㄢˋ ㄊㄡˊ)
a nuclear warhead 亦作「核子彈頭」

核彈攻擊(ㄏㄜˊ ㄉㄢˋ ㄍㄨㄥ ㄐㄧˊ)
nuking

核定(ㄏㄜˊ ㄉㄧㄥˋ)
① to decide after examination ② to fix or approve (a sum, budget, etc.) for a project, etc.; to check and ratify

核奪(ㄏㄜˊ ㄉㄨㄛˊ)
to make your kind decision after examination

核對(ㄏㄜˊ ㄉㄨㄟˋ)
to verify; to check (the facts): 將你的答案與我的核對一下。Check your answers with mine.

核桃(ㄏㄜˊ ·ㄊㄠ)
a walnut

核能(ㄏㄜˊ ㄋㄥˊ)
nuclear energy

核能發電(ㄏㄜˊ ㄋㄥˊ ㄈㄚ ㄉㄧㄢˋ)
nuclear power

核能電廠(ㄏㄜˊ ㄋㄥˊ ㄉㄧㄢˋ ㄔㄤˇ)
a nuclear power station

核果(ㄏㄜˊ ㄍㄨㄛˇ)
a drupe; a stone fruit

核擴散(ㄏㄜˊ ㄎㄨㄛˋ ㄙㄢˋ)
nuclear proliferation

核計(ㄏㄜˊ ㄐㄧˋ)
to examine and calculate

核減(ㄏㄜˊ ㄐㄧㄢˇ)
to cut (a budget, an estimate, etc.) after examination

核銷(ㄏㄜˊ ㄒㄧㄠ)
to verify accounts, budgets, etc. and find them faultless

核效應(ㄏㄜˊ ㄒㄧㄠˋ ㄧㄥˋ)
nuclear effect

核心(ㄏㄜˊ ㄒㄧㄣ)
① the core (of a matter, etc.) ② the inner circle (of a political party, government, etc.)

核心人物(ㄏㄜˊ ㄒㄧㄣ ㄖㄣˊ ㄨˋ)
a key person; a key figure

核准(ㄏㄜˊ ㄓㄨㄣˇ)
to approve; approval: 校長已核准有關該節日的計劃。The principal gave his approval to plans for the holiday.

核實(ㄏㄜˊ ㄕˊ)
to examine the facts; on-the-spot investigation

核示(ㄏㄜˊ ㄕˋ)
to consider or examine a matter and give instructions accordingly

核試驗(ㄏㄜˊ ㄕˋ ㄧㄢˋ)or 核子試爆(ㄏㄜˊ ㄗˇ ㄕˋ ㄅㄠˋ)
a nuclear test

核仁(ㄏㄜˊ ㄖㄣˊ)
① a nucleolus ② the kernel (of a fruit stone)

核融合(ㄏㄜˊ ㄖㄨㄥˊ ㄏㄜˊ)
nuclear fusion

核子(ㄏㄜˊ ㄗˇ)
a nucleus; a nucleon

核子彈頭(ㄏㄜˊ ㄗˇ ㄉㄢˋ ㄊㄡˊ)
a nuclear warhead 亦作「核彈頭」

核子動力船(ㄏㄜˊ ㄗˇ ㄉㄨㄥˋ ㄌㄧˋ ㄔㄨㄢˊ)
a nuclear ship

核子潛艇(ㄏㄜˊ ㄗˇ ㄑㄧㄢˊ ㄊㄧㄥˇ)
a nuclear submarine

核子戰略(ㄏㄜˊ ㄗˇ ㄓㄢˋ ㄌㄩㄝˋ)
nuclear strategy

核子戰爭(ㄏㄜˊ ㄗˇ ㄓㄢˋ ㄓㄥ)
nuclear war

核子武器(ㄏㄜˊ ㄗˇ ㄨˇ ㄑㄧˋ)
nuclear weapons

核算(ㄏㄜˊ ㄙㄨㄢˋ)
to examine and calculate

核兒(ㄏㄜˊㄦ)or(ㄏㄨˊㄦ)
the kernel; the fruit stone

核議(ㄏㄜˊ ㄧˋ)
to decide after consideration

【校】 2429 1. ㄒㄧㄠˋ shiaw xiào

1. a school: 該城有五所學校。There are five schools in the town.
2. field-grade (officers)

校本部(ㄒㄧㄠˋ ㄅㄣˇ ㄅㄨˋ)
the main campus of a school

校門(ㄒㄧㄠˋ ㄇㄣˊ)
a gate of a school or college

校風(ㄒㄧㄠˋ ㄈㄥ)
the characteristic of a particular school; the style of a school; the prevailing atmosphere in a school (especially referring to the conduct of the students); school tradition; school spirit: 他們學習牛津大學的優良校風。They learned from the spirit of Oxford University.

校服(ㄒㄧㄠˋ ㄈㄨˊ)
school uniform

校隊(ㄒㄧㄠˋ ㄉㄨㄟˋ)
the school team

校董(ㄒㄧㄠˋ ㄉㄨㄥˇ)
directors of a school

校董會(ㄒㄧㄠˋ ㄉㄨㄥˇ ㄏㄨㄟˋ)
the board of directors or trustees of a school

校內(ㄒㄧㄠˋ ㄋㄟˋ)
within or inside the school

校歌(ㄒㄧㄠˋ ㄍㄜ)
a school song; a college song

校規(ㄒㄧㄠˋ ㄍㄨㄟ)
school regulations; school discipline: 他違反校規。He broke school regulations.

校官(ㄒㄧㄠˋ ㄍㄨㄢ)
field-grade officers

校刊(ㄒㄧㄠˋ ㄎㄢ)
a school magazine; a school bulletin

校花(ㄒㄧㄠˋ ㄏㄨㄚ)
a campus queen; a school belle

校徽(ㄒㄧㄠˋ ㄏㄨㄟ)
a school emblem; a badge

校際(ㄒㄧㄠˋ ㄐㄧˋ)
interscholastic; intercolle-

giate

校警(ㄒㄧㄠˋ ㄐㄧㄥˇ)
the police guards of a school

校旗(ㄒㄧㄠˋ ㄑㄧˊ)
a school flag

校慶(ㄒㄧㄠˋ ㄑㄧㄥˋ)
anniversary celebrations of a school: 我們慶祝校慶。We celebrate the anniversary of the founding of our school.

校訓(ㄒㄧㄠˋ ㄒㄩㄣˋ)
a school motto

校址(ㄒㄧㄠˋ ㄓˇ)
the location of a school

校長(ㄒㄧㄠˋ ㄓㄤˇ)
a principal; a schoolmaster; the president or chancellor of a university; the commandant of a military academy

校長室(ㄒㄧㄠˋ ㄓㄤˇ ㄕˋ)
the schoolmaster's office; the president's office

校車(ㄒㄧㄠˋ ㄔㄜ)
a school bus

校舍(ㄒㄧㄠˋ ㄕㄜˋ)
school premises; school buildings: 他在這校舍一帶流連。He lingered about the school premises.

校醫(ㄒㄧㄠˋ ㄧ)
a school doctor or physician: 你如生病，即刻去看校醫。If you are ill, go to see a school doctor at once.

校友(ㄒㄧㄠˋ ㄧㄡˇ)
an alumnus or alumna; alumni or alumnae

校友會(ㄒㄧㄠˋ ㄧㄡˇ ㄏㄨㄟˋ)
an alumni association: 他們是這個校友會的會員。They are members of the alumni association.

校務(ㄒㄧㄠˋ ㄨˋ)
school administration; college administration

校外(ㄒㄧㄠˋ ㄨㄞˋ)
outside the school

校譽(ㄒㄧㄠˋ ㄩˋ)
the reputation or prestige of a school or college

校園(ㄒㄧㄠˋ ㄩㄢˊ)
the school ground; the campus

【校】 2429
2. ㄐㄧㄠˋ jiaw jiào

1. to compare
2. to proofread; proofs: 五校 the fifth proof; to proofread for the fifth time
3. to revise (books, etc.); to collate

校本(ㄐㄧㄠˋ ㄅㄣˇ)
an incomplete or deleted edition with addition of words copied from the original version

校訂(ㄐㄧㄠˋ ㄉㄧㄥˋ)
to revise: 他正在校訂手稿。He is revising a manuscript.

校訂本(ㄐㄧㄠˋ ㄉㄧㄥˋ ㄅㄣˇ)
a revised edition

校對(ㄐㄧㄠˋ ㄉㄨㄟˋ)
① to proofread; to correct proofs: 我編寫和校對這些書。I edited and proofed these books. ② a proofreader ③ to calibrate

校理(ㄐㄧㄠˋ ㄌㄧˇ)
① to revise and arrange (a book, etc.) ② a secretarial rank in the Tang Dynasty

校獵(ㄐㄧㄠˋ ㄌㄧㄝˋ)
to hunt animals or birds on grounds enclosed with wooden posts or boards

校改(ㄐㄧㄠˋ ㄍㄞˇ)
to read and correct proofs

校勘(ㄐㄧㄠˋ ㄎㄢ)
to collate; to compare and correct

校正(ㄐㄧㄠˋ ㄓㄥˋ)
to correct; to correct proofs: 我校正我書中的錯字。I corrected misprints in my book.

校準(ㄐㄧㄠˋ ㄓㄨㄣˇ)
calibration: 方位校準 bearing calibration

校讐(ㄐㄧㄠˋ ㄔㄡˊ)
to collate or proofread (books, etc.)

校場(ㄐㄧㄠˋ ㄔㄤˇ)
(in ancient China) a military drill ground

校書(ㄐㄧㄠˋ ㄕㄨ)
① to proofread books ② a euphemism for "prostitute"

校樣(ㄐㄧㄠˋ ㄧㄤˋ)
galley proofs: 我已看完校樣。I have read the proofs.

校閱(ㄐㄧㄠˋ ㄩㄝˋ)
① to examine; to collate; to read and revise ② to inspect troops, honor guards, etc.: 總統校閱軍隊。The president inspected troops.

【栲】 2430
ㄎㄠˇ kao kǎo

(botany) *Castanopsis hystrix*

【根】 2431
ㄍㄣ gen gēn

1. the root of a plant: 他們將那樹連根拔起。They pulled up the tree by the roots.
2. a base; a foundation
3. the beginning, cause, or source of something
4. (mathematics) the root of a number: 2 是 4 的平方根。Two is the square root of four.
5. (chemistry) radical
6. a piece (of string, rope, etc.); a (stick, spear or thing of slender shape)
7. a Chinese family name

根本(ㄍㄣ ㄅㄣˇ)
① a root; a base; an origin; a foundation; a basis ② at all; basically: 這件事根本就不對。This matter is basically wrong.

根本辦法(ㄍㄣ ㄅㄣˇ ㄅㄢˋ ㄈㄚˇ)
basic principles of action; basic methods or measures

根本觀念(ㄍㄣ ㄅㄣˇ ㄍㄨㄢ ㄋㄧㄢˋ)
a radical conception

根本解決(ㄍㄣ ㄅㄣˇ ㄐㄧㄝˇ ㄐㄩㄝˊ)
a radical solution; to settle something once for all

根本上(ㄍㄣ ㄅㄣˇ ˙ㄕㄤ)
basically; fundamentally; radically: 英語根本上是一種日耳曼語。English is radically a Germanic language.

根本問題(ㄍㄣ ㄅㄣˇ ㄨㄣˋ ㄊㄧˊ)
fundamental questions

根部(ㄍㄣ ㄅㄨˋ)
the root of a plant

根末(ㄍㄣ ㄇㄛˋ)
root and branch—throughout; altogether; completely

根毛(ㄍㄣ ㄇㄠˊ)
root hairs

根苗(ㄍㄣ ㄇㄧㄠˊ)
① the root, source or origin ② roots and shoots

根底(ㄍㄣ ㄉㄧˇ)
① the origin, cause and effect, or the ins and outs of something ② a basis; a foundation ③ the possessions or financial standing: 她頗有根

〔木部〕

底。She is quite well-to-do. ④ background learning; early training: 你的根底很好。You have good scholastic training. ⑤ background

根柢(ㄍㄣ ㄉㄧˇ)
① the root of a plant ② a basis; a foundation

根瘤(ㄍㄣ ㄌㄧㄡˊ)
root nodules; root tubercles

根號(ㄍㄣ ㄏㄠˋ)
(mathematics) the radical sign

根基
①(ㄍㄣ ㄐㄧ) ⓐ foundation (in learning): 我要打好英文的根基。I want to lay a solid foundation in English. ⓑ financial standing
②(ㄍㄣ ·ㄐㄧ) behavior or conduct

根脚(ㄍㄣ ㄐㄧㄠˇ)
a foundation; a base

根究(ㄍㄣ ㄐㄧㄡˋ)
to go to the very root or source of something; to get to the bottom of; to probe into: 這事必須根究。This matter must be probed to the bottom.

根莖(ㄍㄣ ㄐㄧㄥ)
a rhizome; a rootstock

根據(ㄍㄣ ㄐㄩˋ)
① a basis; a root, source or origin; grounds: 毫無根據。It is utterly groundless. ② in accordance with (the regulation, etc.); on the strength of; in the light of: 根據天氣預報，將要下雨。According to the weather forecast, it will rain.

根據地(ㄍㄣ ㄐㄩˋ ㄉㄧˋ)
a base (of operations); a home base

根絕(ㄍㄣ ㄐㄩㄝˊ)
to root out (a problem, vice, etc.); to exterminate completely

根器(ㄍㄣ ㄑㄧˋ)
natural gift or inclination for (religious faith and achievement, etc.)

根鬚(ㄍㄣ ㄒㄩ)
fibrous roots

根治(ㄍㄣ ㄓˋ)
a radical treatment (for a disease, etc.); to cure (a disease) for good

根插(ㄍㄣ ㄔㄚ)
root cutting

根除(ㄍㄣ ㄔㄨˊ)
thoroughly to do away with; to eradicate; to root out; to eliminate; to exterminate; to uproot (social evils); to effect a cure (of disease): 我們將根除水患。We'll eliminate the scourge of floods.

根深蒂固(ㄍㄣ ㄕㄣ ㄉㄧˋ ㄍㄨˋ)
deep-rooted; time-honored; firmly established; deeply entrenched

根深葉茂(ㄍㄣ ㄕㄣ ㄧㄝˋ ㄇㄠˋ)
The root is deep and leaves are many.—to be well established and vigorously developing; flourishing for a long time

根生土長(ㄍㄣ ㄕㄥ ㄊㄨˇ ㄓㄤˇ)
to be born and raised in a place: 他是根生土長的中國人。He was born and raised in China.

根數(ㄍㄣ ㄕㄨˋ)
(mathematics) radical

根子(ㄍㄣ ·ㄗ) or 根兒(ㄍㄜㄦ)
① the root of a plant; the base ② a source; an origin: 這個問題的根子是什麼? What's the source of the trouble?

根芽(ㄍㄣ ㄧㄚˊ)
a radicle

根由(ㄍㄣ ㄧㄡˊ)
the source, origin or cause of something

根源(ㄍㄣ ㄩㄢˊ)
the cause, source or origin of something: 貪財爲百禍之根源。The greed of money is the root of all evil.

【桁】 2432 1. ㄏㄥˊ herng héng

the purlins of a roof

桁桷(ㄏㄥˊ ㄐㄩㄝˊ)
purlins and rafters

【桁】 2432 2. ㄏㄤˊ harng háng

a big wooden collar (for punishing a criminal)

桁楊(ㄏㄤˊ ㄧㄤˊ)
a cangue

【桁】 2432 3. ㄏㄤˋ hanq hàng

a rack for hanging clothes

【格】 2433 ㄍㄜˊ ger gé

1. to correct; to adjust or regulate
2. to reach; to come or go to
3. to influence
4. to resist; to attack; to fight
5. to obstruct; to block
6. to study thoroughly; to search to the very source; to investigate
7. a standard; a form; a rule; a pattern; a style: 他的小說獨創一格。His fiction was original in style.
8. a frame; a trellis
9. squares formed by crossed lines
10. a Chinese family name

格非(ㄍㄜˊ ㄈㄟ)
to correct the wrong and evil ways

格鬥(ㄍㄜˊ ㄉㄡˋ)
a brawl; a hand-to-hand fight; a free-for-all; fisticuffs: 孩子們在格鬥。The boys are fighting hand to hand.

格調(ㄍㄜˊ ㄉㄧㄠˋ)
① literary or artistic style; form; pattern: 他的小說格調豪放。His novels have a vigorous and flowing style. ② personality

格度(ㄍㄜˊ ㄉㄨˋ)
one's moral character and bearing

格拉斯哥(ㄍㄜˊ ㄌㄚ ㄙ ㄍㄜ)
Glasgow, a city in Scotland

格蘭姆(ㄍㄜˊ ㄌㄢˊ ㄇㄨˇ)
gram, metric unit of weight 亦作「克」

格林威治(ㄍㄜˊ ㄌㄧㄣˊ ㄨㄟ ㄓˋ)
Greenwich

格林威治時間(ㄍㄜˊ ㄌㄧㄣˊ ㄨㄟ ㄓˋ ㄕˊ ㄐㄧㄢ)
Greenwich Mean Time (GMT)

格陵蘭(ㄍㄜˊ ㄌㄧㄥˊ ㄌㄢˊ)
Greenland

格律(ㄍㄜˊ ㄌㄩˋ)
① standard; form; pattern ② the meter of poetry, etc., with special emphasis on the number of words, rhymes, etc.

格格不入(ㄍㄜˊ ㄍㄜˊ ㄅㄨˋ ㄖㄨˋ)
totally incompatible with; to be out of tune with; to be

like a square peg in a round hole; cannot get along with

格格(ㄍㄜˊ·ㄍㄜ)
a princess in the Ching Dynasty

格局(ㄍㄜˊ ㄐㄩˊ)
structure and form; style; setup

格心(ㄍㄜˊ ㄒㄧㄣ)
to correct one's heart (and lead him to the ways of the good)

格致(ㄍㄜˊ ㄓˋ)
① to investigate things and extend knowledge to the utmost ② an old name for physics

格式(ㄍㄜˊ ㄕˋ)
form; patterns; format: 他懂得公文格式。He knows of the form of an official document.

格殺(ㄍㄜˊ ㄕㄚ)
to kill in fighting

格殺勿論(ㄍㄜˊ ㄕㄚ ㄨˋ ㄌㄨㄣˋ)
to kill on sight; to shoot on sight; to execute summarily

格瑞那達(ㄍㄜˊ ㄖㄨㄟˋ ㄋㄚˋ ㄉㄚˊ)
Grenada

格子(ㄍㄜˊ·ㄗ) or 格兒(ㄍㄜˊㄦ)
a square frame or blank; a trellis; a lattice

格子布(ㄍㄜˊ·ㄗ ㄅㄨˋ)
checkered or checked cloth

格子窗(ㄍㄜˊ·ㄗ ㄔㄨㄤ)
a lattice window

格言(ㄍㄜˊ ㄧㄢˊ)
a proverb; a motto; an aphorism; a maxim

格物致知(ㄍㄜˊ ㄨˋ ㄓˋ ㄓ)
to investigate things and to extend knowledge to the utmost

格外(ㄍㄜˊ ㄨㄞˋ)
exceptions; exceptional; extraordinary; unusual; exceptionally; unusually; extraordinarily; especially

格外開恩(ㄍㄜˊ ㄨㄞˋ ㄎㄞ ㄣ)
to pardon an offender; to punish an offender lightly

格於規定(ㄍㄜˊ ㄩˊ ㄍㄨㄟ ㄉㄧㄥˋ)
(not permissible) because of existing regulations; to be barred by regulations

【桀】 2434
ㄐㄧㄝˊ jye jié

1. ferocious and cruel
2. name of the last ruler of the Hsia Dynasty
3. same as 傑, outstanding and brave
4. a Chinese family name

桀犬吠堯(ㄐㄧㄝˊ ㄑㄩㄢˇ ㄈㄟˋ ㄧㄠˊ)
(literally) The dog of Chieh (the symbol of evil) barked at Yao (the symbol of good). —Each faithfully serves his own master.

桀黠(ㄐㄧㄝˊ ㄒㄧㄚˊ)
crooked and cruel; cruel and crafty

桀紂(ㄐㄧㄝˊ ㄓㄡˋ)
Chieh and Chou, two typical tyrants, the last rulers of the Hsia and the Shang Dynasties respectively—used as a synonymous term for a tyrant

桀驁(ㄐㄧㄝˊ ㄠˋ)
tyrannical and haughty

桀驁不馴(ㄐㄧㄝˊ ㄠˋ ㄅㄨˋ ㄒㄩㄣˊ)
obstinate and unruly; wild and intractable

【案】 2435
ㄢˋ ann àn

1. a narrow, long table
2. according to; on the strength of; following this precedent
3. a legal case; legal records; a legal offense: 此事有案可查。This matter was on record.
4. to press 亦作「按」

案板(ㄢˋ ㄅㄢˇ)
a chopping or kneading board

案發(ㄢˋ ㄈㄚ)
a crime or conspiracy coming to the open

案奉(ㄢˋ ㄈㄥˋ)
(a documentary terminology used to begin a reply or a circular, etc.) on the strength of instructions from a higher government office

案牘(ㄢˋ ㄉㄨˊ)
official correspondence or documents

案頭(ㄢˋ ㄊㄡˊ)
on the desk: 案頭放着一套百科全書。There is a set of encyclopedia on the desk.

案件(ㄢˋ ㄐㄧㄢˋ)
a legal case; a crime: 這是民事案件。This is a civil case.

案據(ㄢˋ ㄐㄩˋ)
(a documentary terminology used to begin a report, etc.) according to information furnished by a subordinate government office

案卷(ㄢˋ ㄐㄩㄢˋ)
official files; archives

案情(ㄢˋ ㄑㄧㄥˊ)
the record of a case; the ins and outs of a crime

案情大白(ㄢˋ ㄑㄧㄥˊ ㄉㄚˋ ㄅㄞˊ)
The riddle of a puzzling case has been completely unraveled.

案桌(ㄢˋ ㄓㄨㄛ)
a narrow, long table

案准(ㄢˋ ㄓㄨㄣˇ)
a beginning term in documentary usage for correspondence, memo, etc. between government offices of the same or equal standing

案子(ㄢˋ·ㄗ)
① a legal case; a crime: 這是一樁謀殺案子。This is a murder case. ② a large-size table (usually used in shops)

案問 or 按問(ㄢˋ ㄨㄣˋ)
to question; to test

案語 or 按語(ㄢˋ ㄩˇ)
the editor's comments or remarks

【桌】 2436
(棹) ㄓㄨㄛ juo zhuō

1. a table; a desk
2. dishes for guests around the table—usually consisting of 20 courses
3. a tableful of guests (10 to 12 persons at a round table)

桌布(ㄓㄨㄛ ㄅㄨˋ)
a tablecloth

桌面(ㄓㄨㄛ ㄇㄧㄢˋ)
the top of a table

桌燈(ㄓㄨㄛ ㄉㄥ)
a desk lamp

桌球(ㄓㄨㄛ ㄑㄧㄡˊ)
table tennis; ping-pong

桌扇(ㄓㄨㄛ ㄕㄢˋ)
a desk fan

桌子(ㄓㄨㄛ·ㄗ) or 桌兒(ㄓㄨㄛㄦ)
a table; a desk

桌椅板櫈(ㄓㄨㄛ ㄧˇ ㄅㄢˇ ㄉㄥˋ)
tables, desks, chairs and benches—household furni-

〔木部〕

ture in general

【桑】 2437 ㄙㄤ sang sāng

1. the mulberry tree: 我的花園中有一棵桑樹。There is a mulberry tree in my garden.
2. a Chinese family name

桑麻(ㄙㄤ ㄇㄚˊ)
mulberry leaves and hemp—the life on a farm

桑田(ㄙㄤ ㄊㄧㄢˊ)
a plantation of mulberry trees

桑土
①(ㄙㄤ ㄊㄨˇ) mulberry fields; mulberry grounds
②(ㄙㄤ ㄉㄨˋ) the roots of the mulberry tree

桑果(ㄙㄤ ㄍㄨㄛˇ)
sorosis; the berry of a mulberry

桑間濮上(ㄙㄤ ㄐㄧㄢ ㄆㄨˊ ㄕㄤˋ)
a place notorious for profligacy

桑中之樂(ㄙㄤ ㄓㄨㄥ ㄓ ㄌㄜˋ)
illicit love

桑中之會(ㄙㄤ ㄓㄨㄥ ㄓ ㄏㄨㄟˋ)
(literally) a meeting in Sang-chung (桑中); a meeting amid mulberry trees—(figuratively) the lovers' rendezvous

桑葚(ㄙㄤ ㄕㄣˋ)
a mulberry; mulberry fruit

桑樹(ㄙㄤ ㄕㄨˋ)
a mulberry tree

桑梓(ㄙㄤ ㄗˇ)
one's native place or hometown

桑梓之情(ㄙㄤ ㄗˇ ㄓ ㄑㄧㄥˊ)
the friendship of natives or inhabitants of a particular region

桑蠶(ㄙㄤ ㄘㄢˊ)
a silkworm

桑葉(ㄙㄤ ㄧㄝˋ)
mulberry leaves (for feeding silkworms)

桑榆(ㄙㄤ ㄩˊ)
①the west ②the closing years of one's life

桑榆暮景(ㄙㄤ ㄩˊ ㄇㄨˋ ㄐㄧㄥˇ)
old age; the closing years of one's life; the evening of one's life

桑園(ㄙㄤ ㄩㄢˊ)
mulberry fields

【栽】 2438 ㄗㄞ tzai zāi

1. to plant
2. to care; to assist
3. to fall; to fail
4. young trees, saplings, cuttings for planting

栽培(ㄗㄞ ㄆㄟˊ)
①to plant and cultivate; to tend ②to educate people ③to give special favor; to receive special favor

栽倒(ㄗㄞ ㄉㄠˇ)
to fall: 他從窗上栽倒下來。He fell out of the window.

栽跟頭(ㄗㄞ ㄍㄣ ·ㄊㄡ)
①to stumble (both literally and figuratively) ②to be greatly embarrassed

栽植(ㄗㄞ ㄓˊ)
to plant; to raise: 她在花園裡栽植玫瑰。She planted roses in the garden.

栽種(ㄗㄞ ㄓㄨㄥˋ)
to plant; to grow

栽贓(ㄗㄞ ㄗㄤ)
to place stolen goods in somebody's place with the intention of incriminating him; to frame somebody; to fabricate a charge against somebody; to plant: 那些毒品不是我的，是他們栽贓給我。Those drugs aren't mine; they planted them on me.

栽秧(ㄗㄞ ㄧㄤ)
to transplant rice seedlings

【桂】 2439 ㄍㄨㄟˋ guey guì

1. cassia or cinnamon
2. a short name of Kwangsi Province
3. a Chinese family name

桂皮(ㄍㄨㄟˋ ㄆㄧˊ)
cinnamon bark

桂林(ㄍㄨㄟˋ ㄌㄧㄣˊ)
Kweilin, capital of Kwangsi Province

桂冠(ㄍㄨㄟˋ ㄍㄨㄢ)
①laurels (as an emblem of victory, success and distinction) ② a garland made of laurel flowers

桂冠詩人(ㄍㄨㄟˋ ㄍㄨㄢ ㄕ ㄖㄣˊ)
a poet laureate, or a laureate

桂花(ㄍㄨㄟˋ ㄏㄨㄚ)
sweet osmanthus

桂子(ㄍㄨㄟˋ ㄗˇ)
①cassia buds ②famous and talented sons (a polite term referring to another's children)

桂子蘭孫(ㄍㄨㄟˋ ㄗˇ ㄌㄢˊ ㄙㄨㄣ)
famous and capable posterity

桂月(ㄍㄨㄟˋ ㄩㄝˋ)
the eighth month of the lunar calendar

桂圓(ㄍㄨㄟˋ ㄩㄢˊ)
①a longan ②dried longan

【桃】 2440 ㄊㄠˊ taur táo

1. a peach
2. a Chinese family name

桃符(ㄊㄠˊ ㄈㄨˊ)or 桃板(ㄊㄠˊ ㄅㄢˇ)
①the peachwood charm, used to drive away evil spirits ②couplets or scrolls pasted on Lunar New Year

桃符換舊(ㄊㄠˊ ㄈㄨˊ ㄏㄨㄢˋ ㄐㄧㄡˋ)
the time when old "scrolls" are replaced by new ones—the Lunar New Year's Day

桃脯(ㄊㄠˊ ㄈㄨˇ)
peaches preserved in honey

桃李(ㄊㄠˊ ㄌㄧˇ)
①(literally) peaches and plums—one's students or pupils ②the beauty of a woman

桃李不言，下自成蹊(ㄊㄠˊ ㄌㄧˇ ㄅㄨˋ ㄧㄢˊ, ㄒㄧㄚˋ ㄗˋ ㄔㄥˊ ㄒㄧ)
Peaches and plums do not have to talk, yet people beat a path to them.—(figuratively) quiet but attractive 或 Where there is real ability, there is fame.

桃李滿門(ㄊㄠˊ ㄌㄧˇ ㄇㄢˇ ㄇㄣˊ)
(said of a master) to have many pupils

桃李滿天下(ㄊㄠˊ ㄌㄧˇ ㄇㄢˇ ㄊㄧㄢ ㄒㄧㄚˋ)
(said of a master or teacher) His students have spread throughout the world.

桃李門牆(ㄊㄠˊ ㄌㄧˇ ㄇㄣˊ ㄑㄧㄤˊ)
disciples and students of a master

桃李年(ㄊㄠˊ ㄌㄧˇ ㄋㄧㄢˊ)
one's youth or prime; a girl's blooming age

桃李爭春(ㄊㄠˊ ㄌㄧˇ ㄓㄥ ㄔㄨㄣ)

Peaches and plums emulate each other in springtime.

桃李盈庭(ㄊㄠˊ ㄌㄧˇ ㄧㄥˊ ㄊㄧㄥˊ)
Peaches and plums fill up the courtyard. —(said of a master) to have many students

桃核(ㄊㄠˊ ㄏㄜˊ)
a peach stone

桃花(ㄊㄠˊ ㄏㄨㄚ)
the peach blossom: 人面桃花相映紅。The young girl's face and the peach flowers reflect each other's glow.

桃花臉(ㄊㄠˊ ㄏㄨㄚ ㄌㄧㄢˇ)
rosy cheeks; the peach-blossom face of a beauty

桃花心木(ㄊㄠˊ ㄏㄨㄚ ㄒㄧㄣ ㄇㄨˋ)
mahogany

桃花癬(ㄊㄠˊ ㄏㄨㄚ ㄒㄩㄢˇ)
a kind of ringworm shaped like a peach blossom, usually infecting the cheeks of young women or girls

桃花汛(ㄊㄠˊ ㄏㄨㄚ ㄒㄩㄣˋ)
spring freshets; spring floods

桃花水(ㄊㄠˊ ㄏㄨㄚ ㄕㄨㄟˇ)
spring freshets—the water from melting snow when the peach trees are in full blossom in spring

桃花源(ㄊㄠˊ ㄏㄨㄚ ㄩㄢˊ)or 桃源(ㄊㄠˊ ㄩㄢˊ)
Peach Flower Spring — a utopia (originally from a story by Tao Yüan-ming (陶淵明), one of China's most celebrated poets, where people live in peace, oblivious of the passing of time)

桃花運(ㄊㄠˊ ㄏㄨㄚ ㄩㄣˋ)
a duration in a man's life when he is particularly lucky or popular with women; luck in love; a romance

桃紅(ㄊㄠˊ ㄏㄨㄥˊ)
pink; light red

桃紅柳綠(ㄊㄠˊ ㄏㄨㄥˊ ㄌㄧㄡˇ ㄌㄩˋ)
(literally) The peach blossoms and the willow turns green.—a description of the beautiful scenes of spring

桃金孃(ㄊㄠˊ ㄐㄧㄣ ㄋㄧㄤˊ)
(botany) *Rhodomyrtus tomentosa*, a myrtle

桃樹(ㄊㄠˊ ㄕㄨˋ)
a peach tree

桃仁(ㄊㄠˊ ㄖㄣˊ)
the dried meat of a walnut; a shelled walnut; peach kernels

桃瓤兒(ㄊㄠˊ ㄖㄤˊㄦ)
the dried meat of a walnut; a shelled walnut

桃子(ㄊㄠˊ ·ㄗ)or 桃兒(ㄊㄠˊㄦ)
a peach: 我較喜歡桃子而不喜歡蘋果。I like peaches better than apples.

桃色(ㄊㄠˊ ㄙㄜˋ)
① peach color ② the symbol of romances

桃色新聞(ㄊㄠˊ ㄙㄜˋ ㄒㄧㄣ ㄨㄣˊ)
news of illicit love; newspaper stories of love and sex

桃色案(ㄊㄠˊ ㄙㄜˋ ㄢˋ)
a criminal case involving sex; crimes of passion

桃腮杏眼(ㄊㄠˊ ㄙㄞ ㄒㄧㄥˋ ㄧㄢˇ)
large eyes and rosy cheeks of a beauty

桃夭迨吉(ㄊㄠˊ ㄧㄠ ㄉㄞˋ ㄐㄧˊ)
the right age for marriage

桃月(ㄊㄠˊ ㄩㄝˋ)
the third month of the lunar year

桃園結義(ㄊㄠˊ ㄩㄢˊ ㄐㄧㄝˊ ㄧˋ)
① In the Epoch of the Three Kingdoms, the three men —Liu Pei (劉備), who later became ruler of Shu, Kuan Yü (關羽) and Chang Fei (張飛) —swore as brothers in a peach orchard. ② (said of friends) to become sworn brothers

【桄】 2441
ㄍㄨㄤˋ guanq guàng

1. a crossbeam
2. a reel

【桅】 2442
ㄨㄟˊ wei wéi

the mast of a ship: 這船有三根桅桿。The ship has three masts.

桅竿(ㄨㄟˊ ㄍㄢ)
the mast of a boat

桅檣(ㄨㄟˊ ㄑㄧㄤˊ)
a mast

【框】 2443
ㄎㄨㄤˋ kuanq kuàng
(又讀 ㄎㄨㄤ kuang kuāng)

1. a door frame
2. a frame; to frame
3. the skeleton (of a lantern, etc.)

框框(ㄎㄨㄤˋ ·ㄎㄨㄤ)
① a frame; a circle ② restriction; convention; to set a pattern

框子(ㄎㄨㄤˋ ·ㄗ)or 框兒(ㄎㄨㄤˋㄦ)
a frame; a framework

【桎】 2444
ㄓˋ jyh zhì

1. fetters; shackles; to fetter
2. to suffocate

桎梏(ㄓˋ ㄍㄨˋ)
shackles

【桐】 2445
ㄊㄨㄥˊ torng tóng

1. a paulownia
2. a Chinese family name

桐棺(ㄊㄨㄥˊ ㄍㄨㄢ)
a coffin made of the timber of a paulownia, considered to be of very inferior quality

桐城派(ㄊㄨㄥˊ ㄔㄥˊ ㄆㄞˋ)
the Tungcheng School, a literary school in the Ching Dynasty led by Fang Pao (方苞) and Yao Nai (姚鼐) whose hometown was Tungcheng, Anhwei

桐樹(ㄊㄨㄥˊ ㄕㄨˋ)
a tung tree

桐人(ㄊㄨㄥˊ ㄖㄣˊ)
(in ancient China) carved human figures to be buried with the deceased

桐葉(ㄊㄨㄥˊ ㄧㄝˋ)
leaves of a paulownia

桐油(ㄊㄨㄥˊ ㄧㄡˊ)
tung oil; wood oil obtained from the seeds of a paulownia

桐月(ㄊㄨㄥˊ ㄩㄝˋ)
the seventh month of the lunar year

【桓】 2446
ㄏㄨㄢˊ hwan huán

1. a tree with leaves like a willow and white bark
2. a Chinese family name
3. greatly; effectively

桓公(ㄏㄨㄢˊ ㄍㄨㄥ)
Duke Huan of Chi, died 643 B.C., the most celebrated among the five leading chieftains who held power in China during the 7th century B.C.

〔木部〕

桓桓武夫(ㄏㄨㄢ ㄏㄨㄢ ㄨˇ ㄈㄨ)
a martial military man

【桔】 2447
1. ㄐㄧㄝˊ jye jié
a well sweep

桔槔(ㄐㄧㄝˊ ㄍㄠ)
a well sweep, a device with a water bucket raised and lowered in a well by means of a lever

桔梗(ㄐㄧㄝˊ ㄍㄥˇ)
Platycodon grandiflorum, a Chinese bellflower

【桔】 2447
2. ㄐㄩˊ jyu jú
an abbreviated form of 橘, a mandarin orange or tangerine

桔餅(ㄐㄩˊ ㄅㄧㄥˇ)
a dried orange flattened like a cake

桔子(ㄐㄩˊ ·ㄗ)
a small mandarin orange

【桚】 2448
(拶) ㄗㄚˊ tzar zá
(又讀 ㄗㄢˇ tzaan zǎn)
to press; to squeeze

桚指(ㄗㄢˇ ㄓˇ)
a torture by squeezing the fingers in former times

桚子(ㄗㄢˇ ·ㄗ)
a torture instrument for squeezing a prisoner's fingers 亦作「指枷」

【桕】 2449
ㄐㄧㄡˋ jiow jiù
the tallow tree (*Sapium sebiferum*)

【栱】 2450
ㄍㄨㄥˇ goong gǒng
a big peg or stake; a post; a prop

七畫

【桴】 2451
ㄈㄨˊ fwu fú
1. the ridge pole on a roof
2. a drumstick
3. a raft (of wood or bamboo)

桴鼓相應(ㄈㄨˊ ㄍㄨˇ ㄒㄧㄤ ㄧㄥˋ)
to render mutual support or assistance

桴鼓助戰(ㄈㄨˊ ㄍㄨˇ ㄓㄨˋ ㄓㄢˋ)
women assisting in fighting

【桫】 2452
ㄙㄨㄛ suo suō
1. a horse chestnut (*Stewartia pseudocamellia*)
2. sal (*Cyathea spinulosa*)

桫欏(ㄙㄨㄛ ㄌㄨㄛˊ)
① the horse chestnut (*Stewartia pseudocamellia*) ② sal (*Cyathea spinulosa*)

【梧】 2453
ㄨˊ wu wú
1. a firmiana (*Firmiana platanifolia*)
2. a support; a prop
3. to support; to prop up
4. a Chinese family name

梧桐(ㄨˊ ㄊㄨㄥˊ)
a firmiana; a Chinese parasol (tree)

梧州(ㄨˊ ㄓㄡ)
Wuchow, an important city in Kwangsi Province

梧鼠技窮(ㄨˊ ㄕㄨˇ ㄐㄧˋ ㄑㄩㄥˊ)
at one's wits' end; at the end of one's rope

【桶】 2454
ㄊㄨㄥˇ toong tǒng
a bucket; a tub; a pail; a barrel; a keg; a cask

桶鋪(ㄊㄨㄥˇ ㄆㄨˋ)
a coopery

桶匠(ㄊㄨㄥˇ ㄐㄧㄤˋ)
a cooper

桶子(ㄊㄨㄥˇ ·ㄗ)
a bucket; a pail; a barrel; a keg

【桷】 2455
ㄐㄩㄝˊ jyue jué
1. a rafter
2. (botany) *Malus toringo*

【梁】 2456
ㄌㄧㄤˊ liang liáng
1. a bridge
2. beams of a house
3. a ridge; a swelling
4. Liang, name of a dynasty (502 to 557 A.D.)
5. a state during the Epoch of Warring States , also known as Wei (魏)
6. a Chinese family name

梁孟(ㄌㄧㄤˊ ㄇㄥˋ)
an abbreviation for Liang Hung (梁鴻) and Meng Kuang (孟光) of the Han Dynasty, whose married life served as a paragon for all married couple

梁木其壞(ㄌㄧㄤˊ ㄇㄨˋ ㄑㄧˊ ㄏㄨㄞˋ)
(literally) The beams are rotten.—the death of a virtuous person

梁麗(ㄌㄧㄤˊ ㄌㄧˋ)
① beams on a roof ② (now rarely) a small boat

梁惠王(ㄌㄧㄤˊ ㄏㄨㄟˋ ㄨㄤˊ)
① name of a king of the Liang State during the Epoch of Warring States ② the title of a chapter in *The works of Mencius* (孟子)

梁紅玉(ㄌㄧㄤˊ ㄏㄨㄥˊ ㄩˋ)
Liang Hung-yü, wife of General Han Shih-chung (韓世忠) of the Sung Dynasty (When her husband was engaged in a life-and-death battle with Nüchen troops, she beat the military drum to urge the defenders on.)

梁啓超(ㄌㄧㄤˊ ㄑㄧˇ ㄔㄠ)
Liang Chi-chao, 1873-1929, one of the major advocates of political reform in China in the late 19th century

梁山泊(ㄌㄧㄤˊ ㄕㄢ ㄅㄛˊ)
the home base of a gang of hero-bandits in *All Men Are Brothers* (水滸傳), a very popular work of fiction written by Shih Nai-an (施耐庵)

梁上君子 or 樑上君子(ㄌㄧㄤˊ ㄕㄤˋ ㄐㄩㄣ ㄗˇ)
(literally) gentlemen up on the beams—burglars

梁武帝(ㄌㄧㄤˊ ㄨˇ ㄉㄧˋ)
Emperor Wu of the Liang Dynasty (464 to 549 A.D.)

【梃】 2457
ㄊㄧㄥˇ tiing tǐng
1. a club; a cudgel; a stick; a cane
2. a stalk; a branch; a stem
3. straight and strong

梃杖(ㄊㄧㄥˇ ㄓㄤˋ)
a club; a stick

【梅】 2458
ㄇㄟˊ mei méi
1. plums; prunes
2. a Chinese family name

梅妃(ㄇㄟˊ ㄈㄟ)
a concubine of Emperor Ming of the Tang Dynasty, so called because she loved plum blossoms

梅毒(ㄇㄟˊ ㄉㄨˊ)
syphilis

梅毒菌(ㄇㄟˊ ㄉㄨˊ ㄐㄩㄣˋ)

the spirochete which causes syphilis

梅特涅(ㄇㄟˊ ㄊㄜˋ ㄋㄧㄝˋ)
Prince Klemens Wenzel Metternich, 1773-1859, Austrian prime minister

梅林止渴(ㄇㄟˊ ㄌㄧㄣˊ ㄓˇ ㄎㄜˇ)
When one visits the orchard of plums, he never feels thirsty.

梅花(ㄇㄟˊ ㄏㄨㄚ)
① a plum blossom ② a wintersweet

梅花大鼓(ㄇㄟˊ ㄏㄨㄚ ㄉㄚˋ ㄍㄨˇ)
a kind of storytelling by singing to the accompaniment of a drum and various stringed instruments

梅花鹿(ㄇㄟˊ ㄏㄨㄚ ㄌㄨˋ)
a sika deer; a spotted deer; a kind of deer with white spots

梅花雀(ㄇㄟˊ ㄏㄨㄚ ㄑㄩㄝˋ)
an avadavat

梅紅(ㄇㄟˊ ㄏㄨㄥˊ)
a light red color

梅妻鶴子(ㄇㄟˊ ㄑㄧ ㄏㄜˋ ㄗˇ)
the story of Lin Pu (林逋), who took plum trees as his wife and cranes for children —the life of a hermit

梅縣(ㄇㄟˊ ㄒㄧㄢˋ)
name of a county in Kwangtung Province, home of the Hakkas

梅香(ㄇㄟˊ ㄒㄧㄤ)
a name usually given to a maid or slave-girl in former times, now used as a synonym for a maid servant

梅子(ㄇㄟˊ ˙ㄗ)
plums: 我喜歡梅子勝於桃子。I like plums better than peaches.

梅雨(ㄇㄟˊ ㄩˇ)
the rainy season in early summer when plums are ripening

梅月(ㄇㄟˊ ㄩㄝˋ)
the fourth month of the lunar year

【梓】 2459 ㄗˇ tzyy zǐ

1. *Catalpa ovata,* a tall, stately tree with palm-shaped leaves and yellow flowers in summer
2. one's native place or hometown
3. to make furniture; furniture
4. to carve words on a woodboard; printing blocks: 他最近的著作已付梓。His latest work has been sent to the printers.
5. (now rarely) a Chinese family name

梓里(ㄗˇ ㄌㄧˇ)
one's native place or hometown

梓宮(ㄗˇ ㄍㄨㄥ)
the coffin for an emperor

梓匠輪輿(ㄗˇ ㄐㄧㄤˋ ㄌㄨㄣˊ ㄩˊ)
carpenters and wheelwrights

梓器(ㄗˇ ㄑㄧˋ)
a coffin

梓人(ㄗˇ ㄖㄣˊ)
a carpenter; a wood engraver; a builder; an architect

【梏】 2460 1. ㄍㄨˋ guh gù

1. hand-shackles; handcuffs; manacles
2. to detain; to imprison

梏亡(ㄍㄨˋ ㄨㄤˊ)
to be fettered in mind by greed

【梏】 2460 2. ㄐㄩㄝˊ jyue jué

1. great
2. straightforward; upright

【梔】 2461 (栀) ㄓ jy zhī

a gardenia

梔子(ㄓ ˙ㄗ)
a gardenia

梔子花(ㄓ ˙ㄗ ㄏㄨㄚ)
Cape jasmine

【梗】 2462 ㄍㄥˇ geeng gěng

1. the branch or stem of a plant
2. to prick or pierce with a thorn; thorny
3. an outline; a synopsis; a summary
4. to block; to obstruct: 他從中作梗。He placed obstacles in the way.
5. stubborn; stiff
6. fierce and fearless
7. an ailment; bane; distress
8. to straighten: 他梗着脖子。He straightened up his neck.
9. honest; straight

梗概(ㄍㄥˇ ㄍㄞˋ)
an outline; a summary; a synopsis

梗化(ㄍㄥˇ ㄏㄨㄚˋ)
to obstruct education; to hinder cultural development

梗直(ㄍㄥˇ ㄓˊ)
straight and honest; outspoken

梗阻(ㄍㄥˇ ㄗㄨˇ)
to block; to obstruct; to hamper: 他梗阻我們的計劃。He obstructed our plan.

梗塞(ㄍㄥˇ ㄙㄜˋ)
to obstruct; to block

梗礙(ㄍㄥˇ ㄞˋ)
to obstruct: 樹木梗礙了視野。Trees obstructed the view.

梗兒(ㄍㄥˇㄦ)
a stem or branch

【條】 2463 ㄊㄧㄠˊ tyau tiáo

1. an article, section, clause, etc. of an agreement, pact, treaty, law, etc.
2. in good order; (to present) one by one
3. a numerary adjunct for something narrow and long, as roads, fish, ropes, dogs, snakes, etc.
4. stripes

條碼(ㄊㄧㄠˊ ㄇㄚˇ)
(computers) a bar code

條目(ㄊㄧㄠˊ ㄇㄨˋ)
clauses or articles of an agreement, etc.; particulars or details

條分縷析(ㄊㄧㄠˊ ㄈㄣ ㄌㄩˇ ㄒㄧ)
to analyze to the last detail; detailed presentation

條幅(ㄊㄧㄠˊ ㄈㄨˊ)
a vertical hanging scroll of calligraphy or painting

條達(ㄊㄧㄠˊ ㄉㄚˊ)
① reasonable; logical; orderly ② a bracelet

條對(ㄊㄧㄠˊ ㄉㄨㄟˋ)
to give answers to every question asked

條頓(ㄊㄧㄠˊ ㄉㄨㄣˋ)
the Teutons

條條(ㄊㄧㄠˊ ㄊㄧㄠˊ)
in good order; reasonable; logical

條條大道通羅馬(ㄊㄧㄠˊ ㄊㄧㄠˊ ㄉㄚˋ ㄉㄠˋ ㄊㄨㄥ ㄌㄨㄛˊ ㄇㄚˇ)

Every road leads to Rome.
條理(ㄊㄧㄠˊ ㄌㄧˇ)
①reasonable; logical ② orderly; (to present) in good order; methodical: 他的文章條理清楚。His articles are well-organized.
條理井然(ㄊㄧㄠˊ ㄌㄧˇ ㄐㄧㄥˇ ㄖㄢˊ)
in good order and with good reasoning
條例(ㄊㄧㄠˊ ㄌㄧˋ)
rules, regulations, or laws
條列(ㄊㄧㄠˊ ㄌㄧㄝˋ)
to list item by item
條規(ㄊㄧㄠˊ ㄍㄨㄟ)
rules and regulations: 遵守這遊戲的條規。Obey the rules and regulations of the game.
條貫(ㄊㄧㄠˊ ㄍㄨㄢˋ)
to present reasons, analyses, etc. in good order and with logic
條款(ㄊㄧㄠˊ ㄎㄨㄢˇ)
an article of laws; a section, chapter, or clause of agreements, regulations, provisions, etc.
條件(ㄊㄧㄠˊ ㄐㄧㄢˋ)
① conditions; conditional; terms: 才能與努力是成功的條件。Ability and effort are conditions of success. ② articles, clauses, etc. in an agreement, etc.
條件句(ㄊㄧㄠˊ ㄐㄧㄢˋ ㄐㄩˋ)
(grammar) a conditional clause
條陳(ㄊㄧㄠˊ ㄔㄣˊ)
① to present item by item ② such a written presentation
條暢 or 條鬯(ㄊㄧㄠˊ ㄔㄤˋ)
clear and smooth (writing, etc.)
條子(ㄊㄧㄠˊ ·ㄗ)
① a short letter; a note ② an order; a memo (often from a superior): 我們老板給我們下條子。Our boss gave us a written order. ③ a summons for prostitutes
條案(ㄊㄧㄠˊ ㄢˋ)
a long and narrow table
條文(ㄊㄧㄠˊ ㄨㄣˊ)
the text of a treaty, regulation, law, etc.
條紋(ㄊㄧㄠˊ ㄨㄣˊ)
stripes; streaks; the grain (of wood)
條約(ㄊㄧㄠˊ ㄩㄝ)
a treaty (between nations)
條約港(ㄊㄧㄠˊ ㄩㄝ ㄍㄤˇ)
a treaty port
條約國(ㄊㄧㄠˊ ㄩㄝ ㄍㄨㄛˊ)
Treaty Powers

【梟】2464
ㄒㄧㄠ shiau xiāo

1. an owl; a legendary bird said to eat its own mother
2. a smuggler of contraband, narcotics, etc.
3. brave and unscrupulous

梟哺(ㄒㄧㄠ ㄅㄨˇ)
a reformed son
梟匪(ㄒㄧㄠ ㄈㄟˇ) or 梟販(ㄒㄧㄠ ㄈㄢˋ)
smugglers of contraband, narcotics, etc.
梟鳥(ㄒㄧㄠ ㄋㄧㄠˇ)
an owl
梟亂(ㄒㄧㄠ ㄌㄨㄢˋ)
to confuse; to cause turmoil
梟騎(ㄒㄧㄠ ㄐㄧˋ)
élite cavalry units: 梟騎騎馬進入市區。The élite cavalry rode into the city.
梟將(ㄒㄧㄠ ㄐㄧㄤˋ)
a brave leader of troops; a brave general: 他是一員梟將。He was a brave general.
梟獍(ㄒㄧㄠ ㄐㄧㄥˋ)
(literally) the mother-eater and the father-eater—disobedient children; ungrateful persons
梟雄(ㄒㄧㄠ ㄒㄩㄥˊ)
an unscrupulous, brave and capable person; a fierce, ambitious man: 他是一代梟雄。He was a fierce and ambitious person in his time.
梟示(ㄒㄧㄠ ㄕˋ)
to display the head of a decapitated person (as a warning to others)
梟首(ㄒㄧㄠ ㄕㄡˇ)
to decapitate a person and hang his head on a pole

【梵】2465
ㄈㄢˋ fann fàn

1. clean and pure
2. Sanskrit
3. a Brahman
4. anything pertaining to Buddhism

梵唄(ㄈㄢˋ ㄅㄞˋ)
Buddhist chanting of prayers
梵諦岡(ㄈㄢˋ ㄉㄧˋ ㄍㄤ)
the Vatican
梵諦岡城(ㄈㄢˋ ㄉㄧˋ ㄍㄤ ㄔㄥˊ)
the Vatican City
梵宮(ㄈㄢˋ ㄍㄨㄥ)
a Buddhist temple
梵學(ㄈㄢˋ ㄒㄩㄝˊ)
Buddhism (as a kind of learning)
梵衆(ㄈㄢˋ ㄓㄨㄥˋ)
Buddhist monks
梵剎(ㄈㄢˋ ㄔㄚˋ)
a Buddhist temple: 我們參觀了一座梵剎。We visited a Buddhist temple.
梵唱(ㄈㄢˋ ㄔㄤˋ)
Buddhist chanting
梵師(ㄈㄢˋ ㄕ)
a salutation for a Buddhist monk
梵書(ㄈㄢˋ ㄕㄨ)
① Buddhist scriptures ② the Sanskrit
梵字(ㄈㄢˋ ㄗˋ)
the written Sanskrit
梵音(ㄈㄢˋ ㄧㄣ)
the chanting of the Buddhist scriptures
梵文(ㄈㄢˋ ㄨㄣˊ)
the written Sanskrit
梵宇(ㄈㄢˋ ㄩˇ)
a Buddhist temple
梵語(ㄈㄢˋ ㄩˇ)
the spoken Sanskrit

【梯】2466
ㄊㄧ ti tī

1. a ladder; steps; stairs: 這段短樓梯通到二樓。The short stair leads to the second floor.
2. something to lean or depend on
3. terraced
4. private; intimate
5. a phase (in the induction of military draftees)

梯隊(ㄊㄧ ㄉㄨㄟˋ)
echelon formation; echelon
梯田(ㄊㄧ ㄊㄧㄢˊ)
terraced paddies on a slope
梯級(ㄊㄧ ㄐㄧˊ)
a stair; a step
梯己(ㄊㄧ ·ㄐㄧ)
① private property that is not known to others ② close

〔木部〕

and intimate conversations or persons 亦作「體己」
梯階(ㄊㄧ ㄐㄧㄝ)
①steps of a ladder ②keys to accomplish something; means to achieve a result
梯形(ㄊㄧ ㄒㄧㄥˊ)
①(geometry) trapezoid ②a flat raised piece of land in gardens
梯山航海(ㄊㄧ ㄕㄢ ㄏㄤˊ ㄏㄞˇ)
scaling mountains and crossing seas—to travel along a long and difficult road 亦作「梯航」
梯子(ㄊㄧ ·ㄗ)
a ladder or steps; a stepladder
梯次(ㄊㄧ ㄘˋ)
phases (in the induction of military draftees)

【械】 2467 ㄒㄧㄝˋ shieh xiè (又讀 ㄐㄧㄝˋ jieh jiè)
1. weapons
2. implements; machinery; machines
3. shackles; fetters
4. to arrest and put in prison
械鬥(ㄒㄧㄝˋ ㄉㄡˋ)
(said of mobs or gangsters) to fight with arms or implements; to fight with weapons between groups of people
械彈(ㄒㄧㄝˋ ㄉㄢˋ)
weapons and ammunition
械繫(ㄒㄧㄝˋ ㄒㄧˋ)
to shackle a prisoner
械用(ㄒㄧㄝˋ ㄩㄥˋ)
implements

【棁】 2468 ㄓㄨㄛˊ jwo zhuó
1. a joist
2. a club or cane

【梠】 2469 ㄌㄩˇ leu lǔ
a small beam supporting the rafters at the eaves

【梢】 2470 ㄕㄠ shau shāo
1. the tip of a branch or things of similar shape
2. the end of something—the result, etc.
3. the rudder
4. (now rarely) the sound of wind
梢婆(ㄕㄠ ㄆㄛˊ)
a boatwoman
梢末(ㄕㄠ ㄇㄛˋ)
the extreme end of a thing
梢頭(ㄕㄠ ㄊㄡˊ)
①the tip of a tree: 一隻鳥棲在樹梢頭。A bird perched on the tip of a tree. ②the close of spring
梢公 or 艄公(ㄕㄠ ㄍㄨㄥ)
a helmsman; a boatman; a rudder: 梢公帶旅客過渡頭。The boat rudder rowed the travelers over the ferry.
梢長大漢(ㄕㄠ ㄔㄤˊ ㄉㄚˋ ㄏㄢˋ)
a tall and big fellow
梢子(ㄕㄠ ·ㄗ)or 梢兒(ㄕㄠㄦ)
①the tip of a branch or anything of similar shape ②a boatman ③short pants

【梭】 2471 ㄙㄨㄛ suo suō
1. a weaver's shuttle
2. to move to and fro; to shuttle: 飛機穿梭於波士頓與紐約之間。The airplane shuttles from Boston to New York.
3. swift
梭哈(ㄙㄨㄛ ·ㄏㄚ)
a kind of card game
梭巡(ㄙㄨㄛ ㄒㄩㄣˊ)
to patrol to and fro
梭子(ㄙㄨㄛ ·ㄗ)
a weaver's shuttle

【梆】 2472 ㄅㄤ bang bāng
a watchman's rattle made of wood or bamboo
梆子(ㄅㄤ ·ㄗ)
①a watchman's rattle ②a kind of Chinese opera originated in Shensi (陝西)
梆子腔(ㄅㄤ ·ㄗ ㄑㄧㄤ)
a type of Chinese opera originated in Shensi (陝西)

【梳】 2473 (梳) ㄕㄨ shu shū
1. a comb; a coarse comb
2. to comb: 他用手指頭梳他紅而長的鬍子。He was combing his fingers through his long red beard.
梳篦(ㄕㄨ ㄅㄧˋ)
to dress up one's hair
梳頭(ㄕㄨ ㄊㄡˊ)
to comb one's hair
梳理(ㄕㄨ ㄌㄧˇ)
①(textile) carding ②combing
梳攏(ㄕㄨ ·ㄌㄨㄥ)
(said of a maiden sold to a whorehouse) to receive patron for the first time
梳裹(ㄕㄨ ㄍㄨㄛˇ)
(formerly) to comb the hair and bind the feet (referring to women's small feet)
梳洗(ㄕㄨ ㄒㄧˇ)
to comb one's hair and wash up
梳粧(ㄕㄨ ㄓㄨㄤ)
(said of a woman) to doll up; to dress and make up
梳粧打扮(ㄕㄨ ㄓㄨㄤ ㄉㄚˇ ㄅㄢˋ)
to dress smartly; to be dressed up
梳粧臺(ㄕㄨ ㄓㄨㄤ ㄊㄞˊ)
a dressing table where cosmetics, toilet requisites, etc. are laid out for use
梳齒(ㄕㄨ ㄔˇ)
the teeth of a comb
梳子(ㄕㄨ ·ㄗ)or 梳兒(ㄕㄨㄦ)
a comb

【桿】 2474 ㄍㄢˇ gaan gǎn
a wooden pole, cane, stick, or club
桿撥(ㄍㄢˇ ㄅㄛ)
a thin piece of wood for plucking a *pi-pa* (琵琶) or a Chinese moon guitar (月琴), now fingers are used instead
桿棒(ㄍㄢˇ ㄅㄤˋ)
a club used as a weapon in ancient warfare
桿弟(ㄍㄢˇ ㄉㄧˋ)
a caddy; a caddie
桿菌(ㄍㄢˇ ㄐㄩㄣˋ)or 桿狀菌(ㄍㄢˇ ㄓㄨㄤˋ ㄐㄩㄣˋ)
a bacillus; bacilli
桿子(ㄍㄢˇ ·ㄗ)
a club; a stick

八畫

【梨】 2475 (棃) ㄌㄧˊ li lí
1. a pear
2. Chinese opera
梨頭(ㄌㄧˊ ㄊㄡˊ)
a variety of small pear
梨乾兒(ㄌㄧˊ ㄍㄚㄦ)
dried pears

梨膏(ㄌㄧˊ ㄍㄠ)
a heavy syrup of pear juice and honey

梨糕(ㄌㄧˊ ㄍㄠ)
hard candy with malt sugar and sesame as main ingredients

梨果(ㄌㄧˊ ㄍㄨㄛˇ)
(botany) pome

梨花大鼓(ㄌㄧˊ ㄏㄨㄚ ㄉㄚˋ ㄍㄨˇ)
a type of folksong in Shantung Province, usually accompanied by a drum and two brass pieces to punctuate the narrative song

梨花簡(ㄌㄧˊ ㄏㄨㄚ ㄐㄧㄢˇ)
the crescent brass pieces used in 梨花大鼓

梨花槍(ㄌㄧˊ ㄏㄨㄚ ㄑㄧㄤ)
a set of combat techniques featuring the use of spear in ancient China

梨樹(ㄌㄧˊ ㄕㄨˋ)
the pear tree

梨棗(ㄌㄧˊ ㄗㄠˇ)
the pear and the date, whose wood is used for cutting printing blocks; printing blocks

梨兒(ㄌㄧㄜˊㄦ)
pears

梨渦(ㄌㄧˊ ㄨㄛ)
dimples: 這個美麗的女子兩頰都有梨渦。This pretty girl has dimples on her cheeks.

梨園(ㄌㄧˊ ㄩㄢˊ)
the operatic circle

梨園子弟(ㄌㄧˊ ㄩㄢˊ ㄗˇ ㄉㄧˋ)
operatic players

【棄】 2476
(弃) ㄑㄧˋ chih qì

1. to discard; to cast aside
2. to reject; to abandon; to desert; to forsake: 他放棄運動研究醫學。He forsook sports to study medicine.
3. to forget
4. to throw away one's own life

棄背(ㄑㄧˋ ㄅㄟˋ)
the death of one's parents; to suffer loss of one's parents

棄婦(ㄑㄧˋ ㄈㄨˋ)
a woman who is divorced or deserted by her husband

棄短取長(ㄑㄧˋ ㄉㄨㄢˇ ㄑㄩˇ ㄔㄤˊ)
to eliminate the defects or shortcomings and adopt the good points of others

棄官(ㄑㄧˋ ㄍㄨㄢ)
to give up one's office; to abandon official life

棄甲曳兵(ㄑㄧˋ ㄐㄧㄚˇ ㄧˋ ㄅㄧㄥ)
(said of military troops) to be totally defeated; to throw away their armor and trail their weapons behind them

棄舊迎新(ㄑㄧˋ ㄐㄧㄡˋ ㄧㄥˊ ㄒㄧㄣ)
to reject the old and welcome the new—as in the case of taking a second wife

棄井(ㄑㄧˋ ㄐㄧㄥˇ)
(literally) to stop the digging of a well before water is reached—all the past accomplishments coming to naught

棄捐(ㄑㄧˋ ㄐㄩㄢ)
to cast aside; to reject; to abandon; to fall out of favor; to be neglected

棄妻(ㄑㄧˋ ㄑㄧ)
① a woman divorced by her husband ②(formerly) to divorce one's wife

棄權(ㄑㄧˋ ㄑㄩㄢˊ)
(in voting) to abstain; to waive a right; a waiver

棄邪歸正(ㄑㄧˋ ㄒㄧㄝˊ ㄍㄨㄟ ㄓㄥˋ)
to reject evil ways and start on the right track

棄之可惜(ㄑㄧˋ ㄓ ㄎㄜˇ ㄒㄧ)
It is a waste to discard it.

棄之如敝屣(ㄑㄧˋ ㄓ ㄖㄨˊ ㄅㄧˋ ㄒㄧˇ)
to reject something as if it were worthless

棄職潛逃(ㄑㄧˋ ㄓˊ ㄑㄧㄢˊ ㄊㄠˊ)
to desert one's post and take flight

棄置(ㄑㄧˋ ㄓˋ)
to cast aside

棄世(ㄑㄧˋ ㄕˋ)
① to die ② to lift one's head above ordinary things; to look far and high; to abandon worldly life

棄市(ㄑㄧˋ ㄕˋ)
to be executed; public execution

棄暗投明(ㄑㄧˋ ㄢˋ ㄊㄡˊ ㄇㄧㄥˊ)
(literally) to forsake darkness and come to the light —to renounce a bad cause and join the camp of justice (often used by defectors for self-justification)

棄兒(ㄑㄧˋ ㄦˊ)
an abandoned child; a foundling

棄言(ㄑㄧˋ ㄧㄢˊ)
① to be unable to keep one's promise ② words which have become obsolete and no longer in circulation

棄養(ㄑㄧˋ ㄧㄤˇ)
the death of one's parents

棄嬰(ㄑㄧˋ ㄧㄥ)
an abandoned infant; a foundling

棄物(ㄑㄧˋ ㄨˋ)
trash; discarded useless things

棄文就武(ㄑㄧˋ ㄨㄣˊ ㄐㄧㄡˋ ㄨˇ)
to quit civilian life and join the military

【棉】 2477
ㄇㄧㄢˊ mian mián

cotton: 這件襯衫是棉製品。This shirt is made of cotton.

棉薄 or 緜薄(ㄇㄧㄢˊ ㄅㄛˊ)
meager or trivial: 他靠每月棉薄的薪資過生活。He lives on his meager pay per month.

棉被(ㄇㄧㄢˊ ㄅㄟˋ)
a cotton quilt

棉布(ㄇㄧㄢˊ ㄅㄨˋ)
a cotton cloth

棉袍(ㄇㄧㄢˊ ㄆㄠˊ)
a cotton-wadded long gown

棉毛衫(ㄇㄧㄢˊ ㄇㄠˊ ㄕㄢ)
a cotton sweater or T-shirt; a cotton jersey

棉紡(ㄇㄧㄢˊ ㄈㄤˇ)
cotton spinning

棉紡廠(ㄇㄧㄢˊ ㄈㄤˇ ㄔㄤˇ)
a cotton spinning and weaving mill; a cotton mill

棉套(ㄇㄧㄢˊ ㄊㄠˋ)
a cotton-wadded covering for keeping something warm

棉條(ㄇㄧㄢˊ ㄊㄧㄠˊ)
a sliver

棉田(ㄇㄧㄢˊ ㄊㄧㄢˊ)
cotton fields

棉褲(ㄇㄧㄢˊ ㄎㄨˋ)
cotton-padded trousers

棉花(ㄇㄧㄢˊ ㄏㄨㄚ)
cotton: 他們把棉花紡成紗。They spun cotton into yarn.

棉線(ㄇㄧㄢˊ ㄒㄧㄢˋ)
cotton thread; cotton
棉絮(ㄇㄧㄢˊ ㄒㄩˋ)
fluffed cotton; cotton batting
棉織物(ㄇㄧㄢˊ ㄓ ㄨˋ)or 棉織品(ㄇㄧㄢˊ ㄓ ㄆㄧㄣˇ)
cotton goods or cotton piece goods; cotton textiles; cotton fabrics
棉紙(ㄇㄧㄢˊ ㄓˇ)
a kind of thin and soft paper
棉紗(ㄇㄧㄢˊ ㄕㄚ)
cotton yarn
棉繩(ㄇㄧㄢˊ ㄕㄥˊ)
cotton cord
棉子油(ㄇㄧㄢˊ ㄗˇ ㄧㄡˊ)
cottonseed oil
棉襖(ㄇㄧㄢˊ ㄠˇ)
a cotton-padded Chinese jacket
棉衣(ㄇㄧㄢˊ ㄧ)
cotton clothes: 他花費很多錢在棉衣上。He spends a lot of money on cotton clothes.

【棋】 2478 (棊、碁) ㄑㄧˊ chyi qí
1. any piece used in the game of chess
2. chess or other similar games
棋卜(ㄑㄧˊ ㄅㄨˇ)
to divine with chess
棋布(ㄑㄧˊ ㄅㄨˋ)
to spread out (something) in great numbers like stones or chessmen on a chessboard
棋盤(ㄑㄧˊ ㄆㄢˊ)or 棋枰(ㄑㄧˊ ㄆㄧㄥˊ)
a chessboard
棋品(ㄑㄧˊ ㄆㄧㄣˇ)
one's demeanor while playing chess; character of a chess player
棋譜(ㄑㄧˊ ㄆㄨˇ)
a manual on chess; a collection of records of famous chess plays between experts, contemporary and ancient
棋迷(ㄑㄧˊ ㄇㄧˊ)
a chess fan; a chess enthusiast
棋逢敵手(ㄑㄧˊ ㄈㄥˊ ㄉㄧˊ ㄕㄡˇ)
a good match; to be well-matched in a contest
棋段(ㄑㄧˊ ㄉㄨㄢˋ)
grades of the skill of chess playing
棋列(ㄑㄧˊ ㄌㄧㄝˋ)
to spread out (something) in great numbers like stones or chessmen on a chessboard
棋格(ㄑㄧˊ ㄍㄜˊ)
one's rating in chess-playing skill
棋高一著(ㄑㄧˊ ㄍㄠ ㄧˋ ㄓㄠ)
to be superior in intelligence, stratagem, skill, etc. than one's opponent
棋局(ㄑㄧˊ ㄐㄩˊ)
① the chessboard with the pieces arranged ② a game of chess
棋峙(ㄑㄧˊ ㄓˋ)
(said of partitioning of land by warlords, etc.) to exist side by side; to confront each other; to match in power as rivals (as in the Epoch of the Three Kingdoms)
棋戰(ㄑㄧˊ ㄓㄢˋ)
to fight it out in chess; a game of chess
棋士(ㄑㄧˊ ㄕˋ)
a professional chess player
棋手(ㄑㄧˊ ㄕㄡˇ)
a high-graded chess player
棋聖(ㄑㄧˊ ㄕㄥˋ)
an expert among chess experts; a national champion at chess
棋子(ㄑㄧˊ ㄗˇ)
chess pieces
棋子兒(ㄑㄧˊ ㄗㄜˇㄦ)
chessmen; stones (in *go* game)
棋王(ㄑㄧˊ ㄨㄤˊ)
a chess champion

【棍】 2479 ㄍㄨㄣˋ guenn gùn
1. a club; a stick; a cudgel; a truncheon
2. a rascal; a villain; a ruffian: 他被一群惡棍攻擊。He was attacked by a band of ruffians.
棍棒(ㄍㄨㄣˋ ㄅㄤˋ)
clubs; sticks: 他用棍棒打人。He beat the man with a stick.
棍騙(ㄍㄨㄣˋ ㄆㄧㄢˋ)
to swindle; to cheat; to wheedle
棍徒(ㄍㄨㄣˋ ㄊㄨˊ)
rascals, villains, ruffians, rowdies, etc.
棍子(ㄍㄨㄣˋ ·ㄗ)or 棍兒(ㄍㄨㄜˋㄦ)
① a club, stick, cudgel, etc. ② (when preceded by a noun, as party, information, etc.) an unprincipled small fry; a paw

【棒】 2480 ㄅㄤˋ banq bàng
1. a club; a stick; a truncheon
2. to hit with a club
3. good; strong; wonderful: 她字寫得眞棒。She writes a good hand.
棒棒糖(ㄅㄤˋ ·ㄅㄤ ㄊㄤˊ)
a lollipop
棒棒雞(ㄅㄤˋ ·ㄅㄤ ㄐㄧ)
boneless chicken with heavy seasoning (a specialty in Szechwan restaurants)
棒冰(ㄅㄤˋ ㄅㄧㄥ)
an ice-cream stick, usually a sherbet stick
棒打薄情郎(ㄅㄤˋ ㄉㄚˇ ㄅㄛˊ ㄑㄧㄥˊ ㄌㄤˊ)
to hit a fickle male lover with a club
棒頭出孝子(ㄅㄤˋ ㄊㄡˊ ㄔㄨ ㄒㄧㄠˋ ㄗˇ)
(a Chinese saying) Dutiful sons are the products of the rod.—Children must be disciplined whenever necessary. 或 Parents must be very severe while educating their children.
棒喝(ㄅㄤˋ ㄏㄜˋ)
① to bang and bawl in rebuke of a student ② to arouse a person from his evil ways—as if by using a club: 給他來個當頭棒喝。Let's give him a direct sharp warning.
棒喝團(ㄅㄤˋ ㄏㄜˋ ㄊㄨㄢˊ)
another name for Fascisti, an Italian political organization (1919 to 1943) founded by Benito Mussolini
棒球(ㄅㄤˋ ㄑㄧㄡˊ)
baseball: 棒球是美國全國性的運動。Baseball is the national game of the U.S.A.
棒球場(ㄅㄤˋ ㄑㄧㄡˊ ㄔㄤˇ)or(ㄅㄤˋ ㄑㄧㄡˊ ㄔㄤˊ)
a baseball diamond; a baseball stadium

棒杵(ㄅㄤˋ ㄔㄨˇ)or 棒槌(ㄅㄤˋ ㄔㄨㄟˊ)
a club used to pound clothes
棒瘡(ㄅㄤˋ ㄔㄨㄤ)
inflammations, lesions, etc. as a result of punishment by caning
棒子(ㄅㄤˋ ·ㄗ)
① a short and thick club: 他用棒子打我。He hit me with a club. ② Indian corn
棒子麵兒(ㄅㄤˋ ·ㄗ ㄇㄧㄚˋㄦ)
cornmeal 亦作「玉米麵」

【棗】 2481 ㄗㄠˇ tzao zǎo
1. jujube (*Zizyphus vulgaris*), commonly called date
2. a Chinese family name
棗木(ㄗㄠˇ ㄇㄨˋ)
jujube (trees)
棗脯(ㄗㄠˇ ㄈㄨˇ)
dried dates preserved in honey; dried dates
棗泥(ㄗㄠˇ ㄋㄧˊ)
jujube paste, used as stuffing for pastry or dumplings
棗(兒)糕(ㄗㄠˇ(ㄦ) ㄍㄠ)
date-dumplings; steamed cake with dates
棗核兒(ㄗㄠˇ ㄏㄜˊㄦ)
date stones
棗樹(ㄗㄠˇ ㄕㄨˋ)
a jujube tree
棗仁(ㄗㄠˇ ㄖㄣˊ)
kernels of the date
棗子(ㄗㄠˇ ·ㄗ)or 棗兒(ㄗㄠˇㄦ)
dates

【棘】 2482 ㄐㄧˊ jyi jí
1. buckthorns; thorny brambles: 小心那荆棘叢。Be careful of that thorn bush.
2. urgent
3. a Chinese family name
棘皮動物(ㄐㄧˊ ㄆㄧˊ ㄉㄨㄥˋ ㄨˋ)
an echinoderm
棘林(ㄐㄧˊ ㄌㄧㄣˊ)
a forest of buckthorns, brambles, etc.
棘卿(ㄐㄧˊ ㄑㄧㄥ)
(in ancient China) the president of the Supreme Court
棘心(ㄐㄧˊ ㄒㄧㄣ)
a term of self-reference for a son when speaking of his parents
棘針(ㄐㄧˊ ㄓㄣ)
buckthorns
棘楚(ㄐㄧˊ ㄔㄨˇ)
troubles; problems; thorns
棘手(ㄐㄧˊ ㄕㄡˇ)
thorny (matters); difficult to handle
棘人(ㄐㄧˊ ㄖㄣˊ)
a term of self-reference during the mourning period for one's parent
棘闈(ㄐㄧˊ ㄨㄟˊ)or 棘院(ㄐㄧˊ ㄩㄢˋ)
the examination hall in old China—the surrounding walls were covered with thorns

【棖】 2483 ㄔㄥˊ cherng chéng
1. doorposts
2. to stop
3. to touch
4. a Chinese family name
棖撥(ㄔㄥˊ ㄅㄛ)
to push aside
棖觸(ㄔㄥˊ ㄔㄨˋ)
① to be sentimentally moved or touched ② to touch with one's hand

【棧】 2484 ㄓㄢˋ jann zhàn
1. a storehouse; a warehouse: 他把商品儲存於貨棧中。He stored the goods in the warehouse.
2. a tavern; an inn
3. a road made along a cliff
4. (now rarely) a pen or stable
5. a Chinese family name
棧房(ㄓㄢˋ ㄈㄤˊ)
①a storehouse; a warehouse; a godown②a tavern; an inn
棧道(ㄓㄢˋ ㄉㄠˋ)or 棧閣(ㄓㄢˋ ㄍㄜˊ)
a log-formed road along a steep cliff
棧單(ㄓㄢˋ ㄉㄢ)
a warrant (a receipt for goods in storage)
棧橋(ㄓㄢˋ ㄑㄧㄠˊ)
a pier for loading and unloading purposes; a landing pier

【棟】 2485 ㄉㄨㄥˋ donq dòng
the main beam of a house
棟梁 or 棟樑(ㄉㄨㄥˋ ㄌㄧㄤˊ)
① the ridgepole and beams ②(figuratively) a man of great ability 參看「棟樑之才」
棟梁之器 or 棟樑之器(ㄉㄨㄥˋ ㄌㄧㄤˊ ㄓ ㄑㄧˋ)
a man of great ability and tremendous promise
棟梁之才 or 棟樑之才(ㄉㄨㄥˋ ㄌㄧㄤˊ ㄓ ㄘㄞˊ)
a man of tremendous promise; a man of great statesmanship
棟折榱崩(ㄉㄨㄥˋ ㄓㄜˊ ㄘㄨㄟ ㄅㄥ)
(literally) The beams are broken and rafters destroyed.—The state is falling apart.
棟宇(ㄉㄨㄥˋ ㄩˇ)
a house

【棚】 2486 ㄆㄥˊ perng péng
a tent; a shed; an awning; a mat awning
棚鋪(ㄆㄥˊ ㄆㄨˋ)
a tent shop
棚戶(ㄆㄥˊ ㄏㄨˋ)
(literally) people who live in tents—refugees or poor families; squatters; slum dwellers
棚匠(ㄆㄥˊ ㄐㄧㄤˋ)
a person who erects tents or mat awnings as a profession
棚車(ㄆㄥˊ ㄔㄜ)
a covered cart (usually with canvas, etc.); a wagon (used by early Americans in their travel to the West)
棚子(ㄆㄥˊ ·ㄗ)or 棚兒(ㄆㄥˊㄦ)
a small tent; a shed

【棣】 2487 ㄉㄧˋ dih dì
1. a mountain tree, as a cherry, etc.
2. same as 弟—a kid brother
3. a Chinese family name
棣棠(ㄉㄧˋ ㄊㄤˊ)
a shrub with yellow flowers (*Kerria japonica*)
棣華(ㄉㄧˋ ㄏㄨㄚˊ)
brothers
棣鄂 or 棣萼(ㄉㄧˋ ㄜˋ)
love between brothers; fraternity

【棠】 2488 ㄊㄤˊ tarng táng
the sweet pear tree; the wild plum
棠棣(ㄊㄤˊ ㄉㄧˋ)
① *Prunus japonica,* the wild plum ② brothers

【棨】 2489 ㄑㄧˇ chii qǐ

(in ancient China) a tally or wooden pass used by a messenger as his credentials in passing through a guarded gate, checkpoint, etc.
棨戟(ㄑㄧˇ ㄐㄧˇ)
(in ancient China) a black cloth draped over a spear used to herald the arrival of an official so that people will step aside to let him pass

【棻】 2490
ㄈㄣ fen fēn
a kind of fragrant tree used to produce perfume by burning it

【棐】 2491
ㄈㄟˇ feei fěi
1. a species of yew found in North China
2. bamboo products
3. to assist

【棼】 2492
ㄈㄣˊ fern fén
1. beams on the roof of a house
2. a kind of linen
3. confused; disarrayed; disordered
棼亂(ㄈㄣˊ ㄌㄨㄢˋ)
in confusion

【森】 2493
ㄙㄣ sen sēn
1. luxuriant vegetation or luxuriant growth of trees
2. dark and obscure; severe
3. serene; majestic
森巴舞(ㄙㄣ ㄅㄚ ㄨˇ)
samba, a ballroom dance that originated in Brazil
森列(ㄙㄣ ㄌㄧㄝˋ)
(said of mountain peaks) rising in ranks
森林(ㄙㄣ ㄌㄧㄣˊ)
forest
森林資源(ㄙㄣ ㄌㄧㄣˊ ㄗ ㄩㄢˊ)
forest reserves
森林浴(ㄙㄣ ㄌㄧㄣˊ ㄩˋ)
a green shower
森羅殿(ㄙㄣ ㄌㄨㄛˊ ㄉㄧㄢˋ)
(in Chinese mythology) the palace of the ruler of the underworld; the palace of the King of Hell
森羅萬象(ㄙㄣ ㄌㄨㄛˊ ㄨㄢˋ ㄒㄧㄤˋ)
the phenomena of the universe
森豎(ㄙㄣ ㄕㄨˋ)
one's hair standing on end —for fear
森然(ㄙㄣ ㄖㄢˊ)
①(said of tall trees) dense; thick: 那公園林木森然。The park is thickly wooded with tall trees. ② awe-inspiring; trembling
森森(ㄙㄣ ㄙㄣ)
①luxuriant growth of vegetation; dense; thick ②trembling; fearful; dark: 鬧鬼的古堡陰森森的。The haunted castle was very dark.
森聳(ㄙㄣ ㄙㄨㄥˇ)
to rise high and majestic
森嚴(ㄙㄣ ㄧㄢˊ)
stern and severe; forbidden (looks); awe-inspiring
森衛(ㄙㄣ ㄨㄟˋ)
closely guarded
森鬱(ㄙㄣ ㄩˋ)
thickly overgrown; dense

【椒】 2494
ㄐㄧㄠ jiau jiāo
1. pepper: 在菜裡加點胡椒。Add some pepper to the dish.
2. mountaintops
椒餅(ㄐㄧㄠ ㄅㄧㄥˇ)
pepper cake
椒目(ㄐㄧㄠ ㄇㄨˋ)
the dark seeds of pepper fruit
椒粉(ㄐㄧㄠ ㄈㄣˇ)
pepper
椒房(ㄐㄧㄠ ㄈㄤˊ)or 椒屋(ㄐㄧㄠ ㄨ)or 椒殿(ㄐㄧㄠ ㄉㄧㄢˋ)
the palace of the queen; private apartments of the empress
椒蘭(ㄐㄧㄠ ㄌㄢˊ)
① persons of low moral standing; unprincipled persons ② relatives of the nobility
椒酒(ㄐㄧㄠ ㄐㄧㄡˇ)
wine soaked with pepper which one used to offer his seniors on the Lunar New Year's Day in former times
椒鹽(ㄐㄧㄠ ㄧㄢˊ)
a condiment made of powdered roast prickly ash and salt

【棫】 2495
ㄩˋ yuh yù
a thorny shrub with yellow flowers and dark fruit
棫樸(ㄩˋ ㄆㄨˊ)
① the title of a poem in *The Book of Poetry* ② a multitude of talented persons ③ names of two kinds of trees —*yü* and *pu*

【棬】 2496
ㄑㄩㄢ chiuan quān
a wooden bowl
棬樞(ㄑㄩㄢ ㄕㄨ)
(literally) a door peg made of warped wood—a very poor family

【棲】 2497
ㄑㄧ chi qī
(又讀 ㄒㄧ shi xī)
1. to rest; to stay; to perch; to settle: 一隻烏鴉棲息在樹頂。A crow perched on the treetop.
2. the place one stays
3. (now rarely) a bed
棲遁 or 棲遯(ㄑㄧ ㄉㄨㄣˋ)
to live in seclusion: 她遠離朋友，過棲遁生活。She lives in seclusion apart from her friends.
棲流所(ㄑㄧ ㄌㄧㄡˊ ㄙㄨㄛˇ)
a refuge for vagrants or the homeless (mostly for women)
棲遑(ㄑㄧ ㄏㄨㄤˊ)
in a hurry; hasty
棲居(ㄑㄧ ㄐㄩ)
to dwell; to live
棲棲(ㄑㄧ ㄑㄧ)
anxious; jittery; jumpy
棲棲遑遑(ㄑㄧ ㄑㄧ ㄏㄨㄤˊ ㄏㄨㄤˊ)
anxious; nervous; jumpy
棲息(ㄑㄧ ㄒㄧˊ)
to rest; to stay; to perch: 有許多麻雀棲息在電線上。A great number of sparrows perched on the wires.
棲止(ㄑㄧ ㄓˇ)
to settle (at a place)
棲遲(ㄑㄧ ㄔˊ)
to sojourn; to travel and rest
棲處
①(ㄑㄧ ㄔㄨˇ) to stay (at a place)
②(ㄑㄧ ㄔㄨˋ) an abode (usually temporarily)
棲身(ㄑㄧ ㄕㄣ)
to live; to stay; to dwell: 這

〔木部〕

些難民無處棲身。These refugees have no place to stay.

棲神(ㄑㄧ ㄕㄣˊ)
(Taoism) a way to discipline one's mind

棲宿(ㄑㄧ ㄙㄨˋ)
to rest or stay for the night

棲泊(ㄒㄧ ㄅㄛˊ)
to come to anchor; to stay temporarily

【棺】 2498 ㄍㄨㄢ guan guān
a coffin (usually made of wood in China)

棺木(ㄍㄨㄢ ㄇㄨˋ)
a coffin 亦作「棺材」: 他們把棺木放進墓穴。They lowered the coffin into the grave.

棺殮(ㄍㄨㄢ ㄌㄧㄢˋ)
① coffin and graveclothes ② to put a shrouded corpse into a coffin

棺蓋(ㄍㄨㄢ ㄍㄞˋ)
the lid of a coffin

棺槨(ㄍㄨㄢ ㄍㄨㄛˇ)
inner and outer coffins in ancient times

棺罩(ㄍㄨㄢ ㄓㄠˋ)
a pall (for covering a coffin)

棺材(ㄍㄨㄢ ˙ㄘㄞ)
a coffin: 他用釘子釘自己的棺材(他自尋滅亡)。He drove a nail into his coffin.

【棵】 2499 ㄎㄜ ke kē
a numerary adjunct for trees: 一棵大樹遮著房子。A large tree shaded the house.

【植】 2500 ㄓˊ jyr zhí
1. to plant; to set up; to erect
2. (now rarely) to lean on
3. plants; vegetation

植病害(ㄓˊ ㄅㄧㄥˋ ㄏㄞˋ)
plant disease

植黨營私(ㄓˊ ㄉㄤˇ ㄧㄥˊ ㄙ)
to form a faction for selfish ends: 他們植黨營私。They form political cliques for the benefit of themselves.

植立(ㄓˊ ㄌㄧˋ)
to set up; to erect

植樹(ㄓˊ ㄕㄨˋ)
to plant trees: 他在花園裡植樹。He planted trees in his garden.

植樹節(ㄓˊ ㄕㄨˋ ㄐㄧㄝˊ)
Arbor Day on March 12, death anniversary of Dr. Sun Yat-sen

植字(ㄓˊ ㄗˋ)
to set type for printing

植字板(ㄓˊ ㄗˋ ㄅㄢˇ)
a printing plate of setting type

植物(ㄓˊ ㄨˋ)
vegetables; plants; flora: 樹是大型植物。Trees are large plants.

植物標本(ㄓˊ ㄨˋ ㄅㄧㄠ ㄅㄣˇ)
a herbarium; a botanical specimen

植物病理學(ㄓˊ ㄨˋ ㄅㄧㄥˋ ㄌㄧˇ ㄒㄩㄝˊ)
phytopathology

植物發育學(ㄓˊ ㄨˋ ㄈㄚ ㄩˋ ㄒㄩㄝˊ)
vegetable embryology

植物分類學(ㄓˊ ㄨˋ ㄈㄣ ㄌㄟˋ ㄒㄩㄝˊ)
classificatory botany

植物化學(ㄓˊ ㄨˋ ㄏㄨㄚˋ ㄒㄩㄝˊ)
phytochemistry

植物界(ㄓˊ ㄨˋ ㄐㄧㄝˋ)
the vegetable kingdom

植物群落(ㄓˊ ㄨˋ ㄑㄩㄣˊ ㄌㄨㄛˋ)
a plant community

植物形態學(ㄓˊ ㄨˋ ㄒㄧㄥˊ ㄊㄞˋ ㄒㄩㄝˊ)
morphological botany

植物學(ㄓˊ ㄨˋ ㄒㄩㄝˊ)
botany: 他研究植物學。He studies botany.

植物學家(ㄓˊ ㄨˋ ㄒㄩㄝˊ ㄐㄧㄚ)
a botanist: 他父親是植物學家。His father was a botanist.

植物生態學(ㄓˊ ㄨˋ ㄕㄥ ㄊㄞˋ ㄒㄩㄝˊ)
plantation ecology; vegetable ecology

植物人(ㄓˊ ㄨˋ ㄖㄣˊ)
a vegetable

植物油(ㄓˊ ㄨˋ ㄧㄡˊ)
vegetable oil

植物岩(ㄓˊ ㄨˋ ㄧㄢˊ)
phytogenic rocks

植物園(ㄓˊ ㄨˋ ㄩㄢˊ)
a botanical garden; an arboretum: 台北有一座植物園。There is an arboretum in Taipei.

【椎】 2501 ㄓㄨㄟ juei zhuī (又讀 ㄔㄨㄟˊ chwei chuí)
1. a hammer; a mallet; a bludgeon; a mace
2. to beat; to hammer; to hit; to strike
3. a vertebra

椎剽(ㄓㄨㄟ ㄆㄧㄠˋ)
to kill a person and rob him

椎埋(ㄓㄨㄟ ㄇㄞˊ)
① to kill someone and bury his body ② to dig graves

椎牛(ㄓㄨㄟ ㄋㄧㄡˊ)
to kill an ox

椎魯(ㄓㄨㄟ ㄌㄨˇ)
dull and stupid

椎輪(ㄓㄨㄟ ㄌㄨㄣˊ)
a wheel without the hub—something at its initial state and leaving much to be desired or done

椎骨(ㄓㄨㄟ ㄍㄨˇ)
a vertebra: 他椎骨痛。He has a pain in his vertebrae.

椎擊(ㄓㄨㄟ ㄐㄧˊ)
to strike with a mallet, hammer, etc.

椎髻(ㄓㄨㄟ ㄐㄧˋ)
(in hairdressing) a tiny bum shaped like a mallet

椎心泣血(ㄓㄨㄟ ㄒㄧㄣ ㄑㄧˋ ㄒㄧㄝˇ)
deep sorrow; extreme grief; excruciating pains

椎殺(ㄓㄨㄟ ㄕㄚ)
to kill with a mallet, hammer, etc.

【棹】 2502 1. (桌) ㄓㄨㄛ juo zhuō
a table

【棹】 2502 2. (櫂) ㄓㄠˋ jaw zhào
1. an oar or scull
2. a boat: 他鼓棹而進。He rowed his boat forward.

【椅】 2503 ㄧˇ yii yǐ
1. a chair; a bench: 他們坐在公園的長椅上。They sat on the bench in the park.
2. *Idesia polycarpa* 即「山桐子」

椅背(ㄧˇ ㄅㄟˋ)
the back of a chair

椅披(ㄧˇ ㄆㄧ)
a colorful silk drapery at the back of a chair

椅墊子(ㄧˇ ㄉㄧㄢˋ ˙ㄗ)
a chair cushion

椅套(ㄧˇ ㄊㄠˋ)
chair covers

椅靠(ㄧˇ ㄎㄠˋ)
the back of a chair 參看「椅背」
椅子(ㄧˇ ·ㄗ)
a chair

【椁】 2504
(槨) ㄍㄨㄛˇ guoo guǒ
an outer coffin

【椏】 2505
ㄧㄚ ia yā
the forking branch of a tree
椏枝(ㄧㄚ ㄓ)
a forking branch

【椓】 2506
ㄓㄨㄛˊ jwo zhuó
1. to strike; to hammer
2. (an ancient punishment) to castrate; castration
3. to slander; to injury

【棕】 2507
(椶) ㄗㄨㄥ tzong zōng
the palm tree
棕綳兒(ㄗㄨㄥ ㄅㄥㄦ)
a wooden frame with stretched coir ropes to be placed on a bedstead
棕毛(ㄗㄨㄥ ㄇㄠˊ)
palm coir or fibers
棕毯(ㄗㄨㄥ ㄊㄢˇ)
coir matting
棕櫚(ㄗㄨㄥ ㄌㄩˊ)or棕櫚樹(ㄗㄨㄥ ㄌㄩˊ ㄕㄨˋ)
the palm tree
棕櫚科(ㄗㄨㄥ ㄌㄩˊ ㄎㄜ)
Palmae
棕竹(ㄗㄨㄥ ㄓㄨˊ)
Rhapis humilis, a variety of black bamboo
棕種(ㄗㄨㄥ ㄓㄨㄥˇ)
the Brown Race
棕繩(ㄗㄨㄥ ㄕㄥˊ)
coir rope
棕樹(ㄗㄨㄥ ㄕㄨˋ)
a palm
棕色(ㄗㄨㄥ ㄙㄜˋ)
brown, the color of palm fibers: 我有一套棕色的衣服。I have a brown suit.
棕簑(ㄗㄨㄥ ㄙㄨㄛ)
a coir rain-cape; a coir raincoat
棕筍(ㄗㄨㄥ ㄙㄨㄣˇ)
clusters of the flower buds of palms

九畫

【椹】 2508
ㄓㄣ jen zhēn
a chopping board; a block
椹板(ㄓㄣ ㄅㄢˇ)
a chopping board
椹質(ㄓㄣ ㄓˊ)
a wooden block used in beheading a death convict

【椳】 2509
ㄨㄟ uei wēi
sockets which hold doors in place

【椷】 2510
1. ㄐㄧㄢ jian jiān
1. a wooden box or chest
2. same as 緘—a letter

【椷】 2510
2. ㄒㄧㄢˊ shyan xián
a goblet

【椽】 2511
ㄔㄨㄢˊ chwan chuán
a beam; a rafter
椽筆(ㄔㄨㄢˊ ㄅㄧˇ)
your masterly writing
椽柱(ㄔㄨㄢˊ ㄓㄨˋ)
a pillar
椽子(ㄔㄨㄢˊ ·ㄗ)
a beam; a rafter

【椰】 2512
ㄧㄝˊ ye yé
a coconut; a coconut palm; a coconut tree
椰乾(ㄧㄝˊ ㄍㄢ)
copra, coppra, coprah, or copperah
椰殼(ㄧㄝˊ ㄎㄜˊ)
a coconut shell
椰肉(ㄧㄝˊ ㄖㄡˋ)
coconut meat: 椰肉用來做蛋糕。The coconut meat is used for making a cake.
椰子(ㄧㄝˊ ·ㄗ)
a coconut
椰菜(ㄧㄝˊ ㄘㄞˋ)
a savoy
椰油(ㄧㄝˊ ㄧㄡˊ)
coconut oil; coconut butter

【椿】 2513
ㄔㄨㄣ chuen chūn
1. one's father
2. *Cedrela sinensis*
椿庭(ㄔㄨㄣ ㄊㄧㄥˊ)
one's father
椿齡(ㄔㄨㄣ ㄌㄧㄥˊ)or 椿壽(ㄔㄨㄣ ㄕㄡˋ)or 椿年(ㄔㄨㄣ ㄋㄧㄢˊ)
venerable age; great age; long life
椿象(ㄔㄨㄣ ㄒㄧㄤˋ)
Aenaria lewisi, a kind of beetle sucking the juice from rice and wheat stalks; a stinkbug; a shieldbug
椿萱(ㄔㄨㄣ ㄒㄩㄢ)
one's parents
椿萱並茂(ㄔㄨㄣ ㄒㄩㄢ ㄅㄧㄥˋ ㄇㄠˋ)
Both parents are alive and well.

【楂】 2514
ㄓㄚ ja zhā
1. a species of hawthorn
2. a wooden raft
楂楂(ㄓㄚ ㄓㄚ)
the sound of magpies crowing

【楓】 2515
ㄈㄥ feng fēng
a maple
楓糖(ㄈㄥ ㄊㄤˊ)
maple sugar
楓橋(ㄈㄥ ㄑㄧㄠˊ)
name of a bridge at Soochow, Kiangsu Province
楓宸(ㄈㄥ ㄔㄣˊ)
an emperor's residence
楓樹(ㄈㄥ ㄕㄨˋ)
a maple: 楓樹到秋天就變紅了。Maples turn red in fall.

【楊】 2516
ㄧㄤˊ yang yáng
1. a poplar
2. a willow
3. a Chinese family name
楊白頭(ㄧㄤˊ ㄅㄞˊ ㄊㄡˊ)
an albino
楊墨(ㄧㄤˊ ㄇㄛˋ)
Yang Chu, an egoist, and Mo Ti, a philanthropist, both were contemporaries of Mencius
楊梅(ㄧㄤˊ ㄇㄟˊ)
(botany) an arbutus
楊梅瘡(ㄧㄤˊ ㄇㄟˊ ㄔㄨㄤ)
syphilis 亦作「梅毒」
楊太眞(ㄧㄤˊ ㄊㄞˋ ㄓㄣ)or楊玉環(ㄧㄤˊ ㄩˋ ㄏㄨㄢˊ)
Yang Yü-huan (719-756), a concubine of Emperor Hsüan Tsung of the Tang Dynasty 亦作「楊貴妃」
楊桃(ㄧㄤˊ ㄊㄠˊ)
a carambola or star fruit
楊柳(ㄧㄤˊ ㄌㄧㄡˇ)
a willow
楊花(ㄧㄤˊ ㄏㄨㄚ)
poplar blossoms; poplar fila-

ments
楊朱(ㄧㄤˊ ㄓㄨ)
Yang Chu, a contemporary of Mencius and advocate of egoism

〔木部〕

【楔】 2517 ㄒㄧㄝˋ shieh xiè
1. to wedge
2. a gatepost
3. a wedge
楔緊(ㄒㄧㄝˋ ㄐㄧㄣˇ)
to wedge it tight
楔形葉(ㄒㄧㄝˋ ㄒㄧㄥˊ ㄧㄝˋ)
a cuneate leaf
楔形文字(ㄒㄧㄝˋ ㄒㄧㄥˊ ㄨㄣˊ ㄗˋ)
cuneiform; sphenogram
楔子(ㄒㄧㄝˋ ·ㄗ)
① a wedge ② a preface; a foreword; a prologue

【楙】 2518 ㄇㄠˋ maw mào
1. (said of vegetation) luxuriant; lush
2. name of a plant

【楛】 2519 1. ㄏㄨˋ huh hù
the arrow-thorn—name of a plant
楛矢(ㄏㄨˋ ㄕˇ)
an arrow with a shaft made of this particular wood

【楛】 2519 2. ㄎㄨˇ kuu kǔ
crude and easy to break

【楞】 2520 1. ㄌㄥˊ leng léng
1. angular
2. an edge
3. Ceylon (used in Buddhist books)
楞伽(ㄌㄥˊ ㄑㄧㄝˊ)
① Lanka, a mountain in the southeast part of Ceylon, now called Adam's Peak ② the island of Ceylon
楞伽經(ㄌㄥˊ ㄑㄧㄝˊ ㄐㄧㄥ)
the *Lankavatara* sutra
楞嚴經(ㄌㄥˊ ㄧㄢˊ ㄐㄧㄥ)
the Surangama sutra

【楞】 2520 2. (愣) ㄌㄥˋ lenq lèng
stupid; imbecile; rude

【楡】 2521 ㄩˊ yu yú
an elm
楡皮(ㄩˊ ㄆㄧˊ)
elm bark (used as medicine)
楡林港(ㄩˊ ㄌㄧㄣˊ ㄍㄤˇ)
Yülin, a seaport on Hainan Island
楡關(ㄩˊ ㄍㄨㄢ)
Elm Pass, another name of Shanhaikwan(山海關), eastern end of the Great Wall
楡科(ㄩˊ ㄎㄜ)
Ulmaceae, the elm family
楡火(ㄩˊ ㄏㄨㄛˇ)
a fire produced by rubbing pieces of elm wood
楡莢(ㄩˊ ㄐㄧㄚˊ)
elm seeds
楡莢雨(ㄩˊ ㄐㄧㄚˊ ㄩˇ)
spring rain
楡錢兒糕(ㄩˊ ㄑㄧㄚˊㄦ ㄍㄠ)
elm-seed cake
楡錢(ㄩˊ ㄑㄧㄢˊ)or 楡錢兒(ㄩˊ ㄑㄧㄚˊㄦ)
elm seeds 參看「楡莢」
楡樹(ㄩˊ ㄕㄨˋ)
an elm; an elm tree
楡塞(ㄩˊ ㄙㄞˋ)
a frontier stronghold

【楝】 2522 ㄌㄧㄢˋ liann liàn
a kind of tree (*Melia azedarach*); chinaberry
楝樹(ㄌㄧㄢˋ ㄕㄨˋ)
chinaberry

【楢】 2523 ㄧㄡˊ you yóu
a kind of tree (*Quercus glandulifera*)

【楰】 2524 ㄩˊ yu yú
Yü (name of a plant)

【楚】 2525 ㄔㄨˇ chuu chǔ
1. name of a powerful feudal state which existed 740-330 B. C.
2. a Chinese family name
3. clear; neat
4. distress; suffering
楚霸王(ㄔㄨˇ ㄅㄚˋ ㄨㄤˊ)
the title adopted by Hsiang Yü(項羽), who overthrew the Chin Dynasty
楚歌(ㄔㄨˇ ㄍㄜ)
the songs of the people of Chu(楚) 參看「四面楚歌」
楚國(ㄔㄨˇ ㄍㄨㄛˊ)
a powerful feudal state that existed 740-330 B. C.
楚館秦樓(ㄔㄨˇ ㄍㄨㄢˇ ㄑㄧㄣˊ ㄌㄡˊ)
places for pleasure; brothels
楚弓楚得(ㄔㄨˇ ㄍㄨㄥ ㄔㄨˇ ㄉㄜˊ)
Loss of a possession within one's own state is no cause for regret because it will come into the possession of a fellow countryman, not of an alien.
楚狂(ㄔㄨˇ ㄎㄨㄤˊ)
a lunatic
楚河漢界(ㄔㄨˇ ㄏㄜˊ ㄏㄢˋ ㄐㄧㄝˋ)
the border of two opposing powers
楚囚(ㄔㄨˇ ㄑㄧㄡˊ)
① a prisoner ② a man in great straits
楚囚對泣(ㄔㄨˇ ㄑㄧㄡˊ ㄉㄨㄟˋ ㄑㄧˋ)
to lament a common misery
楚楚(ㄔㄨˇ ㄔㄨˇ)
① touching; pathetic ② bright and clear ③ tidy; neat
楚楚動人(ㄔㄨˇ ㄔㄨˇ ㄉㄨㄥˋ ㄖㄣˊ)
(said of a young woman) lovingly pathetic; delicate and attractive
楚楚可憐(ㄔㄨˇ ㄔㄨˇ ㄎㄜˇ ㄌㄧㄢˊ)
pathetically delicate; tender and pathetic: 那女孩子楚楚可憐。That girl was delicate and touching.
楚聲(ㄔㄨˇ ㄕㄥ)
the songs of the people of Chu(楚)
楚辭(ㄔㄨˇ ㄘˊ)
a collection of poems compiled by Liu Hsiang(劉向)
楚材晉用(ㄔㄨˇ ㄘㄞˊ ㄐㄧㄣˋ ㄩㄥˋ)
(literally) Chu's talents are employed by Tsin—(figuratively) Talents of one country are employed by other countries.
楚騷(ㄔㄨˇ ㄙㄠ)
Li-sao, a representative work by the patriotic poet Chü Yüan (屈原) of the state of Chu
楚腰(ㄔㄨˇ ㄧㄠ)
(literally) the waist of Chu—the slim waist of a woman

【業】 2526 ㄧㄝˋ yeh yè
1. work; occupations; professions; vocations; callings; trades: 他已經失業一年了。He has been out of work for a year.
2. estate; property
3. already

業荒於嬉(ㄧㄝˋ ㄏㄨㄤ ㄩˊ ㄒㄧ)
Distraction deprives work of excellence.
業績(ㄧㄝˋ ㄐㄧ)
the track record
業經(ㄧㄝˋ ㄐㄧㄥ)
to have already been: 你的求職申請書業經批准。Your application for the position has already been approved.
業精於勤(ㄧㄝˋ ㄐㄧㄥ ㄩˊ ㄑㄧㄣˊ)
Excellence in work is possible only with diligence.
業障(ㄧㄝˋ ㄓㄤˋ)
(Buddhism) the past sin as a present obstacle; karma
業主(ㄧㄝˋ ㄓㄨˇ)
the proprietor; the owner
業種(ㄧㄝˋ ㄓㄨㄥˇ)
son of a concubine; a bastard
業師(ㄧㄝˋ ㄕ)
one's teacher
業已(ㄧㄝˋ ㄧˇ)
already: 他的老板業已病故。His boss has already died of illness.
業務(ㄧㄝˋ ㄨˋ)
official functions; business activities: 這家公司恢復正常業務。This company resumed normal business.
業餘(ㄧㄝˋ ㄩˊ)
① nonprofessional; amateur ② spare time: 他利用業餘時間幫朋友修手錶。He repaired wrist watches for his friends during his spare time.

【楣】 2527 ㄇㄟˊ mei méi
the lintel (over a door)
楣式(ㄇㄟˊ ㄕˋ)
the lintel style

【楨】 2528 ㄓㄣ jen zhēn (又讀 ㄓㄥ jeng zhēng)
1. sturdy wood
2. posts at ends of walls

【楫】 2529 ㄐㄧˊ jyi jí
1. an oar
2. a boat
楫師(ㄐㄧˊ ㄕ)
a boatman; a ferryman

【楬】 2530 ㄐㄧㄝˊ jye jié
a signpost

【極】 2531 ㄐㄧˊ jyi jí
1. to exhaust
2. extreme; extremely; highest; topmost; farthest; utmost: 此事極為重要。This is a matter of the utmost importance.
3. poles: 北極與南極 the North and South Poles
4. to reach; to arrive at
極表同情(ㄐㄧˊ ㄅㄧㄠˇ ㄊㄨㄥˊ ㄑㄧㄥˊ)
very sympathetic
極品(ㄐㄧˊ ㄆㄧㄣˇ)
a thing of the highest grade
極目(ㄐㄧˊ ㄇㄨˋ)
to look as far as possible
極峯(ㄐㄧˊ ㄈㄥ)
the topmost figure (of a nation)
極大(ㄐㄧˊ ㄉㄚˋ)
maximum
極地(ㄐㄧˊ ㄉㄧˋ)
the polar regions
極點(ㄐㄧˊ ㄉㄧㄢˇ) or 極頂(ㄐㄧˊ ㄉㄧㄥˇ)
an extremity; the topmost point; the zenith; the apex; the height; the climax: 他走運到了極點。He was at the apex of his fortunes.
極度(ㄐㄧˊ ㄉㄨˋ)
extremely; exceedingly: 我極度疲勞。I was extremely tired.
極多(ㄐㄧˊ ㄉㄨㄛ)
extremely numerous
極端(ㄐㄧˊ ㄉㄨㄢ)
an extreme; an extreme act; extremely: 他極端負責的態度令老闆讚賞。His extreme sense of responsibility was appreciated by his boss.
極東(ㄐㄧˊ ㄉㄨㄥ)
the Far East
極樂世界(ㄐㄧˊ ㄌㄜˋ ㄕˋ ㄐㄧㄝˋ)
(Buddhism) Paradise; Pure Land
極力(ㄐㄧˊ ㄌㄧˋ)
to make every effort; to make the utmost effort: 我們應極力避免犯錯。We ought to make the utmost effort to avoid mistakes.
極流(ㄐㄧˊ ㄌㄧㄡˊ)
polar currents 亦作「寒流」
極量(ㄐㄧˊ ㄌㄧㄤˋ)
(pharmacology) the maximum dose
極光(ㄐㄧˊ ㄍㄨㄤ)
the auroras (or aurorae); the polar lights: 北極光 the northern lights 南極光 the southern lights
極口稱讚(ㄐㄧˊ ㄎㄡˇ ㄔㄥ ㄗㄢˋ)
to speak in the highest terms; to praise lavishly
極好(ㄐㄧˊ ㄏㄠˇ)
very good; extremely good; superb; excellent: 這演員表演得極好。The actor gave a superb performance.
極化(ㄐㄧˊ ㄏㄨㄚˋ)
polarization; to polarize: 社會極化成兩個階級。Society has polarized into two classes.
極壞(ㄐㄧˊ ㄏㄨㄞˋ)
the worst
極盡(ㄐㄧˊ ㄐㄧㄣˋ)
to use to the utmost
極距(ㄐㄧˊ ㄐㄩˋ)
(astronomy) polar distance
極其(ㄐㄧˊ ㄑㄧˊ)
very; exceedingly; highly: 王小姐是一個極其美麗的女孩。Miss Wang is a girl of exceeding beauty.
極圈(ㄐㄧˊ ㄑㄩㄢ)
the polar circles
極權國家(ㄐㄧˊ ㄑㄩㄢˊ ㄍㄨㄛˊ ㄐㄧㄚ)
a dictatorial nation; a dictatorship; a totalitarian nation
極權主義(ㄐㄧˊ ㄑㄩㄢˊ ㄓㄨˇ ㄧˋ)
dictatorship; totalitarianism
極限(ㄐㄧˊ ㄒㄧㄢˋ)
(mathematics) a limit
極刑(ㄐㄧˊ ㄒㄧㄥˊ)
death penalty; capital punishment
極行(ㄐㄧˊ ㄒㄧㄥˊ)
the best deed
極選(ㄐㄧˊ ㄒㄩㄢˇ)
the best choice
極致(ㄐㄧˊ ㄓˋ)
the ultimate attainment; the acme
極軸(ㄐㄧˊ ㄓㄡˊ)
(mathematics) a polar axis
極處(ㄐㄧˊ ㄔㄨˋ)
extremity; the farthest point
極盛(ㄐㄧˊ ㄕㄥˋ)
the heyday; the prime; the zenith; the acme; the golden age: 羅馬在極盛時期統治了整個文明的歐洲。Rome ruled all of civilized Europe at the

zenith of its power.
極尊(ㄐㄧˊ ㄗㄨㄣ)
parents
極惡(ㄐㄧˊ ㄜˋ)
extreme atrocity
極爲(ㄐㄧˊ ㄨㄟˊ)
extremely; exceedingly; highly

【楮】 2532 ㄔㄨˇ chuu chǔ
paper mulberry
楮幣(ㄔㄨˇ ㄅㄧˋ)or 楮券(ㄔㄨˇ ㄑㄩㄢˋ)
(formerly) a bank note
楮墨(ㄔㄨˇ ㄇㄛˋ)
paper and ink
楮錢(ㄔㄨˇ ㄑㄧㄢˊ)or 楮鏹(ㄔㄨˇ ㄑㄧㄤˇ)
imitation paper money burned for the dead
楮知白(ㄔㄨˇ ㄓ ㄅㄛˊ)
another name of paper

【楷】 2533 ㄎㄞˇ kae kǎi
1. regular; standard
2. a model; a norm
3. (calligraphy) standard script: 請用正楷寫你的名字。Please write your name in standard script.
楷模(ㄎㄞˇ ㄇㄛˊ)
a model (for imitation): 他是勤勞的楷模。He's a model of industry.
楷法(ㄎㄞˇ ㄈㄚˇ)
techniques of standard handwriting
楷範(ㄎㄞˇ ㄈㄢˋ)
a model for others in conduct, etc.
楷體(ㄎㄞˇ ㄊㄧˇ)
the standard style of handwriting in Chinese, as block letters in English
楷書(ㄎㄞˇ ㄕㄨ)
standard script of handwriting; regular script
楷則(ㄎㄞˇ ㄗㄜˊ)
a model; a norm

【楸】 2534 ㄑㄧㄡ chiou qiū
Chinese catalpa (*Mallotus japonicus*), a kind of hard wood used for making chessboards
楸枰(ㄑㄧㄡ ㄆㄧㄥˊ)
a chessboard

【楹】 2535 ㄧㄥˊ yng yíng
a pillar; a column:
楹聯(ㄧㄥˊ ㄌㄧㄢˊ)
the scrolls hung on a pillar; the literary couplet on a pillar or wall
楹鼓(ㄧㄥˊ ㄍㄨˇ)
a large drum strengthened with a cross bar
楹柱(ㄧㄥˊ ㄓㄨˋ)
a pillar; a column

【楯】 2536 ㄕㄨㄣˇ shoen shǔn
1. the horizontal bar of a railing
2. same as 盾—a shield used in battle

【楩】 2537 ㄆㄧㄢˊ pyan pián
a kind of tree

十畫

【榕】 2538 ㄖㄨㄥˊ rong róng
a banyan tree
榕城(ㄖㄨㄥˊ ㄔㄥˊ)
another name of Foochow (福州), noted for its banyan trees
榕樹(ㄖㄨㄥˊ ㄕㄨˋ)
a banyan tree

【榔】 2539 ㄌㄤˊ lang láng
1. a betel palm
2. a betel nut
榔頭(ㄌㄤˊ ·ㄊㄡ)
a hammer

【榛】 2540 ㄓㄣ jen zhēn
a hazel
榛莽(ㄓㄣ ㄇㄤˇ)
thickets; bushes; thick underbrush or undergrowth
榛榛 (ㄓㄣ ㄓㄣ)
overgrown with wild plants
榛子(ㄓㄣ ·ㄗ)
a hazelnut
榛蕪(ㄓㄣ ㄨˊ)
① bushy and weedy ② a wilderness ③ humble; inferior

【榦】 2541 1. (幹) ㄍㄢˋ gann gàn
1. a tree trunk
2. posts, or supports, at ends of walls

【榦】 2541 2. (幹) ㄏㄢˊ harn hán
railings around a well

【榖】 2542 ㄍㄨˇ guu gǔ
a kind of tree (*Broussonetia papyrifera*)

【槔】 2543 ㄍㄠ gau gāo
a well sweep

【榭】 2544 ㄒㄧㄝˋ shieh xiè
a pavilion; an arbor; a kiosk: 水榭 a pavilion surrounded by water

【榫】 2545 ㄙㄨㄣˇ soen sǔn
tenon and mortise
榫頭(ㄙㄨㄣˇ ·ㄊㄡ)
a tenon
榫子(ㄙㄨㄣˇ ·ㄗ)or 榫兒(ㄙㄨㄜˇㄦ)
tenon and mortise
榫牙(ㄙㄨㄣˇ ㄧㄚˊ)
a tenon
榫眼(ㄙㄨㄣˇ ㄧㄢˇ)
a mortise

【榨】 2546 ㄓㄚˋ jah zhà
to squeeze or press (for juice); to extract: 他把檸檬榨乾。He squeezed a lemon dry.
榨取(ㄓㄚˋ ㄑㄩˇ)
exploitation; to exploit; to extort; to squeeze: 榨取遊客會破壞商業。Exploitation of the tourist destroys trade.
榨牀(ㄓㄚˋ ㄔㄨㄤˊ)
a press for extracting oil or juice
榨菜(ㄓㄚˋ ㄘㄞˋ)
preserved mustard seasoned with salt and hot pepper
榨油(ㄓㄚˋ ㄧㄡˊ)
to extract oil: 我們可自橄欖中榨油。We can extract oil from olives.
榨油水(ㄓㄚˋ ㄧㄡˊ ㄕㄨㄟˇ)
to extort money from people

【榜】 2547 1. ㄅㄤˇ baang bǎng
a publicly posted roll of successful examinees
榜牌(ㄅㄤˇ ㄆㄞˊ)
a bulletin board
榜帖(ㄅㄤˇ ㄊㄧㄝˇ)
① a list of successful examinees ② a bulletin; a public

notice
榜示(ㄅㄤˇ ㄕˋ)
to post for public attention
榜首(ㄅㄤˇ ㄕㄡˇ)
the top candidate of an examination
榜上無名(ㄅㄤˇ ㄕㄤˋ ㄨˊ ㄇㄧㄥˊ)
to fail in an examination
榜額(ㄅㄤˇ ㄜˊ)
a horizontal tablet
榜眼(ㄅㄤˇ ㄧㄢˇ)
the second best of the successful examinees in the imperial examination
榜樣(ㄅㄤˇ ㄧㄤˋ)
an example; a model
榜文(ㄅㄤˇ ㄨㄣˊ)
the writing in a public notice

【榜】 2547 2. ㄅㄥˋ benq bèng
1. to oar
2. a whip; a rod
榜女(ㄅㄥˋ ㄋㄩˇ)
a boatwoman
榜掠(ㄅㄥˋ ㄌㄩㄝˋ)
to whip; to flog
榜歌(ㄅㄥˋ ㄍㄜ)
a boatman's song
榜笞(ㄅㄥˋ ㄔ)
to beat; to flog; to whip
榜楚(ㄅㄥˋ ㄔㄨˇ)
to beat; to flog; to whip
榜箠(ㄅㄥˋ ㄔㄨㄟˊ)
a cane for torturing criminals
榜人(ㄅㄥˋ ㄖㄣˊ)
a boatman; a ferryman

【榱】 2548 ㄘㄨㄟ tsuei cuī
a rafter

【榻】 2549 ㄊㄚˋ tah tà
a couch; a bed
榻布(ㄊㄚˋ ㄅㄨˋ)
a kind of coarse cloth
榻登(ㄊㄚˋ ㄉㄥ)
a rug placed on a low-legged stool beside a bed
榻榻米(ㄊㄚˋ ㄊㄚˋ ㄇㄧˇ)
(Japanese) tatami—① any of a number of thick, woven straw mats of uniform dimensions, about three feet by six feet, used in Japanese houses ② a measure of living space equal to about 18 square feet

【榴】 2550 ㄌㄧㄡˊ liou liú
a pomegranate
榴彈(ㄌㄧㄡˊ ㄉㄢˋ)
a grenade; a high explosive shell
榴彈礮(ㄌㄧㄡˊ ㄉㄢˋ ㄆㄠˋ)
a howitzer
榴火(ㄌㄧㄡˊ ㄏㄨㄛˇ)
fiery red of pomegranate blossoms

【榮】 2551 ㄖㄨㄥˊ rong róng
1. glory; honor: 他是讓全國引以爲榮的人。He is an honor to his country.
2. luxuriant; lush; teeming; leafy: 草春榮冬枯。Grass grows in spring and withers in winter.
3. a Chinese family name
榮民(ㄖㄨㄥˊ ㄇㄧㄣˊ)
retired servicemen; veterans
榮名(ㄖㄨㄥˊ ㄇㄧㄥˊ)
honor and fame
榮典(ㄖㄨㄥˊ ㄉㄧㄢˇ)
a honorary reward
榮祿(ㄖㄨㄥˊ ㄌㄨˋ)
Jung Lu, a high ranking Manchu official, who helped Empress Dowager Tzu Hsi thwart the political reform movement during the last years of the 19th century
榮祿大夫(ㄖㄨㄥˊ ㄌㄨˋ ㄉㄞˋ ㄈㄨ)
a rank in government service in former times
榮歸(ㄖㄨㄥˊ ㄍㄨㄟ)
①(said of a high official) to retire in glory ② to return home in triumph
榮光(ㄖㄨㄥˊ ㄍㄨㄤ)
glory; splendor
榮枯(ㄖㄨㄥˊ ㄎㄨ)
①(said of vegetation) flourishing and withering ②rise and fall; ups and downs; vicissitudes: 我們應該榮枯與共。We should share our vicissitudes.
榮華富貴(ㄖㄨㄥˊ ㄏㄨㄚˊ ㄈㄨˋ ㄍㄨㄟˋ)
honor and wealth
榮獲(ㄖㄨㄥˊ ㄏㄨㄛˋ)
to get or win the honor：此次比賽他榮獲冠軍。He won the championship in the contest.
榮顯(ㄖㄨㄥˊ ㄒㄧㄢˇ)
honor and high position
榮幸(ㄖㄨㄥˊ ㄒㄧㄥˋ)
honored; to have the honor of: 很榮幸能與你共餐。It is a great honor to dine with you.
榮恥(ㄖㄨㄥˊ ㄔˇ)
honor and dishonor
榮寵(ㄖㄨㄥˊ ㄔㄨㄥˇ)
glorious favor
榮施(ㄖㄨㄥˊ ㄕ)
glorious giving
榮任(ㄖㄨㄥˊ ㄖㄣˋ)
to have the honor of being appointed (to a post)
榮辱(ㄖㄨㄥˊ ㄖㄨˇ)
honor and dishonor
榮宗耀祖(ㄖㄨㄥˊ ㄗㄨㄥ ㄧㄠˋ ㄗㄨˇ)
to bring glory to one's family and ancestors; to redound to the glory of one's ancestors
榮悴(ㄖㄨㄥˊ ㄘㄨㄟˋ)
① flourishing and withering (of vegetation) ② ups and downs; vicissitudes
榮哀錄(ㄖㄨㄥˊ ㄞ ㄌㄨˋ)
a collection of eulogies and commemorative writings in honor of an illustrious figure
榮耀(ㄖㄨㄥˊ ㄧㄠˋ)
glory; honor; splendor
榮養(ㄖㄨㄥˊ ㄧㄤˇ)
to support one's parents
榮膺(ㄖㄨㄥˊ ㄧㄥ)
to have the honor of being appointed (to a post)
榮譽(ㄖㄨㄥˊ ㄩˋ)
honor: 他的成功爲學校贏得榮譽。His success won honor for his school.
榮譽軍人(ㄖㄨㄥˊ ㄩˋ ㄐㄩㄣ ㄖㄣˊ)
servicemen wounded in action

【槃】 2552 (盤) ㄆㄢˊ parn pán
1. a wooden tray
2. great
槃根錯節(ㄆㄢˊ ㄍㄣ ㄘㄨㄛˋ ㄐㄧㄝˊ)
① very complicated; difficult to solve or explain ② (said of old social forces) deep-rooted 亦作「盤根錯節」
槃才(ㄆㄢˊ ㄘㄞˊ)
a person of great talent
槃匜(ㄆㄢˊ ㄧˊ)

〔木部〕

a basin; a tray; a washing-bowl

【槊】2553 ㄕㄨㄛˋ shuoh shuò
a spear; a lance

【槁】2554 (稾) ㄍㄠˇ gao gǎo
withered; dead; rotten: 長期臥病使這病人形容枯槁。A long illness has emaciated the invalid.

槁木死灰(ㄍㄠˇ ㄇㄨˋ ㄙˇ ㄏㄨㄟ)
(literally) rotten wood and cold ashes—a person utterly without vitality or ambition; completely apathetic

槁骨(ㄍㄠˇ ㄍㄨˇ)
bones of the deceased

槁梧(ㄍㄠˇ ㄨˊ)
name of a stringed instrument in Chinese music

【構】2555 ㄍㄡˋ gow gòu
to frame; to form; to build; to establish; to constitute; to scheme: 雙親與孩子構成一個家庭。Parents and children form a family.

構兵(ㄍㄡˋ ㄅㄧㄥ)
to be at war; to have a clash of arms; to wage war

構圖(ㄍㄡˋ ㄊㄨˊ)
composition (in drawing): 他的畫構圖甚美。The composition of his picture is beautiful.

構難(ㄍㄡˋ ㄋㄢˋ)
to bring trouble

構亂(ㄍㄡˋ ㄌㄨㄢˋ)
to stir up disorder

構禍(ㄍㄡˋ ㄏㄨㄛˋ)
to bring disaster

構會(ㄍㄡˋ ㄏㄨㄟˋ)
to incriminate unjustly

構精(ㄍㄡˋ ㄐㄧㄥ)
① to have sexual union ② to concentrate attention

構陷(ㄍㄡˋ ㄒㄧㄢˋ)
to frame a charge against someone; to incriminate unjustly

構釁(ㄍㄡˋ ㄒㄧㄣˋ)
to be at feud

構想(ㄍㄡˋ ㄒㄧㄤˇ)
an idea; a conception; a plan; a scheme

構築(ㄍㄡˋ ㄓㄨˊ)
to construct; to build: 我們構築防禦工事。We construct our fortifications.

構成(ㄍㄡˋ ㄔㄥˊ)
to constitute; to form; a contexture

構造(ㄍㄡˋ ㄗㄠˋ)
structure; construction; organization: 人體是個奇妙的構造。Human body is a wonderful structure.

構造心理學(ㄍㄡˋ ㄗㄠˋ ㄒㄧㄣ ㄌㄧˇ ㄒㄩㄝˊ)
structural psychology

構造式(ㄍㄡˋ ㄗㄠˋ ㄕˋ)
constitutional formula (of a chemical compound)

構思(ㄍㄡˋ ㄙ)
① to weigh something mentally ② to plot; a plot

構怨(ㄍㄡˋ ㄩㄢˋ)
to be at feud; to contract hatred against

【槌】2556 ㄔㄨㄟˊ chwei chuí
a hammer

槌兒(ㄔㄨㄟˊㄦ)
a hammer

槌骨(ㄔㄨㄟˊ ㄍㄨˇ)
a malleus

槌鼓(ㄔㄨㄟˊ ㄍㄨˇ)
to beat a drum

槌擊(ㄔㄨㄟˊ ㄐㄧˊ)
to beat with a hammer

槌球(ㄔㄨㄟˊ ㄑㄧㄡˊ)
croquet

【槍】2557 ㄑㄧㄤ chiang qiāng
1.a spear; a lance; a javelin
2.a rifle; a pistol; a gun

槍斃(ㄑㄧㄤ ㄅㄧˋ)or槍決(ㄑㄧㄤ ㄐㄩㄝˊ)
to execute by shooting; to shoot to death

槍炮(ㄑㄧㄤ ㄆㄠˋ)
firearms; guns

槍法(ㄑㄧㄤ ㄈㄚˇ)
① marksmanship ② art of using spears

槍刀劍戟(ㄑㄧㄤ ㄉㄠ ㄐㄧㄢˋ ㄐㄧˇ)
arms; weapons

槍彈(ㄑㄧㄤ ㄉㄢˋ)
a cartridge; a shell; a bullet

槍頭兒(ㄑㄧㄤ ㄊㄡˊㄦ)
a spearhead

槍膛(ㄑㄧㄤ ㄊㄤˊ)
a bore

槍替(ㄑㄧㄤ ㄊㄧˋ)
to serve as a substitute examinee; to take an examination in place of the real examinee

槍托(ㄑㄧㄤ ㄊㄨㄛ)
the rifle butt; the gun stock

槍榴彈(ㄑㄧㄤ ㄌㄧㄡˊ ㄉㄢˋ)
a rifle grenade

槍林彈雨(ㄑㄧㄤ ㄌㄧㄣˊ ㄉㄢˋ ㄩˇ)
a fierce battle (in which one faces a rain of bullets and artillery shells): 戰士們冒着槍林彈雨衝鋒陷陣。The soldiers charged under a hail of bullets.

槍桿(ㄑㄧㄤ ㄍㄢˇ)
① the shaft of a spear ② a rifle; arms

槍口(ㄑㄧㄤ ㄎㄡˇ)
a muzzle (of a rifle, pistol, etc.)

槍機(ㄑㄧㄤ ㄐㄧ)
a trigger

槍尖(ㄑㄧㄤ ㄐㄧㄢ)
a spearhead

槍械(ㄑㄧㄤ ㄒㄧㄝˋ)
weapons

槍枝(ㄑㄧㄤ ㄓ)
rifles

槍戰(ㄑㄧㄤ ㄓㄢˋ)
a gun battle; exchange of fire; a shootout: 他們都是在槍戰時受傷。They are all wounded in the gun battle.

槍殺(ㄑㄧㄤ ㄕㄚ)
to shoot

槍手
①(ㄑㄧㄤ ㄕㄡˇ) a rifleman; a gunman; a hired gunman
②(ㄑㄧㄤ ·ㄕㄡ) ⓐ a substitute examinee; a hired examinee; one who takes an examination in place of the real examinee ⓑ a ghost writer

槍傷(ㄑㄧㄤ ㄕㄤ)
bullet (or gunshot) wounds

槍聲(ㄑㄧㄤ ㄕㄥ)
the report or crack of a gun; a shot

槍刺(ㄑㄧㄤ ㄘˋ)
to thrust with a spear

【槐】2558 ㄏㄨㄞˊ hwai huái
a locust tree (*Sophora japonica*) similar to the ash; an

acacia; a Chinese scholar-tree

槐鼎(ㄏㄨㄞˊ ㄉㄧㄥˇ)
the three top officials of the state in ancient times

槐火(ㄏㄨㄞˊ ㄏㄨㄛˇ)
a fire made by drilling a piece of locust wood

槐序(ㄏㄨㄞˊ ㄒㄩˋ)
summer

槐月(ㄏㄨㄞˊ ㄩㄝˋ)
the fourth moon of the lunar year

【槎】 2559 ㄔㄚˊ char chá
1. a raft
2. to hew; to chop; to cut

【槓】 2560 ㄍㄤˋ ganq gàng
1. a lever; a carrying pole
2. (sports) a bar
3. to sharpen (a knife)
4. to argue; to dispute
5. to cross out

槓夫(ㄍㄤˋ ㄈㄨ)
a coffin bearer

槓刀(ㄍㄤˋ ㄉㄠ)
to sharpen a knife

槓刀布(ㄍㄤˋ ㄉㄠ ㄅㄨˋ)
a coarse cloth for sharpening a razor

槓頭(ㄍㄤˋ ㄊㄡˊ)
① the head coffin bearer ② an argumentative person

槓鈴(ㄍㄤˋ ㄌㄧㄥˊ)
(sports) a barbell

槓桿(ㄍㄤˋ ㄍㄢˇ)
a lever; a pry: 工人用槓桿移動巖石。The worker is levering at the rock.

槓桿定律(ㄍㄤˋ ㄍㄢˇ ㄉㄧㄥˋ ㄌㄩˋ)
(physics) law of lever

槓子(ㄍㄤˋ ˙ㄗ)
① horizontal or parallel bars: 他會玩槓子。He can take gymnastic exercises on bars. ② a stout carrying pole

【榷】 2561 ㄑㄩㄝˋ chiueh què
1. to monopolize
2. to levy taxes

榷利(ㄑㄩㄝˋ ㄌㄧˋ)
to enjoy monopoly

榷酤(ㄑㄩㄝˋ ㄍㄨ)
to monopolize the sale of alcoholic beverages

榷茶(ㄑㄩㄝˋ ㄔㄚˊ)
to levy tea taxes

榷鹽(ㄑㄩㄝˋ ㄧㄢˊ)
to levy salt taxes

榷運局(ㄑㄩㄝˋ ㄩㄣˋ ㄐㄩˊ)
a government agency in charge of salt taxes

【榧】 2562 ㄈㄟˇ feei fěi
a species of yew (*Torreya nucifera*)

【榾】 2563 ㄍㄨˇ guu gǔ
chopped pieces of wood

榾柮(ㄍㄨˇ ㄉㄨㄛˋ)
chopped pieces of wood

【槅】 2564 ㄍㄜˊ ger gé
a semicircular wooden collar at the end of the shafts of a large carriage; a yoke for harnessing animals

十一畫

【槥】 2565 ㄏㄨㄟˋ huey huì
a small coffin

【槭】 2566 ㄗㄨˊ tzwu zú
a kind of maple (*Acer palmatum*)

槭樹(ㄗㄨˊ ㄕㄨˋ)
a maple

【槱】 2567 ㄧㄡˇ yeou yǒu
1. an ancient rite of building fires in worship
2. to supply firewood for building fires

【概】 2568 (槩) ㄍㄞˋ gay gài
1. general; overall; roughly: 大概地說物價仍在上漲。Overall, prices are rising.
2. without exception; categorically
3. the manner of carrying oneself; deportment

概不考慮(ㄍㄞˋ ㄅㄨˋ ㄎㄠˇ ㄌㄩˋ)
No consideration will be given to all requests, suggestions, etc.

概不賒欠(ㄍㄞˋ ㄅㄨˋ ㄕㄜ ㄑㄧㄢˋ)
No sale on credit under all circumstances, conditions, etc. 或 No chits.

概不容情(ㄍㄞˋ ㄅㄨˋ ㄖㄨㄥˊ ㄑㄧㄥˊ)
No leniency toward any offence, mistake, etc.

概貌(ㄍㄞˋ ㄇㄠˋ)
a general picture

概念(ㄍㄞˋ ㄋㄧㄢˋ)
a concept; a conception; a general idea

概論(ㄍㄞˋ ㄌㄨㄣˋ)
a general discussion; an outline

概略(ㄍㄞˋ ㄌㄩㄝˋ)
an outline; a summary: 他已告訴我這篇故事的概略。He has already told me the outline of the story.

概觀(ㄍㄞˋ ㄍㄨㄢ)
a general view; a bird's-eye view; a conspectus

概括(ㄍㄞˋ ㄎㄨㄛˋ)
to summarize; to sum up; to generalize: 我把我的看法概括地講一講。I'll give my views in broad outline.

概括性(ㄍㄞˋ ㄎㄨㄛˋ ㄒㄧㄥˋ)
generality

概況(ㄍㄞˋ ㄎㄨㄤˋ)
a general situation; an overall condition: 我已把前線的概況報告他了。I have reported the general situation of the front to him.

概見(ㄍㄞˋ ㄐㄧㄢˋ)
to have a general look

概算(ㄍㄞˋ ㄙㄨㄢˋ)
① to compute roughly; to make a rough estimate of ② a preliminary government budget; a rough estimate

概而不論(ㄍㄞˋ ㄦˊ ㄅㄨˊ ㄌㄨㄣˋ)
to do without careful consideration; to be headlong

概要(ㄍㄞˋ ㄧㄠˋ)
a summary; an outline; a synopsis; a résumé

概予(ㄍㄞˋ ㄩˇ) or 概行(ㄍㄞˋ ㄒㄧㄥˊ)
to do something without exception

【槧】 2569 ㄑㄧㄢˋ chiann qiàn
1. a wooden tablet for writing
2. an edition, or version, of a book
3. a letter

槧本(ㄑㄧㄢˋ ㄅㄣˇ)
a book printed by engravings

【槳】 2570
ㄐㄧㄤˇ jeang jiǎng
an oar

【樂】 2571
1. ㄩㄝˋ yueh yuè

〔木部〕

1. music: 她喜愛各種音樂。She likes every kind of music.
2. a Chinese family name

樂譜(ㄩㄝˋ ㄆㄨˇ)
a score (of music); musical notes; music: 他一張一張地翻樂譜。He leafed through the music.

樂府(ㄩㄝˋ ㄈㄨˇ)
①(in ancient times) a government agency for collecting songs ②a collection of songs and poems

樂隊(ㄩㄝˋ ㄉㄨㄟˋ)
a band; an orchestra: 我們學校的樂隊是新組成的。The band of our school is newly organized.

樂團(ㄩㄝˋ ㄊㄨㄢˊ)
①a philharmonic society ②a philharmonic orchestra

樂理(ㄩㄝˋ ㄌㄧˇ)
musicology

樂歌(ㄩㄝˋ ㄍㄜ)
playing music and singing songs

樂官(ㄩㄝˋ ㄍㄨㄢ)
(formerly) the official in charge of music

樂工(ㄩㄝˋ ㄍㄨㄥ)
a musician

樂戶(ㄩㄝˋ ㄏㄨˋ)
(formerly) a government-operated whorehouse

樂經(ㄩㄝˋ ㄐㄧㄥ)
the *Book of Music* (one of the *Six Classics*, supposedly lost when the First Emperor of the Chin Dynasty burned books)

樂器(ㄩㄝˋ ㄑㄧˋ)
a musical instrument

樂曲(ㄩㄝˋ ㄑㄩˇ)
a piece of music; a musical composition

樂章(ㄩㄝˋ ㄓㄤ)
a movement (of a symphony, sonata, etc.)

樂師(ㄩㄝˋ ㄕ)
musicians

樂音(ㄩㄝˋ ㄧㄣ)
a musical tone; a musical sound

樂舞(ㄩㄝˋ ㄨˇ)
a dance accompanied by music

【樂】 2571
2. ㄌㄜˋ leh lè

1. happy; glad; joyful; joyous; cheerful; elated; content; delighted; pleased; willing: 孩子們似乎很快樂。The children seem very happy.
2. pleasant; agreeable; enjoyable; pleasing; comfortable

樂不可支(ㄌㄜˋ ˙ㄅㄨ ㄎㄜˇ ㄓ)
to be beside oneself with happiness; to be overwhelmed with joy

樂不思蜀(ㄌㄜˋ ˙ㄅㄨ ㄙ ㄕㄨˇ)
too happy to think of home —an allusion to Liu Chan (劉禪), who felt happy in Loyang (洛陽) after he was captured as a prisoner by Ssu-Ma Chao (司馬昭)

樂得(ㄌㄜˋ ㄉㄜˊ)
to be very glad to; to do something willingly (because of sure reward for doing it)

樂陶陶(ㄌㄜˋ ㄊㄠˊ ㄊㄠˊ)
cheerful; happy; joyful

樂天(ㄌㄜˋ ㄊㄧㄢ)
to be content with one's lot; to be optimistic; to be easygoing; happy-go-lucky

樂天派(ㄌㄜˋ ㄊㄧㄢ ㄆㄞˋ)
an optimist; an easygoing person; a happy-go-lucky person

樂天知命(ㄌㄜˋ ㄊㄧㄢ ㄓ ㄇㄧㄥˋ)
to be content with what one is; happy-go-lucky: 樂天知命的人沒煩惱。Those who are contented with their lot have nothing to worry about.

樂天主義(ㄌㄜˋ ㄊㄧㄢ ㄓㄨˇ ㄧˋ)
optimism

樂土(ㄌㄜˋ ㄊㄨˇ)
a land of comfort; a paradise

樂觀(ㄌㄜˋ ㄍㄨㄢ)
optimistic: 我們對國家的前途很樂觀。We are optimistic about the future of our country.

樂觀主義(ㄌㄜˋ ㄍㄨㄢ ㄓㄨˇ ㄧˋ)
optimism

樂呵呵(ㄌㄜˋ ㄏㄜ ㄏㄜ)
buoyant; happy and gay: 他成天總是樂呵呵的。He is always cheerful and gay.

樂禍(ㄌㄜˋ ㄏㄨㄛˋ)
to take delight in others' disaster

樂壞了(ㄌㄜˋ ㄏㄨㄞˋ ˙ㄌㄜ)
very happy: 他樂壞了。He was very happy.

樂極生悲(ㄌㄜˋ ㄐㄧˊ ㄕㄥ ㄅㄟ)
Happiness is followed by sorrow when it reaches an extreme.

樂境(ㄌㄜˋ ㄐㄧㄥˋ)
state of happiness; happiness

樂捐(ㄌㄜˋ ㄐㄩㄢ)
to donate voluntarily

樂趣(ㄌㄜˋ ㄑㄩˋ)
delight; pleasure; joy; fun

樂嘻嘻的(ㄌㄜˋ ˙ㄒㄧ ㄒㄧ ˙ㄉㄜ)
pleased; delighted; glad; joyous

樂助(ㄌㄜˋ ㄓㄨˋ)
willing to help

樂處(ㄌㄜˋ ㄔㄨˋ)
a source of delight; pleasures; happiness

樂施(ㄌㄜˋ ㄕ)
willing to give to the poor; charitable; generous; benevolent

樂事(ㄌㄜˋ ㄕˋ)
a pleasant thing or matter; a source of joy: 他以助人爲樂事。He found a source of joy in helping others.

樂善好施(ㄌㄜˋ ㄕㄢˋ ㄏㄠˋ ㄕ)
willing to do good and give help to the poor; fond of doing philanthropic work; charitable; benevolent

樂輸(ㄌㄜˋ ㄕㄨ)
willing to pay or contribute

樂滋滋(ㄌㄜˋ ㄗ ㄗ)
contented; pleased

樂子(ㄌㄜˋ ˙ㄗ)
①joy; fun; joy derived from a joke: 他尋我的樂子。He joked with me. ②an awkward predicament

樂此不疲(ㄌㄜˋ ㄘˇ ㄅㄨˋ ㄆㄧˊ) or 樂此不倦(ㄌㄜˋ ㄘˇ ㄅㄨˋ ㄐㄩㄢˋ)
to delight in a thing and never get tired of it

樂從(ㄌㄜˋ ㄘㄨㄥˊ)

willing to obey; obedient; willing to follow
樂兒(ㄌㄜˋㄦ)
①happy laughter ②an enjoyable thing: 這不是什麼樂兒。This is nothing enjoyable.
樂而不淫(ㄌㄜˋ ㄦˊ ㄅㄨˋ ㄧㄣˊ)
pleasant but not obscene
樂而忘返(ㄌㄜˋ ㄦˊ ㄨㄤˋ ㄈㄢˇ)
to be a slave of pleasure
樂以忘憂(ㄌㄜˋ ㄧˇ ㄨㄤˋ ㄧㄡ)
to seek pleasure in order to free oneself from care
樂易(ㄌㄜˋ ㄧˋ)
pleasant; agreeable
樂意(ㄌㄜˋ ㄧˋ)
① willing: 我樂意幫你的忙。I am willing to help you. ② pleased: 她聽了這話有點樂意。She seemed somewhat pleased with that remark.
樂業(ㄌㄜˋ ㄧㄝˋ)
to like one's job or trade
樂紋兒(ㄌㄜˋ ㄨㄜˊㄦ)
a dimple
樂聞(ㄌㄜˋ ㄨㄣˊ)
happy to hear about
樂於(ㄌㄜˋ ㄩˊ)
to like or love (doing something): 他樂於幫助他人。He likes to help others.
樂育(ㄌㄜˋ ㄩˋ)
to be happy in teaching
樂園(ㄌㄜˋ ㄩㄢˊ)
a paradise; Eden; Elysium: 香港是購物者的樂園。Hong Kong is a paradise for shoppers.

【樂】 2571
3. ㄧㄠˋ yaw yào
to love; to be fond of; to delight in
樂羣(ㄧㄠˋ ㄑㄩㄣˊ) or (ㄌㄜˋ ㄑㄩㄣˊ)
fond of company and learning from one's friends

【槲】 2572
ㄏㄨˊ hwu hú
a species of oak (*Quercus dentata*)

【槿】 2573
ㄐㄧㄣˇ jiin jǐn
1. a hibiscus
2. as in 朝槿—morning-glories

【槽】 2574
ㄘㄠˊ tsaur cáo
1. a manger
2. a trough; a flume; a chute
3. as in 跳槽—to jump on another bandwagon
槽櫪(ㄘㄠˊ ㄌㄧˋ)
a stable
槽子(ㄘㄠˊ ·ㄗ)
a trough; a manger 亦作「槽頭」
槽兒(ㄘㄠˊㄦ)
①a depression or groove in a surface ②(formerly) a term for addressing the wine waiter

【樁】 2575
ㄓㄨㄤ juang zhuāng
1. a stake; a post; a pile
2. a numerary auxiliary for affairs or matters

【樅】 2576
ㄘㄨㄥ tsong cōng
a fir; a fir tree (*Abies firma*): 樅木是一種常綠樹。The fir is an evergreen tree.

【樟】 2577
ㄓㄤ jang zhāng
a camphor tree
樟木(ㄓㄤ ㄇㄨˋ)
①a camphor tree ②the wood of a camphor tree
樟腦(ㄓㄤ ㄋㄠˇ)
camphor
樟腦酊(ㄓㄤ ㄋㄠˇ ㄉㄧㄥ)
tincture of camphor
樟腦精(ㄓㄤ ㄋㄠˇ ㄐㄧㄥ)
camphene; spirit of camphor; essence of camphor
樟腦油(ㄓㄤ ㄋㄠˇ ㄧㄡˊ)
camphor oil
樟腦丸(ㄓㄤ ㄋㄠˇ ㄨㄢˊ)
a camphor ball; a mothball
樟科(ㄓㄤ ㄎㄜ)
the camphor family (*Lauraceae*)
樟樹(ㄓㄤ ㄕㄨˋ)
a camphor tree
樟蠶(ㄓㄤ ㄘㄢˊ)
Caligula japonica, a kind of silkworm

【樗】 2578
ㄕㄨ shu shū
Ailanthus altissima
樗蒲(ㄕㄨ ㄆㄨˊ)
an ancient gambling game
樗櫟之材(ㄕㄨ ㄌㄧˋ ㄓ ㄘㄞˊ)
the timber of the ailanthus and the chestnut oak —a useless person
樗材(ㄕㄨ ㄘㄞˊ)
(a self-reference in polite conversation) a useless person; a good-for-nothing
樗散(ㄕㄨ ㄙㄢˇ)
to have talent without being recognized or employed

【樊】 2579
ㄈㄢˊ farn fán
1. a bird cage
2. disorderly; confused; messy
3. a Chinese family name
樊籬(ㄈㄢˊ ㄌㄧˊ)
① the fence ②(figuratively) something preventing progress or approach, etc.
樊籠(ㄈㄢˊ ㄌㄨㄥˊ)
①a cage to confine birds or wild beasts ②(figuratively) the place or condition of confinement
樊然(ㄈㄢˊ ㄖㄢˊ)
disorderly; confused; messy

【樓】 2580
ㄌㄡˊ lou lóu
a building of two stories or more; a tower
樓板(ㄌㄡˊ ㄅㄢˇ)
wooden planks used to build a floor (above the ground floor)
樓房(ㄌㄡˊ ㄈㄤˊ)
a building of two stories or more
樓底下(ㄌㄡˊ ㄉㄧˇ ·ㄒㄧㄚ)
the ground floor; downstairs
樓頂(ㄌㄡˊ ㄉㄧㄥˇ)
the top of a tall building
樓臺(ㄌㄡˊ ㄊㄞˊ)
a tower
樓梯(ㄌㄡˊ ㄊㄧ)
a staircase: 外邊的樓梯通到花園。The outside staircase leads to the garden.
樓櫓(ㄌㄡˊ ㄌㄨˇ)
a watchtower; a donjon
樓鴿(ㄌㄡˊ ㄍㄜ)
pigeons nesting in buildings
樓閣(ㄌㄡˊ ㄍㄜˊ)
a tower
樓下(ㄌㄡˊ ㄒㄧㄚˋ)
downstairs: 她在樓下等候。She is waiting downstairs.
樓船(ㄌㄡˊ ㄔㄨㄢˊ)
a large turreted boat
樓上(ㄌㄡˊ ㄕㄤˋ)

〔木部〕

〔木部〕

upstairs: 樓上住着一位退休的老工人。A retired worker lives upstairs.

【標】 2581 ㄅㄧㄠ biau biāo

1. to show; to indicate; to mark; to symbolize; to put a mark, tag or label on: 這藥的成分標在瓶上。The ingredients of the medicine are marked on the bottle.
2. a mark; a sign; a symbol; an indication; a label
3. a model; a paragon
4. to bid; to tender

標本(ㄅㄧㄠ ㄅㄣˇ)
①a specimen ②appearance and substance

標榜(ㄅㄧㄠ ㄅㄤˇ)
①to glorify; to uphold: 他們標榜自由平等。They uphold liberty and equality. ②to profess; to declare ③to boost: 他們互相標榜。They boosted each other.

標賣(ㄅㄧㄠ ㄇㄞˋ)
to sell by tender

標名(ㄅㄧㄠ ㄇㄧㄥˊ)
a label; a title

標明(ㄅㄧㄠ ㄇㄧㄥˊ)
to label; to indicate; to mark clearly: 紙箱上標明「小心輕放」。The carton is marked "Handle with care."

標的(ㄅㄧㄠ ㄉㄧˋ)
a target; an objective; a purpose; an aim

標點(ㄅㄧㄠ ㄉㄧㄢˇ)
punctuation

標點符號(ㄅㄧㄠ ㄉㄧㄢˇ ㄈㄨˊ ㄏㄠˋ)
a punctuation mark

標題(ㄅㄧㄠ ㄊㄧˊ)
a heading; a title; a headline

標題音樂(ㄅㄧㄠ ㄊㄧˊ ㄧㄣ ㄩㄝˋ)
program music

標統(ㄅㄧㄠ ㄊㄨㄥˇ)
(Ching Dynasty) a regiment commander

標格(ㄅㄧㄠ ㄍㄜˊ)
an example; a model

標高(ㄅㄧㄠ ㄍㄠ)
elevation; the vertical distance between the top of an object and the sea level: 此山標高是五千呎。The elevation of the mountain is 5,000 feet.

標購(ㄅㄧㄠ ㄍㄡˋ)
to buy at public bidding

標竿(ㄅㄧㄠ ㄍㄢ)
a guidepost

標會(ㄅㄧㄠ ㄏㄨㄟˋ)
to draw lots to determine who should get the loan from a private loan association

標記(ㄅㄧㄠ ㄐㄧˋ)
a mark; an indication; a sign: 他已在有地雷的地方做了一個標記。He has put a mark on the spot where there is a land mine.

標價(ㄅㄧㄠ ㄐㄧㄚˋ)
①the tag price; the listed price ②to indicate the price of a commodity on a tag

標籤(ㄅㄧㄠ ㄑㄧㄢ)
a label; a tag: 我在盒子上貼了一張標籤。I put a label on the box.

標槍(ㄅㄧㄠ ㄑㄧㄤ)
a javelin; a spear; a lance

標新立異(ㄅㄧㄠ ㄒㄧㄣ ㄌㄧˋ ㄧˋ)
to try to be fanciful; to try to be original; to do something unconventional or unorthodox

標致 or 標緻(ㄅㄧㄠ ㄓˋ)
(said of females) good-looking; handsome

標幟(ㄅㄧㄠ ㄓˋ)
a mark or sign made for distinction

標識 or 標誌(ㄅㄧㄠ ㄓˋ)
a mark; a symbol; a sign

標注(ㄅㄧㄠ ㄓㄨˋ)
to mark (for calling attention or avoiding confusion)

標準(ㄅㄧㄠ ㄓㄨㄣˇ)
①a standard; a criterion: 我們學校有極高的教學標準。Our school has high standards of teaching. ②typical

標準桿(ㄅㄧㄠ ㄓㄨㄣˇ ㄍㄢˇ)
(golf) par

標準國語(ㄅㄧㄠ ㄓㄨㄣˇ ㄍㄨㄛˊ ㄩˇ) or 標準語(ㄅㄧㄠ ㄓㄨㄣˇ ㄩˇ)
Mandarin Chinese; Mandarin

標準化(ㄅㄧㄠ ㄓㄨㄣˇ ㄏㄨㄚˋ)
to standardize; standardization: 汽車零件是標準化的。The parts of an automobile are standardized.

標準局(ㄅㄧㄠ ㄓㄨㄣˇ ㄐㄩˊ)
the National Bureau of Standards

標準氣壓(ㄅㄧㄠ ㄓㄨㄣˇ ㄑㄧˋ ㄧㄚ)
standard atmospheric pressure

標準制(ㄅㄧㄠ ㄓㄨㄣˇ ㄓˋ)
the metric system

標準燭光(ㄅㄧㄠ ㄓㄨㄣˇ ㄓㄨˊ ㄍㄨㄤ)
standard (or mean) candle power: 標準燭光測量光之強度。A standard candle measures the intensity of a light.

標準時(ㄅㄧㄠ ㄓㄨㄣˇ ㄕˊ)
standard time

標準音(ㄅㄧㄠ ㄓㄨㄣˇ ㄧㄣ)
standard pronunciation

標售(ㄅㄧㄠ ㄕㄡˋ)
to sell by tender: 這些貨物要公開標售。These goods are to be sold through open tender.

標語(ㄅㄧㄠ ㄩˇ)
a slogan; a motto: 他們在牆上張貼標語。They paste up slogans on the wall.

【樛】 2582 ㄐㄧㄡ jiou jiū

1. drooping branches
2. twisted; distorted

樛木(ㄐㄧㄡ ㄇㄨˋ)
①a tree with hanging branches ②(figuratively) a man of position who is benevolent to the humble and the underprivileged

樛結(ㄐㄧㄡ ㄐㄧㄝˊ)
twisted; entangled

【樞】 2583 ㄕㄨ shu shū

1. a hinge; a pivot
2. a kind of tree

樞密使(ㄕㄨ ㄇㄧˋ ㄕˇ) or 樞史(ㄕㄨ ㄕˇ) or 樞相(ㄕㄨ ㄒㄧㄤˋ)
a lord chancellor, or prime minister, of the late Tang Dynasty and the Sung Dynasty

樞密院(ㄕㄨ ㄇㄧˋ ㄩㄢˋ) or 樞府(ㄕㄨ ㄈㄨˇ)
the Privy Council, or Cabinet, of the late Tang Dynasty and the Sung Dynasty

樞紐(ㄕㄨ ㄋㄧㄡˇ)
the vital point; the key; the pivot: 這火車站是這個小鎮的交通樞紐。The railway sta-

tion is the pivot of the communication of the small town.
樞路(ㄕㄨ ㄌㄨˋ)
a key road
樞機(ㄕㄨ ㄐㄧ)
①the vital element ② important government posts 亦作「樞衡」
樞機主教(ㄕㄨ ㄐㄧ ㄓㄨˇ ㄐㄧㄠˋ)
a cardinal of the Catholic Church
樞軸(ㄕㄨ ㄓㄡˊ)
the center of administration
樞臣(ㄕㄨ ㄔㄣˊ)
a chief courtier; a prime minister; a premier
樞奧(ㄕㄨ ㄠˋ)
confidential information or affairs
樞要(ㄕㄨ ㄧㄠˋ)
the center of administration
樞務(ㄕㄨ ㄨˋ)
the duty of the premier; state affairs

【模】 2584
1. ㄇㄛˊ mo mó
1. a model; a norm: 我給他買了一個船模型。I bought him a model of a ship.
2. to imitate; to copy
模表(ㄇㄛˊ ㄅㄧㄠˇ)
an exemplary thing; an example; a model
模模糊糊(ㄇㄛˊ ·ㄇㄛ ·ㄏㄨ ·ㄏㄨ)
vague; ambiguous; dim; hazy; unintelligible: 在霧中一切東西都顯得模模糊糊的。In a fog everything looks vague.
模範(ㄇㄛˊ ㄈㄢˋ)
an exemplary thing; an example; a model
模範生(ㄇㄛˊ ㄈㄢˋ ㄕㄥ)
a model student
模仿(ㄇㄛˊ ㄈㄤˇ)
to imitate; to copy; to model oneself on: 這小男孩模仿他的父親。The little boy imitated his father.
模倣性(ㄇㄛˊ ㄈㄤˇ ㄒㄧㄥˋ)
imitativeness
模特兒(ㄇㄛˊ ㄊㄜˋ ㄦˊ)
a model (for artists, photographers, etc.); a manikin or mannequin
模擬(ㄇㄛˊ ㄋㄧˇ)
to simulate; to imitate
模稜兩可(ㄇㄛˊ ㄌㄥˊ ㄌㄧㄤˇ ㄎㄜˇ)
equivocal; ambiguous
模里西斯(ㄇㄛˊ ㄌㄧˇ ㄒㄧ ㄙ)
Mauritius
模楷(ㄇㄛˊ ㄎㄞˇ)
a model; a norm; an exemplary thing; an example; to take something as a model 亦作「楷模」: 這個學生是勤勉的模楷。The student is a model of diligence.
模糊(ㄇㄛˊ ·ㄏㄨ)
①dim; vague; ambiguous; unintelligible: 此句意義模糊。This sentence is ambiguous in sense. ②to obscure; to blur: 眼淚使我視線模糊。Tears blurred my sight.
模寫(ㄇㄛˊ ㄒㄧㄝˇ)
to transcribe; to copy
模寫教授(ㄇㄛˊ ㄒㄧㄝˇ ㄐㄧㄠˋ ㄕㄡˋ)
presentative instruction
模型(ㄇㄛˊ ㄒㄧㄥˊ)
a miniature; a model
模式(ㄇㄛˊ ㄕˋ)
a model; a formula; a pattern
模數(ㄇㄛˊ ·ㄕㄨ)
(mathematics) modulus
模造紙(ㄇㄛˊ ㄗㄠˋ ㄓˇ)
simile paper: 我要買一張模造紙。I want to buy a piece of simile paper.
模斯(ㄇㄛˊ ㄙ)
Samuel F.B. Morse (1791-1872), inventor of telegraph

【模】 2584
2. ㄇㄨˊ mu mú
a mold; a form; a matrix
模子(ㄇㄨˊ ·ㄗ)
a mold; a form
模樣(ㄇㄨˊ ㄧㄤˋ)
①appearances; looks: 他的模樣很高尚。He is a man of noble appearance. ②about; around: 那女的有30歲模樣。The woman was around thirty.

【樣】 2585
ㄧㄤˋ yanq yàng
1. appearances; looks
2. a style; a pattern; a mode; a form
3. a sort; a kind; a variety
4. a sample
樣板(ㄧㄤˋ ㄅㄢˇ)
①a sample plate ②a template ③a model; a prototype; an example
樣本(ㄧㄤˋ ㄅㄣˇ)
a sample (of printed material): 它和樣本相符。It comes up to sample.
樣品(ㄧㄤˋ ㄆㄧㄣˇ)
a specimen; a sample (of a commodity): 讓我看看布匹的樣品。Show me samples of cloths.
樣張(ㄧㄤˋ ㄓㄤ)
a specimen sheet
樣册子(ㄧㄤˋ ㄘㄜˋ ·ㄗ) or 樣册兒(ㄧㄤˋ ㄘㄜˋㄦ)
a book used to hold patterns for embroidery
樣式(ㄧㄤˋ ㄕˋ)
style; modes; patterns
樣子(ㄧㄤˋ ·ㄗ) or 樣兒(ㄧㄤˋㄦ)
①appearances; looks ②style; modes; patterns ③a sample ④a proof sheet
樣樣(ㄧㄤˋ ㄧㄤˋ)
each and every; all; every kind: 那孩子樣樣都好。That child is developing in every way.
樣樣宗宗(ㄧㄤˋ ㄧㄤˋ ㄗㄨㄥ ㄗㄨㄥ)
of all sorts; varied; diversified
樣樣兒(ㄧㄤˋ ㄧㄤˋㄦ)
every sort; every variety

【樠】 2586
ㄇㄢˊ man mán
a kind of tree

十二畫

【樸】 2587
ㄆㄨˊ pwu pú
1. (said of dress, clothing, literary style, etc.) plain; simple
2. the substance of things; things in the rough
3. honest; sincere; simple
4. *Aphananthe aspera*, a tree of the elm family
樸樸實實(ㄆㄨˊ ·ㄆㄨ ㄕˊ ㄕˊ) or 樸實(ㄆㄨˊ ㄕˊ)
①(said of dresses, style, etc.) simple; plain ②honest; sincere; simple in taste
樸馬(ㄆㄨˊ ㄇㄚˇ)
an untrained horse; a horse that has not been broken in
樸鈍(ㄆㄨˊ ㄉㄨㄣˋ)

〔木部〕

①(said of tools, knives, etc.) blunt ②(said of one's natural endowments) dull; slow; stupid

樸厚(ㄆㄨˊ ㄏㄡˋ)
simple and sincere; simple-mindedness: 此地民風樸厚。The people here are simple and sincere.

樸學(ㄆㄨˊ ㄒㄩㄝˊ)
textual study of the Chinese classics, advocated by scholars during the Han Dynasty 亦作「漢學」

樸直(ㄆㄨˊ ㄓˊ)
simple-minded; honest; sincerity

樸質(ㄆㄨˊ ㄓˊ)
not ornamented; unadorned

樸拙(ㄆㄨˊ ㄓㄨㄛˊ)
simple and naive

樸素(ㄆㄨˊ ㄙㄨˋ)
(said of dresses, etc.) simple and plain: 她的衣着樸素。She dresses simply.

樸野(ㄆㄨˊ ㄧㄝˇ)
simple; rustic

【樵】 2588 ㄑㄧㄠˊ chyau qiáo
1. firewood; fuel
2. to gather fuel or firewood
3. a woodcutter
4. to burn
5. a tower; a lookout

樵夫(ㄑㄧㄠˊ ㄈㄨ) or 樵客(ㄑㄧㄠˊ ㄎㄜˋ) or 樵子(ㄑㄧㄠˊ ㄗˇ)
a woodcutter

樵斧(ㄑㄧㄠˊ ㄈㄨˇ)
an axe

樵歌(ㄑㄧㄠˊ ㄍㄜ)
① songs of the woodcutters 亦作「樵唱」② the title of a three-volume collection of poems, etc. by Chu Tun-ju (朱敦儒) of the Sung Dynasty 亦作「太平樵唱」

樵戶(ㄑㄧㄠˊ ㄏㄨˋ)
a family which lives on woodcutting or gathering firewood

樵薪(ㄑㄧㄠˊ ㄒㄧㄣ)
to gather fuel or firewood

樵叟(ㄑㄧㄠˊ ㄙㄡˇ)
an old woodcutter

樵蘇(ㄑㄧㄠˊ ㄙㄨ)
to gather firewood and weed

樵隱(ㄑㄧㄠˊ ㄧㄣˇ)
a recluse or hermit who leads a woodcutter's life

【樺】 2589 ㄏㄨㄚˋ huah huà
a birch

樺科(ㄏㄨㄚˋ ㄎㄜ)
Betulaceae

樺燭(ㄏㄨㄚˋ ㄓㄨˊ)
a torch or candle made by rolling the bark of birch around beeswax

【樨】 2590 ㄒㄧ shi xī
a cassia tree

【橄】 2591 ㄍㄢˇ gaan gǎn
an olive

橄欖(ㄍㄢˇ ㄌㄢˇ)
olives: 橄欖是和平的象徵。An olive is the symbol of peace.

橄欖球(ㄍㄢˇ ㄌㄢˇ ㄑㄧㄡˊ)
American football; rugby: 你喜歡玩橄欖球嗎? Do you like playing American football?

橄欖枝(ㄍㄢˇ ㄌㄢˇ ㄓ)
the olive branch (a symbol of peace)

橄欖油(ㄍㄢˇ ㄌㄢˇ ㄧㄡˊ)
olive oil

【樾】 2592 ㄩㄝˋ yueh yuè
the shade of trees

樾蔭(ㄩㄝˋ ㄧㄣˋ)
the protection from the powerful

【樽】 2593 ㄗㄨㄣ tzuen zūn
1. a wine vessel; a goblet; a bottle; a wine jar
2. (said of vegetation) luxuriant

樽俎(ㄗㄨㄣ ㄗㄨˇ)
a goblet; a wine vessel (used in rituals)

樽俎折衝(ㄗㄨㄣ ㄗㄨˇ ㄓㄜˊ ㄔㄨㄥ)
to talk or negotiate over cups of wine—to discharge the duties of a diplomat

【橐】 2594 ㄊㄨㄛˊ two tuó
a bag or sack

橐筆(ㄊㄨㄛˊ ㄅㄧˇ)
living on writing

橐駝(ㄊㄨㄛˊ ㄊㄨㄛˊ)
① a camel ② a hunchback

橐橐(ㄊㄨㄛˊ ㄊㄨㄛˊ)
the sound of footsteps or rattles

橐囊(ㄊㄨㄛˊ ㄋㄤˊ)
sacks or bags

橐中裝(ㄊㄨㄛˊ ㄓㄨㄥ ㄓㄨㄤ)
gems; jewels; valuables

橐笥(ㄊㄨㄛˊ ㄙˋ)
a bag; a satchel

橐籥(ㄊㄨㄛˊ ㄩㄝˋ)
a tube for blowing up the fire in a furnace, etc.

【樹】 2595 ㄕㄨˋ shuh shù
1. trees
2. to plant; to cultivate; to grow: 十年樹木，百年樹人。It takes ten years to grow trees, but a hundred years to rear people.
3. to erect; to establish
4. (now rarely) a door screen

樹碑(ㄕㄨˋ ㄅㄟ)
to erect a memorial tablet

樹碑立傳(ㄕㄨˋ ㄅㄟ ㄌㄧˋ ㄓㄨㄢˋ)
to erect a monument and write a biography to glorify somebody—to build up somebody's public image

樹本(ㄕㄨˋ ㄅㄣˇ)
① the root of a tree ② to build a good foundation for something

樹皮(ㄕㄨˋ ㄆㄧˊ)
bark

樹末(ㄕㄨˋ ㄇㄛˋ) or 樹梢(ㄕㄨˋ ㄕㄠ)
the tip of a tree 亦作「樹杪」

樹苗(ㄕㄨˋ ㄇㄧㄠˊ)
a seedling; a sapling

樹木(ㄕㄨˋ ㄇㄨˋ)
① trees ② to plant a tree

樹大根深(ㄕㄨˋ ㄉㄚˋ ㄍㄣ ㄕㄣ)
(literally) The tree is big, and the root, deep.—① A famous personality wields great and deep-rooted influence. ② This big concern has a good foundation of long standing.

樹大招風(ㄕㄨˋ ㄉㄚˋ ㄓㄠ ㄈㄥ)
(literally) High trees attract the wind.—Famous persons attract criticisms easily.

樹大蔭大(ㄕㄨˋ ㄉㄚˋ ㄧㄣˋ ㄉㄚˋ)
(literally) The bigger the tree, the bigger the shade.—A powerful man can easily help or shield his follower.

樹德(ㄕㄨˋ ㄉㄜˊ)

to establish one's virtues; to exemplify one's integrity
樹倒猢猻散(ㄕㄨˋ ㄉㄠˇ ㄏㄨˊ ㄙㄨㄣ ㄙㄢˋ)
(literally) When a big tree comes down, all the monkeys on it will disperse. —When a big family fortune comes to nil, all who live on it will run away. 或 When a high official is dismissed from office, all his underlings will break up and run away.
樹黨(ㄕㄨˋ ㄉㄤˇ)
to form a clique, gang, faction, party, etc.
樹敵(ㄕㄨˋ ㄉㄧˊ)
to make an enemy of; to make enemy; to antagonize: 我們不應樹敵太多。We should not make too many enemies.
樹巔(ㄕㄨˋ ㄉㄧㄢ)
the top of a tree; the highest point of a tree 亦作「樹頂」
樹梃(ㄕㄨˋ ㄊㄧㄥˇ)
the trunk of a tree
樹立(ㄕㄨˋ ㄌㄧˋ)
to establish (a reputation, etc.)
樹林(ㄕㄨˋ ㄌㄧㄣˊ)
a forest; a grove of trees; woods
樹幹(ㄕㄨˋ ㄍㄢˋ)
the trunk of a tree
樹根(ㄕㄨˋ ㄍㄣ)
the root of a tree
樹節(ㄕㄨˋ ㄐㄧㄝˊ)
to establish one's virtue; to preserve one's integrity
樹介(ㄕㄨˋ ㄐㄧㄝˋ)
icicles on a tree
樹膠(ㄕㄨˋ ㄐㄧㄠ)
resin; gum
樹教(ㄕㄨˋ ㄐㄧㄠˋ)
to establish a religion
樹起筋骨(ㄕㄨˋ ㄑㄧˇ ㄐㄧㄣ ㄍㄨˇ)
to pull oneself together (for a task, etc.)
樹下(ㄕㄨˋ ㄒㄧㄚˋ)
under the tree
樹勳(ㄕㄨˋ ㄒㄩㄣ)
to establish one's name by great accomplishments
樹汁(ㄕㄨˋ ㄓ)
sap
樹枝(ㄕㄨˋ ㄓ)
boughs or branches of a tree: 樹枝在微風中搖曳。The branches waved in the breeze.
樹脂(ㄕㄨˋ ㄓ)
resin
樹樁子(ㄕㄨˋ ㄓㄨㄤ ·ㄗ)
the stump of a tree: 獵人坐在樹樁子上。The hunter sat on a stump.
樹杈兒(ㄕㄨˋ ㄔㄚˋㄦ)
the fork of a tree; a crotch: 她正坐在一棵樹杈兒上。She is sitting in the crotch of a tree.
樹身(ㄕㄨˋ ㄕㄣ)
① the trunk of a tree ② to establish one's virtue; to preserve one's integrity
樹上(ㄕㄨˋ ㄕㄤˋ)
on the tree; above the tree: 鳥兒棲息於樹上。The bird perched on the tree.
樹薯粉(ㄕㄨˋ ㄕㄨˇ ㄈㄣˇ)
cassava
樹人(ㄕㄨˋ ㄖㄣˊ)
to cultivate young persons; to educate the young
樹叢(ㄕㄨˋ ㄘㄨㄥˊ)
a grove of trees
樹恩(ㄕㄨˋ ㄣ)
to give favors; to befriend
樹葉(ㄕㄨˋ ㄧㄝˋ) or 樹葉子(ㄕㄨˋ ㄧㄝˋ ·ㄗ) or 樹葉兒(ㄕㄨˋ ㄧㄜˋㄦ)
the leaves of a tree; foliage
樹腰(ㄕㄨˋ ㄧㄠ)
the middle of a tree trunk
樹陰(ㄕㄨˋ ㄧㄣ) or 樹蔭(ㄕㄨˋ ㄧㄣˋ)
the shade of a tree: 我在樹蔭下休息。I took a rest in the shade of a tree.
樹影(ㄕㄨˋ ㄧㄥˇ)
the shadow of a tree
樹威(ㄕㄨˋ ㄨㄟ)
to establish one's reputation, awe-inspiring name, or great influence
樹欲靜而風不止(ㄕㄨˋ ㄩˋ ㄐㄧㄥˋ ㄦˊ ㄈㄥ ㄅㄨˋ ㄓˇ)
(literally) The tree wants to remain quiet, but the winds won't stop.—I'd like to do something, but circumstances won't allow it.
樹怨(ㄕㄨˋ ㄩㄢˋ)
to make an enemy of; to make enemy; to antagonize: 他的政策使得市民和他樹怨。His policy antagonized the people of the town.

2596
【橇】 ㄘㄨㄟˋ tsuey cuì (又讀 ㄑㄧㄠ chiau qiāo)
a sledge for transportation over mud or snow; a sleigh

2597
【橈】 ㄋㄠˊ nau náo
1. crooked or bent wood
2. to enfeeble; to weaken; to sap; to devitalize
3. to disperse; to scatter
4. to wrong or be wronged
橈敗(ㄋㄠˊ ㄅㄞˋ)
defeated as troops
橈骨(ㄋㄠˊ ㄍㄨˇ)
(anatomy) the radius of the forearm
橈足(ㄋㄠˊ ㄗㄨˊ)
(zoology) pleopod, a swimmeret 亦作「腹肢」
橈足類(ㄋㄠˊ ㄗㄨˊ ㄌㄟˋ)
(zoology) copepoda

2598
【橋】 ㄑㄧㄠˊ chyau qiáo
1. a bridge; any bridge-like structure: 河上架着一座橋。A bridge was built across the river.
2. beams of a structure
3. (now rarely) cross-grained
4. tall; high; elevated
5. a Chinese family name
橋牌(ㄑㄧㄠˊ ㄆㄞˊ)
(card games) bridge
橋墩(ㄑㄧㄠˊ ㄉㄨㄣ)
the buttresses of a bridge
橋洞(ㄑㄧㄠˊ ㄉㄨㄥˋ)
the arches of a bridge
橋頭(ㄑㄧㄠˊ ㄊㄡˊ)
either end of a bridge
橋頭堡(ㄑㄧㄠˊ ㄊㄡˊ ㄅㄠˇ)
①(military) a bridgehead ② (construction) a bridge tower
橋欄杆(ㄑㄧㄠˊ ㄌㄢˊ ·ㄍㄢ)
railings or balustrades of a bridge
橋梁(ㄑㄧㄠˊ ㄌㄧㄤˊ)
any material which forms the span of a bridge
橋拱(ㄑㄧㄠˊ ㄍㄨㄥˇ)
a bridge arch
橋下(ㄑㄧㄠˊ ㄒㄧㄚˋ)

〔木部〕

below the bridge
橋上(ㄑㄧㄠˊ ㄕㄤˋ)
on the bridge

2599
【橙】 ㄔㄥˊ cherng chéng (語音 ㄔㄣˊ chern chén)
the orange: 柳橙產於溫暖的地方。Oranges are produced in warm districts.
橙皮(ㄔㄥˊ ㄆㄧˊ)
orange peel—used in Chinese herbal medicine
橙皮菓醬(ㄔㄥˊ ㄆㄧˊ ㄍㄨㄛˇ ㄐㄧㄤˋ)
marmalade
橙黃橘綠(ㄔㄥˊ ㄏㄨㄤˊ ㄐㄩˊ ㄌㄩˋ)
the autumn season (when the oranges mellow)
橙黃色(ㄔㄥˊ ㄏㄨㄤˊ ㄙㄜˋ)
orange (color)
橙汁(ㄔㄥˊ ㄓ)
orange juice
橙子(ㄔㄥˊ ·ㄗ)
oranges

2600
【橘】 ㄐㄩˊ jyu jú
the mandarin orange; the Chinese orange; a tangerine
橘餅(ㄐㄩˊ ㄅㄧㄥˇ)
flattened orange seasoned with honey
橘皮(ㄐㄩˊ ㄆㄧˊ)or 橘紅(ㄐㄩˊ ㄏㄨㄥˊ)
the peel of mandarin orange—used in Chinese herbal medicine
橘化爲枳(ㄐㄩˊ ㄏㄨㄚˋ ㄨㄟˊ ㄓˇ)
The orange in the south of the River Huai becomes its another variety when it is transplanted into the north of the River Huai.—(figuratively) Things will turn out differently in different localities or surroundings.
橘黃(ㄐㄩˊ ㄏㄨㄤˊ)
an orange color
橘紅(ㄐㄩˊ ㄏㄨㄥˊ)
① tangerine (color) ② (Chinese medicine) dried tangerine peel
橘樹(ㄐㄩˊ ㄕㄨˋ)
the mandarin orange tree
橘子(ㄐㄩˊ ·ㄗ)
mandarin oranges; tangerines
橘子汁(ㄐㄩˊ ·ㄗ ㄓ)
orange juice: 我喜歡喝橘子汁。I like orange juice.

2601
【橡】 ㄒㄧㄤˋ shianq xiàng
an acorn
橡皮(ㄒㄧㄤˋ ㄆㄧˊ)
① a rubber; an eraser: 這枝鉛筆有橡皮。The pencil has a rubber. ② rubber
橡皮圖章(ㄒㄧㄤˋ ㄆㄧˊ ㄊㄨˊ ㄓㄤ)
a rubber stamp
橡皮膏(ㄒㄧㄤˋ ㄆㄧˊ ㄍㄠ)
adhesive plaster
橡皮筋(ㄒㄧㄤˋ ㄆㄧˊ ㄐㄧㄣ)
rubber bands
橡栗(ㄒㄧㄤˋ ㄌㄧˋ)
oak chestnuts
橡膠(ㄒㄧㄤˋ ㄐㄧㄠ)
rubber
橡膠樹(ㄒㄧㄤˋ ㄐㄧㄠ ㄕㄨˋ)
a rubber tree
橡膠園(ㄒㄧㄤˋ ㄐㄧㄠ ㄩㄢˊ)
a plantation of trees that produce latex
橡實(ㄒㄧㄤˋ ㄕˊ)or 橡子(ㄒㄧㄤˋ ㄗˇ)
an acorn
橡樹(ㄒㄧㄤˋ ㄕㄨˋ)
an oak

2602
【橢】 ㄊㄨㄛˇ tuoo tuǒ
oval; oblong; elliptical
橢圓(ㄊㄨㄛˇ ㄩㄢˊ)
(mathematics) an ellipse
橢圓體(ㄊㄨㄛˇ ㄩㄢˊ ㄊㄧˇ)
an ellipsoid
橢圓規(ㄊㄨㄛˇ ㄩㄢˊ ㄍㄨㄟ)
an ellipsograph; elliptical compasses
橢圓形的(ㄊㄨㄛˇ ㄩㄢˊ ㄒㄧㄥˊ ·ㄉㄜ)
oval; elliptical

2603
【橦】 ㄊㄨㄥˊ torng tóng
a species of tree grown in Yunnan (雲南) whose flowers are used to make a kind of cloth
橦布(ㄊㄨㄥˊ ㄅㄨˋ)
the cloth made from the flowers of 橦

2604
【槾】 ㄇㄤˇ maang mǎng
a mango

2605
【機】 ㄐㄧ ji jī
1. mechanics; machinery
2. opportune; opportunity
3. a crucial point; a pivot
4. tricky; cunning
5. an aircraft; a plane; an airplane: 你要坐飛機去嗎? Are you going by plane?
機堡(ㄐㄧ ㄅㄠˇ)
revetment (for parking an airplane)
機變(ㄐㄧ ㄅㄧㄢˋ)
① to adapt oneself to environment, etc.; flexibility ② cunning and shrewd; contrivances and versatile schemes
機變百出(ㄐㄧ ㄅㄧㄢˋ ㄅㄞˇ ㄔㄨ)
with a thousand tricks up one's sleeves
機謀(ㄐㄧ ㄇㄡˊ)
① shrewdness; cunning; quick-witted and full of tricks; tricky ② a stratagem
機米(ㄐㄧ ㄇㄧˇ)
machine-polished rice
機密(ㄐㄧ ㄇㄧˋ)
secret; confidential; classified: 我們應嚴守國防機密。We should strictly guard national defense secrets.
機密消息(ㄐㄧ ㄇㄧˋ ㄒㄧㄠ ·ㄒㄧ)
classified information
機密文件(ㄐㄧ ㄇㄧˋ ㄨㄣˊ ㄐㄧㄢˋ)
secret or confidential documents: 這是絕對機密文件。This is strictly confidential documents.
機敏(ㄐㄧ ㄇㄧㄣˇ)
sharp; quick-witted; shrewdness; cleverness; perspicacity; resourceful
機房(ㄐㄧ ㄈㄤˊ)
① a storage for textile machinery ② an engine room
機動(ㄐㄧ ㄉㄨㄥˋ)
mobile
機動性(ㄐㄧ ㄉㄨㄥˋ ㄒㄧㄥˋ)
(military) mobility
機動車(ㄐㄧ ㄉㄨㄥˋ ㄔㄜ)
motorized vehicles
機頭(ㄐㄧ ㄊㄡˊ)
the nose section of an airplane
機能(ㄐㄧ ㄋㄥˊ)
functions; functional (ailments, etc.)
機鈕(ㄐㄧ ㄋㄧㄡˇ)
① a button that controls a machine ② a key point in something or development
機靈(ㄐㄧ ㄌㄧㄥˊ)
clever; smart; sharp; intelli-

gent: 她是一個機靈的學生。She is a smart student.
機伶(ㄐㄧ ˙ㄌㄧㄥ)
quick-witted; clever; readily responsive 參看「機靈」
機伶鬼兒(ㄐㄧ ˙ㄌㄧㄥ ㄍㄨㄜˇㄦ)
a quick-witted or clever fellow
機率(ㄐㄧ ㄌㄩˋ)
the probability 亦作「或然率」
機構(ㄐㄧ ㄍㄡˋ)
an organization
機關(ㄐㄧ ㄍㄨㄢ)
①an organization; an institution ②a machine ③a stratagem; an intrigue
機關報(ㄐㄧ ㄍㄨㄢ ㄅㄠˋ)
a government party paper; an official mouthpiece
機關槍(ㄐㄧ ㄍㄨㄢ ㄑㄧㄤ)
a machine gun
機關車(ㄐㄧ ㄍㄨㄢ ㄔㄜ)
a locomotive; an engine
機工(ㄐㄧ ㄍㄨㄥ)
①a mechanic; a worker in a textile mill ②short for mechanical engineering
機庫(ㄐㄧ ㄎㄨˋ)
a hangar
機括(ㄐㄧ ㄎㄨㄛˋ)
①a mechanism; a mechanical contrivance ②a catch or trigger
機會(ㄐㄧ ㄏㄨㄟˋ)
opportunity: 此種機會不應失去。Such opportunities should not be missed.
機會均等(ㄐㄧ ㄏㄨㄟˋ ㄐㄩㄣ ㄉㄥˇ)
equal opportunity
機會主義(ㄐㄧ ㄏㄨㄟˋ ㄓㄨˇ ㄧˋ)
opportunism
機會主義者(ㄐㄧ ㄏㄨㄟˋ ㄓㄨˇ ㄧˋ ㄓㄜˇ)
an opportunist
機捷(ㄐㄧ ㄐㄧㄝˊ)
witty; quick-witted; cleverness
機件(ㄐㄧ ㄐㄧㄢˋ)
machine parts or works; component parts of a machine
機近(ㄐㄧ ㄐㄧㄣˋ)
secret and strategic (positions, places, points, etc.)
機警(ㄐㄧ ㄐㄧㄥˇ)
alert; alertness; sharp and quick-witted: 他很機警。He has an alert mind.
機器(ㄐㄧ ㄑㄧˋ)
machinery; a machine: 一個工廠有許多機器。A factory contains much machinery.
機器人(ㄐㄧ ㄑㄧˋ ㄖㄣˊ)
a robot
機巧(ㄐㄧ ㄑㄧㄠˇ)
tact; tactful; clever; cleverness; shrewd; shrewdness
機槍(ㄐㄧ ㄑㄧㄤ)
a machine gun
機槍手(ㄐㄧ ㄑㄧㄤ ㄕㄡˇ)
a machine gunner
機羣(ㄐㄧ ㄑㄩㄣˊ)
an air armada; a fleet of airplanes
機械(ㄐㄧ ㄒㄧㄝˋ)
①a machine; machinery ②mechanical: 我不喜歡機械般的勞動。I don't like mechanical labor. ③(said of persons) cunning or shrewd
機械工程(ㄐㄧ ㄒㄧㄝˋ ㄍㄨㄥ ㄔㄥˊ)
mechanical engineering
機械化(ㄐㄧ ㄒㄧㄝˋ ㄏㄨㄚˋ)
mechanization
機械化部隊(ㄐㄧ ㄒㄧㄝˋ ㄏㄨㄚˋ ㄅㄨˋ ㄉㄨㄟˋ)
motorized troops; mechanized troops
機械性(ㄐㄧ ㄒㄧㄝˋ ㄒㄧㄥˋ)
of a mechanical nature; mechanical: 她的誦讀很機械性。Her reading is very mechanical.
機械學(ㄐㄧ ㄒㄧㄝˋ ㄒㄩㄝˊ)
mechanics
機械油(ㄐㄧ ㄒㄧㄝˋ ㄧㄡˊ)
lubricants for machines
機先(ㄐㄧ ㄒㄧㄢ)
(to take) the initiative or steps in advance
機心(ㄐㄧ ㄒㄧㄣ)
a shrewd and cunning mind: 他是個有機心的政客。He is a shrewd politician.
機型(ㄐㄧ ㄒㄧㄥˊ)
①the type (of an aircraft) ②the model (of a machine): 他的車子是去年的機型。His car is last year's model.
機織(ㄐㄧ ㄓ)
machine-woven; woven by a machine
機製(ㄐㄧ ㄓˋ)
made by a machine; machine-made
機智(ㄐㄧ ㄓˋ)
alertness; quick wit; ready responsiveness; skillful; tact: 簡潔乃機智的靈魂。Brevity is the soul of wit.
機詐(ㄐㄧ ㄓㄚˋ)
cunningness; cunning; tricky; crafty; sly
機軸(ㄐㄧ ㄓㄡˊ)
a pivot; an axis
機長(ㄐㄧ ㄓㄤˇ)
an aircraft (or crew) commander
機杼(ㄐㄧ ㄓㄨˋ)
①the shuttle of a loom ②the construction of an essay
機車(ㄐㄧ ㄔㄜ)
①motorcycles: 他騎機車上工。He goes to work by motorcycle. ②a locomotive
機場(ㄐㄧ ㄔㄤˇ)or(ㄐㄧ ㄔㄤˊ)
an airport; an airfield
機床(ㄐㄧ ㄔㄨㄤˊ)
a machine tool
機師(ㄐㄧ ㄕ)
a pilot (of an airplane)
機身(ㄐㄧ ㄕㄣ)
the fuselage
機組(ㄐㄧ ㄗㄨˇ)
①(machinery) a unit; a set ②the aircrew; the flight crew
機座(ㄐㄧ ㄗㄨㄛˋ)
machine base; machine foundation
機艙(ㄐㄧ ㄘㄤ)
the cockpit of a small airplane; the cabin of an airliner
機宜(ㄐㄧ ㄧˊ)
a matter and its arrangements; a line of action; guidelines; a policy
機翼(ㄐㄧ ㄧˋ)
wings of an airplane: 機翼在飛行中折斷。The wings of an airplane were broken in the flight.
機要(ㄐㄧ ㄧㄠˋ)
confidential and important (matters, etc.)
機要秘書(ㄐㄧ ㄧㄠˋ ㄇㄧˋ ㄕㄨ)
a confidential secretary
機油(ㄐㄧ ㄧㄡˊ)
lubricating oil; lubricant: 上

油的時候試試這種機油。When it's time to lubricate, try this lubricant.

機務(ㄐㄧ ㄨˋ)
①important matters ②mechanical work

機尾(ㄐㄧ ㄨㄟˇ)
the tail section of an airplane

機遇(ㄐㄧ ㄩˋ)
chance; opportunity; luck

機員(ㄐㄧ ㄩㄢˊ)
a member of an aircraft crew

機緣(ㄐㄧ ㄩㄢˊ)
chance and opportunity: 偶然的機緣導致鑽石礦的發現。Chance led to the finding of the diamond mine.

機運(ㄐㄧ ㄩㄣˋ)
luck; fate: 凡事都有機運。There is luck in everything.

【橫】2606
1. ㄏㄥˊ herng héng

1. horizontal; crosswise; lateral
2. east to west or vice versa
3. by the side of; sideways
4. to move crosswise; to traverse: 這條鐵路橫貫沙漠數百哩。This railway traverses hundreds of miles of the desert.
5. unrestrainedly; turbulently: 江河橫溢。Waters overflow turbulently.
6. a Chinese family name

橫波(ㄏㄥˊ ㄅㄛ)
①the sideway glances (of a beauty, etc.) ②a transverse wave

橫濱(ㄏㄥˊ ㄅㄧㄣ)
Yokohama, Japan

橫披(ㄏㄥˊ ㄆㄧ)
the horizontal scroll of painting or calligraphic work

橫眉瞪眼(ㄏㄥˊ ㄇㄟˊ ㄉㄥˋ ㄧㄢˇ)
angry looks; to look angrily at 亦作「橫眉立目」

橫目(ㄏㄥˊ ㄇㄨˋ)
①angry eyes; to look angrily at ②(now rarely) human kind

橫幅(ㄏㄥˊ ㄈㄨˊ)
①a horizontal scroll of painting or calligraphy ②a banner

橫刀奪愛(ㄏㄥˊ ㄉㄠ ㄉㄨㄛˊ ㄞˋ)
to take away another's woman by force

橫笛(ㄏㄥˊ ㄉㄧˊ)
the common flute (to be played horizontally)

橫渡(ㄏㄥˊ ㄉㄨˋ)
to cross (a river, ocean, etc.)

橫隊(ㄏㄥˊ ㄉㄨㄟˋ)
a rank; a row

橫斷面(ㄏㄥˊ ㄉㄨㄢˋ ㄇㄧㄢˋ)
the cross section

橫斷山脈(ㄏㄥˊ ㄉㄨㄢˋ ㄕㄢ ㄇㄞˋ) or 橫貫山脈(ㄏㄥˊ ㄍㄨㄢˋ ㄕㄢ ㄇㄞˋ)
①a mountain range that runs from east to west ②name of a mountain range in Sikang(西康) stretching to Szechwan(四川) and Yunnan(雲南)

橫躺豎臥(ㄏㄥˊ ㄊㄤˇ ㄕㄨˋ ㄨㄛˋ)
(said of persons) lying in total disorder

橫了心(ㄏㄥˊ ·ㄌㄜ ㄒㄧㄣ)
to steel one's heart (as a result of anger; an indication of determination, etc.); in desperation

橫攔豎遮(ㄏㄥˊ ㄌㄢˊ ㄕㄨˋ ㄓㄜ)
to place obstructions at every possible point

橫列(ㄏㄥˊ ㄌㄧㄝˋ)
to arrange in a horizontal line

橫流(ㄏㄥˊ ㄌㄧㄡˊ)
(said of a river) to overflow; to run out of the accustomed course

橫梁(ㄏㄥˊ ㄌㄧㄤˊ)
a crossbeam

橫膈膜(ㄏㄥˊ ㄍㄜˊ ㄇㄛˊ)
the diaphragm

橫亙(ㄏㄥˊ ㄍㄣˋ)
①crosswise; horizontal; from east to west or vice versa ②to span; to traverse: 一座美麗的大橋橫亙在河上。A beautiful bridge traversed the river.

橫貫公路(ㄏㄥˊ ㄍㄨㄢˋ ㄍㄨㄥ ㄌㄨˋ)
①any highway that runs from east to west ②the Cross-Island or East-West Highway in Taiwan

橫跨(ㄏㄥˊ ㄎㄨㄚˋ)
to stretch over or across: 一道彩虹橫跨天際。A rainbow stretched across the sky.

橫截(ㄏㄥˊ ㄐㄧㄝˊ)
to cut across

橫截面(ㄏㄥˊ ㄐㄧㄝˊ ㄇㄧㄢˋ)
a cross section

橫七豎八(ㄏㄥˊ ㄑㄧ ㄕㄨˋ ㄅㄚ)
in total disorder or disarray; to be cluttered: 那房間橫七豎八地堆滿了書和雜誌。The room was cluttered up with books and magazines.

橫起來(ㄏㄥˊ ㄑㄧˇ ·ㄌㄞ)
①to place things horizontally ②to shoulder the responsibility of

橫渠學派(ㄏㄥˊ ㄑㄩˊ ㄒㄩㄝˊ ㄆㄞˋ)
a school of learning founded by Chang Tsai(張載) of the Northern Sung Dynasty stressing on emulating ancient styles

橫寫(ㄏㄥˊ ㄒㄧㄝˇ)
to write horizontally (as distinct from the traditional Chinese way of writing from top to bottom)

橫行(ㄏㄥˊ ㄒㄧㄥˊ)
①to run wild; to proceed on ways other than proper (usually evil) ②to move sideways—as crabs

橫行霸道(ㄏㄥˊ ㄒㄧㄥˊ ㄅㄚˋ ㄉㄠˋ)
to bully; to terrorize; to act tyrannically; to behave in total disregard of law

橫行介士(ㄏㄥˊ ㄒㄧㄥˊ ㄐㄧㄝˋ ㄕˋ)
the crab

橫行文字(ㄏㄥˊ ㄒㄧㄥˊ ㄨㄣˊ ㄗˋ)
the Romanized languages—English, French, German, etc. that go horizontally

橫須賀(ㄏㄥˊ ㄒㄩ ㄏㄜˋ)
Yokosuka, the biggest Japanese naval base

橫軸(ㄏㄥˊ ㄓㄡˊ)
①a horizontal scroll (of calligraphy, picture, etc.) ②a transversal axis, or the axis of an abscissa

橫振動(ㄏㄥˊ ㄓㄣˋ ㄉㄨㄥˋ)
transverse vibration

橫征暴斂(ㄏㄥˊ ㄓㄥ ㄅㄠˋ ㄌㄧㄢˋ)
to impose or force unbearable taxes on the people: 國王橫征暴斂。A king imposed unbearable taxes on the peo-

ple.

横陳(ㄏㄥˊ ㄔㄣˊ)
to lie down with limbs fully stretched

横衝直撞(ㄏㄥˊ ㄔㄨㄥ ㄓˊ ㄓㄨㄤˋ)
(said of a bull, car, truck, etc.) to bump; to jostle and elbow one's way right and left

横生(ㄏㄥˊ ㄕㄥ)
① to arise from every side ② to be full of; to brim (with happiness, interest, etc.): 他的演說妙趣横生。His speech was full of wit and humor. ③ all beings except human beings

横生枝節(ㄏㄥˊ ㄕㄥ ㄓ ㄐㄧㄝˊ)
① side issues or new problems that come or appear unexpectedly ② to raise obstacles; to complicate an issue deliberately

横豎
①(ㄏㄥˊ ㄕㄨˋ) in any case; anyway
②(ㄏㄥˊ ˙ㄕㄨ) horizontal and perpendicular; in every direction

横說豎說(ㄏㄥˊ ㄕㄨㄛ ㄕㄨˋ ㄕㄨㄛ)
to persuade repeatedly and insistently; to exhaust oneself with persuasion

横槊賦詩(ㄏㄥˊ ㄕㄨㄛˋ ㄈㄨˋ ㄕ)
(literally) to compose poems while holding the lance horizontally in the saddle—to indulge in literary pursuits while in war

横閂(ㄏㄥˊ ㄕㄨㄢ)
a door latch or bolt

横肉(ㄏㄥˊ ㄖㄡˋ)
(said of a person's appearance) fierce-looking: 他一臉横肉。He is fierce-looking.

横坐標(ㄏㄥˊ ㄗㄨㄛˋ ㄅㄧㄠ)
(mathematics) an abscissa

横財(ㄏㄥˊ ㄘㄞˊ)
a fortune which one doesn't deserve; a windfall; illegal gains: 他發了横財。He made a windfall.

横掃(ㄏㄥˊ ㄙㄠˇ)
to sweep away; to make a clean sweep of; to roll back

横三豎四(ㄏㄥˊ ㄙㄢ ㄕㄨˋ ㄙˋ)
disorderly; in disarray; confusion

横兒(ㄏㄥˊ ㄦ)
①(calligraphy) a horizontal stroke ② a horizontal scroll or picture

横溢(ㄏㄥˊ ㄧˋ)
① brimming; overflowing; abundant ② to brim; to overflow: 河水横溢兩岸。The river overflowed its banks.

横紋肌(ㄏㄥˊ ㄨㄣˊ ㄐㄧ)
the striped muscle

【横】 2606
2. ㄏㄥˋ henq hèng
1. cross-grained; perverse
2. presumptuous and unreasonable
3. unexpected; uncalled for
4. violent; cross

横暴(ㄏㄥˋ ㄅㄠˋ)
perverse and tyrannical

横逆(ㄏㄥˋ ㄋㄧˋ)
perverse and unreasonable; unreasonableness

横流(ㄏㄥˋ ㄌㄧㄡˊ)
water flowing out of its proper course; an overflowing of (evil tides, etc.)

横話(ㄏㄥˋ ㄏㄨㄚˋ)
① unlucky words or utterances ② stiff and stern language; harsh words

横禍(ㄏㄥˋ ㄏㄨㄛˋ)
unexpected misfortune or disaster

横政(ㄏㄥˋ ㄓㄥˋ)
tyrannical rule or administration

横事(ㄏㄥˋ ㄕˋ)
a bad accident; unlucky happenings

横恣(ㄏㄥˋ ㄗˋ)
arrogant and presumptuous

横死(ㄏㄥˋ ㄙˇ)
an unnatural death; a violent death; to meet with a sudden death

横議(ㄏㄥˋ ㄧˋ)
extreme views; radical statements; far-fetched arguments

横夭(ㄏㄥˋ ㄧㄠˇ)
an unnatural death

十三畫

【檀】 2607
ㄊㄢˊ tarn tán
1. sandalwood
2. a Chinese family name

檀板(ㄊㄢˊ ㄅㄢˇ)
pieces (usually three) of hardwood for beating time; castanets

檀島(ㄊㄢˊ ㄉㄠˇ)
the Hawaiian Islands

檀郎(ㄊㄢˊ ㄌㄤˊ)
(formerly) a term of address for one's husband or lover

檀林(ㄊㄢˊ ㄌㄧㄣˊ)
a Buddhist monastery

檀口(ㄊㄢˊ ㄎㄡˇ)
the red lips of a pretty girl

檀香(ㄊㄢˊ ㄒㄧㄤ)
① incense made of sandalwood ② *Santalum album*

檀香山(ㄊㄢˊ ㄒㄧㄤ ㄕㄢ)
Honolulu

檀越(ㄊㄢˊ ㄩㄝˋ)
Danapati, an almsgiver, or a patron (a salutation used by Buddhist monks in addressing one who bestows alms)

【檄】 2608
ㄒㄧˊ shyi xí
a summons to arms in ancient times

檄文(ㄒㄧˊ ㄨㄣˊ)
a written summons to arms for a cause; a manifesto listing the crimes of a tyrant

【檐】 2609
(簷) ㄧㄢˊ yan yán
1. eaves of a house
2. the brim: 請抓住你的帽檐兒。Please hold the brim of your cap.

【檔】 2610
ㄉㄤˇ daang dǎng
(又讀 ㄉㄤˋ danq dàng)
1. an abbreviation for 檔案 (files)
2. shelves; pigeonholes
3. a wooden crosspiece, as the rung of a ladder, etc.
4. (now rarely) a wooden chair

檔卷(ㄉㄤˇ ㄐㄩㄢˋ)
official files

檔期(ㄉㄤˇ ㄑㄧˊ)
a schedule for showing motion pictures in a theater

檔子(ㄉㄤˇ ˙ㄗ) or 檔兒(ㄉㄤˇ ㄦ)
① one (thing, matter) ② a group of (persons, etc.)

〔木部〕

〔木部〕

檔册(ㄉㄤˇ ㄘㄜˋ)
records; files
檔案(ㄉㄤˇ ㄢˋ)
official files (of government offices); archives: 他們調閱了所有檔案。They consulted all the files.

【檉】2611
ㄔㄥ cheng chēng
a tamarisk
檉柳(ㄔㄥ ㄌㄧㄡˇ)
a tamarisk

【檜】2612
ㄎㄨㄞˋ kuay kuài
(又讀 ㄍㄨㄟˋ guey guì)
the Chinese juniper or cypress
檜柏(ㄎㄨㄞˋ ㄅㄛˊ)
a Chinese cypress
檜木(ㄎㄨㄞˋ ㄇㄨˋ)
timber of a Chinese cypress or juniper

【檎】2613
ㄑㄧㄣˊ chyn qín
a small red apple (*Malus asiatica*)

【檟】2614
ㄐㄧㄚˇ jea jiǎ
1. an ancient version of 茶, tea
2. a small evergreen shrub (*Mallotus japonicus*)

【檢】2615
ㄐㄧㄢˇ jean jiǎn
1. a book label
2. to sort; to gather
3. to inspect; to check up; to collate
4. to discuss thoroughly: 我們檢討利弊得失。We discussed thoroughly the merits and demerits.
5. a form; a pattern
6. to restrict; to regulate
檢波器(ㄐㄧㄢˇ ㄅㄛ ㄑㄧˋ)
a detector (for testing conductivity of electric currents)
檢點(ㄐㄧㄢˇ ㄉㄧㄢˇ)
①to behave (oneself) ②to inspect and arrange; to check ③(in ancient China) a bodyguard; an orderly ④to be cautious; to be careful: 他的言行有失檢點。He was careless about his words and acts.
檢定(ㄐㄧㄢˇ ㄉㄧㄥˋ)
①to inspect and approve (or sanction) ②inspection
檢定考試(ㄐㄧㄢˇ ㄉㄧㄥˋ ㄎㄠˇ ㄕˋ)
an examination held to determine the qualification of government employees and teachers who have not received regular training for the posts they are to hold
檢討(ㄐㄧㄢˇ ㄊㄠˇ)
to review and discuss (past performances, etc.); to make self-examination or soul-searching
檢討會(ㄐㄧㄢˇ ㄊㄠˇ ㄏㄨㄟˋ)
a conference held for reviewing and discussing past performances, plans, etc.
檢校(ㄐㄧㄢˇ ㄐㄧㄠˋ)
①to collate and correct; to examine ②to evaluate or grade the performance of government officials
檢舉(ㄐㄧㄢˇ ㄐㄩˇ)
to lay bare evidences of a corrupt official, etc.; to inform the authorities of an unlawful act, plot, etc.; to inform against an offender, etc.: 人人應該檢舉罪犯。Everyone should inform against a criminal.
檢修(ㄐㄧㄢˇ ㄒㄧㄡ)
to examine and repair; to overhaul: 他正在檢修汽車引擎。He is overhauling the engine of a car.
檢查(ㄐㄧㄢˇ ㄔㄚˊ)
to inspect; to examine; to test (a machine, etc.); (physical) checkup: 我已作了身體檢查。I have had a physical examination.
檢查站(ㄐㄧㄢˇ ㄔㄚˊ ㄓㄢˋ)
a checkpoint; an inspection station
檢查人員(ㄐㄧㄢˇ ㄔㄚˊ ㄖㄣˊ ㄩㄢˊ)
an inspector (as a customs officer, etc.); a person authorized to search, inspect, etc.
檢察(ㄐㄧㄢˇ ㄔㄚˊ)
①to inspect ②inspection
檢察官(ㄐㄧㄢˇ ㄔㄚˊ ㄍㄨㄢ)
a court prosecutor; an attorney general; a procurator
檢察長(ㄐㄧㄢˇ ㄔㄚˊ ㄓㄤˇ)
the procurator general (of the Supreme Court)
檢察處(ㄐㄧㄢˇ ㄔㄚˊ ㄔㄨˋ)
a judicial office where court prosecutors institute prosecutions in criminal cases; a procuratorate
檢束(ㄐㄧㄢˇ ㄕㄨˋ)
to discipline; to restrain: 她無法檢束孩子們惡作劇。She could not restrain her children from mischief.
檢字(ㄐㄧㄢˇ ㄗˋ)
①a table or index in a dictionary to help find a word ②to censor or screen writings
檢字法(ㄐㄧㄢˇ ㄗˋ ㄈㄚˇ)
the method for using the table or index in a dictionary for finding words
檢疫(ㄐㄧㄢˇ ㄧˋ)
quarantine
檢疫所(ㄐㄧㄢˇ ㄧˋ ㄙㄨㄛˇ)
the quarantine office
檢驗(ㄐㄧㄢˇ ㄧㄢˋ)
to inspect and examine; inspection
檢溫器(ㄐㄧㄢˇ ㄨㄣ ㄑㄧˋ)
a medical thermometer
檢閱(ㄐㄧㄢˇ ㄩㄝˋ)
to inspect or review (troops); a military review: 將軍正在檢閱儀仗隊。The general is reviewing a guard of honor.

【檣】2616
ㄑㄧㄤˊ chyang qiáng
the mast of a ship: 這船有三根桅檣。The ship has three masts.
檣傾楫摧(ㄑㄧㄤˊ ㄑㄧㄥ ㄐㄧˊ ㄘㄨㄟ)
a totally wrecked boat

【檁】2617
ㄌㄧㄣˇ liin lǐn
a crossbeam in a house
檁子(ㄌㄧㄣˇ ・ㄗ)
purlins; crossbeams

【檥】2618
ㄧˇ yii yǐ
to moor a boat to the bank

【檝】2619
(楫) ㄐㄧˊ jyi jí
an oar or paddle

十四畫

【檸】 2620 ㄋㄧㄥˊ ning níng
lemon
檸檬(ㄋㄧㄥˊ ㄇㄥˊ)
lemon: 我喜歡在茶裡加檸檬。I like lemon in my tea.
檸檬水(ㄋㄧㄥˊ ㄇㄥˊ ㄕㄨㄟˇ)
lemonade
檸檬色(ㄋㄧㄥˊ ㄇㄥˊ ㄙㄜˋ)
citrine
檸檬素(ㄋㄧㄥˊ ㄇㄥˊ ㄙㄨˋ)
citrin
檸檬酸(ㄋㄧㄥˊ ㄇㄥˊ ㄙㄨㄢ)
citric acid
檸檬酸鹽(ㄋㄧㄥˊ ㄇㄥˊ ㄙㄨㄢ ㄧㄢˊ)
citrate

【檬】 2621 ㄇㄥˊ meng méng
1. a kind of locust or acacia
2. lemon
檬果(ㄇㄥˊ ㄍㄨㄛˇ)
a mango 亦作「芒果」

【檮】 2622 ㄊㄠˊ taur táo
ignorant and stupid; a blockhead
檮昧(ㄊㄠˊ ㄇㄟˋ)
ignorant and naive; dull and stupid
檮杌(ㄊㄠˊ ㄨˋ)
① a legendary fierce animal ② villainous

【檻】 2623 1. ㄐㄧㄢˋ jiann jiàn
railings; bars, as window or door bars
檻車(ㄐㄧㄢˋ ㄔㄜ)
a cart with a cage for animals or prisoners
檻羊(ㄐㄧㄢˋ ㄧㄤˊ)
(figuratively) at the mercy of others like a caged lamb

【檻】 2623 2. ㄎㄢˇ kaan kǎn
a doorsill; a threshold

【櫃】 2624 ㄍㄨㄟˋ guey guì
1. a cabinet; a wardrobe; a cupboard
2. a shop counter
櫃面兒(ㄍㄨㄟˋ ㄇㄧㄢˋㄦ)
a shop counter
櫃房(ㄍㄨㄟˋ ㄈㄤˊ)
① the cashier's room in a shop ② the cashier in a shop ③ a counting house
櫃臺(ㄍㄨㄟˋ ㄊㄞˊ)
the counter in a store: 店員站在櫃臺後面。The clerk stood behind the counter.
櫃櫥(ㄍㄨㄟˋ ㄔㄨˊ)
a cabinet; a cupboard; a sideboard
櫃子(ㄍㄨㄟˋ ·ㄗ) or 櫃兒(ㄍㄨㄜˋㄦ)
a cabinet; a sideboard

【檯】 2625 ㄊㄞˊ tair tái
a table
檯布(ㄊㄞˊ ㄅㄨˋ)
a tablecloth
檯面(ㄊㄞˊ ㄇㄧㄢˋ)
(gambling) stakes
檯燈(ㄊㄞˊ ㄉㄥ)
a table lamp: 請打開檯燈。Please turn on the table lamp.
檯球(ㄊㄞˊ ㄑㄧㄡˊ)
table tennis

【檳】 2626 ㄅㄧㄣ bin bīn
the areca; the betel; the areca nut; the betel nut
檳榔(ㄅㄧㄣ ㄌㄤˊ)
the areca nut; the betel nut
檳榔糕(ㄅㄧㄣ ㄌㄤˊ ㄍㄠ)
sweets made of betel nut and sugar
檳榔嶼(ㄅㄧㄣ ㄌㄤˊ ㄩˇ)
Penang, Malaysia

【櫂】 2627 (棹) ㄓㄠˋ jaw zhào
1. an oar; a paddle
2. to row
3. a general name of boat
櫂歌(ㄓㄠˋ ㄍㄜ)
a boat-song; to chant a boat-song
櫂槳(ㄓㄠˋ ㄐㄧㄤˇ)
to pull an oar
櫂船(ㄓㄠˋ ㄔㄨㄢˊ)
to row a boat

十五畫

【櫚】 2628 ㄌㄩˊ liu lǘ
a palm; the Chinese coir palm

【櫟】 2629 ㄌㄧˋ lih lì
the chestnut-leaved oak (*Quercus chinensis* and *serrata*)
櫟散(ㄌㄧˋ ㄙㄢˇ)
useless materials

【櫓】 2630 (艣) ㄌㄨˇ luu lǔ
1. an oar; a scull; a sweep
2. (in ancient warfare) a big shield; a long spear
3. (now rarely) a lookout tower on a city wall
櫓夫(ㄌㄨˇ ㄈㄨ)
an oarsman

【櫛】 2631 ㄐㄧㄝˊ jye jié
1. a comb; a comb of many fine teeth
2. to comb the hair
3. to weed out; to eliminate; to delete
櫛比(ㄐㄧㄝˊ ㄅㄧˋ)
(said of houses) placed closely together like the teeth of a comb; joined closely together: 那些房子鱗次櫛比。Those houses close together in serrated formation.
櫛風沐雨(ㄐㄧㄝˊ ㄈㄥ ㄇㄨˋ ㄩˇ)
(literally) combed by the wind and bathed by the rain—to be exposed to hardships; hardworking; industrious
櫛工(ㄐㄧㄝˊ ㄍㄨㄥ)
a barber; a hairdresser
櫛櫛(ㄐㄧㄝˊ ㄐㄧㄝˊ)
placed very closely together as teeth of a comb (often said of masts of boats in a fishing harbor, etc.)

【櫝】 2632 ㄉㄨˊ dwu dú
1. a closet; a wardrobe; a cabinet; a sideboard or cupboard
2. a coffin
3. a scabbard
4. to hide; to conceal

【櫥】 2633 (廚) ㄔㄨˊ chwu chú
a closet; a cabinet; a sideboard; a cupboard, etc.
櫥櫃(ㄔㄨˊ ㄍㄨㄟˋ)
a closet; a cabinet; a night table with drawers, etc.
櫥窗(ㄔㄨˊ ㄔㄨㄤ)
a show window; a showcase; a display window

十六畫

〔木部〕

【櫪】 2634 ㄌㄧˋ lih lì
1. a stable; a manger
2. *Quercus serrata*
3. a wooden device used to torture a criminal by pressing his fingers
櫪馬(ㄌㄧˋ ㄇㄚˇ)
stablehorse
櫪撕(ㄌㄧˋ ㄒㄧ)
a wooden device used to torture a criminal by pressing his fingers

【櫬】 2635 ㄔㄣˋ chenn chèn
1. a coffin
2. a tung tree

【櫨】 2636 ㄌㄨˊ lu lú
1. the square peck-shaped box half way up a staff or mast
2. the name of a plant
櫨薄(ㄌㄨˊ ㄅㄛˊ)
the square peck-shaped box half way up a staff or mast

【櫳】 2637 (櫳) ㄌㄨㄥˊ long lóng
1. window with bars
2. a pen or cage for animals
櫳檻(ㄌㄨㄥˊ ㄐㄧㄢˋ)
a pen or cage for animals

【櫱】 2638 ㄋㄧㄝˋ nieh niè
sprouts grown from the stump of a tree

【櫫】 2639 ㄓㄨ ju zhū
a wooden peg; a post; a stalk or stick

十七畫

【櫺】 2640 ㄌㄧㄥˊ ling líng
1. carved or patterned window-railings, sills
2. the wooden planks which join eaves with a house
櫺牀(ㄌㄧㄥˊ ㄔㄨㄤˊ)
a bed with railings

【欄】 2641 ㄌㄢˊ lan lán
1. a railing; a balustrade; a fence: 此馬跳過了柵欄。The horse jumped over the fence.
2. a pen for domesticated animals
欄杆(ㄌㄢˊ ㄍㄢ)
① a railing; a balustrade ② silk trimming for girls
欄杆兒(ㄌㄢˊ ·ㄍㄚㄦ)
① a railing or balustrade ② (in Chinese opera company) a horizontal bar for developing muscular strength of players

【櫻】 2642 ㄧㄥ ing yīng
the cherry; the cherry blossoms
櫻桃(ㄧㄥ ㄊㄠˊ)
cherries
櫻脣(ㄧㄥ ㄔㄨㄣˊ)
the small, beautiful mouth of a woman
櫻草(ㄧㄥ ㄘㄠˇ)or 櫻草花(ㄧㄥ ㄘㄠˇ ㄏㄨㄚ)
a primrose

【欅】 2643 ㄐㄩˇ jeu jǔ
a kind of elm, with fine-grained wood (*Zelkova serrata*)

【欃】 2644 ㄔㄢˊ charn chán
1. sandalwood
2. a comet

【欂】 2645 ㄅㄛˊ bor bó
參看「欂櫨」
欂櫨(ㄅㄛˊ ㄌㄨˊ)
a square wooden block at the top of a column

【檃】 2646 ㄧㄣˇ yiin yǐn
1. to straighten bent wood (by heat, etc.)
2. to correct or adjust
檃括(ㄧㄣˇ ㄍㄨㄚ)
a piece of wood used in straightening bent wood

十八畫

【權】 2647 ㄑㄩㄢˊ chyuan quán
1. to weigh (the significance, etc.); to assess
2. power; authority; inherent rights; jurisdiction; influence
3. an expedient way; expediency; alternative
4. temporarily; for the time being
5. a Chinese family name
權變(ㄑㄩㄢˊ ㄅㄧㄢˋ)
to adjust oneself to changing situations, conditions, etc.
權柄(ㄑㄩㄢˊ ㄅㄧㄥˇ)or(ㄑㄩㄢˊ ㄅㄧㄥˋ)
authority; power: 我掌握權柄。I was in power.
權謀(ㄑㄩㄢˊ ㄇㄡˊ)
schemes and power; the use of schemes and power
權門(ㄑㄩㄢˊ ㄇㄣˊ)
powerful families; the households of powerful ministers
權代(ㄑㄩㄢˊ ㄉㄞˋ)
to act in another's place temporarily; to substitute for another for the time being: 他權代經理。He acted as manager for the time being.
權典(ㄑㄩㄢˊ ㄉㄧㄢˇ)
a provisional law; temporary regulations
權能(ㄑㄩㄢˊ ㄋㄥˊ)
① authority; powers and functions ②(law) the exercise of one's rights
權能分開(ㄑㄩㄢˊ ㄋㄥˊ ㄈㄣ ㄎㄞ)
the division of people's rights and the powers of the government in a democratic constitution
權佞(ㄑㄩㄢˊ ㄋㄧㄥˋ)
a mean politician in power
權利(ㄑㄩㄢˊ ㄌㄧˋ)
rights; some right or advantage enjoyed by common consent
權利法案(ㄑㄩㄢˊ ㄌㄧˋ ㄈㄚˇ ㄢˋ)
Bill of Rights
權力(ㄑㄩㄢˊ ㄌㄧˋ)
power; authority
權力結構(ㄑㄩㄢˊ ㄌㄧˋ ㄐㄧㄝˊ ㄍㄡˋ)
power structure
權略(ㄑㄩㄢˊ ㄌㄩㄝˋ)
schemes or measures to meet exigencies
權貴(ㄑㄩㄢˊ ㄍㄨㄟˋ)
highly-placed personalities; ranking officials; influential figures; the mighty
權衡(ㄑㄩㄢˊ ㄏㄥˊ)
to weigh, consider or assess: 我們權衡利弊。We weighed the advantages and disadvantages.

權且(ㄑㄩㄢˊ ㄑㄧㄝˇ)
for the time being; temporarily; in the mean time; interim: 我們權且如此辦理。 Let's carry it out as interim measure.
權限(ㄑㄩㄢˊ ㄒㄧㄢˋ)
limitation of power or authority; jurisdiction within certain limits
權詐(ㄑㄩㄢˊ ㄓㄚˋ)
crafty and dishonest; expediency in disregard of morality
權杖(ㄑㄩㄢˊ ㄓㄤˋ)
a baton or staff borne as a symbol of office
權重(ㄑㄩㄢˊ ㄓㄨㄥˋ)
to be in power
權臣(ㄑㄩㄢˊ ㄔㄣˊ)
powerful courtiers: 權臣欺君。Powerful courtiers insult their king.
權寵(ㄑㄩㄢˊ ㄔㄨㄥˇ)
to gain powers through favor from the emperor, etc.
權勢(ㄑㄩㄢˊ ㄕˋ)
power and influence
權術(ㄑㄩㄢˊ ㄕㄨˋ)
craft or tact (in handling political things, etc.); political trickery; politics: 他喜歡玩弄權術。He likes to play politics.
權數(ㄑㄩㄢˊ ㄕㄨˋ)
the talent to meet exigencies
權宜(ㄑㄩㄢˊ ㄧˊ)
expedient; temporary (measures, etc.)
權宜之計(ㄑㄩㄢˊ ㄧˊ ㄓ ㄐㄧˋ)
an expedient; a makeshift
權益(ㄑㄩㄢˊ ㄧˋ)
rights and interests
權要(ㄑㄩㄢˊ ㄧㄠˋ)
① bigwigs; top dogs; powerful persons ② confidential matter
權右(ㄑㄩㄢˊ ㄧㄡˋ)
bigwigs; top dogs; highly-placed personalities
權威(ㄑㄩㄢˊ ㄨㄟ)
① an authority (in certain sphere of knowledge): 他是一個語音學權威。He is an authority on phonetics. ② power and prestige
權輿(ㄑㄩㄢˊ ㄩˊ)
the beginning

十九畫

【欒】 2648
ㄌㄨㄢˊ luan luán
1. *Koelreuteria paniculata*, name of a small tree with tiny leaves and yellow flowers
2. the two corners at the mouth of a Chinese bell
3. a Chinese family name

二十一畫

【欖】 2649
ㄌㄢˇ laan lǎn
the olive

欠部
ㄑㄧㄢ chiann qiàn

【欠】 2650
ㄑㄧㄢˋ chiann qiàn
1. to owe; to owe money
2. deficient; lacking; short of; not enough: 他的寫作文字欠佳。His writing is not good enough.
3. to raise slightly (a part of the body)
4. to yawn

欠妥(ㄑㄧㄢˋ ㄊㄨㄛˇ)
not very proper or appropriate; not satisfactory or dependable: 他的文章措詞欠妥。His essay was not properly worded.
欠款(ㄑㄧㄢˋ ㄎㄨㄢˇ)
① to owe money ② debts; the amount of money owed
欠佳(ㄑㄧㄢˋ ㄐㄧㄚ)
not satisfactory: 結果欠佳。The result was not satisfactory.
欠繳(ㄑㄧㄢˋ ㄐㄧㄠˇ)
to have not paid (one's due, tax, etc.)
欠據(ㄑㄧㄢˋ ㄐㄩˋ)
an I.O.U. note
欠錢(ㄑㄧㄢˋ ㄑㄧㄢˊ)
① to owe money ② to be short of money
欠情(ㄑㄧㄢˋ ㄑㄧㄥˊ)
to owe favors; favors not returned or repaid
欠缺(ㄑㄧㄢˋ ㄑㄩㄝ)
① to lack; deficient; short of: 他們仍欠缺經驗。They are still lacking in experience. ② shortcomings: 我的工作還有很多欠缺。There are still many shortcomings in my job.
欠薪(ㄑㄧㄢˋ ㄒㄧㄣ)
overdue wages; back pay
欠債(ㄑㄧㄢˋ ㄓㄞˋ)
to be in debt; to owe money
欠賬(ㄑㄧㄢˋ ㄓㄤˋ)
① to owe money; to buy on credit ② overdue bills
欠伸(ㄑㄧㄢˋ ㄕㄣ)
to yawn
欠身(ㄑㄧㄢˋ ㄕㄣ)
to get ready to stand up as a gesture of courtesy
欠稅(ㄑㄧㄢˋ ㄕㄨㄟˋ)
tax arrears
欠資郵票(ㄑㄧㄢˋ ㄗ ㄧㄡˊ ㄆㄧㄠˋ)
a postage-due stamp
欠安(ㄑㄧㄢˋ ㄢ)
not at ease at heart; not feeling well physically

二畫

【次】 2651
ㄘˋ tsyh cì
1. the next in order; secondary
2. inferior; lower
3. vice or deputy (ministers, etc.)
4. a place where one stops for rest on a trip; a place
5. to stop at a place
6. by; at (the feast, table, etc.); in the midst
7. a grade; grading; order; sequence
8. (chemistry) the prefix "hypo"
9. time (each occasion of a recurring action or event)

次品(ㄘˋ ㄆㄧㄣˇ)
goods of inferior quality
次等(ㄘˋ ㄉㄥˇ)or 次一等(ㄘˋ ㄧ ㄉㄥˇ)
a lower or inferior class or category; of the second grade or quality
次等貨(ㄘˋ ㄉㄥˇ ㄏㄨㄛˋ)
seconds
次第(ㄘˋ ㄉㄧˋ)

① order; grade; sequence ② in order; one by one; one after another

次年(ㄘˋ ㄋㄧㄢˊ)
the next year; the following year

次女(ㄘˋ ㄋㄩˇ)
the second daughter

次女高音(ㄘˋ ㄋㄩˇ ㄍㄠ ㄧㄣ)
a mezzo-soprano

次席(ㄘˋ ㄒㄧˊ)
① the seat next to the guest of honor or the person in command ② a bamboo mat

次序(ㄘˋ ㄒㄩˋ)
order, sequence, succession, etc.: 這些書是按照大小次序排列的。The books are arranged in order of size.

次殖民地(ㄘˋ ㄓˊ ㄇㄧㄣˊ ㄉㄧˋ)
a country with the important part of its sovereignty usurped by foreign powers and is therefore in a worse situation than a colony

次長(ㄘˋ ㄓㄤˇ)
a vice minister; a deputy minister: 他是參謀次長。He is a Deputy Chief of the General Staff.

次中音(ㄘˋ ㄓㄨㄥ ㄧㄣ)
(music) submediant

次室(ㄘˋ ㄕˋ)
a concubine

次數(ㄘˋ ㄕㄨˋ)
the number of times

次日(ㄘˋ ㄖˋ)
the next day; the following day: 他於次日來見我。He came to see me the next day.

次子(ㄘˋ ㄗˇ)or 次男(ㄘˋ ㄋㄢˊ)
the second son

次早(ㄘˋ ㄗㄠˇ)
the next morning

次次(ㄘˋ ㄘˋ)
① every time ② uneasy

次要(ㄘˋ ㄧㄠˋ)
secondary; not very important: 你使這個問題退居次要地位。You relegated the problem to a secondary position.

次於(ㄘˋ ㄩˊ)
next to...; inferior to...

次韻(ㄘˋ ㄩㄣˋ)
(poetry) to rhyme one's poem in accordance with another's

四畫

【欣】 2652 ㄒㄧㄣ shin xīn
glad; gladly; joyful; joyfully; delighted; happy: 這消息使全國歡欣鼓舞。The news delighted the whole nation.

欣忭(ㄒㄧㄣ ㄅㄧㄢˋ)
delight; joy

欣逢(ㄒㄧㄣ ㄈㄥˊ)
happy to be present (on a joyful occasion)

欣戴(ㄒㄧㄣ ㄉㄞˋ)
to support (a leader, cause, etc.) gladly

欣悉(ㄒㄧㄣ ㄒㄧ)
delighted to learn; to have happily learned that

欣喜(ㄒㄧㄣ ㄒㄧˇ)or 欣懌(ㄒㄧㄣ ㄧˋ)
joyful; happy; delight

欣喜欲狂(ㄒㄧㄣ ㄒㄧˇ ㄩˋ ㄎㄨㄤˊ)or 欣喜若狂(ㄒㄧㄣ ㄒㄧˇ ㄖㄨㄛˋ ㄎㄨㄤˊ)
to be beside oneself with joy: 他欣喜若狂。He was beside himself with joy.

欣羡(ㄒㄧㄣ ㄒㄧㄢˋ)
to admire or envy

欣欣向榮(ㄒㄧㄣ ㄒㄧㄣ ㄒㄧㄤˋ ㄖㄨㄥˊ)
①(said of flowers in spring) blossoming ②(said of business, financial situations, etc.) prospering; flourishing; thriving: 我國國民經濟正欣欣向榮。Our national economy is prospering.

欣欣然(ㄒㄧㄣ ㄒㄧㄣ ㄖㄢˊ)
happy; joyful; complacent

欣賞(ㄒㄧㄣ ㄕㄤˇ)
to appreciate; to enjoy; to admire: 她欣賞藝術與音樂。She has an appreciation of art and music.

欣然(ㄒㄧㄣ ㄖㄢˊ)
gladly; with pleasure: 他欣然接受禮物。He accepted the present with pleasure.

欣慰(ㄒㄧㄣ ㄨㄟˋ)
gratified; delighted; satisfied; comforted; contented; satisfaction; to joy: 我看到你如此成功而感欣慰。I joy to see you so successful.

欣悅(ㄒㄧㄣ ㄩㄝˋ)
delighted; joyous; joyful; glad; happy

欣躍(ㄒㄧㄣ ㄩㄝˋ)
dancing with glee

六畫

【欬】 2653 1. (咳) ㄎㄜˊ ker ké
1. to cough: 他欬得很厲害。He coughs badly.
2. the sound of laughing

【欬】 2653 2. ㄎㄞˋ kay kài
asthma and coughing

七畫

【欲】 2654 ㄩˋ yuh yù
1. to desire; to intend; to long for; to want; wish; desire; expectation; longing: 他暢所欲言。He poured out what he wished to say.
2. (now rarely) love; to love
3. (now rarely) genial and amiable
4. about to; on the point of; on the verge of: 這座大廟，搖搖欲墜。This temple is on the verge of collapse.

欲罷不能(ㄩˋ ㄅㄚˋ ㄅㄨˋ ㄋㄥˊ)
unable to stop even if one wants to

欲不可從 or 欲不可縱(ㄩˋ ㄅㄨˋ ㄎㄜˇ ㄗㄨㄥˋ)
Desire must be kept under control.

欲待(ㄩˋ ㄉㄞˋ)
to intend to; to want to

欲蓋彌彰(ㄩˋ ㄍㄞˋ ㄇㄧˊ ㄓㄤ)
The more one tries to cover up (a secret, etc.), the better-known it will become.

欲海難填(ㄩˋ ㄏㄞˇ ㄋㄢˊ ㄊㄧㄢˊ)
One's desires are insatiable.

欲火 or 慾火(ㄩˋ ㄏㄨㄛˇ)
the fire of desire—sexual desire

欲加之罪，何患無詞(ㄩˋ ㄐㄧㄚ ㄓ ㄗㄨㄟˋ，ㄏㄜˊ ㄏㄨㄢˋ ㄨˊ ㄘˊ)
If you want to condemn somebody, you can always trump up a charge.

欲界(ㄩˋ ㄐㄧㄝˋ)
(Buddhism) *Kamadhatu*; the realm or realms of desire for food, sleep and sex

欲箭(ㄩˋ ㄐㄧㄢˋ)
(Buddhism) the arrow of five desires—that can harm all living beings

欲塹(ㄩˋ ㄑㄧㄢˋ)
the gulf of human desires —deep and hard to get across

欲擒故縱(ㄩˋ ㄑㄧㄣˊ ㄍㄨˋ ㄗㄨㄥˋ)
(literally) If one wants to catch somebody, he may need to let loose the noose for a while.—to try to get something by feigning uninterestedness or making concessions

欲心(ㄩˋ ㄒㄧㄣ)
one's desires

欲想(ㄩˋ ㄒㄧㄤˇ)
desires for wealth and women

欲障(ㄩˋ ㄓㄤˋ)
desires that pose as one's obstacles to salvation

欲速不達(ㄩˋ ㄙㄨˋ ㄅㄨˋ ㄉㄚˊ)
Haste makes waste. 或 More haste, less speed.

欲愛(ㄩˋ ㄞˋ)
passion-love; love inspired by desire, through any of the five senses

欲要(ㄩˋ ㄧㄠˋ)
to desire; to want to

欲言又止(ㄩˋ ㄧㄢˊ ㄧㄡˋ ㄓˇ)
to wish to speak but keep silent on second thought

欲望(ㄩˋ ㄨㄤˋ)
desires; to long for; longings: 這年輕人有求名的欲望。The young man had a desire for fame.

【欸】 2655
1. ㄞˇ ae ǎi

1. the sound of answering
2. sighs
3. the sound of rowing a boat

欸乃(ㄞˇ ㄋㄞˇ)
the sound of rowing a boat

【欸】 2655
2. ㄟˋ ey èi

an exclamation indicating promise or affirmation: 欸，我就來! Yes, I'll come in a moment.

【欷】 2656
ㄒㄧ shi xī

to sob

欷歔(ㄒㄧ ㄒㄩ)
to sob

八畫

【款】 2657
(欵) ㄎㄨㄢˇ koan kuǎn

1. sincerity; sincere; sincerely
2. an article, an item, etc. (in a contract, treaty, etc.)
3. to entertain; to treat well
4. slowly; slow
5. to knock (at a door)
6. a fund; a sum of money; money
7. empty (words, etc.)

款步(ㄎㄨㄢˇ ㄅㄨˋ)
(often said of women) to move or proceed slowly; to walk in slow steps: 她款步而行。She walked in slow steps.

款門(ㄎㄨㄢˇ ㄇㄣˊ)
to knock at the door

款密(ㄎㄨㄢˇ ㄇㄧˋ)
intimate

款目(ㄎㄨㄢˇ ㄇㄨˋ)
① an article or item in a contract, treaty, etc. ② an entry in an account; a sum of money

款服(ㄎㄨㄢˇ ㄈㄨˊ)
to submit to or obey willingly; to admire

款附(ㄎㄨㄢˇ ㄈㄨˋ)
to submit to or obey with true loyalty; to follow willingly

款待(ㄎㄨㄢˇ ㄉㄞˋ)
to entertain with courtesy and warmth; hospitality

款段(ㄎㄨㄢˇ ㄉㄨㄢˋ)
(said of horses) to proceed slowly

款冬(ㄎㄨㄢˇ ㄉㄨㄥ)
(botany) a coltsfoot (*Tussilago farfara*)

款留(ㄎㄨㄢˇ ㄌㄧㄡˊ)
to try sincerely to make a guest stay longer in order to offer greater hospitality

款客(ㄎㄨㄢˇ ㄎㄜˋ)
to entertain guests

款款(ㄎㄨㄢˇ ㄎㄨㄢˇ)
① sincerely ② slowly

款接(ㄎㄨㄢˇ ㄐㄧㄝ)
to entertain (guests, etc.); to receive (visitors, etc.)

款交(ㄎㄨㄢˇ ㄐㄧㄠ)
sincere friendship

款襟(ㄎㄨㄢˇ ㄐㄧㄣ)
to talk to one's heart's content

款啓(ㄎㄨㄢˇ ㄑㄧˇ)
limited views; provincialism

款洽(ㄎㄨㄢˇ ㄑㄧㄚˋ)or(ㄎㄨㄢˇ ㄒㄧㄚˊ)
a meeting of minds; on very agreeable terms

款曲(ㄎㄨㄢˇ ㄑㄩ)
① secrets in one's heart; heartfelt feelings ② to conduct oneself with great tact in social gatherings

款項(ㄎㄨㄢˇ ㄒㄧㄤˋ)
a sum of money; a fund; money: 他出一大筆款項買了這幢房子。He paid a large sum for the house.

款識(ㄎㄨㄢˇ ㄓˋ)
① words engraved on tripods, bells, etc. ② the name, signature, etc. in a painting or calligraphy

款式(ㄎㄨㄢˇ ㄕˋ)
fashions; styles; patterns: 這些皮鞋是最新的款式。These are the latest style in shoes.

款子(ㄎㄨㄢˇ ˙ㄗ)
money; a sum of money

款額(ㄎㄨㄢˇ ㄜˊ)
the amount of money involved

款言(ㄎㄨㄢˇ ㄧㄢˊ)
empty words: 款言不聽。Do not listen to empty words.

款引(ㄎㄨㄢˇ ㄧㄣˇ)
to confess; to admit

款語(ㄎㄨㄢˇ ㄩˇ)
gentle and persuasive conversation

【欽】 2658
ㄑㄧㄣ chin qīn

1. to respect; respectful; to admire
2. a term used to address a monarch in ancient China —Your Majesty
3. a Chinese family name

欽佩(ㄑㄧㄣ ㄆㄟˋ)
to admire; to respect; to agree wholeheartedly: 我欽佩你的坦白。I admire your frankness.

欽命(ㄑㄧㄣ ㄇㄧㄥˋ)
①(by) imperial orders ② an

imperial emissary
欽慕(ㄑㄧㄣ ㄇㄨˋ)
to admire; to look up to: 他的聰明爲人所欽慕。His cleverness is much admired.
欽點(ㄑㄧㄣ ㄉㄧㄢˇ)
designated by the emperor as members of the Imperial Academy
欽定(ㄑㄧㄣ ㄉㄧㄥˋ)
(said of books, etc.) compiled and published by imperial orders; compiled or edited by the emperor
欽天監(ㄑㄧㄣ ㄊㄧㄢ ㄐㄧㄢˋ)
(in old China) a government post in charge of astronomy, astrology, divination and related sciences
欽敬(ㄑㄧㄣ ㄐㄧㄥˋ)
to admire and respect
欽遲(ㄑㄧㄣ ㄔˊ)
to admire; to look up to
欽差大臣(ㄑㄧㄣ ㄔㄞ ㄉㄚˋ ㄔㄣˊ)
(in old China) officials sent to the provinces on specific missions by order of the emperor; imperial inspector generals
欽此(ㄑㄧㄣ ㄘˇ)
an expression making the end of imperial orders in old China
欽賜(ㄑㄧㄣ ㄙˋ)
granted or bestowed by the emperor (for meritorious service, etc.)
欽挹(ㄑㄧㄣ ㄧˋ)
to admire and respect; to look up to
欽仰(ㄑㄧㄣ ㄧㄤˇ)
to admire and respect; to look up to

【欺】 2659
ㄑㄧ chi qī
1. to cheat; to deceive; to swindle; to impose on; to take advantage of
2. to disregard the dictates of one's own conscience
3. to insult; to bully

欺騙(ㄑㄧ ㄆㄧㄢˋ)
to cheat; to deceive; to swindle
欺瞞(ㄑㄧ ㄇㄢˊ)
to deceive; to cheat
欺矇(ㄑㄧ ㄇㄥˊ)
to cheat; to defraud; to hide the truth (from superiors, etc.)
欺負(ㄑㄧ ·ㄈㄨ)
to bully; to oppress; to insult; to ridicule
欺誕(ㄑㄧ ㄉㄢˋ)
to cheat by exaggerating
欺凌(ㄑㄧ ㄌㄧㄥˊ)
to mistreat; to insult; to bully
欺君(ㄑㄧ ㄐㄩㄣ)
to withhold truth from the emperor
欺下罔上(ㄑㄧ ㄒㄧㄚˋ ㄨㄤˇ ㄕㄤˋ)
to oppress the people and hide the truth from higher authorities
欺心(ㄑㄧ ㄒㄧㄣ)
to disregard the dictates of one's own conscience; unconscionable
欺詐(ㄑㄧ ㄓㄚˋ)
to swindle; to defraud; to cheat: 誠實的商人不欺詐顧客。Honest merchants do not swindle their customers.
欺世盜名(ㄑㄧ ㄕˋ ㄉㄠˋ ㄇㄧㄥˊ)
to win fame by cheating the world
欺善怕惡(ㄑㄧ ㄕㄢˋ ㄆㄚˋ ㄜˋ)
to oppress the good and timid and fear the wicked
欺上瞞下(ㄑㄧ ㄕㄤˋ ㄇㄢˊ ㄒㄧㄚˋ)
to cheat one's superiors and defraud one's subordinates
欺人太甚(ㄑㄧ ㄖㄣˊ ㄊㄞˋ ㄕㄣˋ)
It's really too much! 或 You have insulted me beyond the limit.或 That's going too far.
欺人之談(ㄑㄧ ㄖㄣˊ ㄓ ㄊㄢˊ)
a lie
欺人自欺(ㄑㄧ ㄖㄣˊ ㄗˋ ㄑㄧ)
to cheat oneself and others
欺軟怕硬(ㄑㄧ ㄖㄨㄢˇ ㄆㄚˋ ㄧㄥˋ)
to bully the weak and fear the strong
欺壓(ㄑㄧ ㄧㄚ)
to cheat and oppress
欺侮(ㄑㄧ ㄨˇ)
to insult or ridicule; to bully: 他欺侮他的弟弟。He bullies his younger brother.
欺罔(ㄑㄧ ㄨㄤˇ)or 欺誑(ㄑㄧ ㄎㄨㄤˊ)
to cheat

【欻】 2660
1. ㄏㄨ hu hū
sudden; suddenly; abruptly
欻忽(ㄏㄨ ㄏㄨ)
quickly; swiftly

【欻】 2660
2. ㄔㄨㄚ chua chuā
descriptive of the sound

【歁】 2661
ㄎㄢˇ kaan kǎn
1. discontented with oneself
2. sad and gloomy

歁然(ㄎㄢˇ ㄖㄢˊ)
① dissatisfied; discontented ② without elation

【猗欠】 2662
(猗) ㄧ i yī
an interjection of pleasure—Bravo! Good!

欹歟盛哉(ㄧ ㄩˊ ㄕㄥˋ ㄗㄞ)
What a grand occasion! 或 What a grand sight!

九畫

【歇】 2663
ㄒㄧㄝ shie xiē
1. to rest
2. to sleep
3. to come to an end; to stop
4. to lodge

歇泊(ㄒㄧㄝ ㄅㄛˊ)
to lie at anchor
歇拍(ㄒㄧㄝ ㄆㄞ)
the ending of a lyrical song (詞)
歇馬(ㄒㄧㄝ ㄇㄚˇ)
① to dismount and take a rest ② to stop working
歇乏(ㄒㄧㄝ ㄈㄚˊ)
a rest after toiling
歇店(ㄒㄧㄝ ㄉㄧㄢˋ)
① to stay or lodge at an inn: 他歇店住了一星期。He stayed at an inn for a week. ② an inn
歇頂(ㄒㄧㄝ ㄉㄧㄥˇ)
to get bald as one gets older
歇腿兒(ㄒㄧㄝ ㄊㄨㄟˇㄦ)
① to rest one's feet after a long walk ② to rest at a place; to stay at an inn
歇工(ㄒㄧㄝ ㄍㄨㄥ)
to stop work
歇後(ㄒㄧㄝ ㄏㄡˋ)
to omit the last part of a common expression
歇後語(ㄒㄧㄝ ㄏㄡˋ ㄩˇ)
a common expression whose

last part is omitted; a riddle thus made, for example, 泥菩薩過河—自身難保。A clay idol fords a river.—It is hard for one to save himself (let alone help others).

歇脚(ㄒㄧㄝ ㄐㄧㄠˇ)
to rest the feet after walking

歇息(ㄒㄧㄝ ㄒㄧˊ)
①to take a rest ②to put up for the night; to stay at an inn

歇夏(ㄒㄧㄝ ㄒㄧㄚˋ)
(said of an opera company, etc.) to stop performance in summer; to take a vacation in summer

歇歇兒(ㄒㄧㄝ ·ㄒㄧㄝㄦ)
to take a little rest: 勞苦工作後歇歇兒是必須的。Rest is necessary after hard work.

歇心(ㄒㄧㄝ ㄒㄧㄣ)
not to indulge in fancy or desire; not to worry or care

歇手(ㄒㄧㄝ ㄕㄡˇ)
to discontinue (an operation, work, etc.); to stop doing something

歇晌兒(ㄒㄧㄝ ㄕㄤˇㄦ)
a rest after lunch; to take a nap or siesta after noon: 他每天午後歇晌兒。He takes a nap every afternoon.

歇坐(ㄒㄧㄝ ㄗㄨㄛˋ)
(in a Chinese feast) to take a brief rest after three rounds of drink

歇嘴(ㄒㄧㄝ ㄗㄨㄟˇ)
to stop talking; to shut up

歇斯的里(ㄒㄧㄝ ㄙ ㄉㄧˋ ㄌㄧˇ)
hysteria

歇宿(ㄒㄧㄝ ㄙㄨˋ)
to spend the night; to stay for the night; to make an overnight stop: 他來此歇宿。He came here to make an overnight stop.

歇一宿(ㄒㄧㄝ ㄧˋ ㄒㄧㄡˇ)
to stay or rest for the night

歇一歇(ㄒㄧㄝ ·ㄧ ·ㄒㄧㄝ)or 歇歇(ㄒㄧㄝ ·ㄒㄧㄝ)
to take a rest or break

歇業(ㄒㄧㄝ ㄧㄝˋ)
to close shop

【歆】 2664
ㄒㄧㄣ shin xīn

1. (said of gods, etc.) to accept offerings, etc.
2. to admire; to submit to willingly
3. to move

歆慕 or 欣慕(ㄒㄧㄣ ㄇㄨˋ)
to cherish

歆羨(ㄒㄧㄣ ㄒㄧㄢˋ)
to admire; to envy (another's beauty or luck)

歆艷(ㄒㄧㄣ ㄧㄢˋ)
to envy; to admire

【歃】 2665
ㄕㄚˋ shah shà

to drink blood; to smear the mouth with blood of an animal in oath-taking

歃血(ㄕㄚˋ ㄒㄩㄝˋ)
(an ancient practice) to smear the mouth with blood in oath-taking

十畫

【歉】 2666
ㄑㄧㄢˋ chiann qiàn

1. deficient; insufficient; deficiency
2. a poor crop or harvest
3. to regret; sorry
4. an apology; apologetic

歉收(ㄑㄧㄢˋ ㄕㄡ)
a bad harvest

歉然(ㄑㄧㄢˋ ㄖㄢˊ)
to regret; to feel sorry

歉仄(ㄑㄧㄢˋ ㄗㄜˋ)
very sorry; regrettable

歉歲(ㄑㄧㄢˋ ㄙㄨㄟˋ)
a year of poor harvest

歉意(ㄑㄧㄢˋ ㄧˋ)
regrets; apologies: 我表示歉意。I expressed my regret.

【歌】 2667
ㄍㄜ ge gē

1. to sing; to chant
2. to praise
3. a song
4. poems with rhythms and rhymes suitable for use as lyrics in songs

歌譜(ㄍㄜ ㄆㄨˇ)
music scores

歌德(ㄍㄜ ㄉㄜˊ)
① to praise the virtues, achievements, etc. of someone (often one's superior) ② Johann Wolfgang von Goethe (1749-1832), German poet and dramatist

歌臺舞榭(ㄍㄜ ㄊㄞˊ ㄨˇ ㄒㄧㄝˋ)
the stage—where songs and dances are performed; places of amusement

歌廳(ㄍㄜ ㄊㄧㄥ)
an entertainment establishment where popular songs are sung by professional singers

歌女(ㄍㄜ ㄋㄩˇ)
a songstress; a female singer

歌功頌德(ㄍㄜ ㄍㄨㄥ ㄙㄨㄥˋ ㄉㄜˊ)
①to praise another (usually one's superior) for his achievements and virtues ② to flatter; to give undeserved praises

歌喉(ㄍㄜ ㄏㄡˊ)
one's singing voice; one's vocal talent as a singer

歌后(ㄍㄜ ㄏㄡˋ)
a very accomplished female vocalist

歌集(ㄍㄜ ㄐㄧˊ)or 歌本(ㄍㄜ ㄅㄣˇ)
a collection of songs; a songbook

歌妓(ㄍㄜ ㄐㄧˋ)
(formerly) female entertainers somewhat like the geisha girls in Japan

歌劇(ㄍㄜ ㄐㄩˋ)
operas

歌曲(ㄍㄜ ㄑㄩˇ)
a song; a tune; a ballad: 她唱了一首流行歌曲。She sang a popular song.

歌星(ㄍㄜ ㄒㄧㄥ)
a singing star; an accomplished vocalist

歌詩(ㄍㄜ ㄕ)
① songs ② to sing poems

歌唱(ㄍㄜ ㄔㄤˋ)
to sing; to chant

歌唱家(ㄍㄜ ㄔㄤˋ ㄐㄧㄚ)
a vocalist; an acclaimed singer

歌吹(ㄍㄜ ㄔㄨㄟˋ)
singing and musical accompaniments; the singing and the playing of musical instruments

歌手(ㄍㄜ ㄕㄡˇ)
a songster; a vocalist

歌聲(ㄍㄜ ㄕㄥ)
the singing voice; the vocal part in a performance: 歌聲

〔欠部〕

盈耳。The sound of singing fills the ear.
歌聲繞梁(ㄍㄜ ㄕㄥ ㄖㄠˋ ㄌㄧㄤˊ)
The voice of singing reverberates round the beams of a house for days. (an expression to describe the superb performance of a vocalist)
歌詞(ㄍㄜ ㄘˊ)
lyrics or words of a song
歌頌(ㄍㄜ ㄙㄨㄥˋ)
to sing praises: 我們歌頌她的美德。We chant the praise of her virtues.
歌誦(ㄍㄜ ㄙㄨㄥˋ)
① to read a book aloud musically ② to sing praises
歌兒(ㄍㄜㄦ)
a song; a tune
歌謠(ㄍㄜ ㄧㄠˊ)
a ballad; a folk song
歌筵(ㄍㄜ ㄧㄢˊ)
a feast enlivened by a singing performance
歌舞(ㄍㄜ ㄨˇ)
singing and dancing; song and dance
歌舞伎(ㄍㄜ ㄨˇ ㄐㄧˋ)
a geisha (especially in Japan)
歌舞劇(ㄍㄜ ㄨˇ ㄐㄩˋ)
a light opera; a musical; an operetta
歌舞場(ㄍㄜ ㄨˇ ㄔㄤˊ)
places of amusement or entertainment—stages and cabarets
歌舞昇平(ㄍㄜ ㄨˇ ㄕㄥ ㄆㄧㄥˊ)
reign of peace and prosperity (when people can rejoice with singing and dancing)
歌王(ㄍㄜ ㄨㄤˊ)
a very accomplished male vocalist
歌詠(ㄍㄜ ㄩㄥˇ)
to sing praises; to sing; to eulogize: 他們歌詠聖賢。They eulogized the sages.

十一畫

【歎】 2668
(嘆) ㄊㄢˋ tann tàn
to sigh in wonderment or lamentation; to exclaim
歎美(ㄊㄢˋ ㄇㄟˇ)
to praise
歎服(ㄊㄢˋ ㄈㄨˊ)
to praise and admire
歎號(ㄊㄢˋ ㄏㄠˋ)
(punctuation) the exclamation mark (!)
歎氣(ㄊㄢˋ ㄑㄧˋ)
to sigh: 那老人唉聲嘆氣。The old man sighed in despair.
歎息(ㄊㄢˋ ㄒㄧˊ)
① to sigh in lamentation; to lament ② to exclaim ③ a sigh: 他深深發出一聲歎息。He heaved a great sigh.
歎惜(ㄊㄢˋ ㄒㄧˊ)
to sigh with regret; to lament
歎傷(ㄊㄢˋ ㄕㄤ)
to lament: 她爲何歎傷? Why does she lament?
歎賞(ㄊㄢˋ ㄕㄤˇ)
to praise and admire; to exclaim in appreciation
歎詞(ㄊㄢˋ ㄘˊ)
(grammar) an interjection
歎愕(ㄊㄢˋ ㄜˋ)
to exclaim in surprise or wonder
歎一口氣(ㄊㄢˋ ㄧˋ ㄎㄡˇ ㄑㄧˋ)
to heave a sigh
歎爲觀止(ㄊㄢˋ ㄨㄟˊ ㄍㄨㄢ ㄓˇ)
the most magnificent sight of all; an unrivaled sight; a sight never to be forgotten
歎惋(ㄊㄢˋ ㄨㄢˇ)
to sigh in lamentation; to sigh with regret

【歐】 2669
ㄡ ou ōu
1. Europe; European
2. same as 嘔—to vomit
3. same as 毆—to beat
4. same as 謳—to sing
5. (electricity) ohm, the SI unit of electrical resistance
6. a Chinese family name
歐美(ㄡ ㄇㄟˇ)
Europe and America—the West; Western
歐姆(ㄡ ㄇㄨˇ)
Georg Simon Ohm (1787—1854), German physicist
歐姆定律(ㄡ ㄇㄨˇ ㄉㄧㄥˋ ㄌㄩˋ)
Ohm's law
歐風美雨(ㄡ ㄈㄥ ㄇㄟˇ ㄩˇ)
the influences of Western culture and civilization
歐羅巴(ㄡ ㄌㄨㄛˊ ㄅㄚ)
① the European continent ② (Greek mythology) Europa
歐化(ㄡ ㄏㄨㄚˋ)
Europeanization; westernized
歐幾里得(ㄡ ㄐㄧ ㄌㄧˇ ㄉㄜˊ)
Euclid (330-275 B.C.?), Greek mathematician
歐幾里得原理(ㄡ ㄐㄧ ㄌㄧˇ ㄉㄜˊ ㄩㄢˊ ㄌㄧˇ)
the Elements of Euclid
歐西(ㄡ ㄒㄧ)
the Western world; the West
歐洲(ㄡ ㄓㄡ)
Europe
歐洲共同市場(ㄡ ㄓㄡ ㄍㄨㄥˋ ㄊㄨㄥˊ ㄕˋ ㄔㄤˇ)
European Common Market (ECM)
歐戰(ㄡ ㄓㄢˋ)
World War I (which was largely confined in Europe)
歐氏管(ㄡ ㄕˋ ㄍㄨㄢˇ)
(anatomy) the Eustachian tube 亦作「耳氣管」
歐亞(ㄡ ㄧㄚˇ)
Europe and Asia; Eurasia
歐亞混血兒(ㄡ ㄧㄚˇ ㄏㄨㄣˋ ㄒㄧㄝˇ ㄦˊ)
a Eurasian
歐陽(ㄡ ㄧㄤˊ)
a Chinese family name
歐陽修(ㄡ ㄧㄤˊ ㄒㄧㄡ)
Ou-Yang Hsiu (1007-1072), a famous conservative official and man of letters of the Sung Dynasty

【歑】 2670
ㄏㄨ hu hū
to blow; to exhale

【歒】 2671
ㄧㄣˇ yiin yǐn
the ancient version of 飲—to drink

十二畫

【歙】 2672
1. ㄒㄧˋ shih xì
to suck; to inhale

【歙】 2672
2. ㄕㄜˋ sheh shè
name of a county in Anhwei Province

【歔】 2673
ㄒㄩ shiu xū
1. to exhale from the nose

2. to sob
歔欷(ㄒㄩ ㄒㄧ)
to sob; to sniffle—as after crying

【歗】 2674 (嘯) ㄒㄧㄠˋ shiaw xiào
1. to scream or whistle; a whistling or hissing sound
2. to sigh; to groan

十三畫

【歕】 2675 (噴) ㄆㄣ pen pēn
1. to spurt; to blow
2. to snort; to puff

【歜】 2676 ㄔㄨˋ chuh chù
furious; wrathful

【歛】 2677 ㄌㄧㄢˋ liann liàn
1. to collect; to gather
2. to hold together
3. to deduct; to subtract
4. to desire; to ask for something

十四畫

【歟】 2678 ㄩˊ yu yú
a final particle indicating doubt, surprise, exclamation, etc.

十五畫

【歠】 2679 ㄔㄨㄛˋ chuoh chuò
to drink; to sip; to suck

十八畫

【歡】 2680 ㄏㄨㄢ huan huān
1. pleased; glad; jubilant
2. pleasures; joys
3. a lover
4. active and energetic; quick; in full swing
5. a Chinese family name
歡伯(ㄏㄨㄢ ㄅㄛˊ)
wine and liquor
歡蹦亂跳(ㄏㄨㄢ ㄅㄥˋ ㄌㄨㄢˋ ㄊㄧㄠˋ)
skipping or jumping about with joy; gamboling
歡抃(ㄏㄨㄢ ㄅㄧㄢˋ)
happy; joyful
歡抃(ㄏㄨㄢ ㄅㄧㄢˋ)
to clap hands as a result of joy
歡騰(ㄏㄨㄢ ㄊㄥˊ)
great rejoicing; jubilation
歡天喜地(ㄏㄨㄢ ㄊㄧㄢ ㄒㄧˇ ㄉㄧˋ)
overjoyed; very much pleased: 我們歡天喜地的迎接國慶。We greeted National Day with boundless joy.
歡樂(ㄏㄨㄢ ㄌㄜˋ)
joy; happiness; gaiety
歡樂場(ㄏㄨㄢ ㄌㄜˋ ㄔㄤˇ)or 歡場(ㄏㄨㄢ ㄔㄤˇ)
gay establishments; places where people seek carnal pleasure
歡呼(ㄏㄨㄢ ㄏㄨ)
to cheer with jubilation; to shout for joy; to hurrah
歡會(ㄏㄨㄢ ㄏㄨㄟˋ)
a happy reunion
歡聚(ㄏㄨㄢ ㄐㄩˋ)
①a happy reunion; a joyful meeting; a happy get-together ② to gather together happily: 我們歡聚一堂。We happily gathered under the same roof.
歡喜(ㄏㄨㄢ ㄒㄧˇ)
joyful; happy: 小孩子歡歡喜喜的過新年。Children spent a joyful New Year.
歡喜佛(ㄏㄨㄢ ㄒㄧˇ ㄈㄛˊ)or 歡喜天(ㄏㄨㄢ ㄒㄧˇ ㄊㄧㄢ)
devas of pleasure; two human figures with elephant heads, one a male and the other a female, shown in an obscene act, which are found in the secret chambers of some Lamaist temples—a symbol of the good, represented by the female, subduing the forces of evil and violence, represented by the male
歡喜錢兒(ㄏㄨㄢ ㄒㄧˇ ㄑㄧㄚˊㄦ)
money given on happy occasions, such as a wedding, birthday party, etc.
歡洽(ㄏㄨㄢ ㄒㄧㄚˋ)
friendly; harmoniously
歡笑(ㄏㄨㄢ ㄒㄧㄠˋ)
cheer and laughter—great joy; jubilation
歡心(ㄏㄨㄢ ㄒㄧㄣ)
(to win another's) favor or heart; love
歡欣(ㄏㄨㄢ ㄒㄧㄣ)
jubilation; joy
歡欣鼓舞(ㄏㄨㄢ ㄒㄧㄣ ㄍㄨˇ ㄨˇ)
to be overjoyed; very pleased; to be beside oneself with joy; dancing with joy; to be filled with exultation
歡敍(ㄏㄨㄢ ㄒㄩˋ)
to meet in joy; to talk about old times happily
歡暢(ㄏㄨㄢ ㄔㄤˋ)
thoroughly delighted; elated
歡聲雷動(ㄏㄨㄢ ㄕㄥ ㄌㄟˊ ㄉㄨㄥˋ)
to cheer thunderously; roaring applause: 全場觀衆歡聲雷動。The audience broke into roaring applause.
歡送(ㄏㄨㄢ ㄙㄨㄥˋ)
to send off; to give a farewell party
歡顏(ㄏㄨㄢ ㄧㄢˊ)
happy looks or appearances
歡宴(ㄏㄨㄢ ㄧㄢˋ)
to dine a guest in a friendly manner
歡迎(ㄏㄨㄢ ㄧㄥˊ)
to welcome; a welcome
歡娛(ㄏㄨㄢ ㄩˊ)
joy and pleasure
歡悅(ㄏㄨㄢ ㄩㄝˋ)
joy and happiness; very pleased
歡躍(ㄏㄨㄢ ㄩㄝˋ)
overjoyed; very pleased; dancing with joy: 母親對她兒子的成功十分歡躍。The mother is very pleased with her son's success.

止部
ㄓˇ jyy zhǐ

【止】 2681 ㄓˇ jyy zhǐ
1. to stop; to desist; to still: 他停止吸煙。He stopped smoking.
2. to rest in; to stay
3. deportment
4. to detain
5. to prohibit
6. to come to; to arrive at

7. still; calm; stagnant
8. only

止泊(ㄓˇ ㄅㄛˊ)
to stay and rest

止謗(ㄓˇ ㄅㄤˋ)
to stop libels or slanders

止步(ㄓˇ ㄅㄨˋ)
to stop; to stand still; to go no further: 遊客止步。No visitors. 或 Out of bounds.

止付(ㄓˇ ㄈㄨˋ)
(economics) to stop payment

止妒(ㄓˇ ㄉㄨˋ)
to suppress jealousy

止痛(ㄓˇ ㄊㄨㄥˋ)
to stop pain; to kill pain

止痛藥(ㄓˇ ㄊㄨㄥˋ ㄧㄠˋ)
the anodyne drug; the anodyne; the painkiller

止怒(ㄓˇ ㄋㄨˋ)
to stop or check anger

止戈爲武(ㄓˇ ㄍㄜ ㄨㄟˊ ㄨˇ)
Military forces are to be used for the maintenance of peace and order.

止咳(ㄓˇ ㄎㄜˊ)
to stop coughing

止渴(ㄓˇ ㄎㄜˇ)
to quench thirst

止境(ㄓˇ ㄐㄧㄥˋ)
limits; the terminal point; the end: 他的貪心是無止境的。His greed knows no limits.

止息(ㄓˇ ㄒㄧˊ)
to cease; to stop

止血(ㄓˇ ㄒㄧㄝˇ)
to stop bleeding or hemorrhage

止血帶(ㄓˇ ㄒㄧㄝˇ ㄉㄞˋ)
a tourniquet

止血藥(ㄓˇ ㄒㄧㄝˇ ㄧㄠˋ)
a styptic

止瀉(ㄓˇ ㄒㄧㄝˋ)
to stop diarrhea

止住(ㄓˇ ㄓㄨˋ)
to stop; to halt; to desist

止是 or 祇是(ㄓˇ ㄕˋ)
only that; it is only

止水(ㄓˇ ㄕㄨㄟˇ)
stagnant water; still water

止詞(ㄓˇ ㄘˊ)
(grammar) the object of a preposition or transitive verb

止宿(ㄓˇ ㄙㄨˋ)
to stay at

止遏(ㄓˇ ㄜˋ)
to stop; to suppress; to quench (thirst); to put (a fire) under control; to ward off (the enemy attack)

止癢(ㄓˇ ㄧㄤˇ)
to stop or alleviate itching

止於(ㄓˇ ㄩˊ)
to stop at; this far and no further

止於至善(ㄓˇ ㄩˊ ㄓˋ ㄕㄢˋ)
to arrive at supreme goodness; to attain perfection or *summum bonum*

一畫

【正】 2682
1. ㄓㄥˋ jenq zhèng

1. the obverse side; the right side
2. appropriate; proper
3. formal
4. to rectify; to correct
5. pure; not contaminated
6. straightforward and unbending; honest and virtuous
7. the person in charge; the person in command; the principal (as against the secondary)
8. to mete out punishment for a criminal
9. original (texts, etc.)
10. exactly; just; right: 這正是你們所需要的東西。This is exactly what you want.
11. positively
12. main; principal
13. sharp; punctually: 九點正來。Come at nine o'clock sharp.
14. just; unbiased
15. a Chinese family name

正北(ㄓㄥˋ ㄅㄟˇ)
due north: 這風是向正北吹。The wind is due north.

正本(ㄓㄥˋ ㄅㄣˇ)
the original copy: 我已將正本送至檔案庫存放了。I deposited the original in the archives.

正本清源(ㄓㄥˋ ㄅㄣˇ ㄑㄧㄥ ㄩㄢˊ)
to effect radical reform; to overhaul thoroughly

正比例(ㄓㄥˋ ㄅㄧˇ ㄌㄧˋ) or 正比(ㄓㄥˋ ㄅㄧˇ)
direct proportion

正步(ㄓㄥˋ ㄅㄨˋ)
the goose step; the parade step: 正步走！Parade step, march!

正牌兒(ㄓㄥˋ ㄆㄞˊㄦ)
the original or real thing; the original brand (as distinct from the imitation product)

正派(ㄓㄥˋ ㄆㄞˋ)
honest, proper and straightforward; virtuous; upright

正門(ㄓㄥˋ ㄇㄣˊ)
the front door; the front gate; the main entrance

正面(ㄓㄥˋ ㄇㄧㄢˋ)
① the right side; the obverse side; the head (of a coin); the front ② directly: 有建議請正面提出來。Please offer your suggestion directly. ③ positive

正面攻擊(ㄓㄥˋ ㄇㄧㄢˋ ㄍㄨㄥ ㄐㄧˊ)
a frontal attack

正名(ㄓㄥˋ ㄇㄧㄥˊ)
to give a right or good name to a cause; rectification of name

正法(ㄓㄥˋ ㄈㄚˇ)
① the proper law or rule ② to execute (a death convict); execution

正反(ㄓㄥˋ ㄈㄢˇ)
positive and negative

正反合(ㄓㄥˋ ㄈㄢˇ ㄏㄜˊ)
(dialectic) thesis-antithesis-synthesis

正犯(ㄓㄥˋ ㄈㄢˋ)
the principal criminal (as opposed to accessories): 正犯被警察逮捕。The principal criminal was arrested by the policeman.

正方(ㄓㄥˋ ㄈㄤ)
① to adjust to the right course ② a square

正方形(ㄓㄥˋ ㄈㄤ ㄒㄧㄥˊ)
(geometry) a square

正房(ㄓㄥˋ ㄈㄤˊ)
① the main rooms in a compound with houses around a courtyard ② one's legal wife (as contrasted with a concubine) 參看「上房」

正負(ㄓㄥˋ ㄈㄨˋ)
positive and negative

正大(ㄓㄥˋ ㄉㄚˋ)
just and fair; honest; above-

board
正大光明(ㄓㄥˋ ㄉㄚˋ ㄍㄨㄤ ㄇㄧㄥˊ)
fair and frank; just and pure of mind; open and aboveboard
正道(ㄓㄥˋ ㄉㄠˋ)or 正路(ㄓㄥˋ ㄌㄨˋ)
the right course; the proper way; the correct path
正旦(ㄓㄥˋ ㄉㄢˋ)
①the female role in Chinese opera; the prima donna virtuoso ②the first day of a year
正當
①(ㄓㄥ ㄉㄤ)just at that time; right at that time; just when: 正當秋收之時。It is just the time for autumn harvest.
②(ㄓㄥˋ ㄉㄤˋ)proper; appropriate; justifiable; legitimate
正當年(ㄓㄥ ㄉㄤ ㄋㄧㄢˊ)
in the prime of one's life; the golden years of one's life
正當中(ㄓㄥ ㄉㄤ ㄓㄨㄥ)
right in the middle
正當理由(ㄓㄥˋ ㄉㄤˋ ㄌㄧˇ ㄧㄡˊ)
proper reasons
正當行爲(ㄓㄥˋ ㄉㄤˋ ㄒㄧㄥˊ ㄨㄟˊ)
proper conduct
正當要求(ㄓㄥˋ ㄉㄤˋ ㄧㄠ ㄑㄧㄡˊ)
an appropriate request; a justifiable demand
正殿(ㄓㄥˋ ㄉㄧㄢˋ)
the main hall; the hall in the middle
正對(ㄓㄥˋ ㄉㄨㄟˋ)
directly across; face to face; directly opposite: 太陽光正對着我們照射。The sun was shining in our faces.
正東(ㄓㄥˋ ㄉㄨㄥ)
due east
正頭香主(ㄓㄥˋ ㄊㄡˊ ㄒㄧㄤ ㄓㄨˇ)
one's male heirs
正題(ㄓㄥˋ ㄊㄧˊ)
①the subject (or topic) of a talk or an essay: 他的演說轉入正題。His speech came to the subject. ②(philosophy) a thesis
正體字(ㄓㄥˋ ㄊㄧˇ ㄗˋ)
the standard Chinese character (as distinct from the simplified character and the running and manuscript styles of writing)
正廳(ㄓㄥˋ ㄊㄧㄥ)
①the main hall ②stalls (in a theater)
正途(ㄓㄥˋ ㄊㄨˊ)
the proper way or course: 他偏離正途。He digressed from the proper way.
正統(ㄓㄥˋ ㄊㄨㄥˇ)
orthodox; authorized
正統派(ㄓㄥˋ ㄊㄨㄥˇ ㄆㄞˋ)
the orthodox school (of thought)
正南(ㄓㄥˋ ㄋㄢˊ)
due south
正路(ㄓㄥˋ ㄌㄨˋ)
the right path; the straight path
正論(ㄓㄥˋ ㄌㄨㄣˋ)
the reasonable or appropriate opinion; the sound statement
正割(ㄓㄥˋ ㄍㄜ)
(mathematics) secant
正格(ㄓㄥˋ ㄍㄜˊ)
the orthodox style of Chinese poetry
正該(ㄓㄥˋ ㄍㄞ)
should; must; it's proper...
正趕上(ㄓㄥˋ ㄍㄢˇ ˙ㄕㄤ)
just in time for...: 我昨天正趕上汽船。I was just in time for the steamer yesterday.
正果(ㄓㄥˋ ㄍㄨㄛˇ)
(Buddhism) spiritual progress through practicing Buddhism
正規軍(ㄓㄥˋ ㄍㄨㄟ ㄐㄩㄣ)
the regular army: 他加入正規軍。He entered the regular army.
正軌(ㄓㄥˋ ㄍㄨㄟˇ)
the right track; the proper way or course
正宮(ㄓㄥˋ ㄍㄨㄥ)
①the queen's apartment in the palace ②the queen consort
正宮娘娘(ㄓㄥˋ ㄍㄨㄥ ㄋㄧㄤˊ ˙ㄋㄧㄤ)
the queen consort; the emperor's legal wife
正課(ㄓㄥˋ ㄎㄜˋ)
taxes and revenues
正楷(ㄓㄥˋ ㄎㄞˇ)
the standard script (in Chinese calligraphy)
正合式 or 正合適(ㄓㄥˋ ㄏㄜˊ ㄕˋ)
exactly right or appropriate; to fit exactly; to fit like a glove
正合我意(ㄓㄥˋ ㄏㄜˊ ㄨㄛˇ ㄧˋ)
It's exactly what I am hoping for. 他的回答正合我意。His answer was exactly what I was hoping for.
正好(ㄓㄥˋ ㄏㄠˇ)
exactly (at the right moment); exactly right; it just happened that...; just enough: 這套衣服我穿正好。This suit fits me nicely.
正號(ㄓㄥˋ ㄏㄠˋ)
(mathematics) the plus sign, or the positive sign
正貨(ㄓㄥˋ ㄏㄨㄛˋ)
the legal tender; the hard currency
正極(ㄓㄥˋ ㄐㄧˊ)
(electricity) the positive electrode; the positive pole; the anode
正襟危坐(ㄓㄥˋ ㄐㄧㄣ ㄨㄟˊ ㄗㄨㄛˋ)
to straighten one's lapels and sit up stiffly; to sit upright and look straight ahead
正經(ㄓㄥˋ ㄐㄧㄥ)
(said of manners, conduct, etc.) very proper; respectable; serious
正經八百(ㄓㄥˋ ㄐㄧㄥ ㄅㄚ ㄅㄞˇ)
serious; earnest: 選擇職業是件正經八百的事。The selection of one's occupation is a serious matter.
正妻(ㄓㄥˋ ㄑㄧ)
one's legal wife
正氣(ㄓㄥˋ ㄑㄧˋ)
righteousness; the spiritual strength for the right and just
正氣歌(ㄓㄥˋ ㄑㄧˋ ㄍㄜ)
The Song of Righteousness —authored by Wen Tien-hsiang (文天祥) of the Sung Dynasty after being taken prisoner by the Mongols
正切(ㄓㄥˋ ㄑㄧㄝ)
(mathematics) tangent
正巧(ㄓㄥˋ ㄑㄧㄠˇ)
exactly; it happens that...; exactly when..., coincidence: 他來訪時，正巧我出去了。I happened to be out when he

〔止部〕

called.

正寢(ㄓㄥˋ ㄑㄧㄣˇ)
the main room in a house

正取(ㄓㄥˋ ㄑㄩˇ)
(said of students, etc. through entrance or qualifying examinations) to be formally admitted, as contrasted to those admitted on the list of alternative candidates

正取生(ㄓㄥˋ ㄑㄩˇ ㄕㄥ)
a student formally admitted 參看「正取」

正確(ㄓㄥˋ ㄑㄩㄝˋ)
accurate; correct; right; proper; appropriate

正確性(ㄓㄥˋ ㄑㄩㄝˋ ㄒㄧㄥˋ)
accuracy; correctness

正西(ㄓㄥˋ ㄒㄧ)
due west

正席(ㄓㄥˋ ㄒㄧˊ)
the table of honor in a grand feast

正弦(ㄓㄥˋ ㄒㄧㄢˊ)
(mathematics) sine

正相反(ㄓㄥˋ ㄒㄧㄤ ㄈㄢˇ)
on the contrary

正學(ㄓㄥˋ ㄒㄩㄝˊ)
the orthodox learning

正直(ㄓㄥˋ ㄓˊ)
upright and honest; straightforward and unbiased; candid and fair: 他爲人正直。He is straightforward and unbiased.

正値(ㄓㄥˋ ㄓˊ)
just at that time; exactly during; it happened just when...

正著(ㄓㄥˋ ㄓㄠˊ)
(to run into somebody) face to face; (to score) the bull's eye; (to smash) right into something

正中(ㄓㄥˋ ㄓㄨㄥ)
right in the middle; right in the center: 請把花瓶放在桌子的正中。Please put the vase right in the middle of the table.

正中下懷(ㄓㄥˋ ㄓㄨㄥˋ ㄒㄧㄚˋ ㄏㄨㄞˊ)
to fit in exactly with one's wishes; exactly as one wishes or hopes for: 此事正中下懷。It is just what I hope for.

正常(ㄓㄥˋ ㄔㄤˊ)
normal; normally; common; commonly; usual; usually: 機器運作正常。The machine is functioning normally.

正常價格(ㄓㄥˋ ㄔㄤˊ ㄐㄧㄚˋ ㄍㄜˊ)
regular price

正長石(ㄓㄥˋ ㄔㄤˊ ㄕˊ)
orthoclase

正出(ㄓㄥˋ ㄔㄨ)
children born by the legal wife

正史(ㄓㄥˋ ㄕˇ)
official history as contrasted to legends, etc.

正是(ㄓㄥˋ ㄕˋ)
① yes, exactly so: 正是如此。Just so! ② an expression introducing a common saying which ends a chapter in the old Chinese novel

正式(ㄓㄥˋ ㄕˋ)
formal; formally; official; officially; legally or lawfully: 他們正式宣告訂婚。They formally announced their engagement.

正室(ㄓㄥˋ ㄕˋ)
① one's legal wife ② one's male heir

正事(ㄓㄥˋ ㄕˋ)
① one's job; one's duty or obligation ② serious business: 我們開始談正事吧。Let's begin to talk business.

正視(ㄓㄥˋ ㄕˋ)
to look straight in the eye; to look at something without bias or distortion: 我們應該正視現實。We should look at the facts without bias.

正身(ㄓㄥˋ ㄕㄣ)
one's real self; one's real person

正數(ㄓㄥˋ ㄕㄨˋ)
a positive number

正人君子(ㄓㄥˋ ㄖㄣˊ ㄐㄩㄣ ㄗˇ)
a gentleman; a just and upright man

正字(ㄓㄥˋ ㄗˋ)
①to correct a wrongly written character ② the standard script

正則(ㄓㄥˋ ㄗㄜˊ)
①the proper ways or methods ② to adjust the rules and regulations, etc.

正在(ㄓㄥˋ ㄗㄞˋ)
①(said of a position) exactly at ② used before a verb to form a progressive tense: 我們正在聊天。We're having a chat.

正坐(ㄓㄥˋ ㄗㄨㄛˋ)
to sit straight

正宗(ㄓㄥˋ ㄗㄨㄥ)
orthodox; handed down directly from the founder, master, etc.

正色(ㄓㄥˋ ㄙㄜˋ)
① stern and serious facial expression ② cardinal colors —blue, yellow, red, white and black

正義(ㄓㄥˋ ㄧˋ)
righteousness; justice: 我們爲正義而戰。We fight for justice.

正義感(ㄓㄥˋ ㄧˋ ㄍㄢˇ)
the sense of justice or righteousness: 這年輕人具有正義感。The young man has a sense of justice.

正業(ㄓㄥˋ ㄧㄝˋ)
①a respectable job; a regular occupation; proper duties: 他的兒子不務正業。His son didn't attend to his duties. ② one's main job as contrasted to his side-jobs

正顏厲色(ㄓㄥˋ ㄧㄢˊ ㄌㄧˋ ㄙㄜˋ)
a stern and severe look; a serious manner

正音(ㄓㄥˋ ㄧㄣ)
to correct pronunciation: 他爲我正音。He corrected my pronunciation.

正午(ㄓㄥˋ ㄨˇ)
high noon; noon

正誤(ㄓㄥˋ ㄨˋ)
to correct mistakes

正味(ㄓㄥˋ ㄨㄟˋ)
the original and unmodified taste

正位(ㄓㄥˋ ㄨㄟˋ)
the principal seat; the seat of honor

正文(ㄓㄥˋ ㄨㄣˊ)
text; key paragraphs of an article

正用(ㄓㄥˋ ㄩㄥˋ)
(for) legitimate or proper use

【正】 2682
2. ㄓㄥ jeng zhēng

the first in the lunar calendar
正朔(ㄓㄥ ㄕㄨㄛˋ)
①the first day of the first lunar month ②(formerly) the calendar officially promulgated by the emperor
正月(ㄓㄥ ㄩㄝˋ)
the first month of the lunar year

二畫

【此】 2683 ㄘˇ tsyy cǐ
1. this; these
2. such; thus: 他用功讀書,因此獲得高分數。He studied hard; thus he got high marks.
3. if so; in this case
4. here

此輩(ㄘˇ ㄅㄟˋ)
people of this type; such people
此仆彼起(ㄘˇ ㄆㄨ ㄅㄧˇ ㄑㄧˇ)
here falling and there rising (said of the voices of chanting crowds, jumping fish, etc.)
此番(ㄘˇ ㄈㄢ)
this time
此覆(ㄘˇ ㄈㄨˋ)
I hereby reply as above. (an expression used at the end of the official correspondence addressed to a man of the equal footing)
此道(ㄘˇ ㄉㄠˋ)
(often used derogatively) things like this; this pursuit, hobby, work, etc.
此等(ㄘˇ ㄉㄥˇ)
this kind; this type; such
此地(ㄘˇ ㄉㄧˋ)
this place; here
此地無銀三百兩(ㄘˇ ㄉㄧˋ ㄨˊ ㄧㄣˊ ㄙㄢ ㄅㄞˇ ㄌㄧㄤˇ)
In a folk tale, a person buried 300 taels of silver in the ground and posted a sign there declaring,"No 300 taels of silver buried here."
此老(ㄘˇ ㄌㄠˇ)
this old man (used in a comic sense)
此路不通(ㄘˇ ㄌㄨˋ ㄅㄨˋ ㄊㄨㄥ)
This road is blocked.—please detour
此公(ㄘˇ ㄍㄨㄥ)
this fellow
此刻(ㄘˇ ㄎㄜˋ)
at this moment; at present; presently
此後(ㄘˇ ㄏㄡˋ)
from now on; hereafter; henceforth
此際(ㄘˇ ㄐㄧˋ)
at this time ; at the moment
此間(ㄘˇ ㄐㄧㄢ)
this place; within this; here: 此間已有傳聞。It has been so rumored here.
此舉(ㄘˇ ㄐㄩˇ)
this action; this undertaking; this move
此君(ㄘˇ ㄐㄩㄣ)
① this gentleman ② bamboo (from 晉書王羲之傳—徽之但嘯咏,指竹曰:「何可一日無此君耶!」)
此起彼落(ㄘˇ ㄑㄧˇ ㄅㄧˇ ㄌㄨㄛˋ)
(said of voices) rising and falling; continuously
此致(ㄘˇ ㄓˋ)
(the form closing a letter) Thus I inform you.
此中(ㄘˇ ㄓㄨㄥ)
in this
此處(ㄘˇ ㄔㄨˋ)
this place; here: 請從此處走。Come this way, please.
此時此地(ㄘˇ ㄕˊ ㄘˇ ㄉㄧˋ)
here and now; under the present circumstances
此時此刻(ㄘˇ ㄕˊ ㄘˇ ㄎㄜˋ)
at the (very) moment
此事(ㄘˇ ㄕˋ)
this matter: 此事無關緊要。This matter is not important.
此上(ㄘˇ ㄕㄤˋ)
I hereby submit the above. (an expression used at the end of a letter addressed to a superior or an elder)
此生(ㄘˇ ㄕㄥ)
(in) this life: 他此生很有成就。He has had a successful life.
此日(ㄘˇ ㄖˋ)
this day; this very day
此人(ㄘˇ ㄖㄣˊ)
this man; this fellow: 此人是誰? Who is this?
此一時,彼一時(ㄘˇ ㄧ ㄕˊ,ㄅㄧˇ ㄧ ㄕˊ)
Time has changed. (Therefore, one must think or do things differently.) 或 Circumstances have changed with the passage of time.
此外(ㄘˇ ㄨㄞˋ)
besides; aside from this; in addition: 你需要錢和時間,此外你還需要努力。You need money and time. In addition, you need diligence.

三畫

【步】 2684 ㄅㄨˋ buh bù
1. a pace; a step: 這是邁向成功的第一步。It was the first step toward success.
2. to walk; on foot: 他經常在公園散步。He often walks in the park.
3. situation; state; degree: 事情怎麼會發展到如此駭人的地步? How did things get into such an appalling state?
4. banks of rivers, ponds, etc.
5. fortune; doom
6. a unit of length in ancient China of about 5.5 feet
7. a Chinese family name

步兵(ㄅㄨˋ ㄅㄧㄥ)
foot soldiers; infantry
步步(ㄅㄨˋ ㄅㄨˋ)
①step by step; pace after pace ② gradually; progressively; steadily: 敵軍正在步步逼進中。Our enemy troops are pressing forward steadily.
步步高陞(ㄅㄨˋ ㄅㄨˋ ㄍㄠ ㄕㄥ)
to get promotion step by step or continuously; to attain eminence step by step
步步生蓮花(ㄅㄨˋ ㄅㄨˋ ㄕㄥ ㄌㄧㄢˊ ㄏㄨㄚ)
the mincing steps of a beautiful woman (a term in reference to the concubine of 南齊東昏侯 who was made to walk on the golden lotus flowers laid on the floor)
步步爲營(ㄅㄨˋ ㄅㄨˋ ㄨㄟˊ ㄧㄥˊ)
to consolidate every position occupied before the troops push forward again; to move carefully every step on the way

〔止部〕

步伐(ㄅㄨˋ ㄈㄚˊ)or(ㄅㄨˋ ㄈㄚ)
steps or paces (in the military drill, parade, review, etc.): 他們以一致的步伐行走。They were walking in step.
步法(ㄅㄨˋ ㄈㄚˇ)
(dancing) footwork
步道(ㄅㄨˋ ㄉㄠˋ)
a sidewalk; a footpath
步調(ㄅㄨˋ ㄉㄧㄠˋ)
marching order; gaits: 他以快速的步調行走。He took a fast gait.
步調一致(ㄅㄨˋ ㄉㄧㄠˋ ㄧˊ ㄓˋ)
to be united in action; to act in unison; to keep in step
步隊(ㄅㄨˋ ㄉㄨㄟˋ)
a formation of foot soldiers; infantry
步態(ㄅㄨˋ ㄊㄞˋ)
a gait; a pace
步履(ㄅㄨˋ ㄌㄩˇ)
to walk; to move on foot
步履維艱(ㄅㄨˋ ㄌㄩˇ ㄨㄟˊ ㄐㄧㄢ)
to walk with difficulty
步鎗 or 步槍(ㄅㄨˋ ㄑㄧㄤ)
a rifle
步趨(ㄅㄨˋ ㄑㄩ)
to follow or pattern after (an example, etc.)
步行(ㄅㄨˋ ㄒㄧㄥˊ)
to walk; to march on foot
步哨(ㄅㄨˋ ㄕㄠˋ)
a sentry; the watch; a guard
步人後塵(ㄅㄨˋ ㄖㄣˊ ㄏㄡˋ ㄔㄣˊ)
to follow in another's footsteps; to trail along behind others 亦作「步其後塵」
步子(ㄅㄨˋ ·ㄗ)
a step; a pace: 他們步子輕快。They walked with springy steps.
步驟(ㄅㄨˋ ㄗㄡˋ)
procedure, or sequence of doing something; measures or steps taken: 他們正在採取適當的步驟。They are taking proper steps.
步測(ㄅㄨˋ ㄘㄜˋ)
to measure distance by counting paces; to pace off
步搖(ㄅㄨˋ ㄧㄠˊ)
a dangling ornament worn by women in ancient China (which sways when the wearer walks)亦作「步步搖」
步月(ㄅㄨˋ ㄩㄝˋ)
to stroll under the moon
步韻(ㄅㄨˋ ㄩㄣˋ)
to compose a poem by using the rhymes of a poem by another

四畫

【歧】 2685 ㄑㄧˊ chyi qí

1. a path branching out from the main road; a forked road
2. forked; divergent; strayed: 他們的意見分歧。They are divided in opinion.
3. anything that goes astray

歧途(ㄑㄧˊ ㄊㄨˊ)or 歧路(ㄑㄧˊ ㄌㄨˋ)
①a path branching out from the main road ②the wrong way; the road of evil
歧念(ㄑㄧˊ ㄋㄧㄢˋ)
evil thoughts or ideas
歧路徬徨(ㄑㄧˊ ㄌㄨˋ ㄆㄤˊ ㄏㄨㄤˊ)
to be hesitant or indecisive at a road junction
歧路亡羊(ㄑㄧˊ ㄌㄨˋ ㄨㄤˊ ㄧㄤˊ)
(literally) Sheep will easily get lost when there're too many forked roads.—One who seeks truth is apt to get lost when confronted with too many choices.
歧黃 or 岐黃(ㄑㄧˊ ㄏㄨㄤˊ)
① medical science ② names of two legendary herb doctors — Chi Po (歧伯) and Huang Ti (黃帝)
歧見(ㄑㄧˊ ㄐㄧㄢˋ)
different opinions or interpretations; conflicting ideas
歧出(ㄑㄧˊ ㄔㄨ)
① branching out ② conflicting and confusing
歧視(ㄑㄧˊ ㄕˋ)
to give different kinds of treatment to people; to act biasedly; to discriminate against; discrimination
歧義(ㄑㄧˊ ㄧˋ)
ambiguity; different meanings; various interpretations
歧異(ㄑㄧˊ ㄧˋ)
different; discrepancies; conflicts

【武】 2686 ㄨˇ wuu wǔ

1. force; military
2. warlike; martial
3. footprints; steps
4. the length of half a pace
5. the string of an ancient hat
6. to inherit
7. a Chinese family name

武備(ㄨˇ ㄅㄟˋ)
armaments and military provisions
武編(ㄨˇ ㄅㄧㄢ)
the title of a 10-volume book in two parts on major wars in Chinese history and military strategies and tactics, authored by Tang Shun-chih (唐順之) of the Ming Dynasty
武弁(ㄨˇ ㄅㄧㄢˋ)
①a hat for a military man ②a military man
武廟(ㄨˇ ㄇㄧㄠˋ)
temples built in honor of Generals Kuan Yü (關羽) and Yüeh Fei (岳飛)
武夫(ㄨˇ ㄈㄨ)
a person of great physical strength; military men; a warrior: 他乃一介武夫。He was a warrior.
武德(ㄨˇ ㄉㄜˊ)
soldierly virtues
武鬥(ㄨˇ ㄉㄡˋ)
to resort to violence; to use force
武旦(ㄨˇ ㄉㄢˋ)
a Chinese opera actress who plays the role of a lady warrior
武當派(ㄨˇ ㄉㄤ ㄆㄞˋ)
the Wutang School of Chinese boxing, which stresses the use of internal force (內功)
武斷(ㄨˇ ㄉㄨㄢˋ)
to jump to a conclusion without regard to reason, logic, propriety, etc.; to decide arbitrarily
武力(ㄨˇ ㄌㄧˋ)
military might; naked power; (by) force; force of arms
武力干涉(ㄨˇ ㄌㄧˋ ㄍㄢ ㄕㄜˋ)
to interfere through the use of force
武力解決(ㄨˇ ㄌㄧˋ ㄐㄧㄝˇ ㄐㄩㄝˊ)

solution through the use of force; to settle differences through force
武力鎮壓(ㄨˇ ㄌㄧˋ ㄓㄣˋ ㄧㄚ)
armed suppression
武林(ㄨˇ ㄌㄧˊㄣ)
the circle of boxers
武官(ㄨˇ ㄍㄨㄢ)
① a military officer ② a military attaché in an embassy: 他是一位海軍武官。He is a naval attaché.
武工(ㄨˇ ㄍㄨㄥ)
(usually said of players in Chinese operas) acrobatic skills
武功(ㄨˇ ㄍㄨㄥ)
① military achievements ② fighting skills; a feat of arms ③ name of a county and a mountain in Shensi Province
武科(ㄨˇ ㄎㄜ)
(formerly) subjects used to test or qualify military personnel
武庫(ㄨˇ ㄎㄨˋ)
① an arsenal or a general storeroom in ancient China ② name of a constellation, also known as 奎
武侯(ㄨˇ ㄏㄡˊ)
the Count of Wu, Chu-Ko Liang (諸葛亮), in the Epoch of the Three Kingdoms
武漢(ㄨˇ ㄏㄢˋ)
Wuhan—Wuchang (武昌) and Hankow (漢口), sometimes the city of Hanyang (漢陽) is included
武行(ㄨˇ ㄏㄤˊ)
(in Chinese opera) actors and actresses who play acrobatic roles or the role of warriors
武將(ㄨˇ ㄐㄧㄤˋ)
field commanders; ranking military officers
武舉(ㄨˇ ㄐㄩˇ)or 武舉人(ㄨˇ ㄐㄩˇ ㄖㄣˊ)
(formerly) successful candidates of provincial examinations of military officers
武器(ㄨˇ ㄑㄧˋ)
weapons; arms
武戲(ㄨˇ ㄒㄧˋ)
a Chinese opera that consists chiefly of fighting scenes
武俠(ㄨˇ ㄒㄧㄚˊ)
chivalry
武俠小說(ㄨˇ ㄒㄧㄚˊ ㄒㄧㄠˇ ㄕㄨㄛ)
a novel of swordsmen
武俠片(ㄨˇ ㄒㄧㄚˊ ㄆㄧㄢˋ)
motion pictures depicting the chivalry and prowess of ancient swordsmen
武秀才(ㄨˇ ㄒㄧㄡˋ ㄘㄞˊ)
a county qualified military officer
武仙座(ㄨˇ ㄒㄧㄢ ㄗㄨㄛˋ)
(astronomy) Hercules
武訓(ㄨˇ ㄒㄩㄣˋ)
Wu Hsün, 1838-1896, a beggar who founded several schools with his savings from mendicancy
武職(ㄨˇ ㄓˊ)
military offices or posts
武裝(ㄨˇ ㄓㄨㄤ)
① armed; to arm; armament ② military uniform
武裝部隊(ㄨˇ ㄓㄨㄤ ㄅㄨˋ ㄉㄨㄟˋ)
armed forces
武裝和平(ㄨˇ ㄓㄨㄤ ㄏㄜˊ ㄆㄧㄥˊ)
armed peace; peace maintained precariously by the balance of power
武裝侵略(ㄨˇ ㄓㄨㄤ ㄑㄧㄣ ㄌㄩㄝˋ)
armed aggression
武裝衝突(ㄨˇ ㄓㄨㄤ ㄔㄨㄥ ㄊㄨˊ)
an armed conflict; open hostilities; an armed clash
武狀元(ㄨˇ ㄓㄨㄤˋ ㄩㄢˊ)
the candidate who came out top in Imperial Examinations for military personnel in old China
武昌(ㄨˇ ㄔㄤ)
Wuchang, one of the three cities in the Wuhan (武漢) industrial complex in central China
武昌起義(ㄨˇ ㄔㄤ ㄑㄧˇ ㄧˋ)
The Wuchang Uprising on October 10, 1911, which led to the downfall of the Ching Dynasty and the birth of the Republic of China
武場(ㄨˇ ㄔㄤˇ)or(ㄨˇ ㄔㄤˊ)
①(in Chinese opera) music produced by percussion instruments such as gongs, drums and cymbals, which accompanies fighting scenes, gestures, etc. 參看「文場」② a practicing ground in a military camp in old China
武師(ㄨˇ ㄕ)
① a person skilled in martial arts ② troops
武士(ㄨˇ ㄕˋ)
① a brave man of fighting skill; a warrior ② a samurai ③ a knight or cavalier: 他頗有武士氣慨。He had knightly qualities.
武士道(ㄨˇ ㄕˋ ㄉㄠˋ)
the samurai spirit; the samurai code; (Japanese) Bushido
武生(ㄨˇ ㄕㄥ)
a male actor in Peking opera who plays the role of a young warrior or acrobat
武術(ㄨˇ ㄕㄨˋ)
martial arts; skills in boxing, fencing, etc.; fighting skills or feats
武人(ㄨˇ ㄖㄣˊ)
① an army man 參看「文人」 ② a warlord; a warrior; a leader
武則天(ㄨˇ ㄗㄜˊ ㄊㄧㄢ)or 武后(ㄨˇ ㄏㄡˋ)
Empress Wu (625-705) of the Tang Dynasty, who usurped the throne, famous for her lasciviousness and statecraft
武夷(ㄨˇ ㄧˊ)
Mount Wu Yi in Fukien, where the famous black tea *Bohea* (Fukienese pronunciation of Wu Yi) is grown
武藝(ㄨˇ ㄧˋ)
fighting skills or feats

五畫

【歪】 2687
ㄨㄞ uai wāi

1. aslant; askew; crooked; tilted; awry; out of the perpendicular: 那道牆歪了。The wall is out of the perpendicular.
2. depraved; evil
3. to lie down on one side for a brief nap
4. to shirk one's responsibility and try to involve others

歪憋(ㄨㄞ ㄅㄧㄝ)
to make trouble

〔止部〕

歪門邪道(ㄨㄞ ㄇㄣˊ ㄒㄧㄝˊ ㄉㄠˋ)
crooked ways; dishonest practices 亦作「邪魔外道」

歪風(ㄨㄞ ㄈㄥ)
an evil wind; an unhealthy trend

歪打正著(ㄨㄞ ㄉㄚˇ ㄓㄥˋ ㄓㄠˊ)
to do something unintentionally, but harvest exactly what one wishes; to hit the mark by a fluke

歪念頭(ㄨㄞ ㄋㄧㄢˋ ·ㄊㄡ)or 歪主意(ㄨㄞ ㄓㄨˇ ㄧˋ)
evil ideas; crooked ideas; depraved thoughts

歪貨(ㄨㄞ ㄏㄨㄛˋ)
a rotten apple; fallen angels or wanton girls

歪七扭八(ㄨㄞ ㄑㄧ ㄋㄧㄡˇ ㄅㄚ)
not straight or upright; aslant; askew; very untidy; to twist around

歪曲(ㄨㄞ ㄑㄩ)
to twist or confuse (things, facts, etc.) intentionally; to distort: 他歪曲我的話，以便造成一種錯誤印象。He twisted what I said so as to give a wrong impression.

歪曲事實(ㄨㄞ ㄑㄩ ㄕˋ ㄕˊ)
to twist or distort facts; fact-fudging; to fudge a fact: 他歪曲事實，使之聳人聽聞。He distorted the fact to make it sensational.

歪斜(ㄨㄞ ㄒㄧㄝˊ)
aslant; askew; crooked

歪心(ㄨㄞ ㄒㄧㄣ)
a twisted mind; a crooked mind; an evil mind

歪纏(ㄨㄞ ㄔㄢˊ)
to tangle people with lengthy and nonsensical talks; to harass another (with endless and meaningless conversation)

歪詩(ㄨㄞ ㄕ)
doggerel; inelegant verses

歪嘴(ㄨㄞ ㄗㄨㄟˇ)
a wry mouth; wry-mouthed

歪歪扭扭(ㄨㄞ ·ㄨㄞ ㄋㄧㄡˇ ㄋㄧㄡˇ)
crooked and twisted; not straight

九畫

【歲】 2688
ㄙㄨㄟˋ suey suì

1. a year; age (of a person): 一個人到二十一歲即成年。A man comes of age at twenty-one.
2. harvest

歲不我與(ㄙㄨㄟˋ ㄅㄨˋ ㄨㄛˇ ㄩˇ)
I can't help getting old.或 Time and tide wait for no one.

歲杪(ㄙㄨㄟˋ ㄇㄧㄠˇ)
the end of a year

歲暮(ㄙㄨㄟˋ ㄇㄨˋ)
① the late season of a year: 歲暮天寒。Cold weather sets in as the year draws to its end. ② the closing years of one's life

歲闌(ㄙㄨㄟˋ ㄌㄢˊ)
the late season of a year

歲貢(ㄙㄨㄟˋ ㄍㄨㄥˋ)
(in ancient China) the annual tribute offered by a vassal state or protectorate, etc.

歲寒三友(ㄙㄨㄟˋ ㄏㄢˊ ㄙㄢ ㄧㄡˇ)
the three friends in the cold of the year—the pine, the bamboo, and the plum, which do not wither in winter

歲寒松柏(ㄙㄨㄟˋ ㄏㄢˊ ㄙㄨㄥ ㄅㄛˊ)
virtuous persons (whose fortitude and uprightness are best revealed in time of trouble or when the going is rough)

歲華(ㄙㄨㄟˋ ㄏㄨㄚˊ)
time of year; the procession of the seasons

歲計(ㄙㄨㄟˋ ㄐㄧˋ)
the annual budget

歲夕(ㄙㄨㄟˋ ㄒㄧˋ)
New Year's Eve

歲差(ㄙㄨㄟˋ ㄔㄚ)
the precession of the equinoxes

歲出(ㄙㄨㄟˋ ㄔㄨ)
annual expenditures

歲除(ㄙㄨㄟˋ ㄔㄨˊ)
the close of a year; New Year's Eve

歲時(ㄙㄨㄟˋ ㄕˊ)
time of year; times and seasons

歲收(ㄙㄨㄟˋ ㄕㄡ)
the annual income

歲首(ㄙㄨㄟˋ ㄕㄡˇ)
the beginning of a year

歲數(ㄙㄨㄟˋ ㄕㄨˋ)
age (of a person); years: 他看來比實際歲數年輕。He looks young for his age.

歲入(ㄙㄨㄟˋ ㄖㄨˋ)
the annual income

歲次(ㄙㄨㄟˋ ㄘˋ)
the year of (followed by the year identified by its cyclic name consisting of a celestial stem (天干) and a terrestrial branch (地支))

歲歲年年(ㄙㄨㄟˋ ㄙㄨㄟˋ ㄋㄧㄢˊ ㄋㄧㄢˊ)
year after year; every year

歲夜(ㄙㄨㄟˋ ㄧㄝˋ)
New Year's Eve

歲月(ㄙㄨㄟˋ ㄩㄝˋ)
times and seasons; time:歲月會證明誰是對的。Time will show who is right.

歲月如流(ㄙㄨㄟˋ ㄩㄝˋ ㄖㄨˊ ㄌㄧㄡˊ)or 歲月不居(ㄙㄨㄟˋ ㄩㄝˋ ㄅㄨˋ ㄐㄩ)or 歲月無情(ㄙㄨㄟˋ ㄩㄝˋ ㄨˊ ㄑㄧㄥˊ)
Time and tide wait for no man. 或 Time flies! 或 Tempus fugit.

歲運(ㄙㄨㄟˋ ㄩㄣˋ)
the luck for the year

十二畫

【歷】 2689
ㄌㄧˋ lih lì

1. to pass; to elapse
2. to undergo; to go through; to experience: 探險者經歷很多痛苦。The explorers underwent much suffering.
3. things or duration that had come to pass
4. all previous (occasions, sessions); what has taken place
5. through; throughout; successive: 他歷任五年市長。He has been mayor for five successive years.
6. to last (a certain period of time)

歷代(ㄌㄧˋ ㄉㄞˋ)
successive generations; throughout the ages; the dynasties in their successive order: 這些是歷代名畫。These are famous paintings through the ages.

歷年(ㄌㄧˋ ㄋㄧㄢˊ)
through the years; in the years past
歷來(ㄌㄧˋ ㄌㄞˊ)
hitherto; till now; heretofore; from the old days; since a long time ago: 這是一個歷來無人知道的事實。It is a fact hitherto unknown.
歷覽(ㄌㄧˋ ㄌㄢˇ)
to travel and see; to view during a tour; to visit
歷歷(ㄌㄧˋ ㄌㄧˋ)
distinctly; clearly; vividly: 往事歷歷在心頭。Past events remain fresh in my memory.
歷歷落落(ㄌㄧˋ ㄌㄧˋ ㄌㄨㄛˋ ㄌㄨㄛˋ)
confused; disorderly
歷歷如繪(ㄌㄧˋ ㄌㄧˋ ㄖㄨˊ ㄏㄨㄟˋ)
(to tell a story or experience) vividly; distinctly
歷歷在目(ㄌㄧˋ ㄌㄧˋ ㄗㄞˋ ㄇㄨˋ)
(said of recollecting a past event or experience) as if it were taking place right before one's eyes; vividly
歷練(ㄌㄧˋ ˙ㄌㄧㄢ)
to practice and experience
歷落(ㄌㄧˋ ㄌㄨㄛˋ)
① noisy ② disorderly; disarray ③ dashing and elegant (manner, deportment, etc.)
歷亂(ㄌㄧˋ ㄌㄨㄢˋ)
confused and disorderly; in turmoil
歷劫(ㄌㄧˋ ㄐㄧㄝˊ)
① to experience many mishaps and misfortunes; to pass through one crisis after another ② to pass through years and decades
歷屆(ㄌㄧˋ ㄐㄧㄝˋ)
successive (or all) previous (meetings, games, elections, etc.): 那是個歷屆畢業生的聚會。It's a party for graduates of all previous years.
歷久不衰(ㄌㄧˋ ㄐㄧㄡˇ ㄅㄨˋ ㄕㄨㄞ)
(said of writing, reputation, a school of thought, etc.) long-lasting
歷久彌堅(ㄌㄧˋ ㄐㄧㄡˇ ㄇㄧˊ ㄐㄧㄢ)
(said of one's faith, belief, conviction, etc.) to remain unshakable and become even firmer as time goes by
歷盡艱難(ㄌㄧˋ ㄐㄧㄣˋ ㄐㄧㄢ ㄋㄢˊ)
to have gone through all kinds of hardships and difficulties
歷經(ㄌㄧˋ ㄐㄧㄥ)
to have experienced, undergone or encountered many times: 他們歷經千辛萬苦。They have experienced great hardships and pains.
歷險(ㄌㄧˋ ㄒㄧㄢˇ)
to undergo or experience adventures and dangers; to have had a narrow escape
歷朝(ㄌㄧˋ ㄔㄠˊ)
down through the dynasties; through the successive dynasties
歷程(ㄌㄧˋ ㄔㄥˊ)
process; course: 他們回顧戰爭的歷程。They looked back on the course of the war.
歷時(ㄌㄧˋ ㄕˊ)
to last (a certain period of time): 會議歷時三個鐘頭。The meeting lasted three hours.
歷史(ㄌㄧˋ ㄕˇ)
history: 中國是歷史悠久的國家。China is a richly historied land.
歷史的(ㄌㄧˋ ㄕˇ ˙ㄉㄜ)
historical: 這些是歷史的眞實事件和人物。These are historical events and people.
歷史的眞實性(ㄌㄧˋ ㄕˇ ˙ㄉㄜ ㄓㄣ ㄕˊ ㄒㄧㄥˋ)
historicity
歷史地理(ㄌㄧˋ ㄕˇ ㄉㄧˋ ㄌㄧˇ)
historical geography
歷史觀(ㄌㄧˋ ㄕˇ ㄍㄨㄢ)
the historical view or concept
歷史家(ㄌㄧˋ ㄕˇ ㄐㄧㄚ)
a historian; a historiographer: 他是位著名的歷史家。He is an eminent historian.
歷史性的(ㄌㄧˋ ㄕˇ ㄒㄧㄥˋ ˙ㄉㄜ)
historic: 那是一場歷史性的勝利。It's a historic victory.
歷史學(ㄌㄧˋ ㄕˇ ㄒㄩㄝˊ)
the science of history; historiography
歷史眼光(ㄌㄧˋ ㄕˇ ㄧㄢˇ ㄍㄨㄤ)
in the light of history; historically
歷稔(ㄌㄧˋ ㄖㄣˇ)
down through the years
歷任(ㄌㄧˋ ㄖㄣˋ)
① to have held the following posts ② (those who) have held the same post
歷次(ㄌㄧˋ ㄘˋ)
all previous or past (occasions, etc.)
歷有年所(ㄌㄧˋ ㄧㄡˇ ㄋㄧㄢˊ ㄙㄨㄛˇ)
It has been many years (since a certain event occurred).

十四畫

【歸】 2690
ㄍㄨㄟ guei guī
1. to come back; to return: 他下班遲歸。He returned from work late.
2. to return (something to its owner): 物歸原主。Return the thing to its rightful owner.
3. (said of a woman) to marry
4. to pledge allegiance to
5. to belong; to attribute: 這些書歸我所有。These books belong to me.
6. to turn over to; to put in somebody's charge: 這事應歸他管。This matter should be turned over to him.
7. a Chinese family name

歸併(ㄍㄨㄟ ㄅㄧㄥˋ)
to merge into; to unite with; to put together; to annex; to incorporate into:一些小銀行歸併成一個大組織。The small banks were merged into one large organization.
歸附(ㄍㄨㄟ ㄈㄨˋ)
to follow (a leader in a revolution, etc.); to pledge allegiance to
歸檔(ㄍㄨㄟ ㄉㄤˇ)
to return (a document, materials, etc.) back to file; to file away: 把這些信件仔細地歸檔。File these letters carefully.
歸隊(ㄍㄨㄟ ㄉㄨㄟˋ)
(said of stragglers, individual members of an organization) to return to the ranks; to rejoin the group; to go back to the unit
歸天(ㄍㄨㄟ ㄊㄧㄢ)or 歸西(ㄍㄨㄟ ㄒㄧ)
(literally) to return to heaven—to pass away

止部

歸田(ㄍㄨㄟ ㄊㄧㄢˊ)
①(in ancient China) one was allotted farmland at 20 and would return the land to the state at 60—having reached 60 years of age ② to return to one's hometown after serving the government for years—to retire from public life

歸途(ㄍㄨㄟ ㄊㄨˊ)
on the way home; the homeward journey: 我在歸途中遇到他。I met him on my way home.

歸納(ㄍㄨㄟ ㄋㄚˋ)
to induct (a theory, natural law, etc.); to sum up: 他歸納出一些自然法則。He inducted some physical laws.

歸納法(ㄍㄨㄟ ㄋㄚˋ ㄈㄚˇ)
the inductive method; induction: 所有歸納法的推論都是一種猜測。Every induction is a speculation.

歸寧(ㄍㄨㄟ ㄋㄧㄥˊ)
(said of a woman) to visit her parents after marriage

歸類(ㄍㄨㄟ ㄌㄟˋ)
to categorize; to classify

歸老(ㄍㄨㄟ ㄌㄠˇ)
to retire on account of age

歸攏(ㄍㄨㄟ ㄌㄨㄥˇ)
to unite with; to collaborate with: 請把東西歸攏起來。Please put the things together.

歸根結底(ㄍㄨㄟ ㄍㄣ ㄐㄧㄝˊ ㄉㄧˇ)
fundamentally; basically; finally; in the end; in the final analysis: 歸根結底，和平豈非即爲人權? Is not peace, in the final analysis, a matter of human rights?

歸耕(ㄍㄨㄟ ㄍㄥ)
to retire from public service and return home

歸骨(ㄍㄨㄟ ㄍㄨˇ)
to bring home one's remains for burial

歸國(ㄍㄨㄟ ㄍㄨㄛˊ)
to return to one's fatherland

歸功於(ㄍㄨㄟ ㄍㄨㄥ ㄩˊ)
to give the credit to; to attribute the success to: 我們一切的成就都歸功於他的幫忙。We attribute all our achievements to his help.

歸戶(ㄍㄨㄟ ㄏㄨˋ)
(said of tax officials) to add undivided dividend to the income of a taxpayer

歸化(ㄍㄨㄟ ㄏㄨㄚˋ)
① to be naturalized as a citizen: 他歸化爲中國人。He was naturalized as a Chinese citizen. ②(said of a protectorate state, etc.) to pledge allegiance to

歸還(ㄍㄨㄟ ㄏㄨㄢˊ)
① to return (something to its owner): 請把那本書歸還圖書館。Return that book to the library, please. ② to come home

歸寂(ㄍㄨㄟ ㄐㄧˊ)
(Buddhism) to die

歸計(ㄍㄨㄟ ㄐㄧˋ)
plans for going home; to go home

歸家(ㄍㄨㄟ ㄐㄧㄚ)
to return home; homecoming

歸結(ㄍㄨㄟ ㄐㄧㄝˊ)
the end or conclusion of a matter; to sum up; to put in a nutshell: 歸結起來(一句話)，我們結婚了。In a nutshell, we got married.

歸咎(ㄍㄨㄟ ㄐㄧㄡˋ)
to lay the blame on…; to impute: 不要把你的貧窮歸咎於運氣不好。Don't impute your poverty to bad luck.

歸期(ㄍㄨㄟ ㄑㄧˊ)
the date of one's return

歸齊(ㄍㄨㄟ ㄑㄧˊ)
① to amount to; to total ② in the end; fundamentally; basically

歸僑(ㄍㄨㄟ ㄑㄧㄠˊ)
returned overseas Chinese 亦作「歸國華僑」

歸休(ㄍㄨㄟ ㄒㄧㄡ)
① to take a leave for rest ② to die

歸心(ㄍㄨㄟ ㄒㄧㄣ)
① to submit heart and soul (to a cause, leader, etc.) ② the thought or idea of returning home; homesickness

歸心似箭(ㄍㄨㄟ ㄒㄧㄣ ㄙˋ ㄐㄧㄢˋ)
to be anxious or eager to return home; with one's heart set on speeding home: 他歸心似箭。He was anxious to return home as soon as possible.

歸降(ㄍㄨㄟ ㄒㄧㄤˊ)
to yield; to pledge allegiance; to surrender

歸向(ㄍㄨㄟ ㄒㄧㄤˋ)
① the direction of movement ②to turn toward (the righteous side); to incline to

歸省(ㄍㄨㄟ ㄒㄧㄥˇ)
to return home to visit one's parents

歸趙(ㄍㄨㄟ ㄓㄠˋ)
to return something to its rightful owner

歸眞(ㄍㄨㄟ ㄓㄣ)
① to revert to one's natural self ②(in Buddhist terminology) to die

歸正(ㄍㄨㄟ ㄓㄥˋ)
to return to the right cause; (said of rebellious elements, etc.) to return to the side of the government

歸主(ㄍㄨㄟ ㄓㄨˇ)
to return to the Lord—conversion

歸著
①(ㄍㄨㄟ ㄓㄨㄛˊ) a place to stay, develop, etc.; a home base ②(ㄍㄨㄟ˙ㄓㄜ) to make arrangements; to put in order; to tidy up

歸程(ㄍㄨㄟ ㄔㄥˊ)
the homeward journey

歸除(ㄍㄨㄟ ㄔㄨˊ)
(in abacus calculation) division of a number consisting of three or more digits

歸屬(ㄍㄨㄟ ㄕㄨˇ)
① ownership ② to belong

歸順(ㄍㄨㄟ ㄕㄨㄣˋ)
①to yield; to submit; to surrender ② name of an old region in Yunnan Province

歸入(ㄍㄨㄟ ㄖㄨˋ)
to classify; to include: 這些書可歸入同一類。These books may be classified in the same category.

歸葬(ㄍㄨㄟ ㄗㄤˋ)
to bring back one's remains home for burial

歸罪(ㄍㄨㄟ ㄗㄨㄟˋ)
to lay the blame on another; to hold someone responsible

for a mistake; to impute: 他把你的失敗歸罪於懶惰。He imputed your failure to laziness.

歸宗(ㄍㄨㄟ ㄗㄨㄥ)
to return an adopted son to his original ancestral lineage

歸宿(ㄍㄨㄟ ㄙㄨˋ)
① one's final settling place; a home to return to ② (said of a woman) marriage: 她終於找到歸宿了。She was finally married. ③ conclusions

歸綏(ㄍㄨㄟ ㄙㄨㄟ)
Kweisui, capital city of Suiyüan Province

歸案(ㄍㄨㄟ ㄢˋ)
to arrest a criminal and bring him to court for prosecution: 他已被緝拿歸案。He was arrested and brought to justice.

歸依(ㄍㄨㄟ ㄧ)
to follow Buddhist faith; to become a Buddhist disciple, monk or nun 亦作「皈依」: 他已經歸依佛教。He has become a Buddhist disciple.

歸隱(ㄍㄨㄟ ㄧㄣˇ)
to retire; retirement

歸於(ㄍㄨㄟ ㄩˊ)
① to belong to; to be attributed to ② to result in; to end in

歸獄(ㄍㄨㄟ ㄩˋ)
(said of prisoners) to return to jail after a home leave

歹 部
ㄉㄞˇ dae dǎi

【歹】 2691
1. ㄉㄞˇ dae dǎi
bad; wicked; evil; crooked; depraved; vicious: 他常為非作歹。He often did evil.

歹毒(ㄉㄞˇ ㄉㄨˊ)
vicious; viciousness; malicious; malice

歹徒(ㄉㄞˇ ㄊㄨˊ)
hoodlums; bad guys; ruffians; scoundrels; evil fellows

歹念(ㄉㄞˇ ㄋㄧㄢˋ)
evil thoughts: 歹念佔據了他的心。Evil thoughts occupy his mind.

歹心(ㄉㄞˇ ㄒㄧㄣ)
evil intent

歹人(ㄉㄞˇ ㄖㄣˊ)
① evil persons ② thieves or burglars

歹意(ㄉㄞˇ ㄧˋ)
malice; malicious intent; bad intentions

【歹】 2691
2. (歺) ㄜˋ eh è
(now rarely) the remains of a person

二畫

【死】 2692
ㄙˇ syy sǐ
1. to die; to die for; dead; death: 人皆有死。Death comes to all men.
2. used as an intensive or superlative; very; extremely: 她高興死了。She was extremely happy.
3. condemned (persons whose lives are numbered, as criminals on the death row)
4. inanimate; dull and stupid; inert; insensible; lifeless
5. obstinate or stubborn; persevering; resolute; resolutely
6. rigid, fixed or unchangeable (regulations, etc.); immovable (drawers, etc.): 那是個死規矩。It's a rigid rule.
7. impassable; closed

死板(ㄙˇ ㄅㄢˇ)
wooden (persons); rigid (regulations); fixed and unchangeable (methods, etc.); monotonous (work, life, etc.): 他辦事死板板的。He worked in a mechanical way.

死別(ㄙˇ ㄅㄧㄝˊ)
to be parted by death; death-partings

死不瞑目(ㄙˇ ·ㄅㄨ ㄇㄧㄥˊ ㄇㄨˋ)
to be unwilling to die (because of some unfinished tasks, unfulfilled wishes, intensive grudges, etc.)

死不了(ㄙˇ ·ㄅㄨ ㄌㄧㄠˇ)
cannot die; will not die

死不悔改(ㄙˇ ㄅㄨˋ ㄏㄨㄟˇ ㄍㄞˇ)
absolutely unrepentant; incorrigible

死不認錯(ㄙˇ ·ㄅㄨ ㄖㄣˋ ㄘㄨㄛˋ)
stubbornly refuse to admit one's guilt or mistake

死不足惜(ㄙˇ ·ㄅㄨ ㄗㄨˊ ㄒㄧˊ)
Death is not to be regretted (if it serves a purpose).

死不要臉(ㄙˇ ·ㄅㄨ ㄧㄠˋ ㄌㄧㄢˇ)
extremely shameless; utterly shameless; brazen-faced

死皮賴臉(ㄙˇ ㄆㄧˊ ㄌㄞˋ ㄌㄧㄢˇ)
brazen-faced and unreasonable; to importune shamelessly

死拼(ㄙˇ ㄆㄧㄣ)
to fight to the death: 他們將死拼到底。They will fight to the death.

死馬當作活馬醫(ㄙˇ ㄇㄚˇ ㄉㄤˋ ㄗㄨㄛˋ ㄏㄨㄛˊ ㄇㄚˇ ㄧ)
to do what one can to solve an apparently unsolvable problem or reverse a seemingly hopeless situation

死眉瞪眼(ㄙˇ ㄇㄟˊ ㄉㄥˋ ㄧㄢˇ)
① a wooden expression that infuriates ② inanimate

死命(ㄙˇ ㄇㄧㄥˋ)
① with all the power and strength at one's command; desperately: 他死命掙扎。He struggled desperately. ② to cause to die: 他制敵於死命。He sent the enemy to his doom.

死法子(ㄙˇ ㄈㄚˇ ·ㄗ)
a rigid and unimaginative way of doing things

死得其所(ㄙˇ ㄉㄜˊ ㄑㄧˊ ㄙㄨㄛˇ)
to die a worthy death

死鬪(ㄙˇ ㄉㄡˋ)
to fight to death

死黨(ㄙˇ ㄉㄤˇ)
sworn confederates; sworn followers; a gang of diehards sticking together till death shall they part

死擋(ㄙˇ ㄉㄤˇ)
to resist to death

死等(ㄙˇ ㄉㄥˇ)
to wait indefinitely without giving up hope; to wait forever

死敵(ㄙˇ ㄉㄧˊ)
a mortal enemy; an arch adversary; an implacable

foe; a deadly enemy
死地(ㄙˇ ㄉㄧˋ)
①a hopeless situation ②a "dead" locality or site (in the geomantic sense) ③the place of death
死店活人開(ㄙˇ ㄉㄧㄢˋ ㄏㄨㄛˊ ㄖㄣˊ ㄎㄞ)
Everything depends on how one manages it. 或 Man's action and thought determine the success of an endeavor.
死讀書(ㄙˇ ㄉㄨˊ ㄕㄨ)
to study mechanically; to read (a book) without thinking
死對頭(ㄙˇ ㄉㄨㄟˋ ·ㄊㄡ)
arch enemies or rivals; bitter opponents
死胎(ㄙˇ ㄊㄞ)
a stillbirth; a dead fetus
死腦筋(ㄙˇ ㄋㄠˇ ㄐㄧㄣ)
a one-track mind
死難(ㄙˇ ㄋㄢˋ)
to die a martyr's death
死拉活拽(ㄙˇ ㄌㄚ ㄏㄨㄛˊ ㄓㄨㄞˋ)
to drag and pull with all one's strength
死裏逃生(ㄙˇ ㄌㄧˇ ㄊㄠˊ ㄕㄥ)
to escape death by a narrow margin; to have a close bout with death; to escape by the skin of one's teeth
死力(ㄙˇ ㄌㄧˋ)
to strive with all one's efforts
死路(ㄙˇ ㄌㄨˋ)
①a blind alley; a dead end ②a fatal route
死路一條(ㄙˇ ㄌㄨˋ ㄧˋ ㄊㄧㄠˊ)
no way out; doomed
死溝(ㄙˇ ㄍㄡ)
a blocked up ditch or gutter
死狗(ㄙˇ ㄍㄡˇ)
a dead dog (a term used in name-calling)
死規矩(ㄙˇ ㄍㄨㄟ ·ㄐㄩ)
rigid, stiff, unchangeable, and sometimes unreasonable rules
死鬼(ㄙˇ ㄍㄨㄟˇ)
You devil! (a term often used by Chinese women to scold their husbands)
死光(ㄙˇ ㄍㄨㄤ)
① death rays ② all dead; without survivors
死工夫(ㄙˇ ㄍㄨㄥ ·ㄈㄨ)
sheer hard work (in which luck or talent plays no part)
死摳兒(ㄙˇ ㄎㄡㄦ)
①obstinate; stubborn ②to dedicate oneself (to a study) ③stingy; tight-fisted
死海(ㄙˇ ㄏㄞˇ)
Dead Sea between Israel and Jordan
死後(ㄙˇ ㄏㄡˋ)
after death; postmortem
死衚衕兒(ㄙˇ ㄏㄨˊ ㄊㄨㄥˋㄦ)
a dead-end alley
死活(ㄙˇ ㄏㄨㄛˊ)
①dead or alive ②no matter what; in any case; anyway; simply
死火山(ㄙˇ ㄏㄨㄛˇ ㄕㄢ)
an extinct volcano
死灰(ㄙˇ ㄏㄨㄟ)
cold ashes of a fire—(figuratively) discouraged or lonely
死灰復燃(ㄙˇ ㄏㄨㄟ ㄈㄨˋ ㄖㄢˊ)
(said of emotion, especially love, crushed rebellious force, dormant ideas, etc.) rekindled; rejuvenated
死肌(ㄙˇ ㄐㄧ)
muscles that have lost functioning power due to rheumatism, etc.
死寂(ㄙˇ ㄐㄧˊ)
deathly stillness
死忌(ㄙˇ ㄐㄧˋ)
death anniversaries
死記(ㄙˇ ㄐㄧˋ)
to memorize by rote; mechanical memorizing
死勁兒(ㄙˇ ㄐㄧㄜˋㄦ)
①all one's strength; all one's might ②with all one's strength (or might); for all one is worth: 她死勁兒跑。She ran for all she was worth.
死節(ㄙˇ ㄐㄧㄝˊ)
to die a martyr's death; to die for honor
死結(ㄙˇ ㄐㄧㄝˊ)
①a fast knot (as opposed to slip knots) ②a problem or issue that defies solution; an impasse
死角(ㄙˇ ㄐㄧㄠˇ)
a dead angle; the defiladed space
死諫(ㄙˇ ㄐㄧㄢˋ)
to risk one's life in pressing a point on the emperor
死井(ㄙˇ ㄐㄧㄥˇ)
a dried-up well
死期(ㄙˇ ㄑㄧˊ)
the time of death; the hour of doom
死棋(ㄙˇ ㄑㄧˊ)
①a dead piece in a game of chess ②(figuratively) a hopeless case
死乞白賴(ㄙˇ ㄑㄧˇ ㄅㄞˊ ㄌㄞˋ)
to entangle without stop; to be importunate; to lie shamelessly
死氣沉沉(ㄙˇ ㄑㄧˋ ㄔㄣˊ ㄔㄣˊ)
a dead atmosphere; hopeless and gloomy; dull and despondent; lifeless air; stagnant: 那是場死氣沉沉的表演。It's a lifeless performance.
死囚(ㄙˇ ㄑㄧㄡˊ)
a death convict
死前(ㄙˇ ㄑㄧㄢˊ)
before death; before one dies: 他死前立下遺言。He made a will before his death.
死去活來(ㄙˇ ㄑㄩˋ ㄏㄨㄛˊ ㄌㄞˊ)
in extreme pain or distress; half dead
死心(ㄙˇ ㄒㄧㄣ)
to give up one's hope for good; to think no more of something
死心塌地(ㄙˇ ㄒㄧㄣ ㄊㄚ ㄉㄧˋ)
unreservedly; wholeheartedly; to be dead set; head over heels
死心眼兒(ㄙˇ ㄒㄧㄣ ㄧㄚˇㄦ)
obstinate and simple-minded
死信(ㄙˇ ㄒㄧㄣˋ)
undeliverable letters; dead letters
死巷(ㄙˇ ㄒㄧㄤˋ)or 死胡同(ㄙˇ ㄏㄨˊ ㄊㄨㄥˋ)
a dead-end alley (also used figuratively)
死相(ㄙˇ ㄒㄧㄤˋ)
(literally) a cadaverous look—a dull and inanimate look (often used by a wife to scold her husband)
死刑(ㄙˇ ㄒㄧㄥˊ)
a capital punishment; a death penalty
死性(ㄙˇ ·ㄒㄧㄥ)

①obstinacy; stubbornness ②an over-candid disposition that knows neither refinement nor tact in dealing with people

死訊(ㄙˇ ㄒㄩㄣˋ)
news of someone's death

死者(ㄙˇ ㄓㄜˇ)
the dead; the deceased; the departed soul: 他們哀悼死者。They mourned for the dead.

死戰(ㄙˇ ㄓㄢˋ)
to battle to the last

死中求生(ㄙˇ ㄓㄨㄥ ㄑㄧㄡˊ ㄕㄥ)
to struggle in a desperate or hopeless situation for survival

死纏活纏(ㄙˇ ㄔㄢˊ ㄏㄨㄛˊ ㄔㄢˊ)
to importune or entangle a person incessantly

死屍(ㄙˇ ㄕ)
a corpse

死守(ㄙˇ ㄕㄡˇ)
to defend (a position, city, etc.) to the last: 英勇的戰士死守陣地。The brave soldiers defended the position to the last.

死傷(ㄙˇ ㄕㄤ)
the dead and wounded; casualties

死傷枕藉(ㄙˇ ㄕㄤ ㄓㄣˇ ㄐㄧㄝˋ)
heavy casualties

死生有命(ㄙˇ ㄕㄥ ㄧㄡˇ ㄇㄧㄥˋ)
Life and death are predetermined. 或 Life and death lie in the lap of the gods.或 A person's life and death are matters of fate.

死說活說(ㄙˇ ㄕㄨㄛ ㄏㄨㄛˊ ㄕㄨㄛ)
to persuade by all means; to importune incessantly

死水(ㄙˇ ㄕㄨㄟˇ)
stagnant water; stagnating water

死水坑子(ㄙˇ ㄕㄨㄟˇ ㄎㄥ ˙ㄗ)
a low-lying point where drainage of water is difficult

死人(ㄙˇ ㄖㄣˊ)
①a dead person ②You blockhead! 或 You stupid! 或 You fool!

死字(ㄙˇ ㄗˋ)
a word which is no longer in use or circulation; an obsolete word

死罪(ㄙˇ ㄗㄨㄟˋ)
①the capital punishment; sentence of death ②(in ancient China) a term of apology used in correspondence ③(in ancient China) a conventional phrase used in writing memorials to the emperor

死喪(ㄙˇ ㄙㄤ)
death and burial

死而復甦(ㄙˇ ㄦˊ ㄈㄨˋ ㄙㄨ)
to wake up from death; to resurrect

死而後已(ㄙˇ ㄦˊ ㄏㄡˋ ㄧˇ)
to stop only upon death

死而無怨(ㄙˇ ㄦˊ ㄨˊ ㄩㄢˋ)
to die without a grudge

死要面子(ㄙˇ ㄧㄠˋ ㄇㄧㄢˋ ˙ㄗ)
to try to preserve one's face at all costs

死有餘辜(ㄙˇ ㄧㄡˇ ㄩˊ ㄍㄨ)
Death will not expiate all his crimes. 他眞是死有餘辜。He deserves to die many times for his crimes.

死因(ㄙˇ ㄧㄣ)
the cause of death: 他的死因不明。The cause of his death is still unknown.

死樣(ㄙˇ ˙ㄧㄤ)
stupid and dull; wooden; doltish

死硬(ㄙˇ ㄧㄥˋ)
intransigent; very obstinate; irreconcilable; stiff and unbending

死硬派(ㄙˇ ㄧㄥˋ ㄆㄞˋ)
diehards

死無對證(ㄙˇ ㄨˊ ㄉㄨㄟˋ ㄓㄥˋ)
to lack evidence because of the death of a principal witness

死無葬身之地(ㄙˇ ㄨˊ ㄗㄤˋ ㄕㄣ ㄓ ㄉㄧˋ)
to die without a place for burial (a phrase usually used as a warning to somebody)

死無遺憾(ㄙˇ ㄨˊ ㄧˊ ㄏㄢˋ)
to die without regret

死文字(ㄙˇ ㄨㄣˊ ㄗˋ)
dead languages—languages which are no longer in common usage, as Greek, Latin, etc.

死亡(ㄙˇ ㄨㄤˊ)
to die; death: 他因傷死亡。He died from a wound.

死亡保險(ㄙˇ ㄨㄤˊ ㄅㄠˇ ㄒㄧㄢˇ)
life insurance 亦作「壽險」or「人壽保險」

死亡通告(ㄙˇ ㄨㄤˊ ㄊㄨㄥ ㄍㄠˋ)
an obituary; a death notice 亦作「訃聞」

死亡率(ㄙˇ ㄨㄤˊ ㄌㄩˋ)
death rate; mortality

死亡學(ㄙˇ ㄨㄤˊ ㄒㄩㄝˊ)
thanatology

死亡證書(ㄙˇ ㄨㄤˊ ㄓㄥˋ ㄕㄨ)
a death certificate

死於非命(ㄙˇ ㄩˊ ㄈㄟ ㄇㄧㄥˋ)
to die an unnatural death: 他昨夜死於非命。He died an unnatural death last night.

四畫

【歿】 2693
(殁) ㄇㄛˋ moh mò
to die; death: 他於一九五六年病歿。He died of illness in 1956.

歿世不忘(ㄇㄛˋ ㄕˋ ㄅㄨˋ ㄨㄤˋ)
shall never forget

歿存均感(ㄇㄛˋ ㄘㄨㄣˊ ㄐㄩㄣ ㄍㄢˇ)
Both the dead and the living shall be grateful.

【殀】 2694
ㄧㄠˇ yeau yǎo
1. to die young or untimely
2. to be wronged or aggrieved

五畫

【殆】 2695
ㄉㄞˋ day dài
1. precarious; dangerous; danger; perilous: 他處於危殆之中。He is in great danger.
2. tired
3. afraid
4. nearly; almost: 存款殆盡。The cash is almost exhausted.
5. only; merely; even

殆不可能(ㄉㄞˋ ㄅㄨˋ ㄎㄜˇ ㄋㄥˊ)
almost impossible

殆矣哉(ㄉㄞˋ ㄧˇ ㄗㄞ)
in grave danger; very dangerous indeed

殆已無望(ㄉㄞˋ ㄧˇ ㄨˊ ㄨㄤˋ)
nearly hopeless

【殄】 2696
ㄊㄧㄢˇ tean tiǎn
1. to end; to terminate
2. to exterminate; to extirpate;

to weed out; to wipe out
3. to waste

殄滅(ㄊㄧㄢˇ ㄇㄧㄝˋ)
to exterminate thoroughly; to extirpate; to commit genocide

殄難(ㄊㄧㄢˇ ㄋㄢˋ)
to exterminate dangers; to eliminate dangers and hardships

殄絕(ㄊㄧㄢˇ ㄐㄩㄝˊ)
to bring to termination; to bring to an end

殄墜(ㄊㄧㄢˇ ㄓㄨㄟˋ)
(said of a dynasty, reign, etc.) to be eliminated; to come to an end

殄瘁(ㄊㄧㄢˇ ㄘㄨㄟˋ)
misfortune and poverty; ruin

【殃】 2697
ㄧㄤ iang yāng

1. disaster; misfortune; calamities: 戰爭是可怕的災殃。War is a frightful calamity.
2. the return of the spirit of the deceased

殃民(ㄧㄤ ㄇㄧㄣˊ)
to wrong and suppress the people; to bring disaster to the people

殃禍(ㄧㄤ ㄏㄨㄛˋ)
disasters and calamities

殃及池魚(ㄧㄤ ㄐㄧˊ ㄔˊ ㄩˊ)
(literally) (When the city gate catches fire,) the disaster even extends to the fish in the moat—to cause trouble or bring disaster to innocent people

殃及無辜(ㄧㄤ ㄐㄧˊ ㄨˊ ㄍㄨ)
Trouble involves the innocent people.

【殂】 2698
ㄘㄨˊ tswu cú

to die; dead; death

殂沒(ㄘㄨˊ ㄇㄛˋ)
to die; to perish; death

殂落(ㄘㄨˊ ㄌㄨㄛˋ)or 殂謝(ㄘㄨˊ ㄒㄧㄝˋ)
to pass away; to demise

殂殞(ㄘㄨˊ ㄩㄣˇ)
to die; death (of usually an eminent figure)

六畫

【殉】 2699
ㄒㄩㄣˋ shiunn xùn

1. to die for a cause
2. (originally) to be buried with the dead (usually said of slaves, loyal servants, concubines, etc.)

殉名(ㄒㄩㄣˋ ㄇㄧㄥˊ)
to win fame at the expense of one's life

殉道(ㄒㄩㄣˋ ㄉㄠˋ)
to die for the right cause; to die a martyr's death

殉道精神(ㄒㄩㄣˋ ㄉㄠˋ ㄐㄧㄥ ㄕㄣˊ)
martyrdom

殉道者(ㄒㄩㄣˋ ㄉㄠˋ ㄓㄜˇ)
a martyr

殉難(ㄒㄩㄣˋ ㄋㄢˋ)
to die for one's country: 他父親爲國殉難。His father died for his country.

殉利(ㄒㄩㄣˋ ㄌㄧˋ)or 殉財(ㄒㄩㄣˋ ㄘㄞˊ)
to die for money

殉國(ㄒㄩㄣˋ ㄍㄨㄛˊ)
to die for one's country; to die a martyr's death

殉節(ㄒㄩㄣˋ ㄐㄧㄝˊ)
to die to protect one's virtue or for the sake of honor

殉教(ㄒㄩㄣˋ ㄐㄧㄠˋ)
to die for a religious cause

殉情(ㄒㄩㄣˋ ㄑㄧㄥˊ)
to die for love

殉職(ㄒㄩㄣˋ ㄓˊ)
to die on one's job; to die while performing one's work: 他因公殉職了。He died at his post.

殉身(ㄒㄩㄣˋ ㄕㄣ)
to die for a cause, faith, etc.

殉葬(ㄒㄩㄣˋ ㄗㄤˋ)
to bury the living, jewels, vessels, etc. with the dead

【殊】 2700
ㄕㄨ shu shū

1. different; special; strange
2. distinguished; outstanding
3. extremely; very
4. really; indeed: 此事殊難解決。This matter is indeed difficult to settle
5. still; yet
6. exceed; over

殊不可解(ㄕㄨ ˙ㄅㄨ ㄎㄜˇ ㄐㄧㄝˇ)
really difficult to understand

殊不知(ㄕㄨ ˙ㄅㄨ ㄓ)
Who knows that....; really don't know

殊方(ㄕㄨ ㄈㄤ)
strange lands; foreign lands

殊途同歸(ㄕㄨ ㄊㄨˊ ㄊㄨㄥˊ ㄍㄨㄟ)
to reach the same destination (or goal) by different routes; to reach the same decision or conclusion by different means or ways

殊禮(ㄕㄨ ㄌㄧˇ)
a very polite reception; utmost courtesy

殊功(ㄕㄨ ㄍㄨㄥ)
extraordinary achievements; distinguished services

殊堪嘉尚(ㄕㄨ ㄎㄢ ㄐㄧㄚ ㄕㄤˋ)
richly deserving commendation (a cliché often found in official citations)

殊行(ㄕㄨ ㄒㄧㄥˊ)
remarkable behavior or conduct; extraordinary actions

殊勳(ㄕㄨ ㄒㄩㄣ)
extraordinary achievements or merits

殊寵(ㄕㄨ ㄔㄨㄥˇ)
special favor

殊深(ㄕㄨ ㄕㄣ)
extremely; profoundly; deeply

殊勝(ㄕㄨ ㄕㄥˋ)
remarkable and outstanding

殊容(ㄕㄨ ㄖㄨㄥˊ)
a stunningly beautiful face; extraordinary beauty

殊榮(ㄕㄨ ㄖㄨㄥˊ)
special honors

殊死(ㄕㄨ ㄙˇ)
desperate; life-and-death: 那是一場殊死的搏鬥。That was a life-and-death struggle.

殊死戰(ㄕㄨ ㄙˇ ㄓㄢˋ)
to fight to the last man; a life-or-death battle; a desperate fight: 他們作殊死戰。They fought a last-ditch battle.

殊俗(ㄕㄨ ㄙㄨˊ)
① strange customs ② different from common practices; extraordinary

殊異(ㄕㄨ ㄧˋ)
special; extraordinary

殊未(ㄕㄨ ㄨㄟˋ)
not yet

殊文(ㄕㄨ ㄨㄣˊ)
a strange language (especially written); a different language

殊遇(ㄕㄨ ㄩˋ)
special treatment; special kindness
殊域(ㄕㄨ ㄩˋ)
strange lands

七畫

【殍】2701
ㄆㄧㄠˇ peau piǎo
1. to starve to death
2. a person who died from starvation 亦作「莩」

八畫

【殖】2702
ㄓˊ jyr zhí
1. to grow in abundance; to prosper; to reproduce; to propagate: 大多數植物靠種子繁殖。Most plants reproduce by seeds.
2. to plant
3. to become wealthy
4. to colonize; colonization
殖民(ㄓˊ ㄇㄧㄣˊ)
to colonize; to settle people in a less developed area
殖民地(ㄓˊ ㄇㄧㄣˊ ㄉㄧˋ)
a colony
殖民教育(ㄓˊ ㄇㄧㄣˊ ㄐㄧㄠˋ ㄩˋ)
colonial education
殖民政策(ㄓˊ ㄇㄧㄣˊ ㄓㄥˋ ㄘㄜˋ)
the colonial policy; colonialism
殖利(ㄓˊ ㄌㄧˋ)
to make profits
殖穀(ㄓˊ ㄍㄨˇ)
to plant rice
殖貨(ㄓˊ ㄏㄨㄛˋ)
to prosper in commercial dealings; to increase one's possessions in property and goods
殖產(ㄓˊ ㄔㄢˇ)
to increase one's property and holdings

【殘】2703
ㄘㄢˊ tsarn cán
1. to destroy; to injure; to damage; to spoil
2. to wither
3. cruel and fierce; heartless and relentless: 他生性凶殘。He was cruel by nature.
4. crippled; disfigured: 他在一次車禍中變成殘廢。He was crippled in a motorcar accident.
5. remnants or residues; the little amount of something left
6. incomplete: 這是他的殘稿。This is his incomplete manuscript.
7. to kill
殘杯冷炙(ㄘㄢˊ ㄅㄟ ㄌㄥˇ ㄓˋ)
the dregs of wine and cold meat—what is left of a feast
殘暴(ㄘㄢˊ ㄅㄠˋ)
cruel and heartless; cold-blooded; cruelty; ruthlessness; brutal: 殘暴的士兵，毆打他們的俘虜。Brutal soldiers beat their prisoners.
殘兵敗將(ㄘㄢˊ ㄅㄧㄥ ㄅㄞˋ ㄐㄧㄤˋ)
the remnants of a defeated army
殘部(ㄘㄢˊ ㄅㄨˋ)
the remnants of defeated troops, bandit groups, etc.
殘破(ㄘㄢˊ ㄆㄛˋ)
① damaged; spoiled; dilapidated: 傢俱由於使用而殘破。Furniture is dilapidated by use. ② not complete; deficient
殘篇斷簡(ㄘㄢˊ ㄆㄧㄢ ㄉㄨㄢˋ ㄐㄧㄢˇ)
books with missing pages, chapters, volumes, etc.; fragments
殘夢(ㄘㄢˊ ㄇㄥˋ)
an unfinished dream
殘民自肥(ㄘㄢˊ ㄇㄧㄣˊ ㄗˋ ㄈㄟˊ)
to fatten oneself by exploiting the people
殘廢(ㄘㄢˊ ㄈㄟˋ)
crippled, maimed, or disabled: 他在戰爭中受重傷而殘廢。He was seriously maimed in the war.
殘燈復明(ㄘㄢˊ ㄉㄥ ㄈㄨˋ ㄇㄧㄥˊ)
(figuratively) the last flicker of life in a dying man
殘冬(ㄘㄢˊ ㄉㄨㄥ)
the last days of winter
殘年(ㄘㄢˊ ㄋㄧㄢˊ) or 殘歲(ㄘㄢˊ ㄙㄨㄟˋ)
① the closing days of the year ② one's closing years; the evening of life
殘虐(ㄘㄢˊ ㄋㄩㄝˋ)
cruelty and torture; cold-bloodedness
殘留(ㄘㄢˊ ㄌㄧㄡˊ)
to remain; to be left over
殘羹剩飯(ㄘㄢˊ ㄍㄥ ㄕㄥˋ ㄈㄢˋ)
the remains of a meal; leftovers
殘酷(ㄘㄢˊ ㄎㄨˋ)
cruelty; heartlessness; cold-bloodedness; savagery: 那是一場殘酷的戰爭。That was a cruel war.
殘骸(ㄘㄢˊ ㄏㄞˊ)
① incomplete remains ② the wreckage (of an airplane, ship or truck): 那是飛機的殘骸。It was the wreckage of an airplane.
殘害(ㄘㄢˊ ㄏㄞˋ)
to oppress cruelly; to injure heartlessly; to slaughter
殘痕(ㄘㄢˊ ㄏㄣˊ)
traces or marks left
殘花敗柳(ㄘㄢˊ ㄏㄨㄚ ㄅㄞˋ ㄌㄧㄡˇ)
(literally) faded flowers and withered willows—fallen angels; prostitutes
殘紅(ㄘㄢˊ ㄏㄨㄥˊ)
fallen flowers
殘疾(ㄘㄢˊ ㄐㄧˊ)
physical deformity—crippled, deformed, maimed, etc.
殘局(ㄘㄢˊ ㄐㄩˊ)
① the aftermath of war, revolution or great upheaval ② an unfinished chess game
殘卷(ㄘㄢˊ ㄐㄩㄢˋ)
a volume with many missing pages; a volume that used to be part of a complete book
殘缺 or 殘闕(ㄘㄢˊ ㄑㄩㄝ)
incomplete; fragmentary
殘席(ㄘㄢˊ ㄒㄧˊ)
a table after a feast
殘照(ㄘㄢˊ ㄓㄠˋ)
① the setting sun ② the evening glow
殘燭(ㄘㄢˊ ㄓㄨˊ)
an expiring candle
殘喘(ㄘㄢˊ ㄔㄨㄢˇ)
agonized breathing just before dying
殘春(ㄘㄢˊ ㄔㄨㄣ)
the last days of spring
殘殺(ㄘㄢˊ ㄕㄚ)
to kill indiscriminately or savagely; to massacre; to slaughter

〔歹部〕

〔歹部〕

殘山賸水(ㄘㄢˊ ㄕㄢ ㄕㄥˋ ㄕㄨㄟˇ)
the reduced territories of a nation after aggression by a foreign power
殘生(ㄘㄢˊ ㄕㄥ)
the closing years of one's life; one's remaining years
殘暑(ㄘㄢˊ ㄕㄨˇ)
the lingering heat of late summer
殘忍(ㄘㄢˊ ㄖㄣˇ)
cruelty; heartlessness; brutality; cruel; heartless; brutal; savage: 我不喜歡殘忍的人。I do not like cruel people.
殘賊(ㄘㄢˊ ㄗㄜˊ)
①to injure; to spoil ②a ravening thief
殘存(ㄘㄢˊ ㄘㄨㄣˊ)
surviving
殘而不廢(ㄘㄢˊ ㄦˊ ㄅㄨˋ ㄈㄟˋ)
disabled but useful; crippled but leading an active life
殘陽(ㄘㄢˊ ㄧㄤˊ)
the setting sun; the evening glow
殘餘(ㄘㄢˊ ㄩˊ)
remnants; survivals; remains; vestiges; residues
殘月(ㄘㄢˊ ㄩㄝˋ)
the waning moon

九畫

【殛】2704 ㄐㄧˊ jyi jí
to put to death

十畫

【殞】2705 ㄩㄣˇ yeun yǔn
1. to die; to perish
2. same as 隕—to fall
殞沒(ㄩㄣˇ ㄇㄛˋ)
to perish; to die
殞滅(ㄩㄣˇ ㄇㄧㄝˋ)
to exterminate; to annihilate; to wipe out
殞命(ㄩㄣˇ ㄇㄧㄥˋ)
to perish; to die
殞落(ㄩㄣˇ ㄌㄨㄛˋ)or 殞墜(ㄩㄣˇ ㄓㄨㄟˋ)
to fall
殞石(ㄩㄣˇ ㄕˊ)
a meteorite

十一畫

【殣】2706 ㄐㄧㄣˇ jiin jǐn
1. to starve to death
2. to bury

【殤】2707 ㄕㄤ shang shāng
1. to die young; to die prematurely
2. national mourning

【殢】2708 ㄊㄧˋ tih tì
greatly distressed
殢酒(ㄊㄧˋ ㄐㄧㄡˇ)
to suffer from alcoholism

十二畫

【殪】2709 ㄧˋ yih yì
1. to die
2. to kill

【殫】2710 ㄉㄢ dan dān
to use up; to exhaust
殫悶(ㄉㄢ ㄇㄣˋ)
to swoon; to lose consciousness; to faint
殫力(ㄉㄢ ㄌㄧˋ)
to strive; to endeavor
殫竭其力(ㄉㄢ ㄐㄧㄝˊ ㄑㄧˊ ㄌㄧˋ)
to give all of one's strength
殫見洽聞(ㄉㄢ ㄐㄧㄢˋ ㄒㄧㄚˊ ㄨㄣˊ)
to have vast knowledge and experience; to have seen all and heard all
殫精竭慮(ㄉㄢ ㄐㄧㄥ ㄐㄧㄝˊ ㄌㄩˋ)
to devote one's entire energy and thought; to think with all one's energies or powers
殫洽(ㄉㄢ ㄒㄧㄚˊ)
very erudite
殫心(ㄉㄢ ㄒㄧㄣ)
to devote one's entire mind
殫殘(ㄉㄢ ㄘㄢˊ)
to destroy
殫思極慮(ㄉㄢ ㄙ ㄐㄧˊ ㄌㄩˋ)or 殫精極慮(ㄉㄢ ㄐㄧㄥ ㄐㄧˊ ㄌㄩˋ)
to devote one's entire thought; to rack one's brains

十三畫

【殭】2711 ㄐㄧㄤ jiang jiāng
dead and stiff
殭巴(ㄐㄧㄤ ·ㄅㄚ)
shriveled
殭尸 or 殭屍(ㄐㄧㄤ ㄕ)
a vampire; a reanimated corpse
殭蠶(ㄐㄧㄤ ㄘㄢˊ)
the silkworm dead before producing the cocoon; a stiffened silkworm
殭硬(ㄐㄧㄤ ㄧㄥˋ)
stiff

【殮】2712 ㄌㄧㄢˋ liann liàn
to prepare a body for the coffin; to encoffin
殮埋(ㄌㄧㄢˋ ㄇㄞˊ)or 殮葬(ㄌㄧㄢˋ ㄗㄤˋ)
to shroud and bury
殮具(ㄌㄧㄢˋ ㄐㄩˋ)
articles for preparing the body for the coffin

十四畫

【殯】2713 ㄅㄧㄣˋ binn bìn
1. to lay a coffin in a memorial hall
2. to carry to the grave
殯殮(ㄅㄧㄣˋ ㄌㄧㄢˋ)
a funeral
殯車(ㄅㄧㄣˋ ㄔㄜ)
a hearse
殯葬(ㄅㄧㄣˋ ㄗㄤˋ)
a burial; a funeral
殯儀館(ㄅㄧㄣˋ ㄧˊ ㄍㄨㄢˇ)
a funeral parlor

十七畫

【殲】2714 ㄐㄧㄢ jian jiān
to annihilate; to exterminate; to destroy
殲滅(ㄐㄧㄢ ㄇㄧㄝˋ)
to annihilate; to exterminate; to wipe out
殲滅戰(ㄐㄧㄢ ㄇㄧㄝˋ ㄓㄢˋ)
a large-scale military operation designed to wipe out enemy forces; a war or battle of annihilation
殲敵(ㄐㄧㄢ ㄉㄧˊ)
to destroy the enemy

殳部
ㄕㄨ shu shū

【殳】 2715
ㄕㄨ shu shū
a halberd; a kind of ancient weapon made of bamboo
殳書(ㄕㄨ ㄕㄨ)
a style of handwriting in Chin (秦) Dynasty (used for inscriptions on weapons)

五畫

【段】 2716
ㄉㄨㄢˋ duann duàn
1. a section; a division; a part; a paragraph
2. a stage
3. a Chinese family name
段落(ㄉㄨㄢˋ ㄌㄨㄛˋ)
①end (of a paragraph, stage, etc.): 這事已暫時告一段落。This matter has come to an end for the time being. ②a paragraph ③a phase

六畫

【殷】 2717
1. ㄧㄣ in yīn
1. abundant; flourishing; thriving; prosperous; rich
2. polite; courteous; civil; hospitable
3. sad; sorrowful; mournful
4. eager; eagerly
5. an alternative name for the latter half of the Shang(商) Dynasty
殷富(ㄧㄣ ㄈㄨˋ)
wealthy; prosperous; well-off
殷鑑(ㄧㄣ ㄐㄧㄢˋ)
(literally) a warning for the Yin people—a predecessor's failure as a warning
殷鑑不遠(ㄧㄣ ㄐㄧㄢˋ ㄅㄨˋ ㄩㄢˇ)
The beacon of Yin is not far distant.—(figuratively) The lesson (of failure) can be found in recent time. 或 One need not look far for a lesson.
殷契(ㄧㄣ ㄑㄧˋ)
the oracle-bone writing
殷切(ㄧㄣ ㄑㄧㄝˋ)
ardent; eager
殷勤 or 慇懃(ㄧㄣ ㄑㄧㄣˊ)
courteous; polite; civil: 他們對客人很慇懃。They are very courteous to their guests.
殷墟(ㄧㄣ ㄒㄩ)
the dwelling place of the Yin people (before 1200 B.C.) found in what is today's Anyang County (安陽縣), Honan Province (河南省), once the capital of the Yin Dynasty
殷墟書契(ㄧㄣ ㄒㄩ ㄕㄨ ㄑㄧˋ)or 殷墟文字(ㄧㄣ ㄒㄩ ㄨㄣˊ ㄗˋ)
the oracle-bone writing found in the dwelling place of the Yin people
殷實(ㄧㄣ ㄕˊ)
prosperous; well-off; substantial: 這是家殷實商店。It's a substantial store.
殷商(ㄧㄣ ㄕㄤ)
①the Shang Dynasty (c. 1800-1200 B.C.) which was later renamed Yin Dynasty ②a prosperous merchant: 他是一名殷商。He is a prosperous merchant.
殷盛(ㄧㄣ ㄕㄥˋ)
thriving; flourishing; prosperous; abundant
殷憂啓聖(ㄧㄣ ㄧㄡ ㄑㄧˇ ㄕㄥˋ)
Deep sorrow leads to enlightenment.
殷殷(ㄧㄣ ㄧㄣ)
① prosperous; thriving; rich; abundant ②courteous; polite; civil ③ sorrowful; sad; mournful
殷殷垂誡(ㄧㄣ ㄧㄣ ㄔㄨㄟˊ ㄐㄧㄝˋ)
to admonish sincerely

【殷】 2717
2. ㄧㄢ ian yān
dark red
殷紅(ㄧㄢ ㄏㄨㄥˊ)
dark red

七畫

【殺】 2718
1. ㄕㄚ sha shā
1. to kill; to put to death; to slaughter; to destroy: 殺生容易，回生難。It's easy to kill, but impossible to restore life.
2. exceedingly; extremely: 他的行爲眞是笑殺人。His conduct is extremely ridiculous.
3. to weaken; to deflate: 你最好殺殺他的威風。You'd better deflate his arrogance.
4. to fight: 他殺出敵人重圍。He fought his way out of the enemy's heavy siege.
殺伐(ㄕㄚ ㄈㄚˊ)or(ㄕㄚ ㄈㄚ)
fighting; war: 殺伐之聲 a noise of fighting
殺風景(ㄕㄚ ㄈㄥ ㄐㄧㄥˇ)
to dampen interest; to make dull; to spoil or ruin happiness; to kill joy; to do something to spoil one's enthusiasm
殺敵(ㄕㄚ ㄉㄧˊ)
to fight the enemy
殺敵致果(ㄕㄚ ㄉㄧˊ ㄓˋ ㄍㄨㄛˇ)
to serve with distinction in war
殺頭(ㄕㄚ ㄊㄡˊ)
to perform decapitation; to behead: 他因叛國罪被殺頭。He was beheaded for high treason.
殺退(ㄕㄚ ㄊㄨㄟˋ)
to put to flight; to rout
殺戮(ㄕㄚ ㄌㄨˋ)
to kill; to slay
殺掠(ㄕㄚ ㄌㄩㄝˋ)
to kill and plunder
殺光(ㄕㄚ ㄍㄨㄤ)
to kill all
殺害(ㄕㄚ ㄏㄞˋ)
to murder; to kill: 她被殺害了。She was murdered.
殺機(ㄕㄚ ㄐㄧ)
intention to murder
殺雞警猴(ㄕㄚ ㄐㄧ ㄐㄧㄥˇ ㄏㄡˊ)
to kill the chicken to intimidate the monkey—to punish somebody as a warning to others 亦作「殺雞駭猴」
殺雞取卵(ㄕㄚ ㄐㄧ ㄑㄩˇ ㄌㄨㄢˇ)
to kill the hen to get eggs —a very foolish act
殺雞焉用牛刀(ㄕㄚ ㄐㄧ ㄧㄢ ㄩㄥˋ ㄋㄧㄡˊ ㄉㄠ)
(literally) Why use a cattle knife for a chicken?—Great talent can be used for better purposes or for greater results.
殺價(ㄕㄚ ㄐㄧㄚˋ)
to reduce prices; to cut price

〔殳部〕

down
殺戒(ㄕㄚ ㄐㄧㄝˋ)
the Buddhist prohibition against killing
殺盡斬絕(ㄕㄚ ㄐㄧㄣˋ ㄓㄢˇ ㄐㄩㄝˊ)
to kill all; to give no quarter
殺菌(ㄕㄚ ㄐㄩㄣˋ)
to kill germs; to sterilize; to decontaminate; to disinfect
殺菌燈(ㄕㄚ ㄐㄩㄣˋ ㄉㄥ)
an ultraviolet lamp
殺氣(ㄕㄚ ㄑㄧˋ)
① (said of a sight or scene) a very severe or chilling appearance ② a murderous atmosphere; a furious look
殺氣騰騰(ㄕㄚ ㄑㄧˋ ㄊㄥˊ ㄊㄥˊ)
There is a prevailing thirst for blood.—with a murderous look on one's face
殺青(ㄕㄚ ㄑㄧㄥ)
(said of films, books, etc.) to be completed: 這部電影將於明年六月殺青。The movie will be completed next June.
殺蟲劑(ㄕㄚ ㄔㄨㄥˊ ㄐㄧˋ)
the insecticide
殺蟲藥(ㄕㄚ ㄔㄨㄥˊ ㄧㄠˋ)
anthelmintic (against intestinal parasites)
殺手(ㄕㄚ ㄕㄡˇ)
a hit man; a killer
殺身之禍(ㄕㄚ ㄕㄣ ㄓ ㄏㄨㄛˋ)
a fatal disaster; a lethal misfortune: 他的財富和聲望招致殺身之禍。His wealth and reputation caused a fatal misfortune to him.
殺身成仁(ㄕㄚ ㄕㄣ ㄔㄥˊ ㄖㄣˊ)
to fulfil justice at the cost of one's own life; to sacrifice one's own life for justice
殺傷(ㄕㄚ ㄕㄤ)
to kill and wound; to inflict wounds upon: 這種地雷殺傷力很強。This is a powerful antipersonnel mine.
殺生(ㄕㄚ ㄕㄥ)
killing
殺牲(ㄕㄚ ㄕㄥ)
to butcher domestic animals other than cats and dogs
殺人(ㄕㄚ ㄖㄣˊ)
to kill a person; to murder: 汝不可殺人！Thou shalt not kill!
殺人不見血(ㄕㄚ ㄖㄣˊ ㄅㄨˋ ㄐㄧㄢˋ ㄒㄧㄝˇ)
(said of a devious act) able to kill without bloodshed—to kill with subtle means
殺人不眨眼(ㄕㄚ ㄖㄣˊ ㄅㄨˋ ㄓㄚˇ ㄧㄢˇ)
capable of killing without even a blink of the eyes—hardhearted, cold-blooded, or very cruel
殺人犯(ㄕㄚ ㄖㄣˊ ㄈㄢˋ)
a murder convict; a murderer; a homicide
殺人者死(ㄕㄚ ㄖㄣˊ ㄓㄜˇ ㄙˇ)
Murder is punishable by death.
殺人如麻(ㄕㄚ ㄖㄣˊ ㄖㄨˊ ㄇㄚˊ)
to kill people as if they were just hemp; to have killed many people
殺人罪(ㄕㄚ ㄖㄣˊ ㄗㄨㄟˋ)
homicide; murder
殺人盈野(ㄕㄚ ㄖㄣˊ ㄧㄥˊ ㄧㄝˇ)
Bodies of the killed lie everywhere.
殺人未遂(ㄕㄚ ㄖㄣˊ ㄨㄟˋ ㄙㄨㄟˋ)
an attempted murder
殺人越貨(ㄕㄚ ㄖㄣˊ ㄩㄝˋ ㄏㄨㄛˋ)
to kill and rob
殺死(ㄕㄚ ㄙˇ)
to kill; to slay; to murder
殺一警百(ㄕㄚ ㄧ ㄐㄧㄥˇ ㄅㄞˇ)
to kill one as a warning to a hundred
殺威棒(ㄕㄚ ㄨㄟ ㄅㄤˋ)
a flogging administered to a culprit upon his first appearance before the magistrate with the intention of crushing his spirit
殺尾(ㄕㄚ ㄨㄟˇ)
to come to a conclusion

【殺】 2718
2. ㄕㄞˋ shay shài
to degrade; to decline; to diminish; to abate: 風勢稍殺。The winds have abated.

八畫

【殼】 2719
(殻、壳) ㄑㄩㄝˋ chiueh què
(又讀 ㄎㄜˊ ker ké)
(語音 ㄑㄧㄠˋ chiaw qiào)
shells; husks; coverings
殼斗(ㄎㄜˊ ㄉㄡˇ)
cupule
殼果(ㄎㄜˊ ㄍㄨㄛˇ)
a nut
殼子(ㄎㄜˊ ·ㄗ) or 殼兒(ㄎㄜˊㄦ)
a shell; a hard covering (of an animal, or of an egg, fruit, nut or seed); the outer surface (as opposed to the contents or substance)
殼菜(ㄎㄜˊ ㄘㄞˋ)
a kind of mussel with edible meat (*Mytilus crassitesta*) 亦作「淡菜」

【殽】 2720
ㄧㄠˊ yau yáo
1. confusion; disorder; mess
2. dishes
殽亂(ㄧㄠˊ ㄌㄨㄢˋ)
disorderly; confused; messy
殽核(ㄧㄠˊ ㄏㄜˊ)
dishes and fruit
殽舛(ㄧㄠˊ ㄔㄨㄢˇ)
disorderly; confused; messy
殽雜(ㄧㄠˊ ㄗㄚˊ)
disorderly; messy

九畫

【殿】 2721
ㄉㄧㄢˋ diann diàn
1. a palace; a palace hall; a temple; a sanctuary: 神殿 the temple of gods
2. the rear; the rear guard
殿版(ㄉㄧㄢˋ ㄅㄢˇ)
the edition of classics and other works printed by imperial decree in the early Ching Dynasty
殿本(ㄉㄧㄢˋ ㄅㄣˇ)
a copy or the edition of classics and other works printed by imperial order in the early Ching Dynasty
殿堂(ㄉㄧㄢˋ ㄊㄤˊ) or 殿宇(ㄉㄧㄢˋ ㄩˇ)
a palace; a palace hall; a temple; a sanctuary
殿後(ㄉㄧㄢˋ ㄏㄡˋ)
the rear, or rear guard (of marching troops); to bring up the rear
殿軍(ㄉㄧㄢˋ ㄐㄩㄣ)
① the rear guard (of marching troops) ② the last-placed winner in a contest
殿下(ㄉㄧㄢˋ ㄒㄧㄚˋ)

① Your, His, or Her Highness ② Your, or His Majesty (in the Wei and Tsin Dynasties)

殿試(ㄉㄧㄢˋ ㄕˋ)
the civil service examination held in the presence of the emperor at his court

殿元(ㄉㄧㄢˋ ㄩㄢˊ)
the candidate who won the first place in a civil service examination held in the presence of the emperor

【毀】 2722 ㄏㄨㄟˇ hoei huǐ

1. to destroy; to ruin; to damage; to injure: 他自毀前程。He destroyed his own career.
2. to libel; to slander; to abuse; to revile; to defame; to blame excessively

毀敗(ㄏㄨㄟˇ ㄅㄞˋ)
to destroy; to ruin

毀謗(ㄏㄨㄟˇ ㄅㄤˋ)
to libel; to slander; to malign; a libel or slander; calumniation: 他不在乎他人惡意的毀謗。He doesn't care about others' malicious slanders.

毀滅(ㄏㄨㄟˇ ㄇㄧㄝˋ)
to destroy; to ruin; to demolish: 你將毀滅你的前途。You will ruin your prospects.

毀詆(ㄏㄨㄟˇ ㄉㄧˇ)
to slander; to libel

毀短(ㄏㄨㄟˇ ㄉㄨㄢˇ)
to disparage; to denounce; to run down; to speak ill of

毀害(ㄏㄨㄟˇ ㄏㄞˋ)
to injure; to damage: 不要毀害他人。Don't injure other people.

毀壞(ㄏㄨㄟˇ ㄏㄨㄞˋ)
to destroy; to injure; to damage

毀家紓難(ㄏㄨㄟˇ ㄐㄧㄚ ㄕㄨ ㄋㄢˋ)
to donate all one has for the sake of the nation in a crisis; to offer all one has for charity

毀棄(ㄏㄨㄟˇ ㄑㄧˋ)
to abrogate; to repeal; to dissolve; to annul; to rescind

毀傷(ㄏㄨㄟˇ ㄕㄤ)
to damage; to injure: 他的名譽受到毀傷。He has a damaged reputation.

毀容(ㄏㄨㄟˇ ㄖㄨㄥˊ)
to disfigure

毀訾(ㄏㄨㄟˇ ㄗˇ)
to revile; to abuse

毀損(ㄏㄨㄟˇ ㄙㄨㄣˇ)
to damage; to injure; to disfigure

毀於一旦(ㄏㄨㄟˇ ㄩˊ ㄧˊ ㄉㄢˋ)
to be ruined or destroyed in one day

毀譽(ㄏㄨㄟˇ ㄩˋ)
praise and dispraise: 他不計毀譽。He was indifferent to people's praise or dispraise.

毀譽參半(ㄏㄨㄟˇ ㄩˋ ㄘㄢ ㄅㄢˋ)
to give a mixture of praise and dispraise; to draw both praises and criticisms; to be as much censured as praised: 此人毀譽參半。The man got both praise and dispraise.

毀約(ㄏㄨㄟˇ ㄩㄝ)
to break one's promise: 他從不毀約。He never breaks his promise.

十一畫

【毅】 2723 ㄧˋ yih yì

firm; resolute; endurance; fortitude

毅力(ㄧˋ ㄌㄧˋ)
perseverance; determination; resoluteness; indomitability; firmness; stamina: 這個年輕人缺乏毅力。The youth lacks stamina.

毅然(ㄧˋ ㄖㄢˊ)
firmly; courageously

毅然決然(ㄧˋ ㄖㄢˊ ㄐㄩㄝˊ ㄖㄢˊ)
in a determined manner; with determination; resolutely; firmly

毅勇(ㄧˋ ㄩㄥˇ)
firm courage; fortitude

【毆】 2724 ㄡ ou ōu

to beat; to hit; a blow: 他們吵嘴後互毆。They exchanged blows after a hot argument.

毆斃(ㄡ ㄅㄧˋ)
to beat to death

毆打(ㄡ ㄉㄚˇ)
to have a fist fight; to fisticuff; to beat a person with fists or clubs; to come to blows: 他用拳頭毆打我。He struck me with his fist.

毆擊(ㄡ ㄐㄧˊ)
to fisticuff; to beat someone with fists or clubs

毆殺(ㄡ ㄕㄚ)
to beat to death 參看「毆斃」

毆傷(ㄡ ㄕㄤ)
to injure by beating

毆辱(ㄡ ㄖㄨˇ)
to beat and insult

毋部 ㄨˊ wu wú

【毋】 2725 ㄨˊ wu wú

1. (imperative) do not; no: 毋誤前途。Do not hurt your career.
2. a Chinese family name

毋寧(ㄨˊ ㄋㄧㄥˊ)
rather... (than); (not so much...) as: 與其說他是個學者,毋寧說他是個教師。He is rather a teacher than a scholar.

毋需(ㄨˊ ㄒㄩ)
do not need: 你今天毋需工作。You do not need to work today.

毋忘在莒(ㄨˊ ㄨㄤˋ ㄗㄞˋ ㄐㄩˇ)
Do not forget national humiliation in time of peace and security.

毋庸(ㄨˊ ㄩㄥ)
need not: 應毋庸議。This need not be considered.

毋庸諱言(ㄨˊ ㄩㄥ ㄏㄨㄟˋ ㄧㄢˊ)
There's no need for reticence.

一畫

【母】 2726 ㄇㄨˇ muu mǔ

1. one's mother; one's female parent: 家母今年八十歲。My mother is 80 years old.
2. mother—(figuratively) the origin: 需要爲發明之母。Necessity is the mother of invention.

〔毋部〕

3. female
母馬(ㄇㄨˇ ㄇㄚˇ)
a mare
母貓(ㄇㄨˇ ㄇㄠ)
a tabby (as opposed to a tomcat)
母法(ㄇㄨˇ ㄈㄚˇ)
a foreign law from which a domestic law is copied or patterned after
母範(ㄇㄨˇ ㄈㄢˋ)
a model for mothers
母的(ㄇㄨˇ ˙ㄉㄜ)
female
母黨(ㄇㄨˇ ㄉㄤˇ)
maternal relatives
母弟(ㄇㄨˇ ㄉㄧˋ)
one's younger brother born of the same mother
母體(ㄇㄨˇ ㄊㄧˇ)
the mother body
母兔(ㄇㄨˇ ㄊㄨˋ)
a doe
母難日(ㄇㄨˇ ㄋㄢˋ ㄖˋ)
my birthday (a day when mother underwent a crisis and excruciating pains in giving birth)
母牛(ㄇㄨˇ ㄋㄧㄡˊ)
a cow
母女(ㄇㄨˇ ㄋㄩˇ)
mother and daughter
母老虎(ㄇㄨˇ ㄌㄠˇ ㄏㄨˇ)
① a shrew; a termagant ② a tigress
母狼(ㄇㄨˇ ㄌㄤˊ)
a she-wolf
母鹿(ㄇㄨˇ ㄌㄨˋ)
a roe deer; a roe
母狗(ㄇㄨˇ ㄍㄡˇ)
a bitch
母國(ㄇㄨˇ ㄍㄨㄛˊ)
one's mother country; one's motherland
母公司(ㄇㄨˇ ㄍㄨㄥ ㄙ)
a parent company
母后(ㄇㄨˇ ㄏㄡˋ)
① the queen ② the queen mother
母機(ㄇㄨˇ ㄐㄧ)
a mother machine; a machine that makes other machines
母雞(ㄇㄨˇ ㄐㄧ)
a hen
母姊會(ㄇㄨˇ ㄐㄧㄝˇ ㄏㄨㄟˋ)
a mother-sister conference
母教(ㄇㄨˇ ㄐㄧㄠˋ)
one's mother's teachings
母舅(ㄇㄨˇ ㄐㄧㄡˋ)
a maternal uncle; one's mother's brother
母艦(ㄇㄨˇ ㄐㄧㄢˋ)
mother ship; a carrier: 航空母艦 an aircraft carrier
母錢(ㄇㄨˇ ㄑㄧㄢˊ)
capital (for business)
母親(ㄇㄨˇ ㄑㄧㄣ)
mother
母親節(ㄇㄨˇ ㄑㄧㄣ ㄐㄧㄝˊ)
Mother's Day, on the second Sunday in May
母權(ㄇㄨˇ ㄑㄩㄢˊ)
matriarchal power
母系(ㄇㄨˇ ㄒㄧˋ)
① the maternal side ② matriarchal
母系制度(ㄇㄨˇ ㄒㄧˋ ㄓˋ ㄉㄨˋ)
matriarchy
母系社會(ㄇㄨˇ ㄒㄧˋ ㄕㄜˋ ㄏㄨㄟˋ)
a matriarchal society
母校(ㄇㄨˇ ㄒㄧㄠˋ)
one's alma mater; Alma Mater: 我們必須為母校爭光。We must try to reflect credit on our alma mater.
母象(ㄇㄨˇ ㄒㄧㄤˋ)
a female elephant
母性(ㄇㄨˇ ㄒㄧㄥˋ)
motherliness; maternity; maternal instinct; the mother: 那件事引出了她的母性。It brought out the mother in her.
母兄(ㄇㄨˇ ㄒㄩㄥ)
one's elder brother born of the same mother
母豬(ㄇㄨˇ ㄓㄨ)
a sow
母獅(ㄇㄨˇ ㄕ)
a lioness
母山羊(ㄇㄨˇ ㄕㄢ ㄧㄤˊ)
a she-goat, or nanny goat
母數(ㄇㄨˇ ㄕㄨˋ)
a denominator (in arithmetic)
母子(ㄇㄨˇ ㄗˇ)
① mother and son ② principal and interest
母子之情(ㄇㄨˇ ㄗˇ ㄓ ㄑㄧㄥˊ)
love between mother and son
母鵝(ㄇㄨˇ ㄜˊ)
a goose (as opposed to a gander)
母愛(ㄇㄨˇ ㄞˋ)
mother love; maternal affection; maternal love
母儀(ㄇㄨˇ ㄧˊ)
the paragon of motherhood
母以子貴(ㄇㄨˇ ㄧˇ ㄗˇ ㄍㄨㄟˋ)
A mother's social position is elevated by the success of her sons.
母鴨(ㄇㄨˇ ㄧㄚ)
a duck (as opposed to a drake)
母液(ㄇㄨˇ ㄧㄝˋ)
(chemistry) mother liquid
母夜叉(ㄇㄨˇ ㄧㄝˋ ㄔㄚ)
① an ugly female devil ② an ugly and fierce woman
母岩(ㄇㄨˇ ㄧㄢˊ)
mother rock
母音(ㄇㄨˇ ㄧㄣ)
a vowel 亦作「元音」
母羊(ㄇㄨˇ ㄧㄤˊ)
a ewe
母語(ㄇㄨˇ ㄩˇ)
① one's mother tongue; one's native language ② a parent language

三畫

【每】 2727 ㄇㄟˇ meei měi
every; each; per: 我們每人都有自己的責任。Each one of us has his duty.
每每(ㄇㄟˇ ㄇㄟˇ)
repeatedly; often: 他每每不在家。He is often not at home.
每飯不忘(ㄇㄟˇ ㄈㄢˋ ㄅㄨˋ ㄨㄤˋ)
to be remembered at every meal
每逢(ㄇㄟˇ ㄈㄥˊ)
every time or whenever (a season, festival or some specific occasion comes)
每逢佳節倍思親(ㄇㄟˇ ㄈㄥˊ ㄐㄧㄚ ㄐㄧㄝˊ ㄅㄟˋ ㄙ ㄑㄧㄣ)
On the happy festival, more than ever we think of our relatives far away.
每當(ㄇㄟˇ ㄉㄤ)
whenever; every time
每天(ㄇㄟˇ ㄊㄧㄢ)

every day; daily: 他們每天見面。They saw each other every day.

每年(ㄇㄟˇ ㄋㄧㄢˊ)
every year; annually; per annum; yearly; each year

每隔(ㄇㄟˇ ㄍㄜˊ)
every (three hours, five days, two feet, etc.): 他們每隔二週見一次面。They saw each other every two weeks.

每下愈況(ㄇㄟˇ ㄒㄧㄚˋ ㄩˋ ㄎㄨㄤˋ)or 每況愈下(ㄇㄟˇ ㄎㄨㄤˋ ㄩˋ ㄒㄧㄚˋ)
progressively worse; steadily worse; getting worse and worse; going from bad to worse: 現在一切的事情每況愈下。Things are going from bad to worse nowadays.

每處(ㄇㄟˇ ㄔㄨˋ)
everywhere

每日(ㄇㄟˇ ㄖˋ)
every day; daily: 大多數的報紙每日出版。Most newspapers appear daily.

每人(ㄇㄟˇ ㄖㄣˊ)
everybody; each one; everyone: 每人可以試兩次。Each man may try twice.

每次(ㄇㄟˇ ㄘˋ)
every time; each time: 他常常聽到這個故事，但他每次都笑。He has heard the story often but he laughs every time.

每月(ㄇㄟˇ ㄩㄝˋ)
each month; every month; monthly: 他每月來一次。He comes here monthly.

【毐】 2728 ㄞˇ ae ǎi
adulterous

四畫

【毒】 2729 ㄉㄨˊ dwu dú
1. poison; toxins: 對甲是良藥對乙却是劇毒。One man's meat is another man's poison.
2. poisonous; noxious: 那是隻毒蜘蛛。It's a poisonous spider.
3. to poison

毒品(ㄉㄨˊ ㄆㄧㄣˇ)
narcotic drugs; narcotics

毒罵(ㄉㄨˊ ㄇㄚˋ)
to scold ferociously and maliciously; to revile; to rail at madly

毒打(ㄉㄨˊ ㄉㄚˇ)
to beat cruelly or savagely

毒辣(ㄉㄨˊ ㄌㄚˋ)
cruel; malicious; spiteful: 他這樣謀害孩童眞是毒辣。It's cruel of him to murder the child.

毒癘(ㄉㄨˊ ㄌㄧˋ)
① an ulcer ② an epidemic

毒瘤(ㄉㄨˊ ㄌㄧㄡˊ)
malignant growth; cancer growth

毒害(ㄉㄨˊ ㄏㄞˋ)
to injure atrociously; to murder

毒狠(ㄉㄨˊ ㄏㄣˇ)
atrocious; heinous; cruel: 他眞毒狠! How cruel he is!

毒卉(ㄉㄨˊ ㄏㄨㄟˋ)
the poppy

毒計(ㄉㄨˊ ㄐㄧˋ)
a malicious scheme; a deadly trap

毒酒(ㄉㄨˊ ㄐㄧㄡˇ)
poisoned wine

毒氣(ㄉㄨˊ ㄑㄧˋ)
poisonous gas; noxious gas

毒氣彈(ㄉㄨˊ ㄑㄧˋ ㄉㄢˋ)
a gas bomb

毒刑(ㄉㄨˊ ㄒㄧㄥˊ)
cruel punishment; brutal torture

毒性(ㄉㄨˊ ㄒㄧㄥˋ)
toxicity; poisonousness: 他正在研究殺蟲劑的毒性。He is studying the toxicity of insecticides.

毒汁(ㄉㄨˊ ㄓ)
poisonous fluid

毒質(ㄉㄨˊ ㄓˊ)
poisonous matter

毒著兒(ㄉㄨˊ ㄓㄠ ㄦ)
a dirty trick; an odious scheme; venomous means; a murderous plan

毒瘴(ㄉㄨˊ ㄓㄤˋ)
miasmas 亦作「瘴氣」

毒蟲(ㄉㄨˊ ㄔㄨㄥˊ)
a poisonous insect

毒殺(ㄉㄨˊ ㄕㄚ)
to poison to death; to kill by poisoning

毒砂(ㄉㄨˊ ㄕㄚ)
(mining) arsenopyrite

毒蛇(ㄉㄨˊ ㄕㄜˊ)or 毒虺(ㄉㄨˊ ㄏㄨㄟˇ)
a venomous snake: 他被毒蛇咬傷了。He was bitten by a venomous snake.

毒手(ㄉㄨˊ ㄕㄡˇ)
an atrocious act; a venomous action; a murderous scheme (or hand): 他對她下了毒手。He laid murderous hands on her.

毒刺(ㄉㄨˊ ㄘˋ)
a venomous sting; a poisonous prick

毒草(ㄉㄨˊ ㄘㄠˇ)
poisonous herbs

毒死(ㄉㄨˊ ㄙˇ)or 毒斃(ㄉㄨˊ ㄅㄧˋ)
to poison to death

毒素(ㄉㄨˊ ㄙㄨˋ)
poisonous matter; toxins

毒餌(ㄉㄨˊ ㄦˇ)
poison bait

毒牙(ㄉㄨˊ ㄧㄚˊ)
a poison fang

毒藥(ㄉㄨˊ ㄧㄠˋ)
poisonous drugs; poison

毒物(ㄉㄨˊ ㄨˋ)
poisonous substance; poison

毒瓦斯(ㄉㄨˊ ㄨㄚˇ ㄙ)
toxic gas; poison gas

九畫

【毓】 2730 ㄩˋ yuh yù
1. to bring up; to rear; to nurture; to nurse
2. to grow

比部
ㄅㄧˇ bii bǐ

【比】 2731 1. ㄅㄧˇ bii bǐ
1. to compare with; to be comparable to: 我的畫不能與你的比。My painting cannot be compared with yours.
2. to liken; to compare to: 人生常被比喻爲朝聖之旅程。Life is often likened to a pilgrimage.
3. to compete
4. than: 我比他年輕。I am younger than he.
5. to: 我隊以五比二勝他隊。Our

〔比部〕

team beat their team (by a score of) five to two.

比並(ㄅㄧˇ ㄅㄧㄥˋ)
to liken; to compare to

比不得(ㄅㄧˇ ·ㄅㄨ ·ㄉㄜ)
not to be compared; beyond all comparison

比不上(ㄅㄧˇ ·ㄅㄨ ㄕㄤˋ)
to be inferior to; to be no peer for: 我的英文比不上他。My English cannot compare with his.

比目魚(ㄅㄧˇ ㄇㄨˋ ㄩˊ)
a flatfish; a sole

比分(ㄅㄧˇ ㄈㄣ)
(sports) score: 現在比分是六比五。The score is 6 to 5.

比方(ㄅㄧˇ ·ㄈㄤ)
to liken; to compare to

比方說(ㄅㄧˇ ·ㄈㄤ ㄕㄨㄛ)
for example; for instance

比附(ㄅㄧˇ ㄈㄨˋ)
to liken; to compare to

比對(ㄅㄧˇ ㄉㄨㄟˋ)
to compare and check; to collate

比擬(ㄅㄧˇ ㄋㄧˇ)
①to liken; to compare to: 她把他的詩比擬爲彎曲的溪流。She compared his poetry to a meandering stream. ②a parallel: 這種比擬是不當的。It is improper to draw such a parallel.

比例(ㄅㄧˇ ㄌㄧˋ)
ratio; proportion: 人的智慧和年齡成比例嗎? Are men wise in proportion to their age?

比例尺(ㄅㄧˇ ㄌㄧˋ ㄔˇ)
scale (of a map, model, etc.)

比率(ㄅㄧˇ ㄌㄩˋ)
ratio; proportion: 出生與人口的比率 the proportion of births to the population

比個高低(ㄅㄧˇ ·ㄍㄜ ㄍㄠ ㄉㄧ)
to determine by competition who is the better or stronger of two or more contestants

比號(ㄅㄧˇ ㄏㄠˋ)
the sign of ratio(:)

比畫(ㄅㄧˇ ·ㄏㄨㄚ)
①to gesticulate; to gesture; to use sign language 亦作「比手畫脚」: 她比手畫脚地說著。She made herself understood with the help of gestures. ②to come to blows

比基尼(ㄅㄧˇ ㄐㄧ ㄋㄧˊ)
Bikini Island, a site of many atomic tests

比基尼泳裝(ㄅㄧˇ ㄐㄧ ㄋㄧˊ ㄩㄥˇ ㄓㄨㄤ)
bikini (a very small 2-piece bathing suit for women)

比加(ㄅㄧˇ ㄐㄧㄚ)
belga (a former monetary unit of Belgium)

比價(ㄅㄧˇ ㄐㄧㄚˋ)
to compare prices or bids

比較(ㄅㄧˇ ㄐㄧㄠˇ)or(ㄅㄧˇ ㄐㄧㄠˋ)
①comparative; comparatively; relatively: 近來他的生活過得比較舒適。He lived in comparative comfort recently.②to compare: 把你的車跟他的車比較一下。Compare your car with his.

比較級(ㄅㄧˇ ㄐㄧㄠˇ ㄐㄧˊ)
(grammar) the comparative degree

比較值(ㄅㄧˇ ㄐㄧㄠˇ ㄓˊ)
comparative value

比較文學(ㄅㄧˇ ㄐㄧㄠˋ ㄨㄣˊ ㄒㄩㄝˊ)
comparative literature: 嚴先生專攻比較文學。Mr. Yen majors in comparative literature.

比較語言學(ㄅㄧˇ ㄐㄧㄠˋ ㄩˇ ㄧㄢˊ ㄒㄩㄝˊ)
comparative linguistics

比丘(ㄅㄧˇ ㄑㄧㄡ)
a Buddhist monk

比丘尼(ㄅㄧˇ ㄑㄧㄡ ㄋㄧˊ)
a Buddhist nun

比照(ㄅㄧˇ ㄓㄠˋ)
according to; in the light of: 我們可以比照他們的經驗來擬定我們的計畫。We can draw up our plan in the light of their experience.

比重(ㄅㄧˇ ㄓㄨㄥˋ)
specific gravity

比重瓶(ㄅㄧˇ ㄓㄨㄥˋ ㄆㄧㄥˊ)
a pycnometer

比重計(ㄅㄧˇ ㄓㄨㄥˋ ㄐㄧˋ)
a hydrometer

比試(ㄅㄧˇ ·ㄕ)
①have a competition ②to measure with one's hand or arm; to make a gesture of measuring

比上不足，比下有餘(ㄅㄧˇ ㄕㄤˋ ㄅㄨˋ ㄗㄨˊ, ㄅㄧˇ ㄒㄧㄚˋ ㄧㄡˇ ㄩˊ)
to be worse off than some but better off than many; to fall short of the best but be better than the worst

比熱(ㄅㄧˇ ㄖㄜˋ)
(physics) specific heat

比如(ㄅㄧˇ ㄖㄨˊ)
such as; like

比薩斜塔(ㄅㄧˇ ㄙㄚˋ ㄒㄧㄝˊ ㄊㄚˇ)
the (Leaning) Tower of Pisa

比賽(ㄅㄧˇ ㄙㄞˋ)
a contest; a match; a tournament; to compete in contest: 他參加了射擊比賽。He took part in the shooting contest.

比塞大(ㄅㄧˇ ㄙㄞˋ ㄉㄚˋ)
Bizerta or Bizerte, a North African seaport

比翼(ㄅㄧˇ ㄧˋ)
(to fly) wing to wing—inseparable (said of lovers, or a married couple)

比翼鳥(ㄅㄧˇ ㄧˋ ㄋㄧㄠˇ)
①a spoonbill 亦作「鶼鶼」②a pair of lovebirds; a pair of birds with the wings of one—a devoted couple

比翼雙飛(ㄅㄧˇ ㄧˋ ㄕㄨㄤ ㄈㄟ)
to fly side by side

比一比(ㄅㄧˇ ·ㄧ ·ㄅㄧ)
①to make a comparison ②to engage in a contest; to have a contest

比武(ㄅㄧˇ ㄨˇ)
to demonstrate fighting skills in a tournament; to contest in physical prowess

比喻(ㄅㄧˇ ㄩˋ)
①a metaphor; a figure of speech; a simile: 這不過是個比喻之辭。This is just a figure of speech. ②to compare to; to liken: 人生常被比喻成海上的旅程。Man's life is often likened to a sea voyage.

【比】 2731
2. ㄅㄧˋ bih bì

1. close; near; neighboring
2. to stand side by side

比比皆是(ㄅㄧˋ ㄅㄧˋ ㄐㄧㄝ ㄕˋ)
to be found or seen everywhere—very common; a common sight: 中國的名詩人比比皆是。Famous Chinese poets can be found everywhere.

比匪(ㄅㄧˋ ㄈㄟˇ)
to associate with bad characters

比年(ㄅㄧˋ ㄋㄧㄢˊ)or 比歲(ㄅㄧˋ ㄙㄨㄟˋ)
① recent years ② every year

比來(ㄅㄧˋ ㄌㄞˊ)
recently; lately

比聯(ㄅㄧˋ ㄌㄧㄢˊ)
to adjoin each other (as lands, etc.)

比鄰(ㄅㄧˋ ㄌㄧㄣˊ)
close neighbors

比及(ㄅㄧˋ ㄐㄧˊ)
up to the time when; by the time when

比肩(ㄅㄧˋ ㄐㄧㄢ)
side by side; shoulder to shoulder: 他們比肩而行。They walked side by side.

比肩作戰(ㄅㄧˋ ㄐㄧㄢ ㄗㄨㄛˋ ㄓㄢˋ)
to fight shoulder to shoulder

比親(ㄅㄧˋ ㄑㄧㄣ)
intimate; close

比舍(ㄅㄧˋ ㄕㄜˋ)
the next-door house; the neighboring house; the adjacent house

比屋(ㄅㄧˋ ㄨ)
houses adjoining each other

五畫

【毖】 2732
ㄅㄧˋ bih bì
1. cautious; caution; to guard against; judicious
2. (said of springs) flowing; gushing

【毗】 2733
ㄆㄧˊ pyi pí
1. to assist
2. to adjoin: 運動場與學校毗連。The playing field adjoins the school.

毗尼(ㄆㄧˊ ㄋㄧˊ)
(Buddhism) vinaya; the precepts and commands of moral asceticism and monastic discipline (said to have been given by Buddha)

毗連(ㄆㄧˊ ㄌㄧㄢˊ)
(of lands) to adjoin each other; adjacent to: 加拿大和美國毗連。Canada adjoins the United States.

毗倚(ㄆㄧˊ ㄧˇ)
to depend upon; to rely upon

十三畫

【毚】 2734
ㄔㄢˊ charn chán
1. cunning; crafty
2. greedy

毚兔(ㄔㄢˊ ㄊㄨˋ)
a crafty hare

毚欲(ㄔㄢˊ ㄩˋ)
greed; avarice

毛部
ㄇㄠˊ mau máo

【毛】 2735
ㄇㄠˊ mau máo
1. hair; fur; feathers; down: 我的狗長得一身好毛。My dog has a good coat of hair.
2. vegetation
3. ten cents; a dime: 他們幾乎連一毛錢也沒有賺到。They made hardly a dime.
4. gross; untouched; unpolished
5. panic-stricken; scared; flurried: 他心裡直發毛。He felt scared.
6. very young; little: 他只是個毛孩子。He's only a little child.
7. a Chinese family name

毛玻璃(ㄇㄠˊ ㄅㄛ ·ㄌㄧ)
frosted glass

毛包(ㄇㄠˊ ㄅㄠ)
a simple, unpolished person

毛筆(ㄇㄠˊ ㄅㄧˇ)
a writing brush; a hair pencil

毛筆畫(ㄇㄠˊ ㄅㄧˇ ㄏㄨㄚˋ)
drawings done with a writing brush

毛邊紙(ㄇㄠˊ ㄅㄧㄢ ㄓˇ)
a kind of paper made from bamboo pulp, which was widely used in old China

毛病(ㄇㄠˊ ㄅㄧㄥˋ)
① fault; defects; shortcoming; blemish: 這篇文章有小毛病。There are some small mistakes in the article.② trouble; disorder: 這架電視機有點毛病。There's something wrong with the television.③ disease; illness; trouble: 她胃有毛病。She has stomach trouble.

毛病百出(ㄇㄠˊ ㄅㄧㄥˋ ㄅㄞˇ ㄔㄨ)
glitched-filled

毛坯(ㄇㄠˊ ㄆㄧ)
① earthenware that is not baked yet ② a half-finished product; raw products

毛皮(ㄇㄠˊ ㄆㄧˊ)
fur; pelt

毛毛蟲(ㄇㄠˊ ·ㄇㄠ ㄔㄨㄥˊ)
a caterpillar 亦作「毛蟲」

毛毛雨(ㄇㄠˊ ·ㄇㄠ ㄩˇ)
drizzle

毛髮(ㄇㄠˊ ㄈㄚˇ)
body hairs and hair

毛紡廠(ㄇㄠˊ ㄈㄤˇ ㄔㄤˇ)
a woolen textile mill

毛豆(ㄇㄠˊ ㄉㄡˋ)
① green or tender soybeans ② young soybeans

毛桃(ㄇㄠˊ ㄊㄠˊ)
a kind of small peach; a wild peach

毛頭(ㄇㄠˊ ·ㄊㄡ)
a youngster; a child

毛毯(ㄇㄠˊ ㄊㄢˇ)
a woolen blanket: 他圍着一條毛毯。He wrapped his woolen blanket around him.

毛里斯(ㄇㄠˊ ㄌㄧˇ ㄙ)
Mauritius Island, off the east African coast 亦作「模里西斯」

毛利(ㄇㄠˊ ㄌㄧˋ)
gross earnings; gross profit

毛料(ㄇㄠˊ ㄌㄧㄠˋ)
woolen material

毛驢(ㄇㄠˊ ㄌㄩˊ)
a young donkey

毛莨(ㄇㄠˊ ㄍㄣˋ)
(botany) a crowfoot; a buttercup

毛骨悚然(ㄇㄠˊ ㄍㄨˇ ㄙㄨㄥˇ ㄖㄢˊ)
to shudder with fear; to be horror-stricken; to make one's hair stand on end

毛公鼎(ㄇㄠˊ ㄍㄨㄥ ㄉㄧㄥˇ)
name of a bronze tripod cast in the Chou Dynasty, famed for its inscribed characters

毛褲(ㄇㄠˊ ㄎㄨˋ)
long woolen underwear

毛孔(ㄇㄠˊ ㄎㄨㄥˇ)
pores (of the skin): 汗由皮膚上的毛孔流出來。Sweat comes through the pores in the

〔毛部〕

skin.

毛孩子(ㄇㄠˊ ㄏㄞˊ ˙ㄗ)
a child

毛巾(ㄇㄠˊ ㄐㄧㄣ)
①a towel: 我用毛巾擦乾自己。I dried myself on a towel. ②a woolen muffler

毛舉(ㄇㄠˊ ㄐㄩˇ)
①to cite at random ②to list or cite trifles

毛奇(ㄇㄠˊ ㄑㄧˊ)
Helmuth Karl Bernhard, Count von Moltke, 1800-1891, a famous Prussian general

毛嬙西施(ㄇㄠˊ ㄑㄧㄤˊ ㄒㄧ ㄕ)
Mao Chiang and Hsi Shih, famous beauties in ancient China, now used as synonymous terms of very beautiful women

毛細管(ㄇㄠˊ ㄒㄧˋ ㄍㄨㄢˇ)
a capillary tube; a capillary

毛細現象(ㄇㄠˊ ㄒㄧˋ ㄒㄧㄢˋ ㄒㄧㄤˋ)
capillary action; capillary attraction and repulsion

毛線(ㄇㄠˊ ㄒㄧㄢˋ)
woolen yarn; knitting wool

毛線衣(ㄇㄠˊ ㄒㄧㄢˋ ㄧ)
a knitted woolen garment; a sweater; wool: 他冬天穿毛線衣。He wears wool in winter.

毛織物(ㄇㄠˊ ㄓ ㄨˋ)or 毛織品(ㄇㄠˊ ㄓ ㄆㄧㄣˇ)
woolen textiles; woolen goods; woolen stuff; woolen fabrics; wool: 我們通常在冬天穿毛織品。We usually wear wool in winter.

毛氈(ㄇㄠˊ ㄓㄢ)
①a woolen carpet ②felt: 那是用毛氈製的。It is made of felt.

毛蟲(ㄇㄠˊ ㄔㄨㄥˊ)
①a caterpillar ②wild beasts

毛蝨(ㄇㄠˊ ㄕ)
a crab louse

毛詩(ㄇㄠˊ ㄕ)
the *Book of Odes* as edited by Mao Heng (毛亨)in the Han Dynasty

毛手毛脚(ㄇㄠˊ ㄕㄡˇ ㄇㄠˊ ㄐㄧㄠˇ)
①restless; uneasy; unquiet ②to take liberties with a woman by the actions of one's hands

毛茸(ㄇㄠˊ ㄖㄨㄥˊ)
hair on a plant

毛茸茸(ㄇㄠˊ ㄖㄨㄥˊ ㄖㄨㄥˊ)
hairy; downy: 他有雙毛茸茸的手。He has hairy hands.

毛子(ㄇㄠˊ ˙ㄗ)
①a hairy fellow—a Westerner ②the tuft of hair on a child's head

毛躁(ㄇㄠˊ ˙ㄗㄠ)
①irritable: 她近來毛躁得很。She has been very irritable lately. ②rash and restless: 他是個毛躁的年輕人。He's a rash young man.

毛瑟鎗(ㄇㄠˊ ㄙㄜˋ ㄑㄧㄤ)
a mauser

毛遂自薦(ㄇㄠˊ ㄙㄨㄟˋ ㄗˋ ㄐㄧㄢˋ)
to recommend oneself; to volunteer for a task—a common allusion to Mao Sui (毛遂) of the Warring States Period, who recommended himself to a post

毛筍(ㄇㄠˊ ㄙㄨㄣˇ)
the shoot of a variety of bamboo

毛兒(ㄇㄠˊ ㄦ)
hairs

毛衣(ㄇㄠˊ ㄧ)
woolen sweaters; sweaters: 我的毛衣是羊毛製的。My sweater is made of wool.

毛丫頭(ㄇㄠˊ ㄧㄚ ˙ㄊㄡ)
a little girl

毛穎(ㄇㄠˊ ㄧㄥˇ)
a writing brush

毛襪(ㄇㄠˊ ㄨㄚˋ)
woolen stockings

毛羽(ㄇㄠˊ ㄩˇ)
fur and feathers

六畫

【毧】 2736
ㄖㄨㄥˊ rong róng

1. fine hair; down
2. felt

毧帽(ㄖㄨㄥˊ ㄇㄠˋ)
a felt cap or hat

毧鞋(ㄖㄨㄥˊ ㄒㄧㄝˊ)
felt shoes

七畫

【毫】 2737
ㄏㄠˊ haur háo

1. fine hair
2. a measure of length
3. a writing brush: 狼毫 a writing brush made of wolf's hair
4. a dime
5. a measure of weight
6. a Chinese family name

毫巴(ㄏㄠˊ ㄅㄚ)
(meteorology) millibar, a unit of atmospheric pressure

毫不(ㄏㄠˊ ㄅㄨˋ)
not at all; not in the least: 這個消息毫不足怪。This news is not at all surprising.

毫不相干(ㄏㄠˊ ˙ㄅㄨ ㄒㄧㄤ ㄍㄢ)
totally unrelated; completely irrelevant

毫不在乎(ㄏㄠˊ ˙ㄅㄨ ㄗㄞˋ ˙ㄏㄨ)
completely unperturbed; not at all perturbed; do not mind or care at all

毫末(ㄏㄠˊ ㄇㄛˋ)
extremely small parts; minute elements

毫毛(ㄏㄠˊ ㄇㄠˊ)
the fine hair on human skin: 他們的威脅無損於我們一根毫毛。Their threats can't harm a single hair of our head.

毫芒(ㄏㄠˊ ㄇㄤˊ)
extremely tiny parts

毫米(ㄏㄠˊ ㄇㄧˇ)
millimeter (mm.), a unit of length

毫秒(ㄏㄠˊ ㄇㄧㄠˇ)
a millisecond

毫髮(ㄏㄠˊ ㄈㄚˇ)
extremely little

毫髮不爽(ㄏㄠˊ ㄈㄚˇ ㄅㄨˋ ㄕㄨㄤˇ)
There is not even slightest deviation. 或 It does not deviate a hair's breath. 或It's perfectly accurate.

毫釐(ㄏㄠˊ ㄌㄧˊ)
extremely small space; hairbreadth; an iota

毫釐不差(ㄏㄠˊ ㄌㄧˊ ㄅㄨˋ ㄔㄚ)
without the slightest error

毫釐千里(ㄏㄠˊ ㄌㄧˊ ㄑㄧㄢ ㄌㄧˇ)
An error by a hairbreadth may eventually result in an error of a thousand miles.

毫克(ㄏㄠˊ ㄎㄜˋ)
milligram (mg.), a unit of mass or weight

毫升(ㄏㄠˊ ㄕㄥ)

milliliter (ml.), a unit of capacity
毫素(ㄏㄠˊ ㄙㄨˋ)
the writing brush and writing paper
毫無(ㄏㄠˊ ㄨˊ)
not at all; not in the least
毫無可取(ㄏㄠˊ ㄨˊ ㄎㄜˇ ㄑㄩˇ)
totally worthless
毫無價值(ㄏㄠˊ ㄨˊ ㄐㄧㄚˋ ㄓˊ)
good for nothing: 一支破了的溫度計是毫無價值的。A broken thermometer is good for nothing.
毫無誠意(ㄏㄠˊ ㄨˊ ㄔㄥˊ ㄧˋ)
to have no sincerity at all
毫無疑問(ㄏㄠˊ ㄨˊ ㄧˊ ㄨㄣˋ)
There is no doubt.

【毬】 2738 ㄑㄧㄡˊ chyou qiú
a ball; a sphere
毬果(ㄑㄧㄡˊ ㄍㄨㄛˇ)
cones (of pines, spruces, etc.); strobiles

八畫

【毯】 2739 ㄊㄢˇ taan tǎn
a rug; a carpet; a blanket: 地板上鋪着地毯。The floor is covered with a carpet.
毯子(ㄊㄢˇ ·ㄗ)
a rug; a carpet; a blanket: 他圍上一條厚毛毯子。He wrapped a woolen rug around him.

【毳】 2740 ㄘㄨㄟˋ tsuey cuì
fine feathers or fur
毳毛(ㄘㄨㄟˋ ㄇㄠˊ)
fine feathers or fur
毳冕(ㄘㄨㄟˋ ㄇㄧㄢˇ)
imperial costume for worship of nature
毳幕(ㄘㄨㄟˋ ㄇㄨˋ)or 毳帳(ㄘㄨㄟˋ ㄓㄤˋ)
a felt curtain; a felt tent
毳衣(ㄘㄨㄟˋ ㄧ)
①a kind of elaborate garment woven of down or fur ② a garment woven of feathers and worn by Buddhist monks

九畫

【毽】 2741 ㄐㄧㄢˋ jiann jiàn
a shuttlecock: 雞毛毽 a shuttlecock made of chicken feathers
毽子(ㄐㄧㄢˋ ·ㄗ)or 毽兒 (ㄐㄧㄚˋㄦ)
a shuttlecock

十一畫

【氂】 2742 ㄌㄧˊ li lí (又讀 ㄇㄠˊ mau máo)
1. a horse tail
2. long hair; thick hair
3. a yak
氂牛(ㄇㄠˊ ㄋㄧㄡˊ)
a yak 亦作「犛牛」

十二畫

【氅】 2743 ㄔㄤˇ chaang chǎng
a garment woven of down
氅衣(ㄔㄤˇ ㄧ)
① an outer garment; a coat ② the costume of the Taoist priest

【氄】 2744 ㄖㄨㄥˇ roong rǒng
1. fine hair
2. fine; soft
氄毛兒(ㄖㄨㄥˇ ㄇㄠˊㄦ)
fine hair
氄刺(ㄖㄨㄥˇ ㄘˋ)
fine fishbones

十三畫

【氈】 2745 (毡、氊) ㄓㄢ jan zhān
1. felt
2. a blanket
氈帽(ㄓㄢ ㄇㄠˋ)
a felt cap or hat
氈幕(ㄓㄢ ㄇㄨˋ)
a felt tent
氈毯(ㄓㄢ ㄊㄢˇ)
a felt rug
氈笠(ㄓㄢ ㄌㄧˋ)
a felt hat with broad rim
氈裘(ㄓㄢ ㄑㄧㄡˊ)
① a felt garment worn by the nomad people in the north ② the chieftain of the nomads
氈裘之君(ㄓㄢ ㄑㄧㄡˊ ㄓ ㄐㄩㄣ)
a nomad chieftain
氈鞋(ㄓㄢ ㄒㄧㄝˊ)
felt shoes
氈子(ㄓㄢ ·ㄗ)
felt

氏部
ㄕˋ shyh shì

【氏】 2746 1. ㄕˋ shyh shì
1. family name; surname: 陳氏兄弟 the Chen brothers
2. a character placed after a married woman's maiden name; née: 夫人林氏 his wife née Lin
3. the title of a government position in former times
氏譜(ㄕˋ ㄆㄨˇ)
a family tree; lineage; a genealogy
氏族(ㄕˋ ㄗㄨˊ)
a family; a clan
氏族制度(ㄕˋ ㄗㄨˊ ㄓˋ ㄉㄨˋ)
the clan system

【氏】 2746 2. ㄓ jy zhī
name of an ancient barbarian tribe 參看「月氏」

一畫

【氐】 2747 1. ㄉㄧ di dī
1. name of an ancient barbarian tribe to the west
2. same as 低—low
氐羌(ㄉㄧ ㄑㄧㄤ)
ancient barbarian tribes to the west

【氐】 2747 2. ㄉㄧˇ dii dǐ
1. foundation
2. same as 抵—on the whole

【民】 2748 ㄇㄧㄣˊ min mín
1. the people; the subject; the populace; the public: 他們爲民除害。They rid the people of a scourge.
2. civilians: 我們實施軍民聯防。We are making joint defense by army and civilians.

〔氏部〕

3. a Chinese family name
民胞物與(ㄇㄧㄣˊ ㄅㄠ ㄨˋ ㄩˇ)
to be kind to people and animals
民辦(ㄇㄧㄣˊ ㄅㄢˋ)
privately operated; privately owned; nongovernmental: 那是一所民辦中學。That is a high school run by the local people.
民本主義(ㄇㄧㄣˊ ㄅㄣˇ ㄓㄨˇ ㄧˋ)
democracy
民兵(ㄇㄧㄣˊ ㄅㄧㄥ)
① a militiaman ② a militia force
民不聊生(ㄇㄧㄣˊ ㄅㄨˋ ㄌㄧㄠˊ ㄕㄥ)
The people cannot live in peace. 或 The people are living in misery.
民不堪命(ㄇㄧㄣˊ ㄅㄨˋ ㄎㄢ ㄇㄧㄥˋ)
The people cannot stand the pressure of the government. 或 The people are hard pressed.
民瘼(ㄇㄧㄣˊ ㄇㄛˋ)
sufferings of the people
民母(ㄇㄧㄣˊ ㄇㄨˇ)
① the queen ② my mother (a reference used in speaking to judges in former times)
民法(ㄇㄧㄣˊ ㄈㄚˇ)
the civil law; the civil code
民憤(ㄇㄧㄣˊ ㄈㄣˋ)
public wrath; popular hatred: 此事引起極大的民憤。It has aroused the bitter indignation of the people.
民房(ㄇㄧㄣˊ ㄈㄤˊ)
a private house; a civilian house
民風(ㄇㄧㄣˊ ㄈㄥ)
customs of the people; popular customs
民夫(ㄇㄧㄣˊ ㄈㄨ)
① a laborer drafted for government service ② my husband (a reference used in speaking to judges in former times)
民田(ㄇㄧㄣˊ ㄊㄧㄢˊ)
people's farmland
民庭(ㄇㄧㄣˊ ㄊㄧㄥˊ)
a civil court 亦作「民事法庭」
民團(ㄇㄧㄣˊ ㄊㄨㄢˊ)
a posse; a paramilitary unit organized by a community for self-defense
民力(ㄇㄧㄣˊ ㄌㄧˋ)
① the means of the people ② people's labor
民歌(ㄇㄧㄣˊ ㄍㄜ)
a folk song; a ballad
民國(ㄇㄧㄣˊ ㄍㄨㄛˊ)
① a republic; a democracy ② the Republic of China, founded in 1912
民貴君輕(ㄇㄧㄣˊ ㄍㄨㄟˋ ㄐㄩㄣ ㄑㄧㄥ)
The people are more important than the ruler. (a concept upheld by Mencius)
民可使由之，不可使知之(ㄇㄧㄣˊ ㄎㄜˇ ㄕˇ ㄧㄡˊ ㄓ, ㄅㄨˋ ㄎㄜˇ ㄕˇ ㄓ ㄓ)
The people should be told to do this or that without telling them why.
民害(ㄇㄧㄣˊ ㄏㄞˋ)
a scourge or calamity to the people; evils to the common people
民航(ㄇㄧㄣˊ ㄏㄤˊ)
civil aviation
民航機(ㄇㄧㄣˊ ㄏㄤˊ ㄐㄧ)
an airliner; a civil airplane (or aircraft)
民航局(ㄇㄧㄣˊ ㄏㄤˊ ㄐㄩˊ)
Civil Aeronautics Administration (CAA)
民間(ㄇㄧㄣˊ ㄐㄧㄢ)
among the people: 這首歌謠長久地在民間流傳。For generations this ballad has circulated among the people.
民間故事(ㄇㄧㄣˊ ㄐㄧㄢ ㄍㄨˋ ˙ㄕ)
folktales; folklore
民間疾苦(ㄇㄧㄣˊ ㄐㄧㄢ ㄐㄧˊ ㄎㄨˇ)
the hardships of the people: 他深知民間疾苦。He understood the hardships of the people.
民間藝術(ㄇㄧㄣˊ ㄐㄧㄢ ㄧˋ ㄕㄨˋ)
folk art
民間音樂(ㄇㄧㄣˊ ㄐㄧㄢ ㄧㄣ ㄩㄝˋ)
folk music
民間文學(ㄇㄧㄣˊ ㄐㄧㄢ ㄨㄣˊ ㄒㄩㄝˊ)
folk literature; popular literature
民妻(ㄇㄧㄣˊ ㄑㄧ)
my wife (a reference used in speaking to judges in former times)
民氣(ㄇㄧㄣˊ ㄑㄧˋ)
morale or spirit of the people
民情(ㄇㄧㄣˊ ㄑㄧㄥˊ)
the condition of the people
民權(ㄇㄧㄣˊ ㄑㄩㄢˊ)
civil rights; people's rights
民權主義(ㄇㄧㄣˊ ㄑㄩㄢˊ ㄓㄨˇ ㄧˋ)
The Principle of the People's Rights (one of *The Three Principles of the People*)
民權初步(ㄇㄧㄣˊ ㄑㄩㄢˊ ㄔㄨ ㄅㄨˋ)
The Fundamental Knowledge in Democracy, a book dealing with the procedures of the parliamentary rule, authored by Dr. Sun Yat-sen
民窮財盡(ㄇㄧㄣˊ ㄑㄩㄥˊ ㄘㄞˊ ㄐㄧㄣˋ)
The means of the people have been used up (due to government exploitation or heavy spending).
民心(ㄇㄧㄣˊ ㄒㄧㄣ)
popular sentiments; popular support: 他深得民心。He wins the ardent support of the people.
民選(ㄇㄧㄣˊ ㄒㄩㄢˇ)
popularly elected
民脂民膏(ㄇㄧㄣˊ ㄓ ㄇㄧㄣˊ ㄍㄠ)
the hard-won possessions of the people; the fruits of people's toil
民治(ㄇㄧㄣˊ ㄓˋ)
government by the people
民智(ㄇㄧㄣˊ ㄓˋ)
intelligence of the people
民政(ㄇㄧㄣˊ ㄓㄥˋ)
civil administration
民政廳(ㄇㄧㄣˊ ㄓㄥˋ ㄊㄧㄥ)
Department of Civil Affairs
民主(ㄇㄧㄣˊ ㄓㄨˇ)
democratic; democracy: 美國的學校是民主的。Schools in the United States are democratic.
民主黨(ㄇㄧㄣˊ ㄓㄨˇ ㄉㄤˇ)
Democratic Party (of the United States)
民主政體(ㄇㄧㄣˊ ㄓㄨˇ ㄓㄥˋ ㄊㄧˇ)
democratic government; democracy
民主政治(ㄇㄧㄣˊ ㄓㄨˇ ㄓㄥˋ ㄓˋ)
democracy
民主主義(ㄇㄧㄣˊ ㄓㄨˇ ㄓㄨˇ ㄧˋ)
democratism
民主潮流(ㄇㄧㄣˊ ㄓㄨˇ ㄔㄠˊ ㄌㄧㄡˊ)
the tide of democracy

民主社會黨(ㄇㄧㄣˊ ㄓㄨˇ ㄕㄜˋ ㄏㄨㄟˋ ㄉㄤˇ)or民社黨(ㄇㄧㄣˊ ㄕㄜˋ ㄉㄤˇ)
China Democratic Socialist Party

民衆(ㄇㄧㄣˊ ㄓㄨㄥˋ)
the people; the common people; the multitude; the masses; the populace

民衆團體(ㄇㄧㄣˊ ㄓㄨㄥˋ ㄊㄨㄢˊ ㄊㄧˇ)
a civic organization; a mass organization; a civic body

民衆教育(ㄇㄧㄣˊ ㄓㄨㄥˋ ㄐㄧㄠˋ ㄩˋ)
education of the masses; adult education

民初(ㄇㄧㄣˊ ㄔㄨ)
in the early republican years; in the early days of the Republic of China

民師(ㄇㄧㄣˊ ㄕ)
a model or teacher of the people

民食(ㄇㄧㄣˊ ㄕˊ)
foodstuff for the people; provisions for the people

民時(ㄇㄧㄣˊ ㄕˊ)
the farming season

民事(ㄇㄧㄣˊ ㄕˋ)
① civil affairs ② agricultural affairs

民事訴訟法(ㄇㄧㄣˊ ㄕˋ ㄙㄨˋ ㄙㄨㄥˋ ㄈㄚˇ)
the code of civil procedures

民生(ㄇㄧㄣˊ ㄕㄥ)
the people's livelihood: 戰爭使得民生凋敝。The war has reduced the people to destitution.

民生主義(ㄇㄧㄣˊ ㄕㄥ ㄓㄨˇ ㄧˋ)
The Principle of the People's Livelihood (one of *The Three Principles of the People*)

民生在勤(ㄇㄧㄣˊ ㄕㄥ ㄗㄞˋ ㄑㄧㄣˊ)
To live well, one must work diligently.

民生物資(ㄇㄧㄣˊ ㄕㄥ ㄨˋ ㄗ)
daily necessities; goods essential to daily living

民生問題(ㄇㄧㄣˊ ㄕㄥ ㄨㄣˋ ㄊㄧˊ)
problems of the people's livelihood

民賊(ㄇㄧㄣˊ ㄗㄟˊ)
a public enemy; a traitor to the people

民族(ㄇㄧㄣˊ ㄗㄨˊ)
a nation; a people: 中國人是個勤勞的民族。The Chinese are a hard-working people.

民族革命(ㄇㄧㄣˊ ㄗㄨˊ ㄍㄜˊ ㄇㄧㄥˋ)
a national revolution

民族性(ㄇㄧㄣˊ ㄗㄨˊ ㄒㄧㄥˋ)
national character

民族學(ㄇㄧㄣˊ ㄗㄨˊ ㄒㄩㄝˊ)
ethnology

民族至上(ㄇㄧㄣˊ ㄗㄨˊ ㄓˋ ㄕㄤˋ)
(slogan) the nation above all

民族主義(ㄇㄧㄣˊ ㄗㄨˊ ㄓㄨˇ ㄧˋ)
① *The Principle of Nationalism* (one of The *Three Principles of the People*) ② nationalism

民族自決(ㄇㄧㄣˊ ㄗㄨˊ ㄗˋ ㄐㄩㄝˊ)
national self-determination

民族意識(ㄇㄧㄣˊ ㄗㄨˊ ㄧˋ ㄕˋ)
national consciousness

民族英雄(ㄇㄧㄣˊ ㄗㄨˊ ㄧㄥ ㄒㄩㄥˊ)
a national hero: 他是位民族英雄。He was a national hero.

民族舞蹈(ㄇㄧㄣˊ ㄗㄨˊ ㄨˇ ㄉㄠˋ)
race dance

民族運動(ㄇㄧㄣˊ ㄗㄨˊ ㄩㄣˋ ㄉㄨㄥˋ)
a national movement

民俗(ㄇㄧㄣˊ ㄙㄨˊ)
folkways; customs and practices of the people

民俗學(ㄇㄧㄣˊ ㄙㄨˊ ㄒㄩㄝˊ)
folklore

民以食爲天(ㄇㄧㄣˊ ㄧˇ ㄕˊ ㄨㄟˊ ㄊㄧㄢ)
To the people foodstuff is all-important.

民意(ㄇㄧㄣˊ ㄧˋ)
popular sentiments; public opinion; the will of the people

民意代表(ㄇㄧㄣˊ ㄧˋ ㄉㄞˋ ㄅㄧㄠˇ)
people's representatives; parliamentarians

民意機關(ㄇㄧㄣˊ ㄧˋ ㄐㄧ ㄍㄨㄢ)
the people's representative body

民意測驗(ㄇㄧㄣˊ ㄧˋ ㄘㄜˋ ㄧㄢˋ)
a poll; polltaking; a public opinion survey

民謠(ㄇㄧㄣˊ ㄧㄠˊ)
a folk song

民有，民治，民享(ㄇㄧㄣˊ ㄧㄡˇ, ㄇㄧㄣˊ ㄓˋ, ㄇㄧㄣˊ ㄒㄧㄤˇ)
of the people, by the people, and for the people

民隱(ㄇㄧㄣˊ ㄧㄣˇ)
the distress of the people unknown to the authorities

民營(ㄇㄧㄣˊ ㄧㄥˊ)
privately owned

民惟邦本 or 民爲邦本(ㄇㄧㄣˊ ㄨㄟˊ ㄅㄤ ㄅㄣˇ)
The people are the foundation of the state.

民望(ㄇㄧㄣˊ ㄨㄤˋ)
① popular expectation; popularity among the people ② an example to be observed by people

民約論(ㄇㄧㄣˊ ㄩㄝ ㄌㄨㄣˋ)
the *Doctrine of Social Contract* by Jean Jacques Rousseau

民怨沸騰(ㄇㄧㄣˊ ㄩㄢˋ ㄈㄟˋ ㄊㄥˊ)
Discontent among the people is boiling. 或 Public resentment is seething.

民運(ㄇㄧㄣˊ ㄩㄣˋ)
① civil transport ② democratic movement

民用機場(ㄇㄧㄣˊ ㄩㄥˋ ㄐㄧ ㄔㄤˇ)or(ㄇㄧㄣˊ ㄩㄥˋ ㄐㄧ ㄔㄤˊ)
a civil airport

四畫

【氓】 2749
1. (甿) ㄇㄥˊ meng méng

the people; the populace

氓隸(ㄇㄥˊ ㄌㄧˋ)
people who are engaged in laborious work

【氓】 2749
2. ㄇㄤˊ mang máng

a rascal; a vagabond: 他們是城裏的流氓。They are city rascals.

气部
ㄑㄧˋ chih qì

二畫

【氖】 2750
ㄋㄞˇ nae nǎi

neon

氖燈(ㄋㄞˇ ㄉㄥ)
a neon lamp; a neon light; a neon sign 亦作「霓虹燈」

〔气部〕

〔气部〕

四畫

【氛】 2751
ㄈㄣ fen fēn

air; atmosphere; prevailing mood: 鄉下有一種寧靜的氣氛。There's an atmosphere of peace in the country.

氛厲(ㄈㄣ ㄌㄧˋ)
disasters; calamities

氛邪(ㄈㄣ ㄒㄧㄝˊ)
an evil air

氛翳(ㄈㄣ ㄧˋ)
an inauspicious and foreboding atmosphere

氛圍(ㄈㄣ ㄨㄟˊ)
air; atmosphere; mood

氛氳(ㄈㄣ ㄩㄣ)
the spirit, or atmosphere, of prosperity or propitiousness; a vigorous spirit; a vigorous atmosphere

五畫

【氟】 2752
ㄈㄨˊ fwu fú

fluorine

氟化作用(ㄈㄨˊ ㄏㄨㄚˋ ㄗㄨㄛˋ ㄩㄥˋ)
fluorination

氟化物(ㄈㄨˊ ㄏㄨㄚˋ ㄨˋ)
(chemistry) fluoride

六畫

【氣】 2753
ㄑㄧˋ chih qì

1. air; gas; vapor; the atmosphere: 我們必須呼吸新鮮空氣。We must breathe fresh air.
2. breath: 他深深地吸了一口氣。He took a deep breath.
3. spirit; morale: 士氣消沈(or 極佳)。The morale of the troops is low (or perfect).
4. influence
5. bearing; manner
6. smells; odors: 玫瑰發出香氣。Roses smell sweet.
7. to be angry; to be indignant; rage; anger: 他氣得直哆嗦。He trembled with rage.
8. to provoke; to goad; to make angry; to annoy: 他故意氣你一下。He was deliberately to annoy you.
9. weather: 秋高氣爽 fine autumn weather

氣瓣(ㄑㄧˋ ㄅㄢˋ)
an air valve

氣不平(ㄑㄧˋ ˙ㄅㄨ ㄆㄧㄥˊ)
to be indignant about unfairness or injustice

氣魄(ㄑㄧˋ ㄆㄛˋ)
spirit; vigor; broadness of mind; moral strength

氣派(ㄑㄧˋ ˙ㄆㄞ)
a dignified air; an impressive style or manner

氣泡(ㄑㄧˋ ㄆㄠˋ)
air bubbles: 氣泡破了。The bubble has burst.

氣門(ㄑㄧˋ ㄇㄣˊ)
① an air valve; an air escape ② (zoology) a stigma

氣悶(ㄑㄧˋ ㄇㄣˋ)
stifling; sultry; oppressive

氣氛(ㄑㄧˋ ㄈㄣ)
atmosphere; mood: 研討會的氣氛始終很熱烈。The atmosphere was lively throughout the seminar.

氣忿 or 氣憤(ㄑㄧˋ ㄈㄣˋ)
to be angry; to be furious; to be enraged; to be indignant: 大家對這樣的誣告感到氣憤。Everybody was indignant at such a false accusation.

氣忿忿(ㄑㄧˋ ㄈㄣˋ ㄈㄣˋ)
furious; angry; enraged; mad; wrathful

氣墊(ㄑㄧˋ ㄉㄧㄢˋ)
an air cushion (or mattress)

氣度(ㄑㄧˋ ㄉㄨˋ)
① spirit; air; bearing; manner: 他氣度非凡。He has an impressive manner. ② capacity for tolerance

氣短(ㄑㄧˋ ㄉㄨㄢˇ)
① to be short of breath; to pant ② to be disappointed; to be discouraged: 失敗並未使林先生氣短。Mr. Lin was not discouraged by failure.

氣頭兒上(ㄑㄧˋ ㄊㄡˊㄦ ˙ㄕㄤ)
right in the middle of one's fit of rage

氣體(ㄑㄧˋ ㄊㄧˇ)
gas; the gaseous body; vapor: 空氣是許多氣體的混合物。Air is a mixture of gases.

氣體動力論(ㄑㄧˋ ㄊㄧˇ ㄉㄨㄥˋ ㄌㄧˋ ㄌㄨㄣˋ)
the kinetic theory of gases

氣體動力學(ㄑㄧˋ ㄊㄧˇ ㄉㄨㄥˋ ㄌㄧˋ ㄒㄩㄝˊ)or 氣體力學(ㄑㄧˋ ㄊㄧˇ ㄌㄧˋ ㄒㄩㄝˊ)
aerodynamics; pneumatics

氣團(ㄑㄧˋ ㄊㄨㄢˊ)
a mass of cold or hot air: 冷氣團 a cold air mass

氣吞山河(ㄑㄧˋ ㄊㄨㄣ ㄕㄢ ㄏㄜˊ)
(descriptive of warriors) to be filled with vehemence that can conquer mountains and rivers—full of daring

氣筒(ㄑㄧˋ ㄊㄨㄥˇ)or 氣筒子(ㄑㄧˋ ㄊㄨㄥˇ ˙ㄗ)
an air pump; an inflator; a bicycle pump

氣餒(ㄑㄧˋ ㄋㄟˇ)
discouraged; despondent; crestfallen: 失敗並沒有使她氣餒。She was not discouraged by failure.

氣惱(ㄑㄧˋ ㄋㄠˇ)
to be sulky; to be sullen; to take offense; to be resentful: 不要因細故而氣惱。Don't be sulky about trifles.

氣囊(ㄑㄧˋ ㄋㄤˊ)
the air bladder (of fish); the air sac (of birds or plants); the gasbag or envelope (of a dirigible)

氣逆(ㄑㄧˋ ㄋㄧˋ)
(Chinese herb medicine) the supposed upward motion of the spirit

氣力(ㄑㄧˋ ㄌㄧˋ)
strength; effort; energy: 他們花了很大的氣力完成了這項任務。They exerted great efforts to accomplish the duty.

氣流(ㄑㄧˋ ㄌㄧㄡˊ)
an airflow; an air current; an atmospheric current

氣量大(ㄑㄧˋ ㄌㄧㄤˋ ㄉㄚˋ)
magnanimous; generous; tolerant; broad-minded: 他是一位氣量大的統治者。He was a magnanimous ruler.

氣量小(ㄑㄧˋ ㄌㄧㄤˋ ㄒㄧㄠˇ)
narrow-minded: 他是個氣量小的法官。He is a narrow-minded judge.

氣格(ㄑㄧˋ ㄍㄜˊ)
character; personality

氣概(ㄑㄧˋ ㄍㄞˋ)
spirit; air; bearing; manner:

他具有英雄氣概。He is a man of heroic spirit.

氣根(ㄑㄧˋ ㄍㄣ)
a clinging root; an aerial root

氣骨(ㄑㄧˋ ㄍㄨˇ)
one's natural character

氣管(ㄑㄧˋ ㄍㄨㄢˇ)
trachea; windpipe

氣管炎(ㄑㄧˋ ㄍㄨㄢˇ ㄧㄢˊ)
tracheitis

氣貫長虹(ㄑㄧˋ ㄍㄨㄢˋ ㄔㄤˊ ㄏㄨㄥˊ)
(descriptive of warriors) to be filled with a spirit as lofty as the rainbow spanning the sky—full of noble aspiration and daring

氣功(ㄑㄧˋ ㄍㄨㄥ)
(Chinese boxing) the ability to use one's inner strength such as control of muscle and breathing; a system of deep breathing exercises

氣孔(ㄑㄧˋ ㄎㄨㄥˇ)
pores (on the skin); stomas (on a leaf); the spiracle or blowhole (of a whale); vesicles (of the igneous rock)

氣候(ㄑㄧˋ ㄏㄡˋ)
①climate; weather: 我喜歡乾燥氣候。I like an arid climate. ② situations: 政治氣候 the political situation (or climate)

氣候學(ㄑㄧˋ ㄏㄡˋ ㄒㄩㄝˊ)
climatology

氣恨(ㄑㄧˋ ㄏㄣˋ)
to be angry; to be resentful; to be hateful; to be bitter

氣哼哼(ㄑㄧˋ ㄏㄥ ㄏㄥ)
angry; mad; enraged; furious

氣呼呼(ㄑㄧˋ ㄏㄨ ㄏㄨ)
panting with rage

氣化(ㄑㄧˋ ㄏㄨㄚˋ)
to evaporate; to gasify; to vaporize; gasification

氣化熱(ㄑㄧˋ ㄏㄨㄚˋ ㄖㄜˋ)
evaporation heat

氣昏了(ㄑㄧˋ ㄏㄨㄣ ˙ㄌㄜ)
to be driven mad by anger

氣急敗壞(ㄑㄧˋ ㄐㄧˊ ㄅㄞˋ ㄏㄨㄞˋ)
desperate and low-spirited

氣結(ㄑㄧˋ ㄐㄧㄝˊ)
①(Chinese herb medicine) supposed clogging of the spirit ② depressed; despondent; low-spirited

氣節(ㄑㄧˋ ㄐㄧㄝˊ)
① moral principle; righteousness: 他的確是個有氣節的人。He is indeed a man of righteousness. ②a season; the 24 solar periods of the year

氣界(ㄑㄧˋ ㄐㄧㄝˋ)
the atmosphere (surrounding the earth)

氣盡(ㄑㄧˋ ㄐㄧㄣˋ)
to run out of vitality

氣沮(ㄑㄧˋ ㄐㄩˇ)
dispirited; depressed

氣絕(ㄑㄧˋ ㄐㄩㄝˊ)
to breathe one's last; at one's last gasp: 他到達時，他父親剛剛氣絕了。He arrived just after his father had breathed his last.

氣球(ㄑㄧˋ ㄑㄧㄡˊ)
a balloon

氣槍(ㄑㄧˋ ㄑㄧㄤ)
an air gun; an air rifle: 你能用氣槍打下一隻鳥嗎? Can you shoot down a bird with an air gun?

氣圈(ㄑㄧˋ ㄑㄩㄢ)
the atmosphere (around the earth)

氣息(ㄑㄧˋ ㄒㄧˊ)
① breath: 今天有點春天的氣息。There is a breath of spring in the air today.② the spirit (of writings): 他的作品毫無氣息。His writings totally lack of spirit.

氣息奄奄(ㄑㄧˋ ㄒㄧˊ ㄧㄢˇ ㄧㄢˇ)
The breath is dying out. —dying; at one's last gasp

氣象(ㄑㄧˋ ㄒㄧㄤˋ)
①meteorology; weather; climates ②the prevailing spirit; atmosphere: 這是生氣蓬勃的新氣象。This is a new and dynamic atmosphere.

氣象報告(ㄑㄧˋ ㄒㄧㄤˋ ㄅㄠˋ ㄍㄠˋ)or 氣象預報(ㄑㄧˋ ㄒㄧㄤˋ ㄩˋ ㄅㄠˋ)
a weather forecast

氣象臺(ㄑㄧˋ ㄒㄧㄤˋ ㄊㄞˊ)
a weather station; a meteorological observatory

氣象局(ㄑㄧˋ ㄒㄧㄤˋ ㄐㄩˊ)
a weather bureau

氣象學(ㄑㄧˋ ㄒㄧㄤˋ ㄒㄩㄝˊ)
meteorology

氣象衛星(ㄑㄧˋ ㄒㄧㄤˋ ㄨㄟˋ ㄒㄧㄥ)
a weather satellite

氣象萬千(ㄑㄧˋ ㄒㄧㄤˋ ㄨㄢˋ ㄑㄧㄢ)
Nature abounds in changes. 或 Things change in countless ways.

氣性(ㄑㄧˋ ㄒㄧㄥˋ)
temper; dispositions

氣虛(ㄑㄧˋ ㄒㄩ)
physically weak; deficiency of vital energy

氣吁吁(ㄑㄧˋ ㄒㄩ ㄒㄩ)
gasping for breath

氣質(ㄑㄧˋ ㄓˊ)
dispositions; temperament: 這兩兄弟的氣質完全不同。The two brothers have entirely different temperaments.

氣壯山河(ㄑㄧˋ ㄓㄨㄤˋ ㄕㄢ ㄏㄜˊ)
The spirit is so vigorous that it affects even the mountains and the rivers.

氣成岩(ㄑㄧˋ ㄔㄥˊ ㄧㄢˊ)
aerial rock

氣喘(ㄑㄧˋ ㄔㄨㄢˇ)
①to pant; to gasp; to be out of breath: 他跑得太快，而氣喘不已。He ran so fast that he was out of breath.② asthma: 陣發性氣喘 spasmodic asthma

氣喘如牛(ㄑㄧˋ ㄔㄨㄢˇ ㄖㄨˊ ㄋㄧㄡˊ)
to pant like an ox

氣窗(ㄑㄧˋ ㄔㄨㄤ)
a transom; a ventilation window; a louver window; a fanlight

氣沖斗牛(ㄑㄧˋ ㄔㄨㄥ ㄉㄡˇ ㄋㄧㄡˊ)
(literally) The anger even affects the northern stars. —very angry

氣沖沖(ㄑㄧˋ ㄔㄨㄥ ㄔㄨㄥ)
furious; to fly into a rage

氣勢(ㄑㄧˋ ㄕˋ)
vehemence; fervor; imposing manner: 明年我想參觀氣勢雄偉的萬里長城。I wish to visit the imposing Great Wall next year.

氣勢磅礴(ㄑㄧˋ ㄕˋ ㄆㄤˊ ㄅㄛˊ)
of great momentum; powerful

氣盛(ㄑㄧˋ ㄕㄥˋ)
overbearing; arrogant

氣數(ㄑㄧˋ ㄕㄨˋ)or 氣運(ㄑㄧˋ ㄩㄣˋ)
destiny; fate; fortune

氣層(ㄑㄧˋ ㄘㄥˊ)
the atmosphere (around the earth)

〔水部〕

氣死人(ㄑㄧˋ ㄙˇ ㄖㄣˊ)
infuriating; maddening; exasperating
氣色(ㄑㄧˋ ㄙㄜˋ)
complexion; color: 他的氣色很好。He has a good complexion. 或 He has a rosy complexion. 他的氣色不好。He looks pale.
氣昂昂(ㄑㄧˋ ㄤˊ ㄤˊ)
in high spirits; elated
氣壓(ㄑㄧˋ ㄧㄚ)
air pressure; atmospheric pressure; barometric pressure: 高氣壓 high pressure
氣壓計(ㄑㄧˋ ㄧㄚ ㄐㄧˋ)
a barometer; an air gauge 亦作「風雨表」or「晴雨表」
氣燄(ㄑㄧˋ ㄧㄢˋ)
hauteur; arrogance: 他的氣燄囂張。He was swollen with arrogance.
氣味(ㄑㄧˋ ㄨㄟˋ)or氣味兒(ㄑㄧˋ ㄨㄜˋㄦ)
smacks; smells; odors: 這氣味眞好! What a nice smell!
氣味相投(ㄑㄧˋ ㄨㄟˋ ㄒㄧㄤ ㄊㄡˊ)
having the same tastes and temperament; congenial; to be birds of a feather
氣溫(ㄑㄧˋ ㄨㄣ)
the atmospheric temperature; the temperature
氣宇(ㄑㄧˋ ㄩˇ)
dignified and inspiring looks; the manner of a person's carriage
氣宇軒昂(ㄑㄧˋ ㄩˇ ㄒㄩㄢ ㄤˊ)
dignified; exalted; manly
氣韻(ㄑㄧˋ ㄩㄣˋ)
the tone or style (of a work of art, literature, etc.)

【氤】2754
ㄧㄣ in yin
the spirit of harmony (between heaven and earth) 參看「氤氳」
氤氳(ㄧㄣ ㄩㄣ)
① the spirit of harmony (between heaven and earth)
② misty; cloudy; dense; thick
③ the spirit of vigor or prosperity

【氧】2755
ㄧㄤˇ yeang yǎng
oxygen: 水含有氫和氧。Water contains hydrogen and oxygen.
氧化(ㄧㄤˇ ㄏㄨㄚˋ)
to oxidize or be oxidized; oxidation
氧化碳(ㄧㄤˇ ㄏㄨㄚˋ ㄊㄢˋ)
carbon oxide
氧化鐵(ㄧㄤˇ ㄏㄨㄚˋ ㄊㄧㄝˇ)
ferric oxide
氧化銅(ㄧㄤˇ ㄏㄨㄚˋ ㄊㄨㄥˊ)
cupric oxide; cuprite
氧化鋁(ㄧㄤˇ ㄏㄨㄚˋ ㄌㄩˇ)
aluminum oxide
氧化鈣(ㄧㄤˇ ㄏㄨㄚˋ ㄍㄞˋ)
calcium oxide
氧化汞(ㄧㄤˇ ㄏㄨㄚˋ ㄍㄨㄥˇ)
mercuric oxide
氧化劑(ㄧㄤˇ ㄏㄨㄚˋ ㄐㄧˋ)
an oxidizing agent; an oxidizer
氧化金(ㄧㄤˇ ㄏㄨㄚˋ ㄐㄧㄣ)
gold oxide
氧化鉛(ㄧㄤˇ ㄏㄨㄚˋ ㄑㄧㄢ)
plumbic oxide
氧化錫(ㄧㄤˇ ㄏㄨㄚˋ ㄒㄧˊ)
stannic oxide
氧化矽(ㄧㄤˇ ㄏㄨㄚˋ ㄒㄧˋ)
silica
氧化鋅(ㄧㄤˇ ㄏㄨㄚˋ ㄒㄧㄣ)
zinc oxide
氧化焰(ㄧㄤˇ ㄏㄨㄚˋ ㄧㄢˋ)
oxidizing flame
氧化銀(ㄧㄤˇ ㄏㄨㄚˋ ㄧㄣˊ)
oxidized silver
氧化物(ㄧㄤˇ ㄏㄨㄚˋ ㄨˋ)
the oxide
氧氣(ㄧㄤˇ ㄑㄧˋ)
oxygen

【氦】2756
ㄏㄞˋ hay hài
helium

七畫

【氫】2757
ㄑㄧㄥ ching qīng
hydrogen
氫彈(ㄑㄧㄥ ㄉㄢˋ)
hydrogen bombs
氫化(ㄑㄧㄥ ㄏㄨㄚˋ)
hydrogenation
氫化作用(ㄑㄧㄥ ㄏㄨㄚˋ ㄗㄨㄛˋ ㄩㄥˋ)
hydrogenation
氫化物(ㄑㄧㄥ ㄏㄨㄚˋ ㄨˋ)
the hydride
氫氣(ㄑㄧㄥ ㄑㄧˋ)
hydrogen
氫酸(ㄑㄧㄥ ㄙㄨㄢ)
hydracid
氫氧化鈉(ㄑㄧㄥ ㄧㄤˇ ㄏㄨㄚˋ ㄋㄚˋ)
sodium hydroxide
氫氧化鈣(ㄑㄧㄥ ㄧㄤˇ ㄏㄨㄚˋ ㄍㄞˋ)
calcium hydroxide
氫氧化物(ㄑㄧㄥ ㄧㄤˇ ㄏㄨㄚˋ ㄨˋ)
hydroxide
氫氧基(ㄑㄧㄥ ㄧㄤˇ ㄐㄧ)or 氫氧根(ㄑㄧㄥ ㄧㄤˇ ㄍㄣ)
hydroxyl
氫氧吹管(ㄑㄧㄥ ㄧㄤˇ ㄔㄨㄟ ㄍㄨㄢˇ)
an oxyhydrogen blowpipe

八畫

【氯】2758
ㄌㄩˋ liuh lǜ
chlorine
氯化鈉(ㄌㄩˋ ㄏㄨㄚˋ ㄋㄚˋ)
sodium chloride
氯化鈣(ㄌㄩˋ ㄏㄨㄚˋ ㄍㄞˋ)
calcium chloride
氯化鉀(ㄌㄩˋ ㄏㄨㄚˋ ㄐㄧㄚˇ)
potassium chloride
氯化金(ㄌㄩˋ ㄏㄨㄚˋ ㄐㄧㄣ)
auric chloride
氯化物(ㄌㄩˋ ㄏㄨㄚˋ ㄨˋ)
the chloride
氯氣(ㄌㄩˋ ㄑㄧˋ)
chlorine; chlorine gas
氯水(ㄌㄩˋ ㄕㄨㄟˇ)
chlorine water

【氮】2759
ㄉㄢˋ dann dàn
nitrogen
氮肥(ㄉㄢˋ ㄈㄟˊ)
nitrogenous fertilizers
氮氣固定法(ㄉㄢˋ ㄑㄧˋ ㄍㄨˋ ㄉㄧㄥˋ ㄈㄚˇ)
the nitrogen fixation

十畫

【氳】2760
ㄩㄣ iun yūn
the atmosphere of harmony; the spirit of prosperity or vigor 參看「氤氳」

水部
ㄕㄨㄟˇ shoei shuǐ

【水】 2761 ㄕㄨㄟˇ shoei shuǐ

1. water: 活水 flowing water 死水 stagnant water
2. a general term for seas, lakes, rivers, etc.
3. liquid; juice: 檸檬水 lemonade 墨水 ink
4. flood disaster; flood
5. a Chinese family name

水壩(ㄕㄨㄟˇ ㄅㄚˋ)
a dam: 尼羅河上有好幾個水壩。There are several dams across the Nile.

水玻璃(ㄕㄨㄟˇ ㄅㄛ ·ㄌㄧ)
sodium silicate; water glass

水表(ㄕㄨㄟˇ ㄅㄧㄠˇ)
a water meter; a hydrometer; a water gauge

水濱(ㄕㄨㄟˇ ㄅㄧㄣ)or 水邊(ㄕㄨㄟˇ ㄅㄧㄢ)
the waterside; the shore

水兵(ㄕㄨㄟˇ ㄅㄧㄥ)
① a sailor; a bluejacket ② an old name of the navy

水波(ㄕㄨㄟˇ ㄆㄛ)
ripples of water

水牌(ㄕㄨㄟˇ ㄆㄞˊ)
a blackboard in stores for temporary recording of bills

水泡(ㄕㄨㄟˇ ㄆㄠˋ)
① foam; a bubble ② a blister; to blister 亦作「水疱」: 她的脚很嬌嫩,容易起水泡。Her feet are tender and blister easily.

水畔(ㄕㄨㄟˇ ㄆㄢˋ)
beside of the water; the shore

水盆(ㄕㄨㄟˇ ㄆㄣˊ)
a basin: 在水盆內洗手。Wash your hands in the basin.

水瓢(ㄕㄨㄟˇ ㄆㄧㄠˊ)
a dipper; a water ladle

水萍(ㄕㄨㄟˇ ㄆㄧㄥˊ)
(botany) duckweed

水平(ㄕㄨㄟˇ ㄆㄧㄥˊ)
horizontal

水平面(ㄕㄨㄟˇ ㄆㄧㄥˊ ㄇㄧㄢˋ)
a level surface

水平舵(ㄕㄨㄟˇ ㄆㄧㄥˊ ㄉㄨㄛˋ)
a horizontal rudder; a stabilizer

水平線(ㄕㄨㄟˇ ㄆㄧㄥˊ ㄒㄧㄢˋ)
a horizontal line

水瓶座(ㄕㄨㄟˇ ㄆㄧㄥˊ ㄗㄨㄛˋ)
(astrology) Aquarius (or Water Carrier) 亦作「寶瓶座」

水平儀(ㄕㄨㄟˇ ㄆㄧㄥˊ ㄧˊ)
leveling instrument; a level

水磨
① (ㄕㄨㄟˇ ㄇㄛˊ) fine work on jade, etc. polished with waterstone
②(ㄕㄨㄟˇ ㄇㄛˋ) a water mill

水磨工夫(ㄕㄨㄟˇ ㄇㄛˊ ㄍㄨㄥ ·ㄈㄨ)
the fine workmanship

水脈(ㄕㄨㄟˇ ㄇㄛˋ)or(ㄕㄨㄟˇ ㄇㄞˋ)
river channel; stream course

水墨畫(ㄕㄨㄟˇ ㄇㄛˋ ㄏㄨㄚˋ)
a painting done with ink and water to bring out different shades of darkness

水沫子(ㄕㄨㄟˇ ㄇㄛˋ ·ㄗ)
foam; froth

水門(ㄕㄨㄟˇ ㄇㄣˊ)
a floodgate; a water gate; a sluice

水門汀(ㄕㄨㄟˇ ㄇㄣˊ ㄊㄧㄥ)
cement 亦作「水泥」

水蜜桃(ㄕㄨㄟˇ ㄇㄧˋ ㄊㄠˊ)
a honey peach

水面(ㄕㄨㄟˇ ㄇㄧㄢˋ)
the water surface; the water level

水母(ㄕㄨㄟˇ ㄇㄨˇ)
Aurelia aurita, a jellyfish

水肥(ㄕㄨㄟˇ ㄈㄟˊ)
collected human body waste (used as fertilizer)

水分(ㄕㄨㄟˇ ㄈㄣˋ)
moisture; dampness; water content; humidity: 海上吹來的風通常含有水分。Winds from the sea are usually moist.

水夫(ㄕㄨㄟˇ ㄈㄨ)
a water bearer

水道(ㄕㄨㄟˇ ㄉㄠˋ)
① a watercourse; a waterway ②(by) water: 這回我想打水道去花蓮。This time I'll go to Hualien by water.

水稻(ㄕㄨㄟˇ ㄉㄠˋ)
aquatic rice (as opposed to hill rice)

水到渠成(ㄕㄨㄟˇ ㄉㄠˋ ㄑㄩˊ ㄔㄥˊ)
(literally) As water comes, it forms a channel automatically.—When conditions are ripe, success will come. 或 The thing takes care of itself.

水痘(ㄕㄨㄟˇ ㄉㄡˋ)
chicken pox; varicella

水滴(ㄕㄨㄟˇ ㄉㄧ)
water drops

水滴石穿(ㄕㄨㄟˇ ㄉㄧ ㄕˊ ㄔㄨㄢ)
(literally) Dripping water can wear through a stone. —Persistent effort can solve any problem. 或 Constant effort brings success.

水底(ㄕㄨㄟˇ ㄉㄧˇ)
at the bottom of water

水底電纜(ㄕㄨㄟˇ ㄉㄧˇ ㄉㄧㄢˋ ㄌㄢˇ)
cable (laid across oceans); submarine cable

水電(ㄕㄨㄟˇ ㄉㄧㄢˋ)
water and electricity

水電費(ㄕㄨㄟˇ ㄉㄧㄢˋ ㄈㄟˋ)
charges for water and electricity

水碓(ㄕㄨㄟˇ ㄉㄨㄟˋ)
a rice-polishing device using water power

水塔(ㄕㄨㄟˇ ㄊㄚˇ)
a water tower

水獺(ㄕㄨㄟˇ ㄊㄚˇ)
an otter (*Lutra lutra*)

水潭(ㄕㄨㄟˇ ㄊㄢˊ)
a pool; a pond

水塘(ㄕㄨㄟˇ ㄊㄤˊ)
a pool; a pond: 一隻青蛙跳入水塘中。A frog jumped into the pond.

水天一色(ㄕㄨㄟˇ ㄊㄧㄢ ㄧˊ ㄙㄜˋ)
The water and the sky merge in one color. 或 A vast expanse of blue water directly adjoins the blue sky.

水田(ㄕㄨㄟˇ ㄊㄧㄢˊ)
the paddy field; the rice field

水土(ㄕㄨㄟˇ ㄊㄨˇ)
① the natural environment ② soil and water

水土保持(ㄕㄨㄟˇ ㄊㄨˇ ㄅㄠˇ ㄔˊ)
soil conservation

水土不服(ㄕㄨㄟˇ ㄊㄨˇ ㄅㄨˋ ㄈㄨˊ)
one's system disagreeing with a new natural environment; to fail to acclimate oneself in a new natural environment

水桶(ㄕㄨㄟˇ ㄊㄨㄥˇ)
a bucket; a pail: 他們用水桶提水。They carried water in

〔水部〕

〔水部〕

buckets.

水泥(ㄕㄨㄟˇ ㄋㄧˊ)
cement: 水泥是由石灰石做的。Cement is made from limestone.

水泥攪拌機(ㄕㄨㄟˇ ㄋㄧˊ ㄐㄧㄠˇ ㄅㄢˋ ㄐㄧ)
a concrete mixer

水鳥(ㄕㄨㄟˇ ㄋㄧㄠˇ)
water birds; waterfowls; aquatic birds

水牛(ㄕㄨㄟˇ ㄋㄧㄡˊ)
a water buffalo: 這農夫有三隻水牛。The farmer has three water buffaloes.

水牛城(ㄕㄨㄟˇ ㄋㄧㄡˊ ㄔㄥˊ)
Buffalo, a port in West New York

水牛兒(ㄕㄨㄟˇ ㄋㄧㄡˊㄦ)
a snail

水來土掩(ㄕㄨㄟˇ ㄌㄞˊ ㄊㄨˇ ㄧㄢˇ)
to attempt to stop any onslaught

水雷(ㄕㄨㄟˇ ㄌㄟˊ)
a mine (against the ship): 水雷用以炸敵船。A mine is used to blow up enemy ships.

水雷艇(ㄕㄨㄟˇ ㄌㄟˊ ㄊㄧㄥˇ)
① a minelayer ② a torpedo boat

水漏(ㄕㄨㄟˇ ㄌㄡˋ)
a water clock; a clepsydra

水力(ㄕㄨㄟˇ ㄌㄧˋ)
hydraulic power; water power

水力發電(ㄕㄨㄟˇ ㄌㄧˋ ㄈㄚ ㄉㄧㄢˋ)
hydraulic power generation

水力發電廠(ㄕㄨㄟˇ ㄌㄧˋ ㄈㄚ ㄉㄧㄢˋ ㄔㄤˇ)
a hydraulic power plant

水力起重機(ㄕㄨㄟˇ ㄌㄧˋ ㄑㄧˇ ㄓㄨㄥˋ ㄐㄧ)
a hydraulic crane

水力學(ㄕㄨㄟˇ ㄌㄧˋ ㄒㄩㄝˊ)
hydraulics

水力昇降機(ㄕㄨㄟˇ ㄌㄧˋ ㄕㄥ ㄐㄧㄤˋ ㄐㄧ)
a hydraulic lift

水利(ㄕㄨㄟˇ ㄌㄧˋ)
water conservancy

水利工程(ㄕㄨㄟˇ ㄌㄧˋ ㄍㄨㄥ ㄔㄥˊ)or 水利工程學(ㄕㄨㄟˇ ㄌㄧˋ ㄍㄨㄥ ㄔㄥˊ ㄒㄩㄝˊ)
hydraulic engineering

水利局(ㄕㄨㄟˇ ㄌㄧˋ ㄐㄩˊ)
Water Conservancy Bureau

水利設施(ㄕㄨㄟˇ ㄌㄧˋ ㄕㄜˋ ㄕ)
water conservancy facilities

水療(ㄕㄨㄟˇ ㄌㄧㄠˊ)
hydrotherapy; hydropathic treatment

水流(ㄕㄨㄟˇ ㄌㄧㄡˊ)
water current; water flow: 他順著水流游泳。He swimmed with the current.

水簾(ㄕㄨㄟˇ ㄌㄧㄢˊ)
a waterfall; a cascade

水量(ㄕㄨㄟˇ ㄌㄧㄤˋ)
water volume; amount of water

水靈(ㄕㄨㄟˇ ·ㄌㄧㄥ)
①(said of fruit, vegetables, etc.) fresh and juicy ②(said of appearances) bright and beautiful; radiant and vivacious

水路(ㄕㄨㄟˇ ㄌㄨˋ)
① a waterway; a watercourse ②(by) water: 那批貨物是由水路運送的。The goods were shipped by water.

水路圖(ㄕㄨㄟˇ ㄌㄨˋ ㄊㄨˊ)
a hydrographic map

水陸(ㄕㄨㄟˇ ㄌㄨˋ)
land and water

水陸並進(ㄕㄨㄟˇ ㄌㄨˋ ㄅㄧㄥˋ ㄐㄧㄣˋ)
to send troops to a place by sea and over land simultaneously

水陸兩棲動物(ㄕㄨㄟˇ ㄌㄨˋ ㄌㄧㄤˇ ㄑㄧ ㄉㄨㄥˋ ㄨˋ)
an amphibian

水陸兩用(ㄕㄨㄟˇ ㄌㄨˋ ㄌㄧㄤˇ ㄩㄥˋ)
amphibious: 那是一輛水陸兩用坦克。It's an amphibious tank.

水淥淥的(ㄕㄨㄟˇ ㄌㄨˋ ㄌㄨˋ ·ㄉㄜ)
drenched; wet all over; dripping: 他一身水淥淥的。He is drenched to the skin.

水落石出(ㄕㄨㄟˇ ㄌㄨㄛˋ ㄕˊ ㄔㄨ)
(literally) Stones come into view with the drop of the water surface.—The truth comes into light eventually. 眞象一定會水落石出的。Doubts will clear up when facts are known.

水輪(ㄕㄨㄟˇ ㄌㄨㄣˊ)
a water wheel

水輪機(ㄕㄨㄟˇ ㄌㄨㄣˊ ㄐㄧ)
a machine powered by water wheels

水龍(ㄕㄨㄟˇ ㄌㄨㄥˊ)
① a fire engine ② a kind of water plant

水龍頭(ㄕㄨㄟˇ ㄌㄨㄥˊ ㄊㄡˊ)
a faucet; a cock; a tap: 請打開水龍頭。Please turn the tap on.

水綠(ㄕㄨㄟˇ ㄌㄩˋ)
light green

水閣(ㄕㄨㄟˇ ㄍㄜˊ)
a pavilion or tower by the water

水溝(ㄕㄨㄟˇ ㄍㄡ)
a ditch; a drain; a gutter

水缸(ㄕㄨㄟˇ ㄍㄤ)
a large pottery jug for holding water

水耕法(ㄕㄨㄟˇ ㄍㄥ ㄈㄚˇ)
hydroponics亦作「無土栽培法」

水國(ㄕㄨㄟˇ ㄍㄨㄛˊ)
a watery region

水果(ㄕㄨㄟˇ ㄍㄨㄛˇ)
fruit: 那些是多汁的水果。They are juicy fruits.

水鬼(ㄕㄨㄟˇ ㄍㄨㄟˇ)
① a water goblin ②(slang) a frogman

水管(ㄕㄨㄟˇ ㄍㄨㄢˇ)
a water pipe

水罐(ㄕㄨㄟˇ ㄍㄨㄢˋ)
a water pot; a canteen

水光(ㄕㄨㄟˇ ㄍㄨㄤ)
the light on the water

水坑(ㄕㄨㄟˇ ㄎㄥ)
a water hole; a pool: 汚水坑 a cesspit or cesspool

水庫(ㄕㄨㄟˇ ㄎㄨˋ)
a reservoir

水痕(ㄕㄨㄟˇ ㄏㄣˊ)
water stains; watermarks

水壺(ㄕㄨㄟˇ ㄏㄨˊ)
a canteen: 那是個軍人的水壺。That's a soldier's canteen.

水滸傳(ㄕㄨㄟˇ ㄏㄨˇ ㄓㄨㄢˋ)
All Men Are Brothers, a popular novel by Shih Nai-an (施耐庵)

水花(ㄕㄨㄟˇ ㄏㄨㄚ)
① foam; froth; spray: 瀑布的水花 the spray of a waterfall ② a flower blooming in water

水火(ㄕㄨㄟˇ ㄏㄨㄛˇ)
① water and fire — essen-

tials of life ② incompatible (things) ③disaster; miseries: 他們生活於水火之中。They live in untold miseries.

水火不相容(ㄕㄨㄟˇ ㄏㄨㄛˇ ㄅㄨˋ ㄒㄧㄤ ㄖㄨㄥˊ)
Water and fire cannot coexist. —(figuratively) incompatible; irreconcilable: 他們兩人水火不相容。Both of them are incompatible as fire and water.

水火無情(ㄕㄨㄟˇ ㄏㄨㄛˇ ㄨˊ ㄑㄧㄥˊ)
Water and fire are merciless. 或 Floods and fires have no mercy for anybody.

水患(ㄕㄨㄟˇ ㄏㄨㄢˋ)
floods; flood disaster: 豪雨在這城的低窪處造成水患。The rainstorm caused floods in the low-lying parts of the town.

水紅(ㄕㄨㄟˇ ㄏㄨㄥˊ)
pink

水解(ㄕㄨㄟˇ ㄐㄧㄝˇ)
hydrolysis

水脚(ㄕㄨㄟˇ ㄐㄧㄠˇ)
freight

水餃兒(ㄕㄨㄟˇ ㄐㄧㄠˇㄦ)
Chinese ravioli; boiled dumplings

水酒(ㄕㄨㄟˇ ㄐㄧㄡˇ)
diluted wine

水晶(ㄕㄨㄟˇ ㄐㄧㄥ)
crystal; crystallized quartz

水晶體(ㄕㄨㄟˇ ㄐㄧㄥ ㄊㄧˇ)
①(anatomy) the lens (of eyes) ② the crystalline lens

水晶宮(ㄕㄨㄟˇ ㄐㄧㄥ ㄍㄨㄥ)
the crystal palace, abode of the legendary Dragon King

水晶球(ㄕㄨㄟˇ ㄐㄧㄥ ㄑㄧㄡˊ)
a crystal ball

水晶石(ㄕㄨㄟˇ ㄐㄧㄥ ㄕˊ)
cryolite

水精鹽(ㄕㄨㄟˇ ㄐㄧㄥ ㄧㄢˊ)
natural salt

水井(ㄕㄨㄟˇ ㄐㄧㄥˇ)
a well: 這口水井乾涸了。The well is dry.

水居(ㄕㄨㄟˇ ㄐㄩ)
①(said of person) to make one's home on rivers, lakes, or waterways ② fishes and mollusks

水軍(ㄕㄨㄟˇ ㄐㄩㄣ)
(formerly) the navy; naval units

水汽(ㄕㄨㄟˇ ㄑㄧˋ)
water vapor; moisture; steam

水球(ㄕㄨㄟˇ ㄑㄧㄡˊ)
(sports) water polo

水鉛鑛(ㄕㄨㄟˇ ㄑㄧㄢ ㄎㄨㄤˋ)
wulfenite

水禽(ㄕㄨㄟˇ ㄑㄧㄣˊ)
aquatic birds; waterfowls

水芹(ㄕㄨㄟˇ ㄑㄧㄣˊ)
water celery

水槍(ㄕㄨㄟˇ ㄑㄧㄤ)
a squirt gun

水清無魚(ㄕㄨㄟˇ ㄑㄧㄥ ㄨˊ ㄩˊ)
(literally) There is no fish in clear water.—An overly pure-minded person has few friends.

水螅(ㄕㄨㄟˇ ㄒㄧ)
a polyp; a hydra

水系(ㄕㄨㄟˇ ㄒㄧˋ)
the river system; the hydrographic net

水下(ㄕㄨㄟˇ ㄒㄧㄚˋ)
under water; submerged: 潛艇潛入水下去了。The submarine submerged.

水蠍(ㄕㄨㄟˇ ㄒㄧㄝ)
a water scorpion

水榭(ㄕㄨㄟˇ ㄒㄧㄝˋ)
a pavilion or bower surrounded by water

水瀉(ㄕㄨㄟˇ ㄒㄧㄝˋ)
diarrhoea

水泄不通(ㄕㄨㄟˇ ㄒㄧㄝˋ ㄅㄨˋ ㄊㄨㄥ)
so crowded, or so carefully guarded, that it is impossible even for water to seep through: 此路擠得水泄不通。The road is so crowded as to be impassable.

水袖(ㄕㄨㄟˇ ㄒㄧㄡˋ)
the long white fabric sewed to the lower end of sleeves of robes worn in Chinese opera

水銹(ㄕㄨㄟˇ ㄒㄧㄡˋ)
① rust; watermarks ② scale; incrustation

水仙花(ㄕㄨㄟˇ ㄒㄧㄢ ㄏㄨㄚ)
a narcissus; a daffodil

水險(ㄕㄨㄟˇ ㄒㄧㄢˇ)
marine insurance

水鄉(ㄕㄨㄟˇ ㄒㄧㄤ)
a place near a lake, sea or river; swampy regions

水箱(ㄕㄨㄟˇ ㄒㄧㄤ)
a water tank

水星(ㄕㄨㄟˇ ㄒㄧㄥ)
the planet Mercury

水性(ㄕㄨㄟˇ ㄒㄧㄥˋ)
① an unpredictable temperament ② the water condition (of a river, etc., as affecting a swimmer): 他不習水性。He was an inexperienced swimmer.

水性楊花(ㄕㄨㄟˇ ㄒㄧㄥˋ ㄧㄤˊ ㄏㄨㄚ)
(said of women) fickle and lascivious

水質(ㄕㄨㄟˇ ㄓˋ)
properties of particular specimens of water

水蛭(ㄕㄨㄟˇ ㄓˋ)
a leech

水閘(ㄕㄨㄟˇ ㄓㄚˊ)
a floodgate; a water gate; a sluice; a lock (of a canal)

水柵(ㄕㄨㄟˇ ㄓㄚˋ)
a water barrier; a weir

水戰(ㄕㄨㄟˇ ㄓㄢˋ)
a naval warfare

水漲船高(ㄕㄨㄟˇ ㄓㄤˇ ㄔㄨㄢˊ ㄍㄠ)
(literally) When water rises, the boat rises with it.—① When the person one relies on rises in the world, one rises with him. ② When the production cost rises, the commodity price rises with it.

水脹(ㄕㄨㄟˇ ㄓㄤˋ)
(medicine) edema

水蒸氣(ㄕㄨㄟˇ ㄓㄥ ㄑㄧˋ)
water vapor; steam; vapor: 水蒸氣推動機器。Steam drives machinery.

水珠子(ㄕㄨㄟˇ ㄓㄨ ·ㄗ)
(colloquial) drops of water

水柱(ㄕㄨㄟˇ ㄓㄨˋ)
a water column

水準(ㄕㄨㄟˇ ㄓㄨㄣˇ)
a standard; a level

水準器(ㄕㄨㄟˇ ㄓㄨㄣˇ ㄑㄧˋ)
a level (an instrument)

水中撈月(ㄕㄨㄟˇ ㄓㄨㄥ ㄌㄠ ㄩㄝˋ)
(literally) to try to fish the moon out of water—to make obviously futile efforts

水腫(ㄕㄨㄟˇ ㄓㄨㄥˇ)
dropsy; hydrophilic swelling

水池(ㄕㄨㄟˇ ㄔˊ)or 水池子(ㄕㄨㄟˇ ㄔˊ ˙ㄗ)
a pool; a pond; a water tank: 他在野外跌入水池中。He fell into the pool in the field.

水車(ㄕㄨㄟˇ ㄔㄜ)
① a water wheel ② a water cart; a water wagon

水產(ㄕㄨㄟˇ ㄔㄢˇ)
marine products

水產學(ㄕㄨㄟˇ ㄔㄢˇ ㄒㄩㄝˊ)
fishery science

水產學校(ㄕㄨㄟˇ ㄔㄢˇ ㄒㄩㄝˊ ㄒㄧㄠˋ)
the school for training of fishery workers

水產資源(ㄕㄨㄟˇ ㄔㄢˇ ㄗ ㄩㄢˊ)
aquatic resources

水產業(ㄕㄨㄟˇ ㄔㄢˇ ㄧㄝˋ)
fishery; fishing industry

水廠(ㄕㄨㄟˇ ㄔㄤˇ)
waterworks

水程(ㄕㄨㄟˇ ㄔㄥˊ)
sea voyage; voyage by water

水成岩(ㄕㄨㄟˇ ㄔㄥˊ ㄧㄢˊ)
sedimentary rock; aqueous rock

水師(ㄕㄨㄟˇ ㄕ)
①(formerly) the navy; naval units ② a sailor; a boatman

水蝕(ㄕㄨㄟˇ ㄕˊ)
water erosion

水勢(ㄕㄨㄟˇ ㄕˋ)
① the flow of the water ② the direction of flowing water

水蛇(ㄕㄨㄟˇ ㄕㄜˊ)
a water snake; an aquatic snake

水蛇腰(ㄕㄨㄟˇ ㄕㄜˊ ㄧㄠ)
an extremely slender waist

水手(ㄕㄨㄟˇ ㄕㄡˇ)
a sailor; a mariner

水深(ㄕㄨㄟˇ ㄕㄣ)
the depth of water

水深火熱(ㄕㄨㄟˇ ㄕㄣ ㄏㄨㄛˇ ㄖㄜˋ)
an abyss of suffering; misery caused by government oppression: 他們過去生活在水深火熱之中。They lived in an abyss of misery in the past.

水上芭蕾舞(ㄕㄨㄟˇ ㄕㄤˋ ㄅㄚ ㄌㄟˇ ㄨˇ)
water ballet; synchronized swimming

水上飛機(ㄕㄨㄟˇ ㄕㄤˋ ㄈㄟ ㄐㄧ)
a seaplane; a hydroplane

水上警察(ㄕㄨㄟˇ ㄕㄤˋ ㄐㄧㄥˇ ㄔㄚˊ) or 水警(ㄕㄨㄟˇ ㄐㄧㄥˇ)
the water police; the marine police

水上人家(ㄕㄨㄟˇ ㄕㄤˋ ㄖㄣˊ ㄐㄧㄚ)
boat dwellers

水上運動(ㄕㄨㄟˇ ㄕㄤˋ ㄩㄣˋ ㄉㄨㄥˋ)
water sports; aquatic sports

水生植物(ㄕㄨㄟˇ ㄕㄥ ㄓˊ ㄨˋ)
the aquatic plants

水栓(ㄕㄨㄟˇ ㄕㄨㄢ)
a hydrant

水乳交融(ㄕㄨㄟˇ ㄖㄨˇ ㄐㄧㄠ ㄖㄨㄥˊ)
in harmony like water and milk

水溶性(ㄕㄨㄟˇ ㄖㄨㄥˊ ㄒㄧㄥˋ)
water soluble; solubility

水漬(ㄕㄨㄟˇ ㄗˋ)
① to drench ② water stains; watermarks

水漬貨(ㄕㄨㄟˇ ㄗˋ ㄏㄨㄛˋ)
goods with water stains; water damaged commodities

水災(ㄕㄨㄟˇ ㄗㄞ)
flood disaster; floods: 在水災地區建立臨時流動餐館。Canteens were set up in the flooded areas.

水藻(ㄕㄨㄟˇ ㄗㄠˇ)
algae

水葬(ㄕㄨㄟˇ ㄗㄤˋ)
burial at sea; burial in the sea

水族(ㄕㄨㄟˇ ㄗㄨˊ)
aquatic animals

水族館(ㄕㄨㄟˇ ㄗㄨˊ ㄍㄨㄢˇ)
an aquarium

水鑽(ㄕㄨㄟˇ ㄗㄨㄢˋ)
① a hydraulic drill ② a diamond

水彩(ㄕㄨㄟˇ ㄘㄞˇ)
watercolor

水彩畫(ㄕㄨㄟˇ ㄘㄞˇ ㄏㄨㄚˋ)
a watercolor painting; a watercolor

水彩畫家(ㄕㄨㄟˇ ㄘㄞˇ ㄏㄨㄚˋ ㄐㄧㄚ)
a watercolorist

水槽(ㄕㄨㄟˇ ㄘㄠˊ)
a water trough; a water tank

水草(ㄕㄨㄟˇ ㄘㄠˇ)
① waterweeds; water plants ② water and grass

水葱(ㄕㄨㄟˇ ㄘㄨㄥ)
a water onion

水葱兒似的(ㄕㄨㄟˇ ㄘㄨㄥㄦ ㄙˋ ˙ㄉㄜ)
(said of girls) bright and beautiful

水速(ㄕㄨㄟˇ ㄙㄨˋ)
the speed of a water current

水速表(ㄕㄨㄟˇ ㄙㄨˋ ㄅㄧㄠˇ)
a tachometer

水鴨(ㄕㄨㄟˇ ㄧㄚ)
a teal

水鴨子(ㄕㄨㄟˇ ㄧㄚ ˙ㄗ)
(slang) a small naval craft for beach operations

水壓(ㄕㄨㄟˇ ㄧㄚ)
water pressure

水壓機(ㄕㄨㄟˇ ㄧㄚ ㄐㄧ)
a hydraulic press

水舀子(ㄕㄨㄟˇ ㄧㄠˇ ˙ㄗ)
a dipper; a ladle

水曜日(ㄕㄨㄟˇ ㄧㄠˋ ㄖˋ)
Wednesday

水煙(ㄕㄨㄟˇ ㄧㄢ)
tobacco for the hookah

水煙袋(ㄕㄨㄟˇ ㄧㄢ ㄉㄞˋ)
a hookah; a hubble-bubble

水銀(ㄕㄨㄟˇ ㄧㄣˊ)
mercury (an element)

水銀燈(ㄕㄨㄟˇ ㄧㄣˊ ㄉㄥ)
a mercury lamp

水銀柱(ㄕㄨㄟˇ ㄧㄣˊ ㄓㄨˋ)
a mercury column

水印(ㄕㄨㄟˇ ㄧㄣˋ)
the seal or chop of a business firm

水污染(ㄕㄨㄟˇ ㄨ ㄖㄢˇ)
water pollution

水位(ㄕㄨㄟˇ ㄨㄟˋ)
the water stage; the water level; the watermark

水文(ㄕㄨㄟˇ ㄨㄣˊ)or 水文學(ㄕㄨㄟˇ ㄨㄣˊ ㄒㄩㄝˊ)
hydrology

水汪汪的(ㄕㄨㄟˇ ㄨㄤ ㄨㄤ ˙ㄉㄜ)
(said of women's eyes) bright and attractive

水芋(ㄕㄨㄟˇ ㄩˋ)
a calla (or calla lily)

水域(ㄕㄨㄟˇ ㄩˋ)
waters; a water area: 熱帶水域 a tropical water area

水源(ㄕㄨㄟˇ ㄩㄢˊ)
① the riverhead; the waterhead; headwaters ② a source of water: 他們正在尋找新水源。They were seeking new sources of water.

水運(ㄕㄨㄟˇ ㄩㄣˋ)
transportation by water

〔水部〕

一畫

【永】2762 ㄩㄥˇ yeong yǒng
long in time; everlasting; eternal; permanent
永保太平(ㄩㄥˇ ㄅㄠˇ ㄊㄞˋ ㄆㄧㄥˊ)
to remain peaceful for all time
永保青春(ㄩㄥˇ ㄅㄠˇ ㄑㄧㄥ ㄔㄨㄣ)
to remain youthful forever
永別(ㄩㄥˇ ㄅㄧㄝˊ)
to part for good; to die
永不(ㄩㄥˇ ㄅㄨˋ)
will never: 他永不改變心意。He will never change his mind.
永不分離(ㄩㄥˇ ㄅㄨˋ ㄈㄣ ㄌㄧˊ)
never to be separated
永不敍用(ㄩㄥˇ ㄅㄨˋ ㄒㄩˋ ㄩㄥˋ)
(said of a disgraced official) never to be employed again
永命(ㄩㄥˇ ㄇㄧㄥˋ)
a long life; longevity
永斷葛藤(ㄩㄥˇ ㄉㄨㄢˋ ㄍㄜˊ ㄊㄥˊ)
to sever relations forever
永年(ㄩㄥˇ ㄋㄧㄢˊ)
a long life; longevity
永樂大典(ㄩㄥˇ ㄌㄜˋ ㄉㄚˋ ㄉㄧㄢˇ)
Encyclopedia Sinica, a 22,877-volume collection of books compiled by order of Emperor Cheng Tsu of the Ming Dynasty (明成祖)
永古(ㄩㄥˇ ㄍㄨˇ)
time immemorial
永固(ㄩㄥˇ ㄍㄨˋ)
to remain secure forever
永恒(ㄩㄥˇ ㄏㄥˊ)
eternity; eternal; perpetual; everlasting
永久(ㄩㄥˇ ㄐㄧㄡˇ)
permanent; perpetual; eternal; lasting; everlasting; unending; endless
永久地址(ㄩㄥˇ ㄐㄧㄡˇ ㄉㄧˋ ㄓˇ)
a permanent address
永久和平(ㄩㄥˇ ㄐㄧㄡˇ ㄏㄜˊ ㄆㄧㄥˊ)
everlasting peace; permanent peace
永久中立國(ㄩㄥˇ ㄐㄧㄡˇ ㄓㄨㄥ ㄌㄧˋ ㄍㄨㄛˊ)
a permanent neutral power
永久齒(ㄩㄥˇ ㄐㄧㄡˇ ㄔˇ)
permanent teeth
永久組織(ㄩㄥˇ ㄐㄧㄡˇ ㄗㄨˇ ㄓ)
a permanent organization
永訣(ㄩㄥˇ ㄐㄩㄝˊ)
to be gone forever—to die
永享(ㄩㄥˇ ㄒㄧㄤˇ)
to enjoy forever
永誌不忘(ㄩㄥˇ ㄓˋ ㄅㄨˋ ㄨㄤˋ)
to bear in mind forever; to remember forever
永晝(ㄩㄥˇ ㄓㄡˋ)
a long day
永垂不朽(ㄩㄥˇ ㄔㄨㄟˊ ㄅㄨˋ ㄒㄧㄡˇ)
to be remembered forever by posterity; immortal (fame, accomplishment, etc.): 他已獲得永垂不朽的聲名。He has achieved immortality.
永世(ㄩㄥˇ ㄕˋ)
① forever; eternity: 我對那事永世難忘。I will never forget it for my life. ② the whole lifetime
永逝(ㄩㄥˇ ㄕˋ)
to be gone forever—to die
永生(ㄩㄥˇ ㄕㄥ)
① for ever: 我將永生永世愛她。I shall love her for ever and ever. ② eternal life: 基督教許諾永生嗎? Does the Christian religion promise eternal life?
永日(ㄩㄥˇ ㄖˋ)
a long day; all the day
永字八法(ㄩㄥˇ ㄗˋ ㄅㄚ ㄈㄚˇ)
the eight representative strokes as contained in the character 永 (側, 勒, 努, 趯, 策, 掠, 啄, 磔)
永存(ㄩㄥˇ ㄘㄨㄣˊ)
to remain forever; to live for ever and ever
永逸(ㄩㄥˇ ㄧˋ)
to be at ease and free from trouble forever: 一勞永逸 to do all that is required so that one never has to do it again
永夜(ㄩㄥˇ ㄧㄝˋ)
a long night
永言(ㄩㄥˇ ㄧㄢˊ)
to be remembered forever
永無寧日(ㄩㄥˇ ㄨˊ ㄋㄧㄥˊ ㄖˋ)
Never will there be days of peace.
永遠(ㄩㄥˇ ㄩㄢˇ)
forever; eternally; perpetually: 他永遠離開了。He went away forever.

二畫

【汆】2763 1. ㄊㄨㄣˇ toen tǔn
the action of water moving or pushing an object
【汆】2763 2. ㄘㄨㄢ tsuan cuān
(cooking) to boil (food)
汆湯(ㄘㄨㄢ ㄊㄤ)
to prepare a soup
汆子(ㄘㄨㄢ ˙ㄗ)or 汆兒(ㄘㄨㄚㄦ)
a kind of metal kettle
【氾】2764 ㄈㄢˋ fann fàn
1. to spread; to fill everywhere
2. extensive; vast; boundless
3. floating
氾博(ㄈㄢˋ ㄅㄛˊ)
vast; broad; extensive; immense
氾氾(ㄈㄢˋ ㄈㄢˋ)
afloat
氾濫(ㄈㄢˋ ㄌㄢˋ)
① to overflow; in flood: 湖水氾濫。The lake overflowed. ② to spread far and wide
氾論(ㄈㄢˋ ㄌㄨㄣˋ)
general discussion
【汁】2765 ㄓ jy zhī
juice; the natural fluid; sap
汁水兒(ㄓ ㄕㄨㄜˇㄦ)or 汁兒(ㄓㄜㄦ)
juice; fluid; sap: 這種水果汁水兒很多。This fruit is juicy.
汁液(ㄓ ㄧㄝˋ)
juice; sap
【汀】2766 ㄊㄧㄥ ting tīng
1. a low, level land along a river; beach
2. a shoal
汀曲(ㄊㄧㄥ ㄑㄩ)
a bend in a stream
汀洲(ㄊㄧㄥ ㄓㄡ)
an islet in a stream; a shoal
汀渚(ㄊㄧㄥ ㄓㄨˇ)
an islet in a stream; a shoal
【求】2767 ㄑㄧㄡˊ chyou qiú
1. to solicit; to ask for; to pray for; to beg: 求您幫個忙, 好嗎? May I ask you a favor?
2. demand: 供不應求。The sup-

〔水部〕

ply falls short of the demand.
3. to seek: 大多數人尋求財富，每個人都追求幸福。Most men seek wealth; all men seek happiness.
4. to covet; to desire

求備(ㄑㄧㄡˊ ㄅㄟˋ)
to seek completeness

求名求利(ㄑㄧㄡˊ ㄇㄧㄥˊ ㄑㄧㄡˊ ㄌㄧˋ)
to seek fame and wealth

求福免禍(ㄑㄧㄡˊ ㄈㄨˊ ㄇㄧㄢˇ ㄏㄨㄛˋ)
to seek happiness and avoid calamity

求代(ㄑㄧㄡˊ ㄉㄞˋ)
to seek a substitute to do a duty

求貸(ㄑㄧㄡˊ ㄉㄞˋ)
to ask for loan

求田問舍(ㄑㄧㄡˊ ㄊㄧㄢˊ ㄨㄣˋ ㄕㄜˋ)
interested exclusively in the acquisition of one's estate—not interested in more ambitious things

求告(ㄑㄧㄡˊ ㄍㄠˋ)
to implore; to beseech; to entreat; to supplicate

求過於供(ㄑㄧㄡˊ ㄍㄨㄛˋ ㄩˊ ㄍㄨㄥ)
The demand exceeds the supply.

求和(ㄑㄧㄡˊ ㄏㄜˊ)or 求成(ㄑㄧㄡˊ ㄔㄥˊ)
to seek peace with an enemy; to try to end hostilities

求化(ㄑㄧㄡˊ ㄏㄨㄚˋ)
(said of Buddhist monks) to beg for alms: 僧侶們沿街求化。The monks beg for alms from street to street.

求歡(ㄑㄧㄡˊ ㄏㄨㄢ)
to seek the consent of a woman for a sexual intercourse

求婚(ㄑㄧㄡˊ ㄏㄨㄣ)or 求親(ㄑㄧㄡˊ ㄑㄧㄣ)
to propose (to a woman): 他已下定決心要向她求婚。He has made up his mind to propose marriage to her.

求凰(ㄑㄧㄡˊ ㄏㄨㄤˊ)
to seek a wife

求解(ㄑㄧㄡˊ ㄐㄧㄝˇ)
① to seek help in distress ② to seek the solution to a mathematical problem

求教(ㄑㄧㄡˊ ㄐㄧㄠˋ)
to seek instruction; to seek advice: 向他求教。Ask him for advice.

求救(ㄑㄧㄡˊ ㄐㄧㄡˋ)
to seek relief; to ask for rescue: 他們發出求救信號。They signaled for help.或 They signaled an SOS.

求見(ㄑㄧㄡˊ ㄐㄧㄢˋ)
to seek an interview

求漿得酒(ㄑㄧㄡˊ ㄐㄧㄤ ㄉㄜˊ ㄐㄧㄡˇ)
to get more than one has asked for

求乞(ㄑㄧㄡˊ ㄑㄧˇ)
to beg for food or money: 他沿門求乞。He begs his bread from door to door.

求籤(ㄑㄧㄡˊ ㄑㄧㄢ)
to seek divine guidance by drawing lots

求親(ㄑㄧㄡˊ ㄑㄧㄣ)
① to seek a marriage alliance ② to ask for help from relatives

求親告友(ㄑㄧㄡˊ ㄑㄧㄣ ㄍㄠˋ ㄧㄡˇ)
to ask favors of relatives and friends

求情(ㄑㄧㄡˊ ㄑㄧㄥˊ)
① to ask for mercy or leniency; to intercede; to plead ② to ask for a favor

求全(ㄑㄧㄡˊ ㄑㄩㄢˊ)
① to seek a satisfactory result; to demand perfection: 萬事莫求全。Don't ask for perfection. ② to try to preserve oneself

求全之毀(ㄑㄧㄡˊ ㄑㄩㄢˊ ㄓ ㄏㄨㄟˇ)
to try to be perfect only to receive reproaches

求全責備(ㄑㄧㄡˊ ㄑㄩㄢˊ ㄗㄜˊ ㄅㄟˋ)
to criticize so that everything will become perfect; to demand perfection: 他事事求全責備。He demands perfection in everything.

求仙(ㄑㄧㄡˊ ㄒㄧㄢ)
to seek an immortal (usually in mountains)

求賢若渴(ㄑㄧㄡˊ ㄒㄧㄢˊ ㄖㄨㄛˋ ㄎㄜˇ)
to seek talent with eagerness

求心力(ㄑㄧㄡˊ ㄒㄧㄣ ㄌㄧˋ)
centripetal force

求學(ㄑㄧㄡˊ ㄒㄩㄝˊ)
to receive education; to study

求知(ㄑㄧㄡˊ ㄓ)
to seek knowledge

求知慾(ㄑㄧㄡˊ ㄓ ㄩˋ)
a thirst (or craving) for knowledge

求之不得(ㄑㄧㄡˊ ㄓ ㄅㄨˋ ㄉㄜˊ)
to be exactly what has been sought eagerly; most welcome: 這是求之不得的好機會。This is a most welcome opportunity.

求職(ㄑㄧㄡˊ ㄓˊ)
positions wanted

求證(ㄑㄧㄡˊ ㄓㄥˋ)
to seek verification or confirmation

求助(ㄑㄧㄡˊ ㄓㄨˋ)
to resort to; to seek help; to seek aid

求成(ㄑㄧㄡˊ ㄔㄥˊ)
① to hope for success: 他急於求成。He is impatient for success. ② to seek peace with an enemy 參看「求和」

求神問卜(ㄑㄧㄡˊ ㄕㄣˊ ㄨㄣˋ ㄅㄨˇ)
to seek divine advice

求生(ㄑㄧㄡˊ ㄕㄥ)
to seek to survive; to try to remain alive

求勝(ㄑㄧㄡˊ ㄕㄥˋ)
to strive for victory: 他們求勝心切。They strove to gain victory.

求饒(ㄑㄧㄡˊ ㄖㄠˊ)
to ask for forgiveness; to seek pardon; to beg for mercy

求人(ㄑㄧㄡˊ ㄖㄣˊ)
① to ask for help ② to look for talents

求人不如求己(ㄑㄧㄡˊ ㄖㄣˊ ㄅㄨˋ ㄖㄨˊ ㄑㄧㄡˊ ㄐㄧˇ)
Relying upon oneself is better than relying upon others.

求仁得仁(ㄑㄧㄡˊ ㄖㄣˊ ㄉㄜˊ ㄖㄣˊ)
to seek for virtue and get virtue — to want something and succeed in getting it

求容(ㄑㄧㄡˊ ㄖㄨㄥˊ)
to seek room or space for oneself

求子(ㄑㄧㄡˊ ㄗˇ)
(said of a childless couple) to pray for a son

求才(ㄑㄧㄡˊ ㄘㄞˊ)
positions vacant

求愛(ㄑㄧㄡˊ ㄞˋ)
to woo; to court

求偶(ㄑㄧㄡˊ ㄡˇ)
to seek a spouse
求雨(ㄑㄧㄡˊ ㄩˇ)
to pray for rain
求援(ㄑㄧㄡˊ ㄩㄢˊ)
to seek relief; to ask for help

三畫

【汊】 2768 ㄔㄚˋ chah chà
a branching stream
汊流(ㄔㄚˋ ㄌㄧㄡˊ)
a tributary of a river or current
汊港(ㄔㄚˋ ㄍㄤˇ)
a branching point of a stream

【汎】 2769 ㄈㄢˋ fann fàn
1. afloat; to float
2. extensive; widespread

汎美航空公司(ㄈㄢˋ ㄇㄟˇ ㄏㄤˊ ㄎㄨㄥ ㄍㄨㄥ ㄙ)
Pan American World Airways
汎美洲主義(ㄈㄢˋ ㄇㄟˇ ㄓㄡ ㄓㄨˇ ㄧˋ)
Pan-Americanism
汎汎(ㄈㄢˋ ㄈㄢˋ)
going downstream smoothly
汎濫(ㄈㄢˋ ㄌㄢˋ)
to overflow; to spread; to flood; to inundate
汎理論(ㄈㄢˋ ㄌㄧˇ ㄌㄨㄣˋ)
panlogism
汎論(ㄈㄢˋ ㄌㄨㄣˋ)
general discussion
汎心論(ㄈㄢˋ ㄒㄧㄣ ㄌㄨㄣˋ)
panpsychism
汎舟(ㄈㄢˋ ㄓㄡ)
to row a boat; boating: 他喜歡汎舟和游泳。He enjoys boating and swimming.
汎稱(ㄈㄢˋ ㄔㄥ)
a collective name; generally called
汎愛(ㄈㄢˋ ㄞˋ)
philanthropy; to overflow in love to all

【汕】 2770 ㄕㄢˋ shann shàn
a basket for catching fish
汕頭(ㄕㄢˋ ㄊㄡˊ)
Swatow, a city in Kwangtung Province

【汐】 2771 ㄒㄧˋ shih xì
the flow of the tide at night

【汗】 2772 1. ㄏㄢˋ hann hàn
sweat; perspiration
汗斑(ㄏㄢˋ ㄅㄢ)
dark spots on the skin supposed to be caused by obstructed perspiration
汗馬功勞(ㄏㄢˋ ㄇㄚˇ ㄍㄨㄥ ㄌㄠˊ)
distinguished services in war
汗毛(ㄏㄢˋ ㄇㄠˊ)
down; the soft, fine hair on the human body
汗毛孔(ㄏㄢˋ ㄇㄠˊ ㄎㄨㄥˇ)
pores in the skin
汗漫(ㄏㄢˋ ㄇㄢˋ)
① a wide expanse of water ② large but empty ③ unconventional and uninhibited
汗牛充棟(ㄏㄢˋ ㄋㄧㄡˊ ㄔㄨㄥ ㄉㄨㄥˋ)
(said of books, particularly those dealing with the same subject) numerous; overabundant; truckload of
汗流滿面(ㄏㄢˋ ㄌㄧㄡˊ ㄇㄢˇ ㄇㄧㄢˋ)
to perspire all over one's face
汗流浹背(ㄏㄢˋ ㄌㄧㄡˊ ㄐㄧㄚˊ ㄅㄟˋ)
to perspire all over (because of fear of punishment); bathed in sweat; soaked with sweat (from fear or physical exertion): 他全身汗流浹背。He was bathed in sweat.
汗垢(ㄏㄢˋ ㄍㄡˋ)
sweat mixed with dirt
汗脚(ㄏㄢˋ ㄐㄧㄠˇ)
feet that tend to perspire
汗巾(ㄏㄢˋ ㄐㄧㄣ)
a girdle; a sash
汗青(ㄏㄢˋ ㄑㄧㄥ)
(literally) to sweat bamboo pieces by heat for use in writing—① to put something in writing ② history
汗腺(ㄏㄢˋ ㄒㄧㄢˋ)
a sweat gland
汗疹(ㄏㄢˋ ㄓㄣˇ)
sudamina
汗珠子(ㄏㄢˋ ㄓㄨ ˙ㄗ)
beads of perspiration
汗手(ㄏㄢˋ ㄕㄡˇ)
hands wet with perspiration
汗衫(ㄏㄢˋ ㄕㄢ)
a T-shirt
汗如雨下(ㄏㄢˋ ㄖㄨˊ ㄩˇ ㄒㄧㄚˋ)
to sweat profusely
汗液(ㄏㄢˋ ㄧㄝˋ)
perspiration; sweat: 胖人流很多汗液。Fat persons perspire heavily.
汗顏(ㄏㄢˋ ㄧㄢˊ)
to perspire from embarrassment or shame

【汗】 2772 2. ㄏㄢˊ harn hán
as in 可汗—a khan

【池】 2773 ㄔˊ chyr chí
1. a pond; a pool; a moat: 我們學校有一游泳池。Our school has a swimming pool.
2. an enclosed space with raised sides: 舞池 a dance floor
3. a Chinese family name

池塘(ㄔˊ ㄊㄤˊ)
a pond: 綠色的浮渣漂在池塘上面。Green scum floated on the top of the pond.
池隍(ㄔˊ ㄏㄨㄤˊ)
a moat
池榭(ㄔˊ ㄒㄧㄝˋ)
a bower or pavilion on a pond
池心(ㄔˊ ㄒㄧㄣ)
the middle or center of a pond
池沼(ㄔˊ ㄓㄠˇ)
ponds and swamps
池中物(ㄔˊ ㄓㄨㄥ ㄨˋ)
(literally) common stuff that can be found in a pond—a mediocre person
池水(ㄔˊ ㄕㄨㄟˇ)
pond water
池子(ㄔˊ ˙ㄗ)
① a pond ② orchestra stalls in a theater
池鹽(ㄔˊ ㄧㄢˊ)
lake salt
池魚(ㄔˊ ㄩˊ)
the fish in the moat—According to the folktale, when the gate of a city in the State of Sung was on fire, people drew water from the moat to put out the fire. Therefore, the moat was soon dried and the fish in the moat died.

池魚之殃(ㄔˊ ㄩˊ ㄓ ㄧㄤ)
disasters suffered by outsiders or innocent people; disasters brought on by others 參看「池魚」

【汜】 2774 ㄙˋ syh sì
a stream that branches and afterwards merges again

【汝】 2775 ㄖㄨˇ ruu rǔ
you; thou; thee; thy: 汝意為何? What do you aim at?

汝輩(ㄖㄨˇ ㄅㄟˋ)or 汝曹(ㄖㄨˇ ㄘㄠˊ)or 汝等(ㄖㄨˇ ㄉㄥˇ)
(plural) ye (used in addressing inferiors); you: 汝曹好學。You all are fond of studying.

汝窯(ㄖㄨˇ ㄧㄠˊ)
name of a famous porcelain kiln in the Sung Dynasty at Juchou (汝州), in Honan

【江】 2776 ㄐㄧㄤ jiang jiāng
1. a large river
2. the Yangtze River
3. a Chinese family name

江北(ㄐㄧㄤ ㄅㄟˇ)
the area north of the Yangtze River (particularly referring to northern Kiangsu)

江表(ㄐㄧㄤ ㄅㄧㄠˇ)
the area south of the Yangtze River

江畔(ㄐㄧㄤ ㄆㄢˋ)
the river bank; beside the river

江防(ㄐㄧㄤ ㄈㄤˊ)
① river control works for the Yangtze River ② defense works along the Yangtze River

江東(ㄐㄧㄤ ㄉㄨㄥ)
the Kiangsu area; the lower reaches of the Yangtze River

江南(ㄐㄧㄤ ㄋㄢˊ)
the entire area south of the Yangtze River (particularly referring to southern Kiangsu)

江郎才盡(ㄐㄧㄤ ㄌㄤˊ ㄘㄞˊ ㄐㄧㄣˋ)
to have used up one's literary talent or energy—the reference is about Chiang Yen(江淹)

江輪(ㄐㄧㄤ ㄌㄨㄣˊ)
a river steamship

江河行地(ㄐㄧㄤ ㄏㄜˊ ㄒㄧㄥˊ ㄉㄧˋ)
unalterable (like rivers flowing through on the surface of the earth)

江河日下(ㄐㄧㄤ ㄏㄜˊ ㄖˋ ㄒㄧㄚˋ)
to decline steadily (as river water flows downstream); to go from bad to worse

江湖(ㄐㄧㄤ ㄏㄨˊ)
① rivers and lakes ② wandering; vagrant; vagabond: 他曾流落江湖。He once lived a vagabond life. ③ sophisticated and shrewd ④ practicing quackery; a quack

江湖客(ㄐㄧㄤ ㄏㄨˊ ㄎㄜˋ)
an itinerant

江湖氣(ㄐㄧㄤ ㄏㄨˊ ㄑㄧˋ)
insincere; sly; sleekly

江淮(ㄐㄧㄤ ㄏㄨㄞˊ)
① the Yangtze River and the Huai River (淮河) ② Kiangsu and Anhwei provinces

江西(ㄐㄧㄤ ㄒㄧ)
Kiangsi Province

江心(ㄐㄧㄤ ㄒㄧㄣ)
the middle of a river (as opposed to portions near the banks)

江心補漏(ㄐㄧㄤ ㄒㄧㄣ ㄅㄨˇ ㄌㄡˋ)
(literally) to mend a leak in midstream—to try to prevent a disaster when it is too late

江浙(ㄐㄧㄤ ㄓㄜˋ)
Kiangsu (江蘇) and Chekiang (浙江)

江浙菜(ㄐㄧㄤ ㄓㄜˋ ㄘㄞˋ)
cuisine of the Kiangsu-Chekiang area

江山(ㄐㄧㄤ ㄕㄢ)
the mountains and rivers of a country—the land; the throne; the national territory or authority over it: 那君王已失江山。That King has lost his political power.

江山美人(ㄐㄧㄤ ㄕㄢ ㄇㄟˇ ㄖㄣˊ)
the throne and the beauty

江山易改，本性難移(ㄐㄧㄤ ㄕㄢ ㄧˋ ㄍㄞˇ, ㄅㄣˇ ㄒㄧㄥˋ ㄋㄢˊ ㄧˊ)
Changing one's nature is harder than changing mountains and rivers. 或 A fox may grow gray, but never good. 或 A leopard never changes his spots.

江水(ㄐㄧㄤ ㄕㄨㄟˇ)
river water

江左(ㄐㄧㄤ ㄗㄨㄛˇ)
the Kiangsu area

江蘇(ㄐㄧㄤ ㄙㄨ)
Kiangsu Province

江瑤柱(ㄐㄧㄤ ㄧㄠˊ ㄓㄨˋ)
a scallop

江右(ㄐㄧㄤ ㄧㄡˋ)
the Kiangsi area

江淹(ㄐㄧㄤ ㄧㄢ)
Chiang Yen(444-505), famous for his achievement in literature, but his talent exhausted in old age

江洋大盜(ㄐㄧㄤ ㄧㄤˊ ㄉㄚˋ ㄉㄠˋ)
a notorious bandit leader

江月(ㄐㄧㄤ ㄩㄝˋ)
the moon's reflection on a river

【汛】 2777 ㄒㄩㄣˋ shiunn xùn
1. to sprinkle
2. abundant water; a flood
3. menses; menstruation

汛期(ㄒㄩㄣˋ ㄑㄧˊ)
(irrigation) the flood season

【汞】 2778 ㄍㄨㄥˇ goong gǒng (又讀 ㄏㄨㄥˋ honq hòng)
mercury (an element)

汞粉(ㄍㄨㄥˇ ㄈㄣˇ)
calomel

汞膏(ㄍㄨㄥˇ ㄍㄠ)
amalgam 亦作「貢齊」

汞化物(ㄍㄨㄥˇ ㄏㄨㄚˋ ㄨˋ)
mercuride

汞養 or 汞氧(ㄍㄨㄥˇ ㄧㄤˇ)
oxide of mercury

【汚】 2779 (汙、污) ㄨ u wū
1. dirty; filthy
2. to stain; to mar; to insult; to slander: 殘酷玷汚了他的品性。His character was stained by cruelty.
3. corrupt: 汚吏接受了該賄款。The corrupt official accepted the money.

汚衊(ㄨ ㄇㄧㄝˋ)
to libel; to slander

汚名(ㄨ ㄇㄧㄥˊ)
infamy; dishonor

汚點(ㄨ ㄉㄧㄢˇ)

a blot; a stain; a smear; a flaw; a defect: 他的品性是沒有汚點的。His character is without a stain.

汚泥(ㄨ ㄋㄧˊ)
mud: 他的上衣染有汚泥。He has mud stains on his coat.

汚吏(ㄨ ㄌㄧˋ)
a corrupt official

汚垢(ㄨ ㄍㄡˋ)
dirt; filth: 我怎樣除去牆上的汚垢呢? How can I get the dirt off the walls?

汚穢(ㄨ ㄏㄨㄟˋ)
dirty; filthy: 那是條汚穢的街道。That's a filthy street.

汚穢不堪(ㄨ ㄏㄨㄟˋ ㄅㄨˋ ㄎㄢ)
intolerably dirty or filthy

汚跡(ㄨ ㄐㄧ)
stains; smears; smudges

汚臭(ㄨ ㄒㄧㄡˋ)
a foul odor

汚濁(ㄨ ㄓㄨㄛˊ)
muddy; dirty; foul; filthy: 那是條汚濁的溪流。It is a muddy stream.

汚水(ㄨ ㄕㄨㄟˇ)
sewage; filthy water

汚水處理(ㄨ ㄕㄨㄟˇ ㄔㄨˇ ㄌㄧˇ)
sewage disposal; sewage treatment

汚染(ㄨ ㄖㄢˇ)
to stain; to contaminate; to pollute; contamination; pollution: 我們應謹愼避免供水的汚染。We must be careful to avoid contamination of our water supply.

汚辱(ㄨ ㄖㄨˇ)
①to insult; to shame; to humiliate ②to rape

汚俗(ㄨ ㄙㄨˊ)
vulgar custom

汚損(ㄨ ㄙㄨㄣˇ)
to stain and damage; to contaminate

四畫

【汨】2780 ㄇㄧˋ mih mì
name of a river in Hunan Province

汨羅(ㄇㄧˋ ㄌㄨㄛˊ)or 汨羅江(ㄇㄧˋ ㄌㄨㄛˊ ㄐㄧㄤ)
a river in Hunan Province (where the ancient poet, Chü Yüan(屈原)drowned himself)

【汩】2781 1. ㄍㄨˇ guu gǔ
1. to dredge(a channel, etc.)
2. confused; disorderly
3. the sound of waves
4. a Chinese family name

汩沒(ㄍㄨˇ ㄇㄛˋ)
to sink; to decline

汩亂(ㄍㄨˇ ㄌㄨㄢˋ)
to cause disorder

汩汩(ㄍㄨˇ ㄍㄨˇ)
①the sound of waves: 那溪流繞著石頭汩汩地流著。The stream gurgled around the rocks. ②panicky; in confusion

【汩】2781 2. ㄩˋ yuh yù
rapid; fleeting

汩流(ㄩˋ ㄌㄧㄡˊ)
rapids

【汭】2782 ㄖㄨㄟˋ ruey ruì
a bend in a stream

【汰】2783 ㄊㄞˋ tay tài
1. excessive
2. to sift; to eliminate; to remove

汰揀(ㄊㄞˋ ㄐㄧㄢˇ)
to wash and polish

汰去(ㄊㄞˋ ㄑㄩˋ)
to eliminate; to remove

汰侈(ㄊㄞˋ ㄔˇ)
excessive luxury; too extravagant

汰沙(ㄊㄞˋ ㄕㄚ)
①to sift sand ②to eliminate useless stuff

汰弱留強(ㄊㄞˋ ㄖㄨㄛˋ ㄌㄧㄡˊ ㄑㄧㄤˊ)
to weed out the weak and retain the strong

【汪】2784 ㄨㄤ uang wāng
1. (said of water) deep and extensive
2. a puddle: 一汪雨水 a puddle of rainwater
3. (said of liquid) to soak; to collect; to accumulate: 連蓆子都汪著水。Even the straw mat was soaked.
4. a Chinese family name

汪達爾(ㄨㄤ ㄉㄚˊ ㄦˇ)
the Vandals

汪精衞(ㄨㄤ ㄐㄧㄥ ㄨㄟˋ)
Wang Ching-wei, 1883-1944, who once tried to assassinate Tsai Li (載灃), the regent of the Ching Dynasty, and was thus put in prison until the revolution of 1911 in Wuchang

汪洋(ㄨㄤ ㄧㄤˊ)
a vast expanse of water: 汪洋浩瀚the vast expanse of the ocean

汪洋大海(ㄨㄤ ㄧㄤˊ ㄉㄚˋ ㄏㄞˇ)
the vast expanse of the sea or ocean

汪汪(ㄨㄤ ㄨㄤ)
①(said of water)deep and extensive ②the barking of dogs; a bowwow: 這隻黑狗汪汪地叫着。The black dog is barking. ③ brimming with tears: 一股油然而生的憐憫之情使他淚眼汪汪。Sudden pity teared his sight.

【汲】2785 ㄐㄧˊ jyi jí
1. to draw water or liquid: 他從池裡汲水。He drew water from the pond.
2. a Chinese family name

汲道(ㄐㄧˊ ㄉㄠˋ)
a road for drawing water

汲古(ㄐㄧˊ ㄍㄨˇ)
to explore the classics

汲古閣(ㄐㄧˊ ㄍㄨˇ ㄍㄜˊ)
the library of Mao Chin (毛晉) in the Ming Dynasty, with a collection of more than 80,000 volumes, besides many books reprinted under his personal supervision

汲汲(ㄐㄧˊ ㄐㄧˊ)
anxious; avid; restless(ly); to crave: 勿汲汲於個人名利。Do not crave personal fame and gain.

汲酒(ㄐㄧˊ ㄐㄧㄡˇ)
to draw wine from a barrel

汲取(ㄐㄧˊ ㄑㄩˇ)
to draw; to derive: 他由讀書中汲取快樂。He derived pleasure from reading.

汲水(ㄐㄧˊ ㄕㄨㄟˇ)
to draw water

汲水機(ㄐㄧˊ ㄕㄨㄟˇ ㄐㄧ)
a device for drawing water

汲水唧筒(ㄐㄧˊ ㄕㄨㄟˇ ㄐㄧˊ ㄊㄨㄥˇ)
a pump

〔水部〕

汲引(ㄐㄧˊ ㄧㄣˇ)
to employ people of talent: 汲引後進 to employ and promote younger talents to higher positions

【決】 2786
(決) ㄐㄩㄝˊ jyue jué

1. to decide; to conclude; to judge: 他將決定誰先去。He'll decide who goes first.
2. (said of a dike) to burst; to break
3. certain; sure; definite
4. to put someone to death; to execute a person: 他們槍決了那個犯人。They executed that prisoner by shooting.

決不(ㄐㄩㄝˊ ㄅㄨˋ)
never: 我們決不退讓。We will never give in.

決不寬貸(ㄐㄩㄝˊ ˙ㄅㄨ ㄎㄨㄢ ㄉㄞˋ)
On no account will leniency be shown.

決不至於(ㄐㄩㄝˊ ˙ㄅㄨ ㄓˋ ㄩˊ)
will certainly not be so (bad or good)

決不食言(ㄐㄩㄝˊ ˙ㄅㄨ ㄕˊ ㄧㄢˊ)
never to break a promise

決非(ㄐㄩㄝˊ ㄈㄟ)
by no means; in no way: 他們臉色黝黑，但決非難看。They are dark-faced, but by no means bad-looking.

決防(ㄐㄩㄝˊ ㄈㄤˊ)
the breach or rupture of a dike

決鬥 or 決鬭(ㄐㄩㄝˊ ㄉㄡˋ)
a duel; to fight a duel: 我向你挑釁作一決鬥。I challenge you to a duel.

決定(ㄐㄩㄝˊ ㄉㄧㄥˋ)
to determine; to decide; to resolve; a decision: 他決定更用功。He resolved to work harder.

決定權(ㄐㄩㄝˊ ㄉㄧㄥˋ ㄑㄩㄢˊ)
the say; the power to make decisions

決定性的(ㄐㄩㄝˊ ㄉㄧㄥˋ ㄒㄧㄥˋ ˙ㄉㄜ)
decisive: 我們贏得決定性的戰役。We won a decisive battle.

決斷(ㄐㄩㄝˊ ㄉㄨㄢˋ)
to decide; to make a decision; to conclude

決堤(ㄐㄩㄝˊ ㄊㄧˊ)
the collapse of an embankment or a dyke

決裂(ㄐㄩㄝˊ ㄌㄧㄝˋ)
① to burst open; to suffer a rupture ② to break; to break off relations; a rupture: 他們的友情決裂了。Their friendship was broken off.

決口(ㄐㄩㄝˊ ㄎㄡˇ)
a rupture; an opening

決計(ㄐㄩㄝˊ ㄐㄧˋ)
① to make up one's mind; to decide: 我決計要去加拿大。I have decided to leave for Canada. ② absolutely; certainly: 咱們這麼辦決計沒錯兒。We absolutely can't go wrong if we do it this way.

決絕(ㄐㄩㄝˊ ㄐㄩㄝˊ)
① to sever relations firmly ② to part forever

決心(ㄐㄩㄝˊ ㄒㄧㄣ)
to make up one's mind; to resolve; determination; determined: 他決心改正自己的錯誤。He is determined to correct his own mistakes.

決選(ㄐㄩㄝˊ ㄒㄩㄢˇ)
a runoff election; a runoff

決戰(ㄐㄩㄝˊ ㄓㄢˋ)
a decisive battle; to fight a decisive battle

決勝(ㄐㄩㄝˊ ㄕㄥˋ)
① certain to bring victory ② to decide a contest

決然(ㄐㄩㄝˊ ㄖㄢˊ)
resolutely; firmly; in a determined manner

決眥(ㄐㄩㄝˊ ㄗˋ)
to have a lesion in the eye (in consequence of an angry stare)

決擇(ㄐㄩㄝˊ ㄗㄜˊ)
to make a final resolution between possible alternatives

決雌雄(ㄐㄩㄝˊ ㄘˊ ㄒㄩㄥˊ)
to fight a decisive battle

決策(ㄐㄩㄝˊ ㄘㄜˋ)
an adopted policy; a decision

決策機構(ㄐㄩㄝˊ ㄘㄜˋ ㄐㄧ ㄍㄡˋ)
a policy-making agency

決死(ㄐㄩㄝˊ ㄙˇ)
life-and-death: 那是一場決死的戰鬥。That was a life-and-death struggle.

決賽(ㄐㄩㄝˊ ㄙㄞˋ)
the final (of a contest, race, etc.): 他將參加網球決賽。He will take part in the tennis finals.

決算(ㄐㄩㄝˊ ㄙㄨㄢˋ)
a final financial statement

決疑(ㄐㄩㄝˊ ㄧˊ)
to settle a doubtful point; to dispel doubts

決意(ㄐㄩㄝˊ ㄧˋ)
to make up one's mind; to decide; to resolve

決議(ㄐㄩㄝˊ ㄧˋ)
a resolution (reached at a meeting); a decision; to decide; to resolve

決議案(ㄐㄩㄝˊ ㄧˋ ㄢˋ)
a resolution (reached at a meeting)

決無(ㄐㄩㄝˊ ㄨˊ)
never; by no means; impossible: 那是決無可能的事啊! What an impossible story!

決獄(ㄐㄩㄝˊ ㄩˋ)
to decide a legal case

【汶】 2787
ㄨㄣˋ wenn wèn

name of a river in Shantung

汶水(ㄨㄣˋ ㄕㄨㄟˇ)
name of a river in Shantung

【汴】 2788
ㄅㄧㄢˋ biann biàn

1. an alternative name for Honan
2. the ancient name of a river in Honan

汴京(ㄅㄧㄢˋ ㄐㄧㄥ) or 汴梁(ㄅㄧㄢˋ ㄌㄧㄤˊ)
the capital of the Northern Sung Dynasty, at what is Kaifeng(開封)today

汴水(ㄅㄧㄢˋ ㄕㄨㄟˇ)
the ancient name of a river in Honan

【汾】 2789
ㄈㄣˊ fern fén

name of a tributary of the Yellow River

汾酒(ㄈㄣˊ ㄐㄧㄡˇ)
kaoliang wine made in the Fen River(汾水)area

汾水(ㄈㄣˊ ㄕㄨㄟˇ) or 汾河(ㄈㄣˊ ㄏㄜˊ)
name of a tributary of the Yellow River

【沁】 2790
ㄑㄧㄣˋ chinn qìn

to soak; to seep; to percolate; to permeate; to ooze; to exude: 他的額上沁出了汗珠。His forehead was oozing sweat.

沁水(ㄑㄧㄣˋ ㄕㄨㄟˇ)
a county in Shansi Province

沁人心脾(ㄑㄧㄣˋ ㄖㄣˊ ㄒㄧㄣ ㄆㄧˊ)
to affect people deeply; to touch one's heart

沁入(ㄑㄧㄣˋ ㄖㄨˋ)
to soak into; to soak through; to permeate: 水會沁入土中。Water will soak through the earth.

【沂】2791 ㄧˊ yi yí
names of four rivers originating in Shantung

沂水(ㄧˊ ㄕㄨㄟˇ)
① name of a county in Shantung ② names of the rivers originating in Shantung

【沅】2792 ㄩㄢˊ yuan yuán
name of a river flowing through Hunan

沅水(ㄩㄢˊ ㄕㄨㄟˇ)or 沅江(ㄩㄢˊ ㄐㄧㄤ)
name of a river flowing through Hunan

【沃】2793 ㄨㄛˋ woh wò
1. to irrigate: 沃田 to irrigate farmland
2. (said of land) fertile: 這塊土地很肥沃。The land is fertile.

沃土(ㄨㄛˋ ㄊㄨˇ)
fertile land

沃饒(ㄨㄛˋ ㄖㄠˊ)
fertile and productive

沃壤(ㄨㄛˋ ㄖㄤˇ)
fertile soil

沃潤(ㄨㄛˋ ㄖㄨㄣˋ)
fertile and moist

沃野千里(ㄨㄛˋ ㄧㄝˇ ㄑㄧㄢ ㄌㄧˇ)
an endless expanse of fertile land

沃衍(ㄨㄛˋ ㄧㄢˇ)
a fertile area

沃腴(ㄨㄛˋ ㄩˊ)
fertile

【汽】2794 ㄑㄧˋ chih qì
gas; steam; vapor

汽表(ㄑㄧˋ ㄅㄧㄠˇ)
a steam gauge

汽泡(ㄑㄧˋ ㄆㄠˋ)
bubbles

汽門(ㄑㄧˋ ㄇㄣˊ)
a steam valve

汽笛(ㄑㄧˋ ㄉㄧˊ)
a steam whistle; a siren

汽艇(ㄑㄧˋ ㄊㄧㄥˇ)
a motorboat; a steam launch

汽缸(ㄑㄧˋ ㄍㄤ)
cylinders (in automobiles, motorcycles, etc.)

汽鍋(ㄑㄧˋ ㄍㄨㄛ)
a boiler; a steam boiler

汽管(ㄑㄧˋ ㄍㄨㄢˇ)
a steam pipe

汽焊(ㄑㄧˋ ㄏㄢˋ)
oxyacetylene welding

汽化(ㄑㄧˋ ㄏㄨㄚˋ)
vaporization; to vaporize: 水煮沸時就汽化。Water vaporizes when boiled.

汽機(ㄑㄧˋ ㄐㄧ)
a steam engine

汽槍(ㄑㄧˋ ㄑㄧㄤ)
an air gun

汽車(ㄑㄧˋ ㄔㄜ)
an automobile: 警察吹警笛令汽車停止。The policeman whistled for the automobile to stop.

汽車旅館(ㄑㄧˋ ㄔㄜ ㄌㄩˇ ㄍㄨㄢˇ)
a motel

汽車工業(ㄑㄧˋ ㄔㄜ ㄍㄨㄥ ㄧㄝˋ)
the auto industry

汽車間(ㄑㄧˋ ㄔㄜ ㄐㄧㄢ)
a garage: 我租了一幢有汽車間的房子。I rented a house with a garage.

汽船(ㄑㄧˋ ㄔㄨㄢˊ)
a steamship; a steamboat; a steamer

汽水(ㄑㄧˋ ㄕㄨㄟˇ)or 汽水兒(ㄑㄧˋ ㄕㄨㄟˇㄦ)
soda water; soft drinks or soda pop: 她喝了一杯汽水。She drank a glass of soda.

汽壓(ㄑㄧˋ ㄧㄚ)
steam pressure

汽油(ㄑㄧˋ ㄧㄡˊ)
gasoline; gas: 我的汽油用完了。I've run out of gas.

汽油彈(ㄑㄧˋ ㄧㄡˊ ㄉㄢˋ)
① a napalm bomb ② a fire bomb or Molotov cocktail

汽油引擎(ㄑㄧˋ ㄧㄡˊ ㄧㄣˇ ㄑㄧㄥˊ)
a gasoline engine

【沇】2795 ㄧㄢˇ yean yǎn
flowing and engulfing; overflowing and brimming

沇水(ㄧㄢˇ ㄕㄨㄟˇ)
① the Chi River(濟水), in Honan(河南) ② the Yen River in Shansi (山西)

【沆】2796 1. ㄏㄤˊ harng háng
to ferry; a ferry

【沆】2796 2. ㄏㄤˋ hanq hàng
1. a vast expanse of water
2. mist; fog
3. flowing

沆茫(ㄏㄤˋ ㄇㄤˊ)or 沆漭(ㄏㄤˋ ㄇㄤˇ)
an expanse of water; water everywhere

沆溉(ㄏㄤˋ ㄍㄞˋ)
moderately flowing waters

沆瀣一氣(ㄏㄤˋ ㄒㄧㄝˋ ㄧˊ ㄑㄧˋ)
(to talk, think, etc.) in the same vein; the meeting of minds; to gang up for an objective

沆瀁(ㄏㄤˋ ㄧㄤ)
expansive waters

【沌】2797 ㄉㄨㄣˋ duenn dùn
turbid; unclear; chaotic: 混沌 the chaotic world in prehistoric times

【沈】2798 1. (沉) ㄔㄣˊ chern chén
1. to sink; to be drawn deep into; to submerge; to set: 太陽沈到山後。The sun sank behind the mountain.
2. to indulge in; to be addicted to: 他沈迷於吸煙。He is addicted to smoking.
3. (said of sleep) deep; sound; fast: 他睡得很沈。He was in a deep sleep.
4. persistent and lasting; for a long time
5. delaying; postponement
6. heavy (in weight): 這包沙太沈了。This sack of sand is too heavy.
7. latent; hidden
8. to straighten (one's face); to put on a grave expression: 他把臉一沈。He put on a grave expression.
9. to retain (one's composure); to restrain (oneself from

〔水部〕

rashness, etc.); to contain: 他沈得住氣。He contained his anger.

沈博絕麗(ㄔㄣˊ ㄅㄛˊ ㄐㄩㄝˊ ㄌㄧˋ)
(said of literary works) profound in substance and beautiful in style

沈不住氣(ㄔㄣˊ ˙ㄅㄨ ㄓㄨˋ ㄑㄧˋ)
to be rash; easily excited; excitable; cannot remain calm

沈沒(ㄔㄣˊ ㄇㄛˋ)
to sink

沈默(ㄔㄣˊ ㄇㄛˋ)
silence; silent; reticent: 沈默即同意。Silence gives consent.

沈默寡言(ㄔㄣˊ ㄇㄛˋ ㄍㄨㄚˇ ㄧㄢˊ)
taciturn; reticent: 他是個沈默寡言的人。He is a taciturn person.

沈默是金(ㄔㄣˊ ㄇㄛˋ ㄕˋ ㄐㄧㄣ)
Silence is golden.

沈悶(ㄔㄣˊ ㄇㄣˋ)
① depressed; heavy at heart: 他的心情沈悶。He felt depressed. ② dull and heavy (atmosphere); hot and humid

沈迷(ㄔㄣˊ ㄇㄧˊ)
to indulge in; to wallow in: 他沈迷於金錢。He is wallowing in money.

沈迷不醒(ㄔㄣˊ ㄇㄧˊ ㄅㄨˋ ㄒㄧㄥˇ)or 沈迷不悟(ㄔㄣˊ ㄇㄧˊ ㄅㄨˋ ㄨˋ)
deeply addicted to, imbibed or infatuated in (vice, sinful ways, etc.)

沈綿(ㄔㄣˊ ㄇㄧㄢˊ)
chronic (diseases); persistent and lasting

沈湎(ㄔㄣˊ ㄇㄧㄢˇ)
to wallow in; to be abandoned (or given) to: 他沈湎於賭博。He was given to gambling.

沈湎酒色(ㄔㄣˊ ㄇㄧㄢˇ ㄐㄧㄡˇ ㄙㄜˋ)
to overindulge oneself in wine and women; to sink deeply into the world of wine and sex

沈冥(ㄔㄣˊ ㄇㄧㄥˊ)
to leave without a trace; traceless

沈伏(ㄔㄣˊ ㄈㄨˊ)
① latent; hidden; not obvious ② dull and slow ③ a low official rank that does not command attention

沈浮(ㄔㄣˊ ㄈㄨˊ)
① ups and downs in a person's life ② to follow or change with prevailing customs, practices, etc. ③ (now rarely) very many

沈達(ㄔㄣˊ ㄉㄚˊ)
quiet and understanding; silent but aboveboard

沈得住氣(ㄔㄣˊ ˙ㄉㄜ ㄓㄨˋ ㄑㄧˋ)
to retain one's composure; to be able to restrain oneself even in an emotional crisis; calm: 他總是沈得住氣。He always keeps his composure.

沈甸甸的(ㄔㄣˊ ㄉㄧㄢ ㄉㄧㄢ ˙ㄉㄜ)
①(said of swords, pens, chopsticks or tools) heavy and not easy to wield ② heavy: 這一袋麵粉沈甸甸的。This sack of flour is pretty heavy. ③ heavy (at heart); serious (looks)

沈澱(ㄔㄣˊ ㄉㄧㄢˋ)
to precipitate; to settle; sedimentation

沈澱物(ㄔㄣˊ ㄉㄧㄢˋ ㄨˋ)
sediment: 茶中有沈澱物。There's some sediment in the tea.

沈痛(ㄔㄣˊ ㄊㄨㄥˋ)
① to be deeply grieved; to be heavy or painful at heart: 她母親的去世使她感到非常沈痛。She was deeply grieved at her mother's death. ② bitter: 這是個沈痛的教訓。It is a bitter lesson.

沈溺(ㄔㄣˊ ㄋㄧˋ)
① to be imbibed or to indulge in (vices, etc.); to immerse in: 他沈溺於一本書中。He was immersed in a book. ② to sink and submerge in water

沈落(ㄔㄣˊ ㄌㄨㄛˋ)
to sink; to fall down

沈淪(ㄔㄣˊ ㄌㄨㄣˊ)
to drown and perish (in water, sins, etc.)

沈痼(ㄔㄣˊ ㄍㄨˋ)
① a chronic disease or ailment; a serious illness ② a bad habit from which one cannot withdraw

沈厚(ㄔㄣˊ ㄏㄡˋ)
① calm and sincere ② profundity

沈酣(ㄔㄣˊ ㄏㄢ)
① to be comfortably drunk ② to indulge oneself or be imbibed in (an amusement, pastime, hobby, etc.)

沈酣經史(ㄔㄣˊ ㄏㄢ ㄐㄧㄥ ㄕˇ)
deeply absorbed in the study of classics

沈積岩(ㄔㄣˊ ㄐㄧ ㄧㄢˊ)
sedimentary rocks

沈機觀變(ㄔㄣˊ ㄐㄧ ㄍㄨㄢ ㄅㄧㄢˋ)
to watch calmly the changes and turns of affairs

沈寂(ㄔㄣˊ ㄐㄧˊ)
① quiet; silent; hush; hushed: 房間陷入一片沈寂。A hush fell over the room. ② newsless; traceless ③ to lie low

沈浸(ㄔㄣˊ ㄐㄧㄣˋ)
① to permeate; to be immersed in; to submerge; to be steeped in: 她沈浸在快樂的回憶裏。She was immersed in happy memories. ② very erudite

沈降(ㄔㄣˊ ㄐㄧㄤˋ)
to subside

沈靜(ㄔㄣˊ ㄐㄧㄥˋ)
calm; quiet; placid: 他心情沈靜。He was in a placid mood.

沈潛(ㄔㄣˊ ㄑㄧㄢˊ)
of a thoughtful and calm disposition; reserved and retiring

沈西(ㄔㄣˊ ㄒㄧ)
(literally) to sink in the west—sunset

沈下臉來(ㄔㄣˊ ㄒㄧㄚˋ ㄌㄧㄢˇ ˙ㄌㄞ)
to straighten one's face—to turn on an angry look; to pull a long face

沈陷(ㄔㄣˊ ㄒㄧㄢˋ)
① to sink; to cave in: 地震使土地沈陷了。The earthquake made the ground cave in. ② (construction) settlement

沈心(ㄔㄣˊ ㄒㄧㄣ)
① to get angry through misunderstanding ② to think deeply and consider carefully

沈香(ㄔㄣˊ ㄒㄧㄤ)or 沈香木(ㄔㄣˊ ㄒㄧㄤ ㄇㄨˋ)
aloeswood; agalloch eaglewood

沈酗(ㄔㄣˊ ㄒㄩˋ)
to be addicted to liquor;

〔水部〕

alcoholism; dead drunk

沈滯(ㄔㄣˊ ㄓˋ)
① stagnant; stalemated ② to feel bad and miserable ③ to remain in an inferior position for a long time

沈舟破釜(ㄔㄣˊ ㄓㄡ ㄆㄛˋ ㄈㄨˇ)
to cast the dice; to reach the point of no return; to cross the Rubicon 參看「破斧沈舟」

沈住氣(ㄔㄣˊ ㄓㄨˋ ㄑㄧˋ)
Steady (on)! 或 to restrain oneself; to control one's temper; to remain calm or composed

沈著(ㄔㄣˊ ㄓㄨㄛˊ)
calm and steady; slow but sure; serene; composed

沈重(ㄔㄣˊ ㄓㄨㄥˋ)
① heavy (in weight) ② heavy (at heart); serious (looks) ③ calm, steady and graceful; dignified

沈沈(ㄔㄣˊ ㄔㄣˊ)
① heavy: 玉蜀黍穗沈沈地垂下來。The ears of corn hang heavy on the stalks. ② deep: 他已沈沈入睡。He has sunk into a deep sleep. ③ dull; gloomy; dark; dreary: 暮氣沈沈 lifeless; lethargic

沈船(ㄔㄣˊ ㄔㄨㄢˊ)
① a sunken ship; a shipwreck ② to scuttle a ship

沈睡(ㄔㄣˊ ㄕㄨㄟˋ) or 沈眠(ㄔㄣˊ ㄇㄧㄢˊ)
deep slumber; sound sleep

沈醉(ㄔㄣˊ ㄗㄨㄟˋ)
① dead-drunk ② to become intoxicated

沈猜(ㄔㄣˊ ㄘㄞ)
to be very suspicious

沈思(ㄔㄣˊ ㄙ)
to ponder; to meditate; to contemplate; meditation; contemplation

沈思凝想(ㄔㄣˊ ㄙ ㄋㄧㄥˊ ㄒㄧㄤˇ)
to ponder; to think deeply or profoundly

沈邃(ㄔㄣˊ ㄙㄨㄟˋ)
deep and profound; deep and obscure

沈疴(ㄔㄣˊ ㄜ) or 沈痼(ㄔㄣˊ ㄍㄨˋ)
a chronic disease; a serious ailment of long standing

沈疑(ㄔㄣˊ ㄧˊ)
hesitant, suspicious and deep-thinking

沈抑(ㄔㄣˊ ㄧˋ)
(said of talents, etc.) buried or submerged

沈毅(ㄔㄣˊ ㄧˋ)
steady and sturdy; plucky

沈壓(ㄔㄣˊ ㄧㄚ)
buried and submerged (talents, etc.)

沈憂(ㄔㄣˊ ㄧㄡ)
deep worries and anxiety; melancholic

沈吟(ㄔㄣˊ ㄧㄣˊ)
① to hesitate ② to ponder; to think deeply

沈飲(ㄔㄣˊ ㄧㄣˇ)
to drink heavily

沈魚落雁(ㄔㄣˊ ㄩˊ ㄌㄨㄛˋ ㄧㄢˋ)
(said of women) extremely beautiful

沈鬱(ㄔㄣˊ ㄩˋ)
deeply depressed; downcast; gloomy

沈鬱頓挫(ㄔㄣˊ ㄩˋ ㄉㄨㄣˋ ㄘㄨㄛˋ)
(said of literary works) profound and forceful

沈寃(ㄔㄣˊ ㄩㄢ)
an unredressed wrong or grievance of long standing; a grievous wrong: 他沈寃莫白。He suffered a grievous wrong.

沈遠(ㄔㄣˊ ㄩㄢˇ)
far and great (ambitions, objectives, etc.)

沈勇(ㄔㄣˊ ㄩㄥˇ)
calm, steady and courageous

【沈】 2798
2. ㄕㄣˇ sheen shěn

a Chinese family name

沈周(ㄕㄣˇ ㄓㄡ) or 沈石田(ㄕㄣˇ ㄕˊ ㄊㄧㄢˊ)
Shen Chou, 1472-1509, a noted landscape painter in the Ming Dynasty

沈腰(ㄕㄣˇ ㄧㄠ)
slender waist—the reference is about Shen Yüeh (沈約)

沈腰潘鬢(ㄕㄣˇ ㄧㄠ ㄆㄢ ㄅㄧㄣˋ)
to have a slender waist and hoary hair, the reference is about Shen Yüeh (沈約) and Pan Yüeh (潘岳)

沈約(ㄕㄣˇ ㄩㄝ)
Shen Yüeh, 441-513, an official and scholar of the Liang Dynasty, best remembered for his 四聲譜, an epoch-making work in phonology

【沐】 2799
ㄇㄨˋ muh mù

1. to shampoo; to wash; to bathe; to cleanse
2. a holiday; a leave; to take a leave
3. to receive favor
4. a Chinese family name

沐猴(ㄇㄨˋ ㄏㄡˊ)
a macaque

沐猴而冠(ㄇㄨˋ ㄏㄡˊ ㄦˊ ㄍㄨㄢˋ)
(literally) to dress up a monkey, trying to fool people into believing that it's a man—A worthless fellow is a worthless fellow, no matter what he wears. 或 Beautiful clothes can't hide one's ugliness inside. 或 Clothes do not make the man.

沐櫛(ㄇㄨˋ ㄐㄧㄝˊ)
to shampoo and comb

沐日(ㄇㄨˋ ㄖˋ)
① a day of rest; a holiday ② sunbathing

沐恩(ㄇㄨˋ ㄣ)
① to receive favor ② (formerly) a self reference used by low-ranking officers in speaking to their superiors

沐雨櫛風(ㄇㄨˋ ㄩˇ ㄐㄧㄝˊ ㄈㄥ)
to work and toil; to work very hard regardless of weather

沐浴(ㄇㄨˋ ㄩˋ) or 沐洗(ㄇㄨˋ ㄒㄧˇ)
① to bathe ② to steep in or receive favor ③ to soak in

沐浴清化(ㄇㄨˋ ㄩˋ ㄑㄧㄥ ㄏㄨㄚˋ)
enriched by your kindness and transformed by your purity

【沔】 2800
ㄇㄧㄢˇ mean miǎn

1. overflowing (water); a flood
2. name of a river

沔水(ㄇㄧㄢˇ ㄕㄨㄟˇ)
Mian River, or Han River, in Shansi Province

【沖】 2801
(冲) ㄔㄨㄥ chong chōng

1. to wash away; to wash with running water; to rinse; to flush: 這艘船被沖上岸來。The boat was washed ashore.

〔水部〕

2. to soar; to rise rapidly or shoot up
3. to pour water (to powder, etc.); to make beverages, etc.; to infuse: 沖泡茶水 to infuse tea leaves in hot water to make tea
4. empty; void
5. to dash against; to clash with
6. childhood
7. to neutralize; to make void

沖犯(ㄔㄨㄥ ㄈㄢˋ)
to offend (a superior, an elder, etc.): 我希望我一點也沒有沖犯了您。I hope I haven't offended you in any way.

沖服(ㄔㄨㄥ ㄈㄨˊ)
(medicine) to infuse with water and drink

沖倒了(ㄔㄨㄥ ㄉㄠˇ ˙ㄌㄜ)
to be crushed or knocked down by flood

沖淡(ㄔㄨㄥ ㄉㄢˋ)
① to dilute with water, etc. ② to play down; to mitigate the intensity of a situation or statement ③ to make few demands on life

沖塌(ㄔㄨㄥ ㄊㄚ)
to be destroyed by floods

沖天(ㄔㄨㄥ ㄊㄧㄢ) or 沖霄(ㄔㄨㄥ ㄒㄧㄠ)
to shoot up to the sky

沖退(ㄔㄨㄥ ㄊㄨㄟˋ)
to defer to; to be submissive

沖牛奶(ㄔㄨㄥ ㄋㄧㄡˊ ㄋㄞˇ)
to make milk from powdered milk by pouring boiling water

沖齡(ㄔㄨㄥ ㄌㄧㄥˊ)
childhood

沖開水(ㄔㄨㄥ ㄎㄞ ㄕㄨㄟˇ)
① to pour boiled water on; to infuse (tea, etc.); to pour boiling water in a thermos bottle ②(Shanghai dialect) to buy boiling water from a shop

沖口而出(ㄔㄨㄥ ㄎㄡˇ ㄦˊ ㄔㄨ)
to say something without thinking; to blurt out

沖和(ㄔㄨㄥ ㄏㄜˊ)
to diffuse; to dilute; to mix liquids

沖壞(ㄔㄨㄥ ㄏㄨㄞˋ)
to be damaged or destroyed by lashing waters or by flood: 堤防被暴風雨沖壞了。The embankment was washed out by the storm.

沖昏頭腦(ㄔㄨㄥ ㄏㄨㄣ ㄊㄡˊ ㄋㄠˇ)
to turn someone's head; dizzy

沖積(ㄔㄨㄥ ㄐㄧ)
alluviation

沖積期(ㄔㄨㄥ ㄐㄧ ㄑㄧˊ)
the alluvial epoch

沖積扇(ㄔㄨㄥ ㄐㄧ ㄕㄢˋ)
(geology) alluvial fan

沖積層(ㄔㄨㄥ ㄐㄧ ㄘㄥˊ)
an alluvium; an alluvial stratum; alluvial deposits

沖積物(ㄔㄨㄥ ㄐㄧ ㄨˋ)
sediment; deposit

沖擊(ㄔㄨㄥ ㄐㄧˊ)
(said of waves or floods) to lash or pound against: 海浪不斷地沖擊岩石。The sea waves continuously lashed at the rocks.

沖襟(ㄔㄨㄥ ㄐㄧㄣ)
open-minded and at peace with oneself and the world

沖洗(ㄔㄨㄥ ㄒㄧˇ)
① to flush; to wash with running water; flush: 這水管堵住了,好好把它沖洗一下。The pipe is blocked; give it a good flush. ②(photography) to develop or process negatives: 他在暗室沖洗底片。He was in the darkroom developing his films.

沖喜(ㄔㄨㄥ ㄒㄧˇ)
(an old Chinese custom) to arrange a wedding for a young man who was seriously ill with the hope that the "event of great joy" would drive away his bad luck and hasten his recovery

沖虛(ㄔㄨㄥ ㄒㄩ)
① carefree; devoid of ambition ② to soar; to rise high

沖帳 or 沖賬(ㄔㄨㄥ ㄓㄤˋ)
(accounting) to cancel out an expenditure

沖撞(ㄔㄨㄥ ㄓㄨㄤˋ)
to offend (especially a superior, an elder, etc.): 你說的話真的沖撞了你的上司。What you said really offended your boss.

沖茶(ㄔㄨㄥ ㄔㄚˊ)
to make tea

沖沖(ㄔㄨㄥ ㄔㄨㄥ)
① tinklings of pendants ② the sound of breaking ice ③ an infuriated expression

沖繩(ㄔㄨㄥ ㄕㄥˊ)
Okinawa

沖刷(ㄔㄨㄥ ㄕㄨㄚ)
erosion; to scour; to wash out (or away): 將銹跡沖刷掉。Scour the rust off.

沖散(ㄔㄨㄥ ㄙㄢˋ)
to disperse by the use of force; (said of a family in war or other great upheaval) to be scattered or separated in confusion: 警察將人羣沖散。The police dispersed the crowd.

【沙】 2802 ㄕㄚ sha shā

1. sand; tiny gravel or pebbles: 孩子們喜歡在沙地上玩。Children enjoy playing on the sands.
2. the land around water; a beach; a sandbank; a desert
3. to pick, select, sort or sift
4. (said of fruit, especially melons) overripe
5. (said of the human voice) hoarse: 他一直喊叫到聲音沙啞了。He shouted until he was hoarse.
6. sandy—not glossy or smooth; granular
7. a kind of clay for making utensils, vessels, etc.
8. a Chinese family name

沙巴(ㄕㄚ ㄅㄚ)
Sabah, a state of Malaysia

沙包(ㄕㄚ ㄅㄠ)
① sandbags ② a porcelain vessel shaped like a small jug

沙暴(ㄕㄚ ㄅㄠˋ)
a sandstorm

沙盤演習(ㄕㄚ ㄆㄢˊ ㄧㄢˇ ㄒㄧˊ) or 沙盤作業(ㄕㄚ ㄆㄢˊ ㄗㄨㄛˋ ㄧㄝˋ)
(military) sand table exercises

沙模(ㄕㄚ ㄇㄛˊ)
a sand mold

沙漠(ㄕㄚ ㄇㄛˋ)
a desert: 那是沙漠中的綠洲。That is an oasis in the desert.

沙漠之舟(ㄕㄚ ㄇㄛˋ ㄓ ㄓㄡ)

the ship of the desert—the camel

沙門(ㄕㄚ ㄇㄣˊ)
①(Buddhism) a monk or a nun ②name of an islet off the Shantung coast

沙彌(ㄕㄚ ㄇㄧˊ)or 沙僧(ㄕㄚ ㄙㄥ)
a Buddhist novice

沙彌子(ㄕㄚ ㄇㄧ ㄗˇ)
a monk who entered the temple or monastery at a very young age; a Buddhist novice

沙發(ㄕㄚ ㄈㄚ)
a sofa: 她在裝沙發套。She was upholstering the sofa.

沙袋(ㄕㄚ ㄉㄞˋ)
①sandbags ②an instrument of torture in ancient China made of layers of leather sewed together and stuffed with sand

沙丁魚(ㄕㄚ ㄉㄧㄥ ㄩˊ)
a sardine: 他們擠得像沙丁魚一樣。They were packed like sardines.

沙堆(ㄕㄚ ㄉㄨㄟ)
a sand dune; a sand hill

沙汰(ㄕㄚ ㄊㄞˋ)
to sift; to eliminate (as in a contest)

沙灘(ㄕㄚ ㄊㄢ)
a piece of sandy land around water; a sandbank; a sandy beach

沙糖(ㄕㄚ ㄊㄤˊ)
crystal sugar; granular sugar; brown sugar; powdered sugar

沙隄(ㄕㄚ ㄊㄧˊ)
a sand bar

沙田(ㄕㄚ ㄊㄧㄢˊ)
farmland converted from tideland

沙田柚(ㄕㄚ ㄊㄧㄢˊ ㄧㄡˋ)
pomelos produced in Kwangsi, especially in Junghsien(容縣)

沙土(ㄕㄚ ㄊㄨˇ)
a mixture of sand and clay; sandy soil

沙拉(ㄕㄚ ㄌㄚ)
salad: 水果沙拉 fruit salad

沙拉醬(ㄕㄚ ㄌㄚ ㄐㄧㄤˋ)
salad dressing

沙拉油(ㄕㄚ ㄌㄚ ㄧㄡˊ)
salad oil

沙勞越(ㄕㄚ ㄌㄠˊ ㄩㄝˋ)
Sarawak, a state of Malaysia

沙漏(ㄕㄚ ㄌㄡˋ)
①an hourglass ②a sand filter

沙裏淘金(ㄕㄚ ㄌㄧˇ ㄊㄠˊ ㄐㄧㄣ)
①to sift gold from sand ②to pick the best from a vast quantity ③time-consuming

沙粒(ㄕㄚ ㄌㄧˋ)
sand grains

沙礫(ㄕㄚ ㄌㄧˋ)
pebbles; gravel; grit: 沙礫跑進我的鞋子裏。I have got grit in my shoe.

沙龍(ㄕㄚ ㄌㄨㄥˊ)
a salon

沙籠(ㄕㄚ ㄌㄨㄥˊ)
a sarong

沙濾(ㄕㄚ ㄌㄩˋ)or 沙濾器(ㄕㄚ ㄌㄩˋ ㄑㄧˋ)
a sand filter

沙鍋(ㄕㄚ ㄍㄨㄛ)
①an earthenware cooking pot ② food cooked and served in such a pot

沙果兒(ㄕㄚ ㄍㄨㄛˇㄦ)
a kind of small apples; the crab apple

沙坑(ㄕㄚ ㄎㄥ)
a sand pit

沙皇(ㄕㄚ ㄏㄨㄤˊ)
a czar or a tsar (of Russia)

沙金(ㄕㄚ ㄐㄧㄣ)
alluvial gold

沙磧(ㄕㄚ ㄑㄧˋ)
a desert

沙丘(ㄕㄚ ㄑㄧㄡ)
a sand dune; a sand hill

沙紙(ㄕㄚ ㄓˇ)
sandpaper; emery paper

沙洲(ㄕㄚ ㄓㄡ)
a shoal; a sand bar; a sandbank

沙渚(ㄕㄚ ㄓㄨˇ)
a sandy islet; a sandbank; a sand bar

沙場(ㄕㄚ ㄔㄤˇ)
a battlefield: 他戰死於沙場。He died on the battlefield.

沙石(ㄕㄚ ㄕˊ)
①gravel ②sandstone

沙士(ㄕㄚ ㄕˋ)
sarsaparilla

沙沙(ㄕㄚ ㄕㄚ)
to rustle; a rustle: 樹葉在微風中發出沙沙聲。Leaves rustled in the breeze.

沙沙聲響(ㄕㄚ ㄕㄚ ㄕㄥ ㄒㄧㄤˇ)
a light chafing sound; a rustle: 我們聽見樹葉的沙沙聲響。We have heard a rustle of leaves.

沙手(ㄕㄚ ㄕㄡˇ)
(Chinese boxing) hands toughened by rubbing daily with green beans and then iron sand, which are capable of performing unusual feats

沙子(ㄕㄚ ˙ㄗ)
sand

沙俄(ㄕㄚ ㄜˋ)
czarist Russia

沙鷗(ㄕㄚ ㄡ)
a sea gull

沙啞(ㄕㄚ ㄧㄚˇ)
(said of the voice) husky; hoarse: 他唱了一小時後嗓子都沙啞了。He is hoarse after singing for an hour.

沙燕兒(ㄕㄚ ㄧㄢˋㄦ)
the common kite, looking like a swallow

沙岩(ㄕㄚ ㄧㄢˊ)
sandstone

沙眼(ㄕㄚ ㄧㄢˇ)
trachoma

沙烏地阿拉伯(ㄕㄚ ㄨ ㄉㄧˋ ㄚ ㄌㄚ ㄅㄛˊ)
Saudi Arabia

沙文主義(ㄕㄚ ㄨㄣˊ ㄓㄨˇ ㄧˋ)
chauvinism

沙魚(ㄕㄚ ㄩˊ)
the shark

【沒】 2803
1. ㄇㄛˋ moh mò

1. to sink; to submerge: 潛艇沒入水中。The submarine submerged.
2. to overflow; to rise beyond
3. to disappear
4. to go into oblivion: 在我們的歷史中, 許多英雄被埋沒了。Many heroes went into oblivion.
5. none; exhausted
6. eliminated
7. finished; completed
8. to take property away from another; to confiscate
9. to die; dead

沒沒無聞(ㄇㄛˋ ㄇㄛˋ ㄨˊ ㄨㄣˊ)

〔水部〕

(said of a person) unknown; nameless; obscure: 他是個沒沒無聞的作家。He was a nameless writer.
沒頂(ㄇㄛˋ ㄉㄧㄥˇ)
to drown
沒奈何 (ㄇㄛˋ ㄋㄞˋ ㄏㄜˊ) or (ㄇㄟˊ ㄋㄞˋ ㄏㄜˊ)
to have no alternative; to have to; cannot but(do)
沒落(ㄇㄛˋ ㄌㄨㄛˋ)
① to sink ② the fall or decline (of an empire, etc.): 羅馬帝國的沒落 the decline of the Rome Empire
沒骨畫(ㄇㄛˋ ㄍㄨˇ ㄏㄨㄚˋ)
(in old China) a school of painting resembling today's watercolor
沒官(ㄇㄛˋ ㄍㄨㄢ)
to be confiscated by the government
沒齒(ㄇㄛˋ ㄔˇ)
to the end of one's life
沒齒難忘(ㄇㄛˋ ㄔˇ ㄋㄢˊ ㄨㄤˋ)
to remember (a favor) as long as one lives: 你這個恩情叫我沒齒難忘。I always feel indebted to you for this favor.
沒世(ㄇㄛˋ ㄕˋ)
① through one's lifetime ② eternal; forever; everlasting
沒收(ㄇㄛˋ ㄕㄡ)
to confiscate; confiscation: 政府將所有叛國者的財產沒收了。The government confiscated the property of all traitors.
沒入(ㄇㄛˋ ㄖㄨˋ)
to confiscate

【沒】 2803
2. ㄇㄟˊ mei méi

1. none; nothing; no: 我的財富一點也沒給我帶來快樂。I am none the happier for my wealth.
2. not yet; negative
沒把鼻(ㄇㄟˊ ㄅㄚˇ ㄅㄧˊ)
groundless; without a basis; without any hold on (another, etc.)
沒把握(ㄇㄟˊ ㄅㄚˇ ㄨㄛˋ)
not sure; not certain; uncertain: 他沒把握會成功。He is uncertain of success.
沒皮沒臉(ㄇㄟˊ ㄆㄧˊ ㄇㄟˊ ㄌㄧㄢˇ)
shameless; shamelessly
沒皮賴臉(ㄇㄟˊ ㄆㄧˊ ㄌㄞˋ ㄌㄧㄢˇ)
brazen-faced; brazen-facedly
沒譜兒(ㄇㄟˊ ㄆㄨˇㄦ)
without any standard or criterion; to be unsure; to have no idea: 關於如何幫助他，我們還沒譜兒呢! We have no idea yet as to how to help him.
沒門兒(ㄇㄟˊ ㄇㄜˊㄦ)
① to have no access to something; to have no means of doing something ② no go
沒命(ㄇㄟˊ ㄇㄧㄥˋ)
① regardless of life; with one's all-out effort ② to die; dead
沒法兒(ㄇㄟˊ ㄈㄚˇㄦ) or 沒法子(ㄇㄟˊ ㄈㄚˇ ·ㄗ)
no way out; no alternative (but…); without a way; to have to
沒分曉(ㄇㄟˊ ㄈㄣ ㄒㄧㄠˇ)
foolish
沒縫兒(ㄇㄟˊ ㄈㄥˋㄦ)
without a crack or loophole
沒大沒小(ㄇㄟˊ ㄉㄚˋ ㄇㄟˊ ㄒㄧㄠˇ)
ill-mannered or rude to one's elders
沒德行(ㄇㄟˊ ㄉㄜˊ ·ㄒㄧㄥ)
mean; nasty
沒道理(ㄇㄟˊ ㄉㄠˋ ㄌㄧˇ)
unreasonable; not justified
沒地兒(ㄇㄟˊ ㄉㄧˋㄦ)
no seat or place for
沒多少(ㄇㄟˊ ㄉㄨㄛ ㄕㄠˇ)
not much; not many
沒對兒(ㄇㄟˊ ㄉㄨㄟˋㄦ)
matchless; peerless
沒斷(ㄇㄟˊ ㄉㄨㄢˋ)
incessant; continuous; continuously; ceaselessly: 雨沒斷地下了一星期。We've had a week of incessant rain.
沒頭沒腦(ㄇㄟˊ ㄊㄡˊ ㄇㄟˊ ㄋㄠˇ)
(to utter, do, etc. something) all of a sudden; abruptly; inexplicably; illogical
沒頭帖(ㄇㄟˊ ㄊㄡˊ ㄊㄧㄝˇ)
an unsigned or unnamed (invitation, etc.) card
沒頭腦(ㄇㄟˊ ㄊㄡˊ ㄋㄠˇ)
without brains; stupid; ignorant
沒頭案子(ㄇㄟˊ ㄊㄡˊ ㄢˋ ·ㄗ)
a criminal case without a clue for the police to work on
沒聽提(ㄇㄟˊ ㄊㄧㄥ ㄊㄧˊ)
to take no notice of; to pay no attention to
沒了(ㄇㄟˊ ·ㄌㄜ)
① to disappear; to vanish ② without: 我們沒了他不成。We cannot do without him.
沒來(ㄇㄟˊ ㄌㄞˊ)
to have not come; to fail to show up: 她還沒來。She has not come yet.
沒來由(ㄇㄟˊ ㄌㄞˊ ㄧㄡˊ)
without any cause or reason; uncalled-for; unprovoked
沒落子(ㄇㄟˊ ㄌㄠˋ ·ㄗ) or 沒落兒(ㄇㄟˊ ㄌㄠˋㄦ)
with no means of making a living
沒了期(ㄇㄟˊ ㄌㄧㄠˇ ㄑㄧˊ)
(said of misery or misfortune) to have no end; endless
沒臉(ㄇㄟˊ ㄌㄧㄢˇ)
too ashamed to (do a thing); to lose face
沒良心(ㄇㄟˊ ㄌㄧㄤˊ ·ㄒㄧㄣ)
without conscience; unconscionable; ungrateful
沒路(ㄇㄟˊ ㄌㄨˋ)
at the end of one's rope; at one's wits' end
沒籠頭的馬(ㄇㄟˊ ㄌㄨㄥˊ ·ㄊㄡ ·ㄉㄜ ㄇㄚˇ)
unharnessed horse—(figuratively) without restraints of any kind; unbridled
沒骨頭(ㄇㄟˊ ㄍㄨˇ ·ㄊㄡ) or 沒骨氣(ㄇㄟˊ ㄍㄨˇ ㄑㄧˋ)
spineless; chicken-hearted
沒規矩(ㄇㄟˊ ㄍㄨㄟ ·ㄐㄩ)
not observing proper rules or manners; improper; inappropriate; impudent
沒關係(ㄇㄟˊ ㄍㄨㄢ ·ㄒㄧ)
It does not matter. 或 Never mind.
沒開過眼(ㄇㄟˊ ㄎㄞ ·ㄍㄨㄛ ㄧㄢˇ)
rustic; unsophisticated; to have seen little of the world
沒勁兒(ㄇㄟˊ ㄐㄧㄣˋㄦ)
① to have no interest in, or desire for, anything ② listless
沒結沒完(ㄇㄟˊ ㄐㄧㄝˊ ㄇㄟˊ ㄨㄢˊ)

incessant and continuous; endless

沒見過世面(ㄇㄟˊ ㄐㄧㄢˋ ·ㄍㄨㄛ ㄕˋ ·ㄇㄧㄢ)
green and inexperienced; unsophisticated

沒見識(ㄇㄟˊ ㄐㄧㄢˋ ·ㄕ)
inexperienced and ignorant; unlearned and provincial

沒講究(ㄇㄟˊ ㄐㄧㄤˇ ·ㄐㄧㄡ)
①nothing particular to think about ②to discard formalities

沒精打彩(ㄇㄟˊ ㄐㄧㄥ ㄉㄚˇ ㄘㄞˇ)
listless; dispirited: 病後幾週他一直沒精打彩。He remained listless for weeks after his illness.

沒輕沒重(ㄇㄟˊ ㄑㄧㄥ ㄇㄟˊ ㄓㄨㄥˋ)
①(said of behavior) without manners ②(said of utterances) untimely or thoughtless; rash and rude

沒去(ㄇㄟˊ ㄑㄩˋ)
didn't go; to have not left: 他沒去那裏。He did not go there.

沒趣兒(ㄇㄟˊ ㄑㄩˋㄦ)
① uninteresting; unpleasant or awkward situation ② rebuke; snub; rebuff; reprimand: 他自討沒趣兒。He received a rebuff.

沒下梢(ㄇㄟˊ ㄒㄧㄚˋ ㄕㄠ)
to have a tragic end; to have no happy ending

沒羞沒臊(ㄇㄟˊ ㄒㄧㄡ ㄇㄟˊ ㄙㄠˋ)
brazen-faced; shameless

沒心沒肺(ㄇㄟˊ ㄒㄧㄣ ㄇㄟˊ ㄈㄟˋ)
careless; inattentive

沒心腸(ㄇㄟˊ ㄒㄧㄣ ·ㄔㄤ)
no heart for; not interested in

沒心眼兒(ㄇㄟˊ ㄒㄧㄣ ㄧㄚˇㄦ)
①careless ②frank; candid

沒想到(ㄇㄟˊ ㄒㄧㄤˇ ㄉㄠˋ)
to have not expected; to have not thought about; unexpectedly

沒指望(ㄇㄟˊ ㄓˇ ㄨㄤˋ)
hopeless: 這情況似乎已沒指望。It seems to be a hopeless case.

沒志氣(ㄇㄟˊ ㄓˋ ·ㄑㄧ)
(said of a person) without ambition; marked by defeatism

沒轍(ㄇㄟˊ ㄓㄜˊ)
Nothing can be done about it.

沒治兒(ㄇㄟˊ ㄓˋㄦ)
unmanageable

沒主意(ㄇㄟˊ ㄓㄨˇ ·ㄧ)or(ㄇㄟˊ ㄓㄨˊ ·ㄧ)
to lose one's head; cannot make up one's mind

沒準兒(ㄇㄟˊ ㄓㄨㄣˇㄦ)
uncertain; unsure; doubtful; maybe

沒種(ㄇㄟˊ ㄓㄨㄥˇ)
cowardly

沒尺寸(ㄇㄟˊ ㄔˇ ·ㄘㄨㄣ)
rash and thoughtless; illmannered

沒出息(ㄇㄟˊ ㄔㄨ ·ㄒㄧ)
(said of persons) not promising; useless; good-for-nothing

沒事(ㄇㄟˊ ㄕˋ)or 沒事兒(ㄇㄟˊ ㄕˋㄦ)
①nothing wrong; all right; O.K.: 我保你沒事。I guarantee that nothing will happen to you. ② without anything to do; nothing important

沒事找事(ㄇㄟˊ ㄕˋ ㄓㄠˇ ㄕˋ)
①to ask for trouble; to ask for it ②to try hard to find fault; to cavil

沒甚麼(ㄇㄟˊ ㄕㄜˊ ·ㄇㄜ)
① Nothing! 或 Never mind! 或 It's all right.② not important; not difficult, bad, etc.: 這事對我們沒甚麼重要的。The matter is of little importance to us.

沒深沒淺(ㄇㄟˊ ㄕㄣ ㄇㄟˊ ㄑㄧㄢˇ)
ignorant and rash; impudent and thoughtless

沒商量(ㄇㄟˊ ㄕㄤ ·ㄌㄧㄤ)
nothing to discuss or negotiate—already decided

沒日沒夜(ㄇㄟˊ ㄖˋ ㄇㄟˊ ㄧㄝˋ)
day and night

沒日子(ㄇㄟˊ ㄖˋ ·ㄗ)
①the date not set yet; the time undecided ②not long in the future; in the near future

沒早沒晚(ㄇㄟˊ ㄗㄠˇ ㄇㄟˊ ㄨㄢˇ)
day and night; without regard to the time of day

沒造化(ㄇㄟˊ ㄗㄠˋ ·ㄏㄨㄚ)
unlucky; out of luck

沒詞兒(ㄇㄟˊ ㄘˊㄦ)
to be short of words—unable to respond; to lose in a debate, an argument, etc.

沒錯兒(ㄇㄟˊ ㄘㄨㄛˋㄦ)
① I'm quite sure. 或 You can rest assured. ② can't go wrong

沒意思(ㄇㄟˊ ㄧˋ ·ㄙ)
weary; bored; not interesting

沒有(ㄇㄟˊ ㄧㄡˇ)
no; not; not yet; do not have; without: 教室裡沒有人。There isn't anyone in the classroom.

沒有的話(ㄇㄟˊ ㄧㄡˇ ·ㄉㄜ ㄏㄨㄚˋ)
not true; nothing of the kind; it can not be

沒有的事兒(ㄇㄟˊ ㄧㄡˇ ·ㄉㄜ ㄕˋㄦ)
Nothing of that sort! 或 It's impossible.

沒有說的(ㄇㄟˊ ㄧㄡˇ ㄕㄨㄛ ·ㄉㄜ)
① really good ② it goes without saying; needless to say

沒影兒(ㄇㄟˊ ㄧㄥˇㄦ)
① not even a shadow—without trace ② groundless; not true ③ to vanish ④ to get far away

沒味兒(ㄇㄟˊ ㄨㄟˋㄦ)
(literally) tasteless—① not delicious ② not interesting

沒胃口(ㄇㄟˊ ㄨㄟˋ ㄎㄡˇ)
① to have lost one's appetite ② to have no interest in something

沒完(ㄇㄟˊ ㄨㄢˊ)
① incessant; continuous; without end: 他的困苦經歷好像沒完沒了似的。The story of his troubles seemed (to be) endless. ② There will be no end to this.

沒王法(ㄇㄟˊ ㄨㄤˊ ㄈㄚˇ)
lawless; without justice; to act lawlessly

沒緣(ㄇㄟˊ ㄩㄢˊ)
Fate has decided against (people's meeting again, etc.). 或 no opportunity of

沒用(ㄇㄟˊ ㄩㄥˋ)
useless; of no use: 抱怨也沒用。It's no use complaining (or to complain).

【沚】 2804 ㄓˇ jyy zhǐ

a sandy islet in a stream; a small sandbank

〔水部〕

【沏】 2805
1. ㄑㄧ chi qī
1. to infuse
2. (said of the flowing water) rapidly; turbulently

沏茶(ㄑㄧ ㄔㄚˊ)
to infuse tea; to make tea: 她用開水沏茶。She was infusing tea leaves in boiling water to make tea.

【沏】 2805
2. ㄑㄩ chiu qū
to drench with water

【沓】 2806
ㄊㄚˋ tah tà
1. repeated; reiterated
2. crowded together; joined or connected; piled up
3. lax
4. talkative

沓沓(ㄊㄚˋ ㄊㄚˋ)
① lax ② chattering and talkative ③ running quickly

沓合(ㄊㄚˋ ㄏㄜˊ)
to pile one upon another; to superimpose

沓至(ㄊㄚˋ ㄓˋ)
to come one after another without stop

沓雜(ㄊㄚˋ ㄗㄚˊ)
crowded and mixed; confused

【沛】 2807
ㄆㄟˋ pey pèi
1. copious; abundance; full of; much: 他活力充沛。He is full of vitality.
2. quickly; rapidly; sudden
3. to fall prostrate
4. to reserve water for irrigation
5. tall; high; great

沛沛(ㄆㄟˋ ㄆㄟˋ)
a great flow of water; flowing copiously

沛公(ㄆㄟˋ ㄍㄨㄥ)
Liu Pang (劉邦), the founding emperor of the Han Dynasty, who started his uprising at his native town of Pei (沛)

沛然(ㄆㄟˋ ㄖㄢˊ)
①(said of rain) copious ② great or vast

沛澤(ㄆㄟˋ ㄗㄜˊ)
thickets and marshes

沛艾(ㄆㄟˋ ㄞˋ)
(said of horses) tall and strong

五畫

【沫】 2808
ㄇㄛˋ moh mò
1. tiny bubbles on the surface of water; froth; suds; lather: 啤酒倒出時起泡沫。Beer froths when it is poured out.
2. saliva
3. (now rarely) to end; to finish

沫子(ㄇㄛˋ ·ㄗ) or 沫兒(ㄇㄛˋㄦ)
froth; suds; tiny bubbles

沫雨(ㄇㄛˋ ㄩˇ)
rains that cause floods

【沬】 2809
ㄇㄟˋ mey mèi
1. dusk
2. name of a river
3. (in ancient China) name of a town in the state of Wei, in today's Honan Province

沬血(ㄇㄟˋ ㄒㄧㄝˇ)
blood flowing in one's face; a bleeding face

【沮】 2810
1. ㄐㄩ jiu jū
1. name of a river in Shantung Province; name of a river in Shansi Province
2. a Chinese family name

沮蒼(ㄐㄩ ㄘㄤ)
Chü Sung (沮誦) and Tsang Chieh (倉頡), legendary figures credited with the invention of Chinese characters

沮誦 or 沮頌(ㄐㄩ ㄙㄨㄥˋ)
name of a legendary person in the reign of Huang Ti (Yellow Emperor), who helped create the Chinese written language

【沮】 2810
2. ㄐㄩˇ jeu jǔ
1. to stop; to abate
2. to lose; to be defeated
3. to spoil; to injure; to destroy or damage

沮短(ㄐㄩˇ ㄉㄨㄢˇ)
to slander; to gossip; to backbite

沮駭(ㄐㄩˇ ㄏㄞˋ)
to frighten by a threat of destruction; to intimidate

沮壞(ㄐㄩˇ ㄏㄨㄞˋ)
ruined; damaged

沮泄(ㄐㄩˇ ㄒㄧㄝˋ)
to leak (secrets, information, etc.)

沮舍(ㄐㄩˇ ㄕㄜˋ)
a damaged, ruined or dilapidated house

沮喪(ㄐㄩˇ ㄙㄤˋ)
discouraged and disappointed; crestfallen; despondent; downcast; low-spirited

【沮】 2810
3. ㄐㄩˋ jiuh jù
damp, low-lying land; marshy

沮洳(ㄐㄩˋ ㄖㄨˋ)
damp, low-lying land

沮澤(ㄐㄩˋ ㄗㄜˊ)
swamps; marsh

【沭】 2811
ㄕㄨˋ shuh shù
short for 沭水

沭水(ㄕㄨˋ ㄕㄨㄟˇ)
name of a river in Shantung Province

【沱】 2812
ㄊㄨㄛˊ two tuó
1. waterways; rivers; streams
2. name of a river
3. continuous heavy rains

沱茶(ㄊㄨㄛˊ ㄔㄚˊ)
a bowl-shaped compressed mass of tea leaves

沱若(ㄊㄨㄛˊ ㄖㄨㄛˋ)
(said of tears, etc.) flowing down

【沴】 2813
ㄌㄧˋ lih lì
1. miasmas; foul and poisonous air
2. dislocation

沴孽(ㄌㄧˋ ㄋㄧㄝˋ)
evil spirits

沴氣(ㄌㄧˋ ㄑㄧˋ)
miasmas; poisonous vapor

【沸】 2814
ㄈㄟˋ fey fèi
1. boiling (water,etc.)
2. to gush; bubbling up

沸沸(ㄈㄟˋ ㄈㄟˋ)
water gushing out from a spring (usually used figuratively)

沸沸揚揚(ㄈㄟˋ ㄈㄟˋ ㄧㄤˊ ㄧㄤˊ)
to bubble with noise; in a hubbub

沸點(ㄈㄟˋ ㄉㄧㄢˇ)
the boiling point

沸鼎(ㄈㄟˋ ㄉㄧㄥˇ)
a cauldron holding boiling water
沸湯(ㄈㄟˋ ㄊㄤ)
boiling water
沸騰(ㄈㄟˋ ㄊㄥˊ)
①boiling—when liquids turn to steam: 壺水因沸騰而溢出。The pot is boiling over.② bubbling and boiling—unrest; seething: 他的熱血沸騰。His blood is bubbling and boiling.
沸泉(ㄈㄟˋ ㄑㄩㄢˊ)
a bubbling spring
沸石(ㄈㄟˋ ㄕˊ)
zeolite
沸水(ㄈㄟˋ ㄕㄨㄟˇ)
boiling water

【油】 2815
ㄧㄡˊ you yóu

1. a general name for oil, fat, grease, either animal or vegetable: 油水不相容。Oil and water have an antipathy.
2. anything in liquid form which is inflammable, as petroleum, gasoline, etc.
3. to oil: 他給脚踏車上油。He oiled his bicycle.
4. to varnish; to paint: 請油一油大門。Varnish the gate, please.
5. greasy: 她不喜歡油膩的食物。She disliked greasy food.
6. polished and over-experienced; sly; sleeky
7. luxuriant; prospering; flourishing

油杯(ㄧㄡˊ ㄅㄟ)or 油壺(ㄧㄡˊ ㄏㄨˊ)
an oilcup
油餅(ㄧㄡˊ ㄅㄧㄥˇ)
fried salty pancakes
油布(ㄧㄡˊ ㄅㄨˋ)
oilcloth (used as a waterproof covering)
油瓶(ㄧㄡˊ ㄆㄧㄥˊ)
① a bottle for storing oil ② a woman's children by previous marriage
油墨(ㄧㄡˊ ㄇㄛˋ)
printing ink
油門(ㄧㄡˊ ㄇㄣˊ)
① a throttle ② an accelerator: 公車司機踩油門加速。The bus driver stepped on the accelerator.
油坊(ㄧㄡˊ ㄈㄤˊ)
an oil extracting mill
油豆腐(ㄧㄡˊ ㄉㄡˋ ·ㄈㄨ)
fried bean curd
油燈(ㄧㄡˊ ㄉㄥ)
an oil lamp
油點子(ㄧㄡˊ ㄉㄧㄢˇ ·ㄗ)or 油點兒(ㄧㄡˊ ㄉㄧㄚˇㄦ)
greasy spots; oil stains
油頭粉面(ㄧㄡˊ ㄊㄡˊ ㄈㄣˇ ㄇㄧㄢˋ)
pomaded hair and powdered face — descriptive of a frivolous youngster
油頭滑腦(ㄧㄡˊ ㄊㄡˊ ㄏㄨㄚˊ ㄋㄠˇ)
slick; flippant
油條(ㄧㄡˊ ㄊㄧㄠˊ)
① fritters of twisted dough—a Chinese specialty usually for breakfast ② a suave, well-oiled person, long on experience but short on sincerity: 他是個老油條。He is a well-oiled fellow.
油田(ㄧㄡˊ ㄊㄧㄢˊ)
an oil field
油桶(ㄧㄡˊ ㄊㄨㄥˇ)
an oil drum
油泥(ㄧㄡˊ ㄋㄧˊ)
greasy dirt: 擦掉你手錶上的油泥。Clean the greasy dirt on your watch.
油膩(ㄧㄡˊ ㄋㄧˋ)
(said of food) fatty; oily; greasy: 這食物油膩。The food was greasy.
油簍(ㄧㄡˊ ㄌㄡˇ)
a willow basket covered with oilcloth, etc. for storage of liquids
油料(ㄧㄡˊ ㄌㄧㄠˋ)
petroleum, oil and lubricant (POL)
油料庫(ㄧㄡˊ ㄌㄧㄠˋ ㄎㄨˋ)
an oil depot; a POL depot
油亮(ㄧㄡˊ ㄌㄧㄤˋ)
glossy; shiny: 這桌面非常的油亮。The top of this table is very glossy.
油輪(ㄧㄡˊ ㄌㄨㄣˊ)
an oil tanker; a tanker; an oiler
油綠(ㄧㄡˊ ㄌㄩˋ)
dark green
油膏(ㄧㄡˊ ㄍㄠ)
ointment
油鍋(ㄧㄡˊ ㄍㄨㄛ)
① an oil pan for frying or cooking ② a cauldron of oil—a punishment for evil spirits in the legendary hell
油管(ㄧㄡˊ ㄍㄨㄢˇ)
oil pipes; oil pipelines: 他們在鋪設油管。They were laying oil pipes.
油罐(ㄧㄡˊ ㄍㄨㄢˋ)
an oilcan; an oil tank
油光(ㄧㄡˊ ㄍㄨㄤ)
glossy; shiny; varnished: 他的鞋子油光晶亮。His shoes are shiny.
油礦(ㄧㄡˊ ㄎㄨㄤˋ)
an oil field; oil deposit
油葫蘆(ㄧㄡˊ ㄏㄨˊ ㄌㄨˊ)
a kind of cricket (*Gryllodes miltratus*)
油滑(ㄧㄡˊ ㄏㄨㄚˊ)
slippery and sly; suave and crafty; sleeky: 他是個油滑的政客。He is a crafty politician.
油畫(ㄧㄡˊ ㄏㄨㄚˋ)
oil paintings
油灰(ㄧㄡˊ ㄏㄨㄟ)
putty
油跡(ㄧㄡˊ ㄐㄧ)
oil stains; greasy spots: 油跡易除。Oil stains are easy to remove.
油煎(ㄧㄡˊ ㄐㄧㄢ)
to fry in oil or fat
油井(ㄧㄡˊ ㄐㄧㄥˇ)
an oil well: 他們鑽了一口油井。They drilled (or bored) an oil well.
油漆(ㄧㄡˊ ㄑㄧ)
① paint; varnish; oil paint: 油漆未乾! Wet (or Fresh) Paint! ② to paint: 請把大門油漆一下。Please have the gate painted.
油漆匠(ㄧㄡˊ ㄑㄧ ㄐㄧㄤˋ)
a house painter; an oil painter
油腔滑調(ㄧㄡˊ ㄑㄧㄤ ㄏㄨㄚˊ ㄉㄧㄠˋ)
oily and fishy; polished and slippery; suave and sly; utterly insincere; glib
油裙(ㄧㄡˊ ㄑㄩㄣˊ)
an apron used during cooking
油箱(ㄧㄡˊ ㄒㄧㄤ)
a fuel tank
油星(子)(ㄧㄡˊ ㄒㄧㄥ (·ㄗ))or 油杵

〔水部〕

〔水部〕

子(ㄧㄡˊ ㄔˇ ㄧㄡˇ ·ㄗ)
droplets of oil, that may shoot out during frying, etc.
油脂(ㄧㄡˊ ㄓ)
①(chemistry) olein ② oil and grease; fats
油紙(ㄧㄡˊ ㄓˇ)
oilpaper
油渣(ㄧㄡˊ ㄓㄚ)
① dregs of fat ② oil residue
油渣餅(ㄧㄡˊ ㄓㄚ ㄅㄧㄥˇ)
oil cake
油渣粉(ㄧㄡˊ ㄓㄚ ㄈㄣˇ)
oil meal
油炸果(ㄧㄡˊ ㄓㄚˊ ㄍㄨㄛˇ)or 油炸鬼(ㄧㄡˊ ㄓㄚˊ ㄍㄨㄟˇ)
fritters of twisted dough
油榨機(ㄧㄡˊ ㄓㄚˋ ㄐㄧ)
an oil press
油毡(ㄧㄡˊ ㄓㄢ)
asphalt roofing
油廠(ㄧㄡˊ ㄔㄤˇ)
① an oil refinery ② an oil extracting mill
油商(ㄧㄡˊ ㄕㄤ)
an oil dealer; an oil businessman; an oilman
油水兒(ㄧㄡˊ ㄕㄨㄟˇㄦ)
① the cream or essence of something ② side profit or outside gains in a deal—as kickbacks, etc.
油然(ㄧㄡˊ ㄖㄢˊ)
① copious; luxuriant; flourishing; abundantly ② (now rarely) not moving ahead; halting
油然而生(ㄧㄡˊ ㄖㄢˊ ㄦˊ ㄕㄥ)
(said of love, admiration, sympathy, etc.) to grow in abundance and somewhat suddenly; to well up: 同情之心，油然而生。Sympathy wells up in one's heart.
油子(ㄧㄡˊ ·ㄗ)
① a sleeky person; a sly fellow ② any black sticky substance
油嘴(ㄧㄡˊ ㄗㄨㄟˇ)
glib-tongued; oily-tongued
油嘴滑舌(ㄧㄡˊ ㄗㄨㄟˇ ㄏㄨㄚˊ ㄕㄜˊ)
sweet and smooth words which are not backed by sincerity: 他是個油嘴滑舌的政客。He was a politician with a well-oiled tongue.

油彩(ㄧㄡˊ ㄘㄞˇ)
greasepaint; paint
油菜(ㄧㄡˊ ㄘㄞˋ)
rape
油層(ㄧㄡˊ ㄘㄥˊ)
an oil reservoir; an oil layer; an oil horizon
油頁岩(ㄧㄡˊ ㄧㄝˋ ㄧㄢˊ)
oil shale
油油(ㄧㄡˊ ㄧㄡˊ)
① luxuriant and glossy—as new leaves in spring ②(said of water) flowing
油煙(ㄧㄡˊ ㄧㄢ)
soot; lampblack
油煙子(ㄧㄡˊ ㄧㄢ ·ㄗ)
greasy dirt produced from heating oil
油鹽店(ㄧㄡˊ ㄧㄢˊ ㄉㄧㄢˋ)
a grocery store
油鹽醬醋(ㄧㄡˊ ㄧㄢˊ ㄐㄧㄤˋ ㄘㄨˋ)
oils, salt, soybean sauce and vinegar—daily necessaries
油印(ㄧㄡˊ ㄧㄣˋ)
to mimeograph: 他油印了六十份宣傳資料。He mimeographed sixty copies of propaganda.
油印本(ㄧㄡˊ ㄧㄣˋ ㄅㄣˇ)
a mimeographed booklet, pamphlet, etc.
油印機(ㄧㄡˊ ㄧㄣˋ ㄐㄧ)
a mimeograph
油污(ㄧㄡˊ ㄨ)
greasy dirt

【河】 2816 ㄏㄜˊ her hé

1. a general name for rivers, streams, and waterways: 這河注入湖內。The river runs into a lake.
2. Ho, the Yellow River in northern China, 2,700 miles long

河壩(ㄏㄜˊ ㄅㄚˋ)
dikes; embankments; levees
河伯娶婦(ㄏㄜˊ ㄅㄛˊ ㄑㄩˇ ㄈㄨˋ)
(in ancient China) a local custom of offering a young girl to the god of the Yellow River as his bride—by throwing her into the river
河北(ㄏㄜˊ ㄅㄟˇ)
① north of the river ② Hopeh Province
河蚌(ㄏㄜˊ ㄅㄤˋ)
bivalves grown in rivers and lakes; mussels
河邊(ㄏㄜˊ ㄅㄧㄢ)or 河邊兒(ㄏㄜˊ ㄅㄧㄚㄦ)
the riverside; by the side of the river: 我們沿著河邊走。We walked along the riverside.
河邊的(ㄏㄜˊ ㄅㄧㄢ ·ㄉㄜ)
riverain; riverine: 河邊的村落顯得特別的寧靜。Riverine villages appear especially calm.
河濱(ㄏㄜˊ ㄅㄧㄣ)
the riverbanks; the riverside; the waterfront
河畔(ㄏㄜˊ ·ㄆㄢ)
riverbanks; by the side of the river; the riverside
河馬(ㄏㄜˊ ㄇㄚˇ)
a hippopotamus, or a hippo
河防(ㄏㄜˊ ㄈㄤˊ)
embankments or levees along the Yellow River
河道(ㄏㄜˊ ㄉㄠˋ)
the course of a river; a waterway; the channel of a river: 他們沿該國的河道逆流而上。They went up the riverways of the country.
河隄or河堤(ㄏㄜˊ ㄉㄧ)or(ㄏㄜˊ ㄊㄧˊ)
embankments; dikes; levees
河東(ㄏㄜˊ ㄉㄨㄥ)
① the area east of the Yellow River in Shansi Province (山西) ② the southwestern part of Shansi Province
河東獅吼(ㄏㄜˊ ㄉㄨㄥ ㄕ ㄏㄡˇ)
the display of shrewishness; the outburst of a virago
河東獅子(ㄏㄜˊ ㄉㄨㄥ ㄕ ·ㄗ)
a shrew; a virago; a fishwife
河套(ㄏㄜˊ ㄊㄠˋ)
the Great Bend of the Yellow River Inner in Mongolia
河灘(ㄏㄜˊ ㄊㄢ)
the sand dune along a river
河圖洛書(ㄏㄜˊ ㄊㄨˊ ㄌㄨㄛˋ ㄕㄨ)
(according to Chinese legends) mystic signs and markings revealed to Fu Hsi (伏羲) and Yü the Great (大禹) thousands of years ago
河豚(ㄏㄜˊ ㄊㄨㄣˊ)
the globefish; a blowfish; a puffer
河內(ㄏㄜˊ ㄋㄟˋ)
① Hanoi, North Vietnam ② the old name of a region

north of the Yellow River, including the northern part of Honan and the southern part of Shansi
河南(ㄏㄜˊ ㄋㄢˊ)
Honan Province
河南墜子(ㄏㄜˊ ㄋㄢˊ ㄓㄨㄟˋ ·ㄗ)
Honan opera featuring narration and singing to the accompaniment of stringed and percussion instruments
河流(ㄏㄜˊ ㄌㄧㄡˊ)
streams, waterways, rivers or channels of water
河梁(ㄏㄜˊ ㄌㄧㄤˊ)
① a bridge spanning a river ② the parting place
河洛(ㄏㄜˊ ㄌㄨㄛˋ)
① the basin between the Yellow River and the River Lo ② short for 河圖洛書
河工(ㄏㄜˊ ㄍㄨㄥ)
river engineering; river works
河公(ㄏㄜˊ ㄍㄨㄥ) or 河伯(ㄏㄜˊ ㄅㄛˊ)
the god of the Yellow River
河口(ㄏㄜˊ ㄎㄡˇ)
a river mouth; a stream outlet
河海不擇細流(ㄏㄜˊ ㄏㄞˇ ㄅㄨˋ ㄗㄜˊ ㄒㄧˋ ㄌㄧㄡˊ)
Profound learning is an accumulation of bits of knowledge.
河漢(ㄏㄜˊ ㄏㄢˋ)
the Milky Way
河漢斯言(ㄏㄜˊ ㄏㄢˋ ㄙ ㄧㄢˊ)
statements that are too far-fetched to gain credulity
河清(ㄏㄜˊ ㄑㄧㄥ)
clear water in the Yellow River (which is always muddy), regarded as a harbinger of some great happy event
河清難俟(ㄏㄜˊ ㄑㄧㄥ ㄋㄢˊ ㄙˋ)
It takes too long to wait, and life is short.
河清海晏(ㄏㄜˊ ㄑㄧㄥ ㄏㄞˇ ㄧㄢˋ)
halcyon days; time of peace and prosperity
河渠(ㄏㄜˊ ㄑㄩˊ)
the place where water is reserved; a reservoir; waterways
河西(ㄏㄜˊ ㄒㄧ)
west of the Yellow River
河心(ㄏㄜˊ ㄒㄧㄣ)
the middle of a river
河州 or 河洲(ㄏㄜˊ ㄓㄡ)
a sand bar or islet in a river
河牀(ㄏㄜˊ ㄔㄨㄤˊ)
the riverbed; the floor of a river
河山(ㄏㄜˊ ㄕㄢ)
rivers and mountains—the territory of a country
河山變色(ㄏㄜˊ ㄕㄢ ㄅㄧㄢˋ ㄙㄜˋ)
The situation of the land is greatly changed.
河身(ㄏㄜˊ ㄕㄣ)
water volume of a river
河神(ㄏㄜˊ ㄕㄣˊ)
a river-god
河朔(ㄏㄜˊ ㄕㄨㄛˋ)
① the northern bank of the Yellow River ② the part of China north of the Yellow River
河水不犯井水(ㄏㄜˊ ㄕㄨㄟˇ ㄅㄨˋ ㄈㄢˋ ㄐㄧㄥˇ ㄕㄨㄟˇ)
not to interfere with one another 或 Everyone minds his own business.
河岸(ㄏㄜˊ ㄢˋ)
the riverbank; the riverside
河魚腹疾(ㄏㄜˊ ㄩˊ ㄈㄨˋ ㄐㄧˊ) or 河魚之疾(ㄏㄜˊ ㄩˊ ㄓ ㄐㄧˊ)
diarrhea
河嶽(ㄏㄜˊ ㄩㄝˋ)
the Yellow River and the Five Sacred Mountains of China
河源(ㄏㄜˊ ㄩㄢˊ)
① the source of the Yellow River—in Tsinghai Province ② name of a county in Kwangtung Province

【沼】 2817 ㄓㄠˇ jao zhǎo

a lake; a pond; a pool; a marsh
沼氣(ㄓㄠˇ ㄑㄧˋ)
marsh gas; methane
沼澤(ㄓㄠˇ ㄗㄜˊ)
a marsh; a swamp; a bog; lakes and ponds

【沽】 2818 ㄍㄨ gu gū

1. to buy
2. to sell
3. crude; inferior (quality)
4. (now rare) negligent

沽名釣譽(ㄍㄨ ㄇㄧㄥˊ ㄉㄧㄠˋ ㄩˋ)
to do something, not for the sake of achievement, but for the sake of fishing for a good reputation or fame; to seek publicity
沽河(ㄍㄨ ㄏㄜˊ)
also known as the Pai River (白河) near Tientsin
沽激(ㄍㄨ ㄐㄧ)
to behave unnaturally for the sake of a good reputation
沽酒(ㄍㄨ ㄐㄧㄡˇ)
① to buy wine ② wine or spirits bought from stores
沽售(ㄍㄨ ㄕㄡˋ)
to buy and sell

【治】 2819 ㄓˋ jyh zhì (動詞讀音 ㄔˊ chyr chí)

1. to administer; to control; to govern; to manage; to rule: 他統治這國家有二十年。He ruled the country for twenty years.
2. to regulate; to harness (a river)
3. the seat of the local government: 縣治 the county seat
4. to treat (a disease); to cure: 牙醫師在治療我的牙齒。The dentist is treating my teeth.
5. to study; to research: 他專治農業。He makes a study in agriculture.
6. to punish
7. peaceful and orderly
8. a Chinese family name

治辦(ㄓˋ ㄅㄢˋ)
successful discharge of duties
治本(ㄓˋ ㄅㄣˇ)
to deal with (or cure) a trouble, etc. at the source; to treat a matter thoroughly
治標(ㄓˋ ㄅㄧㄠ)
to cope with the symptoms only (as opposed to 治本)
治兵(ㄓˋ ㄅㄧㄥ)
to lead troops; to direct military affairs
治病(ㄓˋ ㄅㄧㄥˋ)
to treat a disease or ailment: 我是來治病的。I am here to cure.
治平(ㄓˋ ㄆㄧㄥˊ)
① to govern the nation and

〔水部〕

bring peace to the world ② peace and prosperity as a result of enlightened government

治命(ㄓˋ ㄇㄧㄥˋ)
the sensible orders or instructions left by a dead man

治理(ㄓˋ ㄌㄧˇ)
① to administer; to regulate; to manage; to govern: 總統治理國家。The President governs the country. ② to harness; to regulate; to bring under control; to put in order

治療(ㄓˋ ㄌㄧㄠˊ)
to treat or cure (a disease); cure; treatment; therapy

治亂(ㄓˋ ㄌㄨㄢˋ)
order and disorder; peace and upheaval

治亂興亡(ㄓˋ ㄌㄨㄢˋ ㄒㄧㄥ ㄨㄤˊ)
the rise and fall of a nation; order and prosperity on the one hand and confusion and decline on the other

治亂之道(ㄓˋ ㄌㄨㄢˋ ㄓ ㄉㄠˋ)
the proper way of government

治國(ㄓˋ ㄍㄨㄛˊ)
to govern a nation; to administer national affairs; to rule a country: 治國平天下 to rule the country and give peace to the world

治功(ㄓˋ ㄍㄨㄥ)
the achievement of managing national affairs

治好了(ㄓˋ ㄏㄠˇ ·ㄌㄜ)
(said of a disease) cured: 她的病不久就治好了。She was soon cured of her illness.

治化(ㄓˋ ㄏㄨㄚˋ)
to train the people with better (or more civilized) ways of life with enlightened government

治淮(ㄓˋ ㄏㄨㄞˊ)
to regulate the Huai River (which is particularly troublesome)

治黃(ㄓˋ ㄏㄨㄤˊ)
to regulate the Yellow River (which is particularly troublesome)

治績(ㄓˋ ㄐㄧ)
the merits or achievements of an administration

治家(ㄓˋ ㄐㄧㄚ)
to manage a household; to regulate a family

治經(ㄓˋ ㄐㄧㄥ)
to study classics

治軍(ㄓˋ ㄐㄩㄣ)
to direct military affairs; to direct troops

治權(ㄓˋ ㄑㄩㄢˊ)
the power of governing, as opposed to people's political rights

治下(ㄓˋ ㄒㄧㄚˋ)
① under the rule, control, or jurisdiction of ② a self-reference when reporting to a superior or a local chief

治學(ㄓˋ ㄒㄩㄝˊ)
to study; to devote oneself to learning

治裝(ㄓˋ ㄓㄨㄤ)
to pack or arrange one's baggage before taking a trip; to buy new clothing before embarking on a long journey

治產(ㄓˋ ㄔㄢˇ)
to manage property; to buy real estate

治世(ㄓˋ ㄕˋ)
a time of peace and order as a result of enlightened government

治事(ㄓˋ ㄕˋ)
to transact business

治生(ㄓˋ ㄕㄥ)
to make a living

治術(ㄓˋ ㄕㄨˋ)
the ways and means of a good government

治水(ㄓˋ ㄕㄨㄟˇ)
to regulate waterways, rivers, etc. to prevent them from flooding; river control; flood control

治戎(ㄓˋ ㄖㄨㄥˊ)
to use the military forces

治罪(ㄓˋ ㄗㄨㄟˋ)
to punish a criminal according to law; to bring to justice

治絲而棼(ㄓˋ ㄙ ㄦˊ ㄈㄣˊ)
to mess up something because of mishandling

治喪(ㄓˋ ㄙㄤ)
to manage a funeral; to take care of the funeral rites

治喪委員會(ㄓˋ ㄙㄤ ㄨㄟˇ ㄩㄢˊ ㄏㄨㄟˋ)
a funeral committee

治安(ㄓˋ ㄢ)
public security; peace and order of a society or a nation

治安機關(ㄓˋ ㄢ ㄐㄧ ㄍㄨㄢ)
the public-security organization; law-enforcement agencies

治外法權(ㄓˋ ㄨㄞˋ ㄈㄚˇ ㄑㄩㄢˊ)
extraterritoriality; extrality

治愈 or 治癒(ㄓˋ ㄩˋ)
to succeed in curing a disease; to restore health to a patient; to heal: 此病很快就治癒了。It soon healed up.

【沾】 2820
ㄓㄢ jan zhān

1. to moisten; to wet
2. to tinge; to stain; to contaminate
3. to be imbued with; to be infected with
4. to benefit from
5. to touch: 他煙酒不沾。He touched neither tobacco nor alcohol.

沾邊(ㄓㄢ ㄅㄧㄢ)
① to touch on (or upon) only lightly: 別和那種事沾邊。Don't touch that kind of business. ② to be close to what it should be; to be relevant: 你講的一點兒也不沾邊。What you say is not relevant at all.

沾便宜(ㄓㄢ ㄆㄧㄢˊ ·ㄧ)
① to reap benefits from a deal etc.; to gain small advantage or profit ② to tease someone in order to get some verbal advantage

沾溉(ㄓㄢ ㄍㄞˋ)
① to moisten and irrigate (the land) ② favors

沾光(ㄓㄢ ㄍㄨㄤ)
to benefit from the support or influence of someone; to ride on someone's coattails to success

沾花惹草(ㄓㄢ ㄏㄨㄚ ㄖㄜˇ ㄘㄠˇ)
to fool around with women

沾襟(ㄓㄢ ㄐㄧㄣ)
to moisten sleeves with tears

沾親帶故(ㄓㄢ ㄑㄧㄣ ㄉㄞˋ ㄍㄨˋ)

①with blood or marital relationship; having personal connections, close or remote ②to rub off some glory on friends and relatives
沾沾自喜(ㄓㄢ ㄓㄢ ㄗˋ ㄒㄧˇ)
smug and complacent
沾濕(ㄓㄢ ㄕ)
①to make wet; to moisten; damp or wet ②steeped in; imbued with
沾手(ㄓㄢ ㄕㄡˇ)
①to touch with the hand ②to play a role in something; to have a finger in the pie
沾水(ㄓㄢ ㄕㄨㄟˇ)
to soak in water
沾脣(ㄓㄢ ㄔㄨㄣˊ)
(said of food or drink) to touch the lips: 她一向酒不沾脣。She has never let wine touch her lips.
沾染(ㄓㄢ ㄖㄢˇ)
to be steeped in; to become addicted to (bad habits, practices, etc.): 他沾染了惡習。He was steeped in vice.
沾染習氣(ㄓㄢ ㄖㄢˇ ㄒㄧˊ ㄑㄧˋ)
to be corrupted by prevailing bad customs or practices
沾染世俗(ㄓㄢ ㄖㄢˇ ㄕˋ ㄙㄨˊ)
corrupted by worldly ways
沾潤(ㄓㄢ ㄖㄨㄣˋ)
①to moisten; to wet ②to harvest benefits from the side
沾漬(ㄓㄢ ㄗˋ)
imbued with; to soak in

【況】 2821
(况) ㄎㄨㄤˋ kuanq kuàng
1. moreover; in addition; not to mention...
2. to compare; comparative: 以古況今to compare the present with the past
3. situations; conditions; circumstances: 您的近況如何? How have you been recently?
4. to visit; to call on
5. a Chinese family name
況兼(ㄎㄨㄤˋ ㄐㄧㄢ)
besides; moreover; in addition; not to mention the fact that…
況且(ㄎㄨㄤˋ ㄑㄧㄝˇ)
moreover; besides; furthermore: 我太疲倦不能出去，況且時候也太晚了。I am too tired to go; besides, it's too late.
況又(ㄎㄨㄤˋ ㄧㄡˋ)
furthermore
況味(ㄎㄨㄤˋ ㄨㄟˋ)
①situations; conditions; circumstances ②flavor

【泂】 2822
ㄐㄩㄥˇ jeong jiǒng
1. (said of water) clear and deep
2. far and wide
泂泂(ㄐㄩㄥˇ ㄐㄩㄥˇ)
clear and deep

【沿】 2823
1. ㄧㄢˊ yan yán
1. to follow; to go along; along: 我沿著街道走。I walked along the street.
2. to hand down; to continue: 相沿成習。A custom has come down from the past and become customary.
3. successive; continuous
沿波討源(ㄧㄢˊ ㄅㄛ ㄊㄠˇ ㄩㄢˊ)
(literally) to trace the water and search for its source—to get into the very source of something
沿邊兒(ㄧㄢˊ ㄅㄧㄚㄦ)
along the edge
沿門托鉢(ㄧㄢˊ ㄇㄣˊ ㄊㄨㄛ ㄅㄛ)
(Buddhism) to beg for alms from door to door
沿途(ㄧㄢˊ ㄊㄨˊ)
along the way; throughout the journey: 我們沿途受到熱情的接待。We were warmly received throughout our journey.
沿例(ㄧㄢˊ ㄌㄧˋ)
to follow a precedent or prevailing practice
沿路(ㄧㄢˊ ㄌㄨˋ)
along the road; along the way: 我們沿路看到許多野生動物。We saw many wild animals along the way.
沿革(ㄧㄢˊ ㄍㄜˊ)
successive changes; vicissitudes or history (of a system, institution, etc.); evolution: 社會風習的沿革 the evolution of social customs
沿河(ㄧㄢˊ ㄏㄜˊ)
along the river
沿海(ㄧㄢˊ ㄏㄞˇ)
①along the coast ②offshore
沿海一帶(ㄧㄢˊ ㄏㄞˇ ㄧˊ ㄉㄞˋ)
along the coastal region; in the seaboard region or coastal area
沿襲(ㄧㄢˊ ㄒㄧˊ)
to follow the old or traditional (practices, customs, precedents, etc.): 切勿沿襲陳規。Do not follow the old conventions.
沿線(ㄧㄢˊ ㄒㄧㄢˋ)
along a railway or highway: 這些是鐵路沿線的村鎮。These are the villages and towns along the railway.
沿著(ㄧㄢˊ ·ㄓㄜ)
to follow or go along…: 我們沿著河岸走。We went along the riverside.
沿才授職(ㄧㄢˊ ㄘㄞˊ ㄕㄡˋ ㄓˊ)
to confer an office, position, etc. on a person according to his ability; assignment on merit basis
沿岸(ㄧㄢˊ ㄢˋ)
along the coast of…; littoral: 我們沿岸散步。We take a walk along the shore.
沿用(ㄧㄢˊ ㄩㄥˋ)
to continue following the old practices, customs, etc.: 我們仍沿用舊有的習俗。We continued following the old customs.

【沿】 2823
2. ㄧㄢˋ yann yàn
the edge of something; the brim: 邊沿 the edge or border of anything

【泄】 2824
1. ㄒㄧㄝˋ shieh xiè
1. to leak out; to reveal
2. to vent
3. to scatter; to disperse
4. a Chinese family name
泄憤(ㄒㄧㄝˋ ㄈㄣˋ)
to vent one's anger
泄涕(ㄒㄧㄝˋ ㄊㄧˋ)
to come to tears; to cry
泄漏(ㄒㄧㄝˋ ㄌㄡˋ) or 泄露(ㄒㄧㄝˋ ㄌㄨˋ)
to leak out (secrets, etc.): 消息已泄漏出去了。The information has leaked out.
泄痢(ㄒㄧㄝˋ ㄌㄧˋ)
diarrhoea 參看「泄瀉」
泄露(ㄒㄧㄝˋ ㄌㄨˋ)

〔水部〕

to leak out (information, secrets, etc.); to reveal or expose unintentionally

泄恨(ㄒㄧㄝˋ ㄏㄣˋ)
to vent one's hatred or anger

泄勁(ㄒㄧㄝˋ ㄐㄧㄣˋ)
to be discouraged; to be disheartened; to slacken one's efforts

泄瀉(ㄒㄧㄝˋ ㄒㄧㄝˋ)
diarrhoea; to have loose bowels

泄水(ㄒㄧㄝˋ ㄕㄨㄟˇ)
(said of water) to seep out from cracks; sluicing

泄水道(ㄒㄧㄝˋ ㄕㄨㄟˇ ㄉㄠˋ)
sluiceway

【泄】2824
2. ㄧˋ yih yì
1. mild and easy
2. many; crowded

泄沓(ㄧˋ ㄊㄚˋ)
① garrulous and disorderly ② easygoing; lax in moral attitude 亦作「泄泄沓沓」

泄泄(ㄧˋ ㄧˋ)
① to flap wings ② many (people); crowded

【泆】2825
ㄧˋ yih yì
1. dissipated and licentious; libertine
2. flooding; overflowing

【泐】2826
ㄌㄜˋ leh lè
1. rocks splitting
2. to write letters
3. to carve
4. to condense; to coagulate

泐布(ㄌㄜˋ ㄅㄨˋ)
to report by letter

泐覆(ㄌㄜˋ ㄈㄨˋ)
to reply by letter

泐達(ㄌㄜˋ ㄉㄚˊ)
to notify or report by letter

泐石(ㄌㄜˋ ㄕˊ)
① to carve on a rock ② rock splitting up

泐此(ㄌㄜˋ ㄘˇ)
a concluding expression used at the end of a letter in old China

【泊】2827
ㄅㄛˊ bor bó
(又讀 ㄆㄛˋ poh pò)
1. to stay; to anchor a ship; to moor: 這船停泊在岸邊。The ship anchored along the shore.
2. to drift
3. tranquil and quiet
4. a lake; a body of water: 此一湖泊魚產甚豐。The lake teems with fish.

泊泊(ㄅㄛˊ ㄅㄛˊ)
ripples (of water)

泊船(ㄅㄛˊ ㄔㄨㄢˊ)
to moor a boat

泊岸(ㄅㄛˊ ㄢˋ)
to anchor alongside the river

【泅】2828
ㄑㄧㄡˊ chyou qiú
to swim: 他不費力地泅過這條河。He swam across the river easily.

泅渡(ㄑㄧㄡˊ ㄉㄨˋ)
to swim across

泅水(ㄑㄧㄡˊ ㄕㄨㄟˇ)
to swim

【泌】2829
1. ㄅㄧˋ bih bì
1. swift and easy gushing of water
2. name of a river in Honan Province

泌水(ㄅㄧˋ ㄕㄨㄟˇ)
the Pi River in Honan Province

【泌】2829
2. ㄇㄧˋ mih mì
to seep out; to excrete; to secrete

泌尿管(ㄇㄧˋ ㄋㄧㄠˋ ㄍㄨㄢˇ)or(ㄇㄧˋ ㄙㄨㄟ ㄍㄨㄢˇ)
the uropoietic passage; the urinary canal

泌尿科(ㄇㄧˋ ㄋㄧㄠˋ ㄎㄜ)or(ㄇㄧˋ ㄙㄨㄟ ㄎㄜ)
the urological department

泌尿器官(ㄇㄧˋ ㄋㄧㄠˋ ㄑㄧˋ ㄍㄨㄢ)or(ㄇㄧˋ ㄙㄨㄟ ㄑㄧˋ ㄍㄨㄢ)
(physiology) uropoietic organs; urinary organs

泌尿學(ㄇㄧˋ ㄋㄧㄠˋ ㄒㄩㄝˊ)
urology

【泔】2830
ㄍㄢ gan gān
1. the water from washing rice
2. a way of cooking
3. (said of food) stale

泔水(ㄍㄢ ㄕㄨㄟˇ)
the water from washing rice; hogwash

泔水桶(ㄍㄢ ㄕㄨㄟˇ ㄊㄨㄥˇ)
a bucket for hogwash

【泓】2831
ㄏㄨㄥˊ horng hóng
1. clear, deep water; limpid water
2. the ancient name of a stream in Honan Province

泓泓(ㄏㄨㄥˊ ㄏㄨㄥˊ)
very deep

泓宏(ㄏㄨㄥˊ ㄏㄨㄥˊ)
very loud; roaring

【法】2832
1. (灋) ㄈㄚˇ faa fǎ
1. an institution
2. law; regulations; rules; the statutes; legal: 守法是人人的義務。It is the duty of everybody to obey the law.
3. methods; ways of doing things: 他的教法很好。His teaching method is very good.
4. to pattern or model after; to emulate: 他勤讀以效法那位名作家。He studied hard in emulating the famous writer.
5. (Buddhism) the "way"—doctrines, etc.
6. tricks; magic arts: 請解釋這戲法。Please explain the trick.
7. expert or standard (calligraphy, painting, etc.)
8. penalty; punishment
9. a Chinese family name

法寶(ㄈㄚˇ ㄅㄠˇ)
① *dharmaratna,* one of the three Buddhist treasures ② something of uncanny or occult power—for killing or subduing the enemy ③ a standby; something that one always brings along—as saw, nails, hammer to a carpenter; pencil and paper to a reporter: 這字典是他的隨身法寶。This dictionary is his standby.

法辦(ㄈㄚˇ ㄅㄢˋ)
to bring (someone) to justice; to punish according to the law: 謀殺兇手已送法辦。The murderer was brought to justice.

法幣(ㄈㄚˇ ㄅㄧˋ)
the legal tender

法部(ㄈㄚˇ ㄅㄨˋ)or 法務部(ㄈㄚˇ ㄨˋ ㄅㄨˋ)

the Ministry of Justice

法碼(ㄈㄚˇ ㄇㄚˇ)
standard weights

法門(ㄈㄚˇ ㄇㄣˊ)
①(in ancient China) the south gate ② *dharmaparyaya;* the doctrines or wisdom of Buddha regarded as the door to enlightenment ③ the way, or method of learning something: 勤儉是成功的不二法門。Industry and thrift are the only correct method to success.

法名(ㄈㄚˇ ㄇㄧㄥˊ)
the name one assumes upon becoming a Buddhist monk or nun

法服(ㄈㄚˇ ㄈㄨˊ)
① ceremonial dress; dress for official functions ② gowns or robes worn by Buddhist monks or nuns

法典(ㄈㄚˇ ㄉㄧㄢˇ)
① a code of laws; a statute book ② the scriptures of Buddhism

法定(ㄈㄚˇ ㄉㄧㄥˋ)
stipulated by law; legal; legally-provided; determined or prescribed by law

法定代理人(ㄈㄚˇ ㄉㄧㄥˋ ㄉㄞˋ ㄌㄧˇ ㄖㄣˊ)
a legal representative

法定年齡(ㄈㄚˇ ㄉㄧㄥˋ ㄋㄧㄢˊ ㄌㄧㄥˊ)
legal age

法定人數(ㄈㄚˇ ㄉㄧㄥˋ ㄖㄣˊ ㄕㄨˋ)
a quorum — the number of members of a group or organization required to be present to transact business legally, usually a majority: 我們現在已足法定人數。We have a quorum now.

法度(ㄈㄚˇ ㄉㄨˋ)
laws and institutions

法臺(ㄈㄚˇ ㄊㄞˊ)
a platform on which a Buddhist monk or Taoist priest performs rites

法堂(ㄈㄚˇ ㄊㄤˊ)
a court of law in former times

法帖(ㄈㄚˇ ㄊㄧㄝˋ)
a model copy book of calligraphy

法條(ㄈㄚˇ ㄊㄧㄠˊ)
items or articles of law

法庭(ㄈㄚˇ ㄊㄧㄥˊ)
a law court; a courtroom; a tribunal: 此事將由法庭裁決。The court will rule on the matter.

法徒(ㄈㄚˇ ㄊㄨˊ)
the Buddhist monk

法統(ㄈㄚˇ ㄊㄨㄥˇ)
the system of justice

法臘(ㄈㄚˇ ㄌㄚˋ)
the end of the Buddhist monk's year after the summer retreat; a Buddhist year (the number of 夏臘 or 戒臘 or discipline years, indicating the years since a monk's ordination)

法老(ㄈㄚˇ ㄌㄠˇ)
Pharaoh, title of an ancient Egyptian king

法理(ㄈㄚˇ ㄌㄧˇ)
① the principle or theory of law ② the doctrines of Buddhism

法理學(ㄈㄚˇ ㄌㄧˇ ㄒㄩㄝˊ)
jurisprudence

法力(ㄈㄚˇ ㄌㄧˋ)
① power of Buddhist doctrines ② black magic; supernatural power

法吏(ㄈㄚˇ ㄌㄧˋ)
a warden; a prison-guard; court clerks

法令(ㄈㄚˇ ㄌㄧㄥˋ)
a general term for laws and regulations

法螺(ㄈㄚˇ ㄌㄨㄛˊ)
① a horn made of sea shell, used originally in the ancient army, now also used in Buddhist and Taoist rituals ②(figuratively) as in 吹法螺—to brag; to boast; to make boasts

法輪(ㄈㄚˇ ㄌㄨㄣˊ)
(Buddhism) *dharmacakra;* the Wheel of the Law; the Buddha truth which is capable of crushing all evil and all opposition, like Indra's wheel, and which rolls on from man to man, place to place, age to age

法律(ㄈㄚˇ ㄌㄩˋ)
laws

法律顧問(ㄈㄚˇ ㄌㄩˋ ㄍㄨˋ ㄨㄣˋ)
a legal advisor

法律行爲(ㄈㄚˇ ㄌㄩˋ ㄒㄧㄥˊ ㄨㄟˊ)
a legal act

法律學(ㄈㄚˇ ㄌㄩˋ ㄒㄩㄝˊ)
jurisprudence; law; the science of law 亦作「法學」

法律學系(ㄈㄚˇ ㄌㄩˋ ㄒㄩㄝˊ ㄒㄧˋ)or 法律系(ㄈㄚˇ ㄌㄩˋ ㄒㄧˋ)
the Department of Law (at a university)

法律制裁(ㄈㄚˇ ㄌㄩˋ ㄓˋ ㄘㄞˊ)
legal sanctions

法規(ㄈㄚˇ ㄍㄨㄟ)
laws and regulations

法官(ㄈㄚˇ ㄍㄨㄢ)
a judge (at court); a judicial official; a justice: 這法官很仁慈。The judge was very kind.

法冠(ㄈㄚˇ ㄍㄨㄢ)
① a cap worn by judicial officials in ancient times ② the cap of a Taoist high priest

法科(ㄈㄚˇ ㄎㄜ)
the law department of a college; the department of human sciences—including law, economics, political science

法號(ㄈㄚˇ ㄏㄠˋ)
the religious name of a Buddhist monk or nun

法籍(ㄈㄚˇ ㄐㄧˊ)
law books

法紀(ㄈㄚˇ ㄐㄧˋ)
law and discipline: 他目無法紀。He acted in utter disregard of law and discipline.

法家(ㄈㄚˇ ㄐㄧㄚ)
① the Legalist School, one of the nine schools of learning in ancient China, stressing law and punishment ② a great master; a leading authority

法家拂士(ㄈㄚˇ ㄐㄧㄚ ㄅㄧˋ ㄕˋ)
(originally in Mencius) officials and advisors of high moral standing and ability

法警(ㄈㄚˇ ㄐㄧㄥˇ)
① the judicial police ② a bailiff

法器(ㄈㄚˇ ㄑㄧˋ)
① implements used in worship ② one who obeys Buddha ③ a vessel of the law

法權(ㄈㄚˇ ㄑㄩㄢˊ)
jurisdiction

〔水部〕

法新(ㄈㄚˇ ㄒㄧㄣ)
(British coin) a farthing
法相(ㄈㄚˇ ㄒㄧㄤˋ)
(Buddhism) the aspects or characteristics of things — All things are of monadic nature but differ in form.
法學博士(ㄈㄚˇ ㄒㄩㄝˊ ㄅㄛˊ ㄕˋ)
a Doctor of Laws (LL.D.)
法學家(ㄈㄚˇ ㄒㄩㄝˊ ㄐㄧㄚ)
a jurist
法學士(ㄈㄚˇ ㄒㄩㄝˊ ㄕˋ)
a Bachelor of Laws (LL.B.)
法治(ㄈㄚˇ ㄓˋ)
rule of law
法制(ㄈㄚˇ ㄓˋ)
the legal system; laws and institutions: 我們要加強民主法制。Let's strengthen the democratic legal system.
法制室(ㄈㄚˇ ㄓˋ ㄕˋ)
a bureau in the early days of the Republic responsible for the drafting of statutes and laws
法場(ㄈㄚˇ ㄔㄤˇ)or(ㄈㄚˇ ㄔㄤˊ)
① an execution ground; the place of execution ② any place set aside for religious practices
法師(ㄈㄚˇ ㄕ)
① a salutation for a Buddhist monk ② a Taoist high priest
法施(ㄈㄚˇ ㄕ)
to teach the principles of Buddhism
法式(ㄈㄚˇ ㄕˋ)
① a pattern; a model; something to emulate; a standard ② legal ways or forms
法事(ㄈㄚˇ ㄕˋ)
Buddhist rituals performed on special occasions
法身(ㄈㄚˇ ㄕㄣ)
(Buddhism) *dharmakaya;* embodiment of truth and law; the spiritual or true body; essential Buddhahood; the essence of being; the absolute; the norm of the universe
法書(ㄈㄚˇ ㄕㄨ)
① masterpieces of calligraphy ② a volume on institutions and systems
法術(ㄈㄚˇ ㄕㄨˋ)
① an uncanny, occult, or supernatural feat, usually performed by a Buddhist or Taoist, for a purpose—as curing of the sick, etc. ② the black art
法數(ㄈㄚˇ ㄕㄨˋ)
(mathematics) an addend, subtrahend, multiplier or divisor
法人(ㄈㄚˇ ㄖㄣˊ)
a juridical person; a corporate person; a legal person; *legalis homo*
法則(ㄈㄚˇ ㄗㄜˊ)
① a way or method; a pattern or model considered as a standard ② a formula in mathematics ③ an agreement which has the same binding force as law
法藏(ㄈㄚˇ ㄗㄤˋ)
the doctrines in Buddhist scriptures
法座(ㄈㄚˇ ㄗㄨㄛˋ)
①the seat of the chief, as a throne in court ②a rendezvous for listening to Buddhist's lecture
法曹(ㄈㄚˇ ㄘㄠˊ)
judges
法案(ㄈㄚˇ ㄢˋ)
a bill which has been passed by parliament; a law; a statute
法衣(ㄈㄚˇ ㄧ)
robes or gowns worn by Buddhist monks or judges or lawyers
法醫(ㄈㄚˇ ㄧ)
an expert in forensic medicine employed by a court of law, such as a coroner
法醫學(ㄈㄚˇ ㄧ ㄒㄩㄝˊ)
forensic medicine; medical jurisprudence
法益(ㄈㄚˇ ㄧˋ)
interests provided in the law or protected by the law
法外施恩(ㄈㄚˇ ㄨㄞˋ ㄕ ㄣ)
to be lenient within the limits of the law
法網(ㄈㄚˇ ㄨㄤˇ)
the dragnet or the arms of law
法院(ㄈㄚˇ ㄩㄢˋ)
a court of justice; a court of law: 犯人被押到法院受審。The prisoner was brought to court for trial.

【法】 2832
2. ㄈㄚˊ far fá
法碼兒(ㄈㄚˊ ·ㄇㄚㄦ)
weights of a scale 亦作「砝碼」
法子(ㄈㄚˊ ·ㄗ)
a method; a way: 他採用同一法子。He adopted the same method.

【法】 2832
3. ㄈㄚ fa fā
a way, especially used in 沒法兒"No way out."

【法】 2832
4. ㄈㄚˋ fah fà
1. the Frank
2. France; French
法蘭西(ㄈㄚˋ ㄌㄢˊ ㄒㄧ)
France
法蘭絨(ㄈㄚˋ ㄌㄢˊ ㄖㄨㄥˊ)
flannel
法郎(ㄈㄚˋ ㄌㄤˊ)
(a monetary unit of France) franc 亦作「佛郎」: 這本書值十五法郎。This book costs 15 francs.
法國(ㄈㄚˋ ㄍㄨㄛˊ)
France: 法國的首都是巴黎。The capital of France is Paris.
法國大革命(ㄈㄚˋ ㄍㄨㄛˊ ㄉㄚˋ ㄍㄜˊ ㄇㄧㄥˋ)
the French Revolution (1789-1799)
法國人(ㄈㄚˋ ㄍㄨㄛˊ ㄖㄣˊ)
the French; a Frenchman
法籍(ㄈㄚˋ ㄐㄧˊ)
of French nationality
法西斯分子(ㄈㄚˋ ㄒㄧ ㄙ ㄈㄣˋ ㄗˇ)
Fascists
法西斯主義(ㄈㄚˋ ㄒㄧ ㄙ ㄓㄨˇ ㄧˋ)
Fascism
法新社(ㄈㄚˋ ㄒㄧㄣ ㄕㄜˋ)
Agence France Presse (AFP)
法文(ㄈㄚˋ ㄨㄣˊ)
the French language
法語(ㄈㄚˋ ㄩˇ)
the spoken French; French: 我母親會說法語。My mother speaks French.

【泗】 2833
ㄙˋ syh sì
1. snivel; nasal mucus

2. name of a river
3. name of a county
泗水(ㄙˋ ㄕㄨㄟˇ)
①name of a county in Shantung ②Surabaya, a seaport on Java

【泖】2834 ㄇㄠˇ mao mǎo
1. still waters
2. name of a river in Kiangsu Province

【泚】2835 ㄘˇ tsyy cǐ
1. clear waters
2. bright and brilliant
3. sweating

【泝】2836 ㄙㄨˋ suh sù
same as 溯—to go upstream or to trace up to the source
泝流(ㄙㄨˋ ㄌㄧㄡˊ)
to go against the current; to go upstream
泝洄(ㄙㄨˋ ㄏㄨㄟˊ)
to go against the stream
泝游(ㄙㄨˋ ㄧㄡˊ)
to go down the stream
泝沿(ㄙㄨˋ ㄧㄢˊ)
①to follow the stream or current ②to follow along a course
泝源(ㄙㄨˋ ㄩㄢˊ)
to trace up to the source

【泠】2837 ㄌㄧㄥˊ ling líng
1. clear sounds
2. mild and comfortable
3. same as 伶—a drama performer; an actor; an actress
4. a Chinese family name
泠風(ㄌㄧㄥˊ ㄈㄥ)
mild winds; breezes
泠冽(ㄌㄧㄥˊ ㄌㄧㄝˋ)
clear
泠泠(ㄌㄧㄥˊ ㄌㄧㄥˊ)
①gurgling sound ②cool ③clear and crisp sound
泠然(ㄌㄧㄥˊ ㄖㄢˊ)
①gentle and charming ②to understand; to realize ③cool ④a clear and crisp sound

【泛】2838 ㄈㄢˋ fann fàn
1. to float; to drift
2. not exact or precise; not practical
3. not sincere; not intimate
4. generally (speaking); as a whole; pan-: 泛美 Pan-American
5. to be suffused with
泛美航空公司(ㄈㄢˋ ㄇㄟˇ ㄏㄤˊ ㄎㄨㄥ ㄍㄨㄥ ㄙ)
the Pan American World Airways Inc.
泛泛(ㄈㄢˋ ㄈㄢˋ)
①not close or intimate ②in generalities ③to float
泛泛之交(ㄈㄢˋ ㄈㄢˋ ㄓ ㄐㄧㄠ)
a nodding acquaintance; a casual acquaintance
泛覽(ㄈㄢˋ ㄌㄢˇ)or 泛觀(ㄈㄢˋ ㄍㄨㄢ)
a quick and general glance; to see or view briefly
泛濫成災(ㄈㄢˋ ㄌㄢˋ ㄔㄥˊ ㄗㄞ)
a disaster caused by flooding waters; a disastrous flood
泛論(ㄈㄢˋ ㄌㄨㄣˋ)
to discuss generally; a general survey or review
泛指(ㄈㄢˋ ㄓˇ)
to generally indicate; vague reference or allusion: 他的說明是泛指一般人的。His explanation refers to people in general.
泛舟(ㄈㄢˋ ㄓㄡ)
to row a boat; boating: 我們去泛舟。Let's go boating now.
泛常(ㄈㄢˋ ㄔㄤˊ)
①usually; frequently; often ②not close or intimate
泛稱(ㄈㄢˋ ㄔㄥ)
generally called…
泛神論(ㄈㄢˋ ㄕㄣˊ ㄌㄨㄣˋ)
pantheism
泛音(ㄈㄢˋ ㄧㄣ)
(music) overtones
泛問(ㄈㄢˋ ㄨㄣˋ)
a question which does not concern a particular person or thing

【波】2839 ㄅㄛ bo bō (又讀 ㄆㄛ po pō)
1. waves; breakers: 波浪很高。The waves were high.
2. to undulate; undulation; to fluctuate; fluctuations
3. to affect; to involve; to implicate; to entangle
波峯(ㄅㄛ ㄈㄥ)
the wave crest
波幅(ㄅㄛ ㄈㄨˊ)
the range of undulations or fluctuations
波蕩(ㄅㄛ ㄉㄤˋ)
unstable; turmoil
波多黎各(ㄅㄛ ㄉㄨㄛ ㄌㄧˊ ㄍㄜˋ)
Puerto Rico
波段(ㄅㄛ ㄉㄨㄢˋ)
a wave band
波動(ㄅㄛ ㄉㄨㄥˋ)
①undulation ②(said of prices) fluctuations; to fluctuate: 物價年年波動。Prices fluctuate from year to year.
波濤(ㄅㄛ ㄊㄠˊ)
billows; breakers; large waves
波濤起伏(ㄅㄛ ㄊㄠˊ ㄑㄧˇ ㄈㄨˊ)
(said of sea waves) swelling, heaving and subsiding—also used figuratively to describe tumultuous situations, instability, etc.
波濤洶湧(ㄅㄛ ㄊㄠˊ ㄒㄩㄥ ㄩㄥˇ)
roaring waves and billows that swell up to heaven; to billow—a term used figuratively to describe tumultuous situations
波累(ㄅㄛ ㄌㄟˇ)
to involve in a trouble
波蘭(ㄅㄛ ㄌㄢˊ)
Poland: 華沙是波蘭的首都。Warsaw is the capital of Poland.
波蘭人(ㄅㄛ ㄌㄢˊ ㄖㄣˊ)
a Pole; the Poles
波瀾(ㄅㄛ ㄌㄢˊ)
①waves or billows ②the turns and twists of a piece of writing
波瀾起伏(ㄅㄛ ㄌㄢˊ ㄑㄧˇ ㄈㄨˊ)
(said of a piece of writing) with one climax following another
波瀾壯闊(ㄅㄛ ㄌㄢˊ ㄓㄨㄤˋ ㄎㄨㄛˋ)
surging forward with great momentum; unfolding on a magnificent scale
波浪(ㄅㄛ ㄌㄤˋ)
billows; breakers; waves: 波浪在岸邊起伏。The waves rose and fell on the shore.
波浪鼓(ㄅㄛ ㄌㄤˋ ㄍㄨˇ)
a kind of toy-drum for children with a long handle and

〔水部〕

one pendant on each side which hits the drum when the handle is twisted 亦作「博浪鼓」
波羅門(ㄅㄛ ㄌㄨㄛˊ ㄇㄣˊ)
(Hinduism) Brahman, or Brahmin, a member of the highest, or priestly, class among the Hindus
波羅的海(ㄅㄛ ㄌㄨㄛˊ ㄉㄧˋ ㄏㄞˇ)
the Baltic Sea, in northern Europe
波谷(ㄅㄛ ㄍㄨˇ)
the trough of the waves
波光(ㄅㄛ ㄍㄨㄤ)
the glistening light of waves
波河(ㄅㄛ ㄏㄜˊ)
the Po River, in northern Italy
波及(ㄅㄛ ㄐㄧˊ)
① to affect; to involve: 經濟危機波及了全世界。The economic crisis affected the entire world. ②(said of a fire) to engulf; to spread to
波心(ㄅㄛ ㄒㄧㄣ)
① the center of a water-ring ② the heart of a trouble, instability, etc.
波札那(ㄅㄛ ㄓㄚˊ ㄋㄚˇ)
Botswana
波折(ㄅㄛ ㄓㄜˊ)
twists and turns of a matter; obstructions or obstacles: 事情發生了波折。Things took an unexpected turn.
波磔(ㄅㄛ ㄓㄜˊ)
(Chinese calligraphy) a long downward stroke to the left or right
波狀葉(ㄅㄛ ㄓㄨㄤˋ ㄧㄝˋ)
sinuate leaves
波臣(ㄅㄛ ㄔㄣˊ)
① denizens of water ② victims of drowning
波長(ㄅㄛ ㄔㄤˊ)
(physics) wavelength
波士頓(ㄅㄛ ㄕˋ ㄉㄨㄣˋ)
Boston
波神(ㄅㄛ ㄕㄣˊ)
a nymph; the deity of a river
波茨坦宣言(ㄅㄛ ㄘˊ ㄊㄢˇ ㄒㄩㄢ ㄧㄢˊ)
the Potsdam Declaration signed by China, Great Britain and the U.S. in 1945
波斯(ㄅㄛ ㄙ)
Persia
波斯貓(ㄅㄛ ㄙ ㄇㄠ)
a Persian cat
波斯帝國(ㄅㄛ ㄙ ㄉㄧˋ ㄍㄨㄛˊ)
the Persian Empire
波斯菊(ㄅㄛ ㄙ ㄐㄩˊ)
coreopsis
波斯灣(ㄅㄛ ㄙ ㄨㄢ)
the Persian Gulf
波昂(ㄅㄛ ㄤˊ)
Bonn, capital of West Germany
波義耳定律(ㄅㄛ ㄧˋ ㄦˇ ㄉㄧㄥˋ ㄌㄩˋ)
Boyle's Law
波紋(ㄅㄛ ㄨㄣˊ)
ripples; a water-ring

【泣】 2840
ㄑㄧˋ chih qì

to weep; to come to tears without crying: 她泣不成聲。She choked with sobs.
泣別(ㄑㄧˋ ㄅㄧㄝˊ)
to part in tears
泣涕(ㄑㄧˋ ㄊㄧˋ)
to come to tears for sorrow; to weep
泣辜(ㄑㄧˋ ㄍㄨ)
to commiserate a criminal as Yü the Great (大禹) did, descending from the carriage to do so 參看「泣罪」
泣鬼神(ㄑㄧˋ ㄍㄨㄟˇ ㄕㄣˊ)
to move, or touch not only men, but the spirits and gods as well: 動天地而泣鬼神 to move the universe and cause the gods to weep—very moving
泣叩(ㄑㄧˋ ㄎㄡˋ)
a concluding expression used after one's name in a mourning notice
泣諫(ㄑㄧˋ ㄐㄧㄢˋ)
to counsel (a superior, king, or emperor) in tears indicating absolute sincerity
泣下沾襟(ㄑㄧˋ ㄒㄧㄚˋ ㄓㄢ ㄐㄧㄣ)
to weep so much that the tears make the front part of the garment dripping wet
泣下數行(ㄑㄧˋ ㄒㄧㄚˋ ㄕㄨˋ ㄏㄤˊ)
tears coursing down the cheeks
泣下如雨(ㄑㄧˋ ㄒㄧㄚˋ ㄖㄨˊ ㄩˇ)
One's tears fall down like rain.
泣血(ㄑㄧˋ ㄒㄩㄝˋ)
to weep blood (an expression used especially after one's name in a mourning notice for one's parents)
泣血稽顙(ㄑㄧˋ ㄒㄩㄝˋ ㄑㄧˇ ㄙㄤˇ)
weeping blood and knocking the head—in mourning for one's parents (an expression used in an obituary)
泣血三年(ㄑㄧˋ ㄒㄩㄝˋ ㄙㄢ ㄋㄧㄢˊ)
to mourn for one's parents for three years
泣杖(ㄑㄧˋ ㄓㄤˋ)
to cry over the stick (said of a filial son, Han Po-yü (韓伯俞) of the Han Dynasty, who wept because the stick used by his mother to punish him was making lighter strokes and he drew the conclusion that his mother was getting weaker)
泣珠(ㄑㄧˋ ㄓㄨ)
to weep pearly tears—with reference to a Chinese mythical tale of how a generous person repaid his host by weeping pearls instead of tears to be presented to the host
泣罪(ㄑㄧˋ ㄗㄨㄟˋ)
to weep for a criminal's evil-doing 亦作「泣辜」
泣訴(ㄑㄧˋ ㄙㄨˋ)
to tell one's sorrows or grievances in tears; to accuse while weeping

【泡】 2841
1. ㄆㄠˋ paw pào

1. bubbles; suds; froth; foam: 他用肥皂水吹氣泡。He blows bubbles with soap water.
2. a blister
3. to steep; to soak; to dip; to infuse (tea, etc.): 她把麵包泡在牛奶中。She soaked bread in milk.
4. (slang) to dawdle; to fool around (especially with women)

泡泡糖(ㄆㄠˋ ·ㄆㄠ ㄊㄤˊ)
bubble gum
泡沫(ㄆㄠˋ ㄇㄛˋ)
suds; foam; froth: 浪花衝擊海岸造成泡沫。The foam is made by waves breaking on the shore.
泡沫乳膠(ㄆㄠˋ ㄇㄛˋ ㄖㄨˇ ㄐㄧㄠ)

foam rubber
泡飯(ㄆㄠˋ ㄈㄢˋ)
to heat cooked rice with boiling water for eating
泡湯(ㄆㄠˋ ㄊㄤ)
① to make soup by infusing in hot water ②(said of a dream) busted; (said of money) wasted; (said of hope) dashed
泡幻(ㄆㄠˋ ㄏㄨㄢˋ)
visionary; empty bubbles
泡茶(ㄆㄠˋ ㄔㄚˊ)
to infuse tea; to make tea
泡水(ㄆㄠˋ ㄕㄨㄟˇ)
to soak in water
泡菜(ㄆㄠˋ ㄘㄞˋ)
vegetables preserved in salted water; Chinese pickles
泡兒(ㄆㄠˋㄦ)
① bubbles; foam: 水開時就起氣泡兒。When water boils, bubbles form. ② blisters: 我的脚起泡兒了。I've got blisters on my feet.
泡影(ㄆㄠˋ ㄧㄥˇ)
the shadow of bubbles—unreality; pie in the sky

【泡】 2841
2. ㄆㄠ pau pāo

1. loose and soft; spongy
2. an amount of excrement or urine: 小孩兒撒一泡尿。The child urinated.

【泥】 2842
1. ㄋㄧˊ ni ní

1. mud; mire; earth; soil; clay: 我的上衣沾滿汚泥。My coat is covered with mud.
2. to paste; to plaster: 這工人正在泥牆。The worker was plastering the wall.
3. mashed vegetables or fruit; paste: 棗泥 jujube paste

泥巴(ㄋㄧˊ ˙ㄅㄚ)
mud; mire; earth; clay
泥盆紀(ㄋㄧˊ ㄆㄣˊ ㄐㄧˋ)
(geology) the Devonian Period
泥菩薩(ㄋㄧˊ ㄆㄨˊ ㄙㄚˋ)
a clay idol: 他像泥菩薩過江，自身難保。He is like a clay idol wading across a river—hardly able to save himself (let alone anyone else).
泥封(ㄋㄧˊ ㄈㄥ)
to seal (a wine jug, jars, etc.) with mud or clay
泥點兒(ㄋㄧˊ ㄉㄧㄚˇㄦ)or 泥點子(ㄋㄧˊ ㄉㄧㄢˇ ˙ㄗ)
droplets of mud
泥多佛大(ㄋㄧˊ ㄉㄨㄛ ㄈㄛˊ ㄉㄚˋ)
(literally) The more the clay, the bigger the statue of Buddha.—The more the supporters, the greater the achievements of the leader.
泥胎(ㄋㄧˊ ㄊㄞ)
statues of gods made of mud
泥炭(ㄋㄧˊ ㄊㄢˋ)
peat 亦作「泥煤」
泥塘(ㄋㄧˊ ㄊㄤˊ)or 泥潭(ㄋㄧˊ ㄊㄢˊ)
a pond of mire; a morass
泥塗(ㄋㄧˊ ㄊㄨˊ)
① the ground soaked in rain water; mire ② filthy; dirty ③ the masses; the unknown; the humble
泥土(ㄋㄧˊ ㄊㄨˇ)
mud; clay; earth; soil: 把它埋在泥土裏。Bury it in the earth.
泥淖(ㄋㄧˊ ㄋㄠˋ)
mud; quagmires: 車子陷在泥淖中。The cart was bogged in the mud.
泥牛入海(ㄋㄧˊ ㄋㄧㄡˊ ㄖㄨˋ ㄏㄞˇ)
(literally) A mud ox goes into the sea.—never to return
泥濘(ㄋㄧˊ ㄋㄧㄥˋ)
muddy: 那是一條泥濘的路。It is a muddy road.
泥潦(ㄋㄧˊ ㄌㄠˇ)
a marshy ground; a quagmire
泥垢(ㄋㄧˊ ㄍㄡˋ)
mud and dirt—especially those on the human body: 洗掉你手上的泥垢。Wash the dirt off your hands.
泥坑(ㄋㄧˊ ㄎㄥ)
a mud pit; a quagmire; a morass: 不要陷入悲觀主義的泥坑裏。Don't fall into the quagmire of pessimism.
泥灰土(ㄋㄧˊ ㄏㄨㄟ ㄊㄨˇ)
marly soil
泥漿(ㄋㄧˊ ㄐㄧㄤ)
mire: 我們在滿是泥漿的足球場上踢球。We played on a football field that was thick with mire.
泥鰍 or 泥鰌(ㄋㄧˊ ˙ㄑㄧㄡ)
a loach; a mudfish
泥像(ㄋㄧˊ ㄒㄧㄤˋ)
a statue or image of a god, made of mud or clay
泥沼(ㄋㄧˊ ㄓㄠˇ)
mire; swamp; morasses; sloughs
泥磚(ㄋㄧˊ ㄓㄨㄢ)
sun-dried mud bricks
泥船渡河(ㄋㄧˊ ㄔㄨㄢˊ ㄉㄨˋ ㄏㄜˊ)
(originally in the Buddhist scripture) to cross a river in a boat of mud—How dangerous is the world where temptations lurk everywhere.
泥沙(ㄋㄧˊ ㄕㄚ)
① mud and sand; silt ② something worthless ③ to sink to the bottom
泥沙俱下(ㄋㄧˊ ㄕㄚ ㄐㄩˋ ㄒㄧㄚˋ)
Mud and sand are carried along.—There is a mingling of good and bad.
泥首(ㄋㄧˊ ㄕㄡˇ)
to kowtow with the head touching the ground
泥水活(ㄋㄧˊ ㄕㄨㄟˇ ㄏㄨㄛˊ)
the work of a bricklayer and plasterer
泥水匠(ㄋㄧˊ ㄕㄨㄟˇ ㄐㄧㄤˋ)
a bricklayer; a plasterer
泥人(ㄋㄧˊ ㄖㄣˊ)
a clay doll
泥滓(ㄋㄧˊ ㄗˇ)
① dirty or filthy ② low and inferior ③ the world
泥足深陷(ㄋㄧˊ ㄗㄨˊ ㄕㄣ ㄒㄧㄢˋ)
to sink deep in the mire; to get into real trouble; to bog down
泥醉(ㄋㄧˊ ㄗㄨㄟˋ)
dead drunk
泥塑(ㄋㄧˊ ㄙㄨˋ)
a clay sculpture
泥塑木雕(ㄋㄧˊ ㄙㄨˋ ㄇㄨˋ ㄉㄧㄠ)
(literally) made of clay or carved from wood—① idols ② one who is devoid of emotions
泥塑人(ㄋㄧˊ ㄙㄨˋ ㄖㄣˊ)
(literally) a person of clay—a person without motion of any kind, as after a shock or in great embarrassment
泥娃娃(ㄋㄧˊ ㄨㄚˊ ˙ㄨㄚ)
a clay doll (often found in the temple of the goddess of

〔水部〕

propagation ready to be stolen by those women believers who wish to beget a son)

〔水部〕

【泥】 2842
2. ㄋㄧˋ nih nì

1. to be tied down by conventions, old practices; very conservative
2. to request with sweet words
3. inapplicable

泥古(ㄋㄧˋ ㄍㄨˇ)
very conservative; to stick to ancient ways and thoughts

泥滯(ㄋㄧˋ ㄓˋ)
①bigoted and conservative ②to stay somewhere without obvious reason ③to be mired

泥飲(ㄋㄧˋ ㄧㄣˇ)
to compel others to drink

【泮】 2843
ㄆㄢˋ pann pàn

1. (in ancient China) an institution of higher learning
2. (now rarely) to dissolve; to melt

泮宮(ㄆㄢˋ ㄍㄨㄥ)
an institution of higher learning in ancient China

泮汗(ㄆㄢˋ ㄏㄢˋ)
(said of flooding waters) expansive

泮渙(ㄆㄢˋ ㄏㄨㄢˋ)
to dissolve (like floes)

泮水(ㄆㄢˋ ㄕㄨㄟˇ)
a semicircular pool on the premises of an institution of higher learning in former times

【泯】 2844
ㄇㄧㄣˇ miin mǐn

to destroy; to eliminate; to put an end to; to vanish

泯滅(ㄇㄧㄣˇ ㄇㄧㄝˋ)or 泯沒(ㄇㄧㄣˇ ㄇㄛˋ)
to vanish without a trace; to sink into oblivion: 他們的貢獻永遠不會泯沒的。Their contributions will never sink into oblivion.

泯泯(ㄇㄧㄣˇ ㄇㄧㄣˇ)
①vague and gloomy; very low visibility ②clear (water) ③tumultuous; confusing and disorderly

泯絕(ㄇㄧㄣˇ ㄐㄩㄝˊ)
to be lost for ever; extinguished

【注】 2845
ㄓㄨˋ juh zhù

1. to pour (liquid): 雷電過後,大雨如注。After lightning and thunder came a heavy downpour.
2. to concentrate; to engross; preoccupation: 她全神貫注於一篇有趣的故事。She was engrossed in an interesting story.
3. same as 註—to annotate: 有的人一面讀書一面做批注。Some people annotate as they read.
4. stakes (in gambling): 孤注一擲 to stake all on a single throw of the dice

注明(ㄓㄨˋ ㄇㄧㄥˊ)
to make a footnote; to mark out 亦作「註明」: 你應該注明出處。You should give sources of your quotations.

注目(ㄓㄨˋ ㄇㄨˋ)
to look attentively; to focus one's look on; to gaze at; to stare at

注目禮(ㄓㄨˋ ㄇㄨˋ ㄌㄧˇ)
(military) parade salute

注帶(ㄓㄨˋ ㄉㄞˋ)
casting

注定(ㄓㄨˋ ㄉㄧㄥˋ)
to be doomed; to be destined: 他注定要失敗。He is doomed to failure.

注解(ㄓㄨˋ ㄐㄧㄝˇ)
①to annotate ②footnotes; annotations 亦作「註解」

注脚(ㄓㄨˋ ㄐㄧㄠˇ)
footnotes; annotations 亦作「註脚」

注銷(ㄓㄨˋ ㄒㄧㄠ)
to make void; to nullify; to annul; to cancel; to be written off: 賬已注銷。The account has been written off.

注心(ㄓㄨˋ ㄒㄧㄣ)
to concentrate attention; to focus attention

注重(ㄓㄨˋ ㄓㄨㄥˋ)
to attach great importance to; to consider to be important; to lay stress on; to emphasize: 本辭典特別注重文法。This dictionary puts a special emphasis on grammar.

注釋(ㄓㄨˋ ㄕˋ)
①to annotate ②footnotes; annotations 亦作「註釋」

注視(ㄓㄨˋ ㄕˋ)
to look attentively; to watch; to focus one's look on; to gaze at: 他注視着太陽漸漸落到樹後。He watched the sun setting behind the trees.

注射(ㄓㄨˋ ㄕㄜˋ)
to inject; injection; to get a shot: 傷寒預防注射 a typhoid shot

注射器(ㄓㄨˋ ㄕㄜˋ ㄑㄧˋ)
a syringe (for injection)

注疏(ㄓㄨˋ ㄕㄨ)or(ㄓㄨˋ ㄕㄨˋ)
notes and commentaries

注水(ㄓㄨˋ ㄕㄨㄟˇ)
water flooding

注入(ㄓㄨˋ ㄖㄨˋ)
to pour into; to empty into: 河水注入海。The waters of the river pour into the sea.

注入式(ㄓㄨˋ ㄖㄨˋ ㄕˋ)
(education) a spoonfeeding method or a cramming method (as opposed to a developmental method)

注子(ㄓㄨˋ ·ㄗ)
a wine vessel

注意(ㄓㄨˋ ㄧˋ)
to pay attention to; to watch: 過街時要注意車輛。Watch out for cars when you cross the street.

注意力(ㄓㄨˋ ㄧˋ ㄌㄧˋ)
attention

注音(ㄓㄨˋ ㄧㄣ)
to make phonetic transcriptions: 本文有注音嗎? Is the text marked with phonetic symbols?

注音符號(ㄓㄨˋ ㄧㄣ ㄈㄨˊ ㄏㄠˋ)
the National Phonetic Symbols (for Mandarin)

【泱】 2846
ㄧㄤ iang yāng

1. great; profound
2. (said of clouds) turbulent

泱漭無際(ㄧㄤ ㄇㄤˇ ㄨˊ ㄐㄧˋ)
vast without limit

泱泱(ㄧㄤ ㄧㄤ)
①great; magnificent; broad and deep ②(said of clouds) turbulent

泱泱大風(ㄧㄤ ㄧㄤ ㄉㄚˋ ㄈㄥ)
the impressive manner of a

great country
泱泱大國(丨ㄤ 丨ㄤ ㄉㄚˋ ㄍㄨㄛˊ)
a great country

【泳】 2847
ㄩㄥˇ yeong yǒng
1. to swim: 他游泳過河。He swam across the river.
2. types or methods of swimming: 蛙泳 breaststroke

【泉】 2848
ㄑㄩㄢˊ chyuan quán
1. a spring; a fountain
2. money (archaic)
3. a Chinese family name
泉幣(ㄑㄩㄢˊ ㄅㄧˋ)or泉布(ㄑㄩㄢˊ ㄅㄨˋ)
money, or currency (archaic terms)
泉脈(ㄑㄩㄢˊ ㄇㄞˋ)or(ㄑㄩㄢˊ ㄇㄛˋ)
ground water channels
泉臺(ㄑㄩㄢˊ ㄊㄞˊ)
a grave; a tomb
泉林(ㄑㄩㄢˊ ㄌㄧㄣˊ)
① natural scenery ② the abode of a recluse
泉路(ㄑㄩㄢˊ ㄌㄨˋ)
the way to Hades
泉下(ㄑㄩㄢˊ ㄒㄧㄚˋ)
the world of the dead; Hades
泉州(ㄑㄩㄢˊ ㄓㄡ)
Chuanchow, Fukien Province
泉州灣(ㄑㄩㄢˊ ㄓㄡ ㄨㄢ)
name of the estuary of the Tsin River in Fukien
泉石(ㄑㄩㄢˊ ㄕˊ)
springs and rocks—the beauty of nature
泉石膏肓(ㄑㄩㄢˊ ㄕˊ ㄍㄠ ㄏㄨㄤ)
inveterate love of outing; an obsession with nature
泉水(ㄑㄩㄢˊ ㄕㄨㄟˇ)
spring water
泉壤(ㄑㄩㄢˊ ㄖㄤˇ)
the world of the dead; Hades
泉源(ㄑㄩㄢˊ ㄩㄢˊ)
a fountainhead; a springhead; a source; a wellspring: 知識是智慧的泉源。Knowledge is the source of wisdom.

【泰】 2849
ㄊㄞˋ tay tài
1. great; big
2. quiet; calm; peace; ease: 國泰民安。The country is prosperous at peace, and the people live in happiness.
3. Thailand
4. good luck
5. same as 太—very; much; too; excessive
泰半(ㄊㄞˋ ㄅㄢˋ)
more than half; the greater part; the majority
泰斗(ㄊㄞˋ ㄉㄡˇ)
① Mountain Tai and the Dipper ② a leading authority (in certain field or discipline)
泰戈爾(ㄊㄞˋ ㄍㄜ ㄦˇ)
Rabindranath Tagore, 1861-1941, an Indian poet
泰國(ㄊㄞˋ ㄍㄨㄛˊ)
Thailand: 泰國首都是曼谷。The capital of Thailand is Bangkok.
泰國人(ㄊㄞˋ ㄍㄨㄛˊ ㄖㄣˊ)
a Thai; a Thailander
泰西(ㄊㄞˋ ㄒㄧ)
the Western countries; the West; the Occident
泰山(ㄊㄞˋ ㄕㄢ)
① Mountain Tai (in Shantung, one of the Five Sacred Mountains) ② (figuratively) great importance ③ one's father-in-law (one's wife's father) ④ Tarzan
泰山北斗(ㄊㄞˋ ㄕㄢ ㄅㄟˇ ㄉㄡˇ)
① Mountain Tai and the Dipper ② an eminent authority (in a learned field)
泰山不讓土壤(ㄊㄞˋ ㄕㄢ ㄅㄨˋ ㄖㄤˋ ㄊㄨˇ ㄖㄤˇ)
A learned man never stops his pursuit of knowledge.
泰山梁木(ㄊㄞˋ ㄕㄢ ㄌㄧㄤˊ ㄇㄨˋ)
a sage
泰山刻石(ㄊㄞˋ ㄕㄢ ㄎㄜˋ ㄕˊ)
the Mountain Tai inscription (attributed to 秦始皇)
泰山鴻毛(ㄊㄞˋ ㄕㄢ ㄏㄨㄥˊ ㄇㄠˊ)
the difference between Mountain Tai and a feather — very great difference (especially used in describing the manner of one's death—to die for a noble cause or for a trifle reason)
泰山其頹(ㄊㄞˋ ㄕㄢ ㄑㄧˊ ㄊㄨㄟˊ)
The revered man is dead.
泰山壓卵(ㄊㄞˋ ㄕㄢ ㄧㄚ ㄌㄨㄢˇ)or 泰山壓頂(ㄊㄞˋ ㄕㄢ ㄧㄚ ㄉㄧㄥˇ)
(literally) It is like Mountain Tai crushing an egg.—It is a big mismatch. 或 overwhelming force
泰水(ㄊㄞˋ ㄕㄨㄟˇ)
one's mother-in-law (one's wife's mother)
泰然(ㄊㄞˋ ㄖㄢˊ)or 泰然自若(ㄊㄞˋ ㄖㄢˊ ㄗˋ ㄖㄨㄛˋ)
unperturbed; unagitated; unalarmed; self-possessed; composed; equanimous
泰晤士報(ㄊㄞˋ ㄨˋ ㄕˋ ㄅㄠˋ)
the *Times*, published in London since 1785
泰晤士河(ㄊㄞˋ ㄨˋ ㄕˋ ㄏㄜˊ)
the Thames River

六畫

【洄】 2850
ㄏㄨㄟˊ hwei huí
(said of water) whirling
洄洑(ㄏㄨㄟˊ ㄈㄨˊ)
(said of water) whirling
洄瀾(ㄏㄨㄟˊ ㄌㄢˊ)
eddies

【洎】 2851
ㄐㄧˋ jih jì
1. until; till; up to
2. soup; meat broth
3. to soak; to drench
洎乎(ㄐㄧˋ ㄏㄨ)
until; till; up to

【洑】 2852
ㄈㄨˊ fwu fú
1. a whirlpool; a vortex
2. an undercurrent

【洌】 2853
ㄌㄧㄝˋ lieh liè
(said of liquid) clear and transparent

【洋】 2854
ㄧㄤˊ yang yáng
1. an ocean
2. foreign; Western; Occidental
3. imported
洋布(ㄧㄤˊ ㄅㄨˋ)
machine-made piece goods
洋房(ㄧㄤˊ ㄈㄤˊ)
a Western-style house
洋服(ㄧㄤˊ ㄈㄨˊ)
Western clothes; Occidental dress
洋釘(ㄧㄤˊ ㄉㄧㄥ)
a nail

〔水部〕

洋鐵(ㄧㄤˊ ㄊㄧㄝˇ)
tin plate; galvanized iron
洋鐵罐兒(ㄧㄤˊ ㄊㄧㄝˇ ㄍㄨㄚˋㄦ)
a tin, or tin can
洋奴(ㄧㄤˊ ㄋㄨˊ)
a slave of a foreign master; a flunkey of the Occident; a worshipper of everything foreign
洋蠟(ㄧㄤˊ ㄌㄚˋ)
a candle
洋樓(ㄧㄤˊ ㄌㄡˊ)
a Western-style building of two stories or more
洋流(ㄧㄤˊ ㄌㄧㄡˊ)
the marine current
洋狗(ㄧㄤˊ ㄍㄡˇ)
a dog of foreign breed
洋鬼子(ㄧㄤˊ ㄍㄨㄟˇ ˙ㄗ)
a foreign devil (a derogatory term referring to a foreigner, especially a Westerner)
洋廣雜貨(ㄧㄤˊ ㄍㄨㄤˇ ㄗㄚˊ ㄏㄨㄛˋ)
foreign goods (imported through Kwangtung)
洋行(ㄧㄤˊ ㄏㄤˊ)
a foreign business firm
洋化(ㄧㄤˊ ㄏㄨㄚˋ)
to be westernized
洋火(ㄧㄤˊ ㄏㄨㄛˇ)
matches (for making a fire) 亦作「火柴」
洋貨(ㄧㄤˊ ㄏㄨㄛˋ)
foreign goods; imported products
洋槐(ㄧㄤˊ ㄏㄨㄞˊ)
an acacia; a locust tree
洋灰(ㄧㄤˊ ㄏㄨㄟ)
cement
洋紅(ㄧㄤˊ ㄏㄨㄥˊ)
carmine
洋酒(ㄧㄤˊ ㄐㄧㄡˇ)
imported wine and spirits
洋涇浜(ㄧㄤˊ ㄐㄧㄥ ㄅㄤ)
①the concessions in Shanghai before World War II ② pidgin English 亦作「洋涇浜英語」
洋錢(ㄧㄤˊ ㄑㄧㄢˊ)
silver dollars; Mexican dollars
洋琴(ㄧㄤˊ ㄑㄧㄣˊ)
a piano
洋琴鬼(ㄧㄤˊ ㄑㄧㄣˊ ㄍㄨㄟˇ)
(derogatory term) a bandsman
洋鎗大砲(ㄧㄤˊ ㄑㄧㄤ ㄉㄚˋ ㄆㄠˋ)
firearms; guns
洋繡球(ㄧㄤˊ ㄒㄧㄡˋ ㄑㄧㄡˊ)
a hydrangea
洋相(ㄧㄤˊ ㄒㄧㄤˋ)
to make an exhibition of oneself: 你是在當衆出洋相。You are making an exhibition of yourself.
洋裝(ㄧㄤˊ ㄓㄨㄤ)
① Western dress ② Western binding (for books)
洋車(ㄧㄤˊ ㄔㄜ)
a rickshaw or ricksha
洋場(ㄧㄤˊ ㄔㄤˇ)
① old foreign settlement, usually referring to old Shanghai ② a prosperous metropolis
洋式(ㄧㄤˊ ㄕˋ)
the Western style
洋水仙(ㄧㄤˊ ㄕㄨㄟˇ ㄒㄧㄢ)
hyacinth (an aquatic plant) 亦作「風信子」
洋人(ㄧㄤˊ ㄖㄣˊ)
a Westerner; a foreigner
洋財(ㄧㄤˊ ㄘㄞˊ)
a big fortune; a windfall
洋菜(ㄧㄤˊ ㄘㄞˋ)
thin strips of agar-agar extracted from *Gracilaria*, used as a dish; agar 亦作「石花菜」
洋葱(ㄧㄤˊ ㄘㄨㄥ)
an onion: 我們在後院種洋葱。We grow onions in the backyard.
洋傘(ㄧㄤˊ ㄙㄢˇ)
an (Western-style) umbrella
洋溢(ㄧㄤˊ ㄧˋ)
to be filled or fraught with; to brim with
洋油(ㄧㄤˊ ㄧㄡˊ)
kerosene
洋煙(ㄧㄤˊ ㄧㄢ)or 洋烟捲兒(ㄧㄤˊ ㄧㄢ ㄐㄩㄢˇㄦ)
cigarettes; imported cigarettes or tobacco
洋銀(ㄧㄤˊ ㄧㄣˊ)
German silver, the alloy of Cu 40-65%, Ni 6-35%, Zn 15-35%
洋洋(ㄧㄤˊ ㄧㄤˊ)
① full of water ② vast; extensive; great ③ in high spirits; elated
洋洋大觀(ㄧㄤˊ ㄧㄤˊ ㄉㄚˋ ㄍㄨㄢ)
imposing; grand; magnificent
洋洋得意(ㄧㄤˊ ㄧㄤˊ ㄉㄜˊ ㄧˋ)
in high spirits; proud and happy; elated: 他聽到這消息而洋洋得意。He was elated over the news.
洋洋自得(ㄧㄤˊ ㄧㄤˊ ㄗˋ ㄉㄜˊ)
self-satisfied
洋洋灑灑(ㄧㄤˊ ㄧㄤˊ ㄙㄚˇ ㄙㄚˇ)
(said of expository writing, etc.) copious and fluent
洋務(ㄧㄤˊ ㄨˋ)
foreign affairs or business
洋娃娃(ㄧㄤˊ ㄨㄚˊ ˙ㄨㄚ)
a doll: 這女孩有個漂亮的洋娃娃。The little girl has a pretty doll.
洋爲中用(ㄧㄤˊ ㄨㄟˊ ㄓㄨㄥ ㄩㄥˋ)
to make foreign things serve China
洋文(ㄧㄤˊ ㄨㄣˊ)
a foreign language
洋芋(ㄧㄤˊ ㄩˋ)
a potato: 洋芋長在地下。Potatoes grow under the ground.

【洒】 2855
1. ㄙㄚˇ saa sǎ
1. I; me
2. to pour; to sprinkle
洒家(ㄙㄚˇ ㄐㄧㄚ)
I; me
洒掃(ㄙㄚˇ ㄙㄠˇ)
to sprinkle water and sweep away the dirt; to clean up 亦作「灑掃」

【洒】 2855
2. ㄒㄧㄢˇ shean xiǎn
1. respectful
2. deep
3. alarmed; surprised
洒然(ㄒㄧㄢˇ ㄖㄢˊ)
① alarmed; surprised ② cold
洒如(ㄒㄧㄢˇ ㄖㄨˊ)
respectful; deferential

【洒】 2855
3. ㄒㄧˇ shii xǐ
same as 洗—to wash

【洗】 2856
1. ㄒㄧˇ shii xǐ
1. to wash; to rinse; to cleanse; to clean; to clear: 飯前把手洗乾淨。Wash your hands clean before each meal.
2. to baptize: 他受洗禮入基督教。He was baptized into the

Christian faith.
洗不掉(ㄒㄧˇ ˙ㄅㄨ ㄉㄧㄠˋ)
incapable of being washed off; indelible
洗不淸(ㄒㄧˇ ˙ㄅㄨ ㄑㄧㄥ)
unable to vindicate oneself
洗牌(ㄒㄧˇ ㄆㄞˊ)
to shuffle playing cards or mah-jong pieces; a shuffle
洗髮粉(ㄒㄧˇ ㄈㄚˇ ㄈㄣˇ)
shampoo powder
洗髮水(ㄒㄧˇ ㄈㄚˇ ㄕㄨㄟˇ)
liquid shampoo
洗盪(ㄒㄧˇ ㄉㄤˋ)
to wash or purify
洗滌(ㄒㄧˇ ㄉㄧˊ)
to wash; to cleanse; to rinse
洗滌劑(ㄒㄧˇ ㄉㄧˊ ㄐㄧˋ)
a detergent; washing fluid
洗頭(ㄒㄧˇ ㄊㄡˊ)or 洗頭髮(ㄒㄧˇ ㄊㄡˊ ˙ㄈㄚ)
to shampoo; to wash one's hair; to have one's hair washed
洗腦(ㄒㄧˇ ㄋㄠˇ)
to brainwash; to indoctrinate
洗禮(ㄒㄧˇ ㄌㄧˇ)
①to baptize or be baptized; baptism: 他受洗禮成爲天主教徒。He was baptized a Catholic. ②a severe test: 他受過戰爭的洗禮。He has gone through the test of battle.
洗臉(ㄒㄧˇ ㄌㄧㄢˇ)
to wash one's face; to wash oneself: 他在洗臉。He's washing his face now.
洗臉盆(ㄒㄧˇ ㄌㄧㄢˇ ㄆㄣˊ)
a washbasin 亦作「臉盆」
洗煉(ㄒㄧˇ ㄌㄧㄢˋ)
(said of literary writings) refined; polished; elegant
洗刮(ㄒㄧˇ ㄍㄨㄚ)
to wash and scrape
洗甲(ㄒㄧˇ ㄐㄧㄚˇ)or 洗兵(ㄒㄧˇ ㄅㄧㄥ)
to end hostilities; to have a truce
洗刼(ㄒㄧˇ ㄐㄧㄝˊ)
to sack everything; to sack a place without leaving anything behind: 士兵洗刼這城。The soldiers sacked the town.
洗脚(ㄒㄧˇ ㄐㄧㄠˇ)
to wash one's feet
洗淨(ㄒㄧˇ ㄐㄧㄥˋ)
to wash something until it's clean: 把它們洗(乾)淨。Wash them clean.
洗錢(ㄒㄧˇ ㄑㄧㄢˊ)
to launder money; money laundering
洗心革面(ㄒㄧˇ ㄒㄧㄣ ㄍㄜˊ ㄇㄧㄢˋ)
to reform oneself; to reform: 如果給他機會，他答應洗心革面。He promised to reform if given a chance.
洗削(ㄒㄧˇ ㄒㄩㄝ)
to wipe away (disgrace, etc.)
洗雪(ㄒㄧˇ ㄒㄩㄝˇ)or(ㄒㄧˇ ㄒㄩㄝˋ)
①to cleanse (both literally and figuratively) ②to revenge; to vindicate
洗濯(ㄒㄧˇ ㄓㄨㄛˊ)
to wash; to rinse
洗塵(ㄒㄧˇ ㄔㄣˊ)or 洗泥(ㄒㄧˇ ㄋㄧˊ)
to give a welcome dinner (for someone arriving after a long trip)
洗腸(ㄒㄧˇ ㄔㄤˊ)
to purge the bowels; to remove poison from one's stomach by means of laxatives or saline
洗晒(ㄒㄧˇ ㄕㄞˋ)
to wash and dry in the sun
洗手(ㄒㄧˇ ㄕㄡˇ)
①to wash one's hands: 你飯前要洗手。You have to wash (your hands) before dinner. ②to wash one's hands of evil ways
洗手不幹(ㄒㄧˇ ㄕㄡˇ ㄅㄨˋ ㄍㄢˋ)
to wash one's hands of an evil practice; to quit committing crimes
洗手間(ㄒㄧˇ ㄕㄡˇ ㄐㄧㄢ)
a toilet; a water closet; a rest room; a lavatory
洗腎(ㄒㄧˇ ㄕㄣˋ)
dialysis or hemodialysis
洗刷(ㄒㄧˇ ㄕㄨㄚ)
①a scrub; to scrub; to clean: 他將地板洗刷乾淨。He scrubbed the floor clean ②to vindicate oneself
洗刷不淸(ㄒㄧˇ ㄕㄨㄚ ㄅㄨˋ ㄑㄧㄥ)
unable to vindicate oneself
洗澡(ㄒㄧˇ ㄗㄠˇ)
to take a bath: 我們在湖裡洗澡。We bathed in the lake.
洗澡盆(ㄒㄧˇ ㄗㄠˇ ㄆㄣˊ)
a bathtub 亦作「浴盆」
洗澡塘(ㄒㄧˇ ㄗㄠˇ ㄊㄤˊ)
a bath pool
洗澡間(ㄒㄧˇ ㄗㄠˇ ㄐㄧㄢ)
a bathroom 亦作「浴室」: 我能借用你的洗澡間嗎? May I use your bathroom?
洗擦(ㄒㄧˇ ㄘㄚ)
to wash and scrub
洗耳恭聽(ㄒㄧˇ ㄦˇ ㄍㄨㄥ ㄊㄧㄥ)
to listen respectfully
洗衣(ㄒㄧˇ ㄧ)or 洗衣服(ㄒㄧˇ ㄧ ˙ㄈㄨ)
to wash clothes; to do one's washing: 她每天上午洗衣。She does her washing every morning.
洗衣店(ㄒㄧˇ ㄧ ㄉㄧㄢˋ)
a laundry shop: 將這些襯衫送到洗衣店去。Send these shirts to the laundry.
洗衣機(ㄒㄧˇ ㄧ ㄐㄧ)
a washing machine; a laundry machine
洗衣作(ㄒㄧˇ ㄧ ㄗㄨㄛˋ)
a laundry shop
洗胃(ㄒㄧˇ ㄨㄟˋ)
(medicine) gastric lavage
洗碗碟(ㄒㄧˇ ㄨㄢˇ ㄉㄧㄝˊ)
to do the dishes
洗碗機(ㄒㄧˇ ㄨㄢˇ ㄐㄧ)
a dishwasher
洗浴(ㄒㄧˇ ㄩˋ)
to take a bath
洗冤(ㄒㄧˇ ㄩㄢ)
to clear oneself of a false charge; to vindicate oneself: 見證人的證詞爲被告洗冤。The testimony of witnesses vindicated the defendant.
洗熨(ㄒㄧˇ ㄩㄣˋ)
to launder; to wash and iron (clothes)

【洗】 2856 2. ㄒㄧㄢˇ shean xiǎn

a Chinese family name
洗馬(ㄒㄧㄢˇ ㄇㄚˇ)
an official title given to the crown prince's herald

【洙】 2857 ㄓㄨ ju zhū (又讀 ㄕㄨ shu shū)

name of a river in Shantung
洙水(ㄓㄨ ㄕㄨㄟˇ)
name of a river in Shantung
洙泗(ㄓㄨ ㄙˋ)
names of two rivers in

〔水部〕

Shantung

【洟】 2858 ㄧˊ yi yí
nasal mucus; snivel
洟涕(ㄧˊ ㄊㄧˋ)
nasal mucus; snivel

〔水部〕

【洞】 2859 ㄉㄨㄥˋ donq dòng
1. a cave; a hole: 我的鞋子破了個洞。There is a hole in my shoe.
2. to penetrate; to see through
洞房(ㄉㄨㄥˋ ㄈㄤˊ)
①an inner chamber ②a nuptial chamber
洞房花燭夜(ㄉㄨㄥˋ ㄈㄤˊ ㄏㄨㄚ ㄓㄨˊ ㄧㄝˋ)
wedding night; the night of wedding
洞府(ㄉㄨㄥˋ ㄈㄨˇ)
the abode of a mountain genie or a Taoist priest
洞達(ㄉㄨㄥˋ ㄉㄚˊ)
having insight; to understand thoroughly
洞天(ㄉㄨㄥˋ ㄊㄧㄢ)
①a hidden but beautiful spot (or world) ②a cavern as the abode of the fairies
洞天福地(ㄉㄨㄥˋ ㄊㄧㄢ ㄈㄨˊ ㄉㄧˋ)
mountains inhabited by Taoist priests
洞庭(ㄉㄨㄥˋ ㄊㄧㄥˊ) or 洞庭湖(ㄉㄨㄥˋ ㄊㄧㄥˊ ㄏㄨˊ)
Lake Tungting (in northern Hunan)
洞貫(ㄉㄨㄥˋ ㄍㄨㄢˋ)
① to penetrate through ② to understand fully
洞開(ㄉㄨㄥˋ ㄎㄞ)
wide open
洞窟(ㄉㄨㄥˋ ㄎㄨ)
a cave; a cavern
洞鑒(ㄉㄨㄥˋ ㄐㄧㄢˋ)
to see clearly
洞見癥結(ㄉㄨㄥˋ ㄐㄧㄢˋ ㄓㄥ ㄐㄧㄝˊ)
to see clearly the hidden cause of a problem; to get to the heart of the problem
洞悉(ㄉㄨㄥˋ ㄒㄧ)
to see clearly and understand thoroughly
洞悉無遺(ㄉㄨㄥˋ ㄒㄧ ㄨˊ ㄧˊ)
to see and know completely
洞簫(ㄉㄨㄥˋ ㄒㄧㄠ)
a kind of flute; a bamboo flageolet
洞曉(ㄉㄨㄥˋ ㄒㄧㄠˇ)
to know clearly
洞僊(ㄉㄨㄥˋ ㄒㄧㄢ)
genies living in caves
洞穴(ㄉㄨㄥˋ ㄒㄩㄝˋ)
a cave; a cavern
洞察(ㄉㄨㄥˋ ㄔㄚˊ)
to see and understand clearly; to have an insight into: 他能洞察那事件的是非。He saw clearly the rights and wrongs of the case.
洞徹(ㄉㄨㄥˋ ㄔㄜˋ)
to understand thoroughly
洞穿(ㄉㄨㄥˋ ㄔㄨㄢ)
to pierce through: 子彈洞穿了他的帽子。The shot pierced his hat.
洞若觀火(ㄉㄨㄥˋ ㄖㄨㄛˋ ㄍㄨㄢ ㄏㄨㄛˇ)
to see clearly as if one were seeing fire
洞兒(ㄉㄨㄥˋㄦ)
a cave; a hole; a pit

【洛】 2860 ㄌㄨㄛˋ luoh luò
name of a river
洛克斐勒(ㄌㄨㄛˋ ㄎㄜˋ ㄈㄟˇ ㄌㄜˋ)
John D. Rockefeller, 1839-1937, American oil magnate and philanthropist
洛迦諾(ㄌㄨㄛˋ ㄐㄧㄚ ㄋㄨㄛˋ)
Locarno, Switzerland
洛神(ㄌㄨㄛˋ ㄕㄣˊ)
the Goddess of the Lo River
洛神賦(ㄌㄨㄛˋ ㄕㄣˊ ㄈㄨˋ)
Ode to the Goddess of the Lo River, by Tsao Chih (曹植) (192-232 A. D.)
洛書(ㄌㄨㄛˋ ㄕㄨ)
the characters supposedly devised by Emperor Yü (禹) of the Hsia Dynasty (2205-1782 B. C.) in imitation of the shell pattern of a divine tortoise in the Lo River
洛桑(ㄌㄨㄛˋ ㄙㄤ)
Lausanne, Switzerland
洛誦(ㄌㄨㄛˋ ㄙㄨㄥˋ)
to read repeatedly in order to commit to memory
洛邑(ㄌㄨㄛˋ ㄧˋ)
an ancient city in what is Loyang, Honan, today
洛陽(ㄌㄨㄛˋ ㄧㄤˊ)
Loyang, in Honan, capital of the Eastern Han Dynasty
洛陽花(ㄌㄨㄛˋ ㄧㄤˊ ㄏㄨㄚ)
a white peony
洛陽紙貴(ㄌㄨㄛˋ ㄧㄤˊ ㄓˇ ㄍㄨㄟˋ)
to become a best seller

【津】 2861 ㄐㄧㄣ jin jīn
1. a ferry
2. juicy; tasty
3. saliva
4. to sweat; to perspire
5. as in 指點迷津 (to show one how to get to the right path)
6. short for Tientsin
津巴布韋(ㄐㄧㄣ ㄅㄚ ㄅㄨˋ ㄨㄟˊ)
Zimbabwe 亦作「辛巴威」
津浦鐵路(ㄐㄧㄣ ㄆㄨˇ ㄊㄧㄝˇ ㄌㄨˋ)
the Tientsin-Pukou Railway
津門(ㄐㄧㄣ ㄇㄣˊ)
①a checkpoint at a ferry ② another name of Tientsin (天津)
津筏(ㄐㄧㄣ ㄈㄚˊ)
a ferry raft; a ferryboat
津逮(ㄐㄧㄣ ㄉㄞˋ)
to arrive at a place through a ferry
津渡(ㄐㄧㄣ ㄉㄨˋ)
a ferry
津貼(ㄐㄧㄣ ㄊㄧㄝ)
an allowance; a subsidy; to subsidize; to help out with money: 他們受到政府的津貼。They were subsidized by the government.
津梁(ㄐㄧㄣ ㄌㄧㄤˊ)
a bridge (both literally and figuratively)
津關(ㄐㄧㄣ ㄍㄨㄢ)
a checkpoint
津津樂道(ㄐㄧㄣ ㄐㄧㄣ ㄌㄜˋ ㄉㄠˋ)
to talk with great relish: 這他對自己的成就津津樂道。He relishes talking about his achievement.
津津有味(ㄐㄧㄣ ㄐㄧㄣ ㄧㄡˇ ㄨㄟˋ)
①(to do something) with great relish or interest; with gusto ② very tasty; very agreeable to the palate
津人(ㄐㄧㄣ ㄖㄣˊ)
a ferryman
津潤(ㄐㄧㄣ ㄖㄨㄣˋ)
juicy and nourishing
津涯(ㄐㄧㄣ ㄧㄚˊ)
the waterside; shores
津液(ㄐㄧㄣ ㄧㄝˋ)
saliva

津要(ㄐㄧㄣ ㄧㄠˋ)
① key places or locations ② key posts

【洧】2862 ㄨㄟˇ woei wěi
name of a river in Honan
洧水(ㄨㄟˇ ㄕㄨㄟˇ)or 洧河(ㄨㄟˇ ㄏㄜˊ)
name of a river in Honan

【洫】2863 ㄒㄩˋ shiuh xù
a ditch; a moat

【洩】2864 ㄒㄧㄝˋ shieh xiè
to drain; to vent; to let out; to dissipate; to leak out: 秘密已經外洩。The secret has leaked out.
洩忿 or 洩憤(ㄒㄧㄝˋ ㄈㄣˋ)
to give vent to one's anger
洩底(ㄒㄧㄝˋ ㄉㄧˇ)
to disclose a secret
洩漏(ㄒㄧㄝˋ ㄌㄡˋ)
to make known; to disclose; to divulge; to reveal; to leak out; leakage: 這消息洩漏出去了。The news has leaked out.
洩漏秘密(ㄒㄧㄝˋ ㄌㄡˋ ㄇㄧˋ ㄇㄧˋ)
to disclose a secret; to divulge a secret
洩漏天機(ㄒㄧㄝˋ ㄌㄡˋ ㄊㄧㄢ ㄐㄧ)
to disclose a divine secret
洩露(ㄒㄧㄝˋ ㄌㄨˋ)
to disclose; to reveal; to divulge: 永不要洩露我的秘密。Never reveal my secret.
洩恨(ㄒㄧㄝˋ ㄏㄣˋ)
to give vent to one's resentment; to vent one's grudge
洩洪(ㄒㄧㄝˋ ㄏㄨㄥˊ)
to let water flow out from the reservoir; to release excessive water from a reservoir
洩氣(ㄒㄧㄝˋ ㄑㄧˋ)
① to lose strength, momentum, etc. ② discouraging; disappointing; discouraged; disappointed: 再試試！不要因爲一次失敗就洩氣。Try again! Don't let one failure discourage you. ③ to give vent to one's pent-up resentment, frustration, etc.

【洪】2865 ㄏㄨㄥˊ horng hóng
1. great; immense; magnificent
2. floods; turbulent waters; torrents: 山洪淹沒了田野。The mountain torrent flooded the fields.
3. a Chinese family name
洪波(ㄏㄨㄥˊ ㄅㄛ)or 洪濤(ㄏㄨㄥˊ ㄊㄠ)
turbulent waves; big waves
洪門(ㄏㄨㄥˊ ㄇㄣˊ)
a secret society originally dedicated to the cause of overthrowing the Manchus and the restoration of the Ming Dynasty 亦作「紅幫」
洪峯(ㄏㄨㄥˊ ㄈㄥ)
the high point of a flood
洪福(ㄏㄨㄥˊ ㄈㄨˊ)
great happiness; bliss; blessing
洪福齊天(ㄏㄨㄥˊ ㄈㄨˊ ㄑㄧˊ ㄊㄧㄢ)
great happiness; boundless bliss
洪大(ㄏㄨㄥˊ ㄉㄚˋ)
great; massive; immense
洪流(ㄏㄨㄥˊ ㄌㄧㄡˊ)
① a torrent ② a powerful current: 民主的洪流洶湧澎湃。The powerful current of democracy is surging forward.
洪亮(ㄏㄨㄥˊ ㄌㄧㄤˋ)
loud and clear; sonorous: 這歌者的嗓音洪亮。The singer has a sonorous voice.
洪量(ㄏㄨㄥˊ ㄌㄧㄤˋ)
① magnanimity ② great capacity for drinking
洪鑪 or 洪爐(ㄏㄨㄥˊ ㄌㄨˊ)
① a large furnace; a smelting oven ② (figuratively) mighty furnace
洪荒(ㄏㄨㄥˊ ㄏㄨㄤ)
primitive; chaotic
洪積期(ㄏㄨㄥˊ ㄐㄧ ㄑㄧˊ)
(geology) the Pleistocene Epoch; the Diluvial Epoch
洪積層(ㄏㄨㄥˊ ㄐㄧ ㄘㄥˊ)
(geology) diluviums
洪秀全(ㄏㄨㄥˊ ㄒㄧㄡˋ ㄑㄩㄢˊ)
Hung Hsiu-chüan, 1812-1864, leader of the Taiping rebels
洪憲(ㄏㄨㄥˊ ㄒㄧㄢˋ)
the reigning title adopted by Yüan Shih-kai(袁世凱), which lasted less than three months in 1915
洪鐘(ㄏㄨㄥˊ ㄓㄨㄥ)
① a large bell ② (said of a voice) stentorian; very loud or powerful: 他聲如洪鐘。He has a stentorian voice.
洪水(ㄏㄨㄥˊ ㄕㄨㄟˇ)
a flood; a deluge: 洪水淹沒了整個地區。The flood inundated the whole district.
洪水猛獸(ㄏㄨㄥˊ ㄕㄨㄟˇ ㄇㄥˇ ㄕㄡˋ)
disaster; calamity; a catastrophe
洪水位(ㄏㄨㄥˊ ㄕㄨㄟˇ ㄨㄟˋ)
the high water mark; the high water level; the flood level
洪澤湖(ㄏㄨㄥˊ ㄗㄜˊ ㄏㄨˊ)
name of a lake between Anhwei and Kiangsu
洪才大略(ㄏㄨㄥˊ ㄘㄞˊ ㄉㄚˋ ㄌㄩㄝˋ)
a great mind with great schemes
洪儒(ㄏㄨㄥˊ ㄖㄨˊ)
a great scholar
洪恩(ㄏㄨㄥˊ ㄣ)
great kindness
洪楊之亂(ㄏㄨㄥˊ ㄧㄤˊ ㄓ ㄌㄨㄢˋ)
the Taiping Rebellion (1851-1864), led by Hung Hsiu-chüan (洪秀全) and Yang Hsiu-ching (楊秀清)

【洱】2866 ㄦˇ eel ěr
1. name of a lake in Yunnan
2. name of a river in Yunnan
洱海(ㄦˇ ㄏㄞˇ)
name of a lake in Yunnan
洱水(ㄦˇ ㄕㄨㄟˇ)
name of a river in Yunnan

【洳】2867 ㄖㄨˋ ruh rù
damp; moist; oozy

【洲】2868 ㄓㄡ jou zhōu
1. an island in a river
2. a continent
洲汀(ㄓㄡ ㄊㄧㄥ)
an island in a river
洲際彈道飛彈(ㄓㄡ ㄐㄧˋ ㄉㄢˋ ㄉㄠˋ ㄈㄟ ㄉㄢˋ)
the intercontinental ballistic missile; the ICBM
洲沚(ㄓㄡ ㄓˇ)
an island in a river
洲渚(ㄓㄡ ㄓㄨˇ)
an island in a river
洲嶼(ㄓㄡ ㄩˇ)
an island in a river

【洮】2869 1. ㄊㄠˊ taur táo

name of a river in Kansu

洮河(ㄊㄠˊ ㄏㄜˊ)
name of a river in Kansu

【洮】 2869
2. ㄧㄠˊ yau yáo
name of a lake in Kiangsu

洮湖(ㄧㄠˊ ㄏㄨˊ)
name of a lake in Kiangsu

【洵】 2870
ㄒㄩㄣˊ shyun xún
true; real; truly; really; certainly

洵河(ㄒㄩㄣˊ ㄏㄜˊ)
name of a river in Shensi

洵屬(ㄒㄩㄣˊ ㄕㄨˇ)
truly; certainly

【洶】 2871
ㄒㄩㄥ shiong xiōng
1. unquiet; restless; turbulent; tumultuous
2. noisy; uproarious; clamorous

洶動(ㄒㄩㄥ ㄉㄨㄥˋ)
unquiet; restless; disturbed

洶洶(ㄒㄩㄥ ㄒㄩㄥ)
tumultuous; turbulent; agitated; truculent

洶湧 or 洶涌(ㄒㄩㄥ ㄩㄥˇ)
(said of water) tumultuous; turbulent: 河流洶湧地滾滾流去。The river rolls turbulently.

洶湧澎湃(ㄒㄩㄥ ㄩㄥˇ ㄆㄥ ㄆㄞˋ)
surging; turbulent; tempestuous

【洽】 2872
ㄒㄧㄚˊ shya xiá
(又讀 ㄑㄧㄚˋ chiah qià)
1. to spread; to diffuse
2. harmony; agreement
3. to negotiate; to consult

洽博(ㄒㄧㄚˊ ㄅㄛˊ)
of wide experience and knowledge

洽辦(ㄒㄧㄚˊ ㄅㄢˋ)
to handle an assignment through negotiation

洽談(ㄒㄧㄚˊ ㄊㄢˊ)
to discuss or consult (problems) together

洽化(ㄒㄧㄚˊ ㄏㄨㄚˋ)
to diffuse virtuous influence

洽商(ㄒㄧㄚˊ ㄕㄤ)
to discuss (details of a contract, etc.)

洽聞(ㄒㄧㄚˊ ㄨㄣˊ)
of wide knowledge; learned; widely read

【活】 2873
ㄏㄨㄛˊ hwo huó
1. to live; to survive; to be alive
2. to save the life of
3. active; lively; vivacious
4. movable; mobile; flexible
5. work

活靶(ㄏㄨㄛˊ ㄅㄚˇ)
a maneuvering target

活剝生吞(ㄏㄨㄛˊ ㄅㄛ ㄕㄥ ㄊㄨㄣ)
(literally) to skin an animal alive and eat the meat raw without chewing—to make unimaginative use of ready-made ideas (especially in writing)

活寶(ㄏㄨㄛˊ ㄅㄠˇ)
a lively person; one who behaves clownishly

活版(ㄏㄨㄛˊ ㄅㄢˇ)
a printing plate with movable type

活不了(ㄏㄨㄛˊ ·ㄅㄨ ㄌㄧㄠˇ)
unlikely to survive

活不下去(ㄏㄨㄛˊ ·ㄅㄨ ㄒㄧㄚˋ ㄑㄩˋ)
to lack the means, strength, or courage to live on

活潑潑地(ㄏㄨㄛˊ ㄆㄛ ㄆㄛ ·ㄉㄜ)
actively; vivaciously; with sprightliness

活潑(ㄏㄨㄛˊ ·ㄆㄛ)
active; lively; sprightly; full of life; vivacious (especially said of children): 她是個活潑的小孩。She is a lively child.

活埋(ㄏㄨㄛˊ ㄇㄞˊ)
to bury alive

活賣(ㄏㄨㄛˊ ㄇㄞˋ)
to pawn; to pledge; to mortgage

活門(ㄏㄨㄛˊ ㄇㄣˊ)or 活瓣(ㄏㄨㄛˊ ㄅㄢˋ)
a valve

活命(ㄏㄨㄛˊ ㄇㄧㄥˋ)
① to survive; to live ② life

活佛(ㄏㄨㄛˊ ㄈㄛˊ)
(Lamaism) a Buddha incarnate

活的(ㄏㄨㄛˊ ·ㄉㄜ)
living; live; alive: 它是條活的魚。It's a living fish.

活得不耐煩(ㄏㄨㄛˊ ·ㄉㄜ ㄅㄨˋ ㄋㄞˋ ㄈㄢˊ)
getting tired of living (a sarcastic expression)

活到老，學不了(ㄏㄨㄛˊ ㄉㄠˋ ㄌㄠˇ, ㄒㄩㄝˊ ·ㄅㄨ ㄌㄧㄠˇ)
There is still much to learn after one has grown old. 或 The pursuit of knowledge is an endless effort.

活到老，學到老(ㄏㄨㄛˊ ㄉㄠˋ ㄌㄠˇ, ㄒㄩㄝˊ ㄉㄠˋ ㄌㄠˇ)
One is never too old to learn. 或 No dog is too old to learn new tricks.

活動房屋(ㄏㄨㄛˊ ㄉㄨㄥˋ ㄈㄤˊ ㄨ)
a movable building

活動(ㄏㄨㄛˊ ·ㄉㄨㄥ)
① activities: 我們喜歡戶外活動。We are fond of outdoor activities. ② active; lively ③ to try to get help or support for an objective; to lobby; to canvass: 他正在替她活動。He is trying to get help for her. ④ movable; mobile ⑤ loose ⑥ to exercise; to limber; to move about: 站起來活動活動。Stand up and move about.

活脫(ㄏㄨㄛˊ ㄊㄨㄛ)
(to be) remarkably like

活力(ㄏㄨㄛˊ ㄌㄧˋ)
vitality; vigor

活力素(ㄏㄨㄛˊ ㄌㄧˋ ㄙㄨˋ)
vitamins 亦作「維生素」

活靈活現(ㄏㄨㄛˊ ㄌㄧㄥˊ ㄏㄨㄛˊ ㄒㄧㄢˋ)
vivid; lifelike: 他說得活靈活現的。He gave a vivid description. 亦作「活龍活現」

活路(ㄏㄨㄛˊ ㄌㄨˋ)
① an unblocked passage ② a feasible approach or course of action; a way out ③ a way to make a living

活絡(ㄏㄨㄛˊ ㄌㄨㄛˋ)
① loose ② noncommittal; indefinite

活龍活現(ㄏㄨㄛˊ ㄌㄨㄥˊ ㄏㄨㄛˊ ㄒㄧㄢˋ)
vividly; as if it were taking place here and now

活該(ㄏㄨㄛˊ ㄍㄞ)
It serves you (him, them) right. 要是她不再跟你講話，那是你活該。It will serve you right if she never speaks to you again.

活口(ㄏㄨㄛˊ ㄎㄡˇ)
① a captive; a prisoner ② to support a dependent or dependents

活活(ㄏㄨㄛˊ ㄏㄨㄛˊ)or 活活的(ㄏㄨㄛˊ

ㄏㄨㄛˊ ˙ㄌㄜ
alive; live; living: 他們被活活燒死了。They were burnt alive.
活火山(ㄏㄨㄛˊ ㄏㄨㄛˇ ㄕㄢ)
an active volcano
活計(ㄏㄨㄛˊ ˙ㄐㄧ)
① one's way to make a living ② needlework; handiwork: 她喜歡坐著做活計。She likes to sit at needlework.
活見鬼(ㄏㄨㄛˊ ㄐㄧㄢˋ ㄍㄨㄟˇ)
absurd; preposterous
活劇(ㄏㄨㄛˊ ㄐㄩˋ)
a living drama; a drama in real life
活期(ㄏㄨㄛˊ ㄑㄧˊ)
due on demand
活期存款(ㄏㄨㄛˊ ㄑㄧˊ ㄘㄨㄣˊ ㄎㄨㄢˇ)
a demand deposit; a current deposit
活期存款帳戶(ㄏㄨㄛˊ ㄑㄧˊ ㄘㄨㄣˊ ㄎㄨㄢˇ ㄓㄤˋ ㄏㄨˋ)
a current account
活現(ㄏㄨㄛˊ ㄒㄧㄢˋ)
to appear vividly; to come alive
活性碳(ㄏㄨㄛˊ ㄒㄧㄥˋ ㄊㄢˋ)
active carbon
活像(ㄏㄨㄛˊ ㄒㄧㄤˋ)
to look like a reincarnation of; to be quite like; to be image of: 長得活像他父親。He is the image of his father.
活捉(ㄏㄨㄛˊ ㄓㄨㄛ)
to catch alive; to capture alive: 他們被活捉。They were captured alive.
活世壽人(ㄏㄨㄛˊ ㄕˋ ㄕㄡˋ ㄖㄣˊ)
to benefit the world and mankind
活受罪(ㄏㄨㄛˊ ㄕㄡˋ ㄗㄨㄟˋ)
to feel as if one were just living to suffer; to suffer greatly
活生生(ㄏㄨㄛˊ ㄕㄥ ㄕㄥ)
very much alive; alive and kicking: 它是個活生生的例子。It's a living example.
活水(ㄏㄨㄛˊ ㄕㄨㄟˇ)
flowing water; running water
活人(ㄏㄨㄛˊ ㄖㄣˊ)
a living person; a person who is still alive
活人無算(ㄏㄨㄛˊ ㄖㄣˊ ㄨˊ ㄙㄨㄢˋ)
(especially said of a doctor) to have saved innumerable lives
活字版(ㄏㄨㄛˊ ㄗˋ ㄅㄢˇ)
movable type
活字金(ㄏㄨㄛˊ ㄗˋ ㄐㄧㄣ)
type metal
活死人(ㄏㄨㄛˊ ㄙˇ ㄖㄣˊ)
a living corpse
活塞(ㄏㄨㄛˊ ㄙㄜˋ)
a piston
活兒(ㄏㄨㄛˊㄦ)
① jobs; work; labor: 他一個人做兩個人的活兒。He does the work of two men. ② products: 這些活兒做得好。These products are well made.
活頁 or 活葉(ㄏㄨㄛˊ ㄧㄝˋ)
loose or detachable leaves (of notebooks, etc.)
活躍(ㄏㄨㄛˊ ㄩㄝˋ)or(ㄏㄨㄛˊ ㄧㄠˋ)
active; actively: 市面很活躍。The market is very active.
活用(ㄏㄨㄛˊ ㄩㄥˋ)
to use or apply knowledge with imagination or ingenuity

【派】 2874 ㄆㄞˋ pay pài

1. a tributary; a branch
2. a division; a school (of philosophy, art, etc.); a party:他是一個老派人物。He is a gentleman of the old school.
3. a faction: 該黨分爲幾個小派系。The party split into petty factions.
4. to assign; to dispatch; to send: 他派女僕去請醫生。He sent the maid for a doctor.

派別(ㄆㄞˋ ㄅㄧㄝˊ)
① factions ② schools (of thought)
派兵(ㄆㄞˋ ㄅㄧㄥ)
to send troops; to dispatch troops
派兵遣將(ㄆㄞˋ ㄅㄧㄥ ㄑㄧㄢˇ ㄐㄧㄤˋ)
to dispatch troops and send generals
派不是(ㄆㄞˋ ㄅㄨˋ ˙ㄕ)
to criticize one for a mistake; to blame one for a fault: 他們派他不是。They blamed him for his faults.
派發(ㄆㄞˋ ㄈㄚ)
to distribute
派代表(ㄆㄞˋ ㄉㄞˋ ㄅㄧㄠˇ)
to send a delegate; to dispatch a representative
派對(ㄆㄞˋ ㄉㄨㄟˋ)
a party (for social entertainment)
派頭(ㄆㄞˋ ㄊㄡˊ)
manner; air; the way one acts and speaks: 我叔父派頭十足。My uncle has a conceited manner.
派令(ㄆㄞˋ ㄌㄧㄥˋ)
orders of appointment in written form
派遣(ㄆㄞˋ ㄑㄧㄢˇ)
to dispatch: 美國派遣使者到中國。The United States dispatched a messenger to China.
派遣軍(ㄆㄞˋ ㄑㄧㄢˇ ㄐㄩㄣ)
an expeditionary force
派系(ㄆㄞˋ ㄒㄧˋ)
① factions (within a political party, etc.) ② affiliation with (a school or party)
派駐(ㄆㄞˋ ㄓㄨˋ)
to accredit
派差(ㄆㄞˋ ㄔㄞ)
to assign work; to send one on an errand
派出所(ㄆㄞˋ ㄔㄨ ㄙㄨㄛˇ)
a police station
派司(ㄆㄞˋ ㄙ)
a pass; a safe-conduct
派員(ㄆㄞˋ ㄩㄢˊ)
to send a staffer or officer
派用場(ㄆㄞˋ ㄩㄥˋ ㄔㄤˇ)or(ㄆㄞˋ ㄩㄥˋ ㄔㄤˊ)
to assign work; to use something for a specific purpose

【流】 2875 ㄌㄧㄡˊ liou liú

1. to flow; to discharge: 水向低處流。Water flows to the lowest level.
2. to wander; to stray
3. a branch; a division
4. a class; a rank: 上流人士和普通民衆都喜歡他。He is liked by the classes and the masses.
5. unsettled; unfixed; mobile

流波(ㄌㄧㄡˊ ㄅㄛ)
① (said of a beautiful woman) a turn of the eyes in one direction ② flowing water; current

流輩(ㄌㄧㄡˊ ㄅㄟˋ)
people of the same rank

流弊(ㄌㄧㄡˊ ㄅㄧˋ)
long accumulated evil effect; abuses

流別(ㄌㄧㄡˊ ㄅㄧㄝˊ)
branches; schools; divisions

流變(ㄌㄧㄡˊ ㄅㄧㄢˋ)
later developments

流逋(ㄌㄧㄡˊ ㄅㄨ)
to be exiled

流布(ㄌㄧㄡˊ ㄅㄨˋ)
to be transmitted; to spread

流派(ㄌㄧㄡˊ ㄆㄞˋ)
① branches; divisions; schools ② a tributary

流配(ㄌㄧㄡˊ ㄆㄟˋ)
to banish; to exile

流盼(ㄌㄧㄡˊ ㄆㄢˋ)
to turn the eyes

流品(ㄌㄧㄡˊ ㄆㄧㄣˇ)
social status

流馬(ㄌㄧㄡˊ ㄇㄚˇ)
a device for hauling supplies devised by Chu-Ko Liang (諸葛亮) in the Epoch of the Three Kingdoms

流沫(ㄌㄧㄡˊ ㄇㄛˋ)
foam; froth

流氓(ㄌㄧㄡˊ ㄇㄤˊ)
a hoodlum; a hooligan; a villain; a rascal: 他在耍流氓。He behaved like a hoodlum.

流湎(ㄌㄧㄡˊ ㄇㄧㄢˇ)
① to be addicted to alcoholic drinks ② to indulge

流眄(ㄌㄧㄡˊ ㄇㄧㄢˇ)or 流目(ㄌㄧㄡˊ ㄇㄨˋ)
to turn the eyes

流民(ㄌㄧㄡˊ ㄇㄧㄣˊ)
refugees

流芳(ㄌㄧㄡˊ ㄈㄤ)
to hand down a fine reputation through history; to be honored by posterity

流芳百世(ㄌㄧㄡˊ ㄈㄤ ㄅㄞˇ ㄕˋ)or 流芳千古(ㄌㄧㄡˊ ㄈㄤ ㄑㄧㄢ ㄍㄨˇ)
to hand down a fine reputation through generations; to be honored by all generations

流放(ㄌㄧㄡˊ ㄈㄤˋ)
to exile; to banish: 他被流放到西伯利亞。He was banished to Siberia.

流風(ㄌㄧㄡˊ ㄈㄥ)
traditional customs

流彈(ㄌㄧㄡˊ ㄉㄢˋ)
a stray bullet

流宕(ㄌㄧㄡˊ ㄉㄤˋ)
① to loaf about ②(said of a piece of writing) fluent and uninhibited

流蕩(ㄌㄧㄡˊ ㄉㄤˋ)
to loaf about; to roam

流當(ㄌㄧㄡˊ ㄉㄤˋ)
to fail to reclaim pawned articles within the specified time

流當品(ㄌㄧㄡˊ ㄉㄤˋ ㄆㄧㄣˇ)
unclaimed or unredeemed articles in a pawnshop

流電(ㄌㄧㄡˊ ㄉㄧㄢˋ)
lightning speed; extreme swiftness

流毒(ㄌㄧㄡˊ ㄉㄨˊ)
detrimental effect; harm

流動(ㄌㄧㄡˊ ㄉㄨㄥˋ)
① to be in flowing motion: 河水緩緩地流動。The river is flowing sluggishly. ② on the move ③ mobile; itinerant; going from place to place

流動投資(ㄌㄧㄡˊ ㄉㄨㄥˋ ㄊㄡˊ ㄗ)
current investment

流動戶口(ㄌㄧㄡˊ ㄉㄨㄥˋ ㄏㄨˋ ㄎㄡˇ)
the registered temporary domicile

流動金(ㄌㄧㄡˊ ㄉㄨㄥˋ ㄐㄧㄣ)or 流動基金(ㄌㄧㄡˊ ㄉㄨㄥˋ ㄐㄧ ㄐㄧㄣ)
revolving funds; working capital

流動性(ㄌㄧㄡˊ ㄉㄨㄥˋ ㄒㄧㄥˋ)
mobility; fluidity

流動商店(ㄌㄧㄡˊ ㄉㄨㄥˋ ㄕㄤ ㄉㄧㄢˋ)
a mobile shop

流動人口(ㄌㄧㄡˊ ㄉㄨㄥˋ ㄖㄣˊ ㄎㄡˇ)
transient population or residents; the floating population

流動資本(ㄌㄧㄡˊ ㄉㄨㄥˋ ㄗ ㄅㄣˇ)
floating capital; circulating capital

流動資產(ㄌㄧㄡˊ ㄉㄨㄥˋ ㄗ ㄔㄢˇ)
(accounting) accrued assets; circulating assets

流體(ㄌㄧㄡˊ ㄊㄧˇ)
fluid: 空氣是流體，不是液體。Air is a fluid but not a liquid.

流涕(ㄌㄧㄡˊ ㄊㄧˋ)
to shed tears

流鐵槽(ㄌㄧㄡˊ ㄊㄧㄝˇ ㄘㄠˊ)
(metallurgy) an iron runner

流通(ㄌㄧㄡˊ ㄊㄨㄥ)
in circulation; to circulate; to ventilate: 我們開窗以使空氣流通。We ventilate a room by opening windows.

流年(ㄌㄧㄡˊ ㄋㄧㄢˊ)
① years that flow by one after another; fleeting time: 似水流年。Time passes swiftly like flowing water. ② the change of one's fortune in a given year

流年不利(ㄌㄧㄡˊ ㄋㄧㄢˊ ㄅㄨˋ ㄌㄧˋ)
to have a year of ill luck; an unlucky year

流淚(ㄌㄧㄡˊ ㄌㄟˋ)
to shed tears: 這女孩流淚了。The girl shed tears.

流覽(ㄌㄧㄡˊ ㄌㄢˇ)
① to take a comprehensive look; to survey ② to skim over; to read through

流浪(ㄌㄧㄡˊ ㄌㄤˋ)
to wander about; to roam about; to rove: 這小女孩流浪街頭。The little girl wandered the street.

流浪漢(ㄌㄧㄡˊ ㄌㄤˋ ㄏㄢˋ)
a vagabond; a bum; a drifter: 他是個無家可歸的流浪漢。He is a homeless vagabond.

流離失所(ㄌㄧㄡˊ ㄌㄧˊ ㄕ ㄙㄨㄛˇ)
homeless and wandering from place to place: 戰爭使許多人流離失所。The war forced thousands of people to wander about as refugees.

流理台(ㄌㄧㄡˊ ㄌㄧˇ ㄊㄞˊ)
a set of kitchen units including such items as a kitchen sink, a range, etc.

流利(ㄌㄧㄡˊ ㄌㄧˋ)
flowing smoothly; fluent: 你的英語相當流利。Your English is rather fluent.

流麗(ㄌㄧㄡˊ ㄌㄧˋ)
(said of literary writings) fluent and elegant

流里流氣(ㄌㄧㄡˊ ˙ㄌㄧ ㄌㄧㄡˊ ㄑㄧˋ)
rascally

流連(ㄌㄧㄡˊ ㄌㄧㄢˊ)
reluctant to leave; reluctant to end a pleasant experience; to tarry; to linger on

流連忘返(ㄌㄧㄡˊ ㄌㄧㄢˊ ㄨㄤˋ ㄈㄢˇ)
to forget to go home because of pleasures elsewhere

流量(ㄌㄧㄡˊ ㄌㄧㄤˋ)
(hydrology) flow capacity; discharge

流露(ㄌㄧㄡˊ ㄌㄨˋ)
to reveal unknowingly; to betray; to manifest: 他眞情流露。He revealed his sentiment.

流落(ㄌㄧㄡˊ ㄌㄨㄛˋ)
to become an outcast in a strange land; to become a wanderer in a faraway land owing to lack of money for the home trip: 她流落異鄉。She wandered destitute far from home.

流丐(ㄌㄧㄡˊ ㄍㄞˋ)
a vagrant beggar; a vagabond

流官(ㄌㄧㄡˊ ㄍㄨㄢ)
(during the Ching Dynasty) a local official appointed by the Central Government (as opposed to those holding inherited titles)

流光(ㄌㄧㄡˊ ㄍㄨㄤ)
① the swift flow of time ② moonlight reflected on flowing water

流寇(ㄌㄧㄡˊ ㄎㄡˋ)
wandering bandits; bandits without a permanent base

流汗(ㄌㄧㄡˊ ㄏㄢˋ)
to perspire; to sweat: 天氣很熱時，我們會流汗。We sweat when it is very hot.

流戶(ㄌㄧㄡˊ ㄏㄨˋ)
homeless families

流滑(ㄌㄧㄡˊ ·ㄏㄨㄚ)
crafty; cunning

流火(ㄌㄧㄡˊ ㄏㄨㄛˇ)
① summer heat ② (Chinese medicine) inflammatory disease with redness of skin

流金鑠石(ㄌㄧㄡˊ ㄐㄧㄣ ㄕㄨㄛˋ ㄕˊ)
scorching heat in the summer sun

流氣(ㄌㄧㄡˊ ㄑㄧˋ)
hooliganism; rascally behavior

流徙(ㄌㄧㄡˊ ㄒㄧˇ)
to exile

流霞(ㄌㄧㄡˊ ㄒㄧㄚˊ)
flowing vapor

流血(ㄌㄧㄡˊ ㄒㄧㄝˇ)
to shed blood; to bleed; bloodshed; bleeding: 有人說政治是不流血的戰爭。It is said politics is war without bloodshed.

流涎(ㄌㄧㄡˊ ㄒㄧㄢˊ)
to drivel; to drool

流線型(ㄌㄧㄡˊ ㄒㄧㄢˋ ㄒㄧㄥˊ)
streamlined

流星(ㄌㄧㄡˊ ㄒㄧㄥ)
(astronomy) a meteor

流星雨(ㄌㄧㄡˊ ㄒㄧㄥ ㄩˇ)
a meteoric shower

流刑(ㄌㄧㄡˊ ㄒㄧㄥˊ)
(in old China) banishment or exile as a form of punishment

流行(ㄌㄧㄡˊ ㄒㄧㄥˊ)
① to be in fashion; to be popular; to be in vogue; fashionable; prevalent:這是現今流行的論調。This argument is prevalent now. ②(said of a contagious disease) to spread, rage, or be rampant: 疾病在該村流行著。Sickness was rampant in the village.

流行病(ㄌㄧㄡˊ ㄒㄧㄥˊ ㄅㄧㄥˋ)
an epidemic (disease)

流行性感冒(ㄌㄧㄡˊ ㄒㄧㄥˊ ㄒㄧㄥˋ ㄍㄢˇ ㄇㄠˋ)
influenza; flu; epidemic catarrh

流質(ㄌㄧㄡˊ ㄓˋ)
liquid

流注(ㄌㄧㄡˊ ㄓㄨˋ)
(said of a river) to flow into a lake or sea

流轉(ㄌㄧㄡˊ ㄓㄨㄢˇ)
① to wander about; to move from place to place ② to spread; to transmit, or be transmitted (from person to person, or from generation to generation) ③ to alternate

流產(ㄌㄧㄡˊ ㄔㄢˇ)
① to have a miscarriage; abortion ② to prove abortive; to fail to materialize: 她的計劃流產了。Her plan proved abortive.

流娼(ㄌㄧㄡˊ ㄔㄤ)
a streetwalker

流暢(ㄌㄧㄡˊ ㄔㄤˋ)
(usually said of the style of writing) fluent; smooth

流程(ㄌㄧㄡˊ ㄔㄥˊ)
① technological process ② (mining) circuits

流傳(ㄌㄧㄡˊ ㄔㄨㄢˊ)
to transmit, or be transmitted, from person to person, or from generation to generation; to spread: 這消息很快地流傳開來。The news soon spread.

流失(ㄌㄧㄡˊ ㄕ)
to run off; to be washed away

流逝(ㄌㄧㄡˊ ㄕˋ)
(said of time) to pass; to elapse; passage

流沙(ㄌㄧㄡˊ ㄕㄚ)
① sediment (in rivers) ② the quicksand

流說(ㄌㄧㄡˊ ㄕㄨㄛ)
heretical assertion

流水(ㄌㄧㄡˊ ㄕㄨㄟˇ)
flowing water; current: 他順著流水游泳。He swam with the current.

流水賬(ㄌㄧㄡˊ ㄕㄨㄟˇ ㄓㄤˋ)
running account; journal account

流人(ㄌㄧㄡˊ ㄖㄣˊ)
① a refugee ② an exile

流刺網(ㄌㄧㄡˊ ㄘˋ ㄨㄤˇ)
a drift net

流竄(ㄌㄧㄡˊ ㄘㄨㄢˋ)
(said of bandits or rebel troops) to roam about

流蘇(ㄌㄧㄡˊ ㄙㄨ)
tassels (of flags)

流俗(ㄌㄧㄡˊ ㄙㄨˊ)
popular customs

流速(ㄌㄧㄡˊ ㄙㄨˋ)
the speed of current; current velocity

流速計(ㄌㄧㄡˊ ㄙㄨˋ ㄐㄧˋ)
a current meter

流言(ㄌㄧㄡˊ ㄧㄢˊ)
groundless statement; idle talk; rumor; hearsay

流言止於智者(ㄌㄧㄡˊ ㄧㄢˊ ㄓˇ ㄩˊ ㄓˋ ㄓㄜˇ)
A wise man does not believe in rumors.

流音(ㄌㄧㄡˊ ㄧㄣ)
(phonetics) a glide; the transitional sound

〔水部〕

流鶯(ㄌㄧㄡˊ ㄧㄥ)
a streetwalker
流螢(ㄌㄧㄡˊ ㄧㄥˊ)
a firefly
流亡(ㄌㄧㄡˊ ㄨㄤˊ)
to be exiled; to wander in a strange land: 他終生流亡國外。He was exiled for life.
流亡政府(ㄌㄧㄡˊ ㄨㄤˊ ㄓㄥˋ ㄈㄨˇ)
a government in exile
流於形式(ㄌㄧㄡˊ ㄩˊ ㄒㄧㄥˊ ㄕˋ)
to have become a matter of formality
流域(ㄌㄧㄡˊ ㄩˋ)
drainage basin; drainage area; catchment area; catchment basin; river basin; valley
流寓(ㄌㄧㄡˊ ㄩˋ)
to live here and there in a strange land; to have no permanent home
流用(ㄌㄧㄡˊ ㄩㄥˋ)
to put a thing to a use not originally intended

【洏】 2876
ㄦˊ erl ér
1. tearful; weeping
2. to cook food thoroughly

【洸】 2877
ㄍㄨㄤ guang guāng
1. name of a river in Shantung
2. (said of water) to glitter
3. cavalierly; bravely; to be martial-looking

七畫

【浙】 2878
ㄓㄜˋ jeh zhè
1. Chekiang
2. name of a river
浙東(ㄓㄜˋ ㄉㄨㄥ)
eastern Chekiang
浙江(ㄓㄜˋ ㄐㄧㄤ)
①Chekiang Province ②name of a river in Chekiang
浙江潮(ㄓㄜˋ ㄐㄧㄤ ㄔㄠˊ)
the tide at the mouth of the Chientang River (錢塘江) in Chekiang
浙西(ㄓㄜˋ ㄒㄧ)
western Chekiang

【浚】 2879
ㄐㄩㄣˋ jiunn jùn
1. to dredge
2. deep
浚泥機(ㄐㄩㄣˋ ㄋㄧˊ ㄐㄧ)
a dredge
浚利(ㄐㄩㄣˋ ㄌㄧˋ)
(said of a waterway) unobstructed

【浜】 2880
ㄅㄤ bang bāng
a small stream

【浡】 2881
ㄅㄛˊ bor bó
to rise; excited
浡然(ㄅㄛˊ ㄖㄢˊ)
① rising ② flourishingly

【浣】 2882
ㄏㄨㄢˇ hoan huǎn
(又讀 ㄨㄢˇ woan wǎn)
1. to wash; to rinse
2. ten days; any of the three ten-day divisions of a month: 上浣 the first ten days of a month
浣滌(ㄏㄨㄢˇ ㄉㄧˊ)
to wash; to rinse
浣花溪(ㄏㄨㄢˇ ㄏㄨㄚ ㄒㄧ)
name of a place in Szechwan(四川), known as the home of the poet Tu Fu
浣熊(ㄏㄨㄢˇ ㄒㄩㄥˊ)
a racoon
浣濯(ㄏㄨㄢˇ ㄓㄨㄛˊ)
to wash; to rinse
浣紗溪(ㄏㄨㄢˇ ㄕㄚ ㄒㄧ)
name of a river in Chekiang, where the famed beauty, Hsi Shih (西施), washed cotton yarn when she was a country girl
浣衣(ㄏㄨㄢˇ ㄧ)
to wash clothes

【浩】 2883
ㄏㄠˋ haw hào
1. massive; great; vast
2. many; much
3. a Chinese family name
浩博(ㄏㄠˋ ㄅㄛˊ)
many; much
浩漫(ㄏㄠˋ ㄇㄢˋ)
many; numerous
浩茫(ㄏㄠˋ ㄇㄤˊ)
(said of a body of water) vast or extensive
浩渺 or 浩淼(ㄏㄠˋ ㄇㄧㄠˇ)
(said of a body of water) vast or extensive; extending into the distance
浩繁(ㄏㄠˋ ㄈㄢˊ)
① many; numerous ② (said of duties, etc.) heavy: 這是一筆浩繁的開銷。This is a heavy expenditure.
浩大(ㄏㄠˋ ㄉㄚˋ)
great; vast
浩蕩(ㄏㄠˋ ㄉㄤˋ)
vast and restless
浩歎(ㄏㄠˋ ㄊㄢˋ)
to give a deep emotional sigh; to heave a deep sigh
浩歌(ㄏㄠˋ ㄍㄜ)
to sing aloud
浩浩(ㄏㄠˋ ㄏㄠˋ)
①(said of water) vast ②(said of time) infinitive ③(said of the heaven) vast
浩浩蕩蕩(ㄏㄠˋ ㄏㄠˋ ㄉㄤˋ ㄉㄤˋ)
(said of an army in march) moving in an imposing manner; surging ahead; overwhelming
浩瀚(ㄏㄠˋ ㄏㄢˋ)
huge quantities; vast
浩劫(ㄏㄠˋ ㄐㄧㄝˊ)
great disaster; a catastrophe; a calamity
浩氣(ㄏㄠˋ ㄑㄧˋ)
the Great Spirit (the aim of self-cultivation preached by Mencius)
浩氣長存(ㄏㄠˋ ㄑㄧˋ ㄔㄤˊ ㄘㄨㄣˊ)
imperishable noble spirit
浩然(ㄏㄠˋ ㄖㄢˊ)
great; overwhelming
浩然之氣(ㄏㄠˋ ㄖㄢˊ ㄓ ㄑㄧˋ)
the Great Spirit (the aim of self-cultivation preached by Mencius)
浩壤(ㄏㄠˋ ㄖㄤˇ)
vast land
浩如烟海(ㄏㄠˋ ㄖㄨˊ ㄧㄢ ㄏㄞˇ)
as vast as a misty ocean
浩飲(ㄏㄠˋ ㄧㄣˇ)
to drink without inhibition; to drink like a fish

【浥】 2884
ㄧˋ yih yì
wet, moist; to moisten
浥濕(ㄧˋ ㄕ)
wet; moist
浥潤(ㄧˋ ㄖㄨㄣˋ)
wet; moist
浥浥(ㄧˋ ㄧˋ)
moist

【浦】 2885
ㄆㄨˇ puu pǔ
1. the shore; the beach; the

riverside
2. a Chinese family name
浦東(ㄆㄨˇ ㄉㄨㄥ)
that part of Shanghai east of the Huangpu River
浦口(ㄆㄨˇ ㄎㄡˇ)
a city opposite Nanking on the Yangtze River

【浬】 2886
ㄌㄧˇ lii lǐ
(a unit of distance used chiefly in navigation) a nautical mile; a geographic mile; a sea mile

【浪】 2887
1. ㄌㄤˋ lanq làng
1. waves; billows; breakers: 白浪滔天 white breakers sweeping across the sky 巨浪打在我們身上。Great waves surged over us. 海浪拍擊著海岸。The waves beat upon the shore.
2. dissolute; debauched; unrestrained; rash
浪板(ㄌㄤˋ ㄅㄢˇ)
a plastic roofing board
浪婆(ㄌㄤˋ ㄆㄛˊ)
the goddess of the waves
浪漫(ㄌㄤˋ ㄇㄢˋ)
① dissolute; debauched ② romantic
浪漫派(ㄌㄤˋ ㄇㄢˋ ㄆㄞˋ)
romanticism
浪漫的(ㄌㄤˋ ㄇㄢˋ ·ㄉㄜ)
romantic
浪漫主義(ㄌㄤˋ ㄇㄢˋ ㄓㄨˇ ㄧˋ)
romanticism
浪莽(ㄌㄤˋ ㄇㄤˇ)
unrestrained
浪孟(ㄌㄤˋ ㄇㄥˋ)
① discouraged; dejected ② aloud
浪費(ㄌㄤˋ ㄈㄟˋ)
to waste; to lavish; waste: 他在不重要的事情上面浪費許多時間。 He wastes a lot of time on things that have no importance.
浪放(ㄌㄤˋ ㄈㄤˋ)
uninhibited; unrestrained 亦作「放浪」
浪蕩(ㄌㄤˋ ㄉㄤˋ)
to debauch; to dissipate: 他的生活浪蕩。He led a debauched life.
浪頭(ㄌㄤˋ ㄊㄡˊ)
the crest of a wave: 此時浪頭很高。Now the crests of the waves are high.
浪花(ㄌㄤˋ ㄏㄨㄚ)
spray of breaking waves: 我們被海水的浪花濺濕。We were wet with the sea spray.
浪迹(ㄌㄤˋ ㄐㄧ)
wandering; vagrant
浪迹天涯(ㄌㄤˋ ㄐㄧ ㄊㄧㄢ ㄧㄚˊ)
to wander about far away from home
浪橋(ㄌㄤˋ ㄑㄧㄠˊ)
a swing bridge
浪信(ㄌㄤˋ ㄒㄧㄣˋ)
gullible; to believe unwisely: 他浪信人言。He unwisely believed in others' words.
浪職(ㄌㄤˋ ㄓˊ)
to neglect one's duty
浪潮(ㄌㄤˋ ㄔㄠˊ)
① tide; waves ② (figuratively) tide; tendency
浪闖(ㄌㄤˋ ㄔㄨㄤˇ)
to beat about pointlessly
浪士(ㄌㄤˋ ㄕˋ)
a debauchee
浪人(ㄌㄤˋ ㄖㄣˊ)
① a vagrant ② a dismissed courtier ③ an unemployed person; a jobless person
浪子(ㄌㄤˋ ㄗˇ)
a prodigal; a debauchee; a loafer
浪子回頭(ㄌㄤˋ ㄗˇ ㄏㄨㄟˊ ㄊㄡˊ)
the return of the prodigal son
浪遊(ㄌㄤˋ ㄧㄡˊ)
to roam for pleasure; to make a tour: 那攝影家浪遊世界。The photographer roamed about the world.
浪語(ㄌㄤˋ ㄩˇ)
a nonsensical joke

【浪】 2887
2. ㄌㄤˊ lang láng
flowing; fluent
浪浪(ㄌㄤˊ ㄌㄤˊ)
flowing

【浭】 2888
ㄍㄥ geng gēng
name of a river in Hopeh
浭水(ㄍㄥ ㄕㄨㄟˇ)
a river in Hopeh

【浴】 2889
ㄩˋ yuh yù
1. to bathe; to wash: 他用熱水沐浴。He bathed himself in hot water.
2. a bath
浴盆(ㄩˋ ㄆㄣˊ)
a bath; a bathtub
浴佛(ㄩˋ ㄈㄛˊ)
to bathe Buddha's image (as a Buddhist rite in celebration of the Buddha's birthday)
浴佛節(ㄩˋ ㄈㄛˊ ㄐㄧㄝˊ)
the Buddha Bathing Festival (on the eighth day of the fourth moon, when Buddha's image is bathed in celebration of his birthday)
浴德(ㄩˋ ㄉㄜˊ)
to cultivate one's virtue
浴堂(ㄩˋ ㄊㄤˊ)
a bathhouse; a public bath
浴巾(ㄩˋ ㄐㄧㄣ)
a bath towel
浴像(ㄩˋ ㄒㄧㄤˋ)
to bathe Buddha's image (as a Buddhist rite)
浴血苦戰(ㄩˋ ㄒㄩㄝˋ ㄎㄨˇ ㄓㄢˋ)
to be at bay in a fierce battle; to fight a bloody battle
浴池(ㄩˋ ㄔˊ)
a bath pool
浴場(ㄩˋ ㄔㄤˇ)or(ㄩˋ ㄔㄤˊ)
a bathing beach: 去年夏天他常去那個海水浴場。Last summer he often went to that bathing beach.
浴屍(ㄩˋ ㄕ)
to bathe a corpse (in preparation for funeral service)
浴室(ㄩˋ ㄕˋ)
a bathroom
浴日(ㄩˋ ㄖˋ)
① bright sunrise ② great distinction; great exploits; eminent contributions
浴衣(ㄩˋ ㄧ)
a bathrobe; bathing dress; bathing costume; a bathing gown

【浮】 2890
ㄈㄨˊ fwu fú
(又讀 ㄈㄡˊ four fóu)
1. to float; to waft
2. to overflow; to exceed
3. empty; superficial; unsubstantial; unfounded; groundless
浮薄(ㄈㄨˊ ㄅㄛˊ)
insincere; untruthful; unsta-

〔水部〕

〔水部〕

ble; frivolous; flippant: 他是個浮薄少年。He's an unstable youth.

浮報(ㄈㄨˊ ㄅㄠˋ)
to report more than the actual amount spent

浮標(ㄈㄨˊ ㄅㄧㄠ)
a buoy

浮冰(ㄈㄨˊ ㄅㄧㄥ)
floating ice; (ice) floes

浮萍(ㄈㄨˊ ㄆㄧㄥˊ)
duckweed

浮冒(ㄈㄨˊ ㄇㄠˋ)
reckless and untruthful (in accounts)

浮靡(ㄈㄨˊ ㄇㄧˇ)
decadent

浮面(ㄈㄨˊ ㄇㄧㄢˋ)
the surface: 他把浮面的一層泥刮去。He scraped the mud off the surface.

浮名(ㄈㄨˊ ㄇㄧㄥˊ)
an empty name or honor

浮費(ㄈㄨˊ ㄈㄟˋ)
to waste; to lavish

浮泛(ㄈㄨˊ ㄈㄢˋ)
① to boat ② superficial: 他的報告內容浮泛。His report was superficial and full of generalities.

浮雕(ㄈㄨˊ ㄉㄧㄠ)
(sculpture) relief

浮動(ㄈㄨˊ ㄉㄨㄥˋ)
① to waft; to float; to drift ② to be unsteady; to fluctuate

浮屠 or 浮圖(ㄈㄨˊ ㄊㄨˊ)
① Buddha ② a pagoda; a stupa

浮浪(ㄈㄨˊ ㄌㄤˋ)
to loaf about

浮浪人(ㄈㄨˊ ㄌㄤˋ ㄖㄣˊ)
a loafer

浮浪子弟(ㄈㄨˊ ㄌㄤˋ ㄗˇ ㄉㄧˋ)
vagrant or unemployed persons

浮力(ㄈㄨˊ ㄌㄧˋ)
(physics) buoyancy: 木頭的浮力大於鐵。Wood has more buoyancy than iron.

浮利(ㄈㄨˊ ㄌㄧˋ)
empty profit

浮梗(ㄈㄨˊ ㄍㄥˇ)
duckweed stalks

浮瓜沈李(ㄈㄨˊ ㄍㄨㄚ ㄔㄣˊ ㄌㄧˇ)
to pursue summer joys or pleasures

浮光掠影(ㄈㄨˊ ㄍㄨㄤ ㄌㄩㄝˋ ㄧㄥˇ)
floating light and passing shadow—superficial opinions, descriptions, sketches, etc.

浮誇(ㄈㄨˊ ㄎㄨㄚ)
boastfully vain; vainglorious: 他很浮誇地說他所做過的事。He speaks boastfully of what he has done.

浮華(ㄈㄨˊ ㄏㄨㄚˊ)
vanity; superficial beauty: 他過著浮華的人生。He led a life of vanity.

浮滑(ㄈㄨˊ ㄏㄨㄚˊ)
fickle and crafty

浮家泛宅(ㄈㄨˊ ㄐㄧㄚ ㄈㄢˋ ㄓㄞˊ)
to dwell on a boat

浮氣(ㄈㄨˊ ㄑㄧˋ)
flippancy; frivolity

浮橋(ㄈㄨˊ ㄑㄧㄠˊ) or 浮梁(ㄈㄨˊ ㄌㄧㄤˊ)
a pontoon bridge

浮簽(ㄈㄨˊ ㄑㄧㄢ)
a piece of paper intended to be detached eventually

浮淺(ㄈㄨˊ ㄑㄧㄢˇ)
superficial; shallow

浮囂(ㄈㄨˊ ㄒㄧㄠ)
fickle and excitable: 他們是浮囂之輩。They are fickle and excitable fellows.

浮現(ㄈㄨˊ ㄒㄧㄢˋ)
(said of memories, etc.) to rise before one's mind; to appear in one's mind's eye

浮腫(ㄈㄨˊ ㄓㄨㄥˇ)
① (medicine) dropsy; edema ② bloated; swollen; dropsical

浮沈(ㄈㄨˊ ㄔㄣˊ)
① rise and fall; vicissitudes ② to follow the trend: 他與世浮沈。He followed the crowd without his own principles.

浮沈子(ㄈㄨˊ ㄔㄣˊ ㄗˇ)
(physics) a Cartesian diver

浮塵(ㄈㄨˊ ㄔㄣˊ) or 浮埃(ㄈㄨˊ ㄞ)
floating dust

浮秤(ㄈㄨˊ ㄔㄥˋ)
a hydrometer

浮屍(ㄈㄨˊ ㄕ)
a floating corpse

浮石(ㄈㄨˊ ㄕˊ)
(mining) pumice (stone)

浮士德(ㄈㄨˊ ㄕˋ ㄉㄜˊ)
① Johann Faust, German magician, ?-C.1538 ② Faust (in medieval legend, a philosopher, represented as selling his soul to a devil, Mephistopheles, for wisdom and power, the main character of Goethe's *Faust* and Marlowe's *Dr. Faustus*.)

浮世繪(ㄈㄨˊ ㄕˋ ㄏㄨㄟˋ)
a (Japanese) woodcut

浮生六記(ㄈㄨˊ ㄕㄥ ㄌㄧㄡˋ ㄐㄧˋ)
Six Unforgettable Chapters of My Life, by Shen San-pai (沈三白) of the Ching Dynasty

浮生若夢(ㄈㄨˊ ㄕㄥ ㄖㄨㄛˋ ㄇㄥˋ)
Life is like a dream.

浮說(ㄈㄨˊ ㄕㄨㄛ)
groundless remarks

浮水(ㄈㄨˊ ㄕㄨㄟˇ)
(dialect) to float; to waft; to swim

浮榮(ㄈㄨˊ ㄖㄨㄥˊ)
vanity

浮躁(ㄈㄨˊ ㄗㄠˋ)
restless; impatient; rash

浮辭(ㄈㄨˊ ㄘˊ)
untruthful remarks; unfounded statements; high-sounding remarks

浮財(ㄈㄨˊ ㄘㄞˊ)
wealth (which is transient and has no intrinsic value)

浮額(ㄈㄨˊ ㄜˊ)
an amount in excess; an extra number or sum

浮一大白(ㄈㄨˊ ㄧˊ ㄉㄚˋ ㄅㄞˊ)
to empty a full glass of wine or liquor at one drink

浮游(ㄈㄨˊ ㄧㄡˊ)
an ephemera

浮游生物(ㄈㄨˊ ㄧㄡˊ ㄕㄥ ㄨˋ)
plankton

浮言(ㄈㄨˊ ㄧㄢˊ)
unfounded remarks; groundless statements

浮艷(ㄈㄨˊ ㄧㄢˋ)
pompous and unsubstantial

浮揚(ㄈㄨˊ ㄧㄤˊ)
to soar

浮影(ㄈㄨˊ ㄧㄥˇ)
floating shadows; visions

浮文(ㄈㄨˊ ㄨㄣˊ)
empty writing

浮譽(ㄈㄨˊ ㄩˋ)
empty honor
浮雲(ㄈㄨˊ ㄩㄣˊ)
floating clouds
浮雲朝露(ㄈㄨˊ ㄩㄣˊ ㄓㄠ ㄌㄨˋ)
(literally) floating cloud and morning dew—fleeting; ephemeral; brief

【海】 2891
ㄏㄞˇ hae hǎi

1. the sea; the ocean:我在海中游泳。I swam in the sea.
2. a great number of people or things coming together —(figuratively) a huge gathering
3. an area; a field: 學海無涯。The field of learning is boundless.
4. great; unlimited
5. a Chinese family name

海拔(ㄏㄞˇ ㄅㄚˊ)
the elevation or height above sea level: 這山高海拔三千九百米。The mountain is 3,900 meters above sea level.
海豹(ㄏㄞˇ ㄅㄠˋ)
a seal (a sea animal): 某些種類的海豹已近乎絕種。Some kinds of seals are nearly extinct.
海報(ㄏㄞˇ ㄅㄠˋ)
a theater poster
海邦(ㄏㄞˇ ㄅㄤ)
a maritime nation
海表(ㄏㄞˇ ㄅㄧㄠˇ)
overseas lands
海邊(ㄏㄞˇ ㄅㄧㄢ)or 海邊兒(ㄏㄞˇ ㄅㄧㄚㄦ)
the seashore; the seaside; the beach: 孩子們在海邊到處奔跑。Children were running about on the beach.
海濱(ㄏㄞˇ ㄅㄧㄣ)
the seashore; the beach: 我們在海濱度假。We spent our holidays by the seashore.
海不揚波(ㄏㄞˇ ㄅㄨˋ ㄧㄤˊ ㄅㄛ)
The sea is calm.—The world is in peace.
海派(ㄏㄞˇ ㄆㄞˋ)
the Shanghai style (of opera, living, etc.), as opposed to the Peking style
海泡石(ㄏㄞˇ ㄆㄠˋ ㄕˊ)
(mining) sepiolite
海盤車(ㄏㄞˇ ㄆㄢˊ ㄔㄜ)
an asteroid; a starfish
海平面(ㄏㄞˇ ㄆㄧㄥˊ ㄇㄧㄢˋ)
sea level: 這座山高出海平面一萬英尺。The mountain is 10,000 feet above sea level.
海埔(ㄏㄞˇ ㄆㄨˇ)
the seaside
海埔新生地(ㄏㄞˇ ㄆㄨˇ ㄒㄧㄣ ㄕㄥ ㄉㄧˋ)
the tidal land
海馬(ㄏㄞˇ ㄇㄚˇ)
① hippocampus ② a sea horse
海罵(ㄏㄞˇ ㄇㄚˋ)
to accuse or slander an unnamed person
海鰻(ㄏㄞˇ ㄇㄢˊ)
a conger pike; a sea eel
海綿(ㄏㄞˇ ㄇㄧㄢˊ)
sponge
海面(ㄏㄞˇ ㄇㄧㄢˋ)
the sea surface
海防(ㄏㄞˇ ㄈㄤˊ)
① coastal defense: 海防十分鞏固。The coastal defense is very strong. ② Haiphong, North Viet Nam
海防部隊(ㄏㄞˇ ㄈㄤˊ ㄅㄨˋ ㄉㄨㄟˋ)
coastal defense forces
海風(ㄏㄞˇ ㄈㄥ)
a sea wind; a sea breeze: 海風自北方吹來。A sea wind was blowing from the north.
海帶(ㄏㄞˇ ㄉㄞˋ)
kelp; a sea tangle
海島(ㄏㄞˇ ㄉㄠˇ)
an island (in the sea): 臺灣是一個海島。Taiwan is an island.
海盜(ㄏㄞˇ ㄉㄠˋ)
a pirate; a sea rover; a sea robber
海盜船(ㄏㄞˇ ㄉㄠˋ ㄔㄨㄢˊ)
a pirate ship; a sea rover
海膽(ㄏㄞˇ ㄉㄢˇ)
a sea urchin
海底(ㄏㄞˇ ㄉㄧˇ)
the bed or bottom of the sea
海底電線(ㄏㄞˇ ㄉㄧˇ ㄉㄧㄢˋ ㄒㄧㄢˋ)or 海底電纜(ㄏㄞˇ ㄉㄧˇ ㄉㄧㄢˋ ㄌㄢˇ)
a submarine cable
海底撈針(ㄏㄞˇ ㄉㄧˇ ㄌㄠ ㄓㄣ)
(literally) to try to recover a needle from the bottom of the sea—to make a futile search
海底撈月(ㄏㄞˇ ㄉㄧˇ ㄌㄠ ㄩㄝˋ)
to try to fish out the moon from the bottom of the sea —to strive in vain
海底鑽探(ㄏㄞˇ ㄉㄧˇ ㄗㄨㄢ ㄊㄢˋ)
offshore drilling
海地(ㄏㄞˇ ㄉㄧˋ)
Haiti
海地人(ㄏㄞˇ ㄉㄧˋ ㄖㄣˊ)
a Haitian
海釣(ㄏㄞˇ ㄉㄧㄠˋ)
offshore angling
海頓(ㄏㄞˇ ㄉㄨㄣˋ)
Franz Joseph Haydn, 1732-1809, Austrian composer
海獺(ㄏㄞˇ ㄊㄚˇ)
a sea otter; a beaver: 動物園裡有三隻海獺。There are three beavers in the zoo.
海濤(ㄏㄞˇ ㄊㄠ)
sea waves; billows
海灘(ㄏㄞˇ ㄊㄢ)
the seashore; the beach
海棠(ㄏㄞˇ ㄊㄤˊ)
Malus spectabilis; Chinese flowering apple
海塘(ㄏㄞˇ ㄊㄤˊ)or 海堤(ㄏㄞˇ ㄊㄧˊ)
sea wall; sea embankment
海圖(ㄏㄞˇ ㄊㄨˊ)
a sea or marine chart
海豚(ㄏㄞˇ ㄊㄨㄣˊ)
a dolphin
海內(ㄏㄞˇ ㄋㄟˋ)
within the four seas; within the country
海內清平(ㄏㄞˇ ㄋㄟˋ ㄑㄧㄥ ㄆㄧㄥˊ)
The country is in peace and good order.
海內存知己(ㄏㄞˇ ㄋㄟˋ ㄘㄨㄣˊ ㄓ ㄐㄧˇ)
"A real friend cannot be wanting in this wide world." (a line from 王勃)
海內晏如(ㄏㄞˇ ㄋㄟˋ ㄧㄢˋ ㄖㄨˊ)
Peace reigns throughout the land.
海內無雙(ㄏㄞˇ ㄋㄟˋ ㄨˊ ㄕㄨㄤ)
unequaled or peerless in the whole country
海南島(ㄏㄞˇ ㄋㄢˊ ㄉㄠˇ)
Hainan (an island off South China)
海難(ㄏㄞˇ ㄋㄢˋ)
a disaster at sea; a wreck: 那次暴風雨引起了許多海難。The storm caused many

〔水部〕

wrecks.

海鳥(ㄏㄞˇ ㄋㄧㄠˇ)
a seafowl; a sea crow

海蘭泡(ㄏㄞˇ ㄌㄢˊ ㄆㄠˋ)
Blagoveshchensk

海浪(ㄏㄞˇ ㄌㄤˋ)
seas; sea waves: 海浪很高。Sea waves are very high.

海狸(ㄏㄞˇ ㄌㄧˊ)
a beaver

海里(ㄏㄞˇ ㄌㄧˇ)
nautical mile, a unit of distance used chiefly in navigation

海流(ㄏㄞˇ ㄌㄧㄡˊ)
the ocean current

海量(ㄏㄞˇ ㄌㄧㄤˋ)
① a mind with the broadness of the sea; great magnanimity; magnanimous ② great capacity for alcoholic drinks

海路(ㄏㄞˇ ㄌㄨˋ)
a sea route; a sea lane; a seaway

海螺(ㄏㄞˇ ㄌㄨㄛˊ)
a sea univalve; a conch

海洛因(ㄏㄞˇ ㄌㄨㄛˋ ㄧㄣ)
heroin

海輪(ㄏㄞˇ ㄌㄨㄣˊ)
a seagoing (or oceangoing) ship

海倫凱勒(ㄏㄞˇ ㄌㄨㄣˊ ㄎㄞˇ ㄌㄜˋ)
Helen Adams Keller, 1880-1968

海龍王(ㄏㄞˇ ㄌㄨㄥˊ ㄨㄤˊ)
Dragon King, the Chinese equivalent of Neptune

海溝(ㄏㄞˇ ㄍㄡ)
(oceanic) trenches

海狗(ㄏㄞˇ ㄍㄡˇ)
a seal

海港(ㄏㄞˇ ㄍㄤˇ)
a seaport; a harbor: 這島上有個良好的海港。The island has a fine harbor.

海國(ㄏㄞˇ ㄍㄨㄛˊ)
a maritime nation

海龜(ㄏㄞˇ ㄍㄨㄟ)
a green turtle (*Chelonia mydas*)

海關(ㄏㄞˇ ㄍㄨㄢ)
the customs; a custom house: 通過海關的檢查花了一小時。It took an hour to pass the customs.

海關檢查(ㄏㄞˇ ㄍㄨㄢ ㄐㄧㄢˇ ㄔㄚˊ)
customs inspection

海關人員(ㄏㄞˇ ㄍㄨㄢ ㄖㄣˊ ㄩㄢˊ)
customs officers

海口(ㄏㄞˇ ㄎㄡˇ)
① a seaport ② bragging; exaggerated statements

海枯石爛(ㄏㄞˇ ㄎㄨ ㄕˊ ㄌㄢˋ)
(I will remain faithful to you) even if the sea dries and stones rot

海闊天空(ㄏㄞˇ ㄎㄨㄛˋ ㄊㄧㄢ ㄎㄨㄥ)
endlessly vast; boundless

海葵(ㄏㄞˇ ㄎㄨㄟˊ)
(zoology) a sea anemone

海涵(ㄏㄞˇ ㄏㄢˊ)
great magnanimity; broadmindedness; forgiveness

海話(ㄏㄞˇ ㄏㄨㄚˋ)
boasts; exaggerations; bragging

海貨(ㄏㄞˇ ㄏㄨㄛˋ)
marine goods

海岬(ㄏㄞˇ ㄐㄧㄚˇ)
a cape

海角天涯(ㄏㄞˇ ㄐㄧㄠˇ ㄊㄧㄢ ㄧㄚˊ)
the farthest end of the earth

海徼(ㄏㄞˇ ㄐㄧㄠˋ)
remote coastal regions

海禁(ㄏㄞˇ ㄐㄧㄣˋ)
restrictions at ports of entry and exit

海禁大開(ㄏㄞˇ ㄐㄧㄣˋ ㄉㄚˋ ㄎㄞ)
to drastically ease restrictions at ports of entry and exit

海疆(ㄏㄞˇ ㄐㄧㄤ)
coastal areas and territorial seas

海景(ㄏㄞˇ ㄐㄧㄥˇ)
the seascape: 海景悅目。The seascape pleases the eyes.

海軍(ㄏㄞˇ ㄐㄩㄣ)
the navy; naval: 他服務於海軍。He serves in the navy.

海軍部(ㄏㄞˇ ㄐㄩㄣ ㄅㄨˋ)
Department of the Navy (especially of the United States)

海軍部長(ㄏㄞˇ ㄐㄩㄣ ㄅㄨˋ ㄓㄤˇ)
the Secretary of the Navy (especially of the United States)

海軍陸戰隊(ㄏㄞˇ ㄐㄩㄣ ㄌㄨˋ ㄓㄢˋ ㄉㄨㄟˋ)
the Marine Corps

海軍陸戰隊司令(ㄏㄞˇ ㄐㄩㄣ ㄌㄨˋ ㄓㄢˋ ㄉㄨㄟˋ ㄙ ㄌㄧㄥˋ)
the commandant of the Marine Corps

海軍官校(ㄏㄞˇ ㄐㄩㄣ ㄍㄨㄢ ㄒㄧㄠˋ)
a naval academy: 他在海軍官校讀書。He studies at the naval academy now.

海軍中將(ㄏㄞˇ ㄐㄩㄣ ㄓㄨㄥ ㄐㄧㄤˋ)
vice-admiral

海軍中校(ㄏㄞˇ ㄐㄩㄣ ㄓㄨㄥ ㄒㄧㄠˋ)
commander (above lieutenant commander)

海軍中尉(ㄏㄞˇ ㄐㄩㄣ ㄓㄨㄥ ㄨㄟˋ)
lieutenant junior grade

海軍少將(ㄏㄞˇ ㄐㄩㄣ ㄕㄠˋ ㄐㄧㄤˋ)
rear admiral

海軍少校(ㄏㄞˇ ㄐㄩㄣ ㄕㄠˋ ㄒㄧㄠˋ)
lieutenant commander

海軍少尉(ㄏㄞˇ ㄐㄩㄣ ㄕㄠˋ ㄨㄟˋ)
ensign

海軍上將(ㄏㄞˇ ㄐㄩㄣ ㄕㄤˋ ㄐㄧㄤˋ)
admiral

海軍上校(ㄏㄞˇ ㄐㄩㄣ ㄕㄤˋ ㄒㄧㄠˋ)
captain (just below rear admiral)

海軍上尉(ㄏㄞˇ ㄐㄩㄣ ㄕㄤˋ ㄨㄟˋ)
lieutenant (just below lieutenant commander)

海軍總司令(ㄏㄞˇ ㄐㄩㄣ ㄗㄨㄥˇ ㄙ ㄌㄧㄥˋ)
the commander in chief of the navy; (in the U.S.) the chief of naval operations

海軍演習(ㄏㄞˇ ㄐㄩㄣ ㄧㄢˇ ㄒㄧˊ)
naval maneuvers

海鞘(ㄏㄞˇ ㄑㄧㄠˋ)
a sea squirt

海權(ㄏㄞˇ ㄑㄩㄢˊ)
sea power

海峽(ㄏㄞˇ ㄒㄧㄚˊ)
straits; a channel: 台灣海峽 the Taiwan Straits

海嘯(ㄏㄞˇ ㄒㄧㄠˋ)
a tidal wave; a tsunami

海鮮(ㄏㄞˇ ㄒㄧㄢ)
fresh seafood; marine delicacies: 我喜歡吃海鮮。I like seafood.

海象(ㄏㄞˇ ㄒㄧㄤˋ)
a sea elephant; a walrus

海星(ㄏㄞˇ ㄒㄧㄥ)
the starfish

海蜇(ㄏㄞˇ ㄓㄜˊ)
a sea blubber; a jellyfish

海戰(ㄏㄞˇ ㄓㄢˋ)
a naval battle; a sea encounter
海潮(ㄏㄞˇ ㄔㄠˊ)
ocean tides
海產(ㄏㄞˇ ㄔㄢˇ)
marine products; seafood
海船(ㄏㄞˇ ㄔㄨㄢˊ)
a seagoing ship
海獅(ㄏㄞˇ ㄕ)
a sea lion
海事(ㄏㄞˇ ㄕˋ)
marine affairs; maritime affairs
海誓山盟(ㄏㄞˇ ㄕˋ ㄕㄢ ㄇㄥˊ)
to vow eternal love
海市蜃樓(ㄏㄞˇ ㄕˋ ㄕㄣˋ ㄌㄡˊ)
a mirage
海蛇(ㄏㄞˇ ㄕㄜˊ)
a sea serpent
海獸(ㄏㄞˇ ㄕㄡˋ)
a sea animal
海扇(ㄏㄞˇ ㄕㄢˋ)
a scallop
海參(ㄏㄞˇ ㄕㄣ)
a trepang; a sea cucumber; a sea slug; *bêche-de-mer*
海參崴(ㄏㄞˇ ㄕㄣ ㄨㄟ)
Vladivostok
海神(ㄏㄞˇ ㄕㄣˊ)
Neptune; Poseidon
海商(ㄏㄞˇ ㄕㄤ)
marine commerce
海上保險(ㄏㄞˇ ㄕㄤˋ ㄅㄠˇ ㄒㄧㄢˇ)
marine insurance
海上保險單(ㄏㄞˇ ㄕㄤˋ ㄅㄠˇ ㄒㄧㄢˇ ㄉㄢ)
a marine policy
海上貿易(ㄏㄞˇ ㄕㄤˋ ㄇㄠˋ ㄧˋ)
seaborne commerce
海上法(ㄏㄞˇ ㄕㄤˋ ㄈㄚˇ)or 海洋法(ㄏㄞˇ ㄧㄤˊ ㄈㄚˇ)
marine law; maritime law; the law of the sea
海上作業(ㄏㄞˇ ㄕㄤˋ ㄗㄨㄛˋ ㄧㄝˋ)
operations on the sea
海上運輸(ㄏㄞˇ ㄕㄤˋ ㄩㄣˋ ㄕㄨ)
marine transportation
海水不可斗量(ㄏㄞˇ ㄕㄨㄟˇ ㄅㄨˋ ㄎㄜˇ ㄉㄡˇ ㄌㄧㄤˊ)
Sea water is immeasurable.—Great minds cannot be fathomed.
海水汚染(ㄏㄞˇ ㄕㄨㄟˇ ㄨ ㄖㄢˇ)
sea water pollution
海水浴(ㄏㄞˇ ㄕㄨㄟˇ ㄩˋ)
sea bathing
海藻(ㄏㄞˇ ㄗㄠˇ)
seaweed
海葬(ㄏㄞˇ ㄗㄤˋ)
burial at sea
海菜(ㄏㄞˇ ㄘㄞˋ)
(botany) an edible seaweed
海鷗(ㄏㄞˇ ㄡ)
a sea gull
海岸(ㄏㄞˇ ㄢˋ)
the coast; the seaside; the seashore: 海岸的土地貧瘠。The land is barren on the coast.
海岸線(ㄏㄞˇ ㄢˋ ㄒㄧㄢˋ)
the coastal line
海牙(ㄏㄞˇ ㄧㄚˊ)
The Hague: 國際法庭位於海牙。The International Court of Justice is at The Hague.
海鹽(ㄏㄞˇ ㄧㄢˊ)
sea salt
海燕(ㄏㄞˇ ㄧㄢˋ)
a petrel
海晏河清(ㄏㄞˇ ㄧㄢˋ ㄏㄜˊ ㄑㄧㄥ)
time of peace and calm
海洋(ㄏㄞˇ ㄧㄤˊ)
seas and oceans; the ocean
海洋大學(ㄏㄞˇ ㄧㄤˊ ㄉㄚˋ ㄒㄩㄝˊ)
a university on the sea
海洋童子軍(ㄏㄞˇ ㄧㄤˊ ㄊㄨㄥˊ ㄗˇ ㄐㄩㄣ)
a sea scout
海洋公約(ㄏㄞˇ ㄧㄤˊ ㄍㄨㄥ ㄩㄝ)
a maritime convention
海洋性氣候(ㄏㄞˇ ㄧㄤˊ ㄒㄧㄥˋ ㄑㄧˋ ㄏㄡˋ)
the oceanic (or marine) climate
海洋學(ㄏㄞˇ ㄧㄤˊ ㄒㄩㄝˊ)
oceanography
海洋洲(ㄏㄞˇ ㄧㄤˊ ㄓㄡ)
Oceania
海洋生物(ㄏㄞˇ ㄧㄤˊ ㄕㄥ ㄨˋ)
a marine organism
海洋資源(ㄏㄞˇ ㄧㄤˊ ㄗ ㄩㄢˊ)
marine resources
海屋添籌(ㄏㄞˇ ㄨ ㄊㄧㄢ ㄔㄡˊ)
(literally) to add another counter as the ocean once again turned into dry land —a conventional phrase for wishing an aged person a happy birthday
海霧(ㄏㄞˇ ㄨˋ)
sea fog
海外(ㄏㄞˇ ㄨㄞˋ)
overseas; abroad
海外僑胞(ㄏㄞˇ ㄨㄞˋ ㄑㄧㄠˊ ㄅㄠ)
overseas Chinese: 海外僑胞慶祝雙十節國慶日。Overseas Chinese celebrate the Double Tenth, our National Day.
海味(ㄏㄞˇ ㄨㄟˋ)
seafood
海灣(ㄏㄞˇ ㄨㄢ)
a bay; a gulf
海碗(ㄏㄞˇ ㄨㄢˇ)
a big bowl
海王(ㄏㄞˇ ㄨㄤˊ)
a dominant sea power; the king of the sea
海王星(ㄏㄞˇ ㄨㄤˊ ㄒㄧㄥ)
the planet Neptune
海隅(ㄏㄞˇ ㄩˊ)
remote regions by the sea
海芋(ㄏㄞˇ ㄩˋ)
a common calla; a lily-of-the-Nile 亦作「馬蹄蓮」
海域(ㄏㄞˇ ㄩˋ)
a sea area; a marine area; sea waters
海員(ㄏㄞˇ ㄩㄢˊ)
a sailor; a seaman; a mariner
海員法庭(ㄏㄞˇ ㄩㄢˊ ㄈㄚˇ ㄊㄧㄥˊ)
a marine court
海運(ㄏㄞˇ ㄩㄣˋ)
marine transportation; sea transportation

【浸】 2892
ㄐㄧㄣˋ jinn jìn
1. to dip; to immerse; to soak; to permeate; to percolate
2. gradual; gradually
浸不透(ㄐㄧㄣˋ ·ㄅㄨ ㄊㄡˋ)
impervious to water; cannot be soaked through
浸泡(ㄐㄧㄣˋ ㄆㄠˋ)
to soak; to immerse
浸透(ㄐㄧㄣˋ ㄊㄡˋ)
to permeate; to percolate; soaked through: 雨水浸透了她的衣裳。Her clothes were soaked with rain.
浸禮(ㄐㄧㄣˋ ㄌㄧˇ)
baptism by immersion (not by sprinkling)
浸禮會(ㄐㄧㄣˋ ㄌㄧˇ ㄏㄨㄟˋ)
the Baptist Church
浸假(ㄐㄧㄣˋ ㄐㄧㄚˇ)
gradually
浸漸(ㄐㄧㄣˋ ㄐㄧㄢˋ)
gradually; step by step; little

〔水部〕

by little: 他浸漸致富。He has become rich little by little.
浸信會(ㄐㄧㄣˋ ㄒㄧㄣˋ ㄏㄨㄟˋ)
the Baptist Church
浸尋(ㄐㄧㄣˋ ㄒㄩㄣˊ)
gradually
浸濕(ㄐㄧㄣˋ ㄕ)
to soak: 洗衣前先將衣服浸濕。Soak clothes before washing.
浸蝕(ㄐㄧㄣˋ ㄕˊ)
erosion; to erode: 流水浸蝕土壤與巖石。Running water erodes soil and rocks.
浸水(ㄐㄧㄣˋ ㄕㄨㄟˇ)
to immerse or dip in water; flooded; deluged; inundated: 她將頭浸水。She dipped her head in the water.
浸染(ㄐㄧㄣˋ ㄖㄢˇ)
to contaminate or be contaminated gradually
浸入(ㄐㄧㄣˋ ㄖㄨˋ)
to permeate; to percolate: 水能浸入吸墨紙中。Water will permeate blotting paper.
浸潤(ㄐㄧㄣˋ ㄖㄨㄣˋ)
to pass in gradually; to soak: 雨水浸潤著大地。The rain is soaking into the earth.
浸漬(ㄐㄧㄣˋ ㄗˋ)
to soak or be soaked
浸淫(ㄐㄧㄣˋ ㄧㄣˊ)
① to stain gradually ② to be familiar with
浸淫羣籍(ㄐㄧㄣˋ ㄧㄣˊ ㄑㄩㄣˊ ㄐㄧˊ)
to read extensively over a long period of time

【浼】 2893
ㄇㄟˇ meei měi
1. to stain; to soil; to contaminate; to defile
2. full of water
3. to entrust
浼人說項(ㄇㄟˇ ㄖㄣˊ ㄕㄨㄛ ㄒㄧㄤˋ)
to request one to say a good word for
浼汚(ㄇㄟˇ ㄨ)
to soil, besmirch (someone's reputation, etc.)

【涇】 2894
ㄐㄧㄥ jing jīng
name of a river in Shensi (陝西)
涇河(ㄐㄧㄥ ㄏㄜˊ)
name of a river in Shensi (陝西)
涇渭(ㄐㄧㄥ ㄨㄟˋ)
two merging rivers in Shensi, of which one is muddy and the other is clear
涇渭不分(ㄐㄧㄥ ㄨㄟˋ ㄅㄨˋ ㄈㄣ)
unable to distinguish between the clear and the muddy; unable to distinguish between good and evil
涇渭分明(ㄐㄧㄥ ㄨㄟˋ ㄈㄣ ㄇㄧㄥˊ)
as different as the waters of the Ching and the Wei—to be entirely different

【涅】 2895
(湼) ㄋㄧㄝˋ nieh niè
1. to blacken; to dye black
2. to block up
涅白(ㄋㄧㄝˋ ㄅㄞˊ)
opaque
涅槃(ㄋㄧㄝˋ ㄆㄢˊ)
Nirvana
涅面(ㄋㄧㄝˋ ㄇㄧㄢˋ)
to tattoo the face
涅齒(ㄋㄧㄝˋ ㄔˇ)
to blacken the teeth
涅字(ㄋㄧㄝˋ ㄗˋ)
tattooed letters or characters

【涉】 2896
ㄕㄜˋ sheh shè
1. to wade: 他們涉水過河。They waded across the river.
2. to cross
3. to experience
4. to involve; to entangle; to implicate
5. a Chinese family name
涉筆(ㄕㄜˋ ㄅㄧˇ)
to start to write
涉覽(ㄕㄜˋ ㄌㄢˇ)
to read casually; to skim
涉覽群書(ㄕㄜˋ ㄌㄢˇ ㄑㄩㄣˊ ㄕㄨ)
to read widely
涉歷(ㄕㄜˋ ㄌㄧˋ)
one's past experience
涉獵(ㄕㄜˋ ㄌㄧㄝˋ)
to study haphazardly; to dabble in; to browse; to read cursorily
涉及(ㄕㄜˋ ㄐㄧˊ)
to involve; to relate to; to deal with
涉禽類(ㄕㄜˋ ㄑㄧㄣˊ ㄌㄟˋ)
Gallatores
涉嫌(ㄕㄜˋ ㄒㄧㄢˊ)
to come under suspicion; to be involved (in a crime)
涉險(ㄕㄜˋ ㄒㄧㄢˇ)
to be engaged in an adventure; to adventure: 除了他以外，沒有人敢涉險做這件事。No man would adventure it except him.
涉想(ㄕㄜˋ ㄒㄧㄤˇ)
to think about
涉事(ㄕㄜˋ ㄕˋ)
to give a narration
涉世(ㄕㄜˋ ㄕˋ)
to make one's way through the world; to get along in the world
涉世未深(ㄕㄜˋ ㄕˋ ㄨㄟˋ ㄕㄣ)
inexperienced in affairs of the world
涉足(ㄕㄜˋ ㄗㄨˊ)
to set foot in: 永遠不要涉足我們的地產。Never set foot in our property again.
涉足花叢(ㄕㄜˋ ㄗㄨˊ ㄏㄨㄚ ㄘㄨㄥˊ)
to fool around with women; to visit brothels
涉足其間(ㄕㄜˋ ㄗㄨˊ ㄑㄧˊ ㄐㄧㄢ)
to set foot there
涉訟(ㄕㄜˋ ㄙㄨㄥˋ)
to get involved in a lawsuit

【消】 2897
ㄒㄧㄠ shiau xiāo
1. to vanish; to disappear; to die out
2. to disperse; to eliminate; to remove; to alleviate; to allay; to extinguish; to quench
3. to need; to take: 來回只消三天。It takes only three days to get there and back.
消磨(ㄒㄧㄠ ㄇㄛˊ)
to while away (time): 孩子們在海灘上消磨許多下午。The children while away many afternoons on the beach.
消磨時間(ㄒㄧㄠ ㄇㄛˊ ㄕˊ ㄐㄧㄢ)
to kill time; to pass the time
消弭(ㄒㄧㄠ ㄇㄧˇ)
to put an end to; to terminate; to bring to an end
消弭禍患(ㄒㄧㄠ ㄇㄧˇ ㄏㄨㄛˋ ㄏㄨㄢˋ)
to soothe catastrophes
消滅(ㄒㄧㄠ ㄇㄧㄝˋ)
① to annihilate; to exterminate; to destroy; extermination; annihilation ② to die out

消費(ㄒㄧㄠ ㄈㄟˋ)
consumption; to consume
消費品(ㄒㄧㄠ ㄈㄟˋ ㄆㄧㄣˇ)
consumer goods; expendable materials
消費合作社(ㄒㄧㄠ ㄈㄟˋ ㄏㄜˊ ㄗㄨㄛˋ ㄕㄜˋ)
a consumers' cooperative
消費者(ㄒㄧㄠ ㄈㄟˋ ㄓㄜˇ)
a consumer: 生產者設法供應消費者的需要。Producers try to supply the demand of consumers.
消費水準(ㄒㄧㄠ ㄈㄟˋ ㄕㄨㄟˇ ㄓㄨㄣˇ)
the standard of consumption
消防(ㄒㄧㄠ ㄈㄤˊ)
fire fighting; prevention and extinction of fires
消防隊(ㄒㄧㄠ ㄈㄤˊ ㄉㄨㄟˋ)
a fire brigade; a fire department
消防隊員(ㄒㄧㄠ ㄈㄤˊ ㄉㄨㄟˋ ㄩㄢˊ)or 消防人員(ㄒㄧㄠ ㄈㄤˊ ㄖㄣˊ ㄩㄢˊ)
a fireman; a fire fighter
消防車(ㄒㄧㄠ ㄈㄤˊ ㄔㄜ)
a fire engine
消防雲梯(ㄒㄧㄠ ㄈㄤˊ ㄩㄣˊ ㄊㄧ)
a ladder truck
消毒(ㄒㄧㄠ ㄉㄨˊ)
to disinfect; to sterilize; to pasteurize; to decontaminate
消毒劑(ㄒㄧㄠ ㄉㄨˊ ㄐㄧˋ)
disinfectant
消毒水(ㄒㄧㄠ ㄉㄨˊ ㄕㄨㄟˇ)
antiseptic solution
消毒藥(ㄒㄧㄠ ㄉㄨˊ ㄧㄠˋ)
disinfectant; antiseptic
消停(ㄒㄧㄠ ㄊㄧㄥˊ)
to stop; to pause
消耗(ㄒㄧㄠ ㄏㄠˋ)
to consume; to expend; to exhaust
消耗品(ㄒㄧㄠ ㄏㄠˋ ㄆㄧㄣˇ)
expendables; consumables
消耗戰(ㄒㄧㄠ ㄏㄠˋ ㄓㄢˋ)
a war of attrition
消化(ㄒㄧㄠ ㄏㄨㄚˋ)
① to digest (food); digestion: 有些食物比其他食物容易消化。Some foods are digested more easily than others. ② to absorb mentally
消化不良(ㄒㄧㄠ ㄏㄨㄚˋ ㄅㄨˋ ㄌㄧㄤˊ)
indigestion; dyspepsia: 他患消化不良症。He suffers from indigestion.
消化道(ㄒㄧㄠ ㄏㄨㄚˋ ㄉㄠˋ)
the alimentary canal; the digestive tract
消化器官(ㄒㄧㄠ ㄏㄨㄚˋ ㄑㄧˋ ㄍㄨㄢ)
the digestive organs
消化系統(ㄒㄧㄠ ㄏㄨㄚˋ ㄒㄧˋ ㄊㄨㄥˇ)
the digestive apparatus or system
消火唧筒(ㄒㄧㄠ ㄏㄨㄛˇ ㄐㄧ ㄊㄨㄥˇ)
a fire engine
消火劑(ㄒㄧㄠ ㄏㄨㄛˇ ㄐㄧˋ)
fire-extinguishing chemicals
消火器(ㄒㄧㄠ ㄏㄨㄛˇ ㄑㄧˋ)
a fire extinguisher
消火栓(ㄒㄧㄠ ㄏㄨㄛˇ ㄕㄨㄢ)or 消防栓(ㄒㄧㄠ ㄈㄤˊ ㄕㄨㄢ)
a fireplug; a hydrant
消魂 or 銷魂(ㄒㄧㄠ ㄏㄨㄣˊ)
to be held spellbound (by a beautiful woman)
消極(ㄒㄧㄠ ㄐㄧˊ)
negative; pessimistic; passive
消極抵抗(ㄒㄧㄠ ㄐㄧˊ ㄉㄧˇ ㄎㄤˋ)
passive resistance
消極主義(ㄒㄧㄠ ㄐㄧˊ ㄓㄨˇ ㄧˋ)
pessimism; negativism; passivism
消解(ㄒㄧㄠ ㄐㄧㄝˇ)
to clear up; to dispel
消減(ㄒㄧㄠ ㄐㄧㄢˇ)
to decrease; to lessen; to diminish; to abate; to reduce: 他的興趣消減。His interest decreases.
消金窟(ㄒㄧㄠ ㄐㄧㄣ ㄎㄨ)
cabarets or brothels (where money is spent freely)
消氣(ㄒㄧㄠ ㄑㄧˋ)
to allay one's anger
消遣(ㄒㄧㄠ ㄑㄧㄢˇ)
pastimes; diversions; recreation: 他有時打牌消遣。He sometimes plays cards as a pastime.
消卻(ㄒㄧㄠ ㄑㄩㄝˋ)
to eliminate; to get rid of
消息(ㄒㄧㄠ ˙ㄒㄧ)
news; tidings; information: 我很久沒他的消息了。I have had no news from him for a long time.
消息靈通(ㄒㄧㄠ ˙ㄒㄧ ㄌㄧㄥˊ ㄊㄨㄥ)
well-informed: 他消息靈通。He's well-informed.
消夏(ㄒㄧㄠ ㄒㄧㄚˋ)
to relieve summer heat; to take a summer vacation 亦作「消暑」
消歇(ㄒㄧㄠ ㄒㄧㄝ)
to become extinct; to subside: 暴風雨已消歇。The storm has subsided.
消閒(ㄒㄧㄠ ㄒㄧㄢˊ)
to kill the leisure time: 他藉著看小說來消閒。He kills the leisure time by reading a novel.
消長(ㄒㄧㄠ ㄓㄤˇ)
rise and fall; vicissitudes; ups and downs; waning and waxing
消腫(ㄒㄧㄠ ㄓㄨㄥˇ)
to remove or reduce a swelling
消愁解悶(ㄒㄧㄠ ㄔㄡˊ ㄐㄧㄝˇ ㄇㄣˋ)
to quench sorrow and dissipate worry
消沈(ㄒㄧㄠ ㄔㄣˊ)
depressed; dejected; low-spirited: 雨天總是使我消沈。The rainy days always depressed me.
消除(ㄒㄧㄠ ㄔㄨˊ)
to eliminate; to get rid of
消除噪音(ㄒㄧㄠ ㄔㄨˊ ㄗㄠˋ ㄧㄣ)
abatement of noise
消失(ㄒㄧㄠ ㄕ)
to vanish; to disappear; to die out: 船消失於地平線之外。The ship vanished beyond the horizon.
消石灰(ㄒㄧㄠ ㄕˊ ㄏㄨㄟ)
slaked lime
消逝(ㄒㄧㄠ ㄕˋ)
to die away; to vanish; to elapse: 音樂慢慢消逝了。The music slowly died away.
消釋(ㄒㄧㄠ ㄕˋ)
to clear up; to dispel
消受(ㄒㄧㄠ ㄕㄡˋ)
① to endure: 我無法消受他。I can't endure him. ② to enjoy
消瘦(ㄒㄧㄠ ㄕㄡˋ)
skinny; emaciated; wasted
消暑(ㄒㄧㄠ ㄕㄨˇ)
to relieve summer heat; to take a summer vacation
消暑止渴(ㄒㄧㄠ ㄕㄨˇ ㄓˇ ㄎㄜˇ)
(said of a drink) to relieve summer heat and quench thirst
消鎔 or 消溶(ㄒㄧㄠ ㄖㄨㄥˊ)

(said of substances) to melt
消融(ㄒㄧㄠ ㄖㄨㄥˊ)
to melt: 在溫暖的春天冰雪全消融了。The ice melts in the warmth of spring.
消災(ㄒㄧㄠ ㄗㄞ)
to prevent or forestall calamities
消散(ㄒㄧㄠ ㄙㄢˋ)
to scatter and disappear; to dissipate
消夜 or 宵夜(ㄒㄧㄠ ㄧㄝˋ)
a midnight snack
消炎(ㄒㄧㄠ ㄧㄢˊ)
to reduce or eliminate inflammation
消炎片(ㄒㄧㄠ ㄧㄢˊ ㄆㄧㄢˋ)
sulfaguanidine tablets; anti-inflammation pills
消炎粉(ㄒㄧㄠ ㄧㄢˊ ㄈㄣˇ)
sulfadiazine powder; anti-inflammation powder
消音器(ㄒㄧㄠ ㄧㄣ ㄑㄧˋ)
a silencer; a muffler 亦作「消聲器」

【涑】 2898 ㄙㄨˋ suh sù
name of a tributary of the Yellow River
涑水(ㄙㄨˋ ㄕㄨㄟˇ)
name of a tributary of the Yellow River

【涓】 2899 ㄐㄩㄢ jiuan juān
a small stream; a rivulet; a brook
涓滴(ㄐㄩㄢ ㄉㄧ)
trickles; drips
涓滴歸公(ㄐㄩㄢ ㄉㄧ ㄍㄨㄟ ㄍㄨㄥ)
(said of an honest official) to hand over every cent of public money to the government treasury
涓流(ㄐㄩㄢ ㄌㄧㄡˊ)
a small stream; a rivulet; a brook
涓毫(ㄐㄩㄢ ㄏㄠˊ)
a modicum; a drop or a grain
涓涓(ㄐㄩㄢ ㄐㄩㄢ)
trickles; a small stream
涓塵(ㄐㄩㄢ ㄔㄣˊ)or 涓埃(ㄐㄩㄢ ㄞ)
① tiny fragments; particles ② insignificant; negligible; the least

【涎】 2900 ㄒㄧㄢˊ shyan xián
saliva
涎皮賴臉(ㄒㄧㄢˊ ㄆㄧˊ ㄌㄞˋ ㄌㄧㄢˇ)or 涎皮涎臉(ㄒㄧㄢˊ ㄆㄧˊ ㄒㄧㄢˊ ㄌㄧㄢˇ)
shameless; brazen
涎沫(ㄒㄧㄢˊ ㄇㄛˋ)
saliva 亦作「涎水」
涎臉(ㄒㄧㄢˊ ·ㄌㄧㄢ)
shameless; brazen
涎涎(ㄒㄧㄢˊ ㄒㄧㄢˊ)
shiny; glossy

【涔】 2901 ㄘㄣˊ tsern cén
1. a puddle
2. tearful
涔涔(ㄘㄣˊ ㄘㄣˊ)
① rainy ② distressed ③ dusky; shadowy ④ tearful
涔涔淚下(ㄘㄣˊ ㄘㄣˊ ㄌㄟˋ ㄒㄧㄚˋ)
in tears: 我發覺她涔涔淚下。I found her in tears.

【涕】 2902 ㄊㄧˋ tih tì
1. tears
2. snivel
涕淚(ㄊㄧˋ ㄌㄟˋ)
tears: 涕淚從她的面頰流下。The tears rolled down her cheeks.
涕零(ㄊㄧˋ ㄌㄧㄥˊ)
to shed tears
涕零如雨(ㄊㄧˋ ㄌㄧㄥˊ ㄖㄨˊ ㄩˇ)
tears streaming down like raindrops
涕泣(ㄊㄧˋ ㄑㄧˋ)
to weep; to cry: 她爲她悲慘的命運而涕泣。She wept her sad fate.
涕泣沾襟(ㄊㄧˋ ㄑㄧˋ ㄓㄢ ㄐㄧㄣ)
to wet the front part of one's garment with tears
涕泗滂沱(ㄊㄧˋ ㄙˋ ㄆㄤ ㄊㄨㄛˊ)
drenched with tears and snivel
涕泗交流(ㄊㄧˋ ㄙˋ ㄐㄧㄠ ㄌㄧㄡˊ)
Tears and snivel fall down at the same time.—crying bitterly
涕洟(ㄊㄧˋ ㄧˊ)
tears and snivel

【洚】 2903 ㄐㄧㄤˋ jiang jiàng
a flood
洚水(ㄐㄧㄤˋ ㄕㄨㄟˇ)
floodwater; a flood

【涖】 2904 ㄌㄧˋ lih lì
1. to arrive
2. the murmur of flowing water
涖止(ㄌㄧˋ ㄓˇ)or 涖臨(ㄌㄧˋ ㄌㄧㄣˊ)
to arrive; to be present
涖政(ㄌㄧˋ ㄓㄥˋ)
to administer the government

【浞】 2905 ㄓㄨㄛˊ jwo zhuó
to soak

【浯】 2906 ㄨˊ wu wú
name of a river in Shantung
浯水(ㄨˊ ㄕㄨㄟˇ)
name of a river in Shantung

【涌】 2907 ㄩㄥˇ yeong yǒng
to rise; to spring; to gush out; to pour out; to surge
涌湍(ㄩㄥˇ ㄊㄨㄢ)
(said of flowing water) rapid and turbulent
涌進(ㄩㄥˇ ㄐㄧㄣˋ)
to rush into; to swarm into
涌泉(ㄩㄥˇ ㄑㄩㄢˊ)
a bubbling fountain
涌出(ㄩㄥˇ ㄔㄨ)
to gush out

八畫

【涯】 2908 ㄧㄚˊ ya yá
1. water's edge; waterfront; a bank
2. a limit
3. faraway places
涯際(ㄧㄚˊ ㄐㄧˋ)
the edge; the limit: 他的貪心是無涯際的。His greed knows no limits.
涯涘(ㄧㄚˊ ㄙˋ)
① the edge of a body of water ② limits
涯岸(ㄧㄚˊ ㄢˋ)
the edge; the limit: 別走得太近涯岸。Don't walk too near the edge.

【液】 2909 ㄧㄝˋ yeh yè (讀音 ㄧˋ yih yì)
liquid; juices; secretions; sap
液態(ㄧㄝˋ ㄊㄞˋ)
(physics) the liquid state
液體(ㄧㄝˋ ㄊㄧˇ)
liquid
液體比重計(ㄧㄝˋ ㄊㄧˇ ㄅㄧˇ ㄓㄨㄥˋ ㄐㄧˋ)

an areometer; a hydrometer
液體動力學(ㄧㄝˋ ㄊㄧˇ ㄉㄨㄥˋ ㄌㄧˋ ㄒㄩㄝˊ)
hydrodynamics
液體靜力學(ㄧㄝˋ ㄊㄧˇ ㄐㄧㄥˋ ㄌㄧˋ ㄒㄩㄝˊ)
hydrostatics
液體燃料(ㄧㄝˋ ㄊㄧˇ ㄖㄢˊ ㄌㄧㄠˋ)
liquid fuel
液化(ㄧㄝˋ ㄏㄨㄚˋ)
to liquefy or be liquefied; liquefaction
液化天然氣(ㄧㄝˋ ㄏㄨㄚˋ ㄊㄧㄢ ㄖㄢˊ ㄑㄧˋ)
liquefied natural gas
液汁(ㄧㄝˋ ㄓ)
liquid; fluid; juices; sap

【涪】 2910 ㄈㄨˊ fwu fú
1. name of a river in Szechwan Province
2. name of an old administrative district
涪江(ㄈㄨˊ ㄐㄧㄤ)
name of a river in Szechwan Province

【涵】 2911 ㄏㄢˊ harn hán
1. wet, damp and marshy
2. to contain
3. lenient and broad-minded
涵洞(ㄏㄢˊ ㄉㄨㄥˋ)
a culvert
涵管(ㄏㄢˊ ㄍㄨㄢˇ)
a drainage pipe
涵煦(ㄏㄢˊ ㄒㄩˇ)
to protect and raise (children, etc.); to cherish and nourish
涵蓄 or 含蓄(ㄏㄢˊ ㄒㄩˋ)
(said of manners, speeches, etc.) reserved
涵濡(ㄏㄢˊ ㄖㄨˊ)
to set a good moral example to the younger generation
涵容(ㄏㄢˊ ㄖㄨㄥˊ)
① to contain; capable of holding ② tolerant
涵義(ㄏㄢˊ ㄧˋ)
meaning; implication 亦作「含義」
涵養(ㄏㄢˊ ㄧㄤˇ)
① capability to be kind, patient, lenient, tolerant or broad-minded under all circumstances ② to cherish and nourish
涵泳(ㄏㄢˊ ㄩㄥˇ)
to swim

【涸】 2912 ㄏㄜˊ her hé (語音 ㄏㄠˋ haw hào)
drying up; dried-up; exhausted
涸鮒(ㄏㄜˊ ㄈㄨˋ)
in dire poverty
涸轍(ㄏㄜˊ ㄔㄜˋ)
(literally) fish in a dried rut—men in dire poverty
涸澤(ㄏㄜˊ ㄗㄜˊ)
a dried-up lake; to dry up a lake: 久旱涸澤。The long drought dried up a lake.
涸乾(ㄏㄠˋ ㄍㄢ)
dried-up; exhausted

【涿】 2913 ㄓㄨㄛ juo zhuō
1. to drip; to trickle
2. old and current names of counties, rivers, mountains in various places
涿鹿(ㄓㄨㄛ ㄌㄨˋ)
① name of a county in Chahar(察哈爾) ② name of a mountain southeast of the county mentioned above, where Huang Ti (黃帝) or the Yellow Emperor, killed Chih Yu (蚩尤), the enemy chieftain, after a decisive battle
涿水(ㄓㄨㄛ ㄕㄨㄟˇ)
ancient name of a river west of today's Cho County(涿縣) in Hopeh Province

【淀】 2914 ㄉㄧㄢˋ diann diàn
shallow water
淀河(ㄉㄧㄢˋ ㄏㄜˊ)
also known as Ta Ching River (大清河) in Hopeh Province

【淄】 2915 ㄗ tzy zī
1. black
2. name of a river in Shantung Province
淄水(ㄗ ㄕㄨㄟˇ)
a river in Shantung Province

【涼】 2916 ㄌㄧㄤˊ liang liáng
1. cool; chilly; cold
2. thin
3. discouraged; disappointed
4. name of one of the 16 states during the Eastern Tsin
5. a Chinese family name
涼拌(ㄌㄧㄤˊ ㄅㄢˋ)
(said of food) cold and dressed with sauce
涼棚(ㄌㄧㄤˊ ㄆㄥˊ)
a shed, awning, etc. to provide shade in the sun: 他們最近蓋了一個涼棚。They built a shed recently.
涼帽(ㄌㄧㄤˊ ㄇㄠˋ)
a straw hat; a summer hat: 他戴上涼帽出去了。He put on his straw hat and went out.
涼粉兒(ㄌㄧㄤˊ ㄈㄜˇㄦ)
gelatin or jelly made from agar-agar, bean flour, etc.
涼風(ㄌㄧㄤˊ ㄈㄥ)
a cool breeze; a cool wind from the southwest
涼德(ㄌㄧㄤˊ ㄉㄜˊ)
(having) very little virtue
涼臺(ㄌㄧㄤˊ ㄊㄞˊ)
a balcony; a veranda
涼亭(ㄌㄧㄤˊ ㄊㄧㄥˊ)
(formerly) a shed along a highway or country road, to provide a place of rest for travelers
涼了(ㄌㄧㄤˊ ·ㄌㄜ)
① already cold ② disappointed or discouraged
涼了半截兒(ㄌㄧㄤˊ ·ㄌㄜ ㄅㄢˋ ㄐㄧㄝˊㄦ)
to be greatly disappointed or discouraged; half-beaten psychologically
涼糕(ㄌㄧㄤˊ ㄍㄠ)
a kind of cake made of glutinous rice served cold in summer
涼開水(ㄌㄧㄤˊ ㄎㄞ ㄕㄨㄟˇ)
cold boiled water: 我喜歡涼開水。I like cold boiled water.
涼快(ㄌㄧㄤˊ ㄎㄨㄞˋ)
① cool and comfortable ② to cool oneself
涼氣(ㄌㄧㄤˊ ㄑㄧˋ)
chilly air
涼蓆(ㄌㄧㄤˊ ㄒㄧˊ)
a sleeping mat (usually made of straw or bamboo) used in summer
涼鞋(ㄌㄧㄤˊ ㄒㄧㄝˊ)
sandals; summer shoes; slippers

涼著了(ㄌㄧㄤˊ ㄓㄠˊ ˙ㄌㄜ)
to have caught cold: 我涼著了。I have caught cold.
涼州(ㄌㄧㄤˊ ㄓㄡ)
name of the former capital of Kansu Province
涼茶(ㄌㄧㄤˊ ㄔㄚˊ)
①cold tea ②(Chinese medicine) a concoction drink of many herbal ingredients to drive off the "heat" in human body
涼水(ㄌㄧㄤˊ ㄕㄨㄟˇ)
cold water
涼爽(ㄌㄧㄤˊ ㄕㄨㄤˇ)
cool and comfortable; refreshing
涼菜(ㄌㄧㄤˊ ㄘㄞˋ)
vegetables eaten uncooked; cold dishes
涼颼颼的(ㄌㄧㄤˊ ㄙㄡ ㄙㄡ ˙ㄉㄜ)
chilly: 不穿外套，我覺得涼颼颼的。Without my coat I feel chilly.
涼傘(ㄌㄧㄤˊ ㄙㄢˇ)
a parasol
涼陰(ㄌㄧㄤˊ ㄢ)
(said of an emperor) in mourning; royal mourning 亦作「諒闇」
涼意(ㄌㄧㄤˊ ㄧˋ)
to be getting chilly

【淅】 2917 ㄒㄧ shi xī
1. water for washing rice; to wash rice
2. name of a river in Honan Province
淅米(ㄒㄧ ㄇㄧˇ)
to wash rice
淅瀝(ㄒㄧ ㄌㄧˋ)
①the pattering of sleet; the sound of raindrops ②the sound of falling leaves in the wind
淅淅(ㄒㄧ ㄒㄧ)
the sound of the mild wind
淅颯(ㄒㄧ ㄙㄚˋ)
the sound of light or gentle movements

【淆】 2918 ㄧㄠˊ yau yáo
confused and disorderly; mixed
淆亂(ㄧㄠˊ ㄌㄨㄢˋ)
to confuse; to mislead
淆亂視聽(ㄧㄠˊ ㄌㄨㄢˋ ㄕˋ ㄊㄧㄥ)
to confuse and muddle the truth; to mislead the public 亦作「混淆視聽」
淆雜(ㄧㄠˊ ㄗㄚˊ)
mixed; miscellaneous

【洴】 2919 ㄆㄧㄥˊ pyng píng
1. the sound of silk, etc. floating in the wind
2. to wash; to bleach
洴澼(ㄆㄧㄥˊ ㄆㄧˋ)
the sound of silk flapping in the wind
洴澼絖(ㄆㄧㄥˊ ㄆㄧˋ ㄎㄨㄤˋ)
to float silk on water; the washing of silk

【淌】 2920 ㄊㄤˇ taang tǎng
to flow down; to trickle; to drip
淌汗(ㄊㄤˇ ㄏㄢˋ)
to perspire
淌眼抹淚(ㄊㄤˇ ㄧㄢˇ ㄇㄛˇ ㄌㄟˋ)
to cry; to weep
淌眼淚(ㄊㄤˇ ㄧㄢˇ ㄌㄟˋ)
to shed tears; to be in tears

【淖】 2921 ㄋㄠˋ naw nào
slush; mud
淖濘(ㄋㄠˋ ㄋㄧㄥˋ)
slushy mud

【淑】 2922 ㄕㄨˊ shwu shú
1. good; pure; virtuous
2. (said of women) beautiful or charming
3. clear
淑美(ㄕㄨˊ ㄇㄟˇ)
beautiful; beautiful and virtuous
淑妃(ㄕㄨˊ ㄈㄟ)
a general name for the emperor's concubines
淑範(ㄕㄨˊ ㄈㄢˋ)
a paragon of female virtues
淑德(ㄕㄨˊ ㄉㄜˊ)
female virtues—especially chastity
淑弟(ㄕㄨˊ ㄉㄧˋ)
my good kid brother
淑女(ㄕㄨˊ ㄋㄩˇ)
gentlewomen; ladies; unmarried girls of respectable reputation
淑候(ㄕㄨˊ ㄏㄡˋ)
a greeting (used in letters addressed to women)
淑華(ㄕㄨˊ ㄏㄨㄚˊ)
fine and outstanding
淑化(ㄕㄨˊ ㄏㄨㄚˋ)
teachings of virtues and goodness
淑景(ㄕㄨˊ ㄐㄧㄥˇ)
beautiful scenery
淑均(ㄕㄨˊ ㄐㄩㄣ)
fine and fair
淑氣(ㄕㄨˊ ㄑㄧˋ)
the mild air in spring
淑清(ㄕㄨˊ ㄑㄧㄥ)
(said of the sun, the moon, the sky, etc.) clear and bright
淑心(ㄕㄨˊ ㄒㄧㄣ)
a pure heart
淑行(ㄕㄨˊ ㄒㄧㄥˋ)
virtuous conduct or behavior
淑性(ㄕㄨˊ ㄒㄧㄥˋ)
a gentle disposition or temperament
淑善君子(ㄕㄨˊ ㄕㄢˋ ㄐㄩㄣ ㄗˇ)
a good man; a gentleman; a virtuous man
淑慎(ㄕㄨˊ ㄕㄣˋ)
(said of women) gentle and respectful: 那護士甚爲淑愼。The nurse is very gentle and respectful.
淑人(ㄕㄨˊ ㄖㄣˊ)
①a good man; a virtuous man ②an honorary title bestowed on wives of ranking officials in ancient China
淑姿(ㄕㄨˊ ㄗ)
graceful manner; graceful deportment
淑儀(ㄕㄨˊ ㄧˊ)
a rank of court ladies in ancient China
淑婉(ㄕㄨˊ ㄨㄢˇ)
good and gentle; elegant; refined
淑郁(ㄕㄨˊ ㄩˋ)
aromatic
淑媛(ㄕㄨˊ ㄩㄢˋ)
①a rank of court ladies in ancient China ②ladies; gentlewomen; virtuous women

【淒】 2923 ㄑㄧ chi qī
1. cloudy and rainy
2. cold and chilly
3. sorrow; sorrowful; miserable; desolate

淒迷(ㄑㄧ ㄇㄧˊ)
①(said of sights) cheerless; desolate; dreary ②(said of the mood) despondent; depressed
淒風苦雨(ㄑㄧ ㄈㄥ ㄎㄨˇ ㄩˇ)
chilly winds and cold rains that inspire sadness in a person's mind
淒冷(ㄑㄧ ㄌㄥˇ)
desolate; bleak
淒厲(ㄑㄧ ㄌㄧˋ)
① sad and sorrowful ② bleak and harsh
淒涼(ㄑㄧ ㄌㄧㄤˊ)or 淒淒涼涼(ㄑㄧ ˙ㄑㄧ ㄌㄧㄤˊ ㄌㄧㄤˊ)
desolate and sorrowful; lonely; lonesome: 這個老人過着淒涼的生活。The old man led a lonesome life.
淒惶(ㄑㄧ ㄏㄨㄤˊ)
very anxious about
淒緊(ㄑㄧ ㄐㄧㄣˇ)
harsh blowing of chilly winds
淒淒(ㄑㄧ ㄑㄧ)
① descriptive of the coldness of wind and rain; chilly ② the rising of clouds ③ flowing (tears, etc.)
淒其(ㄑㄧ ㄑㄧˊ)
cold and chilly
淒切(ㄑㄧ ㄑㄧㄝˋ)or 淒淒切切(ㄑㄧ ㄑㄧ ㄑㄧㄝˋ ㄑㄧㄝˋ)
bitter and sorrowful
淒切動人(ㄑㄧ ㄑㄧㄝˋ ㄉㄨㄥˋ ㄖㄣˊ)
sadly moving
淒楚(ㄑㄧ ㄔㄨˇ)
sad and sorrowful; heartrending; heartbreaking
淒愴(ㄑㄧ ㄔㄨㄤˋ)
heartrending; heartbreaking 亦作「悽愴」
淒然(ㄑㄧ ㄖㄢˊ)
very sorrowful; very sad
淒慘(ㄑㄧ ㄘㄢˇ)or 淒淒慘慘(ㄑㄧ ˙ㄑㄧ ㄘㄢˇ ㄘㄢˇ)
heartrending; heartbreaking
淒咽(ㄑㄧ ㄧㄝˋ)
a low and sad voice; to sob while speaking
淒豔(ㄑㄧ ㄧㄢˋ)
(said of a love story) sad and beautiful

【淋】 2924
1. ㄌㄧㄣˊ lin lín
1. to soak with water; to drip
2. gonorrhea
淋巴(ㄌㄧㄣˊ ㄅㄚ)
lymph
淋巴管(ㄌㄧㄣˊ ㄅㄚ ㄍㄨㄢˇ)
lymphatic ducts; lymphatics
淋巴腺(ㄌㄧㄣˊ ㄅㄚ ㄒㄧㄢˋ)
lymphatic glands
淋巴腺結核(ㄌㄧㄣˊ ㄅㄚ ㄒㄧㄢˋ ㄐㄧㄝˊ ㄏㄜˊ)
lymphadenitis tuberculosis
淋巴腺炎(ㄌㄧㄣˊ ㄅㄚ ㄒㄧㄢˋ ㄧㄢˊ)
lymphadenitis
淋病(ㄌㄧㄣˊ ㄅㄧㄥˋ)
gonorrhea 亦作「淋症」
淋漓(ㄌㄧㄣˊ ㄌㄧˊ)
dripping wet
淋離(ㄌㄧㄣˊ ㄌㄧˊ)
① dripping wet ②(now rarely) long
淋漓盡致(ㄌㄧㄣˊ ㄌㄧˊ ㄐㄧㄣˋ ㄓˋ)
(to narrate, describe, argue, etc.) thoroughly; completely
淋淋(ㄌㄧㄣˊ ㄌㄧㄣˊ)
dripping wet; pouring (rain, etc.)
淋鈴(ㄌㄧㄣˊ ㄌㄧㄥˊ)
the sound of splattering rains
淋漉(ㄌㄧㄣˊ ㄌㄨˋ)
dripping wet; pouring (rain, etc.)
淋菌(ㄌㄧㄣˊ ㄐㄩㄣˋ)
gonococci
淋濕(ㄌㄧㄣˊ ㄕ)or(ㄌㄩㄣˊ ㄕ)
to be soaked, splashed wet (by rain, etc.): 我們渾身淋濕了。Our clothes were soaked through.
淋雨(ㄌㄧㄣˊ ㄩˇ)or(ㄌㄩㄣˊ ㄩˇ)
to get wet in the rain; to be exposed to the rain
淋浴(ㄌㄧㄣˊ ㄩˋ)
a shower; a shower bath: 他們在早晨淋浴。They have a shower in the morning.亦作「淋雨浴」

【淋】 2924
2. ㄌㄧㄣˋ linn lìn
to filter; to strain
淋酒(ㄌㄧㄣˋ ㄐㄧㄡˇ)
to strain wine

【淘】 2925
ㄊㄠˊ taur táo
1. to wash (especially rice); to wash in a sieve
2. to dredge; to scour
3. to eliminate the inferior (by exams, contests, etc.)
淘米(ㄊㄠˊ ㄇㄧˇ)
to wash rice
淘汰(ㄊㄠˊ ㄊㄞˋ)
① to eliminate inferior contestants, goods, etc. ② elimination
淘汰法(ㄊㄠˊ ㄊㄞˋ ㄈㄚˇ)
(mining) concentration
淘汰賽(ㄊㄠˊ ㄊㄞˋ ㄙㄞˋ)
elimination series
淘淘(ㄊㄠˊ ㄊㄠˊ)
① water flowing ② to wash
淘漉(ㄊㄠˊ ㄌㄨˋ)
① to dredge ② to wash
淘換(ㄊㄠˊ ㄏㄨㄢˋ)
to search for; to select; to choose
淘金(ㄊㄠˊ ㄐㄧㄣ)
① to pan gold ② to make quick bucks or high profits
淘金者(ㄊㄠˊ ㄐㄧㄣ ㄓㄜˇ)
a gold digger
淘井(ㄊㄠˊ ㄐㄧㄥˇ)
to wash or scour a well
淘氣(ㄊㄠˊ ㄑㄧˋ)
naughty, mischievous or annoying (children): 他弟弟像猴子一樣淘氣。His brother is as mischievous as a monkey.
淘氣鬼(ㄊㄠˊ ㄑㄧˋ ㄍㄨㄟˇ)
a mischievous imp
淘沙揀金(ㄊㄠˊ ㄕㄚ ㄐㄧㄢˇ ㄐㄧㄣ)
to wash the sand for gold—to choose or search for the very best
淘神(ㄊㄠˊ ㄕㄣˊ)
① annoyed as a result of a child's naughtiness or mischief ② worrying; irritating; troublesome

【淚】 2926
(泪) ㄌㄟˋ ley lèi
tears
淚滴(ㄌㄟˋ ㄉㄧ)
teardrops 亦作「淚點」
淚囊(ㄌㄟˋ ㄋㄤˊ)
a lachrymal sac
淚河(ㄌㄟˋ ㄏㄜˊ)
a river of tears—very sad; deep sorrow
淚痕(ㄌㄟˋ ㄏㄣˊ)
traces of tears
淚下沾襟(ㄌㄟˋ ㄒㄧㄚˋ ㄓㄢ ㄐㄧㄣ)

to wet the front part of one's garment with tears
淚腺(ㄌㄟˋ ㄒㄧㄢˋ)
a lachrymal gland
淚珠(ㄌㄟˋ ㄓㄨ)
teardrops: 淚珠從她臉頰流下。Teardrops fell down her cheeks.
淚竹(ㄌㄟˋ ㄓㄨˊ)
another name of 斑竹, the speckled bamboo
淚水(ㄌㄟˋ ㄕㄨㄟˇ)
tears
淚人兒(ㄌㄟˋ ㄖㄣˊㄦ)
one who is crying bitterly; a weeping Niobe; one who is all tears
淚如泉湧(ㄌㄟˋ ㄖㄨˊ ㄑㄩㄢˊ ㄩㄥˇ)
tears welling up like a fountain: 她淚如泉湧。Her tears well up like a fountain.
淚如雨下(ㄌㄟˋ ㄖㄨˊ ㄩˇ ㄒㄧㄚˋ)
The tears come down like rain.
淚容滿面(ㄌㄟˋ ㄖㄨㄥˊ ㄇㄢˇ ㄇㄧㄢˋ)
tearful look; lachrymal countenance
淚涔涔(ㄌㄟˋ ㄘㄣˊ ㄘㄣˊ)
tears falling down abundantly
淚眼(ㄌㄟˋ ㄧㄢˇ)
teary eyes
淚眼模糊(ㄌㄟˋ ㄧㄢˇ ㄇㄛˊ ㄏㄨˊ)
eyes blurred by tears
淚汪汪的(ㄌㄟˋ ㄨㄤ ㄨㄤ ˙ㄉㄜ)
tearful; brimming with tears

【淝】 2927
ㄈㄟˊ feir féi
name of a river in Anhwei Province
淝水(ㄈㄟˊ ㄕㄨㄟˇ)
the Fei River in Anhwei Province
淝水之戰(ㄈㄟˊ ㄕㄨㄟˇ ㄓ ㄓㄢˋ)
the Battle of the Fei River in which Hsieh Hsüan(謝玄) defeated Fu Chien(苻堅), thus ensuring the security of the Eastern Tsin(東晉) Dynasty against invasion from the north

【淙】 2928
ㄘㄨㄥˊ tsorng cóng
1. the sound of flowing water
2. water flowing
淙琤(ㄘㄨㄥˊ ㄔㄥ)or 淙靜(ㄘㄨㄥˊ ㄐㄧㄥˋ)
the tinkling sound of gems
淙淙(ㄘㄨㄥˊ ㄘㄨㄥˊ)
① the gurgling sound of flowing water—especially a creek ② the tinkling sound of metals or gems

【淟】 2929
ㄊㄧㄢˇ tean tiǎn
turbid; muddy
淟汩(ㄊㄧㄢˇ ㄇㄧˋ)
to submerge
淟涊(ㄊㄧㄢˇ ㄋㄧㄢˇ)
dirty; filthy

【淞】 2930
ㄙㄨㄥ song sōng
name of a river in Kiangsu Province
淞江(ㄙㄨㄥ ㄐㄧㄤ)
the Sung River in Kiangsu

【淡】 2931
ㄉㄢˋ dann dàn
1. weak or thin (tea, coffee, etc.)
2. tasteless; without enough salt; insipid
3. off-season—when business is poor; dull; slack
4. light (in color); slight
5. without worldly desires
6. same as 氮—nitrogen
淡泊(ㄉㄢˋ ㄅㄛˊ)
to lead a tranquil life without worldly desires
淡泊名利(ㄉㄢˋ ㄅㄛˊ ㄇㄧㄥˊ ㄌㄧˋ)
to be indifferent to fame and wealth 亦作「澹泊名利」
淡薄(ㄉㄢˋ ㄅㄛˊ)
① thin; weak; deficient; light ② to become indifferent; to flag ③ dim; faint
淡漠(ㄉㄢˋ ㄇㄛˋ)
indifference; aloofness; not interested or enthusiastic: 她對他很淡漠。She treated him with indifference.
淡墨(ㄉㄢˋ ㄇㄛˋ)
light ink
淡飯(ㄉㄢˋ ㄈㄢˋ)
simple food
淡淡(ㄉㄢˋ ㄉㄢˋ)
① light; slight ②(now rarely) water flowing smoothly
淡綠(ㄉㄢˋ ㄌㄩˋ)
light green
淡化(ㄉㄢˋ ㄏㄨㄚˋ)
① desalination ② to play down; to water down
淡話(ㄉㄢˋ ㄏㄨㄚˋ)
an insipid talk or conversation
淡黃(ㄉㄢˋ ㄏㄨㄤˊ)
light yellow
淡紅(ㄉㄢˋ ㄏㄨㄥˊ)
light red; pink: 她穿淡紅色的衣服。She is dressed in pink.
淡紅銀礦(ㄉㄢˋ ㄏㄨㄥˊ ㄧㄣˊ ㄎㄨㄤˋ)
proustite
淡季(ㄉㄢˋ ㄐㄧˋ)
slack seasons or off-seasons (for business): 淡季旅館收費較低。Hotel charges are lower in the slack season.
淡酒(ㄉㄢˋ ㄐㄧㄡˇ)
weak wine
淡江大學(ㄉㄢˋ ㄐㄧㄤ ㄉㄚˋ ㄒㄩㄝˊ)
Tamkang University
淡妝濃抹(ㄉㄢˋ ㄓㄨㄤ ㄋㄨㄥˊ ㄇㄛˇ)
a woman's make-up—originally from a line of a poem by Su Shih (蘇軾): "Whether *in light or heavy make-up*, she looks as becoming as ever."
淡水(ㄉㄢˋ ㄕㄨㄟˇ)
① fresh water—as opposite to salt water or seawater ② Tamsui, a seaside resort in northern Taiwan
淡水湖(ㄉㄢˋ ㄕㄨㄟˇ ㄏㄨˊ)
freshwater lakes
淡水魚(ㄉㄢˋ ㄕㄨㄟˇ ㄩˊ)
fishes grown in fresh water
淡水漁業(ㄉㄢˋ ㄕㄨㄟˇ ㄩˊ ㄧㄝˋ)
freshwater fishing
淡然(ㄉㄢˋ ㄖㄢˊ)
indifferent; not to care
淡然置之(ㄉㄢˋ ㄖㄢˊ ㄓˋ ㄓ)
to care very little about the matter; to take it easy; unruffled
淡菜(ㄉㄢˋ ㄘㄞˋ)
dried meat of a species of mussel, *Mytilus crassitesta*
淡色(ㄉㄢˋ ㄙㄜˋ)
a light color; light-colored: 他喜歡淡色的衣服。He likes light-colored clothes.
淡掃娥眉(ㄉㄢˋ ㄙㄠˇ ㄜˊ ㄇㄟˊ)
(said of a woman) to apply a light make-up
淡而無味(ㄉㄢˋ ㄦˊ ㄨˊ ㄨㄟˋ)
① tasteless (food, etc.) ② insipid (stories, talks, conversations, etc.)

淤雅(ㄉㄢˋ ㄧㄚˇ)
(said of attire, decoration, etc.) light, simple but graceful or elegant
淡忘(ㄉㄢˋ ㄨㄤˋ)
to fade from one's memory
淡月(ㄉㄢˋ ㄩㄝˋ)
a slack month (for business, etc.)

【淤】2932 ㄩ iu yū
1. muddy sediment; mud; sediment
2. stalemated; blocked; to silt up
淤點(ㄩ ㄉㄧㄢˇ)
(pathology) petechiae
淤泥(ㄩ ㄋㄧˊ)
sediment at the bottom of a river, ditch, etc.; silt: 港口爲淤泥所塞。The harbor is being choked up with silt.
淤漑(ㄩ ㄍㄞˋ)
to irrigate farmland with muddy water which is nourishing to the plants
淤河(ㄩ ㄏㄜˊ)
rivers or streams choked up by silt of mud and sand
淤積(ㄩ ㄐㄧ)
to silt up; to clog up: 沙土淤積於麥田上。Sand silted over wheat fields.
淤血(ㄩ ㄒㄧㄝˇ)
blood clot
淤滯(ㄩ ㄓˋ)
clogged; choked
淤濁(ㄩ ㄓㄨㄛˊ)
muddy and turbid
淤沙(ㄩ ㄕㄚ)
silt
淤塞(ㄩ ㄙㄜˋ)
to silt up; to block; blocked or choked by silt
淤閼(ㄩ ㄜˋ)
blocked or choked by silt
淤鬱(ㄩ ㄩˋ)
silted; blocked

【淦】2933 ㄍㄢˋ gann gàn
1. water leaking into a boat
2. name of a river in Kiangsi Province

【淥】2934 ㄌㄨˋ luh lù
1. clear water
2. to drip; to strain
3. name of a tributary of the Hsiang River (湘江) in Hunan Province
4. a Chinese family name
淥淥(ㄌㄨˋ ㄌㄨˋ)
damp and wet; dripping
淥水(ㄌㄨˋ ㄕㄨㄟˇ)
name of a tributary of the Hsiang River (湘江) in Hunan Province

【淩】2935 (凌) ㄌㄧㄥˊ ling líng
1. to pass; to traverse; to cross
2. to intrude; to insult or bully
3. a Chinese family name

【淪】2936 ㄌㄨㄣˊ luen lún
1. to sink into oblivion, ruin, etc.; to fall; engulfed or lost; submerged
2. ripples; eddying water
淪敗(ㄌㄨㄣˊ ㄅㄞˋ)
(said of a nation) to fall; lost or ruined
淪滅(ㄌㄨㄣˊ ㄇㄧㄝˋ)
totally lost or ruined; to sink into total disintegration
淪替(ㄌㄨㄣˊ ㄊㄧˋ)
to get weaker and disintegrate gradually
淪落(ㄌㄨㄣˊ ㄌㄨㄛˋ)
to get lost (in a strange land, etc.)
淪迴(ㄌㄨㄣˊ ㄏㄨㄟˊ)
an eddy
淪棄(ㄌㄨㄣˊ ㄑㄧˋ)
rejected and discarded
淪陷(ㄌㄨㄣˊ ㄒㄧㄢˋ)
(said of a territory) occupied by or lost to the enemy
淪陷區(ㄌㄨㄣˊ ㄒㄧㄢˋ ㄑㄩ)
territory occupied by the enemy; enemy occupied area
淪胥(ㄌㄨㄣˊ ㄒㄩ)
to drag each other to total ruin; to be involved in ruin together
淪入風塵(ㄌㄨㄣˊ ㄖㄨˋ ㄈㄥ ㄔㄣˊ)
(said of women) to fall into professions not socially respectable—as prostitution, etc.
淪喪(ㄌㄨㄣˊ ㄙㄤˋ)
to be lost or ruined
淪爲(ㄌㄨㄣˊ ㄨㄟˊ)
to become what is way below the social position one used to occupy
淪亡(ㄌㄨㄣˊ ㄨㄤˊ)
lost or ruined

【淨】2937 ㄐㄧㄥˋ jinq jìng
1. clean; pure; to cleanse; to purify
2. empty; vain
3. a role in Chinese opera with a heavily painted face
4. completely; totally
5. only; merely; nothing but
6. net (income, profit, etc.)
淨本(ㄐㄧㄥˋ ㄅㄣˇ)
(Tang Dynasty) a clean and neat copy of an original work
淨瓶(ㄐㄧㄥˋ ㄆㄧㄥˊ)
a vessel used by Buddhists for washing hands
淨面(ㄐㄧㄥˋ ㄇㄧㄢˋ)
to wash one's face
淨土(ㄐㄧㄥˋ ㄊㄨˇ)
sukhavati; the land of the pure—the land of Buddha
淨土宗(ㄐㄧㄥˋ ㄊㄨˇ ㄗㄨㄥ)
the Pure-land Sect of Buddhism whose chief tenet is salvation by faith in *Amitabha*, also known as the Lotus Sect (蓮花宗 or 蓮宗)
淨利(ㄐㄧㄥˋ ㄌㄧˋ)
net profit
淨化(ㄐㄧㄥˋ ㄏㄨㄚˋ)
to purify
淨價(ㄐㄧㄥˋ ㄐㄧㄚˋ)
a net price
淨角(ㄐㄧㄥˋ ㄐㄧㄠˇ)
a male role in Chinese opera with a heavily painted face
淨盡(ㄐㄧㄥˋ ㄐㄧㄣˋ)
completely exhausted (as stocks, supplies, etc.)
淨君(ㄐㄧㄥˋ ㄐㄩㄣ)
another name of a broom
淨値(ㄐㄧㄥˋ ㄓˊ)
net value
淨宅(ㄐㄧㄥˋ ㄓㄞˊ)
to exorcize evil spirits from a haunted house
淨賺(ㄐㄧㄥˋ ㄓㄨㄢˋ)
net earnings
淨重(ㄐㄧㄥˋ ㄓㄨㄥˋ)
net weight 亦作「淨量」
淨手(ㄐㄧㄥˋ ㄕㄡˇ)
① to wash one's hands ② to

〔水部〕

relieve oneself
淨身(ㄐㄧㄥˋ ㄕㄣ)
to castrate; castration
淨身人(ㄐㄧㄥˋ ㄕㄣ ㄖㄣˊ)
a castrated man
淨剩(ㄐㄧㄥˋ ㄕㄥˋ)
only: 屋裡淨剩他一個人。Only he is left in the room.
淨水(ㄐㄧㄥˋ ㄕㄨㄟˇ)
clean water
淨存(ㄐㄧㄥˋ ㄘㄨㄣˊ)or 淨餘(ㄐㄧㄥˋ ㄩˊ)
net balance
淨眼(ㄐㄧㄥˋ ㄧㄢˇ)
eyes which can see gods and deities

【淬】 2938 ㄘㄨㄟˋ tsuey cuì
1. to temper iron or steel for making swords, etc. (also used figuratively)
2. to dip into water; to soak; to dye
淬勉(ㄘㄨㄟˋ ㄇㄧㄢˇ)
to persuade; to urge and advise; to arouse to action: 他淬勉我努力用功。He persuaded me to work hard.
淬勵(ㄘㄨㄟˋ ㄌㄧˋ)
to arouse to action; to encourage
淬礪(ㄘㄨㄟˋ ㄌㄧˋ)
① to temper and grind ② to train or discipline oneself (toward a goal)

【淮】 2939 ㄏㄨㄞˊ hwai huái
name of a river flowing from West China into the Gulf of Pohai
淮南(ㄏㄨㄞˊ ㄋㄢˊ)
the region south of the Huai River
淮南鷄犬(ㄏㄨㄞˊ ㄋㄢˊ ㄐㄧ ㄑㄩㄢˇ)
humble followers waiting for a pull from their superior—Legend has it that Liu An, King of Huai Nan(淮南王劉安), achieved immortality and that his chickens and dogs, having eaten the leftovers of his elixir, followed him into heaven.
淮南子(ㄏㄨㄞˊ ㄋㄢˊ ㄗˇ)
the title of a book on philosophy by Liu An, King of Huai Nan (淮南王劉安) of the Han Dynasty
淮軍(ㄏㄨㄞˊ ㄐㄩㄣ)
a military force trained and commanded by Li Hung-chang (李鴻章), which played a major role in the suppression of the Taiping Rebellion (so named because the soldiers were recruited in the valley of the Huai River)
淮枳(ㄏㄨㄞˊ ㄓˇ)
Things appear differently under different situations.
淮水(ㄏㄨㄞˊ ㄕㄨㄟˇ)or 淮河(ㄏㄨㄞˊ ㄏㄜˊ)
the Huai River, which begins in Honan Province, runs through Anhwei and empties into the sea on the Kiangsu coast
淮鹽(ㄏㄨㄞˊ ㄧㄢˊ)
salt produced in the Huai region
淮陰侯(ㄏㄨㄞˊ ㄧㄣ ㄏㄡˊ)
General Han Hsin (韓信) of the Han Dynasty, who was conferred the title Marquis of Huai Yin

【淫】 2940 ㄧㄣˊ yn yín
1. licentious; lewd; lascivious; libidinous; dissolute
2. obscene; pornographic
3. to seduce; to debauch; to tempt; temptation
4. things related to sexual desire and behavior
淫奔(ㄧㄣˊ ㄅㄣ)
to elope; elopement
淫朋狎友(ㄧㄣˊ ㄆㄥˊ ㄒㄧㄚˊ ㄧㄡˇ)
debauching company
淫靡(ㄧㄣˊ ㄇㄧˇ)
extravagant; extravagance
淫放(ㄧㄣˊ ㄈㄤˋ)
to give free rein to the passion
淫風(ㄧㄣˊ ㄈㄥ)
wanton customs; libidinous practices; dissoluteness and debauchery that prevail
淫風甚熾(ㄧㄣˊ ㄈㄥ ㄕㄣˋ ㄔˋ)
Wanton custom is in a blaze.
淫夫淫婦(ㄧㄣˊ ㄈㄨ ㄧㄣˊ ㄈㄨˋ)
a man and a woman having illicit liaison; adulterers and adulteresses
淫蕩(ㄧㄣˊ ㄉㄤˋ)
(especially said of women) lewd and libidinous; lascivious and wanton; profligate
淫慝(ㄧㄣˊ ㄊㄜˋ)
wanton and debauching
淫念(ㄧㄣˊ ㄋㄧㄢˋ)
carnal desires; lust
淫謔(ㄧㄣˊ ㄋㄩㄝˋ)
obscene jesting
淫樂(ㄧㄣˊ ㄌㄜˋ)
to give free rein to sexual desire; wantonness; carnal pleasures
淫潦(ㄧㄣˊ ㄌㄠˇ)
floods caused by excessive rains or overflowing rivers
淫亂(ㄧㄣˊ ㄌㄨㄢˋ)
debauchery
淫畫(ㄧㄣˊ ㄏㄨㄚˋ)
pornographic or obscene pictures
淫穢(ㄧㄣˊ ㄏㄨㄟˋ)
dirty (books, pictures, language, scenes); obscene
淫巧(ㄧㄣˊ ㄑㄧㄠˇ)
clever in improper ways; lewdly suave
淫戲(ㄧㄣˊ ㄒㄧˋ)
① sexual intercourse ② pornographic plays, shows, etc.
淫刑(ㄧㄣˊ ㄒㄧㄥˊ)
to mete out punishments freely or without any consideration; punishments meted out in this manner
淫行(ㄧㄣˊ ㄒㄧㄥˋ)
licentious conduct
淫學(ㄧㄣˊ ㄒㄩㄝˊ)
improper learning; unorthodox learning
淫視(ㄧㄣˊ ㄕˋ)
to make sheep's eyes; a come-hither look; lascivious looks
淫書(ㄧㄣˊ ㄕㄨ)
obscene books
淫水(ㄧㄣˊ ㄕㄨㄟˇ)
① flooding waters ② saliva-like excretion during or before sexual intercourse
淫人妻女(ㄧㄣˊ ㄖㄣˊ ㄑㄧ ㄋㄩˇ)
to violate another's wife and daughters (will have one's own violated)
淫辭(ㄧㄣˊ ㄘˊ)

obscene expressions; wanton language
淫泆(ㄧㄣˊ ㄧˋ)
debauchery; wantonness
淫業(ㄧㄣˊ ㄧㄝˋ)
the profession of prostitution
淫娃蕩子(ㄧㄣˊ ㄨㄚˊ ㄉㄤˋ ㄗˇ)
fast women and lewd men
淫威(ㄧㄣˊ ㄨㄟ)
① imposing or awe-inspiring power ② excessive use of powers and punishments
淫雨(ㄧㄣˊ ㄩˇ)
incessant rains; excessive rains: 淫雨爲災。Excessive rains become a calamity.
淫慾(ㄧㄣˊ ㄩˋ)
wanton desires; sexual desire
淫慾過度(ㄧㄣˊ ㄩˋ ㄍㄨㄛˋ ㄉㄨˋ)
to abandon oneself to the passion; excessive indulgence in the pursuit of pleasures

【淳】 2941
ㄔㄨㄣˊ chwen chún
1. pure; clean; simple; sincere; honest
2. a couple or pair (of chariots)
3. big; great
淳樸(ㄔㄨㄣˊ ㄆㄨˊ)
sincere and simple (villagers, etc.); honest; unsophisticated: 他是個淳樸的莊稼人。He is an honest peasant.
淳風(ㄔㄨㄣˊ ㄈㄥ)
simple and sincere tradition or custom
淳良(ㄔㄨㄣˊ ㄌㄧㄤˊ)
pure, simple and honest
淳古(ㄔㄨㄣˊ ㄍㄨˇ)
as simple and pure as in ancient times
淳和(ㄔㄨㄣˊ ㄏㄜˊ)
simple and gentle
淳厚(ㄔㄨㄣˊ ㄏㄡˋ)
simple and sincere
淳質(ㄔㄨㄣˊ ㄓˋ)
the quality of being simple and pure
淳粹(ㄔㄨㄣˊ ㄘㄨㄟˋ)
pure; unadulterated

【淵】 2942
ㄩㄢ iuan yuān
1. deep waters; a gulf; an abyss
2. profound (learning); depth; profundity; erudition; extensive
3. a Chinese family name
淵博(ㄩㄢ ㄅㄛˊ)
(said of learning) erudite; erudition; profound and extensive: 他的學問淵博。He has profound and extensive knowledge.
淵海(ㄩㄢ ㄏㄞˇ)
(literally) deep sea—deep and vast; profound and extensive
淵泓(ㄩㄢ ㄏㄨㄥˊ)
profound and vast; deep and extensive
淵玄(ㄩㄢ ㄒㄩㄢˊ)
profundity; depth
淵沖(ㄩㄢ ㄔㄨㄥ)
deep but open-minded
淵識(ㄩㄢ ㄕˋ)
erudite and sophisticated; well versed in learning and rich in experience
淵藪(ㄩㄢ ㄙㄡˇ)
the place where things or persons flock together—a haunt or hotbed
淵詣(ㄩㄢ ㄧˋ)
deep or profound meaning
淵源(ㄩㄢ ㄩㄢˊ)
① the source; the origin or background ② relationship
淵遠(ㄩㄢ ㄩㄢˇ)
deep; profound

【深】 2943
ㄕㄣ shen shēn
1. deep; depth
2. profound; mysterious; difficult; abstruse
3. close; intimate
4. very; extremely
深壁高壘(ㄕㄣ ㄅㄧˋ ㄍㄠ ㄌㄟˇ)
strong defense works
深表同情(ㄕㄣ ㄅㄧㄠˇ ㄊㄨㄥˊ ㄑㄧㄥˊ)
to sympathize with; very sympathetic to; to express deep sympathy: 我對你的傷心事深表同情。I sympathize with you in your grief.
深不可測(ㄕㄣ ㄅㄨˋ ㄎㄜˇ ㄘㄜˋ)
immeasurable depth or profundity; extremely abstruse; unfathomable; to be an enigma
深謀遠慮(ㄕㄣ ㄇㄡˊ ㄩㄢˇ ㄌㄩˋ)
to think and plan far ahead; great prudence; foresight
深莽(ㄕㄣ ㄇㄤˇ)
land with dense tall grass
深渺(ㄕㄣ ㄇㄧㄠˇ)
deep and far
深妙(ㄕㄣ ㄇㄧㄠˋ)
abstruse and uncanny; profound
深明大義(ㄕㄣ ㄇㄧㄥˊ ㄉㄚˋ ㄧˋ)
to have a firm grasp of what is right and wrong; to forget self-interest in the face of an event of great significance
深得民心(ㄕㄣ ㄉㄜˊ ㄇㄧㄣˊ ㄒㄧㄣ)
well-received; to win strong popular support: 我們政府深得民心。Our government wins strong popular support.
深度(ㄕㄣ ㄉㄨˋ)
① depth (of a river, box, tank, etc.) ② profundity (of learning, etc.) ③ understanding (of the ways of the world); sophistication
深談(ㄕㄣ ㄊㄢˊ)
intimate talks
深痛(ㄕㄣ ㄊㄨㄥˋ)
deep grief; to lament deeply
深念(ㄕㄣ ㄋㄧㄢˋ)
to remember or consider; to think deeply
深藍(ㄕㄣ ㄌㄢˊ)
dark blue
深慮(ㄕㄣ ㄌㄩˋ)
deep worry or consideration; to think far ahead
深溝高壘(ㄕㄣ ㄍㄡ ㄍㄠ ㄌㄟˇ) or 深塹高壘(ㄕㄣ ㄑㄧㄢˋ ㄍㄠ ㄌㄟˇ)
a deep ditch and a high wall—strong defense works or fortifications
深感(ㄕㄣ ㄍㄢˇ)
to feel keenly or deeply
深耕(ㄕㄣ ㄍㄥ)
to plow deep
深更半夜(ㄕㄣ ㄍㄥ ㄅㄢˋ ㄧㄝˋ)
deep in the night; midnight: 他們工作至深更半夜。They worked until midnight.
深痼(ㄕㄣ ㄍㄨˋ)
chronic or deep-rooted (disease, habit, etc.)

深閨(ㄕㄣ ㄍㄨㄟ)
inner chambers or apartments where the women of the house live

深宮(ㄕㄣ ㄍㄨㄥ)
the forbidden palace; the harem

深刻(ㄕㄣ ㄎㄜˋ)
① deeply meaningful; profound significance ② penetrating (views, comments, etc.); poignant; incisive: 他的批評很深刻。His criticism is very penetrating. ③ to carve deep (in my heart); deep (impression, etc.)

深坑(ㄕㄣ ㄎㄥ)
a deep pit; an abyss

深海(ㄕㄣ ㄏㄞˇ)
deep sea

深海動物(ㄕㄣ ㄏㄞˇ ㄉㄨㄥˋ ㄨˋ)
abyssal faunae

深海漁業(ㄕㄣ ㄏㄞˇ ㄩˊ ㄧㄝˋ)
deep-sea fishery

深厚(ㄕㄣ ㄏㄡˋ)
① long and close (friendship, relationship, etc.): 我們有深厚的友誼。We have long and close friendship. ② profound (learning, training, etc.) ③ deep-seated; solid

深恨(ㄕㄣ ㄏㄣˋ)
① deep hatred ② to regret very much

深呼吸(ㄕㄣ ㄏㄨ ㄒㄧ)
a deep breath; to breathe deeply

深紅(ㄕㄣ ㄏㄨㄥˊ)
dark red

深交(ㄕㄣ ㄐㄧㄠ)
long, intimate friendship

深究(ㄕㄣ ㄐㄧㄡˋ)
to study, deliberate, search or delve into something deeply: 對這個問題不必深究。You don't have to delve into the subject deeply.

深井(ㄕㄣ ㄐㄧㄥˇ)
a deep well

深居簡出(ㄕㄣ ㄐㄩ ㄐㄧㄢˇ ㄔㄨ)
to lead a secluded life; to live in seclusion or solitude

深切(ㄕㄣ ㄑㄧㄝˋ)
deeply; sincerely; penetrating; intensively; thorough; intensely

深秋(ㄕㄣ ㄑㄧㄡ)
late fall; late autumn

深淺(ㄕㄣ ㄑㄧㄢˇ)
① deep or shallow; depth ② (said of colors) deep or light ③ (good or evil) intentions

深情(ㄕㄣ ㄑㄧㄥˊ)
deep affection or love: 他對他太太懷著深情。He has deep affection for his wife.

深情厚誼(ㄕㄣ ㄑㄧㄥˊ ㄏㄡˋ ㄧˋ)
long and close friendship

深趣(ㄕㄣ ㄑㄩˋ)
deep interest; enthusiasm: 我對音樂有深趣。I have deep interest in music.

深悉(ㄕㄣ ㄒㄧ)
to realize fully; to know thoroughly; fully aware

深宵(ㄕㄣ ㄒㄧㄠ)
deep in the night

深心(ㄕㄣ ㄒㄧㄣ)
deep in one's heart; deep thoughts; profound meaning

深信(ㄕㄣ ㄒㄧㄣˋ)
to believe strongly; deep faith; firmly convinced

深信不疑(ㄕㄣ ㄒㄧㄣˋ ㄅㄨˋ ㄧˊ)
to believe without a shadow of doubt

深省(ㄕㄣ ㄒㄧㄥˇ)
to understand after soul-searching; to make a thorough self-examination

深知(ㄕㄣ ㄓ)
to know thoroughly; well aware; to realize fully: 他深知其錯。He fully realizes his error.

深致(ㄕㄣ ㄓˋ)
to convey or express sincerely or deeply

深摯(ㄕㄣ ㄓˋ)
close or intimate (friendship, etc.); deep (affection); sincere: 他們兩友誼深摯。There was intimate friendship between them.

深宅大院(ㄕㄣ ㄓㄞˊ ㄉㄚˋ ㄩㄢˋ)
a large house and a big yard—the house of the wealthy

深池(ㄕㄣ ㄔˊ)
① a deep pond ② a deep moat

深讎 or 深仇(ㄕㄣ ㄔㄡˊ)
deep animosity or hatred

深仇大恨(ㄕㄣ ㄔㄡˊ ㄉㄚˋ ㄏㄣˋ)
a deep-seated hatred

深沈(ㄕㄣ ㄔㄣˊ)
① dark: 天色漸深沈。It is getting dark. ② (said of a person) reserved; impenetrable; unfathomable; calm; composed; serious: 她這人很深沈。She is impenetrable.

深長(ㄕㄣ ㄔㄤˊ)
profound (significance, meaning, etc.): 這篇文章意義深長。This article is profound in meaning.

深成岩(ㄕㄣ ㄔㄥˊ ㄧㄢˊ)
plutonic rocks

深處(ㄕㄣ ㄔㄨˋ)
the deep, inner or obscure part (of woods, heart, etc.)

深識(ㄕㄣ ㄕˋ)
farsight; profound understanding: 他是有深識的人。He is a man of farsight.

深室(ㄕㄣ ㄕˋ)
a prison cell

深山(ㄕㄣ ㄕㄢ)
deep in the mountain

深深(ㄕㄣ ㄕㄣ)
very deeply

深水(ㄕㄣ ㄕㄨㄟˇ)
deep waters

深水炸彈(ㄕㄣ ㄕㄨㄟˇ ㄓㄚˋ ㄉㄢˋ)
a depth charge bomb

深入(ㄕㄣ ㄖㄨˋ)
(to research, study, delve, etc.) deeply or thoroughly into something; to reach or penetrate deep (into enemy territory)

深入不毛(ㄕㄣ ㄖㄨˋ ㄅㄨˋ ㄇㄠˊ)
to penetrate deep into wilderness or uncivilized regions

深入淺出(ㄕㄣ ㄖㄨˋ ㄑㄧㄢˇ ㄔㄨ)
to explain in everyday language the results of a profound study, research, etc.

深入人心(ㄕㄣ ㄖㄨˋ ㄖㄣˊ ㄒㄧㄣ)
to impress deeply upon everyone's mind: 這觀念深入人心。The idea impressed deeply upon everyone's mind.

深造(ㄕㄣ ㄗㄠˋ)
to pursue advanced study

深藏不露(ㄕㄣ ㄘㄤˊ ㄅㄨˋ ㄌㄡˋ)
Real knowledge is not showy.

深藏若虛(ㄕㄣ ㄘㄤˊ ㄖㄨㄛˋ ㄒㄩ)
(literally) to bosom a trea-

sure and act as if one had nothing with him—very reserved and humble
深叢(ㄕㄣ ㄘㄨㄥˊ)
deep in the woods
深思(ㄕㄣ ㄙ)
deep thought; contemplation; to think deeply; to ponder: 他坐在那裏深思。He sat there deep in contemplation.
深思熟慮(ㄕㄣ ㄙ ㄕㄨˊ ㄌㄩˋ)
careful deliberation; to think and contemplate thoroughly; to ponder: 他對此事深思熟慮。He ponders deeply over the matter.
深邃(ㄕㄣ ㄙㄨㄟˋ)
deep and far; profound and abstruse
深算(ㄕㄣ ㄙㄨㄢˋ)
careful deliberation, calculation or planning
深奧(ㄕㄣ ㄠˋ)
deep; abstruse; profound; recondite: 這是一本深奧的書。This is a profound book.
深黯(ㄕㄣ ㄢˋ)
dark; dark and obscure: 顏色深黯。The color is dark.
深恩(ㄕㄣ ㄣ)
great favors: 他的深恩令人難忘。His great favors are unforgettable.
深意(ㄕㄣ ㄧˋ)
deep or abstruse meaning
深夜(ㄕㄣ ㄧㄝˋ)
deep in the night
深憂(ㄕㄣ ㄧㄡ)
deep worries: 深憂使他不能入睡。Deep worries kept him awake.
深言(ㄕㄣ ㄧㄢˊ)or 深語(ㄕㄣ ㄩˇ)
a confidential or intimate talk
深惡痛絕(ㄕㄣ ㄨˋ ㄊㄨㄥˋ ㄐㄩㄝˊ)
to shun like poison; to detest extremely; to have a great aversion(to something or someone): 他對酗酒深惡痛絕。He regards drunkenness with great aversion.
深爲(ㄕㄣ ㄨㄟˊ)
greatly; deeply; highly: 他深爲吃驚。He was greatly surprised.
深文奧義(ㄕㄣ ㄨㄣˊ ㄠˋ ㄧˋ)
(said of writings) hard to understand; abstruse
深淵(ㄕㄣ ㄩㄢ)
an abyss; a very dangerous place: 他陷入苦難的深淵。He fell into the abyss of misery.
深遠(ㄕㄣ ㄩㄢˇ)
deep and far (in meaning, significance, etc.)
深院(ㄕㄣ ㄩㄢˋ)
a large courtyard—the house of a rich family
深願(ㄕㄣ ㄩㄢˋ)
to be very willingly; would be very glad to…

2944
【淶】ㄌㄞˊ lai lái
name of a river in Hopeh Province 亦作「淶水」
淶水(ㄌㄞˊ ㄕㄨㄟˇ)
參看「淶」

2945
【混】1. ㄏㄨㄣˋ huenn hùn
1. disorderly; confused
2. to mix; mixed; to mingle or blend
3. to fool around; just to get along
4. to do things at random or without purpose
混不過去(ㄏㄨㄣˋ ·ㄅㄨ ㄍㄨㄛˋ ㄑㄩˋ)
unable to fool others
混不下去(ㄏㄨㄣˋ ·ㄅㄨ ㄒㄧㄚˋ ㄑㄩˋ)
cannot stay on the job any longer; unable to get along smoothly due to many handicaps, etc.
混飯吃(ㄏㄨㄣˋ ㄈㄢˋ ㄔ)
just to make ends meet; just to get along
混紡(ㄏㄨㄣˋ ㄈㄤˇ)
(said of textiles) mixture of natural and synthetic fibers
混沌(ㄏㄨㄣˋ ㄉㄨㄣˋ)or 混混沌沌(ㄏㄨㄣˋ ㄏㄨㄣˋ ㄉㄨㄣˋ ㄉㄨㄣˋ)
① the chaotic world in prehistoric times ② ignorant and dumb
混沌初開(ㄏㄨㄣˋ ㄉㄨㄣˋ ㄔㄨ ㄎㄞ)
at the dawn of civilization
混同(ㄏㄨㄣˋ ㄊㄨㄥˊ)
to merge; to combine: 油和水不容易混同。Oil and water do not readily combine.
混凝土(ㄏㄨㄣˋ ㄋㄧㄥˊ ㄊㄨˇ)
concrete
混亂(ㄏㄨㄣˋ ㄌㄨㄢˋ)
confusion; chaos: 軍隊陷於混亂。The army were thrown into confusion.
混汞法(ㄏㄨㄣˋ ㄍㄨㄥˇ ㄈㄚˇ)
(chemistry) amalgamation
混合(ㄏㄨㄣˋ ㄏㄜˊ)
to mix together; to mingle or blend together
混合法(ㄏㄨㄣˋ ㄏㄜˊ ㄈㄚˇ)
syncretic theories; mixture
混合列車(ㄏㄨㄣˋ ㄏㄜˊ ㄌㄧㄝˋ ㄔㄜ)
a mixed train (with both freight cars and passenger coaches)
混合花序(ㄏㄨㄣˋ ㄏㄜˊ ㄏㄨㄚ ㄒㄩˋ)
mixed inflorescence
混合機(ㄏㄨㄣˋ ㄏㄜˊ ㄐㄧ)
a concrete mixer; a mixer
混合雙打(ㄏㄨㄣˋ ㄏㄜˊ ㄕㄨㄤ ㄉㄚˇ)
mixed doubles
混合物(ㄏㄨㄣˋ ㄏㄜˊ ㄨˋ)
a mixture; a blend: 空氣是氣體的混合物, 不是化合物。Air is a mixture, not a compound of gases.
混號(ㄏㄨㄣˋ ㄏㄠˋ)or 混名(ㄏㄨㄣˋ ㄇㄧㄥˊ)
a nickname
混混(ㄏㄨㄣˋ ㄏㄨㄣˋ)
① dark; opaque; blackened ② to drift through(life) ③ a hoodlum; a hooligan; a villain; a rascal
混跡(ㄏㄨㄣˋ ㄐㄧ)
to mix or hide oneself in a company, crowd, society, organization, etc: 他正混跡人群中。He is hiding himself in the crowd.
混進(ㄏㄨㄣˋ ㄐㄧㄣˋ)
to infiltrate; to sneak into
混血(ㄏㄨㄣˋ ㄒㄧㄝˇ)
hybridization
混血兒(ㄏㄨㄣˋ ㄒㄧㄝˇ ㄦˊ)
a human hybrid; a mixed-blood; a child of an interracial marriage
混戰(ㄏㄨㄣˋ ㄓㄢˋ)
a melee; a wild battle
混帳 or 混賬(ㄏㄨㄣˋ ㄓㄤˋ)
That good-for-nothing! 或 That s.o.b! 或 Scoundrel! 或 Rascal!
混成(ㄏㄨㄣˋ ㄔㄥˊ)
to mix together; to blend together

〔水部〕

混成旅(ㄏㄨㄣˋ ㄔㄥˊ ㄌㄩˇ)
(military) a mixed or composite brigade
混充(ㄏㄨㄣˋ ㄔㄨㄥ)
to pretend to be (someone else); to masquerade or pose (as someone else): 他混充音樂家。He pretends to be a musician.
混世魔王(ㄏㄨㄣˋ ㄕˋ ㄇㄛˊ ㄨㄤˊ)
a fiendish person who causes an upheaval in the world—like Hitler, etc.
混說(ㄏㄨㄣˋ ㄕㄨㄛ)
to talk nonsense; to talk at random: 別混說! Don't talk nonsense!
混日子(ㄏㄨㄣˋ ㄖˋ ·ㄗ)
just to make a living; just to get along (without any plan, ambition, etc. for the future)
混然(ㄏㄨㄣˋ ㄖㄢˊ)
mixed and indistinguishable
混入(ㄏㄨㄣˋ ㄖㄨˋ)
to mix oneself inside a body of people, an organization; to get into an organization or restricted area without undergoing the proper procedures
混資格(ㄏㄨㄣˋ ㄗ ㄍㄜˊ)
to study or receive a training not for the sake of knowledge but for the academic degree or diploma
混子(ㄏㄨㄣˋ ·ㄗ)
one who fools around in a respectable profession; a quack
混雜(ㄏㄨㄣˋ ㄗㄚˊ)
① to blend; to mix: 不要把糖和沙混雜在一起。Don't mix sand with the sugar. ② motley; heterogeneous; mixed ③ disorderly; chaotic; confused
混一(ㄏㄨㄣˋ ㄧ)
unification
混一混(ㄏㄨㄣˋ ·ㄧ ·ㄏㄨㄣ)or 混混(ㄏㄨㄣˋ ·ㄏㄨㄣ)
just to get along
混爲一談(ㄏㄨㄣˋ ㄨㄟˊ ㄧˊ ㄊㄢˊ)
to lump together; to confuse something with something else

【混】 2945
2. (渾) ㄏㄨㄣˊ hwen hún
turbid; muddy; not clear
混蛋(ㄏㄨㄣˊ ㄉㄢˋ)
Bloody fool!
混濁(ㄏㄨㄣˊ ㄓㄨㄛˊ)
turbid; not clean or pure: 這是條混濁的河。This is a turbid river.
混水(ㄏㄨㄣˊ ㄕㄨㄟˇ)
① turbid water ② troubled waters ③ improper undertakings; illegal activities
混水摸魚(ㄏㄨㄣˊ ㄕㄨㄟˇ ㄇㄛ ㄩˊ)
to fish in troubled waters

【混】 2945
3. ㄏㄨㄣˇ hoen hǔn
confused and not distinguishable
混亂(ㄏㄨㄣˇ ㄌㄨㄢˋ)
confusion; disorder; chaos: 他的房間一片混亂。His room was in great disorder.
混淆(ㄏㄨㄣˇ ㄧㄠˊ)
mixed, confused and indistinguishable
混淆是非(ㄏㄨㄣˇ ㄧㄠˊ ㄕˋ ㄈㄟ)
to confound right and wrong
混淆視聽(ㄏㄨㄣˇ ㄧㄠˊ ㄕˋ ㄊㄧㄥ)
to confuse public opinion

【清】 2946
ㄑㄧㄥ ching qīng
1. pure; clean; clear
2. brief; scarce
3. virtuous; honest
4. to arrange; to place in order
5. to conclude; to terminate; to repay (debts); to settle
6. clear, simple and easily understandable
7. Ching Dynasty (1644-1911)
8. to clean
清白(ㄑㄧㄥ ㄅㄞˊ)
(said of a person's character, family background) clean; unsoiled; unimpeachable; innocent
清班(ㄑㄧㄥ ㄅㄢ)or 清秩(ㄑㄧㄥ ㄓˋ)
virtuous officials collectively
清標(ㄑㄧㄥ ㄅㄧㄠ)
① a pure and austere look ② the bright moon
清兵(ㄑㄧㄥ ㄅㄧㄥ)
Manchu troops
清貧(ㄑㄧㄥ ㄆㄧㄣˊ)
poor and virtuous: 他很清貧。He is very poor and virtuous.
清平(ㄑㄧㄥ ㄆㄧㄥˊ)
① peace and justice ② (said of a disposition) pure, honest and peace-loving ③ name of counties in Shantung and Kweichow
清平世界(ㄑㄧㄥ ㄆㄧㄥˊ ㄕˋ ㄐㄧㄝˋ)
a peaceful and orderly world
清門(ㄑㄧㄥ ㄇㄣˊ)
a poor family
清廟(ㄑㄧㄥ ㄇㄧㄠˋ)
① (Chou Dynasty) the temple for worshipping King Wen (文王) ② an ancestral shrine
清名(ㄑㄧㄥ ㄇㄧㄥˊ)
an unimpeachable reputation; an unsoiled name
清明(ㄑㄧㄥ ㄇㄧㄥˊ)
① clean and just (administration) ② one of the 24 solar periods in a year which falls on April 5 or 6 when people visit their ancestral tombs, also known as Tomb-Sweeping Day
清芬(ㄑㄧㄥ ㄈㄣ)
① soothing aroma ② virtues
清風(ㄑㄧㄥ ㄈㄥ)
① cool breezes; soothing wind ② (said of an official) to remain poor and clean at retirement
清風明月(ㄑㄧㄥ ㄈㄥ ㄇㄧㄥˊ ㄩㄝˋ)
(literally) the soothing wind and the bright moon —aloof
清風兩袖(ㄑㄧㄥ ㄈㄥ ㄌㄧㄤˇ ㄒㄧㄡˋ)
(said of an honest official) to remain poor upon retirement
清風徐來(ㄑㄧㄥ ㄈㄥ ㄒㄩˊ ㄌㄞˊ)
The soothing breezes slowly blow this way.
清福(ㄑㄧㄥ ㄈㄨˊ)
a kind of happiness with the absence of worries and cares; an easy and carefree life
清道(ㄑㄧㄥ ㄉㄠˋ)
① to sweep the road; to clear the way ② (in former times) before the passing of the sedan chair of a high official, magistrate, etc. guardsmen would first clear the way and warn the peo-

ple of his imminent arrival
清道夫(ㄑㄧㄥ ㄉㄠˋ ㄈㄨ)
a scavenger
清單(ㄑㄧㄥ ㄉㄢ)
a detailed list of items which serves as a receipt, statement, etc.; a statement of account
清淡(ㄑㄧㄥ ㄉㄢˋ)
① not enthusiastic; calm ② dull or sluggish (markets); slack: 這一季生意清淡。Business is slack at this season. ③(said of food) simple; without grease or heavy seasoning
清黨(ㄑㄧㄥ ㄉㄤˇ)
a purge within a political party; to purge undesirable elements from a political party
清點(ㄑㄧㄥ ㄉㄧㄢˇ)
to check; to make an inventory; to sort and count
清燉(ㄑㄧㄥ ㄉㄨㄣˋ)
to stew or steam meat without seasoning
清談(ㄑㄧㄥ ㄊㄢˊ)
① pure theoretical talks based on the teachings of Lao-tzu (老子) ② a polite reference to the utterances of others
清談誤國(ㄑㄧㄥ ㄊㄢˊ ㄨˋ ㄍㄨㄛˊ)
(said of intellectuals) Pure theories and talks without action will get the nation into trouble.
清湯(ㄑㄧㄥ ㄊㄤ)
consommé; clear soup; light soup
清天(ㄑㄧㄥ ㄊㄧㄢ)
① a clear sky: 清天無雲。There were no clouds in the clear sky. ②a virtuous official (often used as a salutation to the judge in former times)
清恬(ㄑㄧㄥ ㄊㄧㄢˊ)
pure and quiet (life); tranquil and comfortable
清聽(ㄑㄧㄥ ㄊㄧㄥ)
your kind listening
清廷(ㄑㄧㄥ ㄊㄧㄥˊ)
the Ching government; the Manchu court
清通(ㄑㄧㄥ ㄊㄨㄥ)
(said of writings, etc.) clear and smooth style; clearly understandable
清朗(ㄑㄧㄥ ㄌㄤˇ)
① clear and loud (sound, voice, etc.) ② clear and crisp (weather): 天氣清朗。The weather is clear and crisp.
清冷(ㄑㄧㄥ ㄌㄥˇ)
① cool; refreshing ② deserted
清理(ㄑㄧㄥ ㄌㄧˇ)
① to settle (accounts, etc.); clearance (of sales, etc.) ② to arrange; to tidy up
清麗(ㄑㄧㄥ ㄌㄧˋ)
(said of writings, etc.) a clear and attractive style
清冽(ㄑㄧㄥ ㄌㄧㄝˋ)
clear and cold (water): 水甚清冽。The water is clear and cold.
清寥(ㄑㄧㄥ ㄌㄧㄠˊ)
clear and open (space, fields, etc.)
清流(ㄑㄧㄥ ㄌㄧㄡˊ)
① a clear stream ② virtuous scholars ③(now rarely) an air current ④ name of a county in Fukien Province
清漣(ㄑㄧㄥ ㄌㄧㄢˊ)
clear, rippled waters in a pond, etc.
清廉(ㄑㄧㄥ ㄌㄧㄢˊ)
clean, honest and capable (officials, etc.); free from corruption
清涼(ㄑㄧㄥ ㄌㄧㄤˊ)
① nice and cool; refreshing (weather, water, etc.): 天氣清涼。It is nice and cool. ② name of a hill in Nanking
清涼劑(ㄑㄧㄥ ㄌㄧㄤˊ ㄐㄧˋ)
a herbal concoction that is supposed to relieve the latent "heat" in the human body
清涼飲料(ㄑㄧㄥ ㄌㄧㄤˊ ㄧㄣˇ ㄌㄧㄠˋ)
a cold drink; a cooler
清亮(ㄑㄧㄥ ㄌㄧㄤˋ)
clear and bright (eyes): 她眼睛清亮。Her eyes are clear and bright.
清歌(ㄑㄧㄥ ㄍㄜ)
singing without an instrumental accompaniment
清歌妙舞(ㄑㄧㄥ ㄍㄜ ㄇㄧㄠˋ ㄨˇ)
good songs and wonderful dances—the stage; a good song-and-dance performance
清高(ㄑㄧㄥ ㄍㄠ)
morally lofty or upright; not interested in politics or other worldly things
清高絕俗(ㄑㄧㄥ ㄍㄠ ㄐㄩㄝˊ ㄙㄨˊ)
extremely aloof from mundane affairs
清規(ㄑㄧㄥ ㄍㄨㄟ)
Buddhist rules; discipline among Buddhist monks and nuns
清貴(ㄑㄧㄥ ㄍㄨㄟˋ)
① pure and valuable ② the Hanlin Academy (翰林院), often referred to as 清貴衙門
清官(ㄑㄧㄥ ㄍㄨㄢ)
honest officials
清宮(ㄑㄧㄥ ㄍㄨㄥ)
① to clean or sweep the palace chambers ② the palace of the Ching rulers
清客(ㄑㄧㄥ ㄎㄜˋ)
① proteges of the powerful who stay with their benefactors like parasites ② another name of plum blossoms
清苦(ㄑㄧㄥ ㄎㄨˇ)
poor but clean and honest
清寒(ㄑㄧㄥ ㄏㄢˊ)
① poor but clean and honest ②(said of weather, etc.) cold and crisp ③(said of moonlight) cold and bright
清華(ㄑㄧㄥ ㄏㄨㄚˊ)
①(literary style) outstanding and beautiful ② eminent and honest gentlemen ③ moonlight ④ enchanting views
清華大學(ㄑㄧㄥ ㄏㄨㄚˊ ㄉㄚˋ ㄒㄩㄝˊ)
National Tsing Hua University
清華園(ㄑㄧㄥ ㄏㄨㄚˊ ㄩㄢˊ)
name of a garden in suburban Peking
清化(ㄑㄧㄥ ㄏㄨㄚˋ)
moral influence or education
清季(ㄑㄧㄥ ㄐㄧˋ)
the last years of the Ching Dynasty
清潔(ㄑㄧㄥ ㄐㄧㄝˊ)
clean; sanitary
清潔隊(ㄑㄧㄥ ㄐㄧㄝˊ ㄉㄨㄟˋ)
a cleaning squad

〔水部〕

清潔工人(ㄑㄧㄥ ㄐㄧㄝˊ ㄍㄨㄥ ㄖㄣˊ)
sanitation workers; street cleaners
清潔劑(ㄑㄧㄥ ㄐㄧㄝˊ ㄐㄧˋ)
a detergent
清介(ㄑㄧㄥ ㄐㄧㄝˋ)
pure, virtuous and not mixing with the ordinary run of life
清剿(ㄑㄧㄥ ㄐㄧㄠˇ)
to wipe out (bandits or rebel troops) completely
清教徒(ㄑㄧㄥ ㄐㄧㄠˋ ㄊㄨˊ)
the Puritans
清酒(ㄑㄧㄥ ㄐㄧㄡˇ)
①wine used in ancestral worshipping or in offerings; pure spirits ②a kind of rice wine; sake
清減(ㄑㄧㄥ ㄐㄧㄢˇ)
to get thin; to lose weight
清淨(ㄑㄧㄥ ㄐㄧㄥˋ)
clean and pure
清淨無爲(ㄑㄧㄥ ㄐㄧㄥˋ ㄨˊ ㄨㄟˊ)
to discard all desires and worries from one's mind—Taoist teachings
清靜(ㄑㄧㄥ ㄐㄧㄥˋ)
quiet (houses, surroundings, etc.): 咱們找個清靜的地方休息。Let's find a quiet place for a rest.
清欠(ㄑㄧㄥ ㄑㄧㄢˋ)
to repay all one's debts
清癯(ㄑㄧㄥ ㄑㄩˊ)
thin but healthy; lean and sprightly
清曲(ㄑㄧㄥ ㄑㄩˇ)
singing without dialogues 亦作「散曲」
清泉(ㄑㄧㄥ ㄑㄩㄢˊ)
①a crystal-clear fountain ②old name of a county in Hunan, now merged into Hengyang city
清晰(ㄑㄧㄥ ㄒㄧ)
①loud and clear (in radio reception, talking, listening, etc.): 這小女孩發音清晰。The little girl's pronunciation is clear. ②clearly
清洗(ㄑㄧㄥ ㄒㄧˇ)
to wash clean: 他在清洗炊具。He is cleaning cooking utensils.
清曉(ㄑㄧㄥ ㄒㄧㄠˇ)
dawn: 他清曉即起。He got up at dawn.
清修(ㄑㄧㄥ ㄒㄧㄡ)
to lead a life of few wants and ambitions
清秀(ㄑㄧㄥ ㄒㄧㄡˋ)
good-looking; with clear-cut features; well-shaped; handsome without the aid of cosmetics
清閒(ㄑㄧㄥ ㄒㄧㄢˊ)
at leisure; to have all the time one needs
清新(ㄑㄧㄥ ㄒㄧㄣ)
refreshing (style, fashion, etc.); fresh
清心寡慾(ㄑㄧㄥ ㄒㄧㄣ ㄍㄨㄚˇ ㄩˋ)
to purge one's mind of desires and ambitions
清香(ㄑㄧㄥ ㄒㄧㄤ)
mild fragrance (as distinct from strong aroma)
清香撲鼻(ㄑㄧㄥ ㄒㄧㄤ ㄆㄨ ㄅㄧˊ)
A sweet scent assails one's nostrils.
清鄉(ㄑㄧㄥ ㄒㄧㄤ)
to get rid of bandits from the countryside
清醒(ㄑㄧㄥ ㄒㄧㄥˇ)
①to come to; wide awake: 病人已經清醒過來。The patient has come to. ②clear-minded; sober
清興(ㄑㄧㄥ ㄒㄧㄥˋ)
pleasure: 他一直過着清興的生活。He has always lived a life of pleasure.
清虛(ㄑㄧㄥ ㄒㄩ)
high and mild; refined and nonaggressive
清眞(ㄑㄧㄥ ㄓㄣ)
①Mohammedan or Islamic ②pure; purity
清眞館(ㄑㄧㄥ ㄓㄣ ㄍㄨㄢˇ)or 清眞食堂(ㄑㄧㄥ ㄓㄣ ㄕˊ ㄊㄤˊ)
a Mohammedan restaurant where no pork is served
清眞教(ㄑㄧㄥ ㄓㄣ ㄐㄧㄠˋ)
Mohammedanism or Islamism
清眞寺(ㄑㄧㄥ ㄓㄣ ㄙˋ)
a mosque
清賬(ㄑㄧㄥ ㄓㄤˋ)
to pay off all one's debts; to settle all one's accounts
清蒸(ㄑㄧㄥ ㄓㄥ)
(a form of cooking) to steam; steamed
清正(ㄑㄧㄥ ㄓㄥˋ)
clean, honest and just
清濁(ㄑㄧㄥ ㄓㄨㄛˊ)
①(some water) clear and (some water) turbid ②(said of people) honest and dishonest
清濁不分(ㄑㄧㄥ ㄓㄨㄛˊ ㄅㄨˋ ㄈㄣ)
to be unable to distinguish the clear from the muddy
清茶(ㄑㄧㄥ ㄔㄚˊ)
①green tea ②(to entertain) with nothing but tea
清查(ㄑㄧㄥ ㄔㄚˊ)
to check, investigate, survey thoroughly; a thorough checkup
清澈(ㄑㄧㄥ ㄔㄜˋ)
crystal-clear; limpid (water)
清朝(ㄑㄧㄥ ㄔㄠˊ)
①the Ching or Manchu Dynasty (1644-1911) ②an enlightened reign
清晨(ㄑㄧㄥ ㄔㄣˊ)
early in the morning; dawn: 我清晨起床。I got up at dawn.
清償(ㄑㄧㄥ ㄔㄤˊ)
to pay off all one's debts
清場(ㄑㄧㄥ ㄔㄤˊ)or(ㄑㄧㄥ ㄔㄤˇ)
(said of movie theaters) to have every moviegoer out before the next show starts
清唱(ㄑㄧㄥ ㄔㄤˋ)
to sing Chinese opera without wearing costume or makeup
清除(ㄑㄧㄥ ㄔㄨˊ)
①to eliminate, rid of, clear away, liquidate, purge, or remove ②to clean or tidy up (a house)
清楚(ㄑㄧㄥ ㄔㄨˇ)or 清清楚楚(ㄑㄧㄥ ·ㄑㄧㄥ ㄔㄨˇ ㄔㄨˇ)
①clear; without ambiguity ②to know thoroughly; to understand: 這個問題你清楚嗎? Do you understand this question?
清創術(ㄑㄧㄥ ㄔㄨㄤ ㄕㄨˋ)
(medicine) *débridement*
清士(ㄑㄧㄥ ㄕˋ)
a man of honesty and unimpeachable integrity
清室(ㄑㄧㄥ ㄕˋ)
the royal family of the Ching Dynasty
清瘦(ㄑㄧㄥ ㄕㄡˋ)

thin and lean: 你看起來很清瘦。You look rather thin.
清尙(ㄑㄧㄥ ㄕㄤˋ)
high-class; high-society
清聲(ㄑㄧㄥ ㄕㄥ)
voiceless consonants
清水(ㄑㄧㄥ ㄕㄨㄟˇ)
clear (or fresh) water
清水貨(ㄑㄧㄥ ㄕㄨㄟˇ ㄏㄨㄛˋ)
① unadulterated goods ② (slang) a virgin
清爽(ㄑㄧㄥ ㄕㄨㄤˇ)
① sober ② quiet and comfortable; cooling and refreshing ③ clear and easy to understand ④ to have everything (debts, etc.) settled; relieved; relaxed
清早(ㄑㄧㄥ ㄗㄠˇ)
early in the morning; dawn
清册(ㄑㄧㄥ ㄘㄜˋ)
a long list or volume containing all details or items to be handed over to the successor, to an office, etc.
清操(ㄑㄧㄥ ㄘㄠ)
virtuous disposition and behavior
清倉查庫(ㄑㄧㄥ ㄘㄤ ㄔㄚˊ ㄎㄨˋ)
to make an inventory of warehouses
清脆(ㄑㄧㄥ ㄘㄨㄟˋ)
clear and crisp (note, sound, etc.); sharp and loud (slapping sound, etc.)
清掃戰場(ㄑㄧㄥ ㄙㄠˋ ㄓㄢˋ ㄔㄤˇ)or (ㄑㄧㄥ ㄙㄠˇ ㄓㄢˋ ㄔㄤˇ)
to mop up the remnants of the enemy on battlefield
清算(ㄑㄧㄥ ㄙㄨㄢˋ)
① to liquidate; liquidation ② to purge
清一色(ㄑㄧㄥ ㄧˊ ㄙㄜˋ)
①(in mah-jong) the series of 13 or 16 blocks belonging to the same pattern which is equivalent to a hand of royal flush in poker and a grand slam in bridge ② uniformly; homogeneous
清議(ㄑㄧㄥ ㄧˋ)
comments among the honest and scholarly
清雅(ㄑㄧㄥ ㄧㄚˇ)
neat and refined (taste, adornment, etc.); graceful: 此爲清雅設計。It is a neat and refined design.
清夜(ㄑㄧㄥ ㄧㄝˋ)
in the still of the night
清夜捫心(ㄑㄧㄥ ㄧㄝˋ ㄇㄣˊ ㄒㄧㄣ)
to make self-examination in the still of the night
清幽(ㄑㄧㄥ ㄧㄡ)
quiet and secluded: 此地十分清幽。This place is quiet and secluded.
清油(ㄑㄧㄥ ㄧㄡˊ)
(dialect) ① vegetable oil ② tea oil
清揚(ㄑㄧㄥ ㄧㄤˊ)
① fine-featured; beautiful or handsome (especially said of eyes and eyebrows) ②(Buddhism) clear and resonant
清玩(ㄑㄧㄥ ㄨㄢˊ)
curios; small decorative articles
清望(ㄑㄧㄥ ㄨㄤˋ)
fine prestige; untarnished reputation

【淺】 2947 ㄑㄧㄢˇ chean qiǎn

1. shallow; superficial
2. easy; simple
3. (color) light
4. (said of land) narrow and small

淺薄(ㄑㄧㄢˇ ㄅㄛˊ)
superficial; superficiality; shallow; meager
淺謀(ㄑㄧㄢˇ ㄇㄡˊ)
a scheme which can be easily detected or discovered
淺明(ㄑㄧㄢˇ ㄇㄧㄥˊ)
easy and clear (readings, ideas, etc.): 他的思想淺明。His ideas are easy and clear.
淺灘(ㄑㄧㄢˇ ㄊㄢ)
a shoal: 該船在淺灘失事。The ship was wrecked on the shoals.
淺陋(ㄑㄧㄢˇ ㄌㄡˋ)
vulgar; crude; shallow
淺陋不堪(ㄑㄧㄢˇ ㄌㄡˋ ㄅㄨˋ ㄎㄢ)
very shallow and detestable
淺海(ㄑㄧㄢˇ ㄏㄞˇ)
a shallow sea; an epeiric sea
淺紅(ㄑㄧㄢˇ ㄏㄨㄥˊ)
light red
淺交(ㄑㄧㄢˇ ㄐㄧㄠ)
not on intimate terms
淺見(ㄑㄧㄢˇ ㄐㄧㄢˋ)
① a superficial or shallow view; a short-sighted view ②(a polite expression) my shallow view: 這是我的淺見。This is my shallow view.
淺近(ㄑㄧㄢˇ ㄐㄧㄣˋ)
easy to understand; fundamental; simple
淺笑(ㄑㄧㄢˇ ㄒㄧㄠˋ)
a smile; to smile
淺鮮(ㄑㄧㄢˇ ㄒㄧㄢˇ)
slight; insignificant
淺顯(ㄑㄧㄢˇ ㄒㄧㄢˇ)
obvious; easily understandable: 這是很淺顯的。It is quite obvious.
淺學(ㄑㄧㄢˇ ㄒㄩㄝˊ)
shallow or superficial learning
淺斟低唱(ㄑㄧㄢˇ ㄓㄣ ㄉㄧ ㄔㄤˋ)
(literally) to drink light and hum low—a scene of a merrymaking party in the company of prostitutes or disreputable women
淺嘗輒止(ㄑㄧㄢˇ ㄔㄤˊ ㄓㄜˊ ㄓˇ)
(literally) to stop after a sip or nibble—to refuse to make a deeper study; do not study further or deeper; to make a superficial study only
淺說(ㄑㄧㄢˇ ㄕㄨㄛ)
a layman's description or talk; an explanation of a theory, etc. in layman's language
淺睡(ㄑㄧㄢˇ ㄕㄨㄟˋ)
a dogsleep 亦作「假寐」
淺人(ㄑㄧㄢˇ ㄖㄣˊ)
a shallow or superficial person; a person without much deep thought
淺色(ㄑㄧㄢˇ ㄙㄜˋ)
light colors: 她穿著一件淺色的衣服。She wore a light-colored dress.
淺而易見(ㄑㄧㄢˇ ㄦˊ ㄧˋ ㄐㄧㄢˋ)
apparent; obvious; easily understood
淺易(ㄑㄧㄢˇ ㄧˋ)
very easy or simple (to learn, understand, etc.)
淺聞(ㄑㄧㄢˇ ㄨㄣˊ)
narrow or shallow learning or experience

【淹】 2948
ㄧㄢ ian yān

1. to submerge; to drown; to soak; to steep in; to flood
2. to delay; to procrastinate
3. to stay; to be stranded
4. (now rarely) deep; well-versed; erudite; profound
5. (now rarely) discomfort caused by perspiration or liquids on skin

淹博(ㄧㄢ ㄅㄛˊ)
erudite; erudition

淹沒(ㄧㄢ ㄇㄛˋ)
① submerged; inundated; drowned ② to waste a talent as if by submerging it

淹通(ㄧㄢ ㄊㄨㄥ)
to be well-versed; to have attained profundity or depth

淹通古今(ㄧㄢ ㄊㄨㄥ ㄍㄨˇ ㄐㄧㄣ)
to be thoroughly acquainted with the old and modern

淹留(ㄧㄢ ㄌㄧㄡˊ)
to stay for a long period

淹該(ㄧㄢ ㄍㄞ)
erudite and well-versed

淹貫(ㄧㄢ ㄍㄨㄢˋ)
well-versed; widely-read

淹滯(ㄧㄢ ㄓˋ)
talented persons holding inferior posts

淹遲(ㄧㄢ ㄔˊ)
slow; dilatory

淹沈(ㄧㄢ ㄔㄣˊ)
① to be bed-ridden for a long time ② to procrastinate

淹識(ㄧㄢ ㄕˋ)
profundity; erudition

淹潤(ㄧㄢ ㄖㄨㄣˋ)
intimate but shy; amiable but timid

淹死(ㄧㄢ ㄙˇ)
drowned: 他跌入海裡淹死了。He fell into the sea and was drowned.

淹雅(ㄧㄢ ㄧㄚˇ)
(said of a scholar of profound learning) deep and refined

【添】 2949
ㄊㄧㄢ tian tiān

1. to add to; to increase; to replenish (stock, etc.)
2. to have a baby

添本(ㄊㄧㄢ ㄅㄣˇ)
to increase capital: 他們決定添本。They decided to increase capital.

添兵(ㄊㄧㄢ ㄅㄧㄥ)
to reinforce

添補(ㄊㄧㄢ ㄅㄨˇ)
to make complete; to complete what is lacking

添飯(ㄊㄧㄢ ㄈㄢˋ)
to have another helping (or bowl) of rice

添墳(ㄊㄧㄢ ㄈㄣˊ)
to add earth to the graves of the deceased, especially on the Tomb-Sweeping Day (清明)

添房(ㄊㄧㄢ ㄈㄤˊ)
(old usage) presents sent to the family which is marrying off a daughter

添福添壽(ㄊㄧㄢ ㄈㄨˊ ㄊㄧㄢ ㄕㄡˋ)
(a well-wishing expression) to add to your happiness and your longevity

添附(ㄊㄧㄢ ㄈㄨˋ)
to enclose; to supplement; to add to; additional

添丁(ㄊㄧㄢ ㄉㄧㄥ)
to beget a son: 他添丁了。He begot a son.

添丁發財(ㄊㄧㄢ ㄉㄧㄥ ㄈㄚ ㄘㄞˊ)
May you have an increase in your family and be prosperous by becoming wealthy.

添多(ㄊㄧㄢ ㄉㄨㄛ)
to add more; to increase: 這城市人口添多了。The town is increasing in population.

添改(ㄊㄧㄢ ㄍㄞˇ)
to add and change; to make additions and alterations

添購(ㄊㄧㄢ ㄍㄡˋ)
to purchase; to make additional purchase of: 她添購了許多新衣服。She purchases a lot of new dresses.

添貨(ㄊㄧㄢ ㄏㄨㄛˋ)
(said of a store) to replenish stock

添加(ㄊㄧㄢ ㄐㄧㄚ)
to add to; to increase

添加劑(ㄊㄧㄢ ㄐㄧㄚ ㄐㄧˋ)
(chemistry) an additive

添價(ㄊㄧㄢ ㄐㄧㄚˋ)
to raise the price (of something): 商人添價。Merchants raise prices.

添箱(ㄊㄧㄢ ㄒㄧㄤ)or 添妝(ㄊㄧㄢ ㄓㄨㄤ)
wedding presents sent to the bride's family

添枝添葉(ㄊㄧㄢ ㄓ ㄊㄧㄢ ㄧㄝˋ)or 添枝加葉(ㄊㄧㄢ ㄓ ㄐㄧㄚ ㄧㄝˋ)
(literally) to add branches and leaves—to blow up or embellish a story, report, etc.

添置(ㄊㄧㄢ ㄓˋ)
to purchase additionally: 我要添置家具。I want to buy more furniture.

添製衣服(ㄊㄧㄢ ㄓˋ ㄧ ˙ㄈㄨ)
to make or purchase additional clothes

添註(ㄊㄧㄢ ㄓㄨˋ)
to fill (a blank form, etc.)

添設(ㄊㄧㄢ ㄕㄜˋ)
to set up additionally

添上(ㄊㄧㄢ ˙ㄕㄤ)
① to add to ② besides; in addition to

添造(ㄊㄧㄢ ㄗㄠˋ)
to build more; to construct; to expand

添菜(ㄊㄧㄢ ㄘㄞˋ)
to have additional dishes

添油加醋(ㄊㄧㄢ ㄧㄡˊ ㄐㄧㄚ ㄘㄨˋ)or 添油加醬(ㄊㄧㄢ ㄧㄡˊ ㄐㄧㄚ ㄐㄧㄤˋ)
(literally) to add oil and vinegar—to embellish or blow up a story or report with something which is usually not true

【涴】 2950
ㄨㄛˋ woh wò
to stain; to soil

【淇】 2951
ㄑㄧˊ chyi qí
name of a river in Honan

淇水(ㄑㄧˊ ㄕㄨㄟˇ)
name of a river in Honan

【涮】 2952
ㄕㄨㄢˋ shuann shuàn

1. to rinse (a container, etc.)
2. to boil in a chafing pot
3. to cheat with lies

涮洗(ㄕㄨㄢˋ ㄒㄧˇ)
to rinse

涮羊肉(ㄕㄨㄢˋ ㄧㄤˊ ㄖㄡˋ)or 涮鍋子(ㄕㄨㄢˋ ㄍㄨㄛ ˙ㄗ)
mutton cooked in a chafing pot

【淴】 2953
ㄏㄨ hu hū

the sound of flowing waters
淴浴(ㄏㄨ ㄩˋ)
(dialect) to take a bath

【淼】 2954
ㄇㄧㄠˇ meau miǎo
(said of water) extensive or overwhelming
淼茫(ㄇㄧㄠˇ ㄇㄤˊ) or 淼漫(ㄇㄧㄠˇ ㄇㄢˋ) or 淼淼(ㄇㄧㄠˇ ㄇㄧㄠˇ)
(said of an expanse of water) stretching as far as the eye can see

九畫

【渙】 2955
ㄏㄨㄢˋ huann huàn
1. scattered; dispersed
2. name of a river
渙發(ㄏㄨㄢˋ ㄈㄚ)
high-spirited
渙然(ㄏㄨㄢˋ ㄖㄢˊ)
scattered; dispersed
渙然冰釋(ㄏㄨㄢˋ ㄖㄢˊ ㄅㄧㄥ ㄕˋ)
(said of a grudge, misunderstanding, etc.) to disappear as melting ice; to vanish: 他的疑慮渙然冰釋。His misgivings have melted away.
渙散(ㄏㄨㄢˋ ㄙㄢˋ)
① lacking concentration or organization ② (said of morale) to collapse

【渚】 2956
ㄓㄨˇ juu zhǔ
a sand bar in river

【渟】 2957
ㄊㄧㄥˊ tyng tíng
1. (said of water) not flowing; still
2. (said of water) clear

【渝】 2958
ㄩˊ yu yú
1. to change one's mind
2. another name of Chungking
3. another name of the Chialing River in Szechwan

【減】 2959
ㄐㄧㄢˇ jean jiǎn
1. to decrease; to reduce; to lessen; to diminish; to subtract; to deduct; to cut
2. a Chinese family name
減半(ㄐㄧㄢˇ ㄅㄢˋ)
to reduce to a half
減筆字(ㄐㄧㄢˇ ㄅㄧˇ ㄗˋ)
a simplified Chinese character
減免(ㄐㄧㄢˇ ㄇㄧㄢˇ)
① to mitigate or annul (a punishment) ② to reduce or remit (taxation, etc.)
減法(ㄐㄧㄢˇ ㄈㄚˇ)
(arithmetic) subtraction
減肥(ㄐㄧㄢˇ ㄈㄟˊ)
to reduce (weight); to lose weight
減俸(ㄐㄧㄢˇ ㄈㄥˋ) or 減薪(ㄐㄧㄢˇ ㄒㄧㄣ)
a pay cut; a salary reduction
減低(ㄐㄧㄢˇ ㄉㄧ)
to decrease; to reduce; to lessen; to lower
減退(ㄐㄧㄢˇ ㄊㄨㄟˋ)
to reduce; to fall; to abate; to decrease; to lessen; to diminish
減號(ㄐㄧㄢˇ ㄏㄠˋ)
the minus sign (—)
減緩(ㄐㄧㄢˇ ㄏㄨㄢˇ)
to retard; to slow down
減價(ㄐㄧㄢˇ ㄐㄧㄚˋ)
to cut down prices; to reduce prices; to mark down
減輕(ㄐㄧㄢˇ ㄑㄧㄥ)
to lighten; to lessen; to reduce; to diminish; to mitigate
減去(ㄐㄧㄢˇ ㄑㄩˋ)
to subtract; to deduct; to take away
減息(ㄐㄧㄢˇ ㄒㄧˊ)
to lower interest rate
減刑(ㄐㄧㄢˇ ㄒㄧㄥˊ)
① to commute a sentence ② a commutation of sentence; mitigation of penalty
減產(ㄐㄧㄢˇ ㄔㄢˇ)
to cut production or output; a drop in production or output
減少(ㄐㄧㄢˇ ㄕㄠˇ)
to decrease; to diminish; to lessen; to reduce
減收(ㄐㄧㄢˇ ㄕㄡ)
① a decrease in income or receipt ② a drop in harvest
減省(ㄐㄧㄢˇ ㄕㄥˇ)
to reduce waste; to save; to be frugal; to economize
減數(ㄐㄧㄢˇ ㄕㄨˋ)
(mathematics) subtrahend
減稅(ㄐㄧㄢˇ ㄕㄨㄟˋ)
to reduce, cut, or lower taxes
減弱(ㄐㄧㄢˇ ㄖㄨㄛˋ)
to weaken; to subside; to reduce in strength or intensity: 風勢減弱了。The wind has subsided.
減竈(ㄐㄧㄢˇ ㄗㄠˋ)
to make a deceptive show of weakness or decline, as Sun Pin (孫臏) of the Epoch of Warring States did by leaving fewer and fewer cooking ovens behind as his troops retreated
減租(ㄐㄧㄢˇ ㄗㄨ)
to reduce, cut, or lower rent
減色(ㄐㄧㄢˇ ㄙㄜˋ)
to fade or pale (literally and figuratively); to impair the excellence of
減速(ㄐㄧㄢˇ ㄙㄨˋ)
to slow down; to decelerate
減縮(ㄐㄧㄢˇ ㄙㄨㄛ)
① to retrench ② to abbreviate

【渡】 2960
ㄉㄨˋ duh dù
1. to cross (a river or ocean)
2. a ferry
渡頭(ㄉㄨˋ ㄊㄡˊ)
a ferry
渡輪(ㄉㄨˋ ㄌㄨㄣˊ)
a ferry steamer
渡過難關(ㄉㄨˋ ㄍㄨㄛˋ ㄋㄢˊ ㄍㄨㄢ)
to tide over a difficulty
渡口(ㄉㄨˋ ㄎㄡˇ)
a ferry
渡河(ㄉㄨˋ ㄏㄜˊ)
to cross a river: 我們可以用渡船渡河。We can cross the river by ferry.
渡海(ㄉㄨˋ ㄏㄞˇ)
to sail across a sea
渡航(ㄉㄨˋ ㄏㄤˊ)
to sail across a river or a sea
渡假(ㄉㄨˋ ㄐㄧㄚˋ)
to spend one's holidays
渡江(ㄉㄨˋ ㄐㄧㄤ)
to cross a large river
渡船(ㄉㄨˋ ㄔㄨㄢˊ)
a ferryboat

【渣】 2961
ㄓㄚ ja zhā
dregs; lees; grounds; sediment
渣滓(ㄓㄚ ㄗˇ)

〔水部〕

〔水部〕

dregs; lees; grounds; sediment

渣子(ㄓㄚ ˙ㄗ)or 渣兒(ㄓㄚㄦ)
dregs; lees; grounds; sediment

【渠】 2962 ㄑㄩˊ chyu qú
1. a drain; a channel; a ditch
2. great; deep
3. he; she
4. a Chinese family name

渠輩(ㄑㄩˊ ㄅㄟˋ)
they; them

渠道(ㄑㄩˊ ㄉㄠˋ)
①an irrigation ditch ②a medium of communication; a channel

渠魁(ㄑㄩˊ ㄎㄨㄟˊ)or 渠帥(ㄑㄩˊ ㄕㄨㄞˋ)
chief criminals

【渤】 2963 ㄅㄛˊ bor bó
(said of water) swelling or rising

渤海(ㄅㄛˊ ㄏㄞˇ)
Pohai, a gulf of the Yellow Sea

【渥】 2964 ㄨㄛˋ woh wò
1. to dye
2. great (kindness)

渥丹(ㄨㄛˋ ㄉㄢ)
①to dye red ②deep red; vermilion

渥太華(ㄨㄛˋ ㄊㄞˋ ㄏㄨㄚˊ)
Ottawa, capital of Canada

渥惠(ㄨㄛˋ ㄏㄨㄟˋ)
great kindness; profound benefaction

渥澤(ㄨㄛˋ ㄗㄜˊ)
great kindness; profound benefaction

渥恩(ㄨㄛˋ ㄣ)
profound benefaction; great kindness

渥味(ㄨㄛˋ ㄨㄟˋ)
strong flavor

【渦】 2965 1. ㄨㄛ uo wō
a whirlpool; an eddy

渦電流(ㄨㄛ ㄉㄧㄢˋ ㄌㄧㄡˊ)
eddy current

渦流(ㄨㄛ ㄌㄧㄡˊ)
①(geography) the circular movement of a fluid; a whirling fluid; an eddy ②(physics) eddy current; vortex flow

渦輪發電機(ㄨㄛ ㄌㄨㄣˊ ㄈㄚ ㄉㄧㄢˋ ㄐㄧ)
a turbine generator

渦輪機(ㄨㄛ ㄌㄨㄣˊ ㄐㄧ)
a turbine

渦旋(ㄨㄛ ㄒㄩㄢˊ)
to whirl: 樹葉在風中渦旋。The leaves whirled in the wind.

【渦】 2965 2. ㄍㄨㄛ guo guō
name of a river

渦河(ㄍㄨㄛ ㄏㄜˊ)
name of a river flowing through Anhwei(安徽)

【渭】 2966 ㄨㄟˋ wey wèi
name of a river

渭河(ㄨㄟˋ ㄏㄜˊ)
Wei River, a tributary of the Yellow River

【港】 2967 ㄍㄤˇ gaang gǎng
1. a harbor; a seaport
2. a bay; a gulf
3. short for Hongkong

港幣(ㄍㄤˇ ㄅㄧˋ)
Hongkong currency

港督(ㄍㄤˇ ㄉㄨ)
the governor of Hongkong

港口(ㄍㄤˇ ㄎㄡˇ)
a harbor; a seaport; a port

港九(ㄍㄤˇ ㄐㄧㄡˇ)
Hongkong and Kowloon

港警(ㄍㄤˇ ㄐㄧㄥˇ)
the harbor police

港紙(ㄍㄤˇ ㄓˇ)
paper money circulated in Hongkong

港市(ㄍㄤˇ ㄕˋ)
a port

港澳(ㄍㄤˇ ㄠˋ)
Hongkong and Macao

港務局(ㄍㄤˇ ㄨˋ ㄐㄩˊ)
the harbor bureau

港灣(ㄍㄤˇ ㄨㄢ)
①a harbor ②a bay; a gulf

【渲】 2968 ㄒㄩㄢˋ shiuann xuàn
to color with paint

渲染(ㄒㄩㄢˋ ㄖㄢˇ)
①to color with paint ②to make exaggerated additions in a story or report; to play up

【測】 2969 ㄘㄜˋ tseh cè
to measure; to survey

測不透(ㄘㄜˋ ˙ㄅㄨ ㄊㄡˋ)
hard to understand; incomprehensible; unable to understand; unable to figure out

測地學(ㄘㄜˋ ㄉㄧˋ ㄒㄩㄝˊ)
geodesy

測定(ㄘㄜˋ ㄉㄧㄥˋ)
to determine

測度(ㄘㄜˋ ㄉㄨㄛˊ)
to infer; to speculate; to conjecture; to guess

測雷器(ㄘㄜˋ ㄌㄟˊ ㄑㄧˋ)
a mine detector

測力計(ㄘㄜˋ ㄌㄧˋ ㄐㄧˋ)
a hand-dynamometer 亦作「握力計」

測量(ㄘㄜˋ ㄌㄧㄤˊ)
①geodetic survey ②to survey

測量地形(ㄘㄜˋ ㄌㄧㄤˊ ㄉㄧˋ ㄒㄧㄥˊ)
to survey the topography

測量隊(ㄘㄜˋ ㄌㄧㄤˊ ㄉㄨㄟˋ)
a survey party

測量局(ㄘㄜˋ ㄌㄧㄤˊ ㄐㄩˊ)
a survey office

測量學(ㄘㄜˋ ㄌㄧㄤˊ ㄒㄩㄝˊ)
surveying

測量術(ㄘㄜˋ ㄌㄧㄤˊ ㄕㄨˋ)
geodetic surveying; surveying

測量水深(ㄘㄜˋ ㄌㄧㄤˊ ㄕㄨㄟˇ ㄕㄣ)
to strike soundings

測量員(ㄘㄜˋ ㄌㄧㄤˊ ㄩㄢˊ)
a land surveyor; a surveyor 亦作「測繪員」

測候(ㄘㄜˋ ㄏㄡˋ)
astronomical or meteorological observation

測繪(ㄘㄜˋ ㄏㄨㄟˋ)
to survey and map

測繪員(ㄘㄜˋ ㄏㄨㄟˋ ㄩㄢˊ)
a land surveyor; a surveyor

測謊(ㄘㄜˋ ㄏㄨㄤˇ)
a polygraph test

測謊器(ㄘㄜˋ ㄏㄨㄤˇ ㄑㄧˋ)
a lie detector; a polygraph

測角器(ㄘㄜˋ ㄐㄧㄠˇ ㄑㄧˋ)
a goniometer; a protractor

測徑器(ㄘㄜˋ ㄐㄧㄥˋ ㄑㄧˋ)
calipers

測深器(ㄘㄜˋ ㄕㄣ ㄑㄧˋ)
a sounder

測字(ㄘㄜˋ ㄗˋ)
to tell someone's fortune by analyzing the component

parts of the character he picks at random 亦作「拆字」
測字攤(ㄘㄜˋ ㄗˋ ㄊㄢ)
a curbside stand where a fortuneteller tells customers' fortune by 測字
測驗(ㄘㄜˋ ㄧㄢˋ)
①to test; to examine ②a quiz or test: 老師明天要測驗我們算術。The teacher will give us a test in arithmetic tomorrow.
測音器(ㄘㄜˋ ㄧㄣ ㄑㄧˋ)
a sound locator; an acoustimeter
測圓法(ㄘㄜˋ ㄩㄢˊ ㄈㄚˇ)
cyclometry
測圓器(ㄘㄜˋ ㄩㄢˊ ㄑㄧˋ)
a cyclometer

【渴】2970 ㄎㄜˇ kee kě
1. thirsty
2. to long; to crave; to pine
渴筆(ㄎㄜˇ ㄅㄧˇ)
①a dry brush ②a style in Chinese landscape painting done with a dry brush
渴病(ㄎㄜˇ ㄅㄧㄥˋ)
diabetes
渴慕(ㄎㄜˇ ㄇㄨˋ)
to long for; to aspire after
渴得很(ㄎㄜˇ ·ㄉㄜ ㄏㄣˇ)
very thirsty: 我覺得渴得很。I feel very thirsty.
渴念(ㄎㄜˇ ㄋㄧㄢˋ)
to miss very much; to yearn for
渴求(ㄎㄜˇ ㄑㄧㄡˊ)
to search for earnestly; to crave for
渴想(ㄎㄜˇ ㄒㄧㄤˇ)
to miss very much; to long for; to crave for
渴賞(ㄎㄜˇ ㄕㄤˇ)
eager for a reward
渴睡(ㄎㄜˇ ㄕㄨㄟˋ)
①a doze; a cat nap; to doze ②sleepy
渴死(ㄎㄜˇ ㄙˇ)
extremely thirsty
渴仰(ㄎㄜˇ ㄧㄤˇ)
to adore; to admire
渴望(ㄎㄜˇ ㄨㄤˋ)
to long for; to be thirsty for; to crave for; to aspire after: 他們渴望發財。They aspire after wealth.
渴雨(ㄎㄜˇ ㄩˇ)
(said of land) thirsty for rain
渴欲(ㄎㄜˇ ㄩˋ)
to aspire to

【湃】2971 ㄆㄞˋ pay pài
billowy; turbulent

【湣】2972 ㄇㄧㄣˇ miin mǐn
mixed; confused

【渺】2973 ㄇㄧㄠˇ meau miǎo
1. endlessly long or vast; far
2. tiny; infinitesimal
3. indistinct; blurred
渺不足道(ㄇㄧㄠˇ ·ㄅㄨ ㄗㄨˊ ㄉㄠˋ)
too small for mention
渺漫(ㄇㄧㄠˇ ㄇㄢˋ)
endlessly long or vast
渺茫(ㄇㄧㄠˇ ㄇㄤˊ)
①endlessly vast; boundless ②remote and vague; indistinct
渺渺(ㄇㄧㄠˇ ㄇㄧㄠˇ)
blurred; indistinct
渺乎其微(ㄇㄧㄠˇ ㄏㄨ ㄑㄧˊ ㄨㄟˊ)
too small to be measured; infinitesimal
渺小(ㄇㄧㄠˇ ㄒㄧㄠˇ)
very small; tiny; infinitesimal; insignificant
渺然(ㄇㄧㄠˇ ㄖㄢˊ)
vast; boundless; endless
渺無人跡(ㄇㄧㄠˇ ㄨˊ ㄖㄣˊ ㄐㄧ)
remote and uninhabited

【游】2974 ㄧㄡˊ you yóu
1. to swim; to float; to waft; to drift
2. same as 遊—to wander about
3. part of a river
4. a Chinese family name
游民(ㄧㄡˊ ㄇㄧㄣˊ)
idle people; idlers
游牧(ㄧㄡˊ ㄇㄨˋ)
nomadic
游牧民族(ㄧㄡˊ ㄇㄨˋ ㄇㄧㄣˊ ㄗㄨˊ)
nomadic people; nomads
游目騁懷(ㄧㄡˊ ㄇㄨˋ ㄔㄥˇ ㄏㄨㄞˊ)
to feel spiritual uplift before a thrilling view of nature
游蕩(ㄧㄡˊ ㄉㄤˋ)
to loaf; loafing
游動(ㄧㄡˊ ㄉㄨㄥˋ)
to move about
游談(ㄧㄡˊ ㄊㄢˊ)
①to go canvassing; to canvass ②to play and talk
游離(ㄧㄡˊ ㄌㄧˊ)
(of a radical, valency, nucleus, etc., in chemistry) free; ionization; liberation
游離分子(ㄧㄡˊ ㄌㄧˊ ㄈㄣ ㄗˇ)
one who quits the collective
游宦(ㄧㄡˊ ㄏㄨㄢˋ)
to serve as an official away from home
游擊(ㄧㄡˊ ㄐㄧˊ)
①a military rank in former times ②a guerrilla attack; a hit-and-run attack
游擊隊(ㄧㄡˊ ㄐㄧˊ ㄉㄨㄟˋ)
a guerrilla band; guerrillas
游擊戰(ㄧㄡˊ ㄐㄧˊ ㄓㄢˋ)
a guerrilla warfare
游擊手(ㄧㄡˊ ㄐㄧˊ ㄕㄡˇ)
(baseball) a shortstop
游騎兵(ㄧㄡˊ ㄐㄧˋ ㄅㄧㄥ)
a ranger
游戲(ㄧㄡˊ ㄒㄧˋ)
a game; play (also written 遊戲)
游戲人間(ㄧㄡˊ ㄒㄧˋ ㄖㄣˊ ㄐㄧㄢ)
①to play through life ②a world of fun and frolic
游俠(ㄧㄡˊ ㄒㄧㄚˊ)
a traveling swordsman; a traveling champion of justice
游學(ㄧㄡˊ ㄒㄩㄝˊ)
to study in a strange land
游塵(ㄧㄡˊ ㄔㄣˊ)
①floating particles of dust ②trivial things
游食(ㄧㄡˊ ㄕˊ)
to live like a parasite
游士(ㄧㄡˊ ㄕˋ)
a free-lancing scholar
游手好閒(ㄧㄡˊ ㄕㄡˇ ㄏㄠˋ ㄒㄧㄢˊ)
loitering about and doing nothing; loafing 亦作「遊手好閒」
游山玩水(ㄧㄡˊ ㄕㄢ ㄨㄢˊ ㄕㄨㄟˇ)
to roam in hills and play with water
游說(ㄧㄡˊ ㄕㄨㄟˋ)
to lobby; to canvass (for a cause, project, etc.); to drum up support
游刃有餘(ㄧㄡˊ ㄖㄣˋ ㄧㄡˇ ㄩˊ)
more than capable of doing something; highly competent

〔水部〕

游資(ㄧㄡˊ ㄗ)
idle capital; idle money
游子(ㄧㄡˊ ㄗˇ)
① an ion ② a wandering son
游子思親(ㄧㄡˊ ㄗˇ ㄙ ㄑㄧㄣ)
A wandering son thinks of his parents.
游辭(ㄧㄡˊ ㄘˊ)
① unfounded remarks; a groundless statement ② a joke; a jest
游絲(ㄧㄡˊ ㄙ)
gossamer
游移不定(ㄧㄡˊ ㄧˊ ㄅㄨˋ ㄉㄧㄥˋ)
undecided; wavering; hesitating; vacillating
游移其詞(ㄧㄡˊ ㄧˊ ㄑㄧˊ ㄘˊ)
to hesitate in words
游弋 or 游奕(ㄧㄡˊ ㄧˋ)
(said of naval vessels) to patrol
游言(ㄧㄡˊ ㄧㄢˊ)
unfounded remarks; rumors
游泳(ㄧㄡˊ ㄩㄥˇ)or 游水(ㄧㄡˊ ㄕㄨㄟˇ)
swimming
游泳池(ㄧㄡˊ ㄩㄥˇ ㄔˊ)
a swimming pool
游泳衣(ㄧㄡˊ ㄩㄥˇ ㄧ)
a swimming suit

【渾】 2975 1. ㄏㄨㄣˊ hwen hún

1. entire; complete
2. to blend; to merge
3. muddy; turbid

渾名(ㄏㄨㄣˊ ㄇㄧㄥˊ)
a nickname
渾蛋(ㄏㄨㄣˊ ㄉㄢˋ)
"rotten egg"—(abusive language) a blackguard; a wretch; a scoundrel; a bastard; a skunk 亦作「混蛋」
渾天儀(ㄏㄨㄣˊ ㄊㄧㄢ ㄧˊ)
(astronomy) an armillary sphere
渾厚(ㄏㄨㄣˊ ㄏㄡˋ)
①(said of one's character) simple and honest ②(said of writing, painting, etc.) simple and vigorous
渾涵(ㄏㄨㄣˊ ㄏㄢˊ)
to include; to contain; to embrace
渾渾噩噩(ㄏㄨㄣˊ ㄏㄨㄣˊ ㄜˋ ㄜˋ)or 渾噩(ㄏㄨㄣˊ ㄜˋ)
① simple and honest ② ignorant; muddle-headed
渾家(ㄏㄨㄣˊ ㄐㄧㄚ)
① the whole family ②(a polite expression) my wife
渾球(ㄏㄨㄣˊ ㄑㄧㄡˊ)
a zany
渾象(ㄏㄨㄣˊ ㄒㄧㄤˋ)
(astronomy) a celestial globe
渾濁(ㄏㄨㄣˊ ㄓㄨㄛˊ)
turbid; muddy
渾成(ㄏㄨㄣˊ ㄔㄥˊ)
to blend or merge into (something new)
渾身(ㄏㄨㄣˊ ㄕㄣ)
one's entire body; from head to toe: 他渾身都是傷。He was wounded from head to toe.
渾身解數(ㄏㄨㄣˊ ㄕㄣ ㄐㄧㄝˇ ㄕㄨˋ)
① every means of solution ② charm (of women)
渾身是膽(ㄏㄨㄣˊ ㄕㄣ ㄕˋ ㄉㄢˇ)
very daring; fearless
渾水(ㄏㄨㄣˊ ㄕㄨㄟˇ)
muddy water
渾水摸魚(ㄏㄨㄣˊ ㄕㄨㄟˇ ㄇㄛ ㄩˊ)
to fish in troubled waters
渾然(ㄏㄨㄣˊ ㄖㄢˊ)
① completely: 我渾然不覺冷。I don't feel cold at all. ② without leaving a trace
渾然一體(ㄏㄨㄣˊ ㄖㄢˊ ㄧ ㄊㄧˇ)
a unified entity; an integral whole
渾人(ㄏㄨㄣˊ ㄖㄣˊ)
an unreasonable fellow
渾似(ㄏㄨㄣˊ ㄙˋ)
as if; as though; very much alike
渾圓(ㄏㄨㄣˊ ㄩㄢˊ)
① tactful; sophisticated ② a sphere ③ perfectly round

【渾】 2975 2. ㄏㄨㄣˋ huenn hùn

chaotic; confused; messy
渾沌(ㄏㄨㄣˋ ㄉㄨㄣˋ)
chaos; confusion; mess
渾沌初開(ㄏㄨㄣˋ ㄉㄨㄣˋ ㄔㄨ ㄎㄞ)
when the universe was taking shape
渾天儀(ㄏㄨㄣˋ ㄊㄧㄢ ㄧˊ)
a celestial globe; an armillary sphere

【湄】 2976 ㄇㄟˊ mei méi

shore; bank; the margin (of the water)
湄公河(ㄇㄟˊ ㄍㄨㄥ ㄏㄜˊ)
the Mekong River

【湊】 2977 (凑)ㄘㄡˋ tsow cöu

1. to put together
2. to raise (fund)
3. to happen by chance
4. to move close to; to press near

湊不齊(ㄘㄡˋ ˙ㄅㄨ ㄑㄧˊ)
① unable to gather enough people together for a game ② unable to get all the parts together to form the whole
湊不出(ㄘㄡˋ ˙ㄅㄨ ㄔㄨ)
unable to get a necessary sum of money ready; unable to raise the amount of (money)
湊分子(ㄘㄡˋ ㄈㄣˋ ˙ㄗ)
to raise money from among several people for a joint gift or a social party
湊膽子(ㄘㄡˋ ㄉㄢˇ ˙ㄗ)
to seek company so as to lessen fear or to boost courage
湊攏(ㄘㄡˋ ㄌㄨㄥˇ)
to manage to collect or gather together
湊空兒(ㄘㄡˋ ㄎㄨㄥˋㄦ)
to take advantage of leisure to do something
湊合(ㄘㄡˋ ˙ㄏㄜ)
① to manage to collect or gather together ② to make do with what is available ③ to improvise ④ not too bad; passable
湊集(ㄘㄡˋ ㄐㄧˊ)
to scrape together; to manage to gather or collect together
湊近(ㄘㄡˋ ㄐㄧㄣˋ)
to get near; to approach; to come closer
湊齊(ㄘㄡˋ ㄑㄧˊ)
① to manage to line up enough people for a game ② to manage to collect all the parts to form the whole
湊巧(ㄘㄡˋ ㄑㄧㄠˇ)
by chance; by coincidence: 我湊巧遇到他。I met him by chance.
湊趣兒(ㄘㄡˋ ㄑㄩˋㄦ)

①to make fun; to poke fun: 別拿他湊趣兒。Don't poke fun at him. ②to cater to another's taste

湊成(ㄘㄡˋ ㄔㄥˊ)
to succeed in putting together

湊數(ㄘㄡˋ ㄕㄨˋ)
①to make up the proper number ②to play second fiddle; to play an unimportant role

湊熱鬧(ㄘㄡˋ ㄖㄜˋ ·ㄋㄠ)
①to take part in merriment; to help make merry ②to add trouble to

湊在一起(ㄘㄡˋ ㄗㄞˋ ㄧˋ ㄑㄧˇ)
①to put together ②(said of people) to gang up; to team up

湊足(ㄘㄡˋ ㄗㄨˊ)
①to manage to raise enough money for a purpose ②to manage to line up enough people for a game

【湎】 2978
ㄇㄧㄢˇ mean miǎn
1. drunk
2. unaware
3. changing

湎於酒(ㄇㄧㄢˇ ㄩˊ ㄐㄧㄡˇ)
to be addicted to intoxicants

【湍】 2979
ㄊㄨㄢ tuan tuān
rapidly flowing

湍瀨(ㄊㄨㄢ ㄌㄞˋ)
shallow rapids

湍流(ㄊㄨㄢ ㄌㄧㄡˊ)
rapids; torrent; swift current: 他逆著湍流游泳。He swam against the swift current.

湍激(ㄊㄨㄢ ㄐㄧ)
(said of water) rapid

湍急(ㄊㄨㄢ ㄐㄧˊ)
(said of water) swift; rapid: 水流湍急。The current is rapid.

【湓】 2980
ㄆㄣˊ pern pén
name of a river in Kiangsi

湓水(ㄆㄣˊ ㄕㄨㄟˇ)
name of a river in Kiangsi

【湔】 2981
ㄐㄧㄢ jian jiān
to wash

湔洗(ㄐㄧㄢ ㄒㄧˇ)
to wash

湔雪(ㄐㄧㄢ ㄒㄩㄝˇ)
to wipe away (disgrace, etc.)

湔濯(ㄐㄧㄢ ㄓㄨㄛˊ)
to wash

【湜】 2982
ㄕˊ shyr shí
(said of water) transparent

【湧】 2983
ㄩㄥˇ yeong yǒng
1. to gush; to pour
2. to rise

湧進(ㄩㄥˇ ㄐㄧㄣˋ)
to swarm into; to sweep into: 人們湧進電影院。People swarmed into the cinema.

湧泉(ㄩㄥˇ ㄑㄩㄢˊ)
a fountain; a spring

湧現(ㄩㄥˇ ㄒㄧㄢˋ)
to crop up (in one's mind, etc.); to emerge: 新問題不斷湧現。New problems are constantly emerging.

湧至(ㄩㄥˇ ㄓˋ)
to arrive like a flood

湧出(ㄩㄥˇ ㄔㄨ)
to well out; to spring out

湧上來(ㄩㄥˇ ㄕㄤˋ ·ㄌㄞ)
①to well up: 她的眼淚湧上來。Tears welled up in her eyes. ②to come in a sweep

湧上心來(ㄩㄥˇ ㄕㄤˋ ㄒㄧㄣ ·ㄌㄞ)
to come up in the mind like a ground swell

【湖】 2984
ㄏㄨˊ hwu hú
1. a lake
2. a Chinese family name

湖泊(ㄏㄨˊ ㄅㄛˊ)
lakes

湖北(ㄏㄨˊ ㄅㄟˇ)
Hupeh Province

湖筆(ㄏㄨˊ ㄅㄧˇ)
a writing brush made at Huchow(湖州), Chekiang

湖邊(ㄏㄨˊ ㄅㄧㄢ) or 湖畔(ㄏㄨˊ ㄆㄢˋ)
beside the lake; the shore of a lake

湖畔詩人(ㄏㄨˊ ㄆㄢˋ ㄕ ㄖㄣˊ)
the Lake Poets (in English literature)

湖南(ㄏㄨˊ ㄋㄢˊ)
Hunan Province

湖光山色(ㄏㄨˊ ㄍㄨㄤ ㄕㄢ ㄙㄜˋ)
the natural beauty of lakes and mountains

湖廣(ㄏㄨˊ ㄍㄨㄤˇ)
name of an ancient province covering parts of Hunan, Hupeh, Kwangtung and Kwangsi

湖廣熟天下足(ㄏㄨˊ ㄍㄨㄤˇ ㄕㄡˊ ㄊㄧㄢ ㄒㄧㄚˋ ㄗㄨˊ)
When Hukwang has a bumper crop, the country will be free from hunger.

湖海之士(ㄏㄨˊ ㄏㄞˇ ㄓ ㄕˋ)
a man with a great mind

湖心(ㄏㄨˊ ㄒㄧㄣ)
the middle of a lake

湖心亭(ㄏㄨˊ ㄒㄧㄣ ㄊㄧㄥˊ)
a pavilion in the middle of a lake

湖沼(ㄏㄨˊ ㄓㄠˇ)
lakes and marshes

湖州(ㄏㄨˊ ㄓㄡ)
Huchow, an old prefecture in Chekiang

湖縐(ㄏㄨˊ ㄓㄡˋ)
a kind of silk produced at Huchow(湖州), Chekiang

湖水(ㄏㄨˊ ㄕㄨㄟˇ)
lake water: 湖水甚清。The lake water is clear.

湖澤(ㄏㄨˊ ㄗㄜˊ)
lakes

湖煙(ㄏㄨˊ ㄧㄢ)
mist on a lake

【湘】 2985
ㄒㄧㄤ shiang xiāng
1. name of a river flowing through Hunan
2. an alternative name of Hunan

湘妃(ㄒㄧㄤ ㄈㄟ)
the two wives of the legendary Emperor Shun (舜)

湘妃竹(ㄒㄧㄤ ㄈㄟ ㄓㄨˊ)
speckled bamboo

湘夫人(ㄒㄧㄤ ㄈㄨ ㄖㄣˊ)
the nymph of the Hsiang River

湘女多情(ㄒㄧㄤ ㄋㄩˇ ㄉㄨㄛ ㄑㄧㄥˊ)
Girls of Hunan are affectionate.

湘簾(ㄒㄧㄤ ㄌㄧㄢˊ)
a bamboo curtain made of speckled bamboo

湘江(ㄒㄧㄤ ㄐㄧㄤ) or 湘水(ㄒㄧㄤ ㄕㄨㄟˇ)
the Hsiang River, flowing through Hunan

湘君(ㄒㄧㄤ ㄐㄩㄣ)

〔水部〕

〔水部〕

a deity of the Hsiang River in Hunan
湘軍(ㄒㄧㄤ ㄐㄩㄣ)
the army organized by Tseng Kuo-fan (曾國藩) toward the end of the Ching Dynasty to put down the Taiping Rebellion, so called because the soldiers were mostly from Hunan.
湘繡(ㄒㄧㄤ ㄒㄧㄡˋ)
embroideries from Hunan; Hunan-style embroideries
湘竹(ㄒㄧㄤ ㄓㄨˊ)
speckled bamboo
湘中(ㄒㄧㄤ ㄓㄨㄥ)
an alternative name of Hunan

【湛】 2986
ㄓㄢˋ jann zhàn
1. dewy
2. deep; profound
3. same as 沈—to sink
4. a Chinese family name
湛藍(ㄓㄢˋ ㄌㄢˊ)
dark blue; azure
湛新(ㄓㄢˋ ㄒㄧㄣ)
brand-new: 這是湛新的車子。This is a brand-new car.
湛湛(ㄓㄢˋ ㄓㄢˋ)
① dewy ② deep; profound
湛然(ㄓㄢˋ ㄖㄢˊ)
①(said of water) transparent: 水清湛然。The water is clean and transparent. ② quiet; calm
湛恩(ㄓㄢˋ ㄣ)
great kindness
湛憂(ㄓㄢˋ ㄧㄡ)
deep worry

【湮】 2987
ㄧㄣ in yīn
1. to bury
2. to block
3. long (in time)
湮沒(ㄧㄣ ㄇㄛˋ)
to bury or be buried
湮沒不彰(ㄧㄣ ㄇㄛˋ ㄅㄨˋ ㄓㄤ)
to fall into the shade
湮沒無聞(ㄧㄣ ㄇㄛˋ ㄨˊ ㄨㄣˊ)
to remain unknown; to remain obscure; to pass into oblivion
湮滅(ㄧㄣ ㄇㄧㄝˋ)
to bury; to destroy (evidence): 他們湮滅證據。They destroyed the evidence.
湮沈(ㄧㄣ ㄔㄣˊ)
to have no chance to rise in the world
湮阨(ㄧㄣ ㄜˋ)
clogged; blocked
湮遠(ㄧㄣ ㄩㄢˇ)
very long (in time)

【湫】 2988
1. ㄐㄧㄡ jiou jiū
1. name of a river in Kansu Province
2. a small pond

【湫】 2988
2. ㄐㄧㄠˇ jeau jiǎo
damp and narrow
湫隘(ㄐㄧㄠˇ ㄞˋ)
a damp and narrow place

【湯】 2989
1. ㄊㄤ tang tāng
1. hot water
2. soup; broth
3. a Chinese family name
湯餅筵(ㄊㄤ ㄅㄧㄥˇ ㄧㄢˊ)
a dinner party given on the third day after the birth of a baby 亦作「湯餅之喜」
湯婆子(ㄊㄤ ㄆㄛˊ ˙ㄗ)
a hot-water bedwarmer, made of copper or pewter 亦作「湯壺」
湯麪(ㄊㄤ ㄇㄧㄢˋ)
noodles with soup
湯沐(ㄊㄤ ㄇㄨˋ)
to bathe; to take a bath: 他每晨湯沐。He takes a bath every morning.
湯頭(ㄊㄤ ㄊㄡˊ)
a prescription of herbal medicines
湯糰(ㄊㄤ ㄊㄨㄢˊ)
balls of glutinous rice
湯鍋(ㄊㄤ ㄍㄨㄛ)
a soup pot
湯火(ㄊㄤ ㄏㄨㄛˇ)
hot water and burning fire —dangerous things
湯鑊(ㄊㄤ ㄏㄨㄛˋ)
a cauldron for boiling criminals in ancient China
湯池(ㄊㄤ ㄔˊ)
①(literally) a city moat filled with boiling water —impenetrable defense works ② hot springs
湯池之固(ㄊㄤ ㄔˊ ㄓ ㄍㄨˋ)
impenetrable defense works
湯匙(ㄊㄤ ㄔˊ)
a spoon
湯勺(ㄊㄤ ㄕㄠˊ)
a soup ladle
湯水(ㄊㄤ ㄕㄨㄟˇ)
① name of a river in Honan ② soup ③ financial means ④ troublesome
湯若望(ㄊㄤ ㄖㄨㄛˋ ㄨㄤˋ)
Joannes Adam Schall von Bell (1591-1666), German Jesuit missionary who introduced the solar calendar to China
湯藥(ㄊㄤ ㄧㄠˋ)
decoction of Chinese medicine 亦作「湯液」
湯武(ㄊㄤ ㄨˇ)
Tang and Wu, founders of the Shang and Chou dynasties respectively
湯武革命(ㄊㄤ ㄨˇ ㄍㄜˊ ㄇㄧㄥˋ)
the revolutions by which Tang founded the Dynasty Shang and Wu founded the Dynasty Chou
湯碗(ㄊㄤ ㄨㄢˇ)
a large bowl for holding soup
湯圓(ㄊㄤ ㄩㄢˊ)
balls of glutinous rice

【湯】 2989
2. ㄕㄤ shang shāng
(said of water) flowing
湯湯(ㄕㄤ ㄕㄤ)
(said of water) flowing turbulently

【湟】 2990
ㄏㄨㄤˊ hwang huáng
1. a mean, dirty place
2. name of a river

【渫】 2991
ㄒㄧㄝˋ shieh xiè
to remove; to eliminate

【湲】 2992
ㄩㄢˊ yuan yuán
(said of water) flowing

【湑】 2993
ㄒㄩˇ sheu xǔ
luxuriant; rich

【湢】 2994
ㄅㄧˋ bih bì
1. a bathroom
2. neat; orderly

【渨】 2995
ㄨㄟ uei wēi

a bend on a river

【渰】 2996 ㄧㄢˇ yean yǎn
(said of clouds) forming or rising

【湉】 2997 ㄊㄧㄢ tyan tián
to flow placidly

十畫

【溫】 2998 (温) ㄨㄣ uen wēn
1. warm; mild; lukewarm; to warm: 請把酒溫一下。Please warm up the wine.
2. to review; to revise
3. temperature
4. a Chinese family name

溫飽(ㄨㄣ ㄅㄠˇ)
adequately fed and clothed
溫帶(ㄨㄣ ㄉㄞˋ)
the Temperate Zone
溫帶氣候(ㄨㄣ ㄉㄞˋ ㄑㄧˋ ㄏㄡˋ)
temperate climate
溫帶植物(ㄨㄣ ㄉㄞˋ ㄓˊ ㄨˋ)
the flora of the Temperate Zone
溫度(ㄨㄣ ㄉㄨˋ)
temperature
溫度計(ㄨㄣ ㄉㄨˋ ㄐㄧˋ)or 溫度表(ㄨㄣ ㄉㄨˋ ㄅㄧㄠˇ)
a thermometer: 華氏溫度表 the Fahrenheit thermometer 攝氏溫度表 the Celsius thermometer
溫尼伯(ㄨㄣ ㄋㄧˊ ㄅㄛˊ)
Winnipeg, a city in Canada
溫暖(ㄨㄣ ㄋㄨㄢˇ)
warm; warmth: 這件外衣可以使你保持溫暖。This coat will keep you warm.
溫良(ㄨㄣ ㄌㄧㄤˊ)
good-natured
溫哥華(ㄨㄣ ㄍㄜ ㄏㄨㄚˊ)
Vancouver, a city in Canada
溫故知新(ㄨㄣ ㄍㄨˋ ㄓ ㄒㄧㄣ)
to learn new things by reviewing old things
溫恭自虛(ㄨㄣ ㄍㄨㄥ ㄗˋ ㄒㄩ)
gentle and modest
溫開水(ㄨㄣ ㄎㄞ ㄕㄨㄟˇ)
lukewarm boiled water
溫炕(ㄨㄣ ㄎㄤˋ)
a brick or earthen bed warmed by a fire underneath (in North China)
溫和(ㄨㄣ ㄏㄜˊ)
gentle; mild; temperate; warm: 天氣還溫和呢。The weather is still warm.
溫和派(ㄨㄣ ㄏㄜˊ ㄆㄞˋ)
the moderate faction; a moderate (as opposed to a radical)
溫厚(ㄨㄣ ㄏㄡˋ)
gentle and sincere
溫酒(ㄨㄣ ㄐㄧㄡˇ)
to heat wine; lukewarm wine
溫居(ㄨㄣ ㄐㄩ)
① to congratulate someone on moving into a new residence ② a housewarming
溫覺(ㄨㄣ ㄐㄩㄝˊ)
the faculty to feel hot or cold
溫情(ㄨㄣ ㄑㄧㄥˊ)
kindness; warm-heartedness; a warm feelings
溫情主義(ㄨㄣ ㄑㄧㄥˊ ㄓㄨˇ ㄧˋ)
① paternalism ② soft-heartedness; excessive tender-heartedness
溫泉(ㄨㄣ ㄑㄩㄢˊ)
a hot spring; a mineral spring; a spa
溫泉浴(ㄨㄣ ㄑㄩㄢˊ ㄩˋ)
a hot-spring bath
溫習(ㄨㄣ ㄒㄧˊ)
to review (what has been learned): 他溫習功課。He reviews his lessons.
溫血動物(ㄨㄣ ㄒㄧㄝˇ ㄉㄨㄥˋ ㄨˋ)
a warm-blooded animal
溫馨(ㄨㄣ ㄒㄧㄣ)
warm and fragrant
溫煦(ㄨㄣ ㄒㄩˇ)
mild and warm
溫馴(ㄨㄣ ㄒㄩㄣˊ)
easily controlled; docile; meek; tame
溫州(ㄨㄣ ㄓㄡ)
Wenchow, Chekiang
溫州灣(ㄨㄣ ㄓㄡ ㄨㄢ)
Wenchow Bay (off Wenchow, Chekiang)
溫差(ㄨㄣ ㄔㄚ)
difference in temperature; the range of temperature
溫牀(ㄨㄣ ㄔㄨㄤˊ)
a hotbed
溫室(ㄨㄣ ㄕˋ)
a greenhouse
溫書(ㄨㄣ ㄕㄨ)
to read familiar books again
溫水(ㄨㄣ ㄕㄨㄟˇ)
lukewarm water
溫水浴(ㄨㄣ ㄕㄨㄟˇ ㄩˋ)
a warm water bath; a hot water bath
溫順(ㄨㄣ ㄕㄨㄣˋ)
gentle; good-natured; docile; obedient: 她常常騎溫順的馬。She always rides a docile horse.
溫柔(ㄨㄣ ㄖㄡˊ)
warm and tender; sweet-natured
溫柔敦厚(ㄨㄣ ㄖㄡˊ ㄉㄨㄣ ㄏㄡˋ)
tender and gentle
溫柔鄉(ㄨㄣ ㄖㄡˊ ㄒㄧㄤ)
(literally) land of the tender — ① a brothel ② the enthralling experience of enjoying female charms in an intimate manner
溫潤(ㄨㄣ ㄖㄨㄣˋ)
① mild and smooth ② beautiful and tender
溫辭(ㄨㄣ ㄘˊ)
mild or gentle words
溫存(ㄨㄣ ㄘㄨㄣˊ)
tender; loving; caressing
溫存話兒(ㄨㄣ ㄘㄨㄣˊ ㄏㄨㄚˋㄦ)
loving words
溫雅(ㄨㄣ ㄧㄚˇ)
gentle and graceful
溫顏(ㄨㄣ ㄧㄢˊ)
a happy and agreeable look
溫婉(ㄨㄣ ㄨㄢˇ)
gentle; obedient
溫文(ㄨㄣ ㄨㄣˊ)
gentle and polite
溫文爾雅(ㄨㄣ ㄨㄣˊ ㄦˇ ㄧㄚˇ)
gentle and graceful

【源】 2999 ㄩㄢˊ yuan yuán
a source; a head (of a stream)

源頭(ㄩㄢˊ ㄊㄡˊ)
a head or a source (of a stream)
源流(ㄩㄢˊ ㄌㄧㄡˊ)
full particulars; all the details; the whole story
源清流清(ㄩㄢˊ ㄑㄧㄥ ㄌㄧㄡˊ ㄑㄧㄥ)or 源清流潔(ㄩㄢˊ ㄑㄧㄥ ㄌㄧㄡˊ ㄐㄧㄝˊ)
(literally) If a stream is

〔水部〕

clear, it is because the source is clear.—If the leader is good, his followers will be good.

源泉(ㄩㄢˊ ㄑㄩㄢˊ)
an original source; a fountainhead

源水(ㄩㄢˊ ㄕㄨㄟˇ)
a fountainhead

源委 or 原委(ㄩㄢˊ ㄨㄟˇ)
full particulars; all the details; the whole story: 請你告訴我源委。Please let me know all the details.

源源本本 or 元元本本(ㄩㄢˊ ㄩㄢˊ ㄅㄣˇ ㄅㄣˇ)
from beginning to end; without omissions; the whole story

源源不絕(ㄩㄢˊ ㄩㄢˊ ㄅㄨˋ ㄐㄩㄝˊ)
to continue without end

源源而來(ㄩㄢˊ ㄩㄢˊ ㄦˊ ㄌㄞˊ)
to come in an endless flow

源遠流長(ㄩㄢˊ ㄩㄢˇ ㄌㄧㄡˊ ㄔㄤˊ)
(literally) to have a long course originating in a remote source—to have a long history

【溘】 3000
ㄎㄜˋ keh kè

sudden; abrupt; unexpected

溘謝(ㄎㄜˋ ㄒㄧㄝˋ)
to die suddenly

溘逝(ㄎㄜˋ ㄕˋ)or 溘然長逝(ㄎㄜˋ ㄖㄢˊ ㄔㄤˊ ㄕˋ)
to die suddenly: 他溘然長逝。He died suddenly.

溘然(ㄎㄜˋ ㄖㄢˊ)
suddenly; unexpectedly; all of a sudden

【溟】 3001
ㄇㄧㄥˊ ming míng

1. drizzle
2. vast; boundless
3. the sea; the ocean

溟漭(ㄇㄧㄥˊ ㄇㄤˇ)
endlessly vast; boundless

溟濛(ㄇㄧㄥˊ ㄇㄥˊ)
① drizzle ② gloomy; dim; obscure

溟溟(ㄇㄧㄥˊ ㄇㄧㄥˊ)
① drizzling ② gloomy; dim; dark

溟島(ㄇㄧㄥˊ ㄉㄠˇ)
an island in the sea

溟海(ㄇㄧㄥˊ ㄏㄞˇ)
a dark sea

溟池(ㄇㄧㄥˊ ㄔˊ)
the northern sea

【溝】 3002
ㄍㄡ gou gōu

1. a ditch; a waterway; a moat
2. a groove; a rut

溝瀆(ㄍㄡ ㄉㄨˊ)
a ditch; a channel; a drain

溝通(ㄍㄡ ㄊㄨㄥ)
to bring about an unobstructed interflow of (feelings, ideas, etc.); to act as an intermediary for the promotion of mutual understanding; to facilitate the flow of (culture, etc.)

溝壑(ㄍㄡ ㄏㄨㄛˋ)
a valley, gorge, or canyon

溝渠(ㄍㄡ ㄑㄩˊ)
a ditch; a drain; a channel; a gutter

溝洫(ㄍㄡ ㄒㄩˋ)
an irrigation ditch

溝中瘠(ㄍㄡ ㄓㄨㄥ ㄐㄧˊ)
a poor person found dead in a ditch

溝子(ㄍㄡ ·ㄗ)or 溝兒(ㄍㄡㄦ)
① a ditch; a drain; a channel; a gutter ② a groove

【溜】 3003
1. ㄌㄧㄡˋ liow liù

1. rapids
2. a row; a column
3. surroundings; neighborhood

溜溜 or 遛遛(ㄌㄧㄡˋ ·ㄌㄧㄡ)
① to take a stroll; to stroll; to ramble: 我們溜溜去。Let's take a stroll. ② the murmur of flowing waters

溜兒(ㄌㄧㄡˋㄦ)
a row; a column

【溜】 3003
2. ㄌㄧㄡ liou liū

1. to go secretly and quietly
2. to slip; to slide

溜邊兒(ㄌㄧㄡ ㄅㄧㄚㄦ)
to go stealthily

溜冰(ㄌㄧㄡ ㄅㄧㄥ)
to skate; skating

溜冰鞋(ㄌㄧㄡ ㄅㄧㄥ ㄒㄧㄝˊ)
a pair of skates; skating shoes; roller skates: 他買了一雙溜冰鞋。He bought a pair of skates.

溜冰場(ㄌㄧㄡ ㄅㄧㄥ ㄔㄤˇ)or(ㄌㄧㄡ ㄅㄧㄥ ㄔㄤˊ)
a skating rink

溜門子的(ㄌㄧㄡ ㄇㄣˊ ·ㄗ ·ㄉㄜ)
a sneak thief

溜達(ㄌㄧㄡ ·ㄉㄚ)or(ㄌㄧㄡˋ ·ㄉㄚ)
to stroll; to ramble: 我們在鎮上溜達溜達。We rambled about the town.

溜光(ㄌㄧㄡ ㄍㄨㄤ)
① smooth ② (said of people) to have all gone away

溜口(ㄌㄧㄡ ㄎㄡˇ)
a slip of the tongue; to divulge a secret unintentionally; to blurt out

溜滑(ㄌㄧㄡ ㄏㄨㄚˊ)
① slippery ② cunning; crafty

溜滑板(ㄌㄧㄡ ㄏㄨㄚˊ ㄅㄢˇ)
to skate with a skateboard

溜之大吉(ㄌㄧㄡ ㄓ ㄉㄚˋ ㄐㄧˊ)
to leave stealthily; to leave without notifying others; to slip out

溜走(ㄌㄧㄡ ㄗㄡˇ)
to leave stealthily; to slip away: 他偷偷地溜走沒被人看見。He slipped away without being seen.

【準】 3004
ㄓㄨㄣˇ joen zhǔn

1. level; even
2. a rule; a criterion; a standard; accurate; accuracy: 你的工作未達標準。Your work is below (the) standard.
3. to aim; to sight
4. would-be (bride, son-in-law, etc.); to-be
5. (law) quasi-
6. certainly: 他明天準去。He'll certainly be there tomorrow.

準兒(ㄓㄨㄜˇㄦ)
certain; sure: 這種天氣沒準兒。No one can be sure about this kind of weather.

準備(ㄓㄨㄣˇ ㄅㄟˋ)
① to prepare; to get ready; preparation: 妳準備好了嗎? Are you ready? ② to plan: 他們準備下星期三開始試驗。They plan to start the experiment next Wednesday.

準備活動(ㄓㄨㄣˇ ㄅㄟˋ ㄏㄨㄛˊ ㄉㄨㄥˋ)
a warming-up exercise; a limbering-up exercise

準備金(ㄓㄨㄣˇ ㄅㄟˋ ㄐㄧㄣ)
① preparatory funds ② (banking) reserve

準不準(ㄓㄨㄣˇ ·ㄅㄨ ㄓㄨㄣˇ)

Is it accurate? 或Is it correct? 或 Is it true? 或Does the clock keep good time?

準犯罪(ㄓㄨㄣˇ ㄈㄢˋ ㄗㄨㄟˋ)
(law) quasi-offense

準的(ㄓㄨㄣˇ ㄉㄧˋ)
a standard; a criterion

準定(ㄓㄨㄣˇ ㄉㄧㄥˋ)
definitely 亦作「一定」

準頭(ㄓㄨㄣˇ ·ㄊㄡ)
accuracy; a standard: 他做事沒有準頭。There is no standard in what he does.

準禁治產者(ㄓㄨㄣˇ ㄐㄧㄣˋ ㄓˋ ㄔㄢˇ ㄓㄜˇ)
(law) a quasi-incompetent person

準據(ㄓㄨㄣˇ ㄐㄩˋ)
a basis: 這信念沒任何科學的準據。The belief has no scientific basis whatever.

準確(ㄓㄨㄣˇ ㄑㄩㄝˋ)
correct; accurate; precise; exact: 這句子不大準確。This sentence is not quite correct.

準確性(ㄓㄨㄣˇ ㄑㄩㄝˋ ㄒㄧㄥˋ)
accuracy

準新娘(ㄓㄨㄣˇ ㄒㄧㄣ ㄋㄧㄤˊ)
a would-be bride; a bride-to-be

準新郎(ㄓㄨㄣˇ ㄒㄧㄣ ㄌㄤˊ)
a would-be bridegroom; a bridegroom-to-be

準星(ㄓㄨㄣˇ ㄒㄧㄥ)
the front sight (of a gun)

準成(ㄓㄨㄣˇ ㄔㄥˊ)
reliable; dependable

準時(ㄓㄨㄣˇ ㄕˊ)
punctual; punctually; punctuality; on time: 請準時出席。You are requested to come punctually.

準式(ㄓㄨㄣˇ ㄕˋ)
a rule; a regulation; a criterion

準繩(ㄓㄨㄣˇ ㄕㄥˊ)
①(carpenter's) marking line
②a criterion; a standard: 我們學校有很高的教學準繩。Our school has a high standard of teaching.

準則(ㄓㄨㄣˇ ㄗㄜˊ)
a rule; a criterion; a standard

【溢】 3005 ㄧˋ yih yì

1. to flow over; to brim over
2. excessive

溢美(ㄧˋ ㄇㄟˇ)
to praise excessively

溢美之言(ㄧˋ ㄇㄟˇ ㄓ ㄧㄢˊ)
words of fulsome praise

溢滿(ㄧˋ ㄇㄢˇ)
to brim over; to overflow

溢目(ㄧˋ ㄇㄨˋ)
to crowd one's sight; to be too numerous to be fully seen

溢洪道(ㄧˋ ㄏㄨㄥˊ ㄉㄠˋ)
a spillway

溢價(ㄧˋ ㄐㄧㄚˋ)
to soar beyond the original price

溢出(ㄧˋ ㄔㄨ)
to brim over; to flow over; to overflow; to spill over: 這河水溢出兩岸。The river flowed over its banks.

溢收(ㄧˋ ㄕㄡ)
to earn more than planned

溢額(ㄧˋ ㄜˊ)
the amount in excess; excess; overage

溢惡(ㄧˋ ㄜˋ)
to be excessively abusive

溢於言表(ㄧˋ ㄩˊ ㄧㄢˊ ㄅㄧㄠˇ)
(said of emotions or inner feelings) to show clearly in one's utterances and manners

溢譽(ㄧˋ ㄩˋ)
flattery; excessive praises; to flatter; to praise excessively: 別為她的溢譽所騙。Don't be deceived by her flatteries.

【溥】 3006 ㄆㄨˇ puu pǔ

1. great; wide; vast
2. universal

溥博(ㄆㄨˇ ㄅㄛˊ)
inclusive and extensive

溥被(ㄆㄨˇ ㄅㄟˋ)
to spread widely

溥天同慶(ㄆㄨˇ ㄊㄧㄢ ㄊㄨㄥˊ ㄑㄧㄥˋ)
simultaneously celebrated everywhere under the sun; universally celebrated

溥天之下(ㄆㄨˇ ㄊㄧㄢ ㄓ ㄒㄧㄚˋ)
everywhere under the sun

溥儀(ㄆㄨˇ ㄧˊ)
Pu-yi, the last emperor of the Ching Dynasty

溥原(ㄆㄨˇ ㄩㄢˊ)
an extensive plain; a prairie

【溧】 3007 ㄌㄧˋ lih lì

1. name of a river flowing through Anhwei and Kiangsu
2. name of a county in Kiangsu

溧烈(ㄌㄧˋ ㄌㄧㄝˋ)
biting cold

溧水(ㄌㄧˋ ㄕㄨㄟˇ)
name of a county and a river in Kiangsu

【溯】 3008 ㄙㄨˋ suh sù

1. to go upstream; to go against a stream
2. to trace; to recall

溯洄(ㄙㄨˋ ㄏㄨㄟˊ)
to go upstream

溯江而上(ㄙㄨˋ ㄐㄧㄤ ㄦˊ ㄕㄤˋ)
to go upstream in a boat

溯自(ㄙㄨˋ ㄗˋ)
ever since

溯游(ㄙㄨˋ ㄧㄡˊ)
to go upstream

溯源(ㄙㄨˋ ㄩㄢˊ)
to trace back to the source

【溪】 3009 ㄒㄧ shi xī (又讀 ㄑㄧ chi qī)

a mountain stream

溪流(ㄒㄧ ㄌㄧㄡˊ)
a (mountain) stream; a brook

溪谷(ㄒㄧ ㄍㄨˇ)
a valley; a dale; a canyon; a gorge

溪口(ㄒㄧ ㄎㄡˇ)
a town in Chekiang, where President Chiang Kai-shek was born

溪澗(ㄒㄧ ㄐㄧㄢˋ)
a mountain stream

溪水(ㄒㄧ ㄕㄨㄟˇ)
the water of a mountain stream; mountain streams

【溲】 3010 ㄙㄡ sou sōu

1. to urinate
2. to immerse; to soak; to drench

溲便(ㄙㄡ ㄅㄧㄢˋ)
to urinate

溲溺(ㄙㄡ ㄋㄧㄠˋ)
to urinate

溲箕(ㄙㄡ ㄐㄧ)
a basket for washing rice

溲器(ㄙㄡ ㄑㄧˋ)

〔水部〕

a urinal

【溴】 3011 ㄒㄧㄡˋ shiow xiù
bromine
溴化鈉(ㄒㄧㄡˋ ㄏㄨㄚˋ ㄋㄚˋ)
sodium bromide
溴化鉀(ㄒㄧㄡˋ ㄏㄨㄚˋ ㄐㄧㄚˇ)
potassium bromide
溴化氫(ㄒㄧㄡˋ ㄏㄨㄚˋ ㄑㄧㄥ)
hydrogen bromide
溴化銀(ㄒㄧㄡˋ ㄏㄨㄚˋ ㄧㄣˊ)
silver bromide
溴水(ㄒㄧㄡˋ ㄕㄨㄟˇ)
bromine water
溴酸(ㄒㄧㄡˋ ㄙㄨㄢ)
bromic acid

【溷】 3012 ㄏㄨㄣˋ huenn hùn
1. dirty
2. messy
溷跡(ㄏㄨㄣˋ ㄐㄧ)
to conceal
溷汁(ㄏㄨㄣˋ ㄓ)
dirty water; sewage
溷濁(ㄏㄨㄣˋ ㄓㄨㄛˊ)
dirty; muddy
溷廁(ㄏㄨㄣˋ ㄘˋ)
a water closet; a lavatory
溷肴(ㄏㄨㄣˋ ㄧㄠˊ)
messy; confused; chaotic: 他已經溷肴了。He became confused.

【溺】 3013 1. ㄋㄧˋ nih nì
1. to drown
2. to indulge
溺女(ㄋㄧˋ ㄋㄩˇ)
to drown a daughter at birth (in former times when daughters were unwanted in poor families)
溺鬼(ㄋㄧˋ ㄍㄨㄟˇ)
the ghost of the drowned
溺職(ㄋㄧˋ ㄓˊ)
to neglect one's duty
溺志(ㄋㄧˋ ㄓˋ)
to indulge (in an enjoyment, pursuit, etc.)
溺死(ㄋㄧˋ ㄙˇ)or 溺斃(ㄋㄧˋ ㄅㄧˋ)
to be drowned: 那男人溺死了。The man was drowned.
溺愛(ㄋㄧˋ ㄞˋ)
to lavish one's love upon (a child); to pamper: 他溺愛孩子。He pampers his child.
溺於酒色(ㄋㄧˋ ㄩˊ ㄐㄧㄡˇ ㄙㄜˋ)
to indulge in wine and women

【溺】 3013 2. ㄋㄧㄠˋ niaw niào
to urinate
溺褲(ㄋㄧㄠˋ ㄎㄨˋ)
to wet oneself
溺器(ㄋㄧㄠˋ ㄑㄧˋ)
a urinal; a bedpan
溺牀(ㄋㄧㄠˋ ㄔㄨㄤˊ)
to wet the bed
溺尿(ㄋㄧㄠˋ ㄙㄨㄟ)or(ㄋㄧㄠˋ ㄋㄧㄠˋ)
to urinate; to make water

【溶】 3014 ㄖㄨㄥˊ rong róng
1. to dissolve; to melt
2. (said of rivers) having much water
溶媒(ㄖㄨㄥˊ ㄇㄟˊ)
a solvent
溶點(ㄖㄨㄥˊ ㄉㄧㄢˇ)
the melting point
溶化(ㄖㄨㄥˊ ㄏㄨㄚˋ)
to dissolve; to melt: 冰全溶化了。The ice had all melted.
溶劑(ㄖㄨㄥˊ ㄐㄧˋ)
a dissolvent; a solvent: 水是糖及鹽的溶劑。Water is a solvent of suger and salt.
溶解(ㄖㄨㄥˊ ㄐㄧㄝˇ)
to dissolve; to melt
溶解度(ㄖㄨㄥˊ ㄐㄧㄝˇ ㄉㄨˋ)
solubility
溶解力(ㄖㄨㄥˊ ㄐㄧㄝˇ ㄌㄧˋ)
(chemistry) solvency
溶解性(ㄖㄨㄥˊ ㄐㄧㄝˇ ㄒㄧㄥˋ)
solvability
溶解熱(ㄖㄨㄥˊ ㄐㄧㄝˇ ㄖㄜˋ)
the heat of dissolution
溶質(ㄖㄨㄥˊ ㄓˊ)
a solute: 鹽是海水中的溶質。Salt is a solute in sea water.
溶入(ㄖㄨㄥˊ ㄖㄨˋ)
to dissolve into
溶溶(ㄖㄨㄥˊ ㄖㄨㄥˊ)
①(said of a river) having much water; full of water ② vast; extensive; broad
溶液(ㄖㄨㄥˊ ㄧˋ)
(chemistry) solution

【溽】 3015 ㄖㄨˋ ruh rù
moist; humid
溽氣(ㄖㄨˋ ㄑㄧˋ)
the muggy vapor
溽氣蒸騰(ㄖㄨˋ ㄑㄧˋ ㄓㄥ ㄊㄥˊ)
sweltering
溽暑(ㄖㄨˋ ㄕㄨˇ)
sweltering summer weather

【滁】 3016 ㄔㄨˊ chwu chú
name of a tributary of the Yangtze River
滁河(ㄔㄨˊ ㄏㄜˊ)
name of a tributary of the Yangtze River
滁水(ㄔㄨˊ ㄕㄨㄟˇ)
name of a river in Anhwei

【滃】 3017 ㄨㄥˇ woeng wěng
(said of rivers and clouds) swelling or rising
滃鬱(ㄨㄥˇ ㄩˋ)
filled with vapor

【滂】 3018 ㄆㄤ pang pāng
torrential; overwhelming
滂渤(ㄆㄤ ㄅㄛˊ)
(said of moving water) turbulent
滂湃(ㄆㄤ ㄆㄞˋ)
torrential; overwhelming; surging
滂沛(ㄆㄤ ㄆㄟˋ)
①(said of rain) torrential ② surging; sweeping
滂沱(ㄆㄤ ㄊㄨㄛˊ)
①(said of rain) torrential: 大雨滂沱。The rain came down in torrents. ②(said of tears) streaming
滂澤(ㄆㄤ ㄗㄜˊ)
great kindness
滂洋(ㄆㄤ ㄧㄤˊ)
vast; extensive

【滄】 3019 ㄘㄤ tsang cāng
blue; azure; green
滄波(ㄘㄤ ㄅㄛ)
the blue waves
滄茫(ㄘㄤ ㄇㄤˊ)
endlessly vast; boundless; blurred by vast distance
滄溟(ㄘㄤ ㄇㄧㄥˊ)
the blue sea
滄浪(ㄘㄤ ㄌㄤˊ)
azure water
滄海(ㄘㄤ ㄏㄞˇ)
the blue sea
滄海橫流(ㄘㄤ ㄏㄞˇ ㄏㄥˊ ㄌㄧㄡˊ)
the chaos of the world
滄海桑田(ㄘㄤ ㄏㄞˇ ㄙㄤ ㄊㄧㄢˊ)or 滄桑(ㄘㄤ ㄙㄤ)
the swift changes of the

world; the vicissitudes of life
滄海遺珠(ㄘㄤ ㄏㄞˇ ㄧˊ ㄓㄨ)
a pearl left in the boundless sea—undiscovered talent
滄海一粟(ㄘㄤ ㄏㄞˇ ㄧˊ ㄙㄨˋ)
a grain in the boundless sea; a pebble in the boundless ocean—infinitely small
滄江(ㄘㄤ ㄐㄧㄤ)
the blue river
滄洲(ㄘㄤ ㄓㄡ)
the silvan waterside (often in reference to the abode of a hermit)
滄滄涼涼(ㄘㄤ ㄘㄤ ㄌㄧㄤˊ ㄌㄧㄤˊ)
(said of atmosphere) cold
滄瀛(ㄘㄤ ㄧㄥˊ)
the blue sea

【滅】 3020 ㄇㄧㄝˋ mieh miè

1. to destroy; to ruin; to wipe out; to exterminate
2. to put out; to extinguish; to go out

滅沒(ㄇㄧㄝˋ ㄇㄛˋ)
to vanish; to disappear
滅門(ㄇㄧㄝˋ ㄇㄣˊ)
to put a whole family to death
滅門之禍(ㄇㄧㄝˋ ㄇㄣˊ ㄓ ㄏㄨㄛˋ)
(in ancient China) the disaster of having a whole family beheaded when a member of the family committed high treason, rebellion, etc.
滅燈(ㄇㄧㄝˋ ㄉㄥ)
to turn off lights; to blow out the lamp: 別滅燈。Don't blow out the lamp.
滅掉(ㄇㄧㄝˋ ㄉㄧㄠˋ)
to destroy; to ruin
滅頂(ㄇㄧㄝˋ ㄉㄧㄥˇ)
to be drowned
滅度(ㄇㄧㄝˋ ㄉㄨˋ)
(Buddhism) *Nirvana*
滅裂(ㄇㄧㄝˋ ㄌㄧㄝˋ)
to manage things in a slapdash, irresponsible manner
滅良心(ㄇㄧㄝˋ ㄌㄧㄤˊ ·ㄒㄧㄣ)
to go against conscience
滅口(ㄇㄧㄝˋ ㄎㄡˇ)
to kill a person to prevent him from disclosing a secret
滅戶(ㄇㄧㄝˋ ㄏㄨˋ)
to exterminate a family
滅火劑(ㄇㄧㄝˋ ㄏㄨㄛˇ ㄐㄧˋ)
fire-extinguishing chemicals (or agents)
滅火器(ㄇㄧㄝˋ ㄏㄨㄛˇ ㄑㄧˋ)
a fire extinguisher
滅火沙(ㄇㄧㄝˋ ㄏㄨㄛˇ ㄕㄚ)
sand for extinguishing a fire
滅跡(ㄇㄧㄝˋ ㄐㄧ)
to destroy evidence
滅盡天良(ㄇㄧㄝˋ ㄐㄧㄣˋ ㄊㄧㄢ ㄌㄧㄤˊ)
to destroy utterly one's conscience
滅絕(ㄇㄧㄝˋ ㄐㄩㄝˊ)
to exterminate; to annihilate; to wipe out
滅心(ㄇㄧㄝˋ ㄒㄧㄣ)
to go against conscience
滅性(ㄇㄧㄝˋ ㄒㄧㄥˋ)
to lose life
滅種(ㄇㄧㄝˋ ㄓㄨㄥˇ)
to commit genocide
滅屍(ㄇㄧㄝˋ ㄕ)
to destroy a corpse so as to leave no traces of the crime
滅族(ㄇㄧㄝˋ ㄗㄨˊ)
to wipe out an entire clan; genocide
滅此朝食(ㄇㄧㄝˋ ㄘˇ ㄓㄠ ㄕˊ)
eager to destroy the enemy
滅音器(ㄇㄧㄝˋ ㄧㄣ ㄑㄧˋ)
the muffler (of an engine)
滅亡(ㄇㄧㄝˋ ㄨㄤˊ)
(said of a country) to lose independence status and become a mere geographic name; to perish; to be doomed

【滇】 3021 ㄉㄧㄢ dian diān (又讀 ㄊㄧㄢˊ tyan tián)

an alternative name of Yünnan
滇湎鐵路(ㄉㄧㄢ ㄇㄧㄢˇ ㄊㄧㄝˇ ㄌㄨˋ)
a railway linking Yünnan and Burma
滇緬公路(ㄉㄧㄢ ㄇㄧㄢˇ ㄍㄨㄥ ㄌㄨˋ)
the Burma Road (from Kunming to Ledo)
滇池(ㄉㄧㄢ ㄔˊ)
name of a lake in Yünnan
滇越鐵路(ㄉㄧㄢ ㄩㄝˋ ㄊㄧㄝˇ ㄌㄨˋ)
a railway linking Yünnan and Vietnam

【滋】 3022 ㄗ tzy zī

1. to grow
2. to increase; to multiply
3. to nourish
4. to give rise to
5. to spurt out
6. juice; sap

滋補(ㄗ ㄅㄨˇ)
to nourish; nutritious; tonic: 人參是滋補身體的名藥。Ginseng is a famous tonic medicine.
滋茂(ㄗ ㄇㄠˋ)
luxuriant; lush; teeming: 兩岸草木滋茂。Lush grass grows along the river banks.
滋蔓(ㄗ ㄇㄢˋ)
lush; teeming; to grow and spread: 田裏雜草滋蔓。Weeds grow and spread in the field.
滋蔓難圖(ㄗ ㄇㄢˋ ㄋㄢˊ ㄊㄨˊ)
It will be too late to deal with an enemy if he is allowed to grow in strength.
滋多(ㄗ ㄉㄨㄛ)
to increase; to multiply
滋息(ㄗ ㄒㄧˊ)
to bear interest
滋殖(ㄗ ㄓˊ)
to reproduce in large numbers
滋長(ㄗ ㄓㄤˇ)
to grow; to thrive: 花沒有日光就不會滋長。Flowers will not thrive without sunshine.
滋事(ㄗ ㄕˋ)
to create trouble; to disturb peace: 他因滋事被捕。He was arrested for disturbing peace.
滋生(ㄗ ㄕㄥ)
to reproduce in large numbers; to multiply
滋擾(ㄗ ㄖㄠˇ)
to disturb peace and order; to harass
滋潤(ㄗ ㄖㄨㄣˋ)
① to freshen; to enrich ② to moisten; moist; juicy
滋嘴兒(ㄗ ㄗㄨㄟˇㄦ)
to smile; to grin
滋芽兒(ㄗ ㄧㄚˊㄦ)
to sprout
滋養(ㄗ ㄧㄤˇ)
to nourish: 用牛奶滋養嬰孩。Babies are nourished with milk.
滋養品(ㄗ ㄧㄤˇ ㄆㄧㄣˇ)
nourishing food; nutritive food; nutrient; nourishment

〔水部〕

滋養分(ㄗ ㄧㄤˇ ㄈㄣˋ)or 滋養料(ㄗ ㄧㄤˇ ㄌㄧㄠˋ)
nourishment; nutrition
滋味(ㄗ ㄨㄟˋ)
taste; flavor
滋腴(ㄗ ㄩˊ)
greasy food
滋育(ㄗ ㄩˋ)
to reproduce in large numbers; to multiply

【滑】 3023 ㄏㄨㄚˊ hwa huá
1. to slip; to slide; to glide
2. smooth; slippery
3. insincere; dishonest; cunning
滑板(ㄏㄨㄚˊ ㄅㄢˇ)
①(machinery) a slide ②(table tennis) feint play ③a skateboard
滑瓣(ㄏㄨㄚˊ ㄅㄢˋ)
a sliding valve
滑冰(ㄏㄨㄚˊ ㄅㄧㄥ)
to skate
滑冰場(ㄏㄨㄚˊ ㄅㄧㄥ ㄔㄤˇ)
a skating rink
滑坡(ㄏㄨㄚˊ ㄆㄛ)
landslide; landslip
滑門(ㄏㄨㄚˊ ㄇㄣˊ)
a sliding door
滑倒(ㄏㄨㄚˊ ㄉㄠˇ)
to slip and fall: 他在冰上滑倒。He slipped on the ice.
滑道(ㄏㄨㄚˊ ㄉㄠˋ)
a chute; a slide
滑頂(ㄏㄨㄚˊ ㄉㄧㄥˇ)
the sliding roof (of an automobile)
滑動(ㄏㄨㄚˊ ㄉㄨㄥˋ)
(physics) to slide
滑頭(ㄏㄨㄚˊ ㄊㄡˊ)
a crafty person; a cunning person
滑頭滑腦(ㄏㄨㄚˊ ㄊㄡˊ ㄏㄨㄚˊ ㄋㄠˇ)
sly; crafty; guile
滑梯(ㄏㄨㄚˊ ㄊㄧ)
a slideway (for children's amusement)
滑鐵盧(ㄏㄨㄚˊ ㄊㄧㄝˇ ㄌㄨˊ)
Waterloo, a village in central Belgium (Napoleon decisively defeated here on June 18, 1815)
滑膩(ㄏㄨㄚˊ ㄋㄧˋ)
smooth and lustrous
滑了一跤(ㄏㄨㄚˊ ·ㄌㄜ ㄧˋ ㄐㄧㄠ)
to have a slip when walking
滑壘(ㄏㄨㄚˊ ㄌㄟˇ)
(baseball) base sliding
滑溜兒(ㄏㄨㄚˊ ㄌㄧㄡㄦ)
smooth and shiny
滑輪(ㄏㄨㄚˊ ㄌㄨㄣˊ)
①a roller ②a pulley
滑竿(ㄏㄨㄚˊ ㄍㄢ)
an uncovered sedan chair in Szechwan
滑桿(ㄏㄨㄚˊ ㄍㄢˇ)
(mechanics) a sliding bar
滑口(ㄏㄨㄚˊ ㄎㄡˇ)
glib; voluble
滑稽(ㄏㄨㄚˊ ㄐㄧ)or(ㄍㄨˇ ㄐㄧ)
ludicrous; funny; comical; ridiculous: 多麼滑稽的故事！What a funny story!
滑稽劇(ㄏㄨㄚˊ ㄐㄧ ㄐㄩˋ)or(ㄍㄨˇ ㄐㄧ ㄐㄩˋ)
comedy; burlesque; farce
滑劑(ㄏㄨㄚˊ ㄐㄧˋ)
lubricant
滑精(ㄏㄨㄚˊ ㄐㄧㄥ)
involuntary emission of semen; spermatorrhea
滑翔(ㄏㄨㄚˊ ㄒㄧㄤˊ)
to glide
滑翔機(ㄏㄨㄚˊ ㄒㄧㄤˊ ㄐㄧ)
a glider
滑翔翼(ㄏㄨㄚˊ ㄒㄧㄤˊ ㄧˋ)
a hang glider
滑翔運動(ㄏㄨㄚˊ ㄒㄧㄤˊ ㄩㄣˋ ㄉㄨㄥˋ)
exercise in glider manipulation; glider sports
滑行(ㄏㄨㄚˊ ㄒㄧㄥˊ)
to slide; to coast; to taxi
滑雪(ㄏㄨㄚˊ ㄒㄩㄝˇ)
to ski; to slide or travel on skis
滑車(ㄏㄨㄚˊ ㄔㄜ)
a pulley; a winch
滑石(ㄏㄨㄚˊ ㄕˊ)
talc or talcum
滑石粉(ㄏㄨㄚˊ ㄕˊ ㄈㄣˇ)
talcum powder
滑水(ㄏㄨㄚˊ ㄕㄨㄟˇ)
water skiing
滑潤(ㄏㄨㄚˊ ㄖㄨㄣˋ)
smooth; well-lubricated
滑澤(ㄏㄨㄚˊ ㄗㄜˊ)
smooth and lustrous
滑草運動(ㄏㄨㄚˊ ㄘㄠˇ ㄩㄣˋ ㄉㄨㄥˋ)
grass skiing

【滔】 3024 ㄊㄠ tau tāo
1. fluent
2. to fill; to prevail
滔滔(ㄊㄠ ㄊㄠ)
flowing smoothly; fluent
滔滔不絕(ㄊㄠ ㄊㄠ ㄅㄨˋ ㄐㄩㄝˊ)
talking fluently and endlessly
滔滔善辯(ㄊㄠ ㄊㄠ ㄕㄢˋ ㄅㄧㄢˋ)
eloquent; skilled in debating
滔天大罪(ㄊㄠ ㄊㄧㄢ ㄉㄚˋ ㄗㄨㄟˋ)
heinous crimes; an extremely serious offense

【滓】 3025 ㄗˇ tzyy zǐ
dregs; lees; sediment

【滎】 3026 ㄧㄥˊ yng yíng
(said of waves) rising
滎澤(ㄧㄥˊ ㄗㄜˊ)
name of an ancient lake in Honan
滎陽(ㄧㄥˊ ㄧㄤˊ)
name of a county in Honan

【溎】 3027 ㄍㄨㄟˋ guey guì
name of a river

【滕】 3028 ㄊㄥˊ terng téng
name of a state during the Spring and Autumn Age
滕文公(ㄊㄥˊ ㄨㄣˊ ㄍㄨㄥ)
name of a king of the state of 滕 during the Spring and Autumn Age
滕王閣(ㄊㄥˊ ㄨㄤˊ ㄍㄜˊ)
a renowned tower in Nanchang, Kiangsi, built in the Tang Dynasty

十一畫

【滬】 3029 ㄏㄨˋ huh hù
an alternative name of Shanghai
滬寧鐵路(ㄏㄨˋ ㄋㄧㄥˊ ㄊㄧㄝˇ ㄌㄨˋ)
old name of the Shanghai-Nanking Railway
滬杭鐵路(ㄏㄨˋ ㄏㄤˊ ㄊㄧㄝˇ ㄌㄨˋ)
the Shanghai-Hangchow Railway
滬杭甬鐵路(ㄏㄨˋ ㄏㄤˊ ㄩㄥˇ ㄊㄧㄝˇ ㄌㄨˋ)
the Shanghai-Hangchow-Ningpo Railway
滬江(ㄏㄨˋ ㄐㄧㄤ)
an alternative name of Shanghai
滬市(ㄏㄨˋ ㄕˋ)

Shanghai

【滌】3030 ㄉㄧˊ dyi dí
1. to wash; to cleanse
2. to sweep
滌蕩(ㄉㄧˊ ㄉㄤˋ) ①to wash off ②to spread out
滌慮(ㄉㄧˊ ㄌㄩˋ) to free the mind from worries
滌去(ㄉㄧˊ ㄑㄩˋ) to wash off; to wash away: 滌去牆上的污跡。Wash those dirty marks off the wall.
滌瑕(ㄉㄧˊ ㄒㄧㄚˊ) to cleanse away a stain; to mend one's ways
滌塵(ㄉㄧˊ ㄔㄣˊ) to wash off dust
滌場(ㄉㄧˊ ㄔㄤˇ)or(ㄉㄧˊ ㄔㄤˊ) to sweep the yard
滌除(ㄉㄧˊ ㄔㄨˊ) ①to wash off; to wash away ②to sweep away ③to do away with
滌硯(ㄉㄧˊ ㄧㄢˋ) to wash the ink-slab—to prepare for study

【滯】3031 ㄓˋ jyh zhì
at a standstill; stagnant; impeded; blocked; stationary
滯悶(ㄓˋ ㄇㄣˋ) to have pent-up feeling
滯伏(ㄓˋ ㄈㄨˊ) ①to lie hidden ②to lack ambition
滯泥(ㄓˋ ㄋㄧˋ) to adhere too closely; stubborn and inflexible
滯累(ㄓˋ ㄌㄟˇ) the burden of the temporal world
滯留(ㄓˋ ㄌㄧㄡˊ) ①to remain at a standstill ②to loiter; to detain: 他因事滯留在辦公室。He was detained in the office by business. ③to overstay
滯留鋒(ㄓˋ ㄌㄧㄡˊ ㄈㄥ) stagnant atmospheric masses; stationary front
滯固(ㄓˋ ㄍㄨˋ) obstinate; inflexible
滯貨(ㄓˋ ㄏㄨㄛˋ)or 滯銷貨(ㄓˋ ㄒㄧㄠ ㄏㄨㄛˋ) unsaleable goods; dead stock
滯氣(ㄓˋ ㄑㄧˋ) stagnant humor
滯銷(ㄓˋ ㄒㄧㄠ) sales slump
滯住(ㄓˋ ㄓㄨˋ) impeded; stopped; detained
滯塞不通(ㄓˋ ㄙㄜˋ ㄅㄨˋ ㄊㄨㄥ) obstructed and impeded
滯訟(ㄓˋ ㄙㄨㄥˋ)or 滯獄(ㄓˋ ㄩˋ) a prolonged lawsuit
滯礙(ㄓˋ ㄞˋ) to obstruct; to impede: 他工作受到滯礙。He was impeded in his work.
滯淹(ㄓˋ ㄧㄢ) to remain at a standstill
滯淫(ㄓˋ ㄧㄣˊ) ①to remain at a standstill ②stagnation; stagnancy
滯胃(ㄓˋ ㄨㄟˋ) indigestion
滯運(ㄓˋ ㄩㄣˋ) bad fortune; adversity

【滲】3032 ㄕㄣˋ shenn shèn
to permeate; to percolate; to infiltrate; to seep; to ooze: 雨水滲入砂中。The rain has permeated the sand.
滲透(ㄕㄣˋ ㄊㄡˋ) to infiltrate; to permeate; to percolate; to seep through: 水滲透到泥土裏面。The water permeated through the soil.
滲透性(ㄕㄣˋ ㄊㄡˋ ㄒㄧㄥˋ) permeability; osmosis (or osmose)
滲透作用(ㄕㄣˋ ㄊㄡˋ ㄗㄨㄛˋ ㄩㄥˋ) osmosis; permeation
滲透壓力(ㄕㄣˋ ㄊㄡˋ ㄧㄚ ㄌㄧˋ) osmotic pressure
滲漏(ㄕㄣˋ ㄌㄡˋ) to seep out; to ooze out
滲出(ㄕㄣˋ ㄔㄨ) to seep out; to ooze out: 泉水自石中滲出。The spring oozes out of a rock.
滲入(ㄕㄣˋ ㄖㄨˋ) ①to permeate; to seep into: 雨水滲入地下。The rain permeated the ground. ②(said of influence, etc.) to penetrate; to infiltrate

【滴】3033 ㄉㄧ di dī
1. water drops
2. to drip
滴答(ㄉㄧ ㄉㄚ) ticktack (or other similar recurring sound)
滴滴(ㄉㄧ ㄉㄧ) in drops; drop by drop
滴滴答答(ㄉㄧ ㄉㄧ ㄉㄚ ㄉㄚ) to ticktack; ticktack: 霰滴滴答答地打在窗上。Sleet ticktacked against the window panes.
滴定法(ㄉㄧ ㄉㄧㄥˋ ㄈㄚˇ) (chemistry) titration
滴瀝(ㄉㄧ ㄌㄧˋ) the pattering sound of raindrops
滴里搭拉的(ㄉㄧ ·ㄌㄧ ㄉㄚ ㄌㄚ ·ㄉㄜ) the pattering of raindrops
滴溜溜(ㄉㄧ ㄌㄧㄡ ㄌㄧㄡ) round; going round and round
滴管(ㄉㄧ ㄍㄨㄢˇ) a medicine dropper; a pipette
滴灌(ㄉㄧ ㄍㄨㄢˋ) (agriculture) drip irrigation; trickle irrigation
滴下(ㄉㄧ ㄒㄧㄚˋ) to drip: 雨從傘上滴下。Rain drips from the umbrella.
滴血(ㄉㄧ ㄒㄧㄝˇ) (in former times) to drop blood in water in a test to decide kinship
滴水穿石(ㄉㄧ ㄕㄨㄟˇ ㄔㄨㄢ ㄕˊ) (literally) Constant dropping wears away a stone.—Persistent efforts can overcome any difficulty.

【滹】3034 ㄏㄨ hu hū
name of a river flowing through Hopeh
滹沱(ㄏㄨ ㄊㄨㄛˊ) name of a river flowing through Hopeh

【滸】3035 ㄏㄨˇ huu hǔ
waterside; shore

【滾】3036 (滚) ㄍㄨㄣˇ goen gun
1. to turn round and round; to roll; to rotate: 很多石頭從山坡上滾下來。Many stones came rolling down the slope.
2. boiling: 茶壺中的水滾了。The

〔水部〕

pot is boiling.
滾邊(ㄍㄨㄣˇ ㄅㄧㄢ)
①an embroidered hem ②to stitch a hem around a border
滾翻(ㄍㄨㄣˇ ㄈㄢ)
(sports) a roll; to roll
滾蛋(ㄍㄨㄣˇ ㄉㄢˋ)
Get out! 或Go to hell! 或Beat it!
滾地球(ㄍㄨㄣˇ ㄉㄧˋ ㄑㄧㄡˊ)
(baseball) ground ball
滾動摩擦(ㄍㄨㄣˇ ㄉㄨㄥˋ ㄇㄛˊ ㄘㄚ)
rolling friction
滾湯(ㄍㄨㄣˇ ㄊㄤ)
boiled water
滾燙(ㄍㄨㄣˇ ㄊㄤˋ)
boiling; steaming hot; piping hot: 水滾燙。The water is steaming hot.
滾筒印刷機(ㄍㄨㄣˇ ㄊㄨㄥˇ ㄧㄣˋ ㄕㄨㄚ ㄐㄧ)
a rotary press
滾利(ㄍㄨㄣˇ ㄌㄧˋ)
to yield compound interest
滾路機(ㄍㄨㄣˇ ㄌㄨˋ ㄐㄧ)
a road roller
滾瓜爛熟(ㄍㄨㄣˇ ㄍㄨㄚ ㄌㄢˋ ㄕㄨˊ)
learned very thoroughly; committed to memory firmly
滾滾(ㄍㄨㄣˇ ㄍㄨㄣˇ)
①(said of flowing waters) rolling; torrential; billowing: 滾滾的濃煙向上升起。The billowing smoke rose up. ②to pour into: 財源滾滾到我家。Profits pour into my home from all sides.
滾滾東流(ㄍㄨㄣˇ ㄍㄨㄣˇ ㄉㄨㄥ ㄌㄧㄡˊ)
rolling eastward (as most rivers in China)
滾滾流出(ㄍㄨㄣˇ ㄍㄨㄣˇ ㄌㄧㄡˊ ㄔㄨ)
to flow out plentifully; to gush out
滾滾而來(ㄍㄨㄣˇ ㄍㄨㄣˇ ㄦˊ ㄌㄞˊ)
to come in torrents
滾開(ㄍㄨㄣˇ ・ㄎㄞ)
Get away! 或Get out! 或Beat it!
滾起來(ㄍㄨㄣˇ ㄑㄧˇ ・ㄌㄞ)
①to start a fist fight ②Get up! (used abusively) ③to start boiling
滾球兒(ㄍㄨㄣˇ ㄑㄧㄡˊ ㄦ)
Go away!
滾下去(ㄍㄨㄣˇ ㄒㄧㄚˋ ・ㄑㄩ)
①to roll down ②Get out! 或Beat it!
滾雪球(ㄍㄨㄣˇ ㄒㄩㄝ ㄑㄧㄡˊ)
①to roll a snowball ②to snowball
滾出去(ㄍㄨㄣˇ ㄔㄨ ・ㄑㄩ)
①to roll out ②Get out!
滾石不生苔(ㄍㄨㄣˇ ㄕˊ ㄅㄨˋ ㄕㄥ ㄊㄞˊ)
A rolling stone gathers no moss.
滾水(ㄍㄨㄣˇ ㄕㄨㄟˇ)
boiling water
滾熱(ㄍㄨㄣˇ ㄖㄜˋ)or滾熱兒的(ㄍㄨㄣˇ ㄖㄜˋㄦ ・ㄉㄜ)
piping hot
滾子(ㄍㄨㄣˇ ・ㄗ)
a roller
滾兒(ㄍㄨㄜˇㄦ)
a turn; a roll
滾圓(ㄍㄨㄣˇ ㄩㄢˊ)
perfectly round

【滿】 3037 ㄇㄢˇ maan mǎn

1. full; filled: 這箱子滿了。The box is full.
2. plentiful; abundant
3. proud; haughty
4. to expire: 他的任期將滿。His term of office will soon expire.
5. completely; entirely; perfectly
6. Manchu
7. a Chinese family name

滿杯(ㄇㄢˇ ㄅㄟ)
a full cup: 他喝滿杯的酒。He drank a full cup of wine.
滿不在乎(ㄇㄢˇ ・ㄅㄨ ㄗㄞˋ ・ㄏㄨ)
completely unperturbed; do not care at all; nonchalant
滿瓶不動半瓶搖(ㄇㄢˇ ㄆㄧㄥˊ ㄅㄨˋ ㄉㄨㄥˋ ㄅㄢˋ ㄆㄧㄥˊ ㄧㄠˊ)
Full vessels give the least sound.
滿沒聽提(ㄇㄢˇ ㄇㄟˊ ㄊㄧㄥ ㄊㄧˊ)or 滿不聽提(ㄇㄢˇ ㄅㄨˋ ㄊㄧㄥ ㄊㄧˊ)
to pay no attention at all
滿滿的(ㄇㄢˇ ㄇㄢˇ ・ㄉㄜ)
full to the brim; brimful: 杯子滿滿的。The glass is full to the brim.
滿滿當當(ㄇㄢˇ ㄇㄢˇ ㄉㄤ ㄉㄤ)
full; plentiful
滿門(ㄇㄢˇ ㄇㄣˊ)
the whole family
滿門桃李(ㄇㄢˇ ㄇㄣˊ ㄊㄠˊ ㄌㄧˇ)
a lot of students
滿面怒容(ㄇㄢˇ ㄇㄧㄢˋ ㄋㄨˋ ㄖㄨㄥˊ)
red with anger; to look furious
滿面笑容(ㄇㄢˇ ㄇㄧㄢˋ ㄒㄧㄠˋ ㄖㄨㄥˊ)
looking happy and cheerful; all smiles
滿面春風(ㄇㄢˇ ㄇㄧㄢˋ ㄔㄨㄣ ㄈㄥ)
looking happy and cheerful; beaming with pleasure
滿目蕭然(ㄇㄢˇ ㄇㄨˋ ㄒㄧㄠ ㄖㄢˊ)
Desolation spreads as far as the eye can reach.
滿目瘡痍(ㄇㄢˇ ㄇㄨˋ ㄔㄨㄤ ㄧˊ)
Misery and suffering greets the eye everywhere.
滿帆(ㄇㄢˇ ㄈㄢˊ)
full sails
滿分(ㄇㄢˇ ㄈㄣ)or滿分兒(ㄇㄢˇ ㄈㄜㄦ)
a perfect score; full marks
滿服(ㄇㄢˇ ㄈㄨˊ)
to complete a mourning period
滿腹牢騷(ㄇㄢˇ ㄈㄨˋ ㄌㄠˊ ㄙㄠ)
to have a heart full of discontents, grievances, complaints, etc.
滿腹狐疑(ㄇㄢˇ ㄈㄨˋ ㄏㄨˊ ㄧˊ)
to be filled with suspicion; extremely suspicious
滿腹經綸(ㄇㄢˇ ㄈㄨˋ ㄐㄧㄥ ㄌㄨㄣˊ)
very erudite; very much learned
滿打算(ㄇㄢˇ ㄉㄚˇ ・ㄙㄨㄢ)
to have intended
滿地(ㄇㄢˇ ㄉㄧˋ)
all over the ground; everywhere
滿頭大汗(ㄇㄢˇ ㄊㄡˊ ㄉㄚˋ ㄏㄢˋ)
with one's brow beaded with perspiration
滿堂紅(ㄇㄢˇ ㄊㄤˊ ㄏㄨㄥˊ)
①conventional decorations in red for the drawing room on an auspicious occasion ②all-round victory; success in every field
滿天下(ㄇㄢˇ ㄊㄧㄢ ㄒㄧㄚˋ)
all over the world; everywhere
滿天星(ㄇㄢˇ ㄊㄧㄢ ㄒㄧㄥ)
①(botany) *Serissa foetida; Enkianthus japonicus* ②the sky filled with stars
滿天星斗(ㄇㄢˇ ㄊㄧㄢ ㄒㄧㄥ ㄉㄡˇ)
a clear sky full of stars
滿腦子(ㄇㄢˇ ㄋㄠˇ ・ㄗ)

to have one's mind stuffed with
滿擬(ㄇㄢˇ ㄋㄧˇ)
to have had the intention of
滿壘(ㄇㄢˇ ㄌㄟˇ)
bases loaded; full base
滿臉風塵(ㄇㄢˇ ㄌㄧㄢˇ ㄈㄥ ㄔㄣˊ)
a face covered with traveling dust—the indication of having undergone hardship
滿臉通紅(ㄇㄢˇ ㄌㄧㄢˇ ㄊㄨㄥ ㄏㄨㄥˊ)
The face reddens all over.
滿臉晦氣(ㄇㄢˇ ㄌㄧㄢˇ ㄏㄨㄟˋ ㄑㄧˋ)
to look very depressed
滿臉殺氣(ㄇㄢˇ ㄌㄧㄢˇ ㄕㄚ ㄑㄧˋ)
to look like one in a murderous mood
滿臉俗氣(ㄇㄢˇ ㄌㄧㄢˇ ㄙㄨˊ ㄑㄧˋ)
to look very vulgar: 那記者滿臉俗氣。The reporter looks very vulgar.
滿貫(ㄇㄢˇ ㄍㄨㄢˋ)
① to reach the utmost ② (mah-jong game) full marks; a perfect score
滿口胡説(ㄇㄢˇ ㄎㄡˇ ㄏㄨˊ ㄕㄨㄛ)
to talk irresponsibly; to talk nonsense或Nonsense! 或Rubbish! 或 Baloney!
滿口稱讚(ㄇㄢˇ ㄎㄡˇ ㄔㄥ ㄗㄢˋ)
to praise unreservedly
滿口應承(ㄇㄢˇ ㄎㄡˇ ㄧㄥ ㄔㄥˊ)or 滿口答應(ㄇㄢˇ ㄎㄡˇ ㄉㄚ ㄧㄥˋ)
to promise with great readiness
滿坑滿谷(ㄇㄢˇ ㄎㄥ ㄇㄢˇ ㄍㄨˇ)
(literally) numerous enough to fill the pit or the valley — exceedingly numerous
滿漢(ㄇㄢˇ ㄏㄢˋ)
the Manchus and the Chinese
滿漢全席(ㄇㄢˇ ㄏㄢˋ ㄑㄩㄢˊ ㄒㄧˊ)
the complete Manchu and Chinese banquet, featuring numerous courses and delicacies, which lasts as long as one or two days
滿懷(ㄇㄢˇ ㄏㄨㄞˊ)
a heart full of (enthusiasm, sorrow, etc.)
滿假(ㄇㄢˇ ㄐㄧㄚˋ)
Leave of absence expires.
滿街(ㄇㄢˇ ㄐㄧㄝ)
all over the street
滿江紅(ㄇㄢˇ ㄐㄧㄤ ㄏㄨㄥˊ)
① a kind of flowerless plant (*Azolla imbricata*) ②a poetic form (made famous by Gen. Yüeh Fei of the Sung Dynasty)
滿期(ㄇㄢˇ ㄑㄧˊ)
the expiration of a given period; to expire
滿腔熱血(ㄇㄢˇ ㄑㄧㄤ ㄖㄜˋ ㄒㄧㄝˇ)
full of patriotic fervor
滿腔熱忱(ㄇㄢˇ ㄑㄧㄤ ㄖㄜˋ ㄔㄣˊ)
to be filled with ardor and sincerity
滿清(ㄇㄢˇ ㄑㄧㄥ)
the Ching Dynasty (1644-1911)
滿孝(ㄇㄢˇ ㄒㄧㄠˋ)
to complete a period of mourning
滿限(ㄇㄢˇ ㄒㄧㄢˋ)
to have reached the deadline
滿心(ㄇㄢˇ ㄒㄧㄣ)
wholeheartedly
滿心歡喜(ㄇㄢˇ ㄒㄧㄣ ㄏㄨㄢ ㄒㄧˇ)
to be filled with joy
滿紙(ㄇㄢˇ ㄓˇ)
all over a page or letter sheet
滿招損，謙受益(ㄇㄢˇ ㄓㄠ ㄙㄨㄣˇ, ㄑㄧㄢ ㄕㄡˋ ㄧˋ)
Haughtiness invites losses while modesty brings profits.
滿洲(ㄇㄢˇ ㄓㄡ)
Manchuria
滿洲八旗(ㄇㄢˇ ㄓㄡ ㄅㄚ ㄑㄧˊ)
the eight army divisions organized by the Manchus during the Ching Dynasty with each division identified by the color of its banner
滿洲國(ㄇㄢˇ ㄓㄡ ㄍㄨㄛˊ)
the puppet Manchukuo set up by the Japanese in Manchuria, lasting from 1932 to 1945
滿洲語(ㄇㄢˇ ㄓㄡ ㄩˇ)
Manchu (the Tungusic language of the Manchus)
滿張羅(ㄇㄢˇ ㄓㄤ ·ㄌㄨㄛ)
very thoughtful in the reception of guests
滿裝(ㄇㄢˇ ㄓㄨㄤ)
① Manchu clothing ② filled with; loaded with: 貨車滿裝着貨物。The cart was loaded with goods.
滿朝文武(ㄇㄢˇ ㄔㄠˊ ㄨㄣˊ ㄨˇ)
all the ministers and generals in the imperial court
滿場(ㄇㄢˇ ㄔㄤˊ)or(ㄇㄢˇ ㄔㄤˇ)
① the whole assembly ② Tickets sold out!
滿城風雨(ㄇㄢˇ ㄔㄥˊ ㄈㄥ ㄩˇ)
widespread excitement over a scandal, an incident, etc.; the talk of the town
滿處(ㄇㄢˇ ㄔㄨˋ)
all over the place: 滿處是人。People are everywhere.
滿市街(ㄇㄢˇ ㄕˋ ㄐㄧㄝ)
all over the city; everywhere
滿身(ㄇㄢˇ ㄕㄣ)
the whole body
滿身是汗(ㄇㄢˇ ㄕㄣ ㄕˋ ㄏㄢˋ)
to sweat all over
滿人(ㄇㄢˇ ㄖㄣˊ)
①the Manchus ②(Buddhism) a perfect man; one who does good deeds
滿載(ㄇㄢˇ ㄗㄞˋ)
fully laden
滿載而歸(ㄇㄢˇ ㄗㄞˋ ㄦˊ ㄍㄨㄟ)
to return home fully laden with riches, gifts, etc.
滿足(ㄇㄢˇ ㄗㄨˊ)
to satisfy or be satisfied; to gratify or be gratified; to meet; content; satisfaction; gratification
滿族(ㄇㄢˇ ㄗㄨˊ)
the Manchu people; the Manchus
滿座(ㄇㄢˇ ㄗㄨㄛˋ)
① all the people present; all the audience; all the attendants ② a capacity audience
滿座高朋(ㄇㄢˇ ㄗㄨㄛˋ ㄍㄠ ㄆㄥˊ)
The whole audience is lofty and intelligent.
滿嘴(ㄇㄢˇ ㄗㄨㄟˇ)
to have a mouthful of (food, honeyed words, etc.)
滿額(ㄇㄢˇ ㄜˊ)
to have reached the fixed amount or quota
滿而不溢(ㄇㄢˇ ㄦˊ ㄅㄨˋ ㄧˋ)
(literally) full without flowing over—very much accomplished but behaving modestly
滿耳(ㄇㄢˇ ㄦˇ)
to have one's ears filled

〔水部〕

〔水部〕

with (sound or voice)
滿以為(ㄇㄢˇ ㄧˇ ㄨㄟˊ)
to have counted on or expected something to happen (but it did not)
滿意(ㄇㄢˇ ㄧˋ)
satisfied; content: 大家對你的進步都很滿意。Everyone was satisfied with your progress.
滿眼(ㄇㄢˇ ㄧㄢˇ)
① to have one's eyes filled with ② to meet the eye on every side
滿文(ㄇㄢˇ ㄨㄣˊ) or 滿洲文字(ㄇㄢˇ ㄓㄡ ㄨㄣˊ ㄗˋ)
written Manchu language
滿月(ㄇㄢˇ ㄩㄝˋ)
① a full moon 亦作「望月」② (of a baby) to be one month old
滿園春色(ㄇㄢˇ ㄩㄢˊ ㄔㄨㄣ ㄙㄜˋ)
The garden is filled with the brightness of spring.

【漁】 3038 ㄩˊ yu yú
1. to fish
2. to seek; to pursue
3. to seize; to acquire forcibly
漁婆(ㄩˊ ㄆㄛˊ)
a fisherwoman
漁民(ㄩˊ ㄇㄧㄣˊ)
the fishing population; fishermen
漁夫(ㄩˊ ㄈㄨ)
a fisherman: 漁夫捉到一條大魚。The fisherman caught a big fish.
漁艇(ㄩˊ ㄊㄧㄥˇ)
a fishing boat: 我們乘漁艇去吧。Let us go by fishing boat.
漁撈科(ㄩˊ ㄌㄠ ㄎㄜ)
the department of fishery
漁郎(ㄩˊ ㄌㄤˊ)
a fisherman
漁利(ㄩˊ ㄌㄧˋ)
to seek profits or gains by unethical means; profiteering
漁獵(ㄩˊ ㄌㄧㄝˋ)
① fishing and hunting ② to seek (illegal gains)
漁獵時代(ㄩˊ ㄌㄧㄝˋ ㄕˊ ㄉㄞˋ)
the fishing and hunting age
漁歌(ㄩˊ ㄍㄜ)
fishermen's songs 參看「漁唱」
漁港(ㄩˊ ㄍㄤˇ)
a fishing harbor
漁戶(ㄩˊ ㄏㄨˋ)
fishing families; fishermen
漁火(ㄩˊ ㄏㄨㄛˇ)
lights on fishing boats
漁獲量(ㄩˊ ㄏㄨㄛˋ ㄌㄧㄤˋ)
a catch
漁會(ㄩˊ ㄏㄨㄟˋ)
a fishermen's association
漁家(ㄩˊ ㄐㄧㄚ)
fishing families; fishermen
漁具(ㄩˊ ㄐㄩˋ)
a fishing outfit
漁樵耕讀(ㄩˊ ㄑㄧㄠˊ ㄍㄥ ㄉㄨˊ)
the fisherman, the woodcutter, the farmer, and the scholar (the four respectable occupations in old China)
漁權(ㄩˊ ㄑㄩㄢˊ)
a piscary 亦作「捕漁權」
漁汛(ㄩˊ ㄒㄩㄣˋ)
fishing seasons
漁舟(ㄩˊ ㄓㄡ) or 漁船(ㄩˊ ㄔㄨㄢˊ)
a fishing boat
漁產(ㄩˊ ㄔㄢˇ)
aquatic products
漁場(ㄩˊ ㄔㄤˇ) or (ㄩˊ ㄔㄤˊ)
fishing grounds
漁唱(ㄩˊ ㄔㄤˋ)
fishermen's songs 參看「漁歌」
漁食(ㄩˊ ㄕˊ)
to get sustenance forcibly as a fisherman gets fish
漁人(ㄩˊ ㄖㄣˊ)
a fisherman
漁人得利(ㄩˊ ㄖㄣˊ ㄉㄜˊ ㄌㄧˋ) or 漁翁得利(ㄩˊ ㄨㄥ ㄉㄜˊ ㄌㄧˋ)
The fisherman catches both (while the snipe and the clam are locked in a fight). 或(While two dogs fight for a bone,) a third runs away with it.
漁村(ㄩˊ ㄘㄨㄣ)
a fishing village
漁色(ㄩˊ ㄙㄜˋ)
to seek carnal pleasure
漁色之徒(ㄩˊ ㄙㄜˋ ㄓ ㄊㄨˊ)
a fellow of excessive lust
漁業(ㄩˊ ㄧㄝˋ)
fishery
漁業公司(ㄩˊ ㄧㄝˋ ㄍㄨㄥ ㄙ)
a fishing company; a marine products company
漁業區(ㄩˊ ㄧㄝˋ ㄑㄩ)
a fishing zone
漁網(ㄩˊ ㄨㄤˇ)
a fishing net
漁翁(ㄩˊ ㄨㄥ) or 漁父(ㄩˊ ㄈㄨˇ)
an old fisherman

【漈】 3039 ㄐㄧˋ jih jì
shore; waterside

【漉】 3040 ㄌㄨˋ luh lù
1. to remove sediment by filtering
2. wet; dripping

【漂】 3041 1. ㄆㄧㄠ piau piāo
to drift; to float; to be tossed about
漂泊(ㄆㄧㄠ ㄅㄛˊ)
to drift; to wander: 我像朵孤雲般漂泊。I wandered lonely as a cloud.
漂泊異鄉(ㄆㄧㄠ ㄅㄛˊ ㄧˋ ㄒㄧㄤ)
to wander in a strange land
漂萍(ㄆㄧㄠ ㄆㄧㄥˊ)
duckweed
漂浮(ㄆㄧㄠ ㄈㄨˊ)
to drift; to float
漂蕩(ㄆㄧㄠ ㄉㄤˋ)
① to drift about; to be tossed (by waves): 船在波浪中漂蕩。The ship is tossed by the wave. ② to wander; to ramble about
漂流(ㄆㄧㄠ ㄌㄧㄡˊ)
to drift
漂流無定(ㄆㄧㄠ ㄌㄧㄡˊ ㄨˊ ㄉㄧㄥˋ)
to drift about; to wander aimlessly
漂流物(ㄆㄧㄠ ㄌㄧㄡˊ ㄨˋ)
flotsam
漂零(ㄆㄧㄠ ㄌㄧㄥˊ)
① (said of leaves) to be scattered about ② to live a lone wandering life
漂淪(ㄆㄧㄠ ㄌㄨㄣˊ)
to be a pitiable lone wanderer
漂海(ㄆㄧㄠ ㄏㄞˇ)
to take a long voyage
漂絮(ㄆㄧㄠ ㄒㄩˋ)
to wander about like catkins floating in the air
漂兒(ㄆㄧㄠㄦ)
a buoy; afloat
漂搖(ㄆㄧㄠ ㄧㄠˊ)
to be tossed about in wind or water; to wave; to flutter
漂洋(ㄆㄧㄠ ㄧㄤˊ)

to take a long voyage
漂絮(ㄆㄧㄠ ㄒㄩˋ)
to wander about like catkins floating in the air
漂兒(ㄆㄧㄠㄦ)
a buoy; a float
漂搖(ㄆㄧㄠ ㄧㄠˊ)
to be tossed about in wind or water; to wave; to flutter
漂洋(ㄆㄧㄠ ㄧㄤˊ)
to take a long voyage
漂洋過海(ㄆㄧㄠ ㄧㄤˊ ㄍㄨㄛˋ ㄏㄞˇ)
to sail across an ocean

【漂】 3041
2. ㄆㄧㄠˇ peau piǎo
to bleach
漂白(ㄆㄧㄠˇ ㄅㄞˊ)
to bleach
漂白粉(ㄆㄧㄠˇ ㄅㄞˊ ㄈㄣˇ)
bleaching powder
漂白劑(ㄆㄧㄠˇ ㄅㄞˊ ㄐㄧˋ)
a bleaching agent; a decolorant
漂布(ㄆㄧㄠˇ ㄅㄨˋ)
①to bleach linen ②bleached linen

【漂】 3041
3. ㄆㄧㄠˋ piaw piào
pretty; nice; sleek
漂亮(ㄆㄧㄠˋ •ㄌㄧㄤ)
① pretty; handsome ② wise in worldly ways ③ brilliant; beautiful

【漆】 3042
1. ㄑㄧ chi qī
1. a varnish tree; a lacquer tree
2. varnish; lacquer
3. to varnish; to lacquer; to paint: 他把門漆成紅色。He painted the door red.
漆工(ㄑㄧ ㄍㄨㄥ)or 漆匠(ㄑㄧ •ㄐㄧㄤ)
a painter; a varnisher: 他是個房屋漆工。He is a house painter.
漆器(ㄑㄧ ㄑㄧˋ)
lacquer wares: 小販廉價出售漆器。The peddler sold his lacquer wares cheap.
漆書(ㄑㄧ ㄕㄨ)
to write in varnish on bamboo tablets
漆樹(ㄑㄧ ㄕㄨˋ)
the varnish tree

【漆】 3042
2. ㄑㄩ chiuh qù
pitch-black
漆黑(ㄑㄩ ㄏㄟ)
pitch-black; coal black; raven
漆黑一團(ㄑㄩ ㄏㄟ ㄧˊ ㄊㄨㄢˊ)
complete darkness

【漏】 3043
ㄌㄡˋ low lòu
1. to divulge; to disclose: 他洩漏了秘密。He disclosed the secret.
2. leak; to leak: 管子在漏水。Water is leaking out of the pipe.
3. to slip or omit unintentionally; to neglect; to forget; to be missing: 漏了兩行。Two lines are missing.
4. a water clock; an hourglass
漏報(ㄌㄡˋ ㄅㄠˋ)
to fail to include something in a report intentionally or unintentionally
漏排(ㄌㄡˋ ㄆㄞˊ)
to omit some words or passages in printing due to carelessness
漏風(ㄌㄡˋ ㄈㄥ)
not airtight: 風箱漏風了。The bellows is not airtight.
漏風聲(ㄌㄡˋ ㄈㄥ ㄕㄥ)
to disclose a secret; to leak out a secret: 這封信漏了風聲。This letter discloses a secret.
漏脯充飢(ㄌㄡˋ ㄈㄨˇ ㄔㄨㄥ ㄐㄧ)
to care only for the present regardless of future consequences
漏斗(ㄌㄡˋ ㄉㄡˇ)
a funnel
漏斗狀花冠(ㄌㄡˋ ㄉㄡˇ ㄓㄨㄤˋ ㄏㄨㄚ ㄍㄨㄢ)
a funnel-shaped corolla
漏底(ㄌㄡˋ ㄉㄧˇ)
① a leak in the bottom of a vessel for liquids ② to disclose a secret
漏掉(ㄌㄡˋ ㄉㄧㄠˋ)
to be missing or left out
漏電(ㄌㄡˋ ㄉㄧㄢˋ)
electric leakage
漏洞(ㄌㄡˋ ㄉㄨㄥˋ)
a shortcoming; a loophole: 任何法律都有漏洞。Every law has a loophole.
漏脫(ㄌㄡˋ ㄊㄨㄛ)
to be left out inadvertently
漏列(ㄌㄡˋ ㄌㄧㄝˋ)
to fail to include or list due to oversight
漏鼓(ㄌㄡˋ ㄍㄨˇ)
a drum for announcing the watches or hours of the day
漏刻(ㄌㄡˋ ㄎㄜˋ)
a water clock; a clepsydra
漏孔(ㄌㄡˋ ㄎㄨㄥˇ)
a small hole through which air or water leaks out
漏壺(ㄌㄡˋ ㄏㄨˊ)
a water clock; a clepsydra
漏接(ㄌㄡˋ ㄐㄧㄝ)
(baseball) passed ball
漏箭(ㄌㄡˋ ㄐㄧㄢˋ)
an arrow, or a needle, for indicating time in a clepsydra
漏盡(ㄌㄡˋ ㄐㄧㄣˋ)
The night has run its course.
漏精(ㄌㄡˋ ㄐㄧㄥ)
involuntary emission of semen; spermatorrhea
漏氣(ㄌㄡˋ ㄑㄧˋ)
(said of air) to leak out; not airtight
漏洩 or 漏泄(ㄌㄡˋ ㄒㄧㄝˋ)
to leak out: 這消息已漏洩出去了。The news has leaked out.
漏卮(ㄌㄡˋ ㄓ)
① a leaky wine-cup ② leakage of interest ③ one who can drink much liquor
漏出來(ㄌㄡˋ ㄔㄨ •ㄌㄞ)
to leak out
漏師(ㄌㄡˋ ㄕ)
to leak out military secrets
漏杓(ㄌㄡˋ ㄕㄠˊ)
a skimmer; a skimming ladle
漏水(ㄌㄡˋ ㄕㄨㄟˇ)
(said of containers, holds, etc.) leaking: 這船漏水了。This boat leaks.
漏稅(ㄌㄡˋ ㄕㄨㄟˋ)
tax evasion; to evade tax payment
漏子(ㄌㄡˋ •ㄗ)
① a funnel ② a shortcoming; a weak point 亦作「漏兒」
漏夜(ㄌㄡˋ ㄧㄝˋ)
in the dead of night: 他們漏夜工作。They worked in the

dead of night.
漏屋(ㄌㄡˋ ㄨ)
a leaky house
漏網之魚(ㄌㄡˋ ㄨㄤˇ ㄓ ㄩˊ)
a fish that has escaped the net—a criminal who has escaped punishment
漏雨(ㄌㄡˋ ㄩˇ)
(said of a roof) leaking

〔水部〕

【漓】 3044 ㄌㄧˊ li lí
1. dripping wet
2. thin

【漑】 3045 ㄍㄞˋ gay gài
1. to water; to irrigate
2. to wash
漑滌(ㄍㄞˋ ㄉㄧˊ)
to wash
漑田(ㄍㄞˋ ㄊㄧㄢˊ)
to irrigate fields: 農夫漑田。The farmers irrigate fields.

【漚】 3046 1. ㄡ ou ōu
foam; bubbles; froth

【漚】 3046 2. ㄡˋ ow òu
to soak
漚麻(ㄡˋ ㄇㄚˊ)
to soak hemp in water (so that it can be split easily)
漚鬱(ㄡ ㄩˋ)
(said of fragrance) rich

【演】 3047 ㄧㄢˇ yean yǎn
1. to perform for entertainment; to act; to play
2. to expound
3. to exercise; to practice
4. to evolve; to develop
演變(ㄧㄢˇ ㄅㄧㄢˋ)
to develop and change; to evolve; evolutionary changes
演練(ㄧㄢˇ ㄌㄧㄢˋ)
drill
演化(ㄧㄢˇ ㄏㄨㄚˋ)
to develop and change; to evolve; evolution
演技(ㄧㄢˇ ㄐㄧˋ)
acting
演進(ㄧㄢˇ ㄐㄧㄣˋ)
to evolve; to develop
演講(ㄧㄢˇ ㄐㄧㄤˇ)
to deliver a speech; to orate; to speak; to address
演講比賽(ㄧㄢˇ ㄐㄧㄤˇ ㄅㄧˇ ㄙㄞˋ)
an oratorical contest
演講稿(ㄧㄢˇ ㄐㄧㄤˇ ㄍㄠˇ)
written text of a speech
演劇(ㄧㄢˇ ㄐㄩˋ)
① drama ② to act in a play
演習(ㄧㄢˇ ㄒㄧˊ)
military exercises; maneuvers; a war game
演戲(ㄧㄢˇ ㄒㄧˋ)
① to act in a play ② to play-act: 別再演戲了。Stop playacting.
演唱(ㄧㄢˇ ㄔㄤˋ)
to sing before an audience; to sing onstage
演出(ㄧㄢˇ ㄔㄨ)
(said of entertainers) to perform; to present (a play): 我們班上演出一劇。Our class presented a play.
演示(ㄧㄢˇ ㄕˋ)
to demonstrate (skills, techniques, etc.)
演說(ㄧㄢˇ ㄕㄨㄛ)
to give a speech; to deliver a speech; to speak; to address; to orate
演說家(ㄧㄢˇ ㄕㄨㄛ ㄐㄧㄚ)
an orator
演說者(ㄧㄢˇ ㄕㄨㄛ ㄓㄜˇ)
a speaker
演奏(ㄧㄢˇ ㄗㄡˋ)
(said of musicians) to perform
演奏會(ㄧㄢˇ ㄗㄡˋ ㄏㄨㄟˋ)
a concert; a recital
演算(ㄧㄢˇ ㄙㄨㄢˋ)
mathematical exercises; to do mathematical problems
演義(ㄧㄢˇ ㄧˋ)
a historical novel
演繹(ㄧㄢˇ ㄧˋ)
to deduce
演繹法(ㄧㄢˇ ㄧˋ ㄈㄚˇ)
deduction; the deductive method
演武場(ㄧㄢˇ ㄨˇ ㄔㄤˇ) or (ㄧㄢˇ ㄨˇ ㄔㄤˊ)
a parade ground
演員(ㄧㄢˇ ㄩㄢˊ)
an actor or actress

【漕】 3048 ㄘㄠˊ tsaur cáo
to transport grain by water
漕糧(ㄘㄠˊ ㄌㄧㄤˊ)
rice transported to the capital by water as farm tax in kind during the Ching Dynasty
漕溝(ㄘㄠˊ ㄍㄡ)
a canal
漕轉(ㄘㄠˊ ㄓㄨㄢˇ)
transportation of rice to the capital by water and by land
漕司(ㄘㄠˊ ㄙ)
(Sung Dynasty) an official post in charge of water transportation of rice to the capital
漕銀(ㄘㄠˊ ㄧㄣˊ)
money paid to the government in place of tribute rice
漕運(ㄘㄠˊ ㄩㄣˋ)
to transport grain to the capital by water

【漠】 3049 ㄇㄛˋ moh mò
1. a desert
2. indifferent; unconcerned
3. quiet; silent
漠北(ㄇㄛˋ ㄅㄟˇ)
north of the Gobi Desert—Outer Mongolia
漠不關心(ㄇㄛˋ ˙ㄅㄨ ㄍㄨㄢ ㄒㄧㄣ)
to pay no attention at all; do not care at all; completely indifferent
漠不相關(ㄇㄛˋ ˙ㄅㄨ ㄒㄧㄤ ㄍㄨㄢ)
totally unrelated
漠漠(ㄇㄛˋ ㄇㄛˋ)
①overcast ②silent; quiet ③ misty; foggy ④ vast and lonely
漠南(ㄇㄛˋ ㄋㄢˊ)
south of the Gobi Desert—Inner Mongolia
漠視(ㄇㄛˋ ㄕˋ)
① to despise; to hold in contempt ② to ignore; to pay no heed to ③ to consider unimportant; to underestimate; to treat with indifference
漠然(ㄇㄛˋ ㄖㄢˊ)
① indifferent; unaffected; unmoved ② completely ignorant; at a loss
漠然不動(ㄇㄛˋ ㄖㄢˊ ㄅㄨˋ ㄉㄨㄥˋ)
not in the least moved; quite unaffected; completely indifferent

【漣】 3050 ㄌㄧㄢˊ lian lián
1. ripples
2. weeping

漣漣(ㄌㄧㄢˊ ㄌㄧㄢˊ)
weeping
漣洏(ㄌㄧㄢˊ ㄖㄨˊ)
weeping
漣漪(ㄌㄧㄢˊ ㄧ)
ripples: 月光在漣漪上閃耀。The moon danced on the ripples.

【漪】 3051
ㄧ i yī
ripples
漪瀾(ㄧ ㄌㄢˊ)
ripples

【漩】 3052
ㄒㄩㄢˊ shyuan xuán
(又讀 ㄒㄩㄢˋ shiuann xuàn)
a whirlpool
漩渦(ㄒㄩㄢˊ ㄨㄛ)
① a whirlpool ② a dispute; a quarrel

【漢】 3053
ㄏㄢˋ hann hàn
1. of the Han Dynasty (206 B.C.-220 A.D.)
2. of the Chinese people or language
3. a man; a fellow
4. name of a tributary of the Yangtze River
漢碑(ㄏㄢˋ ㄅㄟ)
tablets with inscriptions of the Han Dynasty
漢堡(ㄏㄢˋ ㄅㄠˇ)
① Hamburg, Germany ② a hamburger
漢方(ㄏㄢˋ ㄈㄤ)
Chinese medicinal art
漢代(ㄏㄢˋ ㄉㄞˋ)
the Han Dynasty (206 B.C.-220 A.D.)
漢調(ㄏㄢˋ ㄉㄧㄠˋ)
a style of Chinese opera prevalent in Hupeh
漢土(ㄏㄢˋ ㄊㄨˇ)
the land of the Han people—China
漢尼拔(ㄏㄢˋ ㄋㄧˊ ㄅㄚˊ)
Hannibal, 247-183B.C., general of Carthage
漢女(ㄏㄢˋ ㄋㄩˇ)
the goddess of the Han River (a tributary of the Yangtze)
漢高祖(ㄏㄢˋ ㄍㄠ ㄗㄨˇ)
the dynastic title of Liu Pang (劉邦), 247-195B.C., founder of the Han Dynasty (206 B.C.-220 A.D.)
漢光武帝(ㄏㄢˋ ㄍㄨㄤ ㄨˇ ㄉㄧˋ)
Emperor Kuang Wu, who restored the Han Dynasty in 25 A.D. after the usurpation by Wang Mang (王莽)
漢口(ㄏㄢˋ ㄎㄡˇ)
Hankow, Hupeh
漢化(ㄏㄢˋ ㄏㄨㄚˋ)
sinicized; assimilated by the Chinese
漢奸(ㄏㄢˋ ㄐㄧㄢ)
a traitor (to China)
漢江(ㄏㄢˋ ㄐㄧㄤ)
the Han River
漢軍(ㄏㄢˋ ㄐㄩㄣ)
the Manchu troops composed of defected Chinese people in the early Ching Dynasty
漢獻帝(ㄏㄢˋ ㄒㄧㄢˋ ㄉㄧˋ)
Emperor Hsien (181-234 A.D.), the last ruler of the Eastern Han Dynasty
漢姓(ㄏㄢˋ ㄒㄧㄥˋ)
a Chinese surname adopted by an alien
漢學(ㄏㄢˋ ㄒㄩㄝˊ)
① Sinology: 他專攻漢學。He majors in Sinology. ② textual study of classics (prevalent in the Han Dynasty)
漢學家(ㄏㄢˋ ㄒㄩㄝˊ ㄐㄧㄚ)
① a Sinologue or Sinologist ② an expert in the textual study of classics
漢朝(ㄏㄢˋ ㄔㄠˊ)
the Han Dynasty (206 B.C.-220 A.D.)
漢城(ㄏㄢˋ ㄔㄥˊ)
Seoul, capital of South Korea
漢室(ㄏㄢˋ ㄕˋ)
the House of Liu, which ruled China during the Han Dynasty (206 B.C.-220 A.D.)
漢書(ㄏㄢˋ ㄕㄨ)
the *History of the Han Dynasty*, prepared by Pan Ku (班固) during the latter half of the Han Dynasty (also known as 前漢書, covering the 239 years from 漢高祖 to the death of 王莽)
漢水(ㄏㄢˋ ㄕㄨㄟˇ)
the Han River, a tributary of the Yangtze
漢人(ㄏㄢˋ ㄖㄣˊ)
the Han people—the predominant ethnic group in China
漢字(ㄏㄢˋ ㄗˋ)
the Chinese characters
漢子(ㄏㄢˋ ˙ㄗ)
① a man ② a husband
漢族(ㄏㄢˋ ㄗㄨˊ)
the Han people—the largest ethnic group of the Chinese race
漢醫(ㄏㄢˋ ㄧ)
① a Chinese medicine ② a Chinese herb doctor
漢譯(ㄏㄢˋ ㄧˋ)
translated into Chinese; a Chinese rendering of a book: 這是哈姆雷特的漢譯。This is a Chinese translation of *Hamlet*.
漢陽(ㄏㄢˋ ㄧㄤˊ)
Hanyang, a city on the Yangtze River opposite Hankow
漢英詞典(ㄏㄢˋ ㄧㄥ ㄘˊ ㄉㄧㄢˇ)
a Chinese-English dictionary
漢武帝(ㄏㄢˋ ㄨˇ ㄉㄧˋ)
Emperor Wu (157-87 B.C.), whose reign marked the culmination of the Han Dynasty
漢文(ㄏㄢˋ ㄨㄣˊ)
①written Chinese ② the Chinese language or literature
漢語(ㄏㄢˋ ㄩˇ)
the Chinese language

【漫】 3054
1. ㄇㄢˋ mann màn
1. overflowing
2. uncontrolled; uninhibited
3. reckless; wild
4. unsystematic; aimless
5. to spread or extend over
6. all over the place; everywhere
7. a Chinese family name
漫筆(ㄇㄢˋ ㄅㄧˇ)
a familiar essay; a causerie
漫步(ㄇㄢˋ ㄅㄨˋ)
to ramble; to stroll
漫不經心(ㄇㄢˋ ˙ㄅㄨ ㄐㄧㄥ ㄒㄧㄣ)
heedless; unmindful; inattentive; unconcerned
漫評(ㄇㄢˋ ㄆㄧㄥˊ)
rambling comments
漫罵(ㄇㄢˋ ㄇㄚˋ)

〔水部〕

to abuse or slander with abandon
漫漫(ㄇㄢˋ ㄇㄢˋ)
unrestrained; uninhibited
漫談(ㄇㄢˋ ㄊㄢˊ)
casual comments; rambling talks
漫條斯理 or 慢條斯理 (ㄇㄢˋ ㄊㄧㄠˊ ㄙ ㄌㄧˇ)
leisurely; calmly
漫浪(ㄇㄢˋ ㄌㄤˋ)
morally reckless or loose
漫汗(ㄇㄢˋ ㄏㄢˋ)
vast; boundless
漫畫(ㄇㄢˋ ㄏㄨㄚˋ)
a cartoon; a caricature
漫畫家(ㄇㄢˋ ㄏㄨㄚˋ ㄐㄧㄚ)
a cartoonist; a caricaturist
漫漶(ㄇㄢˋ ㄏㄨㄢˋ)
indecipherable; illegible
漫長(ㄇㄢˋ ㄔㄤˊ)
endless; infinite
漫射(ㄇㄢˋ ㄕㄜˋ)
diffused reflection or diffusion
漫山遍野(ㄇㄢˋ ㄕㄢ ㄅㄧㄢˋ ㄧㄝˇ)
so numerous as to cover the mountains and the plains; to be found everywhere
漫溢(ㄇㄢˋ ㄧˋ)
to overflow; to brim over
漫遊(ㄇㄢˋ ㄧㄡˊ)
to tour without a serious purpose; to travel about for pleasure
漫言(ㄇㄢˋ ㄧㄢˊ)
words uttered without much thought; unsupported remarks
漫衍(ㄇㄢˋ ㄧㄢˇ)
① to extend endlessly ② to wander from place to place; to have no fixed home
漫無邊際(ㄇㄢˋ ㄨˊ ㄅㄧㄢ ㄐㄧˋ)
① boundless; limitless ② straying far from the point; rambling; discursive
漫無目標(ㄇㄢˋ ㄨˊ ㄇㄨˋ ㄅㄧㄠ)
aimless; at random
漫無限制(ㄇㄢˋ ㄨˊ ㄒㄧㄢˋ ㄓˋ)
with no restrictions whatsoever
漫無止境(ㄇㄢˋ ㄨˊ ㄓˇ ㄐㄧㄥˋ)
extending or continuing endlessly; boundless
漫語(ㄇㄢˋ ㄩˇ)
words uttered without much thought; unsupported or unfounded remarks

【漫】 3054
2. ㄇㄢˊ man mán
(said of an expanse of water) vast or endless
漫漫(ㄇㄢˊ ㄇㄢˊ)
extending endlessly
漫漫長夜(ㄇㄢˊ ㄇㄢˊ ㄔㄤˊ ㄧㄝˋ)
a long, long night which seems to have no end
漫天(ㄇㄢˊ ㄊㄧㄢ)
so vast as to cover the heavens
漫天大謊(ㄇㄢˊ ㄊㄧㄢ ㄉㄚˋ ㄏㄨㄤˇ)
a monstrous lie
漫天討價(ㄇㄢˊ ㄊㄧㄢ ㄊㄠˇ ㄐㄧㄚˋ) or 漫天要價(ㄇㄢˊ ㄊㄧㄢ ㄧㄠˋ ㄐㄧㄚˋ)
to quote an exorbitant price in anticipation of haggling

【漬】 3055
ㄗˋ tzyh zì
1. to soak
2. to dye
3. to be caked with
漬痕(ㄗˋ ㄏㄣˊ)
a stain; a spot; a smear
漬染(ㄗˋ ㄖㄢˇ)
to dye: 這布容易漬染。This cloth dyes easily.

【漯】 3056
ㄊㄚˋ tah tà
name of a river flowing through Shantung
漯河(ㄊㄚˋ ㄏㄜˊ)
name of a river flowing through Shantung

【漱】 3057
ㄕㄨˋ shuh shù
(讀音 ㄙㄡˋ sow sòu)
1. to rinse; to gargle
2. to wash
漱口(ㄕㄨˋ ㄎㄡˇ)
to rinse the mouth; to gargle the throat
漱口水(ㄕㄨˋ ㄎㄡˇ ㄕㄨㄟˇ)
a gargle; a mouthwash
漱口藥水(ㄕㄨˋ ㄎㄡˇ ㄧㄠˋ ㄕㄨㄟˇ)
a mouthwash
漱口盂(ㄕㄨˋ ㄎㄡˇ ㄩˊ) or 漱口杯(ㄕㄨˋ ㄎㄡˇ ㄅㄟ)
a mouth washing cup; a mug
漱滌(ㄙㄡˋ ㄉㄧˊ)
to wash; to rinse

【漵】 3058
ㄒㄩˋ shiuh xù
name of a river in Hunan

【漳】 3059
ㄓㄤ jang zhāng
1. name of a river in Fukien
2. name of a river in Honan
漳緞(ㄓㄤ ㄉㄨㄢˋ)
brocade produced in Changchou, Fukien
漳泥(ㄓㄤ ㄋㄧˊ)
seal ink produced in Changchou
漳河(ㄓㄤ ㄏㄜˊ)
name of a river in Honan
漳廈鐵路(ㄓㄤ ㄒㄧㄚˋ ㄊㄧㄝˇ ㄌㄨˋ)
the Changchou-Amoy Railway in Fukien
漳州(ㄓㄤ ㄓㄡ)
Changchou, Fukien

【漲】 3060
1. ㄓㄤˇ janq zhǎng
to swell; to expand
漲潮(ㄓㄤˇ ㄔㄠˊ)
(said of the tide) to flow
漲水(ㄓㄤˇ ㄕㄨㄟˇ)
the swell of a river; to swell: 河因下雨而漲水。The river is swollen by rain.
漲縮(ㄓㄤˇ ㄙㄨㄛ)
swelling and shrinking; elasticity
漲溢(ㄓㄤˇ ㄧˋ)
(said of a river) to overflow

【漲】 3060
2. ㄓㄤˇ jaang zhǎng
to go up or rise (as prices, water, etc.): 河水暴漲。The river suddenly rose.
漲風(ㄓㄤˇ ㄈㄥ)
the upward trend of commodity prices and service charges
漲幅(ㄓㄤˇ ㄈㄨˊ)
(said of commodity prices, stocks, etc.) the rate of increase or rise
漲跌(ㄓㄤˇ ㄉㄧㄝˊ)
price fluctuation
漲落(ㄓㄤˇ ㄌㄠˋ) or (ㄓㄤˇ ㄌㄨㄛˋ)
① price fluctuation ② rising and dropping (of water stage)
漲價(ㄓㄤˇ ㄐㄧㄚˋ)
to register a price hike; to raise prices; appreciation

【漾】 3061
ㄧㄤˋ yanq yàng
1. to ripple

〔水部〕

2. to brim over
3. to throw up; to vomit
漾波(ㄧㄤˋ ㄅㄛ)
ripples
漾舟(ㄧㄤˋ ㄓㄡ)
to enjoy boating
漾漾(ㄧㄤˋ ㄧㄤˋ)
rippling

【漸】 3062
1. ㄐㄧㄢˋ jiann jiàn
gradually; little by little; by degrees
漸減(ㄐㄧㄢˋ ㄐㄧㄢˇ)
to decrease gradually: 他對這科目的興趣漸減。His interest in this subject gradually decreases.
漸漸(ㄐㄧㄢˋ ㄐㄧㄢˋ)
gradually; little by little: 你會漸漸習慣它的。You will get used to it gradually.
漸進(ㄐㄧㄢˋ ㄐㄧㄣˋ)
to advance little by little; to make gradual progress
漸強音(ㄐㄧㄢˋ ㄑㄧㄤˊ ㄧㄣ)
(music) a crescendo
漸入佳境(ㄐㄧㄢˋ ㄖㄨˋ ㄐㄧㄚ ㄐㄧㄥˋ)
to get better and better
漸增(ㄐㄧㄢˋ ㄗㄥ)
to increase gradually: 駕駛員漸增速度。The driver increased speed gradually.
漸次(ㄐㄧㄢˋ ㄘˋ)
gradually; little by little; by degrees: 水面漸次上升。The water level rose little by little.

【漸】 3062
2. ㄐㄧㄢ jian jiān
1. to soak; to permeate
2. (said of the territory) to reach
漸染(ㄐㄧㄢ ㄖㄢˇ)
to soak; to imbue
漸洳(ㄐㄧㄢ ㄖㄨˋ)
to soak
漸漬(ㄐㄧㄢ ㄗˋ)
to soak; to imbue

【漶】 3063
ㄏㄨㄢˋ huann huàn
to wear out beyond recognition

【滷】 3064
ㄌㄨˇ luu lǔ
1. gravy; broth; sauce
2. salty; salted
滷麵(ㄌㄨˇ ㄇㄧㄢˋ)
noodles served with gravy
滷蛋(ㄌㄨˇ ㄉㄢˋ)
a hard-boiled egg stewed in gravy; a marinated egg
滷湖(ㄌㄨˇ ㄏㄨˊ)
a salt lake
滷鷄(ㄌㄨˇ ㄐㄧ)
chicken stewed in soybean sauce; marinated chicken
滷蝦(ㄌㄨˇ ㄒㄧㄚ)
salted shrimp gravy
滷汁(ㄌㄨˇ ㄓ)
marinade
滷水(ㄌㄨˇ ㄕㄨㄟˇ)
salt brine
滷肉(ㄌㄨˇ ㄖㄡˋ)
meat stewed in soybean sauce; marinated meat
滷菜(ㄌㄨˇ ㄘㄞˋ)
marinated vegetables, meat, etc.
滷鴨(ㄌㄨˇ ㄧㄚ)
marinated duck

【滺】 3065
ㄧㄡ iou yōu
(said of water) flowing

【漦】 3066
ㄌㄧˊ li lí
1. saliva; spittle
2. flowing downstream

【漿】 3067
ㄐㄧㄤ jiang jiāng
1. thick fluid; starch
2. to starch
漿果(ㄐㄧㄤ ㄍㄨㄛˇ)
a berry
漿糊(ㄐㄧㄤ ·ㄏㄨ)
paste: 他用漿糊把信封封住。He sealed the envelope with paste.
漿洗衣服(ㄐㄧㄤ ㄒㄧˇ ㄧ ㄈㄨˊ)
to wash and starch clothes
漿水(ㄐㄧㄤ ㄕㄨㄟˇ)
starch solution; mixed starch

【潁】 3068
ㄧㄥˇ yiing yǐng
name of a river and a place in Anhwei
潁河(ㄧㄥˇ ㄏㄜˊ)
name of a river in Anhwei
潁上(ㄧㄥˇ ㄕㄤˋ)
name of a county in Anhwei

【漻】 3069
ㄌㄧㄠˊ liau liáo
deep and clear

十二畫

【漭】 3070
ㄇㄤˇ maang mǎng
vast; expansive

【潔】 3071
ㄐㄧㄝˊ jye jié
1. clean; spotless; pure; stainless; immaculate: 他心地純潔。He is pure in heart.
2. to clean; to keep clean
潔白(ㄐㄧㄝˊ ㄅㄞˊ)
clean and white; immaculate; spotless
潔癖(ㄐㄧㄝˊ ㄆㄧˋ)
a morbid fear of getting dirty; mysophobia
潔婦(ㄐㄧㄝˊ ㄈㄨˋ)
a chaste woman
潔朗(ㄐㄧㄝˊ ㄌㄤˇ)
clean and bright
潔廉(ㄐㄧㄝˊ ㄌㄧㄢˊ)
incorruptible; clean: 潔廉的人不會受賄。The incorruptible man could not be bribed.
潔己(ㄐㄧㄝˊ ㄐㄧˇ)
to keep oneself free from immorality
潔淨(ㄐㄧㄝˊ ㄐㄧㄥˋ)
clean; untarnished; untainted; stainless: 他雙手潔淨。His hands are clean.
潔身自好(ㄐㄧㄝˊ ㄕㄣ ㄗˋ ㄏㄠˋ)or 潔身自愛(ㄐㄧㄝˊ ㄕㄣ ㄗˋ ㄞˋ)
to exercise self-control so as to protect oneself from immorality
潔樽候教(ㄐㄧㄝˊ ㄗㄨㄣ ㄏㄡˋ ㄐㄧㄠˋ)
I am looking forward to your visit with wine-cups washed clean. (a conventional phrase often printed on an invitation to dinner)

【潑】 3072
ㄆㄛ po pō
1. to pour; to sprinkle; to spill
2. ferocious; fierce; spiteful; villainous
潑皮(ㄆㄛ ㄆㄧˊ)
a ruffian; a villain
潑墨山水(ㄆㄛ ㄇㄛˋ ㄕㄢ ㄕㄨㄟˇ)
landscape painting done with splashes of ink; splash-ink landscape
潑婦(ㄆㄛ ㄈㄨˋ)
a virago; a shrew; a termagant
潑婦罵街(ㄆㄛ ㄈㄨˋ ㄇㄚˋ ㄐㄧㄝ)
(literally) a virago yelling

水部

in the street—to utter abusive language loudly and freely without much provocation or justification

潑天富貴(ㄆㄛ ㄊㄧㄢ ㄈㄨˋ ㄍㄨㄟˋ)
extreme wealth

潑天大禍(ㄆㄛ ㄊㄧㄢ ㄉㄚˋ ㄏㄨㄛˋ)
extreme disaster

潑剌(ㄆㄛ ㄌㄚˋ)
splashing sound of fish jumping out of water

潑辣(ㄆㄛ ˙ㄌㄚ)
① fierce; ferocious; spiteful ② pungent: 這份評論寫得很潑辣。The critique is written in a pungent style.

潑辣貨(ㄆㄛ ˙ㄌㄚ ㄏㄨㄛˋ)
a ferocious woman: 她是個潑辣貨。She is a ferocious woman.

潑賴(ㄆㄛ ㄌㄞˋ)
villainous; knavish

潑冷水(ㄆㄛ ㄌㄥˇ ㄕㄨㄟˇ)
to pour or to throw cold water on—(figuratively) to dampen the enthusiasm of

潑街(ㄆㄛ ㄐㄧㄝ)
to water the street

潑水難收(ㄆㄛ ㄕㄨㄟˇ ㄋㄢˊ ㄕㄡ)
(literally) Spilled water cannot be retrieved.—One cannot undo an accomplished fact.

潑水節(ㄆㄛ ㄕㄨㄟˇ ㄐㄧㄝˊ)
the Water-Sprinkling Festival of Thailand, Laos, Burma and some minority nationalities in China

【潛】 3073 ㄑㄧㄢˊ chyan qián

1. to hide; to conceal
2. to dive
3. hidden; secret; latent

潛伏(ㄑㄧㄢˊ ㄈㄨˊ)
① to be in hiding; to lie hidden ② latent; hidden; concealed

潛伏期(ㄑㄧㄢˊ ㄈㄨˊ ㄑㄧˊ)
an incubation period; a latent period

潛伏性(ㄑㄧㄢˊ ㄈㄨˊ ㄒㄧㄥˋ)
latency

潛德(ㄑㄧㄢˊ ㄉㄜˊ)
hidden virtues; unnoticed virtues

潛邸(ㄑㄧㄢˊ ㄉㄧˇ)
the residence of an emperor before ascending the throne

潛遁(ㄑㄧㄢˊ ㄉㄨㄣˋ)
to escape secretly; to slip away: 他們潛遁了。They slipped away.

潛逃(ㄑㄧㄢˊ ㄊㄠˊ)
to flee secretly; to slip away; to abscond

潛艇(ㄑㄧㄢˊ ㄊㄧㄥˇ)
a submarine

潛艇補給艦(ㄑㄧㄢˊ ㄊㄧㄥˇ ㄅㄨˇ ㄐㄧˇ ㄐㄧㄢˋ)
a submarine tender

潛能(ㄑㄧㄢˊ ㄋㄥˊ)
potential energy; potentiality

潛匿(ㄑㄧㄢˊ ㄋㄧˋ)
to go into hiding; to hide oneself

潛力(ㄑㄧㄢˊ ㄌㄧˋ)
potential; hidden force; unused strength: 他似乎具有領導者的潛力。He seems to have potential as a leader.

潛龍(ㄑㄧㄢˊ ㄌㄨㄥˊ)
a hidden dragon—an unrecognized sage

潛居(ㄑㄧㄢˊ ㄐㄩ)
to live in seclusion; to live in a hiding place

潛修(ㄑㄧㄢˊ ㄒㄧㄡ)
to cultivate oneself in quiet privacy

潛心(ㄑㄧㄢˊ ㄒㄧㄣ)
to have a quiet concentrated mind

潛心研究(ㄑㄧㄢˊ ㄒㄧㄣ ㄧㄢˊ ㄐㄧㄡˋ)
to study diligently with a quiet mind: 他潛心研究歷史。He devotes himself to the study of history.

潛行(ㄑㄧㄢˊ ㄒㄧㄥˊ)
to go secretly

潛虛(ㄑㄧㄢˊ ㄒㄩ)
to live in seclusion

潛師(ㄑㄧㄢˊ ㄕ)
to move troops secretly

潛勢力(ㄑㄧㄢˊ ㄕˋ ㄌㄧˋ)
latent power

潛水(ㄑㄧㄢˊ ㄕㄨㄟˇ)
① to dive ② name of a river flowing through Anhwei (安徽) and Kiangsu (江蘇)

潛水底(ㄑㄧㄢˊ ㄕㄨㄟˇ ㄉㄧˇ)
to explore a riverbed, sea bottom, etc., by diving

潛水艇(ㄑㄧㄢˊ ㄕㄨㄟˇ ㄊㄧㄥˇ)
a submarine: 潛水艇潛水了。The submarine dived.

潛水炸彈(ㄑㄧㄢˊ ㄕㄨㄟˇ ㄓㄚˋ ㄉㄢˋ)
a depth charge

潛水衣(ㄑㄧㄢˊ ㄕㄨㄟˇ ㄧ)
a diving suit

潛水員(ㄑㄧㄢˊ ㄕㄨㄟˇ ㄩㄢˊ)or 潛水夫(ㄑㄧㄢˊ ㄕㄨㄟˇ ㄈㄨ)
a diver

潛熱(ㄑㄧㄢˊ ㄖㄜˋ)
latent heat

潛入(ㄑㄧㄢˊ ㄖㄨˋ)
① to enter secretly; to slip in ② to dive into (water)

潛滋暗長(ㄑㄧㄢˊ ㄗ ㄢˋ ㄓㄤˇ)
to grow and develop secretly

潛在(ㄑㄧㄢˊ ㄗㄞˋ)
latent

潛在能力(ㄑㄧㄢˊ ㄗㄞˋ ㄋㄥˊ ㄌㄧˋ)or 潛力(ㄑㄧㄢˊ ㄌㄧˋ)
potentiality

潛在意識(ㄑㄧㄢˊ ㄗㄞˋ ㄧˋ ㄕˋ)or 潛意識(ㄑㄧㄢˊ ㄧˋ ㄕˋ)
subconsciousness

潛藏(ㄑㄧㄢˊ ㄘㄤˊ)
to be in hiding

潛移默化(ㄑㄧㄢˊ ㄧˊ ㄇㄛˋ ㄏㄨㄚˋ)
to change and influence unobtrusively and imperceptibly

潛望鏡(ㄑㄧㄢˊ ㄨㄤˋ ㄐㄧㄥˋ)
a periscope

【潘】 3074 ㄆㄢ pan pān

1. a Chinese family name
2. water in which rice has been washed

潘金蓮(ㄆㄢ ㄐㄧㄣ ㄌㄧㄢˊ)
Pan Chin-lien, a female character of loose morals in the novel *All Men Are Brothers* (水滸傳)

【澙】 3075 ㄒㄧˋ shih xì

saline land

澙湖(ㄒㄧˋ ㄏㄨˊ)
(geography) a lagoon

【潞】 3076 ㄌㄨˋ luh lù

name of several rivers in Northern China

【潢】 3077 ㄏㄨㄤˊ hwang huáng

a lake or a pond

潢池(ㄏㄨㄤˊ ㄔˊ)
a pond

瀇洋(ㄏㄨㄤˇ ㄧㄤˊ)
deep and expansive
瀇漾(ㄏㄨㄤˇ ㄧㄤˋ)
(said of a body of water) boundless

【澗】 3078 ㄐㄧㄢˋ jiann jiàn
a mountain stream
澗流(ㄐㄧㄢˋ ㄌㄧㄡˊ)
a mountain stream; a stream in a valley
澗河(ㄐㄧㄢˋ ㄏㄜˊ)
name of a river originating in Honan
澗壑(ㄐㄧㄢˋ ㄏㄨㄛˋ)
a valley; a ravine
澗溪(ㄐㄧㄢˋ ㄒㄧ)
a mountain stream; a stream in a valley: 我們順著澗溪而下。We went down the mountain stream.
澗峽(ㄐㄧㄢˋ ㄒㄧㄚˊ)
a gorge
澗水(ㄐㄧㄢˋ ㄕㄨㄟˇ)
a mountain stream: 他跳過澗水。He jumped across the mountain stream.

【潦】 3079 1. (澇) ㄌㄠˋ law lào
to flood; floods

【潦】 3079 2. ㄌㄠˇ lao lǎo
a puddle

【潦】 3079 3. ㄌㄧㄠˊ liau liáo
1. disheartened; disappointed
2. without care
潦倒(ㄌㄧㄠˊ ㄉㄠˇ)
disappointed; unhappy; down in luck: 他過着潦倒的生活。He led an unhappy life.
潦草(ㄌㄧㄠˊ ㄘㄠˇ)or潦潦草草(ㄌㄧㄠˊ ㄌㄧㄠˊ ㄘㄠˇ ㄘㄠˇ)
① in a careless, irresponsible manner; perfunctory ② (said of handwriting) hasty and careless; illegible
潦草塞責(ㄌㄧㄠˊ ㄘㄠˇ ㄙㄜˋ ㄗㄜˊ)
to do a duty perfunctorily

【潤】 3080 ㄖㄨㄣˋ ruenn rùn
1. moist; glossy; fresh
2. to moisten; to freshen
3. to enrich; to benefit
4. to embellish
潤筆(ㄖㄨㄣˋ ㄅㄧˇ)or 潤毫(ㄖㄨㄣˋ ㄏㄠˊ)
remuneration (or fee) for writing or painting
潤肺(ㄖㄨㄣˋ ㄈㄟˋ)
(Chinese herb medicine) to moisten supposedly dry lungs
潤膩(ㄖㄨㄣˋ ㄋㄧˋ)
fine and smooth
潤滑(ㄖㄨㄣˋ ㄏㄨㄚˊ)
① to lubricate ② smooth
潤滑劑(ㄖㄨㄣˋ ㄏㄨㄚˊ ㄐㄧˋ)
a lubricant
潤滑油(ㄖㄨㄣˋ ㄏㄨㄚˊ ㄧㄡˊ)
lubricating oil
潤腸(ㄖㄨㄣˋ ㄔㄤˊ)
(Chinese herb medicine) to moisten the supposedly dry digestive apparatus
潤濕(ㄖㄨㄣˋ ㄕ)
moist and fresh: 草因露水而潤濕。Grasses were moist with dew.
潤飾(ㄖㄨㄣˋ ㄕˋ)
to add color; to embellish or polish a writing
潤飾之詞(ㄖㄨㄣˋ ㄕˋ ㄓ ㄘˊ)
ornamental words that gloss over fault
潤身(ㄖㄨㄣˋ ㄕㄣ)
to invigorate or enrich oneself with virtues
潤資(ㄖㄨㄣˋ ㄗ)
fee for writing or painting
潤澤(ㄖㄨㄣˋ ㄗㄜˊ)
① moist and glossy; fresh; vigorous: 她有一頭潤澤有光的頭髮。She has sleek and glossy hair. ② to moisten; to freshen; to invigorate
潤色(ㄖㄨㄣˋ ㄙㄜˋ)
to add color; to embellish or polish a writing: 你的作文需要潤色一下。Your composition needs polishing.
潤益(ㄖㄨㄣˋ ㄧˋ)
profit; benefit; dividend
潤屋(ㄖㄨㄣˋ ㄨ)
to enrich the house with material wealth

【潭】 3081 ㄊㄢˊ tarn tán
1. deep water; a deep pool
2. deep; profound
潭府(ㄊㄢˊ ㄈㄨˇ)
your residence or house (a polite expression)
潭第(ㄊㄢˊ ㄉㄧˋ)
your mansion (a polite expression)
潭腿(ㄊㄢˊ ㄊㄨㄟˇ)
one of the northern schools of boxing, founded by the monks of the Temple of Dragon Pond (龍潭寺)
潭祉(ㄊㄢˊ ㄓˇ)
great happiness (a term used in letter writing)
潭水(ㄊㄢˊ ㄕㄨㄟˇ)
deep water
潭奧(ㄊㄢˊ ㄠˋ)
profound; deep
潭影(ㄊㄢˊ ㄧㄥˇ)
the reflection in a deep pond

【潮】 3082 ㄔㄠˊ chaur cháo
1. the tide
2. damp; moist; wet
3. (now rarely, said of gold, silver, etc.) inferior in skill or fineness
潮流(ㄔㄠˊ ㄌㄧㄡˊ)
① tides; tidal currents ② a current; a trend; a tendency
潮解(ㄔㄠˊ ㄐㄧㄝˇ)
to deliquesce; deliquescence
潮氣(ㄔㄠˊ ㄑㄧˋ)
dampness; high humidity; moist; moisture
潮汐(ㄔㄠˊ ㄒㄧˋ)
morning tide and evening tide; tides
潮信(ㄔㄠˊ ㄒㄧㄣˋ)
① the fixed time of the tides ② menstruation; period; the time of menstruating
潮州(ㄔㄠˊ ㄓㄡ)
Chaochow, Kwantung Province
潮濕(ㄔㄠˊ ㄕ)
humid; damp: 我不喜歡潮濕的天氣。I don't like damp weather.
潮水(ㄔㄠˊ ㄕㄨㄟˇ)
the tide
潮音(ㄔㄠˊ ㄧㄣ)
the chanting of Buddhist scriptures by the monks

【潯】 3083 ㄒㄩㄣˊ shyun xún
1. a steep bank by the stream
2. an alternative name of Chiuchiang (九江) in Kiangsi
潯江(ㄒㄩㄣˊ ㄐㄧㄤ)

〔水部〕

name of a river in Kwangsi
潯陽(ㄒㄩㄣˊ ㄧㄤˊ)
name of a river near Chiuchiang

【潼】 3084
ㄊㄨㄥˊ torng tóng
1. high and lofty
2. a tributary of the Yellow River
3. a county in Shensi Province
潼關(ㄊㄨㄥˊ ㄍㄨㄢ)
name of a strategic point and a county in Shensi Province, a gateway between Northwest and Central China

【潺】 3085
ㄔㄢˊ charn chán
the sound of water flowing
潺潺(ㄔㄢˊ ㄔㄢˊ)
the gurgling of water flowing; the murmuring of flowing water
潺湲(ㄔㄢˊ ㄩㄢˊ)
① water flowing ② tears streaming down

【潸】 3086
ㄕㄢ shan shān
tears flowing; to weep
潸泫(ㄕㄢ ㄒㄩㄢˋ)
tears flowing; weeping
潸潸(ㄕㄢ ㄕㄢ)
to weep continually
潸然(ㄕㄢ ㄖㄢˊ)
tears falling

【潰】 3087
ㄎㄨㄟˋ kuey kuì
1. a river overflowing its banks
2. broken up; scattered
3. (military) defeated
4. (said of a dike or dam) to burst
潰敗(ㄎㄨㄟˋ ㄅㄞˋ)
(military) defeated and scattered; routed; a rout: 撤退變成潰敗。The retreat became a rout.
潰不成軍(ㄎㄨㄟˋ ·ㄅㄨ ㄔㄥˊ ㄐㄩㄣ)
defeated and broken up to such a state that it can no longer be called an army; completely routed
潰破(ㄎㄨㄟˋ ㄆㄛˋ)
(said of dikes) broken up; (said of the army) defeated; (said of abscesses) bursting
潰盟(ㄎㄨㄟˋ ㄇㄥˊ)
to violate an agreement or treaty; a breach of faith
潰敵(ㄎㄨㄟˋ ㄉㄧˊ)
to defeat the enemy; to put the enemy to rout
潰逃(ㄎㄨㄟˋ ㄊㄠˊ)
to escape in disorder; to flee pell-mell; to run helter-skelter: 敵人潰逃。The enemies fled pell-mell.
潰退(ㄎㄨㄟˋ ㄊㄨㄟˋ)
to retreat as a result of defeat
潰爛(ㄎㄨㄟˋ ㄌㄢˋ)
bursting of an abscess; inflamed; inflammation
潰決(ㄎㄨㄟˋ ㄐㄩㄝˊ)
floods overflowing or breaking up levees, embankments, etc.
潰走(ㄎㄨㄟˋ ㄗㄡˇ)
(said of a defeated army) to scatter and run for life
潰散(ㄎㄨㄟˋ ㄙㄢˋ)
defeated and dispersed
潰瘍(ㄎㄨㄟˋ ㄧㄤˊ)
an ulcer
潰圍(ㄎㄨㄟˋ ㄨㄟˊ)
to break the enemy encirclement and get away

【澄】 3088
ㄔㄥˊ cherng chéng
(語音 ㄉㄥˋ denq dèng)
1. clear and still (water)
2. to purify water by letting the impurities settle down to the bottom
3. to pacify
澄明(ㄔㄥˊ ㄇㄧㄥˊ)
clear and bright
澄空(ㄔㄥˊ ㄎㄨㄥ)
a clear sky
澄清(ㄔㄥˊ ㄑㄧㄥ)
①to purify water by letting the impurities settle down to the bottom ② to quell disturbances in the world; to put in order; to set right ③ to clarify ④ clear
澄清天下(ㄔㄥˊ ㄑㄧㄥ ㄊㄧㄢ ㄒㄧㄚˋ)
to rid the world of all troubles and disturbances
澄清事實(ㄔㄥˊ ㄑㄧㄥ ㄕˋ ㄕˊ)
to clarify some facts
澄心(ㄔㄥˊ ㄒㄧㄣ)
to calm one's mind
澄澈(ㄔㄥˊ ㄔㄜˋ)
crystal clear.
澄淵(ㄔㄥˊ ㄩㄢ)
clear, deep water

【澈】 3089
ㄔㄜˋ cheh chè
1. thoroughly; completely
2. clear water
3. to understand
澈底(ㄔㄜˋ ㄉㄧˇ)
thoroughly; completely; thoroughgoing
澈頭澈尾(ㄔㄜˋ ㄊㄡˊ ㄔㄜˋ ㄨㄟˇ)
out and out; thoroughly
澈查(ㄔㄜˋ ㄔㄚˊ)
to investigate thoroughly
澈悟(ㄔㄜˋ ㄨˋ)
to realize or understand completely

【澎】 3090
1. ㄆㄥ peng pēng
the roaring of colliding billows
澎湃(ㄆㄥ ㄆㄞˋ)
the roaring of billows; to surge: 大海中波濤澎湃。Waves surge in the sea.

【澎】 3090
2. ㄆㄥˊ perng péng
the Pescadores
澎湖(ㄆㄥˊ ㄏㄨˊ)
the Penghus, or the Pescadores, in the Taiwan Straits

【澍】 3091
ㄕㄨˋ shuh shù
1. seasonal rains; timely rain
2. (said of plants, etc.) saturated with rainwater

【澆】 3092
ㄐㄧㄠ jiau jiāo
1. to water (plants, flowers, etc.)
2. to sprinkle water on
3. perfidious; faithless; ungrateful
澆薄(ㄐㄧㄠ ㄅㄛˊ)
rash and perfidious; faithless and ungrateful
澆薄之世(ㄐㄧㄠ ㄅㄛˊ ㄓ ㄕˋ)
the age of demoralization
澆浮(ㄐㄧㄠ ㄈㄨˊ)
rash and faithless
澆奠(ㄐㄧㄠ ㄉㄧㄢˋ)
to pour out a libation
澆冷水(ㄐㄧㄠ ㄌㄥˇ ㄕㄨㄟˇ)
to dampen enthusiasm; to discourage; to throw cold water on

澆灌(ㄐㄧㄠ ㄍㄨㄢˋ)
to water (plants, etc.); to pour water: 她每天早晨澆灌花草。She waters plants every morning.
澆花(ㄐㄧㄠ ㄏㄨㄚ)
to water flowers: 那女孩正在澆花。The girl is watering flowers.
澆愁(ㄐㄧㄠ ㄔㄡˊ)
to wash away sorrows with wine
澆水(ㄐㄧㄠ ㄕㄨㄟˇ)
to water; to pour water on

【潲】 3093 ㄕㄠˋ shaw shào
(said of rain) to fall slantwise
潲進來(ㄕㄠˋ ㄐㄧㄣˋ ·ㄌㄞ)
(said of the rainwater) splashing in with the wind
潲濕了(ㄕㄠˋ ㄕ ·ㄌㄜ)
to get wet by the rainwater splashing in with the wind
潲雨(ㄕㄠˋ ㄩˇ)
① rain slanted by wind ② to get wet by the slanting rain

【澇】 3094 ㄌㄠˋ law lào
1. (said of farm crops) to rot in the field owing to floods; waterlogged
2. torrents; floods

【澮】 3095 ㄍㄨㄟ guei guī
name of a river in Yung-chi County (永濟縣) Shansi Province

【澌】 3096 ㄙ sy sī
1. to exhaust; to drain out
2. the sound of breaking or scattering
澌滅(ㄙ ㄇㄧㄝˋ)
to vanish
澌盡(ㄙ ㄐㄧㄣˋ)
to exhaust; to drain out
澌澌(ㄙ ㄙ)
the sound of the pouring rain or the heaving wind

【澉】 3097 ㄍㄢˇ gaan gǎn
to wash
澉浦(ㄍㄢˇ ㄆㄨˇ)
name of a town in Chekiang (浙江)

【澔】 3098 ㄏㄠˋ haw hào
radiance of gems

【澂】 3099 ㄔㄥˊ cherng chéng
same as 澄—clear and still water
澂江(ㄔㄥˊ ㄐㄧㄤ)
name of a county in Yunnan Province

十三畫

【澠】 3100 1. ㄕㄥˊ sherng shéng
name of a river in Shantung Province
澠水(ㄕㄥˊ ㄕㄨㄟˇ)
name of a river in Shantung Province

【澠】 3100 2. ㄇㄧㄣˇ miin mǐn
1. the ancient name of a place in Honan Province where the kings of Chin (秦) and Chao (趙) of the Epoch of Warring States held their summit conference
2. name of a river and a county in Honan Province
澠河(ㄇㄧㄣˇ ㄏㄜˊ)
name of a river in Honan Province

【澥】 3101 ㄒㄧㄝˋ shieh xiè
1. a blocked stream
2. to stop the flow of water
3. another name of Pohai (渤海)

【澡】 3102 ㄗㄠˇ tzao zǎo
to wash; to bathe
澡盆(ㄗㄠˇ ㄆㄣˊ)
a bathtub
澡堂 or 澡塘(ㄗㄠˇ ㄊㄤˊ)
a bathhouse; a public bath
澡身(ㄗㄠˇ ㄕㄣ)
to take a bath
澡身浴德(ㄗㄠˇ ㄕㄣ ㄩˋ ㄉㄜˊ)
(literally) to bathe oneself in water and in virtues—to cleanse both physically and morally

【澧】 3103 ㄌㄧˇ lii lǐ
1. a fountain; a spring
2. name of a county in Hunan Province

【澮】 3104 ㄎㄨㄞˋ kuay kuài
1. ditches on farmland
2. name of a river in Shansi and Honan provinces
澮水(ㄎㄨㄞˋ ㄕㄨㄟˇ)
① name of a river in Shansi
② name of a river in Honan

【澨】 3105 ㄕˋ shyh shì
1. the waterside; the waterfront
2. name of a river in Hupeh Province
澨水(ㄕˋ ㄕㄨㄟˇ)
name of a river in Hupeh Province

【澤】 3106 ㄗㄜˊ tzer zé
1. the place where water gathers; a marsh
2. grace; favors; kindness
3. brilliance; radiance; luster; bright; glossy; smooth
4. to benefit; to enrich
澤被(ㄗㄜˊ ㄅㄟˋ)
to extend benefit
澤被天下(ㄗㄜˊ ㄅㄟˋ ㄊㄧㄢ ㄒㄧㄚˋ)
Benefits spread to all people.
澤民(ㄗㄜˊ ㄇㄧㄣˊ)
to benefit the people
澤鹵(ㄗㄜˊ ㄌㄨˇ)
salty land that grows no crops
澤國(ㄗㄜˊ ㄍㄨㄛˊ)
land submerged or inundated by water; a marsh or swamp
澤及枯骨(ㄗㄜˊ ㄐㄧˊ ㄎㄨ ㄍㄨˇ)
to benefit even the dead
澤及萬世(ㄗㄜˊ ㄐㄧˊ ㄨㄢˋ ㄕˋ)
The good grace or benevolence will be felt for countless generations to come.

【澱】 3107 ㄉㄧㄢˋ diann diàn
1. sediment; dregs; precipitate
2. indigo
澱粉(ㄉㄧㄢˋ ㄈㄣˇ)
starch

【澳】 3108 ㄠˋ aw ào
1. deep waters—where seagoing vessels can moor
2. name of various places (see below)
澳門(ㄠˋ ㄇㄣˊ)
Macao

澳大利亞(ㄠˋ ㄉㄚˋ ㄌㄧˋ ㄧㄚˇ)
Australia
澳洲(ㄠˋ ㄓㄡ)
Australia 參看「澳大利亞」

〔水部〕

【澼】 3109
ㄆㄧˋ pih pì
to wash; to launder

【澹】 3110
1. ㄉㄢˋ dann dàn
quiet and tranquil
澹泊(ㄉㄢˋ ㄅㄛˊ)
having no worldly desires or ambitions 亦作「淡泊」
澹泊名利(ㄉㄢˋ ㄅㄛˊ ㄇㄧㄥˊ ㄌㄧˋ)
to be indifferent toward fame and wealth
澹泊明志(ㄉㄢˋ ㄅㄛˊ ㄇㄧㄥˊ ㄓˋ)
to live a simple life to show one's will and moral fortitude
澹漠(ㄉㄢˋ ㄇㄛˋ)
indifference; indifferent; placid and dispassionate
澹澉(ㄉㄢˋ ㄍㄢˇ)
to wash
澹然(ㄉㄢˋ ㄖㄢˊ)
tranquil and calm
澹雅(ㄉㄢˋ ㄧㄚˇ)
quiet and refined

【澹】 3110
2. ㄊㄢˊ tarn tán
澹臺(ㄊㄢˊ ㄊㄞˊ)
①a double-surname ②name of a lake in Kiangsu (江蘇)

【澶】 3111
ㄔㄢˊ charn chán
1. (said of the water) placid, calm and tranquil
2. name of a river
澶州(ㄔㄢˊ ㄓㄡ)
the ancient name of a political region in the Tang Dynasty in today's Ching Feng County (清豐縣) of Hopeh Province

【激】 3112
ㄐㄧ ji jī
1. to stir up; to rouse; to arouse; to urge; to excite
2. sudden; great; very
3. heated (debate, battle, etc.); fierce; angry; vexed
4. abnormal; unusual; drastic
5. to turn back the current—as a dike
激變(ㄐㄧ ㄅㄧㄢˋ)
an upheaval; a sudden change of a situation (such as mutiny, coup, etc.)
激辯(ㄐㄧ ㄅㄧㄢˋ)
a heated argument or debate
激發(ㄐㄧ ㄈㄚ)
to stir up; to arouse; to spur to action
激發天良(ㄐㄧ ㄈㄚ ㄊㄧㄢ ㄌㄧㄤˊ)
to arouse one's conscience
激憤(ㄐㄧ ㄈㄣˋ)
wrathful; indignant: 群衆心情激憤。The crowd are filled with indignation.
激盪(ㄐㄧ ㄉㄤˋ)
to surge; turmoil; stirring; in drastic motion or change
激動(ㄐㄧ ㄉㄨㄥˋ)
aroused; stimulated; excited; agitated
激湍(ㄐㄧ ㄊㄨㄢ)
(said of the flow of water) swift and torrential
激痛(ㄐㄧ ㄊㄨㄥˋ)
very painful; severe pain; painfully excited or stimulated
激怒(ㄐㄧ ㄋㄨˋ)
to irritate; to infuriate; to provoke; to enrage
激浪(ㄐㄧ ㄌㄤˋ)
heaving breakers or billows
激厲(ㄐㄧ ㄌㄧˋ)
to arouse to high emotional response; to stimulate and urge
激勵(ㄐㄧ ㄌㄧˋ)
to arouse and encourage ; to impel: 他的一番演說激勵我們更加努力。His speech impelled us to greater efforts.
激勵士氣(ㄐㄧ ㄌㄧˋ ㄕˋ ㄑㄧˋ)
to boost the morale (of the army or people)
激烈(ㄐㄧ ㄌㄧㄝˋ)
heated (debates, battles, etc.); drastic (measures, means, etc.); violent (actions, speeches, etc.); radical or extremist (parties, etc.); fierce (combats)
激烈手段(ㄐㄧ ㄌㄧㄝˋ ㄕㄡˇ ㄉㄨㄢˋ)
drastic actions or measures; violent means
激流(ㄐㄧ ㄌㄧㄡˊ)
strong currents; rapids
激論(ㄐㄧ ㄌㄨㄣˋ)
heated discussions or comments
激聒(ㄐㄧ ㄍㄨㄚ)
to chatter incessantly
激減(ㄐㄧ ㄐㄧㄢˇ)
to decrease or lessen drastically
激進(ㄐㄧ ㄐㄧㄣˋ)
radical
激進派(ㄐㄧ ㄐㄧㄣˋ ㄆㄞˋ)
a radical or extremist party or faction
激進分子(ㄐㄧ ㄐㄧㄣˋ ㄈㄣˋ ㄗˇ)or 激烈分子(ㄐㄧ ㄌㄧㄝˋ ㄈㄣˋ ㄗˇ)
radicals; extremists
激將(ㄐㄧ ㄐㄧㄤˋ)
to taunt someone into doing something which he will not do under ordinary circumstances
激將法(ㄐㄧ ㄐㄧㄤˋ ㄈㄚˇ)
urging or prodding somebody by derision, sarcasm, etc.
激劇(ㄐㄧ ㄐㄩˋ)
very excited; extremely agitated
激起(ㄐㄧ ㄑㄧˇ)
to arouse; to excite; to stir up
激起公憤(ㄐㄧ ㄑㄧˇ ㄍㄨㄥ ㄈㄣˋ)
to arouse public indignation
激切(ㄐㄧ ㄑㄧㄝˋ)
to talk so candidly and honestly that it hurts
激情(ㄐㄧ ㄑㄧㄥˊ)
fervor; ardor; passion; enthusiasm
激勸(ㄐㄧ ㄑㄩㄢˋ)
to excite and encourage; to arouse and persuade
激戰(ㄐㄧ ㄓㄢˋ)
a heated battle; a fierce combat
激濁揚清(ㄐㄧ ㄓㄨㄛˊ ㄧㄤˊ ㄑㄧㄥ)
to rid of the evil and hail the virtuous
激楚(ㄐㄧ ㄔㄨˇ)
voices that rend the heart and rouse the spirit
激賞(ㄐㄧ ㄕㄤˇ)
to appreciate tremendously; to heap high praise on (a work, person, etc.)
激增(ㄐㄧ ㄗㄥ)
to shoot up; to increase sharply
激素 (ㄐㄧ ㄙㄨˋ)

(physiology) hormone 亦作「荷爾蒙」
激昂(ㄐㄧˊ ㄤˊ)or激昂慷慨(ㄐㄧ ㄤˊ ㄎㄤ ㄎㄞˇ)
high-spirited; tremendously excited; passionate
激揚(ㄐㄧ ㄧㄤˊ)
to be moved to renewed courage or determination; to be aroused to a new lease of spirit
激於義憤(ㄐㄧ ㄩˊ ㄧˋ ㄈㄣˋ)
to be aroused by one's sense of justice
激越(ㄐㄧ ㄩㄝˋ)
sonorous; stentorian

【濁】 3113
ㄓㄨㄛˊ jwo zhuó
1. (said of water) turbid or muddy
2. (said of the world) tumultuous, evil, corrupt
3. (said of a person) stupid and idiotic
4. name of a constellation
濁醪(ㄓㄨㄛˊ ㄌㄠˊ)
unstrained wine
濁浪(ㄓㄨㄛˊ ㄌㄤˋ)
muddy waves
濁流(ㄓㄨㄛˊ ㄌㄧㄡˊ)
a turbid stream
濁酒(ㄓㄨㄛˊ ㄐㄧㄡˇ)
unstrained wine or liquor
濁井(ㄓㄨㄛˊ ㄐㄧㄥˇ)
a muddy well
濁氣(ㄓㄨㄛˊ ㄑㄧˋ)
foul smell, breath or air; bad breath
濁漳(ㄓㄨㄛˊ ㄓㄤ)
another name of the Chang River in Honan Province
濁世(ㄓㄨㄛˊ ㄕˋ)
①(Buddhism) the human world ②the tumultuous world
濁聲(ㄓㄨㄛˊ ㄕㄥ)
voiced sounds
濁水(ㄓㄨㄛˊ ㄕㄨㄟˇ)
turbid or muddy water
濁水溪(ㄓㄨㄛˊ ㄕㄨㄟˇ ㄒㄧ)
①a muddy river ②name of a river in Taiwan
濁人(ㄓㄨㄛˊ ㄖㄣˊ)
a stupid, mixed-up person; a muddle-headed person
濁音(ㄓㄨㄛˊ ㄧㄣ)
a voiced sound
濁物(ㄓㄨㄛˊ ㄨˋ)
a bloody fool; an idiot; a blockhead

【濂】 3114
ㄌㄧㄢˊ lian lián
name of a river in Hunan Province
濂洛關閩(ㄌㄧㄢˊ ㄌㄨㄛˋ ㄍㄨㄢ ㄇㄧㄣˊ)
the four most influential branches of the Li School of Thought(理學), led by Chou Tun-yi of Lien-hsi(濂溪周敦頤), Cheng Hao & Cheng Yi of Loyang(洛陽程顥程頤), Chang Tsai of Kuan-chung (關中張載) and Chu Hsi of Min(閩中朱熹), in the Sung Dynasty
濂溪(ㄌㄧㄢˊ ㄒㄧ)
the River Lien, in Hunan Province
濂溪學派(ㄌㄧㄢˊ ㄒㄧ ㄒㄩㄝˊ ㄆㄞˋ)
the Lien Hsi branch of the Li School 參看「濂洛關閩」

【濃】 3115
ㄋㄨㄥˊ nong nóng
1. (said of drinks, liquids, etc.) thick; strong; heavy; concentrated: 血濃於水。Blood is thicker than water.
2. (said of colors) deep; dark
3. dense
4. (said of a smell) strong; heavy: 梔子花香味很濃。The capejasmine has a heavy fragrance.
濃抹(ㄋㄨㄥˊ ㄇㄛˇ)
to wear heavy make-up
濃墨(ㄋㄨㄥˊ ㄇㄛˋ)
heavy (Chinese) ink; thick ink
濃眉大眼(ㄋㄨㄥˊ ㄇㄟˊ ㄉㄚˋ ㄧㄢˇ)
bushy eyebrows and big eyes
濃密(ㄋㄨㄥˊ ㄇㄧˋ)
(said of the growth of vegetation, beard, hair, etc.) dense; thick; luxuriant: 她有一頭濃密的頭髮。She has thick hair.
濃淡(ㄋㄨㄥˊ ㄉㄢˋ)
①(said of color) deep or light ②(said of drinks) strong or weak ③(said of make-up) heavy or light ④(said of liquid generally) concentrated or diluted
濃度(ㄋㄨㄥˊ ㄉㄨˋ)
①(chemistry) concentration ②density
濃湯(ㄋㄨㄥˊ ㄊㄤ)
thick soup
濃綠(ㄋㄨㄥˊ ㄌㄩˋ)
dark green
濃厚(ㄋㄨㄥˊ ㄏㄡˋ)
①(said of material things) thick and dense ②(said of feelings, interest, etc.) deep; great
濃酒(ㄋㄨㄥˊ ㄐㄧㄡˇ)
strong drink
濃情(ㄋㄨㄥˊ ㄑㄧㄥˊ)
passionate feeling; affectionate regard
濃情蜜意(ㄋㄨㄥˊ ㄑㄧㄥˊ ㄇㄧˋ ㄧˋ)
strong affection and deep love
濃妝 or 濃粧(ㄋㄨㄥˊ ㄓㄨㄤ)
heavy make-up; gorgeously dressed
濃妝艷抹(ㄋㄨㄥˊ ㄓㄨㄤ ㄧㄢˋ ㄇㄛˇ)
to wear heavy make-up
濃茶(ㄋㄨㄥˊ ㄔㄚˊ)
strong tea
濃睡(ㄋㄨㄥˊ ㄕㄨㄟˋ)
a sound sleep; deep slumbers
濃縮(ㄋㄨㄥˊ ㄙㄨㄛ)
①to condense; condensed; to concentrate: 他把一段濃縮爲一行。He condensed the paragraph into one line. ② to enrich; enriched
濃縮果汁(ㄋㄨㄥˊ ㄙㄨㄛ ㄍㄨㄛˇ ㄓ)
condensed fruit juices
濃煙(ㄋㄨㄥˊ ㄧㄢ)
thick smoke; heavy smoke
濃豔 or 濃艷(ㄋㄨㄥˊ ㄧㄢˋ)
gorgeous; bright-colored
濃蔭(ㄋㄨㄥˊ ㄧㄣˋ)
the dark shade under a big tree with thick foliage or in a dense forest
濃蔭蔽空(ㄋㄨㄥˊ ㄧㄣˋ ㄅㄧˋ ㄎㄨㄥ)
The thick branches and leaves seem to blot out the sky.
濃霧(ㄋㄨㄥˊ ㄨˋ)
heavy fog; dense mist: 倫敦以濃霧聞名。London is famous for its dense fog.
濃郁(ㄋㄨㄥˊ ㄩˋ)
strong; heavy; rich: 這些故事具有濃郁的浪漫氣息。These stories have a strong flavor

水部

of romance.

濃雲密佈(ㄋㄨㄥˊ ㄩㄣˊ ㄇㄧˋ ㄅㄨˋ)
Dark clouds stretch all over the sky.—a sign of an impending storm

【濊】3116 1. ㄏㄨㄟˋ huey huì
water plentiful

【濊】3116 2. ㄨㄟˋ wey wèi
1. deep and expansive
2. dirty
3. name of a river

濊水(ㄨㄟˋ ㄕㄨㄟˇ)
name of an old river in Hopeh, now silted

【澟】3117 ㄌㄧㄣˇ liin lǐn
1. desolate; deserted
2. cold; chilly

澟冽(ㄌㄧㄣˇ ㄌㄧㄝˋ)
ice-cold; bone-chilling: 北風澟冽。The north wind is ice-cold.

澟然(ㄌㄧㄣˇ ㄖㄢˊ)
awe-inspiring; commanding respect

【澣】3118 (浣) ㄏㄨㄢˇ hoan huǎn (又讀 ㄨㄢˇ woan wǎn)
1. to wash
2. (Tang Dynasty) ten days

十四畫

【濘】3119 1. ㄋㄧㄥˋ ninq nìng
muddy; miry

濘淖(ㄋㄧㄥˋ ㄋㄠˋ)
mud; muddy; covered with mud: 汽車陷入濘淖中。The car stuck in the mud of the road.

濘滯(ㄋㄧㄥˋ ㄓˋ)
muddy roads that make traveling difficult

【濘】3119 2. ㄋㄥˋ nenq nèng
pasty; soft and mashy

濘泥(ㄋㄥˋ ㄋㄧˊ)
mire; mud

【濛】3120 ㄇㄥˊ meng méng
misty; drizzly

濛濛(ㄇㄥˊ ㄇㄥˊ)
misty

濛濛細雨(ㄇㄥˊ ㄇㄥˊ ㄒㄧˋ ㄩˇ)
drizzle; to drizzle

濛鬆雨(ㄇㄥˊ ㄙㄨㄥ ㄩˇ)
drizzle

濛霧(ㄇㄥˊ ㄨˋ)
mist; fog: 濛霧全消散了。The mist has entirely cleared off.

【澀】3121 (澁) ㄙㄜˋ seh sè
1. rough; harsh; not smooth
2. a slightly bitter taste that numbs the tongue—as some unripened fruits; puckery
3. (said of writing, reading, etc.) difficult or jolting
4. slow of tongue

澀體(ㄙㄜˋ ㄊㄧˇ)
(Tang Dynasty) a style of literary writing which is difficult to read

澀訥(ㄙㄜˋ ㄋㄜˋ) or 澀吶(ㄙㄜˋ ㄋㄚˋ)
slow of tongue

澀滯(ㄙㄜˋ ㄓˋ)
not smooth; obstructed

澀賬 or 澀帳(ㄙㄜˋ ㄓㄤˋ)
bad debts

澀縮(ㄙㄜˋ ㄙㄨㄛ)
not straightforward

澀味(ㄙㄜˋ ㄨㄟˋ)
astringent taste

【濠】3122 ㄏㄠˊ haur háo
a moat; a trench or ditch

濠梁(ㄏㄠˊ ㄌㄧㄤˊ)
a bridge spanning a small creek

濠溝(ㄏㄠˊ ㄍㄡ)
a trench: 他們挖條濠溝。They dug a trench.

濠塹(ㄏㄠˊ ㄑㄧㄢˋ)
a moat; a canal or ditch around the city wall

【濟】3123 1. ㄐㄧˋ jih jì
1. to relieve; to aid: 同舟共濟。Being in the same boat, the refugees help one another.
2. to cross a stream
3. to succeed; to be up to standard
4. to benefit; benefits
5. a ford

濟貧(ㄐㄧˋ ㄆㄧㄣˊ)
to aid or relieve the poor

濟度(ㄐㄧˋ ㄉㄨˋ)
(Buddhism) to provide salvation for the masses

濟溺(ㄐㄧˋ ㄋㄧˋ)
to help or relieve others in great difficulty

濟困扶危(ㄐㄧˋ ㄎㄨㄣˋ ㄈㄨˊ ㄨㄟˊ)
(literally) to relieve the less privileged and help the endangered—philanthropic; compassionate

濟急(ㄐㄧˋ ㄐㄧˊ)
to aid the people in urgent need

濟世(ㄐㄧˋ ㄕˋ)
to benefit the world

濟世安民(ㄐㄧˋ ㄕˋ ㄢ ㄇㄧㄣˊ)
to benefit the age and pacify the masses

濟事(ㄐㄧˋ ㄕˋ)
to help the matter; to be useful in coping with a situation, etc.: 光哭是不濟事的。Crying won't help the matter.

濟燃眉之急(ㄐㄧˋ ㄖㄢˊ ㄇㄟˊ ㄓ ㄐㄧˊ)
to help meet an urgent need

濟弱扶傾(ㄐㄧˋ ㄖㄨㄛˋ ㄈㄨˊ ㄑㄧㄥ)
to help the weak and aid the needy

濟私(ㄐㄧˋ ㄙ)
to benefit one's own end; to serve a selfish purpose

濟惡(ㄐㄧˋ ㄜˋ)
to help an evil cause

濟危(ㄐㄧˋ ㄨㄟˊ)
to aid the endangered or needy

【濟】3123 2. ㄐㄧˇ jii jǐ
1. various; varied; numerous
2. elegant and dignified
3. name of various counties and a river

濟南(ㄐㄧˇ ㄋㄢˊ)
Tsinan, capital of Shantung Province

濟濟(ㄐㄧˇ ㄐㄧˇ)
① multitudinous; numerous ② magnificent ③ beautiful

濟濟多士(ㄐㄧˇ ㄐㄧˇ ㄉㄨㄛ ㄕˋ)
Numerous are talented persons.

濟濟一堂(ㄐㄧˇ ㄐㄧˇ ㄧˋ ㄊㄤˊ)
to gather together or congregate in this hall

濟水(ㄐㄧˇ ㄕㄨㄟˇ)
name of a stream which empties into the Yellow River from Honan Province

【濤】3124 ㄊㄠˊ taur táo
(又讀 ㄊㄠ tau tāo)
a big wave; a billow; a heavy swell
濤波(ㄊㄠˊ ㄅㄛ)or 濤瀾(ㄊㄠˊ ㄌㄢˊ)
billows; great waves
濤聲(ㄊㄠˊ ㄕㄥ)
the sound of roaring billows: 我們聽到遠處的濤聲。We heard the sound of roaring billows in the distance.

【濡】3125 ㄖㄨˊ ru rú
1. to moisten; to immerse; to wet
2. to linger; to procrastinate
3. glossy; smooth
4. to tolerate; to endure
濡筆(ㄖㄨˊ ㄅㄧˇ)or 濡毫(ㄖㄨˊ ㄏㄠˊ)
to moisten the (Chinese) writing or painting brush
濡翰(ㄖㄨˊ ㄏㄢˋ)
to moisten the brush
濡跡(ㄖㄨˊ ㄐㄧ)
to linger at (a place, etc.)
濡滯(ㄖㄨˊ ㄓˋ)
slow; to procrastinate
濡濕(ㄖㄨˊ ㄕ)
to soak by immersion; to make wet
濡染(ㄖㄨˊ ㄖㄢˇ)
to dye; to be imbued with
濡忍(ㄖㄨˊ ㄖㄣˇ)
to endure; to bear with patience
濡潤(ㄖㄨˊ ㄖㄨㄣˋ)
glossy

【濫】3126 ㄌㄢˋ lann làn
1. to overflow; to flood; to inundate; inundation
2. to do things without plans; reckless
3. to practice no self-restraint; to give way to unbridled license
4. to abuse (one's power, influence, etc.)
5. false; not true
6. superfluous words or expressions
濫發(ㄌㄢˋ ㄈㄚ)
to issue an excessive amount of (bank notes, invitations, etc.)
濫罰(ㄌㄢˋ ㄈㄚˊ)
excessive or undue penalty or punishment
濫伐(ㄌㄢˋ ㄈㄚˊ)
excessive felling of trees
濫伐森林(ㄌㄢˋ ㄈㄚˊ ㄙㄣ ㄌㄧㄣˊ)
to log without (or not according to) plan; excessive felling of trees
濫費(ㄌㄢˋ ㄈㄟˋ)
to go to excess in expenditure; to waste (money)
濫調(ㄌㄢˋ ㄉㄧㄠˋ)
platitudes; clichés; hackneyed expressions; worn-out themes
濫套(ㄌㄢˋ ㄊㄠˋ)
truisms; clichés; trite or superfluous expressions
濫頭寸(ㄌㄢˋ ㄊㄡˊ ㄘㄨㄣˋ)
idle money in the bank
濫墾(ㄌㄢˋ ㄎㄣˇ)
to cultivate farms in areas where soil conservation should be maintained
濫交(ㄌㄢˋ ㄐㄧㄠ)
to befriend at random; to make friends indiscriminately
濫取(ㄌㄢˋ ㄑㄩˇ)
to take what one does not deserve; to take excessively
濫刑(ㄌㄢˋ ㄒㄧㄥˊ)
excessive punishment
濫殺(ㄌㄢˋ ㄕㄚ)
to kill at random; to kill indiscriminately
濫收(ㄌㄢˋ ㄕㄡ)
to receive or take what one should not; to receive or take too much; to charge too much
濫觴(ㄌㄢˋ ㄕㄤ)
the very origin or source (of a practice, tradition, etc.); the beginning
濫惡(ㄌㄢˋ ㄜˋ)
big evils
濫汚(ㄌㄢˋ ㄨ)
dirty; tricky; unchaste
濫竽充數(ㄌㄢˋ ㄩˊ ㄔㄨㄥ ㄕㄨˋ)
to hold a post without the necessary qualifications just to make up the number
濫用(ㄌㄢˋ ㄩㄥˋ)
① to spend excessively; to expend too much ② to misuse; to abuse
濫用公款(ㄌㄢˋ ㄩㄥˋ ㄍㄨㄥ ㄎㄨㄢˇ)
irregularities in use of public funds
濫用職權(ㄌㄢˋ ㄩㄥˋ ㄓˊ ㄑㄩㄢˊ)
to misuse one's powers; to abuse one's authority
濫用藥物(ㄌㄢˋ ㄩㄥˋ ㄧㄠˋ ㄨˋ)
drug abuse

【濯】3127 ㄓㄨㄛˊ jwo zhuó
1. to wash
2. to eliminate vices
3. grand; magnificent
4. a Chinese family name
濯濯(ㄓㄨㄛˊ ㄓㄨㄛˊ)
① bright and brilliant ② (said of mountains) denuded; bare; bald: 童山濯濯。That mountain is bald. ③ to be fat and sleek
濯纓濯足(ㄓㄨㄛˊ ㄧㄥ ㄓㄨㄛˊ ㄗㄨˊ)
Whether one is received with respect or despite depends on his own conduct.

【濮】3128 ㄆㄨˊ pwu pú
1. name of an ancient river in today's Honan Province
2. name of an ancient barbarian tribe
3. a Chinese family name
濮上(ㄆㄨˊ ㄕㄤˋ)
a place where debauchery is prevalent
濮上之音(ㄆㄨˊ ㄕㄤˋ ㄓ ㄧㄣ)
lewd and debauching music
濮水(ㄆㄨˊ ㄕㄨㄟˇ)
name of an ancient stream in Honan and Hupeh

【濬】3129 ㄐㄩㄣˋ jiunn jùn
1. to dredge a waterway; to dig or wash (a well, etc.)
2. deep; profound
濬哲(ㄐㄩㄣˋ ㄓㄜˊ)
profound wisdom: 他的言行表現其濬哲。He showed great wisdom in what he said and did.

【濰】3130 ㄨㄟˊ wei wéi
name of a river in Shantung Province
濰水(ㄨㄟˊ ㄕㄨㄟˇ)
the Wei River, in Shantung Province

【濱】3131 ㄅㄧㄣ bin bīn
1. water's edge; to border on

〔水部〕

〔水部〕

2. same as 瀕—near at hand
3. (military) a low, level seacoast

濱臨大海(ㄅㄧㄣ ㄌㄧㄣˊ ㄉㄚˋ ㄏㄞˇ)
on the brink of the sea

濱海地區(ㄅㄧㄣ ㄏㄞˇ ㄉㄧˋ ㄑㄩ)
the coastal region; the coast

濱近(ㄅㄧㄣ ㄐㄧㄣˋ)
close to; near to: 我家濱近車站。My house is close to the station.

濱江(ㄅㄧㄣ ㄐㄧㄤ)
the former name of Harbin (哈爾濱), capital of Sungkiang Province

濱死(ㄅㄧㄣ ㄙˇ)
to be near to death; dying; to have one foot in the grave

濱危(ㄅㄧㄣ ㄨㄟˊ)
to have a close encounter with great danger; dying; close to death

【濩】 3132
ㄏㄨㄛˋ huoh huò
1. turbulent water
2. (now rarely) to cook; to boil

【濕】 3133
(溼) ㄕ shy shī
1. damp; moist; wet; humid; to get wet
2. (Chinese medicine) ailments caused by high humidity

濕地(ㄕ ㄉㄧˋ)
a damp place; a marsh or swamp: 濕地有很多青蛙。There are a lot of frogs in the marsh.

濕電池(ㄕ ㄉㄧㄢˋ ㄔˊ)
a galvanic battery

濕度(ㄕ ㄉㄨˋ)
humidity

濕度表(ㄕ ㄉㄨˋ ㄅㄧㄠˇ)
a hygrometer

濕透(ㄕ ㄊㄡˋ)
to be drenched; dripping wet; soaking wet: 你的上裝濕透了。Your coat is dripping wet.

濕漉漉(ㄕ ㄌㄨˋ ㄌㄨˋ)
dripping wet

濕季(ㄕ ㄐㄧˋ)
a rainy season; a monsoon

濕津津(ㄕ ㄐㄧㄣ ㄐㄧㄣ)
damp and wet: 我不喜歡濕津津的天氣。I don't like damp and wet weather.

濕氣(ㄕ ㄑㄧˋ)
①(Chinese medicine) ailments caused by high humidity, such as rashes, pustules, rheumatism, athlete's foot, etc. ② humidity; dampness; moisture

濕疹(ㄕ ㄓㄣˇ)
eczema

濕熱(ㄕ ㄖㄜˋ)
damp and hot

濕潤(ㄕ ㄖㄨㄣˋ)
damp; to moisten

濕窪(ㄕ ㄨㄚ)
swampy regions; swamp

十五畫

【濺】 3134
ㄐㄧㄢˋ jiann jiàn
to splash; to sprinkle; to spray; to spill: 我被濺了一身水。I was splashed with water all over.

濺沫(ㄐㄧㄢˋ ㄇㄛˋ)
to splash saliva around (especially when one talks excitedly or vehemently)

濺泥(ㄐㄧㄢˋ ㄋㄧˊ)
to splash mud

濺濺(ㄐㄧㄢ ㄐㄧㄢ)
the gurgling sound of flowing water

濺血(ㄐㄧㄢˋ ㄒㄧㄝ)
to splash with drops of blood

濺水(ㄐㄧㄢˋ ㄕㄨㄟˇ)
to splash water

【濼】 3135
1. ㄌㄨㄛˋ luoh luò
name of a stream in Shantung Province

【濼】 3135
2. ㄅㄛˊ bor bó
a lake

【瀆】 3136
ㄉㄨˊ dwu dú
1. a ditch
2. a river
3. to desecrate; to profane; to blaspheme; to be rude and disrespectful
4. to annoy

瀆犯(ㄉㄨˊ ㄈㄢˋ)
to be rude and profane; to desecrate; to be sacrilegious

瀆職(ㄉㄨˊ ㄓˊ)
malfeasance; irregularity or misconduct in office; dereliction of duty

瀆職罪(ㄉㄨˊ ㄓˊ ㄗㄨㄟˋ)
guilt for malfeasance

瀆神(ㄉㄨˊ ㄕㄣˊ)
① to desecrate the god ② to disturb (your) peace of mind (an expression often used in asking someone for a favor)

【濾】 3137
ㄌㄩˋ liuh lǜ
to filter; to strain out

濾波器(ㄌㄩˋ ㄅㄛ ㄑㄧˋ)
a wave filter

濾過性病毒(ㄌㄩˋ ㄍㄨㄛˋ ㄒㄧㄥˋ ㄅㄧㄥˋ ㄉㄨˊ) or 濾過性病原體(ㄌㄩˋ ㄍㄨㄛˋ ㄒㄧㄥˋ ㄅㄧㄥˋ ㄩㄢˊ ㄊㄧˇ)
virus—a living thing even smaller than bacteria which causes infectious disease in the body, in plants, etc.

濾管(ㄌㄩˋ ㄍㄨㄢˇ)
a filter pipe

濾器(ㄌㄩˋ ㄑㄧˋ)
a filter: 用濾器把水濾清。Clean the water with a filter.

濾紙(ㄌㄩˋ ㄓˇ)
a filter paper

濾水池(ㄌㄩˋ ㄕㄨㄟˇ ㄔˊ)
a settling pond; a depositing reservoir; a filter bed

濾嘴香烟(ㄌㄩˋ ㄗㄨㄟˇ ㄒㄧㄤ ㄧㄢ)
filter-tipped cigarettes

【瀑】 3138
1. ㄆㄨˋ puh pù
a waterfall; a cascade; a cataract

瀑布(ㄆㄨˋ ㄅㄨˋ)
a waterfall; a cascade; a cataract

瀑流(ㄆㄨˋ ㄌㄧㄡˊ)
a cascade; a waterfall; a cataract

【瀑】 3138
2. ㄅㄠˋ baw bào
a pouring rain which comes all of a sudden; a sudden shower

【瀉】 3139
ㄒㄧㄝˋ shieh xiè
1. to drain; water flowing down: 一瀉千里 to flow a thousand *li* at one plunge
2. diarrhea; to have loose

bowels

瀉肚(ㄒㄧㄝˋ ㄉㄨˋ)or 瀉肚子(ㄒㄧㄝˋ ㄉㄨˋ ˙ㄗ)
diarrhea; to have loose bowels: 他瀉肚子。He has diarrhea.

瀉痢(ㄒㄧㄝˋ ㄌㄧˋ)
diarrhea

瀉利鹽(ㄒㄧㄝˋ ㄌㄧˋ ㄧㄢˊ)
Epsom salts (magnesium sulfate)

瀉鹵(ㄒㄧㄝˋ ㄌㄨˇ)
barren, salty land

瀉出(ㄒㄧㄝˋ ㄔㄨ)
to leak out; to spurt out: 汽油瀉出。The gasoline leaks out.

瀉藥(ㄒㄧㄝˋ ㄧㄠˋ)or 瀉劑(ㄒㄧㄝˋ ㄐㄧˋ)
cathartics, laxatives or purgatives

瀉鹽(ㄒㄧㄝˋ ㄧㄢˊ)
Epsom salts (magnesium sulfate)亦作「瀉利鹽」

【瀋】 3140
ㄕㄣˇ sheen shěn

1. juice; fluid; liquid; water
2. short for Shenyang (Mukden), capital of Liaoning Province

瀋陽(ㄕㄣˇ ㄧㄤˊ)
Mukden (Shenyang), capital of Liaoning Province

瀋陽事變(ㄕㄣˇ ㄧㄤˊ ㄕˋ ㄅㄧㄢˋ)
The Mukden Incident on September 18, 1931, which ended in the occupation of Manchuria by the Japanese militarists

【瀏】 3141
ㄌㄧㄡˊ liou liú

1. (said of water) clear; bright and clear; the appearance of a clear stream
2. a fast-blowing wind; a cool wind
3. to get away secretly; to take French leave

瀏覽(ㄌㄧㄡˊ ㄌㄢˇ)
to glance over; to thumb through; to take a casual look at (a scene); to skim through

瀏亮(ㄌㄧㄡˊ ㄌㄧㄤˋ)
(said of the sky, etc.) bright and clear

【瀅】 3142
ㄧㄥˊ yng yíng

(said of water) clear; bright and clear; glossy

【瀍】 3143
ㄔㄢˊ charn chán

name of a river in Honan

瀍水(ㄔㄢˊ ㄕㄨㄟˇ)
the Chan River, a tributary of the Lo River in Honan

【瀁】 3144
ㄧㄤˇ yeang yǎng

1. water in motion
2. to move a boat or something in water
3. ripples; waves; rapids
4. to overflow—too much or too many
5. name of a stream in Shensi Province

十六畫

【瀘】 3145
ㄌㄨˊ lu lú

1. name of a river in Yunnan Province
2. name of a river in Szechwan Province

瀘水(ㄌㄨˊ ㄕㄨㄟˇ)
① name of a river in Szechwan Province ② name of a river in Yunnan Province

【瀕】 3146
ㄅㄧㄣ bin bīn

1. near; close to; to border
2. water's edge

瀕臨(ㄅㄧㄣ ㄌㄧㄣˊ)
near; on the brink of

瀕河(ㄅㄧㄣ ㄏㄜˊ)
on the bank of the river; riverside

瀕海(ㄅㄧㄣ ㄏㄞˇ)
close to the sea; along the coast

瀕行(ㄅㄧㄣ ㄒㄧㄥˊ)
upon leaving; about to leave

瀕死(ㄅㄧㄣ ㄙˇ)or 瀕於死亡(ㄅㄧㄣ ㄩˊ ㄙˇ ㄨㄤˊ)
on the brink of death

瀕危(ㄅㄧㄣ ㄨㄟˊ)
on the verge of death or great danger

瀕於破產(ㄅㄧㄣ ㄩˊ ㄆㄛˋ ㄔㄢˇ)
on the verge of bankruptcy

瀕於毀滅(ㄅㄧㄣ ㄩˊ ㄏㄨㄟˇ ㄇㄧㄝˋ)
on the brink of ruin

瀕於絕境(ㄅㄧㄣ ㄩˊ ㄐㄩㄝˊ ㄐㄧㄥˋ)
to face an impasse

【瀚】 3147
ㄏㄢˋ hann hàn

vast; expansive

瀚海(ㄏㄢˋ ㄏㄞˇ)
the Gobi Desert

瀚瀚(ㄏㄢˋ ㄏㄢˋ)
vast and expansive

【瀝】 3148
ㄌㄧˋ lih lì

1. to fall down by drops; to drip; to trickle
2. remaining drops of wine
3. to strain water or liquids

瀝膽披肝(ㄌㄧˋ ㄉㄢˇ ㄆㄧ ㄍㄢ)
absolutely sincere and loyal

瀝瀝(ㄌㄧˋ ㄌㄧˋ)
① the sound of flowing waters ② the sound of heaving wind ③ to drip; to trickle

瀝懇(ㄌㄧˋ ㄎㄣˇ)
to beseech; to request earnestly

瀝酒(ㄌㄧˋ ㄐㄧㄡˇ)
to strain wine

瀝青(ㄌㄧˋ ㄑㄧㄥ)
① asphalt; pitch ② another name of resin

瀝青路(ㄌㄧˋ ㄑㄧㄥ ㄌㄨˋ)
a bituminous road; an asphalt road

瀝青岩(ㄌㄧˋ ㄑㄧㄥ ㄧㄢˊ)
a pitchstone 亦作「松脂岩」

瀝血(ㄌㄧˋ ㄒㄧㄝˇ)or(ㄌㄧˋ ㄒㄩㄝˋ)
① to drip blood ② to take a blood-oath ③ very loyal and sincere

瀝陳(ㄌㄧˋ ㄔㄣˊ)
to state honestly in detail

瀝液(ㄌㄧˋ ㄧㄝˋ)
a small amount of flowing waters

【瀟】 3149
ㄒㄧㄠ shiau xiāo

1. the sound of beating rain and whistling wind; the roar of a strong wind
2. name of a stream in Hunan

瀟瀟(ㄒㄧㄠ ㄒㄧㄠ)
a rushing rain and whistling wind; the roar of gusts

瀟湘(ㄒㄧㄠ ㄒㄧㄤ)
① the Hsiao River and Hsiang River ② name of a town in Hunan, north of Ling Ling, where the two rivers meet

瀟灑 or 瀟洒(ㄒㄧㄠ ㄙㄚˇ)
(usually said of a man's

〔水部〕

manner) casual and elegant; dashing and refined

【瀛】 3150
ㄧㄥˊ yng yíng
1. the sea; the ocean
2. within the lake

瀛臺(ㄧㄥˊ ㄊㄞˊ)
a spot within the Forbidden City in Peking, which was surrounded on three sides by water, where the young Emperor Kuang Hsü (光緒) was imprisoned by Queen Dowager Tzu Hsi (慈禧太后) after the abortive political reform movement in the late 19th century

瀛海(ㄧㄥˊ ㄏㄞˇ)
the sea; the ocean

瀛寰(ㄧㄥˊ ㄏㄨㄢˊ)
the globe; the world

瀛眷(ㄧㄥˊ ㄐㄩㄢˋ)
your dependents; your family (a polite expression)

瀛洲(ㄧㄥˊ ㄓㄡ)
(in old Chinese legend) the Holy Mountain in the East Sea, where the immortals dwell

【瀨】 3151
ㄌㄞˋ lay lài
1. a torrent; a swift current
2. water flowing over shallows
3. name of a stream in Kwangsi, also known as the River Li
4. name of a stream in Kiangsu

瀨水(ㄌㄞˋ ㄕㄨㄟˇ)
① also known as the River Li (荔江), a stream in Kwangsi ② name of a stream in Kiangsu

【瀧】 3152
1. ㄌㄨㄥˊ long lóng
1. raining; rainy
2. wet; soaked; saturated
3. a swift current
4. (in Japanese) a waterfall

【瀧】 3152
2. ㄕㄨㄤ shuang shuāng
name of a river in Hunan

瀧岡(ㄕㄨㄤ ㄍㄤ)
name of a hill in Yung-feng County (永豐縣) of Kiangsi

【瀣】 3153
ㄒㄧㄝˋ shieh xiè
mist; vapor

【瀦】 3154
ㄓㄨ ju zhū
a pool; a pond

【瀠】 3155
ㄧㄥˊ yng yíng
參看「瀠洄」

瀠洄(ㄧㄥˊ ㄏㄨㄟˊ)
the whirling of water

十七畫

【瀰】 3156
ㄇㄧˊ mi mí
(said of water) brimming; overflowing

瀰漫(ㄇㄧˊ ㄇㄢˋ)
① brimming, overflowing water ② to permeate

【瀹】 3157
ㄩㄝˋ yueh yuè
1. to cook or to boil with soup
2. to soak
3. to clear the courses of rivers

【瀾】 3158
1. ㄌㄢˊ lan lán
a great wave; a huge billow

瀾翻(ㄌㄢˊ ㄈㄢ)
(said of a piece of writing or a speech) with numerous turns and twists

瀾滄江(ㄌㄢˊ ㄘㄤ ㄐㄧㄤ)
the Lantsang River in Yunnan, one of the tributaries of the Mekong River

【瀾】 3158
2. ㄌㄢˋ lann làn
1. overflowing; dripping wet; a vast expanse of water
2. thin rice paste

瀾漫(ㄌㄢˋ ㄇㄢˋ)
① overflowing; inundating ② dripping wet; wet through ③ sprightly; carefree: 這些孩子天眞瀾漫。These childern are innocent and carefree. ④ disorderly

瀾汗(ㄌㄢˋ ㄏㄢˋ)
descriptive of a vast expanse of water

【瀲】 3159
ㄌㄧㄢˋ liann liàn
1. (said of water) overflowing
2. the edge of a large body of water

瀲瀲(ㄌㄧㄢˋ ㄌㄧㄢˋ)
overflowing; inundating

瀲灩(ㄌㄧㄢˋ ㄧㄢˋ)
(said of water or wine) overflowing

十八畫

【灉】 3160
ㄩㄥ iong yōng
1. the flowing back of flooding waters
2. name of a stream in Shantung Province

灉水(ㄩㄥ ㄕㄨㄟˇ)
name of a stream in Shantung Province

【灃】 3161
ㄈㄥ feng fēng
name of a river in Shensi Province

灃沛(ㄈㄥ ㄆㄟˋ)
① brimming; overflowing; abundant ② copious rain

灃水(ㄈㄥ ㄕㄨㄟˇ)
the Feng River, in Shensi Province

【灌】 3162
ㄍㄨㄢˋ guann guàn
1. to water; to fill; to pour (on, into, at); to irrigate
2. to offer a libation
3. shrubs; bushy clumps

灌片子(ㄍㄨㄢˋ ㄆㄧㄢˋ ·ㄗ) or 灌唱片(ㄍㄨㄢˋ ㄔㄤˋ ㄆㄧㄢˋ)
to cut a record

灌莽(ㄍㄨㄢˋ ㄇㄤˇ)
grassy and bushy land

灌迷湯(ㄍㄨㄢˋ ㄇㄧˊ ㄊㄤ)
to flatter; (said of a woman) to utter sweet words to a man for ulterior purposes

灌木(ㄍㄨㄢˋ ㄇㄨˋ)
shrubs

灌佛(ㄍㄨㄢˋ ㄈㄛˊ)
to wash a Buddha's image with scented water

灌地(ㄍㄨㄢˋ ㄉㄧˋ)
to offer a libation by pouring wine on the ground

灌頂(ㄍㄨㄢˋ ㄉㄧㄥˇ)
(Buddhism) *abhisecani; murdhabhisitka* (inauguration or consecration by sprinkling or pouring water on the head)

灌溉(ㄍㄨㄢˋ ㄍㄞˋ)
to irrigate; irrigation

灌溉渠(ㄍㄨㄢˋ ㄍㄞˋ ㄑㄩˊ)

an irrigation canal
灌溉系統(ㄍㄨㄢˋ ㄍㄞˋ ㄒㄧˋ ㄊㄨㄥˇ)
an irrigation system
灌救(ㄍㄨㄢˋ ㄐㄧㄡˋ)
to save life by forcing medicine down the throat of a dying person
灌漿(ㄍㄨㄢˋ ㄐㄧㄤ)
to fill the crevices between bricks, etc. with mortar to make the foundation, wall, or pavement secure
灌注(ㄍㄨㄢˋ ㄓㄨˋ)
① to pour into ② to teach; to inculcate; to instill ③ to concentrate (attention) on
灌腸(ㄍㄨㄢˋ ㄔㄤˊ)
to give an enema or clyster
灌腸劑(ㄍㄨㄢˋ ㄔㄤˊ ㄐㄧˋ)
a clyster; an enema
灌腸器(ㄍㄨㄢˋ ㄔㄤˊ ㄑㄧˋ)
an enema syringe; a clyster pipe
灌唱片(ㄍㄨㄢˋ ㄔㄤˋ ㄆㄧㄢˋ)
參看「灌片子」
灌輸(ㄍㄨㄢˋ ㄕㄨ)
to instill; to teach; to impart (knowledge to someone); to inculcate
灌水(ㄍㄨㄢˋ ㄕㄨㄟˇ)
to inject water into (meat, chicken, etc.) so as to increase weight before marketing; to pour water into something
灌醉(ㄍㄨㄢˋ ㄗㄨㄟˋ)
to force someone to drink until he is drunk
灌叢(ㄍㄨㄢˋ ㄘㄨㄥˊ)
dense shrubs and thick undergrowth
灌藥(ㄍㄨㄢˋ ㄧㄠˋ)
to force one to take medicine
灌音(ㄍㄨㄢˋ ㄧㄣ)
to cut a record

十九畫

【灑】 3163
(洒) ㄙㄚˇ saa sǎ
1. to splash; to spill; to sprinkle (liquids)
2. to wash
灑脫(ㄙㄚˇ ㄊㄨㄛ)
casual and carefree; graceful; free and easy
灑淚(ㄙㄚˇ ㄌㄟˋ)
to shed tears: 她灑淚公堂。She shed tears in court.
灑落(ㄙㄚˇ ㄌㄨㄛˋ)
① casual and elegant ② desolate; dilapidated ③ to give the cold shoulder to; to be rude to
灑汗(ㄙㄚˇ ㄏㄢˋ)
to perspire; to sweat
灑家(ㄙㄚˇ ㄐㄧㄚ)
I; me 亦作「洒家」
灑泣(ㄙㄚˇ ㄑㄧˋ)
to shed tears
灑水(ㄙㄚˇ ㄕㄨㄟˇ)
to spill water; to sprinkle water: 他灑水於街上。He sprinkles the street with water.
灑水車(ㄙㄚˇ ㄕㄨㄟˇ ㄔㄜ)
a sprinkler truck
灑然(ㄙㄚˇ ㄖㄢˊ)
shocked; frightened
灑灑(ㄙㄚˇ ㄙㄚˇ)
continuously; incessantly
灑掃(ㄙㄚˇ ㄙㄠˇ)
to sprinkle water and sweep

【灘】 3164
ㄊㄢ tan tān
a beach; a sandbank; a shoal
灘頭陣地(ㄊㄢ ㄊㄡˊ ㄓㄣˋ ㄉㄧˋ)or 灘頭堡(ㄊㄢ ㄊㄡˊ ㄅㄠˇ)
a beachhead
灘簧(ㄊㄢ ㄏㄨㄤˊ)
Soochow opera
灘船(ㄊㄢ ㄔㄨㄢˊ)
a small boat without an awning or cover

二十一畫

【灝】 3165
ㄏㄠˋ haw hào
bean soup

【灞】 3166
ㄅㄚˋ bah bà
name of a river in Shensi
灞橋(ㄅㄚˋ ㄑㄧㄠˊ)
name of a bridge over the Pa River, where ancient people in Changan (長安), the old capital, often bade their friends good-bye
灞橋折柳(ㄅㄚˋ ㄑㄧㄠˊ ㄓㄜˊ ㄌㄧㄡˇ)
to part from friends; to bid farewell
灞水(ㄅㄚˋ ㄕㄨㄟˇ)
name of a river near Changan (長安), Shensi (陝西)

二十二畫

【灣】 3167
ㄨㄢ uan wān
1. a bay; a gulf; a cove
2. the bend of a stream
3. to anchor; to moor
灣流(ㄨㄢ ㄌㄧㄡˊ)
a gulf stream
灣轉(ㄨㄢ ·ㄓㄨㄢ)
to get by indirect means; to hunt for (something) in a painstaking way
灣子(ㄨㄢ ·ㄗ)
a curve

二十三畫

【灤】 3168
ㄌㄨㄢˊ luan luán
name of a river in northern China
灤河(ㄌㄨㄢˊ ㄏㄜˊ)
name of a river in northern China

二十四畫

【灨】 3169
ㄍㄢˋ gann gàn
the Kan River in Kiangsi (江西) Province
灨江(ㄍㄢˋ ㄐㄧㄤ)
the Kan River in Kiangsi (江西) Province

二十八畫

【灩】 3170
(灔) ㄧㄢˋ yann yàn
overflowing; inundating
灩澦堆(ㄧㄢˋ ㄩˋ ㄉㄨㄟ)
a steep cliff in the middle of the Yangtze River in Szechwan (四川), a navigator's nightmare

火部
ㄏㄨㄛˇ huoo huǒ

火部

【火】 3171 ㄏㄨㄛˇ huoo huǒ

1. fire; flames; to burn with fire
2. fury; anger; temper
3. urgency; urgent; imminent; pressing
4. (Chinese herbal medicine) the latent "heat" in human body
5. (now rarely) a group (of people)
6. a Chinese family name

火拔子(ㄏㄨㄛˇ ㄅㄚˊ ·ㄗ)
(Chinese medicine) cupping; a suction cup (used to suck "moisture" from the human body, with the cup made vacuum by burning thin paper, etc. inside)亦作「拔火罐兒」

火把(ㄏㄨㄛˇ ㄅㄚˇ)
a torch: 火把點燃了。The torch was lighted.

火鉢(ㄏㄨㄛˇ ㄅㄛ)
a brazier; a fire pan; a fire bowl

火玻璃(ㄏㄨㄛˇ ㄅㄛ ·ㄌㄧ)
flint glass; fireproof glass

火爆(ㄏㄨㄛˇ ㄅㄠˋ)
(dialect) fiery; irritable

火伴 or 伙伴(ㄏㄨㄛˇ ㄅㄢˋ) or 伙伴兒(ㄏㄨㄛˇ ㄅㄚˋㄦ)
buddies; companions

火棒(ㄏㄨㄛˇ ㄅㄤˋ)
① a torch made of a club tipped with alcohol-drenched cloth for twirling in darkness ② a poker

火併(ㄏㄨㄛˇ ㄅㄧㄥˋ)
an intramural fight

火砲(ㄏㄨㄛˇ ㄆㄠˋ)
artillery pieces

火盆(ㄏㄨㄛˇ ㄆㄣˊ)
a brazier; a fire pan

火門(ㄏㄨㄛˇ ㄇㄣˊ)
a fire hole

火苗子(ㄏㄨㄛˇ ㄇㄧㄠˊ ·ㄗ) or 火苗兒(ㄏㄨㄛˇ ㄇㄧㄠˊㄦ)
tongues of flame; flames

火棉(ㄏㄨㄛˇ ㄇㄧㄢˊ) or 火藥棉(ㄏㄨㄛˇ ㄧㄠˋ ㄇㄧㄢˊ)
guncotton

火房 or 伙房(ㄏㄨㄛˇ ㄈㄤˊ)
a kitchen: 她在火房裏烹飪。She is cooking in the kitchen.

火夫 or 火伕(ㄏㄨㄛˇ ㄈㄨ)
a kitchen assistant; (military) a cook

火底(ㄏㄨㄛˇ ㄉㄧˇ)
ashes, etc. after a fire

火頭(ㄏㄨㄛˇ ㄊㄡˊ)
① the person responsible for the start of a fire ②(in old China) a cook ③ the duration and degree of heating, cooking, etc.

火頭軍(ㄏㄨㄛˇ ㄊㄡˊ ㄐㄩㄣ)
a mess sergeant; a military cook

火腿(ㄏㄨㄛˇ ㄊㄨㄟˇ)
Chinese ham

火腿蛋(ㄏㄨㄛˇ ㄊㄨㄟˇ ㄉㄢˋ)
ham and egg

火腿三明治(ㄏㄨㄛˇ ㄊㄨㄟˇ ㄙㄢ ㄇㄧㄥˊ ㄓˋ)
a ham sandwich

火牛(ㄏㄨㄛˇ ㄋㄧㄡˊ)
(in ancient China) to attach burning reeds, etc. to the tails of oxen to overwhelm the enemy defense 參看「火牛計」

火牛計(ㄏㄨㄛˇ ㄋㄧㄡˊ ㄐㄧˋ)
tactics in this manner used by General Tien Tan(田單) of Chi(齊) during the Warring States period 參看「火牛」

火奴魯魯(ㄏㄨㄛˇ ㄋㄨˊ ㄌㄨˇ ㄌㄨˇ)
Honolulu 亦作「檀香山」

火辣辣(ㄏㄨㄛˇ ㄌㄚˋ ㄌㄚˋ)
burning

火力(ㄏㄨㄛˇ ㄌㄧˋ)
① firepower: 砲兵的火力比步兵的大。The artillery has more firepower than the infantry. ② thermal

火力發電廠(ㄏㄨㄛˇ ㄌㄧˋ ㄈㄚ ㄉㄧㄢˋ ㄔㄤˇ)
a thermoelectric plant; a thermo-power plant

火力集中(ㄏㄨㄛˇ ㄌㄧˋ ㄐㄧˊ ㄓㄨㄥ)
concentration of fire

火爐子(ㄏㄨㄛˇ ㄌㄨˊ ·ㄗ)
a stove

火輪(ㄏㄨㄛˇ ㄌㄨㄣˊ)
① a steamship ② the sun

火龍(ㄏㄨㄛˇ ㄌㄨㄥˊ) or 火蛇(ㄏㄨㄛˇ ㄕㄜˊ)
a firedrake; a mythical fiery dragon

火耕水耨(ㄏㄨㄛˇ ㄍㄥ ㄕㄨㄟˇ ㄋㄡˋ)
to burn straws and weeds and water the land—an ancient way to fertilize the land

火鍋(ㄏㄨㄛˇ ㄍㄨㄛ)
a chafing pot; a chafing dish

火光(ㄏㄨㄛˇ ㄍㄨㄤ)
the light or glow of fire

火光冲天(ㄏㄨㄛˇ ㄍㄨㄤ ㄔㄨㄥ ㄊㄧㄢ)
The glow of fire lit up the sky.

火攻(ㄏㄨㄛˇ ㄍㄨㄥ)
to attack by setting fire to enemy ships or camps

火口(ㄏㄨㄛˇ ㄎㄡˇ)
a volcanic crater

火炕(ㄏㄨㄛˇ ㄎㄤˋ)
(in North China) a bed of bricks with a fire built underneath to keep warm

火坑(ㄏㄨㄛˇ ㄎㄥ)
① a situation of extreme hardship or difficulty ② prostitution: 她掉入火坑。She has fallen into prostitution.

火筷子(ㄏㄨㄛˇ ㄎㄨㄞˋ ·ㄗ)
a pair of fire-tongs; a poker

火鶴(ㄏㄨㄛˇ ㄏㄜˋ)
a flamingo

火海(ㄏㄨㄛˇ ㄏㄞˇ)
a great fire; a conflagration

火海戰術(ㄏㄨㄛˇ ㄏㄞˇ ㄓㄢˋ ㄕㄨˋ)
the tactics featuring intensive firepower to counter the human-sea tactics

火候(ㄏㄨㄛˇ ㄏㄡˋ)
① the time used in cooking a certain food ② scholastic achievement ③Taoist alchemy

火候未到(ㄏㄨㄛˇ ㄏㄡˋ ㄨㄟˋ ㄉㄠˋ)
(said of cooking time, training, etc.) not yet up to the required standard

火狐(ㄏㄨㄛˇ ㄏㄨˊ)
a red fox

火花(ㄏㄨㄛˇ ㄏㄨㄚ)
sparks: 火花從營火中迸出。Sparks were flying from the campfire.

火花放電(ㄏㄨㄛˇ ㄏㄨㄚ ㄈㄤˋ ㄉㄧㄢˋ)
spark discharge

火花四濺(ㄏㄨㄛˇ ㄏㄨㄚ ㄙˋ ㄐㄧㄢˋ)
Sparks fly off in all directions.

火化(ㄏㄨㄛˇ ㄏㄨㄚˋ)
to cremate; cremation

火患(ㄏㄨㄛˇ ㄏㄨㄢˋ)
fire hazards

火紅(ㄏㄨㄛˇ ㄏㄨㄥˊ)
red as fire; fiery; flaming

火雞(ㄏㄨㄛˇ ㄐㄧ)
a turkey

火急(ㄏㄨㄛˇ ㄐㄧˊ)
very urgent; imminent

火計 or 伙計(ㄏㄨㄛˇ ・ㄐㄧ)
waiters; assistants in a store; salesmen; shop clerks

火教(ㄏㄨㄛˇ ㄐㄧㄠˋ)
Parseeism

火酒(ㄏㄨㄛˇ ㄐㄧㄡˇ)
alcohol

火剪(ㄏㄨㄛˇ ㄐㄧㄢˇ)
①a pair of fire-tongs for poking or moving burning coals ②(formerly) a pair of fire-tongs for curling hair

火箭(ㄏㄨㄛˇ ㄐㄧㄢˋ)
①a rocket: 火箭被發射到月球。The rocket was launched to the moon. ②an arrow with a burning substance attached

火箭砲(ㄏㄨㄛˇ ㄐㄧㄢˋ ㄆㄠˋ)
a bazooka; a rocket launcher

火箭發射臺(ㄏㄨㄛˇ ㄐㄧㄢˋ ㄈㄚ ㄕㄜˋ ㄊㄞˊ)
a rocket launching pad

火箭飛機(ㄏㄨㄛˇ ㄐㄧㄢˋ ㄈㄟ ㄐㄧ)
a rocket-propelled plane

火警(ㄏㄨㄛˇ ㄐㄧㄥˇ)or 火警警報(ㄏㄨㄛˇ ㄐㄧㄥˇ ㄐㄧㄥˇ ㄅㄠˋ)
a fire alarm; a signal that warns that a fire has started

火炬(ㄏㄨㄛˇ ㄐㄩˋ)
a torch; a link

火漆(ㄏㄨㄛˇ ㄑㄧ)
sealing wax

火氣(ㄏㄨㄛˇ ㄑㄧˋ)
①(Chinese medicine) internal heat (as a cause of disease) ②temper; the boiling point (of a person): 他火氣很大。He has a quick temper.

火器(ㄏㄨㄛˇ ㄑㄧˋ)
firearms

火球(ㄏㄨㄛˇ ㄑㄧㄡˊ)
a meteor; a fireball

火鉗(ㄏㄨㄛˇ ㄑㄧㄢˊ)
a pair of fire-tongs; fire irons 亦作「火箸」

火槍(ㄏㄨㄛˇ ㄑㄧㄤ)
a firelock; a flintlock

火線(ㄏㄨㄛˇ ㄒㄧㄢˋ)
the battlefront; a firing line; a fighting line

火巷(ㄏㄨㄛˇ ㄒㄧㄤˋ)
a fire lane

火星(ㄏㄨㄛˇ ㄒㄧㄥ)
①the planet Mars ②sparks

火星人(ㄏㄨㄛˇ ㄒㄧㄥ ㄖㄣˊ)
a Martian

火刑(ㄏㄨㄛˇ ㄒㄧㄥˊ)
death by fire

火性(ㄏㄨㄛˇ ㄒㄧㄥˋ)
quick-tempered; the low boiling point (of a person)

火紙媒兒(ㄏㄨㄛˇ ㄓˇ ㄇㄜˊㄦ)or 火紙捻兒(ㄏㄨㄛˇ ㄓˇ ㄋㄧㄚˇㄦ)
a thin roll of touch paper used for lighting in water-pipe smoking

火燭(ㄏㄨㄛˇ ㄓㄨˊ)
①candlelight ②an inflammable substance; a combustible substance

火燭小心(ㄏㄨㄛˇ ㄓㄨˊ ㄒㄧㄠˇ ㄒㄧㄣ)
Be careful with fire!

火主(ㄏㄨㄛˇ ㄓㄨˇ)
the owner or lodger of a house where a fire first started

火磚(ㄏㄨㄛˇ ㄓㄨㄢ)
firebricks

火中取栗(ㄏㄨㄛˇ ㄓㄨㄥ ㄑㄩˇ ㄌㄧˋ)
to pull chestnuts out of the fire

火種(ㄏㄨㄛˇ ㄓㄨㄥˇ)
①tinder; embers kept for starting a new fire ②any burning object which causes a fire disaster

火熾(ㄏㄨㄛˇ ㄔˋ)
white-hot (also used figuratively to describe passion)

火車(ㄏㄨㄛˇ ㄔㄜ)
a train

火車票(ㄏㄨㄛˇ ㄔㄜ ㄆㄧㄠˋ)
train tickets: 請替我買火車票。Please buy the train tickets for me.

火車頭(ㄏㄨㄛˇ ㄔㄜ ㄊㄡˊ)
a locomotive; a railway engine for drawing a train

火車站(ㄏㄨㄛˇ ㄔㄜ ㄓㄢˋ)
a railway station

火車時間表(ㄏㄨㄛˇ ㄔㄜ ㄕˊ ㄐㄧㄢ ㄅㄧㄠˇ)
a railway schedule; a train schedule

火柴(ㄏㄨㄛˇ ㄔㄞˊ)
a match

火柴盒(ㄏㄨㄛˇ ㄔㄞˊ ㄏㄜˊ)
a matchbox

火場(ㄏㄨㄛˇ ㄔㄤˇ)or(ㄏㄨㄛˇ ㄔㄤˊ)
the scene of a fire

火成岩(ㄏㄨㄛˇ ㄔㄥˊ ㄧㄢˊ)
igneous rocks

火石(ㄏㄨㄛˇ ㄕˊ)
flint

火勢(ㄏㄨㄛˇ ㄕˋ)
the intensity and scope of a fire

火食 or 伙食(ㄏㄨㄛˇ ・ㄕ)
meals; board

火食費(ㄏㄨㄛˇ ・ㄕ ㄈㄟˋ)
a boarding fee

火舌(ㄏㄨㄛˇ ㄕㄜˊ)
licking flame; tongues of flame

火燒
①(ㄏㄨㄛˇ ㄕㄠ)a fire disaster ②(ㄏㄨㄛˇ ・ㄕㄠ)baked wheaten cake

火燒眉毛(ㄏㄨㄛˇ ㄕㄠ ㄇㄟˊ ㄇㄠˊ)
(literally) like fire burning the eyebrows—very urgent or imminent

火燒心(ㄏㄨㄛˇ ㄕㄠ ㄒㄧㄣ)
(literally) like fire burning the heart—very anxious or worried

火燒雲(ㄏㄨㄛˇ ㄕㄠ ㄩㄣˊ)
red clouds—as at sunset

火首(ㄏㄨㄛˇ ㄕㄡˇ)
one whose house is the first to catch fire

火山(ㄏㄨㄛˇ ㄕㄢ)
a volcano

火山爆發(ㄏㄨㄛˇ ㄕㄢ ㄅㄠˋ ㄈㄚ)
a volcanic eruption

火山脈(ㄏㄨㄛˇ ㄕㄢ ㄇㄞˋ)
a volcanic range

火山地震(ㄏㄨㄛˇ ㄕㄢ ㄉㄧˋ ㄓㄣˋ)
an earthquake caused by the eruption of a volcano

火山口(ㄏㄨㄛˇ ㄕㄢ ㄎㄡˇ)
a volcanic crater

火山灰(ㄏㄨㄛˇ ㄕㄢ ㄏㄨㄟ)
volcanic ashes; lapillus

火山熔岩(ㄏㄨㄛˇ ㄕㄢ ㄖㄨㄥˊ ㄧㄢˊ)
lava

火山岩(ㄏㄨㄛˇ ㄕㄢ ㄧㄢˊ)
volcanic rocks

火神(ㄏㄨㄛˇ ㄕㄣˊ)
(Chinese mythology) the god of fire

火傷(ㄏㄨㄛˇ ㄕㄤ)
a burn; a blister caused by burning

火上加油(ㄏㄨㄛˇ ㄕㄤˋ ㄐㄧㄚ ㄧㄡˊ)
(literally) to pour oil on the flame—to make things worse; to aggravate

火樹銀花(ㄏㄨㄛˇ ㄕㄨˋ ㄧㄣˊ ㄏㄨㄚ)
spluttering fireworks—bright lights and illuminations of a big city at night

火熱(ㄏㄨㄛˇ ㄖㄜˋ)
passionate; enthusiastic; intimate

火災(ㄏㄨㄛˇ ㄗㄞ)
a fire disaster

火災保險(ㄏㄨㄛˇ ㄗㄞ ㄅㄠˇ ㄒㄧㄢˇ)or 火險(ㄏㄨㄛˇ ㄒㄧㄢˇ)
fire insurance

火災保險費(ㄏㄨㄛˇ ㄗㄞ ㄅㄠˇ ㄒㄧㄢˇ ㄈㄟˋ)
a premium for fire insurance

火災保險單(ㄏㄨㄛˇ ㄗㄞ ㄅㄠˇ ㄒㄧㄢˇ ㄉㄢ)or 火險保單(ㄏㄨㄛˇ ㄒㄧㄢˇ ㄅㄠˇ ㄉㄢ)
a fire insurance policy

火葬(ㄏㄨㄛˇ ㄗㄤˋ)
to cremate; cremation

火葬爐(ㄏㄨㄛˇ ㄗㄤˋ ㄌㄨˊ)
a cremator

火葬場(ㄏㄨㄛˇ ㄗㄤˋ ㄔㄤˊ)or(ㄏㄨㄛˇ ㄗㄤˋ ㄔㄤˇ)
a crematory; a crematorium

火傘(ㄏㄨㄛˇ ㄙㄢˇ)
the white-hot sunshine in summer

火傘高張(ㄏㄨㄛˇ ㄙㄢˇ ㄍㄠ ㄓㄤ)
the scorching sunshine in summer—like a fully spread umbrella of fire

火速(ㄏㄨㄛˇ ㄙㄨˋ)
urgently; with the greatest urgency; imminent; urgent; posthaste: 食物必須火速送給那些災民。It's urgent that food must be sent to the sufferers.

火兒(ㄏㄨㄛˇㄦ)
① fire ② anger

火兒了(ㄏㄨㄛˇㄦ ˙ㄌㄜ)or 火了(ㄏㄨㄛˇ ˙ㄌㄜ)
to get mad; to become angry

火藥(ㄏㄨㄛˇ ㄧㄠˋ)
gunpowder: 我們需要火藥。We are in need of gunpowder.

火藥庫(ㄏㄨㄛˇ ㄧㄠˋ ㄎㄨˋ)
a powder magazine; an ammunition depot

火藥味(ㄏㄨㄛˇ ㄧㄠˋ ㄨㄟˋ)or 火藥氣息(ㄏㄨㄛˇ ㄧㄠˋ ㄑㄧˋ ㄒㄧ)
the smell of gunpowder—a tense situation which can easily erupt into open hostilities

火曜日(ㄏㄨㄛˇ ㄧㄠˋ ㄖˋ)
Tuesday

火油(ㄏㄨㄛˇ ㄧㄡˊ)
kerosene

火眼金睛(ㄏㄨㄛˇ ㄧㄢˇ ㄐㄧㄣ ㄐㄧㄥ)
fierce-looking; awe-inspiring (looks)

火燄(ㄏㄨㄛˇ ㄧㄢˋ)
flames

火燄噴射器(ㄏㄨㄛˇ ㄧㄢˋ ㄆㄣ ㄕㄜˋ ㄑㄧˋ)
a flame thrower

火印(ㄏㄨㄛˇ ㄧㄣˋ)
a firemark; a seal made by hot iron; a brand

火網(ㄏㄨㄛˇ ㄨㄤˇ)
(literally) the net of fire—intense shooting in battle; cross fire

二畫

【灰】 3172
ㄏㄨㄟ huei huī

1. ashes; dust
2. lime
3. gray (color)
4. disheartened; disappointed or discouraged
5. (now rarely) to break into tiny pieces or particles

灰白(ㄏㄨㄟ ㄅㄞˊ)
pale; ashen: 她臉色灰白。She turned pale.

灰白質(ㄏㄨㄟ ㄅㄞˊ ㄓˊ)
the gray matter (the outer cortex of nerve cells) and the white matter (the inner mass of nerve fibers); the cinereum matter

灰蒙蒙(ㄏㄨㄟ ㄇㄥˊ ㄇㄥˊ)
dusky; overcast: 灰蒙蒙的夜色 a dusky night scene

灰錳氧(ㄏㄨㄟ ㄇㄥˇ ㄧㄤˇ)
potassium permanganate

灰滅(ㄏㄨㄟ ㄇㄧㄝˋ)
to destroy; to wipe out; to vanish: 他所有的希望都灰滅了。All his hopes were destroyed.

灰分(ㄏㄨㄟ ㄈㄣˋ)
(biology) inorganic substance in a plant; ashes

灰頭土面(ㄏㄨㄟ ㄊㄡˊ ㄊㄨˇ ㄇㄧㄢˋ)
dusty and dirty in appearance—a sloven

灰頭土臉兒(ㄏㄨㄟ ㄊㄡˊ ㄊㄨˇ ㄌㄧㄚˇㄦ)
① to be covered with dust all over the face ② to lose face

灰銻礦(ㄏㄨㄟ ㄊㄧˋ ㄎㄨㄤˋ)
gray antimony

灰土(ㄏㄨㄟ ㄊㄨˇ)
dust; dirt

灰姑娘(ㄏㄨㄟ ㄍㄨ ˙ㄋㄧㄤ)
① Cinderella, the heroine of a fairy tale ② a person who achieves unexpected or sudden success or recognition, especially after obscurity, neglect or misery

灰燼(ㄏㄨㄟ ㄐㄧㄣˋ)
ashes; ember

灰心(ㄏㄨㄟ ㄒㄧㄣ)
disappointed; discouraged; disheartened: 不要因一次失敗而灰心。Don't be disheartened by a single failure.

灰心喪氣(ㄏㄨㄟ ㄒㄧㄣ ㄙㄤˋ ㄑㄧˋ)
crestfallen and disheartened

灰汁(ㄏㄨㄟ ㄓ)or 灰水(ㄏㄨㄟ ㄕㄨㄟˇ)
lye

灰指甲(ㄏㄨㄟ ㄓ ˙ㄐㄧㄚ)
leuconychia

灰塵(ㄏㄨㄟ ㄔㄣˊ)
dust: 馬路上積了厚厚的灰塵。Dust lay thick on the road.

灰長石(ㄏㄨㄟ ㄔㄤˊ ㄕˊ)
anorthite

灰吹法(ㄏㄨㄟ ㄔㄨㄟ ㄈㄚˇ)
cupellation

灰石(ㄏㄨㄟ ㄕˊ)
limestone

灰沙(ㄏㄨㄟ ㄕㄚ)
sand and dust

灰鼠(ㄏㄨㄟ ㄕㄨˇ)
the squirrel

灰曹長石(ㄏㄨㄟ ㄘㄠˊ ㄔㄤˊ ㄕˊ)
labradorite

灰色(ㄏㄨㄟ ㄙㄜˋ)or(ㄏㄨㄟ ˙ㄕㄞ)
gray color

灰色人生觀(ㄏㄨㄟ ㄙㄜˋ ㄖㄣˊ ㄕㄥ ㄍㄨㄢ)

pessimistic attitude toward life

灰暗(ㄏㄨㄟ ㄢˋ)
murky gray; gloomy: 灰暗的天空使人發愁。The gloomy sky makes people sad.

三畫

【灸】3173 ㄐㄧㄡˇ jeou jiǔ
(Chinese medicine) to cauterize by burning moxa; moxa cautery; moxibustion

灸治(ㄐㄧㄡˇ ㄓˋ)
to treat by moxa cautery or moxibustion

灸刺(ㄐㄧㄡˇ ㄘˋ)
cautery and acupuncture

【灼】3174 ㄓㄨㄛˊ jwo zhuó
1. to burn; to cauterize
2. bright; clear; luminous; brilliant
3. flowers in full bloom

灼爛(ㄓㄨㄛˊ ㄌㄢˋ)
badly burned

灼骨(ㄓㄨㄛˊ ㄍㄨˇ)
to burn the bones—a method of divination in ancient times

灼見(ㄓㄨㄛˊ ㄐㄧㄢˋ)
brilliant views; clear views: 你對這一題目有何灼見? What are your brilliant views on the subject?

灼灼(ㄓㄨㄛˊ ㄓㄨㄛˊ)
① bright and brilliant ② blooming ③ (figuratively) of uncommon brilliance

灼傷(ㄓㄨㄛˊ ㄕㄤ)
burn

灼爍(ㄓㄨㄛˊ ㄕㄨㄛˋ)
① bright and luminous ② splendorous

灼熱(ㄓㄨㄛˊ ㄖㄜˋ)
intense heat; red-hot

灼然(ㄓㄨㄛˊ ㄖㄢˊ)
crystal-clear; obvious

【災】3175 (灾、菑、烖) ㄗㄞ tzai zāi
a disaster; a calamity; a catastrophe

災變(ㄗㄞ ㄅㄧㄢˋ)
a disaster; a calamity

災民(ㄗㄞ ㄇㄧㄣˊ)
refugees created by disasters

災難(ㄗㄞ ㄋㄢˋ)
disasters; calamities; catastrophes

災黎(ㄗㄞ ㄌㄧˊ)
refugees created by disasters or calamities

災黎遍野(ㄗㄞ ㄌㄧˊ ㄅㄧㄢˋ ㄧㄝˇ)
The land is filled with disaster-stricken refugees.

災戾(ㄗㄞ ㄌㄧˋ)
disasters; calamities: 戰爭是可怕的災戾。War is a frightful calamity.

災沴(ㄗㄞ ㄌㄧˋ)
disasters (like droughts or floods)

災害(ㄗㄞ ㄏㄞˋ)
disasters; calamities; damage or casualties caused by disasters

災禍(ㄗㄞ ㄏㄨㄛˋ)
disasters or calamities; catastrophes

災禍臨頭(ㄗㄞ ㄏㄨㄛˋ ㄌㄧㄣˊ ㄊㄡˊ)
A great disaster is imminent.

災患(ㄗㄞ ㄏㄨㄢˋ)
disasters or calamities

災荒(ㄗㄞ ㄏㄨㄤ)
famine caused by floods or droughts

災情(ㄗㄞ ㄑㄧㄥˊ)
the extent of a disaster or calamity

災情慘重(ㄗㄞ ㄑㄧㄥˊ ㄘㄢˇ ㄓㄨㄥˋ)
① The situation in the afflicted area is serious. ② (now often used comically) heavy losses; big damages

災區(ㄗㄞ ㄑㄩ)
the area affected by a disaster or calamity; the afflicted area; the disaster area

災祥(ㄗㄞ ㄒㄧㄤˊ)
an omen of good or bad; a disaster or blessing

災星(ㄗㄞ ㄒㄧㄥ)
(literally) the star of calamity—disasters or calamities

災疫(ㄗㄞ ㄧˋ)
a pestilence: 災疫正在東方肆虐。A pestilence is raging in the East.

災殃(ㄗㄞ ㄧㄤ)
a disaster; a calamity; a catastrophe

災阨(ㄗㄞ ㄜˋ)
disasters or calamities; catastrophes

四畫

【炎】3176 ㄧㄢˊ yan yán
1. burning; hot; sultry
2. to blaze; to flame; to flare up
3. inflammation

炎方(ㄧㄢˊ ㄈㄤ)
the south (where the weather is very hot)

炎帝(ㄧㄢˊ ㄉㄧˋ)
Yen Ti, who supposedly lived from 2737 to 2697 B. C. 亦作「神農」

炎天(ㄧㄢˊ ㄊㄧㄢ)
a hot day; dog days

炎土(ㄧㄢˊ ㄊㄨˇ)
the region in the southwestern China, where the weather is very hot

炎涼(ㄧㄢˊ ㄌㄧㄤˊ)
① (said of weather) hot and cold ② snobbishness

炎涼世態(ㄧㄢˊ ㄌㄧㄤˊ ㄕˋ ㄊㄞˋ)
the aspect of worldly affairs, now hot and now cold

炎漢(ㄧㄢˊ ㄏㄢˋ) or 炎劉(ㄧㄢˊ ㄌㄧㄡˊ)
the Han Dynasty (206 B. C. to 220 A. D.)

炎荒(ㄧㄢˊ ㄏㄨㄤ)
the southern frontiers, where the weather is very hot

炎黃(ㄧㄢˊ ㄏㄨㄤˊ)
Yen Ti and Huang Ti (or the Yellow Emperor), two of the earliest rulers of China

炎黃子孫(ㄧㄢˊ ㄏㄨㄤˊ ㄗˇ ㄙㄨㄣ)
the Chinese people, who are supposed to be descendants of Yen Ti (炎帝) and Huang Ti (黃帝)

炎徼(ㄧㄢˊ ㄐㄧㄠˋ)
the southern frontiers

炎夏(ㄧㄢˊ ㄒㄧㄚˋ)
hot summer; summer at its hottest

炎瘴(ㄧㄢˊ ㄓㄤˋ)
the far south frontiers where miasma and malaria prevail

炎症(ㄧㄢˊ ㄓㄥˋ)

〔火部〕

inflammation
炎暑(ㄧㄢˊ ㄕㄨˇ)
hot summer; summer heat; summer at its hottest
炎熱(ㄧㄢˊ ㄖㄜˋ)
(said of weather) very hot: 天氣炎熱。The weather has been very hot.
炎宋(ㄧㄢˊ ㄙㄨㄥˋ)
the Sung Dynasty (the House of Chao)
炎炎(ㄧㄢˊ ㄧㄢˊ)
① impressive and imposing; awe-inspiring ② very hot
炎陽(ㄧㄢˊ ㄧㄤˊ)
the scorching sun
炎威(ㄧㄢˊ ㄨㄟ)
oppressively imposing; oppressiveness

【炊】 3177 ㄔㄨㄟ chuei chuī
to cook: 巧婦難爲無米之炊。Even a skillful wife cannot cook a meal without rice.
炊餅(ㄔㄨㄟ ㄅㄧㄥˇ)
steamed cake
炊骨易子(ㄔㄨㄟ ㄍㄨˇ ㄧˋ ㄗˇ)
(literally) to cook with the bones as fuel and to exchange children for eating —sufferings during a severe famine
炊桂(ㄔㄨㄟ ㄍㄨㄟˋ)
scarcity of firewood
炊火(ㄔㄨㄟ ㄏㄨㄛˇ)
a cooking fire which indicates presence of human habitation
炊金饌玉(ㄔㄨㄟ ㄐㄧㄣ ㄓㄨㄢˋ ㄩˋ)
the finest delicacies—as expensive as gold and gems
炊具(ㄔㄨㄟ ㄐㄩˋ)
cooking utensils 亦作「炊事用具」
炊帚(ㄔㄨㄟ ˙ㄓㄡ)
a brush for washing kitchen utensils
炊事(ㄔㄨㄟ ㄕˋ)
cooking
炊事兵(ㄔㄨㄟ ㄕˋ ㄅㄧㄥ)
a military cook
炊沙作飯(ㄔㄨㄟ ㄕㄚ ㄗㄨㄛˋ ㄈㄢˋ)
(literally) to cook the sand for food—a useless or meaningless attempt
炊爨(ㄔㄨㄟ ㄘㄨㄢˋ)
to prepare meals
炊烟(ㄔㄨㄟ ㄧㄢ)
the smoke from a kitchen fire
炊烟裊裊(ㄔㄨㄟ ㄧㄢ ㄋㄧㄠˇ ㄋㄧㄠˇ)
smoke spiraling from kitchens
炊烟四起(ㄔㄨㄟ ㄧㄢ ㄙˋ ㄑㄧˇ)
cooking smoke all around —It's about mealtime.

【炕】 3178 ㄎㄤˋ kanq kàng
1. dry; to dry
2. hot
3. *kang,* a brick bed warmed by a fire underneath (in North China)
炕面甎(ㄎㄤˋ ㄇㄧㄢˋ ㄓㄨㄢ)
square bricks that surface a brick bed
炕洞(ㄎㄤˋ ㄉㄨㄥˋ)
the hole under the brick bed for taking out or putting in the stove that warms; the flue of a brick bed
炕爐子(ㄎㄤˋ ㄌㄨˊ ˙ㄗ)
a squat stove or oven used specially for warming the brick bed
炕牀(ㄎㄤˋ ㄔㄨㄤˊ)
a brick bed warmed by a fire underneath
炕沿兒(ㄎㄤˋ ㄧㄚˊㄦ)
the outer edge of a brick bed

【炖】 3179 ㄉㄨㄣˋ duenn dùn
fire burning intensely

【炘】 3180 ㄒㄧㄣ shin xīn
1. brilliant and bright
2. to scorch; scorching hot
炘炘(ㄒㄧㄣ ㄒㄧㄣ)
brilliant and bright

【炙】 3181 ㄓˋ jyh zhì
to burn; to cauterize; to roast; to broil; to heat
炙背(ㄓˋ ㄅㄟˋ)
to expose the back to the sun
炙乾(ㄓˋ ㄍㄢ)
to dry by applying heat
炙炒(ㄓˋ ㄔㄠˇ)
to broil
炙手可熱(ㄓˋ ㄕㄡˇ ㄎㄜˇ ㄖㄜˋ)
very influential and powerful

【炒】 3182 ㄔㄠˇ chao chǎo
to fry; to stir-fry
炒米粉(ㄔㄠˇ ㄇㄧˇ ㄈㄣˇ)
to fry rice noodles; fried rice noodles
炒麵(ㄔㄠˇ ㄇㄧㄢˋ)
to fry noodles; fried noodles
炒飯(ㄔㄠˇ ㄈㄢˋ)
to fry rice; fried rice
炒蛋(ㄔㄠˇ ㄉㄢˋ)
scrambled eggs
炒地皮(ㄔㄠˇ ㄉㄧˋ ㄆㄧˊ)
to engage in land speculation
炒冷飯(ㄔㄠˇ ㄌㄥˇ ㄈㄢˋ)
to fry leftover rice—to do the same old thing without new contents
炒肝兒(ㄔㄠˇ ㄍㄚㄦ)
stir-fried liver
炒股票(ㄔㄠˇ ㄍㄨˇ ㄆㄧㄠˋ)
(colloquial) to manipulate stock trading
炒勺(ㄔㄠˇ ㄕㄠˊ)
a flat cooking ladle
炒熱(ㄔㄠˇ ㄖㄜˋ)
① to jack up the price of stocks by manipulation ② to make an ordinary news event a top story by sensational reporting
炒肉絲(ㄔㄠˇ ㄖㄡˋ ㄙ)
stir-fried meat slices; to stir-fry meat slices
炒菜(ㄔㄠˇ ㄘㄞˋ)
to fry vegetables or meat; fried dishes (as distinct from steamed or stewed dishes)
炒魷魚(ㄔㄠˇ ㄧㄡˊ ㄩˊ)
(slang) to be fired: 他因不誠實而被炒魷魚。He was fired for dishonesty.

五畫

【炫】 3183 ㄒㄩㄢˋ shiuann xuàn
1. to show off; to display; to flaunt
2. dazzling; bright; shining
炫目(ㄒㄩㄢˋ ㄇㄨˋ)
to dazzle the eyes
炫怪(ㄒㄩㄢˋ ㄍㄨㄞˋ)
to try to attract others' attention by sensationalism

炫惑(ㄒㄩㄢˋ ㄏㄨㄛˋ)
to dazzle and confuse
炫晝縞夜(ㄒㄩㄢˋ ㄓㄡˋ ㄍㄠˇ ㄧㄝˋ)
to illuminate day and night
炫俗(ㄒㄩㄢˋ ㄙㄨˊ)
to show off; to flaunt
炫耀(ㄒㄩㄢˋ ㄧㄠˋ)
① to flaunt; to show off: 這女孩炫耀她的新衣服。The girl flaunted her new clothes. ② bright and brilliant

【炬】 3184 ㄐㄩˋ jiuh jù
1. a torch
2. fire

【炮】 3185 1. ㄆㄠˊ paur páo
to refine medicinal herbs
炮鳳烹龍(ㄆㄠˊ ㄈㄥˋ ㄆㄥ ㄌㄨㄥˊ)
to cook a pheasant and a white horse as sacrifices when the emperors of old China officiated at grand ceremonies
炮煉(ㄆㄠˊ ㄌㄧㄢˋ)
to refine or decoct (medicine) by applying heat
炮烙(ㄆㄠˊ ㄌㄨㄛˋ)
an ancient Chinese torture
炮烙之刑(ㄆㄠˊ ㄌㄨㄛˋ ㄓ ㄒㄧㄥˊ)
an ancient torture or punishment by ordering a prisoner to walk on a slippery metal beam kept hot by coal underneath
炮製(ㄆㄠˊ ㄓˋ)
to refine or decoct (herbal medicine); the process of refining herbal medicine

【炮】 3185 2. (砲) ㄆㄠˋ paw pào
a big gun, cannon, etc.
炮火(ㄆㄠˋ ㄏㄨㄛˇ)
gunfire 亦作「砲火」

【炮】 3185 3. (炰) ㄅㄠ bau bāo
1. to roast or bake
2. to dry by heat
炮肉(ㄅㄠ ㄖㄡˋ)
roasted meat; to roast or barbecue meat

【炯】 3186 (烱) ㄐㄩㄥˇ jeong jiong
bright; brightness; clear
炯晃(ㄐㄩㄥˇ ㄏㄨㄤˇ)
bright and clear
炯戒(ㄐㄩㄥˇ ㄐㄧㄝˋ)
a clear warning
炯鑒(ㄐㄩㄥˇ ㄐㄧㄢˋ)
clear reflection; clear understanding
炯炯(ㄐㄩㄥˇ ㄐㄩㄥˇ)
① clear and bright (eyes, etc.): 他有一雙炯炯有神的眼睛。He has a pair of bright piercing eyes. ② discerning
炯心(ㄐㄩㄥˇ ㄒㄧㄣ)
clear conscience

【炳】 3187 ㄅㄧㄥˇ biing bǐng
bright; luminous
炳燭 or 秉燭(ㄅㄧㄥˇ ㄓㄨˊ)
(to take a night trip, stroll, etc.) by the bright candlelight
炳著(ㄅㄧㄥˇ ㄓㄨˋ)
eminent; renowned
炳然(ㄅㄧㄥˇ ㄖㄢˊ)
bright
炳耀(ㄅㄧㄥˇ ㄧㄠˋ)
bright and luminous
炳蔚(ㄅㄧㄥˇ ㄨㄟˋ)
deep and luminous

【炷】 3188 ㄓㄨˋ juh zhù
1. the wick (of a candle, lamp, etc.)
2. a stick (of incense, etc.)
3. to burn; to cauterize
炷香(ㄓㄨˋ ㄒㄧㄤ)
① to burn incense ② a stick of incense

【炸】 3189 1. ㄓㄚˋ jah zhà
1. to explode; to burst; to bomb
2. to get mad
3. to disperse boisterously; to flee in terror
炸彈(ㄓㄚˋ ㄉㄢˋ)
bombs
炸裂(ㄓㄚˋ ㄌㄧㄝˋ)
to split , blast or break by explosion or bombing; to develop cracks as a result of explosion
炸燬(ㄓㄚˋ ㄏㄨㄟˇ)
to destroy by bombing or explosion; to blow up; to blast
炸傷(ㄓㄚˋ ㄕㄤ)
to be injured in bombing or explosion
炸死(ㄓㄚˋ ·ㄙ)
to kill by bombing; to be killed in bombing or explosion
炸藥(ㄓㄚˋ ㄧㄠˋ)
dynamite; explosives

【炸】 3189 2. ㄓㄚˊ jar zhá
to fry in oil or fat; to deep-fry
炸麻花兒(ㄓㄚˊ ㄇㄚˊ ㄏㄨㄚㄦ)
sweet twisted pastry-strips fried in oil
炸糕(ㄓㄚˊ ㄍㄠ)
stuffed glutinous rice cakes fried in oil
炸雞(ㄓㄚˊ ㄐㄧ)
to fry chicken; fried chicken
炸醬(ㄓㄚˊ ㄐㄧㄤˋ)
fried bean sauce (usually with mince-meat)
炸醬麵(ㄓㄚˊ ㄐㄧㄤˋ ㄇㄧㄢˋ)
a kind of noodles served with fried bean sauce and mince-meat
炸圈兒(ㄓㄚˊ ㄑㄩㄚㄦ)
fried large hog intestines
炸油條(ㄓㄚˊ ㄧㄡˊ ㄊㄧㄠˊ)
to fry twisted dough-strips
炸丸子(ㄓㄚˊ ㄨㄢˊ ·ㄗ)
fried meat balls; to fry meat balls

【炭】 3190 ㄊㄢˋ tann tàn
1. charcoal
2. coal
3. (chemistry) C—carbon
炭筆(ㄊㄢˋ ㄅㄧˇ)
charcoal for drawing
炭田(ㄊㄢˋ ㄊㄧㄢˊ)
a coal field
炭爐(ㄊㄢˋ ㄌㄨˊ)
a charcoal stove
炭坑(ㄊㄢˋ ㄎㄥ)
(mining) a coal pit
炭化(ㄊㄢˋ ㄏㄨㄚˋ)
to carbonize; carbonization; to carburet; carburetion
炭化鈣(ㄊㄢˋ ㄏㄨㄚˋ ㄍㄞˋ)
calcium carbide (CaC_2)
炭化作用(ㄊㄢˋ ㄏㄨㄚˋ ㄗㄨㄛˋ ㄩㄥˋ)
carbonization
炭化物(ㄊㄢˋ ㄏㄨㄚˋ ㄨˋ)
carbides
炭畫(ㄊㄢˋ ㄏㄨㄚˋ)
charcoal drawings
炭火(ㄊㄢˋ ㄏㄨㄛˇ)

charcoal fires
炭灰(ㄊㄢˋ ㄏㄨㄟ)
ashes
炭精(ㄊㄢˋ ㄐㄧㄥ)
pure carbon
炭紙(ㄊㄢˋ ㄓˇ) or 炭精紙(ㄊㄢˋ ㄐㄧㄥ ㄓˇ)
carbon paper 亦作「複寫紙」
炭商(ㄊㄢˋ ㄕㄤ)
a coal or charcoal dealer
炭水化合物(ㄊㄢˋ ㄕㄨㄟˇ ㄏㄨㄚˋ ㄏㄜˊ ㄨˋ)
carbohydrate
炭素(ㄊㄢˋ ㄙㄨˋ)
carbon
炭酸(ㄊㄢˋ ㄙㄨㄢ)
carbonic acid
炭酸飽和(ㄊㄢˋ ㄙㄨㄢ ㄅㄠˇ ㄏㄜˊ)
carbonation
炭酸氣(ㄊㄢˋ ㄙㄨㄢ ㄑㄧˋ)
carbonic-acid gas
炭酸石灰(ㄊㄢˋ ㄙㄨㄢ ㄕˊ ㄏㄨㄟ)
carbonate of lime
炭酸水(ㄊㄢˋ ㄙㄨㄢ ㄕㄨㄟˇ)
carbonated water; soda water; aerated water
炭酸鹽(ㄊㄢˋ ㄙㄨㄢ ㄧㄢˊ)
carbonate

【炤】 3191
ㄓㄠˋ jaw jhào
formerly interchangeable with 照—to shine

【为】 3192
1. ㄨㄟˊ wei wéi
simplified form of 爲—to be; to do; to make

【为】 3192
2. ㄨㄟˋ wey wèi
simplified form of 爲—for

六畫

【烏】 3193
ㄨ u wū
1. a crow, raven or rook
2. dark color
3. how; what; when
4. Alas!
5. (now rarely) the sun
6. a Chinese family name

烏鬢(ㄨ ㄅㄧㄣˋ)
young people (whose hair is black)
烏哺(ㄨ ㄅㄨˇ)
to provide for or support one's parents when they get old (According to Chinese legend, the raven feeds its parents when they get too old to find food outside.)
烏梅(ㄨ ㄇㄟˊ)
dried plums
烏帽(ㄨ ㄇㄠˋ)
the costume of a hermit or of one who chooses to live in seclusion
烏木(ㄨ ㄇㄨˋ)
ebony
烏髮(ㄨ ㄈㄚˇ)
① dark hair; raven hair ② to dye the hair black
烏飛兔走(ㄨ ㄈㄟ ㄊㄨˋ ㄗㄡˇ)
How time flies!
烏豆(ㄨ ㄉㄡˋ)
the black beans—a variety of soybeans, usually used in herbal medicine
烏兔(ㄨ ㄊㄨˋ)
the sun and the moon
烏托邦(ㄨ ㄊㄨㄛ ㄅㄤ)
① utopia—an ideal place or state; any visionary system of political or social perfection ② *Utopia*
烏托邦社會主義(ㄨ ㄊㄨㄛ ㄅㄤ ㄕㄜˋ ㄏㄨㄟˋ ㄓㄨˇ ㄧˋ)
utopian socialism
烏鳥私情(ㄨ ㄋㄧㄠˇ ㄙ ㄑㄧㄥˊ)
filial piety 參看「烏哺」
烏拉圭(ㄨ ㄌㄚ ㄍㄨㄟ)
Uruguay
烏拉山(ㄨ ㄌㄚ ㄕㄢ)
the Ural Mountains
烏拉草(ㄨ ㄌㄚ ㄘㄠˇ)
name of a reed produced in Kirin Province, usually used as lining or padding in winter shoes to warm the feet
烏裏烏塗(ㄨ ·ㄌㄧ ㄨ ·ㄊㄨ) or 烏塗(ㄨ ·ㄊㄨ)
① lukewarm ②(said of persons) dumb and dull ③ vain (effort); in vain ④ tangled; muddled; ambiguous
烏溜溜(ㄨ ㄌㄧㄡ ㄌㄧㄡ)
(said of eyes) dark and liquid: 她有一雙烏溜溜的眼睛。She has dark and liquid eyes.
烏梁海(ㄨ ㄌㄧㄤˊ ㄏㄞˇ)
Uriankhai, a Mongolian tribe 亦作「兀良哈」
烏亮(ㄨ ㄌㄧㄤˋ)
glossy black; jet-black: 烏亮的頭髮 jet-black hair
烏魯木齊(ㄨ ㄌㄨˇ ㄇㄨˋ ㄑㄧˊ)
Urumchi, old name of Tihwa (廸化), in Sinkiang (新疆)
烏龍茶(ㄨ ㄌㄨㄥˊ ㄔㄚˊ)
oolong (a variety of semifermented brown or amber tea from Taiwan)
烏干達(ㄨ ㄍㄢ ㄉㄚˊ)
Uganda
烏龜(ㄨ ㄍㄨㄟ)
① a turtle; a tortoise ② a cuckold; a man who is two-timed by his wife
烏克蘭(ㄨ ㄎㄜˋ ㄌㄢˊ)
Ukraine, Russia
烏合之衆(ㄨ ㄏㄜˊ ㄓ ㄓㄨㄥˋ)
a band of rebels or bandits characterized by lack of discipline and tight organization; a mob; a rabble
烏黑(ㄨ ㄏㄟ)
pitch-dark (night); raven black (hair)
烏呼 or 烏虖 or 烏嘑 or 嗚呼(ㄨ ㄏㄨ)
Alas!
烏鷄(ㄨ ㄐㄧ) or 烏骨鷄(ㄨ ㄍㄨˇ ㄐㄧ)
dark-boned and dark-skinned chicken (believed to be of more nutritious value than the ordinary species)
烏脚病(ㄨ ㄐㄧㄠˇ ㄅㄧㄥˋ)
the black foot disease, a kind of endemic ailment in southern Taiwan
烏桕 or 烏臼(ㄨ ㄐㄧㄡˋ)
Sapium sebiferum, the Chinese tallow tree
烏巾(ㄨ ㄐㄧㄣ)
a hat worn by an official in ancient China
烏江(ㄨ ㄐㄧㄤ)
① name of a stream in Anhwei, where Hsiang Yü(項羽), an arch rival of Liu Pang (劉邦), committed suicide ② former name of Chienchiang (黔江), the biggest river in Kweichow Province
烏七八糟(ㄨ ㄑㄧ ㄅㄚ ㄗㄠ)
in total disorder, confusion or pandemonium
烏騅(ㄨ ㄓㄨㄟ)
a dark stallion
烏紗帽(ㄨ ㄕㄚ ㄇㄠˋ)
a hat worn by officials in

ancient China (now used as a synonym of a government post)

烏賊(ㄨ ㄗㄟˊ)
the cuttlefish; the inkfish

烏蘇里江(ㄨ ㄙㄨ ㄌㄧˇ ㄐㄧㄤ)
the Ussuri River, a tributary of Heilungkiang

烏孫(ㄨ ㄙㄨㄣ)
name of an ancient state, west of the Han Empire

烏衣巷(ㄨ ㄧ ㄒㄧㄤˋ)
Black Gown Lane, a special residential area of the nobility in the Tsin (晉) Dynasty, southeast of today's Nanking

烏鴉(ㄨ ㄧㄚ)
a crow; a raven

烏鴉座(ㄨ ㄧㄚ ㄗㄨㄛˋ)
(astronomy) Corvus

烏有(ㄨ ㄧㄡˇ)
nothingness

烏有先生(ㄨ ㄧㄡˇ ㄒㄧㄢ ˙ㄕㄥ)
Mr. Nobody—a fictitious character created by Su-Ma Hsiang-ju (司馬相如)

烏烟瘴氣(ㄨ ㄧㄢ ㄓㄤˋ ㄑㄧˋ)
(said of air) heavily polluted; now also used figuratively to indicate corruption, confusion, etc.

烏焉成馬(ㄨ ㄧㄢ ㄔㄥˊ ㄇㄚˇ)
Copying begets mistakes, as 烏 and 焉 are erroneously written as 馬 after being copied repeatedly.

烏魚(ㄨ ㄩˊ)
black mullet

烏魚子(ㄨ ㄩˊ ㄗˇ)
mullet's roe

烏雲(ㄨ ㄩㄣˊ)
① dark clouds ② (figuratively) a woman's black hair

烏雲密佈(ㄨ ㄩㄣˊ ㄇㄧˋ ㄅㄨˋ)
as dark clouds mass up—A heavy downpour is in the making or the situation is getting dangerous or imminent.

【烈】 3194 ㄌㄧㄝˋ lieh liè

1. fiery; acute; vehement; fierce; strong; violent
2. honest and virtuous; just and straightforward; chaste
3. merits; achievements
4. a Chinese family name

烈風(ㄌㄧㄝˋ ㄈㄥ)
a strong wind

烈婦(ㄌㄧㄝˋ ㄈㄨˋ)
① a woman who kills herself after her husband's death ② a woman or girl who dies to defend her chastity

烈女(ㄌㄧㄝˋ ㄋㄩˇ)
a girl of virtuous upbringing

烈烈(ㄌㄧㄝˋ ㄌㄧㄝˋ)
① majestic and imposing ② sad ③ cold ④ blazing

烈火(ㄌㄧㄝˋ ㄏㄨㄛˇ)
a blazing fire; a fierce fire

烈火轟雷(ㄌㄧㄝˋ ㄏㄨㄛˇ ㄏㄨㄥ ㄌㄟˊ)
quick-tempered; violent; ferocious

烈火見眞金(ㄌㄧㄝˋ ㄏㄨㄛˇ ㄐㄧㄢˋ ㄓㄣ ㄐㄧㄣ)
Pure gold proves its worth in a blazing fire.—Truth is ultimately louder than lies or slanders.或 True loyalty can stand the test of adversity.

烈酒(ㄌㄧㄝˋ ㄐㄧㄡˇ)
strong drink; a stiff drink

烈性(ㄌㄧㄝˋ ㄒㄧㄥˋ)
a straightforward but violent disposition

烈士(ㄌㄧㄝˋ ㄕˋ)or 烈漢(ㄌㄧㄝˋ ㄏㄢˋ)
martyrs; noble-hearted men who bow to neither intimidation nor temptation: 他們是革命烈士。They are revolutionary martyrs.

烈士殉名(ㄌㄧㄝˋ ㄕˋ ㄒㄩㄣˋ ㄇㄧㄥˊ)
An upright man dies in defense of his name.

烈暑(ㄌㄧㄝˋ ㄕㄨˇ)
summer at its hottest

烈日(ㄌㄧㄝˋ ㄖˋ)
the scorching sun

烈日當空(ㄌㄧㄝˋ ㄖˋ ㄉㄤ ㄎㄨㄥ)
the scorching sun high up in the sky

烈祖(ㄌㄧㄝˋ ㄗㄨˇ)
an illustrious ancestor

烈焰(ㄌㄧㄝˋ ㄧㄢˋ)
blazing flames; a violent or fierce fire

【烝】 3195 ㄓㄥ jeng zhēng

1. to rise—as steam
2. many; numerous
3. lewdness, incest, etc. among the older generation
4. to steam 亦作「蒸」

烝民(ㄓㄥ ㄇㄧㄣˊ)
the people; the masses

烝黎(ㄓㄥ ㄌㄧˊ)
the people; the masses

烝烝(ㄓㄥ ㄓㄥ)
① rising and flourishing ② (now rarely) sincere and filial

【烊】 3196 ㄧㄤˊ yang yáng

to smelt; to melt

烊金(ㄧㄤˊ ㄐㄧㄣ)
molten metal; molten metal ores

【烘】 3197 ㄏㄨㄥ hong hōng

1. to bake; to roast
2. to dry or warm near a fire

烘焙(ㄏㄨㄥ ㄅㄟˋ)
to dry (herbal medicine) over a fire

烘托(ㄏㄨㄥ ㄊㄨㄛ)
(said of writing or painting) to make conspicuous by contrast

烘暖(ㄏㄨㄥ ㄋㄨㄢˇ)
to warm by fire

烘爐(ㄏㄨㄥ ㄌㄨˊ)
a baking oven; a portable stove or furnace

烘乾(ㄏㄨㄥ ㄍㄢ)
to dry beside or over a fire

烘乾機(ㄏㄨㄥ ㄍㄢ ㄐㄧ)
a clothing dryer

烘烤(ㄏㄨㄥ ㄎㄠˇ)or 烘焙(ㄏㄨㄥ ㄅㄟˋ)
to bake; to roast; to warm or dry by the fire

烘烘(ㄏㄨㄥ ㄏㄨㄥ)
① warm and cozy ② (said of a fire) blazing ③ (said of a crowd) noisy and jubilant

烘焦(ㄏㄨㄥ ㄐㄧㄠ)
(said of cloth, paper, etc.) to get partially burned because of over-heating near the fire

烘襯(ㄏㄨㄥ ㄔㄣˋ)
(said of writing or painting) to make conspicuous by contrast or other means

烘染(ㄏㄨㄥ ㄖㄢˇ)
to emphasize the most important point by elaboration

烘雲托月(ㄏㄨㄥ ㄩㄣˊ ㄊㄨㄛ ㄩㄝˋ)
to bring something out with the help of a favorable background; to make something more noticeable by contrast

【烤】 3198 ㄎㄠˇ kao kǎo
1. to roast; to bake; to toast
2. to warm by a fire
3. scorching

烤餅(ㄎㄠˇ ㄅㄧㄥˇ)
to bake a cake

烤麵包(ㄎㄠˇ ㄇㄧㄢˋ ㄅㄠ)
to bake bread; to toast bread

烤麵包機(ㄎㄠˇ ㄇㄧㄢˋ ㄅㄠ ㄐㄧ)
a toaster

烤爐(ㄎㄠˇ ㄌㄨˊ)
an oven

烤火(ㄎㄠˇ ㄏㄨㄛˇ)
to warm by the fire

烤焦(ㄎㄠˇ ㄐㄧㄠ)
burned in roasting or baking

烤箱(ㄎㄠˇ ㄒㄧㄤ)
an oven for baking

烤肉(ㄎㄠˇ ㄖㄡˋ)
① to roast meat; to barbecue: 我們烤肉和馬鈴薯。We roasted meat and potatoes. ② barbecue; meat roasted before an open fire

烤一烤(ㄎㄠˇ ·ㄧ ㄎㄠˇ)
① to warm or dry near a fire ② to roast for a little while

烤鴨(ㄎㄠˇ ㄧㄚ)
① to roast duck ② roasted duck

【烟】 3199 ㄧㄢ ian yān
simplified form of 煙

【烙】 3200 ㄌㄠˋ law lào (讀音 ㄌㄨㄛˋ luoh luò)
1. to burn
2. to brand; to iron
3. to bake in a pan

烙餅(ㄌㄠˋ ㄅㄧㄥˇ)
① a kind of thick, hard pancake ② the baking of such a cake

烙鐵(ㄌㄠˋ ㄊㄧㄝˇ)
an iron; a branding iron

烙印(ㄌㄠˋ ㄧㄣˋ)
to brand; a brand

七畫

【烽】 3201 ㄈㄥ feng fēng
(in ancient China) a tall structure (on a city wall, etc.) where fire was made to signal enemy invasion or presence of bandits

烽鼓(ㄈㄥ ㄍㄨˇ)
signal fires and drums—war

烽候(ㄈㄥ ㄏㄡˋ)
to erect a watchtower to detect enemy's presence

烽火(ㄈㄥ ㄏㄨㄛˇ)
signal fires; beacon fires

烽火臺(ㄈㄥ ㄏㄨㄛˇ ㄊㄞˊ)
a tall structure for lighting a signal or beacon fire

烽火連年(ㄈㄥ ㄏㄨㄛˇ ㄌㄧㄢˊ ㄋㄧㄢˊ)
continuous wars

烽燧(ㄈㄥ ㄙㄨㄟˋ)
fire and smoke used as warning signals during night and day respectively

烽烟(ㄈㄥ ㄧㄢ)
smoke used as a warning signal

烽烟遍地(ㄈㄥ ㄧㄢ ㄅㄧㄢˋ ㄉㄧˋ)
Beacon fires are found everywhere.

烽烟四起(ㄈㄥ ㄧㄢ ㄙˋ ㄑㄧˇ)
a land or country beset by war

【烹】 3202 ㄆㄥ peng pēng
1. to cook; to boil; to decoct
2. (cooking) to add bean sauce and dressing after frying
3. (slang) to frighten (away)

烹調(ㄆㄥ ㄊㄧㄠˊ)
to cook or prepare (food); cooking

烹醢(ㄆㄥ ㄏㄞˇ)
the most frightening tortures for prisoners in ancient China

烹煮(ㄆㄥ ㄓㄨˇ)
to cook; to boil

烹茶(ㄆㄥ ㄔㄚˊ)
to make tea: 她爲客人烹茶。She makes tea for the guests.

烹飪(ㄆㄥ ㄖㄣˋ)
to cook; cooking

烹飪法(ㄆㄥ ㄖㄣˋ ㄈㄚˇ)
a culinary art; cookery; a recipe

【焄】 3203 ㄒㄩㄣ shiun xūn
1. rising flames or fumes
2. aroma

【焉】 3204 ㄧㄢ ian yān
1. an interrogative—how, why, when, etc.
2. a pronoun—it
3. an adverb—there; here
4. a conjunctive—and so; so that
5. a final particle indicating numerous senses

焉得(ㄧㄢ ㄉㄜˊ)
How can one be (or attain)...?

焉能(ㄧㄢ ㄋㄥˊ)
How can (one do it, succeed,etc.)?

焉敢(ㄧㄢ ㄍㄢˇ)
How dare...?

焉支(ㄧㄢ ㄓ)
name of a mountain in Kansu Province

焉知(ㄧㄢ ㄓ)
How could one know...?

焉知非福(ㄧㄢ ㄓ ㄈㄟ ㄈㄨˊ)
How could you know it is not a blessing?

焉有(ㄧㄢ ㄧㄡˇ)
How could there be such...?

焉用(ㄧㄢ ㄩㄥˋ)
Why is it necessary to use...? 或 Is it needed?

【烺】 3205 ㄌㄤˇ laang lǎng
(said of fire) bright

【烷】 3206 ㄨㄢˊ wan wán
1. fire
2. alkane

烷基(ㄨㄢˊ ㄐㄧ)
(chemistry) alkyl

【烯】 3207 ㄒㄧ shi xī
1. the color of fire
2. alkene

八畫

【焙】 3208 ㄅㄟˋ bey bèi
to dry or heat near a fire; to toast; to bake

焙粉(ㄅㄟˋ ㄈㄣˇ)

baking powder 亦作「發粉」
焙爐(ㄅㄟˋ ㄌㄨˊ)
an oven; a toaster
焙乾(ㄅㄟˋ ㄍㄢ)
to dry by fire
焙茶(ㄅㄟˋ ㄔㄚˊ)
to dry tea by fire

【焮】3209
ㄒㄧㄣˋ shinn xìn
1. to burn; to heat; to cauterize
2. "heat" in Chinese medicine
焮天(ㄒㄧㄣˋ ㄊㄧㄢ)
(said of a big fire) fiercely burning
焮腫(ㄒㄧㄣˋ ㄓㄨㄥˇ)
(medicine) a skin swelling or inflammation

【焯】3210
ㄓㄨㄛˊ jwo zhuó
1. same as 灼—to burn
2. bright and brilliant

【焚】3211
ㄈㄣˊ fern fén
to burn; to set fire to
焚斃(ㄈㄣˊ ㄅㄧˋ)
to burn to death; to be burned to death
焚滅(ㄈㄣˊ ㄇㄧㄝˋ)
to burn down to nothing; to destroy by fire
焚溺(ㄈㄣˊ ㄋㄧˋ)
to be burned or drowned—to be in great difficulty
焚掠(ㄈㄣˊ ㄌㄩㄝˋ)
to burn and loot; burning and pillaging
焚膏繼晷(ㄈㄣˊ ㄍㄠ ㄐㄧˋ ㄍㄨㄟˇ)
to burn the midnight oil—(figuratively) to be very diligent in study
焚化(ㄈㄣˊ ㄏㄨㄚˋ)
① to cremate ② to burn (offerings, etc.) for the dead ③ to put to fire
焚化爐(ㄈㄣˊ ㄏㄨㄚˋ ㄌㄨˊ)
an incinerator
焚毀(ㄈㄣˊ ㄏㄨㄟˇ)
to burn up; to destroy by fire; to consume by burning
焚刼(ㄈㄣˊ ㄐㄧㄝˊ)
to burn and loot; burning and pillaging
焚琴煮鶴(ㄈㄣˊ ㄑㄧㄣˊ ㄓㄨˇ ㄏㄜˋ)
to burn the *chin* (a musical instrument) and cook the crane—(figuratively) to pour cold water on something interesting or exciting; to spoil the fun
焚修(ㄈㄣˊ ㄒㄧㄡ)
to burn incense and discipline oneself according to the strict rules of Buddhism or Taoism
焚香(ㄈㄣˊ ㄒㄧㄤ)
to burn incense (in worship, offering, etc.)
焚香膜拜(ㄈㄣˊ ㄒㄧㄤ ㄇㄛˊ ㄅㄞˋ)
to worship at temples
焚芝(ㄈㄣˊ ㄓ)
good people or virtuous persons being involved in trouble or incriminated with trumped-up charges
焚舟(ㄈㄣˊ ㄓㄡ)
to burn the boat after crossing the river; to cross the Rubicon—There's no going back.
焚燒(ㄈㄣˊ ㄕㄠ)
to consume by fire; to burn; to destroy by burning: 他焚燒他所有的信。He burned all his letters.
焚身(ㄈㄣˊ ㄕㄣ)
to bring ruin to oneself because of greediness
焚書坑儒(ㄈㄣˊ ㄕㄨ ㄎㄥ ㄖㄨˊ)
to burn the books and bury the scholars alive—said of Shih Huang of the Chin (秦) Dynasty
焚如(ㄈㄣˊ ㄖㄨˊ)
a fire disaster
焚硯 or 焚研(ㄈㄣˊ ㄧㄢˋ)
to destroy the ink-slab—to write no more because others write so much better

【焱】3212
(燄) ㄧㄢˋ yann yàn
flames

【焦】3213
ㄐㄧㄠ jiau jiāo
1. scorched or burned; charred
2. the smell or stench of things burned
3. worried and anxious
4. a Chinese family name
焦不離孟，孟不離焦(ㄐㄧㄠ ㄅㄨˋ ㄌㄧˊ ㄇㄥˋ, ㄇㄥˋ ㄅㄨˋ ㄌㄧˊ ㄐㄧㄠ)
Damon and Pythias
焦平面(ㄐㄧㄠ ㄆㄧㄥˊ ㄇㄧㄢˋ)
a focal plane
焦煤(ㄐㄧㄠ ㄇㄟˊ)
coke
焦悶(ㄐㄧㄠ ㄇㄣˋ)
①(said of weather) hot and humid or oppressive ② worried and anxious; harassed; a depressive mood
焦點(ㄐㄧㄠ ㄉㄧㄢˇ)
① focus ② a burning point; a point of tremendous significance; a focal point
焦頭爛額(ㄐㄧㄠ ㄊㄡˊ ㄌㄢˋ ㄜˊ)
(literally) to suffer burns on head and forehead when fighting a fire—in great trouble or difficulty; in straits; in bad shape
焦炭(ㄐㄧㄠ ㄊㄢˋ)
coke
焦土(ㄐㄧㄠ ㄊㄨˇ)
scorched earth—ravages of war
焦土抗戰(ㄐㄧㄠ ㄊㄨˇ ㄎㄤˋ ㄓㄢˋ)
to adopt a scorched earth policy in fighting the invading enemy
焦土政策(ㄐㄧㄠ ㄊㄨˇ ㄓㄥˋ ㄘㄜˋ)
the scorched earth policy
焦桐(ㄐㄧㄠ ㄊㄨㄥˊ)
a Chinese lute or lyre
焦勞(ㄐㄧㄠ ㄌㄠˊ)
worried and worn down by hard work
焦慮(ㄐㄧㄠ ㄌㄩˋ)
deeply worried and anxious
焦慮不安(ㄐㄧㄠ ㄌㄩˋ ㄅㄨˋ ㄢ)
to be on pins and needles
焦渴(ㄐㄧㄠ ㄎㄜˇ)
① very thirsty ② very anxious
焦枯(ㄐㄧㄠ ㄎㄨ)
withered (by heat)
焦黃(ㄐㄧㄠ ㄏㄨㄤˊ)
pale yellow
焦急(ㄐㄧㄠ ㄐㄧˊ)
very anxious; in deep anxiety
焦竭(ㄐㄧㄠ ㄐㄧㄝˊ)
worried and exhausted
焦距(ㄐㄧㄠ ㄐㄩˋ)
(physics) focal length or focal distance; focus: 這相片對準了焦距。This photograph is in focus.
焦心(ㄐㄧㄠ ㄒㄧㄣ)
anxious; worried

焦灼(ㄐㄧㄠ ㄓㄨㄛˊ)
①burned by fire ②anxious; worried
焦熱(ㄐㄧㄠ ㄖㄜˋ)
burning heat; scorching hot
焦熱電現象(ㄐㄧㄠ ㄖㄜˋ ㄉㄧㄢˋ ㄒㄧㄢˋ ㄒㄧㄤˋ)
pyroelectricity
焦棗兒(ㄐㄧㄠ ㄗㄠˇㄦ)
fire-dried dates—a specialty in Northern China
焦躁(ㄐㄧㄠ ㄗㄠˋ)
worried, anxious and getting impatient; getting restless because of anxiety
焦思(ㄐㄧㄠ ㄙ)
deep worry: 焦思使她不能入睡。Deep worry kept her awake.
焦散面(ㄐㄧㄠ ㄙㄢˋ ㄇㄧㄢˋ)
(optics) the caustic surface
焦爾定律 or 焦耳定律(ㄐㄧㄠ ㄦˇ ㄉㄧㄥˋ ㄌㄩˋ)
(physics) Joule's Law
焦爾熱 or 焦耳熱(ㄐㄧㄠ ㄦˇ ㄖㄜˋ)
Joule's heat
焦油(ㄐㄧㄠ ㄧㄡˊ)
tar
焦油腦(ㄐㄧㄠ ㄧㄡˊ ㄋㄠˇ)
naphthalene

【無】 3214 ㄨˊ wu wú

1. negative; not; no; none
2. without; destitute of; wanting; to lack; to have not
3. no matter what (or how); not yet
4. a Chinese family name

無巴鼻(ㄨˊ ㄅㄚ ㄅㄧˊ)
to have nothing to hold on; unreal
無備(ㄨˊ ㄅㄟˋ)
unprepared; without preparation
無被花(ㄨˊ ㄅㄟˋ ㄏㄨㄚ)
an achlamydeous flower
無報酬(ㄨˊ ㄅㄠˋ ㄔㄡˊ)
without pay, recompense or reward; gratuitous
無比(ㄨˊ ㄅㄧˇ)
incomparable; incomparably; extremely; without peer; peerless; matchless
無裨(ㄨˊ ㄅㄧˋ)
won't help; useless
無邊(ㄨˊ ㄅㄧㄢ)
limitless; vast and expansive
無邊風月(ㄨˊ ㄅㄧㄢ ㄈㄥ ㄩㄝˋ)
boundless natural charms
無邊無際(ㄨˊ ㄅㄧㄢ ㄨˊ ㄐㄧˋ)
boundless; limitless; vast
無邊無礙(ㄨˊ ㄅㄧㄢ ㄨˊ ㄞˋ)
without restraints of any sort
無病呻吟(ㄨˊ ㄅㄧㄥˋ ㄕㄣ ㄧㄣˊ)
(literally) to groan when there is no physical pain—① to groan for no reason; to complain without a cause ② (said of writing) affected sentimentality
無病自灸(ㄨˊ ㄅㄧㄥˋ ㄗˋ ㄐㄧㄡˇ)
to bring trouble to oneself by making uncalled-for moves
無補(ㄨˊ ㄅㄨˇ)
useless; of no avail or use; won't help: 空談無補於事實。Mere words won't help facts.
無不(ㄨˊ ㄅㄨˋ)
all without exception; invariably
無不如意(ㄨˊ ㄅㄨˋ ㄖㄨˊ ㄧˋ)
to have everything go one's way
無朋(ㄨˊ ㄆㄥˊ)
incomparable; incomparably; peerless; matchless
無偏無頗(ㄨˊ ㄆㄧㄢ ㄨˊ ㄆㄛ)
very just; unbiased; impartial: 法律應該一視同仁無偏無頗。Law shall be uniform and impartial.
無米之炊(ㄨˊ ㄇㄧˇ ㄓ ㄔㄨㄟ)
(Even a capable woman cannot prepare) a meal without rice—impossible for lacking the most essential
無明(ㄨˊ ㄇㄧㄥˊ)
(Buddhism) *avidya*, ignorance, nescience, unknowing—the primary or fundamental root of all evil and suffering in the world
無明火(ㄨˊ ㄇㄧㄥˊ ㄏㄨㄛˇ)
fury; wrath; anger
無名小卒(ㄨˊ ㄇㄧㄥˊ ㄒㄧㄠˇ ㄗㄨˊ)
a nobody; an unimportant person; small fry
無名指(ㄨˊ ㄇㄧㄥˊ ㄓˇ)
the ring finger
無名氏(ㄨˊ ㄇㄧㄥˊ ㄕˋ)
Mr. Anonymous—usually used by a person who contributes to a charitable cause without revealing his name
無名作家(ㄨˊ ㄇㄧㄥˊ ㄗㄨㄛˋ ㄐㄧㄚ)
①an anonymous writer ②an unknown writer
無名業火(ㄨˊ ㄇㄧㄥˊ ㄧㄝˋ ㄏㄨㄛˇ)
irrepressible anger
無名英雄(ㄨˊ ㄇㄧㄥˊ ㄧㄥ ㄒㄩㄥˊ)
an unsung hero; an unknown soldier (for a cause)
無目的(ㄨˊ ㄇㄨˋ ㄉㄧˋ)
aimless; without objective; at random: 他過着無目的的生活。He leads an aimless life.
無法(ㄨˊ ㄈㄚˇ)
unable; incapable: 我們無法應付困難。We are unable to cope with difficulties.
無法可想(ㄨˊ ㄈㄚˇ ㄎㄜˇ ㄒㄧㄤˇ)
no way out; no alternative; at the end of one's rope; powerless
無法形容(ㄨˊ ㄈㄚˇ ㄒㄧㄥˊ ㄖㄨㄥˊ)
beyond description
無法可施(ㄨˊ ㄈㄚˇ ㄎㄜˇ ㄕ)
unable to do anything about it
無法無天(ㄨˊ ㄈㄚˇ ㄨˊ ㄊㄧㄢ)
lawless and godless; to be totally devoid of conscience and respect for law; recklessly
無非(ㄨˊ ㄈㄟ)
no other than; only; no more than; nothing but: 無非是好壞兩種後果。There are only two consequences, a good one and a bad one.
無分彼此(ㄨˊ ㄈㄣ ㄅㄧˇ ㄘˇ)
one for all and all for one
無分軒輊(ㄨˊ ㄈㄣ ㄒㄩㄢ ㄓˋ)
a draw or tie; well-matched
無分(ㄨˊ ㄈㄣˋ)
①to have nothing to do with it ②to be denied a share
無方(ㄨˊ ㄈㄤ)
①no set rules, regulations, or precedents; no set pattern ②not the right method; the wrong way (of bringing up a child)
無妨(ㄨˊ ㄈㄤˊ)
①doesn't matter; unimpor-

火部

tant ② do not constitute an obstacle or obstruction; there's no harm

無風(ㄨˊ ㄈㄥ)
(meteorology) calm: 昨天海上無風。The sea was calm yesterday.

無風不起浪(ㄨˊ ㄈㄥ ㄅㄨˋ ㄑㄧˇ ㄌㄤˋ)
(literally) There won't be billows when there's no wind.—There must be a cause or reason for this.

無風起浪(ㄨˊ ㄈㄥ ㄑㄧˇ ㄌㄤˋ)
to start a big trouble out of nothing

無風三尺浪(ㄨˊ ㄈㄥ ㄙㄢ ㄔˇ ㄌㄤˋ)
(literally) There are billows three feet high (on the sea) even if there is no wind.—A sea voyage is full of risks.

無道(ㄨˊ ㄉㄠˋ)
tyranny; tyrannical; injustice; unjust

無黨無派(ㄨˊ ㄉㄤˇ ㄨˊ ㄆㄞˋ)
without party affiliation of any sort; nonpartisan

無敵(ㄨˊ ㄉㄧˊ)
without match; matchless; invincible

無敵不克(ㄨˊ ㄉㄧˊ ㄅㄨˋ ㄎㄜˋ)
to make conquests on all sides; to smash whoever stands in the way

無敵艦隊(ㄨˊ ㄉㄧˊ ㄐㄧㄢˋ ㄉㄨㄟˋ)
the Invincible Armada

無底洞(ㄨˊ ㄉㄧˇ ㄉㄨㄥˋ)
(literally) the bottomless pit—human greed or desires (which can never be fully satisfied); any hobby or pursuit which requires an inexhaustible supply of funds

無抵抗主義(ㄨˊ ㄉㄧˇ ㄎㄤˋ ㄓㄨˇ ㄧˋ)
the Principle of Nonresistance, initiated by Lev Nikolaevich Tolstoy, 1828-1910, also known as Tolstoyism

無的放矢(ㄨˊ ㄉㄧˋ ㄈㄤˋ ㄕˇ)
(literally) to shoot without a target—indiscriminate; to attack without a cause; to make unfounded charges or accusations

無地自容(ㄨˊ ㄉㄧˋ ㄗˋ ㄖㄨㄥˊ)
(literally) no place to hide—extremely embarrassed or ashamed: 他因他所做的事無地自容。He is extremely ashamed of what he did.

無定形(ㄨˊ ㄉㄧㄥˋ ㄒㄧㄥˊ)
amorphous; formless

無毒(ㄨˊ ㄉㄨˊ)
poisonless; harmless: 有些蛇無毒。Some snakes are poisonless.

無毒不丈夫(ㄨˊ ㄉㄨˊ ㄅㄨˋ ㄓㄤˋ ㄈㄨ)
Ruthlessness is the mark of a truly great man. 或 One who is not ruthless is not a truly great man.

無獨有偶(ㄨˊ ㄉㄨˊ ㄧㄡˇ ㄡˇ)
It happens that there is a similar case. 或 by coincidence

無度(ㄨˊ ㄉㄨˋ)
without restraints; very indulgent: 他飲酒無度。He drank without restraints.

無多有少(ㄨˊ ㄉㄨㄛ ㄧㄡˇ ㄕㄠˇ)
(said of a contribution to a charity) It doesn't matter how much.

無端(ㄨˊ ㄉㄨㄢ)
without cause or reason; unprovoked; unjustified: 他無端生氣。He was angry without cause.

無冬無夏(ㄨˊ ㄉㄨㄥ ㄨˊ ㄒㄧㄚˋ)
It doesn't matter whether it is summer or winter.

無動於衷(ㄨˊ ㄉㄨㄥˋ ㄩˊ ㄓㄨㄥ)
① unmoved; flinty-hearted; callous: 她對我的忠告無動於衷。She is callous to my advice. ② to remain firm; to stand pat

無頭案(ㄨˊ ㄊㄡˊ ㄢˋ)
a criminal case without any clues

無頭無腦(ㄨˊ ㄊㄡˊ ㄨˊ ㄋㄠˇ)
disorderly and confused; muddled and mixed-up

無頭無尾(ㄨˊ ㄊㄡˊ ㄨˊ ㄨㄟˇ)
without head or tail—confused, muddled or mixed-up

無題(ㄨˊ ㄊㄧˊ)
(usually serving as a title of a poem) "Without a Title"—a poem which says more than a title can contain

無條件投降(ㄨˊ ㄊㄧㄠˊ ㄐㄧㄢˋ ㄊㄡˊ ㄒㄧㄤˊ)
unconditional surrender: 中國接受日本無條件投降。China accepted Japan's unconditional surrender.

無忝所生(ㄨˊ ㄊㄧㄢˇ ㄙㄨㄛˇ ㄕㄥ)
Don't do anything to bring shame on your parents!

無他(ㄨˊ ㄊㄨㄛ)
① nothing else; for no other reason than ② loyal; dedicated ③ in good health; safe 亦作「無恙」

無痛分娩法(ㄨˊ ㄊㄨㄥˋ ㄈㄣ ㄇㄧㄢˇ ㄈㄚˇ)
painless delivery

無奈(ㄨˊ ㄋㄞˋ)
can't help it; having no alternative

無能(ㄨˊ ㄋㄥˊ)
incompetent; inefficient; incapable; without talent

無能爲力(ㄨˊ ㄋㄥˊ ㄨㄟˊ ㄌㄧˋ)
unable to help; can't do anything about it; powerless

無寧(ㄨˊ ㄋㄧㄥˊ)
to prefer; rather...

無賴(ㄨˊ ㄌㄞˋ)
a villain; a rascal

無漏(ㄨˊ ㄌㄡˋ)
(Buddhism) *anasrava*, no drip, leak or flow—passionless; outside the passion stream

無理(ㄨˊ ㄌㄧˇ)
unreasonable; unjustifiable

無理方程式(ㄨˊ ㄌㄧˇ ㄈㄤ ㄔㄥˊ ㄕˋ)
an irrational equation

無理函數(ㄨˊ ㄌㄧˇ ㄏㄢˊ ㄕㄨˋ)
(mathematics) an irrational quantity

無理取鬧(ㄨˊ ㄌㄧˇ ㄑㄩˇ ㄋㄠˋ)
to make trouble without a cause; to make trouble out of nothing

無理要求(ㄨˊ ㄌㄧˇ ㄧㄠ ㄑㄧㄡˊ)
unjustifiable demands

無力(ㄨˊ ㄌㄧˋ)
① feeble; weak ② cannot afford; too poor to do something: 我無力在台北購買房子。I cannot afford to buy a house in Taipei.

無利可圖(ㄨˊ ㄌㄧˋ ㄎㄜˇ ㄊㄨˊ)
profitless: 這是無利可圖的買賣。This is a profitless business.

無立錐之地(ㄨˊ ㄌㄧˋ ㄓㄨㄟ ㄓ ㄉㄧˋ)
very poor; stark poverty: 他

〔火部〕

窮得無立錐之地。He is very poor.

無聊(ㄨˊ ㄌㄧㄠˊ)
①listless; ennui; boring; boredom; (feeling) indifferent and uninteresting ②nonsensical; silly: 不要講這種無聊話。Don't make such silly remarks.

無聊賴(ㄨˊ ㄌㄧㄠˊ ㄌㄞˋ)
disappointed and discouraged

無良(ㄨˊ ㄌㄧㄤˊ)
no good; without virtue or principle

無兩(ㄨˊ ㄌㄧㄤˇ)or 無二(ㄨˊ ㄦˋ)
matchless; without match; unique: 這幅圖畫被認爲是獨一無二的。The picture is thought to be unique.

無量(ㄨˊ ㄌㄧㄤˋ)
limitless; boundless

無量佛(ㄨˊ ㄌㄧㄤˋ ㄈㄛˊ)or 無量壽(ㄨˊ ㄌㄧㄤˋ ㄕㄡˋ)
①boundless, infinite life ②a name of Amitabha

無路可走(ㄨˊ ㄌㄨˋ ㄎㄜˇ ㄗㄡˇ)
at the end of one's rope; at one's wit's end; no way out; to come to a dead end

無論(ㄨˊ ㄌㄨㄣˋ)
①no matter; whatever; regardless: 無論誰都不能違法。Nobody is supposed to break laws, no matter who he is. ②not to mention the fact that; let alone; to say nothing of

無論如何(ㄨˊ ㄌㄨㄣˋ ㄖㄨˊ ㄏㄜˊ)
no matter what; anyway; in any case; under all circumstances; come what may

無告(ㄨˊ ㄍㄠˋ)
with no one to turn to for help

無垢(ㄨˊ ㄍㄡˋ)
spotless

無干(ㄨˊ ㄍㄢ)
no concern (of mine, yours, etc.); nothing to do (with you, me, him, etc.): 這事與我無干。It has nothing to do with me.

無根無蒂(ㄨˊ ㄍㄣ ㄨˊ ㄉㄧˋ)
without ground; groundless; with nothing to rely on

無辜(ㄨˊ ㄍㄨ)
innocent; guiltless; the innocent: 這司機並非無辜。The driver was not guiltless.

無骨(ㄨˊ ㄍㄨˇ)
①(literally) without a bone —without the backbone ②(said of a girl dancing, etc.) soft and graceful (as if she were without a bone in her body)

無故(ㄨˊ ㄍㄨˋ)
without cause or reason; uncalled-for: 學生不得無故缺席。Students may not be absent without reason.

無怪(ㄨˊ ㄍㄨㄞˋ)or 無怪乎(ㄨˊ ㄍㄨㄞˋ ㄏㄨ)
It's not strange that.... 或 no wonder that; naturally: 無怪乎他會失敗。No wonder that he has failed.

無軌電車(ㄨˊ ㄍㄨㄟˇ ㄉㄧㄢˋ ㄔㄜ)
a trolley car; a trolley bus

無軌可循(ㄨˊ ㄍㄨㄟˇ ㄎㄜˇ ㄒㄩㄣˊ)
no precedent to follow

無鬼論(ㄨˊ ㄍㄨㄟˇ ㄌㄨㄣˋ)
a theory refuting the existence of ghosts or spirits advanced by Juan Chan (阮瞻) of the Tsin Dynasty

無關(ㄨˊ ㄍㄨㄢ)
no relationship; no concern; no connection; irrelevant; to have nothing to do with: 此事與我們無關。It has nothing to do with us.

無關痛癢(ㄨˊ ㄍㄨㄢ ㄊㄨㄥˋ ㄧㄤˇ)
not important at all; of no concern or consequence

無關宏旨(ㄨˊ ㄍㄨㄢ ㄏㄨㄥˊ ㄓˇ)
insignificant; of no consequence; unimportant

無關緊要(ㄨˊ ㄍㄨㄢ ㄐㄧㄣˇ ㄧㄠˋ)
not important; of no consequence or significance: 這事無關緊要。This matter is not important.

無官一身輕(ㄨˊ ㄍㄨㄢ ㄧˋ ㄕㄣ ㄑㄧㄥ)
One feels carefree when he is relieved of official duties.

無功受祿(ㄨˊ ㄍㄨㄥ ㄕㄡˋ ㄌㄨˋ)
to get the reward without real achievements or contributions

無可奈何(ㄨˊ ㄎㄜˇ ㄋㄞˋ ㄏㄜˊ)or 無可如何(ㄨˊ ㄎㄜˇ ㄖㄨˊ ㄏㄜˊ)
having no alternative; to have to; powerless

無可厚非(ㄨˊ ㄎㄜˇ ㄏㄡˋ ㄈㄟ)
shouldn't be blamed too much for that—no serious mistakes committed

無可救藥(ㄨˊ ㄎㄜˇ ㄐㄧㄡˋ ㄧㄠˋ)
incorrigible; incurable

無可置疑(ㄨˊ ㄎㄜˇ ㄓˋ ㄧˊ)
beyond doubt; cannot be doubted: 他的誠意是無可置疑的。His honesty is beyond doubt.

無可爭辯(ㄨˊ ㄎㄜˇ ㄓㄥ ㄅㄧㄢˋ)
indisputable: 這是無可爭辯的事實。This is an indisputable fact.

無可無不可(ㄨˊ ㄎㄜˇ ㄨˊ ㄅㄨˋ ㄎㄜˇ)
yes and no (an expression used to indicate an ambiguous attitude)

無愧(ㄨˊ ㄎㄨㄟˋ)
with a clear conscience; able to look people straight in the eye

無愧色(ㄨˊ ㄎㄨㄟˋ ㄙㄜˋ)
without any expression of shame, regret or embarrassment

無孔不入(ㄨˊ ㄎㄨㄥˇ ㄅㄨˊ ㄖㄨˋ)
to let no opportunity slip by (in the pursuit of one's selfish ends); (to serve self-interest) by hook or by crook; to exploit every crack or loophole one can find

無何有之鄉(ㄨˊ ㄏㄜˊ ㄧㄡˇ ㄓ ㄒㄧㄤ)
(originally from *Chuang Tzu*) a world where nothing really exists

無害(ㄨˊ ㄏㄞˋ)
harmless; not injurious

無後(ㄨˊ ㄏㄡˋ)
heirless; without posterity

無後座力砲(ㄨˊ ㄏㄡˋ ㄗㄨㄛˋ ㄌㄧˋ ㄆㄠˋ)
a recoilless gun

無後爲大(ㄨˊ ㄏㄡˋ ㄨㄟˊ ㄉㄚˋ)
Having no male heir is the gravest of the three cardinal offenses against filial piety. 參看「不孝有三」

無恆(ㄨˊ ㄏㄥˊ)or 無恆心(ㄨˊ ㄏㄥˊ ㄒㄧㄣ)
lacking perseverance; without persistency; without patience; without consistency

無花果(ㄨˊ ㄏㄨㄚ ㄍㄨㄛˇ)

the fig

無話不談(ㄨˊ ㄏㄨㄚˋ ㄅㄨˋ ㄊㄢˊ)
to keep no secrets from each other

無毀無譽(ㄨˊ ㄏㄨㄟˇ ㄨˊ ㄩˋ)
(literally) neither criticism nor praise—just so-so; passable; merely acceptable

無稽(ㄨˊ ㄐㄧ)
wild (talks, rumors, etc.); groundless

無稽之談(ㄨˊ ㄐㄧ ㄓ ㄊㄢˊ)or 無稽之言(ㄨˊ ㄐㄧ ㄓ ㄧㄢˊ)
groundless utterances; wild talks; rumors; sheer nonsense

無機(ㄨˊ ㄐㄧ)
(chemistry) inorganic

無機體(ㄨˊ ㄐㄧ ㄊㄧˇ)or 無機物(ㄨˊ ㄐㄧ ㄨˋ)
inorganic matters; inorganic substances

無機化合物(ㄨˊ ㄐㄧ ㄏㄨㄚˋ ㄏㄜˊ ㄨˋ)
inorganic compounds

無機化學(ㄨˊ ㄐㄧ ㄏㄨㄚˋ ㄒㄩㄝˊ)
inorganic chemistry

無極(ㄨˊ ㄐㄧˊ)
①a mind completely devoid of worries, thought or desires (a philosophical theory initiated by Chou Tun-yi (周敦頤) of the Sung Dynasty) ②name of a county in Hopeh Province

無疾而終(ㄨˊ ㄐㄧˊ ㄦˊ ㄓㄨㄥ)
to die without any apparent ailment or disease

無籍游民(ㄨˊ ㄐㄧˊ ㄧㄡˊ ㄇㄧㄣˊ)
vagrants without homes

無幾(ㄨˊ ㄐㄧˇ)
①not much; not many; little; almost the same: 我們兩人年齡相差無幾。We are almost the same age. ②not long afterwards; shortly

無給職(ㄨˊ ㄐㄧˇ ㄓˊ)
a position without pay; an honorary post

無際(ㄨˊ ㄐㄧˋ)
(said of space) boundless: 我喜歡一望無際的海洋。I like the boundless ocean.

無記(ㄨˊ ㄐㄧˋ)
(Buddhism) unrecordable (either as good or bad)

無記名投票(ㄨˊ ㄐㄧˋ ㄇㄧㄥˊ ㄊㄡˊ ㄆㄧㄠˋ)
secret ballot

無計可施(ㄨˊ ㄐㄧˋ ㄎㄜˇ ㄕ)
at the end of one's rope; helpless; powerless; at one's wit's end: 我對此事無計可施。I am quite powerless in the matter.

無濟於事(ㄨˊ ㄐㄧˋ ㄩˊ ㄕˋ)
won't help the matter; not enough by a long shot; inadequate; to no avail; to no effect; of no avail

無家可歸(ㄨˊ ㄐㄧㄚ ㄎㄜˇ ㄍㄨㄟ)
homeless; without a home to go back to

無價之寶(ㄨˊ ㄐㄧㄚˋ ㄓ ㄅㄠˇ)
a priceless treasure; an invaluable asset: 那件藝術品是無價之寶。That is a priceless work of art.

無解(ㄨˊ ㄐㄧㄝˇ)
insolvable

無噍類(ㄨˊ ㄐㄧㄠˋ ㄌㄟˋ)
all dead—no survivors

無堅不摧(ㄨˊ ㄐㄧㄢ ㄅㄨˋ ㄘㄨㄟ)
to overrun all fortifications; to be all-conquering

無間(ㄨˊ ㄐㄧㄢˋ)
①nonstop; continuous: 兩國合作無間。The two countries cooperated continuously. ②close and intimate

無盡藏(ㄨˊ ㄐㄧㄣˋ ㄗㄤˋ)
(Buddhism) virtue that encompasses all

無盡無休(ㄨˊ ㄐㄧㄣˋ ㄨˊ ㄒㄧㄡ)
continuous; endlessly; boundless; limitless

無疆(ㄨˊ ㄐㄧㄤ)
boundless; limitless

無精打采(ㄨˊ ㄐㄧㄥ ㄉㄚˇ ㄘㄞˇ)
listless; indifferent; low-spirited; not interested; discouraged or disappointed; despondent; dejected: 他們無精打采地握握手。They shook hands rather listlessly.

無莖植物(ㄨˊ ㄐㄧㄥ ㄓˊ ㄨˋ)
plants without stems—a general name for all varieties of fungi and algae

無拘無束(ㄨˊ ㄐㄩ ㄨˊ ㄕㄨˋ)or 無拘束(ㄨˊ ㄐㄩ ㄕㄨˋ)
unconstrained; carefree; without a worry or care in the world; to feel at home; to have a completely free hand in...; completely without restraints; freely

無期(ㄨˊ ㄑㄧˊ)
no definite term or date; with no end in sight

無期徒刑(ㄨˊ ㄑㄧˊ ㄊㄨˊ ㄒㄧㄥˊ)
life imprisonment: 他被判無期徒刑。He was sentenced to imprisonment for life.

無奇不有(ㄨˊ ㄑㄧˊ ㄅㄨˋ ㄧㄡˇ)
Nothing is too strange (in the world, this school, etc.).

無巧不巧(ㄨˊ ㄑㄧㄠˇ ㄅㄨˋ ㄑㄧㄠˇ)
by coincidence; coincidentally

無巧不成書(ㄨˊ ㄑㄧㄠˇ ㄅㄨˋ ㄔㄥˊ ㄕㄨ)
There would have been no story to tell if not for that coincidence.—It happened that....

無牽無掛(ㄨˊ ㄑㄧㄢ ㄨˊ ㄍㄨㄚˋ)
to have no cares

無前(ㄨˊ ㄑㄧㄢˊ)
(used to describe a brave and skillful fighter) matchless; peerless

無情(ㄨˊ ㄑㄧㄥˊ)
callous; heartless; ruthless; devoid of emotions or feelings: 他是無情的人。He is a heartless man.

無情無緒(ㄨˊ ㄑㄧㄥˊ ㄨˊ ㄒㄩˋ)
listless and indifferent; bored

無權(ㄨˊ ㄑㄩㄢˊ)
to have no right

無拳無勇(ㄨˊ ㄑㄩㄢˊ ㄨˊ ㄩㄥˇ)
to have neither fighting skill nor courage—a weakling

無窮(ㄨˊ ㄑㄩㄥˊ)
endless; boundless; limitless; inexhaustible; interminable; infinite: 他似乎有無窮的智慧和力量。It seems that he has inexhaustible wisdom and power.

無窮大(ㄨˊ ㄑㄩㄥˊ ㄉㄚˋ)
(mathematics) infinite; infinitely great

無窮小(ㄨˊ ㄑㄩㄥˊ ㄒㄧㄠˇ)
(mathematics) infinitesimal

無窮無盡(ㄨˊ ㄑㄩㄥˊ ㄨˊ ㄐㄧㄣˋ)
endless; infinite; boundless; limitless; interminable

無錫(ㄨˊ ㄒㄧˊ)
name of a county in Kiangsu Province famous for its production of wheat flour,

cotton yarn and farm products

無息貸款(ㄨˊ ㄒㄧˊ ㄉㄞˋ ㄎㄨㄢˇ)
an interest-free loan

無隙可乘(ㄨˊ ㄒㄧˋ ㄎㄜˇ ㄔㄥˊ)
to have no vulnerability or weakness to exploit; to have no loophole to exploit

無瑕(ㄨˊ ㄒㄧㄚˊ)
without blemish, defect or fault—perfect: 他的行爲無瑕。His behavior was perfect.

無暇(ㄨˊ ㄒㄧㄚˊ)
to have no time; without leisure

無下箸處(ㄨˊ ㄒㄧㄚˋ ㄓㄨˋ ㄔㄨˋ)
(literally) no place to ply the chopsticks (said of the rich who are too particular about their food)

無懈可擊(ㄨˊ ㄒㄧㄝˋ ㄎㄜˇ ㄐㄧ)
flawless; unimpeachable; unassailable; invulnerable

無效(ㄨˊ ㄒㄧㄠˋ)
①ineffective; useless; to no avail ②invalid; not valid; null and void: 他們宣佈合約無效。They declared the contract invalid.

無休止(ㄨˊ ㄒㄧㄡ ㄓˇ)
ceaseless; endless; on and on: 他們無休止地爭論。They argued on and on.

無限(ㄨˊ ㄒㄧㄢˋ)
limitless; boundless; infinite; unlimited; immeasurable: 他是個有無限野心的獨裁者。He is a dictator with limitless ambitions.

無限公司(ㄨˊ ㄒㄧㄢˋ ㄍㄨㄥ ㄙ)
an unlimited company

無限花序(ㄨˊ ㄒㄧㄢˋ ㄏㄨㄚ ㄒㄩˋ)
indefinite inflorescence

無限制(ㄨˊ ㄒㄧㄢˋ ㄓˋ)
unlimited; without qualifications or restrictions; unbridled

無線電(ㄨˊ ㄒㄧㄢˋ ㄉㄧㄢˋ)
radio; wireless

無線電報(ㄨˊ ㄒㄧㄢˋ ㄉㄧㄢˋ ㄅㄠˋ)
a telegram; a wireless cable

無線電變壓器(ㄨˊ ㄒㄧㄢˋ ㄉㄧㄢˋ ㄅㄧㄢˋ ㄧㄚ ㄑㄧˋ)
a radio transformer

無線電天線(ㄨˊ ㄒㄧㄢˋ ㄉㄧㄢˋ ㄊㄧㄢ ㄒㄧㄢˋ)
a radio antenna

無線電桿(ㄨˊ ㄒㄧㄢˋ ㄉㄧㄢˋ ㄍㄢˇ)
a wireless mast

無線電廣播站(ㄨˊ ㄒㄧㄢˋ ㄉㄧㄢˋ ㄍㄨㄤˇ ㄅㄛ ㄓㄢˋ)
a radio station

無線電廣播員(ㄨˊ ㄒㄧㄢˋ ㄉㄧㄢˋ ㄍㄨㄤˇ ㄅㄛ ㄩㄢˊ)
a radiobroadcaster

無線電擴大器(ㄨˊ ㄒㄧㄢˋ ㄉㄧㄢˋ ㄎㄨㄛˋ ㄉㄚˋ ㄑㄧˋ)
a radio amplifier

無線電話(ㄨˊ ㄒㄧㄢˋ ㄉㄧㄢˋ ㄏㄨㄚˋ)
radiophone

無線電傳眞(ㄨˊ ㄒㄧㄢˋ ㄉㄧㄢˋ ㄔㄨㄢˊ ㄓㄣ)
fax (facsimile)

無心(ㄨˊ ㄒㄧㄣ)
①unintentional; unintentionally; inadvertently ②in no mood

無信(ㄨˊ ㄒㄧㄣˋ)
faithless; devoid of faith

無形(ㄨˊ ㄒㄧㄥˊ)
without leaving a trace; without taking a form; invisible

無形中(ㄨˊ ㄒㄧㄥˊ ㄓㄨㄥ)
imperceptibly; insidiously; unknowingly: 這無形中成了慣例。This has imperceptibly become a common practice.

無行爲能力人(ㄨˊ ㄒㄧㄥˊ ㄨㄟˊ ㄋㄥˊ ㄌㄧˋ ㄖㄣˊ)
(law) a person without disposing capacity

無行(ㄨˊ ㄒㄧㄥˋ)
indulgent in evil ways; to have no moral scruples

無性(ㄨˊ ㄒㄧㄥˋ)
(biology) asexual

無性生殖(ㄨˊ ㄒㄧㄥˋ ㄕㄥ ㄓˊ)
(biology) asexual reproduction or propagation; cloning

無須(ㄨˊ ㄒㄩ) or 無須乎(ㄨˊ ㄒㄩ ㄏㄨ)
unnecessary; not necessary; no need to: 無須解釋。It's unnecessary to explain it.

無知(ㄨˊ ㄓ)
ignorant; ignorance; (said of a child) innocent

無止境(ㄨˊ ㄓˇ ㄐㄧㄥˋ)
to have no limits or boundary; (said of knowledge) to know no end: 他的貪心是無止境的。His greed has no limits.

無遮大會(ㄨˊ ㄓㄜ ㄉㄚˋ ㄏㄨㄟˋ)
(Buddhism) *panca (varsika)-parisad,* the quinquennial assembly for having all things in common, and for confession, penance and remission

無照(ㄨˊ ㄓㄠˋ)
(to engage in a business) without a license: 無照駕駛是違法的。It is illegal to drive without a license.

無長物(ㄨˊ ㄓㄤˋ ㄨˋ)
to have no extra things

無徵不信(ㄨˊ ㄓㄥ ㄅㄨˋ ㄒㄧㄣˋ)
not credible unless supported by evidence or reference

無政府主義(ㄨˊ ㄓㄥˋ ㄈㄨˇ ㄓㄨˇ ㄧˋ)
anarchism

無政府狀態(ㄨˊ ㄓㄥˋ ㄈㄨˇ ㄓㄨㄤˋ ㄊㄞˋ)
anarchy

無主見(ㄨˊ ㄓㄨˇ ㄐㄧㄢˋ)
indecisive; cannot make up one's mind about anything

無著(ㄨˊ ㄓㄨㄛˊ)
①cannot locate; cannot find ②(Buddhism) name of Buddhist saint Asanga, brother of Vasubandhu ③a term referring to Buddha

無狀(ㄨˊ ㄓㄨㄤˋ)
ill-mannered

無中生有(ㄨˊ ㄓㄨㄥ ㄕㄥ ㄧㄡˇ)
(literally) to make something out of nothing—to fabricate; to imagine; to invent; to frame up; purely fictitious

無恥(ㄨˊ ㄔˇ)
shameless; brazen; impudent

無恥之尤(ㄨˊ ㄔˇ ㄓ ㄧㄡˊ)
utterly shameless; most brazen; completely devoid of a sense of shame

無產階級(ㄨˊ ㄔㄢˇ ㄐㄧㄝ ㄐㄧˊ)
the proletarian class; the proletariat

無產階級專政(ㄨˊ ㄔㄢˇ ㄐㄧㄝ ㄐㄧˊ ㄓㄨㄢ ㄓㄥˋ)
the dictatorship of the proletariat; proletarian dictatorship

無產階級文化大革命(ㄨˊ ㄔㄢˇ ㄐㄧㄝ ㄐㄧˊ ㄨㄣˊ ㄏㄨㄚˋ ㄉㄚˋ ㄍㄜˊ ㄇㄧㄥˋ)
the Great Proletarian Cultural Revolution on the Chinese mainland (1966-1976)

無常(ㄨˊ ㄔㄤˊ)

①ever-changing; capricious; variable: 他是個反覆無常的人。He is a man of capricious temper. ②(Buddhism) *anitya*, impermanent ③(Chinese mythology) name of a ghost or spirit that heralds a person's death ④death

無腸公子(ㄨˊ ㄔㄤˊ ㄍㄨㄥ ㄗˇ)
a crab

無出(ㄨˊ ㄔㄨ)
without any offspring or children

無出其右(ㄨˊ ㄔㄨ ㄑㄧˊ ㄧㄡˋ)
Nobody can better him. 或 second to none; peerless; matchless; unequaled

無師自通(ㄨˊ ㄕ ㄗˋ ㄊㄨㄥ)
to acquire a skill without being taught

無時無地(ㄨˊ ㄕˊ ㄨˊ ㄉㄧˋ)
every minute and everywhere

無時無刻(ㄨˊ ㄕˊ ㄨˊ ㄎㄜˋ)
every minute and every moment; always; constantly; all the time

無始(ㄨˊ ㄕˇ)
(Buddhism) without beginning, as is the chain of transmigration

無始無邊(ㄨˊ ㄕˇ ㄨˊ ㄅㄧㄢ)
vastly expansive and everlasting

無視(ㄨˊ ㄕˋ)
to consider as unimportant; to pay no attention to; to have no high opinion of; to disregard

無事不登三寶殿(ㄨˊ ㄕˋ ㄅㄨˋ ㄉㄥ ㄙㄢ ㄅㄠˇ ㄉㄧㄢˋ)
One never goes to a Buddhist temple for nothing. —One would not go to somebody's place except on business or for help. 或I wouldn't come to you if I hadn't something to ask of you.

無事忙(ㄨˊ ㄕˋ ㄇㄤˊ)
to be busy for nothing; a busybody

無事生非(ㄨˊ ㄕˋ ㄕㄥ ㄈㄟ)
to make trouble out of nothing

無涉(ㄨˊ ㄕㄜˋ)
no concern; no business (of his, yours, mine, etc.); not involved; to have nothing to do with

無神論(ㄨˊ ㄕㄣˊ ㄌㄨㄣˋ)
atheism

無神論者(ㄨˊ ㄕㄣˊ ㄌㄨㄣˋ ㄓㄜˇ)
an atheist

無傷(ㄨˊ ㄕㄤ)
no harm; doesn't matter

無傷大雅(ㄨˊ ㄕㄤ ㄉㄚˋ ㄧㄚˇ)
No serious harm is done. 或 It means no offense. 或 It doesn't matter. 他們說的話無傷大雅。What they said means no offense.

無上光榮(ㄨˊ ㄕㄤˋ ㄍㄨㄤ ㄖㄨㄥˊ)
matchless honor; the highest honor

無生(ㄨˊ ㄕㄥ)
(Buddhism) immortal; subject neither to birth nor to death

無生物(ㄨˊ ㄕㄥ ㄨˋ)
an inanimate object; a nonliving matter

無聲(ㄨˊ ㄕㄥ)
noiseless; silent: 鳥在樹上悄然無聲。The birds were silent in the trees.

無聲電影(ㄨˊ ㄕㄥ ㄉㄧㄢˋ ㄧㄥˇ)
a silent movie (or film)

無聲無臭(ㄨˊ ㄕㄥ ㄨˊ ㄒㄧㄡˋ)
①a nobody; small fry or potatoes ②quietly and without leaving a trace

無殊(ㄨˊ ㄕㄨ)
not different from; tantamount to

無數(ㄨˊ ㄕㄨˋ)
①countless; numerous ②an uncertain number of; do not know for certain

無雙(ㄨˊ ㄕㄨㄤ) or 無二(ㄨˊ ㄦˋ)
peerless; matchless; unique; unrivaled; unparalleled: 他的辯才無雙。His eloquence is unrivaled.

無雙國士(ㄨˊ ㄕㄨㄤ ㄍㄨㄛˊ ㄕˋ)
a man of superior talent or ability

無日(ㄨˊ ㄖˋ)
①not a single day ②soon

無人過問(ㄨˊ ㄖㄣˊ ㄍㄨㄛˋ ㄨㄣˋ)
(literally) Nobody asks about it. 或 Nobody cares about it. 或 Nobody shows any interest in it.

無人駕駛飛機(ㄨˊ ㄖㄣˊ ㄐㄧㄚˋ ㄕˇ ㄈㄟ ㄐㄧ)
a pilotless plane

無任感激(ㄨˊ ㄖㄣˋ ㄍㄢˇ ㄐㄧ)
to appreciate very much

無任歡迎(ㄨˊ ㄖㄣˋ ㄏㄨㄢ ㄧㄥˊ)
most welcome: 如蒙光臨,無任歡迎。Your visit will be most welcome.

無任所大使(ㄨˊ ㄖㄣˋ ㄙㄨㄛˇ ㄉㄚˋ ㄕˇ)
a roving ambassador

無如(ㄨˊ ㄖㄨˊ)
It's a pity that....或 couldn't help that...

無足輕重(ㄨˊ ㄗㄨˊ ㄑㄧㄥ ㄓㄨㄥˋ)
of little significance; of no consequence; of little importance

無罪(ㄨˊ ㄗㄨㄟˋ)
innocent; guiltless; not guilty

無疵(ㄨˊ ㄘ)
flawless; without blemish or defect: 他的推理完美無疵。His reasoning is flawless.

無猜(ㄨˊ ㄘㄞ)
childlike innocence; unsuspicious

無措(ㄨˊ ㄘㄨㄛˋ)
①to act strangely, without propriety, etc. ②jumpy

無從(ㄨˊ ㄘㄨㄥˊ)
to have no place (or no way) to lay hands on or begin with

無私(ㄨˊ ㄙ)
selfless; disinterested; unselfish: 他是個無私的官員。He is a selfless official.

無私有弊(ㄨˊ ㄙ ㄧㄡˇ ㄅㄧˋ)
(said of the performance of government officials) susceptible to accusations of irregularities owing to poor handling although no irregularities are involved

無所不至(ㄨˊ ㄙㄨㄛˇ ㄅㄨˋ ㄓˋ)
①omnipresent; omnipresence; ubiquitous; present everywhere ②very thorough; very attentive; very thoughtful

無所不在(ㄨˊ ㄙㄨㄛˇ ㄅㄨˋ ㄗㄞˋ)
omnipresent; ubiquitous

無所不用其極(ㄨˊ ㄙㄨㄛˇ ㄅㄨˋ ㄩㄥˋ ㄑㄧˊ ㄐㄧˊ)
to go to extremes in every

measure or on every count; to pursue everything to its brutal end; to stop at nothing

無所不包(ㄨˊ ㄙㄨㄛˇ ㄅㄨˋ ㄅㄠ)
Nothing is left out. 或 all-encompassing; all-embracing

無所不能(ㄨˊ ㄙㄨㄛˇ ㄅㄨˋ ㄋㄥˊ)
omnipotent; omnipotence; almighty; capable of doing anything: 沒有人是無所不能的。None is omnipotent.

無所不知(ㄨˊ ㄙㄨㄛˇ ㄅㄨˋ ㄓ)
omniscient; omniscience; to know everything

無所不有(ㄨˊ ㄙㄨㄛˇ ㄅㄨˋ ㄧㄡˇ)
omnifarious; to have all

無所不爲(ㄨˊ ㄙㄨㄛˇ ㄅㄨˋ ㄨㄟˊ)
ready to do anything, however bad it may be; to stop at nothing 或 No act is considered too evil or too cruel.

無所住(ㄨˊ ㄙㄨㄛˇ ㄓㄨˋ)
(Buddhism) *apratisthita*, no means of staying; nonabiding

無所事事(ㄨˊ ㄙㄨㄛˇ ㄕˋ ㄕˋ)
to do nothing; to be at a loose end; to idle away one's time

無所適從(ㄨˊ ㄙㄨㄛˇ ㄕˋ ㄘㄨㄥˊ)
don't know where to turn to; indecisive; no set plan or principle to follow; don't know whose suggestion to follow

無所謂(ㄨˊ ㄙㄨㄛˇ ㄨㄟˋ)
don't mind—one way or the other; do not care: 他來不來我都無所謂。I don't mind whether he comes or not.

無所畏懼(ㄨˊ ㄙㄨㄛˇ ㄨㄟˋ ㄐㄩˋ)
fearless; dauntless

無算(ㄨˊ ㄙㄨㄢˋ)
① countless; cannot be counted ② of an uncertain number

無惡不作(ㄨˊ ㄜˋ ㄅㄨˋ ㄗㄨㄛˋ)
capable of committing every crime under the sun; to stop at nothing in doing evil

無礙(ㄨˊ ㄞˋ)
① do not matter; no harm; not in the way; all right ② (Buddhism) *apratihata* (unhindered; without obstacle; permeating everywhere)

無一不備(ㄨˊ ㄧ ㄅㄨˋ ㄅㄟˋ)
Everything is available. 或 Nothing is missing.

無一不通(ㄨˊ ㄧ ㄅㄨˋ ㄊㄨㄥ)
to know all; extremely versatile

無一不能(ㄨˊ ㄧ ㄅㄨˋ ㄋㄥˊ)
almighty; extremely versatile; to be able to handle everything (at hand)

無一不精(ㄨˊ ㄧ ㄅㄨˋ ㄐㄧㄥ)
to be an expert in everything; versatility plus virtuosity

無依無靠(ㄨˊ ㄧ ㄨˊ ㄎㄠˋ)
with no one to turn to or rely on; completely helpless

無疑(ㄨˊ ㄧˊ)
without doubt; undoubtedly; unquestionably: 那無疑是眞的。That is undoubtedly true.

無已(ㄨˊ ㄧˇ)
① endlessly ② cannot help but...

無以復加(ㄨˊ ㄧˇ ㄈㄨˋ ㄐㄧㄚ)
extremely; utterly; utmost; cannot be surpassed; the last word in (beauty, brutality, etc.)

無以自解(ㄨˊ ㄧˇ ㄗˋ ㄐㄧㄝˇ)
unable to explain oneself away; cannot extricate oneself from; unable to give an excuse

無以爲繼(ㄨˊ ㄧˇ ㄨㄟˊ ㄐㄧˋ)
to be hard put to find a sequel

無益(ㄨˊ ㄧˋ)
won't serve any purpose; useless; without benefit; unprofitable; no good: 多談無益。It is useless to keep talking.

無異(ㄨˊ ㄧˋ)
not different from; tantamount to; the same as: 你的回答無異是拒絕。Your answer is tantamount to a refusal.

無異議(ㄨˊ ㄧˋ ㄧˋ)
without a dissenting voice; unanimous

無異議通過(ㄨˊ ㄧˋ ㄧˋ ㄊㄨㄥ ㄍㄨㄛˋ)
to pass unanimously

無意(ㄨˊ ㄧˋ)
to have no interest in; to have no intention (of doing something)

無意犯(ㄨˊ ㄧˋ ㄈㄢˋ)
a person who commits an offense unintentionally

無意中(ㄨˊ ㄧˋ ㄓㄨㄥ) or 無意間(ㄨˊ ㄧˋ ㄐㄧㄢ)
unexpectedly; unintentionally; accidentally; by accident

無意識(ㄨˊ ㄧˋ ㄕˋ)
①(psychology) unconsciousness ② unintentional

無涯(ㄨˊ ㄧㄚˊ)
boundless; limitless; endless

無業遊民(ㄨˊ ㄧㄝˋ ㄧㄡˊ ㄇㄧㄣˊ)
a vagrant

無憂無慮(ㄨˊ ㄧㄡ ㄨˊ ㄌㄩˋ)
carefree; without a worry and care in the world

無由(ㄨˊ ㄧㄡˊ)
no way to; in no position to; unable to

無有(ㄨˊ ㄧㄡˇ)
none; nothing

無煙煤(ㄨˊ ㄧㄢ ㄇㄟˊ)
anthracite, or hard coal

無煙火藥(ㄨˊ ㄧㄢ ㄏㄨㄛˇ ㄧㄠˋ)
smokeless powder; ballistite

無顏見江東父老(ㄨˊ ㄧㄢˊ ㄐㄧㄢˋ ㄐㄧㄤ ㄉㄨㄥ ㄈㄨˋ ㄌㄠˇ)
to have no face or to be too ashamed to go back home to see one's elders (after defeat, failure, etc.)

無厭(ㄨˊ ㄧㄢˋ)
insatiable (as man's greed, desires, etc.); never tire of

無因(ㄨˊ ㄧㄣ)
① without cause or reason ② no way to; in no position to; unable to

無垠(ㄨˊ ㄧㄣˊ)
(said of space) boundless; limitless; extremely expansive: 我們看到了一望無垠的草原。We saw a boundless prairie.

無恙(ㄨˊ ㄧㄤˋ)
to feel well; all right; (usually used in the opening paragraph of a letter); in good health; safe: 別來無恙? Have you been all right since we last met?

無影無蹤(ㄨˊ ㄧㄥˇ ㄨˊ ㄗㄨㄥ)
(to vanish or disappear) without a trace

無誤(ㄨˊ ㄨˋ)

correct; right; verified and found correct

無我(ㄨˊ ㄨㄛˇ)
(Buddhism) *anatman*, no individual independent existence

無為(ㄨˊ ㄨㄟˊ)
to let things take their own course; inaction; inactivity

無為而治(ㄨˊ ㄨㄟˊ ㄦˊ ㄓˋ)
(literally) to govern by doing nothing—according to Lao-tzu(老子), enlightened administration is possible only when the ruler can set a good example for the people to follow instead of proclaiming restrictive laws and regulations which tend to interfere with the orderly life of the masses

無微不至(ㄨˊ ㄨㄟ ㄅㄨˋ ㄓˋ)
down to the very last detail; very thoughtful; to considerate in every way

無味(ㄨˊ ㄨㄟˋ)
① tasteless; not interesting; dull; dry; unattractive (offers, etc.) ② unpalatable; unappetizing

無謂(ㄨˊ ㄨㄟˋ)
① don't presume ② senseless; meaningless; pointless

無畏(ㄨˊ ㄨㄟˋ)
dauntless; without fear

無畏艦(ㄨˊ ㄨㄟˋ ㄐㄧㄢˋ)
Dreadnaught (name of a class of warships)

無畏施(ㄨˊ ㄨㄟˋ ㄕ)
abhayyapradana, the bestowing of confidence by every true Buddhist, i.e. that none may fear him

無往不利(ㄨˊ ㄨㄤˇ ㄅㄨˋ ㄌㄧˋ)
lucky in every endeavor; successful in whatever one does

無望(ㄨˊ ㄨㄤˋ)
① hopeless; to despair of; without hope ② do not expect that... ③ without boundary line or marks

無妄之災(ㄨˊ ㄨㄤˋ ㄓ ㄗㄞ)
unexpected misfortunes; uncalled-for disasters or calamities

無虞匱乏(ㄨˊ ㄩˊ ㄎㄨㄟˋ ㄈㄚˊ)
no fear of deficiency; sufficient; abundant

無與倫比(ㄨˊ ㄩˇ ㄌㄨㄣˊ ㄅㄧˇ)
beyond comparison; peerless; head and shoulders above others; without equal; unique; unparalleled

無欲則剛(ㄨˊ ㄩˋ ㄗㄜˊ ㄍㄤ)
One can be upright if he has no selfish desires.

無緣(ㄨˊ ㄩㄢˊ)
① no opportunity or chance ② no way to; unable to ③ an inexplicable animosity toward somebody

無緣無故(ㄨˊ ㄩㄢˊ ㄨˊ ㄍㄨˋ)
without cause or reason; uncalled-for; for no reason at all

無遠弗屆(ㄨˊ ㄩㄢˇ ㄈㄨˊ ㄐㄧㄝˋ)
No place is too far away to be reached.或 to reach everywhere: 他的美名傳遍天下，無遠弗屆。His good reputation reached everywhere.

無韻詩(ㄨˊ ㄩㄣˋ ㄕ)
(poetry) blank verse: 這個劇本是用無韻詩寫的。The play is written in blank verse.

無庸(ㄨˊ ㄩㄥ)
no need to; unnecessary

無庸置疑(ㄨˊ ㄩㄥ ㄓˋ ㄧˊ)
unquestionable

無用(ㄨˊ ㄩㄥˋ)
useless; of no use: 汽車沒有汽油即無用。A car is useless without gasoline.

【然】 3215
ㄖㄢˊ ran rán

1. yes; most certainly; permission; right; correct
2. however; but; still; nevertheless; on the other hand
3. really; if so
4. same as 燃— to burn
5. a Chinese family name

然眉之急(ㄖㄢˊ ㄇㄟˊ ㄓ ㄐㄧˊ)
extremely urgent—as if the eyebrows were on fire 亦作「燃眉之急」

然否(ㄖㄢˊ ㄈㄡˇ)
Yes or no?或 Is it correct?或 Is it so?

然諾(ㄖㄢˊ ㄋㄨㄛˋ)
a promise; to give one's word: 他是重然諾的人。He is serious about making and keeping a promise.

然後(ㄖㄢˊ ㄏㄡˋ)
then; afterward; later

然乎(ㄖㄢˊ ㄏㄨ)
Isn't it so?

然信(ㄖㄢˊ ㄒㄧㄣˋ)
to pledge to keep a promise

然則(ㄖㄢˊ ㄗㄜˊ)
but; but then; in that case

然而(ㄖㄢˊ ㄦˊ)
however; but; nevertheless; on the other hand

【焰】 3216
(燄) ㄧㄢˋ yann yàn
(又讀 ㄧㄢˊ yan yán)

1. flames; blazes
2. glowing; brilliant

焰火(ㄧㄢˋ ㄏㄨㄛˇ)
fireworks 亦作「煙火」

焰焰(ㄧㄢˋ ㄧㄢˋ)
blazing

九畫

【煌】 3217
ㄏㄨㄤˊ hwang huáng

bright and brilliant

煌煌(ㄏㄨㄤˊ ㄏㄨㄤˊ)
(said of stars, etc.) bright and scintillating

【煉】 3218
ㄌㄧㄢˋ liann liàn

1. to smelt; to refine; to condense (milk); to temper (a metal) with fire
2. (Chinese medicine) to keep herbs, etc. boiling for a long time
3. to train; to form character by hardship

煉丹(ㄌㄧㄢˋ ㄉㄢ)
(Taoism) to refine (by heating) concoctions for special purposes; to make pills of immortality

煉鐵法(ㄌㄧㄢˋ ㄊㄧㄝˇ ㄈㄚˇ)
puddling

煉鐵爐(ㄌㄧㄢˋ ㄊㄧㄝˇ ㄌㄨˊ)
a bloomery; a puddling furnace

煉鐵廠(ㄌㄧㄢˋ ㄊㄧㄝˇ ㄔㄤˇ)
a blooming mill; an ironworks

煉鋼(ㄌㄧㄢˋ ㄍㄤ)
to refine steel; steelmaking

煉鋼廠(ㄌㄧㄢˋ ㄍㄤ ㄔㄤˇ)
a steel refinery; a steel mill

煉焦(ㄌㄧㄢˋ ㄐㄧㄠ)

to make coke
煉焦爐(ㄌㄧㄢˋ ㄐㄧㄠ ㄌㄨˊ)
a coke furnace
煉指(ㄌㄧㄢˋ ㄓˇ)
finger-burning (an ascetic act of Buddhists)
煉製(ㄌㄧㄢˋ ㄓˋ)
to refine
煉石補天 or 鍊石補天(ㄌㄧㄢˋ ㄕˊ ㄅㄨˇ ㄊㄧㄢ)
to smelt stones to mend the sky (a feat performed by 女媧氏, a mythological character)
煉乳(ㄌㄧㄢˋ ㄖㄨˇ)
condensed milk
煉油廠(ㄌㄧㄢˋ ㄧㄡˊ ㄔㄤˇ)
an oil refinery
煉獄(ㄌㄧㄢˋ ㄩˋ)
the purgatory

【煒】 3219 ㄨㄟˇ woei wěi
1. dark red
2. glowing; bright

【煖】 3220 (暖) ㄋㄨㄢˇ noan nuǎn
warm; to warm; genial (weather)
煖風徐來(ㄋㄨㄢˇ ㄈㄥ ㄒㄩˊ ㄌㄞˊ)
The genial breeze blows gently.
煖衣飽食(ㄋㄨㄢˇ ㄧ ㄅㄠˇ ㄕˊ)
well-clad and well-fed

【煜】 3221 ㄩˋ yuh yù
1. bright and brilliant
2. flames or blazes
3. to illuminate; to shine
煜煜(ㄩˋ ㄩˋ)
bright and shining

【煙】 3222 (烟) ㄧㄢ ian yān
1. smoke; fumes
2. tobacco; a smoke; a cigarette
3. mist; vapor
4. opium
5. a Chinese family name
煙波(ㄧㄢ ㄅㄛ)
lakes; mist-covered waters
煙煤(ㄧㄢ ㄇㄟˊ)
bituminous coal; soft coal
煙幕(ㄧㄢ ㄇㄨˋ)
①a smoke screen ②(figuratively) anything that serves to hide a ship, airplane, etc. from the enemy
煙幕彈(ㄧㄢ ㄇㄨˋ ㄉㄢˋ)
a smoke bomb
煙袋(ㄧㄢ ㄉㄞˋ)
a smoking pipe: 水煙袋 a pipe with a water compartment for filtering tobacco
煙袋荷包(ㄧㄢ ㄉㄞˋ ㄏㄜˊ ·ㄅㄠ)
a tobacco pouch
煙斗(ㄧㄢ ㄉㄡˇ)
a pipe (for smoking)
煙燈(ㄧㄢ ㄉㄥ)
a tiny lamp for opium-smoking
煙蒂(ㄧㄢ ㄉㄧˋ)
a cigarette butt: 不要到處亂丟煙蒂。Don't throw away cigarette butts anywhere.
煙毒(ㄧㄢ ㄉㄨˊ)
the poisoning effect of opium-smoking
煙臺(ㄧㄢ ㄊㄞˊ)
Yentai, or Chefoo, in Shantung
煙頭(ㄧㄢ ㄊㄡˊ)
a cigarette butt (or end, stub, stump)
煙突(ㄧㄢ ㄊㄨˊ)
a pipe; a chimney
煙土(ㄧㄢ ㄊㄨˇ)
raw or crude opium
煙筒(ㄧㄢ ·ㄊㄨㄥ)
a chimney; a ventilating pipe for a stove; a funnel; a stovepipe
煙嵐(ㄧㄢ ㄌㄢˊ)
mountain mists or vapor
煙膏(ㄧㄢ ㄍㄠ)
processed opium in paste form
煙鬼(ㄧㄢ ㄍㄨㄟˇ)
an opium smoker or addict; a heavy smoker
煙館(ㄧㄢ ㄍㄨㄢˇ)
a house for opium smoking
煙海(ㄧㄢ ㄏㄞˇ)
(literally) mists over the sea—many, numerous; huge and voluminous: 我們的資料浩如煙海。We have a huge amount of data.
煙花(ㄧㄢ ㄏㄨㄚ)
① prostitutes ② fanfare; prosperity ③ a mist of flowers—beautiful scenery of spring flowers
煙花巷(ㄧㄢ ㄏㄨㄚ ㄒㄧㄤˋ) or 煙花柳巷(ㄧㄢ ㄏㄨㄚ ㄌㄧㄡˇ ㄒㄧㄤˋ)
a red-light district; a zone where brothels are located
煙火(ㄧㄢ ㄏㄨㄛˇ)
① kitchen smoke which suggests presence of humans ② cooked food (as distinct from herbs and fruits which are supposed to be the food of immortals) ③ a signal fire or beacon ④ fireworks: 他們在廣場放煙火。They put on a display of fireworks in the square. ⑤ smoke and fire: 嚴禁煙火。Smoking or lighting fires strictly forbidden.
煙火氣(ㄧㄢ ㄏㄨㄛˇ ㄑㄧˋ)
(Taoism) the worldly ways, customs, etc.
煙灰(ㄧㄢ ㄏㄨㄟ)
cigarette ashes; cigar ashes
煙灰缸(ㄧㄢ ㄏㄨㄟ ㄍㄤ)
an ashtray
煙酒稅 or 菸酒稅(ㄧㄢ ㄐㄧㄡˇ ㄕㄨㄟˋ)
wine and tobacco tax
煙鹼(ㄧㄢ ㄐㄧㄢˇ)
nicotine
煙禁(ㄧㄢ ㄐㄧㄣˋ)
prohibition of opium smoking
煙景(ㄧㄢ ㄐㄧㄥˇ)
① beautiful scenes of a fine day ② changing clouds and mists ③ vapor over a lake
煙捲兒(ㄧㄢ ㄐㄩㄢˇㄦ)
a cigarette
煙槍(ㄧㄢ ㄑㄧㄤ)
① a pipe for opium smoking; an opium pipe ② a chain smoker
煙霞癖(ㄧㄢ ㄒㄧㄚˊ ㄆㄧˇ)
① a deep love for natural charms—mountains, lakes, etc. ②(comically) opium addiction
煙霞痼疾(ㄧㄢ ㄒㄧㄚˊ ㄍㄨˋ ㄐㄧˊ)
a deep-rooted love for natural charms
煙消火滅(ㄧㄢ ㄒㄧㄠ ㄏㄨㄛˇ ㄇㄧㄝˋ)
to vanish or disappear; to come to an end
煙消雲散(ㄧㄢ ㄒㄧㄠ ㄩㄣˊ ㄙㄢˋ)
to vanish like mist and smoke—to vanish completely; to disappear
煙瘴(ㄧㄢ ㄓㄤˋ)

〔火部〕

miasmas
煙塵(ㄧㄢ ㄔㄣˊ)
①smoke and dust; air pollution ②the smoke and dust of battle
煙士披利純(ㄧㄢ ㄕˋ ㄆㄧ ㄌㄧˋ ㄔㄨㄣˊ)
inspiration 亦作「靈感」
煙嘴兒(ㄧㄢ ㄗㄨㄜˇㄦ)
a cigarette holder
煙草 or 菸草(ㄧㄢ ㄘㄠˇ)
tobacco; the tobacco plant
煙囪(ㄧㄢ ㄘㄨㄥ)
a chimney; a stack; a funnel; a stovepipe
煙絲(ㄧㄢ ㄙ)
cut-tobacco for pipe smoking
煙靄(ㄧㄢ ㄞˇ)
mist and vapor; clouds
煙兒(ㄧㄚㄦ)
smoke
煙葉(ㄧㄢ ㄧㄝˋ)
tobacco (leaves)
煙癮(ㄧㄢ ㄧㄣˇ)
①opium or tobacco addiction ②a craving for tobacco
煙霧(ㄧㄢ ㄨˋ)
smoke; mist; vapor; misty; smog
煙雲過眼(ㄧㄢ ㄩㄣˊ ㄍㄨㄛˋ ㄧㄢˇ)
ephemeral; transient

【煤】 3223 ㄇㄟˊ mei méi
1. coal; charcoal; coke
2. carbon; soot
煤末(ㄇㄟˊ ㄇㄛˋ)
coal dust
煤袋(ㄇㄟˊ ㄉㄞˋ)
a coal sack
煤毒(ㄇㄟˊ ㄉㄨˊ)
carbon monoxide (CO)
煤炭(ㄇㄟˊ ㄊㄢˋ)
coal; anthracite; hard coal; coke: 我們貯備煤炭過冬。We lay in coals for the winter.
煤炭店(ㄇㄟˊ ㄊㄢˋ ㄉㄧㄢˋ)
a shop selling coal, firewood, etc.
煤田(ㄇㄟˊ ㄊㄧㄢˊ)
a coal field; a coal bed
煤爐子(ㄇㄟˊ ㄌㄨˊ ˙ㄗ)
a coal stove
煤坑(ㄇㄟˊ ㄎㄥ)
a coal pit
煤礦(ㄇㄟˊ ㄎㄨㄤˋ)
①a coal mine: 他們在地裏開採煤礦。They mined the earth for coal. ②a coal shaft
煤礦工人(ㄇㄟˊ ㄎㄨㄤˋ ㄍㄨㄥ ㄖㄣˊ)
a coal miner: 他的父親是煤礦工人。His father is a coal miner.
煤焦油(ㄇㄟˊ ㄐㄧㄠ ㄧㄡˊ)
coal tar
煤氣(ㄇㄟˊ ㄑㄧˋ)
gas (for lighting or heating); coal gas
煤氣表(ㄇㄟˊ ㄑㄧˋ ㄅㄧㄠˇ)
a gas meter 亦作「瓦斯表」
煤氣燈(ㄇㄟˊ ㄑㄧˋ ㄉㄥ)
a gas lamp; a gas light
煤氣炭(ㄇㄟˊ ㄑㄧˋ ㄊㄢˋ)
gas carbon
煤氣爐(ㄇㄟˊ ㄑㄧˋ ㄌㄨˊ)
a gas stove; a gas furnace
煤氣管(ㄇㄟˊ ㄑㄧˋ ㄍㄨㄢˇ)
gas pipes
煤氣公司(ㄇㄟˊ ㄑㄧˋ ㄍㄨㄥ ㄙ)
a gas company
煤氣機(ㄇㄟˊ ㄑㄧˋ ㄐㄧ)
a coal gas engine
煤氣中毒(ㄇㄟˊ ㄑㄧˋ ㄓㄨㄥˋ ㄉㄨˊ)
carbon monoxide poisoning; gas poisoning
煤球(ㄇㄟˊ ㄑㄧㄡˊ)
coal balls (made of coal dust and clay); briquets
煤屑(ㄇㄟˊ ㄒㄧㄝˋ)
coal dust; coal splinters
煤箱(ㄇㄟˊ ㄒㄧㄤ)
a coal scuttle; a coal hod
煤渣(ㄇㄟˊ ㄓㄚ)
coal cinders; coal slag
煤車(ㄇㄟˊ ㄔㄜ)
a coal car
煤塵爆炸(ㄇㄟˊ ㄔㄣˊ ㄅㄠˋ ㄓㄚˋ)
a coal-dust explosion
煤商(ㄇㄟˊ ㄕㄤ)
a coal dealer; a coalman
煤倉(ㄇㄟˊ ㄘㄤ)
a coal bunker
煤層(ㄇㄟˊ ㄘㄥˊ)
a coal seam; a coal bed; coal measures
煤油(ㄇㄟˊ ㄧㄡˊ)
kerosene: 這個爐子燒煤油。This stove burns kerosene.
煤油燈(ㄇㄟˊ ㄧㄡˊ ㄉㄥ)
a kerosene lamp
煤油爐(ㄇㄟˊ ㄧㄡˊ ㄌㄨˊ)
a kerosene stove
煤油罐(ㄇㄟˊ ㄧㄡˊ ㄍㄨㄢˋ)
a kerosene can or container
煤煙(ㄇㄟˊ ㄧㄢ)
soot

【煥】 3224 ㄏㄨㄢˋ huann huàn
1. bright; brilliant; lustrous; luminous
2. (said of an appearance) shining; vigorous and elegant
煥發(ㄏㄨㄢˋ ㄈㄚ)
brilliant and luminous; scintillating; shining; radiant; vivacious; glowing: 他容光煥發。His face is glowing with health.
煥爛(ㄏㄨㄢˋ ㄌㄢˋ)
very bright and luminous; shining and flourishing
煥煥(ㄏㄨㄢˋ ㄏㄨㄢˋ)
①bright and shining; scintillating ②glorious; remarkable; prominent
煥然一新(ㄏㄨㄢˋ ㄖㄢˊ ㄧˋ ㄒㄧㄣ)
brand-new; renovated from top to bottom; to take on an entirely new look
煥曜(ㄏㄨㄢˋ ㄧㄠˋ)
bright and luminous; shining and flourishing

【煨】 3225 ㄨㄟ uei wei
to bake; to stew; to simmer; to burn in ashes; to roast (sweet potatoes, etc.) in fresh cinders
煨乾避濕(ㄨㄟ ㄍㄢ ㄅㄧˋ ㄕ)
(literally) to sleep on a bed sheet wet by a child and let the child sleep where the sheet is dry—the loving care a mother gives to her child
煨燼(ㄨㄟ ㄐㄧㄣˋ)
ashes
煨肉(ㄨㄟ ㄖㄡˋ)
to stew meat

【煩】 3226 ㄈㄢˊ farn fán
1. to vex; to annoy; to worry
2. annoying
3. to trouble
4. superfluous and confusing
煩悶 or 煩懣(ㄈㄢˊ ㄇㄣˋ)
annoyed; vexed; depressed; downcast; bored; worried: 他爲何那麼煩悶？Why is he so worried?

〔火部〕

煩法(ㄈㄢˊ ㄈㄚˇ)
irritating petty laws and regulations; red tape

煩費(ㄈㄢˊ ㄈㄟˋ)
to cause trouble and expenses

煩惱(ㄈㄢˊ ㄋㄠˇ)
worries; cares; worried

煩難(ㄈㄢˊ ㄋㄢˊ)
complicated and difficult to handle

煩了(ㄈㄢˊ ˙ㄌㄜ)
tired of; bored

煩勞(ㄈㄢˊ ㄌㄠˊ)
to ask someone to do something

煩亂(ㄈㄢˊ ㄌㄨㄢˋ)
confusing

煩苛(ㄈㄢˊ ㄎㄜ)
petty and harassing (regulations, taxation, etc.)

煩交(ㄈㄢˊ ㄐㄧㄠ)
please deliver to

煩請(ㄈㄢˊ ㄑㄧㄥˇ)
Would you mind...? 或 Please be so kind as to....

煩細(ㄈㄢˊ ㄒㄧˋ)
petty details; petty and detailed

煩囂(ㄈㄢˊ ㄒㄧㄠ)
① the hubbub of a noisy place ② cares and worries of this world

煩心(ㄈㄢˊ ㄒㄧㄣ)
to trouble or worry the mind; vexation

煩想(ㄈㄢˊ ㄒㄧㄤˇ)
worries

煩絮(ㄈㄢˊ ㄒㄩˋ)
verbose; verbosity; long-winded; prolix

煩數(ㄈㄢˊ ㄕㄨㄛˋ)
frequency

煩熱(ㄈㄢˊ ㄖㄜˋ)
oppressively hot; oppressive heat; sultry

煩擾(ㄈㄢˊ ㄖㄠˇ)
to trouble with petty things; to annoy; to harass; to feel disturbed: 蚊子在夏天煩擾我們。Mosquitoes annoy us in the summer.

煩冗(ㄈㄢˊ ㄖㄨㄥˇ)
lengthy and tedious; petty, disorderly and busy; diverse and complicated

煩雜(ㄈㄢˊ ㄗㄚˊ)
petty and varied; confusing and disorderly

煩躁(ㄈㄢˊ ㄗㄠˋ)
annoyed and impatient; vexed; short-tempered; agitated

煩瑣(ㄈㄢˊ ㄙㄨㄛˇ)
petty and multitudinous; tedious

煩碎(ㄈㄢˊ ㄙㄨㄟˋ)
petty and overdetailed

煩言(ㄈㄢˊ ㄧㄢˊ)
complaints

煩猥(ㄈㄢˊ ㄨㄟˇ)
multitudinous and petty

煩文縟節(ㄈㄢˊ ㄨㄣˊ ㄖㄨˋ ㄐㄧㄝˊ)
petty formalities; red tape

【煬】 3227
1. ㄧㄤˊ yang yáng
same as 烊—to smelt or melt (metals)

煬帝(ㄧㄤˊ ㄉㄧˋ)
Emperor Yang of the Sui Dynasty, who ordered the digging of the Grand Canal in the early seventh century

【煬】 3227
2. ㄧㄤˋ yanq yàng
1. (said of fire) roaring or blazing
2. to put before the fire

【煮】 3228
(煑) ㄓㄨˇ juu zhǔ
to cook; to boil; to stew; to decoct

煮茗(ㄓㄨˇ ㄇㄧㄥˊ)
to boil tea; to infuse tea

煮沸(ㄓㄨˇ ㄈㄟˋ)
to boil; to heat water or soup until it boils

煮飯(ㄓㄨˇ ㄈㄢˋ)
to cook rice; to cook meals

煮豆燃萁(ㄓㄨˇ ㄉㄡˋ ㄖㄢˊ ㄑㄧˊ)
(literally) to make a fire of beanstalks for boiling beans—fraternal persecution; the conflict among brothers

煮爛(ㄓㄨˇ ㄌㄢˋ)
to stew something until it's tender

煮鶴焚琴(ㄓㄨˇ ㄏㄜˋ ㄈㄣˊ ㄑㄧㄣˊ)
to destroy something fine by behaving rudely

煮海爲鹽(ㄓㄨˇ ㄏㄞˇ ㄨㄟˊ ㄧㄢˊ)
to boil seawater for salt

煮餃子(ㄓㄨˇ ㄐㄧㄠˇ ˙ㄗ)
to boil ravioli (or stuffed dumplings)

煮粥(ㄓㄨˇ ㄓㄡ)
to cook congee

煮熟(ㄓㄨˇ ㄕㄡˊ)
to cook thoroughly

煮肉(ㄓㄨˇ ㄖㄡˋ)
to cook meat

煮字療飢(ㄓㄨˇ ㄗˋ ㄌㄧㄠˊ ㄐㄧ)
to live on writing; to have a writer's career

煮菜(ㄓㄨˇ ㄘㄞˋ)
to prepare food or dishes

煮鹽(ㄓㄨˇ ㄧㄢˊ)
to get salt by evaporation of seawater

【煎】 3229
ㄐㄧㄢ jian jiān
1. to fry in fat or oil
2. to decoct
3. (figuratively) to torment; to kill

煎逼(ㄐㄧㄢ ㄅㄧ) or 煎迫(ㄐㄧㄢ ㄆㄛˋ)
to torture; to persecute

煎餅(ㄐㄧㄢ ˙ㄅㄧㄥ)
pancakes: 他常以煎餅當早餐。He usually has pancakes for breakfast.

煎蛋(ㄐㄧㄢ ㄉㄢˋ)
①to fry eggs: 他正用平底鍋煎蛋。He is frying the egg in the pan. ② fried eggs

煎心(ㄐㄧㄢ ㄒㄧㄣ)
(literally) to fry the heart—very worried

煎炒(ㄐㄧㄢ ㄔㄠˇ)
to fry; to stir-fry

煎熬(ㄐㄧㄢ ㄠˊ)
① to decoct until almost dry ② to put somebody in hot water; to make someone suffer; to torture; to torment

煎藥(ㄐㄧㄢ ㄧㄠˋ)
to make a decoction of herbal medicines

煎魚(ㄐㄧㄢ ㄩˊ)
to fry fish

【煞】 3230
1. ㄕㄚˋ shah shà
1. a fierce god; a malignant deity; an evil spirit; a goblin
2. very; much; extremely
3. to bring to an end; to conclude

煞筆(ㄕㄚˋ ㄅㄧˇ)
(said of a piece of writing or a speech) ① to come to a

conclusion; to write the final line ② concluding lines of an article

煞費工夫(ㄕㄚˋ ㄈㄟˋ ㄍㄨㄥ ㄈㄨ)
to take much trouble

煞費苦心(ㄕㄚˋ ㄈㄟˋ ㄎㄨˇ ㄒㄧㄣ)
to have made painstaking effort; to take great pains: 他煞費苦心做事。 He did the work with great pains.

煞風景(ㄕㄚˋ ㄈㄥ ㄐㄧㄥˇ)
to throw a wet blanket; to spoil pleasure

煞後兒(ㄕㄚˋ ㄏㄡˋㄦ)
timid; shy; not aggressive

煞脚(ㄕㄚˋ ㄐㄧㄠˇ)
to stop or halt; to come to a conclusion

煞氣(ㄕㄚˋ ㄑㄧˋ)
a fierce attitude; an ominous look

煞星(ㄕㄚˋ ㄒㄧㄥ)
a malignant star—(usually said of a person) that brings wars, deaths, calamities, disasters

煞著步兒(ㄕㄚ ·ㄓㄜ ㄅㄨˋㄦ)
to halt one's pace

煞是(ㄕㄚˋ ㄕˋ)
very (interesting, encouraging, etc.): 他的話煞是有趣。 What he said was very funny.

煞神(ㄕㄚˋ ㄕㄣˊ)
an ominous deity or malignant god who brings catastrophes

煞尾(ㄕㄚˋ ㄨㄟˇ)
① the conclusion or ending paragraph of an article ② a final stage; an end; an ending ③ to come to an end; to wind up

【煞】 3230
2. ㄕㄚ sha shā

1. to tighten; to bind
2. to offset; to reduce; to mitigate
3. an auxiliary particle in old usage
4. to brake; to stop; to bring to a close

煞氣(ㄕㄚ ㄑㄧˋ)
to vent one's anger on an innocent party; to take it out on somebody or something

煞性子(ㄕㄚ ㄒㄧㄥˋ ·ㄗ)
to vent one's anger on an innocent party

煞賬(ㄕㄚ ㄓㄤˋ)
(said of an accountant) to make out a statement

煞住(ㄕㄚ ㄓㄨˋ)
to stop; to hold it

煞車(ㄕㄚ ㄔㄜ)
① to fasten goods on a truck or cart with ropes ② to apply the brakes; to brake

【煦】 3231
ㄒㄩˇ sheu xǔ

1. warm and cozy
2. favors; kindness; good graces; kind and gracious

煦沫(ㄒㄩˇ ㄇㄛˋ)
to drool

煦煦(ㄒㄩˇ ㄒㄩˇ)
①kind; gracious; benevolent ②(said of weather) warm and fine; balmy: 煦煦春風使人昏昏欲睡。The balmy spring breeze makes us sleepy.

煦日(ㄒㄩˇ ㄖˋ)
① the warm sun ② a warm and fine day

【照】 3232
ㄓㄠˋ jaw zhào

1. to shine upon; to light or illumine
2. a certificate or license
3. in accordance with; according to; to pattern on or after
4. to compare, collate, survey, etc.
5. to photograph; to take a picture; to shoot
6. to look after; to take care of
7. to notify or proclaim
8. sunshine
9. a picture
10. a Chinese family name

照搬(ㄓㄠˋ ㄅㄢ)
to imitate; to copy

照辦(ㄓㄠˋ ㄅㄢˋ)
to take actions, etc. accordingly; to act upon; to comply with; to manage, or handle something according to instructions, orders, etc.

照本宣科(ㄓㄠˋ ㄅㄣˇ ㄒㄩㄢ ㄎㄜ)
to read item by item from the text; to repeat what the book says

照本出售(ㄓㄠˋ ㄅㄣˇ ㄔㄨ ㄕㄡˋ)
to sell at cost price (a common sales slogan in a Chinese shop)

照壁(ㄓㄠˋ ㄅㄧˋ)
a wall immediately outside the front door

照片(ㄓㄠˋ ㄆㄧㄢˋ)
a photograph; a snapshot

照碼對折(ㄓㄠˋ ㄇㄚˇ ㄉㄨㄟˋ ㄓㄜˊ)
(a common sales slogan) to offer a 50 percent discount on the tagged prices

照面(ㄓㄠˋ ㄇㄧㄢˋ)
to meet; to come face to face: 讓我們彼此打個照面。 Let's come face to face with each other.

照明(ㄓㄠˋ ㄇㄧㄥˊ)
(said of photography, etc.) lighting

照明彈(ㄓㄠˋ ㄇㄧㄥˊ ㄉㄢˋ)
a flare

照明設備(ㄓㄠˋ ㄇㄧㄥˊ ㄕㄜˋ ㄅㄟˋ)
illuminating equipment; photo flash equipment

照拂(ㄓㄠˋ ㄈㄨˊ)
to look after; to care for: 請多照拂她。 Please be so kind as to take good care of her.

照付(ㄓㄠˋ ㄈㄨˋ)
to pay the full amount according to the price tag, receipt, notice, IOU, etc.

照度(ㄓㄠˋ ㄉㄨˋ)
(physics) illumination

照例(ㄓㄠˋ ㄌㄧˋ)
to follow precedents or usual practices; as a rule

照料(ㄓㄠˋ ㄌㄧㄠˋ)
to take care of; to look after: 你不在時家裏的事有我們照料。We'll take care of things at home while you're away.

照臨(ㄓㄠˋ ㄌㄧㄣˊ)
①(polite usage, said of a guest) your much honored arrival (at our place) ② the visits of a king or emperor ③ to shine on: 曙光照臨大地。 The early sun shines on the land. ④(figuratively) to enlighten and rule

照錄(ㄓㄠˋ ㄌㄨˋ) or 照抄(ㄓㄠˋ ㄔㄠ)
to record or copy exactly as what is said or written

〔火部〕

照顧(ㄓㄠˋ ㄍㄨˋ)
①to look after; to take care of; care ②to patronize ③to give consideration to; to consider; to take something into account

照管(ㄓㄠˋ ㄍㄨㄢˇ)
to take care of; to manage; to be in charge of; to look after: 她在家照管孩子。She looks after children at home.

照看(ㄓㄠˋ ㄎㄢˋ)
to look after; to keep an eye on: 請幫我照看一下小孩。Will you please keep an eye on my child?

照空燈(ㄓㄠˋ ㄎㄨㄥ ㄉㄥ)
a searchlight

照會(ㄓㄠˋ ㄏㄨㄟˋ)
diplomatic notes; memoranda: 提出照會 to present a note

照價收買(ㄓㄠˋ ㄐㄧㄚˋ ㄕㄡ ㄇㄞˇ)
to buy or requisition (land) according to the price declared by the owner

照繳(ㄓㄠˋ ㄐㄧㄠˇ)
to pay (taxes, fines, etc.) according to the stipulated amount

照舊(ㄓㄠˋ ㄐㄧㄡˋ)
as usual; as before: 他照舊在晚餐前回到了家。He came home before dinner as usual.

照鏡自憐(ㄓㄠˋ ㄐㄧㄥˋ ㄗˋ ㄌㄧㄢˊ)
to sympathize with oneself in the mirror

照鏡子(ㄓㄠˋ ㄐㄧㄥˋ ·ㄗ)
to see oneself in the mirror

照牆(ㄓㄠˋ ㄑㄧㄤˊ)
a wall immediately outside the front door

照相(ㄓㄠˋ ㄒㄧㄤˋ)
to take a picture or photograph: 我們週末照相去。Let's go and take photographs this weekend.

照相板(ㄓㄠˋ ㄒㄧㄤˋ ㄅㄢˇ)
a phototype; a photogravure

照相館(ㄓㄠˋ ㄒㄧㄤˋ ㄍㄨㄢˇ)
a photostudio

照相機(ㄓㄠˋ ㄒㄧㄤˋ ㄐㄧ)
a camera

照相師(ㄓㄠˋ ㄒㄧㄤˋ ㄕ)
a photographer

照相術(ㄓㄠˋ ㄒㄧㄤˋ ㄕㄨˋ)
photography

照直說(ㄓㄠˋ ㄓˊ ㄕㄨㄛ)
to speak frankly; to talk bluntly

照章辦理(ㄓㄠˋ ㄓㄤ ㄅㄢˋ ㄌㄧˇ)
to carry on, operate, or manage according to rules, regulations, etc.

照准(ㄓㄠˋ ㄓㄨㄣˇ)
to approve (a request); to grant; to give approval (to a request); approved: 請假一天照准。Your request for a day off is granted.

照常(ㄓㄠˋ ㄔㄤˊ)
as usual

照射(ㄓㄠˋ ㄕㄜˋ)
to shine or light upon; to illuminate; to radiate; to irradiate

照收(ㄓㄠˋ ㄕㄡ)
①to duly receive; duly received ②to accept accordingly

照身鏡(ㄓㄠˋ ㄕㄣ ㄐㄧㄥˋ)
a cheval glass; a long mirror that reflects the whole length of the body

照數(ㄓㄠˋ ㄕㄨˋ)
according to the listed sum, number, etc.

照說(ㄓㄠˋ ㄕㄨㄛ)
as a rule: 照說這時候該冷了。As a rule, it should be cold by now.

照此類推(ㄓㄠˋ ㄘˇ ㄌㄟˋ ㄊㄨㄟ)
to draw analogous conclusions

照算(ㄓㄠˋ ㄙㄨㄢˋ)
①to calculate or charge (the listed items) accordingly ②to charge without deduction, discount, etc.

照妖鏡(ㄓㄠˋ ㄧㄠ ㄐㄧㄥˋ)
①(a Taoist superstition) a tiny mirror hung on the back to frighten away evil spirits ②a mirror said to make evil spirits appearing in human form show their original forms

照耀(ㄓㄠˋ ㄧㄠˋ)
to radiate; to light up; to shine; to illuminate: 那是陽光照耀的美麗早晨。It was a beautiful morning with the sun shining.

照樣(ㄓㄠˋ ㄧㄤˋ)
①to pattern after; to copy ②as usual; in the old manner; all the same

照應(ㄓㄠˋ ㄧㄥˋ)
①to take care of; to look after: 請照應一下我的小孩。Please take care of my child for a moment. ②to correlate

照原價(ㄓㄠˋ ㄩㄢˊ ㄐㄧㄚˋ)
according to the old price (although there has been a price hike)

【煢】 3233 ㄑㄩㄥˊ chyong qióng

to be all alone; without friends or relatives; solitary

煢單(ㄑㄩㄥˊ ㄉㄢ)
to be all alone in the whole wide world

煢獨(ㄑㄩㄥˊ ㄉㄨˊ)
alone; friendless and childless

煢居(ㄑㄩㄥˊ ㄐㄩ)
to live alone

煢煢(ㄑㄩㄥˊ ㄑㄩㄥˊ)
desolate and alone; lonely

十畫

【熙】 3234 ㄒㄧ shi xī

1. bright and brilliant; glorious
2. expansive; spacious
3. flourishing; prosperous; booming
4. peaceful and happy

熙來壤往 or 熙來攘往(ㄒㄧ ㄌㄞˊ ㄖㄤˇ ㄨㄤˇ)
the hustle and bustle of large crowds

熙熙(ㄒㄧ ㄒㄧ)
peaceful and happy

熙熙壤壤 or 熙熙攘攘(ㄒㄧ ㄒㄧ ㄖㄤˇ ㄖㄤˇ)
coming and going busily; crowded and noisy; hustle and bustle

熙洽(ㄒㄧ ㄒㄧㄚˊ)
(said of times) peaceful and prosperous

熙笑(ㄒㄧ ㄒㄧㄠˋ)
to laugh happily

熙朝(ㄒㄧ ㄔㄠˊ)
a prosperous reign or age (in old China, a reference to

the dynasty in which one lived)
熙春(ㄒㄧ ㄔㄨㄣ)
spring; springtime
熙怡(ㄒㄧ ㄧˊ)
amiable and cordial

【熊】 3235 ㄒㄩㄥˊ shyong xióng
1. a bear
2. shining bright
3. a Chinese family name
熊白(ㄒㄩㄥˊ ㄅㄞˊ)
the fatty portion on the back of a bear which tastes delicious
熊羆(ㄒㄩㄥˊ ㄆㄧˊ)
① name of two fierce animals used as a synonym of men of enormous strength ② name of an ancient Chinese (in the *Book of Shu*)
熊羆入夢(ㄒㄩㄥˊ ㄆㄧˊ ㄖㄨˋ ㄇㄥˋ)
May you bear a son!—a congratulatory greeting to a friend when he begets a son
熊貓(ㄒㄩㄥˊ ㄇㄠ)
a panda
熊蹯(ㄒㄩㄥˊ ㄈㄢˊ)
the palm of a bear (a rare delicacy in Chinese feasts)亦作「熊掌」
熊膽(ㄒㄩㄥˊ ㄉㄢˇ)
the gall secretion of a bear (used in Chinese medicine)
熊虎(ㄒㄩㄥˊ ㄏㄨˇ)
the bear and the tiger —intrepid; fierce
熊心豹膽(ㄒㄩㄥˊ ㄒㄧㄣ ㄅㄠˋ ㄉㄢˇ)
(literally) the heart of a bear and the gall of a leopard — tremendous bravery or courage
熊熊(ㄒㄩㄥˊ ㄒㄩㄥˊ)
bright and brilliant; flaming and glorious; shining
熊熊大火(ㄒㄩㄥˊ ㄒㄩㄥˊ ㄉㄚˋ ㄏㄨㄛˇ)
a blazing fire
熊掌(ㄒㄩㄥˊ ㄓㄤˇ)
the palms or soles of a bear (a rare delicacy in Chinese feasts)
熊腰虎背(ㄒㄩㄥˊ ㄧㄠ ㄏㄨˇ ㄅㄟˋ)
the waist of a bear and the back of a tiger—heavy and muscular build of the body

【熏】 3236 (燻) ㄒㄩㄣ shiun xūn
1. smoke; to smoke; to burn; smoked (meat, fish, etc.)
2. (said of smell) to assail nostrils: 臭氣熏人。The stench is assailing our nostrils.
3. warm; mild
4. to move or touch
5. same as 曛 or 薰
6. to scent; to fumigate
熏沐(ㄒㄩㄣ ㄇㄨˋ)
to bathe and apply perfume
熏風(ㄒㄩㄣ ㄈㄥ)
southeast (warm) winds
熏天(ㄒㄩㄣ ㄊㄧㄢ)
overwhelming
熏爐(ㄒㄩㄣ ㄌㄨˊ)
a portable stove for burning incense or warming; a brazier
熏黑(ㄒㄩㄣ ㄏㄟ)
to blacken by smoke
熏夕(ㄒㄩㄣ ㄒㄧˋ)
evening time; dusk
熏香(ㄒㄩㄣ ㄒㄧㄤ)
a kind of incense used especially for perfuming clothing, bedding, rooms, etc.
熏炙(ㄒㄩㄣ ㄓˋ)
to cauterize
熏灼四方(ㄒㄩㄣ ㄓㄨㄛˊ ㄙˋ ㄈㄤ)
(said of powerful officials) to terrorize or bully people
熏肉(ㄒㄩㄣ ㄖㄡˋ)
to smoke meat; smoked meat; bacon
熏染(ㄒㄩㄣ ㄖㄢˇ)
to influence
熏死(ㄒㄩㄣ ㄙˇ)
suffocated to death (by fumes, stench, etc.)
熏衣(ㄒㄩㄣ ㄧ)
to fumigate clothing with aromatic smoke
熏魚(ㄒㄩㄣ ㄩˊ)
to smoke fish; smoked fish

【熄】 3237 ㄒㄧˊ shyi xí
1. to extinguish (a fire); to put out (a light): 把燈熄了。Put out the light.
2. to quash; to destroy; to obliterate
熄滅(ㄒㄧˊ ㄇㄧㄝˋ)
to extinguish (a fire); to put out (a light); to die out
熄燈(ㄒㄧˊ ㄉㄥ)
to put out the light; to turn or switch off the light: 你離開時請熄燈。Please turn off the light (or lamp) as you leave.
熄火(ㄒㄧˊ ㄏㄨㄛˇ)
①(usually said of factories, steamships, etc.) to stop the fire (in the boiler)—to stop operation ② to turn off the lamp or light
熄火器(ㄒㄧˊ ㄏㄨㄛˇ ㄑㄧˋ)
a fire extinguisher 亦作「滅火器」

【熗】 3238 ㄑㄧㄤˋ chianq qiàng
1. a way of cooking in which foods (especially bivalves and some vegetables) are eaten right after being brought to a boil
2. to fry something quickly in hot oil, then cook it with sauce and water
3. same as 嗆—to choke with smoke, etc.

【煽】 3239 ㄕㄢ shan shān
1. to stir up; to instigate; to incite; to fan
2. flaming; blazing; to flame
煽動(ㄕㄢ ㄉㄨㄥˋ)
to incite; to stir up (a strike, uprising, etc.): 他們企圖煽動群衆。They tried to stir up trouble among the masses.
煽火(ㄕㄢ ㄏㄨㄛˇ)
to fan the fire; to fan the flame
煽惑(ㄕㄢ ㄏㄨㄛˋ)
to incite; to agitate; to rouse with words or lies: 不要煽惑人心。Don't agitate people by demagogy.

【熔】 3240 (鎔) ㄖㄨㄥˊ rong róng
1. to smelt; to weld or fuse metals; to melt
2. a die; a mold
3. a spear-like weapon
熔點(ㄖㄨㄥˊ ㄉㄧㄢˇ)
a melting or fusion point
熔度(ㄖㄨㄥˊ ㄉㄨˋ)
fusibility
熔爐(ㄖㄨㄥˊ ㄌㄨˊ)
a smelting furnace; a melting pot: 美國常被稱爲熔爐。America is often called a

melting pot.

熔化(ㄖㄨㄥˊ ㄏㄨㄚˋ)
to turn metals into liquid by heating; to smelt; to melt

熔劑(ㄖㄨㄥˊ ㄐㄧˋ)
flux

熔接(ㄖㄨㄥˊ ㄐㄧㄝ)
to weld: 銅很容易熔接。Copper welds easily.

熔解(ㄖㄨㄥˊ ㄐㄧㄝˇ)
to turn metals into liquid by heating; to smelt; to melt; to fuse; fusion or melting

熔解熱(ㄖㄨㄥˊ ㄐㄧㄝˇ ㄖㄜˋ)
① the quantity of heat energy needed to turn a cubic centimeter of solid metals into liquid ② latent heat of fusion

熔鑄(ㄖㄨㄥˊ ㄓㄨˋ)
founding; casting

熔冶(ㄖㄨㄥˊ ㄧㄝˇ)
to smelt; to melt

熔岩(ㄖㄨㄥˊ ㄧㄢˊ)
lava

【熒】 3241 ㄧㄥˊ yng yíng

1. bright; shining; luminous
2. dazzling; glittering; sparkling; glimmering
3. to doubt; to suspect

熒燎(ㄧㄥˊ ㄌㄧㄠˊ)
light of fire

熒光(ㄧㄥˊ ㄍㄨㄤ)
(physics) fluorescence; fluorescent light

熒惑(ㄧㄥˊ ㄏㄨㄛˋ)
① to confuse or fool others with smooth talks, etc. ② the god of fire ③ another name of Mars

熒熒(ㄧㄥˊ ㄧㄥˊ)
① bright and brilliant; luminous ② twinkling; glimmering; sparkling

十一畫

【熠】 3242 ㄧˋ yih yì

bright and brilliant; luminous

熠熠(ㄧˋ ㄧˋ)
bright and luminous: 星光熠熠。The stars are bright and luminous.

熠燿(ㄧˋ ㄧㄠˋ)
① bright and luminous ② a glowworm; a firefly

【熟】 3243 ㄕㄨˊ shwu shú (讀音 ㄕㄡˊ shour shóu)

1. cooked or well-done (as opposed to raw); prepared or processed
2. ripe (fruit); to ripen
3. very familiar; well versed; experienced; conversant
4. careful or painstaking survey, study, inspection, etc.)
5. deep or sound (sleep)

熟皮(ㄕㄨˊ ㄆㄧˊ)
leather; processed hides

熟寐(ㄕㄨˊ ㄇㄟˋ)
a sound sleep or slumber

熟苗(ㄕㄨˊ ㄇㄧㄠˊ)
the part of Miao people (a minority race in China) who have been assimilated to the Han (Chinese) ways of life and observe government laws

熟眠(ㄕㄨˊ ㄇㄧㄢˊ)
a deep sleep or slumber: 嬰兒在搖籃裏熟眠。The baby slumbered in his cradle.

熟番(ㄕㄨˊ ㄈㄢ)
assimilated border tribes

熟飯(ㄕㄨˊ ㄈㄢˋ)or(ㄕㄡˊ ㄈㄢˋ)
cooked rice

熟道(ㄕㄨˊ ㄉㄠˋ)or 熟路(ㄕㄡˊ ㄌㄨˋ)
a familiar road or route

熟地(ㄕㄨˊ ㄉㄧˋ)
① the root of foxglove — *Rehmannia glutinosa* — used in Chinese medicine ② cultivated land

熟讀(ㄕㄨˊ ㄉㄨˊ)or(ㄕㄡˊ ㄉㄨˊ)
to be well versed in; to read thoroughly; to memorize by rote

熟透(ㄕㄨˊ ㄊㄡˋ)or(ㄕㄡˊ ㄊㄡˋ)
① well-cooked ② thoroughly ripe ③ very familiar with

熟炭(ㄕㄨˊ ㄊㄢˋ)
coke; charcoal

熟鐵(ㄕㄨˊ ㄊㄧㄝˇ)
wrought iron

熟脫(ㄕㄨˊ ㄊㄨㄛ)
well versed; very familiar with

熟銅(ㄕㄨˊ ㄊㄨㄥˊ)
wrought brass or copper

熟能生巧(ㄕㄨˊ ㄋㄥˊ ㄕㄥ ㄑㄧㄠˇ)
Skill comes from long experience. 或 Dexterity is the product of long practice. 或 Practice makes perfect.

熟年(ㄕㄨˊ ㄋㄧㄢˊ)
a plentiful year; a year of good harvests

熟了(ㄕㄨˊ ·ㄌㄜ)or(ㄕㄡˊ ·ㄌㄜ)
①ripe: 蘋果已經熟了。The apple is ripe. ②well prepared (lessons) ③ well cooked or done: 肉已經煮熟了。The meat is well cooked.

熟臉兒(ㄕㄨˊ ㄌㄧㄚˇㄦ)or 熟面孔(ㄕㄨˊ ㄇㄧㄢˋ ㄎㄨㄥˇ)
a familiar face

熟料(ㄕㄨˊ ㄌㄧㄠˋ)
① timber which has been sawed and cut to required sizes for construction purposes ② cooked or prepared ingredients

熟練(ㄕㄨˊ ㄌㄧㄢˋ)
experienced, skilled or dexterous

熟練工人(ㄕㄨˊ ㄌㄧㄢˋ ㄍㄨㄥ ㄖㄣˊ)
experienced or skilled workers

熟路(ㄕㄨˊ ㄌㄨˋ)
a familiar route

熟慮(ㄕㄨˊ ㄌㄩˋ)
to consider or ponder carefully

熟客(ㄕㄨˊ ㄎㄜˋ)or(ㄕㄡˊ ㄎㄜˋ)
an old customer or patron; a frequent visitor

熟貨(ㄕㄨˊ ㄏㄨㄛˋ)or(ㄕㄡˊ ㄏㄨㄛˋ)
processed commodities or goods; finished products

熟悉(ㄕㄨˊ ㄒㄧ)
very familiar with; conversant with; to have an intimate knowledge of: 他熟悉此事。He has an intimate knowledge of the matter.

熟習(ㄕㄨˊ ㄒㄧˊ)
to learn by heart; to be well versed in; to be skilled in

熟知(ㄕㄨˊ ㄓ)
well acquainted or familiar with; to be well versed in; to know well

熟主顧(ㄕㄨˊ ㄓㄨˇ ㄍㄨˋ)
an old customer or patron

熟食(ㄕㄨˊ ㄕˊ)

①cooked food ②the habit of eating cooked food instead of raw or uncooked food

熟石灰(ㄕㄨˊ ㄕˊ ㄏㄨㄟ)
slaked lime

熟視(ㄕㄨˊ ㄕˋ)
to look carefully and for a long time; to scrutinize

熟視無睹(ㄕㄨˊ ㄕˋ ㄨˊ ㄉㄨˇ)
to look at but pay no attention to; to regard as of no consequence; to turn a blind eye to

熟識(ㄕㄨˊ ㄕˋ)
to know well; very familiar with

熟手(ㄕㄨˊ ㄕㄡˇ)or(ㄕㄡˊ ㄕㄡˇ)
an experienced or skilled hand

熟睡(ㄕㄨˊ ㄕㄨㄟˋ)
a sound sleep; to sleep soundly

熟肉(ㄕㄨˊ ㄖㄡˋ)or(ㄕㄡˊ ㄖㄡˋ)
cooked meat; well-done meat

熟人(ㄕㄨˊ ㄖㄣˊ)or(ㄕㄡˊ ㄖㄣˊ)
an old acquaintance

熟字(ㄕㄨˊ ㄗˋ)or(ㄕㄡˊ ㄗˋ)
a familiar word; a word one knows

熟思(ㄕㄨˊ ㄙ)
to think over or consider carefully; to ponder deeply; to deliberate: 答覆之前，他熟思這問題。He deliberated the question before he made an answer.

熟菜(ㄕㄨˊ ㄘㄞˋ)or(ㄕㄡˊ ㄘㄞˋ)
cooked dishes or food

熟諳(ㄕㄨˊ ㄢ)
well-experienced; to be well versed in; to be an expert in: 他熟諳水性。He is an expert in swimming.

【熬】 3244
1. ㄠˊ aur ɑ́o

1. to extract (oil, etc.) by applying heat
2. to cook; to stew or simmer
3. to endure with perseverance; to suffer with patience (an ordeal, etc.); to sustain

熬不過(ㄠˊ ·ㄅㄨ ㄍㄨㄛˋ)
to be unable to sustain or endure; cannot survive a grave illness (after a given time)

熬頭兒(ㄠˊ ·ㄊㄡㄦ)
the reward obtained from long ordeals, sufferings, etc.

熬湯(ㄠˊ ㄊㄤ)
to stew or simmer (meat) for broth

熬煉(ㄠˊ ㄌㄧㄢˋ)
to boil and smelt—strict discipline

熬膏(ㄠˊ ㄍㄠ)
①to simmer (raw opium) to paste, readying it for smoking ②to prepare (herbal medicine) in paste form, mostly for external use

熬枯受淡(ㄠˊ ㄎㄨ ㄕㄡˋ ㄉㄢˋ)
to have undergone the whole ordeal of ennui and dull life

熬煎(ㄠˊ ㄐㄧㄢ)
a tremendous ordeal; suffering

熬刑(ㄠˊ ㄒㄧㄥˊ)
(said of a prisoner) to insist on innocence under torture

熬粥(ㄠˊ ㄓㄡ)
to cook congee or gruel by simmering

熬出來(ㄠˊ ㄔㄨ ·ㄌㄞ)or 熬出頭(ㄠˊ ㄔㄨ ㄊㄡˊ)
to have gone through all sorts of ordeal

熬日子(ㄠˊ ㄖˋ ·ㄗ)
to go through hard times

熬夜(ㄠˊ ㄧㄝˋ)
to work (or gamble) until deep into the night; to burn the midnight oil

熬藥(ㄠˊ ㄧㄠˋ)
to decoct medicinal herbs

熬油(ㄠˊ ㄧㄡˊ)
①to waste lamp oil by staying up at night ②to extract oil (as lard, etc.) by heating

【熬】 3244
2. ㄠ au ɑo

1. to cook; to stew
2. to be worn down by worries, cares; discouraged or despondent; dejected

熬惱(ㄠ ㄋㄠˇ)
unhappy and dejected

熬心(ㄠ ㄒㄧㄣ)
annoying; vexing; unhappy

熬菜(ㄠ ㄘㄞˋ)
to cook food (with water)

【熱】 3245
ㄖㄜˋ reh rè

1. hot; heated; burning; to heat: 房間熱得像火爐。The room was as hot as an oven.
2. fever
3. earnest; ardent; zealous; enthusiastic; passionate: 他是個熱心的工作者。He is a zealous worker.

熱病(ㄖㄜˋ ㄅㄧㄥˋ)
fever

熱門(ㄖㄜˋ ㄇㄣˊ)
something very much in vogue or fashion; something everyone is after or interested in; a craze: 駕滑翔機是最近的熱門玩意兒。Gliding is the latest craze.

熱門貨(ㄖㄜˋ ㄇㄣˊ ㄏㄨㄛˋ)
a commodity which is enjoying a brisk sale

熱敷法(ㄖㄜˋ ㄈㄨ ㄈㄚˇ)
(medicine) hot compresses

熱帶(ㄖㄜˋ ㄉㄞˋ)
the tropics; the Torrid Zone: 熱帶地方是很熱的。It's hot in the tropics.

熱帶植物(ㄖㄜˋ ㄉㄞˋ ㄓˊ ㄨˋ)
tropical plants

熱帶魚(ㄖㄜˋ ㄉㄞˋ ㄩˊ)
tropical fish

熱帶雨林(ㄖㄜˋ ㄉㄞˋ ㄩˇ ㄌㄧㄣˊ)
a tropical rain forest

熱度(ㄖㄜˋ ㄉㄨˋ)
①heat; temperature: 他的熱度降下去了嗎? Has his temperature come down? ②enthusiasm

熱湯(ㄖㄜˋ ㄊㄤ)
hot soup

熱騰騰(ㄖㄜˋ ㄊㄥ ㄊㄥ)
piping hot; steaming hot

熱天(ㄖㄜˋ ㄊㄧㄢ)
hot weather; dog days

熱那亞(ㄖㄜˋ ㄋㄚˋ ㄧㄚˋ)
Genoa, Italy

熱鬧(ㄖㄜˋ ·ㄋㄠ)
①bustling; thronged; populous; noisy; hustle and bustle: 這個市場很熱鬧。The market is bustling with activity. ②prosperous; flourishing; thriving ③lively; animated; cheerful; cheery; merry; gay

熱鬧兒(ㄖㄜˋ ·ㄋㄠㄦ)
merriment; merrymaking;

mirth; fun; hilarity
熱能(ㄖㄜˋ ㄋㄥˊ)
thermal energy
熱刺刺的(ㄖㄜˋ ㄘㄚˋ ㄘㄚˋ ·ㄉㄜ)
① impassioned; passionate ② burning hot; scorching: 太陽熱刺刺的。The sun is burning hot.
熱淚盈眶(ㄖㄜˋ ㄌㄟˋ ㄧㄥˊ ㄎㄨㄤ)
tearful; eyes moistening
熱浪(ㄖㄜˋ ㄌㄤˋ)
a heat wave; a hot wave
熱力(ㄖㄜˋ ㄌㄧˋ)
heat energy; thermal energy
熱力學(ㄖㄜˋ ㄌㄧˋ ㄒㄩㄝˊ)
thermodynamics
熱烈(ㄖㄜˋ ㄌㄧㄝˋ)
fervent; passionate; vehement; fiery; enthusiastic; rousing (welcomes): 大家對他的建議反應很熱烈。Everybody responded enthusiastically to his proposal.
熱戀(ㄖㄜˋ ㄌㄧㄢˋ)
to be passionately in love; to be head over heels in love
熱量(ㄖㄜˋ ㄌㄧㄤˋ)
the quantity of heat; calories
熱絡(ㄖㄜˋ ㄌㄨㄛˋ)
very intimate; on friendly terms: 他們是很熱絡的朋友。They are very intimate friends.
熱狗(ㄖㄜˋ ㄍㄡˇ)
a hot dog
熱鍋上的螞蟻(ㄖㄜˋ ㄍㄨㄛ ·ㄕㄤ ·ㄉㄜ ㄇㄚˇ ·ㄧ)
(literally) an ant on a hot pan—one in extreme anxiety; restless or fidgeting due to deep worry: 他們急得像熱鍋上的螞蟻。They were as restless as ants on a hot pan.
熱炕(ㄖㄜˋ ㄎㄤˋ)
a brick bed warmed by fire
熱狂(ㄖㄜˋ ㄎㄨㄤˊ)
wild with excitement; hot-headed; frantic; fanatical
熱河(ㄖㄜˋ ㄏㄜˊ)
Jehol Province
熱海(ㄖㄜˋ ㄏㄞˇ)
①Issiq Köl, or Issyk-Kul, a lake in Soviet Central Asia ② Atami, Japan
熱呼呼的(ㄖㄜˋ ㄏㄨ ㄏㄨ ·ㄉㄜ)
piping hot; warm: 他心裏感到熱呼呼的。He felt it heart-warming.
熱和(ㄖㄜˋ ·ㄏㄨㄛ)
① warm ② gentle; friendly; amiable ③ intimate; close
熱烘烘的(ㄖㄜˋ ㄏㄨㄥ ㄏㄨㄥ ·ㄉㄜ)
glowing with heat; red-hot; white-hot
熱氣(ㄖㄜˋ ㄑㄧˋ)
hot vapor; hot gas; hot air; heat
熱氣騰騰(ㄖㄜˋ ㄑㄧˋ ㄊㄥˊ ㄊㄥˊ)
piping hot; steaming hot
熱切(ㄖㄜˋ ㄑㄧㄝˋ)
fervent; earnest; sincerely; earnestly
熱情(ㄖㄜˋ ㄑㄧㄥˊ)
passion; ardor; fervor; passionate; fervent; ardent
熱血(ㄖㄜˋ ㄒㄧㄝˇ)
hot-blooded; fiery-spirited; fervent; zealous; righteous ardor
熱血沸騰(ㄖㄜˋ ㄒㄧㄝˇ ㄈㄟˋ ㄊㄥˊ)
to seethe with fervor; to have a boiling passion
熱血動物(ㄖㄜˋ ㄒㄧㄝˇ ㄉㄨㄥˋ ㄨˋ)
a warm-blooded animal
熱心(ㄖㄜˋ ㄒㄧㄣ) or 熱心腸兒(ㄖㄜˋ ㄒㄧㄣ ㄔㄤˊㄦ)
enthusiastic; eager; ardent; zealous; warm-hearted: 他熱心公益事業。He is enthusiastic in promoting public welfare.
熱著(ㄖㄜˋ ·ㄓㄠ)
to suffer heatstroke
熱戰(ㄖㄜˋ ㄓㄢˋ)
a hot war; a shooting war (as distinct from a cold war)
熱脹冷縮(ㄖㄜˋ ㄓㄤˋ ㄌㄥˇ ㄙㄨㄛ)
to expand when hot and to shrink when cold
熱中名利(ㄖㄜˋ ㄓㄨㄥ ㄇㄧㄥˊ ㄌㄧˋ)
to pursue fame and wealth with fervor
熱潮(ㄖㄜˋ ㄔㄠˊ)
① great mass fervor ② an upsurge
熱忱(ㄖㄜˋ ㄔㄣˊ)
enthusiasm; sincerity; earnest: 我們受到熱忱的歡迎。We are received with great enthusiasm.
熱腸(ㄖㄜˋ ㄔㄤˊ)
enthusiastic; eager; ardent; zealous
熱誠(ㄖㄜˋ ㄔㄥˊ)
eager devotion; earnestness; sincerity
熱身運動(ㄖㄜˋ ㄕㄣ ㄩㄣˋ ㄉㄨㄥˋ)
warm-up exercise
熱水瓶(ㄖㄜˋ ㄕㄨㄟˇ ㄆㄧㄥˊ)
a thermos (bottle); a thermos flask
熱水器(ㄖㄜˋ ㄕㄨㄟˇ ㄑㄧˋ)
a water heater
熱容量(ㄖㄜˋ ㄖㄨㄥˊ ㄌㄧㄤˋ)
heat capacity
熱竈(ㄖㄜˋ ㄗㄠˋ)
(figuratively) a man in power
熱愛(ㄖㄜˋ ㄞˋ)
to love passionately; to love fervently; passionate love; deep attachment
熱一句，冷一句(ㄖㄜˋ ㄧˊ ㄐㄩˋ, ㄌㄥˇ ㄧˊ ㄐㄩˋ)
to fling hot words and cold words alternately
熱飲(ㄖㄜˋ ㄧㄣˇ)
hot drinks
熱望(ㄖㄜˋ ㄨㄤˋ)
to hope earnestly; to wish ardently: 我們熱望他會成功。We hoped earnestly that he would succeed.

【熰】 3246
(㮛 ㄧㄡˇ yeou yǒu)
to burn piled firewood

【熨】 3247
1. ㄩㄣˋ yunn yùn
to iron (clothes or cloth)
熨平(ㄩㄣˋ ㄆㄧㄥˊ)
to iron (clothes or cloth)
熨斗(ㄩㄣˋ ㄉㄡˇ)
an iron (for pressing clothes)
熨衣服(ㄩㄣˋ ㄧ ·ㄈㄨ)
to iron clothes: 她一下午都在熨衣服。She's been ironing all afternoon.

【熨】 3247
2. ㄩˋ yuh yù
to settle (matters)
熨貼(ㄩˋ ㄊㄧㄝ)
(said of matters) settled, or taken care of

【熛】 3248
ㄅㄧㄠ biau biāo
1. to cultivate fields
2. valiant; vigorous

十二畫

【熾】 3249 ㄔˋ chyh chì

1. intense; vigorous; energetic
2. burning hot; flaming

熾茂(ㄔˋ ㄇㄠˋ)
luxuriant; teeming; lush

熾烈(ㄔˋ ㄌㄧㄝˋ)
blazing; burning vigorously: 爐火熾烈。The stove is burning fiercely.

熾盛(ㄔˋ ㄕㄥˋ)
thriving; flourishing

熾熱(ㄔˋ ㄖㄜˋ)
intense heat; intensely hot; blazing: 工人在熾熱的陽光下辛苦工作。The workers labored under a blazing sun.

【燈】 3250 ㄉㄥ deng dēng

1. a lamp; a lantern; a burner
2. Buddha dharma; the Buddhist doctrine
3. a valve; a tube

燈泡兒(ㄉㄥ ㄆㄠˋㄦ)
an electric bulb; a light bulb

燈謎(ㄉㄥ ㄇㄧˊ) or 燈虎(ㄉㄥ ㄏㄨˇ)
riddles written on lanterns (in public contests in which prizes are offered); lantern riddles

燈塔(ㄉㄥ ㄊㄚˇ)
a lighthouse

燈臺(ㄉㄥ ㄊㄞˊ)
① a lighthouse ② a lampstand

燈頭(ㄉㄥ ㄊㄡˊ)
a socket for an electric bulb

燈籠褲(ㄉㄥ ㄌㄨㄥˊ ㄎㄨˋ)
baggy pants worn by athletes; knickerbockers

燈籠(ㄉㄥ ·ㄌㄨㄥ)
a lantern

燈光(ㄉㄥ ㄍㄨㄤ)
lamplight; lights; illumination

燈花(ㄉㄥ ㄏㄨㄚ)
snuff (of wick)

燈火(ㄉㄥ ㄏㄨㄛˇ)
lamplight; lights; illumination

燈火管制(ㄉㄥ ㄏㄨㄛˇ ㄍㄨㄢˇ ㄓˋ)
a blackout or dim-out (against air raiders, etc.)

燈紅酒綠(ㄉㄥ ㄏㄨㄥˊ ㄐㄧㄡˇ ㄌㄩˋ)
(literally) red lanterns and green wine—a scene of debauchery

燈架(ㄉㄥ ㄐㄧㄚˋ)
a lamp holder

燈節(ㄉㄥ ㄐㄧㄝˊ)
the Lantern Festival (falling on the 15th day of the first lunar month)

燈下(ㄉㄥ ㄒㄧㄚˋ)
by lamplight—by night

燈心(ㄉㄥ ㄒㄧㄣ) or 燈蕊(ㄉㄥ ㄖㄨㄟˇ)
lampwick; candlewick; wick

燈心絨(ㄉㄥ ㄒㄧㄣ ㄖㄨㄥˊ)
corduroy

燈心草(ㄉㄥ ㄒㄧㄣ ㄘㄠˇ)
a rush

燈罩(ㄉㄥ ㄓㄠˋ)
a lampshade: 燈罩上灰塵積聚。Dust accumulated on the lampshade.

燈盞(ㄉㄥ ㄓㄢˇ)
oil lamps

燈燭輝煌(ㄉㄥ ㄓㄨˊ ㄏㄨㄟ ㄏㄨㄤˊ)
blazing with lights 或 The lights are glittering with splendor.

燈船(ㄉㄥ ㄔㄨㄢˊ)
a lightship

燈座(ㄉㄥ ㄗㄨㄛˋ)
a lampstand

燈蛾(ㄉㄥ ㄜˊ)
moths attracted by lamplight

燈蛾撲火(ㄉㄥ ㄜˊ ㄆㄨ ㄏㄨㄛˇ)
(literally) Moths dash into the flame.—an act of self-destruction; a suicidal act

燈油(ㄉㄥ ㄧㄡˊ)
lamp oil

【燃】 3251 ㄖㄢˊ ran rán

to burn; to ignite; to light

燃眉之急(ㄖㄢˊ ㄇㄟˊ ㄓ ㄐㄧˊ)
a matter as urgent as if the eyebrows had caught fire

燃放(ㄖㄢˊ ㄈㄤˋ)
to set off (fireworks, etc.)

燃燈(ㄖㄢˊ ㄉㄥ)
to light a lamp

燃料(ㄖㄢˊ ㄌㄧㄠˋ)
fuel: 汽油不再是廉價燃料。Gasoline is no longer a cheap fuel.

燃料庫(ㄖㄢˊ ㄌㄧㄠˋ ㄎㄨˋ)
a fuel depot; a fuel reservoir

燃料礦物(ㄖㄢˊ ㄌㄧㄠˋ ㄎㄨㄤˋ ㄨˋ)
mineral fuels

燃燭(ㄖㄢˊ ㄓㄨˊ)
to light a candle

燃燒(ㄖㄢˊ ㄕㄠ)
to burn; to be on fire; to be in flames; combustion: 乾柴容易燃燒。Dry wood burns easily.

燃燒彈(ㄖㄢˊ ㄕㄠ ㄉㄢˋ)
an incendiary shell or bomb

燃燒點(ㄖㄢˊ ㄕㄠ ㄉㄧㄢˇ)
the point of combustion

燃燒熱(ㄖㄢˊ ㄕㄠ ㄖㄜˋ)
heat of combustion

【燎】 3252 1. ㄌㄧㄠˋ liaw liào

1. to burn over a wider and wider area; to set fire to
2. to be brilliant

燎朗(ㄌㄧㄠˋ ㄌㄤˇ)
bright; luminous

燎獵(ㄌㄧㄠˋ ㄌㄧㄝˋ)
to hunt by setting fire to the bushes in the field

燎炬(ㄌㄧㄠˋ ㄐㄩˋ)
a torch

燎原(ㄌㄧㄠˋ ㄩㄢˊ)
① to set the prairie ablaze: 星星之火可以燎原。A little spark can set a blazing prairie fire. ② to get out of control like a prairie fire

【燎】 3252 2. ㄌㄧㄠˇ leau liǎo

to singe

燎毛(ㄌㄧㄠˇ ㄇㄠˊ)
to singe hair—a thing that can be done very easily

燎髮(ㄌㄧㄠˇ ㄈㄚˇ)
to singe hair—a thing that can be done very easily

【燉】 3253 1. ㄉㄨㄣˋ duenn dùn

1. to stew; to simmer
2. to warm

燉爛(ㄉㄨㄣˋ ㄌㄢˋ)
to stew until it is soft

燉雞(ㄉㄨㄣˋ ㄐㄧ)
① to stew chicken ② stewed chicken

燉熟(ㄉㄨㄣˋ ㄕㄡˊ)
to stew until it is done

燉肉(ㄉㄨㄣˋ ㄖㄡˋ)
① stewed meat ② to stew meat

燉藥(ㄉㄨㄣˋ ㄧㄠˋ)

to make concoction by simmering

【燉】 3253
2. ㄉㄨㄣ duen dūn
Tunhwang, Kansu 參看「燉煌」

燉煌 or 敦煌(ㄉㄨㄣ ㄏㄨㄤˊ)
Tunhwang, Kansu (甘肅), a site of many caves housing vast quantities of Buddhist arts and scriptures of ancient China

【燒】 3254
ㄕㄠ shau shāo
1. to burn
2. to roast; to stew
3. to boil; to heat: 水燒開了。The water is boiling.
4. to run a fever; to have a temperature
5. a fever: 他的燒退了。His fever is down.

燒杯(ㄕㄠ ㄅㄟ)
a beaker

燒餅(ㄕㄠ ㄅㄧㄥˇ)
a sesame seed cake

燒盤兒(ㄕㄠ ㄆㄚˊㄦ)
(figuratively) a face red with shame or embarrassment

燒瓶(ㄕㄠ ㄆㄧㄥˊ)
a flask

燒賣(ㄕㄠ ·ㄇㄞ)
a kind of steamed pie stuffed with meat

燒刀子(ㄕㄠ ㄉㄠ ·ㄗ)
a kind of strong alcoholic drink

燒頭香(ㄕㄠ ㄊㄡˊ ㄒㄧㄤ)
to burn the first incense stick of the day (at a temple on a festival)

燒鳥(ㄕㄠ ㄋㄧㄠˇ)
roast bird

燒冷竈(ㄕㄠ ㄌㄥˇ ㄗㄠˋ)
to engage in an unpopular activity or to cultivate the friendship of someone temporary out of luck in the hope of eventually profiting therefrom

燒煉(ㄕㄠ ㄌㄧㄢˋ)
Taoist technique of making the elixir of life; to practice alchemy

燒烤(ㄕㄠ ㄎㄠˇ)
to roast

燒化(ㄕㄠ ㄏㄨㄚˋ)
to reduce to ashes; to melt down by fire; to cremate

燒活(ㄕㄠ ㄏㄨㄛˊ)
paper structures burned in a funeral

燒火(ㄕㄠ ㄏㄨㄛˇ)
to build a fire; to make a fire

燒灰(ㄕㄠ ㄏㄨㄟ)
to reduce to ashes

燒燬(ㄕㄠ ㄏㄨㄟˇ)
to burn down; to destroy in fire

燒焦(ㄕㄠ ㄐㄧㄠ)
to scorch; to sear; to singe

燒酒(ㄕㄠ ㄐㄧㄡˇ)
a kind of strong alcoholic drink; white spirits

燒鹼 or 燒碱 (ㄕㄠ ㄐㄧㄢˇ)
caustic soda

燒錢化紙(ㄕㄠ ㄑㄧㄢˊ ㄏㄨㄚˋ ㄓˇ)
to perform the rite of burning imitation paper money for the dead

燒心(ㄕㄠ ㄒㄧㄣ)
fretful; uneasy; anxious; apprehensive

燒香(ㄕㄠ ㄒㄧㄤ)
to burn joss sticks in worship

燒指(ㄕㄠ ㄓˇ)
to burn fingers in the Buddhist rite of self-torture

燒紙引鬼(ㄕㄠ ㄓˇ ㄧㄣˇ ㄍㄨㄟˇ)
(literally) to invite ghosts unintentionally by burning imitation paper money—to invite trouble by showing civility or kindness

燒殺(ㄕㄠ ㄕㄚ)
burning and killing; atrocities committed by enemy troops, bandits, etc.

燒傷(ㄕㄠ ㄕㄤ)
burns: 他受到三級燒傷。He suffered from third-degree burns.

燒水(ㄕㄠ ㄕㄨㄟˇ)
to boil water; to heat water

燒死(ㄕㄠ ㄙˇ)or(ㄕㄠ ·ㄙ)
to burn to death

燒夷彈(ㄕㄠ ㄧˊ ㄉㄢˋ)
an incendiary shell or bomb

燒窰(ㄕㄠ ㄧㄠˊ)
to build fire in a pottery or porcelain kiln

燒尾(ㄕㄠ ㄨㄟˇ)
celebrating banquets held by the scholars of the Tang and Sung dynasties who had just passed the imperial civil service examination

【燐】 3255
(磷) ㄌㄧㄣˊ lin lín
phosphorus

燐肥(ㄌㄧㄣˊ ㄈㄟˊ)
phosphorus fertilizer; phosphorite

燐光(ㄌㄧㄣˊ ㄍㄨㄤ)
phosphorescence

燐火(ㄌㄧㄣˊ ㄏㄨㄛˇ)
a jack-o'-lantern; a will-o'-the-wisp; a phosphorescent light

燐灰石(ㄌㄧㄣˊ ㄏㄨㄟ ㄕˊ)
apatite

燐酸(ㄌㄧㄣˊ ㄙㄨㄢ)
phosphoric acid

燐酸鈣(ㄌㄧㄣˊ ㄙㄨㄢ ㄍㄞˋ)
calcium phosphate

【燔】 3256
ㄈㄢˊ farn fán
1. roast meat for offering
2. to burn; to roast

燔柴(ㄈㄢˊ ㄔㄞˊ)
a holocaust (an ancient rite of worshiping Heaven)

燔肉(ㄈㄢˊ ㄖㄡˋ)
roast meat for offering

【熹】 3257
(熺) ㄒㄧ shi xī
1. faint sunlight; dawn
2. giving out faint light

熹微(ㄒㄧ ㄨㄟˊ)
① faint light at dawn ② (said of morning sunlight) dim; pale

【燕】 3258
1. ㄧㄢˋ yann yàn
1. a swallow
2. comfort; ease
3. to feast; to enjoy

燕麥(ㄧㄢˋ ㄇㄞˋ)
oats

燕麥片(ㄧㄢˋ ㄇㄞˋ ㄆㄧㄢˋ)
oatmeal

燕婉之私(ㄧㄢˋ ㄋㄧˇ ㄓ ㄙ)
conjugal happiness

燕女(ㄧㄢˋ ㄋㄩˇ)
to delight in women

燕樂
①(ㄧㄢˋ ㄌㄜˋ) to entertain; to

please
②(ㄧㄢˋ ㄩㄝˋ) ⓐ music played in the banquet ⓑ popular music (as distinct from classical music)

燕侶(ㄧㄢˋ ㄌㄩˇ)
a married couple; husband and wife

燕侶鶯儔(ㄧㄢˋ ㄌㄩˇ ㄧㄥ ㄔㄡˊ)
a happily married couple; a devoted couple

燕賀(ㄧㄢˋ ㄏㄜˋ)
to offer congratulations on the completion of a new residence

燕好(ㄧㄢˋ ㄏㄠˇ)
(said of husband and wife) very fond of each other

燕頷虎頸(ㄧㄢˋ ㄏㄢˋ ㄏㄨˇ ㄐㄧㄥˇ)
a noble look; a dignified appearance

燕几(ㄧㄢˋ ㄐㄧˇ)
a stool much used at one's leisure

燕居(ㄧㄢˋ ㄐㄩ)
to live at leisure; to live at ease

燕雀兒(ㄧㄢˋ ㄑㄧㄠˇㄦ)
a finch

燕寢(ㄧㄢˋ ㄑㄧㄣˇ)
a place for rest

燕雀處堂(ㄧㄢˋ ㄑㄩㄝˋ ㄔㄨˇ ㄊㄤˊ)
to be oblivious of danger in the comfort of an easy life

燕雀安知鴻鵠志(ㄧㄢˋ ㄑㄩㄝˋ ㄢ ㄓ ㄏㄨㄥˊ ㄏㄨˊ ㄓˋ)
(literally) How can a swallow understand the mind of a swan?—How can a common fellow read the mind of a great man?

燕巢幕上(ㄧㄢˋ ㄔㄠˊ ㄇㄨˋ ㄕㄤˋ)
(literally) a swallow's nest built on a curtain—a very precarious situation

燕出(ㄧㄢˋ ㄔㄨ)
(said of a ruler) to go out in secrecy

燕瘦環肥(ㄧㄢˋ ㄕㄡˋ ㄏㄨㄢˊ ㄈㄟˊ)
(literally) Chao Fei-yen (趙飛燕) was skinny while Yang Yü-huan (楊玉環) was plump. (Both were imperial concubines of unusual beauty.)—beautiful women, each of whom is attractive in her own way

燕子(ㄧㄢˋ ·ㄗ)or 燕兒(ㄧㄚˋㄦ)
a swallow

燕子磯(ㄧㄢˋ ·ㄗ ㄐㄧ)
name of a hill to the north of Nanking overlooking the Yangtze River

燕菜(ㄧㄢˋ ㄘㄞˋ)
a rare delicacy prepared from swallows' nests found on seaside cliffs, etc., built of seaweed and a certain secretion from swallows

燕安(ㄧㄢˋ ㄢ)
comfort; ease; peace

燕爾新婚(ㄧㄢˋ ㄦˇ ㄒㄧㄣ ㄏㄨㄣ)
marital happiness; conjugal bliss

燕遊(ㄧㄢˋ ㄧㄡˊ)
to make pleasure trips

燕燕于飛(ㄧㄢˋ ㄧㄢˋ ㄩˊ ㄈㄟ)
The swallows go flying together.— (said of husband and wife) deeply attached to each other

燕飲(ㄧㄢˋ ㄧㄣˇ)
to feast: 他們坐在那裏, 燕飲終日。They sat there feasting all day long.

燕窩(ㄧㄢˋ ㄨㄛ)
swallows' nests found on seaside cliffs, etc., built of seaweed and a certain secretion by swallows, used as an ingredient for a highly valued Chinese dish

燕尾服(ㄧㄢˋ ㄨㄟˇ ㄈㄨˊ)
a swallow-tailed coat; a swallowtail; a tailcoat; a full-dress coat; tails

燕婉(ㄧㄢˋ ㄨㄢˇ)
friendly; genial

燕語(呢喃)(ㄧㄢˋ ㄩˇ (ㄋㄧˊ ㄋㄢˊ))
the soft chirping of swallows

【燕】 3258
2. ㄧㄢ ian yān

a state in what is Hopeh (河北) today during the Epoch of Warring States

燕京(ㄧㄢ ㄐㄧㄥ)
ancient name of Peking

燕京大學(ㄧㄢ ㄐㄧㄥ ㄉㄚˋ ㄒㄩㄝˊ)
Yenching University, Peking

燕趙(ㄧㄢ ㄓㄠˋ)
the state of Yen and the state of Chao, now used in reference to northern China

燕山(ㄧㄢ ㄕㄢ)
a mountain range in Hopeh

燕說(ㄧㄢ ㄕㄨㄛ)
distorted remarks; slanted views; twisted interpretations

燕然山(ㄧㄢ ㄖㄢˊ ㄕㄢ)
ancient name of what is today's Hangai Mountain (杭愛山) in Outer Mongolia

燕雲十六州(ㄧㄢ ㄩㄣˊ ㄕˊ ㄌㄧㄡˋ ㄓㄡ)
the 16 provinces roughly corresponding to what is today's Hopeh (河北), northern Shensi (陝西) and Chahar (察哈爾) that were ceded to the Kitans in the 10th century A.D. by Shih Ching-tang(石敬塘), the first ruler of the Later Tsin Dynasty, as a price for their assistance in obtaining his throne

【燙】 3259
ㄊㄤˋ tanq tàng

1. to scald; to burn
2. to heat; to warm
3. very hot: 這湯眞燙。The soup is boiling hot.
4. to iron

燙麪(ㄊㄤˋ ㄇㄧㄢˋ)
dough kneaded with hot water; to knead dough with hot water

燙髮(ㄊㄤˋ ㄈㄚˇ)
to have a permanent wave; to have a permanent

燙酒(ㄊㄤˋ ㄐㄧㄡˇ)
to heat wine or liquor in hot water

燙金(ㄊㄤˋ ㄐㄧㄣ)
gilding; bronzing

燙手(ㄊㄤˋ ㄕㄡˇ)
① to scald one's hand ② difficult to handle or manage

燙傷(ㄊㄤˋ ㄕㄤ)
① a burn; a scald ② to scald: 他被熱水燙傷。He was scalded with hot water.

燙衣服(ㄊㄤˋ ㄧ ·ㄈㄨ)
to iron clothes

燙一燙(ㄊㄤˋ ·ㄧ ㄊㄤˋ)
to have (something) heated, scalded, or ironed

【燊】 3260
ㄕㄣ shen shēn

vigorous

〔火部〕

〔火部〕

【燋】 3261 1. ㄐㄧㄠ jiau jiāo
1. a torch
2. same as 焦 — to scorch; to scald

【燋】 3261 2. (憔) ㄑㄧㄠˊ chyan qiáo
haggard; worn; emaciated

【燜】 3262 ㄇㄣˋ menn mèn (又讀 ㄇㄣ mhen mēn)
to cook with mild heat in a closed vessel; to cook in a casserole
燜飯(ㄇㄣˋ ㄈㄢˋ)
to cook rice over a slow fire
燜肉(ㄇㄣˋ ㄖㄡˋ)
meat cooked in a casserole

【燁】 3263 ㄧㄝˋ yeh yè
blazing; splendid; glorious

十三畫

【營】 3264 ㄧㄥˊ yng yíng
1. military barracks; a camp: 集中營 a concentration camp
2. a battalion: 騎兵營 a cavalry battalion
3. to manage; to administer; to handle; to operate; to run
營販(ㄧㄥˊ ㄈㄢˋ)
to manage sale business
營房(ㄧㄥˊ ㄈㄤˊ)
barracks
營地(ㄧㄥˊ ㄉㄧˋ)
a campsite; a camping ground
營田(ㄧㄥˊ ㄊㄧㄢˊ)
① to engage in farming ② to employ refugees or vagrants to cultivate public land
營利(ㄧㄥˊ ㄌㄧˋ)
to engage in making profit
營火(ㄧㄥˊ ㄏㄨㄛˇ)
a campfire—an outdoor fire in a camp for warmth or cooking
營火會(ㄧㄥˊ ㄏㄨㄛˇ ㄏㄨㄟˋ)
a campfire —a social gathering of soldiers, scouts, etc.
營妓(ㄧㄥˊ ㄐㄧˋ)
publicly provided prostitutes at military barracks; a camp follower
營救(ㄧㄥˊ ㄐㄧㄡˋ)
to rescue or deliver
營建(ㄧㄥˊ ㄐㄧㄢˋ)
to manage or handle the construction of; to construct
營求(ㄧㄥˊ ㄑㄧㄡˊ)
to seek
營寨(ㄧㄥˊ ㄓㄞˋ)
barracks; a military post
營長(ㄧㄥˊ ㄓㄤˇ)
a battalion commander
營帳(ㄧㄥˊ ㄓㄤˋ)
tents used as military barracks
營繕(ㄧㄥˊ ㄕㄢˋ)
civil engineering activities
營生(ㄧㄥˊ ㄕㄥ)
to make a living: 他靠賣水果營生。He earns a living as a fruiterer.
營造(ㄧㄥˊ ㄗㄠˋ)
to construct; to build: 建築者職司營造。A builder is one who builds.
營造尺(ㄧㄥˊ ㄗㄠˋ ㄔˇ)
the standard foot adopted by the Public Works Ministry during the Ming and Ching dynasties
營造廠(ㄧㄥˊ ㄗㄠˋ ㄔㄤˇ)
a construction firm; a building contractor; a contractor
營造商(ㄧㄥˊ ㄗㄠˋ ㄕㄤ)
a building contractor; a contractor
營葬(ㄧㄥˊ ㄗㄤˋ)
to manage a funeral
營私(ㄧㄥˊ ㄙ)
to seek personal gain (especially through a public post)
營私舞弊(ㄧㄥˊ ㄙ ㄨˇ ㄅㄧˋ)
to seek personal gain illicitly while holding a public post; to practice graft
營業(ㄧㄥˊ ㄧㄝˋ)
to engage in business; business operation
營業開支(ㄧㄥˊ ㄧㄝˋ ㄎㄞ ㄓ)
management and general expenses
營業執照(ㄧㄥˊ ㄧㄝˋ ㄓˊ ㄓㄠˋ)
a business license
營業時間(ㄧㄥˊ ㄧㄝˋ ㄕˊ ㄐㄧㄢ)
business hours: 營業時間是上午八時到下午六時。Business hours, 8 a.m. to 6 p.m.
營業收入(ㄧㄥˊ ㄧㄝˋ ㄕㄡ ㄖㄨˋ)
operating revenue
營業稅(ㄧㄥˊ ㄧㄝˋ ㄕㄨㄟˋ)
business tax
營業額(ㄧㄥˊ ㄧㄝˋ ㄜˊ)
the volume of business
營養(ㄧㄥˊ ㄧㄤˇ)
nutrition; nourishment: 均衡的食物使你的身體獲得營養。A balanced diet provides nutrition for your body.
營養不良(ㄧㄥˊ ㄧㄤˇ ㄅㄨˋ ㄌㄧㄤˊ)
malnutrition; undernourishment: 不適當的食物會引起營養不良。Improper food can cause malnutrition.
營養品(ㄧㄥˊ ㄧㄤˇ ㄆㄧㄣˇ)
nutriment
營養價值(ㄧㄥˊ ㄧㄤˇ ㄐㄧㄚˋ ㄓˊ)
nutritive value
營養學(ㄧㄥˊ ㄧㄤˇ ㄒㄩㄝˊ)
nutriology
營養素(ㄧㄥˊ ㄧㄤˇ ㄙㄨˋ)
nutrients (a collective term for protein, carbonhydrates, fat, vitamins, and minerals)
營務(ㄧㄥˊ ㄨˋ)
military matters

【燧】 3265 ㄙㄨㄟˋ suey suì
1. a flint
2. a beacon
燧石(ㄙㄨㄟˋ ㄕˊ)
flint
燧人氏(ㄙㄨㄟˋ ㄖㄣˊ ㄕˋ)
a legendary ruler said to be the first to discover fire

【燠】 3266 1. ㄩˋ yuh yù
warm

【燠】 3266 2. ㄠˋ aw ào
very hot; sweltering
燠熱(ㄠˋ ㄖㄜˋ)
very hot: 天氣這麼燠熱，我什麼事也不想做。It's so hot that I do not want to do anything.

【燠】 3266 3. ㄧㄡ iou yōu
as in 燠休— to comfort or to soothe (the distressed or afflicted)

【燦】 3267 ㄘㄢˋ tsann càn
bright; brilliant; resplendent

燦爛(ㄘㄢˋ ㄌㄢˋ)
resplendent; brilliant; glorious: 金剛鑽閃耀著燦爛的光輝。The diamond sparkles with brilliant light.
燦然(ㄘㄢˋ ㄖㄢˊ)
brilliantly; brightly; gloriously

【燬】 3268 ㄏㄨㄟˇ hoei huǐ
1. fire; a blaze
2. to destroy by fire; to burn away; to burn down: 這幢房子燒燬了。The house was burnt down.

【燥】 3269 ㄗㄠˋ tzaw zào
1. arid; dry; parched: 天氣發燥。The weather is dry.
2. impatient; restless
燥烈(ㄗㄠˋ ㄌㄧㄝˋ)
(said of food or drug) burning
燥渴(ㄗㄠˋ ㄎㄜˇ)
very thirsty
燥灼(ㄗㄠˋ ㄓㄨㄛˊ)
very uneasy; very anxious
燥濕(ㄗㄠˋ ㄕ)
dryness and wetness
燥熱(ㄗㄠˋ ㄖㄜˋ)
dry and hot: 這些時天氣很燥熱。The weather has been very dry and hot.

【燴】 3270 ㄏㄨㄟˋ huey huì
1. to put (a variety of materials) together and cook; to braise
2. to serve (noodles, rice, etc.) with a topping of meat, vegetables, etc., in gravy

【燭】 3271 ㄓㄨˊ jwu zhú
1. a candle
2. to illuminate; to shine upon: 火光燭天。Leaping flames lit up the sky.
燭臺(ㄓㄨˊ ㄊㄞˊ)
a candlestick; a candlestand
燭奴(ㄓㄨˊ ㄋㄨˊ)
a large wooden candlestand carved in the shape of a boy
燭淚(ㄓㄨˊ ㄌㄟˋ)
the guttering of a candle
燭光(ㄓㄨˊ ㄍㄨㄤ)
①(physics) candle power: 這是六十燭光的燈泡。This is a 60-watt bulb. ② candlelight
燭花(ㄓㄨˊ ㄏㄨㄚ)
snuff: 她在剪燭花。She is trimming off the snuff.
燭架(ㄓㄨˊ ㄐㄧㄚˋ)
a candlestick; a candlestand
燭心 or 燭芯(ㄓㄨˊ ㄒㄧㄣ)
candlewick

【燮】 3272 ㄒㄧㄝˋ shieh xiè
to blend; to harmonize; harmonious
燮理(ㄒㄧㄝˋ ㄌㄧˇ)
to harmonize; to adapt; to adjust; well-regulated
燮和(ㄒㄧㄝˋ ㄏㄜˊ)
to harmonize; living in harmony
燮友(ㄒㄧㄝˋ ㄧㄡˇ)
gentle; good-natured

十四畫

【燹】 3273 ㄒㄧㄢˇ shean xiǎn
1. fires set off by troops or shells
2. outdoor fire

【燾】 3274 ㄊㄠˊ taur táo (又讀 ㄉㄠˋ daw dào)
1. to illuminate extensively
2. to cover like a canopy
燾育(ㄊㄠˊ ㄩˋ)
(said of Heaven) to nurse all the things on earth

【燼】 3275 ㄐㄧㄣˋ jinn jìn
1. embers; ashes; cinders
2. victims of disasters

【燿】 3276 ㄧㄠˋ yaw yào
same as 耀—to shine brilliantly

十五畫

【爆】 3277 ㄅㄠˋ baw bào
1. to explode; to burst; to crack; to pop
2. to quick-boil; to quick-fry
爆破(ㄅㄠˋ ㄆㄛˋ)
to demolish by explosives; demolition
爆米花(ㄅㄠˋ ㄇㄧˇ ㄏㄨㄚ)
popcorn
爆發(ㄅㄠˋ ㄈㄚ)
① to explode; to blow up ② to break out; to erupt; to flare up: 抗日戰爭在一九三七年爆發。The war of Resistance against Japan broke out in 1937.
爆肚兒(ㄅㄠˋ ㄉㄨˇㄦ)
cooked tripe of sheep (regarded as a delicacy in North China)
爆裂(ㄅㄠˋ ㄌㄧㄝˋ)
to burst; to erupt; to pop open; to crack
爆性(ㄅㄠˋ ㄒㄧㄥˋ)
quick-tempered; hot-tempered
爆炸(ㄅㄠˋ ㄓㄚˋ)
to explode; to blow up; explosion; blast
爆炸力(ㄅㄠˋ ㄓㄚˋ ㄌㄧˋ)
explosive force; the impact of explosion
爆炸物(ㄅㄠˋ ㄓㄚˋ ㄨˋ)
an explosive
爆仗(ㄅㄠˋ ㄓㄤˋ)
firecrackers
爆竹(ㄅㄠˋ ㄓㄨˊ)
firecrackers: 孩子們在燃放爆竹。The children are letting off firecrackers.

【爍】 3278 ㄕㄨㄛˋ shuoh shuò
1. to glitter; to glisten; to sparkle
2. to melt: 衆口爍金。People's gossip is enough to melt metals.—People's gossip is enough to destroy anybody.
爍亮(ㄕㄨㄛˋ ㄌㄧㄤˋ)
glittering; glistening; sparkling
爍爍(ㄕㄨㄛˋ ㄕㄨㄛˋ)
glittering; glistening; sparkling

【爇】 3279 ㄖㄨㄛˋ ruoh ruò (又讀 ㄖㄜˋ reh rè)
to burn

十六畫

【爐】 3280 ㄌㄨˊ lu lú
a stove; an oven; a furnace; a fireplace; a hearth
爐邊(ㄌㄨˊ ㄅㄧㄢ)
the fireside; a hearth
爐邊談話(ㄌㄨˊ ㄅㄧㄢ ㄊㄢˊ ㄏㄨㄚˋ)
a fireside chat

爐餅(ㄌㄨˊ ㄅㄧㄥˇ)
a kind of baked cake
爐門兒(ㄌㄨˊ ㄇㄜˊㄦ)
the draft and ash hole of a stove
爐臺兒(ㄌㄨˊ ㄊㄞˊㄦ)
a mantel
爐條(ㄌㄨˊ ㄊㄧㄠˊ)
the grill of a stove or oven
爐坑(ㄌㄨˊ ㄎㄥ)
space for collecting ashes in a stove
爐火純青(ㄌㄨˊ ㄏㄨㄛˇ ㄔㄨㄣˊ ㄑㄧㄥ)
(literally) The stove fire for concocting the elixir of life begins to give a pure glow. — The skill is mature. 或 the consummation of skill or learning
爐灰(ㄌㄨˊ ㄏㄨㄟ)
ashes from a stove
爐子(ㄌㄨˊ ·ㄗ)
a stove; a fireplace; a furnace; a kiln
爐竈(ㄌㄨˊ ㄗㄠˋ)
① a cooking stove; a cooking range ② (figuratively) a start; an enterprise: 你計畫另起爐竈嗎? Do you plan to make a fresh start?
爐鴨(ㄌㄨˊ ㄧㄚ)
a roast duck
爐冶(ㄌㄨˊ ㄧㄝˇ)
metallurgical works

十七畫

【爛】 3281 ㄌㄢˋ lann làn
1. overripe; rotten; to rot; to fester: 傷口爛了。The wound is festering.
2. cooked soft; well cooked: 肉煮爛了。The meat is boiled soft.
3. bright; brilliant
4. to scald; to burn; to scorch
5. worn-out: 鞋子穿爛了。The shoes are worn-out.
6. dissolute; messy

爛漫(ㄌㄢˋ ㄇㄢˋ)
① brilliant; resplendent: 山花爛漫。The bright mountain flowers are in full bloom. ② dissipated; debauched ③ fast asleep ④ naive; simple-minded: 她是個天眞爛漫的小女孩。She is a naive (or an innocent) little girl.
爛得很(ㄌㄢˋ ·ㄉㄜ ㄏㄣˇ)
lousy
爛攤子(ㄌㄢˋ ㄊㄢ ·ㄗ)
a shambles
爛泥(ㄌㄢˋ ㄋㄧˊ)
soft mud; mire
爛爛(ㄌㄢˋ ㄌㄢˋ)
bright; brilliant
爛好人(ㄌㄢˋ ㄏㄠˇ ㄖㄣˊ)
one who cannot say no to requests for help or favor; one who is ever ready to help others indiscriminately; a goody-goody: 他眞是個爛好人。He is such a goody-goody fellow.
爛糊(ㄌㄢˋ ·ㄏㄨ)
(said of food) very soft, well cooked, or overripe
爛貨(ㄌㄢˋ ㄏㄨㄛˋ)
① (abusive language) a fast woman; a woman of easy virtue ② worthless goods; goods of poor quality
爛紙(ㄌㄢˋ ㄓˇ)
wastepaper
爛賬(ㄌㄢˋ ㄓㄤˋ)
uncollectable debts
爛熟(ㄌㄢˋ ㄕㄡˊ)
① very well cooked; very ripe ② thoroughly familiar: 她的台詞背得爛熟。She learns her lines thoroughly.
爛然(ㄌㄢˋ ㄖㄢˊ)
bright; brilliant
爛醉(ㄌㄢˋ ㄗㄨㄟˋ)
dead drunk
爛醉如泥(ㄌㄢˋ ㄗㄨㄟˋ ㄖㄨˊ ㄋㄧˊ)
dead drunk; drunk as a lord
爛羊頭(ㄌㄢˋ ㄧㄤˊ ㄊㄡˊ)
(literally) a rotten sheep head—official titles that are wantonly conferred upon unworthy persons

十八畫

【爝】 3282 ㄐㄩㄝˊ jyue jué
a torch
爝火(ㄐㄩㄝˊ ㄏㄨㄛˇ)
torch fire

二十五畫

【爨】 3283 ㄘㄨㄢˋ tsuann cuàn
1. to cook
2. a cooking stove
爨婢(ㄘㄨㄢˋ ㄅㄧˋ)
a kitchenmaid
爨婦(ㄘㄨㄢˋ ㄈㄨˋ)
a female cook
爨室(ㄘㄨㄢˋ ㄕˋ)
a kitchen

爪 部
ㄓㄠˇ jao zhǎo

【爪】 3284 1. ㄓㄠˇ jao zhǎo
1. a nail
2. a claw; a talon
爪士(ㄓㄠˇ ㄕˋ)
retainers; lackeys
爪牙(ㄓㄠˇ ㄧㄚˊ)
nails and teeth — retainers; lackeys; cat's-paws
爪牙吏(ㄓㄠˇ ㄧㄚˊ ㄌㄧˋ)
officials serving as tools of a tyrannical ruler
爪牙官(ㄓㄠˇ ㄧㄚˊ ㄍㄨㄢ)
lackeys of a ruthless ruler
爪牙鷹犬(ㄓㄠˇ ㄧㄚˊ ㄧㄥ ㄑㄩㄢˇ)
lackeys and hired ruffians
爪印(ㄓㄠˇ ㄧㄣˋ)
a nail mark; a trace; a print
爪哇(ㄓㄠˇ ㄨㄚ)
Java, island of Indonesia

【爪】 3284 2. ㄓㄨㄚˇ joa zhuǎ
claw
爪子(ㄓㄨㄚˇ ·ㄗ)
a claw; a paw; a talon

四畫

【爬】 3285 ㄆㄚˊ par pá
1. to creep; to crawl
2. to climb; to clamber
3. to scratch
4. to lie face downwards
爬不動(ㄆㄚˊ ·ㄅㄨ ㄉㄨㄥˋ)
unable to crawl or climb
爬不起來(ㄆㄚˊ ·ㄅㄨ ㄑㄧˇ ㄌㄞˊ)
unable to get up (from a lying position or a bed)

爬飯(ㄆㄚˊ ㄈㄢˋ)
to rake rice into the mouth with chopsticks

爬得高跌得重(ㄆㄚˊ ˙ㄉㄜ ㄍㄠ ㄉㄧㄝ ˙ㄉㄜ ㄓㄨㄥˋ)
The higher one climbs, the harder one falls.

爬剔(ㄆㄚˊ ㄊㄧ)
to exploit; to squeeze

爬羅剔抉(ㄆㄚˊ ㄌㄨㄛˊ ㄊㄧ ㄐㄩㄝˊ)
to dig up and rake up everything—to exploit thoroughly

爬高枝兒(ㄆㄚˊ ㄍㄠ ㄓㄜㄦ)
to be a hanger-on of glory; to jump on the bandwagon of the powerful; to cling to the wealthy and influential

爬櫛(ㄆㄚˊ ㄐㄧㄝˊ)
to comb; to straighten out; to put in order

爬起來(ㄆㄚˊ ㄑㄧˇ ㄌㄞˊ)
to get up

爬牆(ㄆㄚˊ ㄑㄧㄤˊ)
to climb a fence; to scale a wall

爬行(ㄆㄚˊ ㄒㄧㄥˊ)
① to crawl; to creep ② a crawl

爬行運動(ㄆㄚˊ ㄒㄧㄥˊ ㄩㄣˋ ㄉㄨㄥˋ)
creeping movement

爬出來(ㄆㄚˊ ㄔㄨ ˙ㄌㄞ)
to climb out: 小孩從車子裏爬出來。The child climbed out of the car.

爬蟲(ㄆㄚˊ ㄔㄨㄥˊ)
a reptile

爬蟲類(ㄆㄚˊ ㄔㄨㄥˊ ㄌㄟˋ)
Reptilia

爬山(ㄆㄚˊ ㄕㄢ)
to climb mountains

爬山虎(ㄆㄚˊ ㄕㄢ ㄏㄨˇ)
(botany) Virginia creeper

爬山者(ㄆㄚˊ ㄕㄢ ㄓㄜˇ)
an alpinist; a mountaineer: 他是老經驗的爬山者。He is an experienced mountaineer.

爬山鼠(ㄆㄚˊ ㄕㄢ ㄕㄨˇ)
a field mouse

爬山運動(ㄆㄚˊ ㄕㄢ ㄩㄣˋ ㄉㄨㄥˋ)
mountain climbing; mountaineering; alpinism

爬上(ㄆㄚˊ ˙ㄕㄤ)
to climb up: 我看見他爬上一棵樹。I saw him climbing up a tree.

爬梳(ㄆㄚˊ ㄕㄨ)
to comb; to straighten out; to tidy up

爬搔(ㄆㄚˊ ㄙㄠ)
to scratch

【爭】 3286
ㄓㄥ jeng zhēng

1. to contend; to struggle; to strive
2. to fight; to dispute; to argue; to quarrel: 他們在爭什麼? What are they arguing about?
3. short of; to lack; to be deficient in
4. same as 怎—how; why

爭霸(ㄓㄥ ㄅㄚˋ)
to contend (or struggle) for hegemony; to scramble (or strive) for supremacy

爭霸戰(ㄓㄥ ㄅㄚˋ ㄓㄢˋ)
a struggle for power; a power struggle; a fight for hegemony

爭辯(ㄓㄥ ㄅㄧㄢˋ)
to argue; to debate; to dispute

爭面子(ㄓㄥ ㄇㄧㄢˋ ˙ㄗ)
to try to win or excel for the sake of face

爭鳴(ㄓㄥ ㄇㄧㄥˊ)
to contend

爭名奪利(ㄓㄥ ㄇㄧㄥˊ ㄉㄨㄛˊ ㄌㄧˋ)
to struggle for fame and wealth

爭風吃醋(ㄓㄥ ㄈㄥ ㄔ ㄘㄨˋ)
to quarrel from jealousy; to fight for the affection of a man or woman

爭得(ㄓㄥ ㄉㄜˊ)
① to win ② How can it be?

爭鬥 or 爭鬭(ㄓㄥ ㄉㄡˋ)
to struggle; to contend; to conflict

爭奪(ㄓㄥ ㄉㄨㄛˊ)
to struggle for; to contend for; to scramble for; to fight for; to vie with somebody for something

爭奪戰(ㄓㄥ ㄉㄨㄛˊ ㄓㄢˋ)
a battle over a city, strategic point, etc.

爭端(ㄓㄥ ㄉㄨㄢ)
the cause of dispute, quarrel, or fight

爭論(ㄓㄥ ㄌㄨㄣˋ)
to argue; to dispute; debate; dispute

爭光(ㄓㄥ ㄍㄨㄤ)
to win glory

爭功(ㄓㄥ ㄍㄨㄥ)
to contend for credit

爭衡(ㄓㄥ ㄏㄥˊ)
to vie for superiority; to scramble for advantage

爭競(ㄓㄥ ㄐㄧㄥˋ)
to compete; to vie

爭氣(ㄓㄥ ㄑㄧˋ)
don't let down; to strive to excel; to try to win credit for

爭強(ㄓㄥ ㄑㄧㄤˊ)
to struggle for supremacy

爭強鬥勝(ㄓㄥ ㄑㄧㄤˊ ㄉㄡˋ ㄕㄥˋ)
to desire to excel over others; to fight for the leading role

爭取(ㄓㄥ ㄑㄩˇ)
to try to get; to win over; to strive for; to compete for

爭取時間(ㄓㄥ ㄑㄩˇ ㄕˊ ㄐㄧㄢ)
① to endeavor to avoid waste of time; to act quickly ② to stall for time

爭權奪利(ㄓㄥ ㄑㄩㄢˊ ㄉㄨㄛˊ ㄌㄧˋ)
to fight for selfish gains; to scramble for personal gains

爭席(ㄓㄥ ㄒㄧˊ)
to contend for a seat

爭先恐後(ㄓㄥ ㄒㄧㄢ ㄎㄨㄥˇ ㄏㄡˋ)
anxious to be ahead of others; afraid to fall behind others

爭閒氣(ㄓㄥ ㄒㄧㄢˊ ㄑㄧˋ)
to argue or dispute over trifles

爭相羅致(ㄓㄥ ㄒㄧㄤ ㄌㄨㄛˊ ㄓˋ)
engaged in a frantic competition to secure employment of (talent); to compete for the service of (a capable person)

爭雄(ㄓㄥ ㄒㄩㄥˊ)
to struggle or contend for supremacy

爭執(ㄓㄥ ㄓˊ)or 爭持(ㄓㄥ ㄔˊ)
to contest; to argue or dispute obstinately; to wrangle; to refuse to give in; argument; wrangling dispute

爭執不下(ㄓㄥ ㄓˊ ㄅㄨˋ ㄒㄧㄚˋ)
Each sticks to his own stand.

爭吵(ㄓㄥ ㄔㄠˇ)

〔爪部〕

to quarrel; to wrangle; to altercate; to squabble

爭產(ㄓㄥ ㄔㄢˇ)
(especially said of brothers) to fight for inheritance

爭長競短(ㄓㄥ ㄔㄤˊ ㄐㄧㄥˋ ㄉㄨㄢˇ)
to squabble over trifles

爭城奪地(ㄓㄥ ㄔㄥˊ ㄉㄨㄛˊ ㄉㄧˋ)
to conquer cities and capture territories by force of arms

爭勝(ㄓㄥ ㄕㄥˋ)
to struggle or contend for the upper hand

爭嘴(ㄓㄥ ㄗㄨㄟˇ)
① to fight for food ② to argue in self-defense

爭訟(ㄓㄥ ㄙㄨㄥˋ)
to dispute through a lawsuit; litigation

爭議(ㄓㄥ ㄧˋ)
to engage in a controversy; to dispute; to argue

爭一口氣(ㄓㄥ ㄧˋ ㄎㄡˇ ㄑㄧˋ)
to strive for a vindication; to struggle for honor or success to prove one's worth

爭妍鬥艷(ㄓㄥ ㄧㄢˊ ㄉㄡˋ ㄧㄢˋ)
to contend in beauty and fascination

五畫

【爰】 3287
ㄩㄢˊ yuan yuán
thereupon; therefore; accordingly

爰歷(ㄩㄢˊ ㄌㄧˋ)
an ancient wordbook by Chao Kao (趙高) of the Chin (秦) Dynasty

爰於(ㄩㄢˊ ㄩˊ)
Accordingly, (I took such and such an action on a certain date.)

八畫

【爲】 3288
1.(為) ㄨㄟˊ wei wéi

1. to do; to act
2. to manage; to handle; to exercise; to administer; to govern
3. to serve as
4. to become
5. to be

爲盼(ㄨㄟˊ ㄆㄢˋ)
That is what I, or we, expect. (a conventional phrase often used to close a formal letter)

爲憑(ㄨㄟˊ ㄆㄧㄥˊ)or 爲據(ㄨㄟˊ ㄐㄩˋ)
to use as proof; to use as evidence: 以郵戳爲憑。The postmark will serve as a proof.

爲民前鋒(ㄨㄟˊ ㄇㄧㄣˊ ㄑㄧㄢˊ ㄈㄥ)
to be the vanguard of the people

爲法自斃(ㄨㄟˊ ㄈㄚˇ ㄗˋ ㄅㄧˋ)
to suffer from one's own schemes

爲非作歹(ㄨㄟˊ ㄈㄟ ㄗㄨㄛˋ ㄉㄞˇ)
to do evil; to perpetrate outrages

爲富不仁(ㄨㄟˊ ㄈㄨˋ ㄅㄨˋ ㄖㄣˊ)
wealthy but unkind; rich but immoral

爲禱(ㄨㄟˊ ㄉㄠˇ)
That is what I, or we, humbly pray for. (a conventional phrase frequently used to close a formal letter)

爲頭(ㄨㄟˊ ㄊㄡˊ)or 爲首(ㄨㄟˊ ㄕㄡˇ)
① to be the head or leader ② headed by; led by

爲難(ㄨㄟˊ ㄋㄢˊ)
① awkward; troubled; distressed; in difficulties or a dilemma: 他問了個很爲難的問題。He asked a very awkward question. ② to make things difficult (for another): 他似乎故意爲難我。It seems that he deliberately makes things difficult for me.

爲力(ㄨㄟˊ ㄌㄧˋ)
to endeavor; to make efforts; to strive

爲鬼爲蜮(ㄨㄟˊ ㄍㄨㄟˇ ㄨㄟˊ ㄩˋ)
to injure others in secret

爲荷(ㄨㄟˊ ㄏㄜˋ)or 爲感(ㄨㄟˊ ㄍㄢˇ)
I, or we, will highly appreciate your kindness. (a conventional phrase frequently used to close a formal letter of request)

爲患(ㄨㄟˊ ㄏㄨㄢˋ)or 爲害(ㄨㄟˊ ㄏㄞˋ)
to be a cause of trouble; to bring trouble

爲期(ㄨㄟˊ ㄑㄧˊ)
to serve as the date (for an occasion) or deadline: 展覽爲期一週。The exhibition is scheduled to last a week.

爲期不遠(ㄨㄟˊ ㄑㄧˊ ㄅㄨˋ ㄩㄢˇ)
in the near future; soon

爲限(ㄨㄟˊ ㄒㄧㄢˋ)
to serve as a limit; exclusively; not to exceed

爲幸(ㄨㄟˊ ㄒㄧㄥˋ)
It would be fortunate indeed. (a conventional phrase often used to close a formal letter of request)

爲學(ㄨㄟˊ ㄒㄩㄝˊ)
to engage in studies

爲止(ㄨㄟˊ ㄓˇ)
① until; till; up to: 他賭到把錢都輸光爲止。He gambled till he had lost all his money. ② no further: 我們的討論到此爲止。That's all for our discussion.

爲證(ㄨㄟˊ ㄓㄥˋ)
to serve as proof; to serve as evidence

爲政不在多言(ㄨㄟˊ ㄓㄥˋ ㄅㄨˋ ㄗㄞˋ ㄉㄨㄛ ㄧㄢˊ)
Acts speak louder than words in government administration. 或 True statesmanship does not lie in empty talks. 或 Mere talking does not give birth to efficient administration.

爲主(ㄨㄟˊ ㄓㄨˇ)
mainly; to be the most important; to be the chief or principal (element, component, etc.)

爲重(ㄨㄟˊ ㄓㄨㄥˋ)
to attach most importance to: 你必須以大局爲重。You must put the general interest first.

爲時過早(ㄨㄟˊ ㄕˊ ㄍㄨㄛˋ ㄗㄠˇ)
earlier than is expected; premature; too early; too soon: 現在下結論爲時過早。It's still too early to reach a conclusion.

爲壽(ㄨㄟˊ ㄕㄡˋ)
to offer congratulations on birthdays

爲山九仞，功虧一簣(ㄨㄟˊ ㄕㄢ ㄐㄧㄡˇ ㄖㄣˋ, ㄍㄨㄥ ㄎㄨㄟ ㄧˊ ㄎㄨㄟˋ)
(literally) The lack of one basketful of earth spoils the

entire effort to build a nine-*jen* mountain.—The whole plan is ruined by a last-minute mistake or negligence.

爲善(ㄨㄟˊ ㄕㄢˋ)
to do good

爲善最樂(ㄨㄟˊ ㄕㄢˋ ㄗㄨㄟˋ ㄌㄜˋ)
Doing good is the greatest source of happiness.

爲生(ㄨㄟˊ ㄕㄥ)
to make a living: 他以當店員爲生。He makes a living as a salesman.

爲數不多(ㄨㄟˊ ㄕㄨˋ ㄅㄨˋ ㄉㄨㄛ)
limited in number; not many: 我有幾個，但爲數不多。I have a few, but not many.

爲數不少(ㄨㄟˊ ㄕㄨˋ ㄅㄨˋ ㄕㄠˇ)
many; quite a number of: 考試不及格的學生爲數不少。Many a student fails to pass in the examination.

爲人(ㄨㄟˊ ㄖㄣˊ)
one's personality, temperament, or character; to behave; to conduct oneself: 他爲人高尚。He conducts himself nobly.

爲人師表(ㄨㄟˊ ㄖㄣˊ ㄕ ㄅㄧㄠˇ)
to be a model of virtue for others

爲人在世(ㄨㄟˊ ㄖㄣˊ ㄗㄞˋ ㄕˋ)
to live in this world

爲所欲爲(ㄨㄟˊ ㄙㄨㄛˇ ㄩˋ ㄨㄟˊ)
to have one's way; to do as one pleases; unscrupulous

爲惡(ㄨㄟˊ ㄜˋ)
to do evil

爲業(ㄨㄟˊ ㄧㄝˋ)
as a means of livelihood

爲要(ㄨㄟˊ ㄧㄠˋ)
It's very important that you do what I have told you. (a conventional phrase for closing a formal letter of injunction)

爲伍(ㄨㄟˊ ㄨˇ)
to associate or mix (with)

【爲】 3288
2.(為) ㄨㄟˋ wey wèi

for; for the good of; for the sake of

爲民喉舌(ㄨㄟˋ ㄇㄧㄣˊ ㄏㄡˊ ㄕㄜˊ)
to speak for the people

爲民請命(ㄨㄟˋ ㄇㄧㄣˊ ㄑㄧㄥˇ ㄇㄧㄥˋ)
to plead for the people; to appeal for the people

爲民除害(ㄨㄟˋ ㄇㄧㄣˊ ㄔㄨˊ ㄏㄞˋ)
to remove the evils from the people; to eliminate a public scourge; to destroy a public enemy

爲名爲利(ㄨㄟˋ ㄇㄧㄥˊ ㄨㄟˋ ㄌㄧˋ)
for fame and for wealth

爲的是(ㄨㄟˋ ˙ㄉㄜ ㄕˋ)
for the sake of; for the purpose of

爲了(ㄨㄟˋ ˙ㄌㄜ)
for; for the sake of: 爲了和平，我們必須有耐心。We must be patient for the sake of peace.

爲國捐軀(ㄨㄟˋ ㄍㄨㄛˊ ㄐㄩㄢ ㄑㄩ)
to sacrifice one's life for the fatherland

爲國爭光(ㄨㄟˋ ㄍㄨㄛˊ ㄓㄥ ㄍㄨㄤ)
to struggle for the glory of one's country

爲公(ㄨㄟˋ ㄍㄨㄥ)
for public good

爲何(ㄨㄟˋ ㄏㄜˊ)
What for? 或 Why? 或 for what reason: 你知道他爲何遲到嗎? Do you know why he was late?

爲虎傅翼(ㄨㄟˋ ㄏㄨˇ ㄈㄨˋ ㄧˋ) or 爲虎添翼(ㄨㄟˋ ㄏㄨˇ ㄊㄧㄢ ㄧˋ)
(literally) to give wings to a tiger—to help a villain do evil

爲虎作倀(ㄨㄟˋ ㄏㄨˇ ㄗㄨㄛˋ ㄔㄤ)
to help an evil person do evil; to make common cause with an evildoer

爲己(ㄨㄟˋ ㄐㄧˇ)
for personal interest

爲…起見(ㄨㄟˋ…ㄑㄧˇ ㄐㄧㄢˋ)
in order to...; for the purpose of...

爲小失大(ㄨㄟˋ ㄒㄧㄠˇ ㄕ ㄉㄚˋ)
to lose a pound in trying to save a penny

爲之動容(ㄨㄟˋ ㄓ ㄉㄨㄥˋ ㄖㄨㄥˊ)
to show interest in (something)

爲甚麼(ㄨㄟˋ ㄕㄜˊ ˙ㄇㄜ)
What for? 或 Why? 爲甚麼猶豫不決呢? Why hesitate?

爲人(ㄨㄟˋ ㄖㄣˊ)
for others' interest; for the sake of others

爲人說項(ㄨㄟˋ ㄖㄣˊ ㄕㄨㄛ ㄒㄧㄤˋ)
to say a good word for someone

爲人作伐(ㄨㄟˋ ㄖㄣˊ ㄗㄨㄛˋ ㄈㄚˊ)
to act as a matchmaker

爲人作嫁(ㄨㄟˋ ㄖㄣˊ ㄗㄨㄛˋ ㄐㄧㄚˋ)
to work for others without profiting oneself

爲此(ㄨㄟˋ ㄘˇ)
because of this; for this reason: 我們都爲此感動不已。We all were deeply moved by this.

爲私(ㄨㄟˋ ㄙ)
for one's personal interest

爲我(ㄨㄟˋ ㄨㄛˇ)
egoistic; selfish

十四畫

【爵】 3289
ㄐㄩㄝˊ jyue jué

1. a degree or a title of nobility; peerage; the rank or dignity of a peer
2. an ancient wine pitcher with three legs and a loop handle

爵弁(ㄐㄩㄝˊ ㄅㄧㄢˋ)
a kind of ceremonial cap in the Chou Dynasty

爵服(ㄐㄩㄝˊ ㄈㄨˊ)
the degree and costume of nobility

爵土(ㄐㄩㄝˊ ㄊㄨˇ)
land conferred along with a degree of nobility

爵祿(ㄐㄩㄝˊ ㄌㄨˋ)
the degree and emolument of nobility

爵高者憂深(ㄐㄩㄝˊ ㄍㄠ ㄓㄜˇ ㄧㄡ ㄕㄣ)
The higher one's position is, the greater one's care will be. 或 *noblesse oblige*

爵章(ㄐㄩㄝˊ ㄓㄤ)
badges of nobility conferred on noblemen in Mongolia, Tibet and Mohammedan districts after the birth of the Republic

爵主(ㄐㄩㄝˊ ㄓㄨˇ)
an heir apparent to a title of nobility

爵士(ㄐㄩㄝˊ ㄕˋ)
Sir (a title of nobility)

爵士音樂(ㄐㄩㄝˊ ㄕˋ ㄧㄣ ㄩㄝˋ)
jazz; jazz music

爵士樂隊(ㄐㄩㄝˊ ㄕˋ ㄩㄝˋ ㄉㄨㄟˋ)
a jazz band

爵位(ㄐㄩㄝˊ ㄨㄟˋ)

a degree of nobility

父部
ㄈㄨˋ fuh fù

【父】 3290
1. ㄈㄨˋ fuh fù

1. father: 有其父必有其子。Like father, like son.
2. a male relative of an elder generation: 伯父 uncle 祖父 grandfather
3. to do father's duties

父輩(ㄈㄨˋ ㄅㄟˋ)
the elder generation; the senior generation

父不父，子不子(ㄈㄨˋ ㄅㄨˋ ㄈㄨˋ, ㄗˇ ㄅㄨˋ ㄗˇ)
Fathers neglect their duties as fathers while sons neglect their duties as sons.

父命(ㄈㄨˋ ㄇㄧㄥˋ)
father's orders; father's commands: 父命不可違。Father's orders must be obeyed.

父母(ㄈㄨˋ ㄇㄨˇ)
parents; father and mother

父母國(ㄈㄨˋ ㄇㄨˇ ㄍㄨㄛˊ)
fatherland; mother country

父母官(ㄈㄨˋ ㄇㄨˇ ㄍㄨㄢ)
a local official; a magistrate

父母劬勞(ㄈㄨˋ ㄇㄨˇ ㄑㄩˊ ㄌㄠˊ)
the hardships of parents in bringing up children

父母之邦(ㄈㄨˋ ㄇㄨˇ ㄓ ㄅㄤ)
one's own country; one's native land

父父子子(ㄈㄨˋ ㄈㄨˋ ㄗˇ ㄗˇ)
Fathers do their duties as fathers and sons do their duties as sons.

父黨(ㄈㄨˋ ㄉㄤˇ)
one's kinsfolk on the paternal side

父臺(ㄈㄨˋ ㄊㄞˊ)
a polite way of addressing a local official in former times

父天母地(ㄈㄨˋ ㄊㄧㄢ ㄇㄨˇ ㄉㄧˋ)
the son of Heaven and Earth—the emperor

父老(ㄈㄨˋ ㄌㄠˇ)
elders

父親(ㄈㄨˋ ㄑㄧㄣ)
father: 他一直像父親一般待我。He has been like a father to me.

父親節(ㄈㄨˋ ㄑㄧㄣ ㄐㄧㄝˊ)
Father's Day (falling on August 8)

父權(ㄈㄨˋ ㄑㄩㄢˊ)
paternal power; patriarchate

父系制度(ㄈㄨˋ ㄒㄧˋ ㄓˋ ㄉㄨˋ)
patriarchy

父兄(ㄈㄨˋ ㄒㄩㄥ)
male seniors in a family; father and elder brothers

父執(ㄈㄨˋ ㄓˊ)
father's friends

父債子還(ㄈㄨˋ ㄓㄞˋ ㄗˇ ㄏㄨㄢˊ)
According to Chinese customs, the son is bound to pay his father's debts.

父事(ㄈㄨˋ ㄕˋ)
to attend upon someone as one attends upon one's own father

父子(ㄈㄨˋ ㄗˇ)
father and son

父子兵(ㄈㄨˋ ㄗˇ ㄅㄧㄥ)
troops bound together like father and son

父子相傳(ㄈㄨˋ ㄗˇ ㄒㄧㄤ ㄔㄨㄢˊ)
passed down through generations by fathers to sons

父作子述(ㄈㄨˋ ㄗㄨㄛˋ ㄗˇ ㄕㄨˋ)
What the father founded, the son developed.

父慈子孝(ㄈㄨˋ ㄘˊ ㄗˇ ㄒㄧㄠˋ)
The father is affectionate and the son is filial.

父嚴母慈(ㄈㄨˋ ㄧㄢˊ ㄇㄨˇ ㄘˊ)
The father is stern and the mother is gentle.

父蔭(ㄈㄨˋ ㄧㄣˋ)
father's influence and protection

父王(ㄈㄨˋ ㄨㄤˊ)
my imperial father

【父】 3290
2. ㄈㄨˇ fuu fǔ

a respectful term for an elderly man in ancient times: 漁父 a fisherman

四畫

【爸】 3291
ㄅㄚˋ bah bà

father

爸爸(ㄅㄚˋ ·ㄅㄚ)
father; papa

六畫

【爹】 3292
ㄉㄧㄝ die diē

father: 乾爹 an adoptive father

爹媽(ㄉㄧㄝ ㄇㄚ)
father and mother; parents

爹爹(ㄉㄧㄝ ·ㄉㄧㄝ)
father

爹娘 or 爹孃(ㄉㄧㄝ ㄋㄧㄤˊ)
father and mother; parents

九畫

【爺】 3293
ㄧㄝˊ ye yé

1. father
2. master; sir
3. god: 老天爺 God; Heaven

爺們(ㄧㄝˊ ·ㄇㄣ)
men; gentlemen

爺娘 or 爺孃(ㄧㄝˊ ㄋㄧㄤˊ)
father and mother; parents

爺兒們(ㄧㄝˊㄦ ·ㄇㄣ)
men and boys

爺兒倆(ㄧㄝˊㄦ ㄌㄧㄚˇ)
father and son; father and daughter

爺爺(ㄧㄝˊ ·ㄧㄝ)
① grandfather; grandpa ② sir

爻部
ㄧㄠˊ yau yáo

3294
【爻】 ㄧㄠˊ yau yáo
(讀音 ㄒㄧㄠˊ shyau xiáo)

single and divided lines in eight groups of three lines each as specified in the *Book of Changes*: 陽爻 *yang yao*—the long line(—) 陰爻 *yin yao*—two broken short lines(--)

爻象(ㄧㄠˊ ㄒㄧㄤˋ)
diagrams for divination

爻辭(ㄧㄠˊ ㄘˊ)
explanations of diagrams for divination

七畫

【爽】 3295 ㄕㄨㄤˇ shoang shuǎng

1. refreshing; bracing; crisp; agreeable; pleasant; brisk: 秋高氣爽 the clear and crisp autumn climate
2. to feel well: 他感到身體不爽。He does not feel well.
3. straightforward; frank; open-hearted: 他爲人豪爽。He is straightforward.
4. to fail; to miss; to lose
5. to be in error

爽法(ㄕㄨㄤˇ ㄈㄚˇ)
to break regulations; to disregard the law; to violate the law

爽德(ㄕㄨㄤˇ ㄉㄜˊ)
to lose virtue; to depart from virtue; to forfeit one's virtue

爽當(ㄕㄨㄤˇ ㄉㄤ)
brisk; agile

爽朗(ㄕㄨㄤˇ ㄌㄤˇ)
①(said of weather, etc.) refreshing: 我喜歡鄉間爽朗的天氣。I like the refreshing weather in the countryside. ② open-minded; straightforward

爽利(ㄕㄨㄤˇ ㄌㄧˋ)
agile; brisk and neat; speedy; alert: 他辦事爽利。He is brisk and neat in his work.

爽塏(ㄕㄨㄤˇ ㄎㄞˇ)
high and dry ground

爽口(ㄕㄨㄤˇ ㄎㄡˇ)
palatable; tasty

爽快(ㄕㄨㄤˇ ㄎㄨㄞˋ)
① straightforward; frank; open-hearted: 他對人很爽快。He is open-hearted with everybody. ② readily and briskly; with alacrity ③ comfortable; pleasant; refreshing

爽氣(ㄕㄨㄤˇ ㄑㄧˋ)
① refreshing air; a bracing atmosphere ② straightforward; open-hearted

爽心(ㄕㄨㄤˇ ㄒㄧㄣ)
gratified; satisfied; pleased; cheerful

爽心悅目(ㄕㄨㄤˇ ㄒㄧㄣ ㄩㄝˋ ㄇㄨˋ)
refreshing to the heart and pleasing to the eye

爽信(ㄕㄨㄤˇ ㄒㄧㄣˋ)
to fail to keep a promise: 不可爽信於人。One should not fail to keep one's promise.

爽性(ㄕㄨㄤˇ ·ㄒㄧㄥ)
might just as well: 我們爽性做完再休息。We might as well finish it before we have a rest.

爽直(ㄕㄨㄤˇ ㄓˊ)
outspoken; frank; straightforward; open-hearted: 他說話很爽直。He is very outspoken.

爽失(ㄕㄨㄤˇ ㄕ)
to fail to keep or honor (a pledge, etc.)

爽身粉(ㄕㄨㄤˇ ㄕㄣ ㄈㄣˇ)
talcum powder

爽神(ㄕㄨㄤˇ ㄕㄣˊ)
refreshing

爽然(ㄕㄨㄤˇ ㄖㄢˊ)
discouraged; disappointed; dejected

爽然若失(ㄕㄨㄤˇ ㄖㄢˊ ㄖㄨㄛˋ ㄕ)
dejected as if one had made a mistake

爽脆(ㄕㄨㄤˇ ㄘㄨㄟˋ)
brisk; keen and energetic

爽約(ㄕㄨㄤˇ ㄩㄝ)
to fail to keep a promise; to break an appointment

十畫

【爾】 3296 ㄦˇ eel ěr

1. you; thou
2. that; this; those; these; such; so: 果爾 if so
3. after adjectives: 率爾 hastily; thoughtless
4. only

爾等(ㄦˇ ㄉㄥˇ)
you all

爾來(ㄦˇ ㄌㄞˊ)
until now; up to the present

爾後(ㄦˇ ㄏㄡˋ)
thereafter; afterwards; subsequently

爾時(ㄦˇ ㄕˊ)
at that time; then

爾日(ㄦˇ ㄖˋ)
that day

爾汝(ㄦˇ ㄖㄨˇ)
to address each other intimately; on first name basis

爾汝交(ㄦˇ ㄖㄨˇ ㄐㄧㄠ)
intimate friendship

爾曹(ㄦˇ ㄘㄠˊ)
you all; you people

爾爾(ㄦˇ ㄦˇ)
so-so; not so outstanding: 生意不過爾爾。Business is only just so-so.

爾雅(ㄦˇ ㄧㄚˇ)
① an ancient book containing commentaries on classics, names, etc. ② graceful and correct

爾爲爾，我爲我(ㄦˇ ㄨㄟˊ ㄦˇ, ㄨㄛˇ ㄨㄟˊ ㄨㄛˇ)
(literally) You are you and I am I. —(figuratively) Let everybody mind his own business.

爿部
ㄑㄧㄤˊ chyang qiáng

四畫

【牀】 3297 (床) ㄔㄨㄤˊ chwang chuáng

1. a bed; a couch: 單人牀 a single bed 雙人牀 a double bed
2. the ground under a body of water: 河床 a riverbed

牀鋪(ㄔㄨㄤˊ ㄆㄨˋ)
a bed and bedding

牀單(ㄔㄨㄤˊ ㄉㄢ)
bed linen; a bedsheet; sheets

牀墊(ㄔㄨㄤˊ ㄉㄧㄢˋ)
a mattress

牀榻(ㄔㄨㄤˊ ㄊㄚˋ)
a bed; a couch

牀頭(ㄔㄨㄤˊ ㄊㄡˊ)
the head of a bed; bedside

牀頭金盡(ㄔㄨㄤˊ ㄊㄡˊ ㄐㄧㄣ ㄐㄧㄣˋ)
impoverished by frequent visits to whorehouses or by association with disreputable women

牀頭人(ㄔㄨㄤˊ ㄊㄡˊ ㄖㄣˊ)
one's wife

牀公牀婆(ㄔㄨㄤˊ ㄍㄨㄥ ㄔㄨㄤˊ ㄆㄛˊ)

the god and goddess of the bed

牀架(ㄔㄨㄤˊ ㄐㄧㄚˋ)
a bedstead

牀脚(ㄔㄨㄤˊ ㄐㄧㄠˇ)
the foot of the bed

牀罩(ㄔㄨㄤˊ ㄓㄠˋ)
a bedspread

牀帳子(ㄔㄨㄤˊ ㄓㄤˋ ·ㄗ)
a mosquito net 亦作「帳子」

牀蝨(ㄔㄨㄤˊ ㄕ)
bedbugs; a cimex

牀上(ㄔㄨㄤˊ ·ㄕㄤ)
on a bed or a couch: 他還在牀上睡覺。He is still in bed.

牀上安牀(ㄔㄨㄤˊ ㄕㄤˋ ㄢ ㄔㄨㄤˊ)
duplication; overlapping; to duplicate; to overlap

牀蓐(ㄔㄨㄤˊ ㄖㄨˋ)
bedding; bedclothes

牀褥子(ㄔㄨㄤˊ ㄖㄨˋ ·ㄗ)
a mattress

牀笫(ㄔㄨㄤˊ ㄗˇ)
privacy of the bed

牀笫之間(ㄔㄨㄤˊ ㄗˇ ㄓ ㄐㄧㄢ)
on the conjugal bed

牀笫之言(ㄔㄨㄤˊ ㄗˇ ㄓ ㄧㄢˊ)
private talks between husband and wife

牀沿(ㄔㄨㄤˊ ㄧㄢˊ)
edge of the bed

牀位(ㄔㄨㄤˊ ㄨㄟˋ)
berths or bunks (in a ship or on a train)

五畫

【牁】 3298
ㄍㄜ ge gē
a stake to which a boat may be moored

六畫

【牂】 3299
ㄗㄤ tzang zāng
a ewe

牂牁(ㄗㄤ ㄍㄜ)
①ancient name of Kweichow (貴州) and its vicinity today ② stakes to which boats are moored

牂雲(ㄗㄤ ㄩㄣˊ)
dog-shaped clouds

十三畫

【牆】 3300
(墻) ㄑㄧㄤˊ chyang qiáng
a wall; a fence: 隔牆有耳。Walls have ears.

牆壁(ㄑㄧㄤˊ ㄅㄧˋ)
a wall (of a building)

牆頭(ㄑㄧㄤˊ ㄊㄡˊ)
the top or crest of a fence or wall

牆頭草，風吹兩邊倒(ㄑㄧㄤˊ ㄊㄡˊ ㄘㄠˇ, ㄈㄥ ㄔㄨㄟ ㄌㄧㄤˇ ㄅㄧㄢ ㄉㄠˇ)
The grass on the top of a wall sways with every wind. —A person acts as the occasion dictates.

牆根(ㄑㄧㄤˊ ㄍㄣ)
the foot of a wall or fence; foundations of a wall

牆角(ㄑㄧㄤˊ ㄐㄧㄠˇ)
a corner between two walls: 他們躲在牆角裏。They hid in the corner between two walls.

牆脚(ㄑㄧㄤˊ ㄐㄧㄠˇ)
the foot of a wall

牆外漢(ㄑㄧㄤˊ ㄨㄞˋ ㄏㄢˋ)
an outsider; an amateur

牆宇(ㄑㄧㄤˊ ㄩˇ)
①dwelling; walled building ②capacity for tolerance

牆垣(ㄑㄧㄤˊ ㄩㄢˊ)
a wall; a fence: 有些古老的城市周圍有牆垣。Some old towns have walls right round them.

片部
ㄆㄧㄢˋ piann piàn

【片】 3301
1. ㄆㄧㄢˋ piann piàn
a piece; a slice; a fragment; a chip

片片(ㄆㄧㄢˋ ㄆㄧㄢˋ)
in pieces; in fragments

片麻岩(ㄆㄧㄢˋ ㄇㄚˊ ㄧㄢˊ)
(geology) gneiss

片面(ㄆㄧㄢˋ ㄇㄧㄢˋ)
① unilateral: 他們片面撕毀協議。They tore up the agreement unilaterally. ② unfair: 你不能片面地看問題。You should not take an unfair approach to problems.

片面之交(ㄆㄧㄢˋ ㄇㄧㄢˋ ㄓ ㄐㄧㄠ)
a casual acquaintance

片面之言(ㄆㄧㄢˋ ㄇㄧㄢˋ ㄓ ㄧㄢˊ) or 片面之詞(ㄆㄧㄢˋ ㄇㄧㄢˋ ㄓ ㄘˊ)
one-sided remarks

片名(ㄆㄧㄢˋ ㄇㄧㄥˊ)
title of a motion picture

片段(ㄆㄧㄢˋ ㄉㄨㄢˋ)
①passages or fragments of a writing; extracts ②parts; fragments: 生活的片段 a part of life

片頭(ㄆㄧㄢˋ ㄊㄡˊ)
titles (of a motion picture)

片刻(ㄆㄧㄢˋ ㄎㄜˋ)
a little while; a brief space of time; a moment; an instant: 請稍候片刻。Please wait for a little while.

片甲不留(ㄆㄧㄢˋ ㄐㄧㄚˇ ㄅㄨˋ ㄌㄧㄡˊ)
(literally) to have not even a fragment of armor remaining — ① to wipe out the enemy to a man ② to suffer a crushing defeat

片假名(ㄆㄧㄢˋ ㄐㄧㄚˇ ㄇㄧㄥˊ)
the square Japanese syllabary; katakana

片紙隻字(ㄆㄧㄢˋ ㄓˇ ㄓ ㄗˋ)
a brief piece of writing; a brief note or letter

片酬(ㄆㄧㄢˋ ㄔㄡˊ)
remuneration for a movie actor or actress for starring in a film

片長(ㄆㄧㄢˋ ㄔㄤˊ)
the length of a motion picture in terms of showing time

片時(ㄆㄧㄢˋ ㄕˊ)
a brief space of time; a short while: 我片時即回。I'll be back in a short while.

片晌(ㄆㄧㄢˋ ㄕㄤˇ)
a short space of time; a short while

片子(ㄆㄧㄢˋ ·ㄗ)
①a motion picture or a film ②a calling card

片租(ㄆㄧㄢˋ ㄗㄨ)
a film rent

片兒(ㄆㄧㄚˋ ㄦ)
①a thin flat piece ②a calling card; a visiting card 亦

作「名片」
片兒湯(ㄆㄧˋㄦ ㄊㄤ)
flat pieces of dough served with soup
片岩(ㄆㄧㄢˋ ㄧㄢˊ)
schistose rocks
片言(ㄆㄧㄢˋ ㄧㄢˊ)
a few words: 他能片言解紛。He can settle a dispute with just a few words.
片言折獄(ㄆㄧㄢˋ ㄧㄢˊ ㄓㄜˊ ㄩˋ)
A single word uttered by a wise man can decide a legal case.

【片】 3301
2. ㄆㄧㄢ pian piān
1. a photograph
2. a phonograph record

四畫

【版】 3302
ㄅㄢˇ baan bǎn
1. household registers
2. printing plate
3. edition: 平裝版 a paperback edition 精裝版 a hardback edition
4. supporting boards used in building walls

版版六十四(ㄅㄢˇ ㄅㄢˇ ㄌㄧㄡˋ ㄕˊ ㄙˋ)
very conservative; inflexible
版本(ㄅㄢˇ ㄅㄣˇ)
edition: 這是最新的版本。This is the newest edition.
版面(ㄅㄢˇ ㄇㄧㄢˋ)
① space of a whole page ② layout of a printed sheet
版圖(ㄅㄢˇ ㄊㄨˊ)
① household registers and maps; population and territory ② territory; dominion: 南沙群島是中國的版圖。The Spratly Islands are Chinese territory.
版畫(ㄅㄢˇ ㄏㄨㄚˋ)
a picture printed from an engraved or etched plate; a print
版籍(ㄅㄢˇ ㄐㄧˊ)
① books ② household registers; a census
版權(ㄅㄢˇ ㄑㄩㄢˊ)
copyright
版權法(ㄅㄢˇ ㄑㄩㄢˊ ㄈㄚˇ)
copyright law
版權所有(ㄅㄢˇ ㄑㄩㄢˊ ㄙㄨㄛˇ ㄧㄡˇ)
all rights reserved (as stated by the publisher in a book)
版築(ㄅㄢˇ ㄓㄨˊ)
① to build (walls with the aid of supporting boards) ② to build; to construct
版稅(ㄅㄢˇ ㄕㄨㄟˋ)
royalties (on books)

八畫

【牌】 3303
ㄆㄞˊ pair pái
1. a bulletin board
2. a tablet; a signboard; a plate: 門牌 a doorplate 招牌 a signboard
3. a card; a tag; a label
4. a trademark; a brand: 他喜歡買名牌貨。He likes to buy goods of a well-known brand.

牌榜(ㄆㄞˊ ㄅㄤˇ)
a bulletin board
牌匾(ㄆㄞˊ ㄅㄧㄢˇ)
a tablet; a signboard; a plaque
牌坊(ㄆㄞˊ ˙ㄈㄤ)
an honorific arch or portal
牌樓(ㄆㄞˊ ㄌㄡˊ)
a celebration arch; a ceremonial arch
牌號(ㄆㄞˊ ㄏㄠˋ)
a store name appearing on the signboard; a trademark; a brand
牌九(ㄆㄞˊ ㄐㄧㄡˇ)
Chinese dominoes
牌局(ㄆㄞˊ ㄐㄩˊ)
a gambling game
牌照(ㄆㄞˊ ㄓㄠˋ)
a license plate; a license
牌示(ㄆㄞˊ ㄕˋ)
a public notice; a bulletin
牌子(ㄆㄞˊ ˙ㄗ)
① a bulletin board ② a card; a tag; a label ③ a brand (of commodities): 這是牌子極好的咖啡。This is an excellent brand of coffee. ④ reputation ⑤ a signboard; a plate
牌子老(ㄆㄞˊ ˙ㄗ ㄌㄠˇ)
a brand or a trademark which has been in use for a long time (which means the merchandise concerned must be very good)
牌額(ㄆㄞˊ ㄜˊ)
a tablet (bearing inscriptions, written characters, etc.)
牌位(ㄆㄞˊ ㄨㄟˋ)
an ancestral tablet; a memorial tablet

九畫

【牒】 3304
ㄉㄧㄝˊ dye dié
1. official documents
2. certificates
3. records of a family pedigree

牒籍(ㄉㄧㄝˊ ㄐㄧˊ)
ancient books and records: 牒籍上有記載。It was recorded in the ancient books.
牒狀(ㄉㄧㄝˊ ㄓㄨㄤˋ)
documents pertaining to a lawsuit
牒文(ㄉㄧㄝˊ ㄨㄣˊ)
official dispatches

十畫

【牓】 3305
(榜) ㄅㄤˇ baang bǎng
1. a tablet; a plaque
2. a public notice

牓示(ㄅㄤˇ ㄕˋ)
to announce by putting up a notice
牓書(ㄅㄤˇ ㄕㄨ)
large characters on a tablet
牓子(ㄅㄤˇ ˙ㄗ)
folded paper listing one's biographic data or the reason for calling when he is about to be received by a superior or ruler

十一畫

【牖】 3306
ㄧㄡˇ yeou yǒu
1. a window
2. to guide; to educate; to enlighten

牖民(ㄧㄡˇ ㄇㄧㄣˊ)
to guide the people; to educate the people
牖里(ㄧㄡˇ ㄌㄧˇ)
the place where King Wen of the Chou Dynasty (周文王) was held prisoner by King Chou of the Shang Dynasty

(商紂)

十五畫

【牘】 3307 ㄉㄨˊ dwu dú
1. a wooden writing tablet
2. documents; archives; letters
3. a hollow pole used to strike the ground to mark the beat of music in ancient times

牘箋(ㄉㄨˊ ㄐㄧㄢ)
letters

牘尾(ㄉㄨˊ ㄨㄟˇ)
the closing part of a letter

牙部
ㄧㄚˊ ya yá

【牙】 3308 ㄧㄚˊ ya yá
1. teeth: 蛀牙 a decayed tooth
2. to bite
3. ivory articles
4. a broker

牙白口清(ㄧㄚˊ ㄅㄞˊ ㄎㄡˇ ㄑㄧㄥ)
able to speak articulately

牙買加(ㄧㄚˊ ㄇㄞˇ ㄐㄧㄚ)
Jamaica

牙粉(ㄧㄚˊ ㄈㄣˇ)
dentifrice; tooth powder

牙縫兒(ㄧㄚˊ ㄈㄥˋㄦ)
space between the teeth

牙疼(ㄧㄚˊ ㄊㄥˊ)or 牙痛(ㄧㄚˊ ㄊㄨㄥˋ)
toothache

牙帖(ㄧㄚˊ ㄊㄧㄝˇ)
a business license of a brokerage firm

牙膏(ㄧㄚˊ ㄍㄠ)
toothpaste

牙垢(ㄧㄚˊ ㄍㄡˋ)
tartar on the teeth

牙根(ㄧㄚˊ ㄍㄣ)
base of the teeth

牙關(ㄧㄚˊ ㄍㄨㄢ)
a mandibular joint

牙科(ㄧㄚˊ ㄎㄜ)
dentistry

牙科醫生(ㄧㄚˊ ㄎㄜ ㄧ ㄕㄥ)or 牙醫(ㄧㄚˊ ㄧ)
a dentist: 我明天跟牙醫有約。I have an appointment with the dentist tomorrow.

牙行(ㄧㄚˊ ㄏㄤˊ)
a commission agency of a broker; a brokerage firm

牙慧(ㄧㄚˊ ㄏㄨㄟˋ)
what others have said or written; a stale expression

牙祭(ㄧㄚˊ ㄐㄧˋ)
as in 打牙祭—to have a rare sumptuous meal; to have something special to eat

牙將(ㄧㄚˊ ㄐㄧㄤˋ)
a low-ranking military officer

牙籤(兒)(ㄧㄚˊ ㄑㄧㄢ (ㄦ))
a toothpick

牙線(ㄧㄚˊ ㄒㄧㄢˋ)
dental floss

牙周病(ㄧㄚˊ ㄓㄡ ㄅㄧㄥˋ)
periodontosis; rapidly advancing juvenile periodontitis

牙章(ㄧㄚˊ ㄓㄤ)
an ivory seal or chop

牙筯(ㄧㄚˊ ㄓㄨˋ)or 牙筷(ㄧㄚˊ ㄎㄨㄞˋ)
chopsticks made of ivory

牙齒(ㄧㄚˊ ㄔˇ)
a tooth or teeth: 我昨天拔了一顆牙齒。I had a tooth pulled out yesterday.

牙牀(ㄧㄚˊ ㄔㄨㄤˊ)
① teethridge; gum ② an ivory bedstead

牙刷(ㄧㄚˊ ㄕㄨㄚ)
a toothbrush: 你每餐之後都要用牙刷刷牙。Brush your teeth with a toothbrush after every meal.

牙人(ㄧㄚˊ ㄖㄣˊ)
a sales agent; a broker

牙磁(ㄧㄚˊ ㄘˊ)
enamel

牙牙學語(ㄧㄚˊ ㄧㄚˊ ㄒㄩㄝˊ ㄩˇ)
(said of an infant) to begin to babble, prattle, or lisp

牙音(ㄧㄚˊ ㄧㄣ)
gutturals or velars (in traditional Chinese phonology)

牙齦(ㄧㄚˊ ㄧㄣˊ)
gums

八畫

【掌】 3309 (撐) ㄔㄥ cheng chēng
to prop; to support

牛部
ㄋㄧㄡˊ niou niú

【牛】 3310 ㄋㄧㄡˊ niou niú
1. an ox; cattle; a cow; a bull: 水牛 a water buffalo 乳牛 a milk cow
2. a Chinese family name
3. (said of a person) stubborn; headstrong

牛排(ㄋㄧㄡˊ ㄆㄞˊ)
steak; beefsteak

牛皮(ㄋㄧㄡˊ ㄆㄧˊ)
① cowhide ② as in 吹牛皮—to talk big; to brag

牛脾氣(ㄋㄧㄡˊ ㄆㄧˊ ·ㄑㄧ)
stubbornness; obstinacy

牛皮紙(ㄋㄧㄡˊ ㄆㄧˊ ㄓˇ)
kraft paper; brown paper

牛馬(ㄋㄧㄡˊ ㄇㄚˇ)
① cattle and horses ② people who are being overworked like beasts of burden: 莫爲兒孫作牛馬。Do not slave for your children.

牛馬不如(ㄋㄧㄡˊ ㄇㄚˇ ㄅㄨˋ ㄖㄨˊ)
to be worked even harder than cattle and horses

牛馬生活(ㄋㄧㄡˊ ㄇㄚˇ ㄕㄥ ㄏㄨㄛˊ)
a life of drudgery

牛毛(ㄋㄧㄡˊ ㄇㄠˊ)
hairs of an ox—numerous: 他的問題多如牛毛。He has numerous problems.

牛毛雨(ㄋㄧㄡˊ ㄇㄠˊ ㄩˇ)or 牛毛細雨(ㄋㄧㄡˊ ㄇㄠˊ ㄒㄧˋ ㄩˇ)
fine drizzling rain

牛虻 or 牛蝱(ㄋㄧㄡˊ ㄇㄥˊ)
a gadfly

牛眠吉壤(ㄋㄧㄡˊ ㄇㄧㄢˊ ㄐㄧˊ ㄖㄤˇ)
an ideal burial ground (in the superstitious sense)

牛糞(ㄋㄧㄡˊ ㄈㄣˋ)
cow dung

牛蜂(ㄋㄧㄡˊ ㄈㄥ)
a hornet

牛刀(ㄋㄧㄡˊ ㄉㄠ)
a butcher knife for cattle

牛刀小試(ㄋㄧㄡˊ ㄉㄠ ㄒㄧㄠˇ ㄕˋ)
①(literally) to use a large butcher knife to cut a little

thing—to try to kill a fly with a long spear ② the first small display of a master hand

牛痘(ㄋㄧㄡˊ ㄉㄡˋ)
cowpox; vaccinia

牛鼎烹雞(ㄋㄧㄡˊ ㄉㄧㄥˇ ㄆㄥ ㄐㄧ)
(literally) to boil a fowl in the great cauldron for cooking an ox—to kill a fly with a long spear; to employ a steam hammer to crack a nut

牛犢(子)(ㄋㄧㄡˊ ㄉㄨˊ (·ㄗ))
a calf

牛肚子(ㄋㄧㄡˊ ㄉㄨˇ ·ㄗ)
the stomach of an ox

牛頓(ㄋㄧㄡˊ ㄉㄨㄣˋ)
Sir Isaac Newton (1642-1727), English philosopher and mathematician

牛頓運動定律(ㄋㄧㄡˊ ㄉㄨㄣˋ ㄩㄣˋ ㄉㄨㄥˋ ㄉㄧㄥˋ ㄌㄩˋ)
Newton's law of motion

牛頭不對馬嘴(ㄋㄧㄡˊ ㄊㄡˊ ㄅㄨˋ ㄉㄨㄟˋ ㄇㄚˇ ㄗㄨㄟˇ)
(literally) The head of an ox does not match the mouth of a horse.—irrelevant; not to the point; unconnected; incongruous

牛頭馬面(ㄋㄧㄡˊ ㄊㄡˊ ㄇㄚˇ ㄇㄧㄢˋ)
ox-headed and horse-faced demons in Hades

牛奶(ㄋㄧㄡˊ ㄋㄞˇ)
(cow's) milk

牛奶糖(ㄋㄧㄡˊ ㄋㄞˇ ㄊㄤˊ)
butter candy; toffee; taffy

牛奶公司(ㄋㄧㄡˊ ㄋㄞˇ ㄍㄨㄥ ㄙ)
a dairy company

牛腩(ㄋㄧㄡˊ ㄋㄢˇ)
sirloin; tenderloin

牛酪(ㄋㄧㄡˊ ㄌㄠˋ)
butter and cheese; yogurt

牛郎(ㄋㄧㄡˊ ㄌㄤˊ)
a cowboy: 他在電影裏飾演牛郎。He acted as a cowboy in the film.

牛郎織女(ㄋㄧㄡˊ ㄌㄤˊ ㄓ ㄋㄩˇ)
the Cowherd and the Weaving Maid who, according to Chinese folklore, meet once a year on the seventh day of the seventh moon over a bridge across the Milky Way formed by sympathetic magpies 亦作「牽牛織女」

牛骨(ㄋㄧㄡˊ ㄍㄨˇ)
bones of an ox

牛鬼蛇神(ㄋㄧㄡˊ ㄍㄨㄟˇ ㄕㄜˊ ㄕㄣˊ)
(literally) demons with the head of an ox and spirits with the body of a serpent—① absurdities ② forces of evil

牛後(ㄋㄧㄡˊ ㄏㄡˋ)
(literally) buttocks of an ox—people content to follow the great: 寧爲雞口，毋爲牛後。Better to reign in hell than serve in heaven.

牛黃(ㄋㄧㄡˊ ㄏㄨㄤˊ)
bezoar taken from an ox (used as a medicine)

牛驥同皁(ㄋㄧㄡˊ ㄐㄧˋ ㄊㄨㄥˊ ㄗㄠˋ)
(literally) a cow and a thoroughbred horse sharing the same trough—to make no distinction between the wise and the foolish

牛角(ㄋㄧㄡˊ ㄐㄧㄠˇ)
horns of cattle

牛角尖(ㄋㄧㄡˊ ㄐㄧㄠˇ ㄐㄧㄢ)
the tip of a horn—an insignificant problem: 鑽牛角尖 to get oneself into a dead-end alley through sheer stubbornness

牛津(ㄋㄧㄡˊ ㄐㄧㄣ)
Oxford, a city in England

牛津大學(ㄋㄧㄡˊ ㄐㄧㄣ ㄉㄚˋ ㄒㄩㄝˊ)
Oxford University

牛筋(ㄋㄧㄡˊ ㄐㄧㄣ)
a cattle tendon

牛勁(ㄋㄧㄡˊ ㄐㄧㄣˋ)or 牛勁兒(ㄋㄧㄡˊ ㄐㄧㄜˋㄦ)
① very stubborn; stubbornness; headstrong: 這小伙子有股牛勁。The lad is headstrong. ② great strength

牛氣(ㄋㄧㄡˊ ·ㄑㄧ)
self-conceit; pride; haughtiness

牛群(ㄋㄧㄡˊ ㄑㄩㄣˊ)
a herd of cattle

牛心(ㄋㄧㄡˊ ㄒㄧㄣ)
① the heart of an ox ② stubbornness

牛性(ㄋㄧㄡˊ ㄒㄧㄥˋ)
stubbornness

牛車(ㄋㄧㄡˊ ㄔㄜ)
an oxcart; an ox-drawn cart

牛舌(ㄋㄧㄡˊ ㄕㄜˊ)
the tongue of an ox

牛舍(ㄋㄧㄡˊ ㄕㄜˋ)or 牛棚(ㄋㄧㄡˊ ㄆㄥˊ) or 牛欄(ㄋㄧㄡˊ ㄌㄢˊ)
a cattle pen, shed, or yard

牛山濯濯(ㄋㄧㄡˊ ㄕㄢ ㄓㄨㄛˊ ㄓㄨㄛˊ)
(literally) a treeless mountain—a bald head

牛肉(ㄋㄧㄡˊ ㄖㄡˋ)
beef

牛肉麪(ㄋㄧㄡˊ ㄖㄡˋ ㄇㄧㄢˋ)
noodles served with stewed beef

牛肉店(ㄋㄧㄡˊ ㄖㄡˋ ㄉㄧㄢˋ)
a beef store

牛肉湯(ㄋㄧㄡˊ ㄖㄡˋ ㄊㄤ)
beef soup

牛肉乾(ㄋㄧㄡˊ ㄖㄡˋ ㄍㄢ)
dried roast beef

牛肉汁(ㄋㄧㄡˊ ㄖㄡˋ ㄓ)
beef extract

牛乳(ㄋㄧㄡˊ ㄖㄨˇ)
cow milk

牛仔(ㄋㄧㄡˊ ㄗㄞˇ)
a cowboy

牛仔褲(ㄋㄧㄡˊ ㄗㄞˇ ㄎㄨˋ)
blue jeans; jeans: 男孩子穿着牛仔褲或卡其褲。The boys wore jeans or khakis.

牛溲馬勃(ㄋㄧㄡˊ ㄙㄡ ㄇㄚˇ ㄅㄛˊ)
trivial but useful things

牛耳(ㄋㄧㄡˊ ㄦˇ)
the ears of a bull: 執牛耳 to hold the bull's ear—to play the leading role; to be in a dominant position

牛衣對泣(ㄋㄧㄡˊ ㄧ ㄉㄨㄟˋ ㄑㄧˋ)
(literally) to weep together in coarse clothes—(said of a married couple) to live in extreme poverty

牛疫(ㄋㄧㄡˊ ㄧˋ)or 牛瘟(ㄋㄧㄡˊ ㄨㄣ)
rinderpest; a cattle plague

牛腰(ㄋㄧㄡˊ ㄧㄠ)
kidneys of an ox

牛油(ㄋㄧㄡˊ ㄧㄡˊ)
① butter ② tallow ③ butter oil

牛油麪包(ㄋㄧㄡˊ ㄧㄡˊ ㄇㄧㄢˋ ㄅㄠ)
butter and bread

牛飲(ㄋㄧㄡˊ ㄧㄣˇ)
to drink heavily; to drink like a fish

牛蛙(ㄋㄧㄡˊ ㄨㄚ)
a bullfrog

牛尾湯(ㄋㄧㄡˊ ㄨㄟˇ ㄊㄤ)
an oxtail broth

(牛部)

二畫

【牝】3311 ㄆㄧㄣˋ pinn pìn
female of an animal
牝馬(ㄆㄧㄣˋ ㄇㄚˇ)
a mare
牝貓(ㄆㄧㄣˋ ㄇㄠ)
a tabby (as distinct from a tomcat)
牝牡驪黃(ㄆㄧㄣˋ ㄇㄨˇ ㄌㄧˊ ㄏㄨㄤˊ)
One's real worth is more valuable than his looks. 或 to judge not by the superficial aspects of things
牝犢(ㄆㄧㄣˋ ㄉㄨˊ)
a female calf; a young cow; a heifer
牝兔(ㄆㄧㄣˋ ㄊㄨˋ)
a female rabbit; a doe
牝鹿(ㄆㄧㄣˋ ㄌㄨˋ)
a female deer; a doe; a roe, or a roe deer
牝雞(ㄆㄧㄣˋ ㄐㄧ)
a hen: 我們養牝雞生蛋。We raised hens to get eggs.
牝雞司晨(ㄆㄧㄣˋ ㄐㄧ ㄙ ㄔㄣˊ)
(literally) the hen crowing at dawn—a woman usurping man's power 或 The gray mare is the better horse.
牝豬(ㄆㄧㄣˋ ㄓㄨ)
a she-pig; a sow
牝朝(ㄆㄧㄣˋ ㄔㄠˊ)
the Female Era (the reign of Empress Wu from 690 to 705 A.D.)
牝鵝(ㄆㄧㄣˋ ㄜˊ)
a goose (as opposed to a gander)
牝羊(ㄆㄧㄣˋ ㄧㄤˊ)
a ewe

【牟】3312 ㄇㄡˊ mou móu
1. to seek
2. to bellow (or low)
3. a Chinese family name
牟尼(ㄇㄡˊ ㄋㄧˊ)
(Buddhism) *muni*; peace
牟利(ㄇㄡˊ ㄌㄧˋ)
to seek profits
牟取(ㄇㄡˊ ㄑㄩˇ)
to seek; to obtain: 有些商人牟取暴利。Some merchants seek exorbitant profits.

三畫

【牡】3313 ㄇㄨˇ muu mǔ (又讀 ㄇㄡˇ moou mǒu)
a male animal
牡馬(ㄇㄨˇ ㄇㄚˇ)
a stallion
牡丹(ㄇㄨˇ ㄉㄢ)
a peony
牡丹江(ㄇㄨˇ ㄉㄢ ㄐㄧㄤ)
the Mutankiang (a river in Kirin Province(吉林省))
牡牛(ㄇㄨˇ ㄋㄧㄡˊ)
a bull; an ox
牡蠣(ㄇㄨˇ ㄌㄧˋ)
an oyster
牡鹿(ㄇㄨˇ ㄌㄨˋ)
a stag
牡齒(ㄇㄨˇ ㄔˇ)
lower teeth

【牠】3314 ㄊㄚ ta tā (讀音 ㄊㄨㄛ tuo tuō) (又讀 ㄊㄜ te tē)
it

【牢】3315 ㄌㄠˊ lau láo
1. a pen; a stable; a cage
2. a jail; a prison
3. secure; stable; firm; fast
4. worried; concerned
5. sacrifice
牢不可破(ㄌㄠˊ ㄅㄨˋ ㄎㄜˇ ㄆㄛˋ)
impregnable; invulnerable; very secure; unbreakable; unshakable
牢牢(ㄌㄠˊ ㄌㄠˊ)
firmly; fast: 我把小船牢牢繫在木柱上。I made the boat fast to the post.
牢籠(ㄌㄠˊ ㄌㄨㄥˊ)
① to cover; to include ② to captivate; to ensnare; to win over by schemes ③ a pen; a cage; a prison
牢籠計(ㄌㄠˊ ㄌㄨㄥˊ ㄐㄧˋ)
a scheme to entrap; a trick
牢固(ㄌㄠˊ ㄍㄨˋ)
secure; firm
牢靠(ㄌㄠˊ ㄎㄠˋ)
① firm; stable; secure; sturdy ② reliable; trustworthy; dependable
牢記(ㄌㄠˊ ㄐㄧˋ)
to keep firmly in mind
牢檻(ㄌㄠˊ ㄐㄧㄢˋ)
a jail; a prison
牢什子(ㄌㄠˊ ㄕˊ ·ㄗ)
a nuisance; an eyesore
牢卒(ㄌㄠˊ ㄗㄨˊ)
a jailer
牢騷(ㄌㄠˊ ㄙㄠ)
discontent; grumbling; complaint: 不要發牢騷。Don't grumble!
牢穩(ㄌㄠˊ ㄨㄣˇ)
secure; stable; firm: 這門牢穩嗎? Is the door secure?
牢獄(ㄌㄠˊ ㄩˋ)
a jail; a prison

四畫

【牧】3316 ㄇㄨˋ muh mù
1. to pasture; to shepherd
2. pasture
3. to govern
4. a magistrate; a public administrator
牧馬(ㄇㄨˋ ㄇㄚˇ)
to pasture horses
牧馬中原(ㄇㄨˋ ㄇㄚˇ ㄓㄨㄥ ㄩㄢˊ)
to become master of the country
牧民(ㄇㄨˋ ㄇㄧㄣˊ)
to shepherd the people; to govern the people
牧夫(ㄇㄨˋ ㄈㄨ)
officials in charge of civil administration
牧笛(ㄇㄨˋ ㄉㄧˊ)
a shepherd's pipe
牧地(ㄇㄨˋ ㄉㄧˋ)
a pasture; a grazing area
牧童(ㄇㄨˋ ㄊㄨㄥˊ)
a cowboy; a shepherd boy
牧牛(ㄇㄨˋ ㄋㄧㄡˊ)
to pasture cattle; to herd cows: 他在草地上牧牛。He pastured cattle.
牧歌(ㄇㄨˋ ㄍㄜ)
a pastoral song; a shepherd song
牧者(ㄇㄨˋ ㄓㄜˇ)
a shepherd
牧豬奴(ㄇㄨˋ ㄓㄨ ㄋㄨˊ)
① a swineherd ② a gambler
牧場(ㄇㄨˋ ㄔㄤˇ)

a pasture; a ranch; a stock farm

牧畜(ㄇㄨˋ ㄔㄨˋ)
pasturage; stock farming

牧師(ㄇㄨˋ ㄕ)
a pastor; a preacher; a clergyman

牧守(ㄇㄨˋ ㄕㄡˇ)
a provincial magistrate during the Han Dynasty

牧草(ㄇㄨˋ ㄘㄠˇ)
herbage; pasture: 這些地方有好的牧草。These lands afford good pasture.

牧羊(ㄇㄨˋ ㄧㄤˊ)
to pasture sheep; to tend sheep

牧羊犬(ㄇㄨˋ ㄧㄤˊ ㄑㄩㄢˇ)
a shepherd dog; a collie

牧羊人(ㄇㄨˋ ㄧㄤˊ ㄖㄣˊ)
a shepherd: 牧羊人帶羊下山。The shepherd guided his sheep down the hill.

【物】 3317 ㄨˋ wuh wù

1. a thing; matter; a being
2. content; substance: 他的演說言之無物。There was no substance in his speech.
3. the physical world; nature
4. other people

物薄情厚(ㄨˋ ㄅㄛˊ ㄑㄧㄥˊ ㄏㄡˋ)
The gift is of small value but the thoughtfulness behind it is immense.

物品(ㄨˋ ㄆㄧㄣˇ)
things; articles

物莫如新，友莫如故(ㄨˋ ㄇㄛˋ ㄖㄨˊ ㄒㄧㄣ, ㄧㄡˇ ㄇㄛˋ ㄖㄨˊ ㄍㄨˋ)
Things are good when new, but friendship is good when old.

物美價廉(ㄨˋ ㄇㄟˇ ㄐㄧㄚˋ ㄌㄧㄢˊ)
(said of merchandise) excellent quality and reasonable price

物腐蟲生(ㄨˋ ㄈㄨˇ ㄔㄨㄥˊ ㄕㄥ)
(literally) Worms breed only when things have already started rotting. —Ruin befalls only those who have weaknesses. 或 A nation falls only when it has already been on the decline.

物阜民康(ㄨˋ ㄈㄨˋ ㄇㄧㄣˊ ㄎㄤ)
Goods are plentiful and the people are happy.

物體(ㄨˋ ㄊㄧˇ)
(physics) a body; a substance; an object

物累(ㄨˋ ㄌㄟˇ)
the burden of material things

物離鄉貴(ㄨˋ ㄌㄧˊ ㄒㄧㄤ ㄍㄨㄟˋ)
A commodity commands a higher price where it is not grown or manufactured.

物理(ㄨˋ ㄌㄧˇ)
① the law of nature ② physics

物理變化(ㄨˋ ㄌㄧˇ ㄅㄧㄢˋ ㄏㄨㄚˋ)
physical changes

物理學(ㄨˋ ㄌㄧˇ ㄒㄩㄝˊ)
physics

物理學家(ㄨˋ ㄌㄧˇ ㄒㄩㄝˊ ㄐㄧㄚ)
a physicist

物力(ㄨˋ ㄌㄧˋ)
material means or resources: 我們要節約財力物力。We must use financial and material resources sparingly.

物料(ㄨˋ ㄌㄧㄠˋ)
materials; stuff

物論(ㄨˋ ㄌㄨㄣˋ)
public opinion

物各有主(ㄨˋ ㄍㄜˋ ㄧㄡˇ ㄓㄨˇ)
Everything has its owner.

物故(ㄨˋ ㄍㄨˋ)
dead; deceased; to pass away; to die: 這位小說家已物故多年。The novelist has been dead for several years.

物歸原主(ㄨˋ ㄍㄨㄟ ㄩㄢˊ ㄓㄨˇ)
Things return to their proper owners.

物華(ㄨˋ ㄏㄨㄚˊ)
① the essence of things ② beautiful scenes

物華天寶(ㄨˋ ㄏㄨㄚˊ ㄊㄧㄢ ㄅㄠˇ)
Good products from the earth are nature's treasures.

物化(ㄨˋ ㄏㄨㄚˋ)
① changes of matters in nature ② death

物換星移(ㄨˋ ㄏㄨㄢˋ ㄒㄧㄥ ㄧˊ)
(literally) Things change and stars move.—vicissitudes of human affairs with the elapse of time

物極則反(ㄨˋ ㄐㄧˊ ㄗㄜˊ ㄈㄢˇ) or 物極必反(ㄨˋ ㄐㄧˊ ㄅㄧˋ ㄈㄢˇ)
As soon as a thing reaches its extremity, it reverses its course.

物價(ㄨˋ ㄐㄧㄚˋ)
commodity prices: 物價平落。Prices drop to normal.

物價波動(ㄨˋ ㄐㄧㄚˋ ㄅㄛ ㄉㄨㄥˋ)
price fluctuations

物價指數(ㄨˋ ㄐㄧㄚˋ ㄓˇ ㄕㄨˋ)
a price index

物價穩定(ㄨˋ ㄐㄧㄚˋ ㄨㄣˇ ㄉㄧㄥˋ)
stability of commodity prices; price stability

物件(ㄨˋ ㄐㄧㄢˋ)
articles; things

物盡其用(ㄨˋ ㄐㄧㄣˋ ㄑㄧˊ ㄩㄥˋ)
The utility of things should be exhausted.

物鏡(ㄨˋ ㄐㄧㄥˋ)
the objective (of a microscope)

物競天擇(ㄨˋ ㄐㄧㄥˋ ㄊㄧㄢ ㄗㄜˊ)
the struggle for survival among things by the law of natural selection

物象(ㄨˋ ㄒㄧㄤˋ)
① physical phenomena; natural phenomena ② the shape and appearance of things

物質(ㄨˋ ㄓˊ)
(physics) matter

物質不滅律(ㄨˋ ㄓˊ ㄅㄨˋ ㄇㄧㄝˋ ㄌㄩˋ)
the law of conservation of matter

物質名詞(ㄨˋ ㄓˊ ㄇㄧㄥˊ ㄘˊ)
a material noun

物質建設(ㄨˋ ㄓˊ ㄐㄧㄢˋ ㄕㄜˋ)
material development or progress (of a community, country, etc.)

物質生活(ㄨˋ ㄓˊ ㄕㄥ ㄏㄨㄛˊ)
physical life; material life

物質三態(ㄨˋ ㄓˊ ㄙㄢ ㄊㄞˋ)
the three states of matter —solid, liquid and gas

物質文明(ㄨˋ ㄓˊ ㄨㄣˊ ㄇㄧㄥˊ)
material civilization

物證(ㄨˋ ㄓㄥˋ)
material evidence

物主(ㄨˋ ㄓㄨˇ)
the owner (of a thing): 誰是這些物品的物主? Who is the owner of these articles?

物產(ㄨˋ ㄔㄢˇ)
natural resources

物傷其類(ㄨˋ ㄕㄤ ㄑㄧˊ ㄌㄟˋ)
All beings grieve for the death of their fellow beings.

物資(ㄨˋ ㄗ)
materials; supplies; goods
物色(ㄨˋ ㄙㄜˋ)
to seek (talent); to scout for (talent); to look for (a son-in-law, mate, etc.)
物以類聚(ㄨˋ ㄧˇ ㄌㄟˋ ㄐㄩˋ)
Birds of a feather flock together.
物以稀爲貴(ㄨˋ ㄧˇ ㄒㄧ ㄨㄟˊ ㄍㄨㄟˋ)
A thing is valued if it is rare. 或 When a thing is scarce, it is precious.
物役(ㄨˋ ㄧˋ)
to be a slave of material things
物議(ㄨˋ ㄧˋ)
public criticisms; public censure
物有本末，事有終始(ㄨˋ ㄧㄡˇ ㄅㄣˇ ㄇㄛˋ, ㄕˋ ㄧㄡˇ ㄓㄨㄥ ㄕˇ)
Things have their root and branches; affairs have their end and beginning.
物物交換(ㄨˋ ㄨˋ ㄐㄧㄠ ㄏㄨㄢˋ)
to barter one thing for another
物我兩忘(ㄨˋ ㄨㄛˇ ㄌㄧㄤˇ ㄨㄤˋ)
to become unconscious of the boundary between oneself and the external world
物外(ㄨˋ ㄨㄞˋ)
beyond the physical world
物望(ㄨˋ ㄨㄤˋ)
the object of popular admiration
物慾(ㄨˋ ㄩˋ)
worldly desires; craving for material things

五畫

【牯】3318 ㄍㄨˇ guu gǔ
1. a cow
2. a castrated bull
牯牛(ㄍㄨˇ ㄋㄧㄡˊ)
① a cow ② a castrated bull
牯嶺(ㄍㄨˇ ㄌㄧㄥˇ)
Kuling, a summer resort in Kiangsi

【牲】3319 ㄕㄥ sheng shēng
livestock
牲口(ㄕㄥ ·ㄎㄡ)
livestock
牲畜(ㄕㄥ ㄔㄨˋ)
livestock

【牴】3320 ㄉㄧˇ dii dǐ
to gore
牴觸(ㄉㄧˇ ㄔㄨˋ)
to contradict; to conflict
牴牾(ㄉㄧˇ ㄨˇ)
to contradict; to conflict 參看「牴觸」

六畫

【特】3321 ㄊㄜˋ teh tè
1. special; unique; peculiar; particular; extraordinary; unusual; outstanding; distinguished; exclusive: 這種食物有奇特的味道。This food has a peculiar taste.
2. just; merely; only: 不特如此 not only that
3. a bull
特別(ㄊㄜˋ ㄅㄧㄝˊ)
① special; peculiar; particular; unique; unusual; extraordinary: 嬰兒需要特別的食物。Babies need special food. ② especially; particularly
特別法(ㄊㄜˋ ㄅㄧㄝˊ ㄈㄚˇ)
special law
特別費(ㄊㄜˋ ㄅㄧㄝˊ ㄈㄟˋ)
extraordinary expenses; special expenses
特別黨部(ㄊㄜˋ ㄅㄧㄝˊ ㄉㄤˇ ㄅㄨˋ)
non-regional party headquarters of the Kuomintang formed in the various professions or various branches of government-operated enterprises
特別開支(ㄊㄜˋ ㄅㄧㄝˊ ㄎㄞ ㄓ)
special expenses
特別快車(ㄊㄜˋ ㄅㄧㄝˊ ㄎㄨㄞˋ ㄔㄜ)or 特快車(ㄊㄜˋ ㄎㄨㄞˋ ㄔㄜ)
a special express train; a special express: 這是上午八時去台北的特別快車。This is the 8:00 a.m. special express to Taipei.
特別區域(ㄊㄜˋ ㄅㄧㄝˊ ㄑㄩ ㄩˋ)
special administrative districts (such as Jehol, Suiyüan, etc. before they became provinces)
特別市(ㄊㄜˋ ㄅㄧㄝˊ ㄕˋ)
a special municipality (directly under the jurisdiction of the Central Government)
特派(ㄊㄜˋ ㄆㄞˋ)
specially despatched or appointed; to commission specially
特派記者(ㄊㄜˋ ㄆㄞˋ ㄐㄧˋ ㄓㄜˇ)
a special correspondent; an accredited journalist
特派員(ㄊㄜˋ ㄆㄞˋ ㄩㄢˊ)
a correspondent (of a news agency, newspaper, etc.): 王先生是我們駐倫敦的特派員。Mr. Wang is our London correspondent.
特命全權大使(ㄊㄜˋ ㄇㄧㄥˋ ㄑㄩㄢˊ ㄑㄩㄢˊ ㄉㄚˋ ㄕˇ)
an ambassador extraordinary and plenipotentiary
特命全權公使(ㄊㄜˋ ㄇㄧㄥˋ ㄑㄩㄢˊ ㄑㄩㄢˊ ㄍㄨㄥ ㄕˇ)
an envoy extraordinary and minister plenipotentiary
特大(ㄊㄜˋ ㄉㄚˋ)
exceptionally big; the most
特大號(ㄊㄜˋ ㄉㄚˋ ㄏㄠˋ)
king-size; extra large size: 我們都很羨慕他那特大號的床。We all admire his king-size bed.
特等(ㄊㄜˋ ㄉㄥˇ)
of the special class or grade
特等艙(ㄊㄜˋ ㄉㄥˇ ㄘㄤ)
a stateroom
特地(ㄊㄜˋ ㄉㄧˋ)
on purpose; specially; designedly; exclusively: 我們是特地來向你學習的。We came specially to learn from you.
特點(ㄊㄜˋ ㄉㄧㄢˇ)
special features; peculiarities; characteristics
特定(ㄊㄜˋ ㄉㄧㄥˋ)
① specially designated ② specific; specified; given
特拉瓦(ㄊㄜˋ ㄌㄚ ㄨㄚˇ)
Delaware, a state in U.S.A.
特拉維夫(ㄊㄜˋ ㄌㄚ ㄨㄟˊ ㄈㄨ)
Tel Aviv
特例(ㄊㄜˋ ㄌㄧˋ)
a special case; a special instance; an exceptional case
特立獨行(ㄊㄜˋ ㄌㄧˋ ㄉㄨˊ ㄒㄧㄥˊ)
to be self-reliant; to be one's own master
特洛伊(ㄊㄜˋ ㄌㄨㄛˋ ㄧ)
Troy

特故(ㄊㄜˋ ㄍㄨˋ)
on purpose; intentionally

特工(ㄊㄜˋ ㄍㄨㄥ)
secret service

特攻隊(ㄊㄜˋ ㄍㄨㄥ ㄉㄨㄟˋ)
commando units; rangers

特工人員(ㄊㄜˋ ㄍㄨㄥ ㄖㄣˊ ㄩㄢˊ)
a special agent

特刊(ㄊㄜˋ ㄎㄢ)
the extra edition, special edition or special supplement (of a newspaper or magazine)

特惠關稅(ㄊㄜˋ ㄏㄨㄟˋ ㄍㄨㄢ ㄕㄨㄟˋ)
preferential tariffs

特急(ㄊㄜˋ ㄐㄧˊ)
of special urgency

特級(ㄊㄜˋ ㄐㄧˊ)
of the special class or grade; superfine: 他送我一些特級烏龍茶。He gave me some superfine oolong tea.

特級上將(ㄊㄜˋ ㄐㄧˊ ㄕㄤˋ ㄐㄧㄤˋ)
a five-star general or admiral

特技(ㄊㄜˋ ㄐㄧˋ)
special skills; stunts; aerobatics

特家新聞(ㄊㄜˋ ㄐㄧㄚ ㄒㄧㄣ ㄨㄣˊ)or 特家報導(ㄊㄜˋ ㄐㄧㄚ ㄅㄠˋ ㄉㄠˇ)
an exclusive report or story by a news medium; a scoop 亦作「獨家報導」

特價(ㄊㄜˋ ㄐㄧㄚˋ)
a specially reduced price; a bargain price: 我們這些東西都是特價出售的。We'll sell these articles at a bargain price.

特獎(ㄊㄜˋ ㄐㄧㄤˇ)
a special prize; a grand prize

特遣隊(ㄊㄜˋ ㄑㄧㄢˇ ㄉㄨㄟˋ)
a task force

特權(ㄊㄜˋ ㄑㄩㄢˊ)
privileges: 繳半費之特權 the privilege of paying half fare

特權階級(ㄊㄜˋ ㄑㄩㄢˊ ㄐㄧㄝ ㄐㄧˊ)
the privileged class

特寫(ㄊㄜˋ ㄒㄧㄝˇ)
① a feature story (in a newspaper or magazine) ② a close-up (in a movie)

特效(ㄊㄜˋ ㄒㄧㄠˋ)
special virtue or efficacy (of a medicine, etc.)

特效藥(ㄊㄜˋ ㄒㄧㄠˋ ㄧㄠˋ)
a specific; a wonder drug; a patent medicine

特性(ㄊㄜˋ ㄒㄧㄥˋ)
characteristics; peculiarities; distinctive features; defining features: 每個地區都有它的特性。Every region has its own characteristics.

特許(ㄊㄜˋ ㄒㄩˇ)
to permit as a special case; to charter; special mission

特許權(ㄊㄜˋ ㄒㄩˇ ㄑㄩㄢˊ)
a patent

特許狀(ㄊㄜˋ ㄒㄩˇ ㄓㄨㄤˋ)
a charter

特選(ㄊㄜˋ ㄒㄩㄢˇ)
carefully chosen; handpicked

特支費(ㄊㄜˋ ㄓ ㄈㄟˋ)
a special allowance for a government agency or its chief to meet contingent expenses

特質(ㄊㄜˋ ㄓˋ)
special qualities; characteristics; peculiarities

特指(ㄊㄜˋ ㄓˇ)
to refer particularly to

特製(ㄊㄜˋ ㄓˋ)
manufactured for a specific purpose; manufactured with a special process or extra care

特徵(ㄊㄜˋ ㄓㄥ)
defining qualities; distinctive features; characteristics; unique qualities: 他們有一共同的特徵。They have one characteristic in common.

特准(ㄊㄜˋ ㄓㄨㄣˇ)
a special permit; to permit as a special case

特種(ㄊㄜˋ ㄓㄨㄥˇ)
of a special kind

特種部隊(ㄊㄜˋ ㄓㄨㄥˇ ㄅㄨˋ ㄉㄨㄟˋ)
special forces

特種營業(ㄊㄜˋ ㄓㄨㄥˇ ㄧㄥˊ ㄧㄝˋ)
special business operations (such as cabarets, bars, wine-houses, etc.)

特產(ㄊㄜˋ ㄔㄢˇ)
unique or special products (of a place)

特長(ㄊㄜˋ ㄔㄤˊ)
special merits; strong points; a specialty; a special skill: 舞蹈是我的特長。Dancing is my strong point.

特稱(ㄊㄜˋ ㄔㄥ)
(logic) particular (as opposed to universal)

特出(ㄊㄜˋ ㄔㄨ)
outstanding; distinguished; eminent; prominent: 他證明自己是位特出的政治家。He proved himself an eminent statesman.

特使(ㄊㄜˋ ㄕˇ)or(ㄊㄜˋ ㄕˋ)
a special envoy

特赦(ㄊㄜˋ ㄕㄜˋ)
special pardon; an amnesty

特殊(ㄊㄜˋ ㄕㄨ)
special; unusual; unique: 在我的一生中，這是一個特殊的日子。This is a special day in my life.

特殊分子(ㄊㄜˋ ㄕㄨ ㄈㄣˋ ㄗˇ)
special members

特殊教育(ㄊㄜˋ ㄕㄨ ㄐㄧㄠˋ ㄩˋ)
special education (as for the blind, etc.)

特任(ㄊㄜˋ ㄖㄣˋ)
special appointment rank, the highest of the four civil service grades in China

特任官(ㄊㄜˋ ㄖㄣˋ ㄍㄨㄢ)
an official holding a post of the special appointment rank

特操(ㄊㄜˋ ㄘㄠ)
extraordinary moral conduct or righteousness

特色(ㄊㄜˋ ㄙㄜˋ)
unique features; special features; characteristics: 你的計劃有何特色? What are the unique features of your plan?

特恩(ㄊㄜˋ ㄣ)
special favor or kindness

特意(ㄊㄜˋ ㄧˋ)
on purpose; intentionally

特異(ㄊㄜˋ ㄧˋ)
peculiar; singular; unusual; strange

特藝彩色(ㄊㄜˋ ㄧˋ ㄘㄞˇ ㄙㄜˋ)
deluxe colors (of motion pictures)

特優(ㄊㄜˋ ㄧㄡ)
(said of performance) excellent; extraordinary

特有(ㄊㄜˋ ㄧㄡˇ)
to have exclusively; unique;

peculiar; special: 香蕉有其特有的香味。Bananas have their own special smell.

特宥(ㄊㄜˋ ㄧㄡˋ)
special pardon or leniency

特務(ㄊㄜˋ ㄨˋ)
a secret agent

特爲(ㄊㄜˋ ㄨㄟˋ)
for this particular reason; particularly for the sake of: 我特爲此事而來。I come specially for this purpose.

特約(ㄊㄜˋ ㄩㄝ)
①a special agreement or contract ②specially or exclusively engaged

特約記者(ㄊㄜˋ ㄩㄝ ㄐㄧˋ ㄓㄜˇ)
a stringer or a special correspondent (of a newspaper, etc.)

特約診所(ㄊㄜˋ ㄩㄝ ㄓㄣˇ ㄙㄨㄛˇ)
a clinic exclusively engaged by an organization

特約撰稿人(ㄊㄜˋ ㄩㄝ ㄓㄨㄢˋ ㄍㄠˇ ㄖㄣˊ)
a special contributor

特約醫院(ㄊㄜˋ ㄩㄝ ㄧ ㄩㄢˋ)
a hospital exclusively engaged by an organization

【牷】 3322 ㄑㄩㄢˊ chyuan quán
1. an ox of one color
2. (said of a sacrifice) intact

【牸】 3323 ㄗˋ tzyh zì
1. female animals
2. a cow

七畫

【牽】 3324 ㄑㄧㄢ chian qiān
1. to lead along; to drag; to pull; to tug; to haul
2. to involve; to affect
3. to control; to restrain

牽動(ㄑㄧㄢ ㄉㄨㄥˋ)
to affect as if a tugging action had been applied; to influence

牽牛花(ㄑㄧㄢ ㄋㄧㄡˊ ㄏㄨㄚ)
morning glory

牽牛星(ㄑㄧㄢ ㄋㄧㄡˊ ㄒㄧㄥ)
the star Altair

牽念(ㄑㄧㄢ ㄋㄧㄢˋ)
to feel anxious about; to be concerned for: 我如晚回，請勿牽念。Don't be anxious if I am late.

牽累(ㄑㄧㄢ ㄌㄟˋ)
to drag (into trouble); to involve

牽連(ㄑㄧㄢ ㄌㄧㄢˊ)
to involve (in trouble); to implicate

牽蘿補屋(ㄑㄧㄢ ㄌㄨㄛˊ ㄅㄨˇ ㄨ)
(literally) to mend a leaky roof with vines—in financial straits

牽掛(ㄑㄧㄢ ㄍㄨㄚˋ)
to be concerned for; to feel anxious about; to worry about: 她牽掛她丈夫的安危。She worried about her husband's safety.

牽合(ㄑㄧㄢ ㄏㄜˊ)
to couple by force; to match by force

牽強(ㄑㄧㄢ ㄑㄧㄤˇ)
(said of an interpretation, etc.) forced; unnatural; far-fetched: 他的比擬有些牽強。His comparison is somewhat far-fetched.

牽強附會(ㄑㄧㄢ ㄑㄧㄤˇ ㄈㄨˋ ㄏㄨㄟˋ)
to give a forced interpretation; to distort the meaning; to make a far-fetched interpretation; to draw a forced analogy

牽線(ㄑㄧㄢ ㄒㄧㄢˋ)
①to pull strings; to use indirect influence to gain one's ends, etc.; to control from behind the scenes ②to act as a go-between

牽制(ㄑㄧㄢ ㄓˋ)
①to restrain; to curb; to check: 戰爭牽制了我們的計劃。The war gave a check to our plan.②to divert (enemy attention)

牽制行動(ㄑㄧㄢ ㄓˋ ㄒㄧㄥˊ ㄉㄨㄥˋ)
(military) a diversionary action or move

牽著鼻子走(ㄑㄧㄢ ˙ㄓㄜ ㄅㄧˊ ˙ㄗ ㄗㄡˇ)
to lead by the nose: 不要讓任何人牽著鼻子走。Don't let anyone lead you by the nose.

牽扯(ㄑㄧㄢ ㄔㄜˇ)
complication (of a matter); to involve; to implicate

牽掣(ㄑㄧㄢ ㄔㄜˋ)
to restrain; to get bogged down; to curb; to check; to impede: 不要被枝節問題牽掣住。Don't get bogged down in minor issues.

牽腸掛肚(ㄑㄧㄢ ㄔㄤˊ ㄍㄨㄚˋ ㄉㄨˋ)or 牽腸割肚(ㄑㄧㄢ ㄔㄤˊ ㄍㄜ ㄉㄨˋ)
to be deeply concerned; to be very worried about

牽涉(ㄑㄧㄢ ㄕㄜˋ)
to involve; to affect; to implicate

牽手(ㄑㄧㄢ ㄕㄡˇ)
①to lead by the hand ②one's wife

牽絲(ㄑㄧㄢ ㄙ)
①to enter government service (in days of feudalism) ②to draw lots by pulling at one of the silk threads

牽絲扳藤(ㄑㄧㄢ ㄙ ㄅㄢ ㄊㄥˊ)
to harass or annoy persistently

牽一髮而動全身(ㄑㄧㄢ ㄧˋ ㄈㄚˇ ㄦˊ ㄉㄨㄥˋ ㄑㄩㄢˊ ㄕㄣ)
The pull of one hair may move the whole body. —What happens to a small part may affect the whole.

牽引(ㄑㄧㄢ ㄧㄣˇ)
①to involve (in trouble); to drag (into trouble) ②to draw

牽引機(ㄑㄧㄢ ㄧㄣˇ ㄐㄧ)
a tractor

牽挽(ㄑㄧㄢ ㄨㄢˇ)
to drag; to tug; to pull

【牾】 3325 ㄨˇ wuu wǔ
1. to oppose
2. to gore

八畫

【犂】 3326 (犁) ㄌㄧˊ li lí
1. to till; to plough
2. a plough

犂田(ㄌㄧˊ ㄊㄧㄢˊ)
to plough (or plow) a field

犂庭掃穴(ㄌㄧˊ ㄊㄧㄥˊ ㄙㄠˇ ㄒㄩㄝˋ)or 犂庭掃閭(ㄌㄧˊ ㄊㄧㄥˊ ㄙㄠˇ ㄌㄩˊ)
to annihilate the enemy

【犀】 3327 ㄒㄧ shi xī
1. (said of armor, weapons, etc.) sharp-edged and hard
2. a rhinoceros

犀兵(ㄒㄧ ㄅㄧㄥ)
sharp weapons
犀牛(ㄒㄧ ㄋㄧㄡˊ)
the rhinoceros
犀利(ㄒㄧ ㄌㄧˋ)
① hard and sharp ② trenchant; sharp: 他的文筆犀利。He has a trenchant pen.
犀甲(ㄒㄧ ㄐㄧㄚˇ)
armor made of rhinoceros hide
犀角(ㄒㄧ ㄐㄧㄠˇ)
① a rhinoceros horn ② bone of the forehead
犀照(ㄒㄧ ㄓㄠˋ)
very discerning

【犄】 3328 ㄐㄧ ji jī
a horn
犄角(ㄐㄧ ·ㄐㄧㄠ)
① a horn ② a corner: 屋子犄角裏有一張書桌。There is a desk in a corner of the room.

【犉】 3329 ㄖㄨㄣˊ ruen rún
1. an ox with yellow hair and a black mouth
2. an ox seven feet tall

【犇】 3330 ㄅㄣ ben bēn
an ancient variant of 奔— to run away; to be in a hurry

九畫

【犍】 3331 ㄐㄧㄢ jian jiān
a castrated bull
犍牛(ㄐㄧㄢ ㄋㄧㄡˊ)
a bullock

十畫

【犒】 3332 ㄎㄠˋ kaw kào
to reward (soldiers, laborers, etc.)
犒勞(ㄎㄠˋ ㄌㄠˋ)
① to reward or cheer troops with food, money, gifts, etc. ② food, money, gifts, etc. used to cheer troops
犒師(ㄎㄠˋ ㄕ)or 犒軍(ㄎㄠˋ ㄐㄩㄣ)
to cheer troops with material gifts
犒賞(ㄎㄠˋ ㄕㄤˇ)
to reward (one for contributions) with money or gifts

【犖】 3333 ㄌㄨㄛˋ luoh luò
1. a spotted ox
2. of many colors
犖犖(ㄌㄨㄛˋ ㄌㄨㄛˋ)
clear; evident; apparent
犖犖大者(ㄌㄨㄛˋ ㄌㄨㄛˋ ㄉㄚˋ ㄓㄜˇ)
the evident and major instances, cases, examples, etc.
犖确(ㄌㄨㄛˋ ㄑㄩㄝˋ)
rugged or craggy (mountains)

十一畫

【犛】 3334 ㄌㄧˊ li lí
1. a black ox
2. a yak
犛牛(ㄌㄧˊ ㄋㄧㄡˊ)
a yak

十五畫

【犢】 3335 ㄉㄨˊ dwu dú
a calf: 初生之犢不畏虎。A newborn calf fears not the tiger.
犢鼻(ㄉㄨˊ ㄅㄧˊ)
(Chinese herb medicine) a point susceptible to acupuncture under the kneecap
犢鼻褌(ㄉㄨˊ ㄅㄧˊ ㄎㄨㄣ)
knee breeches; shorts

十六畫

【犧】 3336 ㄒㄧ shi xī
1. sacrifice (as homage to a deity); a beast of a uniform color for sacrifice
2. to give up (for the sake of something of greater value); to sacrifice
犧牲(ㄒㄧ ㄕㄥ)
① sacrifice (offered to a deity) ② to sacrifice (something valued for the sake of something else): 他英勇爲國犧牲。He died a heroic death for his country.
犧牲品(ㄒㄧ ㄕㄥ ㄆㄧㄣˇ)
① a loss leader—a popular article sold for a fraction of its normal price ② a sacrificial lamb
犧牲打(ㄒㄧ ㄕㄥ ㄉㄚˇ)
a sacrifice hit
犧牲者(ㄒㄧ ㄕㄥ ㄓㄜˇ)
victim(s)
犧尊(ㄒㄧ ㄗㄨㄣ)
a wooden wine cup shaped like an ox

【犨】 3337 ㄔㄡ chou chōu
the panting of an ox

犬部
ㄑㄩㄢˇ cheuan quǎn

【犬】 3338 ㄑㄩㄢˇ cheuan quǎn
a dog; a canine
犬舖(ㄑㄩㄢˇ ㄆㄨˋ)or 犬窩(ㄑㄩㄢˇ ㄨㄛ)
a doghouse; a kennel
犬馬之勞(ㄑㄩㄢˇ ㄇㄚˇ ㄓ ㄌㄠˊ)
(literally) labor of a dog or a horse—one's own service (a self-depreciatory term): 我願效犬馬之勞。I'll serve you loyally.
犬吠(ㄑㄩㄢˇ ㄈㄟˋ)
the bark of a dog
犬禍(ㄑㄩㄢˇ ㄏㄨㄛˋ)
prevalence of rabies
犬彘(ㄑㄩㄢˇ ㄓˋ)
a beast or brute (used as a term of abuse)
犬齒(ㄑㄩㄢˇ ㄔˇ)or 犬牙(ㄑㄩㄢˇ ㄧㄚˊ)
a cuspid; a canine tooth
犬儒學派(ㄑㄩㄢˇ ㄖㄨˊ ㄒㄩㄝˊ ㄆㄞˋ)
the Cynics (in Greek philosophy)
犬儒主義(ㄑㄩㄢˇ ㄖㄨˊ ㄓㄨˇ ㄧˋ)
Cynicism
犬戎(ㄑㄩㄢˇ ㄖㄨㄥˊ)
name of a barbarian tribe to the west in ancient times
犬子(ㄑㄩㄢˇ ㄗˇ)
my son (a self-depreciatory term): 請原諒犬子無知。Please excuse my son's ignorance.
犬牙相制(ㄑㄩㄢˇ ㄧㄚˊ ㄒㄧㄤ ㄓˋ)
①(said of two countries) to adjoin each other along a

zigzag borderline ②(said of two forces) to face each other across a zigzag front

犬牙相錯(ㄑㄩㄢˇ ㄧㄚˊ ㄒㄧㄤ ㄘㄨㄛˋ)or 犬牙交錯(ㄑㄩㄢˇ ㄧㄚˊ ㄐㄧㄠ ㄘㄨㄛˋ)
to adjoin each other along a zigzag borderline; interlocking

一畫

【犮】 3339 ㄅㄛˊ bor bó
the way a dog walks

二畫

【犯】 3340 ㄈㄢˋ fann fàn
1. to violate; to offend; to break (regulations or laws)
2. to commit (crimes, etc.)
3. to invade; to attack; to work against
4. a criminal
5. to have a recurrence of; to revert to

犯病(ㄈㄢˋ ㄅㄧㄥˋ)
to fall back into an old illness or a bad habit; to have a relapse: 他昨天又犯病了。He had a relapse yesterday.

犯不著(ㄈㄢˋ ·ㄅㄨ ㄓㄠˊ)or 犯不上(ㄈㄢˋ ·ㄅㄨ ㄕㄤˋ)
not worthwhile: 犯不著和這小孩爭辯。It is not worthwhile arguing with this child.

犯脾氣(ㄈㄢˋ ㄆㄧˊ ·ㄑㄧ)
to lose one's temper

犯法(ㄈㄢˋ ㄈㄚˇ)
to violate the law; to break the law

犯得著(ㄈㄢˋ ·ㄉㄜ ㄓㄠˊ)or 犯得上(ㄈㄢˋ ·ㄉㄜ ㄕㄤˋ)
worthwhile: 犯得著跟他吵嗎? Is it worthwhile quarreling with him?

犯土(ㄈㄢˋ ㄊㄨˇ)
to offend the deity of a locality (as through some construction project)

犯難(ㄈㄢˋ ㄋㄢˊ)
to risk danger

犯鱗(ㄈㄢˋ ㄌㄧㄣˊ)
to advise or admonish the emperor bluntly

犯規(ㄈㄢˋ ㄍㄨㄟ)
(sports) to commit a foul; to violate a rule or regulation

犯規者(ㄈㄢˋ ㄍㄨㄟ ㄓㄜˇ)
an offender

犯科(ㄈㄢˋ ㄎㄜ)
to break the law; to commit an offense

犯諱(ㄈㄢˋ ㄏㄨㄟˋ)
(in old China) to use a word which is part of the name of an emperor or an elder

犯忌諱(ㄈㄢˋ ㄐㄧˋ ㄏㄨㄟˋ)
to violate a taboo; to do something proscribed by superstitions

犯戒(ㄈㄢˋ ㄐㄧㄝˋ)
to violate a religious prohibition

犯界(ㄈㄢˋ ㄐㄧㄝˋ)
to cross the frontiers of another country illegally or by force

犯禁(ㄈㄢˋ ㄐㄧㄣˋ)
to violate prohibitions (laid down by the proper authorities)

犯境(ㄈㄢˋ ㄐㄧㄥˋ)
to invade the territory; to aggress upon the territory of another country

犯闕(ㄈㄢˋ ㄑㄩㄝˋ)
(said of rebels) to invade the imperial palace; to attack the capital

犯舌(ㄈㄢˋ ㄕㄜˊ)
to talk too much; to blab

犯上(ㄈㄢˋ ㄕㄤˋ)
to offend against one's superiors

犯上作亂(ㄈㄢˋ ㄕㄤˋ ㄗㄨㄛˋ ㄌㄨㄢˋ)
to rebel against authority

犯人(ㄈㄢˋ ㄖㄣˊ)
a criminal; a prisoner

犯罪(ㄈㄢˋ ㄗㄨㄟˋ)
(to commit) a crime, an offense or a sin: 他因犯罪而下獄。He was sent to prison for his crimes.

犯罪心理學(ㄈㄢˋ ㄗㄨㄟˋ ㄒㄧㄣ ㄌㄧˇ ㄒㄩㄝˊ)
criminal psychology

犯罪行爲(ㄈㄢˋ ㄗㄨㄟˋ ㄒㄧㄥˊ ㄨㄟˊ)
a criminal act; a criminality; crime: 謀殺和詐騙是犯罪行爲。Murder and swindling are criminal acts.

犯罪學(ㄈㄢˋ ㄗㄨㄟˋ ㄒㄩㄝˊ)
criminology

犯錯誤(ㄈㄢˋ ㄘㄨㄛˋ ㄨˋ)or 犯錯(ㄈㄢˋ ㄘㄨㄛˋ)
to make a mistake; to err: 犯錯是人之常情，寬恕是超凡的。To err is human, to forgive divine.

犯死罪(ㄈㄢˋ ㄙˇ ㄗㄨㄟˋ)
to commit a crime punishable by death

犯案(ㄈㄢˋ ㄢˋ)
to commit a crime; to commit an offense

犯疑(ㄈㄢˋ ㄧˊ)or 犯疑心(ㄈㄢˋ ㄧˊ ㄒㄧㄣ)
to be suspicious: 無知者犯疑。The ignorant are suspicious.

犯意(ㄈㄢˋ ㄧˋ)
criminal intent

犯顏(ㄈㄢˋ ㄧㄢˊ)
to incur the displeasure of an elder or superior with words

三畫

【犴】 3341 ㄢˋ ann àn
1. a prison; a jail
2. a species of dog with black mouth and nose

四畫

【狀】 3342 ㄓㄨㄤˋ juanq zhuàng
1. appearance; look; shape; form
2. condition; state; situation
3. written appeal
4. a certificate: 獎狀 a certificate of commendation
5. to describe; to narrate; description

狀貌(ㄓㄨㄤˋ ㄇㄠˋ)
appearance; look

狀態(ㄓㄨㄤˋ ㄊㄞˋ)
situation; state; condition: 我們處於戰爭狀態。We are in a state of war.

狀況(ㄓㄨㄤˋ ㄎㄨㄤˋ)
situation; circumstances; condition

狀況證據(ㄓㄨㄤˋ ㄎㄨㄤˋ ㄓㄥˋ ㄐㄩˋ)
circumstantial evidence

狀紙(ㄓㄨㄤˋ ㄓˇ)
an official form for filing a lawsuit

狀子(ㄓㄨㄤˋ・ㄗ)
a written complaint; a plaint

狀詞(ㄓㄨㄤˋ ㄘˊ)
the contents of an accusation

狀元(ㄓㄨㄤˋ ㄩㄢˊ) or 狀頭(ㄓㄨㄤˋ ㄊㄡˊ)
① the top successful candidate in the imperial examination ② the very best: 行行出狀元。Every trade has its master. 或 One may distinguish himself in any trade.

狀元紅(ㄓㄨㄤˋ ㄩㄢˊ ㄏㄨㄥˊ)
a kind of high-quality Shaohsing wine

【狂】 3343
ㄎㄨㄤˊ kwang kuáng

1. crazy; mad; mentally deranged
2. violent
3. unrestrained; uninhibited; wild
4. haughty

狂暴(ㄎㄨㄤˊ ㄅㄠˋ)
wild; fierce; furious; ferocious; brutal

狂奔(ㄎㄨㄤˊ ㄅㄣ)
to run about wildly; to run about madly

狂飆(ㄎㄨㄤˊ ㄅㄧㄠ)
a hurricane

狂吠(ㄎㄨㄤˊ ㄈㄟˋ)
① to bark wildly ② to utter wild words; to yell like a mad dog; to yell nonsense

狂放(ㄎㄨㄤˊ ㄈㄤˋ)
wild; unrestrained

狂風暴雨(ㄎㄨㄤˊ ㄈㄥ ㄅㄠˋ ㄩˇ)
violent wind and rain; a violent storm: 這場狂風暴雨造成很大的損害。The violent storm did a lot of harm.

狂風怒號(ㄎㄨㄤˊ ㄈㄥ ㄋㄨˋ ㄏㄠˊ)
A violent wind is howling wildly.

狂蜂浪蝶(ㄎㄨㄤˊ ㄈㄥ ㄌㄤˋ ㄉㄧㄝˊ)
lascivious men

狂夫(ㄎㄨㄤˊ ㄈㄨ)
a bohemian; one who cares nothing about conventions or decorum

狂蕩(ㄎㄨㄤˊ ㄉㄤˋ)
to debauch; to dissipate; debauchery

狂態(ㄎㄨㄤˊ ㄊㄞˋ)
① a scandalous scene; a display of wild manners ② insolent and conceited manners

狂瀾(ㄎㄨㄤˊ ㄌㄢˊ)
① violent waves ② violent disturbances: 力挽狂瀾 to do one's utmost to stem violent disturbances

狂亂(ㄎㄨㄤˊ ㄌㄨㄢˋ)
wild; frenzied; frantic; mad; frenzy

狂歌(ㄎㄨㄤˊ ㄍㄜ)
to sing with wild joy

狂客(ㄎㄨㄤˊ ㄎㄜˋ)
① a bohemian ② poplar catkins ③ peach blossoms

狂呼(ㄎㄨㄤˊ ㄏㄨ)
to shout in wild excitement

狂歡(ㄎㄨㄤˊ ㄏㄨㄢ)
to rejoice with wild excitement; to be carried away by wild pleasure or joy; to revel

狂歡節(ㄎㄨㄤˊ ㄏㄨㄢ ㄐㄧㄝˊ)
a carnival 亦作「嘉年華會」

狂狷(ㄎㄨㄤˊ ㄐㄩㄢˋ)
radicals and ultraconservatives

狂犬病(ㄎㄨㄤˊ ㄑㄩㄢˇ ㄅㄧㄥˋ)
rabies; hydrophobia

狂喜(ㄎㄨㄤˊ ㄒㄧˇ)
to show wild joy; to rejoice with wild excitement

狂笑(ㄎㄨㄤˊ ㄒㄧㄠˋ)
to give wild laughter

狂想曲(ㄎㄨㄤˊ ㄒㄧㄤˇ ㄑㄩˇ)
(music) a rhapsody

狂相(ㄎㄨㄤˊ ㄒㄧㄤˋ)
a display of unrestraint, of excessive haughtiness, or of excessive frivolity

狂士(ㄎㄨㄤˊ ㄕˋ)
an idiosyncratic gentleman; a bohemian scholar; a self-conceited scholar

狂生(ㄎㄨㄤˊ ㄕㄥ)
a bohemian young scholar

狂熱(ㄎㄨㄤˊ ㄖㄜˋ)
fanatical; feverish; unreasonably enthusiastic; wildly zealous

狂人(ㄎㄨㄤˊ ㄖㄣˊ)
① a lunatic ② an extremely conceited fellow

狂恣(ㄎㄨㄤˊ ㄗˋ)
unrestrained; uninhibited; dissolute; profligate

狂走(ㄎㄨㄤˊ ㄗㄡˇ)
to run about madly; to run about wildly

狂草(ㄎㄨㄤˊ ㄘㄠˇ)
a wild scribble; an excessively free cursive style (in Chinese calligraphy)

狂傲(ㄎㄨㄤˊ ㄠˋ)
unreasonably haughty; improperly domineering

狂藥(ㄎㄨㄤˊ ㄧㄠˋ)
alcoholic beverages

狂言(ㄎㄨㄤˊ ㄧㄢˊ)
wild words; boastful talks; brag

狂妄(ㄎㄨㄤˊ ㄨㄤˋ)
① wild; irrational; crazy; mentally deranged; out of one's right mind ② extremely conceited: 他是個狂妄的畫家。He is an extremely conceited painter.

狂妄無知(ㄎㄨㄤˊ ㄨㄤˋ ㄨˊ ㄓ)
conceited and ignorant

【狄】 3344
ㄉㄧˊ dyi dí

1. name of a barbarian tribe to the north of ancient China
2. a Chinese family name

狄更斯(ㄉㄧˊ ㄍㄥ ㄙ)
Charles Dickens, 1812-1870, English novelist

狄克推多(ㄉㄧˊ ㄎㄜˋ ㄊㄨㄟ ㄉㄨㄛ)
① a dictator 亦作「獨裁者」② dictatorship 亦作「獨裁」

狄青(ㄉㄧˊ ㄑㄧㄥ)
Ti Ching, 1008-1057, a general in the Sung Dynasty

狄斯耐樂園(ㄉㄧˊ ㄙ ㄋㄞˋ ㄌㄜˋ ㄩㄢˊ)
Disneyland, U. S. A.

狄斯可(ㄉㄧˊ ㄙ ㄎㄜˇ)
disco 亦作「迪斯可」

【狁】 3345
ㄩㄣˇ yeun yŭn

name of a barbarian tribe to the north of ancient China

【狃】 3346
ㄋㄧㄡˇ neou niŭ

1. to covet
2. to be accustomed to
3. to hold the post of
4. avaricious; greedy

狃於陋習(ㄋㄧㄡˇ ㄩˊ ㄌㄡˋ ㄒㄧˊ)

to be accustomed to bad habits

狃於成見(ㄋㄧㄡˇ ㄩˊ ㄔㄥˊ ㄐㄧㄢˋ)
to be a slave of preconceived ideas; opinionated

五畫

【狎】 3347 ㄒㄧㄚˊ shya xiá

to show familiarity, intimacy, or disrespect

狎暱(ㄒㄧㄚˊ ㄋㄧˋ)
very intimate; very familiar

狎弄(ㄒㄧㄚˊ ㄌㄨㄥˋ)
to show improper familiarity with; to be rude to; to be impolite to

狎客(ㄒㄧㄚˊ ㄎㄜˋ)
① a rude person; an impolite person; a disrespectful person ② prostitute's customers

狎妓(ㄒㄧㄚˊ ㄐㄧˋ)
to visit a brothel

狎近(ㄒㄧㄚˊ ㄐㄧㄣˋ)
to be very intimate; to be very familiar

狎邪(ㄒㄧㄚˊ ㄒㄧㄝˊ)
① to indulge in vice; to visit a brothel ② improper

狎侮(ㄒㄧㄚˊ ㄨˇ)
to show improper intimacy with; to be impolite to; to treat with disrespect

狎翫(ㄒㄧㄚˊ ㄨㄢˋ)
to show disrespect from familiarity

【狗】 3348 ㄍㄡˇ goou gǒu

1. a dog
2. (figuratively) a lackey; a footman; a servile person; a follower
3. damned; cursed

狗屁(ㄍㄡˇ ㄆㄧˋ) or 狗屁不通(ㄍㄡˇ ㄆㄧˋ ㄅㄨˋ ㄊㄨㄥ)
Nonsense! 或 Rubbish! 或 Baloney!

狗命(ㄍㄡˇ ㄇㄧㄥˋ)
a life worth as little as a dog's; a life of little worth

狗母(ㄍㄡˇ ㄇㄨˇ)
lizard fish 亦作「蜥蜴魚」

狗吠(ㄍㄡˇ ㄈㄟˋ)
the bark of a dog

狗膽(ㄍㄡˇ ㄉㄢˇ) or 狗膽包天(ㄍㄡˇ ㄉㄢˇ ㄅㄠ ㄊㄧㄢ)
monstrous audacity; boldness; bold; daring

狗顛屁股(ㄍㄡˇ ㄉㄧㄢ ㄆㄧˋ ˙ㄍㄨ)
obsequious; subservient

狗頭(ㄍㄡˇ ㄊㄡˊ)
a dog's head (a term of abuse)

狗頭軍師(ㄍㄡˇ ㄊㄡˊ ㄐㄩㄣ ㄕ)
a person who offers bad advice; a good-for-nothing adviser

狗腿子(ㄍㄡˇ ㄊㄨㄟˇ ˙ㄗ)
a dog's leg—(figuratively) a person who slavishly does legwork for others; a hired thug; a henchman

狗拿耗子，多管閒事(ㄍㄡˇ ㄋㄚˊ ㄏㄠˋ ˙ㄗ, ㄉㄨㄛ ㄍㄨㄢˇ ㄒㄧㄢˊ ㄕˋ)
a dog trying to catch mice—to meddle; to poke one's nose into other's business

狗男女(ㄍㄡˇ ㄋㄢˊ ㄋㄩˇ)
adulterers and adulteresses

狗急跳牆(ㄍㄡˇ ㄐㄧˊ ㄊㄧㄠˋ ㄑㄧㄤˊ)
A cornered beast will do something desperate.—A person takes desperate measures in a critical situation.

狗監(ㄍㄡˇ ㄐㄧㄢ)
an emperor's attendant in charge of hunting dogs (during the Han Dynasty)

狗氣(ㄍㄡˇ ˙ㄑㄧ)
(literally) a dog's temperament—the attitude of flattering superiors and bullying subordinates

狗血噴頭(ㄍㄡˇ ㄒㄧㄝˇ ㄆㄣ ㄊㄡˊ)
(literally) to get a spray of dog's blood on the head—to be scolded in a very humiliating fashion

狗熊(ㄍㄡˇ ㄒㄩㄥˊ)
① a bear ② (figuratively) a coward

狗彘不若(ㄍㄡˇ ㄓˋ ㄅㄨˋ ㄖㄨㄛˋ)
even more despicable than a beast

狗彘不食(ㄍㄡˇ ㄓˋ ㄅㄨˋ ㄕˊ)
a very bad man (so bad that even beasts avoid eating his flesh after his death)

狗仗人勢(ㄍㄡˇ ㄓㄤˋ ㄖㄣˊ ㄕˋ)
(literally) to behave like a dog relying upon the power of its master—to use the influence of one's master in bullying others

狗吃屎(ㄍㄡˇ ㄔ ㄕˇ)
a dog eating dung—(figuratively) face down: 他跌了個狗吃屎。He stumbled and fell to the ground face down.

狗食(ㄍㄡˇ ㄕˊ)
dog food (a term of abuse)

狗屎(ㄍㄡˇ ㄕˇ)
(literally) dog's droppings—utterly worthless

狗肉(ㄍㄡˇ ㄖㄡˋ)
dog meat

狗嘴長不出象牙來(ㄍㄡˇ ㄗㄨㄟˇ ㄓㄤˇ ㄅㄨˋ ㄔㄨ ㄒㄧㄤˋ ㄧㄚˊ ˙ㄌㄞ)
(literally) One cannot expect to find elephant tusks in the mouth of a dog.—A mean fellow never speaks nice things.

狗才(ㄍㄡˇ ㄘㄞˊ)
(literally) a man with a dog's talent—a man of little competence

狗咬呂洞賓(ㄍㄡˇ ㄧㄠˇ ㄌㄩˇ ㄉㄨㄥˋ ㄅㄧㄣ)
to snarl and snap at Lü Tung-pin (one of the Eight Immortals of Taoism)—to mistake a good man for a bad one

狗眼看人低(ㄍㄡˇ ㄧㄢˇ ㄎㄢˋ ㄖㄣˊ ㄉㄧ)
to act like a snob

狗尾續貂(ㄍㄡˇ ㄨㄟˇ ㄒㄩˋ ㄉㄧㄠ)
(literally) to put a dog's tail to a marten's body—to complete a masterpiece with poor writing (a self-depreciatory expression)

狗尾草(ㄍㄡˇ ㄨㄟˇ ㄘㄠˇ)
foxtail

【狐】 3349 ㄏㄨˊ hwu hú

the fox

狐步舞(ㄏㄨˊ ㄅㄨˋ ㄨˇ)
a fox trot

狐朋狗友(ㄏㄨˊ ㄆㄥˊ ㄍㄡˇ ㄧㄡˇ)
a bunch of rogues

狐埋狐搰(ㄏㄨˊ ㄇㄞˊ ㄏㄨˊ ㄏㄨˊ)
to be hesitant to achieve success

狐媚(ㄏㄨˊ ㄇㄟˋ)
to charm by flattery; to be sycophantic; to bewitch by cajolery

狐狸(ㄏㄨˊ ˙ㄌㄧ)
a fox

狐狸狗(ㄏㄨˊ ·ㄌㄧ ㄍㄡˇ)
a spitz, or Pomeranian

狐狸精(ㄏㄨˊ ·ㄌㄧ ㄐㄧㄥ)
a woman of easy virtue (supposed to be a fox in disguise); an enchantress; a vixen

狐狸尾巴(ㄏㄨˊ ·ㄌㄧ ㄨㄟˇ ·ㄅㄚ)
a fox's tail—something that reveals one's true form or evil intentions; a cloven hoof: 狐狸尾巴總是要露出來的。The devil can't hide his cloven hoof.

狐猴(ㄏㄨˊ ㄏㄡˊ)
a lemur

狐假虎威(ㄏㄨˊ ㄐㄧㄚˇ ㄏㄨˇ ㄨㄟ)
(literally) to behave like the fox that borrowed the terror of the tiger—to be an ass in a lion's skin; to bully the weak because of one's association with the powerful

狐裘羔袖(ㄏㄨˊ ㄑㄧㄡˊ ㄍㄠ ㄒㄧㄡˋ)
(literally) a fox-fur robe with lamb-skin sleeves —good on the whole but not perfect

狐羣狗黨(ㄏㄨˊ ㄑㄩㄣˊ ㄍㄡˇ ㄉㄤˇ)
a bunch of rogues; a gang of scoundrels

狐仙(ㄏㄨˊ ㄒㄧㄢ)
a fairy fox

狐臭(ㄏㄨˊ ㄔㄡˋ) or 狐騷(ㄏㄨˊ ㄙㄠ)
an armpit odor

狐死兔泣(ㄏㄨˊ ㄙˇ ㄊㄨˋ ㄑㄧˋ) or 狐死兔悲(ㄏㄨˊ ㄙˇ ㄊㄨˋ ㄅㄟ)
When the fox dies, the hare grieves.—One grieves for one's kind.

狐疑(ㄏㄨˊ ㄧˊ)
suspicious; doubt; suspicion: 他似乎滿腹狐疑。He seemed to be very suspicious.

狐疑不決(ㄏㄨˊ ㄧˊ ㄅㄨˋ ㄐㄩㄝˊ)
hesitant; undecided

【狒】 3350 ㄈㄟˋ fey fèi
the baboon

狒狒(ㄈㄟˋ ㄈㄟˋ)
the baboon

【狙】 3351 ㄐㄩ jiu jū
1. a monkey; an ape
2. to lie in ambush

狙伏(ㄐㄩ ㄈㄨˊ)
to lie in ambush

狙擊(ㄐㄩ ㄐㄧˊ)
to launch a sneak attack; to attack by surprise; to snipe

狙擊手(ㄐㄩ ㄐㄧˊ ㄕㄡˇ)
a sniper

狙詐(ㄐㄩ ㄓㄚˋ)
a trick; a ruse; a wile: 不可狙詐待人。You should not treat others with tricks.

狙伺(ㄐㄩ ㄙˋ)
to spy; to reconnoiter in secret

六畫

【狠】 3352 ㄏㄣˇ heen hěn
1. vicious; cruel; atrocious
2. severe(ly); extreme(ly)

狠命(ㄏㄣˇ ㄇㄧㄥˋ)
to make a desperate effort; to use all the strength

狠毒(ㄏㄣˇ ㄉㄨˊ)
atrocious; cruel; brutal; malicious: 他對待犯人非常狠毒。He is very brutal to the prisoners.

狠戾(ㄏㄣˇ ㄌㄧˋ)
vicious; cruel; atrocious

狠狠地(ㄏㄣˇ ㄏㄣˇ ·ㄉㄜ)
in cold blood; mercilessly; cruelly; brutally; severely

狠心(ㄏㄣˇ ㄒㄧㄣ)
heartless; pitiless; merciless; cruel

【狡】 3353 ㄐㄧㄠˇ jeau jiǎo
1. cunning; crafty; sly; wily; artful; shrewd
2. suspicion; to suspect

狡辯(ㄐㄧㄠˇ ㄅㄧㄢˋ)
to use sophisticated argument in self-defense; to defend oneself in a devious way; artful self-defense; to quibble

狡憤(ㄐㄧㄠˇ ㄈㄣˋ)
to fly into a rage; to rage

狡徒(ㄐㄧㄠˇ ㄊㄨˊ)
a swindler; a crook; a crafty person

狡兔死，走狗烹(ㄐㄧㄠˇ ㄊㄨˋ ㄙˇ, ㄗㄡˇ ㄍㄡˇ ㄆㄥ)
(literally) After the cunning hare is killed, the hound is boiled.—After work is done, those who did the work are discarded.

狡兔三窟(ㄐㄧㄠˇ ㄊㄨˋ ㄙㄢ ㄎㄨ)
(literally) A wily rabbit has three burrows. —elaborate precautions made for self-protection

狡脫(ㄐㄧㄠˇ ㄊㄨㄛ)
to evade smartly

狡童(ㄐㄧㄠˇ ㄊㄨㄥˊ)
① a crafty youth ② a youth handsome but worthless

狡賴(ㄐㄧㄠˇ ㄌㄞˋ)
to prevaricate; to give a false alibi

狡獪(ㄐㄧㄠˇ ㄎㄨㄞˋ)
crafty; cunning; deceitful; treacherous; artful

狡猾(ㄐㄧㄠˇ ㄏㄨㄚˊ)
cunning; crafty; sly; wily; artful

狡計(ㄐㄧㄠˇ ㄐㄧˋ)
a clever scheme; a cunning plot

狡黠(ㄐㄧㄠˇ ㄒㄧㄚˊ)
deceitful; treacherous; sly; crafty

狡詐(ㄐㄧㄠˇ ㄓㄚˋ)
deceitful; cunning; swindling; wily

狡飾(ㄐㄧㄠˇ ㄕˋ)
to cover up the truth; to deceive; to lie

狡僞(ㄐㄧㄠˇ ㄨㄟˇ)
deceitful; treacherous; crafty

【狩】 3354 ㄕㄡˋ show shòu
1. to hunt in winter
2. an imperial tour

狩獵(ㄕㄡˋ ㄌㄧㄝˋ)
hunting; to hunt or trap game

七畫

【狴】 3355 ㄅㄧˋ bih bì
1. a legendary beast looking like a tiger
2. a prison

狴犴(ㄅㄧˋ ㄢˋ)
①a legendary beast looking like a tiger ②a prison or penitentiary

【狼】 3356 ㄌㄤˊ lang láng
1. the wolf
2. a heartless, cruel person;

cruel and heartless; cunning and crafty
3. name of a constellation
4. a Chinese family name

〔犬部〕

狼狽(ㄌㄤˊ ㄅㄟˋ)
①helplessly dependent; desperate ②in a difficult position: 他們處境狼狽。They are in a difficult position. ③ill at ease; embarrassed: 他感到很狼狽。He felt quite embarrassed. ④heartless and cruel persons

狼狽不堪(ㄌㄤˊ ㄅㄟˋ ㄅㄨˋ ㄎㄢ)
in utter disorder or confusion; to be in great distress or embarrassment; very troubled

狼狽爲奸(ㄌㄤˊ ㄅㄟˋ ㄨㄟˊ ㄐㄧㄢ)
to work hand in glove (in evil ways); to gang up with somebody

狼多肉少(ㄌㄤˊ ㄉㄨㄛ ㄖㄡˋ ㄕㄠˇ)
(literally) There is too little meat for so many wolves. —too many looters for the limited wealth, resources, etc.

狼貪(ㄌㄤˊ ㄊㄢ)
greedy; avaricious

狼吞虎嚥(ㄌㄤˊ ㄊㄨㄣ ㄏㄨˇ ㄧㄢˋ)
to devour (food) like a wolf and a tiger—to gobble up; to wolf down; to devour ravenously

狼狗(ㄌㄤˊ ㄍㄡˇ)
a German shepherd; a wolfhound

狼顧(ㄌㄤˊ ㄍㄨˋ)
(literally) to turn back one's head from time to time as a wolf does—very suspicious

狼毫(ㄌㄤˊ ㄏㄠˊ)
a Chinese writing brush made of wolf's hair

狼嗥鬼叫(ㄌㄤˊ ㄏㄠˊ ㄍㄨㄟˇ ㄐㄧㄠˋ)
pathetic cries; bloodcurdling shrieks

狼藉 or 狼籍(ㄌㄤˊ ㄐㄧˊ)
①in total disorder or disarray; in pandemonium: 杯盤狼藉。Empty glasses and plates are scattered all over. ②as in 聲名狼藉—notorious

狼犬(ㄌㄤˊ ㄑㄩㄢˇ)
the German shepherd dog; a police dog

狼心狗肺(ㄌㄤˊ ㄒㄧㄣ ㄍㄡˇ ㄈㄟˋ)
heartless and cruel; rotten to the core

狼人(ㄌㄤˊ ㄖㄣˊ)
a wolf man

狼子野心(ㄌㄤˊ ㄗˇ ㄧㄝˇ ㄒㄧㄣ)
a cruel and heartless character

狼崽子(ㄌㄤˊ ㄗㄞˇ ·ㄗ)
an ingrate; a greedy and coldblooded s.o.b.

狼煙(ㄌㄤˊ ㄧㄢ)
(in ancient China) a smoke signal; smoke from burning wolf excrement as a signal to alert troops against invaders

【狽】 3357
ㄅㄟˋ bey bèi

a kind of wolf with shorter forelegs

【狷】 3358
ㄐㄩㄢˋ jiuann juàn

1. rash; quick-tempered
2. honest and straightforward

狷忿(ㄐㄩㄢˋ ㄈㄣˋ)
easily impatient and angry

狷急(ㄐㄩㄢˋ ㄐㄧˊ)
a rigid and candid disposition which cannot be easily bent

狷介(ㄐㄩㄢˋ ㄐㄧㄝˋ)
honest and straightforward; incorruptible; upright

狷狹(ㄐㄩㄢˋ ㄒㄧㄚˊ)or 狷隘(ㄐㄩㄢˋ ㄞˋ)
narrow-minded; parochial; narrow

【狸】 3359
(貍) ㄌㄧˊ li lí

1. a fox
2. a racoon dog

狸貓(ㄌㄧˊ ㄇㄠ)
a kind of wild cat

狸德(ㄌㄧˊ ㄉㄜˊ)
as greedy as a fox

【狹】 3360
ㄒㄧㄚˊ shya xiá

narrow; narrow-minded

狹陋(ㄒㄧㄚˊ ㄌㄡˋ)
(usually said of a house, room, etc.) narrow and dingy

狹路(ㄒㄧㄚˊ ㄌㄨˋ)or 狹徑(ㄒㄧㄚˊ ㄐㄧㄥˋ)
a narrow path or road

狹路相逢(ㄒㄧㄚˊ ㄌㄨˋ ㄒㄧㄤ ㄈㄥˊ)
(literally) to meet on a narrow path—enemies or rivals coming face to face

狹小(ㄒㄧㄚˊ ㄒㄧㄠˇ)
(said of rooms, etc.) narrow and small: 他正想走出狹小的圈子。He is trying to step out of his narrow circle.

狹心症(ㄒㄧㄚˊ ㄒㄧㄣ ㄓㄥˋ)
angina pectoris

狹窄(ㄒㄧㄚˊ ㄓㄞˇ)
narrow; cramped: 他的見識狹窄。He is limited in knowledge and narrow in experience.

狹長(ㄒㄧㄚˊ ㄔㄤˊ)
long and narrow

狹隘(ㄒㄧㄚˊ ㄞˋ)
narrow-minded; narrow; parochial: 我不喜歡你狹隘的看法。I don't like your narrow view.

狹義(ㄒㄧㄚˊ ㄧˋ)
the narrow sense

狹韻(ㄒㄧㄚˊ ㄩㄣˋ)
a rhyme that encompasses only a few characters

【狺】 3361
ㄧㄣˊ yn yín

the snarling of dogs

狺狺(ㄧㄣˊ ㄧㄣˊ)
to yelp

八畫

【猖】 3362
ㄔㄤ chang chāng

wild; mad; impudent; unruly; reckless

猖披(ㄔㄤ ㄆㄧ)
to act wildly as one pleases; to act without restraints of any sort; unbridled and ungovernable

猖厲(ㄔㄤ ㄌㄧˋ)
wild and severe; mad and violent

猖亂(ㄔㄤ ㄌㄨㄢˋ)
wild and disorderly

猖狂(ㄔㄤ ㄎㄨㄤˊ)
wild; ungovernable; unrestrained; unbridled; unruly: 我們擊退猖狂的敵人。We defeated unrestrained enemy.

猖獗(ㄔㄤ ㄐㄩㄝˊ)
rampant; on the rampage; raging

【猗】 3363
1. ㄧ i yī
1. an exclamation indicating admiration
2. an adverbial particle
猗靡(ㄧ ㄇㄧˇ)
flowing and fluttering with the wind
猗猗(ㄧ ㄧ)
splendid and flourishing

【猗】 3363
2. ㄜ ee ē
gentle, soft and pliant
猗儺(ㄜ ㄋㄨㄛˊ)
gentle; soft and pliant

【猊】 3364
ㄋㄧˊ ni ní
1. the lion
2. a wild beast or wild horse

【猙】 3365
ㄓㄥ jeng zhēng
fierce-looking; hideous; repulsive
猙獰(ㄓㄥ ㄋㄧㄥˊ)
fierce-looking; hideous; repulsive: 那人看起來相貌猙獰。That man looks hideous.

【猛】 3366
ㄇㄥˇ meeng měng
1. bold; brave; fierce; violent
2. sudden and quick (strikes, thrusts, etc.)
3. severe; strict; stringent
4. a Chinese family name
猛不防(ㄇㄥˇ ㄅㄨˋ ㄈㄤˊ)
unexpectedly; unawares
猛拍(ㄇㄥˇ ㄆㄞ)
to lunge at something with force; to attack fiercely
猛力(ㄇㄥˇ ㄌㄧˋ)
vigorously; with great force
猛戾(ㄇㄥˇ ㄌㄧˋ)
fierce and violent; ferocious and unruly
猛烈(ㄇㄥˇ ㄌㄧㄝˋ)
fierce; violent and savage
猛攻(ㄇㄥˇ ㄍㄨㄥ)
a powerful or fierce attack; to attack in full force or savagely; a furious assault
猛可(ㄇㄥˇ ㄎㄜˇ)
suddenly; all of a sudden: 他猛可想起他的母親。All of a sudden he thought of his mother.
猛虎(ㄇㄥˇ ㄏㄨˇ)
a ferocious tiger
猛火(ㄇㄥˇ ㄏㄨㄛˇ)
a raging fire
猛擊(ㄇㄥˇ ㄐㄧˊ)
a furious blow; a sudden and violent attack or thrust; to attack with full force
猛劑(ㄇㄥˇ ㄐㄧˋ)
very potent drugs
猛進(ㄇㄥˇ ㄐㄧㄣˋ)
to advance in quick and big strides; remarkable improvement or progress: 我們正在突飛猛進。We are advancing by leaps and bounds.
猛將(ㄇㄥˇ ㄐㄧㄤˋ)
a brave or courageous general: 我們的猛將如雲。We have a great many brave generals.
猛決(ㄇㄥˇ ㄐㄩㄝˊ)
brave and determined
猛禽(ㄇㄥˇ ㄑㄧㄣˊ)
fierce birds (as eagles, hawks, etc.); birds of prey: 鷹是一種猛禽。The eagle is a bird of prey.
猛犬(ㄇㄥˇ ㄑㄩㄢˇ)
fierce dogs; vicious dogs; bulldogs
猛襲(ㄇㄥˇ ㄒㄧˊ)
to attack ferociously
猛省 or 猛醒(ㄇㄥˇ ㄒㄧㄥˇ)
a sudden realization; to awake or realize all of a sudden
猛追(ㄇㄥˇ ㄓㄨㄟ)
to be in hot pursuit of: 狗猛追兔子。The dog is in hot pursuit of the rabbits.
猛撞(ㄇㄥˇ ㄓㄨㄤˋ)
to ram or bump suddenly and with force: 那輛卡車猛撞他的汽車。That truck bumped his car with force.
猛士(ㄇㄥˇ ㄕˋ)
brave men; warriors
猛獸(ㄇㄥˇ ㄕㄡˋ)
fierce wild beasts
猛然(ㄇㄥˇ ㄖㄢˊ)
suddenly; abruptly: 他的聲音和態度猛然改變。His voice and manner changed suddenly.
猛以濟寬(ㄇㄥˇ ㄧˇ ㄐㄧˋ ㄎㄨㄢ)
Strictness is to correct the weakness of laxity.

【猜】 3367
ㄘㄞ tsai cāi
1. to guess; to suspect; to doubt: 她猜對了。She guessed right.
2. cruel and suspicious
猜不透(ㄘㄞ ·ㄅㄨ ㄊㄡˋ)
unable to guess; unable to make out (what's on his mind, etc.)
猜不著(ㄘㄞ ·ㄅㄨ ㄓㄠˊ)or 猜不出(ㄘㄞ ·ㄅㄨ ㄔㄨ)
cannot guess; unable to make out or find the right answer
猜破(ㄘㄞ ㄆㄛˋ)
to make out or unearth mentally what's on another's mind
猜謎(ㄘㄞ ㄇㄧˊ)or 猜謎兒(ㄘㄞ ㄇㄧㄜˊㄦ)
① to solve riddles ② to guess
猜防(ㄘㄞ ㄈㄤˊ)
to suspect and be on guard
猜燈(ㄘㄞ ㄉㄥ)
to solve riddles (on Lantern Festival)
猜度(ㄘㄞ ㄉㄨㄛˋ)
to guess and assess; to surmise; to conjecture
猜忌(ㄘㄞ ㄐㄧˋ)
to be jealous and suspicious
猜懼(ㄘㄞ ㄐㄩˋ)
to suspect and fear; suspicious and apprehensive
猜拳(ㄘㄞ ㄑㄩㄢˊ)
to play the finger-guessing game (usually in drinking)
猜嫌(ㄘㄞ ㄒㄧㄢˊ)
jealous and suspicious
猜想(ㄘㄞ ㄒㄧㄤˇ)
to guess; to conjecture; to surmise
猜著(ㄘㄞ ㄓㄠˊ)or 猜中(ㄘㄞ ㄓㄨㄥˋ)
to guess correctly; to make out; to solve (a riddle)
猜測(ㄘㄞ ㄘㄜˋ)
to guess; to assess; to surmise; to speculate; to conjecture: 這個謠言引起很多的猜測。The rumor raised much conjecture.
猜貳(ㄘㄞ ㄦˋ)
to suspect; suspicion; to doubt
猜疑(ㄘㄞ ㄧˊ)
suspicion; to suspect; to

〔犬部〕

doubt: 甚至他母親也有猜疑。Even his mother suspected him.

【猓】 3368 ㄍㄨㄛˇ guoo guǒ

name of a tribe spread over Yunnan, Kweichow and Szechwan provinces

猓玀(ㄍㄨㄛˇ ㄌㄨㄛˊ)

參看「猓」

【猝】 3369 ㄘㄨˋ tsuh cù

sudden; abrupt; hurried; unexpected

猝不及防(ㄘㄨˋ ·ㄅㄨ ㄐㄧˊ ㄈㄤˊ)

to be caught unprepared; to be caught off one's guard

猝然(ㄘㄨˋ ㄖㄢˊ)

sudden; suddenly; abruptly; unexpectedly: 天氣猝然起變化。There was a sudden change in the weather.

【猋】 3370 ㄅㄧㄠ biau biāo

1. same as 飆—a storm, gale or hurricane
2. (said of dogs) running fast
3. swift; quick; rapid

九畫

【猢】 3371 ㄏㄨˊ hwu hú

a monkey

猢猻(ㄏㄨˊ ㄙㄨㄣ)

monkeys (also used figuratively): 樹倒猢猻散。When the tree falls, the monkeys scatter. —When a person falls from power, his followers leave him.

猢猻入布袋(ㄏㄨˊ ㄙㄨㄣ ㄖㄨˋ ㄅㄨˋ ㄉㄞˋ)

to submit to discipline reluctantly (like monkeys being confined in a bag)

猢猻王(ㄏㄨˊ ㄙㄨㄣ ㄨㄤˊ)

(literally) the king of monkeys—(formerly) a teacher of a private village school

【猥】 3372 ㄨㄟˇ woei wěi

1. vulgar; wanton; low; lewd and licentious
2. many; numerous; varied; multitudinous
3. the bark of a dog

猥官(ㄨㄟˇ ㄍㄨㄢ)

low-ranking officials at various levels

猥妓(ㄨㄟˇ ㄐㄧˋ)

prostitutes

猥賤(ㄨㄟˇ ㄐㄧㄢˋ)

low and vulgar; lowly; humble: 他出身猥賤。He is a man of humble birth.

猥褻(ㄨㄟˇ ㄒㄧㄝˋ)

obscene; obscenity; lewd; to act indecently toward (a woman): 他的想法猥褻。What an obscene mind he has!

猥褻行爲(ㄨㄟˇ ㄒㄧㄝˋ ㄒㄧㄥˊ ㄨㄟˊ)

obscene or indecent acts (or behavior)

猥雜(ㄨㄟˇ ㄗㄚˊ)

numerous and varied

猥瑣(ㄨㄟˇ ㄙㄨㄛˇ)

low and petty

【猶】 3373 ㄧㄡˊ you yóu

1. like; similar to; tantamount to; as if
2. still; yet; even; especially; while: 此事記憶猶新。It is still fresh in my memory.
3. a kind of monkey
4. a Chinese family name
5. strategy; scheme; plot

猶大(ㄧㄡˊ ㄉㄚˋ)

Judas

猶他(ㄧㄡˊ ㄊㄚ)

the state of Utah, U. S. A.

猶太(ㄧㄡˊ ㄊㄞˋ)

① Jews or Hebrews; Jewish ② Judaea, name of an ancient state in today's Southern Palestine ③(comically) stingy or tight-fisted; miserly; parsimonious

猶太的(ㄧㄡˊ ㄊㄞˋ ·ㄉㄜ)

Jewish

猶太教(ㄧㄡˊ ㄊㄞˋ ㄐㄧㄠˋ)

Judaism

猶太人(ㄧㄡˊ ㄊㄞˋ ㄖㄣˊ)

the Jewish people; Jews

猶女(ㄧㄡˊ ㄋㄩˇ)

a niece

猶可(ㄧㄡˊ ㄎㄜˇ)

still all right; probably (negotiable, etc.)

猶之乎(ㄧㄡˊ ㄓ ㄏㄨ)

like; similar to

猶然(ㄧㄡˊ ㄖㄢˊ)

①just like; just as if ② still ③(now rarely) easy-going; lax ④(now rarely) laughingly; smiling

猶如(ㄧㄡˊ ㄖㄨˊ)

just like: 教室燈火輝煌, 猶如白晝。The classroom was lit up as bright as day.

猶若(ㄧㄡˊ ㄖㄨㄛˋ)

just like; almost like; tantamount to

猶子(ㄧㄡˊ ㄗˇ)

① a nephew ② just like a son

猶自(ㄧㄡˊ ㄗˋ)

still (as an adverb)

猶孫(ㄧㄡˊ ㄙㄨㄣ)

sons of a nephew

猶疑(ㄧㄡˊ ㄧˊ)

undecided; to hesitate: 猶疑不決的人不會成功。He who hesitates is lost.

猶有可爲(ㄧㄡˊ ㄧㄡˇ ㄎㄜˇ ㄨㄟˊ)

(said of a bad situation) still retrievable, reversible, salvable, etc.

猶有餘悸(ㄧㄡˊ ㄧㄡˇ ㄩˊ ㄐㄧˋ)

Even now I am scared.

猶未定(ㄧㄡˊ ㄨㄟˋ ㄉㄧㄥˋ)

not decided yet

猶未可知(ㄧㄡˊ ㄨㄟˋ ㄎㄜˇ ㄓ)

do not know yet; maybe

猶豫(ㄧㄡˊ ㄩˋ)or 猶猶豫豫(ㄧㄡˊ ㄧㄡˊ ㄩˋ ㄩˋ)

hesitant; undecided

【猩】 3374 ㄒㄧㄥ shing xīng

1. scarlet; red
2. a yellow-haired ape

猩紅(ㄒㄧㄥ ㄏㄨㄥˊ)

scarlet

猩紅熱(ㄒㄧㄥ ㄏㄨㄥˊ ㄖㄜˋ)

scarlet fever

猩猩(ㄒㄧㄥ ㄒㄧㄥ)

a yellow-haired ape; a chimpanzee; an orangutan

猩猩能言，不離禽獸(ㄒㄧㄥ ㄒㄧㄥ ㄋㄥˊ ㄧㄢˊ, ㄅㄨˋ ㄌㄧˊ ㄑㄧㄣˊ ㄕㄡˋ)

Though a chimpanzee is able to talk, it is still an animal.

猩脣(ㄒㄧㄥ ㄔㄨㄣˊ)

① red lips ② the ape's lips (one of the eight rare delicacies in Chinese cookery)

【猱】 3375 ㄋㄠˊ nau náo

1. a yellow-haired monkey
2. to scratch

猱升(ㄋㄠˊ ㄕㄥ)

the monkey climbs a tree
猱雜(ㄋㄠˊ ㄗㄚˊ)
noisily and cynically; comical and restless
猱兒(ㄋㄠˊ ㄦˊ)
prostitutes

【猴】3376 ㄏㄡˊ hour hóu
1. the monkey
2. naughty or impish (child)
猴類(ㄏㄡˊ ㄌㄟˋ)
quadrumana
猴急(ㄏㄡˊ ㄐㄧˊ)
very impatient: 你爲何如此猴急? Why are you so impatient?
猴戲(ㄏㄡˊ ㄒㄧˋ)
a monkey show (in a circus, a zoo, etc.)
猴子(ㄏㄡˊ ·ㄗ)or 猴兒(ㄏㄡˊㄦ)
①a monkey ②a clever person with a glib and sharp tongue
猴棗(ㄏㄡˊ ㄗㄠˇ)
①a kind of bezoar taken from monkeys ② a kind of persimmon
猴猻王(ㄏㄡˊ ㄙㄨㄣ ㄨㄤˊ)
(literally) the king of the monkeys—a satirical term referring to village tutors in ancient China

【猷】3377 ㄧㄡˊ you yóu
1. a plan; a program; a scheme
2. a way or path
3. to draw or paint
4. like; similar to
5. (now rarely) an opening particle

十畫

【猺】3378 (傜) ㄧㄠˊ yau yáo
1. a jackal
2. name of a tribe in Kwangtung, Hunan, Kwangsi and Yunnan
猺峝(ㄧㄠˊ ㄉㄨㄥˋ)
caves in which the Yao tribesmen live
猺山(ㄧㄠˊ ㄕㄢ)
name of a mountain range in Kwangsi
猺族(ㄧㄠˊ ㄗㄨˊ)
the Yao tribe in Kwangtung, Kwangsi, Hunan and Yunnan

【猿】3379 (猨) ㄩㄢˊ yuan yuán
an ape; a gibbon
猿臂(ㄩㄢˊ ㄅㄧˋ)
①the ape's arms ②long arms
猿啼(ㄩㄢˊ ㄊㄧˊ)
the gibbon's howling
猿類(ㄩㄢˊ ㄌㄟˋ)
anthropoid
猿號(ㄩㄢˊ ㄏㄠˊ)
an ape's call; a gibbon's howls
猿猴(ㄩㄢˊ ㄏㄡˊ)
apes and monkeys
猿人(ㄩㄢˊ ㄖㄣˊ)
the ape; anthropoid apes; a gorilla

【獅】3380 ㄕ shy shī
the lion: 獅子是萬獸之王。The lion is the king of beasts.
獅猴(ㄕ ㄏㄡˊ)
a kind of lion-like animal with a roundish head and long, soft and thick hair
獅身人面像(ㄕ ㄕㄣ ㄖㄣˊ ㄇㄧㄢˋ ㄒㄧㄤˋ)
the Sphinx
獅子(ㄕ ·ㄗ)
the lion
獅子搏兎(ㄕ ·ㄗ ㄅㄛˊ ㄊㄨˋ)
(literally) A lion fights a hare.—to use a lot of strength to perform a small feat
獅子鼻(ㄕ ·ㄗ ㄅㄧˊ)
a snub nose
獅子猫(ㄕ ·ㄗ ㄇㄠ)
the Siamese cat
獅子頭(ㄕ ·ㄗ ㄊㄡˊ)
stewed meat balls
獅子狗(ㄕ ·ㄗ ㄍㄡˇ)
a poodle
獅子國(ㄕ ·ㄗ ㄍㄨㄛˊ)
Ceylon or Sri Lanka
獅子吼(ㄕ ·ㄗ ㄏㄡˇ)
①the howls of a shrew ②(Buddhism) the preaching of Buddha that shakes the world—like a lion's roars
獅子會(ㄕ ·ㄗ ㄏㄨㄟˋ)
International Association of Lions Clubs亦作「國際獅子會」
獅子山(ㄕ ·ㄗ ㄕㄢ)
①Sierra Leone ②name of a strategic hill overlooking the Yangtze River, northwest of Nanking
獅子座(ㄕ ·ㄗ ㄗㄨㄛˋ)
①(astronomy) Leo ②(Buddhism) the Lion's Seat—where Buddha sat
獅子鷹(ㄕ ·ㄗ ㄧㄥ)
the screech-owl

【猾】3381 ㄏㄨㄚˊ hwa huá
cunning; shrewd; crafty: 他狡猾如狐狸。He is as cunning as a fox.
猾伯(ㄏㄨㄚˊ ㄅㄛˊ)
a master in cunningness
猾吏(ㄏㄨㄚˊ ㄌㄧˋ)
a cunning and wicked official
猾亂(ㄏㄨㄚˊ ㄌㄨㄢˋ)
to cause turmoil or upheaval
猾賊(ㄏㄨㄚˊ ㄗㄟˊ)
a glib rascal

【猻】3382 ㄙㄨㄣ suen sūn
a monkey

【獃】3383 (呆) ㄉㄞ dai dāi (又讀 ㄞˊ air ái)
1. stupid; silly; foolish; idiotic; a fool: 你 眞 是 獃! What a fool you were!
2. maladroit; awkward; clumsy; bungling
3. to stay: 我每天都獃在家裏。I stay at home every day.
獃板(ㄉㄞ ㄅㄢˇ)
dull and mechanical; without flexibility
獃獃地(ㄉㄞ ㄉㄞ ·ㄉㄜ)
stupidly; idiotically
獃頭獃腦(ㄉㄞ ㄊㄡˊ ㄉㄞ ㄋㄠˇ)
a silly or clumsy appearance; a rustic and stupid look; looking like an idiot
獃磕磕(ㄉㄞ ·ㄎㄜ ㄎㄜ)
vacant and stupid; dumbfounded
獃話(ㄉㄞ ㄏㄨㄚˋ)
stupid nonsense: 不要聽他的獃話。Don't listen to his stupid nonsense.
獃氣(ㄉㄞ ㄑㄧˋ)
a silly look; idiotic
獃相(ㄉㄞ ㄒㄧㄤˋ)
a silly look

〔犬部〕

獃住了(ㄉㄞ ㄓㄨˋ ˙ㄌㄜ)
dumbfounded: 聽他這麼說，她獃住了。She was dumbfounded to hear him say so.
獃若木鷄(ㄉㄞ ㄖㄨㄛˋ ㄇㄨˋ ㄐㄧ)
as dull as a wooden chicken—very dull or stupid
獃子(ㄉㄞ ˙ㄗ)
an idiot; a stupid person

【獄】 3384 ㄩˋ yuh yù
1. jail; prison
2. a lawsuit: 折獄 to decide a lawsuit
獄吏(ㄩˋ ㄌㄧˋ)
a jailer; a warden
獄官(ㄩˋ ㄍㄨㄢ)
a warden: 他當了二十年的獄官。He has been a warden for twenty years.
獄警(ㄩˋ ㄐㄧㄥˇ)
the prison police; prison guards
獄囚(ㄩˋ ㄑㄧㄡˊ)
prisoners
獄卒(ㄩˋ ㄗㄨˊ) or 獄丁(ㄩˋ ㄉㄧㄥ)
low-ranking employees who help run a prison; jailers; gaolers
獄訟(ㄩˋ ㄙㄨㄥˋ)
a lawsuit

十一畫

【獒】 3385 ㄠˊ aur áo
a large fierce dog; a mastiff

【獏】 3386 ㄇㄨˊ mu mú
Mu, name of a tribe in Hopu, Kwangtung Province 亦作「獏貊」

【獐】 3387 ㄓㄤ jang zhāng
the roe deer; the hornless river deer
獐頭鼠目(ㄓㄤ ㄊㄡˊ ㄕㄨˇ ㄇㄨˋ)
facial features suggesting cunning and meanness

十二畫

【獠】 3388 ㄌㄧㄠˊ liau liáo
1. also known as 夷, a primitive tribe in Southwest China
2. (said of one's looks) fierce
3. nocturnal hunting
4. a monster; a wicked person
獠面(ㄌㄧㄠˊ ㄇㄧㄢˋ)
a fierce appearance; terrifying looks
獠牙(ㄌㄧㄠˊ ㄧㄚˊ)
long protruding teeth; buckteeth; fangs: 青面獠牙 with a green face and ferocious fangs

【獞】 3389 (僮) ㄊㄨㄥˊ torng tóng
Tung, name of a primitive tribe in Kwangtung and Kwangsi
獞人(ㄊㄨㄥˊ ㄖㄣˊ)
the tribesmen of Tung
獞族(ㄊㄨㄥˊ ㄗㄨˊ)
the Tung tribe

【獗】 3390 ㄐㄩㄝˊ jyue jué
unruly; lawless and wild; rampant

十三畫

【獨】 3391 ㄉㄨˊ dwu dú
1. alone; solitary; single
2. only
3. to monopolize
4. to be old and without a son
5. how; Is it possible?
獨覇一方(ㄉㄨˊ ㄅㄚˋ ㄧˋ ㄈㄤ)
to wield absolute power in a part of a country, province, etc.
獨白(ㄉㄨˊ ㄅㄞˊ)
(dramatics) monologue; soliloquy
獨臂盜(ㄉㄨˊ ㄅㄧˋ ㄉㄠˋ)
a one-armed robber
獨步(ㄉㄨˊ ㄅㄨˋ)
unrivaled; peerless; without match; unique
獨步古今(ㄉㄨˊ ㄅㄨˋ ㄍㄨˇ ㄐㄧㄣ)
to be equaled neither in ancient times nor in modern times
獨排衆議(ㄉㄨˊ ㄆㄞˊ ㄓㄨㄥˋ ㄧˋ)
to hold one's own opinion against that of the majority (often said of a person of unique ability)
獨門兒(ㄉㄨˊ ㄇㄜˊㄦ)
the special skill transmitted from generation to generation exclusively inside a family
獨門獨院(ㄉㄨˊ ㄇㄣˊ ㄉㄨˊ ㄩㄢˋ)
a single house which has its own entrance and courtyard (as distinct from apartment houses)
獨木不成林(ㄉㄨˊ ㄇㄨˋ ㄅㄨˋ ㄔㄥˊ ㄌㄧㄣˊ)
(literally) A single tree can not make a forest.—One person cannot handle all the tasks by himself.
獨木難支(ㄉㄨˊ ㄇㄨˋ ㄋㄢˊ ㄓ)
One cannot sustain or stem the adversity all by himself.
獨幕劇(ㄉㄨˊ ㄇㄨˋ ㄐㄩˋ)
a one-act play
獨木橋(ㄉㄨˊ ㄇㄨˋ ㄑㄧㄠˊ)
a single-plank bridge
獨木舟(ㄉㄨˊ ㄇㄨˋ ㄓㄡ)
a canoe
獨峯駝(ㄉㄨˊ ㄈㄥ ㄊㄨㄛˊ)
the single-humped camel—the dromedary
獨夫(ㄉㄨˊ ㄈㄨ)
a merciless autocrat; a cruel ruler
獨到(ㄉㄨˊ ㄉㄠˋ)
original: 他有很多獨到的見解。He is rich in original views.
獨到之處(ㄉㄨˊ ㄉㄠˋ ㄓ ㄔㄨˋ)
originality (of ideas); special merits
獨當一面(ㄉㄨˊ ㄉㄤ ㄧˊ ㄇㄧㄢˋ)
to handle a major task or assignment unaided; to head a large organization: 她已經可以獨當一面了。She can now handle a major task by herself.
獨斷獨行(ㄉㄨˊ ㄉㄨㄢˋ ㄉㄨˊ ㄒㄧㄥˊ)
to decide and act on one's own; to act arbitrarily
獨特(ㄉㄨˊ ㄊㄜˋ)
unique
獨吞(ㄉㄨˊ ㄊㄨㄣ)
to pocket (profit) without sharing (it) with anyone else
獨攬大權(ㄉㄨˊ ㄌㄢˇ ㄉㄚˋ ㄑㄩㄢˊ)
to grasp at authority by oneself; to arrogate all power to oneself
獨立(ㄉㄨˊ ㄌㄧˋ)
independence; independent
獨立旅(ㄉㄨˊ ㄌㄧˋ ㄌㄩˇ)
(military) a brigade which forms an independent fight-

ing unit and is not subordinate to the command of a division or corps

獨立國(ㄉㄨˊ ㄌㄧˋ ㄍㄨㄛˊ)or 獨立國家(ㄉㄨˊ ㄌㄧˋ ㄍㄨㄛˊ ㄐㄧㄚ)
an independent nation or country

獨立紀念日(ㄉㄨˊ ㄌㄧˋ ㄐㄧˋ ㄋㄧㄢˋ ㄖˋ)
Independence Day (U.S.), the Fourth of July, the anniversary of the adoption of the Declaration of Independence

獨立精神(ㄉㄨˊ ㄌㄧˋ ㄐㄧㄥ ㄕㄣˊ)
the spirit of independence; independent-minded

獨立宣言(ㄉㄨˊ ㄌㄧˋ ㄒㄩㄢ ㄧㄢˊ)
the Declaration of Independence of the U.S.A.

獨立師(ㄉㄨˊ ㄌㄧˋ ㄕ)
(military) a division as an independent fighting force which is not subordinate to the command of a corps

獨立自主(ㄉㄨˊ ㄌㄧˋ ㄗˋ ㄓㄨˇ)
① the independence of sovereignty ② to act independently and with the initiative in one's own hands

獨力(ㄉㄨˊ ㄌㄧˋ)
single-handed; all by oneself; on one's own: 你能獨力做此工作嗎? Can you do the work on your own?

獨力支持(ㄉㄨˊ ㄌㄧˋ ㄓ ㄔˊ)
to support single-handedly

獨輪車(ㄉㄨˊ ㄌㄨㄣˊ ㄔㄜ)
a monocycle

獨家經營(ㄉㄨˊ ㄐㄧㄚ ㄐㄧㄥ ㄧㄥˊ)
to engage in a line of business without competition

獨家新聞(ㄉㄨˊ ㄐㄧㄚ ㄒㄧㄣ ㄨㄣˊ)
an exclusive news report; a scoop

獨脚戲(ㄉㄨˊ ㄐㄧㄠˇ ㄒㄧˋ)
a one-man show

獨角獸(ㄉㄨˊ ㄐㄧㄠˇ ㄕㄡˋ)
a unicorn (a legendary animal)

獨居(ㄉㄨˊ ㄐㄩ)
to live alone

獨居石(ㄉㄨˊ ㄐㄩ ㄕˊ)
(mineral) monazite

獨具匠心(ㄉㄨˊ ㄐㄩˋ ㄐㄧㄤˋ ㄒㄧㄣ)
to have originality

獨具隻眼(ㄉㄨˊ ㄐㄩˋ ㄓ ㄧㄢˇ)or 獨具慧眼 (ㄉㄨˊ ㄐㄩˋ ㄏㄨㄟˋ ㄧㄢˇ)
to have a remarkable view; to have clairvoyance; to see things in a different light

獨清獨醒(ㄉㄨˊ ㄑㄧㄥ ㄉㄨˊ ㄒㄧㄥˇ)
to remain sane and sober and realize the lurking dangers in time of outward peace and prosperity when others live in a false sense of security

獨秀(ㄉㄨˊ ㄒㄧㄡˋ)
to be outstanding at a given time

獨弦哀歌(ㄉㄨˊ ㄒㄧㄢˊ ㄞ ㄍㄜ)
to pretend to be unique and outstanding in one's statements or actions

獨行(ㄉㄨˊ ㄒㄧㄥˊ)
① to walk alone ② to insist on one's ways in doing things

獨行盜(ㄉㄨˊ ㄒㄧㄥˊ ㄉㄠˋ)
a lone robber; a robber who acts alone

獨占 or 獨佔(ㄉㄨˊ ㄓㄢˋ)
to monopolize; monopoly

獨占花魁(ㄉㄨˊ ㄓㄢˋ ㄏㄨㄚ ㄎㄨㄟˊ)
to be the lucky man in winning the pretty courtesan's hand

獨占鼇頭(ㄉㄨˊ ㄓㄢˋ ㄠˊ ㄊㄡˊ)
① to emerge first in the civil service examination in former times ②to come out first; to be the champion

獨掌(ㄉㄨˊ ㄓㄤˇ)
to head or to be in charge of (a department, etc.)

獨酌(ㄉㄨˊ ㄓㄨㄛˊ)
to drink without company

獨持異議(ㄉㄨˊ ㄔˊ ㄧˋ ㄧˋ)
to hold an opinion different from that of the majority on a controversial issue

獨唱(ㄉㄨˊ ㄔㄤˋ)
singing solo; a vocal recital

獨出心裁(ㄉㄨˊ ㄔㄨ ㄒㄧㄣ ㄘㄞˊ)
to be unique or original in one's planning and design

獨處(ㄉㄨˊ ㄔㄨˇ)
to stay alone

獨創(ㄉㄨˊ ㄔㄨㄤˋ)
(literally) to create all by oneself—unique; original

獨善其身(ㄉㄨˊ ㄕㄢˋ ㄑㄧˊ ㄕㄣ)
to keep oneself clean and pure; to conduct oneself virtuously

獨身(ㄉㄨˊ ㄕㄣ)
unmarried; single

獨身主義(ㄉㄨˊ ㄕㄣ ㄓㄨˇ ㄧˋ)
the belief in the merits of remaining unmarried (as distinct from religious celibacy)

獨生女(ㄉㄨˊ ㄕㄥ ㄋㄩˇ)
the only daughter

獨生子(ㄉㄨˊ ㄕㄥ ㄗˇ)or 獨子(ㄉㄨˊ ㄗˇ)
the only son

獨樹一幟(ㄉㄨˊ ㄕㄨˋ ㄧˊ ㄓˋ)
(literally) to set up a separate flag—to take a distinctive course or attitude of one's own

獨資經營(ㄉㄨˊ ㄗ ㄐㄧㄥ ㄧㄥˊ)
to operate a business setup entirely with one's own capital: 他獨資經營這家商店。He is the sole owner of the store.

獨自(ㄉㄨˊ ㄗˋ)or 獨自個(ㄉㄨˊ ㄗˋ ㄍㄜˋ)
alone; single-handedly; personally

獨奏(ㄉㄨˊ ㄗㄡˋ)
(music) a solo performance: 他將獨奏喇叭。He's going to solo on the trumpet.

獨坐(ㄉㄨˊ ㄗㄨㄛˋ)
to sit all by oneself

獨裁(ㄉㄨˊ ㄘㄞˊ)
dictatorship; dictatorial

獨裁政治(ㄉㄨˊ ㄘㄞˊ ㄓㄥˋ ㄓˋ)
dictatorship; autocracy

獨一無二(ㄉㄨˊ ㄧ ㄨˊ ㄦˋ)
the one and the only one; unique; to stand alone

獨眼龍(ㄉㄨˊ ㄧㄢˇ ㄌㄨㄥˊ)
(comically) a one-eyed person or a person with a defective eye

獨往獨來(ㄉㄨˊ ㄨㄤˇ ㄉㄨˊ ㄌㄞˊ)
(literally) to come and go alone—to act independently without seeking company

【獪】 3392 ㄎㄨㄞˋ kuay kuài

cunning; artful; crafty: 狐狸非常狡獪。A fox has a great deal of cunning.

獪猾(ㄎㄨㄞˋ ㄏㄨㄚˊ)
cunning: 他是個獪猾的政客。He is a crafty politician.

【獬】 3393 ㄒㄧㄝˋ shieh xiè

〔犬部〕

1. a Pekingese dog
2. a mythical animal which was supposed to know the difference between right and wrong

十四畫

【獲】 3394 ㄏㄨㄛˋ huoh huò

1. to get; to obtain; to incur; to capture; to catch; to reap: 我們去年喜獲豐收。We happily reaped a bumper harvest last year.
2. can; able: 不獲善終 to be not able to die a natural death
3. a slave-girl

獲得(ㄏㄨㄛˋ ㄉㄜˊ)
to get or obtain; to acquire: 他將獲得所要的東西。He will obtain what he wants.

獲麟(ㄏㄨㄛˋ ㄌㄧㄣˊ)
① the capture of a unicorn (When Confucius had written about the capture of a *lin* (a female unicorn), he concluded his *Spring and Autumn Annals*—the only book he authored.) ② (figuratively) All affairs come to an end.

獲咎(ㄏㄨㄛˋ ㄐㄧㄡˋ)
to incur blame

獲救(ㄏㄨㄛˋ ㄐㄧㄡˋ)
to be rescued or saved from (death, disaster, etc.)

獲獎(ㄏㄨㄛˋ ㄐㄧㄤˇ)
to win a prize

獲赦(ㄏㄨㄛˋ ㄕㄜˋ)
to be pardoned

獲勝(ㄏㄨㄛˋ ㄕㄥˋ)
to triumph; to obtain victory; to win: 甲隊以三比一獲勝。Team A won the match three to one.

獲罪(ㄏㄨㄛˋ ㄗㄨㄟˋ)
to be blamed; to offend; to commit a crime or sin

獲益(ㄏㄨㄛˋ ㄧˋ)
to get profit: 他學習英文頗有獲益。He has studied English to his profit.

【獮】 3395 ㄒㄧㄢˇ shean xiǎn

1. to hunt; to kill
2. autumn hunting by ancient emperors

【獯】 3396 ㄒㄩㄣ shiun xūn

name of a northern barbarian tribe in ancient China known as the Huns(匈奴) during the Han Dynasty

獯鬻(ㄒㄩㄣ ㄩˋ)
參看「獯」

【獰】 3397 ㄋㄧㄥˊ ning níng

a fierce appearance; an awe-inspiring look

獰笑(ㄋㄧㄥˊ ㄒㄧㄠˋ)
① a laugh with malignant intent; a frightening laugh ② to laugh malignantly

獰惡可怖(ㄋㄧㄥˊ ㄜˋ ㄎㄜˇ ㄅㄨˋ)
(said of a person's appearance) fierce and terrifying

十五畫

【獵】 3398 ㄌㄧㄝˋ lieh liè

to hunt; to chase; field sports

獵名(ㄌㄧㄝˋ ㄇㄧㄥˊ)
to hunt for a good name or a good reputation; to be after fame: 他此舉乃為獵名。He did this to hunt for a good name.

獵狗(ㄌㄧㄝˋ ㄍㄡˇ)
a pointer; a hunting dog; a hound: 獵狗迫近獵物。The hounds got nearer to their game.

獵戶(ㄌㄧㄝˋ ㄏㄨˋ)
hunters; huntsmen

獵戶座(ㄌㄧㄝˋ ㄏㄨˋ ㄗㄨㄛˋ)
(astronomy) Orion

獵獲(ㄌㄧㄝˋ ㄏㄨㄛˋ)
to catch in hunting; to bag: 我們昨天獵獲兩三隻野兎。We bagged a couple of hares yesterday.

獵奇(ㄌㄧㄝˋ ㄑㄧˊ)
① to hunt for the strange or uncommon ② a record of what is strange or uncommon

獵槍(ㄌㄧㄝˋ ㄑㄧㄤ)
a hunting gun; a fowling piece; a shotgun

獵取(ㄌㄧㄝˋ ㄑㄩˇ)
to chase after; to pursue; to hunt

獵取功名(ㄌㄧㄝˋ ㄑㄩˇ ㄍㄨㄥ ㄇㄧㄥˊ)
to try to win a degree in civil examination

獵犬(ㄌㄧㄝˋ ㄑㄩㄢˇ)
a hunting dog; a pointer, dachshund, etc.: 獵犬追逐野獸。The hunting dogs chased wild animals.

獵犬座(ㄌㄧㄝˋ ㄑㄩㄢˇ ㄗㄨㄛˋ)
Canes Venatici

獵裝(ㄌㄧㄝˋ ㄓㄨㄤ)
hunting dress

獵場(ㄌㄧㄝˋ ㄔㄤˇ)
a hunting ground; a hunting field

獵食(ㄌㄧㄝˋ ㄕˊ)
to hunt for food: 狼成群獵食。Wolves hunt in packs.

獵人(ㄌㄧㄝˋ ㄖㄣˊ)
a hunter; a huntsman

獵艷(ㄌㄧㄝˋ ㄧㄢˋ)
to chase after pretty women

獵鷹(ㄌㄧㄝˋ ㄧㄥ)
a falcon

獵物(ㄌㄧㄝˋ ㄨˋ)
game; a quarry

【獷】 3399 ㄍㄨㄤˇ goang guǎng

fierce and rude; uncivilized

獷敵(ㄍㄨㄤˇ ㄉㄧˊ)
a savage enemy; a deadly rival

獷悍(ㄍㄨㄤˇ ㄏㄢˋ)
rude and brutal

獷俗(ㄍㄨㄤˇ ㄙㄨˊ)
uncivilized customs; barbarian ways

【獸】 3400 ㄕㄡˋ show shòu

1. a general name for quadruped; a beast or animal
2. bestial; beastly

獸皮(ㄕㄡˋ ㄆㄧˊ)
animal skin or hide

獸面(ㄕㄡˋ ㄇㄧㄢˋ)
(in ancient China) a mask of an animal head worn by a player

獸類(ㄕㄡˋ ㄌㄟˋ)
animals; beasts

獸力(ㄕㄡˋ ㄌㄧˋ)
animal power (especially said of beasts of burden)

獸爐(ㄕㄡˋ ㄌㄨˊ)
a vessel for burning incense usually shaped like an animal

獸工(ㄕㄡˋ ㄍㄨㄥ)
a tanner
獸環(ㄕㄡˋ ㄏㄨㄢˊ)
a doorknob shaped like the head of an animal with a ring for a knocking purpose
獸姦(ㄕㄡˋ ㄐㄧㄢ)
sodomy; buggery
獸檻(ㄕㄡˋ ㄐㄧㄢˋ)
a pen or cage for animals亦作「獸圈」
獸聚鳥散(ㄕㄡˋ ㄐㄩˋ ㄋㄧㄠˇ ㄙㄢˋ)
(usually said of bandits, etc.) to get together and disperse like animals and birds
獸圈(ㄕㄡˋ ㄐㄩㄢˋ)
a pen or cage for animals
獸心(ㄕㄡˋ ㄒㄧㄣ)
bestiality; beastliness
獸行(ㄕㄡˋ ㄒㄧㄥˊ)
bestial or beastly acts or conduct; atrocities
獸性(ㄕㄡˋ ㄒㄧㄥˋ)
① bestiality; beastliness ② animal passions or desires
獸性大發(ㄕㄡˋ ㄒㄧㄥˋ ㄉㄚˋ ㄈㄚ)
to raise one's animal disposition
獸中之王(ㄕㄡˋ ㄓㄨㄥ ㄓ ㄨㄤˊ)
the king of beasts—the lion
獸醫(ㄕㄡˋ ㄧ)
a veterinarian
獸醫學(ㄕㄡˋ ㄧ ㄒㄩㄝˊ)
veterinary science; zoopathology
獸慾(ㄕㄡˋ ㄩˋ)
carnal desire; lust; bestial urge (especially referring to rape)

十六畫

【獺】 3401
ㄊㄚˋ tah tà
an otter
獺祭(ㄊㄚˋ ㄐㄧˋ)
to write an article by heaping up quotations and allusions from a large number of books

【獻】 3402
ㄒㄧㄢˋ shiann xiàn
1. to present; to forward; to offer; to dedicate; to donate
2. to display; to show; to stage
3. to curry (favor, etc.); to flatter or cater to

獻寶(ㄒㄧㄢˋ ㄅㄠˇ)
① to present a treasure ② to offer a scheme or one's valuable experience ③ to show off what one treasures
獻曝(ㄒㄧㄢˋ ㄆㄨˋ)
(a polite expression) to offer my humble gift or advice
獻媚(ㄒㄧㄢˋ ㄇㄟˋ)
① to act coquettishly ② to curry favor; to toady; to act obsequiously
獻俘(ㄒㄧㄢˋ ㄈㄨˊ)
(in ancient China) to offer prisoners of war at the national shrine after the triumphal conclusion of a war
獻禮(ㄒㄧㄢˋ ㄌㄧˇ)
① the ceremony of offering presents ② to present a gift
獻花(ㄒㄧㄢˋ ㄏㄨㄚ)
to present flowers or bouquets; to lay a wreath: 小姐們向英雄獻花。The girls presented flowers to the heroes.
獻機(ㄒㄧㄢˋ ㄐㄧ)
to contribute money for the procurement of warplanes as a gift to the country
獻技(ㄒㄧㄢˋ ㄐㄧˋ)
to display one's feat; to stage a performance of special skills or feats: 他到國外獻技去了。He went abroad to perform feats.
獻計(ㄒㄧㄢˋ ㄐㄧˋ)
to present or offer advice or a scheme for adoption; to make suggestions
獻捷(ㄒㄧㄢˋ ㄐㄧㄝˊ)
to send prisoners of war to an ally as a gesture of friendship upon the victorious conclusion of a war
獻酒(ㄒㄧㄢˋ ㄐㄧㄡˇ)
to offer wine
獻艦(ㄒㄧㄢˋ ㄐㄧㄢˋ)
to contribute money for the procurement of warships as a gift to the country
獻金(ㄒㄧㄢˋ ㄐㄧㄣ)
① to contribute (money) ② money contributed
獻旗(ㄒㄧㄢˋ ㄑㄧˊ)
to present flags or pennants

獻芹(ㄒㄧㄢˋ ㄑㄧㄣˊ)
to offer my humble gift
獻醜(ㄒㄧㄢˋ ㄔㄡˇ)or 獻拙(ㄒㄧㄢˋ ㄓㄨㄛˊ)
to show my poor skill or talent (a polite expression)
獻身(ㄒㄧㄢˋ ㄕㄣ)
to offer or dedicate oneself (to a cause, one's nation, etc.): 他一生獻身學術。He dedicated all his life to learning.
獻身社會(ㄒㄧㄢˋ ㄕㄣ ㄕㄜˋ ㄏㄨㄟˋ)
to offer oneself to social work; to dedicate oneself to public services
獻詞(ㄒㄧㄢˋ ㄘˊ)
a dedication; a dedication speech
獻策(ㄒㄧㄢˋ ㄘㄜˋ)
① to offer a plan, scheme, etc.; to advise ② a plan; advice
獻歲(ㄒㄧㄢˋ ㄙㄨㄟˋ)
the beginning of a new year
獻藝(ㄒㄧㄢˋ ㄧˋ)
① to exhibit one's skill ② (said of actors) to appear on stage for performances: 電影明星將來此登臺獻藝。The movie star will come here and appear on stage.
獻殷勤(ㄒㄧㄢˋ ㄧㄣ ㄑㄧㄣˊ)
to flatter; to make oneself liked; to ingratiate

十七畫

【獼】 3403
ㄇㄧˊ mi mí
a rhesus monkey
獼猴(ㄇㄧˊ ㄏㄡˊ)
a rhesus monkey; a macaque

十九畫

【玀】 3404
ㄌㄨㄛˊ luo luó
a primitive tribe 參看「猓玀」

二十畫

【獮】 3405
(獫)ㄒㄧㄢˇ shean xiǎn
a dog with a long snout or muzzle
獮狁(ㄒㄧㄢˇ ㄩㄣˇ)

Hsien-yün, a barbarian tribe known as the Huns (匈奴) during the Chin and the Han dynasties

玄部
ㄒㄩㄢˊ shyuan xuán

【玄】 3406
ㄒㄩㄢˊ shyuan xuán

1. far and obscure; occult or mystic
2. dark or black
3. deep and profound; abstruse and subtle: 這太玄了。This is getting too abstruse.
4. silent and meditative
5. pretending
6. a Chinese family name

玄默(ㄒㄩㄢˊ ㄇㄛˋ)
taciturn and meditative

玄謀(ㄒㄩㄢˊ ㄇㄡˊ)
a subtle and profound scheme

玄門(ㄒㄩㄢˊ ㄇㄣˊ)
① Buddhism ② Taoism

玄妙(ㄒㄩㄢˊ ㄇㄧㄠˋ)
profound, abstruse and subtle; mysterious: 這些是很玄妙的問題。These are very abstruse questions.

玄服(ㄒㄩㄢˊ ㄈㄨˊ)
dark dress or clothing

玄德(ㄒㄩㄢˊ ㄉㄜˊ)
① latent or hidden virtues ②(Buddhism) the fabulous and subtle faith

玄談(ㄒㄩㄢˊ ㄊㄢˊ)
① the profound, abstruse words of Lao-tzu ② the foreword or introduction to a Buddhist scripture

玄鳥(ㄒㄩㄢˊ ㄋㄧㄠˇ)
① a swallow ② a crane

玄覽(ㄒㄩㄢˊ ㄌㄢˇ)
to view all with a tranquil mind

玄理(ㄒㄩㄢˊ ㄌㄧˇ)
profound or abstruse reasoning or theory

玄關(ㄒㄩㄢˊ ㄍㄨㄢ)
① the entrance to Buddhism ② the door of a house ③ a vestibule

玄黃(ㄒㄩㄢˊ ㄏㄨㄤˊ)
① heaven and earth ② dark yellow

玄機(ㄒㄩㄢˊ ㄐㄧ)
(Taoism) the profound and mysterious truth

玄教(ㄒㄩㄢˊ ㄐㄧㄠˋ)
Taoism

玄酒(ㄒㄩㄢˊ ㄐㄧㄡˇ)
①(in ancient China) the water used in worshiping ② diluted wine

玄穹(ㄒㄩㄢˊ ㄑㄩㄥ)
the sky; heaven

玄象(ㄒㄩㄢˊ ㄒㄧㄤˋ)
the phenomena of celestial bodies

玄虛(ㄒㄩㄢˊ ㄒㄩ)
① empty and without substance; mysterious; mystic: 他爲何故弄玄虛? Why was he deliberately mysterious? ②cunning and evil schemes; tricks

玄學(ㄒㄩㄢˊ ㄒㄩㄝˊ)
① metaphysics: 玄學討論抽象的概念。Metaphysics deals with abstractions. ② Taoism ③ Buddhism ④ spiritualism (as opposed to materialism)

玄學家(ㄒㄩㄢˊ ㄒㄩㄝˊ ㄐㄧㄚ)
a spiritualist; a metaphysicist

玄之又玄(ㄒㄩㄢˊ ㄓ ㄧㄡˋ ㄒㄩㄢˊ)
① occult; the most mysterious of the mysterious ② nonsense

玄眞(ㄒㄩㄢˊ ㄓㄣ)
jade

玄著(ㄒㄩㄢˊ ㄓㄨˋ)
profound or abstruse writings

玄奘(ㄒㄩㄢˊ ㄗㄤˋ)
Hsüan Tsang, 596-664, a Buddhist monk in the Tang Dynasty, who toured India for more than 10 years and brought back 600-odd Buddhist scriptures, 75 of which he and his disciples translated into Chinese

玄宗(ㄒㄩㄢˊ ㄗㄨㄥ)
the Buddhist religion

玄孫(ㄒㄩㄢˊ ㄙㄨㄣ)
great-great-grandson

玄奧(ㄒㄩㄢˊ ㄠˋ)
① abstruse and subtle; difficult to comprehend ② mysteries; profundities

玄武湖(ㄒㄩㄢˊ ㄨˇ ㄏㄨˊ)
a famous lake in Nanking

玄武岩(ㄒㄩㄢˊ ㄨˇ ㄧㄢˊ)
basalt

玄悟(ㄒㄩㄢˊ ㄨˋ)
a profound understanding of an abstruse theory

玄月(ㄒㄩㄢˊ ㄩㄝˋ)
the ninth moon in the lunar calendar

六畫

【率】 3407
1. ㄕㄨㄞˋ shuay shuài

1. to lead (troops, a team, etc.); to command
2. to follow; to act in accordance with
3. rash and hasty
4. generally; in general; usually
5. simple and candid; frank; straightforward; to the point
6. (said of men) dashing

率部(ㄕㄨㄞˋ ㄅㄨˋ)or 率兵(ㄕㄨㄞˋ ㄅㄧㄥ)
to lead troops

率土之濱(ㄕㄨㄞˋ ㄊㄨˇ ㄓ ㄅㄧㄣ)
within the sea-boundaries of the land—within the territory of a state

率同(ㄕㄨㄞˋ ㄊㄨㄥˊ)
accompanied by; to lead all the others in (visiting, inspecting, etc.)

率領(ㄕㄨㄞˋ ㄌㄧㄥˇ)
to lead (troops, a team, etc.); to head (a mission, etc.): 將軍率領軍隊衝鋒。The general led his armies in the charge.

率先(ㄕㄨㄞˋ ㄒㄧㄢ)
to be the first; to take the lead: 由誰率先開始? Who takes the lead?

率性(ㄕㄨㄞˋ ㄒㄧㄥˋ)
① one's natural disposition ② to act according to the dictates of one's conscience

率直(ㄕㄨㄞˋ ㄓˊ)
candid; frank; straight; honest

率眞(ㄕㄨㄞˋ ㄓㄣ)
candid; frank; honest

率衆(ㄕㄨㄞˋ ㄓㄨㄥˋ)

to lead a crowd; to lead a large group of people

率師(ㄕㄨㄞˋ ㄕ)
to lead troops

率獸食人(ㄕㄨㄞˋ ㄕㄡˋ ㄕˊ ㄖㄣˊ)
to lead on beasts to devour men—tyranny of government

率然(ㄕㄨㄞˋ ㄖㄢˊ)
randomly; casually

率爾(ㄕㄨㄞˋ ㄦˇ)
casually; rashly; at random: 你不應該率爾行事。You should not do everything rashly.

率爾操觚(ㄕㄨㄞˋ ㄦˇ ㄘㄠ ㄍㄨ)
to write at random or desultorily

率意(ㄕㄨㄞˋ ㄧˋ)
①to act on the spur of the moment; to follow one's inclination: 不可率意孤行。You should not act on the spur of the moment. ②with all one's sincerity

率由(ㄕㄨㄞˋ ㄧㄡˊ)
to follow; to act according to

率由舊章(ㄕㄨㄞˋ ㄧㄡˊ ㄐㄧㄡˋ ㄓㄤ)
to follow old practices or precedents

率允(ㄕㄨㄞˋ ㄩㄣˇ)
to promise at random or carelessly

【率】 3407
2. ㄌㄩˋ liuh lǜ

1. (mathematics) ratio
2. a suffix used to indicate a measure or rate
3. to calculate

玉 部
ㄩˋ yuh yù

【玉】 3408
ㄩˋ yuh yù

1. a precious stone—especially jade; a gem
2. a polite expression for "your"
3. a designation of things belonging to a girl or young woman
4. (said of a person, especially a woman) pure; fair; beautiful
5. a Chinese family name

玉撥(ㄩˋ ㄅㄛ)
a jade hairpin

玉帛(ㄩˋ ㄅㄛˊ)
①gems and silk (used as state gifts in ancient China) ②(figuratively) friendship

玉杯(ㄩˋ ㄅㄟ)
①a jade cup ②name of a book authored by Tung Chung-shu (董仲舒) of the Han Dynasty

玉臂(ㄩˋ ㄅㄧˋ)
a girl's arms; a pretty woman's arms

玉陛(ㄩˋ ㄅㄧˋ)
the steps of white jade leading to the throne

玉鬢(ㄩˋ ㄅㄧㄣˋ)
white hair

玉步(ㄩˋ ㄅㄨˋ)
①your footsteps ②the footsteps of a pretty girl

玉不琢不成器(ㄩˋ ㄅㄨˋ ㄓㄨㄛˊ ㄅㄨˋ ㄔㄥˊ ㄑㄧˋ)
(literally) Jade must be cut and chiseled to make it a useful vessel.—A person must be disciplined and educated to be a useful citizen.

玉佩(ㄩˋ ㄆㄟˋ)
jade pendants on a girdle

玉盤(ㄩˋ ㄆㄢˊ)
①a jade plate or tray ②(figuratively) the moon ③a variety of chrysanthemum with protruding yellow center and whitish green edge

玉貌(ㄩˋ ㄇㄠˋ) or 玉面(ㄩˋ ㄇㄧㄢˋ)
①a fair face; the face of a pretty girl ②your face

玉門關(ㄩˋ ㄇㄣˊ ㄍㄨㄢ) or 玉塞(ㄩˋ ㄙㄞˋ) or 玉關(ㄩˋ ㄍㄨㄢ)
the Yü-men Pass—a gate on the Great Wall in Kansu Province, a strategic gateway to the Western Regions (西域)

玉米(ㄩˋ ㄇㄧˇ)
Indian corn; maize

玉米花兒(ㄩˋ ㄇㄧˇ ㄏㄨㄚㄦ)
popcorn

玉面朱唇(ㄩˋ ㄇㄧㄢˋ ㄓㄨ ㄔㄨㄣˊ)
a beautiful and fashionable woman

玉帶(ㄩˋ ㄉㄞˋ)
a jade-studded belt worn by high-ranking officials in ancient China

玉雕(ㄩˋ ㄉㄧㄠ)
jade carving; jade sculpture

玉敦(ㄩˋ ㄉㄨㄟˋ)
a jade vessel used to hold blood during the oath-taking ceremony in ancient China

玉堂(ㄩˋ ㄊㄤˊ)
①a rich and powerful family ②an imperial harem ③name of an office in the Han Dynasty

玉體(ㄩˋ ㄊㄧˇ)
①yourself; your person: 請保重玉體。Please take good care of yourself. ②the nude body of a girl

玉體橫陳(ㄩˋ ㄊㄧˇ ㄏㄥˊ ㄔㄣˊ)
(said of a girl or a young woman) the beautiful nude body lying in full view

玉體違和(ㄩˋ ㄊㄧˇ ㄨㄟˊ ㄏㄜˊ)
a term referring to someone who is out of sorts

玉兔(ㄩˋ ㄊㄨˋ)
①(Chinese mythology) the jade hare in the moon ②the moon

玉兔東升(ㄩˋ ㄊㄨˋ ㄉㄨㄥ ㄕㄥ)
The moon rises in the east.

玉輦(ㄩˋ ㄋㄧㄢˇ)
the imperial carriage

玉女(ㄩˋ ㄋㄩˇ)
①a young and beautiful girl ②your daughter ③an angel in the fairyland

玉樓(ㄩˋ ㄌㄡˊ)
①the fairyland; paradise ②a jade tower ③(Taoism) the shoulder

玉樓赴召(ㄩˋ ㄌㄡˊ ㄈㄨˋ ㄓㄠˋ)
(said of a young scholar) to die

玉漏(ㄩˋ ㄌㄡˋ)
a jade hourglass

玉蘭(ㄩˋ ㄌㄢˊ)
a magnolia

玉露(ㄩˋ ㄌㄨˋ)
①dewdrops ②the best green tea

玉鉤 or 玉鈎(ㄩˋ ㄍㄡ)
①the crescent moon; the new moon ②the jade hook

玉粳(ㄩˋ ㄍㄥ)
a neat row of sparkling

〔玉部〕

〔玉部〕

teeth
玉骨冰肌(ㄩˋ ㄍㄨˇ ㄅㄧㄥ ㄐㄧ)
elegant demeanor and high personality
玉衡(ㄩˋ ㄏㄥˊ)
an ancient instrument for observing heavenly bodies
玉壺(ㄩˋ ㄏㄨˊ)
①a jade wine-cup, symbolic of spiritual purity ②honest and virtuous ③a jade hour-glass
玉笏(ㄩˋ ㄏㄨˋ)
a jade tablet held by a high official to attend the imperial court session in the early morning
玉環(ㄩˋ ㄏㄨㄢˊ)
①jade rings or bracelets ②the moon
玉皇大帝(ㄩˋ ㄏㄨㄤˊ ㄉㄚˋ ㄉㄧˋ)or 玉帝(ㄩˋ ㄉㄧˋ)
the Jade Emperor, the supreme deity in Taoism
玉潔冰清(ㄩˋ ㄐㄧㄝˊ ㄅㄧㄥ ㄑㄧㄥ)
pure like jade, clear like ice —pure and virtuous
玉尖(ㄩˋ ㄐㄧㄢ)
①tapering fingers of a beautiful woman ②mountain peaks
玉減香消(ㄩˋ ㄐㄧㄢˇ ㄒㄧㄤ ㄒㄧㄠ)
(said of a beauty) to become emaciated
玉漿(ㄩˋ ㄐㄧㄤ)
good wine
玉器(ㄩˋ ㄑㄧˋ)
jade articles
玉磬(ㄩˋ ㄑㄧㄥˋ)
an ancient musical instrument
玉闕(ㄩˋ ㄑㄩㄝˋ)
①the holy city ②the gate to a holy land
玉泉山(ㄩˋ ㄑㄩㄢˊ ㄕㄢ)
name of a hill northwest of Peking, near the Summer Palace
玉璽(ㄩˋ ㄒㄧˇ)
the imperial seal
玉匣(ㄩˋ ㄒㄧㄚˊ)
①a jade box for jewels ②a coffin for emperors in the Han Dynasty
玉屑(ㄩˋ ㄒㄧㄝˋ)
①broken jade ②snow ③exquisite writing
玉簫(ㄩˋ ㄒㄧㄠ)
a jade flute
玉心(ㄩˋ ㄒㄧㄣ)
a heart as pure as jade
玉虛(ㄩˋ ㄒㄩ)
the fairyland
玉巵(ㄩˋ ㄓ)
a jade cup
玉質(ㄩˋ ㄓˊ)
of jade
玉趾(ㄩˋ ㄓˇ)
(a term of respect) your footsteps
玉札(ㄩˋ ㄓㄚˊ)
name of a herb used in Chinese medicine
玉照(ㄩˋ ㄓㄠˋ)
your photograph or picture
玉展(ㄩˋ ㄓㄢˇ)
for your perusal (a polite expression following the name of a person to whom a letter is addressed)
玉筯(ㄩˋ ㄓㄨˋ)
①chopsticks made of jade ②snivel; tears ③a style of calligraphy known as "small seal" (小篆)
玉鐲(ㄩˋ ㄓㄨㄛˊ)
a jade bracelet
玉池(ㄩˋ ㄔˊ)
(Taoism) the mouth
玉齒(ㄩˋ ㄔˇ)
sparkling teeth
玉蟾(ㄩˋ ㄔㄢˊ)
the jade toad—the moon
玉成其事(ㄩˋ ㄔㄥˊ ㄑㄧˊ ㄕˋ)
to assist another in accomplishing a task or attaining a goal
玉食(ㄩˋ ㄕˊ)
delicacies; dainties
玉食錦衣(ㄩˋ ㄕˊ ㄐㄧㄣˇ ㄧ)
sumptuous food and luxurious clothing
玉石俱焚(ㄩˋ ㄕˊ ㄐㄩˋ ㄈㄣˊ)
to destroy indiscriminately, be it jade or rock
玉手(ㄩˋ ㄕㄡˇ)
fair hands; hands of a pretty lady
玉手纖纖(ㄩˋ ㄕㄡˇ ㄒㄧㄢ ㄒㄧㄢ)
the slender hands of a pretty young woman
玉山(ㄩˋ ㄕㄢ)
①Mt. Yü, the highest mountain peak in Taiwan ②elegant and majestic ③name of a county in Kiangsi
玉蜀黍(ㄩˋ ㄕㄨˇ ㄕㄨˇ)
Indian corn; maize: 玉蜀黍差不多可以收成了。The corn is nearly ready for harvesting.
玉樹(ㄩˋ ㄕㄨˋ)
①a young person with talent and good looks ②a locust tree
玉人(ㄩˋ ㄖㄣˊ)
①a beautiful woman ②a lapidary
玉潤珠圓(ㄩˋ ㄖㄨㄣˋ ㄓㄨ ㄩㄢˊ)
(said of a singing voice) smooth and soft
玉容(ㄩˋ ㄖㄨㄥˊ)
a beautiful face
玉容花貌(ㄩˋ ㄖㄨㄥˊ ㄏㄨㄚ ㄇㄠˋ)
a fair face and elegant form
玉簪(ㄩˋ ㄗㄢ)
①a jade hairpin ②(botany) tuberose
玉慘花愁(ㄩˋ ㄘㄢˇ ㄏㄨㄚ ㄔㄡˊ)
(said of a pretty woman) sad; crying
玉色(ㄩˋ ㄙㄜˋ)
①a color that never changes as jade ②virtuous and pure ③fair (faces) ④(color) jade green
玉搔頭(ㄩˋ ㄙㄠ ㄊㄡˊ)
a jade hairpin 亦作「玉簪」
玉髓(ㄩˋ ㄙㄨㄟˇ)
①exquisite wine ②(mineral) chalcedony
玉碎珠沉(ㄩˋ ㄙㄨㄟˋ ㄓㄨ ㄔㄣˊ)
the death of a beauty
玉筍(ㄩˋ ㄙㄨㄣˇ)
①fingers of a beautiful woman ②talents as many as bamboo shoots
玉案(ㄩˋ ㄢˋ)
①a jade plate for food ②a narrow jade table ③name of a mountain in Yunnan Province
玉儀(ㄩˋ ㄧˊ)
①a complexion as smooth as jade ②a jade-ornamented instrument for observing heavenly bodies
玉液瓊漿(ㄩˋ ㄧㄝˋ ㄑㄩㄥˊ ㄐㄧㄤ)or 玉液(ㄩˋ ㄧㄝˋ)
top-quality wine
玉顏(ㄩˋ ㄧㄢˊ)

a fair complexion

玉豔(ㄩˋ ㄧㄢˋ)
a complexion as smooth as jade

玉音(ㄩˋ ㄧㄣ)
① valuable words ② imperial decrees ③your esteemed reply ④jadelike music—beautiful sound

玉英(ㄩˋ ㄧㄥ)
①jade of best quality ② cactus flowers

玉腕(ㄩˋ ㄨㄢˋ)
the wrist and forearm of a beautiful woman

玉宇(ㄩˋ ㄩˇ)
①a splendid hall—as if made of jade ② the palace of the legendary Jade Emperor

玉殞香消(ㄩˋ ㄩㄣˇ ㄒㄧㄤ ㄒㄧㄠ)
the death of a woman

【王】 3409

1. ㄨㄤˊ wang wáng

1. a king; a ruler
2. a prince, the highest rank of nobility
3. great; of a tremendous size
4. the strongest or most powerful
5. a salutation of respect
6. an audience with the ruler or emperor
7. a Chinese family name

王八 or 忘八(ㄨㄤˊ ˙ㄅㄚ)
①a turtle; a tortoise ②a cuckold ③a man who works in a brothel ④ an s.o.b.

王八蛋(ㄨㄤˊ ˙ㄅㄚ ㄉㄢˋ)
a term of revilement similar to "s.o.b."

王八羔子(ㄨㄤˊ ˙ㄅㄚ ㄍㄠ ˙ㄗ)
a term of revilement similar to "s.o.b."

王霸(ㄨㄤˊ ㄅㄚˋ)
the business of being a king or ruler

王牌(ㄨㄤˊ ㄆㄞˊ)
a trump card

王莽(ㄨㄤˊ ㄇㄤˇ)
Wang Mang (45 B.C.–23 A.D.), a prime minister of the Western Han Dynasty who introduced many reforms after he usurped the throne

王命(ㄨㄤˊ ㄇㄧㄥˋ)
the emperor's orders; the royal decrees

王母(ㄨㄤˊ ㄇㄨˇ)
① the grandmother ② the leading Taoist goddess

王法(ㄨㄤˊ ㄈㄚˇ)
the King's law—the laws of the land; the law

王妃(ㄨㄤˊ ㄈㄟ)
a prince's concubine

王府(ㄨㄤˊ ㄈㄨˇ)
the palace of a prince

王父(ㄨㄤˊ ㄈㄨˋ)
the grandfather

王大父(ㄨㄤˊ ㄉㄚˋ ㄈㄨˋ)
the great grandfather

王道(ㄨㄤˊ ㄉㄠˋ)
the ways of an enlightened ruler; an enlightened reign of righteousness (as opposed to tyranny); royal government

王庭(ㄨㄤˊ ㄊㄧㄥˊ)
the king's court; the imperial court

王綱(ㄨㄤˊ ㄍㄤ)
laws, regulations, institutions, etc. of a reign

王國(ㄨㄤˊ ㄍㄨㄛˊ)
a kingdom

王冠(ㄨㄤˊ ㄍㄨㄢ)
a crown

王宮(ㄨㄤˊ ㄍㄨㄥ)
a royal palace

王公(ㄨㄤˊ ㄍㄨㄥ)or 王公大人(ㄨㄤˊ ㄍㄨㄥ ㄉㄚˋ ㄖㄣˊ)
princes and nobles

王侯(ㄨㄤˊ ㄏㄡˊ)
princes and marquises—the nobility

王侯將相(ㄨㄤˊ ㄏㄡˊ ㄐㄧㄤˋ ㄒㄧㄤˋ)
princes, nobles, generals and ministers—the ruling class

王后(ㄨㄤˊ ㄏㄡˋ)
the queen

王化(ㄨㄤˊ ㄏㄨㄚˋ)
civilizing influence; sovereign grace

王畿(ㄨㄤˊ ㄐㄧ)
the suburbs of the capital of an empire

王駕(ㄨㄤˊ ㄐㄧㄚˋ)
① the king's carriage ② the king or emperor

王權(ㄨㄤˊ ㄑㄩㄢˊ)
the authority of a king; imperial powers; the throne

王羲之(ㄨㄤˊ ㄒㄧ ㄓ)
Wang Hsi-chih (321-379), the greatest of Chinese calligraphers

王謝(ㄨㄤˊ ㄒㄧㄝˋ)
Wang and Hsieh, both prospering families during the period of the Six Dynasties, now used as a synonym of influential families

王者(ㄨㄤˊ ㄓㄜˇ)
① an emperor or king ② a true royal sovereign

王昭君(ㄨㄤˊ ㄓㄠ ㄐㄩㄣ)
another name of Wang Chiang (王嬙), a court lady during the Han Dynasty, who was given to the chieftain of a barbarian tribe as his wife in the performance of matrimonial diplomacy

王朝(ㄨㄤˊ ㄔㄠˊ)
a dynasty

王臣(ㄨㄤˊ ㄔㄣˊ)
king's servants

王儲(ㄨㄤˊ ㄔㄨˇ)
a crown prince

王師(ㄨㄤˊ ㄕ)
the king's troops; the emperor's troops

王事(ㄨㄤˊ ㄕˋ)
royal affairs

王室(ㄨㄤˊ ㄕˋ)
① the royal family; the ruling house ② the imperial or royal court

王水(ㄨㄤˊ ㄕㄨㄟˇ)
(chemistry) aqua regia

王子(ㄨㄤˊ ㄗˇ)
a prince

王族(ㄨㄤˊ ㄗㄨˊ)
the royal family; persons of royal lineage

王佐之才(ㄨㄤˊ ㄗㄨㄛˇ ㄓ ㄘㄞˊ)
the capabilities of a prime minister: 此人具有王佐之才。This man has the capabilities of a prime minister.

王孫(ㄨㄤˊ ㄙㄨㄣ)
① descendants of the nobility ② a cricket ③ a monkey ④ a Chinese family name

王孫公子(ㄨㄤˊ ㄙㄨㄣ ㄍㄨㄥ ㄗˇ)
blue-blooded young men; aristocrats

王安石(ㄨㄤˊ ㄢ ㄕˊ)

Wang An-shih (1021-1086), a prime minister during the reign of Emperor Shen Tzung (神宗), part of whose "new deal" is still being practiced today
王爾德(ㄨㄤˊ ㄦˇ ㄉㄜˊ)
Oscar Wilde (1856-1900), English novelist and playwright
王業(ㄨㄤˊ ㄧㄝˋ)
the country (regarded as the monarch's private property)
王爺(ㄨㄤˊ ˙ㄧㄝ)
① a nobleman ② Your Imperial Highness
王陽明(ㄨㄤˊ ㄧㄤˊ ㄇㄧㄥˊ) or 王守仁(ㄨㄤˊ ㄕㄡˇ ㄖㄣˊ)
Wang Yang-ming (1472-1528), who advocated the theory that action should go along with knowledge or theory
王維(ㄨㄤˊ ㄨㄟˊ)
Wang Wei (699-759), a famous painter and poet in the Tang Dynasty
王位(ㄨㄤˊ ㄨㄟˋ)
the throne; the crown

【王】 3409 2. ㄨㄤˋ wanq wàng
to rule; to govern
王天下(ㄨㄤˋ ㄊㄧㄢ ㄒㄧㄚˋ)
to rule over the empire

二畫

【玎】 3410 ㄉㄧㄥ ding dīng
the jingling or tinkling sound
玎璫(ㄉㄧㄥ ㄉㄤ)
ding-dong; the jingling or tinkling sound: 鐘玎璫地響。The bell goes ding-dong.
玎玲(ㄉㄧㄥ ㄌㄧㄥˊ)
the jingling or tinkling sound

三畫

【玕】 3411 ㄍㄢ gan gān
a kind of inferior gem; a stone slightly inferior in quality to jade

【玖】 3412 ㄐㄧㄡˇ jeou jiǔ
1. a black jade stone
2. an elaborate form of 九, nine, used in checks, etc. to prevent fraud

四畫

【玫】 3413 ㄇㄟˊ mei méi
1. the rose
2. another name of black mica—a sparkling red gem

玫瑰(ㄇㄟˊ ˙ㄍㄨㄟ)
① the rose (blossoms) ② black mica—a sparkling red gem
玫瑰露(ㄇㄟˊ ˙ㄍㄨㄟ ㄌㄨˋ)
mild and sweetened kaoliang wine
玫瑰紅(ㄇㄟˊ ˙ㄍㄨㄟ ㄏㄨㄥˊ)
①rose red ②rose-red: 她穿上玫瑰紅的衣服。She put on rose-red clothes.
玫瑰紫(ㄇㄟˊ ˙ㄍㄨㄟ ㄗˇ)
dark red; rose purple
玫瑰油(ㄇㄟˊ ˙ㄍㄨㄟ ㄧㄡˊ)
attar of roses

【玦】 3414 ㄐㄩㄝˊ jyue jué
a jade ring with a small segment cut off

【玩】 3415 1. ㄨㄢˊ wan wán
1. to play with; to play; to toy with: 孩子們在玩。The children are at play.
2. to amuse oneself with; to find pleasure in

玩兒(ㄨㄚˊㄦ)
to play; to play or toy with
玩兒票(ㄨㄚˊㄦ ㄆㄧㄠˋ) or 玩票(ㄨㄢˊ ㄆㄧㄠˋ)
① to amuse oneself by playing parts in Chinese operas as an amateur ② to do a payless job
玩兒命(ㄨㄚˊㄦ ㄇㄧㄥˋ)
to play with one's life at stake; to do daredevil tricks; to toy with one's life
玩兒話(ㄨㄚˊㄦ ㄏㄨㄚˋ)
jokes; utterances which are not said or taken seriously
玩把戲(ㄨㄢˊ ㄅㄚˇ ㄒㄧˋ)
to play little tricks; to juggle
玩不得(ㄨㄢˊ ˙ㄅㄨ ˙ㄉㄜ)
(literally) (It's) not something to play with—something serious or important
玩不動(ㄨㄢˊ ˙ㄅㄨ ㄉㄨㄥˋ)
too exhausted or too weak to play
玩弄(ㄨㄢˊ ㄋㄨㄥˋ)
to toy with: 她玩弄她的一串珠子。She toyed with her string of beads.
玩花樣(ㄨㄢˊ ㄏㄨㄚ ㄧㄤˋ)
to play tricks; to cheat
玩火(ㄨㄢˊ ㄏㄨㄛˇ)
to play with fire—a dangerous game
玩火自焚(ㄨㄢˊ ㄏㄨㄛˇ ㄗˋ ㄈㄣˊ)
Whoever plays with fire will get burnt. 或 Whoever plays with fire will perish by fire.
玩具(ㄨㄢˊ ㄐㄩˋ)
toys
玩具店(ㄨㄢˊ ㄐㄩˋ ㄉㄧㄢˋ)
a toy shop
玩笑(ㄨㄢˊ ㄒㄧㄠˋ)
① jokes; jesting ② to take something less seriously than it deserves
玩手段(ㄨㄢˊ ㄕㄡˇ ㄉㄨㄢˋ)
to resort to scheming; to manipulate
玩賞(ㄨㄢˊ ㄕㄤˇ)
to amuse by viewing; to enjoy or appreciate the beauty of something
玩耍(ㄨㄢˊ ㄕㄨㄚˇ)
to play; to have fun
玩偶(ㄨㄢˊ ㄡˇ)
dolls
玩意兒 or 玩藝兒(ㄨㄢˊ ㄧㄜˋㄦ)
① toys ② activities for entertainment or relaxation ③ a thing ④ (slang) a louse
玩物(ㄨㄢˊ ㄨˋ)
a plaything; something to play with; a toy

【玩】 3415 2. ㄨㄢˋ wann wàn
1. to joke; to take things lightly; to toy with
2. something to amuse oneself—as antiques, etc.
3. (now rarely) to learn

玩法(ㄨㄢˋ ㄈㄚˇ)
to toy with laws; to take laws and regulations lightly
玩弄(ㄨㄢˋ ㄌㄨㄥˋ)
① to juggle with: 他喜歡玩弄詞句。He likes to juggle with words. ② to play jokes on;

to fool: 不要再玩弄他。Don't fool him any longer.
玩愒(ㄨㄢˊ ㄎㄞˋ)or 玩歲愒日(ㄨㄢˊ ㄙㄨㄟˋ ㄎㄞˋ ㄖˋ)
to fritter away one's time
玩好(ㄨㄢˋ ㄏㄠˋ)
something one adopts as a hobby or one amuses oneself with
玩忽(ㄨㄢˊ ㄏㄨ)
to take things lightly; to neglect (official duties, laws and regulations)
玩習(ㄨㄢˊ ㄒㄧˊ)
to learn and practice
玩視(ㄨㄢˊ ㄕˋ)
to take laws and regulations lightly as if they were something to toy with
玩世不恭(ㄨㄢˊ ㄕˋ ㄅㄨˋ ㄍㄨㄥ)
to be a cynic, beatnik or hippie; to take everything lightly; to disdain worldly affairs
玩物喪志(ㄨㄢˊ ㄨˋ ㄙㄤˋ ㄓˋ)
to apply oneself too much to trifles, petty amusements, etc. so that one's fortitude and will power are eroded away 或 Riding a hobby saps one's will to make progress. 或 Excessive attention to trivia saps the will.
玩味(ㄨㄢˊ ㄨㄟˋ)
to ponder; to digest food for thought: 這個問題頗值玩味。This problem is worth pondering.
玩月(ㄨㄢˊ ㄩㄝˋ)
to enjoy the moonlight

【玨】 3416
(珏) ㄐㄩㄝˊ jyue jué
two pieces of jade fastened together

【玠】 3417
ㄐㄧㄝˋ jieh jiè
a large jade tablet

五畫

【玲】 3418
ㄌㄧㄥˊ ling líng
the tinkling of jade pendants
玲玎(ㄌㄧㄥˊ ㄌㄧㄥ)
①the tinkling of jade pendants ②the sound of waves pounding on rocks
玲琅(ㄌㄧㄥˊ ㄌㄤˊ)
the tinkling of jades
玲玲(ㄌㄧㄥˊ ㄌㄧㄥˊ)
the tinkling of jade pendants
玲瓏(ㄌㄧㄥˊ ㄌㄨㄥˊ)
① pleasing; delicate; cute; fine; regular ② bright ③ tinkling of jades
玲瓏剔透(ㄌㄧㄥˊ ㄌㄨㄥˊ ㄊㄧ ㄊㄡˋ)
①exquisitely carved ②(said of a person) very bright

【玷】 3419
ㄉㄧㄢˋ diann diàn
1. a flaw or blemish in a piece of jade; a stain; a defect; a spot
2. to stain; to blemish; to disgrace
玷辱(ㄉㄧㄢˋ ㄖㄨˋ)
to disgrace (one's family name, etc.)
玷汙(ㄉㄧㄢˋ ㄨ)
a stain (in one's reputation, etc.); a blot on the scutcheon; to stain: 殘酷玷汙他的品性。His character was stained by cruelty.

【玳】 3420
ㄉㄞˋ day dài
the tortoise shell
玳瑁(ㄉㄞˋ ㄇㄟˋ)
a hawksbill turtle, or hawksbill
玳瑁眼鏡(ㄉㄞˋ ㄇㄟˋ ㄧㄢˇ ㄐㄧㄥˋ)
hawksbill shell-rimmed eyeglasses

【珉】 3421
ㄇㄧㄣˊ min mín
a stone resembling jade

【珂】 3422
ㄎㄜ ke kē
1. a stone resembling jade
2. a decorative article on a bridle
3. a kind of cowry
珂里(ㄎㄜ ㄌㄧˇ)or 珂鄉(ㄎㄜ ㄒㄧㄤ)
(a polite expression) your hometown
珂羅版(ㄎㄜ ㄌㄨㄛˊ ㄅㄢˇ)
collotype

【玼】 3423
ㄘˇ tsyy cǐ
1. a blemish; a flaw
2. brilliant

【珊】 3424
ㄕㄢ shan shān
1. coral
2. the tinkling of pendants
珊瑚(ㄕㄢ ㄏㄨˊ)
coral: 她戴着珊瑚戒指。She wears a coral ring.
珊瑚島(ㄕㄢ ㄏㄨˊ ㄉㄠˇ)
a coral island; an atoll
珊瑚礁(ㄕㄢ ㄏㄨˊ ㄐㄧㄠ)
coral reefs
珊瑚蟲(ㄕㄢ ㄏㄨˊ ㄔㄨㄥˊ)
a coral polyp
珊瑚樹(ㄕㄢ ㄏㄨˊ ㄕㄨˋ)
a kind of evergreen tree (*Viburnum odoratissimum*)
珊珊(ㄕㄢ ㄕㄢ)
the tinkling of jade pendants

【珍】 3425
ㄓㄣ jen zhēn
1. precious; rare; very valuable
2. valuables; treasures
3. delicacies; dainties
珍寶(ㄓㄣ ㄅㄠˇ)
jewelry and valuables
珍本(ㄓㄣ ㄅㄣˇ)
a rare or precious edition of an ancient book; a rare book
珍品(ㄓㄣ ㄆㄧㄣˇ)
delicacies; treasures or valuables; precious objects
珍祕(ㄓㄣ ㄇㄧˋ)
a treasure or precious thing which one is reluctant to let others know
珍怪(ㄓㄣ ㄍㄨㄞˋ)
rarities; strange happenings
珍貴(ㄓㄣ ㄍㄨㄟˋ)
valuable; treasurable; precious
珍奇(ㄓㄣ ㄑㄧˊ)
rare and precious
珍禽(ㄓㄣ ㄑㄧㄣˊ)
a rare bird
珍禽異獸(ㄓㄣ ㄑㄧㄣˊ ㄧˋ ㄕㄡˋ)
rare birds and animals
珍惜(ㄓㄣ ㄒㄧˊ)
to treasure; to consider very precious; to prize
珍羞 or 珍饈(ㄓㄣ ㄒㄧㄡ)
rare delicacies; dainties
珍珠(ㄓㄣ ㄓㄨ)
pearls
珍珠米(ㄓㄣ ㄓㄨ ㄇㄧˇ)
maize; (Indian) corn
珍珠港(ㄓㄣ ㄓㄨ ㄍㄤˇ)
Pearl Harbor
珍重(ㄓㄣ ㄓㄨㄥˋ)
to take good care of (your-

self); to think much of; to value highly
珍視(ㄓㄣ ㄕˋ)
to value highly; to have a high opinion of (something); to treasure
珍攝(ㄓㄣ ㄕㄜˋ)
to take good care of one's health
珍賞(ㄓㄣ ㄕㄤˇ)
to treasure and enjoy (a collection, etc.)
珍藏(ㄓㄣ ㄘㄤˊ)
to treasure; to keep something as a treasure (usually said of rare books and works of art)
珍藏密斂(ㄓㄣ ㄘㄤˊ ㄇㄧˋ ㄌㄧㄢˋ)
to hide or keep in a very safe place
珍愛(ㄓㄣ ㄞˋ)
to value; to treasure; to love dearly: 她珍愛她媽媽送給她的針線包。She treasures the sewing kit her mother gave her.
珍異(ㄓㄣ ㄧˋ)
rare and precious
珍物(ㄓㄣ ㄨˋ)
① treasures; valuables: 她將珍物藏在保險箱裏。She kept her valuables in a safe. ② delicacies
珍味(ㄓㄣ ㄨㄟˋ)
rare delicacies
珍玩(ㄓㄣ ㄨㄢˊ)
curios of great value: 他買了許多珍玩。He bought a lot of curios.
珍聞(ㄓㄣ ㄨㄣˊ)
rare news or information; very valuable information
珍御(ㄓㄣ ㄩˋ)
expensive items of clothing

【玻】 3426 ㄅㄛ bo bō
glass
玻璃(ㄅㄛ ·ㄌㄧ)
glass: 玻璃易碎。Glass breaks easily.
玻璃杯(ㄅㄛ ·ㄌㄧ ㄅㄟ)
a glass; a tumbler
玻璃版(ㄅㄛ ·ㄌㄧ ㄅㄢˇ)
collotype
玻璃板(ㄅㄛ ·ㄌㄧ ㄅㄢˇ)
a glass plate; plate glass
玻璃片(ㄅㄛ ·ㄌㄧ ㄆㄧㄢˋ)
window glass; sheet glass
玻璃瓶(ㄅㄛ ·ㄌㄧ ㄆㄧㄥˊ)
a glass bottle
玻璃體(ㄅㄛ ·ㄌㄧ ㄊㄧˇ)
(anatomy) vitreous body
玻璃匠(ㄅㄛ ·ㄌㄧ ㄐㄧㄤˋ)
① a glassblower ② a glazier; a glass cutter; a workman who fixes window glass or plate glass
玻璃球(ㄅㄛ ·ㄌㄧ ㄑㄧㄡˊ)
glass beads; glass balls
玻璃圈(ㄅㄛ ·ㄌㄧ ㄑㄩㄢ)
(slang) the gay circle; the world of male homosexuals
玻璃紙(ㄅㄛ ·ㄌㄧ ㄓˇ)
cellophane
玻璃窗(ㄅㄛ ·ㄌㄧ ㄔㄨㄤ)
a glass window
玻利維亞(ㄅㄛ ㄌㄧˋ ㄨㄟˊ ㄧㄚˋ)
Bolivia

【珀】 3427 ㄆㄛˋ poh pò
amber

【珈】 3428 ㄐㄧㄚ jia jiā
a kind of jewelry

六畫

【珙】 3429 ㄍㄨㄥˇ goong gǒng
a large piece of jadestone

【珥】 3430 ㄦˇ eel ěr
1. an ear ornament of pearl or jade
2. to stick; to insert

【珞】 3431 ㄌㄨㄛˋ luoh luò
jade ornaments for the neck

【珠】 3432 ㄓㄨ ju zhū
1. a pearl
2. a bead; a drop
3. the pupil of the eye
4. a Chinese family name
珠箔(ㄓㄨ ㄅㄛˊ)
a curtain of pearls; a screen of beads
珠寶(ㄓㄨ ㄅㄠˇ)
jewelry; pearls and valuables; gems
珠蚌(ㄓㄨ ㄅㄤˋ)
the oysters or mollusks that produce pearls; the pearl oyster
珠母(ㄓㄨ ㄇㄨˇ)
the pearl oyster
珠胎暗結(ㄓㄨ ㄊㄞ ㄢˋ ㄐㄧㄝˊ)
to be pregnant (as a result of a love affair)
珠淚(ㄓㄨ ㄌㄟˋ)
tears
珠簾(ㄓㄨ ㄌㄧㄢˊ)
a curtain or screen of pearls or beads
珠聯璧合(ㄓㄨ ㄌㄧㄢˊ ㄅㄧˋ ㄏㄜˊ)
an excellent match (especially referring to marriage); a perfect pair; a happy combination
珠履(ㄓㄨ ㄌㄩˇ)
shoes with pearls as ornament
珠光寶氣(ㄓㄨ ㄍㄨㄤ ㄅㄠˇ ㄑㄧˋ)
(said of wealthy women) sparkling with pearls and precious stones; to be richly bejeweled
珠宮貝闕(ㄓㄨ ㄍㄨㄥ ㄅㄟˋ ㄑㄩㄝˋ)
the palace for the god of water
珠喉(ㄓㄨ ㄏㄡˊ)
the smooth and sweet voice of a vocalist
珠汗(ㄓㄨ ㄏㄢˋ)
beads of perspiration
珠還合浦(ㄓㄨ ㄏㄨㄢˊ ㄏㄜˊ ㄆㄨˇ)
the return of a valuable thing to its rightful owner
珠鷄(ㄓㄨ ㄐㄧ)
a guinea fowl (*Numida meleagris*)
珠璣(ㄓㄨ ㄐㄧ)
exquisite or excellent wording of a piece of writing
珠江(ㄓㄨ ㄐㄧㄤ)
the Pearl River in Kwangtung Province
珠江三角洲(ㄓㄨ ㄐㄧㄤ ㄙㄢ ㄐㄧㄠˇ ㄓㄡ)
the delta of the Pearl River
珠子(ㄓㄨ ·ㄗ)
pearls; beads: 這串珠子多少錢? How much is this string of beads?
珠翠(ㄓㄨ ㄘㄨㄟˋ)
pearls and jades—head ornaments of a woman
珠算(ㄓㄨ ㄙㄨㄢˋ)
calculation with an abacus
珠兒(ㄓㄨㄦ)
beads

珠圍翠繞(ㄓㄨ ㄨㄟˊ ㄘㄨㄟˋ ㄖㄠˋ)
①(said of women) richly ornamented ②surrounded by pretty waiting maids

珠玉(ㄓㄨ ㄩˋ)
①beautifully written verses or articles ②elegant and stately (in appearance)

珠圓玉潤(ㄓㄨ ㄩㄢˊ ㄩˋ ㄖㄨㄣˋ)
①smooth and sweet (voice) ②smooth and easy (style in writing)

【珩】 3433
ㄏㄥˊ herng héng
the top gem of the pendants from a girdle

【班】 3434
ㄅㄢ ban bān
1. a grade; a seat or position
2. a class or company; a set; a group
3. a squad (of soldiers)
4. to distribute
5. to return
6. same as 斑 — variegated; of different colors
7. of equal rank, same generation, etc.
8. a shift; duty
9. scheduled runs (of the bus, etc.)
10. a Chinese family name

班駁(ㄅㄢ ㄅㄛˊ) or 班駁陸離(ㄅㄢ ㄅㄛˊ ㄌㄨˋ ㄌㄧˊ)
variegated; of different colors

班白 or 斑白(ㄅㄢ ㄅㄞˊ) or (ㄅㄢ ㄅㄛˊ)
gray-headed; graying: 他的頭髮已經班白。His hair has turned gray.

班班(ㄅㄢ ㄅㄢ)
①clear and apparent ②the noise of moving wagons

班門弄斧(ㄅㄢ ㄇㄣˊ ㄋㄨㄥˋ ㄈㄨˇ)
to show off one's talent or skill before an expert: 我不敢在他面前班門弄斧。I dare not show off my skill before him.

班底(ㄅㄢ ㄉㄧˇ)
①ordinary members of a theatrical troupe ②(in politics, etc.) loyal supporters; hard-core followers

班頭(ㄅㄢ ㄊㄡˊ)
the leader of longshoremen or pedicab drivers at a specific locality

班列(ㄅㄢ ㄌㄧㄝˋ)
relative ranks; order or sequence

班固(ㄅㄢ ㄍㄨˋ)
Pan Ku (32-92 A.D.), who completed the *History of the Han Dynasty* begun by his father

班行(ㄅㄢ ㄏㄤˊ)
in the same rank

班機(ㄅㄢ ㄐㄧ)
an airliner on the scheduled flight: 這是快速班機。This is a fast airliner.

班級(ㄅㄢ ㄐㄧˊ)
a grade; a form; a class

班昭(ㄅㄢ ㄓㄠ)
Pan Chao (c. 49-120), sister of 班固, a famous authoress

班長(ㄅㄢ ㄓㄤˇ)
①(military) a squad leader ②(in school) the leader of a class; a dux; a class monitor

班車(ㄅㄢ ㄔㄜ)
a regular bus

班超(ㄅㄢ ㄔㄠ)
Pan Ch'ao (32-102 A.D.), a younger brother of Pan Ku (班固), known for his exploits in the Western Regions (西域)

班禪(ㄅㄢ ㄔㄢˊ)
the Panchen Lama (of Tibet)

班師(ㄅㄢ ㄕ)
to withdraw troops after a victorious campaign

班子(ㄅㄢ ˙ㄗ)
①an operatic company ②a brothel

班次(ㄅㄢ ㄘˋ)
①the flight number of an airliner ②the designated number of a scheduled train ③the grade or class (of a student): 在學校時，他的班次比我高。At school he is in a higher class than I. ④sequence

【珪】 3435
(圭) ㄍㄨㄟ guei guī
a jade tablet worn by feudal princes as a symbol of authority

【珣】 3436
ㄒㄩㄣˊ shyun xún
name of a kind of jade

【珮】 3437
(佩) ㄆㄟˋ pey pèi
jade pendants

【琉】 3438
ㄌㄧㄡˊ liou liú
1. a glossy and bright stone
2. glazed

琉璃(ㄌㄧㄡˊ ˙ㄌㄧ)
①glass ②a glasslike substance; porcelain ③colored glaze ④glossy gems

琉璃廠(ㄌㄧㄡˊ ˙ㄌㄧ ㄔㄤˇ)
a place in Peking where bookstores are concentrated —so named because it was originally the site of a porcelain kiln

琉璃草(ㄌㄧㄡˊ ˙ㄌㄧ ㄘㄠˇ)
a forget-me-not 亦作「毋忘我草」

琉璃瓦(ㄌㄧㄡˊ ˙ㄌㄧ ㄨㄚˇ)
encaustic tiles; glazed tiles

琉球(ㄌㄧㄡˊ ㄑㄧㄡˊ)
Ryukyu

七畫

【現】 3439
ㄒㄧㄢˋ shiann xiàn
1. to emerge; to appear; to reveal
2. current; now; present; modern
3. in time of need; extempore
4. cash
5. ready; available
6. actual

現批(ㄒㄧㄢˋ ㄆㄧ)
to make purchases in cash

現買現賣(ㄒㄧㄢˋ ㄇㄞˇ ㄒㄧㄢˋ ㄇㄞˋ)
to sell something right after it is bought

現代(ㄒㄧㄢˋ ㄉㄞˋ)
modern; current; present; in modern times; the present world; the present age

現代化(ㄒㄧㄢˋ ㄉㄞˋ ㄏㄨㄚˋ)
to modernize; modernization

現代史(ㄒㄧㄢˋ ㄉㄞˋ ㄕˇ)
contemporary history; modern history

現代作家(ㄒㄧㄢˋ ㄉㄞˋ ㄗㄨㄛˋ ㄐㄧㄚ)
a contemporary writer; a modern writer

現代音樂(ㄒㄧㄢˋ ㄉㄞˋ ㄧㄣ ㄩㄝˋ)
modern music

現代五項運動(ㄒㄧㄢˋ ㄉㄞˋ ㄨˇ ㄒㄧㄤˋ

ㄩㄣˋ ㄌㄨㄥˇ)
modern pentathlon
現代文學(ㄒㄧㄢˋ ㄉㄞˋ ㄨㄣˊ ㄒㄩㄝˊ)
contemporary literature; modern literature
現露(ㄒㄧㄢˋ ㄌㄨˋ)
to reveal; to come to the open; to unveil
現款(ㄒㄧㄢˋ ㄎㄨㄢˇ)
cash; ready money
現貨(ㄒㄧㄢˋ ㄏㄨㄛˋ)
stock goods; goods on hand; spots
現貨交易(ㄒㄧㄢˋ ㄏㄨㄛˋ ㄐㄧㄠ ㄧˋ)
spot transactions
現貨市場(ㄒㄧㄢˋ ㄏㄨㄛˋ ㄕˋ ㄔㄤˇ)
the spot market
現階段(ㄒㄧㄢˋ ㄐㄧㄝ ㄉㄨㄢˋ)
the present stage
現今(ㄒㄧㄢˋ ㄐㄧㄣ)
nowadays; at present; now
現金(ㄒㄧㄢˋ ㄐㄧㄣ) or 現錢(ㄒㄧㄢˋ ㄑㄧㄢˊ)
cash; ready money
現金買賣(ㄒㄧㄢˋ ㄐㄧㄣ ㄇㄞˇ ㄇㄞˋ)or 現金交易(ㄒㄧㄢˋ ㄐㄧㄣ ㄐㄧㄠ ㄧˋ)
business transactions in cash; cash transactions
現下(ㄒㄧㄢˋ ㄒㄧㄚˋ)
now; at present
現象(ㄒㄧㄢˋ ㄒㄧㄤˋ)
phenomena; appearances
現象界(ㄒㄧㄢˋ ㄒㄧㄤˋ ㄐㄧㄝˋ)
the phenomenal world
現象學(ㄒㄧㄢˋ ㄒㄧㄤˋ ㄒㄩㄝˊ)
the phenomenology
現形(ㄒㄧㄢˋ ㄒㄧㄥˊ)
to reveal one's true colors, form, character, etc.
現行(ㄒㄧㄢˋ ㄒㄧㄥˊ)
existing; presently valid or effective; in force: 我們將維持現行政策。We'll maintain the existing policies.
現行法(ㄒㄧㄢˋ ㄒㄧㄥˊ ㄈㄚˇ)
the law actually in force; the existing law
現行犯(ㄒㄧㄢˋ ㄒㄧㄥˊ ㄈㄢˋ)
a person caught *flagrante delicto*
現職(ㄒㄧㄢˋ ㄓˊ)
the present job; a current post or position
現狀(ㄒㄧㄢˋ ㄓㄨㄤˋ)
things as they are; the *status quo*: 他們企圖維持現狀。They seek to preserve the *status quo*.
現場(ㄒㄧㄢˋ ㄔㄤˇ)
the scene (of an incident); a site; a spot: 警察匆忙趕到作案現場。The police hurried to the scene of the crime.
現場表演(ㄒㄧㄢˋ ㄔㄤˇ ㄅㄧㄠˇ ㄧㄢˇ)
①to reenact a crime by a criminal at the same scene after he is caught ②a live show
現場採訪(ㄒㄧㄢˋ ㄔㄤˇ ㄘㄞˇ ㄈㄤˇ)
spot coverage
現成(ㄒㄧㄢˋ ㄔㄥˊ)
ready; ready-made; at hand: 他常買現成的衣服。He often buys ready-made clothes.
現成飯(ㄒㄧㄢˋ ㄔㄥˊ ㄈㄢˋ)
(literally) food which has already been prepared—benefits, etc. that one can readily reap without exertion
現成話(ㄒㄧㄢˋ ㄔㄥˊ ㄏㄨㄚˋ)
I-told-you-so remarks; an onlooker's unsolicited comments
現實(ㄒㄧㄢˋ ㄕˊ)
①reality; things as they are: 你不知道人生的現實。You do not know the realities of life. ② practical; pragmatic; real; actual
現實主義(ㄒㄧㄢˋ ㄕˊ ㄓㄨˇ ㄧˋ)
realism; pragmatism
現實生活(ㄒㄧㄢˋ ㄕˊ ㄕㄥ ㄏㄨㄛˊ)
the real life; the actual life
現勢(ㄒㄧㄢˋ ㄕˋ)
the present situation; the current situation
現世(ㄒㄧㄢˋ ㄕˋ)
①the world nowadays; present; this life ②to be disgraced; to bring shame on oneself
現世報(ㄒㄧㄢˋ ㄕˋ ㄅㄠˋ)
retribution in one's own lifetime
現身說法(ㄒㄧㄢˋ ㄕㄣ ㄕㄨㄛ ㄈㄚˇ)
to act as an example to others; to give a demonstration in person
現任(ㄒㄧㄢˋ ㄖㄣˋ)
present (position, job, or employment); incumbent: 現任校長過去是教師。The present principal used to be a teacher.
現在(ㄒㄧㄢˋ ㄗㄞˋ)
now; at present
現在完成式(ㄒㄧㄢˋ ㄗㄞˋ ㄨㄢˊ ㄔㄥˊ ㄕˋ)
(English grammar) the present perfect tense
現存(ㄒㄧㄢˋ ㄘㄨㄣˊ)
in stock; on hand; available
現役(ㄒㄧㄢˋ ㄧˋ)
active (military) service; active duty
現役軍人(ㄒㄧㄢˋ ㄧˋ ㄐㄩㄣ ㄖㄣˊ)
military personnel on active service
現有(ㄒㄧㄢˋ ㄧㄡˇ)
to have on hand; available; existing
現眼(ㄒㄧㄢˋ ㄧㄢˇ)
to lose face; to be embarrassed; to make a scene; to cut a sorry figure: 他在衆人面前丟人現眼。He made a fool of himself in public.
現銀(ㄒㄧㄢˋ ㄧㄣˊ)
ready cash (originally referring to silver coins)
現洋(ㄒㄧㄢˋ ㄧㄤˊ)
① silver dollars 亦作「現大洋」 ② ready cash

【球】 3440 ㄑㄧㄡˊ chyou qiú

1. a ball or anything shaped like a ball: 請把球傳給我。Please pass me the ball.
2. the globe; the earth: 全球戰略 the global strategy

球板(ㄑㄧㄡˊ ㄅㄢˇ)
paddles (for hitting ping-pong, etc.)
球拍(ㄑㄧㄡˊ ㄆㄞ)
rackets (for tennis, etc.)
球門(ㄑㄧㄡˊ ㄇㄣˊ)
(in football, etc.) the goal
球門球(ㄑㄧㄡˊ ㄇㄣˊ ㄑㄧㄡˊ)
(football) goal kick
球迷(ㄑㄧㄡˊ ㄇㄧˊ)
fans of ball games: 我弟弟是棒球迷。My younger brother is a baseball fan.
球面(ㄑㄧㄡˊ ㄇㄧㄢˋ)
(mathematics) spherical surface
球面幾何學(ㄑㄧㄡˊ ㄇㄧㄢˋ ㄐㄧˇ ㄏㄜˊ ㄒㄩㄝˊ)
spherical geometry
球房(ㄑㄧㄡˊ ㄈㄤˊ)
a gym where ball games

〔玉部〕

(especially table tennis) are played

球膽(ㄑㄧㄡˊ ㄉㄢˇ)
a ball bladder

球隊(ㄑㄧㄡˊ ㄉㄨㄟˋ)
teams for playing ball games: 我不是任何足球隊的球員。I am not on any football team.

球僮(ㄑㄧㄡˊ ㄊㄨㄥˊ)
a caddy

球類(ㄑㄧㄡˊ ㄌㄟˋ)
kinds of balls—football, basketball, baseball, etc.

球根(ㄑㄧㄡˊ ㄍㄣ)
bulbous roots

球莖(ㄑㄧㄡˊ ㄐㄧㄥ)
bulbs or corms

球徑(ㄑㄧㄡˊ ㄐㄧㄥˋ)
the diameter of a sphere

球徑器(ㄑㄧㄡˊ ㄐㄧㄥˋ ㄑㄧˋ)
a spherometer

球戲(ㄑㄧㄡˊ ㄒㄧˋ)
a ball game

球鞋(ㄑㄧㄡˊ ㄒㄧㄝˊ)
tennis shoes; sneakers: 她每天都穿球鞋。She wears a pair of tennis shoes every day.

球形(ㄑㄧㄡˊ ㄒㄧㄥˊ)
spherical; globular; bulbous: 他建了一棟球形小屋。He has built a little globular house.

球穴(ㄑㄧㄡˊ ㄒㄩㄝˋ)
a hole

球證(ㄑㄧㄡˊ ㄓㄥˋ)
a referee or an umpire of a ball game

球狀花序(ㄑㄧㄡˊ ㄓㄨㄤˋ ㄏㄨㄚ ㄒㄩˋ)
(botany) strobilus

球狀菌(ㄑㄧㄡˊ ㄓㄨㄤˋ ㄐㄩㄣˋ)or 球菌(ㄑㄧㄡˊ ㄐㄩㄣˋ)
(microbiology) coccus

球場(ㄑㄧㄡˊ ㄔㄤˇ)or(ㄑㄧㄡˊ ㄔㄤˊ)
a playground for ball games

球賽(ㄑㄧㄡˊ ㄙㄞˋ)
a ball game

球兒(ㄑㄧㄡˊㄦ)
a ball: 他把球兒踢開。He kicked the ball away.

球衣(ㄑㄧㄡˊ ㄧ)
the jacket for a ballplayer

球員(ㄑㄧㄡˊ ㄩㄢˊ)
a ballplayer

球運(ㄑㄧㄡˊ ㄩㄣˋ)
① the luck of a team during a ball game ② movements or drives for the promotion of ball games

【理】 3441 ㄌㄧˇ lii li

1. reason; logic; cause; truth; right; righteousness
2. law; principles; doctrine; theory; science
3. to arrange
4. to administer; to govern; to operate; to regulate; to manage; to run
5. to reply or answer; to respond
6. texture; grain (in wood, skin, etc.)
7. name of a religious sect
8. a Chinese family name

理賠(ㄌㄧˇ ㄆㄟˊ)
(insurance) adjustment

理髮(ㄌㄧˇ ㄈㄚˇ)
to cut the hair; to have a haircut: 他昨天去理髮。He had his hair cut yesterday.

理髮店(ㄌㄧˇ ㄈㄚˇ ㄉㄧㄢˋ)or 理髮廳(ㄌㄧˇ ㄈㄚˇ ㄊㄧㄥ)or 理髮館(ㄌㄧˇ ㄈㄚˇ ㄍㄨㄢˇ)
a barbershop: 昨天我到理髮店理髮。I had a haircut at the barbershop yesterday.

理髮小姐(ㄌㄧˇ ㄈㄚˇ ㄒㄧㄠˇ ㄐㄧㄝˇ)
a woman barber

理髮師(ㄌㄧˇ ㄈㄚˇ ㄕ)
a barber; a hairdresser

理藩院(ㄌㄧˇ ㄈㄢ ㄩㄢˋ)
the Ministry of Tribal Affairs in the Ching Dynasty, roughly equivalent to the Commission on Mongolian and Tibetan Affairs of the republican era

理當(ㄌㄧˇ ㄉㄤ)
ought to; to be obliged to; should; duty-bound: 理當如此。That's just as it should be.

理短(ㄌㄧˇ ㄉㄨㄢˇ)
to be on the wrong side; to have no justification

理念(ㄌㄧˇ ㄋㄧㄢˋ)
a rational concept; an idea

理路(ㄌㄧˇ ㄌㄨˋ)
logical thinking

理亂(ㄌㄧˇ ㄌㄨㄢˋ)
① to put in order; to wipe out confusion with sound administration ② orderliness and confusion; peace and turmoil

理論(ㄌㄧˇ ㄌㄨㄣˋ)
① theory; theoretical ② to argue; to debate: 我和我的老闆理論。I argued with my boss.

理論科學(ㄌㄧˇ ㄌㄨㄣˋ ㄎㄜ ㄒㄩㄝˊ)
theoretical or pure sciences

理論家(ㄌㄧˇ ㄌㄨㄣˋ ㄐㄧㄚ)
theoreticians: 他是軍事理論家。He is a military theoretician.

理論與實際(ㄌㄧˇ ㄌㄨㄣˋ ㄩˇ ㄕˊ ㄐㄧˋ)
theory and reality; ideals and facts

理該(ㄌㄧˇ ㄍㄞ)
duty-bound; should; ought to: 他理該幫助他兄弟。He was duty-bound to help his brother.

理工科(ㄌㄧˇ ㄍㄨㄥ ㄎㄜ)
departments of natural sciences and engineering in a college

理科(ㄌㄧˇ ㄎㄜ)
departments of natural sciences in a college or university

理虧(ㄌㄧˇ ㄎㄨㄟ)
to be on the wrong side; to be in the wrong; to have no justification: 他承認自己理虧。He admitted that he was in the wrong.

理合(ㄌㄧˇ ㄏㄜˊ)
good reasons dictate that…; (in documentary usage) ought to…; duty-bound; as a matter of course

理化(ㄌㄧˇ ㄏㄨㄚˋ)
① physics and chemistry ② politics and education; to govern and educate

理會(ㄌㄧˇ ㄏㄨㄟˋ)
① to understand; to comprehend: 這很難理會。It's difficult to understand. ② to care; to heed; to take notice of; to pay attention to: 不要理會他們。Don't pay attention to them.

理家(ㄌㄧˇ ㄐㄧㄚ)
to manage domestic affairs; to housekeep

理解(ㄌㄧˇ ㄐㄧㄝˇ)
to comprehend; to under-

stand: 請用孩子能夠理解的字眼。Please use words that the child can comprehend.

理解力(ㄌㄧˇ ㄐㄧㄝˇ ㄌㄧˋ)
the faculty of comprehension; understanding; perception: 這問題超出我的理解力。The problem is beyond my comprehension.

理教(ㄌㄧˇ ㄐㄧㄠˋ)
name of a religious sect founded by Yang lai-ju (羊來如) of the early Ching Dynasty, which advocates clean living

理屈(ㄌㄧˇ ㄑㄩ)
to be on the wrong side; cannot appeal to good reasoning

理屈詞窮(ㄌㄧˇ ㄑㄩ ㄘˊ ㄑㄩㄥˊ)
to be on the wrong side and unable to say a word in self-defense

理想(ㄌㄧˇ ㄒㄧㄤˇ)
① ideal: 這種天氣玩棒球很理想。This weather is ideal for playing baseball. ② ideas; thought

理想的(ㄌㄧˇ ㄒㄧㄤˇ ·ㄉㄜ)
ideal; ideally; theoretically

理想國(ㄌㄧˇ ㄒㄧㄤˇ ㄍㄨㄛˊ)
① Utopia, an imaginary island described in Sir Thomas More's *Utopia* ② a utopia; an ideal state

理想化(ㄌㄧˇ ㄒㄧㄤˇ ㄏㄨㄚˋ)
to idealize

理想家(ㄌㄧˇ ㄒㄧㄤˇ ㄐㄧㄚ)
idealists

理想主義(ㄌㄧˇ ㄒㄧㄤˇ ㄓㄨˇ ㄧˋ)
idealism

理性(ㄌㄧˇ ㄒㄧㄥˋ)
(philosophy) reason; rationality: 他似乎失去理性。It seems that he has lost his reason.

理性主義(ㄌㄧˇ ㄒㄧㄥˋ ㄓㄨˇ ㄧˋ)
rationalism

理學(ㄌㄧˇ ㄒㄩㄝˊ)
① natural sciences ② a school of learning in the Sung Dynasty devoted to the study of the classics with a rational approach

理學博士(ㄌㄧˇ ㄒㄩㄝˊ ㄅㄛˊ ㄕˋ)
Doctor of Science (D. Sc.)

理學家(ㄌㄧˇ ㄒㄩㄝˊ ㄐㄧㄚ)
a scholar devoted to the study of the classics with a philosophical approach

理學學士(ㄌㄧˇ ㄒㄩㄝˊ ㄒㄩㄝˊ ㄕˋ)
Bachelor of Science (B. Sc.)

理學碩士(ㄌㄧˇ ㄒㄩㄝˊ ㄕㄨㄛˋ ㄕˋ)
Master of Science (M. Sc.)

理直氣壯(ㄌㄧˇ ㄓˊ ㄑㄧˋ ㄓㄨㄤˋ)
(to speak, act, etc.) with confidence for one knows that he is in the right; to be fearless with the knowledge that one is on the side of justice: 他理直氣壯地回答。He replied with perfect assurance.

理智(ㄌㄧˇ ㄓˋ)
intellect; reason (as opposed to emotion): 他已喪失理智。He has lost his reason.

理查(ㄌㄧˇ ㄔㄚˊ)
transliteration of Richard

理查遜(ㄌㄧˇ ㄔㄚˊ ㄙㄨㄣˋ)
transliteration of Richardson

理事(ㄌㄧˇ ㄕˋ)
① to manage or administer affairs: 他病得太嚴重，不能理事。He is too sick to manage affairs. ② an administrator ③ board directors (of a company)

理事國(ㄌㄧˇ ㄕˋ ㄍㄨㄛˊ)
a member country of the Security Council of the United Nations

理事會(ㄌㄧˇ ㄕˋ ㄏㄨㄟˋ)
the board of directors; a council

理事長(ㄌㄧˇ ㄕˋ ㄓㄤˇ)
the board chairman; chairman of the board of directors

理則學(ㄌㄧˇ ㄗㄜˊ ㄒㄩㄝˊ)
logic 亦作「邏輯學」

理財(ㄌㄧˇ ㄘㄞˊ)
to manage or administer finances; to conduct financial transactions

理財家(ㄌㄧˇ ㄘㄞˊ ㄐㄧㄚ)
a financier

理睬(ㄌㄧˇ ㄘㄞˇ)
to pay attention to; to care; to heed: 沒人理睬他。Nobody pays any attention to him.

理塞(ㄌㄧˇ ㄙㄜˋ)
to be in the wrong; to have no excuse

理所當然(ㄌㄧˇ ㄙㄨㄛˇ ㄉㄤ ㄖㄢˊ)
as a matter of course; naturally; natural

理由(ㄌㄧˇ ㄧㄡˊ)
reasons; grounds; causes; explanations: 我有充分理由相信你是對的。I have every reason to believe that you are right.

理由書(ㄌㄧˇ ㄧㄡˊ ㄕㄨ)
(law) a statement in which one states one's reasons, causes or grounds for a certain action

理應(ㄌㄧˇ ㄧㄥ)
duty-bound; as a matter of course; ought to; obliged to: 我理應向他致謝。I'm in duty-bound to thank him.

理喻(ㄌㄧˇ ㄩˋ)
to appeal with reason

【琅】 3442 ㄌㄤˊ lang láng

1. a kind of stone resembling jade
2. clean and white; pure; spotless
3. a Chinese family name

琅璫入獄(ㄌㄤˊ ㄉㄤ ㄖㄨˋ ㄩˋ)
to be put in jail clanking with manacles

琅琅(ㄌㄤˊ ㄌㄤˊ)
the tinkling or jingling of metals and jades

琅琅書聲(ㄌㄤˊ ㄌㄤˊ ㄕㄨ ㄕㄥ)
the sound of reading aloud

琅玕(ㄌㄤˊ ㄍㄢ)
a stone resembling jade

琅函(ㄌㄤˊ ㄏㄢˊ)
① a bookcase ② (a polite expression) your letter

琅簡蘂書(ㄌㄤˊ ㄐㄧㄢˇ ㄖㄨㄟˇ ㄕㄨ)
Taoist scriptures

琅書(ㄌㄤˊ ㄕㄨ)
Taoist scriptures

琅邪 or 琅琊(ㄌㄤˊ ㄧㄝˊ)
ancient name of Chiaochou (膠州), including the eastern part of Shantung (山東)

【琊】 3443 ㄧㄝˊ ye yé

used in 琅琊, ancient name of the eastern portion of Shantung (山東); also name of a mountain in eastern Shantung

八畫

【琖】 3444 (盞) ㄓㄢˇ jaan zhǎn
a jade wine-cup or chalice

【琛】 3445 ㄔㄣ chen chēn
treasures; jewelry or valuables

【琢】 3446 ㄓㄨㄛˊ jwo zhuó
1. to cut, chisel or polish jade, gems
2. to improve (literary works); to polish; to refine

琢磨(ㄓㄨㄛˊ ㄇㄛˊ)
①to cut and polish ②to study and improve; to mold (oneself) ③to ponder over; to consider

琢句(ㄓㄨㄛˊ ㄐㄩˋ)
sentence formation; to write and polish phrases and sentences

【琚】 3447 ㄐㄩ jiu jū
a gem worn at the girdle-pendant

【琤】 3448 ㄔㄥ cheng chēng
a tinkling sound—descriptive of jangling, twanging, or gurgling (of flowing water)

琤琤(ㄔㄥ ㄔㄥ)
①the sound of plucking stringed musical instrument ②the sound of flowing water or stream

琤瑽(ㄔㄥ ㄘㄨㄥ)
the tinkling of jade pendants

【琦】 3449 ㄑㄧˊ chyi qí
1. a kind of jade
2. same as 奇—strange
3. outstanding; extraordinary; distinguished; admirable

琦瑋(ㄑㄧˊ ㄨㄟˇ)
① fine jades ② distinguished

【琨】 3450 ㄎㄨㄣ kuen kūn
fine rocks next to jade in quality

琨庭(ㄎㄨㄣ ㄊㄧㄥˊ)
a yard dotted with white stones

【琪】 3451 ㄑㄧˊ chyi qí
a piece of jade; a jadelike precious stone; a white gem

琪花瑤草(ㄑㄧˊ ㄏㄨㄚ ㄧㄠˊ ㄘㄠˇ)
blossoms and vegetation in the fairyland

琪樹(ㄑㄧˊ ㄕㄨˋ)
①a jade tree in myth ②a tree whose branches hang down like willows and bear berries

【琥】 3452 ㄏㄨˇ huu hǔ
1. a jade ornament in the shape of a tiger
2. amber

琥珀(ㄏㄨˇ ㄆㄛˋ)
amber

琥珀酸(ㄏㄨˇ ㄆㄛˋ ㄙㄨㄢ)
succinic acid

【琺】 3453 ㄈㄚˋ fah fà
enamel; enamelware

琺瑯(ㄈㄚˋ ㄌㄤˊ)
enamel

琺瑯質(ㄈㄚˋ ㄌㄤˊ ㄓˊ)
enamel—especially referring to the hard, white glossy coating of teeth

【琬】 3454 ㄨㄢˇ woan wǎn
1. a kind of jade tablet slightly tapering at the top
2. the virtue of a gentleman

琬圭(ㄨㄢˇ ㄍㄨㄟ)
a kind of jade tablet held by feudal princes during the audience with the emperor

琬琰之章(ㄨㄢˇ ㄧㄢˇ ㄓ ㄓㄤ)
an esteemed letter

【琮】 3455 ㄘㄨㄥˊ tsorng cóng
an octagonal jade piece with a round hole in the center

【琴】 3456 ㄑㄧㄣˊ chyn qín
1. *chin,* a Chinese fretted instrument with seven or five strings somewhat similar to the zither
2. a musical instrument—especially stringed, as the piano, the violin, etc.
3. a Chinese family name

琴譜(ㄑㄧㄣˊ ㄆㄨˇ)
a score for the lute, the guitar, the piano or other stringed instruments

琴囊(ㄑㄧㄣˊ ㄋㄤˊ)
a cloth bag for a *chin* (琴)

琴鳥(ㄑㄧㄣˊ ㄋㄧㄠˇ)
a lyrebird (*Menura superba*)

琴歌(ㄑㄧㄣˊ ㄍㄜ)
①a tune for stringed instruments ②to play stringed instruments and sing

琴鍵(ㄑㄧㄣˊ ㄐㄧㄢˋ)
a key

琴劍飄零(ㄑㄧㄣˊ ㄐㄧㄢˋ ㄆㄧㄠ ㄌㄧㄥˊ)
(said of impoverished men of letters) wandering from place to place

琴棋書畫(ㄑㄧㄣˊ ㄑㄧˊ ㄕㄨ ㄏㄨㄚˋ)
music, chess, calligraphy and painting—the secondary accomplishments of an all-round scholar

琴弦(ㄑㄧㄣˊ ㄒㄧㄢˊ)
the string of a stringed instrument: 她將小提琴的琴弦上緊。She tightened the strings of her violin.

琴心(ㄑㄧㄣˊ ㄒㄧㄣ)
the emotional appeal through lute playing

琴心劍膽(ㄑㄧㄣˊ ㄒㄧㄣ ㄐㄧㄢˋ ㄉㄢˇ)
music and swordsmanship—the qualities of an accomplished scholar

琴牀(ㄑㄧㄣˊ ㄔㄨㄤˊ)
a stand or prop for a stringed instrument

琴師(ㄑㄧㄣˊ ㄕ)
a player of the stringed instrument; a pianist

琴手(ㄑㄧㄣˊ ㄕㄡˇ)
a player of the stringed instrument

琴操(ㄑㄧㄣˊ ㄘㄠ)
①the music of a lute ②title of a music book ③name of a prostitute in the Sung Dynasty

琴瑟(ㄑㄧㄣˊ ㄙㄜˋ)
①*chin* and *se,* two Chinese instruments ②a married couple

琴瑟不調(ㄑㄧㄣˊ ㄙㄜˋ ㄅㄨˋ ㄊㄧㄠˊ)
discord between husband and wife; a marriage on the rocks

琴瑟調和(ㄑㄧㄣˊ ㄙㄜˋ ㄊㄧㄠˊ ㄏㄜˊ)
a happy married life; conjugal harmony

〔玉部〕

琴瑟和鳴(ㄑㄧㄣˊ ㄙㄜˋ ㄏㄜˊ ㄇㄧㄥˊ)
marital harmony; conjugal bliss

【琵】 3457 ㄆㄧˊ pyi pí
the four-stringed guitar or the balloon-guitar

琵琶(ㄆㄧˊ ·ㄆㄚ)
pi-pa—a short-necked fretted lute of Chinese origin

琵琶撥(ㄆㄧˊ ·ㄆㄚ ㄅㄛ)
a plectrum

琵琶別抱(ㄆㄧˊ ·ㄆㄚ ㄅㄧㄝˊ ㄅㄠˋ)
the remarriage of a woman; to marry another husband

琵琶骨(ㄆㄧˊ ·ㄆㄚ ㄍㄨˇ)
the collarbone

琵琶記(ㄆㄧˊ ·ㄆㄚ ㄐㄧˋ)
name of a well-known Chinese drama

【琶】 3458 ㄆㄚˊ par pá (語音 ·ㄆㄚ ·pa pɑ)
a four-stringed guitar or balloon-guitar

【琳】 3459 ㄌㄧㄣˊ lin lín
a fine piece of jade; a gem

琳琅 or 琳瑯(ㄌㄧㄣˊ ㄌㄤˊ)
① fine jades ② people of outstanding talent ③ precious collection of books ④ the tinkling of jade pendants

琳琅滿目(ㄌㄧㄣˊ ㄌㄤˊ ㄇㄢˇ ㄇㄨˋ)
(literally) Good gems fill the eyes.—a vast array of beautiful and fine things

琳宮(ㄌㄧㄣˊ ㄍㄨㄥ) or 琳宇(ㄌㄧㄣˊ ㄩˇ)
a Taoist monastery

【琰】 3460 ㄧㄢˇ yean yǎn
the glitter of gems

琰圭(ㄧㄢˇ ㄍㄨㄟ)
a jade tablet with a pointed top

【琯】 3461 ㄍㄨㄢˇ goan guǎn
1. a jade tube used as an instrument in ancient times
2. to polish precious metals or stones

九畫

【瑟】 3462 ㄙㄜˋ seh sè
1. *se*, a large horizontal musical instrument, about nine feet long, originally with 50 strings which was later reduced to 25 with movable bridges for tuning
2. varied and many
3. elegant and stately; majestic
4. bright and clear; pure and clean
5. same as 索—alone; lonely; solitary

瑟堡(ㄙㄜˋ ㄅㄠˇ)
Cherbourg, a French port

瑟調(ㄙㄜˋ ㄉㄧㄠˋ)
a form in Chinese "Collection of Tunes"(樂府) consisting of 38 tunes, played with seven musical instruments

瑟瑟(ㄙㄜˋ ㄙㄜˋ)
① the heaving sound of wind ② the turquoise

瑟縮(ㄙㄜˋ ㄙㄨㄛ)
① stiff and numb—as from cold ② timid and trembling; to shrink—as from fear ③ the heaving sound of wind

【瑁】 3463 1. ㄇㄟˋ mey mèi
a tortoise shell

【瑁】 3463 2. ㄇㄠˋ maw mào
a very precious piece of jade worn by ancient emperors to match tablets borne by the nobles

【瑋】 3464 ㄨㄟˇ woei wěi
1. a kind of jade
2. rare; precious; splendorous

【瑄】 3465 ㄒㄩㄢ shiuan xuān
an ornamental piece of jade about 6.5 inches in diameter

【瑑】 3466 ㄓㄨㄢˋ juann zhuàn
engraving on a jade tablet

【瑕】 3467 ㄒㄧㄚˊ shya xiá
1. a flaw, spot, or blemish in a piece of jade
2. a fault, error, blemish or flaw

瑕病(ㄒㄧㄚˊ ㄅㄧㄥˋ)
a blemish; a flaw

瑕不掩瑜(ㄒㄧㄚˊ ㄅㄨˋ ㄧㄢˇ ㄩˊ)
The defects do not outweigh the merits.

瑕玷(ㄒㄧㄚˊ ㄉㄧㄢˋ)
flaws and defects

瑕釁(ㄒㄧㄚˊ ㄒㄧㄣˋ)
faults and errors

瑕謫(ㄒㄧㄚˊ ㄓㄜˊ)
blemishes and flaws; errors

瑕疵(ㄒㄧㄚˊ ㄘ)
defects; flaws; blemishes

瑕瑜(ㄒㄧㄚˊ ㄩˊ)
good and bad points; virtues and flaws

瑕瑜互見(ㄒㄧㄚˊ ㄩˊ ㄏㄨˋ ㄐㄧㄢˋ)
(said of a single person) to have both good and bad qualities; (said of two measures, persons, etc.) each having strong and weak points

【瑙】 3468 ㄋㄠˇ nao nǎo
agate; cornelian

【瑛】 3469 ㄧㄥ ing yīng
1. the glitter or sheen of jade
2. a transparent piece of jade; a crystal

【瑜】 3470 ㄩˊ yu yú
1. a fine and flawless piece of jade; a perfect gem
2. the brilliancy of jade; the luster of gems
3. excellences; virtues
4. yoga, a mystic and ascetic practice in Hindu philosophy

瑜不掩瑕(ㄩˊ ㄅㄨˋ ㄧㄢˇ ㄒㄧㄚˊ)
The merits do not outweigh the defects.

瑜伽(ㄩˊ ㄑㄧㄝˊ)
yoga, a mystic and ascetic practice in Hindu philosophy 亦作「瑜珈」

瑜伽派(ㄩˊ ㄑㄧㄝˊ ㄆㄞˋ)
the yoga sect of the Hindu philosophy 亦作「瑜珈派」

瑜伽宗(ㄩˊ ㄑㄧㄝˊ ㄗㄨㄥ)
the Yogacara, or esoteric sect (The principles of yoga are accredited to Patanjali in the second century B.C., later founded as a school in Buddhism by Asanga, fourth century A.D. Hsüan Tsang (玄奘) became a disciple and advocate of this school.) 亦作「瑜珈宗」

【瑞】 3471 ㄖㄨㄟˋ ruey ruì
1. something portending good

luck or fortune; good omen : 吉瑞 signs of good luck
2. lucky; auspicious; fortunate
3. a jade tablet given to feudal princes on their investiture, as a sign of authority and rank
4. a Chinese family name

瑞符(ㄖㄨㄟˋ ㄈㄨˊ)
a credential tally in ancient China issued to the commander, etc. authorizing him to launch military operations

瑞典(ㄖㄨㄟˋ ㄉㄧㄢˇ)
Sweden

瑞典人(ㄖㄨㄟˋ ㄉㄧㄢˇ ㄖㄣˊ)
the Swedes

瑞圖(ㄖㄨㄟˋ ㄊㄨˊ)
a drawing, or picture portending luck, good fortune, etc.

瑞腦(ㄖㄨㄟˋ ㄋㄠˇ)
camphor from Borneo

瑞鳥(ㄖㄨㄟˋ ㄋㄧㄠˇ)
an auspicious bird—a bird of good omen (in Chinese legends, known as 鸞)

瑞禾(ㄖㄨㄟˋ ㄏㄜˊ)
an excellent crop 亦作「嘉禾」

瑞祥(ㄖㄨㄟˋ ㄒㄧㄤˊ)
good luck; good fortune; good omen ; auspiciousness

瑞雪(ㄖㄨㄟˋ ㄒㄩㄝˇ)
① a timely snow in late winter or early spring; a seasonable snow that will kill pests and that portends a bumper crop in the coming year ②a Chinese medicinal herb 亦作「栝樓根」

瑞雪兆豐年(ㄖㄨㄟˋ ㄒㄩㄝˇ ㄓㄠˋ ㄈㄥ ㄋㄧㄢˊ)
A timely snow promises a good harvest.

瑞士(ㄖㄨㄟˋ ㄕˋ)
Switzerland

瑞士人(ㄖㄨㄟˋ ㄕˋ ㄖㄣˊ)
a Swiss; the Swiss people

瑞草(ㄖㄨㄟˋ ㄘㄠˇ)
a legendary shrub, regarded as a good omen; the shrub of luck-tea

瑞應(ㄖㄨㄟˋ ㄧㄥˋ)
the appearance of precious, rare and auspicious things as Heaven's response to the high virtue of the reigning monarch

瑞玉(ㄖㄨㄟˋ ㄩˋ)
a piece of jade serving as the credentials of a feudal lord

瑞雲(ㄖㄨㄟˋ ㄩㄣˊ)
auspicious clouds

【瑚】 3472 ㄏㄨˊ hwu hú
coral

瑚璉(ㄏㄨˊ ㄌㄧㄢˇ)
a sacrificial vessel for grains in the imperial ancestral shrine—a person of virtue and quality

【琿】 3473 ㄏㄨㄣˊ hwen hún
a kind of precious jade

【瑗】 3474 ㄩㄢˋ yuann yuàn
1. a huge ring of fine jade
2. name of a kind of jade

【瑀】 3475 ㄩˇ yeu yǔ
a jadelike stone

十畫

【瑩】 3476 ㄧㄥˊ yng yíng
1. the luster of jade
2. a jadelike pebble
3. smooth and glossy; clean and shining; bright and brilliant
4. transparent; pure
5. (said of a person) bright and clever

瑩潔(ㄧㄥˊ ㄐㄧㄝˊ)
clean and lustrous; pure and clear

瑩鏡(ㄧㄥˊ ㄐㄧㄥˋ)
a clear mirror

瑩徹(ㄧㄥˊ ㄔㄜˋ)
clear and transparent

瑩潤(ㄧㄥˊ ㄖㄨㄣˋ)
polished and glossy; clear and lustrous

瑩澤(ㄧㄥˊ ㄗㄜˊ)
transparent and shiny

【瑤】 3477 ㄧㄠˊ yau yáo
1. a precious jade or stone
2. clean, pure and white
3. treasurable; valuable; precious

瑤碧(ㄧㄠˊ ㄅㄧˋ)
agate with a greenish luster

瑤圃(ㄧㄠˊ ㄆㄨˇ)
the place where immortals live; a fairyland

瑤臺(ㄧㄠˊ ㄊㄞˊ)
① a towerlike building ornamented with gems ② a fairyland ③ a beautiful terrace

瑤花(ㄧㄠˊ ㄏㄨㄚ)
rare flowers

瑤華
①(ㄧㄠˊ ㄏㄨㄚ) blossoms as white and pure as jade
②(ㄧㄠˊ ㄏㄨㄚˊ) ⓐ treasurable; precious ⓑ fine jade

瑤箋(ㄧㄠˊ ㄐㄧㄢ) or 瑤函(ㄧㄠˊ ㄏㄢˊ)
(a polite expression) your letter

瑤琴(ㄧㄠˊ ㄑㄧㄣˊ)
a lute studded or ornamented with gems

瑤池(ㄧㄠˊ ㄔˊ)
the place where immortals live; a fairyland

瑤觴(ㄧㄠˊ ㄕㄤ)
a jade wine-cup

瑤英(ㄧㄠˊ ㄧㄥ)
the most precious kind of jade

【瑣】 3478 ㄙㄨㄛˇ suoo suǒ
1. trifles; petty; frivolous; trifling
2. troublesome; annoying
3. a jade chain
4. a palace gate

瑣瀆(ㄙㄨㄛˇ ㄉㄨˊ)
to bother others with trifle matters

瑣細(ㄙㄨㄛˇ ㄒㄧˋ)
① petty; trifling; frivolous ② troublesome

瑣屑(ㄙㄨㄛˇ ㄒㄧㄝˋ)
petty; unimportant; insignificant; small

瑣事(ㄙㄨㄛˇ ㄕˋ)
trifles; trivial matters

瑣辭(ㄙㄨㄛˇ ㄘˊ)
petty or trivial talks; superfluous wording; annoying and uncalled-for utterances

瑣才(ㄙㄨㄛˇ ㄘㄞˊ)
(said of persons) of little capability or talent

瑣碎(ㄙㄨㄛˇ ㄙㄨㄟˋ)
① trifling; petty and varied:

他認爲那是瑣碎之事。He takes it as a trifling matter. ②a slight indisposition or ailment

瑣務(ㄙㄨㄛˇ ㄨˋ)
trifling matters

瑣尾流離(ㄙㄨㄛˇ ㄨㄟˇ ㄌㄧㄡˊ ㄌㄧˊ)
to begin (a career, life, etc.) happily but end in failure

瑣聞(ㄙㄨㄛˇ ㄨㄣˊ)
bits of unimportant information; sundry news or anecdotes

【瑯】 3479
(琅) ㄌㄤˊ lang láng
a stone resembling jade, pure and white

瑯嬛福地(ㄌㄤˊ ㄏㄨㄢˊ ㄈㄨˊ ㄉㄧˋ)
library of a fairyland, where rare ancient books were stored

瑯琊(ㄌㄤˊ ㄧㄝˊ)
①name of an ancient region in today's eastern Shantung Province ②name of a mountain in Shantung

【瑰】 3480
ㄍㄨㄟ guei guī
1. fabulous; great; extraordinary
2. a stone which is a little less valuable than jade; a kind of jasper

瑰寶(ㄍㄨㄟ ㄅㄠˇ)
a treasure; a gem

瑰麗(ㄍㄨㄟ ㄌㄧˋ)
fabulously beautiful; magnificent: 這座宮殿眞是雄偉瑰麗。The palace is indeed magnificent.

瑰姿(ㄍㄨㄟ ㄗ)
(said of a person) extraordinary or preeminent appearance

瑰岸(ㄍㄨㄟ ㄢˋ)
tall and strong

瑰異(ㄍㄨㄟ ㄧˋ)
fabulous and extraordinary things

瑰意琦行(ㄍㄨㄟ ㄧˋ ㄑㄧˊ ㄒㄧㄥˋ)
outstanding in thinking and action

瑰瑋(ㄍㄨㄟ ㄨㄟˇ)
rare and precious; treasurable

【瑱】 3481
1. ㄊㄧㄢˋ tiann tiàn
earplugs of jade

【瑱】 3481
2. ㄓㄣˋ jenn zhèn
to weight; to press

【瑪】 3482
ㄇㄚˇ maa mǎ
agate; cornelian

瑪瑙(ㄇㄚˇ ㄋㄠˇ)
agate; cornelian

瑪麗 or 瑪利(ㄇㄚˇ ㄌㄧˋ)
Mary

瑪志尼(ㄇㄚˇ ㄓˋ ㄋㄧˊ)
Giuseppe Mazzini (1805-1872), Italian patriot 亦作「馬志尼」

瑪賽克(ㄇㄚˇ ㄙㄞˋ ㄎㄜˋ)
mosaic 亦作「馬賽克」

瑪雅人(ㄇㄚˇ ㄧㄚˇ ㄖㄣˊ)
Maya

【瑳】 3483
ㄘㄨㄛˇ tsuoo cuǒ
1. the luster and purity of jade
2. bright and flourishing
3. the brilliant white appearance of the teeth

【瑲】 3484
ㄑㄧㄤ chiang qiāng
the tinkling of jade pendants

瑲瑲(ㄑㄧㄤ ㄑㄧㄤ)
the jingling or chiming of bells

【瑨】 3485
ㄐㄧㄣˋ jinn jìn
a fine piece of jade

十一畫

【瑽】 3486
ㄘㄨㄥ tsong cōng
the tinkling of metal ornaments and jade pendants

【瑾】 3487
ㄐㄧㄣˇ jiin jǐn
fine jade

瑾瑜(ㄐㄧㄣˇ ㄩˊ)
a fine piece of jade

瑾瑜匿瑕(ㄐㄧㄣˇ ㄩˊ ㄋㄧˋ ㄒㄧㄚˊ)
flaws hidden in a beautiful gem

【璀】 3488
ㄘㄨㄟˇ tsoei cuǐ
the luster or glitter of jade and gems

璀璨(ㄘㄨㄟˇ ㄘㄢˋ)
the brilliancy and luster of pearls and precious stones: 她的鑽戒璀璨奪目。Her diamond ring dazzled with brilliancy.

璀錯(ㄘㄨㄟˇ ㄘㄨㄛˋ)
many and varied

璀璀(ㄘㄨㄟˇ ㄘㄨㄟˇ)
bright and clear

【璇】 3489
ㄒㄩㄢˊ shyuan xuán
1. fine jade
2. name of a constellation

璇閨(ㄒㄩㄢˊ ㄍㄨㄟ)
an exquisite, cozy boudoir ornamented with fine jade

璇宮(ㄒㄩㄢˊ ㄍㄨㄥ)
an exquisite room ornamented with fine gems; a swanky palace; a luxuriously-furnished hall

璇花(ㄒㄩㄢˊ ㄏㄨㄚ)
blossoms as pure and white as jade

璇璣(ㄒㄩㄢˊ ㄐㄧ)
①the North Star ②an ancient astronomical instrument of the time of Shun (舜) (2255-2205 B.C.)

璇室(ㄒㄩㄢˊ ㄕˋ)
a gem-studded room

【璃】 3490
ㄌㄧˊ li lí
glass; a glassy substance 參看「琉璃」

【璉】 3491
ㄌㄧㄢˊ lian lián
a vessel used to hold grain offerings for the imperial sacrifice

【璈】 3492
ㄠˊ aur áo
name of an ancient musical instrument

【璋】 3493
ㄓㄤ jang zhāng
an ancient jade ornament used in state ceremonies; a jade tablet

【璁】 3494
ㄘㄨㄥ tsong cōng
a jadelike stone

璁琤(ㄘㄨㄥ ㄔㄥ)
the sound of music instruments; the tinkling of jades

十二畫

【璟】 3495
ㄐㄧㄥˇ jiing jǐng
the luster of jade

【璘】 3496
ㄌㄧㄣˊ lin lín

the brilliance of jade

【璜】3497 ㄏㄨㄤˊ hwang huang

an ancient jade ornament, semicircular in shape, hung up as a tinkling pendant

【璞】3498 ㄆㄨˊ pwu pu

1. an uncarved or unpolished jade or gem
2. (figuratively) natural; unadorned: 返璞歸眞 to revert to one's natural self

璞玉渾金(ㄆㄨˊ ㄩˋ ㄏㄨㄣˊ ㄐㄧㄣ)
(literally) uncarved jade and unrefined gold—The real value of things lies in what they are made of, not what they appear to be.

【璣】3499 ㄐㄧ ji ji

1. pearls, jade, etc. which are not quite circular
2. as in 旋璣 or 璿璣—an ancient astronomical instrument
3. name of a constellation

【璠】3500 ㄈㄢˊ farn fan

a piece of precious jade

【璐】3501 ㄌㄨˋ luh lu

fine jade

十三畫

【璦】3502 ㄞˋ ay ai

fine jade

璦琿(ㄞˋ ㄏㄨㄣˊ)
Ai Hun, a county in Heilungkiang (黑龍江) in Northeast China

璦琿條約(ㄞˋ ㄏㄨㄣˊ ㄊㄧㄠˊ ㄩㄝ)
the Sino-Russian treaty concluded in 1858 at Ai Hun, in which the present boundaries between the two nations were defined

【璧】3503 ㄅㄧˋ bih bi

1. a round and flat piece of jade with a circular hole in it
2. a general name of all kinds of jade, jade-wares and ornaments

璧田(ㄅㄧˋ ㄊㄧㄢˊ)
good farmland

璧合(ㄅㄧˋ ㄏㄜˊ)
a perfect match

璧還(ㄅㄧˋ ㄏㄨㄢˊ)
to return a gift or present; to decline a present with thanks

璧謝(ㄅㄧˋ ㄒㄧㄝˋ)
to return a present with thanks

璧趙(ㄅㄧˋ ㄓㄠˋ)
to return something valuable to its original owner

璧水(ㄅㄧˋ ㄕㄨㄟˇ)
(in ancient China) a semicircular pool within the precincts of a college

璧人(ㄅㄧˋ ㄖㄣˊ)
a person as beautiful or handsome as jade; a fine-looking person

璧玉(ㄅㄧˋ ㄩˋ)
a round and flat piece of jade with a circular hole in it

璧月(ㄅㄧˋ ㄩㄝˋ)
a full moon

【環】3504 ㄏㄨㄢˊ hwan huan

1. a jade ring or bracelet; a ring; a bracelet
2. earrings for women; ear-ornaments
3. around; round; to surround; surrounding; to encircle: 台北四面環山。Taipei is surrounded by mountains.
4. a link: 這是最弱的一環。This is the weakest link.
5. (sports) a ring: 命中三環 to hit the three-point ring
6. a Chinese family name

環拜(ㄏㄨㄢˊ ㄅㄞˋ)
to bow around

環保(ㄏㄨㄢˊ ㄅㄠˇ)
short for 環境保護

環保局(ㄏㄨㄢˊ ㄅㄠˇ ㄐㄩˊ)
the Bureau of Environmental Protection (BEP) in the local government

環保署(ㄏㄨㄢˊ ㄅㄠˇ ㄕㄨˋ)
the Environmental Protection Agency (EPA) in the Central Government

環抱(ㄏㄨㄢˊ ㄅㄠˋ)
to surround; to encircle; to hem in; to encincture: 羣山環抱著村莊。A ring of hills encinctured the village.

環佩(ㄏㄨㄢˊ ㄆㄟˋ)
ornaments for women

環肥燕瘦(ㄏㄨㄢˊ ㄈㄟˊ ㄧㄢˋ ㄕㄡˋ)
(literally) Yang Yü-huan (楊玉環) was plump, while Chao Fei-yen (趙飛燕) was skinny. (Both were imperial concubines of unusual beauty.)— beautiful women, each of whom is attractive in her own way 亦作「燕瘦環肥」

環島(ㄏㄨㄢˊ ㄉㄠˇ)
around-the-island

環堵蕭然(ㄏㄨㄢˊ ㄉㄨˇ ㄒㄧㄠ ㄖㄢˊ)
(literally) nothing within the four walls—abject poverty

環列(ㄏㄨㄢˊ ㄌㄧㄝˋ)
to place in a circle; to surround on all sides

環流(ㄏㄨㄢˊ ㄌㄧㄡˊ)
① to flow or travel around in circles ② circulation; circumfluence

環顧(ㄏㄨㄢˊ ㄍㄨˋ)
① to look around ② to review; to take stock of: 環顧國際局勢 to take stock of the world situation

環顧四週(ㄏㄨㄢˊ ㄍㄨˋ ㄙˋ ㄓㄡ)
to look around

環河(ㄏㄨㄢˊ ㄏㄜˊ)
along a river bend

環海(ㄏㄨㄢˊ ㄏㄞˇ)
within the seven seas—China

環節(ㄏㄨㄢˊ ㄐㄧㄝˊ)
a segment; a link: 這不是主要的環節。This is not the key link.

環節動物(ㄏㄨㄢˊ ㄐㄧㄝˊ ㄉㄨㄥˋ ㄨˋ)
the annulata

環境(ㄏㄨㄢˊ ㄐㄧㄥˋ)
surroundings; environment; circumstances

環境保護(ㄏㄨㄢˊ ㄐㄧㄥˋ ㄅㄠˇ ㄏㄨˋ)
environmental protection

環境污染(ㄏㄨㄢˊ ㄐㄧㄥˋ ㄨ ㄖㄢˇ)
pollution of the environment; environmental pollution

環境衛生(ㄏㄨㄢˊ ㄐㄧㄥˋ ㄨㄟˋ ㄕㄥ)
environmental sanitation

環球(ㄏㄨㄢˊ ㄑㄧㄡˊ)

〔玉部〕

around the globe; throughout the world; universal
環城(ㄏㄨㄢˊ ㄔㄥˊ)
around the city
環蝕(ㄏㄨㄢˊ ㄕˊ)
(astronomy) annular eclipse
環視(ㄏㄨㄢˊ ㄕˋ)
to look around
環繞(ㄏㄨㄢˊ ㄖㄠˋ)
to revolve round; to circle; to move round; to surround
環子(ㄏㄨㄢˊ ·ㄗ) or 環兒(ㄏㄨㄚˊㄦ)
a ring
環遊世界(ㄏㄨㄢˊ ㄧㄡˊ ㄕˋ ㄐㄧㄝˋ)
to take a round-the-world tour
環衛(ㄏㄨㄢˊ ㄨㄟˋ)
the imperial guards
環暈(ㄏㄨㄢˊ ㄩㄣˋ)
the lunar or solar halo

【璨】 3505 ㄘㄢˋ tsann càn
bright and brilliant; lustrous and luminous

【璫】 3506 ㄉㄤ dang dāng
1. richly ornamented
2. pearls for filling up ear punctures to prevent the holes from closing
3. ancient headgear

【璩】 3507 ㄑㄩˊ chyu qú
1. a ringed ornament—earrings, rings for fingers
2. a Chinese family name

十四畫

【璽】 3508 ㄒㄧˇ shii xǐ
1. the seal of an emperor or a king
2. the formal seal of a state; the national emblem
璽綬(ㄒㄧˇ ㄕㄡˋ)
the imperial seal and the attached cordon
璽書(ㄒㄧˇ ㄕㄨ)
documents sealed with personal or official seals

【璵】 3509 ㄩˊ yu yú
fine jade

【璿】 3510 ㄒㄩㄢˊ shyuan xuán
fine jade
璿圖(ㄒㄩㄢˊ ㄊㄨˊ)
the state; the nation
璿宮(ㄒㄩㄢˊ ㄍㄨㄥ)
a gem-studded chamber
璿璣玉衡(ㄒㄩㄢˊ ㄐㄧ ㄩˋ ㄏㄥˊ)
an ancient astronomical instrument

【璺】 3511 ㄨㄣˋ wenn wèn
a crack in jade (or on glassware or earthenware)

十五畫

【瓊】 3512 ㄑㄩㄥˊ chyong qióng
1. fine jade or agate
2. excellent; beautiful; fabulous
瓊杯(ㄑㄩㄥˊ ㄅㄟ)
a jade wine-cup
瓊葩(ㄑㄩㄥˊ ㄆㄚ)
blossoms as pure and white as jade
瓊麻(ㄑㄩㄥˊ ㄇㄚˊ)
sisal: 這條繩子是用瓊麻製成的。The rope is made of sisal.
瓊島(ㄑㄩㄥˊ ㄉㄠˇ)
① Hainan Island (海南島) ② also known as Chiung Hua Islet (瓊華島), one of the eight scenic spots in Peking
瓊樓玉宇(ㄑㄩㄥˊ ㄌㄡˊ ㄩˋ ㄩˇ)
①(Chinese mythology) the Palace of the Moon ② a magnificent or splendid building
瓊粒(ㄑㄩㄥˊ ㄌㄧˋ)
ricegrains in a year of famine (which are as precious as jade)
瓊林(ㄑㄩㄥˊ ㄌㄧㄣˊ)
a collection of rare and valuable things (usually referring to books)
瓊林宴(ㄑㄩㄥˊ ㄌㄧㄣˊ ㄧㄢˋ)
(in the Ching Dynasty) a feast hosted by the emperor in honor of the successful candidates of imperial examination the day after the examination
瓊花(ㄑㄩㄥˊ ㄏㄨㄚ)
a rare flower said to confer immortality when eaten
瓊華(ㄑㄩㄥˊ ㄏㄨㄚˊ)
fine jade; beautiful gems
瓊玖(ㄑㄩㄥˊ ㄐㄧㄡˇ)
fine jade
瓊漿(ㄑㄩㄥˊ ㄐㄧㄤ)
good wine
瓊琚(ㄑㄩㄥˊ ㄐㄩ)
fine jade
瓊枝玉葉(ㄑㄩㄥˊ ㄓ ㄩˋ ㄧㄝˋ)
lineal imperial descendants
瓊州海峽(ㄑㄩㄥˊ ㄓㄡ ㄏㄞˇ ㄒㄧㄚˊ)
the Hainan Straits
瓊姿(ㄑㄩㄥˊ ㄗ)
an elegant or a graceful appearance
瓊斯(ㄑㄩㄥˊ ㄙ)
transliteration of Jones
瓊瑤(ㄑㄩㄥˊ ㄧㄠˊ)
① fine jade ② your letter ③ a gift or literary piece written for others
瓊筵(ㄑㄩㄥˊ ㄧㄢˊ)
a banquet; an elaborate feast
瓊音(ㄑㄩㄥˊ ㄧㄣ)
a clear and crisp sound
瓊英(ㄑㄩㄥˊ ㄧㄥ)
a beautiful stone resembling jade

十六畫

【瓏】 3513 ㄌㄨㄥˊ long lóng
1. a clear and crisp sound
2. dry; parched
3. the rumbling of cart
4. the tinkling of metals or jades
5. dusky

【瓌】 3514 ㄍㄨㄟ guei guī
1. same as 瑰, a kind of jasper
2. extraordinary; fabulous or admirable
瓌寶(ㄍㄨㄟ ㄅㄠˇ)
an extraordinary treasure
瓌奇(ㄍㄨㄟ ㄑㄧˊ)
rare and precious things

十七畫

【瓔】 3515 ㄧㄥ ing yīng
a necklace of precious stones
瓔珞(ㄧㄥ ㄌㄨㄛˋ)
a necklace of precious stones

〔玉部〕

瓔珞棗兒(ㄧㄥ ㄌㄨㄛˋ ㄗㄠˇㄦ)
a kind of oblong jujube

瓜 部
ㄍㄨㄚ gua guā

【瓜】 3516
ㄍㄨㄚ gua guā
melons, gourds, cucumbers, etc.
瓜瓣(ㄍㄨㄚ ㄅㄢˋ)
melon seed
瓜剖豆分(ㄍㄨㄚ ㄆㄡˇ ㄉㄡˋ ㄈㄣ)
(said of a country) to be divided or split like a melon or a bean; to be partitioned
瓜棚(ㄍㄨㄚ ㄆㄥˊ)
the framework for melon vines
瓜皮帽(ㄍㄨㄚ ㄆㄧˊ ㄇㄠˋ)
a small round skullcap much worn in former times
瓜皮艇(ㄍㄨㄚ ㄆㄧˊ ㄊㄧㄥˇ)
a small skiff
瓜緜(ㄍㄨㄚ ㄇㄧㄢˊ)
to have prosperous descendants 參看「瓜瓞緜緜」
瓜分(ㄍㄨㄚ ㄈㄣ)
to divide and distribute; to apportion; to partition; to dismember
瓜達康納爾(ㄍㄨㄚ ㄉㄚˊ ㄎㄤ ㄋㄚˋ ㄦˇ)
Guadalcanal Island in the Pacific
瓜代(ㄍㄨㄚ ㄉㄞˋ)
to relieve or replace (an official) upon the expiration of his term of office
瓜地馬拉(ㄍㄨㄚ ㄉㄧˋ ㄇㄚˇ ㄌㄚ)
Guatemala
瓜瓞緜緜(ㄍㄨㄚ ㄉㄧㄝˊ ㄇㄧㄢˊ ㄇㄧㄢˊ)
to have prosperous descendants (an expression of felicitation printed on a marriage certificate) 亦作「緜緜瓜瓞」
瓜條(ㄍㄨㄚ ㄊㄧㄠˊ)
melon rind cut into thin strips and sweetened
瓜田李下(ㄍㄨㄚ ㄊㄧㄢˊ ㄌㄧˇ ㄒㄧㄚˋ)
(literally) in a melon field (where one may be suspected of stealing melons if one ties one's shoestrings) and under a plum tree (where one may be suspected of stealing plums if one arranges one's hat)—a position that invites suspicion
瓜葛(ㄍㄨㄚ ㄍㄜˊ)
melon vines—a multitude of relatives; to get mixed up; connected; involved; related; complications
瓜果(ㄍㄨㄚ ㄍㄨㄛˇ)
melons and fruits: 瓜果有益健康。Melons and fruits are good for the health.
瓜熟蒂落(ㄍㄨㄚ ㄕㄨˊ ㄉㄧˋ ㄌㄨㄛˋ)
(literally) When a melon is ripe, it falls of its own accord.—Things take care of themselves when the right time comes. 或 Everything can be done easily at the right time.
瓜仁(ㄍㄨㄚ ㄖㄣˊ) or 瓜仁兒(ㄍㄨㄚ ㄖㄜˊㄦ)
the edible part of a melon seed; the kernel of a melon seed
瓜瓤(ㄍㄨㄚ ㄖㄤˊ)
the pulp of a melon
瓜子(ㄍㄨㄚ ㄗˇ) or 瓜子兒(ㄍㄨㄚ ㄗㄜˇㄦ)
melon seeds
瓜子臉(ㄍㄨㄚ ㄗˇ ㄌㄧㄢˇ)
an oval face (usually said of a pretty woman): 這女孩有張瓜子臉。The girl has an oval face.

五畫

【瓞】 3517
ㄉㄧㄝˊ dye dié
a kind of small melons

六畫

【瓠】 3518
ㄏㄨˋ huh hù
a gourd; a calabash
瓠肥(ㄏㄨˋ ㄈㄟˊ)
obese; fat
瓠落(ㄏㄨˋ ㄌㄨㄛˋ)
(said of a vessel) flat and shallow—large but useless
瓠果(ㄏㄨˋ ㄍㄨㄛˇ)
pepos

十一畫

【瓢】 3519
ㄆㄧㄠˊ pyau piáo
a ladle (often made of a dried calabash or gourd)
瓢蟲(ㄆㄧㄠˊ ㄔㄨㄥˊ)
a ladybug; a ladybird
瓢兒(ㄆㄧㄠˊㄦ)
① a ladle (often made of a dried calabash or gourd) ② (jocular usage) human head

十四畫

【瓣】 3520
ㄅㄢˋ bann bàn
1. petals (of a flower)
2. sections (as of oranges)
3. a valve; a lamella
4. fragments; pieces
瓣兒(ㄅㄚˋㄦ)
① petals (of flowers) ② sections (as of oranges)
瓣香(ㄅㄢˋ ㄒㄧㄤ)
① petallike incense used in worship of Buddha ② the worship or admiration of someone

十七畫

【瓤】 3521
ㄖㄤˊ rang ráng
1. the pulp of a fruit; a section of an orange, a tangerine, etc.
2. the interior part of certain things
瓤兒(ㄖㄤˊㄦ)
the pulp of a fruit; a section of an orange, a tangerine, etc.

瓦 部
ㄨㄚˇ woa wǎ

【瓦】 3522
1. ㄨㄚˇ woa wǎ
1. earthenware; pottery
2. a tile
3. watt, the SI unit of power
4. a Chinese family name
瓦房(ㄨㄚˇ ㄈㄤˊ)
a tiled house: 他住在一所瓦房子裏。He lives in a tiled

〔瓜·瓦部〕

house.
瓦釜雷鳴(ㄨㄚˇ ㄈㄨˇ ㄌㄟˊ ㄇㄧㄥˊ)
(literally) an earthen pot sounding like thunder—an unworthy man creating sensations and enjoying popularity
瓦當(ㄨㄚˇ ㄉㄤ)
tiles with a circular facade at one end used along the edge of palace eaves during the Han Dynasty
瓦當文(ㄨㄚˇ ㄉㄤ ㄨㄣˊ)
inscriptions on the circular facade of a tile參看「瓦當」
瓦特(ㄨㄚˇ ㄊㄜˋ)
① James Watt, 1736-1819, Scottish inventor ②(electricity) watt
瓦楞紙(ㄨㄚˇ ㄌㄥˊ ㄓˇ)
corrugated paper
瓦礫(ㄨㄚˇ ㄌㄧˋ)
① rubble; ruin ② worthless things
瓦裂(ㄨㄚˇ ㄌㄧㄝˋ)
broken like a tile
瓦鱗(ㄨㄚˇ ㄌㄧㄣˊ)
tiles overlapping like scales
瓦鍋(ㄨㄚˇ ㄍㄨㄛ)
an earthen pot
瓦棺(ㄨㄚˇ ㄍㄨㄢ)
a pottery coffin
瓦罐(ㄨㄚˇ ㄍㄨㄢˋ)
an earthen jar; a pottery container
瓦塊(ㄨㄚˇ ㄎㄨㄞˋ)
fragments of a tile
瓦合(ㄨㄚˇ ㄏㄜˊ)
loosely put together
瓦解(ㄨㄚˇ ㄐㄧㄝˇ)
to fall apart; to disintegrate; to collapse; to crumble
瓦解冰銷(ㄨㄚˇ ㄐㄧㄝˇ ㄅㄧㄥ ㄒㄧㄠ)
to disintegrate like tiles and to dissolve like ice
瓦解土崩(ㄨㄚˇ ㄐㄧㄝˇ ㄊㄨˇ ㄅㄥ)
to fall completely apart; to disintegrate completely
瓦匠(ㄨㄚˇ ㄐㄧㄤˋ)
a bricklayer; a plasterer
瓦器(ㄨㄚˇ ㄑㄧˋ)
earthenware; pottery
瓦全(ㄨㄚˇ ㄑㄩㄢˊ)
to choose life rather than death when it would be more honorable to die; to compromise one's principles for self-preservation: 寧爲玉碎，不爲瓦全。One would rather be a broken piece of jade than be a whole piece of tile.—One would rather die with honor than survive with dishonor.
瓦時(ㄨㄚˇ ㄕˊ)
(electricity) watt-hour
瓦時計(ㄨㄚˇ ㄕˊ ㄐㄧˋ)
a watt-hour meter
瓦作(ㄨㄚˇ ·ㄗㄨㄛ)
a bricklayer; a plasterer
瓦斯(ㄨㄚˇ ㄙ)
gas; poisonous gas used in war
瓦斯彈(ㄨㄚˇ ㄙ ㄉㄢˋ)
a gas bomb; a gas shell
瓦斯筒(ㄨㄚˇ ㄙ ㄊㄨㄥˇ)
a gas cylinder
瓦窰(ㄨㄚˇ ㄧㄠˊ)
a pottery or tile kiln

【瓦】3522 2. ㄨㄚˋ wah wà
to cover a roof with tiles; to tile

五畫

【瓴】3523 ㄌㄧㄥˊ ling líng
1. the concave channels of tiling
2. a bottle with a handle

六畫

【瓷】3524 ㄘˊ tsyr cí
porcelain; chinaware
瓷胎(ㄘˊ ㄊㄞ)
porcelain not yet baked
瓷土(ㄘˊ ㄊㄨˇ)
kaolin(e); porcelain clay
瓷器(ㄘˊ ㄑㄧˋ)
porcelain; porcelain ware; chinaware; china: 她買了一套精美的瓷器。She bought a set of fine china.
瓷甎 or 瓷磚(ㄘˊ ㄓㄨㄢ)
small porcelain tiles used for wall paneling or floor pavement
瓷窰(ㄘˊ ㄧㄠˊ)
a porcelain kiln
瓷瓦兒(ㄘˊ ㄨㄚˇㄦ)
fragments of porcelain

八畫

【瓿】3525 ㄆㄡˇ poou pǒu
a jar; a pot

【瓶】3526 (甁、缾) ㄆㄧㄥˊ pyng píng
a bottle; a pitcher; a jug; a vase
瓶鉢(ㄆㄧㄥˊ ㄅㄛ)
a Buddhist monk's rice bowl
瓶頸(ㄆㄧㄥˊ ㄐㄧㄥˇ)
a bottleneck
瓶裝(ㄆㄧㄥˊ ㄓㄨㄤ)
bottled
瓶子(ㄆㄧㄥˊ·ㄗ)or 瓶兒(ㄆㄧㄥˊㄦ)
a bottle; a jar; a vase
瓶塞兒(ㄆㄧㄥˊ ㄙㄞㄦ)
a bottle stopper or plug; a cork

九畫

【甄】3527 ㄓㄣ jen zhēn
1. a potter's wheel
2. to make pottery ware
3. to examine; to discern
4. to grade (competence, etc.) by examinations
5. to make clear
6. a Chinese family name
甄拔(ㄓㄣ ㄅㄚˊ)
to select (talent) by a competitive examination
甄別(ㄓㄣ ㄅㄧㄝˊ)
to grade (competence, aptitude, etc. by an examination); to screen
甄別考試(ㄓㄣ ㄅㄧㄝˊ ㄎㄠˇ ㄕˋ)
an examination for grading abilities, screening, etc.
甄汰(ㄓㄣ ㄊㄞˋ)
to eliminate by an examination
甄選(ㄓㄣ ㄒㄩㄢˇ)
to select (talented people, etc.)
甄審(ㄓㄣ ㄕㄣˇ)
to screen and select (candidates)
甄用(ㄓㄣ ㄩㄥˋ)
to employ by an examination

【甃】 3528 ㄓㄡˋ jow zhòu
1. the brick wall of a well; a tile
2. to build a well
3. to construct with bricks

十一畫

【甌】 3529 ㄡ ou ōu
1. a cup; a bowl
2. a Chinese family name

甌脫(ㄡ ㄊㄨㄛ)
①entrenchments on the frontiers ②no man's land on the border

甌越(ㄡ ㄩㄝˋ)
eastern Chekiang

【甎】 3530 (磚、塼) ㄓㄨㄢ juan zhuān
brick

甎頭(ㄓㄨㄢ ㄊㄡˊ)
bricks: 他們用甎頭造房子。They built their houses with bricks.

甎廠(ㄓㄨㄢ ㄔㄤˇ)
a brickfield; a brickyard

甎窰(ㄓㄨㄢ ㄧㄠˊ)
a brick kiln

甎瓦(ㄓㄨㄢ ㄨㄚˇ)
bricks and tiles

【甍】 3531 ㄇㄥˊ meng méng
rafters

十二畫

【甑】 3532 ㄗㄥˋ tzenq zèng
earthenware for cooking

甑塵釜魚(ㄗㄥˋ ㄔㄣˊ ㄈㄨˇ ㄩˊ)
(literally) Dust has covered kitchen utensils and fish has spawned in cooking vessels because of long disuse.—a state of stark poverty

甑兒糕(ㄗㄥˋㄦ ㄍㄠ)
a kind of steamed rice cake with stuffing

十三畫

【甕】 3533 ㄨㄥˋ wenq wèng
a jar; a jug; a pot; an urn

甕天(ㄨㄥˋ ㄊㄧㄢ)
(literally) to see the sky from inside a jar—to know very little of the world

甕計(ㄨㄥˋ ㄐㄧˋ)
counting chickens before they are hatched

甕中之鼈(ㄨㄥˋ ㄓㄨㄥ ㄓ ㄅㄧㄝ)
(literally) the turtle inside a jar—something that can be caught easily

甕中捉鼈(ㄨㄥˋ ㄓㄨㄥ ㄓㄨㄛ ㄅㄧㄝ)
(literally) to catch the turtle inside a jar—to catch something that has no way of escape

甕牖(ㄨㄥˋ ㄧㄡˇ)
(literally) a small round window like the mouth of a jar; a window made of the mouth of a broken jar—the mark of a needy family

【甓】 3534 ㄆㄧˋ pih pì
a brick; a tile

十六畫

【甗】 3535 ㄧㄢˇ yean yǎn
an earthenware vessel in two parts, of which one is for steaming and the other is for boiling; an ancient double boiler

甘部
ㄍㄢ gan gān

【甘】 3536 ㄍㄢ gan gān
1. tasty; luscious; delicious
2. sweet
3. willing: 我不甘落後。I was unwilling to lag behind.
4. to enjoy
5. pleasant; pleasing
6. a Chinese family name

甘拜下風(ㄍㄢ ㄅㄞˋ ㄒㄧㄚˋ ㄈㄥ)
willing to take an inferior position; to admit defeat willingly

甘比亞(ㄍㄢ ㄅㄧˇ ㄧㄚˋ)
Gambia, a river in W Africa, flowing W to the Atlantic

甘美(ㄍㄢ ㄇㄟˇ)
delicious; tasty; palatable

甘地(ㄍㄢ ㄉㄧˋ)
Mahatma Gandhi (Mohandas Karamchand Gandhi), 1869-1948, the spiritual leader of India in its independence movement

甘地主義(ㄍㄢ ㄉㄧˋ ㄓㄨˇ ㄧˋ)
Gandhism

甘棠遺愛(ㄍㄢ ㄊㄤˊ ㄧˊ ㄞˋ)
the memory left behind by a virtuous and capable official

甘迺廸(ㄍㄢ ㄋㄞˇ ㄉㄧˊ)
John Fitzgerald Kennedy, 1917-1963, the 35th President of the United States

甘藍(ㄍㄢ ㄌㄢˊ) or 甘藍菜(ㄍㄢ ㄌㄢˊ ㄘㄞˋ)
a kale; a cabbage: 他在菜園種甘藍菜。He grows cabbages in his garden.

甘霖(ㄍㄢ ㄌㄧㄣˊ)
a seasonable rain; a timely rain

甘霖普降(ㄍㄢ ㄌㄧㄣˊ ㄆㄨˇ ㄐㄧㄤˋ)
Seasonable rain has fallen everywhere.

甘露(ㄍㄢ ㄌㄨˋ)
sweet dew

甘羅(ㄍㄢ ㄌㄨㄛˊ)
Kan Lo, a child prodigy in the state of Chin, who was given a high official rank at the age of 12 in the Epoch of Warring States

甘瓜苦蒂(ㄍㄢ ㄍㄨㄚ ㄎㄨˇ ㄉㄧˋ)
(literally) a sweet melon with a bitter peduncle—a flaw in a precious stone 或 Nothing can be perfect.

甘汞(ㄍㄢ ㄍㄨㄥˇ)
calomel

甘苦(ㄍㄢ ㄎㄨˇ)
①sweetness and bitterness; happiness and suffering; prosperity and adversity ②hardships and difficulties experienced in work

甘苦備嘗(ㄍㄢ ㄎㄨˇ ㄅㄟˋ ㄔㄤˊ)
to have tasted both sweetness and bitterness; to have known both happiness and suffering

甘苦同受(ㄍㄢ ㄎㄨˇ ㄊㄨㄥˊ ㄕㄡˋ)
to share not only the sweets but also the bitters; to share both enjoyment and suffer-

ing
甘結(ㄍㄢ ㄐㄧㄝˊ)
an affidavit pledging that what is stated therein is absolutely true
甘蕉(ㄍㄢ ㄐㄧㄠ)
a banana 亦作「香蕉」
甘井先竭(ㄍㄢ ㄐㄧㄥˇ ㄒㄧㄢ ㄐㄧㄝˊ)
(literally) A sweet well dries early.—Men of talent decay faster.
甘寢(ㄍㄢ ㄑㄧㄣˇ)
to sleep soundly
甘泉(ㄍㄢ ㄑㄩㄢˊ)
① a fresh spring ② name of a county in Shensi
甘休(ㄍㄢ ㄒㄧㄡ)
willing to stop or halt: 他不肯與他們善罷甘休。He won't stop quarreling with them.
甘心(ㄍㄢ ㄒㄧㄣ)
① willingly; willing ② joyous; happy ③ to be wearied in mind
甘心瞑目(ㄍㄢ ㄒㄧㄣ ㄇㄧㄥˊ ㄇㄨˋ)
to die without dissatisfaction
甘心情願(ㄍㄢ ㄒㄧㄣ ㄑㄧㄥˊ ㄩㄢˋ)
perfectly willing
甘心忍受(ㄍㄢ ㄒㄧㄣ ㄖㄣˇ ㄕㄡˋ)
willing to endure
甘之如飴(ㄍㄢ ㄓ ㄖㄨˊ ㄧˊ)
to be quite content even in adversity
甘旨(ㄍㄢ ㄓˇ)
delicious or tasty food
甘蔗(ㄍㄢ ㄓㄜˋ)
sugarcane: 甘蔗沒有兩頭甜。A sugarcane is never sweet at both ends.—One can't have it both ways.
甘蔗板(ㄍㄢ ㄓㄜˋ ㄅㄢˇ)
a bagasse board
甘薯 or 甘藷(ㄍㄢ ㄕㄨˇ)
sweet potatoes
甘草(ㄍㄢ ㄘㄠˇ)
licorice
甘脆(ㄍㄢ ㄘㄨㄟˋ)
delicacies
甘肅(ㄍㄢ ㄙㄨˋ)
Kansu Province
甘油(ㄍㄢ ㄧㄡˊ)
glycerine
甘言(ㄍㄢ ㄧㄢˊ)
honeyed words
甘爲戎首(ㄍㄢ ㄨㄟˊ ㄖㄨㄥˊ ㄕㄡˇ)
not to hesitate in starting a war
甘味(ㄍㄢ ㄨㄟˋ)
sweetness; lusciousness
甘於(ㄍㄢ ㄩˊ)
to be willing to; to be happy to
甘雨(ㄍㄢ ㄩˇ)
a seasonable rain
甘願(ㄍㄢ ㄩㄢˋ)
willing; willingly; readily: 他甘願做任何事情。He was willing to do anything.

四畫

【甚】 3537 1. ㄕㄣˋ shenn shèn
1. to a great extent; to a high degree; very; exceedingly
2. more than
甚多(ㄕㄣˋ ㄉㄨㄛ)
very much or many
甚好(ㄕㄣˋ ㄏㄠˇ)or 甚佳(ㄕㄣˋ ㄐㄧㄚ)
very good; very well
甚急(ㄕㄣˋ ㄐㄧˊ)
① very anxious ② very urgent
甚囂塵上(ㄕㄣˋ ㄒㄧㄠ ㄔㄣˊ ㄕㄤˋ)
(literally) much noise amid a cloud of dust—very much talked about; widely reported or speculated
甚至(ㄕㄣˋ ㄓˋ)or 甚至於(ㄕㄣˋ ㄓˋ ㄩˊ)
though it may seem improbable (emphasizing the limit of what is possible or probable); even; even to the extent that...; to go so far as...
甚是(ㄕㄣˋ ㄕˋ)
very; exceedingly; extremely
甚少(ㄕㄣˋ ㄕㄠˇ)
very few; very little: 甚少人知道他的名字。Very few people know his name.
甚早(ㄕㄣˋ ㄗㄠˇ)
very early
甚而(ㄕㄣˋ ㄦˊ)
so much so that...
甚殷(ㄕㄣˋ ㄧㄣ)
very sincerely; very badly
甚爲(ㄕㄣˋ ㄨㄟˊ)
very; much: 我聞此消息甚爲欣喜。I was very pleased to hear the news.
甚爲不解(ㄕㄣˋ ㄨㄟˊ ㄅㄨˋ ㄐㄧㄝˇ)
much perplexed; completely at a loss
甚於(ㄕㄣˋ ㄩˊ)
(to be worse, harder, better, etc.) than...
甚遠(ㄕㄣˋ ㄩㄢˇ)
very far

【甚】 3537 2.(什) ㄕㄜˊ sher shé
what
甚麼(ㄕㄜˊ ·ㄇㄜ)
what: 你讀過甚麼書? What books have you read?
甚麼的(ㄕㄜˊ ·ㄇㄜ ·ㄉㄜ)
① and what not; and so forth 亦作「等等」 ② what
甚麼地方(ㄕㄜˊ ·ㄇㄜ ㄉㄧˋ ·ㄈㄤ)
where: 你住在甚麼地方? Where do you live?
甚麼話(ㄕㄜˊ ·ㄇㄜ ㄏㄨㄚˋ)
What nonsense! 或 Bosh!
甚麼事(ㄕㄜˊ ·ㄇㄜ ㄕˋ)
① What's the matter? ② no matter what; whatever it is
甚麼人(ㄕㄜˊ ·ㄇㄜ ㄖㄣˊ)
① Who? 還有甚麼人在那裡? Who else was there? ② no matter who; whoever it is
甚麼樣(ㄕㄜˊ ·ㄇㄜ ㄧㄤˋ)
What kind? 或 What sort? 他是甚麼樣的人? What is he like?

六畫

【甜】 3538 ㄊㄧㄢˊ tyan tián
1. sweet; luscious: 這蛋糕太甜了。This cake is too sweet.
2. agreeable; pleasant
甜美(ㄊㄧㄢˊ ㄇㄟˇ)
① sweet; luscious ② pleasant; refreshing
甜蜜(ㄊㄧㄢˊ ㄇㄧˋ)
sweet as honey; honeyed; affectionate; fond; happy
甜麵醬(ㄊㄧㄢˊ ㄇㄧㄢˋ ㄐㄧㄤˋ)
sweetened soybean paste
甜點(ㄊㄧㄢˊ ㄉㄧㄢˇ)
sweet; dessert: 甜點隨後就送來。The sweets will be served next.
甜頭(ㄊㄧㄢˊ ·ㄊㄡ)
① sweet taste; pleasant flavor ② good; benefit
甜甘(ㄊㄧㄢˊ ·ㄍㄢ)
sweet, honeyed, or pleasing:

〔甘部〕

這種茶甜甘。This kind of tea is sweet.

甜瓜(ㄊㄧㄢˊ ㄍㄨㄚ)
a sweet melon

甜酒釀(ㄊㄧㄢˊ ㄐㄧㄡˇ ㄋㄧㄤˋ)
fermented rice

甜津津的(ㄊㄧㄢˊ ㄐㄧㄣ ㄐㄧㄣ ˙ㄉㄜ)
very sweet; very agreeable

甜情蜜意(ㄊㄧㄢˊ ㄑㄧㄥˊ ㄇㄧˋ ㄧˋ)
tender affections or love between man and woman

甜心(ㄊㄧㄢˊ ㄒㄧㄣ)
a sweetheart

甜香(ㄊㄧㄢˊ ㄒㄧㄤ)
sweet and fragrant

甜食(ㄊㄧㄢˊ ㄕˊ)
sweet food; sweetmeats: 她愛吃甜食。She likes sweet things.

甜睡(ㄊㄧㄢˊ ㄕㄨㄟˋ)
sleeping soundly

甜菜(ㄊㄧㄢˊ ㄘㄞˋ)
a sugar beet

甜菜糖(ㄊㄧㄢˊ ㄘㄞˋ ㄊㄤˊ)
beet sugar

甜酸苦辣(ㄊㄧㄢˊ ㄙㄨㄢ ㄎㄨˇ ㄌㄚˋ)
(literally) sweetness, sourness, bitterness and hotness—all sorts of joys and sorrows: 我嘗遍了人生的甜酸苦辣。I have experienced all sorts of joys and sorrows.

甜言蜜語(ㄊㄧㄢˊ ㄧㄢˊ ㄇㄧˋ ㄩˇ)
honeyed words; cajolery; flattery

甜玉米(ㄊㄧㄢˊ ㄩˋ ㄇㄧˇ)
sweet corn; sugar corn

甜味(ㄊㄧㄢˊ ㄨㄟˋ)
sweet taste: 這麵包有點甜味。This bread tastes sweet.

生部
ㄕㄥ sheng shēng

【生】 3539
ㄕㄥ sheng shēng

1. to live; life; living; livelihood; alive: 她過着幸福的生活。She leads a happy life.
2. to be born; to come into being; to come into existence: 我在台北出生和長大。I was born and bred in Taipei.
3. to breed; to bear; to beget; to produce; to create; to give rise to; to cause
4. uncooked; raw; unripe; crude: 蕃茄可以生吃。Tomatoes can be eaten raw.
5. unfamiliar; strange; unknown: 這小孩不會認生。This child is not shy with strangers.
6. savage; untamed; barbarian; uncultured
7. a pupil; a student
8. the male character type in Chinese opera
9. creatures
10. a Chinese family name

生病(ㄕㄥ ㄅㄧㄥˋ)
to get sick; to fall ill: 她正照料著生病的父親。She is taking care of her sick father.

生不帶來，死不帶去(ㄕㄥ ㄅㄨˋ ㄉㄞˋ ㄌㄞˊ, ㄙˇ ㄅㄨˋ ㄉㄞˋ ㄑㄩˋ)
One does not bring anything when one comes into this world, nor does one take anything when one leaves it.

生不逢辰(ㄕㄥ ㄅㄨˋ ㄈㄥˊ ㄔㄣˊ)
to be born at a wrong time; luckless; unlucky: 我生不逢辰。I was born under an unlucky star.

生怕(ㄕㄥ ㄆㄚˋ)
very anxious; very apprehensive

生皮(ㄕㄥ ㄆㄧˊ)
raw hide; untanned hide

生啤酒(ㄕㄥ ㄆㄧˊ ㄐㄧㄡˇ)
draught beer

生僻(ㄕㄥ ㄆㄧˋ)
not frequently seen; strange; unusual; uncommon

生平(ㄕㄥ ㄆㄧㄥˊ)
① one's brief biographical sketch ② in the course of life

生煤(ㄕㄥ ㄇㄟˊ)
bituminous coal; soft coal

生米煮成熟飯(ㄕㄥ ㄇㄧˇ ㄓㄨˇ ㄔㄥˊ ㄕㄡˊ ㄈㄢˋ)
(literally) The rice has been boiled.—What is done cannot be undone.

生苗(ㄕㄥ ㄇㄧㄠˊ)
the savage Miao people in remote southwestern China as distinct from those relatively cultured

生民(ㄕㄥ ㄇㄧㄣˊ)
the people; the populace

生命(ㄕㄥ ㄇㄧㄥˋ)
life: 生命短促，藝術流長。Art is long; life is short.

生命力(ㄕㄥ ㄇㄧㄥˋ ㄌㄧˋ)
vitality: 她的生命力因爲病痛而減弱了。Her vitality was lessened by illness.

生命線(ㄕㄥ ㄇㄧㄥˋ ㄒㄧㄢˋ)
a lifeline (in a figurative sense)

生母(ㄕㄥ ㄇㄨˇ)
a real mother (as distinct from a foster mother)

生髮油(ㄕㄥ ㄈㄚˇ ㄧㄡˊ)
hair tonic

生佛(ㄕㄥ ㄈㄛˊ)
① all living creatures and Buddha ② a living Buddha

生番(ㄕㄥ ㄈㄢ)
savages; barbarians

生飯(ㄕㄥ ㄈㄢˋ)
(Buddhism) symbolic offering of food to all creatures before a meal

生分(ㄕㄥ ˙ㄈㄣ)
unfriendly; strange; unfamiliar

生父(ㄕㄥ ㄈㄨˋ)
a real father (as distinct from a foster father): 他是我的生父。He is my real father.

生旦淨末丑(ㄕㄥ ㄉㄢˋ ㄐㄧㄥˋ ㄇㄛˋ ㄔㄡˇ)
the major types of characters in Chinese opera—the male roles, female roles, painted-face roles, and clownish roles

生的米突(ㄕㄥ ㄉㄧˋ ㄇㄧˇ ㄊㄨˊ)
centimeter 亦作「公分」

生動(ㄕㄥ ㄉㄨㄥˋ)
vivid; lively; lifelike

生態(ㄕㄥ ㄊㄞˋ)
the relations and interactions between organisms and their environment, including other organisms

生態學(ㄕㄥ ㄊㄞˋ ㄒㄩㄝˊ)
ecology

生疼(ㄕㄥ ㄊㄥˊ)
very painful

生鐵(ㄕㄥ ㄊㄧㄝˇ)
pig iron; crude iron

生徒(ㄕㄥ ㄊㄨˊ)
pupils; students

〔生部〕

生吞活剝(ㄕㄥ ㄊㄨㄣ ㄏㄨㄛˊ ㄅㄛ)
to make awkward use of stock expressions in one's compositions; to use someone's ideas without fully understanding them

生銅(ㄕㄥ ㄊㄨㄥˊ)
unprocessed copper; brass: 這是生銅製的。This is made of unprocessed copper.

生年月日(ㄕㄥ ㄋㄧㄢˊ ㄩㄝˋ ㄖˋ)
the date of birth

生拉硬拽(ㄕㄥ ㄌㄚ ㄧㄥˋ ㄓㄨㄞˋ)
① to obtain reluctant obedience or compliance ② irrelevant; far-fetched; unnatural

生來(ㄕㄥ ㄌㄞˊ)
① since one's birth ② by nature; inborn: 他們是生來就喜歡惡作劇的孩子。They are children with an inborn love of mischief.

生老病死(ㄕㄥ ㄌㄠˇ ㄅㄧㄥˋ ㄙˇ)
(Buddhism) birth, age, disease, and death—the four miseries, or sufferings in the course of human life

生冷(ㄕㄥ ㄌㄥˇ)
(said of food) uncooked and cold

生離死別(ㄕㄥ ㄌㄧˊ ㄙˇ ㄅㄧㄝˊ)
separation in life and parting at death—the bitterest sorrows to man

生理(ㄕㄥ ㄌㄧˇ)
physiological functions and processes; physiology: 消化是一種生理過程。Digestion is a physiological process.

生理學(ㄕㄥ ㄌㄧˇ ㄒㄩㄝˊ)
physiological science; physiology

生利息(ㄕㄥ ㄌㄧˋ ˙ㄒㄧ)
to bear interest; to yield interest

生力軍(ㄕㄥ ㄌㄧˋ ㄐㄩㄣ)
fresh troops; a vital new force: 他們是文藝界的一支生力軍。They are a vital new force in the field of art and literature.

生料(ㄕㄥ ㄌㄧㄠˋ)
unprocessed goods

生靈塗炭(ㄕㄥ ㄌㄧㄥˊ ㄊㄨˊ ㄊㄢˋ)
The people are suffering from extreme privation (during wartime).

生路(ㄕㄥ ㄌㄨˋ)
① a way to make a living; a way to survive: 他不得不另謀生路。He cannot but try to find another job. ② an unfamiliar road; a strange road

生龍活虎(ㄕㄥ ㄌㄨㄥˊ ㄏㄨㄛˊ ㄏㄨˇ)
(like) a live dragon or a live tiger—full of vigor and vitality: 年青人幹起活來眞是生龍活虎。When the youth work, they do it with furious energy.

生根(ㄕㄥ ㄍㄣ)
to root: 植物很快地生根。The plant roots quickly.

生公說法(ㄕㄥ ㄍㄨㄥ ㄕㄨㄛ ㄈㄚˇ)
(said of orations) very touching or convincing; emotion-arousing

生客(ㄕㄥ ㄎㄜˋ)
a new guest; an unfamiliar guest

生恐(ㄕㄥ ㄎㄨㄥˇ)
very anxious; very apprehensive

生虎子(ㄕㄥ ㄏㄨˇ ˙ㄗ)
a beginner; a novice; a greenhorn

生花妙筆(ㄕㄥ ㄏㄨㄚ ㄇㄧㄠˋ ㄅㄧˇ)
ability for exquisite writing; admirable writing skill

生活(ㄕㄥ ㄏㄨㄛˊ)
① life: 日常生活 daily life ② to live: 我與我太太幸福地生活著。I live happily with my wife.

生活必需品(ㄕㄥ ㄏㄨㄛˊ ㄅㄧˋ ㄒㄩ ㄆㄧㄣˇ)
necessities of life: 這些是生活必需品。These are necessities of life.

生活費(ㄕㄥ ㄏㄨㄛˊ ㄈㄟˋ)
living expenses

生活方式(ㄕㄥ ㄏㄨㄛˊ ㄈㄤ ㄕˋ)
the ways of living; the modes of living

生活指數(ㄕㄥ ㄏㄨㄛˊ ㄓˇ ㄕㄨˋ)
the index of living cost

生活程度(ㄕㄥ ㄏㄨㄛˊ ㄔㄥˊ ㄉㄨˋ)
① the standard of living ② the cost of living: 東京生活程度高。The cost of living in Tokyo is high.

生活水準(ㄕㄥ ㄏㄨㄛˊ ㄕㄨㄟˇ ㄓㄨㄣˇ)
the standard of living

生活問題(ㄕㄥ ㄏㄨㄛˊ ㄨㄣˋ ㄊㄧˊ)
the problems of livelihood

生火(ㄕㄥ ㄏㄨㄛˇ)
to make a fire; to build a fire: 生火吧! Make a fire.

生還(ㄕㄥ ㄏㄨㄢˊ)
to come back alive; to survive

生還者(ㄕㄥ ㄏㄨㄢˊ ㄓㄜˇ)
a survivor

生機(ㄕㄥ ㄐㄧ)
① vitality; liveliness: 整個天地間似乎充滿了生機。All nature seemed to be full of life. ② the chance of survival

生計(ㄕㄥ ㄐㄧˋ)
livelihood; living: 我另謀生計。I tried to find some other means of livelihood.

生寄死歸(ㄕㄥ ㄐㄧˋ ㄙˇ ㄍㄨㄟ)
To live is like being a lodger in the world, and to die is like returning home.

生就的(ㄕㄥ ㄐㄧㄡˋ ˙ㄉㄜ)
inborn; by nature: 他生就的懶。He is lazy by nature.

生薑(ㄕㄥ ㄐㄧㄤ)
green ginger

生聚教訓(ㄕㄥ ㄐㄩˋ ㄐㄧㄠˋ ㄒㄩㄣˋ)
the pooling and training of manpower (for a sacred war)

生絹(ㄕㄥ ㄐㄩㄢˋ)
raw silk

生漆(ㄕㄥ ㄑㄧ)
crude lacquer

生氣(ㄕㄥ ㄑㄧˋ)
① vitality; liveliness: 年輕人充滿了生氣。Young people are full of vitality. ② to get angry; to get mad

生氣蓬勃(ㄕㄥ ㄑㄧˋ ㄆㄥˊ ㄅㄛˊ)
vigorous; active; lively: 那老人依然生氣蓬勃。The old man is still vigorous and lively.

生前(ㄕㄥ ㄑㄧㄢˊ)
during one's lifetime; before one's death; while one was alive

生擒(ㄕㄥ ㄑㄧㄣˊ)
to take (a prisoner) alive; to capture alive

生趣(ㄕㄥ ㄑㄩˋ)
the pleasure of life

生全(ㄕㄥ ㄑㄩㄢˊ)
the salvation of life

生息(ㄕㄥ ㄒㄧˊ)
①to bear interest; to yield interest ②to reproduce and multiply ③to live; living

生肖(ㄕㄥ ㄒㄧㄠˋ)
the relation of the year of one's birth to one of the 12 animals (the mouse, the ox, the tiger, the rabbit, the dragon, the snake, the horse, the sheep, the monkey, the fowl, the dog, and the pig)亦作「屬相」

生效(ㄕㄥ ㄒㄧㄠˋ)
to go into effect; to be effective or valid

生銹(ㄕㄥ ㄒㄧㄡˋ)
to rust: 我的刀生銹了。My knife rusted.

生性(ㄕㄥ ㄒㄧㄥˋ)
①natural disposition; nature ②aloof; unfriendly

生殖(ㄕㄥ ㄓˊ)
(biology) reproduction

生殖力(ㄕㄥ ㄓˊ ㄌㄧˋ)
fecundity

生殖器(ㄕㄥ ㄓˊ ㄑㄧˋ)
reproductive organs; genitals

生張熟魏(ㄕㄥ ㄓㄤ ㄕㄡˊ ㄨㄟˋ)
①old acquaintances and new customers received alike by the prostitutes—promiscuous ②to be unacquainted with each other

生長(ㄕㄥ ㄓㄤˇ)
to grow; to develop; growth

生長激素(ㄕㄥ ㄓㄤˇ ㄐㄧ ㄙㄨˋ)
growth hormone

生衆食寡(ㄕㄥ ㄓㄨㄥˋ ㄕˊ ㄍㄨㄚˇ)
Production surpasses consumption.

生吃(ㄕㄥ ㄔ)
to eat (something) raw; to eat (something) without cooking: 他生吃蔬菜。He eats vegetables raw.

生產(ㄕㄥ ㄔㄢˇ)
①to produce; production: 這個工廠生產汽車。This factory produces cars.②to give birth to; childbirth: 我姐姐快生產了。My sister will be having her baby soon.

生產部(ㄕㄥ ㄔㄢˇ ㄅㄨˋ)
a productive department

生產力(ㄕㄥ ㄔㄢˇ ㄌㄧˋ)
productivity

生產量(ㄕㄥ ㄔㄢˇ ㄌㄧㄤˋ)
the productive output

生產率(ㄕㄥ ㄔㄢˇ ㄌㄩˋ)
the production rate

生產過程(ㄕㄥ ㄔㄢˇ ㄍㄨㄛˋ ㄔㄥˊ)
production process

生產過剩(ㄕㄥ ㄔㄢˇ ㄍㄨㄛˋ ㄕㄥˋ)
overproduction

生產合作社(ㄕㄥ ㄔㄢˇ ㄏㄜˊ ㄗㄨㄛˋ ㄕㄜˋ)
a producers' guild; a producers' cooperative

生產機關(ㄕㄥ ㄔㄢˇ ㄐㄧ ㄍㄨㄢ)
①production organization ②(economics) the means of production

生產計畫(ㄕㄥ ㄔㄢˇ ㄐㄧˋ ㄏㄨㄚˋ)
a production plan

生產技術(ㄕㄥ ㄔㄢˇ ㄐㄧˋ ㄕㄨˋ)
production technique

生產效率(ㄕㄥ ㄔㄢˇ ㄒㄧㄠˋ ㄌㄩˋ)
production efficiency

生產線(ㄕㄥ ㄔㄢˇ ㄒㄧㄢˋ)
production line

生產中心(ㄕㄥ ㄔㄢˇ ㄓㄨㄥ ㄒㄧㄣ)
a production center

生產成本(ㄕㄥ ㄔㄢˇ ㄔㄥˊ ㄅㄣˇ)
(accounting) the cost of production; production cost

生產額(ㄕㄥ ㄔㄢˇ ㄜˊ)
(accounting) the volume of production

生辰(ㄕㄥ ㄔㄣˊ)
birthday

生成(ㄕㄥ ㄔㄥˊ)
①to grow to ②inborn; by nature

生石灰(ㄕㄥ ㄕˊ ㄏㄨㄟ)
quicklime; unslaked lime

生事(ㄕㄥ ㄕˋ)
①to create trouble; to give rise to disturbance ②livelihood

生殺予奪(ㄕㄥ ㄕㄚ ㄩˇ ㄉㄨㄛˊ)
to spare, kill, give,. and take at will; to wield absolute power

生手(ㄕㄥ ㄕㄡˇ)
a beginner; a novice: 生手很可能出錯。Novices are likely to make some mistakes.

生身父母(ㄕㄥ ㄕㄣ ㄈㄨˋ ㄇㄨˇ)
real parents (as distinct from foster parents)

生生不息(ㄕㄥ ㄕㄥ ㄅㄨˋ ㄒㄧˊ)or 生生不已(ㄕㄥ ㄕㄥ ㄅㄨˋ ㄧˇ)
to multiply endlessly; to breed in endless succession

生疎 or 生疏(ㄕㄥ ㄕㄨ)
①unfamiliar; unskilled; pretty rusty ②strange; not on intimate terms: 我在此人地生疏。I'm quite strange here.

生水(ㄕㄥ ㄕㄨㄟˇ)
unboiled water

生日(ㄕㄥ ㄖˋ)
birthday: 我的生日是五月二十日。My birthday is May 20.

生人(ㄕㄥ ㄖㄣˊ)
①a living person ②a stranger: 一個陌生人和我講話。A stranger spoke to me.

生榮死哀(ㄕㄥ ㄖㄨㄥˊ ㄙˇ ㄞ)
respected while living and mourned when dead

生字(ㄕㄥ ㄗˋ)
a new word; an unfamiliar word: 不要用艱澀的生字。Do not use difficult new words.

生詞(ㄕㄥ ㄘˊ)
a new word

生財(ㄕㄥ ㄘㄞˊ)
the furniture and office equipment of a shop or business firm

生財有道(ㄕㄥ ㄘㄞˊ ㄧㄡˇ ㄉㄠˋ)
to be expert in making money

生菜(ㄕㄥ ㄘㄞˋ)
raw vegetables; salad: 我點了一份生菜沙拉。I ordered a helping of vegetable salad.

生存(ㄕㄥ ㄘㄨㄣˊ)
to survive; survival; existence

生存空間(ㄕㄥ ㄘㄨㄣˊ ㄎㄨㄥ ㄐㄧㄢ)
living space; lebensraum

生存競爭(ㄕㄥ ㄘㄨㄣˊ ㄐㄧㄥˋ ㄓㄥ)
the struggle for existence

生存權(ㄕㄥ ㄘㄨㄣˊ ㄑㄩㄢˊ)
the right to life

生絲(ㄕㄥ ㄙ)
raw silk

生死關頭(ㄕㄥ ㄙˇ ㄍㄨㄢ ㄊㄡˊ)
a life-and-death crisis

生死之交(ㄕㄥ ㄙˇ ㄓ ㄐㄧㄠ)
deep friendship (implying the sharing of each other's fate)

生死肉骨(ㄕㄥ ㄙˇ ㄖㄡˋ ㄍㄨˇ)
(literally) to revive the dead and flesh a skeleton—to provide miraculous relief

生死以之(ㄕㄥ ㄙˇ ㄧˇ ㄓ)
willing to sacrifice one's life for the attainment of an objective
生色(ㄕㄥ ㄙㄜˋ)
①to add color; to add splendor ②a mild harmony appearing in the countenance
生澀(ㄕㄥ ㄙㄜˋ)
(said of a piece of writing) difficult to read or understand
生而知之(ㄕㄥ ㄦˊ ㄓ ㄓ)
to know from birth; to know without learning
生兒育女(ㄕㄥ ㄦˊ ㄩˋ ㄋㄩˇ)
to give birth to children and rear them
生疑(ㄕㄥ ㄧˊ)
to become suspicious
生意(ㄕㄥ ㄧˋ)
①business; trade: 生意清淡。Business is dull. ②vitality: 春天的大地充滿生意。Spring has filled the earth with vitality.
生意經(ㄕㄥ ˙ㄧ ㄐㄧㄥ)
businessmen's talk
生涯(ㄕㄥ ㄧㄚˊ)
①a career; a life ②livelihood
生油(ㄕㄥ ㄧㄡˊ)
①uncooked edible oil ②peanut oil
生厭(ㄕㄥ ㄧㄢˋ)
to become bored or tired of something
生硬(ㄕㄥ ㄧㄥˋ)
awkward; stiff: 她生硬地鞠著躬。She made a stiff bow.
生物(ㄕㄥ ㄨˋ)
①a living thing; animal and plant life; an organism ②biology
生物標本(ㄕㄥ ㄨˋ ㄅㄧㄠ ㄅㄣˇ)
a biological specimen
生物化學(ㄕㄥ ㄨˋ ㄏㄨㄚˋ ㄒㄩㄝˊ)
biochemistry
生物界(ㄕㄥ ㄨˋ ㄐㄧㄝˋ)
the biological world; the kingdom of fauna and flora; the world of living things
生物圈(ㄕㄥ ㄨˋ ㄑㄩㄢ)
the biosphere
生物學(ㄕㄥ ㄨˋ ㄒㄩㄝˊ)
biology: 植物學和動物學是生物學的部分。Botany and zoology are branches of biology.
生於憂患，死於安樂(ㄕㄥ ㄩˊ ㄧㄡ ㄏㄨㄢˋ, ㄙˇ ㄩˊ ㄢ ㄌㄜˋ)
Life springs from sorrow and calamity, and death from ease and pleasure.—to thrive in adversity and to perish in soft living
生育(ㄕㄥ ㄩˋ)
to give birth to; childbirth
生育限制(ㄕㄥ ㄩˋ ㄒㄧㄢˋ ㄓˋ)
birth control; family planning
生員(ㄕㄥ ㄩㄢˊ)
①successful candidates in local examinations under the former civil service system ②(in old times) students

五畫

【甡】 3540 ㄕㄣ shen shēn
1. numerous; many
2. crowded

六畫

【產】 3541 ㄔㄢˇ chaan chǎn
1. to bear (offspring); to lay (eggs)
2. to produce; to bring about: 耕作是有生產價值的勞動。Farming is productive labor.

產婆(ㄔㄢˇ ㄆㄛˊ)
a midwife
產品(ㄔㄢˇ ㄆㄧㄣˇ)
products
產品成本(ㄔㄢˇ ㄆㄧㄣˇ ㄔㄥˊ ㄅㄣˇ)
product cost
產門(ㄔㄢˇ ㄇㄣˊ)
(anatomy) the vagina
產房(ㄔㄢˇ ㄈㄤˊ)
a lying-in room; a maternity room; a delivery ward
產婦(ㄔㄢˇ ㄈㄨˋ)
a lying-in woman; a woman who has just given birth to a baby
產地(ㄔㄢˇ ㄉㄧˋ)
a producing center; a growing district; a breeding center
產地證明書(ㄔㄢˇ ㄉㄧˋ ㄓㄥˋ ㄇㄧㄥˊ ㄕㄨ)
the certificate of origin
產量(ㄔㄢˇ ㄌㄧㄤˋ)
production; output; yield: 過去三十年中農產品產量劇增。Over the last thirty years crop yields have increased sharply.
產卵(ㄔㄢˇ ㄌㄨㄢˇ)
to lay eggs; to spawn
產卵管(ㄔㄢˇ ㄌㄨㄢˇ ㄍㄨㄢˇ) or 產卵器(ㄔㄢˇ ㄌㄨㄢˇ ㄑㄧˋ)
(zoology) the ovipositor
產卵期(ㄔㄢˇ ㄌㄨㄢˇ ㄑㄧˊ)
the breeding season; the spawning season
產科(ㄔㄢˇ ㄎㄜ)
obstetrics
產科醫生(ㄔㄢˇ ㄎㄜ ㄧ ㄕㄥ)
an obstetrician
產科醫院(ㄔㄢˇ ㄎㄜ ㄧ ㄩㄢˋ)
a lying-in hospital; a maternity hospital
產後(ㄔㄢˇ ㄏㄡˋ)
after childbirth; postnatal
產假(ㄔㄢˇ ㄐㄧㄚˋ)
maternity leave: 她請產假。She asked for maternity leave.
產期(ㄔㄢˇ ㄑㄧˊ)
time of childbirth
產前(ㄔㄢˇ ㄑㄧㄢˊ)
before childbirth; prenatal
產權(ㄔㄢˇ ㄑㄩㄢˊ)
ownership (of real estate)
產銷(ㄔㄢˇ ㄒㄧㄠ)
production and marketing
產銷合一(ㄔㄢˇ ㄒㄧㄠ ㄏㄜˊ ㄧ) or 產銷一元化(ㄔㄢˇ ㄒㄧㄠ ㄧˋ ㄩㄢˊ ㄏㄨㄚˋ)
integration of production and marketing operations
產生(ㄔㄢˇ ㄕㄥ)
to produce; to give rise to; to cause; to bring about: 那一世紀產生的偉人很少。The century produced few great men.
產蓐 or 產褥(ㄔㄢˇ ㄖㄨˋ)
lying-in
產褥熱(ㄔㄢˇ ㄖㄨˋ ㄖㄜˋ)
puerperal fever
產額(ㄔㄢˇ ㄜˊ)
the amount of production; output
產兒(ㄔㄢˇ ㄦˊ)
a newborn infant
產業(ㄔㄢˇ ㄧㄝˋ)

①property; estate: 他有一大片產業。He has a large estate. ②industry

產業革命(ㄔㄢˇ ㄧㄝˋ ㄍㄜˊ ㄇㄧㄥˋ)
the Industrial Revolution

產物(ㄔㄢˇ ㄨˋ)
products; outcomes

七畫

【甥】 3542
ㄕㄥ sheng shēng

1. a nephew (son of a sister)
2. a son-in-law who assumes one's own name and lives under one's own roof

甥女(ㄕㄥ ㄋㄩˇ)
a niece (daughter of a sister)

甥舘(ㄕㄥ ㄍㄨㄢˇ)
the room for a son-in-law who assumes his father-in-law's name and lives under his father-in-law's roof

甥兒(ㄕㄥ ㄦˊ)
a nephew; a sister's son

【甦】 3543
ㄙㄨ su sū

to come back to life; to rise from the dead; to revive; to resurrect; to regain consciousness

甦醒(ㄙㄨ ㄒㄧㄥˇ)
to come back to life; to revive; to come to: 他使昏迷的孩子甦醒。He revived a senseless child.

【甤】 3544
ㄖㄨㄟˊ ruei ruí

(plants) drooping with fruit

用 部
ㄩㄥˋ yonq yòng

【用】 3545
ㄩㄥˋ yonq yòng

1. to use; to employ: 誰都不應使用暴力。Nobody should use force.
2. to exert
3. use: 那架電視仍在使用。The television set is still in use.
4. effect
5. finance
6. to need; need: 不用擔心。Do not worry.
7. to eat; to drink: 請用甜點。Have some sweets, please.

用畢(ㄩㄥˋ ㄅㄧˋ)
after using (durable articles)

用兵(ㄩㄥˋ ㄅㄧㄥ)
to make use of troops; to manipulate troops: 他善於用兵。He is well versed in the art of war.

用不得(ㄩㄥˋ ·ㄅㄨ ·ㄉㄜ)
①unfit for use ②(said of a person) cannot be employed without resulting in harm

用不了(ㄩㄥˋ ·ㄅㄨ ㄌㄧㄠˇ)
①more than enough for the purpose: 我把用不了的錢存放在銀行裏。I put the spare money in the bank. ②can be done with less

用不慣(ㄩㄥˋ ·ㄅㄨ ㄍㄨㄢˋ)
unaccustomed to the use of

用不著(ㄩㄥˋ ·ㄅㄨ ㄓㄠˊ)
①to have no use for ② there is no need to; it is unnecessary to

用不完(ㄩㄥˋ ·ㄅㄨ ㄨㄢˊ)
too many or too much for use; cannot be used up

用品(ㄩㄥˋ ㄆㄧㄣˇ)
articles for use: 這些是辦公用品。These are articles for office use.

用命(ㄩㄥˋ ㄇㄧㄥˋ)
to obey orders

用法(ㄩㄥˋ ㄈㄚˇ)
the way to use a thing; directions for using or operating something

用非所學(ㄩㄥˋ ㄈㄟ ㄙㄨㄛˇ ㄒㄩㄝˊ)
to be engaged in an occupation not related to one's training

用非所長(ㄩㄥˋ ㄈㄟ ㄙㄨㄛˇ ㄔㄤˊ)
to be engaged in an occupation having nothing to do with one's speciality

用飯(ㄩㄥˋ ㄈㄢˋ)
to have a meal; to take a meal; to eat a meal

用得着(ㄩㄥˋ ·ㄉㄜ ㄓㄠˊ)
①to find something useful; to need ②there is need to; it is necessary to: 你用得著立刻出發嗎? Is it necessary that you start at once?

用地(ㄩㄥˋ ㄉㄧˋ)
land for a specific use

用度(ㄩㄥˋ ㄉㄨˋ)
expenses; expenditure: 他的用度浩繁。His expenditure is multifarious.

用特(ㄩㄥˋ ㄊㄜˋ)
Therefore, I specially.... (a conventional phrase in formal letters)

用頭(ㄩㄥˋ ·ㄊㄡ)
use (to which a thing can be put); a purpose (for which a thing may be employed)

用途(ㄩㄥˋ ㄊㄨˊ)
a purpose (for which a thing may be employed); use: 今日石油的用途很廣。Nowadays petroleum has many uses.

用力(ㄩㄥˋ ㄌㄧˋ)
to exert oneself; to make an effort; to put forth one's strength: 我用力把車推了一下。I gave the car a hard push.

用力過度(ㄩㄥˋ ㄌㄧˋ ㄍㄨㄛˋ ㄉㄨˋ)
to exert oneself too strenuously; to make too strenuous efforts

用光(ㄩㄥˋ ㄍㄨㄤ)
to use up; to run out of; to exhaust: 他用光了所有的錢。He exhausted all his money.

用功(ㄩㄥˋ ㄍㄨㄥ)
to study diligently; to work hard; to study hard

用工夫(ㄩㄥˋ ㄍㄨㄥ ·ㄈㄨ)
to practice or study diligently; to work hard

用戶(ㄩㄥˋ ㄏㄨˋ)
a customer (of a utility); a user; a consumer: 公司徵求用戶意見。The company asked for consumers' opinions.

用計(ㄩㄥˋ ㄐㄧˋ)
to use tricks; to employ schemes: 他用計陷害人。He used tricks for getting another in trouble.

用盡(ㄩㄥˋ ㄐㄧㄣˋ)
to exhaust (strength, etc.)

用盡方法(ㄩㄥˋ ㄐㄧㄣˋ ㄈㄤ ㄈㄚˇ)
to exhaust one's wits; to resort to every available means; to do something by hook or by crook

用盡心機(ㄩㄥˋ ㄐㄧㄣˋ ㄒㄧㄣ ㄐㄧ)
to have tried every means; to have left no stone unturned: 他用盡心機賺錢。He has tried every means to earn money.

用具(ㄩㄥˋ ㄐㄩˋ)
a tool; an appliance; an implement

用錢(ㄩㄥˋ ㄑㄧㄢˊ)
① to spend money ② middleman's fees; commission

用錢如水(ㄩㄥˋ ㄑㄧㄢˊ ㄖㄨˊ ㄕㄨㄟˇ)
to spend money like water; to spend money carelessly or extravagantly

用情(ㄩㄥˋ ㄑㄧㄥˊ)
to appeal to emotion; to feel serious about a love affair

用情不專(ㄩㄥˋ ㄑㄧㄥˊ ㄅㄨˋ ㄓㄨㄢ)
to be frivolous in affairs of the heart

用去(ㄩㄥˋ ㄑㄩˋ)
to have spent or used

用賢(ㄩㄥˋ ㄒㄧㄢˊ)
to employ men of wisdom and virtue

用心(ㄩㄥˋ ㄒㄧㄣ)
to be careful; to exercise caution; to take care; to pay attention: 你當用心讀書。You must pay attention to your study.

用心良苦(ㄩㄥˋ ㄒㄧㄣ ㄌㄧㄤˊ ㄎㄨˇ)
well-intentioned but little understood; to lay oneself out

用刑(ㄩㄥˋ ㄒㄧㄥˊ)
to torture

用之不竭(ㄩㄥˋ ㄓ ㄅㄨˋ ㄐㄧㄝˊ)
It cannot be used up. 或 It is inexhaustible.

用場(ㄩㄥˋ ㄔㄤˇ) or 用處(ㄩㄥˋ ㄔㄨˋ)
a purpose (for which a thing may be employed); use: 用處甚大。The usefulness is great.

用世(ㄩㄥˋ ㄕˋ)
to be employed in a way in which one can do good to the world

用事(ㄩㄥˋ ㄕˋ)
① to be in power ② to manage things; to handle things; to act: 你別意氣用事。Don't be swayed by your feelings and act rashly.

用是(ㄩㄥˋ ㄕˋ)
therefore; for this reason

用水(ㄩㄥˋ ㄕㄨㄟˇ)
① to use water ② water for a specific use

用人(ㄩㄥˋ ㄖㄣˊ)
① to employ people ② a servant

用字(ㄩㄥˋ ㄗˋ)
wording

用以(ㄩㄥˋ ㄧˇ)
in order to; so as to

用意(ㄩㄥˋ ㄧˋ)
an intention; a purpose; an idea: 他用意甚善。He is well-intended.

用印(ㄩㄥˋ ㄧㄣˋ)
to put a stamp or seal on a document; to stamp

用武(ㄩㄥˋ ㄨˇ)
① to resort to force; to use violence ② to display one's abilities or talents

用完(ㄩㄥˋ ㄨㄢˊ)
to use up; to exhaust

用語(ㄩㄥˋ ㄩˇ)
terminology; phraseology: 我不懂法律用語。I don't understand legal phraseology.

用韻(ㄩㄥˋ ㄩㄣˋ)
to use rhyme

【甩】 3546 ㄕㄨㄞˇ shoai shuǎi

1. to throw away; to discard; to cast away
2. to leave (somebody) behind
3. to swing: 不要甩你的手臂。Don't swing your arms.

甩不掉(ㄕㄨㄞˇ ˙ㄅㄨ ㄉㄧㄠˋ) or 甩不脫(ㄕㄨㄞˇ ˙ㄅㄨ ㄊㄨㄛ)
cannot get rid of; cannot shake off

甩了(ㄕㄨㄞˇ ˙ㄌㄜ)
to have thrown away; to have cast away: 他被女朋友甩了。He was thrown overboard by his girl friend.

甩手(ㄕㄨㄞˇ ㄕㄡˇ)
to take no heed; to ignore; to wash one's hands of

二畫

【甫】 3547 ㄈㄨˇ fuu fǔ

1. (euphemism) a man
2. (euphemism) father
3. then and only then
4. just; immediately after; a short while ago
5. barely
6. a Chinese family name

甫能(ㄈㄨˇ ㄋㄥˊ)
able then and only then

【甬】 3548 ㄩㄥˇ yeong yǒng

1. a measure of capacity (equal to 10 斗)
2. alternative name of Ningpo, Chekiang

甬道(ㄩㄥˇ ㄉㄠˋ) or 甬路(ㄩㄥˇ ㄌㄨˋ)
① the central path in a hall ② a road flanked by walls ③ a corridor

四畫

【甭】 3549 ㄅㄥˊ berng béng

unnecessary; do not have to: 甭再說了。Don't say anymore.

七畫

【甯】 3550 1. ㄋㄧㄥˋ ninq nìng

a Chinese family name

【甯】 3550 2. ㄋㄧㄥˊ ning níng

same as 寧—peaceful; rather

田部
ㄊㄧㄢˊ tyan tián

【田】 3551 ㄊㄧㄢˊ tyan tián

1. agricultural land; cultivated land; a field; a rice field; farmland; cropland: 他星期天在田地裏工作。He works in the field on Sunday.
2. to hunt game
3. a Chinese family name

田夫(ㄊㄧㄢˊ ㄈㄨ)
a farmer; a husbandman

田父(ㄊㄧㄢˊ ㄈㄨˇ)
an old farmer; an aged farmer

田賦(ㄊㄧㄢˊ ㄈㄨˋ)
taxes on agricultural land

田單(ㄊㄧㄢˊ ㄉㄢ)
① title deeds (for agricul-

tural land) ② General Tien Tan of the Chi State (齊國) during the Epoch of Warring States, who recovered his fatherland from the hands of Yen (燕) invaders

田地(ㄊㄧㄢˊ ㄉㄧˋ)
① agricultural land ② position; condition; state of affairs; a plight: 我怎麼落到這步田地。How did I get into such a plight?

田頭(ㄊㄧㄢˊ ㄊㄡˊ)
a manager of agricultural land

田納西(ㄊㄧㄢˊ ㄋㄚˋ ㄒㄧ)
Tennessee, U.S.A.

田里(ㄊㄧㄢˊ ㄌㄧˇ)
a rural area; a rural community

田獵(ㄊㄧㄢˊ ㄌㄧㄝˋ)
to hunt game

田廬(ㄊㄧㄢˊ ㄌㄨˊ)
a farmhouse

田螺(ㄊㄧㄢˊ ㄌㄨㄛˊ)
a mud-snail; a pond-snail

田埂(ㄊㄧㄢˊ ㄍㄥˇ)
ridges between plots of farmland

田戶(ㄊㄧㄢˊ ㄏㄨˋ)
a land tiller; a farmer

田鷄(ㄊㄧㄢˊ ㄐㄧ)
a frog

田家(ㄊㄧㄢˊ ㄐㄧㄚ)
a farming family; a peasant family; a cottage

田家子(ㄊㄧㄢˊ ㄐㄧㄚ ㄗˇ)
farmers; farming people; peasants

田間(ㄊㄧㄢˊ ㄐㄧㄢ)
in the field

田徑賽(ㄊㄧㄢˊ ㄐㄧㄥˋ ㄙㄞˋ)
track and field events

田契(ㄊㄧㄢˊ ㄑㄧˋ)
a title deed for agricultural land

田器(ㄊㄧㄢˊ ㄑㄧˋ)
agricultural tools; farming implements

田主(ㄊㄧㄢˊ ㄓㄨˇ)
a landlord (of agricultural land)

田莊(ㄊㄧㄢˊ ㄓㄨㄤ)
a farmhouse; a farmstead: 我祖父有一座田莊。My grandfather had a farmhouse.

田中義一(ㄊㄧㄢˊ ㄓㄨㄥ ㄧˋ ㄧ)
Giichi Tanaka (1863-1929), Japanese prime minister (1927-1929), a military and political leader known for masterminding the invasion of China

田疇(ㄊㄧㄢˊ ㄔㄡˊ)
agricultural land; farmland

田產(ㄊㄧㄢˊ ㄔㄢˇ)
real estate

田舍(ㄊㄧㄢˊ ㄕㄜˋ)
a farmhouse

田舍奴(ㄊㄧㄢˊ ㄕㄜˋ ㄋㄨˊ) or 田舍漢(ㄊㄧㄢˊ ㄕㄜˋ ㄏㄢˋ) or 田舍兒(ㄊㄧㄢˊ ㄕㄜˋ ㄦˊ)
a country bumpkin; a yokel; a rustic

田舍翁(ㄊㄧㄢˊ ㄕㄜˋ ㄨㄥ)
an old countryman

田鼠(ㄊㄧㄢˊ ㄕㄨˇ)
the field mouse

田租(ㄊㄧㄢˊ ㄗㄨ)
the land rental paid by a tenant farmer

田賽(ㄊㄧㄢˊ ㄙㄞˋ)
field sports; field events

田叟(ㄊㄧㄢˊ ㄙㄡˇ)
old farmers; aged farmers

田岸(ㄊㄧㄢˊ ㄢˋ)
ridges between plots of farmland

田野(ㄊㄧㄢˊ ㄧㄝˇ)
fields; cultivated lands

田月桑時(ㄊㄧㄢˊ ㄩㄝˋ ㄙㄤ ㄕˊ)
the farming season

田園(ㄊㄧㄢˊ ㄩㄢˊ)
① fields and gardens ② rural; pastoral; bucolic

田園詩人(ㄊㄧㄢˊ ㄩㄢˊ ㄕ ㄖㄣˊ)
a pastoral poet; an idyllist

田園文學(ㄊㄧㄢˊ ㄩㄢˊ ㄨㄣˊ ㄒㄩㄝˊ)
pastoral literature; idyllic literature

【由】 3552 ㄧㄡˊ you yóu

1. reason; cause; a source; derivation
2. from: 鋼是由鐵製成的。Steel is made from iron.
3. up to (someone to make a decision): 事不由己。Things are getting out of hand.
4. by; through: 請由大門出去。Please exit by the main door.
5. a Chinese family name

由不得(ㄧㄡˊ ·ㄅㄨ ·ㄉㄜ)
involuntarily; unable to do as one pleases: 這件事由不得你。The matter is not up to you.

由他去罷(ㄧㄡˊ ㄊㄚ ㄑㄩˋ ·ㄅㄚ)
Leave him alone. 或 Let him be.

由天而降(ㄧㄡˊ ㄊㄧㄢ ㄦˊ ㄐㄧㄤˋ)
to come down from heaven; to come from nowhere

由你(ㄧㄡˊ ㄋㄧˇ)
as you please; as you like; whatever you say

由你決定(ㄧㄡˊ ㄋㄧˇ ㄐㄩㄝˊ ㄉㄧㄥˋ)
It's up to you to make the decision. 此事由你決定。This matter is up to you to make the decision.

由來(ㄧㄡˊ ㄌㄞˊ)
① derivation; a source ② so far; up to now

由來已久(ㄧㄡˊ ㄌㄞˊ ㄧˇ ㄐㄧㄡˇ)
It has been so for quite some time. 或 long-standing; time-honored: 這種風俗由來已久。This is a long-standing custom.

由儉入奢易(ㄧㄡˊ ㄐㄧㄢˇ ㄖㄨˋ ㄕㄜ ㄧˋ)
It is easy to go from frugality to extravagance.

由簡而繁(ㄧㄡˊ ㄐㄧㄢˇ ㄦˊ ㄈㄢˊ)
to go from the simple to the complex

由近及遠(ㄧㄡˊ ㄐㄧㄣˋ ㄐㄧˊ ㄩㄢˇ)
to go from the near to the distant

由淺入深(ㄧㄡˊ ㄑㄧㄢˇ ㄖㄨˋ ㄕㄣ)
to go from the easy to the difficult and complicated

由衷(ㄧㄡˊ ㄓㄨㄥ)
from the depth of one's heart; heartfelt: 我們表示由衷的感激。We extended our heartfelt thanks.

由衷之言(ㄧㄡˊ ㄓㄨㄥ ㄓ ㄧㄢˊ)
words uttered in sincerity; words spoken from the bottom of one's heart

由奢入儉難(ㄧㄡˊ ㄕㄜ ㄖㄨˋ ㄐㄧㄢˇ ㄋㄢˊ)
It is difficult to go from extravagance to frugality.

由此(ㄧㄡˊ ㄘˇ)
hence; from this; therefore

由此觀之(ㄧㄡˊ ㄘˇ ㄍㄨㄢ ㄓ)
judging from this; looking at

the matter from this viewpoint

由此可見(ㄧㄡˊ ㄘˇ ㄎㄜˇ ㄐㄧㄢˋ)
thus it can be seen; this shows; that proves

由此前往(ㄧㄡˊ ㄘˇ ㄑㄧㄢˊ ㄨㄤˇ)
to go from here

由於(ㄧㄡˊ ㄩˊ)
because of; owing to; due to; as a result of: 由於你的協助,工作進行得很順利。Owing to your assistance, work is going on smoothly.

【甲】 3553 ㄐㄧㄚˇ jea jiǎ

1. the first of the Ten Celestial Stems
2. armor; shell; crust
3. most outstanding
4. a measure of land in Taiwan (equal to 0.97 hectare)
5. a tithing—a group of ten families under the Tithing System introduced by Wang An-shih(王安石)of the Sung Dynasty

甲板(ㄐㄧㄚˇ ㄅㄢˇ)
the deck (of a ship)

甲苯(ㄐㄧㄚˇ ㄅㄣˇ)
toluene, or methylbenzene

甲榜(ㄐㄧㄚˇ ㄅㄤˇ)
a successful candidate in an imperial examination under the former civil service examination system

甲兵(ㄐㄧㄚˇ ㄅㄧㄥ)or 甲士(ㄐㄧㄚˇ ㄕˋ) or 甲卒(ㄐㄧㄚˇ ㄗㄨˊ)
an armed soldier

甲部(ㄐㄧㄚˇ ㄅㄨˋ)
the Classics (one of the four traditional library divisions) 亦作「經部」

甲等(ㄐㄧㄚˇ ㄉㄥˇ)
grade-A (said of student papers scoring 80 points or more)

甲第(ㄐㄧㄚˇ ㄉㄧˋ)
①a mansion; a hall: 甲第連雲。Large and high houses are towering to the clouds. ②a top successful candidate in an examination

甲天下(ㄐㄧㄚˇ ㄊㄧㄢ ㄒㄧㄚˋ)
to be unequaled in the world: 桂林山水甲天下。The mountains and rivers of Kweilin are the finest under heaven.

甲骨文(ㄐㄧㄚˇ ㄍㄨˇ ㄨㄣˊ)
oracle-bone scriptures

甲科(ㄐㄧㄚˇ ㄎㄜ)
the highest category in the civil service examinations before the Republic

甲殼(ㄐㄧㄚˇ ㄎㄜˊ)
a shell

甲殼類(ㄐㄧㄚˇ ㄎㄜˊ ㄌㄟˋ)
the crustacean: 螃蟹、龍蝦、蝦子等是甲殼類。Crabs, lobsters, shrimps, etc. are crustaceans.

甲基(ㄐㄧㄚˇ ㄐㄧ)
methyl

甲醛(ㄐㄧㄚˇ ㄑㄩㄢˊ)
formaldehyde, or methanal

甲胄(ㄐㄧㄚˇ ㄓㄡˋ)
armor; a panoply

甲長(ㄐㄧㄚˇ ㄓㄤˇ)
a head of a tithing

甲狀腺(ㄐㄧㄚˇ ㄓㄨㄤˋ ㄒㄧㄢˋ)
thyroid

甲狀腺切除手術(ㄐㄧㄚˇ ㄓㄨㄤˋ ㄒㄧㄢˋ ㄑㄧㄝ ㄔㄨˊ ㄕㄡˇ ㄕㄨˋ)
thyroidectomy

甲狀腺腫(ㄐㄧㄚˇ ㄓㄨㄤˋ ㄒㄧㄢˋ ㄓㄨㄥˇ)
goiter

甲狀腺素(ㄐㄧㄚˇ ㄓㄨㄤˋ ㄒㄧㄢˋ ㄙㄨˋ)
thyroxine; thyroiodine

甲狀腺炎(ㄐㄧㄚˇ ㄓㄨㄤˋ ㄒㄧㄢˋ ㄧㄢˊ)
thyroiditis

甲狀軟骨(ㄐㄧㄚˇ ㄓㄨㄤˋ ㄖㄨㄢˇ ㄍㄨˇ)
the thyroid cartilage

甲醇(ㄐㄧㄚˇ ㄔㄨㄣˊ)
methyl alcohol or methanol

甲蟲(ㄐㄧㄚˇ ㄔㄨㄥˊ)
a beetle

甲申之役(ㄐㄧㄚˇ ㄕㄣ ㄓ ㄧˋ)
the Sino-French War (in 1884)

甲子(ㄐㄧㄚˇ ㄗˇ)
①the first year in a sexagenary cycle of which each year is designated by a combination of one of the Ten Celestial Stems and one of the Twelve Terrestrial Branches ②one's age

甲族(ㄐㄧㄚˇ ㄗㄨˊ)
influential families of long standing

甲乙(ㄐㄧㄚˇ ㄧˇ)
the first and second of the Ten Celestial Stems—the sequence or order of things

甲午之戰(ㄐㄧㄚˇ ㄨˇ ㄓ ㄓㄢˋ)
the Sino-Japanese War of 1894

甲烷(ㄐㄧㄚˇ ㄨㄢˊ)
methane

甲魚(ㄐㄧㄚˇ ㄩˊ)
a green turtle (*Trionyx sinensis*)

甲於天下(ㄐㄧㄚˇ ㄩˊ ㄊㄧㄢ ㄒㄧㄚˋ)
unequaled in the world

【申】 3554 ㄕㄣ shen shēn

1. the ninth of the Twelve Terrestrial Branches
2. to appeal; to plead
3. to state; to set forth; to explain; to explicate
4. to extend; to expand
5. to inculcate (especially repeatedly)
6. a brief name of Shanghai
7. a Chinese family name

申包胥(ㄕㄣ ㄅㄠ ㄒㄩ)
a minister of the state of Chu (楚) during the Epoch of Spring and Autumn, whose real name was Kung - Sun Pao-hsü (公孫包胥)

申報(ㄕㄣ ㄅㄠˋ)
①to declare; to file (tax returns) ②name of a newspaper formerly published in Shanghai

申報戶口(ㄕㄣ ㄅㄠˋ ㄏㄨˋ ㄎㄡˇ)
to report one's address for the domiciliary register

申辯(ㄕㄣ ㄅㄧㄢˋ)
to argue; to contend; to defend oneself; to explain one's conduct: 你將需要律師爲你申辯。You will need lawyers to defend you.

申明(ㄕㄣ ㄇㄧㄥˊ)
to set forth; to explain; to expound; to explicate

申覆(ㄕㄣ ㄈㄨˋ)
to reply to a superior

申旦(ㄕㄣ ㄉㄢˋ)
from night till morning

申討(ㄕㄣ ㄊㄠˇ)
openly condemn; to denounce

申理(ㄕㄣ ㄌㄧˇ)
to redress wrong

申令(ㄕㄣ ㄌㄧㄥˋ)
to decree; to order

申告(ㄕㄣ ㄍㄠˋ)
to file a complaint (in a

court of law); to appeal to a court of law
申告鈴(ㄕㄣ ㄍㄠˋ ㄌㄧㄥˊ)
a bell to be rung when appealing to a court of law
申誡(ㄕㄣ ㄐㄧㄝˋ)
① a reprimand; a rebuke ② to rebuke; to reprimand
申請(ㄕㄣ ㄑㄧㄥˇ)
to request or to apply (to some authorities for something); application; request: 他向銀行申請貸款。He applied to the bank for a loan.
申請書(ㄕㄣ ㄑㄧㄥˇ ㄕㄨ)
an application form; a written request
申請人(ㄕㄣ ㄑㄧㄥˇ ㄖㄣˊ)
an applicant; one who makes a request to the higher authorities
申謝(ㄕㄣ ㄒㄧㄝˋ)
to extend one's thanks; to express gratitude
申斥(ㄕㄣ ㄔˋ)
to reprimand; to rebuke
申飭(ㄕㄣ ㄔˋ)
to reprimand; to rebuke
申時(ㄕㄣ ㄕˊ)
3-5 p.m.
申述(ㄕㄣ ㄕㄨˋ)
to state; to explain in detail
申說(ㄕㄣ ㄕㄨㄛ)
to explain; to explicate; to set forth; to expound
申訴(ㄕㄣ ㄙㄨˋ)
to present one's case (in a law court, etc.); to appeal; to lodge a complaint: 我向上級法院提出申訴。I appealed to the higher court.
申冤(ㄕㄣ ㄩㄢ)
to appeal for justice regarding a false charge

二畫

【男】 3555
ㄋㄢˊ nan nán
1. a human male; a man; a boy; a son
2. a baron
男扮女裝(ㄋㄢˊ ㄅㄢˋ ㄋㄩˇ ㄓㄨㄤ)
disguised as a woman
男儐相(ㄋㄢˊ ㄅㄧㄣ ㄒㄧㄤˋ)
a best man (at a wedding)
男朋友(ㄋㄢˊ ㄆㄥˊ ㄧㄡˇ)
a boyfriend: 從來沒有人看見她有男朋友。She is never seen with a boy.
男僕(ㄋㄢˊ ㄆㄨˊ)
a male servant
男方(ㄋㄢˊ ㄈㄤ)
the bridegroom's family, relatives and friends collectively
男大當婚，女大當嫁(ㄋㄢˊ ㄉㄚˋ ㄉㄤ ㄏㄨㄣ, ㄋㄩˇ ㄉㄚˋ ㄉㄤ ㄐㄧㄚˋ)
Upon growing up, every male should take a wife and every female should take a husband.
男盜女娼(ㄋㄢˊ ㄉㄠˋ ㄋㄩˇ ㄔㄤ)
The male are robbers and the female harlots.
男低音(ㄋㄢˊ ㄉㄧ ㄧㄣ)
(music) ① bass (the lowest male voice) ② a bass (a singer with the lowest male voice)
男女(ㄋㄢˊ ㄋㄩˇ)
① male and female; men and women; both sexes ② one's children ③ attendants; servants
男女平等(ㄋㄢˊ ㄋㄩˇ ㄆㄧㄥˊ ㄉㄥˇ)
equal rights for both sexes
男女同校(ㄋㄢˊ ㄋㄩˇ ㄊㄨㄥˊ ㄒㄧㄠˋ)
coeducation
男女老幼(ㄋㄢˊ ㄋㄩˇ ㄌㄠˇ ㄧㄡˋ)
males and females of all ages; all people regardless of age and sex
男女關係(ㄋㄢˊ ㄋㄩˇ ㄍㄨㄢ ㄒㄧˋ)
relations between the two sexes
男女授受不親(ㄋㄢˊ ㄋㄩˇ ㄕㄡˋ ㄕㄡˋ ㄅㄨˋ ㄑㄧㄣ)
A man and a woman unless related by blood or marriage should not touch hands when giving and taking things. (according to the code of conduct before the republican era)
男女有別(ㄋㄢˊ ㄋㄩˇ ㄧㄡˇ ㄅㄧㄝˊ)
Males and females should be treated differently. 或 Males and females should be distinguished.
男高音(ㄋㄢˊ ㄍㄠ ㄧㄣ)
(music) ① tenor (the highest male voice) ② a tenor (a singer with the highest male voice)
男耕女織(ㄋㄢˊ ㄍㄥ ㄋㄩˇ ㄓ)
(said of an agricultural society) The men plow and the women weave.
男孩子(ㄋㄢˊ ㄏㄞˊ ·ㄗ) or 男孩兒(ㄋㄢˊ ㄏㄚˊㄦ)
a boy
男歡女愛(ㄋㄢˊ ㄏㄨㄢ ㄋㄩˇ ㄞˋ)
The couple are enraptured with love.
男婚女嫁(ㄋㄢˊ ㄏㄨㄣ ㄋㄩˇ ㄐㄧㄚˋ)
A man should take a wife and a woman should take a husband.
男家(ㄋㄢˊ ㄐㄧㄚ)
the bridegroom's family
男爵(ㄋㄢˊ ㄐㄩㄝˊ)
a baron
男爵夫人(ㄋㄢˊ ㄐㄩㄝˊ ㄈㄨ ㄖㄣˊ)
a baroness
男系(ㄋㄢˊ ㄒㄧˋ)
the male line; the spear side
男性(ㄋㄢˊ ㄒㄧㄥˋ)
① the male sex ② the masculine gender
男性荷爾蒙(ㄋㄢˊ ㄒㄧㄥˋ ㄏㄜˊ ㄦˇ ㄇㄥˊ)
(biochemistry) androgen
男性化(ㄋㄢˊ ㄒㄧㄥˋ ㄏㄨㄚˋ)
(said of a girl or a woman) acting or behaving like a man
男裝(ㄋㄢˊ ㄓㄨㄤ)
male costume; men's clothing
男中音(ㄋㄢˊ ㄓㄨㄥ ㄧㄣ)
(music) ① baritone, or barytone (the male singing voice lower than tenor and higher than bass) ② a baritone, or a barytone (a man with such a singing voice)
男生(ㄋㄢˊ ㄕㄥ)
a boy student
男子(ㄋㄢˊ ㄗˇ) or 男人(ㄋㄢˊ ㄖㄣˊ)
a man: 他沒有男子氣。He's only half a man.
男子漢(ㄋㄢˊ ㄗˇ ㄏㄢˋ)
a manly man: 我們怎樣使他成爲男子漢? How can we make a manly man of him?
男子生殖器(ㄋㄢˊ ㄗˇ ㄕㄥ ㄓˊ ㄑㄧˋ)
the male genitals; the male reproductive organs
男左女右(ㄋㄢˊ ㄗㄨㄛˇ ㄋㄩˇ ㄧㄡˋ)
(a popular concept) The left

represents the male and the right represents the female.

男尊女卑(ㄋㄢˊ ㄗㄨㄣ ㄋㄩˇ ㄅㄟ)
the treatment of females as inferior to males

男廁所(ㄋㄢˊ ㄘㄜˋ ㄙㄨㄛˇ)
men's room

男才女貌(ㄋㄢˊ ㄘㄞˊ ㄋㄩˇ ㄇㄠˋ)
The man is able and the woman is beautiful. —an ideal couple

男色(ㄋㄢˊ ㄙㄜˋ)or 男寵(ㄋㄢˊ ㄔㄨㄥˇ)
sodomy; buggery

男兒(ㄋㄢˊ ㄦˊ)
①a boy; a son ②a man (emphasizing the manliness)

男兒本色(ㄋㄢˊ ㄦˊ ㄅㄣˇ ㄙㄜˋ)
the manliness of a man

【甸】 3556 ㄉㄧㄢˋ diann diàn

1. suburbs or outskirts of the capital
2. to govern; to rule
3. farm crops

甸服(ㄉㄧㄢˋ ㄈㄨˊ)
areas within 500 *li* of the capital in the Hsia Dynasty

甸地(ㄉㄧㄢˋ ㄉㄧˋ)
the suburbs or outskirts of the capital

甸甸(ㄉㄧㄢˋ ㄉㄧㄢˋ)
the sound of horses and carriages in motion

甸侯(ㄉㄧㄢˋ ㄏㄡˊ)
feudal lord within 500 *li* of the imperial capital in the Hsia Dynasty

甸人(ㄉㄧㄢˋ ㄖㄣˊ)
an ancient official title

甸役(ㄉㄧㄢˋ ㄧˋ)
hunting

甸萬姓(ㄉㄧㄢˋ ㄨㄢˋ ㄒㄧㄥˋ)
to govern the people

【町】 3557 1. ㄊㄧㄥˇ tiing tǐng

the boundary between agricultural land

町畽(ㄊㄧㄥˇ ㄊㄨㄢˇ)
waste land; a paddock

町畦(ㄊㄧㄥˇ ㄒㄧˊ)
a low bank of earth between fields

【町】 3557 2. ㄉㄧㄥ ding dīng

(in Japan) a street; a city block

三畫

【甿】 3558 ㄇㄥˊ meng méng

farming population

【畀】 3559 ㄅㄧˋ bih bì

to confer; to bestow; to give to

四畫

【界】 3560 ㄐㄧㄝˋ jieh jiè

1. a boundary
2. to limit; to demarcate; to define; to delimit
3. world

界碑(ㄐㄧㄝˋ ㄅㄟ)
a landmark; a boundary stone

界畫(ㄐㄧㄝˋ ㄏㄨㄚˋ)
to draw lines with the aid of a ruler in drawing palatial buildings 亦作「匠畫」

界限(ㄐㄧㄝˋ ㄒㄧㄢˋ)
①outer limits; a border ②to limit; to restrict

界線(ㄐㄧㄝˋ ㄒㄧㄢˋ)
a boundary; a borderline; a dividing line; a demarcation line

界尺(ㄐㄧㄝˋ ㄔˇ)
a ruler (for ruling a line)

界石(ㄐㄧㄝˋ ㄕˊ)
a boundary stone; a landmark

界說(ㄐㄧㄝˋ ㄕㄨㄛ)
a definition

界外球(ㄐㄧㄝˋ ㄨㄞˋ ㄑㄧㄡˊ)
(sports) out-of-bounds

界約(ㄐㄧㄝˋ ㄩㄝ)
a frontier agreement (between two countries)

【畏】 3561 ㄨㄟˋ wey wèi

1. to stand in awe of; to fear; to dread; to be afraid of; to be scared of
2. to revere; to respect

畏避(ㄨㄟˋ ㄅㄧˋ)
to evade because of fear

畏怕(ㄨㄟˋ ㄆㄚˋ)
to fear; to dread; to stand in awe of

畏法(ㄨㄟˋ ㄈㄚˇ)
to fear the law

畏服(ㄨㄟˋ ㄈㄨˊ)
to submit from fear; to yield from awe

畏憚(ㄨㄟˋ ㄉㄢˋ)
to have scruples about

畏途(ㄨㄟˋ ㄊㄨˊ)
①a difficult path deserving fear; a dangerous path ②a task shirked by everybody

畏難(ㄨㄟˋ ㄋㄢˊ)
to fear difficulty

畏光(ㄨㄟˋ ㄍㄨㄤ)
(medicine) photophobia

畏忌(ㄨㄟˋ ㄐㄧˋ)
to have scruples about

畏敬(ㄨㄟˋ ㄐㄧㄥˋ)
to stand in awe of

畏懼(ㄨㄟˋ ㄐㄩˋ)
to dread; to be scared of; to fear

畏怯(ㄨㄟˋ ㄑㄧㄝˋ)
to fear; to be scared of

畏葸退縮(ㄨㄟˋ ㄒㄧˇ ㄊㄨㄟˋ ㄙㄨㄛ)
to recoil from fear

畏首畏尾(ㄨㄟˋ ㄕㄡˇ ㄨㄟˋ ㄨㄟˇ)
to have too many fears; to harbor fear fore and aft

畏日(ㄨㄟˋ ㄖˋ)
the scorching sun in summer

畏罪(ㄨㄟˋ ㄗㄨㄟˋ)
to be afraid of punishment

畏罪自殺(ㄨㄟˋ ㄗㄨㄟˋ ㄗˋ ㄕㄚ)
to kill oneself from fear of punishment

畏死(ㄨㄟˋ ㄙˇ)
to be afraid of dying; to fear death

畏縮(ㄨㄟˋ ㄙㄨㄛ)
to shrink; to recoil; to cringe; to flinch

畏友(ㄨㄟˋ ㄧㄡˇ)
a friend of stern moral integrity; a respectable friend

【畋】 3562 ㄊㄧㄢˊ tyan tián

1. to cultivate land
2. to hunt game

畋獵(ㄊㄧㄢˊ ㄌㄧㄝˋ)
hunting

【畎】 3563 ㄑㄩㄢˇ cheuan quǎn

1. an irrigation ditch
2. a valley; a dale; a canyon

畎畝(ㄑㄩㄢˇ ㄇㄨˇ)

the fields
畎澮(ㄑㄩㄢˇ ㄎㄨㄞˋ)
ditches in the fields

五畫

【畔】 3564 ㄆㄢˋ pann pàn
1. a boundary between fields
2. a side; a bank
3. same as 叛 — to rebel; to betray

畔岸(ㄆㄢˋ ㄢˋ)
① limits; a boundary ② self-indulgent

【畛】 3565 ㄓㄣˇ jeen zhěn
1. footpaths between fields; dikes along watercourses in fields
2. a boundary; limits

畛域(ㄓㄣˇ ㄩˋ)
range; scope; a boundary; (figuratively) distinction: 我們不分畛域。We make no distinctions.

【畚】 3566 ㄅㄣˇ been běn
a bamboo basket for carrying earth

畚箕(ㄅㄣˇ ㄐㄧ)
a bamboo basket for carrying earth or dirt

【畜】 3567 1. ㄔㄨˋ chuh chù
1. a dumb creature; an animal
2. livestock

畜類(ㄔㄨˋ ㄌㄟˋ)
dumb creatures; animals

畜力(ㄔㄨˋ ㄌㄧˋ)
animal power

畜生(ㄔㄨˋ ㄕㄥ)
① dumb creatures; animals ② a beast (a reviling term)

畜疫(ㄔㄨˋ ㄧˋ)
epidemic disease of domestic animals

【畜】 3567 2. ㄒㄩˋ shiuh xù
1. to rear or raise (livestock or children)
2. a Chinese family name

畜牧(ㄒㄩˋ ㄇㄨˋ)
animal husbandry; livestock industry

畜牧學(ㄒㄩˋ ㄇㄨˋ ㄒㄩㄝˊ)
animal husbandry; zootechny

畜牧場(ㄒㄩˋ ㄇㄨˋ ㄔㄤˇ)or(ㄒㄩˋ ㄇㄨˋ ㄔㄤˊ)
a livestock farm; a range; a grazing ground

畜牧時代(ㄒㄩˋ ㄇㄨˋ ㄕˊ ㄉㄞˋ)
the pastoral age

畜產(ㄒㄩˋ ㄔㄢˇ)
products of animal husbandry

畜養(ㄒㄩˋ ㄧㄤˇ)
to rear or raise (livestock): 他畜養家畜。He raised domestic animals.

【畝】 3568 ㄇㄨˇ muu mǔ
mu, a Chinese land measure (equal to 733 ½ square yards)

【留】 3569 (畱) ㄌㄧㄡˊ liou liú
1. to remain; to stay; to be at a standstill
2. to ask somebody to stay
3. to detain; to obstruct; to keep; to delay
4. to leave
5. to preserve; to reserve

留別(ㄌㄧㄡˊ ㄅㄧㄝˊ)
to give something to (or to write a poem for) a friend as a souvenir on parting

留別紀念(ㄌㄧㄡˊ ㄅㄧㄝˊ ㄐㄧˋ ㄋㄧㄢˋ)
a souvenir or keepsake

留步(ㄌㄧㄡˊ ㄅㄨˋ)
(Please) do not trouble yourself by accompanying me to the door (a visitor's remark to the host on leaving)

留不住(ㄌㄧㄡˊ ˙ㄅㄨ ㄓㄨˋ)
unable to detain; unable to make someone stay

留名(ㄌㄧㄡˊ ㄇㄧㄥˊ)
to leave behind a good reputation

留得青山在，不愁沒柴燒(ㄌㄧㄡˊ ㄉㄜˊ ㄑㄧㄥ ㄕㄢ ㄗㄞˋ, ㄅㄨˋ ㄔㄡˊ ㄇㄟˊ ㄔㄞˊ ㄕㄠ)
As long as the mountain is green, there will be firewood.—As long as there is life, there is hope.

留待(ㄌㄧㄡˊ ㄉㄞˋ)
to wait until

留地步(ㄌㄧㄡˊ ㄉㄧˋ ㄅㄨˋ)
not to push one's advantage too far; not to go to extremes

留頭髮(ㄌㄧㄡˊ ㄊㄡˊ ˙ㄈㄚ)
to allow the hair to grow

留退步(ㄌㄧㄡˊ ㄊㄨㄟˋ ㄅㄨˋ)or 留後步(ㄌㄧㄡˊ ㄏㄡˋ ㄅㄨˋ)
to leave ground for retreat

留難(ㄌㄧㄡˊ ㄋㄢˊ)
to make things difficult (for another); to put obstacles in somebody's way: 他老是留難我。He always puts obstacles in my way.

留鳥(ㄌㄧㄡˊ ㄋㄧㄠˇ)
a stationary bird; a resident bird

留念(ㄌㄧㄡˊ ㄋㄧㄢˋ)
as a keepsake or souvenir

留連(ㄌㄧㄡˊ ㄌㄧㄢˊ)
reluctant to leave; unwilling to part with

留連忘返(ㄌㄧㄡˊ ㄌㄧㄢˊ ㄨㄤˋ ㄈㄢˇ)
so enchanted as to forget about home

留戀(ㄌㄧㄡˊ ㄌㄧㄢˋ)
unwilling to leave; reluctant to part with

留客(ㄌㄧㄡˊ ㄎㄜˋ)
to detain a guest; to ask a guest to stay

留侯(ㄌㄧㄡˊ ㄏㄡˊ)
the title conferred upon Chang Liang (張良), the strategist who played a significant role in the founding of the Han Dynasty

留後路(ㄌㄧㄡˊ ㄏㄡˋ ㄌㄨˋ)
to keep a way open for retreat; to leave a way out: 你該給自己留條後路。You should leave yourself a way out.

留鬍子(ㄌㄧㄡˊ ㄏㄨˊ ˙ㄗ)
to grow a mustache or a beard

留話(ㄌㄧㄡˊ ㄏㄨㄚˋ)
to leave a message

留級(ㄌㄧㄡˊ ㄐㄧˊ)
to repeat the year's work; to fail to get promoted to the next grade at school

留居(ㄌㄧㄡˊ ㄐㄩ)
to stay on or settle down in a place

留情(ㄌㄧㄡˊ ㄑㄧㄥˊ)
to show mercy; to relent: 他對別人毫不留情。He shows others no mercy.

〔田部〕

留取(ㄌㄧㄡˊ ㄑㄩˇ)
to preserve; to leave

留下(ㄌㄧㄡˊ ㄒㄧㄚˋ)
①to leave: 那傷口留下一個疤。The wound left a scar. ② to detain; to stop ③to remain; to stay ④to preserve

留校察看(ㄌㄧㄡˊ ㄒㄧㄠˋ ㄔㄚˊ ㄎㄢˋ)
(said of a misbehaving student) to be kept in school but placed under surveillance

留心(ㄌㄧㄡˊ ㄒㄧㄣ)
to pay attention; to take heed; to be careful; to exercise caution

留鬚(ㄌㄧㄡˊ ㄒㄩ)
to grow a beard: 那老人留鬚。That old man grows a beard.

留學(ㄌㄧㄡˊ ㄒㄩㄝˊ)
to study abroad; to study in a foreign country

留學生(ㄌㄧㄡˊ ㄒㄩㄝˊ ㄕㄥ)
a student studying abroad

留職停薪(ㄌㄧㄡˊ ㄓˊ ㄊㄧㄥˊ ㄒㄧㄣ)
leave without pay

留置(ㄌㄧㄡˊ ㄓˋ)
to detain; to put aside

留滯(ㄌㄧㄡˊ ㄓˋ)
to remain at a standstill; to stay

留中不發(ㄌㄧㄡˊ ㄓㄨㄥ ㄅㄨˋ ㄈㄚ)
(said of a memorial 奏摺) to be kept at the imperial palace without an answer; to be shelved

留住(ㄌㄧㄡˊ ˙ㄓㄨ)
to succeed in making someone stay

留呈(ㄌㄧㄡˊ ㄔㄥˊ)
to leave (a written message) behind for an elder or superior

留守(ㄌㄧㄡˊ ㄕㄡˇ)
①to act for the emperor during his absence from the capital ②(said of troops) to remain stationed at a camp in the rear

留守處(ㄌㄧㄡˊ ㄕㄡˇ ㄔㄨˋ)
a liaison office left in the rear by troops fighting on the front

留神(ㄌㄧㄡˊ ㄕㄣˊ)
to pay attention; to be careful; to exercise caution: 過街時要留神。Be careful when you are crossing the street.

留聲機(ㄌㄧㄡˊ ㄕㄥ ㄐㄧ)
a phonograph

留任(ㄌㄧㄡˊ ㄖㄣˋ)
to stay in a position for another term

留存(ㄌㄧㄡˊ ㄘㄨㄣˊ)
①to preserve; to keep ②to remain; to be extant

留宿(ㄌㄧㄡˊ ㄙㄨˋ)
to keep (a guest) overnight

留意(ㄌㄧㄡˊ ㄧˋ)
to pay attention; to be careful; to be cautious; to take care; to exercise caution

留一手(ㄌㄧㄡˊ ㄧˋ ㄕㄡˇ)or 留後手(ㄌㄧㄡˊ ㄏㄡˋ ㄕㄡˇ)
to hold back a trick or two (in teaching a trade or skill)

留言(ㄌㄧㄡˊ ㄧㄢˊ)
to leave one's comments; to leave a message

留養(ㄌㄧㄡˊ ㄧㄤˋ)
to stay at home to look after one's parents

留影(ㄌㄧㄡˊ ㄧㄥˇ)
to take a photo as a memento; to have a picture taken as a souvenir

留餘地(ㄌㄧㄡˊ ㄩˊ ㄉㄧˋ)
to refrain from going to extremes; not to push one's advantage too far; to allow for unforeseen circumstances

留寓(ㄌㄧㄡˊ ㄩˋ)
to be long absent from home

留用(ㄌㄧㄡˊ ㄩㄥˋ)
①to give employment to someone ②to keep for use by oneself

六畫

【畦】 3570 ㄒㄧ shi xī (語音 ㄑㄧˊ chyi qí)

1. land of 50 *mu*(畝)
2. a plot, piece, or parcel of land
3. a farmer; a laborer

畦徑(ㄒㄧ ㄐㄧㄥˋ)
①a bypath②a way; a method

畦畛(ㄒㄧ ㄓㄣˇ)
①scope; range ②prejudice

【畤】 3571 ㄓˋ jyh zhì

a place for worshipping Heaven, Earth, and the five sage kings in ancient times

【略】 3572 (畧) ㄌㄩㄝˋ liueh lüè

1. approximate; rough; brief
2. slight; small in extent
3. to scheme; to plan
4. strategy: 他是一個戰略家。He is a person skilled in strategy.
5. to invade; to seize
6. to omit; to leave out: 這一章可以略去。This chapter may be omitted.
7. to survey the boundaries
8. a Chinese family name

略賣(ㄌㄩㄝˋ ㄇㄞˋ)
to sell women or children kidnapped or seduced from their homes

略地(ㄌㄩㄝˋ ㄉㄧˋ)
①to invade territory ②to inspect a frontier

略奪(ㄌㄩㄝˋ ㄉㄨㄛˊ)
to rob; to take by force

略圖(ㄌㄩㄝˋ ㄊㄨˊ)
a rough drawing; a sketch; a rough sketch; a sketch map; a rough plan: 他畫了一張這個鎮的略圖。He made a sketch of the town.

略同(ㄌㄩㄝˋ ㄊㄨㄥˊ)
approximately the same; about the same; similar

略歷(ㄌㄩㄝˋ ㄌㄧˋ)
a brief personal record; a biographical sketch

略略(ㄌㄩㄝˋ ㄌㄩㄝˋ)
briefly; slightly; a little; somewhat

略可(ㄌㄩㄝˋ ㄎㄜˇ)
acceptable in general; all right on the whole

略取(ㄌㄩㄝˋ ㄑㄩˇ)
to take by force

略去(ㄌㄩㄝˋ ㄑㄩˋ)
to omit; to leave out; to delete

略知一二(ㄌㄩㄝˋ ㄓ ㄧ ㄦˋ)
to know or understand just a little

略傳(ㄌㄩㄝˋ ㄓㄨㄢˋ)
a biographical sketch; a brief personal history

略識之無(ㄌㄩㄝˋ ㄕˋ ㄓ ㄨˊ)

only slightly literate

略勝一籌(ㄌㄩㄝˋ ㄕㄥˋ ㄧˋ ㄔㄡˊ)
slightly better; slightly superior; a cut above

略述(ㄌㄩㄝˋ ㄕㄨˋ)
to describe briefly; to give a short description of; to outline

略說(ㄌㄩㄝˋ ㄕㄨㄛ)
to say a few words about; briefly refer to

略字(ㄌㄩㄝˋ ㄗˋ)
abbreviated form of a word; abbreviation

略有門徑(ㄌㄩㄝˋ ㄧㄡˇ ㄇㄣˊ ㄐㄧㄥˋ)
to have some rough understanding of a subject

略有所聞(ㄌㄩㄝˋ ㄧㄡˇ ㄙㄨㄛˇ ㄨㄣˊ)
to have heard something (about it): 此事我略有所聞。I have heard something about this matter.

略誘(ㄌㄩㄝˋ ㄧㄡˋ)
(law) to seduce or force a minor to leave his family or guardian; abduction; kidnapping

略言之(ㄌㄩㄝˋ ㄧㄢˊ ㄓ)
to state briefly; in short: 略言之，他不接受我的勸告。In short, he did not take my advice.

略微(ㄌㄩㄝˋ ㄨㄟˊ)
slightly; a little; somewhat: 她略微有點頭痛。She has a slight headache.

【畢】 3573 ㄅㄧˋ bih bì

1. to complete; to finish; to end
2. whole; total; complete
3. a Chinese family name

畢命(ㄅㄧˋ ㄇㄧㄥˋ)
to end one's life; to die

畢達哥拉斯(ㄅㄧˋ ㄉㄚˊ ㄍㄜ ㄌㄚ ㄙ)
Pythagoras, 582-500 B.C., Greek philosopher and mathematician

畢卡索(ㄅㄧˋ ㄎㄚˇ ㄙㄨㄛˇ)
Pablo Picasso, 1881-1973, Spanish painter

畢集(ㄅㄧˋ ㄐㄧˊ)
to gather or assemble completely

畢竟(ㄅㄧˋ ㄐㄧㄥˋ)
after all; in the long run; ultimately

畢其功於一役(ㄅㄧˋ ㄑㄧˊ ㄍㄨㄥ ㄩˊ ㄧˊ ㄧˋ)
to accomplish the whole task at one stroke

畢肖(ㄅㄧˋ ㄒㄧㄠˋ)
similar; completely alike; closely resembling

畢生(ㄅㄧˋ ㄕㄥ)
in one's whole life; throughout one's lifetime; lifelong: 他以畢生的精力從事語言研究。He devoted a lifetime to the study of language.

畢昇(ㄅㄧˋ ㄕㄥ)
Pi Sheng (c. 11th century), inventor of the movable type during the Sung Dynasty

畢業(ㄅㄧˋ ㄧㄝˋ)
to be graduated; to graduate; graduation: 在牛津大學讀了三年，他畢業了。After three years at Oxford, he graduated.

畢業班(ㄅㄧˋ ㄧㄝˋ ㄅㄢ)
the graduating class

畢業典禮(ㄅㄧˋ ㄧㄝˋ ㄉㄧㄢˇ ㄌㄧˇ)
commencement exercises; a commencement亦作「畢業式」

畢業年限(ㄅㄧˋ ㄧㄝˋ ㄋㄧㄢˊ ㄒㄧㄢˋ)
a required number of years for graduation

畢業論文(ㄅㄧˋ ㄧㄝˋ ㄌㄨㄣˋ ㄨㄣˊ)
a thesis

畢業考試(ㄅㄧˋ ㄧㄝˋ ㄎㄠˇ ㄕˋ)
a graduation examination

畢業照片(ㄅㄧˋ ㄧㄝˋ ㄓㄠˋ ㄆㄧㄢˋ)
a photograph of all the graduating students and their teachers taken together on the commencement day

畢業證書(ㄅㄧˋ ㄧㄝˋ ㄓㄥˋ ㄕㄨ)or 畢業文憑(ㄅㄧˋ ㄧㄝˋ ㄨㄣˊ ㄆㄧㄥˊ)
a diploma

畢業式(ㄅㄧˋ ㄧㄝˋ ㄕˋ)
commencement exercises; a commencement

畢業生(ㄅㄧˋ ㄧㄝˋ ㄕㄥ)
a graduate: 我是耶魯大學的畢業生。I'm a graduate of Yale University.

【異】 3574 (异) ㄧˋ yih yì

1. different; difference
2. peculiar; extraordinary; unusual; strange; uncommon
3. foreign; unfamiliar; unknown
4. to marvel; to wonder
5. to separate

異邦(ㄧˋ ㄅㄤ)
a foreign country

異稟(ㄧˋ ㄅㄧㄥˇ)
extraordinary endowments; extraordinary talent

異名(ㄧˋ ㄇㄧㄥˊ)
a different name

異母兄弟(ㄧˋ ㄇㄨˇ ㄒㄩㄥ ㄉㄧˋ)
brothers born of different mothers; half brothers

異方殊俗(ㄧˋ ㄈㄤ ㄕㄨ ㄙㄨˊ)
different customs in alien countries

異服(ㄧˋ ㄈㄨˊ)
outlandish costume; strange clothing: 他喜歡穿奇裝異服。He likes to wear an outlandish dress.

異代(ㄧˋ ㄉㄞˋ)
a different age or era

異代交(ㄧˋ ㄉㄞˋ ㄐㄧㄠ)
admiration for historical personalities

異地(ㄧˋ ㄉㄧˋ)
a strange land; a foreign land

異端(ㄧˋ ㄉㄨㄢ)
strange doctrines

異端邪說(ㄧˋ ㄉㄨㄢ ㄒㄧㄝˊ ㄕㄨㄛ)
heretical beliefs; heresy

異態(ㄧˋ ㄊㄞˋ)
strange bearing or manner

異體字(ㄧˋ ㄊㄧˇ ㄗˋ)
a variant form of a Chinese character

異途同歸(ㄧˋ ㄊㄨˊ ㄊㄨㄥˊ ㄍㄨㄟ)
(literally) to arrive at an identical point through different courses—to reach an identical conclusion through different procedures of separate studies; to attain the same objective through different efforts

異同(ㄧˋ ㄊㄨㄥˊ)
① differences and similarities ② inconsistent

異能(ㄧˋ ㄋㄥˊ)
extraordinary talent; genius: 他是一個有奇才異能的人。He has extraordinary talents and abilities.

異類(ㄧˋ ㄌㄟˋ)
① those of a different class or kind ② nonhuman ③

〔田部〕

aliens; a different tribe or race

異國(ㄧˋ ㄍㄨㄛˊ)
a foreign country

異國情調(ㄧˋ ㄍㄨㄛˊ ㄑㄧㄥˊ ㄉㄧㄠˋ)
an exotic touch or mood on a foreign land

異客(ㄧˋ ㄎㄜˋ)
a stranger

異口同聲(ㄧˋ ㄎㄡˇ ㄊㄨㄥˊ ㄕㄥ) or 異口同音(ㄧˋ ㄎㄡˇ ㄊㄨㄥˊ ㄧㄣ)
The same thing is said by different mouths. 或 People are unanimous in their opinion.

異乎尋常(ㄧˋ ㄏㄨ ㄒㄩㄣˊ ㄔㄤˊ)
unusual; extraordinary

異花受精(ㄧˋ ㄏㄨㄚ ㄕㄡˋ ㄐㄧㄥ)
allogamy; cross-fertilization

異化(ㄧˋ ㄏㄨㄚˋ)
①(philosophy) alienation ②(linguistics) dissimilation

異化作用(ㄧˋ ㄏㄨㄚˋ ㄗㄨㄛˋ ㄩㄥˋ)
catabolism

異己(ㄧˋ ㄐㄧˇ)
those who differ from or disagree with oneself; a dissident

異教(ㄧˋ ㄐㄧㄠˋ)
heathenism; paganism

異教徒(ㄧˋ ㄐㄧㄠˋ ㄊㄨˊ)
a heathen; a pagan

異軍突起(ㄧˋ ㄐㄩㄣ ㄊㄨˊ ㄑㄧˇ)
(literally) A new army appears all of a sudden (to change the situation).—the unexpected appearance of a new talent, factor, stratagem, etc. that upsets the status quo

異曲同工(ㄧˋ ㄑㄩˇ ㄊㄨㄥˊ ㄍㄨㄥ)
(literally) Different songs are sung with the same excellence.—The writings are different, but the excellence is the same.

異趣(ㄧˋ ㄑㄩˋ)
①different tastes or interests ②extraordinary taste

異心(ㄧˋ ㄒㄧㄣ)
dishonesty; infidelity; disloyalty; insincerity; treachery

異香(ㄧˋ ㄒㄧㄤ)
rare fragrance; unusually sweet smell

異香異氣(ㄧˋ ㄒㄧㄤ ㄧˋ ㄑㄧˋ)
an unusual kind of pleasant smell

異鄉(ㄧˋ ㄒㄧㄤ)
a strange community; a strange land; a foreign land; away from one's home

異想天開(ㄧˋ ㄒㄧㄤˇ ㄊㄧㄢ ㄎㄞ)
to have fantastic notions

異相(ㄧˋ ㄒㄧㄤˋ)
①a strange physiognomy ②to differ in appearance

異象(ㄧˋ ㄒㄧㄤˋ)
strange phenomena

異形(ㄧˋ ㄒㄧㄥˊ)
a strange form or shape

異性(ㄧˋ ㄒㄧㄥˋ)
①of the other sex; the opposite sex ②of a different nature

異性戀(ㄧˋ ㄒㄧㄥˋ ㄌㄧㄢˋ)
heterosexuality

異姓(ㄧˋ ㄒㄧㄥˋ)
those with different surnames

異質(ㄧˋ ㄓˊ)
of a different nature; of a different quality

異質體(ㄧˋ ㄓˊ ㄊㄧˇ)
a heterogeneous body

異質同像(ㄧˋ ㄓˊ ㄊㄨㄥˊ ㄒㄧㄤˋ)
isomorphism

異常(ㄧˋ ㄔㄤˊ)
extraordinary; unusual; strange: 天氣異常寒冷。It was unusually cold.

異事(ㄧˋ ㄕˋ)
①a peculiar affair ②a different matter; another affair ③to be engaged in different occupations

異數(ㄧˋ ㄕㄨˋ)
①different rank ②courteous reception; unusual favor

異說(ㄧˋ ㄕㄨㄛ)
①heresies ②a different interpretation; a different theory

異日(ㄧˋ ㄖˋ)
①another day; some other day ②bygone days

異人(ㄧˋ ㄖㄣˊ)
①an extraordinary person; an idiosyncratic person ②a stranger ③another person; somebody else

異哉(ㄧˋ ㄗㄞ)
How strange! 或 What a strange thing it is!

異族(ㄧˋ ㄗㄨˊ)
a different clan, tribe, or race

異辭(ㄧˋ ㄘˊ)
dissenting statements

異才(ㄧˋ ㄘㄞˊ)
unusual talent; genius

異彩(ㄧˋ ㄘㄞˇ)
extraordinary (or radiant) splendor

異爨(ㄧˋ ㄘㄨㄢˋ)
(said of brothers) to form separate families

異俗(ㄧˋ ㄙㄨˊ)
①different custom ②bad custom

異議(ㄧˋ ㄧˋ)
dissent; objections

異議分子(ㄧˋ ㄧˋ ㄈㄣˋ ㄗˇ)
a dissident

異樣(ㄧˋ ㄧㄤˋ)
unusual; extraordinary; peculiar; strange; differences

異物(ㄧˋ ㄨˋ)
①a rare treasure; an extremely valuable object ②a peculiar thing; a strange thing; an uncommon thing ③the dead

異味(ㄧˋ ㄨㄟˋ)
extraordinarily pleasant flavor; uncommonly sweet taste

異聞(ㄧˋ ㄨㄣˊ)
①unusual news; a strange story; a strange tale ②a different report

異域(ㄧˋ ㄩˋ)
a foreign land; a strange land

七畫

【番】 3575
1. ㄈㄢ fan fān

1. to take turns
2. order in series
3. a time: 他三番兩次的打擾她。He disturbed her time and again.
4. a kind of; a sort of
5. barbarians

番邦(ㄈㄢ ㄅㄤ)
a barbarian state

番代(ㄈㄢ ㄉㄞˋ)
to take turns

番地(ㄈㄢ ㄉㄧˋ)

a strange land; a foreign land
番瓜(ㄈㄢ ㄍㄨㄚ)
a pumpkin 亦作「南瓜」: 番瓜用來做餅。A pumpkin is used for making pies.
番鬼(ㄈㄢ ㄍㄨㄟˇ)
a foreign devil (an abusive term)
番號(ㄈㄢ ㄏㄠˋ)
a numerical designation of a military unit
番紅花(ㄈㄢ ㄏㄨㄥˊ ㄏㄨㄚ)
a saffron
番椒(ㄈㄢ ㄐㄧㄠ)
pepper; capsicum 亦作「辣椒」
番茄(ㄈㄢ ㄑㄧㄝˊ)
a tomato
番茄醬(ㄈㄢ ㄑㄧㄝˊ ㄐㄧㄤˋ)
tomato ketchup
番茄汁(ㄈㄢ ㄑㄧㄝˊ ㄓ)
tomato juice
番休(ㄈㄢ ㄒㄧㄡ)
to take a leave by turns 亦作「輪休」
番石榴(ㄈㄢ ㄕˊ ˙ㄌㄧㄡ)
a guava
番薯(ㄈㄢ ㄕㄨˇ)
a sweet potato
番戍(ㄈㄢ ㄕㄨˋ)
to keep watch by turns
番人(ㄈㄢ ㄖㄣˊ)
aborigines; savages; barbarians
番子(ㄈㄢ ˙ㄗ)
a barbarian—a foreigner; an alien
番菜(ㄈㄢ ㄘㄞˋ)
western-style meals
番銀(ㄈㄢ ㄧㄣˊ)
Mexican silver dollars
番語(ㄈㄢ ㄩˇ)
foreign languages

【番】 3575
2. ㄆㄢ pan pān
1. a county in Kwangtung
2. a Chinese family name
番禺(ㄆㄢ ㄩˊ)
a county in Kwangtung (廣東)

【番】 3575
3. ㄅㄛ bo bō
martial-like

【畬】 3576
ㄩˊ yu yú
land cultivated for two or three years

【畬】 3577
ㄕㄜ she shē
1. name of a backward people in southern China
2. to cultivate land by first setting fire to it
畬蠻(ㄕㄜ ㄇㄢˊ)
name of a backward people in southern China

【畫】 3578
ㄏㄨㄚˋ huah huà
1. to paint or draw (a picture); a painting; a drawing: 牆上有幅畫。There's a painting on the wall.
2. to mark off; to delimit
3. to plan; to design; a plan
4. a stroke in a Chinese character
畫報(ㄏㄨㄚˋ ㄅㄠˋ)
a pictorial
畫板(ㄏㄨㄚˋ ㄅㄢˇ)
a drawing board; a drafting board
畫筆(ㄏㄨㄚˋ ㄅㄧˇ)
a painting brush
畫壁(ㄏㄨㄚˋ ㄅㄧˋ)
a wall with murals
畫餅(ㄏㄨㄚˋ ㄅㄧㄥˇ)
pie in the sky; illusion
畫餅充飢(ㄏㄨㄚˋ ㄅㄧㄥˇ ㄔㄨㄥ ㄐㄧ)
(literally) to try to satisfy hunger by drawing cakes—to value empty names; empty solace
畫布(ㄏㄨㄚˋ ㄅㄨˋ)
a canvas (for painting)
畫癖(ㄏㄨㄚˋ ㄆㄧˇ)
a craze for painting
畫片兒(ㄏㄨㄚˋ ㄆㄧㄚˋㄦ)
printed pictures; picture postcards
畫品(ㄏㄨㄚˋ ㄆㄧㄣˇ)
the grade of paintings
畫屏(ㄏㄨㄚˋ ㄆㄧㄥˊ)
a screen decorated with paintings
畫譜(ㄏㄨㄚˋ ㄆㄨˇ)
① a picture copybook ② commentaries on painting
畫眉(ㄏㄨㄚˋ ㄇㄟˊ)
① to blacken eyebrows ② the thrush
畫眉鳥(ㄏㄨㄚˋ ㄇㄟˊ ㄋㄧㄠˇ)
the thrush
畫卯(ㄏㄨㄚˋ ㄇㄠˇ)
(said of officials in former times) to report for work early in the morning
畫面(ㄏㄨㄚˋ ㄇㄧㄢˋ)
① the full length and breadth of a picture ② (geometry) a picture plane
畫法(ㄏㄨㄚˋ ㄈㄚˇ)
a method of painting or drawing
畫分 or 劃分(ㄏㄨㄚˋ ㄈㄣ)
to mark off; to divide; to demarcate
畫舫(ㄏㄨㄚˋ ㄈㄤˇ)
a pleasure boat decorated with pictures and elaborate wood lacework
畫符(ㄏㄨㄚˋ ㄈㄨˊ)
(said of Taoist priests) to draw spells or charms
畫符念咒(ㄏㄨㄚˋ ㄈㄨˊ ㄋㄧㄢˋ ㄓㄡˋ)
(said of Taoist priests) to draw spells and mumble incantations
畫到(ㄏㄨㄚˋ ㄉㄠˋ)
(said of an employee) to sign one's name in the roll when reporting for work in the morning; to clock in
畫荻教子(ㄏㄨㄚˋ ㄉㄧˊ ㄐㄧㄠˋ ㄗˇ)
(literally) to teach the child by drawing characters on the ground with a reed (the story is about the mother of Ou-Yang Hsiu (歐陽修))—to teach one's children with great maternal patience
畫地自限(ㄏㄨㄚˋ ㄉㄧˋ ㄗˋ ㄒㄧㄢˋ)
to try to limit oneself; to impose restrictions on oneself
畫地爲牢(ㄏㄨㄚˋ ㄉㄧˋ ㄨㄟˊ ㄌㄠˊ)
to draw a circle on the ground to serve as a prison
畫棟雕梁(ㄏㄨㄚˋ ㄉㄨㄥˋ ㄉㄧㄠ ㄌㄧㄤˊ)
(said of ornate buildings) painted rafters and carved beams
畫堂(ㄏㄨㄚˋ ㄊㄤˊ)
a beautifully decorated room or house
畫帖(ㄏㄨㄚˋ ㄊㄧㄝˋ)
a copybook for art students
畫圖(ㄏㄨㄚˋ ㄊㄨˊ)
① to paint pictures; to draw pictures ② a picture; a painting; a drawing
畫圖器(ㄏㄨㄚˋ ㄊㄨˊ ㄑㄧˋ)

drawing instruments

畫諾(ㄏㄨㄚˋ ㄋㄨㄛˋ)
to sign one's name to express consent; to endorse a document

畫廊(ㄏㄨㄚˋ ㄌㄤˊ)
a gallery (for paintings)

畫龍點睛(ㄏㄨㄚˋ ㄌㄨㄥˊ ㄉㄧㄢˇ ㄐㄧㄥ)
(literally) to add eyeballs to the picture of a dragon—to enliven the whole composition by the skillful use of a couple of sentences; to add the punch line; to add the finishing touch

畫稿(ㄏㄨㄚˋ ㄍㄠˇ)
① drafts for paintings or drawings: 他正在做畫稿。He's making a draft for his painting. ② to endorse the draft of a document

畫工(ㄏㄨㄚˋ ㄍㄨㄥ)
a painter (in the sense of a craftsman as distinct from an accomplished artist)

畫供(ㄏㄨㄚˋ ㄍㄨㄥˋ)
to sign a written confession to a crime by the accused

畫刊(ㄏㄨㄚˋ ㄎㄢ)
a pictorial magazine

畫框(ㄏㄨㄚˋ ㄎㄨㄤ)
a picture frame

畫虎類狗(ㄏㄨㄚˋ ㄏㄨˇ ㄌㄟˋ ㄍㄡˇ)
(literally) to try to draw a tiger and end up with a dog—to fail because of undue ambition

畫畫兒(ㄏㄨㄚˋ ㄏㄨㄚˋㄦ)
to paint pictures; to draw pictures: 他的孩子會畫畫兒。His child can paint pictures.

畫戟(ㄏㄨㄚˋ ㄐㄧˇ)
a halberd decorated with pictures

畫家(ㄏㄨㄚˋ ㄐㄧㄚ)
a painter; an artist

畫架(ㄏㄨㄚˋ ㄐㄧㄚˋ)
an easel

畫界(ㄏㄨㄚˋ ㄐㄧㄝˋ)
to delimit; to mark boundaries; to demarcate

畫匠(ㄏㄨㄚˋ ㄐㄧㄤˋ)
a painter (in the sense of a craftsman as distinct from an artist) 參看「畫工」

畫境(ㄏㄨㄚˋ ㄐㄧㄥˋ)
the world created by the painter

畫具(ㄏㄨㄚˋ ㄐㄩˋ)
articles used for painting; painting tools

畫像(ㄏㄨㄚˋ ㄒㄧㄤˋ)
① to paint a portrait ② a portrait ③ a portrayal in words

畫行(ㄏㄨㄚˋ ㄒㄧㄥˊ)
to write down the character 行 on a document to show one's approval

畫學(ㄏㄨㄚˋ ㄒㄩㄝˊ)
① a painting school; an art school ② the art of painting

畫展(ㄏㄨㄚˋ ㄓㄢˇ)
an art exhibition; a painting exhibition

畫中有詩(ㄏㄨㄚˋ ㄓㄨㄥ ㄧㄡˇ ㄕ)
There is poetry in a painting.

畫師(ㄏㄨㄚˋ ㄕ)
a painter; an artist

畫史(ㄏㄨㄚˋ ㄕˇ)
a book by Mi Fei (米芾) of the Sung Dynasty commenting on the authenticity of well-known paintings

畫室(ㄏㄨㄚˋ ㄕˋ)
an artist's studio

畫蛇添足(ㄏㄨㄚˋ ㄕㄜˊ ㄊㄧㄢ ㄗㄨˊ)
(literally) to add feet to a snake while painting it—to make undesirable additions; superfluous

畫聖(ㄏㄨㄚˋ ㄕㄥˋ)
the Divine Master of Painting, the title accorded by posterity to the Tang Dynasty painter Wu Tao-tzu (吳道子)

畫册(ㄏㄨㄚˋ ㄘㄜˋ)
a picture or painting album

畫策(ㄏㄨㄚˋ ㄘㄜˋ)
to plan; to scheme

畫兒(ㄏㄨㄚˋㄦ)
a painting; a drawing: 這是一張好畫兒。This is a good drawing.

畫一 or 劃一(ㄏㄨㄚˋ ㄧ)
① uniform ② to make uniform

畫一組織 or 劃一組織(ㄏㄨㄚˋ ㄧ ㄗㄨˇ ㄓ)
to have a uniform organization

畫意(ㄏㄨㄚˋ ㄧˋ)
the mood of a painting

畫押(ㄏㄨㄚˋ ㄧㄚ)
to sign a contract or agreement

畫頁(ㄏㄨㄚˋ ㄧㄝˋ)
a picture sheet; a picture page

畫影圖形(ㄏㄨㄚˋ ㄧㄥˇ ㄊㄨˊ ㄒㄧㄥˊ)
to draw the likenesses of a criminal at large for posting in various places

【畯】 3579 ㄐㄩㄣˋ jiunn jùn

1. the official in charge of farmland in ancient times
2. rustic; crude

八畫

【畹】 3580 ㄨㄢˇ woan wǎn

a measure of land equaling 12 or 30 *mu* (畝)

【畸】 3581 ㄐㄧ ji jī

1. fields with irregular boundaries
2. malformed; misshapen; deformity
3. fractional remainders

畸態(ㄐㄧ ㄊㄞˋ)
abnormality; oddity

畸零(ㄐㄧ ㄌㄧㄥˊ)
① fractional remainders ② a solitary person; a lonely person

畸角子(ㄐㄧ ㄐㄧㄠˇ ·ㄗ) or 畸角兒(ㄐㄧ ㄐㄧㄠˇㄦ)
a corner

畸輕畸重(ㄐㄧ ㄑㄧㄥ ㄐㄧ ㄓㄨㄥˋ)
to place either too little or too great emphasis on a matter; to attach too much weight to this and too little weight to that

畸形(ㄐㄧ ㄒㄧㄥˊ)
malformation; deformity; abnormality; abnormal; deformed

畸形發展(ㄐㄧ ㄒㄧㄥˊ ㄈㄚ ㄓㄢˇ)
abnormal development

畸人(ㄐㄧ ㄖㄣˊ)
an odd person; an idiosyncratic person

【當】 3582 1. ㄉㄤ dang dāng

1. to undertake or assume (responsibilities, etc.); to

accept
2. to face: 他當著我的面扯了個謊。He told me a lie to my face.
3. equal; well-matched: 我們實力相當。We are well-matched in strength.
4. the very same (place, year, day, etc.)
5. ought to; should; must: 你當遵守諾言。You should keep your promise.
6. just at (a time or a place)
7. to work as; to serve as

當班(ㄉㄤ ㄅㄢ)
to be on duty by turns

當兵(ㄉㄤ ㄅㄧㄥ)
to serve in the army; to be a soldier

當兵的(ㄉㄤ ㄅㄧㄥ ˙ㄉㄜ)
a soldier; a serviceman

當不起(ㄉㄤ ˙ㄅㄨ ㄑㄧˇ)
unequal to (a responsibility, honor, etc.); dare not accept: 我可當不起這樣的獎賞。I just don't deserve such a prize.

當面(ㄉㄤ ㄇㄧㄢˋ)
right in one's face; right in one's presence; face to face: 他當面說好話，背後中傷我。He says nice things to my face, then stabs me in the back.

當面鑼對面鼓(ㄉㄤ ㄇㄧㄢˋ ㄌㄨㄛˊ ㄉㄨㄟˋ ㄇㄧㄢˋ ㄍㄨˇ)
right in one's face; in one's presence

當面言明(ㄉㄤ ㄇㄧㄢˋ ㄧㄢˊ ㄇㄧㄥˊ)
to state clearly in one's presence

當番(ㄉㄤ ㄈㄢ)
to do a duty by turns; to be on duty

當代(ㄉㄤ ㄉㄞˋ)
in the present age

當道(ㄉㄤ ㄉㄠˋ)
① men holding the reins of government; to be in power ② to block one's way

當地(ㄉㄤ ㄉㄧˋ)
this place; local

當斷不斷(ㄉㄤ ㄉㄨㄢˋ ㄅㄨˊ ㄉㄨㄢˋ)
to be indecisive when decision is needed

當頭(ㄉㄤ ㄊㄡˊ)
① right overhead; right on somebody's head; head-on ② to face with (difficulties, etc.); imminent

當頭棒喝(ㄉㄤ ㄊㄡˊ ㄅㄤˋ ㄏㄜˋ)
① to arouse a person from stupidity by drastic means ② to give an aggressor a stunning blow at the start

當頭人(ㄉㄤ ㄊㄡˊ ㄖㄣˊ)
husband (used by wives in speaking of their husbands)

當天(ㄉㄤ ㄊㄧㄢ)
on the same day; on that very day: 這事必須當天做完。The work must be done on the very day.

當年(ㄉㄤ ㄋㄧㄢˊ)
① that year; the year in question ② bygone years; in those days: 她的美貌不減當年。She is as beautiful as ever.

當量(ㄉㄤ ㄌㄧㄤˋ)
(chemistry) equivalent

當令(ㄉㄤ ㄌㄧㄥˋ)
seasonable; fashionable

當盧 or 當壚(ㄉㄤ ㄌㄨˊ)
to sell alcoholic drinks

當爐(ㄉㄤ ㄌㄨˊ)
to sit before a fire

當路(ㄉㄤ ㄌㄨˋ)
① people holding the reins of government ② to obstruct one's way

當國(ㄉㄤ ㄍㄨㄛˊ)
to hold the reins of government; to rule the country

當歸(ㄉㄤ ㄍㄨㄟ)
ligusticum, or levisticum, whose root is used as medicine

當歸鴨(ㄉㄤ ㄍㄨㄟ ㄧㄚ)
a dish of duck seasoned with ligusticum

當官(ㄉㄤ ㄍㄨㄢ)
① to fill an office; to be an official: 他已不當官了。He is no longer in office. ② in the presence of an official

當關(ㄉㄤ ㄍㄨㄢ)
① to guard a pass or checkpoint ② a doorkeeper

當口(ㄉㄤ ㄎㄡˇ)
the critical moment; the crucial point

當行出色(ㄉㄤ ㄏㄤˊ ㄔㄨ ㄙㄜˋ)
excellent and opportune; to be an expert; to be in one's element

當機立斷(ㄉㄤ ㄐㄧ ㄌㄧˋ ㄉㄨㄢˋ)
to make quick decisions in the face of problems

當即(ㄉㄤ ㄐㄧˊ)
immediately; with dispatch; promptly; right away: 我當即表示贊同。I gave my approval immediately.

當家(ㄉㄤ ㄐㄧㄚ)
to housekeep; to manage household affairs; to be the master of a family, an organization, etc.

當家的(ㄉㄤ ㄐㄧㄚ ˙ㄉㄜ)
① my husband ② a housekeeper ③ the head monk of a temple

當間兒(ㄉㄤ ㄐㄧㄚˋㄦ)
in the middle

當街(ㄉㄤ ㄐㄧㄝ)
in the street: 他當街行乞。He begs in the street.

當今(ㄉㄤ ㄐㄧㄣ)
① the present time; today ② the reigning emperor

當局(ㄉㄤ ㄐㄩˊ)
the authorities

當局者迷，旁觀者清(ㄉㄤ ㄐㄩˊ ㄓㄜˇ ㄇㄧˊ, ㄆㄤˊ ㄍㄨㄢ ㄓㄜˇ ㄑㄧㄥ)
The onlooker sees the game more clearly than the players. 或 Those who are involved cannot see things as clearly as outsiders do.

當前(ㄉㄤ ㄑㄧㄢˊ)
① before one; facing one ② present; current

當權(ㄉㄤ ㄑㄩㄢˊ)
to exercise authority; to be in power

當下(ㄉㄤ ㄒㄧㄚˋ)
presently; immediately

當先(ㄉㄤ ㄒㄧㄢ)
① to be in the front ② formerly; previously

當心(ㄉㄤ ㄒㄧㄣ)
to be careful; to be cautious; to take care: 當心不要打破雞蛋。Be careful not to break the eggs.

當心扒手(ㄉㄤ ㄒㄧㄣ ㄆㄚˊ ㄕㄡˇ)
Watch out for pickpockets! 或 Beware of pickpockets!

當心火車(ㄉㄤ ㄒㄧㄣ ㄏㄨㄛˇ ㄔㄜ)
Beware of trains!

當選(ㄉㄤ ㄒㄩㄢˇ)
to get elected; to be elected;

〔田部〕

to win an election: 他當選爲主席。He was elected chairman.
當選證書(ㄉㄤ ㄒㄩㄢˇ ㄓㄥˋ ㄕㄨ)
certificates issued to the successful candidates of an election
當選人(ㄉㄤ ㄒㄩㄢˇ ㄖㄣˊ)
as in 總統當選人 (the president-elect)
當之無愧(ㄉㄤ ㄓ ㄨˊ ㄎㄨㄟˋ)
fully deserve (a title, an honor, etc.); to be worthy of: 英雄的稱號，他當之無愧。He fully deserves the title of a hero.
當值(ㄉㄤ ㄓˊ)
to take one's turn on duty; to be on duty by turns
當中(ㄉㄤ ㄓㄨㄥ)
right in the middle
當衆(ㄉㄤ ㄓㄨㄥˋ)
in the presence of all
當衆宣佈(ㄉㄤ ㄓㄨㄥˋ ㄒㄩㄢ ㄅㄨˋ)
to announce before a crowd; to announce publicly
當差(ㄉㄤ ㄔㄞ)
to do a duty; to be on duty
當差的(ㄉㄤ ㄔㄞ ·ㄉㄜ)
① a servant ② a government employee
當朝(ㄉㄤ ㄔㄠˊ)
① during the present reign ② the present emperor
當娼(ㄉㄤ ㄔㄤ)
to be a prostitute
當場(ㄉㄤ ㄔㄤˇ)or(ㄉㄤ ㄔㄤˊ)
on the spot; then and there: 我當場拒絕了他們的幫助。I turned down their help on the spot.
當場交貨(ㄉㄤ ㄔㄤˇ ㄐㄧㄠ ㄏㄨㄛˋ)or(ㄉㄤ ㄔㄤˊ ㄐㄧㄠ ㄏㄨㄛˋ)
delivery on the spot upon payment
當場出醜(ㄉㄤ ㄔㄤˇ ㄔㄨ ㄔㄡˇ)or(ㄉㄤ ㄔㄤˊ ㄔㄨ ㄔㄡˇ)
to suffer embarrassment right before a crowd
當初(ㄉㄤ ㄔㄨ)
at first; in the beginning
當時(ㄉㄤ ㄕˊ)
① at that time; then; in those days ② at the very moment; immediately
當世(ㄉㄤ ㄕˋ)
① the present age; the present time ② to be a ruler
當事(ㄉㄤ ㄕˋ)
① to deal with a matter; to take charge of a matter ② the authorities
當事者(ㄉㄤ ㄕˋ ㄓㄜˇ)or 當事人(ㄉㄤ ㄕˋ ㄖㄣˊ)
the party concerned; those directly involved
當日(ㄉㄤ ㄖˋ)
on the same day; on that very day: 此文件當日有效。This document is valid on the same day.
當然(ㄉㄤ ㄖㄢˊ)
① of course; naturally ② as it should be; only natural: 那是理所當然。That is just as it should be.
當然委員(ㄉㄤ ㄖㄢˊ ㄨㄟˇ ㄩㄢˊ)
an ex-officio member of a committee, council or commission
當仁不讓(ㄉㄤ ㄖㄣˊ ㄅㄨˋ ㄖㄤˋ)
① to yield to nobody when one is doing what is right ② do not refuse to accept a reward or position which one deserves ③ to be behind none in the desire to benefit mankind
當夜(ㄉㄤ ㄧㄝˋ)
on the same night; on that very night
當陽(ㄉㄤ ㄧㄤˊ)
①(literally) to face the sun or the south—to rule ② a county in Hupeh
當午(ㄉㄤ ㄨˇ)
noon; noontide; midday
當務之急(ㄉㄤ ㄨˋ ㄓ ㄐㄧˊ)
a business or task of the greatest urgency at present
當晚(ㄉㄤ ㄨㄢˇ)
on the same night; on that very night

【當】 3582
2. ㄉㄤˋ danq dàng
1. proper; appropriate
2. to pawn; to mortgage; to pledge
3. to take as; to regard as; to consider as
當票(ㄉㄤˋ ㄆㄧㄠˋ)
a pawn ticket
當鋪(ㄉㄤˋ ·ㄆㄨ)
a pawnbroker's shop; a pawnshop
當當(ㄉㄤˋ ㄉㄤˋ)
to pawn something at a pawnshop
當頭(ㄉㄤˋ ·ㄊㄡ)
something pawned; a pledge
當眞(ㄉㄤˋ ㄓㄣ)
① true; real; really: 這話當眞? Is it really true? ② to be serious; no joking
當作 or 當做(ㄉㄤˋ ㄗㄨㄛˋ)
to regard as; to treat as
當耳邊風(ㄉㄤˋ ㄦˇ ㄅㄧㄢ ㄈㄥ)
(literally) to regard as nothing but a wind blowing past the ear—to take no serious heed to (advice, etc.)
當押(ㄉㄤˋ ㄧㄚ)
to pawn; to mortgage

【當】 3582
3. ㄉㄤˇ daang dǎng
to mistake something for another
當是(ㄉㄤˇ ㄕˋ)
to mistake something for another; to think that...: 我把她當是她的姐姐。I mistook her for her sister.

十畫

【畿】 3583
ㄐㄧ ji jī
(又讀 ㄑㄧˊ chyi qí)
areas near the capital; the royal domain
畿輔(ㄐㄧ ㄈㄨˇ)or 畿甸(ㄐㄧ ㄉㄧㄢˋ)
areas near the capital
畿輦(ㄐㄧ ㄋㄧㄢˇ)
the capital

十四畫

【疆】 3584
ㄐㄧㄤ jiang jiāng
1. the boundary; the border; the frontier
2. a limit
疆土(ㄐㄧㄤ ㄊㄨˇ)
territory
疆吏(ㄐㄧㄤ ㄌㄧˋ)
a frontier official
疆界(ㄐㄧㄤ ㄐㄧㄝˋ)
borders; frontiers
疆徼(ㄐㄧㄤ ㄐㄧㄠˋ)
frontiers; borders

疆場(ㄐㄧㄤ ㄔㄤˊ)
a battlefield: 他戰死疆場。He died on the battlefield.

疆埸(ㄐㄧㄤ ㄧˋ)
① national borders ② field borders

疆域(ㄐㄧㄤ ㄩˋ)
territory

【疇】 3585 ㄔㄡˊ chour chóu

1. agricultural land; fields
2. who
3. formerly; previously
4. a class; a category; a rank

疇輩(ㄔㄡˊ ㄅㄟˋ)
people of the same generation or position

疇類(ㄔㄡˊ ㄌㄟˋ)
of the same class or category

疇昔(ㄔㄡˊ ㄒㄧˊ)
formerly; previously; in the past; yesterday

疇日(ㄔㄡˊ ㄖˋ)
in the past; in former times

疇人(ㄔㄡˊ ㄖㄣˊ)
an astrologist

十七畫

【疊】 3586 (曡) ㄉㄧㄝˊ dye dié

1. to fold up
2. to pile up
3. to repeat; to duplicate
4. a stack of (bank notes)

疊羅漢(ㄉㄧㄝˊ ㄌㄨㄛˊ ㄏㄢˋ)
(sports) pyramid

疊騎(ㄉㄧㄝˊ ㄐㄧˋ)
to ride side by side

疊句(ㄉㄧㄝˊ ㄐㄩˋ)
a refrain

疊起(ㄉㄧㄝˊ ㄑㄧˇ)
① to fold up: 百葉窗可以疊起來。The window shutters fold back. ② to pile up

疊置法(ㄉㄧㄝˊ ㄓˋ ㄈㄚˇ)
(mathematics) superposition

疊嶂(ㄉㄧㄝˊ ㄓㄤˋ)
rows of peaks

疊牀架屋(ㄉㄧㄝˊ ㄔㄨㄤˊ ㄐㄧㄚˋ ㄨ)
to be repetitious; redundant; overlapping

疊字(ㄉㄧㄝˊ ㄗˋ)
(linguistics) reiterative locution; reduplication

疊韻(ㄉㄧㄝˊ ㄩㄣˋ)
① two words of the same rhyme ② to repeat a rhyme

疋部
ㄆㄧˇ pii pǐ

【疋】 3587 ㄆㄧˇ pii pǐ

a roll (of cloth); a bolt (of cloth)

疋頭(ㄆㄧˇ ㄊㄡˊ)
cloth; fabrics; piece goods

疋練(ㄆㄧˇ ㄌㄧㄢˋ)
a cascade

六畫

【疏】 3588 (疎, 或疏, 七畫) 1. ㄕㄨ shu shū

1. thin; sparse; few: 那老人有疏疏的幾根鬍子。That old man has a sparse beard.
2. unfamiliar; distant; unfriendly: 他們在台北人地生疏。They are unfamiliar with Taipei and its people.
3. careless; neglectful: 他疏忽了他的健康。He neglected his health.
4. to channel; to remove obstructions
5. coarse

疏布(ㄕㄨ ㄅㄨˋ)
coarse cloth

疏慢(ㄕㄨ ㄇㄢˋ)
to neglect inadvertently

疏密(ㄕㄨ ㄇㄧˋ)
① looseness and density ② neglect and watchfulness

疏防(ㄕㄨ ㄈㄤˊ)or 疏於防範(ㄕㄨ ㄩˊ ㄈㄤˊ ㄈㄢˋ)
to fail to take precautions; to be neglectful of necessary precautions

疏放(ㄕㄨ ㄈㄤˋ)
careless; lax; loose

疏導(ㄕㄨ ㄉㄠˇ)or(ㄕㄨ ㄉㄠˋ)
① to channel ② to enlighten

疏宕(ㄕㄨ ㄉㄤˋ)
open-minded; carefree; free and easy

疏通(ㄕㄨ ㄊㄨㄥ)
① to clean or dredge (a waterway) ② to improve (relations, etc.); to bring about an understanding or reconciliation; to bridge different views

疏漏(ㄕㄨ ㄌㄡˋ)
careless omissions; slips; oversights

疏懶(ㄕㄨ ㄌㄢˇ)
idle; lazy; loose; lax: 他是一個疏懶的人。He is an idle fellow.

疏朗(ㄕㄨ ㄌㄤˇ)
clear

疏理(ㄕㄨ ㄌㄧˇ)
① to dredge and improve (a waterway) ② to put (matters) in order

疏落(ㄕㄨ ㄌㄨㄛˋ)or 疏疏落落(ㄕㄨ ㄕㄨ ㄌㄨㄛˋ ㄌㄨㄛˋ)
sparse; few

疏略(ㄕㄨ ㄌㄩㄝˋ)
to neglect inadvertently

疏闊(ㄕㄨ ㄎㄨㄛˋ)
① lacking precision; inaccurate; rough ②(said of relations) distant; cold; to estrange; to alienate

疏狂(ㄕㄨ ㄎㄨㄤˊ)
unrestrained; uninhibited

疏忽(ㄕㄨ ㄏㄨ)
carelessness; careless; inadvertent; remiss; negligent; oversight; to neglect: 他一時疏忽，弄錯了。He made the mistake through an oversight.

疏濬(ㄕㄨ ㄐㄩㄣˋ)
to clean or dredge (waterways): 港口正在疏濬中。The harbor is being dredged.

疏懈(ㄕㄨ ㄒㄧㄝˋ)
negligent; neglectful; idle; lazy

疏星(ㄕㄨ ㄒㄧㄥ)
sparse stars

疏失(ㄕㄨ ㄕ)
remiss; at fault; negligent; negligence

疏食(ㄕㄨ ㄕˊ)
coarse meal

疏神(ㄕㄨ ㄕㄣˊ)
careless; inadvertent; inadvertence: 他的錯誤只是一時疏神。His error was a mere inadvertence.

疏率(ㄕㄨ ㄕㄨㄞˋ)

careless and rash; heedless
疏財仗義(ㄕㄨ ㄘㄞˊ ㄓㄤˋ ㄧˋ)
to give generously and be a champion of justice; generous and ready to extend a helping hand
疏散(ㄕㄨ ㄙㄢˋ)
to disperse; dispersion
疏鬆(ㄕㄨ ㄙㄨㄥ)
① loose: 土質疏鬆。The soil is loose. ② to loosen ③ puffy
疏而不漏(ㄕㄨ ㄦˊ ㄅㄨˋ ㄌㄡˋ)
(said of the meshes of justice) to be loose but never miss
疏野(ㄕㄨ ㄧㄝˇ)
rude; impolite
疏影(ㄕㄨ ㄧㄥˇ)
scattered shadows as of plum blossoms
疏於職守(ㄕㄨ ㄩˊ ㄓˊ ㄕㄡˇ)
to neglect one's duty
疏瀹(ㄕㄨ ㄩㄝˋ)
to clean or dredge (waterways)
疏遠(ㄕㄨ ㄩㄢˇ) or 疏逖(ㄕㄨ ㄊㄧˋ)
(said of relations) not close; cold; to make a stranger of; to alienate or estrange: 爭吵使他與其家人疏遠。A quarrel had estranged him from his family.

【疏】 3588
2. ㄕㄨˋ shuh shù
1. to present point by point
2. to explicate; to annotate

九畫

【疑】 3589
ㄧˊ yi yí
1. doubtful; dubious; skeptical; doubt; to doubt; to question
2. suspicious; to suspect
3. strange; incomprehensible; mysterious; questionable
4. sham; dummy; false
疑謗(ㄧˊ ㄅㄤˋ)
suspected and slandered
疑兵(ㄧˊ ㄅㄧㄥ)
troops deployed to mislead the enemy
疑犯(ㄧˊ ㄈㄢˋ)
a criminal suspect
疑竇(ㄧˊ ㄉㄡˋ)
suspicion; doubt: 此事啓人疑竇。This matter aroused our suspicion.
疑點(ㄧˊ ㄉㄧㄢˇ)
① a doubtful or questionable point ② a suspicious point
疑團(ㄧˊ ㄊㄨㄢˊ)
clogging suspicions; a maze of suspicions: 他滿腹疑團。He was full of doubts and suspicions.
疑團冰釋(ㄧˊ ㄊㄨㄢˊ ㄅㄧㄥ ㄕˋ)
The suspicions have dissolved completely.
疑難(ㄧˊ ㄋㄢˊ)
a question; a problem; a puzzle; things one cannot understand or problems one cannot solve; uncertainty
疑慮(ㄧˊ ㄌㄩˋ)
apprehension; anxiety; misgivings; to misgive: 他覺得疑慮不安。His mind misgave him.
疑古(ㄧˊ ㄍㄨˇ)
to be skeptical of antiquity
疑惑(ㄧˊ ㄏㄨㄛˋ)
① to doubt ② to suspect ③ to puzzle
疑忌(ㄧˊ ㄐㄧˋ)
suspicious and jealous
疑懼(ㄧˊ ㄐㄩˋ)
suspicious and fearful
疑心(ㄧˊ ㄒㄧㄣ)
① to doubt ② suspicion: 我對他起疑心。I have a feeling of suspicion about him.
疑心病(ㄧˊ ㄒㄧㄣ ㄅㄧㄥˋ)
① hypochondria ② skepticism
疑心生暗鬼(ㄧˊ ㄒㄧㄣ ㄕㄥ ㄢˋ ㄍㄨㄟˇ)
A suspicious heart will see imaginary ghosts. 或 Suspicions create imaginary fears.
疑信參半(ㄧˊ ㄒㄧㄣˋ ㄘㄢ ㄅㄢˋ)
half in belief and half in doubt; do not believe entirely
疑兇(ㄧˊ ㄒㄩㄥ)
a suspected murderer or assailant: 警察逮捕了疑兇。The police have arrested this suspected murderer.
疑塚(ㄧˊ ㄓㄨㄥˇ)
false graves (for distracting the attention of body snatchers or tomb sackers)
疑城(ㄧˊ ㄔㄥˊ)
sham castles (for deceiving the enemy)
疑神疑鬼(ㄧˊ ㄕㄣˊ ㄧˊ ㄍㄨㄟˇ)
to have unnecessary suspicions; to be even afraid of one's own shadow: 他終日疑神疑鬼的。He was even afraid of his own shadow all day.
疑則勿用，用則勿疑(ㄧˊ ㄗㄜˊ ㄨˋ ㄩㄥˋ, ㄩㄥˋ ㄗㄜˊ ㄨˋ ㄧˊ)
Do not employ a person one distrusts, but one must trust the person one employs.
疑猜(ㄧˊ ㄘㄞ)
to suspect; to guess; to conjecture
疑似(ㄧˊ ㄙˋ)
could be; suspected to be
疑案(ㄧˊ ㄢˋ)
an unsettled case; an uncertain case; a puzzling case
疑貳(ㄧˊ ㄦˋ)
to become double-minded because of suspicion
疑義(ㄧˊ ㄧˋ)
dubious interpretation
疑問(ㄧˊ ㄨㄣˋ)
a question; doubt; uncertainty: 你有什麼疑問? Do you have any questions?
疑問代名詞(ㄧˊ ㄨㄣˋ ㄉㄞˋ ㄇㄧㄥˊ ㄘˊ)
interrogative pronouns
疑問號(ㄧˊ ㄨㄣˋ ㄏㄠˋ)
a question mark
疑問句(ㄧˊ ㄨㄣˋ ㄐㄩˋ)
an interrogative sentence
疑獄(ㄧˊ ㄩˋ)
an uncertain criminal case; a mysterious criminal case; a puzzling case
疑雲(ㄧˊ ㄩㄣˊ)
clouds of suspicion or misgivings (darkening one's mind): 疑雲頓刻消散。The misgivings were dispelled at once.

【疐】 3590
ㄓˋ jyh zhì
to suffer a fall; to fall; to trip; to stumble

疒部
ㄔㄨㄤ chwang chuáng

二畫

【疔】 3591 ㄉㄧㄥ ding dīng
a boil; a carbuncle
疔毒(ㄉㄧㄥ ㄉㄨˊ)
carbuncular infection
疔瘡(ㄉㄧㄥ ㄔㄨㄤ)
(pathology) a boil; a carbuncle; furuncle

三畫

【疙】 3592 ㄍㄜ ge gē
a wart; a pustule; a pimple
疙瘩(ㄍㄜ ˙ㄉㄚ)
①a wart; a pustule; a pimple ②a round lump; a knot (of rope, string, thread,etc.) ③a knot in one's heart; hang-up: 他的勸告解開了我心上的疙瘩。His advice got rid of my hang-up.
疙瘩兒湯(ㄍㄜ ˙ㄉㄚㄦ ㄊㄤ)
small round lumps of dough served with soup
疙裏疙瘩的(ㄍㄜ ˙ㄌㄧ ㄍㄜ ˙ㄉㄚ ˙ㄉㄜ)
①troublesome; not smooth ②faultfinding; hard to please
疙疙瘩瘩(ㄍㄜ ˙ㄍㄜ ㄉㄚ ㄉㄚ)
rough; bumpy

【疚】 3593 ㄐㄧㄡˋ jiow jiù
1. prolonged illness
2. mental discomfort
3. a guilty conscience
疚懷(ㄐㄧㄡˋ ㄏㄨㄞˊ)
ashamed
疚心(ㄐㄧㄡˋ ㄒㄧㄣ)
ashamed

【疝】 3594 ㄕㄢˋ shann shàn
hernia
疝痛(ㄕㄢˋ ㄊㄨㄥˋ)
colic
疝氣(ㄕㄢˋ ㄑㄧˋ)
hernia

四畫

【疤】 3595 ㄅㄚ ba bā
1. a scar
2. a birthmark
疤瘌(ㄅㄚ ˙ㄌㄚ)
①a scar ②a birthmark
疤瘌鬢(ㄅㄚ ˙ㄌㄚ ㄅㄧㄣˋ)
a birthmark at the temple (considered undesirable for a woman)
疤瘌眼(ㄅㄚ ˙ㄌㄚ ㄧㄢˇ)
a scarred eyelid
疤臉(ㄅㄚ ㄌㄧㄢˇ)
a scarred face
疤痕(ㄅㄚ ㄏㄣˊ)
a scar

【疥】 3596 ㄐㄧㄝˋ jieh jiè
scabies
疥癬(ㄐㄧㄝˋ ㄒㄩㄢˇ)
scabies; the itch; mange; ringworm
疥癬蟲(ㄐㄧㄝˋ ㄒㄩㄢˇ ㄔㄨㄥˊ)
a scab mite; an itch mite
疥瘡(ㄐㄧㄝˋ ㄔㄨㄤ)
sores from scabies

【疫】 3597 ㄧˋ yih yì
an epidemic; a plague; a pestilence
疫病傳染(ㄧˋ ㄅㄧㄥˋ ㄔㄨㄢˊ ㄖㄢˇ)
contagion
疫苗(ㄧˋ ㄇㄧㄠˊ)
vaccine
疫癘(ㄧˋ ㄌㄧˋ)
bubonic plague; a plague; pestilence
疫症(ㄧˋ ㄓㄥˋ)
an epidemic
疫症學(ㄧˋ ㄓㄥˋ ㄒㄩㄝˊ)
epidemiology

【疣】 3598 ㄧㄡˊ you yóu
a wart; a papule

五畫

【疲】 3599 ㄆㄧˊ pyi pí
weary; tired; fatigued; exhausted
疲憊(ㄆㄧˊ ㄅㄟˋ)
fatigued; tired; weary
疲憊不堪(ㄆㄧˊ ㄅㄟˋ ㄅㄨˋ ㄎㄢ)
extremely tired; about to collapse from exhaustion
疲敝(ㄆㄧˊ ㄅㄧˋ)
weak from exhaustion; weary and weak
疲乏(ㄆㄧˊ ㄈㄚˊ)
tired; weary; exhausted: 我太疲乏，不能再向前走了。I'm too tired to go any further.
疲鈍(ㄆㄧˊ ㄉㄨㄣˋ)
weary and slow; slothful from exhaustion
疲勞(ㄆㄧˊ ㄌㄠˊ)
fatigue; exhaustion; weariness: 他很疲勞。He suffered fatigue.
疲勞過度(ㄆㄧˊ ㄌㄠˊ ㄍㄨㄛˋ ㄉㄨˋ)
excessive fatigue
疲勞轟炸(ㄆㄧˊ ㄌㄠˊ ㄏㄨㄥ ㄓㄚˋ)
①harassing air raids ②a long and tedious harangue
疲倦(ㄆㄧˊ ㄐㄩㄢˋ)
weary; tired; fatigued
疲弱(ㄆㄧˊ ㄖㄨㄛˋ)
①weary and weak; weak from exhaustion ②(of commodities) to decrease in demand
疲軟(ㄆㄧˊ ㄖㄨㄢˇ)
①tired and feeble ②(of commodities) to decrease in demand ③(of finance) to weaken
疲玩(ㄆㄧˊ ㄨㄢˊ)
remiss; negligent; not alert
疲於奔命(ㄆㄧˊ ㄩˊ ㄅㄣ ㄇㄧㄥˋ)
tired from running around —wearied of coping with many problemes at the same time

【疳】 3600 ㄍㄢ gan gān
1. a kind of infantile disease caused by digestive trouble or malnutrition
2. a kind of infectious venereal disease
疳積(ㄍㄢ ㄐㄧ)
an infantile disease caused by digestive trouble or malnutrition

【疸】 3601 ㄉㄢˇ daan dǎn
jaundice

【疴】 3602 (痾) ㄜ e ē
(又讀 ㄎㄜ ke kē)

sickness; disease

【疹】 3603
ㄓㄣˇ jeen zhěn
rashes

疹子(ㄓㄣˇ ·ㄗ)
measles; carbuncles

【疽】 3604
ㄐㄩ jiu jū
ulcer

【疼】 3605
ㄊㄥˊ terng téng

1. to ache; to hurt; pain; sore: 她的腿疼。She has a pain in the leg.
2. to dote on; to be fond of (a child)

疼痛(ㄊㄥˊ ㄊㄨㄥˋ)
to ache

疼熱(ㄊㄥˊ ㄖㄜˋ)
to suffer pain and fever

疼愛(ㄊㄥˊ ㄞˋ)
to be fond of (a child): 她非常疼愛她的小孩。She is very fond of her children.

【疾】 3606
ㄐㄧˊ jyi jí

1. disease; suffering: 疾病通常由病菌而起。Disease is usually caused by germs.
2. to hate; to detest
3. swift; rapid; quick; fast

疾病(ㄐㄧˊ ㄅㄧㄥˋ)
diseases: 醫生的職責爲預防和治療疾病。The business of doctors is to prevent and cure diseases.

疾風知勁草(ㄐㄧˊ ㄈㄥ ㄓ ㄐㄧㄥˋ ㄘㄠˇ)
(literally) Strong winds test the sturdiness of grass. —Adversity tests the character of a man.

疾雷(ㄐㄧˊ ㄌㄟˊ)
① a sudden clap of thunder ② a swift action

疾雷不及掩耳(ㄐㄧˊ ㄌㄟˊ ㄅㄨˋ ㄐㄧˊ ㄧㄢˇ ㄦˇ)
(literally) a clap of thunder so sudden that there is no time for covering one's ears —an action so swift that there is no time to prepare to meet it

疾苦(ㄐㄧˊ ㄎㄨˇ)
suffering (especially under an oppressive government)

疾呼(ㄐㄧˊ ㄏㄨ)
to call out loudly; to shout

疾駛(ㄐㄧˊ ㄕˇ) or 疾馳(ㄐㄧˊ ㄔˊ)
to move swiftly; to dart; to fleet; to drive very fast: 船乘風疾駛。The ship was driving very fast before the wind.

疾視(ㄐㄧˊ ㄕˋ)
to look at someone angrily

疾首(ㄐㄧˊ ㄕㄡˇ)
headache caused by rage

疾甚(ㄐㄧˊ ㄕㄣˋ)
to be seriously ill

疾走(ㄐㄧˊ ㄗㄡˇ)
to move or march swiftly; to walk quickly; to run

疾足先登(ㄐㄧˊ ㄗㄨˊ ㄒㄧㄢ ㄉㄥ)
He who has fast legs will get there first. 或 He who acts fast will succeed first. 亦作「捷足先登」

疾惡如仇(ㄐㄧˊ ㄜˋ ㄖㄨˊ ㄔㄡˊ)
to hate evil as much as one hates an enemy

疾言厲色(ㄐㄧˊ ㄧㄢˊ ㄌㄧˋ ㄙㄜˋ)
(literally) to speak fast with a harsh look—to lecture severely

疾言遽色(ㄐㄧˊ ㄧㄢˊ ㄐㄩˋ ㄙㄜˋ)
speaking hastily and looking flurried

【病】 3607
ㄅㄧㄥˋ binq bìng

1. illness; disease; ailment
2. to be ill
3. blemish; fault: 此不足爲病。It cannot be counted as a fault.
4. to injure; to harm
5. to worry
6. to hate
7. to insult

病包兒(ㄅㄧㄥˋ ㄅㄠㄦ)
a sickly person

病變(ㄅㄧㄥˋ ㄅㄧㄢˋ)
pathological changes

病魔(ㄅㄧㄥˋ ㄇㄛˊ)
the demon of ill health; the curse of disease

病沒 or 病歿(ㄅㄧㄥˋ ㄇㄛˋ)
to die of illness; to succumb to a disease

病發(ㄅㄧㄥˋ ㄈㄚ)
to fall ill

病廢(ㄅㄧㄥˋ ㄈㄟˋ)
to be disabled by disease

病房(ㄅㄧㄥˋ ㄈㄤˊ)
a sickroom; a ward: 醫生正在巡查病房。The doctor is visiting the ward.

病夫(ㄅㄧㄥˋ ㄈㄨ)
a man who is sick most of the time

病倒(ㄅㄧㄥˋ ㄉㄠˇ)
to fall ill; to be confined in bed due to illness: 他的妻子病倒了。His wife fell sick.

病毒(ㄅㄧㄥˋ ㄉㄨˊ)
viruses

病篤(ㄅㄧㄥˋ ㄉㄨˇ)
dying of illness: 這老人病篤。The old man was dying of illness.

病榻(ㄅㄧㄥˋ ㄊㄚˋ)
a sickbed 參看「病床」

病態(ㄅㄧㄥˋ ㄊㄞˋ)
morbid (or abnormal) state

病痛(ㄅㄧㄥˋ ㄊㄨㄥˋ)
slight illness; indisposition

病理學(ㄅㄧㄥˋ ㄌㄧˇ ㄒㄩㄝˊ)
pathology

病例(ㄅㄧㄥˋ ㄌㄧˋ)
number of cases of a particular disease

病歷(ㄅㄧㄥˋ ㄌㄧˋ)
case history; medical history (of a patient)

病根(ㄅㄧㄥˋ ㄍㄣ)
① cause of a disease; the origin of a disease ② the cause of trouble: 自私是他的病根。Selfishness is the cause of his trouble.

病根子(ㄅㄧㄥˋ ㄍㄣ ·ㄗ)
a constitutional disease; a chronic disease; an old complaint

病骨(ㄅㄧㄥˋ ㄍㄨˇ)
to get skinny due to a disease; to be emaciated from disease

病故(ㄅㄧㄥˋ ㄍㄨˋ)
to die of illness: 她父親病故於中風。Her father died of apoplexy.

病國病民(ㄅㄧㄥˋ ㄍㄨㄛˊ ㄅㄧㄥˋ ㄇㄧㄣˊ)
to injure both the state and the people

病況(ㄅㄧㄥˋ ㄎㄨㄤˋ)
the condition of a patient

病號(ㄅㄧㄥˋ ㄏㄠˋ)
a hospitalized patient who is numbered for easy identification

病後(ㄅㄧㄥˋ ㄏㄡˋ)
after an illness; during convalescence

病革(ㄅㄧㄥˋ ㄐㄧˊ)

about to die of an illness
病疾(ㄅㄧㄥˋ ㄐㄧˊ)
sickness; disease; illness
病急亂投醫(ㄅㄧㄥˋ ㄐㄧˊ ㄌㄨㄢˋ ㄊㄡˊ ㄧ)
to turn to any doctor or prescription one can find when critically ill—to try anything when in a desperate situation
病家(ㄅㄧㄥˋ ㄐㄧㄚ)
a patient
病假(ㄅㄧㄥˋ ㄐㄧㄚˋ)
sick leave: 她請病假。She asked for sick leave.
病劇(ㄅㄧㄥˋ ㄐㄩˋ)
seriously ill; far advanced in one's illness; in a critical condition
病菌(ㄅㄧㄥˋ ㄐㄩㄣˋ)
germs; bacteria; viruses: 這牛奶沒有病菌嗎? Is this milk free from germs?
病情(ㄅㄧㄥˋ ㄑㄧㄥˊ)
the condition of a patient: 這嬰兒的病情有好轉。The baby's condition took a favorable turn.
病軀(ㄅㄧㄥˋ ㄑㄩ)
a sick body
病徵(ㄅㄧㄥˋ ㄓㄥ)
symptoms of a disease
病症(ㄅㄧㄥˋ ㄓㄥˋ)
① a disease; an ailment ② symptoms of a disease
病狀(ㄅㄧㄥˋ ㄓㄨㄤˋ)
symptoms of a disease
病重(ㄅㄧㄥˋ ㄓㄨㄥˋ)
seriously ill; in a critical condition
病牀(ㄅㄧㄥˋ ㄔㄨㄤˊ)
a sickbed: 這所醫院有五百張病牀。The hospital has five hundred sickbeds.
病蟲害(ㄅㄧㄥˋ ㄔㄨㄥˊ ㄏㄞˋ)
blight
病室(ㄅㄧㄥˋ ㄕˋ)
a sickroom; a ward
病勢(ㄅㄧㄥˋ ㄕˋ)
the condition of a patient
病人(ㄅㄧㄥˋ ㄖㄣˊ)
a sick man; a patient
病入膏肓(ㄅㄧㄥˋ ㄖㄨˋ ㄍㄠ ㄏㄨㄤ)
so advanced in one's disease as to be past remedy
病容(ㄅㄧㄥˋ ㄖㄨㄥˊ)
a sickly look; an emaciated look
病從口入(ㄅㄧㄥˋ ㄘㄨㄥˊ ㄎㄡˇ ㄖㄨˋ)
Diseases enter by the mouth. (Therefore, one should be careful in his diet or eating habits.): 病從口入，禍從口出。Diseases enter by the mouth; misfortunes issue from it.
病死(ㄅㄧㄥˋ ㄙˇ)
to die of an illness
病因(ㄅㄧㄥˋ ㄧㄣ)
the cause of a disease; the origin of a disease
病危(ㄅㄧㄥˋ ㄨㄟˊ)
dying of an illness; about to die of an illness
病愈 or 病癒(ㄅㄧㄥˋ ㄩˋ)
to recover from illness; to get well
病原(ㄅㄧㄥˋ ㄩㄢˊ)
the cause of a disease; the origin of a disease
病原體(ㄅㄧㄥˋ ㄩㄢˊ ㄊㄧˇ)
viruses
病院(ㄅㄧㄥˋ ㄩㄢˋ)
a hospital: 他仍在精神病院裡。He is still in a mental hospital.

【症】 3608
ㄓㄥˋ jenq zhèng
1. disease; an ailment
2. symptoms or manifestations of a disease
症候(ㄓㄥˋ ㄏㄡˋ) or 症狀(ㄓㄥˋ ㄓㄨㄤˋ)
symptoms or manifestations of a disease

【痃】 3609
ㄒㄧㄢˊ shyan xián
(pathology) bubo

【痀】 3610
ㄐㄩ jiu jū
a hunchback; a humpback
痀僂(ㄐㄩ ㄌㄡˊ) or 痀瘻(ㄐㄩ ㄌㄡˋ)
hunchback; humpback

【痂】 3611
ㄐㄧㄚ jia jiā
scab over a sore

【疱】 3612
(皰) ㄆㄠˋ paw pào
acne
疱疹(ㄆㄠˋ ㄓㄣˇ)
① a bleb ② herpes

【痁】 3613
ㄉㄧㄢˋ diann diàn
chronic malaria

【痄】 3614
ㄓㄚˋ jah zhà
scrofulous swellings and sores
痄腮(ㄓㄚˋ ㄙㄞ)
mumps

【疵】 3615
ㄘ tsy cī
(又讀 ㄘˊ tsyr cí)
a defect; a flaw; a mistake
疵點(ㄘ ㄉㄧㄢˇ)
a flaw; a fault; a defect
疵癘(ㄘ ㄌㄧˋ)
① disease ② disaster
疵瑕(ㄘ ㄒㄧㄚˊ)
a fault; a mistake; an error

六畫

【恫】 3616
ㄊㄨㄥ tong tōng
aching; painful
恫瘝(ㄊㄨㄥ ㄍㄨㄢ)
suffering; disease
恫瘝在抱(ㄊㄨㄥ ㄍㄨㄢ ㄗㄞˋ ㄅㄠˋ)
to have a constant concern for the suffering of the people

【痍】 3617
ㄧˊ yi yí
a wound; a bruise; a sore

【痊】 3618
ㄑㄩㄢˊ chyuan quán
healed; cured; recovery
痊可(ㄑㄩㄢˊ ㄎㄜˇ)
to have been cured; to have recovered from illness
痊愈 or 痊癒(ㄑㄩㄢˊ ㄩˋ)
to have been cured; to have recovered from illness

【痏】 3619
ㄨㄟˇ woei wěi
a mark on the skin; a scar

【痕】 3620
ㄏㄣˊ hern hén
a mark; a scar; a trace: 他的面頰上有一道傷痕。He had a scar on his cheek.
痕跡(ㄏㄣˊ ㄐㄧ)
a trace: 露營者除去所有營火的痕跡。The campers removed all traces of their fire.

【痔】 3621
ㄓˋ jyh zhì
piles; hemorrhoids
痔漏 or 痔瘻(ㄓˋ ㄌㄡˋ)
an anal fistula
痔核(ㄓˋ ㄏㄜˊ)
blind piles

〔疒部〕

〔疒部〕

痔瘡(ㄓˋ ˙ㄔㄨㄤ)
piles; hemorrhoids

七畫

【痛】 3622 ㄊㄨㄥˋ tonq tòng
1. painful; aching
2. sorrowful; sad; bitter; poignant; bitterly
3. heartily; to one's heart's content

痛不欲生(ㄊㄨㄥˋ ˙ㄅㄨ ㄩˋ ㄕㄥ)
to grieve to the extent of wishing to die

痛罵(ㄊㄨㄥˋ ㄇㄚˋ)
to berate; to revile; to vituperate; to give a good dressing-down

痛風(ㄊㄨㄥˋ ㄈㄥ)
gout (a disease)

痛打(ㄊㄨㄥˋ ㄉㄚˇ)
to beat soundly; to give a severe thrashing

痛悼(ㄊㄨㄥˋ ㄉㄠˋ)
to grieve over the death of someone bitterly

痛詆(ㄊㄨㄥˋ ㄉㄧˇ)
to berate; to revile; to vituperate: 他痛詆他兒子。He berated his son.

痛定思痛(ㄊㄨㄥˋ ㄉㄧㄥˋ ㄙ ㄊㄨㄥˋ)
to recall the past with pangs in the heart; to feel pangs over a past defeat, failure, mistake, etc.

痛改前非(ㄊㄨㄥˋ ㄍㄞˇ ㄑㄧㄢˊ ㄈㄟ)
to repent past mistakes

痛哭(ㄊㄨㄥˋ ㄎㄨ)
to weep bitterly: 她痛哭。She wept bitter tears.

痛哭流涕(ㄊㄨㄥˋ ㄎㄨ ㄌㄧㄡˊ ㄊㄧˋ)
to shed tears in bitter sorrow; to shed tears of anguish

痛苦(ㄊㄨㄥˋ ㄎㄨˇ)
painful; suffering; pain; anguish

痛快(ㄊㄨㄥˋ ˙ㄎㄨㄞ)or 痛痛快快(ㄊㄨㄥˋ ˙ㄊㄨㄥ ˙ㄎㄨㄞ ˙ㄎㄨㄞ)
① delighted; very happy ② straightforward ③ to one's heart's content

痛快淋漓(ㄊㄨㄥˋ ㄎㄨㄞˋ ㄌㄧㄣˊ ㄌㄧˊ)
satisfying in every respect

痛恨(ㄊㄨㄥˋ ㄏㄣˋ)
to detest; to hate deeply

痛悔(ㄊㄨㄥˋ ㄏㄨㄟˇ)
to repent bitterly

痛擊(ㄊㄨㄥˋ ㄐㄧˊ)
to give a hard blow

痛覺(ㄊㄨㄥˋ ㄐㄩㄝˊ)
a sense of pain

痛切(ㄊㄨㄥˋ ㄑㄧㄝˋ)
sharply painful to the feelings; poignant; pungent

痛惜(ㄊㄨㄥˋ ㄒㄧˊ)
to regret deeply

痛心(ㄊㄨㄥˋ ㄒㄧㄣ)
heartbroken; very sorry

痛心疾首(ㄊㄨㄥˋ ㄒㄧㄣ ㄐㄧˊ ㄕㄡˇ)
to hate deeply; to feel bitter about...

痛斥(ㄊㄨㄥˋ ㄔˋ)
to scold severely; scathingly denounce

痛楚(ㄊㄨㄥˋ ㄔㄨˇ)
pain; suffering; anguish

痛處(ㄊㄨㄥˋ ㄔㄨˋ)
a sore spot; a tender spot

痛入骨髓(ㄊㄨㄥˋ ㄖㄨˋ ㄍㄨˇ ㄙㄨㄟˇ)
The pain penetrates even into the marrow.

痛自悔改(ㄊㄨㄥˋ ㄗˋ ㄏㄨㄟˇ ㄍㄞˇ)
to show deep repentance

痛責(ㄊㄨㄥˋ ㄗㄜˊ)
to scold severely

痛愛(ㄊㄨㄥˋ ㄞˋ)
to love deeply; to love passionately

痛毆(ㄊㄨㄥˋ ㄡ)
to beat savagely; to give a sounding beating

痛飲(ㄊㄨㄥˋ ㄧㄣˇ)
to drink to one's heart's content

痛飲黃龍(ㄊㄨㄥˋ ㄧㄣˇ ㄏㄨㄤˊ ㄌㄨㄥˊ)
to drink for victory in the heart of conquered enemy territory

痛癢(ㄊㄨㄥˋ ㄧㄤˇ)
① sufferings; difficulties ② importance: 那無關痛癢。It is of no importance.

痛癢相關(ㄊㄨㄥˋ ㄧㄤˇ ㄒㄧㄤ ㄍㄨㄢ)
to have loving concern for each other; to share a common lot: 我們痛癢相關。We shared a common lot.

痛惡(ㄊㄨㄥˋ ㄨˋ)
to hate bitterly; to detest; to abhor; disgusting: 我痛惡每天必須早起。I detest having to rise early every day.

【痘】 3623 ㄉㄡˋ dow dòu
smallpox 亦作「天花」

痘疤(ㄉㄡˋ ㄅㄚ)
smallpox scabs

痘苗(ㄉㄡˋ ㄇㄧㄠˊ)
vaccine; lymph

痘瘡(ㄉㄡˋ ㄔㄨㄤ)
smallpox

【痙】 3624 ㄐㄧㄥˋ jinq jìng
spasm; convulsions

痙攣(ㄐㄧㄥˋ ㄌㄩㄢˊ)
convulsions; spasm; cramp; a jerk

【痢】 3625 ㄌㄧˋ lih lì
dysentery; diarrhea

痢疾(ㄌㄧˋ ㄐㄧˊ)
dysentery; diarrhea: 他患痢疾。He has diarrhea.

【痧】 3626 ㄕㄚ sha shā
1. cholera
2. measles

痧子(ㄕㄚ ˙ㄗ)
measles

【痣】 3627 ㄓˋ jyh zhì
moles; nevus: 她下巴上有顆痣。She has a mole on her chin.

【痠】 3628 ㄙㄨㄢ suan suān
muscular pains

痠疼(ㄙㄨㄢ ㄊㄥˊ)or 痠痛(ㄙㄨㄢ ㄊㄨㄥˋ)
(said of muscles, bones, etc.) to ache 參看「酸疼」: 我的骨頭痠疼。 My bones ache.

痠懶(ㄙㄨㄢ ㄌㄢˇ)
sore and weary

痠軟(ㄙㄨㄢ ㄖㄨㄢˇ)
sore and weak: 我的四肢痠軟。My limbs are sore and weak.

【痡】 3629 ㄆㄨ pu pū
a disease; an ailment

【痞】 3630 ㄆㄧˇ pii pǐ
1. dyspepsia; a spleen infection
2. a ruffian; a scoundrel

痞棍(ㄆㄧˇ ㄍㄨㄣˋ)or 痞子(ㄆㄧˇ ˙ㄗ)
a rascal; a scoundrel

痞塊(ㄆㄧˇ ㄎㄨㄞˋ)
a swelling of the abdomen due to constipation

【痤】 3631 ㄘㄨㄛˊ tswo cuó
1. a boil or carbuncle on the face
2. minor swelling; an abscess

八畫

【痰】 3632 ㄊㄢˊ tarn tán
phlegm; expectoration; sputum
痰迷心竅(ㄊㄢˊ ㄇㄧˊ ㄒㄧㄣ ㄑㄧㄠˋ)
confused; foolish; befuddled
痰桶(ㄊㄢˊ ㄊㄨㄥˇ)
a spittoon
痰涎(ㄊㄢˊ ㄒㄧㄢˊ)
phlegm; spittle; expectoration
痰喘(ㄊㄢˊ ㄔㄨㄢˇ)
asthma
痰盂(ㄊㄢˊ ㄩˊ)or痰罐(ㄊㄢˊ ㄍㄨㄢˋ)
a spittoon

【痱】 3633 (疿) ㄈㄟˋ fey fèi
heat rashes; heat spots; prickly heat
痱子(ㄈㄟˋ ·ㄗ)
heat rashes; heat spots; prickly heat: 這孩子生痱子。The child has heat rashes.
痱子粉(ㄈㄟˋ ·ㄗ ㄈㄣˇ)
talcum powder; baby powder

【痳】 3634 (淋) ㄌㄧㄣˊ lin lín
gonorrhea
痳病(ㄌㄧㄣˊ ㄅㄧㄥˋ)
gonorrhea 參看「淋病」
痳症(ㄌㄧㄣˊ ㄓㄥˋ)
gonorrhea

【痲】 3635 ㄇㄚˊ ma má
1. measles
2. leprosy
3. to stupefy; to benumb; to anesthetize; to paralyze
4. a pockmark
痲痹(ㄇㄚˊ ㄅㄧˋ)
paralysis; palsy; numbness
痲面(ㄇㄚˊ ㄇㄧㄢˋ)
a pockmarked face
痲瘋(ㄇㄚˊ ㄈㄥ)
leprosy
痲瘋院(ㄇㄚˊ ㄈㄥ ㄩㄢˋ)
a leprosarium; a lazaretto; a leper house
痲臉婆(ㄇㄚˊ ㄌㄧㄢˇ ㄆㄛˊ)
a woman with a pockmarked face
痲疹(ㄇㄚˊ ㄓㄣˇ)
measles: 痲疹是小孩生的病。Measles is a children's disease.
痲子(ㄇㄚˊ ·ㄗ)
① pockmarks ② a person with a pockmarked face

【痹】 3636 ㄅㄧˋ bih bì
paralysis

【痼】 3637 ㄍㄨˋ guh gù
a chronic disease: 痼病不治。A chronic disease is incurable.
痼癖(ㄍㄨˋ ㄆㄧˇ)
an addiction; a fondness
痼疾(ㄍㄨˋ ㄐㄧˊ)
an incurable chronic disease: 我是來治痼疾的。I am here to cure my chronic disease.
痼習(ㄍㄨˋ ㄒㄧˊ)
a deep-rooted habit

【瘀】 3638 ㄩ iu yū
a hematoma
瘀膿(ㄩ ㄋㄨㄥˊ)
pus
瘀血(ㄩ ㄒㄧㄝˇ)
a hematoma
瘀傷(ㄩ ㄕㄤ)
a contusion; a bruise: 他的腿瘀傷了。He received a bruise on his leg.
瘀肉(ㄩ ㄖㄡˋ)
gangrene

【痿】 3639 ㄨㄟˇ woei wěi
paralysis; impotent
痿痹(ㄨㄟˇ ㄅㄧˋ)
paralysis
痿症(ㄨㄟˇ ㄓㄥˋ)
(Chinese medicine) the flaccidity-syndrome; flaccid paralysis

【瘁】 3640 ㄘㄨㄟˋ tsuey cuì
1. disease; illness
2. overfatigued; toil

【痴】 3641 ㄔ chy chī
the simplified form of 癡, 參看「癡」

九畫

【瘍】 3642 ㄧㄤˊ yang yáng
skin diseases or infections; sores; an ulcer

【瘋】 3643 ㄈㄥ feng fēng
insane; crazy; mad; mentally deranged; lunatic; wild
瘋癲(ㄈㄥ ㄉㄧㄢ)or瘋瘋癲癲(ㄈㄥ ·ㄈㄥ ㄉㄧㄢ ㄉㄧㄢ)
mentally deranged; insane
瘋狗(ㄈㄥ ㄍㄡˇ)or瘋犬(ㄈㄥ ㄑㄩㄢˇ)
a mad dog; a rabid dog
瘋狂(ㄈㄥ ㄎㄨㄤˊ)
crazy; mad; insane; wild; irrational: 她因過分悲傷而導致瘋狂。She went insane from the tragedy.
瘋話(ㄈㄥ ㄏㄨㄚˋ)
gibberish; jargon
瘋犬病(ㄈㄥ ㄑㄩㄢˇ ㄅㄧㄥˋ)
rabies; hydrophobia
瘋人(ㄈㄥ ㄖㄣˊ)or瘋子(ㄈㄥ ·ㄗ)
a lunatic; a madman; a maniac
瘋人院(ㄈㄥ ㄖㄣˊ ㄩㄢˋ)
a mental hospital; a mental institution; an insane asylum

【瘓】 3644 ㄏㄨㄢˋ huann huàn
paralysis: 他的左臂癱瘓了。His left arm was paralyzed.

【瘖】 3645 ㄧㄣ in yīn
dumb; mute
瘖啞(ㄧㄣ ㄧㄚˇ)
dumb; mute

【瘌】 3646 ㄌㄚˋ lah là
favus
瘌痢 or 鬎鬁(ㄌㄚˋ ㄌㄧˋ)
favus
瘌痢頭(ㄌㄚˋ ㄌㄧˋ ㄊㄡˊ)
a head made bald by favus

【瘉】 3647 ㄩˋ yuh yù
1. same as 愈—healed; cured
2. ill; sick

【瘧】 3648 ㄋㄩㄝˋ niueh nüè
malaria
瘧疾(ㄋㄩㄝˋ ㄐㄧˊ)
malaria
瘧疾原蟲(ㄋㄩㄝˋ ㄐㄧˊ ㄩㄢˊ ㄔㄨㄥˊ)

〔疒部〕

a plasmodium
瘧蚊(ㄋㄩㄝ ㄨㄣˊ)
an anopheles

十畫

【瘝】 3649 ㄍㄨㄢ guan guān
sick; ill; ailing

【瘟】 3650 ㄨㄣ uen wēn
an epidemic; a plague; a pestilence
瘟氣(ㄨㄣ ㄑㄧˋ)
pestilential vapor
瘟神(ㄨㄣ ㄕㄣˊ)
① the god of pestilence ② a fellow who brings disaster to mankind
瘟生(ㄨㄣ ㄕㄥ)
(Shanghai dialect) a sucker
瘟疫(ㄨㄣ ㄧˋ)
an epidemic; a plague; a pestilence: 瘟疫正流行於那個城。The plague is now prevailing in that city.

【瘡】 3651 ㄔㄨㄤ chuang chuāng
1. an ulcer; a sore; a boil
2. a wound
瘡疤(ㄔㄨㄤ ㄅㄚ)
the scar of an ulcer; wound scars
瘡癆(ㄔㄨㄤ ㄌㄠˊ)
a chronic ulcer
瘡口(ㄔㄨㄤ ㄎㄡˇ)
an opening of an ulcer or a sore
瘡痍(ㄔㄨㄤ ㄧˊ)or瘡痏(ㄔㄨㄤ ㄨㄟˇ)
① an ulcer; a sore ② suffering; hardship; privation
瘡痍滿目(ㄔㄨㄤ ㄧˊ ㄇㄢˇ ㄇㄨˋ)
One sees suffering everywhere.

【瘦】 3652 ㄕㄡˋ show shòu
thin; lean; slim; meager; scrawny; emaciated
瘦巴(ㄕㄡˋ ·ㄅㄚ)
skinny; lean
瘦馬(ㄕㄡˋ ㄇㄚˇ)
a lean horse
瘦骨嶙峋(ㄕㄡˋ ㄍㄨˇ ㄌㄧㄣˊ ㄒㄩㄣˊ)
very skinny
瘦果(ㄕㄡˋ ㄍㄨㄛˇ)
an achene
瘦瘠(ㄕㄡˋ ㄐㄧˊ)
(said of soil) unproductive; barren
瘦筋巴骨(ㄕㄡˋ ㄐㄧㄣ ㄅㄚ ㄍㄨˇ)
skinny; very lean; very thin
瘦金書(ㄕㄡˋ ㄐㄧㄣ ㄕㄨ)
a style of Chinese calligraphy, originated by Emperor Hui Tsung (徽宗) of the Sung Dynasty, featuring thin and sturdy strokes
瘦小(ㄕㄡˋ ㄒㄧㄠˇ)
thin and small
瘦削(ㄕㄡˋ ㄒㄩㄝˋ)
slim: 胖的女孩羨慕瘦削的女孩。Fat girls envy slim girls.
瘦長(ㄕㄡˋ ㄔㄤˊ)
skinny and tall; tall and lean
瘦肉(ㄕㄡˋ ㄖㄡˋ)
lean meat
瘦弱(ㄕㄡˋ ㄖㄨㄛˋ)
thin and weak; emaciated and frail: 生病後，她看來瘦弱。She looked thin and weak after her illness.
瘦子(ㄕㄡˋ ·ㄗ)
a thin person; a living skeleton
瘦硬(ㄕㄡˋ ㄧㄥˋ)
(said of a handwriting) fine and forceful

【瘠】 3653 ㄐㄧˊ jyi jí
1. thin; lean; meager; emaciated
2. (said of land) sterile, infertile, or unproductive; barren
瘠地(ㄐㄧˊ ㄉㄧˋ)
sterile, or unproductive land
瘠土(ㄐㄧˊ ㄊㄨˇ)
sterile soil; infertile soil
瘠瘦(ㄐㄧˊ ㄕㄡˋ)
emaciated; lean and weak

【瘢】 3654 ㄅㄢ ban bān
a scar; a freckle
瘢點(ㄅㄢ ㄉㄧㄢˇ)
a black spot on the skin; a scar
瘢痕(ㄅㄢ ㄏㄣˊ)
a scar

【瘥】 3655 1. ㄔㄞˋ chay chài
cured; healed; recovered

【瘥】 3655 2. ㄘㄨㄛˊ tswo cuó
sick; ill; ailing; affliction

【瘩】 3656 ·ㄉㄚ ·da da (又讀 ㄉㄚˊ dar dá)
a boil; a pimple; a wart

【瘞】 3657 ㄧˋ yih yì
to bury

【瘤】 3658 (瘤) ㄌㄧㄡˊ liou liú
a tumor; a swelling; a lump
瘤胃(ㄌㄧㄡˊ ㄨㄟˋ)
a rumen

十一畫

【瘴】 3659 ㄓㄤˋ janq zhàng
miasma; swamp vapor
瘴母(ㄓㄤˋ ㄇㄨˇ)
masses of miasma
瘴地(ㄓㄤˋ ㄉㄧˋ)
a miasmal place
瘴癘(ㄓㄤˋ ㄌㄧˋ)
disease or epidemic attributed to miasma; poisonous vapor
瘴氣(ㄓㄤˋ ㄑㄧˋ)
miasma; pestilential vapor
瘴煙毒霧(ㄓㄤˋ ㄧㄢ ㄉㄨˊ ㄨˋ)
clouds of pestilential vapor; miasmal clouds
瘴雨蠻煙(ㄓㄤˋ ㄩˇ ㄇㄢˊ ㄧㄢ)
pestilential rain and unhealthy mist

【瘳】 3660 ㄔㄡ chou chōu
1. cured; healed
2. to harm; to hurt

【瘵】 3661 ㄓㄞˋ jay zhài
1. tuberculosis
2. distress

【瘻】 3662 1. ㄌㄩˊ liu lǘ
a hunchback; a humpback

【瘻】 3662 2. ㄌㄡˋ low lòu
goiter; scrofula

【瘸】 3663 ㄑㄩㄝˊ chyue qué
1. a cripple
2. to be lame: 我的右腿瘸了。I am lame in the right leg.
瘸腿(ㄑㄩㄝˊ ㄊㄨㄟˇ)
crippled; lame
瘸子(ㄑㄩㄝˊ ·ㄗ)
a lame man; a cripple

【瘼】 3664 ㄇㄛˋ moh mò
1. disease; illness; an ailment
2. suffering; hardship; privation

十二畫

【療】 3665 ㄌㄧㄠˊ liau liáo
to treat (a disease); to relieve; to heal
療貧(ㄌㄧㄠˊ ㄆㄧㄣˊ)
to relieve the poor
療法(ㄌㄧㄠˊ ㄈㄚˇ)
a cure; a therapy
療毒(ㄌㄧㄠˊ ㄉㄨˊ)
to remove poison from human body
療妒(ㄌㄧㄠˊ ㄉㄨˋ)
to cure jealousy
療飢(ㄌㄧㄠˊ ㄐㄧ)
to relieve hunger
療效(ㄌㄧㄠˊ ㄒㄧㄠˋ)
curative effect
療治(ㄌㄧㄠˊ ㄓˋ)
to treat (a disease)
療養(ㄌㄧㄠˊ ㄧㄤˇ)
to recuperate; to convalesce: 他正在療養中。He is convalescent now.
療養院(ㄌㄧㄠˊ ㄧㄤˇ ㄩㄢˋ)
a sanatorium; a sanitarium; a rest home

【癃】 3666 ㄌㄨㄥˊ long lóng
1. humping of the back in old age
2. anuria
癃疾(ㄌㄨㄥˊ ㄐㄧˊ)
① humping of the back in old age ② anuria

【癌】 3667 ㄧㄢˊ yan yán (又讀 ㄞˊ air ái)
cancer: 他死於胃癌。He died of stomach cancer.
癌細胞(ㄧㄢˊ ㄒㄧˋ ㄅㄠ)
cancer cells
癌症(ㄧㄢˊ ㄓㄥˋ)
cancer
癌腫(ㄧㄢˊ ㄓㄨㄥˇ)
a malignant tumor; cancer

【癆】 3668 ㄌㄠˊ lau láo
tuberculosis; consumption
癆病(ㄌㄠˊ ㄅㄧㄥˋ) or 癆症(ㄌㄠˊ ㄓㄥˋ)
tuberculosis; consumption
癆傷(ㄌㄠˊ ㄕㄤ)
weakened by overexertion

【癇】 3669 ㄒㄧㄢˊ shyan xián
epilepsy
癇風(ㄒㄧㄢˊ ㄈㄥ)
epilepsy

【癉】 3670 ㄉㄢˋ dann dàn
1. to hate bitterly; to detest
2. illness caused by overexhaustion; distress

【瘢】 3671 ㄅㄢ ban bān
unhealthy marks on the skin; a blotch

十三畫

【癖】 3672 ㄆㄧˇ pii pǐ
1. chronic swelling of the spleen
2. addiction; a habitual inclination
癖好(ㄆㄧˇ ㄏㄠˋ)
a habitual inclination; addiction; a propensity
癖性(ㄆㄧˇ ㄒㄧㄥˋ)
a propensity; a habitual inclination; a habitual tendency

【癘】 3673 ㄌㄧˋ lih lì
1. an ulcer
2. pestilential vapor; pestilence

【癒】 3674 (瘉) ㄩˋ yuh yù
healed; cured

十四畫

【癟】 3675 (癟) ㄅㄧㄝˇ biee biě
flat; sunken; not full
癟螺痧(ㄅㄧㄝˇ ㄌㄨㄛˊ ㄕㄚ)
cholera
癟着肚子(ㄅㄧㄝˇ ·ㄓㄜ ㄉㄨˋ ·ㄗ)
with an empty stomach
癟子(ㄅㄧㄝˇ ·ㄗ)
a setback; a blow
癟嘴子(ㄅㄧㄝˇ ㄗㄨㄟˇ ·ㄗ)
a person who has lost all teeth
癟三(ㄅㄧㄝˇ ㄙㄢ)
(Wu or Shanghai dialect) a bum; a tramp

【癡】 3676 (痴) ㄔ chy chī
1. idiotic; silly; foolish; stupid; senseless; crazy; insane
2. to besot: 她的美麗使他如醉如癡。Her beauty besotted him.
癡迷(ㄔ ㄇㄧˊ)
infatuated; besotted
癡肥(ㄔ ㄈㄟˊ)
very fat and looking stupid; obese
癡福(ㄔ ㄈㄨˊ)
the bliss of imbecility; idiotic happiness
癡鈍(ㄔ ㄉㄨㄣˋ)
dull; imbecile; stupid
癡男(ㄔ ㄋㄢˊ)
a man blinded by love; an infatuated man
癡念(ㄔ ㄋㄧㄢˋ)
stupid notions; foolish ideas; idiotic thoughts
癡狂(ㄔ ㄎㄨㄤˊ)
nonsensical; irrational; silly; senseless; idiotic
癡漢(ㄔ ㄏㄢˋ)
a fool; a simpleton; an idiot
癡情(ㄔ ㄑㄧㄥˊ)
blind love; blind passion; infatuation
癡笑(ㄔ ㄒㄧㄠˋ)
to giggle; to titter
癡心(ㄔ ㄒㄧㄣ)
① blind love; blind passion; infatuation ② a silly wish
癡心女子負心漢(ㄔ ㄒㄧㄣ ㄋㄩˇ ㄗˇ ㄈㄨˋ ㄒㄧㄣ ㄏㄢˋ)
the common story of an infatuated girl deserted by a heartless man
癡心妄想(ㄔ ㄒㄧㄣ ㄨㄤˋ ㄒㄧㄤˇ)
silly and fantastic notions; daydreaming: 許多人喜歡癡心妄想。There are people who are fond of daydreaming.
癡想(ㄔ ㄒㄧㄤˇ)
silly thoughts; idiotic ideas; to daydream; to indulge in wishful thinking
癡人(ㄔ ㄖㄣˊ)
an idiot; a fool; a foolish man
癡人說夢(ㄔ ㄖㄣˊ ㄕㄨㄛ ㄇㄥˋ)
an idiot's gibberish; nonsense
癡子(ㄔ ·ㄗ)
an idiot; a simpleton; a fool

癡騃(ㄔ ㄞˊ)or 癡呆(ㄔ ㄉㄞ)
stupid; foolish; imbecile; idiotic; dull; silly
癡物(ㄔ ㄨˋ)
a fool; an idiot; a simpleton

十五畫

【癢】 3677 (痒) ㄧㄤˇ yeang yǎng
to itch; to tickle: 我的鼻子癢。My nose tickles.
癢癢(ㄧㄤˇ ˙ㄧㄤ)
itchy; ticklish; to itch terribly

【癤】 3678 1. ㄐㄧㄝˊ jye jié
a small sore; a pimple

【癤】 3678 2. ㄐㄧㄝ jie jiē
a gnarl
癤子(ㄐㄧㄝ ˙ㄗ)
a gnarl

【癥】 3679 ㄓㄥ jeng zhēng
obstruction of the bowels
癥結(ㄓㄥ ㄐㄧㄝˊ)
① obstruction of the bowels ② a difficult point (of a problem); a bottleneck; the ultimate source of trouble; a crux; a basic problem: 問題的癥結在此。The crux of the matter is this.

十六畫

【癩】 3680 ㄌㄞˋ lay lài
1. leprosy
2. favus; scabies
3. bad
癩皮狗(ㄌㄞˋ ㄆㄧˊ ㄍㄡˇ)
① a mangy dog ② a disgusting creature
癩頭(ㄌㄞˋ ㄊㄡˊ)
a favus-infected head
癩頭瘡(ㄌㄞˋ ㄊㄡˊ ㄔㄨㄤ)
scabies on the head
癩蝦蟆(ㄌㄞˋ ㄏㄚˊ ˙ㄇㄚ)
the toad
癩蝦蟆想吃天鵝肉(ㄌㄞˋ ㄏㄚˊ ˙ㄇㄚ ㄒㄧㄤˇ ㄔ ㄊㄧㄢ ㄜˊ ㄖㄡˋ)
(literally) for a toad to think of eating a swan's meat—to have wishes above one's social or financial position, or beyond one's ability to realize (especially said of a man's marital aspiration)
癩癬(ㄌㄞˋ ㄒㄩㄢˇ)
favus; ringworm
癩瘡(ㄌㄞˋ ㄔㄨㄤ)
scabies
癩子(ㄌㄞˋ ˙ㄗ)
one whose head is made bald or scarred by favus

十七畫

【癭】 3681 ㄧㄥˇ yiing yǐng
1. a reddish swelling on the neck
2. a gnarl

【癮】 3682 ㄧㄣˇ yiin yǐn
1. addiction; a habitual craving: 他是一個有毒癮的人。He is a drug addict.
2. strong interest (in a sport or pastime): 她看電影看上癮了。She takes a strong interest in movies.
癮頭(ㄧㄣˇ ˙ㄊㄡ)
addiction
癮君子(ㄧㄣˇ ㄐㄩㄣ ㄗˇ)
an opium eater; a heavy smoker

【癬】 3683 ㄒㄩㄢˇ sheuan xuǎn (讀音 ㄒㄧㄢˇ shean xiǎn)
ringworm; tetter

十八畫

【癰】 3684 ㄩㄥ iong yōng
a carbuncle
癰疽(ㄩㄥ ㄐㄩ)
a carbuncle
癰腫(ㄩㄥ ㄓㄨㄥˇ)
an abscess
癰瘡(ㄩㄥ ㄔㄨㄤ)
a carbuncle

【癯】 3685 ㄑㄩˊ chyu qú
emaciated; thin; lean

十九畫

【癲】 3686 ㄉㄧㄢ dian diān
mentally deranged; insane; mad; crazy; lunatic
癲狂(ㄉㄧㄢ ㄎㄨㄤˊ)
mentally deranged; insane; mad; crazy; lunatic
癲癇(ㄉㄧㄢ ㄒㄧㄢˊ)
epilepsy

【癱】 3687 ㄊㄢ tan tān
paralysis
癱瘓(ㄊㄢ ㄏㄨㄢˋ)
paralyzed; standstill
癱軟(ㄊㄢ ㄖㄨㄢˇ)
(said of arms, legs, etc.) weak and limp
癱子(ㄊㄢ ˙ㄗ)
a paralytic

癶 部
ㄅㄛ bo bō

四畫

【癸】 3688 ㄍㄨㄟˇ goei guǐ
the last of the Ten Celestial Stems

七畫

【登】 3689 ㄉㄥ deng dēng
1. to ascend; to climb; to rise
2. to record; to register; to enter
3. to take; to employ
4. to board
5. to step on; to tread
登報(ㄉㄥ ㄅㄠˋ)
to make an announcement in the newspaper
登報聲明(ㄉㄥ ㄅㄠˋ ㄕㄥ ㄇㄧㄥˊ)
to clarify or announce by a newspaper advertisement
登榜(ㄉㄥ ㄅㄤˇ)
to succeed, or be announced as a successful candidate (in a competitive examination); to pass a competitive examination
登陴(ㄉㄥ ㄆㄧˊ)
to guard the city wall
登門(ㄉㄥ ㄇㄣˊ)

to pay a special visit to another's house
登門拜訪(ㄉㄥ ㄇㄣˊ ㄅㄞˋ ㄈㄤˇ)
to make a special call on another at his house; to visit
登門答謝(ㄉㄥ ㄇㄣˊ ㄉㄚˊ ㄒㄧㄝˋ)
to make a special call on another at his house to express gratitude
登峯造極(ㄉㄥ ㄈㄥ ㄗㄠˋ ㄐㄧˊ)
to reach the summit of achievement; to reach the acme; to achieve the highest attainments
登第(ㄉㄥ ㄉㄧˋ)
to pass a competitive examination; to succeed in a competitive examination
登臺(ㄉㄥ ㄊㄞˊ)
①to mount a platform ②to go on the stage: 她要登臺。She wants to go on the stage.
登臺演說(ㄉㄥ ㄊㄞˊ ㄧㄢˇ ㄕㄨㄛ)
to deliver a speech from a platform
登壇拜將(ㄉㄥ ㄊㄢˊ ㄅㄞˋ ㄐㄧㄤˋ)
(in ancient times) to go through the ceremonies of appointing a commander-in-chief
登堂入室(ㄉㄥ ㄊㄤˊ ㄖㄨˋ ㄕˋ)
to ascend to the hall and reach the inner room — to master learning or skill
登天(ㄉㄥ ㄊㄧㄢ)
(literally) climbing to heaven—something very difficult
登徒子(ㄉㄥ ㄊㄨˊ ㄗˇ)
a lecher; a debauchee
登樓(ㄉㄥ ㄌㄡˊ)
to climb a flight of stairs; to go toward an upper floor; to go upstairs
登臨(ㄉㄥ ㄌㄧㄣˊ)
to climb a hill, a tall building, etc. which commands a broad view
登陸(ㄉㄥ ㄌㄨˋ)
to go ashore; to land: 敵軍登陸我海岸。The enemy landed on our shore.
登陸部隊(ㄉㄥ ㄌㄨˋ ㄅㄨˋ ㄉㄨㄟˋ)
landing troops
登陸艇(ㄉㄥ ㄌㄨˋ ㄊㄧㄥˇ)
landing craft; landing ship tank (LST)
登陸戰(ㄉㄥ ㄌㄨˋ ㄓㄢˋ)
landing operations
登錄(ㄉㄥ ㄌㄨˋ)
to register
登錄號(ㄉㄥ ㄌㄨˋ ㄏㄠˋ)
the registered mark or number
登輪(ㄉㄥ ㄌㄨㄣˊ)
to board a steamship
登龍門(ㄉㄥ ㄌㄨㄥˊ ㄇㄣˊ)
to enter a successful career with the help of an influential person
登龍有術(ㄉㄥ ㄌㄨㄥˊ ㄧㄡˇ ㄕㄨˋ)
very skillful in finding a powerful patron to advance one's career
登革熱(ㄉㄥ ㄍㄜˊ ㄖㄜˋ)
(medicine) dengue fever
登高(ㄉㄥ ㄍㄠ)
to ascend heights; to climb mountains
登高節(ㄉㄥ ㄍㄠ ㄐㄧㄝˊ)
the Mountain Climbing Festival (on the 9th of the 9th moon)
登高自卑(ㄉㄥ ㄍㄠ ㄗˋ ㄅㄟ)
To reach a high position, one must start from a low position.
登高一呼(ㄉㄥ ㄍㄠ ㄧˋ ㄏㄨ)
to rally for a just cause; to arouse for action
登科(ㄉㄥ ㄎㄜ)
to pass the civil service examination in former times
登科錄(ㄉㄥ ㄎㄜ ㄌㄨˋ)
a roster of successful candidates of the civil service examination in former times
登基(ㄉㄥ ㄐㄧ)
to ascend the throne
登機(ㄉㄥ ㄐㄧ)
to board a plane
登極(ㄉㄥ ㄐㄧˊ)
to ascend the throne
登記(ㄉㄥ ㄐㄧˋ)
to register; to check in; to enter one's name; registration
登記簿(ㄉㄥ ㄐㄧˋ ㄅㄨˋ)
a register
登記處(ㄉㄥ ㄐㄧˋ ㄔㄨˋ)
a registry; a registration office
登進(ㄉㄥ ㄐㄧㄣˋ)
to be promoted in rank; to get a promotion
登遐 or 登假(ㄉㄥ ㄒㄧㄚˊ)
the death of the emperor
登仙(ㄉㄥ ㄒㄧㄢ)
①to become an immortal ②to die
登舟(ㄉㄥ ㄓㄡ)
to take a boat ride
登賬 or 登帳(ㄉㄥ ㄓㄤˋ)
to enter in the accounts
登場(ㄉㄥ ㄔㄤˊ)
①(said of actors, entertainers, etc.) to appear on the stage ②(said of products) to appear in the market ③to be gathered and taken to the threshing ground
登程(ㄉㄥ ㄔㄥˊ)
to start a journey; to set out
登船(ㄉㄥ ㄔㄨㄢˊ)
to take a boat; to take a ride aboard a ship: 我在高雄登船往歐洲。At Kaohsiung I took a boat for Europe.
登春臺(ㄉㄥ ㄔㄨㄣ ㄊㄞˊ)
the peace and happiness of people in a prosperous age
登時(ㄉㄥ ㄕˊ)
immediately; forthwith; at once
登山(ㄉㄥ ㄕㄢ)
to climb a mountain; to mountaineer: 他很喜歡登山。He is very fond of mountaineering.
登山隊(ㄉㄥ ㄕㄢ ㄉㄨㄟˋ)
a mountaineering party
登山協會(ㄉㄥ ㄕㄢ ㄒㄧㄝˊ ㄏㄨㄟˋ)
an alpine club or association
登山陟嶺(ㄉㄥ ㄕㄢ ㄓˋ ㄌㄧㄥˇ)
to go over hills and mountains
登載(ㄉㄥ ㄗㄞˇ)
(said of a periodical or newspaper) to carry (an article); to publish (a news story)
登岸(ㄉㄥ ㄢˋ)
to go ashore; to land: 乘客均已登岸。The passengers have landed.
登瀛州(ㄉㄥ ㄧㄥˊ ㄓㄡ)
to reach the paradise of immortals
登位(ㄉㄥ ㄨㄟˋ)

〔癶部〕

to ascend the throne
登庸人才(ㄉㄥ ㄩㄥ ㄖㄣ ㄘㄞ)
to employ talents

【發】 3690
ㄈㄚ fa fā
1. to shoot; to launch
2. to issue; to publish
3. to begin; to start; to initiate; to originate
4. to reveal; to disclose; to uncover
5. to become; to come to be
6. to utter; to express; to speak
7. to set off; to set out
8. to illuminate; to help out

發白(ㄈㄚ ㄅㄞ)
to turn white; to turn pale: 她的臉色發白。She turns pale.
發包(ㄈㄚ ㄅㄠ)
to contract with a contractor for a construction program
發報(ㄈㄚ ㄅㄠˋ)
to transmit messages
發報機(ㄈㄚ ㄅㄠˋ ㄐㄧ)
a telegraph transmitter
發榜(ㄈㄚ ㄅㄤˇ)
to publish the result of a competitive examination
發表(ㄈㄚ ㄅㄧㄠˇ)
to make (a statement); to make known; to make public; to publish; to announce; to deliver (a speech)
發邊(ㄈㄚ ㄅㄧㄢ)
to banish to the frontiers
發兵(ㄈㄚ ㄅㄧㄥ)
to dispatch troops
發病(ㄈㄚ ㄅㄧㄥˋ)
to get sick; to fall ill
發布 or 發佈(ㄈㄚ ㄅㄨˋ)
to announce; to promulgate: 國王發佈了一項命令。The king promulgated a decree.
發排(ㄈㄚ ㄆㄞˊ)
to send (manuscripts) to the composing room
發牌(ㄈㄚ ㄆㄞˊ)
to deal cards: 是誰發的牌? Who dealt the cards?
發配(ㄈㄚ ㄆㄟˋ)
to banish (a criminal) to a frontier garrison
發砲(ㄈㄚ ㄆㄠˋ)
to fire artillery pieces
發胖(ㄈㄚ ㄆㄤˋ)
to put on (or gain) weight; to get fat
發脾氣(ㄈㄚ ㄆㄧˊ ·ㄑㄧ)
to lose one's temper; to get angry; to get mad
發票(ㄈㄚ ㄆㄧㄠˋ)
a bill of sale; an invoice
發麻(ㄈㄚ ㄇㄚˊ)
numb; benumbed: 我的雙手因冷而發麻。My hands are numb with cold.
發賣(ㄈㄚ ㄇㄞˋ)
to put on sale
發邁(ㄈㄚ ㄇㄞˋ)
to embark on a long journey
發霉(ㄈㄚ ㄇㄟˊ)
to get mildewed; to mildew
發毛(ㄈㄚ ㄇㄠˊ)
to feel a shudder; to have the feeling of the hair standing on end (with horror, etc.): 他看見血便發毛。He felt a shudder at the sight of blood.
發悶
①(ㄈㄚ ㄇㄣ) (said of the weather) to become oppressive
②(ㄈㄚ ㄇㄣˋ) to become depressed, dejected, or low-spirited
發蒙(ㄈㄚ ㄇㄥˊ)
① to teach a child to read and write ② to enlighten
發麵(ㄈㄚ ㄇㄧㄢˋ)
① to make dough rise; to leaven dough ② leavened dough
發明(ㄈㄚ ㄇㄧㄥˊ)
① to invent; to innovate; to devise: 蒸汽機是何時發明的? When was the steam engine invented? ② an invention
發明家(ㄈㄚ ㄇㄧㄥˊ ㄐㄧㄚ)
an inventor: 愛迪生是一個著名的發明家。Edison was a famous inventor.
發命令(ㄈㄚ ㄇㄧㄥˋ ㄌㄧㄥˋ)
to issue orders; to give orders
發木(ㄈㄚ ㄇㄨˋ)
to be numbed; to be benumbed; to be inactive
發凡(ㄈㄚ ㄈㄢˊ)
an introduction; a preface; a foreword
發煩(ㄈㄚ ㄈㄢˊ)
to get impatient; to become irritable; to feel annoyed
發粉(ㄈㄚ ㄈㄣˇ) or 發酵粉(ㄈㄚ ㄒㄧㄠˋ ㄈㄣˇ)
baking powder
發憤(ㄈㄚ ㄈㄣˋ)
to be roused to action; to be spurred
發憤圖強(ㄈㄚ ㄈㄣˋ ㄊㄨˊ ㄑㄧㄤˊ)
(said of a nation) to strive for progress with determination 亦作「發奮圖強」
發憤忘食(ㄈㄚ ㄈㄣˋ ㄨㄤˋ ㄕˊ)
to be roused to such diligence as to forget one's meals
發放(ㄈㄚ ㄈㄤˋ)
① to issue; to distribute; to provide; to extend ② to dispose of
發瘋(ㄈㄚ ㄈㄥ)
to go mad; to lose one's senses; to lose one's mind; to become insane
發福(ㄈㄚ ㄈㄨˊ)
① to become rich and happy ② (jocularly) to become fat
發付(ㄈㄚ ㄈㄨˋ)
to send on an errand; to dispatch
發達(ㄈㄚ ㄉㄚˊ)
to develop; to evolve; to grow; developed; prosperous; thriving; booming
發獃(ㄈㄚ ㄉㄞ)
to look absent-minded; to look like an idiot; to be lost in reverie
發抖(ㄈㄚ ㄉㄡˇ)
to tremble; to shudder; to shiver
發單(ㄈㄚ ㄉㄢ)
an invoice; a bill of sale
發電(ㄈㄚ ㄉㄧㄢˋ)
① to generate electric power ② to send a telegram
發電體(ㄈㄚ ㄉㄧㄢˋ ㄊㄧˇ)
a charged body; an electrified body
發電機(ㄈㄚ ㄉㄧㄢˋ ㄐㄧ)
a generator; a dynamo: 發電機產生電力。A dynamo generates electricity.
發電廠(ㄈㄚ ㄉㄧㄢˋ ㄔㄤˇ)
a power plant
發電所(ㄈㄚ ㄉㄧㄢˋ ㄙㄨㄛˇ)

a powerhouse
發端(ㄈㄚ ㄉㄨㄢ)
to originate; to begin; to stem
發動(ㄈㄚ ㄉㄨㄥˋ)
to start; to launch; to initiate: 我不能使它發動。I can't make it start.
發動機(ㄈㄚ ㄉㄨㄥˋ ㄐㄧ)
a motor; an engine
發條(ㄈㄚ ㄊㄧㄠˊ)
a spring (of a mechanical device): 這玩具是用發條轉動。The toy is worked by a spring.
發難(ㄈㄚ ㄋㄢˋ)
① to spearhead a rebellion or revolution ② to ask difficult questions
發黏(ㄈㄚ ㄋㄧㄢˊ)
to become sticky
發怒(ㄈㄚ ㄋㄨˋ)
to become angry; to get mad; to lose one's temper
發擂(ㄈㄚ ㄌㄟˊ)
to start beating (drums, gongs, etc.)
發牢騷(ㄈㄚ ㄌㄠˊ ·ㄙㄠ)
to grumble; to complain: 不要發牢騷! Don't grumble!
發懶(ㄈㄚ ㄌㄢˇ)
to become indolent or lazy
發冷(ㄈㄚ ㄌㄥˇ)
to feel a chill; to feel chilly
發楞(ㄈㄚ ㄌㄥˋ)
to stare vacantly into space
發利市(ㄈㄚ ㄌㄧˋ ㄕˋ)
to do a good business; to do a brisk business
發亮(ㄈㄚ ㄌㄧㄤˋ)
to shine; to glitter; to shimmer; to gleam: 她的黑髮閃閃發亮。Her black hair shone glisteningly.
發落(ㄈㄚ ㄌㄨㄛˋ)
to deal with (an offender): 法官對少年犯從輕發落。The judge dealt with the juvenile delinquent leniently.
發給(ㄈㄚ ㄍㄟˇ)
to issue (supplies, allowances, etc.): 將口糧發給士兵們了。Food rations were issued to the soldiers.
發糕(ㄈㄚ ㄍㄠ)
a steamed sponge cake (usually sweetened)
發稿(ㄈㄚ ㄍㄠˇ)
(journalism) to send out a story or report for publication
發乾(ㄈㄚ ㄍㄢ)
to become dry
發光(ㄈㄚ ㄍㄨㄤ)
to shine; to glitter; to twinkle; to gleam; to emit light
發光體(ㄈㄚ ㄍㄨㄤ ㄊㄧˇ)
a luminous body: 太陽與星星都是發光體。The sun and stars are luminous bodies.
發光顏料(ㄈㄚ ㄍㄨㄤ ㄧㄢˊ ㄌㄧㄠˋ)
luminescent pigment
發刊(ㄈㄚ ㄎㄢ)
to start or launch (a magazine, newspaper, etc.); to bring out the first issue
發刊詞(ㄈㄚ ㄎㄢ ㄘˊ)
editor's opening statement for a new magazine, newspaper, etc.
發狂(ㄈㄚ ㄎㄨㄤˊ)
to go crazy; to become mentally deranged
發號施令(ㄈㄚ ㄏㄠˋ ㄕ ㄌㄧㄥˋ)
to give commands; to issue orders
發汗(ㄈㄚ ㄏㄢˋ)
①to perspire or sweat ②diaphoresis; to induce perspiration (as by drugs)
發汗劑(ㄈㄚ ㄏㄢˋ ㄐㄧˋ)
a diaphoretic; a sudorific
發狠(ㄈㄚ ㄏㄣˇ)
① to make a tremendous effort; to exert oneself ② to show anger
發橫(ㄈㄚ ㄏㄥˋ)
to turn villainous
發乎情，止乎禮(ㄈㄚ ㄏㄨ ㄑㄧㄥˊ, ㄓˇ ㄏㄨ ㄌㄧˇ)
An action impelled by emotion should stop within the limit of propriety.
發話器(ㄈㄚ ㄏㄨㄚˋ ㄑㄧˋ)
a telephone transmitter
發火(ㄈㄚ ㄏㄨㄛˇ)
① to become angry; to show anger; to get mad ② to burst into flames ③ to go off
發火點(ㄈㄚ ㄏㄨㄛˇ ㄉㄧㄢˇ)
a flash point; an ignition point
發貨(ㄈㄚ ㄏㄨㄛˋ)
to send off goods; to send out goods; to forward goods
發揮(ㄈㄚ ㄏㄨㄟ)
to bring (skill, talent, etc.) into full play: 我們應該發揮集體智慧。We should bring our collective wisdom into full play.
發揮作用(ㄈㄚ ㄏㄨㄟ ㄗㄨㄛˋ ㄩㄥˋ)
to produce a marked effect; to be effective; to produce a result; (said of effect) to tell
發回(ㄈㄚ ㄏㄨㄟˊ)
to send back; to return
發回更審(ㄈㄚ ㄏㄨㄟˊ ㄍㄥ ㄕㄣˇ)
to order a lower court to make a new trial
發還(ㄈㄚ ㄏㄨㄢˊ)
to send back; to return
發昏(ㄈㄚ ㄏㄨㄣ)
① to be giddy; to faint ② to lose one's head; to become confused
發慌(ㄈㄚ ㄏㄨㄤ)
to lose one's composure; to become panicky; to be jittery; to feel nervous; to get flustered; to get flurried
發皇(ㄈㄚ ㄏㄨㄤˊ)
to flourish; to thrive; to prosper
發洪(ㄈㄚ ㄏㄨㄥˊ)
to swell into a flood
發迹(ㄈㄚ ㄐㄧ)
to rise (in business, career, etc.); to gain fame and fortune
發急(ㄈㄚ ㄐㄧˊ)
to become nervous; to fret; to chafe; to grow impatient: 我等朋友等得發急。I am impatient for a friend's arrival.
發交(ㄈㄚ ㄐㄧㄠ)
to hand over; to turn over; to deliver
發酒瘋(ㄈㄚ ㄐㄧㄡˇ ㄈㄥ)
to get drunk and behave irrationally
發姦擿伏(ㄈㄚ ㄐㄧㄢ ㄊㄧˋ ㄈㄨˊ)
to uncover hidden iniquities
發掘(ㄈㄚ ㄐㄩㄝˊ)
to unearth; to dig out; to excavate: 我由一大堆的報告中發掘眞象。I dug out the truth from a mass of information.
發噱(ㄈㄚ ㄐㄩㄝˊ)

〔癶部〕

to laugh
發覺(ㄈㄚ ㄐㄩㄝˊ)
①to realize; to come to know; to discover; to find: 我們發覺我們做錯了。We found that we had made a mistake. ②(said of crimes, plots, etc.) to be brought to light; to be uncovered
發起(ㄈㄚ ㄑㄧˇ)
to initiate; to start; to originate: 這計畫是誰發起的? With whom did the scheme originate?
發起人(ㄈㄚ ㄑㄧˇ ㄖㄣˊ)
an originator; an initiator; a promoter
發球(ㄈㄚ ㄑㄧㄡˊ)
to serve a ball (in tennis, handball, etc.): 該你發球了。It's your turn to serve the ball.
發遣(ㄈㄚ ㄑㄧㄢˇ)
to send away
發情期(ㄈㄚ ㄑㄧㄥˊ ㄑㄧˊ)
①puberty ②rut or heat (of some animals)
發下(ㄈㄚ ㄒㄧㄚˋ)
to issue (orders, supplies, etc.)
發泄 or 發洩(ㄈㄚ ㄒㄧㄝˋ)
to give vent to; to vent; to let out
發笑(ㄈㄚ ㄒㄧㄠˋ)
to laugh
發酵(ㄈㄚ ㄒㄧㄠˋ)
to ferment; fermentation
發酵乳(ㄈㄚ ㄒㄧㄠˋ ㄖㄨˇ)
ferment milk; yogurt
發現 or 發見(ㄈㄚ ㄒㄧㄢˋ)
to discover; to find; discovery: 在他和我的交往中，我發現他是誠實的。I've found him honest in his dealings with me.
發薪水(ㄈㄚ ㄒㄧㄣ ㄕㄨㄟˇ)
to hand out paychecks to employees
發信(ㄈㄚ ㄒㄧㄣˋ)
to mail a letter; to send or post a letter: 他發信給他的朋友。He sent a letter to his friend.
發祥地(ㄈㄚ ㄒㄧㄤˊ ㄉㄧˋ)
the place of a thing's beginning or early development; the cradle; a birthplace
發餉(ㄈㄚ ㄒㄧㄤˇ)
to issue pay (especially to soldiers)
發行
①(ㄈㄚ ㄒㄧㄥˊ) (said of currency, bonds, books, etc.) to issue; to publish; to distribute; to put on sale; to release: 政府發行債券。The government issues bonds.
②(ㄈㄚ ㄏㄤˊ) ⓐ to sell wholesale ⓑ a wholesaler
發行量(ㄈㄚ ㄒㄧㄥˊ ㄌㄧㄤˋ)
the volume of circulation
發行人(ㄈㄚ ㄒㄧㄥˊ ㄖㄣˊ) or 發行者(ㄈㄚ ㄒㄧㄥˊ ㄓㄜˇ)
a publisher
發咒(ㄈㄚ ㄓㄡˋ)
to take an oath; to vow; to swear
發展(ㄈㄚ ㄓㄢˇ)
to develop; to grow; to expand; development
發展中國家(ㄈㄚ ㄓㄢˇ ㄓㄨㄥ ㄍㄨㄛˊ ㄐㄧㄚ)
a developing country
發顫(ㄈㄚ ㄓㄢˋ)
to tremble; to shudder; to shiver
發疹子(ㄈㄚ ㄓㄣˇ ·ㄗ)
to have rashes; to have measles
發脹(ㄈㄚ ㄓㄤˋ)
①to swell; to bloat ②to have a glutted feeling
發冢(ㄈㄚ ㄓㄨㄥˇ)
to open graves
發癡(ㄈㄚ ㄔ)
to stare vacantly into space; to appear absent-minded
發潮(ㄈㄚ ㄔㄠˊ)
to become damp: 我的襯衫有點兒發潮。My shirt became a bit damp.
發愁(ㄈㄚ ㄔㄡˊ)
to worry; to be anxious or troubled: 他為還債的事發愁。He was worried about paying the debts.
發出(ㄈㄚ ㄔㄨ)
to send forth; to generate; to issue; to emit: 玫瑰花發出宜人的香氣。The roses send forth delightful fragrance.
發怵(ㄈㄚ ㄔㄨˋ)
to become fearful; to be seized with fear
發喘(ㄈㄚ ㄔㄨㄢˇ)
to run short of breath
發矢(ㄈㄚ ㄕˇ)
to shoot an arrow; to discharge an arrow
發市(ㄈㄚ ㄕˋ)
to begin business
發誓(ㄈㄚ ㄕˋ)
to vow; to swear; to take an oath: 他發誓效忠國王。He vowed that he would be loyal to the king.
發痧(ㄈㄚ ㄕㄚ)
to contract cholera
發射(ㄈㄚ ㄕㄜˋ)
to launch; to shoot; to catapult: 我們將發射人造衛星。We will launch a man-made satellite.
發射臺(ㄈㄚ ㄕㄜˋ ㄊㄞˊ)
a launching pad
發燒(ㄈㄚ ㄕㄠ)
to have a temperature; to run a temperature; to have a fever
發售(ㄈㄚ ㄕㄡˋ)
to go on sale
發身(ㄈㄚ ㄕㄣ)
to reach puberty
發神經(ㄈㄚ ㄕㄣˊ ㄐㄧㄥ)
to go crazy; to lose sanity
發生(ㄈㄚ ㄕㄥ)
to happen; to occur; to arise: 可能有什麼事要發生。Some thing is likely to happen.
發生關係(ㄈㄚ ㄕㄥ ㄍㄨㄢ ·ㄒㄧ)
①to establish relationship; to have something to do with ②to have an affair with
發生心理學(ㄈㄚ ㄕㄥ ㄒㄧㄣ ㄌㄧˇ ㄒㄩㄝˊ)
genetic psychology
發生學(ㄈㄚ ㄕㄥ ㄒㄩㄝˊ)
embryology
發生衝突(ㄈㄚ ㄕㄥ ㄔㄨㄥ ㄊㄨˊ)
to have a conflict; to come to a clash; to develop into a fight
發聲(ㄈㄚ ㄕㄥ)
to give off sound
發聲器(ㄈㄚ ㄕㄥ ㄑㄧˋ)
①a vocal organ ②a sounder (of a telegraph)
發攄(ㄈㄚ ㄕㄨ)
to bring into full play
發熱(ㄈㄚ ㄖㄜˋ)

to have a temperature; to run a temperature; to have a fever
發人深省(ㄈㄚ ㄖㄣˊ ㄕㄣ ㄒㄧㄥˇ)
to stimulate deep thought; to provide food for thought
發軔(ㄈㄚ ㄖㄣˋ)
the beginning (or origin) of a thing
發躁(ㄈㄚ ㄗㄠˋ)
to become irritable; to get impatient
發作(ㄈㄚ ㄗㄨㄛˋ)
① to go into action; to show effect; to break out: 毒性開始發作。The poison began to show its effect. ② to have a fit (of anger) ③(said of illness) to have a relapse; to have an attack of disease: 他的心臟病又發作了。He's had another heart attack. ④ (said of a crime or a plot) to be exposed
發慈悲(ㄈㄚ ㄘˊ ㄅㄟ)
to show mercy or pity
發財(ㄈㄚ ㄘㄞˊ)
to make a fortune; to acquire wealth; to become rich
發散(ㄈㄚ ㄙㄢˋ)
to disperse; to dissipate; to scatter
發散透鏡(ㄈㄚ ㄙㄢˋ ㄊㄡˋ ㄐㄧㄥˋ)
a divergent lens
發喪(ㄈㄚ ㄙㄤ)
to inform relatives and friends of a death
發酸(ㄈㄚ ㄙㄨㄢ)
① to become sour; to sour ② (said of muscles) to ache from exertion
發送(ㄈㄚ ㄙㄨㄥˋ)
① to send: 報務員會發送密碼電報。Telegraphists can transmit a coded message. ② to hold a funeral service
發呆(ㄈㄚ ㄞˊ)or(ㄈㄚ ㄉㄞ)
to look absent-minded; to stare vacantly
發芽(ㄈㄚ ㄧㄚˊ)
to sprout: 雨水使小麥發芽。The rain has sprouted the wheat.
發啞(ㄈㄚ ㄧㄚˇ)
to become hoarse: 他由於傷風而聲音發啞。He was hoarse from a cold.
發瘧子(ㄈㄚ ㄧㄠˋ ·ㄗ)
to have an attack of malaria
發煙硫酸(ㄈㄚ ㄧㄢ ㄌㄧㄡˊ ㄙㄨㄢ)
fuming sulfuric acid
發煙硝酸(ㄈㄚ ㄧㄢ ㄒㄧㄠ ㄙㄨㄢ)
fuming nitric acid
發炎(ㄈㄚ ㄧㄢˊ)
to become inflamed; to become infected: 我的傷口發炎了。My wound has become inflamed.
發言(ㄈㄚ ㄧㄢˊ)
to speak; to voice one's views: 我要求發言。I ask to be heard.
發言權(ㄈㄚ ㄧㄢˊ ㄑㄩㄢˊ)
right of speaking; voice (in a conference or meeting)
發言人(ㄈㄚ ㄧㄢˊ ㄖㄣˊ)
a spokesman: 他是政府發言人。He was the government spokesman.
發音(ㄈㄚ ㄧㄣ)
to pronounce; pronunciation; articulation; to enunciate; enunciation
發音器官(ㄈㄚ ㄧㄣ ㄑㄧˋ ㄍㄨㄢ)
vocal organs
發音學(ㄈㄚ ㄧㄣ ㄒㄩㄝˊ)
orthoepy
發引(ㄈㄚ ㄧㄣˇ)
(said of a funeral procession) to leave for the place of burial
發揚(ㄈㄚ ㄧㄤˊ)
to exalt; to enhance; to encourage; to add glory to
發揚蹈厲(ㄈㄚ ㄧㄤˊ ㄉㄠˋ ㄌㄧˋ)
to show a dauntless spirit
發揚光大(ㄈㄚ ㄧㄤˊ ㄍㄨㄤ ㄉㄚˋ)
to enhance and glorify
發洋財(ㄈㄚ ㄧㄤˊ ㄘㄞˊ)
to make a big fortune; to make a strike
發癢(ㄈㄚ ㄧㄤˇ)
to itch: 我的背部發癢。My back itches.
發威(ㄈㄚ ㄨㄟ)
to fly into a rage; to rage
發問(ㄈㄚ ㄨㄣˋ)
to ask questions; to raise questions
發往(ㄈㄚ ㄨㄤˇ)
to send or dispatch to (a place)
發語詞(ㄈㄚ ㄩˇ ㄘˊ)
an introductory particle
發育(ㄈㄚ ㄩˋ)
① to grow up; to develop: 植物是由種子發育而成的。Plants develop from seeds. ②to send forth and nourish
發育不良(ㄈㄚ ㄩˋ ㄅㄨˋ ㄌㄧㄤˊ)
maldevelopment
發越(ㄈㄚ ㄩㄝˋ)
① swift; quick ②(said of a pleasant smell, etc.) to diffuse
發源(ㄈㄚ ㄩㄢˊ)
①an origin; a source: 這河發源於這湖。The river takes its source from the lake. ② to originate
發源地(ㄈㄚ ㄩㄢˊ ㄉㄧˋ)
(said of rivers, etc.) the place of origin
發願(ㄈㄚ ㄩㄢˋ)
to vow to achieve an objective
發怨言(ㄈㄚ ㄩㄢˋ ㄧㄢˊ)
to grumble; to complain
發暈(ㄈㄚ ㄩㄣ)
to feel dizzy or giddy

九畫

【凳】 3691
(櫈) ㄉㄥˋ denq dèng
a stool
凳子(ㄉㄥˋ ·ㄗ)or凳兒(ㄉㄥˋㄦ)
a stool

白 部
ㄅㄛˊ bor bó

【白】 3692
ㄅㄞˊ bair bái
(讀音 ㄅㄛˊ bor bó)
1. white; clear; bright; clean; pure; plain
2. empty; blank
3. in vain; for nothing
4. free of charge; gratis
5. the spoken part in an opera, etc.
6. to state; to explain
7. a Chinese family name
白白地(ㄅㄞˊ ㄅㄞˊ ·ㄉㄜ)
in vain; to no purpose; to

(or of) no avail; for nothing
白百合花(ㄅㄞˊ ㄅㄞˇ ㄏㄜˊ ㄏㄨㄚ)or 白水仙(ㄅㄞˊ ㄕㄨㄟˇ ㄒㄧㄢ)
a Madonna lily
白斑(ㄅㄞˊ ㄅㄢ)or(ㄅㄛˊ ㄅㄢ)
white specks; white spots
白斑症(ㄅㄞˊ ㄅㄢ ㄓㄥˋ)
vitiligo; leukoderma
白璧微瑕(ㄅㄞˊ ㄅㄧˋ ㄨㄟ ㄒㄧㄚˊ)
a trivial flaw on a jade; a small defect
白布(ㄅㄞˊ ㄅㄨˋ)
plain white cloth; calico
白跑一趟(ㄅㄞˊ ㄆㄠˇ ㄧˊ ㄊㄤˋ)
to make a futile trip
白砒(ㄅㄞˊ ㄆㄧ)
arsenic 亦作「砒霜」
白皮書(ㄅㄞˊ ㄆㄧˊ ㄕㄨ)
a white paper (in the sense of an official government report)
白葡萄酒(ㄅㄞˊ ㄆㄨˊ ·ㄊㄠ ㄐㄧㄡˇ)
sherry: 白葡萄酒是由葡萄做成的。Sherry is made from grapes.
白馬非馬論(ㄅㄞˊ ㄇㄚˇ ㄈㄟ ㄇㄚˇ ㄌㄨㄣˋ)
the argument that a white horse is not entirely the same as a horse, advanced by Kung-Sun Lung (公孫龍) of the Epoch of Warring States
白馬寺(ㄅㄞˊ ㄇㄚˇ ㄙˋ)
the White Horse Temple, the oldest Buddhist temple in China (in Honan) built in the first century
白螞蟻(ㄅㄞˊ ㄇㄚˇ ㄧˇ)
a termite
白墨(ㄅㄞˊ ㄇㄛˋ)
chalk
白沫子(ㄅㄞˊ ㄇㄛˋ ·ㄗ)
white froth or foam: 啤酒倒出時會起白沫子。Beer froths when it is poured out.
白煤(ㄅㄞˊ ㄇㄟˊ)
anthracite; hard coal; smokeless coal
白黴(ㄅㄞˊ ㄇㄟˊ)
mold; mildew
白茅(ㄅㄞˊ ㄇㄠˊ)or(ㄅㄛˊ ㄇㄠˊ)
an edible wild grass (*Imperata cylindrica*), whose root is used in Chinese herbal medicine
白忙(ㄅㄞˊ ㄇㄤˊ)
to busy oneself to no purpose
白茫茫(ㄅㄞˊ ㄇㄤˊ ㄇㄤˊ)
showing a vast expanse of whiteness
白米(ㄅㄞˊ ㄇㄧˇ)or(ㄅㄛˊ ㄇㄧˇ)
white polished rice
白蜜(ㄅㄞˊ ㄇㄧˋ)or(ㄅㄛˊ ㄇㄧˋ)
whitish honey
白麵兒(ㄅㄞˊ ㄇㄧㄚˋㄦ)
heroin 亦作「海洛因」
白描(ㄅㄞˊ ㄇㄧㄠˊ)or(ㄅㄛˊ ㄇㄧㄠˊ)
a kind of Chinese outline drawing; a sketch
白面書生(ㄅㄞˊ ㄇㄧㄢˋ ㄕㄨ ㄕㄥ)
①a fair-complexioned young scholar ②an inexperienced young scholar
白牡丹(ㄅㄞˊ ㄇㄨˇ ㄉㄢ)
a white peony: 我們園中有棵白牡丹。There is a white peony in our garden.
白木耳(ㄅㄞˊ ㄇㄨˋ ㄦˇ)
a kind of white-colored edible fungus (*Tremella fuciformis*)亦作「銀耳」
白髮蒼蒼(ㄅㄞˊ ㄈㄚˇ ㄘㄤ ㄘㄤ)
hoary-headed
白費(ㄅㄞˊ ㄈㄟˋ)
to use up or spend without profit; to waste: 我白費力氣。I waste my energy.
白費心機(ㄅㄞˊ ㄈㄟˋ ㄒㄧㄣ ㄐㄧ)
to scheme in vain; to make plans to no avail
白礬(ㄅㄞˊ ㄈㄢˊ)or(ㄅㄛˊ ㄈㄢˊ)
alum 亦作「明礬」
白飯(ㄅㄞˊ ㄈㄢˋ)or(ㄅㄛˊ ㄈㄢˋ)
cooked white rice (especially if not mixed with any other food): 中國人喜吃白飯。The Chinese like to eat cooked white rice.
白搭(ㄅㄞˊ ㄉㄚ)
futile; fruitless; in vain; to no avail; no use: 和她辯也是白搭。It is no use arguing with her.
白帶(ㄅㄞˊ ㄉㄞˋ)
(medicine) leucorrhea; white flow
白刀子進，紅刀子出(ㄅㄞˊ ㄉㄠ ·ㄗ ㄐㄧㄣˋ, ㄏㄨㄥˊ ㄉㄠ ·ㄗ ㄔㄨ)
(literally) The knife is white upon entry and red upon exit. —A murder takes place.
白帝城(ㄅㄞˊ ㄉㄧˋ ㄔㄥˊ)
White God City—a strategic point in Szechwan during the Epoch of the Three Kingdoms
白丁(ㄅㄞˊ ㄉㄧㄥ)or 白民(ㄅㄞˊ ㄇㄧㄣˊ)
a commoner
白頭(ㄅㄞˊ ㄊㄡˊ)or(ㄅㄛˊ ㄊㄡˊ)
a hoary head
白頭偕老(ㄅㄞˊ ㄊㄡˊ ㄒㄧㄝˊ ㄌㄠˇ)
(said of a married couple) to stick to each other to the end of their lives
白頭如新(ㄅㄞˊ ㄊㄡˊ ㄖㄨˊ ㄒㄧㄣ)
to remain aloof from each other though associated for a long time
白頭翁(ㄅㄞˊ ㄊㄡˊ ㄨㄥ)
①(zoology) a grackle; a grey starling ②(botany) an anemone (*Anemone camphor*)
白糖(ㄅㄞˊ ㄊㄤˊ)
white sugar; refined sugar: 在咖啡中加些白糖。Put some refined sugar in the coffee.
白鐵(ㄅㄞˊ ㄊㄧㄝˇ)
galvanized iron; tinplate
白天(ㄅㄞˊ ㄊㄧㄢ)
daytime
白兎(ㄅㄞˊ ㄊㄨˋ)or(ㄅㄛˊ ㄊㄨˋ)
①a white rabbit ②the rabbit in the moon—the moon
白銅(ㄅㄞˊ ㄊㄨㄥˊ)
tutenag
白內障(ㄅㄞˊ ㄋㄟˋ ㄓㄤˋ)
(medicine) cataract
白鑞(ㄅㄞˊ ㄌㄚˋ)
pewter; solder
白蠟(ㄅㄞˊ ㄌㄚˋ)
white wax (*Cire blanche*), a kind of insect secretion
白蠟蟲(ㄅㄞˊ ㄌㄚˋ ㄔㄨㄥˊ)
a lanternfly (*Flata limbata*)
白蘭地(ㄅㄞˊ ㄌㄢˊ ㄉㄧˋ)
brandy
白浪滔天(ㄅㄞˊ ㄌㄤˋ ㄊㄠ ㄊㄧㄢ)
white breakers sweeping across the sky
白梨(ㄅㄞˊ ㄌㄧˊ)
a kind of light-skinned pear (grown in the Peking area)
白痢(ㄅㄞˊ ㄌㄧˋ)
white dysentery (dysentery characterized by white mucous stool)
白蓮教(ㄅㄞˊ ㄌㄧㄢˊ ㄐㄧㄠˋ)

the White Lotus Society, set up near the end of the Yüan Dynasty, announcing the coming of Maitreya, the opening of his white lotus, and the day of salvation at hand (It developed into a revolution which resulted in the expulsion of the Mongols and establishment of the Ming Dynasty. Under the Ching Dynasty it was resurrected under a variety of names, and caused various uprisings.)

白蓮社(ㄅㄞˊ ㄌㄧㄢˊ ㄕㄜˋ)
a society formed in the Tsin Dynasty early in the fourth century A.D. by Hui Yüan (慧遠), who with 123 notable literati, swore to a life of purity before the image of Amitabha, and planted white lotuses in symbol

白練(ㄅㄞˊ ㄌㄧㄢˋ)
① white silk ② a cascade

白領階級(ㄅㄞˊ ㄌㄧㄥˇ ㄐㄧㄝ ㄐㄧˊ)
the white-collar class

白令海峽(ㄅㄞˊ ㄌㄧㄥˋ ㄏㄞˇ ㄒㄧㄚˊ)
the Bering Strait

白露(ㄅㄞˊ ㄌㄨˋ)or(ㄅㄛˊ ㄌㄨˋ)
① one of the 24 climatic periods of the lunar year (beginning on September 8 or 9) ② white dew

白鷺(ㄅㄞˊ ㄌㄨˋ)or(ㄅㄛˊ ㄌㄨˋ)
an egret

白鹿洞(ㄅㄞˊ ㄌㄨˋ ㄉㄨㄥˋ)
a place in Kiangsi where Confucian scholar Chu Hsi (朱熹) of the Sung Dynasty ran his school

白龍魚服(ㄅㄞˊ ㄌㄨㄥˊ ㄩˊ ㄈㄨˊ)
a ranking government official in ordeal while traveling incognito

白乾兒 or 白干兒(ㄅㄞˊ ㄍㄚㄦ)
pure kaoliang wine

白鴿(ㄅㄞˊ ㄍㄜ)
a pigeon

白給(ㄅㄞˊ ㄍㄟˇ)
to give for nothing

白骨(ㄅㄞˊ ㄍㄨˇ)
bones of the dead

白果(ㄅㄞˊ ㄍㄨㄛˇ)
a ginkgo nut, or a gingko nut

白圭之玷(ㄅㄞˊ ㄍㄨㄟ ㄓ ㄉㄧㄢˋ)
(literally) a flaw in a piece of jade—damage suffered through careless speech

白桂油(ㄅㄞˊ ㄍㄨㄟˋ ㄧㄡˊ)
canella

白宮(ㄅㄞˊ ㄍㄨㄥ)
the White House, Washington D.C.

白開水(ㄅㄞˊ ㄎㄞ ㄕㄨㄟˇ)
boiled water

白喉(ㄅㄞˊ ㄏㄡˊ)
diphtheria

白喉菌(ㄅㄞˊ ㄏㄡˊ ㄐㄩㄣˋ)
a diphtherial bacillus

白虎(ㄅㄞˊ ㄏㄨˇ)
① general name of seven stars in the western sky ② (slang) a woman's reproductive organ without hairs

白虎星(ㄅㄞˊ ㄏㄨˇ ㄒㄧㄥ)
(said of a woman) a jinx

白花
①(ㄅㄞˊ ㄏㄨㄚ) ⓐto spend (time, or money) without results ⓑ white flowers
②(ㄅㄞˊ ·ㄏㄨㄚ) sweet words to console

白花狗(ㄅㄞˊ ㄏㄨㄚ ㄍㄡˇ)
Dalmatian (a dog)

白花花(ㄅㄞˊ ㄏㄨㄚ ㄏㄨㄚ)
shining white

白花蛇(ㄅㄞˊ ㄏㄨㄚ ㄕㄜˊ)
a spotted venomous snake (*Agkistrodon acutus*)

白話(ㄅㄞˊ ㄏㄨㄚˋ)
spoken Chinese; vernacular Chinese: 這故事以白話寫成。The story is written in spoken Chinese.

白話小說(ㄅㄞˊ ㄏㄨㄚˋ ㄒㄧㄠˇ ㄕㄨㄛ)
novels in vernacular Chinese

白話詩(ㄅㄞˊ ㄏㄨㄚˋ ㄕ)
verses in vernacular Chinese

白話詞(ㄅㄞˊ ㄏㄨㄚˋ ㄘˊ)
verses of irregular lines in vernacular Chinese

白話文(ㄅㄞˊ ㄏㄨㄚˋ ㄨㄣˊ)
writing in vernacular Chinese

白話文學(ㄅㄞˊ ㄏㄨㄚˋ ㄨㄣˊ ㄒㄩㄝˊ)
vernacular Chinese literature; vernacular literature

白樺(ㄅㄞˊ ㄏㄨㄚˋ)
the white birch

白灰(ㄅㄞˊ ㄏㄨㄟ)or(ㄅㄛˊ ㄏㄨㄟ)
lime

白芥子(ㄅㄞˊ ㄐㄧㄝˋ ㄗˇ)
mustard seed

白酒(ㄅㄞˊ ㄐㄧㄡˇ)
spirits usually distilled from sorghum or maize; white spirits

白金(ㄅㄞˊ ㄐㄧㄣ)
① platinum ② silver

白金漢宮(ㄅㄞˊ ㄐㄧㄣ ㄏㄢˋ ㄍㄨㄥ)
Buckingham Palace, England

白淨(ㄅㄞˊ ·ㄐㄧㄥ)
perfectly clean; immaculate

白駒過隙(ㄅㄞˊ ㄐㄩ ㄍㄨㄛˋ ㄒㄧˋ)
(literally) a fleeting horse seen from a crevice—the swiftness of the lapse of time

白居易(ㄅㄞˊ ㄐㄩ ㄧˋ)
Pai Chü-i (772-846), a poet of the Tang Dynasty

白菊花(ㄅㄞˊ ㄐㄩˊ ㄏㄨㄚ)
a feverfew

白卷兒(ㄅㄞˊ ㄐㄩㄚˋㄦ)or白卷子(ㄅㄞˊ ㄐㄩㄢˋ ·ㄗ)
an examination paper handed in with all the questions unanswered: 他繳白卷子。He handed in a blank examination paper.

白鉛礦(ㄅㄞˊ ㄑㄧㄢ ㄎㄨㄤˋ)
cerussite

白屈菜(ㄅㄞˊ ㄑㄩ ㄘㄞˋ)
a celandine

白皙(ㄅㄞˊ ㄒㄧ)or(ㄅㄛˊ ㄒㄧ)
white-skinned: 他有白皙的皮膚。He is a white-skinned person.

白血病(ㄅㄞˊ ㄒㄧㄝˇ ㄅㄧㄥˋ)
leukemia

白血球(ㄅㄞˊ ㄒㄧㄝˇ ㄑㄧㄡˊ)
white blood cells; leucocytes

白信石(ㄅㄞˊ ㄒㄧㄣˋ ㄕˊ)
white arsenic

白相(ㄅㄞˊ ㄒㄧㄤˋ)or(ㄅㄛˊ ㄒㄧㄤˋ)
(the Wu or Shanghai dialect) to play

白相人(ㄅㄞˊ ㄒㄧㄤˋ ㄖㄣˊ)
(the Wu or Shanghai dialect) a loafer

白癬(ㄅㄞˊ ㄒㄩㄢˇ)
favus; honeycomb ringworm

白熊(ㄅㄞˊ ㄒㄩㄥˊ)or(ㄅㄛˊ ㄒㄩㄥˊ)
a polar bear: 白熊生活在北極區。Polar bears are living in the arctic regions.

〔白部〕

白芷(ㄅㄞˊ ㄓˇ)
dahurian angelica (root)
白摺子(ㄅㄞˊ ㄓㄜˊ ·ㄗ)
a writing pad of plain white paper used for practicing calligraphy
白齋(ㄅㄞˊ ㄓㄞ)
a diet of unflavored food
白晝(ㄅㄞˊ ㄓㄡˋ)or(ㄅㄛˊ ㄓㄡˋ)
broad daylight: 他們在白晝搶刼他。They robbed him in broad daytime.
白晝見鬼(ㄅㄞˊ ㄓㄡˋ ㄐㄧㄢˋ ㄍㄨㄟˇ)
to see a ghost in broad daylight; to have a fantasy
白晝宣淫(ㄅㄞˊ ㄓㄡˋ ㄒㄩㄢ ㄧㄣˊ)
to indulge in lascivious acts in broad daylight
白煮(ㄅㄞˊ ㄓㄨˇ)
to boil in plain water
白紵(ㄅㄞˊ ㄓㄨˋ)or(ㄅㄛˊ ㄓㄨˋ)
fine white linen: 那一家備有很多白紵織物。The house has a good stock of fine white linen.
白濁(ㄅㄞˊ ㄓㄨㄛˊ)
gonorrhea; gonoblennorrhoea 亦作「淋病」
白賺(ㄅㄞˊ ㄓㄨㄢˋ)
to earn with little or no effort
白種人(ㄅㄞˊ ㄓㄨㄥˇ ㄖㄣˊ)
the white people; the Caucasians
白吃(ㄅㄞˊ ㄔ)
to eat without payment: 他白吃了一頓大餐。He ate a big dinner without payment.
白癡(ㄅㄞˊ ㄔ)or(ㄅㄛˊ ㄔ)
an idiot: 他的舉動像白癡。He is behaving like an idiot.
白菖蒲(ㄅㄞˊ ㄔㄤ ㄆㄨˊ)
Acorus calamus, a sweet flag
白氅(ㄅㄞˊ ㄔㄤˇ)or(ㄅㄛˊ ㄔㄤˇ)
a uniform made of down worn by a guard in ancient times
白食(ㄅㄞˊ ㄕˊ)
a free meal
白士(ㄅㄞˊ ㄕˋ)or(ㄅㄛˊ ㄕˋ)
a needy but morally clean scholar
白蛇傳(ㄅㄞˊ ㄕㄜˊ ㄓㄨㄢˋ)
a legend of a white-snake fairy Pai Su-chen (白素貞), who fell in love with and married a mortal man Hsü Hsien (許仙)
白首(ㄅㄞˊ ㄕㄡˇ)or(ㄅㄛˊ ㄕㄡˇ)
a hoary head—the old age
白首窮經(ㄅㄞˊ ㄕㄡˇ ㄑㄩㄥˊ ㄐㄧㄥ)
to continue to study even in old age
白手成家(ㄅㄞˊ ㄕㄡˇ ㄔㄥˊ ㄐㄧㄚ)or白手起家(ㄅㄞˊ ㄕㄡˇ ㄑㄧˇ ㄐㄧㄚ)
to rise in life by one's own efforts; to become rich from scratch; from rags to riches
白山黑水(ㄅㄞˊ ㄕㄢ ㄏㄟ ㄕㄨㄟˇ)
Mt. Changpai (長白山) and the Amur River (黑龍江), which dominate the landscape of Manchuria
白身(ㄅㄞˊ ㄕㄣ)or(ㄅㄛˊ ㄕㄣ)
not holding any government office
白鼠(ㄅㄞˊ ㄕㄨˇ)
a white mouse (commonly believed to be divine); an albino rat: 我以白鼠做實驗。I made experiments on white mice.
白薯(ㄅㄞˊ ㄕㄨˇ)
a sweet potato
白蜀葵(ㄅㄞˊ ㄕㄨˇ ㄎㄨㄟˊ)
candytuft
白說(ㄅㄞˊ ㄕㄨㄛ)
to waste one's breath; to speak in vain
白水(ㄅㄞˊ ㄕㄨㄟˇ)or(ㄅㄛˊ ㄕㄨㄟˇ)
plain water
白日(ㄅㄞˊ ㄖˋ)or(ㄅㄛˊ ㄖˋ)
① daytime; daylight ② the sun
白日夢(ㄅㄞˊ ㄖˋ ㄇㄥˋ)
a daydream; reverie
白日鬼(ㄅㄞˊ ㄖˋ ㄍㄨㄟˇ)
a swindler; a cheater; a trickster; a burglar
白日昇天(ㄅㄞˊ ㄖˋ ㄕㄥ ㄊㄧㄢ)
① to become an immortal ② to rise abruptly in the world
白熱(ㄅㄞˊ ㄖㄜˋ)
white-hot
白熱化(ㄅㄞˊ ㄖㄜˋ ㄏㄨㄚˋ)
(said of a contest, movement, etc.) to reach the white-hot point; to reach the climax
白人(ㄅㄞˊ ㄖㄣˊ)
a white man or woman
白刃(ㄅㄞˊ ㄖㄣˋ)or(ㄅㄛˊ ㄖㄣˋ)
naked blades
白刃戰(ㄅㄞˊ ㄖㄣˋ ㄓㄢˋ)
a bayonet fight; a hand-to-hand combat
白扔(ㄅㄞˊ ㄖㄥ)
to spend without proper return; to waste
白字(ㄅㄞˊ ㄗˋ)
misused homophonous characters; wrongly written or mispronounced characters: 他寫得白字連篇。He wrote pages and pages of wrongly written characters.
白菜(ㄅㄞˊ ㄘㄞˋ)
① *Brassica pekinensis*, Chinese cabbage ② white rape
白醋(ㄅㄞˊ ㄘㄨˋ)
plain vinegar
白色(ㄅㄞˊ ㄙㄜˋ)
white
白色人種(ㄅㄞˊ ㄙㄜˋ ㄖㄣˊ ㄓㄨㄥˇ)
the white race
白松香(ㄅㄞˊ ㄙㄨㄥ ㄒㄧㄤ)
galbanum
白送(ㄅㄞˊ ㄙㄨㄥˋ)
to give away; to give gratis; to send (a gift) with nothing in return
白鵝(ㄅㄞˊ ㄜˊ)
a white goose
白俄(ㄅㄞˊ ㄜˋ)
White Russian; Byelorussian
白俄羅斯(ㄅㄞˊ ㄜˋ ㄌㄨㄛˊ ㄙ)
White Russia; Byelorussia
白堊(ㄅㄞˊ ㄜˋ)
(geology) chalk
白堊紀(ㄅㄞˊ ㄜˋ ㄐㄧˋ)
the Cretaceous period
白皚皚(ㄅㄞˊ ㄞˊ ㄞˊ)
(usually said of snow) white and clean
白衣大士(ㄅㄞˊ ㄧ ㄉㄚˋ ㄕˋ)
the Goddess of Mercy (in Buddhism)
白衣天使(ㄅㄞˊ ㄧ ㄊㄧㄢ ㄕˇ)
angels in white—nurses
白蟻(ㄅㄞˊ ㄧˇ)
a termite
白眼(ㄅㄞˊ ㄧㄢˇ)or(ㄅㄛˊ ㄧㄢˇ)
① the whites of the eyes ② disdain; contempt: 他遭人白眼。He was treated with disdain.
白眼圈(ㄅㄞˊ ㄧㄢˇ ㄑㄩㄢ)

the white-eye (a bird)
白眼珠兒(ㄅㄞˊ ㄧㄢˇ ㄓㄨㄦ)
the whites of the eye
白銀(ㄅㄞˊ ㄧㄣˊ)or(ㄅㄛˊ ㄧㄣˊ)
silver: 這戒指是白銀製的。The ring is made of silver.
白楊(ㄅㄞˊ ㄧㄤˊ)or(ㄅㄛˊ ㄧㄤˊ)
a poplar; an aspen; an abele
白鸚鵡(ㄅㄞˊ ㄧㄥ ㄨˇ)
a cacatua; a kakatoe
白尾鷹(ㄅㄞˊ ㄨㄟˇ ㄧㄥ)
a sea eagle
白文(ㄅㄞˊ ㄨㄣˊ)or(ㄅㄛˊ ㄨㄣˊ)
plain text without annotations
白榆(ㄅㄞˊ ㄩˊ)or(ㄅㄛˊ ㄩˊ)
an elm with whitish bark
白玉(ㄅㄞˊ ㄩˋ)or(ㄅㄛˊ ㄩˋ)
white jade
白玉微瑕(ㄅㄞˊ ㄩˋ ㄨㄟˊ ㄒㄧㄚˊ)
(literally) a tiny flaw in a piece of white jade—a small defect
白雲(ㄅㄞˊ ㄩㄣˊ)
white clouds
白雲母(ㄅㄞˊ ㄩㄣˊ ㄇㄨˇ)
white mica; muscovite
白雲觀(ㄅㄞˊ ㄩㄣˊ ㄍㄨㄢˋ)or(ㄅㄛˊ ㄩㄣˊ ㄍㄨㄢˋ)
a Taoist temple near Peking
白雲石(ㄅㄞˊ ㄩㄣˊ ㄕˊ)
dolomite
白雲蒼狗(ㄅㄞˊ ㄩㄣˊ ㄘㄤ ㄍㄡˇ)
(literally) A white cloud at one moment may look like a gray dog the next moment. —Things change in an unpredictable manner.
白用心機(ㄅㄞˊ ㄩㄥˋ ㄒㄧㄣ ㄐㄧ)
to scheme in vain; to fail in one's designs

一畫

【百】 3693 ㄅㄞˇ bae bǎi
(讀音 ㄅㄛˊ bor bó)

1. hundred
2. many; numerous
3. all

百拜(ㄅㄞˇ ㄅㄞˋ)
much courtesy
百倍(ㄅㄞˇ ㄅㄟˋ)
one hundred times
百寶箱(ㄅㄞˇ ㄅㄠˇ ㄒㄧㄤ)
a jewel case; a jewel box
百般(ㄅㄞˇ ㄅㄢ)
all sorts; every kind
百般殷勤(ㄅㄞˇ ㄅㄢ ㄧㄣ ㄑㄧㄣˊ)
courtesy expressed in numerous ways
百弊(ㄅㄞˇ ㄅㄧˋ)
all the ill effects
百弊叢生(ㄅㄞˇ ㄅㄧˋ ㄘㄨㄥˊ ㄕㄥ)
All the ill effects appear.
百不得一(ㄅㄞˇ ㄅㄨˋ ㄉㄜˊ ㄧ)
Not one out of a hundred is acceptable. 或 Less than 1% is qualified.
百不失一(ㄅㄞˇ ㄅㄨˋ ㄕ ㄧ)
There is not a single miss in a hundred tries.
百步穿楊(ㄅㄞˇ ㄅㄨˋ ㄔㄨㄢ ㄧㄤˊ)
(archery) superior marksmanship: 他是一個百步穿楊的射手。He is a superior marksman.
百朋之錫(ㄅㄞˇ ㄆㄥˊ ㄓ ㄒㄧˊ)
a very expensive gift; a handsome reward
百美圖(ㄅㄞˇ ㄇㄟˇ ㄊㄨˊ)
a picture showing large numbers of beautiful women
百米賽跑(ㄅㄞˇ ㄇㄧˇ ㄙㄞˋ ㄆㄠˇ)
the 100-meter dash
百慕達羣島(ㄅㄞˇ ㄇㄨˋ ㄉㄚˊ ㄑㄩㄣˊ ㄉㄠˇ)
the Bermuda Islands
百發百中(ㄅㄞˇ ㄈㄚ ㄅㄞˇ ㄓㄨㄥˋ)
to hit the target at every shot: 那射手百發百中。That archer hits the target at every shot.
百廢待興(ㄅㄞˇ ㄈㄟˋ ㄉㄞˋ ㄒㄧㄥ)
(said of government administration) All neglected matters are yet to be dealt with.
百廢俱舉(ㄅㄞˇ ㄈㄟˋ ㄐㄩˋ ㄐㄩˇ)or(ㄅㄞˇ ㄈㄟˋ ㄐㄩ ㄐㄩˇ)
(said of government administration) All neglected matters have been taken care of.
百分比(ㄅㄞˇ ㄈㄣ ㄅㄧˇ)or百分率(ㄅㄞˇ ㄈㄣ ㄌㄩˋ)
a percentage
百分法(ㄅㄞˇ ㄈㄣ ㄈㄚˇ)
statement or expression in percentage
百分之百(ㄅㄞˇ ㄈㄣ ㄓ ㄅㄞˇ)
a hundred per cent; out and out; absolutely
百分數(ㄅㄞˇ ㄈㄣ ㄕㄨˋ)
a percentage
百夫長(ㄅㄞˇ ㄈㄨ ㄓㄤˇ)
① a centurion (of the Roman Empire) ② a low-ranking military officer (in ancient China)
百讀不厭(ㄅㄞˇ ㄉㄨˊ ㄅㄨˋ ㄧㄢˋ)
(said of a book)not boring even after repeated reading; very interesting: 這本書百讀不厭。I never get tired of reading this book.
百端(ㄅㄞˇ ㄉㄨㄢ)
all matters
百聽不厭(ㄅㄞˇ ㄊㄧㄥ ㄅㄨˋ ㄧㄢˋ)
worth hearing a hundred times: 這個故事令我百聽不厭。I never get tired of hearing this story.
百衲(ㄅㄞˇ ㄋㄚˋ)
full of patches—said of a Buddhist monk's robe
百衲本(ㄅㄞˇ ㄋㄚˋ ㄅㄣˇ)
a book made complete by assembling many different rare editions or fragments
百衲衣(ㄅㄞˇ ㄋㄚˋ ㄧ)
①clothes with many patches ② a Buddhist monk's robe full of patches
百鳥(ㄅㄞˇ ㄋㄧㄠˇ)
all species of birds
百年(ㄅㄞˇ ㄋㄧㄢˊ)
① a hundred years; a century: 這是百年罕見的大水災。It's the biggest flood in the century. ② a lifetime
百年大計(ㄅㄞˇ ㄋㄧㄢˊ ㄉㄚˋ ㄐㄧˋ)
a project of vital and lasting importance; a great plan covering a very long period; a long-range program
百年好合(ㄅㄞˇ ㄋㄧㄢˊ ㄏㄠˇ ㄏㄜˊ)
a harmonious union lasting a hundred years (a conventional congratulatory message on a wedding)
百年後(ㄅㄞˇ ㄋㄧㄢˊ ㄏㄡˋ)
after death
百年紀念(ㄅㄞˇ ㄋㄧㄢˊ ㄐㄧˋ ㄋㄧㄢˋ)
the centennial, or centenary
百年戰爭(ㄅㄞˇ ㄋㄧㄢˊ ㄓㄢˋ ㄓㄥ)
the Hundred Years' War, 1337-1453, between England and France
百年樹人(ㄅㄞˇ ㄋㄧㄢˊ ㄕㄨˋ ㄖㄣˊ)
It takes one hundred years to cultivate a man. 或 Educa-

tion of the people takes a hundred years to bear fruit.

百裏挑一(ㄅㄞˇ ㄌㄧˇ ㄊㄧㄠ ㄧ)
(literally) to pick one out of a hundred—very few

百里侯(ㄅㄞˇ ㄌㄧˇ ㄏㄡˊ)
the magistrate of a county in former times

百里才(ㄅㄞˇ ㄌㄧˇ ㄘㄞˊ)
talent barely good enough for a county magistrate

百僚(ㄅㄞˇ ㄌㄧㄠˊ)
all the officials

百鍊鋼 or 百鍊剛(ㄅㄞˇ ㄌㄧㄢˋ ㄍㄤ)
well-tempered steel

百鍊金(ㄅㄞˇ ㄌㄧㄢˋ ㄐㄧㄣ)
well-tempered gold

百鍊成鋼(ㄅㄞˇ ㄌㄧㄢˋ ㄔㄥˊ ㄍㄤ)
Mastery comes from long training. 或 Expertise is the result of long and hard practice.

百伶百俐(ㄅㄞˇ ㄌㄧㄥˊ ㄅㄞˇ ㄌㄧˋ)
very clever; very intelligent

百靈鳥(ㄅㄞˇ ㄌㄧㄥˊ ㄋㄧㄠˇ)
a lark; the Mongolian lark

百感交集(ㄅㄞˇ ㄍㄢˇ ㄐㄧㄠ ㄐㄧˊ)
Lots of emotions crowd into the heart.

百穀(ㄅㄞˇ ㄍㄨˇ)
all kinds of grain

百果(ㄅㄞˇ ㄍㄨㄛˇ)
all kinds of fruits

百官(ㄅㄞˇ ㄍㄨㄢ)
officials of all ranks and descriptions

百工(ㄅㄞˇ ㄍㄨㄥ)
①all sorts of officers ②all sorts of handicraftsmen

百科全書(ㄅㄞˇ ㄎㄜ ㄑㄩㄢˊ ㄕㄨ)or 百科辭典(ㄅㄞˇ ㄎㄜ ㄘˊ ㄉㄧㄢˇ)
an encyclopedia

百口莫辯(ㄅㄞˇ ㄎㄡˇ ㄇㄛˋ ㄅㄧㄢˋ)
There is no room for verbal defense.—unable to give a convincing explanation for self-defense

百揆(ㄅㄞˇ ㄎㄨㄟˊ)or(ㄅㄛˊ ㄎㄨㄟˊ)
the chief minister of a state

百孔千瘡(ㄅㄞˇ ㄎㄨㄥˇ ㄑㄧㄢ ㄔㄨㄤ)
(literally) honeycombed or riddled with holes—in a state of ruin or extreme distress; in very bad shape

百合(ㄅㄞˇ ˙ㄏㄜ)
the lily

百合花(ㄅㄞˇ ㄏㄜˊ ㄏㄨㄚ)
the lily

百花(ㄅㄞˇ ㄏㄨㄚ)
all sorts of flowers

百花齊放(ㄅㄞˇ ㄏㄨㄚ ㄑㄧˊ ㄈㄤˋ)
All flowers are in bloom.

百花洲(ㄅㄞˇ ㄏㄨㄚ ㄓㄡ)
a place in Nanchang, Kiangsi, a naval training center during the Sung Dynasty

百花生日(ㄅㄞˇ ㄏㄨㄚ ㄕㄥ ㄖˋ)
the birthday of all flowers (the 12th day of the second lunar month)

百花王(ㄅㄞˇ ㄏㄨㄚ ㄨㄤˊ)
the Queen of Flowers—the peony

百貨公司(ㄅㄞˇ ㄏㄨㄛˋ ㄍㄨㄥ ㄙ)
a department store

百貨商場(ㄅㄞˇ ㄏㄨㄛˋ ㄕㄤ ㄔㄤˇ)or (ㄅㄞˇ ㄏㄨㄛˋ ㄕㄤ ㄔㄤˊ)
an emporium

百計千方(ㄅㄞˇ ㄐㄧˋ ㄑㄧㄢ ㄈㄤ)
all sorts of tricks and stratagems

百家(ㄅㄞˇ ㄐㄧㄚ)
①the various schools of thinkers ②various families

百家姓(ㄅㄞˇ ㄐㄧㄚ ㄒㄧㄥˋ)
the *Book of Family Names*

百家爭鳴(ㄅㄞˇ ㄐㄧㄚ ㄓㄥ ㄇㄧㄥˊ)
All schools of thoughts contend for attention.

百結衣(ㄅㄞˇ ㄐㄧㄝˊ ㄧ)
clothes full of patches

百星不如一月(ㄅㄞˇ ㄒㄧㄥ ㄅㄨˋ ㄖㄨˊ ㄧˊ ㄩㄝˋ)
(literally) A single moon is better than one hundred stars.—Quality is more important than quantity.

百姓(ㄅㄞˇ ㄒㄧㄥˋ)
①the common people; the people ②all existing family names

百折不撓(ㄅㄞˇ ㄓㄜˊ ㄅㄨˋ ㄋㄠˊ)
unflinching despite repeated setbacks; indomitable; unswerving; unshakable

百折不回(ㄅㄞˇ ㄓㄜˊ ㄅㄨˋ ㄏㄨㄟˊ)
pushing forward despite repeated frustrations

百褶裙(ㄅㄞˇ ㄓㄜˊ ㄑㄩㄣˊ)or 百襉裙(ㄅㄞˇ ㄐㄧㄢˇ ㄑㄩㄣˊ)
a pleated skirt

百戰百勝(ㄅㄞˇ ㄓㄢˋ ㄅㄞˇ ㄕㄥˋ)
victorious in every battle

百中無一(ㄅㄞˇ ㄓㄨㄥ ㄨˊ ㄧ)
not one in a hundred; very few

百尺竿頭(ㄅㄞˇ ㄔˇ ㄍㄢ ㄊㄡˊ)
(literally) the top of a hundred-foot pole—the highest achievement

百尺竿頭，更進一步(ㄅㄞˇ ㄔˇ ㄍㄢ ㄊㄡˊ, ㄍㄥˋ ㄐㄧㄣˋ ㄧˊ ㄅㄨˋ)
to make still further progress

百川滙宗(ㄅㄞˇ ㄔㄨㄢ ㄏㄨㄟˋ ㄗㄨㄥ)
(literally) A hundred rivers may merge in one.—Divergence ends in uniformity or agreement.

百十來個(ㄅㄞˇ ㄕˊ ㄌㄞˊ ˙ㄍㄜ)
around a hundred; a hundred or so

百世(ㄅㄞˇ ㄕˋ)
a period of a hundred generations—a very long period of time

百世師(ㄅㄞˇ ㄕˋ ㄕ)
a teacher for a hundred generations—a sage

百事通(ㄅㄞˇ ㄕˋ ㄊㄨㄥ)
an expert in everything; an all-rounder; a knowledgeable person

百事俱廢(ㄅㄞˇ ㄕˋ ㄐㄩˋ ㄈㄟˋ)
Everything is neglected.

百舌(ㄅㄞˇ ㄕㄜˊ)or(ㄅㄛˊ ㄕㄜˊ)or 百舌鳥(ㄅㄞˇ ㄕㄜˊ ㄋㄧㄠˇ)
a shrike 亦作「反舌鳥」or「伯勞鳥」

百壽圖(ㄅㄞˇ ㄕㄡˋ ㄊㄨˊ)
a pattern composed of a hundred different styles of the character 壽 and presented as a birthday gift

百獸之王(ㄅㄞˇ ㄕㄡˋ ㄓ ㄨㄤˊ)
the king of all animals—the lion

百善孝爲先(ㄅㄞˇ ㄕㄢˋ ㄒㄧㄠˋ ㄨㄟˊ ㄒㄧㄢ)
Filial piety is the most important of all virtues.

百身莫贖(ㄅㄞˇ ㄕㄣ ㄇㄛˋ ㄕㄨˊ)
A dead person cannot be made alive again by any means.

百乘之家(ㄅㄞˇ ㄕㄥˋ ㄓ ㄐㄧㄚ)
a house with a hundred carriages—a family of an official during the Chou Dynas-

ty
百日(ㄅㄞˇ ㄖˋ)
the hundredth day after one's death
百日咳(ㄅㄞˇ ㄖˋ ㄎㄜˊ)
whooping cough
百日紅(ㄅㄞˇ ㄖˋ ㄏㄨㄥˊ)
crape myrtle
百日草(ㄅㄞˇ ㄖˋ ㄘㄠˇ)
(botany) youth-and-old-age
百忍(ㄅㄞˇ ㄖㄣˇ)
great endurance; great forbearance
百子圖(ㄅㄞˇ ㄗˇ ㄊㄨˊ)
a picture showing numerous children either drawn or embroidered (given as a wish that the recipient will have numerous offspring)
百子全書(ㄅㄞˇ ㄗˇ ㄑㄩㄢˊ ㄕㄨ)
a complete collection of all schools of thoughts from ancient times, compiled during the Ching Dynasty
百足之蟲，死而不殭(ㄅㄞˇ ㄗㄨˊ ㄓ ㄔㄨㄥˊ, ㄙˇ ㄦˊ ㄅㄨˋ ㄐㄧㄤ)
(literally) A centipede dies hard.—The influence of a powerful man lingers on after his downfall.
百縱千隨(ㄅㄞˇ ㄗㄨㄥˋ ㄑㄧㄢ ㄙㄨㄟˊ)
to yield to all the wishes (of a child, etc.)
百思莫解(ㄅㄞˇ ㄙ ㄇㄛˋ ㄐㄧㄝˇ)
incomprehensible; inexplicable: 此事我百思莫解。I remain puzzled after pondering over the matter a hundred times.
百依百順(ㄅㄞˇ ㄧ ㄅㄞˇ ㄕㄨㄣˋ)
to yield to all the wishes (of a child, etc.) 亦作「百縱千隨」
百葉箱(ㄅㄞˇ ㄧㄝˋ ㄒㄧㄤ)
a thermometer screen
百葉窗(ㄅㄞˇ ㄧㄝˋ ㄔㄨㄤ)
Venetian blinds
百憂(ㄅㄞˇ ㄧㄡ)
all worries or sorrows
百無聊賴(ㄅㄞˇ ㄨˊ ㄌㄧㄠˊ ㄌㄞˋ)
very much bored
百無禁忌(ㄅㄞˇ ㄨˊ ㄐㄧㄣˋ ㄐㄧˋ)
There are no taboos or restrictions at all.
百無一長(ㄅㄞˇ ㄨˊ ㄧˋ ㄔㄤˊ)
skilled in nothing; good-for-nothing
百無一失(ㄅㄞˇ ㄨˊ ㄧˋ ㄕ)
(literally) There is not a single miss in a hundred tries.—sure to succeed if certain rules are followed
百物(ㄅㄞˇ ㄨˋ)
all things
百萬(ㄅㄞˇ ㄨㄢˋ)
a million
百萬富翁(ㄅㄞˇ ㄨㄢˋ ㄈㄨˋ ㄨㄥ)
a millionaire
百聞不如一見(ㄅㄞˇ ㄨㄣˊ ㄅㄨˋ ㄖㄨˊ ㄧˊ ㄐㄧㄢˋ)
There is nothing like seeing for oneself. 或 Seeing is believing.
百喻經(ㄅㄞˇ ㄩˋ ㄐㄧㄥ)
the sutra of the 100 parables, translated by Gunarddhi, in the late fifth century
百越(ㄅㄞˇ ㄩㄝˋ)
Yüeh—ancient name of the area of what is Chekiang, Fukien, and Kwangtung today

二畫

【皁】 3694 (皂) ㄗㄠˋ tzaw zào
1. black
2. menial labor
3. a menial; a lictor
4. soap

皁白(ㄗㄠˋ ㄅㄞˊ)
black and white—right and wrong
皁白不分(ㄗㄠˋ ㄅㄞˊ ㄅㄨˋ ㄈㄣ)
to fail to distinguish between right and wrong
皁隸(ㄗㄠˋ ㄌㄧˋ)
a government-employed laborer, messenger, etc. in ancient times
皁櫪(ㄗㄠˋ ㄌㄧˋ)
a stable 亦作「馬廐」
皁莢(ㄗㄠˋ ㄐㄧㄚˊ)
a honey locust

【皂】 3695 ㄗㄠˋ tzaw zào
soap

三畫

【的】 3696 1. ㄉㄧˋ dih dì
1. clear; manifest
2. a target; a goal

的的(ㄉㄧˋ ㄉㄧˋ)
clear; distinct
的曆 or 的皪(ㄉㄧˋ ㄌㄧˋ)
bright; lustrous

【的】 3696 2. ㄉㄧˊ dyi dí
accurate; exact; proper
的當(ㄉㄧˊ ㄉㄤˋ)
accurate; proper
的款(ㄉㄧˊ ㄎㄨㄢˇ)
a surely available sum of money
的確(ㄉㄧˊ ㄑㄩㄝˋ)
certainly; surely

【的】 3696 3. ˙ㄉㄜ ˙de de
1. a bound subordinate particle translatable by "'s" or with terms interchanged by "of": 這是我姊姊的皮包。This is my elder sister's purse.
2. by "-ly"
3. by an adjectival ending, a prepositional phrase, or a relative: 玫瑰花開了，有紅的，有黃的。The roses are in bloom; some are red and some yellow.

四畫

【皆】 3697 ㄐㄧㄝ jie jiē
all; every; entire: 四海之內，皆兄弟也。Within the four seas all people are brothers.
皆大歡喜(ㄐㄧㄝ ㄉㄚˋ ㄏㄨㄢ ㄒㄧˇ)
Everybody is satisfied.
皆可(ㄐㄧㄝ ㄎㄜˇ)
all acceptable
皆知(ㄐㄧㄝ ㄓ)
all aware
皆是(ㄐㄧㄝ ㄕˋ)
(they) all are
皆屬(ㄐㄧㄝ ㄕㄨˇ)
(they) all belong to
皆因(ㄐㄧㄝ ㄧㄣ)
only because; just because; all because

【皇】 3698 ㄏㄨㄤˊ hwang huáng
1. imperial; royal
2. an emperor
3. beautiful; brilliant
4. uneasy; anxious
5. a term of respect for an ancestor

皇妣(ㄏㄨㄤˊ ㄅㄧˇ)
one's deceased mother

皇辟(ㄏㄨㄤˊ ㄅㄧˋ)
① the emperor ② my late husband
皇甫(ㄏㄨㄤˊ ㄈㄨˇ)
a Chinese family name
皇帝(ㄏㄨㄤˊ ㄉㄧˋ)
an emperor
皇都(ㄏㄨㄤˊ ㄉㄨ)
the imperial capital
皇太后(ㄏㄨㄤˊ ㄊㄞˋ ㄏㄡˋ)
the empress dowager
皇太子(ㄏㄨㄤˊ ㄊㄞˋ ㄗˇ)
the crown prince 參看「皇儲」
皇天后土(ㄏㄨㄤˊ ㄊㄧㄢ ㄏㄡˋ ㄊㄨˇ)
Heaven and Earth
皇圖(ㄏㄨㄤˊ ㄊㄨˊ)
the domain of an empire
皇統(ㄏㄨㄤˊ ㄊㄨㄥˇ)
imperial lineage
皇陵(ㄏㄨㄤˊ ㄌㄧㄥˊ)
an imperial mausoleum
皇冠(ㄏㄨㄤˊ ㄍㄨㄢ)
an imperial crown
皇宮(ㄏㄨㄤˊ ㄍㄨㄥ)
an imperial palace
皇考(ㄏㄨㄤˊ ㄎㄠˇ)
one's deceased father
皇后(ㄏㄨㄤˊ ㄏㄡˋ)
an empress
皇皇(ㄏㄨㄤˊ ㄏㄨㄤˊ)
① brilliant ② uneasy; anxious; restless
皇皇巨著(ㄏㄨㄤˊ ㄏㄨㄤˊ ㄐㄩˋ ㄓㄨˋ)
a great brilliant work
皇極(ㄏㄨㄤˊ ㄐㄧˊ)
the rules established by the emperor for public observance
皇家(ㄏㄨㄤˊ ㄐㄧㄚ)
the imperial family (or house)
皇親國戚(ㄏㄨㄤˊ ㄑㄧㄣ ㄍㄨㄛˊ ˙ㄑㄧ)
relatives of the emperor
皇清經解(ㄏㄨㄤˊ ㄑㄧㄥ ㄐㄧㄥ ㄐㄧㄝˇ)
a huge collection of commentaries on classics compiled by Juan Yüan (阮元) during the Ching Dynasty
皇城(ㄏㄨㄤˊ ㄔㄥˊ)
the Imperial City (the inner part of Peking)
皇儲(ㄏㄨㄤˊ ㄔㄨˊ)
the crown prince 亦作「皇太子」
皇室(ㄏㄨㄤˊ ㄕˋ)
the imperial household; the royal household
皇上(ㄏㄨㄤˊ ㄕㄤˋ)
His Majesty
皇族(ㄏㄨㄤˊ ㄗㄨˊ)
the imperial family; the royal family
皇祖(ㄏㄨㄤˊ ㄗㄨˇ)
the imperial ancestors before the founder of the dynasty
皇祖妣(ㄏㄨㄤˊ ㄗㄨˇ ㄅㄧˇ)
one's deceased grandmother
皇祖考(ㄏㄨㄤˊ ㄗㄨˇ ㄎㄠˇ)
one's deceased grandfather
皇恩(ㄏㄨㄤˊ ㄣ)
imperial favor or kindness

【皈】 3699 ㄍㄨㄟ guei guī
to follow
皈依(ㄍㄨㄟ ㄧ)
to be converted to (Buddhism)

五畫

【皋】 3700 (皐) ㄍㄠ gau gāo
1. a marsh; a swamp
2. a shore
皋比(ㄍㄠ ㄆㄧˊ)
① a tiger's skin ② a teacher's seat; a teacher's position
皋門(ㄍㄠ ㄇㄣˊ)
a palace gate
皋隰(ㄍㄠ ㄒㄧˊ)
a swamp; a marsh
皋壤(ㄍㄠ ㄖㄤˇ)
land by a marsh or swamp
皋陶(ㄍㄠ ㄧㄠˊ)
name of the man who served as a chief judicial officer for the legendary ruler Shun (舜)
皋月(ㄍㄠ ㄩㄝˋ)
the fifth month of the lunar year

六畫

【皎】 3701 ㄐㄧㄠˇ jeau jiǎo
1. white; clean
2. bright; lustrous; brilliant: 皎月當空。The bright moon hung in the sky.
皎白(ㄐㄧㄠˇ ㄅㄞˊ)
brightly white
皎厲(ㄐㄧㄠˇ ㄌㄧˋ)
proud
皎潔(ㄐㄧㄠˇ ㄐㄧㄝˊ)
brightly clean
皎皎(ㄐㄧㄠˇ ㄐㄧㄠˇ)
① very white ② bright
皎如日星(ㄐㄧㄠˇ ㄖㄨˊ ㄖˋ ㄒㄧㄥ)
as bright as the heavenly bodies

七畫

【皓】 3702 ㄏㄠˋ haw hào
white and bright
皓魄(ㄏㄠˋ ㄆㄛˋ)
the moon or moonlight
皓礬(ㄏㄠˋ ㄈㄢˊ)
white vitriol or goslarite
皓天 or 昊天(ㄏㄠˋ ㄊㄧㄢ)
① a summer sky ② the sky; heaven
皓皓(ㄏㄠˋ ㄏㄠˋ)
bright; brilliant; glistening; gleaming
皓齒(ㄏㄠˋ ㄔˇ)
white teeth; sparkling teeth
皓首(ㄏㄠˋ ㄕㄡˇ)
a hoary head—old age
皓首窮經(ㄏㄠˋ ㄕㄡˇ ㄑㄩㄥˊ ㄐㄧㄥ)
to continue to study even in old age
皓腕(ㄏㄠˋ ㄨㄢˋ)
an attractive white arm (of a woman)
皓月當空(ㄏㄠˋ ㄩㄝˋ ㄉㄤ ㄎㄨㄥ)
The bright moon hangs in the sky.

【皖】 3703 ㄨㄢˇ woan wǎn
1. name of an ancient state in what is today's Anhwei
2. an alternative name of Anhwei
皖北(ㄨㄢˇ ㄅㄟˇ)
the part of Anhwei north of the Yangtze River
皖南(ㄨㄢˇ ㄋㄢˊ)
the part of Anhwei south of the Yangtze River
皖水(ㄨㄢˇ ㄕㄨㄟˇ)
a tributary of the Yangtze River originating in Anhwei

【皕】 3704 ㄅㄧˋ bih bì
two hundred

八畫

【皙】 3705
ㄒㄧ shi xī
1. white skin
2. a kind of dates

十畫

【皚】 3706
ㄞˊ air ái
pure white; white and clean; brightly white
皚皚(ㄞˊ ㄞˊ)
brightly white: 白雪皚皚 an expanse of white snow

【皜】 3707
ㄏㄠˋ haw hào
white; bright
皜皜(ㄏㄠˋ ㄏㄠˋ)
white and glistening

十二畫

【皤】 3708
ㄆㄛˊ por pó
1. (said of an old man) hoary-headed
2. white
3. a vast belly
皤皤(ㄆㄛˊ ㄆㄛˊ)
white; hoary
皤然(ㄆㄛˊ ㄖㄢˊ)
white; hoary

皮部
ㄆㄧˊ pyi pí

【皮】 3709
ㄆㄧˊ pyi pí
1. skin; fur; hide; leather; rind; peltry; bark
2. a thin sheet
3. naughty
4. a Chinese family name
皮包(ㄆㄧˊ ㄅㄠ)
a handbag or purse (especially one made of leather): 她從皮包裡拿出錢來。She took money from her handbag.
皮包骨(ㄆㄧˊ ㄅㄠ ㄍㄨˇ)or 皮包骨頭(ㄆㄧˊ ㄅㄠ ㄍㄨˇ ·ㄊㄡ)
skinny; only skin and bones: 他瘦得皮包骨。He is only skin and bones.
皮弁(ㄆㄧˊ ㄅㄧㄢˋ)
an ancient cap made of a deer's hide
皮破血流(ㄆㄧˊ ㄆㄛˋ ㄒㄧㄝˇ ㄌㄧㄡˊ)
wounded and bleeding
皮袍(ㄆㄧˊ ㄆㄠˊ)
a fur gown
皮膜組織(ㄆㄧˊ ㄇㄛˊ ㄗㄨˇ ㄓ)
(anatomy) epithelium
皮毛(ㄆㄧˊ ㄇㄠˊ)
superficial knowledge
皮毛之見(ㄆㄧˊ ㄇㄠˊ ㄓ ㄐㄧㄢˋ)
a superficial view or opinion
皮面(ㄆㄧˊ ㄇㄧㄢˋ)
① the outer skin; epidermis ② to remove the skin; to skin ③ a leather cover
皮筏(ㄆㄧˊ ㄈㄚˊ)
a kayak
皮膚(ㄆㄧˊ ㄈㄨ)
skin
皮膚病(ㄆㄧˊ ㄈㄨ ㄅㄧㄥˋ)
skin disease
皮膚科(ㄆㄧˊ ㄈㄨ ㄎㄜ)
dermatology
皮膚科醫生(ㄆㄧˊ ㄈㄨ ㄎㄜ ㄧ ㄕㄥ)
a dermatologist
皮膚科醫院(ㄆㄧˊ ㄈㄨ ㄎㄜ ㄧ ㄩㄢˋ)
a dermatological clinic
皮膚炎(ㄆㄧˊ ㄈㄨ ㄧㄢˊ)
dermatitis
皮膚癌(ㄆㄧˊ ㄈㄨ ㄧㄢˊ)
skin cancer
皮袋(ㄆㄧˊ ㄉㄞˋ)
a leather bag or purse
皮帶(ㄆㄧˊ ㄉㄞˋ)
a leather belt
皮蛋(ㄆㄧˊ ㄉㄢˋ)
duck's eggs preserved in lime
皮條(ㄆㄧˊ ㄊㄧㄠˊ)
thongs
皮條客(ㄆㄧˊ ㄊㄧㄠˊ ㄎㄜˋ)
a pimp
皮條縴(ㄆㄧˊ ㄊㄧㄠˊ ㄑㄧㄢˋ)
the service rendered by a pander
皮艇(ㄆㄧˊ ㄊㄧㄥˇ)
a skin boat
皮囊(ㄆㄧˊ ㄋㄤˊ)
a leather bag
皮裏抽肉(ㄆㄧˊ ㄌㄧˇ ㄔㄡ ㄖㄡˋ)
skinny; emaciated
皮裏春秋(ㄆㄧˊ ㄌㄧˇ ㄔㄨㄣ ㄑㄧㄡ)or 皮裏陽秋(ㄆㄧˊ ㄌㄧˇ ㄧㄤˊ ㄑㄧㄡ)
to have an unexpressed opinion about the worth of a person or thing; to criticize mentally
皮臉(ㄆㄧˊ ㄌㄧㄢˇ)
shameless; brazen
皮革(ㄆㄧˊ ㄍㄜˊ)
leather
皮革工廠(ㄆㄧˊ ㄍㄜˊ ㄍㄨㄥ ㄔㄤˇ)
a tannery
皮開肉綻(ㄆㄧˊ ㄎㄞ ㄖㄡˋ ㄓㄢˋ)
The skin ruptures and the flesh bursts.—the effect of severe beating
皮厚(ㄆㄧˊ ㄏㄡˋ)
thick-skinned: 她剝了一個皮厚的柳橙。She peeled a thick-skinned orange.
皮花科(ㄆㄧˊ ㄏㄨㄚ ㄎㄜ)
the department of dermatology and syphilology
皮貨(ㄆㄧˊ ㄏㄨㄛˋ)
furs
皮黃(ㄆㄧˊ ㄏㄨㄤˊ)
a Peking opera tune; Peking opera
皮夾子(ㄆㄧˊ ㄐㄧㄚˊ ·ㄗ)or 皮夾兒(ㄆㄧˊ ㄐㄧㄚˊㄦ)
a wallet (especially of leather)
皮夾克(ㄆㄧˊ ㄐㄧㄚˊ ㄎㄜˋ)
a leather jacket, or Windbreaker
皮匠(ㄆㄧˊ ·ㄐㄧㄤ)
a cobbler
皮球(ㄆㄧˊ ㄑㄧㄡˊ)
a rubber ball
皮下注射(ㄆㄧˊ ㄒㄧㄚˋ ㄓㄨˋ ㄕㄜˋ)
① a hypodermic injection, or subcutaneous injection ② to skin-pop
皮鞋(ㄆㄧˊ ㄒㄧㄝˊ)
leather shoes
皮笑肉不笑(ㄆㄧˊ ㄒㄧㄠˋ ㄖㄡˋ ㄅㄨˋ ㄒㄧㄠˋ)
treacherous; crafty; putting on a false smile
皮箱(ㄆㄧˊ ㄒㄧㄤ)
a suitcase or valise (especially of leather)
皮相(ㄆㄧˊ ㄒㄧㄤˋ)
an external appearance
皮相之談(ㄆㄧˊ ㄒㄧㄤˋ ㄓ ㄊㄢˊ)
a superficial talk or opinion

〔皿部〕

皮靴(ㄆㄧˊ ㄒㄩㄝ)
leather boots: 她穿着一雙長筒的皮靴。She was in a pair of leather boots.
皮之不存，毛將焉附(ㄆㄧˊ ㄓ ㄅㄨˋ ㄘㄨㄣˊ, ㄇㄠˊ ㄐㄧㄤ ㄧㄢ ㄈㄨˋ)
(literally) Where can the hair grow when there is no skin?—How can one live as a free man when one's country loses its sovereignty?
皮紙(ㄆㄧˊ ㄓˇ)
heavy wrapping paper
皮裝書(ㄆㄧˊ ㄓㄨㄤ ㄕㄨ)
a leather-bound book
皮尺(ㄆㄧˊ ㄔˇ)
a tape measure; a tape
皮肉生涯(ㄆㄧˊ ㄖㄡˋ ㄕㄥ ㄧㄚˊ)
prostitution
皮子(ㄆㄧˊ ·ㄗ)
① skin; rind ② leather; hide ③ the cover or jacket (of a book)
皮草(ㄆㄧˊ ㄘㄠˇ)
furs
皮層(ㄆㄧˊ ㄘㄥˊ)
a cortex
皮鬆肉緊(ㄆㄧˊ ㄙㄨㄥ ㄖㄡˋ ㄐㄧㄣˇ)
idle; inactive
皮襖(ㄆㄧˊ ㄠˇ)
a fur coat; a leather coat
皮衣(ㄆㄧˊ ㄧ)
fur clothing: 她穿着非常昂貴的皮衣。She was wearing very expensive furs.
皮影戲(ㄆㄧˊ ㄧㄥˇ ㄒㄧˋ)
the shadow show

五畫

【皰】 3710 (疱) ㄆㄠˋ paw pào
pimples

七畫

【皴】 3711 ㄘㄨㄣ tsuen cūn
1. (said of the skin) to crack or chap from cold
2. (Chinese painting) a technique of representing irregular surfaces
皴法(ㄘㄨㄣ ㄈㄚˇ)
(Chinese painting) a technique of representing irregular surfaces

九畫

【皸】 3712 ㄐㄩㄣ jiun jūn
(said of the skin) to crack or chap from cold or dryness
皸裂(ㄐㄩㄣ ㄌㄧㄝˋ)
(said of the skin) to chap or crack from cold or dryness

十畫

【皺】 3713 ㄓㄡˋ jow zhòu
1. wrinkles; creases; folds; rumples
2. to wrinkle; to fold; to contract; to crease; to crumple
皺彆(ㄓㄡˋ ·ㄅㄧㄝ)
unpleasantly narrow; close; confining
皺眉(ㄓㄡˋ ㄇㄟˊ) or 皺眉頭(ㄓㄡˋ ㄇㄟˊ ·ㄊㄡ)
to frown; to knit the brows
皺摺(ㄓㄡˋ ㄓㄜˊ)
creases; folds
皺皺巴巴(ㄓㄡˋ ·ㄓㄡ ㄅㄚ ㄅㄚ)
not smooth; full of creases; creasy; crumpled; shriveled
皺胃(ㄓㄡˋ ㄨㄟˋ)
an abomasum
皺紋(ㄓㄡˋ ㄨㄣˊ)
wrinkles; creases; folds; rumples

皿部 ㄇㄧㄣˇ miin mǐn

【皿】 3714 ㄇㄧㄣˇ miin mǐn (又讀 ㄇㄧㄥˇ miing mǐng)
a shallow container (such as a dish, plate, saucer, etc.)

三畫

【盂】 3715 ㄩˊ yu yú
1. a basin; a broad-mouthed receptacle for holding liquid; a jar
2. a party for hunting
盂蘭盆會(ㄩˊ ㄌㄢˊ ㄆㄣˊ ㄏㄨㄟˋ)
the Buddhist name of the Ghost Festival (the 15th of the seventh moon), being a transliteration from Sanskrit *ullambana* (deliverance)

四畫

【盅】 3716 ㄓㄨㄥ jong zhōng
a small cup
【盆】 3717 ㄆㄣˊ pern pén
a bowl; a basin; a tub
盆地(ㄆㄣˊ ㄉㄧˋ)
(geology) a basin
盆景(ㄆㄣˊ ㄐㄧㄥˇ)
a potted plant; a bonsai
盆子(ㄆㄣˊ ·ㄗ) or 盆兒(ㄆㄜˊㄦ)
a bowl; a basin; a tub
盆栽(ㄆㄣˊ ㄗㄞ)
a potted plant; to plant in a pot; a bonsai 亦作「盆景」
【盈】 3718 ㄧㄥˊ yng yíng
to fill; to become full
盈把(ㄧㄥˊ ㄅㄚˇ)
a handful
盈滿(ㄧㄥˊ ㄇㄢˇ)
filled; full
盈利(ㄧㄥˊ ㄌㄧˋ)
profit; gains: 盈利一百萬元 to net a profit of one million dollars
盈貫(ㄧㄥˊ ㄍㄨㄢˋ)
(said of a bow) drawn to the fullest extent
盈虧(ㄧㄥˊ ㄎㄨㄟ)
①(said of the moon) waxing and waning ② profits and losses
盈千累萬(ㄧㄥˊ ㄑㄧㄢ ㄌㄟˇ ㄨㄢˋ)
thousands upon thousands
盈缺(ㄧㄥˊ ㄑㄩㄝ)
(said of the moon) waxing and waning
盈箱累篋(ㄧㄥˊ ㄒㄧㄤ ㄌㄟˇ ㄑㄧㄝˋ)
(said of treasures, etc.) to fill boxes and baskets to the brim
盈虛(ㄧㄥˊ ㄒㄩ)
waxing and waning; fullness and emptiness; ups and downs
盈則必虧(ㄧㄥˊ ㄗㄜˊ ㄅㄧˋ ㄎㄨㄟ)

When the fullest extent is reached, the decline begins.
盈溢(ㄧㄥˊ ㄧˋ)
to brim over
盈盈(ㄧㄥˊ ㄧㄥˊ)
①(said of water) clear and abundant②(said of a woman's bearing) easy and graceful
盈餘(ㄧㄥˊ ㄩˊ)
a surplus; profit
盈餘滾存(ㄧㄥˊ ㄩˊ ㄍㄨㄣˇ ㄘㄨㄣˊ)
to enter the surplus in the accounts
盈月(ㄧㄥˊ ㄩㄝˋ)
a full moon

【盃】 3719
(杯) ㄅㄟ bei bēi
a cup; a tumbler

五畫

【益】 3720
ㄧˋ yih yì
1. to increase; to add to; to augment
2. in a higher degree; to a greater extent; more
3. benefit; profit; advantage: 這是對他有益的。 It is to his advantage.
益發(ㄧˋ ㄈㄚ)
increasingly; more and more; all the more; ever more: 工作益發困難了。The work is getting increasingly difficult.
益鳥(ㄧˋ ㄋㄧㄠˇ)
beneficial birds; insectivorous birds
益加(ㄧˋ ㄐㄧㄚ)
increasingly; more and more; all the more; ever more
益智(ㄧˋ ㄓˋ)
① to grow in intelligence or wisdom ② the longan
益者三友(ㄧˋ ㄓㄜˇ ㄙㄢ ㄧㄡˇ)
There are three kinds of beneficial friends—honest friends, understanding friends, and learned friends.
益州(ㄧˋ ㄓㄡ)
an ancient province in what is Szechwan today
益處(ㄧˋ ㄔㄨˋ)or(ㄧˋ ·ㄔㄨ)
advantages; benefit; profit
益蟲(ㄧˋ ㄔㄨㄥˊ)
beneficial insects
益壽(ㄧˋ ㄕㄡˋ)
to lengthen or prolong one's life: 據說此藥可延年益壽。It is said that the medicine may prolong one's life.
益友(ㄧˋ ㄧㄡˇ)
helpful friends; beneficial friends; useful friends

【盍】 3721
ㄏㄜˊ her hé
1. what
2. why not
3. to get together
盍興乎來(ㄏㄜˊ ㄒㄧㄥ ㄏㄨ ㄌㄞˊ)
Why not rise and join us?

【盎】 3722
ㄤˋ anq àng
1. a basin; a pot; a bowl
2. abundant; plentiful; rich
盎格羅薩克森(ㄤˋ ㄍㄜˊ ㄌㄨㄛˊ ㄙㄚˋ ㄎㄜˋ ㄙㄣ)
the Anglo-Saxons
盎然(ㄤˋ ㄖㄢˊ)
abundant; full; exuberant: 趣味盎然 full of interest
盎斯(ㄤˋ ㄙ)
an ounce 亦作「盎司」
盎盎(ㄤˋ ㄤˋ)
plentiful; full

【盌】 3723
ㄨㄢˇ woan wǎn
same as 碗—a bowl

六畫

【盒】 3724
ㄏㄜˊ her hé
a small box; a case: 他吃了一整盒糖。He ate a whole box of candy.
盒子(ㄏㄜˊ ·ㄗ)or 盒兒(ㄏㄜˊㄦ)
a small case; a small box
盒子礮(ㄏㄜˊ ·ㄗ ㄆㄠˋ)
a mauser pistol

【盔】 3725
ㄎㄨㄟ kuei kuī
1. a helmet
2. a basin; a pot
盔頭(ㄎㄨㄟ ㄊㄡˊ)
caps formerly worn by actors in Chinese opera
盔甲(ㄎㄨㄟ ㄐㄧㄚˇ)
helmets and mail; armor

七畫

【盛】 3726
1. ㄕㄥˋ shenq shèng
1. abundant; rich; exuberant; flourishing; prosperous
2. (said of fire, storm, etc.)to rage: 火勢很盛。The fire is raging.
3. a Chinese family name
盛名(ㄕㄥˋ ㄇㄧㄥˊ)
a glorious name; great reputation
盛名難副(ㄕㄥˋ ㄇㄧㄥˊ ㄋㄢˊ ㄈㄨˋ)
to have a fame greater than one deserves 或 It is hard to live up to a great reputation.
盛名之累(ㄕㄥˋ ㄇㄧㄥˊ ㄓ ㄌㄟˇ)
the trouble of being a famous personality
盛服(ㄕㄥˋ ㄈㄨˊ)
in all one's robes; in full dress
盛大(ㄕㄥˋ ㄉㄚˋ)
grand; magnificent; majestic
盛德大業(ㄕㄥˋ ㄉㄜˊ ㄉㄚˋ ㄧㄝˋ)
great virtues and magnificent achievements (of a ruler, etc.)
盛典(ㄕㄥˋ ㄉㄧㄢˇ)
a grand occasion; a big ceremony
盛冬(ㄕㄥˋ ㄉㄨㄥ)
midwinter
盛唐(ㄕㄥˋ ㄊㄤˊ)
the period of full literary grandeur in the Tang Dynasty, corresponding to most of the 8th century
盛年(ㄕㄥˋ ㄋㄧㄢˊ)
the prime of one's life: 他在盛年時期去世。He died in the prime of his life.
盛怒(ㄕㄥˋ ㄋㄨˋ)
in great anger; wrath
盛開(ㄕㄥˋ ㄎㄞ)
in full bloom: 櫻花盛開。The cherry trees are in full bloom.
盛況空前(ㄕㄥˋ ㄎㄨㄤˋ ㄎㄨㄥ ㄑㄧㄢˊ)
unprecedented in grandeur, festivity, etc.
盛會(ㄕㄥˋ ㄏㄨㄟˋ)
a grand gathering; a magnificent assembly
盛極必衰(ㄕㄥˋ ㄐㄧˊ ㄅㄧˋ ㄕㄨㄞ)
Everything starts to fall after it has reached the ze-

〔皿部〕

〔皿部〕

nith.

盛極一時(ㄕㄥˋ ㄐㄧˊ ㄧˋ ㄕˊ)
to be in vogue for a time; to be all the rage at the moment

盛舉(ㄕㄥˋ ㄐㄩˇ)
a great undertaking or enterprise; a worthy project: 讓我們共襄盛舉。Let's cooperated in this great project.

盛氣(ㄕㄥˋ ㄑㄧˋ)
① exploding anger or rage ②arrogant; haughty ③full of spirit

盛氣凌人(ㄕㄥˋ ㄑㄧˋ ㄌㄧㄥˊ ㄖㄣˊ)
to treat others rudely through arrogance

盛情(ㄕㄥˋ ㄑㄧㄥˊ)
warm thoughtfulness; a very warm heart; utmost sincerity

盛情難卻(ㄕㄥˋ ㄑㄧㄥˊ ㄋㄢˊ ㄑㄩㄝˋ)
It is hard to turn down the offer made with such warm-heartedness.

盛夏(ㄕㄥˋ ㄒㄧㄚˋ)
midsummer

盛行(ㄕㄥˋ ㄒㄧㄥˊ)
(said of things) to be popular or in vogue: 這些衣服曾經盛行一時。These clothes were in vogue for a time.

盛饌(ㄕㄥˋ ㄓㄨㄢˋ)
a sumptuous meal; a feast

盛裝(ㄕㄥˋ ㄓㄨㄤ)
in full dress; in rich attire

盛產(ㄕㄥˋ ㄔㄢˇ)
to abound in; to teem with; to be rich in: 中東盛產石油。The Middle East is rich in oil.

盛世(ㄕㄥˋ ㄕˋ)
a prosperous age or period; halcyon days

盛事(ㄕㄥˋ ㄕˋ)
a grand affair or occasion

盛暑(ㄕㄥˋ ㄕㄨˇ)
midsummer; intense heat

盛衰(ㄕㄥˋ ㄕㄨㄞ)
rise and fall; ups and downs; vicissitudes

盛衰興廢(ㄕㄥˋ ㄕㄨㄞ ㄒㄧㄥ ㄈㄟˋ)
vicissitudes; ups and downs; waning and waxing; rise and fall

盛讚(ㄕㄥˋ ㄗㄢˋ)
to praise profusely; to pay high compliments

盛意(ㄕㄥˋ ㄧˋ)
warm-heartedness; thoughtfulness; generosity: 我們對他的盛意表示感謝。We thanked him for his generosities.

盛顏(ㄕㄥˋ ㄧㄢˊ)
one's look in the prime of his life

盛筵(ㄕㄥˋ ㄧㄢˊ)
a sumptuous feast: 我們參加了那個盛筵。We went to the sumptuous feast.

盛筵難再(ㄕㄥˋ ㄧㄢˊ ㄋㄢˊ ㄗㄞˋ)
Sumptuous feasts are not repeated often. 或 Grand gatherings do not take place every day.

盛宴(ㄕㄥˋ ㄧㄢˋ)
a grand banquet; a splendid meal 亦作「盛筵」

盛王(ㄕㄥˋ ㄨㄤˊ)
a ruler of great virtue

盛譽(ㄕㄥˋ ㄩˋ)
great fame; high reputation

【盛】 3726
2. ㄔㄥˊ cherng chéng

to take (loose material) into a bowl or basin; to hold; to contain

盛飯(ㄔㄥˊ ㄈㄢˋ)
to take cooked rice out of a cooker into a bowl

盛殮(ㄔㄥˊ ㄌㄧㄢˋ)
to place a body in a coffin

【盗】 3727
ㄉㄠˋ daw dào

to steal; to rob; to misappropriate

盗版(ㄉㄠˋ ㄅㄢˇ)
a pirated edition

盗賣(ㄉㄠˋ ㄇㄞˋ)
to misappropriate and sell

盗名(ㄉㄠˋ ㄇㄧㄥˊ)
to steal glory one does not deserve; to seek undeserved publicity

盗墓(ㄉㄠˋ ㄇㄨˋ)
to steal from graves; to sack tombs; to plunder graves

盗伐(ㄉㄠˋ ㄈㄚˊ)
to fell trees unlawfully

盗匪(ㄉㄠˋ ㄈㄟˇ)
robbers; bandits; brigands

盗壘(ㄉㄠˋ ㄌㄟˇ)
base stealing (as of baseball)

盗錄(ㄉㄠˋ ㄌㄨˋ)
to pirate (a videocassette, record, etc.)

盗魁(ㄉㄠˋ ㄎㄨㄟˊ)or 盗首(ㄉㄠˋ ㄕㄡˇ)
the leader of a gang of robbers or bandits; a ringleader

盗汗(ㄉㄠˋ ㄏㄢˋ)
(pathology) night sweats

盗竊(ㄉㄠˋ ㄑㄧㄝˋ)
theft; larceny; misappropriation: 他因盗竊而被關進獄中。He was put in prison for theft.

盗取(ㄉㄠˋ ㄑㄩˇ)
to take unlawfully; to steal; to pilfer; to purloin

盗儒(ㄉㄠˋ ㄖㄨˊ)
a corrupt scholar; an immoral intellectual

盗賊(ㄉㄠˋ ㄗㄜˊ)
a thief; a robber; a bandit

盗賊蠭起(ㄉㄠˋ ㄗㄜˊ ㄈㄥ ㄑㄧˇ)
to be infested with robbers and thieves

盗憎主人(ㄉㄠˋ ㄗㄥ ㄓㄨˇ ㄖㄣˊ)
① to bully the weak; to usurp power ② Thieves are angry with the master.

盗藪(ㄉㄠˋ ㄙㄡˇ)
a den of robbers

盗案(ㄉㄠˋ ㄢˋ)
a theft case

盗亦有道(ㄉㄠˋ ㄧˋ ㄧㄡˇ ㄉㄠˋ)
Even robbers have a code of conduct.

盗印(ㄉㄠˋ ㄧㄣˋ)
to pirate; piracy

盗用(ㄉㄠˋ ㄩㄥˋ)
to embezzle; to usurp

八畫

【盞】 3728
ㄓㄢˇ jaan zhǎn

1. a small shallow container; a small cup
2. a numerical adjunct denoting lamps

【盟】 3729
ㄇㄥˊ meng méng

1. a covenant; an oath; a vow; to covenant; to ally: 許多國家將與我國締盟。Many foreign powers will ally with us.
2. a Mongol league

盟邦(ㄇㄥˊ ㄅㄤ)
an allied country; allies
盟府(ㄇㄥˊ ㄈㄨˇ)
(in ancient China) the repository of covenants; a place for safekeeping records of an alliance
盟國(ㄇㄥˊ ㄍㄨㄛˊ)
allied powers; allies
盟機(ㄇㄥˊ ㄐㄧ)
allied warplanes
盟軍(ㄇㄥˊ ㄐㄩㄣ)
allied troops; allied forces
盟心(ㄇㄥˊ ㄒㄧㄣ)
to swear mutual devotion
盟兄弟(ㄇㄥˊ ㄒㄩㄥ ㄉㄧˋ)
sworn brothers (not linked by kinship)
盟長(ㄇㄥˊ ㄓㄤˇ)
the chief of a Mongol league composed of several tribes
盟主(ㄇㄥˊ ㄓㄨˇ)
the leader of an alliance
盟誓(ㄇㄥˊ ㄕˋ)
an oath of mutual devotion; to take an oath; to make a pledge
盟友(ㄇㄥˊ ㄧㄡˇ)
an ally
盟約(ㄇㄥˊ ㄩㄝ)
a treaty of alliance

九畫

【盡】 3730 ㄐㄧㄣˋ jinn jìn

1. to exhaust; to use up
2. to put to the best use
3. to complete; to finish; to accomplish
4. all; entirely; totally; completely; wholly
5. the utmost

盡本分(ㄐㄧㄣˋ ㄅㄣˇ ·ㄈㄣ)
to play one's proper role; to do what one is supposed to do, no more and no less
盡命(ㄐㄧㄣˋ ㄇㄧㄥˋ)
to sacrifice one's own life
盡付東流(ㄐㄧㄣˋ ㄈㄨˋ ㄉㄨㄥ ㄌㄧㄡˊ)
(literally) all gone with the eastward stream—all in vain
盡頭(ㄐㄧㄣˋ ㄊㄡˊ)
the extremity; the end
盡年(ㄐㄧㄣˋ ㄋㄧㄢˊ)
to live out a natural life span; to complete the whole of the allotted span of life
盡禮(ㄐㄧㄣˋ ㄌㄧˇ)
very polite; the full observance of the rules of propriety
盡力(ㄐㄧㄣˋ ㄌㄧˋ)
to make efforts; to exert oneself; to do all one can; to do one's best: 我們將盡力支援你。We'll do our best to help you.
盡力而爲(ㄐㄧㄣˋ ㄌㄧˋ ㄦˊ ㄨㄟˊ)or 盡力爲之(ㄐㄧㄣˋ ㄌㄧˋ ㄨㄟˊ ㄓ)
to execute or perform with effort; to do one's best
盡量(ㄐㄧㄣˋ ㄌㄧㄤˋ)
as much as possible; to the utmost 亦作「儘量」
盡歡而散(ㄐㄧㄣˋ ㄏㄨㄢ ㄦˊ ㄙㄢˋ)
to leave only after each has enjoyed himself to the utmost
盡節(ㄐㄧㄣˋ ㄐㄧㄝˊ)
to die for chastity
盡淨(ㄐㄧㄣˋ ㄐㄧㄥˋ)
completely; all together
盡其在我(ㄐㄧㄣˋ ㄑㄧˊ ㄗㄞˋ ㄨㄛˇ)
to do one's best; to do what one can (and leave the rest to God or Heaven)
盡其所長(ㄐㄧㄣˋ ㄑㄧˊ ㄙㄨㄛˇ ㄔㄤˊ)
to work or endeavor to the best of one's ability
盡其所有(ㄐㄧㄣˋ ㄑㄧˊ ㄙㄨㄛˇ ㄧㄡˇ)
to give all one has
盡棄(ㄐㄧㄣˋ ㄑㄧˋ)
① all wasted; all in vain ② all forgotten
盡情(ㄐㄧㄣˋ ㄑㄧㄥˊ)
to one's heart's content
盡孝(ㄐㄧㄣˋ ㄒㄧㄠˋ)
to do one's filial duty: 不要忘記對父母盡孝。Don't forget your duty to your parents.
盡心(ㄐㄧㄣˋ ㄒㄧㄣ)
to devote all one's energies: 他盡心做一件工作。He devoted his energies to a task.
盡心竭力(ㄐㄧㄣˋ ㄒㄧㄣ ㄐㄧㄝˊ ㄌㄧˋ)
to devote all the mental and physical energy one can muster; to do one's utmost
盡信書則不如無書(ㄐㄧㄣˋ ㄒㄧㄣˋ ㄕㄨ ㄗㄜˊ ㄅㄨˋ ㄖㄨˊ ㄨˊ ㄕㄨ)
Believing everything in books is worse than having no books at all.
盡性(ㄐㄧㄣˋ ㄒㄧㄥˋ)
to fulfill one's nature
盡興(ㄐㄧㄣˋ ㄒㄧㄥˋ)
to enjoy to one's heart's content: 我們盡興而歸。We returned after thoroughly enjoying ourselves.
盡職(ㄐㄧㄣˋ ㄓˊ)
to do one's duty; having a sense of responsibility; conscientious: 她工作很盡職。She is a conscientious worker.
盡忠(ㄐㄧㄣˋ ㄓㄨㄥ)
to do one's duty as a subject; to be loyal to the ruler: 他爲國盡忠。He was loyal to his country.
盡忠報國(ㄐㄧㄣˋ ㄓㄨㄥ ㄅㄠˋ ㄍㄨㄛˊ)
to devote oneself to one's country
盡是(ㄐㄧㄣˋ ㄕˋ)
all are; without exception; to be full of
盡善盡美(ㄐㄧㄣˋ ㄕㄢˋ ㄐㄧㄣˋ ㄇㄟˇ)
perfectly satisfactory; perfectly good; flawless; perfect
盡述(ㄐㄧㄣˋ ㄕㄨˋ)
to tell a complete story
盡數(ㄐㄧㄣˋ ㄕㄨˋ)
fully; the whole; the whole amount
盡日(ㄐㄧㄣˋ ㄖˋ)
the whole day; all day long
盡人情(ㄐㄧㄣˋ ㄖㄣˊ ㄑㄧㄥˊ)
to do what friendship or other human relations dictate
盡人事(ㄐㄧㄣˋ ㄖㄣˊ ㄕˋ)
to do everything one ought to do (and hope that fate will take care of the rest)
盡人事以聽天命(ㄐㄧㄣˋ ㄖㄣˊ ㄕˋ ㄧˇ ㄊㄧㄥ ㄊㄧㄢ ㄇㄧㄥˋ)
One does one's best and leaves the rest to Heaven.
盡責任(ㄐㄧㄣˋ ㄗㄜˊ ㄖㄣˋ)
to do one's duty: 每個人都應該盡責任。Every man should do his duty.
盡瘁(ㄐㄧㄣˋ ㄘㄨㄟˋ)
to exhaust one's mental energy
盡意(ㄐㄧㄣˋ ㄧˋ)
① to give full expression to one's ideas ② to one's heart's content
盡義務(ㄐㄧㄣˋ ㄧˋ ㄨˋ)

①to fulfill one's duty: 我們應盡義務。We should fulfill our duty. ②to work without pay

盡言(ㄐㄧㄣˋ ㄧㄢˊ)
to speak out; to speak up; to admonish without reserve

【監】 3731
1. ㄐㄧㄢ jian jiān

1. to supervise; to superintend; to oversee; to direct; to inspect
2. to confine; to keep in custody; to imprison

監謗(ㄐㄧㄢ ㄅㄤˋ)
to watch over libelers or detractors

監票(ㄐㄧㄢ ㄆㄧㄠˋ)
(in elections) to watch for irregularities in a voting; to scrutinize a ballot

監票人(ㄐㄧㄢ ㄆㄧㄠˋ ㄖㄣˊ)or 監票員(ㄐㄧㄢ ㄆㄧㄠˋ ㄩㄢˊ)
a ballot supervisor; a scrutineer

監犯(ㄐㄧㄢ ㄈㄢˋ)
a prisoner; a jailbird

監房(ㄐㄧㄢ ㄈㄤˊ)
a prison cell

監督(ㄐㄧㄢ ㄉㄨ)
to supervise; to superintend; to oversee

監聽(ㄐㄧㄢ ㄊㄧㄥ)
to monitor

監牢(ㄐㄧㄢ ㄌㄠˊ)
a prison; a jail

監臨(ㄐㄧㄢ ㄌㄧㄣˊ)
to supervise or proctor (a civil service examination in former times)

監國(ㄐㄧㄢ ㄍㄨㄛˊ)
a regent

監管(ㄐㄧㄢ ㄍㄨㄢˇ)
to take charge of

監工(ㄐㄧㄢ ㄍㄨㄥ)
① a superintendent or supervisor of a construction project ②to superintend or supervise work: 他親自監工。He superintended all their work personally.

監考(ㄐㄧㄢ ㄎㄠˇ)
to proctor or invigilate an examination

監考員(ㄐㄧㄢ ㄎㄠˇ ㄩㄢˊ)
a proctor; an invigilator

監護(ㄐㄧㄢ ㄏㄨˋ)
custody; to act as the guardian of: 父母對年幼兒女有監護之責。Parents have the custody of their young children.

監護人(ㄐㄧㄢ ㄏㄨˋ ㄖㄣˊ)
a guardian (of a minor)

監交(ㄐㄧㄢ ㄐㄧㄠ)
to supervise or witness the handover (of duties or public property between officials)

監禁(ㄐㄧㄢ ㄐㄧㄣˋ)
①to confine; to imprison; to immure ②custody; confinement; imprisonment

監軍(ㄐㄧㄢ ㄐㄩㄣ)
an inspector—the general of an army in former times

監修(ㄐㄧㄢ ㄒㄧㄡ)
①to direct or supervise the compilation or editing (of books) ②to direct or supervise repair work

監製(ㄐㄧㄢ ㄓˋ)
to direct or supervise the manufacture of

監斬(ㄐㄧㄢ ㄓㄢˇ)
to supervise the decapitation of criminals in former times

監察(ㄐㄧㄢ ㄔㄚˊ)
to supervise; to control; control

監察權(ㄐㄧㄢ ㄔㄚˊ ㄑㄩㄢˊ)
the power of control (one of the five powers of the government specified in the Constitution of the Republic of China)

監察使(ㄐㄧㄢ ㄔㄚˊ ㄕˇ)or(ㄐㄧㄢ ㄔㄚˊ ㄕˋ)
a controlling inspector (appointed to help exercise the power of control in the early years of the Republic of China)

監察人(ㄐㄧㄢ ㄔㄚˊ ㄖㄣˊ)
an auditor (in a corporation)

監察委員(ㄐㄧㄢ ㄔㄚˊ ㄨㄟˇ ㄩㄢˊ)
a member of the Control Yüan: 他父親做過監察委員。His father was a member of the Control Yüan.

監察御史(ㄐㄧㄢ ㄔㄚˊ ㄩˋ ㄕˇ)
an official in charge of the discipline of public functionaries in former times

監察員(ㄐㄧㄢ ㄔㄚˊ ㄩㄢˊ)
an inspector

監察院(ㄐㄧㄢ ㄔㄚˊ ㄩㄢˋ)
Control Yüan (one of the five major branches of the government of the Republic of China)

監場(ㄐㄧㄢ ㄔㄤˇ)or(ㄐㄧㄢ ㄔㄤˊ)
①to proctor or invigilate an examination ②a proctor; an invigilator

監視(ㄐㄧㄢ ㄕˋ)
①to keep a watchful eye on; to watch; to keep under surveillance: 警察嚴密監視那罪犯。The police kept the criminal under strict surveillance. ②to monitor

監視器(ㄐㄧㄢ ㄕˋ ㄑㄧˋ)
a watchdog

監試(ㄐㄧㄢ ㄕˋ)
to invigilate; to keep watch over students at an examination

監事(ㄐㄧㄢ ㄕˋ)
a supervisor (of a corporation)

監事會(ㄐㄧㄢ ㄕˋ ㄏㄨㄟˋ)
a board of supervisors (of a corporation)

監守自盜(ㄐㄧㄢ ㄕㄡˇ ㄗˋ ㄉㄠˋ)
embezzlement; to pilfer public property one is entrusted to safeguard

監押(ㄐㄧㄢ ㄧㄚ)
to keep (a person) in custody

監印(ㄐㄧㄢ ㄧㄣˋ)
an official in charge of the official seal

監獄(ㄐㄧㄢ ㄩˋ)
a prison; a jail: 他們因偷錢被送進監獄。They were taken to prison for stealing money.

【監】 3731
2. ㄐㄧㄢˋ jiann jiàn

1. an official position in former times
2. a government establishment (such as a school) in former times
3. a eunuch

監本(ㄐㄧㄢˋ ㄅㄣˇ)
books issued by the Imperial Academy (國子監) during the various dynasties

監生(ㄐㄧㄢˋ ㄕㄥ)

a student of the Imperial Academy (國子監) during the Ming and Ching dynasties

十畫

【盤】 3732 ㄆㄢˊ parn pán

1. a tray; a plate; a dish
2. twisted; entangled; entwined; intricate; winding; to entangle; to entwine
3. to investigate; to interrogate
4. (said of a chess match, etc.) a round

盤剝取利(ㄆㄢˊ ㄅㄛ ㄑㄩˇ ㄌㄧˋ)
to be a Shylock; to exploit

盤駁(ㄆㄢˊ ㄅㄛˊ)
to interrogate and refute

盤礴(ㄆㄢˊ ㄅㄛˊ)
vast; extensive

盤馬彎弓(ㄆㄢˊ ㄇㄚˇ ㄨㄢ ㄍㄨㄥ)
to make a show of readiness to fight; to rattle the saber

盤費(ㄆㄢˊ ·ㄈㄟ)
traveling expenses

盤點(ㄆㄢˊ ㄉㄧㄢˇ)
to check; to make an inventory of

盤腿(ㄆㄢˊ ㄊㄨㄟˇ)
to sit with the legs crossed

盤尼西林(ㄆㄢˊ ㄋㄧˊ ㄒㄧ ㄌㄧㄣˊ)
penicillin

盤弄(ㄆㄢˊ ㄋㄨㄥˋ)
① to tamper with ② to provoke

盤根錯節(ㄆㄢˊ ㄍㄣ ㄘㄨㄛˋ ㄐㄧㄝˊ)
(literally) twisted roots and intricate gnarls—great complexity; very complicated

盤庚(ㄆㄢˊ ㄍㄥ)
name of a ruler in the Shang Dynasty

盤古(ㄆㄢˊ ㄍㄨˇ)
Pan Ku, the legendary creator and first ruler of the universe

盤互(ㄆㄢˊ ㄏㄨˋ)
to entangle each other

盤貨(ㄆㄢˊ ㄏㄨㄛˋ)
to make an inventory of stock; to take stock

盤獲(ㄆㄢˊ ㄏㄨㄛˋ)
to catch (a criminal) through investigation

盤桓(ㄆㄢˊ ㄏㄨㄢˊ)
to linger: 我們在東京盤桓了幾天,遊覽了各處名勝。We lingered a few days sightseeing in Tokyo.

盤結(ㄆㄢˊ ㄐㄧㄝˊ)
to join in a coil

盤詰(ㄆㄢˊ ㄐㄧㄝˊ)
to interrogate closely

盤踞(ㄆㄢˊ ㄐㄩˋ)
① to squat with the legs crossed ② to take a fixed position; to be entrenched; to occupy: 敵人盤踞我們的堡壘。The enemy occupied our fort.

盤據(ㄆㄢˊ ㄐㄩˋ)
to occupy and hold a place (usually said of enemy troops, rebels or bandits)

盤曲(ㄆㄢˊ ㄑㄩ)
winding; spiraling; coiling

盤膝(ㄆㄢˊ ㄒㄧ)
to sit with the legs crossed: 他盤膝而坐。He sat with his legs crossed.

盤香(ㄆㄢˊ ㄒㄧㄤ)
coiled incense

盤旋(ㄆㄢˊ ㄒㄩㄢˊ)
to circle; to hover around: 兩隻鷹在頭頂盤旋。Two hawks were hovering overhead.

盤賬(ㄆㄢˊ ㄓㄤˋ)
to examine the account

盤查(ㄆㄢˊ ㄔㄚˊ)
to question; to cross-examine; to interrogate and search: 警察盤查可疑的人。The policemen questioned a suspicious person.

盤纏(ㄆㄢˊ ·ㄔㄢ)
traveling expenses

盤川(ㄆㄢˊ ㄔㄨㄢ)
traveling expenses

盤石(ㄆㄢˊ ㄕˊ)
a huge circular stone

盤繞(ㄆㄢˊ ㄖㄠˋ)
to twine; to wind round: 藤葛盤繞在樹幹上。The vines twine round the tree trunk.

盤子(ㄆㄢˊ ·ㄗ) or 盤兒(ㄆㄚˊㄦ)
a tray; a plate; a dish

盤餐(ㄆㄢˊ ㄘㄢ)
dishes of food

盤錯(ㄆㄢˊ ㄘㄨㄛˋ)
entwined; entangled

盤存(ㄆㄢˊ ㄘㄨㄣˊ)
to take an inventory of

盤算(ㄆㄢˊ ·ㄙㄨㄢ)
to make a mental calculation; to figure

盤飧(ㄆㄢˊ ㄙㄨㄣ)
dishes; the food in a dish

盤渦(ㄆㄢˊ ㄨㄛ)
a whirlpool; an eddy

盤問(ㄆㄢˊ ㄨㄣˋ)
to interrogate closely

盤紆(ㄆㄢˊ ㄩ)
winding; circuitous

盤鬱(ㄆㄢˊ ㄩˋ)
(said of scenic spots) winding and enchanting

盤運(ㄆㄢˊ ㄩㄣˋ)
to convey; to transport

十一畫

【盥】 3733 ㄍㄨㄢˋ guann guàn

1. to wash one's hands
2. to wash

盥櫛(ㄍㄨㄢˋ ㄐㄧㄝˊ)
to wash one's face and comb one's hair

盥洗(ㄍㄨㄢˋ ㄒㄧˇ)
to wash oneself

盥洗室(ㄍㄨㄢˋ ㄒㄧˇ ㄕˋ)
a washroom; a restroom; a lavatory

盥濯(ㄍㄨㄢˋ ㄓㄨㄛˊ)
to wash; to rinse

盥漱(ㄍㄨㄢˋ ㄙㄡˋ)
to wash the hands and rinse the mouth

【盦】 3734 ㄢ an ān

1. the lid of a caldron
2. a Buddhist cloister for nuns 亦作「庵」

【盧】 3735 ㄌㄨˊ lu lú

1. black
2. a Chinese family name

盧比(ㄌㄨˊ ㄅㄧˇ)
rupee (a monetary unit of India, etc.)

盧布(ㄌㄨˊ ㄅㄨˋ)
ruble (a monetary unit of the Soviet Union)

盧溝橋 or 蘆溝橋(ㄌㄨˊ ㄍㄡ ㄑㄧㄠˊ)
the Marco Polo Bridge (near Peking, where on July 7, 1937, a clash between the Japanese and Chinese troops

triggered the Sino-Japanese War of 1937-1945)

盧森堡(ㄌㄨˊ ㄙㄣ ㄅㄠˇ)
Luxemburg, Europe

盧梭(ㄌㄨˊ ㄙㄨㄛ)
Jean Jacques Rousseau, 1712-1778, French philosopher

盧安達(ㄌㄨˊ ㄢ ㄉㄚˊ)
Rwanda

盧昂(ㄌㄨˊ ㄤˊ)
Rouen, France

十二畫

【盩】 3736 ㄓㄡ jou zhōu
the turn of a mountain range

盩厔(ㄓㄡ ㄓˋ)
name of a county in Shensi

【盪】 3737 ㄉㄤˋ danq dàng
1. to toss about; to swing
2. to wash

盪盪(ㄉㄤˋ ㄉㄤˋ)
vast; extensive

盪滌(ㄉㄤˋ ㄉㄧˊ)
to wash; to rinse; to refresh: 美景可以盪滌你心。The beautiful scenery can refresh your mind.

盪槳(ㄉㄤˋ ㄐㄧㄤˇ)
to row a boat

盪秋千(ㄉㄤˋ ㄑㄧㄡ ㄑㄧㄢ)
to swing (in a swing)

盪舟(ㄉㄤˋ ㄓㄡ)
① to boat ② to move a boat along upon the land

盪漾(ㄉㄤˋ ㄧㄤˋ)
① to be gently tossed about ② to ripple: 綠油油的稻子在微風中盪漾。The green rice rippled in the breeze.

十四畫

【盬】 3738 ㄍㄨˇ guu gǔ
1. a salt pit
2. incompact
3. leisure
4. to drink by sucking

目部
ㄇㄨˋ muh mù

【目】 3739 ㄇㄨˋ muh mù
1. the eye: 他雙目失明。He is blind in both eyes.
2. to look; to regard; to see: 此事被目爲奇蹟。It was regarded as a miracle.
3. a table of contents; a category

目波(ㄇㄨˋ ㄅㄛ)
glances as bright as dancing waves

目標(ㄇㄨˋ ㄅㄧㄠ)
① an objective; a target; to target ② an aim; a goal: 他的人生目標是當個大作家。His goal in life is to become a great writer.

目不窺園(ㄇㄨˋ ㄅㄨˋ ㄎㄨㄟ ㄩㄢˊ)
completely absorbed in study

目不交睫(ㄇㄨˋ ㄅㄨˋ ㄐㄧㄠ ㄐㄧㄝˊ)
to go completely without sleep

目不見睫(ㄇㄨˋ ㄅㄨˋ ㄐㄧㄢˋ ㄐㄧㄝˊ)
(literally) The eyes cannot see the eyelashes.—One does not have a correct appraisal of his own ability.

目不暇給(ㄇㄨˋ ㄅㄨˋ ㄒㄧㄚˊ ㄐㄧˇ) or 目不暇接(ㄇㄨˋ ㄅㄨˋ ㄒㄧㄚˊ ㄐㄧㄝ)
So many things come into sight that the eyes are kept fully occupied.

目不斜視(ㄇㄨˋ ㄅㄨˋ ㄒㄧㄝˊ ㄕˋ)
to look steadily forward; to look straight ahead

目不轉睛(ㄇㄨˋ ㄅㄨˋ ㄓㄨㄢˇ ㄐㄧㄥ)
to gaze steadily; to look attentively

目不識丁(ㄇㄨˋ ㄅㄨˋ ㄕˋ ㄉㄧㄥ)
(literally) to recognize not even the character 丁—completely illiterate

目迷五色(ㄇㄨˋ ㄇㄧˊ ㄨˇ ㄙㄜˋ)
so dazzled as to lose clear vision; bewildered by a complicated situation

目瞪口呆(ㄇㄨˋ ㄉㄥˋ ㄎㄡˇ ㄉㄞ)
dumbfounded; stupefied

目的(ㄇㄨˋ ㄉㄧˋ)
a purpose; an objective; an end; an aim

目的地(ㄇㄨˋ ㄉㄧˋ ㄉㄧˋ)
a destination

目的論(ㄇㄨˋ ㄉㄧˋ ㄌㄨㄣˋ)
(philosophy) teleology

目的物(ㄇㄨˋ ㄉㄧˋ ㄨˋ)
an objective; an aim

目睹 or 目覩(ㄇㄨˋ ㄉㄨˇ)
to see directly; to witness; to see with one's own eyes: 他目睹此意外事件。He witnessed the accident.

目逃(ㄇㄨˋ ㄊㄠˊ)
to look away in shame or awe

目挑心招(ㄇㄨˋ ㄊㄧㄠ ㄒㄧㄣ ㄓㄠ)
(said of prostitutes) to seduce; to behave coquettishly

目聽(ㄇㄨˋ ㄊㄧㄥ)
(literally) to hear with the eyes—to know what one is about to say by looking at him

目逆(ㄇㄨˋ ㄋㄧˋ)
to greet someone with the eyes on his (or her) approach

目力(ㄇㄨˋ ㄌㄧˋ)
eyesight; vision: 我的目力不佳。I have poor eyesight.

目連救母(ㄇㄨˋ ㄌㄧㄢˊ ㄐㄧㄡˋ ㄇㄨˇ)
the legend of Moginlin(目犍連), a disciple of Buddha, entering Hell to rescue his own mother

目錄(ㄇㄨˋ ㄌㄨˋ)
① a table of contents; contents ② a list; a catalogue

目錄學(ㄇㄨˋ ㄌㄨˋ ㄒㄩㄝˊ)
bibliography

目耕(ㄇㄨˋ ㄍㄥ)
to read as diligently as someone plows the field

目光(ㄇㄨˋ ㄍㄨㄤ)
insight; vision; sight: 那是目光短淺的計畫。It is a shortsighted plan.

目光炯炯(ㄇㄨˋ ㄍㄨㄤ ㄐㄩㄥˇ ㄐㄩㄥˇ)
to have eyes with a piercing gleam

目光如豆(ㄇㄨˋ ㄍㄨㄤ ㄖㄨˊ ㄉㄡˋ)
to lack insight or vision; shortsighted: 目光如豆的人永不會成功。Those who are shortsighted will never suc-

ceed.

目光如炬(ㄇㄨˋ ㄍㄨㄤ ㄖㄨˊ ㄐㄩˋ)
to have great insight or vision; farsighted

目光銳利(ㄇㄨˋ ㄍㄨㄤ ㄖㄨㄟˋ ㄌㄧˋ)
to have a penetrating sight; sharp-eyed; sharp-sighted: 他是目光銳利的人。He is a sharp-eyed person.

目眶(ㄇㄨˋ ㄎㄨㄤˋ)
the eye sockets

目空一切(ㄇㄨˋ ㄎㄨㄥ ㄧˊ ㄑㄧㄝˋ)
so self-conceited that nothing enters one's eyes; to consider everybody and everything beneath one's notice; to look down on everyone or everything; to be supercilious or arrogant

目擊(ㄇㄨˋ ㄐㄧˊ)
to see personally; to witness: 他目擊此意外。He witnessed the accident.

目今(ㄇㄨˋ ㄐㄧㄣ)
now; the present

目禁(ㄇㄨˋ ㄐㄧㄣˋ)
to restrain (someone) by winks or blinks

目鏡(ㄇㄨˋ ㄐㄧㄥˋ)
the ocular, or eyepiece (of a microscope)

目前(ㄇㄨˋ ㄑㄧㄢˊ)
now; at present: 到目前爲止,我沒有得到他一點音信。I have heard nothing from him up to now.

目下(ㄇㄨˋ ㄒㄧㄚˋ)
at the moment; now; at present

目笑(ㄇㄨˋ ㄒㄧㄠˋ)
to cast a derisive look

目眩(ㄇㄨˋ ㄒㄩㄢˋ)
dazzled

目指氣使(ㄇㄨˋ ㄓˇ ㄑㄧˋ ㄕˇ)
arrogant; haughty

目中無人(ㄇㄨˋ ㄓㄨㄥ ㄨˊ ㄖㄣˊ)
so arrogant that no one is important in his eyes; to be supercilious; to be overweening

目使頤令(ㄇㄨˋ ㄕˇ ㄧˊ ㄌㄧㄥˋ)
(literally) giving orders by a look or glance—arrogant; conceited

目濡耳染(ㄇㄨˋ ㄖㄨˊ ㄦˇ ㄖㄢˇ)
to become familiar with something because of long exposure to it

目眥欲裂(ㄇㄨˋ ㄗˋ ㄩˋ ㄌㄧㄝˋ)
to show such anger in the eyes that it appears as if they were bursting

目次(ㄇㄨˋ ㄘˋ)
a table of contents

目測(ㄇㄨˋ ㄘㄜˋ)
to measure distance with the eyes

目送(ㄇㄨˋ ㄙㄨㄥˋ)
to follow with the eyes; to gaze after

目迎目送(ㄇㄨˋ ㄧㄥˊ ㄇㄨˋ ㄙㄨㄥˋ)
to salute an officer with the eyes

目無法紀(ㄇㄨˋ ㄨˊ ㄈㄚˇ ㄐㄧˋ)
to disregard all laws and regulations; lawless

目無全牛(ㄇㄨˋ ㄨˊ ㄑㄩㄢˊ ㄋㄧㄡˊ)
(said of an experienced butcher) to see an ox not as a whole (but only as parts to be cut)—to be supremely skilled; dexterous

目無尊長(ㄇㄨˋ ㄨˊ ㄗㄨㄣ ㄓㄤˇ)
to show no respect to elders and superiors

目無餘子(ㄇㄨˋ ㄨˊ ㄩˊ ㄗˇ)
to despise all others

目語(ㄇㄨˋ ㄩˇ)
to converse with the eyes for fear of speaking out under tyranny

二畫

【盯】 3740
ㄉㄧㄥ ding dīng
to stare at; to gaze at; to fix one's eyes on; to keep a close watch: 他兩眼盯着電視。His eyes were fixed on the TV.

盯梢(ㄉㄧㄥ ㄕㄠ)
to shadow somebody; to tail somebody

三畫

【盱】 3741
ㄒㄩ shiu xū
1. to open the eyes wide
2. worried; uneasy; anxious

盱衡(ㄒㄩ ㄏㄥˊ)
①to look with eyes wide open ②to make a general survey

盱盱(ㄒㄩ ㄒㄩ)
①staring with eyes wide open ②proud and haughty

【盲】 3742
ㄇㄤˊ mang máng
1. blind; to blind
2. deluded

盲目(ㄇㄤˊ ㄇㄨˋ)
①blind ②lacking insight or understanding ③reckless; aimless

盲目不盲心(ㄇㄤˊ ㄇㄨˋ ㄅㄨˋ ㄇㄤˊ ㄒㄧㄣ)
blind in the eye but not in the mind

盲目飛行(ㄇㄤˊ ㄇㄨˋ ㄈㄟ ㄒㄧㄥˊ)
instrument flying

盲點(ㄇㄤˊ ㄉㄧㄢˇ) or 盲斑(ㄇㄤˊ ㄅㄢ)
(anatomy) a blind spot; a scotoma

盲動(ㄇㄤˊ ㄉㄨㄥˋ)
to act blindly or rashly

盲腸(ㄇㄤˊ ㄔㄤˊ)
the cecum, or caecum; the vermiform appendix

盲腸割除手術(ㄇㄤˊ ㄔㄤˊ ㄍㄜ ㄔㄨˊ ㄕㄡˇ ㄕㄨˋ)
an appendectomy 亦作「闌尾切除手術」

盲腸炎(ㄇㄤˊ ㄔㄤˊ ㄧㄢˊ)
appendicitis

盲人(ㄇㄤˊ ㄖㄣˊ)
a blind person

盲人摸象(ㄇㄤˊ ㄖㄣˊ ㄇㄛ ㄒㄧㄤˋ)
to draw a conclusion from incomplete data (as some blind men did about the elephant, each touching merely a small part of the elephant's body)

盲人教育(ㄇㄤˊ ㄖㄣˊ ㄐㄧㄠˋ ㄩˋ)
the education of the blind

盲人騎瞎馬(ㄇㄤˊ ㄖㄣˊ ㄑㄧˊ ㄒㄧㄚ ㄇㄚˇ)
(literally) A blind man rides a blind horse.—a very dangerous act

盲從(ㄇㄤˊ ㄘㄨㄥˊ)
to follow blindly: 他們盲從他們的領袖。They followed their leaders blindly.

盲啞學校(ㄇㄤˊ ㄧㄚˇ ㄒㄩㄝˊ ㄒㄧㄠˋ)
a school for the blind and the mute

盲文(ㄇㄤˊ ㄨㄣˊ) or 盲字(ㄇㄤˊ ㄗˋ)
braille 亦作「點字」

【直】 3743
ㄓˊ jyr zhí

1. straight; to straighten: 站直！Stand up straight!
2. upright and honest; fair; unbiased
3. vertical; longitudinal; from top to bottom
4. outspoken; frank; straightforward: 請你直說吧。Please speak frankly.
5. directly; firsthand: 我直接獲知此事。I learned it firsthand.
6. continuous; uninterrupted
7. stiff; numb: 天太冷，我的手指都凍直了。It was so cold that my fingers were frozen stiff.
8. just; simply; only; merely
9. a vertical stroke (in Chinese characters)

直筆(ㄓˊ ㄅㄧˇ)
unprejudiced or straightforward writing; to write in an unprejudiced or straightforward way

直布羅陀(ㄓˊ ㄅㄨˋ ㄌㄨㄛˊ ㄊㄨㄛˊ)
Gibraltar

直布羅陀海峽(ㄓˊ ㄅㄨˋ ㄌㄨㄛˊ ㄊㄨㄛˊ ㄏㄞˇ ㄒㄧㄚˊ)
Strait of Gibraltar

直脾氣(ㄓˊ ㄆㄧˊ ˙ㄑㄧ)
outspoken; frank

直眉瞪眼(ㄓˊ ㄇㄟˊ ㄉㄥˋ ㄧㄢˇ)
①to look angry ②to look stupid; to stare blankly; to be stupefied

直髮種(ㄓˊ ㄈㄚˇ ㄓㄨㄥˇ)
the Mongolian race (characterized by straight hair)

直奉戰爭(ㄓˊ ㄈㄥˋ ㄓㄢˋ ㄓㄥ)
the war between warlords, Tsao Kun (曹錕) and Chang Tso-lin (張作霖) in 1923-1924

直達(ㄓˊ ㄉㄚˊ)
to go nonstop to; through: 請買兩張直達車票。Please buy two through tickets.

直達車(ㄓˊ ㄉㄚˊ ㄔㄜ)
a nonstop express; a through train, bus, etc.

直待(ㄓˊ ㄉㄞˋ)
to go on waiting

直搗黃龍(ㄓˊ ㄉㄠˇ ㄏㄨㄤˊ ㄌㄨㄥˊ)
to march to the enemy's heartland

直到(ㄓˊ ㄉㄠˋ)
①till; until ②up to

直挺挺(ㄓˊ ㄊㄧㄥˇ ㄊㄧㄥˇ)
stiff; straight; stiffly: 他直挺挺地站着。He stands straight.

直通(ㄓˊ ㄊㄨㄥ)
to lead directly to; to reach directly

直隸(ㄓˊ ㄌㄧˋ)
①to be directly under the jurisdiction of ②former name of Hopeh(河北)

直立(ㄓˊ ㄌㄧˋ)
to stand erect

直立莖(ㄓˊ ㄌㄧˋ ㄐㄧㄥ)
(botany) an erect stem

直流(ㄓˊ ㄌㄧㄡˊ)
(electricity) direct current

直流發電機(ㄓˊ ㄌㄧㄡˊ ㄈㄚ ㄉㄧㄢˋ ㄐㄧ)
a direct-current dynamo; a direct-current generator

直流電(ㄓˊ ㄌㄧㄡˊ ㄉㄧㄢˋ)
direct current (D.C.)

直話(ㄓˊ ㄏㄨㄚˋ)
outspoken remarks; a frank speech

直接(ㄓˊ ㄐㄧㄝ)
direct; firsthand; directly: 火車直接開往那裏。The train goes there direct.

直接推理(ㄓˊ ㄐㄧㄝ ㄊㄨㄟ ㄌㄧˇ)
immediate reasoning

直接交涉(ㄓˊ ㄐㄧㄝ ㄐㄧㄠ ㄕㄜˋ)
direct negotiations: 他們直接交涉和約。They negotiated a peace treaty directly.

直接交易(ㄓˊ ㄐㄧㄝ ㄐㄧㄠ ㄧˋ)
direct transaction

直接教學法(ㄓˊ ㄐㄧㄝ ㄐㄧㄠˋ ㄒㄩㄝˊ ㄈㄚˇ)
(pedagogy) the direct method

直接選舉(ㄓˊ ㄐㄧㄝ ㄒㄩㄢˇ ㄐㄩˇ)
direct election (as distinct from election by an electoral college)

直接證據(ㄓˊ ㄐㄧㄝ ㄓㄥˋ ㄐㄩˋ)
direct evidence

直接政治(ㄓˊ ㄐㄧㄝ ㄓㄥˋ ㄓˋ)
direct government

直接稅(ㄓˊ ㄐㄧㄝ ㄕㄨㄟˋ)
a direct tax: 所得稅是一種直接稅。A tax on income is a direct tax.

直捷(ㄓˊ ㄐㄧㄝˊ)
simple and direct; straightforward

直截了當(ㄓˊ ㄐㄧㄝˊ ㄌㄧㄠˇ ㄉㄤˋ)
straightforward; flatly; blunt; simple and direct: 你直截了當地說好了。Come straight to the point.

直交(ㄓˊ ㄐㄧㄠ)
(mathematics) orthogonal

直角(ㄓˊ ㄐㄧㄠˇ)
a right angle: 那部車向北作直角轉彎。The car right-angled sharply north.

直角體(ㄓˊ ㄐㄧㄠˇ ㄊㄧˇ)
(mathematics) a cuboid

直角三角形(ㄓˊ ㄐㄧㄠˇ ㄙㄢ ㄐㄧㄠˇ ㄒㄧㄥˊ)
a right-angled triangle

直諫(ㄓˊ ㄐㄧㄢˋ)
to admonish without reserve

直講(ㄓˊ ㄐㄧㄤˇ)
to explain (classics) in the vernacular

直徑(ㄓˊ ㄐㄧㄥˋ)
①a diameter ②a straight path

直覺(ㄓˊ ㄐㄩㄝˊ)
intuition: 她憑著女人的直覺去了解他。She understood him by woman's intuition.

直前(ㄓˊ ㄑㄧㄢˊ)
to go straightforward

直去直來(ㄓˊ ㄑㄩˋ ㄓˊ ㄌㄞˊ)
to go and return without undue delay

直系親屬(ㄓˊ ㄒㄧˋ ㄑㄧㄣ ㄕㄨˇ)
a direct or lineal relation (as opposed to a collateral relation): 孫子是祖父的直系親屬。A grandson is a lineal descendant of his grandfather.

直轄(ㄓˊ ㄒㄧㄚˊ)
to be under the direct control or jurisdiction of

直轄市(ㄓˊ ㄒㄧㄚˊ ㄕˋ)
a special municipality (under the direct jurisdiction of the Central Government like a province)

直下(ㄓˊ ㄒㄧㄚˋ)
to deteriorate steadily

直銷(ㄓˊ ㄒㄧㄠ)
to sell directly or direct sale by a manufacturer instead of through an agent

直線(ㄓˊ ㄒㄧㄢˋ)
①a straight line ②steep; sharp: 現在物價直線上漲。Nowadays, prices rise sharply.

直線形(ㄓˊ ㄒㄧㄢˋ ㄒㄧㄥˊ)
a rectilinear figure

直心眼兒(ㄓˊ ㄒㄧㄣ ㄧㄚˇㄦ)
honest; upright
直性兒(ㄓˊ ㄒㄧㄥˋㄦ)or 直性子(ㄓˊ ㄒㄧㄥˋ ·ㄗ)
straightforward; honest; frank
直須(ㄓˊ ㄒㄩ)
should then; should immediately
直直腰兒(ㄓˊ ·ㄓ ㄧㄠㄦ)
to give the waist a stretch—to take a rest
直尺(ㄓˊ ㄔˇ)
a straightedge
直臣(ㄓˊ ㄔㄣˊ)
an outspoken subject or courtier
直陳(ㄓˊ ㄔㄣˊ)
to describe truthfully; to state frankly
直腸(ㄓˊ ㄔㄤˊ)
the rectum
直腸直肚(ㄓˊ ㄔㄤˊ ㄓˊ ㄉㄨˋ)
outspoken; straightforward; frank
直腸癌(ㄓˊ ㄔㄤˊ ㄧㄢˊ)
cancer of the rectum
直腸炎(ㄓˊ ㄔㄤˊ ㄧㄢˊ)
rectitis; proctitis
直是(ㄓˊ ㄕˋ)
it is always
直視(ㄓˊ ㄕˋ)
to look steadily at
直受兒(ㄓˊ ㄕㄡˋㄦ)
①to accept oppression meekly ②to fail to return a salutation or gift
直上青雲(ㄓˊ ㄕㄤˋ ㄑㄧㄥ ㄩㄣˊ)
to hit the highest literary honors
直上直下(ㄓˊ ㄕㄤˋ ㄓˊ ㄒㄧㄚˋ)
very steep
直昇機(ㄓˊ ㄕㄥ ㄐㄧ)
a helicopter
直昇機坪(ㄓˊ ㄕㄥ ㄐㄧ ㄆㄧㄥˊ)or 直昇機場(ㄓˊ ㄕㄥ ㄐㄧ ㄔㄤˇ)
a heliport; a helipad
直書(ㄓˊ ㄕㄨ)
to write straightforwardly
直抒己見(ㄓˊ ㄕㄨ ㄐㄧˇ ㄐㄧㄢˋ)
to state one's opinions straightforwardly
直屬(ㄓˊ ㄕㄨˇ)
to be under the direct control or jurisdiction of
直率(ㄓˊ ㄕㄨㄞˋ)
frank; outspoken; straightforward; candid: 請直率地告訴我。Please tell me frankly.
直爽(ㄓˊ ㄕㄨㄤˇ)
straightforward; frank; forthright: 他的性格直爽。He has a forthright character.
直認不諱(ㄓˊ ㄖㄣˋ ㄅㄨˋ ㄏㄨㄟˋ)
to plead guilty to a charge
直入(ㄓˊ ㄖㄨˋ)
to go right in
直譯(ㄓˊ ㄧˋ)
literal translation; verbatim translation; word-for-word translation
直言(ㄓˊ ㄧㄢˊ)
①to speak out; to speak bluntly: 恕我直言。Excuse me for speaking bluntly. ②outspoken remarks; frank statement
直言不諱(ㄓˊ ㄧㄢˊ ㄅㄨˋ ㄏㄨㄟˋ)
to speak plainly and frankly; not to mince words
直言無隱(ㄓˊ ㄧㄢˊ ㄨˊ ㄧㄣˇ)
to tell the truth without reservation
直皖戰爭(ㄓˊ ㄨㄢˇ ㄓㄢˋ ㄓㄥ)
the war between warlords Tsao Kun (曹錕) and Tuan Chi-jui (段祺瑞) in 1920
直喩(ㄓˊ ㄩˋ)
a simile 亦作「明喩」

四畫

【相】 3744
1. ㄒㄧㄤ shiang xiāng

1. each other; one another; mutually; reciprocal: 我們兩人素不相識。We do not know each other.
2. substance

相伴(ㄒㄧㄤ ㄅㄢˋ)
to accompany somebody; to be a companion of each other
相比(ㄒㄧㄤ ㄅㄧˇ)
to compare with each other: 兩者相差懸殊，無法相比。There's no comparison between the two.
相並(ㄒㄧㄤ ㄅㄧㄥˋ)
abreast; side by side
相陪(ㄒㄧㄤ ㄆㄟˊ)
in the company of; accompanied by
相配(ㄒㄧㄤ ㄆㄟˋ)
to match well: 他們是很相配的一對夫妻。They are a well-matched couple.
相撲(ㄒㄧㄤ ㄆㄨ)
to wrestle with each other
相罵(ㄒㄧㄤ ㄇㄚˋ)
to revile each other; to abuse each other
相煩(ㄒㄧㄤ ㄈㄢˊ)
to trouble someone with requests; to ask for a favor
相反(ㄒㄧㄤ ㄈㄢˇ)
contrary; opposed to each other; contradictory: 結果與我們預期的相反。The result was contrary to our expectations.
相反相成(ㄒㄧㄤ ㄈㄢˇ ㄒㄧㄤ ㄔㄥˊ)
(said of two things) to be both contrary and complementary to each other; to oppose each other and yet also complement each other
相反詞(ㄒㄧㄤ ㄈㄢˇ ㄘˊ)
an antonym
相仿(ㄒㄧㄤ ㄈㄤˇ)
alike; similar: 他們年紀相仿。They are about the same age.
相逢(ㄒㄧㄤ ㄈㄥˊ)
to meet each other; to come across: 他們的車子在狹路相逢。Their cars met on the narrow road.
相符(ㄒㄧㄤ ㄈㄨˊ)
to tally; to correspond; to agree; to match: 他的陳述與事實相符。His statement tallies with the facts.
相輔相成(ㄒㄧㄤ ㄈㄨˇ ㄒㄧㄤ ㄔㄥˊ)
to complement each other; to reciprocate and complement
相打(ㄒㄧㄤ ㄉㄚˇ)
to have a fight: 你們爲何又相打了? Why did you have a fight again?
相得(ㄒㄧㄤ ㄉㄜˊ)
harmonious; friendly
相得益彰(ㄒㄧㄤ ㄉㄜˊ ㄧˋ ㄓㄤ)
Each gains in appearance from the presence of the other. 或 Each complements the other.
相待(ㄒㄧㄤ ㄉㄞˋ)
to treat (a person): 請別把我

當小孩相待。Please don't treat me as a child.

相當(ㄒㄧㄤ ㄉㄤ)
①to balance; equivalent; to match; to correspond to: 得失相當。The gains balance the losses. ②considerable; to a great extent ③appropriate; fit; suitable

相等(ㄒㄧㄤ ㄉㄥˇ)
equal; equivalent: 他把蛋糕切成相等的兩分。He divided the cake into two equal parts.

相抵(ㄒㄧㄤ ㄉㄧˇ)
to offset; to cancel each other; to counterbalance: 這兩個數彼此相抵。These two figures cancel each other.

相對(ㄒㄧㄤ ㄉㄨㄟˋ)
①corresponding ②relative ③opposite; face to face: 這兩個男孩相對而坐。The two boys sit opposite each other.

相對論(ㄒㄧㄤ ㄉㄨㄟˋ ㄌㄨㄣˋ)
the theory of relativity

相對基金(ㄒㄧㄤ ㄉㄨㄟˋ ㄐㄧ ㄐㄧㄣ)
a counterpart fund

相投(ㄒㄧㄤ ㄊㄡˊ)
congenial; compatible

相談(ㄒㄧㄤ ㄊㄢˊ)
to converse; to talk together: 他們相談了一會兒。They talked together for a short time.

相提並論(ㄒㄧㄤ ㄊㄧˊ ㄅㄧㄥˋ ㄌㄨㄣˋ)
mentioned and discussed as related things; to mention (two things or persons of different worth) in the same breath: 這兩件事不能相提並論。These two things cannot be mentioned in the same breath.

相托(ㄒㄧㄤ ㄊㄨㄛ)
to entrust

相通(ㄒㄧㄤ ㄊㄨㄥ)
to communicate with each other; to be interlinked: 這兩個房間有門相通。The two rooms open into each other.

相同(ㄒㄧㄤ ㄊㄨㄥˊ)
①the same; identical: 這兩個學生在這個問題上觀點相同。The two students have the same views on this question. ②similar; alike

相賴(ㄒㄧㄤ ㄌㄞˋ)
to depend on each other

相連(ㄒㄧㄤ ㄌㄧㄢˊ)
connected; joined; linked: 兩地有橋樑相連。The two places are linked by a bridge.

相隔(ㄒㄧㄤ ㄍㄜˊ)
to be separated by; to be apart; to be at a distance of: 這個小鎮與市區相隔十哩。The small town is ten miles apart from downtown.

相告(ㄒㄧㄤ ㄍㄠˋ)
to tell; to pass information

相干(ㄒㄧㄤ ㄍㄢ)
related; connected; to have to do with: 這兩個問題互不相干。The two problems are not related to each other.

相顧失色(ㄒㄧㄤ ㄍㄨˋ ㄕ ㄙㄜˋ)
to look at each other in dismay

相關(ㄒㄧㄤ ㄍㄨㄢ)
related; connected: 公共衛生和國民健康密切相關。Public health has a direct bearing on the citizens' health.

相尅(ㄒㄧㄤ ㄎㄜˋ)
mutually destructive

相看(ㄒㄧㄤ ㄎㄢˋ)
①to look at each other ②to appraise each other (said of a man and a woman in a meeting arranged by the matchmaker)

相好(ㄒㄧㄤ ㄏㄠˇ)
①to be on friendly terms ②a good friend; a lover; a sweetheart ③to have an affair with

相互(ㄒㄧㄤ ㄏㄨˋ)
each other; one another; mutually; reciprocally; mutual; reciprocal: 這次的討論會增進相互的了解。The discussion meeting promoted mutual understanding.

相互關係(ㄒㄧㄤ ㄏㄨˋ ㄍㄨㄢ ㄒㄧˋ)
mutual relation; correlation: 氣候與農作物間有極密切的相互關係。There is a close correlation between climate and crops.

相互信任(ㄒㄧㄤ ㄏㄨˋ ㄒㄧㄣˋ ㄖㄣˋ)
mutual credits

相會(ㄒㄧㄤ ㄏㄨㄟˋ)
to meet together; to meet each other

相繼(ㄒㄧㄤ ㄐㄧˋ)
in succession; one after another: 代表們相繼發言。The representatives spoke in succession.

相偕(ㄒㄧㄤ ㄐㄧㄝ)or(ㄒㄧㄤ ㄒㄧㄝˊ)
both; together

相交(ㄒㄧㄤ ㄐㄧㄠ)
①to intersect: 這條路與主要街道相交。This road intersects main streets. ②to make friends with each other; to become associated with each other: 他們相交有年。They have made friends with each other for years.

相較(ㄒㄧㄤ ㄐㄧㄠˋ)
to compare with each other

相救(ㄒㄧㄤ ㄐㄧㄡˋ)
to rescue; to help out of difficulty

相煎太急(ㄒㄧㄤ ㄐㄧㄢ ㄊㄞˋ ㄐㄧˊ)
to torment a person too hard

相間(ㄒㄧㄤ ㄐㄧㄢˋ)
spaced in-between; to alternate

相見恨晚(ㄒㄧㄤ ㄐㄧㄢˋ ㄏㄣˋ ㄨㄢˇ)
to regret having not met earlier

相近(ㄒㄧㄤ ㄐㄧㄣˋ)
close (in amount, degree, quality, etc.); approximate: 得分相近。The score was very close.

相將(ㄒㄧㄤ ㄐㄧㄤ)
together; both

相敬如賓(ㄒㄧㄤ ㄐㄧㄥˋ ㄖㄨˊ ㄅㄧㄣ)
(said of a married couple) to respect each other as if the other were a guest

相距(ㄒㄧㄤ ㄐㄩˋ)
distance between two points; away from: 這兩棵樹相距二十公尺。The distance between the two trees is 20 meters.

相聚(ㄒㄧㄤ ㄐㄩˋ)
to meet together; to assemble

相切(ㄒㄧㄤ ㄑㄧㄝ)
(geometry) to be tangent

相求(ㄒㄧㄤ ㄑㄧㄡˊ)
to ask for a favor; to beg; to entreat: 他有事相求於我。He entreated a favor of me.

相親相愛(ㄒㄧㄤ ㄑㄧㄣ ㄒㄧㄤ ㄞˋ)
to be kind to each other and love each other

相去無幾(ㄒㄧㄤ ㄑㄩˋ ㄨˊ ㄐㄧˇ)
The difference is insignificant.

相覷(ㄒㄧㄤ ㄑㄩˋ)
to look at each other

相勸(ㄒㄧㄤ ㄑㄩㄢˋ)
to persuade; to offer advice: 她昨天對他好言相勸。She offered him well-meaning advice yesterday.

相信(ㄒㄧㄤ ㄒㄧㄣˋ)
to believe ; to have faith in: 我不能十分相信他。I can't quite believe him.

相向(ㄒㄧㄤ ㄒㄧㄤˋ)
to face each other

相像(ㄒㄧㄤ ㄒㄧㄤˋ)
to resemble; to be similar; to be alike: 這兩幅畫很相像。These two pictures are very much alike.

相形見絀(ㄒㄧㄤ ㄒㄧㄥˊ ㄐㄧㄢˋ ㄔㄨˋ)
found to be inferior by comparison; to be outshone

相形之下(ㄒㄧㄤ ㄒㄧㄥˊ ㄓ ㄒㄧㄚˋ)
by comparison; when compared; in comparison with

相續(ㄒㄧㄤ ㄒㄩˋ)
① to inherit ② to continue or succeed one after another

相知(ㄒㄧㄤ ㄓ)
① bosom friends; great friends ② to know each other well: 相知恨晚。It is much regretted that we have not known earlier.

相爭(ㄒㄧㄤ ㄓㄥ)
to fight each other over something; to quarrel; to argue vehemently

相助(ㄒㄧㄤ ㄓㄨˋ)
to help; to help each other: 多謝你大力相助。Thank you very much for your great help.

相撞(ㄒㄧㄤ ㄓㄨㄤˋ)
to collide with each other

相持不下(ㄒㄧㄤ ㄔˊ ㄅㄨˋ ㄒㄧㄚˋ)
persistently opposing each other with neither giving way; to be at a stalemate (or deadlock): 這兩派相持不下。The two parties are at a deadlock.

相差(ㄒㄧㄤ ㄔㄚ)
to differ

相稱(ㄒㄧㄤ ㄔㄣˋ)
to fit each other; to match each other; to be symmetrical: 這兩種布配在一起很相稱。The two kinds of cloth match very well.

相處(ㄒㄧㄤ ㄔㄨˇ)
to spend time together; to live together; to get along with: 他這個人不好相處。He is difficult to get along with.

相傳(ㄒㄧㄤ ㄔㄨㄢˊ)
①(said of a report) to be transmitted from person to person或It is said that.... 或 Legend has it that.... ② to be passed or handed down from generation to generation

相視(ㄒㄧㄤ ㄕˋ)
to look at each other

相識(ㄒㄧㄤ ㄕˋ)
① to know each other; to be acquainted with each other: 我們素不相識。We are not acquainted with each other. ② an acquaintance: 他是我們的老相識。He is our old acquaintance.

相善(ㄒㄧㄤ ㄕㄢˋ)
on friendly terms; on good terms

相商(ㄒㄧㄤ ㄕㄤ)
to confer; to exchange views; to consult: 我有要事相商。I have something important to consult with you.

相生相剋(ㄒㄧㄤ ㄕㄥ ㄒㄧㄤ ㄎㄜˋ)
mutual production and destruction (as among the five elements); mutual promotion and restraint

相率(ㄒㄧㄤ ㄕㄨㄞˋ)
leading one another; together

相濡以沫(ㄒㄧㄤ ㄖㄨˊ ㄧˇ ㄇㄛˋ)
to help each other when both are in humble circumstances

相若(ㄒㄧㄤ ㄖㄨㄛˋ)
similar; alike: 這兩兄弟長相相若。The two brothers look alike.

相贈(ㄒㄧㄤ ㄗㄥˋ)
to present a gift; to give a present: 他以金錶相贈。He presented me with a gold watch.

相左(ㄒㄧㄤ ㄗㄨㄛˇ)
to disagree; to differ; to be at odds with; to conflict with each other

相思(ㄒㄧㄤ ㄙ)
to pine for each other; to miss each other; to be in love with each other

相思病(ㄒㄧㄤ ㄙ ㄅㄧㄥˋ)
lovesickness

相思鳥(ㄒㄧㄤ ㄙ ㄋㄧㄠˇ)
a lovebird (any of small parrots that show great affection for their mates)

相思樹(ㄒㄧㄤ ㄙ ㄕㄨˋ)
① *Abrus precatorius* ② an acacia

相思子(ㄒㄧㄤ ㄙ ㄗˇ)or 相思豆(ㄒㄧㄤ ㄙ ㄉㄡˋ)
red beans; seeds of *Abrus precatorius*; jequirities; love peas 亦作「紅豆」

相似(ㄒㄧㄤ ㄙˋ)
alike; similar: 他們面貌相似。They look alike.

相似字(ㄒㄧㄤ ㄙˋ ㄗˋ)
a synonym

相似詞(ㄒㄧㄤ ㄙˋ ㄘˊ)
a synonymous phrase; a synonym

相愛(ㄒㄧㄤ ㄞˋ)
to love each other

相安無事(ㄒㄧㄤ ㄢ ㄨˊ ㄕˋ)
at peace with each other

相依(ㄒㄧㄤ ㄧ)
to depend on each other; to be interdependent: 我們唇齒相依。We are as closely related to each other as lips and teeth.

相依爲命(ㄒㄧㄤ ㄧ ㄨㄟˊ ㄇㄧㄥˋ)
to rely upon each other for life

相宜(ㄒㄧㄤ ㄧˊ)
fitting; proper; appropriate

相邀(ㄒㄧㄤ ㄧㄠ)
to invite

相沿(ㄒㄧㄤ ㄧㄢˊ)
to pass down from generation to generation without change

相沿成習(ㄒㄧㄤ ㄧㄢˊ ㄔㄥˊ ㄒㄧˊ)
to have come down from the past and become customary

相印(ㄒㄧㄤ ㄧㄣˋ)
① to bear testimony or witness for each other ② to fit

目部

〔目部〕

or match each other completely (as two hearts)

相迎(ㄒㄧㄤ ㄧㄥˊ)
to welcome; to greet

相應(ㄒㄧㄤ ㄧㄥˋ)
①(documentary usage) should ②to support each other ③corresponding; relevant

相應不理(ㄒㄧㄤ ㄧㄥˋ ㄅㄨˋ ㄌㄧˇ)
to disregard another's request (a phrase common in official communications); to ignore; to pay no heed to

相映成趣(ㄒㄧㄤ ㄧㄥˋ ㄔㄥˊ ㄑㄩˋ)
to form an interesting or delightful contrast

相違(ㄒㄧㄤ ㄨㄟˊ)
①to disagree; to differ ②to be parted; to be separated

相維(ㄒㄧㄤ ㄨㄟˊ)
to support each other

相與(ㄒㄧㄤ ㄩˇ)
①to get along with: 他這個人極難相與。He is extremely difficult to get along with. ②a friend ③together

相遇(ㄒㄧㄤ ㄩˋ)
to meet each other

相約(ㄒㄧㄤ ㄩㄝ)
to reach an agreement; to make an appointment

【相】 3744
2. ㄒㄧㄤˋ shianq xiàng

1. to examine; to study; to read
2. a countenance; facial features; looks; an appearance; bearing; posture: 這個人一臉福相。The man has a countenance of good luck.
3. the prime minister (in feudal times)
4. to assist; to help

相片(ㄒㄧㄤˋ ㄆㄧㄢˋ)
a photograph; a photo

相貌(ㄒㄧㄤˋ ㄇㄠˋ)
a countenance; a physiognomy; a face; facial features: 他的相貌很端正。He has very regular features.

相貌堂堂(ㄒㄧㄤˋ ㄇㄠˋ ㄊㄤˊ ㄊㄤˊ)
to have a dignified appearance

相面(ㄒㄧㄤˋ ㄇㄧㄢˋ)
to practice physiognomy; to tell somebody's fortune by reading his face

相命(ㄒㄧㄤˋ ㄇㄧㄥˋ)
fortunetelling

相法(ㄒㄧㄤˋ ㄈㄚˇ)
physiognomy

相夫教子(ㄒㄧㄤˋ ㄈㄨ ㄐㄧㄠˋ ㄗˇ)
to help the husband and teach the children—the duty of a wife

相府(ㄒㄧㄤˋ ㄈㄨˇ)
an influential courtier's mansion; a prime minister's residence

相臺(ㄒㄧㄤˋ ㄊㄞˊ)
a tower built by Tsao Tsao (曹操) in what is Honan today

相體裁衣(ㄒㄧㄤˋ ㄊㄧˇ ㄘㄞˊ ㄧ)
to decide the quantity of materials needed before proceeding to do something

相女配夫(ㄒㄧㄤˋ ㄋㄩˇ ㄆㄟˋ ㄈㄨ)
Study your own daughter properly when finding her a husband.

相國(ㄒㄧㄤˋ ㄍㄨㄛˊ)
the prime minister (a term of respect)

相公
①(ㄒㄧㄤˋ ㄍㄨㄥ) the premier
②(ㄒㄧㄤˋ ˙ㄍㄨㄥ) ⓐ a young gentleman (a term common in operas and old novels) ⓑ (slang) a catamite ⓒ a mahjong player who unintentionally takes in the wrong number of dominos and is thus disqualified in a game

相機(ㄒㄧㄤˋ ㄐㄧ)
①to watch for the good chance for action ②a camera

相機行事(ㄒㄧㄤˋ ㄐㄧ ㄒㄧㄥˊ ㄕˋ)
to act as circumstances dictate

相親(ㄒㄧㄤˋ ㄑㄧㄣ)
an interview prior to marriage; to size up a prospective mate in an arranged meeting

相紙(ㄒㄧㄤˋ ㄓˇ)
(photography) printing paper; photographic paper

相士(ㄒㄧㄤˋ ㄕˋ)
①a fortune-teller: 他從不相信相士的話。He never believes the fortune-teller's words. ②to appraise a person's latent ability

相手術(ㄒㄧㄤˋ ㄕㄡˇ ㄕㄨˋ)
palmistry

相聲(ㄒㄧㄤˋ ㄕㄥ)
a Chinese comic dialogue; a cross talk

相術(ㄒㄧㄤˋ ㄕㄨˋ)
physiognomy

相人(ㄒㄧㄤˋ ㄖㄣˊ)
to practice physiognomy

相爺(ㄒㄧㄤˋ ㄧㄝˊ)
the prime minister

相印(ㄒㄧㄤˋ ㄧㄣˋ)
the prime minister's seal

【盻】 3745
ㄒㄧˋ shih xì

to look in anger

【盼】 3746
ㄆㄢˋ pann pàn

1. to look
2. (descriptive of the black and white of the eyes) well defined
3. to hope; to look for; to expect

盼禱(ㄆㄢˋ ㄉㄠˇ)
(a conventional phrase in formal letters) to hope

盼頭(ㄆㄢˋ ˙ㄊㄡ)
hope; good prospects 亦作「盼兒」: 我覺得這事有盼頭了。I feel this business is looking hopeful now.

盼念(ㄆㄢˋ ㄋㄧㄢˋ)
to hope; to long for

盼望(ㄆㄢˋ ㄨㄤˋ)
to hope; to wish

【眄】 3747
ㄇㄧㄢˇ mean miǎn

1. to look askance; to ogle
2. to look

眄眄(ㄇㄧㄢˇ ㄇㄧㄢˇ)
①looking askance ②looking dull

眄睨(ㄇㄧㄢˇ ㄋㄧˋ)
to look askance

眄睞(ㄇㄧㄢˇ ㄌㄞˋ)
looking concerned

【眇】 3748
ㄇㄧㄠˇ meau miǎo

1. tiny; fine; small; unimportant
2. blind in one eye

眇眇(ㄇㄧㄠˇ ㄇㄧㄠˇ)
①tiny ②far; distant; high

眇眇忽忽(ㄇㄧㄠˇ ㄇㄧㄠˇ ㄏㄨ ㄏㄨ)

indistinct; too small to identify

眇乎其小(ㄇㄧㄠˇ ㄏㄨ ㄑㄧˊ ㄒㄧㄠˇ)
How small it is! 或 How insignificant it is!

眇小(ㄇㄧㄠˇ ㄒㄧㄠˇ)
very small; tiny; insignificant: 他們成功的希望很眇小。There is small hope of success for them.

【眈】 3749
ㄉㄢ dan dān
to look downward

眈眈(ㄉㄢ ㄉㄢ)
eyeing gloatingly; looking at greedily; staring

【眊】 3750
ㄇㄠˋ maw mào
1. dim-sighted; eyes not seeing very clearly; dull and mixed-up
2. same as 耄—aged

眊眊(ㄇㄠˋ ㄇㄠˋ)
① unable to see clearly ② dull and mixed-up, probably because of old age

眊聵(ㄇㄠˋ ㄎㄨㄟˋ)
dim-sighted and hard of hearing

【盹】 3751
ㄉㄨㄣˇ doen duň
to doze: 他伏在書上打盹。He dozed over a book.

盹兒(ㄉㄨㄜˇㄦ)
a doze; a nap: 他總是在上課時打盹兒。He always fell into a doze in his classes.

盹睡(ㄉㄨㄣˇ ㄕㄨㄟˋ)
to doze; to nod; a nap

【盾】 3752
ㄕㄨㄣˇ shoen shuň
(又讀 ㄉㄨㄣˋ duenn duǹ)
1. a shield; a buckler
2. a guilder, a monetary unit in Holland

盾牌(ㄉㄨㄣˋ ㄆㄞˊ)
① a shield ② (figuratively) a pretext; an excuse

【省】 3753
1. ㄕㄥˇ sheeng shěng
1. a province; provincial
2. economical; frugal; to economize: 學生應當能省則省。Students should economize wherever possible.
3. to save; to omit; to reduce; to avoid; to abridge: 這個字不能省。The word cannot be omitted.

省不下(ㄕㄥˇ ·ㄅㄨ ㄒㄧㄚˋ)
unable to economize any further

省分(ㄕㄥˇ ㄈㄣˋ)
a province

省得(ㄕㄥˇ ·ㄉㄜ)
① lest ② to avoid; to save (trouble, etc.)

省道(ㄕㄥˇ ㄉㄠˋ)
a provincial highway; an interprovincial highway

省黨部(ㄕㄥˇ ㄉㄤˇ ㄅㄨˋ)
provincial headquarters of a political party

省力(ㄕㄥˇ ㄌㄧˋ)
to save energy or labor; labor-saving: 這種機器省力不少。The machine saves a lot of labor.

省立學校(ㄕㄥˇ ㄌㄧˋ ㄒㄩㄝˊ ㄒㄧㄠˋ)
a provincial school

省料(ㄕㄥˇ ㄌㄧㄠˋ)
to save material

省令(ㄕㄥˇ ㄌㄧㄥˋ)
orders issued by the provincial government

省略(ㄕㄥˇ ㄌㄩㄝˋ)
to omit; to abridge; omission; abridgment

省略符號(ㄕㄥˇ ㄌㄩㄝˋ ㄈㄨˊ ㄏㄠˋ)
① an ellipsis (...); an apostrophe(') ② (music) an abbreviation

省略推理(ㄕㄥˇ ㄌㄩㄝˋ ㄊㄨㄟ ㄌㄧˇ)
(logic) an enthymeme

省略算(ㄕㄥˇ ㄌㄩㄝˋ ㄙㄨㄢˋ)
(mathematics) an approximation

省工夫兒(ㄕㄥˇ ㄍㄨㄥ ·ㄈㄨㄦ)
to save time

省會(ㄕㄥˇ ㄏㄨㄟˋ)
the seat of the provincial government; a provincial capital; the capital city of a province

省界(ㄕㄥˇ ㄐㄧㄝˋ)
provincial boundaries

省減(ㄕㄥˇ ㄐㄧㄢˇ)
to reduce; to cut (expenses, a budget, etc.); to lessen; to practice austerity; to economize

省儉(ㄕㄥˇ ㄐㄧㄢˇ)
frugal; frugality; thrifty

省錢(ㄕㄥˇ ㄑㄧㄢˊ)
to save money; economical

省卻(ㄕㄥˇ ㄑㄩㄝˋ)
to avoid (trouble, etc.); to save (time, etc.): 此書爲教師省卻許多麻煩。The book saves the teacher much trouble.

省下(ㄕㄥˇ ㄒㄧㄚˋ)
to save (money)

省心(ㄕㄥˇ ㄒㄧㄣ)
to save cares or worries; to save further thought

省治(ㄕㄥˇ ㄓˋ)
the seat of the provincial government; the capital city of a province

省長(ㄕㄥˇ ㄓㄤˇ)
the governor of a province in the early republican years

省政府(ㄕㄥˇ ㄓㄥˋ ㄈㄨˇ)
the provincial government

省主席(ㄕㄥˇ ㄓㄨˇ ㄒㄧˊ)
the governor of a province

省吃儉用(ㄕㄥˇ ㄔ ㄐㄧㄢˇ ㄩㄥˋ)
frugal and thrifty; to practice austerity in every respect

省城(ㄕㄥˇ ㄔㄥˊ)
the city in which the provincial government is located; a provincial capital

省時(ㄕㄥˇ ㄕˊ)
to save time; timesaving: 開車比走路省時。It will save time if we drive the car instead of walking.

省事(ㄕㄥˇ ㄕˋ)
① to save trouble: 這樣可以省事不少。This can save me a lot of trouble. ② easy

省試(ㄕㄥˇ ㄕˋ)
a provincial examination (for civil officials, etc.)

省議會(ㄕㄥˇ ㄧˋ ㄏㄨㄟˋ)
the provincial assembly

省議員(ㄕㄥˇ ㄧˋ ㄩㄢˊ)
a provincial assemblyman; a member of a provincial assembly

省油(ㄕㄥˇ ㄧㄡˊ)
low in fuel consumption; to save fuel

省油燈(ㄕㄥˇ ㄧㄡˊ ㄉㄥ)
(slang) an oil-saving lamp—a fellow who causes the least trouble

〔目部〕

省文(ㄕㄥˇ ㄨㄣˊ)
an abridged expression; elliptical
省垣(ㄕㄥˇ ㄩㄢˊ)
the seat of the provincial government; the capital city of a province
省用(ㄕㄥˇ ㄩㄥˋ)
to save; to economize

【省】 3753
2. ㄒㄧㄥˇ shiing xǐng

1. to examine (oneself, etc.); to reflect; to introspect; to consider
2. to understand; to know
3. to visit (one's seniors, etc.)
4. to test; an examination
5. memory

省墓(ㄒㄧㄥˇ ㄇㄨˋ)
to visit the graves of one's ancestors
省會(ㄒㄧㄥˇ ㄏㄨㄟˋ)
① to instruct; to exhort ② to understand; to know
省親(ㄒㄧㄥˇ ㄑㄧㄣ)
to visit one's senior relatives —especially parents
省察(ㄒㄧㄥˇ ㄔㄚˊ)
① to examine; to study; to observe ② to introspect; to make self-examination
省事(ㄒㄧㄥˇ ㄕˋ)
clever and understanding; perceptive and alert—observant; conscious
省視(ㄒㄧㄥˇ ㄕˋ)
to examine; to survey; to inspect; to visit
省悟(ㄒㄧㄥˇ ㄨˋ)
to realize; realization; to awaken to (truth, etc.); awakening

【眉】 3754
ㄇㄟˊ mei méi

1. eyebrows
2. the side
3. the top margin of a printed page in a book
4. a rare Chinese family name

眉筆(ㄇㄟˊ ㄅㄧˇ)
an eyebrow pencil
眉批(ㄇㄟˊ ㄆㄧ)
the running comment on the upper margin of a printed page in a book
眉毛(ㄇㄟˊ ·ㄇㄠ)
the eyebrows
眉目(ㄇㄟˊ ㄇㄨˋ)
① a general facial appearance ② arrangement, order or sequence of things; a general sketch or idea of things: 我的論文已有眉目了。I have had a general sketch for my treatise. ③ close or near at hand ④ the sign of a positive outcome: 我的計畫有眉目了。My plan is beginning to take shape.
眉目傳情(ㄇㄟˊ ㄇㄨˋ ㄔㄨㄢˊ ㄑㄧㄥˊ)
to make sheep's eyes (at someone); to converse with eyes (between a man and a woman); eloquent eyes
眉目如畫(ㄇㄟˊ ㄇㄨˋ ㄖㄨˊ ㄏㄨㄚˋ)
as pretty as a picture
眉飛色舞(ㄇㄟˊ ㄈㄟ ㄙㄜˋ ㄨˇ)
to be beside oneself with joy; to be overjoyed; to be enraptured; to be exultant
眉黛(ㄇㄟˊ ㄉㄞˋ)
painted eyebrows; pretty eyebrows
眉頭(ㄇㄟˊ ㄊㄡˊ)
the space between the eyebrows
眉頭不展(ㄇㄟˊ ㄊㄡˊ ㄅㄨˋ ㄓㄢˇ)
with knitted brows—worried; unhappy
眉來眼去(ㄇㄟˊ ㄌㄞˊ ㄧㄢˇ ㄑㄩˋ)
(between a man and a woman) to converse with eyes; to make passes both ways
眉高眼低(ㄇㄟˊ ㄍㄠ ㄧㄢˇ ㄉㄧ)
a kind of facial expression
眉開眼笑(ㄇㄟˊ ㄎㄞ ㄧㄢˇ ㄒㄧㄠˋ)or 眉花眼笑(ㄇㄟˊ ㄏㄨㄚ ㄧㄢˇ ㄒㄧㄠˋ)
very happy, joyful or jubilant
眉急(ㄇㄟˊ ㄐㄧˊ)
very urgent or imminent (predicaments)
眉睫(ㄇㄟˊ ㄐㄧㄝˊ)
① very close, imminent or urgent: 這危險迫在眉睫。This is an imminent danger. ② eyebrows and eyelashes
眉蘚(ㄇㄟˊ ㄐㄧㄢˇ)
to knit one's eyebrows—pensive, sad or worried
眉清目秀(ㄇㄟˊ ㄑㄧㄥ ㄇㄨˋ ㄒㄧㄡˋ)or 眉目清秀(ㄇㄟˊ ㄇㄨˋ ㄑㄧㄥ ㄒㄧㄡˋ)
good-looking; to look clean and pretty; pleasant facial features
眉心(ㄇㄟˊ ㄒㄧㄣ)
the space between the eyebrows
眉史(ㄇㄟˊ ㄕˇ)
(euphemism) a prostitute
眉梢(ㄇㄟˊ ㄕㄠ)
the ends of the eyebrows
眉壽(ㄇㄟˊ ㄕㄡˋ)
bushy eyebrows—longevity; a long life
眉山(ㄇㄟˊ ㄕㄢ)
Meishan, a county in Szechwan Province
眉眼(ㄇㄟˊ ㄧㄢˇ)
facial expression
眉宇(ㄇㄟˊ ㄩˇ)
① a facial appearance ② the forehead
眉語(ㄇㄟˊ ㄩˇ)
(literally) to speak with the eyebrows—to signal with eyebrows
眉月(ㄇㄟˊ ㄩㄝˋ)
crescent-shaped eyebrows

【看】 3755
1. ㄎㄢˋ kann kàn

1. to see; to look at; to observe; to watch; to look in the direction of; to read: 她看書看得睡着了。She read herself to sleep.
2. to examine; to consider; to think: 我看他這個人不可靠。I don't think he is reliable.
3. to visit; to call on: 我下週會去看你的。I will visit you next week.
4. to present (tea, wine, etc.)
5. to depend on

看病(ㄎㄢˋ ㄅㄧㄥˋ)
① to see a doctor: 他明天要去看病。He's going to see a doctor tomorrow. ② to examine the patient; to take a look at the patient; to practice medicine: 醫生出門給人看病去了。The doctor's gone to see a patient.
看不得(ㄎㄢˋ ·ㄅㄨ ·ㄉㄜ)
① should not see ② unnecessary to see; not worth seeing
看不透(ㄎㄢˋ ·ㄅㄨ ㄊㄡˋ)
① unable to see through; unable to understand or gain a full understanding of something or somebody; unable to assess the full (potential,

etc.) ② unable to face a situation or accept a fact with resignation
看不來(ㄎㄢˋ ˙ㄅㄨ ㄌㄞˊ)
①not willing to see ②unable to see
看不過(ㄎㄢˋ ˙ㄅㄨ ㄍㄨㄛˋ)
(in a case of exceptionally intolerable, cruel, etc. situation) cannot help but (give him a helping hand, etc.); one's heart is not steely enough to see
看不慣(ㄎㄢˋ ˙ㄅㄨ ㄍㄨㄢˋ)
to detest; to disdain
看不起(ㄎㄢˋ ˙ㄅㄨ ㄑㄧˇ)
to look down upon; to despise
看不下去(ㄎㄢˋ ˙ㄅㄨ ㄒㄧㄚˋ ㄑㄩˋ)
①unable to continue seeing ②cannot help but... 亦作「看不過」③ugly; utterly not worth seeing
看不出(ㄎㄢˋ ˙ㄅㄨ ㄔㄨ)
unable to perceive, detect, foresee, etc.
看不上(ㄎㄢˋ ˙ㄅㄨ ㄕㄤˋ)or 看不上眼(ㄎㄢˋ ˙ㄅㄨ ㄕㄤˋ ㄧㄢˇ)
①not up to one's standard; not to one's taste ② to detest; to disdain; to despise
看破(ㄎㄢˋ ㄆㄛˋ)
①to see through a thing ② to be resigned to what is inevitable
看破紅塵(ㄎㄢˋ ㄆㄛˋ ㄏㄨㄥˊ ㄔㄣˊ)
to see through the vanity of life (and to become a Buddhist monk or nun); to be disillusioned with the mortal world
看面子(ㄎㄢˋ ㄇㄧㄢˋ ˙ㄗ)
for the sake of (a person who recommended, requested, etc.)
看法(ㄎㄢˋ ㄈㄚˇ)
an opinion; a viewpoint
看風頭(ㄎㄢˋ ㄈㄥ ˙ㄊㄡ)
to see which way the wind blows (so that one can manage to stay in an advantageous position)
看風轉舵(ㄎㄢˋ ㄈㄥ ㄓㄨㄢˇ ㄉㄨㄛˋ)or 看風使帆(ㄎㄢˋ ㄈㄥ ㄕˇ ㄈㄢ)
to adapt oneself to circumstances; to trim one's sails
看風水(ㄎㄢˋ ㄈㄥ ㄕㄨㄟˇ)
to practice geomancy (in selecting a site for a tomb or building)
看得透(ㄎㄢˋ ˙ㄉㄜ ㄊㄡˋ)
①to be able to see through or understand: 這個人我看得透。I can see through the man. ②to be able to face a situation or accept a fact with resignation
看得來(ㄎㄢˋ ˙ㄉㄜ ㄌㄞˊ)
worth seeing; presentable
看得過(ㄎㄢˋ ˙ㄉㄜ ㄍㄨㄛˋ)
presentable; passable
看得過去(ㄎㄢˋ ˙ㄉㄜ ㄍㄨㄛˋ ㄑㄩˋ)
barely presentable; barely worth seeing
看得起(ㄎㄢˋ ˙ㄉㄜ ㄑㄧˇ)
to think highly of; to have a high opinion of; to respect
看得上(ㄎㄢˋ ˙ㄉㄜ ㄕㄤˋ)
to one's taste; presentable; up to standard
看待(ㄎㄢˋ ㄉㄞˋ)
to treat (another, a child, friend, etc.); treatment
看到(ㄎㄢˋ ㄉㄠˋ)
to catch sight of; to see
看臺(ㄎㄢˋ ㄊㄞˊ)
(sports) a deck or stand for observers or spectators; bleachers
看透(ㄎㄢˋ ㄊㄡˋ)
①to see through (a trick, conspiracy, etc.) ②to be resigned to what is inevitable
看頭兒(ㄎㄢˋ ˙ㄊㄡㄦ)or 看頭(ㄎㄢˋ ˙ㄊㄡ)
that which is worth seeing or reading: 這篇報導很有看頭。This report is well worth reading.
看天田(ㄎㄢˋ ㄊㄧㄢ ㄊㄧㄢˊ)
paddies without dependable irrigation water
看膩了(ㄎㄢˋ ㄋㄧˋ ˙ㄌㄜ)
to be tired of seeing or watching
看來(ㄎㄢˋ ㄌㄞˊ)
it looks as if; evidently: 這工作看來今天可以做完。It looks as if we'll be able to finish this job today.
看個飽(ㄎㄢˋ ˙ㄍㄜ ㄅㄠˇ)or 看個夠(ㄎㄢˋ ˙ㄍㄜ ㄍㄡˋ)
to see or watch to one's heart's content
看顧(ㄎㄢˋ ㄍㄨˋ)
to look after
看過(ㄎㄢˋ ㄍㄨㄛˋ)
①to take a look at ②to make a perusal of ③to have seen or read: 你看過這新戲沒有? Have you seen the new play?
看官(ㄎㄢˋ ㄍㄨㄢ)
①(in old Chinese novels) dear readers ② the audience
看慣(ㄎㄢˋ ㄍㄨㄢˋ)
to be used to seeing; to become accustomed to seeing
看看(ㄎㄢˋ ˙ㄎㄢ)
①to take a look at: 仔細看看我。Watch me carefully. ② to examine and survey ③to visit or call on: 我想你應該去看看他。I think you ought to call on him. ④to see the sights ⑤to thumb through (a book, etc.)
看機會(ㄎㄢˋ ㄐㄧ ㄏㄨㄟˋ)
to look for a chance or an opportunity; to watch for an opportunity
看見(ㄎㄢˋ ˙ㄐㄧㄢ)
to see (with one's eyes); to catch sight of: 我們看見有人站在門口。We saw someone standing in the doorway.
看齊(ㄎㄢˋ ㄑㄧˊ)
①(military) to dress: 向右看齊! Right face!或Right dress! ②to follow the example of; to emulate (someone)
看輕(ㄎㄢˋ ㄑㄧㄥ)
to despise; to underestimate
看清楚(ㄎㄢˋ ㄑㄧㄥ ˙ㄔㄨ)
to see clearly; to have a clear look at
看情形(ㄎㄢˋ ㄑㄧㄥˊ ˙ㄒㄧㄥ)
depending on circumstances
看取(ㄎㄢˋ ㄑㄩˇ)
Let's see....
看戲(ㄎㄢˋ ㄒㄧˋ)
to watch a show: 我們去看戲吧。Let's go to the play.
看相(ㄎㄢˋ ㄒㄧㄤˋ)
①to visit a physiognomist or fortuneteller ② to practice physiognomy
看著辦(ㄎㄢˋ ˙ㄓㄜ ㄅㄢˋ)
to see what happens and act accordingly; to manage

〔目部〕

things according to the prevailing situation

看朱成碧(ㄎㄢˋ ㄓㄨ ㄔㄥˊ ㄅㄧˋ)
(literally) to take red for green—dim-sighted; dazzled

看中(ㄎㄢˋ ㄓㄨㄥˋ)
to feel satisfied with; to favor (a choice); to choose; to settle on; to prefer; to like

看重(ㄎㄢˋ ㄓㄨㄥˋ)
to esteem; to respect; to regard as important; to value

看成(ㄎㄢˋ ㄔㄥˊ)
to look upon as; to regard as

看出(ㄎㄢˋ ㄔㄨ)
to make out; to see: 我已看出問題在那裏。I have seen where the trouble is.

看穿(ㄎㄢˋ ㄔㄨㄢ)
to see through (a trick): 我們立即看穿他的詭計。We at once saw through his trick.

看事做事(ㄎㄢˋ ㄕˋ ㄗㄨㄛˋ ㄕˋ)
to make no decision beforehand but take appropriate actions as the situation warrants

看手相(ㄎㄢˋ ㄕㄡˇ ㄒㄧㄤˋ)
to read palms as a means of fortunetelling; to practice palmistry

看上(ㄎㄢˋ ㄕㄤˋ)
① to favor; to be satisfied with; to choose ② to be absorbed (in reading, etc.) ③ to take a fancy to: 他看上一位美麗的姑娘。He took a fancy to a beautiful girl.

看書(ㄎㄢˋ ㄕㄨ)
to read a book: 我沒有足夠的時間看書。I haven't enough time to read.

看熱鬧(ㄎㄢˋ ㄖㄜˋ ˙ㄋㄠ)
① to go where the crowds are (for fun or excitement): 他不喜歡看熱鬧。He hates to go where the crowds are. ② to watch others' failure with secret delight

看人(ㄎㄢˋ ㄖㄣˊ)
① depending on who the person is ② to visit or see someone

看人眉睫(ㄎㄢˋ ㄖㄣˊ ㄇㄟˊ ㄐㄧㄝˊ)
to be subservient as a yes-man; to watch for the expression of another so that one knows how to act to please him

看人嘴臉(ㄎㄢˋ ㄖㄣˊ ㄗㄨㄟˇ ㄌㄧㄢˇ)
to be subservient or obedient; to live on another's favor; to depend on another

看作(ㄎㄢˋ ㄗㄨㄛˋ)
to regard as; to consider to be; to treat as

看錯(ㄎㄢˋ ㄘㄨㄛˋ)
① to mistake someone or something for another ② to misjudge someone's ability, character, etc.

看醫生(ㄎㄢˋ ㄧ ㄕㄥ)
to consult a doctor or physician

看一看(ㄎㄢˋ ˙ㄧ ˙ㄎㄢ)
to take a look; to have a look: 讓我們看一看你的字典。Let's have a look at your dictionary.

看樣子(ㄎㄢˋ ㄧㄤˋ ˙ㄗ)
it seems; it looks as if: 看樣子，他是不會來了。It seems that he will not come.

看望(ㄎㄢˋ ˙ㄨㄤ)
to visit or call on

【看】 3755
2. ㄎㄢ kan kān

1. to watch; to mind; to look after
2. to guard; to keep under surveillance

看馬(ㄎㄢ ㄇㄚˇ)
to tend horses; to look after horses

看門(ㄎㄢ ㄇㄣˊ)
① a doorkeeper or gatekeeper; a watchman; a janitor ② to watch or guard the door

看牛(ㄎㄢ ㄋㄧㄡˊ)
① a cowherd ② to herd or take care of cattle

看更(ㄎㄢ ㄍㄥ)
① to beat the night watch ② a night watchman

看管(ㄎㄢ ㄍㄨㄢˇ)
① to take into custody; to guard; to safeguard ② a custodian

看護(ㄎㄢ ㄏㄨˋ)
① to nurse; to take care: 她看護病人。She nursed the sick. ② a nurse (in hospital)

看護婦(ㄎㄢ ㄏㄨˋ ㄈㄨˋ)
a hospital nurse

看家(ㄎㄢ ㄐㄧㄚ)
① to stay at home and look after the house ② a house-guard ③ (money, etc.) saved for a rainy day

看家本領(ㄎㄢ ㄐㄧㄚ ㄅㄣˇ ㄌㄧㄥˇ)
one's specialty or special skill

看家狗(ㄎㄢ ㄐㄧㄚ ㄍㄡˇ)
a watchdog

看守(ㄎㄢ ㄕㄡˇ)
① to watch or guard: 這條狗日夜看守着這個小孩。The dog guarded the child day and night. ② to detain

看守所(ㄎㄢ ㄕㄡˇ ㄙㄨㄛˇ)
a detention house for prisoners awaiting trials

看座兒的(ㄎㄢ ㄗㄨㄛˋㄦ ˙ㄉㄜ)
a steward in a Chinese opera theater

看財奴(ㄎㄢ ㄘㄞˊ ㄋㄨˊ)
a miser

看押(ㄎㄢ ㄧㄚ)
to detain (for questioning, awaiting trial, etc.); to put under guard or custody

五畫

【眙】 3756
1. ㄔˋ chyh chì

1. to stare; to look in the face
2. to look in astonishment; to look with the eyes wide open

【眙】 3756
2. ㄧˊ yi yí

as in 盱眙—name of a county

【眣】 3757
ㄉㄧㄝˊ dye dié

squinting eyes

【眛】 3758
ㄇㄟˋ mey mèi

dim-sighted; poor-visioned

眛良心(ㄇㄟˋ ㄌㄧㄤˊ ˙ㄒㄧㄣ)
to disregard one's conscience

眛於(ㄇㄟˋ ㄩˊ)
blind to: 他們眛於事實。They are blind to the facts.

【眠】 3759
ㄇㄧㄢˊ mian mián

1. to sleep; sleep: 那晚我失眠通宵。I lay all that night sleepless.
2. to hibernate; hibernation: 有些熊冬眠。Some bears hibernate.

眠花宿柳(ㄇㄧㄢˊ ㄏㄨㄚ ㄙㄨˋ ㄌㄧㄡˇ)
to sleep with prostitutes; to visit a brothel

眠思夢想(ㄇㄧㄢˊ ㄙ ㄇㄥˋ ㄒㄧㄤˇ)
to think day and night

眠雲(ㄇㄧㄢˊ ㄩㄣˊ)
(literally) to sleep in the clouds — to live in a hill or mountain

【眩】 3760 ㄒㄩㄢˋ shiuann xuàn
1. to confuse; to dazzle
2. dizzy; giddy; confused vision

眩惑(ㄒㄩㄢˋ ㄏㄨㄛˋ)
to confuse and cheat (the people); to mislead

眩耀(ㄒㄩㄢˋ ㄧㄠˋ)
dazzling; to dazzle

眩暈(ㄒㄩㄢˋ ㄩㄣˋ)
vertigo; giddiness; dizziness

【眨】 3761 ㄓㄚˇ jaa zhǎ
to wink; to blink: 那女孩對我眨了眨眼。The girl winked at me.

眨巴眼兒(ㄓㄚˇ ·ㄅㄚ ㄧㄚˇㄦ)
to wink one's eyes in quick succession

眨眼(ㄓㄚˇ ㄧㄢˇ)
to wink

眨眼間(ㄓㄚˇ ㄧㄢˇ ㄐㄧㄢ)
in the twinkling of an eye; a very short time: 這種事情眨眼間就過去了。It will pass away in a very short while.

【眞】 3762 (真) ㄓㄣ jen zhēn
1. true; real; factual; genuine; actual; substantial; really; truly: 美即是眞，眞即是美。Beauty is truth, truth beauty.
2. the highest sincerity one is capable of
3. a Chinese family name

眞皮(ㄓㄣ ㄆㄧˊ)
① dermis ② genuine leather

眞憑實據(ㄓㄣ ㄆㄧㄥˊ ㄕˊ ㄐㄩˋ)
concrete proof and genuine evidence; indisputable proof

眞面目(ㄓㄣ ㄇㄧㄢˋ ㄇㄨˋ)
(literally) the real face —true colors; true character; the actual thing behind a false front: 我已認清他的眞面目。I see him in his true colors.

眞分數(ㄓㄣ ㄈㄣ ㄕㄨˋ)
a proper fraction

眞刀眞槍(ㄓㄣ ㄉㄠ ㄓㄣ ㄑㄧㄤ)
genuine swords and spears (in theatrical performance or stage show)—the real thing: 他們眞刀眞槍地幹起來了。They started in real earnest.

眞諦(ㄓㄣ ㄉㄧˋ)
the real meaning; the essence: 他要講演人生的眞諦。He will speak on the real meaning of life.

眞理(ㄓㄣ ㄌㄧˇ)
① truth ② righteousness

眞格的(ㄓㄣ ㄍㄜˊ ·ㄉㄜ)
real; true: 別再開玩笑啦，說眞格的吧。Stop making a joke and tell me the truth.

眞箇(ㄓㄣ ㄍㄜˋ)
really; actually: 他眞箇了不起。He is really wonderful.

眞果(ㄓㄣ ㄍㄨㄛˇ)
(botany) true fruit

眞工夫(ㄓㄣ ㄍㄨㄥ ·ㄈㄨ)
a true skill or accomplishment

眞空(ㄓㄣ ㄎㄨㄥ)
vacuum

眞空地帶(ㄓㄣ ㄎㄨㄥ ㄉㄧˋ ㄉㄞˋ)
① a region where no authority is exercised by any party ②(military) no man's land

眞空管(ㄓㄣ ㄎㄨㄥ ㄍㄨㄢˇ)
① a vacuum tube ② tubes used in radio receivers, etc.

眞空計(ㄓㄣ ㄎㄨㄥ ㄐㄧˋ)
a vacuum gauge

眞空吸塵器(ㄓㄣ ㄎㄨㄥ ㄒㄧ ㄔㄣˊ ㄑㄧˋ)
a vacuum cleaner

眞話(ㄓㄣ ㄏㄨㄚˋ)
the truth; true or factual statements: 他說的根本不是眞話。There is not a particle of truth in what he says.

眞迹(ㄓㄣ ㄐㄧ)
real handwriting, paintings, etc. (as opposed to forgeries or fakes); authentic works

眞假(ㄓㄣ ㄐㄧㄚˇ)
true and false; real and fake

眞金不怕火煉(ㄓㄣ ㄐㄧㄣ ㄅㄨˋ ㄆㄚˋ ㄏㄨㄛˇ ㄌㄧㄢˋ)
(literally) Genuine gold is not afraid of fire.—Truth is ultimately louder than lies or slanders. 或 True loyalty can stand the test of adversity.

眞君(ㄓㄣ ㄐㄩㄣ)
a deferential title of an immortal

眞切(ㄓㄣ ㄑㄧㄝˋ)
① true and concise; vivid ② (to see or hear) clearly

眞槍實彈(ㄓㄣ ㄑㄧㄤ ㄕˊ ㄉㄢˋ)
real guns and bullets; live ammunition

眞情(ㄓㄣ ㄑㄧㄥˊ)
① actual happenings (of an incident, etc.); the true state of affairs ② real affections; true feelings; sincerity: 她的信眞情流露。Her letter reveals her true feelings.

眞確(ㄓㄣ ㄑㄩㄝˋ)
authentic; true; real; accurate; clear; distinct: 他帶來眞確的消息。He brought authentic news.

眞詮(ㄓㄣ ㄑㄩㄢˊ)
the correct meaning or explanation

眞心(ㄓㄣ ㄒㄧㄣ)
from the bottom of one's heart; real or actual intention; sincere; sincerity; wholehearted

眞心話(ㄓㄣ ㄒㄧㄣ ㄏㄨㄚˋ)
sincere talks; words from the bottom of one's heart

眞心實意(ㄓㄣ ㄒㄧㄣ ㄕˊ ㄧˋ)or 眞心誠意(ㄓㄣ ㄒㄧㄣ ㄔㄥˊ ㄧˋ)
genuinely and sincerely; truly and wholeheartedly; wholeheartedly; sincerely

眞相(ㄓㄣ ㄒㄧㄤˋ)
the truth (about a happening, etc.); the real situation; the actual state of affairs: 他掩蓋眞相。He covered up the facts.

眞相畢露(ㄓㄣ ㄒㄧㄤˋ ㄅㄧˋ ㄌㄨˋ)
to have one's true face or colors completely exposed

眞相大白(ㄓㄣ ㄒㄧㄤˋ ㄉㄚˋ ㄅㄞˊ)
The truth is out.

眞像(ㄓㄣ ㄒㄧㄤˋ)

(optics) the real image
眞性(ㄓㄣ ㄒㄧㄥˋ)
①the natural property ② one's natural disposition
眞知灼見(ㄓㄣ ㄓ ㄓㄨㄛˊ ㄐㄧㄢˋ)
correct and penetrating views
眞摯(ㄓㄣ ㄓˋ)
sincere; sincerity; faithful; true; truly: 他們的友誼是眞摯的。Their friendship is sincere.
眞正(ㄓㄣ ㄓㄥˋ)
① actual; actually; real; really; precisely ② genuine
眞珠(ㄓㄣ ㄓㄨ)
natural pearls (as distinct from cultured pearls or imitation pearls)
眞珠岩(ㄓㄣ ㄓㄨ ㄧㄢˊ)
perlite, or pearlite
眞誠(ㄓㄣ ㄔㄥˊ)
sincere; genuine; true: 眞誠的友誼應永恆不渝。True friendship should last forever.
眞除(ㄓㄣ ㄔㄨˊ)
the formal appointment to an office (as opposed to an acting capacity)
眞實(ㄓㄣ ㄕˊ)
actual; true; truth; real; factual: 這是一篇眞實的故事。This is a story of real life.
眞實性(ㄓㄣ ㄕˊ ㄒㄧㄥˋ)
reliability; truthfulness
眞善美(ㄓㄣ ㄕㄢˋ ㄇㄟˇ)
truth, goodness and beauty; the true, the good, and the beautiful
眞書(ㄓㄣ ㄕㄨ)
the standard or regular style of Chinese calligraphy 亦作「楷書」
眞率(ㄓㄣ ㄕㄨㄞˋ)
frank and honest; straightforward; unaffected
眞人(ㄓㄣ ㄖㄣˊ)
①(Taoism) the Immortal —also used as a title of respect in addressing Taoists ②a real person
眞人不露相(ㄓㄣ ㄖㄣˊ ㄅㄨˋ ㄌㄡˋ ㄒㄧㄤˋ)
A man of substance does not like to show off (or reveal his true worth).
眞人眞事(ㄓㄣ ㄖㄣˊ ㄓㄣ ㄕˋ)
The characters are real, and the story is true. 或 real people and real events
眞宰(ㄓㄣ ㄗㄞˇ)
the Almighty; Heaven; the true lord of the universe
眞贓(ㄓㄣ ㄗㄤ)
stolen goods; loot
眞贓實犯(ㄓㄣ ㄗㄤ ㄕˊ ㄈㄢˋ)
concrete evidence; irrefutable proof of guilt
眞材實料(ㄓㄣ ㄘㄞˊ ㄕˊ ㄌㄧㄠˋ)
genuine material and solid substance
眞才實學(ㄓㄣ ㄘㄞˊ ㄕˊ ㄒㄩㄝˊ)
①solid learning; genuine talent ②truly learned; highly competent
眞草(ㄓㄣ ㄘㄠˇ)
the standard style and script style in Chinese calligraphy
眞愛(ㄓㄣ ㄞˋ)
true love
眞意(ㄓㄣ ㄧˋ)
true intent and real meaning
眞贋(ㄓㄣ ㄧㄢˋ)
true or false; genuine or fake
眞僞(ㄓㄣ ㄨㄟˇ)
true and false
眞僞莫辨(ㄓㄣ ㄨㄟˇ ㄇㄛˋ ㄅㄧㄢˋ)
cannot distinguish whether it's genuine or fake, true or false

【眚】3763 ㄕㄥˇ sheeng shěng
1. an eye-ailment or disease
2. a blunder; a fault; a mistake; an error
3. corruption
4. to reduce; to save (the trouble, etc.)
5. calamity; disaster
眚災(ㄕㄥˇ ㄗㄞ)
faults and misfortunes

【眥】3764 (眦) ㄗˋ tzyh zì
eye sockets
眥目(ㄗˋ ㄇㄨˋ)
to open eyes wide
眥裂(ㄗˋ ㄌㄧㄝˋ)
to open eyes wide, as in anger

六畫

【眯】3765 ㄇㄧˇ mii mǐ
1. a foreign body getting into the eye
2. to close one's eyes into narrow slits

【眱】3766 ㄧˊ yi yí
to stare at someone for a long time without talking

【眶】3767 ㄎㄨㄤˋ kuanq kuàng
the socket of the eye; the rim of the eye: 她熱淚盈眶。Her eyes filled with tears.

【眸】3768 ㄇㄡˊ mou móu
the pupil of the eye — the eyes
眸子(ㄇㄡˊ ·ㄗ)
the eyes; the pupil of the eye

【眼】3769 ㄧㄢˇ yean yǎn
1. the eye: 我親眼看見了。I saw it with my own eyes.
2. a look; a glance: 她瞪了我一眼。She gave me a hard look.
3. a tiny hole; an opening; an orifice; an aperture
4. a key point
眼巴巴(ㄧㄢˇ ㄅㄚ ㄅㄚ)
① expectantly; anxiously; eagerly: 大家眼巴巴盼着你的來臨。We were eagerly looking forward to your arrival. ②helplessly (watching something unpleasant happen)
眼波(ㄧㄢˇ ㄅㄛ)
eyesight; vision; bright-eyed —like the ripples on a stream
眼不見，心不煩(ㄧㄢˇ ㄅㄨˋ ㄐㄧㄢˋ, ㄒㄧㄣ ·ㄅㄨ ㄈㄢˊ)
One who avoids seeing trouble does not have to worry about trouble.
眼不見爲淨(ㄧㄢˇ ㄅㄨˋ ㄐㄧㄢˋ ㄨㄟˊ ㄐㄧㄥˋ)
If one wants to avoid seeing dirtiness, he should turn his eyes away.—a passive way to stay out of trouble 或 Out of sight, out of mind.
眼不觀邪(ㄧㄢˇ ㄅㄨˋ ㄍㄨㄢ ㄒㄧㄝˊ)
to see no evil; to turn eyes away from evils
眼皮(ㄧㄢˇ ㄆㄧˊ)
eyelids

眼明手快(ㄧㄢˇ ㄇㄧㄥˊ ㄕㄡˇ ㄎㄨㄞˋ)
to be sharp of sight and quick of hand; to see things clearly and act speedily; sharp-eyed and quick-moving

眼目(ㄧㄢˇ ㄇㄨˋ)
① the eyes ② to serve as the eye of another; a spy ③ essential points or parts

眼福(ㄧㄢˇ ㄈㄨˊ)
a feast to the eye; joy to the eye; delight to the eye

眼到手到(ㄧㄢˇ ㄉㄠˋ ㄕㄡˇ ㄉㄠˋ)
to take down notes while reading, as a diligent scholar does

眼跳(ㄧㄢˇ ㄊㄧㄠˋ)
twitching of the eyelid (believed to portend trouble or disaster)

眼淚(ㄧㄢˇ ㄌㄟˋ)
tears: 擦乾你的眼淚。Wipe away your tears.

眼淚汪汪(ㄧㄢˇ ㄌㄟˋ ㄨㄤ ㄨㄤ)
eyes brimming with tears; tearful

眼裏(ㄧㄢˇ ㄌㄧˇ)
within one's vision; in one's eyes: 他看在眼裏，記在心裏。He bears in mind what he sees.

眼力(ㄧㄢˇ ㄌㄧˋ)
① eyesight; vision ② discerning ability; the power of judgment

眼簾(ㄧㄢˇ ㄌㄧㄢˊ)
the iris

眼亮(ㄧㄢˇ ㄌㄧㄤˋ)
clear-sighted; sharp-sighted

眼高手低(ㄧㄢˇ ㄍㄠ ㄕㄡˇ ㄉㄧ)
to criticize the performance of others when oneself cannot equal or better; to have great aims but poor abilities; to be conceited but incompetent

眼觀鼻，鼻觀心(ㄧㄢˇ ㄍㄨㄢ ㄅㄧˊ, ㄅㄧˊ ㄍㄨㄢ ㄒㄧㄣ)
to sit quietly without looking sideways

眼光(ㄧㄢˇ ㄍㄨㄤ)
sight; insight; vision; eye—discerning ability; power of judgment: 我們的眼光都集中到她身上。We turned our eyes on her.

眼光短淺(ㄧㄢˇ ㄍㄨㄤ ㄉㄨㄢˇ ㄑㄧㄢˇ)
shortsighted

眼光遠大(ㄧㄢˇ ㄍㄨㄤ ㄩㄢˇ ㄉㄚˋ)
farsighted

眼科(ㄧㄢˇ ㄎㄜ)
ophthalmology

眼科大夫(ㄧㄢˇ ㄎㄜ ㄉㄞˋ ˙ㄈㄨ)or 眼科醫生(ㄧㄢˇ ㄎㄜ ㄧ ㄕㄥ)
an ophthalmologist; an oculist; an eye doctor

眼科醫院(ㄧㄢˇ ㄎㄜ ㄧ ㄩㄢˋ)
a hospital of ophthalmology

眼看(ㄧㄢˇ ㄎㄢˋ)or 眼看著(ㄧㄢˇ ㄎㄢˋ ˙ㄓㄜ)
① imminent; soon: 眼看天就要黑了。It'll be dark soon. ② to see something happening ③ to watch helplessly

眼庫(ㄧㄢˇ ㄎㄨˋ)
an eye bank

眼眶(ㄧㄢˇ ㄎㄨㄤˋ)
an eye socket: 她眼眶裏含着熱淚。Her eyes were filled with tears.

眼孔(ㄧㄢˇ ㄎㄨㄥˇ)
an eyelet; an orifice

眼黑(ㄧㄢˇ ㄏㄟ)
greedy; avarice

眼花(ㄧㄢˇ ㄏㄨㄚ)
eyesight blurred; dim of sight; giddy or dizzy

眼花撩亂(ㄧㄢˇ ㄏㄨㄚ ㄌㄧㄠˊ ㄌㄨㄢˋ)
(scenes so varied and confusing as) to dazzle the eyes

眼紅(ㄧㄢˇ ㄏㄨㄥˊ)
① red-eyed ② covetous; envious ③ angry

眼睫毛(ㄧㄢˇ ㄐㄧㄝˊ ㄇㄠˊ)
eyelashes

眼界(ㄧㄢˇ ㄐㄧㄝˋ)
one's field of vision; an outlook

眼界高(ㄧㄢˇ ㄐㄧㄝˋ ㄍㄠ)
to have one's standard set high

眼尖(ㄧㄢˇ ㄐㄧㄢ)
sharp-eyed; quick of sight

眼瞼(ㄧㄢˇ ㄐㄧㄢˇ)
eyelids

眼鏡(ㄧㄢˇ ㄐㄧㄥˋ)
glasses; spectacles

眼鏡舖子(ㄧㄢˇ ㄐㄧㄥˋ ㄆㄨˋ ˙ㄗ)
an optician's shop

眼鏡盒(ㄧㄢˇ ㄐㄧㄥˋ ㄏㄜˊ)
a case for glasses

眼鏡蛇(ㄧㄢˇ ㄐㄧㄥˋ ㄕㄜˊ)
a cobra

眼睛(ㄧㄢˇ ˙ㄐㄧㄥ)
the eyes

眼球(ㄧㄢˇ ㄑㄧㄡˊ)
eyeballs

眼球筋(ㄧㄢˇ ㄑㄧㄡˊ ㄐㄧㄣ)
ocular muscles

眼前(ㄧㄢˇ ㄑㄧㄢˊ)
① right before one's eyes: 眼前是一片水域。Before our eyes was a stretch of water. ② at this moment; now; at present

眼圈子(ㄧㄢˇ ㄑㄩㄢ ˙ㄗ)or 眼圈兒(ㄧㄢˇ ㄑㄩㄚㄦ)
the rim of the eye; an eye socket

眼下(ㄧㄢˇ ㄒㄧㄚˋ)
at present; currently; at the moment: 眼下我們必須安於現狀。At present, we must be content with matters as they stand.

眼線(ㄧㄢˇ ㄒㄧㄢˋ)
(said of crime investigation) a contact, a stool pigeon, or an informer

眼罩(ㄧㄢˇ ㄓㄠˋ)
① an eyeshade ② blinkers (for a horse)

眼睜睜(ㄧㄢˇ ㄓㄥ ㄓㄥ)
① right before one's eyes; publicly; openly; in broad daylight ② watchful; attentively ③ to watch helplessly

眼珠(ㄧㄢˇ ㄓㄨ)
eyeballs

眼珠子(ㄧㄢˇ ㄓㄨ ˙ㄗ)or 眼珠兒(ㄧㄢˇ ㄓㄨㄦ)
① eyeballs ②(figuratively) vision

眼拙(ㄧㄢˇ ㄓㄨㄛˊ)
(usually a polite expression) dim or shortsighted (for not knowing you before)

眼中釘(ㄧㄢˇ ㄓㄨㄥ ㄉㄧㄥ)or 眼中刺(ㄧㄢˇ ㄓㄨㄥ ㄘˋ)
(literally) a thorn in the eye—the most hated person; an eyesore

眼中人(ㄧㄢˇ ㄓㄨㄥ ㄖㄣˊ)
the loved one; the person after one's heart

眼中無人(ㄧㄢˇ ㄓㄨㄥ ㄨˊ ㄖㄣˊ)
haughty; arrogant

眼岔(ㄧㄢˇ ㄔㄚˋ)

confusing vision; eyesight blurred; to mistake one for another

眼饞(ㄧㄢˇ ㄔㄢˊ)
covetous; envious

眼穿(ㄧㄢˇ ㄔㄨㄢ)
anxiously awaiting; eagerly expecting

眼屎(ㄧㄢˇ ㄕˇ)
secretions of the eyes

眼神(ㄧㄢˇ ㄕㄣˊ)
expression of the eyes; gleams of the eyes

眼生(ㄧㄢˇ ㄕㄥ)
unfamiliar by sight: 這個人我瞧著眼生。The man is unfamiliar to me.

眼熟(ㄧㄢˇ ㄕㄨˊ)
to seem to know; seemingly familiar by sight: 來客看來很眼熟。The visitor looks familiar.

眼如秋水(ㄧㄢˇ ㄖㄨˊ ㄑㄧㄡ ㄕㄨㄟˇ)
bright-eyed

眼子(ㄧㄢˇ ·ㄗ)
a small hole; an orifice

眼色(ㄧㄢˇ ㄙㄜˋ)
the expression of one's eyes (indicating one's intention, wish, etc.); a hint or a cue given with the eyes

眼兒(ㄧㄢˇㄦ)
① the eye ② a tiny hole; an orifice

眼藥水(ㄧㄢˇ ㄧㄠˋ ㄕㄨㄟˇ)
eyewash; eyewater; eyedrops

眼窩(ㄧㄢˇ ㄨㄛ)
an orbit; an eye socket

眼語(ㄧㄢˇ ㄩˇ)
(literally) the eye-talk—to indicate or hint with one's eyes

眼暈(ㄧㄢˇ ㄩㄣˋ)
① dazzled; blurring vision; dizzy ② (cosmetics) eye-shadow

【眺】 3770
ㄊㄧㄠˋ tiaw tiào

to look far away; to take a look at faraway things; to look far into the distance

眺望(ㄊㄧㄠˋ ㄨㄤˋ)
to look far away

【眵】 3771
ㄔ chy chī

caking of eye secretions; secretions

【眾】 3772
(衆) ㄓㄨㄥˋ jonq zhòng

1. many; numerous
2. a crowd; a multitude; all; the masses
3. public or popular (opinion, views, etc.)

眾叛親離(ㄓㄨㄥˋ ㄆㄢˋ ㄑㄧㄣ ㄌㄧˊ)
(said of a dictator at his downfall) opposed by the masses and deserted by followers—to be utterly isolated

眾目睽睽(ㄓㄨㄥˋ ㄇㄨˋ ㄎㄨㄟˊ ㄎㄨㄟˊ)
the glare of the public; the public gaze

眾目昭彰(ㄓㄨㄥˋ ㄇㄨˋ ㄓㄠ ㄓㄤ)
the stare or watchful eyes of the public

眾多(ㄓㄨㄥˋ ㄉㄨㄛ)
numerous

眾怒難犯(ㄓㄨㄥˋ ㄋㄨˋ ㄋㄢˊ ㄈㄢˋ)
It's unwise to offend the public. 或 It's dangerous to antagonize the masses.

眾寡不敵(ㄓㄨㄥˋ ㄍㄨㄚˇ ㄅㄨˋ ㄉㄧˊ)
One is no match for a crowd. 或 being outnumbered

眾寡懸殊(ㄓㄨㄥˋ ㄍㄨㄚˇ ㄒㄩㄢˊ ㄕㄨ)
The disparity of numerical strength is too great.

眾口難調(ㄓㄨㄥˋ ㄎㄡˇ ㄋㄢˊ ㄊㄧㄠˊ)
It's difficult to obtain unanimity from a crowd.

眾口鑠金(ㄓㄨㄥˋ ㄎㄡˇ ㄕㄨㄛˋ ㄐㄧㄣ)
Too many rumors can confuse what is right or wrong.

眾口一詞(ㄓㄨㄥˋ ㄎㄡˇ ㄧˋ ㄘˊ)
(said of many persons) to speak out with one voice; unanimously

眾擎易舉(ㄓㄨㄥˋ ㄑㄧㄥˊ ㄧˋ ㄐㄩˇ)
Cooperation and unity make difficult things easy.

眾志成城(ㄓㄨㄥˋ ㄓˋ ㄔㄥˊ ㄔㄥˊ)or 眾心成城(ㄓㄨㄥˋ ㄒㄧㄣ ㄔㄥˊ ㄔㄥˊ)
Unity of purpose is a formidable force.

眾矢之的(ㄓㄨㄥˋ ㄕˇ ㄓ ㄉㄧˋ)
(literally) the target of many arrows—the target of public attacks (or censure)

眾生(ㄓㄨㄥˋ ㄕㄥ)
① all living creatures ② beasts or animals

眾生相(ㄓㄨㄥˋ ㄕㄥ ㄒㄧㄤˋ)
(Buddhism) the idea that all the living are produced by the *skandhas*

眾庶(ㄓㄨㄥˋ ㄕㄨˋ)
the masses; the people

眾說紛紜(ㄓㄨㄥˋ ㄕㄨㄛ ㄈㄣ ㄩㄣˊ)
Opinions vary. 眾說紛紜，莫衷一是。As opinions vary, no conclusion can be reached.

眾人(ㄓㄨㄥˋ ㄖㄣˊ)
many people; all people; the multitude: 這是一齣吸引眾人的戲劇。It's a play that appeals to the multitude.

眾所週知(ㄓㄨㄥˋ ㄙㄨㄛˇ ㄓㄡ ㄓ)
universally known; as everyone knows; as is known to all; it is common knowledge that

眾議紛紜(ㄓㄨㄥˋ ㄧˋ ㄈㄣ ㄩㄣˊ)
Public opinions or views are divergent. 或There's no agreement among many views.

眾議院(ㄓㄨㄥˋ ㄧˋ ㄩㄢˋ)or 眾院(ㄓㄨㄥˋ ㄩㄢˋ)
the Lower House of a Parliament; the House of Commons; the House

眾望(ㄓㄨㄥˋ ㄨㄤˋ)
public support or confidence; popularity (of a leader); people's expectations: 這位領袖不孚眾望。The leader fell short of people's confidence.

眾望所歸(ㄓㄨㄥˋ ㄨㄤˋ ㄙㄨㄛˇ ㄍㄨㄟ)
to enjoy public confidence; to command public respect and support

【眷】 3773
ㄐㄩㄢˋ jiuann juàn

1. to look back—to regard; to care for; to concern
2. to admire; to love
3. relatives; dependents

眷念(ㄐㄩㄢˋ ㄋㄧㄢˋ)
to think of or remember with affection; to feel nostalgic about

眷戀(ㄐㄩㄢˋ ㄌㄧㄢˋ)
to admire; to be attached to someone

眷糧(ㄐㄩㄢˋ ㄌㄧㄤˊ)
food allowances for dependents or military personnel or public functionaries

眷顧(ㄐㄩㄢˋ ㄍㄨˋ)
to care for; to concern; to

regard; regards
眷口(ㄐㄩㄢˋ ㄎㄡˇ)
family; dependents
眷懷(ㄐㄩㄢˋ ㄏㄨㄞˊ)
to remember; to cherish the memory of
眷眷(ㄐㄩㄢˋ ㄐㄩㄢˋ)
to remember with tender feelings
眷注(ㄐㄩㄢˋ ㄓㄨˋ)
to concern with affection; to care for
眷屬(ㄐㄩㄢˋ ㄕㄨˇ)
dependents; family
眷村(ㄐㄩㄢˋ ㄘㄨㄣ)
a military dependents' village
眷愛(ㄐㄩㄢˋ ㄞˋ)
to care for; to love; to regard with affection
眷佑(ㄐㄩㄢˋ ㄧㄡˋ)
to care for and assist

七畫

【睇】 3774
ㄉㄧˋ dih dì
1. to take a casual look at
2. to look sideways; to look askance; to cast a sidelong glance

【睏】 3775
ㄎㄨㄣˋ kuenn kùn
drowsy; sleepy

【着】 3776
ㄓㄨㄛˊ jwo zhuó
ㄓㄠˊ jaur zháo
ㄓㄠ jau zhāo
˙ㄓㄜ ˙je zhe
same as 著

八畫

【睛】 3777
ㄐㄧㄥ jing jīng
1. the pupil of the eye
2. eyes
睛球(ㄐㄧㄥ ㄑㄧㄡˊ)
the eyeball; the pupil of the eye
睛珠(ㄐㄧㄥ ㄓㄨ)
the eyeball; the pupil of the eye

【睞】 3778
ㄌㄞˋ lay lài
1. to look at; to glance
2. to squint; cockeyed

【睡】 3779
ㄕㄨㄟˋ shuey shuì
to sleep; to rest with eyes closed: 柔和的音樂使他入睡。The soft music put him to sleep.
睡袍(ㄕㄨㄟˋ ㄆㄠˊ)
a sleeping gown
睡魔(ㄕㄨㄟˋ ㄇㄛˊ)
extreme sleepiness
睡美人(ㄕㄨㄟˋ ㄇㄟˇ ㄖㄣˊ)
a sleeping beauty
睡夢(ㄕㄨㄟˋ ㄇㄥˋ)
in sleep; in one's dreams
睡眠(ㄕㄨㄟˋ ㄇㄧㄢˊ)
sleep: 你需要幾小時的睡眠? How many hours' sleep do you need?
睡眠不足(ㄕㄨㄟˋ ㄇㄧㄢˊ ㄅㄨˋ ㄗㄨˊ)
insufficient sleep; want of sleep
睡眠曲(ㄕㄨㄟˋ ㄇㄧㄢˊ ㄑㄩˇ)
a lullaby
睡眠時間(ㄕㄨㄟˋ ㄇㄧㄢˊ ㄕˊ ㄐㄧㄢ)
① the length of one's sleep
② one's bedtime
睡袋(ㄕㄨㄟˋ ㄉㄞˋ)
a sleeping bag
睡懶覺(ㄕㄨㄟˋ ㄌㄢˇ ㄐㄧㄠˋ)
to get up late; to sleep in
睡蓮(ㄕㄨㄟˋ ㄌㄧㄢˊ)
a water lily
睡覺(ㄕㄨㄟˋ ㄐㄧㄠˋ)
to sleep; to go to bed: 你該睡覺了。It's time for you to go to bed.
睡鄉(ㄕㄨㄟˋ ㄒㄧㄤ)
dreamland
睡醒(ㄕㄨㄟˋ ㄒㄧㄥˇ)
to wake up from sleep
睡著(ㄕㄨㄟˋ ㄓㄠˊ)
to have fallen asleep: 小嬰兒已經睡著了。The little baby has fallen asleep.
睡車(ㄕㄨㄟˋ ㄔㄜ)
a sleeping car; a sleeper
睡獅(ㄕㄨㄟˋ ㄕ)
(literally) a sleeping lion—a big country lacking vitality
睡熟(ㄕㄨㄟˋ ㄕㄨˊ)or(ㄕㄨㄟˋ ㄕㄡˊ)
to sleep soundly
睡衣(ㄕㄨㄟˋ ㄧ)
pajamas; a sleeping gown; night clothes
睡意(ㄕㄨㄟˋ ㄧˋ)
sleepiness; drowsiness: 他似乎已有幾分睡意。He seems to be somewhat sleepy.
睡遊病(ㄕㄨㄟˋ ㄧㄡˊ ㄅㄧㄥˋ)
somnambulism
睡眼朦朧(ㄕㄨㄟˋ ㄧㄢˇ ㄇㄥˊ ㄌㄨㄥˊ)
sleepy-eyed; eyes heavy with slumber
睡眼惺忪(ㄕㄨㄟˋ ㄧㄢˇ ㄒㄧㄥ ㄙㄨㄥ)
to have a drowsy look
睡午覺(ㄕㄨㄟˋ ㄨˇ ㄐㄧㄠˋ)
to take a siesta or afternoon nap

【睢】 3780
ㄙㄨㄟ suei suī
1. to raise one's eyes
2. freely or without thought of others; at random
3. a Chinese family name
睢陽(ㄙㄨㄟ ㄧㄤˊ)
name of an ancient region in today's Shangchiu County (商邱) of Honan Province—It was defended to the last man against rebels led by An Lu-shan (安祿山) in the Tang Dynasty.

【睜】 3781
ㄓㄥ jeng zhēng
to open the eyes
睜開眼睛(ㄓㄥ ㄎㄞ ㄧㄢˇ ˙ㄐㄧㄥ)
to open the eyes
睜開眼睛說瞎話(ㄓㄥ ㄎㄞ ㄧㄢˇ ㄐㄧㄥ ㄕㄨㄛ ㄒㄧㄚ ㄏㄨㄚˋ)
to tell a barefaced lie
睜眼(ㄓㄥ ㄧㄢˇ)
to open the eyes
睜一隻眼,閉一隻眼(ㄓㄥ ㄧˋ ㄓ ㄧㄢˇ, ㄅㄧˋ ㄧˋ ㄓ ㄧㄢˇ)
to turn a blind eye to something; to pretend not to see—to overlook purposely

【睥】 3782
ㄅㄧˋ bih bì
1. to look askance; a scornful look
2. battlements atop city walls
睥睨(ㄅㄧˋ ㄋㄧˋ)
to look askance—an expression of disdain; overweening

【睨】 3783
ㄋㄧˋ nih nì
1. to look askance—an expression of disdain or arrogance
2. to slant

【睦】 3784
ㄇㄨˋ muh mù
1. friendly; amiable; to befriend; to be on friendly

〔目部〕

terms
2. a Chinese family name

睦鄰(ㄇㄨˋ ㄌㄧㄣˊ)
to remain on friendly terms with the neighbors (often referring to neighboring countries)

睦親(ㄇㄨˋ ㄑㄧㄣ)
close relatives

睦誼(ㄇㄨˋ ㄧˋ)
cordiality or friendship (usually referring to that between nations)

【睫】 3785 ㄐㄧㄝˊ jye jié
1. eyelashes
2. to blink; to wink

睫毛(ㄐㄧㄝˊ ㄇㄠˊ)
eyelashes

【睬】 3786 ㄘㄞˇ tsae cǎi
1. to look; to watch
2. to notice; to pay attention to

【督】 3787 ㄉㄨ du dū
1. to oversee; to superintend; to supervise
2. to reprove; to censure
3. a marshal; a general
4. a viceroy or governor-general
5. a Chinese family name

督辦(ㄉㄨ ㄅㄢˋ)
①to superintend an operation; to supervise and manage ②an official rank—a director, superintendent, or supervisor

督撫(ㄉㄨ ㄈㄨˇ)
the viceroy and inspector-general

督導(ㄉㄨ ㄉㄠˋ)or(ㄉㄨ ㄉㄠˇ)
to direct and supervise

督理(ㄉㄨ ㄌㄧˇ)
to supervise and manage

督勵(ㄉㄨ ㄌㄧˋ)
to urge and encourage

督過(ㄉㄨ ㄍㄨㄛˋ)
to reprove; to censure

督工(ㄉㄨ ㄍㄨㄥ)
①to oversee working; to superintend workers ②an overseer; a foreman 亦作「監工」

督課(ㄉㄨ ㄎㄜˋ)
to supervise one's work; to direct a job or task

督軍(ㄉㄨ ㄐㄩㄣ)
(in the early days of the Republic) the highest military commander as well as the governor in a province

督學(ㄉㄨ ㄒㄩㄝˊ)
an inspector of educational establishments

督戰(ㄉㄨ ㄓㄢˋ)
to direct military operations

督飭(ㄉㄨ ㄔˋ)
to supervise and direct

督察(ㄉㄨ ㄔㄚˊ)
①to superintend and oversee; to act as a watchdog ②an inspector

督師(ㄉㄨ ㄕ)
to lead the army

督署(ㄉㄨ ㄕㄨˇ)
the office of the viceroy, governor, etc.

督率(ㄉㄨ ㄕㄨㄞˋ)
to direct and lead

督責(ㄉㄨ ㄗㄜˊ)
to supervise and urge on

督造(ㄉㄨ ㄗㄠˋ)
to supervise the manufacture of (weapons, cars, etc.)

督促(ㄉㄨ ㄘㄨˋ)
to urge; to press (a person to complete a task in time, etc.): 工頭督促工人努力工作。The foreman urged his workmen on.

督郵(ㄉㄨ ㄧㄡˊ)
(in ancient China) an assistant to the chief of a prefecture

【睪】 3788 (睾) ㄍㄠ gau gāo
1. the marsh 亦作「皐」
2. high; lofty
3. the testicle, or testis

睪丸(ㄍㄠ ㄨㄢˊ)
the testicle, or testis

【睠】 3789 ㄐㄩㄢˋ jiuann juàn
1. to look back
2. same as 眷—to care for

九畫

【睹】 3790 (覩) ㄉㄨˇ duu dǔ
to witness; to see; to look at; to observe; to gaze at

睹物思人(ㄉㄨˇ ㄨˋ ㄙ ㄖㄣˊ)
to see the things one is reminded of the owner; to think of a person as one sees the thing(s) he has left behind

【睽】 3791 ㄎㄨㄟˊ kwei kuí
1. separated 亦作「暌」
2. in opposition
3. to squint
4. to stare at
5. unusual; strange

睽離(ㄎㄨㄟˊ ㄌㄧˊ)
long separation; separated for a long time: 她睽離母親二十年。She was separated from her mother for twenty years.

睽隔(ㄎㄨㄟˊ ㄍㄜˊ)
sundered; separated

睽孤(ㄎㄨㄟˊ ㄍㄨ)
eccentric and unsociable

睽睽(ㄎㄨㄟˊ ㄎㄨㄟˊ)
to stare; staring

睽疑(ㄎㄨㄟˊ ㄧˊ)
to suspect; to feel strange

睽違(ㄎㄨㄟˊ ㄨㄟˊ)
to separate; separation

【瞅】 3792 ㄔㄡˇ choou chǒu
to look at; to see; to gaze

瞅不得(ㄔㄡˇ ·ㄅㄨ ·ㄉㄜ)
①should not be seen ②not worth seeing

瞅不見(ㄔㄡˇ ·ㄅㄨ ㄐㄧㄢˋ)
unable to see; to look but unable to see

瞅了一眼(ㄔㄡˇ ·ㄌㄜ ㄧˊ ㄧㄢˇ)
to take a look at

瞅見(ㄔㄡˇ ㄐㄧㄢˋ)
to see

瞅睬(ㄔㄡˇ ㄘㄞˇ)
to notice; to look: 她全不瞅睬他。She won't pay any attention to him.

【瞄】 3793 ㄇㄧㄠˊ miau miáo
to aim at; to take aim; to look at attentively

瞄準(ㄇㄧㄠˊ ㄓㄨㄣˇ)
to take aim; to aim at; to train upon; to take sight: 把砲瞄準敵人的船隻。Train guns upon the enemy ships.

瞄準器(ㄇㄧㄠˊ ㄓㄨㄣˇ ㄑㄧˋ)
a sighting device; gun sights

【睿】 3794 ㄖㄨㄟˋ ruey ruì
1. to understand thoroughly; quick or keen of perception
2. wise and clever; astute and discreet; perspicacious
3. the profoundest (learning); the divine sagacity of sages
睿圖(ㄖㄨㄟˋ ㄊㄨˊ)
①plans designed by the emperor ②a portrait of Confucius
睿覽(ㄖㄨㄟˋ ㄌㄢˇ)
for the emperor's perusal
睿智 or 睿知(ㄖㄨㄟˋ ㄓˋ)
the divine sagacity of sages; superior intelligence
睿哲(ㄖㄨㄟˋ ㄓㄜˊ)
①saintly wisdom; superior intelligence ②His Majesty
睿藻(ㄖㄨㄟˋ ㄗㄠˇ)
poems or articles written by the emperor, the empress or imperial concubines

【瞀】 3795 ㄇㄠˋ maw mào (又讀 ㄇㄡˋ mow mòu)
1. dim-sighted; nearsighted; indistinct vision
2. illiterate; ignorant; feeble-minded
3. confused; confusion; dazzled
瞀亂(ㄇㄠˋ ㄌㄨㄢˋ)
confused and feeble-minded
瞀儒(ㄇㄠˋ ㄖㄨˊ)
a stupid or ignorant scholar

十畫

【瞋】 3796 ㄔㄣ chen chen
1. angry; anger 亦作「嗔」
2. to open the eyes
瞋目(ㄔㄣ ㄇㄨˋ)
①to glare; an angry look; angry eyes ②to open one's eyes wide
瞋怒(ㄔㄣ ㄋㄨˋ)
to be beside oneself with anger
瞋視(ㄔㄣ ㄕˋ)
to look with angry eyes; to look angrily at

【瞎】 3797 ㄒㄧㄚ shia xiā
1. blind; blindly
2. reckless; heedless; rash; (to do things, etc.) without purpose or reason; at random; groundlessly
3. (dialect) to become tangled (said of thread, etc.)
瞎掰(ㄒㄧㄚ ㄅㄞ)
to make a futile effort; to work to no avail
瞎捧(ㄒㄧㄚ ㄆㄥˇ)
to heap praises on someone blindly
瞎貓逮死耗子(ㄒㄧㄚ ㄇㄠ ㄉㄞˇ ㄙˇ ㄏㄠˋ ·ㄗ)
(literally) A blind cat caught a dead rat.—a pure coincidence; a lucky hit
瞎忙(ㄒㄧㄚ ㄇㄤˊ)
to mess about; to be busy for nothing; to be busy without purpose or objective
瞎鬧(ㄒㄧㄚ ㄋㄠˋ)
to make nonsense; to cause meaningless trouble; to make a loud fuss over nothing; to fool around: 別瞎鬧，趕快往前走。Go ahead quickly and don't fool around.
瞎弄(ㄒㄧㄚ ㄋㄨㄥˋ)
to throw into disorder or confusion; to manage or operate without any method or plan
瞎了(ㄒㄧㄚ ·ㄌㄜ)
to be blinded; to lose one's vision
瞎了眼睛(ㄒㄧㄚ ·ㄌㄜ ㄧㄢˇ ·ㄐㄧㄥ)
①Blind fool! ②to become blind
瞎賴(ㄒㄧㄚ ㄌㄞˋ)
to put blame on others without the slightest justification
瞎聊(ㄒㄧㄚ ㄌㄧㄠˊ)
to converse at random; to talk nonsense; to jaw; to chat idly
瞎攪 or 瞎搞(ㄒㄧㄚ ㄍㄠˇ)
to do a thing without any plan or method
瞎話(ㄒㄧㄚ ㄏㄨㄚˋ)
lies; a nonsensical remark
瞎抓(ㄒㄧㄚ ㄓㄨㄚ)
to grasp anything within reach without knowing what to do with it
瞎扯(ㄒㄧㄚ ㄔㄜˇ)
to talk recklessly; to tell lies; to speak nonsense
瞎吹(ㄒㄧㄚ ㄔㄨㄟ)
to brag; to make wild boasts
瞎闖(ㄒㄧㄚ ㄔㄨㄤˇ)
to move ahead without a set direction or purpose; to make reckless or rash moves
瞎說(ㄒㄧㄚ ㄕㄨㄛ)
to speak groundlessly; to talk nonsense; wild talks: 別瞎說。Don't speak groundlessly.
瞎說八道(ㄒㄧㄚ ㄕㄨㄛ ㄅㄚˊ ㄉㄠˋ)
to talk through one's hat; to make reckless or irresponsible utterances; to tell lies or talk nonsense
瞎字不識(ㄒㄧㄚ ㄗˋ ㄅㄨˋ ㄕˋ)
illiterate; unable to read a single word
瞎子(ㄒㄧㄚ ·ㄗ)
a blind man
瞎子摸象(ㄒㄧㄚ ·ㄗ ㄇㄛ ㄒㄧㄤˋ)
(literally) The blindman feels an elephant.—unable to learn the whole picture
瞎猜(ㄒㄧㄚ ㄘㄞ)
to guess wildly; to make a wild guess; to make a random guess
瞎眼(ㄒㄧㄚ ㄧㄢˇ)
blind

【瞍】 3798 ㄙㄡˇ soou sǒu
to have eyes without pupils; blind

【瞑】 3799 1. ㄇㄧㄥˊ ming míng (又讀 ㄇㄧㄥˇ miing mǐng)
to close the eyes
瞑瞑(ㄇㄧㄥˊ ㄇㄧㄥˊ)
to look but see nothing; vision obscured
瞑目(ㄇㄧㄥˊ ㄇㄨˋ)
①to close the eyes ②to die without regret or in peace

【瞑】 3799 2. ㄇㄧㄢˋ miann miàn
to throw into a state of confusion 參看「瞑眩」
瞑眩(ㄇㄧㄢˋ ㄒㄩㄢˋ)
①to feel dizzy and upset ②medicine in its beneficial operation, yet causing distress; dizziness, nausea, etc. as a side effect of drugs

【瞌】 3800 ㄎㄜ ke kē

to be tired and to doze off

瞌睡(ㄎㄜ ㄕㄨㄟˋ)
to doze off while sitting: 他伏在書上打瞌睡。He dozed over a book.

【瞇】3801 ㄇㄧ mhi mī
1. to keep one's eyes half closed; to narrow the eyes: 她瞇着眼睛笑。She narrowed her eyes into a smile.
2. (dialect) to take a nap: 我剛才瞇了一會兒。I took a short nap just now.

瞇縫眼兒(ㄇㄧ ·ㄈㄥ ㄧㄚˇㄦ)
① slit eyes ② slit-eyed; half-closed (eyes)

十一畫

【瞞】3802 ㄇㄢˊ man mán
1. to hide the truth; to fool others by lying; to deceive
2. dim-sighted; poor vision

瞞不了人(ㄇㄢˊ ·ㄅㄨ ㄌㄧㄠˇ ㄖㄣˊ)
cannot hide the truth from others; cannot deceive others

瞞騙(ㄇㄢˊ ㄆㄧㄢˋ)
to deceive and lie; to hide the truth by lying

瞞得過(ㄇㄢˊ ·ㄉㄜ ㄍㄨㄛˋ)
(said of secrets, truth, etc.) can be concealed or hidden—with lies, etc.

瞞天過海(ㄇㄢˊ ㄊㄧㄢ ㄍㄨㄛˋ ㄏㄞˇ)
very clever and daring in deceiving others

瞞哄(ㄇㄢˊ ㄏㄨㄥˇ)
to deceive and cheat; to hide (the truth) and cheat

瞞心昧己(ㄇㄢˊ ㄒㄧㄣ ㄇㄟˋ ㄐㄧˇ)
unconscionable and self-deceiving; very mean

瞞上欺下(ㄇㄢˊ ㄕㄤˋ ㄑㄧ ㄒㄧㄚˋ)
to hide the truth from higher authorities and oppress the people

【瞟】3803 ㄆㄧㄠˇ peau piǎo
to look askance at

瞟眇(ㄆㄧㄠˇ ㄇㄧㄠˇ)
① obscure and indistinct—due to distance, mists, etc. ② very undependable or unreliable ③ having little chance 亦作「縹緲」

瞟了他一眼(ㄆㄧㄠˇ ·ㄌㄜ ㄊㄚ ㄧˋ ㄧㄢˇ)
to give him a side glance

【瞠】3804 ㄔㄥ cheng chēng
to look straight at; to stare at

瞠目(ㄔㄥ ㄇㄨˋ)
to gaze at fixedly; wide-eyed

瞠目結舌(ㄔㄥ ㄇㄨˋ ㄐㄧㄝˊ ㄕㄜˊ)
wide-eyed and tongue-tied; amazed and speechless

瞠乎其後(ㄔㄥ ㄏㄨ ㄑㄧˊ ㄏㄡˋ)
far behind, without any hope of catching up

【瞢】3805 ㄇㄥˊ meng méng
1. dim-sighted; poor vision
2. obscure; not bright
3. ashamed
4. grief

瞢然(ㄇㄥˊ ㄖㄢˊ)
dark and obscure

【瞖】3806 ㄧˋ yih yì
cataract

十二畫

【瞬】3807 ㄕㄨㄣˋ shuenn shùn
1. to blink, wink or twinkle
2. a very short time; in the twinkling of an eye

瞬華(ㄕㄨㄣˋ ㄏㄨㄚˊ)
time flying away; ephemeral

瞬間(ㄕㄨㄣˋ ㄐㄧㄢ)
in the twinkling of an eye; in an instant: 就在那一瞬間，電話響了。At that instant the telephone rang.

瞬息(ㄕㄨㄣˋ ㄒㄧˊ)or瞬息之間(ㄕㄨㄣˋ ㄒㄧˊ ㄓ ㄐㄧㄢ)
in a wink; in the twinkling of an eye

瞬息萬變(ㄕㄨㄣˋ ㄒㄧˊ ㄨㄢˋ ㄅㄧㄢˋ)
(literally) ten thousand changes in the twinkling of an eye—many changes within a short time

瞬霎(ㄕㄨㄣˋ ㄕㄚˋ)
in a blink; in a twinkling

【瞰】3808 ㄎㄢˋ kann kàn
1. to watch; to look far away
2. to overlook (from a high ground)

瞰臨(ㄎㄢˋ ㄌㄧㄣˊ)
to overlook; to watch from above

瞰望(ㄎㄢˋ ㄨㄤˋ)
to overlook; to observe or look from above; to have a bird's-eye view

【瞳】3809 ㄊㄨㄥˊ torng tóng
1. the pupil of the eye
2. stupid; ignorant

瞳矇(ㄊㄨㄥˊ ㄇㄥˊ)
ignorant

瞳孔(ㄊㄨㄥˊ ㄎㄨㄥˇ)
the pupil of the eye

瞳孔散大(ㄊㄨㄥˊ ㄎㄨㄥˇ ㄙㄢˇ ㄉㄚˋ)
mydriasis (the dilation of the pupil)

瞳孔縮小(ㄊㄨㄥˊ ㄎㄨㄥˇ ㄙㄨㄛ ㄒㄧㄠˇ)
the contraction of the pupil

瞳人(ㄊㄨㄥˊ ㄖㄣˊ)
the pupil of the eye

瞳子(ㄊㄨㄥˊ ㄗˇ)
the pupil of the eye

【瞪】3810 ㄉㄥˋ denq dèng
to stare at; to open (one's eyes) wide; to glare at

瞪視(ㄉㄥˋ ㄕˋ)
to stare one in the face

瞪眼(ㄉㄥˋ ㄧㄢˇ)
① to stare at angrily ② to look straight ahead; to make a fishy glance

【瞭】3811 1. ㄌㄧㄠˇ leau liǎo
1. to understand
2. clear and bright

瞭亮(ㄌㄧㄠˇ ㄌㄧㄤˋ)
to understand; to be clear about

瞭解(ㄌㄧㄠˇ ㄐㄧㄝˇ)
to comprehend; to understand; understanding

瞭然(ㄌㄧㄠˇ ㄖㄢˊ)
clear and evident; plain and fully understandable

瞭如指掌(ㄌㄧㄠˇ ㄖㄨˊ ㄓˇ ㄓㄤˇ)
to know or understand thoroughly—as clear as if one were looking at one's own palms and fingers

【瞭】3811 2. ㄌㄧㄠˋ liaw liào
to look down from a higher place

瞭望(ㄌㄧㄠˋ ㄨㄤˋ)
to look down from a higher place

瞭望臺(ㄌㄧㄠˋ ㄨㄤˋ ㄊㄞˊ)

a watchtower; a lookout (post)

【瞶】 3812 ㄍㄨㄟˋ guey guì

1. a blind man
2. stupid; ignorant

【瞧】 3813 ㄑㄧㄠˊ chyau qiáo

1. to see; to look at: 等着瞧吧。Wait and see.
2. to steal a glance; to glance quickly

瞧病(ㄑㄧㄠˊ ㄅㄧㄥˋ)
①(said of a patient) to see a doctor ②(said of a doctor) to take a look at a patient

瞧不得(ㄑㄧㄠˊ ˙ㄅㄨ ˙ㄉㄜ)
should not be seen; not worth seeing; unnecessary to see

瞧不透(ㄑㄧㄠˊ ˙ㄅㄨ ㄊㄡˋ)
unable to see through; not able to understand: 我眞瞧不透他爲何如此做。I can't understand why he did so.

瞧不過(ㄑㄧㄠˊ ˙ㄅㄨ ㄍㄨㄛˋ)
(in the case of exceptionally cruel, etc. scenes) not hard-hearted enough to see something to its brutal end

瞧不慣(ㄑㄧㄠˊ ˙ㄅㄨ ㄍㄨㄢˋ)
not used to seeing or witnessing (cruel scenes, practices, etc.)

瞧不起(ㄑㄧㄠˊ ˙ㄅㄨ ㄑㄧˇ)
to look down upon; to despise; to hold in contempt: 我們都瞧不起他。We all look down upon him.

瞧不上眼(ㄑㄧㄠˊ ˙ㄅㄨ ㄕㄤˋ ㄧㄢˇ)
not worth seeing — well beneath one's standard or ideal ①(said of commodities, etc.) not up to one's (fine) taste ②(said of a person) to turn one's nose up at

瞧得透(ㄑㄧㄠˊ ˙ㄉㄜ ㄊㄡˋ)
to see through; to understand thoroughly

瞧得起(ㄑㄧㄠˊ ˙ㄉㄜ ㄑㄧˇ)
to esteem or respect; to value; to think much (or highly) of somebody

瞧得上(ㄑㄧㄠˊ ˙ㄉㄜ ㄕㄤˋ)
good enough to suit one's taste

瞧見(ㄑㄧㄠˊ ㄐㄧㄢˋ)
to see; to catch sight of

瞧著(ㄑㄧㄠˊ ˙ㄓㄜ)
① while looking ② Let's see. 或 Let's consider. 或 Let's wait and see.

瞧著辦(ㄑㄧㄠˊ ˙ㄓㄜ ㄅㄢˋ)
Let's wait and see what happens and plan our strategy, countermeasure, etc. then.

瞧熱鬧兒(ㄑㄧㄠˊ ㄖㄜˋ ˙ㄋㄠㄦ)
① to go and see where the fanfare is—as in a festival, etc. ② to be a bystander in fights, fires, etc. ③ to watch the failure or disaster of others with secret delight

瞧一瞧(ㄑㄧㄠˊ ˙ㄧ ˙ㄑㄧㄠ)
to take a look: 讓我們瞧一瞧你的字典。Let's have a look at your dictionary.

【瞵】 3814 ㄌㄧㄣˊ lin lín

1. to look at; to stare at
2. (said of eyes) clear and bright

瞵盼(ㄌㄧㄣˊ ㄆㄢˋ)
to look around

【瞥】 3815 ㄆㄧㄝ pie piē

to have a casual and short glance; to catch a glimpse of

瞥了一眼(ㄆㄧㄝ ˙ㄌㄜ ㄧˋ ㄧㄢˇ)
to cast a casual and brief glance

瞥見(ㄆㄧㄝ ㄐㄧㄢˋ)
to catch a glimpse of; to catch sight of

十三畫

【瞻】 3816 ㄓㄢ jan zhān

1. to look; to look up
2. to regard respectfully; to reverence

瞻對(ㄓㄢ ㄉㄨㄟˋ)
① to respond to the emperor during a court audience ② name of a tribal district in Sikang(西康)

瞻禮日(ㄓㄢ ㄌㄧˇ ㄖˋ)
Sunday

瞻前顧後(ㄓㄢ ㄑㄧㄢˊ ㄍㄨˋ ㄏㄡˋ)
(literally) to look forward and backward—very cautious: 做這種工作不要太過瞻前顧後。Don't be too cautious over this work.

瞻徇(ㄓㄢ ㄒㄩㄣˊ)
to practice favoritism; to be unduly lenient in the enforcement of law

瞻視(ㄓㄢ ㄕˋ)
to look; to behold; to look up to

瞻依(ㄓㄢ ㄧ)
to look up to one's father as an example and to depend on one's mother while one is growing up

瞻仰 or 瞻卬(ㄓㄢ ㄧㄤˇ)
① to look up respectfully; to pay respects to ② to look up to

瞻望(ㄓㄢ ㄨㄤˋ)
①to look forward to a faraway place; to raise one's head and look far ahead ② to adore; to worship

【瞼】 3817 ㄐㄧㄢˇ jean jiǎn

the eyelids

【瞽】 3818 ㄍㄨˇ guu gǔ

1. blind
2. (in ancient China) blind musicians
3. having no discerning ability; lacking the power of judgment

瞽矇(ㄍㄨˇ ㄇㄥˊ)
the official rank of court musicians in ancient China

瞽者(ㄍㄨˇ ㄓㄜˇ)
the blind; a blind person

瞽史(ㄍㄨˇ ㄕˇ)
the two official posts in the Chou Dynasty, one in charge of music, and the other in charge of rites and astrology

瞽說(ㄍㄨˇ ㄕㄨㄛ)or 瞽言(ㄍㄨˇ ㄧㄢˊ)
shallow and unreasonable talks; wild talks

瞽瞍(ㄍㄨˇ ㄙㄡˇ)
Ku-sou—"The Blind Man", a nickname of the father of Shun (舜), so called for his attempt to kill his son who eventually became a sage king

瞽議(ㄍㄨˇ ㄧˋ)
wild talks; groundless statements

〔矛部〕

【瞿】3819 1. ㄑㄩ chiu qū (又讀 ㄑㄩˊ chyu qú)
a Chinese family name
瞿曇(ㄑㄩ ㄊㄢˊ)
Gautama, the family name of Buddha
瞿唐峽(ㄑㄩ ㄊㄤˊ ㄒㄧㄚˊ)
the Chü Tang Gorge, one of the three gorges along the Yangtze River and a gateway to Szechwan

【瞿】3819 2. ㄐㄩˋ jiuh jù
1. shocked or scared
2. (said of hawks and falcons) to look around
瞿然(ㄐㄩˋ ㄖㄢˊ)
alarmed

十四畫

【矇】3820 1. ㄇㄥˊ meng méng
1. blind
2. (figuratively) ignorant; stupid and obstinate
矇蔽(ㄇㄥˊ ㄅㄧˋ)
to hide the truth from a superior
矇昧(ㄇㄥˊ ㄇㄟˋ)
① stupid and obstinate ② dim-sighted
矇矇(ㄇㄥˊ ㄇㄥˊ)
obscure and dim; unclear
矇矓(ㄇㄥˊ ㄌㄨㄥˊ)
①hazy; sight-blurred: 矇矓的景色頗有詩意。A hazy view is quite poetic. ② half-asleep; drowsy; somnolent
矇聵(ㄇㄥˊ ㄎㄨㄟˋ)
① blind and deaf ② ignorant and stupid
矇瞍(ㄇㄥˊ ㄙㄡˇ)
① a blind person ② blind musicians in ancient China

【矇】3820 2. ㄇㄥ mheng mēng
1. to deceive; to cheat
2. lucky
矇騙(ㄇㄥ ㄆㄧㄢˋ)
to deceive and cheat
矇混(ㄇㄥ ㄏㄨㄣˋ)
to fake and cheat
矇著(ㄇㄥ ·ㄓㄜ)
to obtain or achieve something through sheer luck
矇住(ㄇㄥ ㄓㄨˋ)
① to hide the truth and deceive others ② to get confused or befuddled

十五畫

【矍】3821 ㄐㄩㄝˊ jyue jué
1. to watch in fright; scared
2. old but healthy
矍鑠(ㄐㄩㄝˊ ㄕㄨㄛˋ)
to be old but healthy and spry; to be hale and hearty
矍然(ㄐㄩㄝˊ ㄖㄢˊ)
looking around in fear

十六畫

【矓】3822 ㄌㄨㄥˊ long lóng
hazy; blurred: 霧氣使群山矇矓不清。Mists blurred the hills.

十九畫

【矗】3823 ㄔㄨˋ chuh chù
1. rising sharply; steep
2. lofty; upright; straight
3. luxuriant growth
矗立(ㄔㄨˋ ㄌㄧˋ)
rising up steeply; to stand high; to stick up; to tower up
矗矗(ㄔㄨˋ ㄔㄨˋ)
steep and lofty

二十畫

【矙】3824 ㄎㄢˋ kann kàn
1. to watch; to spy
2. to overlook; to look downward

二十一畫

【矚】3825 ㄓㄨˇ juu zhǔ
to watch; to observe or gaze at carefully or steadily; to pay attention
矚目(ㄓㄨˇ ㄇㄨˋ)
to watch or stare at with great interest; to look at eagerly; to be the focus of attention
矚望(ㄓㄨˇ ㄨㄤˋ)
to watch and expect eagerly; to look forward to

矛部
ㄇㄠˊ mau máo

【矛】3826 ㄇㄠˊ mau máo
a lance; a spear
矛兵(ㄇㄠˊ ㄅㄧㄥ)
a lancer; a pikeman
矛盾(ㄇㄠˊ ㄉㄨㄣˋ)or(ㄇㄠˊ ㄕㄨㄣˇ)
to contradict; contradiction; inconsistency: 他的話與事實矛盾。His statement contradicts with the facts.
矛盾律(ㄇㄠˊ ㄉㄨㄣˋ ㄌㄩˋ)
the law of contradiction
矛頭(ㄇㄠˊ ㄊㄡˊ)
a spearhead
矛戟(ㄇㄠˊ ㄐㄧˇ)
lances and spears
矛槍(ㄇㄠˊ ㄑㄧㄤ)
spears and javelins

四畫

【矜】3827 1. ㄐㄧㄣ jin jīn
1. to feel sorry for; to pity; to commiserate with; to be sympathetic with; to compassionate
2. to brag; to boast; arrogant; conceited: 他的行爲舉止顯現驕矜之氣。His manner revealed his arrogant airs.
3. self-esteem; self-control; self-discipline; dignified
4. to emulate
矜免(ㄐㄧㄣ ㄇㄧㄢˇ)
to commute the sentence of a criminal for humanitarian reasons
矜憫(ㄐㄧㄣ ㄇㄧㄣˇ)
to pity; to sympathize; to compassionate
矜伐(ㄐㄧㄣ ㄈㄚˊ)
to be arrogant due to one's accomplishments
矜大(ㄐㄧㄣ ㄉㄚˋ)
proud and bragging; arrogant and exaggerative

矜憐(ㄐㄧㄣ ㄌㄧㄢˊ)
to commiserate with; to pity; to feel sorry for

矜貴(ㄐㄧㄣ ㄍㄨㄟˋ)
to boast of one's high position, blue blood, etc.

矜誇(ㄐㄧㄣ ㄎㄨㄚ)
to brag or boast about one's accomplishments: 她從不矜誇自己的才能。She never boasted about her talent.

矜惜(ㄐㄧㄣ ㄒㄧˊ)
to value; to treasure

矜恤(ㄐㄧㄣ ㄒㄩˋ)
to sympathize with; to have pity on

矜重(ㄐㄧㄣ ㄓㄨㄥˋ)
dignified; self-control or self-esteem

矜持(ㄐㄧㄣ ㄔˊ)
to carry oneself with dignity and reserve; to conduct oneself with circumspection: 他的舉止矜持。He conducted himself with circumspection.

矜寵(ㄐㄧㄣ ㄔㄨㄥˇ)
to presume on the favor of the boss

矜式(ㄐㄧㄣ ㄕˋ)
to emulate or pattern after; to respect as a model

矜飾(ㄐㄧㄣ ㄕˋ)
to brag and pretend

矜人(ㄐㄧㄣ ㄖㄣˊ)
men in a pitiable case

【矜】 3827
2. ㄍㄨㄢ guan guān
a widower 亦作「鰥」

矜寡孤獨(ㄍㄨㄢ ㄍㄨㄚˇ ㄍㄨ ㄉㄨˊ)
(literally) the widower, the widow, the orphan and the childless—the less privileged group or unfortunate lot

七畫

【矞】 3828
ㄩˋ yuh yù
1. bright and brilliant; charming
2. nature bursting into life
3. clouds of many hues

矞皇(ㄩˋ ㄏㄨㄤˊ)
① bright and beautiful ② name of a deity

矞矞(ㄩˋ ㄩˋ)
nature bursting into life

矞雲(ㄩˋ ㄩㄣˊ)
clouds of many hues

矢部
ㄕˇ shyy shǐ

【矢】 3829
ㄕˇ shyy shǐ
1. an arrow; a dart
2. to vow; to take an oath; to pledge
3. to display
4. straightforward

矢服(ㄕˇ ㄈㄨˊ)
a quiver for holding arrows

矢口不移(ㄕˇ ㄎㄡˇ ㄅㄨˋ ㄧˊ)
to stick to one's original statement

矢口否認(ㄕˇ ㄎㄡˇ ㄈㄡˇ ㄖㄣˋ)
to deny flatly

矢志不移(ㄕˇ ㄓˋ ㄅㄨˋ ㄧˊ)
to swear that one will stick to something; to take an oath not to change one's mind: 我對妳的愛矢志不移。I swear I'll love you forever.

矢志靡他(ㄕˇ ㄓˋ ㄇㄧˇ ㄊㄚ)
to swear that one would stick it out

矢車菊(ㄕˇ ㄔㄜ ㄐㄩˊ)
bluebottle; cornflower; bachelor's button

矢石(ㄕˇ ㄕˊ)
arrows and rocks used as weapons in ancient warfare; bullets and bombs in modern warfare

矢誓(ㄕˇ ㄕˋ)
to take an oath

矢人(ㄕˇ ㄖㄣˊ)
a maker of arrows

矢如雨下(ㄕˇ ㄖㄨˊ ㄩˇ ㄒㄧㄚˋ)
The arrows come down like a shower.

矢在弦上(ㄕˇ ㄗㄞˋ ㄒㄧㄢˊ ㄕㄤˋ)
(literally) The arrow is on the strained cord.—imminent; cannot be stopped

矢言(ㄕˇ ㄧㄢˊ)
an oath; a solemn vow; to make a vow

二畫

【矣】 3830
ㄧˇ yii yǐ
1. a final particle denoting the perfect tense: 悔之晚矣。It's too late to repent.
2. an auxiliary denoting determination
3. (in usage) both particles or auxiliaries indicating exclamations or questions 亦作「哉」or「乎」

三畫

【知】 3831
1. ㄓ jy zhī
1. knowledge
2. to know; to understand; to feel; to recognize; to be aware of: 若要人不知，除非己莫爲。If you don't want others to know it, don't do it.
3. to acquaint; to be familiar with; to befriend
4. to control; to operate; to direct
5. to wait on

知白守黑(ㄓ ㄅㄛˊ ㄕㄡˇ ㄏㄟ)
(literally) to stick to obscurity for a reason, even if one knows that light is something valuable (from Laotzu)—to be content with retirement and to let others enjoy the limelight

知賓(ㄓ ㄅㄧㄣ)
a receptionist

知兵(ㄓ ㄅㄧㄥ)
to be well versed in military arts

知名(ㄓ ㄇㄧㄥˊ)
well-known

知名度(ㄓ ㄇㄧㄥˊ ㄉㄨˋ)
name recognition; name familiarity

知名之士(ㄓ ㄇㄧㄥˊ ㄓ ㄕˋ)or 知名人士(ㄓ ㄇㄧㄥˊ ㄖㄣˊ ㄕˋ)
a well-known personality; a famous person; a public figure; a celebrity

知命之年(ㄓ ㄇㄧㄥˋ ㄓ ㄋㄧㄢˊ)
50 years of age

知法犯法(ㄓ ㄈㄚˇ ㄈㄢˋ ㄈㄚˇ)
to transgress a law knowingly

知府(ㄓ ㄈㄨˇ)
the magistrate of a prefec-

〔矢部〕

ture
知道(ㄓ ˙ㄉㄠ)
to know; to realize; to understand: 他眞的不知道這件事。He really knows nothing about it.
知難行易(ㄓ ㄋㄢˊ ㄒㄧㄥˊ ㄧˋ)
It's easier to do a thing than to know the why. (a theory advanced by Dr. Sun Yat-sen, in rebutting the popular belief to the contrary)
知難而退(ㄓ ㄋㄢˊ ㄦˊ ㄊㄨㄟˋ)
to withdraw or quit after learning of the difficulties, hardships, etc. involved
知禮(ㄓ ㄌㄧˇ)
to say and act in proper manners ; to know the rules of propriety
知了(ㄓ ㄌㄧㄠˇ)
the cicada, or broad locust
知根知底(ㄓ ㄍㄣ ㄓ ㄉㄧˇ)
to know (somebody or something) to the very root or source; to know through and through
知更雀(ㄓ ㄍㄥ ㄑㄩㄝˋ)or 知更鳥(ㄓ ㄍㄥ ㄋㄧㄠˇ)
the robin
知過(ㄓ ㄍㄨㄛˋ)
to realize (or know) one's mistake
知過必改(ㄓ ㄍㄨㄛˋ ㄅㄧˋ ㄍㄞˇ)
One should correct his faults once he is aware of them.
知客(ㄓ ㄎㄜˋ)
①a reception monk in a Buddhist temple ②a person in charge of reception at ceremonies
知幾(ㄓ ㄐㄧ)
to know or detect something before it takes shape; to discover something at its very beginning
知己(ㄓ ㄐㄧˇ)
①a close or intimate friend: 他是我的知己。He is my bosom (or intimate) friend. ②intimate: 我和她很知己。I am on intimate terms with her. ③to know oneself
知己知彼，百戰百勝(ㄓ ㄐㄧˇ ㄓ ㄅㄧˇ, ㄅㄞˇ ㄓㄢˋ ㄅㄞˇ ㄕㄥˋ)
Knowing one's own situation and that of the enemy guarantees victory in every battle.
知交(ㄓ ㄐㄧㄠ)
intimate and close friends: 他和我父親是多年知交。He and my father are intimate friends for many years.
知覺(ㄓ ㄐㄩㄝˊ)
①consciousness: 我們在睡眠時沒有知覺。We have no consciousness during sleep. ②perception
知覺神經(ㄓ ㄐㄩㄝˊ ㄕㄣˊ ㄐㄧㄥ)
sensory nerves
知其不可爲而爲之(ㄓ ㄑㄧˊ ㄅㄨˋ ㄎㄜˇ ㄨㄟˊ ㄦˊ ㄨㄟˊ ㄓ)
to do something even though one knows it is impossible to succeed
知其一不知其二(ㄓ ㄑㄧˊ ㄧ ㄅㄨˋ ㄓ ㄑㄧˊ ㄦˋ)
to know only a part of the story; to have only a partial understanding of a situation
知情(ㄓ ㄑㄧㄥˊ)
to be aware of (usually referring to a secret, plot, etc.); to be in the know: 知情不報將受罰。Those who conceal what they know of a case will be punished.
知趣(ㄓ ㄑㄩˋ)
sensible; having a sense of propriety; knowing what to do in a delicate situation
知悉(ㄓ ㄒㄧ)
to know; to learn of; to be aware of : 我們尙未知悉他是否安全到達。We have not yet learned whether he arrived safely.
知曉(ㄓ ㄒㄧㄠˇ)
to know; to be aware of; to learn of; to understand
知縣(ㄓ ㄒㄧㄢˋ)
a county magistrate in former times
知心(ㄓ ㄒㄧㄣ)
①meeting of minds; bosom (friends) ②to know what's on the mind of another person
知心話(ㄓ ㄒㄧㄣ ㄏㄨㄚˋ)
intimate talks or words; secrets from the bottom of one's heart
知心人(ㄓ ㄒㄧㄣ ㄖㄣˊ)
a bosom friend: 她終於找到知心人了。She has finally found a bosom friend.
知行合一(ㄓ ㄒㄧㄥˊ ㄏㄜˊ ㄧ)
(literally) Knowledge and action should go hand in hand.—Action without knowledge serves no purpose, while knowledge without action is futile. (a theory advocated by Wang Yang-ming (王陽明) of the Ming Dynasty)
知之爲知之，不知爲不知，是知也(ㄓ ㄓ ㄨㄟˊ ㄓ ㄓ, ㄅㄨˋ ㄓ ㄨㄟˊ ㄅㄨˋ ㄓ, ㄕˋ ㄓ ㄧㄝˇ)
When you know a thing, to hold that you know it; and when you do not know a thing, to allow that you do not know it;—this is knowledge. (論語・爲政)
知止(ㄓ ㄓˇ)
to know where to stop
知制誥(ㄓ ㄓˋ ㄍㄠˋ)
an official in ancient China in charge of secretarial matters
知照(ㄓ ㄓㄠˋ)
①to notify; to tell ②(a Chinese documentary usage to a subordinate organization) for your information
知州(ㄓ ㄓㄡ)
(in ancient China) the chief of a prefecture
知政(ㄓ ㄓㄥˋ)
to administer the government; to handle state affairs
知恥(ㄓ ㄔˇ)
to have a sense of shame
知恥近乎勇(ㄓ ㄔˇ ㄐㄧㄣˋ ㄏㄨ ㄩㄥˇ)
Knowing shame is akin to courage.
知事(ㄓ ㄕˋ)
①a former official post equivalent to today's county magistrate ②to know things when one grows up
知識(ㄓ ㄕˋ)
knowledge; learning; information: 知識即力量。Knowledge is power.
知識分子(ㄓ ㄕˋ ㄈㄣˋ ㄗˇ)
intellectuals; the intelligentsia
知識論(ㄓ ㄕˋ ㄌㄨㄣˋ)
(philosophy) epistemology;

the theory of knowledge 亦作「認識論」

知識階級(ㄓ ㄕˋ ㄐㄧㄝ ㄐㄧˊ)
the intelligentsia; the intellectual class

知人(ㄓ ㄖㄣˊ)
to know people—the ability to understand people, their moral standing, integrity, ability, etc.

知人知面不知心(ㄓ ㄖㄣˊ ㄓ ㄇㄧㄢˋ ㄅㄨˋ ㄓ ㄒㄧㄣ)
(literally) One may know a person by his face, but one cannot read his mind.—Do not trust people too easily.

知人善任(ㄓ ㄖㄣˊ ㄕㄢˋ ㄖㄣˋ)
to be expert in judging people's worth and to know how to employ them to the best advantage

知子莫若父(ㄓ ㄗˇ ㄇㄛˋ ㄖㄨㄛˋ ㄈㄨˋ)
Father knows his sons best.

知足(ㄓ ㄗㄨˊ)
to be content with what one has had

知足常樂(ㄓ ㄗㄨˊ ㄔㄤˊ ㄌㄜˋ)
Contentment brings happiness.

知友(ㄓ ㄧㄡˇ)
a close or intimate friend

知言(ㄓ ㄧㄢˊ)
① words of wisdom ② to know the true meaning of one's words

知音(ㄓ ㄧㄣ)
① a close or intimate friend ② one who is well versed in music

知無不言(ㄓ ㄨˊ ㄅㄨˋ ㄧㄢˊ)
to hide nothing; to be very frank

知無不言，言無不盡(ㄓ ㄨˊ ㄅㄨˋ ㄧㄢˊ, ㄧㄢˊ ㄨˊ ㄅㄨˋ ㄐㄧㄣˋ)
One says all one knows and says it without reserve.

知我罪我(ㄓ ㄨㄛˇ ㄗㄨㄟˋ ㄨㄛˇ)
If you understand me, well and good. If not, I don't care a bit.

知遇(ㄓ ㄩˋ)
to have found a patron or superior who appreciates one's ability

知遇之恩(ㄓ ㄩˋ ㄓ ㄣ)
the debt one owes to somebody who understands him and has treated him well

【知】 3831
2. (智) ㄓˋ jyh zhì
the learned; the wise; brains

知能(ㄓˋ ㄋㄥˊ)
intellectual capacity

知者不惑(ㄓˋ ㄓㄜˇ ㄅㄨˋ ㄏㄨㄛˋ)
The wise harbor no doubts.

知者樂水(ㄓˋ ㄓㄜˇ ㄧㄠˋ ㄕㄨㄟˇ)
The wise enjoy water.

四畫

【矧】 3832
ㄕㄣˇ sheen shěn
1. still more
2. also
3. gums

【矦】 3833
(侯) ㄏㄡˊ hour hóu
1. the second of the five grades of the nobility; a marquis
2. a bull's-eye
3. beautiful
4. an opening particle—but
5. why
6. a Chinese family name

五畫

【矩】 3834
ㄐㄩˇ jeu jǔ
1. a carpenter's square
2. a rule; a regulation; a pattern
3. to carve

矩步(ㄐㄩˇ ㄅㄨˋ)
to behave in a cautious manner

矩度(ㄐㄩˇ ㄉㄨˋ)
laws and regulations; a pattern or model

矩矱(ㄐㄩˇ ㄏㄨㄛˋ)
regulations; rules

矩形(ㄐㄩˇ ㄒㄧㄥˊ)
a rectangle; rectangular

矩形體(ㄐㄩˇ ㄒㄧㄥˊ ㄊㄧˇ)
a rectangular parallelepiped

矩尺(ㄐㄩˇ ㄔˇ)
a carpenter's square

七畫

【矬】 3835
ㄘㄨㄛˊ tswo cuó
short; dwarf

矬子(ㄘㄨㄛˊ ·ㄗ)
a dwarf; a shortie

【短】 3836
ㄉㄨㄢˇ doan duǎn
1. short; brief: 冬季晝短夜長。In winter the days are short and the nights long.
2. to be deficient; to want; to lack; to owe
3. shortcomings; faults; mistakes: 勿道人之短。Don't talk about people's shortcomings.

短波(ㄉㄨㄢˇ ㄅㄛ)
(said of radio, etc.) shortwave

短兵(ㄉㄨㄢˇ ㄅㄧㄥ)
knives and swords, etc. (as opposed to lances and spears)

短兵相接(ㄉㄨㄢˇ ㄅㄧㄥ ㄒㄧㄤ ㄐㄧㄝ)
(military) to fight at close quarters; hand-to-hand combat

短不了(ㄉㄨㄢˇ ·ㄅㄨ ㄌㄧㄠˇ)
① cannot do without: 人短不了水。People cannot do without water. ② cannot avoid; to have to

短跑(ㄉㄨㄢˇ ㄆㄠˇ)
a short-distance race; a sprint; a dash

短跑健將(ㄉㄨㄢˇ ㄆㄠˇ ㄐㄧㄢˋ ㄐㄧㄤˋ)
a sprinter; a short-distance runner: 他弟弟是著名的短跑健將。His younger brother is a famous sprinter.

短篇小說(ㄉㄨㄢˇ ㄆㄧㄢ ㄒㄧㄠˇ ㄕㄨㄛ)
short stories: 我喜歡有關科學的短篇小說。I like short stories about science.

短片(ㄉㄨㄢˇ ㄆㄧㄢˋ)
(film) a short film

短評(ㄉㄨㄢˇ ㄆㄧㄥˊ)
a short comment or critique; a brief commentary

短命(ㄉㄨㄢˇ ㄇㄧㄥˋ)
to die early; short-lived; to die young

短打(ㄉㄨㄢˇ ㄉㄚˇ)
① short clothes (as opposed to long gowns) ②(drama) a hand-to-hand fight in tights ③(baseball) to bunt; a bunt

短大衣(ㄉㄨㄢˇ ㄉㄚˋ ㄧ)
a short overcoat

短刀(ㄉㄨㄢˇ ㄉㄠ)
a short sword; a dagger

短笛(ㄉㄨㄢˇ ㄉㄧˊ)

a piccolo
短短(ㄉㄨㄢˇ ㄉㄨㄢˇ)
brief; short: 她給他寫了一封短短的謝函。She wrote him a brief letter of thanks.
短噸(ㄉㄨㄢˇ ㄉㄨㄣˋ)
short ton
短亭長亭(ㄉㄨㄢˇ ㄊㄧㄥˊ ㄔㄤˊ ㄊㄧㄥˊ)
small pavilions outside every city in ancient China, a smaller one in every 5 *li*, and a larger one in every 10 *li*
短禮(ㄉㄨㄢˇ ㄌㄧˇ)
to lack courtesy
短路(ㄉㄨㄢˇ ㄌㄨˋ)
① an improper or unlawful way of making a living—as robbery, burglary, etc. ② (electricity) short circuit
短綆汲深(ㄉㄨㄢˇ ㄍㄥˇ ㄐㄧˊ ㄕㄣ)
(literally) to draw water from a deep well with a short rope—to do something beyond one's capability
短工(ㄉㄨㄢˇ ㄍㄨㄥ)
a temporary worker; a handy man; a temporary employee: 他要我幫他找一位短工。He asked me to find a temporary worker for him.
短褲(ㄉㄨㄢˇ ㄎㄨˋ)
knee pants; shorts; short pants
短褐(ㄉㄨㄢˇ ㄏㄜˋ)
the clothing of the poor
短計(ㄉㄨㄢˇ ㄐㄧˋ)
unsound plans or measures; bad policies
短見(ㄉㄨㄢˇ ㄐㄧㄢˋ)
① shortsightedness ② suicide: 老人昨晚尋短見。The old man attempted suicide last night.
短劍(ㄉㄨㄢˇ ㄐㄧㄢˋ)
a dagger
短距離(ㄉㄨㄢˇ ㄐㄩˋ ㄌㄧˊ)
short distance; close range
短期(ㄉㄨㄢˇ ㄑㄧˊ)
short-term (bonds, loans, etc.); a short period: 我要申請一筆短期貸款。I want to apply for a short-term loan.
短期投資(ㄉㄨㄢˇ ㄑㄧˊ ㄊㄡˊ ㄗ)
liquid investment; temporary investment; short-term investment
短期計劃(ㄉㄨㄢˇ ㄑㄧˊ ㄐㄧˋ ㄏㄨㄚˋ)
a short-term project
短期信貸(ㄉㄨㄢˇ ㄑㄧˊ ㄒㄧㄣˋ ㄉㄞˋ)
short-term credit
短期銀行貸款(ㄉㄨㄢˇ ㄑㄧˊ ㄧㄣˊ ㄏㄤˊ ㄉㄞˋ ㄎㄨㄢˇ)
short-term bank loans
短氣(ㄉㄨㄢˇ ㄑㄧˋ)
to lose courage or heart; despondent and discouraged; depressed; in low spirits
短欠(ㄉㄨㄢˇ ㄑㄧㄢˋ)
to be short by...; to fall short; to owe
短缺(ㄉㄨㄢˇ ㄑㄩㄝ)
to fall short; deficient; deficiency; shortage: 在戰爭時，常常發生糧食短缺的情形。Food shortages often occur in time of war.
短小(ㄉㄨㄢˇ ㄒㄧㄠˇ)
short and small: 他的身材短小。He is a person of short and small stature.
短小精悍(ㄉㄨㄢˇ ㄒㄧㄠˇ ㄐㄧㄥ ㄏㄢˋ)
short but energetic; short in physical stature but long in stamina
短訓班(ㄉㄨㄢˇ ㄒㄩㄣˋ ㄅㄢ)
a short-term training course
短折(ㄉㄨㄢˇ ㄓㄜˊ)
to die young; short-lived
短暫(ㄉㄨㄢˇ ㄓㄢˋ)
transient; brief; a short period: 這數學天才的一生是短暫而光榮的。The mathematical genius' life was short but glorious.
短針(ㄉㄨㄢˇ ㄓㄣ)
the hour hand
短裝(ㄉㄨㄢˇ ㄓㄨㄤ)
short clothes
短長(ㄉㄨㄢˇ ㄔㄤˊ)
① shortcomings and good points ② good and evil ③ life and death
短程(ㄉㄨㄢˇ ㄔㄥˊ)
short distance; short range
短絀(ㄉㄨㄢˇ ㄔㄨˋ)
to fall short by...; deficient; deficiency
短處(ㄉㄨㄢˇ ·ㄔㄨ)
shortcomings; faults; defects; weak points: 不守時間是他最大的短處。Not being punctual is his greatest shortcoming.
短時間(ㄉㄨㄢˇ ㄕˊ ㄐㄧㄢ)
a short time or period
短視(ㄉㄨㄢˇ ㄕˋ)
shortsighted; to lack foresight: 政府的政策是短視的。The government's policy is shortsighted.
短少(ㄉㄨㄢˇ ㄕㄠˇ)
to fall short by...; deficient; deficiency; missing: 這本書短少一頁。There is one page missing in this book.
短衫(ㄉㄨㄢˇ ㄕㄢ)
a shirt; a jacket
短促(ㄉㄨㄢˇ ㄘㄨˋ)
①(said of time) short; brief; transient; ephemeral ② of short duration: 如是結束了這個短促的旅程。Thus ended the journey of short duration.
短音階(ㄉㄨㄢˇ ㄧㄣ ㄐㄧㄝ)
(music) the minor scale
短音程(ㄉㄨㄢˇ ㄧㄣ ㄔㄥˊ)
(music) a minor interval
短襪(ㄉㄨㄢˇ ㄨㄚˋ)
socks
短文(ㄉㄨㄢˇ ㄨㄣˊ)
a short essay
短語(ㄉㄨㄢˇ ㄩˇ)
phrases

八畫

【矮】 3837
ㄞˇ ae ǎi
1. a short person; a dwarf
2. short; low; low-ranking: 他比他姐姐矮一個頭。He's a head shorter than his sister.
矮柏(ㄞˇ ㄅㄞˇ)
a tree resembling a cedar or a cypress but much shorter, usually planted in gardens
矮胖(ㄞˇ ㄆㄤˋ)
short and fat
矮櫈子(ㄞˇ ㄉㄥˋ ·ㄗ) or 矮櫈(ㄞˇ ㄉㄥˋ)
a low bench or stool
矮奴(ㄞˇ ㄋㄨˊ)
①(derogatively) the Japs ② Ainus (a race of dwarfs)
矮個兒(ㄞˇ ㄍㄜˋㄦ) or 矮個子(ㄞˇ ㄍㄜˋ ·ㄗ)
a person of short stature; short-statured
矮牆淺屋(ㄞˇ ㄑㄧㄤˊ ㄑㄧㄢˇ ㄨ)
The wall is low and house small.—a poor family
矮小(ㄞˇ ㄒㄧㄠˇ)

short-statured; undersized; low (houses, trees, etc.): 他的身材矮小。He is short and slight in figure.
矮樹(ㄞˇ ㄕㄨˋ)
a low tree; bushes
矮人觀場(ㄞˇ ㄖㄣˊ ㄍㄨㄢ ㄔㄤˇ)or 矮人看場(ㄞˇ ㄖㄣˊ ㄎㄢˋ ㄔㄤˇ)
(literally) the dwarf seeing a show—seeing nothing but applauding with the others
矮子(ㄞˇ ·ㄗ)
a short person; a dwarf
矮子看戲(ㄞˇ ·ㄗ ㄎㄢˋ ㄒㄧˋ)
to follow the reaction of others without an opinion of one's own 參看「矮人看場」
矮矬子(ㄞˇ ㄘㄨㄛˊ ·ㄗ)
a short person; a dwarf
矮屋(ㄞˇ ㄨ)
a house with a low ceiling; a low house

十二畫

【矯】3838 ㄐㄧㄠˇ jeau jiǎo
1. to straighten; to correct; to rectify
2. to falsify; to forge; to fake; to pretend
3. strong and powerful; vigorous; brave
4. to raise (one's head) high
5. a Chinese family name
矯託(ㄐㄧㄠˇ ㄊㄨㄛ)
to fake; to take...as an excuse or a pretext
矯亢(ㄐㄧㄠˇ ㄎㄤˋ)
to affect superiority by acting or talking in a manner different from others'
矯捷(ㄐㄧㄠˇ ㄐㄧㄝˊ)
agile; vigorous and nimble; brisk
矯矯不羣(ㄐㄧㄠˇ ㄐㄧㄠˇ ㄅㄨˋ ㄑㄩㄣˊ)
outstanding; peerless; remarkable
矯健(ㄐㄧㄠˇ ㄐㄧㄢˋ)
strong and vigorous: 他踏著矯健的步伐。He walks with vigorous strides.
矯情(ㄐㄧㄠˇ ㄑㄧㄥˊ)
to talk or act against customs or common practices in order to advertise one's self-styled superiority; to be affectedly unconventional
矯形(ㄐㄧㄠˇ ㄒㄧㄥˊ)
(medicine) orthopaedic
矯制(ㄐㄧㄠˇ ㄓˋ)
to fake orders from above
矯詔(ㄐㄧㄠˇ ㄓㄠˋ)
to forge or fake an imperial decree
矯正(ㄐㄧㄠˇ ㄓㄥˋ)
to correct or rectify
矯世(ㄐㄧㄠˇ ㄕˋ)
to reform or correct social customs or practices by personally setting examples
矯飾(ㄐㄧㄠˇ ㄕˋ)
to affect; affected; affectation
矯揉造作(ㄐㄧㄠˇ ㄖㄡˊ ㄗㄠˋ ㄗㄨㄛˋ)
affectation; to behave in an affected manner
矯枉過正(ㄐㄧㄠˇ ㄨㄤˇ ㄍㄨㄛˋ ㄓㄥˋ)
to be overstrict in correcting mistakes, faults, etc.; to exceed the proper limits in righting a wrong

【矰】3839 ㄗㄥ tzeng zēng
an arrow, dart, etc. attached to a silk cord or string for shooting birds, etc.
矰繳(ㄗㄥ ㄓㄨㄛˊ)
a bird-shooting device (see above)

十四畫

【矱】3840 ㄏㄨㄛˋ huoh huò
a measure; a criterion

石部
ㄕˊ shyr shí

【石】3841 1. ㄕˊ shyr shí
1. rocks; stones; minerals, etc.: 滾石不生苔。A rolling stone gathers no moss.
2. a calculus, as a kidney calculus (commonly known as a kidney stone)
3. stone tablets
4. medicines
5. barren, as a barren woman
6. name of an ancient musical instrument
7. a Chinese family name
石碑(ㄕˊ ㄅㄟ)
a stone tablet; a stele
石斑魚(ㄕˊ ㄅㄢ ㄩˊ)
a spotted grouper; a cabrilla
石板(ㄕˊ ㄅㄢˇ)
a slate; a stone slab; a flagstone
石版(ㄕˊ ㄅㄢˇ)
① a lithographic stoneplate ② stone slabs or slates—usually for construction purposes ③ a slate
石版畫(ㄕˊ ㄅㄢˇ ㄏㄨㄚˋ)
a lithograph
石版石(ㄕˊ ㄅㄢˇ ㄕˊ)
a lithographic stone
石本(ㄕˊ ㄅㄣˇ)
rubbing from stone inscriptions
石筆(ㄕˊ ㄅㄧˇ)
a slate pencil
石壁(ㄕˊ ㄅㄧˋ)
a stone wall; a precipice
石破天驚(ㄕˊ ㄆㄛˋ ㄊㄧㄢ ㄐㄧㄥ)
(said of music, statements, writings, etc.) world-shaking; sensational; remarkably original and forceful
石癖(ㄕˊ ㄆㄧˇ)
a love for rocks and stones
石馬(ㄕˊ ㄇㄚˇ)
stone horses — as those beside a grave or tomb
石墨(ㄕˊ ㄇㄛˋ)
graphite; black lead; plumbago
石磨(ㄕˊ ㄇㄛˋ)
a millstone; a grindstone
石煤(ㄕˊ ㄇㄟˊ)
hard coal; stone coal; bone coal
石門水庫(ㄕˊ ㄇㄣˊ ㄕㄨㄟˇ ㄎㄨˋ)
the Shih-men Reservoir in northern Taiwan
石綿(ㄕˊ ㄇㄧㄢˊ)
asbestos
石綿板(ㄕˊ ㄇㄧㄢˊ ㄅㄢˇ)
an asbestos board
石綿瓦(ㄕˊ ㄇㄧㄢˊ ㄨㄚˇ)
an asbestos shingle; an asbestos tile
石民(ㄕˊ ㄇㄧㄣˊ)
civilians

石縫(ㄕˊ ㄈㄥˋ)
a crevice in stone or between rocks

石達開(ㄕˊ ㄉㄚˊ ㄎㄞ)
Shih Ta-kai (?-1863) a scholar-general who fought the Manchus during the Taiping Rebellion

石埭(ㄕˊ ㄉㄞˋ)
①a dike or embankment of stone ②name of a county in Anhwei Province

石磴(ㄕˊ ㄉㄥˋ)
stone steps

石雕(ㄕˊ ㄉㄧㄠ)
①stone carving ②carved stone

石墩(ㄕˊ ㄉㄨㄣ)
①a stone pier ②a block of stone used as a seat

石洞(ㄕˊ ㄉㄨㄥˋ)
a stone cave

石頭(ㄕˊ ㄊㄡˊ)or(ㄕˊ ˙ㄊㄡ)
stone; a rock

石頭記(ㄕˊ ㄊㄡˊ ㄐㄧˋ)
another title of the Chinese novel 紅樓夢 (*The Dream of the Red Chamber*)

石頭城(ㄕˊ ㄊㄡˊ ㄔㄥˊ)
name of an ancient city west of Nanking

石炭(ㄕˊ ㄊㄢˋ)
coal

石炭酸(ㄕˊ ㄊㄢˋ ㄙㄨㄢ)
carbolic acid; phenol

石田(ㄕˊ ㄊㄧㄢˊ)
barren land; a field which is not arable

石楠(ㄕˊ ㄋㄢˊ)
a rhododendron

石女(ㄕˊ ㄋㄩˇ)
a barren woman; a woman with a defective reproductive organ

石蠟(ㄕˊ ㄌㄚˋ)
paraffin (wax)

石礫(ㄕˊ ㄌㄧˋ)
gravel

石榴(ㄕˊ ˙ㄌㄧㄡ)or(ㄕˊ ㄌㄧㄡˊ)
a pomegranate

石榴裙(ㄕˊ ㄌㄧㄡˊ ㄑㄩㄣˊ)
①a red skirt; a woman's petticoat ②(now figuratively) feminine charms

石榴石(ㄕˊ ㄌㄧㄡˊ ㄕˊ)
a garnet

石路(ㄕˊ ㄌㄨˋ)
a stone-paved road; a pebble road; a gravel road

石膏(ㄕˊ ㄍㄠ)
gypsum; plaster

石膏像(ㄕˊ ㄍㄠ ㄒㄧㄤˋ)
a plaster bust; a plaster statue

石敢當(ㄕˊ ㄍㄢˇ ㄉㄤ)
a stone tablet, erected at the entrance of a lane, etc. to drive away misfortune or evil spirits

石鼓(ㄕˊ ㄍㄨˇ)
drum-shaped stones of the Epoch of Warring States, ten of which have been preserved

石鼓文(ㄕˊ ㄍㄨˇ ㄨㄣˊ)
ancient characters engraved on the drum-shaped stones

石棺(ㄕˊ ㄍㄨㄢ)
a stone coffin; a sarcophagus

石工(ㄕˊ ㄍㄨㄥ)
a mason; masonry: 他的職業是石工。He's a mason by trade.

石刻(ㄕˊ ㄎㄜˋ)
stone engraving; stone carving; stone inscriptions

石窟(ㄕˊ ㄎㄨ)
a grotto

石塊(ㄕˊ ㄎㄨㄞˋ)
a piece of stone or rock; a pebble; a boulder: 石塊與碎石正自山上滾下。Rocks and stones were rolling down the hill.

石斛蘭(ㄕˊ ㄏㄨˊ ㄌㄢˊ)
dendrobium

石花菜(ㄕˊ ㄏㄨㄚ ㄘㄞˋ)
Gelidium amansii, a gelatinous seaweed which is used as a dish after cooking亦作「洋菜」

石化工業(ㄕˊ ㄏㄨㄚˋ ㄍㄨㄥ ㄧㄝˋ)
the petrochemical industries

石灰(ㄕˊ ㄏㄨㄟ)
lime: 熟石灰 slaked lime 生石灰 quick lime

石灰粉末(ㄕˊ ㄏㄨㄟ ㄈㄣˇ ㄇㄛˋ)
slaked lime

石灰石(ㄕˊ ㄏㄨㄟ ㄕˊ)
limestone

石灰水(ㄕˊ ㄏㄨㄟ ㄕㄨㄟˇ)
limewater; aqua calcis

石灰岩(ㄕˊ ㄏㄨㄟ ㄧㄢˊ)
limestone

石黃(ㄕˊ ㄏㄨㄤˊ)
hartite

石階(ㄕˊ ㄐㄧㄝ)
stone steps: 一段石階往上通到房子。A flight of stone steps leads up to the house.

石交(ㄕˊ ㄐㄧㄠ)
friendship or ties as strong as stone; close and intimate friendship

石鹼(ㄕˊ ㄐㄧㄢˇ)
soap

石鹼石(ㄕˊ ㄐㄧㄢˇ ㄕˊ)
soapstone

石匠(ㄕˊ ˙ㄐㄧㄤ)
a stonemason: 蘇格拉底曾做過石匠和雕刻匠。Socrates was a stonemason and carver.

石晶(ㄕˊ ㄐㄧㄥ)
rock crystal

石經(ㄕˊ ㄐㄧㄥ)
classics engraved on stone tablets in various dynasties after exhaustive verification and research, made usually by orders of the emperors

石決明(ㄕˊ ㄐㄩㄝˊ ㄇㄧㄥˊ)
an abalone; the shell of an abalone or sea-ear

石器(ㄕˊ ㄑㄧˋ)
stoneware; stone implements; a stone artifact; a stone vessel

石器時代(ㄕˊ ㄑㄧˋ ㄕˊ ㄉㄞˋ)
the Stone Age

石牆(ㄕˊ ㄑㄧㄤˊ)
a stone wall

石像(ㄕˊ ㄒㄧㄤˋ)
a statue or bust of stone

石竹(ㄕˊ ㄓㄨˊ)
a carnation

石柱(ㄕˊ ㄓㄨˋ)
a stone pillar

石鐘乳(ㄕˊ ㄓㄨㄥ ㄖㄨˇ)or 石乳(ㄕˊ ㄖㄨˇ)
stalactites 亦作「鐘乳石」

石沈大海(ㄕˊ ㄔㄣˊ ㄉㄚˋ ㄏㄞˇ)
(literally) rocks falling into the sea—completely without information or response; no news at all; without a trace; to disappear forever

石室(ㄕˊ ㄕˋ)
①a stone house—very

strong and safe ②a stone chamber for keeping books ③a stone tomb or vault

石蕊試紙(ㄕˊ ㄖㄨㄟˇ ㄕˋ ㄓˇ)
litmus paper

石蕊試藥(ㄕˊ ㄖㄨㄟˇ ㄕˋ ㄧㄠˋ)
litmus

石絨(ㄕˊ ㄖㄨㄥˊ)
asbestos

石子(ㄕˊ ㄗˇ)or 石子兒(ㄕˊ ㄗㄜˇㄦ)or 石頭子兒(ㄕˊ ㄊㄡˊ ㄗㄜˇㄦ)
pieces of stone; pebbles

石子路(ㄕˊ ㄗˇ ㄌㄨˋ)
a graveled path; a macadam road: 有一條石子路通到花園。There is a graveled path leading to the garden.

石髓(ㄕˊ ㄙㄨㄟˇ)
stalactites

石筍(ㄕˊ ㄙㄨㄣˇ)
a stalagmite: 這個洞裏有許多石筍。There are many stalagmites in the cave.

石油(ㄕˊ ㄧㄡˊ)
crude oil; petroleum: 石油價格又上漲了。The price of petroleum has gone up again.

石油公司(ㄕˊ ㄧㄡˊ ㄍㄨㄥ ㄙ)
a petroleum company

石油工業(ㄕˊ ㄧㄡˊ ㄍㄨㄥ ㄧㄝˋ)
petroleum industry

石油化工廠(ㄕˊ ㄧㄡˊ ㄏㄨㄚˋ ㄍㄨㄥ ㄔㄤˇ)
a petrochemical works

石油化學(ㄕˊ ㄧㄡˊ ㄏㄨㄚˋ ㄒㄩㄝˊ)
petrochemistry

石油化學工業(ㄕˊ ㄧㄡˊ ㄏㄨㄚˋ ㄒㄩㄝˊ ㄍㄨㄥ ㄧㄝˋ)
the petrochemical industries

石油精(ㄕˊ ㄧㄡˊ ㄐㄧㄥ)
benzine

石油井(ㄕˊ ㄧㄡˊ ㄐㄧㄥˇ)
(petroleum) an oil well

石鹽(ㄕˊ ㄧㄢˊ)
mineral salt; rock salt

石印(ㄕˊ ㄧㄣˋ)
lithography

石印本(ㄕˊ ㄧㄣˋ ㄅㄣˇ)
a lithographic edition or copy

石英(ㄕˊ ㄧㄥ)
quartz

石英鐘(ㄕˊ ㄧㄥ ㄓㄨㄥ)
a quartz clock

石屋(ㄕˊ ㄨ)
a stone house

【石】 3841
2. ㄉㄢˋ dann dàn

1. a dry measure for grains roughly equivalent to 120-160 pounds; picul
2. a weight measure equivalent to about 110 pounds

三畫

【矽】 3842
ㄒㄧˋ shih xì

silicon (Si)

矽鋼(ㄒㄧˋ ㄍㄤ)
silicon steel

矽谷(ㄒㄧˋ ㄍㄨˇ)
Silicon Valley in California

矽石(ㄒㄧˋ ㄕˊ)
silex

矽砂(ㄒㄧˋ ㄕㄚ)
quartz sand

矽藻(ㄒㄧˋ ㄗㄠˇ)
diatom

矽酸(ㄒㄧˋ ㄙㄨㄢ)
silicic acid

矽酸鈉(ㄒㄧˋ ㄙㄨㄢ ㄋㄚˋ)
sodium silicate

矽酸鋁(ㄒㄧˋ ㄙㄨㄢ ㄌㄩˇ)
aluminium silicate

矽酸鈣(ㄒㄧˋ ㄙㄨㄢ ㄍㄞˋ)
calcium silicate

矽酸鉀(ㄒㄧˋ ㄙㄨㄢ ㄐㄧㄚˇ)
potassium silicate

矽酸鹽(ㄒㄧˋ ㄙㄨㄢ ㄧㄢˊ)
silicate

【矻】 3843
ㄎㄨˋ kuh kù

1. stone
2. diligent; industrious
3. very tired

矻矻(ㄎㄨˋ ㄎㄨˋ)
①diligent; industrious ②very tired

四畫

【砉】 3844
ㄏㄨㄛˋ huoh huò

a splitting sound; a cracking sound

【砂】 3845
ㄕㄚ sha shā

1. sand; coarse sand; gravel: 孩子們喜歡在砂裏玩。Children enjoy playing on the sands.
2. coarse—not smooth
3. infinitesimal

砂布(ㄕㄚ ㄅㄨˋ)
emery cloth; abrasive cloth

砂糖(ㄕㄚ ㄊㄤˊ)
crude sugar; brown sugar

砂鐵(ㄕㄚ ㄊㄧㄝˇ)
magnetic sand

砂土(ㄕㄚ ㄊㄨˇ)
a sandy soil

砂囊(ㄕㄚ ㄋㄤˊ)
a gizzard

砂礫(ㄕㄚ ㄌㄧˋ)
gravel; pebbles

砂輪(ㄕㄚ ㄌㄨㄣˊ)
an emery wheel; grindstone

砂濾器(ㄕㄚ ㄌㄩˋ ㄑㄧˋ)
a sand filter

砂礦(ㄕㄚ ㄎㄨㄤˋ)
minerals in the form of sand

砂礁(ㄕㄚ ㄐㄧㄠ)
sandy shoals

砂金(ㄕㄚ ㄐㄧㄣ)
gold dust; placer gold; alluvial gold

砂金石(ㄕㄚ ㄐㄧㄣ ㄕˊ)
aventurine

砂質(ㄕㄚ ㄓˊ)
sandy: 這條河流是砂質底。The river is of a sandy bottom.

砂紙(ㄕㄚ ㄓˇ)
sandpaper; emery paper

砂岩(ㄕㄚ ㄧㄢˊ)
sandstone

砂眼(ㄕㄚ ㄧㄢˇ)
(medicine) trachoma 亦作「沙眼」

砂浴(ㄕㄚ ㄩˋ)
(chemistry) sand bath

【砌】 3846
ㄑㄧˋ chih qì

1. to lay (bricks, etc.); to pave; to raise in layers; to build
2. steps

砌路(ㄑㄧˋ ㄌㄨˋ)
to build or pave a road

砌牆(ㄑㄧˋ ㄑㄧㄤˊ)
to build a wall

砌磚工人(ㄑㄧˋ ㄓㄨㄢ ㄍㄨㄥ ㄖㄣˊ)
a bricklayer

砌詞捏控(ㄑㄧˋ ㄘˊ ㄋㄧㄝ ㄎㄨㄥˋ)
to fabricate or trump up charges; to frame

【砍】 3847
ㄎㄢˇ kaan kǎn

1. to chop; to hack; to fell (trees, etc.); to cut down:

他們把路邊的樹砍倒。They felled these roadside trees.
2. to throw at
砍伐(ㄎㄢˇ ㄈㄚˊ)
to fell (trees, etc.)
砍斷(ㄎㄢˇ ㄉㄨㄢˋ)
to break apart by chopping; to cut something in two
砍頭(ㄎㄢˇ ㄊㄡˊ)
to behead; to decapitate
砍下來(ㄎㄢˇ ㄒㄧㄚˋ ·ㄌㄞ)
to chop or cut down: 他把這些樹枝砍下來。He chops down the branches.
砍柴(ㄎㄢˇ ㄔㄞˊ)
to chop or cut firewood
砍殺(ㄎㄢˇ ㄕㄚ)
to hack to death; to hack and kill
砍傷(ㄎㄢˇ ㄕㄤ)
to wound by hacking or cutting
砍死(ㄎㄢˇ ㄙˇ)
to hack to death: 他被強盜砍死。He was hacked to death by a robber.

〔石部〕

【砒】 3848
ㄆㄧ pi pī
arsenic
砒霜(ㄆㄧ ㄕㄨㄤ)
arsenic trioxide(As_2O_3)
砒酸(ㄆㄧ ㄙㄨㄢ)
arsenic acid

五畫

【砥】 3849
ㄉㄧˇ dii dǐ
(又讀 ㄓˇ jyy zhǐ)
1. a whetstone; a grindstone
2. to discipline; to polish
砥礪(ㄉㄧˇ ㄌㄧˋ)
to discipline and polish; to temper; to encourage
砥柱(ㄉㄧˇ ㄓㄨˋ)
① name of a mountain through which the Yellow River was supposedly channeled ② an indomitable person
砥石(ㄉㄧˇ ㄕˊ)
a fine grindstone; a whetstone

【砧】 3850
ㄓㄣ jen zhēn
1. a rock with a flat top on which the laundry is beaten and washed; an anvil
2. an ancient instrument for torture
砧板(ㄓㄣ ㄅㄢˇ)
a chopping block
砧斧(ㄓㄣ ㄈㄨˇ)
ancient weapons or instruments for killing
砧骨(ㄓㄣ ㄍㄨˇ)
(anatomy) an incus
砧鑕(ㄓㄣ ㄓˋ)
an ancient instrument for torture
砧杵(ㄓㄣ ㄔㄨˇ)
the stone block and wooden club for laundering clothes; anvil and pestle

【砭】 3851
ㄅㄧㄢ bian biān
1. a stone probe; a stone needle used in acupuncture in ancient China
2. to advise or exhort; to admonish
3. to pierce
砭骨(ㄅㄧㄢ ㄍㄨˇ)
(literally) to pierce the bone —extremely painful or cold
砭灸(ㄅㄧㄢ ㄐㄧㄡˇ)
to acupuncture and cauterize
砭人肌骨(ㄅㄧㄢ ㄖㄣˊ ㄐㄧ ㄍㄨˇ)
(said of cold, pain, etc.) bone-piercing

【砰】 3852
ㄆㄥ peng pēng
1. the sound of crashing stones
2. Bang! a loud sound; deafening: 他砰的一聲把門關上。He shut the door with a bang.
砰磅(ㄆㄥ ㄆㄤ)
① Bing-bang!—the sound of falling stones ② the roars of raging water
砰砰(ㄆㄥ ㄆㄥ)
① the sound of drumbeats ② Bang! Bang!—the sound of gunfire
砰磷(ㄆㄥ ㄌㄧㄣˊ)
① high and steep ② thunder
砰訇(ㄆㄥ ㄏㄨㄥ)
loud or deafening
砰然(ㄆㄥ ㄖㄢˊ)
loud; deafening; roaring; banging

【砝】 3853
ㄈㄚˊ far fá
standard weights used in scales; steelyard weights
砝碼(兒)(ㄈㄚˊ ·ㄇㄚ(ㄦ))
standard weights used in scales; steelyard weights

【破】 3854
ㄆㄛˋ poh pò
1. to break
2. dilapidated; ruined; destroyed
3. to defeat; to beat (the enemy); to capture (enemy territory)
4. to expose; exposed; to lay bare; (to see) through
5. to spend (money, etc.)
6. to solve or break (a murder case, etc.); to analyze
7. to come to an end
8. paltry
破敗(ㄆㄛˋ ㄅㄞˋ)
destroyed; ruined; dilapidated; beaten: 這棟房子已經破敗不堪。The house is dilapidated.
破壁飛去(ㄆㄛˋ ㄅㄧˋ ㄈㄟ ㄑㄩˋ)
to rocket into fame and fortune; to become wealthy and influential all of a sudden
破冰船(ㄆㄛˋ ㄅㄧㄥ ㄔㄨㄢˊ)
an icebreaker
破布(ㄆㄛˋ ㄅㄨˋ)
rags
破破爛爛(ㄆㄛˋ ·ㄆㄛ ㄌㄢˋ ㄌㄢˋ)
tattered; tumble-down; dilapidated: 他穿着破破爛爛的衣服。He is dressed in tatters.
破盤(ㄆㄛˋ ㄆㄢˊ)
① broken dishes ② the baring of a secret or plot
破片(ㄆㄛˋ ㄆㄧㄢˋ)
fragments; broken pieces
破門(ㄆㄛˋ ㄇㄣˊ)
excommunication
破門而入(ㄆㄛˋ ㄇㄣˊ ㄦˊ ㄖㄨˋ)
to break into a house; to force one's way into a house
破謎兒(ㄆㄛˋ ㄇㄧˊㄦ)
to solve a riddle
破滅(ㄆㄛˋ ㄇㄧㄝˋ)
to come to nil; ruined or destroyed; to fall through; to be shattered; to disillusion: 我們的希望破滅了。Our hopes were shattered.
破廟(ㄆㄛˋ ㄇㄧㄠˋ)
a dilapidated temple
破費(ㄆㄛˋ ·ㄈㄟ)

to spend money; to go to some expense; (used in polite conversation) to waste your money

破釜沈舟(ㄆㄛˋ ㄈㄨˇ ㄔㄣˊ ㄓㄡ)
(literally) to destroy the cooking pots and scuttle the ships—no turning back; determined; to cut off all means of retreat 參看「沈舟破釜」

破腹(ㄆㄛˋ ㄈㄨˋ)
diarrhea

破膽(ㄆㄛˋ ㄉㄢˇ)
to be scared out of one's wits; very frightened

破敵(ㄆㄛˋ ㄉㄧˊ)
to defeat the enemy (or one's opponents)

破的(ㄆㄛˋ ㄉㄧˋ)
to the point; to hit the bull's eye; to hit the nail on the head

破題(ㄆㄛˋ ㄊㄧˊ)
to analyze the meaning of the title or subject (of a composition) in the first two sentences of their writings by writers of the eight-legged essays (八股文) in the Ming and Ching dynasties

破題兒第一遭(ㄆㄛˋ ㄊㄧˊㄦ ㄉㄧˋ ㄧ ㄗㄠ)
for the first time

破體字(ㄆㄛˋ ㄊㄧˇ ㄗˋ)
a character written in an unorthodox form

破涕爲笑(ㄆㄛˋ ㄊㄧˋ ㄨㄟˊ ㄒㄧㄠˋ)
to break into laughter while still crying (upon learning of cheering news, etc.); to smile through tears

破天荒(ㄆㄛˋ ㄊㄧㄢ ㄏㄨㄤ)
never before—for the first time; unprecedented; history-making

破土(ㄆㄛˋ ㄊㄨˇ)
① to break the ground (for a building project) ②(said of a seedling) to break through the soil

破土典禮(ㄆㄛˋ ㄊㄨˇ ㄉㄧㄢˇ ㄌㄧˇ)
a ground-breaking ceremony

破爛兒(ㄆㄛˋ ㄌㄚˋㄦ)
rags and rubbish; wastes or refuse; junk

破浪(ㄆㄛˋ ㄌㄤˋ)
(literally) to break the waves—to set sail; to embark on a sea voyage

破例(ㄆㄛˋ ㄌㄧˋ)
to make an exception (to a rule, common practices, etc.); to break a rule

破裂(ㄆㄛˋ ㄌㄧㄝˋ)
① to end in a rupture; to break off; rupture; severance: 洪水導致水壩破裂。The flood led to the rupture of the dam. ② broken; cracked

破臉(ㄆㄛˋ ㄌㄧㄢˇ)
to quarrel openly; to turn against (an acquaintance or associate); to fall out: 我不願同朋友破臉。I don't like to fall out with my friends.

破落(ㄆㄛˋ ㄌㄨㄛˋ)
the decline (of wealth and position, etc.); to fall into reduced circumstances

破落戶(ㄆㄛˋ ㄌㄨㄛˋ ㄏㄨˋ)
① a fallen family ② rascals or vagrants coming from once wealthy and influential families

破格(ㄆㄛˋ ㄍㄜˊ)
exceptions to a rule or practice; to make an exception

破格錄用(ㄆㄛˋ ㄍㄜˊ ㄌㄨˋ ㄩㄥˋ)
to employ (usually a person of remarkable ability) in defiance of rules, practices, etc.

破瓜(ㄆㄛˋ ㄍㄨㄚ) or **破瓜之年**(ㄆㄛˋ ㄍㄨㄚ ㄓ ㄋㄧㄢˊ)
①(said of a girl) reaching 16 years of age ②to deflower a virgin ③(said of a man) 64 years of age

破罐子(ㄆㄛˋ ㄍㄨㄢˋ ˙ㄗ)
(literally) a broken vessel, jar, etc.—① an unchaste woman ② a person of poor health

破工夫(ㄆㄛˋ ㄍㄨㄥ ˙ㄈㄨ)
to take time

破口大罵(ㄆㄛˋ ㄎㄡˇ ㄉㄚˋ ㄇㄚˋ)
to abuse freely and loudly; to shout with abuse; to let loose a torrent of invective

破獲(ㄆㄛˋ ㄏㄨㄛˋ)
to break (into a secret hideout) and capture (criminals, loots, etc.); to uncover (a plot, criminal activities, etc.)

破壞(ㄆㄛˋ ㄏㄨㄞˋ)
to ruin; to destroy; to violate; to break

破壞名譽(ㄆㄛˋ ㄏㄨㄞˋ ㄇㄧㄥˊ ㄩˋ)
to ruin one's reputation; to libel; to slander

破壞力(ㄆㄛˋ ㄏㄨㄞˋ ㄌㄧˋ)
destructive power

破壞秩序(ㄆㄛˋ ㄏㄨㄞˋ ㄓˋ ㄒㄩˋ)
to cause damage or disruption to public order; the violation of public order

破壞中立(ㄆㄛˋ ㄏㄨㄞˋ ㄓㄨㄥ ㄌㄧˋ)
the violation of neutrality

破紀錄(ㄆㄛˋ ㄐㄧˋ ㄌㄨˋ)
to break a record; record-breaking; record-shattering

破家(ㄆㄛˋ ㄐㄧㄚ)
① to exhaust one's family property ② to ruin one's family

破戒(ㄆㄛˋ ㄐㄧㄝˋ)
①(usually said of monks, nuns, etc.) to break the rules; to break a religious precept ②to make an exception; to break one's vow

破舊(ㄆㄛˋ ㄐㄧㄡˋ)
shabby; worn-out; disreputable; dilapidated

破鏡重圓(ㄆㄛˋ ㄐㄧㄥˋ ㄔㄨㄥˊ ㄩㄢˊ)
(said of a divorced or separated couple) reunion and reconciliation

破鞋(ㄆㄛˋ ㄒㄧㄝˊ)
(literally) worn-out shoes—unlicensed prostitutes; loose women

破曉(ㄆㄛˋ ㄒㄧㄠˇ)
daybreak; dawn

破相(ㄆㄛˋ ㄒㄧㄤˋ)
①(said of facial features) to be marred by a scar, etc. ② to make a fool of oneself

破折號(ㄆㄛˋ ㄓㄜˊ ㄏㄠˋ)
a dash (a punctuation mark)

破綻(ㄆㄛˋ ˙ㄓㄢ)
a slip, flaw or weak point; a loophole: 他們的證詞破綻百出。Their testimony is full of flaws.

破竹之勢(ㄆㄛˋ ㄓㄨˊ ㄓ ㄕˋ)
overwhelming force; irresistible; able to overcome all

obstacles with great ease —as splitting a bamboo pole

破鈔(ㄆㄛˋ ㄔㄠˋ)or(ㄆㄛˋ ㄔㄠ)
to spend money; (in polite usage) to waste your money

破產(ㄆㄛˋ ㄔㄢˇ)
① bankruptcy; insolvency; to go bankrupt; to bankrupt; insolvent; to go bust: 胡亂的花費將使他破產。Foolish expenditures will bankrupt him. ② to come to naught; to fall through

破除(ㄆㄛˋ ㄔㄨˊ)
to eliminate; to get rid of

破除迷信(ㄆㄛˋ ㄔㄨˊ ㄇㄧˊ ㄒㄧㄣˋ)
to get rid of superstition

破船(ㄆㄛˋ ㄔㄨㄢˊ)
a broken-down ship

破船偏遇打頭風(ㄆㄛˋ ㄔㄨㄢˊ ㄆㄧㄢ ㄩˋ ㄉㄚˇ ㄊㄡˊ ㄈㄥ)
(literally) As luck would have it, a broken-down ship should encounter a headwind. —dogged by oil on the fire of misfortune

破身(ㄆㄛˋ ㄕㄣ)
the first sexual intercourse of a man or woman

破傷風(ㄆㄛˋ ㄕㄤ ㄈㄥ)
tetanus

破財(ㄆㄛˋ ㄘㄞˊ)
to lose money

破財消災(ㄆㄛˋ ㄘㄞˊ ㄒㄧㄠ ㄗㄞ)
to suffer unexpected financial losses and forestall calamities

破碎(ㄆㄛˋ ㄙㄨㄟˋ)
①broken (heart, hope, etc.) ②to come to pieces; to shatter

破損(ㄆㄛˋ ㄙㄨㄣˇ)
broken or damaged; ruined: 這棟房子已經破損了。This house has been damaged.

破案(ㄆㄛˋ ㄢˋ)
to break a criminal case; to solve a case

破衣裳(ㄆㄛˋ ㄧ ˙ㄕㄤ)or 破衣(ㄆㄛˋ ㄧ)
rags; ragged garments or clothing: 他穿著破衣。He was clad in rags.

破顏(ㄆㄛˋ ㄧㄢˊ)
to break into a smile

破音字(ㄆㄛˋ ㄧㄣ ㄗˋ)or 破字(ㄆㄛˋ ㄗˋ) or 破音(ㄆㄛˋ ㄧㄣ)
a character which is not pronounced in the usual way because of a different meaning it carries

【砷】 3855 ㄕㄣ shen shēn
arsenic

砷化氫(ㄕㄣ ㄏㄨㄚˋ ㄑㄧㄥ)
hydrogen arsenide

【砸】 3856 ㄗㄚˊ tzar zá
1. to crash and break; to squash; to smash; to knock; to pound: 玻璃杯掉在地板上砸了。The glass smashed on the floor.
2. to ruin; to fail; to be bungled: 他把事情搞砸了。The job was bungled by him.
3. to mash; to beat to a pulp

砸飯碗(ㄗㄚˊ ㄈㄢˋ ㄨㄢˇ)
(literally) to break one's rice bowl—to lose one's job

砸了(ㄗㄚˊ ˙ㄌㄜ)
① to knock and break: 她把茶壺砸了。She dropped the teapot and broke it. ② to fail; to bungle; busted

砸爛(ㄗㄚˊ ㄌㄢˋ)
to crush to a mash

砸鍋(ㄗㄚˊ ㄍㄨㄛ)
to fail in a task or an attempt

砸傷(ㄗㄚˊ ㄕㄤ)
to be injured by a crashing object

砸死(ㄗㄚˊ ㄙˇ)
① to be crushed to death ② (used comically) to hand a person an impossible task to perform

砸碎(ㄗㄚˊ ㄙㄨㄟˋ)
to break to pieces; to smash

【砮】 3857 ㄋㄨˇ nuu nǔ
flint arrowheads

【砦】 3858 ㄓㄞˋ jay zhài
a stockade; a military outpost

【砲】 3859 ㄆㄠˋ paw pào
a simplified form of 礮 —artillery

砲艦(ㄆㄠˋ ㄐㄧㄢˋ)
a gunboat

六畫

【硃】 3860 ㄓㄨ ju zhū
1. vermilion
2. imperial (the signature and instructions of an emperor were written in red)

硃筆(ㄓㄨ ㄅㄧˇ)
a vermilion writing brush

硃批(ㄓㄨ ㄆㄧ)
an imperial rescript

硃卷(ㄓㄨ ㄐㄩㄢˋ)
the red-ink copy of test papers used in civil service examinations in former times

硃砂(ㄓㄨ ㄕㄚ)
cinnabar

硃砂痣(ㄓㄨ ㄕㄚ ㄓˋ)
a red mole

硃諭(ㄓㄨ ㄩˋ)or 硃批諭旨(ㄓㄨ ㄆㄧ ㄩˋ ㄓˇ)
imperial decrees, mandates, instructions, etc.

【硌】 3861 ㄍㄜˋ geh gè
damage or injuries caused by being squeezed or pressed on a rough surface

硌得慌(ㄍㄜˋ ˙ㄉㄜ ˙ㄏㄨㄤ)
to feel uncomfortable over some bumpy surface

【硒】 3862 ㄒㄧ shi xī
selenium (Se)

【硫】 3863 ㄌㄧㄡˊ liou liú
sulphur, or sulfur

硫苦土(ㄌㄧㄡˊ ㄎㄨˇ ㄊㄨˇ)or 硫酸鎂(ㄌㄧㄡˊ ㄙㄨㄢ ㄇㄟˇ)
magnesium sulfate

硫化物(ㄌㄧㄡˊ ㄏㄨㄚˋ ㄨˋ)
a sulfide; a sulfuret

硫磺(ㄌㄧㄡˊ ㄏㄨㄤˊ)
sulphur, or sulfur; brimstone

硫磺島(ㄌㄧㄡˊ ㄏㄨㄤˊ ㄉㄠˇ)
Iwo Jima, one of the Volcano Islands

硫磺礦(ㄌㄧㄡˊ ㄏㄨㄤˊ ㄎㄨㄤˋ)
a sulfur or brimstone mine: 陽明山有豐富的硫磺礦。Yangmingshan is rich in sulfur mines.

硫磺泉(ㄌㄧㄡˊ ㄏㄨㄤˊ ㄑㄩㄢˊ)
a sulfur spring

硫酸(ㄌㄧㄡˊ ㄙㄨㄢ)
sulfuric acid

硫酸鎂(ㄌㄧㄡˊ ㄙㄨㄢ ㄇㄟˇ)
magnesium sulfate ($MgSO_4$)

硫酸銅(ㄌㄧㄡˊ ㄙㄨㄢ ㄊㄨㄥˊ)
cupric sulfate ($CuSO_4$)亦作「膽礬」

硫酸鈉(ㄌㄧㄡˊ ㄙㄨㄢ ㄋㄚˋ)
sodium sulfate (Na_2SO_4)

硫酸化合物(ㄌㄧㄡˊ ㄙㄨㄢ ㄏㄨㄚˋ ㄏㄜˊ ㄨˋ)
sulfates

硫酸銨(ㄌㄧㄡˊ ㄙㄨㄢ ㄢ)
ammonium sulfate

硫酸鹽(ㄌㄧㄡˊ ㄙㄨㄢ ㄧㄢˊ)
sulfate

【研】 3864
(硏) ㄧㄢˊ yan yán

1. to go to the very source; to study; to investigate; to research; to examine; to search into carefully
2. to grind; to powder

研磨(ㄧㄢˊ ㄇㄛˊ)
①to grind; to pestle ②to abrade; to polish

研墨(ㄧㄢˊ ㄇㄛˋ)
to rub an ink stick on an ink-slab (for brush writing)

研討(ㄧㄢˊ ㄊㄠˇ)
to study and discuss; to investigate and research

研討會(ㄧㄢˊ ㄊㄠˇ ㄏㄨㄟˋ)
a study group; a workshop; a seminar; a symposium

研覈(ㄧㄢˊ ㄏㄜˊ)
to examine with great care

研究(ㄧㄢˊ ㄐㄧㄡˋ)
to study and research; studies; researches; to go to the very source of: 他的研究工作很成功。His researches have been successful.

研究費(ㄧㄢˊ ㄐㄧㄡˋ ㄈㄟˋ)
research funds; research expenditure

研究計畫(ㄧㄢˊ ㄐㄧㄡˋ ㄐㄧˋ ㄏㄨㄚˋ)
a research project

研究室(ㄧㄢˊ ㄐㄧㄡˋ ㄕˋ)
a research laboratory; a research chamber

研究生(ㄧㄢˊ ㄐㄧㄡˋ ㄕㄥ)
a graduate student

研究所(ㄧㄢˊ ㄐㄧㄡˋ ㄙㄨㄛˇ)
a research laboratory; a research institute; a graduate school

研究員(ㄧㄢˊ ㄐㄧㄡˋ ㄩㄢˊ)
a researcher; a research worker; a research fellow: 研究員正在研究此問題。Research workers are examining the problem.

研究院(ㄧㄢˊ ㄐㄧㄡˋ ㄩㄢˋ)
a research institute

研求(ㄧㄢˊ ㄑㄧㄡˊ)
to research and examine; to study; to examine into; to explore

研習(ㄧㄢˊ ㄒㄧˊ)
to research and study; to examine and study

研習會(ㄧㄢˊ ㄒㄧˊ ㄏㄨㄟˋ)
a study meeting or conference; a symposium; a seminar; a workshop

研製(ㄧㄢˊ ㄓˋ)
①to prepare; to manufacture; to develop ②(Chinese medicine) to prepare medicinal powder by grinding

研鑽(ㄧㄢˊ ㄗㄨㄢ)
to examine into; to closely study and investigate; to research into

研碎(ㄧㄢˊ ㄙㄨㄟˋ)
to grind to pieces: 他們將咖啡豆研碎。They grind coffee beans to pieces.

七畫

【硜】 3865
ㄎㄥ keng kēng

the sound of pebbles or stones rubbing or knocking together

硜硜(ㄎㄥ ㄎㄥ)
stubborn; obstinate

硜硜自守(ㄎㄥ ㄎㄥ ㄗˋ ㄕㄡˇ)
shallow and obstinate

【硬】 3866
ㄧㄥˋ yinq yìng

1. hard; stiff; solid; firm
2. stiff; rigid; inflexible; obstinate; very insistent; unyielding
3. to harden; to solidify; to stiffen
4. by force; to manage to do something in a forced manner
5. (said of quality) good
6. able (person)

硬玻璃(ㄧㄥˋ ㄅㄛ ·ㄌㄧ)
hard glass

硬幫幫(ㄧㄥˋ ㄅㄤ ㄅㄤ)
①hard and firm ②rigid and inflexible; stiff: 這些規則硬幫幫的。The rules are rigid and inflexible.

硬逼(ㄧㄥˋ ㄅㄧ)
to compel or force; to press hard; hard-pressed

硬幣(ㄧㄥˋ ㄅㄧˋ)
hard money (as opposed to paper money); coins; specie

硬碰硬(ㄧㄥˋ ㄆㄥˋ ㄧㄥˋ)
①to meet force with force ②100 per cent (genuine) ③extremely rigid or inflexible; fixed ④(said of a job) tough; painstaking：這是硬碰硬的差事。This is an extremely tough job.

硬煤(ㄧㄥˋ ㄇㄟˊ)
hard coal; anthracite

硬木(ㄧㄥˋ ㄇㄨˋ)
hardwood

硬度(ㄧㄥˋ ㄉㄨˋ)
hardness: 這塊板子的硬度不夠。The board is not hard enough.

硬頭貨(ㄧㄥˋ ㄊㄡˊ ㄏㄨㄛˋ)
①foods not easily digested ②money (especially hard cash)

硬體(ㄧㄥˋ ㄊㄧˇ)
(computers) hardware

硬挺(ㄧㄥˋ ㄊㄧㄥˇ)
to endure with one's best; to put up with all one's might; to stick out

硬來(ㄧㄥˋ ㄌㄞˊ)
to do something forcibly: 他做事常常硬來。He often does things forcibly.

硬朗(ㄧㄥˋ ·ㄌㄤ)
(said of the aged) sturdy and strong: 他七十多了，身體還挺硬朗的。He's over seventy but still sturdy and strong.

硬裏子(ㄧㄥˋ ㄌㄧˇ ·ㄗ)
a good supporting player, actor, or actress

硬領子(ㄧㄥˋ ㄌㄧㄥˇ ·ㄗ)
a hard collar starched or lined with celluloid

硬幹(ㄧㄥˋ ㄍㄢˋ)
to do something in disregard of obstacles

硬骨頭(ㄧㄥˋ ㄍㄨˇ ·ㄊㄡ)
a hard bone—an incorrupt-

〔石部〕

ible person; a person of moral fortitude; a dauntless, unyielding person

硬漢(ㄧㄥˋ ㄏㄢˋ)
a hardened man; a courageous man; a man of fortitude

硬話(ㄧㄥˋ ㄏㄨㄚˋ)
a defiant talk; a big talk

硬化(ㄧㄥˋ ㄏㄨㄚˋ)
①to harden; to stiffen; to solidify ②(medicine) sclerosis; cirrhosis

硬氣(ㄧㄥˋ ˙ㄑㄧ)
①to feel no qualm in the knowledge that one is on the side of righteousness ②firm and manly; sportsmanlike

硬橡皮(ㄧㄥˋ ㄒㄧㄤˋ ㄆㄧˊ)
ebonite; hard rubber

硬性(ㄧㄥˋ ㄒㄧㄥˋ)
①a stubborn or obstinate disposition ②(said of materials) hardness

硬性規定(ㄧㄥˋ ㄒㄧㄥˋ ㄍㄨㄟ ㄉㄧㄥˋ)
rigid and inflexible ruling; hard-and-fast rules

硬脂(ㄧㄥˋ ㄓ)
stearin

硬脂酸(ㄧㄥˋ ㄓ ㄙㄨㄢ)
stearic acid

硬紙板(ㄧㄥˋ ㄓˇ ㄅㄢˇ)
cardboard

硬著頭皮(ㄧㄥˋ ˙ㄓㄜ ㄊㄡˊ ㄆㄧˊ)
to do something against one's will; to force oneself to: 我硬着頭皮去見她。I forced myself to see her.

硬著心(ㄧㄥˋ ˙ㄓㄜ ㄒㄧㄣ)
to steel one's heart

硬仗(ㄧㄥˋ ㄓㄤˋ)
a showdown battle; a formidable task; a fierce fight; an all-out battle

硬撐(ㄧㄥˋ ㄔㄥ)
to hold on firmly despite extreme adversity, pain, etc.; to keep on doing something without regard to one's own strength

硬石膏(ㄧㄥˋ ㄕˊ ㄍㄠ)
anhydrite

硬是(ㄧㄥˋ ㄕˋ)
(dialect)①actually; really ②just; simply

硬手(ㄧㄥˋ ㄕㄡˇ)
an expert; an efficient or capable person

硬說(ㄧㄥˋ ㄕㄨㄛ)
to insist on saying; to assert; to stand on one's views: 他硬說自己的判斷是對的。He obstinately asserted that his judgment was right.

硬水(ㄧㄥˋ ㄕㄨㄟˇ)
hard water

硬彩(ㄧㄥˋ ㄘㄞˇ)
deep or dark colors on porcelain

硬要(ㄧㄥˋ ㄧㄠˋ)
to want or demand insistently: 他們硬要我收下這些禮物。They demanded insistently that I accept these gifts.

硬文學(ㄧㄥˋ ㄨㄣˊ ㄒㄩㄝˊ)
(literally) hard literature—academic writings; literature with a bold and raw style that stirs up the inner feelings or fighting spirit of the readers

硬玉(ㄧㄥˋ ㄩˋ)
jadeite

【硝】 3867 ㄒㄧㄠ shiau xiāo

1. niter; saltpeter
2. to tan leather

硝化(ㄒㄧㄠ ㄏㄨㄚˋ)
nitration

硝化甘油(ㄒㄧㄠ ㄏㄨㄚˋ ㄍㄢ ㄧㄡˊ)
nitroglycerine

硝基(ㄒㄧㄠ ㄐㄧ)
nitro

硝鏹水(ㄒㄧㄠ ㄑㄧㄤˊ ㄕㄨㄟˇ)or 硝酸(ㄒㄧㄠ ㄙㄨㄢ)
nitric acid

硝石(ㄒㄧㄠ ㄕˊ)
saltpeter, or niter

硝酸鈉(ㄒㄧㄠ ㄙㄨㄢ ㄋㄚˋ)
sodium nitrate

硝酸鉀(ㄒㄧㄠ ㄙㄨㄢ ㄐㄧㄚˇ)
potassium nitrate

硝酸鹽(ㄒㄧㄠ ㄙㄨㄢ ㄧㄢˊ)
nitrate

【硯】 3868 ㄧㄢˋ yann yàn

an inkstone

硯臺(ㄧㄢˋ ˙ㄊㄞ)
an ink-slab; an inkstone

硯田(ㄧㄢˋ ㄊㄧㄢˊ)
(literally) the ink-slab farm—writing as a means of making a living

硯耕(ㄧㄢˋ ㄍㄥ)
(literally) to plough the field of the ink-slab—to live by writing

硯盒(ㄧㄢˋ ㄏㄜˊ)or 硯室(ㄧㄢˋ ㄕˋ)
a case for an ink-slab

硯兄(ㄧㄢˋ ㄒㄩㄥ)
a polite reference to fellow students who are older than oneself

硯池(ㄧㄢˋ ㄔˊ)
①the depression for water on an ink-slab ②a pool for washing the ink-slab

硯友(ㄧㄢˋ ㄧㄡˇ)
fellow students; classmates

硯瓦(ㄧㄢˋ ㄨㄚˇ)
an ink-slab

【硭】 3869 ㄇㄤˊ mang máng

sodium sulphate

硭硝(ㄇㄤˊ ㄒㄧㄠ)
sodium sulphate

【确】 3870 ㄑㄩㄝˋ chiueh què

1. hard stone
2. (said of land) barren; unproductive

八畫

【硎】 3871 ㄒㄧㄥˊ shyng xíng

a whetstone; a grindstone

【硼】 3872 1. ㄆㄥˊ perng péng

1. (chemistry) boron
2. borax

硼化物(ㄆㄥˊ ㄏㄨㄚˋ ㄨˋ)
boride

硼砂(ㄆㄥˊ ㄕㄚ)
borax

硼酸(ㄆㄥˊ ㄙㄨㄢ)
boric acid

硼酸綿(ㄆㄥˊ ㄙㄨㄢ ㄇㄧㄢˊ)
cotton immersed in boric acid

硼酸鹽(ㄆㄥˊ ㄙㄨㄢ ㄧㄢˊ)
borate

【硼】 3872 2. ㄆㄥ peng pēng

the sound of splashing

硼硼(ㄆㄥ ㄆㄥ)
the sound of water splashing or sloshing

【碌】 3873 ㄌㄨˋ luh lù

1. mediocre; common
2. busy; occupied
3. a kind of stone roller

碌碡(ㄌㄨˋ ㄉㄨˊ)
a kind of stone roller

碌碌(ㄌㄨˋ ㄌㄨˋ)
① mediocre; commonplace; incompetent: 他是個碌碌無能的辦事員。He is an incompetent clerk. ② busy; occupied: 他整天忙忙碌碌的。He is busy going about his work all day long. ③ the color of jade

【碑】 3874
ㄅㄟ bei bēi

a stone tablet

碑版(ㄅㄟ ㄅㄢˇ)
stone tablets; steles

碑銘(ㄅㄟ ㄇㄧㄥˊ)
a part of an inscription on a tablet, usually in rhyme

碑帖(ㄅㄟ ㄊㄧㄝˋ)
the rubbings of inscriptions from stone tablets used as calligraphic models

碑亭(ㄅㄟ ㄊㄧㄥˊ)
a pavilion built over a stone tablet

碑林(ㄅㄟ ㄌㄧㄣˊ)
a large collection of stone tablets, especially that of Sian (西安) which includes more than 600 items

碑記(ㄅㄟ ㄐㄧˋ)
an inscriptional record; an inscription

碑碣(ㄅㄟ ㄐㄧㄝˊ)
stone tablets; steles

碑誌(ㄅㄟ ㄓˋ)
an inscription on a tablet

碑額(ㄅㄟ ㄜˊ)
the head of a stone tablet; the top part of a tablet

碑陰(ㄅㄟ ㄧㄣ)
the back of a stone tablet

碑文(ㄅㄟ ㄨㄣˊ)
an inscription on a tablet

【碎】 3875
ㄙㄨㄟˋ suey suì

1. broken; smashed; torn; to break to pieces; to smash
2. trivial; unimportant; trifling
3. garrulous; gabby

碎冰斧(ㄙㄨㄟˋ ㄅㄧㄥ ㄈㄨˇ)
an ice ax

碎冰船(ㄙㄨㄟˋ ㄅㄧㄥ ㄔㄨㄢˊ)
an icebreaker

碎步兒(ㄙㄨㄟˋ ㄅㄨˋㄦ)
short quick steps

碎片(ㄙㄨㄟˋ ㄆㄧㄢˋ)
fragments; splinters; shreds; chips: 鏡子破成碎片。The mirror broke into splinters.

碎煤(ㄙㄨㄟˋ ㄇㄟˊ)
slack coal

碎密(ㄙㄨㄟˋ ㄇㄧˋ)
complicated and disorderly

碎紛紛(ㄙㄨㄟˋ ㄈㄣ ㄈㄣ)
broken to pieces

碎爛(ㄙㄨㄟˋ ㄌㄢˋ)
smashed or broken beyond recognition

碎裂(ㄙㄨㄟˋ ㄌㄧㄝˋ)
torn or broken to pieces

碎工(ㄙㄨㄟˋ ㄍㄨㄥ)
odd jobs

碎貨(ㄙㄨㄟˋ ㄏㄨㄛˋ)
retail goods

碎金(ㄙㄨㄟˋ ㄐㄧㄣ)
brief literary masterpieces

碎屑(ㄙㄨㄟˋ ㄒㄧㄝˋ)
very small broken pieces

碎小(ㄙㄨㄟˋ ㄒㄧㄠˇ)
one's dependents

碎屍萬段(ㄙㄨㄟˋ ㄕ ㄨㄢˋ ㄉㄨㄢˋ)
(literally) to tear the body to thousands of pieces—to inflict severe punishment

碎石(ㄙㄨㄟˋ ㄕˊ)
(construction) macadam; crushed stones; broken stones

碎石路(ㄙㄨㄟˋ ㄕˊ ㄌㄨˋ)
a macadam pavement; a gravel road; a broken stone road

碎石機(ㄙㄨㄟˋ ㄕˊ ㄐㄧ)
a crusher; a stone breaker

碎石子(ㄙㄨㄟˋ ㄕˊ ㄗˇ)
gravel; macadam

碎嘴子(ㄙㄨㄟˋ ㄗㄨㄟˇ ˙ㄗ)
① a chatterbox; a garrulous person ② to chatter; to talk too much; to prate

碎瓷(ㄙㄨㄟˋ ㄘˊ)
the crackleware; the porcelainware with a smashed-ice design

碎銀(ㄙㄨㄟˋ ㄧㄣˊ)
small bits of silver

碎務(ㄙㄨㄟˋ ㄨˋ)
chores

碎玉(ㄙㄨㄟˋ ㄩˋ)
① broken jade ② beautiful white teeth

【碉】 3876
ㄉㄧㄠ diau diāo

a stone chamber

碉堡(ㄉㄧㄠ ㄅㄠˇ)
a fort; a pillbox; a blockhouse

【碓】 3877
ㄉㄨㄟˋ duey duì

a pestle (for husking grain)

碓房(ㄉㄨㄟˋ ㄈㄤˊ)
an establishment for hulling grain

碓臼(ㄉㄨㄟˋ ㄐㄧㄡˋ)
pestles and mortars

【碇】 3878
ㄉㄧㄥˋ dinq dìng

an anchor (for a ship)

【碰】 3879
(掽) ㄆㄥˋ penq pèng

1. to collide; to hit; to touch; to bump: 我用力碰他。I hit hard against him.
2. to meet unexpectedly; to run into: 我沒碰着她。I didn't meet her.
3. to take one's chance: 我要去那兒碰碰機會。I want to go there to take a chance.

碰杯(ㄆㄥˋ ㄅㄟ)
to clink glasses

碰壁(ㄆㄥˋ ㄅㄧˋ)
① to meet rejection ② to encounter difficulties; to run into a blind alley

碰面(ㄆㄥˋ ㄇㄧㄢˋ)
to meet; to come face to face

碰翻(ㄆㄥˋ ㄈㄢ)
to tip over after being hit by something

碰倒(ㄆㄥˋ ㄉㄠˇ)
to tumble down after being hit by something

碰到(ㄆㄥˋ ㄉㄠˋ)
① to meet someone unexpectedly ② to touch something

碰釘子(ㄆㄥˋ ㄉㄧㄥ ˙ㄗ)
to meet rejection; to be rebuffed; to be rebuked

碰頭(ㄆㄥˋ ㄊㄡˊ)
① to meet someone; to rendezvous ② to have one's head hit accidentally

碰壞(ㄆㄥˋ ㄏㄨㄞˋ)

to be damaged by collision
碰見(ㄆㄥˋ ㄐㄧㄢˋ)
to meet or encounter someone unexpectedly; to run into
碰巧(ㄆㄥˋ ㄑㄧㄠˇ)
by coincidence; accidentally; to happen to: 我碰巧在公車上遇見她。I happened to meet her in the bus.
碰撞(ㄆㄥˋ ㄓㄨㄤˋ)
to hit; to run into: 一輛巴士從後面碰撞了一部汽車。A bus ran into a car from behind.
碰傷(ㄆㄥˋ ㄕㄤ)
to be injured or damaged after being hit by something
碰一鼻子灰(ㄆㄥˋ ㄧˋ ㄅㄧˊ ·ㄗ ㄏㄨㄟ)
to meet rejection; to meet with a rebuff
碰運氣(ㄆㄥˋ ㄩㄣˋ ·ㄑㄧ)
① to try one's luck ② sheer luck; a lucky stroke; a fluke

【碚】 3880 ㄅㄟˋ bey bèi
1. as in 蝦蟆碚—a place in Hupeh
2. as in 碚礧—a bud

【碘】 3881 ㄉㄧㄢˇ dean diǎn
iodine
碘化物(ㄉㄧㄢˇ ㄏㄨㄚˋ ㄨˋ)
an iodide
碘酒(ㄉㄧㄢˇ ㄐㄧㄡˇ) or 碘酊(ㄉㄧㄢˇ ㄉㄧㄥ)
iodine tincture: 他在傷口上擦些碘酒。He applied some iodine tincture on the wound.
碘酸(ㄉㄧㄢˇ ㄙㄨㄢ)
iodic acid
碘銀礦(ㄉㄧㄢˇ ㄧㄣˊ ㄎㄨㄤˋ)
iodyrite

【碏】 3882 ㄑㄩㄝˋ chiueh què
(said of stone) many-colored

【碡】 3883 ㄉㄨˊ dwu dú
a kind of stone roller

【碁】 3884 (棋)ㄑㄧˊ chyi qí
1. any Oriental game played on a checkered board, like Chinese chess, *go*, etc.
2. any piece used in the game of chess

【碍】 3885 ㄞˋ ay ài
a simplified form of 礙—to obstruct; to hinder: 無知爲進步之障礙。Ignorance is an obstruction to progress.

【碗】 3886 (盌、椀) ㄨㄢˇ woan wǎn
a bowl (especially a small one): 他把碗打破了。He broke his bowl.
碗碟(ㄨㄢˇ ㄉㄧㄝˊ)
bowls and dishes
碗櫃(ㄨㄢˇ ㄍㄨㄟˋ) or 碗碟櫃(ㄨㄢˇ ㄉㄧㄝˊ ㄍㄨㄟˋ)
a cupboard
碗筷(ㄨㄢˇ ㄎㄨㄞˋ)
bowls and chopsticks

九畫

【碧】 3887 ㄅㄧˋ bih bì
1. green; blue; verdant; emerald green
2. jasper; emerald
碧桃(ㄅㄧˋ ㄊㄠˊ)
a kind of peach tree that does not bear fruit 亦作「千葉桃」
碧潭(ㄅㄧˋ ㄊㄢˊ)
the Green Lake(in suburban Taipei,Taiwan)
碧落(ㄅㄧˋ ㄌㄨㄛˋ)
the sky; the blue realm
碧綠(ㄅㄧˋ ㄌㄩˋ)
verdant; emerald green: 田野長滿碧綠的青草。The field was covered with verdant grass.
碧空(ㄅㄧˋ ㄎㄨㄥ)
a blue sky; an azure sky
碧海青天(ㄅㄧˋ ㄏㄞˇ ㄑㄧㄥ ㄊㄧㄢ)
the emerald sea under the blue sky
碧漢(ㄅㄧˋ ㄏㄢˋ)
a blue sky; an azure sky
碧血(ㄅㄧˋ ㄒㄧㄝˇ)or(ㄅㄧˋ ㄒㄩㄝˋ)
bloodshed for patriotism or loyalty, from the legend of Chang Hung (萇弘) of the Chou Dynasty whose blood turned to jasper three years after his death in battle
碧血丹心(ㄅㄧˋ ㄒㄧㄝˇ ㄉㄢ ㄒㄧㄣ)or(ㄅㄧˋ ㄒㄩㄝˋ ㄉㄢ ㄒㄧㄣ)
deep patriotism
碧水(ㄅㄧˋ ㄕㄨㄟˇ)
blue waters
碧草(ㄅㄧˋ ㄘㄠˇ)
verdant grass; green grass
碧草如茵(ㄅㄧˋ ㄘㄠˇ ㄖㄨˊ ㄧㄣ)
The expanse of verdant grass seems like a pleasant mat. 或a carpet of green grass
碧眼兒(ㄅㄧˋ ㄧㄚˇㄦ)
(literally) men with blue eyes—Westerners
碧瑤(ㄅㄧˋ ㄧㄠˊ)
Baguio, the Philippines
碧眼(ㄅㄧˋ ㄧㄢˇ)
blue-eyed
碧瓦(ㄅㄧˋ ㄨㄚˇ)
emerald green glazed tiles
碧玉(ㄅㄧˋ ㄩˋ)
jasper; emerald
碧雲寺(ㄅㄧˋ ㄩㄣˊ ㄙˋ)
a famed Buddhist temple in the Western Hills(西山)near Peking

【碣】 3888 ㄐㄧㄝˊ jye jié
a stone tablet (especially one with a round outline)

【碩】 3889 ㄕˊ shyr shí (語音 ㄕㄨㄛˋ shuoh shuò)
great; large
碩大無朋(ㄕˊ ㄉㄚˋ ㄨˊ ㄆㄥˊ)
unequaled in huge size; mammoth; gigantic
碩老(ㄕˊ ㄌㄠˇ)
a learned elder; an old venerable scholar
碩果僅存(ㄕˊ ㄍㄨㄛˇ ㄐㄧㄣˇ ㄘㄨㄣˊ)
the only remaining of the great; the only one of its kind to have survived; the rare survival
碩學通儒(ㄕˊ ㄒㄩㄝˊ ㄊㄨㄥ ㄖㄨˊ)or 碩學鴻儒(ㄕˊ ㄒㄩㄝˊ ㄏㄨㄥˊ ㄖㄨˊ)
an erudite and wise scholar
碩士
①(ㄕˊ ㄕˋ) a wise man
②(ㄕㄨㄛˋ ㄕˋ) a holder of the master's degree
碩儒(ㄕˊ ㄖㄨˊ)
a great Confucian scholar; a great scholar
碩言(ㄕˊ ㄧㄢˊ)
boastful talks; grand words
碩彥(ㄕˊ ㄧㄢˋ)

a man of great talent; a learned scholar

碩望(ㄕˋ ㄨㄤˋ)

a much respected man; a man of great fame

【碳】 3890
ㄊㄢˋ tann tàn

carbon 亦作「炭」

碳化(ㄊㄢˋ ㄏㄨㄚˋ)

to carbonize; to carbonate; carbonization

碳化物(ㄊㄢˋ ㄏㄨㄚˋ ㄨˋ)

carbide

碳水化合物(ㄊㄢˋ ㄕㄨㄟˇ ㄏㄨㄚˋ ㄏㄜˊ ㄨˋ)

carbohydrate

碳酸(ㄊㄢˋ ㄙㄨㄢ)

carbonic acid

碳酸鈉(ㄊㄢˋ ㄙㄨㄢ ㄋㄚˋ)

sodium carbonate

碳酸鈣(ㄊㄢˋ ㄙㄨㄢ ㄍㄞˋ)

calcium carbonate

碳酸氣(ㄊㄢˋ ㄙㄨㄢ ㄑㄧˋ)

carbonic-acid gas; carbon dioxide 亦作「二氧化碳」

碳酸中毒(ㄊㄢˋ ㄙㄨㄢ ㄓㄨㄥˋ ㄉㄨˊ)

poisoning from carbonic acid

【碴】 3891
ㄔㄚˊ char chá

1. chips, fragments or splinters (of glass, china, etc.)
2. to be cut (by broken glass, china, etc.)

碴兒(ㄔㄚˊㄦ)

① chips, fragments or splinters(of glass, china, etc.) ② the cause of a trouble; a quarrel: 別找他的碴兒。Do not pick a quarrel with him.

【碟】 3892
ㄉㄧㄝˊ dye dié

a dish or plate (especially a small one)

碟兒(ㄉㄧㄝˊㄦ)or 碟子(ㄉㄧㄝˊ ·ㄗ)

a dish or plate (especially a small one)

碟影片(ㄉㄧㄝˊ ㄧㄥˇ ㄆㄧㄢˋ)

a videodisc

碟影機(ㄉㄧㄝˊ ㄧㄥˇ ㄐㄧ)

a videodisc player

十畫

【確】 3893
ㄑㄩㄝˋ chiueh què

1. sure; certain; secure; real; true; valid: 我確信他會來。I am sure that he will come.
2. firm; firmly

確保(ㄑㄩㄝˋ ㄅㄠˇ)

to secure; to insure; to be sure to

確非(ㄑㄩㄝˋ ㄈㄟ)

actually not; really not; truly not

確否待考(ㄑㄩㄝˋ ㄈㄡˇ ㄉㄞˋ ㄎㄠˇ)or 確否待查(ㄑㄩㄝˋ ㄈㄡˇ ㄉㄞˋ ㄔㄚˊ)

Whether it's true or not remains to be verified.

確當(ㄑㄩㄝˋ ㄉㄤˋ)

fitting; proper and correct

確定(ㄑㄩㄝˋ ㄉㄧㄥˋ)

① to decide; to fix; to settle; to determine ② certain; sure; definite

確立(ㄑㄩㄝˋ ㄌㄧˋ)

to establish firmly

確論(ㄑㄩㄝˋ ㄌㄨㄣˋ)

a sound statement; a definite view

確耗(ㄑㄩㄝˋ ㄏㄠˋ)

reliable information

確乎(ㄑㄩㄝˋ ㄏㄨ)

certainly; surely; assuredly; undoubtedly

確據(ㄑㄩㄝˋ ㄐㄩˋ)

sure proof; reliable evidence

確切(ㄑㄩㄝˋ ㄑㄧㄝˋ)

valid; sound; right; accurate; exact; precise; clear and unambiguous: 你必須確切地執行命令。You must carry out an order exactly to the letter.

確信(ㄑㄩㄝˋ ㄒㄧㄣˋ)

to be convinced; to believe firmly; to be certain of: 我確信他會成功。I was certain of his succeeding.

確訊(ㄑㄩㄝˋ ㄒㄩㄣˋ)

reliable information; reliable report

確知(ㄑㄩㄝˋ ㄓ)

to know for sure: 你確知全部實情嗎? Do you know the whole truth for sure?

確證(ㄑㄩㄝˋ ㄓㄥˋ)

convincing proof; conclusive evidence; ironclad proof

確實(ㄑㄩㄝˋ ㄕˊ)

real; true; certain: 這確實是個好主意。This is really a good idea.

確實性(ㄑㄩㄝˋ ㄕˊ ㄒㄧㄥˋ)

reliability; authenticity

確然(ㄑㄩㄝˋ ㄖㄢˊ)

certain; sure; without doubt

確認(ㄑㄩㄝˋ ㄖㄣˋ)

to certify; to identify with certainty; to affirm; to confirm

確鑿(ㄑㄩㄝˋ ㄗㄨㄛˊ)

accurate; precise; beyond any doubt; authentic; conclusive; irrefutable: 你能提出確鑿證據嗎? Can you give me conclusive proof?

確有其事(ㄑㄩㄝˋ ㄧㄡˇ ㄑㄧˊ ㄕˋ)

It actually happened.

確有其人(ㄑㄩㄝˋ ㄧㄡˇ ㄑㄧˊ ㄖㄣˊ)

There is (or was) indeed such a person.

【碾】 3894
ㄋㄧㄢˇ nean niǎn

1. a stone roller
2. to mill; to roll; to crush

碾米(ㄋㄧㄢˇ ㄇㄧˇ)

to husk rice

碾米機(ㄋㄧㄢˇ ㄇㄧˇ ㄐㄧ)

a rice-husking machine

碾米廠(ㄋㄧㄢˇ ㄇㄧˇ ㄔㄤˇ)

a rice-husking mill

碾子(ㄋㄧㄢˇ ·ㄗ)

a stone roller for hulling grain, etc.

碾碎(ㄋㄧㄢˇ ㄙㄨㄟˋ)

to pulverize

【碼】 3895
ㄇㄚˇ maa mǎ

1. yard (a measure of length)
2. a symbol; a code; a sign or thing indicating number

碼頭(ㄇㄚˇ ·ㄊㄡ)

① a dock; a quay; a wharf; a pier ② a port city ③ bailiwick or sphere of influence (of gangsters)

碼頭工人(ㄇㄚˇ ·ㄊㄡ ㄍㄨㄥ ㄖㄣˊ)

a stevedore; a longshoreman

碼頭稅(ㄇㄚˇ ·ㄊㄡ ㄕㄨㄟˋ)or 碼頭費(ㄇㄚˇ ·ㄊㄡ ㄈㄟˋ)

wharfage; quayage; pier dues

碼子(ㄇㄚˇ ·ㄗ)or 碼兒(ㄇㄚˇㄦ)

a system of numerical symbols used in business

【磁】 3896
ㄘˊ tsyr cí

1. magnetic; magnetism
2. porcelain; china

磁暴(ㄘˊ ㄅㄠˋ)

(physics) a magnetic storm

磁片(ㄘˊ ㄆㄧㄢˋ)or 磁碟片(ㄘˊ ㄉㄧㄝˊ ㄆㄧㄢˋ)
(computers) a diskette; a floppy disc
磁帶(ㄘˊ ㄉㄞˋ)
a magnetic tape
磁頭(ㄘˊ ㄊㄡˊ)
a magnetic head
磁鐵(ㄘˊ ㄊㄧㄝˇ)
a magnet; magnetic iron
磁鐵礦(ㄘˊ ㄊㄧㄝˇ ㄎㄨㄤˋ)
magnetite; loadstone
磁力(ㄘˊ ㄌㄧˋ)
magnetic force; magnetism: 這塊鐵已失去磁力。The iron has lost its magnetic force.
磁感應(ㄘˊ ㄍㄢˇ ㄧㄥˋ)
magnetic induction
磁化(ㄘˊ ㄏㄨㄚˋ)
to magnetize; magnetization
磁婚(ㄘˊ ㄏㄨㄣ)
china wedding, the 20th wedding anniversary
磁極(ㄘˊ ㄐㄧˊ)
magnetic poles
磁圈(ㄘˊ ㄑㄩㄢ)
the magnetic field
磁性(ㄘˊ ㄒㄧㄥˋ)
magnetism
磁針(ㄘˊ ㄓㄣ)
a magnetic needle: 磁針指向南方。The magnetic needle points south.
磁場(ㄘˊ ㄔㄤˊ)or(ㄘˊ ㄔㄤˇ)
the magnetic field
磁石(ㄘˊ ㄕˊ)
a magnet; a loadstone: 地球中心是一塊天然磁石。The center of the earth is a natural magnet.

【磋】 3897 ㄘㄨㄛ tsuo cuō

to file; to polish (jade, stone, horn, etc.)
磋磨(ㄘㄨㄛ ㄇㄛˊ)
①to polish (jade, horn, stone, etc.) ②to learn through discussions with others
磋商(ㄘㄨㄛ ㄕㄤ)
to exchange views; to hold a discussion or consultation

【磅】 3898 1. ㄅㄤˋ banq bàng

1. a pound
2. scales
3. to weigh

磅秤(ㄅㄤˋ ㄔㄥˋ)
scales giving the weight in avoirdupois

【磅】 3898 2. ㄆㄤ pang pāng

the noise of stone crashing
磅礴(ㄆㄤ ㄅㄛˊ)
boundless; majestic; extensive; filling all space

【磔】 3899 ㄓㄜˊ jer zhé

1. to dismember a human being (an ancient punishment)
2. (Chinese calligraphy) a downward stroke sliding to the right

【磕】 3900 ㄎㄜ ke kē

to strike; to bump; to collide; to knock
磕碰(ㄎㄜ ㄆㄥˋ)
to bump against; to hit against; to collide with
磕頭(ㄎㄜ ㄊㄡˊ)
to kowtow
磕頭碰腦(ㄎㄜ ㄊㄡˊ ㄆㄥˋ ㄋㄠˇ)
to bump against things on every side (as in a room full of furniture); to bump against one another (as in a crowd)
磕磕巴巴(ㄎㄜ ˙ㄎㄜ ㄅㄚ ㄅㄚ)
stammering; stuttering
磕磕撞撞(ㄎㄜ ˙ㄎㄜ ㄓㄨㄤˋ ㄓㄨㄤˋ)
to walk unsteadily; to stumble or stagger along
磕牙(ㄎㄜ ㄧㄚˊ)
to chat; to jabber; to palaver; to prate; to gossip: 別坐在那兒與她閒磕牙兒了。Don't sit there prating and making fun of her.

【磊】 3901 ㄌㄟˇ leei lěi

1. a heap of stones
2. great; massive

磊磊(ㄌㄟˇ ㄌㄟˇ)
①(said of stones) innumerable ②rolling
磊磊落落(ㄌㄟˇ ˙ㄌㄟ ㄌㄨㄛˋ ㄌㄨㄛˋ)
①clear; distinct ②open-hearted; candid; unaffected; free and easy
磊落(ㄌㄟˇ ㄌㄨㄛˋ)
①a lot of ②open-hearted; candid; unaffected; open and aboveboard; free and easy: 他的行爲光明磊落。He acts openly and aboveboard.
磊塊 or 壘塊(ㄌㄟˇ ㄎㄨㄞˋ)
one's grievances

【磒】 3902 ㄩㄣˇ yeun yǔn

to fall down
磒石(ㄩㄣˇ ㄕˊ)or 磒星(ㄩㄣˇ ㄒㄧㄥ)
a meteor; a meteorite: 無聲的磒石滑過夜空。The silent meteor slides in the night sky.

【磐】 3903 ㄆㄢˊ parn pán

1. a massive rock
2. to linger around
3. to league together

磐礴(ㄆㄢˊ ㄅㄛˊ)
extensive; vast; imposing; great
磐石(ㄆㄢˊ ㄕˊ)
a massive rock: 他們的愛情堅若磐石。Their love is as steady as a massive rock.
磐石之安(ㄆㄢˊ ㄕˊ ㄓ ㄢ)
as stable and secure as a massive rock
磐牙 or 盤牙(ㄆㄢˊ ㄧㄚˊ)
to league together (as bandits)

十一畫

【磨】 3904 1. ㄇㄛˊ mo mó

1. to dawdle; to waste time; to while away
2. to rub; to grind; to polish; to wear: 我的脚上磨了泡。My feet were blistered from the rubbing.
3. sufferings; obstacles; setbacks: 好事多磨。The road to happiness is strewn with setbacks.

磨墨(ㄇㄛˊ ㄇㄛˋ)
to prepare liquid ink from an ink stick; to rub down an ink stick
磨滅(ㄇㄛˊ ㄇㄧㄝˋ)
①to wear out ②to obliterate; delible: 他在我心中留下不可磨滅的印象。He left an indelible impression on my mind.
磨刀(ㄇㄛˊ ㄉㄠ)
to sharpen a knife

磨刀石(ㄇㄛˊ ㄉㄠ ㄕˊ)
a whetstone; a grindstone

磨難(ㄇㄛˊ ㄋㄢˋ)
① sufferings; privations; tribulations; difficulties; obstacles ②to cause to suffer; to give a hard time

磨礪 or 磨厲(ㄇㄛˊ ㄌㄧˋ)
① to sharpen (a knife) ② to train; to harden; to temper; to discipline oneself

磨礪以須 or 磨厲以須(ㄇㄛˊ ㄌㄧˋ ㄧˇ ㄒㄩ)
to be combat-ready; to sharpen weapons in anticipation of war

磨鍊(ㄇㄛˊ ㄌㄧㄢˋ)
①to forge or temper (metal) ②to train; to harden; to discipline

磨光(ㄇㄛˊ ㄍㄨㄤ)
to polish; to burnish

磨功夫(ㄇㄛˊ ㄍㄨㄥ ·ㄈㄨ)
to waste time; time-consuming: 刺繡是件磨功夫的活兒。Embroidering is a time-consuming job.

磨勘(ㄇㄛˊ ㄎㄢ)
① to grade; to rate ② to review (examination papers under the former civil service examination system) ③ to study hard in search of truth

磨勁兒(ㄇㄛˊ ㄐㄧㄣˋㄦ)
persistence; perseverance; persistent; persevering

磨鏡(ㄇㄛˊ ㄐㄧㄥˋ)
to polish pieces of metal into mirrors

磨鏡子(ㄇㄛˊ ㄐㄧㄥˋ ·ㄗ)
(slang) homosexual act between two women; lesbianism

磨拳擦掌(ㄇㄛˊ ㄑㄩㄢˊ ㄘㄚ ㄓㄤˇ)
saber-rattling; ready for fight

磨折(ㄇㄛˊ ㄓㄜˊ)
tribulations; privations; sufferings; to cause to suffer; to give a hard time; to wear down; to reduce (a person) to a worse condition

磨琢(ㄇㄛˊ ㄓㄨㄛˊ)
(literally) to grind and to carve—to educate; to train; to study

磨杵成針(ㄇㄛˊ ㄔㄨˇ ㄔㄥˊ ㄓㄣ)
(literally) A pestle can be rubbed into a needle.—Persistent efforts can achieve difficult things.

磨穿鐵硯(ㄇㄛˊ ㄔㄨㄢ ㄊㄧㄝˇ ㄧㄢˋ)
(literally) to wear through an iron ink-slab—to apply oneself to literary work with persistent efforts

磨石子地(ㄇㄛˊ ㄕˊ ·ㄗ ㄉㄧˋ)
terrazzo floor

磨擦(ㄇㄛˊ ㄘㄚ)
① to rub ② friction

磨蹭(ㄇㄛˊ ·ㄘㄥ)
to be tardy; to be slow; to dawdle: 不要磨磨蹭蹭的，趕快做你的事。Stop dawdling and do your work quickly.

磨損(ㄇㄛˊ ㄙㄨㄣˇ)
wear and tear; to wear away

磨牙(ㄇㄛˊ ㄧㄚˊ)
① to be talkative and argumentative ② to grind one's teeth

【磨】 3904
2. ㄇㄛˋ moh mò
1. a mill
2. to turn around
3. to grind (grain, etc.)

磨磐(ㄇㄛˋ ㄆㄢˊ)
a millstone; a mill

磨坊(ㄇㄛˋ ㄈㄤˊ)or 磨房(ㄇㄛˋ ㄈㄤˊ)
a mill (referring to the building)

磨豆腐(ㄇㄛˋ ㄉㄡˋ ·ㄈㄨ)
to grind beans to make bean curd

【罄】 3905
ㄑㄧㄥˋ chinq qìng
a kind of musical instrument (made by hollowing out a hard sonorous stone, etc.); a musical stone

罄竭(ㄑㄧㄥˋ ㄐㄧㄝˊ)
used up; exhausted; emptied

罄折(ㄑㄧㄥˋ ㄓㄜˊ)
humpbacked or bent as a chiming-stone

罄氏(ㄑㄧㄥˋ ㄕˋ)
a workman who makes musical stones

【磧】 3906
ㄑㄧˋ chih qì
1. gravel and sand in shallow waters
2. a desert

磧鹵(ㄑㄧˋ ㄌㄨˇ)
sandy and saline land; barren land

【磚】 3907
ㄓㄨㄢ juan zhuān
bricks 亦作「甎」

十二畫

【磯】 3908
ㄐㄧ ji jī
1. a rocky cliff on the water's edge; water-surrounded rocks
2. rocks that water pounds against; stones in a river, interrupting and fretting the current

【磴】 3909
ㄉㄥˋ denq dèng
steps on rock

磴道(ㄉㄥˋ ㄉㄠˋ)
a rocky mountain path

【磷】 3910
1. ㄌㄧㄣˊ lin lín
1. phosphorus 亦作「燐」
2. water flowing between stones

磷磷(ㄌㄧㄣˊ ㄌㄧㄣˊ)
① the sound of water and stone beating against each other ② brilliance of precious stones

磷礦(ㄌㄧㄣˊ ㄎㄨㄤˋ)
phosphate rock

【磷】 3910
2. ㄌㄧㄣˋ linn lìn
thin (as opposed to thick)

【磺】 3911
ㄏㄨㄤˊ hwang huáng
sulfur; brimstone

磺酸(ㄏㄨㄤˊ ㄙㄨㄢ)
sulfonic acid

磺胺藥類(ㄏㄨㄤˊ ㄢ ㄧㄠˋ ㄌㄟˋ)
sulfa drugs

【磽】 3912
ㄑㄧㄠ chiau qiāo
hard barren land; poor in soil

磽薄(ㄑㄧㄠ ㄅㄛˊ)
hard and barren; hard and infertile

磽瘠(ㄑㄧㄠ ㄐㄧˊ)
hard and barren; hard and infertile

磽埆(ㄑㄧㄠ ㄑㄩㄝ)
①hard and barren land ②

〔石部〕

〔石部〕

hard (as opposed to soft)

【礁】 3913 ㄐㄧㄠ jiau jiāo
a reef
礁石(ㄐㄧㄠ ㄕˊ)
a reef

十三畫

【礎】 3914 ㄔㄨˇ chuu chǔ
a plinth
礎石(ㄔㄨˇ ㄕˊ)
the stone base of a column
礎潤而雨(ㄔㄨˇ ㄖㄨㄣˋ ㄦˊ ㄩˇ)
(literally) A damp plinth foretells rain.—Insignificant signs reveal big events ahead.

十四畫

【礙】 3915 (碍) ㄞˋ ay ài
1. to obstruct; to hinder; to be in the way
2. harmful; detrimental: 缺乏睡眠有礙身體健康。Lack of sleep is detrimental to one's health.
礙道(ㄞˋ ㄉㄠˋ)
to obstruct the way
礙難照准(ㄞˋ ㄋㄢˊ ㄓㄠˋ ㄓㄨㄣˇ)
It is impossible for this office to grant the permission. (a conventional phrase in official communications)
礙口(ㄞˋ ㄎㄡˇ)
unpleasant to talk about: 這種事有點礙口。It is unpleasant to talk about such a thing.
礙事(ㄞˋ ㄕˋ)
to be in the way; to be an obstacle to work; to be a problem: 只擦破皮，不礙事。It is just a graze, nothing serious.
礙手礙脚(ㄞˋ ㄕㄡˇ ㄞˋ ㄐㄧㄠˇ)
to be very much in the way
礙眼(ㄞˋ ㄧㄢˇ)or 礙目(ㄞˋ ㄇㄨˋ)
unpleasant to the eye; to offend the eye; to be an eyesore
礙於情面(ㄞˋ ㄩˊ ㄑㄧㄥˊ ㄇㄧㄢˋ)
for fear of hurting somebody's feelings

十五畫

【礫】 3916 ㄌㄧˋ lih lì
gravel; a pebble; shingle
礫石(ㄌㄧˋ ㄕˊ)
gravel; a pebble
礫岩(ㄌㄧˋ ㄧㄢˊ)
(geology) conglomerate

【礪】 3917 ㄌㄧˋ lih lì
1. a whetstone
2. to sharpen (a knife)
礪石(ㄌㄧˋ ㄕˊ)
a whetstone

【礬】 3918 ㄈㄢˊ farn fán
alum; vitriol
礬土(ㄈㄢˊ ㄊㄨˇ)
alumina
礬石(ㄈㄢˊ ㄕˊ)
alunite

【礦】 3919 (鑛) ㄎㄨㄤˋ kuanq kuàng
1. a mineral; ore
2. mining
3. a mine—(figuratively) a rich source
礦脈(ㄎㄨㄤˋ ㄇㄞˋ)
an ore vein; an ore lode
礦苗(ㄎㄨㄤˋ ㄇㄧㄠˊ)
the outcrop of a mineral; ore
礦工(ㄎㄨㄤˋ ㄍㄨㄥ)or 礦夫(ㄎㄨㄤˋ ㄈㄨ)
a miner
礦坑(ㄎㄨㄤˋ ㄎㄥ)
a mining shaft; a pit; 這附近有一個舊礦坑。There's an old pit near here.
礦區(ㄎㄨㄤˋ ㄑㄩ)
a mining district; an ore field
礦泉(ㄎㄨㄤˋ ㄑㄩㄢˊ)
a mineral spring
礦泉水(ㄎㄨㄤˋ ㄑㄩㄢˊ ㄕㄨㄟˇ)
mineral water
礦產(ㄎㄨㄤˋ ㄔㄢˇ)
mineral resources: 臺灣礦產並不豐富。Taiwan is not rich in mineral resources.
礦牀(ㄎㄨㄤˋ ㄔㄨㄤˊ)
the bed (of a mineral); mineral deposit; ore beds
礦石(ㄎㄨㄤˋ ㄕˊ)
a mineral; ore
礦石收音機(ㄎㄨㄤˋ ㄕˊ ㄕㄡ ㄧㄣ ㄐㄧ)
a crystal radio set
礦砂(ㄎㄨㄤˋ ㄕㄚ)
the ore in sand form
礦山(ㄎㄨㄤˋ ㄕㄢ)
mountains containing mineral deposits; a mine
礦藏(ㄎㄨㄤˋ ㄘㄤˊ)
mineral reserves; mineral resources: 中國礦藏豐富。China is rich in mineral resources.
礦層(ㄎㄨㄤˋ ㄘㄥˊ)
the bed or stratum (of a mineral); mineral deposits; a seam
礦業(ㄎㄨㄤˋ ㄧㄝˋ)
mining industry; mining
礦物(ㄎㄨㄤˋ ㄨˋ)
a mineral
礦物學(ㄎㄨㄤˋ ㄨˋ ㄒㄩㄝˊ)
mineralogy
礦物學家(ㄎㄨㄤˋ ㄨˋ ㄒㄩㄝˊ ㄐㄧㄚ)
a mineralogist
礦物油(ㄎㄨㄤˋ ㄨˋ ㄧㄡˊ)
mineral oil

十六畫

【礮】 3920 (砲) ㄆㄠˋ paw pào
1. a catapult
2. an artillery piece; a cannon; a gun
礮兵(ㄆㄠˋ ㄅㄧㄥ)
① an artilleryman; a gunner
② artillery (as a branch of the armed forces): 礮兵轟擊該城。The artillery bombarded the town.
礮兵部隊(ㄆㄠˋ ㄅㄧㄥ ㄅㄨˋ ㄉㄨㄟˋ)
artillery units
礮兵陣地(ㄆㄠˋ ㄅㄧㄥ ㄓㄣˋ ㄉㄧˋ)
an artillery position or emplacement
礮彈(ㄆㄠˋ ㄉㄢˋ)
a cannon ball; a shell; a cannon shot
礮塔(ㄆㄠˋ ㄊㄚˇ)
a turret; a barbette; a gunhouse: 他們極力守護著礮塔。They tried hard to guard the turret.
礮臺(ㄆㄠˋ ㄊㄞˊ)
a gun emplacement; a battery; a fort

礮艇(ㄆㄠˋ ㄊㄧㄥˇ)
a gunboat
礮火(ㄆㄠˋ ㄏㄨㄛˇ)
artillery fire; gunfire
礮灰(ㄆㄠˋ ㄏㄨㄟ)
cannon fodder
礮轟(ㄆㄠˋ ㄏㄨㄥ)
① to bombard with artillery fire; to cannonade ② concentrated verbal attacks
礮擊(ㄆㄠˋ ㄐㄧˊ)
a cannonade; bombardment; to bombard with artillery fire; to shell: 我們的戰艦礮擊他們的堡壘。Our ships bombarded their fortress.
礮艦(ㄆㄠˋ ㄐㄧㄢˋ)
a gunboat
礮車(ㄆㄠˋ ㄔㄜ)
a gun carriage
礮手(ㄆㄠˋ ㄕㄡˇ)
a gunner; a cannoneer; an artilleryman: 他在戰時是礮手。He was a gunner during the war.
礮身(ㄆㄠˋ ㄕㄣ)
the gun barrel
礮聲(ㄆㄠˋ ㄕㄥ)
the roaring of artillery pieces; the thunder of cannonade
礮座(ㄆㄠˋ ㄗㄨㄛˋ)
a gun platform; a barbette
礮衣(ㄆㄠˋ ㄧ)
canvas covering of an artillery piece; a gun cover
礮位(ㄆㄠˋ ㄨㄟˋ)
an artillery park; a gun pit; an emplacement

【礱】 3921 ㄌㄨㄥˊ long lóng
1. to grind
2. a kind of mill

十七畫

【礴】 3922 ㄅㄛˊ bor bó
filling all space; extensive

示部 ㄕˋ shyh shì

【示】 3923 ㄕˋ shyh shì
1. to show; to indicate
2. to make known; to notify; a notice
3. to instruct
4. to demonstrate

示範(ㄕˋ ㄈㄢˋ)
① to set an example ② to demonstrate (how a thing works, etc.)
示範表演(ㄕˋ ㄈㄢˋ ㄅㄧㄠˇ ㄧㄢˇ)
demonstration (of a skill)
示覆(ㄕˋ ㄈㄨˋ)
to reply to an inquiry (a conventional phrase in formal communications when asking the other party to reply)
示疾(ㄕˋ ㄐㄧˊ)
illness (of a Buddhist priest)
示寂(ㄕˋ ㄐㄧˋ)
(said of a Buddhist priest) to indicate the way to Nirvana; to die
示警(ㄕˋ ㄐㄧㄥˇ)
to give a warning: 他們在街上鳴鑼示警。They gave a warning by beating gongs in the street.
示知(ㄕˋ ㄓ)
to inform; to notify
示衆(ㄕˋ ㄓㄨㄥˋ)
to exhibit to the public; to show to the public
示人(ㄕˋ ㄖㄣˊ)
to make known; to show others; to let others have a look at
示弱(ㄕˋ ㄖㄨㄛˋ)
to show weakness; to yield; to give in: 他不甘示弱而再試一次。He didn't give in and tried again.
示愛(ㄕˋ ㄞˋ)
to show one's tender feeling to one of the opposite sex
示意(ㄕˋ ㄧˋ)
to indicate one's wish or intention (usually by facial expressions or gestures); to drop a hint; to motion: 他示意我進去。He motioned me to enter.
示威(ㄕˋ ㄨㄟ)
① to demonstrate (by a mass meeting or parade) ② to make a show of force
示威遊行(ㄕˋ ㄨㄟ ㄧㄡˊ ㄒㄧㄥˊ)
demonstration
示威運動(ㄕˋ ㄨㄟ ㄩㄣˋ ㄉㄨㄥˋ)
demonstration (by a mass meeting or parade)

二畫

【礽】 3924 ㄖㄥˊ reng réng
a blessing; happiness; bliss

三畫

【社】 3925 ㄕㄜˋ sheh shè
1. the god of land
2. an association; an organization; a corporation; an agency
3. society; a community

社評(ㄕㄜˋ ㄆㄧㄥˊ)
an editorial
社土(ㄕㄜˋ ㄊㄨˇ)
land conferred upon a feudal lord by the emperor
社團(ㄕㄜˋ ㄊㄨㄢˊ)
an association; a corporation; a civic organization: 他們組成協助盲人的社團。They formed an association to help blind people.
社論(ㄕㄜˋ ㄌㄨㄣˋ)
an editorial
社會(ㄕㄜˋ ㄏㄨㄟˋ)
society; community: 他爲社會的利益而做那件事。He did it for the interests of society.
社會變遷(ㄕㄜˋ ㄏㄨㄟˋ ㄅㄧㄢˋ ㄑㄧㄢ)
social change
社會名流(ㄕㄜˋ ㄏㄨㄟˋ ㄇㄧㄥˊ ㄌㄧㄡˊ)
noted public figures; socialites
社會發展(ㄕㄜˋ ㄏㄨㄟˋ ㄈㄚ ㄓㄢˇ)
social development
社會福利(ㄕㄜˋ ㄏㄨㄟˋ ㄈㄨˊ ㄌㄧˋ)
social welfare
社會福利事業保險(ㄕㄜˋ ㄏㄨㄟˋ ㄈㄨˊ ㄌㄧˋ ㄕˋ ㄧㄝˋ ㄅㄠˇ ㄒㄧㄢˇ)
social welfare insurance
社會服務(ㄕㄜˋ ㄏㄨㄟˋ ㄈㄨˊ ㄨˋ)
social services
社會黨(ㄕㄜˋ ㄏㄨㄟˋ ㄉㄤˇ)
Socialist Party
社會地位(ㄕㄜˋ ㄏㄨㄟˋ ㄉㄧˋ ㄨㄟˋ)
social status; social position;

〔示部〕

social standing
社會倫理(ㄕㄜˋ ㄏㄨㄟˋ ㄌㄨㄣˊ ㄌㄧˇ)
social ethics
社會改革(ㄕㄜˋ ㄏㄨㄟˋ ㄍㄞˇ ㄍㄜˊ)
social reform
社會工作(ㄕㄜˋ ㄏㄨㄟˋ ㄍㄨㄥ ㄗㄨㄛˋ)
social work
社會工作者(ㄕㄜˋ ㄏㄨㄟˋ ㄍㄨㄥ ㄗㄨㄛˋ ㄓㄜˇ)
a social worker
社會科學(ㄕㄜˋ ㄏㄨㄟˋ ㄎㄜ ㄒㄩㄝˊ)
social science
社會教育(ㄕㄜˋ ㄏㄨㄟˋ ㄐㄧㄠˋ ㄩˋ)
social education
社會進步(ㄕㄜˋ ㄏㄨㄟˋ ㄐㄧㄣˋ ㄅㄨˋ)
social progress
社會進化(ㄕㄜˋ ㄏㄨㄟˋ ㄐㄧㄣˋ ㄏㄨㄚˋ)
social evolution
社會局(ㄕㄜˋ ㄏㄨㄟˋ ㄐㄩˊ)
the bureau of social affairs (under a city or county government)
社會角色(ㄕㄜˋ ㄏㄨㄟˋ ㄐㄩㄝˊ ㄙㄜˋ)
a social role
社會現象(ㄕㄜˋ ㄏㄨㄟˋ ㄒㄧㄢˋ ㄒㄧㄤˋ)
social phenomena
社會心理(ㄕㄜˋ ㄏㄨㄟˋ ㄒㄧㄣ ㄌㄧˇ)
social psychology (as a phenomenon)
社會心理學(ㄕㄜˋ ㄏㄨㄟˋ ㄒㄧㄣ ㄌㄧˇ ㄒㄩㄝˊ)
social psychology (as a science)
社會新聞(ㄕㄜˋ ㄏㄨㄟˋ ㄒㄧㄣ ㄨㄣˊ)
human interest stories or crime stories (as distinct from political, military, or educational news items)
社會學(ㄕㄜˋ ㄏㄨㄟˋ ㄒㄩㄝˊ)
sociology
社會秩序(ㄕㄜˋ ㄏㄨㄟˋ ㄓˋ ㄒㄩˋ)
social order
社會主義(ㄕㄜˋ ㄏㄨㄟˋ ㄓㄨˇ ㄧˋ)
socialism
社會事業(ㄕㄜˋ ㄏㄨㄟˋ ㄕˋ ㄧㄝˋ)
social work; social service; public welfare projects
社會生活(ㄕㄜˋ ㄏㄨㄟˋ ㄕㄥ ㄏㄨㄛˊ)
social life; community life
社會組織(ㄕㄜˋ ㄏㄨㄟˋ ㄗㄨˇ ㄓ)
social organization
社會壓力(ㄕㄜˋ ㄏㄨㄟˋ ㄧㄚ ㄌㄧˋ)
social pressure
社會問題(ㄕㄜˋ ㄏㄨㄟˋ ㄨㄣˋ ㄊㄧˊ)
a social problem
社會運動(ㄕㄜˋ ㄏㄨㄟˋ ㄩㄣˋ ㄉㄨㄥˋ)
social movement
社稷(ㄕㄜˋ ㄐㄧˋ)
the god of land and the god of grain—a country
社稷之臣(ㄕㄜˋ ㄐㄧˋ ㄓ ㄔㄣˊ)
a key minister; an important courtier
社交(ㄕㄜˋ ㄐㄧㄠ)
social intercourse; sociality
社交公開(ㄕㄜˋ ㄐㄧㄠ ㄍㄨㄥ ㄎㄞ)
free social intercourse between men and women
社交生活(ㄕㄜˋ ㄐㄧㄠ ㄕㄥ ㄏㄨㄛˊ)
social life
社交舞(ㄕㄜˋ ㄐㄧㄠ ㄨˇ)
social dancing; ballroom dancing
社區(ㄕㄜˋ ㄑㄩ)
a community
社區發展(ㄕㄜˋ ㄑㄩ ㄈㄚ ㄓㄢˇ)
community development
社區規劃(ㄕㄜˋ ㄑㄩ ㄍㄨㄟ ㄏㄨㄚˋ)
community planning
社學(ㄕㄜˋ ㄒㄩㄝˊ)
a community school (in the Ming and Ching dynasties)
社長(ㄕㄜˋ ㄓㄤˇ)
the president or director (of an association, newspaper, etc.): 他已經當了六年的社長了。He has been the president of the association for six years.
社鼠(ㄕㄜˋ ㄕㄨˇ)
(literally) mice in a temple —wicked people under the protection of a powerful man
社友(ㄕㄜˋ ㄧㄡˇ)
a fellow member (of a society, association, etc.): 歡迎所有社友參加此一活動。All fellow members are welcome to take part in the activity.
社務(ㄕㄜˋ ㄨˋ)
affairs or business of an association, newspaper office, etc.
社員(ㄕㄜˋ ㄩㄢˊ)
a member (of an association, society, etc.)
社員大會(ㄕㄜˋ ㄩㄢˊ ㄉㄚˋ ㄏㄨㄟˋ)
a general convention of an association, society, etc.

【祁】 3926 ㄑㄧˊ chyi qí

vigorous; thriving; to be large
祁門(ㄑㄧˊ ㄇㄣˊ)
name of a county in Anhwei, famous for its black tea
祁連山(ㄑㄧˊ ㄌㄧㄢˊ ㄕㄢ)
name of a mountain in Kansu
祁寒酷暑(ㄑㄧˊ ㄏㄢˊ ㄎㄨˋ ㄕㄨˇ)
severe cold and intense heat
祁山(ㄑㄧˊ ㄕㄢ)
name of a mountain in Kansu used as a staging area by Chu-Ko Liang (諸葛亮) in the war against Wei (魏) during the Epoch of the Three Kingdoms

【祀】 3927 ㄙˋ syh sì

to worship; to offer sacrifices to
祀奉(ㄙˋ ㄈㄥˋ)
to worship: 中國人祀奉祖先。The Chinese worship their ancestors.
祀典(ㄙˋ ㄉㄧㄢˇ)
religious rites or services; rites of offering sacrifices
祀天(ㄙˋ ㄊㄧㄢ)
to worship, or offer sacrifices to Heaven
祀孔(ㄙˋ ㄎㄨㄥˇ)
to worship Confucius in ceremonies held on his birth anniversary on September 28
祀事(ㄙˋ ㄕˋ)
religious rites or services
祀神(ㄙˋ ㄕㄣˊ)
to worship gods
祀竈(ㄙˋ ㄗㄠˋ)
to worship the kitchen god (done on the 23rd of the 12th moon)
祀祖(ㄙˋ ㄗㄨˇ)
to worship ancestors

四畫

【祆】 3928 ㄒㄧㄢ shian xiān

Ormazd, the supreme deity in Zoroastrianism
祆教(ㄒㄧㄢ ㄐㄧㄠˋ)
Zoroastrianism

【祅】 3929 ㄧㄠ iau yāo

1. calamity due to terrestrial disturbances (as distinct from 災—disaster which is sent down from above)
2. bizarre

【祇】 3930 1. ㄑㄧˊ chyi qí
1. the god of the earth
2. peace; serenity; to be at rest

祇悔(ㄑㄧˊ ㄏㄨㄟˇ)
great regret; deep remorse

【祇】 3930 2.(只、祇) ㄓˇ jyy zhǐ (原讀 ㄓ jy zhī)
only; merely

祇得(ㄓˇ ㄉㄟˇ)
to have to; to have no alternative

祇好(ㄓˇ ㄏㄠˇ)
to have to; to have no other choice

祇要(ㄓˇ ㄧㄠˋ)
only if

【祈】 3931 ㄑㄧˊ chyi qí
1. to pray
2. to beg; to entreat; to beseech; to supplicate; to request respectfully: 敬祈指導。We respectfully request your guidance.

祈福(ㄑㄧˊ ㄈㄨˊ)
to pray for blessings

祈禱(ㄑㄧˊ ㄉㄠˇ)
to pray; to offer a prayer

祈禱者(ㄑㄧˊ ㄉㄠˇ ㄓㄜˇ)
a person praying; a prayer

祈禱文(ㄑㄧˊ ㄉㄠˇ ㄨㄣˊ)
prayers

祈年(ㄑㄧˊ ㄋㄧㄢˊ)
to pray for a bumper crop

祈年殿(ㄑㄧˊ ㄋㄧㄢˊ ㄉㄧㄢˋ) or 祈穀壇(ㄑㄧˊ ㄍㄨˇ ㄊㄢˊ)
name of a shrine in the Temple of Heaven in Peking

祈年宮(ㄑㄧˊ ㄋㄧㄢˊ ㄍㄨㄥ)
name of an ancient palace in Shensi

祈祈(ㄑㄧˊ ㄑㄧˊ)
slowly

祈求(ㄑㄧˊ ㄑㄧㄡˊ)
to pray for; to appeal for; to ask humbly for; to supplicate for: 他祈求上帝幫助。He prayed to God for help.

祈請(ㄑㄧˊ ㄑㄧㄥˇ)
to beg; to beseech; to entreat

祈禳(ㄑㄧˊ ㄖㄤˊ)
to pray for protection against calamities

祈雨(ㄑㄧˊ ㄩˇ)
to pray for rain: 農民正在祈雨。The farmers are praying for rain.

【祉】 3932 ㄓˇ jyy zhǐ
happiness; blessings; blessedness; welfare

祉祿(ㄓˇ ㄌㄨˋ)
happiness and wealth

五畫

【祐】 3933 ㄧㄡˋ yow yòu
divine help

祐助(ㄧㄡˋ ㄓㄨˋ)
(said of a deity) to help (a mortal)

【祓】 3934 ㄈㄨˊ fwu fú
1. to exorcise
2. to cleanse; to clean

祓禊(ㄈㄨˊ ㄒㄧˋ)
exorcism by a bath; ablutions

祓濯(ㄈㄨˊ ㄓㄨㄛˊ)
to cleanse; to purify

祓除(ㄈㄨˊ ㄔㄨˊ)
to exorcise

祓飾(ㄈㄨˊ ㄕˋ)
to refresh; to renew

【祔】 3935 ㄈㄨˋ fuh fù
1. to enshrine in the ancestral temple
2. to bury in the family tomb

【祕】 3936 (秘) ㄇㄧˋ mih mì (又讀 ㄅㄧˋ bih bì)
secret; confidential; hidden; unknown; mysterious: 你必須爲此事保守祕密。You must keep the matter a secret.

祕寶(ㄇㄧˋ ㄅㄠˇ)
a rare treasure

祕本(ㄇㄧˋ ㄅㄣˇ)
① a rare book ② a secret book

祕密(ㄇㄧˋ ㄇㄧˋ)
secret; confidential; hidden; clandestine; a secret

祕密投票(ㄇㄧˋ ㄇㄧˋ ㄊㄡˊ ㄆㄧㄠˋ)
a secret ballot

祕密條約(ㄇㄧˋ ㄇㄧˋ ㄊㄧㄠˊ ㄩㄝ)
a secret treaty

祕密會議(ㄇㄧˋ ㄇㄧˋ ㄏㄨㄟˋ ㄧˋ)
a secret conference; a closed-door meeting; a conclave; a clandestine meeting: 他們在祕密會議裏碰頭。They met at a clandestine meeting.

祕密結婚(ㄇㄧˋ ㄇㄧˋ ㄐㄧㄝˊ ㄏㄨㄣ)
a secret wedding; a clandestine marriage

祕密結社(ㄇㄧˋ ㄇㄧˋ ㄐㄧㄝˊ ㄕㄜˋ)
to form a secret society

祕密警察(ㄇㄧˋ ㄇㄧˋ ㄐㄧㄥˇ ㄔㄚˊ)
the secret police; the Gestapo

祕密消息(ㄇㄧˋ ㄇㄧˋ ㄒㄧㄠ ˙ㄒㄧ)
confidential information; classified information

祕密外交(ㄇㄧˋ ㄇㄧˋ ㄨㄞˋ ㄐㄧㄠ)
secret diplomacy

祕密文件(ㄇㄧˋ ㄇㄧˋ ㄨㄣˊ ㄐㄧㄢˋ)
a secret document; a classified document

祕方(ㄇㄧˋ ㄈㄤ)
a secret recipe

祕府(ㄇㄧˋ ㄈㄨˇ)
① a secret repository ② a secretariat in former times

祕魯(ㄇㄧˋ ㄌㄨˇ) or (ㄅㄧˋ ㄌㄨˇ)
Peru; Peruvian

祕閣(ㄇㄧˋ ㄍㄜˊ)
① a place in the imperial palace to file confidential documents ② an armrest (used when one is writing)

祕笈(ㄇㄧˋ ㄐㄧˊ)
an extraordinary book

祕籍(ㄇㄧˋ ㄐㄧˊ)
① a rare book ② a secret book

祕訣(ㄇㄧˋ ㄐㄩㄝˊ)
a knack; secrets (of success, etc.); the key (to the solution of a problem): 你能否告訴我們你的成功祕訣? Can you tell us the secret of your success?

祕製(ㄇㄧˋ ㄓˋ)
to prepare from a secret recipe

祕傳(ㄇㄧˋ ㄔㄨㄢˊ)
to transmit from generation to generation exclusively inside a family

祕書(ㄇㄧˋ ㄕㄨ)
a secretary: 他是董事長的祕書。He is secretary to the President.

祕書省(ㄇㄧˋ ㄕㄨ ㄕㄥˇ)
the emperor's secretariat

祕奧(ㄇㄧˋ ㄠˋ)
the inner mysteries

祕而不宣(ㄇㄧˋ ㄦˊ ㄅㄨˋ ㄒㄩㄢ)
to keep (things) secret; to refrain from making an announcement

祕要(ㄇㄧˋ ㄧㄠˋ)
(said of government papers, etc.) classified

祕文(ㄇㄧˋ ㄨㄣˊ)
secret writing; a secret book

祕聞(ㄇㄧˋ ㄨㄣˊ)
exclusively inmost news

【祖】 3937 ㄗㄨˇ tzuu zǔ

1. one's grandfather or grandmother: 外祖 one's maternal grandfather
2. ancestors; forebears: 遠祖 remote ancestors
3. a founder; an originator
4. to follow the example of; to imitate
5. a Chinese family name

祖輩(ㄗㄨˇ ㄅㄟˋ)
ancestors; forefathers

祖妣(ㄗㄨˇ ㄅㄧˇ)
one's deceased grandmother

祖鞭(ㄗㄨˇ ㄅㄧㄢ)
to strive for achievements (a reference to 祖逖)

祖廟(ㄗㄨˇ ㄇㄧㄠˋ)
an ancestral shrine or temple

祖母(ㄗㄨˇ ㄇㄨˇ)
one's grandmother: 他小時候住在祖母家。He lived in his grandmother's home when he was young.

祖墳(ㄗㄨˇ ㄈㄣˊ)
an ancestral grave

祖父(ㄗㄨˇ ㄈㄨˋ)
one's grandfather: 他已經當祖父了。He's a grandfather now.

祖德(ㄗㄨˇ ㄉㄜˊ)
the virtuous deeds of one's ancestors

祖逖(ㄗㄨˇ ㄊㄧˋ)
Tsu Ti, 266-321 A.D., a patriotic general of the Tsin Dynasty

祖國(ㄗㄨˇ ㄍㄨㄛˊ)
one's fatherland; one's mother country; one's homeland

祖考(ㄗㄨˇ ㄎㄠˇ)
① one's deceased grandfather ② ancestors

祖籍(ㄗㄨˇ ㄐㄧˊ)
one's ancestral home; the land of one's ancestors: 我們祖籍廣東。Our ancestral home is in Kwangtung.

祖餞(ㄗㄨˇ ㄐㄧㄢˋ)
to give a farewell dinner or luncheon

祖居(ㄗㄨˇ ㄐㄩ)
one's ancestral home

祖先(ㄗㄨˇ ㄒㄧㄢ)
ancestors; forebears; forefathers

祖帳(ㄗㄨˇ ㄓㄤˋ)
to give a farewell dinner or luncheon

祖產(ㄗㄨˇ ㄔㄢˇ)
ancestral estate

祖傳(ㄗㄨˇ ㄔㄨㄢˊ)
handed down by one's ancestors; inherited from one's ancestors; hereditary

祖沖之(ㄗㄨˇ ㄔㄨㄥ ㄓ)
Tsu Chung-chih, 429-500, a scholar and inventor

祖師(ㄗㄨˇ ㄕ)
① the founder of a sect, especially Bodhidharma (達摩) of the Zen sect ② the originator of a craft or trade

祖上(ㄗㄨˇ ㄕㄤˋ)
ancestors; forebears; forefathers

祖述(ㄗㄨˇ ㄕㄨˋ)
to hand down as if from one's ancestors

祖宗(ㄗㄨˇ ㄗㄨㄥ)
ancestors; forefathers; forebears

祖孫(ㄗㄨˇ ㄙㄨㄣ)
ancestors and descendants

祖送(ㄗㄨˇ ㄙㄨㄥˋ)
to give a farewell luncheon or dinner party

祖業(ㄗㄨˇ ㄧㄝˋ)
① property inherited from one's ancestors ② a trade or business inherited from one's ancestors

【祗】 3938 ㄓ jy zhī

1. to respect; to revere
2. only; but; just 亦作「衹」

祗奉(ㄓ ㄈㄥˋ)
① to respect; to hold in great respect ② to accept with respect

祗候(ㄓ ㄏㄡˋ)
① to wait upon respectfully ② an official receptionist in the Sung Dynasty

祗承(ㄓ ㄔㄥˊ)
to accept with respect

祗遵(ㄓ ㄗㄨㄣ)
to observe or follow with respect

祗肅(ㄓ ㄙㄨˋ)
respectful; reverent

祗仰(ㄓ ㄧㄤˇ)
to respect; to revere; to hold in high esteem

【祜】 3939 ㄏㄨˋ huh hù

a blessing

【祛】 3940 ㄑㄩ chiu qū

to dispel; to expel; to remove

祛祛(ㄑㄩ ㄑㄩ)
healthy and strong; stout

祛災(ㄑㄩ ㄗㄞ)
to dispel disasters

祛疑(ㄑㄩ ㄧˊ)
to dispel doubt

【祚】 3941 ㄗㄨㄛˋ tzuoh zuò

1. a blessing
2. the throne
3. the year

祚命(ㄗㄨㄛˋ ㄇㄧㄥˋ)
a heavenly blessing

祚胤(ㄗㄨㄛˋ ㄧㄣˋ)
to grant happiness and dignity to one's posterity

【祝】 3942 ㄓㄨˋ juh zhù

1. to wish someone happiness; to pray for happiness: 祝你旅途愉快。I wish you a pleasant journey. 或 Bon voyage!
2. to congratulate; to felicitate
3. to celebrate
4. a Chinese family name

祝福(ㄓㄨˋ ㄈㄨˊ)
① to bless ② to wish happiness to ③ new year's sacri-

fice (an old custom in certain parts of Chekiang Province)

祝典(ㄓㄨˋ ㄉㄧㄢˇ)
a celebration

祝告(ㄓㄨˋ ㄍㄠˋ)
to invoke; to implore in prayer

祝嘏(ㄓㄨˋ ㄍㄨˇ)
to wish someone a happy birthday

祝賀(ㄓㄨˋ ㄏㄜˋ)
congratulations; to congratulate; to felicitate: 請接受我的祝賀。Please accept my congratulations.

祝捷(ㄓㄨˋ ㄐㄧㄝˊ)
to celebrate victory; to send a congratulatory message to a victorious army or sports team

祝壽(ㄓㄨˋ ㄕㄡˋ)
to celebrate someone's birthday; to wish someone a happy birthday

祝融(ㄓㄨˋ ㄖㄨㄥˊ)
the god of fire

祝融爲虐(ㄓㄨˋ ㄖㄨㄥˊ ㄨㄟˊ ㄋㄩㄝˋ)
The god of fire wrought great havoc.

祝詞 or 祝辭(ㄓㄨˋ ㄘˊ)
① a congratulatory message ② prayers at sacrificial rites in ancient times

祝頌(ㄓㄨˋ ㄙㄨㄥˋ)
to congratulate and commend

祝文(ㄓㄨˋ ㄨㄣˊ)
a congratulatory message

【神】 3943
ㄕㄣˊ shern shén

1. gods; deities; immortals; spiritual beings
2. soul; mind; spirit
3. appearances; looks; expressions; airs
4. supernatural; marvelous; wondrous; miraculous; mysterious; mystical
5. smart; clever

神兵(ㄕㄣˊ ㄅㄧㄥ)
divine troops

神不知鬼不覺(ㄕㄣˊ ㄅㄨˋ ㄓ ㄍㄨㄟˇ ㄅㄨˋ ㄐㄩㄝˊ)
unknown even to gods and spirits—cloaked in extreme secrecy; extremely stealthy

神不守舍(ㄕㄣˊ ㄅㄨˋ ㄕㄡˇ ㄕㄜˋ)
out of one's wits; mentally wandering; delirious

神品(ㄕㄣˊ ㄆㄧㄣˇ)
sublime works (of art, literature, etc.); works of genius

神謀魔道(ㄕㄣˊ ㄇㄡˊ ㄇㄛˊ ㄉㄠˋ)
as if urged by gods or demons

神秘 or 神祕(ㄕㄣˊ ㄇㄧˋ)
mysterious; mystical; mystery: 他是位神秘人物。He's a mysterious person.

神妙(ㄕㄣˊ ㄇㄧㄠˋ)
marvelous; wondrous; wonderful: 他的筆法神妙。His style of writing is wonderful.

神廟(ㄕㄣˊ ㄇㄧㄠˋ)
a temple of the gods

神明(ㄕㄣˊ ㄇㄧㄥˊ)
the gods; deities; divinities

神明保佑(ㄕㄣˊ ㄇㄧㄥˊ ㄅㄠˇ ㄧㄡˋ)
to have divine help

神木(ㄕㄣˊ ㄇㄨˋ)
a divine tree

神峯(ㄕㄣˊ ㄈㄥ)
outstanding dignity

神鋒(ㄕㄣˊ ㄈㄥ)
a sword

神風隊(ㄕㄣˊ ㄈㄥ ㄉㄨㄟˋ)or 神風特攻隊(ㄕㄣˊ ㄈㄥ ㄊㄜˋ ㄍㄨㄥ ㄉㄨㄟˋ)
kamikaze, Japan's suicide pilots at the end of World War II

神福(ㄕㄣˊ ㄈㄨˊ)
① to pray for happiness ② offerings to the gods

神父(ㄕㄣˊ ㄈㄨˋ)
a Catholic father 亦作「神甫」

神殿(ㄕㄣˊ ㄉㄧㄢˋ)
a sanctuary

神都(ㄕㄣˊ ㄉㄨ)
① China ② the imperial capital

神態(ㄕㄣˊ ㄊㄞˋ)
looks; appearances; airs; facial expressions: 他的神態悠閒。He looks perfectly relaxed.

神頭鬼面(ㄕㄣˊ ㄊㄡˊ ㄍㄨㄟˇ ㄇㄧㄢˋ)
monstrosities

神通(ㄕㄣˊ ㄊㄨㄥ)
ubiquitous supernatural power, especially of the Buddha

神通廣大(ㄕㄣˊ ㄊㄨㄥ ㄍㄨㄤˇ ㄉㄚˋ)
possessing marvelous abilities; very resourceful

神童(ㄕㄣˊ ㄊㄨㄥˊ)
a child prodigy

神鳥(ㄕㄣˊ ㄋㄧㄠˇ)
the phoenix

神農(ㄕㄣˊ ㄋㄨㄥˊ)
Shen Nung, a legendary ruler supposed to have introduced agriculture and herbal medicine

神女(ㄕㄣˊ ㄋㄩˇ)
a prostitute; a harlot

神來之筆(ㄕㄣˊ ㄌㄞˊ ㄓ ㄅㄧˇ)
a stroke of genius (as if it were the result of divine inspiration)

神力(ㄕㄣˊ ㄌㄧˋ)
divine power; marvelous ability; supernatural strength

神靈(ㄕㄣˊ ㄌㄧㄥˊ)
① gods; spirits ② marvelous; prodigious

神怪(ㄕㄣˊ ㄍㄨㄞˋ)
mysterious; mystical; supernatural

神龜(ㄕㄣˊ ㄍㄨㄟ)
a supernatural tortoise

神鬼(ㄕㄣˊ ㄍㄨㄟˇ)
gods and ghosts

神功(ㄕㄣˊ ㄍㄨㄥ)
a prodigious feat; a supernatural accomplishment; a miracle

神工鬼斧(ㄕㄣˊ ㄍㄨㄥ ㄍㄨㄟˇ ㄈㄨˇ)
prodigious skill; supernatural skill 參看「鬼斧神工」

神龕(ㄕㄣˊ ㄎㄢ)
a sanctuary; a shrine for idols or ancestral tablets

神乎其神(ㄕㄣˊ ㄏㄨ ㄑㄧˊ ㄕㄣˊ)
How marvelous! 或 How wondrous! 或 fantastic; wonderful; miraculous

神戶(ㄕㄣˊ ㄏㄨˋ)
Kobe, Japan

神化(ㄕㄣˊ ㄏㄨㄚˋ)
to deify; deified; deification; to make a god of

神話(ㄕㄣˊ ㄏㄨㄚˋ)
a myth; mythology

神話學(ㄕㄣˊ ㄏㄨㄚˋ ㄒㄩㄝˊ)
mythology

神話時代(ㄕㄣˊ ㄏㄨㄚˋ ㄕˊ ㄉㄞˋ)
the mythological age

〔示部〕

〔示部〕

神魂(ㄕㄣˊㄏㄨㄣˊ)
①the soul ②a state of mind: 他顯得神魂不定。He appeared to be deeply perturbed.
神魂顛倒(ㄕㄣˊㄏㄨㄣˊㄉㄧㄢ ㄉㄠˇ)
to be fascinated head over heels; to be carried away; to be transported; to be infatuated; to be held spellbound
神迹 or 神蹟(ㄕㄣˊㄐㄧ)
a marvelous event; a miracle: 過去從未發生這種神蹟。Such a miracle has never occurred before.
神機(ㄕㄣˊㄐㄧ)
①a God-given chance ②the divine plan
神機妙算(ㄕㄣˊㄐㄧ ㄇㄧㄠˋㄙㄨㄢˋ)
①stratagems so wonderful that they seem to be conceived by divine beings ②wonderful foresight (in military operations, etc.)
神交(ㄕㄣˊㄐㄧㄠ)
①friendship grown out of mutual admiration without having met once ②spiritual communication
神經(ㄕㄣˊㄐㄧㄥ)
nerve, any of the threadlike parts of the body which form a system to carry feelings and messages to and from the brain
神經病(ㄕㄣˊㄐㄧㄥㄅㄧㄥˋ)
①neurosis; mental disorder ②a neurotic
神經痛(ㄕㄣˊㄐㄧㄥㄊㄨㄥˋ)
neuralgia
神經過敏(ㄕㄣˊㄐㄧㄥㄍㄨㄛˋㄇㄧㄣˇ)
①morbidly sensitive; excessively sensitive ②(medicine) hyperaesthesia
神經緊張(ㄕㄣˊㄐㄧㄥㄐㄧㄣˇㄓㄤ)
nervous: 有些人在黑暗處會神經緊張。Some are nervous in the dark.
神經系(ㄕㄣˊㄐㄧㄥㄒㄧˋ)
the nervous system
神經細胞(ㄕㄣˊㄐㄧㄥㄒㄧˋㄅㄠ)
nerve cells; neurocyte
神經纖維(ㄕㄣˊㄐㄧㄥㄒㄧㄢㄨㄟˊ)
nerve fibers
神經質(ㄕㄣˊㄐㄧㄥㄓˋ)
a nervous temperament; nervosity: 她的母親是個神經質的人。Her mother has a nervous temperament.
神經戰(ㄕㄣˊㄐㄧㄥㄓㄢˋ)
a war of nerves; psychological warfare
神經中樞(ㄕㄣˊㄐㄧㄥㄓㄨㄥㄕㄨ)
the nerve center: 腦是身體的神經中樞。The brain is the nerve center of the body.
神經梢(ㄕㄣˊㄐㄧㄥㄕㄠ)
nerve endings
神經衰弱(ㄕㄣˊㄐㄧㄥㄕㄨㄞㄖㄨㄛˋ)
neurasthenia
神經組織(ㄕㄣˊㄐㄧㄥㄗㄨˇㄓ)
nerve tissue
神經錯亂(ㄕㄣˊㄐㄧㄥㄘㄨㄛˋㄌㄨㄢˋ)
nervous disorder; mental disorder
神經炎(ㄕㄣˊㄐㄧㄥㄧㄢˊ)
neuritis
神劇(ㄕㄣˊㄐㄩˋ)
an oratorio
神奇(ㄕㄣˊㄑㄧˊ)
marvelous; wondrous; mysterious; miraculous
神祇(ㄕㄣˊㄑㄧˊ)
the gods; the spirits
神氣
①(ㄕㄣˊㄑㄧˋ) divine atmosphere ②(ㄕㄣˊ ·ㄑㄧ) ⓐdignified; imposing ⓑto put on airs; overweening: 呵！這老人倒神氣起來了。Humph! What airs the old man gives himself! ⓒan appearance; an air; an expression: 男孩臉上顯出得意的神氣。The boy had an air of complacency.
神氣活現(ㄕㄣˊ·ㄑㄧㄏㄨㄛˊㄒㄧㄢˋ)
very cocky; as proud as a peacock
神器(ㄕㄣˊㄑㄧˋ)
the throne
神槍手(ㄕㄣˊㄑㄧㄤㄕㄡˇ)
a sharpshooter; a marksman
神情(ㄕㄣˊㄑㄧㄥˊ)
a facial expression; a look; an appearance; an air: 他臉上露出愉快的神情。He wore a happy expression.
神曲(ㄕㄣˊㄑㄩˇ)
the *Divine Comedy*, by Dante Alighieri, 1265-1321
神權(ㄕㄣˊㄑㄩㄢˊ)
①the divine right (of kings) ②religious authority
神效(ㄕㄣˊㄒㄧㄠˋ)
marvelous effect; wondrous efficacy
神仙(ㄕㄣˊㄒㄧㄢ)
an immortal; a supernatural being; a celestial being
神仙魚(ㄕㄣˊㄒㄧㄢㄩˊ)
an angelfish (a species of tropical fish)
神像(ㄕㄣˊㄒㄧㄤˋ)
①an image of a dead person ②an idol; the picture or the statue of a god or the Buddha
神學(ㄕㄣˊㄒㄩㄝˊ)
theology: 他是研究神學的學生。He is a student of theology.
神學博士(ㄕㄣˊㄒㄩㄝˊㄅㄛˊㄕˋ)
a doctor of divinity (D.D.)
神學院(ㄕㄣˊㄒㄩㄝˊㄩㄢˋ)
a seminary (for training priests or ministers)
神職人員(ㄕㄣˊㄓˊㄖㄣˊㄩㄢˊ)
the clergy
神紙(ㄕㄣˊㄓˇ)
paper burned in worship
神志(ㄕㄣˊㄓˋ)
①mind ②consciousness
神志不清(ㄕㄣˊㄓˋㄅㄨˋㄑㄧㄥ)
unconscious; in a state of a coma
神智(ㄕㄣˊㄓˋ)
①mind ②intelligence
神智不清(ㄕㄣˊㄓˋㄅㄨˋㄑㄧㄥ)
clouded in the mind; incapable of clear thinking; muddleheaded
神州(ㄕㄣˊㄓㄡ)
①China ②the imperial capital
神主(ㄕㄣˊㄓㄨˇ)
a wooden tablet used as a symbol of the deceased
神馳(ㄕㄣˊㄔˊ)
to allow the thoughts to fly to an adored person
神差鬼使(ㄕㄣˊㄔㄞㄍㄨㄟˇㄕˇ)
as though urged by gods and demons (said of someone doing something inexplicably)
神出鬼沒(ㄕㄣˊㄔㄨㄍㄨㄟˇㄇㄛˋ)
to appear and disappear quite unpredictably like gods and demons; to appear unexpectedly in a moment

and to disappear completely in the next (usually said of guerrillas); to come and go like a shadow: 這個間諜神出鬼沒的。The spy comes and goes like a shadow.
神社(ㄕㄣˊ ㄕㄜˋ)
a Shinto shrine
神聖(ㄕㄣˊ ㄕㄥˋ)
holy; sacred; divine: 保護國土是軍人的神聖職責。Defending territory is soldiers' sacred duty.
神聖不可侵犯(ㄕㄣˊ ㄕㄥˋ ㄅㄨˋ ㄎㄜˇ ㄑㄧㄣ ㄈㄢˋ)
sacred and not to be violated; holy and inviolable
神聖羅馬帝國(ㄕㄣˊ ㄕㄥˋ ㄌㄨㄛˊ ㄇㄚˇ ㄉㄧˋ ㄍㄨㄛˊ)
the Holy Roman Empire
神術(ㄕㄣˊ ㄕㄨˋ)
marvelous technique; wondrous tricks
神人(ㄕㄣˊ ㄖㄣˊ)
① one who has discovered truth; a holy man ② man with a very dignified look ③ gods and men
神人共憤(ㄕㄣˊ ㄖㄣˊ ㄍㄨㄥˋ ㄈㄣˋ)
to be hated by immortals and mortals alike—to incur the wrath or indignation of all
神彩(ㄕㄣˊ ㄘㄞˇ)
a countenance; a look; an expression
神采煥發(ㄕㄣˊ ㄘㄞˇ ㄏㄨㄢˋ ㄈㄚ)
a happy look; gay
神采奕奕(ㄕㄣˊ ㄘㄞˇ ㄧˋ ㄧˋ)
① beaming; in high spirits ② glowing with health and radiating vigor
神思(ㄕㄣˊ ㄙ)
thoughts; a state of mind; a mental state
神似(ㄕㄣˊ ㄙˋ)
lifelike; to be alike in spirit; to be an excellent likeness
神色(ㄕㄣˊ ㄙㄜˋ)
a look; an expression
神色自若(ㄕㄣˊ ㄙㄜˋ ㄗˋ ㄖㄨㄛˋ)
to look unperturbed
神速(ㄕㄣˊ ㄙㄨˋ)
marvelously fast; wondrously quick; lightning speed: 收效神速 to yield marvelously quick results

神髓(ㄕㄣˊ ㄙㄨㄟˇ)
essence; quintessence
神算(ㄕㄣˊ ㄙㄨㄢˋ)
① a very clever plan ② miraculous foresight; marvelous prediction
神恩(ㄕㄣˊ ㄣ)
divine favor
神兒(ㄕㄜˊㄦ)
a look; an expression; an air
神醫(ㄕㄣˊ ㄧ)
a marvelous physician; a great doctor
神異(ㄕㄣˊ ㄧˋ)
① miraculous; marvelous; wondrous ② gods and spirits
神意(ㄕㄣˊ ㄧˋ)
the will of God; divine will
神遊(ㄕㄣˊ ㄧㄡˊ)
to tour (a place) by imagination; to make a mental travel
神佑(ㄕㄣˊ ㄧㄡˋ)
divine help
神鷹(ㄕㄣˊ ㄧㄥ)
①(literally) a divine eagle —a patriotic way of saying "our air force" or "our air force planes" ② a condor
神武(ㄕㄣˊ ㄨˇ)
intelligent and courageous
神物(ㄕㄣˊ ㄨˋ)
① a supernatural being; an immortal; a deity ② a wonder; a prodigy; a phenomenon
神悟(ㄕㄣˊ ㄨˋ)
marvelously quick understanding
神位(ㄕㄣˊ ㄨㄟˋ)
a sacred tablet used as the symbol of a deity
神往(ㄕㄣˊ ㄨㄤˇ)
to have one's thoughts or imagination absorbed in some wonderful thing or place: 日月潭的景色令人神往。The scenery of the Sun Moon Lake is enchanting.
神宇(ㄕㄣˊ ㄩˇ)
an appearance; a look
神韻(ㄕㄣˊ ㄩㄣˋ)
① (said of a person) an appearance and a carriage; an impression; an air ②(said of paintings or calligraphic works) poetic quality; charm

神勇(ㄕㄣˊ ㄩㄥˇ)
superhuman bravery; extraordinarily brave

【祠】 3944 ㄘˊ tsyr cí
1. a temple; a shrine
2. the spring worship
祠堂(ㄘˊ ㄊㄤˊ)
a shrine; an ancestral hall (or temple); a memorial temple
祠官(ㄘˊ ㄍㄨㄢ)
an official in charge of the spring worship
祠祝(ㄘˊ ㄓㄨˋ)
a custodian of a temple or shrine
祠宇(ㄘˊ ㄩˇ)
a shrine; a temple

【祟】 3945 ㄙㄨㄟˋ suey suì
1. the evil influence of gods or demons
2. (said of ghosts or evil spirits) to haunt; to afflict
祟惑(ㄙㄨㄟˋ ㄏㄨㄛˋ)
to confuse by evil influence

六畫

【祥】 3946 ㄒㄧㄤˊ shyang xiáng
auspicious; propitious; favorable
祥麟(ㄒㄧㄤˊ ㄌㄧㄣˊ)
a legendary horse-like animal resembling the unicorn, whose appearance was regarded in ancient times as an auspicious omen
祥兆(ㄒㄧㄤˊ ㄓㄠˋ)
a good omen
祥瑞(ㄒㄧㄤˊ ㄖㄨㄟˋ)
a good omen; an auspicious omen; auspiciousness
祥雲(ㄒㄧㄤˊ ㄩㄣˊ)
auspicious clouds

【祧】 3947 ㄊㄧㄠ tiau tiāo
1. an ancestral temple (especially of distant ancestors)
2. to be or become heir to

【票】 3948 ㄆㄧㄠˋ piaw piào
1. a bill; a note

〔示部〕

2. a ticket: 憑票入場。Admission by ticket only.
3. a ballot
4. a hostage
5. amateur performance

票面(ㄆㄧㄠˋ ㄇㄧㄢˋ)
the face value of a note, bond, etc.

票面值(ㄆㄧㄠˋ ㄇㄧㄢˋ ㄓˊ)or 票面額(ㄆㄧㄠˋ ㄇㄧㄢˋ ㄜˊ)
face value; nominal value; par value

票房(ㄆㄧㄠˋ ㄈㄤˊ)
①a box office; a ticket window ②a club of amateur Peking opera actors ③box office—(figuratively) the power of a show or performer to attract an audience

票根(ㄆㄧㄠˋ ㄍㄣ)
a ticket stub; a counterfoil

票匭(ㄆㄧㄠˋ ㄍㄨㄟˇ)
①a ticket box ②a ballot box

票價(ㄆㄧㄠˋ ㄐㄧㄚˋ)
the price of a ticket; an admission (or entrance) fee

票據(ㄆㄧㄠˋ ㄐㄩˋ)
negotiable instruments; bills; notes; vouchers; receipts

票據法(ㄆㄧㄠˋ ㄐㄩˋ ㄈㄚˇ)
Law of Negotiable Instruments

票據交換所(ㄆㄧㄠˋ ㄐㄩˋ ㄐㄧㄠ ㄏㄨㄢˋ ㄙㄨㄛˇ)
a clearing house

票決(ㄆㄧㄠˋ ㄐㄩㄝˊ)
to decide by casting ballots: 讓我們付諸票決。Let's decide by casting ballots.

票箱(ㄆㄧㄠˋ ㄒㄧㄤ)
a ballot box

票選(ㄆㄧㄠˋ ㄒㄩㄢˇ)
to elect by casting ballots

票傳(ㄆㄧㄠˋ ㄔㄨㄢˊ)
to serve a summons on someone

票數(ㄆㄧㄠˋ ㄕㄨˋ)
the number of votes or ballots

票子(ㄆㄧㄠˋ ·ㄗ)or 票兒(ㄆㄧㄠˋㄦ)
a ticket; a note; a bill; paper money: 我有許多票子要付款。I have many bills to pay.

票存(ㄆㄧㄠˋ ㄘㄨㄣˊ)
cash reserves against notes issued

票額(ㄆㄧㄠˋ ㄜˊ)
the sum stated on a check or bill; face value

票友兒(ㄆㄧㄠˋ ㄧㄡˇㄦ)
an amateur actor or actress of Peking opera

【祭】 3949 ㄐㄧˋ jih jì

1. to worship; to offer sacrifices to; to honor by a rite or service
2. to wield

祭品(ㄐㄧˋ ㄆㄧㄣˇ)
offerings; sacrificial articles; sacrifices

祭服(ㄐㄧˋ ㄈㄨˊ)
a robe worn for a religious rite

祭地(ㄐㄧˋ ㄉㄧˋ)
annual services of offering sacrifices to the earth

祭典(ㄐㄧˋ ㄉㄧㄢˇ)
services or ceremonies of offering sacrifices

祭奠(ㄐㄧˋ ㄉㄧㄢˋ)
to offer sacrifices to the spirit of a deceased person

祭壇(ㄐㄧˋ ㄊㄢˊ)
an altar

祭天(ㄐㄧˋ ㄊㄧㄢ)
annual services of offering sacrifices to Heaven

祭田(ㄐㄧˋ ㄊㄧㄢˊ)
fields set apart for maintaining annual sacrifices

祭禮(ㄐㄧˋ ㄌㄧˇ)
sacrifices offered to gods or the deceased; sacrificial offerings

祭告(ㄐㄧˋ ㄍㄠˋ)
to inform (the gods of important national events) through a rite or service

祭冠(ㄐㄧˋ ㄍㄨㄢ)
a cap worn in a major religious service

祭酒(ㄐㄧˋ ㄐㄧㄡˇ)
①(in ancient times) the person who performs the libation before a banquet ②a respectable elder; the most senior and respected person of a profession

祭獻(ㄐㄧˋ ㄒㄧㄢˋ)
to offer (sacrifices)

祭主(ㄐㄧˋ ㄓㄨˇ)
an officiant at a religious rite or service

祭竈(ㄐㄧˋ ㄗㄠˋ)
the worship of the kitchen god (performed on the 23rd day of the 12th lunar month)

祭祖(ㄐㄧˋ ㄗㄨˇ)
to perform rites in honor of ancestors

祭司(ㄐㄧˋ ㄙ)or 祭師(ㄐㄧˋ ㄕ)
an officiant at a religious service; a high priest

祭祀(ㄐㄧˋ ㄙˋ)
to worship; to honor by a service or rite; to offer sacrifices to

祭掃(ㄐㄧˋ ㄙㄠˇ)
to clean and offer sacrifices at a tomb

祭物(ㄐㄧˋ ㄨˋ)
sacrifices

祭文(ㄐㄧˋ ㄨㄣˊ)
a written message offered (to the gods and the deceased, etc.) in worship; sacrificial writing; an elegiac address

七畫

【祲】 3950 ㄐㄧㄣ jin jīn

1. ominous or sinister spirits
2. vigorous

八畫

【祺】 3951 ㄑㄧˊ chyi qí

1. lucky; propitious; auspicious
2. peaceful; serene

祺祥(ㄑㄧˊ ㄒㄧㄤˊ)
fortunate; lucky; auspicious; propitious

祺然(ㄑㄧˊ ㄖㄢˊ)
peaceful; serene

【祿】 3952 ㄌㄨˋ luh lù

1. happiness; prosperity
2. official pay; salary

祿命(ㄌㄨˋ ㄇㄧㄥˋ)
a person's lot through life

祿俸(ㄌㄨˋ ㄈㄥˋ)
official pay

祿蠹(ㄌㄨˋ ㄉㄨˋ)
a sinecurist

祿秩(ㄌㄨˋ ㄓˋ)
official rank and pay

祿食(ㄌㄨˋ ㄕˊ)
official pay

祿餌(ㄌㄨˋ ㄦˇ)
official pay as a bait (for talent)

祿養(ㄌㄨˋ ㄧㄤˇ)
to support (dependents) with official pay

祿位(ㄌㄨˋ ㄨㄟˋ)
official salary and rank

【祼】 3953
ㄍㄨㄢˋ guann guàn
to pour out a libation

【禁】 3954
1. ㄐㄧㄣˋ jinn jìn

1. to prohibit; to forbid; to ban: 禁止在這湖內游泳。Swimming is banned in this lake.
2. to confine; to imprison; to detain: 他們把我監禁起來。They imprisoned me.
3. secret
4. a royal residence: 紫禁城 the Forbidden City in Peking

禁閉(ㄐㄧㄣˋ ㄅㄧˋ)
①to prohibit entry into government services ② to imprison; to confine; to lock up: 他被關禁閉。He was placed in confinement.

禁閉室(ㄐㄧㄣˋ ㄅㄧˋ ㄕˋ)
a confinement cell

禁品(ㄐㄧㄣˋ ㄆㄧㄣˇ)
contraband; prohibited merchandise

禁方(ㄐㄧㄣˋ ㄈㄤ)
a secret medical prescription

禁地(ㄐㄧㄣˋ ㄉㄧˋ)
a forbidden ground; an area declared out of bounds

禁賭(ㄐㄧㄣˋ ㄉㄨˇ)
to prohibit gambling

禁屠(ㄐㄧㄣˋ ㄊㄨˊ)
to prohibit slaughter of animals

禁例(ㄐㄧㄣˋ ㄌㄧˋ)
an official prohibition or restraint; an interdict

禁獵(ㄐㄧㄣˋ ㄌㄧㄝˋ)
a ban on hunting

禁令(ㄐㄧㄣˋ ㄌㄧㄥˋ)
a prohibition; a ban; an interdict

禁臠(ㄐㄧㄣˋ ㄌㄨㄢˊ)
①a forbidden thing; one's exclusive domain ②a precious thing

禁錮(ㄐㄧㄣˋ ㄍㄨˋ)
① confinement; imprisonment ②to prohibit entry into government services

禁菓(ㄐㄧㄣˋ ㄍㄨㄛˇ)
the forbidden fruit: 夏娃吃了禁菓。Eve ate the forbidden fruit.

禁火(ㄐㄧㄣˋ ㄏㄨㄛˇ)
to prohibit cooking (on March 3 in the lunar calendar)

禁忌(ㄐㄧㄣˋ ㄐㄧˋ)
① a taboo; to taboo ② to avoid; to abstain from

禁酒(ㄐㄧㄣˋ ㄐㄧㄡˇ)
to prohibit the use of alcoholic drinks

禁軍(ㄐㄧㄣˋ ㄐㄩㄣ)
imperial guards

禁區(ㄐㄧㄣˋ ㄑㄩ)
① a forbidden region; a restricted zone ② a preserve; a reserve ③(football) the penalty area ④(basketball) the restricted area

禁止(ㄐㄧㄣˋ ㄓˇ)
to forbid; to prohibit; to ban; to taboo: 禁止在火車內吸煙。Smoking is banned in the train.

禁止倒垃圾(ㄐㄧㄣˋ ㄓˇ ㄉㄠˋ ㄌㄜˋ ㄙㄜˋ)
Do not leave garbage here.

禁止停車(ㄐㄧㄣˋ ㄓˇ ㄊㄧㄥˊ ㄔㄜ)
No parking.

禁止關稅(ㄐㄧㄣˋ ㄓˇ ㄍㄨㄢ ㄕㄨㄟˋ)
a prohibitive tariff

禁止吸煙(ㄐㄧㄣˋ ㄓˇ ㄒㄧ ㄧㄢ)
No smoking.

禁止招貼(ㄐㄧㄣˋ ㄓˇ ㄓㄠ ㄊㄧㄝ)
Post no bills.

禁止車輛通行(ㄐㄧㄣˋ ㄓˇ ㄔㄜ ㄌㄧㄤˋ ㄊㄨㄥ ㄒㄧㄥˊ)
No vehicles allowed. 或 No thoroughfare. 或 Closed to traffic.

禁止設攤(ㄐㄧㄣˋ ㄓˇ ㄕㄜˋ ㄊㄢ)
Do not set up stands here.

禁止入內(ㄐㄧㄣˋ ㄓˇ ㄖㄨˋ ㄋㄟˋ)
No admittance.

禁止按喇叭(ㄐㄧㄣˋ ㄓˇ ㄢˋ ㄌㄚˇ ˙ㄅㄚ)
Do not sound horns. 或 No honking.

禁治產(ㄐㄧㄣˋ ㄓˋ ㄔㄢˇ)
(law) incompetency (to manage one's own property)

禁中(ㄐㄧㄣˋ ㄓㄨㄥ)
the emperor's living quarters

禁城(ㄐㄧㄣˋ ㄔㄥˊ)
the forbidden city

禁食(ㄐㄧㄣˋ ㄕˊ)
fast; to fast

禁書(ㄐㄧㄣˋ ㄕㄨ)
banned books

禁足(ㄐㄧㄣˋ ㄗㄨˊ)
to forbid a soldier to leave the barracks on holidays as a form of punishment

禁坐(ㄐㄧㄣˋ ㄗㄨㄛˋ)
the throne

禁夜(ㄐㄧㄣˋ ㄧㄝˋ)
the curfew

禁煙(ㄐㄧㄣˋ ㄧㄢ)
① to prohibit opium ② to prohibit cooking ③ smoke rising from the imperial palace

禁煙節(ㄐㄧㄣˋ ㄧㄢ ㄐㄧㄝˊ)
Opium Prohibition Day, on June 3

禁衛軍(ㄐㄧㄣˋ ㄨㄟˋ ㄐㄩㄣ)
imperial guards 亦作「禁軍」

禁慾(ㄐㄧㄣˋ ㄩˋ)
to be ascetic; abstinence

禁苑(ㄐㄧㄣˋ ㄩㄢˋ)
an imperial garden

禁運(ㄐㄧㄣˋ ㄩㄣˋ)
to embargo; an embargo

【禁】 3954
2. ㄐㄧㄣ jin jīn
to endure; to bear; to withstand; to stand

禁不起(ㄐㄧㄣ ˙ㄅㄨ ㄑㄧˇ)
unable to endure; unable to withstand; unable to help; unable to stand: 他禁不起誘惑。He failed to withstand the temptation.

禁不住(ㄐㄧㄣ ˙ㄅㄨ ㄓㄨˋ)
① unable to endure; unable to withstand; unable to stand; unable to avoid: 他禁不住一點批評。He can't stand a little bit of criticism. ② can not help: 她禁不住哭了起來。She could not help crying.

禁得起(ㄐㄧㄣ ˙ㄉㄜ ㄑㄧˇ)
able to withstand; able to stand; able to endure; able to avoid: 他禁得起嚴厲的考

驗。He was able to stand severe tests.
禁得住(ㄐㄧㄣ ˙ㄉㄜ ㄓㄨˋ)
able to withstand; able to endure; able to refrain from

〔示部〕

九畫

【禍】3955
ㄏㄨㄛˋ huoh huò
1. calamity; disaster; misfortune; evil: 戰爭是可怕的災禍。War is a frightful calamity.
2. to bring disaster upon; to harm; to injure; to do evil to
3. to punish
禍不單行(ㄏㄨㄛˋ ㄅㄨˋ ㄉㄢ ㄒㄧㄥˊ)
Misfortunes never come singly(or single).
禍福倚伏(ㄏㄨㄛˋ ㄈㄨˊ ㄧˇ ㄈㄨˊ)
Fortune and misfortune are interrelated.
禍福無門(ㄏㄨㄛˋ ㄈㄨˊ ㄨˊ ㄇㄣˊ)
(literally) Fortune and misfortune do not come through a definite door.—The arrival of fortune or misfortune is unpredictable.
禍端(ㄏㄨㄛˋ ㄉㄨㄢ)
the cause of a misfortune or disaster
禍胎(ㄏㄨㄛˋ ㄊㄞ)
a source of disaster
禍亂(ㄏㄨㄛˋ ㄌㄨㄢˋ)
disturbances; disastrous disorder
禍根(ㄏㄨㄛˋ ㄍㄣ)
seeds of misfortune; a source of disaster
禍國殃民(ㄏㄨㄛˋ ㄍㄨㄛˊ ㄧㄤ ㄇㄧㄣˊ)
to bring disaster upon the state and the people; to harm the state and injure the people
禍害(ㄏㄨㄛˋ ㄏㄞˋ)
harm; injury; evil
禍患(ㄏㄨㄛˋ ㄏㄨㄢˋ)
misfortune; disaster; harm; evil
禍起蕭牆(ㄏㄨㄛˋ ㄑㄧˇ ㄒㄧㄠ ㄑㄧㄤˊ)
Disaster arises from the very inside.
禍心(ㄏㄨㄛˋ ㄒㄧㄣ)
evil intention; malice: 此人包藏禍心。This man harbors evil intentions (or thoughts).
禍兆(ㄏㄨㄛˋ ㄓㄠˋ)
evil omens or portents
禍種(ㄏㄨㄛˋ ㄓㄨㄥˇ)
seeds of trouble in the future
禍事(ㄏㄨㄛˋ ㄕˋ)
disaster; calamity; mishap; misfortune; catastrophe
禍首(ㄏㄨㄛˋ ㄕㄡˇ)
the one who starts the trouble; a chief culprit
禍水(ㄏㄨㄛˋ ㄕㄨㄟˇ)
a woman who is often the source of troubles
禍棗災梨(ㄏㄨㄛˋ ㄗㄠˇ ㄗㄞ ㄌㄧˊ)
to print worthless writings; to publish useless books
禍從天降(ㄏㄨㄛˋ ㄘㄨㄥˊ ㄊㄧㄢ ㄐㄧㄤˋ)
(literally) A calamity descended from the sky.—an unexpected disaster
禍從口出(ㄏㄨㄛˋ ㄘㄨㄥˊ ㄎㄡˇ ㄔㄨ)
(literally) The mouth is the primary source of calamities.—Careless talks may land one in trouble.

【福】3956
ㄈㄨˊ fwu fú
happiness; good fortune; good luck; a blessing; bliss: 我祝你婚姻幸福。I wish you felicity in marriage.
福薄(ㄈㄨˊ ㄅㄛˊ)
luckless; unlucky; hapless; unfortunate
福庇(ㄈㄨˊ ㄅㄧˋ)
(a complimentary phrase) your fortunate protection
福命(ㄈㄨˊ ㄇㄧㄥˋ)
one's lot through life
福分(ㄈㄨˊ ˙ㄈㄣ)
share of happiness allotted by destiny
福地洞天(ㄈㄨˊ ㄉㄧˋ ㄉㄨㄥˋ ㄊㄧㄢ)
a paradise
福特(ㄈㄨˊ ㄊㄜˋ)
① Henry Ford, 1863-1947, American inventor of the automobile and philanthropist ② Gerald Rudolph Ford, born 1913, 38th U.S. President (1974-77)
福特基金會(ㄈㄨˊ ㄊㄜˋ ㄐㄧ ㄐㄧㄣ ㄏㄨㄟˋ)
Ford Foundation
福體(ㄈㄨˊ ㄊㄧˇ)
your health (a respectful expression used in addressing one's elders)
福利(ㄈㄨˊ ㄌㄧˋ)
welfare; good; prosperity; well-being; fringe benefits for employees: 我們要爲人民謀福利。We should work for the well-being of the people.
福利社(ㄈㄨˊ ㄌㄧˋ ㄕㄜˋ)
a store doing business on the premises of a school, factory, government agency, etc.
福祿特爾(ㄈㄨˊ ㄌㄨˋ ㄊㄜˋ ㄦˇ)
Marie Arouet Voltaire, 1694-1778, French thinker and writer
福祿壽(ㄈㄨˊ ㄌㄨˋ ㄕㄡˋ)
happiness, wealth, and longevity (which are the ingredients of a happy life)
福過災生(ㄈㄨˊ ㄍㄨㄛˋ ㄗㄞ ㄕㄥ)
When fortune passes, misfortune follows.
福躬(ㄈㄨˊ ㄍㄨㄥ)
(a complimentary phrase) your happy or fortunate person
福克蘭群島(ㄈㄨˊ ㄎㄜˋ ㄌㄢˊ ㄑㄩㄣˊ ㄉㄠˇ)
the Falkland Islands
福建(ㄈㄨˊ ㄐㄧㄢˋ)
Fukien Province
福晉(ㄈㄨˊ ㄐㄧㄣˋ)
a Manchurian term for "wife"
福氣(ㄈㄨˊ ˙ㄑㄧ)
good luck
福相(ㄈㄨˊ ㄒㄧㄤˋ)
a countenance of good luck
福星高照(ㄈㄨˊ ㄒㄧㄥ ㄍㄠ ㄓㄠˋ)
The lucky star is in the ascendant.—to ride the high tide of good luck
福至心靈(ㄈㄨˊ ㄓˋ ㄒㄧㄣ ㄌㄧㄥˊ)
The mind works more efficiently when good fortune comes.
福州(ㄈㄨˊ ㄓㄡ)
Foochow, Fukien
福壽全歸(ㄈㄨˊ ㄕㄡˋ ㄑㄩㄢˊ ㄍㄨㄟ)
to have enjoyed both happiness and longevity (a laudatory expression about a person who died at a venerable age)
福壽雙全(ㄈㄨˊ ㄕㄡˋ ㄕㄨㄤ ㄑㄩㄢˊ)
to enjoy both happiness and longevity

福善禍淫(ㄈㄨˊ ㄕㄢˋ ㄏㄨㄛˋ ｜ㄣˊ)
Heaven blesses the virtuous and punishes the evil.
福如東海(ㄈㄨˊ ㄖㄨˊ ㄉㄨㄥ ㄏㄞˇ)
happiness as immense as the eastern sea
福澤(ㄈㄨˊ ㄗㄜˊ)
good fortune; happiness; blessedness
福音(ㄈㄨˊ ｜ㄣ)
① good news; welcome news ② the gospel: 他是個福音傳道者。He's a minister of the gospel.
福音堂(ㄈㄨˊ ｜ㄣ ㄊㄤˊ)
a chapel
福音主義(ㄈㄨˊ ｜ㄣ ㄓㄨˇ ｜ˋ)
evangelism
福蔭(ㄈㄨˊ ｜ㄣˋ)
(a complimentary phrase) your fortunate protection
福無雙至(ㄈㄨˊ ㄨˊ ㄕㄨㄤ ㄓˋ)
Blessings never come in pairs.
福王(ㄈㄨˊ ㄨㄤˊ)
one of the last princes of the Ming Dynasty, executed by the Manchus

【禋】 3957 ｜ㄣ in yīn
1. to worship with sincerity and reverence
2. to offer sacrifices to Heaven

【禊】 3958 ㄒ｜ˋ shih xì
semiannual exorcism performed at the water's edge in ancient times
禊帖(ㄒ｜ˋ ㄊ｜ㄝˇ)
the "Gathering at Orchid Pavilion" (蘭亭帖) by Wang Hsi-chih (王羲之), considered to be the most valuable calligraphic work

【禔】 3959 ㄊ｜ˊ tyi tí
happiness; good fortune; good luck; blessings

【禎】 3960 ㄓㄣ jen zhēn
1. auspicious; a good omen
2. a Chinese family name
禎祥(ㄓㄣ ㄒ｜ㄤˊ)
a good omen; a lucky omen

【禕】 3961 ｜ i yī
excellent

【禘】 3962 ㄉ｜ˋ dih dì
imperial sacrifice made once every five years
禘郊(ㄉ｜ˋ ㄐ｜ㄠ)
imperial sacrifice held in the countryside

十畫

【禡】 3963 ㄇㄚˋ mah mà
sacrifice to the god of war offered by troops on the eve of a battle
禡祭(ㄇㄚˋ ㄐ｜ˋ)
the ritual of offering sacrifices to the god of war by troops on the eve of a battle

【禛】 3964 ㄓㄣ jen zhēn
to be blessed because of one's sincerity

十一畫

【禦】 3965 ㄩˋ yuh yù
to guard against; to take precautions against: 攻擊爲最佳之防禦。The best defense is to attack.
禦敵(ㄩˋ ㄉ｜ˊ)
to guard against the enemy
禦寇(ㄩˋ ㄎㄡˋ)
to guard against bandits; to take precautions against invaders
禦寒(ㄩˋ ㄏㄢˊ)
to protect oneself from cold; to take precautions against cold
禦侮(ㄩˋ ㄨˇ)
to guard against the insults of foreign powers

【禩】 3966 ㄙˋ syh sì
same as 祀—to worship; to offer sacrifices

十二畫

【禧】 3967 ㄒ｜ shi xī (又讀 ㄒ｜ˇ shii xǐ)
happiness; blessings; auspiciousness: 恭賀新禧。Happy New Year!

【禪】 3968 1. ㄔㄢˊ charn chán
1. Zen Buddhism
2. meditation; intense contemplation
禪房(ㄔㄢˊ ㄈㄤˊ)
a hermitage; a monastery
禪堂(ㄔㄢˊ ㄊㄤˊ)
a meditation hall or room
禪林(ㄔㄢˊ ㄌ｜ㄣˊ)
a grove of meditation—a monastery
禪機(ㄔㄢˊ ㄐ｜)
subtleties of Zen principles
禪寂(ㄔㄢˊ ㄐ｜ˊ)
(Buddhism) the ideal peace of mind
禪偈(ㄔㄢˊ ㄐ｜ˋ)
utterances of a Zen master, in the form of verse, often a recapitulation of what he has just said
禪牀(ㄔㄢˊ ㄔㄨㄤˊ)
(Buddhism) a seat for meditation
禪師(ㄔㄢˊ ㄕ)
a master, or teacher, of meditation, or of the Zen school
禪宗(ㄔㄢˊ ㄗㄨㄥ)
the Zen sect of Buddhism, said to be established in China by Bodhidharma (達摩)
禪寺(ㄔㄢˊ ㄙˋ)
a Buddhist temple
禪椅(ㄔㄢˊ ｜ˇ)
(Buddhism) a seat for meditation
禪悟(ㄔㄢˊ ㄨˋ)
to realize truth through meditation; a full realization of truth through meditation
禪味(ㄔㄢˊ ㄨㄟˋ)
(Buddhism) pleasant effect of meditation
禪悅(ㄔㄢˊ ㄩㄝˋ)
(Buddhism) joy of the mystic trance

【禪】 3968 2. ㄕㄢˋ shann shàn
to abdicate (the throne)
禪讓(ㄕㄢˋ ㄖㄤˋ)
to abdicate the throne
禪位(ㄕㄢˋ ㄨㄟˋ)
to abdicate the throne

【禨】 3969 ㄐ｜ ji jī

〔示部〕

to seek blessings from ghosts

十三畫

〔示部〕

【禮】 3970 ㄌㄧˇ lii lǐ
1. courtesy; propriety; decorum; politeness; civility; etiquette: 他對老師總是彬彬有禮。He is always courteous to the teachers.
2. rites; ceremony
3. a gift; a present
4. a Chinese family name

禮拜(ㄌㄧˇ ㄅㄞˋ)
① church service; worship ② a week: 她生病臥床已經一個禮拜了。She has been sick in bed for a week.

禮拜堂(ㄌㄧˇ ㄅㄞˋ ㄊㄤˊ)
a chapel; a church

禮拜天(ㄌㄧˇ ㄅㄞˋ ㄊㄧㄢ)or 禮拜日(ㄌㄧˇ ㄅㄞˋ ㄖˋ)
Sunday 亦作「星期天」

禮拜寺(ㄌㄧˇ ㄅㄞˋ ㄙˋ)
a mosque

禮部(ㄌㄧˇ ㄅㄨˋ)
(in former times) Ministry of Rites and Education

禮部試(ㄌㄧˇ ㄅㄨˋ ㄕˋ)
general civil service examinations in former times, administered by the Ministry of Rites and Education

禮礮 or 禮砲(ㄌㄧˇ ㄆㄠˋ)
a gun salute; a salvo

禮品(ㄌㄧˇ ㄆㄧㄣˇ)
a gift; a present

禮聘(ㄌㄧˇ ㄆㄧㄣˋ)
to cordially invite the service of; to enlist the service of someone with handsome gifts

禮帽(ㄌㄧˇ ㄇㄠˋ)
a ceremonial hat or cap; a hat or cap worn by men on a formal occasion or ceremony

禮貌(ㄌㄧˇ ㄇㄠˋ)
etiquette; politeness; good manners; civility; decorum: 對人要有禮貌。Be polite to others.

禮門義路(ㄌㄧˇ ㄇㄣˊ ㄧˋ ㄌㄨˋ)
Decorum is an obligatory road to all men.

禮法(ㄌㄧˇ ㄈㄚˇ)
decorum; rules of politeness

禮服(ㄌㄧˇ ㄈㄨˊ)
ceremonial dress; full dress; a dress suit; a formal dress: 她穿着一件漂亮的禮服。She wears a beautiful formal dress.

禮單(ㄌㄧˇ ㄉㄢ)
a list of presents

禮度(ㄌㄧˇ ㄉㄨˋ)
rules of decorum; etiquette

禮多人不怪(ㄌㄧˇ ㄉㄨㄛ ㄖㄣˊ ㄅㄨˋ ㄍㄨㄞˋ)
Nobody blames excessive politeness.

禮堂(ㄌㄧˇ ㄊㄤˊ)
① an auditorium ② a hall decorated for a wedding ceremony or funeral service

禮記(ㄌㄧˇ ㄐㄧˋ)
the *Book of Rites*, one of the Thirteen Classics

禮節(ㄌㄧˇ ㄐㄧㄝˊ)
etiquette; requirements of decorum; rules of politeness; courtesy; protocol; civility

禮教(ㄌㄧˇ ㄐㄧㄠˋ)
ethical education

禮金(ㄌㄧˇ ㄐㄧㄣ)
a cash gift

禮器(ㄌㄧˇ ㄑㄧˋ)
instruments for sacrificial ceremonies

禮輕人意重(ㄌㄧˇ ㄑㄧㄥ ㄖㄣˊ ㄧˋ ㄓㄨㄥˋ)
The thoughtfulness is worth far more than the gift itself. 或 The gift is trifling, but the feeling is profound.

禮券(ㄌㄧˇ ㄑㄩㄢˋ)
gift coupons sold by a shop, which the recipient may convert into goods (or cash) at the shop in question

禮賢下士(ㄌㄧˇ ㄒㄧㄢˊ ㄒㄧㄚˋ ㄕˋ)
(said of a ruler) courteous to the wise and condescending to the scholarly

禮制(ㄌㄧˇ ㄓˋ)
a system of ceremonial forms

禮成(ㄌㄧˇ ㄔㄥˊ)
Ceremony is over.

禮尙往來(ㄌㄧˇ ㄕㄤˋ ㄨㄤˇ ㄌㄞˊ)
Courtesy emphasizes reciprocity.

禮數(ㄌㄧˇ ㄕㄨˋ)
different grades of courtesy due to differences in rank

禮讓(ㄌㄧˇ ㄖㄤˋ)
to make way humbly or modestly

禮讚(ㄌㄧˇ ㄗㄢˋ)
to praise; to worship; to idolize; to adore; to glorify: 他們唱聖詩禮讚上帝。They sing hymns to glorify God.

禮葬(ㄌㄧˇ ㄗㄤˋ)
to bury with pomp

禮俗(ㄌㄧˇ ㄙㄨˊ)
manners and custom (of a people)

禮所當然(ㄌㄧˇ ㄙㄨㄛˇ ㄉㄤ ㄖㄢˊ)
Etiquette requires it.

禮儀(ㄌㄧˇ ㄧˊ)
ceremonies for courtesy; etiquette; protocol; decorum

禮儀之邦(ㄌㄧˇ ㄧˊ ㄓ ㄅㄤ)
a state of ceremonies

禮義廉恥(ㄌㄧˇ ㄧˋ ㄌㄧㄢˊ ㄔˇ)
propriety, justice, honesty, and a sense of shame—the four cardinal virtues of the people

禮無不答(ㄌㄧˇ ㄨˊ ㄅㄨˋ ㄉㄚˊ)
Courtesy must be reciprocated.

禮物(ㄌㄧˇ ㄨˋ)
① a gift; a present: 我有一份禮物送給您。I have a present for you. ② products of a culture

禮遇(ㄌㄧˇ ㄩˋ)
to treat with courtesy; to treat with respect: 他受到禮遇。He was accorded courteous reception.

禮樂射御書數(ㄌㄧˇ ㄩㄝˋ ㄕㄜˋ ㄩˋ ㄕㄨ ㄕㄨˋ)
rites, music, archery, driving a chariot, learning and mathematics (known together as "six arts", which ancient scholars were required to master)

十四畫

【禰】 3971 1. ㄋㄧˇ nii nǐ
the shrine where one's father's sacred tablet is kept

【禰】 3971 2. ㄇㄧˊ mi mí

a Chinese family name

【禱】 3972 ㄉㄠˇ dao dǎo
to pray; to beseech; to plead; to entreat: 她祈禱兒子歸來。She prayed for her son's return.
禱告(ㄉㄠˇ ㄍㄠˋ)
a prayer; to pray: 他向上帝禱告求助。He prayed to God for help.
禱祀(ㄉㄠˇ ㄙˋ)
to perform a sacrifice and pray for happiness

十七畫

【禳】 3973 ㄖㄤˊ rang ráng
1. a form of sacrifice performed for exorcism
2. to exorcise

【禴】 3974 ㄩㄝˋ yueh yuè
a kind of annual sacrifice

内部
ㄖㄡˊ rou róu

四畫

【禹】 3975 ㄩˇ yeu yǔ
1. Yü, the legendary founder of the Hsia (夏) Dynasty (21st-16th century B.C.)
2. a Chinese family name
禹碑(ㄩˇ ㄅㄟ)
a tablet with inscriptions supposedly set up by the legendary ruler Yü (禹)
禹甸(ㄩˇ ㄉㄧㄢˋ)
the domain of China in prehistoric times
禹陵(ㄩˇ ㄌㄧㄥˊ)
the monument of the legendary ruler Yü (禹) (in Chekiang)
禹貢(ㄩˇ ㄍㄨㄥˋ)
China's oldest known book of geography
禹跡(ㄩˇ ㄐㄧ)
the area where the legendary ruler Yü (禹) traversed
禹穴(ㄩˇ ㄒㄩㄝˋ)
①a cave in Chekiang supposedly used as a repository of books by the legendary ruler Yü (禹) ②a place in Shensi supposedly used as an abode by the legendary ruler Yü (禹) when he tamed the Yellow River

【禺】 3976 1. ㄩ yu yú
name of a mountain in Chekiang

【禺】 3976 2. ㄩˇ yuh yǔ
a monkey

八畫

【禽】 3977 ㄑㄧㄣˊ chyn qín
1. birds; fowls
2. same as 擒 — to catch; to capture
禽鳥(ㄑㄧㄣˊ ㄋㄧㄠˇ)
birds; fowls
禽獵(ㄑㄧㄣˊ ㄌㄧㄝˋ)
to hunt
禽荒(ㄑㄧㄣˊ ㄏㄨㄤ)
obsessed with hunting
禽獸(ㄑㄧㄣˊ ㄕㄡˋ)
①dumb creatures ②birds and beasts

禾部
ㄏㄜˊ her hé

【禾】 3978 ㄏㄜˊ her hé
1. grains still on the stalk
2. the rice crop
禾本科(ㄏㄜˊ ㄅㄣˇ ㄎㄜ)
the grass family
禾苗(ㄏㄜˊ ㄇㄧㄠˊ)
rice seedlings
禾稈(ㄏㄜˊ ㄍㄢˇ)
the stalk of a rice plant
禾黍(ㄏㄜˊ ㄕㄨˇ)
millet; corn
禾穗(ㄏㄜˊ ㄙㄨㄟˋ)
an ear of grain

二畫

【禿】 3979 (秃) ㄊㄨ tu tū
bald; bare: 這棵樹光禿禿的。This tree is bare (or leafless).
禿筆(ㄊㄨ ㄅㄧˇ)
① a worn-down writing brush ②(a self-depreciatory term) poor writing skill
禿髮症(ㄊㄨ ㄈㄚˇ ㄓㄥˋ)
alopecia 亦作「禿髮病」
禿頂(ㄊㄨ ㄉㄧㄥˇ)
bald at the top of the head; baldheaded
禿頭(ㄊㄨ ㄊㄡˊ)
baldheaded; bald; a bald head
禿驢(ㄊㄨ ㄌㄩˊ)
a bald ass (an abusive term applied to a Buddhist monk)
禿鷲(ㄊㄨ ㄐㄧㄡˋ)
a vulture; a condor
禿瘡(ㄊㄨ ㄔㄨㄤ)
(pathology) favus
禿山(ㄊㄨ ㄕㄢ)
a bare hill; a barren hill
禿子(ㄊㄨ ·ㄗ)
a baldhead; a baldpate
禿友(ㄊㄨ ㄧㄡˇ)
a pen or writing brush

【秀】 3980 ㄒㄧㄡˋ shiow xiù
1. brilliant; excellent; competent; outstanding
2. beautiful; elegant; graceful; delicate; fine
3. (said of grain crops) to put forth new flowers or ears
秀拔(ㄒㄧㄡˋ ㄅㄚˊ)
(said of a calligraphic style) fine
秀眉(ㄒㄧㄡˋ ㄇㄟˊ)
long hairs in the eyebrows of an aged person
秀美(ㄒㄧㄡˋ ㄇㄟˇ)
elegant; graceful; beautiful; fine: 她寫的字極爲秀美。Her handwriting is very beautiful.
秀發(ㄒㄧㄡˋ ㄈㄚ)
① blooming ② good-looking; fine-looking; handsome
秀頂(ㄒㄧㄡˋ ㄉㄧㄥˇ)
a bald head; baldheaded
秀女(ㄒㄧㄡˋ ㄋㄩˇ)
(during the Ching Dynasty) women in the emperor's

harem
秀麗(ㄒㄧㄡˋ ㄌㄧˋ)
elegant; beautiful; graceful; fine
秀氣
①(ㄒㄧㄡˋ ㄑㄧˋ) the invigorating sight of a marvelous landscape
②(ㄒㄧㄡˋ ·ㄑㄧ) fine; elegant; graceful
秀出(ㄒㄧㄡˋ ㄔㄨ)
outstanding
秀士(ㄒㄧㄡˋ ㄕˋ)
① a man of outstanding ability and virtue ② the lowest degree conferred upon successful candidates under the former civil service examination system
秀才(ㄒㄧㄡˋ ㄘㄞˊ)
① the lowest degree conferred upon successful candidates under the former civil service examination system ② fine talent ③ a scholar; a skillful writer
秀才人情紙半張(ㄒㄧㄡˋ ㄘㄞˊ ㄖㄣˊ ㄑㄧㄥˊ ㄓˇ ㄅㄢˋ ㄓㄤ)
(literally) A gift costs a scholar no more than a half sheet of paper.—Because scholars value literary products as gifts, their friendship is inexpensive.
秀色可餐(ㄒㄧㄡˋ ㄙㄜˋ ㄎㄜˇ ㄘㄢ)
(said of a woman) beauty that is the feast of the eye—very attractive
秀而不實(ㄒㄧㄡˋ ㄦˊ ㄅㄨˋ ㄕˊ)
(literally) flowering but bearing no fruit—beautiful in appearance but empty in substance
秀異(ㄒㄧㄡˋ ㄧˋ)
outstanding; striking
秀雅(ㄒㄧㄡˋ ㄧㄚˇ)
graceful; elegant; fine
秀外慧中(ㄒㄧㄡˋ ㄨㄞˋ ㄏㄨㄟˋ ㄓㄨㄥ)
beautiful and intelligent: 她是位秀外慧中的女孩。She's a beautiful and intelligent girl.

【私】 3981 ㄙ sy sī

1. private; personal; person-to-person
2. secret; clandestine
3. to have illicit relations or an affair with
4. contraband
5. prejudice; biased; to favor
6. selfish; selfishly
7. reproductive organs of both sexes

私奔(ㄙ ㄅㄣ)
to elope; elopement: 那女孩子與情人私奔。That girl eloped with her lover.
私弊(ㄙ ㄅㄧˋ)
dishonest practice; irregularities
私門(ㄙ ㄇㄣˊ)
① powerful or influential families ② one's home or hometown ③ an unlicensed brothel
私名號(ㄙ ㄇㄧㄥˊ ㄏㄠˋ)
(in Chinese punctuation marks) the line along either side of a word or words to indicate a proper noun
私販(ㄙ ㄈㄢˋ)
dealers in contraband goods; smugglers
私房(ㄙ ㄈㄤˊ)
①private or personal (pocket, etc.) ② personal or private savings (usually of married women)
私房錢(ㄙ ㄈㄤˊ ㄑㄧㄢˊ)
private savings (usually of married women)
私訪(ㄙ ㄈㄤˇ)
(said of officials in old times) to travel incognito in order to get in touch with the public for its opinions, views, etc.
私德(ㄙ ㄉㄜˊ)
personal virtue; private conduct; personal morals
私鬥(ㄙ ㄉㄡˋ)
a private or personal fight; a brawl
私底下(ㄙ ㄉㄧˇ ·ㄒㄧㄚ)
privately; secretly
私第(ㄙ ㄉㄧˋ)
a private residence
私定終身(ㄙ ㄉㄧㄥˋ ㄓㄨㄥ ㄕㄣ)
(in old China) to pledge to marry without the permission of parents
私逃(ㄙ ㄊㄠˊ)
to escape or run away secretly; to elope; to abscond
私談(ㄙ ㄊㄢˊ)
to talk in private; private talks; confidential talks
私帑(ㄙ ㄊㄤˇ)
personal or private property of the emperor
私田(ㄙ ㄊㄧㄢˊ)
privately owned farmland
私通(ㄙ ㄊㄨㄥ)
① to collaborate with enemy forces or a foreign country ② to have an illicit affair with parties other than one's spouse; adultery
私囊(ㄙ ㄋㄤˊ)
private pocket (as opposed to the public coffers)
私暱(ㄙ ㄋㄧˋ)
to favor privately; to have an affair with
私釀(ㄙ ㄋㄧㄤˋ)
to bootleg; to brew alcoholic drinks illegally
私累(ㄙ ㄌㄟˇ)
a personal burden—such as the family
私立(ㄙ ㄌㄧˋ)
(usually said of schools, hospitals, etc.) established and operated by private funds: 他在一所私立學校求學。He studies at a private school.
私利(ㄙ ㄌㄧˋ)
private interests; personal gains: 只圖個人私利是自私的行爲。It is selfish to pursue only private ends.
私和(ㄙ ㄏㄜˊ)
private settlement of a criminal case
私話(ㄙ ㄏㄨㄚˋ)
secret or personal words or talks; confidential talks
私貨(ㄙ ㄏㄨㄛˋ)
① smuggled goods ② goods whose source cannot be traced, usually referring to stolen articles
私會(ㄙ ㄏㄨㄟˋ)
a secret rendezvous
私積(ㄙ ㄐㄧ)
private savings
私家偵探(ㄙ ㄐㄧㄚ ㄓㄣ ㄊㄢˋ)
a private detective; a private eye
私家車(ㄙ ㄐㄧㄚ ㄔㄜ)
a private car
私交(ㄙ ㄐㄧㄠ)

personal friendship (as distinct from official association)
私酒(ㄙ ㄐㄧㄡˇ)
alcoholic beverages produced by unlicensed breweries; untaxed liquors; bootleg; moonshine
私見(ㄙ ㄐㄧㄢˋ)
a personal opinion or view; bias
私情(ㄙ ㄑㄧㄥˊ)
① private feelings; personal preference ② illicit love
私下(ㄙ ㄒㄧㄚˋ) or 私下裏(ㄙ ㄒㄧㄚˋ ˙ㄌㄧ)
privately; secretly: 我希望私下同你談談。I wish to talk with you in private.
私梟(ㄙ ㄒㄧㄠ)
a smuggler
私心(ㄙ ㄒㄧㄣ)
selfishness; private or selfish motive; favoritism: 他腦裏充滿著私心雜念。He was full of selfish ideas and personal considerations.
私信(ㄙ ㄒㄧㄣˋ)
personal letters, mail or correspondence
私相授受(ㄙ ㄒㄧㄤ ㄕㄡˋ ㄕㄡˋ)
to transfer offices or ownership of public properties without going through legal procedure: 不可拿公家的東西私相授受。There must be no illicit transfer of public property.
私刑(ㄙ ㄒㄧㄥˊ)
to lynch; lynching
私蓄(ㄙ ㄒㄩˋ)
personal savings
私宅(ㄙ ㄓㄞˊ)
a private residence
私債(ㄙ ㄓㄞˋ)
personal debts
私章(ㄙ ㄓㄤ)
a personal seal; a private chop
私鑄(ㄙ ㄓㄨˋ)
(in old China) to mint coins illegally
私衷(ㄙ ㄓㄨㄥ)
a private view; a personal wish 亦作「私悃」
私仇(ㄙ ㄔㄡˊ)
a personal grudge
私產(ㄙ ㄔㄢˇ)
private property; personal estate
私娼(ㄙ ㄔㄤ)
unlicensed prostitutes or brothels
私處(ㄙ ㄔㄨˋ)
private parts; reproductive organs of both sexes
私室(ㄙ ㄕˋ)
a private room
私事(ㄙ ㄕˋ) or 私務(ㄙ ㄨˋ)
personal affairs; private affairs: 不要干涉我的私事。Don't interfere in my personal affairs.
私設(ㄙ ㄕㄜˋ)
established without authorization
私生活(ㄙ ㄕㄥ ㄏㄨㄛˊ)
one's private life
私生子(ㄙ ㄕㄥ ㄗˇ)
an illegitimate child; a bastard; a bastard son
私塾(ㄙ ㄕㄨˊ)
(formerly) a village school supported by private means
私淑(ㄙ ㄕㄨˊ)
to learn not directly from the master himself
私淑弟子(ㄙ ㄕㄨˊ ㄉㄧˋ ㄗˇ)
a disciple who has not taken lessons directly under the master himself
私人(ㄙ ㄖㄣˊ)
① individual; personal; private: 別問私人的事。Don't ask personal questions. ② persons employed not because of their merits but because of their personal relationship with the boss
私人秘書(ㄙ ㄖㄣˊ ㄇㄧˋ ㄕㄨ)
a private secretary; a personal secretary
私人企業(ㄙ ㄖㄣˊ ㄑㄧˇ ㄧㄝˋ)
private enterprises
私人資格(ㄙ ㄖㄣˊ ㄗ ㄍㄜˊ)
in one's personal capacity; as an individual
私自(ㄙ ㄗˋ)
personally; privately; doing something without permission
私藏(ㄙ ㄘㄤˊ)
① private collection ② to keep something against the law
私謁(ㄙ ㄧㄝˋ)
to call on someone to ask for a personal favor
私有(ㄙ ㄧㄡˇ)
privately-owned; private: 這部車是他的私有財產。The car is his private property.
私有土地(ㄙ ㄧㄡˇ ㄊㄨˇ ㄉㄧˋ)
privately-owned land; private land
私有林(ㄙ ㄧㄡˇ ㄌㄧㄣˊ)
privately-owned forests or woodland
私有公物(ㄙ ㄧㄡˇ ㄍㄨㄥ ㄨˋ)
(law) to offer private possessions for public uses
私有制(ㄙ ㄧㄡˇ ㄓˋ)
private ownership of property
私有財產(ㄙ ㄧㄡˇ ㄘㄞˊ ㄔㄢˇ)
private property or possessions
私鹽(ㄙ ㄧㄢˊ)
untaxed salt
私印(ㄙ ㄧㄣˋ)
a private seal; a personal chop
私營(ㄙ ㄧㄥˊ)
privately-operated; privately-run
私語(ㄙ ㄩˇ)
① private talks; intimate and soothing words ② to whisper or talk in a very low voice: 他們在竊竊私語。They were talking in whispers.
私欲 or 私慾(ㄙ ㄩˋ)
① personal or selfish desires ② greediness
私怨(ㄙ ㄩㄢˋ)
a personal grudge: 我對你沒有私怨。I owe you no grudge.
私願(ㄙ ㄩㄢˋ)
a personal wish or desire
私運(ㄙ ㄩㄣˋ)
to smuggle
私用(ㄙ ㄩㄥˋ)
①(for) personal use ② illegal use (of public property, etc.)

三畫

【秉】 3982
ㄅㄧㄥˇ biing bǐng

1. to hold in hand
2. to take charge of; to rule
3. authority
4. an ancient grain measure; a measure for liquid
5. a Chinese family name

秉筆(ㄅㄧㄥˇ ㄅㄧˇ)
to hold a pen

秉賦(ㄅㄧㄥˇ ㄈㄨˋ)
one's natural endowments

秉鐸(ㄅㄧㄥˇ ㄉㄨㄛˊ)
an instructor

秉國(ㄅㄧㄥˇ ㄍㄨㄛˊ)
to rule a nation; to exercise authority over a nation

秉公辦理(ㄅㄧㄥˇ ㄍㄨㄥ ㄅㄢˋ ㄌㄧˇ)
① to act strictly according to official procedures ② to handle a matter impartially

秉鈞(ㄅㄧㄥˇ ㄐㄩㄣ) or 秉軸(ㄅㄧㄥˇ ㄓㄡˊ)
to be in power; to rule a nation

秉性 or 稟性(ㄅㄧㄥˇ ㄒㄧㄥˋ)
nature; a natural disposition or temperament

秉直(ㄅㄧㄥˇ ㄓˊ)
① to adhere to correct principles ② frank and honest

秉燭夜遊(ㄅㄧㄥˇ ㄓㄨˊ ㄧㄝˋ ㄧㄡˊ)
(literally) to hold a candle for a night excursion—Life being short, one cannot afford to let time flee without making use of it.

秉持(ㄅㄧㄥˇ ㄔˊ)
① to hold on to or to adhere to (one's principles, etc.) ② to hold in hand (a spear, etc.)

秉鉞(ㄅㄧㄥˇ ㄩㄝˋ)
to wield military power

四畫

【秋】 3983
(秌) ㄑㄧㄡ chiou qiū

1. autumn; fall: 秋去冬來。Winter comes after autumn.
2. time; a period: 多事之秋 an eventful period
3. a season
4. a year: 千秋萬歲 for thousands of years
5. ripening of grains; a harvest
6. a Chinese family name

秋波(ㄑㄧㄡ ㄅㄛ)
bewitching eyes of a woman

秋波暗送(ㄑㄧㄡ ㄅㄛ ㄢˋ ㄙㄨㄥˋ)
to send silent and endearing messages with bewitching eyes 亦作「暗送秋波」

秋波微轉(ㄑㄧㄡ ㄅㄛ ㄨㄟˊ ㄓㄨㄢˇ)
a slight turn of her bewitching eyes; eloquent eyes that send a silent message

秋末(ㄑㄧㄡ ㄇㄛˋ)
late autumn; the last days of autumn

秋分(ㄑㄧㄡ ㄈㄣ)
the autumnal equinox (or point), one of the 24 climatic transitions in a solar year, which falls on September 23 or 24

秋風(ㄑㄧㄡ ㄈㄥ)
① autumn wind ② presents or gift money obtained on pretexts, such as one's birthday, etc.

秋風過耳(ㄑㄧㄡ ㄈㄥ ㄍㄨㄛˋ ㄦˇ)
like an autumn breeze passing by the ear—something heard but not given much attention

秋刀魚(ㄑㄧㄡ ㄉㄠ ㄩˊ)
a saury

秋天(ㄑㄧㄡ ㄊㄧㄢ)
autumn; fall

秋娘(ㄑㄧㄡ ㄋㄧㄤˊ)
an aged woman (whose beauty has disappeared with youth)

秋老虎(ㄑㄧㄡ ㄌㄠˇ ㄏㄨˇ)
scorching heat in early autumn

秋涼(ㄑㄧㄡ ㄌㄧㄤˊ)
chilliness in autumn

秋羅(ㄑㄧㄡ ㄌㄨㄛˊ)
a kind of thin, light and striped silk fabric

秋高馬肥(ㄑㄧㄡ ㄍㄠ ㄇㄚˇ ㄈㄟˊ)
(literally) when the autumn skies are high and the horses are fat—time fit for starting a campaign in ancient times

秋高氣爽(ㄑㄧㄡ ㄍㄠ ㄑㄧˋ ㄕㄨㄤˇ)
the clear and crisp autumn climate

秋海棠(ㄑㄧㄡ ㄏㄞˇ ㄊㄤˊ)
(botany) a begonia

秋毫(ㄑㄧㄡ ㄏㄠˊ)
① a very tiny thing; trifles ② a writing brush

秋毫無犯(ㄑㄧㄡ ㄏㄠˊ ㄨˊ ㄈㄢˋ)
(said of troops) not to cause the slightest trouble to the people

秋後(ㄑㄧㄡ ㄏㄡˋ)
after the "Beginning of Autumn", one of the 24 climatic transitions in a lunar year which falls on August 7 or 8

秋季(ㄑㄧㄡ ㄐㄧˋ)
autumn (season)

秋節(ㄑㄧㄡ ㄐㄧㄝˊ)
① the Moon Festival on the 15th of the eighth lunar month ② the Mountain Climbing Festival on the ninth of the ninth lunar month

秋瑾(ㄑㄧㄡ ㄐㄧㄣˇ)
Chiu Chin (1875-1907), a woman revolutionary executed by the Manchus

秋氣(ㄑㄧㄡ ㄑㄧˋ)
① the desolate air of autumn ② dilapidated or desolate

秋千 or 鞦韆(ㄑㄧㄡ ㄑㄧㄢ)
a swing: 他在那兒打秋千。He was having a swing over there.

秋汛(ㄑㄧㄡ ㄒㄩㄣˋ)
the overflowing of rivers in the early part of autumn

秋蟬(ㄑㄧㄡ ㄔㄢˊ)
the autumn cicada which hums in the evening

秋成(ㄑㄧㄡ ㄔㄥˊ)
the autumn harvest

秋蟲(ㄑㄧㄡ ㄔㄨㄥˊ)
autumn insects—often referring to crickets

秋實(ㄑㄧㄡ ㄕˊ)
fruits in autumn (as a result of flowering in spring)

秋試(ㄑㄧㄡ ㄕˋ) or 秋闈(ㄑㄧㄡ ㄨㄟˊ)
(in ancient China) the civil service examination held in autumn

秋事(ㄑㄧㄡ ㄕˋ)
the autumn harvest

秋社(ㄑㄧㄡ ㄕㄜˋ)
Chinese Thanksgiving Day in autumn

秋收(ㄑㄧㄡ ㄕㄡ)
the autumn harvest

秋扇(ㄑㄧㄡ ㄕㄢˋ)
(literally) fans in autumn—deserted women
秋扇見捐(ㄑㄧㄡ ㄕㄢˋ ㄐㄧㄢˋ ㄐㄩㄢ)
(said of women) to be deserted as fans are cast away in autumn
秋聲(ㄑㄧㄡ ㄕㄥ)
the sound of winds sweeping through withered leaves in autumn; the autumnal sough
秋水(ㄑㄧㄡ ㄕㄨㄟˇ)
① autumn waters—clear and bright ② the bewitching eyes of a woman ③ (said of complexion) clear and bright ④ the flashing of swords
秋水伊人(ㄑㄧㄡ ㄕㄨㄟˇ ㄧ ㄖㄣˊ)
thinking of an old acquaintance on seeing a familiar scene
秋霜(ㄑㄧㄡ ㄕㄨㄤ)
① autumn frost—(figuratively) snowy hair ② severity; sternness
秋思(ㄑㄧㄡ ㄙ)
(literally) autumn thought—a lonesome and desolate mood
秋色(ㄑㄧㄡ ㄙㄜˋ)
autumn scenes; autumnal colors
秋色宜人(ㄑㄧㄡ ㄙㄜˋ ㄧˊ ㄖㄣˊ)
delightful autumn scenery
秋意(ㄑㄧㄡ ㄧˋ)
cool and a little chilly, indicating the presence of autumn
秋顏(ㄑㄧㄡ ㄧㄢˊ)
fading beauty
秋雨(ㄑㄧㄡ ㄩˇ)
autumn rain
秋月春風(ㄑㄧㄡ ㄩㄝˋ ㄔㄨㄣ ㄈㄥ)
(literally) the autumn moon and spring breezes—the beauty of nature

【科】 3984
ㄎㄜ ke kē

1. a department
2. a section
3. a class; a variety; a family (of plants or animals)
4. rules; laws
5. the action in Chinese opera
6. a subject in the civil service examination of former times
7. a branch of academic or vocational studies
8. to mete out (prison terms, etc.); to levy (taxes, etc.); to fine someone

科白(ㄎㄜ ㄅㄞˊ)
dialogue and acting in Chinese opera
科班(ㄎㄜ ㄅㄢ)
① a Chinese operatic company which operates a class to train young pupils ② very formal or orthodox training one received when young
科班出身(ㄎㄜ ㄅㄢ ㄔㄨ ㄕㄣ)
having received professional training for what one is doing
科名(ㄎㄜ ㄇㄧㄥˊ)
to establish one's name and position under the civil service examination system in monarchical China
科目(ㄎㄜ ㄇㄨˋ)
① subjects, courses, classifications of academic studies ② the civil examination system in former times
科斗 or 蝌蚪(ㄎㄜ ㄉㄡˇ)
the tadpole
科斗文(ㄎㄜ ㄉㄡˇ ㄨㄣˊ)
Chinese characters in the Chou Dynasty (1125-255B.C.) which resemble tadpoles in shape
科令(ㄎㄜ ㄌㄧㄥˋ)
laws and regulations
科羅拉多(ㄎㄜ ㄌㄨㄛˊ ㄌㄚ ㄉㄨㄛ)
the state of Colorado, U.S.A.
科倫坡(ㄎㄜ ㄌㄨㄣˊ ㄆㄛ)
Colombo, the capital of Sri Lanka 今譯作「可倫坡」
科隆(ㄎㄜ ㄌㄨㄥˊ)
Cologne, a German city
科幻小說(ㄎㄜ ㄏㄨㄢˋ ㄒㄧㄠˇ ㄕㄨㄛ)
science fiction 亦作「科學幻想小說」
科諢(ㄎㄜ ㄏㄨㄣˋ)
(Chinese opera) a comical part—including jokes and clownish acts
科技(ㄎㄜ ㄐㄧˋ)
science and technology
科際整合(ㄎㄜ ㄐㄧˋ ㄓㄥˇ ㄏㄜˊ)
interdisciplinary integration
科舉(ㄎㄜ ㄐㄩˇ) or 科甲(ㄎㄜ ㄐㄧㄚˇ) or 科第(ㄎㄜ ㄉㄧˋ)
the civil service examination system in ancient China
科西嘉(ㄎㄜ ㄒㄧ ㄐㄧㄚ)
Corsica
科刑(ㄎㄜ ㄒㄧㄥˊ) or 科罪(ㄎㄜ ㄗㄨㄟˋ)
to mete out punishment
科學(ㄎㄜ ㄒㄩㄝˊ)
science: 他決定研究科學。He decided to study science.
科學方法(ㄎㄜ ㄒㄩㄝˊ ㄈㄤ ㄈㄚˇ)
scientific methods, ways or approaches
科學的(ㄎㄜ ㄒㄩㄝˊ ˙ㄉㄜ)
scientific: 她具有科學的頭腦。She has a scientific mind.
科學管理(ㄎㄜ ㄒㄩㄝˊ ㄍㄨㄢˇ ㄌㄧˇ) or 科學化管理(ㄎㄜ ㄒㄩㄝˊ ㄏㄨㄚˋ ㄍㄨㄢˇ ㄌㄧˇ)
scientific management
科學工業園區(ㄎㄜ ㄒㄩㄝˊ ㄍㄨㄥ ㄧㄝˋ ㄩㄢˊ ㄑㄩ)
the Science Industrial District
科學化(ㄎㄜ ㄒㄩㄝˊ ㄏㄨㄚˋ)
to scientize
科學家(ㄎㄜ ㄒㄩㄝˊ ㄐㄧㄚ)
scientists
科學界(ㄎㄜ ㄒㄩㄝˊ ㄐㄧㄝˋ)
① the world of science ② the community of scientists
科學教育(ㄎㄜ ㄒㄩㄝˊ ㄐㄧㄠˋ ㄩˋ)
science education
科學知識(ㄎㄜ ㄒㄩㄝˊ ㄓ ㄕˋ)
scientific knowledge
科學時代(ㄎㄜ ㄒㄩㄝˊ ㄕˊ ㄉㄞˋ)
the era of science
科學儀器(ㄎㄜ ㄒㄩㄝˊ ㄧˊ ㄑㄧˋ)
scientific instruments
科學萬能(ㄎㄜ ㄒㄩㄝˊ ㄨㄢˋ ㄋㄥˊ)
There is nothing science cannot accomplish.
科長(ㄎㄜ ㄓㄤˇ)
a section chief in various government agencies
科場(ㄎㄜ ㄔㄤˇ)
a site of the civil service examination in ancient China
科任教員(ㄎㄜ ㄖㄣˋ ㄐㄧㄠˋ ㄩㄢˊ)
a teacher who is employed to teach a specific subject or course of study, as math., literature, etc. (as opposed to those employed to oversee a class)
科則(ㄎㄜ ㄗㄜˊ)
classifications, grades, etc.

in taxation and compulsory services, etc.

科以罰金(ㄎㄜ ㄧˇ ㄈㄚˊ ㄐㄧㄣ)
to impose a fine on someone

科威特(ㄎㄜ ㄨㄟ ㄊㄜˋ)
Kuwait

科員(ㄎㄜ ㄩㄢˊ)
a junior government employee

【秒】 3985 ㄇㄧㄠˇ meau miǎo

1. (said of time or a degree) a second
2. the beard of grain

秒錶(ㄇㄧㄠˇ ㄅㄧㄠˇ)
a stopwatch; a chronograph 亦作「碼錶」

秒忽(ㄇㄧㄠˇ ㄏㄨ)
an infinitesimal number

秒針(ㄇㄧㄠˇ ㄓㄣ)
the second hand (on the dial of a clock or watch)

【秕】 3986 ㄅㄧˇ bii bǐ

1. husks; grains not fully grown; blasted grains
2. mean; no good; not qualified or competent

秕謬(ㄅㄧˇ ㄇㄧㄡˋ)
to go against good reasoning or sense; mistaken; erroneous

秕穀(ㄅㄧˇ ㄍㄨˇ)
rice grains not fully grown

秕糠 or 粃糠(ㄅㄧˇ ㄎㄤ)
① chaff ② worthless stuff; leavings

秕政(ㄅㄧˇ ㄓㄥˋ)
bad administration or government

秕滓(ㄅㄧˇ ㄗˇ)
husks, chaff or refuse

【种】 3987 ㄔㄨㄥˊ chorng chóng

1. naive; naivete
2. a Chinese family name
3. a simplified form of 種

【秔】 3988 (稉、粳) ㄍㄥ geng gēng (語音 ㄐㄧㄥ jing jīng)

non-glutinous rice

秔米(ㄍㄥ ㄇㄧˇ)
non-glutinous rice 亦作「粳米」

秔稻(ㄍㄥ ㄉㄠˋ)
non-glutinous rice which ripens a little late 亦作「粳稻」

五畫

【秦】 3989 ㄑㄧㄣˊ chyn qín

1. the feudal state of Chin (879-221 B.C.) in the Chou Dynasty, which later unified the whole country under the Chin Dynasty (221-206 B.C.)
2. another name of Shensi Province
3. the ancient name of China as known to the people of the Western Region (西域)
4. a Chinese family name

秦庭之哭(ㄑㄧㄣˊ ㄊㄧㄥˊ ㄓ ㄎㄨ)
begging in tears for assistance in desperation (a reference to the episode of Shen Pao-hsü (申包胥) in the Epoch of Warring States)

秦樓楚館(ㄑㄧㄣˊ ㄌㄡˊ ㄔㄨˇ ㄍㄨㄢˇ)
brothels

秦良玉(ㄑㄧㄣˊ ㄌㄧㄤˊ ㄩˋ)
Chin Liang-yü, the wife of Ma Chien-cheng (馬千乘), a ranking military officer in the Ming Dynasty, whose military acumen was so superb that she was given a field command in her own right

秦嶺(ㄑㄧㄣˊ ㄌㄧㄥˇ)
also known as Mt. Chin (秦山), or the Southern Mountain (終南山), which soars up in Kansu and ends in Honan

秦觀(ㄑㄧㄣˊ ㄍㄨㄢ)
Chin Kuan, alias Shao-yü (少游), 1049-1100, a famous poet and essayist in the Sung Dynasty

秦檜(ㄑㄧㄣˊ ㄎㄨㄞˋ) or (ㄑㄧㄣˊ ㄍㄨㄟˋ)
Chin Kuei (1090-1155), a prime minister of the Sung Dynasty, regarded as a traitor by posterity for his part in executing General Yüeh Fei (岳飛), an outstanding field commander

秦火(ㄑㄧㄣˊ ㄏㄨㄛˇ)
the fire of Chin—a reference to the burning of books ordered by the First Emperor (始皇帝)

秦淮(ㄑㄧㄣˊ ㄏㄨㄞˊ)
the Chinhuai River that flows through Nanking City, formerly, a merrymaking center

秦皇島(ㄑㄧㄣˊ ㄏㄨㄤˊ ㄉㄠˇ)
Chinhuangtao, a port in Hopeh Province, which was opened as a commercial port in 1898

秦晉之好(ㄑㄧㄣˊ ㄐㄧㄣˋ ㄓ ㄏㄠˇ)
Chin and Tsin, the two powerful states in the Epoch of Warring States, which maintained close ties for generations through matrimonial diplomacy—a phrase now used as a congratulatory expression on wedding

秦鏡高懸(ㄑㄧㄣˊ ㄐㄧㄥˋ ㄍㄠ ㄒㄩㄢˊ)
(literally) The all-discerning mirror in the palace of Chin hangs high.— Nothing escapes the discerning eyes of the presiding judge.

秦腔(ㄑㄧㄣˊ ㄑㄧㄤ)
a kind of opera popular in part of northern China, also known as 梆子

秦中(ㄑㄧㄣˊ ㄓㄨㄥ)
another name of Shensi Province

秦始皇(ㄑㄧㄣˊ ㄕˇ ㄏㄨㄤˊ)
Chin Shih Huang, or the First Emperor of Chin, 259-210 B.C., who unified China under the Chin Dynasty, which he hoped to last forever

秦聲(ㄑㄧㄣˊ ㄕㄥ)
tunes and songs of Chin

秦二世(ㄑㄧㄣˊ ㄦˋ ㄕˋ)
the second son of the First Emperor, who was killed after a three-year reign

【租】 3990 ㄗㄨ tzu zū

1. to rent; to lease; to let; to hire; to charter
2. rent; rental
3. taxes; to tax

租米(ㄗㄨ ㄇㄧˇ)
the percentage of a crop yield given to the landlord as farm rental

租費(ㄗㄨ ㄈㄟˋ)
royalties

租賃(ㄗㄨ ㄌㄧㄣˋ)

to rent (a house, etc.); to lease: 他租賃了服裝和道具。He rented costumes and stage properties.
租賃契約(ㄗㄨ ㄌㄧㄣˋ ㄑㄧˋ ㄩㄝ)
a lease contract
租戶(ㄗㄨ ㄏㄨˋ)
a tenant
租價(ㄗㄨ ㄐㄧㄚˋ)
rent, or rental
租界(ㄗㄨ ㄐㄧㄝˋ)
a foreign settlement or concession
租借(ㄗㄨ ㄐㄧㄝˋ)
lend-lease; to rent: 我們租借公寓。We rented an apartment.
租借法案(ㄗㄨ ㄐㄧㄝˋ ㄈㄚˇ ㄢˋ)
the Lend-Lease Act of the U.S. in World War II
租借地(ㄗㄨ ㄐㄧㄝˋ ㄉㄧˋ)
a settlement or concession granted to a foreign nation (usually as a result of military defeat) for a specified time; leased territory
租金(ㄗㄨ ㄐㄧㄣ)or 租錢(ㄗㄨ ㄑㄧㄢˊ)
rent or rental: 我得去收租金。I must collect the rent.
租金收入(ㄗㄨ ㄐㄧㄣ ㄕㄡ ㄖㄨˋ)
rental receipts
租契(ㄗㄨ ㄑㄧˋ)
a lease or rental agreement
租出(ㄗㄨ ㄔㄨ)
to let
租售(ㄗㄨ ㄕㄡˋ)
for rent or sale
租書處(ㄗㄨ ㄕㄨ ㄔㄨˋ)
a rental library
租稅(ㄗㄨ ㄕㄨㄟˋ)
taxes paid to the government
租傜(ㄗㄨ ㄧㄠˊ)
taxes and compulsory services
租約(ㄗㄨ ㄩㄝ)
a lease: 租約何時期滿? When does the lease expire?
租用(ㄗㄨ ㄩㄥˋ)
to rent for use; to rent from others; to be tenanted: 我租用她的房子。I rented the house from her.

【秧】 3991
ㄧㄤ iang yang
1. rice seedlings
2. tree saplings; very young plants for transplanting
3. fry
4. (now rarely) to cultivate; to grow
秧苗(ㄧㄤ ㄇㄧㄠˊ)
rice seedlings: 農夫在移植秧苗。The farmer was setting out rice seedlings.
秧田(ㄧㄤ ㄊㄧㄢˊ)
a water field for the cultivation of rice seedlings
秧歌(ㄧㄤ ㄍㄜ)
songs sung by farmers when transplanting rice seedlings
秧針(ㄧㄤ ㄓㄣ)
the first sprouts of rice seedlings

【秤】 3992
1. ㄔㄥˋ chenq cheng
1. a weighing scale; a balance; a steelyard
2. to weigh with a scale, etc.
秤平斗滿(ㄔㄥˋ ㄆㄧㄥˊ ㄉㄡˇ ㄇㄢˇ)
(literally) even balances and full measures—fair dealings; honest business transactions
秤量貨幣(ㄔㄥˋ ㄌㄧㄤˊ ㄏㄨㄛˋ ㄅㄧˋ)
money by weight (used before the appearance of standardized coins)
秤桿兒(ㄔㄥˋ ㄍㄚˇㄦ)
the beam of a steelyard
秤鉤兒(ㄔㄥˋ ㄍㄡㄦ)
the hook at the end of a steelyard
秤薪而爨(ㄔㄥˋ ㄒㄧㄣ ㄦˊ ㄘㄨㄢˋ)
① extremely stingy ② overemphasis on trifles
秤星(ㄔㄥˋ ㄒㄧㄥ)
the brass marks on a steelyard
秤錘(ㄔㄥˋ ㄔㄨㄟˊ)or 秤砣(ㄔㄥˋ ㄊㄨㄛˊ)
the weight used with a steelyard; the sliding weight of a steelyard

【秤】 3992
2. ㄆㄧㄥˊ pyng ping
scales for measuring weight

【秩】 3993
ㄓˋ jyh zhi
1. order; orderly
2. official ranks
3. official salaries
4. a decade
秩滿(ㄓˋ ㄇㄢˇ)
to have completed the tenure of a public post
秩祿(ㄓˋ ㄌㄨˋ)
official salaries
秩序(ㄓˋ ㄒㄩˋ)
① order ② arrangement
秩序大亂(ㄓˋ ㄒㄩˋ ㄉㄚˋ ㄌㄨㄢˋ)
in pandemonium; in total (or great) disorder
秩序井然(ㄓˋ ㄒㄩˋ ㄐㄧㄥˇ ㄖㄢˊ)
in perfect or apple-pie order
秩然有序(ㄓˋ ㄖㄢˊ ㄧㄡˇ ㄒㄩˋ)
orderly; neat and well arranged; shipshape

【秣】 3994
ㄇㄛˋ moh mo
1. horse feed; fodder
2. to feed a horse
秣馬厲兵(ㄇㄛˋ ㄇㄚˇ ㄌㄧˋ ㄅㄧㄥ)
(literally) to feed the horses and drill the soldiers—to prepare for war
秣陵(ㄇㄛˋ ㄌㄧㄥˊ)
name of an old city near Nanking

【秭】 3995
ㄗˇ tzyy zi
one trillion—1,000,000,000,000

【秬】 3996
ㄐㄩˋ jiuh ju
the black millet
秬酒(ㄐㄩˋ ㄐㄧㄡˇ)
liquor made from black millet
秬鬯(ㄐㄩˋ ㄔㄤˋ)
a sacrificial wine made from millet and fragrant herbs, and given as an imperial favor

【秫】 3997
ㄕㄨˊ shwu shu
a glutinous variety of millet; kaoliang; sorghum
秫米(ㄕㄨˊ ㄇㄧˇ)
another name of glutinous rice; husked sorghum
秫稭(ㄕㄨˊ ·ㄐㄧㄝ)or 秫秕(ㄕㄨˊ ㄅㄧˇ)
the stalk of millet
秫酒(ㄕㄨˊ ㄐㄧㄡˇ)
wine made from glutinous rice

六畫

【移】 3998
ㄧˊ yi yi
1. to change; to alter; to influence; to affect
2. to shift; to move: 他把沙發移到左邊。He moved the sofa to the left.

〔禾部〕

3. to forward; to transmit; to transfer; to transplant; to convey: 工廠將被移到基隆。The factory will be transferred to Keelung.
4. to give; to endow

移步(ㄧˊ ㄅㄨˋ)
to move one's steps; to walk

移民(ㄧˊ ㄇㄧㄣˊ)
① to immigrate; immigration ② to emigrate; to settle people (in a new region, etc.); to colonize ③ an immigrant; an immigration ④ an emigrant

移民法(ㄧˊ ㄇㄧㄣˊ ㄈㄚˇ)
the immigration laws

移民局(ㄧˊ ㄇㄧㄣˊ ㄐㄩˊ)
the immigration office

移民區(ㄧˊ ㄇㄧㄣˊ ㄑㄩ)
a settlement; a colony

移民政策(ㄧˊ ㄇㄧㄣˊ ㄓㄥˋ ㄘㄜˋ)
an emigration or immigration policy; a colonization policy

移風易俗(ㄧˊ ㄈㄥ ㄧˋ ㄙㄨˊ)
to make changes in customs and traditions; to improve public morals

移牒(ㄧˊ ㄉㄧㄝˊ)
a formal notification addressed to another government organization of corresponding level in a foreign country

移調(ㄧˊ ㄉㄧㄠˋ)
(music) transposition

移鼎(ㄧˊ ㄉㄧㄥˇ)
the change of a regime or dynasty

移東就西(ㄧˊ ㄉㄨㄥ ㄐㄧㄡˋ ㄒㄧ)
to make up a deficit or insufficiency in one place with a surplus from somewhere else

移動(ㄧˊ ㄉㄨㄥˋ)
to move; to shift; to change: 不要移動我桌上的東西。Don't move the things on my table.

移天易日(ㄧˊ ㄊㄧㄢ ㄧˋ ㄖˋ)
to usurp political power; to usurp the throne

移挪(ㄧˊ ㄋㄨㄛˊ)
to use money for a purpose not originally intended

移靈(ㄧˊ ㄌㄧㄥˊ)
to move a corpse to a funeral parlor

移國(ㄧˊ ㄍㄨㄛˊ)
to usurp the political power of a nation; to usurp the throne

移晷(ㄧˊ ㄍㄨㄟˇ)
the moving of shadows under the sun-(figuratively) the passage of time

移宮換羽(ㄧˊ ㄍㄨㄥ ㄏㄨㄢˋ ㄩˇ)
the variation of a musical composition

移開(ㄧˊ ㄎㄞ)
to move away: 他們把桌子移開了。They moved the table away.

移花接木(ㄧˊ ㄏㄨㄚ ㄐㄧㄝ ㄇㄨˋ)
① to cheat by sleight of hand ② to graft; to graft one twig on another

移禍(ㄧˊ ㄏㄨㄛˋ)
to shift trouble or calamity to another; to shirk one's responsibility, etc. by incriminating another person

移交(ㄧˊ ㄐㄧㄠ)
to turn over; to hand over (responsibility, public property, etc.) to another person or organization: 這些儀器已經移交給學校了。These instruments have been turned over to the school.

移居(ㄧˊ ㄐㄩ)
to move one's place of dwelling; to move to another town, country, etc. for settlement: 他們已移居鄉下。They moved to the country.

移情別戀(ㄧˊ ㄑㄧㄥˊ ㄅㄧㄝˊ ㄌㄧㄢˋ)
to shift one's love to another person; to have a new sweetheart

移徙(ㄧˊ ㄒㄧˇ)
to move and settle (people) in an undeveloped place

移孝作忠(ㄧˊ ㄒㄧㄠˋ ㄗㄨㄛˋ ㄓㄨㄥ)
to replace filial piety with loyalty to the country

移植(ㄧˊ ㄓˊ)
① to transplant: 我們把花移植到花園裡。We transplanted the flowers to the garden. ② grafting; transplanting

移殖(ㄧˊ ㄓˊ)
to move people for colonization

移住(ㄧˊ ㄓㄨˋ)
to change one's place of dwelling; to move and settle down in another land

移轉(ㄧˊ ㄓㄨㄢˇ)
to transfer (certain rights, holdings, etc.)

移充(ㄧˊ ㄔㄨㄥ)
to use money or something for a purpose not originally intended

移時(ㄧˊ ㄕˊ)
a little while; a brief period of time

移山倒海(ㄧˊ ㄕㄢ ㄉㄠˇ ㄏㄞˇ)
very capable; very resourceful

移審(ㄧˊ ㄕㄣˇ)
to transfer a legal case to an appellate court

移書(ㄧˊ ㄕㄨ)
to write a letter to someone

移樽就教(ㄧˊ ㄗㄨㄣ ㄐㄧㄡˋ ㄐㄧㄠˋ)
① to go to another's place in order to seek his advice ② accommodating

移液管(ㄧˊ ㄧㄝˋ ㄍㄨㄢˇ)
a pipette

移玉(ㄧˊ ㄩˋ)
(a polite expression in a letter of invitation) May I request your company at…?

七畫

【稍】 3999
ㄕㄠ shau shāo

1. slightly; a little; slight: 你不要稍待片刻嗎? Won't you stay a little while?
2. somewhat; rather: 天氣稍熱。The weather is rather hot.
3. gradually

稍淡(ㄕㄠ ㄉㄢˋ)
(said of a liquid) a little too thin; (said of taste) a little too weak; (said of a color) a little too pale

稍濃(ㄕㄠ ㄋㄨㄥˊ)
(said of a color or liquid) a little too thick; (said of smell or taste) rather strong

稍可(ㄕㄠ ㄎㄜˇ)
slightly better; moderately successful

稍可即止(ㄕㄠ ㄎㄜˇ ㄐㄧˊ ㄓˇ)

to stop after being moderately successful—don't be too ambitious for...

稍後(ㄕㄠ ㄏㄡˋ)
shortly afterward; soon afterward: 我稍後寫了一封信給他。I wrote him a letter soon afterward.

稍候(ㄕㄠ ㄏㄡˋ)
to wait for a while (or moment)亦作「稍等」: 請稍候一會兒。Please wait a moment.

稍緩(ㄕㄠ ㄏㄨㄢˇ)
a little slower; not so fast; to put off for a while

稍加(ㄕㄠ ㄐㄧㄚ)
slightly more; to make some addition

稍佳(ㄕㄠ ㄐㄧㄚ)
a little better

稍覺(ㄕㄠ ㄐㄩㄝˊ)
to feel slightly

稍息(ㄕㄠ ㄒㄧˊ)
(military) to stand at ease: 稍息! (a word of command) At ease!

稍暇(ㄕㄠ ㄒㄧㄚˊ)
to have a little leisure

稍懈(ㄕㄠ ㄒㄧㄝˋ)
① to relax a little ② to slow down slightly

稍嫌(ㄕㄠ ㄒㄧㄢˊ)
slightly more or less than the ideal state or amount

稍稍(ㄕㄠ ㄕㄠ)
① briefly ② gradually ③ just a little

稍縱即逝(ㄕㄠ ㄗㄨㄥˋ ㄐㄧˊ ㄕˋ)
transient; fleeting: 莫錯失了這稍縱即逝的機會。Don't miss this fleeting opportunity.

稍次(ㄕㄠ ㄘˋ)
slightly inferior in quality

稍異(ㄕㄠ ㄧˋ)
slightly different; somewhat different

稍有更動(ㄕㄠ ㄧㄡˇ ㄍㄥ ㄉㄨㄥˋ)
some slight changes

稍微(ㄕㄠ ㄨㄟˊ) or 稍許(ㄕㄠ ㄒㄩˇ)
slightly; a little; a bit; rather: 明天會稍微有點冷。It will be rather chilly tomorrow.

【稀】 4000
ㄒㄧ shi xi

1. thin (liquids, etc.); watery; diluted: 這酒精加水變稀了。The alcohol is diluted with water.
2. rare; scarce; uncommon: 物以稀爲貴。A thing is valued if it is rare.
3. scattered; sparse
4. open; loose (as texture)

稀薄(ㄒㄧ ㄅㄛˊ)
①(said of air) thin or rare: 高地空氣稀薄。The air is thin on heights. ②(said of liquids) diluted

稀飯(ㄒㄧ ㄈㄢˋ)
congee; gruel; porridge

稀爛(ㄒㄧ ㄌㄢˋ)
① completely mashed; like paste; pulpy ② crumbled; smashed to pieces

稀硫酸(ㄒㄧ ㄌㄧㄡˊ ㄙㄨㄢ)
diluted sulphuric acid

稀亂八糟(ㄒㄧ ㄌㄨㄢˋ ㄅㄚ ㄗㄠ)
in total disorder; in a pandemonium

稀客(ㄒㄧ ㄎㄜˋ)
a guest who seldom comes to visit; a visitor the host hasn't seen for a long time

稀罕(ㄒㄧ ㄏㄢˇ)
① rare; rarity; scarce: 在那個國家, 雪是稀罕的。Snow is a rarity in that country. ② to care: 誰稀罕? Who cares?

稀奇(ㄒㄧ ㄑㄧˊ)
① strange; rare: 他的拜訪實屬稀奇。His visits are rather rare. ② to care

稀奇古怪(ㄒㄧ ㄑㄧˊ ㄍㄨˇ ㄍㄨㄞˋ)
strange; bizarre; odd

稀世(ㄒㄧ ㄕˋ)
extremely rare or precious

稀釋(ㄒㄧ ㄕˋ)
to dilute (liquids)

稀少(ㄒㄧ ㄕㄠˇ)
few; little; scarce; rare; sparse: 聽衆稀少。The audience was few.

稀疏(ㄒㄧ ㄕㄨ)
scattered or dispersed; thin; sparse

稀糟(ㄒㄧ ㄗㄠ)
extremely rotten; very bad

稀鬆(ㄒㄧ ㄙㄨㄥ)
① indifferent; not interested: 他把那活兒看得稀鬆。He is indifferent to the work. ② not important; common; trivial ③ loose

稀有(ㄒㄧ ㄧㄡˇ)
rare; one in a million: 她是世上稀有的美女。She is a rare beauty.

稀鹽酸(ㄒㄧ ㄧㄢˊ ㄙㄨㄢ)
diluted hydrochloric acid

【稅】 4001
ㄕㄨㄟˋ shuey shuì

1. taxes; duties on commodities: 他們被課以重稅。They are heavily taxed.
2. (now rarely) to lay; to place
3. (now rarely) to present another with

稅票(ㄕㄨㄟˋ ㄆㄧㄠˋ)
receipts for taxes paid

稅目(ㄕㄨㄟˋ ㄇㄨˋ)
a tax designation

稅法(ㄕㄨㄟˋ ㄈㄚˇ)
tax law

稅單(ㄕㄨㄟˋ ㄉㄢ)
① a transit pass for imports; a tax invoice ② a tax form

稅吏(ㄕㄨㄟˋ ㄌㄧˋ)
tax collectors; tax officials 亦作「稅務員」

稅率(ㄕㄨㄟˋ ㄌㄩˋ)
tax rates; duty rates

稅關(ㄕㄨㄟˋ ㄍㄨㄢ)
the customhouse; the Customs

稅款(ㄕㄨㄟˋ ㄎㄨㄢˇ)
tax money

稅金(ㄕㄨㄟˋ ㄐㄧㄣ)
tax money; tax dues

稅捐(ㄕㄨㄟˋ ㄐㄩㄢ)
taxes and surtaxes

稅捐稽徵處(ㄕㄨㄟˋ ㄐㄩㄢ ㄐㄧ ㄓㄥ ㄔㄨˋ)
a tax collection office

稅契(ㄕㄨㄟˋ ㄑㄧˋ)
receipts issued by a tax office for taxes paid on deeds to newly purchased real estate

稅制(ㄕㄨㄟˋ ㄓˋ)
the tax system: 累進稅制 progressive taxation

稅收(ㄕㄨㄟˋ ㄕㄡ)
tax revenue

稅則(ㄕㄨㄟˋ ㄗㄜˊ)
a customs tariff; a customs order; a customs table

稅額(ㄕㄨㄟˋ ㄜˊ)
an amount of tax

〔禾部〕

稅務(ㄕㄨㄟˋ ㄨˋ)
tax administration; affairs pertaining to taxation
稅務機關(ㄕㄨㄟˋ ㄨˋ ㄐㄧ ㄍㄨㄢ)
tax offices
稅務員(ㄕㄨㄟˋ ㄨˋ ㄩㄢˊ)or 稅務人員(ㄕㄨㄟˋ ㄨˋ ㄖㄣˊ ㄩㄢˊ)
revenue officers; tax collectors; tax officials 參看「稅吏」

【稊】 4002
ㄊㄧˊ tyi tí
darnels; tares

【稈】 4003
ㄍㄢˇ gaan gǎn
the stalk of grain; straw: 高粱稈 a sorghum stalk 麥稈床 a bed of straw
稈子(ㄍㄢˇ ·ㄗ)
the stalk of a rice plant; straw

【稂】 4004
ㄌㄤˊ lang láng
weeds or grass which are particularly harmful to the growth of rice seedlings; wolf's-tail grass
稂莠(ㄌㄤˊ ㄧㄡˇ)
weeds and grass

【程】 4005
ㄔㄥˊ cherng chéng
1. a form; a pattern
2. degree; extent
3. a schedule; an agenda; order
4. a course
5. to measure; to assess
6. a journey; a road
7. distance
8. a general name of measurements of all kinds
9. a Chinese family name
程墨(ㄔㄥˊ ㄇㄛˋ)
published standard test papers of civil service examination in former times
程門立雪(ㄔㄥˊ ㄇㄣˊ ㄌㄧˋ ㄒㄩㄝˇ)
(said of pupils) to serve and learn from the master with reverence—a reference to Yu Tso (游酢) and Yang Shih (楊時), who waited at the gate of Cheng Yi (程頤) in snow until it was one foot deep
程邈(ㄔㄥˊ ㄇㄧㄠˇ)
Cheng Miao, a jailer-turned prisoner in the Chin Dynasty, who created the "clerical style" (隸書) of Chinese calligraphy
程度(ㄔㄥˊ ㄉㄨˋ)
① degree; extent; a stage, a state or condition: 學生們表現出不同程度的技巧。The students show various degrees of skill. ② standard; required qualifications or attainments ③ general achievement in academic studies
程顥(ㄔㄥˊ ㄏㄠˋ)
Cheng Hao (1032—1085), a famous scholar in the Sung Dynasty
程序(ㄔㄥˊ ㄒㄩˋ)
procedures; processes: 他熟悉出口程序。He is familiar with export procedure.
程朱(ㄔㄥˊ ㄓㄨ)
Cheng Hao (程顥), Cheng Yi (程頤) and Chu Hsi (朱熹), all famous scholars of the Sung Dynasty
程式(ㄔㄥˊ ㄕˋ)
① standard forms or patterns; standard procedures ② (computers) a program
程式設計(ㄔㄥˊ ㄕˋ ㄕㄜˋ ㄐㄧˋ)
programing
程子(ㄔㄥˊ ㄗˇ)
the Cheng brothers—Cheng Hao (程顥) and Cheng Yi (程頤)—of the Sung Dynasty
程儀(ㄔㄥˊ ㄧˊ)
presents or gifts for a friend embarking on a journey
程頤(ㄔㄥˊ ㄧˊ)
Cheng Yi (1033-1107), a famous scholar of the Sung Dynasty 亦作「伊川先生」

【稌】 4006
ㄊㄨˊ twu tú
(glutinous) rice

八畫

【稟】 4007
ㄅㄧㄥˇ biing bǐng
1. to report to a superior or one's seniors; to petition; to appeal
2. to receive commands; at the behest of
3. one's natural endowments or gifts
稟白(ㄅㄧㄥˇ ㄅㄛˊ)or 稟報(ㄅㄧㄥˇ ㄅㄠˋ)
to report to a superior 參看「稟告」
稟明(ㄅㄧㄥˇ ㄇㄧㄥˊ)
to explain to a superior or elder; to clarify a matter to a superior or elder
稟命(ㄅㄧㄥˇ ㄇㄧㄥˋ)
at the behest of; by order of
稟賦(ㄅㄧㄥˇ ㄈㄨˋ)
a natural endowment, gift or disposition: 他稟賦聰明。He is gifted with keen intelligence.
稟覆(ㄅㄧㄥˇ ㄈㄨˋ)
to make a (verbal or written) reply to a superior
稟告(ㄅㄧㄥˇ ㄍㄠˋ)
to report (to one's superior)
稟性(ㄅㄧㄥˇ ㄒㄧㄥˋ)
a natural disposition or temperament: 此人稟性純厚。The man is simple and honest by nature.
稟陳(ㄅㄧㄥˇ ㄔㄣˊ)
to report to a superior 參看「稟告」
稟承(ㄅㄧㄥˇ ㄔㄥˊ)
(to do something) according to orders of a superior or higher office; to take (orders); to receive (commands): 他稟承其父的旨意。He acted on the orders of his father.
稟受(ㄅㄧㄥˇ ㄕㄡˋ)
① to endure ② nature

【稔】 4008
ㄖㄣˇ reen rěn
1. the ripening of paddy or rice; a harvest
2. a year
3. used to; often
4. to accumulate; to hoard
5. to be familiar with somebody
稔亂(ㄖㄣˇ ㄌㄨㄢˋ)
the turmoil that has been brewed for a long time
稔知(ㄖㄣˇ ㄓ)
to know well; familiar
稔熟(ㄖㄣˇ ㄕㄡˊ)
(said of grain) ripe
稔色(ㄖㄣˇ ㄙㄜˋ)
① beauty or charms ② to have a weakness for women

【稚】 4009
(穉) ㄓˋ jyh zhì
young and tender; small; delicate; immature; childish

稚嫩(ㄓˋ ㄋㄣˋ)
① tender and delicate ② young and tender
稚女(ㄓˋ ㄋㄩˇ)
young girls
稚齡(ㄓˋ ㄌㄧㄥˊ)
tender age (or years)
稚氣(ㄓˋ ㄑㄧˋ)
innocence of a child; childishness
稚齒(ㄓˋ ㄔˇ)
young people; children; toddlers
稚弱(ㄓˋ ㄖㄨㄛˋ)
tender and delicate
稚子(ㄓˋ ㄗˇ)
① young children ② bamboo shoots

【稜】 4010 ㄌㄥˊ leng léng
1. a corner; an angle; an edge
2. a square piece of wood
3. an awe-inspiring air
稜稜(ㄌㄥˊ ㄌㄥˊ)
① chilly or frosty ② awe-inspiring
稜角(ㄌㄥˊ ㄐㄧㄠˇ)
① an angle; a corner ② pointed; pointedness: 挫折可以把你的稜角磨掉。Frustrations could eliminate your pointedness.
稜鏡(ㄌㄥˊ ㄐㄧㄥˋ)
a prism: 三稜鏡 a triangular prism
稜睜(ㄌㄥˊ ㄓㄥ) or 稜稜睜睜(ㄌㄥˊ ㄌㄥˊ ㄓㄥ ㄓㄥ)
① rash; rude ② very cold
稜柱體(ㄌㄥˊ ㄓㄨˋ ㄊㄧˇ)
(mathematics) a prism
稜錐體(ㄌㄥˊ ㄓㄨㄟ ㄊㄧˇ)
a pyramid
稜子(ㄌㄥˊ ·ㄗ) or 稜兒(ㄌㄥˊㄦ)
an angle; a right angle; a corner

【稗】 4011 ㄅㄞˋ bay bài
1. barnyard grass
2. small; little
3. novels, legends, etc.
稗販(ㄅㄞˋ ㄈㄢˋ)
peddlers or hawkers
稗官(ㄅㄞˋ ㄍㄨㄢ)
officials of low ranks
稗官野史(ㄅㄞˋ ㄍㄨㄢ ㄧㄝˇ ㄕˇ)
unofficial historical writings; historical novels
稗史(ㄅㄞˋ ㄕˇ)
unofficial historical writings
稗說(ㄅㄞˋ ㄕㄨㄛ)
novels; stories
稗子(ㄅㄞˋ ·ㄗ)
barnyard grass

【稠】 4012 ㄔㄡˊ chour chóu
1. dense; closely crowded together
2. (said of liquids) thick; viscous
3. a Chinese family name
稠密(ㄔㄡˊ ㄇㄧˋ)
crowded; dense: 這是個人煙稠密的城市。This is a thickly populated city.
稠疊(ㄔㄡˊ ㄉㄧㄝˊ)
overlapping
稠濁(ㄔㄡˊ ㄓㄨㄛˊ)
wordy and confused
稠人廣衆(ㄔㄡˊ ㄖㄣˊ ㄍㄨㄤˇ ㄓㄨㄥˋ)
a large audience; a sea of people
稠雲(ㄔㄡˊ ㄩㄣˊ)
dense clouds

【稞】 4013 ㄎㄜ ke kē
wheat or barley

九畫

【種】 4014 1. ㄓㄨㄥˇ joong zhǒng
1. seeds of grain
2. races (of human beings)
3. descendants; posterity
4. a species; a genus; a kind or sort: 這是柳橙的一種。This is a species of orange.
5. guts; grit: 他沒種做這件事。He has no guts for it.
種別(ㄓㄨㄥˇ ㄅㄧㄝˊ)
classification
種皮(ㄓㄨㄥˇ ㄆㄧˊ)
a seed coat
種馬(ㄓㄨㄥˇ ㄇㄚˇ)
a studhorse; a stallion
種類(ㄓㄨㄥˇ ㄌㄟˋ)
a sort; a kind; a variety; a class: 他有不同種類的玩具。He has toys of different kinds.
種切(ㄓㄨㄥˇ ㄑㄧㄝˋ)
and so on; etc.
種種(ㄓㄨㄥˇ ㄓㄨㄥˇ)
① various kinds ② short-cropped hair ③ simple and sincere (as rural people)
種畜(ㄓㄨㄥˇ ㄔㄨˋ)
domestic animals raised for a breeding purpose
種人(ㄓㄨㄥˇ ㄖㄣˊ)
people of the same race
種子(ㄓㄨㄥˇ ㄗˇ)
a seed
種子隊(ㄓㄨㄥˇ ㄗˇ ㄉㄨㄟˋ)
(sports meetings) a seed team
種族(ㄓㄨㄥˇ ㄗㄨˊ)
(said of people) a race, or tribe
種族革命(ㄓㄨㄥˇ ㄗㄨˊ ㄍㄜˊ ㄇㄧㄥˋ)
racial revolution
種族隔離(ㄓㄨㄥˇ ㄗㄨˊ ㄍㄜˊ ㄌㄧˊ)
racial segregation; apartheid (in South Africa)
種族歧視(ㄓㄨㄥˇ ㄗㄨˊ ㄑㄧˊ ㄕˋ)
racial discrimination
種原論(ㄓㄨㄥˇ ㄩㄢˊ ㄌㄨㄣˋ)
Origin of Species, by Charles R. Darwin

【種】 4014 2. ㄓㄨㄥˋ jonq zhòng
1. to plant; to sow; to cultivate: 農夫在田裏種小麥。The farmer sowed the field with wheat.
2. to vaccinate
種麥得麥(ㄓㄨㄥˋ ㄇㄞˋ ㄉㄜˊ ㄇㄞˋ)
As a man sows, so shall he reap. 或 A man reaps what he sows.
種德(ㄓㄨㄥˋ ㄉㄜˊ)
to accumulate virtuous deeds; to cultivate virtues
種痘(ㄓㄨㄥˋ ㄉㄡˋ) or 種牛痘(ㄓㄨㄥˋ ㄋㄧㄡˊ ㄉㄡˋ)
to vaccinate; vaccination (against smallpox): 這小孩已經種痘了。The child has been vaccinated.
種地(ㄓㄨㄥˋ ㄉㄧˋ)
to farm; to cultivate the land
種田(ㄓㄨㄥˋ ㄊㄧㄢˊ)
to farm; to till the land
種田的(ㄓㄨㄥˋ ㄊㄧㄢˊ ·ㄉㄜ)
a farmer
種瓜得瓜，種豆得豆(ㄓㄨㄥˋ ㄍㄨㄚ ㄉㄜˊ ㄍㄨㄚ, ㄓㄨㄥˋ ㄉㄡˋ ㄉㄜˊ ㄉㄡˋ)
One reaps what he sows. 或 You must reap what you

have sown.

種花(ㄓㄨㄥˋ ㄏㄨㄚ)
to raise, grow or cultivate flowers

種禍(ㄓㄨㄥˋ ㄏㄨㄛˋ)
to sow the seeds of calamity or misfortune

種植(ㄓㄨㄥˋ ㄓˊ)
to plant; to raise or grow (plants); to cultivate

種莊稼(ㄓㄨㄥˋ ㄓㄨㄤ ˙ㄐㄧㄚ)
to till the land; to be a farmer

種菜(ㄓㄨㄥˋ ㄘㄞˋ)
to grow vegetables

種因(ㄓㄨㄥˋ ㄧㄣ)
to do something which eventually becomes the cause of some development (usually undesirable development) in the future

【稱】 4015 1. ㄔㄥ cheng chēng

1. to weigh; to measure weight
2. to claim; to report; to declare
3. to call; to name; a name; an appellation
4. to offer as an excuse (as illness)
5. to say; to tell; to state
6. to speak laudatory words; to praise
7. to take up (arms, etc.)
8. a Chinese family name

稱霸(ㄔㄥ ㄅㄚˋ)
to become the most powerful nation in the world or part of the world; to hold an undisputed position of strength; to occupy the leading position (in certain field of sports, etc.)

稱便(ㄔㄥ ㄅㄧㄢˋ)
(said of new facilities or better services) hailed as a great service to the public; to commend something

稱兵(ㄔㄥ ㄅㄧㄥ)
to take up arms; to be on the warpath; to commence hostilities with

稱病(ㄔㄥ ㄅㄧㄥˋ)
to offer illness as an excuse; to malinger

稱道(ㄔㄥ ㄉㄠˋ)
to praise or acclaim

稱孤道寡(ㄔㄥ ㄍㄨ ㄉㄠˋ ㄍㄨㄚˇ)
to declare or call oneself king or emperor; to claim imperial authority

稱快(ㄔㄥ ㄎㄨㄞˋ)
to express one's gratification; to feel jubilant

稱號(ㄔㄥ ㄏㄠˋ)
an appellation; a title; a designation: 他贏得了多產作家的稱號。He has won the title of prolific writer.

稱呼(ㄔㄥ ㄏㄨ)
a name by which one addresses another; to address; to name: 你怎麼稱呼市長? How do you address the mayor?

稱慶(ㄔㄥ ㄑㄧㄥˋ)
to congratulate; to express joy

稱謝(ㄔㄥ ㄒㄧㄝˋ)
to express thanks: 他對她的幫助稱謝不止。He thanked her again and again for her help.

稱羨不置(ㄔㄥ ㄒㄧㄢˋ ㄅㄨˋ ㄓˋ)
to envy to no end; to admire greatly

稱羨不已(ㄔㄥ ㄒㄧㄢˋ ㄅㄨˋ ㄧˇ)
to express profuse admiration

稱許(ㄔㄥ ㄒㄩˇ)
to approve and praise; approval and praise

稱兄道弟(ㄔㄥ ㄒㄩㄥ ㄉㄠˋ ㄉㄧˋ)
on first-name terms; very intimate

稱雄(ㄔㄥ ㄒㄩㄥˊ)
to claim leadership; to occupy a dominating position; to hold sway over

稱制(ㄔㄥ ㄓˋ)
(said of an empress dowager) to act as regent; to assume regency

稱臣(ㄔㄥ ㄔㄣˊ)
(literally) to declare oneself a vassal—to be subjugated; to concede defeat; to submit to the victor

稱述(ㄔㄥ ㄕㄨˋ)
to praise or laud someone's deeds

稱說(ㄔㄥ ㄕㄨㄛ)
to narrate; to state; to tell

稱字(ㄔㄥ ㄗˋ)
to address another person by his style as a token of respect

稱讚(ㄔㄥ ㄗㄢˋ)
to praise; to acclaim: 老師稱讚他的勤勞。The teacher praised him for his diligence.

稱頌(ㄔㄥ ㄙㄨㄥˋ)
to praise; to extol: 大多數人喜歡被稱頌。Most people like to receive praises.

稱一稱(ㄔㄥ ˙ㄧ ˙ㄔㄥ)
to weigh (something)

稱引(ㄔㄥ ㄧㄣˇ)
to adduce; to cite as an example or precedent

稱揚(ㄔㄥ ㄧㄤˊ)
to praise and extol

稱爲(ㄔㄥ ㄨㄟˊ)
to call; to designate

稱謂(ㄔㄥ ㄨㄟˋ)
name or appellation of a person or thing

稱譽(ㄔㄥ ㄩˋ)
to praise; to acclaim; to extol

【稱】 4015 2. ㄔㄥˋ chenq chèng

1. a steelyard; a weighing machine
2. fit; proper; suitable; well-matched
3. symmetrical; to be equal to; corresponding to

稱不離錘(ㄔㄥˋ ㄅㄨˋ ㄌㄧˊ ㄔㄨㄟˊ)
(literally) The steelyard never goes without the weight.—inseparable亦作「秤不離錘」

稱體裁衣(ㄔㄥˋ ㄊㄧˇ ㄘㄞˊ ㄧ)
exactly matching; perfectly suitable

稱職(ㄔㄥˋ ㄓˊ)
well qualified; competent; equal to the job one is doing: 他是一位稱職的教師。He is a competent teacher.

稱旨(ㄔㄥˋ ㄓˇ)
to be in full accordance with the ideas of the emperor

稱身(ㄔㄥˋ ㄕㄣ)
(said of dresses) to fit perfectly: 這件夾克你穿了挺稱身的。This jacket fits you perfectly.

【稱】 4015
3. ㄔㄣˋ chenn chèn
fit; suitable; in accordance with
稱錢(ㄔㄣˋ ㄑㄧㄢˊ)
rich
稱心(ㄔㄣˋ ㄒㄧㄣ)
to find something satisfactory; to have something as one's wish 亦作「趁心」: 這部車實在很稱心。This car is quite satisfactory—just the thing I want.
稱心如意(ㄔㄣˋ ㄒㄧㄣ ㄖㄨˊ ㄧˋ)
very gratifying and satisfactory; happy and contented
稱意(ㄔㄣˋ ㄧˋ)
agreeable; gratifying; satisfactory
稱願(ㄔㄣˋ ㄩㄢˋ)
just as one wishes

【稭】 4016
ㄐㄧㄝ jie jiē
the stalk of corn, hemp, etc.
稭稈(ㄐㄧㄝ ㄍㄢˇ)
straw

【稨】 4017
ㄅㄧㄢˇ bean biǎn
a lentil

十畫

【穀】 4018
ㄍㄨˇ guu gǔ
1. grain; corn; cereals
2. lucky; happy; favorable; good
3. to live; while alive
穀道(ㄍㄨˇ ㄉㄠˋ)
① the rectum, or alimentary canal ② to stop eating grain as a means to attain immortality
穀旦(ㄍㄨˇ ㄉㄢˋ)
an auspicious (lucky) day; a good day
穀類(ㄍㄨˇ ㄌㄟˋ)
grain and corn; cereals
穀梁傳(ㄍㄨˇ ㄌㄧㄤˊ ㄓㄨㄢˋ)
one of the three expansions of Confucius' *Spring and Autumn Annals*
穀賤傷農(ㄍㄨˇ ㄐㄧㄢˋ ㄕㄤ ㄋㄨㄥˊ)
Low grain price hurts the farmer.—a theory advanced by Chao Tso (鼂錯) of the Han Dynasty
穀場(ㄍㄨˇ ㄔㄤˇ)or(ㄍㄨˇ ㄔㄤˊ)
a yard for sunning or drying grain, corn, etc.
穀日(ㄍㄨˇ ㄖˋ)
the eighth day of the first month in the lunar calendar
穀子(ㄍㄨˇ ·ㄗ)
millet 亦作「粟」or「小米」
穀倉(ㄍㄨˇ ㄘㄤ)
a barn for storing grain; a granary
穀物(ㄍㄨˇ ㄨˋ)
cereals; grain
穀雨(ㄍㄨˇ ㄩˇ)
Grain rains—one of the 24 climatic transitions in a lunar year, which falls on April 20 or 21

【稿】 4019
(槀) ㄍㄠˇ gao gǎo
1. a manuscript; a sketch; a rough draft or copy: 這是演說的草稿。This is a draft for a speech.
2. a pattern or copy book for drawing
3. straw; a stalk of grain
稿本(ㄍㄠˇ ㄅㄣˇ)
① a manuscript or draft of a literary work ② a pattern or copy book for drawing
稿費(ㄍㄠˇ ㄈㄟˋ)
fees paid to the contributor of a published article; payment to a writer on a piecework basis; contribution fees
稿底(ㄍㄠˇ ㄉㄧˇ)
a rough draft of a piece of writing
稿件(ㄍㄠˇ ㄐㄧㄢˋ)
① contribution to a publication; writings ② manuscripts; a sketch; a rough draft
稿紙(ㄍㄠˇ ㄓˇ)
manuscript or draft paper
稿酬(ㄍㄠˇ ㄔㄡˊ)
fees paid to a writer on a piecework basis
稿子(ㄍㄠˇ ·ㄗ)or 稿兒(ㄍㄠˇㄦ)
① manuscripts; drafts: 他正在起個稿子。He is making a draft. ② plans in one's mind; a plan formulated beforehand ③ a pattern or precedent

【稷】 4020
ㄐㄧˋ jih jì
panicled millet

【稼】 4021
ㄐㄧㄚˋ jiah jià
1. to farm, plant, sow or cultivate
2. grain; crops
稼穡(ㄐㄧㄚˋ ㄙㄜˋ)
planting and harvesting of grain; farming; agricultural operations
稼穡艱難(ㄐㄧㄚˋ ㄙㄜˋ ㄐㄧㄢ ㄋㄢˊ)
the toil and hardship of a farmer's life

【稻】 4022
ㄉㄠˋ daw dào
paddy or rice
稻米(ㄉㄠˋ ㄇㄧˇ)
rice or paddy: 中國人以稻米爲主食。The Chinese live on rice.
稻飯(ㄉㄠˋ ㄈㄢˋ)
cooked rice
稻田(ㄉㄠˋ ㄊㄧㄢˊ)
a paddy field; a rice field
稻穀(ㄉㄠˋ ㄍㄨˇ)
paddy
稻場(ㄉㄠˋ ㄔㄤˇ)or(ㄉㄠˋ ㄔㄤˊ)
a yard for sunning or drying unhulled rice
稻熱病(ㄉㄠˋ ㄖㄜˋ ㄅㄧㄥˋ)
rice blast
稻子(ㄉㄠˋ ·ㄗ)
unhulled rice
稻草(ㄉㄠˋ ㄘㄠˇ)
rice straw
稻草堆(ㄉㄠˋ ㄘㄠˇ ㄉㄨㄟ)
a straw stack
稻草人(ㄉㄠˋ ㄘㄠˇ ㄖㄣˊ)
a scarecrow; a jack of straw
稻草褥(ㄉㄠˋ ㄘㄠˇ ㄖㄨˋ)
a straw mattress
稻穗(ㄉㄠˋ ㄙㄨㄟˋ)
the ear or spike of the rice plant
稻孫(ㄉㄠˋ ㄙㄨㄣ)
the aftergrowth of rice plants
稻秧(ㄉㄠˋ ㄧㄤ)
rice seedlings; rice shoots

【稽】 4023
1. ㄐㄧ ji jī
1. to investigate; to examine; to inspect; to verify: 它是有案可稽的。It can be verified. 或 It's verifiable.

2. to stay; to delay or procrastinate
3. a Chinese family name

稽留(ㄐㄧ ㄌㄧㄡˊ)
①to stay; to stay for a long time ②another name of the prison in the Chou Dynasty

稽留熱(ㄐㄧ ㄌㄧㄡˊ ㄖㄜˋ)
remittent fever

稽古(ㄐㄧ ㄍㄨˇ)
to examine and study ancient ways, matters, etc.

稽考(ㄐㄧ ㄎㄠˇ)
to examine; to verify: 那件事無可稽考。It cannot be verified.

稽核(ㄐㄧ ㄏㄜˊ)
to examine and audit; to inspect and audit: 王先生在稽核帳目。Mr. Wang was auditing the accounts.

稽覈(ㄐㄧ ㄏㄜˊ)
to check; to investigate or verify

稽徵處(ㄐㄧ ㄓㄥ ㄔㄨˋ)
an office for auditing (accounts) and levying (taxes)

稽遲(ㄐㄧ ㄔˊ)or 稽時(ㄐㄧ ㄕˊ)
to be delayed or detained; to procrastinate

稽查(ㄐㄧ ㄔㄚˊ)or 稽察(ㄐㄧ ㄔㄚˊ)
to examine and investigate

稽程(ㄐㄧ ㄔㄥˊ)
①the delay in presenting documents, formal reports, etc. ②to delay journey

稽疑(ㄐㄧ ㄧˊ)
to solve doubt by means of divination; to examine by divination

稽延(ㄐㄧ ㄧㄢˊ)
to delay; to procrastinate

【稽】 4023
2. ㄑㄧˇ chii qǐ

to kowtow; to bow to the ground

稽首(ㄑㄧˇ ㄕㄡˇ)
to kowtow—an expression of great respect

稽顙(ㄑㄧˇ ㄙㄤˇ)
to kowtow to those who attend the funeral service of one's parent with one's forehead touching the ground

【稹】 4024
ㄓㄣˇ jeen zhěn

1. circumspect
2. (said of roots) entwined

十一畫

【穈】 4025
ㄇㄣˊ men mén

large-grained millet with red seedlings

【穌】 4026
ㄙㄨ su sū

1. to mow grass
2. to revive; to come to; to rise again

【穎】 4027
(頴) ㄧㄥˇ yiing yǐng

1. outstanding; remarkable; talented; distinguished
2. a sharp point of an awl
3. the point of a writing brush
4. the ears of grain hanging down with their own weight

穎脫(ㄧㄥˇ ㄊㄨㄛ)
to distinguish oneself in performance

穎果(ㄧㄥˇ ㄍㄨㄛˇ)
a caryopsis

穎花(ㄧㄥˇ ㄏㄨㄚ)
Glumales, a glume flower

穎慧(ㄧㄥˇ ㄏㄨㄟˋ)
clever; bright; intelligent

穎秀(ㄧㄥˇ ㄒㄧㄡˋ)
outstandingly talented

穎哲(ㄧㄥˇ ㄓㄜˊ)
clever and wise

穎悟(ㄧㄥˇ ㄨˋ)
very bright; unusually intelligent

【穆】 4028
ㄇㄨˋ muh mù

1. peaceful; serene
2. respectful; reverent
3. profound
4. majestic; solemn
5. the right side of an ancestral shrine
6. a Chinese family name

穆卜(ㄇㄨˋ ㄅㄨˇ)
to consult the oracle reverently

穆民(ㄇㄨˋ ㄇㄧㄣˊ)
a name which the Mohammedans call themselves

穆穆(ㄇㄨˋ ㄇㄨˋ)
①profound ②respectable; majestic; very admirable

穆罕默德(ㄇㄨˋ ㄏㄢˇ ㄇㄛˋ ㄉㄜˊ)
Mohammed (c.570-632), the founder of Mohammedanism

穆清(ㄇㄨˋ ㄑㄧㄥ)
①the Heaven ②peaceful and orderly (world, etc.)

穆然(ㄇㄨˋ ㄖㄢˊ)
①peaceful and respectful ②meditative

【積】 4029
ㄐㄧ ji jī

1. to accumulate; to store up; to amass
2. long (time); old; deep-rooted; longstanding
3. (mathematics) product

積弊(ㄐㄧ ㄅㄧˋ)
deep-rooted evils or corrupt ways

積弊難返(ㄐㄧ ㄅㄧˋ ㄋㄢˊ ㄈㄢˇ)
It's very difficult to uproot deep-entrenched evils or shortcomings.

積冰(ㄐㄧ ㄅㄧㄥ)
ice which exists for a long time

積木(ㄐㄧ ㄇㄨˋ)
building blocks, or wooden blocks (a kind of children's toy)

積分(ㄐㄧ ㄈㄣ)
①accumulated points ②integral calculus

積分學(ㄐㄧ ㄈㄣ ㄒㄩㄝˊ)
(mathematics) integral calculus

積福(ㄐㄧ ㄈㄨˊ)
to accumulate or store up happiness by charitable deeds

積德(ㄐㄧ ㄉㄜˊ)
to make it a point to do good deeds whenever possible

積年累月(ㄐㄧ ㄋㄧㄢˊ ㄌㄟˇ ㄩㄝˋ)
for years and months—a long time

積累(ㄐㄧ ㄌㄟˇ)
to accumulate: 他已積累了豐富的經驗。He has accumulated a wealth of experience.

積勞成疾(ㄐㄧ ㄌㄠˊ ㄔㄥˊ ㄐㄧˊ)
to fall sick from persistent overwork

積穀防饑(ㄐㄧ ㄍㄨˇ ㄈㄤˊ ㄐㄧ)
to store up food in anticipation of famine; to get prepared for a rainy day

積毀銷骨(ㄐㄧ ㄏㄨㄟˇ ㄒㄧㄠ ㄍㄨˇ)
Libels can destroy strong

family ties.

積極(ㄐㄧ ㄐㄧˊ)
active(ly); positive(ly); persistent(ly): 他們採取了積極的措施。They adopted active measures.

積極分子(ㄐㄧ ㄐㄧˊ ㄈㄣˋ ㄗˇ)
an activist; an enthusiast; a radical

積久(ㄐㄧ ㄐㄧㄡˇ)
over a long time

積漸(ㄐㄧ ㄐㄧㄢˋ)
gradually; little by little

積聚(ㄐㄧ ㄐㄩˋ)
to accumulate; to amass; to pile; to store up

積欠(ㄐㄧ ㄑㄧㄢˋ)
accumulated debts; outstanding debts; arrears: 他還清了積欠的錢。He cleared up all outstanding debts.

積習(ㄐㄧ ㄒㄧˊ)
a deep-rooted practice; an old habit

積習難改(ㄐㄧ ㄒㄧˊ ㄋㄢˊ ㄍㄞˇ)
It's very difficult to get rid of an old habit.

積薪(ㄐㄧ ㄒㄧㄣ)
a pile of firewood; the piling of firewood

積蓄(ㄐㄧ ㄒㄩˋ)
savings: 他失去了所有的積蓄。He lost all his savings.

積雪(ㄐㄧ ㄒㄩㄝˇ)
accumulated snow: 積雪盈尺。Accumulated snow is over a foot.

積貯(ㄐㄧ ㄓㄨˇ)
①savings ②to store up

積重難返(ㄐㄧ ㄓㄨㄥˋ ㄋㄢˊ ㄈㄢˇ)
It is very difficult to break a habit of long standing.

積食(ㄐㄧ ㄕˊ)
(medicine) dyspepsia; indigestion

積沙成塔(ㄐㄧ ㄕㄚ ㄔㄥˊ ㄊㄚˇ)
Great things rise from small beginnings.

積少成多(ㄐㄧ ㄕㄠˇ ㄔㄥˊ ㄉㄨㄛ)
Economy in trifles will ensure abundance. 或 Many buckets of water will make a river. 或 Many feathers make a bed.

積善餘慶(ㄐㄧ ㄕㄢˋ ㄩˊ ㄑㄧㄥˋ)
If one does (or accumulates) enough good deeds, one will have more than enough blessings to spare.

積水(ㄐㄧ ㄕㄨㄟˇ)
to accumulate water; accumulated water (in low-lying areas after a shower)

積攢(ㄐㄧ ㄗㄢˇ)
①savings ②to save bit by bit

積存(ㄐㄧ ㄘㄨㄣˊ)
to save; to store; to lay up (or in): 有些動物會積存食物過冬。Some animals store food for the winter.

積惡(ㄐㄧ ㄜˋ)
to practice evils day in and day out; to indulge in evil ways; to commit many crimes

積壓(ㄐㄧ ㄧㄚ)
to neglect handling official papers, legal cases, etc.; to accumulate and hold up official documents

積雨(ㄐㄧ ㄩˇ)
to rain for a long time

積羽沈舟(ㄐㄧ ㄩˇ ㄔㄣˊ ㄓㄡ)
Accumulation of feathers may sink a boat. 或 Accumulation of small particles results in a mountain.

積怨(ㄐㄧ ㄩㄢˋ)
to accumulate animus, malice or hatred; accumulated or deep-rooted animus, malice or hatred: 消除你心中的積怨。Get rid of your accumulated hatred.

【穄】 4030 ㄐㄧˋ jih jì
same as 稷—panicled millet

十二畫

【穗】 4031 ㄙㄨㄟˋ suey suì
1. fruits or grains in a cluster grown at the tip of a stem or stalk
2. the ear of grain
3. another name of Canton
4. a candle snuff; a candlewick

穗狀花序(ㄙㄨㄟˋ ㄓㄨㄤˋ ㄏㄨㄚ ㄒㄩˋ)
the spikes (of flowers)

穗子(ㄙㄨㄟˋ ·ㄗ)or 穗兒(ㄙㄨㄟˋㄦ)
the ear of grain

十三畫

【穡】 4032 ㄙㄜˋ seh sè
1. to harvest grain; to gather in the harvest; to reap
2. same as 嗇—thrifty; stingy; tight-fisted

穡夫(ㄙㄜˋ ㄈㄨ)or 穡人(ㄙㄜˋ ㄖㄣˊ)
a farmer

穡臣(ㄙㄜˋ ㄔㄣˊ)
an official in charge of agriculture in ancient times

穡事(ㄙㄜˋ ㄕˋ)
farming; husbandry

【穢】 4033 ㄏㄨㄟˋ huey huì
1. vile; wicked
2. dirty; filthy
3. obscene; wanton (ways or conduct)
4. ugly and abominable
5. weeds on a farm

穢名(ㄏㄨㄟˋ ㄇㄧㄥˊ)
a notorious reputation

穢德(ㄏㄨㄟˋ ㄉㄜˊ)
debauched ways; filthy deeds

穢土(ㄏㄨㄟˋ ㄊㄨˇ)
①dirty or unclean earth ②(Buddhism) the human world

穢亂(ㄏㄨㄟˋ ㄌㄨㄢˋ)
debauched; wanton

穢氣(ㄏㄨㄟˋ ㄑㄧˋ)
foul air

穢褻(ㄏㄨㄟˋ ㄒㄧㄝˋ)
obscene; pornographic

穢行(ㄏㄨㄟˋ ㄒㄧㄥˊ)
debauched or vile behavior; scandalous conduct

穢史(ㄏㄨㄟˋ ㄕˇ)
①a record of someone's scandalous acts ②the title of a libelous book by Wei Shou(魏收)

穢物(ㄏㄨㄟˋ ㄨˋ)
filth

【穠】 4034 ㄋㄨㄥˊ nong nóng
luxuriant growth of plants

穠纖合度(ㄋㄨㄥˊ ㄒㄧㄢ ㄏㄜˊ ㄉㄨˋ)
(said of a girl's figure) well-proportioned: 她個子雖小，但長得穠纖合度。She is rather small but well-proportioned.

穠艷(ㄋㄨㄥˊ ㄧㄢˋ)

beautiful and glamorous

十四畫

【穩】 4035 ㄨㄣˇ woen wěn

1. stable; stability; steady; firm: 他把桌子放穩。He made the table steady.
2. sure; certain: 這事你拿得穩嗎? Are you quite sure of it?
3. secure; security

穩便(ㄨㄣˇ ㄅㄧㄢˋ)
①safe and convenient ②at will; to proceed as one wishes

穩婆(ㄨㄣˇ ㄆㄛˊ)
a midwife

穩當(ㄨㄣˇ ·ㄉㄤ)
proper and secure; safe and sound: 他想到一個穩當的辦法。He thinks of a proper and secure method.

穩定(ㄨㄣˇ ㄉㄧㄥˋ)
①to stabilize: 政府設法穩定物價。The government tries to stabilize prices. ②stable; steady: 全世界需要穩定的和平。The whole world needs a stable peace.

穩定平衡(ㄨㄣˇ ㄉㄧㄥˋ ㄆㄧㄥˊ ㄏㄥˊ)
(physics) stable equilibrium

穩貼(ㄨㄣˇ ㄊㄧㄝ)
proper and secure; safe and sound

穩妥(ㄨㄣˇ ㄊㄨㄛˇ)
secure and dependable; proper and secure: 他認爲那樣辦更穩妥。He thinks it's safer to do it that way.

穩固(ㄨㄣˇ ㄍㄨˋ)
stable and firm; secure: 它具有穩固的基礎。It has a firm (or solid) foundation.

穩健(ㄨㄣˇ ㄐㄧㄢˋ)
firm and steady (as opposed to rash or whimsical): 他是個穩健的青年。He is a steady young man.

穩健派(ㄨㄣˇ ㄐㄧㄢˋ ㄆㄞˋ)
the moderates (as opposed to radicals)

穩下(ㄨㄣˇ ㄒㄧㄚˋ)
to calm down: 我們試著穩下那個人的怒氣。We tried to calm down the angry man.

穩紮穩打(ㄨㄣˇ ㄓㄚ ㄨㄣˇ ㄉㄚˇ)
to proceed steadily and step by step; to do things steadily without hurrying; to go ahead steadily and strike sure blows

穩住(ㄨㄣˇ ㄓㄨˋ)
①to hold back someone from intervening in one's plans—sometimes with tricks, etc. ②(said of contests, games, battle, etc.) to hold stable or consolidate; to make secure or stable (a situation, etc.)

穩重(ㄨㄣˇ ㄓㄨㄥˋ)
steady, calm, and dignified

穩如泰山(ㄨㄣˇ ㄖㄨˊ ㄊㄞˋ ㄕㄢ)
as stable as Mount Tai —(figuratively) to be in an invincible position

穩穩當當(ㄨㄣˇ ㄨㄣˇ ㄉㄤ ㄉㄤ)
①safe and secure; proper and dependable ②sure and certain

【穫】 4036 ㄏㄨㄛˋ huoh huò

to reap or harvest; to cut grain

十七畫

【穰】 4037 ㄖㄤˊ rang ráng

1. crowded
2. confusing; mixed-up; disturbed (mind, etc.)
3. stalks of cereal grasses
4. luxuriant

穰田(ㄖㄤˊ ㄊㄧㄢˊ)
to offer sacrifices to gods for a good harvest

穰穰(ㄖㄤˊ ㄖㄤˊ)
①in abundant measure ②confused and disturbed ③luxuriant

穴部
ㄒㄩㄝ shiueh xuè

【穴】 4038 ㄒㄩㄝˋ shiueh xuè

1. a cave; a den; a hole: 老鼠在牆上挖洞穴。The mouse made a hole in the wall.
2. points in the human body where acupuncture can be applied
3. (Chinese boxing) points in the human body where nerve centers are supposed to be located, a strike at which may cause paralysis or even death

穴道(ㄒㄩㄝˋ ㄉㄠˋ)
①see 穴 2. and 3. ②an underground channel

穴見(ㄒㄩㄝˋ ㄐㄧㄢˋ)
limited views or horizons

穴居(ㄒㄩㄝˋ ㄐㄩ)
to live in a cave; cave-dwelling

穴居野處(ㄒㄩㄝˋ ㄐㄩ ㄧㄝˇ ㄔㄨˇ)
(said of primitive people) to live in caves in the wilderness

穴隙(ㄒㄩㄝˋ ㄒㄧˋ)
a hole; a crack

二畫

【究】 4039 ㄐㄧㄡˋ jiow jiù (又讀 ㄐㄧㄡ jiou jiū)

1. to examine; to study; to investigate exhaustively; to dig into
2. finally; in the end; after all
3. actually; really

究辦(ㄐㄧㄡˋ ㄅㄢˋ)
to investigate and punish

究根問底(ㄐㄧㄡˋ ㄍㄣ ㄨㄣˋ ㄉㄧˇ)
to get to the bottom of something; to investigate exhaustively

究詰(ㄐㄧㄡˋ ㄐㄧㄝˊ)
to interrogate; to question closely; to cross-examine

究竟(ㄐㄧㄡˋ ㄐㄧㄥˋ)or(ㄐㄧㄡ ㄐㄧㄥˋ)
①the very truth; the very source; the very end; the outcome: 我們都想知道個究竟。We want to know the outcome. ②after all; in the end; finally; at last ③actually; exactly; on earth: 他究竟到那兒去了? Where on earth has he gone?

究細兒(ㄐㄧㄡˋ ㄒㄧˋㄦ)or(ㄐㄧㄡ ㄒㄧˋㄦ)
to dig into; to scrutinize

究查(ㄐㄧㄡˋ ㄔㄚˊ)

to examine; to investigate; to probe

究問(ㄐㄧㄡˋ ㄨㄣˋ)

to study and question; to dig into; to cross-examine

三畫

【穸】 4040 ㄒㄧˋ shih xì

1. a tomb or grave 參看「窀穸」
2. the dead of night

【穹】 4041 ㄑㄩㄥ chiong qiōng (又讀 ㄑㄩㄥˊ chyong qióng)

1. high and vast
2. arched; vaulted
3. deep and spacious
4. the sky

穹冥(ㄑㄩㄥ ㄇㄧㄥˊ)

the sky; the heavens

穹地(ㄑㄩㄥ ㄉㄧˋ)

an area with an elevated center (the opposite of a basin); an elevation

穹靈(ㄑㄩㄥ ㄌㄧㄥˊ)

gods high above

穹廬(ㄑㄩㄥ ㄌㄨˊ)

the Mongolian felt tents with rounded tops; a yurt

穹隆(ㄑㄩㄥ ㄌㄨㄥˊ)

① the arched firmament; vault 亦作「穹窿」② long and winding

穹谷(ㄑㄩㄥ ㄍㄨˇ)

a deep valley or ravine

穹嵌(ㄑㄩㄥ ㄑㄧㄢ)

places high up on a steep hill

穹蒼(ㄑㄩㄥ ㄘㄤ)

the sky; the firmament; the azure vault

【空】 4042 1. ㄎㄨㄥ kong kōng

1. empty; hollow; void: 那箱子完全是空的。The box was quite empty.
2. to empty; to exhaust; to reduce to extremity
3. fictitious; unreal; impractical
4. vain and useless (efforts, etc.); ineffective; fruitless: 她空忙了一陣。She made fruitless efforts.
5. high and vast
6. the sky; space: 天空無雲。There were no clouds in the sky.
7. (Buddhism) sunyata; empty; void; vacant; non-existent
8. merely; only
9. a Chinese family name

空跑一趟(ㄎㄨㄥ ㄆㄠˇ ㄧˊ ㄊㄤˋ)

to take a trip without achieving the purpose: 他空跑一趟。He made a journey for nothing.

空盤(ㄎㄨㄥ ㄆㄢˊ)

① to buy long or sell short; to speculate on the market ② nominal prices

空門(ㄎㄨㄥ ㄇㄣˊ)

① Buddhism ② the teachings which regard everything as unreal, or immaterial ③ the school of unreality, one of the four divisions made by Tien-tai (天台)

空濛(ㄎㄨㄥ ㄇㄥˊ)

the misty atmosphere of rainy days

空明(ㄎㄨㄥ ㄇㄧㄥˊ)

glittering of reflected moonlight in water

空費(ㄎㄨㄥ ㄈㄟˋ)

to waste (time or money) in vain

空泛(ㄎㄨㄥ ㄈㄢˋ)

① hollow; not practical ② too general—not specific

空防(ㄎㄨㄥ ㄈㄤˊ)

air defense

空腹(ㄎㄨㄥ ㄈㄨˋ)

on an empty stomach

空腹高心(ㄎㄨㄥ ㄈㄨˋ ㄍㄠ ㄒㄧㄣ)

poor in talent but very ambitious

空蕩蕩(ㄎㄨㄥ ㄉㄤˋ ㄉㄤˋ)

empty; deserted

空對地飛彈(ㄎㄨㄥ ㄉㄨㄟˋ ㄉㄧˋ ㄈㄟ ㄉㄢˋ)

air-to-ground missiles

空對空飛彈(ㄎㄨㄥ ㄉㄨㄟˋ ㄎㄨㄥ ㄈㄟ ㄉㄢˋ)

air-to-air missiles

空洞(ㄎㄨㄥ ㄉㄨㄥˋ)

① vast and empty ②(said of writings, thought, etc.) empty; hollow; shallow: 那只不過是個空洞的理論。That is nothing but an empty theory.

空投(ㄎㄨㄥ ㄊㄡˊ)

airdrop; to make airdrop; to airdrop

空頭(ㄎㄨㄥ ㄊㄡˊ)or(ㄎㄨㄥˋ ㄊㄡˊ)

①(stock market) to sell short ② phony; armchair: 他是個空頭戰略家。He's an armchair strategist.

空頭支票(ㄎㄨㄥ ㄊㄡˊ ㄓ ㄆㄧㄠˋ)or(ㄎㄨㄥˋ ㄊㄡˊ ㄓ ㄆㄧㄠˋ)

① a rubber check; a check that bounces; a bad check; a dishonored check ② an empty promise; lip service

空頭人情(ㄎㄨㄥ ㄊㄡˊ ㄖㄣˊ ㄑㄧㄥˊ)or(ㄎㄨㄥˋ ㄊㄡˊ ㄖㄣˊ ㄑㄧㄥˊ)

to offer lip service; a friendly gesture which neither costs nor helps anything

空談(ㄎㄨㄥ ㄊㄢˊ)

empty talks; academic talks in total disregard of realities; idle chatter

空談誤國(ㄎㄨㄥ ㄊㄢˊ ㄨˋ ㄍㄨㄛˊ)

(usually said of intellectuals) Empty talks jeopardize national interests.

空桶子(ㄎㄨㄥ ㄊㄨㄥˇ ·ㄗ)or 空桶兒(ㄎㄨㄥ ㄊㄨㄥˇㄦ)

(literally) an empty bucket or barrel—a blockhead

空難(ㄎㄨㄥ ㄋㄢˋ)

an air disaster; a plane crash or collision: 他在一次空難中喪生。He was killed in an air disaster.

空靈(ㄎㄨㄥ ㄌㄧㄥˊ)

cute; lovely; artistic

空論(ㄎㄨㄥ ㄌㄨㄣˋ)

empty talks; shallow talks; impractical statements

空谷足音(ㄎㄨㄥ ㄍㄨˇ ㄗㄨˊ ㄧㄣ)

(literally) the sound of footsteps in an empty valley—a person of unusual talent or virtue who can seldom be found, or a remarkable statement which one does not hear often

空閨獨守(ㄎㄨㄥ ㄍㄨㄟ ㄉㄨˊ ㄕㄡˇ)

to lead the lonely life of a widow or of a deserted wife

空口說白話(ㄎㄨㄥ ㄎㄡˇ ㄕㄨㄛ ㄅㄞˊ ㄏㄨㄚˋ)

to talk without taking action

空口無憑(ㄎㄨㄥ ㄎㄡˇ ㄨˊ ㄆㄧㄥˊ)

(said of a promise or

〔穴部〕

〔穴部〕

pledge) Mere verbal statement has no binding force.

空闊(ㄎㄨㄥ ㄎㄨㄛˋ)
spacious; broad; as far as eyes can reach; open

空匱(ㄎㄨㄥ ㄎㄨㄟˋ)
poor; needy; deficient

空曠(ㄎㄨㄥ ㄎㄨㄤˋ)
expansive; vast and boundless: 那是一片空曠的草原。It's a vast expanse of prairie.

空空(ㄎㄨㄥ ㄎㄨㄥ)
①empty; nothing: 他兩手空空的。His hands are empty. ②(Buddhism) unreality of unreality (When all has been regarded as illusion, or unreal, the abstract idea of unreality itself must be destroyed.)

空空洞洞(ㄎㄨㄥ ㄎㄨㄥ ㄉㄨㄥˋ ㄉㄨㄥˋ)
empty; hollow; nothing or nobody in there

空空如也(ㄎㄨㄥ ㄎㄨㄥ ㄖㄨˊ ㄧㄝˇ)
empty; nothing left

空函(ㄎㄨㄥ ㄏㄢˊ)
①a letter without words ②a letter asking for books or samples, etc. without enclosing return postage

空話(ㄎㄨㄥ ㄏㄨㄚˋ)
empty talks; talks without content: 沒有人喜歡空話。Nobody likes empty talks.

空歡喜(ㄎㄨㄥ ㄏㄨㄢ ㄒㄧˇ)
joy that ends in disappointment

空幻(ㄎㄨㄥ ㄏㄨㄢˋ)
illusory; visionary; unreal; intangible: 海市蜃樓是一空幻景象。A mirage is an illusion.

空際(ㄎㄨㄥ ㄐㄧˋ)
the sky; the horizon

空即是色(ㄎㄨㄥ ㄐㄧˊ ㄕˋ ㄙㄜˋ)
The immaterial is the material. (Sunyata is rupa.)

空架子(ㄎㄨㄥ ㄐㄧㄚˋ ·ㄗ)
a bold front with nothing behind it; a deceptive appearance of power or influence which no longer exists

空劫(ㄎㄨㄥ ㄐㄧㄝˊ)
(Buddhism) the empty kalpa, one of the Four Calamities, which will reduce the world to nothing

空界(ㄎㄨㄥ ㄐㄧㄝˋ)
(Buddhism) the realm of space, one of the Six Realms: earth, water, fire, wind, space and knowledge

空間(ㄎㄨㄥ ㄐㄧㄢ)
space (in the sense of dimensions)

空降(ㄎㄨㄥ ㄐㄧㄤˋ)
to land troops by parachutes

空降部隊(ㄎㄨㄥ ㄐㄧㄤˋ ㄅㄨˋ ㄉㄨㄟˋ)
airborne troops

空降陣地(ㄎㄨㄥ ㄐㄧㄤˋ ㄓㄣˋ ㄉㄧˋ)
an airhead

空軍(ㄎㄨㄥ ㄐㄩㄣ)
the air force

空軍基地(ㄎㄨㄥ ㄐㄩㄣ ㄐㄧ ㄉㄧˋ)
an air base

空軍中將(ㄎㄨㄥ ㄐㄩㄣ ㄓㄨㄥ ㄐㄧㄤˋ)
a lieutenant general of the air force

空軍中校(ㄎㄨㄥ ㄐㄩㄣ ㄓㄨㄥ ㄒㄧㄠˋ)
a lieutenant colonel of the air force

空軍中尉(ㄎㄨㄥ ㄐㄩㄣ ㄓㄨㄥ ㄨㄟˋ)
a first lieutenant of the air force

空軍少將(ㄎㄨㄥ ㄐㄩㄣ ㄕㄠˋ ㄐㄧㄤˋ)
a major general of the air force

空軍少校(ㄎㄨㄥ ㄐㄩㄣ ㄕㄠˋ ㄒㄧㄠˋ)
a major of the air force; a squadron leader

空軍少尉(ㄎㄨㄥ ㄐㄩㄣ ㄕㄠˋ ㄨㄟˋ)
a second lieutenant of the air force

空軍上將(ㄎㄨㄥ ㄐㄩㄣ ㄕㄤˋ ㄐㄧㄤˋ)
a general of the air force

空軍上校(ㄎㄨㄥ ㄐㄩㄣ ㄕㄤˋ ㄒㄧㄠˋ)
an air-force colonel

空軍上尉(ㄎㄨㄥ ㄐㄩㄣ ㄕㄤˋ ㄨㄟˋ)
an air-force captain

空軍武官(ㄎㄨㄥ ㄐㄩㄣ ㄨˇ ㄍㄨㄢ)
an air attaché

空氣(ㄎㄨㄥ ㄑㄧˋ)
air or atmosphere (also used figuratively): 我們必須呼吸新鮮空氣。We must breathe the fresh air.

空氣墊(ㄎㄨㄥ ㄑㄧˋ ㄉㄧㄢˋ)
an air mattress

空氣調節(ㄎㄨㄥ ㄑㄧˋ ㄊㄧㄠˊ ㄐㄧㄝˊ)
air conditioning

空氣囊(ㄎㄨㄥ ㄑㄧˋ ㄋㄤˊ)
an air bag

空氣流通(ㄎㄨㄥ ㄑㄧˋ ㄌㄧㄡˊ ㄊㄨㄥ)
air ventilation; well ventilated; airy; air circulation: 他的房間空氣流通。His room is well ventilated.

空氣傳染(ㄎㄨㄥ ㄑㄧˋ ㄔㄨㄢˊ ㄖㄢˇ)
airborne infection

空氣汚染(ㄎㄨㄥ ㄑㄧˋ ㄨ ㄖㄢˇ)
air pollution

空前(ㄎㄨㄥ ㄑㄧㄢˊ)
unprecedented

空前絕後(ㄎㄨㄥ ㄑㄧㄢˊ ㄐㄩㄝˊ ㄏㄡˋ)
(said of a remarkable achievement, masterpiece, etc.) not equaled before or after

空拳(ㄎㄨㄥ ㄑㄩㄢˊ)
to hold nothing in the hand; barehanded

空襲(ㄎㄨㄥ ㄒㄧˊ)
an air raid; an air attack

空襲警報(ㄎㄨㄥ ㄒㄧˊ ㄐㄧㄥˇ ㄅㄠˋ)
an air-raid alert; an air-raid alarm

空心(ㄎㄨㄥ ㄒㄧㄣ)
①hollow: 這是一株空心的樹。This is a hollow tree. ②nothing in mind

空心大老官(ㄎㄨㄥ ㄒㄧㄣ ㄉㄚˋ ㄌㄠˇ ㄍㄨㄢ)
a vainglorious person without the means or ability to back up his pretensions

空心菜(ㄎㄨㄥ ㄒㄧㄣ ㄘㄞˋ)
a water convolvulus 亦作「蕹菜」

空想(ㄎㄨㄥ ㄒㄧㄤˇ)
①an impractical thought or idea; a daydream ②to daydream

空虛(ㄎㄨㄥ ㄒㄩ)
empty; void; emptiness

空穴來風(ㄎㄨㄥ ㄒㄩㄝˋ ㄌㄞˊ ㄈㄥ)
(said of news, or information) groundless or baseless

空戰(ㄎㄨㄥ ㄓㄢˋ)
an air battle

空中(ㄎㄨㄥ ㄓㄨㄥ)
in the air; in the sky

空中巴士(ㄎㄨㄥ ㄓㄨㄥ ㄅㄚ ㄕˋ)
an air bus

空中飛人(ㄎㄨㄥ ㄓㄨㄥ ㄈㄟ ㄖㄣˊ)
a trapeze show

空中大學(ㄎㄨㄥ ㄓㄨㄥ ㄉㄚˋ ㄒㄩㄝˊ)
an open university

空中樓閣(ㄎㄨㄥ ㄓㄨㄥ ㄌㄡˊ ㄍㄜˊ)
a castle in the air—illusion

空中纜車(ㄎㄨㄥ ㄓㄨㄥ ㄌㄢˇ ㄔㄜ)
a cable car
空中花園(ㄎㄨㄥ ㄓㄨㄥ ㄏㄨㄚ ㄩㄢˊ)
hanging gardens
空中加油(ㄎㄨㄥ ㄓㄨㄥ ㄐㄧㄚ ㄧㄡˊ)
refueling in midair; in-flight refueling
空中陷阱(ㄎㄨㄥ ㄓㄨㄥ ㄒㄧㄢˋ ㄐㄧㄥˇ)
(aviation) an air pocket
空中小姐(ㄎㄨㄥ ㄓㄨㄥ ㄒㄧㄠˇ ㄐㄧㄝˇ)
a stewardess (of a passenger plane); an air hostess
空中學校(ㄎㄨㄥ ㄓㄨㄥ ㄒㄩㄝˊ ㄒㄧㄠˋ)
a school on the air
空中少爺(ㄎㄨㄥ ㄓㄨㄥ ㄕㄠˋ ㄧㄝˊ)
(informal) a male flight attendant
空中預警機(ㄎㄨㄥ ㄓㄨㄥ ㄩˋ ㄐㄧㄥˇ ㄐㄧ)
airborne warning and control system (AWACS)
空城計(ㄎㄨㄥ ㄔㄥˊ ㄐㄧˋ)
①a bluff ②nobody left behind to guard the house
空手(ㄎㄨㄥ ㄕㄡˇ)
empty-handed; unarmed: 他空手而來。He came empty-handed.
空手道(ㄎㄨㄥ ㄕㄡˇ ㄉㄠˋ)
karate, a type of Oriental boxing
空身(ㄎㄨㄥ ㄕㄣ)
to carry nothing except oneself; to carry no baggage, etc.
空身人兒(ㄎㄨㄥ ㄕㄣ ㄖㄜˊㄦ)
a person without any string attached
空說(ㄎㄨㄥ ㄕㄨㄛ)
empty talks; useless talks
空宗(ㄎㄨㄥ ㄗㄨㄥ)
(Buddhism) the Sunyat sects, i.e. those which make the unreality of the ego and things their fundamental tenet
空言(ㄎㄨㄥ ㄧㄢˊ)
empty talks; mere talks
空運(ㄎㄨㄥ ㄩㄣˋ)
air transportation; air freight; an airlift; to transport by air: 裝備將予空運歐洲。The equipment will be airlifted to Europe.

【空】 4042
2. ㄎㄨㄥˋ konq kòng

1. leisure; free time; spare time: 他現在有空。He is at leisure now.
2. blank (space); vacant; vacancy; to leave blank or vacant
3. spacious—implying a sense of awe
4. a chance; an opportunity
5. wanting; deficient; impoverished

空白(ㄎㄨㄥˋ ㄅㄞˊ)
a blank in a paper or form
空白支票(ㄎㄨㄥˋ ㄅㄞˊ ㄓ ㄆㄧㄠˋ)
a blank check
空乏(ㄎㄨㄥˋ ㄈㄚˊ)
wanting; impoverished
空房(ㄎㄨㄥˋ ㄈㄤˊ)
an unoccupied house or room
空檔(ㄎㄨㄥˋ ㄉㄤˋ)
①vacant space in a movie theater schedule②free time; spare time
空地(ㄎㄨㄥˋ ㄉㄧˋ)
a vacant area; a vacant lot; a vacancy
空肚兒(ㄎㄨㄥˋ ㄉㄨˋㄦ)
empty-stomached
空格兒(ㄎㄨㄥˋ ㄍㄜˊㄦ)
the blank in a form (for filling)
空缺(ㄎㄨㄥˋ ㄑㄩㄝ)
①a vacant position; a vacancy: 我們有些空缺的職位。We have some vacant positions. ②scarcity (of food, money, etc.)
空隙(ㄎㄨㄥˋ ㄒㄧˋ)
a vacant space; a crevice; a gap; a loophole
空暇(ㄎㄨㄥˋ ㄒㄧㄚˊ)
free time; spare time; leisure; time free from work
空閒(ㄎㄨㄥˋ ㄒㄧㄢˊ)
leisure; spare time: 我沒有空閒看書。I have no leisure to read.
空額(ㄎㄨㄥˋ ㄜˊ)
a vacancy; an opening; a deficit: 空額已經補上。The vacancy has already been filled.
空兒(ㄎㄨㄥˋㄦ)
①leisure; spare time ②a vacant space; a gap ③an opportunity
空位(ㄎㄨㄥˋ ㄨㄟˋ)or 空座兒(ㄎㄨㄥˋ ㄗㄨㄛˋㄦ)
a vacant or unoccupied seat: 戲院裏有許多空座兒。There are many vacant seats in the theater.

四畫

【穿】 4043
ㄔㄨㄢ chuan chuān

1. to wear (clothes, shoes, etc.)
2. to pierce through; to penetrate or bore through; to thread
3. to cross (a street, etc.)
4. to see through; to bare (a secret, etc.)

穿幫(ㄔㄨㄢ ㄅㄤ)
(informal) accidentally to reveal something very embarrassing which one has tried to conceal
穿鼻(ㄔㄨㄢ ㄅㄧˊ)
to pierce the nose (of a cow, etc.)
穿壁引光(ㄔㄨㄢ ㄅㄧˋ ㄧㄣˇ ㄍㄨㄤ)
(literally) to bore a hole through the wall so that light from the neighbor can be used for studying—very studious and diligent under financial pressure
穿不得(ㄔㄨㄢ ˙ㄅㄨ ˙ㄉㄜ)
(said of clothing, etc.) cannot or shouldn't be worn (because of unfitness or impropriety)
穿不起(ㄔㄨㄢ ˙ㄅㄨ ㄑㄧˇ)
cannot afford to wear it —too expensive
穿不住(ㄔㄨㄢ ˙ㄅㄨ ㄓㄨˋ)
①cannot stand a lot of wear—poor quality ②cannot wear it any longer—due to a rise in temperature
穿房過屋(ㄔㄨㄢ ㄈㄤˊ ㄍㄨㄛˋ ㄨ)
intimate and close (friends)
穿戴(ㄔㄨㄢ ㄉㄞˋ)
to wear (clothes, ornaments, etc.): 他們穿戴整齊。They are neatly dressed.
穿透(ㄔㄨㄢ ㄊㄡˋ)
to penetrate; to pierce through: 子彈穿透木板。The bullet penetrated the board.
穿堂(ㄔㄨㄢ ㄊㄤˊ)

a small room, etc. serving as a passageway in a house
穿堂門兒(ㄔㄨㄢ ㄊㄤˊ ㄇㄜˊㄦ)
a passageway
穿廊(ㄔㄨㄢ ㄌㄤˊ)
a corridor; a covered passageway
穿過去(ㄔㄨㄢ ·ㄍㄨㄛ ·ㄑㄩ)
to penetrate; to thread through: 子彈從他胸膛穿過去。A bullet penetrated his chest.
穿孔(ㄔㄨㄢ ㄎㄨㄥˇ)
① to bore a hole; to perforate; to punch ②(medicine) perforation: 他患了胃穿孔的病。He suffered from gastric perforation.
穿孔機(ㄔㄨㄢ ㄎㄨㄥˇ ㄐㄧ)
a punch; a perforator
穿甲彈(ㄔㄨㄢ ㄐㄧㄚˇ ㄉㄢˋ)
armor-piercing shells
穿鞋(ㄔㄨㄢ ㄒㄧㄝˊ)
to put on shoes
穿孝(ㄔㄨㄢ ㄒㄧㄠˋ)
to wear or put on mourning (clothing)
穿線(ㄔㄨㄢ ㄒㄧㄢˋ)
① to thread a needle: 能幫我穿線嗎? Will you thread this needle for me? ② to serve as a go-between
穿心槓(ㄔㄨㄢ ㄒㄧㄣ ㄍㄤˋ)
a pole with which two persons lift a coffin
穿針(ㄔㄨㄢ ㄓㄣ)
to thread a needle
穿針引線(ㄔㄨㄢ ㄓㄣ ㄧㄣˇ ㄒㄧㄢˋ)
to serve as a go-between
穿著(ㄔㄨㄢ ㄓㄨㄛˊ)
① attire; dress: 他不講究穿著。He is not particular about his dress. ② dressed in: 她穿着黑色衣服。She was dressed in black.
穿插(ㄔㄨㄢ ㄔㄚ)
① to serve as a go-between ② the insertion of an episode or interlude
穿山甲(ㄔㄨㄢ ㄕㄢ ㄐㄧㄚˇ)
① *Manis pentadactyla*, the pangolin 亦作「鯪鯉」②(Chinese medicine) pangolin scales
穿鑿附會(ㄔㄨㄢ ㄗㄨㄛˋ ㄈㄨˋ ㄏㄨㄟˋ)
to offer far-fetched or dubious explanations
穿刺(ㄔㄨㄢ ㄘˋ)
a puncture
穿素(ㄔㄨㄢ ㄙㄨˋ)
(said of descendants of a deceased person) to wear clothes of subdued colors for some time just after the mourning period
穿梭(ㄔㄨㄢ ㄙㄨㄛ)
① busy comings and goings of people ② to shuttle back and forth
穿耳(ㄔㄨㄢ ㄦˇ)
to pierce the ears (for wearing earrings)
穿衣鏡(ㄔㄨㄢ ㄧ ㄐㄧㄥˋ)
a dressing glass; a cheval glass
穿眼(ㄔㄨㄢ ㄧㄢˇ)
to bore a hole; to perforate
穿窬之盜(ㄔㄨㄢ ㄩˊ ㄓ ㄉㄠˋ)
a burglar; a thief
穿越(ㄔㄨㄢ ㄩㄝˋ)
to pass through; to cross (a bridge, street, tunnel, etc.)

【突】 4044 ㄊㄨˊ twu tú

1. abrupt; sudden; unexpected; suddenly; unexpectedly
2. to offend; to go against
3. to break through (enemy encirclement)
4. to project or jut out
5. a chimney

突變(ㄊㄨˊ ㄅㄧㄢˋ)
① an unexpected change ② mutation
突變說(ㄊㄨˊ ㄅㄧㄢˋ ㄕㄨㄛ)
(biology) the mutation theory
突破(ㄊㄨˊ ㄆㄛˋ)
① to break or smash (old records, etc.) ② to break through
突飛猛進(ㄊㄨˊ ㄈㄟ ㄇㄥˇ ㄐㄧㄣˋ)
to advance (or go ahead) by leaps and bounds; to progress rapidly
突突(ㄊㄨˊ ㄊㄨˊ)
the throbs of heartbeats
突尼西亞(ㄊㄨˊ ㄋㄧˊ ㄒㄧ ㄧㄚˋ)
Tunisia, a country in North Africa, capital Tunis
突感(ㄊㄨˊ ㄍㄢˇ)
to feel suddenly
突擊(ㄊㄨˊ ㄐㄧˊ)
to attack (or assault) suddenly; to make a surprise attack; to raid: 警察突擊賭窟。The police raided a gambling house.
突擊隊(ㄊㄨˊ ㄐㄧˊ ㄉㄨㄟˋ)
shock troops; commando units; a shock brigade
突擊檢查(ㄊㄨˊ ㄐㄧˊ ㄐㄧㄢˇ ㄔㄚˊ)
to make a search without prior notice or announcement
突騎(ㄊㄨˊ ㄐㄧˋ)
the sallying cavalry
突將(ㄊㄨˊ ㄐㄧㄤˋ)
a bold general of unusual fighting skill or stamina
突厥(ㄊㄨˊ ㄐㄩㄝˊ)
an ancient name of the Turks
突起(ㄊㄨˊ ㄑㄧˇ)
① to rise up all of a sudden; to rise high; to tower: 奇峰突起。Peaks tower magnificently. ② to break out; suddenly appear: 戰事突起。Hostilities broke out.
突出(ㄊㄨˊ ㄔㄨ)
① outstanding; remarkable ② to jut out
突然(ㄊㄨˊ ㄖㄢˊ)
suddenly; abruptly; unexpectedly; abrupt; sudden: 突然下起雨來。Suddenly it began to rain.
突如其來(ㄊㄨˊ ㄖㄨˊ ㄑㄧˊ ㄌㄞˊ)
suddenly; abruptly; unexpectedly
突兀(ㄊㄨˊ ㄨˋ)
① lofty and steep; high ② suddenly; abruptly; unexpectedly
突圍(ㄊㄨˊ ㄨㄟˊ)
to break through enemy encirclement or siege

【窀】 4045 ㄓㄨㄣ juen zhūn

a pit for the coffin

五畫

【窅】 4046 ㄧㄠˇ yeau yǎo

1. far and deep; mysterious
2. sad

窅眇(ㄧㄠˇ ㄇㄧㄠˇ)
deep; far and deep
窅冥(ㄧㄠˇ ㄇㄧㄥˊ)

① far and deep; obscure and mysterious ② sunken eyes

窅然(ㄧㄠˇ ㄖㄢˊ)
sad; touched

窅靄(ㄧㄠˇ ㄞˇ)
far and deep

窅窅(ㄧㄠˇ ㄧㄠˇ)
① somber ② deep

【窈】 4047 ㄧㄠˇ yeau yǎo

1. deep; obscure; secluded
2. tranquil

窈冥(ㄧㄠˇ ㄇㄧㄥˊ)
① obscure; dusky ② deep; profound; mysterious

窈窕(ㄧㄠˇ ㄊㄧㄠˇ)
①(said of young women) quiet and modest; attractive and charming ② far and deep

窈窕淑女(ㄧㄠˇ ㄊㄧㄠˇ ㄕㄨˊ ㄋㄩˇ)
a quiet and modest maiden

窈藹(ㄧㄠˇ ㄞˇ)
deep, far or obscure

窈窈(ㄧㄠˇ ㄧㄠˇ)
① obscure; dusky ② far and deep; profound

【窄】 4048 ㄓㄞˇ jae jhǎi (又讀 ㄗㄜˊ tzer zé)

1. narrow; contracted; tight
2. narrow-minded; mean: 他心胸狹窄。He is narrow-minded.

窄門(ㄓㄞˇ ㄇㄣˊ)
a narrow door or gate

窄道(ㄓㄞˇ ㄉㄠˋ)
a narrow path

窄小(ㄓㄞˇ ㄒㄧㄠˇ)
①(said of a dress) tight and small ②(said of a room, etc.) narrow and small

窄巷(ㄓㄞˇ ㄒㄧㄤˋ)
a narrow lane

窄韻(ㄗㄜˊ ㄩㄣˋ)
difficult rhyme; the rarest rhyme in verses

【窆】 4049 ㄅㄧㄢˇ bean biǎn

to put the coffin in the grave; to bury

窆石(ㄅㄧㄢˇ ㄕˊ)
(in ancient China) stones used in gliding a coffin down a tunnel

六畫

【窒】 4050 ㄓˋ jyh jhì

to block; to stop up; to obstruct; to stuff up

窒悶(ㄓˋ ㄇㄣˋ)
close; stuffy; badly ventilated

窒息(ㄓˋ ㄒㄧˊ)
to asphyxiate; to suffocate; to smother; asphyxiation; asphyxia; suffocation: 我幾乎被煙窒息了。I am almost suffocated with smoke.

窒息藥(ㄓˋ ㄒㄧˊ ㄧㄠˋ)
an asphyxiant

窒塞(ㄓˋ ㄙㄜˋ)
to block; to obstruct: 大雪窒塞道路。The heavy snowfall blocked the roads.

窒礙(ㄓˋ ㄞˋ)
to obstruct; an obstacle: 樹林窒礙了視野。Trees obstructed the view.

窒欲 or 窒慾(ㄓˋ ㄩˋ)
to restrain one's lusts

【窕】 4051 ㄊㄧㄠˇ teau tiǎo

1. slender
2. quiet and modest; charming and attractive
3. beautiful; wonderful; good

七畫

【窖】 4052 ㄐㄧㄠˋ jiaw jiào

1. a cellar; a vault; a pit: 他把食物貯藏在地窖裏。He stored food in the cellar.
2. to store things in a cellar, etc.

窖冰(ㄐㄧㄠˋ ㄅㄧㄥ)
to keep ice in a cellar, vault or pit

窖果子(ㄐㄧㄠˋ ㄍㄨㄛˇ ˙ㄗ)
to keep fruits in a cellar

窖藏(ㄐㄧㄠˋ ㄘㄤˊ)
to store things in a cellar

【窗】 4053 (窓、窻、牕) ㄔㄨㄤ chuang chuāng

1. a window; a skylight: 誰打破窗戶? Who broke the window?
2. a place where one studies

窗板(ㄔㄨㄤ ㄅㄢˇ)
window shutters

窗楣(ㄔㄨㄤ ㄇㄟˊ)
the lintel of a window

窗幔(ㄔㄨㄤ ㄇㄢˋ) or 窗帷(ㄔㄨㄤ ㄨㄟˊ)
a window curtain or screen

窗明几淨(ㄔㄨㄤ ㄇㄧㄥˊ ㄐㄧ ㄐㄧㄥˋ)
(said of rooms) neat and bright

窗臺(ㄔㄨㄤ ㄊㄞˊ)
a window sill

窗簾 or 窗帘(ㄔㄨㄤ ㄌㄧㄢˊ)
a window curtain, screen or blind

窗櫺(ㄔㄨㄤ ㄌㄧㄥˊ)
the window lattice

窗口(ㄔㄨㄤ ㄎㄡˇ)
① a window: 她坐在窗口。She sat at (or by) the window. ② a wicket; a window

窗框(ㄔㄨㄤ ㄎㄨㄤ)
a window frame

窗戶(ㄔㄨㄤ ˙ㄏㄨ)
a window: 請打開窗戶。Open the window, please.

窗戶紙(ㄔㄨㄤ ˙ㄏㄨ ㄓˇ)
①a kind of thin semi-transparent paper used to cover a window in place of glass ② (said of a person's complexion) pale ③ a thin veil (in a figurative sense)

窗下(ㄔㄨㄤ ㄒㄧㄚˋ)
to study (before the window)

窗紗(ㄔㄨㄤ ㄕㄚ)
gauze used to cover a window

窗子(ㄔㄨㄤ ˙ㄗ) or 窗兒(ㄔㄨㄤㄦ)
a window: 他把窗子關起來然後離開。He shut the window and then left.

窗友(ㄔㄨㄤ ㄧㄡˇ)
fellow students; schoolmates

窗牖(ㄔㄨㄤ ㄧㄡˇ)
windows

窗外(ㄔㄨㄤ ㄨㄞˋ)
outside the window

【窘】 4054 ㄐㄩㄥˇ jeong jiǒng

1. hard-pressed; poverty-stricken
2. to embarrass
3. afflicted; distressed

窘步(ㄐㄩㄥˇ ㄅㄨˋ)
to walk awkwardly because of being hard-pressed

窘迫(ㄐㄩㄥˇ ㄆㄛˋ)
hard-pressed; afflicted in a predicament: 他的處境窘迫。

He found himself in a predicament.
窘態(ㄐㄩㄥˇ ㄊㄞˋ)
an embarrassed look; a distressed look: 她露出窘態。She showed signs of embarrassment.
窘急(ㄐㄩㄥˇ ㄐㄧˊ)
afflicted; in great difficulty; hard-pressed
窘境(ㄐㄩㄥˇ ㄐㄧㄥˋ)
an awkward situation; a predicament; a plight
窘住(ㄐㄩㄥˇ ·ㄓㄨ)
embarrassed; distressed; to embarrass
窘蹙(ㄐㄩㄥˇ ㄘㄨˋ)
hard-pressed; urgent

八畫

【窟】 4055
ㄎㄨ ku kū
1. a hole; a cave; a pit
2. to dig the ground and build underground living quarters
3. a den for wild animals (now also used figuratively, as a gambling den, an opium-smoking den, etc.)

窟窿(ㄎㄨ ·ㄌㄨㄥ)or 窟窿洞(ㄎㄨ ·ㄌㄨㄥ ㄉㄨㄥˋ)or 窟洞(ㄎㄨ ㄉㄨㄥˋ)
holes: 他的鞋底磨了個窟窿。He has worn a hole in the sole of his shoe.
窟窿眼兒(ㄎㄨ ·ㄌㄨㄥ ㄧㄚˇㄦ)
tiny holes
窟窖(ㄎㄨ ㄐㄧㄠˋ)
a cellar or vault: 他放了些酒在窟窖裏。He stored some wine in the cellar.
窟居(ㄎㄨ ㄐㄩ)
to live in caves
窟穴(ㄎㄨ ㄒㄩㄝˋ)
holes
窟宅(ㄎㄨ ㄓㄞˊ)
an underground chamber
窟室(ㄎㄨ ㄕˋ)
an underground room or chamber; a cellar

【窠】 4056
ㄎㄜ ke kē
1. a den; a burrow
2. a nest
3. a hole
4. a dwelling for people

窠臼(ㄎㄜ ㄐㄧㄡˋ)
a set pattern or rule; a stereotype
窠巢(ㄎㄜ ㄔㄠˊ)
a nest

九畫

【窩】 4057
ㄨㄛ uo wō
1. a cave; a den; a nest
2. an apartment; living quarters; a house
3. to hide; to harbor (a criminal, etc.)
4. to bend; to crease
5. a litter; a brood
6. to block; to hold in; to check
7. a hollow part of the human body; a pit

窩風(ㄨㄛ ㄈㄥ)
to shelter or protect from the wind
窩囊(ㄨㄛ ·ㄋㄤ)
① stupid, cowardly and timid; good-for-nothing; useless (person) ② to feel vexed; to be annoyed: 我不願受他的窩囊氣。I'll not put up with his petty annoyances.
窩囊廢(ㄨㄛ ·ㄋㄤ ㄈㄟˋ)
a stupid, cowardly good-for-nothing; a worthless wretch
窩膿(ㄨㄛ ㄋㄨㄥˊ)
to suppurate
窩裏窩囊(ㄨㄛ ·ㄌㄧ ㄨㄛ ·ㄋㄤ)
stupid and cowardly
窩瞘眼(ㄨㄛ ·ㄎㄡ ㄧㄢˇ)
a person with sunken eyes
窩家(ㄨㄛ ㄐㄧㄚ)
a house where stolen goods are hidden—the house of an evil person
窩心(ㄨㄛ ㄒㄧㄣ)
① to suffer an insult which one is powerless to avenge ② (Shanghai dialect) gratifying
窩主(ㄨㄛ ㄓㄨˇ)
one who harbors criminals or keeps stolen goods
窩藏(ㄨㄛ ㄘㄤˊ)
to harbor (outlaws); to keep (stolen goods)
窩兒(ㄨㄛㄦ)
① a place or den one occupies ② a cave; a pit
窩兒裏反(ㄨㄛㄦ ·ㄌㄧ ㄈㄢˇ)
an intramural fight
窩窩頭(ㄨㄛ ·ㄨㄛ ㄊㄡˊ)or 窩頭(ㄨㄛ ㄊㄡˊ)
a kind of steamed dumpling made of corn meal or other cheap cereals and eaten by the poor in northern China

【窪】 4058
ㄨㄚ ua wā
1. deep; hollow; low-lying
2. a pit; a hole; a hollow; a depression: 這些路滿是坑窪。These roads are full of holes.

窪地(ㄨㄚ ㄉㄧˋ)
marsh land; low-lying land
窪田(ㄨㄚ ㄊㄧㄢˊ)
a low-lying field or plantation; marsh land

【窨】 4059
1. ㄧㄣˋ yinn yìn
a cellar; an underground storeroom

【窨】 4059
2. ㄒㄩㄣ shiun xūn
to add aroma to tea by mixing it with jasmine

【窬】 4060
ㄩˊ yu yú
1. a hole in the wall; a small door or window
2. to climb over a wall

十畫

【窮】 4061
ㄑㄩㄥˊ chyong qióng
1. poor; impoverished; destitute: 他窮得沒錢上學。He was too poor to go to school.
2. to exhaust; to trace to the very source
3. distress; affliction
4. the extreme; the farthest; an end
5. thoroughly

窮北(ㄑㄩㄥˊ ㄅㄟˇ)
the extreme north; the farthest north
窮兵黷武(ㄑㄩㄥˊ ㄅㄧㄥ ㄉㄨˊ ㄨˇ)
to wage war frequently; to follow a policy of expansionism by military means; to be a warmonger
窮忙(ㄑㄩㄥˊ ㄇㄤˊ)
to toil all day long just to make both ends meet; to be

busy for nothing: 你整天在窮忙什麼? What are you busy for all day long?

窮民(ㄑㄩㄥˊ ㄇㄧㄣˊ)
poor people; the destitute

窮目(ㄑㄩㄥˊ ㄇㄨˋ)
to see as far as one can

窮乏(ㄑㄩㄥˊ ㄈㄚˊ)
destitute; wanting; poverty-stricken

窮達(ㄑㄩㄥˊ ㄉㄚˊ)
to remain obscure or to become distinguished; obscurity or eminence

窮大手(ㄑㄩㄥˊ ㄉㄚˋ ㄕㄡˇ)
poor but putting on a bold front by spending lavishly

窮到骨(ㄑㄩㄥˊ ㄉㄠˋ ㄍㄨˇ)
stark poverty; extremely poor

窮當益堅(ㄑㄩㄥˊ ㄉㄤ ㄧˋ ㄐㄧㄢ)
The greater one's adversity is, the stronger his fortitude should be.

窮滴滴(ㄑㄩㄥˊ ㄉㄧ ㄉㄧ)
destitute; poor

窮冬(ㄑㄩㄥˊ ㄉㄨㄥ)
deep in winter; winter at its coldest

窮途(ㄑㄩㄥˊ ㄊㄨˊ)or 窮途末路(ㄑㄩㄥˊ ㄊㄨˊ ㄇㄛˋ ㄌㄨˋ)
extremely distressed or difficult state; in straits; at the end of one's rope

窮通(ㄑㄩㄥˊ ㄊㄨㄥ)
failure or success

窮鳥入懷(ㄑㄩㄥˊ ㄋㄧㄠˇ ㄖㄨˋ ㄏㄨㄞˊ)
to become somebody's protégé when one is down in his luck

窮年累月(ㄑㄩㄥˊ ㄋㄧㄢˊ ㄌㄟˇ ㄩㄝˋ)
for a very long time; for years on end; year after year

窮老(ㄑㄩㄥˊ ㄌㄠˇ)
① till one's death ② old and poor; aged and destitute

窮里(ㄑㄩㄥˊ ㄌㄧˇ)
obscure or out-of-the-way places

窮理(ㄑㄩㄥˊ ㄌㄧˇ)
to probe into or trace to the very root of things

窮骨頭(ㄑㄩㄥˊ ㄍㄨˇ ·ㄊㄡ)
(abusively) a poor or stingy person

窮鬼(ㄑㄩㄥˊ ㄍㄨㄟˇ)
a poverty-stricken fellow

窮光蛋(ㄑㄩㄥˊ ㄍㄨㄤ ㄉㄢˋ)
a destitute fellow; a penniless vagrant; a pauper; a poor wretch

窮逛(ㄑㄩㄥˊ ㄍㄨㄤˋ)
to fool around without spending money

窮開心(ㄑㄩㄥˊ ㄎㄞ ㄒㄧㄣ)
to enjoy moments of happiness even in poverty

窮寇勿追(ㄑㄩㄥˊ ㄎㄡˋ ㄨˋ ㄓㄨㄟ)
(originally, from Sun Tzu's *The Art of War*) Don't pursue a desperate enemy (lest he should put up a life-or-death fight that would make the pursuer pay dearly).

窮坑難滿(ㄑㄩㄥˊ ㄎㄥ ㄋㄢˊ ㄇㄢˇ)
The pit of avarice can never be filled.

窮苦(ㄑㄩㄥˊ ㄎㄨˇ)
destitute; poverty; poverty-stricken

窮困(ㄑㄩㄥˊ ㄎㄨㄣˋ)
poverty-stricken; to be beset by poverty; distressed and afflicted: 這對年輕夫婦極爲窮困。The young couple are as poor as church mice.

窮困潦倒(ㄑㄩㄥˊ ㄎㄨㄣˋ ㄌㄧㄠˇ ㄉㄠˇ)
to be penniless and frustrated

窮漢(ㄑㄩㄥˊ ㄏㄢˋ)
a poor man

窮歡樂(ㄑㄩㄥˊ ㄏㄨㄢ ㄌㄜˋ)
to find moments of rejoicing in poverty

窮極(ㄑㄩㄥˊ ㄐㄧˊ)
① extremely; in the extreme ② abjectly poor

窮極思變(ㄑㄩㄥˊ ㄐㄧˊ ㄙ ㄅㄧㄢˋ)
One will start thinking about changes when he is in extreme poverty.

窮極無聊(ㄑㄩㄥˊ ㄐㄧˊ ㄨˊ ㄌㄧㄠˊ)
① to do very foolish things in desperation ② to be utterly bored ③ absolutely senseless; disgusting

窮家富路(ㄑㄩㄥˊ ㄐㄧㄚ ㄈㄨˋ ㄌㄨˋ)
to practice thrift at home but be amply provided while traveling

窮究(ㄑㄩㄥˊ ㄐㄧㄡˋ)
to examine, inquire, study or trace to the very source of something; to make a thorough inquiry

窮盡(ㄑㄩㄥˊ ㄐㄧㄣˋ)
to come to an end; to exhaust: 這場戰爭窮盡了我們的國力。The war exhausted our country.

窮經(ㄑㄩㄥˊ ㄐㄧㄥ)
to study classics exhaustively

窮氣(ㄑㄩㄥˊ ㄑㄧˋ)
an appearance or look of poverty

窮小子(ㄑㄩㄥˊ ㄒㄧㄠˇ ·ㄗ)
a poor bum (a contemptuous expression)

窮嫌富不要(ㄑㄩㄥˊ ㄒㄧㄢˊ ㄈㄨˋ ㄅㄨˋ ㄧㄠˋ)
(said of a commodity, etc.) The poor shun it because of its high price, and the rich dislike it because of its poor quality.

窮鄉僻壤(ㄑㄩㄥˊ ㄒㄧㄤ ㄆㄧˋ ㄖㄤˇ)
out-of-the-way regions; remote areas

窮相(ㄑㄩㄥˊ ㄒㄧㄤˋ)
an appearance or manners, indicating poverty

窮巷(ㄑㄩㄥˊ ㄒㄧㄤˋ)
a lane in a slum area

窮形盡相(ㄑㄩㄥˊ ㄒㄧㄥˊ ㄐㄧㄣˋ ㄒㄧㄤˋ)
① to give a vivid description of something ② mean and distasteful language or conduct

窮凶極惡(ㄑㄩㄥˊ ㄒㄩㄥ ㄐㄧˊ ㄜˋ)
extremely violent and wicked; utterly evil; atrocious; diabolical

窮治(ㄑㄩㄥˊ ㄓˋ)
to manage a matter by first examining into it thoroughly

窮追不捨(ㄑㄩㄥˊ ㄓㄨㄟ ㄅㄨˋ ㄕㄜˇ)
to pursue relentlessly; to go in hot pursuit

窮愁(ㄑㄩㄥˊ ㄔㄡˊ)
dejection caused by poverty and sorrow

窮愁潦倒(ㄑㄩㄥˊ ㄔㄡˊ ㄌㄧㄠˇ ㄉㄠˇ)
to crack up under the strain of poverty and sorrow

窮奢極侈(ㄑㄩㄥˊ ㄕㄜ ㄐㄧˊ ㄔˇ)or 窮奢極慾(ㄑㄩㄥˊ ㄕㄜ ㄐㄧˊ ㄩˋ)
to go to the extreme of extravagance: 他們過着窮奢

〔穴部〕

極侈的生活。They live a life of wanton extravagance.

窮山惡水(ㄑㄩㄥˊ ㄕㄢ ㄜˋ ㄕㄨㄟˇ)
a barren and unwholesome view; the poor, barren land

窮書生(ㄑㄩㄥˊ ㄕㄨ ㄕㄥ)
a poor scholar; a destitute student

窮鼠齧貓(ㄑㄩㄥˊ ㄕㄨˇ ㄋㄧㄝˋ ㄇㄠ)
(literally) A desperate rat will turn back to bite the pursuing cat.—One will fight back out of desperation.

窮日子(ㄑㄩㄥˊ ㄖˋ ·ㄗ)
poverty-stricken days; the miserable life of a poor fellow

窮人(ㄑㄩㄥˊ ㄖㄣˊ)
destitute people; the poor

窮則變，變則通(ㄑㄩㄥˊ ㄗㄜˊ ㄅㄧㄢˋ, ㄅㄧㄢˋ ㄗㄜˊ ㄊㄨㄥ)
Impasse is followed by change, and change will lead to solution.

窮措大(ㄑㄩㄥˊ ㄘㄨㄛˋ ㄉㄚˋ)
a poor scholar

窮酸(ㄑㄩㄥˊ ㄙㄨㄢ)
(said of a scholar) poor, jealous and pedantic

窮酸相(ㄑㄩㄥˊ ㄙㄨㄢ ㄒㄧㄤˋ)
the manners of a destitute scholar

窮源溯流(ㄑㄩㄥˊ ㄩㄢˊ ㄙㄨˋ ㄌㄧㄡˊ)
(literally) to follow a stream to its very source—to trace to the very source of something

【窰】 4062 (窯) ㄧㄠˊ yau yáo

1. a kiln; a brick furnace
2. pottery
3. a pit in a coal mine; a coal shaft
4. a cave—for human dwelling
5. a brothel

窰洞(ㄧㄠˊ ㄉㄨㄥˋ)
①a cave for human dwelling ②the opening of a kiln

窰坑(ㄧㄠˊ ㄎㄥ)
a pit formed by digging for clay in making pottery

窰黑兒(ㄧㄠˊ ㄏㄜㄦ)
coal miners

窰姐兒(ㄧㄠˊ ㄐㄧㄝˇㄦ)
prostitutes

窰子(ㄧㄠˊ ·ㄗ)
①a brothel ②a prostitute

【窳】 4063 ㄩˇ yeu yǔ

1. coarse; crude; of inferior quality
2. lazy
3. weak; fragile
4. bad; mean

窳敗(ㄩˇ ㄅㄞˋ)
to rot; to fall

窳惰(ㄩˇ ㄉㄨㄛˋ)
lazy and dissipated; weak and indolent

窳陋(ㄩˇ ㄌㄡˋ)
crude; coarse; inferior (quality)

窳劣(ㄩˇ ㄌㄧㄝˋ)
bad; poor (quality)

窳楛(ㄩˇ ㄏㄨˋ)
coarse and fragile

十一畫

【窺】 4064 ㄎㄨㄟ kuei kuī

to watch or see in secret; to spy; to peep; to pry into

窺豹一斑(ㄎㄨㄟ ㄅㄠˋ ㄧˋ ㄅㄢ)
(literally) to see only one spot of the leopard—to have only a limited view

窺探(ㄎㄨㄟ ㄊㄢˋ)
to spy on; to peep; to pry into: 不要窺探他人事物。Don't spy into other people's affairs.

窺天鏡(ㄎㄨㄟ ㄊㄧㄢ ㄐㄧㄥˋ)
a telescope

窺見(ㄎㄨㄟ ㄐㄧㄢˋ)
to get (or catch) a glimpse of; to detect

窺察(ㄎㄨㄟ ㄔㄚˊ)
to spy on; to watch

窺視(ㄎㄨㄟ ㄕˋ)
to peep at; to spy on; to watch secretly

窺測(ㄎㄨㄟ ㄘㄜˋ)
to watch and assess (a situation, development, etc.)

窺伺(ㄎㄨㄟ ㄙˋ)
to watch and wait (for a chance to attack, etc.)

窺窬(ㄎㄨㄟ ㄩˊ)
to watch for a weakness (of the adversary)

窺園(ㄎㄨㄟ ㄩㄢˊ)
(literally) to look out occasionally at the garden—to lack concentration while studying

【窶】 4065 ㄐㄩˋ jiuh jù

impoverished; straitened; destitute

窶人子(ㄐㄩˋ ㄖㄣˊ ㄗˇ)
a son from an impoverished family

十二畫

【窾】 4066 ㄎㄨㄢˇ koan kuǎn

1. a hollow; an opening
2. empty; hollow

窾竅(ㄎㄨㄢˇ ㄑㄧㄠˋ) or 窾要(ㄎㄨㄢˇ ㄧㄠˋ)
the main points or the crux of a matter

【窿】 4067 ㄌㄨㄥˊ long lóng

a hole; a cavity

十三畫

【竄】 4068 ㄘㄨㄢˋ tsuann cuàn

1. to escape; to run away; to flee
2. to change or alter (the wording)
3. to banish; to execute

竄伏(ㄘㄨㄢˋ ㄈㄨˊ)
to lie low; to skulk

竄定(ㄘㄨㄢˋ ㄉㄧㄥˋ)
to change or alter the wording of writings for the last time before publication

竄逃(ㄘㄨㄢˋ ㄊㄠˊ)
to flee in disorder: 敵人兵敗竄逃。The enemy was defeated and fled in disorder.

竄匿(ㄘㄨㄢˋ ㄋㄧˋ)
to flee and hide

竄改(ㄘㄨㄢˋ ㄍㄞˇ)
to make changes and alterations in a piece of writing (especially without authority); to interpolate; to tamper

竄改帳目(ㄘㄨㄢˋ ㄍㄞˇ ㄓㄤˋ ㄇㄨˋ)
to fake accounts; to falsify accounts

竄擾(ㄘㄨㄢˋ ㄖㄠˇ)
①(said of bandits) to harass the people ②(said of the enemy) to intrude

竄入(ㄘㄨㄢˋ ㄖㄨˋ)
① to interpolate ② to flee to

竄逸(ㄘㄨㄢˋ ㄧˋ)
to escape; to take to one's heels

【竅】 4069 ㄑㄧㄠˋ chiaw qiào

1. a hole; a cavity
2. apertures
3. the crux, key points, gist of a matter; a knack

竅門(ㄑㄧㄠˋ ㄇㄣˊ)
the secret of doing something successfully; the right way to do something; the key to something; a knack

十五畫

【竇】 4070 ㄉㄡˋ dow dòu

1. a hole; a cavity; a burrow
2. a corrupt practice
3. a Chinese family name

十六畫

【竈】 4071 (灶) ㄗㄠˋ tzaw zào

1. a place for cooking; a kitchen
2. a cooking stove or furnace

竈頭(ㄗㄠˋ ㄊㄡˊ)
a kitchen place

竈間(ㄗㄠˋ ㄐㄧㄢ)
the kitchen

竈君(ㄗㄠˋ ㄐㄩㄣ) or 竈神(ㄗㄠˋ ㄕㄣˊ) or 竈王爺(ㄗㄠˋ ·ㄨㄤ ㄧㄝˊ)
the god of the kitchen

十七畫

【竊】 4072 ㄑㄧㄝˋ chieh qiè

1. to steal; to burglarize
2. a thief; a burglar
3. to usurp
4. stealthy
5. a self-derogatory way of saying "I"

竊柄(ㄑㄧㄝˋ ㄅㄧㄥˇ)
to usurp the power of the state

竊犯(ㄑㄧㄝˋ ㄈㄢˋ)
a thief; a burglar

竊盜狂(ㄑㄧㄝˋ ㄉㄠˋ ㄎㄨㄤˊ)
kleptomania

竊盜罪(ㄑㄧㄝˋ ㄉㄠˋ ㄗㄨㄟˋ)
theft; larceny: 他因竊盜罪被關入獄中。He was put in prison for theft.

竊聽(ㄑㄧㄝˋ ㄊㄧㄥ)
to eavesdrop; eavesdropping

竊聽器(ㄑㄧㄝˋ ㄊㄧㄥ ㄑㄧˋ)
a bugging device; a tapping device; a listening-in device; a bug

竊鉤竊國(ㄑㄧㄝˋ ㄍㄡ ㄑㄧㄝˋ ㄍㄨㄛˊ)
(originally, from *Chuang Tzu* 莊子) Those who steal a hook would be executed, while those who steal (usurp) the throne would become kings.—punishment or reward not depending upon the things one does

竊看(ㄑㄧㄝˋ ㄎㄢˋ)
to peep; to look at something stealthily

竊窺(ㄑㄧㄝˋ ㄎㄨㄟ)
to steal a glance; to spy; to watch stealthily; to peep

竊號(ㄑㄧㄝˋ ㄏㄠˋ)
to usurp the name of the emperor

竊據(ㄑㄧㄝˋ ㄐㄩˋ)
the occupation of an area, or a city by rebels

竊竊私議(ㄑㄧㄝˋ ㄑㄧㄝˋ ㄙ ㄧˋ)
to discuss something in secret; to comment on something in whispers

竊竊私語(ㄑㄧㄝˋ ㄑㄧㄝˋ ㄙ ㄩˇ)
to talk stealthily or in a very low voice; to whisper

竊取(ㄑㄧㄝˋ ㄑㄩˇ)
to steal; to take something which does not lawfully belong to one: 這個間諜想竊取機密情報。The spy tried to steal secret information.

竊笑(ㄑㄧㄝˋ ㄒㄧㄠˋ)
to laugh behind another's back; to laugh in secret

竊視(ㄑㄧㄝˋ ㄕˋ)
to peep

竊賊(ㄑㄧㄝˋ ㄗㄟˊ)
a thief; a burglar: 昨夜竊賊闖入他家。Burglars broke into his house last night.

竊思(ㄑㄧㄝˋ ㄙ)
I think personally that.... 或 My personal view is that.... 或 in my personal opinion

竊案(ㄑㄧㄝˋ ㄢˋ)
a theft or larceny case

竊衣(ㄑㄧㄝˋ ㄧ)
(botany) torilis

竊以爲(ㄑㄧㄝˋ ㄧˇ ㄨㄟˊ)
in my humble opinion; I presume that....

竊謂(ㄑㄧㄝˋ ㄨㄟˋ)
I should say that.... 或 Personally, I am inclined to think that....

竊位(ㄑㄧㄝˋ ㄨㄟˋ)
to occupy a very powerful position without the required talent

竊位素餐(ㄑㄧㄝˋ ㄨㄟˋ ㄙㄨˋ ㄘㄢ)
to hold a high position but do nothing for public interest

竊玉偷香(ㄑㄧㄝˋ ㄩˋ ㄊㄡ ㄒㄧㄤ)
to have an affair with a girl; the ways of Don Juan, or Casanova with women

立部 ㄌㄧˋ lih ㄌㄧˋ

【立】 4073 ㄌㄧˋ lih ㄌㄧˋ

1. to stand
2. to establish; to found; to build; to erect; to create; to start
3. to stand on one's own feet; to live
4. immediately; at once
5. a Chinese family name

立碑(ㄌㄧˋ ㄅㄟ)
to erect a monument

立逼(ㄌㄧˋ ㄅㄧ)
to force someone to do something right away

立品(ㄌㄧˋ ㄆㄧㄣˇ)
to cultivate one's moral character

立馬(ㄌㄧˋ ㄇㄚˇ)
to stop a horse; to rein in a horse

立眉立眼(ㄌㄧˋ ㄇㄟˊ ㄌㄧˋ ㄧㄢˇ)
to get angry; to become furious

立名(ㄌㄧˋ ㄇㄧㄥˊ)
to distinguish oneself; to achieve fame

立命(ㄌㄧˋ ㄇㄧㄥˋ)

〔立部〕

to establish one's Heaven-ordained being
立法(ㄌㄧˋ ㄈㄚˇ)
to legislate; to make laws; to enact laws
立法機關(ㄌㄧˋ ㄈㄚˇ ㄐㄧ ㄍㄨㄢ)
a legislative organ
立法權(ㄌㄧˋ ㄈㄚˇ ㄑㄩㄢˊ)
legislative power
立法委員(ㄌㄧˋ ㄈㄚˇ ㄨㄟˇ ㄩㄢˊ)
a legislator; a lawmaker
立法院(ㄌㄧˋ ㄈㄚˇ ㄩㄢˋ)
Legislative Yuan
立方(ㄌㄧˋ ㄈㄤ)
(mathematics) cube; cubic power
立方根(ㄌㄧˋ ㄈㄤ ㄍㄣ)
(mathematics) a cube root
立方體(ㄌㄧˋ ㄈㄤ ㄊㄧˇ)
(geometry) a cube
立方形的(ㄌㄧˋ ㄈㄤ ㄒㄧㄥˊ ·ㄉㄜ)
cuboid
立德(ㄌㄧˋ ㄉㄜˊ)
to achieve virtue
立等(ㄌㄧˋ ㄉㄥˇ)or 立待(ㄌㄧˋ ㄉㄞˋ)
immediately; at once
立地成佛(ㄌㄧˋ ㄉㄧˋ ㄔㄥˊ ㄈㄛˊ)
to become a Buddha immediately (as soon as one lays down the butcher's knife)
立定(ㄌㄧˋ ㄉㄧㄥˋ)
(word of command) Halt!
立定主意(ㄌㄧˋ ㄉㄧㄥˋ ㄓㄨˇ ㄧˋ)
to make up one's mind; to make a decision: 我已立定主意當個醫生。I've made up my mind to be a doctor.
立冬(ㄌㄧˋ ㄉㄨㄥ)
the Beginning of Winter (the date marking the beginning of one of the 24 seasonal periods in a year, falling normally on November 7 or 8 in the lunar calendar)或 Winter begins.
立陶宛(ㄌㄧˋ ㄊㄠˊ ㄨㄢˇ)
Lithuania
立談之間(ㄌㄧˋ ㄊㄢˊ ㄓ ㄐㄧㄢ)
in a moment; in an instant; in a jiffy
立體(ㄌㄧˋ ㄊㄧˇ)
①a solid body; a solid ② three-dimensional
立體電影(ㄌㄧˋ ㄊㄧˇ ㄉㄧㄢˋ ㄧㄥˇ)
a wide-angle motion picture; a 3-D motion picture; a Cinerama
立體感(ㄌㄧˋ ㄊㄧˇ ㄍㄢˇ)
three-dimensional effects
立體化學(ㄌㄧˋ ㄊㄧˇ ㄏㄨㄚˋ ㄒㄩㄝˊ)
stereochemistry
立體幾何(ㄌㄧˋ ㄊㄧˇ ㄐㄧˇ ㄏㄜˊ)
solid geometry, stereometry, or geometry of space
立體戰爭(ㄌㄧˋ ㄊㄧˇ ㄓㄢˋ ㄓㄥ)
three-dimensional warfare
立體聲音(ㄌㄧˋ ㄊㄧˇ ㄕㄥ ㄧㄣ)
stereophonically reproduced sound; stereophony; stereo: 這是一臺立體聲音唱機。This is a stereo record player.
立體藝術(ㄌㄧˋ ㄊㄧˇ ㄧˋ ㄕㄨˋ)
plastic arts
立突(ㄌㄧˋ ㄊㄨˊ)or 立脫爾(ㄌㄧˋ ㄊㄨㄛ ㄦˇ)
a liter (or litre)亦作「公升」
立論(ㄌㄧˋ ㄌㄨㄣˋ)
an assertion made; a reasoning advanced; to set forth one's views; to present one's argument
立竿見影(ㄌㄧˋ ㄍㄢ ㄐㄧㄢˋ ㄧㄥˇ)
(literally) The moment a pole is erected, it throws its shadow upon the ground. —The outcome may be known immediately.
立國(ㄌㄧˋ ㄍㄨㄛˊ)
to found a state
立櫃(ㄌㄧˋ ㄍㄨㄟˋ)
a chest of drawers; a closet
立功(ㄌㄧˋ ㄍㄨㄥ)
to render distinguished service; to achieve distinction
立功贖罪(ㄌㄧˋ ㄍㄨㄥ ㄕㄨˊ ㄗㄨㄟˋ)
to render meritorious services to make repayment for one's crimes
立刻(ㄌㄧˋ ㄎㄜˋ)or 立即(ㄌㄧˋ ㄐㄧˊ)or 立時(ㄌㄧˋ ㄕˊ)
at once; immediately; promptly; right away: 我立刻就去。 I'll be there right away.
立合同(ㄌㄧˋ ㄏㄜˊ ㄊㄨㄥˊ)
to conclude a contract
立候(ㄌㄧˋ ㄏㄡˋ)
to wait for something to happen immediately
立後(ㄌㄧˋ ㄏㄡˋ)
to adopt an heir
立婚書(ㄌㄧˋ ㄏㄨㄣ ㄕㄨ)
to draw up a marriage contract
立界(ㄌㄧˋ ㄐㄧㄝˋ)
to erect boundary markers; to mark boundary lines
立脚(ㄌㄧˋ ㄐㄧㄠˇ)
to have a footing; to have a standing space: 這懸崖上沒有立脚之處。There was no footing on the cliff.
立脚點(ㄌㄧˋ ㄐㄧㄠˇ ㄉㄧㄢˇ)or 立足點(ㄌㄧˋ ㄗㄨˊ ㄉㄧㄢˇ)
a footing; a foothold
立見(ㄌㄧˋ ㄐㄧㄢˋ)
can be seen immediately
立決(ㄌㄧˋ ㄐㄩㄝˊ)
to sentence and execute summarily
立契(ㄌㄧˋ ㄑㄧˋ)
to make a contract; to conclude an agreement
立秋(ㄌㄧˋ ㄑㄧㄡ)
the Beginning of Autumn (the date marking the beginning of one of the 24 seasonal periods in a year, falling normally on August 8 or 9 in the lunar calendar)或 Autumn begins.
立泉(ㄌㄧˋ ㄑㄩㄢˊ)
a waterfall; a cascade
立下(ㄌㄧˋ ㄒㄧㄚˋ)
to draw up (a legal document,etc.): 我將替你立下這事的計畫。I'll draw up a scheme of it for you.
立夏(ㄌㄧˋ ㄒㄧㄚˋ)
the Beginning of Summer (the date marking the beginning of one of the 24 seasonal periods in a year, falling normally on May 6 or 7 in the lunar calendar)或 Summer begins.
立效(ㄌㄧˋ ㄒㄧㄠˋ)
①to have a desired effect immediately ②to render meritorious service
立憲國(ㄌㄧˋ ㄒㄧㄢˋ ㄍㄨㄛˊ)
a constitutional state
立憲政體(ㄌㄧˋ ㄒㄧㄢˋ ㄓㄥˋ ㄊㄧˇ)
a constitutional government
立像(ㄌㄧˋ ㄒㄧㄤˋ)
①to erect a statue ②a statue in a standing position
立志(ㄌㄧˋ ㄓˋ)
to set an object of pursuit;

to make up one's mind to pursue some object; to resolve; to be determined: 他立志做大事不做大官。He is determined to do great service, not to be an official.

立正(ㄌㄧˋ ㄓㄥˋ)
to stand at attention 或 Attention!

立軸(ㄌㄧˋ ㄓㄡˊ)
①a hanging scroll (of painting or calligraphy) ② (machinery) a vertical shaft; an upright shaft

立錐之地(ㄌㄧˋ ㄓㄨㄟ ㄓ ㄉㄧˋ)
space just enough for the point of a drill—very small space

立朝(ㄌㄧˋ ㄔㄠˊ)
to serve as a courtier

立場(ㄌㄧˋ ㄔㄤˊ)
a position; a stand; an attitude: 他對這件事表明立場。He made his stand clear on this.

立儲(ㄌㄧˋ ㄔㄨˊ)
to designate the crown prince

立春(ㄌㄧˋ ㄔㄨㄣ)
the Beginning of Spring (the date marking the beginning of one of the 24 seasonal periods in a year, falling normally on February 4 or 5 in the lunar calendar) 或 Spring begins.

立誓(ㄌㄧˋ ㄕˋ)
to take an oath; to vow; to swear: 他立誓戒酒。He is under a vow to drink no wine.

立身處世(ㄌㄧˋ ㄕㄣ ㄔㄨˇ ㄕˋ)
to establish oneself and manage to get along in the world

立字(ㄌㄧˋ ㄗˋ)
to make a contract in writing

立足地(ㄌㄧˋ ㄗㄨˊ ㄉㄧˋ)
a foothold; a footing: 我無法在此獲得立足地。I can't gain a foothold here.

立嗣(ㄌㄧˋ ㄙˋ)
to adopt an heir

立案(ㄌㄧˋ ㄢˋ)
to accredit (a school, etc.); to place a case on file for investigation and prosecution

立遺囑(ㄌㄧˋ ㄧˊ ㄓㄨˇ)
to make one's last will and testament

立意(ㄌㄧˋ ㄧˋ)
① to make up one's mind; to resolve ② intention or purpose; conception

立異(ㄌㄧˋ ㄧˋ)
① to dissent ② to be different

立業(ㄌㄧˋ ㄧㄝˋ)
to establish a business; to get a respectable career

立言(ㄌㄧˋ ㄧㄢˊ)
to leave worthy writings to posterity; to achieve glory by writing

立於不敗之地(ㄌㄧˋ ㄩˊ ㄅㄨˋ ㄅㄞˋ ㄓ ㄉㄧˋ)
to establish oneself in an unassailable position

立愈 or 立癒(ㄌㄧˋ ㄩˋ)
to be cured immediately

立約(ㄌㄧˋ ㄩㄝ)
to conclude a treaty; to conclude an agreement; to contract

五畫

【站】 4074
ㄓㄢˋ jann zhàn

1. to stand: 往後站！Stand back!
2. a station; a stop; a center for rendering certain services

站班(ㄓㄢˋ ㄅㄢ)
(said of guards, etc.) to be on duty; to stand guard

站不起來(ㄓㄢˋ ·ㄅㄨ ㄑㄧˇ ·ㄌㄞ)
unable to stand up

站不住(ㄓㄢˋ ·ㄅㄨ ㄓㄨˋ)
① unable to keep standing ②(said of a theory) disputable; full of loopholes

站不住脚(ㄓㄢˋ ·ㄅㄨ ㄓㄨˋ ㄐㄧㄠˇ)
unable to hold one's position

站不穩(ㄓㄢˋ ·ㄅㄨ ㄨㄣˇ)
unable to stand firmly

站排(ㄓㄢˋ ㄆㄞˊ)
to line up

站票(ㄓㄢˋ ㄆㄧㄠˋ)
a ticket for standing room; an SRO (standing room only) ticket

站夫(ㄓㄢˋ ㄈㄨ)
a porter at a railway station

站得住(ㄓㄢˋ ·ㄉㄜ ㄓㄨˋ)
① able to stand; able to hold one's position ②(said of a theory) sound; irrefutable

站定(ㄓㄢˋ ㄉㄧㄥˋ)
to stand still

站隊(ㄓㄢˋ ㄉㄨㄟˋ)
to queue up; to line up; to stand in line

站臺(ㄓㄢˋ ㄊㄞˊ)
a platform (at a railway station)

站立(ㄓㄢˋ ㄌㄧˋ)
to stand

站籠(ㄓㄢˋ ㄌㄨㄥˊ)
a wooden cage for torturing convicts as a form of punishment in former times 亦作「立枷」

站崗(ㄓㄢˋ ㄍㄤˇ)
to stand guard; to act as a sentry; to stand sentry

站起來(ㄓㄢˋ ㄑㄧˇ ·ㄌㄞ)
to stand up; to rise

站長(ㄓㄢˋ ㄓㄤˇ)
the head of a station; a stationmaster; a station agent

站住(ㄓㄢˋ ·ㄓㄨ)
(word of command) Halt! 或 to stop; to stand: 我聽到有人叫我站住。I heard someone calling to me to stop.

站穩(ㄓㄢˋ ㄨㄣˇ)
to stand firm; to take a firm stand

【竚】 4075
(佇) ㄓㄨˋ juh zhù

to stand for a long time

竚候(ㄓㄨˋ ㄏㄡˋ)
to stand and wait

【竝】 4076
(並) ㄅㄧㄥˋ binq bìng

1. also; and
2. to combine; to join

六畫

【竟】 4077
ㄐㄧㄥˋ jinq jìng

1. to come to an end; to terminate; to go through the whole course; to finish; to complete
2. rather unexpectedly; some-

〔立部〕

what to one's surprise; in a way thought to be rather unlikely

竟敢(ㄐㄧㄥˋ ㄍㄢˇ)
to dare somewhat to one's surprise; to have the audacity: 他竟敢侮辱我。He dared to insult me.

竟是(ㄐㄧㄥˋ ㄕˋ)
to turn out to be

竟日(ㄐㄧㄥˋ ㄖˋ)
the whole day; all day long

竟然(ㄐㄧㄥˋ ㄖㄢˊ)
in a way thought to be rather unlikely; somewhat unexpectedly; somewhat to one's surprise

竟然不理(ㄐㄧㄥˋ ㄖㄢˊ ㄅㄨˋ ㄌㄧˇ)
to pay no heed, somewhat to another's surprise

竟然如此(ㄐㄧㄥˋ ㄖㄢˊ ㄖㄨˊ ㄘˇ)
to be so, somewhat to one's surprise

竟自(ㄐㄧㄥˋ ㄗˋ)
somewhat to one's surprise

竟夜(ㄐㄧㄥˋ ㄧㄝˋ)
all night; the whole night

竟有此事(ㄐㄧㄥˋ ㄧㄡˇ ㄘˇ ㄕˋ)
To everyone's surprise, it did happen.

【章】 4078
ㄓㄤ jang zhāng

1. a piece of writing; a chapter; a main division of a book: 全書共三十章。The book has thirty chapters.
2. a system; a statute; an organized body
3. an emblem; a seal; a stamp
4. to make clear; to make known
5. a pattern; an example
6. a Chinese family name

章法(ㄓㄤ ㄈㄚˇ)
① the presentation of ideas in a piece of writing; the art of composition ② orderly ways: 他辦事很有章法。He does everything in orderly ways.

章服(ㄓㄤ ㄈㄨˊ)
ceremonial dress with distinctive colors and designs for rulers and courtiers in ancient times

章臺(ㄓㄤ ㄊㄞˊ)
(euphemism) a brothel; a house of ill fame

章回小說(ㄓㄤ ㄏㄨㄟˊ ㄒㄧㄠˇ ㄕㄨㄛ)
a serial novel; a type of old Chinese novel with each chapter headed by a couplet giving the main points of its content

章節(ㄓㄤ ㄐㄧㄝˊ)
chapters and sections (of a piece of writing)

章句(ㄓㄤ ㄐㄩˋ)
proper division (of an unpunctuated ancient text) into chapters and sentences

章程(ㄓㄤ ㄔㄥˊ)
① a set of regulation; constitution ② a solution; a way

章奏(ㄓㄤ ㄗㄡˋ)
an appeal or report presented to the emperor

章草(ㄓㄤ ㄘㄠˇ)
a style of cursive writing of the "script" type, originated by Shih-yu (史游) of the Han Dynasty, so named because it was chiefly used in 章奏

章魚(ㄓㄤ ㄩˊ)
an octopus

七畫

【童】 4079
ㄊㄨㄥˊ torng tóng

1. a child; a minor; a virgin
2. (said of land, etc.) bare; barren
3. a Chinese family name

童便(ㄊㄨㄥˊ ㄅㄧㄢˋ)
(Chinese medicine) urine of boys

童僕(ㄊㄨㄥˊ ㄆㄨˊ)
a boy servant; a boy; a houseboy; a manservant

童蒙(ㄊㄨㄥˊ ㄇㄥˊ)
innocent childhood; childish ignorance

童男(ㄊㄨㄥˊ ㄋㄢˊ)
a virgin man

童男女(ㄊㄨㄥˊ ㄋㄢˊ ㄋㄩˇ)
minors of both sexes

童牛角馬(ㄊㄨㄥˊ ㄋㄧㄡˊ ㄐㄧㄠˇ ㄇㄚˇ)
(literally) a hornless ox and a horned horse—against common practice; abnormal phenomenon

童年(ㄊㄨㄥˊ ㄋㄧㄢˊ)
childhood; youth: 他們自童年起即爲好友。They are good friends since childhood.

童女(ㄊㄨㄥˊ ㄋㄩˇ)
a virgin

童工(ㄊㄨㄥˊ ㄍㄨㄥ)
child labor; a child laborer

童話(ㄊㄨㄥˊ ㄏㄨㄚˋ)
nursery stories; juvenile stories; fairy tales

童昏(ㄊㄨㄥˊ ㄏㄨㄣ)
young and ignorant; naive and ignorant

童心(ㄊㄨㄥˊ ㄒㄧㄣ)
a childish heart

童心未泯(ㄊㄨㄥˊ ㄒㄧㄣ ㄨㄟˋ ㄇㄧㄣˇ)
to retain a childish heart; still to keep traces of childishness or childlike innocence

童穉(ㄊㄨㄥˊ ㄓˋ)
children

童貞(ㄊㄨㄥˊ ㄓㄣ)
virginity; chastity

童眞(ㄊㄨㄥˊ ㄓㄣ)
a Buddhist novice; a monk (who should have a child's nature of simplicity)

童裝(ㄊㄨㄥˊ ㄓㄨㄤ)
children's garments

童山(ㄊㄨㄥˊ ㄕㄢ)
a bare hill

童山濯濯(ㄊㄨㄥˊ ㄕㄢ ㄓㄨㄛˊ ㄓㄨㄛˊ)
① an unforested mountain ② baldheaded

童身(ㄊㄨㄥˊ ㄕㄣ)
(said of a male adult) to have had no sexual intercourse with a woman

童生(ㄊㄨㄥˊ ㄕㄥ)
a candidate for the lowest degree under the former civil service examination system

童豎(ㄊㄨㄥˊ ㄕㄨˋ)
a toddler

童子(ㄊㄨㄥˊ ㄗˇ) or 童孺(ㄊㄨㄥˊ ㄖㄨˊ)
a minor; a child; a boy; a lad

童子軍(ㄊㄨㄥˊ ㄗˇ ㄐㄩㄣ) or 童軍(ㄊㄨㄥˊ ㄐㄩㄣ)
a boy scout

童子軍大露營(ㄊㄨㄥˊ ㄗˇ ㄐㄩㄣ ㄉㄚˋ ㄌㄨˋ ㄧㄥˊ)
a camporee; a jamboree

童叟(ㄊㄨㄥˊ ㄙㄡˇ)
children and aged people

童叟無欺(ㄊㄨㄥˊ ㄙㄡˇ ㄨˊ ㄑㄧ)

We are honest even to children and aged people. (a shop sign meaning "We are honest with all customers.")

童騃(ㄊㄨㄥˊ ㄞˊ)
young and ignorant

童謠(ㄊㄨㄥˊ ㄧㄠˊ)
nursery rhymes; nursery songs

童幼(ㄊㄨㄥˊ ㄧㄡˋ)
childhood

童顏鶴髮(ㄊㄨㄥˊ ㄧㄢˊ ㄏㄜˋ ㄈㄚˇ)
(literally) a ruddy complexion and a hoary head—to look youthful at an advanced age

童養媳(ㄊㄨㄥˊ ㄧㄤˇ ㄒㄧˊ)
a girl brought up in the family of her future husband; a child daughter-in-law

【竣】 4080
ㄐㄩㄣˋ jiunn jùn
accomplished; completed

竣工(ㄐㄩㄣˋ ㄍㄨㄥ)
(said of a construction project) to be completed

竣事(ㄐㄩㄣˋ ㄕˋ)
(said of a plan, etc.) having been completed

【竦】 4081
ㄙㄨㄥˇ soong sǒng
1. respectful
2. awed

竦然(ㄙㄨㄥˇ ㄖㄢˊ)
fearful; scared

九畫

【竭】 4082
ㄐㄧㄝˊ jye jié
1. to devote, or put forth (efforts, etc.)
2. to exhaust; to use up

竭力(ㄐㄧㄝˊ ㄌㄧˋ)
to do one's utmost; to do one's best; to exert one's utmost strength: 我們竭力幫助他。We do our best to help him.

竭慮(ㄐㄧㄝˊ ㄌㄩˋ)
to devote one's mental energy to the full

竭盡(ㄐㄧㄝˊ ㄐㄧㄣˋ)
to devote to the full; to exhaust; to use up

竭盡棉薄(ㄐㄧㄝˊ ㄐㄧㄣˋ ㄇㄧㄢˊ ㄅㄛˊ)
to do all one can (a polite expression)

竭蹶(ㄐㄧㄝˊ ㄐㄩㄝˊ)
① to stagger; to totter ② to proceed with difficulty ③ destitute; impoverished

竭智盡慮(ㄐㄧㄝˊ ㄓˋ ㄐㄧㄣˋ ㄌㄩˋ)or 竭智(ㄐㄧㄝˊ ㄓˋ)
to devote one's mental resources to the full

竭誠(ㄐㄧㄝˊ ㄔㄥˊ)
wholeheartedly; with all sincerity: 我們竭誠擁護我們的領袖。We support our leader with all sincerity.

竭澤而漁(ㄐㄧㄝˊ ㄗㄜˊ ㄦˊ ㄩˊ)
(literally) to fish by emptying the water of a pond—to make a thorough but unwise exploitation

【端】 4083
ㄉㄨㄢ duan duān
1. an extreme; an end
2. a beginning
3. correct; proper; upright
4. leads; a clue
5. to carry carefully
6. cause

端木(ㄉㄨㄢ ㄇㄨˋ)
a Chinese double family name

端方(ㄉㄨㄢ ㄈㄤ)
upright; righteous

端底(ㄉㄨㄢ ㄉㄧˇ)
after all; in the long run; ultimately: 他雖浪費，端底不失爲一好人。He is a spendthrift. After all, he is a good man.

端的(ㄉㄨㄢ ㄉㄧˋ)
① indeed; actually; as expected ② after all; in the long run

端倪(ㄉㄨㄢ ㄋㄧˊ)
general shape; an outline; a clue; signs: 我們找到這秘密的一點端倪。We found a clue to the mystery.

端凝(ㄉㄨㄢ ㄋㄧㄥˊ)
solemn; dignified

端賴(ㄉㄨㄢ ㄌㄞˋ)
to rely entirely upon

端麗(ㄉㄨㄢ ㄌㄧˋ)
neat and beautiful; graceful; comely

端拱(ㄉㄨㄢ ㄍㄨㄥˇ)
(said of a monarch) to rule without actually governing

端揆(ㄉㄨㄢ ㄎㄨㄟˊ)
a prime minister

端詳(ㄉㄨㄢ ㄒㄧㄤˊ)
① to study or examine in detail; to scrutinize ② details; the whole story: 告訴我事情的端詳吧。Tell me all the details. ③ dignified and serene: 她舉止端詳。She behaves with serene dignity.

端相(ㄉㄨㄢ ㄒㄧㄤˋ)
to look at carefully

端行(ㄉㄨㄢ ㄒㄧㄥˋ)
upright behavior

端緒(ㄉㄨㄢ ㄒㄩˋ)
clues to the handling of a thing

端正(ㄉㄨㄢ ㄓㄥˋ)
① correct; proper ② to correct; to rectify: 我們端正學習態度。We correct our attitude toward study. ③ regular; well-formed; symmetric: 他的五官端正。He has regular features.

端莊(ㄉㄨㄢ ㄓㄨㄤ)
sober; dignified

端重(ㄉㄨㄢ ㄓㄨㄥˋ)
serious; sober; sedate

端士(ㄉㄨㄢ ㄕˋ)
a high-principled man

端視(ㄉㄨㄢ ㄕˋ)
to look steadily

端上(ㄉㄨㄢ ㄕㄤˋ)
to carry (a tray of food, etc.) carefully

端然(ㄉㄨㄢ ㄖㄢˊ)
neat; symmetrical

端坐(ㄉㄨㄢ ㄗㄨㄛˋ)
to sit properly; to sit straight

端陽節(ㄉㄨㄢ ㄧㄤˊ ㄐㄧㄝˊ)or 端午節(ㄉㄨㄢ ㄨˇ ㄐㄧㄝˊ)
the Dragon-Boat Festival (falling on the fifth day of the fifth lunar month)

端陽競渡(ㄉㄨㄢ ㄧㄤˊ ㄐㄧㄥˋ ㄉㄨˋ)
a dragon-boat race on the Dragon-Boat Festival

端委(ㄉㄨㄢ ㄨㄟˇ)
ceremonial robes or dress

端月(ㄉㄨㄢ ㄩㄝˋ)
the first lunar month; the first moon

十五畫

【競】 4084 ㄐㄧㄥˋ jinq jìng
to compete; to vie
競賣(ㄐㄧㄥˋ ㄇㄞˋ)
an auction; to auction off: 他競賣他的傢俱。He auctioned off his furniture.
競渡(ㄐㄧㄥˋ ㄉㄨˋ)
a boat race (especially the one on the Dragon-Boat Festival)
競技(ㄐㄧㄥˋ ㄐㄧˋ)
a race; a contest; a tournament
競進(ㄐㄧㄥˋ ㄐㄧㄣˋ)
to advance side by side
競選(ㄐㄧㄥˋ ㄒㄩㄢˇ)
to vie in an election; to campaign; to run for: 他競選總統。He ran for the presidency.
競爭(ㄐㄧㄥˋ ㄓㄥ)
to compete; to vie; competition
競爭心(ㄐㄧㄥˋ ㄓㄥ ㄒㄧㄣ)
competitive spirit; the spirit to excel
競爭性(ㄐㄧㄥˋ ㄓㄥ ㄒㄧㄥˋ)
competitiveness
競爭者(ㄐㄧㄥˋ ㄓㄥ ㄓㄜˇ)
a competitor
競走(ㄐㄧㄥˋ ㄗㄡˇ)
a foot race; a walkathon
競賽(ㄐㄧㄥˋ ㄙㄞˋ)
a race; a contest

竹部
ㄓㄨˊ jwu zhú

【竹】 4085 ㄓㄨˊ jwu zhú
1. bamboo
2. slips of bamboo for writing
3. a Chinese family name
竹帛(ㄓㄨˊ ㄅㄛˊ)
① bamboo tablets and textiles (both used as paper in ancient times) ② books
竹報平安(ㄓㄨˊ ㄅㄠˋ ㄆㄧㄥˊ ㄢ)
to report in a letter home that everything is well
竹布(ㄓㄨˊ ㄅㄨˋ)
starched light-blue cotton cloth
竹批兒(ㄓㄨˊ ㄆㄧㄜㄦ)
bamboo strips (as material for making baskets, etc.)
竹馬(ㄓㄨˊ ㄇㄚˇ)
a bamboo hobbyhorse: 兒童騎竹馬玩。Children rode on a bamboo hobbyhorse to play.
竹篾(ㄓㄨˊ ㄇㄧㄝˋ)
thin and flat slips of bamboo used for weaving purpose
竹幕(ㄓㄨˊ ㄇㄨˋ)
the Bamboo Curtain (a derogatory reference to socialist states)
竹筏(ㄓㄨˊ ㄈㄚˊ)
a bamboo raft: 他乘竹筏順流而下。He went down the river on a bamboo raft.
竹夫人(ㄓㄨˊ ㄈㄨ ㄖㄣˊ)
a large pillow-shaped bamboo ware used as an armrest and footrest in bed during summer
竹頭木屑(ㄓㄨˊ ㄊㄡˊ ㄇㄨˋ ㄒㄧㄝˋ)
(literally) odd pieces of bamboo and wood—seemingly unimportant but useful things
竹筒(ㄓㄨˊ ㄊㄨㄥˇ)
a bamboo tube
竹籃(ㄓㄨˊ ㄌㄢˊ)
a bamboo basket: 她買了一個竹籃。She bought a bamboo basket.
竹籬茅舍(ㄓㄨˊ ㄌㄧˊ ㄇㄠˊ ㄕㄜˋ)
(literally) a bamboo fence around a thatched cottage —a simple dwelling
竹笠(ㄓㄨˊ ㄌㄧˋ)
a bamboo hat
竹簾(ㄓㄨˊ ㄌㄧㄢˊ)
a bamboo curtain or screen
竹林(ㄓㄨˊ ㄌㄧㄣˊ)
a bamboo grove
竹林七賢(ㄓㄨˊ ㄌㄧㄣˊ ㄑㄧ ㄒㄧㄢˊ)
山濤、阮籍、嵇康、向秀、劉伶、阮咸、王戎, known as the Seven Wise Men of the Bamboo Grove (a group of seven men of letters in the 3th century)
竹林之遊(ㄓㄨˊ ㄌㄧㄣˊ ㄓ ㄧㄡˊ)
association with learned scholars
竹籠(ㄓㄨˊ ㄌㄨㄥˊ)
a bamboo cage; a bamboo basket with a narrow opening
竹竿(ㄓㄨˊ ㄍㄢ) or 竹竿兒(ㄓㄨˊ ㄍㄚㄦ)
a bamboo pole or cane
竹槓(ㄓㄨˊ ㄍㄤˋ)
a bamboo carrying pole
竹工(ㄓㄨˊ ㄍㄨㄥ)
bamboo works
竹雞(ㄓㄨˊ ㄐㄧ)
a bamboo partridge
竹節(ㄓㄨˊ ㄐㄧㄝˊ)
bamboo joints
竹簡(ㄓㄨˊ ㄐㄧㄢˇ)
slips of bamboo for writing
竹器(ㄓㄨˊ ㄑㄧˋ)
bamboo ware
竹蓆子(ㄓㄨˊ ㄒㄧˊ ˙ㄗ)
a mat made of split bamboo
竹枝詞(ㄓㄨˊ ㄓ ㄘˊ)
a kind of verse mainly about the life of the common people, originating in the Tang Dynasty
竹紙(ㄓㄨˊ ㄓˇ)
bamboo paper
竹製品(ㄓㄨˊ ㄓˋ ㄆㄧㄣˇ)
bamboo articles
竹實(ㄓㄨˊ ㄕˊ)
bamboo seeds
竹書(ㄓㄨˊ ㄕㄨ)
a collection of ancient bamboo books, supposedly unearthed from a prince's grave in the 4th century
竹書紀年(ㄓㄨˊ ㄕㄨ ㄐㄧˋ ㄋㄧㄢˊ)
a chronicle book among a collection of ancient bamboo books, supposedly discovered in a prince's grave in the 4th century
竹子(ㄓㄨˊ ˙ㄗ)
bamboo
竹孫(ㄓㄨˊ ㄙㄨㄣ)
bamboo growing out of a side root
竹蓀(ㄓㄨˊ ㄙㄨㄣ)
an edible whitish fungus
竹筍 or 竹笋(ㄓㄨˊ ㄙㄨㄣˇ)
bamboo shoots
竹椅(ㄓㄨˊ ㄧˇ)
a bamboo chair
竹葉青(ㄓㄨˊ ㄧㄝˋ ㄑㄧㄥ)
① three-year-old Shaohsing wine ② a kind of venomous snake

竹輿(ㄓㄨˊ ㄩˊ)
a bamboo sedan chair

二畫

【竺】 4086
ㄓㄨˊ jwu zhú
1. ancient name of India 參看「天竺」
2. a Chinese family name
竺經(ㄓㄨˊ ㄐㄧㄥ)
the Buddhist scriptures; Indian sutras
竺學(ㄓㄨˊ ㄒㄩㄝˊ)
the study of Buddhism

三畫

【竽】 4087
ㄩˊ yu yú
a kind of musical instrument with 36 reeds

【竿】 4088
ㄍㄢ gan gān
1. a bamboo pole; a bamboo rod
2. slips of bamboo for writing
竿頭日上(ㄍㄢ ㄊㄡˊ ㄖˋ ㄕㄤˋ)
to make constant progress in one's studies 亦作「竿頭日進」
竿子(ㄍㄢ ·ㄗ)or 竿兒(ㄍㄚㄦ)
a bamboo pole

四畫

【笆】 4089
ㄅㄚ ba bā
a bamboo fence
笆斗(ㄅㄚ ㄉㄡˇ)
a willow basket for holding grains

【笊】 4090
ㄓㄠˋ jaw zhào
a bamboo skimmer
笊籬(ㄓㄠˋ ·ㄌㄧ)
a bamboo skimmer; a wire strainer; a fisherman's rake for catching clam, etc.

【笏】 4091
ㄏㄨˋ huh hù
a tablet held by a civil official during an audience with the monarch

【笈】 4092
ㄐㄧˊ jyi jí
a bamboo bookcase

【笑】 4093
ㄒㄧㄠˋ shiaw xiào
1. to laugh; to smile; to grin; to giggle; to titter; to chuckle; to snicker
2. to ridicule; to deride; to jeer: 她剛開始學，別笑她。She has just started learning. Don't jeer at her.
笑柄(ㄒㄧㄠˋ ㄅㄧㄥˇ)
a laughingstock; a joke
笑不可仰(ㄒㄧㄠˋ ㄅㄨˋ ㄎㄜˇ ㄧㄤˇ)
to roll with laughter
笑破肚皮(ㄒㄧㄠˋ ㄆㄛˋ ㄉㄨˋ ㄆㄧˊ)
to be overwhelmed with laughter; to roll with laughter
笑罵由他(ㄒㄧㄠˋ ㄇㄚˋ ㄧㄡˊ ㄊㄚ)
Let him ridicule and revile as he likes. (I don't care a bit about his ridicule and abuse.)
笑貌(ㄒㄧㄠˋ ㄇㄠˋ)
a smiling face
笑瞇瞇的(ㄒㄧㄠˋ ㄇㄧ ㄇㄧ ·ㄉㄜ)
to be all smiles; beaming
笑面虎(ㄒㄧㄠˋ ㄇㄧㄢˋ ㄏㄨˇ)
a smiling tiger—(figuratively) a friendly-looking villain; a wolf in sheep's clothing; a treacherous fellow
笑掉大牙(ㄒㄧㄠˋ ㄉㄧㄠˋ ㄉㄚˋ ㄧㄚˊ)
to burst out laughing over the absurdity, ludicrousness, etc. of something
笑談(ㄒㄧㄠˋ ㄊㄢˊ)
① a laughingstock ② laughing conversation; gay conversation ③ to laugh over
笑納(ㄒㄧㄠˋ ㄋㄚˋ)
to accept (a gift) with a laugh over its worthlessness (a conventional expression for asking another to accept a gift): 請笑納。Please accept this small gift of mine.
笑裏藏刀(ㄒㄧㄠˋ ·ㄌㄧ ㄘㄤˊ ㄉㄠ)
(literally) to conceal a dagger behind a smile—very treacherous
笑臉(ㄒㄧㄠˋ ㄌㄧㄢˇ)
a smiling face: 我們對他笑臉相迎。We greeted him with a smiling face.
笑口常開(ㄒㄧㄠˋ ㄎㄡˇ ㄔㄤˊ ㄎㄞ)
grinning all the time
笑哈哈(ㄒㄧㄠˋ ·ㄏㄚ ·ㄏㄚ)or 笑呵呵(ㄒㄧㄠˋ ㄏㄜ ㄏㄜ)
to laugh heartily
笑話百出(ㄒㄧㄠˋ ㄏㄨㄚˋ ㄅㄞˇ ㄔㄨ)
to make many ridiculous mistakes
笑話(ㄒㄧㄠˋ ·ㄏㄨㄚ)or 笑話兒(ㄒㄧㄠˋ ·ㄏㄨㄚㄦ)
① a joke; a funny story: 那是個有趣的笑話。That's a good joke. ② a ridiculous error; a laughable mistake ③ Nonsense! ④ to laugh at; to ridicule: 可別笑話我的表演。Please do not laugh at my performance.
笑氣(ㄒㄧㄠˋ ㄑㄧˋ)
(chemistry) laughing gas; nitrous oxide
笑嘻嘻(ㄒㄧㄠˋ ㄒㄧ ㄒㄧ)
to be all smiles; to look very happy
笑逐顏開(ㄒㄧㄠˋ ㄓㄨˊ ㄧㄢˊ ㄎㄞ)
to beam with smiles; to be wreathed in smiles
笑場(ㄒㄧㄠˋ ㄔㄤˇ)or(ㄒㄧㄠˋ ㄔㄤˊ)
an entertainer's silly laughter during performance
笑出眼淚(ㄒㄧㄠˋ ㄔㄨ ㄧㄢˇ ㄌㄟˋ)
to laugh until tears come
笑殺(ㄒㄧㄠˋ ·ㄕㄚ)or 笑煞(ㄒㄧㄠˋ ㄕㄚˋ)
to be overwhelmed with laughter
笑聲(ㄒㄧㄠˋ ㄕㄥ)
sound of laughter
笑容(ㄒㄧㄠˋ ㄖㄨㄥˊ)
a smile; happy expression; a smiling countenance
笑容可掬(ㄒㄧㄠˋ ㄖㄨㄥˊ ㄎㄜˇ ㄐㄩ)
to show pleasant smiles; to be all smiles; to be radiant with smiles
笑死人(ㄒㄧㄠˋ ㄙˇ ㄖㄣˊ)
to make one laugh to death; extremely ridiculous; ludicrous to the utmost degree
笑一笑(ㄒㄧㄠˋ ·ㄧ ·ㄒㄧㄠ)
to give a smile
笑靨(ㄒㄧㄠˋ ㄧㄝˋ)or 笑渦(ㄒㄧㄠˋ ㄨㄛ)
dimples appearing with a smile
笑微微(ㄒㄧㄠˋ ㄨㄟˊ ㄨㄟˊ)
smiling

五畫

【笙】 4094
ㄕㄥ sheng shēng
a kind of panpipe with 13 reeds

笙歌(ㄕㄥ ㄍㄜ)
music and songs
笙管(ㄕㄥ ㄍㄨㄢˇ)
pipes of a panpipe
笙簧(ㄕㄥ ㄏㄨㄤˊ)
reeds of a panpipe
笙磬同音(ㄕㄥ ㄑㄧㄥˋ ㄊㄨㄥˊ ㄧㄣ)
in complete harmony

【笠】 4095 ㄌㄧˋ lih lì
1. a bamboo hat
2. a bamboo shade or covering

【笛】 4096 ㄉㄧˊ dyi dí
a flute
笛福(ㄉㄧˊ ㄈㄨˊ)
Daniel Defoe, 1659?—1731, English writer and political commentator
笛卡爾(ㄉㄧˊ ㄎㄚˇ ㄦˇ)
René Descartes, 1596-1650, French philosopher and mathematician
笛子(ㄉㄧˊ ·ㄗ)
a flute: 他在吹笛子。He plays (on) the flute.

【笨】 4097 ㄅㄣˋ benn bèn
1. stupid; dull: 他笨透了。He is as stupid as an owl.
2. clumsy; awkward: 你這人笨手笨脚的。You are clumsy.
笨伯(ㄅㄣˋ ㄅㄛˊ)
a fool; a simpleton
笨蛋(ㄅㄣˋ ㄉㄢˋ)
a fool; a simpleton
笨頭笨腦(ㄅㄣˋ ㄊㄡˊ ㄅㄣˋ ㄋㄠˇ)
stupid; muddleheaded; dull; blockheaded
笨瓜(ㄅㄣˋ ㄍㄨㄚ)
a fool
笨工(ㄅㄣˋ ㄍㄨㄥ)
an unskilled workman
笨漢(ㄅㄣˋ ㄏㄢˋ)
a clumsy fellow: 他是個笨漢。He's a clumsy fellow.
笨貨(ㄅㄣˋ ㄏㄨㄛˋ)
a fool; a simpleton; a dullard
笨傢伙(ㄅㄣˋ ㄐㄧㄚ ·ㄏㄨㄛ)
a fool; a simpleton; a clumsy fellow
笨拙(ㄅㄣˋ ㄓㄨㄛˊ)
unskilled; clumsy; awkward: 他行動笨拙。He is clumsy in movement.
笨重(ㄅㄣˋ ㄓㄨㄥˋ)
① cumbersome; heavy; too heavy for convenient handling ② clumsy
笨車(ㄅㄣˋ ㄔㄜ)
a heavy wagon; a heavy cart
笨手笨脚(ㄅㄣˋ ㄕㄡˇ ㄅㄣˋ ㄐㄧㄠˇ)
acting clumsily; all thumbs
笨人(ㄅㄣˋ ㄖㄣˊ)
a fool; a simpleton; a dullard; an idiot
笨賊(ㄅㄣˋ ㄗㄟˊ)
① a fool; a simpleton; a dullard; an idiot ② a stupid burglar

【笞】 4098 ㄔ chy chī
1. a bamboo whip
2. to whip; to flog
笞背(ㄔ ㄅㄟˋ)
to flog the back; to whip the back
笞罵(ㄔ ㄇㄚˋ)
to whip and revile
笞臀(ㄔ ㄊㄨㄣˊ)
to whip the buttocks; to flog the buttocks
笞刑(ㄔ ㄒㄧㄥˊ)
cane punishment; whipping, or flogging (as a form of punishment in former times)
笞辱(ㄔ ㄖㄨˋ)
to whip and insult

【笥】 4099 ㄙˋ syh sì
a bamboo box or chest
笥匱囊空(ㄙˋ ㄎㄨㄟˋ ㄋㄤˊ ㄎㄨㄥ)
(literally) All the boxes and bags are empty.—extremely destitute; dead broke

【笫】 4100 ㄗˇ tzyy zǐ
a bed

【符】 4101 ㄈㄨˊ fwu fú
1. a tally carried for identification, as a warrant, etc.; an identification tag or label
2. an auspicious omen
3. a charm; a talisman; a spell: 有些人信符咒。Some people believe in charms.
4. to match; to tally; to correspond; to accord: 他言不符實。His statement does not tally with facts.
5. a symbol; a sign
6. a Chinese family name
符命(ㄈㄨˊ ㄇㄧㄥˋ)
auspicious omen sent down upon a prince as a token of his appointment to the throne
符頭(ㄈㄨˊ ㄊㄡˊ)
heads of musical notes
符籙(ㄈㄨˊ ㄌㄨˋ)
Taoist secret talismanic writing
符合(ㄈㄨˊ ㄏㄜˊ)
to correspond; to match; to tally: 你的帳目和我的符合。Your account tallies with mine.
符號(ㄈㄨˊ ㄏㄠˋ)
a symbol; a sign: 文字是思想的符號。Words are the signs of ideas.
符號邏輯(ㄈㄨˊ ㄏㄠˋ ㄌㄨㄛˊ ㄐㄧˊ)
symbolic logic
符節(ㄈㄨˊ ㄐㄧㄝˊ)
a tally or a seal consisting of two halves carried for identification, as a warrant, etc.
符璽(ㄈㄨˊ ㄒㄧˇ)
an imperial seal or stamp
符信(ㄈㄨˊ ㄒㄧㄣˋ)
① an identification tag, sign, etc. ② to certify authenticity by matching the tallies
符咒(ㄈㄨˊ ㄓㄡˋ)
a charm; a spell; an amulet: 他被符咒鎮住。He was bound by a spell.
符讖(ㄈㄨˊ ㄔㄣˋ)
Taoist omens and prophecies
符水(ㄈㄨˊ ㄕㄨㄟˇ)
magic words and water for curing diseases
符瑞(ㄈㄨˊ ㄖㄨㄟˋ)
auspices; an auspicious omen
符驗(ㄈㄨˊ ㄧㄢˋ)
to verify through a tally, etc.
符應(ㄈㄨˊ ㄧㄥˋ)
agreement of an omen with the fact
符尾(ㄈㄨˊ ㄨㄟˇ)
tails of musical notes

【第】 4102 ㄉㄧˋ dih dì
1. sequence; order
2. rank; grade; degree

3. a mansion; a residence
4. a Chinese family name

第八藝術(ㄉㄧˋ ㄅㄚ ㄧˋ ㄕㄨˋ)
the eighth art—the movies

第六感(ㄉㄧˋ ㄌㄧㄡˋ ㄍㄢˇ)
the sixth sense; extrasensory perception (ESP)

第宅(ㄉㄧˋ ㄓㄞˊ)
a mansion

第三(ㄉㄧˋ ㄙㄢ)
third; tertiary: 在賽跑中我得到第三名。I got the third prize in the race.

第三帝國(ㄉㄧˋ ㄙㄢ ㄉㄧˋ ㄍㄨㄛˊ)
the Third Reich; the Nazi Germany

第三國際(ㄉㄧˋ ㄙㄢ ㄍㄨㄛˊ ㄐㄧˋ)
the Third International

第三者(ㄉㄧˋ ㄙㄢ ㄓㄜˇ)
a third person; a disinterested person; a third party

第三世界(ㄉㄧˋ ㄙㄢ ㄕˋ ㄐㄧㄝˋ)
the third world (including the developing countries in Asia, Africa, Latin America and elsewhere)

第三人稱(ㄉㄧˋ ㄙㄢ ㄖㄣˊ ㄔㄥ)
(grammar) the third person

第二(ㄉㄧˋ ㄦˋ)
second; secondary: 她是第二個出去的人。She was the second person to go out.

第二國際(ㄉㄧˋ ㄦˋ ㄍㄨㄛˊ ㄐㄧˋ)
the Second International

第二人稱(ㄉㄧˋ ㄦˋ ㄖㄣˊ ㄔㄥ)
(grammar) the second person

第二次世界大戰(ㄉㄧˋ ㄦˋ ㄘˋ ㄕˋ ㄐㄧㄝˋ ㄉㄚˋ ㄓㄢˋ)
the Second World War; World War II

第一(ㄉㄧˋ ㄧ)
first; primary: 他在全班是第一。He is the first in his class.

第一排(ㄉㄧˋ ㄧ ㄆㄞˊ)
the first row

第一天(ㄉㄧˋ ㄧ ㄊㄧㄢ)
the first day

第一流(ㄉㄧˋ ㄧ ㄌㄧㄡˊ)
first-rate; first-class: 他是第一流的作家。He is a first-rate writer.

第一國際(ㄉㄧˋ ㄧ ㄍㄨㄛˊ ㄐㄧˋ)
the First International

第一泉(ㄉㄧˋ ㄧ ㄑㄩㄢˊ)
spring water of the top quality

第一線(ㄉㄧˋ ㄧ ㄒㄧㄢˋ)
the foremost line; the first line; the front

第一手資料(ㄉㄧˋ ㄧ ㄕㄡˇ ㄗ ㄌㄧㄠˋ)
the firsthand material

第一審(ㄉㄧˋ ㄧ ㄕㄣˇ)
the first instance; the first trial; the first hearing

第一人稱(ㄉㄧˋ ㄧ ㄖㄣˊ ㄔㄥ)
(grammar) the first person

第一次(ㄉㄧˋ ㄧ ㄘˋ)
the first time: 這是我生平第一次搭飛機。I took an airplane for the first time.

第一次世界大戰(ㄉㄧˋ ㄧ ㄘˋ ㄕˋ ㄐㄧㄝˋ ㄉㄚˋ ㄓㄢˋ)
the First World War; World War I

第一義(ㄉㄧˋ ㄧ ㄧˋ)
the primary sense

第五縱隊(ㄉㄧˋ ㄨˇ ㄗㄨㄥˋ ㄉㄨㄟˋ)
the fifth column

【笳】 4103
ㄐㄧㄚ jia jiā
a reed leaf whistle; the Tartar pipe

【笯】 4104
ㄋㄨˊ nu nú
a bird cage

【笴】 4105
ㄍㄜˇ gee gě
the stem of an arrow

【笤】 4106
ㄊㄧㄠˊ tyau tiáo
a bamboo broom

笤帚(ㄊㄧㄠˊ ·ㄓㄡ)
a bamboo broom

【笮】 4107
1. ㄗㄜˊ tzer zé
1. pressing
2. boards laid across rafters
3. an arrow bag

【笮】 4107
2. ㄓㄚˋ jah zhà
1. a kind of liquor container
2. to squeeze; to press

【范】 4108
ㄈㄢˋ fann fàn
1. a bamboo form
2. same as 範—a model

六畫

【筆】 4109
ㄅㄧˇ bii bǐ
1. a writing brush; a pen; a pencil
2. writer's skill or style
3. to write
4. a stroke; a touch
5. a unit of amount
6. (formerly) prose
7. a Chinese family name

筆墨(ㄅㄧˇ ㄇㄛˋ)
① pen and ink ② writing; words: 他們激動的心情難以用筆墨來形容。Words can hardly describe how excited they were.

筆墨生涯(ㄅㄧˇ ㄇㄛˋ ㄕㄥ ㄧㄚˊ)
a writing career: 她放棄了筆墨生涯。She abandoned her writing career.

筆帽(ㄅㄧˇ ㄇㄠˋ)
the cap of a pen or writing brush

筆名(ㄅㄧˇ ㄇㄧㄥˊ)
a pen name; *nom de plume*; a pseudonym

筆伐(ㄅㄧˇ ㄈㄚˊ)or(ㄅㄧˇ ㄈㄚˇ)
to attack in writings

筆法(ㄅㄧˇ ㄈㄚˇ)
① a calligraphic style ② a writing style

筆鋒(ㄅㄧˇ ㄈㄥ)
① a penpoint ② forcefulness of writing

筆答(ㄅㄧˇ ㄉㄚˊ)
written answers (in an examination)

筆底下(ㄅㄧˇ ㄉㄧˇ ·ㄒㄧㄚ)
under the sweep of a writer's pen — (figuratively) ability to write: 他筆底下不錯。He wrote well.

筆底生花(ㄅㄧˇ ㄉㄧˇ ㄕㄥ ㄏㄨㄚ)
(literally) to make flowers bloom under one's pen—to produce very fine writings

筆調(ㄅㄧˇ ㄉㄧㄠˋ)
the tone or style (of a writer)

筆套(ㄅㄧˇ ㄊㄠˋ)
the cap of a pen or writing brush

筆頭兒(ㄅㄧˇ ㄊㄡˊㄦ)
① a penpoint; the point of a writing brush ② ability to write; writing skill: 你筆頭兒很好。Your writing skill is very good.

筆談(ㄅㄧˇ ㄊㄢˊ)
to confer by writing

筆挺(ㄅㄧˇ ㄊㄧㄥˇ)
(said of dress) smooth ironed; spick-and-span; trim: 他穿着一身筆挺的制服。He was dressed in a trim uniform.

筆禿墨乾(ㄅㄧˇ ㄊㄨ ㄇㄛˋ ㄍㄢ)
(literally) The writing brush is worn out and the ink slab is dry.—to have written a great deal

筆筒(ㄅㄧˇ ㄊㄨㄥˇ)
a tubular penrack or penholder; a pen container

筆難盡述(ㄅㄧˇ ㄋㄢˊ ㄐㄧㄣˋ ㄕㄨˋ)
to defy full description in writing; too many to be put down in writing

筆力(ㄅㄧˇ ㄌㄧˋ)
① the vigor of style in literary composition ② the vigor of strokes in calligraphy or drawing

筆桿(ㄅㄧˇ ㄍㄢˇ)or 筆管(ㄅㄧˇ ㄍㄨㄢˇ)
the handle of a pen; a penholder

筆耕(ㄅㄧˇ ㄍㄥ)
to make a living by writing

筆酣墨飽(ㄅㄧˇ ㄏㄢ ㄇㄛˋ ㄅㄠˇ)
(literally) The pen is in full swing and the ink is plentiful.—to be in the middle of a creative writing mood

筆畫(ㄅㄧˇ ㄏㄨㄚˋ)
the number of strokes (in a character)

筆會(ㄅㄧˇ ㄏㄨㄟˋ)
P.E.N. (the International Association of Poets, Playwrights, Editors, Essayists, and Novelists)

筆跡(ㄅㄧˇ ㄐㄧ)
one's handwriting: 我核對他的筆跡。I identified his handwriting.

筆記(ㄅㄧˇ ㄐㄧˋ)
notes taken (of lectures, speeches, etc.)

筆記簿(ㄅㄧˇ ㄐㄧˋ ㄅㄨˋ)
a notebook

筆記小說(ㄅㄧˇ ㄐㄧˋ ㄒㄧㄠˇ ㄕㄨㄛ)
literary sketches; a sketchbook

筆架(ㄅㄧˇ ㄐㄧㄚˋ)
a penrack; a penholder

筆尖(ㄅㄧˇ ㄐㄧㄢ)
a penpoint; the point of a writing brush

筆鉛(ㄅㄧˇ ㄑㄧㄢ)
graphite; the lead in a pencil

筆洗(ㄅㄧˇ ㄒㄧˇ)or 筆海(ㄅㄧˇ ㄏㄞˇ)
a writing-brush washer

筆下留情(ㄅㄧˇ ㄒㄧㄚˋ ㄌㄧㄡˊ ㄑㄧㄥˊ)
to have some restraint when attacking others in writing; to be merciful in writing: 請您筆下留情。Please spare me in critical attacks.

筆下超生(ㄅㄧˇ ㄒㄧㄚˋ ㄔㄠ ㄕㄥ)
to relent when writing a verdict (a phrase for asking a judge to refrain from passing a death sentence)

筆心(ㄅㄧˇ ㄒㄧㄣ)
① pencil lead ② a refill (for a ball-point pen)

筆削(ㄅㄧˇ ㄒㄩㄝˋ)
to correct or improve (a composition)

筆之於書(ㄅㄧˇ ㄓ ㄩˊ ㄕㄨ)
to commit it to writing

筆直(ㄅㄧˇ ㄓˊ)
perfectly straight: 他的身子挺得筆直。He stood straight as a ramrod.

筆札(ㄅㄧˇ ㄓㄚˊ)
①writing materials②records

筆者(ㄅㄧˇ ㄓㄜˇ)
the (present) writer: (本文)筆者對它無記憶。It eludes this writer's memory.

筆戰(ㄅㄧˇ ㄓㄢˋ)
① a paper battle; paper warfare; a war of the pen ② to write polemics against (someone)

筆陣(ㄅㄧˇ ㄓㄣˋ)
a pen with a force as overwhelming as battle array

筆牀(ㄅㄧˇ ㄔㄨㄤˊ)
a penrack; a penholder

筆試(ㄅㄧˇ ㄕˋ)
a written examination: 他筆試及格了。He passed the written examination.

筆勢(ㄅㄧˇ ㄕˋ)
the force (of a calligraphy or writing style)

筆述(ㄅㄧˇ ㄕㄨˋ)
to narrate or describe in writing; narration or description in writing

筆順(ㄅㄧˇ ㄕㄨㄣˋ)
stroke order (for characters)

筆資(ㄅㄧˇ ㄗ)or 筆潤(ㄅㄧˇ ㄖㄨㄣˋ)
writer's fees; remuneration for writing

筆走龍蛇(ㄅㄧˇ ㄗㄡˇ ㄌㄨㄥˊ ㄕㄜˊ)
(literally) Dragons and snakes follow his writing brush.— a vigorous calligraphic style

筆算(ㄅㄧˇ ㄙㄨㄢˋ)
arithmetic worked out on paper; written calculation: 他的筆算有錯誤。He made a mistake in his written calculation.

筆意(ㄅㄧˇ ㄧˋ)
① a calligraphic style ② the meaning of a passage or sentence

筆譯(ㄅㄧˇ ㄧˋ)
written translation: 這本書筆譯有錯誤。This book has errors in written translation.

筆友(ㄅㄧˇ ㄧㄡˇ)
pen pals; friends among fellow writers

筆誤(ㄅㄧˇ ㄨˋ)
a slip of the pen: 這篇文章有筆誤。This essay has a slip of the pen.

【筇】 4110
ㄑㄩㄥˊ chyong qióng

a kind of bamboo (commonly used to make walking sticks)

筇杖(ㄑㄩㄥˊ ㄓㄤˋ)
a kind of bamboo stick

【筌】 4111
ㄑㄩㄢˊ chyuan quán

a bamboo fish trap

【筍】 4112
(笋) ㄙㄨㄣˇ soen sǔn

bamboo shoots or sprouts

筍鞭(ㄙㄨㄣˇ ㄅㄧㄢ)
the subterranean stem of bamboo

筍皮(ㄙㄨㄣˇ ㄆㄧˊ)or 筍殼(ㄙㄨㄣˇ ㄎㄜˊ)
the scale-like outer skin of a bamboo shoot

筍乾(ㄙㄨㄣˇ ㄍㄢ)
bamboo shoots cooked and dried for preservation

筍鷄(ㄙㄨㄣˇ ㄐㄧ)
a young chicken

筍尖(ㄙㄨㄣˇ ㄐㄧㄢ)
the tip, or upper part of tender bamboo shoots

筍衣(ㄙㄨㄣˇ ㄧ)
the shell of a bamboo shoot
筍鴨(ㄙㄨㄣˇ ㄧㄚ)
a young duck; a duckling
筍芽(ㄙㄨㄣˇ ㄧㄚˊ)
sprouting bamboo shoots

【等】 4113 ㄉㄥˇ deeng děng

1. rank; grade
2. same; equal
3. to wait: 請等一下。Would you mind waiting a moment?
4. when; till: 等你做完再走。Stay till you're through.
5. and so on; etc.; and the like
6. common

等比(ㄉㄥˇ ㄅㄧˇ)
geometric ratio; the ratio of equality
等比級數(ㄉㄥˇ ㄅㄧˇ ㄐㄧˊ ㄕㄨˋ)
geometric progression
等邊三角形(ㄉㄥˇ ㄅㄧㄢ ㄙㄢ ㄐㄧㄠˇ ㄒㄧㄥˊ)
an equilateral triangle
等不及(ㄉㄥˇ ˙ㄅㄨ ㄐㄧˊ)
①too impatient to wait ② unable to wait any longer
等偏線(ㄉㄥˇ ㄆㄧㄢ ㄒㄧㄢˋ)
an isogonic line; isogonics
等分
①(ㄉㄥˇ ㄈㄣ) division into equal parts; to divide into equal parts
②(ㄉㄥˇ ㄈㄣˋ) equal in quantities
等待(ㄉㄥˇ ㄉㄞˋ)
to wait for; to await
等到(ㄉㄥˇ ㄉㄠˋ)
by the time; when
等等(ㄉㄥˇ ㄉㄥˇ)
and so forth; et cetera; etc.
等等兒(ㄉㄥˇ ˙ㄉㄥㄦ)
to wait a while
等第(ㄉㄥˇ ㄉㄧˋ)
rank; grade
等同(ㄉㄥˇ ㄊㄨㄥˊ)
to equate; to be equal
等列(ㄉㄥˇ ㄌㄧㄝˋ)
①grade; rank ②to rank with
等量齊觀(ㄉㄥˇ ㄌㄧㄤˋ ㄑㄧˊ ㄍㄨㄢ)
to regard, or treat indiscriminately; to equate
等高線(ㄉㄥˇ ㄍㄠ ㄒㄧㄢˋ)
a contour
等號(ㄉㄥˇ ㄏㄠˋ)
the equal mark or sign(=)
等候(ㄉㄥˇ ㄏㄡˋ)
to wait; to await; to expect: 你們等候命令。You waited for instructions.
等級(ㄉㄥˇ ㄐㄧˊ)
grade; rank: A等級牛奶品質最好。Grade A milk is the best milk.
等價(ㄉㄥˇ ㄐㄧㄚˋ)
equal in value or prices
等角線(ㄉㄥˇ ㄐㄧㄠˇ ㄒㄧㄢˋ)
an isogonal line
等角形(ㄉㄥˇ ㄐㄧㄠˇ ㄒㄧㄥˊ)
isogonal figures
等角三角形(ㄉㄥˇ ㄐㄧㄠˇ ㄙㄢ ㄐㄧㄠˇ ㄒㄧㄥˊ)
an equiangular triangle
等距離(ㄉㄥˇ ㄐㄩˋ ㄌㄧˊ)
equal distance; equidistance
等情(ㄉㄥˇ ㄑㄧㄥˊ)
a phrase conventionally used in official communications immediately after a quotation from a letter by a lower agency
等閒(ㄉㄥˇ ㄒㄧㄢˊ)
①negligent; careless; aimlessly: 大好時光，不可等閒度過。Don't waste your precious time aimlessly. ②common; ordinary; usual; commonplace
等閒虛度(ㄉㄥˇ ㄒㄧㄢˊ ㄒㄩ ㄉㄨˋ)
to pass days in a useless or common way
等閒視之(ㄉㄥˇ ㄒㄧㄢˊ ㄕˋ ㄓ)
to regard it as of no importance
等著(ㄉㄥˇ ˙ㄓㄜ)
waiting for: 一封信等著你(來看)。A letter is waiting for you.
等著要(ㄉㄥˇ ˙ㄓㄜ ㄧㄠˋ)
①waiting to (do a thing) ② to want (something) immediately
等差(ㄉㄥˇ ㄔㄚ)
equal difference
等差級數(ㄉㄥˇ ㄔㄚ ㄐㄧˊ ㄕㄨˋ)
arithmetic progression
等式(ㄉㄥˇ ㄕˋ)
an equation; equality
等身(ㄉㄥˇ ㄕㄣ)
equal to one's height; as high as oneself: 他的著作等身。His works piled up as high as himself.
等人(ㄉㄥˇ ㄖㄣˊ)
①people of the same rank or grade ②to wait for someone ③and others
等子(ㄉㄥˇ ˙ㄗ)
small weights used in measuring precious metals, medicines, etc.
等次(ㄉㄥˇ ㄘˋ)
①rank; grade: 我們的產品分等次售出。Our products are sold in grades. ②sequence; order
等速度(ㄉㄥˇ ㄙㄨˋ ㄉㄨˋ)
uniform velocity
等速運動(ㄉㄥˇ ㄙㄨˋ ㄩㄣˋ ㄉㄨㄥˋ)
(physics) uniform motion
等而下之(ㄉㄥˇ ㄦˊ ㄒㄧㄚˋ ㄓ)
from that grade down
等一會兒(ㄉㄥˇ ㄧˋ ㄏㄨㄜˇㄦ)
①to wait a little while: 不要走那麼快！等我一會兒。Don't go so fast! Wait up for me! ②after a little while
等一等(ㄉㄥˇ ˙ㄧ ˙ㄉㄥ)or 等一下(ㄉㄥˇ ㄧˊ ㄒㄧㄚˋ)
to wait a little while
等腰三角形(ㄉㄥˇ ㄧㄠ ㄙㄢ ㄐㄧㄠˇ ㄒㄧㄥˊ)
an isosceles triangle
等由(ㄉㄥˇ ㄧㄡˊ)
a phrase conventionally used in official communications immediately after a quotation from a letter by an agency of the same rank
等因(ㄉㄥˇ ㄧㄣ)
a conventional phrase used in official communications immediately after a quotation from a letter by an agency of a higher rank or the same rank
等因奉此(ㄉㄥˇ ㄧㄣ ㄈㄥˋ ㄘˇ)
①a conventional phrase used in official communications immediately after a quotation from a letter by a superior agency and before a comment thereupon ②to handle official writings; to serve as a common civil servant
等位(ㄉㄥˇ ㄨㄟˋ)
grade; rank
等溫線(ㄉㄥˇ ㄨㄣ ㄒㄧㄢˋ)

〔竹部〕

〔竹部〕

isotherms
等於(ㄉㄥˇ ㄩˊ)
① to be equal to: 十角等於一元。Ten dimes are equal to one dollar. ② tantamount to; the same as: 這等於拒絕幫助我們。This is tantamount to refusal to help us.

【筏】 4114 ㄈㄚˊ far fá
a raft: 他乘木筏順流而下。He went down the river on a raft.
筏子(ㄈㄚˊ ˙ㄗ)
a raft

【筑】 4115 ㄓㄨˊ jwu zhú
a kind of ancient string instrument with five strings, thirteen strings, or twenty-one strings

【筐】 4116 ㄎㄨㄤ kuang kuāng
a rectangular chest or box woven from bamboo strips (or wicker); a shallow basket
筐篋(ㄎㄨㄤ ㄑㄧㄝˋ)
a rectangular box or chest
筐篋中物(ㄎㄨㄤ ㄑㄧㄝˋ ㄓㄨㄥ ㄨˋ)
a commonplace thing
筐子(ㄎㄨㄤ ˙ㄗ)or 筐兒(ㄎㄨㄤㄦ)
a bamboo chest; a wicker chest

【筒】 4117 ㄊㄨㄥˇ toong tǒng (又讀 ㄊㄨㄥˊ torng tóng)
a tube; a pipe; a cylinder: 這圓筒的容積是多少? What is the volume of this cylinder?
筒狀花冠(ㄊㄨㄥˇ ㄓㄨㄤˋ ㄏㄨㄚ ㄍㄨㄢ)
tubiflora
筒子(ㄊㄨㄥˇ ˙ㄗ)
a tube; a pipe

【筋】 4118 ㄐㄧㄣ jin jīn
1. tendons; sinews; muscles
2. veins that stand out under the skin
3. plant fibers resembling a tendon
筋疲力竭(ㄐㄧㄣ ㄆㄧˊ ㄌㄧˋ ㄐㄧㄝˊ)
to be completely exhausted; to have used up all energy
筋斗(ㄐㄧㄣ ㄉㄡˇ)
a somersault 亦作「跟頭」
筋骨(ㄐㄧㄣ ㄍㄨˇ)
① bones and muscles—physique; build (of one's body): 練功夫可以鍛鍊筋骨。Practicing kung fu strengthens the physique. ② strength
筋節(ㄐㄧㄣ ㄐㄧㄝˊ)
①tendons and joints ②forceful transitions between passages in a piece of writing
筋肉(ㄐㄧㄣ ㄖㄡˋ)
muscle
筋肉組織(ㄐㄧㄣ ㄖㄡˋ ㄗㄨˇ ㄓ)
muscular tissue

【答】 4119 1. ㄉㄚˊ dar dá
1. to answer; to reply: 他答覆了我的問題。He answered my question.
2. to reciprocate; to return
答拜(ㄉㄚˊ ㄅㄞˋ)
① to return a courtesy call ② to return a salutation
答辯(ㄉㄚˊ ㄅㄧㄢˋ)
to reply (to a verbal attack); to speak in self-defense; to defend oneself: 這被告有一律師替他答辯。The accused man had a lawyer to defend him.
答辯書(ㄉㄚˊ ㄅㄧㄢˋ ㄕㄨ)
a written answer, reply, or refutation (to a verbal attack or charge)
答不上來(ㄉㄚˊ ˙ㄅㄨ ㄕㄤˋ ㄌㄞˊ)
unable to answer; at a loss to answer
答非所問(ㄉㄚˊ ㄈㄟ ㄙㄨㄛˇ ㄨㄣˋ)
to give an irrelevant answer
答覆(ㄉㄚˊ ㄈㄨˋ)
to reply to, or answer (an inquiry, etc.); an answer; a reply: 我等候你的答覆。I wait for your reply.
答禮(ㄉㄚˊ ㄌㄧˇ)
to reciprocate another's courtesy; to return a salute
答錄機(ㄉㄚˊ ㄌㄨˋ ㄐㄧ)
an answering machine
答話(ㄉㄚˊ ㄏㄨㄚˋ)
to reply orally; an oral reply or answer
答謝(ㄉㄚˊ ㄒㄧㄝˋ)
to acknowledge; to convey one's thanks (for a favor, etc.)
答數(ㄉㄚˊ ㄕㄨˋ)
an answer (to an arithmetic problem)
答辭 or 答詞(ㄉㄚˊ ㄘˊ)
a thank-you speech; an address in reply; an answering speech
答案(ㄉㄚˊ ㄢˋ)
solution, answers (to examination questions, puzzles, etc.): 我找不到問題的答案。I seek no solution for the problem.
答問(ㄉㄚˊ ㄨㄣˋ)
questions and answers; catechism

【答】 4119 2. ㄉㄚ da dā
a variant of 答(ㄉㄚˊ)used only in some phrases
答答(ㄉㄚ ㄉㄚ)
① a crackling sound ② shy; bashful
答理(ㄉㄚ ㄌㄧˇ)
to answer a person; to respond
答腔(ㄉㄚ ㄑㄧㄤ)
a reply; words uttered in reply; to reply; to answer
答碴兒(ㄉㄚ ㄔㄚˊㄦ)
to continue another's utterance or speech
答應(ㄉㄚ ˙ㄧㄥ)
① to assent or agree to (a request); to promise (to do something) ② an answer: 他們按鈴但沒人答應。They rang but got no answer.

【筈】 4120 ㄍㄨㄚ gua guā
the end of an arrow

【笄】 4121 (笄) ㄐㄧ ji jī
a hairpin for fastening the hair (used by women in former times)
笄年(ㄐㄧ ㄋㄧㄢˊ)
(said of a woman) the age to begin wearing the hairpin —the beginning of maturity at 15
笄冠(ㄐㄧ ㄍㄨㄢ)
having just attained maturity

【策】 4122 ㄘㄜˋ tseh cè
1. a whip (for goading horses)
2. expository writings on government affairs
3. orders of appointment

4. a plan; a scheme; a stratagem
5. to whip; to spur; to urge; to impel
6. a Chinese family name

策馬(ㄘㄜˋ ㄇㄚˇ)
to whip a horse; to spur a horse

策命(ㄘㄜˋ ㄇㄧㄥˋ)
orders of appointment to or removal from an office

策反(ㄘㄜˋ ㄈㄢˇ)
to instigate defection in the enemy camp

策動(ㄘㄜˋ ㄉㄨㄥˋ)
to machinate; to maneuver; to instigate

策勵(ㄘㄜˋ ㄌㄧˋ)
to urge; to impel; to spur

策令(ㄘㄜˋ ㄌㄧㄥˋ)
presidential appointment to an office (in the early years of the Republic of China)

策論(ㄘㄜˋ ㄌㄨㄣˋ)
questions and themes (given in former civil service examinations)

策略(ㄘㄜˋ ㄌㄩㄝˋ)
a stratagem; a scheme; tactics

策畫(ㄘㄜˋ ㄏㄨㄚˋ)
to plan; to make plans

策杖(ㄘㄜˋ ㄓㄤˋ)
to use a walking stick

策士(ㄘㄜˋ ㄕˋ)
a scheming person; a schemer; a member of a brain trust

策試(ㄘㄜˋ ㄕˋ)
to test (candidates under the former civil service examination system)

策應(ㄘㄜˋ ㄧㄥˋ)
to act in concert with each other

策源地(ㄘㄜˋ ㄩㄢˊ ㄉㄧˋ)
① a (military) base ② the source (of a stream) ③ the place of origin

【筊】 4123
ㄐㄧㄠˇ jeau jiǎo
1. a rope made of bamboo strips
2. a kind of bamboo device used in divination

七畫

【筠】 4124
ㄩㄣˊ yun yún
the skin of the bamboo

【筥】 4125
ㄐㄩˇ jeu jǔ
a round bamboo basket for holding rice

【筦】 4126
ㄍㄨㄢˇ goan guǎn
1. same as 管—a pipe; a tube
2. a key
3. to be in charge
4. wind instruments made of bamboo (such as flutes, etc.)
5. a Chinese family name

【筩】 4127
ㄊㄨㄥˊ torng tóng
1. a bamboo pipe
2. a hook for fishing

【筮】 4128
ㄕˋ shyh shì
to divine by means of the stalks of the milfoil

筮人(ㄕˋ ㄖㄣˊ)
a fortuneteller

【筯】 4129
ㄓㄨˋ juh zhù
1. chopsticks
2. tongs

【筱】 4130
ㄒㄧㄠˇ sheau xiǎo
1. little slender bamboo
2. little; small

【筲】 4131
ㄕㄠ shau shāo
a basket for holding cooked rice

筲箕(ㄕㄠ ㄐㄧ)
a basket for washing rice

【筴】 4132
1. ㄘㄜˋ tseh cè
1. the milfoil used for divination in ancient times
2. same as 策

【筴】 4132
2. ㄐㄧㄚˊ jya jiá
tongs

【筳】 4133
ㄊㄧㄥˊ tyng tíng
little slender bamboo

【筵】 4134
ㄧㄢˊ yan yán
1. a bamboo mat
2. a feast; a banquet

筵席(ㄧㄢˊ ㄒㄧˊ)
① a mat for sitting on ② a feast; a banquet

【筭】 4135
ㄙㄨㄢˋ suann suàn
1. an ancient device for working with numbers
2. a scheme

【筷】 4136
ㄎㄨㄞˋ kuay kuài
chopsticks

筷子(ㄎㄨㄞˋ ·ㄗ)
chopsticks

【筧】 4137
ㄐㄧㄢˇ jean jiǎn
a bamboo water pipe

筧橋(ㄐㄧㄢˇ ㄑㄧㄠˊ)
a town north of Hangchow, Chekiang, the site of an airfield and an aviation school

八畫

【箋】 4138
(牋) ㄐㄧㄢ jian jiān
1. a commentary; a note
2. fancy note paper, letter paper, or stationery: 蠟箋 glazed note paper
3. letters; correspondence: 我有許多信箋。I have a good deal of correspondence.

箋牘(ㄐㄧㄢ ㄉㄨˊ)
letters; correspondence

箋紙(ㄐㄧㄢ ㄓˇ)
stationery; letter paper

箋札(ㄐㄧㄢ ㄓㄚˊ)
letters; correspondence

箋注(ㄐㄧㄢ ㄓㄨˋ)
notes and commentaries

【箏】 4139
ㄓㄥ jeng zhēng
1. a plucked stringed instrument in some ways similar to the zither
2. a kite: 他在放風箏。He is flying a kite.

【箑】 4140
ㄕㄚˋ shah shà
(又讀 ㄐㄧㄝˊ jye jié)
a fan

【箍】 4141
ㄍㄨ gu gū
1. a hoop
2. to bind round; to hoop

箍桶(ㄍㄨ ㄊㄨㄥˇ)
to fix hoops on a barrel

箍桶店(ㄍㄨ ㄊㄨㄥˇ ㄉㄧㄢˋ)
a coopery

【箔】 4142
ㄅㄛˊ bor bó
1. foil; gilt
2. a curtain

〔竹部〕

〔竹部〕

3. a frame for raising silkworms
4. paper tinsel burnt as offerings to the dead

【箕】 4143 ㄐㄧ ji jī

1. a winnowing basket; a sieve: 竹箕 a bamboo winnowing basket
2. a dust basket; a garbage basket; a dustpan
3. nonspiral lines on a fingertip

箕斗(ㄐㄧ ㄉㄡˇ)
spiral and nonspiral lines on the fingertips

箕斂(ㄐㄧ ㄌㄧㄢˋ)or 箕會(ㄐㄧ ㄏㄨㄟˋ)
to exploit or squeeze by ruthless taxation

箕踞(ㄐㄧ ㄐㄩˋ)
(said of a person) to sit with legs sprawled out

箕裘(ㄐㄧ ㄑㄧㄡˊ)
to carry on the trade of one's father (from 良弓之子必學爲箕，良冶之子必學爲裘, a passage in the *Book of Rites*)

箕帚(ㄐㄧ ㄓㄡˇ)
(literally) a dustpan and a broom—a wife or a concubine

箕踵(ㄐㄧ ㄓㄨㄥˇ)
wide in the front and narrow in the rear

箕山之志(ㄐㄧ ㄕㄢ ㄓ ㄓˋ)
the desire to live the life of a recluse

箕子(ㄐㄧ ㄗˇ)
Chi Tzu, a righteous courtier in the Yin Dynasty, who incurred the displeasure of his monarch Chou(紂王) and feigned madness

箕坐(ㄐㄧ ㄗㄨㄛˋ)
to sit with legs sprawled out

箕尾(ㄐㄧ ㄨㄟˇ)
the constellations Sagittarius and Scorpio

【算】 4144 ㄙㄨㄢˋ suann suàn

1. to count; to figure; to reckon; to compute; to calculate
2. to plan; to scheme
3. to infer; to guess; to foretell
4. to regard; to consider; to deem; to count
5. to be of importance; to be of consequence; to matter
6. a Chinese family name

算不得(ㄙㄨㄢˋ ˙ㄅㄨ ˙ㄉㄜ)
not to be counted or regarded as

算不了(ㄙㄨㄢˋ ˙ㄅㄨ ㄌㄧㄠˇ)
not to be counted or regarded as

算不了什麼(ㄙㄨㄢˋ ˙ㄅㄨ ㄌㄧㄠˇ ㄕㄜˊ ˙ㄇㄜ)
① not so serious or important; nothing to be alarmed or excited about ② not very impressive

算不清(ㄙㄨㄢˋ ˙ㄅㄨ ㄑㄧㄥ)
innumerable; uncountable

算盤(ㄙㄨㄢˋ ˙ㄆㄢ)
an abacus

算盤腦袋(ㄙㄨㄢˋ ˙ㄆㄢ ㄋㄠˇ ˙ㄉㄞ)
a miser

算盤疙瘩(ㄙㄨㄢˋ ˙ㄆㄢ ㄍㄜ ˙ㄉㄚ)
a kind of ornamental knots made in laces or ropes, looking like abacus beads

算盤子兒(ㄙㄨㄢˋ ˙ㄆㄢ ㄗㄜˇㄦ)
abacus beads

算命(ㄙㄨㄢˋ ㄇㄧㄥˋ)
to tell one's fortune

算命的(ㄙㄨㄢˋ ㄇㄧㄥˋ ˙ㄉㄜ)or 算命先生(ㄙㄨㄢˋ ㄇㄧㄥˋ ㄒㄧㄢ ˙ㄕㄥ)
a fortuneteller

算法(ㄙㄨㄢˋ ㄈㄚˇ)
arithmetic; a method of calculation

算得甚麼(ㄙㄨㄢˋ ˙ㄉㄜ ㄕㄜˊ ˙ㄇㄜ)or 算不得甚麼(ㄙㄨㄢˋ ˙ㄅㄨ ˙ㄉㄜ ㄕㄜˊ ˙ㄇㄜ)
of no special account or consequence; trifling; trivial 或 It's nothing. 那算不得甚麼，實在是容易的事。That does not bother me, it's quite simple.

算題(ㄙㄨㄢˋ ㄊㄧˊ)
an arithmetic problem

算了(ㄙㄨㄢˋ ˙ㄌㄜ)
① Forget about it. 或 That's enough! ② settled; (said of a case) concluded

算來(ㄙㄨㄢˋ ㄌㄞ)
by counting (often used in connection with time or money)

算來算去(ㄙㄨㄢˋ ㄌㄞ ㄙㄨㄢˋ ㄑㄩˋ)
to compute or count over and over again

算曆(ㄙㄨㄢˋ ㄌㄧˋ)
arithmetic and the calendar

算卦(ㄙㄨㄢˋ ㄍㄨㄚˋ)
to tell one's fortune

算卦的(ㄙㄨㄢˋ ㄍㄨㄚˋ ˙ㄉㄜ)
a fortuneteller

算計(ㄙㄨㄢˋ ˙ㄐㄧ)
① to consider; to plan: 我正算計着要去歐洲。I am planning a trip to Europe. ② to plot against someone

算計人(ㄙㄨㄢˋ ˙ㄐㄧ ㄖㄣˊ)
to plot against a person: 他暗中算計人。He secretly plotted against others.

算起來(ㄙㄨㄢˋ ㄑㄧˇ ㄌㄞˊ)
in total; all told; in all; in the aggregate

算清(ㄙㄨㄢˋ ㄑㄧㄥ)
to find out the sum, ratio, etc. of

算學(ㄙㄨㄢˋ ㄒㄩㄝˊ)
mathematics

算賬(ㄙㄨㄢˋ ㄓㄤˋ)
① to compute income and expense; to settle an account: 他算帳算得很快。He is quick at accounts. ② to get even (with a person): 回頭同那壞蛋算賬。The scoundrel will pay for this.

算籌(ㄙㄨㄢˋ ㄔㄡˊ)
tallies used for working with numbers

算式(ㄙㄨㄢˋ ㄕˋ)
a mathematical formula

算上(ㄙㄨㄢˋ ㄕㄤˋ)
to count in; to include: 我們今天宴會也算上她。We included her in today's party.

算數(ㄙㄨㄢˋ ㄕㄨˋ)
① to be of importance ② to count; to stand; to mean what one says; valid: 我說話是算數的。I mean what I say.

算術(ㄙㄨㄢˋ ㄕㄨˋ)
arithmetic

算術級數(ㄙㄨㄢˋ ㄕㄨˋ ㄐㄧˊ ㄕㄨˋ)
an arithmetic progression

算無遺策(ㄙㄨㄢˋ ㄨˊ ㄧˊ ㄘㄜˋ)
to plan very carefully with every conceivable possibility taken into account

【箠】 4145 ㄔㄨㄟˊ chwei chuí

1. a whip (for goading horses)
2. whipping or flogging (as a punishment)

箠罵(ㄔㄨㄟˊ ㄇㄚˋ)

to flog and curse

箠楚(ㄔㄨㄟˊ ㄔㄨˇ)
whipping or flogging as a punishment

【箅】 4146
ㄅㄧˋ bih bì

a bamboo grid for steaming food

【箜】 4147
ㄎㄨㄥ kong kōng

a kind of ancient plucked stringed instrument

箜篌(ㄎㄨㄥ ㄏㄡˊ)
a kind of ancient musical instrument with 23 strings

【箝】 4148
ㄑㄧㄢˊ chyan qián

1. tongs; pincers; tweezers: 火箝 firetongs
2. to tweezer

箝口(ㄑㄧㄢˊ ㄎㄡˇ)
①to keep one's mouth shut; to keep silent ②to prevent from talking; to force to keep silent; to gag

箝口結舌(ㄑㄧㄢˊ ㄎㄡˇ ㄐㄧㄝˊ ㄕㄜˊ)
①to keep silent ②to be forced to keep silent

箝緊(ㄑㄧㄢˊ ㄐㄧㄣˇ)
to clasp tightly

箝形攻勢(ㄑㄧㄢˊ ㄒㄧㄥˊ ㄍㄨㄥ ㄕˋ)
(military operations) a pincers movement

箝制(ㄑㄧㄢˊ ㄓˋ)
to use pressure upon; to force; to pin down

箝子(ㄑㄧㄢˊ ˙ㄗ)
tongs; tweezers; pincers

箝語(ㄑㄧㄢˊ ㄩˇ)
to restrict freedom of speech

【管】 4149
ㄍㄨㄢˇ goan guǎn

1. a tube; a pipe; a duct
2. a wind instrument
3. to control; to manage; to take care of; to keep: 他把工廠管得井井有條。He keeps the factory in good order.
4. to heed; to pay attention to
5. to provide
6. to guarantee: 此照相機管用一年。This camera is guaranteed for one year.
7. to meddle in; to interfere in; to bother about: 別管我。Do not interfere with me.
8. a key
9. a Chinese family name

管保(ㄍㄨㄢˇ ㄅㄠˇ)
to guarantee: 我管保他不知道。I'm sure that he does not know.

管鮑(ㄍㄨㄢˇ ㄅㄠˋ)
Kuan Chung (管仲) and Pao Shu-ya (鮑叔牙) of the Epoch of Warring States (equivalent to Damon and Pythias, or David and Jonathan)

管鮑分金(ㄍㄨㄢˇ ㄅㄠˋ ㄈㄣ ㄐㄧㄣ)
a friendship so close as to make no distinction between each other's wealth 參看「管鮑」

管不了(ㄍㄨㄢˇ ˙ㄅㄨ ㄌㄧㄠˇ)
to lack the capacity to control

管不着(ㄍㄨㄢˇ ˙ㄅㄨ ㄓㄠˊ)
to have no authority to interfere in: 我怎麼管不着? Why shouldn't I interfere?

管不住(ㄍㄨㄢˇ ˙ㄅㄨ ㄓㄨˋ)
to be incapable of controlling

管飯(ㄍㄨㄢˇ ㄈㄢˋ)
(said of an employer, etc.) to provide meals: 這雇主不管飯。This employer does not provide meals.

管待(ㄍㄨㄢˇ ㄉㄞˋ)
to entertain; to fete; to show hospitality to

管道(ㄍㄨㄢˇ ㄉㄠˋ)
①a pipeline; piping; a conduit; tubing: 煤氣管道 gas piping ②a channel (for communication, consultation, etc.)

管寧(ㄍㄨㄢˇ ㄋㄧㄥˊ)
Kuan Ning, 158-241, a hermit during the Epoch of the Three Kingdoms

管理(ㄍㄨㄢˇ ㄌㄧˇ)
to manage; to administer; to handle; to take care of; management; administration: 在他的管理下，公司發展得很快。The company developed rapidly under his administration.

管理顧問(ㄍㄨㄢˇ ㄌㄧˇ ㄍㄨˋ ㄨㄣˋ)
a management consultant

管理局(ㄍㄨㄢˇ ㄌㄧˇ ㄐㄩˊ)or 管理處(ㄍㄨㄢˇ ㄌㄧˇ ㄔㄨˋ)
a government agency in charge of the administration of national railways, highways, forestry, etc.; a special administration

管理人(ㄍㄨㄢˇ ㄌㄧˇ ㄖㄣˊ)
an administrator; a manager; a supervisor; a superintendent; a caretaker; a trustee; a custodian; a keeper

管理員(ㄍㄨㄢˇ ㄌㄧˇ ㄩㄢˊ)
a keeper; a caretaker; an administrator; a manager; a custodian; a janitor

管窺蠡測(ㄍㄨㄢˇ ㄎㄨㄟ ㄌㄧˊ ㄘㄜˋ)
(literally) to view the sky through a tube and measure the sea with a calabash — restricted in vision and shallow in understanding

管伙食(ㄍㄨㄢˇ ㄏㄨㄛˇ ㄕˊ)
①to take charge of meals for a whole organization or a group of people ②(said of an employer) to provide meals

管換(ㄍㄨㄢˇ ㄏㄨㄢˋ)
(a phrase commonly used by shopkeepers) responsible for replacing defective merchandise

管家
①(ㄍㄨㄢˇ ㄐㄧㄚ) to housekeep; to run a home
②(ㄍㄨㄢˇ ˙ㄐㄧㄚ) a housekeeper

管家婆(ㄍㄨㄢˇ ㄐㄧㄚ ㄆㄛˊ)
a housekeeper

管教
①(ㄍㄨㄢˇ ㄐㄧㄠˋ) sure to make (a person feel or act in some predicted way): 聽我的話管教你成功。Surely you will succeed if you follow my advice.
②(ㄍㄨㄢˇ ˙ㄐㄧㄠ) to direct and teach (children, students, etc.); to discipline and educate

管見(ㄍㄨㄢˇ ㄐㄧㄢˋ)
my narrow view or opinion; my humble opinion: 請容陳管見。Please allow me to state my humble opinion.

管轄(ㄍㄨㄢˇ ㄒㄧㄚˊ)
to have jurisdiction over; to have control over

管轄權(ㄍㄨㄢˇ ㄒㄧㄚˊ ㄑㄩㄢˊ)
jurisdiction

管下(ㄍㄨㄢˇ ㄒㄧㄚˋ)
subordinates

管絃 or 管弦(ㄍㄨㄢˇ ㄒㄧㄢˊ)
①wind and stringed instruments ②piping and fiddling

管絃樂(ㄍㄨㄢˇ ㄒㄧㄢˊ ㄩㄝˋ)
orchestral music

管絃樂團(ㄍㄨㄢˇ ㄒㄧㄢˊ ㄩㄝˋ ㄊㄨㄢˊ)
an orchestra

管閒事(ㄍㄨㄢˇ ㄒㄧㄢˊ ㄕˋ)
nosy; to meddle; to poke one's nose into others' business

管制(ㄍㄨㄢˇ ㄓˋ)
to control; control

管賬的(ㄍㄨㄢˇ ㄓㄤˋ ˙ㄉㄜ)
a bookkeeper

管狀花(ㄍㄨㄢˇ ㄓㄨㄤˋ ㄏㄨㄚ)
flowers of tubuliflorous plants

管中窺豹(ㄍㄨㄢˇ ㄓㄨㄥ ㄎㄨㄟ ㄅㄠˋ)
(literally) to look at the spots of a leopard through a tube—to have partial knowledge of something

管仲(ㄍㄨㄢˇ ㄓㄨㄥˋ)
Kuan Chung, ?-644 B.C., prime minister of the state of Chi (齊) during the Epoch of Warring States

管事(ㄍㄨㄢˇ ㄕˋ)
①a housekeeper or shopkeeper ②effective; useful; to work ③to take care of; to administer; to be in charge: 那裡誰管事? Who is in charge there?

管事的(ㄍㄨㄢˇ ㄕˋ ˙ㄉㄜ)
a butler

管束(ㄍㄨㄢˇ ㄕㄨˋ)
to control; to restrain; to discipline

管子
①(ㄍㄨㄢˇ ㄗˇ) ⓐ a book authored by Kuan Chung (管仲) and later expanded by others ⓑ Kuan Chung (管仲), ?-644B.C. 亦作「管氏」 ②(ㄍㄨㄢˇ ˙ㄗ) a tube; a pipe; a duct

管兒(ㄍㄨㄚˇㄦ)
a tube; a pipe; a duct

管晏(ㄍㄨㄢˇ ㄧㄢˋ)
Kuan Chung (管仲) and Yen Ying (晏嬰), both famed statesmen in the state of Chi (齊) during the Epoch of Warring States

管籥(ㄍㄨㄢˇ ㄩㄝˋ)
①a flute; a pipe ②a key

管樂(ㄍㄨㄢˇ ㄩㄝˋ)
wind music

管樂隊(ㄍㄨㄢˇ ㄩㄝˋ ㄉㄨㄟˋ)
a wind band; a band

管樂器(ㄍㄨㄢˇ ㄩㄝˋ ㄑㄧˋ)
wind instruments; the wind

管用(ㄍㄨㄢˇ ㄩㄥˋ)
useful; effective; to work: 這藥很管用。This medicine is very effective.

【箚】 4150
ㄓㄚˊ jar zhá

1. correspondence; letters
2. (in former times) written directives or instructions to a lower government agency

箚記(ㄓㄚˊ ㄐㄧˋ)
①a notebook ②to put down by items

箚子(ㄓㄚˊ ˙ㄗ)
(in former times) written directives or instructions from a higher office

【箙】 4151
ㄈㄨˊ fwu fú

a quiver

【箇】 4152
ㄍㄜˋ geh gè

same as 個—a numerary adjunct for practically everything

箇別(ㄍㄜˋ ㄅㄧㄝˊ)
individually; separately

箇體(ㄍㄜˋ ㄊㄧˇ)
an entity

箇性(ㄍㄜˋ ㄒㄧㄥˋ)
individuality; individual traits; personality

箇中秘密(ㄍㄜˋ ㄓㄨㄥ ㄇㄧˋ ㄇㄧˋ)
the inside story

箇人(ㄍㄜˋ ㄖㄣˊ)
①an individual ②I

箇子(ㄍㄜˋ ˙ㄗ)
a person's stature

箇案(ㄍㄜˋ ㄢˋ)
(social work) an individual case as a subject of study

箇位(ㄍㄜˋ ㄨㄟˋ)
a unit

九畫

【箬】 4153
(篛) ㄖㄨㄛˋ ruoh ruò

1. the bamboo cuticle
2. a kind of bamboo with broad leaves which are often used to make various coverings

箬篷(ㄖㄨㄛˋ ㄆㄥˊ)
a hood, or top, made of bamboo leaves (usually for boats)

箬帽芒鞋(ㄖㄨㄛˋ ㄇㄠˋ ㄇㄤˊ ㄒㄧㄝˊ)
a bamboo hat and straw sandals—the clothing of a farmer or hermit

箬笠(ㄖㄨㄛˋ ㄌㄧˋ)or 箬帽(ㄖㄨㄛˋ ㄇㄠˋ)
a wide, conical bamboo hat

箬竹(ㄖㄨㄛˋ ㄓㄨˊ)
a variety of bamboo, with broad leaves that are often used to make hats, etc.

【箱】 4154
ㄒㄧㄤ shiang xiāng

1. a box; a chest; a trunk: 把行李放在行李箱中。Put the baggage in the trunk.
2. the box or body of a carriage

箱底兒(ㄒㄧㄤ ㄉㄧˇㄦ)
minor actors and actresses in a dramatic troupe

箱籠(ㄒㄧㄤ ㄌㄨㄥˊ)
boxes; chests; trunks: 我給他兩箱籠蜜柑。I gave him two boxes of oranges.

箱根(ㄒㄧㄤ ㄍㄣ)
Hakone, Japan

箱篋(ㄒㄧㄤ ㄑㄧㄝˋ)
boxes; chests

箱屍案(ㄒㄧㄤ ㄕ ㄢˋ)
a murder case with the victim's body found in a trunk

箱子(ㄒㄧㄤ ˙ㄗ)
a box; a chest; a trunk: 他用紙板做一個箱子。He made a box with paperboard.

【箭】 4155
ㄐㄧㄢˋ jiann jiàn

1. an arrow
2. a sign which is like an arrow
3. *Sinarundinaria nitida*, a variety of bamboo

箭靶(ㄐㄧㄢˋ ㄅㄚˇ)
a target for archery

箭風(ㄐㄧㄢˋ ㄈㄥ)
a destructive wind

箭搭上弓(ㄐㄧㄢˋ ㄉㄚ ㄕㄤˋ ㄍㄨㄥ)

(literally) The arrow is fitted to the string.—① ready to go ② imminent
箭袋(ㄐㄧㄢ ㄉㄞˋ)or 箭壺(ㄐㄧㄢˋ ㄏㄨˊ)
a quiver
箭頭子(ㄐㄧㄢˋ ㄊㄡˊ ·ㄗ)
an arrowhead—(figuratively) speedily; fast
箭頭文字(ㄐㄧㄢˋ ㄊㄡˊ ㄨㄣˊ ㄗˋ)
cuneiform characters
箭箙(ㄐㄧㄢˋ ㄊㄨㄥˇ)or 箭筒(ㄐㄧㄢˋ ㄊㄨㄥˇ)
a quiver
箭樓(ㄐㄧㄢˋ ㄌㄡˊ)
battlements
箭豬(ㄐㄧㄢˋ ㄓㄨ)
a porcupine
箭如雨下(ㄐㄧㄢˋ ㄖㄨˊ ㄩˇ ㄒㄧㄚˋ)
Arrows descend like a shower.
箭在絃上(ㄐㄧㄢˋ ㄗㄞˋ ㄒㄧㄢˊ ·ㄕㄤ)
(literally) The arrow is already fitted to the string.—① imminent action expected ② There can be no turning back.
箭鏃(ㄐㄧㄢˋ ㄘㄨˊ)
an arrowhead
箭筍(ㄐㄧㄢˋ ㄙㄨㄣˇ)
small bamboo shoots
箭衣(ㄐㄧㄢˋ ㄧ)
uniform for an archer
箭無虛發(ㄐㄧㄢˋ ㄨˊ ㄒㄩ ㄈㄚ)or 箭無空發(ㄐㄧㄢˋ ㄨˊ ㄎㄨㄥ ㄈㄚ)
(literally) No arrow that is shot is wasted.—excellent marksmanship: 他是位箭無虛發的射手。He is an accurate marksman.

【箯】 4156
ㄅㄧㄢ bian bian
a bamboo sedan chair

【箸】 4157
ㄓㄨˋ juh zhù
chopsticks

【箴】 4158
ㄓㄣ jen zhen
1. a probe; a needle
2. to warn; to admonish
箴砭(ㄓㄣ ㄅㄧㄢ)
stone probes (used in acupuncture)
箴銘(ㄓㄣ ㄇㄧㄥˊ)
admonitions or warnings carved on a stone
箴規(ㄓㄣ ㄍㄨㄟ)
warnings; admonitions; to admonish; to exhort: 傳道者箴規其聽衆爲善。The preacher exhorted his congregation to do good.
箴諫(ㄓㄣ ㄐㄧㄢˋ)
to admonish; to exhort; to caution against
箴石(ㄓㄣ ㄕˊ)
stone probes or needles (used in acupuncture)
箴言(ㄓㄣ ㄧㄢˊ)
admonitions; warning words; a maxim:「三思而後行」是一句箴言。"Look before you leap" is a maxim.

【節】 4159
ㄐㄧㄝˊ jye jié
1. a node; a knot; a joint
2. a passage; a paragraph; a section
3. principles; integrity; fidelity; constancy; uprightness
4. a festival; a holiday
5. seasons
6. (music) beats; rhythm; time
7. to restrain; to control; to restrict
8. to curtail; to economize
節本(ㄐㄧㄝˊ ㄅㄣˇ)
an abridged edition
節拍(ㄐㄧㄝˊ ㄆㄞ)
(music) beats, rhythm or time: 他用快節拍演奏。He played in quick rhythm.
節旄(ㄐㄧㄝˊ ㄇㄠˊ)
tassels on a tally
節目(ㄐㄧㄝˊ ㄇㄨˋ)
the events of an entertainment or the like; a program; items on a program: 整個節目都很令人愉快。The entire program was delightful.
節目單(ㄐㄧㄝˊ ㄇㄨˋ ㄉㄢ)
a program (of a concert, show, etc.)
節婦(ㄐㄧㄝˊ ㄈㄨˋ)
① a woman adhering to widowhood ② a woman who dies for protecting her chastity
節電(ㄐㄧㄝˊ ㄉㄧㄢˋ)
to save electricity; to cut down power consumption: 我們應該節電。We should cut down power consumption.
節度(ㄐㄧㄝˊ ㄉㄨˋ)
an official in charge of military supply (set up in the kingdom of Wu during the Epoch of Three Kingdoms)
節度使(ㄐㄧㄝˊ ㄉㄨˋ ㄕˇ)or(ㄐㄧㄝˊ ㄉㄨˋ ㄕˋ)
a governor of one or more provinces in charge of both civil and military affairs during the Tang Dynasty
節勞(ㄐㄧㄝˊ ㄌㄠˊ)
to conserve one's energy
節禮(ㄐㄧㄝˊ ㄌㄧˇ)
presents sent on a festival
節流(ㄐㄧㄝˊ ㄌㄧㄡˊ)
to curtail expenditures; to cut down expenses: 我們必須開源節流。We have to earn more income and cut down expenses.
節令(ㄐㄧㄝˊ ㄌㄧㄥˋ)
festivals
節錄(ㄐㄧㄝˊ ㄌㄨˋ)
① to excerpt ② an excerpt
節略(ㄐㄧㄝˊ ㄌㄩㄝˋ)
an outline; a summary
節概(ㄐㄧㄝˊ ㄍㄞˋ)
principles; integrity; uprightness
節骨眼(ㄐㄧㄝˊ ㄍㄨˇ ㄧㄢˇ)
a critical juncture; a critical moment
節節敗退(ㄐㄧㄝˊ ㄐㄧㄝˊ ㄅㄞˋ ㄊㄨㄟˋ)
to suffer one defeat after another
節節勝利(ㄐㄧㄝˊ ㄐㄧㄝˊ ㄕㄥˋ ㄌㄧˋ)
to score one victory after another
節儉(ㄐㄧㄝˊ ㄐㄧㄢˇ)
to be frugal; to practice austerity; to economize
節敬(ㄐㄧㄝˊ ㄐㄧㄥˋ)
presents sent on festivals
節氣(ㄐㄧㄝˊ ㄑㄧˋ)
the 24 seasonal periods into which the lunar year is divided, each consisting of 15 days
節孝(ㄐㄧㄝˊ ㄒㄧㄠˋ)
wifely fidelity and filial piety
節制(ㄐㄧㄝˊ ㄓˋ)
to restrict; to hold down; to keep within limits; to limit; to control: 他不能節制他的脾氣。He lost control of his temper.
節制生育(ㄐㄧㄝˊ ㄓˋ ㄕㄥ ㄩˋ)
to practice birth control;

〔竹部〕

birth control 亦作「節育」

節制資本(ㄐㄧㄝˊ ㄓˋ ㄗ ㄅㄣˇ)
the restriction of private capital (one of the measures under *The Three Principles of the People* by Dr. Sun Yat-sen)

節食(ㄐㄧㄝˊ ㄕˊ)
to go on a diet: 她太胖，故須節食。She got so fat that she had to diet.

節上生枝(ㄐㄧㄝˊ ㄕㄤˋ ㄕㄥ ㄓ)
one complication arising from another

節省(ㄐㄧㄝˊ ㄕㄥˇ)
to economize; to save; to use with thrift: 機械節省勞工。Machines save labor.

節省費用(ㄐㄧㄝˊ ㄕㄥˇ ㄈㄟˋ ㄩㄥˋ) or 節省開支(ㄐㄧㄝˊ ㄕㄥˇ ㄎㄞ ㄓ)
to cut down expenses; to practice economy; to economize; to be frugal; to be thrifty

節省時間(ㄐㄧㄝˊ ㄕㄥˇ ㄕˊ ㄐㄧㄢ)
to save time

節日(ㄐㄧㄝˊ ㄖˋ)
a festival; a holiday

節子(ㄐㄧㄝˊ ˙ㄗ)
a node; a joint; a knot

節奏(ㄐㄧㄝˊ ㄗㄡˋ)
rhythm: 他以緩慢的節奏演奏。He played in slow rhythm.

節奏樂器(ㄐㄧㄝˊ ㄗㄡˋ ㄩㄝˋ ㄑㄧˋ)
rhythmical instruments (such as drums, triangles, etc.)

節足動物(ㄐㄧㄝˊ ㄗㄨˊ ㄉㄨㄥˋ ㄨˋ)
an arthropod

節操(ㄐㄧㄝˊ ㄘㄠ)
constancy; fidelity; integrity; chastity; moral fortitude

節哀(ㄐㄧㄝˊ ㄞ)
to restrain grief

節哀順變(ㄐㄧㄝˊ ㄞ ㄕㄨㄣˋ ㄅㄧㄢˋ)
to restrain grief and accept the change (common advice to the bereaved)

節兒(ㄐㄧㄜˊㄦ)
① a node; a joint; a knot ② a section or passage (of a piece of writing) ③ a festival

節衣縮食(ㄐㄧㄝˊ ㄧ ㄙㄨㄛ ㄕˊ)
to economize clothing and food; to live a frugal life

節義(ㄐㄧㄝˊ ㄧˋ)
integrity; fidelity; constancy; chastity

節外生枝(ㄐㄧㄝˊ ㄨㄞˋ ㄕㄥ ㄓ)
to bring about extra complications; to run into unexpected difficulty; to hit a snag

節育(ㄐㄧㄝˊ ㄩˋ)
to practice birth control; birth control

節慾(ㄐㄧㄝˊ ㄩˋ)
to restrain or control one's desires; to be ascetic; to practice abstinence

節約(ㄐㄧㄝˊ ㄩㄝ)
to economize; to be frugal; to use with thrift; to save: 我們當厲行節約。We should practice strict economy.

節用(ㄐㄧㄝˊ ㄩㄥˋ)
to cut down expenses; to economize; to practice economy

【篁】 4160 ㄏㄨㄤˊ hwang huáng

bamboo; a bamboo bush; a clump of bamboos; a bamboo grove

【範】 4161 ㄈㄢˋ fann fàn

1. a model; a form; an example; a pattern: 這學生是勤勉的模範。This student is a model of diligence.
2. range; scope; limits
3. to observe the proper rules
4. a Chinese family name

範本(ㄈㄢˋ ㄅㄣˇ)
① a copy or copybook (for penmanship, calligraphy, painting, etc.) ②a model; an example

範例(ㄈㄢˋ ㄌㄧˋ)
an example; a model: 把這個當範例用。Use this as a model.

範疇(ㄈㄢˋ ㄔㄡˊ)
category

範圍(ㄈㄢˋ ㄨㄟˊ)
range; scope; a sphere: 這件事超過我的能力範圍。It is beyond the range of my ability.

範文(ㄈㄢˋ ㄨㄣˊ)
a model essay

【篇】 4162 ㄆㄧㄢ pian piān

1. a numerary adjunct for compositions, poems, etc.: 這是一篇不朽的文章。This is an immortal composition.
2. a chapter; a section; a part
3. a page
4. books; volumes

篇兒(ㄆㄧㄚㄦ)
① a piece (of poetry, etc.); an article ② a page

篇目(ㄆㄧㄢ ㄇㄨˋ)
titles; headings

篇幅(ㄆㄧㄢ ㄈㄨˊ)
① the length (of a piece of writing) ② space (of a periodical or newspaper)

篇籍(ㄆㄧㄢ ㄐㄧˊ)
books

篇章(ㄆㄧㄢ ㄓㄤ)
books; literary compositions; poems

篇什(ㄆㄧㄢ ㄕˊ)
poems

【篆】 4163 ㄓㄨㄢˋ juann zhuàn

1. the seal type, an ancient calligraphic style
2. a seal
3. a Chinese family name

篆刻(ㄓㄨㄢˋ ㄎㄜˋ)
to cut a seal in the seal type

篆章(ㄓㄨㄢˋ ㄓㄤ)
a seal; a chop

篆書(ㄓㄨㄢˋ ㄕㄨ)
the seal type, an ancient calligraphic style

篆字(ㄓㄨㄢˋ ㄗˋ) or 篆文(ㄓㄨㄢˋ ㄨㄣˊ)
characters written in the seal type

篆額(ㄓㄨㄢˋ ㄜˊ)
to inscribe characters on the top of a tablet in the seal type

篆務(ㄓㄨㄢˋ ㄨˋ)
official affairs

【篋】 4164 ㄑㄧㄝˋ chieh qiè

a chest; a box; a trunk

篋篋(ㄑㄧㄝˋ ㄑㄧㄝˋ)
long and thin; slender

篋笥(ㄑㄧㄝˋ ㄙˋ)
a bamboo box for holding books and clothes, etc.

【篌】 4165 ㄏㄡˊ hour hóu

a kind of ancient musical instrument like a lute 參看「箜篌」

十畫

【築】 4166 ㄓㄨˊ jwu zhú
1. to build (out of earth, rock, etc.)
2. a house; a room
築壇(ㄓㄨˊ ㄊㄢˊ)
to build an altar
築堤(ㄓㄨˊ ㄊㄧˊ)
to build a dike or embankment
築土(ㄓㄨˊ ㄊㄨˇ)
to build an earth-fill structure
築路(ㄓㄨˊ ㄌㄨˋ)
to build roads
築路機(ㄓㄨˊ ㄌㄨˋ ㄐㄧ)
a road-building machine; a grader (for grading a roadway)
築牆(ㄓㄨˊ ㄑㄧㄤˊ)
to build walls
築巢(ㄓㄨˊ ㄔㄠˊ)
to build a nest
築城(ㄓㄨˊ ㄔㄥˊ)
to build a castle or city wall
築室道謀(ㄓㄨˊ ㄕˋ ㄉㄠˋ ㄇㄡˊ)
(literally) to consult passers-by about building a house—to seek the advice of those who have little concern for one's problem

【篝】 4167 ㄍㄡ gou gōu
a basket; a cage

【篚】 4168 ㄈㄟˇ feei fěi
a square bamboo basket

【篡】 4169 ㄘㄨㄢˋ tsuann cuàn
to seize (power, the throne, etc.); to usurp
篡奪(ㄘㄨㄢˋ ㄉㄨㄛˊ)
to seize (power, the throne, etc.); to usurp
篡逆(ㄘㄨㄢˋ ㄋㄧˋ)
to rebel; to revolt
篡立(ㄘㄨㄢˋ ㄌㄧˋ)
to become an unlawful ruler
篡改(ㄘㄨㄢˋ ㄍㄞˇ)
to alter a piece of writing with an evil intent; to tamper (with a document, etc.)
篡弒(ㄘㄨㄢˋ ㄕˋ)
to commit regicide
篡賊(ㄘㄨㄢˋ ㄗㄟˊ)
a usurper
篡位(ㄘㄨㄢˋ ㄨㄟˋ)
to seize the throne

【篤】 4170 ㄉㄨˇ duu dǔ
1. deep; much; great; profound
2. dangerous; serious
3. generous
4. to consolidate; to make solid
5. to limit
篤定(ㄉㄨˇ ㄉㄧㄥˋ)
(informally) very confident; assured
篤老(ㄉㄨˇ ㄌㄠˇ)
very old; of a venerable age
篤癃(ㄉㄨˇ ㄌㄨㄥˊ)
an invalid or disabled person
篤厚(ㄉㄨˇ ㄏㄡˋ)
very sincere
篤疾(ㄉㄨˇ ㄐㄧˊ)
a fatal illness; a serious disease
篤敬(ㄉㄨˇ ㄐㄧㄥˋ)
sincerely respectful
篤劇(ㄉㄨˇ ㄐㄩˋ)
seriously ill
篤信(ㄉㄨˇ ㄒㄧㄣˋ)
① to have sincere faith in ② honest; trustworthy
篤行(ㄉㄨˇ ㄒㄧㄥˋ)
honest in behavior
篤學(ㄉㄨˇ ㄒㄩㄝˊ)
to study diligently
篤志(ㄉㄨˇ ㄓˋ)
firm determination
篤實(ㄉㄨˇ ㄕˊ)
① sincere; honest; candid; faithful ② solid; sound
篤守(ㄉㄨˇ ㄕㄡˇ)
to give careful attention to; to observe with great care
篤生(ㄉㄨˇ ㄕㄥ)
to be much blessed by Heaven—much gifted
篤愛(ㄉㄨˇ ㄞˋ)
deep affection

【篙】 4171 ㄍㄠ gau gāo
the pole for punting a boat; a boat pole
篙工(ㄍㄠ ㄍㄨㄥ)
a boatman (who punts a boat)
篙師(ㄍㄠ ㄕ)
a boatman (especially a skilled one) who punts a boat
篙人(ㄍㄠ ㄖㄣˊ)
a boatman

【篩】 4172 ㄕㄞ shai shāi
1. a sieve; a screen; a sifter; a strainer
2. to sieve; to screen; to sift; to strain
篩分(ㄕㄞ ㄈㄣ) or 篩選(ㄕㄞ ㄒㄩㄢˇ)
screening; sieving; sifting
篩鑼(ㄕㄞ ㄌㄨㄛˊ)
① a small gong ② to beat a gong
篩骨(ㄕㄞ ㄍㄨˇ)
an ethmoid bone
篩管(ㄕㄞ ㄍㄨㄢˇ)
(botany) sieve tubes
篩孔(ㄕㄞ ㄎㄨㄥˇ)
sieve meshes
篩子(ㄕㄞ ˙ㄗ)
a sieve; a sifter

【篦】 4173 ㄅㄧˋ bih bì
a comb (especially a fine-toothed one)
篦櫛(ㄅㄧˋ ㄐㄧㄝˊ)
a fine-toothed comb, usually made of bamboo
篦子(ㄅㄧˋ ˙ㄗ)
a double-edged, fine-toothed comb

【篪】 4174 (箎)ㄔˊ chyr chí
a kind of bamboo flute 亦作「篪」

【篨】 4175 ㄔㄨˊ chwu chú
1. a coarse bamboo mat
2. an ugly bloated mass

【箾】 4176 ㄕㄠ shau shāo
a bamboo tube for holding chopsticks

【篘】 4177 ㄔㄡ chou chōu
1. a wine filter
2. to filter wine

【篛】 4178 ㄖㄨㄛˋ ruoh ruò
same as 箬—a kind of broad-leaved bamboo

【簑】 4179 ㄙㄨㄛ suo suō
same as 蓑—a coir raincoat (or cape)

〔竹部〕

十一畫

【篠】 4180 ㄒㄧㄠˇ sheau xiǎo
1. a variety of bamboo with thin and short stems
2. a bamboo basket

【篳】 4181 ㄅㄧˋ bih bì
bamboo, wicker, etc. which can be used to make baskets, bags, etc.

篳門圭竇(ㄅㄧˋ ㄇㄣˊ ㄍㄨㄟ ㄉㄡˋ)
a humble dwelling

篳路藍縷(ㄅㄧˋ ㄌㄨˋ ㄌㄢˊ ㄌㄩˇ)
(literally) firewood carts and rags—the hard life of pioneers

【篼】 4182 ㄉㄡ dou dōu
a mountain sedan chair made of bamboo

篼子(ㄉㄡ ·ㄗ)
a mountain sedan chair

【篾】 4183 (篾) ㄇㄧㄝˋ mieh miè
1. a thin and long strip of bamboo for making baskets, etc.; thin (bamboo) laths
2. name of a variety of bamboo

篾片(ㄇㄧㄝˋ ㄆㄧㄢˋ)
① a thin and long strip of bamboo ② protégés who are good at pleasing the patron

篾匠(ㄇㄧㄝˋ ·ㄐㄧㄤ)
a bamboo craftsman

篾席(ㄇㄧㄝˋ ㄒㄧˊ)
a bamboo bed mat

【篷】 4184 ㄆㄥˊ perng péng
1. a covering; an awning; a tent
2. a sail; a boat

篷布(ㄆㄥˊ ㄅㄨˋ)
a tarpaulin

篷車(ㄆㄥˊ ㄔㄜ)
a wagon

篷窗(ㄆㄥˊ ㄔㄨㄤ)
windows in a boat

【簌】 4185 ㄙㄨˋ suh sù
(said of flower petals) falling in great quantities

簌地(ㄙㄨˋ ㄉㄧˋ)
(said of tears) flowing

簌簌(ㄙㄨˋ ㄙㄨˋ)
① luxuriant growth (of vegetation) ② (onomatopoeia) a very slight sound ③ to shower down

簌簌地(ㄙㄨˋ ㄙㄨˋ ·ㄉㄜ)
a very slight sound of something moving stealthily, flowing, or dropping—as droplets of water, tears, etc.

【簏】 4186 ㄌㄨˋ luh lù
a bamboo trunk

簏簌(ㄌㄨˋ ㄙㄨˋ)
hanging down

【簇】 4187 ㄘㄨˋ tsuh cù
1. a cluster; a crowd; crowded: 有些花是簇生的。Some flowers grow in clusters.
2. an arrowhead
3. a framework on which silkworms spin
4. to crowd together; to cluster together

簇聚(ㄘㄨˋ ㄐㄩˋ)
to cluster or crowd together: 他們簇聚在火爐邊。They crowded round the stove.

簇新(ㄘㄨˋ ㄒㄧㄣ)
brand-new

簇簇(ㄘㄨˋ ㄘㄨˋ)
piled up; in array

簇擁(ㄘㄨˋ ㄩㄥˇ)
attended by a crowd: 他前後簇擁着一大羣人。He was attended by a large crowd in front and behind.

【簃】 4188 ㄧˊ yi yí
a small house attached to a pavilion

【簀】 4189 ㄗㄜˊ tzer zé
1. a bamboo bed mat
2. to be densely collected together

【簋】 4190 ㄍㄨㄟˇ goei guǐ
a round bamboo vessel for holding grains in ancient offerings or feasts; a bronze vessel for holding food in ancient times

【簉】 4191 ㄗㄠˋ tzaw zào
1. deputy; a deputy; an attendant
2. an escorting vehicle
3. a concubine

簉弄(ㄗㄠˋ ㄋㄨㄥˋ)
a ditty; a little tune

簉室(ㄗㄠˋ ㄕˋ)
a concubine

【篹】 4192 1. ㄓㄨㄢˋ juann zhuàn
same as 撰—to collect, edit or write

【篹】 4192 2. ㄙㄨㄢˇ soan suǎn (又讀 ㄗㄨㄢˇ tzoan zuǎn)
a splint basket; a bamboo basket

【簍】 4193 ㄌㄡˇ loou lǒu
a basket made by weaving bamboo slats, wickers or twigs

簍子(ㄌㄡˇ ·ㄗ)
a basket made of bamboo, wickers or twigs

簍兒(ㄌㄡˇㄦ)
① a basket ② a kind of dumpling with stuffing

【篰】 4194 ㄅㄨˋ buh bù
1. a bamboo basket
2. same as 簿—books, volumes, or letters

【箾】 4195 ㄕㄠ shau shāo
1. the tail of a helm
2. to flutter in the wind

【簰】 4196 ㄆㄞˊ pair pái
a raft; a bamboo raft

【篲】 4197 ㄏㄨㄟˋ huey huì
a broom; a bamboo broom

十二畫

【簞】 4198 ㄉㄢ dan dān
a kind of round bamboo ware for holding cooked rice

簞瓢屢空(ㄉㄢ ㄆㄧㄠˊ ㄌㄩˇ ㄎㄨㄥ)
(literally) The basket and gourd are frequently empty. —with no food and water; stark poverty

簞笥(ㄉㄢ ㄙˋ)
① a bamboo box ② vessels for holding food

簞食瓢飲(ㄉㄢ ㄙˋ ㄆㄧㄠˊ ㄧㄣˇ)

to lead a simple life

簞食壺漿(ㄉㄢ ㄙˋ ㄏㄨˊ ㄐㄧㄤ)

(said of the populace) to cheer the troops with food and drink

【簟】 4199
ㄉㄧㄢˋ diann diàn

a bamboo mat

簟竹(ㄉㄧㄢˋ ㄓㄨˊ)

a variety of giant bamboo

【簡】 4200
(简) ㄐㄧㄢˇ jean jiǎn

1. brief; succinct; terse; simple: 他給了我一個簡潔的答覆。He gave me a terse reply.
2. (in ancient China) a slip or tablet of bamboo for writing
3. a letter; a note
4. to treat coolly or impolitely
5. to designate or appoint (an official)
6. to select; to choose
7. a Chinese family name

簡拔(ㄐㄧㄢˇ ㄅㄚˊ)

to select and designate (someone for a post)

簡報(ㄐㄧㄢˇ ㄅㄠˋ)

a briefing

簡筆字(ㄐㄧㄢˇ ㄅㄧˇ ㄗˋ)or 簡體字(ㄐㄧㄢˇ ㄊㄧˇ ㄗˋ)

an abbreviated or simplified form of a character, such as 体 for 體

簡編(ㄐㄧㄢˇ ㄅㄧㄢ)

books; volumes

簡便(ㄐㄧㄢˇ ㄅㄧㄢˋ)

simple and convenient

簡樸(ㄐㄧㄢˇ ㄆㄨˊ)

simple and unadorned; plain: 他過著簡樸生活。He led a simple life.

簡慢(ㄐㄧㄢˇ ㄇㄢˋ)

(a polite expression to say to a guest) to treat impolitely or coolly

簡明(ㄐㄧㄢˇ ㄇㄧㄥˊ)

brief and clear; terse and to the point; concise: 他對會議作了一個簡明的報告。He gave a concise report of the meeting.

簡分數(ㄐㄧㄢˇ ㄈㄣ ㄕㄨˋ)

a simple fraction

簡單(ㄐㄧㄢˇ ㄉㄢ)

① simple; brief: 這個解釋十分簡單。The explanation was quite simple. ② ordinary

簡單明瞭(ㄐㄧㄢˇ ㄉㄢ ㄇㄧㄥˊ ㄌㄧㄠˇ)

brief and clear; simple and to the point

簡單生活(ㄐㄧㄢˇ ㄉㄢ ㄕㄥ ㄏㄨㄛˊ)

a simple life

簡牘(ㄐㄧㄢˇ ㄉㄨˊ)

① books and volumes ② letters or correspondence

簡短(ㄐㄧㄢˇ ㄉㄨㄢˇ)

brief; succinct; terse; short: 林肯的蓋茨堡演講辭簡短有力。Lincoln's Gettysburg Address is terse.

簡圖(ㄐㄧㄢˇ ㄊㄨˊ)

a sketch; a diagram

簡陋(ㄐㄧㄢˇ ㄌㄡˋ)

simple and crude: 這所學校設備簡陋。This school has simple and crude equipment.

簡練(ㄐㄧㄢˇ ㄌㄧㄢˋ)

① to select and study thoroughly ② (said of a piece of writing) refined; succinct

簡略(ㄐㄧㄢˇ ㄌㄩㄝˋ)

brief; sketchy

簡括(ㄐㄧㄢˇ ㄎㄨㄛˋ)

brief but to the point; succinct

簡忽(ㄐㄧㄢˇ ㄏㄨ)

to slight; to treat coolly

簡化(ㄐㄧㄢˇ ㄏㄨㄚˋ)

to simplify; simplification: 這故事已由王先生簡化了。The story has been simplified by Mr. Wang.

簡潔(ㄐㄧㄢˇ ㄐㄧㄝˊ)

(said of a piece of writing) simple and perspicuous; brief and to the point; succinct

簡介(ㄐㄧㄢˇ ㄐㄧㄝˋ)

a brief introduction; a synopsis

簡寫(ㄐㄧㄢˇ ㄒㄧㄝˇ)

① to write a Chinese character in a simplified form ② to simplify a book for beginners

簡直(ㄐㄧㄢˇ ㄓˊ)

① simply; outright; at all: 那簡直是不可能的。That's simply impossible. ② honest; unaffected

簡札(ㄐㄧㄢˇ ㄓㄚˊ)

letters; correspondence

簡章(ㄐㄧㄢˇ ㄓㄤ)

a brief and concise statement of regulations, procedures, etc.

簡擢(ㄐㄧㄢˇ ㄓㄨㄛˊ)

to select and designate (a person for a post)

簡稱(ㄐㄧㄢˇ ㄔㄥ)

to be called or known as... for short

簡任(ㄐㄧㄢˇ ㄖㄣˋ)

the selected appointment rank (the second highest of the four grades in modern Chinese civil service)

簡字(ㄐㄧㄢˇ ㄗˋ)

① an abbreviated or simplified form of a character ② a kind of phonetic signs devised by Lao Nai-hsüan (勞乃宣) of the Ching Dynasty

簡册(ㄐㄧㄢˇ ㄘㄜˋ)

books

簡而言之(ㄐㄧㄢˇ ㄦˊ ㄧㄢˊ ㄓ)

in short; briefly; in a word

簡易(ㄐㄧㄢˇ ㄧˋ)

simple; easy; simple and convenient

簡易科(ㄐㄧㄢˇ ㄧˋ ㄎㄜ)

a short course; a snap course

簡要(ㄐㄧㄢˇ ㄧㄠˋ)

brief and concise; brief and to the point

簡約(ㄐㄧㄢˇ ㄩㄝ)

brief; terse; succinct

【簣】 4201
ㄎㄨㄟˋ kuey kuì

a bamboo basket for carrying earth

【簦】 4202
ㄉㄥ deng dēng

a kind of umbrella used in ancient China

簦笠(ㄉㄥ ㄌㄧˋ)

a kind of large umbrella with a long handle, used for street stalls

【簠】 4203
ㄈㄨˇ fuu fǔ

a square vessel for containing the cooked grain at sacrifices or feasts

簠簋不飭(ㄈㄨˇ ㄍㄨㄟˇ ㄅㄨˋ ㄔˋ)

(literally) Sacrificial items are not laid out in good order. —the abuse of powers

〔竹部〕

〔竹部〕

by greedy officials

【簨】 4204
ㄙㄨㄣˇ soen sŭn
a beam for hanging bells or chime stone

簨簴(ㄙㄨㄣˇ ㄐㄩˋ)
a beam for hanging bells or chime stone

【簪】 4205
ㄗㄢ tzan zān
(又讀 ㄗㄣ tzen zēn)
1. a clasp for clipping the cap and hair together
2. a hairpin for women
3. to stick (in the hair, etc.); to wear

簪筆(ㄗㄢ ㄅㄧˇ)
(said of ancient courtiers) to stick the writing brush in one's hair or behind the ear

簪紱(ㄗㄢ ㄈㄨˊ)
(literally) a cap clasp and hat tassels for an official seal—high position and wealth

簪笏(ㄗㄢ ㄏㄨˋ)
(literally) the cap clasp and the jade tablet (used during an audience with the emperor, etc.)—high officials

簪花(ㄗㄢ ㄏㄨㄚ)
to wear a flower; to stick a flower on one's cap or hat

簪環首飾(ㄗㄢ ㄏㄨㄢˊ ㄕㄡˇ ㄕˋ)
women's hairpins, rings, jewels, etc.

簪裾(ㄗㄢ ㄐㄩ)
dresses and ornaments of the nobility

簪子(ㄗㄢ ·ㄗ)or 簪兒(ㄗㄚㄦ)
a woman's hairpin

簪纓世胄(ㄗㄢ ㄧㄥ ㄕˋ ㄓㄡˋ)
a family producing public officials for successive generations 亦作「華簪」

【簧】 4206
ㄏㄨㄤˊ hwang huáng
1. a reed; the metal tongue in a reed organ
2. a reed organ
3. a spring or catch in a machine: 這沙發裝有鐵絲彈簧。The sofa has wire springs.

簧片(ㄏㄨㄤˊ ㄆㄧㄢˋ)
the metal tongue in a reed organ; a reed

簧鼓(ㄏㄨㄤˊ ㄍㄨˇ)
to dazzle people with sweet talks

簧樂器(ㄏㄨㄤˊ ㄩㄝˋ ㄑㄧˋ)
the reed instruments (in a symphony orchestra)

【簙】 4207
ㄅㄛˊ bor bó
a kind of chess game

【簫】 4208
ㄒㄧㄠ shiau xiāo
a vertical flute of bamboo: 他在吹簫。He plays on the vertical bamboo flute.

簫管(ㄒㄧㄠ ㄍㄨㄢˇ)
a panpipe and a double flute

簫韶(ㄒㄧㄠ ㄕㄠˊ)
the name of the music created by Emperor Shun(舜), 2255 B.C.

十三畫

【簷】 4209
ㄧㄢˊ yan yán
1. the eaves of a house
2. the edge or brim of anything sloping downward—as that of a hat, umbrella, etc.

簷馬(ㄧㄢˊ ㄇㄚˇ)or 簷鐵馬(ㄧㄢˊ ㄊㄧㄝˇ ㄇㄚˇ)
tiny metallic ornaments, bells, etc., hanging down from the eaves and tinkling in the wind

簷霤(ㄧㄢˊ ㄌㄧㄡˋ)or 簷滴(ㄧㄢˊ ㄉㄧ)
dripping water from the eaves

簷前(ㄧㄢˊ ㄑㄧㄢˊ)
the front of the eaves; in front of the eaves

簷下(ㄧㄢˊ ㄒㄧㄚˋ)
under the eaves: 燕子築巢於簷下。The swallows nested under the eaves.

簷牙(ㄧㄢˊ ㄧㄚˊ)
the projecting tiles on the eaves (for the ornamental purpose)

【簸】 4210
1. ㄅㄛˇ boo bǒ
to winnow; to sift (especially rice)

簸盪(ㄅㄛˇ ㄉㄤˋ)
the rocking of a boat; to roll: 那船在浪上簸盪得很厲害。That ship was rolling heavily on the waves.

簸弄(ㄅㄛˇ ㄌㄨㄥˋ)
① to play jokes on; to deceive ② to spread rumors or tell tales; to start rumors and incite incidents

簸揚(ㄅㄛˇ ㄧㄤˊ)
to winnow; to sift

【簸】 4210
2. ㄅㄛˋ boh bò
a winnow

簸箕(ㄅㄛˋ ·ㄐㄧ)
① a winnow ② a container for dust; a dustpan

【簽】 4211
ㄑㄧㄢ chian qiān
1. to sign one's name; to put down one's signature; to subscribe; to endorse: 他忘記簽名。He's forgotten to sign his name.
2. bamboo slips used for drawing lots or divination
3. a label

簽名(ㄑㄧㄢ ㄇㄧㄥˊ)
to sign; to put down one's signature; to autograph; a signature

簽名簿(ㄑㄧㄢ ㄇㄧㄥˊ ㄅㄨˋ)
a book for putting down autographs (of visitors, guests, etc.); a guest book: 這是來賓簽名簿。This is a book for signatures of visitors.

簽到(ㄑㄧㄢ ㄉㄠˋ)
to sign on an attendance book of an office, firm or factory

簽到簿(ㄑㄧㄢ ㄉㄠˋ ㄅㄨˋ)
a book where employees or workers put down their signatures or initials to indicate their presence in time; an attendance book

簽訂(ㄑㄧㄢ ㄉㄧㄥˋ)
to conclude and sign (a treaty, etc.): 昨天晚上他們簽訂了一份合約。They signed an agreement last night.

簽訂條約(ㄑㄧㄢ ㄉㄧㄥˋ ㄊㄧㄠˊ ㄩㄝ)
to sign a treaty

簽訂合同(ㄑㄧㄢ ㄉㄧㄥˋ ㄏㄜˊ ·ㄊㄨㄥ)
to sign a contract

簽條(ㄑㄧㄢ ㄊㄧㄠˊ)
① a label ② an office note; a memo

簽知(ㄑㄧㄢ ㄓ)
to sign or initial on a docu-

ment, etc. to show that one has read the contents therein

簽證(ㄑㄧㄢ ㄓㄥˋ)
a visa; to visa: 他持有過境簽證。He holds a transit visa.

簽註(ㄑㄧㄢ ㄓㄨˋ)or 簽註意見(ㄑㄧㄢ ㄓㄨˋ ㄧˋ ㄐㄧㄢˋ)
to attach a slip of paper to a document with comments on it; to put down one's comments on a document or official correspondence

簽呈(ㄑㄧㄢ ㄔㄥˊ)
a written report addressed to a superior

簽收(ㄑㄧㄢ ㄕㄡ)
to sign after receiving something

簽署(ㄑㄧㄢ ㄕㄨˋ)
to sign or initial (a document)

簽字(ㄑㄧㄢ ㄗˋ)
a signature; to sign or initial: 這合約簽字後立即生效。The contract came into force upon signature.

簽字筆(ㄑㄧㄢ ㄗˋ ㄅㄧˇ)
a felt pen; a felt-tip pen; a felt marker

簽字國(ㄑㄧㄢ ㄗˋ ㄍㄨㄛˊ)
a signatory country

簽押(ㄑㄧㄢ ㄧㄚ)
to sign one's name or put a seal on

簽印(ㄑㄧㄢ ㄧㄣˋ)
to sign or put a seal on

簽約(ㄑㄧㄢ ㄩㄝ)
to sign a contract, treaty, etc.

【簾】 4212
ㄌㄧㄢˊ lian lián
1. a loose hanging screen for a door or window, usually made of stringed beads, bamboo slabs, etc.; blinds; a curtain: 請將窗簾拉上。Please draw the window curtains.
2. a flag as a shop sign: 酒簾 a wineshop sign

簾幕(ㄌㄧㄢˊ ㄇㄨˋ)
screens and blinds

簾內簾外(ㄌㄧㄢˊ ㄋㄟˋ ㄌㄧㄢˊ ㄨㄞˋ)
(literally) within and without the curtain—private and public

簾櫳(ㄌㄧㄢˊ ㄌㄨㄥˊ)
the windows, doors and the screens

簾官(ㄌㄧㄢˊ ㄍㄨㄢ)
officials in charge of the civil service examination in former times

簾眷(ㄌㄧㄢˊ ㄐㄩㄢˋ)
to win the favor of the queen dowager when she acts as regent in the emperor's childhood

簾政(ㄌㄧㄢˊ ㄓㄥˋ)
the regency of an empress-dowager

簾子(ㄌㄧㄢˊ ·ㄗ)or 簾兒(ㄌㄧㄚˊㄦ)
a screen; a curtain; blinds

簾押(ㄌㄧㄢˊ ㄧㄚ)
a curtain ballast

【簴】 4213
(虡) ㄐㄩˋ jiuh jù
pillars beside the crossbeam for hanging bells or drums

【簿】 4214
ㄅㄨˋ buh bù
1. books: 支票簿 a checkbook
2. to record; to register

簿歷(ㄅㄨˋ ㄌㄧˋ)
a person's records, qualifications, etc.

簿錄(ㄅㄨˋ ㄌㄨˋ)
① to confiscate property ② a catalogue of books: 她做了一本簿錄。She makes a catalogue of books.

簿籍(ㄅㄨˋ ㄐㄧˊ)
① a domiciliary register ② account books

簿記(ㄅㄨˋ ㄐㄧˋ)
bookkeeping: 單(複)式簿記 bookkeeping by single (double) entry

簿記學(ㄅㄨˋ ㄐㄧˋ ㄒㄩㄝˊ)
bookkeeping (as a course of study)

簿記學校(ㄅㄨˋ ㄐㄧˋ ㄒㄩㄝˊ ㄒㄧㄠˋ)
a bookkeeping school

簿記員(ㄅㄨˋ ㄐㄧˋ ㄩㄢˊ)
a bookkeeper; a ledger clerk: 她是本公司的簿記員。She is a bookkeeper of our company.

簿子(ㄅㄨˋ ·ㄗ)
a blank book for writing; an exercise book; a notebook

簿冊(ㄅㄨˋ ㄘㄜˋ)
books (for record, registration, etc.) and files; lists or registers

【簳】 4215
ㄍㄢˇ gaan gǎn
young bamboo

【籀】 4216
(籒) ㄓㄡˋ jow zhòu
1. a type of Chinese calligraphy, also known as 大篆——the large seal
2. to deduce

籀篆(ㄓㄡˋ ㄓㄨㄢˋ)or 籀書(ㄓㄡˋ ㄕㄨ)or 籀文(ㄓㄡˋ ㄨㄣˊ)
the "large seal" type of Chinese calligraphy, initiated during the Chou Dynasty by Historian Chou (史籀)

十四畫

【籃】 4217
ㄌㄢˊ lan lán
a basket: 她買了一籃桃子。She bought a basket of peaches.

籃板球(ㄌㄢˊ ㄅㄢˇ ㄑㄧㄡˊ)
(basketball) rebounds

籃球(ㄌㄢˊ ㄑㄧㄡˊ)
basketball

籃球架(ㄌㄢˊ ㄑㄧㄡˊ ㄐㄧㄚˋ)
basketball back stops; basketball stands

籃球賽(ㄌㄢˊ ㄑㄧㄡˊ ㄙㄞˋ)
a basketball game

籃子(ㄌㄢˊ ·ㄗ)or 籃兒(ㄌㄚˊㄦ)
baskets

籃輿(ㄌㄢˊ ㄩˊ)
a bamboo sedan chair

【籌】 4218
ㄔㄡˊ chour chóu
1. chips, tallies, etc. for calculating purposes
2. to plan; to prepare
3. to raise (money)
4. to assess or estimate

籌備(ㄔㄡˊ ㄅㄟˋ)
to prepare and plan; to arrange

籌備費(ㄔㄡˊ ㄅㄟˋ ㄈㄟˋ)
preliminary expenditure

籌備會(ㄔㄡˊ ㄅㄟˋ ㄏㄨㄟˋ)
a preparatory meeting, committee, etc.; an organizing committee

籌備處(ㄔㄡˊ ㄅㄟˋ ㄔㄨˋ)
a preparatory office

籌備委員(ㄔㄡˊ ㄅㄟˋ ㄨㄟˇ ㄩㄢˊ)
members on a preparatory committee

〔竹部〕

〔竹部〕

籌辦(ㄔㄡˊ ㄅㄢˋ)
to plan and sponsor (a show, sports event, school, etc.)
籌邊(ㄔㄡˊ ㄅㄧㄢ)
to make plans for affairs pertaining to a nation's borders
籌碼(ㄔㄡˊ ㄇㄚˇ)
chips (in gambling, etc.); a counter: 這是政治交易的籌碼。This is a bargaining counter in political deals.
籌募(ㄔㄡˊ ㄇㄨˋ)
to raise; to collect (funds)
籌度(ㄔㄡˊ ㄉㄨㄛˋ)
to plan and estimate
籌略(ㄔㄡˊ ㄌㄩㄝˋ)
strategy; plans; tactics
籌款(ㄔㄡˊ ㄎㄨㄢˇ)
to procure money; to raise funds: 他爲一新事業籌款。He raises money for a new undertaking.
籌劃(ㄔㄡˊ ㄏㄨㄚˋ)
to deliberate and plan; a layout
籌建(ㄔㄡˊ ㄐㄧㄢˋ)
to prepare the construction of
籌餉(ㄔㄡˊ ㄒㄧㄤˇ)
to raise money or funds for military payroll
籌商(ㄔㄡˊ ㄕㄤ)or 籌議(ㄔㄡˊ ㄧˋ)
to plan and discuss (means to cope with a certain problem, etc.)
籌策(ㄔㄡˊ ㄘㄜˋ)
to prepare and plan
籌措(ㄔㄡˊ ㄘㄨㄛˋ)
to raise (funds)
籌算(ㄔㄡˊ ㄙㄨㄢˋ)
to calculate with chips marked with figures
籌安會(ㄔㄡˊ ㄢ ㄏㄨㄟˋ)
a political body founded in 1915, whose aim was to make Yüan Shih-kai (袁世凱) emperor

【籍】 4219
ㄐㄧˊ jyi jí
1. books; volumes; reading materials
2. a record or register of population
3. one's hometown or native place: 祖籍 the native land of one's ancestors
4. a Chinese family name
籍沒(ㄐㄧˊ ㄇㄛˋ)
to confiscate someone's possessions
籍隸(ㄐㄧˊ ㄌㄧˋ)
to be a native of; to hail from
籍斂(ㄐㄧˊ ㄌㄧㄢˋ)
to demand or collect illegal taxes
籍貫(ㄐㄧˊ ㄍㄨㄢˋ)
one's native place or hometown: 你的籍貫是那裡? What is your hometown?
籍籍(ㄐㄧˊ ㄐㄧˊ)
① confusing; disorderly ② noisy; vociferous
籍甚(ㄐㄧˊ ㄕㄣˋ)
(said of reputation) widespread

十五畫

【籐】 4220
ㄊㄥˊ terng téng
same as 藤—vines; canes; climbing plants; rattans
籐椅(ㄊㄥˊ ㄧˇ)
a rattan armchair

十六畫

【籙】 4221
ㄌㄨˋ luh lù
1. lists or registers
2. a Taoist amulet or charm

【籜】 4222
ㄊㄨㄛˋ tuoh tuò
the shell of bamboo shoots

【籟】 4223
ㄌㄞˋ lay lài
1. a kind of pipe
2. unspecified sounds

【籠】 4224
ㄌㄨㄥˊ long lóng
(又讀 ㄌㄨㄥˇ loong lǒng)
1. a cage; a coop
2. a tight, storied cagelike bamboo ware for steaming dumplings, etc.; a bamboo food steamer
3. to include; to encompass
籠頭
①(ㄌㄨㄥˊ ㄊㄡˊ) the leader of prisoners in a jail
②(ㄌㄨㄥˊ ·ㄊㄡ) the halter of an animal
籠統(ㄌㄨㄥˇ ㄊㄨㄥˇ)
generalized; general; sweeping; indiscriminate: 這篇敍述太籠統了。The statement is too general.
籠利(ㄌㄨㄥˇ ㄌㄧˋ)
to amass gains; to make profit
籠絡(ㄌㄨㄥˊ ㄌㄨㄛˋ)or(ㄌㄨㄥˇ ㄌㄨㄛˋ)
① to entice, tempt, ensnare or cajole ② to befriend another with a view to winning him over
籠括(ㄌㄨㄥˇ ㄍㄨㄚ)
to encompass; to seize all
籠罩(ㄌㄨㄥˊ ㄓㄠˋ)or(ㄌㄨㄥˇ ㄓㄠˋ)
to cover completely; to permeate; to shroud: 晨霧籠罩着山頭。The mountain is shrouded in morning mist.
籠中鳥(ㄌㄨㄥˊ ㄓㄨㄥ ㄋㄧㄠˇ)
(literally) a bird in a cage—restricted and confined; without much freedom
籠子(ㄌㄨㄥˊ ·ㄗ)
① a cage; a coop ② a bamboo ware

【籞】 4225
ㄩˋ yuh yù
1. the forbidden garden in a palace
2. a fenced place in a pond for keeping fish

十七畫

【籤】 4226
(籖) ㄑㄧㄢ chian qiān
1. a slip of bamboo engraved with signs to be used in gambling or divination; a lot
2. a label
3. a small sharp-pointed stick
籤兒(ㄑㄧㄚㄦ)
① a gambling slip of bamboo engraved with spots to determine the winner ② sticks with pointed ends, used to pierce into bags, etc. to find out the contents therein ③ a label
籤詩(ㄑㄧㄢ ㄕ)or 籤語(ㄑㄧㄢ ㄩˇ)
a doggerel poem or quote foretelling one's fortune as denoted by a divination lot drawn by oneself

【籥】 4227
ㄩㄝˋ yueh yuè
1. a short flute or pipe used in ancient China
2. a key

【籧】 4228
1. ㄑㄩˊ chyu qú
a crude bamboo mat

籧篨(ㄑㄩˊ ㄔㄨˊ)
a kind of ailment, probably of a rheumatic nature, which causes stiff neck and backbone; a vicious bloated mass

【籧】 4228
2. ㄐㄩˇ jeu jǔ
a vessel for raising silkworms

十九畫

【籩】 4229
ㄅㄧㄢ bian biān
a bamboo container for food, also used to hold fruit or dried meat, etc. in sacrifices

籩豆(ㄅㄧㄢ ㄉㄡˋ)
two ancient food containers used at sacrifices

【籬】 4230
ㄌㄧˊ li lí
a bamboo fence; a hedge

籬笆(ㄌㄧˊ ·ㄅㄚ)
a bamboo fence: 那匹馬跳過了籬笆。That horse jumped over the fence.

籬落(ㄌㄧˊ ㄌㄨㄛˋ)
a fence; a hedge

籬根(ㄌㄧˊ ㄍㄣ)
the lower part of a fence

籬菊(ㄌㄧˊ ㄐㄩˊ)
chrysanthemums beside the fence

籬竹(ㄌㄧˊ ㄓㄨˊ)
a fence formed by living bamboos

籬垣(ㄌㄧˊ ㄩㄢˊ)
a fence; a hedge: 在他家前面有一道籬垣。There is a hedge in front of his house.

【籮】 4231
ㄌㄨㄛˊ luo luó
1. a bamboo basket with a square or rectangular bottom and a round top
2. a piece of sieve-like ware with a broad edge

籮筐(ㄌㄨㄛˊ ㄎㄨㄤ)
a large basket made of bamboo

二十六畫

【籲】 4232
ㄩˋ yuh yù
to appeal; to request; to urge; to ask; to implore; to beseech

籲天(ㄩˋ ㄊㄧㄢ)
to cry to Heaven; to appeal to God

籲求(ㄩˋ ㄑㄧㄡˊ)
to urge; to implore

籲請(ㄩˋ ㄑㄧㄥˇ)
to request; to beseech; to urge

米部
ㄇㄧˇ mii mǐ

【米】 4233
ㄇㄧˇ mii mǐ
1. hulled or husked rice; uncooked rice: 中國人靠米爲生。The Chinese live on rice.
2. a shelled or a husked seed: 花生米 a peanut; a peanut kernel
3. meter (the fundamental unit of length in the metric system)
4. a Chinese family name

米芾(ㄇㄧˇ ㄈㄟˊ)or 米南宮(ㄇㄧˇ ㄋㄢˊ ㄍㄨㄥ)
Mi Fei, a renowned painter and calligrapher of the Sung Dynasty

米飯(ㄇㄧˇ ㄈㄢˋ)
rice; cooked rice: 中國人喜歡吃米飯。The Chinese like to eat cooked rice.

米粉(ㄇㄧˇ ㄈㄣˇ)
① rice flour ② thin noodles made of rice flour; rice-flour noodles: 你喜歡吃米粉嗎? Do you like rice-flour noodles?

米粉肉(ㄇㄧˇ ㄈㄣˇ ㄖㄡˋ)
(Chinese cooking) a dish prepared by steaming meat mixed with rice flour; pork steamed with ground glutinous rice

米店(ㄇㄧˇ ㄉㄧㄢˋ)
a shop selling rice (usually along with other kinds of grain)

米湯(ㄇㄧˇ ㄊㄤ)
① rice soup ② flattering words

米突(ㄇㄧˇ ㄊㄨˊ)
① meter, the fundamental unit of length in the metric system ② metric

米突制(ㄇㄧˇ ㄊㄨˊ ㄓˋ)
the metric system 亦作「米制」or「公制」

米突尺(ㄇㄧˇ ㄊㄨˊ ㄔˇ)
a metric ruler

米蘭(ㄇㄧˇ ㄌㄢˊ)
Milan, an industrial city in central Lombardy, in N Italy

米粒(ㄇㄧˇ ㄌㄧˋ)or 米粒兒(ㄇㄧˇ ㄌㄧㄜˋㄦ)
a grain of rice

米糧(ㄇㄧˇ ㄌㄧㄤˊ)
rice and food supplies; provisions

米糕(ㄇㄧˇ ㄍㄠ)
rice cake; rice pudding

米糠(ㄇㄧˇ ㄎㄤ)
rice bran; paddy chaff

米黃(ㄇㄧˇ ㄏㄨㄤˊ)
cream-colored; cream: 她穿着米黃色衣服。She wore a cream dress.

米價(ㄇㄧˇ ㄐㄧㄚˋ)
the price of rice

米酒(ㄇㄧˇ ㄐㄧㄡˇ)
rice wine; rice beer

米粥(ㄇㄧˇ ㄓㄡ)
congee; rice gruel

米珠薪桂(ㄇㄧˇ ㄓㄨ ㄒㄧㄣ ㄍㄨㄟˋ)
(literally) rice as precious as pearls and firewood as expensive as cinnamon—the high cost of living

米食(ㄇㄧˇ ㄕˊ)
a rice diet

米色(ㄇㄧˇ ㄙㄜˋ)
a very light chocolate brown color; cream

三畫

【籽】 4234
ㄗˇ tzyy zǐ
seeds of plants

〔米部〕

〔米部〕

四畫

【粉】 4235
ㄈㄣˇ feen fěn

1. flour
2. powder
3. white (color)
4. to whitewash; to plaster
5. to make up; to doll up; to powder

粉白黛黑(ㄈㄣˇ ㄅㄞˊ ㄉㄞˋ ㄏㄟ)or 粉紅黛綠(ㄈㄣˇ ㄏㄨㄥˊ ㄉㄞˋ ㄌㄩˋ)
①a beauty ②heavy make-up

粉筆(ㄈㄣˇ ㄅㄧˇ)
chalk

粉壁(ㄈㄣˇ ㄅㄧˋ)
a whitewashed wall

粉皮(ㄈㄣˇ ㄆㄧˊ)
①a thin, almost transparent sheet made with ground green beans ②the sheepskin without wool on it

粉撲兒(ㄈㄣˇ ㄆㄨㄦ)
a powder puff

粉末(ㄈㄣˇ ㄇㄛˋ)
fine dust of anything; powder

粉末檢波器(ㄈㄣˇ ㄇㄛˋ ㄐㄧㄢˇ ㄅㄛ ㄑㄧˋ)
a coherer

粉墨(ㄈㄣˇ ㄇㄛˋ)
①(said of theatrical players) to apply make-up ②to polish up or gloss over (a piece of writing)

粉墨登場(ㄈㄣˇ ㄇㄛˋ ㄉㄥ ㄔㄤˇ)
①to make up and go on stage ②(said of a puppet regime) to assume an air of legality

粉面(ㄈㄣˇ ㄇㄧㄢˋ)
①a fair complexion ②a powdered face

粉黛(ㄈㄣˇ ㄉㄞˋ)
beauties

粉蝶(ㄈㄣˇ ㄉㄧㄝˊ)
a white butterfly (*Pieris rapae*)

粉頭(ㄈㄣˇ ㄊㄡˊ)
①prostitutes ②(Chinese opera) white make-up for male players, denoting a crafty or cunning character

粉條兒(ㄈㄣˇ ㄊㄧㄠˊㄦ)
①a food item made with ground green beans ②chalk or crayons for writing

粉團(ㄈㄣˇ ㄊㄨㄢˊ)
fried glutinous rice cakes (usually covered with sesame)

粉嫩(ㄈㄣˇ ㄋㄣˋ)
(usually said of the skin of women or children) fair and tender; blooming and soft

粉盒(ㄈㄣˇ ㄏㄜˊ)
a powder box; a vanity case

粉紅(ㄈㄣˇ ㄏㄨㄥˊ)
pink

粉箋(ㄈㄣˇ ㄐㄧㄢ)
a kind of pink-colored paper

粉牆(ㄈㄣˇ ㄑㄧㄤˊ)
①to plaster or whitewash a wall ②a white wall

粉紙(ㄈㄣˇ ㄓˇ)
①powder paper (a cosmetic item of women) ②a kind of white paper made of bamboo pulp

粉裝玉琢(ㄈㄣˇ ㄓㄨㄤ ㄩˋ ㄓㄨㄛˊ)
(descriptive of a lady) lovely and white-skinned

粉飾(ㄈㄣˇ ㄕˋ)
①to whitewash; to embellish; to touch up ②to make up

粉飾太平(ㄈㄣˇ ㄕˋ ㄊㄞˋ ㄆㄧㄥˊ)
to whitewash or embellish in order to hide a serious trouble or problem; to pretend that everything is going well

粉身碎骨(ㄈㄣˇ ㄕㄣ ㄙㄨㄟˋ ㄍㄨˇ)
(even) at the cost of one's life; great danger or very risky

粉刷(ㄈㄣˇ ㄕㄨㄚ)
to plaster or whitewash (a wall, etc.): 他決定粉刷那道牆。He decided to whitewash the wall.

粉刺(ㄈㄣˇ ㄘˋ)
pimples; acne

粉絲(ㄈㄣˇ ㄙ)
bean flour noodles

粉碎(ㄈㄣˇ ㄙㄨㄟˋ)
①to shatter; to crush up; to smash ②broken into pieces: 茶杯掉下來摔得粉碎。The cup fell and smashed to pieces.

五畫

【粗】 4236
ㄘㄨ tsu cū

1. thick; bulky; big
2. coarse; rough; crude
3. gruff; husky
4. rude; vulgar
5. brief; sketchy

粗脖子(ㄘㄨ ㄅㄛˊ ˙ㄗ)
①an overgrown neck—a symptom of goiter ②to get angry; to get tough or rough

粗暴(ㄘㄨ ㄅㄠˋ)
rude; violent; rough: 他們粗暴地對待囚犯。They treated the prisoners rough.

粗笨(ㄘㄨ ㄅㄣˋ)
awkward; maladroit; clumsy: 他是個粗笨的傢伙。He is a clumsy fellow.

粗鄙(ㄘㄨ ㄅㄧˇ)
vulgar; crude: 他談吐粗鄙。He is vulgar in his speech.

粗布(ㄘㄨ ㄅㄨˋ)
coarse fabric

粗眉大眼(ㄘㄨ ㄇㄟˊ ㄉㄚˋ ㄧㄢˇ)
(literally) thick-eyebrowed and big-eyed — the appearance of a big or rough man

粗米(ㄘㄨ ㄇㄧˇ)
unpolished rice

粗風暴雨(ㄘㄨ ㄈㄥ ㄅㄠˋ ㄩˇ)
a violent storm; strong winds and pouring rain

粗大(ㄘㄨ ㄉㄚˋ)
thick and big: 那次風雨中許多粗大的樹倒了。Many thick and big trees fell in the storm.

粗通(ㄘㄨ ㄊㄨㄥ)
to know a little about (a language, learning, craft, art, etc.)

粗剌剌(ㄘㄨ ㄌㄚ ㄌㄚ)
coarse; rough

粗陋(ㄘㄨ ㄌㄡˋ)
coarse and crude

粗糲(ㄘㄨ ㄌㄧˋ)
coarse rice

粗劣(ㄘㄨ ㄌㄧㄝˋ)
crude; inferior: 手藝粗劣，工資就少。Crude workmanship deserves poor pay.

粗糧(ㄘㄨ ㄌㄧㄤˊ)or 粗糧食(ㄘㄨ ㄌㄧㄤˊ ㄕˊ)
coarse grain (e.g. corn, sorghum, millet, etc. as distinct from wheat and rice)

粗魯 or 粗鹵(ㄘㄨ ㄌㄨˇ)
rude; impolite; rough
粗略(ㄘㄨ ㄌㄩㄝˋ)
cursory; rough; sketchy
粗獷(ㄘㄨ ㄍㄨㄤˇ)
① rough; rude; boorish ② bold and unconstrained; rugged
粗工(ㄘㄨ ㄍㄨㄥ)
① crude work ② an unskilled workman; a laborer: 他是個粗工。He was an unskilled workman.
粗豪(ㄘㄨ ㄏㄠˊ)
manly and straightforward; generous but paying no attention to niceties
粗話(ㄘㄨ ㄏㄨㄚˋ)
obscene language; a vulgar expression
粗活(ㄘㄨ ㄏㄨㄛˊ)
work of a laborer or coolie; work which demands little brains but lots of brawn
粗貨(ㄘㄨ ㄏㄨㄛˋ)
coarse commodities; crude products: 這雕刻品是粗貨。This carving is of coarse work.
粗具規模(ㄘㄨ ㄐㄩˋ ㄍㄨㄟ ㄇㄛˊ)
(said of an undertaking) having just laid a foundation; having begun to take shape; having finished the spadework
粗淺(ㄘㄨ ㄑㄧㄢˇ)
superficial; coarse and shallow; simple
粗細(ㄘㄨ ㄒㄧˋ)
① thickness (of the thread, stick, rope, or anything which is long and round) ② roughness ③ thick and thin ④ crudeness or fineness; quality of work
粗線條作風(ㄘㄨ ㄒㄧㄢˋ ㄊㄧㄠˊ ㄗㄨㄛˋ ㄈㄥ)
(said of one's style of conduct) straightforward; having little regard for niceties; frank but without tact
粗心(ㄘㄨ ㄒㄧㄣ)
careless (in work)
粗心浮氣(ㄘㄨ ㄒㄧㄣ ㄈㄨˊ ㄑㄧˋ)
unthoughtful and rash
粗心大意(ㄘㄨ ㄒㄧㄣ ㄉㄚˋ ㄧˋ)
rash and careless; thoughtless; inadvertency: 錯誤有時純粹由於粗心大意而造成。Mistakes are sometimes due to inadvertency.
粗枝大葉(ㄘㄨ ㄓ ㄉㄚˋ ㄧㄝˋ)
sketchy (description); roughly finished; careless
粗製品(ㄘㄨ ㄓˋ ㄆㄧㄣˇ)
① a semi-finished product that requires further processing ② a product of low quality; a crude or coarse product
粗製濫造(ㄘㄨ ㄓˋ ㄌㄢˋ ㄗㄠˋ)
to turn out (products) in large quantities without any regard for quality; to manufacture in a rough and slipshod way
粗拙(ㄘㄨ ㄓㄨㄛˊ)
crude; coarse
粗壯(ㄘㄨ ㄓㄨㄤˋ)
stout; muscular; sturdy; brawny: 他是個粗壯的小孩。He is a sturdy child.
粗重(ㄘㄨ ㄓㄨㄥˋ)
① bulky (products, etc.) of low value ② work (of a coolie or unskilled laborer) that needs more muscles than brains: 他無法勝任這粗重的工作。He is not adequate to the heavy task.
粗茶淡飯(ㄘㄨ ㄔㄚˊ ㄉㄢˋ ㄈㄢˋ)
simple food; plain fare
粗實(ㄘㄨ ㄕˊ)
big and strong; raw and durable
粗手笨脚(ㄘㄨ ㄕㄡˇ ㄅㄣˋ ㄐㄧㄠˇ)
awkward; maladroit; clumsy
粗疏(ㄘㄨ ㄕㄨ)
① careless ② unpolished or unrefined; rough
粗率(ㄘㄨ ㄕㄨㄞˋ)
① crude and coarse ② careless; rash: 你不應該粗率的許下諾言。You should never make rash promises.
粗人(ㄘㄨ ㄖㄣˊ)
① a person of much muscle but little refinement; a person of little education ② a boor; an unrefined person
粗糙(ㄘㄨ ㄘㄠ)
(said of a surface, etc.) coarse; rough; unpolished: 他的皮膚粗糙。He has a rough skin.
粗俗(ㄘㄨ ㄙㄨˊ)
coarse; vulgar; unrefined: 他說話粗俗。He uses vulgar language.
粗野(ㄘㄨ ㄧㄝˇ)
rough; rude; boorish; unrefined or unpolished; rustic and coarse: 他在遊戲中動作粗野。He played rough in games.

【粒】 4237
ㄌㄧˋ lih lì
1. a grain (of rice, etc.)
2. to get grain to eat
3. a pill; a bead
粒粒皆辛苦(ㄌㄧˋ ㄌㄧˋ ㄐㄧㄝ ㄒㄧㄣ ㄎㄨˇ)
Every (rice) grain is the product of toiling.
粒兒(ㄌㄧˋㄦ)
① a grain (of rice) ② a pill; a bead

【粕】 4238
ㄆㄛˋ poh pò
the lees; dregs; sediment of liquor

【粘】 4239
(黏) ㄋㄧㄢˊ nian nián
to paste up; to attach to; to stick up; to glue: 他用膠水將封面粘在書上。He glued the cover to the book.
粘貼(ㄋㄧㄢˊ ㄊㄧㄝ)
to paste; to stick: 我們在牆上粘貼標語。We pasted slogans on the wall.

六畫

【粟】 4240
ㄙㄨˋ suh sù
1. grain; paddy
2. millet
3. goose flesh; goose pimples; goose bumps; goose skin
4. a Chinese family name
粟帛(ㄙㄨˋ ㄅㄛˊ)
grain and cloth
粟米(ㄙㄨˋ ㄇㄧˇ)
millet; grain
粟飯(ㄙㄨˋ ㄈㄢˋ)
coarse staple food
粟紅貫朽(ㄙㄨˋ ㄏㄨㄥˊ ㄍㄨㄢˋ ㄒㄧㄡˇ)
in time of great prosperity; in a land of plenty
粟倉(ㄙㄨˋ ㄘㄤ)
a granary; a barn for grain

【粢】4241 1. ㄗ tzy zī
1. the millet to be offered in sacrifice
2. the grain
粢盛(ㄗ ㄔㄥˊ)
the millet placed in a sacrificial vessel

【粢】4241 (餈)2. ㄘˊ tsyr cí
rice cakes

【粥】4242 ㄓㄨˋ juh zhù (語音 ㄓㄡ jou zhōu)
congee; rice gruel
粥餳(ㄓㄡ ㄒㄧㄥˊ)
sweetened congee
粥少僧多(ㄓㄡ ㄕㄠˇ ㄙㄥ ㄉㄨㄛ)
(literally) The congee is not enough for the many monks. —not enough for circulation or distribution

【粵】4243 ㄩㄝˋ yueh yuè
1. Kwangtung Province
2. Kwangtung and Kwangsi Provinces
3. an opening particle
粵東(ㄩㄝˋ ㄉㄨㄥ)
Kwangtung Province
粵海(ㄩㄝˋ ㄏㄞˇ)
① the South China Sea ② short for Kwangtung's Customs House
粵漢鐵路(ㄩㄝˋ ㄏㄢˋ ㄊㄧㄝˇ ㄌㄨˋ)
the Canton-Hankow Railway
粵江(ㄩㄝˋ ㄐㄧㄤ)
another name of the Pearl River
粵江流域(ㄩㄝˋ ㄐㄧㄤ ㄌㄧㄡˊ ㄩˋ)
the Pearl River Valley
粵劇(ㄩㄝˋ ㄐㄩˋ)
Canton opera
粵犬吠雪(ㄩㄝˋ ㄑㄩㄢˇ ㄈㄟˋ ㄒㄩㄝˇ)
(literally) A Kwangtung dog barks at the snow. (Kwangtung being a subtropical region)—People are startled by an unusual phenomenon.
粵西(ㄩㄝˋ ㄒㄧ)
the former name of Kwangsi
粵人(ㄩㄝˋ ㄖㄣˊ)
a Cantonese

【粧】4244 (妝) ㄓㄨㄤ juang zhuāng
1. toilet; to adorn; to doll up: 她梳粧打扮後就出門了。She went out after dressing her hair and applying makeup.
2. woman's personal adornments
3. a bride's trousseau
4. to disguise or pretend
粧扮(ㄓㄨㄤ ㄅㄢˋ)
to doll up: 她粧扮得漂漂亮亮的去參加宴會。She was all dolled up for the party.
粧臺(ㄓㄨㄤ ㄊㄞˊ)
a dressing table
粧奩(ㄓㄨㄤ ㄌㄧㄢˊ)
a bride's trousseau; a dowry
粧飾(ㄓㄨㄤ ㄕˋ)
① to adorn; to doll up ② to pretend

七畫

【粲】4245 ㄘㄢˋ tsann càn
1. bright and clear; radiant
2. beautiful; splendid; excellent
3. smiling; laughing
4. well-polished rice
粲爛(ㄘㄢˋ ㄌㄢˋ)
brilliant; sparkling; radiant; bright
粲花(ㄘㄢˋ ㄏㄨㄚ)
good at speech; skilled in talking
粲者(ㄘㄢˋ ㄓㄜˇ)
a beauty; a pretty girl
粲然(ㄘㄢˋ ㄖㄢˊ)
① bright and brilliant ② smiling brightly
粲然一笑(ㄘㄢˋ ㄖㄢˊ ㄧˊ ㄒㄧㄠˋ)
to give a beaming smile
粲粲(ㄘㄢˋ ㄘㄢˋ)
(said of dresses, etc.) bright, splendid and eye-catching

【粱】4246 ㄌㄧㄤˊ liang liáng
maize; grain; sorghums
粱肉(ㄌㄧㄤˊ ㄖㄡˋ)
(literally) grain and meat —a sumptuous meal

【粮】4247 (糧) ㄌㄧㄤˊ liang liáng
provisions; food; grain; rations

【粳】4248 (秔、稉) ㄍㄥ geng gēng (語音 ㄐㄧㄥ jing jīng)
nonglutinous rice

八畫

【精】4249 ㄐㄧㄥ jing jīng
1.polished rice; unmixed rice
2.the essence; the essentials: 薄荷精 essence of peppermint
3.energy; spirits
4.the male sperm; semen
5.fine and delicate; exquisite
6.dedicated; intensive
7.very; extremely; completely
8.keen; smart; sharp; clever; shrewd: 他太精了，我們不過他。He was too smart for me.
9.skilled; to specialize in: 他精於繪畫。He is skilled in painting.
10.a goblin; a spirit; a demon
精白(ㄐㄧㄥ ㄅㄞˊ)
extremely white; very pure
精兵(ㄐㄧㄥ ㄅㄧㄥ)
crack troops
精疲力竭(ㄐㄧㄥ ㄆㄧˊ ㄌㄧˋ ㄐㄧㄝˊ)
exhausted; dog-tired; worn-out: 長途跋涉後他精疲力竭。He was worn-out after the long hike.
精闢(ㄐㄧㄥ ㄆㄧˋ)
penetrating; brilliant; incisive: 這是一篇精闢的評論。This is a brilliant comment.
精品(ㄐㄧㄥ ㄆㄧㄣˇ)
an exquisite article; an article of top quality
精美(ㄐㄧㄥ ㄇㄟˇ)
exquisite; delicate and beautiful: 這花瓶工藝很精美。This vase is a piece of exquisite workmanship.
精密(ㄐㄧㄥ ㄇㄧˋ)
minute or detailed; precise; accurate; careful: 科學家對病菌做精密的觀察。Scientists make accurate observations of germs.
精密儀器(ㄐㄧㄥ ㄇㄧˋ ㄧˊ ㄑㄧˋ)
precision instruments
精妙(ㄐㄧㄥ ㄇㄧㄠˋ)
exquisite and delicate; wonderful; ingenious

精敏(ㄐㄧㄥ ㄇㄧㄣˇ)
keen and active (or energetic)
精明(ㄐㄧㄥ ㄇㄧㄥˊ)
keen or sharp; clever
精明強幹(ㄐㄧㄥ ㄇㄧㄥˊ ㄑㄧㄤˊ ㄍㄢˋ)
shrewd and capable man
精打細算(ㄐㄧㄥ ㄉㄚˇ ㄒㄧˋ ㄙㄨㄢˋ)
calculate carefully and budget strictly
精到(ㄐㄧㄥ ㄉㄠˋ)
keen and cautious; sharp and careful to the very last detail
精當(ㄐㄧㄥ ㄉㄤˋ)
precise and appropriate
精讀(ㄐㄧㄥ ㄉㄨˊ)
to study or read in minute detail; intensive reading
精挑細選(ㄐㄧㄥ ㄊㄧㄠ ㄒㄧˋ ㄒㄩㄢˇ)
very choosy
精通(ㄐㄧㄥ ㄊㄨㄥ)
well versed in; good at; to have an excellent command of; expert at; to master: 他們精通多種語言。They master many languages.
精囊(ㄐㄧㄥ ㄋㄤˊ)
a spermary
精力(ㄐㄧㄥ ㄌㄧˋ)
the sum total of a person's mental and physical strength; stamina; vitality; energy: 不要浪費精力。Don't waste your energy.
精力旺盛(ㄐㄧㄥ ㄌㄧˋ ㄨㄤˋ ㄕㄥˋ)
very energetic and vigorous; to be full of vitality: 他是個精力旺盛的工作者。He is an energetic worker.
精練(ㄐㄧㄥ ㄌㄧㄢˋ)
smart and capable; skillful and experienced
精煉(ㄐㄧㄥ ㄌㄧㄢˋ)
to rectify; to refine; refined: 油及砂糖是精煉過的。Oil and sugar are refined.
精良(ㄐㄧㄥ ㄌㄧㄤˊ)
of very high quality; exquisite; fine; excellent
精靈(ㄐㄧㄥ ㄌㄧㄥˊ)
①an elf; a fairy; goblins, ghosts, spirits, etc. ②(said of children) a very clever and naughty young fellow
精廬(ㄐㄧㄥ ㄌㄨˊ)
①a house decorated with very refined tastes ②a study; a reading room
精怪(ㄐㄧㄥ ㄍㄨㄞˋ)
a general name of demons, monsters, etc.
精光(ㄐㄧㄥ ㄍㄨㄤ)
①stark-naked; without a stitch on; completely nude ②nothing left; exhausted; completely gone: 他把積蓄花得精光。He exhausted his savings.
精工(ㄐㄧㄥ ㄍㄨㄥ)
delicate and painstaking work; exquisite craftsmanship
精覈(ㄐㄧㄥ ㄏㄜˊ)
a careful and intensive examination or survey
精悍(ㄐㄧㄥ ㄏㄢˋ)
strong and unyielding
精華(ㄐㄧㄥ ㄏㄨㄚˊ)
the essence; the essentials; the cream or choicest parts: 最好的學生即是全班的精華。The cream of the class is made up of the best students.
精簡(ㄐㄧㄥ ㄐㄧㄢˇ)
to simplify
精金良玉(ㄐㄧㄥ ㄐㄧㄣ ㄌㄧㄤˊ ㄩˋ)
(said of a person's disposition) pure and kind; virtuous and tolerant
精進(ㄐㄧㄥ ㄐㄧㄣˋ)
①to dedicate oneself to progress; to devote oneself to improvement; to forge ahead vigorously ②(Buddhism) *virya*; courageously progressing in the good and eliminating the evil
精絕(ㄐㄧㄥ ㄐㄩㄝˊ)
exquisite to the very last detail; perfect
精氣(ㄐㄧㄥ ㄑㄧˋ)
①(Chinese medicine) vitality; essence and vital energy ②(Buddhism) vitality; virility
精巧(ㄐㄧㄥ ㄑㄧㄠˇ)
exquisite; fine and delicate (workmanship, etc.): 這是一件精巧的藝術品。This is an exquisite work of art.
精勤(ㄐㄧㄥ ㄑㄧㄣˊ)
dedicated and diligent; devoted and industrious
精確(ㄐㄧㄥ ㄑㄩㄝˋ)
precise; accurate; precision; accuracy: 你做算術一定要精確。You must be accurate in arithmetic.
精細(ㄐㄧㄥ ㄒㄧˋ)
①fine (materials, etc.); delicate and painstaking (workmanship, handicraft, etc.); exquisite ②very careful and attentive; thorough
精心(ㄐㄧㄥ ㄒㄧㄣ)
elaborate; attentive and circumspect; meticulous; to put all one's mind in: 他精心設計一種新型的冰箱。He puts all his mind in designing a new refrigerator.
精心傑作(ㄐㄧㄥ ㄒㄧㄣ ㄐㄧㄝˊ ㄗㄨㄛˋ)
a masterpiece; a brainchild
精選(ㄐㄧㄥ ㄒㄩㄢˇ)
handpicked; choice; to pick the best; to handpick; to select
精緻(ㄐㄧㄥ ㄓˋ)
(said of materials, etc.) fine; exquisite; delicate: 好精緻的刺繡。What a delicate piece of embroidery!
精製(ㄐㄧㄥ ㄓˋ)
specially picked and baked (tea, etc.); highly finished; refined; manufactured with special care
精湛(ㄐㄧㄥ ㄓㄢˋ)
consummate; exquisite; perfect: 這位雕刻家以精湛的技巧聞名。The sculptor is famous for his consummate skill.
精裝本(ㄐㄧㄥ ㄓㄨㄤ ㄅㄣˇ)
(said of books) a deluxe edition: 這本字典是精裝本。This dictionary is a deluxe edition.
精裝品(ㄐㄧㄥ ㄓㄨㄤ ㄆㄧㄣˇ)
articles in deluxe packing
精忠報國(ㄐㄧㄥ ㄓㄨㄥ ㄅㄠˋ ㄍㄨㄛˊ)
to serve one's fatherland with unreserved loyalty
精巢(ㄐㄧㄥ ㄔㄠˊ)
a spermary 亦作「精囊」
精誠(ㄐㄧㄥ ㄔㄥˊ)
purity and sincerity; earnest and sincere
精誠團結(ㄐㄧㄥ ㄔㄥˊ ㄊㄨㄢˊ ㄐㄧㄝˊ)
to unite together with utmost sincerity; gung ho;

〔米部〕

〔米部〕

esprit de corps

精誠所至，金石爲開(ㄐㄧㄥ ㄔㄥˊ ㄙㄨㄛˇ ㄓˋ, ㄐㄧㄣ ㄕˊ ㄨㄟˊ ㄎㄞ)
Where wholehearted dedication is directed, the whole world will step aside to let you by.

精純(ㄐㄧㄥ ㄔㄨㄣˊ)
① pure; unalloyed; unmixed ② to refine; refinement

精蟲(ㄐㄧㄥ ㄔㄨㄥˊ)
spermatozoa

精舍(ㄐㄧㄥ ㄕㄜˋ)
① a study ② a pure abode; a Buddhist temple ③ a villa

精深(ㄐㄧㄥ ㄕㄣ)
profound; profundity

精神(ㄐㄧㄥ ㄕㄣˊ)
① one's spirit: 你今天很沒精神。You lack spirit today. ② lively; vigorous ③ mental

精神飽滿(ㄐㄧㄥ ㄕㄣˊ ㄅㄠˇ ㄇㄢˇ)
in high spirits; vigorous and energetic

精神病(ㄐㄧㄥ ㄕㄣˊ ㄅㄧㄥˋ)
mental illness

精神病學(ㄐㄧㄥ ㄕㄣˊ ㄅㄧㄥˋ ㄒㄩㄝˊ)
psychiatry

精神病院(ㄐㄧㄥ ㄕㄣˊ ㄅㄧㄥˋ ㄩㄢˋ)
a mental hospital or sanitarium; an asylum

精神不死(ㄐㄧㄥ ㄕㄣˊ ㄅㄨˋ ㄙˇ)
The spirit (of martyrs, etc.) will never die.

精神分裂症(ㄐㄧㄥ ㄕㄣˊ ㄈㄣ ㄌㄧㄝˋ ㄓㄥˋ)
schizophrenia

精神分析(ㄐㄧㄥ ㄕㄣˊ ㄈㄣ ㄒㄧ)
psychoanalysis

精神抖擻(ㄐㄧㄥ ㄕㄣˊ ㄉㄡˇ ㄙㄡˇ)
high-spirited; sprightly; vigorous and energetic; enthusiastic

精神感召(ㄐㄧㄥ ㄕㄣˊ ㄍㄢˇ ㄓㄠˋ)
to be moved to emulate a noble example; to be inspired by (a great leader)

精神恍惚(ㄐㄧㄥ ㄕㄣˊ ㄏㄨㄤˇ ㄏㄨ)
absent-minded

精神教育(ㄐㄧㄥ ㄕㄣˊ ㄐㄧㄠˋ ㄩˋ)
moral education

精神狀態(ㄐㄧㄥ ㄕㄣˊ ㄓㄨㄤˋ ㄊㄞˋ)
a state of mind; a mental condition

精神失常(ㄐㄧㄥ ㄕㄣˊ ㄕ ㄔㄤˊ)
mental disorder; mental derangement; out of one's mind

精神生活(ㄐㄧㄥ ㄕㄣˊ ㄕㄥ ㄏㄨㄛˊ)
spiritual life; moral life

精神文明(ㄐㄧㄥ ㄕㄣˊ ㄨㄣˊ ㄇㄧㄥˊ)
spiritual civilization

精銳(ㄐㄧㄥ ㄖㄨㄟˋ)
crack; picked

精銳部隊(ㄐㄧㄥ ㄖㄨㄟˋ ㄅㄨˋ ㄉㄨㄟˋ)
crack troops; picked troops

精子(ㄐㄧㄥ ㄗˇ)
spermatozoa 亦作「精蟲」

精彩(ㄐㄧㄥ ㄘㄞˇ)
① the highlight or climax (of a play, etc.); the most attractive or wonderful part (of something) ② Wonderful! 或 Bravo! 或 Excellent!

精粗(ㄐㄧㄥ ㄘㄨ)
the fineness and coarseness of things

精萃(ㄐㄧㄥ ㄘㄨㄟˋ)
cream; pick

精粹(ㄐㄧㄥ ㄘㄨㄟˋ)
the essence or essentials; refined and pure; the cream—the best part of anything: 這是我國民族文化的精粹。This is the cream of our national culture.

精髓(ㄐㄧㄥ ㄙㄨㄟˇ)
the marrow; the pith; the quintessence; the essence

精一(ㄐㄧㄥ ㄧ)
dedicated; devoted; pure

精義(ㄐㄧㄥ ㄧˋ)
the essential significance; the profound meaning

精益求精(ㄐㄧㄥ ㄧˋ ㄑㄧㄡˊ ㄐㄧㄥ)
Second best is not good enough.—to try for the best; to do still better: 我們凡事精益求精。We endeavored to do everything better.

精液(ㄐㄧㄥ ㄧㄝˋ)
sperm; semen

精要(ㄐㄧㄥ ㄧㄠˋ)
the essentials; the fundamentals

精研(ㄐㄧㄥ ㄧㄢˊ)
to study intensively: 她精研社會學。She studies sociology intensively.

精鹽(ㄐㄧㄥ ㄧㄢˊ)
refined salt; purified salt: 請把精鹽遞給我。Pass me the refined salt, please.

精微(ㄐㄧㄥ ㄨㄟˊ)
deep; profound; profundity

精衛塡海(ㄐㄧㄥ ㄨㄟˋ ㄊㄧㄢˊ ㄏㄞˇ)
Ching-wei, a legendary small bird, supposed to be the metamorphosis of the drowned daughter of Yen Ti (炎帝), was also known as 寃禽(the bird of hate), and as it was often in the habit of dropping bits of wood and stone into the ocean, in the vain hope of filling it, it was looked upon as a symbol of deep and unsatiable hatred.

精於此道(ㄐㄧㄥ ㄩˊ ㄘˇ ㄉㄠˋ)
skilled in this field

【粹】 4250
ㄘㄨㄟˋ tsuey cuì

1. pure; unmixed; perfect; unadulterated
2. the essence; the best

粹白(ㄘㄨㄟˋ ㄅㄞˊ)
pure white

【粺】 4251
ㄅㄞˋ bay bài

polished rice

九畫

【糊】 4252
ㄏㄨˊ hwu hú

1. paste: 請用漿糊把它貼上。Stick it with paste.
2. to paste
3. scorched
4. not clear; blurred; confused; ambiguous; unintelligible

糊塗(ㄏㄨˊ ㄊㄨˊ)or(ㄏㄨˊ ˙ㄊㄨ)
① mixed-up; confused ② stupid; foolish: 別裝糊塗。Do not play the fool.

糊塗蟲(ㄏㄨˊ ㄊㄨˊ ㄔㄨㄥˊ)
a blunderer; a bungler

糊裏糊塗(ㄏㄨˊ ˙ㄌㄧ ㄏㄨˊ ㄊㄨˊ)
(to do something) without thinking; confused or mixed-up; muddled: 他仍然是糊裏糊塗地混日子。He's still muddling on.

糊口(ㄏㄨˊ ㄎㄡˇ)
to make a living; to make both ends meet; to live from hand to mouth 亦作「餬口」: 他以割草糊口。Mowing lawns is his livelihood.

糊精(ㄏㄨˊ ㄐㄧㄥ)
(chemistry) dextrine
糊牆(ㄏㄨˊ ㄑㄧㄤˊ)
to wallpaper; to paper a wall; paperhanging
糊窗(ㄏㄨˊ ㄔㄨㄤ)
to paper a window: 他用紙糊窗。He pasted a sheet of paper over a lattice window.

【糉】4253 (粽) ㄗㄨㄥˋ tzonq zòng
glutinous rice tamale—made by wrapping the rice in broad leaves of reeds and boiled for a few hours—usually with other ingredients, such as dates, meat, oysters, beans, etc.
糉子 or 粽子(ㄗㄨㄥˋ ˙ㄗ)
glutinous rice dumplings; rice tamale

【糅】4254 ㄖㄡˇ roou rǒu
to mix; mixed
糅合(ㄖㄡˇ ㄏㄜˊ)
to mix together; to blend; to form a mixture
糅雜(ㄖㄡˇ ㄗㄚˊ)
mixed; disorderly

十畫

【糗】4255 ㄑㄧㄡˇ cheou qiǔ
parched grain, rice, etc.; dry food; dry rations

【糒】4256 ㄅㄟˋ bey bèi
parched rice—as a dry food for a journey in the days of old

【糕】4257 (餻) ㄍㄠ gau gāo
cakes; pastries; steamed dumplings
糕餅(ㄍㄠ ㄅㄧㄥˇ)
cakes and biscuits
糕餅店(ㄍㄠ ㄅㄧㄥˇ ㄉㄧㄢˋ)
a pastry shop
糕點(ㄍㄠ ㄉㄧㄢˇ)
cakes and pastries

【糖】4258 ㄊㄤˊ tarng táng
sugar
糖分(ㄊㄤˊ ㄈㄣ)
sugar content; the percentage of natural sugar in food items
糖尿病(ㄊㄤˊ ㄋㄧㄠˋ ㄅㄧㄥˋ)
diabetes
糖尿病人(ㄊㄤˊ ㄋㄧㄠˋ ㄅㄧㄥˋ ㄖㄣˊ)
a diabetic
糖類(ㄊㄤˊ ㄌㄟˋ)
(chemistry) carbohydrate
糖蘿蔔(ㄊㄤˊ ㄌㄨㄛˊ ˙ㄅㄛ)
sugar beets; sweet carrots
糖果(ㄊㄤˊ ㄍㄨㄛˇ)
candy; sweets
糖果店(ㄊㄤˊ ㄍㄨㄛˇ ㄉㄧㄢˋ)
a candy shop
糖果錢(ㄊㄤˊ ㄍㄨㄛˇ ㄑㄧㄢˊ)
a child's candy allowance or pocket money
糖葫蘆(ㄊㄤˊ ㄏㄨˊ ˙ㄌㄨ)
sweetened fruit on stick handles; sugarcoated haws on a stick
糖漿(ㄊㄤˊ ㄐㄧㄤ)
syrup; molasses
糖精(ㄊㄤˊ ㄐㄧㄥ)
saccharin; gluside
糖廠(ㄊㄤˊ ㄔㄤˇ)
a sugar mill; a sugar refinery
糖食(ㄊㄤˊ ㄕˊ)
sweetmeats; sugar-sweetened edibles
糖商(ㄊㄤˊ ㄕㄤ)
a sugar merchant
糖水(ㄊㄤˊ ㄕㄨㄟˇ)
sweetened water; sugar solution
糖醋排骨(ㄊㄤˊ ㄘㄨˋ ㄆㄞˊ ㄍㄨˇ)
sweet and sour spareribs
糖醋魚(ㄊㄤˊ ㄘㄨˋ ㄩˊ)
fish in sweet and sour sauce
糖衣(ㄊㄤˊ ㄧ)
sugarcoating
糖業(ㄊㄤˊ ㄧㄝˋ)
the sugar industry

十一畫

【糜】4259 ㄇㄧˊ mi mí
1. congee; porridge; rice gruel
2. mashed; rotten; corrupted
3. to waste
糜費(ㄇㄧˊ ㄈㄟˋ)
extravagant or wasteful; to waste
糜爛(ㄇㄧˊ ㄌㄢˋ)
① rotten; corrupt debauchery: 她生活糜爛。She lived a life of debauchery. ② to oppress and destroy the people (through devious means)
糜粥(ㄇㄧˊ ㄓㄡ)
congee; porridge

【糞】4260 ㄈㄣˋ fenn fèn
1. night soil; manure; dung: 糞被用做肥料。Dung is used as manure.
2. to fertilize the land
3. to sweep; to wipe out
糞便(ㄈㄣˋ ㄅㄧㄢˋ)
excrement; night soil
糞門(ㄈㄣˋ ㄇㄣˊ)
the anus 亦作「肛門」
糞夫(ㄈㄣˋ ㄈㄨ)
one whose vocation is to collect night soil; a nightman
糞堆(ㄈㄣˋ ㄉㄨㄟ)
a dunghill
糞土(ㄈㄣˋ ㄊㄨˇ)or 糞壤(ㄈㄣˋ ㄖㄤˇ)
(literally) dung and earth—something of little value; dirty earth; refuse: 他視金錢如糞土。He looked upon money as dirt.
糞坑(ㄈㄣˋ ㄎㄥ)
a manure pit; a cesspool
糞箕(ㄈㄣˋ ㄐㄧ)
a dustpan 亦作「畚箕」
糞池(ㄈㄣˋ ㄔˊ)
a manure pit; a septic tank 亦作「化糞池」

【糙】4261 ㄘㄠ tsau cāo
1. coarse or unpolished; rough: 這布料有些粗糙。This cloth feels rough.
2. rough; rude; rash; desultory; careless
糙米(ㄘㄠ ㄇㄧˇ)
unpolished rice

【糝】4262 ㄙㄢˇ saan sǎn
1. a grain of rice
2. mixing rice with broth

【糟】4263 ㄗㄠ tzau zāo
1. sediment or dregs of wine: 酒糟 fermented grain mash
2. to soak food items (as fish, meat, etc.) in wine or wine sediment
3. (said of a plan, arrangement, etc.) to become a mess, or in bad shape: 你已

經把這事弄糟了。You've made a mess of the job.
4. decayed; rotten; spoiled: 這桌子糟爛了。This table is rotten.
5. not sturdy or strong
6. lousy; a louse

糟鼻子(ㄗㄠ ㄅㄧˊ ·ㄗ)
a drunkard's nose

糟粕(ㄗㄠ ㄆㄛˋ)
① dregs or sediment of wine ② something of little value; refuse; dregs: 我們剔除糟粕，吸取精華。We discard the dregs and absorb the essence.

糟蹋(ㄗㄠ ·ㄊㄚ)
① to waste (talent, great ability, etc. on trifles); to ruin; to degrade or debase: 剪裁時要留意，別把布料糟蹋了。Cut the cloth carefully. Don't spoil it.② to insult; to affront: 你說話可不要這樣糟蹋人。Do not affront anyone by talking like this.

糟透了(ㄗㄠ ㄊㄡˋ ·ㄌㄜ)
Too bad! 或What a mess!

糟了(ㄗㄠ ·ㄌㄜ)
Too bad! 或 Alas!

糟爛(ㄗㄠ ㄌㄢˋ)
spoiled, rotten or decayed

糟糕(ㄗㄠ ㄍㄠ)
Alas! 或 What a mess! 或 Too bad! 糟糕！我把車子鑰匙搞丟了。Alas! I've lost the car key.

糟糠(ㄗㄠ ㄎㄤ)
① distillers' grains, husks, chaff, etc.—(figuratively) food of a destitute person ② the wife one married in poverty

糟糠之妻(ㄗㄠ ㄎㄤ ㄓ ㄑㄧ)
the wife one married in poverty (should not be discarded in one's affluence)

糟踐(ㄗㄠ ㄐㄧㄢˋ)
① to waste; to debase or degrade; to ruin ② to insult; to libel

糟心(ㄗㄠ ㄒㄧㄣ)
① unlucky ②(said of plans, arrangements, etc.) to get into a mess: 你把事情搞得糟心透了。You got things into such a mess.

糟魚(ㄗㄠ ㄩˊ)
fish pickled with distillers' grains

【糠】 4264
ㄎㄤ kang kāng

1. husks of rice; rice bran or chaff
2. of inferior quality; not sturdy; empty inside; things of no value
3. spongy

糠秕(ㄎㄤ ㄅㄧˇ)
rice bran 亦作「秕糠」

糠糜(ㄎㄤ ㄇㄧˊ)
coarse food

糠蝦(ㄎㄤ ㄒㄧㄚ)
Mysis opossum shrimp, a variety of greyish freshwater shrimp about one inch long

糠市(ㄎㄤ ㄕˋ)
slums; shantytowns

【糢】 4265
(模) ㄇㄛˊ mo mó

blurred; indistinct

糢糊(ㄇㄛˊ ·ㄏㄨ)
blurred; indistinct; unclear; confused: 眼淚使他的眼睛糢糊。Tears blurred his eyes.

【糨】 4266
(糡) ㄐㄧㄤˋ jianq jiàng

1. paste; to paste together; starched; to starch
2. thick

糨糊(ㄐㄧㄤˋ ·ㄏㄨ)or 糨子(ㄐㄧㄤˋ ·ㄗ)
paste; glue

十二畫

【糧】 4267
(粮) ㄌㄧㄤˊ liang liáng

1. grain; food; provisions; rations: 敵軍彈盡糧絕。The enemy ran out of ammunition and food.
2. farm or land taxes

糧票(ㄌㄧㄤˊ ㄆㄧㄠˋ)
a food coupon; a grain coupon

糧秣(ㄌㄧㄤˊ ㄇㄛˋ)
military food supplies

糧米(ㄌㄧㄤˊ ㄇㄧˇ)
foodstuffs

糧道(ㄌㄧㄤˊ ㄉㄠˋ)
①a road for transportation of food ②(formerly) an official in charge of land taxes

糧行(ㄌㄧㄤˊ ㄏㄤˊ)
a store selling grain and provisions

糧餉(ㄌㄧㄤˊ ㄒㄧㄤˇ)
army provisions and payroll

糧船(ㄌㄧㄤˊ ㄔㄨㄢˊ)
boats for transporting grain

糧食(ㄌㄧㄤˊ ㄕˊ)
foodstuffs; provisions; grain for human consumption: 穀類及肉類皆係糧食。Grain and meat are foodstuffs.

糧食局(ㄌㄧㄤˊ ㄕˊ ㄐㄩˊ)
a grain bureau

糧草(ㄌㄧㄤˊ ㄘㄠˇ)
provisions (for men) and fodder (for horses); food supplies for an army; rations and forage

糧倉(ㄌㄧㄤˊ ㄘㄤ)
a granary

十三畫

【糪】 4268
ㄅㄛˊ bor bó

half-cooked rice; parboiled rice

十四畫

【糯】 4269
(穤、稬) ㄋㄨㄛˋ nuoh nuò

glutinous rice

糯米(ㄋㄨㄛˋ ㄇㄧˇ)
polished glutinous rice

糯稻(ㄋㄨㄛˋ ㄉㄠˋ)
unhusked glutinous rice

【糰】 4270
ㄊㄨㄢˊ twan tuán

round dumplings made from wheat or glutinous rice flour

糰子(ㄊㄨㄢˊ ·ㄗ)
a small dough cake

十五畫

【糲】 4271
ㄌㄧˋ lih lì

1. unpolished rice
2. coarse; rough

糲飯(ㄌㄧˋ ㄈㄢˋ)
cooked unpolished rice

糲粱(ㄌㄧˋ ㄌㄧㄤˊ)
coarse or simple food

十六畫

【糴】 4272 ㄉㄧˊ dyi dí

to buy grain

糴米(ㄉㄧˊ ㄇㄧˇ)

to buy rice

十七畫

【糵】 4273 (蘗) ㄋㄧㄝˋ nieh niè

yeast, leaven or barm for making liquors

十九畫

【糶】 4274 ㄊㄧㄠˋ tiaw tiào

to sell grain

糶米(ㄊㄧㄠˋ ㄇㄧˇ)

to sell rice

糸部

ㄇㄧˋ mih mì

一畫

【系】 4275 ㄒㄧˋ shih xì

1. a system; a line; a connecting link; a connection
2. lineage; a genealogy
3. (politics) a clique; a theoretic or party line
4. (in a college or a university) a department or school
5. to relate to; to bear on: 我們成敗系於此舉。We stand or fall by this.
6. to be
7. a Chinese family name

系絆(ㄒㄧˋ ㄅㄢˋ)

to bridle; to tie; to hinder; to fetter; to restrain; to confine

系譜(ㄒㄧˋ ㄆㄨˇ)

a genealogy; lineage; a family tree

系統(ㄒㄧˋ ㄊㄨㄥˇ)

a system; systematic: 這是個有系統的計畫。This is a systematic project.

系統分類學(ㄒㄧˋ ㄊㄨㄥˇ ㄈㄣ ㄌㄟˋ ㄒㄩㄝˊ)

phylogenetic systematics

系統化(ㄒㄧˋ ㄊㄨㄥˇ ㄏㄨㄚˋ)

to systematize; systematized

系列(ㄒㄧˋ ㄌㄧㄝˋ)

①a line or lineage (of thoughts, theories, etc. arranged chronologically) ② a row; a series

系主任(ㄒㄧˋ ㄓㄨˇ ㄖㄣˋ)

the head or chairman of a department (in a college): 他是系主任。He is chairman of the department.

系出名門(ㄒㄧˋ ㄔㄨ ㄇㄧㄥˊ ㄇㄣˊ)

to come of a noble or reputed family

系族(ㄒㄧˋ ㄗㄨˊ)

the family lineage; a genealogy

系孫(ㄒㄧˋ ㄙㄨㄣ)

a grandson of someone of the same family lineage of one's own generation

【糺】 4276 ㄐㄧㄡˇ jeou jiǔ (又讀 ㄐㄧㄡ jiou jiū)

to collaborate; to band together

二畫

【糾】 4277 ㄐㄧㄡ jiou jiū (又讀ㄐㄧㄡˇ jeou jiǔ)

1. to supervise; to inspect; to investigate
2. to correct; to censure; to impeach; to discipline
3. to collaborate; to band together; to bind together; to entangle; to involve; involved

糾謬(ㄐㄧㄡ ㄇㄧㄡˋ)

to correct a mistake, blunder or evil

糾紛(ㄐㄧㄡ ㄈㄣ)

disputes; quarrels; entanglements: 這事與政治糾紛無關。It is independent of political entanglements.

糾彈(ㄐㄧㄡ ㄊㄢˊ)

to censure and impeach (officials)

糾葛(ㄐㄧㄡ ㄍㄜˊ)

a dispute; an endless involvement: 我們之間有一點糾葛。There's a dispute between us.

糾合(ㄐㄧㄡ ㄏㄜˊ)

to band together: 他糾合了一夥流氓。He banded together a bunch of rascals.

糾劾(ㄐㄧㄡ ㄏㄜˊ)

to censure and impeach

糾夥行劫(ㄐㄧㄡ ㄏㄨㄛˇ ㄒㄧㄥˊ ㄐㄧㄝˊ)

to band together and commit robbery

糾集(ㄐㄧㄡ ㄐㄧˊ)

to get together; to muster

糾結(ㄐㄧㄡ ㄐㄧㄝˊ)

to collaborate; to band together

糾正(ㄐㄧㄡ ㄓㄥˋ)

to correct; to check; to discipline; to rectify

糾衆(ㄐㄧㄡ ㄓㄨㄥˋ)

to stir up a mob; to gather a mob

糾察(ㄐㄧㄡ ㄔㄚˊ)

①to discipline; to investigate; to picket ②a disciplinary officer

糾察隊(ㄐㄧㄡ ㄔㄚˊ ㄉㄨㄟˋ)

a disciplinary patrol; pickets

糾察員(ㄐㄧㄡ ㄔㄚˊ ㄩㄢˊ)

a disciplinary officer; an inspector; an officer in charge of maintaining order and discipline

糾纏(ㄐㄧㄡ ㄔㄢˊ)

①to tangle; to involve; entanglement or involvement ②to pester: 她爲了錢屢次糾纏他。She repeatedly pestered him for money.

糾繩(ㄐㄧㄡ ㄕㄥˊ)

to correct; to discipline

三畫

【紀】 4278 ㄐㄧˋ jih jì

1. a historical record; annals; chronicles
2. a period of 12 years
3. a century
4. to arrange; to put in order
5. institutions; laws and regulations; discipline
6. the age of a person
7. a geological period
8. a Chinese family name

紀年(ㄐㄧˋ ㄋㄧㄢˊ)

annals or chronicles
紀念(ㄐㄧˋ ㄋㄧㄢˋ)
to remember; to commemorate: 那是一個值得紀念的日子。It is a memorable day.
紀念碑(ㄐㄧˋ ㄋㄧㄢˋ ㄅㄟ)
a monument; a memorial
紀念品(ㄐㄧˋ ㄋㄧㄢˋ ㄆㄧㄣˇ)
a souvenir; a keepsake; a memento
紀念館(ㄐㄧˋ ㄋㄧㄢˋ ㄍㄨㄢˇ)
a memorial hall; a museum in memory of somebody
紀念會(ㄐㄧˋ ㄋㄧㄢˋ ㄏㄨㄟˋ)
a commemorative meeting or rally
紀念週(ㄐㄧˋ ㄋㄧㄢˋ ㄓㄡ)
a commemorative meeting on every Monday in memory of Dr. Sun Yat-sen, the founder of the Republic of China
紀念章(ㄐㄧˋ ㄋㄧㄢˋ ㄓㄤ)
a commemoration badge or medal
紀念日(ㄐㄧˋ ㄋㄧㄢˋ ㄖˋ)
a commemoration day; a memorial day; an anniversary: 今天是我們的結婚紀念日。Today is our wedding anniversary.
紀念册(ㄐㄧˋ ㄋㄧㄢˋ ㄘㄜˋ)
an autograph book
紀念醫院(ㄐㄧˋ ㄋㄧㄢˋ ㄧ ㄩㄢˋ)
a memorial hospital
紀念郵票(ㄐㄧˋ ㄋㄧㄢˋ ㄧㄡˊ ㄆㄧㄠˋ)
a commemorative stamp
紀念郵戳(ㄐㄧˋ ㄋㄧㄢˋ ㄧㄡˊ ㄔㄨㄛ)
a commemoration postmark
紀錄(ㄐㄧˋ ㄌㄨˋ)
① a record; minutes (of a conference); to take notes: 這事載於會議紀錄中。It is on the minutes. ② one who records; a recording clerk; a recorder
紀錄片(ㄐㄧˋ ㄌㄨˋ ㄆㄧㄢˋ)
a documentary film
紀律(ㄐㄧˋ ㄌㄩˋ)
discipline; laws and regulations
紀綱(ㄐㄧˋ ㄍㄤ)
①institutions; rules and regulations② (obsolete) a servant
紀功(ㄐㄧˋ ㄍㄨㄥ)
to record an accomplishment
紀功碑(ㄐㄧˋ ㄍㄨㄥ ㄅㄟ)
a stone tablet erected in memory of a worthy deed
紀限儀(ㄐㄧˋ ㄒㄧㄢˋ ㄧˊ)
a sextant 亦作「六分儀」
紀傳體(ㄐㄧˋ ㄓㄨㄢˋ ㄊㄧˇ)
a form of historical record that centers on individuals and their performances (as opposed to annals or chronicles)
紀實(ㄐㄧˋ ㄕˊ)
① to record the facts; a recording of facts ② an on-the-spot report
紀事(ㄐㄧˋ ㄕˋ)
to record a happening, an occurrence or an incident; to chronicle
紀事本末體(ㄐㄧˋ ㄕˋ ㄅㄣˇ ㄇㄛˋ ㄊㄧˇ)
a form of historical writing in which every chapter is devoted to the recording of a particular event of significance
紀述(ㄐㄧˋ ㄕㄨˋ)
the objective reporting or recording of facts and phenomena
紀要(ㄐㄧˋ ㄧㄠˋ)
a recording of important facts; a summary
紀元(ㄐㄧˋ ㄩㄢˊ)
the beginning of a new era
紀元後(ㄐㄧˋ ㄩㄢˊ ㄏㄡˋ)
A.D. (anno Domini)
紀元前(ㄐㄧˋ ㄩㄢˊ ㄑㄧㄢˊ)
B.C. (before Christ)

【紂】 4279 ㄓㄡˋ jow zhòu

1. the last emperor of the Yin Dynasty, whose name stands for tyranny
2. the crupper of a saddle

紂王(ㄓㄡˋ ㄨㄤˊ)
see above 1.

【紃】 4280 ㄒㄩㄣˊ shyun xún

a cord

【紆】 4281 ㄩ iu yū

1. to wind; to spiral; to bend; to twist; to distort; to meander
2. a knot in one's heart; melancholy

紆體(ㄩ ㄊㄧˇ)
to bend one's body; to crouch; to bow down
紆廻(ㄩ ㄏㄨㄟˊ)
winding (roads); circuitous; roundabout 亦作「迂廻」
紆緩(ㄩ ㄏㄨㄢˇ)
slow; dilatory
紆金拖玉(ㄩ ㄐㄧㄣ ㄊㄨㄛ ㄩˋ)
dresses and ornaments of prominent officials
紆譎(ㄩ ㄐㄩㄝˊ)
(said of a story) with many twists and turns
紆青拖紫(ㄩ ㄑㄧㄥ ㄊㄨㄛ ㄗˇ)
the dresses and ornaments of high officials
紆曲(ㄩ ㄑㄩ)
① twists and turns; to wind: 我們紆曲行經窄巷。We wound our way through the narrow streets. ② insinuating; to insinuate
紆行(ㄩ ㄒㄧㄥˊ)
to proceed through a winding and twisting path
紆徐(ㄩ ㄒㄩˊ)
to walk slowly: 那老人正在紆徐漫游。The old man is walking slowly.
紆軫(ㄩ ㄓㄣˇ)
①(said of a road) winding and twisting; tortuous ② hidden secrets in one's heart; melancholy
紆尊降貴(ㄩ ㄗㄨㄣ ㄐㄧㄤˋ ㄍㄨㄟˋ)
to condescend; to deign to
紆餘(ㄩ ㄩˊ)
winding and twisting
紆鬱(ㄩ ㄩˋ)
sad; melancholy

【約】 4282 ㄩㄝ iue yuē

1. an agreement; a covenant; a contract; a treaty
2. brief (ly); simply
3. about; around; approximately; estimated: 現在大約是九點。It is about nine o'clock now.
4. a date; an appointment or engagement; a rendezvous; to make an appointment; to date: 我們約好下星期二碰面。We agreed to meet next Tuesday.
5. poor; poverty; hardship; straitened
6. (mathematics) to reduce

7. to bind; to restrain
8. vague(ly)
約莫(ㄩㄝ ㄇㄛˋ)
or so; about; approximately: 這約莫在一天以前發生的。It happened a day or so ago.
約盟(ㄩㄝ ㄇㄥˊ)
a covenant; an agreement; an alliance; a sworn compact
約明(ㄩㄝ ㄇㄧㄥˊ)
to specify in an agreement; with the mutual understanding that...
約法(ㄩㄝ ㄈㄚˇ)
① to bind with rules or regulations ② a provisional constitution
約法三章(ㄩㄝ ㄈㄚˇ ㄙㄢ ㄓㄤ)
① a three-article provisional law promulgated by Emperor Kao Tsu of the Han Dynasty (漢高祖) ② a verbal agreement
約分(ㄩㄝ ㄈㄣ)
(mathematics) reduction; to reduce a fraction
約旦(ㄩㄝ ㄉㄢˋ)
Jordan
約定(ㄩㄝ ㄉㄧㄥˋ)
to agree upon; to agree to: 我們約定會晤地點。We agreed on a meeting place.
約定地點(ㄩㄝ ㄉㄧㄥˋ ㄉㄧˋ ㄉㄧㄢˇ)
an appointed place; a place agreed upon: 我們在約定地點見面。We met at an appointed place.
約定期限(ㄩㄝ ㄉㄧㄥˋ ㄑㄧˊ ㄒㄧㄢˋ)
stipulated duration
約定時間(ㄩㄝ ㄉㄧㄥˋ ㄕˊ ㄐㄧㄢ)
the appointed time; to agree upon a time for doing something: 我們在約定時間內去。We went at the appointed time.
約定俗成(ㄩㄝ ㄉㄧㄥˋ ㄙㄨˊ ㄔㄥˊ)
practices, rules, etc. initiated by a few and later adopted by all as a common practice or recognized precedent
約同(ㄩㄝ ㄊㄨㄥˊ)
to make an appointment; to agree to do something together: 他約同我們去戲院。He agreed to accompany us to the theater.
約略(ㄩㄝ ㄌㄩㄝˋ)
① brief(ly); sketchy ② approximate
約翰(ㄩㄝ ㄏㄢˋ)
a transliteration of John
約翰尼斯堡(ㄩㄝ ㄏㄢˋ ㄋㄧˊ ㄙ ㄅㄠˇ)
Johannesburg, a city in South Africa
約翰孫(ㄩㄝ ㄏㄢˋ ㄙㄨㄣ)
Samuel Johnson, 1709-84, English lexicographer
約會(ㄩㄝ ㄏㄨㄟˋ)
an appointment or engagement; a date: 我明天有個約會。I have an engagement tomorrow.
約計(ㄩㄝ ㄐㄧˋ)
estimated at around...; a rough estimate
約期(ㄩㄝ ㄑㄧˊ)
a date; an appointment or engagement; the appointed time; the term or duration of an agreement; to stipulate a time; to make an appointment
約請(ㄩㄝ ㄑㄧㄥˇ)
to invite: 我約請他到我家裏。I invited him to my house.
約之以禮(ㄩㄝ ㄓ ㄧˇ ㄌㄧˇ)
to control one's conduct in accordance with rites
約章(ㄩㄝ ㄓㄤ)
an international treaty
約束(ㄩㄝ ㄕㄨˋ)
to bind or restrain; restraint; restriction
約數(ㄩㄝ ㄕㄨˋ)
①(mathematics) an exact divisor ② an estimated number
約瑟(ㄩㄝ ㄙㄜˋ)
a transliteration of Joseph
約瑟芬(ㄩㄝ ㄙㄜˋ ㄈㄣ)
a transliteration of Josephine
約言之(ㄩㄝ ㄧㄢˊ ㄓ)
in short; in a word; in brief

4283
【紅】 1. ㄏㄨㄥˊ horng hóng

1. red; vermilion; rosy: 他因憤怒而漲紅了臉。He was red in the face with anger.
2. to blush; to redden: 她不禁臉一紅而洩露了眞相。She could not help blushing the truth.
3. eminent; influential; (said of players) very popular
4. specially favored; a favorite
紅白事(ㄏㄨㄥˊ ㄅㄞˊ ㄕˋ)
weddings and funerals
紅包(ㄏㄨㄥˊ ㄅㄠ)
① a red paper bag containing money as a gift ② a bribe or kickback
紅寶石(ㄏㄨㄥˊ ㄅㄠˇ ㄕˊ)
a ruby
紅斑(ㄏㄨㄥˊ ㄅㄢ)
①(medicine) erythema ②(marine biology) red-spotted grouper
紅幫(ㄏㄨㄥˊ ㄅㄤ)
name of a secret underworld society 亦作「洪幫」
紅砒(ㄏㄨㄥˊ ㄆㄧ)
sulphurated arsenic
紅皮書(ㄏㄨㄥˊ ㄆㄧˊ ㄕㄨ)
(a diplomatic document) a red book
紅墨(ㄏㄨㄥˊ ㄇㄛˋ)
an ink stick made of vermilion
紅墨水(ㄏㄨㄥˊ ㄇㄛˋ ㄕㄨㄟˇ)
red ink
紅毛(ㄏㄨㄥˊ ㄇㄠˊ) or 紅毛番(ㄏㄨㄥˊ ㄇㄠˊ ㄈㄢ)
(in old China) the redhaired barbarians——Westerns (especially the Dutch)
紅毛丹(ㄏㄨㄥˊ ㄇㄠˊ ㄉㄢ)
a rambutan
紅帽子(ㄏㄨㄥˊ ㄇㄠˋ ·ㄗ)
① the redcaps—railway porters ② the label of being a Communist (usually a false accusation)
紅模子(ㄏㄨㄥˊ ㄇㄨˊ ·ㄗ)
a copy book for children in practicing calligraphy in which characters are printed in red to be traced by the pupils
紅木(ㄏㄨㄥˊ ㄇㄨˋ)
a redwood; a padauk
紅番(ㄏㄨㄥˊ ㄈㄢ)
Red Indians
紅粉(ㄏㄨㄥˊ ㄈㄣˇ)
① women; the fair sex ② rouge and powder
紅粉佳人(ㄏㄨㄥˊ ㄈㄣˇ ㄐㄧㄚ ㄖㄣˊ)
a young beauty; a sweet young thing

〔糸部〕

紅粉知己(ㄏㄨㄥˊ ㄈㄣˇ ㄓ ㄐㄧˇ)
a girlfriend; a mistress
紅得發紫(ㄏㄨㄥˊ ˙ㄉㄜ ㄈㄚ ㄗˇ)
①(said of entertainers) very popular ②(said of a government official) very influential; enjoying complete trust of the boss
紅豆(ㄏㄨㄥˊ ㄉㄡˋ)
① *Abrus precatorius*, the red bean —a token of love and endearment; a love pea 亦作「相思子」② *Ormosia*
紅豆相思(ㄏㄨㄥˊ ㄉㄡˋ ㄒㄧㄤ ㄙ)
red beans that inspire the memory of one's love
紅燈(ㄏㄨㄥˊ ㄉㄥ)
① the red traffic light ② a red light
紅頂子(ㄏㄨㄥˊ ㄉㄧㄥˇ ˙ㄗ)
the official hat worn by a high-ranking government official during the Ching Dynasty
紅糖(ㄏㄨㄥˊ ㄊㄤˊ)
brown sugar: 在水裡加些紅糖。Put some brown sugar into the water.
紅帖(子)(ㄏㄨㄥˊ ㄊㄧㄝˇ (˙ㄗ))
a "red card"—a card announcing a happy event (such as a betrothal, a birthday, etc.)
紅鐵礦(ㄏㄨㄥˊ ㄊㄧㄝˇ ㄎㄨㄤˋ)
hematite
紅土(ㄏㄨㄥˊ ㄊㄨˇ)
red clay; red earth
紅通通(ㄏㄨㄥˊ ㄊㄨㄥ ㄊㄨㄥ)
bright red; glowing; aglow 亦作「紅彤彤」: 她因爲害羞臉兒紅通通的。Her face is aglow with shame.
紅銅(ㄏㄨㄥˊ ㄊㄨㄥˊ)
copper: 紅銅導電良好。Copper conducts electricity well.
紅銅礦(ㄏㄨㄥˊ ㄊㄨㄥˊ ㄎㄨㄤˋ)
cuprite
紅男綠女(ㄏㄨㄥˊ ㄋㄢˊ ㄌㄩˋ ㄋㄩˇ)
fashionably dressed men and women
紅娘(ㄏㄨㄥˊ ㄋㄧㄤˊ)
name of a maid in *The West Chamber* (西廂記), who helped unite the hero and the heroine—a nonprofit-making woman go-between for lovers
紅辣椒(ㄏㄨㄥˊ ㄌㄚˋ ㄐㄧㄠ)
the pimiento
紅淚(ㄏㄨㄥˊ ㄌㄟˋ)
tears with blood—tears of sadness
紅樓(ㄏㄨㄥˊ ㄌㄡˊ)or 紅閨(ㄏㄨㄥˊ ㄍㄨㄟ)
a boudoir; women's living quarters
紅樓夢(ㄏㄨㄥˊ ㄌㄡˊ ㄇㄥˋ)
The Dream of the Red Chamber—one of the greatest Chinese novels, authored by Tsao Hsüeh-chin (曹雪芹) of the Ching Dynasty
紅利(ㄏㄨㄥˊ ㄌㄧˋ)
dividends for stockholders; a net profit; a bonus: 這一行生意紅利不大。The net profits in this business are not large.
紅痢(ㄏㄨㄥˊ ㄌㄧˋ)
dysentery (characterized by blood in a patient's excrement)
紅臉(ㄏㄨㄥˊ ㄌㄧㄢˇ)
① a red face; a blushed face; shamefaced ② an angry look ③ the red face, face painting in Chinese opera, traditionally for the heroic or the honest
紅燐(ㄏㄨㄥˊ ㄌㄧㄣˊ)
red phosphorus (usually for making safety matches)
紅羅(ㄏㄨㄥˊ ㄌㄨㄛˊ)
red silk
紅蘿蔔(ㄏㄨㄥˊ ㄌㄨㄛˊ ˙ㄅㄛ)
a radish
紅鸞星動(ㄏㄨㄥˊ ㄌㄨㄢˊ ㄒㄧㄥ ㄉㄨㄥˋ) or 紅鸞照命(ㄏㄨㄥˊ ㄌㄨㄢˊ ㄓㄠˋ ㄇㄧㄥˋ)
(literally) The propitious star governing marriages is in the ascendant. —a wedding being imminent
紅綠燈(ㄏㄨㄥˊ ㄌㄩˋ ㄉㄥ)
traffic lights; red and green lights
紅股(ㄏㄨㄥˊ ㄍㄨˇ)
bonus; stocks given in return for services rendered
紅果樹(ㄏㄨㄥˊ ㄍㄨㄛˇ ㄕㄨˋ)
holly
紅果兒(ㄏㄨㄥˊ ㄍㄨㄛˇㄦ)
the holly haw
紅光滿面(ㄏㄨㄥˊ ㄍㄨㄤ ㄇㄢˇ ㄇㄧㄢˋ)
a healthy and hearty look; in ruddy health
紅鶴(ㄏㄨㄥˊ ㄏㄜˋ)
the ibis
紅海(ㄏㄨㄥˊ ㄏㄞˇ)
Red Sea
紅鬍子(ㄏㄨㄥˊ ㄏㄨˊ ˙ㄗ)
mounted bandits in Manchuria
紅花(ㄏㄨㄥˊ ㄏㄨㄚ)
the safflower
紅花子油(ㄏㄨㄥˊ ㄏㄨㄚ ˙ㄗ ㄧㄡˊ)
safflower oil
紅貨(ㄏㄨㄥˊ ㄏㄨㄛˋ)
jewels, jade, etc.
紅菊花(ㄏㄨㄥˊ ㄐㄩˊ ㄏㄨㄚ)
a red daisy
紅軍(ㄏㄨㄥˊ ㄐㄩㄣ)
Red Army; Communist troops
紅槍會(ㄏㄨㄥˊ ㄑㄧㄤ ㄏㄨㄟˋ)
① Red Spear Society, an outgrowth of the White Lotus Sect, founded in Hunan during the Ching Dynasty ② a name adopted by local militia units in the late 1920's and early 1930's
紅情綠意(ㄏㄨㄥˊ ㄑㄧㄥˊ ㄌㄩˋ ㄧˋ)
tender affections between a couple in love
紅雀(ㄏㄨㄥˊ ㄑㄩㄝˋ)
a linnet; a redbird; a cardinal bird
紅霞(ㄏㄨㄥˊ ㄒㄧㄚˊ)
red clouds; flaming clouds (in the evening)
紅血球(ㄏㄨㄥˊ ㄒㄧㄝˇ ㄑㄧㄡˊ)
red blood cells; erythrocyte; red corpuscles 亦作「紅細胞」
紅繡鞋(ㄏㄨㄥˊ ㄒㄧㄡˋ ㄒㄧㄝˊ)
① an old Chinese torture device—by forcing a criminal to wear red-hot iron shoes ②(in old China) women's embroidered red shoes
紅線(ㄏㄨㄥˊ ㄒㄧㄢˋ)
① name of a heroine in a Tang Dynasty legend ②(in Chinese folklore) the red string that brings a man and his mate together (Cupid's arrow in its Chinese version)
紅心(ㄏㄨㄥˊ ㄒㄧㄣ)

the bull's-eye (of a target): 他用鎗瞄準了紅心。He aimed his gun at the bull's-eye.

紅鋅礦(ㄏㄨㄥˊ ㄒㄧㄣ ㄎㄨㄤˋ)
zincite

紅杏出牆(ㄏㄨㄥˊ ㄒㄧㄥˋ ㄔㄨ ㄑㄧㄤˊ)
(said of a married woman) to have a lover; to commit adultery: 他的妻子紅杏出牆。His wife committed adultery.

紅痣(ㄏㄨㄥˊ ㄓˋ)
a reddish mole

紅疹(ㄏㄨㄥˊ ㄓㄣˇ)
German measles; rubella

紅燭(ㄏㄨㄥˊ ㄓㄨˊ)
red candles

紅磚 or 紅甎(ㄏㄨㄥˊ ㄓㄨㄢ)
red bricks

紅妝(ㄏㄨㄥˊ ㄓㄨㄤ)
① make-up or ornaments for women ② a young woman

紅腫(ㄏㄨㄥˊ ㄓㄨㄥˇ)
a red swelling of the skin

紅種人(ㄏㄨㄥˊ ㄓㄨㄥˇ ㄖㄣˊ)
the Red Man—the American Indian

紅茶(ㄏㄨㄥˊ ㄔㄚˊ)
black tea: 我喜歡紅茶甚於咖啡。I like black tea better than coffee.

紅潮(ㄏㄨㄥˊ ㄔㄠˊ)
① to blush ② the menses

紅塵(ㄏㄨㄥˊ ㄔㄣˊ)
the mundane world; the world of mortals: 他看破紅塵。He saw through the vanity of the world.

紅場(ㄏㄨㄥˊ ㄔㄤˇ)or(ㄏㄨㄥˊ ㄔㄤˊ)
Red Square (in Moscow)

紅十字會(ㄏㄨㄥˊ ㄕˊ ㄗˋ ㄏㄨㄟˋ)
Red Cross Society

紅事(ㄏㄨㄥˊ ㄕˋ)
auspicious occasions, such as weddings, birthdays, etc.

紅痧(ㄏㄨㄥˊ ㄕㄚ)
scarlet fever

紅燒肉(ㄏㄨㄥˊ ㄕㄠ ㄖㄡˋ)
a Chinese dish prepared by cooking and simmering pork with soybean sauce and sugar

紅杉(ㄏㄨㄥˊ ㄕㄢ)
① a redwood 參看「紅木」 ② Chiness larch

紅繩繫足(ㄏㄨㄥˊ ㄕㄥˊ ㄒㄧˋ ㄗㄨˊ)
(said of a young couple) to be engaged to each other

紅薯(ㄏㄨㄥˊ ㄕㄨˇ)
sweet potatoes: 紅薯長在地下。Sweet potatoes grow under the ground.

紅樹(ㄏㄨㄥˊ ㄕㄨˋ)
a mangrove

紅日(ㄏㄨㄥˊ ㄖˋ)
the sun: 紅日自東方升起。The sun rises in the east.

紅熱(ㄏㄨㄥˊ ㄖㄜˋ)
① red heat ② red-hot

紅人(ㄏㄨㄥˊ ㄖㄣˊ)
① the trusted lieutenant of the boss ② Red Indians

紅潤(ㄏㄨㄥˊ ㄖㄨㄣˋ)
(said of the skin, cheeks, etc.) glowing, tender and rosy: 她的臉色健康紅潤。There is a glow of health in her face.

紅字(ㄏㄨㄥˊ ㄗˋ)
① a red mark for failure in an examination ② red entry in budget ③ *The Scarlet Letter* by Nathaniel Hawthorne

紅棗(ㄏㄨㄥˊ ㄗㄠˇ)
red dates

紅色(ㄏㄨㄥˊ ㄙㄜˋ)
red color: 他昨天把大門漆成紅色。He painted the gate red yesterday.

紅松鶴(ㄏㄨㄥˊ ㄙㄨㄥ ㄏㄜˋ)
a moorfowl

紅松雞(ㄏㄨㄥˊ ㄙㄨㄥ ㄐㄧ)
a moorcock; a moorhen

紅衣主教(ㄏㄨㄥˊ ㄧ ㄓㄨˇ ㄐㄧㄠˋ)
(Roman Catholicism) a cardinal

紅夷(ㄏㄨㄥˊ ㄧˊ)
the Westerners

紅葉(ㄏㄨㄥˊ ㄧㄝˋ)
red leaves (of maples, etc.); autumn leaves

紅藥水(ㄏㄨㄥˊ ㄧㄠˋ ㄕㄨㄟˇ)
mercurochrome

紅顏(ㄏㄨㄥˊ ㄧㄢˊ)
① young beauties ② youths ③ rosy cheeks

紅顏薄命(ㄏㄨㄥˊ ㄧㄢˊ ㄅㄛˊ ㄇㄧㄥˋ)
(a popular Chinese saying) Beauties are often ill-fated.

紅顏美少年(ㄏㄨㄥˊ ㄧㄢˊ ㄇㄟˇ ㄕㄠˋ ㄋㄧㄢˊ)
a handsome young man: 他是一個紅顏美少年。He's a handsome young fellow.

紅眼鳥(ㄏㄨㄥˊ ㄧㄢˇ ㄋㄧㄠˇ)
a chewink

紅羊浩劫(ㄏㄨㄥˊ ㄧㄤˊ ㄏㄠˋ ㄐㄧㄝˊ)
the catastrophe of war and rampage of bandits

紅外線(ㄏㄨㄥˊ ㄨㄞˋ ㄒㄧㄢˋ)
infrared rays

紅衛兵(ㄏㄨㄥˊ ㄨㄟˋ ㄅㄧㄥ)
Red Guards (created by Mao Tse-tung as a weapon to fight his political opponents)

紅魚(ㄏㄨㄥˊ ㄩˊ)
the gurnard

紅雨(ㄏㄨㄥˊ ㄩˇ)
the falling of blossoms (which looks like red raindrops)

紅暈(ㄏㄨㄥˊ ㄩㄣˋ)
a blush; a flush

紅運(ㄏㄨㄥˊ ㄩㄣˋ)
good luck; lucky opportunities, etc.

紅運當頭(ㄏㄨㄥˊ ㄩㄣˋ ㄉㄤ ㄊㄡˊ)
Lucky star shines bright.

【紅】 4283
2. ㄍㄨㄥ gong gōng
work; working

紅女(ㄍㄨㄥ ㄋㄩˇ)
working girls

【紇】 4284
1. ㄏㄜˊ her hé
1. silk of an inferior quality
2. name of a barbarian tribe, ancestors of the Huns(匈奴)

【紇】 4284
2. ㄍㄜ ge gē
a knot made of a rope or string

紇繨(ㄍㄜ ˙ㄉㄚ)
a knot made of a rope or string

【紈】 4285
ㄨㄢˊ wan wán
processed fine and light silk

紈袴(ㄨㄢˊ ㄎㄨˋ)
① expensive dresses of children from wealthy families ② a good-for-nothing young man from a wealthy family

紈袴子弟(ㄨㄢˊ ㄎㄨˋ ㄗˇ ㄉㄧˋ)
a good-for-nothing young man from a wealthy family; a playboy; a dandy; a fop; profligate sons of the rich

紈扇(ㄨㄢˊ ㄕㄢˋ)
a round, silk fan

紈素(ㄨㄢˊ ㄙㄨˋ)
fine, white silk

【紉】 4286 ㄖㄣˋ renn rèn
1. to sew; to stitch
2. to tie; to wear
3. to feel deeply
4. to thread a needle

紉佩(ㄖㄣˋ ㄆㄟˋ)
to be very grateful

紉緝(ㄖㄣˋ ㄑㄧˋ)
to mend; to repair

四畫

【紋】 4287 ㄨㄣˊ wen wén
1. stripes; lines; streaks; veins
2. ripples (of water)
3. (finger) prints
4. wrinkles (on the face)
5. to tattoo

紋兒(ㄨㄜˊㄦ)
stripes; streaks; lines; grain

紋理(ㄨㄣˊ ㄌㄧˇ)
lines; stripes; veins; grain: 那大理石的紋理很好看。That marble has a beautiful grain.

紋身(ㄨㄣˊ ㄕㄣ)
tattoo; to tattoo the body

紋絲兒不動(ㄨㄣˊ ㄙㄜㄦ ㄅㄨˋ ㄉㄨㄥˋ)
not to make even the slightest move

紋銀(ㄨㄣˊ ㄧㄣˊ)
a horseshoe-shaped silver ingot with the highest percentage of fineness; fine silver

【納】 4288 ㄋㄚˋ nah nà
1. to receive; to take; to accept; to admit; to adopt
2. to offer as tribute
3. to enjoy; to feel
4. to repress; to restrain
5. to patch old clothes
6. a Chinese family name

納幣(ㄋㄚˋ ㄅㄧˋ)
to present betrothal gifts to the girl's family

納聘(ㄋㄚˋ ㄆㄧㄣˋ)
to give betrothal money or presents to the girl's family

納悶(ㄋㄚˋ ㄇㄣˋ)or 納悶兒(ㄋㄚˋ ㄇㄜˋㄦ)
①to feel depressed ②to feel curious; to wonder

納福(ㄋㄚˋ ㄈㄨˊ)
to have a good time; to enjoy oneself; to live in comfortable circumstances: 他在家納福。He enjoyed a life of comfort at home.

納涼(ㄋㄚˋ ㄌㄧㄤˊ)
to enjoy the cool air; to enjoy the cool night

納貢(ㄋㄚˋ ㄍㄨㄥˋ)
to offer tribute as a vassal state

納款(ㄋㄚˋ ㄎㄨㄢˇ)
(said of an enemy) to surrender in all sincerity

納罕(ㄋㄚˋ ㄏㄢˇ)
to feel curious; to feel surprised: 這消息使我們納罕。We are surprised at the news.

納賄(ㄋㄚˋ ㄏㄨㄟˋ)
①to offer bribes ②to receive bribes

納吉(ㄋㄚˋ ㄐㄧˊ)
one of the six matrimonial rites in ancient China—to divine the good or bad luck of a marriage in a temple and report back to the bride's family

納節(ㄋㄚˋ ㄐㄧㄝˊ)
(in ancient China) to resign from a government office and return the credentials of the office

納交(ㄋㄚˋ ㄐㄧㄠ)
to make friends with; to befriend

納諫(ㄋㄚˋ ㄐㄧㄢˋ)
to accept an admonition; to receive instruction or advice: 他欣然納諫。He takes our advice quite cheerfully.

納妾(ㄋㄚˋ ㄑㄧㄝˋ)or 納寵(ㄋㄚˋ ㄔㄨㄥˇ)
to take a concubine

納稅(ㄋㄚˋ ㄕㄨㄟˋ)
to pay duties or taxes

納稅人(ㄋㄚˋ ㄕㄨㄟˋ ㄖㄣˊ)
the taxpayer

納入(ㄋㄚˋ ㄖㄨˋ)
to bring into

納采(ㄋㄚˋ ㄘㄞˇ)
to present betrothal gifts to the girl's family

納粹黨(ㄋㄚˋ ㄘㄨㄟˋ ㄉㄤˇ)
Nazi party (National Socialist German Workers' Party, NSDAP, 1919-1945) of Germany

納粹主義(ㄋㄚˋ ㄘㄨㄟˋ ㄓㄨˇ ㄧˋ)
Nazism

納粟(ㄋㄚˋ ㄙㄨˋ)
to contribute grain to the government in return for a public post

納爾遜(ㄋㄚˋ ㄦˇ ㄙㄨㄣˋ)
Admiral Horatio Nelson, 1758-1805, of the British Navy

【紐】 4289 ㄋㄧㄡˇ neou niǔ
1. a knot; a tie; a cord
2. a hold (of a vessel) or handle
3. a button
4. a Chinese family name

紐襻(ㄋㄧㄡˇ ㄆㄢˋ)
loops for buttons

紐芬蘭(ㄋㄧㄡˇ ㄈㄣ ㄌㄢˊ)
Newfoundland

紐扣(ㄋㄧㄡˇ ㄎㄡˋ)
a button

紐西蘭(ㄋㄧㄡˇ ㄒㄧ ㄌㄢˊ)
New Zealand

紐約(ㄋㄧㄡˇ ㄩㄝ)
New York

【純】 4290 ㄔㄨㄣˊ chwen chún
1. pure; net (profits, etc.); unalloyed: 這是一杯純淨的水。This is a glass of pure water.
2. sincere; honest; simple; faithful
3. completely; purely; entirely
4. (now rare) great; large
5. (now rare) silk; silk strands or threads

純白(ㄔㄨㄣˊ ㄅㄞˊ)
pure white

純品(ㄔㄨㄣˊ ㄆㄧㄣˇ)
of the purest quality; completely unmixed

純樸(ㄔㄨㄣˊ ㄆㄨˊ)
simple and sincere

純毛(ㄔㄨㄣˊ ㄇㄠˊ)
all-wool; 100% wool

純理論(ㄔㄨㄣˊ ㄌㄧˇ ㄌㄨㄣˋ)
(philosophy) a theory that recognition comes from instinct instead of senses or experience

純利(ㄔㄨㄣˊ ㄌㄧˋ)

net profits: 這一行生意純利不大。The net profits in this business are not large.

純利潤(ㄔㄨㄣˊ ㄌㄧˋ ㄖㄨㄣˋ)
the portion of net profit after paying dividends to the shareholders, etc.

純良(ㄔㄨㄣˊ ㄌㄧㄤˊ)
kind; honest

純潔(ㄔㄨㄣˊ ㄐㄧㄝˊ)
innocent; pure and clean; honest, sincere and faithful

純金(ㄔㄨㄣˊ ㄐㄧㄣ)
pure gold; unalloyed gold

純淨(ㄔㄨㄣˊ ㄐㄧㄥˋ)
pure and clean

純眞(ㄔㄨㄣˊ ㄓㄣ)
pure, sincere and faithful; genuine; unsophisticated: 她是一個純眞無邪的女孩。She is a pure and innocent girl.

純正(ㄔㄨㄣˊ ㄓㄥˋ)
① pure and unadulterated; pure and genuine ② honest; sincere

純種(ㄔㄨㄣˊ ㄓㄨㄥˇ)
thoroughbred; purebred

純熟(ㄔㄨㄣˊ ㄕㄨˊ)
proficient; very skillful; adroit; skill; deft

純屬虛構(ㄔㄨㄣˊ ㄕㄨˇ ㄒㄩ ㄍㄡˋ)
The matter is an out-and-out fabrication. 或 It is a sheer fabrication.

純粹(ㄔㄨㄣˊ ㄘㄨㄟˋ)
① pure; genuine; unadulterated: 它純粹是虛造的事實。It is a pure fabrication. ② completely; entirely

純色(ㄔㄨㄣˊ ㄙㄜˋ)
① of one color (especially referring to textiles) ② (physics) pure colors

純一(ㄔㄨㄣˊ ㄧ)
sincere; simple; unanimous; pure; uniform

純文學(ㄔㄨㄣˊ ㄨㄣˊ ㄒㄩㄝˊ)
belles-lettres; pure literature such as poetry, drama, novels, etc., without extraneous implications, political or otherwise

【紓】 4291
ㄕㄨ shu shū
1. to relax; to slacken; to slow down; to mitigate
2. to free from; to remove (causes of difficulties, poverty, etc.); to extricate from

紓難(ㄕㄨ ㄋㄢˋ)
to extricate from trouble or danger; to free from difficulties or straits; to give relief in time of distress

紓困(ㄕㄨ ㄎㄨㄣˋ)
to provide financial relief

紓禍(ㄕㄨ ㄏㄨㄛˋ)
to extricate from the grip of misfortune or catastrophe

紓憂(ㄕㄨ ㄧㄡ)
to remove worries

【紕】 4292
1. ㄆㄧ pi pī
1. errors; mistakes; blunders
2. (said of cloth, thread, etc.) to become unwoven or untwisted

紕繆(ㄆㄧ ㄇㄧㄡˋ)
mistakes or blunders

紕漏(ㄆㄧ ㄌㄡˋ)
errors or mistakes; something going wrong: 他出了紕漏。He made a small error.

【紕】 4292
2. ㄆㄧˊ pyi pí
hem ornaments

【紘】 4293
ㄏㄨㄥˊ horng hóng
1. a hat string fastened under the chin
2. vast; spacious

【紗】 4294
ㄕㄚ sha shā
1. gauze; thin silk or cloth
2. yarn, as cotton yarn: 他們把棉花紡成紗。They spin cotton into yarn.
3. a thin, netty or meshy sheet of any materials—such as cotton, silk, nylon, wires—that permits the passing of air but prevents mosquitoes, insects, etc.

紗包線(ㄕㄚ ㄅㄠ ㄒㄧㄢˋ)
cotton-covered wire

紗布(ㄕㄚ ㄅㄨˋ)
① gauze ② a bandage

紗帽(ㄕㄚ ㄇㄠˋ)
hats worn by noblemen or high officials in former times

紗錠(ㄕㄚ ㄉㄧㄥˋ)
a spindle

紗籠(ㄕㄚ ㄌㄨㄥˊ)
a sarong

紗罩(ㄕㄚ ㄓㄠˋ)
① a gauze cover stretched over a frame to keep insects away from food items ② a gas mantle

紗帳(ㄕㄚ ㄓㄤˋ)
a mosquito net

紗廠(ㄕㄚ ㄔㄤˇ)
a cotton yarn mill; a cotton mill; a textile mill

紗櫥(ㄕㄚ ㄔㄨˊ)
① a gauze cabinet for keeping food items ② a mosquito net shaped like a cabin

紗窗(ㄕㄚ ㄔㄨㄤ)
a window screen

【紙】 4295
ㄓˇ jyy zhǐ
paper

紙包不住火(ㄓˇ ㄅㄠ ㄅㄨˊ ㄓㄨˋ ㄏㄨㄛˇ)
(literally) Paper can never wrap up fire.—Plots or evil deeds will be exposed sooner or later.

紙版(ㄓˇ ㄅㄢˇ)
(printing) paper shells for a stereotype; a paper matrix

紙板(ㄓˇ ㄅㄢˇ)
cardboard: 這玩具是用硬紙板造的。This toy is made of cardboard.

紙幣(ㄓˇ ㄅㄧˋ)
paper money; bank notes: 把這張紙幣換成零錢。Give me change for this note.

紙牌(ㄓˇ ㄆㄞˊ)
playing cards: 我們來玩紙牌吧。Let's play cards.

紙片(ㄓˇ ㄆㄧㄢˋ)
scraps of paper

紙煤子(ㄓˇ ㄇㄟˊ ·ㄗ) or 紙捻兒(ㄓˇ ㄋㄧㄚˇㄦ)
a rolled or twisted strip of paper, used to light candles, tobacco in a pipe, etc.; a paper spill

紙彈(ㄓˇ ㄉㄢˋ)
① psywar leaflets ② a ballot

紙條(ㄓˇ ㄊㄧㄠˊ)
a slip of paper

紙老虎(ㄓˇ ㄌㄠˇ ㄏㄨˇ) or 紙糊老虎(ㄓˇ ㄏㄨˊ ㄌㄠˇ ㄏㄨˇ)
a paper tiger: 我們的敵人不是紙老虎。Our enemies are not paper tigers.

紙貴洛陽(ㄓˇ ㄍㄨㄟˋ ㄌㄨㄛˋ ㄧㄤˊ)
The copying of a literary

〔糸部〕

〔糸部〕

masterpiece makes the price of paper soar.—A literary masterpiece becomes a best-seller.
紙盒(ㄓˇ ㄏㄜˊ)
a carton; a paper box
紙婚(ㄓˇ ㄏㄨㄣ)
paper wedding; the first wedding anniversary
紙漿(ㄓˇ ㄐㄧㄤ)
paper pulp: 紙是由紙漿做成的。Paper is made from paper pulp.
紙錢兒(ㄓˇ ㄑㄧㄚˊㄦ)
paper money burnt as offerings to the dead
紙型(ㄓˇ ㄒㄧㄥˊ)
a paper mold; a matrix
紙張(ㄓˇ ㄓㄤ)
paper; sheets of paper; stationery
紙扇(ㄓˇ ㄕㄢˋ)
a paper fan
紙上談兵(ㄓˇ ㄕㄤˋ ㄊㄢˊ ㄅㄧㄥ)
impractical schemes; empty talks; academic talks; to be an armchair strategist
紙醉金迷(ㄓˇ ㄗㄨㄟˋ ㄐㄧㄣ ㄇㄧˊ)
to indulge in a wanton life
紙業(ㄓˇ ㄧㄝˋ)
the paper industry or enterprise
紙業公司(ㄓˇ ㄧㄝˋ ㄍㄨㄥ ㄙ)
a pulp and paper mill
紙煙(ㄓˇ ㄧㄢ)
cigarettes
紙鳶(ㄓˇ ㄩㄢ)
kites (of paper): 他在放紙鳶。He is flying a kite.

【紜】 4296
ㄩㄣˊ yun yún
confusing; disorderly
紜紜(ㄩㄣˊ ㄩㄣˊ)
diverse and confused; numerous and disorderly

【紝】 4297
(絍) ㄖㄣˋ reen rèn
(又讀 ㄖㄣˊ ren rén)
to lay the warp; to weave

【級】 4298
ㄐㄧˊ jyi jí
1. a grade; a class (at school)
2. a level; a degree; a mark of merit; a rank
3. a step (of a flight of steps)
4. a decapitated head
級別(ㄐㄧˊ ㄅㄧㄝˊ)
ranks; levels; grades; scales
級會(ㄐㄧˊ ㄏㄨㄟˋ)
a class meeting (at school)
級長(ㄐㄧˊ ㄓㄤˇ)
a class leader; a monitor
級數(ㄐㄧˊ ㄕㄨˋ)
(mathematics) progression
級任(ㄐㄧˊ ㄖㄣˋ)
a class tutor
級任導師(ㄐㄧˊ ㄖㄣˋ ㄉㄠˇ ㄕ)
a homeroom teacher

【紛】 4299
ㄈㄣ fen fēn
1. confused; disorderly: 桌上紛亂不堪。The table was in great disorder.
2. numerous; many; varied
紛披(ㄈㄣ ㄆㄧ)
①to spread out in a disorderly manner ②numerous
紛飛(ㄈㄣ ㄈㄟ)
to whirl around in confusion; to fly all over: 大雪紛飛。The snow fell in a whirl.
紛繁(ㄈㄣ ㄈㄢˊ)
numerous and complicated: 這案子頭緒紛繁。This case is highly complicated.
紛紛(ㄈㄣ ㄈㄣ)
①numerous and disorderly ②(said of people moving) in droves; numerous and in great confusion
紛沓(ㄈㄣ ㄊㄚˋ)
in endless succession
紛呶(ㄈㄣ ㄋㄠˊ)
noisy and disorderly
紛亂(ㄈㄣ ㄌㄨㄢˋ)
confusion; confused or disorderly; chaotic
紛綸(ㄈㄣ ㄌㄨㄣˊ)
①(said of knowledge, learning, etc.) vast and profound ②confusion; chaos
紛紅駭綠(ㄈㄣ ㄏㄨㄥˊ ㄏㄞˋ ㄌㄩˋ)
luxuriant growth of flowers and vegetation swaying (in the wind, etc.)
紛歧(ㄈㄣ ㄑㄧˊ)
greatly divided (in opinions); diversified; disharmonious; in disorder or diverging; disunited: 我們的意見紛歧。Our opinions are divided.
紛至沓來(ㄈㄣ ㄓˋ ㄊㄚˋ ㄌㄞˊ)
to come in continuous succession; (said of people) to flock in endless waves: 客人紛至沓來。The guests came in succession.
紛爭(ㄈㄣ ㄓㄥ)
a dispute; to dispute; to wrangle; to quarrel: 他們對該問題有一場紛爭。They had a dispute over the question.
紛擾(ㄈㄣ ㄖㄠˇ)
to confuse; confused or disorderly; turmoil; disturbance; to disturb
紛然(ㄈㄣ ㄖㄢˊ)
disorderly; chaotic; confused
紛雜(ㄈㄣ ㄗㄚˊ)
numerous and disorderly
紛紜(ㄈㄣ ㄩㄣˊ)
①numerous and disorderly ②(said of opinions) widely divided; diverse and confused
紛縕(ㄈㄣ ㄩㄣˋ)
flourishing in a disorderly manner

【紡】 4300
ㄈㄤˇ faang fǎng
1. to reel; to spin: 她把羊毛紡成毛線。She spun wool into thread.
2. reeled pongee (a kind of thin silk)
紡織(ㄈㄤˇ ㄓ)
to spin and weave; spinning and weaving
紡織娘(ㄈㄤˇ ㄓ ㄋㄧㄤˊ)
Mecopoda nipponensis, a kind of grasshopper; a katydid; a long-horned grasshopper
紡織工人(ㄈㄤˇ ㄓ ㄍㄨㄥ ㄖㄣˊ)
a textile factory worker
紡織公司(ㄈㄤˇ ㄓ ㄍㄨㄥ ㄙ)
a spinning and weaving mill; a textile company
紡織機(ㄈㄤˇ ㄓ ㄐㄧ)
looms; spinning and weaving machines
紡織廠(ㄈㄤˇ ㄓ ㄔㄤˇ)
a (cotton) spinning and weaving mill; a textile mill
紡織業(ㄈㄤˇ ㄓ ㄧㄝˋ)
the textile industry
紡塼(ㄈㄤˇ ㄓㄨㄢ)
tiles used in weaving
紡車(ㄈㄤˇ ㄔㄜ)
a spinning wheel; a spinning

machine
紡綢(ㄈㄤˇ ㄔㄡˊ)
reeled pongee
紡錘(ㄈㄤˇ ㄔㄨㄟˊ)
a spindle
紡紗(ㄈㄤˇ ㄕㄚ)
to spin cotton, etc. into yarn
紡紗機(ㄈㄤˇ ㄕㄚ ㄐㄧ)
a jenny; a spinning jenny
紡紗織布(ㄈㄤˇ ㄕㄚ ㄓ ㄅㄨˋ)
to spin and weave
紡絲(ㄈㄤˇ ㄙ)
spinning

【紊】4301 ㄨㄣˋ wenn wèn
confused; tangled; involved; disorderly
紊亂(ㄨㄣˋ ㄌㄨㄢˋ)
confused; tangled; chaotic; chaos; disorder; confusion:她的房間紊亂不堪。Her room was in great disorder.

【素】4302 ㄙㄨˋ suh sù
1. pure white silk
2. white (color)
3. plain; simple
4. mourning
5. vegetable food; a vegetarian diet
6. heretofore; up to the present
7. usually; generally
8. the original constitution of things; matter; elements
素不相識(ㄙㄨˋ ㄅㄨˋ ㄒㄧㄤ ㄕˋ)
to have never met or seen before; a total stranger: 我們素不相識。We have never met before.
素朴 or 素樸(ㄙㄨˋ ㄆㄨˊ)
plain and simple (clothing, food, taste, etc.)
素昧平生(ㄙㄨˋ ㄇㄟˋ ㄆㄧㄥˊ ㄕㄥ)
to have never known, met or seen before; to be a total stranger
素門(ㄙㄨˋ ㄇㄣˊ)
a poor family
素描(ㄙㄨˋ ㄇㄧㄠˊ)
(said of writing or painting) a sketch
素麪(ㄙㄨˋ ㄇㄧㄢˋ)
a vegetarian preparation of noodles
素面朝天(ㄙㄨˋ ㄇㄧㄢˋ ㄔㄠˊ ㄊㄧㄢ)
(said of a woman) to wear no make-up during an audience with the emperor
素髮(ㄙㄨˋ ㄈㄚˇ)
white hair
素幡(ㄙㄨˋ ㄈㄢ)
white streamers or flags
素飯(ㄙㄨˋ ㄈㄢˋ)
a vegetarian diet
素封(ㄙㄨˋ ㄈㄥ)
to become wealthy without holding a public office
素風(ㄙㄨˋ ㄈㄥ)
① contemporary customs or practices ② one's usual habits or practices
素服(ㄙㄨˋ ㄈㄨˊ)
white dresses or clothing (especially mourning dress): 他身著素服。He is clad in white clothing.
素來(ㄙㄨˋ ㄌㄞˊ)
heretofore; always; up to the present
素練(ㄙㄨˋ ㄌㄧㄢˋ)
① white silk ②(figuratively) a waterfall; a cascade; a cataract
素履(ㄙㄨˋ ㄌㄩˇ)
① a simple life ② a common scholar contented with a quiet and simple life
素故(ㄙㄨˋ ㄍㄨˋ)
an old friend
素官(ㄙㄨˋ ㄍㄨㄢ)
a poor government official (connoting honesty)
素口罵人(ㄙㄨˋ ㄎㄡˇ ㄇㄚˋ ㄖㄣˊ)
(literally) to eat vegetables (as a Buddhist) but freely use abusive language—to practice not what one preaches
素火腿(ㄙㄨˋ ㄏㄨㄛˇ ㄊㄨㄟˇ)
a cold vegetarian dish made of soybean which looks like ham
素懷(ㄙㄨˋ ㄏㄨㄞˊ)
long-cherished ambitions or hopes
素鷄(ㄙㄨˋ ㄐㄧ)
a cold vegetarian dish made of soybean which looks like chicken meat
素節(ㄙㄨˋ ㄐㄧㄝˊ)
① the Moon Festival ② autumn ③ moral fortitude; integrity ④ one's usual behavior or conduct
素交(ㄙㄨˋ ㄐㄧㄠ)
a true old friend; a long-known friend; an old acquaintance
素舊(ㄙㄨˋ ㄐㄧㄡˋ)
old friendship
素檢(ㄙㄨˋ ㄐㄧㄢˇ)
simple and disciplined (life, taste, etc.)
素淨(ㄙㄨˋ ㄐㄧㄥˋ)
① simple, or plain (clothes) ② simple, or not greasy (food)
素車白馬(ㄙㄨˋ ㄐㄩ ㄅㄛˊ ㄇㄚˇ)
a funeral procession—white carriages and white horses
素秋(ㄙㄨˋ ㄑㄧㄡ)
autumn; fall
素琴(ㄙㄨˋ ㄑㄧㄣˊ)
a harp, guitar, etc. without strings
素昔(ㄙㄨˋ ㄒㄧˊ)
usually; ordinarily; regularly; so far
素席(ㄙㄨˋ ㄒㄧˊ)
a vegetarian feast
素心(ㄙㄨˋ ㄒㄧㄣ)
① simple and honest ② one's true mind or conscience
素心蘭(ㄙㄨˋ ㄒㄧㄣ ㄌㄢˊ)
a cymbidium
素馨(ㄙㄨˋ ㄒㄧㄣ)
(botany) a jasmine
素行(ㄙㄨˋ ㄒㄧㄥˋ)
daily conduct or behavior
素性(ㄙㄨˋ ㄒㄧㄥˋ)
one's true disposition or temperament
素知(ㄙㄨˋ ㄓ)
to have known for some time
素質(ㄙㄨˋ ㄓˋ)
① one's true quality; one's natural talent ② white
素志(ㄙㄨˋ ㄓˋ)
a long-cherished ambition or aspiration
素常(ㄙㄨˋ ㄔㄤˊ)
usually; ordinarily; regularly; commonly; so far: 她素常行爲十分良好。Ordinarily she behaved quite well.
素稱(ㄙㄨˋ ㄔㄥ)
usually called; ordinarily or commonly known as; reputed to be

〔糸部〕

素食(ㄙㄨˋ ㄕˊ)
①vegetables; a vegetarian diet; vegetarian food ②daily diets or food; food one eats on ordinary or usual occasions ③to live like a parasite
素士(ㄙㄨˋ ㄕˋ)
a scholar who is not in government service
素事(ㄙㄨˋ ㄕˋ)
funeral matters
素室(ㄙㄨˋ ㄕˋ)
①a plain and simple family—not well-to-do ②a white-walled chamber
素識(ㄙㄨˋ ㄕˋ)
to have known or been familiar with
素手(ㄙㄨˋ ㄕㄡˇ)
①fair hands; white and tender hands ②empty hands; empty-handed
素尙(ㄙㄨˋ ㄕㄤˋ)
simple and plain virtues; simple aspiration: 謙遜是一種素尙美德。Humility is a simple and plain virtue.
素數(ㄙㄨˋ ㄕㄨˋ)
(mathematics) a prime number 亦作「質數」
素日(ㄙㄨˋ ㄖˋ)
usually; commonly; daily; regularly; frequently: 她素日喜愛閒談。She is usually very chatty.
素稔(ㄙㄨˋ ㄖㄣˇ)
to have known or been familiar with
素族(ㄙㄨˋ ㄗㄨˊ)
a commoner
素材(ㄙㄨˋ ㄘㄞˊ)
material; themes (of an artistic work) collected through daily experience
素菜(ㄙㄨˋ ㄘㄞˋ)
vegetable food; vegetarian dishes
素餐(ㄙㄨˋ ㄘㄢ)
to eat the bread of idleness
素餐尸位(ㄙㄨˋ ㄘㄢ ㄕ ㄨㄟˋ)
to occupy a high position without doing anything; a practically sinecure office
素娥(ㄙㄨˋ ㄜˊ)
①(Chinese mythology) the lady of the moon 亦作「嫦娥」 ②beauties
素愛(ㄙㄨˋ ㄞˋ)
usually (love to do something); commonly (read novels, etc.); regularly (eat certain food, etc.); frequently (fool around the gambling joint, etc.)
素一(ㄙㄨˋ ㄧ)
simple and honest
素衣(ㄙㄨˋ ㄧ)
①plain clothes ②white garments—for mourning
素雅(ㄙㄨˋ ㄧㄚˇ)
simple but elegant; unadorned and in good taste
素業(ㄙㄨˋ ㄧㄝˋ)
a former profession or vocation
素油(ㄙㄨˋ ㄧㄡˊ)
vegetable oil: 他們吃素油。They ate vegetable oil.
素友(ㄙㄨˋ ㄧㄡˇ)
an old friend
素筵(ㄙㄨˋ ㄧㄢˊ)
①a vegetarian feast ②food offerings to Buddha
素因數(ㄙㄨˋ ㄧㄣ ㄕㄨˋ)or 素因子(ㄙㄨˋ ㄧㄣ ㄗˇ)
(mathematics) a prime factor 亦作「質因數」
素仰(ㄙㄨˋ ㄧㄤˇ)
to have always looked up to or admired
素養(ㄙㄨˋ ㄧㄤˇ)
one's general capacity and disposition as a result of long and regular self-discipline; accomplishments: 她具有音樂素養。She has a musical accomplishment.
素位(ㄙㄨˋ ㄨㄟˋ)
one's current position or present circumstances
素聞(ㄙㄨˋ ㄨㄣˊ)
to have often heard; to have been frequently told
素望(ㄙㄨˋ ㄨㄤˋ)
one's good reputation and prestige: 他是個素望良好的人。He is a man of good reputation and prestige.
素約(ㄙㄨˋ ㄩㄝ)
an old promise or vow
素月(ㄙㄨˋ ㄩㄝˋ)
the brilliant moon; the chaste moon
素願(ㄙㄨˋ ㄩㄢˋ)
a long-cherished ambition, aspiration or hope

【索】 4303
1. ㄙㄨㄛˇ suoo suǒ
1. a thick rope; a cable
2. alone; lonely; solitary
3. to search or inquire into
4. to exhaust
5. to tighten; to squeeze; to twist
6. laws and regulations; rules
7. to demand; to ask; to exact
8. to need
9. a Chinese family name

索賠(ㄙㄨㄛˇ ㄆㄟˊ)
to demand compensation; to claim
索馬利蘭(ㄙㄨㄛˇ ㄇㄚˇ ㄌㄧˋ ㄌㄢˊ)
Somaliland
索馬利亞(ㄙㄨㄛˇ ㄇㄚˇ ㄌㄧˋ ㄧㄚˋ)
Somalia
索寞(ㄙㄨㄛˇ ㄇㄛˋ)
(said of one's looks) despondent, discouraged or crestfallen
索命(ㄙㄨㄛˇ ㄇㄧㄥˋ)
(usually referring to a ghost, a victim of injustice) to demand one's life
索道(ㄙㄨㄛˇ ㄉㄠˋ)
a cableway; a ropeway
索價(ㄙㄨㄛˇ ㄐㄧㄚˋ)
to demand a price; to state a price; to quote a price
索解(ㄙㄨㄛˇ ㄐㄧㄝˇ)
to search for an explanation or solution
索居(ㄙㄨㄛˇ ㄐㄩ)
to live alone (like a hermit); to go into retreat
索橋(ㄙㄨㄛˇ ㄑㄧㄠˊ)
a suspension bridge
索求(ㄙㄨㄛˇ ㄑㄧㄡˊ)
to seek (persons, jobs, etc.)
索欠(ㄙㄨㄛˇ ㄑㄧㄢˋ)
to demand the repayment of a debt
索取(ㄙㄨㄛˇ ㄑㄩˇ)
①to ask for; to demand: 我們索取樣品。We asked for a sample. ②to exact; to extort
索薪(ㄙㄨㄛˇ ㄒㄧㄣ)
to demand one's wages or salary
索然(ㄙㄨㄛˇ ㄖㄢˊ)

insipid; listless: 這個故事索然寡味。This story was flat and insipid.
索然無味(ㄙㄨㄛˇ ㄖㄢˊ ㄨˊ ㄨㄟˋ)
not interesting; tasteless; listless
索要(ㄙㄨㄛˇ ㄧㄠˋ)
to demand; to ask for
索引(ㄙㄨㄛˇ ㄧㄣˇ)
①the index (of a book)② to bring together
索隱(ㄙㄨㄛˇ ㄧㄣˇ)
to expose, unearth, or expound something concealed, hidden or obscure
索閱(ㄙㄨㄛˇ ㄩㄝˋ)
to ask for (a book, certificate, card, etc.) for reference

【索】 4303
2. ㄙㄨㄛˊ swo suó
to decide to go ahead and do something without any more consideration; may as well; simply
索性(ㄙㄨㄛˊ ·ㄒㄧㄥ)
directly; to go all the way; might as well

五畫

【紮】 4304
1. (紥) ㄓㄚˊ jar zhá
1. to bind, tie or fasten; to make a bundle; a bundle
2. to stop; to station; to post
紮裹(ㄓㄚˊ ㄍㄨㄛˇ)
to mend and tidy up (clothing); to bandage (a wound, etc.); to pack up (belongings, etc.)
紮寨(ㄓㄚˊ ㄓㄞˋ)
to establish barracks; to make camps; to station soldiers
紮營(ㄓㄚˊ ㄧㄥˊ)
to bivouac; to pitch tents; to station troops; to encamp

【紮】 4304
2.(紥) ㄗㄚ tza zā
to bind; to tie; to fasten: 她紮起她的頭髮。She binds her hair up.
紮帶子(ㄗㄚ ㄉㄞˋ ·ㄗ)
to bind with a ribbon; to tie a string; to tighten the girdle
紮好(ㄗㄚ ㄏㄠˇ)
to tie up; to bind together: 她用繃帶紮好他的傷。She bound his wound with a bandage.
紮緊(ㄗㄚ ㄐㄧㄣˇ)
to tighten; to fasten securely
紮綵樓(ㄗㄚ ㄘㄞˇ ㄌㄡˊ)
to pitch up a festooned platform—for a show, exhibition, contest, etc.

【絇】 4305
ㄑㄩ chyu qú
ornaments for the frontal part of shoes

【紫】 4306
ㄗˇ tzyy zǐ
1. purple; violet:紫色是高貴的顏色。Purple is a noble color.
2. a Chinese family name
紫茉莉(ㄗˇ ㄇㄛˋ ㄌㄧˋ)
(botany) a false jalap; a four-o'clock
紫丁香花(ㄗˇ ㄉㄧㄥ ㄒㄧㄤ ㄏㄨㄚ)
a lilac
紫檀(ㄗˇ ㄊㄢˊ)
(botany) red sandalwood
紫藤(ㄗˇ ㄊㄥˊ)
(botany) a wistaria, or a wisteria
紫銅(ㄗˇ ㄊㄨㄥˊ)
red copper
紫羅蘭(ㄗˇ ㄌㄨㄛˊ ㄌㄢˊ)
(botany) the violet; the stock
紫毫(ㄗˇ ㄏㄠˊ)
a fine writing brush made of rabbit's hair
紫紅(ㄗˇ ㄏㄨㄥˊ)
dark red, almost purplish: 我有一套紫紅色的衣服。I have a dark red suit.
紫金牛(ㄗˇ ㄐㄧㄣ ㄋㄧㄡˊ)
(botany) *Ardisia japonica,* Japanese ardisia
紫金山(ㄗˇ ㄐㄧㄣ ㄕㄢ)
name of a hill outside Nanking City
紫禁城(ㄗˇ ㄐㄧㄣˋ ㄔㄥˊ)
the Forbidden City in Peking with four gates and a circumference of approximately four kilometers
紫荊(ㄗˇ ㄐㄧㄥ)
(botany) *Cercis chinensis*, Chinese redbud
紫晶(ㄗˇ ㄐㄧㄥ)or 紫水晶(ㄗˇ ㄕㄨㄟˇ ㄐㄧㄥ)
amethyst: 紫水晶被用來做珠寶。Amethyst is used for jewelry.
紫景天(ㄗˇ ㄐㄧㄥˇ ㄊㄧㄢ)
(botany) live-forever; orpine
紫菊(ㄗˇ ㄐㄩˊ)
China aster
紫闕(ㄗˇ ㄑㄩㄝ)
①elaborate security precautions in an imperial palace ②the abode of immortals
紫虛(ㄗˇ ㄒㄩ)
the sky; the firmament
紫杉(ㄗˇ ㄕㄢ)
(botany) yew tree
紫菜(ㄗˇ ㄘㄞˋ)
(botany) laver
紫翠玉(ㄗˇ ㄘㄨㄟˋ ㄩˋ)
alexandrite
紫色(ㄗˇ ㄙㄜˋ)
purple; violet: 他氣得臉色發紫。His face becomes purple with rage.
紫衣(ㄗˇ ㄧ)
①(botany) purple moss ② the imperial purple ③a purple Buddhist gown presented by the emperor to an accomplished monk ④official dress of high officials in ancient times
紫藥水(ㄗˇ ㄧㄠˋ ㄕㄨㄟˇ)
gentian violet solution
紫陽花(ㄗˇ ㄧㄤˊ ㄏㄨㄚ)
(botany) hydrangea
紫陽書院(ㄗˇ ㄧㄤˊ ㄕㄨ ㄩㄢˋ)
(originally) name of a study on a hill in Anhwei built by Chu Sung(朱松)of the Sung Dynasty, whose famous son, Chu Hsi(朱熹), also studied there
紫外線(ㄗˇ ㄨㄞˋ ㄒㄧㄢˋ)
ultraviolet rays
紫菀(ㄗˇ ㄨㄢˇ)
(botany) aster
紫雲英(ㄗˇ ㄩㄣˊ ㄧㄥ)
Astragalus sinicus, a grassy plant with purple flowers which are plowed into the earth as fertilizer

【累】 4307
1. ㄌㄟˇ leei lěi
1. to accumulate through a length of time
2. to pile up

〔糸 部〕

3. to repeat; repeatedly; successively
累犯(ㄌㄟˇ ㄈㄢˋ)
①to offend or violate the law repeatedly; recidivism ② a repeated lawbreaker; a recidivist
累代(ㄌㄟˇ ㄉㄞˋ)
generation after generation; many generations
累牘連篇(ㄌㄟˇ ㄉㄨˊ ㄌㄧㄢˊ ㄆㄧㄢ)
(said of writings) long and tiresome; redundant; verbose
累年(ㄌㄟˇ ㄋㄧㄢˊ)
in consecutive years; year after year 亦作「累歲」
累累(ㄌㄟˇ ㄌㄟˇ)
① repeatedly; successively; consecutively ② piling up ③ innumerable; countless
累卵(ㄌㄟˇ ㄌㄨㄢˇ)
(literally) like a pile of eggs —a very dangerous or precarious situation
累卵之危(ㄌㄟˇ ㄌㄨㄢˇ ㄓ ㄨㄟˊ)
great, imminent danger
累積(ㄌㄟˇ ㄐㄧ)
accumulation; to accumulate; to pile up
累計(ㄌㄟˇ ㄐㄧˋ)
to include previous figures in the calculation
累加(ㄌㄟˇ ㄐㄧㄚ)
to keep multiplying; to increase; to accumulate
累減(ㄌㄟˇ ㄐㄧㄢˇ)
(law) gradual commutation of sentences
累減稅(ㄌㄟˇ ㄐㄧㄢˇ ㄕㄨㄟˋ)
regressive taxation
累進稅(ㄌㄟˇ ㄐㄧㄣˋ ㄕㄨㄟˋ)
progressive taxation
累遷(ㄌㄟˇ ㄑㄧㄢ)
successive promotion in official position
累行犯(ㄌㄟˇ ㄒㄧㄥˊ ㄈㄢˋ)
a repeated offender (of law); a criminal who has committed offenses many times; a recidivist
累戰(ㄌㄟˇ ㄓㄢˋ)
successive battles; one battle after another
累時(ㄌㄟˇ ㄕˊ)
repeatedly; for a long time
累世(ㄌㄟˇ ㄕˋ)
for successive generations

累日(ㄌㄟˇ ㄖˋ)
for a number of days in succession
累增(ㄌㄟˇ ㄗㄥ)
to increase progressively
累次(ㄌㄟˇ ㄘˋ)
repeatedly; many times: 他累次的努力終於獲得成功。His repeated efforts at last won success.
累次三番(ㄌㄟˇ ㄘˋ ㄙㄢ ㄈㄢ)
repeatedly; time and again
累月經年(ㄌㄟˇ ㄩㄝˋ ㄐㄧㄥ ㄋㄧㄢˊ)
for months and years; for a long time

【累】 4307 2. ㄌㄟˋ ley lèi

1. to involve; involvement; to implicate
2. to owe; to be in debt
3. tired; weary; fatigue
4. (said of eyes) to strain
5. a family burden
累病了(ㄌㄟˋ ㄅㄧㄥˋ ·ㄌㄜ)or 累倒了(ㄌㄟˋ ㄉㄠˇ ·ㄌㄜ)
to become sick owing to hard work
累得慌(ㄌㄟˋ ·ㄉㄜ ·ㄏㄨㄤ)
very tired
累了(ㄌㄟˋ ·ㄌㄜ)
tired: 我累了。I was tired.
累活兒(ㄌㄟˋ ㄏㄨㄛˊㄦ)
a backbreaking job; hard work; toil
累壞了(ㄌㄟˋ ㄏㄨㄞˋ ·ㄌㄜ)
to become ill as a result of backbreaking toil; to be tired out: 你累壞了。You are tired out.
累及他人(ㄌㄟˋ ㄐㄧˊ ㄊㄚ ㄖㄣˊ)
to involve or implicate others
累及無辜(ㄌㄟˋ ㄐㄧˊ ㄨˊ ㄍㄨ)
to involve the innocent
累極了(ㄌㄟˋ ㄐㄧˊ ·ㄌㄜ)
dog-tired; dead tired: 我們累極了。We were dog-tired.
累心(ㄌㄟˋ ㄒㄧㄣ)
to toil one's mind; to cudgel one's brains
累重(ㄌㄟˋ ㄓㄨㄥˋ)
dependents and property
累事(ㄌㄟˋ ㄕˋ)
drudgery; toil
累人(ㄌㄟˋ ㄖㄣˊ)
to make another tired; to wear down; to be tiring

累坐(ㄌㄟˋ ㄗㄨㄛˋ)
to become involved in a crime and suffer the consequences
累死(ㄌㄟˋ ㄙˇ)
very tired

【累】 4307 3. ㄌㄟˊ lei léi

1. a nuisance
2. to fasten; to bind
累贅(ㄌㄟˊ ·ㄓㄨㄟ)
① a nuisance; a burden; a troublesome thing ② wordy; verbose: 這個句子太累贅。This sentence is too wordy.

【紬】 4308 1.(綢) ㄔㄡˊ chour chóu

a kind of silk fabric

【紬】 4308 2. ㄔㄡ chou chōu

1. to draw out
2. to collect and edit
紬次(ㄔㄡ ㄘˋ)
to collect and arrange in order
紬繹(ㄔㄡ ㄧˋ)
to explain

【細】 4309 ㄒㄧˋ shih xì

1. tiny; small; little
2. thin; slender; tall but lean; slim
3. fine
4. petty; trifling; detailed
5. precise; exquisite; delicate (workmanship, etc.)
細胞(ㄒㄧˋ ㄅㄠ)
a cell
細胞膜(ㄒㄧˋ ㄅㄠ ㄇㄛˊ)
the cell membrane
細胞分裂(ㄒㄧˋ ㄅㄠ ㄈㄣ ㄌㄧㄝˋ)
cell division
細胞體(ㄒㄧˋ ㄅㄠ ㄊㄧˇ)
the cell body
細胞核(ㄒㄧˋ ㄅㄠ ㄏㄜˊ)
the cell nucleus
細胞學(ㄒㄧˋ ㄅㄠ ㄒㄩㄝˊ)
cytology
細胞質(ㄒㄧˋ ㄅㄠ ㄓˊ)
cellularity; cytoplasm
細胞組織(ㄒㄧˋ ㄅㄠ ㄗㄨˇ ㄓ)
cellular tissue
細胞液(ㄒㄧˋ ㄅㄠ ㄧㄝˋ)
cell sap
細布(ㄒㄧˋ ㄅㄨˋ)
fine cloth

細部(ㄒㄧˋ ㄅㄨˋ)
details (of a drawing); minute parts

細密(ㄒㄧˋ ㄇㄧˋ)
①(said of materials) fine and delicate ②careful; cautious; circumspective

細民(ㄒㄧˋ ㄇㄧㄣˊ)
commoners; the people; the masses

細目(ㄒㄧˋ ㄇㄨˋ)
detailed items

細大不捐(ㄒㄧˋ ㄉㄚˋ ㄅㄨˋ ㄐㄩㄢ)
not to cast away anything, big or small

細讀(ㄒㄧˋ ㄉㄨˊ)
to read carefully: 我們細讀這本書。We read this book carefully.

細談(ㄒㄧˋ ㄊㄢˊ)
to talk in detail; to go into every minute point in a conversation: 沒有時間細談。There isn't time to talk in detail.

細條條的(ㄒㄧˋ ㄊㄧㄠˊ ㄊㄧㄠˊ ˙ㄉㄜ)or 細挑(ㄒㄧˋ ˙ㄊㄧㄠ)
(said of one's figure) slender; willowy

細嫩(ㄒㄧˋ ㄋㄣˋ)
(said of the skin) fair and tender; delicate

細膩(ㄒㄧˋ ㄋㄧˋ)
① fine and delicate ②(in writings, dramas and movie directing) to take care of even the smallest points; not to overlook any details: 這本小說描寫細膩。This novel has a minute description.

細流(ㄒㄧˋ ㄌㄧㄡˊ)
① a small creek ②(said of water) to trickle

細路(ㄒㄧˋ ㄌㄨˋ)
a narrow path

細論(ㄒㄧˋ ㄌㄨㄣˋ)
to discuss in detail; to elaborate

細縷(ㄒㄧˋ ㄌㄩˇ)
a very fine thread or strand

細高挑兒(ㄒㄧˋ ㄍㄠ ㄊㄧㄠˇㄦ)
a tall person with a slender figure

細故(ㄒㄧˋ ㄍㄨˋ)
trifling matter or cause (which leads to a dispute, etc.)

細工(ㄒㄧˋ ㄍㄨㄥ)
fine and delicate work; fine and delicate craftsmanship

細看(ㄒㄧˋ ㄎㄢˋ)
to look at carefully; to examine in detail: 你必須細看一切事實。You must look at all the facts in detail.

細活(ㄒㄧˋ ㄏㄨㄛˊ)
fine and delicate work

細節(ㄒㄧˋ ㄐㄧㄝˊ)
minor points; trifles; detail

細究(ㄒㄧˋ ㄐㄧㄡˋ)
to examine or study into all details

細謹(ㄒㄧˋ ㄐㄧㄣˇ)
to be overcautious about small points in etiquette

細講(ㄒㄧˋ ㄐㄧㄤˇ)
to state in detail

細君(ㄒㄧˋ ㄐㄩㄣ)
one's wife

細菌(ㄒㄧˋ ㄐㄩㄣˋ)
bacteria; germs

細菌學(ㄒㄧˋ ㄐㄩㄣˋ ㄒㄩㄝˊ)
bacteriology

細菌戰(ㄒㄧˋ ㄐㄩㄣˋ ㄓㄢˋ)
bacteriological warfare

細巧(ㄒㄧˋ ㄑㄧㄠˇ)
fine and delicate (work, etc.); delicate and ingenious (articles)

細情(ㄒㄧˋ ㄑㄧㄥˊ)
details of a matter

細細(ㄒㄧˋ ㄒㄧˋ)
① very low (voice) ② very light ③ very fine or thin ④ fine and delicate

細小(ㄒㄧˋ ㄒㄧㄠˇ)
tiny; little; thin; petty

細心(ㄒㄧˋ ㄒㄧㄣ)
careful; attentive; cautious; circumspective; to think of all aspects of something: 他細心從事工作。He is careful at his work.

細想(ㄒㄧˋ ㄒㄧㄤˇ)
to think over carefully; to give careful thought to; to ponder

細行(ㄒㄧˋ ㄒㄧㄥˊ)
one's behavior in trivial matters

細枝(ㄒㄧˋ ㄓ)
a slender twig; twiggery

細枝末節(ㄒㄧˋ ㄓ ㄇㄛˋ ㄐㄧㄝˊ)
minor details; nonessentials

細緻(ㄒㄧˋ ㄓˋ)
① fine and delicate; exquisite ② careful and thorough; meticulous; painstaking: 她設想極細緻周到。She thought it out carefully and thoroughly.

細針密縷(ㄒㄧˋ ㄓㄣ ㄇㄧˋ ㄌㄩˇ)
delicate and fine needlework

細賬(ㄒㄧˋ ㄓㄤˋ)
a detailed account

細查(ㄒㄧˋ ㄔㄚˊ)
to investigate thoroughly

細察(ㄒㄧˋ ㄔㄚˊ)
to observe carefully or in detail; to examine thoroughly

細長(ㄒㄧˋ ㄔㄤˊ)
slender; thin and long

細事(ㄒㄧˋ ㄕˋ)
trifling matters; trifles; matters of little significance

細沙(ㄒㄧˋ ㄕㄚ)
fine sand

細紗(ㄒㄧˋ ㄕㄚ)
(textile) spun yarn

細聲(ㄒㄧˋ ㄕㄥ)
a very low voice

細聲細氣(ㄒㄧˋ ㄕㄥ ㄒㄧˋ ㄑㄧˋ)
in a soft voice; soft-spoken

細說(ㄒㄧˋ ㄕㄨㄛ)or 細述(ㄒㄧˋ ㄕㄨˋ)
① to give a detailed account; to state in detail ② a one-sided story from a mean fellow

細水長流(ㄒㄧˋ ㄕㄨㄟˇ ㄔㄤˊ ㄌㄧㄡˊ)
(literally) Water flowing out in a trickle takes a long time to exhaust.— ① One will not go broke if he is frugal. ② One will finally prevail if he persists.

細人(ㄒㄧˋ ㄖㄣˊ)
① a person of narrow vision ② a person of low social standing ③ a concubine

細弱(ㄒㄧˋ ㄖㄨㄛˋ)
①(said of physique) slender and weak ② (said of voice) low and weak: 她的聲音細弱無力。She has a low and weak voice.

細軟(ㄒㄧˋ ㄖㄨㄢˇ)
fine clothes and jewels (of a woman); valuables

細字(ㄒㄧˋ ㄗˋ)

fine print; characters of very small size
細則(ㄒㄧˋ ㄗㄜˊ)
bylaws
細作(ㄒㄧˋ ㄗㄨㄛˋ)
(military) spies; agents; underground workers
細瓷(ㄒㄧˋ ㄘˊ)
fine porcelain
細草(ㄒㄧˋ ㄘㄠˇ)
silky grass; fine grass
細絲(ㄒㄧˋ ㄙ)
a fine thread
細瑣(ㄒㄧˋ ㄙㄨㄛˇ)or 細碎(ㄒㄧˋ ㄙㄨㄟˋ)
petty; trifles
細兒(ㄒㄧˋ ㄦˊ)
a young son
細腰(ㄒㄧˋ ㄧㄠ)
① a slender waist ② a slim-waisted wasp
細微(ㄒㄧˋ ㄨㄟˊ)
tiny; minute
細味(ㄒㄧˋ ㄨㄟˋ)
to reflect, think over, or study carefully
細問(ㄒㄧˋ ㄨㄣˋ)
to question in detail
細雨(ㄒㄧˋ ㄩˇ)
a misty rain; drizzle
細語(ㄒㄧˋ ㄩˇ)
low and tender talk; pillow talk

【紱】 4310 ㄈㄨˊ fwu fú

1. ribbons, strands, or sashes
2. ceremonial dress worn during sacrificial rituals

紱冕(ㄈㄨˊ ㄇㄧㄢˇ)
a high-ranking official

【紳】 4311 ㄕㄣ shen shēn

1. the middle class as a group or individuals; the gentry; a gentleman
2. a sash; a girdle
3. to tie

紳董(ㄕㄣ ㄉㄨㄥˇ)
the local gentry
紳宦(ㄕㄣ ㄏㄨㄢˋ)
retired government officials
紳士(ㄕㄣ ㄕˋ)
a gentleman; an esquire
紳士協定(ㄕㄣ ㄕˋ ㄒㄧㄝˊ ㄉㄧㄥˋ)
a gentlemen's agreement
紳商(ㄕㄣ ㄕㄤ)
the gentry and merchant class

【紹】 4312 ㄕㄠˋ shaw shào

1. to bring together; to connect or join
2. to hand down; to continue

紹介(ㄕㄠˋ ㄐㄧㄝˋ)
to serve as a medium or go-between; to introduce; to recommend
紹興(ㄕㄠˋ ㄒㄧㄥ)
Shaohsing in Chekiang, famous for its Shaohsing wine
紹興酒(ㄕㄠˋ ㄒㄧㄥ ㄐㄧㄡˇ)or 紹酒(ㄕㄠˋ ㄐㄧㄡˇ)
the Shaohsing wine, a mild rice brew of a golden yellow color
紹述(ㄕㄠˋ ㄕㄨˋ)
to continue; to follow

【紼】 4313 ㄈㄨˊ fwu fú

1. a large rope
2. the cord or rope attached to a bier or coffin

【紾】 4314 ㄓㄣˇ jeen zhěn

1. turns or twists; to turn or twist
2. to switch

紾臂(ㄓㄣˇ ㄅㄧˋ)
to twist the arm

【絀】 4315 ㄔㄨˋ chuh chù

1. to sew
2. to bend
3. to degrade
4. deficient; wanting; insufficient; inadequate
5. red; a deep red color

【紵】 4316 ㄓㄨˋ juh zhù

boehmeria; ramie; linen; sackcloth

【紺】 4317 ㄍㄢˋ gann gàn

a reddish dark color; a deep purple color

紺坊(ㄍㄢˋ ㄈㄤ)or 紺園(ㄍㄢˋ ㄩㄢˊ)or 紺宇(ㄍㄢˋ ㄩˇ)or 紺殿(ㄍㄢˋ ㄉㄧㄢˋ)
a Buddhist monastery

【絃】 4318 ㄒㄧㄢˊ shyan xián

1. the string of a musical instrument; a cord: 她把小提琴的絃拴緊。She tightened the strings of her violin.
2. first and last quarters of the moon

絃馬(ㄒㄧㄢˊ ㄇㄚˇ)
the bridge of a violin
絃歌不輟(ㄒㄧㄢˊ ㄍㄜ ㄅㄨˋ ㄔㄨㄛˋ)
(literally) The sound of music and singing never ends.—Reading and studying are not interrupted even in times of distress.
絃子(ㄒㄧㄢˊ ˙ㄗ)
a kind of three-stringed musical instrument
絃索(ㄒㄧㄢˊ ㄙㄨㄛˇ)
stringed instruments
絃誦(ㄒㄧㄢˊ ㄙㄨㄥˋ)
the music and sound of reading
絃外之音(ㄒㄧㄢˊ ㄨㄞˋ ㄓ ㄧㄣ)
(literally) sound outside what the string is making —overtones; connotations; suggestion; implied meaning
絃樂(ㄒㄧㄢˊ ㄩㄝˋ)
string music
絃樂隊(ㄒㄧㄢˊ ㄩㄝˋ ㄉㄨㄟˋ)
a string band
絃樂器(ㄒㄧㄢˊ ㄩㄝˋ ㄑㄧˋ)
stringed instruments

【終】 4319 ㄓㄨㄥ jong zhōng

1. the end; to come to the end; the conclusion
2. death; to die or pass away
3. finally; at last; in the end; after all; in the long run
4. whole; all; entire

終篇(ㄓㄨㄥ ㄆㄧㄢ)
to complete writing or finish reading an article
終點(ㄓㄨㄥ ㄉㄧㄢˇ)
① the terminus; the final point; the end; a destination ② (sports) finish
終端(ㄓㄨㄥ ㄉㄨㄢ)
(electricity) a terminal
終端機(ㄓㄨㄥ ㄉㄨㄢ ㄐㄧ)
a teletype machine or similar device for remote input or output of data, as in time-sharing; a terminal
終天(ㄓㄨㄥ ㄊㄧㄢ)
forever: 他抱恨終天。He regrets forever.
終天年(ㄓㄨㄥ ㄊㄧㄢ ㄋㄧㄢˊ)
to live up one's allotted life span
終南捷徑(ㄓㄨㄥ ㄋㄢˊ ㄐㄧㄝˊ ㄐㄧㄥˋ)

a short cut or snap course to officialdom (usually with an implication of sarcasm)
終南山(ㄓㄨㄥ ㄋㄢˊ ㄕㄢ)
name of a mountain in Shensi Province
終年(ㄓㄨㄥ ㄋㄧㄢˊ)
① the whole year; throughout the year ② the age at which one dies: 他終年八十歲。He died at the age of eighty.
終老(ㄓㄨㄥ ㄌㄠˇ)
throughout one's life; until death
終了(ㄓㄨㄥ ㄌㄧㄠˇ)
to end; to complete; to conclude; to terminate: 我們的交往到此終了。Our intercourse is at an end.
終古(ㄓㄨㄥ ㄍㄨˇ)
① for a long time; forever ② in ancient times; through all antiquity
終歸(ㄓㄨㄥ ㄍㄨㄟ)
① the conclusion; to end or conclude ② finally; after all; at last: 她終歸是個孩子。After all she is still a child.
終極(ㄓㄨㄥ ㄐㄧˊ)
the finality or end
終結(ㄓㄨㄥ ㄐㄧㄝˊ)
the end, conclusion, termination, etc.: 這件事得到很好的終結。The affair was brought to a happy termination.
終久(ㄓㄨㄥ ㄐㄧㄡˇ) or 終究(ㄓㄨㄥ ㄐㄧㄡˋ)
after all; in the end; in the long run: 你終究會成功的。In the end you'll succeed.
終竟(ㄓㄨㄥ ㄐㄧㄥˋ)
① finally; after all; in the end; in the long run ② to end; to come to an end
終局(ㄓㄨㄥ ㄐㄩˊ)
①(said of a gambling session, chess game, etc.) the conclusion, end, etc. ②(said of a game, contest, etc.) the result, outcome, etc.
終其一生(ㄓㄨㄥ ㄑㄧˊ ㄧ ㄕㄥ)
throughout one's life
終獻(ㄓㄨㄥ ㄒㄧㄢˋ)
the third wine offering in a sacrificial ceremony
終須(ㄓㄨㄥ ㄒㄩ)
to have to...in the end; unavoidable in the long run 或 There is no escaping of it sooner or later.人終須歸土。Man has to go the way of all the earth in the end.
終止(ㄓㄨㄥ ㄓˇ)
to come to an end or close; to stop; to end: 罷工終止了。The strike is at an end.
終止符(ㄓㄨㄥ ㄓˇ ㄈㄨˊ)
a full stop; a period
終制(ㄓㄨㄥ ㄓˋ)
to complete the three-year mourning for one's parents
終朝(ㄓㄨㄥ ㄓㄠ)
① the whole morning ② the whole day; throughout the day
終站(ㄓㄨㄥ ㄓㄢˋ)
the terminal stop or station: 我們在終站下車。We got off at the terminal stop.
終場(ㄓㄨㄥ ㄔㄤˊ) or (ㄓㄨㄥ ㄔㄤˇ)
① the conclusion of any matter; the end of a show, game, etc. ② the last test under the former civil service examination system
終食(ㄓㄨㄥ ㄕˊ)
the duration of a meal
終始(ㄓㄨㄥ ㄕˇ)
from beginning to end
終身(ㄓㄨㄥ ㄕㄣ)
the whole life:我預料將在此地居留終身。I expect to live here all my life.
終身伴侶(ㄓㄨㄥ ㄕㄣ ㄅㄢˋ ㄌㄩˇ)
a life company—wife or husband
終身不忘(ㄓㄨㄥ ㄕㄣ ㄅㄨˋ ㄨㄤˋ)
to keep in memory throughout one's life span
終身大事(ㄓㄨㄥ ㄕㄣ ㄉㄚˋ ㄕˋ)
a great event affecting one's whole life (especially referring to one's marriage): 婚姻乃終身大事。Marriage is an important event in one's life.
終身職(ㄓㄨㄥ ㄕㄣ ㄓˊ)
an office for life; a lifetime job
終身事業(ㄓㄨㄥ ㄕㄣ ㄕˋ ㄧㄝˋ)
a lifelong career; a career, endeavor, undertaking, etc. to which one dedicates his whole life: 我以教書爲終身事業。I take teaching as my life career.
終審(ㄓㄨㄥ ㄕㄣˇ)
(law) the third, or final trial (which concludes a case once for all)
終審法庭(ㄓㄨㄥ ㄕㄣˇ ㄈㄚˇ ㄊㄧㄥˊ)
a court of the last resort
終生(ㄓㄨㄥ ㄕㄥ)
the whole life; throughout one's life: 他終生都住在倫敦。He has lived in London all his life.
終日(ㄓㄨㄥ ㄖˋ)
from morning till night; throughout the day
終夜(ㄓㄨㄥ ㄧㄝˋ)
throughout the night; the whole night through: 我們終夜看守。We watched all night (long).
終養(ㄓㄨㄥ ㄧㄤˇ)
to resign from one's office to care for one's parents at home
終於(ㄓㄨㄥ ㄩˊ)
in the end; finally; at last
終譽(ㄓㄨㄥ ㄩˋ)
an everlasting name; immortality; a long-lasting fame

【組】 4320 ㄗㄨˇ tzuu zǔ

1. a group; a team; a section; a department; an organization; a union: 每三個人組成一組。Every three persons constitute a group.
2. to organize; to arrange; to unite; to form: 他們組織新的政黨。They organized a new political party.
3. tassels; a fringe; a girdle; a tape

組閣(ㄗㄨˇ ㄍㄜˊ)
(government) to form a cabinet
組合(ㄗㄨˇ ㄏㄜˊ)
①(mathematics) combinations ②to unite; to make up; to form a partnership ③ a company; a corporation; a union
組曲(ㄗㄨˇ ㄑㄩˇ)
(music) a suite
組訓(ㄗㄨˇ ㄒㄩㄣˋ)
to organize and train (militia units or local self-defense units)

〔糸部〕

組織(ㄗㄨˇ ㄓ)
①to organize; to form; to constitute; to found: 那篇小說組織得很好。That novel is well-organized. ②an organization; a formation: 沒有組織的軍隊是無用的。An army without organization would be useless. ③(biology) tissue; texture
組織法(ㄗㄨˇ ㄓ ㄈㄚˇ)
organic law
組織化(ㄗㄨˇ ㄓ ㄏㄨㄚˋ)
to systematize; systematization; organized
組織學(ㄗㄨˇ ㄓ ㄒㄩㄝˊ)
histology
組長(ㄗㄨˇ ㄓㄤˇ)
the chief of a department or section in a government agency
組成(ㄗㄨˇ ㄔㄥˊ)
to form; to compose; to constitute

【絆】 4321
ㄅㄢˋ bann bàn
1. shackles; fetters
2. to stumble; to trip over; to trip: 她被樹根絆了一下。She stumbled over the root of a tree.
絆倒(ㄅㄢˋ ㄉㄠˇ)
to trip over; to trip: 這塊鬆弛的木板把他絆倒。The loose board tripped him.
絆脚(ㄅㄢˋ ㄐㄧㄠˇ)
fettered; hindered
絆脚石(ㄅㄢˋ ㄐㄧㄠˇ ㄕˊ)
a stumbling block
絆住(ㄅㄢˋ ㄓㄨˋ)
to be detained, hindered or held back; to be bogged down
絆創膏(ㄅㄢˋ ㄔㄨㄤ ㄍㄠ)
an adhesive tape

【絅】 4322
ㄐㄩㄥˇ jeong jiǒng
an overall with no lining; a dust coat

【紽】 4323
ㄊㄨㄛˊ two tuó
a strand of silk; braiding

【紩】 4324
ㄓˋ jyh zhì
to sew

【絁】 4325
ㄕ shy shī
a kind of coarse silk fabric

六畫

【結】 4326
1. ㄐㄧㄝˊ jye jié
1. to tie; to knot; to weave: 那條絲帶沒結好。That ribbon doesn't tie well.
2. a knot: 他在繩上打了一個結。He tied a knot in a rope.
3. to unite; to join; to connect
4. to congeal; coagulation: 水結成冰。Water congeals into ice.
5. to form; to found; to constitute
6. to bear fruit; a result; an outcome: 你的研究會有結果。Your study will bear fruit.
7. to pay, or settle (as an account, etc.)
8. a node: 淋巴結 a lymph node
結疤(ㄐㄧㄝˊ ㄅㄚ)
to heal up; to scar; to form a scab: 她的傷口結疤情形良好。Her wound is scarring well.
結拜(ㄐㄧㄝˊ ㄅㄞˋ)
sworn (brothers, or sisters); to pledge in a sworn brotherhood: 他們是結拜兄弟。They were sworn brothers.
結伴(ㄐㄧㄝˊ ㄅㄢˋ)
to accompany; (to tour, play, take a trip, etc.) together, or in a group: 我們結伴而行。We went in a group.
結冰(ㄐㄧㄝˊ ㄅㄧㄥ)
to freeze; to form ice; to turn to ice
結不解仇(ㄐㄧㄝˊ ㄅㄨˋ ㄐㄧㄝˇ ㄔㄡˊ)
to become a sworn enemy of
結不解緣(ㄐㄧㄝˊ ㄅㄨˋ ㄐㄧㄝˇ ㄩㄢˊ)
(said of marriage, love, close association, etc.) to be united by an ironclad bond
結膜(ㄐㄧㄝˊ ㄇㄛˊ)or 結合膜(ㄐㄧㄝˊ ㄏㄜˊ ㄇㄛˊ)
conjunctiva
結膜炎(ㄐㄧㄝˊ ㄇㄛˊ ㄧㄢˊ)
conjunctivitis
結茅(ㄐㄧㄝˊ ㄇㄠˊ)
to build a cottage
結盟(ㄐㄧㄝˊ ㄇㄥˊ)
to form an alliance; to ally with; to enter into an alliance; alignment
結髮(ㄐㄧㄝˊ ㄈㄚˇ)
to knot the hair upon reaching adulthood in former times
結髮夫妻(ㄐㄧㄝˊ ㄈㄚˇ ㄈㄨ ㄑㄧ)
a legally married couple—the first marriage for both husband and wife
結黨營私(ㄐㄧㄝˊ ㄉㄤˇ ㄧㄥˊ ㄙ)
to gang together for clandestine and illegal activities; to form a clique to pursue selfish interests
結隊成羣(ㄐㄧㄝˊ ㄉㄨㄟˋ ㄔㄥˊ ㄑㄩㄣˊ)
in groups and droves
結同心(ㄐㄧㄝˊ ㄊㄨㄥˊ ㄒㄧㄣ)
to be of one mind
結縭(ㄐㄧㄝˊ ㄌㄧˊ)
to be married
結廬(ㄐㄧㄝˊ ㄌㄨˊ)
①to build a house (or hut) ②(figuratively) retirement
結論(ㄐㄧㄝˊ ㄌㄨㄣˋ)
the conclusion (of a meeting, argument, etc.): 不要忙於下結論。Don't jump to conclusions.
結構(ㄐㄧㄝˊ ㄍㄡˋ)
①structure; structural ②(said of a piece of writing) the arrangement of ideas; presentation; composition: 這篇文章的結構很好。The composition of this article is very good.
結果(ㄐㄧㄝˊ ㄍㄨㄛˇ)
①(said of plants) to bear fruit ②the result, outcome or consequence ③in the end; finally
結合(ㄐㄧㄝˊ ㄏㄜˊ)
①to get united; to combine with; to form an alliance; to associate ②to get married; to marry
結合線(ㄐㄧㄝˊ ㄏㄜˊ ㄒㄧㄢˋ)
(said of a music score) a tie
結核(ㄐㄧㄝˊ ㄏㄜˊ)
(pathology) tubercle
結核病(ㄐㄧㄝˊ ㄏㄜˊ ㄅㄧㄥˋ)
tuberculosis
結核病院(ㄐㄧㄝˊ ㄏㄜˊ ㄅㄧㄥˋ ㄩㄢˋ)
a T.B. hospital
結核防治中心(ㄐㄧㄝˊ ㄏㄜˊ ㄈㄤˊ ㄓˋ ㄓㄨㄥ ㄒㄧㄣ)
a T.B. prevention and treatment center
結核菌(ㄐㄧㄝˊ ㄏㄜˊ ㄐㄩㄣˋ)

tubercle bacilli

結核性的(ㄐㄧㄝˊ ㄏㄜˊ ㄒㄧㄥˋ ˙ㄉㄜ)
tuberculated

結好(ㄐㄧㄝˊ ㄏㄠˇ)
to befriend; to be intimate with; to collaborate with; to win favor from

結夥(ㄐㄧㄝˊ ㄏㄨㄛˇ)
to form a band; to gang up; to band together; to collude: 他們結夥抗議。They banded together to protest.

結滙(ㄐㄧㄝˊ ㄏㄨㄟˋ)
to sell foreign exchange to (or to buy it from) banks; foreign exchange settlement

結歡(ㄐㄧㄝˊ ㄏㄨㄢ)
to please; to win favor; to associate with another in order to win his or her heart; to have a lover

結婚(ㄐㄧㄝˊ ㄏㄨㄣ)
marriage; to get married

結婚證書(ㄐㄧㄝˊ ㄏㄨㄣ ㄓㄥˋ ㄕㄨ)
a marriage certificate

結集(ㄐㄧㄝˊ ㄐㄧˊ)
to concentrate (troops, etc.); concentration (of troops, etc.)

結交(ㄐㄧㄝˊ ㄐㄧㄠ)
to associate with; to befriend; to make friends with

結晶(ㄐㄧㄝˊ ㄐㄧㄥ)
to crystallize; crystallization; crystal

結晶體(ㄐㄧㄝˊ ㄐㄧㄥ ㄊㄧˇ)
a crystal; a crystalloid

結晶學(ㄐㄧㄝˊ ㄐㄧㄥ ㄒㄩㄝˊ)
crystallography

結晶岩(ㄐㄧㄝˊ ㄐㄧㄥ ㄧㄢˊ)
crystalline rocks

結局(ㄐㄧㄝˊ ㄐㄩˊ)
the outcome; the result; the end (of an incident, story, etc.); the ending: 這故事有一個快樂的結局。The story has a happy ending.

結契(ㄐㄧㄝˊ ㄑㄧˋ)
to be on very good or intimate terms with

結欠(ㄐㄧㄝˊ ㄑㄧㄢˋ)
to owe after the settlement of accounts; to remain or continue in debt; the balance due; the debit balance in the red

結親(ㄐㄧㄝˊ ㄑㄧㄣ)
to strike up a matrimonial relationship; to unite in marriage

結清(ㄐㄧㄝˊ ㄑㄧㄥ)
to pay up a bill; to settle a debt; to square accounts; all squared: 我們與他結清賬目。We square accounts with him.

結嫌(ㄐㄧㄝˊ ㄒㄧㄢˊ)
to develop suspicion or animosity (between two or more parties)

結帳 or 結賬(ㄐㄧㄝˊ ㄓㄤˋ)
to settle accounts; to pay up; to square accounts

結撰(ㄐㄧㄝˊ ㄓㄨㄢˋ)
to compose or plan writings, reports, etc.

結轍(ㄐㄧㄝˊ ㄔㄜˋ)
heavy traffic of carriages

結仇 or 結讎(ㄐㄧㄝˊ ㄔㄡˊ)
to contract ill will or animus of; to incur hostility or enmity of

結腸(ㄐㄧㄝˊ ㄔㄤˊ)
colons

結石(ㄐㄧㄝˊ ㄕˊ)
(pathology) stone; calculus

結實(ㄐㄧㄝˊ ㄕˊ)
to bear fruit: 這棵梨樹結實纍纍。This pear tree bears fruit in clusters.

結識(ㄐㄧㄝˊ ㄕˋ)
to know or associate with; to strike up an acquaintance with

結舌(ㄐㄧㄝˊ ㄕㄜˊ)
to be tongue-tied (as a result of stage fright, etc.): 他結舌緘口。He was tongue-tied and mouth-sealed.

結社(ㄐㄧㄝˊ ㄕㄜˋ)
to form a union, association, etc.

結繩(ㄐㄧㄝˊ ㄕㄥˊ) or 結繩記事(ㄐㄧㄝˊ ㄕㄥˊ ㄐㄧˋ ㄕˋ)
to tie knots on a string or rope for recording before the invention of written language: 古人結繩記事。The ancients kept records by tying knots.

結束(ㄐㄧㄝˊ ㄕㄨˋ)
to conclude; to end; to wind up: 代表團結束了對日本的訪問。The delegation has concluded its visit to Japan.

結子(ㄐㄧㄝˊ ˙ㄗ)
a knot on a string or rope

結紮(ㄐㄧㄝˊ ㄗㄚ)
(medicine) ligation; ligature; to ligature

結綵(ㄐㄧㄝˊ ㄘㄞˇ)
to festoon; a festoon (for celebration)

結草銜環(ㄐㄧㄝˊ ㄘㄠˇ ㄒㄧㄢˊ ㄏㄨㄢˊ) or 結草(ㄐㄧㄝˊ ㄘㄠˇ)
to repay favors received even after one's death; most sincere thanks and gratitude

結存(ㄐㄧㄝˊ ㄘㄨㄣˊ)
the credit balance; (said of government finance) foreign exchange reserves

結駟連騎(ㄐㄧㄝˊ ㄙˋ ㄌㄧㄢˊ ㄐㄧˋ)
a carriage drawn by four horses—pomposity

結算(ㄐㄧㄝˊ ㄙㄨㄢˋ)
statements of accounts; settlement of accounts; to settle accounts

結案(ㄐㄧㄝˊ ㄢˋ)
to conclude a case

結義兄弟(ㄐㄧㄝˊ ㄧˋ ㄒㄩㄥ ㄉㄧˋ)
sworn brothers: 我們是結義兄弟。We are sworn brothers.

結業(ㄐㄧㄝˊ ㄧㄝˋ)
to graduate; to conclude or complete a training course

結業典禮(ㄐㄧㄝˊ ㄧㄝˋ ㄉㄧㄢˇ ㄌㄧˇ)
a commencement (ceremony); a graduation ceremony

結尾(ㄐㄧㄝˊ ㄨㄟˇ)
the conclusion; the end; the ending; the final part: 他演說的結尾很有力量。His speech has a forceful ending.

結網(ㄐㄧㄝˊ ㄨㄤˇ)
to make a net

結餘(ㄐㄧㄝˊ ㄩˊ)
a cash surplus; a surplus

結約(ㄐㄧㄝˊ ㄩㄝ)
to conclude a treaty, agreement, etc.

結寃(ㄐㄧㄝˊ ㄩㄢ)
to contract animus, enmity, hatred, ill will, etc.: 他和鄰人結寃。He was at enmity with his neighbors.

結緣(ㄐㄧㄝˊ ㄩㄢˊ)
to associate on good terms; to form ties of affection;

〔糸部〕

(Buddhism) to form a connection, e.g. for future salvation

結怨(ㄐㄧㄝˊ ㄩㄢˋ)
to arouse ill will or dislike; to incur hatred: 我從不結怨。I never incurred hatred.

【結】 4326
2. ㄐㄧㄝ jie jiē

1. to stutter; to stammer
2. tough; strong; durable
3. to bear (fruit); to form (seed)

結巴(ㄐㄧㄝ ˙ㄅㄚ)
to stutter; to stammer

結巴頦子(ㄐㄧㄝ ˙ㄅㄚ ㄎㄜ ˙ㄗ)
one who stutters

結結巴巴(ㄐㄧㄝ ˙ㄐㄧㄝ ㄅㄚ ㄅㄚ)
stuttering; stammering: 他結結巴巴的道歉。He stuttered an apology.

結實(ㄐㄧㄝ ˙ㄕ)
① tough; durable; solid; not easily breakable ② strong; sturdy; muscular and healthy

結子(ㄐㄧㄝ ㄗˇ)or 結子兒(ㄐㄧㄝ ㄗㄜˇㄦ)
(said of plants, especially flowers, etc.) to produce seeds; to bear fruit: 此樹不結子兒。This tree bears no fruit.

【絓】 4327
ㄍㄨㄚˋ guah guà

obstructed; hindered

絓礙(ㄍㄨㄚˋ ㄞˋ)
an obstacle

絓誤(ㄍㄨㄚˋ ㄨˋ)
① to be reprimanded for a certain involvement in the mistakes of someone else ② to get others involved in criminal acts by lying 亦作「詿誤」or「罣誤」

【絕】 4328
ㄐㄩㄝˊ jyue jué

1. to sever; to break off; to cut
2. to renounce; to decline
3. to run out of; exhausted; used up; finished
4. without match; peerless; unparalleled; the utmost
5. isolated; to get out of circulation; to separate
6. to discontinue; to terminate; to stop; to cease
7. without posterity; heirless
8. extremely; utmost; most; absolutely
9. to destroy
10. leaving no leeway; making no allowance; uncompromising
11. a poem of four lines

絕版(ㄐㄩㄝˊ ㄅㄢˇ)
out-of-print (books): 這本書絕版了。This book was out-of-print.

絕筆(ㄐㄩㄝˊ ㄅㄧˇ)
① one's last writing (before death) ② to discontinue writing

絕壁(ㄐㄩㄝˊ ㄅㄧˋ)
cliffs: 他由絕壁墜崖而死。He died in a fall from a cliff.

絕不(ㄐㄩㄝˊ ㄅㄨˋ)
never: 她絕不出去。She never goes out.

絕轡(ㄐㄩㄝˊ ㄆㄟˋ)
①(said of horses) fast ② (said of a person) elegant or stately in a casual manner

絕品(ㄐㄩㄝˊ ㄆㄧㄣˇ)
second-to-none commodities; goods of the highest quality or value; an exquisite article

絕妙(ㄐㄩㄝˊ ㄇㄧㄠˋ)
extremely good or wonderful; exquisite

絕妙好辭(ㄐㄩㄝˊ ㄇㄧㄠˋ ㄏㄠˇ ㄘˊ)
quotable quotes; the last say in (wisecracks, quotes, etc.)

絕妙好詞(ㄐㄩㄝˊ ㄇㄧㄠˋ ㄏㄠˇ ㄘˊ)
an anthology edited by Chou Mi (周密) of the Sung Dynasty containing verses and lyrics of 132 contemporary scholars

絕命(ㄐㄩㄝˊ ㄇㄧㄥˋ)
to die; death

絕命書(ㄐㄩㄝˊ ㄇㄧㄥˋ ㄕㄨ)
one's last writing (before death); a suicide note: 他把絕命書留在桌子上。He left a suicide note on the table.

絕命詞(ㄐㄩㄝˊ ㄇㄧㄥˋ ㄘˊ)
a poem one writes just before anticipated death

絕目(ㄐㄩㄝˊ ㄇㄨˋ)
as far as one's eyes can reach

絕乏(ㄐㄩㄝˊ ㄈㄚˊ)
completely empty; absolutely nothing

絕代(ㄐㄩㄝˊ ㄉㄞˋ)
① matchless, unsurpassed or peerless in one's generation ② in times immemorial

絕代佳人(ㄐㄩㄝˊ ㄉㄞˋ ㄐㄧㄚ ㄖㄣˊ)
a matchless beauty; a beauty of beauties: 她是絕代佳人。She is a beauty of beauties.

絕倒(ㄐㄩㄝˊ ㄉㄠˇ)
① to bring the house down; to split one's sides with laughter ② to admire exceedingly ③ to faint on account of deep grief

絕等(ㄐㄩㄝˊ ㄉㄥˇ)
peerless; the utmost (in quality, etc.)

絕地(ㄐㄩㄝˊ ㄉㄧˋ)
①extremely dangerous spots ② a dead end; an impasse; the end of one's rope

絕頂(ㄐㄩㄝˊ ㄉㄧㄥˇ)
① the top of a mountain peak ② extremely; very (used in the positive sense)

絕頂聰明(ㄐㄩㄝˊ ㄉㄧㄥˇ ㄘㄨㄥ ˙ㄇㄧㄥ)
extremely bright, clever or intelligent

絕對(ㄐㄩㄝˊ ㄉㄨㄟˋ)
absolute(ly); definite(ly); positive; unconditional

絕對服從(ㄐㄩㄝˊ ㄉㄨㄟˋ ㄈㄨˊ ㄘㄨㄥˊ)
absolute obedience; to obey without questioning

絕對單位(ㄐㄩㄝˊ ㄉㄨㄟˋ ㄉㄢ ㄨㄟˋ)
an absolute unit

絕對零度(ㄐㄩㄝˊ ㄉㄨㄟˋ ㄌㄧㄥˊ ㄉㄨˋ)
absolute zero—273.16 degrees below zero C.

絕對論(ㄐㄩㄝˊ ㄉㄨㄟˋ ㄌㄨㄣˋ)
absolutism

絕對濕度(ㄐㄩㄝˊ ㄉㄨㄟˋ ㄕ ㄉㄨˋ)
absolute humidity

絕對溫度(ㄐㄩㄝˊ ㄉㄨㄟˋ ㄨㄣ ㄉㄨˋ)
absolute temperature

絕斷(ㄐㄩㄝˊ ㄉㄨㄢˋ)
to sever or cut off (relationship, etc.)

絕粒(ㄐㄩㄝˊ ㄌㄧˋ)
① to take no food; to go on a hunger strike ② to eat no grain (in order to attain immortality)

絕流(ㄐㄩㄝˊ ㄌㄧㄡˊ)

to cross a stream or river
絕糧(ㄐㄩㄝˊ ㄌㄧㄤˊ)
to run out of food supplies
絕路(ㄐㄩㄝˊ ㄌㄨˋ)
a dead end; an impasse; a road of no return (with retreat cut off)
絕倫(ㄐㄩㄝˊ ㄌㄨㄣˊ)
without match; peerless; unparalleled
絕港(ㄐㄩㄝˊ ㄍㄤˇ)
a seaport which has no river to link with the interior
絕國(ㄐㄩㄝˊ ㄍㄨㄛˊ)
an isolated country; a remote country
絕功棄利(ㄐㄩㄝˊ ㄍㄨㄥ ㄑㄧˋ ㄌㄧˋ)
to work for neither money nor prestige
絕口(ㄐㄩㄝˊ ㄎㄡˇ)
①never to mention again: 我絕口不談。I never mentioned it again. ②to stop talking about
絕好(ㄐㄩㄝˊ ㄏㄠˇ)
extremely good; simply excellent
絕後(ㄐㄩㄝˊ ㄏㄡˋ)
①heirless; without posterity ②(said of extremely good writings, paintings, etc.) probably cannot be repeated again
絕戶(ㄐㄩㄝˊ ˙ㄏㄨ)
①heirless; without posterity ②an heirless person
絕迹(ㄐㄩㄝˊ ㄐㄧ)
to vanish completely; to be completely wiped out; to be stamped out
絕技(ㄐㄩㄝˊ ㄐㄧˋ)
a feat or stunt
絕佳(ㄐㄩㄝˊ ㄐㄧㄚ)
extremely good; excellent
絕交(ㄐㄩㄝˊ ㄐㄧㄠ)
to cut off or sever friendship, diplomatic relations, etc.
絕景(ㄐㄩㄝˊ ㄐㄧㄥˇ)
an excellent view; extremely beautiful landscapes or scenes
絕境(ㄐㄩㄝˊ ㄐㄧㄥˋ)
a desperate spot; the end of one's rope; a helpless situation; an impasse: 我們已瀕於絕境。We have faced an impasse.
絕裾(ㄐㄩㄝˊ ㄐㄩ)
to go ahead with determination in disregard of any obstruction, unfavorable response, etc.
絕句(ㄐㄩㄝˊ ㄐㄩˋ)
a four-line verse with five or seven characters to each line
絕羣(ㄐㄩㄝˊ ㄑㄩㄣˊ)
unmatched; peerless
絕響(ㄐㄩㄝˊ ㄒㄧㄤˇ)
①lost arts ②(said of a great musician) cannot be heard again
絕緒(ㄐㄩㄝˊ ㄒㄩˋ)
heirless; without posterity
絕學(ㄐㄩㄝˊ ㄒㄩㄝˊ)
①a lost art ②unique and matchless arts or learning ③to discard conventional or worthless learning
絕招(ㄐㄩㄝˊ ㄓㄠ)
①unique skill ②an unexpected tricky move (as the last resort) ③a master-stroke
絕症(ㄐㄩㄝˊ ㄓㄥˋ)
an incurable disease; a fatal illness
絕種(ㄐㄩㄝˊ ㄓㄨㄥˇ)
(said of species of animals, etc.) extinction; extinct: 許多鳥獸現已絕種。Many birds and beasts are now extinct.
絕塵(ㄐㄩㄝˊ ㄔㄣˊ)
to move faster than the flying dust—very fast
絕長補短(ㄐㄩㄝˊ ㄔㄤˊ ㄅㄨˇ ㄉㄨㄢˇ)
to supplement insufficiency with a surplus
絕唱(ㄐㄩㄝˊ ㄔㄤˋ)
extremely beautiful poems, songs, lyrics, etc.
絕處逢生(ㄐㄩㄝˊ ㄔㄨˋ ㄈㄥˊ ㄕㄥ)
to get saved at a critical moment; to survive a crisis
絕食(ㄐㄩㄝˊ ㄕˊ)
to fast; to go on a hunger strike
絕世(ㄐㄩㄝˊ ㄕˋ)
①unmatched, unrivaled or unparalleled in one's generation ②without posterity—heirless ③to die
絕世獨立(ㄐㄩㄝˊ ㄕˋ ㄉㄨˊ ㄌㄧˋ)
to hold on to one's views, stand, etc. in spite of a world of objection
絕世佳人(ㄐㄩㄝˊ ㄕˋ ㄐㄧㄚ ㄖㄣˊ)
an incomparable beauty; a rare beauty
絕世超倫(ㄐㄩㄝˊ ㄕˋ ㄔㄠ ㄌㄨㄣˊ)
absolutely matchless and unparalleled
絕聖棄智(ㄐㄩㄝˊ ㄕㄥˋ ㄑㄧˋ ㄓˋ)
to prevent enlightenment; to resort to obscurantism
絕早(ㄐㄩㄝˊ ㄗㄠˇ)
very early; soonest
絕才(ㄐㄩㄝˊ ㄘㄞˊ)
incomparable talent or capability: 他眞是個曠世絕才。He is really an incomparable talent.
絕嗣(ㄐㄩㄝˊ ㄙˋ)
without heir or posterity
絕色(ㄐㄩㄝˊ ㄙㄜˋ)
a stunning beauty; an incomparably beautiful girl
絕塞(ㄐㄩㄝˊ ㄙㄞˋ)
the remote border
絕俗(ㄐㄩㄝˊ ㄙㄨˊ)
①above the worldly ways ②to sever oneself from worldly ways or matters
絕詣(ㄐㄩㄝˊ ㄧˋ)
profoundly well-versed
絕藝(ㄐㄩㄝˊ ㄧˋ)
a unique feat, stunt or performance; consummate skill
絕業(ㄐㄩㄝˊ ㄧㄝˋ)
a career or an endeavor, etc. which has been cut short or interrupted
絕垠(ㄐㄩㄝˊ ㄧㄣˊ)
remote, outlandish places; very distant land
絕靷而馳(ㄐㄩㄝˊ ㄧㄣˇ ㄦˊ ㄔˊ)
(said of a talented person) to have a brilliant career after getting a break
絕無(ㄐㄩㄝˊ ㄨˊ)
absolutely negative; nothing; never
絕無僅有(ㄐㄩㄝˊ ㄨˊ ㄐㄧㄣˇ ㄧㄡˇ)
very rare; unique
絕問(ㄐㄩㄝˊ ㄨㄣˋ)
to have no communication with
絕望(ㄐㄩㄝˊ ㄨㄤˋ)
hopeless; hopelessness; des-

〔糸部〕

perate; desperation; despair; to give up hope

絕域(ㄐㄩㄝˊ ㄩˋ)
out-of-the-way or inaccessible places; inaccessible remote areas

絕緣(ㄐㄩㄝˊ ㄩㄢˊ)
to insulate

絕緣體(ㄐㄩㄝˊ ㄩㄢˊ ㄊㄧˇ)
an insulator

〔糸部〕

【絏】 4329
(紲) ㄒㄧㄝˋ shieh xiè

1. reins; ropes for leading animals
2. to bind; fetters; bonds

【絞】 4330
ㄐㄧㄠˇ jeau jiǎo

1. to twist; to twine; to wring
2. to hang (a criminal)
3. rudeness
4. to mix up

絞盤(ㄐㄧㄠˇ ㄆㄢˊ)
a capstan; a windlass

絞痛(ㄐㄧㄠˇ ㄊㄨㄥˋ)
an acute or gripping pain caused by cholera, appendicitis, etc.

絞臉(ㄐㄧㄠˇ ㄌㄧㄢˇ)
to roll twisted threads over the face (of a woman) to root out fine hairs

絞緊(ㄐㄧㄠˇ ㄐㄧㄣˇ)
to twist tight

絞盡腦汁(ㄐㄧㄠˇ ㄐㄧㄣˋ ㄋㄠˇ ㄓ)
to cudgel one's brains: 我絞盡腦汁想記起她的名字。I cudgeled my brains to recall her name.

絞決(ㄐㄧㄠˇ ㄐㄩㄝˊ)
the execution of a death convict by strangulation or hanging

絞刑(ㄐㄧㄠˇ ㄒㄧㄥˊ)
death by hanging or strangulation

絞車(ㄐㄧㄠˇ ㄔㄜ)
a winch: 他們用絞車舉起車子。They used a winch to lift the car.

絞腸痧(ㄐㄧㄠˇ ㄔㄤˊ ㄕㄚ)
acute appendicitis

絞死(ㄐㄧㄠˇ ㄙˇ)
to kill by hanging; death by hanging

【絡】 4331
1. ㄌㄨㄛˋ luoh luò

1. to wrap around; to encompass
2. a net; a web
3. a cellulose structure in fruits, as melons
4. to associate; to unite; connected
5. a halter
6. (said of blood vessels) capillaries
7. to unreel silk
8. cotton fiber
9. hemp
10. a Chinese family name

絡頭(ㄌㄨㄛˋ ㄊㄡˊ)
a halter

絡腮鬍子(ㄌㄨㄛˋ ㄙㄞ ㄏㄨˊ ˙ㄗ)
whiskers

絡繹不絕(ㄌㄨㄛˋ ㄧˋ ㄅㄨˋ ㄐㄩㄝˊ)
(said of people) to come one after another; in uninterrupted succession; continuous: 參觀美術展覽會的人絡繹不絕。A continuous stream of visitors came to the art exhibition.

絡緯(ㄌㄨㄛˋ ㄨㄟˇ)or 絡絲娘(ㄌㄨㄛˋ ㄙ ㄋㄧㄤˊ)
a cricket—whose nocturnal buzzing in summer sounds like unreeled silk

【絡】 4331
2. ㄌㄠˋ law lào

a web or net

絡子(ㄌㄠˋ ˙ㄗ)
a fine thread basket; a small net

【絢】 4332
ㄒㄩㄢˋ shiuann xuàn

bright and brilliant; adorned and stylish

絢爛(ㄒㄩㄢˋ ㄌㄢˋ)
bright and brilliant; glittering; splendid

絢麗(ㄒㄩㄢˋ ㄌㄧˋ)
gorgeous; magnificent

【給】 4333
1. ㄐㄧˇ jii jǐ

1. to provide; provisions; to supply; supplies
2. to award; to approve; to grant
3. sufficiency; affluence
4. glib; eloquent

給假(ㄐㄧˇ ㄐㄧㄚˋ)
to grant a leave of absence: 他要求老闆給假一星期。He asks the boss to grant him a week's leave.

給諫(ㄐㄧˇ ㄐㄧㄢˋ)or 給事中(ㄐㄧˇ ㄕˋ ㄓㄨㄥ)
an official rank in ancient China, roughly equivalent to a censor

給獎(ㄐㄧˇ ㄐㄧㄤˇ)
to award prizes

給水(ㄐㄧˇ ㄕㄨㄟˇ)
a water supply

給足(ㄐㄧˇ ㄗㄨˊ)
sufficiency; affluence

給養(ㄐㄧˇ ㄧㄤˇ)
military provisions and supplies: 我軍給養充足。Our army is abundantly provisioned.

給與(ㄐㄧˇ ㄩˇ)or(ㄍㄟˇ ㄩˇ)
to give: 他給與乞丐一些錢。He gave the beggar some money.

【給】 4333
2. ㄍㄟˇ geei gěi

1. to give: 給我東西喝好嗎? Will you give me something to drink?
2. for; for the benefit of
3. to let; to allow: 給我看看。Let me have a look.
4. used to indicate a passive meaning or voice
5. used after a verb to indicate "giving": 請把奶油遞給我。Please pass me the butter.

給付(ㄍㄟˇ ㄈㄨˋ)or(ㄐㄧˇ ㄈㄨˋ)
to pay

給臉(ㄍㄟˇ ㄌㄧㄢˇ)
to save (another's) face—so as not to embarrass him; to be nice or considerate to others

給以(ㄍㄟˇ ㄧˇ)
to give; to grant

【絨】 4334
ㄖㄨㄥˊ rong róng

1. fine wool; woolen; velvety; velvet
2. any kind of woolen goods or fabric with a felt-like surface
3. fine; furry; flossy

絨布(ㄖㄨㄥˊ ㄅㄨˋ)
flannel; woolen or cotton piece goods with a felt-like surface; felt

絨毛(ㄖㄨㄥˊ ㄇㄠˊ)
down

絨毯(ㄖㄨㄥˊ ㄊㄢˇ)
a woolen blanket or carpet: 這小孩被裹在絨毯裡。The child was wrapped in a woolen blanket.

絨花(ㄖㄨㄥˊ ㄏㄨㄚ)
artificial flowers made of silk
絨線(ㄖㄨㄥˊ ㄒㄧㄢˋ)
woolen yarn; floss for embroidering; knitting wool
絨繩(ㄖㄨㄥˊ ㄕㄥˊ)
woolen yarn for knitting

【絪】 4335
ㄧㄣ in yin
misty; foggy; cloudy
絪縕(ㄧㄣ ㄩㄣ)
misty; foggy 亦作「氤氳」

【絰】 4336
ㄉㄧㄝˊ dye dié
a hemp hat worn in mourning for one's parents

【統】 4337
ㄊㄨㄥˇ toong tǒng
1. to govern; to rule; to control
2. to unify; to unite
3. wholly; totally; completely; generally; all
4. succession; consecutive generations; from generation to generation

統鋪(ㄊㄨㄥˇ ㄆㄨˋ)
a wide bed for a number of people (as in barracks, inns, etc.)
統帶(ㄊㄨㄥˇ ㄉㄞˋ)
(Ching Dynasty) a regiment commander
統統(ㄊㄨㄥˇ ㄊㄨㄥˇ)
wholly; completely; all: 那統統是他的錯。It is completely his fault.
統領(ㄊㄨㄥˇ ㄌㄧㄥˇ)
a commanding officer; a commander of troops
統購統銷(ㄊㄨㄥˇ ㄍㄡˋ ㄊㄨㄥˇ ㄒㄧㄠ)
state purchasing and selling
統括(ㄊㄨㄥˇ ㄍㄨㄚ)
all included; all-encompassing
統共(ㄊㄨㄥˇ ㄍㄨㄥˋ)
all together; total: 旅行的費用統共多少? What is the total cost of the trip?
統計(ㄊㄨㄥˇ ㄐㄧˋ)
① statistics ② to count
統計表(ㄊㄨㄥˇ ㄐㄧˋ ㄅㄧㄠˇ)
a statistical table, chart, graph, etc.
統計圖表(ㄊㄨㄥˇ ㄐㄧˋ ㄊㄨˊ ㄅㄧㄠˇ)
a statistical diagram; a pictograph
統計學(ㄊㄨㄥˇ ㄐㄧˋ ㄒㄩㄝˊ)
statistics (as a science)
統計資料(ㄊㄨㄥˇ ㄐㄧˋ ㄗ ㄌㄧㄠˋ)
statistical data
統轄(ㄊㄨㄥˇ ㄒㄧㄚˊ)
to rule; to govern; to control
統銷(ㄊㄨㄥˇ ㄒㄧㄠ)
to sell jointly; joint marketing
統制(ㄊㄨㄥˇ ㄓˋ)
① a former military rank, equivalent to today's division commander ② to control; to govern and regulate; to exercise control (over): 政府嚴格統制軍用物資。The government strictly controls military supplies.
統制經濟(ㄊㄨㄥˇ ㄓˋ ㄐㄧㄥ ㄐㄧˋ)
planned economy
統治(ㄊㄨㄥˇ ㄓˋ)
to reign; to rule; to govern: 這位國王賢明地統治他的國家。The king governs his country wisely.
統治階級(ㄊㄨㄥˇ ㄓˋ ㄐㄧㄝ ㄐㄧˊ)
the ruling class
統治權(ㄊㄨㄥˇ ㄓˋ ㄑㄩㄢˊ)
sovereign power
統治者(ㄊㄨㄥˇ ㄓˋ ㄓㄜˇ)
the ruler
統籌(ㄊㄨㄥˇ ㄔㄡˊ)
to plan as a whole
統籌辦理(ㄊㄨㄥˇ ㄔㄡˊ ㄅㄢˋ ㄌㄧˇ)
(said of several matters) to be dealt with simultaneously by a single government agency
統籌兼顧(ㄊㄨㄥˇ ㄔㄡˊ ㄐㄧㄢ ㄍㄨˋ)
to plan jointly so as to take into consideration every aspect of a matter
統稱(ㄊㄨㄥˇ ㄔㄥ)
known together as
統攝(ㄊㄨㄥˇ ㄕㄜˋ)
to control; to rule
統帥(ㄊㄨㄥˇ ㄕㄨㄞˋ)
the commander in chief
統率(ㄊㄨㄥˇ ㄕㄨㄞˋ)
to lead (troops, a mission, etc.); to rule; to govern
統艙(ㄊㄨㄥˇ ㄘㄤ)
steerage (of a passenger steamer)
統一(ㄊㄨㄥˇ ㄧ)
to unify; uniform; unitary: 中國是統一的多民族國家。China is a unitary multinational state.
統一發票(ㄊㄨㄥˇ ㄧ ㄈㄚ ㄆㄧㄠˋ)
a uniform invoice
統一天下(ㄊㄨㄥˇ ㄧ ㄊㄧㄢ ㄒㄧㄚˋ)
to unify the whole country
統御 or 統馭(ㄊㄨㄥˇ ㄩˋ)
to reign; to rule; to control; reign: 一個賢明治理者的統御對國家有利。The reign of a wise ruler benefits his country.

【絳】 4338
ㄐㄧㄤˋ jianq jiàng
crimson; a deep red color
絳袍(ㄐㄧㄤˋ ㄆㄠˊ)
a red robe
絳頰(ㄐㄧㄤˋ ㄐㄧㄚˊ)
rosy cheeks; a flushed face
絳帳(ㄐㄧㄤˋ ㄓㄤˋ)
the seat of the teacher—formerly with a red curtain behind it
絳脣(ㄐㄧㄤˋ ㄔㄨㄣˊ)
red lips
絳樹(ㄐㄧㄤˋ ㄕㄨˋ)
① coral ② name of an ancient beauty
絳幘(ㄐㄧㄤˋ ㄗㄜˊ)
(in ancient China) the imperial guards who wear red turbans
絳色(ㄐㄧㄤˋ ㄙㄜˋ)
a deep red color; a red color

【絲】 4339
ㄙ sy si
1. silk
2. very fine thread, fiber, etc. as those making a spider's web
3. a general name of silk fabrics or goods
4. strings of musical instruments
5. infinitesimal; a trace; a thread; a tiny bit: 她的臉上露出一絲笑容。There is a trace of a smile on her face.
6. 1/100,000 of a tael
絲布(ㄙ ㄅㄨˋ)
cloth with silk and cotton yarn as the warp and the woof respectively
絲帕(ㄙ ㄆㄚˋ)
a silk handkerchief: 她掉了她的絲帕。She lost her silk

〔糸部〕

handkerchief.
絲棉(ㄙ ㄇㄧㄢˊ)
silk batting; silk wadding; silk padding
絲髮(ㄙ ㄈㄚˇ)
① glossy, silky hair ② the tiniest bit
絲帶(ㄙ ㄉㄞˋ)
silk ribbons: 她結粉紅色的絲帶在頭髮上。She had a pink ribbon in her hair.
絲桐(ㄙ ㄊㄨㄥˊ)
a Chinese harp or lute
絲來線去(ㄙ ㄌㄞˊ ㄒㄧㄢˋ ㄑㄩˋ)
tangled and involved endlessly
絲淚(ㄙ ㄌㄟˋ)
little teardrops
絲蘿(ㄙ ㄌㄨㄛˊ)
marriage
絲瓜(ㄙ ㄍㄨㄚ)
the sponge gourd (the fruit of a loofah); towel gourds
絲光棉(ㄙ ㄍㄨㄤ ㄇㄧㄢˊ)
mercerized cotton
絲毫(ㄙ ㄏㄠˊ)
the tiniest, slightest, or least bit
絲毫不爽(ㄙ ㄏㄠˊ ㄅㄨˋ ㄕㄨㄤˇ)
perfectly matching; very reliable or accurate
絲線(ㄙ ㄒㄧㄢˋ)
silk thread
絲織品(ㄙ ㄓ ㄆㄧㄣˇ)
silk fabrics; silk goods
絲竹(ㄙ ㄓㄨˊ)
① Chinese musical instruments ② music
絲綢(ㄙ ㄔㄡˊ)
silk cloth; silk
絲綢之路(ㄙ ㄔㄡˊ ㄓ ㄌㄨˋ)or 絲路(ㄙ ㄌㄨˋ)
(history) the Silk Road
絲絨(ㄙ ㄖㄨㄥˊ)
velvet
絲絲(ㄙ ㄙ)
an expression to describe the fineness or thinness of things
絲絲拉拉(ㄙ ㄙ ㄌㄚ ㄌㄚ)
endless tangles and involvement
絲絲入扣(ㄙ ㄙ ㄖㄨˋ ㄎㄡˋ)
ingenious and touching; right on the beat; even the tiniest bits fit (into the whole thing)
絲兒(ㄙㄜˇㄦ)
tender and delicate things
絲恩髮怨(ㄙ ㄣ ㄈㄚˇ ㄩㄢˋ)
gratitude for the slightest favor received or a grudge against the slightest wrong done
絲襪(ㄙ ㄨㄚˋ)
silk stockings; silk socks: 我買了一雙絲襪。I bought a pair of silk stockings.
絲雨(ㄙ ㄩˇ)
drizzle; misty rain

【絮】 4340
ㄒㄩˋ shiuh xù
1. raw, coarse, old, waste cotton or silk
2. wooly; fluffy
3. catkins and similar blossoms
4. padding; cushioning
5. (said of chatter, writing, etc.) windy
6. to wad with cotton
絮煩(ㄒㄩˋ ˙ㄈㄢ)
① windy; talkative ② tired of; weary; bored
絮叨(ㄒㄩˋ ˙ㄉㄠ)or 絮叨叨(ㄒㄩˋ ㄉㄠ ㄉㄠ)or 絮絮叨叨(ㄒㄩˋ ˙ㄒㄩ ㄉㄠ ㄉㄠ)
nagging; tiresomely talkative; to talk endlessly; to nag: 她絮叨得把他煩死了。She nagged him to death.
絮羹(ㄒㄩˋ ㄍㄥ)
to add seasoning into broth
絮聒(ㄒㄩˋ ㄍㄨㄚ)
① windy and tiresome ② to importune incessantly: 他用問題向我絮聒。He importuned me with questions.
絮絮不休(ㄒㄩˋ ㄒㄩˋ ㄅㄨˋ ㄒㄧㄡ)
to din; to chatter; annoyingly talkative: 她絮絮不休地談論她的工作。She was chattering over her work.
絮語(ㄒㄩˋ ㄩˇ)
incessant chatter

【絜】 4341
1. ㄐㄧㄝ jye jie
clean; pure

【絜】 4341
2. ㄒㄧㄝˊ shye xié
1. to assess; to ascertain; to measure
2. to restrain; to regulate
絜矩(ㄒㄧㄝˊ ㄐㄩˇ)
to examine oneself and think of the others so that each will get what he wants

七畫

【條】 4342
(絛) ㄊㄠ tau tāo
a silk band, sash, or ribbon
絛蟲(ㄊㄠ ㄔㄨㄥˊ)
a tapeworm
絛子(ㄊㄠ ˙ㄗ)
lace or embroidery used for hemming

【絹】 4343
ㄐㄩㄢˋ jiuann juàn
1. a kind of thick, loosely-woven raw silk fabric
2. a handkerchief
絹布(ㄐㄩㄢˋ ㄅㄨˋ)
cottonlike lustring
絹畫(ㄐㄩㄢˋ ㄏㄨㄚˋ)
classical Chinese paintings on silk
絹綢(ㄐㄩㄢˋ ㄔㄡˊ)
a kind of silk fabric
絹扇(ㄐㄩㄢˋ ㄕㄢˋ)
a fan made with silk
絹子(ㄐㄩㄢˋ ˙ㄗ)
a handkerchief
絹絲(ㄐㄩㄢˋ ㄙ)
spun silk yarn
絹素(ㄐㄩㄢˋ ㄙㄨˋ)
a kind of white silk for painting or calligraphy

【絺】 4344
ㄔ chy chi
1. a kind of fine hemp cloth; linen
2. a Chinese family name

【綁】 4345
ㄅㄤˇ baang bǎng
to tie; to bind; to fasten: 他們將他的手脚綁起來。They bound him hand and foot.
綁票(ㄅㄤˇ ㄆㄧㄠˋ)
to kidnap for ransoms; kidnapping
綁匪(ㄅㄤˇ ㄈㄟˇ)
a kidnaper
綁赴市曹(ㄅㄤˇ ㄈㄨˋ ㄕˋ ㄘㄠˊ)
to tie the hands of a prisoner behind the back and parade him down the streets to the execution ground
綁腿(ㄅㄤˇ ㄊㄨㄟˇ)
leggings; gaiters

綁架(ㄅㄤˇ ㄐㄧㄚˋ)
to kidnap for ransoms

綁緊(ㄅㄤˇ ㄐㄧㄣˇ)
to bind or fasten tight

綁起來(ㄅㄤˇ ㄑㄧˇ ·ㄌㄞ)
to tie up: 小狗被綁起來了。The dog is tied up.

【綃】 4346 ㄒㄧㄠ shiau xiāo

1. a fabric made of raw silk
2. raw silk

綃頭(ㄒㄧㄠ ㄊㄡˊ)
a silk hood for binding the hair

【綈】 4347 ㄊㄧˊ tyi tí

a glossy thick silk fabric

綈袍(ㄊㄧˊ ㄆㄠˊ)
a robe made of inferior silk —(figuratively) old friendship

【綆】 4348 ㄍㄥˇ geeng gěng

a rope for drawing up water (from a well, stream, etc.)

綆短汲深(ㄍㄥˇ ㄉㄨㄢˇ ㄐㄧˊ ㄕㄣ)
(literally) The rope is short while the well is deep.—unequal to the job

【綏】 4349 ㄙㄨㄟ suei suī (又讀 ㄙㄨㄟˊ swei suí)

1. to repose; to pacify; to appease; to soothe; to tranquilize
2. to retreat
3. a strap to help one mount a carriage, etc.
4. a banner; a flag

綏服(ㄙㄨㄟ ㄈㄨˊ)
one of the five peace-securing domains around the imperial capital in ancient China

綏撫(ㄙㄨㄟ ㄈㄨˇ)
to pacify; to placate; to soothe; to tranquilize

綏靖(ㄙㄨㄟ ㄐㄧㄥˋ)
to pacify; pacification; to restore peace and order

綏靖政策(ㄙㄨㄟ ㄐㄧㄥˋ ㄓㄥˋ ㄘㄜˋ)
an appeasement or pacification policy

綏靖主任(ㄙㄨㄟ ㄐㄧㄥˋ ㄓㄨˇ ㄖㄣˋ)
an official rank established in the early 1930's responsible for directing and controlling troops and the local militia in an area where the Communist insurgents had just been rooted out

綏遠(ㄙㄨㄟ ㄩㄢˇ)
Suiyüan Province

【經】 4350 ㄐㄧㄥ jing jīng

1. classic books; religious scriptures; books of significant value: 他讀佛經。He reads Buddhist scriptures.
2. the warp of a fabric; things running lengthwise
3. common or customary ways, rules, regulations, etc.
4. to plan; to arrange; to regulate; to rule; to manage; to deal in; to engage in: 她經商。She engaged in trade.
5. menses
6. human arteries, etc.
7. as a result; after
8. to pass through or by: 你將經過郵局。You will pass the post office.
9. to stand; to bear; to endure
10. longitude
11. a Chinese family name

經邦(ㄐㄧㄥ ㄅㄤ)
to rule a nation; to govern a country

經閉(ㄐㄧㄥ ㄅㄧˋ)
a stoppage of the menses; amenorrhea

經部(ㄐㄧㄥ ㄅㄨˋ)
the first of the four categories of Chinese classics (經史子集)亦作「甲部」

經脈(ㄐㄧㄥ ㄇㄞˋ)
blood vessels

經費(ㄐㄧㄥ ㄈㄟˋ)
an outlay, or expenditure (within the budget); a budget; funds: 此計畫因缺經費而作罷。The project was abandoned for want of funds.

經典(ㄐㄧㄥ ㄉㄧㄢˇ)
① religious scriptures ② Chinese classics

經度(ㄐㄧㄥ ㄉㄨˋ)
degrees of longitude

經天緯地(ㄐㄧㄥ ㄊㄧㄢ ㄨㄟˇ ㄉㄧˋ)
great ability—capable of governing the universe

經痛(ㄐㄧㄥ ㄊㄨㄥˋ)
dysmenorrhea; painful menstruation

經年(ㄐㄧㄥ ㄋㄧㄢˊ)
① for a whole year ② for years: 他經年在外。He was out for years.

經年累月(ㄐㄧㄥ ㄋㄧㄢˊ ㄌㄟˇ ㄩㄝˋ)
for months and years

經理(ㄐㄧㄥ ㄌㄧˇ)
① a manager (of a company) ② to manage, direct, regulate, etc.

經歷(ㄐㄧㄥ ㄌㄧˋ)
① one's past experiences ② to undergo; to go through

經練(ㄐㄧㄥ ㄌㄧㄢˋ)
(said of somebody) experienced; keen and sharp

經絡(ㄐㄧㄥ ㄌㄨㄛˋ)
(blood) the circulation system of the human body

經綸(ㄐㄧㄥ ㄌㄨㄣˊ)
principles and policies in government administration; statecraft

經略(ㄐㄧㄥ ㄌㄩㄝˋ)
① to plan and operate ② an old official rank responsible for security in border provinces

經過(ㄐㄧㄥ ㄍㄨㄛˋ)
① to pass by or through: 他的車子從我面前經過。His car passed in front of me. ② the ins and outs of an occurrence ③ after; through

經過良好(ㄐㄧㄥ ㄍㄨㄛˋ ㄌㄧㄤˊ ㄏㄠˇ)
to have done without a hitch; to have completed doing something satisfactorily

經官動詞(ㄐㄧㄥ ㄍㄨㄢ ㄉㄨㄥˋ ㄘˊ)
to get involved in a lawsuit

經管(ㄐㄧㄥ ㄍㄨㄢˇ)
to take charge of; to have charge of; to be in charge of: 他經管財務。He took charge of financial affairs.

經籍(ㄐㄧㄥ ㄐㄧˊ)
classic books; religious scriptures

經紀人(ㄐㄧㄥ ㄐㄧˋ ㄖㄣˊ)
① a manager (of entertainers, boxers, etc.) ② a broker; an agent: 他是個房地產經紀人。He is an estate agent.

經濟(ㄐㄧㄥ ㄐㄧˋ)
①economy; economic ②eco-

〔糸部〕

nomical; to economize

經濟崩潰(ㄐㄧㄥ ㄐㄧˋ ㄅㄥ ㄎㄨㄟˋ)
economic disintegration; economic bankruptcy; economic collapse

經濟部(ㄐㄧㄥ ㄐㄧˋ ㄅㄨˋ)
Ministry of Economic Affairs

經濟封鎖(ㄐㄧㄥ ㄐㄧˋ ㄈㄥ ㄙㄨㄛˇ)
an economic blockade; to cut off all commercial or financial relations

經濟復甦(ㄐㄧㄥ ㄐㄧˋ ㄈㄨˋ ㄙㄨ)
economic resurgence

經濟大恐慌(ㄐㄧㄥ ㄐㄧˋ ㄉㄚˋ ㄎㄨㄥˇ ㄏㄨㄤ)
the Great Depression, the economic crisis and period of low business activity in the U. S. and other countries, beginning in October, 1929, and continuing through the 1930's

經濟利益(ㄐㄧㄥ ㄐㄧˋ ㄌㄧˋ ㄧˋ)
economic interests

經濟領域(ㄐㄧㄥ ㄐㄧˋ ㄌㄧㄥˇ ㄩˋ)
an economic sphere

經濟革命(ㄐㄧㄥ ㄐㄧˋ ㄍㄜˊ ㄇㄧㄥˋ)
an economic revolution

經濟寬裕(ㄐㄧㄥ ㄐㄧˋ ㄎㄨㄢ ㄩˋ)
well-off; well-to-do

經濟困難(ㄐㄧㄥ ㄐㄧˋ ㄎㄨㄣˋ ㄋㄢˊ)
financial straits or difficulties

經濟恐慌(ㄐㄧㄥ ㄐㄧˋ ㄎㄨㄥˇ ㄏㄨㄤ)
financial straits; economic depressions; an economic crisis: 經濟恐慌常使勞工階級受苦。Economic depressions usually cause misery among the working classes.

經濟基礎(ㄐㄧㄥ ㄐㄧˋ ㄐㄧ ㄔㄨˇ)
an economic base; an economic basis

經濟結構(ㄐㄧㄥ ㄐㄧˋ ㄐㄧㄝˊ ㄍㄡˋ)
economic structure

經濟建設(ㄐㄧㄥ ㄐㄧˋ ㄐㄧㄢˋ ㄕㄜˋ)
economic construction

經濟絕交(ㄐㄧㄥ ㄐㄧˋ ㄐㄩㄝˊ ㄐㄧㄠ)
to break off economic relations; severance of economic ties

經濟起飛(ㄐㄧㄥ ㄐㄧˋ ㄑㄧˇ ㄈㄟ)
economic takeoff

經濟蕭條(ㄐㄧㄥ ㄐㄧˋ ㄒㄧㄠ ㄊㄧㄠˊ)
economic stagnation

經濟學(ㄐㄧㄥ ㄐㄧˋ ㄒㄩㄝˊ)
economics (as a course of study)

經濟學家(ㄐㄧㄥ ㄐㄧˋ ㄒㄩㄝˊ ㄐㄧㄚ)
an economist

經濟指標(ㄐㄧㄥ ㄐㄧˋ ㄓˇ ㄅㄧㄠ)
an economic indicator

經濟制度(ㄐㄧㄥ ㄐㄧˋ ㄓˋ ㄉㄨˋ)
the economic system

經濟制裁(ㄐㄧㄥ ㄐㄧˋ ㄓˋ ㄘㄞˊ)
economic sanctions

經濟政策(ㄐㄧㄥ ㄐㄧˋ ㄓㄥˋ ㄘㄜˋ)
an economic policy

經濟成長(ㄐㄧㄥ ㄐㄧˋ ㄔㄥˊ ㄓㄤˇ)
economic growth

經濟史觀(ㄐㄧㄥ ㄐㄧˋ ㄕˇ ㄍㄨㄢ)
economic interpretation of history

經濟衰退(ㄐㄧㄥ ㄐㄧˋ ㄕㄨㄞ ㄊㄨㄟˋ)
the economic recession

經濟作物(ㄐㄧㄥ ㄐㄧˋ ㄗㄨㄛˋ ㄨˋ)
the industrial crop; the cash crop

經濟危機(ㄐㄧㄥ ㄐㄧˋ ㄨㄟˊ ㄐㄧ)
economic Dunkirk

經濟援助(ㄐㄧㄥ ㄐㄧˋ ㄩㄢˊ ㄓㄨˋ)
economic aid

經解(ㄐㄧㄥ ㄐㄧㄝˇ)
① notations on the classics ② name of a chapter in the *Book of Rites*

經界(ㄐㄧㄥ ㄐㄧㄝˋ)
boundary markings on the farmland

經久耐用(ㄐㄧㄥ ㄐㄧㄡˇ ㄋㄞˋ ㄩㄥˋ)
(said of goods) durable; sturdy

經期(ㄐㄧㄥ ㄑㄧˊ)
the woman's period

經銷(ㄐㄧㄥ ㄒㄧㄠ)
to sell as a consignee: 李先生經銷外國書籍。Mr. Lee sells foreign books as a consignee.

經線(ㄐㄧㄥ ㄒㄧㄢˋ)
longitude; the meridian

經線儀(ㄐㄧㄥ ㄒㄧㄢˋ ㄧˊ)
a chronometer (a navigational instrument)

經心(ㄐㄧㄥ ㄒㄧㄣ)
very careful and attentive; painstaking

經學(ㄐㄧㄥ ㄒㄩㄝˊ)
learning devoted to the study of the classics

經訓(ㄐㄧㄥ ㄒㄩㄣˋ)
teachings and instructions derived from the classics

經之營之(ㄐㄧㄥ ㄓ ㄧㄥˊ ㄓ)
to devote painstaking efforts (to an undertaking)

經傳(ㄐㄧㄥ ㄓㄨㄢˋ)
classics and books by lesser authors

經常(ㄐㄧㄥ ㄔㄤˊ)
frequently; often; constantly; regularly: 她經常上學遲到。She is often late for school.

經常費(ㄐㄧㄥ ㄔㄤˊ ㄈㄟˋ)
routine outlays or expenditures, including operational expenses (as opposed to extra or special outlays caused by unexpected happenings, etc.); recurrent appropriation; the overheads

經師(ㄐㄧㄥ ㄕ)
① a teacher of classics ② a teacher whose sole concern is to impart book learning to students (as opposed to 人師)

經師易得，人師難求(ㄐㄧㄥ ㄕ ㄧˋ ㄉㄜˊ, ㄖㄣˊ ㄕ ㄋㄢˊ ㄑㄧㄡˊ)
(literally) It's easier to get a teacher of classics than a teacher of man.—It's easier to find a learned scholar than an exemplary man of virtue.

經史子集(ㄐㄧㄥ ㄕˇ ㄗˇ ㄐㄧˊ)
an old classification of ancient Chinese books—classics, history, philosophy, and literary works

經世(ㄐㄧㄥ ㄕˋ)
① to manage affairs ② for a generation

經世濟民(ㄐㄧㄥ ㄕˋ ㄐㄧˋ ㄇㄧㄣˊ)
to govern and benefit the people

經世之才(ㄐㄧㄥ ㄕˋ ㄓ ㄘㄞˊ)
great ability; statesmanship

經手(ㄐㄧㄥ ㄕㄡˇ)
to handle; to deal with; to attend to a matter personally: 這件事是她經手的。She is the one who handled this matter.

經手人(ㄐㄧㄥ ㄕㄡˇ ㄖㄣˊ)
one who is responsible for, or personally attends to a matter

經售(ㄐㄧㄥ ㄕㄡˋ)

to sell under a consignment agreement; to sell; to deal in: 這家公司經售棉織品。This firm deals in cotton goods.

經商(ㄐㄧㄥ ㄕㄤ)
to engage in commercial activities; to go into business; to be a businessman: 他離校後要去經商。He will go to business when he leaves school.

經生(ㄐㄧㄥ ㄕㄥ)
a master of the classics

經書(ㄐㄧㄥ ㄕㄨ)
classic books

經笥(ㄐㄧㄥ ㄙˋ)
erudite; learned

經義(ㄐㄧㄥ ㄧˋ)
① the true meanings of classics ② to take a quotation from the classics as a subject for composition in the civil service examination of former times

經意(ㄐㄧㄥ ㄧˋ)
careful; attentive; advertent

經由(ㄐㄧㄥ ㄧㄡˊ)
by (a person); through or via (a place): 他將經由日本去美國。He will be bound for U.S.A. via Japan.

經驗(ㄐㄧㄥ ㄧㄢˋ)
experience; empirical: 經驗爲良師。Experience is a good teacher.

經驗豐富(ㄐㄧㄥ ㄧㄢˋ ㄈㄥ ㄈㄨˋ)
well-experienced

經驗論(ㄐㄧㄥ ㄧㄢˋ ㄌㄨㄣˋ)
empiricism

經驗之談(ㄐㄧㄥ ㄧㄢˋ ㄓ ㄊㄢˊ)
statements based on personal experience

經驗哲學(ㄐㄧㄥ ㄧㄢˋ ㄓㄜˊ ㄒㄩㄝˊ)
empirical philosophy

經驗主義者(ㄐㄧㄥ ㄧㄢˋ ㄓㄨˇ ㄧˋ ㄓㄜˇ)
an empiricist

經營(ㄐㄧㄥ ㄧㄥˊ)
to operate or manage or carry on (a shop, a business, etc.)

經緯(ㄐㄧㄥ ㄨㄟˇ)
① longitude and latitude ② the warp and the woof ③ logical planning ④ main points of something

經緯儀(ㄐㄧㄥ ㄨㄟˇ ㄧˊ)
a theodolite; a transit instrument

經緯萬端(ㄐㄧㄥ ㄨㄟˇ ㄨㄢˋ ㄉㄨㄢ)
very complicated

經文(ㄐㄧㄥ ㄨㄣˊ)
classical text

經文緯武(ㄐㄧㄥ ㄨㄣˊ ㄨㄟˇ ㄨˇ)
to map and execute government policies and military affairs

【綑】 4351
(捆) ㄎㄨㄣˇ koen kuěn

1. a bundle; to make a bundle; to tie up; to bundle up
2. to weave

綑綁(ㄎㄨㄣˇ ㄅㄤˇ)
to bind; to tie up: 他們把他的手足綑綁起來。They bound him hand and foot.

綑好(ㄎㄨㄣˇ ㄏㄠˇ)
to tie up; to bundle up

綑緊(ㄎㄨㄣˇ ㄐㄧㄣˇ)
to bind tight; to tighten the rope: 把繩子綑緊些。Tighten the ropes a little.

綑起來(ㄎㄨㄣˇ ㄑㄧˇ ˙ㄌㄞ)
to bind; to tie up

【綖】 4352
ㄧㄢˊ yan yán

the hanging flap in front and at the back of a hat in ancient times

八畫

【綜】 4353
ㄗㄨㄥˋ tzonq zòng

1. to sum up; in a nutshell
2. in view of; to take account of
3. to arrange
4. synthesis; synthetic
5. to inquire or examine into

綜覽(ㄗㄨㄥˋ ㄌㄢˇ)
a general or comprehensive survey; to view generally

綜攬(ㄗㄨㄥˋ ㄌㄢˇ)
to be in overall charge

綜理(ㄗㄨㄥˋ ㄌㄧˇ)
to arrange or manage everything; to be in overall charge

綜括(ㄗㄨㄥˋ ㄍㄨㄚ)
to sum up; to encompass all; to recapitulate

綜觀(ㄗㄨㄥˋ ㄍㄨㄢ)
① a general and comprehensive view ② to view the whole situation

綜管(ㄗㄨㄥˋ ㄍㄨㄢˇ)
to arrange and manage all; to be in overall charge

綜合(ㄗㄨㄥˋ ㄏㄜˊ)
synthesis; to synthesize

綜合報導(ㄗㄨㄥˋ ㄏㄜˊ ㄅㄠˋ ㄉㄠˇ)
a comprehensive dispatch

綜合法(ㄗㄨㄥˋ ㄏㄜˊ ㄈㄚˇ)
a method of synthesis; synthesis

綜合雜誌(ㄗㄨㄥˋ ㄏㄜˊ ㄗㄚˊ ㄓˋ)
a catchall magazine; a magazine of general interest

綜合所得稅(ㄗㄨㄥˋ ㄏㄜˊ ㄙㄨㄛˇ ㄉㄜˊ ㄕㄨㄟˋ)
consolidated income tax

綜合藝術(ㄗㄨㄥˋ ㄏㄜˊ ㄧˋ ㄕㄨˋ)
arts which require both the visual sense and hearing to appreciate, such as performing arts

綜核名實(ㄗㄨㄥˋ ㄏㄜˊ ㄇㄧㄥˊ ㄕˊ)
to check and investigate the actual facts

【綠】 4354
1. ㄌㄩˋ liuh lǜ

1. green (color): 那兒有綠油油的秧苗。There are green and lush seedlings.
2. chlorine, which is now written as 氯

綠寶石(ㄌㄩˋ ㄅㄠˇ ㄕˊ)
emerald; beryl: 她戴着綠寶石戒指。She wore an emerald ring.

綠黴素 or 氯黴素(ㄌㄩˋ ㄇㄟˊ ㄙㄨˋ)
chloromycetin

綠帽子(ㄌㄩˋ ㄇㄠˋ ˙ㄗ) or 綠頭巾(ㄌㄩˋ ㄊㄡˊ ㄐㄧㄣ)
(literally) a green hat—the sign of a cuckold

綠肥(ㄌㄩˋ ㄈㄟˊ)
green manure

綠礬(ㄌㄩˋ ㄈㄢˊ)
melanterite, or green vitriol

綠島(ㄌㄩˋ ㄉㄠˇ)
Green Island, off the southeastern Taiwan coast, the site of a reformatory camp

綠豆(ㄌㄩˋ ㄉㄡˋ)
the green beans; green lentils (*Phaseolus mungo var. radiatus*)

綠豆糕(ㄌㄩˋ ㄉㄡˋ ㄍㄠ)
small cakes made with green-bean flour

綠豆粥(ㄌㄩˋ ㄉㄡˋ ㄓㄡ) or 綠豆稀飯

(ㄌㄩˋ ㄉㄡˋ ㄒㄧ ㄈㄢˋ)
congee or rice porridge cooked with green beans
綠豆芽(ㄌㄩˋ ㄉㄡˋ ㄧㄚˊ)
green bean sprouts
綠燈(ㄌㄩˋ ㄉㄥ)
①(transportation) the green light ② permission to go ahead with some project; the green light
綠地(ㄌㄩˋ ㄉㄧˋ)
space reserved for parks, trees or meadows in an urban community
綠內障(ㄌㄩˋ ㄋㄟˋ ㄓㄤˋ)
glaucoma
綠卡(ㄌㄩˋ ㄎㄚˇ)
a green card, permanent residence permit issued by the U.S. government
綠化(ㄌㄩˋ ㄏㄨㄚˋ)
to plant trees, build parks, or lay out lawns in deserts or urban areas; to afforest: 我們綠化安全島。We afforested the safety islands.
綠鉛礦(ㄌㄩˋ ㄑㄧㄢ ㄎㄨㄤˋ)
pyromorphite
綠洲(ㄌㄩˋ ㄓㄡ)
an oasis: 沙漠中的旅客時常停宿於綠洲上。Travelers in the desert often stop at an oasis.
綠柱石(ㄌㄩˋ ㄓㄨˋ ㄕˊ)
(geology) beryl
綠茶(ㄌㄩˋ ㄔㄚˊ)
green tea
綠藻(ㄌㄩˋ ㄗㄠˇ)
algae; chlorophyceae; chlorella
綠草如茵(ㄌㄩˋ ㄘㄠˇ ㄖㄨˊ ㄧㄣ)
The green grass looks like a velvet carpet.
綠野(ㄌㄩˋ ㄧㄝˇ)
the green field
綠油(ㄌㄩˋ ㄧㄡˊ)
anthracene oil
綠油腦(ㄌㄩˋ ㄧㄡˊ ㄋㄠˇ)
anthracene
綠油油(ㄌㄩˋ ㄧㄡˊ ㄧㄡˊ)
bright green
綠蔭(ㄌㄩˋ ㄧㄣˋ)
a green shade; the shade of trees

【綠】 4354
2. 讀音 ㄌㄨˋ luh lù

綠肥紅瘦(ㄌㄨˋ ㄈㄟˊ ㄏㄨㄥˊ ㄕㄡˋ)
① Leaves are growing dark green when flowers are fading in late spring. ② beautiful women of all descriptions
綠林好漢(ㄌㄨˋ ㄌㄧㄣˊ ㄏㄠˇ ㄏㄢˋ)or 綠林豪傑(ㄌㄨˋ ㄌㄧㄣˊ ㄏㄠˊ ㄐㄧㄝˊ)
① heros of the greenwood; outlaws (who live in thick forest as Robin Hood did) ② a band of bandits entrenched in a mountain stronghold; brigands
綠竹(ㄌㄨˋ ㄓㄨˊ)
green bamboos 亦作「菉竹」
綠水(ㄌㄨˋ ㄕㄨㄟˇ)or(ㄌㄩˋ ㄕㄨㄟˇ)
① crystal clear water ② a green river
綠衣使者(ㄌㄨˋ ㄧ ㄕˇ ㄓㄜˇ)or(ㄌㄩˋ ㄧ ㄕˇ ㄓㄜˇ)
① a mailman ② another name of parrots
綠衣人(ㄌㄨˋ ㄧ ㄖㄣˊ)or(ㄌㄩˋ ㄧ ㄖㄣˊ)
a postman; a mailman (Chinese mailmen wear green uniforms.)
綠葉成蔭(ㄌㄨˋ ㄧㄝˋ ㄔㄥˊ ㄧㄣˋ)
(literally) The thick foliage forms a good shade.—She has become a mother of many children.
綠陰(ㄌㄨˋ ㄧㄣ)
the shade of trees
綠營(ㄌㄨˋ ㄧㄥˊ)
(in the Ching Dynasty) Chinese troops identified by green banners, as distinct from Manchu troops identified by banners of white, yellow, red and blue
綠玉(ㄌㄨˋ ㄩˋ)or(ㄌㄩˋ ㄩˋ)
emerald; green jade
綠雲(ㄌㄨˋ ㄩㄣˊ)
the hair of a beautiful girl

【綢】 4355
ㄔㄡˊ chour chóu

1. a general name of all silk fabrics
2. fine and delicate
3. (now rarely) to twine and tangle

綢繆(ㄔㄡˊ ㄇㄡˊ)
①to weave (beforehand)—to get prepared ② sentimentally attached; tender love ③ to consolidate; to strengthen; to make strong ④ luxuriant growth of flowers
綢緞(ㄔㄡˊ ㄉㄨㄢˋ)
a general name of silk goods; silks and satins: 她穿着綢緞製的衣服。She was dressed in silks and satins.
綢緞莊(ㄔㄡˊ ㄉㄨㄢˋ ㄓㄨㄤ)
a mercery; a store selling textiles
綢直(ㄔㄡˊ ㄓˊ)
(said of dispositions) careful, considerate and honest
綢子(ㄔㄡˊ ·ㄗ)
a general name of silk fabrics
綢兒緞兒(ㄔㄡˊㄦ ㄉㄨㄚˋㄦ)
expensive clothing

【綣】 4356
ㄑㄩㄢˇ cheuan quǎn

to make tender love 參看「繾綣③」

【綬】 4357
ㄕㄡˋ show shòu

silk ribbons attached to an official seal or medal—(figuratively) an office seal: 他解綬而去。He returned the office seal and resigned.
綬帶(ㄕㄡˋ ㄉㄞˋ)
a cordon (as a badge of honor)

【維】 4358
ㄨㄟˊ wei wéi

1. to tie; to hold fast; to secure
2. to maintain; to safeguard
3. to unite; to hold together
4. long and slender—as fibers
5. an initial particle — only, but, etc.
6. a pattern or rule

維妙維肖(ㄨㄟˊ ㄇㄧㄠˋ ㄨㄟˊ ㄒㄧㄠˋ)
so skillfully imitated as to be indistinguishable from the original; remarkably true to life
維多利亞(ㄨㄟˊ ㄉㄨㄛ ㄌㄧˋ ㄧㄚˋ)
a transliteration of Victoria
維他命(ㄨㄟˊ ㄊㄚ ㄇㄧㄥˋ)
vitamins
維那斯 or 維納斯(ㄨㄟˊ ㄋㄚˋ ㄙ)
Venus
維恭維謹(ㄨㄟˊ ㄍㄨㄥ ㄨㄟˊ ㄐㄧㄣˇ)
sincere and respectful
維護(ㄨㄟˊ ㄏㄨˋ)
to safeguard; to uphold; to preserve; to protect: 我們必須維護言論自由。We must uphold freedom of speech.

維吉尼亞(ㄨㄟˊ ㄐㄧˊ ㄋㄧˊ ㄧㄚˋ)
the state of Virginia,U.S.A.
維艱(ㄨㄟˊ ㄐㄧㄢ)
very hard or difficult
維繫(ㄨㄟˊ ㄒㄧˋ)
to maintain; to keep; to make secure and bind together
維修(ㄨㄟˊ ㄒㄧㄡ)
to keep in (good) repair; to service; to maintain: 這機器維修得很好。The machine had been kept in good repair.
維新(ㄨㄟˊ ㄒㄧㄣ)
to make political reforms; to reform (government, etc.)
維新派(ㄨㄟˊ ㄒㄧㄣ ㄆㄞˋ)
reformers
維新政治(ㄨㄟˊ ㄒㄧㄣ ㄓㄥˋ ㄓˋ)
to reform politics; political reformation
維縶(ㄨㄟˊ ㄓˊ)
①to tie and tether ②to detain; to hold back
維舟(ㄨㄟˊ ㄓㄡ)
to moor a boat
維持(ㄨㄟˊ ㄔˊ)
to maintain; to keep; to guard and support; to sustain; to preserve: 我們來維持世界和平吧。Let's maintain peace in the world.
維持費(ㄨㄟˊ ㄔˊ ㄈㄟˋ)
maintenance charges; maintenance costs
維持現狀(ㄨㄟˊ ㄔˊ ㄒㄧㄢˋ ㄓㄨㄤˋ)
to maintain the status quo; to maintain the present condition
維持秩序(ㄨㄟˊ ㄔˊ ㄓˋ ㄒㄩˋ)
to maintain order; to keep order
維持治安(ㄨㄟˊ ㄔˊ ㄓˋ ㄢ)
to maintain public order
維持世界和平(ㄨㄟˊ ㄔˊ ㄕˋ ㄐㄧㄝˋ ㄏㄜˊ ㄆㄧㄥˊ)
to maintain or preserve world peace
維生素(ㄨㄟˊ ㄕㄥ ㄙㄨˋ)
vitamins 亦作「維他命」
維斯杜拉河(ㄨㄟˊ ㄙ ㄉㄨˋ ㄌㄚ ㄏㄜˊ)
the Vistula River in central Europe
維蘇威(ㄨㄟˊ ㄙㄨ ㄨㄟ)
Vesuvius, a volcanic mountain in southern Italy
維也納(ㄨㄟˊ ㄧㄝˇ ㄋㄚˋ)
Vienna
維也納會議(ㄨㄟˊ ㄧㄝˇ ㄋㄚˋ ㄏㄨㄟˋ ㄧˋ)
the Vienna Conference (1814-1815) held after the defeat of Napoleon Bonaparte
維吾爾(ㄨㄟˊ ㄨˊ ㄦˇ)
the Uigur tribe in Sinkiang

【綰】 4359 ㄨㄢˇ woan wǎn
to string together; to bind up, as the hair; to coil up: 她把頭髮綰起來。She coiled her hair.

【綱】 4360 ㄍㄤ gang gāng
1. the large rope of a net, round which it is netted, and by which it is drawn
2. main points; an outline
3. a principle; discipline
綱目(ㄍㄤ ㄇㄨˋ)
①the outline and detailed items ②a form of chronicle
綱理(ㄍㄤ ㄌㄧˇ)
to rule; to govern
綱領(ㄍㄤ ㄌㄧㄥˇ)
an outline
綱紀(ㄍㄤ ㄐㄧˋ)
①a principle; discipline; law; order ②a manager; a magistrate
綱紀廢弛(ㄍㄤ ㄐㄧˋ ㄈㄟˋ ㄕˇ)
Discipline is lax.
綱舉目張(ㄍㄤ ㄐㄩˇ ㄇㄨˋ ㄓㄤ)
There is strict order prevailing.
綱常(ㄍㄤ ㄔㄤˊ)
the three bonds (君臣、父子、夫婦—the relations between ruler and subject, father and son, husband and wife) and the five constant virtues (仁、義、禮、智、信—benevolence, righteousness, propriety, knowledge, and faith)
綱要(ㄍㄤ ㄧㄠˋ)
main points; an outline

【網】 4361 ㄨㄤˇ woang wǎng
1. a net; a network; a web: 他們用網捕魚。They caught fish with a net.
2. (figuratively) the dragnet; the arms of law
3. to bring together; to collect
網膜(ㄨㄤˇ ㄇㄛˊ)
a retina
網目(ㄨㄤˇ ㄇㄨˋ)
meshes 參看「網眼」
網漏吞舟之魚(ㄨㄤˇ ㄌㄡˋ ㄊㄨㄣ ㄓㄡ ㄓ ㄩˊ)
(literally) The net has such wide meshes that even fishes large enough to gulp a boat can escape from it.—The law is so lax that even principal criminals are overlooked.
網籃(ㄨㄤˇ ㄌㄢˊ)
a basket covered with a net; a basket with a net on top
網路(ㄨㄤˇ ㄌㄨˋ)
a network
網羅(ㄨㄤˇ ㄌㄨㄛˊ)
①to bring together; to collect; to assemble ②a net (for catching fish or birds) ③to recruit; to enlist the services of
網罟(ㄨㄤˇ ㄍㄨˇ)
nets
網開三面(ㄨㄤˇ ㄎㄞ ㄙㄢ ㄇㄧㄢˋ)
(literally) to open the net on three sides—to be lenient with offenders
網開一面(ㄨㄤˇ ㄎㄞ ㄧˊ ㄇㄧㄢˋ)
to leave one side of the net open—to give a wrongdoer a way out
網球(ㄨㄤˇ ㄑㄧㄡˊ)
tennis: 她喜歡打網球。She likes playing tennis.
網球拍(ㄨㄤˇ ㄑㄧㄡˊ ㄆㄞ)
a racket (for playing tennis)
網球場(ㄨㄤˇ ㄑㄧㄡˊ ㄔㄤˇ)
a tennis court
網狀脈(ㄨㄤˇ ㄓㄨㄤˋ ㄇㄞˋ)
(said of tree leaves) net-veined
網狀葉(ㄨㄤˇ ㄓㄨㄤˋ ㄧㄝˋ)
(botany) a reticulate leaf
網子(ㄨㄤˇ ·ㄗ)
a net
網眼(ㄨㄤˇ ㄧㄢˇ)
meshes of a net: 這個網有半英寸見方的網眼。This net has half-inch meshes.
網魚(ㄨㄤˇ ㄩˊ)
to net fish

【綴】 4362 ㄓㄨㄟˋ juey zhuì
1. to put together; to combine; to compose
2. to mend clothes; to patch

〔糸部〕

〔糸部〕

up; to sew; to stitch
3. to decorate; to stud
綴補(ㄓㄨㄟˋ ㄅㄨˇ)
to patch up (clothes)
綴法(ㄓㄨㄟˋ ㄈㄚˇ)
a lesson on sentence construction and composition
綴輯(ㄓㄨㄟˋ ㄐㄧˊ)
to compile and edit
綴文(ㄓㄨㄟˋ ㄨㄣˊ)
to write a composition

【綵】 4363 ㄘㄞˇ tsae cǎi
1. varicolored silk; a silk festoon
2. motley; varicolored
綵牌樓(ㄘㄞˇ ㄆㄞˊ ㄌㄡˊ)
a varicolored celebration arch
綵棚(ㄘㄞˇ ㄆㄥˊ)
a gaily decorated wooden framework
綵樓(ㄘㄞˇ ㄌㄡˊ)
a gaily decorated tower or pavilion
綵轎(ㄘㄞˇ ㄐㄧㄠˋ)
a gaily decorated sedan chair
綵球(ㄘㄞˇ ㄑㄧㄡˊ)
a ball wound up from varicolored silk
綵綢(ㄘㄞˇ ㄔㄡˊ)
varicolored silk
綵船(ㄘㄞˇ ㄔㄨㄢˊ)
a gaily decorated boat
綵衣娛親(ㄘㄞˇ ㄧ ㄩˊ ㄑㄧㄣ)
to wear a motley to entertain one's parents, a reference about Lao Lai-tzu (老萊子), who at seventy behaved like a child to please his parents—to be a filial son

【綹】 4364 ㄌㄧㄡˇ leou liǔ
a tuft; a lock; a skein (of yarn)

【綸】 4365 1. ㄌㄨㄣˊ luen lún
1. a fishing line
2. a green silk cord
綸繩(ㄌㄨㄣˊ ㄕㄥˊ)
a fishing line
綸音(ㄌㄨㄣˊ ㄧㄣ)
an imperial edict or rescript

【綸】 4365 2. ㄍㄨㄢ guan guān
a kind of ancient cap
綸巾(ㄍㄨㄢ ㄐㄧㄣ)
a kind of ancient cap resembling a ridged roof

【綺】 4366 ㄑㄧˇ chii qǐ
1. beautiful; magnificent; fine; fair; gorgeous; resplendent; elegant
2. twilled silk cloth; figured woven silk material
綺靡(ㄑㄧˇ ㄇㄧˇ)
① extravagantly beautiful ② (said of a literary style) ornate
綺年(ㄑㄧˇ ㄋㄧㄢˊ)or綺歲(ㄑㄧˇ ㄙㄨㄟˋ)
youthful
綺年玉貌(ㄑㄧˇ ㄋㄧㄢˊ ㄩˋ ㄇㄠˋ)
(said of a girl) young and beautiful
綺麗(ㄑㄧˇ ㄌㄧˋ)
beautiful; fair; magnificent; gorgeous; resplendent; enchanting
綺井(ㄑㄧˇ ㄐㄧㄥˇ)
the ceiling (of a house)
綺情(ㄑㄧˇ ㄑㄧㄥˊ)
tender feeling
綺想(ㄑㄧˇ ㄒㄧㄤˇ)
beautiful thoughts
綺室(ㄑㄧˇ ㄕˋ)
a gorgeous room; a magnificent room
綺襦紈袴(ㄑㄧˇ ㄖㄨˊ ㄨㄢˊ ㄎㄨˋ)
fops from a good family
綺思(ㄑㄧˇ ㄙ)
beautiful thoughts (in literature)亦作「綺想」
綺筵(ㄑㄧˇ ㄧㄢˊ)
a magnificent feast
綺語(ㄑㄧˇ ㄩˇ)
① (Buddhism) profane expressions; sexual talks ② literary pieces concerning love and sex

【綻】 4367 ㄓㄢˋ jann zhàn
1. a ripped seam; a crack
2. a flaw or defect (in a scheme, etc.)
綻露(ㄓㄢˋ ㄌㄡˋ)
to reveal a matter
綻裂(ㄓㄢˋ ㄌㄧㄝˋ)
ripped; to split; to rip
綻線(ㄓㄢˋ ㄒㄧㄢˋ)
to have a ripped seam

【綽】 4368 ㄔㄨㄛˋ chuoh chuò
1. spacious; roomy
2. delicate
綽號(ㄔㄨㄛˋ ㄏㄠˋ)or綽名(ㄔㄨㄛˋ ㄇㄧㄥˊ)
a nickname; a sobriquet
綽綽有餘(ㄔㄨㄛˋ ㄔㄨㄛˋ ㄧㄡˇ ㄩˊ)or綽有餘裕(ㄔㄨㄛˋ ㄧㄡˇ ㄩˊ ㄩˋ)or綽綽有裕(ㄔㄨㄛˋ ㄔㄨㄛˋ ㄧㄡˇ ㄩˋ)
① There is enough room to spare. 或It's more than enough. ② generous feeling
綽約多姿(ㄔㄨㄛˋ ㄩㄝ ㄉㄨㄛ ㄗ)
charmingly delicate

【綾】 4369 ㄌㄧㄥˊ ling líng
very fine silk cloth; damask silk
綾羅(ㄌㄧㄥˊ ㄌㄨㄛˊ)
silk gauze
綾羅錦繡(ㄌㄧㄥˊ ㄌㄨㄛˊ ㄐㄧㄣˇ ㄒㄧㄡˋ)
expensive clothes; expensive dress materials

【緇】 4370 ㄗ tzy zī
1. black
2. black silk
緇帶(ㄗ ㄉㄞˋ)
a black belt
緇流(ㄗ ㄌㄧㄡˊ)
Buddhist monks
緇黃(ㄗ ㄏㄨㄤˊ)
Buddhist monks and Taoist priests
緇素(ㄗ ㄙㄨˋ)
Buddhist monks and laymen
緇衣(ㄗ ㄧ)
①black garments (or robes) worn by courtiers on formal occasions in ancient times ② black garments worn by monks

【緅】 4371 ㄗㄡ tzou zōu
1. bluish red; a puce color
2. light red

【綿】 4372 (緜) ㄇㄧㄢˊ mian mián
1. cotton
2. everlasting; endless
3. weak
綿薄(ㄇㄧㄢˊ ㄅㄛˊ)
(a polite expression) my feeble strength, limited power, or poor abilities
綿密(ㄇㄧㄢˊ ㄇㄧˋ)
paying attention to all

details; circumspect
綿邈(ㄇㄧㄢˊㄇㄧㄠˇ)
long (in time)
綿綿(ㄇㄧㄢˊㄇㄧㄢˊ)
continuous; everlasting; to go on and on: 春雨綿綿。The spring rain goes on and on.
綿綿不絕(ㄇㄧㄢˊㄇㄧㄢˊㄅㄨˋㄐㄩㄝˊ)
to last forever; to keep on endlessly
綿綿絮語(ㄇㄧㄢˊㄇㄧㄢˊㄒㄩˋㄩˇ)
to whisper continually
綿篤(ㄇㄧㄢˊㄉㄨˇ)
seriously ill; dangerously ill
綿頓(ㄇㄧㄢˊㄉㄨㄣˋ)
seriously ill
綿裏針(ㄇㄧㄢˊㄌㄧˇㄓㄣ)
(literally) a needle hidden in cotton—cruelty or harshness hidden behind a friendly appearance
綿力(ㄇㄧㄢˊㄌㄧˋ)
(a self-depreciatory term) my limited power
綿亙(ㄇㄧㄢˊㄍㄣˋ)
to stretch in an unbroken chain: 這森林綿亙數英里之長。The forest stretches for miles.
綿絮(ㄇㄧㄢˊㄒㄩˋ)
cotton
綿長(ㄇㄧㄢˊㄔㄤˊ)
lasting forever; very long (in time)
綿軟(ㄇㄧㄢˊㄖㄨㄢˇ)or 綿弱(ㄇㄧㄢˊㄖㄨㄛˋ)
soft; weak: 我覺得兩腿綿軟無力。I feel weak in the legs.
綿延(ㄇㄧㄢˊㄧㄢˊ)
to extend very long; to stretch over a long distance; to be continuous; to go on
綿羊(ㄇㄧㄢˊㄧㄤˊ)
sheep

【綦】 4373
ㄑㄧˊ chyi qí
1. very; exceedingly
2. dark grey
3. shoelaces
綦重(ㄑㄧˊㄓㄨㄥˋ)
very heavy
綦嚴(ㄑㄧˊㄧㄢˊ)
very stringent; very severe

【綮】 4374
1.(棨) ㄑㄧˇ chii qǐ
a sheath for a lance head

【綮】 4374
2. ㄑㄧㄥˋ chinq qìng
as in 肯綮—the main point; the gist

【緊】 4375
ㄐㄧㄣˇ jiin jǐn
1. tight; firm; fast; secure; taut; tense; close
2. urgent; critical; pressing: 任務緊切。The task is urgent.
緊繃(ㄐㄧㄣˇ·ㄅㄥ)
to stretch taut
緊逼(ㄐㄧㄣˇㄅㄧ)
① to press hard; to close in on ② (basketball) press
緊迫(ㄐㄧㄣˇㄆㄛˋ)
urgent; pressing: 他有更緊迫的事情要處理。He has more pressing things to deal with.
緊密(ㄐㄧㄣˇㄇㄧˋ)
① rigidly precise; rigorous ② compact and orderly ③ to close together ④ rapid and intense
緊防(ㄐㄧㄣˇㄈㄤˊ)
to guard closely or tightly; to remain vigilant against
緊鄰(ㄐㄧㄣˇㄌㄧㄣˊ)
a close neighbor
緊鑼密鼓(ㄐㄧㄣˇㄌㄨㄛˊㄇㄧˋㄍㄨˇ)
wildly beating gongs and drums—(figuratively) to publicize a campaign urgently in preparation for some undertaking
緊跟著(ㄐㄧㄣˇㄍㄣ·ㄓㄜ)
on the heels of; close behind; to follow closely or immediately; to keep in step with: 這小孩緊跟著他的母親。This child keeps in step with his mother.
緊急(ㄐㄧㄣˇㄐㄧˊ)
urgent; critical; of an emergency; pressing: 外面情況緊急。The outside situation is critical.
緊急命令(ㄐㄧㄣˇㄐㄧˊㄇㄧㄥˋㄌㄧㄥˋ)
emergent orders; urgent orders
緊急動議(ㄐㄧㄣˇㄐㄧˊㄉㄨㄥˋㄧˋ)
an urgent or emergent motion (in a parliament, etc.)
緊急集合(ㄐㄧㄣˇㄐㄧˊㄐㄧˊㄏㄜˊ)
an emergency muster
緊急警報(ㄐㄧㄣˇㄐㄧˊㄐㄧㄥˇㄅㄠˋ)
an air-raid alarm sounded when enemy planes are near or already overhead
緊急起飛(ㄐㄧㄣˇㄐㄧˊㄑㄧˇㄈㄟ)
a scramble
緊急信號(ㄐㄧㄣˇㄐㄧˊㄒㄧㄣˋㄏㄠˋ)
an emergency signal
緊急着陸(ㄐㄧㄣˇㄐㄧˊㄓㄨㄛˊㄌㄨˋ)
emergency landing
緊接著(ㄐㄧㄣˇㄐㄧㄝ·ㄓㄜ)
to follow close behind; on the heels of; immediately afterward
緊緊(ㄐㄧㄣˇㄐㄧㄣˇ)
tightly; firmly; closely: 他緊緊盯着我。He watched me closely.
緊張(ㄐㄧㄣˇㄓㄤ)
tense; nervous; taut; tight; tension; strained: 昨天英文考試時我有些緊張。I got nervous at the English examination yesterday.
緊身兒(ㄐㄧㄣˇㄕㄜㄦ)
fitting the body closely; tight; close
緊湊(ㄐㄧㄣˇㄘㄡˋ)
①closely and firmly packed; compact ②(said of an entertainment program, a show, a composition, etc.) one climax after another; absorbingly interesting throughout; well-knit; well-organized: 這篇文章寫得很緊湊。It was a well-organized composition.
緊促(ㄐㄧㄣˇㄘㄨˋ)
pressing; urgent: 這件事很緊促。The matter is pressing.
緊縮(ㄐㄧㄣˇㄙㄨㄛ)
to retrench; to curtail; to cut down; to reduce: 我們緊縮開支。We cut down expenses.
緊隨(ㄐㄧㄣˇㄙㄨㄟˊ)
to follow closely
緊要(ㄐㄧㄣˇㄧㄠˋ)
important; urgent; vital; critical: 瞭解自己，對我們很緊要。It's important for us to know ourselves.
緊要關頭(ㄐㄧㄣˇㄧㄠˋㄍㄨㄢㄊㄡˊ)
a critical moment
緊握(ㄐㄧㄣˇㄨㄛˋ)
to grasp firmly; to take a tight hold of (or over): 緊握繩子。Take a tight hold of the rope.

〔糸部〕

〔糸部〕

【緋】4376 ㄈㄟ fei fēi
scarlet; crimson
緋紅(ㄈㄟ ㄏㄨㄥˊ)
scarlet; crimson: 羞愧使得她兩頰緋紅。Shame made her cheeks crimson.
緋聞(ㄈㄟ ㄨㄣˊ)
sexy news 亦作「桃色新聞」

【緌】4377 ㄖㄨㄟˊ ruei ruí
ornamental strings on a hat

【綫】4378 (線) ㄒㄧㄢˋ shiann xiàn
1. a line
2. threads
綫索(ㄒㄧㄢˋ ㄙㄨㄛˇ)
a clue

九畫

【緒】4379 ㄒㄩˋ shiuh xù
1. the end of a thread or string
2. a clue: 一點頭緒也沒有。There is no clue at all.
3. a beginning
4. a task; a cause; an enterprise: 他得續未竟之緒。He continued an unfinished task.
5. a mental or emotional state; mood: 我的情緒不好。I was in a bad mood.
6. remnants; remains; leftovers
緒論(ㄒㄩˋ ㄌㄨㄣˋ)
a preface; a foreword; an introduction
緒戰(ㄒㄩˋ ㄓㄢˋ)
the first battle between two forces
緒業(ㄒㄩˋ ㄧㄝˋ)
business; a calling
緒言(ㄒㄩˋ ㄧㄢˊ)
a preface; a foreword; a preamble; an introduction
緒餘(ㄒㄩˋ ㄩˊ)
the remnants; a surplus

【緘】4380 ㄐㄧㄢ jian jiān
1. to seal; to close
2. a letter
緘默(ㄐㄧㄢ ㄇㄛˋ)
to keep silence
緘封(ㄐㄧㄢ ㄈㄥ)
to seal
緘口(ㄐㄧㄢ ㄎㄡˇ)
to keep the mouth shut
緘札(ㄐㄧㄢ ㄓㄚˊ)
a letter
緘繩(ㄐㄧㄢ ㄕㄥˊ)
a rope for tying up a coffin

【線】4381 (綫) ㄒㄧㄢˋ shiann xiàn
1. a line
2. threads
3. wires
線膨脹(ㄒㄧㄢˋ ㄆㄥˊ ㄓㄤˋ)
(physics) linear expansion
線民(ㄒㄧㄢˋ ㄇㄧㄣˊ)
a stool pigeon; an informer
線粉(ㄒㄧㄢˋ ㄈㄣˇ)
noodles made of bean flour
線頭(ㄒㄧㄢˋ ㄊㄡˊ)
① the end of a thread ② an odd piece of thread ③ beginnings of things
線條(ㄒㄧㄢˋ ㄊㄧㄠˊ)
lines; streaks
線路(ㄒㄧㄢˋ ㄌㄨˋ)
①(electricity) a circuit ② a narrow path
線縷(ㄒㄧㄢˋ ㄌㄩˇ)
threads
線圈(ㄒㄧㄢˋ ㄑㄩㄢ)
a coil
線脹係數(ㄒㄧㄢˋ ㄓㄤˋ ㄒㄧˋ ㄕㄨˋ)
a coefficient of linear expansion
線裝本(ㄒㄧㄢˋ ㄓㄨㄤ ㄅㄣˇ) or 線裝書(ㄒㄧㄢˋ ㄓㄨㄤ ㄕㄨ)
a book bound in the traditional Chinese style
線蟲類(ㄒㄧㄢˋ ㄔㄨㄥˊ ㄌㄟˋ)
Nematoda
線索(ㄒㄧㄢˋ ㄙㄨㄛˇ)
a clue; a lead

【緞】4382 ㄉㄨㄢˋ duann duàn
satin
緞帶(ㄉㄨㄢˋ ㄉㄞˋ)
a satin ribbon
緞子(ㄉㄨㄢˋ ·ㄗ)
satin

【緝】4383 1. ㄑㄧˋ chih qì
1. to order the arrest of; to arrest; to capture
2. to twist and join (cords)
3. to continue
4. to hem clothing
緝辦(ㄑㄧˋ ㄅㄢˋ)
to arrest and punish
緝捕(ㄑㄧˋ ㄅㄨˇ)
to search and arrest; to capture
緝穆(ㄑㄧˋ ㄇㄨˋ)
at peace with each other
緝盜(ㄑㄧˋ ㄉㄠˋ)
to capture thieves
緝拿(ㄑㄧˋ ㄋㄚˊ)
to arrest; to apprehend: 警察緝拿凶手。The police apprehended the murderer.
緝理(ㄑㄧˋ ㄌㄧˇ)
to set in order
緝獲(ㄑㄧˋ ㄏㄨㄛˋ)
to arrest; to capture; to seize
緝熙(ㄑㄧˋ ㄒㄧ)
bright; brilliant
緝私(ㄑㄧˋ ㄙ)
to arrest smugglers
緝私船(ㄑㄧˋ ㄙ ㄔㄨㄢˊ)
a revenue cutter; an anti-smuggling patrol boat

【緝】4383 2. ㄑㄧ chi qī
to sew in close and straight stitches

【緗】4384 ㄒㄧㄤ shiang xiāng
light-yellow silk
緗縹(ㄒㄧㄤ ㄆㄧㄠˇ)
simple, light-yellow clothes
緗帙(ㄒㄧㄤ ㄓˋ)
① a light-yellow book jacket ② a book
緗素(ㄒㄧㄤ ㄙㄨˋ)
① light-yellow silk ② a scroll made of the light-yellow silk

【締】4385 ㄉㄧˋ dih dì
to connect; to join; to unite
締盟(ㄉㄧˋ ㄇㄥˊ)
to form an alliance
締結(ㄉㄧˋ ㄐㄧㄝˊ)
to conclude (treaties, agreements, etc.): 兩國締結和平條約。Two nations concluded a peace treaty.
締交(ㄉㄧˋ ㄐㄧㄠ)
to establish diplomatic ties or friendship
締造(ㄉㄧˋ ㄗㄠˋ)
to construct; to compose; to build; to found; to create

締姻(ㄉㄧˋ ㄧㄣ)
to be united in wedlock
締約(ㄉㄧˋ ㄩㄝ)
to conclude a treaty
締約國(ㄉㄧˋ ㄩㄝ ㄍㄨㄛˊ)
a treaty power; a signatory power

【緍】 4386
(緡) ㄇㄧㄣˊ min mín
1. a fishing line
2. cords for stringing up coins

【緦】 4387
ㄙ sy sī
1. fine jute cloth
2. to spin jute thread or yarn
緦麻服(ㄙ ㄇㄚˊ ㄈㄨˊ)or 緦服(ㄙ ㄈㄨˊ)
mourning dress of the lowest degree, worn for three months for distant relatives

【緣】 4388
ㄩㄢˊ yuan yuán
1. a cause; a reason: 爲何緣故? For what reason?
2. to go along; to follow
3. a hem; a margin; an edge; a fringe
4. relationship by fate; predestined relationship
緣邊(ㄩㄢˊ ㄅㄧㄢ)
a hem; a margin; an edge; a border
緣簿(ㄩㄢˊ ㄅㄨˋ)
records of contributions kept at a Buddhist temple
緣木求魚(ㄩㄢˊ ㄇㄨˋ ㄑㄧㄡˊ ㄩˊ)
(literally) to climb a tree to get fish—to seek something from a wrong source; impossible to succeed
緣法(ㄩㄢˊ ㄈㄚˇ)
① to copy or follow the old laws ② to follow or abide by the law ③ (Buddhism) predestined relationship
緣分(ㄩㄢˊ ㄈㄣˋ)
relationship by fate; predestined relationship; natural affinity among friends: 我們倆又遇到了，眞是緣分。So we meet again. It must be fate.
緣故(ㄩㄢˊ ㄍㄨˋ)
a cause; a reason
緣何(ㄩㄢˊ ㄏㄜˊ)
why
緣起(ㄩㄢˊ ㄑㄧˇ)
① origins ② a preface; a foreword
緣飾(ㄩㄢˊ ㄕˋ)
to embellish with words
緣坐(ㄩㄢˊ ㄗㄨㄛˋ)
to be punished by the law because of one's relationship with the offender 亦作「連坐」
緣由(ㄩㄢˊ ㄧㄡˊ)
a cause; a reason; the whys and wherefores
緣因(ㄩㄢˊ ㄧㄣ)
cause 亦作「原故」

【編】 4389
ㄅㄧㄢ bian bian
1. to knit; to weave
2. to put together; to organize; to form; to arrange
3. to fabricate; to make up; to invent
4. to compile; to edit
5. (part of) a book; a volume
編貝(ㄅㄧㄢ ㄅㄟˋ)
(said of teeth) beautiful and sparkling
編班(ㄅㄧㄢ ㄅㄢ)
① formation of classes (at school) ② to assign (students) to various classes
編排(ㄅㄧㄢ ㄆㄞˊ)
① to arrange in order ② to write and present (a play, etc.)
編派(ㄅㄧㄢ ㄆㄞˋ)
to libel; to vilify
編目(ㄅㄧㄢ ㄇㄨˋ)
to prepare or compile a catalogue; to arrange a table of contents; to catalogue: 新到的書迄今尙未編目。The new books are still uncatalogued.
編髮(ㄅㄧㄢ ㄈㄚˇ)
to braid the hair
編導(ㄅㄧㄢ ㄉㄠˇ)
① to write and direct (a play, film, etc.) ② a director
編訂(ㄅㄧㄢ ㄉㄧㄥˋ)
to compile and to revise
編隊(ㄅㄧㄢ ㄉㄨㄟˋ)
① formation (of aircrafts, etc.): 戰鬥機群編隊飛行。The fighters made a formation flight. ② to organize into groups
編年(ㄅㄧㄢ ㄋㄧㄢˊ)
to prepare a chronological record; to compile annals
編年體(ㄅㄧㄢ ㄋㄧㄢˊ ㄊㄧˇ)
(said of history) chronological style
編年史(ㄅㄧㄢ ㄋㄧㄢˊ ㄕˇ)
chronicles; annals
編類(ㄅㄧㄢ ㄌㄟˋ)
to arrange into categories
編列(ㄅㄧㄢ ㄌㄧㄝˋ)
to arrange systematically; to list (the expenses for a project in the budget); to compile
編練(ㄅㄧㄢ ㄌㄧㄢˋ)
to organize and train (the militia troops, etc.)
編號(ㄅㄧㄢ ㄏㄠˋ)
① to arrange under numbers; to number ② a serial number
編戶(ㄅㄧㄢ ㄏㄨˋ)
families entered in household registers—common people
編輯(ㄅㄧㄢ ㄐㄧˊ)
① to edit; to compile ② an editor
編輯部(ㄅㄧㄢ ㄐㄧˊ ㄅㄨˋ)
an editorial department; the editorial office
編輯者(ㄅㄧㄢ ㄐㄧˊ ㄓㄜˇ)or 編輯人(ㄅㄧㄢ ㄐㄧˊ ㄖㄣˊ)
an editor
編結(ㄅㄧㄢ ㄐㄧㄝˊ)
to knit; to weave
編劇(ㄅㄧㄢ ㄐㄩˋ)
① to write a play ② a playwright
編遣(ㄅㄧㄢ ㄑㄧㄢˇ)
to lay off or discharge personnel after reorganization
編磬(ㄅㄧㄢ ㄑㄧㄥˋ)
an ancient musical instrument with 16 musical stones
編寫(ㄅㄧㄢ ㄒㄧㄝˇ)
① to compile: 編寫字典 to compile a dictionary ② to write; to compose: 她正在編寫歌劇。She is composing an opera.
編修(ㄅㄧㄢ ㄒㄧㄡ)
① to compile; to edit: 請現在停止編修。Stop editing now, please. ② a government compiler (in ancient times)
編選(ㄅㄧㄢ ㄒㄩㄢˇ)
to select and edit; to compile
編織(ㄅㄧㄢ ㄓ)
to knit: 她正用毛線編織手套。She is knitting wool into

〔糸部〕

gloves.

編織機(ㄅㄧㄢ ㄓ ㄐㄧ)
a knitting machine

編制(ㄅㄧㄢ ㄓˋ)
① organic structure; organization ② to work out; to draw up

編制人員(ㄅㄧㄢ ㄓˋ ㄖㄣˊ ㄩㄢˊ)
employees of a government agency specified in its organic law

編者(ㄅㄧㄢ ㄓㄜˇ)
an editor: 他是那份雜誌的運動版編者。He is the sports editor of that magazine.

編著(ㄅㄧㄢ ㄓㄨˋ) or 編撰(ㄅㄧㄢ ㄓㄨㄢˋ)
to edit; to compile: 他父親編著了一册美語讀本。His father compiled an English reader.

編鐘(ㄅㄧㄢ ㄓㄨㄥ)
an ancient musical instrument with 16 bells

編審(ㄅㄧㄢ ㄕㄣˇ)
① to edit and screen (textbooks, etc.) ② a member of the editing and screening committee

編審委員會(ㄅㄧㄢ ㄕㄣˇ ㄨㄟˇ ㄩㄢˊ ㄏㄨㄟˋ)
an editing and screening committee (for textbooks, etc.)

編書(ㄅㄧㄢ ㄕㄨ)
to edit or compile books

編述(ㄅㄧㄢ ㄕㄨˋ)
to arrange and narrate

編入(ㄅㄧㄢ ㄖㄨˋ)
① to include (in a budget) ② to enlist; to recruit

編造(ㄅㄧㄢ ㄗㄠˋ)
① to fabricate ② to form; to prepare (a budget)

編組(ㄅㄧㄢ ㄗㄨˇ)
to organize into groups

編纂(ㄅㄧㄢ ㄗㄨㄢˇ)
to compile

編譯(ㄅㄧㄢ ㄧˋ)
① to translate and compile ② a translator; an interpreter

編譯館(ㄅㄧㄢ ㄧˋ ㄍㄨㄢˇ)
an institute for compilation and translation

編舞(ㄅㄧㄢ ㄨˇ)
to choreograph

編輿(ㄅㄧㄢ ㄩˊ)
a bamboo sedan chair

【緩】 4390
ㄏㄨㄢˇ hoan huǎn

1. slow; gradual; tardy; leisurely; unhurried
2. to delay; to slacken; to put off; to postpone; to defer
3. to revive; to refresh

緩辦(ㄏㄨㄢˇ ㄅㄢˋ)
to delay action; to put off a project

緩兵之計(ㄏㄨㄢˇ ㄅㄧㄥ ㄓ ㄐㄧˋ)
a strategy for gaining time; delaying tactics

緩不濟急(ㄏㄨㄢˇ ㄅㄨˋ ㄐㄧˋ ㄐㄧˊ)
too late to be of use in a crisis 或 Slow action cannot save a critical situation.

緩步(ㄏㄨㄢˇ ㄅㄨˋ)
to walk slowly; to stroll; to ramble

緩慢(ㄏㄨㄢˇ ㄇㄢˋ)
slow: 她行動緩慢。She is slow in action.

緩圖(ㄏㄨㄢˇ ㄊㄨˊ)
to plan slowly and carefully

緩和(ㄏㄨㄢˇ ㄏㄜˊ)
① to allay; to subside; to moderate; to relax; to alleviate: 熱常常能緩和疼痛。Heat often alleviates pain. ② calm; mild; moderate; detente

緩緩(ㄏㄨㄢˇ ㄏㄨㄢˇ)
slowly; gradually; little by little: 請緩緩地說。Please speak slowly.

緩急(ㄏㄨㄢˇ ㄐㄧˊ)
degrees of urgency

緩頰(ㄏㄨㄢˇ ㄐㄧㄚˊ)
to dissuade someone from taking certain punitive action (usually on behalf of someone else); to intercede: 我們爲他緩頰。We interceded for him.

緩決(ㄏㄨㄢˇ ㄐㄩㄝˊ)
to stay the execution (of a death convict)

緩期(ㄏㄨㄢˇ ㄑㄧˊ)
to postpone a deadline; to suspend

緩限(ㄏㄨㄢˇ ㄒㄧㄢˋ)
to put off the deadline; to extend the time limit

緩刑(ㄏㄨㄢˇ ㄒㄧㄥˊ)
to suspend a sentence; to reprieve; a reprieve; probation

緩召(ㄏㄨㄢˇ ㄓㄠˋ)
to defer the draft (of a man for military service)

緩徵(ㄏㄨㄢˇ ㄓㄥ)
①to remit (taxes) ②to defer the draft of (a man for military service)

緩衝(ㄏㄨㄢˇ ㄔㄨㄥ)
to serve as a buffer; to buff

緩衝地帶(ㄏㄨㄢˇ ㄔㄨㄥ ㄉㄧˋ ㄉㄞˋ)
a buffer zone; a neutral zone

緩衝國(ㄏㄨㄢˇ ㄔㄨㄥ ㄍㄨㄛˊ)
a buffer state

緩衝區域(ㄏㄨㄢˇ ㄔㄨㄥ ㄑㄩ ㄩˋ)
a buffer zone

緩衝作用(ㄏㄨㄢˇ ㄔㄨㄥ ㄗㄨㄛˋ ㄩㄥˋ)
buffer reaction

緩役(ㄏㄨㄢˇ ㄧˋ)
draft deferment

緩議(ㄏㄨㄢˇ ㄧˋ)
to defer the discussion

緩一口氣(ㄏㄨㄢˇ ㄧˋ ㄎㄡˇ ㄑㄧˋ)
to get a breathing space

【緲】 4391
ㄇㄧㄠˇ meau miǎo

distant; far and dim—unsubstantial

【緬】 4392
ㄇㄧㄢˇ mean miǎn

1. distant; far; remote
2. to think of something or somebody in the past

緬邈(ㄇㄧㄢˇ ㄇㄧㄠˇ)
far and remote

緬甸(ㄇㄧㄢˇ ㄉㄧㄢˋ)
Burma

緬甸人(ㄇㄧㄢˇ ㄉㄧㄢˋ ㄖㄣˊ)
a Burmese; the Burmese

緬靦(ㄇㄧㄢˇ ㄊㄧㄢˇ)
shy; bashful; shamefaced because of a guilty conscience

緬懷(ㄇㄧㄢˇ ㄏㄨㄞˊ)
to think of; to remember; to cherish the memory of; to recall: 她緬懷過去。She recalled her past.

緬想(ㄇㄧㄢˇ ㄒㄧㄤˇ)
to think of fondly; to remember with affection

緬因(ㄇㄧㄢˇ ㄧㄣ)
the state of Maine, U.S.A.

【緯】 4393
ㄨㄟˇ woei wěi

1. the woof
2. parallels showing latitude

on a map
3. books about charms, omens, etc. circulated as appendices to the classics
緯度(ㄨㄟˇ ㄉㄨˋ)
degrees of latitude (in geography)
緯線(ㄨㄟˇ ㄒㄧㄢˋ)
parallels or latitude on maps
緯書(ㄨㄟˇ ㄕㄨ)
books about charms, omens, etc. circulated as appendices to the classics in the latter years of the Earlier Han Dynasty

【緱】 4394
ㄍㄡ gou gōu
cord binding on the hilt of a sword

【練】 4395
ㄌㄧㄢˋ liann liàn
1. to practice; to train; to exercise: 我每天練習彈鋼琴。I practice on the piano every day.
2. skilled; experienced: 他很老練。He was an experienced man.
3. to soften and whiten raw silk by boiling
練把式(ㄌㄧㄢˋ ㄅㄚˇ ·ㄕ)
to practice Chinese pugilism
練兵(ㄌㄧㄢˋ ㄅㄧㄥ)
to drill troops; to train troops
練達(ㄌㄧㄢˋ ㄉㄚˊ)
experienced; sophisticated: 他是一位練達的學者。He is an experienced scholar.
練功(ㄌㄧㄢˋ ㄍㄨㄥ)
to do exercises in gymnastics, kung fu, etc.; to practice one's skill
練球(ㄌㄧㄢˋ ㄑㄧㄡˊ)
to practice a ball game
練拳(ㄌㄧㄢˋ ㄑㄩㄢˊ)
to practice boxing
練習(ㄌㄧㄢˋ ㄒㄧˊ)
① to train; to practice (so as to gain skill): 我練習造句。I practice making sentences. ② exercises
練習簿(ㄌㄧㄢˋ ㄒㄧˊ ㄅㄨˋ)
an exercise book
練習題(ㄌㄧㄢˋ ㄒㄧˊ ㄊㄧˊ)
exercises
練習艦(ㄌㄧㄢˋ ㄒㄧˊ ㄐㄧㄢˋ)
a training ship
練習生(ㄌㄧㄢˋ ㄒㄧˊ ㄕㄥ)
a trainee; an apprentice
練習所(ㄌㄧㄢˋ ㄒㄧˊ ㄙㄨㄛˇ)
a training school, institute, station, or camp
練武(ㄌㄧㄢˋ ㄨˇ)
to train oneself in martial arts
練勇(ㄌㄧㄢˋ ㄩㄥˇ)
a militiaman

【緹】 4396
ㄊㄧˊ tyi tí
1. reddish yellow silk
2. reddish yellow soil
3. reddish; red
緹騎(ㄊㄧˊ ㄐㄧˋ)
① cavaliers in reddish yellow — officials sent out to arrest lawbreakers ② the retinue of ranking officials
緹縈救父(ㄊㄧˊ ㄧㄥˊ ㄐㄧㄡˋ ㄈㄨˋ)
the story of Ti Ying (緹縈), a devoted daughter in the Han Dynasty, saving her father from a cruel punishment by offering to serve the Emperor Wen (漢文帝) as a lowly housemaid in an appeal to him

【緻】 4397
ㄓˋ jyh zhì
fine; close; dense; delicate
緻密(ㄓˋ ㄇㄧˋ)
① fine; close; delicate; minute ② (said of conduct) appropriate; careful; irreproachable

【緶】 4398
ㄅㄧㄢˋ biann biàn
1. a narrow strip of woven material (such as the hem of a straw hat)
2. to sew up a hem

【緙】 4399
ㄎㄜˋ keh kè
the woof of a woven item
緙絲(ㄎㄜˋ ㄙ)
tapestry

【緜】 4400
(綿) ㄇㄧㄢˊ mian mián
1. soft; downy
2. enduring

十畫

【縈】 4401
ㄧㄥˊ yng yíng
1. to coil; to entwine; to wind around and around; to twine; to round
2. to entangle; to preoccupy; to bog: 他有麻煩縈身。He was preoccupied with trouble.
縈帶(ㄧㄥˊ ㄉㄞˋ) or 縈迴(ㄧㄥˊ ㄏㄨㄟˊ)
to wind around and around; to coil
縈懷(ㄧㄥˊ ㄏㄨㄞˊ)
to linger; to be constantly on one's mind
縈繞(ㄧㄥˊ ㄖㄠˋ)
to linger; to encircle; to wind around: 疑慮仍縈繞在我心中。A doubt still lingers in my mind.
縈紆(ㄧㄥˊ ㄩ)
to wind around

【縣】 4402
1. ㄒㄧㄢˋ shiann xiàn
a county; a prefecture
縣太爺(ㄒㄧㄢˋ ㄊㄞˋ ㄧㄝˊ)
a reference to a county magistrate among the people in former times
縣立學校(ㄒㄧㄢˋ ㄌㄧˋ ㄒㄩㄝˊ ㄒㄧㄠˋ)
a county-operated school; a county school
縣令(ㄒㄧㄢˋ ㄌㄧㄥˋ)
(an official title in former times) a county magistrate
縣官(ㄒㄧㄢˋ ㄍㄨㄢ)
(a popular term in former times) a county magistrate
縣學(ㄒㄧㄢˋ ㄒㄩㄝˊ)
a county school (in former times)
縣知事(ㄒㄧㄢˋ ㄓ ㄕˋ)
a county magistrate (in the early years of the Republic)
縣志(ㄒㄧㄢˋ ㄓˋ)
general records of a county; county annals
縣治(ㄒㄧㄢˋ ㄓˋ)
the district under the jurisdiction of a county government
縣長(ㄒㄧㄢˋ ㄓㄤˇ)
① the hsien (or county) magistrate (in old China) ② the chief hsien (or county) executive; the head of a county (in modern China)
縣政府(ㄒㄧㄢˋ ㄓㄥˋ ㄈㄨˇ)
a county government
縣城(ㄒㄧㄢˋ ㄔㄥˊ)

the seat of a county government; a county town
縣試(ㄒㄧㄢˋ ㄕˋ)
the county examination (as distinct from the provincial and the imperial examinations under the former civil examination system)
縣議會(ㄒㄧㄢˋ ㄧˋ ㄏㄨㄟˋ)
a county council (with members elected periodically by the people)
縣議員(ㄒㄧㄢˋ ㄧˋ ㄩㄢˊ)
members of a district council

【縣】 4402 2.(懸) ㄒㄩㄢˊ shyuan xuán
to hang

【縠】 4403 ㄏㄨˊ hwu hú
crepe

【縋】 4404 ㄓㄨㄟˋ juey zhuì
to hang by a rope; to let down by a rope
縋登(ㄓㄨㄟˋ ㄉㄥ)
to climb by a rope
縋城(ㄓㄨㄟˋ ㄔㄥˊ)
to climb down a city wall by a rope

【縐】 4405 ㄓㄡˋ jow zhòu
1. crepe; crape
2. wrinkled; creased; crinkled
縐布(ㄓㄡˋ ㄅㄨˋ)
crepe; crape
縐絺(ㄓㄡˋ ㄔ)
fine linen cloth; crepe linen
縐綢(ㄓㄡˋ ㄔㄡˊ)
crepe silk
縐紗(ㄓㄡˋ ㄕㄚ)
crepe silk
縐紋(ㄓㄡˋ ㄨㄣˊ)
wrinkles; creases; folds 亦作「皺紋」

【縑】 4406 ㄐㄧㄢ jian jiān
a kind of fine silk
縑帛(ㄐㄧㄢ ㄅㄛˊ)
silk fabric
縑素(ㄐㄧㄢ ㄙㄨˋ)
silk used for painting and calligraphic works

【縗】 4407 ㄘㄨㄟ tsuei cuī
a piece of sackcloth worn on the breast in mourning

【縛】 4408 ㄈㄨˊ fwu fú
to bind; to tie
縛鷄之力(ㄈㄨˊ ㄐㄧ ㄓ ㄌㄧˋ)
the strength for binding a chicken—very limited strength
縛緊(ㄈㄨˊ ㄐㄧㄣˇ)
to tie or bind tightly
縛住(ㄈㄨˊ ㄓㄨˋ)
to tie up; to bind up
縛手縛脚(ㄈㄨˊ ㄕㄡˇ ㄈㄨˊ ㄐㄧㄠˇ)
with too many constraints; unable to act freely

【縉】 4409 ㄐㄧㄣˋ jinn jìn
red silk
縉紳(ㄐㄧㄣˋ ㄕㄣ)
a ranking government official; a government official in retirement; the gentry 亦作「搢紳」

【縕】 4410 ㄩㄣˋ yunn yùn
1. loose hemp; old yarn
2. confused; chaotic
縕袍(ㄩㄣˋ ㄆㄠˊ)
coarse clothing

【縞】 4411 ㄍㄠˇ gao gǎo
plain white raw silk
縞冠(ㄍㄠˇ ㄍㄨㄢ)
a plain white cap worn in mourning
縞素(ㄍㄠˇ ㄙㄨˋ)
① plain white clothes worn in mourning ② white silk
縞衣(ㄍㄠˇ ㄧ)
① plain white clothes worn in mourning ② thin white silks

【縝】 4412 ㄓㄣˇ jeen zhěn
fine; close; minute
縝密(ㄓㄣˇ ㄇㄧˋ)
fine; minute; well considered and planned in every respect; careful; meticulous; deliberate

【縟】 4413 ㄖㄨˋ ruh rù
1. rich ornament
2. excessive formality or ceremony
縟禮(ㄖㄨˋ ㄌㄧˇ)
excessive formality or ceremony
縟節(ㄖㄨˋ ㄐㄧㄝˊ)
excessive formality or ceremony: 我不喜歡繁文縟節。I dislike complex and excessive ceremony.
縟繡(ㄖㄨˋ ㄒㄧㄡˋ)
resplendent; gorgeous; magnificent

【縢】 4414 ㄊㄥˊ terng téng
1. to bind; to tie; to restrict; to restrain
2. a band
縢履(ㄊㄥˊ ㄌㄩˇ)
shoes for bound feet

【縊】 4415 ㄧˋ yih yì
to strangle; to hang: 他自縊。He hanged himself.
縊頸(ㄧˋ ㄐㄧㄥˇ)
to hang oneself
縊殺(ㄧˋ ㄕㄚ)
to strangle to death; to hang
縊死(ㄧˋ ㄙˇ)
to hang oneself

十一畫

【縫】 4416 1. ㄈㄥˊ ferng féng
1. to sew; to stitch
2. to suture
縫補(ㄈㄥˊ ㄅㄨˇ)
to mend (clothes, etc.)
縫工(ㄈㄥˊ ㄍㄨㄥ)
a sewing worker; a sewer; a seamstress
縫合(ㄈㄥˊ ㄏㄜˊ)
(medicine) to join by sewing; to suture; to sew up: 醫生將傷口縫合。The doctor sewed up the wound.
縫合線(ㄈㄥˊ ㄏㄜˊ ㄒㄧㄢˋ)
a suture
縫製(ㄈㄥˊ ㄓˋ)
to make or manufacture (sewed products)
縫綴(ㄈㄥˊ ㄓㄨㄟˋ)
to sew
縫紉(ㄈㄥˊ ㄖㄣˋ)
sewing; needlework
縫紉機(ㄈㄥˊ ㄖㄣˋ ㄐㄧ)
a sewing machine
縫衣婦(ㄈㄥˊ ㄧ ㄈㄨˋ)
a seamstress; a needlewoman
縫衣服(ㄈㄥˊ ㄧ ˙ㄈㄨ)
to sew clothes; to do needle-

work

【縫】 4416
2. ㄈㄥˋ feng fèng

1. a suture
2. a crack; an opening; a fissure; a cleft; a chink; a crevice: 牆上裂了一條縫兒。There is a crack in the wall.

縫隙(ㄈㄥˋ ㄒㄧˋ)
a chink; a crack; a crevice

縫子(ㄈㄥˋ ·ㄗ)or 縫兒(ㄈㄥˋㄦ)
① a suture ② a crack; an opening; a cleft; a chink

【縭】 4417
ㄌㄧˊ li lí

1. a bridal veil; a bride's sash
2. to tie; to bind

【縱】 4418
1. ㄗㄨㄥˋ tzonq zòng

1. to allow to move or work freely; to let go; to let fly
2. to indulge; indulgence
3. even if; although

縱步(ㄗㄨㄥˋ ㄅㄨˋ)
① to stride: 他縱步向前走。He strode forward. ② a jump; a bound: 他一個縱步跳過了小溪。He crossed the stream in a jump.

縱目(ㄗㄨㄥˋ ㄇㄨˋ)
to look as far as one's eyes can see

縱盜(ㄗㄨㄥˋ ㄉㄠˋ)
to overlook thieves

縱談(ㄗㄨㄥˋ ㄊㄢˊ)
to talk without inhibition; to speak freely: 我們縱談夢想和抱負。We spoke freely about our dreams and ambitions.

縱眺(ㄗㄨㄥˋ ㄊㄧㄠˋ)
to look far and wide

縱脫(ㄗㄨㄥˋ ㄊㄨㄛ)
uninhibited; unrestrained

縱覽(ㄗㄨㄥˋ ㄌㄢˇ)
to look freely and extensively

縱浪(ㄗㄨㄥˋ ㄌㄤˋ)
① uninhibited; unrestrained ② profligate; dissolute

縱令(ㄗㄨㄥˋ ㄌㄧㄥˋ)
even if; even though: 縱令我錯了，你也錯了。Even if I am wrong, you are wrong too.

縱觀(ㄗㄨㄥˋ ㄍㄨㄢ)
to take a free, wide look; to take a sweeping look

縱橫馳騁(ㄗㄨㄥˋ ㄏㄥˊ ㄔˊ ㄔㄥˇ)
to move about freely and swiftly; to sweep through the length and breadth of

縱虎歸山(ㄗㄨㄥˋ ㄏㄨˇ ㄍㄨㄟ ㄕㄢ)
(literally) to allow the tiger to return to the mountain —to allow an evildoer to escape

縱火(ㄗㄨㄥˋ ㄏㄨㄛˇ)
to commit arson

縱火犯(ㄗㄨㄥˋ ㄏㄨㄛˇ ㄈㄢˋ)
an arsonist: 他是縱火犯。He is an arsonist.

縱酒(ㄗㄨㄥˋ ㄐㄧㄡˇ)
to drink to excess

縱囚(ㄗㄨㄥˋ ㄑㄧㄡˊ)
to release prisoners

縱情(ㄗㄨㄥˋ ㄑㄧㄥˊ)or 縱性(ㄗㄨㄥˋ ㄒㄧㄥˋ)
to do as one pleases; to follow one's inclinations; to act without self-control; to one's heart's content: 我們縱情的舞蹈。We danced to our hearts' content.

縱使(ㄗㄨㄥˋ ㄕˇ)
even if; even though: 縱使他不來，我也不介意。I shan't mind even if he doesn't come.

縱身(ㄗㄨㄥˋ ㄕㄣ)
to let the body move (upward, forward, etc.) with full force; to jump; to leap: 兵士們縱身上馬。The soldiers leaped onto their horses.

縱聲(ㄗㄨㄥˋ ㄕㄥ)
to shout or laugh at the top of one's voice

縱然(ㄗㄨㄥˋ ㄖㄢˊ)
even if; even though: 縱然成功的希望不大，我也要試試。I'll try even though there is little hope of success.

縱容(ㄗㄨㄥˋ ㄖㄨㄥˊ)
to pass over indulgently; to connive at: 有些警察縱容賭博。Some policemen connive at gambling.

縱恣(ㄗㄨㄥˋ ㄗˋ)
to give free rein to the passions; to behave without restraint; to indulge; indulgence

縱逸(ㄗㄨㄥˋ ㄧˋ)
unrestrained; uninhibited; dissolute

縱有(ㄗㄨㄥˋ ㄧㄡˇ)
even if there is...; even though there is...

縱淫(ㄗㄨㄥˋ ㄧㄣˊ)or 縱慾(ㄗㄨㄥˋ ㄩˋ)
to abandon oneself to carnal desire; to be dissolute; to be debauched: 他有縱淫的氣色。He had the look of a debauched man.

縱飲(ㄗㄨㄥˋ ㄧㄣˇ)
to indulge in drinking; to drink uninhibitedly: 他縱飲無度。He indulges in drinking.

縱慾無度(ㄗㄨㄥˋ ㄩˋ ㄨˊ ㄉㄨˋ)
to indulge in carnal pleasure without restraint

【縱】 4418
2. ㄗㄨㄥ tzong zōng

vertical; longitudinal

縱波(ㄗㄨㄥ ㄅㄛ)
(physics) longitudinal waves

縱隊(ㄗㄨㄥ ㄉㄨㄟˋ)
column (as opposed to rank) of troops: 一路縱隊行軍。A column of troops marched.

縱斷面(ㄗㄨㄥ ㄉㄨㄢˋ ㄇㄧㄢˋ)
a longitudinal or vertical section; a profile

縱谷(ㄗㄨㄥ ㄍㄨˇ)
a longitudinal valley: 他在縱谷中迷失。He got lost in a longitudinal valley.

縱貫(ㄗㄨㄥ ㄍㄨㄢˋ)
to run lengthwise through

縱貫鐵路(ㄗㄨㄥ ㄍㄨㄢˋ ㄊㄧㄝˇ ㄌㄨˋ)
the main north-south railway of Taiwan

縱海岸(ㄗㄨㄥ ㄏㄞˇ ㄢˋ)
(geology) longitudinal coast

縱橫(ㄗㄨㄥ ㄏㄥˊ)
① the horizontal and the vertical; in length and breadth ②(during the Epoch of Warring States) the two opposing principles of a confederacy against Chin and a federation under Chin ③ to roam about without opposition ④ with great ease: 他的筆意縱橫。He wrote with great ease.

縱橫捭闔(ㄗㄨㄥ ㄏㄥˊ ㄅㄞˇ ㄏㄜˊ)
to deal with friends and enemies with skill

縱橫家(ㄗㄨㄥ ㄏㄥˊ ㄐㄧㄚ)
the Political Strategists (in the Epoch of Warring

〔糸部〕

States)

縱橫交錯(ㄗㄨㄥ ㄏㄥˊ ㄐㄧㄠ ㄘㄨㄛˋ)
arranged in a crisscross pattern

縱橫自如(ㄗㄨㄥ ㄏㄥˊ ㄗˋ ㄖㄨˊ)
capable of moving in any direction

縱橫四海(ㄗㄨㄥ ㄏㄥˊ ㄙˋ ㄏㄞˇ)
to overrun the four seas; to overrun the whole China

縱軸(ㄗㄨㄥ ㄓㄡˊ)
the axis of an ordinate

縱深(ㄗㄨㄥ ㄕㄣ)
(military) the depth (of defense works)

縱座標(ㄗㄨㄥ ㄗㄨㄛˋ ㄅㄧㄠ)
the ordinate (as opposed to the abscissa)

【縮】 4419 ㄙㄨㄛ suo suō (讀音 ㄙㄨˋ suh sù)

1. to contract; to shorten; to reduce; to decrease; to shrink
2. to draw back; to recoil; to wince
3. to bind

縮本(ㄙㄨㄛ ㄅㄣˇ)
①a pocket size edition (of a book) ②an abridged edition (of a book)

縮地之術(ㄙㄨㄛ ㄉㄧˋ ㄓ ㄕㄨˋ)
technique of contracting space; magic of reducing distance

縮短(ㄙㄨㄛ ㄉㄨㄢˇ)
to shorten; to cut down; to shrink; to reduce in length; to contract: 我把文章縮短成一半。I cut the article to half its length.

縮頭吐舌(ㄙㄨㄛ ㄊㄡˊ ㄊㄨˇ ㄕㄜˊ)
to shrug and stick out the tongue (as a jocular expression of fear)

縮頭縮腦(ㄙㄨㄛ ㄊㄡˊ ㄙㄨㄛ ㄋㄠˇ)
to cower or shrink from fear; to be hesitant; to be timid; to be fainthearted

縮圖器(ㄙㄨㄛ ㄊㄨˊ ㄑㄧˋ)
a reduction machine

縮合(ㄙㄨㄛ ㄏㄜˊ)
(chemistry) condensation; to condense

縮回(ㄙㄨㄛ ㄏㄨㄟˊ)
to draw back; to wince; to flinch; to recoil

縮減(ㄙㄨㄛ ㄐㄧㄢˇ)
to reduce; to lessen; to decrease; to curtail; to cut down: 日本縮減軍費。Japan cut down military expenditure.

縮寫(ㄙㄨㄛ ㄒㄧㄝˇ)
abbreviation; to abbreviate: 基督教青年會縮寫成Y.M.C.A.。Young Men's Christian Association is commonly abbreviated to Y.M.C.A.

縮小(ㄙㄨㄛ ㄒㄧㄠˇ)
to contract; to lessen; to reduce

縮小範圍(ㄙㄨㄛ ㄒㄧㄠˇ ㄈㄢˋ ㄨㄟˊ)
to reduce the scope

縮尺(ㄙㄨㄛ ㄔˇ)
a scale rule; a tape measure

縮成一團(ㄙㄨㄛ ㄔㄥˊ ㄧˋ ㄊㄨㄢˊ)
to huddle up; to curl up: 我們嚇得縮成一團。We huddled ourselves up with fear.

縮手旁觀(ㄙㄨㄛ ㄕㄡˇ ㄆㄤˊ ㄍㄨㄢ)
to watch from the sideline without interfering; to stand by with folded arms

縮手縮脚(ㄙㄨㄛ ㄕㄡˇ ㄙㄨㄛ ㄐㄧㄠˇ)
①to keep hands and feet drawn (from cold, reluctance to act, etc.) ②timid; overcautious: 不要像隻老鼠縮手縮脚的。Don't be as timid as a rat.

縮水(ㄙㄨㄛ ㄕㄨㄟˇ)
①dehydration ②(said of fabrics) to shrink after washing; shrinkage

縮水劑(ㄙㄨㄛ ㄕㄨㄟˇ ㄐㄧˋ)
a dehydrating agent

縮衣節食(ㄙㄨㄛ ㄧ ㄐㄧㄝˊ ㄕˊ)
to reduce expenses on clothing and food; to practice austerity; to economize: 他爲了出國縮衣節食。He economized on food and clothing in order to go abroad.

縮印(ㄙㄨㄛ ㄧㄣˋ)
to reprint books in a reduced format

縮影(ㄙㄨㄛ ㄧㄥˇ)
a miniature; an epitome

【縵】 4420 ㄇㄢˋ mann màn

1. plain silk
2. plain; unadorned
3. slow

【縲】 4421 ㄌㄟˊ lei léi

black rope (for a criminal)

縲絏(ㄌㄟˊ ㄒㄧㄝˋ)
bonds; rope for binding a criminal—(figuratively) prison

【縴】 4422 ㄑㄧㄢˋ chiann qiàn

a towrope; a towline

縴夫(ㄑㄧㄢˋ ㄈㄨ)
a boat tower

縴戶(ㄑㄧㄢˋ ㄏㄨˋ)
workers who tow boats; boat towers

縴繩(ㄑㄧㄢˋ ㄕㄥˊ)
a towrope; a towline

【縷】 4423 ㄌㄩˇ leu lǚ

1. a thread; yarn
2. a wisp; a strand; a lock: 一縷頭髮 a lock of hair
3. detailed; in detail

縷縷(ㄌㄩˇ ㄌㄩˇ)
continuous; endlessly: 炊烟縷縷上升。Wisps of smoke rose continuously from the chimneys.

縷解(ㄌㄩˇ ㄐㄧㄝˇ)
to explain in detail

縷析(ㄌㄩˇ ㄒㄧ)
to analyze in detail

縷陳(ㄌㄩˇ ㄔㄣˊ)
to state in detail; to go into details

縷述(ㄌㄩˇ ㄕㄨˋ)
to describe or narrate in detail; to go into particulars: 船長縷述他冒險的故事。The captain narrated his adventures in detail.

【縹】 4424 ㄆㄧㄠˇ peau piǎo

1. light-blue silk
2. light blue
3. dim; misty; indistinct

縹縹(ㄆㄧㄠˇ ㄆㄧㄠˇ)
wafting lightly

縹緲(ㄆㄧㄠˇ ㄇㄧㄠˇ)
distant and dim; far and indistinct; intangible and incorporeal

縹囊(ㄆㄧㄠˇ ㄋㄤˊ)
a silk bag for holding books

縹緗(ㄆㄧㄠˇ ㄒㄧㄤ)
valuable books

縹帙(ㄆㄧㄠˇ ㄓˋ)

books
標瓦(ㄆㄧㄠˇ ㄨㄚˇ)
glossy tiles

【總】 4425
ㄗㄨㄥˇ tzoong zǒng
1. to gather; to collect; to assemble; to unite
2. always
3. all; general; overall; complete; total
4. chief; principal; central
5. at any rate; in any event; anyway; after all; sooner or later: 這個事實總是要面對的。We will face the facts sooner or later.

總罷工(ㄗㄨㄥˇ ㄅㄚˋ ㄍㄨㄥ)
a general strike
總包寄遞(ㄗㄨㄥˇ ㄅㄠ ㄐㄧˋ ㄉㄧˋ)
mail of printed materials en masse at reduced postage under a contract with the post office
總辦(ㄗㄨㄥˇ ㄅㄢˋ)
managers or directors (especially of some government agencies toward the end of the Ching Dynasty)
總崩潰(ㄗㄨㄥˇ ㄅㄥ ㄎㄨㄟˋ)
total collapse
總編輯(ㄗㄨㄥˇ ㄅㄧㄢ ㄐㄧˊ)
an editor-in-chief; a managing editor: 他是總編輯。He is the chief editor.
總兵(ㄗㄨㄥˇ ㄅㄧㄥ)
one of the titles of a high-ranking military officer in former times
總部(ㄗㄨㄥˇ ㄅㄨˋ)
headquarters
總批發(ㄗㄨㄥˇ ㄆㄧ ㄈㄚ)
general wholesale distribution (of commodities in a given area)
總評(ㄗㄨㄥˇ ㄆㄧㄥˊ)
general comment; overall appraisal: 他對此結果作了總評。He made a general comment on the results.
總平均(ㄗㄨㄥˇ ㄆㄧㄥˊ ㄐㄩㄣ)
an overall average
總目(ㄗㄨㄥˇ ㄇㄨˋ)
a general index
總髮(ㄗㄨㄥˇ ㄈㄚˇ)
childhood
總得(ㄗㄨㄥˇ ㄉㄟˇ)
to have to; somehow: 我總得設法將其完成。I must get it finished somehow.
總代理(ㄗㄨㄥˇ ㄉㄞˋ ㄌㄧˇ)
(business) a general agent
總督(ㄗㄨㄥˇ ㄉㄨ)
a viceroy; a governor-general
總動員(ㄗㄨㄥˇ ㄉㄨㄥˋ ㄩㄢˊ)
general mobilization
總體戰(ㄗㄨㄥˇ ㄊㄧˇ ㄓㄢˋ)
an all-out war; a total war
總退卻(ㄗㄨㄥˇ ㄊㄨㄟˋ ㄑㄩㄝˋ)
general retreat: 全軍總退卻。The whole army was in full retreat.
總統(ㄗㄨㄥˇ ㄊㄨㄥˇ)
the president (of a state)
總統府(ㄗㄨㄥˇ ㄊㄨㄥˇ ㄈㄨˇ)
the presidential office
總統當選人(ㄗㄨㄥˇ ㄊㄨㄥˇ ㄉㄤ ㄒㄩㄢˇ ㄖㄣˊ)
a president-elect
總統候選人(ㄗㄨㄥˇ ㄊㄨㄥˇ ㄏㄡˋ ㄒㄩㄢˇ ㄖㄣˊ)
a presidential candidate
總統制(ㄗㄨㄥˇ ㄊㄨㄥˇ ㄓˋ)
a political system under which the president is the chief executive
總攬大權(ㄗㄨㄥˇ ㄌㄢˇ ㄉㄚˋ ㄑㄩㄢˊ)
to be in full power; to have full control of the government; to have overall authority
總理(ㄗㄨㄥˇ ㄌㄧˇ)
① a prime minister; a premier ② a president (of a political party, etc.) ③ a reference to Dr. Sun Yat-sen among members of the Kuomintang which he founded
總理衙門(ㄗㄨㄥˇ ㄌㄧˇ ㄧㄚˊ ㄇㄣˊ)
the Ministry or Department of Foreign Affairs, set up toward the end of the Ching Dynasty
總量(ㄗㄨㄥˇ ㄌㄧㄤˋ)
a total amount
總領事(ㄗㄨㄥˇ ㄌㄧㄥˇ ㄕˋ)
a consul general
總領事館(ㄗㄨㄥˇ ㄌㄧㄥˇ ㄕˋ ㄍㄨㄢˇ)
a consulate general
總路線(ㄗㄨㄥˇ ㄌㄨˋ ㄒㄧㄢˋ)
a general line (a Chinese Communist terminology)
總論(ㄗㄨㄥˇ ㄌㄨㄣˋ)
general discussion; a summary; an introduction: 這本歷史書於每章末均有一總論。The history book has a summary at the end of each chapter.
總綱(ㄗㄨㄥˇ ㄍㄤ)
general principles
總括(ㄗㄨㄥˇ ㄍㄨㄚ)
to sum up; to summarize: 總括言之，她是一個可愛的女孩。To sum up, she is a nice girl.
總歸(ㄗㄨㄥˇ ㄍㄨㄟ)
anyhow; eventually; after all: 事實總歸是事實。After all, facts are facts.
總管(ㄗㄨㄥˇ ㄍㄨㄢˇ)
① a superintendent; a supervisor; a director; a manager ② the title of a ranking military officer in ancient times ③ to supervise: 自修室由教師總管。Study halls are supervised by teachers.
總攻擊令(ㄗㄨㄥˇ ㄍㄨㄥ ㄐㄧˊ ㄌㄧㄥˋ)
orders for the general offensive
總工會(ㄗㄨㄥˇ ㄍㄨㄥ ㄏㄨㄟˋ)
a federation of labor unions
總工程師(ㄗㄨㄥˇ ㄍㄨㄥ ㄔㄥˊ ㄕ)
a chief engineer
總共(ㄗㄨㄥˇ ㄍㄨㄥˋ)
altogether; in all; all told: 總共有五十個客人。There were 50 guests all told.
總合(ㄗㄨㄥˇ ㄏㄜˊ)
an assemblage
總和(ㄗㄨㄥˇ ㄏㄜˊ)
the sum total; the total; the grand total; as a whole
總行(ㄗㄨㄥˇ ㄏㄤˊ) or 總店(ㄗㄨㄥˇ ㄉㄧㄢˋ)
a head office (of a business firm)
總會(ㄗㄨㄥˇ ㄏㄨㄟˋ)
① a conglomeration; an assemblage; a collection ② central committee or administrative body (of an association, etc.) ③ a club ④ bound to; inevitable; sure to happen
總滙(ㄗㄨㄥˇ ㄏㄨㄟˋ)
①(said of books) an assemblage; a collection ②(said of

〔糸部〕

rivers) confluence
總機(ㄗㄨㄥˇ ㄐㄧ)
a telephone switchboard
總機關(ㄗㄨㄥˇ ㄐㄧ ㄍㄨㄢ)
① headquarters ② a chief mechanism (of a machine)
總集(ㄗㄨㄥˇ ㄐㄧˊ)
the complete works (of one or more writers)
總計(ㄗㄨㄥˇ ㄐㄧˋ)
the sum total; the total; the grand total: 他的債務總計達二百萬元。His debts reached a total of two million dollars.
總結(ㄗㄨㄥˇ ㄐㄧㄝˊ)
① summation; conclusion; finale ② to sum up: 法官總結證詞。The judge summed up the evidence.
總教練(ㄗㄨㄥˇ ㄐㄧㄠˋ ㄌㄧㄢˋ)
a chief coach (of a sport delegation): 他是我們的足球總教練。He is our chief coach in football.
總教官(ㄗㄨㄥˇ ㄐㄧㄠˋ ㄍㄨㄢ)
a chief instructor (of a service school)
總監(ㄗㄨㄥˇ ㄐㄧㄢ)
an inspector general; a chief inspector
總經理(ㄗㄨㄥˇ ㄐㄧㄥ ㄌㄧˇ)
a general manager
總局(ㄗㄨㄥˇ ㄐㄩˊ)
the head office; headquarters (of the police in a city or county): 他在總局工作。He works in the head office.
總角(ㄗㄨㄥˇ ㄐㄩㄝˊ)
a child's hair bound into a hornlike knot—childhood
總角之交(ㄗㄨㄥˇ ㄐㄩㄝˊ ㄓ ㄐㄧㄠ)
a friend since childhood
總選(ㄗㄨㄥˇ ㄒㄩㄢˇ)
a general election
總之(ㄗㄨㄥˇ ㄓ)
in short; in conclusion; in brief; in a word: 總之, 這就是對於辯論的答覆。This, in brief, is the answer to the argument.
總值(ㄗㄨㄥˇ ㄓˊ)
total value; a total price
總指揮(ㄗㄨㄥˇ ㄓˇ ㄏㄨㄟ)
the commander-in-chief: 他是遠征隊的總指揮。He is the commander-in-chief of an expedition.
總指揮部(ㄗㄨㄥˇ ㄓˇ ㄏㄨㄟ ㄅㄨˋ)
the headquarters of a high command
總鎮(ㄗㄨㄥˇ ㄓㄣˋ)
one of the titles of a high-ranking military officer in former times 亦作「總兵」
總長(ㄗㄨㄥˇ ㄓㄤˇ)
① a cabinet minister in the early years of the Republic ② short for chief of the general staff
總帳(ㄗㄨㄥˇ ㄓㄤˋ)
(bookkeeping) a general ledger; a ledger: 他要看總帳。He wants to see a ledger.
總主筆(ㄗㄨㄥˇ ㄓㄨˇ ㄅㄧˇ)
a chief editorial writer: 他是紐約客的總主筆。He is the chief editorial writer of *New Yorker*.
總狀花序(ㄗㄨㄥˇ ㄓㄨㄤˋ ㄏㄨㄚ ㄒㄩˋ)
(botany) raceme
總重量(ㄗㄨㄥˇ ㄓㄨㄥˋ ㄌㄧㄤˋ)
gross weight
總稱(ㄗㄨㄥˇ ㄔㄥ)
a generic name; a general term
總是(ㄗㄨㄥˇ ㄕˋ)
always; without exception: 他們總是星期六來。They always come on Saturday.
總商會(ㄗㄨㄥˇ ㄕㄤ ㄏㄨㄟˋ)
the general chamber of commerce
總署(ㄗㄨㄥˇ ㄕㄨˋ)
① the Ministry of Foreign Affairs in former times (總理衙門) ② headquarters; the head office
總數(ㄗㄨㄥˇ ㄕㄨˋ)
the total amount; the total; the amount: 總數是一百二十。The total is 120.
總人口(ㄗㄨㄥˇ ㄖㄣˊ ㄎㄡˇ)
total population
總則(ㄗㄨㄥˇ ㄗㄜˊ)
general principles
總總(ㄗㄨㄥˇ ㄗㄨㄥˇ)
numerous; abundant; teeming
總辭職(ㄗㄨㄥˇ ㄘˊ ㄓˊ)
to resign *en bloc* (usually referring to a cabinet): 舊內閣已總辭職。The old cabinet has resigned *en bloc*.
總冊(ㄗㄨㄥˇ ㄘㄜˋ)
a book of general record (as opposed to one carrying specifics)
總裁(ㄗㄨㄥˇ ㄘㄞˊ)
a director general, president or governor (of a bank, political party, etc.): 他是我們銀行的總裁。He is the president of our bank.
總司令(ㄗㄨㄥˇ ㄙ ㄌㄧㄥˋ)
the commander-in-chief: 他是陸軍總司令。He is the commander-in-chief of the army.
總司令部(ㄗㄨㄥˇ ㄙ ㄌㄧㄥˋ ㄅㄨˋ)
general headquarters (of the military service)
總算(ㄗㄨㄥˇ ㄙㄨㄢˋ)
① on the whole; all things considered; in general ② at long last; finally
總額(ㄗㄨㄥˇ ㄜˊ)
the total amount; the sum total
總而言之(ㄗㄨㄥˇ ㄦˊ ㄧㄢˊ ㄓ)
in short; in a word; to sum up: 總而言之, 我們生氣地回家了。In short, we went home angry.
總要(ㄗㄨㄥˇ ㄧㄠˋ)
should always; must always
總務(ㄗㄨㄥˇ ㄨˋ)
general affairs
總預算(ㄗㄨㄥˇ ㄩˋ ㄙㄨㄢˋ)
a general budget

【縶】 4426 ㄓˊ jyr zhí
1. to tie; to bind; to connect
2. to imprison
3. a bridle
縶維(ㄓˊ ㄨㄟˊ)
to retain (a man of talent)

【縻】 4427 ㄇㄧˊ mi mí
to tie; to fasten; to connect

【繁】 4428 1.(緐) ㄈㄢˊ farn fán
1. many; numerous; abundant; prolific
2. complex; complicated; intricate
繁茂(ㄈㄢˊ ㄇㄠˋ)
(said of vegetation) lush or luxuriant
繁忙(ㄈㄢˊ ㄇㄤˊ)
very busy; hectic: 他們的工作很繁忙。They are very busy

with their work.
繁密(ㄈㄢˊ ㄇㄧˋ)
dense; thick
繁分數(ㄈㄢˊ ㄈㄣ ㄕㄨˋ)
a complex fraction
繁富(ㄈㄢˊ ㄈㄨˋ)
many; numerous; abundant: 美國的天然資源繁富。America is abundant in natural resources.
繁複(ㄈㄢˊ ㄈㄨˋ)
complex; complicated; intricate
繁多(ㄈㄢˊ ㄉㄨㄛ)
many; numerous
繁體字(ㄈㄢˊ ㄊㄧˇ ㄗˋ)
the original complex form of a simplified Chinese character
繁難(ㄈㄢˊ ㄋㄢˊ)
complicated and troublesome
繁華(ㄈㄢˊ ㄏㄨㄚˊ)
① prosperous; flourishing; booming; thriving ② pompous; extravagant
繁華世界(ㄈㄢˊ ㄏㄨㄚˊ ㄕˋ ㄐㄧㄝˋ)
this vain world
繁劇(ㄈㄢˊ ㄐㄩˋ)
a very heavy work load
繁缺(ㄈㄢˊ ㄑㄩㄝ)
a post with a very heavy work load
繁細(ㄈㄢˊ ㄒㄧˋ)
detailed in a complicated way; overloaded with details
繁星(ㄈㄢˊ ㄒㄧㄥ)
numerous stars: 我們在夜晚可看見繁星。We can see the numerous stars at night.
繁殖(ㄈㄢˊ ㄓˊ)
to multiply by reproduction; to propagate; to breed: 大多數的鳥在春季繁殖。Most birds breed in the spring.
繁殖力(ㄈㄢˊ ㄓˊ ㄌㄧˋ)
procreative power
繁徵博引(ㄈㄢˊ ㄓㄥ ㄅㄛˊ ㄧㄣˇ)
to use an abundance of proofs; to quote from many sources
繁重(ㄈㄢˊ ㄓㄨㄥˋ)
(said of work loads) heavy; arduous; strenuous
繁盛(ㄈㄢˊ ㄕㄥˋ)
thriving; flourishing; prosperous
繁暑(ㄈㄢˊ ㄕㄨˇ)
intense heat in summer
繁縟(ㄈㄢˊ ㄖㄨˋ)
abundant; prolific
繁榮(ㄈㄢˊ ㄖㄨㄥˊ)
prosperous; flourishing; thriving
繁雜(ㄈㄢˊ ㄗㄚˊ)
complicated; complex; intricate: 他們的教育制度十分繁雜。Their educational system is very complex.
繁瑣(ㄈㄢˊ ㄙㄨㄛˇ)
minute and complicated
繁碎(ㄈㄢˊ ㄙㄨㄟˋ)
detailed in a complicated way
繁衍(ㄈㄢˊ ㄧㄢˇ)
to proliferate; to teem
繁蕪(ㄈㄢˊ ㄨˊ)
loaded with unnecessary words; expressed in too many words; verbose
繁文縟節(ㄈㄢˊ ㄨㄣˊ ㄖㄨˋ ㄐㄧㄝˊ)
excessive ceremony

【繁】 4428 2. ㄆㄛˊ por pó
a Chinese family name

【繄】 4429 ㄧ i yī
1. a phrase-initial particle (in archaic Chinese)
2. a verb functioning like the verb "to be" (in archaic Chinese)
3. alas

【繇】 4430 1. ㄧㄡˊ you yóu
1. same as 由—through; via; by way of
2. same as 悠—to be in a leisurely manner and satisfied with oneself

【繇】 4430 2.(傜) ㄧㄠˊ yau yáo
1. labor service
2. luxuriant
繇賦(ㄧㄠˊ ㄈㄨˋ)
compulsory labor and land tax

【績】 4431 ㄐㄧ ji jī
1. to spin; to twist
2. merit; achievements; exploits; meritorious labor
績麻(ㄐㄧ ㄇㄚˊ)
to spin hemp
績紡(ㄐㄧ ㄈㄤˇ)
to spin
績女(ㄐㄧ ㄋㄩˇ)
a spinster (who spins)
績溪(ㄐㄧ ㄒㄧ)
name of a county in Anhwei
績效(ㄐㄧ ㄒㄧㄠˋ)
results; effects; achievements
績效預算(ㄐㄧ ㄒㄧㄠˋ ㄩˋ ㄙㄨㄢˋ)
performance budgeting
績學(ㄐㄧ ㄒㄩㄝˊ)
to pursue knowledge
績成(ㄐㄧ ㄔㄥˊ)
achievements
績用(ㄐㄧ ㄩㄥˋ)
utility; use

【繅】 4432 ㄙㄠ sau sāo
to draw or unwind (silk from cocoons)
繅繭(ㄙㄠ ㄐㄧㄢˇ)or 繅繭出絲(ㄙㄠ ㄐㄧㄢˇ ㄔㄨ ㄙ)
to draw silk from cocoons
繅絲(ㄙㄠ ㄙ)
to draw silk (from cocoons)

【繃】 4433 1.(絣) ㄅㄥ beng bēng
to bind
繃繃場面(ㄅㄥ ˙ㄅㄥ ㄔㄤˇ ㄇㄧㄢˋ)
to manage somehow to keep up appearances
繃帶(ㄅㄥ ㄉㄞˋ)
a bandage: 他的頭用繃帶紮起。He has his head in bandages.
繃線(ㄅㄥ ㄒㄧㄢˋ)
bastings
繃子(ㄅㄥ ˙ㄗ)
an embroidery frame

【繃】 4433 2.(絣) ㄅㄥˇ beeng běng
1. taut; tense
2. to endure or bear
繃不住(ㄅㄥˇ ˙ㄅㄨ ㄓㄨˋ)
unable to endure or bear
繃著臉(ㄅㄥˇ ˙ㄓㄜ ㄌㄧㄢˇ)
to have a taut face; to assume a serious or displeased look; to pull a long face

【繃】 4433 3.(絣) ㄅㄥˋ benq bèng
to break open; to burst open; to split open; to crack
繃斷(ㄅㄥˋ ㄉㄨㄢˋ)

〔糸部〕

a snap from tension

【繆】 4434 1. ㄇㄡˊ mou móu

precautions; preparations

繆篆(ㄇㄡˊ ㄓㄨㄢˋ)

one of the six styles of characters begun in the reign of Wang Mang (王莽)

【繆】 4434 2. ㄇㄧㄠˋ miaw miào

a Chinese family name

【繆】 4434 3. ㄇㄧㄡˋ miow miù

erroneous; preposterous; absurd; false; an error; a mistake 亦作「謬」

繆巧(ㄇㄧㄡˋ ㄑㄧㄠˇ)

tricks; wiles; ruses

繆種流傳(ㄇㄧㄡˋ ㄓㄨㄥˇ ㄌㄧㄡˊ ㄔㄨㄢˊ)

People of inability become prosperous while the real talents live in obscurity.

繆誤(ㄇㄧㄡˋ ㄨˋ)

an error; a mistake

【繆】 4434 4.(穆) ㄇㄨˋ muh mù

1. beautiful
2. harmonious
3. silent

【縧】 4435 (絛) ㄊㄠ tau tāo

ribbon; flat silk cord

十二畫

【繒】 4436 1. ㄗㄥ tzeng zēng

silk; silk fabrics

繒綾(ㄗㄥ ㄌㄧㄥˊ)

rugged; not smooth

繒繳(ㄗㄥ ㄓㄨㄛˊ)

a string made of raw silk fastened to the arrow

【繒】 4436 2. ㄗㄥˋ tzenq zèng

繒綳(ㄗㄥˋ ㄅㄥˇ)

to fasten tight

【織】 4437 ㄓ jy zhī

to weave; to knit

織補(ㄓ ㄅㄨˇ)

to darn; to mend

織布(ㄓ ㄅㄨˋ)

to weave cloth: 她用織布機織布。She is weaving cloth on the loom.

織布鳥(ㄓ ㄅㄨˋ ㄋㄧㄠˇ)

a Java sparrow

織布娘(ㄓ ㄅㄨˋ ㄋㄧㄤˊ)

Mecopoda nipponensis, a kind of grasshopper

織布機(ㄓ ㄅㄨˋ ㄐㄧ)or 織機(ㄓ ㄐㄧ)

a loom

織布廠(ㄓ ㄅㄨˋ ㄔㄤˇ)

a weaving mill

織女(ㄓ ㄋㄩˇ)

①(Chinese mythology) the three stars representing the three Weaving Sisters, daughters of Celestial Ruler ②a weaving woman

織女星(ㄓ ㄋㄩˇ ㄒㄧㄥ)

the Weaving Damsel—the star Vega in the constellation Lyra

織花(ㄓ ㄏㄨㄚ)

to weave figures into fabrics

織畫(ㄓ ㄏㄨㄚˋ)

woven pictures: 多麼美麗的一幅織畫啊! What a beautiful woven picture!

織錦(ㄓ ㄐㄧㄣˇ)

brocade or silk brocade

織錦迴文(ㄓ ㄐㄧㄣˇ ㄏㄨㄟˊ ㄨㄣˊ)

a palindrome

織蓆(ㄓ ㄒㄧˊ)

to weave a mat

織造(ㄓ ㄗㄠˋ)

a government agency during the Ming and Ching dynasties, responsible for manufacturing silks for the exclusive use of the royal household and imperial palace

織物(ㄓ ㄨˋ)

fabric; cloth; textiles

織襪(ㄓ ㄨㄚˋ)

to knit socks or stockings: 母親正在織襪。Mother is knitting socks.

織紋(ㄓ ㄨㄣˊ)

a woven pattern

【繕】 4438 ㄕㄢˋ shann shàn

1. to mend; to repair: 他正在修繕房子。He is mending his house.
2. to copy; to transcribe

繕補(ㄕㄢˋ ㄅㄨˇ)

to mend: 他繕補壞了的玩具。He mended the broken toy.

繕錄(ㄕㄢˋ ㄌㄨˋ)

to transcribe

繕就(ㄕㄢˋ ㄐㄧㄡˋ)

to copy; to transcribe; to finish copying or transcribing

繕寫(ㄕㄢˋ ㄒㄧㄝˇ)

to transcribe; to copy neatly: 把這幾句繕寫在你的筆記本上。Copy neatly these sentences in your notebook.

繕修(ㄕㄢˋ ㄒㄧㄡ)

to repair; to mend: 一些人在繕修房屋。Some men were repairing the house.

繕正(ㄕㄢˋ ㄓㄥˋ)

to copy neatly; to write a neat copy

【繚】 4439 ㄌㄧㄠˊ liau liáo

to wind round

繚亂(ㄌㄧㄠˊ ㄌㄨㄢˋ)

intricate; tangled; disorderly; confused

繚繞(ㄌㄧㄠˊ ㄖㄠˋ)

winding round and round (usually referring to musical sound or incense smoke)

【繖】 4440 ㄙㄢˇ saan sǎn

an umbrella; a parasol; a canopy

繖房花序(ㄙㄢˇ ㄈㄤˊ ㄏㄨㄚ ㄒㄩˋ)

(botany) corymb

繖形花序(ㄙㄢˇ ㄒㄧㄥˊ ㄏㄨㄚ ㄒㄩˋ)

(botany) umbel

【繙】 4441 ㄈㄢ fan fān

1. to translate; to interpret
2. (said of a flag, etc.) to flutter; to fly

繙蠻(ㄈㄢ ㄇㄢˊ)

to speak an incomprehensible local dialect

繙譯 or 翻譯(ㄈㄢ ㄧˋ)

to translate; to interpret

【繞】 4442 ㄖㄠˋ raw rào

1. to go around; to make a detour
2. to march round; to circle

繞道(ㄖㄠˋ ㄉㄠˋ)or 繞路(ㄖㄠˋ ㄌㄨˋ)

to make a detour; to detour

繞樑三日(ㄖㄠˋ ㄌㄧㄤˊ ㄙㄢ ㄖˋ)

(said of a song, etc.) to linger long in the air

繞過(ㄖㄠˋ ㄍㄨㄛˋ)

to pass over a point by a detour

繞口令兒(ㄖㄠˋ ㄎㄡˇ ㄌㄧㄥˋㄦ)

a tongue twister

繞圈子(ㄖㄠˋ ㄑㄩㄢ ˙ㄗ)or 繞圈兒(ㄖㄠˋ ㄑㄩㄚㄦ)
①to go round and round ②to beat around the bush; to talk in a roundabout way
繞膝承歡(ㄖㄠˋ ㄒㄧ ㄔㄥˊ ㄏㄨㄢ)
to stay with one's parents in order to make them happy
繞行(ㄖㄠˋ ㄒㄧㄥˊ)
①to detour ②to orbit; to revolve around something
繞指柔(ㄖㄠˋ ㄓˇ ㄖㄡˊ)
(said of temperaments) very pliable
繞著彎兒(ㄖㄠˋ ˙ㄓㄜ ㄨㄚㄦ)
①to be circuitous or roundabout ②to make a detour
繞日(ㄖㄠˋ ㄖˋ)
to revolve around the sun: 地球繞日轉。The earth revolves around the sun.
繞嘴(ㄖㄠˋ ㄗㄨㄟˇ)
jawbreaking; to be difficult to articulate: 他的名字很繞嘴。His name is really jawbreaking.
繞彎兒(ㄖㄠˋ ㄨㄚㄦ)
to take a stroll
繞彎子(ㄖㄠˋ ㄨㄢ ˙ㄗ)
①to go round; to make a detour ②to talk in a roundabout way; to beat about the bush
繞遠兒(ㄖㄠˋ ㄩㄚˇㄦ)
to take a circuitous road; to go a long way round
繞越(ㄖㄠˋ ㄩㄝˋ)
to cross or pass by a detour

【繢】 4443
(繪) ㄏㄨㄟˋ huey huì
to draw; to make a sketch of

【繡】 4444
(綉) ㄒㄧㄡˋ shiow xiù
1. to embroider
2. embroidery
繡被(ㄒㄧㄡˋ ㄅㄟˋ)
bedding adorned with embroidery; embroidered bedding
繡補(ㄒㄧㄡˋ ㄅㄨˇ)
to darn
繡佛(ㄒㄧㄡˋ ㄈㄛˊ)
an embroidered Buddha image
繡房(ㄒㄧㄡˋ ㄈㄤˊ)or 繡閣(ㄒㄧㄡˋ ㄍㄜˊ) or 繡戶(ㄒㄧㄡˋ ㄏㄨˋ)
a young lady's chamber; a boudoir
繡工(ㄒㄧㄡˋ ㄍㄨㄥ)or 繡活(ㄒㄧㄡˋ ㄏㄨㄛˊ)
embroidery
繡口(ㄒㄧㄡˋ ㄎㄡˇ)
talented in literary expressions
繡虎(ㄒㄧㄡˋ ㄏㄨˇ)
a literary genius (a sobriquet originally bestowed on 曹植)
繡花(ㄒㄧㄡˋ ㄏㄨㄚ)
embroidery; to embroider: 她在絲巾上繡花。She embroidered flowers on a silk scarf.
繡花鞋(ㄒㄧㄡˋ ㄏㄨㄚ ㄒㄧㄝˊ)
embroidered shoes
繡花針(ㄒㄧㄡˋ ㄏㄨㄚ ㄓㄣ)
an embroidery needle
繡花枕頭(ㄒㄧㄡˋ ㄏㄨㄚ ㄓㄣˇ ˙ㄊㄡ)
(literally) an embroidered pillow—a person impressive in appearance but disappointing in substance
繡畫(ㄒㄧㄡˋ ㄏㄨㄚˋ)
embroidered pictures or designs
繡貨(ㄒㄧㄡˋ ㄏㄨㄛˋ)
embroideries
繡球(ㄒㄧㄡˋ ㄑㄧㄡˊ)
a ball of rolled silk
繡球風(ㄒㄧㄡˋ ㄑㄧㄡˊ ㄈㄥ)
a pruritus scrotum
繡球花(ㄒㄧㄡˋ ㄑㄧㄡˊ ㄏㄨㄚ)
(botany) hydrangea
繡鞋(ㄒㄧㄡˋ ㄒㄧㄝˊ)
embroidered shoes
繡線(ㄒㄧㄡˋ ㄒㄧㄢˋ)
embroidery thread
繡像(ㄒㄧㄡˋ ㄒㄧㄤˋ)
①embroidered images; to embroider images ②a fine figure painting
繡衣直指(ㄒㄧㄡˋ ㄧ ㄓˊ ㄓˇ)
an official post during the Han Dynasty, responsible for censure and justice

十三畫

【繩】 4445
ㄕㄥˊ sherng shéng
1. a rope; a cord; a line
2. to restrain
3. to rectify; to correct
繩墨(ㄕㄥˊ ㄇㄛˋ)
①(carpenter's) marking lines ②rules of conduct: 他總是拘守繩墨。He always sticks to the rules of conduct.
繩髮(ㄕㄥˊ ㄈㄚˇ)
rope-like braids of hair
繩梯(ㄕㄥˊ ㄊㄧ)
a rope ladder: 一條繩梯懸於船側。A rope ladder hung over the ship's side.
繩妓(ㄕㄥˊ ㄐㄧˋ)
a female tightrope walker
繩檢(ㄕㄥˊ ㄐㄧㄢˇ)
to restrain; to exercise self-restraint
繩其祖武(ㄕㄥˊ ㄑㄧˊ ㄗㄨˇ ㄨˇ)
to imitate one's forebears
繩橋(ㄕㄥˊ ㄑㄧㄠˊ)
a suspension bridge: 繩橋已經拆下。The suspension bridge has been taken down.
繩愆糾繆(ㄕㄥˊ ㄑㄧㄢ ㄐㄧㄡ ㄇㄧㄡˋ)
to correct mistakes
繩趨尺步(ㄕㄥˊ ㄑㄩ ㄔˇ ㄅㄨˋ)
to behave according to decorums
繩戲(ㄕㄥˊ ㄒㄧˋ)
the stunt of walking on a tightrope
繩之以法(ㄕㄥˊ ㄓ ㄧˇ ㄈㄚˇ)
to prosecute according to the law: 他被繩之以法。He was prosecuted according to the law.
繩正(ㄕㄥˊ ㄓㄥˋ)
to rectify; to correct: 她繩正錯誤。She rectified errors.
繩尺(ㄕㄥˊ ㄔˇ)
a rule; law; standard; a criterion
繩子(ㄕㄥˊ ˙ㄗ)or 繩兒(ㄕㄥˊㄦ)
a rope; a line; a cord: 我用繩子包紮盒子。I tied up the box with a cord.
繩索(ㄕㄥˊ ㄙㄨㄛˇ)
ropes; cords: 抓住繩索。Grasp the ropes.

【繪】 4446
ㄏㄨㄟˋ huey huì
to draw (pictures)
繪圖(ㄏㄨㄟˋ ㄊㄨˊ)
①to draw pictures: 她正在繪圖。She is drawing a picture. ②to prepare (engineering) drawings
繪圖員(ㄏㄨㄟˋ ㄊㄨˊ ㄩㄢˊ)

〔糸部〕

a draftsman (of an engineering firm)
繪畫(ㄏㄨㄟˋ ㄏㄨㄚˋ)
painting; drawing: 她有繪畫的天才。She has a talent for painting.
繪具(ㄏㄨㄟˋ ㄐㄩˋ)
drawing tools
繪像(ㄏㄨㄟˋ ㄒㄧㄤˋ)
to draw portraits: 他擅長繪像。He is good at drawing portraits.
繪事(ㄏㄨㄟˋ ㄕˋ)
painting; drawing
繪影繪聲(ㄏㄨㄟˋ ㄧㄥˇ ㄏㄨㄟˋ ㄕㄥ) or 繪聲繪影(ㄏㄨㄟˋ ㄕㄥ ㄏㄨㄟˋ ㄧㄥˇ)
(literally) to portray even shadows and sounds—to give a very vivid description

【繮】 4447
(韁) ㄐㄧㄤ jiang jiāng
(又讀 ㄍㄤ gang gāng)
reins; a bridle; a halter
繮繩(ㄐㄧㄤ ㄕㄥˊ)
reins; a bridle; a halter

【繯】 4448
ㄏㄨㄢˊ hwan huán
1. a noose
2. to hang (to death): 她投繯自盡。She hanged herself.

【繳】 4449
1. ㄐㄧㄠˇ jeau jiǎo
1. to surrender (articles); to submit; to lay down: 繳械投降! Lay down your arms!
2. to pay (taxes, tuition, etc.)
繳費(ㄐㄧㄠˇ ㄈㄟˋ)
to pay fees
繳納(ㄐㄧㄠˇ ㄋㄚˋ)
to pay (taxes, tuition, etc.)
繳庫(ㄐㄧㄠˇ ㄎㄨˋ)
to turn (revenues) to the treasury
繳款(ㄐㄧㄠˇ ㄎㄨㄢˇ)
to make payments (to some authorities, etc.)
繳回(ㄐㄧㄠˇ ㄏㄨㄟˊ)
to return (government property issued)
繳交(ㄐㄧㄠˇ ㄐㄧㄠ)
to turn in; to hand over; to surrender; to submit
繳卷(ㄐㄧㄠˇ ㄐㄩㄢˋ)
to hand in examination papers: 他們立刻繳卷。They hand in examination papers at once.
繳械(ㄐㄧㄠˇ ㄒㄧㄝˋ) or 繳槍(ㄐㄧㄠˇ ㄑㄧㄤ)
to surrender arms; to hand over weapons; to disarm
繳稅(ㄐㄧㄠˇ ㄕㄨㄟˋ)
to pay taxes: 他繳稅五十鎊。He paid £50 in taxes.
繳繞(ㄐㄧㄠˇ ㄖㄠˋ)
to harass
繳存(ㄐㄧㄠˇ ㄘㄨㄣˊ)
to hand in for safekeeping
繳驗(ㄐㄧㄠˇ ㄧㄢˋ)
to hand in for inspection

【繳】 4449
2. ㄓㄨㄛˊ jwo zhuó
a string made of raw silk fastened to the arrow

【繨】 4450
·ㄉㄚ ·da da
(又讀 ㄉㄚˊ dar dá)
a knot (of a rope)

【繹】 4451
ㄧˋ yih yì
1. to draw silk
2. continuous; uninterrupted
3. to infer; to deduce
繹如(ㄧˋ ㄖㄨˊ)
continuous

【繫】 4452
1. ㄒㄧˋ shih xì
to connect; to link; to join
繫泊(ㄒㄧˋ ㄅㄛˊ)
to moor (a boat)
繫絆(ㄒㄧˋ ㄅㄢˋ)
to bridle; to hinder: 別繫絆我。Don't hinder me.
繫戀(ㄒㄧˋ ㄌㄧㄢˋ)
to be inextricably in love with; to be reluctant to leave
繫懷(ㄒㄧˋ ㄏㄨㄞˊ)
to have one's heart drawn by
繫囚(ㄒㄧˋ ㄑㄧㄡˊ)
to be imprisoned: 他因何罪繫囚? For what offense was he imprisoned?
繫辭(ㄒㄧˋ ㄘˊ)
① the title of a section of the *Book of Changes* ② a copula (in grammar and logic)
繫獄(ㄒㄧˋ ㄩˋ)
to imprison; to be imprisoned

【繫】 4452
2. ㄐㄧˋ jih jì
to bind; to tie; to hang up
繫鞋帶兒(ㄐㄧˋ ㄒㄧㄝˊ ㄉㄚˋㄦ)
to tie a shoelace

【繭】 4453
ㄐㄧㄢˇ jean jiǎn
1. cocoons; a chrysalis
2. a callus
繭眉(ㄐㄧㄢˇ ㄇㄟˊ)
beautiful eyebrows
繭栗(ㄐㄧㄢˇ ㄌㄧˋ)
① a calf ② moral uprightness ③ the bulb of flowers ④ young bamboo shoots
繭紙(ㄐㄧㄢˇ ㄓˇ)
silk fabric used as paper for drawing or writing
繭綢(ㄐㄧㄢˇ ㄔㄡˊ)
pongee
繭絲(ㄐㄧㄢˇ ㄙ)
taxes; levies
繭衣(ㄐㄧㄢˇ ㄧ)
rough outside of a cocoon

【繰】 4454
1. ㄗㄠˇ tzao zǎo
a kind of silk

【繰】 4454
2. ㄙㄠ sau sāo
to draw silk from cocoons
參看「繅」

十四畫

【辮】 4455
ㄅㄧㄢˋ biann biàn
a braid of hair; a pigtail; a queue
辮髮(ㄅㄧㄢˋ ㄈㄚˇ)
plaited hair
辮子(ㄅㄧㄢˋ ·ㄗ)
a pigtail; a queue; a braid; a plait: 她把她的頭髮梳成辮子。She wears her hair in braids.

【纂】 4456
ㄗㄨㄢˇ tzoan zuǎn
1. a kind of red cloth
2. to compile; to collect
纂輯(ㄗㄨㄢˇ ㄐㄧˊ)
to compile
纂修(ㄗㄨㄢˇ ㄒㄧㄡ)
to compile; to edit

【繻】 4457
ㄒㄩ shiu xū
1. fine gauze
2. pieces of silk used as credentials

【繽】 4458
ㄅㄧㄣ bin bīn

1. abundant; plentiful; thriving
2. disorderly; confused

繽繙(ㄅㄧㄣ ㄈㄢ)
(said of flags) fluttering: 旗幟繽繙。Flags are fluttering.

繽紛(ㄅㄧㄣ ㄈㄣ)
① flourishing; thriving; abundant ② disorderly; chaotic

繽亂(ㄅㄧㄣ ㄌㄨㄢˋ)
chaotic; disorderly; confused

【繼】 4459 ㄐㄧˋ jih jì

1. to continue; to carry on: 本故事下週繼續。The story will be continued next week.
2. then; afterwards: 她初感頭暈，繼而昏倒。She felt dizzy and then fainted.
3. to follow; to inherit; to succeed to

繼配(ㄐㄧˋ ㄆㄟˋ)
a new wife (in place of the deceased)

繼母(ㄐㄧˋ ㄇㄨˇ)
a stepmother

繼父(ㄐㄧˋ ㄈㄨˋ)
a stepfather: 他告訴他繼父實情。He told his stepfather the truth.

繼電器(ㄐㄧˋ ㄉㄧㄢˋ ㄑㄧˋ)
a relay (for electricity)亦作「電驛」

繼起(ㄐㄧˋ ㄑㄧˇ)
to rise as a successor

繼續(ㄐㄧˋ ㄒㄩˋ)
to continue; to last; to go on: 聚會繼續到午夜。The party went on till midnight.

繼續不斷(ㄐㄧˋ ㄒㄩˋ ㄅㄨˊ ㄉㄨㄢˋ)
without a break

繼續犯(ㄐㄧˋ ㄒㄩˋ ㄈㄢˋ)
a continued offense

繼續進行(ㄐㄧˋ ㄒㄩˋ ㄐㄧㄣˋ ㄒㄧㄥˊ)
to continue the process; to maintain the effort; to go on; to keep going

繼志(ㄐㄧˋ ㄓˋ)
to continue the pursuit of the deceased

繼踵(ㄐㄧˋ ㄓㄨㄥˇ)
to follow; to shadow

繼承(ㄐㄧˋ ㄔㄥˊ)
to inherit; to succeed to

繼承權(ㄐㄧˋ ㄔㄥˊ ㄑㄩㄢˊ)
the right of succession; the right of inheritance

繼承人(ㄐㄧˋ ㄔㄥˊ ㄖㄣˊ)
a successor; an heir

繼承財產(ㄐㄧˋ ㄔㄥˊ ㄘㄞˊ ㄔㄢˇ)
to inherit property

繼承遺志(ㄐㄧˋ ㄔㄥˊ ㄧˊ ㄓˋ)
to carry on the unfinished lifework of the deceased

繼室(ㄐㄧˋ ㄕˋ)
a new wife (in place of the deceased)

繼任(ㄐㄧˋ ㄖㄣˋ)
to succeed to an office

繼子(ㄐㄧˋ ㄗˇ)
an adopted heir: 他是我的繼子。He is my adopted heir.

繼則(ㄐㄧˋ ㄗㄜˊ)or 繼而(ㄐㄧˋ ㄦˊ)
and then; next: 他洗個澡，繼而刷牙。He had a bath and then brushed his teeth.

繼武(ㄐㄧˋ ㄨˇ)
to carry on the unfinished task of the deceased

繼位(ㄐㄧˋ ㄨㄟˋ)
to succeed to the throne

繼往開來(ㄐㄧˋ ㄨㄤˇ ㄎㄞ ㄌㄞˊ)
to carry on the heritage so as to pave the way for future generations; to carry forward the past and forge ahead into the future

【繾】 4460 ㄑㄧㄢˇ chean qiǎn

entangled

繾綣(ㄑㄧㄢˇ ㄑㄩㄢˇ)
① entangled; inextricable; inseparable ②(figuratively) a parasite ③ to make tender love

【纁】 4461 ㄒㄩㄣ shiun xūn

light red

纁裳(ㄒㄩㄣ ㄔㄤˊ)
light red dress

十五畫

【纈】 4462 ㄒㄧㄝˊ shye xié

1. to tie a knot
2. silk with patterns or designs woven into it

【纊】 4463 ㄎㄨㄤˋ kuanq kuàng

cotton

【續】 4464 ㄒㄩˋ shiuh xù

1. to continue; to extend; to renew
2. to add; to supply more

續版(ㄒㄩˋ ㄅㄢˇ)
a reprint (of a book)

續篇(ㄒㄩˋ ㄆㄧㄢ)
a sequel; a continuation of a previous book: 你看了那本小說的續篇嗎? Have you read the sequel of that novel?

續聘(ㄒㄩˋ ㄆㄧㄣˋ)
to continue to employ (a person); to renew the contract of employment with (an employee)

續鳧(ㄒㄩˋ ㄈㄨˊ)
(literally) to try to make the legs of a duck longer —to make an absurd and futile effort

續貂(ㄒㄩˋ ㄉㄧㄠ)
① to appoint incompetent persons to important posts ② (a self-depreciatory expression) to continue another's unfinished job with poor skill

續航力(ㄒㄩˋ ㄏㄤˊ ㄌㄧˋ)
(said of an airplane or ship) the duration to stay in the air or on the sea without refueling

續集(ㄒㄩˋ ㄐㄧˊ)
the sequel (of a long movie, etc.)

續假(ㄒㄩˋ ㄐㄧㄚˋ)
to extend a leave of absence

續借(ㄒㄩˋ ㄐㄧㄝˋ)
to renew (a library book)

續絃(ㄒㄩˋ ㄒㄧㄢˊ)or 續娶(ㄒㄩˋ ㄑㄩˇ)
(said of a man) to remarry

續約(ㄒㄩˋ ㄩㄝ)
to renew a contract: 我們必須續約。We must renew our contract.

【纏】 4465 ㄔㄢˊ charn chán

1. to wind round; to twine round; to bind; to wrap; to tangle
2. to bother persistently
3. to pester; to worry: 他纏著向我要錢。He pestered me for money.
4. to deal with: 這小孩眞難纏。This child is really hard to deal with.

纏門纏戶(ㄔㄢˊ ㄇㄣˊ ㄔㄢˊ ㄏㄨˋ)
to be a persistent bother at

〔糸部〕

the door
纏綿(ㄔㄢ ㄇㄧㄢˊ)
tenderly attached to each other; affectionate; inseparable
纏綿病榻(ㄔㄢˊ ㄇㄧㄢˊ ㄅㄧㄥˋ ㄊㄚˋ)
to be bedridden with a lingering illness
纏綿悱惻(ㄔㄢˊ ㄇㄧㄢˊ ㄈㄟˇ ㄘㄜˋ)
(said of a story or narrative) very pathetic; extremely sad; exceedingly sentimental
纏縛(ㄔㄢˊ ㄈㄨˋ)
to bind; to wrap: 他們將他的手足纏縛。They bound him hand and foot.
纏頭(ㄔㄢˊ ㄊㄡˊ)
①a turban ②money and gifts given to a prostitute
纏頭回子(ㄔㄢˊ ㄊㄡˊ ㄏㄨㄟˊ ·ㄗ)
a turbaned Islamic tribe living in Kansu and Sinkiang
纏來纏去(ㄔㄢˊ ㄌㄞˊ ㄔㄢˊ ㄑㄩˋ)
to be a persistent bother
纏裹(ㄔㄢˊ ㄍㄨㄛˇ)
to wrap up; to cover tightly
纏脚(ㄔㄢˊ ㄐㄧㄠˇ)or 纏足(ㄔㄢˊ ㄗㄨˊ)
to bind the feet (as was done by women in former times)
纏住(ㄔㄢˊ ㄓㄨˋ)
entangled; entwined; to wrap tightly; to wind around: 鬆弛的繩子容易纏住。Loose string is easily entangled.
纏身(ㄔㄢˊ ㄕㄣ)
to be delayed; to be held up by or burdened with something
纏擾(ㄔㄢˊ ㄖㄠˇ)
to bother persistently
纏繞(ㄔㄢˊ ㄖㄠˋ)
①to wind round; to twine around: 藤蔓纏繞樹身。The vine twines around the tree. ②to bother persistently
纏繞莖(ㄔㄢˊ ㄖㄠˋ ㄐㄧㄥ)
a twining stem
纏訟(ㄔㄢˊ ㄙㄨㄥˋ)
to be involved in a tangled lawsuit

【纍】 4466
ㄌㄟˊ lei léi
1. strung together
2. a heavy rope
3. to tie; to bind; to twine around; to wind round
纍纍(ㄌㄟˊ ㄌㄟˊ)
①strung together ②tired; exhausted ③dejected; despondent; frustrated; disappointed
纍囚(ㄌㄟˊ ㄑㄧㄡˊ)
a prisoner
纍紲(ㄌㄟˊ ㄒㄧㄝˋ)
rope for tying up a prisoner 亦作「縲絏」
纍臣(ㄌㄟˊ ㄔㄣˊ)
a vassal or subject in captivity

【纇】 4467
ㄌㄟˋ ley lèi
1. a knot on a thread
2. a flaw

十六畫

【纑】 4468
ㄌㄨˊ lu lú
1. thread
2. to soften hemp, etc., by boiling

十七畫

【纔】 4469
ㄘㄞˊ tsair cái
1. just now; just then
2. only: 這個小女孩纔六歲。The little girl is only six.
3. not until; for the first time; then and only then
纔明白(ㄘㄞˊ ㄇㄧㄥˊ ·ㄅㄞ)or 纔知道(ㄘㄞˊ ㄓ ·ㄉㄠ)
to understand for the first time; not to have understood until then
纔到(ㄘㄞˊ ㄉㄠˋ)
①just arrived: 我早上纔到台北。I just arrived at Taipei in the morning. ②to have only reached (after so much time and effort)
纔來(ㄘㄞˊ ㄌㄞˊ)
to have just come; to have just arrived: 我們纔來。We have just arrived.
纔好(ㄘㄞˊ ㄏㄠˇ)
just fine
纔是(ㄘㄞˊ ㄕˋ)
then and only then is (he, it, etc.)...

【纓】 4470
ㄧㄥ ing yīng
1. chin straps for holding a hat
2. a tassel
3. leaves of turnips
纓帽(ㄧㄥ ㄇㄠˋ)
a ceremonial hat with red tassels worn during the Ching Dynasty
纓絡(ㄧㄥ ㄌㄨㄛˋ)
ornamental fringes on a garment
纓冠(ㄧㄥ ㄍㄨㄢ)
to put on a hat hastily (with the chin strap on the head)

【纕】 4471
1. ㄒㄧㄤ shiang xiāng
to wear

【纕】 4471
2. ㄖㄤˊ rang ráng
same as 攘—to roll up one's sleeve to show the arm

【纖】 4472
ㄒㄧㄢ shian xiān
tiny; minute; fine; delicate; slender
纖毛(ㄒㄧㄢ ㄇㄠˊ)
cilia
纖離(ㄒㄧㄢ ㄌㄧˊ)
a species of horse produced in an ancient state in northern China
纖毫(ㄒㄧㄢ ㄏㄠˊ)
tiny; very little; minute; every small detail
纖介(ㄒㄧㄢ ㄐㄧㄝˋ)
minute; very small
纖鉅(ㄒㄧㄢ ㄐㄩˋ)
big and small; hefty and minute
纖巧(ㄒㄧㄢ ㄑㄧㄠˇ)
fine; delicately formed; squeamishly refined
纖悉(ㄒㄧㄢ ㄒㄧ)
to know thoroughly; to be familiar with every detail of
纖細(ㄒㄧㄢ ㄒㄧˋ)or 纖小(ㄒㄧㄢ ㄒㄧㄠˇ)
fine; tiny; minute
纖屑(ㄒㄧㄢ ㄒㄧㄝˋ)
piddling; trivial; frothy (affairs)
纖纖(ㄒㄧㄢ ㄒㄧㄢ)
①delicate; fine; minute ②sharp
纖指(ㄒㄧㄢ ㄓˇ)
slender or delicate fingers (of a woman)
纖手(ㄒㄧㄢ ㄕㄡˇ)

delicate hands (of a woman)
纖瘦(ㄒㄧㄢ ㄕㄡˋ)
delicate and slender: 她是個身材纖瘦的女孩。She is a delicate and slender girl.
纖柔(ㄒㄧㄢ ㄖㄡˊ)
(said of hands) delicate and soft
纖人(ㄒㄧㄢ ㄖㄣˊ)
a fragile person
纖弱(ㄒㄧㄢ ㄖㄨㄛˋ)
fragile; delicate
纖腰(ㄒㄧㄢ ㄧㄠ)
a slender waist (of a woman)
纖妍(ㄒㄧㄢ ㄧㄢˊ)
slim and pretty
纖微(ㄒㄧㄢ ㄨㄟˊ)
very small; tiny; microscopic; infinitesimal
纖維(ㄒㄧㄢ ㄨㄟˊ)
fiber
纖維工業(ㄒㄧㄢ ㄨㄟˊ ㄍㄨㄥ ㄧㄝˋ)
the textile industry
纖維素(ㄒㄧㄢ ㄨㄟˊ ㄙㄨˋ)
cellulose
纖玉(ㄒㄧㄢ ㄩˋ)
delicate jade—a woman's delicate hands

十八畫

【纛】 4473
ㄉㄠˋ daw dào
(又讀 ㄉㄨˊ dwu dú)
a banner; a streamer

十九畫

【纘】 4474
ㄗㄨㄢˇ tzoan zuǎn
to continue; to carry on; to keep up
纘緒(ㄗㄨㄢˇ ㄒㄩˋ)
to continue (especially great enterprises)

二十一畫

【纜】 4475
ㄌㄢˇ laan lǎn
(又讀 ㄌㄢˋ lann làn)
a hawser; a cable
纜車(ㄌㄢˇ ㄔㄜ)
a cable car
纜車道(ㄌㄢˇ ㄔㄜ ㄉㄠˋ)
a cable railroad
纜繩(ㄌㄢˇ ㄕㄥˊ)
cordage; a thick rope

缶部
ㄈㄡˇ foou fǒu

【缶】 4476
ㄈㄡˇ foou fǒu
a crock with a narrow opening

三畫

【缸】 4477
ㄍㄤ gang gāng
a cistern; a crock

四畫

【缺】 4478
ㄑㄩㄝ chiue quē
1. deficient; lacking; short; incomplete; defective
2. a vacancy; an opening
缺筆(ㄑㄩㄝ ㄅㄧˇ)
a stroke or strokes missing from a written character
缺乏(ㄑㄩㄝ ㄈㄚˊ)
to lack; to be without; to be deficient in; to be short of
缺乏人才(ㄑㄩㄝ ㄈㄚˊ ㄖㄣˊ ㄘㄞˊ)
to be short of talents
缺德(ㄑㄩㄝ ㄉㄜˊ)
deficient in the sense of morality; to have no regard for other members of society; mischievous; wicked: 那人這樣做可眞缺德。It's wicked of the fellow to act like that.
缺德鬼(ㄑㄩㄝ ㄉㄜˊ ㄍㄨㄟˇ)
a public nuisance; a mean fellow: 他是缺德鬼。He is a mean fellow.
缺點(ㄑㄩㄝ ㄉㄧㄢˇ)
a defect; a shortcoming; a flaw
缺奶(ㄑㄩㄝ ㄋㄞˇ)
to have dry breasts
缺漏(ㄑㄩㄝ ㄌㄡˋ)
gaps and omissions
缺糧(ㄑㄩㄝ ㄌㄧㄤˊ)
to lack food supplies
缺課(ㄑㄩㄝ ㄎㄜˋ)
to be absent from class
缺刻葉(ㄑㄩㄝ ㄎㄜˋ ㄧㄝˋ)
(botany) dentate leaf; incised leaf
缺口(ㄑㄩㄝ ㄎㄡˇ)
① an indentation; an indenture ② a breach; an opening ③ inadequately fed
缺口兒(ㄑㄩㄝ ㄎㄡˇㄦ) or 缺齒兒(ㄑㄩㄝ ㄔˇㄦ)
an indentation
缺憾(ㄑㄩㄝ ㄏㄢˋ)
a flaw; a shortcoming; a defect
缺貨(ㄑㄩㄝ ㄏㄨㄛˋ)
(merchandise) to run out of stock: 我們缺貨。We've run out of stock.
缺角(ㄑㄩㄝ ㄐㄧㄠˇ)
a knocked-off corner
缺欠(ㄑㄩㄝ ㄑㄧㄢˋ)
a defect; a shortcoming
缺席(ㄑㄩㄝ ㄒㄧˊ)
to be absent (from a meeting, etc.): 他今天缺席。He is absent from the meeting today.
缺陷(ㄑㄩㄝ ㄒㄧㄢˋ)
a defect; a shortcoming; a handicap; inadequacy
缺陷美(ㄑㄩㄝ ㄒㄧㄢˋ ㄇㄟˇ)
attraction of some special characteristic or imperfection
缺吃缺穿(ㄑㄩㄝ ㄔ ㄑㄩㄝ ㄔㄨㄢ)
to have insufficient food and clothing
缺穿缺戴(ㄑㄩㄝ ㄔㄨㄢ ㄑㄩㄝ ㄉㄞˋ)
to have insufficient clothing
缺脣(ㄑㄩㄝ ㄔㄨㄣˊ)
a harelip; a cleft lip
缺食(ㄑㄩㄝ ㄕˊ)
insufficiently fed
缺少(ㄑㄩㄝ ㄕㄠˇ)
to be short of; to lack; to be deficient in: 他缺少勇氣。He is deficient in courage.
缺水(ㄑㄩㄝ ㄕㄨㄟˇ)
inadequately watered or irrigated; to run out of water supply: 我們缺水。We've run out of water supply.
缺字(ㄑㄩㄝ ㄗˋ)
words or characters inadvertently left out

缺額(ㄑㄩㄝ ㄜˊ)
vacancies waiting to be filled
缺疑(ㄑㄩㄝ ㄧˊ)
a dubious point
缺氧(ㄑㄩㄝ ㄧㄤˇ)
(sports physiology) oxygen deficit

八畫

【缾】4479 ㄆㄧㄥˊ pyng píng
a bottle; a pitcher, etc. 亦作「瓶」

十畫

【罃】4480 ㄧㄥ ing yīng
a long-necked bottle

十一畫

【罄】4481 ㄑㄧㄥˋ chinq qìng
to exhaust; to use up; to empty
罄筆難書(ㄑㄧㄥˋ ㄅㄧˇ ㄋㄢˊ ㄕㄨ)
(said of atrocities or misdeeds) too numerous to be cited
罄匱(ㄑㄧㄥˋ ㄎㄨㄟˋ)
used up; exhausted
罄竭(ㄑㄧㄥˋ ㄐㄧㄝˊ)
used up; exhausted
罄盡(ㄑㄧㄥˋ ㄐㄧㄣˋ)
to use up; to exhaust: 我的糖已經罄盡。I have used up my sugar.
罄其所有(ㄑㄧㄥˋ ㄑㄧˊ ㄙㄨㄛˇ ㄧㄡˇ)
to use up all that is available
罄竹難書(ㄑㄧㄥˋ ㄓㄨˊ ㄋㄢˊ ㄕㄨ)
(said usually of one's crimes) too numerous to be recorded fully even if all the available bamboos are used up

【罅】4482 ㄒㄧㄚˋ shiah xià
a crack; a rift; cleft; a fissure; a flaw
罅縫(兒)(ㄒㄧㄚˋ ㄈㄥˋ(ㄦ))
a fissure; cleft; a crack
罅漏(ㄒㄧㄚˋ ㄌㄡˋ)
a flaw; a fault; a short-coming; a defect; a loophole
罅隙(ㄒㄧㄚˋ ㄒㄧˋ)
a crack; a rift; cleft; a fissure; a flaw

十二畫

【罇】4483 ㄗㄨㄣ tzuen zūn
same as 尊、樽—a goblet, a bottle

【罈】4484 ㄊㄢˊ tarn tán
same as 罎—an earthenware jar or jug
罈子(ㄊㄢˊ ˙ㄗ)
an earthen jar

十三畫

【罋】4485 ㄨㄥˋ wenq wèng
same as 甕—an earthen jar

十四畫

【罌】4486 ㄧㄥ ing yīng
a jar with a small mouth
罌粟(ㄧㄥ ㄙㄨˋ)or 罌子粟(ㄧㄥ ㄗˇ ㄙㄨˋ)
an opium poppy

十五畫

【罍】4487 ㄌㄟˊ lei léi
an earthenware wine jar

十六畫

【罎】4488 ㄊㄢˊ tarn tán
an earthenware jar or jug for wine

【罏】4489 ㄌㄨˊ lu lú
an earthen stand for wine jars

十八畫

【罐】4490 ㄍㄨㄢˋ guann guàn
a vessel; a container; a jar; a jug; a can
罐頭(ㄍㄨㄢˋ ˙ㄊㄡ)
canned goods
罐頭工廠(ㄍㄨㄢˋ ˙ㄊㄡ ㄍㄨㄥ ㄔㄤˇ)
a cannery
罐頭食品(ㄍㄨㄢˋ ˙ㄊㄡ ㄕˊ ㄆㄧㄣˇ)
canned food
罐裝(ㄍㄨㄢˋ ㄓㄨㄤ)
canned
罐子(ㄍㄨㄢˋ ˙ㄗ)or 罐兒(ㄍㄨㄚˋㄦ)
a can; a jar; a jug

网部 ㄨㄤˇ woang wǎng

三畫

【罔】4491 ㄨㄤˇ woang wǎng
1. to libel; to slander; to deceive
2. not straight; crooked
3. not
罔不(ㄨㄤˇ ㄅㄨˋ)
there are none that do not...
罔兩(ㄨㄤˇ ㄌㄧㄤˇ)
① spirits, monsters of the mountain rivers亦作「魍魎」,「蝄蜽」,「罔閬」 ②the penumbra
罔顧人道(ㄨㄤˇ ㄍㄨˋ ㄖㄣˊ ㄉㄠˋ)
inhuman; against humanity
罔極(ㄨㄤˇ ㄐㄧˊ)
① infinite ② to transgress; to go to the utmost extent of what is not right
罔效(ㄨㄤˇ ㄒㄧㄠˋ)
ineffective; to (or of) no avail; in vain
罔上(ㄨㄤˇ ㄕㄤˋ)
to deceive the emperor

【罕】4492 ㄏㄢˇ haan hǎn
rare; few; seldom
罕譬而喻(ㄏㄢˇ ㄆㄧˋ ㄦˊ ㄩˋ)
to explain clearly with few illustrations; to draw a striking but easily understood analogy
罕覯(ㄏㄢˇ ㄍㄡˋ)or 罕見(ㄏㄢˇ ㄐㄧㄢˋ)
rarely found; rare: 這些郵票罕見。These stamps are rare.
罕事(ㄏㄢˇ ㄕˋ)
a rare thing or event: 這眞是罕事。This is really a rare

event.

罕有(ㄏㄢˇ ㄧㄡˇ)
rare: 古騰堡版之聖經爲罕有之書。The Gutenberg Bible is a rare book.

罕有其匹(ㄏㄢˇ ㄧㄡˇ ㄑㄧˊ ㄆㄧˇ)
rarely equaled

罕物(ㄏㄢˇ ㄨˋ)
a curiosity; a rare thing: 他買了許多罕物。He bought a lot of curiosities.

罕聞(ㄏㄢˇ ㄨㄣˊ)
seldom heard of

罕用(ㄏㄢˇ ㄩㄥˋ)
seldom used: 他罕用字典。He seldom used the dictionary.

四畫

【罘】 4493 ㄈㄨˊ fwu fú (又讀 ㄈㄡˊ four fóu)
a net for catching rabbits or hares

五畫

【罡】 4494 ㄍㄤ gang gāng
the Taoist name of the Dipper

罡風(ㄍㄤ ㄈㄥ)
(Taoism) winds blowing over high places

【罟】 4495 ㄍㄨˇ guu gǔ
a net

【罝】 4496 ㄐㄩ jiu jū
a net for catching rabbits or hares

六畫

【罣】 4497 ㄍㄨㄚˋ guah guà
1. hindrance; obstruction
2. a sieve
3. to be concerned; to be worried

罣念(ㄍㄨㄚˋ ㄋㄧㄢˋ)
to be concerned; to be worried: 我罣念你的健康。I am concerned about your health.

罣罳(ㄍㄨㄚˋ ㄙ)
a sieve

罣礙(ㄍㄨㄚˋ ㄞˋ)
hindrance; obstruction; to block; to hinder

罣誤(ㄍㄨㄚˋ ㄨˋ)
to be remiss; to be at fault

八畫

【罩】 4498 ㄓㄠˋ jaw zhào
1. a bamboo basket for catching fish
2. to coop; to cover; to wrap
3. a cover; a shade
4. a mantle; a cloak

罩不住(ㄓㄠˋ ˙ㄅㄨ ㄓㄨˋ)
(informal) unable to control a situation

罩袍(ㄓㄠˋ ㄆㄠˊ)
a dust-robe; a dust-gown; an overall

罩子(ㄓㄠˋ ˙ㄗ) or 罩兒(ㄓㄠˋㄦ)
a cover; a shade

【罪】 4499 ㄗㄨㄟˋ tzuey zuì
1. sin; crime; fault; vice; evil; guilt
2. suffering; pain

罪不容誅(ㄗㄨㄟˋ ˙ㄅㄨ ㄖㄨㄥˊ ㄓㄨ)
The crime is so serious that no punishment is adequate for it. 或 to deserve more than death

罪莫大焉(ㄗㄨㄟˋ ㄇㄛˋ ㄉㄚˋ ㄧㄢ)
The crime or sin is too serious.

罪名(ㄗㄨㄟˋ ㄇㄧㄥˊ)
a charge (brought against a person)

罪犯(ㄗㄨㄟˋ ㄈㄢˋ)
a criminal; an offender

罪大惡極(ㄗㄨㄟˋ ㄉㄚˋ ㄜˋ ㄐㄧˊ)
a heinous crime; a capital offense; most vicious

罪孽(ㄗㄨㄟˋ ㄋㄧㄝˋ)
sin: 戰爭是違反人道的罪孽。War is a sin against humanity.

罪孽深重(ㄗㄨㄟˋ ㄋㄧㄝˋ ㄕㄣ ㄓㄨㄥˋ)
The sin is great.

罪戾(ㄗㄨㄟˋ ㄌㄧˋ)
crime; vice; evil

罪該萬死(ㄗㄨㄟˋ ㄍㄞ ㄨㄢˋ ㄙˇ)
The crime deserves death for ten thousand times.

罪過(ㄗㄨㄟˋ ㄍㄨㄛˋ)
fault; sin

罪魁(ㄗㄨㄟˋ ㄎㄨㄟˊ) or 罪魁禍首(ㄗㄨㄟˋ ㄎㄨㄟˊ ㄏㄨㄛˋ ㄕㄡˇ)
a chief offender; a ringleader

罪愆(ㄗㄨㄟˋ ㄑㄧㄢ)
wrongdoing; crime; vice; evil

罪行(ㄗㄨㄟˋ ㄒㄧㄥˊ)
criminal acts; atrocities; offenses

罪刑(ㄗㄨㄟˋ ㄒㄧㄥˊ)
punishment; penalty

罪障(ㄗㄨㄟˋ ㄓㄤˋ)
(Buddhism) sin

罪證(ㄗㄨㄟˋ ㄓㄥˋ)
proof of a crime; evidence of one's guilt

罪狀(ㄗㄨㄟˋ ㄓㄨㄤˋ)
the nature of an offense or crime; a charge (brought against a person)

罪上加罪(ㄗㄨㄟˋ ㄕㄤˋ ㄐㄧㄚ ㄗㄨㄟˋ)
to add an offense on top of another

罪人(ㄗㄨㄟˋ ㄖㄣˊ)
①a criminal; a sinner ②to blame others

罪惡(ㄗㄨㄟˋ ㄜˋ)
sin; crime; vice; evil; guilt

罪惡滔天(ㄗㄨㄟˋ ㄜˋ ㄊㄠ ㄊㄧㄢ)
The list of crimes committed is long enough to reach the heavens.

罪案(ㄗㄨㄟˋ ㄢˋ)
a criminal case: 他把罪案提交法庭。He took the criminal case to court.

罪有應得(ㄗㄨㄟˋ ㄧㄡˇ ㄧㄥ ㄉㄜˊ)
The punishment is well deserved.

罪因(ㄗㄨㄟˋ ㄧㄣ)
the cause of a crime

【置】 4500 ㄓˋ jyh zhì
1. to put; to place
2. to establish; to set
3. to procure; to purchase

置備(ㄓˋ ㄅㄟˋ)
to have (a thing) within convenient reach

置辦(ㄓˋ ㄅㄢˋ)
to procure; to secure

置辯(ㄓˋ ㄅㄧㄢˋ) or 置喙(ㄓˋ ㄏㄨㄟˋ)
to rebut; to refute; to defend (with words); to explain

置酒(ㄓˋ ㄐㄧㄡˇ)
to throw a banquet; to give a feast

置信(ㄓˋ ㄒㄧㄣˋ)

to believe: 此事令人難以置信。It is hard to believe.或 It is difficult to believe.

置之不理(ㄓˋ ㄓ ㄅㄨˋ ㄌㄧˇ)
to disregard it totally; to ignore

置之度外(ㄓˋ ㄓ ㄉㄨˋ ㄨㄞˋ)
to give no thought to; without regard to; to care nothing about; regardless of

置之腦後(ㄓˋ ㄓ ㄋㄠˇ ㄏㄡˋ)
to disregard it; to forget it

置之死地而後生(ㄓˋ ㄓ ㄙˇ ㄉㄧˋ ㄦˊ ㄏㄡˋ ㄕㄥ)
(military strategy) to deploy troops in such a way as to leave no room for a maneuver or a route for escape so that the soldiers will fight for their dear lives out of desperation and eventually win the battle

置產(ㄓˋ ㄔㄢˇ)
to buy an estate: 他在鄉下置產。He bought an estate in the country.

置身度外(ㄓˋ ㄕㄣ ㄉㄨˋ ㄨㄞˋ)
to keep oneself from getting involved; to be indifferent

置身事外(ㄓˋ ㄕㄣ ㄕˋ ㄨㄞˋ)
to stay away from an affair; to keep out of it; to remain aloof: 你怎能置身事外呢? How could you keep yourself out of it?

置若罔聞(ㄓˋ ㄖㄨㄛˋ ㄨㄤˇ ㄨㄣˊ)
to turn a deaf ear to; to disregard completely; to pay no heed to

置辭(ㄓˋ ㄘˊ)
a choice of words; to find words to say

置疑(ㄓˋ ㄧˊ)
doubt: 此案不容置疑。This case allows of no doubt.

九畫

【罰】 4501 ㄈㄚˊ far fá
to punish; to penalize; to fine: 他處事賞罰分明。He is fair in meting out rewards and punishments.

罰立(ㄈㄚˊ ㄌㄧˋ)or 罰站(ㄈㄚˊ ㄓㄢˋ)
to make a person stand as punishment

罰跪(ㄈㄚˊ ㄍㄨㄟˋ)
to keep a person kneeling as punishment

罰款(ㄈㄚˊ ㄎㄨㄢˇ)
a fine; to fine

罰鍰(ㄈㄚˊ ㄏㄨㄢˊ)
a fine

罰酒(ㄈㄚˊ ㄐㄧㄡˇ)
to impose a drinking penalty; the wine to be drunk as a penalty

罰金(ㄈㄚˊ ㄐㄧㄣ)
to impose a fine; a fine

罰球(ㄈㄚˊ ㄑㄧㄡˊ)
(basketball) a penalty shot; (football) a penalty kick

罰則(ㄈㄚˊ ㄗㄜˊ)
penal regulations; punitive provisions

【署】 4502 1. ㄕㄨˇ shuu shǔ
a public office

【署】 4502 2. ㄕㄨˋ shuh shù
1. to arrange
2. to write down; to put down
3. to be a deputy

署辦(ㄕㄨˋ ㄅㄢˋ)
to act as a deputy

署名(ㄕㄨˋ ㄇㄧㄥˊ)
to sign one's name: 所有學生都在海報上署了名。The poster was jointly signed by all the students.

署理(ㄕㄨˋ ㄌㄧˇ)
to administer in an acting capacity

署款(ㄕㄨˋ ㄎㄨㄢˇ)
to sign one's name; to put down one's signature

署簽(ㄕㄨˋ ㄑㄧㄢ)
to inscribe a title-label on a book

署事(ㄕㄨˋ ㄕˋ)
① to deal with public affairs
② public affairs

署字(ㄕㄨˋ ㄗˋ)
to sign on a document: 他忘了署字。He's forgotten to sign on a document.

【罳】 4503 ㄙ sy sī
a screen with meshes or holes

十畫

【罵】 4504 ㄇㄚˋ mah mà
to call names; to swear; to curse; to revile

罵不回口(ㄇㄚˋ ˙ㄅㄨ ㄏㄨㄟˊ ㄎㄡˇ)
to remain silent when verbally abused

罵不絕口(ㄇㄚˋ ˙ㄅㄨ ㄐㄩㄝˊ ㄎㄡˇ)
to curse unceasingly

罵大街(ㄇㄚˋ ㄉㄚˋ ㄐㄧㄝ)or 罵街(ㄇㄚˋ ㄐㄧㄝ)
to curse without naming names

罵題(ㄇㄚˋ ㄊㄧˊ)
①(said of a piece of writing) contents disagreeing with the topic or title ② acting against what one preaches ③ behavior not matching with one's social standing

罵人(ㄇㄚˋ ㄖㄣˊ)
to call names; to scold

罵座(ㄇㄚˋ ㄗㄨㄛˋ)
to curse fellow guests

【罷】 4505 1. ㄅㄚˋ bah bà
to cease; to stop; to finish; to be done with

罷!罷!(ㄅㄚˋ ㄅㄚˋ)
an interjection of exasperating disappointment

罷兵(ㄅㄚˋ ㄅㄧㄥ)
to suspend hostilities

罷免(ㄅㄚˋ ㄇㄧㄢˇ)
to recall (officials by the people)

罷免權(ㄅㄚˋ ㄇㄧㄢˇ ㄑㄩㄢˊ)
the right of recall; the right of removing a public official from office by a vote of the people, specified in the *Three Principles of the People*

罷了(ㄅㄚˋ ˙ㄌㄜ)
①(as a sentence-final phrase) merely; only; that's all ② That is enough. 或 Let's have no more of it. 或 Be done with it.

罷論(ㄅㄚˋ ㄌㄨㄣˋ)
①(said of a proposal) shelved; cancelled: 此案已作罷論。The case has already been shelved. ② an abandoned idea

罷官(ㄅㄚˋ ㄍㄨㄢ)

to remove from office

罷工(ㄅㄚˋ ㄍㄨㄥ)
(said of workers) to stage a strike; to strike; a strike

罷課(ㄅㄚˋ ㄎㄜˋ)
to boycott classes

罷教(ㄅㄚˋ ㄐㄧㄠˋ)
(said of teachers) to stage a strike; to strike; a teacher strike

罷休(ㄅㄚˋ ㄒㄧㄡ)
to cease; to stop: 我不達目的，決不罷休。I'll not stop until I reach my goal.

罷相(ㄅㄚˋ ㄒㄧㄤˋ)
the ouster of a prime minister

罷職(ㄅㄚˋ ㄓˊ)
to remove from office

罷斥(ㄅㄚˋ ㄔˋ)
to reject (an official) by removing him from office

罷黜(ㄅㄚˋ ㄔㄨˋ)
to remove from office; to fire: 他因行賄而被罷黜。He was fired for bribery.

罷市(ㄅㄚˋ ㄕˋ)
to close shops (in protest)

罷手(ㄅㄚˋ ㄕㄡˇ)
to discontinue an action; to stop; to pause; to give up

罷業(ㄅㄚˋ ㄧㄝˋ)
(said of shopkeepers, workers, etc.) to go on strike; to strike

【罷】 4505
2. ˙ㄅㄚ ·ba ba
same as 吧—a sentence-final particle

【罷】 4505
3. ㄆㄧˊ pyi pí
tired; exhausted; weary

罷弊(ㄆㄧˊ ㄅㄧˋ)
exhausted; weary

十一畫

【罹】 4506
ㄌㄧˊ li lí
1. sorrow; grief
2. to meet (disaster, misfortune, etc.); to be stricken by

罹病(ㄌㄧˊ ㄅㄧㄥˋ)
to fall ill; to suffer from disease

罹難(ㄌㄧˊ ㄋㄢˋ)
to fall victim to a disaster

罹禍(ㄌㄧˊ ㄏㄨㄛˋ)
to meet disaster

罹災(ㄌㄧˊ ㄗㄞ)
to meet a disaster; to be stricken by a calamity

罹殃(ㄌㄧˊ ㄧㄤ)
to be victimized by a calamity; to meet a disaster: 他罹殃。He was victimized by a calamity.

十二畫

【罽】 4507
ㄐㄧˋ jih jì
1. a kind of woolen fabric
2. a fishing net

罽賓(ㄐㄧˋ ㄅㄧㄣ)
the ancient name of Cashmere

罽魚(ㄐㄧˋ ㄩˊ)
another name of *siniperca chuatsi* (鱖魚)

十四畫

【羆】 4508
ㄆㄧˊ pyi pí
a kind of bear (*Ursus arctos*)

羆虎(ㄆㄧˊ ㄏㄨˇ)
fierce animals

【羅】 4509
ㄌㄨㄛˊ luo luó
1. thin, light silk
2. a net; a snare
3. to arrange over a wide space
4. a Chinese family name

羅賓漢(ㄌㄨㄛˊ ㄅㄧㄣ ㄏㄢˋ)
Robin Hood

羅布(ㄌㄨㄛˊ ㄅㄨˋ)
to arrange or display over a wide space

羅布泊(ㄌㄨㄛˊ ㄅㄨˋ ㄅㄛˊ)
Lop Nor, a lake in Sinkiang

羅盤(ㄌㄨㄛˊ ㄆㄢˊ)
a compass

羅馬(ㄌㄨㄛˊ ㄇㄚˇ)
Rome: 條條大路通羅馬。All roads lead to Rome.

羅馬不是一天造成的(ㄌㄨㄛˊ ㄇㄚˇ ㄅㄨˊ ㄕˋ ㄧˋ ㄊㄧㄢ ㄗㄠˋ ㄔㄥˊ ˙ㄉㄜ)
Rome was not built in a day.

羅馬法(ㄌㄨㄛˊ ㄇㄚˇ ㄈㄚˇ)
Roman law

羅馬帝國(ㄌㄨㄛˊ ㄇㄚˇ ㄉㄧˋ ㄍㄨㄛˊ)
the Roman Empire

羅馬尼亞(ㄌㄨㄛˊ ㄇㄚˇ ㄋㄧˊ ㄧㄚˇ)
Romania

羅馬教會(ㄌㄨㄛˊ ㄇㄚˇ ㄐㄧㄠˋ ㄏㄨㄟˋ)
the Roman Catholic Church

羅馬教皇(ㄌㄨㄛˊ ㄇㄚˇ ㄐㄧㄠˋ ㄏㄨㄤˊ)
the Pope

羅馬數字(ㄌㄨㄛˊ ㄇㄚˇ ㄕㄨˋ ㄗˋ)
Roman numerals

羅馬人(ㄌㄨㄛˊ ㄇㄚˇ ㄖㄣˊ)
a Roman; the Romans

羅馬字(ㄌㄨㄛˊ ㄇㄚˇ ㄗˋ)
the Roman alphabet

羅曼蒂克(ㄌㄨㄛˊ ㄇㄢˋ ㄉㄧˋ ㄎㄜˋ)
romantic (a transliteration): 他過着羅曼蒂克的生活。He lived a romantic life.

羅曼諾夫(ㄌㄨㄛˊ ㄇㄢˋ ㄋㄨㄛˋ ㄈㄨ)
Romanov dynasty of Russia that ruled from 1613 to 1917

羅曼羅蘭(ㄌㄨㄛˊ ㄇㄢˋ ㄌㄨㄛˊ ㄌㄢˊ)
Romain Rolland, 1866-1944, French playwright and novelist

羅曼斯(ㄌㄨㄛˊ ㄇㄢˋ ㄙ) or 羅曼史(ㄌㄨㄛˊ ㄇㄢˋ ㄕˇ)
a romance; a love affair; a romantic story

羅密歐(ㄌㄨㄛˊ ㄇㄧˋ ㄡ)
Romeo

羅敷有夫(ㄌㄨㄛˊ ㄈㄨ ㄧㄡˇ ㄈㄨ)
(literally) Lady Lo Fu (a beautiful talented woman of the state of Chao (趙) during the Epoch of Warring States) was a married woman.—She is a married woman.

羅浮宮(ㄌㄨㄛˊ ㄈㄨˊ ㄍㄨㄥ)
Louvre, a national museum in Paris

羅德島(ㄌㄨㄛˊ ㄉㄜˊ ㄉㄠˇ)
the state of Rhode Island, U.S.A.

羅德西亞(ㄌㄨㄛˊ ㄉㄜˊ ㄒㄧ ㄧㄚˋ)
Rhodesia

羅蘭夫人(ㄌㄨㄛˊ ㄌㄢˊ ㄈㄨ ㄖㄣˊ)
Madame Roland — Marie Jeanne Roland de la Platière, 1754-1793

羅列(ㄌㄨㄛˊ ㄌㄧㄝˋ)
to arrange for display; to spread out

羅貫中(ㄌㄨㄛˊ ㄍㄨㄢˋ ㄓㄨㄥ)
Lo Kuan-chung, a novelist of the Yüan Dynasty, known

for the *Romance of the Three Kingdoms* (三國演義)

羅漢(ㄌㄨㄛˊ ㄏㄢˋ)
(Buddhism) ① *arhat*, a perfect man of Hinayana ② the sixteen, eighteen, or 500 disciples appointed to witness to Buddhist truth and save the world

羅漢身子(ㄌㄨㄛˊ ㄏㄢˋ ㄕㄣ ˙ㄗ)
a woman with no menstruation in her whole lifetime, hence barren

羅雀掘鼠(ㄌㄨㄛˊ ㄑㄩㄝˋ ㄐㄩㄝˊ ㄕㄨˇ) or 羅掘(ㄌㄨㄛˊ ㄐㄩㄝˊ)
to try very hard to scrape money together

羅裙(ㄌㄨㄛˊ ㄑㄩㄣˊ)
a skirt of thin silk

羅織(ㄌㄨㄛˊ ㄓ)
to bring a false charge against an innocent person; to frame a charge

羅致人才(ㄌㄨㄛˊ ㄓˋ ㄖㄣˊ ㄘㄞˊ)
to recruit talented people

羅帳(ㄌㄨㄛˊ ㄓㄤˋ)
a curtain of thin silk

羅斯福(ㄌㄨㄛˊ ㄙ ㄈㄨˊ)
① Franklin Delano Roosevelt, 1882-1945, 32nd president of the U.S. (1933-1945) ② Theodore Roosevelt, 1858-1919, 26th president of the U.S. (1901-1909)

羅素(ㄌㄨㄛˊ ㄙㄨˋ)
Bertrand Russell, 1872-1970, British philosopher

羅衣(ㄌㄨㄛˊ ㄧ)
a garment of thin silk

羅幃 or 羅帷(ㄌㄨㄛˊ ㄨㄟˊ)
a gauze curtain

羅紋(ㄌㄨㄛˊ ㄨㄣˊ)
① grain (of wood) ② finger prints

羅網(ㄌㄨㄛˊ ㄨㄤˇ)
a net; a snare: 孩子們設羅網捉兎。The boys made snares to catch rabbits.

十七畫

【羇】 4510 ㄐㄧ ji jī
to lodge at somebody's house

羇旅(ㄐㄧ ㄌㄩˇ)
① a lodger; a traveler ② to be traveling

羇客(ㄐㄧ ㄎㄜˋ)
a lodger; a traveler

羇滯(ㄐㄧ ㄓˋ)
to detain (an offender)

羇愁(ㄐㄧ ㄔㄡˊ)
a traveler's depression or sorrow

十九畫

【羈】 4511 ㄐㄧ ji jī
1. a bridle
2. to confine; to restrain; to bind
3. to lodge at another's house
參看「羇」

羈泊(ㄐㄧ ㄅㄛˊ)
to wander about; to travel from place to place; to be without a fixed home

羈絆(ㄐㄧ ㄅㄢˋ)
to restrain; to confine; to fetter; to tie; to shackle

羈縻(ㄐㄧ ㄇㄧˊ)
to control; to bridle

羈勒(ㄐㄧ ㄌㄜˋ)
to bridle; to restrain; to control

羈留(ㄐㄧ ㄌㄧㄡˊ)
① to detain (an offender) ② to stop over

羈旅(ㄐㄧ ㄌㄩˇ)
① a traveler ② traveling

羈宦(ㄐㄧ ㄏㄨㄢˋ)
to travel far to enter government service

羈牽(ㄐㄧ ㄑㄧㄢ)
to restrain; to bind

羈繫(ㄐㄧ ㄒㄧˋ)
to restrain; to bind: 他受到契約的羈繫。He is bound by a contract.

羈紲(ㄐㄧ ㄒㄧㄝˋ)
bridles and reins

羈滯(ㄐㄧ ㄓˋ)
① to detain (an offender) ② to delay; to hold up

羈束(ㄐㄧ ㄕㄨˋ)
to restrain; to bind

羈押(ㄐㄧ ㄧㄚ)
to detain (an offender); to take into custody

羊部
ㄧㄤˊ yang yáng

【羊】 4512 ㄧㄤˊ yang yáng
a sheep; a goat

羊白頭 or 楊白頭(ㄧㄤˊ ㄅㄞˊ ㄊㄡˊ)
an albino

羊皮紙(ㄧㄤˊ ㄆㄧˊ ㄓˇ)
parchment or sheepskin

羊皮襖(ㄧㄤˊ ㄆㄧˊ ㄠˇ)
a sheepskin jacket

羊膜(ㄧㄤˊ ㄇㄛˊ)
an amnion

羊毛(ㄧㄤˊ ㄇㄠˊ)
wool: 我的毛衣是羊毛製的。My sweater is made of wool.

羊毛袋(ㄧㄤˊ ㄇㄠˊ ㄉㄞˋ)
a woolsack

羊毛脂(ㄧㄤˊ ㄇㄠˊ ㄓ)
wool oil

羊毛出在羊身上(ㄧㄤˊ ㄇㄠˊ ㄔㄨ ㄗㄞˋ ㄧㄤˊ ㄕㄣ ㄕㄤˋ)
(literally) Without a sheep, there can be no wool.—The benefit comes, after all, from a price one has paid. 或 Whatever is the expense, somebody is going to pay for it. 或 One has to pay for what he gets.

羊毛衫(ㄧㄤˊ ㄇㄠˊ ㄕㄢ)
a woolen sweater

羊毛商(ㄧㄤˊ ㄇㄠˊ ㄕㄤ)
a wool stapler: 他是個羊毛商。He is a wool stapler.

羊毛衣(ㄧㄤˊ ㄇㄠˊ ㄧ)
woolen wear

羊毛襪(ㄧㄤˊ ㄇㄠˊ ㄨㄚˋ)
woolen socks

羊癲風(ㄧㄤˊ ㄉㄧㄢ ㄈㄥ) or 羊角風(ㄧㄤˊ ㄐㄧㄠˇ ㄈㄥ) or 羊癇風(ㄧㄤˊ ㄒㄧㄢˊ ㄈㄥ)
epilepsy

羊頭(ㄧㄤˊ ㄊㄡˊ)
① a sheep's head ② *Archosargus probatocephalus,* sheepshead

羊欄(ㄧㄤˊ ㄌㄢˊ)
a sheepcot(e); a sheepfold: 羊被趕入羊欄。The sheep are

driven into a sheepfold.

羊羔(ㄧㄤˊ ㄍㄠ)
①a lamb ②a kind of alcoholic beverage

羊羹(ㄧㄤˊ ㄍㄥ)
a sort of cake

羊毫(ㄧㄤˊ ㄏㄠˊ)
a writing brush made of wool

羊角(ㄧㄤˊ ㄐㄧㄠˇ)
①a ram's horns ②a whirlwind; a cyclone

羊叫(ㄧㄤˊ ㄐㄧㄠˋ)
the bleating of a sheep or goat

羊圈(ㄧㄤˊ ㄐㄩㄢˋ)
a sheepfold; a sheepcote; a sheep pen

羊羣(ㄧㄤˊ ㄑㄩㄣˊ)
a flock of sheep or goats

羊脂(ㄧㄤˊ ㄓ)
suet (from a sheep or goat)

羊脂玉(ㄧㄤˊ ㄓ ㄩˋ)
white jade

羊質虎皮(ㄧㄤˊ ㄓˊ ㄏㄨˇ ㄆㄧˊ)
(literally) a sheep in a tiger's skin—impressive in appearance but disappointing in substance

羊齒(ㄧㄤˊ ㄔˇ)
ferns: 地面上佈滿了羊齒。The ground was covered with ferns.

羊齒植物(ㄧㄤˊ ㄔˇ ㄓˊ ㄨˋ)
ferns; pteridophyte

羊腸小徑(ㄧㄤˊ ㄔㄤˊ ㄒㄧㄠˇ ㄐㄧㄥˋ)or 羊腸小道(ㄧㄤˊ ㄔㄤˊ ㄒㄧㄠˇ ㄉㄠˋ)
a narrow, winding path

羊舍(ㄧㄤˊ ㄕㄜˋ)
a sheepfold; a sheepcote

羊水(ㄧㄤˊ ㄕㄨㄟˇ)
amniotic fluid

羊肉(ㄧㄤˊ ㄖㄡˋ)
mutton

羊入虎口(ㄧㄤˊ ㄖㄨˋ ㄏㄨˇ ㄎㄡˇ)or 羊落虎口(ㄧㄤˊ ㄌㄨㄛˋ ㄏㄨˇ ㄎㄡˇ)
(literally) a sheep in a tiger's mouth—a hopelessly perilous situation

羊胃羊頭(ㄧㄤˊ ㄨㄟˋ ㄧㄤˊ ㄊㄡˊ)
the untouchables who hold high government posts

【芈】 4513
ㄇㄧㄝ mhie miē
(讀音 ㄇㄧˇ mii mǐ)
the bleating of a sheep or goat

二畫

【羌】 4514
(羗、羌) ㄑㄧㄤ chiang qiāng
name of an ancient tribe in West China

羌蠻(ㄑㄧㄤ ㄇㄢˊ)
an ancient barbarian people in West China

羌笛(ㄑㄧㄤ ㄉㄧˊ)
a Tartar pipe; the shepherd's flute

羌胡(ㄑㄧㄤ ㄏㄨˊ)
an ancient tribe in West China

羌活(ㄑㄧㄤ ㄏㄨㄛˊ)
angelica 亦作「白芷」

羌羯(ㄑㄧㄤ ㄐㄧㄝˊ)
an ancient tribe in West China

羌無故實(ㄑㄧㄤ ㄨˊ ㄍㄨˋ ㄕˊ)
a poetic expression containing no allusion whatsoever

三畫

【美】 4515
ㄇㄟˇ meei měi
1. beautiful; pretty; fine; fair: 那女孩多美啊！How beautiful the girl is!
2. good; excellent; exquisite; nice
3. to be pleased with oneself
4. to praise

美備(ㄇㄟˇ ㄅㄟˋ)
good in all respects; perfect

美不勝收(ㄇㄟˇ ˙ㄅㄨ ㄕㄥ ㄕㄡ)
(said of landscape, etc.) too many beautiful or excellent things to be fully appreciated; more beauty than one can take in

美盼(ㄇㄟˇ ㄆㄢˋ)
a charming glance

美貌(ㄇㄟˇ ㄇㄠˋ)
a beautiful face (of a woman); beauty

美滿(ㄇㄟˇ ㄇㄢˇ)
(said of a life, home, etc.) happy; sweet

美滿姻緣(ㄇㄟˇ ㄇㄢˇ ㄧㄣ ㄩㄢˊ)
a happy marriage

美夢(ㄇㄟˇ ㄇㄥˋ)
a fond dream; a beautiful dream

美妙(ㄇㄟˇ ㄇㄧㄠˋ)
exquisite; very pleasant

美眄(ㄇㄟˇ ㄇㄧㄢˇ)
a captivating glance

美名(ㄇㄟˇ ㄇㄧㄥˊ)
an impressive title; fame; high prestige; a good reputation; a good name: 美名勝於財富。A good name is better than riches.

美目(ㄇㄟˇ ㄇㄨˋ)
beautiful (or lovely) eyes

美方(ㄇㄟˇ ㄈㄤ)
the American side; on the part of the Americans

美富(ㄇㄟˇ ㄈㄨˋ)
beautiful and abundant

美婦(ㄇㄟˇ ㄈㄨˋ)
a beautiful woman; a fine woman

美德(ㄇㄟˇ ㄉㄜˊ)
virtue: 節儉是一種美德。Frugality is a virtue.

美談(ㄇㄟˇ ㄊㄢˊ)
an instructive anecdote; a story of an exemplary deed

美男子(ㄇㄟˇ ㄋㄢˊ ㄗˇ)
a handsome man; an Adonis: 他是個美男子。He is a handsome man.

美女(ㄇㄟˇ ㄋㄩˇ)
a beautiful woman; a beauty

美女簪花(ㄇㄟˇ ㄋㄩˇ ㄗㄢ ㄏㄨㄚ)
the graceful strokes of calligraphic works

美拉尼西亞(ㄇㄟˇ ㄌㄚ ㄋㄧˊ ㄒㄧ ㄧㄚˇ)
Melanesia

美麗(ㄇㄟˇ ㄌㄧˋ)
beautiful; pretty; fair

美利堅(ㄇㄟˇ ㄌㄧˋ ㄐㄧㄢ)or 美利堅合衆國(ㄇㄟˇ ㄌㄧˋ ㄐㄧㄢ ㄏㄜˊ ㄓㄨㄥˋ ㄍㄨㄛˊ)
the United States of America; America

美輪美奐(ㄇㄟˇ ㄌㄨㄣˊ ㄇㄟˇ ㄏㄨㄢˋ)
splendid and magnificent (a phrase commonly used to congratulate a person on the completion of a new house)

美感(ㄇㄟˇ ㄍㄢˇ)
a sense of the beautiful; the sense of beauty; the esthetic sense

〔羊部〕

美國(ㄇㄟˇ ㄍㄨㄛˊ)
America; the United States; the United States of America

美國的(ㄇㄟˇ ㄍㄨㄛˊ ·ㄉㄜ)
American

美國獨立戰爭(ㄇㄟˇ ㄍㄨㄛˊ ㄉㄨˊ ㄌㄧˋ ㄓㄢˋ ㄓㄥ)
the American Revolution; the American Revolutionary War; the War of (American) Independence

美國南北戰爭(ㄇㄟˇ ㄍㄨㄛˊ ㄋㄢˊ ㄅㄟˇ ㄓㄢˋ ㄓㄥ)
the American Civil War 1861-1865

美國佬(ㄇㄟˇ ㄍㄨㄛˊ ㄌㄠˇ)
a Yankee

美國國會(ㄇㄟˇ ㄍㄨㄛˊ ㄍㄨㄛˊ ㄏㄨㄟˋ)
the American Congress

美國新聞處(ㄇㄟˇ ㄍㄨㄛˊ ㄒㄧㄣ ㄨㄣˊ ㄔㄨˋ)
the United States Information Service (USIS)

美國之音(ㄇㄟˇ ㄍㄨㄛˊ ㄓ ㄧㄣ)
the Voice of America (VOA)

美國中央情報局(ㄇㄟˇ ㄍㄨㄛˊ ㄓㄨㄥ ㄧㄤ ㄑㄧㄥˊ ㄅㄠˋ ㄐㄩˊ)
the Central Intelligence Agency (CIA)

美國人(ㄇㄟˇ ㄍㄨㄛˊ ㄖㄣˊ)
an American; the Americans

美官(ㄇㄟˇ ㄍㄨㄢ)
an impressive government post

美觀(ㄇㄟˇ ㄍㄨㄢ)
pleasant to the eye; beautiful to look at

美觀大方(ㄇㄟˇ ㄍㄨㄢ ㄉㄚˋ ㄈㄤ)
beautiful and dignified

美工(ㄇㄟˇ ㄍㄨㄥ)
① art designing ② an art designer

美好(ㄇㄟˇ ㄏㄠˇ)
exquisite; fine: 多美好的天氣！What a fine day!

美化(ㄇㄟˇ ㄏㄨㄚˋ)
① to beautify; beautification: 花卉美化環境。Flowers beautify environment. ② Americanized; Americanization

美貨(ㄇㄟˇ ㄏㄨㄛˋ)
American merchandise; U. S. products

美機(ㄇㄟˇ ㄐㄧ)
American planes

美籍(ㄇㄟˇ ㄐㄧˊ)
of American nationality

美酒(ㄇㄟˇ ㄐㄧㄡˇ)
good wine; delicious wine

美艦(ㄇㄟˇ ㄐㄧㄢˋ)
an American naval ship: 美艦昨天啓航了。The American naval ship sailed yesterday.

美金(ㄇㄟˇ ㄐㄧㄣ)or 美元(ㄇㄟˇ ㄩㄢˊ)
the (American) dollar

美錦(ㄇㄟˇ ㄐㄧㄣˇ)
beautiful brocade

美景(ㄇㄟˇ ㄐㄧㄥˇ)
beautiful scenery; beautiful landscape

美景良辰(ㄇㄟˇ ㄐㄧㄥˇ ㄌㄧㄤˊ ㄔㄣˊ)
beautiful scenery and a pleasant morning—an enjoyable situation or experience

美舉(ㄇㄟˇ ㄐㄩˇ)
a praiseworthy deed

美軍(ㄇㄟˇ ㄐㄩㄣ)
American troops; U.S. forces

美其名曰(ㄇㄟˇ ㄑㄧˊ ㄇㄧㄥˊ ㄩㄝ)
to give a dignified name to something ugly or condemnable

美妾(ㄇㄟˇ ㄑㄧㄝˋ)
an attractive concubine

美僑(ㄇㄟˇ ㄑㄧㄠˊ)
an American living abroad; an American resident in a foreign country

美缺(ㄇㄟˇ ㄑㄩㄝ)
an attractive opening or vacancy

美秀(ㄇㄟˇ ㄒㄧㄡˋ)
handsome and brilliant; beautiful and intelligent; handsome and accomplished

美學(ㄇㄟˇ ㄒㄩㄝˊ)
esthetics; aesthetics: 美學是哲學的分枝。Esthetics is a branch of philosophy.

美製(ㄇㄟˇ ㄓˋ)
made in U.S.A.; manufactured in the United States

美洲(ㄇㄟˇ ㄓㄡ)
the Americas

美洲杉(ㄇㄟˇ ㄓㄡ ㄕㄢ)
a sequoia

美饌(ㄇㄟˇ ㄓㄨㄢˋ)
a sumptuous meal

美中不足(ㄇㄟˇ ㄓㄨㄥ ㄅㄨˋ ㄗㄨˊ)
a flaw that mars perfection; the only drawback

美齒(ㄇㄟˇ ㄔˇ)
beautiful teeth

美醜(ㄇㄟˇ ㄔㄡˇ)
beauty and ugliness

美稱(ㄇㄟˇ ㄔㄥ)
① an honorific term; a title of respect; an honorific ② a good name

美事(ㄇㄟˇ ㄕˋ)
① a laudable act; a worthy deed ② a happy event

美術(ㄇㄟˇ ㄕㄨˋ)
the fine arts

美術館(ㄇㄟˇ ㄕㄨˋ ㄍㄨㄢˇ)
an art museum (or gallery)

美術家(ㄇㄟˇ ㄕㄨˋ ㄐㄧㄚ)or 畫家(ㄏㄨㄚˋ ㄐㄧㄚ)
an artist; a painter

美術設計(ㄇㄟˇ ㄕㄨˋ ㄕㄜˋ ㄐㄧˋ)
artistic design

美髯公(ㄇㄟˇ ㄖㄢˊ ㄍㄨㄥ)
an old gentleman with a flowing beard

美人(ㄇㄟˇ ㄖㄣˊ)
① a beauty; a belle: 他妹妹是個美人。His younger sister is a beauty. ②(figuratively) a king ③(figuratively) a man of virtue

美人計(ㄇㄟˇ ㄖㄣˊ ㄐㄧˋ)
a snare using a beautiful woman as a bait

美人蕉(ㄇㄟˇ ㄖㄣˊ ㄐㄧㄠ)
a canna

美人遲暮(ㄇㄟˇ ㄖㄣˊ ㄔˊ ㄇㄨˋ)
(literally) a beauty in her old age—the helpless and frustrating feeling of a has-been

美人魚(ㄇㄟˇ ㄖㄣˊ ㄩˊ)
a mermaid

美容(ㄇㄟˇ ㄖㄨㄥˊ)
to apply make-up or undergo plastic surgery

美容師(ㄇㄟˇ ㄖㄨㄥˊ ㄕ)
a beautician

美容術(ㄇㄟˇ ㄖㄨㄥˊ ㄕㄨˋ)
the art of make-up; the technology for improving one's appearance

美容院(ㄇㄟˇ ㄖㄨㄥˊ ㄩㄢˋ)
a beauty parlor

美色(ㄇㄟˇ ㄙㄜˋ)
① an attractive woman ② (woman's) beauty: 美色只是外表而已。Beauty is only (or

but) skin-deep.
美索不達米亞(ㄇㄟˇ ㄙㄨㄛˇ ㄅㄨˋ ㄉㄚˊ ㄇㄧˇ ㄧㄚˋ)
Mesopotamia
美惡(ㄇㄟˇ ㄜˋ)
right and wrong; good and bad
美而賢(ㄇㄟˇ ㄦˊ ㄒㄧㄢˊ)
(said of a woman) beautiful and virtuous
美意(ㄇㄟˇ ㄧˋ)
a kind intention; goodwill
美意延年(ㄇㄟˇ ㄧˋ ㄧㄢˊ ㄋㄧㄢˊ)
(a congratulatory expression) A carefree life insures longevity.
美言(ㄇㄟˇ ㄧㄢˊ)
① a fine saying ② commending remarks
美豔(ㄇㄟˇ ㄧㄢˋ)
beautiful and voluptuous; glamorous
美味(ㄇㄟˇ ㄨㄟˋ)
delicious; tasty
美文(ㄇㄟˇ ㄨㄣˊ)
belles-lettres 譯作「純文學」:「美文」一詞來自法文。The term "belles-lettres" comes from French.
美玉(ㄇㄟˇ ㄩˋ)
fine jade: 他喜歡搜集美玉。He likes to collect fine jades.
美育(ㄇㄟˇ ㄩˋ)
esthetic education: 美育是件重要的事。Esthetic education is an important thing.
美譽(ㄇㄟˇ ㄩˋ)
honor; fame; glory: 他的美譽傳布全國。His fame spread all over the country.
美援(ㄇㄟˇ ㄩㄢˊ)
American aid; U.S. aid
美元集團(ㄇㄟˇ ㄩㄢˊ ㄐㄧˊ ㄊㄨㄢˊ)
the dollar bloc

【羑】 4516
ㄧㄡˇ yeou yǒu
to guide to goodness

【羌】 4517
ㄑㄧㄤ chiang qiāng
same as 羌—an ancient people in West China

四畫

【羔】 4518
ㄍㄠ gau gāo
a lamb
羔皮(ㄍㄠ ㄆㄧˊ)
lambskin
羔雁(ㄍㄠ ㄧㄢˋ)
lamb and wild goose—presents of ceremony from high officials in ancient times
羔羊(ㄍㄠ ㄧㄤˊ)
a lamb: 她如羔羊般溫柔。She is as gentle as a lamb.

【羖】 4519
ㄍㄨˇ guu gǔ
a black ram

【羓】 4520
ㄅㄚ ba bā
salted meat

【羒】 4521
ㄈㄣ fern fén
a white ram

五畫

【羝】 4522
ㄉㄧ di dī
a ram; a he-goat
羝羊(ㄉㄧ ㄧㄤˊ)
a ram; a he-goat
羝羊觸藩(ㄉㄧ ㄧㄤˊ ㄔㄨˋ ㄈㄢ)
to be in a dilemma

【羚】 4523
ㄌㄧㄥˊ ling líng
an antelope
羚羊(ㄌㄧㄥˊ ㄧㄤˊ)
an antelope
羚羊掛角(ㄌㄧㄥˊ ㄧㄤˊ ㄍㄨㄚˋ ㄐㄧㄠˇ)
(literally) the antelope sticks its horns among branches at night—(said of poetic works) the excellent quality or transcendental charm

【羞】 4524
ㄒㄧㄡ shiou xiū
1. ashamed; abashed: 他對他所做的事感到羞恥。He is ashamed of what he has done.
2. shy; bashful: 她因太害羞而沒跟他講話。She was too shy to speak to him.
3. to disgrace; to insult; to shame
羞明(ㄒㄧㄡ ㄇㄧㄥˊ)
① allergic to strong light; afraid of strong light ② (medicine) photophobia
羞憤(ㄒㄧㄡ ㄈㄣˋ)
ashamed and angry
羞答答(ㄒㄧㄡ ㄉㄚ ㄉㄚ)
shy; bashful
羞刀難入鞘(ㄒㄧㄡ ㄉㄠ ㄋㄢˊ ㄖㄨˋ ㄑㄧㄠˋ)
What is done cannot be undone.
羞惱成怒(ㄒㄧㄡ ㄋㄠˇ ㄔㄥˊ ㄋㄨˋ)
to become angry from shame 亦作「惱羞成怒」
羞赧(ㄒㄧㄡ ㄋㄢˇ)
to blush; to redden; blush: 她轉過臉以掩其羞赧。She turned away to hide her blush.
羞愧(ㄒㄧㄡ ㄎㄨㄟˋ)
mortified; disgraced; shamed
羞花閉月(ㄒㄧㄡ ㄏㄨㄚ ㄅㄧˋ ㄩㄝˋ)
(said of a woman) so beautiful as to cause the flowers to blush and the moon to hide 亦作「閉月羞花」
羞怯(ㄒㄧㄡ ㄑㄧㄝˋ)or(ㄒㄧㄡ ㄑㄩㄝˋ)
shy and nervous: 她羞怯得說不出話來。She is too shy and nervous to utter a word.
羞恥(ㄒㄧㄡ ㄔˇ)
a sense of shame
羞手羞脚(ㄒㄧㄡ ㄕㄡˇ ㄒㄧㄡ ㄐㄧㄠˇ)
afraid to go ahead because of shyness; timid
羞人答答(ㄒㄧㄡ ㄖㄣˊ ㄉㄚ ㄉㄚ)
ashamed; abashed; bashful
羞辱(ㄒㄧㄡ ㄖㄨˋ)
to shame; to insult; to disgrace
羞慚(ㄒㄧㄡ ㄘㄢˊ)
ashamed; abashed; mortified; humiliated: 你應該對自己的行爲感到羞慚。You should be ashamed of your conduct.
羞澀(ㄒㄧㄡ ㄙㄜˋ)
① to act awkwardly because of shame ② to be short of
羞澀阮囊(ㄒㄧㄡ ㄙㄜˋ ㄖㄨㄢˇ ㄋㄤˊ)
embarrassed for being short of money; short of cash
羞惡(ㄒㄧㄡ ㄨˋ)
to be ashamed of evil deeds
羞惡之心(ㄒㄧㄡ ㄨˋ ㄓ ㄒㄧㄣ)
the feeling of shame and dislike; the sense of right and wrong
羞於啓齒(ㄒㄧㄡ ㄩˊ ㄑㄧˇ ㄔˇ)
too shy to speak out one's mind
羞與爲伍(ㄒㄧㄡ ㄩˇ ㄨㄟˊ ㄨˇ)
ashamed to associate with somebody

〔羊部〕

六畫

【羢】 4525 ㄖㄨㄥˊ rong róng
fine wool

七畫

【羣】 4526 (群) ㄑㄩㄣˊ chyun qún
a group; a multitude; a host; a crowd; a swarm; a large number; a flock; a herd
羣芳(ㄑㄩㄣˊ ㄈㄤ)
① a multitude of flowers ② a multitude of beauties
羣芳爭豔(ㄑㄩㄣˊ ㄈㄤ ㄓㄥ ㄧㄢˋ)
① Many flowers rival for gorgeousness. ② A host of beautiful women compete for attention.
羣島(ㄑㄩㄣˊ ㄉㄠˇ)
an archipelago; a group of islands
羣體(ㄑㄩㄣˊ ㄊㄧˇ)
a colony (of corals, etc.)
羣體利益(ㄑㄩㄣˊ ㄊㄧˇ ㄌㄧˋ ㄧˋ)
group interest
羣黎(ㄑㄩㄣˊ ㄌㄧˊ)
the masses; the populace
羣僚(ㄑㄩㄣˊ ㄌㄧㄠˊ)
the whole body of courtiers
羣龍無首(ㄑㄩㄣˊ ㄌㄨㄥˊ ㄨˊ ㄕㄡˇ)
a multitude without a leader; leaderless
羣集(ㄑㄩㄣˊ ㄐㄧˊ)
to swarm; to crowd; to gather in great numbers
羣籍(ㄑㄩㄣˊ ㄐㄧˊ)
a host of books; a multitude of books
羣經(ㄑㄩㄣˊ ㄐㄧㄥ)
all the classics
羣居(ㄑㄩㄣˊ ㄐㄩ)
to live as a group; gregarious: 牛羊是羣居的動物。Sheep and cattles are gregarious.
羣居生活(ㄑㄩㄣˊ ㄐㄩ ㄕㄥ ㄏㄨㄛˊ)
gregarious life; social life
羣聚(ㄑㄩㄣˊ ㄐㄩˋ)
to swarm; to crowd; to gather in large numbers
羣起而攻之(ㄑㄩㄣˊ ㄑㄧˇ ㄦˊ ㄍㄨㄥ ㄓ)
People rise in a mass to attack it, him, etc.
羣青(ㄑㄩㄣˊ ㄑㄧㄥ)
ultramarine 亦作「紺青」
羣輕折軸(ㄑㄩㄣˊ ㄑㄧㄥ ㄓㄜˊ ㄓㄡˊ)
A combination of insignificant efforts or resources can work miracles.
羣情(ㄑㄩㄣˊ ㄑㄧㄥˊ)
popular feeling; public sentiment: 羣情激奮。Popular feeling ran high.
羣小(ㄑㄩㄣˊ ㄒㄧㄠˇ)
a mob; mean fellows; seamy characters
羣賢(ㄑㄩㄣˊ ㄒㄧㄢˊ)
a host of wise men; all the wise men: 羣賢畢至。A host of wise men are all present.
羣星(ㄑㄩㄣˊ ㄒㄧㄥ)
① the myriad of stars ② a galaxy (of movie stars, etc.)
羣性(ㄑㄩㄣˊ ㄒㄧㄥˋ) or 羣居性(ㄑㄩㄣˊ ㄐㄩ ㄒㄧㄥˋ)
gregariousness; sociality
羣學(ㄑㄩㄣˊ ㄒㄩㄝˊ)
sociology 亦作「社會學」
羣雄割據(ㄑㄩㄣˊ ㄒㄩㄥˊ ㄍㄜ ㄐㄩˋ)
rivalry among local barons; fragmentation of a country by rivaling warlords
羣衆(ㄑㄩㄣˊ ㄓㄨㄥˋ)
a crowd; a mob: 羣衆聚集在建築物周圍。Mobs gathered round the building.
羣衆心理(ㄑㄩㄣˊ ㄓㄨㄥˋ ㄒㄧㄣ ㄌㄧˇ)
the mental processes, emotions, thoughts, etc. of the mob
羣衆運動(ㄑㄩㄣˊ ㄓㄨㄥˋ ㄩㄣˋ ㄉㄨㄥˋ)
(sociology) mass movement
羣臣(ㄑㄩㄣˊ ㄔㄣˊ)
the entire body of ministers
羣山(ㄑㄩㄣˊ ㄕㄢ)
many mountains
羣山環抱(ㄑㄩㄣˊ ㄕㄢ ㄏㄨㄢˊ ㄅㄠˋ)
to be surrounded by mountains
羣生(ㄑㄩㄣˊ ㄕㄥ)
the people; the masses 亦作「大衆」
羣從(ㄑㄩㄣˊ ㄗㄨㄥˋ)
nephews and nieces collectively
羣策羣力(ㄑㄩㄣˊ ㄘㄜˋ ㄑㄩㄣˊ ㄌㄧˋ)
to join the force and intelligence of the group; to work as a team
羣毆(ㄑㄩㄣˊ ㄡ)
to gather and have a melee
羣蟻附羶(ㄑㄩㄣˊ ㄧˇ ㄈㄨˋ ㄕㄢ)
(literally) a myriad of ants swarming about a piece of meat that smells—a rush (of people) in search of profit
羣有(ㄑㄩㄣˊ ㄧㄡˇ)
all things; all God's creation
羣英(ㄑㄩㄣˊ ㄧㄥ)
a large number of brilliant minds
羣育(ㄑㄩㄣˊ ㄩˋ)
(education) training in group life

【羨】 4527 ㄒㄧㄢˋ shiann xiàn
to envy; to covet
羨慕(ㄒㄧㄢˋ ㄇㄨˋ)
to envy; to covet: 他很羨慕我有這樣的好媽媽。He envies me my good mother.
羨財(ㄒㄧㄢˋ ㄘㄞˊ)
spare money; surplus money

【義】 4528 ㄧˋ yih yì
1. justice; righteousness
2. generosity; charity; philanthropy; chivalry
3. meaning; connotations: 此字有數種意義。The word has several meanings.
4. unreal; artificial; false
5. a Chinese family name
義兵(ㄧˋ ㄅㄧㄥ)
① troops of justice ② volunteers; militiamen
義不容辭(ㄧˋ ㄅㄨˋ ㄖㄨㄥˊ ㄘˊ)
Moral obligation prohibits declination of the call. 或 duty-bound
義僕(ㄧˋ ㄆㄨˊ)
a faithful servant; a royal servant: 他是個義僕。He's a faithful servant.
義賣(ㄧˋ ㄇㄞˋ)
a charity sale; a bazaar
義門(ㄧˋ ㄇㄣˊ)
a family noted for righteousness
義民(ㄧˋ ㄇㄧㄣˊ)
people with a deep sense of justice
義母(ㄧˋ ㄇㄨˇ)
a foster mother
義憤塡膺(ㄧˋ ㄈㄣˋ ㄊㄧㄢˊ ㄧㄥ) or 義憤塡胸(ㄧˋ ㄈㄣˋ ㄊㄧㄢˊ ㄒㄩㄥ)
to feel indignant at the in-

justice; to be filled with righteous indignation
義方(ㄧˋ ㄈㄤ)
the principle of justice
義風(ㄧˋ ㄈㄥ)
a prevailing sense of justice
義父(ㄧˋ ㄈㄨˋ)
a foster father
義大利 or 意大利(ㄧˋ ㄉㄚˋ ㄌㄧˋ)
Italy
義大利麵食(ㄧˋ ㄉㄚˋ ㄌㄧˋ ㄇㄧㄢˋ ㄕˊ)
pasta; spaghetti
義大利脆餅(ㄧˋ ㄉㄚˋ ㄌㄧˋ ㄘㄨㄟˋ ㄅㄧㄥˇ)
a pizza
義弟(ㄧˋ ㄉㄧˋ)
a younger foster brother
義田(ㄧˋ ㄊㄧㄢˊ)
a field leased to others with the rental collected for relief of the needy among one's own clan
義女(ㄧˋ ㄋㄩˇ)
a foster daughter
義理(ㄧˋ ㄌㄧˇ)
principles; reason
義例(ㄧˋ ㄌㄧˋ)
the outline, or scope, of a book
義工(ㄧˋ ㄍㄨㄥ)
a volunteer worker
義和團(ㄧˋ ㄏㄜˊ ㄊㄨㄢˊ)
the Boxers (responsible for the Boxer Uprising of 1900)
義警(ㄧˋ ㄐㄧㄥˇ)
one who volunteers to do police work
義舉(ㄧˋ ㄐㄩˇ)
an act of charity; a chivalrous deed
義軍(ㄧˋ ㄐㄩㄣ)
troops of justice
義旗(ㄧˋ ㄑㄧˊ)
a banner of justice; a flag of the troops of justice
義氣(ㄧˋ ˙ㄑㄧ)
①spirit of justice or righteousness ②loyalty to friends: 他因義氣而受人尊敬。He is respected for his loyalty to friends.
義犬(ㄧˋ ㄑㄩㄢˇ)
a loyal dog; a faithful dog
義俠(ㄧˋ ㄒㄧㄚˊ)
a chivalrous person
義形於色(ㄧˋ ㄒㄧㄥˊ ㄩˊ ㄙㄜˋ)
righteousness manifested in one's appearance
義行(ㄧˋ ㄒㄧㄥˊ)
an act of justice; a chivalrous act: 幫助被壓迫者是種義行。Helping the oppressed is an act of justice.
義學(ㄧˋ ㄒㄩㄝˊ)
①a free private school ②study of philosophic principles (which prevailed in the Sung Dynasty)
義兄(ㄧˋ ㄒㄩㄥ)
an elder foster brother: 他有三位義兄。He has three elder foster brothers.
義肢(ㄧˋ ㄓ)
artificial limbs
義戰(ㄧˋ ㄓㄢˋ)
a war for justice; a holy war
義正辭嚴(ㄧˋ ㄓㄥˋ ㄘˊ ㄧㄢˊ)
speaking sternly and forcefully in the cause of justice
義莊(ㄧˋ ㄓㄨㄤ)
a farmstead leased to others with the rental collected for the relief of the needy among one's own clan
義塚(ㄧˋ ㄓㄨㄥˇ)
a cemetery for burying the remains of unidentified persons
義齒(ㄧˋ ㄔˇ)
artificial teeth
義師(ㄧˋ ㄕ)
troops of justice
義士(ㄧˋ ㄕˋ)
an adherent to justice; a patriot; a freedom-seeker: 他是個義士。He is a patriot.
義手(ㄧˋ ㄕㄡˇ)
an artificial hand
義塾(ㄧˋ ㄕㄨˊ)
a free private school
義疏(ㄧˋ ㄕㄨˋ)
annotations
義乳(ㄧˋ ㄖㄨˇ)
falsies
義子(ㄧˋ ㄗˇ)
a foster son
義足(ㄧˋ ㄗㄨˊ)
an artificial leg: 他有隻脚是義足。One of his legs is an artificial leg.
義倉(ㄧˋ ㄘㄤ)
a public granary for storing surplus grains in time of plenty to be used for the relief of the needy in time of famine
義粟仁漿(ㄧˋ ㄙㄨˋ ㄖㄣˊ ㄐㄧㄤ)
alms; contributions to charity
義演(ㄧˋ ㄧㄢˇ)
a charity performance (by entertainers); a charity show
義無反顧(ㄧˋ ㄨˊ ㄈㄢˇ ㄍㄨˋ)
to pursue justice without ever turning back
義務(ㄧˋ ㄨˋ)
duty; obligation: 他有義務出席這個會議。He has an obligation to attend the meeting.
義務教育(ㄧˋ ㄨˋ ㄐㄧㄠˋ ㄩˋ)
compulsory education; mandatory education: 義務教育是免費的。Compulsory education is free.
義勇(ㄧˋ ㄩㄥˇ)
① righteous and courageous; patriotic: 他乃義勇之人。He is a patriotic man. ②(said of troops, etc.) volunteer
義勇艦隊(ㄧˋ ㄩㄥˇ ㄐㄧㄢˋ ㄉㄨㄟˋ)
merchant marine reorganized into a navy
義勇軍(ㄧˋ ㄩㄥˇ ㄐㄩㄣ)
a volunteer army; the militia: 他加入義勇軍。He joined the volunteer army.

九畫

【羯】 4529
ㄐㄧㄝˊ jye jié
1. a castrated ram
2. name of an ancient barbarian people

羯鼓(ㄐㄧㄝˊ ㄍㄨˇ)
a kind of drum
羯胡(ㄐㄧㄝˊ ㄏㄨˊ)
an ancient barbarian people
羯雞(ㄐㄧㄝˊ ㄐㄧ)
a castrated cock; a capon 亦作「閹雞」

十畫

【羲】 4530
ㄒㄧ shi xī
Fu Hsi(伏羲), a legendary ruler who introduced houses
羲農(ㄒㄧ ㄋㄨㄥˊ)
the legendary rulers Fu Hsi

〔羊部〕

〔羽部〕

(伏羲), who introduced houses, and Shen Nung (神農), who introduced agriculture

羲和(ㄒㄧ ㄏㄜˊ)
two legendary astronomers Hsi (羲氏) and Ho (和氏)

羲黃(ㄒㄧ ㄏㄨㄤˊ)
the legendary rulers Fu Hsi (伏羲) and Huang Ti (黃帝)

羲皇上人(ㄒㄧ ㄏㄨㄤˊ ㄕㄤˋ ㄖㄣˊ)
people who lived before the legendary ruler Fu Hsi (伏羲); the "noble savage"

十二畫

【羴】 4531
ㄕㄢ shan shān
same as 羶—the odor of a sheep or goat

十三畫

【羶】 4532
(羴) ㄕㄢ shan shān
the odor of a sheep or goat

羶氣(ㄕㄢ ㄑㄧˋ)
the odor of a sheep or goat

羶腥(ㄕㄢ ㄒㄧㄥ)
the odor of mutton

羶味(ㄕㄢ ㄨㄟˋ)
the odor of a sheep or goat

【羹】 4533
ㄍㄥ geng gēng
thick soup; broth

羹湯(ㄍㄥ ㄊㄤ)
thick soup; broth

羹匙(ㄍㄥ ㄔˊ)
a spoon

【羸】 4534
ㄌㄟˊ lei léi
1. lean; emaciated
2. weak; feeble
3. to entangle; to bind

羸憊(ㄌㄟˊ ㄅㄟˋ)
very weary; exhausted

羸劣(ㄌㄟˊ ㄌㄧㄝˋ)
lean and weak

羸瘠(ㄌㄟˊ ㄐㄧˊ)
emaciated; lean

羸師(ㄌㄟˊ ㄕ)
a weak army; exhausted troops

羸瘦(ㄌㄟˊ ㄕㄡˋ)
emaciated: 長期臥病使這病人羸瘦了。A long illness had emaciated the invalid.

羸弱(ㄌㄟˊ ㄖㄨㄛˋ)
emaciated and weak

十五畫

【羼】 4535
ㄔㄢˋ chann chàn
to mix; to interpolate

羽部
ㄩˇ yeu yǔ

【羽】 4536
ㄩˇ yeu yǔ
1. feathers; plumes
2. wings of a bird
3. one of the five notes in the Chinese musical scale

羽毛(ㄩˇ ㄇㄠˊ)
feathers; plumes; down

羽毛豐滿(ㄩˇ ㄇㄠˊ ㄈㄥ ㄇㄢˇ)
① having thick feathers ② experienced; mature; full-fledged

羽毛撣(ㄩˇ ㄇㄠˊ ㄉㄢˇ)
a feather duster

羽毛球(ㄩˇ ㄇㄠˊ ㄑㄧㄡˊ)
badminton: 你打羽毛球嗎? Do you play badminton?

羽毛球拍(ㄩˇ ㄇㄠˊ ㄑㄧㄡˊ ㄆㄞ)
a badminton racket

羽毛球場(ㄩˇ ㄇㄠˊ ㄑㄧㄡˊ ㄔㄤˇ)
a badminton court

羽毛球網(ㄩˇ ㄇㄠˊ ㄑㄧㄡˊ ㄨㄤˇ)
a badminton net

羽毛未豐(ㄩˇ ㄇㄠˊ ㄨㄟˋ ㄈㄥ)
still fledgling; inexperienced; immature

羽獵(ㄩˇ ㄌㄧㄝˋ)
to hunt; a hunt

羽林(ㄩˇ ㄌㄧㄣˊ) or 羽林軍(ㄩˇ ㄌㄧㄣˊ ㄐㄩㄣ)
imperial guards 亦作「御林」or「御林軍」

羽量級(ㄩˇ ㄌㄧㄤˋ ㄐㄧˊ)
a bantamweight; featherweight: 他是羽量級的冠軍。He is the bantamweight champion.

羽蓋(ㄩˇ ㄍㄞˋ)
a feathered carriage top

羽客(ㄩˇ ㄎㄜˋ)
a Taoist priest

羽翮(ㄩˇ ㄏㄜˊ)
the shaft of a feather

羽化(ㄩˇ ㄏㄨㄚˋ)
① to ascend to heaven and become a fairy immortal ② (said of a Taoist) to die ③ (zoology) eclosion

羽化登仙(ㄩˇ ㄏㄨㄚˋ ㄉㄥ ㄒㄧㄢ)
to take flight to the land of the immortal

羽檄(ㄩˇ ㄒㄧˊ) or 羽書(ㄩˇ ㄕㄨ)
an urgent message or dispatch (with a feather attached to indicate the urgency) calling men to arms

羽狀脈(ㄩˇ ㄓㄨㄤˋ ㄇㄞˋ)
pinnate veins

羽狀複葉(ㄩˇ ㄓㄨㄤˋ ㄈㄨˋ ㄧㄝˋ)
(botany) pinnate compound leaf

羽士(ㄩˇ ㄕˋ)
a Taoist priest 參看「羽客」or「羽人」

羽扇(ㄩˇ ㄕㄢˋ)
a feather fan

羽扇綸巾(ㄩˇ ㄕㄢˋ ㄍㄨㄢ ㄐㄧㄣ)
(said of a military commander) free from anxiety; calm; composed

羽觴(ㄩˇ ㄕㄤ)
the wine cup

羽人(ㄩˇ ㄖㄣˊ)
a Taoist priest 參看「羽士」or「羽客」

羽族(ㄩˇ ㄗㄨˊ)
the feathered tribe; birds

羽衣(ㄩˇ ㄧ)
a Taoist priest

羽翼(ㄩˇ ㄧˋ)
assistants; helpers

三畫

【羿】 4537
ㄧˋ yih yì
Yi, name of a legendary archer

四畫

【翁】 4538
ㄨㄥ ueng wēng
1. the father
2. the father-in-law
3. an old man
4. a title of respect

5. a Chinese family name
翁同龢(ㄨㄥ ㄊㄨㄥˊ ㄏㄜˊ)
Weng Tung-ho, 1830-1904, a Ching Dynasty scholar and the tutor of two successive emperors
翁姑(ㄨㄥ ㄍㄨ)
a woman's parents-in-law
翁壻(ㄨㄥ ㄒㄩˋ)
father-in-law and son-in-law
翁仲(ㄨㄥ ㄓㄨㄥˋ)
stone statues placed in front of tombs

【翅】 4539 ㄔˋ chyh chì
1. wings
2. fins
翅膀(ㄔˋ ㄅㄤˇ)
wings

【翃】 4540 ㄏㄨㄥˊ horng hóng
(said of insects) flying

五畫

【翊】 4541 ㄧˋ yih yì
1. flying
2. to assist; to help
3. respectful
翊戴(ㄧˋ ㄉㄞˋ)
to assist and support (a ruler)
翊贊(ㄧˋ ㄗㄢˋ)
to assist
翊翊(ㄧˋ ㄧˋ)
respectful

【翎】 4542 ㄌㄧㄥˊ ling líng
feathers; plumes
翎毛(ㄌㄧㄥˊ ㄇㄠˊ)
① feathers ② birds (a term used in Chinese painting)

【翌】 4543 ㄧˋ yih yì
tomorrow
翌朝(ㄧˋ ㄓㄠ)
tomorrow morning: 我翌朝將離開此地。I will leave here tomorrow morning.
翌日(ㄧˋ ㄖˋ)
tomorrow

【習】 4544 ㄒㄧˊ shyi xí
1. to learn; to familiarize oneself with; to receive training in
2. habit; custom; practice
3. to follow; to repeat
4. a Chinese family name
習兵(ㄒㄧˊ ㄅㄧㄥ)
① to train troops ② versed in the art of war
習非(ㄒㄧˊ ㄈㄟ)
accustomed to wrongdoing
習非成是(ㄒㄧˊ ㄈㄟ ㄔㄥˊ ㄕˋ)
Through usage the wrong becomes the right.
習題(ㄒㄧˊ ㄊㄧˊ)
problems to be worked out in the course of study; exercises
習慣(ㄒㄧˊ ㄍㄨㄢˋ)
habit; custom; practice; to get used to; to be accustomed to
習慣法(ㄒㄧˊ ㄍㄨㄢˋ ㄈㄚˇ)
consuetudinary law
習慣性(ㄒㄧˊ ㄍㄨㄢˋ ㄒㄧㄥˋ)
① inertia ② habitual
習慣成自然(ㄒㄧˊ ㄍㄨㄢˋ ㄔㄥˊ ㄗˋ ㄖㄢˊ)
Habit is second nature.
習慣語(ㄒㄧˊ ㄍㄨㄢˋ ㄩˇ)
an idiom
習見(ㄒㄧˊ ㄐㄧㄢˋ)
often or frequently seen
習氣(ㄒㄧˊ ·ㄑㄧ)
bad habit or custom
習習(ㄒㄧˊ ㄒㄧˊ)
① (descriptive of the east wind) blowing gently; breezy; refreshing ② flying; lively
習性(ㄒㄧˊ ㄒㄧㄥˋ)
temperament; dispositions
習尙(ㄒㄧˊ ㄕㄤˋ)
① honored practice or custom ② fashion
習熟(ㄒㄧˊ ㄕㄨˊ)
to be familiar with; to understand
習染(ㄒㄧˊ ㄖㄢˇ)
to be corrupted by (evil practices)
習字(ㄒㄧˊ ㄗˋ)
to learn penmanship or calligraphy
習字帖(ㄒㄧˊ ㄗˋ ㄊㄧㄝˋ)
a copybook
習作(ㄒㄧˊ ㄗㄨㄛˋ)
to learn to do
習俗(ㄒㄧˊ ㄙㄨˊ)
custom; practice
習俗移人(ㄒㄧˊ ㄙㄨˊ ㄧˊ ㄖㄣˊ)
Habit and custom can change one's nature.
習而不察(ㄒㄧˊ ㄦˊ ㄅㄨˋ ㄔㄚˊ)
to do something without studying it first after one has become accustomed to it
習以爲常(ㄒㄧˊ ㄧˇ ㄨㄟˊ ㄔㄤˊ)
to have become a force of habit; to fall into a habit; having been accustomed to it: 他說謊已習以爲常。He has fallen into the habit of telling lies.
習藝(ㄒㄧˊ ㄧˋ)
to learn a skill or trade
習藝所(ㄒㄧˊ ㄧˋ ㄙㄨㄛˇ)
a vocational training institution (for paupers, convicts, etc.)
習與性成(ㄒㄧˊ ㄩˇ ㄒㄧㄥˋ ㄔㄥˊ)
Habit becomes one's second nature.
習用(ㄒㄧˊ ㄩㄥˋ)
to use as a habit

六畫

【翔】 4545 ㄒㄧㄤˊ shyang xiáng
1. to soar
2. same as 詳—detailed
翔集(ㄒㄧㄤˊ ㄐㄧˊ)
to gather the essence from many sources
翔盡(ㄒㄧㄤˊ ㄐㄧㄣˋ)
detailed and complete
翔實(ㄒㄧㄤˊ ㄕˊ)
detailed and accurate
翔泳(ㄒㄧㄤˊ ㄩㄥˇ)
birds and fish

【翕】 4546 ㄒㄧˋ shih xì
1. to fold; to close
2. to draw together; to gather
翕赫(ㄒㄧˋ ㄏㄜˋ)
vigorous; thriving
翕忽(ㄒㄧˋ ㄏㄨ)
swift; agile; nimble
翕霍(ㄒㄧˋ ㄏㄨㄛˋ)
to open and close alternately
翕張(ㄒㄧˋ ㄓㄤ)
to open and close alternately
翕然(ㄒㄧˋ ㄖㄢˊ)
peace and stability
翕翼(ㄒㄧˋ ㄧˋ)
to fold wings

〔羽部〕

八畫

【翟】 4547 1. ㄓㄞˊ jair zhái (讀音 ㄓㄜˊ jer zhé)
a Chinese family name

【翟】 4547 2. ㄉㄧˊ dyi dí
a kind of pheasant with long tail feathers

翟羽(ㄉㄧˊ ㄩˇ)
pheasant feathers

【翠】 4548 ㄘㄨㄟˋ tsuey cuì
1. bluish green
2. green jade
3. a kingfisher

翠波(ㄘㄨㄟˋ ㄅㄛ)
green waves

翠柏(ㄘㄨㄟˋ ㄅㄞˇ)
a bluish green cypress

翠眉(ㄘㄨㄟˋ ㄇㄟˊ)
①blackened eyebrows ②a beauty's eyebrows

翠黛(ㄘㄨㄟˋ ㄉㄞˋ)
①material for blackening eyebrows ②a beauty's eyebrows

翠鳥(ㄘㄨㄟˋ ㄋㄧㄠˇ)
a kingfisher; a halcyon

翠綠(ㄘㄨㄟˋ ㄌㄩˋ)
emerald; bluish green: 那女孩著翠綠色的衣服。The girl dressed in bluish green.

翠亨村(ㄘㄨㄟˋ ㄏㄥ ㄘㄨㄣ)
the village of Tsuiheng in Kwangtung, where Dr. Sun Yat-sen was born

翠華(ㄘㄨㄟˋ ㄏㄨㄚˊ)
an imperial banner adorned with feathers of kingfishers or halcyons

翠鬟(ㄘㄨㄟˋ ㄏㄨㄢˊ)
beautiful dark hair (of a woman)

翠菊(ㄘㄨㄟˋ ㄐㄩˊ)
(botany) a China aster: 翠菊很快就會開了。China asters will come into flower soon.

翠翹(ㄘㄨㄟˋ ㄑㄧㄠˊ)
①feathers of a kingfisher or halcyon ②a kind of ancient headdress for women

翠竹(ㄘㄨㄟˋ ㄓㄨˊ)
green bamboos

翠繞珠圍(ㄘㄨㄟˋ ㄖㄠˋ ㄓㄨ ㄨㄟˊ)
①(said of a woman) to be fully dressed up ②to be surrounded by beauties

翠帷(ㄘㄨㄟˋ ㄨㄟˊ)
a curtain adorned with feathers of kingfishers

翠微(ㄘㄨㄟˋ ㄨㄟˊ)
①the blue-green mountain side ②blue-green mountain vapor

翠羽(ㄘㄨㄟˋ ㄩˇ)
feathers of kingfishers or halcyons

翠玉(ㄘㄨㄟˋ ㄩˋ)
emerald; blue jade: 她喜歡翠玉甚於珍珠。She prefers emerald to pearls.

【翣】 4549 ㄕㄚˋ shah shà
feathers adorning a coffin

【翡】 4550 ㄈㄟˇ feei fěi
1. a kingfisher
2. emerald

翡翠(ㄈㄟˇ ㄘㄨㄟˋ)
①a kingfisher or halcyon ②emerald

九畫

【翦】 4551 ㄐㄧㄢˇ jean jiǎn
same as 剪—to trim; to clip; to cut with scissors

【翥】 4552 ㄓㄨˋ juh zhù
to take off; to soar

【翬】 4553 ㄏㄨㄟ huei huī
1. to fly
2. a multicolored pheasant

【翩】 4554 ㄆㄧㄢ pian piān
to fly swiftly

翩翩(ㄆㄧㄢ ㄆㄧㄢ)
①to fly swiftly; to flutter: 蝴蝶在花叢中翩翩飛舞。The butterfly fluttered among the flowers. ②(descriptive of movement) lightly and swiftly ③complacent ④elegant; stylish

翩翩公子(ㄆㄧㄢ ㄆㄧㄢ ㄍㄨㄥ ㄗˇ) or 翩翩少年(ㄆㄧㄢ ㄆㄧㄢ ㄕㄠˋ ㄋㄧㄢˊ)
a dandy; a beau

翩翻(ㄆㄧㄢ ㄈㄢ)
to flutter about; to fly up and down

翩躚(ㄆㄧㄢ ㄒㄧㄢ)
flying or dancing gracefully

翩然(ㄆㄧㄢ ㄖㄢˊ)
sprightly

翩然而至(ㄆㄧㄢ ㄖㄢˊ ㄦˊ ㄓˋ)
to come trippingly

【翫】 4555 ㄨㄢˋ wann wàn
1. careless or casual due to familiarity
2. to play

翫愒(ㄨㄢˋ ㄎㄞˋ)
to trifle away one's time

翫忽(ㄨㄢˋ ㄏㄨ)
negligent; careless

翫味(ㄨㄢˋ ㄨㄟˋ)
appreciation: 這首詩值得翫味。This poem is worthy appreciation.

十畫

【翱】 4556 ㄠˊ aur áo
same as 翺—to soar

【翮】 4557 ㄏㄜˊ her hé
the shaft of a feather

【翰】 4558 ㄏㄢˋ hann hàn
1. a white horse
2. a long and hard feather
3. a piece of writing

翰墨(ㄏㄢˋ ㄇㄛˋ)
(literally) quill and ink—literary pursuits

翰林(ㄏㄢˋ ㄌㄧㄣˊ)
①the literary circles ②a high literary degree in the former system ③a scholar with a high literary degree in old China

翰林院(ㄏㄢˋ ㄌㄧㄣˊ ㄩㄢˋ)
the National Academy (in former times)

翰海 or 瀚海(ㄏㄢˋ ㄏㄞˇ)
the Gobi Desert in Mongolia

翰札(ㄏㄢˋ ㄓㄚˊ)
letters

翰池(ㄏㄢˋ ㄔˊ)
an inkstone; an ink slab

翰苑(ㄏㄢˋ ㄩㄢˋ)
the literary circles

十一畫

【翳】 4559
丨ˋ yih yì
(又讀 丨 i yī)
1. to screen; to conceal
2. the haziness of objects due to weakened vision
3. the chariot cover made of feathers
4. the film over a diseased eye

翳翳(丨ˋ 丨ˋ)
dim; hazy; obscure; vague

【翼】 4560
丨ˋ yih yì
1. wings
2. fins
3. to assist; to help
4. to protect; to patronize; to harbor

翼蔽(丨ˋ ㄅ丨ˋ)
to cover

翼戴(丨ˋ ㄉㄞˋ)
to assist and support

翼卵(丨ˋ ㄌㄨㄢˇ)
to protect; to patronize

翼然(丨ˋ ㄖㄢˊ)
(said of architectural features) like extended wings aloft

翼贊(丨ˋ ㄗㄢˋ)
to assist and support

翼翼(丨ˋ 丨ˋ)
① cautious; careful ② robust; vigorous

十二畫

【翹】 4561
1. ㄑ丨ㄠˊ chyau qiáo
1. long tail feathers
2. to raise
3. outstanding

翹企(ㄑ丨ㄠˊ ㄑ丨ˋ)
to long eagerly

翹秀(ㄑ丨ㄠˊ ㄒ丨ㄡˋ)or 翹楚(ㄑ丨ㄠˊ ㄔㄨˇ)
a man of outstanding ability

翹首(ㄑ丨ㄠˊ ㄕㄡˇ)
(literally) to raise the head —to long eagerly

翹首而望(ㄑ丨ㄠˊ ㄕㄡˇ ㄦˊ ㄨㄤˋ)
to raise one's head in hope

翹足而待(ㄑ丨ㄠˊ ㄗㄨˊ ㄦˊ ㄉㄞˋ)
to wait on tiptoe—to expect something to be soon forthcoming

翹材(ㄑ丨ㄠˊ ㄘㄞˊ)
a man of outstanding ability 亦作「翹秀」

翹望(ㄑ丨ㄠˊ ㄨㄤˋ)
to long eagerly 亦作「翹思」

【翹】 4561
2. ㄑ丨ㄠˋ chiaw qiào
to project upward; to stick up; to turn upward

翹辮子(ㄑ丨ㄠˋ ㄅ丨ㄢˋ ・ㄗ)
to die; to kick the bucket

翹翹板(ㄑ丨ㄠˋ ㄑ丨ㄠˋ ㄅㄢˇ)
seesaw 亦作「蹺蹺板」

【翻】 4562
ㄈㄢ fan fān
1. to fly; to flutter
2. to turn; to upset; to capsize: 車子翻了。The car turned over.
3. to rummage
4. to translate
5. to fall out; to break up: 我們鬧翻了。We quarreled and broke up.

翻版(ㄈㄢ ㄅㄢˇ)
a reprint of a book (with or without proper permission)

翻本(ㄈㄢ ㄅㄣˇ)or 翻本兒(ㄈㄢ ㄅㄜˇㄦ)
to recover the money lost (in gambling)

翻覆(ㄈㄢ ㄈㄨˋ)
unstable; vacillating 亦作「反覆」

翻覆無常(ㄈㄢ ㄈㄨˋ ㄨˊ ㄔㄤˊ)
vacillating; unstable; capricious; whimsical: 他是個翻覆無常的人。He is a man of capricious temper.

翻騰(ㄈㄢ ・ㄊㄥ)
① to throw into disorder ② to turn over and over (as water); to roll about; to toss: 波濤翻騰。The waves tossed.

翻天覆地(ㄈㄢ ㄊ丨ㄢ ㄈㄨˋ ㄉ丨ˋ)
to turn everything upside down; world-shaking

翻來覆去(ㄈㄢ ㄌㄞˊ ㄈㄨˋ ㄑㄩˋ)
① to turn over and over; to roll about; to toss and turn ② to vacillate

翻老帳(ㄈㄢ ㄌㄠˇ ㄓㄤˋ)
to bring up old scores again

翻臉(ㄈㄢ ㄌ丨ㄢˇ)
to show displeasure; to get angry; to turn hostile

翻臉不認人(ㄈㄢ ㄌ丨ㄢˇ ㄅㄨˋ ㄖㄣˋ ㄖㄣˊ)
to deny a friend; to turn against an old acquaintance

翻臉無情(ㄈㄢ ㄌ丨ㄢˇ ㄨˊ ㄑ丨ㄥˊ)
to turn against a friend and show him no mercy; to be deceptive and ruthless

翻蓋(ㄈㄢ ㄍㄞˋ)
to rebuild (a house)

翻跟頭(ㄈㄢ ㄍㄣ ・ㄊㄡ)or 翻筋斗(ㄈㄢ ㄐ丨ㄣ ㄉㄡˇ)or 翻跟斗(ㄈㄢ ㄍㄣ ㄉㄡˇ)
① to turn a somersault ② (aeronautic) to loop the loop

翻過兒(ㄈㄢ ㄍㄨㄜˋㄦ)
to turn upside down

翻滾(ㄈㄢ ㄍㄨㄣˇ)
to roll; to toss; to tumble

翻供(ㄈㄢ ㄍㄨㄥˋ)
to withdraw a confession; to retract a testimony (at a law court)

翻開(ㄈㄢ ㄎㄞ)
to turn open

翻悔(ㄈㄟ ㄏㄨㄟˇ)
to disavow a statement, commitment, promise, act, etc.

翻江倒海(ㄈㄢ ㄐ丨ㄤ ㄉㄠˇ ㄏㄞˇ)
to overturn the river and upset the sea—overwhelming; convulsive; world-shaking

翻切(ㄈㄢ ㄑ丨ㄝˋ)
(in ancient Chinese phonetics) to indicate the pronunciation of a character by quick enunciation of two other characters 亦作「反切」

翻修(ㄈㄢ ㄒ丨ㄡ)
to rebuild; to overhaul; to remodel: 他想翻修那道牆。He wants to rebuild the wall.

翻新(ㄈㄢ ㄒ丨ㄣ)
to overhaul; to rebuild; to recondition; to revamp: 舊房子可以翻新。Old houses can be reconditioned.

翻箱倒篋(ㄈㄢ ㄒ丨ㄤ ㄉㄠˇ ㄑ丨ㄝˋ)
(literally) to overturn every box and basket—to make a thorough search

翻車(ㄈㄢ ㄔㄜ)
① a scoop wheel ② (said of a vehicle) to overturn; to capsize ③ a kind of snare for birds

翻車魚(ㄈㄢ ㄔㄜ ㄩˊ)
the sunfish

翻船(ㄈㄢ ㄔㄨㄢˊ)

(said of a boat) to capsize

翻砂(ㄈㄢ ㄕㄚ)
(machinery) to cast metal forms in earthen moulds; to found; founding

翻山越嶺(ㄈㄢ ㄕㄢ ㄩㄝˋ ㄌㄧㄥˇ)
to travel over mountains and valleys

翻身(ㄈㄢ ㄕㄣ)
①to turn the body over ②to rise from poverty to affluence; to have a break of fortune: 他沒機會翻身。He has no chance to rise again.

翻然悔悟(ㄈㄢ ㄖㄢˊ ㄏㄨㄟˇ ㄨˋ)
quickly wake up to one's mistakes

翻案(ㄈㄢ ㄢˋ)
to reverse a previous verdict

翻案文章(ㄈㄢ ㄢˋ ㄨㄣˊ ㄓㄤ)
articles expressing a new point of view about historic incidents

翻譯(ㄈㄢ ㄧˋ)
to translate; to interpret

翻譯本(ㄈㄢ ㄧˋ ㄅㄣˇ)
a translation (of a book); a translated version

翻譯官(ㄈㄢ ㄧˋ ㄍㄨㄢ)
an officer whose business is to interpret or translate

翻譯權(ㄈㄢ ㄧˋ ㄑㄩㄢˊ)
the translation right (for a book)

翻譯者(ㄈㄢ ㄧˋ ㄓㄜˇ)
a translator

翻印(ㄈㄢ ㄧㄣˋ)
to reprint (a book with or without proper permission)

翻印必究(ㄈㄢ ㄧㄣˋ ㄅㄧˋ ㄐㄧㄡ)
(said of a book) all rights reserved

翻胃(ㄈㄢ ㄨㄟˋ)
to feel nausea; nauseating

翻閱(ㄈㄢ ㄩㄝˋ)
to browse; to look over; to glance over; to leaf through; to thumb through (a book, magazine, etc.)

翻雲覆雨(ㄈㄢ ㄩㄣˊ ㄈㄨˋ ㄩˇ)
(said of human affections) as changeable as clouds and rain

【翱】 4563
(翺) ㄠˊ aur áo
1. to soar; to fly
2. to roam; to wander

翱翔(ㄠˊ ㄒㄧㄤˊ)
①to soar; to fly ②to roam

十三畫

【翾】 4564
ㄒㄩㄢ shiuan xuān
to flit

翾翾(ㄒㄩㄢ ㄒㄩㄢ)
flitting; flying sprightly

【翽】 4565
ㄏㄨㄟˋ huey huì
sounds of wings flapping

十四畫

【翿】 4566
ㄉㄠˋ daw dào
(又讀 ㄊㄠˊ taur táo)
a kind of streamer or screen adorned with feathers carried by dancers

【耀】 4567
ㄧㄠˋ yaw yào
(又讀 ㄩㄝˋ yueh yuè)
1. to shine; to dazzle
2. to show off

耀光(ㄧㄠˋ ㄍㄨㄤ)
luster (especially of minerals); to sparkle; sparkling

耀耀(ㄧㄠˋ ㄧㄠˋ)
bright

耀眼(ㄧㄠˋ ㄧㄢˇ)
dazzling; to dazzle

耀眼增光(ㄧㄠˋ ㄧㄢˇ ㄗㄥ ㄍㄨㄤ)
dazzling

耀武揚威(ㄧㄠˋ ㄨˇ ㄧㄤˊ ㄨㄟ)
①to parade military prowess ②to show off one's strength or power; to bluff and bluster

老部
ㄌㄠˇ lao lǎo

【老】 4568
ㄌㄠˇ lao lǎo
1. old; aged; venerable: 活到老學到老。There is still much to learn after one has grown old.
2. always: 他老是遲到。He is always late.
3. the youngest
4. very
5. a particle indicating ordinal numbers to designate order of birth
6. parents
7. a particle used before a man's family name to indicate familiarity and friendship
8. (said of meat, etc.) tough; over-cooked: 這塊牛肉太老。The beef is over-cooked.
9. to treat with the reverence to the aged
10. (said of color) dark: 這件外套顏色太老了。This coat is too dark.

老八板兒(ㄌㄠˇ ㄅㄚ ㄅㄢˇㄦ)
an ultraconservative

老把戲(ㄌㄠˇ ㄅㄚˇ ㄒㄧˋ)
an old trick: 他的狗只會玩老把戲。His dog knows only old tricks.

老把勢(ㄌㄠˇ ㄅㄚˇ ·ㄕ)
an old hand

老伴兒(ㄌㄠˇ ㄅㄢˋㄦ)
one's dear old companion—one's spouse in old age

老伯(ㄌㄠˇ ㄅㄛˊ)
(respectful address) uncle; one's father's friend or friend's father

老百姓(ㄌㄠˇ ㄅㄞˇ ㄒㄧㄥˋ)
the people; the common people

老誖(ㄌㄠˇ ㄅㄟˋ)
in dotage; senile

老輩(ㄌㄠˇ ㄅㄟˋ)
one's senior

老鴇(ㄌㄠˇ ㄅㄠˇ)
a procuress

老板 or 老闆(ㄌㄠˇ ㄅㄢˇ)
①a boss; a master ②a keeper; a proprietor

老板娘(ㄌㄠˇ ㄅㄢˇ ㄋㄧㄤˊ)
①a proprietress; proprietor's wife ②boss's wife; a mistress

老半天(ㄌㄠˇ ㄅㄢˋ ㄊㄧㄢ)
quite a while

老本(ㄌㄠˇ ㄅㄣˇ)or 老本兒(ㄌㄠˇ ㄅㄜˇㄦ)
①a principal; a capital; the original investment ②an old edition

老蚌生珠(ㄌㄠˇ ㄅㄤˋ ㄕㄥ ㄓㄨ)
(literally) a pearl from an old oyster—a son born in

one's old age
老婢(ㄌㄠˇ ㄅㄧˋ)
an old housemaid
老表(ㄌㄠˇ ㄅㄧㄠˇ)
①an old (in the sense of "dear") cousin (on the maternal side) ②a common greeting among men in Kiangsi which amounts to something like "old pal" or "buddy"
老兵(ㄌㄠˇ ㄅㄧㄥ)
an old soldier
老病(ㄌㄠˇ ㄅㄧㄥˋ)
①old and ailing ②an old ailment; a chronic disease
老病侵尋(ㄌㄠˇ ㄅㄧㄥˋ ㄑㄧㄣ ㄒㄩㄣˊ)
aging and ailing
老不正經(ㄌㄠˇ ㄅㄨˋ ㄓㄥˋ ·ㄐㄧㄥ)
a gray-haired womanizer; an old philanderer; old but still licentious
老不死的(ㄌㄠˇ ㄅㄨˋ ㄙˇ ·ㄉㄜ)
an old bastard
老不修(ㄌㄠˇ ·ㄅㄨ ㄒㄧㄡ)
an old lecher
老派兒(ㄌㄠˇ ㄆㄚˋㄦ)
a conservative
老婆婆(ㄌㄠˇ ㄆㄛˊ ·ㄆㄛ)
respectful address for an old woman
老婆子(ㄌㄠˇ ㄆㄛˊ ·ㄗ) or 老婆兒(ㄌㄠˇ ㄆㄛˊㄦ)
①an old woman ②an old wife ③an old maid
老婆(ㄌㄠˇ ·ㄆㄛ)
(vulgar usage) a wife
老牌(ㄌㄠˇ ㄆㄞˊ) or 老牌子(ㄌㄠˇ ㄆㄞˊ ·ㄗ) or 老牌兒(ㄌㄠˇ ㄆㄚˊㄦ)
①an old brand ②a veteran (actor or actress)
老彭(ㄌㄠˇ ㄆㄥˊ)
Lao-tzu (老子) and Pengtsu (彭祖)
老朋友(ㄌㄠˇ ㄆㄥˊ ·ㄧㄡ)
an old friend
老僕(ㄌㄠˇ ㄆㄨˊ)
an old servant
老圃(ㄌㄠˇ ㄆㄨˇ)
①an old vegetable garden ②an old vegetable gardener
老譜兒(ㄌㄠˇ ㄆㄨˇㄦ)
old rules
老鋪(ㄌㄠˇ ㄆㄨˋ) or 老店(ㄌㄠˇ ㄉㄧㄢˋ)
an old store
老嬤嬤(ㄌㄠˇ ㄇㄚ ·ㄇㄚ)
an old housemaid
老媽媽論兒(ㄌㄠˇ ㄇㄚ ·ㄇㄚ ㄌㄨㄜˋㄦ)
a set of mostly superstitious rules handed down from generation to generation in former times
老媽子(ㄌㄠˇ ㄇㄚ ·ㄗ)
a housemaid; an amah
老馬識途(ㄌㄠˇ ㄇㄚˇ ㄕˋ ㄊㄨˊ)
(literally) An old horse knows the way.—experienced and capable of leading others wisely
老邁(ㄌㄠˇ ㄇㄞˋ)
senile and weak
老邁無能(ㄌㄠˇ ㄇㄞˋ ㄨˊ ㄋㄥˊ)
old and powerless; aged and impotent
老妹妹(ㄌㄠˇ ㄇㄟˋ ·ㄇㄟ)
the youngest sister
老毛病(ㄌㄠˇ ㄇㄠˊ ·ㄅㄧㄥ)
①an old ailment ②an old weakness
老眊(ㄌㄠˇ ㄇㄠˋ)
①dim sight of the aged ②a person who is more than eighty years old
老耄(ㄌㄠˇ ㄇㄠˋ)
senile
老謀深算(ㄌㄠˇ ㄇㄡˊ ㄕㄣ ㄙㄨㄢˋ)
scheming and calculating; experienced and astute
老米(ㄌㄠˇ ㄇㄧˇ)
(during the Ming and Ching dynasties) the rice shipped from the southern provinces to Peking or Tungchow, which ferments and changes into a brownish color after being kept too long in the barns
老面皮(ㄌㄠˇ ㄇㄧㄢˋ ㄆㄧˊ)
shameless; brazen
老面子(ㄌㄠˇ ㄇㄧㄢˋ ·ㄗ)
①old friendship ②out of respect for the aged
老命(ㄌㄠˇ ㄇㄧㄥˋ)
①the life of an old person ②one's dear life
老母(ㄌㄠˇ ㄇㄨˇ)
one's old mother
老法子(ㄌㄠˇ ㄈㄚˇ ·ㄗ)
an old method
老佛爺(ㄌㄠˇ ㄈㄛˊ ·ㄧㄝ)
①Buddha ②a reference to the late emperor or to the empress dowager in the Ching Dynasty
老廢物(ㄌㄠˇ ㄈㄟˋ ㄨˋ)
①waste matter; waste material ②a good-for-nothing
老方子(ㄌㄠˇ ㄈㄤ ·ㄗ)
an old prescription
老夫(ㄌㄠˇ ㄈㄨ)
①(used by an old man) I; me ②an old husband
老夫老妻(ㄌㄠˇ ㄈㄨ ㄌㄠˇ ㄑㄧ)
an old couple
老夫少妻(ㄌㄠˇ ㄈㄨ ㄕㄠˋ ㄑㄧ)
an old man with a young wife
老夫子(ㄌㄠˇ ㄈㄨ ㄗˇ)
①a private school master (in former times) ②a reference to a confidential secretary in former times
老腐敗(ㄌㄠˇ ㄈㄨˇ ㄅㄞˋ)
a corrupt old fellow
老婦(ㄌㄠˇ ㄈㄨˋ) or 老婦人(ㄌㄠˇ ㄈㄨˋ ㄖㄣˊ)
an old woman
老父台(ㄌㄠˇ ㄈㄨˋ ㄊㄞˊ)
a reference to the local magistrate in old China
老搭檔(ㄌㄠˇ ㄉㄚ ㄉㄤˋ)
an old partner; an old workmate
老大(ㄌㄠˇ ㄉㄚˋ)
①old ②the eldest child; a firstborn ③the leader of a gang ④extremely; exceedingly
老大不小(ㄌㄠˇ ㄉㄚˋ ㄅㄨˋ ㄒㄧㄠˇ)
to have grown up; to have come of age
老大徒傷悲(ㄌㄠˇ ㄉㄚˋ ㄊㄨˊ ㄕㄤ ㄅㄟ)
to grieve vainly in one's old age
老大哥(ㄌㄠˇ ㄉㄚˋ ㄍㄜ)
a reference to one's senior of equal standing; elder brothers
老呆 or 老獃(ㄌㄠˇ ㄉㄞ)
an old fool
老道(ㄌㄠˇ ㄉㄠˋ)
a Taoist priest
老到(ㄌㄠˇ ·ㄉㄠ)
showing much experience; expert; reliable
老豆腐(ㄌㄠˇ ㄉㄡˋ ·ㄈㄨ)
hardened bean curd
老聃(ㄌㄠˇ ㄉㄢ)
another name of Lao-tzu,

604-531 B.C.

老旦(ㄌㄠˇ ㄉㄢˋ)
the role of an old female in Chinese opera

老當益壯(ㄌㄠˇ ㄉㄤ ㄧˋ ㄓㄨㄤˋ)
to gain vigor with age

老等(ㄌㄠˇ ㄉㄥˇ)
to wait patiently

老底子(ㄌㄠˇ ㄉㄧˇ ·ㄗ)or 老底兒(ㄌㄠˇ ㄉㄧˇㄜㄦ)or 老根兒(ㄌㄠˇ ㄍㄜㄦ)
① an inherited fortune ② ancestry; pedigree ③ the unpublicized seamy side of one's life

老弟(ㄌㄠˇ ㄉㄧˋ)
① a reference to one's junior of equal standing ② my dear student; my dear disciple

老爹(ㄌㄠˇ ㄉㄧㄝ)
① one's father ② respectful address for an aged man

老調重彈(ㄌㄠˇ ㄉㄧㄠˋ ㄔㄨㄥˊ ㄊㄢˊ)
to play the same old tune

老掉牙(ㄌㄠˇ ㄉㄧㄠˋ ㄧㄚˊ)
very old; old-fashioned; outdated; obsolete

老店新開(ㄌㄠˇ ㄉㄧㄢˋ ㄒㄧㄣ ㄎㄞ)
① a store reopened after a period of suspension ② the marriage of a couple who have already had sexual intercourse

老杜(ㄌㄠˇ ㄉㄨˋ)
Tu Fu(杜甫), 712-770, a famous poet of the Tang Dynasty

老東西(ㄌㄠˇ ㄉㄨㄥ ·ㄒㄧ)
①old stuff; old things ②an abusive reference to an aged person

老態(ㄌㄠˇ ㄊㄞˋ)
① one's old way ② the appearance, or manner of the aged

老態龍鍾(ㄌㄠˇ ㄊㄞˋ ㄌㄨㄥˊ ㄓㄨㄥ)
the appearance of senility and dotage of the aged

老太婆(ㄌㄠˇ ㄊㄞˋ ㄆㄛˊ)
an old woman

老太太(ㄌㄠˇ ㄊㄞˋ ·ㄊㄞ)
an old lady

老太爺(ㄌㄠˇ ㄊㄞˋ ㄧㄝˊ)
①(in addressing an aged man) venerable sir ② an old gentleman

老饕(ㄌㄠˇ ㄊㄠ)
a glutton

老頭子(ㄌㄠˇ ㄊㄡˊ ·ㄗ)
① an old chap; an old fellow ② one's husband

老頭兒(ㄌㄠˇ ㄊㄡˊㄦ)
① an old fellow; an old chap ② one's father

老頭兒樂(ㄌㄠˇ ㄊㄡˊㄦ ㄌㄜˋ)
① a kind of muskmelon that is soft and mushy ② a kind of cotton shoes

老天(ㄌㄠˇ ㄊㄧㄢ)
Heaven—divine justice: 看在老天的份上，原諒我吧！Please forgive me for Heaven's sake.

老天爺(ㄌㄠˇ ㄊㄧㄢ ㄧㄝˊ)
Heaven: 老天爺不負苦心人。Heaven helps those who help themselves.

老禿翁(ㄌㄠˇ ㄊㄨ ㄨㄥ)
an old baldhead

老童生(ㄌㄠˇ ㄊㄨㄥˊ ㄕㄥ)
an old man who had repeatedly flunked the civil service examination in former times

老衲(ㄌㄠˇ ㄋㄚˋ)
self-reference of an aged Buddhist monk

老腦筋(ㄌㄠˇ ㄋㄠˇ ㄐㄧㄣ)
an old (or outmoded) way of thinking

老牛舐犢(ㄌㄠˇ ㄋㄧㄡˊ ㄕˋ ㄉㄨˊ)
(literally) the old cow licking her calf—a parent's indulgent love

老年(ㄌㄠˇ ㄋㄧㄢˊ)
old age; old life; late years

老年性痴呆症(ㄌㄠˇ ㄋㄧㄢˊ ㄒㄧㄥˋ ㄔ ㄉㄞ ㄓㄥˋ)
(pathology) senile dementia

老年人(ㄌㄠˇ ㄋㄧㄢˊ ㄖㄣˊ)
the aged; the old people

老娘(ㄌㄠˇ ㄋㄧㄤˊ)
① one's old mother ② self-reference of a virago in a quarrel ③ a midwife

老奴(ㄌㄠˇ ㄋㄨˊ)
① self-reference of an old servant ② an abusive reference to an aged man

老農(ㄌㄠˇ ㄋㄨㄥˊ)
an old farmer; a veteran farmer: 這老農經營一個農場。The old farmer runs a farm.

老辣(ㄌㄠˇ ㄌㄚˋ)
① drastic and ruthless ② (said of literary works) incisive; penetrating

老了(ㄌㄠˇ ·ㄌㄜ)
to have grown old: 他已經老了。He has grown old.

老來(ㄌㄠˇ ㄌㄞˊ)
when one gets old: 他老來富。He lives in richness in his old age.

老來俏(ㄌㄠˇ ㄌㄞˊ ㄑㄧㄠˋ)
(said of a woman) to become more attractive as she gets older

老來少(ㄌㄠˇ ㄌㄞˊ ㄕㄠˋ)
① old in age but young in spirit ②(botany) Joseph's coat 亦作「老少年」or「雁來紅」

老來子(ㄌㄠˇ ㄌㄞˊ ㄗˇ)
a son born in one's old age

老萊子(ㄌㄠˇ ㄌㄞˊ ㄗˇ)
Lao Lai-tse, who flourished in the Epoch of Spring and Autumn, was famous for his filial piety, for when he was seventy he still behaved like a child, wearing a motley in the presence of his parents, so as to please them.

老羸(ㄌㄠˇ ㄌㄟˊ)
old and weak

老淚(ㄌㄠˇ ㄌㄟˋ)
tears of an old person

老淚縱橫(ㄌㄠˇ ㄌㄟˋ ㄗㄨㄥˋ ㄏㄥˊ)
(said of an aged person) tearful

老老 or 姥姥(ㄌㄠˇ ·ㄌㄠ)
① one's maternal grandmother ② a midwife

老老實實的(ㄌㄠˇ ·ㄌㄠ ㄕˊ ㄕˊ ·ㄉㄜ)
conscientiously; honest

老例(ㄌㄠˇ ㄌㄧˋ)or 老例兒(ㄌㄠˇ ㄌㄧˋㄜㄦ)
old practices

老吏斷獄(ㄌㄠˇ ㄌㄧˋ ㄉㄨㄢˋ ㄩˋ)
to decide a legal case promptly and correctly

老臉(ㄌㄠˇ ㄌㄧㄢˇ)
① shameless; brazen ② an actor wearing a painted face in Peking opera

老練(ㄌㄠˇ ㄌㄧㄢˋ)
experienced; skilled; expert; veteran: 他車開得很老練。He is expert at driving a car.

老哥(ㄌㄠˇ ㄍㄜ)
my dear friend (used among

males): 老哥，請聽我說。My dear friend, listen to me, please.

老狗(ㄌㄠˇ ㄍㄡˇ)
an old dog (an abusive term for an old person)

老幹部(ㄌㄠˇ ㄍㄢˋ ㄅㄨˋ)
a veteran cadre

老姑娘(ㄌㄠˇ ㄍㄨ ·ㄋㄧㄤ)
an old spinster; an old maid

老骨頭(ㄌㄠˇ ㄍㄨˇ ·ㄊㄡ)
the life of an old person

老古董(ㄌㄠˇ ㄍㄨˇ ㄉㄨㄥˇ)
① antiques; curios ② an ultraconservative

老鴰(ㄌㄠˇ ㄍㄨㄚ)
a crow

老規矩(ㄌㄠˇ ㄍㄨㄟ ㄐㄩˇ)
old rules; old practices

老公(ㄌㄠˇ ㄍㄨㄥ)
① an old man ② one's husband (a vulgar usage)

老公公(ㄌㄠˇ ㄍㄨㄥ ·ㄍㄨㄥ)
① an old man ② a eunuch

老開(ㄌㄠˇ ㄎㄞ)
Laokai, a town in the Vietnamese side of the Sino-Vietnamese border

老好人(ㄌㄠˇ ㄏㄠˇ ㄖㄣˊ)or 老好子(ㄌㄠˇ ㄏㄠˇ ·ㄗ)
a good-natured person; a soft-hearted person

老漢(ㄌㄠˇ ㄏㄢˋ)
an old man: 那老漢笛子吹得好。The old man played well on the flute.

老行家(ㄌㄠˇ ㄏㄤˊ ·ㄐㄧㄚ)
an expert; an old hand

老糊塗(ㄌㄠˇ ㄏㄨˊ ·ㄊㄨ)
a dotard: 他不能十分相信那老糊塗。He can't quite believe the dotard.

老狐狸(ㄌㄠˇ ㄏㄨˊ ·ㄌㄧ)
① an old fox ② a cunning old man

老虎(ㄌㄠˇ ㄏㄨˇ)
a tiger

老虎鉗(ㄌㄠˇ ㄏㄨˇ ㄑㄧㄢˊ)
a vice, or vise

老花子(ㄌㄠˇ ㄏㄨㄚ ·ㄗ)
a beggar

老花眼(ㄌㄠˇ ㄏㄨㄚ ㄧㄢˇ)
presbyopia 亦作「老光」。

老花眼鏡(ㄌㄠˇ ㄏㄨㄚ ㄧㄢˇ ㄐㄧㄥˋ)
convex glasses for one suffering from presbyopia

老花樣(ㄌㄠˇ ㄏㄨㄚ ㄧㄤˋ)
the same old stuff; the same old trick

老滑頭(ㄌㄠˇ ㄏㄨㄚˊ ㄊㄡˊ)
a cunning old fellow

老話(ㄌㄠˇ ㄏㄨㄚˋ)
① an old saying; a saying; an adage ② remarks about the old days

老話兒(ㄌㄠˇ ㄏㄨㄚˋㄦ)
old remarks; oft-repeated remarks

老幾(ㄌㄠˇ ㄐㄧˇ)
① one's seniority among brothers or sisters: 你在家中排行老幾? What's your seniority in your family? ② who; a nobody: 他算老幾。He is a nobody.

老驥伏櫪，志在千里(ㄌㄠˇ ㄐㄧˋ ㄈㄨˊ ㄌㄧˋ, ㄓˋ ㄗㄞˋ ㄑㄧㄢ ㄌㄧˇ)
An old steed hidden in the stable still aspires to gallop a thousand *li*. —(figuratively said of people) aged but still ambitious

老家(ㄌㄠˇ ㄐㄧㄚ)
① one's original home ② hell: 我送你回老家。I'll send you to hell.

老街坊(ㄌㄠˇ ㄐㄧㄝ ·ㄈㄤ)
a neighbor

老街舊鄰(ㄌㄠˇ ㄐㄧㄝ ㄐㄧㄡˋ ㄌㄧㄣˊ)
an old neighbor

老交情(ㄌㄠˇ ㄐㄧㄠ ·ㄑㄧㄥ)
old friendship

老酒(ㄌㄠˇ ㄐㄧㄡˇ)
old wine

老舊(ㄌㄠˇ ㄐㄧㄡˋ)
old-style; old and worn-out; old-fashioned

老奸巨猾(ㄌㄠˇ ㄐㄧㄢ ㄐㄩˋ ㄏㄨㄚˊ)
shrewd and crafty; a crafty old scoundrel

老繭(ㄌㄠˇ ㄐㄧㄢˇ)
calluses

老江湖(ㄌㄠˇ ㄐㄧㄤ ·ㄏㄨ)
a sophisticated old traveler; a worldly-wise person

老將(ㄌㄠˇ ㄐㄧㄤˋ)
① an old general ② a veteran: 他是沙場老將。He is a veteran of battlefield.

老景(ㄌㄠˇ ㄐㄧㄥˇ)
one's lot in old age

老境(ㄌㄠˇ ㄐㄧㄥˋ)
① the late years of one's life ② one's circumstances in old age

老君(ㄌㄠˇ ㄐㄩㄣ)
a respectful name for Laotzu(老子), 604-531 B.C.

老氣(ㄌㄠˇ ·ㄑㄧ)
① an experienced air or style ② old-fashioned ③ (said of colors) plain or dark

老氣橫秋(ㄌㄠˇ ·ㄑㄧ ㄏㄥˊ ㄑㄧㄡ)
① to exhibit much sophistication (though young) ② to be too obtrusively proud because of one's advanced age; arrogant on account of one's seniority

老千(ㄌㄠˇ ㄑㄧㄢ)
a swindler

老慳(ㄌㄠˇ ㄑㄧㄢ)
an old miser

老前輩(ㄌㄠˇ ㄑㄧㄢˊ ㄅㄟˋ)
a term used to address one's senior or an aged person

老親(ㄌㄠˇ ㄑㄧㄣ)
① parents ② old relatives

老槍(ㄌㄠˇ ㄑㄧㄤ)
① a heavy smoker; a chain smoker ② a veteran opium smoker

老去(ㄌㄠˇ ㄑㄩˋ)
to grow old

老拳(ㄌㄠˇ ㄑㄩㄢˊ)
the fist

老小(ㄌㄠˇ ㄒㄧㄠˇ)
① the old and the young ② one's dependents

老羞成怒(ㄌㄠˇ ㄒㄧㄡ ㄔㄥˊ ㄋㄨˋ)
to be angry as a result of embarrassment; to be moved to anger by the feeling of shame

老朽(ㄌㄠˇ ㄒㄧㄡˇ)
① aged and useless ② a polite self-reference of an old man

老先生(ㄌㄠˇ ㄒㄧㄢ ·ㄕㄥ)
①(in addressing an old gentleman) venerable sir ② an old gentleman

老鄉(ㄌㄠˇ ㄒㄧㄤ)
① a fellow villager; a fellow townsman ② a term used to address a (male) stranger

老學究(ㄌㄠˇ ㄒㄩㄝˊ ㄐㄧㄡˋ)
an old pedant

老兄(ㄌㄠˇ ㄒㄩㄥ)

my dear friend (a term used among males of equal standing)

老者(ㄌㄠˇ ㄓㄜˇ)
an old man; the old

老丈(ㄌㄠˇ ㄓㄤˋ)
an old gentleman

老丈人(ㄌㄠˇ ㄓㄤˋ ·ㄖㄣ)
a man's father-in-law

老帳(ㄌㄠˇ ㄓㄤˋ)
① old debts; old bills ② old scores

老主顧(ㄌㄠˇ ㄓㄨˇ ㄍㄨˋ)
an old customer; an old client

老撾(ㄌㄠˇ ㄓㄨㄚ)
Laos

老拙(ㄌㄠˇ ㄓㄨㄛˊ)
old and stupid (depreciatory self-reference of an old person)

老莊(ㄌㄠˇ ㄓㄨㄤ)
the Taoist philosophers Lao-tzu(老子), 604-531 B.C., and Chuang-tzu(莊子), 369-295 B.C.

老巢(ㄌㄠˇ ㄔㄠˊ)
a den (of robbers)

老成(ㄌㄠˇ ㄔㄥˊ)
sophisticated; experienced

老成凋謝(ㄌㄠˇ ㄔㄥˊ ㄉㄧㄠ ㄒㄧㄝˋ)
(a conventional sentence mourning the death of a respected old person) The experienced and accomplished person has passed away.

老成持重(ㄌㄠˇ ㄔㄥˊ ㄔˊ ㄓㄨㄥˋ)
experienced and cautious: 他是個老成持重的人。He is an experienced and cautious person.

老處女(ㄌㄠˇ ㄔㄨˇ ㄋㄩˇ)
an old maid; a spinster

老師(ㄌㄠˇ ㄕ)
a teacher

老師傅(ㄌㄠˇ ㄕ ㄈㄨˋ)
an old master (of a trade)

老師宿儒(ㄌㄠˇ ㄕ ㄙㄨˋ ㄖㄨˊ)
a respectable old scholar

老實(ㄌㄠˇ ㄕˊ)
honest; truthful

老實頭(ㄌㄠˇ ·ㄕ ㄊㄡˊ)
an honest, simple-minded person

老式(ㄌㄠˇ ㄕˋ)
old-fashioned; of an old style

老世交(ㄌㄠˇ ㄕˋ ㄐㄧㄠ)
families on friendly terms for generations

老少咸宜(ㄌㄠˇ ㄕㄠˋ ㄒㄧㄢˊ ㄧˊ)
suitable for both the old and the young

老少無欺(ㄌㄠˇ ㄕㄠˋ ㄨˊ ㄑㄧ)
(literally) to cheat neither the old nor the young—We are honest with our customers.

老手(ㄌㄠˇ ㄕㄡˇ)
an old hand: 他是開車老手。He is an old hand at driving.

老壽星(ㄌㄠˇ ㄕㄡˋ ㄒㄧㄥ)
a term of compliment for an aged person

老身(ㄌㄠˇ ㄕㄣ)
self-reference of an old woman or man

老生(ㄌㄠˇ ㄕㄥ)
① the role of an old man in Chinese opera ② an aged student or scholar

老聲老氣(ㄌㄠˇ ㄕㄥ ㄌㄠˇ ㄑㄧˋ)
the sound and look of an old person

老生常談(ㄌㄠˇ ㄕㄥ ㄔㄤˊ ㄊㄢˊ)
a threadbare argument or talk; a cliché: 他的演講都是老生常談。His speech is full of clichés.

老書(ㄌㄠˇ ㄕㄨ)
① old books (as distinct from new publications) ② books written by the authors in the past

老鼠(ㄌㄠˇ ㄕㄨˇ)
a rat; a mouse

老人(ㄌㄠˇ ㄖㄣˊ)
① an old person ② the original members of an organization; old faces in an organization after a reshuffle

老人家(ㄌㄠˇ ·ㄖㄣ ·ㄐㄧㄚ)
① old persons (a term of respect) ② parents: 老人家好嗎? How are your parents?

老弱(ㄌㄠˇ ㄖㄨㄛˋ)
the old and weak

老弱殘兵(ㄌㄠˇ ㄖㄨㄛˋ ㄘㄢˊ ㄅㄧㄥ)
① old and weak surviving soldiers ②incompetent workers

老資格(ㄌㄠˇ ㄗ ㄍㄜˊ)
an old-timer; a veteran

老子
①(ㄌㄠˇ ㄗˇ) Lao-tzu (or Lao-tse), 604-531 B.C., a renowned philosopher and founder of Taoism
②(ㄌㄠˇ ·ㄗ) ⓐ one's father ⓑ (a term used when one is angry) I

老早(ㄌㄠˇ ㄗㄠˇ)
① very early ② long ago: 他老早就死了。He died long ago.

老祖宗(ㄌㄠˇ ㄗㄨˇ ㄗㄨㄥ)
ancestors; forefathers

老總(ㄌㄠˇ ㄗㄨㄥˇ)
① a reference to soldiers in former times ② the leader

老蠶作繭(ㄌㄠˇ ㄘㄢˊ ㄗㄨㄛˋ ㄐㄧㄢˇ)
to toil for a living in one's old age

老殘遊記(ㄌㄠˇ ㄘㄢˊ ㄧㄡˊ ㄐㄧˋ)
The Travels of Lao Ts'an: A Social Novel—a Ching Dynasty novel by Liu O (劉鶚)

老粗(ㄌㄠˇ ㄘㄨ)
a rude fellow; a boor; an uneducated person

老葱(ㄌㄠˇ ㄘㄨㄥ)
a thick green onion

老死(ㄌㄠˇ ㄙˇ)
① stubborn; obstinate ② to die of old age

老死不相往來(ㄌㄠˇ ㄙˇ ㄅㄨˋ ㄒㄧㄤ ㄨㄤˇ ㄌㄞˊ)
to obstinately refuse all social intercourse; to be completely isolated from each other

老死牖下(ㄌㄠˇ ㄙˇ ㄧㄡˇ ㄒㄧㄚˋ)
to live an insignificant life without any accomplishment

老叟(ㄌㄠˇ ㄙㄡˇ)
an old man

老僧(ㄌㄠˇ ㄙㄥ)
an old priest; the aged priest

老僧入定(ㄌㄠˇ ㄙㄥ ㄖㄨˋ ㄉㄧㄥˋ)
(literally) to sit quietly with eyes closed (like an old Buddhist monk contemplating truth)—very calm and without worldly passions

老蘇(ㄌㄠˇ ㄙㄨ)
the elder Su—Su Hsün (蘇洵), 1009 - 1066, father of

Su Shih (蘇軾) and Su Che (蘇轍)

老宿(ㄌㄠˇ ㄙㄨˋ)
①an aged monk or priest ②an aged scholar

老媼(ㄌㄠˇ ㄠˇ)
an old woman

老兒(ㄌㄠˇ ㄦˊ)
①a comical reference to an old man ②one's husband

老兒子(ㄌㄠˇ ㄦˊ •ㄗ)
the youngest son

老而不死(ㄌㄠˇ ㄦˊ ㄅㄨˋ ㄙˇ)
(an abusive phrase) old but not dead—The world would be better off without that old bastard.

老一輩(ㄌㄠˇ ㄧˊ ㄅㄟˋ)
the older generation

老鴉(ㄌㄠˇ ㄧㄚ)
a crow; a raven

老爺(ㄌㄠˇ •ㄧㄝ)
①sir ②an old man

老爺們(ㄌㄠˇ ㄧㄝˊ •ㄇㄣ)
men; gentlemen

老么(ㄌㄠˇ ㄧㄠ)
①the youngest child of a family ②the youngest one in a group

老油條(ㄌㄠˇ ㄧㄡˊ ㄊㄧㄠˊ)
a person who has learned to be sly; a sleeky fellow

老油子(ㄌㄠˇ ㄧㄡˊ •ㄗ)
an experienced and cunning person

老友(ㄌㄠˇ ㄧㄡˇ)
an old friend: 他是我父親的老友。He is an old friend of my father's.

老幼(ㄌㄠˇ ㄧㄡˋ)
aged people and young children

老眼昏花(ㄌㄠˇ ㄧㄢˇ ㄏㄨㄣ ㄏㄨㄚ)
the blurred vision of an old person

老樣子(ㄌㄠˇ ㄧㄤˋ •ㄗ)or 老樣兒(ㄌㄠˇ ㄧㄤˋㄦ)
the way a thing or person used to look

老鷹(ㄌㄠˇ ㄧㄥ)
the eagle

老吾老以及人之老(ㄌㄠˇ ㄨˊ ㄌㄠˇ ㄧˇ ㄐㄧˊ ㄖㄣˊ ㄓ ㄌㄠˇ)
to take care of one's own aged parents first and then extend the same care to the aged people in general

老物(ㄌㄠˇ ㄨˋ)
(an abusive term) an old person

老外(ㄌㄠˇ ㄨㄞˋ)
(slang) a foreigner

老頑固(ㄌㄠˇ ㄨㄢˊ ㄍㄨˋ)
a stubborn person; an old diehard; a stubborn old person

老王賣瓜，自賣自誇(ㄌㄠˇ ㄨㄤˊ ㄇㄞˋ ㄍㄨㄚ, ㄗˋ ㄇㄞˋ ㄗˋ ㄎㄨㄚ)
(literally) Lao Wang selling melons praises his own goods.—(figuratively) One praises one's own work or wares.

老翁(ㄌㄠˇ ㄨㄥ)
①an old man ②one's father

老嫗(ㄌㄠˇ ㄩˋ)
an old woman

老嫗能解(ㄌㄠˇ ㄩˋ ㄋㄥˊ ㄐㄧㄝˇ)
intelligible even to a senile woman

老玉米(ㄌㄠˇ ㄩˋ •ㄇㄧ)
(Indian) corn

老遠(ㄌㄠˇ ㄩㄢˇ)
a very long way; a very great distance; very far

老運(ㄌㄠˇ ㄩㄣˋ)
one's lot in old age; good luck in one's old age: 他老運亨通。He has good luck in old age.

【考】 4569
(攷) ㄎㄠˇ kao kǎo

1. one's deceased father
2. to test; to examine
3. to check; to investigate; to study

考妣(ㄎㄠˇ ㄅㄧˇ)
one's deceased father and mother

考畢(ㄎㄠˇ ㄅㄧˋ)
to finish an examination

考不取(ㄎㄠˇ •ㄅㄨ ㄑㄩˇ)or 考不上(ㄎㄠˇ •ㄅㄨ ㄕㄤˋ)
to fail in an examination (for admission to a school, employment, etc.)

考訂(ㄎㄠˇ ㄉㄧㄥˋ)
to review (a piece of writing) for correction

考題(ㄎㄠˇ ㄊㄧˊ)
questions on examination papers

考慮(ㄎㄠˇ ㄌㄩˋ)
to consider; to weigh; consideration; to think over

考古(ㄎㄠˇ ㄍㄨˇ)
to study the life and culture of ancient people

考古家(ㄎㄠˇ ㄍㄨˇ ㄐㄧㄚ)or 考古學家(ㄎㄠˇ ㄍㄨˇ ㄒㄩㄝˊ ㄐㄧㄚ)
an archeologist

考古學(ㄎㄠˇ ㄍㄨˇ ㄒㄩㄝˊ)
archeology

考官(ㄎㄠˇ ㄍㄨㄢ)
an examiner (especially under the former civil service examination system)

考課(ㄎㄠˇ ㄎㄜˋ)
to grade the service (of an official)

考覈 or 考核(ㄎㄠˇ ㄏㄜˊ)
to review or assess (a plan, proposal, etc.); to evaluate

考績(ㄎㄠˇ ㄐㄧ)
to grade the service (of an employee)

考校(ㄎㄠˇ ㄐㄧㄠˋ)
to examine; to check; to collate

考究(ㄎㄠˇ ㄐㄧㄡˋ)
①to examine and consider ②elaborate; beautiful ③tasteful; elegant; choosy; particular

考據(ㄎㄠˇ ㄐㄩˋ)
to search for proofs (in textual research)

考據學(ㄎㄠˇ ㄐㄩˋ ㄒㄩㄝˊ)
textual research

考卷(ㄎㄠˇ ㄐㄩㄢˋ)
an examination paper

考求(ㄎㄠˇ ㄑㄧㄡˊ)
to try to find out by investigation

考勤(ㄎㄠˇ ㄑㄧㄣˊ)
to appraise the diligence (of an employee)

考區(ㄎㄠˇ ㄑㄩ)
an examination district

考取(ㄎㄠˇ ㄑㄩˇ)
to pass an examination (for admission to employment, a school, etc.) 亦作「考中」or「考上」

考選(ㄎㄠˇ ㄒㄩㄢˇ)
to select by a competitive examination

考證(ㄎㄠˇ ㄓㄥˋ)
(in textual research) to try

to verify a point
考住了(ㄎㄠˇ ㄓㄨˋ ·ㄌㄜ)
unable to answer a question or solve a problem in an examination; to fail to answer a question asked verbally
考終(ㄎㄠˇ ㄓㄨㄥ)or 考終命(ㄎㄠˇ ㄓㄨㄥ ㄇㄧㄥˋ)
to die a natural death in old age
考中(ㄎㄠˇ ㄓㄨㄥˋ)
to pass an examination (for admission to employment, a school, etc.)參看「考取」
考查(ㄎㄠˇ ㄔㄚˊ)
to examine; to check; to investigate
考察(ㄎㄠˇ ㄔㄚˊ)
to inspect; to examine; to observe; to study
考察團(ㄎㄠˇ ㄔㄚˊ ㄊㄨㄢˊ)
an investigation team; a fact-finding mission
考場(ㄎㄠˇ ㄔㄤˇ)or(ㄎㄠˇ ㄔㄤˊ)
an examination hall or site
考成(ㄎㄠˇ ㄔㄥˊ)
to appraise the service (of an employee)
考試(ㄎㄠˇ ㄕˋ)
an examination; a test; a quiz
考試不及格(ㄎㄠˇ ㄕˋ ㄅㄨˋ ㄐㄧˊ ㄍㄜˊ)
to fail in an examination: 這學生考試不及格。The student failed in the examination.
考試題目(ㄎㄠˇ ㄕˋ ㄊㄧˊ ㄇㄨˋ)
examination questions 亦作「試題」
考試及格(ㄎㄠˇ ㄕˋ ㄐㄧˊ ㄍㄜˊ)
to pass an examination: 他考試及格了。He passed the examination.
考試卷子(ㄎㄠˇ ㄕˋ ㄐㄩㄢˋ ·ㄗ)
examination papers 亦作「試卷」
考試院(ㄎㄠˇ ㄕˋ ㄩㄢˋ)
Examination Yuan (of the Republic of China)
考上(ㄎㄠˇ ·ㄕㄤ)
to pass an examination (for admission to employment, a school, etc.)
考生(ㄎㄠˇ ㄕㄥ)
an examinee; an examination candidate: 考生按時到達。The examinees arrived on time.
考異(ㄎㄠˇ ㄧˋ)
to collate the variants (in textual research)
考驗(ㄎㄠˇ ㄧㄢˋ)
① to test; to try ② a test; a trial
考完(ㄎㄠˇ ㄨㄢˊ)
to finish an examination
考問(ㄎㄠˇ ㄨㄣˋ)
to examine and question; to examine orally
考語(ㄎㄠˇ ㄩˇ)
comments made on the result of an inspection or examination

四畫

【耄】 4570 ㄇㄠˋ maw mào
1. in an extremely old age; in one's eighties or nineties
2. confused
耄耋(ㄇㄠˋ ㄉㄧㄝˊ)
aged
耄齡(ㄇㄠˋ ㄌㄧㄥˊ)
more than 80 or 70 years old
耄勤(ㄇㄠˋ ㄑㄧㄣˊ)
to remain diligent in old age

【耆】 4571 1. ㄑㄧˊ chyi qí
to be in one's sixties; old
耆年碩德(ㄑㄧˊ ㄋㄧㄢˊ ㄕㄨㄛˋ ㄉㄜˊ)
aged and virtuous
耆臘(ㄑㄧˊ ㄌㄚˋ)
an aged Buddhist monk
耆老(ㄑㄧˊ ㄌㄠˇ)
an aged and respected person
耆碩(ㄑㄧˊ ㄕˊ)or 耆宿(ㄑㄧˊ ㄙㄨˋ)
a respected old person
耆儒(ㄑㄧˊ ㄖㄨˊ)
an aged scholar; a learned old person

【耆】 4571 2. ㄓˇ jyy zhǐ
as in 耆定—to bring into effect

【耆】 4571 3. ㄕˋ shyh shì
as in 耆欲—sensory pleasures

五畫

【者】 4572 ㄓㄜˇ jee zhě
1. those who; he who
2. a particle combining with some words to form adverbials

【耇】 4573 (耉) ㄍㄡˇ goou gǒu
old age; the wizened face of age

六畫

【耋】 4574 ㄉㄧㄝˊ dye dié
octogenarians; in one's eighties

而部
ㄦˊ erl ér

【而】 4575 ㄦˊ erl ér
1. accordingly; otherwise
2. and yet; but; nevertheless
3. you
4. on the condition that; supposing that; if
5. and; also
而立之年(ㄦˊ ㄌㄧˋ ㄓ ㄋㄧㄢˊ)
30 years old
而後(ㄦˊ ㄏㄡˋ)
then; afterwards; later; thenceforward; thenceforth; thereafter: 而後他寫了一封信給我。He wrote me a letter afterwards.
而今(ㄦˊ ㄐㄧㄣ)
now: 而今他已是位成功的律師了。He is now a successful lawyer.
而且(ㄦˊ ㄑㄧㄝˇ)
① and: 這房間很寬敞，而且光線充足。The room is spacious and bright. ② moreover; furthermore; besides; in addition: 他很勇敢而且很親切。He is brave; moreover, he is kind.
而已(ㄦˊ ㄧˇ)
merely; only; and that is all: 這只是個託詞而已。It is merely a pretense.
而外(ㄦˊ ㄨㄞˋ)
aside from; apart from; with

the exception of; except; exclusive of

三畫

【耐】 4576 ㄋㄞˋ nay nài
to bear; to endure; to stand; to resist: 他不耐孤寂。He can't bear living alone.
耐不久(ㄋㄞˋ •ㄅㄨ ㄐㄧㄡˇ)
unable to last or endure long
耐不住(ㄋㄞˋ •ㄅㄨ ㄓㄨˋ)
unable to bear, stand, or endure: 他耐不住喧鬧聲。He is unable to bear the noise.
耐磨(ㄋㄞˋ ㄇㄛˊ)
(said of metals) wear-resisting; wearproof
耐煩(ㄋㄞˋ ㄈㄢˊ)
patient
耐冬(ㄋㄞˋ ㄉㄨㄥ)
① able to endure cold ② a kind of evergreen tree
耐勞(ㄋㄞˋ ㄌㄠˊ)
able to endure hard work
耐力(ㄋㄞˋ ㄌㄧˋ)
endurance; staying power; stamina
耐寒(ㄋㄞˋ ㄏㄢˊ)
able to endure cold
耐火(ㄋㄞˋ ㄏㄨㄛˇ)
fireproof
耐火泥(ㄋㄞˋ ㄏㄨㄛˇ ㄋㄧˊ)
fire clay
耐火磚(ㄋㄞˋ ㄏㄨㄛˇ ㄓㄨㄢ)
a firebrick
耐久(ㄋㄞˋ ㄐㄧㄡˇ)
lasting a long time; durable
耐久力(ㄋㄞˋ ㄐㄧㄡˇ ㄌㄧˋ)
durability; endurance
耐心(ㄋㄞˋ ㄒㄧㄣ)
patience; perseverance
耐性(ㄋㄞˋ ㄒㄧㄥˋ)
patience; perseverance
耐熱(ㄋㄞˋ ㄖㄜˋ)
heat-proof
耐人尋味(ㄋㄞˋ ㄖㄣˊ ㄒㄩㄣˊ ㄨㄟˋ)
intriguing; puzzling; perplexing; providing food for thought: 這學者的話很耐人尋味。What the scholar said gives one much food for thought.
耐用(ㄋㄞˋ ㄩㄥˋ)
durable; sturdy; able to stand wear and tear

【耍】 4577 ㄕㄨㄚˇ shoa shuǎ
to play; to sport: 男孩們正在公園裏玩耍。The boys are playing in the park.
耍把戲(ㄕㄨㄚˇ ㄅㄚˇ ㄒㄧˋ)
to juggle; to play tricks: 他以球耍把戲。He juggled with balls.
耍筆桿(ㄕㄨㄚˇ ㄅㄧˇ ㄍㄢˇ)
to be skilled in literary tricks
耍脾氣(ㄕㄨㄚˇ ㄆㄧˊ •ㄑㄧ)
to lose one's temper; to get angry: 他向他哥哥耍脾氣。He got angry with his elder brother.
耍貧嘴 or 耍頻嘴(ㄕㄨㄚˇ ㄆㄧㄣˊ ㄗㄨㄟˇ)
to joke a great deal
耍大牌(ㄕㄨㄚˇ ㄉㄚˋ ㄆㄞˊ)
to display the temper of or behave like a top-billing actor or actress; to act like a prima donna
耍鬧(ㄕㄨㄚˇ ㄋㄠˋ)
to frolic; to sport: 我們在一起耍鬧作樂。We met in frolic and in laughter.
耍賴(ㄕㄨㄚˇ ㄌㄞˋ)
to act shamelessly; to be unreasonable 亦作「耍無賴」
耍懶(ㄕㄨㄚˇ ㄌㄢˇ)
to loiter; to loaf
耍流氓(ㄕㄨㄚˇ ㄌㄧㄡˊ ㄇㄤˊ)
to behave like a hooligan; to act rudely
耍弄(ㄕㄨㄚˇ ㄌㄨㄥˋ)
to make a fool of; to deceive
耍猴兒(ㄕㄨㄚˇ ㄏㄡˊㄦ)
to make a monkey do tricks
耍花槍(ㄕㄨㄚˇ ㄏㄨㄚ ㄑㄧㄤ)
to play sleight of hand; to be dishonest; to cheat
耍花招兒(ㄕㄨㄚˇ ㄏㄨㄚ ㄓㄠㄦ)
① to show off some special skill ② to play tricks: 別耍花招了! Don't try any tricks!
耍錢(ㄕㄨㄚˇ ㄑㄧㄢˊ)
to gamble
耍笑(ㄕㄨㄚˇ ㄒㄧㄠˋ)
to poke fun at
耍心眼兒(ㄕㄨㄚˇ ㄒㄧㄣ ㄧㄚˇㄦ)
to exercise one's wits for personal gain; to be very crafty; to pull a shrewd trick: 他老愛耍心眼兒。He is very crafty.
耍手藝(ㄕㄨㄚˇ ㄕㄡˇ ㄧˋ)
to make a living by some special skill
耍子(ㄕㄨㄚˇ •ㄗ)
to play; to sport
耍嘴皮子(ㄕㄨㄚˇ ㄗㄨㄟˇ ㄆㄧˊ •ㄗ)
to show off one's joking talent; to brag; to talk big
耍威風(ㄕㄨㄚˇ ㄨㄟ ㄈㄥ)
to make a show of authority; to throw one's weight about; to be overbearing

【耑】 4578 1. ㄉㄨㄢ duan duān
same as 端—an end; a tip; a point

【耑】 4578 2. ㄓㄨㄢ juan zhuān
same as 專—for a particular person, occasion, purpose, etc.

耒部
ㄌㄟˇ leei lěi

【耒】 4579 ㄌㄟˇ leei lěi
the wooden handle of a plough
耒耨(ㄌㄟˇ ㄋㄡˋ)
to till; to plough; to cultivate
耒耜(ㄌㄟˇ ㄙˋ)
ploughs

三畫

【耔】 4580 ㄗˇ tzyy zǐ
to hoe up earth around a plant

四畫

【耙】 4581 ㄆㄚˊ par pá
(又讀 ㄅㄚˋ bah bà)
1. a harrow; a drag
2. to rake: 他把田地耙平。He rakes the field.
耙耡(ㄆㄚˊ ㄔㄨˊ)

〔耒部〕

①a harrow ②to plough with a harrow

耙子(ㄆㄚˊ ·ㄗ)
①a harrow; a drag ②a clue (to a matter)

【耕】 4582 ㄍㄥ geng gēng (語音 ㄐㄧㄥ jing jīng)
to till; to plough; to cultivate

耕牧(ㄍㄥ ㄇㄨˋ)
tilling and pasturing

耕地(ㄍㄥ ㄉㄧˋ)
①cultivated land ②to till land

耕田(ㄍㄥ ㄊㄧㄢˊ)
to till land

耕牛(ㄍㄥ ㄋㄧㄡˊ)
an ox used in farming

耕稼(ㄍㄥ ㄐㄧㄚˋ)
tilling and planting

耕織(ㄍㄥ ㄓ)
(the men) tilling and (the women) weaving

耕者有其田(ㄍㄥ ㄓㄜˇ ㄧㄡˇ ㄑㄧˊ ㄊㄧㄢˊ)
land to the tiller (the final phase of the land reform program on Taiwan)

耕種(ㄍㄥ ㄓㄨㄥˋ)
①to plough and sow; to cultivate ②cultivation

耕事(ㄍㄥ ㄕˋ)
farm work

耕作(ㄍㄥ ㄗㄨㄛˋ)
to cultivate land and grow crops

耕鑿(ㄍㄥ ㄗㄨㄛˊ)
tilling land and drilling wells

耕耘(ㄍㄥ ㄩㄣˊ)
to till and weed; ploughing and weeding; to cultivate: 一分耕耘，一分收穫。The more ploughing and weeding, the better the crop. 或 As you sow, so shall you reap.

耕耘機(ㄍㄥ ㄩㄣˊ ㄐㄧ)
a power tiller

【耘】 4583 ㄩㄣˊ yun yún
to weed

耘田(ㄩㄣˊ ㄊㄧㄢˊ)
to weed rice fields

耘人之田(ㄩㄣˊ ㄖㄣˊ ㄓ ㄊㄧㄢˊ)
(literally) to weed the rice fields of others—to manage a business on behalf of others

耘草(ㄩㄣˊ ㄘㄠˇ)
to remove weeds; to weed: 他正忙着耘草。He is busy weeding.

【耗】 4584 ㄏㄠˋ haw hào
1. to expend; to use up; to waste; to squander; to consume
2. news; a report

耗費(ㄏㄠˋ ㄈㄟˋ)
to expend; to squander

耗電量(ㄏㄠˋ ㄉㄧㄢˋ ㄌㄧㄤˋ)
power consumption

耗體力(ㄏㄠˋ ㄊㄧˇ ㄌㄧˋ)
to expend bodily strength

耗竭(ㄏㄠˋ ㄐㄧㄝˊ)
to exhaust; to use up: 所有材料都耗竭了。All the material is used up.

耗減(ㄏㄠˋ ㄐㄧㄢˇ)
to diminish by expending

耗盡(ㄏㄠˋ ㄐㄧㄣˋ)
to exhaust; to use up; to consume entirely: 他耗盡了所有的錢。He exhausted his money.

耗時間(ㄏㄠˋ ㄕˊ ㄐㄧㄢ)
to consume time; time-consuming: 他寫書耗時間又耗精力。He consumed time and energy in writing this book.

耗子(ㄏㄠˋ ·ㄗ)
a mouse; a rat

耗損(ㄏㄠˋ ㄙㄨㄣˇ)
to diminish by expending

五畫

【耜】 4585 ㄙˋ syh sì
a plough

七畫

【耡】 4586 ㄔㄨˊ chwu chú
same as 鋤—to hoe; a hoe

九畫

【耦】 4587 ㄡˇ oou ǒu
1. to plough side by side
2. even (numbers); in pairs
3. a spouse; a mate

耦耕(ㄡˇ ㄍㄥ)
to plough side by side

耦語(ㄡˇ ㄩˇ)
to have a tête-à-tête; to whisper to each other

十畫

【耨】 4588 ㄋㄡˋ now nòu
1. a hoe
2. to weed; to hoe

十五畫

【耰】 4589 ㄧㄡ iou yōu
1. to draw earth over newly-sown grain; to cover the seed
2. a kind of hoe

耳部 ㄦˇ eel ěr

【耳】 4590 ㄦˇ eel ěr
1. ears
2. (a phrase-final particle) only; merely
3. a Chinese family name

耳鼻科(ㄦˇ ㄅㄧˊ ㄎㄜ)
otorhinology

耳鼻喉科(ㄦˇ ㄅㄧˊ ㄏㄡˊ ㄎㄜ)
otorhinolaryngology; otolaryngology

耳邊風(ㄦˇ ㄅㄧㄢ ㄈㄥ) or 耳旁風(ㄦˇ ㄆㄤˊ ㄈㄥ)
(literally) the wind past the ear—a matter of no concern; to turn a deaf ear to something

耳鬢廝磨(ㄦˇ ㄅㄧㄣˋ ㄙ ㄇㄛˊ)
(literally) ears and sideburns rubbing—(usually said of childhood lovers) very intimate

耳門(ㄦˇ ㄇㄣˊ)
①a side door ②the external ear; the earlap; the auricle; the pinna

耳鳴(ㄦˇ ㄇㄧㄥˊ)
buzzing in the ears; tinnitus aurium

耳目(ㄦˇ ㄇㄨˋ)
①ears and eyes ②one's attention or notice ③an informer
耳目衆多(ㄦˇ ㄇㄨˋ ㄓㄨㄥˋ ㄉㄨㄛ)
There are many spies.
耳目一新(ㄦˇ ㄇㄨˋ ㄧˊ ㄒㄧㄣ)
to have a completely new impression
耳糞(ㄦˇ ㄈㄣˋ)or 耳垢(ㄦˇ ㄍㄡˋ)or 耳屎(ㄦˇ ㄕˇ)
earwax; cerumen
耳朵(ㄦˇ ·ㄉㄨㄛ)
ears: 老師扭住學生的耳朵。The teacher seized the student by the ear.
耳朵長(ㄦˇ ·ㄉㄨㄛ ㄔㄤˊ)
capable of hearing much
耳朵軟(ㄦˇ ·ㄉㄨㄛ ㄖㄨㄢˇ)
credulous
耳朵眼兒(ㄦˇ ·ㄉㄨㄛ ㄧㄚˇㄦ)
a hole pierced in the lobe of an ear for earrings
耳提面命(ㄦˇ ㄊㄧˊ ㄇㄧㄢˋ ㄇㄧㄥˋ)
(literally) to hold one's head by the ears when giving him instructions—to give instructions earnestly; to din into one's ears
耳聽八方(ㄦˇ ㄊㄧㄥ ㄅㄚ ㄈㄤ)
very alert; extremely vigilant: 他們耳聽八方。They were very alert.
耳痛(ㄦˇ ㄊㄨㄥˋ)
otalgia
耳漏(ㄦˇ ㄌㄡˋ)
(medicine) the otorrhea
耳力(ㄦˇ ㄌㄧˋ)
the power of hearing; the sense of hearing; audition: 她的耳力不太好。Her sense of hearing is not very good.
耳聾(ㄦˇ ㄌㄨㄥˊ)
deaf: 他變成耳聾。He became deaf.
耳根(ㄦˇ ㄍㄣ)
(Buddhism) the organ of hearing
耳根清靜(ㄦˇ ㄍㄣ ㄑㄧㄥ ㄐㄧㄥˋ)
peace of mind achieved by staying away from nagging, bickering, etc.
耳鼓(ㄦˇ ㄍㄨˇ)
the eardrum; the tympanum
耳刮子(ㄦˇ ㄍㄨㄚ ·ㄗ)or 耳光(ㄦˇ ㄍㄨㄤ)or 耳光子(ㄦˇ ㄍㄨㄤ ·ㄗ)
a box on the ear
耳科(ㄦˇ ㄎㄜ)
otology
耳科醫生(ㄦˇ ㄎㄜ ㄧ ㄕㄥ)
an ear specialist; an aurist; an otologist: 你必須去看耳科醫生。You must see an aurist.
耳殼(ㄦˇ ㄎㄜˊ)
the concha, or auricle
耳孔(ㄦˇ ㄎㄨㄥˇ)
an otic channel
耳環(ㄦˇ ㄏㄨㄢˊ)
earrings: 她在找她的耳環。She is looking for her earrings.
耳機(ㄦˇ ㄐㄧ)
an earphone: 他的耳機性能不佳。His earphone does not function very well.
耳下腺(ㄦˇ ㄒㄧㄚˋ ㄒㄧㄢˋ)
a parotid gland
耳下腺炎(ㄦˇ ㄒㄧㄚˋ ㄒㄧㄢˋ ㄧㄢˊ)
parotitis
耳墜子(ㄦˇ ㄓㄨㄟˋ ·ㄗ)
earrings; an eardrop
耳垂(ㄦˇ ㄔㄨㄟˊ)
an ear lobe; a lobule
耳食(ㄦˇ ㄕˊ)
to taste food with ears —(figuratively) to be apt to believe hearsay because of one's vulgar and superficial knowledge
耳視目聽(ㄦˇ ㄕˋ ㄇㄨˋ ㄊㄧㄥ)
very intelligent
耳生(ㄦˇ ㄕㄥ)
unfamiliar to the ears; rarely heard of: 這首歌聽起來耳生。The song sounds unfamiliar to me.
耳熟(ㄦˇ ㄕㄡˊ)
familiar to the ears; much heard of
耳熟能詳(ㄦˇ ㄕㄡˊ ㄋㄥˊ ㄒㄧㄤˊ)
so frequently heard about that it can be told (in detail or word by word)
耳屬(ㄦˇ ㄕㄨˇ)
to eavesdrop; to listen with effort and attention
耳順之年(ㄦˇ ㄕㄨㄣˋ ㄓ ㄋㄧㄢˊ)
(literally) the age when nothing one hears can be objectionable—60 years old (from the phrase "六十而耳順")
耳熱(ㄦˇ ㄖㄜˋ)
to have a burning sensation in the ears; to have burning ears
耳濡目染(ㄦˇ ㄖㄨˊ ㄇㄨˋ ㄖㄢˇ)
thoroughly imbued with what one frequently hears and sees
耳聰目明(ㄦˇ ㄘㄨㄥ ㄇㄨˋ ㄇㄧㄥˊ)
sharp in hearing and keen in seeing—(figuratively) very clever
耳塞(ㄦˇ ㄙㄞ)
an earplug
耳耳(ㄦˇ ㄦˇ)
①flourishing; thriving; vigorous ②erect; straight ③an exclamation of discontent
耳炎(ㄦˇ ㄧㄢˊ)
inflammation of the ear; otitis
耳挖子(ㄦˇ ㄨㄚ ·ㄗ)
an ear pick
耳聞(ㄦˇ ㄨㄣˊ)
①to hear ②what one hears about; hearsay
耳聞不如目見(ㄦˇ ㄨㄣˊ ㄅㄨˋ ㄖㄨˊ ㄇㄨˋ ㄐㄧㄢˋ)
Seeing for oneself is better than hearing a hundred times. 或 Seeing is believing.
耳聞目睹(ㄦˇ ㄨㄣˊ ㄇㄨˋ ㄉㄨˇ)
what one sees and hears —widely known
耳語(ㄦˇ ㄩˇ)
to whisper into another's ear; whispers

三畫

【耶】 4591
1. ㄧㄝ ye yē
a phrase-final particle for a question: 是耶? 非耶? Is it or isn't it? 或 Yes or no?

【耶】 4591
2. ㄧㄝ ie yē
transliteration of English names
耶誕禮物(ㄧㄝ ㄉㄢˋ ㄌㄧˇ ㄨˋ)
Christmas gifts
耶誕卡(ㄧㄝ ㄉㄢˋ ㄎㄚˇ)or 耶誕卡片(ㄧㄝ ㄉㄢˋ ㄎㄚˇ ㄆㄧㄢˋ)
a Christmas card
耶誕節(ㄧㄝ ㄉㄢˋ ㄐㄧㄝˊ)
Christmas
耶誕樹(ㄧㄝ ㄉㄢˋ ㄕㄨˋ)
a Christmas tree
耶拿(ㄧㄝ ㄋㄚˊ)

〔耳部〕

Jena, a German city
耶魯大學(ㄧㄝ ㄌㄨˇ ㄉㄚˋ ㄒㄩㄝˊ)
Yale University: 他畢業於耶魯大學。He graduated from Yale University.
耶路撒冷(ㄧㄝ ㄌㄨˋ ㄙㄚ ㄌㄥˇ)
Jerusalem
耶和華(ㄧㄝ ㄏㄜˊ ㄏㄨㄚˊ)
Jehovah
耶穌(ㄧㄝ ㄙㄨ)
Jesus
耶穌復活日(ㄧㄝ ㄙㄨ ㄈㄨˋ ㄏㄨㄛˊ ㄖˋ)
Easter
耶穌會(ㄧㄝ ㄙㄨ ㄏㄨㄟˋ)
the Society of Jesus
耶穌基督(ㄧㄝ ㄙㄨ ㄐㄧ ㄉㄨ)
Jesus Christ
耶穌紀元(ㄧㄝ ㄙㄨ ㄐㄧˋ ㄩㄢˊ)
the Christian Era 亦作「公元」or「西元」
耶穌教(ㄧㄝ ㄙㄨ ㄐㄧㄠˋ)
Protestant Christianity (as distinct from Roman Catholicism)
耶穌聖誕(ㄧㄝ ㄙㄨ ㄕㄥˋ ㄉㄢˋ)
Christmas

【耷】 4592
ㄉㄚ da dā
1. big ears
2. the given name of a famous Ching artist, Chu Ta(朱耷)

耷拉(ㄉㄚ ˙ㄌㄚ)
to hang down; to droop

四畫

【耽】 4593
ㄉㄢ dan dān
1. to indulge in; to be addicted to
2. delightful and enduring
3. (said of ears) large and drooping
4. negligent

耽美主義(ㄉㄢ ㄇㄟˇ ㄓㄨˇ ㄧˋ)
estheticism
耽湎(ㄉㄢ ㄇㄧㄢˇ)
addicted to: 他耽湎於酒。He was addicted to alcohol.
耽耽(ㄉㄢ ㄉㄢ)
(said of a tiger's eyes)glaring covetously; eying greedily
耽讀(ㄉㄢ ㄉㄨˊ)
addicted to reading
耽溺(ㄉㄢ ㄋㄧˋ)
to indulge in (evil ways); unable to free oneself from (bad habits): 他耽溺於賭博。He indulges himself in gambling.
耽樂(ㄉㄢ ㄌㄜˋ)
to indulge in pleasure
耽擱(ㄉㄢ ㄍㄜ)
①to stay; to stop over; a stopover ② to delay: 別把婚期給耽擱了。Don't delay the date of wedding.
耽習(ㄉㄢ ㄒㄧˊ)
to be absorbed in study
耽心(ㄉㄢ ㄒㄧㄣ)
to be worried 亦作「擔心」
耽思(ㄉㄢ ㄙ)
to think deeply; to ponder
耽憂(ㄉㄢ ㄧㄡ)
to worry
耽誤(ㄉㄢ ㄨˋ)
to delay; to hold up: 他們耽誤了整個工程。They held up the whole project.

【耿】 4594
ㄍㄥˇ geeng gěng
1. bright
2. upright; incorruptible
3. a Chinese family name

耿耿(ㄍㄥˇ ㄍㄥˇ)
① bright; shining ② concerned; anxious; apprehensive; restless
耿耿於懷(ㄍㄥˇ ㄍㄥˇ ㄩˊ ㄏㄨㄞˊ)
to keep something anxiously in one's mind; to take something to heart
耿介(ㄍㄥˇ ㄐㄧㄝˋ)
① magnificent ② upright; just; righteous
耿直(ㄍㄥˇ ㄓˊ)
honest; upright: 他秉性耿直。He is upright by nature.

【聃】 4595
(聸) ㄉㄢ dan dān
1. another name of Lao-tzu(老子)
2. a deformed ear

【耻】 4596
ㄔˇ chyy chǐ
same as 恥—shame

五畫

【聆】 4597
ㄌㄧㄥˊ ling líng
to listen; to hear

聆聽(ㄌㄧㄥˊ ㄊㄧㄥ)
to listen to
聆教(ㄌㄧㄥˊ ㄐㄧㄠˋ)
to listen to someone's instructions
聆悉(ㄌㄧㄥˊ ㄒㄧ)
to learn; to hear

【聊】 4598
ㄌㄧㄠˊ liau liáo
1. somehow; somewhat; a little
2. to rely; to depend
3. to chat; a chat
4. interest
5. for the time being

聊備一格(ㄌㄧㄠˊ ㄅㄟˋ ㄧˋ ㄍㄜˊ)
may serve as a specimen
聊表微忱(ㄌㄧㄠˊ ㄅㄧㄠˇ ㄨㄟ ㄔㄣˊ)
as a token of respect or good will (an expression often used when presenting somebody with a gift)
聊天(ㄌㄧㄠˊ ㄊㄧㄢ)
to chat; a chat
聊賴(ㄌㄧㄠˊ ㄌㄞˋ)
something to live for; something to rely upon
聊聊(ㄌㄧㄠˊ ˙ㄌㄧㄠ)
to have a chat: 我們到咖啡廳聊聊。Let's have a chat in the coffee shop.
聊啾(ㄌㄧㄠˊ ㄐㄧㄡ)
buzzing in the ears
聊且(ㄌㄧㄠˊ ㄑㄧㄝˇ)
for the time being
聊齋誌異(ㄌㄧㄠˊ ㄓㄞ ㄓˋ ㄧˋ)
Strange Stories from a Chinese Studio (title of a collection of bizarre stories by Pu Sung-ling(蒲松齡) of the Ching Dynasty)
聊生(ㄌㄧㄠˊ ㄕㄥ)
to make a living
聊勝一籌(ㄌㄧㄠˊ ㄕㄥˋ ㄧˋ ㄔㄡˊ)or 聊勝一等(ㄌㄧㄠˊ ㄕㄥˋ ㄧˋ ㄉㄥˇ)
to surpass only a little bit
聊勝於無(ㄌㄧㄠˊ ㄕㄥˋ ㄩˊ ㄨˊ)
at least better than nothing 或 It's better than nothing.
聊以解嘲(ㄌㄧㄠˊ ㄧˇ ㄐㄧㄝˇ ㄔㄠˊ)
to manage somehow to relieve embarrassment
聊以自慰(ㄌㄧㄠˊ ㄧˇ ㄗˋ ㄨㄟˋ)
just to console oneself; to take comfort in
聊以塞責(ㄌㄧㄠˊ ㄧˇ ㄙㄜˋ ㄗㄜˊ)
merely to avoid the charge of a dereliction of duty

六畫

【聒】 4599
ㄍㄨㄚ gua guā
clamorous; uproarious

聒聒(ㄍㄨㄚ ㄍㄨㄚ)
uproarious; clamorous; noisy

聒聒叫(ㄍㄨㄚ ㄍㄨㄚ ㄐㄧㄠˋ)
very good; wonderful; excellent: 他的英文聒聒叫。His English is excellent.

聒絮(ㄍㄨㄚ ㄒㄩˋ)
to keep talking noisily: 他們聒絮不休。They kept talking noisily.

聒噪(ㄍㄨㄚ ㄗㄠˋ)
to be uproarious; to be noisy: 這隻鸚鵡十分聒噪。This parrot is very noisy.

聒耳(ㄍㄨㄚ ㄦˇ)
offensive to the ear

七畫

【聖】 4600
ㄕㄥˋ shenq shèng
1. a sage
2. sacred; holy

聖保羅(ㄕㄥˋ ㄅㄠˇ ㄌㄨㄛˊ)
① St. Paul, U.S.A. ② São Paulo, Brazil

聖彼得(ㄕㄥˋ ㄅㄧˇ ㄉㄜˊ)
St. Peter

聖彼得堡(ㄕㄥˋ ㄅㄧˇ ㄉㄜˊ ㄅㄠˇ)
St. Petersburg, the old name of Leningrad

聖彼得大教堂(ㄕㄥˋ ㄅㄧˇ ㄉㄜˊ ㄉㄚˋ ㄐㄧㄠˋ ㄊㄤˊ)
St. Peter's

聖馬力諾(ㄕㄥˋ ㄇㄚˇ ㄌㄧˋ ㄋㄨㄛˋ)
San Marino

聖廟(ㄕㄥˋ ㄇㄧㄠˋ)
a Confucian temple

聖明(ㄕㄥˋ ㄇㄧㄥˊ)
① His Majesty; His Holiness ②(said of a leader) capable and virtuous

聖母(ㄕㄥˋ ㄇㄨˇ)
① the Virgin Mary; the Holy Mother ② an empress dowager

聖母瑪利亞(ㄕㄥˋ ㄇㄨˇ ㄇㄚˇ ㄌㄧˋ ㄧㄚˇ)
the Virgin Mary

聖母像(ㄕㄥˋ ㄇㄨˇ ㄒㄧㄤˋ)
Madonna; an image of the Virgin Mary

聖墓(ㄕㄥˋ ㄇㄨˋ)
the tomb of a sage or saint

聖誕(ㄕㄥˋ ㄉㄢˋ)
Christmas

聖誕老人(ㄕㄥˋ ㄉㄢˋ ㄌㄠˇ ㄖㄣˊ)
Santa Claus

聖誕禮物(ㄕㄥˋ ㄉㄢˋ ㄌㄧˇ ㄨˋ)
a Christmas present; a Christmas gift

聖誕卡(ㄕㄥˋ ㄉㄢˋ ㄎㄚˇ)
a Christmas card

聖誕紅(ㄕㄥˋ ㄉㄢˋ ㄏㄨㄥˊ)
a poinsettia

聖誕節(ㄕㄥˋ ㄉㄢˋ ㄐㄧㄝˊ)
Christmastide; Christmastime

聖誕前夕(ㄕㄥˋ ㄉㄢˋ ㄑㄧㄢˊ ㄒㄧˋ)
Christmas Eve

聖誕樹(ㄕㄥˋ ㄉㄢˋ ㄕㄨˋ)
a Christmas tree

聖地(ㄕㄥˋ ㄉㄧˋ)
a holy ground

聖地牙哥(ㄕㄥˋ ㄉㄧˋ ㄧㄚˊ ㄍㄜ)
Santiago, capital of Chile

聖多明哥(ㄕㄥˋ ㄉㄨㄛ ㄇㄧㄥˊ ㄍㄜ)
Santo Domingo, the capital of the Dominican Republic and the republic's old name

聖多斯(ㄕㄥˋ ㄉㄨㄛ ㄙ)
Santos, a harbor in Brazil

聖壇(ㄕㄥˋ ㄊㄢˊ)
an altar

聖堂(ㄕㄥˋ ㄊㄤˊ)
a sanctuary

聖徒(ㄕㄥˋ ㄊㄨˊ)
an apostle; a saint

聖林(ㄕㄥˋ ㄌㄧㄣˊ)
the Confucian tomb 亦作「孔林」

聖靈(ㄕㄥˋ ㄌㄧㄥˊ)
the Holy Ghost; the Holy Spirit

聖路易(ㄕㄥˋ ㄌㄨˋ ㄧˋ)
① St. Louis, U.S.A. ② St. Louis, Senegal

聖公會(ㄕㄥˋ ㄍㄨㄥ ㄏㄨㄟˋ)
the Episcopal Church

聖赫勒拿島(ㄕㄥˋ ㄏㄜˋ ㄌㄜˋ ㄋㄚˊ ㄉㄠˇ)
Saint Helena Island 亦作「聖海倫島」

聖湖(ㄕㄥˋ ㄏㄨˊ)
another name of the West Lake (西湖), Hangchow, Chekiang

聖蹟(ㄕㄥˋ ㄐㄧ)
relics of a sage

聖駕(ㄕㄥˋ ㄐㄧㄚˋ)
His Majesty

聖潔(ㄕㄥˋ ㄐㄧㄝˊ)
holy and immaculate

聖教(ㄕㄥˋ ㄐㄧㄠˋ)
Confucianism

聖經(ㄕㄥˋ ㄐㄧㄥ)
① the Bible ② works of a sage (especially Confucius)

聖經賢傳(ㄕㄥˋ ㄐㄧㄥ ㄒㄧㄢˊ ㄓㄨㄢˋ)
the classics of the sages

聖君(ㄕㄥˋ ㄐㄩㄣ)
① His Majesty ② a reference to General Kuan Yü (關羽)

聖賢(ㄕㄥˋ ㄒㄧㄢˊ)
sages and virtuous men; saints

聖心(ㄕㄥˋ ㄒㄧㄣ)
① His Majesty's heart ② the Sacred Heart

聖像(ㄕㄥˋ ㄒㄧㄤˋ)
① sacred images; idols ② an image of Confucius ③ an image of Jesus Christ

聖職(ㄕㄥˋ ㄓˊ)
holy orders; the ministry: 他就任聖職。He takes holy orders.

聖旨(ㄕㄥˋ ㄓˇ)
an imperial decree

聖哲(ㄕㄥˋ ㄓㄜˊ)
① sages and saints ② the wisdom of a sage

聖者(ㄕㄥˋ ㄓㄜˇ)
a sage; a saint

聖戰(ㄕㄥˋ ㄓㄢˋ)
a holy war; a sacred war

聖朝(ㄕㄥˋ ㄔㄠˊ)
the present dynasty

聖城(ㄕㄥˋ ㄔㄥˊ)
the Holy City: 耶路撒冷及麥加是聖城。Jerusalem and Mecca are Holy Cities.

聖詩(ㄕㄥˋ ㄕ)
a psalm

聖手(ㄕㄥˋ ㄕㄡˇ)
a master (of a skill)

聖善(ㄕㄥˋ ㄕㄢˋ)
sacred; holy

聖上(ㄕㄥˋ ㄕㄤˋ)
His Majesty

聖水(ㄕㄥˋ ㄕㄨㄟˇ)
holy water

聖人(ㄕㄥˋ ㄖㄣˊ)
a sage; a saint

聖餐(ㄕㄥˋ ㄘㄢ)

the Lord's Supper
聖恩(ㄕㄥˋ ㄣ)
imperial favor or graciousness
聖裔(ㄕㄥˋ ㄧˋ)
descendants of a sage (especially of Confucius)
聖域(ㄕㄥˋ ㄩˋ)
the state of being a sage or saint
聖諭(ㄕㄥˋ ㄩˋ)
an imperial edict

【聘】 4601
1. ㄆㄧㄣˋ pinn pìn
1. to invite for service; to employ; to engage
2. to be betrothed; to be engaged
3. to pay respect by sending an envoy
4. to ask; to inquire

聘禮(ㄆㄧㄣˋ ㄌㄧˇ)
①a gift for inviting one's service ②presents for betrothal sent to a girl's family
聘金(ㄆㄧㄣˋ ㄐㄧㄣ)
money paid (to the parents of the prospective bride) at a betrothal
聘君(ㄆㄧㄣˋ ㄐㄩㄣ)
a capable scholar recruited by the imperial court for public service
聘妻(ㄆㄧㄣˋ ㄑㄧ)
a fiancée
聘請(ㄆㄧㄣˋ ㄑㄧㄥˇ)
to invite someone for service; to engage; to appoint
聘召(ㄆㄧㄣˋ ㄓㄠˋ)
to invite someone for service (usually with presents)
聘書(ㄆㄧㄣˋ ㄕㄨ)
the formal letter of employment; the letter of appointment
聘任(ㄆㄧㄣˋ ㄖㄣˋ)
to employ or engage for a post
聘物(ㄆㄧㄣˋ ㄨˋ)
presents for betrothal (sent to the parents of the prospective bride)
聘問(ㄆㄧㄣˋ ㄨㄣˋ)
international exchange of visits
聘用(ㄆㄧㄣˋ ㄩㄥˋ)
to employ; to engage

【聘】 4601
2. ㄆㄧㄥˋ pinq pìng
to give (a daughter) in marriage; to marry
聘姑娘(ㄆㄧㄥˋ ㄍㄨ ·ㄋㄧㄤ)
to give a daughter in marriage; to marry a daughter to someone

八畫

【聚】 4602
ㄐㄩˋ jiuh jù
to come or put together; to gather; to assemble; to collect
聚寶盆(ㄐㄩˋ ㄅㄠˇ ㄆㄣˊ)
a legendary earthen pot in which money multiplies
聚賭(ㄐㄩˋ ㄉㄨˇ)
to assemble for gambling
聚斂(ㄐㄩˋ ㄌㄧㄢˋ)
to gather, to collect, or to amass illegally or immorally
聚落(ㄐㄩˋ ㄌㄨㄛˋ)
a place where people live; a village; a town
聚攏(ㄐㄩˋ ㄌㄨㄥˇ)
to gather; to assemble; to come together
聚光鏡(ㄐㄩˋ ㄍㄨㄤ ㄐㄧㄥˋ)
a condensing lens
聚合(ㄐㄩˋ ㄏㄜˊ)
①to gather; to assemble; to come together ②(chemistry) polymerization
聚合體(ㄐㄩˋ ㄏㄜˊ ㄊㄧˇ)
a polymer
聚會(ㄐㄩˋ ㄏㄨㄟˋ)
to assemble; to gather; to meet; to get together: 他們聚會討論問題。They got together to discuss a problem.
聚會所(ㄐㄩˋ ㄏㄨㄟˋ ㄙㄨㄛˇ)
a place for a meeting; a gathering place
聚積(ㄐㄩˋ ㄐㄧ)
to accumulate
聚集(ㄐㄩˋ ㄐㄧˊ)
to gather; to assemble: 學生們在學校禮堂聚集。The students assembled in the school hall.
聚精會神(ㄐㄩˋ ㄐㄧㄥ ㄏㄨㄟˋ ㄕㄣˊ)
to concentrate oneself; with attention: 你應聚精會神讀書。You should read with attention.
聚居(ㄐㄩˋ ㄐㄩ)
to live together
聚齊(ㄐㄩˋ ㄑㄧˊ)
to be all present at a gathering
聚星(ㄐㄩˋ ㄒㄧㄥ)
multiple stars
聚形(ㄐㄩˋ ㄒㄧㄥˊ)
(mineralogy) combination form
聚衆(ㄐㄩˋ ㄓㄨㄥˋ)
to gather a mob; to assemble a crowd
聚沙成塔(ㄐㄩˋ ㄕㄚ ㄔㄥˊ ㄊㄚˇ)
Accumulation of small amounts results in a huge quantity.
聚首(ㄐㄩˋ ㄕㄡˇ)
to get together; to meet: 我們設法至少每一年聚首一次。We try to get together at least once a year.
聚餐(ㄐㄩˋ ㄘㄢ)
to get together for luncheon or dinner
聚散(ㄐㄩˋ ㄙㄢˋ)
meeting and parting
聚散無常(ㄐㄩˋ ㄙㄢˋ ㄨˊ ㄔㄤˊ)
Meeting and departing are irregular.
聚訟(ㄐㄩˋ ㄙㄨㄥˋ)
to hold different views
聚訟紛紜(ㄐㄩˋ ㄙㄨㄥˋ ㄈㄣ ㄩㄣˊ)
Opinions are divided.
聚乙烯(ㄐㄩˋ ㄧˇ ㄒㄧ)
polyethylene
聚蚊成雷(ㄐㄩˋ ㄨㄣˊ ㄔㄥˊ ㄌㄟˊ)
(literally) A swarm of mosquitos may become a thunder.—United strength can be very great.

【聞】 4603
1. ㄨㄣˊ wen wén
1. to hear; to have heard
2. to learn; learning; to understand
3. to convey, forward or transmit (a message, etc.)
4. to smell
5. to make known
6. a Chinese family name

聞報(ㄨㄣˊ ㄅㄠˋ)
to learn of; to hear it reported

聞不得(ㄨㄣˊ ˙ㄅㄨ ˙ㄉㄜ)
too strong to be smelled
聞不見(ㄨㄣˊ ˙ㄅㄨ ㄐㄧㄢˋ)
cannot sense the smell
聞名(ㄨㄣˊ ㄇㄧㄥˊ)
① famous; distinguished: 此地以風景幽美聞名。The place is famous for its scenic beauty. ② to hear of someone's name
聞名不如見面(ㄨㄣˊ ㄇㄧㄥˊ ㄅㄨˋ ㄖㄨˊ ㄐㄧㄢˋ ㄇㄧㄢˋ)
Knowing someone by his reputation is not as good as meeting him in person.
聞名天下(ㄨㄣˊ ㄇㄧㄥˊ ㄊㄧㄢ ㄒㄧㄚˋ)
world-famous; known far and wide
聞名四方(ㄨㄣˊ ㄇㄧㄥˊ ㄙˋ ㄈㄤ)
to become famous throughout the land
聞風逃竄(ㄨㄣˊ ㄈㄥ ㄊㄠˊ ㄘㄨㄢˋ)
to run away or escape upon learning the news
聞風響應(ㄨㄣˊ ㄈㄥ ㄒㄧㄤˇ ㄧㄥˋ)
to hear the news and rise up in response
聞風喪膽(ㄨㄣˊ ㄈㄥ ㄙㄤˋ ㄉㄢˇ)
to become terror-stricken at the news
聞風而起(ㄨㄣˊ ㄈㄥ ㄦˊ ㄑㄧˇ)
to rise up on hearing the news
聞過色喜(ㄨㄣˊ ㄍㄨㄛˋ ㄙㄜˋ ㄒㄧˇ)
to be pleased upon hearing one's own mistakes (the mark of a true gentleman)
聞鷄起舞(ㄨㄣˊ ㄐㄧ ㄑㄧˇ ㄨˇ)
(literally) to rise up upon hearing the crow of a rooster—diligent and full of enthusiasm; highly motivated (the reference is to 祖逖)
聞見(ㄨㄣˊ ㄐㄧㄢˋ)
to have learned (by hearing or seeing)
聞喜宴(ㄨㄣˊ ㄒㄧˇ ㄧㄢˋ)
banquets given in honor of successful candidates of the civil service examination in the Tang Dynasty and the Sung Dynasty
聞訊(ㄨㄣˊ ㄒㄩㄣˋ)
to learn of the news; to hear of the message
聞知(ㄨㄣˊ ㄓ)
to learn; to hear; to know from others
聞所未聞(ㄨㄣˊ ㄙㄨㄛˇ ㄨㄟˋ ㄨㄣˊ)
unheard of
聞一知十(ㄨㄣˊ ㄧ ㄓ ㄕˊ)
(literally) to learn one thing and know ten—a very bright or clever person
聞問(ㄨㄣˊ ㄨㄣˋ)
communications or correspondence between two persons

【聞】 4603 2. ㄨㄣˋ wenn wèn

reputation
聞達(ㄨㄣˋ ㄉㄚˊ)
illustrious; eminent; famous and influential
聞人(ㄨㄣˋ ㄖㄣˊ)
a prominent figure; a famous person

十一畫

【聯】 4604 ㄌㄧㄢˊ lian lián

1. to unite; to ally; to connect; to join; to make an alliance with
2. allied (forces, etc.); joint (effort, etc.); mutual (guaranties, etc.)
3. a couplet

聯播(ㄌㄧㄢˊ ㄅㄛ)
a radio hookup
聯保(ㄌㄧㄢˊ ㄅㄠˇ)
a mutual guarantee (of proper conduct, etc.)
聯邦(ㄌㄧㄢˊ ㄅㄤ)
a federal union; a federal state
聯邦調查局(ㄌㄧㄢˊ ㄅㄤ ㄉㄧㄠˋ ㄔㄚˊ ㄐㄩˊ)
Federal Bureau of Investigation (FBI) of the United States
聯邦制(ㄌㄧㄢˊ ㄅㄤ ㄓˋ)
the federation system
聯票(ㄌㄧㄢˊ ㄆㄧㄠˋ)
① an interline ticket; a through ticket ② bills in set
聯翩(ㄌㄧㄢˊ ㄆㄧㄢ)
① continuously; successively ② continuously and quickly; in quick succession
聯袂(ㄌㄧㄢˊ ㄇㄟˋ)
side by side; together; jointly
聯盟(ㄌㄧㄢˊ ㄇㄥˊ)
an alliance; a union; a league (as the League of Nations); to form an alliance, etc.
聯緜(ㄌㄧㄢˊ ㄇㄧㄢˊ)
continuous or incessant; successive(ly)
聯緜字(ㄌㄧㄢˊ ㄇㄧㄢˊ ㄗˋ)
a Chinese phrase consisting of two characters, often alliterated or rhymed (as 徬徨 or 徘徊)
聯名(ㄌㄧㄢˊ ㄇㄧㄥˊ)
to sign together; to put two or more signatures on a document
聯防(ㄌㄧㄢˊ ㄈㄤˊ)
joint defense; mutual defense
聯防協定(ㄌㄧㄢˊ ㄈㄤˊ ㄒㄧㄝˊ ㄉㄧㄥˋ)
a joint defense treaty
聯單(ㄌㄧㄢˊ ㄉㄢ)
a certificate, document, etc. in duplicate, triplicate, etc.
聯隊(ㄌㄧㄢˊ ㄉㄨㄟˋ)
(said of the air force) a wing
聯立方程式(ㄌㄧㄢˊ ㄌㄧˋ ㄈㄤ ㄔㄥˊ ㄕˋ)
(mathematics) a simultaneous equation
聯絡(ㄌㄧㄢˊ ㄌㄨㄛˋ)
to keep in contact; to communicate with; to contact
聯絡官(ㄌㄧㄢˊ ㄌㄨㄛˋ ㄍㄨㄢ)
a liaison officer
聯貫(ㄌㄧㄢˊ ㄍㄨㄢˋ)
connection; links; relevance; to link or string together
聯貫性(ㄌㄧㄢˊ ㄍㄨㄢˋ ㄒㄧㄥˋ)
continuity
聯合(ㄌㄧㄢˊ ㄏㄜˊ)
to unite; to form an alliance of some kind; joint (effort, etc.)
聯合內閣(ㄌㄧㄢˊ ㄏㄜˊ ㄋㄟˋ ㄍㄜˊ)
a coalition cabinet
聯合國(ㄌㄧㄢˊ ㄏㄜˊ ㄍㄨㄛˊ)
United Nations
聯合國大會(ㄌㄧㄢˊ ㄏㄜˊ ㄍㄨㄛˊ ㄉㄚˋ ㄏㄨㄟˋ)or 聯大(ㄌㄧㄢˊ ㄉㄚˋ)
United Nations General Assembly
聯合國糧農組織(ㄌㄧㄢˊ ㄏㄜˊ ㄍㄨㄛˊ ㄌㄧㄤˊ ㄋㄨㄥˊ ㄗㄨˇ ㄓ)
United Nations Food and Agriculture Organization
聯合國憲章(ㄌㄧㄢˊ ㄏㄜˊ ㄍㄨㄛˊ ㄒㄧㄢˋ ㄓㄤ)

U.N. Charter
聯合國善後救濟總署(ㄌㄧㄢˊ ㄏㄜˊ ㄍㄨㄛˊ ㄕㄢˋ ㄏㄡˋ ㄐㄧㄡˋ ㄐㄧˋ ㄗㄨㄥˇ ㄕㄨˇ)
United Nations Relief and Rehabilitation Administration (UNRRA)
聯合國日(ㄌㄧㄢˊ ㄏㄜˊ ㄍㄨㄛˊ ㄖˋ)
United Nations Day
聯合國安全理事會(ㄌㄧㄢˊ ㄏㄜˊ ㄍㄨㄛˊ ㄢ ㄑㄩㄢˊ ㄌㄧˇ ㄕˋ ㄏㄨㄟˋ)
U.N. Security Council
聯合國文教組織(ㄌㄧㄢˊ ㄏㄜˊ ㄍㄨㄛˊ ㄨㄣˊ ㄐㄧㄠˋ ㄗㄨˇ ㄓ)
United Nations Educational, Scientific, and Cultural Organization (UNESCO)
聯合公報(ㄌㄧㄢˊ ㄏㄜˊ ㄍㄨㄥ ㄅㄠˋ)
a joint communiqué
聯合戰線(ㄌㄧㄢˊ ㄏㄜˊ ㄓㄢˋ ㄒㄧㄢˋ)
a united front
聯合政府(ㄌㄧㄢˊ ㄏㄜˊ ㄓㄥˋ ㄈㄨˇ)
a coalition government
聯合聲明(ㄌㄧㄢˊ ㄏㄜˊ ㄕㄥ ㄇㄧㄥˊ)
a joint statement or declaration: 他們發表聯合聲明。They made a joint statement.
聯號(ㄌㄧㄢˊ ㄏㄠˋ)
① (said of banknotes, tickets, etc.) with contiguous numbers ② an allied company
聯歡會(ㄌㄧㄢˊ ㄏㄨㄢ ㄏㄨㄟˋ)
a get-together; a social gathering; a gay party: 我被邀參加他們的聯歡會。I was invited to their gay party.
聯接(ㄌㄧㄢˊ ㄐㄧㄝ)
to connect; to join together; contiguous: 這兩個城市由鐵路聯接。The two towns are connected by a railway.
聯接代名詞(ㄌㄧㄢˊ ㄐㄧㄝ ㄉㄞˋ ㄇㄧㄥˊ ㄘˊ)
a group of characters which are used after a verb to form a noun, such as "的" in 賣花的 or "者" in 捕蛇者
聯結(ㄌㄧㄢˊ ㄐㄧㄝˊ)
to form an alliance; to join together or gang up
聯句(ㄌㄧㄢˊ ㄐㄩˋ)
joint authorship of poems, with one participant chanting one line to be followed by the next until a poem is completed (a literary game among intellectuals of the past)
聯軍(ㄌㄧㄢˊ ㄐㄩㄣ)
allied forces
聯席會議(ㄌㄧㄢˊ ㄒㄧˊ ㄏㄨㄟˋ ㄧˋ)
a joint meeting or conference; a joint session: 他出席聯席會議。He attended the joint conference.
聯繫(ㄌㄧㄢˊ ㄒㄧˋ)
① to unite; to join together (under a cause, etc.); to link; to relate ② to maintain communications, contact, or liaison; to get in touch with
聯想(ㄌㄧㄢˊ ㄒㄧㄤˇ)
association of ideas; to associate
聯手(ㄌㄧㄢˊ ㄕㄡˇ)
to join hands (with someone); to gang up
聯署(ㄌㄧㄢˊ ㄕㄨˇ)
to sign jointly
聯屬(ㄌㄧㄢˊ ㄕㄨˇ)
continuous; connected; uninterrupted
聯宗(ㄌㄧㄢˊ ㄗㄨㄥ)
to join persons of different ancestors and make them bear the same family name
聯誼(ㄌㄧㄢˊ ㄧˊ)or 聯誼活動(ㄌㄧㄢˊ ㄧˊ ㄏㄨㄛˊ ㄉㄨㄥˋ)
activities for promoting fellowship
聯姻(ㄌㄧㄢˊ ㄧㄣ)
connections through marriage; to unite by marriage: 他們兩家聯姻。The two families are united by marriage.
聯營(ㄌㄧㄢˊ ㄧㄥˊ)
(said of two or more business setups) joint operation; a pool
聯運(ㄌㄧㄢˊ ㄩㄣˋ)
joint transportation, or through transportation via several railroads

【聰】 4605
ㄘㄨㄥ tsong cong

1. clever; astute; bright; quick of apprehension
2. with a good faculty of hearing

聰敏(ㄘㄨㄥ ㄇㄧㄣˇ)
clever and intelligent
聰明(ㄘㄨㄥ ㄇㄧㄥˊ)
① clever; bright; intelligent; quick of comprehension: 聰明反被聰明誤。Clever people may fall victim to their own cleverness. ② sharp hearing and seeing faculties
聰明絕頂(ㄘㄨㄥ ㄇㄧㄥˊ ㄐㄩㄝˊ ㄉㄧㄥˇ)
extremely clever or intelligent: 他是個聰明絕頂的學生。He is an extremely intelligent student.
聰明自誤(ㄘㄨㄥ ㄇㄧㄥˊ ㄗˋ ㄨˋ)
(literally) ruined by one's own cleverness—too smart
聰明一世，糊塗一時(ㄘㄨㄥ ㄇㄧㄥˊ ㄧˊ ㄕˋ, ㄏㄨˊ ㄊㄨˊ ㄧˋ ㄕˊ)
A lifetime of cleverness can be interrupted by moments of stupidity.
聰了(ㄘㄨㄥ ㄌㄧㄠˇ)
bright and quick of comprehension; astute; intelligent; clever
聰慧(ㄘㄨㄥ ㄏㄨㄟˋ)
intelligent; astute; clever: 她是個聰慧的女孩。She is a clever girl.
聰穎(ㄘㄨㄥ ㄧㄥˇ)
clever and bright: 她的聰穎超過她的年齡。She is clever and bright beyond her years.

【聲】 4606
ㄕㄥ sheng sheng

1. sound; voice; a tone
2. music
3. language; a tongue
4. reputation; fame
5. to make known

聲波(ㄕㄥ ㄅㄛ)
sound waves; acoustic waves
聲門(ㄕㄥ ㄇㄣˊ)
the glottis
聲名(ㄕㄥ ㄇㄧㄥˊ)
reputation; fame: 他是個聲名很好的人。He is a man of good (or high) fame.
聲名狼藉(ㄕㄥ ㄇㄧㄥˊ ㄌㄤˊ ㄐㄧˊ)
a notorious reputation
聲明(ㄕㄥ ㄇㄧㄥˊ)
to announce; to declare; to assert; to make a statement; to clarify publicly: 他聲明他的清白。He asserted his innocence.
聲母(ㄕㄥ ㄇㄨˇ)
the 21 Chinese phonetic signs equivalent to the consonants in European languages

聲帶(ㄕㄥ ㄉㄞˋ)
the vocal cords
聲調(ㄕㄥ ㄉㄧㄠˋ)
① a tone (of a voice), as a severe tone ② a tone in Chinese phonetics ③ a melody in a musical composition
聲調兒(ㄕㄥ ㄉㄧㄠˋㄦ)
① the tone of a human voice ② the sound of a musical instrument
聲東擊西(ㄕㄥ ㄉㄨㄥ ㄐㄧˊ ㄒㄧ)
(literally) to make noise in the east while striking in the west—feigning tactics
聲討(ㄕㄥ ㄊㄠˇ)
to condemn or attack (a rebel, traitor, etc.) by words
聲納(ㄕㄥ ㄋㄚˋ)
(physics) sonar
聲淚俱下(ㄕㄥ ㄌㄟˋ ㄐㄩˋ ㄒㄧㄚˋ)
to cry while speaking
聲浪(ㄕㄥ ㄌㄤˋ)
the sound wave
聲律(ㄕㄥ ㄌㄩˋ)
rules governing rhythm of words
聲光(ㄕㄥ ㄍㄨㄤ)
① fame and conditions (of a person, etc.) ② (said of movies) sound and lighting
聲價(ㄕㄥ ㄐㄧㄚˋ)
fame or popularity of a person
聲教(ㄕㄥ ㄐㄧㄠˋ)
imperial cultural education for the people
聲氣(ㄕㄥ ㄑㄧˋ)
① information ② to rouse one's spirit; to spur on troop morale
聲氣相求(ㄕㄥ ㄑㄧˋ ㄒㄧㄤ ㄑㄧㄡˊ)
(said of a group of people) to share the same interests and purpose
聲請(ㄕㄥ ㄑㄧㄥˇ)
to make requests with reasons stated
聲息(ㄕㄥ ㄒㄧˊ)
① sound; voices: 屋子裏一點聲息都沒有。Not a sound was heard in the house. ② news; information
聲響(ㄕㄥ ㄒㄧㄤˇ)
① sound; noise; a tone ② reputation

聲學(ㄕㄥ ㄒㄩㄝˊ)
acoustics
聲張(ㄕㄥ ㄓㄤ)
to make known; to announce or publicize: 不要聲張這件事。Don't make this thing known to anyone.
聲叉(ㄕㄥ ㄔㄚ)
a tuning fork
聲稱(ㄕㄥ ㄔㄥ)
to assert; to declare
聲勢(ㄕㄥ ㄕˋ)
influence; fame; prestige and power
聲勢浩大(ㄕㄥ ㄕˋ ㄏㄠˋ ㄉㄚˋ)
an impressive display of power or influence
聲述(ㄕㄥ ㄕㄨˋ)
to tell; to state or present (reasons); to explain
聲如洪鐘(ㄕㄥ ㄖㄨˊ ㄏㄨㄥˊ ㄓㄨㄥ)
The voice sounds like a roaring bell.
聲嘶力竭(ㄕㄥ ㄙ ㄌㄧˋ ㄐㄧㄝˊ)
The voice gets husky as a result of exhaustion.
聲色(ㄕㄥ ㄙㄜˋ)
① music and women ② the voice and the facial expression
聲色俱厲(ㄕㄥ ㄙㄜˋ ㄐㄩˋ ㄌㄧˋ)
to speak in a harsh tone and with a severe expression
聲色犬馬之樂(ㄕㄥ ㄙㄜˋ ㄑㄩㄢˇ ㄇㄚˇ ㄓ ㄌㄜˋ)
carnal pleasure; sensory enjoyment
聲速(ㄕㄥ ㄙㄨˋ)
the velocity of sound
聲兒(ㄕㄥㄦ)
sound; voice; a tone
聲言(ㄕㄥ ㄧㄢˊ)
to announce; to profess; to claim; to declare
聲音(ㄕㄥ ㄧㄣ)
a sound; a voice: 我們聽到遠處有奇怪的聲音。We heard strange sounds in the distance.
聲威(ㄕㄥ ㄨㄟ)
fame and the influence that goes with it
聲聞於天(ㄕㄥ ㄨㄣˊ ㄩˊ ㄊㄧㄢ)
The voice is heard by Heaven.
聲聞(ㄕㄥ ㄨㄣˊ)
reputation
聲問(ㄕㄥ ㄨㄣˋ)
① reputation ② information
聲望(ㄕㄥ ㄨㄤˋ)
fame; reputation; prestige: 他的聲望提高了。His prestige rose.
聲譽(ㄕㄥ ㄩˋ)
reputation; fame: 他是個聲譽很好的老師。He has a good reputation as a teacher.
聲譽卓著(ㄕㄥ ㄩˋ ㄓㄨㄛˊ ㄓㄨˋ)
① famous; widely known ② (said of a business firm) with a good reputation
聲樂(ㄕㄥ ㄩㄝˋ)
vocal music
聲樂家(ㄕㄥ ㄩㄝˋ ㄐㄧㄚ)
a vocalist
聲援(ㄕㄥ ㄩㄢˊ)
to give moral support: 他聲援我們。He gave us moral support.
聲韻(ㄕㄥ ㄩㄣˋ)
rhymes and tones of words 亦作「音韻」
聲韻學(ㄕㄥ ㄩㄣˋ ㄒㄩㄝˊ)
phonology 亦作「音韻學」

【聳】 4607 ㄙㄨㄥˇ **soong sǒng**
1. to alarm; to alert; to warn; to be sensational
2. to rise up; to stretch up erect or at full length
3. to be born deaf
4. to urge; to egg on

聳動(ㄙㄨㄥˇ ㄉㄨㄥˋ)
① to urge; to egg on ② to be moved or alarmed
聳動視聽(ㄙㄨㄥˇ ㄉㄨㄥˋ ㄕˋ ㄊㄧㄥ)
to create a sensation
聳聽(ㄙㄨㄥˇ ㄊㄧㄥ)
to alarm others with something sensational; to stimulate others
聳立(ㄙㄨㄥˇ ㄌㄧˋ)
to tower aloft; to rise up steeply
聳肩(ㄙㄨㄥˇ ㄐㄧㄢ)
to shrug shoulders
聳峙(ㄙㄨㄥˇ ㄓˋ)
(said of mountains) to rise up high above; to soar skyward; to stab deep into the sky
聳然(ㄙㄨㄥˇ ㄖㄢˊ)
rising in sharp elevation;

cliffy

聳人聽聞(ㄙㄨㄥˇ ㄖㄣˊ ㄊㄧㄥ ㄨㄣˊ)
(often said of news-reporting, etc.) sensational; to cause false alarm; alarmist talk

聳恿(ㄙㄨㄥˇ ㄩㄥˇ)
to urge; to egg on

【聱】 4608 ㄠˊ aur áo

1. hard to read or understand—too many big words and a tortuous style
2. perverse; unruly
3. lying and winding, as snakes, old trees, etc.

聱牙(ㄠˊ ㄧㄚˊ)
(said of writings) full of characters that are difficult to make out and pronounce

十二畫

【職】 4609 ㄓˊ jyr zhí

1. a profession or a vocation; a career
2. a post; a position
3. an office; official duties
4. to govern; to direct; to manage
5. used in place of "I" in documents to a superior
6. only; particularly

職別(ㄓˊ ㄅㄧㄝˊ)
official rank

職分(ㄓˊ ㄈㄣˋ)
official duties; duty

職蜂(ㄓˊ ㄈㄥ)
a worker bee 亦作「工蜂」

職等(ㄓˊ ㄉㄥˇ)
official rank; grade of position

職官(ㄓˊ ㄍㄨㄢ)
① one's official position and duties; profession ② presidents over the different departments of office

職工(ㄓˊ ㄍㄨㄥ)
① officers and workers (in a plant, company, etc.) ② workers with permanent jobs

職工保險基金(ㄓˊ ㄍㄨㄥ ㄅㄠˇ ㄒㄧㄢˇ ㄐㄧ ㄐㄧㄣ)
the employees' insurance funds

職工福利(ㄓˊ ㄍㄨㄥ ㄈㄨˊ ㄌㄧˋ)
employee benefits

職貢(ㄓˊ ㄍㄨㄥˋ)
tributes paid by a vassal state

職前教育(ㄓˊ ㄑㄧㄢˊ ㄐㄧㄠˋ ㄩˋ)
pre-vocational education

職權(ㄓˊ ㄑㄩㄢˊ)
authority for exercising or discharging one's duties

職權範圍(ㄓˊ ㄑㄩㄢˊ ㄈㄢˋ ㄨㄟˊ)
limits or scope of one's functions and powers

職銜(ㄓˊ ㄒㄧㄢˊ)
the official title of a person: 他的職銜是總經理。His official title is general manager.

職志(ㄓˊ ㄓˋ)
① a flag officer in ancient China ② aspiration; long cherished wish or hope ③ a mission; a lifework: 他以興辦教育爲職志。He takes establishment of education as his lifework.

職掌(ㄓˊ ㄓㄤˇ)
① to have charge of; to direct, manage or supervise, etc. as part of one's official duties ② (said of an organization or official post) functions and duties

職稱(ㄓˊ ㄔㄥ)
the name of a position one holds; the title of a technical or professional post (such as engineer, professor, lecturer, academician, etc.)

職是(ㄓˊ ㄕˋ)
It is for (this reason) that....

職守(ㄓˊ ㄕㄡˇ)
one's official duties, charge, etc.: 他因擅離職守而被免職。He was dismissed from office because he left his duties without permission.

職任(ㄓˊ ㄖㄣˋ)
one's position or duties in an office

職責(ㄓˊ ㄗㄜˊ)
one's position and responsibility; charge: 逮捕罪犯是警方的職責。Arresting criminals is the charge of the police.

職責所在(ㄓˊ ㄗㄜˊ ㄙㄨㄛˇ ㄗㄞˋ)
duty-bound

職司(ㄓˊ ㄙ)
one's official duties, charge, etc.

職業(ㄓˊ ㄧㄝˋ)
a profession; a vocation; an occupation

職業病(ㄓˊ ㄧㄝˋ ㄅㄧㄥˋ)
the occupational disease

職業婦女(ㄓˊ ㄧㄝˋ ㄈㄨˋ ㄋㄩˇ)
career women; working girls

職業介紹所(ㄓˊ ㄧㄝˋ ㄐㄧㄝˋ ㄕㄠˋ ㄙㄨㄛˇ)
an employment agency

職業教育(ㄓˊ ㄧㄝˋ ㄐㄧㄠˋ ㄩˋ)
vocational education

職業學校(ㄓˊ ㄧㄝˋ ㄒㄩㄝˊ ㄒㄧㄠˋ)
a vocational school

職業學生(ㄓˊ ㄧㄝˋ ㄒㄩㄝˊ ㄕㄥ)
① political underlings who pose as students in a college for stirring up troubles ② athletes admitted to a school with fat scholarships in return for their services in school teams

職業訓練(ㄓˊ ㄧㄝˋ ㄒㄩㄣˋ ㄌㄧㄢˋ)
vocational training

職業專科學校(ㄓˊ ㄧㄝˋ ㄓㄨㄢ ㄎㄜ ㄒㄩㄝˊ ㄒㄧㄠˋ)
a vocational junior college

職業外交官(ㄓˊ ㄧㄝˋ ㄨㄞˋ ㄐㄧㄠ ㄍㄨㄢ)
a career diplomat

職務(ㄓˊ ㄨˋ)
one's official duties or obligations

職位(ㄓˊ ㄨㄟˋ)
one's office; one's position in an office: 他在政府中擔任高職位。He has a high office in the government.

職員(ㄓˊ ㄩㄢˊ)
staff members or employees of a company, office, etc.: 他是這家公司的正式職員。He is a regular employee of the company.

職員錄(ㄓˊ ㄩㄢˊ ㄌㄨˋ)
a roster of staff members

職員宿舍(ㄓˊ ㄩㄢˊ ㄙㄨˋ ㄕㄜˋ)
company officers' dormitory; apartments or housing units built for employees

【聵】 4610 ㄎㄨㄟˋ kuey kuì

1. deaf; hard of hearing
2. stupid and unreasonable

【聶】 4611 ㄋㄧㄝˋ nieh niè

1. to whisper into another's ear

2. a Chinese family name

十六畫

【聽】 4612
1. ㄊㄧㄥ ting ting
1. to hear; to listen
2. to obey; to follow
3. to wait for
4. a hall

聽不明白(ㄊㄧㄥ ·ㄅㄨ ㄇㄧㄥˊ ·ㄅㄞ)
cannot understand (what the other is talking about); can not hear well or comprehend

聽不得(ㄊㄧㄥ ·ㄅㄨ ·ㄉㄜ)
should not be heard; should not listen to

聽不見(ㄊㄧㄥ ·ㄅㄨ ㄐㄧㄢˋ)
cannot hear (because voice, or sound is too low or far away)

聽不清(ㄊㄧㄥ ·ㄅㄨ ㄑㄧㄥ)
unable to hear distinctly or clearly

聽命(ㄊㄧㄥ ㄇㄧㄥˋ)
to follow orders

聽得入神(ㄊㄧㄥ ·ㄉㄜ ㄖㄨˋ ㄕㄣˊ)
completely absorbed (in music, lectures, etc.)

聽頭(ㄊㄧㄥ ·ㄊㄡ)
worth listening to: 這音樂很有聽頭。The music is worth listening to.

聽筒(ㄊㄧㄥ ㄊㄨㄥˇ)
a telephone receiver

聽膩了(ㄊㄧㄥ ㄋㄧˋ ·ㄌㄜ)
bored with listening to (music or words repeated too often)

聽力(ㄊㄧㄥ ㄌㄧˋ)
① the sense of hearing ② aural comprehension (in language teaching)

聽力試驗(ㄊㄧㄥ ㄌㄧˋ ㄕˋ ㄧㄢˋ)
audiometry; an audiometric test

聽骨(ㄊㄧㄥ ㄍㄨˇ)
ossicula auditus

聽管(ㄊㄧㄥ ㄍㄨㄢˇ)
the auditory canal

聽慣(ㄊㄧㄥ ㄍㄨㄢˋ)
to get used to hearing (such foul language, etc.)

聽課(ㄊㄧㄥ ㄎㄜˋ)
to attend class teaching or lectures

聽候(ㄊㄧㄥ ㄏㄡˋ)
to wait for (instructions, orders, etc.): 他聽候你的命令。He is waiting for your orders.

聽話(ㄊㄧㄥ ㄏㄨㄚˋ)
① to obey; obedient ② to wait for word or a reply

聽見(ㄊㄧㄥ ㄐㄧㄢˋ)
to hear

聽講(ㄊㄧㄥ ㄐㄧㄤˇ)
to listen to a lecture, speech, etc.

聽覺(ㄊㄧㄥ ㄐㄩㄝˊ)
hearing; the sense of hearing

聽起來(ㄊㄧㄥ ·ㄑㄧ ·ㄌㄞ)
to sound; to ring

聽取(ㄊㄧㄥ ㄑㄩˇ)
to listen (with due attention); to hear (a report)

聽勸告(ㄊㄧㄥ ㄑㄩㄢˋ ㄍㄠˋ)
to accept or listen to another's advice

聽戲(ㄊㄧㄥ ㄒㄧˋ)
to see an operatic show (especially referring to an experienced theatergoer who is more interested in the singing than in the spectacles on the stage)

聽寫(ㄊㄧㄥ ㄒㄧㄝˇ)
dictation; to dictate: 老師考學生聽寫。The teacher gave the pupils dictation.

聽信(ㄊㄧㄥ ㄒㄧㄣˋ)
① to listen to and believe (what others said): 不要聽信謠言。Don't believe rumors. ② to wait for news, messages, information, etc.

聽著(ㄊㄧㄥ ·ㄓㄜ)
to listen 或 Listen!

聽診器(ㄊㄧㄥ ㄓㄣˇ ㄑㄧˋ)
a stethoscope

聽衆(ㄊㄧㄥ ㄓㄨㄥˋ)
an audience; listeners: 聽衆感動淚下。The audience were moved to tears.

聽差(ㄊㄧㄥ ㄔㄞ)
a factotum; a servant; an errand man: 他是個好聽差。He is a good servant.

聽事(ㄊㄧㄥ ㄕˋ)
a hall

聽事的(ㄊㄧㄥ ㄕˋ ·ㄉㄜ)
a servant

聽神經(ㄊㄧㄥ ㄕㄣˊ ㄐㄧㄥ)
the auditory nerve

聽審(ㄊㄧㄥ ㄕㄣˇ)
to stand trial; to be tried

聽說(ㄊㄧㄥ ㄕㄨㄛ)
① It is reported that.... 或 It is said that.... 或 according to unconfirmed reports; to hear of ② to obey; obedient

聽錯(ㄊㄧㄥ ㄘㄨㄛˋ)
to hear incorrectly; to misunderstand what someone has said

聽從(ㄊㄧㄥ ㄘㄨㄥˊ)
to listen to (another's advice, etc.); to listen and follow

聽而不聞(ㄊㄧㄥ ㄦˊ ㄅㄨˋ ㄨㄣˊ)
to turn a deaf ear to; to hear without understanding

聽厭了(ㄊㄧㄥ ㄧㄢˋ ·ㄌㄜ)
to be tired of hearing something repeated too often

聽聞(ㄊㄧㄥ ㄨㄣˊ)
what one has heard

【聽】 4612
2. ㄊㄧㄥˋ tinq ting
1. to let
2. to comply with; to submit to
3. to manage; to govern; to rule
4. to judge and decide

聽便(ㄊㄧㄥˋ ㄅㄧㄢˋ)
to suit one's convenience; to leave it to one's own discretion; to have no fixed opinion and act according to the circumstances

聽憑(ㄊㄧㄥˋ ㄆㄧㄥˊ) or 聽任(ㄊㄧㄥˋ ㄖㄣˋ)
to let someone do whatever he likes; to do nothing to stop or reverse a situation; to sit tight and let it happen

聽命(ㄊㄧㄥˋ ㄇㄧㄥˋ)
to submit oneself to the will of Heaven; to be resigned to one's fate

聽斷(ㄊㄧㄥˋ ㄉㄨㄢˋ)
to pass judgment or verdict after hearing the case

聽天由命(ㄊㄧㄥˋ ㄊㄧㄢ ㄧㄡˊ ㄇㄧㄥˋ)
to submit to the will of Heaven and one's fate; to resign oneself to fate

聽其自然(ㄊㄧㄥˋ ㄑㄧˊ ㄗˋ ㄖㄢˊ)
to let things take their course

聽政(ㄊㄧㄥˋ ㄓㄥˋ)

to administer; to govern; to rule
聽使(ㄊㄧㄥ ㄕˇ)
①convenient; suitable for use ②to await instructions or orders and be ready for errands
聽訟(ㄊㄧㄥ ㄙㄨㄥˋ)
to serve as a judge in a lawsuit

【聾】 4613 ㄌㄨㄥˊ long lóng
1. deaf; hard of hearing
2. deaf—stupid and ignorant
聾聵(ㄌㄨㄥˊ ㄎㄨㄟˋ)
①deaf ②ignorant and stupid
聾子(ㄌㄨㄥˊ ·ㄗ)
a deaf person
聾啞(ㄌㄨㄥˊ ㄧㄚˇ)
deaf-and-dumb; a deaf-mute
聾啞學校(ㄌㄨㄥˊ ㄧㄚˇ ㄒㄩㄝˊ ㄒㄧㄠˋ)
a school for deaf-mutes; a deaf-and-dumb school

聿 部
ㄩˋ yuh yù

【聿】 4614 ㄩˋ yuh yù
1. a writing instrument—a pen, a writing brush, etc.
2. a particle, used in introducing a phrase or sentence
3. agile and quick; nimble

七畫

【肄】 4615 ㄧˋ yih yì
1. to study; to learn; to practice
2. to toil; to work hard
3. remnants; leftovers
4. fresh twigs
肄習(ㄧˋ ㄒㄧˊ)
to practice
肄業(ㄧˋ ㄧㄝˋ)
to learn; to study (at a certain school)

【肆】 4616 ㄙˋ syh sì
1. to let loose; to indulge in; to behave without restraint
2. a marketplace; a shop; a place to display goods: 茶肆 a teahouse 酒肆 a wineshop
3. to exhibit; to display
4. to execute a criminal and expose his corpse in the market
5. to extend; to expand
6. to assault; to attack suddenly
7. to use to the utmost; to exhaust
8. an elaborate form of 四 (four) to prevent forgery
肆目(ㄙˋ ㄇㄨˋ)
to stretch one's eyes as far as one can see
肆虐(ㄙˋ ㄋㄩㄝˋ)
①to indulge in atrocities; to do damage unhinderedly ②reckless and oppressive; rampant: 霍亂肆虐此城。Cholera was rampant in this town.
肆力(ㄙˋ ㄌㄧˋ)
to do one's best or utmost: 我必須肆力幫他的忙。I must do my best to help him.
肆掠(ㄙˋ ㄌㄩㄝˋ)
to indulge in looting, robbery, without restraint; rapine
肆口大罵(ㄙˋ ㄎㄡˇ ㄉㄚˋ ㄇㄚˋ)
to abuse someone outrageously and without any restraint
肆刼(ㄙˋ ㄐㄧㄝˊ) or 肆刼無忌(ㄙˋ ㄐㄧㄝˊ ㄨˊ ㄐㄧˋ)
to loot, or rob freely and without any restraint; rapine
肆行(ㄙˋ ㄒㄧㄥˊ)
to act at the dictate of one's own will without any thought for others; to indulge
肆廛(ㄙˋ ㄔㄢˊ)
shops; stores
肆縱(ㄙˋ ㄗㄨㄥˋ)
indulgent and without restraint
肆意(ㄙˋ ㄧˋ)
at will; without any restraint; indulgently; recklessly
肆飲(ㄙˋ ㄧㄣˇ)
to indulge in drinking
肆應(ㄙˋ ㄧㄥˋ)
to be good at dealing with varied matters properly
肆無忌憚(ㄙˋ ㄨˊ ㄐㄧˋ ㄉㄢˋ)
indulgent and reckless; without restraint of any kind; unscrupulous

【肅】 4617 ㄙㄨˋ suh sù
1. respectful; reverential; to pay respects; to salute
2. solemn; serious; majestic; awe-inspiring
3. to usher in
4. neat and quiet
5. to withdraw; to shrink (as in cold weather, etc.)
6. a Chinese family name
肅穆(ㄙㄨˋ ㄇㄨˋ)
①solemn: 他們注視著肅穆的典禮。They watched the solemn ceremony. ②peaceful
肅立(ㄙㄨˋ ㄌㄧˋ)
to stand upright as a mark of respect
肅客(ㄙㄨˋ ㄎㄜˋ)
to receive a guest
肅函(ㄙㄨˋ ㄏㄢˊ)
to write to you in great reverence
肅敬(ㄙㄨˋ ㄐㄧㄥˋ)
respectful
肅靜(ㄙㄨˋ ㄐㄧㄥˋ)
①a solemn silence: 禮堂內肅靜無聲。A solemn silence reigned in the auditorium. ②peaceful
肅靜無譁(ㄙㄨˋ ㄐㄧㄥˋ ㄨˊ ㄏㄨㄚˊ)
strict silence
肅清(ㄙㄨˋ ㄑㄧㄥ)
①to wipe out or eliminate (rebels, enemy troops, etc.): 他們肅清叛徒。They wiped out the rebels. ②cold and solemn—as a winter night
肅殺(ㄙㄨˋ ㄕㄚ)
①an awe-inspiring, stern, forbidding look ②a lonesome scene of late autumn
肅然(ㄙㄨˋ ㄖㄢˊ)
respectfully; reverently
肅然起敬(ㄙㄨˋ ㄖㄢˊ ㄑㄧˇ ㄐㄧㄥˋ)
great respect rising in one's heart
肅坐(ㄙㄨˋ ㄗㄨㄛˋ)
to sit erect and in silence

八畫

【肇】 4618 ㄓㄠˋ jaw zhào

1. to begin; to start; to commence
2. to found; to devise
3. to incur (misfortune, etc.)
4. to adjust; to make right

肇端(ㄓㄠˋ ㄉㄨㄢ)
the beginning; the start; to originate or initiate

肇亂(ㄓㄠˋ ㄌㄨㄢˋ)
to create upheaval or trouble; to start the whole confusion, uprising, etc.

肇國(ㄓㄠˋ ㄍㄨㄛˊ)
to found a nation or state

肇禍(ㄓㄠˋ ㄏㄨㄛˋ)
to incur or court misfortune; to start or stir up trouble: 他肇禍了。He incurred misfortune.

肇基(ㄓㄠˋ ㄐㄧ)
to lay the foundation; to do the spadework; to pave the way

肇建(ㄓㄠˋ ㄐㄧㄢˋ)
to found

肇釁(ㄓㄠˋ ㄒㄧㄣˋ)
to stir up an incident or trouble

肇始(ㄓㄠˋ ㄕˇ)
to begin

肇事(ㄓㄠˋ ㄕˋ)
to stir up trouble or disturbances

肇造(ㄓㄠˋ ㄗㄠˋ)
to found; to first establish

肉部
ㄖㄨˋ ruh rù

【肉】 4619
ㄖㄡˋ row ròu
(讀音 ㄖㄨˋ ruh rù)

1. flesh
2. physical; carnal
3. meat of animals; meat or pulp of fruits, etc.
4. flesh and blood — dearest, as one's children
5. slow-motion

肉搏(ㄖㄡˋ ㄅㄛˊ) or 肉搏戰(ㄖㄡˋ ㄅㄛˊ ㄓㄢˋ)
hand-to-hand combat

肉包子(ㄖㄡˋ ㄅㄠ ˙ㄗ) or 肉包兒(ㄖㄡˋ ㄅㄠㄦ)
meat dumplings; steamed dumplings stuffed with meat

肉餅(ㄖㄡˋ ㄅㄧㄥˇ)
meat cake: 這是自製的肉餅。This is a homemade meat cake.

肉片兒(ㄖㄡˋ ㄆㄧㄚˋㄦ)
slices of meat; sliced meat

肉票(ㄖㄡˋ ㄆㄧㄠˋ)
a hostage kidnapped for a ransom

肉鋪(ㄖㄡˋ ㄆㄨˋ)
a butcher's shop

肉麻(ㄖㄡˋ ㄇㄚˊ)
a creepy feeling; disgusting; revolting; something that gives one goose pimples

肉饅頭(ㄖㄡˋ ㄇㄢˊ ˙ㄊㄡ)
steamed dumplings with meat stuffing

肉脯(ㄖㄡˋ ㄈㄨˇ)
dried meat in threads or sliced form

肉彈(ㄖㄡˋ ㄉㄢˋ)
a buxom beauty; a woman with an hourglass figure; a siren

肉店(ㄖㄡˋ ㄉㄧㄢˋ)
a butcher's shop

肉釘兒(ㄖㄡˋ ㄉㄧㄥㄦ) or 肉丁(ㄖㄡˋ ㄉㄧㄥ)
diced meat

肉胎(ㄖㄡˋ ㄊㄞ)
to make a statue (for worshiping, etc.) by applying layers of lacquer to the body of the deceased

肉袒(ㄖㄡˋ ㄊㄢˇ) or 肉袒負荊(ㄖㄡˋ ㄊㄢˇ ㄈㄨˋ ㄐㄧㄥ) or 肉袒謝罪(ㄖㄡˋ ㄊㄢˇ ㄒㄧㄝˋ ㄗㄨㄟˋ)
(according to an old Chinese story) to strip off the upper garment as a token of sincere apology—ready to submit to any punishment the other party may give

肉體(ㄖㄡˋ ㄊㄧˇ)
flesh and blood; the human body; physical; carnal; sensory

肉跳(ㄖㄡˋ ㄊㄧㄠˋ)
frightening; awesome; apprehensive

肉泥爛醬(ㄖㄡˋ ㄋㄧˊ ㄌㄢˋ ㄐㄧㄤˋ)
the chilling sight of dismembered bodies and mashed flesh

肉類(ㄖㄡˋ ㄌㄟˋ)
meats

肉瘤(ㄖㄡˋ ㄌㄧㄡˊ)
a fleshy tumor

肉林(ㄖㄡˋ ㄌㄧㄣˊ)
vast quantities of meat (stored in palaces)

肉感(ㄖㄡˋ ㄍㄢˇ)
voluptuous; buxom; sexy

肉桂(ㄖㄡˋ ㄍㄨㄟˋ)
cinnamon

肉冠(ㄖㄡˋ ㄍㄨㄢ)
the comb (of a bird)

肉塊(ㄖㄡˋ ㄎㄨㄞˋ)
chopped meat; meat chops

肉醬(ㄖㄡˋ ㄐㄧㄤˋ)
meat pulp; mashed meat cooked with soybean sauce

肉餡(ㄖㄡˋ ㄒㄧㄢˋ)
meat stuffing; chopped or ground meat

肉星兒(ㄖㄡˋ ㄒㄧㄥㄦ)
tiniest bits of meat (along with a good deal of vegetables)—a poor man's diet

肉刑(ㄖㄡˋ ㄒㄧㄥˊ)
corporeal punishment, including mutilation, etc.

肉芝(ㄖㄡˋ ㄓ)
thousand-year-old toads, bats, or swallows which are supposed to make the eater immortal

肉汁(ㄖㄡˋ ㄓ)
meat juice; meat broth; meat extract

肉食(ㄖㄡˋ ㄕˊ)
to eat meat; meat-eating; carnivorous

肉食動物(ㄖㄡˋ ㄕˊ ㄉㄨㄥˋ ㄨˋ)
carnivorous animals

肉食者鄙(ㄖㄡˋ ㄕˊ ㄓㄜˇ ㄅㄧˇ)
(literally) The meat-eaters are vulgar.—High-ranking government officials are mostly stupid and inefficient.

肉食獸(ㄖㄡˋ ㄕˊ ㄕㄡˋ) or 肉食動物(ㄖㄡˋ ㄕˊ ㄉㄨㄥˋ ㄨˋ)
meat-eating animals; carnivorous animals

肉身(ㄖㄡˋ ㄕㄣ)
the physical body; the flesh

肉絲麵(ㄖㄡˋ ㄙ ㄇㄧㄢˋ)
noodles with shredded meat

肉絲兒(ㄖㄡˋ ㄙㄜㄦ)
shredded meat
肉色(ㄖㄡˋ ㄙㄜˋ)
yellowish pink; flesh-colored
肉鬆(ㄖㄡˋ ㄙㄨㄥ)
fried shredded meat; meat fluff
肉眼(ㄖㄡˋ ㄧㄢˇ)
①a layman's eyes; vulgar eyes ②the naked eye
肉眼凡胎(ㄖㄡˋ ㄧㄢˇ ㄈㄢˊ ㄊㄞ)
①a layman—without an immortal bone in him ②vulgar and stupid
肉眼無珠(ㄖㄡˋ ㄧㄢˇ ㄨˊ ㄓㄨ)
(literally) eyes without pupils—stupid; shallow
肉丸子(ㄖㄡˋ ㄨㄢˊ ·ㄗ)
meatballs
肉慾(ㄖㄡˋ ㄩˋ)
carnal desire; sexual desire

一畫

【肊】 4620 ㄧˋ yih yì
1. breastbone
2. same as 臆 — one's mind, heart, disposition, feelings, or views

二畫

【肋】 4621 ㄌㄟˋ ley lèi (讀音 ㄌㄜˋ leh lè)
the ribs; the sides
肋膜(ㄌㄟˋ ㄇㄛˊ)
the pleura
肋膜炎(ㄌㄟˋ ㄇㄛˊ ㄧㄢˊ)
pleurisy
肋條(ㄌㄟˋ ㄊㄧㄠˊ)
the ribs
肋骨(ㄌㄟˋ ㄍㄨˇ)
the ribs: 他跌了一跤摔斷了三根肋骨。He fell and broke three ribs.

【肌】 4622 ㄐㄧ ji jī
1. tissue; muscles; flesh
2. the skin
肌膚(ㄐㄧ ㄈㄨ)
①the skin and flesh ②the intimate relation between man and woman
肌膚之親(ㄐㄧ ㄈㄨ ㄓ ㄑㄧㄣ)
intimacy arising from sexual intercourse
肌體(ㄐㄧ ㄊㄧˇ)
the body
肌理(ㄐㄧ ㄌㄧˇ)
the texture of the skin (as coarse, tender, or delicate)
肌骨(ㄐㄧ ㄍㄨˇ)
muscles and bones
肌肉(ㄐㄧ ㄖㄡˋ)
muscles

三畫

【肖】 4623 ㄒㄧㄠˋ shiaw xiào
to resemble; to be like; alike; similar: 她酷肖其母。She strongly resembles her mother.
肖像(ㄒㄧㄠˋ ㄒㄧㄤˋ)
a portrait; a likeness, either painted or carved, of a person: 這幅肖像看起來很眞實。This portrait looks real.
肖子(ㄒㄧㄠˋ ㄗˇ)
a good (filial) son
肖似(ㄒㄧㄠˋ ㄙˋ)
to look very much alike; to be like (another)

【肘】 4624 ㄓㄡˇ joou zhǒu
1. the elbow
2. to catch one by the elbow
肘關節(ㄓㄡˇ ㄍㄨㄢ ㄐㄧㄝˊ)
the elbow joint
肘子(ㄓㄡˇ ·ㄗ)or 肘兒(ㄓㄡˇㄦ)
①the upper part of a leg of pork ②the elbow
肘腋(ㄓㄡˇ ㄧㄝˋ)
close by; near at hand

【肓】 4625 ㄏㄨㄤ huang huāng
the vitals; the region between the heart and the diaphragm

【肚】 4626 1. ㄉㄨˋ duh dù
the belly; the abdomen; the bowels
肚皮(ㄉㄨˋ ㄆㄧˊ)
the abdomen; the belly
肚皮舞(ㄉㄨˋ ㄆㄧˊ ㄨˇ)
a belly dance
肚裏明白(ㄉㄨˋ ·ㄌㄧ ㄇㄧㄥˊ ·ㄅㄞ)
to know in one's heart; clear to oneself; a tacit understanding
肚量(ㄉㄨˋ ㄌㄧㄤˋ)
capacity for tolerance and forgiveness
肚臍眼(ㄉㄨˋ ㄑㄧˊ ㄧㄢˇ)or 肚臍(ㄉㄨˋ ㄑㄧˊ)
the navel; the belly button
肚腸(ㄉㄨˋ ㄔㄤˊ)
the bowels
肚子(ㄉㄨˋ ·ㄗ)
the belly; the abdomen: 我們肚子餓了。Our bellies are empty.
肚子疼(ㄉㄨˋ ·ㄗ ㄊㄥˊ)
bellyache; celialgia; to suffer from abdominal pain: 他鬧肚子疼。He suffers from abdominal pain.

【肚】 4626 2. ㄉㄨˇ duu dǔ
the stomach: 我肚子痛。I have a pain in my stomach.
肚子(ㄉㄨˇ ·ㄗ)or 肚兒(ㄉㄨˇㄦ)
tripe

【肛】 4627 ㄍㄤ gang gāng
the anus
肛門(ㄍㄤ ㄇㄣˊ)
the anus

【肝】 4628 ㄍㄢ gan gān
the liver: 他患有肝病。He has liver trouble.
肝病(ㄍㄢ ㄅㄧㄥˋ)or 肝疾(ㄍㄢ ㄐㄧˊ)
a liver ailment
肝膽(ㄍㄢ ㄉㄢˇ)
①intimate; intimacy ②sincere; sincerity ③courage; courageous
肝膽俱裂(ㄍㄢ ㄉㄢˇ ㄐㄩˋ ㄌㄧㄝˋ)
extremely frightened; terror-stricken
肝膽相照(ㄍㄢ ㄉㄢˇ ㄒㄧㄤ ㄓㄠˋ)or 肝膽照人(ㄍㄢ ㄉㄢˇ ㄓㄠˋ ㄖㄣˊ)
to show the deepest sincerity
肝膽之交(ㄍㄢ ㄉㄢˇ ㄓ ㄐㄧㄠ)
sincere friendship
肝動脈(ㄍㄢ ㄉㄨㄥˋ ㄇㄞˋ)
a hepatic artery
肝糖(ㄍㄢ ㄊㄤˊ)
glycogen; hepatin
肝腦塗地(ㄍㄢ ㄋㄠˇ ㄊㄨˊ ㄉㄧˋ)
to try one's very best to serve someone, even at the expense of one's own life
肝鬲(ㄍㄢ ㄍㄜˊ)

intimate; sincere
肝火旺(ㄍㄢ ㄏㄨㄛˇ ㄨㄤˋ)
irritable and unpredictable; irascible
肝靜脈(ㄍㄢ ㄐㄧㄥˋ ㄇㄞˋ)
a hepatic vein
肝氣(ㄍㄢ ˙ㄑㄧ)
①(Chinese medicine) a depressed feeling or pain in the general area of the chest ②irritable and unpredictable dispositions
肝蛭(ㄍㄢ ㄓˋ)
Fasciola hepatica, a kind of parasites found in the livers of human beings and some animals
肝腸寸斷(ㄍㄢ ㄔㄤˊ ㄘㄨㄣˋ ㄉㄨㄢˋ)
greatly afflicted; heartbroken; deep sorrow
肝臟(ㄍㄢ ㄗㄤˋ)
the liver
肝臟脫出(ㄍㄢ ㄗㄤˋ ㄊㄨㄛ ㄔㄨ)
hepatocele
肝臟硬化(ㄍㄢ ㄗㄤˋ ㄧㄥˋ ㄏㄨㄚˋ)or 肝硬化(ㄍㄢ ㄧㄥˋ ㄏㄨㄚˋ)
cirrhosis of liver
肝炎(ㄍㄢ ㄧㄢˊ)
hepatitis
肝癌(ㄍㄢ ㄧㄢˊ)
cancer of the liver

【肐】 4629
(胳) ㄍㄜ ge ge
the arm—from the armpit to the wrist
肐膊(ㄍㄜ ˙ㄅㄛ)
the arm
肐膊肘子(ㄍㄜ ˙ㄅㄛ ㄓㄡˇ ˙ㄗ)or 肐膊肘兒(ㄍㄜ ˙ㄅㄛ ㄓㄡˇㄦ)
the elbow
肐膊腕兒(ㄍㄜ ˙ㄅㄛ ㄨㄢˋㄦ)or 肐膊腕子(ㄍㄜ ˙ㄅㄛ ㄨㄢˋ ˙ㄗ)
the wrist
肐臂(ㄍㄜ ˙ㄅㄟ)
the arm
肐肢窩(ㄍㄜ ˙ㄓ ㄨㄛ)
the armpit

【肜】 4630
ㄖㄨㄥˊ rong róng
an ancient sacrificial ritual lasting two successive days

四畫

【股】 4631
ㄍㄨˇ guu gǔ
1. the thigh; the haunches; the hips
2. a department; a section
3. shares; stock
4. a puff; a blast (of hot air)
5. a bunch or band (of bandits)
股本(ㄍㄨˇ ㄅㄣˇ)
subscribed capital (of a business firm)
股票(ㄍㄨˇ ㄆㄧㄠˋ)
a share or stock certificate; stocks: 股票上漲。Stock is going up.
股票交易(ㄍㄨˇ ㄆㄧㄠˋ ㄐㄧㄠ ㄧˋ)
stock deals
股票交易所(ㄍㄨˇ ㄆㄧㄠˋ ㄐㄧㄠ ㄧˋ ㄙㄨㄛˇ)
a stock exchange
股票掮客(ㄍㄨˇ ㄆㄧㄠˋ ㄑㄧㄢˊ ㄎㄜˋ)
a stockbroker
股票市場(ㄍㄨˇ ㄆㄧㄠˋ ㄕˋ ㄔㄤˇ)
the stock market: 股票市場蕭條。The stock market is dull.
股份 or 股分(ㄍㄨˇ ㄈㄣˋ)
shares or stock (in a business concern): 他擁有這公司的一千股份。He owns one thousand shares of the company.
股份有限公司(ㄍㄨˇ ㄈㄣˋ ㄧㄡˇ ㄒㄧㄢˋ ㄍㄨㄥ ㄙ)
a limited liability company
股東(ㄍㄨˇ ㄉㄨㄥ)
a shareholder or stockholder
股東大會(ㄍㄨˇ ㄉㄨㄥ ㄉㄚˋ ㄏㄨㄟˋ)
a shareholders' meeting; a stockholders' conference
股東權益(ㄍㄨˇ ㄉㄨㄥ ㄑㄩㄢˊ ㄧˋ)
stockholders' equity
股利(ㄍㄨˇ ㄌㄧˋ)
interest on shares 參看「股息」
股栗(ㄍㄨˇ ㄌㄧˋ)
trembling with fear
股關節(ㄍㄨˇ ㄍㄨㄢ ㄐㄧㄝˊ)
the hip joint
股肱(ㄍㄨˇ ㄍㄨㄥ)
top aides; a right-hand man
股肱之臣(ㄍㄨˇ ㄍㄨㄥ ㄓ ㄔㄣˊ)
top ministers
股金(ㄍㄨˇ ㄐㄧㄣ)
capitalization (of a company, or corporation); share capital
股權(ㄍㄨˇ ㄑㄩㄢˊ)
the ownership of a share or stock
股券(ㄍㄨˇ ㄑㄩㄢˋ)
a share or stock certificate
股息(ㄍㄨˇ ㄒㄧˊ)
dividends: 該公司去年付出一成股息。The company paid a 10% dividend last year.
股戰(ㄍㄨˇ ㄓㄢˋ)
trembling with fear
股長(ㄍㄨˇ ㄓㄤˇ)
a section chief; the head of a subdivision
股市(ㄍㄨˇ ㄕˋ)
the stock market
股子(ㄍㄨˇ ˙ㄗ)or 股兒(ㄍㄨˇㄦ)
①a share ②a strand or bundle (of hair, thread, etc.)
股員(ㄍㄨˇ ㄩㄢˊ)
a junior office clerk

【肢】 4632
ㄓ jy zhi
1. the four limbs of a person
2. the legs of an animal
3. the wings or feet of a bird
肢體(ㄓ ㄊㄧˇ)
the body
肢骨(ㄓ ㄍㄨˇ)
the bones of one's limbs
肢解(ㄓ ㄐㄧㄝˇ)
to dismember; dismemberment

【肥】 4633
ㄈㄟˊ feir féi
1. fat; plump; portly; obese; corpulent: 你太肥了。You are too fat.
2. fat (of meat)
3. sufficiency; affluence; plenty
4. fertile
5. to fertilize (land)
6. fertilizers
7. baggy
肥胖(ㄈㄟˊ ㄆㄤˋ)
fat; obese: 你變得太肥胖了。You are getting too fat.
肥胖症(ㄈㄟˊ ㄆㄤˋ ㄓㄥˋ)
obesity
肥美(ㄈㄟˊ ㄇㄟˇ)
plump and pretty
肥大(ㄈㄟˊ ㄉㄚˋ)
fat and big; large and wide
肥地(ㄈㄟˊ ㄉㄧˋ)
①to fertilize the land ②a fat land
肥頭胖耳(ㄈㄟˊ ㄊㄡˊ ㄆㄤˋ ㄦˇ)or 肥頭大耳(ㄈㄟˊ ㄊㄡˊ ㄉㄚˋ ㄦˇ)
(said of a person) fat; portly

〔肉部〕

肥田(ㄈㄟˊ ㄊㄧㄢˊ)
①a piece of fertile land ② to fertilize the land: 人造肥料可以肥田。Artificial manures can fertilize the land.

肥田粉(ㄈㄟˊ ㄊㄧㄢˊ ㄈㄣˇ)
chemical fertilizers

肥嫩(ㄈㄟˊ ㄋㄣˋ)
meaty and tender; fleshy and delicate

肥膩(ㄈㄟˊ ㄋㄧˋ)
fatty; greasy

肥料(ㄈㄟˊ ㄌㄧㄠˋ)
fertilizers; manure: 糞被用做肥料。Dung is used as manure.

肥料廠(ㄈㄟˊ ㄌㄧㄠˋ ㄔㄤˇ)
a fertilizer plant

肥甘(ㄈㄟˊ ㄍㄢ)
tasty; palatable

肥厚(ㄈㄟˊ ㄏㄡˋ)
plump; fleshy: 這果肉肥厚美味。The pulp is fleshy and tasty.

肥己(ㄈㄟˊ ㄐㄧˇ)
to enrich oneself

肥瘠(ㄈㄟˊ ㄐㄧˊ)
the fat and the thin; the rich and the poor; the fertile and the barren (fields)

肥缺(ㄈㄟˊ ㄑㄩㄝ)or 肥差(ㄈㄟˊ ㄔㄞ)
a lucrative post; a job which offers many sources of income on the side; a fat job: 這肥缺待遇優厚。The fat job pays well.

肥鮮(ㄈㄟˊ ㄒㄧㄢ)
rich and fresh foods (usually referring to meat)

肥壯(ㄈㄟˊ ㄓㄨㄤˋ)
husky

肥碩(ㄈㄟˊ ㄕㄛˋ)
big and corpulent (persons)

肥瘦(ㄈㄟˊ ㄕㄡˋ)or 肥瘦兒(ㄈㄟˊ ㄕㄡˋㄦ)
①the fat and thin; the rich and poor, etc. ②the sizes of clothing

肥饒(ㄈㄟˊ ㄖㄠˊ)
fertile (land)

肥肉(ㄈㄟˊ ㄖㄡˋ)
fat meat: 你吃太多肥肉。You eat too much fat meat.

肥皂(ㄈㄟˊ ㄗㄠˋ)
soap: 他買了一塊肥皂。He bought a cake of soap.

肥皂泡(ㄈㄟˊ ㄗㄠˋ ㄆㄠˋ)
soap bubbles; suds

肥皂沫(ㄈㄟˊ ㄗㄠˋ ㄇㄛˋ)
suds; lather

肥皂粉(ㄈㄟˊ ㄗㄠˋ ㄈㄣˇ)
detergent powder

肥皂盒(ㄈㄟˊ ㄗㄠˋ ㄏㄜˊ)
a soap container; a soap box

肥皂水(ㄈㄟˊ ㄗㄠˋ ㄕㄨㄟˇ)
suds; soapsuds

肥沃(ㄈㄟˊ ㄨㄛˋ)
fertile (land): 這塊地很肥沃。The land is fertile.

【肩】 4634 ㄐㄧㄢ jian jiān

1. shoulders
2. to shoulder (responsibility, etc.); to sustain
3. to employ; to appoint

肩膀(ㄐㄧㄢ ㄅㄤˇ)
①the shoulder: 他讓小孩子騎在他肩膀上。He gave the child a ride on his shoulders. ②a sense of responsibility

肩摩轂擊(ㄐㄧㄢ ㄇㄛˊ ㄍㄨˇ ㄐㄧˊ)
(literally) shoulders rubbing and carriages knocking at each other—busy traffic

肩負(ㄐㄧㄢ ㄈㄨˋ)
to take on; to undertake; to shoulder; to bear: 我們肩負著光榮的任務。We are undertaking a glorious task.

肩負重任(ㄐㄧㄢ ㄈㄨˋ ㄓㄨㄥˋ ㄖㄣˋ)
to shoulder heavy responsibilities

肩挑背負(ㄐㄧㄢ ㄊㄧㄠ ㄅㄟˋ ㄈㄨˋ)
to carry on the shoulder and back—the work of coolies or peddlers

肩胛(ㄐㄧㄢ ㄐㄧㄚˇ)
the shoulder

肩胛骨(ㄐㄧㄢ ㄐㄧㄚˇ ㄍㄨˇ)
the shoulder blade; the scapula

肩臼(ㄐㄧㄢ ㄐㄧㄡˋ)
a glenoid cavity

肩起(ㄐㄧㄢ ㄑㄧˇ)
to shoulder or take up (the responsibility, etc.): 他應肩起責任。He should shoulder his responsibility.

肩章(ㄐㄧㄢ ㄓㄤ)
an epaulet; a shoulder badge: 學童常帶肩章。School boys usually have shoulder badges.

肩輿(ㄐㄧㄢ ㄩˊ)
a sedan chair 亦作「轎」

【肪】 4635 ㄈㄤˊ farng fáng (又讀 ㄈㄤ fang fāng)

fat

【肫】 4636 ㄓㄨㄣ juen zhūn

1. sincere; earnest
2. the gizzard of a fowl

【肯】 4637 (肎、肻) ㄎㄣˇ keen kěn (又讀 ㄎㄥˇ keeng kěng)

to be willing; to approve of; to consent to; to permit; to agree

肯不肯(ㄎㄣˇ ·ㄅㄨ ㄎㄣˇ)or 肯否(ㄎㄣˇ ㄈㄡˇ)
Are you willing (to do something) or not? 或Do you approve of it or not?

肯定(ㄎㄣˇ ㄉㄧㄥˋ)
affirmative; positive; sure; definite: 我不能肯定他是否生病了。I'm not sure whether he is ill.

肯堂肯構(ㄎㄣˇ ㄊㄤˊ ㄎㄣˇ ㄍㄡˋ)
The deceased father started and the son would complete the endeavor.

肯幹(ㄎㄣˇ ㄍㄢˋ)
willing to put in hard work; indefatigable

肯綮(ㄎㄣˇ ㄑㄧㄥˋ)
the main point; the gist

肯亞(ㄎㄣˇ ㄧㄚˇ)
Kenya

【肱】 4638 ㄍㄨㄥ gong gōng

the forearm

肱骨(ㄍㄨㄥ ㄍㄨˇ)
a humerus

【育】 4639 ㄩˋ yuh yù

1. to produce; to give birth to; to breed
2. to raise; to bring up; to nourish; to nurse
3. to educate

育苗(ㄩˋ ㄇㄧㄠˊ)
to cultivate seedlings; seeding: 他正在育苗。He is cultivating seedlings.

育民(ㄩˋ ㄇㄧㄣˊ)
to educate the people

育德(ㄩˋ ㄉㄜˊ)

to cultivate one's virtue
育種(ㄩˋ ㄓㄨㄥˇ)
breeding
育才(ㄩˋ ㄘㄞˊ)
to cultivate talents; to educate men of ability
育蠶(ㄩˋ ㄘㄢˊ)
to raise silkworms
育兒法(ㄩˋ ㄦˊ ㄈㄚˇ)
proper care and feeding of children or babies
育幼院(ㄩˋ ㄧㄡˋ ㄩㄢˋ)
a nursery school
育嬰堂(ㄩˋ ㄧㄥ ㄊㄤˊ)
a nursery for foundlings; a foundling hospital; an orphanage; child care

【肴】 4640 ㄧㄠˊ yau yáo
cooked food, especially meat and fish; dishes
肴饌(ㄧㄠˊ ㄓㄨㄢˋ)
rich food; sumptuous dishes

【肸】 4641 ㄒㄧˋ shih xì
1. to spread out; dispersed
2. diligent

五畫

【肺】 4642 ㄈㄟˋ fey fèi
the lungs
肺胞(ㄈㄟˋ ㄅㄠ)
a pulmonary vesicle
肺部(ㄈㄟˋ ㄅㄨˋ)
lungs
肺病(ㄈㄟˋ ㄅㄧㄥˋ)
tuberculosis; a lung ailment
肺膜(ㄈㄟˋ ㄇㄛˊ)
a pleura
肺膜炎(ㄈㄟˋ ㄇㄛˊ ㄧㄢˊ)
pulmonary pleurisy
肺腑(ㄈㄟˋ ㄈㄨˇ)
①close or intimate ②from the bottom of one's heart
肺腑之言(ㄈㄟˋ ㄈㄨˇ ㄓ ㄧㄢˊ)
words from the bottom of one's heart
肺動脈(ㄈㄟˋ ㄉㄨㄥˋ ㄇㄞˋ)
a pulmonary artery
肺癆(ㄈㄟˋ ㄌㄠˊ)
tuberculosis; consumption: 她死於肺癆。She died of (or from) consumption.
肺肝(ㄈㄟˋ ㄍㄢ)
(literally) the lungs and liver—the inner thoughts of a person
肺活量(ㄈㄟˋ ㄏㄨㄛˊ ㄌㄧㄤˋ)
vital capacity; lung capacity
肺活量計(ㄈㄟˋ ㄏㄨㄛˊ ㄌㄧㄤˋ ㄐㄧˋ)
a spirometer
肺結核(ㄈㄟˋ ㄐㄧㄝˊ ㄏㄜˊ)
tuberculosis; pulmonary phthisis; consumption: 他罹患肺結核。He suffered from tuberculosis of the lungs.
肺結核防治中心(ㄈㄟˋ ㄐㄧㄝˊ ㄏㄜˊ ㄈㄤˊ ㄓˋ ㄓㄨㄥ ㄒㄧㄣ)
TB Prevention and Treatment Center
肺靜脈(ㄈㄟˋ ㄐㄧㄥˋ ㄇㄞˋ)
a pulmonary vein
肺循環(ㄈㄟˋ ㄒㄩㄣˊ ㄏㄨㄢˊ)
pulmonary circulation
肺出血(ㄈㄟˋ ㄔㄨ ㄒㄧㄝˋ)
pneumonorrhagia
肺臟(ㄈㄟˋ ㄗㄤˋ)
the lungs
肺葉(ㄈㄟˋ ㄧㄝˋ)
the lobes of the lungs
肺炎(ㄈㄟˋ ㄧㄢˊ)
pneumonia: 醫生診斷出此病爲肺炎。The doctor diagnosed the illness as pneumonia.
肺癌(ㄈㄟˋ ㄧㄢˊ)
carcinomas of the lungs; lung cancer

【胥】 4643 ㄒㄩ shiu xū
1. all; together
2. to wait for
3. to assist; to serve as an advisory role
4. to survey; to inspect
5. to keep away from; separated
6. a final particle
7. mutual
8. a variety of official ranks through ancient dynasties
9. a Chinese family name

【胃】 4644 ㄨㄟˋ wey wèi
the stomach; the gizzard (of birds and fowls)
胃病(ㄨㄟˋ ㄅㄧㄥˋ)
a stomach ailment or complaint
胃疼(ㄨㄟˋ ㄊㄥˊ)or 胃痛(ㄨㄟˋ ㄊㄨㄥˋ)
a stomach pain or ache: 他胃痛。He has a stomach ache.
胃口(ㄨㄟˋ ㄎㄡˇ)
appetite: 他的胃口好。He has a good appetite.
胃潰瘍(ㄨㄟˋ ㄎㄨㄟˋ ㄧㄤˊ)or 胃癰(ㄨㄟˋ ㄩㄥ)
a gastric ulcer
胃加答兒(ㄨㄟˋ ㄐㄧㄚ ㄉㄚˊ ㄦ)or 胃炎(ㄨㄟˋ ㄧㄢˊ)
inflammation of the stomach; catarrh of the stomach
胃鏡(ㄨㄟˋ ㄐㄧㄥˋ)
a gastroscope
胃下垂(ㄨㄟˋ ㄒㄧㄚˋ ㄔㄨㄟˊ)
gastroptosis
胃腺(ㄨㄟˋ ㄒㄧㄢˋ)
gastric glands
胃腸(ㄨㄟˋ ㄔㄤˊ)
the stomach and intestines
胃出血(ㄨㄟˋ ㄔㄨ ㄒㄧㄝˋ)
gastrorrhagia
胃臟(ㄨㄟˋ ㄗㄤˋ)
the stomach
胃酸過多(ㄨㄟˋ ㄙㄨㄢ ㄍㄨㄛˋ ㄉㄨㄛ)
hyperacidity of the gastric juice; superacidity
胃液(ㄨㄟˋ ㄧㄝˋ)
gastric juice
胃液素(ㄨㄟˋ ㄧㄝˋ ㄙㄨˋ)
pepsin
胃炎(ㄨㄟˋ ㄧㄢˊ)
gastritis
胃癌(ㄨㄟˋ ㄧㄢˊ)
a gastric carcinoma: 那老人死於胃癌。The old man died of gastric carcinoma.

【冑】 4645 ㄓㄡˋ jow zhòu
1. descendants; posterity; offspring
2. the eldest (son, etc.) 參看冂部「冑」

【背】 4646 1. ㄅㄟˋ bey bèi
1. the back: 他背脊劇痛。He has a terrible pain in the back.
2. the reverse side; the back side
3. to cast away; to turn one's back on; to give up
4. to go against; to rebel: 這與我的原則相背。It goes against my principles.
5. to remember by rote; to commit to memory in detail
6. (now rarely) to faint; to lapse into a coma
背包(ㄅㄟˋ ㄅㄠ)

〔肉部〕

a knapsack

背部(ㄅㄟˋ ㄅㄨˋ)
the back (of a man or an animal, etc.): 他背部受傷。He was hurt on the back.

背叛(ㄅㄟˋ ㄆㄢˋ)
to rebel; to betray; to defect; to apostatize: 他們背叛自己的國家。They betrayed their country.

背盟(ㄅㄟˋ ㄇㄥˊ)
to break a promise, agreement, or treaty; a breach of contract or agreement

背謬(ㄅㄟˋ ㄇㄧㄡˋ)
to go against all good reasons; errors

背面(ㄅㄟˋ ㄇㄧㄢˋ)or 背面兒(ㄅㄟˋ ㄇㄧㄚˋㄦ)
the reverse side; the back side

背風(ㄅㄟˋ ㄈㄥ)
on the lee side; leeward

背負(ㄅㄟˋ ㄈㄨˋ)
to carry on the back

背道而馳(ㄅㄟˋ ㄉㄠˋ ㄦˊ ㄔˊ)
to proceed in opposite directions; to be diametrically opposed to; to run counter to: 他的計劃跟我的計劃背道而馳。His plans run counter to mine.

背地裏(ㄅㄟˋ ㄉㄧˋ ˙ㄌㄧ)
behind one's back; secretly

背地性(ㄅㄟˋ ㄉㄧˋ ㄒㄧㄥˋ)
(botany) negative geotropism

背對背(ㄅㄟˋ ㄉㄨㄟˋ ㄅㄟˋ)
back to back

背累(ㄅㄟˋ ˙ㄌㄟ)
(said of a family, etc.) a burden: 她是家族的背累。She is a burden on (or to) her family.

背離(ㄅㄟˋ ㄌㄧˊ)
to deviate from; to depart from: 他們背離了正道。They deviated from the right path.

背理(ㄅㄟˋ ㄌㄧˇ)
to go against good reason or conscience

背光(ㄅㄟˋ ㄍㄨㄤ)
to be in a poor light; to do something with one's back to the light

背後(ㄅㄟˋ ㄏㄡˋ)
behind one's back; on the back side (of one's body); the rear in secret: 他們在背後批評他。They criticized him behind his back.

背脊骨(ㄅㄟˋ ㄐㄧˇ ㄍㄨˇ)
the backbone; the spine; the spinal column

背教(ㄅㄟˋ ㄐㄧㄠˋ)
to go against what one is taught; to renege; to apostatize

背景(ㄅㄟˋ ㄐㄧㄥˇ)
background: 我們要知道他的家庭背景。We want to know his family background.

背井離鄉(ㄅㄟˋ ㄐㄧㄥˇ ㄌㄧˊ ㄒㄧㄤ)
to leave one's hometown; to stay on a strange land

背棄(ㄅㄟˋ ㄑㄧˋ)
to turn one's back on; to renounce; to betray

背心(ㄅㄟˋ ㄒㄧㄣ)or 背心兒(ㄅㄟˋ ㄒㄧㄜㄦ)
a vest; a waistcoat; a sleeveless jacket

背信(ㄅㄟˋ ㄒㄧㄣˋ)
to break one's word or promise; to be faithless; a breach of faith

背著(ㄅㄟˋ ˙ㄓㄜ)
in secret; to avoid others

背著手(兒)(ㄅㄟˋ ˙ㄓㄜ ㄕㄡˇ(ㄦ))or 背手(ㄅㄟˋ ㄕㄡˇ)
with one's hands clasped behind one's back

背著人(ㄅㄟˋ ˙ㄓㄜ ㄖㄣˊ)
behind other's back; in secret: 他背著人告訴我此事。He told me about the matter in secret.

背馳(ㄅㄟˋ ㄔˊ)
to proceed in opposite directions

背城借一(ㄅㄟˋ ㄔㄥˊ ㄐㄧㄝˋ ㄧ)
to engage in a last-ditch battle; to fight with one's back to the wall

背時(ㄅㄟˋ ㄕˊ)
to be out of luck; unlucky

背山面水(ㄅㄟˋ ㄕㄢ ㄇㄧㄢˋ ㄕㄨㄟˇ)
(literally) with hills at the back and water in front —beautiful scenes or views (usually referring to a building)

背上(ㄅㄟˋ ˙ㄕㄤ)
on the back

背書(ㄅㄟˋ ㄕㄨ)
① to recite a lesson; to commit a lesson to memory: 輪到你背書了。It's your turn to recite. ②to endorse a check ③ endorsement

背水一戰(ㄅㄟˋ ㄕㄨㄟˇ ㄧˊ ㄓㄢˋ)
(literally) to fight with one's back to the river—to fight to the last ditch

背日性(ㄅㄟˋ ㄖˋ ㄒㄧㄥˋ)
(botany) negative heliotropism

背誦(ㄅㄟˋ ㄙㄨㄥˋ)
to recite

背陰(ㄅㄟˋ ㄧㄣ)
in the shade; obscurity

背影(ㄅㄟˋ ㄧㄥˇ)
the sight of one's back

背約(ㄅㄟˋ ㄩㄝ)
a breach of promise or agreement; to break one's promise

背運(ㄅㄟˋ ㄩㄣˋ)
to be out of luck; to be in one's unlucky day, month, year, etc.

【背】 4646
2. ㄅㄟ bei bēi

to bear or shoulder (a load, burden, etc.); to carry on the back

背包袱(ㄅㄟ ㄅㄠ ˙ㄈㄨ)
to have a weight on one's mind; to take on a mental burden

背榜(ㄅㄟ ㄅㄤˇ)
the last on the list of successful candidates of the civil service examination in former times

背不動(ㄅㄟ ˙ㄅㄨ ㄉㄨㄥˋ)
unable to bear it on the back—too heavy

背帶(ㄅㄟ ㄉㄞˋ)
suspenders

背黑鍋(ㄅㄟ ㄏㄟ ㄍㄨㄛ)
to take the blame for another person

背著(ㄅㄟ ˙ㄓㄜ)
to carry on the back

背債(ㄅㄟ ㄓㄞˋ)
to be in debt; to be burdened with debts

背上(ㄅㄟ ˙ㄕㄤ)
to put on the back for carry-

ing
背子(ㄅㄟ •ㄗ)
a device for carrying something on the back

【胎】 4647 ㄊㄞ tai tāi
1. a fetus; an embryo
2. an unpolished, semiprocessed molding of something
胎盤(ㄊㄞ ㄆㄢˊ)or 胎衣(ㄊㄞ ㄧ)or 胎胞(ㄊㄞ ㄅㄠ)
the placenta
胎髮(ㄊㄞ ㄈㄚˇ)
the hair of a newborn baby
胎毒(ㄊㄞ ㄉㄨˊ)
(Chinese medicine) fetal toxins (toxic materials causing infantile infectious diseases)
胎動(ㄊㄞ ㄉㄨㄥˋ)
the quickening of the womb; fetal movement
胎記(ㄊㄞ ㄐㄧˋ)
a birthmark
胎教(ㄊㄞ ㄐㄧㄠˋ)
prenatal education or influences (An expectant mother's conduct is believed to influence the unborn baby.)
胎氣(ㄊㄞ ㄑㄧˋ)
① fetus-energy ② nausea, vomiting and edema of legs during pregnancy
胎生(ㄊㄞ ㄕㄥ)
viviparous
胎生學(ㄊㄞ ㄕㄥ ㄒㄩㄝˊ)
embryology
胎生魚(ㄊㄞ ㄕㄥ ㄩˊ)
viviparous fish, as whales or certain sharks
胎座(ㄊㄞ ㄗㄨㄛˋ)
(botany) placentas (of flowers)
胎死腹中(ㄊㄞ ㄙˇ ㄈㄨˋ ㄓㄨㄥ)
(literally) death in the womb—(said of a plan, or operation) to fail or be discarded before it gets started; abortive
胎兒(ㄊㄞ ㄦˊ)
a fetus; an unborn baby; an embryo
胎位(ㄊㄞ ㄨㄟˋ)
the position of a fetus

【胖】 4648 1. ㄆㄤˋ panq pàng
obese; fat; corpulent
胖病(ㄆㄤˋ ㄅㄧㄥˋ)
obesity
胖腫(ㄆㄤˋ ㄓㄨㄥˇ)
general swelling over the body
胖子(ㄆㄤˋ •ㄗ)
a fat or corpulent person; a fatty

【胖】 4648 2. ㄆㄢˊ parn pán
comfortable

【胙】 4649 ㄗㄨㄛˋ tzuoh zuò
1. flesh, meat offered in sacrifices
2. blessings from Heaven
3. (now rarely) to report

【胛】 4650 ㄐㄧㄚˇ jea jiǎ
the shoulder; the shoulder blade

【胚】 4651 ㄆㄟ pei pēi
1. a three-month-old fetus; three months of pregnancy
2. things in the embryonic stage; unfinished moldings
3. the tender sprouts of plants
胚盤(ㄆㄟ ㄆㄢˊ)
a germinal disk, or blastoderm
胚胎(ㄆㄟ ㄊㄞ)
①the origination or beginning of things ② an embryo
胚胎學(ㄆㄟ ㄊㄞ ㄒㄩㄝˊ)
embryology
胚囊(ㄆㄟ ㄋㄤˊ)
an embryo sac; a gastrula
胚軸(ㄆㄟ ㄓㄡˊ)
(botany) a hypocotyl
胚珠(ㄆㄟ ㄓㄨ)
an ovule
胚乳(ㄆㄟ ㄖㄨˇ)
albumen (in seeds)
胚子(ㄆㄟ •ㄗ)
① seeds ② things in their embryonic stage; an unpolished and unfinished molding
胚芽(ㄆㄟ ㄧㄚˊ)
to germinate; to cause to sprout; a sprout
胚芽米(ㄆㄟ ㄧㄚˊ ㄇㄧˇ)
germinated rice

【胞】 4652 ㄅㄠ bau bāo
1. the placenta
2. children of the same parents
胞妹(ㄅㄠ ㄇㄟˋ)
my younger sister; one's own younger sister
胞弟(ㄅㄠ ㄉㄧˋ)
my kid brother; one's own younger brother
胞姊(ㄅㄠ ㄐㄧㄝˇ)
my elder sister; one's own elder sister
胞兄弟(ㄅㄠ ㄒㄩㄥ ㄉㄧˋ)
brothers by the same parents
胞子(ㄅㄠ ㄗˇ)
(botany) spores
胞子囊(ㄅㄠ ㄗˇ ㄋㄤˊ)
a sporangium
胞衣(ㄅㄠ ㄧ)
the placenta
胞與爲懷(ㄅㄠ ㄩˇ ㄨㄟˊ ㄏㄨㄞˊ)
fraternity; to treat all creatures like one's brothers

【胠】 4653 ㄑㄩ chiu qū
1. to open
2. the armpit
3. (in ancient warfare) the right flank of an army
胠篋(ㄑㄩ ㄑㄧㄝˋ)
① to open a chest and steal ② name of a chapter in *Chuangtze*(莊子)

【胡】 4654 ㄏㄨˊ hwu hú
1. to blunder; reckless; wildly; disorderly
2. stupidly; blindly; confusedly
3. (in ancient China) a general name of the northern tribes (北狄)
4. (an interrogative particle) How? 或 Why? 或 When?
5. (now rarely) long and lasting
6. a Chinese family name
胡餅(ㄏㄨˊ ㄅㄧㄥˇ)
a baked cake of wheat flour usually topped with sesame 亦作「燒餅」
胡麻(ㄏㄨˊ ㄇㄚˊ)
linseed; sesame
胡母(ㄏㄨˊ ㄇㄨˇ)
①(now very rarely) a Chinese family name ② the mother of anyone whose family name is 胡
胡佛(ㄏㄨˊ ㄈㄛˊ)
Hoover, Herbert Clark,

1874-1964, the 3lst American president (1929-33)
胡服(ㄏㄨˊ ㄈㄨˊ)
the clothing of the northern barbarians
胡豆(ㄏㄨˊ ㄉㄡˋ)
lima beans
胡蝶(ㄏㄨˊ ㄉㄧㄝˊ)
a butterfly 亦作「蝴蝶」
胡蝶蘭(ㄏㄨˊ ㄉㄧㄝˊ ㄌㄢˊ)
phalaenopsis 亦作「蝴蝶蘭」
胡桃(ㄏㄨˊ ㄊㄠˊ)
walnuts
胡塗(ㄏㄨˊ ㄊㄨˊ)
confused; muddleheaded; stupid
胡同兒(ㄏㄨˊ ㄊㄨㄥˋㄦ)
a lane 亦作「衚衕兒」
胡鬧(ㄏㄨˊ ㄋㄠˋ)
to make a row or cause a disturbance without obvious reasons; reckless, irresponsible words or actions
胡來(ㄏㄨˊ ㄌㄞˊ)
to proceed (with a matter, etc.) recklessly and without thought
胡虜(ㄏㄨˊ ㄌㄨˇ)
the northern barbarians (北狄), who used to invade China from time to time through the dynasties
胡蘿蔔(ㄏㄨˊ ㄌㄨㄛˊ ·ㄅㄛ)
the carrot
胡亂(ㄏㄨˊ ㄌㄨㄢˋ)
① at will; at random; recklessly ② without being particular; not choosy
胡攪
①(ㄏㄨˊ ㄍㄠˇ) ⓐ to behave at will or at random—without either objective or cause ⓑ to mess things up; to meddle with something 亦作「胡搞」 ②(ㄏㄨˊ ㄐㄧㄠˇ) to cause confusion or a disturbance recklessly
胡瓜(ㄏㄨˊ ㄍㄨㄚ)
a cucumber
胡漢民(ㄏㄨˊ ㄏㄢˋ ㄇㄧㄣˊ)
Hu Han-min, 1879-1936, a follower of Dr. Sun Yat-sen
胡花亂用(ㄏㄨˊ ㄏㄨㄚ ㄌㄨㄢˋ ㄩㄥˋ)
to spend money extravagantly and recklessly
胡混(ㄏㄨˊ ㄏㄨㄣˋ)
to loaf around; to fool around
胡騎(ㄏㄨˊ ㄐㄧˋ)
mounted northern barbarian troops
胡笳(ㄏㄨˊ ㄐㄧㄚ)
a reed pipe, a musical instrument of the Tartars in ancient times
胡椒(ㄏㄨˊ ㄐㄧㄠ)
pepper
胡琴(ㄏㄨˊ ㄑㄧㄣˊ)
the two-stringed violin (a major Chinese musical instrument today, used especially in Peking opera)
胡扯(ㄏㄨˊ ㄔㄜˇ)
① random talk; aimless conversation ② wild talk; lies
胡纏(ㄏㄨˊ ㄔㄢˊ)
endless (and usually aimless) bothering of another person; to harass
胡牀(ㄏㄨˊ ㄔㄨㄤˊ)
a lightweight rope chair which can be readily folded
胡適(ㄏㄨˊ ㄕˋ)
Hu Shih (1891-1962), educator and philosopher, pioneering a new literary movement which made the vernacular the dominating medium in modern Chinese literature
胡哨(ㄏㄨˊ ㄕㄠˋ)
a whistle made by the mouth
胡說(ㄏㄨˊ ㄕㄨㄛ)
Nonsense! 或 wild talk; to talk nonsense
胡說八道(ㄏㄨˊ ㄕㄨㄛ ㄅㄚ ㄉㄠˋ)
to talk nonsense; wild talk; lies
胡人(ㄏㄨˊ ㄖㄣˊ)
the northern barbarian tribes in ancient China
胡謅(ㄏㄨˊ ㄗㄡ)
wild talk; nonsensical talk; to invent (something false); to lie: 你胡謅! You're lying!
胡作非爲(ㄏㄨˊ ㄗㄨㄛˋ ㄈㄟ ㄨㄟˊ)
to bully others as if the law were non-existent; to do as one pleases
胡思亂想(ㄏㄨˊ ㄙ ㄌㄨㄢˋ ㄒㄧㄤˇ)
to daydream; to give one's thoughts free rein
胡兒(ㄏㄨˊ ㄦˊ)
northern barbarians in ancient China
胡言亂語(ㄏㄨˊ ㄧㄢˊ ㄌㄨㄢˋ ㄩˇ)
to talk nonsense; to gibber; to talk incoherently or unintelligibly; lies or wild talk
胡爲(ㄏㄨˊ ㄨㄟˊ)
① why; how ② to act like a bully; to act recklessly

【胤】 4655
ㄧㄣˋ yinn yìn
long successions of descendants; posterity
胤嗣(ㄧㄣˋ ㄙˋ)
descendants

【朐】 4656
ㄑㄩˊ chyu qú
1. dried meat strips
2. far; faraway

【胗】 4657
1.ㄓㄣ jen zhēn
the gizzard of a fowl 亦作「肫」
胗兒(ㄓㄜㄦ)
the gizzard of a fowl

【胗】 4657
2.ㄓㄣˇ jeen zhěn
pustules; a rash; measles 亦作「疹」

【胝】 4658
ㄓ jy zhī
calluses on hands or feet

六畫

【胭】 4659
(臙) ㄧㄢ ian yān
1. cosmetics, especially referring to rouge and face powder
2. the throat 亦作「咽」
胭粉(ㄧㄢ ㄈㄣˇ)
rouge and face powder
胭粉小說(ㄧㄢ ㄈㄣˇ ㄒㄧㄠˇ ㄕㄨㄛ)
novels featuring love or romantic plots
胭脂(ㄧㄢ ㄓ)
rouge
胭脂虎(ㄧㄢ ㄓ ㄏㄨˇ)
a shrew; a virago; a Circe

【胯】 4660
ㄎㄨㄚˋ kuah kuà
space between the legs; the groin
胯部(ㄎㄨㄚˋ ㄅㄨˋ)
the crotch
胯下辱(ㄎㄨㄚˋ ㄒㄧㄚˋ ㄖㄨˋ)
submitting the disgrace of crawling under another's

legs—said of Han Hsin (韓信), a famous general, who helped found the Han Dynasty

【胰】 4661 ㄧˊ yi yí

the pancreas

胰島素(ㄧˊ ㄉㄠˇ ㄙㄨˋ)
(medicine) insulin; pancreatin

胰子(ㄧˊ ·ㄗ)
soap

胰臟(ㄧˊ ㄗㄤˋ)
the pancreas

胰液素(ㄧˊ ㄧㄝˋ ㄙㄨˋ)
pancreatin; insulin

【胱】 4662 ㄍㄨㄤ guang guāng

the bladder

【胴】 4663 ㄉㄨㄥˋ donq dòng

1. the large intestine
2. the trunk; the body

胴體(ㄉㄨㄥˋ ㄊㄧˇ)
the trunk; the body

【胸】 4664 (胷) ㄒㄩㄥ shiong xiōng

1. the chest; the breast; the bosom; the bust; the thorax
2. one's ambition or aspiration
3. the mind (as narrow-minded, etc.); one's capacity

胸部(ㄒㄩㄥ ㄅㄨˋ)
the chest

胸脯兒(ㄒㄩㄥ ㄆㄨˊㄦ)
the breast, or bosom

胸腹(ㄒㄩㄥ ㄈㄨˋ)
the chest and belly—vital points

胸膛(ㄒㄩㄥ ㄊㄤˊ)
the breast or bosom; the thorax

胸肋膜(ㄒㄩㄥ ㄌㄜˋ ㄇㄛˊ)
pleura costalis

胸膈(ㄒㄩㄥ ㄍㄜˊ)
① the diaphragm ② feelings

胸骨(ㄒㄩㄥ ㄍㄨˇ)
the breastbone; the sternum

胸管(ㄒㄩㄥ ㄍㄨㄢˇ)
ductus thoracicus

胸口(ㄒㄩㄥ ㄎㄡˇ)
the middle of the chest; the pit in the upper part of the stomach

胸廓(ㄒㄩㄥ ㄎㄨㄛˋ)or 胸腔(ㄒㄩㄥ ㄑㄧㄤ)
the thorax

胸廓橫肌(ㄒㄩㄥ ㄎㄨㄛˋ ㄏㄥˊ ㄐㄧ)
a transversal muscle of the thorax

胸花(ㄒㄩㄥ ㄏㄨㄚ)
a corsage

胸懷(ㄒㄩㄥ ㄏㄨㄞˊ)or 胸襟(ㄒㄩㄥ ㄐㄧㄣ)or 胸次(ㄒㄩㄥ ㄘˋ)
ambition or aspiration; mind

胸懷磊落(ㄒㄩㄥ ㄏㄨㄞˊ ㄌㄟˇ ㄌㄨㄛˋ)
frank; honest; harboring no evil thought

胸肌(ㄒㄩㄥ ㄐㄧ)
muscles in the general area of one's chest, as those between ribs

胸脊(ㄒㄩㄥ ㄐㄧˇ)
the thoracic vertebrae

胸襟開闊(ㄒㄩㄥ ㄐㄧㄣ ㄎㄞ ㄎㄨㄛˋ)
broad-minded; large-minded

胸前(ㄒㄩㄥ ㄑㄧㄢˊ)
on one's chest or breast; right in front

胸腔(ㄒㄩㄥ ㄑㄧㄤ)
the thoracic cavity

胸針(ㄒㄩㄥ ㄓㄣ)
a brooch

胸章(ㄒㄩㄥ ㄓㄤ)
a badge or a medal worn on the breast

胸中鱗甲(ㄒㄩㄥ ㄓㄨㄥ ㄌㄧㄣˊ ㄐㄧㄚˇ)
treachery and murder in one's mind; treacherous; vicious; mean

胸中甲兵(ㄒㄩㄥ ㄓㄨㄥ ㄐㄧㄚˇ ㄅㄧㄥ)
well-versed in military strategy and tactics

胸衣(ㄒㄩㄥ ㄧ)
corsets

胸臆(ㄒㄩㄥ ㄧˋ)
① the chest ② thoughts; feelings

胸有城府(ㄒㄩㄥ ㄧㄡˇ ㄔㄥˊ ㄈㄨˇ)
scheming; calculating

胸有成竹(ㄒㄩㄥ ㄧㄡˇ ㄔㄥˊ ㄓㄨˊ)
to have had ready or well-thought-out plans or designs in one's mind (in coping with a matter, situation, etc.)

胸無點墨(ㄒㄩㄥ ㄨˊ ㄉㄧㄢˇ ㄇㄛˋ)
unlearned; ignorant; illiterate

胸無城府(ㄒㄩㄥ ㄨˊ ㄔㄥˊ ㄈㄨˇ)
honest; frank; having nothing hidden in the mind

胸無宿物(ㄒㄩㄥ ㄨˊ ㄙㄨˋ ㄨˋ)
frank; straightforward; outspoken

胸圍(ㄒㄩㄥ ㄨㄟˊ)
the measurement around the bust; the first of the vital statistics of a woman

胸宇(ㄒㄩㄥ ㄩˇ)
one's ambition or aspiration

【朓】 4665 ㄊㄧㄠˇ tiaw tiǎo

sacrificial rites

【能】 4666 ㄋㄥˊ neng néng

1. can; to be able to 你明天能來嗎? Will you be able to come tomorrow?
2. capability; talent; competence
3. energy, as atomic energy

能不(ㄋㄥˊ ㄅㄨˋ)
can't help but; how can one not: 對她你能不切切思念嗎? Can you not help thinking of her?

能不能(ㄋㄥˊ ·ㄅㄨ ㄋㄥˊ)
can or can't; may or may not

能名(ㄋㄥˊ ㄇㄧㄥˊ)
famed for great capability

能否(ㄋㄥˊ ㄈㄡˇ)
can or cannot; may or may not

能耐(ㄋㄥˊ ㄋㄞˋ)
skill; capability; ability; resourcefulness

能力(ㄋㄥˊ ㄌㄧˋ)
① power, as the power of the Almighty, etc. ② a faculty; ability; capability

能吏(ㄋㄥˊ ㄌㄧˋ)
a capable official

能量(ㄋㄥˊ ㄌㄧㄤˋ)
①(physics) energy ② capabilities

能量不滅定律(ㄋㄥˊ ㄌㄧㄤˋ ㄅㄨˋ ㄇㄧㄝˋ ㄉㄧㄥˋ ㄌㄩˋ)
the law of conservation of energy

能率(ㄋㄥˊ ㄌㄩˋ)
the rate of work efficiency

能歌善舞(ㄋㄥˊ ㄍㄜ ㄕㄢˋ ㄨˇ)
(usually said of a woman) skilled in both singing and dancing

能夠 or 能彀(ㄋㄥˊ ㄍㄡˋ)
able to; capable of; can;

〔肉部〕

may: 他或許能夠通過考試。He may be able to pass the exam.
能幹(ㄋㄥˊ ㄍㄢˋ)
capable; able; very competent and efficient: 他是一位能幹的律師。He is an able lawyer.
能見度(ㄋㄥˊ ㄐㄧㄢˋ ㄉㄨˋ)
visibility: 在霧中能見度很低。In a fog the visibility is very poor.
能屈能伸(ㄋㄥˊ ㄑㄩ ㄋㄥˊ ㄕㄣ)
adaptable; flexible: 他是個能屈能伸的人。He is an adaptable man.
能之變化(ㄋㄥˊ ㄓ ㄅㄧㄢˋ ㄏㄨㄚˋ)
transformation of energy
能者多勞(ㄋㄥˊ ㄓㄜˇ ㄉㄨㄛ ㄌㄠˊ)
The capable are usually the busy ones. (a compliment to a busy person)
能臣(ㄋㄥˊ ㄔㄣˊ)
a capable minister or high official
能士(ㄋㄥˊ ㄕˋ)
capable or talented persons
能事(ㄋㄥˊ ㄕˋ)
① that which is within one's ability to do ② one's specialty, or special skill
能手(ㄋㄥˊ ㄕㄡˇ)
a capable or competent person; an expert; a good hand: 她是桌球能手。She is a good hand at table tennis.
能說會道(ㄋㄥˊ ㄕㄨㄛ ㄏㄨㄟˋ ㄉㄠˋ)
very eloquent
能人(ㄋㄥˊ ㄖㄣˊ)
a capable or talented person
能忍自安(ㄋㄥˊ ㄖㄣˇ ㄗˋ ㄢ)
Patience brings peace of mind.
能做(ㄋㄥˊ ㄗㄨㄛˋ)
able to do; capable of doing: 他同時能做很多事。He is able to do lots of things at the same time.
能言快語(ㄋㄥˊ ㄧㄢˊ ㄎㄨㄞˋ ㄩˇ)
eloquent and frank (in speaking)
能言善辯(ㄋㄥˊ ㄧㄢˊ ㄕㄢˋ ㄅㄧㄢˋ)
eloquent and glib in argument
能為(ㄋㄥˊ ㄨㄟˊ)
①capable of doing ②capability; ability; talent; resourcefulness
能文能武(ㄋㄥˊ ㄨㄣˊ ㄋㄥˊ ㄨˇ)
gifted in both intellectual and martial arts; efficient in both brainy and brawny activities
能源(ㄋㄥˊ ㄩㄢˊ)
the sources of energy; energy resources; energy
能源計劃(ㄋㄥˊ ㄩㄢˊ ㄐㄧˋ ㄏㄨㄚˋ)
an energy program
能源需求(ㄋㄥˊ ㄩㄢˊ ㄒㄩ ㄑㄧㄡˊ)
energy needs
能源危機(ㄋㄥˊ ㄩㄢˊ ㄨㄟˊ ㄐㄧ)
the energy crisis: 我們必須面對能源危機。We must face the energy crisis.

【胾】 4667 ㄗˋ tzyh zì

meat cuts; minced meat

【脂】 4668 ㄓ jy zhī

1. the fat of animals; grease; lard; tallow
2. the gum or sap of trees; resin
3. to anoint; to grease; to lubricate
4. cosmetics
5. a Chinese family name

脂麻 or 芝麻(ㄓ ·ㄇㄚ)
sesame
脂粉(ㄓ ㄈㄣˇ)
rouge and face powder—cosmetics
脂粉氣(ㄓ ㄈㄣˇ ㄑㄧˋ)
feminine; sissy
脂肪(ㄓ ㄈㄤˊ)
the fat of animals or plants
脂肪腺(ㄓ ㄈㄤˊ ㄒㄧㄢˋ)
sebaceous glands
脂肪組織(ㄓ ㄈㄤˊ ㄗㄨˇ ㄓ)
adipose tissue; fatty tissue
脂肪酸(ㄓ ㄈㄤˊ ㄙㄨㄢ)
fatty acid
脂膏(ㄓ ㄍㄠ)
① fat, grease, etc. ② wealth; affluence ③hard toil; sweat and blood (of the people)
脂光石(ㄓ ㄍㄨㄤ ㄕˊ)
elaeolite
脂澤(ㄓ ㄗㄜˊ)
well-oiled and glossy
脂油(ㄓ ㄧㄡˊ)
lard

【脆】 4669 (胞) ㄘㄨㄟˋ tsuey cuì

1. brittle; fragile; hard but easily broken (as glass, porcelain, etc.): 這紙太脆。The kind of paper is too fragile.
2. crisp: 她的聲音很清脆。Her voice is clear and crisp.
3. light; shallow; thin
4. (said of the operation, etc. of something) easy, quick and convenient; neat: 她回答得很乾脆。She gave a neat answer.

脆薄(ㄘㄨㄟˋ ㄅㄠˊ)
① thin and brittle: 這玻璃是脆薄的。The glass is thin and brittle. ② shallow
脆皮鴨(ㄘㄨㄟˋ ㄆㄧˊ ㄧㄚ)
roasted Peking duck
脆骨(ㄘㄨㄟˋ ㄍㄨˇ)
a cartilage; gristle
脆怯(ㄘㄨㄟˋ ㄑㄧㄝˋ)
timid; cowardly; weak
脆性(ㄘㄨㄟˋ ㄒㄧㄥˋ)
brittleness
脆弱(ㄘㄨㄟˋ ㄖㄨㄛˋ)
weak; fragile; delicate: 他病後覺得很脆弱。He felt very weak after illness.
脆銀鑛(ㄘㄨㄟˋ ㄧㄣˊ ㄎㄨㄤˋ)
stephanite

【脅】 4670 ㄒㄧㄝˊ shye xié

1. the sides of the trunk from armpits to ribs; the flank
2. to threaten with force; to force
3. to shrug (shoulders); to shrink

脅迫(ㄒㄧㄝˊ ㄆㄛˋ)
to threaten with force; to coerce; coercion
脅肩(ㄒㄧㄝˊ ㄐㄧㄢ)
to shrug the shoulders
脅肩纍足(ㄒㄧㄝˊ ㄐㄧㄢ ㄌㄟˇ ㄗㄨˊ)
frightened; apprehensive and nervous; jittery
脅肩諂笑(ㄒㄧㄝˊ ㄐㄧㄢ ㄔㄢˇ ㄒㄧㄠˋ)
to be sycophantic; to act obsequiously
脅息(ㄒㄧㄝˊ ㄒㄧˊ)
trembling and breathing heavily — very afraid or scared; in trepidation or great fright
脅制(ㄒㄧㄝˊ ㄓˋ)
to control with threat of force, etc.; to coerce
脅持(ㄒㄧㄝˊ ㄔˊ)

① to take somebody on both sides by the arms ②to hold somebody by violence

脅從(ㄒㄧㄝˊ ㄗㄨㄥˋ)
to be forced to join (rebellion, banditry, etc.)

脅從罔治(ㄒㄧㄝˊ ㄗㄨㄥˋ ㄨㄤˇ ㄓˋ)
Those who are forced to follow or take part are not to be punished.

【脈】 4671 (衇、脉) ㄇㄛˋ moh mò (又讀 ㄇㄞˋ may mài)
1. the blood vessels; the veins or arteries; the circulation system
2. the pulse
3. a mountain range
4. things that are related and form a system of some kind
5. stipules or stems of a leaf

脈搏(ㄇㄛˋ ㄅㄛˊ)
the pulse; pulsation

脈搏停止(ㄇㄛˋ ㄅㄛˊ ㄊㄧㄥˊ ㄓˇ)
the cessation or stoppage of pulsation

脈脈(ㄇㄛˋ ㄇㄛˋ)
affectionately; lovingly; amorously

脈脈含情(ㄇㄛˋ ㄇㄛˋ ㄏㄢˊ ㄑㄧㄥˊ)
(said of eyes) quietly sending the message of love 亦作「眽眽含情」

脈理(ㄇㄛˋ ㄌㄧˇ)
the relationship between a patient's pulse and his illness

脈絡(ㄇㄛˋ ㄌㄨㄛˋ)
things that are related and form a system of their own (as veins and arteries forming the circulation system)

脈絡膜(ㄇㄛˋ ㄌㄨㄛˋ ㄇㄛˊ)
(anatomy) choroid

脈管(ㄇㄛˋ ㄍㄨㄢˇ)
the artery

脈鑛(ㄇㄛˋ ㄎㄨㄤˋ)
a fissure filling

脈息(ㄇㄛˋ ㄒㄧˊ)
the pulse; pulsation

脈石(ㄇㄛˋ ㄕˊ)
gangue, or vein stuff

脈岩(ㄇㄛˋ ㄧㄢˊ)
a vein rock

【脊】 4672 ㄐㄧˇ jii jǐ (又讀 ㄐㄧˊ jyi jí)
1. the spine; the spinal column
2. the ridge

脊梁(ㄐㄧˇ ㄌㄧㄤˊ)
① the back 亦作「脊背」② (construction) a ridgepole 亦作「棟木」or「棟梁」

脊柱(ㄐㄧˇ ㄓㄨˋ)
the vertebral column

脊椎(ㄐㄧˇ ㄓㄨㄟ)
the vertebrae

脊椎動物(ㄐㄧˇ ㄓㄨㄟ ㄉㄨㄥˋ ㄨˋ)
the vertebrates

脊椎骨(ㄐㄧˇ ㄓㄨㄟ ㄍㄨˇ)
a vertebra; the spine

脊髓(ㄐㄧˇ ㄙㄨㄟˇ)
the spinal cord

脊髓神經(ㄐㄧˇ ㄙㄨㄟˇ ㄕㄣˊ ㄐㄧㄥ)
the spinal nerves

脊髓炎(ㄐㄧˇ ㄙㄨㄟˇ ㄧㄢˊ)
myelitis

【胹】 4673 ㄦˊ erl ér
cooked; well-done

【胳】 4674 ㄍㄜ ge gē
the arms; the armpits 亦作「肐」

胳臂(ㄍㄜ ˙ㄅㄟ)or(ㄍㄜ ㄅㄟˋ)
the upper arm

胳肢窩(ㄍㄜ ㄓ ㄨㄛ)
the armpit

七畫

【脘】 4675 ㄍㄨㄢˇ goan guǎn
the inside of the stomach —the gastric cavity; a duct in the body

【脛】 4676 ㄐㄧㄥˋ jinq jìng
the calf; the part of a leg between the knee and ankle; the shank

脛骨(ㄐㄧㄥˋ ㄍㄨˇ)
the shinbone, or tibia

脛衣(ㄐㄧㄥˋ ㄧ)
trousers with the seat and upper part missing, worn by old folks in former times 亦作「套褲」

【脣】 4677 (唇) ㄔㄨㄣˊ chwen chún
the lips; the labia

脣兒(ㄔㄨㄣˊㄦ)
the lips

脣膏(ㄔㄨㄣˊ ㄍㄠ)
lipstick

脣紅齒白(ㄔㄨㄣˊ ㄏㄨㄥˊ ㄔˇ ㄅㄞˊ)
red lips and white teeth —very handsome or beautiful

脣槍舌劍(ㄔㄨㄣˊ ㄑㄧㄤ ㄕㄜˊ ㄐㄧㄢˋ)
a heated verbal exchange or debate: 雙方脣槍舌劍。There is an exchange of heated words between the two.

脣形花冠(ㄔㄨㄣˊ ㄒㄧㄥˊ ㄏㄨㄚ ㄍㄨㄢ)
a labiate corolla

脣脂(ㄔㄨㄣˊ ㄓ)
lipstick

脣齒(ㄔㄨㄣˊ ㄔˇ)
the lips and teeth—very close neighbors (implying a sense of interdependency)

脣齒相依(ㄔㄨㄣˊ ㄔˇ ㄒㄧㄤ ㄧ)
closely related and mutually dependent like the lips and teeth

脣齒音(ㄔㄨㄣˊ ㄔˇ ㄧㄣ)
(linguistics) labiodental consonants

脣舌(ㄔㄨㄣˊ ㄕㄜˊ)
①eloquence②spoken words; explanation

脣亡齒寒(ㄔㄨㄣˊ ㄨㄤˊ ㄔˇ ㄏㄢˊ)
(literally) When the lips are gone, the teeth will feel the chill.—mutual dependency of neighboring countries (usually small ones) when confronted with a powerful and aggressive enemy

【脩】 4678 ㄒㄧㄡ shiou xiū
1. to do, act, restore, regulate, cultivate, etc. 亦作「修」
2. dried meat
3. salary for a teacher in ancient times
4. a Chinese family name

脩脯(ㄒㄧㄡ ㄈㄨˇ)
dried meat

脩金(ㄒㄧㄡ ㄐㄧㄣ)or 脩敬(ㄒㄧㄡ ㄐㄧㄥˋ)
salary presented to a tutor or teacher

【脫】 4679 ㄊㄨㄛ tuo tuō
1. to strip; to undress; to take off
2. to abandon; to renounce; to cast off
3. to leave; to escape from; to

〔肉部〕

get out of
4. to omit; omission; to miss out
5. to slip off
6. if; in case; perhaps

脫膊(ㄊㄨㄛ ㄅㄛˊ)
to slip to the waist; to be bare from the waist up

脫班(ㄊㄨㄛ ㄅㄢ)
(said of scheduled trains, buses, and airplanes) to be late; to be behind schedule: 火車脫班了。The train was behind schedule.

脫皮(ㄊㄨㄛ ㄆㄧˊ)
①(said of some kinds of reptiles or insects) ecdyses; to molt ②to cast off the skin; to peel

脫毛(ㄊㄨㄛ ㄇㄠˊ)
(said of animals) the falloff of old hair; to molt; to shed

脫帽(ㄊㄨㄛ ㄇㄠˋ)
to take off one's hat—an ancient way of admitting defeat, now a gesture of respect

脫黨(ㄊㄨㄛ ㄉㄤˇ)
to renounce one's party affiliation; to break off from one's party

脫掉(ㄊㄨㄛ ㄉㄧㄠˋ)
to take off (one's garment, etc.)

脫胎換骨(ㄊㄨㄛ ㄊㄞ ㄏㄨㄢˋ ㄍㄨˇ)
①to disembody (and become immortal) ② to change oneself inside out

脫逃(ㄊㄨㄛ ㄊㄠˊ)
to escape from; to withdraw or run away: 犯人從獄中脫逃。The prisoner escaped from the jail.

脫套(ㄊㄨㄛ ㄊㄠˋ)
to drop ceremony or formalities

脫體(ㄊㄨㄛ ㄊㄧˇ)
①(said of illness) to leave one's body ②(Buddhism) to get rid of the body

脫兎(ㄊㄨㄛ ㄊㄨˋ)
speedily; very quickly; in a flash

脫漏(ㄊㄨㄛ ㄌㄡˋ)
to omit; omission; to miss

脫離(ㄊㄨㄛ ㄌㄧˊ)
①to sever one's relation with; to break away ②not within; away from; out of

脫離關係(ㄊㄨㄛ ㄌㄧˊ ㄍㄨㄢ ㄒㄧˋ)
to sever relations; to divorce; to disown

脫離現實(ㄊㄨㄛ ㄌㄧˊ ㄒㄧㄢˋ ㄕˊ)
to be divorced from reality

脫落(ㄊㄨㄛ ㄌㄨㄛˋ)
to drop; to come off; to fall off; to peel off: 牆上油漆逐漸脫落。The paint is peeling off the walls.

脫稿(ㄊㄨㄛ ㄍㄠˇ)
to complete a piece of writing

脫疘 or 脫肛(ㄊㄨㄛ ㄍㄤ)
prolapse of the rectum; proctocele; (said of piles) to slip out of the anus

脫軌(ㄊㄨㄛ ㄍㄨㄟˇ)
to derail: 火車脫軌了。The train was derailed.

脫光(ㄊㄨㄛ ㄍㄨㄤ)
to strip nude: 他上半身衣服被脫光了。He was stripped to the waist.

脫殼(ㄊㄨㄛ ㄎㄜˊ)or(ㄊㄨㄛ ㄑㄧㄠˋ)
① to cast the shell, as insects ② to make an escape (usually with a coup)

脫開(ㄊㄨㄛ ㄎㄞ)
to escape; to withdraw; to untie or extricate (oneself, etc. from bondage, troubles, etc.)

脫口成章(ㄊㄨㄛ ㄎㄡˇ ㄔㄥˊ ㄓㄤ)
to speak beautifully

脫口而出(ㄊㄨㄛ ㄎㄡˇ ㄦˊ ㄔㄨ)
to slip out of one's lips; to speak without thinking of the consequence

脫空(ㄊㄨㄛ ㄎㄨㄥ)
①to work hard without any success ②to lie

脫籍(ㄊㄨㄛ ㄐㄧˊ)
①(said of licensed prostitutes in former times) to get married ②to drop party membership or nationality

脫節(ㄊㄨㄛ ㄐㄧㄝˊ)
① disconnected; irrelevant or incoherent; to come apart; to lose contact ②dislocation; luxation; to dislocate

脫臼(ㄊㄨㄛ ㄐㄧㄡˋ)
to luxate; luxation; dislocation (of the joints)

脫肩(ㄊㄨㄛ ㄐㄧㄢ)
to relinquish or shirk one's responsibility

脫韁野馬(ㄊㄨㄛ ㄐㄧㄤ ㄧㄝˇ ㄇㄚˇ)or 脫韁之馬(ㄊㄨㄛ ㄐㄧㄤ ㄓ ㄇㄚˇ)
(literally) an unbridled wild horse—(usually said of a person's disposition, a style of writing, etc.) wild and unconventional collapse syndrome; forceful and unrestrained

脫去(ㄊㄨㄛ ㄑㄩˋ)
① to take off or strip (one's clothing, etc.); to throw off: 他脫去外套。He took off his coat.② to vindicate (one's bad reputation, etc.)

脫下(ㄊㄨㄛ ㄒㄧㄚˋ)
to take off; to shed or drop (one's clothing, etc.)

脫鞋(ㄊㄨㄛ ㄒㄧㄝˊ)
to remove shoes; to take off shoes

脫卸(ㄊㄨㄛ ㄒㄧㄝˋ)
to relinquish or shirk (one's responsibility)亦作「脫肩」

脫孝(ㄊㄨㄛ ㄒㄧㄠˋ)
(literally) to take off one's mourning clothes—The mourning period is over.

脫險(ㄊㄨㄛ ㄒㄧㄢˇ)
to escape from danger; to be out of danger

脫星(ㄊㄨㄛ ㄒㄧㄥ)
(informal) an actress who dresses scantily on screen

脫序(ㄊㄨㄛ ㄒㄩˋ)
disorderliness; breakdown of discipline

脫靴(ㄊㄨㄛ ㄒㄩㄝ)
①to pull off one's boots ② to keep the boots of a retired or transferred official at the city gate for memory

脫脂棉(ㄊㄨㄛ ㄓ ㄇㄧㄢˊ)
defatted cotton; medicinal cotton; absorbent cotton

脫脂奶(ㄊㄨㄛ ㄓ ㄋㄞˇ)
skim milk

脫脂奶粉(ㄊㄨㄛ ㄓ ㄋㄞˇ ㄈㄣˇ)
nonfat dried milk; defatted milk powder

脫手(ㄊㄨㄛ ㄕㄡˇ)
①(said of goods or stock at

hand) to sell out; to dispose of: 這些貨不好脫手。These goods are difficult to sell out. ②to slip off one's hands

脫售(ㄊㄨㄛ ㄕㄡˋ)
to sell out

脫身(ㄊㄨㄛ ㄕㄣ)
to leave; to get away from; to shake off; to escape

脫水(ㄊㄨㄛ ㄕㄨㄟˇ)
to dehydrate; dehydrated; dehydration

脫水機(ㄊㄨㄛ ㄕㄨㄟˇ ㄐㄧ)
a hydroextractor; a whizzer

脫水劑(ㄊㄨㄛ ㄕㄨㄟˇ ㄐㄧˋ)
a dehydrating agent

脫然無累(ㄊㄨㄛ ㄖㄢˊ ㄨˊ ㄌㄟˋ)
without a worry or care in the world

脫罪(ㄊㄨㄛ ㄗㄨㄟˋ)
to exonerate someone from a charge

脫色(ㄊㄨㄛ ㄙㄜˋ)
①to decolor; to decolorize ②to fade: 這張畫很快就脫色了。This painting fades fast.

脫俗(ㄊㄨㄛ ㄙㄨˊ)
to free oneself from worldly ways; to drop formalities or ceremony; original; free from vulgarity

脫素(ㄊㄨㄛ ㄙㄨˋ)
to live a simple and frugal life

脫粟(ㄊㄨㄛ ㄙㄨˋ)
to unhusk (rice)

脫衣服(ㄊㄨㄛ ㄧ ˙ㄈㄨ)
to remove one's clothing

脫衣舞(ㄊㄨㄛ ㄧ ㄨˇ)
a striptease

脫陽(ㄊㄨㄛ ㄧㄤˊ)
a kind of shock which a male may suffer during orgasm

脫穎而出(ㄊㄨㄛ ㄧㄥˇ ㄦˊ ㄔㄨ)
to pale others by showing one's ability and talents; (in a race, competition, etc.) to overtake others or outscore rival teams; to come to the fore: 那位藝術家脫穎而出。The artist has come to the fore.

脫誤(ㄊㄨㄛ ㄨˋ)
omissions and errors

【脯】 4680
1. ㄈㄨˇ fuu fǔ
1. dried and seasoned meat
2. preserved fruits

【脯】 4680
2. ㄆㄨˊ pwu pú
flesh or meat in the general area of the chest or breast

【脬】 4681
ㄆㄠ pau pāo
the bladder

【脰】 4682
ㄉㄡˋ dow dòu
the neck

【脞】 4683
ㄘㄨㄛˇ tsuoo cuǒ
tiny; petty; little pieces

【脤】 4684
ㄕㄣˋ shenn shèn
1. raw meat for a sacrifice
2. the buttocks; the bottom

【脖】 4685
ㄅㄛˊ bor bó
the neck

脖領兒(ㄅㄛˊ ㄌㄧㄥˇㄦ)
the neck or collar of a garment

脖頸子(ㄅㄛˊ ㄐㄧㄥˇ ˙ㄗ)or 脖頸兒(ㄅㄛˊ ㄐㄧㄥˇㄦ)
the neck

脖子(ㄅㄛˊ ˙ㄗ)
the neck: 他抓住我的脖子。He caught me by the neck.

【脗】 4686
ㄨㄣˇ woen wěn
1. to kiss; a kiss 亦作「吻」
2. to join together; to match; to tally
3. the lips

脗合(ㄨㄣˇ ㄏㄜˊ)
to match; to tally; to be identical: 這兩人所說的相脗合。The stories of the two men tallied.

【脚】 4687
(腳) ㄐㄧㄠˇ jeau jiǎo
1. the foot or feet
2. the base or foundation of anything

八畫

【脹】 4688
ㄓㄤˋ janq zhàng
1. full-stomached; glutted
2. swelling of the skin, etc.
3. to expand; expansion

脹滿(ㄓㄤˋ ㄇㄢˇ)
full; inflated; glutted

脹率(ㄓㄤˋ ㄌㄩˋ)
the rate of expansion

脹氣(ㄓㄤˋ ㄑㄧˋ)
①inflated with air ②(medicine) flatulence

【胼】 4689
(胼) ㄆㄧㄢˊ pyan pián
calluses

胼胝(ㄆㄧㄢˊ ㄓ)or 胼手胝足(ㄆㄧㄢˊ ㄕㄡˇ ㄓ ㄗㄨˊ)
calluses on the hands and feet—to toil or work hard

【腆】 4690
ㄊㄧㄢˇ tean tiǎn
1. prosperous; affluence
2. good; virtuous
3. protruding (as the belly, etc.)
4. bashful; to blush

腆默(ㄊㄧㄢˇ ㄇㄛˋ)
to blush and keep silence

腆贈(ㄊㄧㄢˇ ㄗㄥˋ)
rich gifts; costly presents

【腋】 4691
ㄧㄝˋ yeh yè
(讀音 ㄧˋ yih yì)
the armpits; the part under the forelegs of animals

腋毛(ㄧㄝˋ ㄇㄠˊ)
armpit hair

腋氣(ㄧㄝˋ ㄑㄧˋ)
the odor emanating from under the arms; a body odor

腋下(ㄧㄝˋ ㄒㄧㄚˋ)
under the arms; the armpits

腋臭(ㄧㄝˋ ㄔㄡˋ)
the odor emanating from the armpits; a body odor 亦作「腋氣」or「狐臭」

腋芽(ㄧㄝˋ ㄧㄚˊ)
(plants) an axillary bud

腋窩(ㄧㄝˋ ㄨㄛ)
the armpits

【腌】 4692
1. ㄤ ang āng
(又讀 ㄚ a ā)
unclean; dirty; filthy

腌臢(ㄤ ㄗㄤ)or(ㄚ ˙ㄗㄚ)
unclean; dirty; filthy: 他衣服腌臢。His clothes are filthy.

腌臢貨(ㄤ ㄗㄤ ㄏㄨㄛˋ)
a filthy person; a lousy or vicious fellow: 他是個腌臢貨。He is a filthy person.

【腌】 4692
2.(醃) ㄧㄢ ian yān
to salt; to pickle

〔肉部〕

【脺】 4693 (膵) ㄘㄨㄟˋ tsuey cuì
the pancreas

【腎】 4694 ㄕㄣˋ shenn shèn
1. the kidneys
2. the testicles

腎門(ㄕㄣˋ ㄇㄣˊ)
a hilum renalis

腎動脈(ㄕㄣˋ ㄉㄨㄥˋ ㄇㄞˋ)
a renal artery

腎痛(ㄕㄣˋ ㄊㄨㄥˋ)
nephralgia

腎囊(ㄕㄣˋ ㄋㄤˊ)
the scrotum

腎虧(ㄕㄣˋ ㄎㄨㄟ)
impotence; a general weakness of the male sexual prowess 亦作「腎虛」

腎靜脈(ㄕㄣˋ ㄐㄧㄥˋ ㄇㄞˋ)
a renal vein

腎虛(ㄕㄣˋ ㄒㄩ)
a general weakness of the male sexual prowess

腎上腺(ㄕㄣˋ ㄕㄤˋ ㄒㄧㄢˋ)
adrenals; the adrenal glands

腎臟(ㄕㄣˋ ㄗㄤˋ)
the kidneys

腎臟病(ㄕㄣˋ ㄗㄤˋ ㄅㄧㄥˋ)
a kidney ailment or disease

腎臟結石(ㄕㄣˋ ㄗㄤˋ ㄐㄧㄝˊ ㄕˊ)or 腎結石(ㄕㄣˋ ㄐㄧㄝˊ ㄕˊ)
(pathology) nephrolithiasis; renal calculus; kidney stone

腎臟炎(ㄕㄣˋ ㄗㄤˋ ㄧㄢˊ)
inflammation of the kidneys; nephritis

腎髓(ㄕㄣˋ ㄙㄨㄟˇ)
the purplish tissue that constitutes the inner part of the kidneys

腎盂(ㄕㄣˋ ㄩˊ)
a pelvis

【腐】 4695 ㄈㄨˇ fuu fǔ
1. to decay; to rot; rotten; putrid; to disintegrate; stale
2. corrupt; evil; worthless
3. old; worn-out; useless or worthless
4. to castrate; castration (as a punishment in ancient China)
5. short for 豆腐—bean curd

腐敗(ㄈㄨˇ ㄅㄞˋ)
① corrupt and rotten (practice, administration, etc.) ② putrid; decayed; to decay; to decompose

腐爛(ㄈㄨˇ ㄌㄢˋ)
to rot or decay; to disintegrate or decompose

腐化(ㄈㄨˇ ㄏㄨㄚˋ)
corrupt or rotten; decadent

腐化分子(ㄈㄨˇ ㄏㄨㄚˋ ㄈㄣˋ ㄗˇ)
corrupt or rotten elements; a depraved person

腐舊(ㄈㄨˇ ㄐㄧㄡˋ)
old and worn-out; worthless or useless

腐氣(ㄈㄨˇ ㄑㄧˋ)
① an odor or stench of decaying (foods, etc.) ② pedantic; pigheaded

腐朽(ㄈㄨˇ ㄒㄧㄡˇ)
decayed; rotten

腐心(ㄈㄨˇ ㄒㄧㄣ)
①extreme hatred ②extremely worried or anxious

腐刑(ㄈㄨˇ ㄒㄧㄥˊ)
(in ancient China) punishment by castration

腐植土(ㄈㄨˇ ㄓˊ ㄊㄨˇ)
humic soil; humus soil

腐臭(ㄈㄨˇ ㄔㄡˋ)
decaying and with a bad odor or stench

腐腸之藥(ㄈㄨˇ ㄔㄤˊ ㄓ ㄧㄠˋ)
(figuratively) rich foods

腐蝕(ㄈㄨˇ ㄕˊ)
① to erode; erosion; to corrode; corrosion: 金屬爲酸所腐蝕。Metals are eroded by acids. ②(chemistry) to etch; etching

腐蝕劑(ㄈㄨˇ ㄕˊ ㄐㄧˋ)
a corrodent

腐鼠(ㄈㄨˇ ㄕㄨˇ)
cheap or worthless things but highly treasured by the vulgar

腐肉(ㄈㄨˇ ㄖㄡˋ)
① rotten flesh or meat ② (medicine) slough

腐儒(ㄈㄨˇ ㄖㄨˊ)
pedants; worthless and narrow-minded scholars

腐乳(ㄈㄨˇ ㄖㄨˇ)
bean cheese

【腑】 4696 ㄈㄨˇ fuu fǔ
the bowels; the entrails; the viscera

腑臟(ㄈㄨˇ ㄗㄤˋ)
the bowels; the entrails; the viscera

【腔】 4697 ㄑㄧㄤ chiang qiāng
1. the cavity—especially referring to the chest and belly
2. a cavity in any vessel
3. a tune
4. an accent of one's pronunciation; a tone of one's voice
5. a manner

腔調(ㄑㄧㄤ ㄉㄧㄠˋ)
① a tune; the melody of a tune ② an accent ③ a manner or style of behavior

腔兒(ㄑㄧㄤㄦ)
① a cavity in any vessel ② a tune

【腕】 4698 ㄨㄢˋ wann wàn
the wrist

腕法(ㄨㄢˋ ㄈㄚˇ)
the three positions of the wrist 枕腕, 提腕, 懸腕 in writing Chinese characters

腕力(ㄨㄢˋ ㄌㄧˋ)
the strength of the wrist which is the key factor in forceful penmanship

腕骨(ㄨㄢˋ ㄍㄨˇ)
the wrist bones; the carpus: 他折斷了腕骨。He broke his wrist bones.

腕子(ㄨㄢˋ ˙ㄗ)
the wrist: 我捉住他的腕子。I took him by the wrist.

【脾】 4699 ㄆㄧˊ pyi pí
1. the spleen
2. a temper; a disposition

脾氣(ㄆㄧˊ ˙ㄑㄧ)
a temper or disposition: 他脾氣暴躁。He has a quick temper.

脾臟(ㄆㄧˊ ㄗㄤˋ)
the spleen

脾胃(ㄆㄧˊ ㄨㄟˋ)
① the stomach ② appetite ③ one's temperament or natural inclination

【腊】 4700 1. ㄒㄧˊ shyi xí
1. dried meat
2. very; extremely

【腊】 4700 2. ㄌㄚˋ lah là
an abbreviated form of 臘

腊梅(ㄌㄚˋ ㄇㄟˊ)

plum flowers
臘肉(ㄌㄚˋ ㄖㄡˋ)
salted and dried meat
臘月(ㄌㄚˋ ㄩㄝˋ)
the twelfth month of the lunar year

【腓】 4701 ㄈㄟˊ feir féi
1. the calf (of the leg)
2. (now rarely) sick; ill
3. (now rarely) to avoid
4. (now rarely) to decay
腓特力大帝(ㄈㄟˊ ㄊㄜˋ ㄌㄧˋ ㄉㄚˋ ㄉㄧˋ)
Frederick the Great, 1712-1786, king of Prussia
腓尼基(ㄈㄟˊ ㄋㄧˊ ㄐㄧ)
Phenicia, or Phoenicia
腓骨(ㄈㄟˊ ㄍㄨˇ)
the fibula

九畫

【腠】 4702 ㄘㄡˋ tsow còu
the texture of muscle

【腥】 4703 ㄒㄧㄥ shing xīng
1. raw, undressed meat
2. an offensive smell, especially of fish or blood
腥風血雨(ㄒㄧㄥ ㄈㄥ ㄒㄧㄝˇ ㄩˇ)
(literally) winds carrying an offensive smell of flesh and rain of blood—the carnage of war
腥德(ㄒㄧㄥ ㄉㄜˊ)
evil conduct; debauchery; dissipated ways
腥穢(ㄒㄧㄥ ㄏㄨㄟˋ)or 腥汚(ㄒㄧㄥ ㄨ)
smelly and dirty
腥氣(ㄒㄧㄥ ·ㄑㄧ)
smelly; an offensive smell of meat, fish, blood, etc.
腥臭(ㄒㄧㄥ ㄔㄡˋ)
an offensive smell of fish, meat, blood, etc.
腥羶(ㄒㄧㄥ ㄕㄢ)
the smell of sheep or goats
腥臊(ㄒㄧㄥ ㄙㄠ)
① a bad smell of fish or meat; a stench ② evil (administration, etc.)
腥味兒(ㄒㄧㄥ ㄨㄜˋㄦ)
an offensive smell of fish, etc.
腥聞(ㄒㄧㄥ ㄨㄣˊ)
a malodorous reputation known far and wide; scandalous acts; notoriety; rank odor

【腦】 4704 ㄋㄠˇ nao nǎo
the brain
腦瓢兒(ㄋㄠˇ ㄆㄧㄠˊㄦ)
the top of the head; the plate of the head
腦貧血(ㄋㄠˇ ㄆㄧㄣˊ ㄒㄧㄝˇ)
cerebral anemia
腦膜(ㄋㄠˇ ㄇㄛˊ)
meninges
腦膜炎(ㄋㄠˇ ㄇㄛˊ ㄧㄢˊ)
meningitis
腦滿腸肥(ㄋㄠˇ ㄇㄢˇ ㄔㄤˊ ㄈㄟˊ)
① a fool or stupid fellow—one who gluts his stomach but never uses his brains ② fat like a pig
腦門子(ㄋㄠˇ ㄇㄣˊ ·ㄗ)or 腦門兒(ㄋㄠˇ ㄇㄜˊㄦ)
the forehead
腦袋(ㄋㄠˇ ·ㄉㄞ)or 腦袋瓜子(ㄋㄠˇ ·ㄉㄞ ㄍㄨㄚ ·ㄗ)or 腦袋瓜兒(ㄋㄠˇ ·ㄉㄞ ㄍㄨㄚㄦ)
the head: 他把他的腦袋伸出窗外。He put his head out of the window.
腦電波圖(ㄋㄠˇ ㄉㄧㄢˋ ㄅㄛ ㄊㄨˊ)
an electroencephalogram
腦力(ㄋㄠˇ ㄌㄧˋ)
brains; mental capability; mental exertion
腦蓋(ㄋㄠˇ ㄍㄞˋ)
the top of the skull
腦蓋骨(ㄋㄠˇ ㄍㄞˋ ㄍㄨˇ)
the cranium
腦瓜頂兒(ㄋㄠˇ ㄍㄨㄚ ㄉㄧㄥˇㄦ)
the top of the head
腦殼(ㄋㄠˇ ㄎㄜˊ)
① the head ② a jocular reference to one's general appearance
腦海(ㄋㄠˇ ㄏㄞˇ)
the mind
腦後(ㄋㄠˇ ㄏㄡˋ)
disregard; to disregard: 他把我的警告拋在腦後。He disregarded my warnings.
腦筋(ㄋㄠˇ ㄐㄧㄣ)
brains; mentality; mental capacity: 她腦筋很好。She has a good brain.
腦筋靈敏(ㄋㄠˇ ㄐㄧㄣ ㄌㄧㄥˊ ㄇㄧㄣˇ)
keen and sharp in thinking; brainy; bright
腦漿(ㄋㄠˇ ㄐㄧㄤ)
the cerebrum, the cerebellum and the medulla oblongata collectively when they are exposed after the skull is crushed
腦汁(ㄋㄠˇ ㄓ)
mental effort or exertion—(figuratively) brains: 他爲了答案絞盡腦汁。He racked his brains for the answer.
腦震盪(ㄋㄠˇ ㄓㄣˋ ㄉㄤˋ)
brain concussion
腦脹(ㄋㄠˇ ㄓㄤˋ)
heavy feeling in the brain
腦中風(ㄋㄠˇ ㄓㄨㄥˋ ㄈㄥ)
(pathology) stroke
腦出血(ㄋㄠˇ ㄔㄨ ㄒㄧㄝˇ)
cerebral hemorrhage; an apoplectic stroke; cerebral apoplexy
腦充血(ㄋㄠˇ ㄔㄨㄥ ㄒㄧㄝˇ)
congestion of the brain
腦勺子(ㄋㄠˇ ㄕㄠˊ ·ㄗ)
the back of the head
腦神經(ㄋㄠˇ ㄕㄣˊ ㄐㄧㄥ)
cranial nerves
腦子(ㄋㄠˇ ·ㄗ)
① the brain ② brains; mental capability; the faculty of memory
腦髓(ㄋㄠˇ ㄙㄨㄟˇ)
a general name of the brain—including cerebrum, cerebellum and medulla oblongata
腦兒(ㄋㄠˇㄦ)
① the brains of animals (for food) ② any greyish white substance resembling the brain, as soft bean curd, etc.
腦溢血(ㄋㄠˇ ㄧˋ ㄒㄧㄝˇ)
cerebral hemorrhage; a stroke; apoplexy
腦炎(ㄋㄠˇ ㄧㄢˊ)
encephalitis

【腫】 4705 ㄓㄨㄥˇ joong zhǒng
to swell; a swelling; a boil: 她受傷的指頭腫起來了。Her injured finger swelled.
腫皰(ㄓㄨㄥˇ ㄆㄠˋ)
a pimple; acne
腫大(ㄓㄨㄥˇ ㄉㄚˋ)
to swell up
腫毒(ㄓㄨㄥˇ ㄉㄨˊ)
a swelling; a tumor

〔肉部〕

腫瘤(ㄓㄨㄥˇ ㄌㄧㄡˊ)
(medicine) a tumor: 良(惡)性腫瘤 a benign (malignant) tumor
腫起來(ㄓㄨㄥˇ ㄑㄧˇ ㄌㄞˊ)
to swell up: 他的臉孔開始腫起來。His face began to swell up.
腫脹(ㄓㄨㄥˇ ㄓㄤˋ)
to swell; swelling

【腰】 4706
ㄧㄠ iau yāo
1. the midriff; the waist: 她的腰很細。She has a small waist.
2. the kidneys
3. the middle of something; the waist portion of a region

腰板兒(ㄧㄠ ㄅㄚˇㄦ)
the back of the midriff; the waist and the back
腰包(ㄧㄠ ㄅㄠ)
①a purse; a billfold; a wallet; a girdle with a built-in pocket worn by farmers in former times ② one's money
腰板脖硬(ㄧㄠ ㄅㄢˇ ㄅㄛˊ ㄧㄥˋ)
stiff or rigid in movements
腰部(ㄧㄠ ㄅㄨˋ)
the waist; the small part of the body between the thorax and hips
腰帶(ㄧㄠ ㄉㄞˋ)
① a girdle; a waistband ② (anatomy) a pelvic girdle
腰刀(ㄧㄠ ㄉㄠ)
a saberlike knife carried at the waist in former times
腰疼(ㄧㄠ ㄊㄥˊ)
lumbago
腰腿(ㄧㄠ ㄊㄨㄟˇ)
nimbleness of one's waist and legs
腰痛(ㄧㄠ ㄊㄨㄥˋ)
lumbago; a muscular pain in the lumbar regions
腰骨(ㄧㄠ ㄍㄨˇ)
the five lowest pieces of bone of the spinal column
腰鼓(ㄧㄠ ㄍㄨˇ)
a kind of drum, having a large end stretched over with skin and a slender hollow cylinder
腰果(ㄧㄠ ㄍㄨㄛˇ)
a cashew nut
腰花(ㄧㄠ ㄏㄨㄚ)
hog kidneys cut lightly which will blossom like flowers when cooked
腰肢(ㄧㄠ ㄓ)
the waistline; the circumference of the body at the waist
腰舟(ㄧㄠ ㄓㄡ)
an empty gourd tied to the waist as a kind of life jacket in former times
腰斬(ㄧㄠ ㄓㄢˇ)
(an ancient Chinese punishment) to chop in two at the waist
腰纏(ㄧㄠ ㄔㄢˊ)
money one carries when traveling
腰纏萬貫(ㄧㄠ ㄔㄢˊ ㄨㄢˋ ㄍㄨㄢˋ)
very rich; loaded
腰身(ㄧㄠ ㄕㄣ)
the waist; the waistline (in dress-making); the size of the midriff: 這條裙子腰身太大。The skirt is too big in the waist.
腰子(ㄧㄠ ˙ㄗ)
the kidneys
腰酸背疼(ㄧㄠ ㄙㄨㄢ ㄅㄟˋ ㄊㄥˊ)
a sore waist and an aching back
腰兒(ㄧㄠㄦ)
the waist
腰窩兒(ㄧㄠ ㄨㄛㄦ)
mutton cut from the side of sheep
腰圍(ㄧㄠ ㄨㄟˊ)
① the waist; the waistline; the second of a girl's vital statistics ② a girdle

【腳】 4707
(脚) ㄐㄧㄠˇ jeau jiǎo
(讀音 ㄐㄩㄝˊ jyue jué)
1. the feet
2. the leg or base of something

腳本(ㄐㄧㄠˇ ㄅㄣˇ)
the script of a play, an opera, etc.
腳步(ㄐㄧㄠˇ ㄅㄨˋ)
steps; paces; strides; footfalls; footsteps
腳盆(ㄐㄧㄠˇ ㄆㄣˊ)
a foot tub
腳面(ㄐㄧㄠˇ ㄇㄧㄢˋ)
the instep; the back of a foot
腳夫(ㄐㄧㄠˇ ㄈㄨ)
a porter or coolie
腳燈(ㄐㄧㄠˇ ㄉㄥ)
footlights on a stage
腳櫈(ㄐㄧㄠˇ ㄉㄥˋ)
a footstool; a footrest
腳底板兒(ㄐㄧㄠˇ ㄉㄧˇ ㄅㄚˇㄦ)
the sole of the foot
腳底下(ㄐㄧㄠˇ ㄉㄧˇ ˙ㄒㄧㄚ)
① under the feet ② feet
腳踏板(ㄐㄧㄠˇ ㄊㄚˋ ㄅㄢˇ)
① a footboard ② a pedal
腳踏兩隻船(ㄐㄧㄠˇ ㄊㄚˋ ㄌㄧㄤˇ ㄓ ㄔㄨㄢˊ)
to straddle the fence; to be undecided
腳踏車(ㄐㄧㄠˇ ㄊㄚˋ ㄔㄜ)
a bicycle: 你騎腳踏車嗎? Do you ride a bicycle?
腳踏實地(ㄐㄧㄠˇ ㄊㄚˋ ㄕˊ ㄉㄧˋ)
(literally) to plant one's feet on solid ground—to do a job honestly and with dedication
腳踢(ㄐㄧㄠˇ ㄊㄧ)
to kick
腳力(ㄐㄧㄠˇ ㄌㄧˋ)
① a messenger; an errand-boy ② carriage charges; porterage ③ strength of one's legs
腳鐐(ㄐㄧㄠˇ ㄌㄧㄠˊ)
foot shackles or fetters
腳爐(ㄐㄧㄠˇ ㄌㄨˊ)
a charcoal foot warmer made of metal
腳後跟(ㄐㄧㄠˇ ㄏㄡˋ ㄍㄣ)or 腳跟(ㄐㄧㄠˇ ㄍㄣ)
① the heel of the foot ②(figuratively) foothold
腳行(ㄐㄧㄠˇ ㄏㄤˊ)
(formerly) a transportation company which employed coolies to do the carrying
腳跡(ㄐㄧㄠˇ ㄐㄧ)
footprints; footmarks; footsteps
腳尖兒(ㄐㄧㄠˇ ㄐㄧㄚㄦ)
the point of the foot; tiptoe: 她踮着腳尖兒走。She walks on tiptoe.
腳氣病(ㄐㄧㄠˇ ㄑㄧˋ ㄅㄧㄥˋ)or 腳氣(ㄐㄧㄠˇ ㄑㄧˋ)
beriberi
腳錢(ㄐㄧㄠˇ ㄑㄧㄢˊ)
a fee for the delivery man of a store
腳下(ㄐㄧㄠˇ ㄒㄧㄚˋ)

① under one's feet ② the foot ③ now; presently

腳心(ㄐㄧㄠˇ ㄒㄧㄣ)
the foot arch; the arch of the foot

腳指頭(ㄐㄧㄠˇ ㄓˇ ·ㄊㄡ)or 腳趾(ㄐㄧㄠˇ ㄓˇ)
toes: 我的腳趾很痛。My toe is very sore.

腳指甲(ㄐㄧㄠˇ ㄓˇ ·ㄐㄧㄚ)
toenails

腳掌(ㄐㄧㄠˇ ㄓㄤˇ)
the sole (of the foot)

腳註(ㄐㄧㄠˇ ㄓㄨˋ)
a footnote: 他忘了打上腳註。He forgot to type the footnotes.

腳踩(ㄐㄧㄠˇ ㄘㄞˇ)
to pedal; to trample; to stamp with the feet

腳色(ㄐㄧㄠˇ ㄙㄜˋ)
① a character; a role: 他扮演哈姆雷特的腳色。He played the role of Hamlet. ② personal background of examinees under the old civil service examination system ③ a talented or resourceful person

腳丫縫兒(ㄐㄧㄠˇ ㄧㄚ ㄈㄥˋㄦ)
space between the toes

腳鴨子(ㄐㄧㄠˇ ㄧㄚ ·ㄗ)or 腳鴨兒(ㄐㄧㄠˇ ㄧㄚㄦ)
the foot

腳印兒(ㄐㄧㄠˇ ㄧㄣˋㄦ)
footprints; footmarks; footsteps

腳腕子(ㄐㄧㄠˇ ㄨㄢˋ ·ㄗ)
the ankle

【腱】 4708 ㄐㄧㄢˋ jiann jiàn
(anatomy) tendon

腱子(ㄐㄧㄢˋ ·ㄗ)
tendons (of meat animals)

【腴】 4709 ㄩˊ yu yú
1. fat
2. plump and soft
3. fertile
4. intestines of dogs and hogs
5. rich

【腸】 4710 ㄔㄤˊ charng cháng
the intestines; the bowels

腸肚(ㄔㄤˊ ㄉㄨˋ)
the intestines and the belly —one's heart (good, evil, etc.)

腸斷(ㄔㄤˊ ㄉㄨㄢˋ)
heartbroken; deeply grieved

腸潰瘍(ㄔㄤˊ ㄎㄨㄟˋ ㄧㄤˊ)
an intestinal ulcer

腸子(ㄔㄤˊ ·ㄗ)
the intestines

腸炎(ㄔㄤˊ ㄧㄢˊ)
intestinal or bowel catarrh; enteritis

腸癌(ㄔㄤˊ ㄧㄢˊ)
bowel cancer

腸胃(ㄔㄤˊ ㄨㄟˋ)
intestines and the stomach

腸胃病(ㄔㄤˊ ㄨㄟˋ ㄅㄧㄥˋ)
a digestive ailment; the disease of stomach and bowels

【腹】 4711 ㄈㄨˋ fuh fù
1. the belly; under the chest; the abdomen
2. the front part
3. the inside; inner

腹背(ㄈㄨˋ ㄅㄟˋ)
① in front and behind ② close

腹背之毛(ㄈㄨˋ ㄅㄟˋ ㄓ ㄇㄠˊ)
(literally) feathers on the back and underside (of a bird)—unimportant

腹背受敵(ㄈㄨˋ ㄅㄟˋ ㄕㄡˋ ㄉㄧˊ)
to be attacked from front and rear

腹部(ㄈㄨˋ ㄅㄨˋ)
the abdominal region; the abdomen; the belly

腹部運動(ㄈㄨˋ ㄅㄨˋ ㄩㄣˋ ㄉㄨㄥˋ)
physical exercise for the abdominal region

腹膜(ㄈㄨˋ ㄇㄛˊ)
the peritoneum

腹膜炎(ㄈㄨˋ ㄇㄛˊ ㄧㄢˊ)
peritonitis

腹誹(ㄈㄨˋ ㄈㄟˇ)or 腹非(ㄈㄨˋ ㄈㄟ)
silent curses or disagreement; to criticize in one's mind

腹地(ㄈㄨˋ ㄉㄧˋ)
a hinterland; the interior

腹痛(ㄈㄨˋ ㄊㄨㄥˋ)
bellyache

腹稿(ㄈㄨˋ ㄍㄠˇ)
(literally) a manuscript in the mind—a rough plan or sketch not yet put down in black and white

腹呼吸(ㄈㄨˋ ㄏㄨ ㄒㄧ)
abdominal respiration

腹瀉(ㄈㄨˋ ㄒㄧㄝˋ)
diarrhea

腹心(ㄈㄨˋ ㄒㄧㄣ)
the belly and the heart—(figuratively) ① true thoughts and feelings ② trusted subordinates ③ a close friend

腹心之患(ㄈㄨˋ ㄒㄧㄣ ㄓ ㄏㄨㄢˋ)
danger from within; danger posed by an enemy lurking nearby

腹式呼吸(ㄈㄨˋ ㄕˋ ㄏㄨ ㄒㄧ)or 腹部呼吸(ㄈㄨˋ ㄅㄨˋ ㄏㄨ ㄒㄧ)
deep or abdominal breathing

腹熱心煎(ㄈㄨˋ ㄖㄜˋ ㄒㄧㄣ ㄐㄧㄢ)
to hope anxiously; to look forward to something very eagerly

腹足類動物(ㄈㄨˋ ㄗㄨˊ ㄌㄟˋ ㄉㄨㄥˋ ㄨˋ)
the gastropod

腹議(ㄈㄨˋ ㄧˋ)
a silent censure; to criticize in one's mind

腹有鱗甲(ㄈㄨˋ ㄧㄡˇ ㄌㄧㄣˊ ㄐㄧㄚˇ)
vicious; treacherous

腹語(ㄈㄨˋ ㄩˇ)
ventriloquy, or ventriloquism

【腩】 4712 ㄋㄢˇ naan nǎn
tender beef

【腺】 4713 ㄒㄧㄢˋ shiann xiàn
a gland

腺體(ㄒㄧㄢˋ ㄊㄧˇ)
a gland

【腼】 4714 (靦)ㄇㄧㄢˇ mean miǎn
1. shy; bashful
2. (said of girls) quiet and graceful

腼腆(ㄇㄧㄢˇ ㄊㄧㄢˇ)
bashful; shy: 這孩子見了生人有點腼腆。The child is shy with strangers.

【腭】 4715 (齶)ㄜˋ eh è
the roof of the mouth; the palate

【腮】 4716 (顋)ㄙㄞ sai sāi
the cheeks: 這小孩腮頰緋紅。The boy has rosy cheeks.

腮幫子(ㄙㄞ ㄅㄤ ·ㄗ)
(colloquial) the cheek

〔肉部〕

十畫

【腿】 4717 ㄊㄨㄟˇ toei tuǐ
the legs and the thighs
腿肚子(ㄊㄨㄟˇ ㄉㄨˋ ·ㄗ)
the calf of the leg
腿腳兒(ㄊㄨㄟˇ ㄐㄧㄠˇㄦ)
steps; gaits; strides

【膀】 4718 1. ㄅㄤˇ baang bǎng
the upper arms
膀臂(ㄅㄤˇ ㄅㄧˋ)
① the arms ② capable aides
膀子(ㄅㄤˇ ·ㄗ)
① the shoulder ② the upper arm

【膀】 4718 2. ㄆㄤˊ parng páng
the bladder
膀胱(ㄆㄤˊ ㄍㄨㄤ)
the bladder
膀胱結石(ㄆㄤˊ ㄍㄨㄤ ㄐㄧㄝˊ ㄕˊ)
a calculus of the bladder; a bladder stone
膀胱炎(ㄆㄤˊ ㄍㄨㄤ ㄧㄢˊ)
cystitis; inflammation of the bladder
膀胱癌(ㄆㄤˊ ㄍㄨㄤ ㄧㄢˊ)
bladder cancer

【膀】 4718 3. ㄅㄤˋ banq bàng
to make passes at (used in the phrase 弔膀子)

【膂】 4719 ㄌㄩˇ leu lǚ
1. the spinal column; the backbone
2. one's physical strength
膂力(ㄌㄩˇ ㄌㄧˋ)
one's physical strength

【膈】 4720 ㄍㄜˊ ger gé
the diaphragm

【膏】 4721 1. ㄍㄠ gau gāo
1. fat; grease
2. ointment
3. fertile
4. the region just below the heart
5. grace; favors
6. sweet
7. (Chinese medicine) a paste-like preparation for external use
8. plaster
9. (food and fruit) cooked to a very thick or pasty form
膏沐(ㄍㄠ ㄇㄨˋ)
oil or grease women used to render their hair glossy in former days
膏粱子弟(ㄍㄠ ㄌㄧㄤˊ ㄗˇ ㄉㄧˋ)
piggish and ignorant off-spring of the rich families; fops
膏火(ㄍㄠ ㄏㄨㄛˇ)
lamp oil
膏肓(ㄍㄠ ㄏㄨㄤ)
the vital region between the heart and diaphragm
膏壤(ㄍㄠ ㄖㄤˇ)
fertile land
膏澤(ㄍㄠ ㄗㄜˊ)
good grace; great favors; the blessings
膏藥(ㄍㄠ ㄧㄠˋ)
①medicated plaster attached to pieces of cloth or paper ②propaganda; boastful claims
膏油(ㄍㄠ ㄧㄡˊ)
grease; lard
膏腴之地(ㄍㄠ ㄩˊ ㄓ ㄉㄧˋ)
fertile land
膏雨(ㄍㄠ ㄩˇ)
a timely rain

【膏】 4721 2. ㄍㄠˋ gaw gào
1. to lubricate; to grease; to make smooth or glossy
2. to enrich; to freshen
膏油(ㄍㄠˋ ㄧㄡˊ)
to add lubricating oil

【膆】 4722 ㄙㄨˋ suh sù
1. the crop of a bird or fowl
2. fat
膆囊(ㄙㄨˋ ㄋㄤˊ)
the crop of a fowl

【膊】 4723 ㄅㄛˊ bor bó
the shoulders; the upper arms

十一畫

【膚】 4724 ㄈㄨ fu fū
1. the skin; the surface: 他的皮膚是棕色的。He has a brown skin.
2. skin-deep; shallow; superficial
3. (now rare) great, as achievements or merit
膚皮(ㄈㄨ ㄆㄧˊ)
dry, dandruff-like scales of the dead skin on the body
膚泛(ㄈㄨ ㄈㄢˋ)
(said of a piece of writing, a speech, etc.) shallow and way off the mark; superficial and off the beam
膚覺(ㄈㄨ ㄐㄩㄝˊ)
cutaneous sensation
膚淺(ㄈㄨ ㄑㄧㄢˇ)
shallow or superficial (views, etc.); skin-deep
膚如凝脂(ㄈㄨ ㄖㄨˊ ㄋㄧㄥˊ ㄓ)
a creamy skin
膚色(ㄈㄨ ㄙㄜˋ)
color of the skin
膚色歧視(ㄈㄨ ㄙㄜˋ ㄑㄧˊ ㄕˋ)
racial discrimination

【膜】 4725 1. ㄇㄛˋ moh mò (又讀 ㄇㄛˊ mo mó)
1. membrane: 細胞膜 cell membrane
2. a film; a thin coating
膜翅目(ㄇㄛˋ ㄔˋ ㄇㄨˋ)
(zoology) *Hymenoptera*
膜外(ㄇㄛˋ ㄨㄞˋ)
outside of one's attention, consideration, etc.

【膜】 4725 2. ㄇㄛˊ mo mó
to kneel and worship
膜拜(ㄇㄛˊ ㄅㄞˋ)
to kneel and worship

【膝】 4726 ㄒㄧ shi xī
the knee
膝步(ㄒㄧ ㄅㄨˋ)or 膝行(ㄒㄧ ㄒㄧㄥˊ)
to walk on knees (a gesture of submission)
膝袒(ㄒㄧ ㄊㄢˇ)
to walk on knees and bare one's breast — a gesture of the deepest apology
膝蓋(ㄒㄧ ㄍㄞˋ)
a knee
膝蓋骨(ㄒㄧ ㄍㄞˋ ㄍㄨˇ)
the kneecap; the patella
膝關節(ㄒㄧ ㄍㄨㄢ ㄐㄧㄝˊ)
a knee joint
膝席(ㄒㄧ ㄒㄧˊ)
to kneel on a mat which was used as a substitute of a table in ancient times
膝下(ㄒㄧ ㄒㄧㄚˋ)

respectful address for one's parents in letters

膝下承歡(ㄒㄧ ㄒㄧㄚˋ ㄔㄥˊ ㄏㄨㄢ)
to please one's parents by living with them

膝癢搔背(ㄒㄧ ㄧㄤˇ ㄙㄠ ㄅㄟˋ)
(literally) to scratch the back while the knee is itching—entirely missing the point; irrelevant

【滕】 4727 ㄊㄥˊ terng téng
1. name of a state in the Epoch of Spring and Autumn in today's Shantung Province
2. a Chinese family name

滕王閣(ㄊㄥˊ ㄨㄤˊ ㄍㄜˊ)
a famous resort in Kiangsi Province, where Wang Po (王勃) composed his famous verse of dedication in his teens

【膠】 4728 ㄐㄧㄠ jiau jiāo
1. glue; gum
2. resin; sap
3. anything sticky
4. rubber; plastics
5. to stick on or together; to adhere
6. stubborn; obstinate
7. a Chinese family name

膠版(ㄐㄧㄠ ㄅㄢˇ)
an offset plate

膠布(ㄐㄧㄠ ㄅㄨˋ)
rubber cloth; plastic cloth

膠片(ㄐㄧㄠ ㄆㄧㄢˋ)
film

膠棉(ㄐㄧㄠ ㄇㄧㄢˊ)
collodion

膠附(ㄐㄧㄠ ㄈㄨˋ)
to adhere to; to stick together tightly

膠帶(ㄐㄧㄠ ㄉㄞˋ)
an adhesive tape

膠體物(ㄐㄧㄠ ㄊㄧˇ ㄨˋ)
a colloid

膠囊(ㄐㄧㄠ ㄋㄤˊ)
a medical capsule

膠固(ㄐㄧㄠ ㄍㄨˋ)
① sturdy; strong ② obstinate; stubborn

膠合板(ㄐㄧㄠ ㄏㄜˊ ㄅㄢˇ)
plywood

膠濟鐵路(ㄐㄧㄠ ㄐㄧˋ ㄊㄧㄝˇ ㄌㄨˋ)
the Tsingtao-Tsinan Railway in Shantung Province

膠捲兒(ㄐㄧㄠ ㄐㄩㄚˇㄦ)
unexposed film: 我找到一卷膠捲兒。I found a roll of unexposed film.

膠譎(ㄐㄧㄠ ㄐㄩㄝˊ)
to cheat; to swindle

膠漆(ㄐㄧㄠ ㄑㄧ)
close and intimate; very much in love

膠漆相投(ㄐㄧㄠ ㄑㄧ ㄒㄧㄤ ㄊㄡˊ)
the intimate and complete meeting of minds

膠鞋(ㄐㄧㄠ ㄒㄧㄝˊ)
rubber shoes; galoshes: 我們在下雨天穿膠鞋。We wear galoshes in wet weather.

膠質(ㄐㄧㄠ ㄓˋ)
① gluey; glue ② gelatinous; gelatin

膠州灣(ㄐㄧㄠ ㄓㄡ ㄨㄢ)
the Chaochow Gulf in the Yellow Sea

膠柱鼓瑟(ㄐㄧㄠ ㄓㄨˋ ㄍㄨˇ ㄙㄜˋ)
obstinate; inflexible; very conservative

膠著(ㄐㄧㄠ ㄓㄨㄛˊ)
stalemated; at a stalemate; a standstill: 戰爭情勢已成膠著狀態。The warfare was at a stalemate.

膠著語(ㄐㄧㄠ ㄓㄨㄛˊ ㄩˇ)
an agglutinative language

膠水(ㄐㄧㄠ ㄕㄨㄟˇ)
glue; size: 請用膠水粘。Please stick it with glue.

【膛】 4729 ㄊㄤˊ tarng táng
1. the breast; the chest
2. a cavity
3. the chamber of a firearm

【膣】 4730 ㄓˋ jyh zhì
the vagina

十二畫

【膨】 4731 ㄆㄥˊ perng péng
to expand; to swell; to inflate

膨脝(ㄆㄥˊ ㄏㄥ)
(said of the stomach) full; loaded

膨脹(ㄆㄥˊ ㄓㄤˋ)
expansion; swelling; inflation; bloated; to expand; to swell: 熱使金屬膨脹。Heat expands metals.

膨脹係數(ㄆㄥˊ ㄓㄤˋ ㄒㄧˋ ㄕㄨˋ)
coefficient of expansion

【膩】 4732 ㄋㄧˋ nih nì
1. fatty or greasy (food)
2. smooth
3. dirty
4. bored; tired; weary
5. intimate (friends)

膩煩(ㄋㄧˋ ㄈㄢˊ)
① bored; tired; to be fed up ② to loathe; to hate

膩得慌(ㄋㄧˋ ·ㄉㄜ ·ㄏㄨㄤ)
very depressed and listless

膩人(ㄋㄧˋ ㄖㄣˊ)
① boring; tiresome ② too greasy

膩友(ㄋㄧˋ ㄧㄡˇ)
bosom friends

膩胃(ㄋㄧˋ ㄨㄟˋ)
(said of rich, greasy food) to kill one's appetite

【膳】 4733 (饍) ㄕㄢˋ shann shàn
meals; food; provisions

膳費(ㄕㄢˋ ㄈㄟˋ)
charges for board

膳房(ㄕㄢˋ ㄈㄤˊ)
① the imperial kitchen 亦作「御膳房」 ② a kitchen

膳夫(ㄕㄢˋ ㄈㄨ)
① the chief cook in charge of the royal family's victuals ② a cook

膳廳(ㄕㄢˋ ㄊㄧㄥ) or 膳堂(ㄕㄢˋ ㄊㄤˊ)
a mess hall; a dining hall

膳食(ㄕㄢˋ ㄕˊ)
meat; victuals

膳宿(ㄕㄢˋ ㄙㄨˋ)
food and lodging

膳宿費(ㄕㄢˋ ㄙㄨˋ ㄈㄟˋ)
charges for board and lodging; boarding charges

膳宿生(ㄕㄢˋ ㄙㄨˋ ㄕㄥ)
a boarding student

【膰】 4734 ㄈㄢˊ farn fán
cooked meat for sacrifice or offering

十三畫

【膿】 4735 ㄋㄨㄥˊ nong nóng
pus or purulent matter

〔肉 部〕

膿包(ㄋㄨㄥˊ ㄅㄠ)
①a pustule; an abscess ②a good-for-nothing; a useless person
膿血(ㄋㄨㄥˊ ㄒㄧㄝˇ)
pus and blood
膿汁(ㄋㄨㄥˊ ㄓ)
purulence
膿腫(ㄋㄨㄥˊ ㄓㄨㄥˇ)
purulent swellings
膿瘡(ㄋㄨㄥˊ ㄔㄨㄤ)
an abscess; a boil
膿水(ㄋㄨㄥˊ ㄕㄨㄟˇ)
pus

【膽】 4736 (胆) ㄉㄢˇ daan dǎn
1. the gall
2. courage; bravery; audacity: 他是個有膽量的人。He is a man of courage.
3. the internal parts, etc. of a vessel
4. the tube of a tire, basketball, etc.
膽破(ㄉㄢˇ ㄆㄛˋ)
to be frightened or scared to death
膽瓶(ㄉㄢˇ ㄆㄧㄥˊ)
a hanging-gall-shaped bottle
膽礬(ㄉㄢˇ ㄈㄢˊ)
chalcanthite
膽大(ㄉㄢˇ ㄉㄚˋ)
bold; audacious 亦作「大膽」
膽大包天(ㄉㄢˇ ㄉㄚˋ ㄅㄠ ㄊㄧㄢ)
extremely audacious; recklessly bold
膽大心細(ㄉㄢˇ ㄉㄚˋ ㄒㄧㄣ ㄒㄧˋ)
brave but cautious; courageous but careful or circumspective
膽大妄爲(ㄉㄢˇ ㄉㄚˋ ㄨㄤˋ ㄨㄟˊ)
audacious and reckless
膽囊(ㄉㄢˇ ㄋㄤˊ)
(anatomy) the gall bladder
膽囊炎(ㄉㄢˇ ㄋㄤˊ ㄧㄢˊ)
cholecystitis
膽力(ㄉㄢˇ ㄌㄧˋ)
courage; bravery
膽裂(ㄉㄢˇ ㄌㄧㄝˋ)
scared to death
膽量(ㄉㄢˇ ㄌㄧㄤˋ)
courage; bravery; guts
膽落(ㄉㄢˇ ㄌㄨㄛˋ)
extremely frightened
膽略(ㄉㄢˇ ㄌㄩㄝˋ)
courage and resourcefulness
膽敢(ㄉㄢˇ ㄍㄢˇ)
so audacious as to; reckless to the extent of; to dare
膽固醇(ㄉㄢˇ ㄍㄨˋ ㄔㄨㄣˊ)
cholesterol; cholesterin
膽寒(ㄉㄢˇ ㄏㄢˊ)
scared; to lose one's nerve
膽怯(ㄉㄢˇ ㄑㄧㄝˋ)
frightened; afraid; faint-hearted
膽小(ㄉㄢˇ ㄒㄧㄠˇ)
timid; cowardly
膽小鬼(ㄉㄢˇ ㄒㄧㄠˇ ㄍㄨㄟˇ)
a coward: 沒有人願意被認爲是膽小鬼。No one wants to be thought a coward.
膽小如鼠(ㄉㄢˇ ㄒㄧㄠˇ ㄖㄨˊ ㄕㄨˇ)
as scared as a mouse; as timid as a mouse: 她膽小如鼠。She is as timid as a mouse.
膽虛(ㄉㄢˇ ㄒㄩ)
nervous; jittery; scared
膽汁(ㄉㄢˇ ㄓ)
bile
膽汁質(ㄉㄢˇ ㄓ ㄓˋ) or 膽液質(ㄉㄢˇ ㄧㄝˋ ㄓˋ)
choleric temperament
膽戰心驚(ㄉㄢˇ ㄓㄢˋ ㄒㄧㄣ ㄐㄧㄥ)
scared and jittery; nervous and jumpy; to tremble with fear
膽壯(ㄉㄢˇ ㄓㄨㄤˋ)
to be full of courage; fearless
膽石(ㄉㄢˇ ㄕˊ) or 膽石症(ㄉㄢˇ ㄕˊ ㄓㄥˋ)
a gallstone
膽識(ㄉㄢˇ ㄕˋ)
courage and wisdom
膽子(ㄉㄢˇ ·ㄗ) or 膽兒(ㄉㄚˇㄦ)
courage; bravery; audacity; nerve

【膾】 4737 ㄎㄨㄞˋ kuay kuài
minced meat
膾炙(ㄎㄨㄞˋ ㄓˋ)
minced and roasted—very tasty
膾炙人口(ㄎㄨㄞˋ ㄓˋ ㄖㄣˊ ㄎㄡˇ)
(said of interesting things, good writings, etc.) to be on everybody's lips; to be talked about by everyone: 他的英勇事蹟膾炙人口。His heroic deeds are on everybody's lips.

【膺】 4738 ㄧㄥ ing yīng
1. the breast of a person
2. (now rarely) a belt across the breast of a horse
3. to receive; to be given (a responsibility, etc.); to undertake; to shoulder; to bear; to sustain
4. (now rarely) to punish (the enemy, etc.) by war
膺期(ㄧㄥ ㄑㄧˊ)
to receive or inherit (a title, the throne, etc.)
膺選(ㄧㄥ ㄒㄩㄢˇ)
to be elected
膺任(ㄧㄥ ㄖㄣˋ)
to be appointed to or given (an office, etc.)

【臀】 4739 ㄊㄨㄣˊ twen tún
1. the buttocks; the behind; the bottom; the rump
2. (now rarely) the bottom of a ware or vessel
臀部(ㄊㄨㄣˊ ㄅㄨˋ)
the buttocks; the bottom; the rump

【臂】 4740 ㄅㄧˋ bih bì (又讀 ㄅㄟˋ bey bèi)
the arms (of a human being or a tool, machine, etc.)
臂膊(ㄅㄧˋ ㄅㄛˊ)
the two arms (of a person)
臂膀(ㄅㄧˋ ㄅㄤˇ)
the arm (usually indicating the upper arm and part of the shoulder)
臂環(ㄅㄧˋ ㄏㄨㄢˊ)
bracelets
臂節(ㄅㄧˋ ㄐㄧㄝˊ)
the elbow (of a piece of machinery)
臂章(ㄅㄧˋ ㄓㄤ)
an arm badge; a brassard: 軍人通常帶著臂章。Soldiers usually have arm badges on.
臂助(ㄅㄧˋ ㄓㄨˋ)
a helping hand; help

【臃】 4741 ㄩㄥˇ yeong yǒng (又讀 ㄩㄥ iong yōng)
1. to swell; a swelling
2. fat and clumsy
臃腫(ㄩㄥˇ ㄓㄨㄥˇ)
fat and clumsy

【臆】 4742 ㄧˋ yih yì

1. one's breast, heart, thoughts, etc.
2. one's personal views or feelings

臆度(ㄧˋ ㄉㄨㄛˋ) or 臆測(ㄧˋ ㄘㄜˋ)
to guess or conjecture; speculation

臆斷(ㄧˋ ㄉㄨㄢˋ)
to draw a conclusion from conjecture; an arbitrary judgment

臆說(ㄧˋ ㄕㄨㄛ)
one's personal assumption or conjecture; a hypothesis

臆造(ㄧˋ ㄗㄠˋ)
to fabricate (a story, reason, etc.); to concoct; to make up

【臉】 4743 ㄌㄧㄢˇ lean liǎn

the face (used both in its physical and figurative senses)

臉盤子(ㄌㄧㄢˇ ㄆㄢˊ ·ㄗ) or 臉盤兒(ㄌㄧㄢˇ ㄆㄚˊㄦ)
the shape of one's face; a facial configuration 亦作「臉龐」

臉盆(ㄌㄧㄢˇ ㄆㄣˊ)
a washing basin

臉皮(ㄌㄧㄢˇ ㄆㄧˊ)
the cheek; one's face (in its figurative sense)

臉皮薄(ㄌㄧㄢˇ ㄆㄧˊ ㄅㄠˊ)
very sensitive; easily getting embarrassed or bashful

臉皮厚(ㄌㄧㄢˇ ㄆㄧˊ ㄏㄡˋ)
thick-skinned; brazen; shameless

臉譜(ㄌㄧㄢˇ ㄆㄨˇ)
(Chinese opera) face paintings indicating the personality, dispositions, etc. of the characters

臉面(ㄌㄧㄢˇ ㄇㄧㄢˋ)
face—(figuratively) sake

臉大(ㄌㄧㄢˇ ㄉㄚˋ)
①a big face—rather influential ②(usually said of women) unabashed

臉蛋兒(ㄌㄧㄢˇ ㄉㄚˋㄦ) or 臉蛋子(ㄌㄧㄢˇ ㄉㄢˋ ·ㄗ)
the shape of a woman's face

臉嫩(ㄌㄧㄢˇ ㄋㄣˋ)
bashful; shy; timid

臉孔(ㄌㄧㄢˇ ㄎㄨㄥˇ)
the face: 這次聚會我看到幾張新臉孔。I saw some new faces at the party.

臉憨皮厚(ㄌㄧㄢˇ ㄏㄢ ㄆㄧˊ ㄏㄡˋ)
brazen; shameless

臉紅(ㄌㄧㄢˇ ㄏㄨㄥˊ)
blushing because of embarrassment, anger or shame; a blush; to blush

臉紅脖子粗(ㄌㄧㄢˇ ㄏㄨㄥˊ ㄅㄛˊ·ㄗ ㄘㄨ)
furious; mad

臉頰(ㄌㄧㄢˇ ㄐㄧㄚˊ)
cheeks

臉上(ㄌㄧㄢˇ ·ㄕㄤ)
①in (or on) the face: 陽光直射在我們的臉上。The sun was shining in our faces. ②face (in its figurative sense)

臉水(ㄌㄧㄢˇ ㄕㄨㄟˇ)
water for washing one's face

臉軟(ㄌㄧㄢˇ ㄖㄨㄢˇ)
kindhearted; good-natured; unable to hurt others' feelings

臉色(ㄌㄧㄢˇ ㄙㄜˋ)
① facial expression ② a complexion

臉硬(ㄌㄧㄢˇ ㄧㄥˋ)
flinty; devoid of emotion or compassion; ruthless

【臊】 4744 1. ㄙㄠ sau sāo

a bad odor or smell, as that of decaying fish, meat, fox, sheep, etc.

臊韃子(ㄙㄠ ㄉㄚˊ ·ㄗ)
(an abusive expression for) Mongols

臊根(ㄙㄠ ㄍㄣ)
the penis

臊氣(ㄙㄠ ㄑㄧˋ)
a bad odor or smell; a stench

臊聲(ㄙㄠ ㄕㄥ) or 臊聞(ㄙㄠ ㄨㄣˊ)
notoriety; a scandalous reputation

【臊】 4744 2. ㄙㄠˋ saw sào

1. ashamed; bashful
2. minced meat

臊得慌(ㄙㄠˋ ·ㄉㄜ ·ㄏㄨㄤ)
very much ashamed

【臌】 4745 ㄍㄨˇ guu gǔ

to expand; to swell; swollen

臌脹(ㄍㄨˇ ㄓㄤˋ)
① expansion; to expand; to swell ② dropsy; edema

【賸】 4746 (剩) ㄕㄥˋ shenq shèng

See "賸 5805" under the radical "貝".

【膻】 4747 (羶) ㄕㄢ shan shān

the bad odor of sheep, deer, etc.

十四畫

【臏】 4748 (髕) ㄅㄧㄣˋ binn bìn

1. the kneecap
2. the punishment of removing kneecaps in ancient times

臏骨(ㄅㄧㄣˋ ㄍㄨˇ)
the kneecap

【臍】 4749 ㄑㄧˊ chyi qí

1. the navel; the umbilicus
2. the underside of a crab

臍帶(ㄑㄧˊ ㄉㄞˋ)
the umbilical cord: 臍帶未脫。The umbilical cord is still on.

十五畫

【臘】 4750 ㄌㄚˋ lah là

1. sacrifice at the end of the lunar year
2. the end of the lunar year
3. salted and smoked meat, fish, chicken, etc.
4. the age of a Buddhist monk

臘八(ㄌㄚˋ ㄅㄚ) or 臘八日(ㄌㄚˋ ㄅㄚ ㄖˋ)
the 8th day of the 12th moon in the lunar calendar when Buddha found the truth of life

臘八米(ㄌㄚˋ ㄅㄚ ㄇㄧˇ)
glutinous rice, mixed grains and cereals and dried fruit for cooking 臘八粥

臘八粥(ㄌㄚˋ ㄅㄚ ㄓㄡ)
congee or porridge of glutinous rice, mixed grains and cereals and dried fruit, eaten on the 8th day of the 12th moon, originally in memory of the Buddhist Festival

臘梅(ㄌㄚˋ ㄇㄟˊ)
plum flowers

臘丁(ㄌㄚˋ ㄉㄧㄥ)

Latin 亦作「拉丁」

臘鼓(ㄌㄚˋ ㄍㄨˇ)
drumbeat on the eighth day of the twelfth month by the ancient calendar (for driving off devils causing pestilence)

臘祭(ㄌㄚˋ ㄐㄧˋ)
the ancient winter sacrificial ceremony held three days after the winter solstice(冬至)

臘盡冬殘(ㄌㄚˋ ㄐㄧㄣˋ ㄉㄨㄥ ㄘㄢˊ)
The (lunar) year and the winter are ending.

臘腸(ㄌㄚˋ ㄔㄤˊ)
Chinese sausage made by stuffing salted meat, liver, etc. in casings

臘腸狗(ㄌㄚˋ ㄔㄤˊ ㄍㄡˇ)
a dachshund

臘戍(ㄌㄚˋ ㄕㄨˋ)
Lashio (a town in Nothern Burma, the southwestern terminus of the Burma Road)

臘肉(ㄌㄚˋ ㄖㄡˋ)
salted and dried meat

臘鴨(ㄌㄚˋ ㄧㄚ)
salted and dried duck

臘味(ㄌㄚˋ ㄨㄟˋ)
preserved meat; cured meat, fish, etc.

臘味飯(ㄌㄚˋ ㄨㄟˋ ㄈㄢˋ)
a Cantonese dish consisting of steamed rice and salted meat, sausage, etc.

臘魚(ㄌㄚˋ ㄩˊ)
salted and dried fish

臘月(ㄌㄚˋ ㄩㄝˋ)
the 12th moon of the lunar year

【臕】 4751 (膘) ㄅㄧㄠ biau biāo
fat

十六畫

【臚】 4752 ㄌㄨˊ lu lú
1. to display; to exhibit; to arrange in order
2. the belly
3. the skin
4. to forward; to convey; to announce

臚列(ㄌㄨˊ ㄌㄧㄝˋ)
to display; to arrange in order for exhibit

臚歡(ㄌㄨˊ ㄏㄨㄢ)
to convey one's pleasure; to express one's joy

臚情(ㄌㄨˊ ㄑㄧㄥˊ)
to state one's case, situation, predicament; to report on such

【臙】 4753 (胭) ㄧㄢ ian yān
rouge, face powder or cosmetics

十七畫

【臝】 4754 (裸) ㄌㄨㄛˇ luoo luǒ
to bare; nude

十八畫

【臟】 4755 ㄗㄤˋ tzanq zàng
a general name of all the internal organs in the chest and abdomen; the viscera

臟腑(ㄗㄤˋ ㄈㄨˇ)
① viscera; entrails ② one's integrity, aspirations, etc.

十九畫

【臠】 4756 ㄌㄨㄢˊ luan luán
1. meat chops or cuts
2. lean; thin

【臢】 4757 ㄗㄤ tzang zāng (又讀 ㄗㄚ tza zā)
dirty; filthy

【臡】 4758 ㄋㄧˊ ni ní
pickled, minced meat

臣 部
ㄔㄣˊ chern chén

【臣】 4759 ㄔㄣˊ chern chén
1. a subject; a vassal
2. to subjugate; to conquer
3. a term for "I" used by officials when addressing the king or emperor
4. (in ancient China) a polite term for "I"
5. a minister; an official; a statesman

臣僕(ㄔㄣˊ ㄆㄨˊ)
officials (who serve the king or nation) and servants (who serve the household)

臣民(ㄔㄣˊ ㄇㄧㄣˊ)
subjects of a kingdom; subjects of a feudal ruler

臣服(ㄔㄣˊ ㄈㄨˊ)
① to be subjugated or conquered; to be made a subject ② to serve a king or emperor as his minister

臣孽(ㄔㄣˊ ㄋㄧㄝˋ)
(in ancient China) a self-reference of a prince born by an imperial concubine in speaking to the monarch

臣僚(ㄔㄣˊ ㄌㄧㄠˊ)
officials in a kingdom or monarchy

臣工(ㄔㄣˊ ㄍㄨㄥ)
ministers and officials

臣妾(ㄔㄣˊ ㄑㄧㄝˋ)
slaves; concubines; humble people; female attendants

臣下(ㄔㄣˊ ㄒㄧㄚˋ)
① a term for "I" used by an official when addressing a king or emperor ② ministers

臣事(ㄔㄣˊ ㄕˋ)
to serve a ruler as his minister

臣庶(ㄔㄣˊ ㄕㄨˋ)
subjects

臣子(ㄔㄣˊ ㄗˇ)
a minister of state; officials in ancient China

臣一主二(ㄔㄣˊ ㄧ ㄓㄨˇ ㄦˋ)
One has the right of choosing the ruler he serves.

一畫

【匠】 4760 (頤) ㄧˊ yi yí
the cheeks

二畫

【臥】 4761 ㄨㄛˋ woh wò
1. to lie down; to rest; to sleep

2. to lay or place across; to lie across

臥冰(ㄨㄛˋ ㄅㄧㄥ)
to lie on ice (in order to melt it and catch fish to feed one's parents)—the highest show of filial piety

臥病(ㄨㄛˋ ㄅㄧㄥˋ)
bedridden on account of illness

臥鋪(ㄨㄛˋ ㄆㄨˋ)
a sleeping berth on a train or ship

臥佛(ㄨㄛˋ ㄈㄛˊ)
a statue of Buddha in a lying position

臥房(ㄨㄛˋ ㄈㄤˊ)or 臥屋(ㄨㄛˋ ㄨ)
a bedroom

臥倒(ㄨㄛˋ ㄉㄠˇ)
to lie down (on the ground to escape enemy fire or detection)

臥底(ㄨㄛˋ ㄉㄧˇ)
(said of thieves, etc.) to act from inside, or do an inside job; to act as a stool pigeon

臥榻(ㄨㄛˋ ㄊㄚˋ)or 臥牀(ㄨㄛˋ ㄔㄨㄤˊ)
a bed

臥內(ㄨㄛˋ ㄋㄟˋ)
a bedroom

臥龍(ㄨㄛˋ ㄌㄨㄥˊ)
the sleeping dragon—a remarkable talent who has not been discovered

臥龍岡(ㄨㄛˋ ㄌㄨㄥˊ ㄍㄤ)
the Sleeping Dragon Hill, in Honan Province—where Chu-Ko Kung-ming (諸葛孔明), a brilliant military strategist in the Epoch of the Three Kingdoms, was supposed to have lived before he was recruited by Liu Pei (劉備), the ruler of Shu(蜀)

臥軌自殺(ㄨㄛˋ ㄍㄨㄟˇ ㄗˋ ㄕㄚ)
to commit suicide by throwing oneself on a railroad

臥虎(ㄨㄛˋ ㄏㄨˇ)
①a severe law-enforcing official ②a tyrannical official ③the awe inspired by a high government official ④a brave general

臥具(ㄨㄛˋ ㄐㄩˋ)
bedding

臥起(ㄨㄛˋ ㄑㄧˇ)
to sleep and get up—things pertaining to daily life

臥薪嘗膽(ㄨㄛˋ ㄒㄧㄣ ㄔㄤˊ ㄉㄢˇ)
(literally) to lie on faggots and taste gall—to goad oneself ahead by depriving oneself of all daily comforts and subjecting oneself to life's bitterness (a reference to Kou Chien(勾踐) when he was nursing vengeance)

臥雪(ㄨㄛˋ ㄒㄩㄝˇ)
(literally) to stay at home without bothering others when it snows heavily—the behavior of a man of integrity and superiority

臥治(ㄨㄛˋ ㄓˋ)
to govern without interfering with the people

臥車(ㄨㄛˋ ㄔㄜ)
a railway sleeping car, or sleeper

臥床(ㄨㄛˋ ㄔㄨㄤˊ)
to lie in bed

臥室(ㄨㄛˋ ㄕˋ)
a bedroom

臥姿(ㄨㄛˋ ㄗ)
a prone position; a lying position

臥遊(ㄨㄛˋ ㄧㄡˊ)
to make a vicarious sightseeing tour by viewing landscape paintings or by reading travelogues, etc.

臥雲(ㄨㄛˋ ㄩㄣˊ)
to make clouds one's bed—the life of a hermit

八畫

【臧】 4762
ㄗㄤ tzang zāng
1. good; right; generous
2. a slave; a servant
3. stolen goods or loots 亦作「贓」
4. a Chinese family name

臧否(ㄗㄤ ㄆㄧˇ)
①right or wrong; gain or loss ②to evaluate; to criticize; to pass judgment

臧獲(ㄗㄤ ㄏㄨㄛˋ)
slaves

十一畫

【臨】 4763
ㄌㄧㄣˊ lin lín
1. to look down from above—preside over
2. to approach; to descend; to come to; to reach; to visit: 聖誕節即將來臨。Christmas is approaching.
3. on the point of; near to; during; at; whilst; while
4. to copy; to imitate
5. temporary; provisional
6. a Chinese family name

臨別(ㄌㄧㄣˊ ㄅㄧㄝˊ)
at the time of parting; on departure: 她在臨別時哭了。She cried at the time of parting.

臨別贈言(ㄌㄧㄣˊ ㄅㄧㄝˊ ㄗㄥˋ ㄧㄢˊ)
advice given by one just before parting

臨盆(ㄌㄧㄣˊ ㄆㄣˊ)
parturition; childbirth

臨摹(ㄌㄧㄣˊ ㄇㄛˊ)
to copy or imitate (paintings or calligraphy)

臨命(ㄌㄧㄣˊ ㄇㄧㄥˋ)
on the point of breathing one's last; before death

臨到(ㄌㄧㄣˊ ㄉㄠˋ)
to approach; to come to; to reach; to happen to

臨頭(ㄌㄧㄣˊ ㄊㄡˊ)
(said of disasters) descending; imminent; hovering over the head: 大難臨頭。A great calamity is imminent.

臨帖(ㄌㄧㄣˊ ㄊㄧㄝˋ)
to copy or imitate calligraphy as a way of practice

臨眺(ㄌㄧㄣˊ ㄊㄧㄠˋ)
to view from a high point

臨難(ㄌㄧㄣˊ ㄋㄢˋ)
beset by disasters or troubles; at difficult times

臨年(ㄌㄧㄣˊ ㄋㄧㄢˊ)
at an advanced age

臨了(ㄌㄧㄣˊ ㄌㄧㄠˇ)or 臨了兒(ㄌㄧㄣˊ ㄌㄧㄠˇㄦ)
in the end; at last

臨渴掘井(ㄌㄧㄣˊ ㄎㄜˇ ㄐㄩㄝˊ ㄐㄧㄥˇ)
(literally) to dig a well when one feels thirsty—to do something too late and without preparations; to make no timely preparations

臨畫(ㄌㄧㄣˊ ㄏㄨㄚˋ)
to copy a painting

臨機應變(ㄌㄧㄣˊ ㄐㄧ ㄧㄥˋ ㄅㄧㄢˋ)

to make changes or adjustments as the situation demands; to act according to what the circumstances dictate

〔臣部〕

臨急(ㄌㄧㄣˊ ㄐㄧˊ)
in time of emergency
臨街(ㄌㄧㄣˊ ㄐㄧㄝ)
facing the street
臨界點(ㄌㄧㄣˊ ㄐㄧㄝˋ ㄉㄧㄢˇ)
(physics) a critical point
臨界角(ㄌㄧㄣˊ ㄐㄧㄝˋ ㄐㄧㄠˇ)
(physics) a critical angle
臨界溫度(ㄌㄧㄣˊ ㄐㄧㄝˋ ㄨㄣ ㄉㄨˋ)
(physics) critical temperature
臨近(ㄌㄧㄣˊ ㄐㄧㄣˋ)
close by; close to; close on
臨期(ㄌㄧㄣˊ ㄑㄧˊ)
to come to the moment; to approach the right time; to mature: 期票本日臨期。The bill matures today.
臨歧(ㄌㄧㄣˊ ㄑㄧˊ)
to accompany another to where the road branches out
臨去秋波(ㄌㄧㄣˊ ㄑㄩˋ ㄑㄧㄡ ㄅㄛ)
(literally) to cast a bewitching look on departing—a parting favor; to give others something to remember by before parting
臨行(ㄌㄧㄣˊ ㄒㄧㄥˊ) or 臨走(ㄌㄧㄣˊ ㄗㄡˇ)
on the point of departure; just before parting
臨幸(ㄌㄧㄣˊ ㄒㄧㄥˋ)
a personal visit by the emperor (regarded as a great honor)
臨軒(ㄌㄧㄣˊ ㄒㄩㄢ)
when the emperor was not taking his seat on the throne
臨陣磨鎗 or 臨陣磨槍(ㄌㄧㄣˊ ㄓㄣˋ ㄇㄛˊ ㄑㄧㄤ)
(literally) to grind the spear just before battle—to make preparations at the last moment
臨陣脫逃(ㄌㄧㄣˊ ㄓㄣˋ ㄊㄨㄛ ㄊㄠˊ)
to escape just before engaging the enemy; to absent oneself when one's presence counts
臨終(ㄌㄧㄣˊ ㄓㄨㄥ) or 臨死(ㄌㄧㄣˊ ㄙˇ)
at one's deathbed; just before dying; about to breathe one's last
臨池(ㄌㄧㄣˊ ㄔˊ)
to diligently practice calligraphy (a reference to Wang Hsi-chih (王羲之), China's greatest calligrapher who was said to have blackened the water in a pond in practicing calligraphy)
臨朝(ㄌㄧㄣˊ ㄔㄠˊ)
① to sit on the throne and govern the nation ② (said of an empress dowager) to govern the nation as regent
臨產(ㄌㄧㄣˊ ㄔㄢˇ)
in childbirth; about to give birth to a child
臨牀(ㄌㄧㄣˊ ㄔㄨㄤˊ)
clinical
臨牀經驗(ㄌㄧㄣˊ ㄔㄨㄤˊ ㄐㄧㄥ ㄧㄢˋ)
clinical experience: 他有豐富的臨牀經驗。He has rich clinical experience.
臨時(ㄌㄧㄣˊ ㄕˊ)
for the time being; temporary; provisional
臨時抱佛脚(ㄌㄧㄣˊ ㄕˊ ㄅㄠˋ ㄈㄛˊ ㄐㄧㄠˇ)
(literally) to embrace Buddha's feet and pray for help in time of emergency—to do something too late and without preparation
臨時大總統(ㄌㄧㄣˊ ㄕˊ ㄉㄚˋ ㄗㄨㄥˇ ㄊㄨㄥˇ)
the president of a provisional government; a provisional president
臨時代辦(ㄌㄧㄣˊ ㄕˊ ㄉㄞˋ ㄅㄢˋ)
chargé d'affaires ad interim
臨時動議(ㄌㄧㄣˊ ㄕˊ ㄉㄨㄥˋ ㄧˋ)
an extraordinary motion
臨時工(ㄌㄧㄣˊ ㄕˊ ㄍㄨㄥ)
a short-term worker; a rush-season worker; an odd-job worker
臨時會(ㄌㄧㄣˊ ㄕˊ ㄏㄨㄟˋ)
an extraordinary meeting; an unscheduled meeting: 俱樂部召開一次臨時會。The club held an unscheduled meeting.
臨時執照(ㄌㄧㄣˊ ㄕˊ ㄓˊ ㄓㄠˋ)
a temporary or provisional license
臨時執政(ㄌㄧㄣˊ ㄕˊ ㄓˊ ㄓㄥˋ)
to govern (the nation) provisionally; a provisional government
臨時政府(ㄌㄧㄣˊ ㄕˊ ㄓㄥˋ ㄈㄨˇ)
a provisional government
臨時事故(ㄌㄧㄣˊ ㄕˊ ㄕˋ ㄍㄨˋ)
an unforeseen matter; an incident; an accident: 這是一樁臨時事故。It was quite an accident.
臨時議會(ㄌㄧㄣˊ ㄕˊ ㄧˋ ㄏㄨㄟˋ)
a provisional assembly
臨時演員(ㄌㄧㄣˊ ㄕˊ ㄧㄢˇ ㄩㄢˊ)
an extra
臨時約法(ㄌㄧㄣˊ ㄕˊ ㄩㄝ ㄈㄚˇ)
the provisional constitution of the Republic of China in the early years of the Republic
臨視(ㄌㄧㄣˊ ㄕˋ)
(usually said of a bigwig) to investigate something in person; to inspect
臨深履薄(ㄌㄧㄣˊ ㄕㄣ ㄌㄩˇ ㄅㄛˊ)
wading in deep water and treading on thin ice—very cautious or careful
臨睡(ㄌㄧㄣˊ ㄕㄨㄟˋ)
before sleep
臨蓐(ㄌㄧㄣˊ ㄖㄨˋ)
in childbirth; childbirth; lying-in: 她在臨蓐時神經緊張。She got nervous in childbirth.
臨財毋苟得，臨難毋苟免
(ㄌㄧㄣˊ ㄘㄞˊ ㄨˊ ㄍㄡˇ ㄉㄜˊ, ㄌㄧㄣˊ ㄋㄢˋ ㄨˊ ㄍㄡˇ ㄇㄧㄢˇ)
Don't be unscrupulous in money matters; don't shrink in face of disaster. (from the *Book of Rites*)
臨安(ㄌㄧㄣˊ ㄢ)
old name of Hangchow (杭州), capital of the Southern Sung Dynasty
臨崖勒馬(ㄌㄧㄣˊ ㄧㄞˊ ㄌㄜˋ ㄇㄚˇ)
(literally) to rein in the horse at the edge of a cliff—to practice self-restraint at a crucial moment
臨危(ㄌㄧㄣˊ ㄨㄟˊ)
① in face of great danger or emergency ② at one's deathbed; just before dying
臨危授命(ㄌㄧㄣˊ ㄨㄟˊ ㄕㄡˋ ㄇㄧㄥˋ)
to give a very important assignment in time of a national emergency
臨文(ㄌㄧㄣˊ ㄨㄣˊ)

when one is writing or composing (an article, etc.): 他在臨文時常抽煙。He used to smoke when he was writing.

臨問(ㄌㄧㄣˊ ㄨㄣˋ)
(said of a dignitary) to visit, cheer up or comfort in person

臨月(ㄌㄧㄣˊ ㄩㄝˋ)
the month when the childbirth is due

臨淵羨魚(ㄌㄧㄣˊ ㄩㄢ ㄒㄧㄢˋ ㄩˊ)
(literally) to covet the fish by merely staring into the water—to envy the store of great wealth (but never plan a way to get it)

自 部
ㄗˋ tzyh zì

【自】 4764 ㄗˋ tzyh zì

1. self; personal; private; in person; personally
2. from
3. natural; naturally
4. a Chinese family name

自拔(ㄗˋ ㄅㄚˊ)
to free oneself (from pain or evildoing); to extricate oneself

自白(ㄗˋ ㄅㄞˊ)or(ㄗˋ ㄅㄛˊ)
confession; to make a personal statement

自白書(ㄗˋ ㄅㄞˊ ㄕㄨ)
an affidavit; a written confession

自卑(ㄗˋ ㄅㄟ)
to slight oneself; to despise oneself; to underestimate oneself

自卑感(ㄗˋ ㄅㄟ ㄍㄢˇ)or **自卑情結**(ㄗˋ ㄅㄟ ㄑㄧㄥˊ ㄐㄧㄝˊ)
inferiority complex; a sense of inferiority

自備(ㄗˋ ㄅㄟˋ)
self-provided; to provide oneself

自暴自棄(ㄗˋ ㄅㄠˋ ㄗˋ ㄑㄧˋ)
to abandon oneself to a dissipated life; to have no ambition at all

自本自力(ㄗˋ ㄅㄣˇ ㄗˋ ㄌㄧˋ)
with one's own capital and effort; to do something alone

自必(ㄗˋ ㄅㄧˋ)
naturally; unavoidably; certainly; surely: 我們的球隊自必獲勝。Certainly our team will win the game.

自斃(ㄗˋ ㄅㄧˋ)
to destroy oneself; self-destruction

自閉症(ㄗˋ ㄅㄧˋ ㄓㄥˋ)
(psychiatry) autism

自便(ㄗˋ ㄅㄧㄢˋ)
as one wishes: 聽其自便。Let her do as she wishes.

自不量力(ㄗˋ ㄅㄨˋ ㄌㄧㄤˋ ㄌㄧˋ)
not to recognize one's own limited strength or resources; to do something beyond one's ability

自賣自誇(ㄗˋ ㄇㄞˋ ㄗˋ ㄎㄨㄚ)
to praise the goods one sells; to blow one's own trumpet

自滿(ㄗˋ ㄇㄢˇ)
complacency; to be sátisfied with oneself

自民黨(ㄗˋ ㄇㄧㄣˊ ㄉㄤˇ)
Liberal Democratic Party in Japan

自鳴得意(ㄗˋ ㄇㄧㄥˊ ㄉㄜˊ ㄧˋ)
to be very much pleased with what one has done or what one has achieved; smug

自鳴清高(ㄗˋ ㄇㄧㄥˊ ㄑㄧㄥ ㄍㄠ)
to consider oneself morally superior to others; to look down on all others as vulgar or dishonest

自鳴鐘(ㄗˋ ㄇㄧㄥˊ ㄓㄨㄥ)
a striking clock

自命不凡(ㄗˋ ㄇㄧㄥˋ ㄅㄨˋ ㄈㄢˊ)
conceited; to have a very high opinion of oneself

自發(ㄗˋ ㄈㄚ)
to work without being prodded; to take the initiative; spontaneous

自伐(ㄗˋ ㄈㄚˊ)
① to abuse oneself ② to be conceited

自肥(ㄗˋ ㄈㄟˊ)
to fatten oneself; to enrich oneself

自費(ㄗˋ ㄈㄟˋ)
to pay one's own expenses; self-provided: 他這次是自費旅行。This time he traveled at his own expense.

自反(ㄗˋ ㄈㄢˇ)
to introspect; introspection; to examine one's own conduct; self-examination

自焚(ㄗˋ ㄈㄣˊ)
to burn oneself to death—self-immolation

自分(ㄗˋ ㄈㄣˋ)
to anticipate; to think or believe; to figure

自封(ㄗˋ ㄈㄥ)
① to be conservative ② to enrich oneself without regard for others

自奉(ㄗˋ ㄈㄥˋ)
to treat oneself (especially in material matter as food, etc.)

自負(ㄗˋ ㄈㄨˋ)
to have a very high opinion of oneself; conceited: 他極其自負。He's full of conceit.

自負盈虧(ㄗˋ ㄈㄨˋ ㄧㄥˊ ㄎㄨㄟ)
(said of an enterprise) to assume sole responsibility for its profits or losses

自達達人(ㄗˋ ㄉㄚˊ ㄉㄚˊ ㄖㄣˊ)
One must be enlightened oneself before one can enlighten others.

自大(ㄗˋ ㄉㄚˋ)
conceited; egomaniacal; egotistic

自得(ㄗˋ ㄉㄜˊ)
① conceited; complacent; to feel satisfied with oneself ② to find joy in one's life

自得其樂(ㄗˋ ㄉㄜˊ ㄑㄧˊ ㄌㄜˋ)
to find joy in one's own way (no matter what others may think)

自蹈法網(ㄗˋ ㄉㄠˋ ㄈㄚˇ ㄨㄤˇ)
to break the law out of free will

自當(ㄗˋ ㄉㄤ)
should naturally: 兒童自當服從他們的父母。Children should naturally obey their parents.

自頂至踵(ㄗˋ ㄉㄧㄥˇ ㄓˋ ㄓㄨㄥˇ)
from head to foot

自瀆(ㄗˋ ㄉㄨˊ)
self-abuse; masturbation

〔自部〕

自度曲(ㄗˋ ㄉㄨˋ ㄑㄩˇ)
a self-composed musical piece; a musical composition which does not follow the old rules or scores

自動(ㄗˋ ㄉㄨㄥˋ)
① voluntary; of one's own free will ② automatic

自動步槍(ㄗˋ ㄉㄨㄥˋ ㄅㄨˋ ㄑㄧㄤ)
an automatic rifle

自動販賣機(ㄗˋ ㄉㄨㄥˋ ㄈㄢˋ ㄇㄞˋ ㄐㄧ)
a vending machine: 她從自動販賣機買了一罐可口可樂。She bought a can of Coca-Cola from a vending machine.

自動電話(ㄗˋ ㄉㄨㄥˋ ㄉㄧㄢˋ ㄏㄨㄚˋ)
a dial telephone; an automatic telephone

自動電信機(ㄗˋ ㄉㄨㄥˋ ㄉㄧㄢˋ ㄒㄧㄣˋ ㄐㄧ)
an autokinetic telegraph

自動提款機(ㄗˋ ㄉㄨㄥˋ ㄊㄧˊ ㄎㄨㄢˇ ㄐㄧ)
a cashomat 參看「自動櫃員機」

自動櫃員機(ㄗˋ ㄉㄨㄥˋ ㄍㄨㄟˋ ㄩㄢˊ ㄐㄧ)
an automated-teller machine

自動開關(ㄗˋ ㄉㄨㄥˋ ㄎㄞ ㄍㄨㄢ)
an automatic switch

自動化(ㄗˋ ㄉㄨㄥˋ ㄏㄨㄚˋ)
automation; to automate

自動檢波器(ㄗˋ ㄉㄨㄥˋ ㄐㄧㄢˇ ㄅㄛ ㄑㄧˋ)
an autocoherer

自動鉛筆(ㄗˋ ㄉㄨㄥˋ ㄑㄧㄢ ㄅㄧˇ)
a mechanical pencil

自動車(ㄗˋ ㄉㄨㄥˋ ㄔㄜ)
automotive vehicles

自動售貨機(ㄗˋ ㄉㄨㄥˋ ㄕㄡˋ ㄏㄨㄛˋ ㄐㄧ)
a vending machine

自討沒趣(ㄗˋ ㄊㄠˇ ㄇㄟˊ ㄑㄩˋ)
"You ask for it!"—to get an insult unnecessarily

自討苦吃(ㄗˋ ㄊㄠˇ ㄎㄨˇ ㄔ)
to ask for trouble

自投羅網(ㄗˋ ㄊㄡˊ ㄌㄨㄛˊ ㄨㄤˇ)
to walk right into a trap

自歎(ㄗˋ ㄊㄢˋ)
to pity oneself; to regret; to sigh to oneself

自歎不如(ㄗˋ ㄊㄢˋ ㄅㄨˋ ㄖㄨˊ)
to admit with regret that one is not as good; to concede that the other fellow is better qualified

自餒(ㄗˋ ㄋㄟˇ)
to hold defeatist views; to think that one cannot do the job without even trying; to lack confidence: 怯懦者自餒。A coward lacks confidence.

自拉自唱(ㄗˋ ㄌㄚ ㄗˋ ㄔㄤˋ)
(literally) to sing while playing the two-stringed violin as an accompaniment all by oneself—①to praise one's own effort or achievement ② to do something all by oneself

自來火(ㄗˋ ㄌㄞˊ ㄏㄨㄛˇ)
①a safety match ② a gaslight ③ a cigarette lighter

自來水(ㄗˋ ㄌㄞˊ ㄕㄨㄟˇ)
running water; tap water

自來水筆(ㄗˋ ㄌㄞˊ ㄕㄨㄟˇ ㄅㄧˇ)
a fountain pen

自來水錶(ㄗˋ ㄌㄞˊ ㄕㄨㄟˇ ㄅㄧㄠˇ)
a water meter

自來水龍頭(ㄗˋ ㄌㄞˊ ㄕㄨㄟˇ ㄌㄨㄥˊ ㄊㄡˊ)
a faucet

自來水管(ㄗˋ ㄌㄞˊ ㄕㄨㄟˇ ㄍㄨㄢˇ)
water pipes

自來水廠(ㄗˋ ㄌㄞˊ ㄕㄨㄟˇ ㄔㄤˇ)
a waterworks

自立(ㄗˋ ㄌㄧˋ)
independent; self-supporting

自立門戶(ㄗˋ ㄌㄧˋ ㄇㄣˊ ㄏㄨˋ)
to establish one's own school of thought or clique

自利(ㄗˋ ㄌㄧˋ)
① to think of nothing but one's own gain ② (Buddhism) *atmahitam*, self-profit; beneficial to oneself

自力更生(ㄗˋ ㄌㄧˋ ㄍㄥ ㄕㄥ)
to achieve self-renewal with one's own effort; self-reliance

自力救濟(ㄗˋ ㄌㄧˋ ㄐㄧㄡˋ ㄐㄧˋ)
to redress a perceived wrong by taking the law into one's own hands

自了(ㄗˋ ㄌㄧㄠˇ)
to be able to conclude or complete something all by oneself

自了漢(ㄗˋ ㄌㄧㄠˇ ㄏㄢˋ)
a selfish person

自料(ㄗˋ ㄌㄧㄠˋ)
to figure; to anticipate; to think or believe

自流井(ㄗˋ ㄌㄧㄡˊ ㄐㄧㄥˇ)
① name of a district of Tzukung(自貢) in Szechwan, a site of more than 4,000 wells of high salt contents ② an artesian well

自戀(ㄗˋ ㄌㄧㄢˋ)
narcissism

自量(ㄗˋ ㄌㄧㄤˋ)
to measure oneself; to have a general idea of one's own abilities or resources; to make a self-assessment

自律(ㄗˋ ㄌㄩˋ)
① to control oneself; to exercise self-restraint or self-control; self-discipline: 她不能自律。She has no control of herself. ②(ethics) autonomy

自個兒(ㄗˋ ㄍㄜˇㄦ)
oneself: 人不應該專爲自個兒而活。One should not live for oneself alone.

自告奮勇(ㄗˋ ㄍㄠˋ ㄈㄣˋ ㄩㄥˇ)
to volunteer

自甘墮落(ㄗˋ ㄍㄢ ㄉㄨㄛˋ ㄌㄨㄛˋ)
to abandon oneself to wanton ways; to indulge in debauchery out of one's own free will

自感應(ㄗˋ ㄍㄢˇ ㄧㄥˋ)
self-induction

自耕農(ㄗˋ ㄍㄥ ㄋㄨㄥˊ)
farmers who till the land they own; owner-farmers

自古及今(ㄗˋ ㄍㄨˇ ㄐㄧˊ ㄐㄧㄣ)
from ancient times till the present; since time immemorial

自古如此(ㄗˋ ㄍㄨˇ ㄖㄨˊ ㄘˇ)
It has been this way since the beginning of time.

自古以來(ㄗˋ ㄍㄨˇ ㄧˇ ㄌㄞˊ)
since ancient times; since time immemorial; down through the ages

自顧不暇(ㄗˋ ㄍㄨˋ ㄅㄨˋ ㄒㄧㄚˊ)
to have trouble even in taking care of oneself

自顧自(ㄗˋ ㄍㄨˋ ㄗˋ)
① selfish ② to mind one's business ③ everyone for himself

自苦(ㄗˋ ㄎㄨˇ)
to look for trouble; to give oneself unnecessary pains

自誇(ㄗˋ ㄎㄨㄚ)
to brag; to boast

自鄶以下(ㄗˋ ㄎㄨㄞˋ ㄧˇ ㄒㄧㄚˋ)
Except so-and-so, none of them was worth a dime. (an

expression used in commenting on historic personalities)

自寬(ㄗˋ ㄎㄨㄢ)
to comfort oneself; self-consolation

自況(ㄗˋ ㄎㄨㄤˋ)
to compare oneself with another person

自豪(ㄗˋ ㄏㄠˊ)
to feel proud of; to pride oneself on; to take pride in

自好(ㄗˋ ㄏㄠˋ)
self-respect; self-esteem

自後(ㄗˋ ㄏㄡˋ)
from now on; henceforth: 我許諾自後不再喝醉。I promise never to get drunk henceforth.

自花受精(ㄗˋ ㄏㄨㄚ ㄕㄡˋ ㄐㄧㄥ)
self-fertilization

自畫像(ㄗˋ ㄏㄨㄚˋ ㄒㄧㄤˋ)
a self-portrait

自毀長城(ㄗˋ ㄏㄨㄟˇ ㄔㄤˊ ㄔㄥˊ)or 自壞長城(ㄗˋ ㄏㄨㄞˋ ㄔㄤˊ ㄔㄥˊ)
to get rid of a capable lieutenant

自己(ㄗˋ ㄐㄧˇ)
self; oneself; one's person: 讓我們為自己乾一杯。Let us drink a toast to ourselves.

自己人(ㄗˋ ㄐㄧˇ ㄖㄣˊ)
persons within the same circle; persons closely related with each other

自給自足(ㄗˋ ㄐㄧˇ ㄗˋ ㄗㄨˊ)
self-sufficient; self-supporting; self-sufficiency: 他們的糧食自給自足。They are self-sufficient in grain.

自家(ㄗˋ ㄐㄧㄚ)
(colloquial) oneself

自家人(ㄗˋ ㄐㄧㄚ ㄖㄣˊ)
persons within the same circle or closely related with each other in some way

自解(ㄗˋ ㄐㄧㄝˇ)
①to explain to oneself; self-explanation ②to extricate oneself (from certain bondage, etc.)

自救(ㄗˋ ㄐㄧㄡˋ)
self-salvation; to rescue oneself (from evil ways): 讓我們團結自救。Let us get united for our own salvation.

自薦(ㄗˋ ㄐㄧㄢˋ)
to introduce or recommend oneself; to volunteer

自今(ㄗˋ ㄐㄧㄣ)
from now on; henceforth: 自今以後他將在另一處工作。From now on he will work in another office.

自矜(ㄗˋ ㄐㄧㄣ)
to brag: 他自矜其財富。He bragged his wealth.

自盡(ㄗˋ ㄐㄧㄣˋ)
to commit suicide; to kill oneself

自經(ㄗˋ ㄐㄧㄥ)
①to hang oneself ②to commit suicide

自剄(ㄗˋ ㄐㄧㄥˇ)
to commit suicide by cutting the throat

自居(ㄗˋ ㄐㄩ)
to consider oneself to be (a genius, VIP, famous figure, etc.)

自決(ㄗˋ ㄐㄩㄝˊ)
to decide or solve (a problem, etc.) by oneself; self-determination

自絕(ㄗˋ ㄐㄩㄝˊ)
①to isolate oneself ②to seek self-destruction

自覺(ㄗˋ ㄐㄩㄝˊ)
①self-consciousness; self-realization ②to feel something concerning oneself; aware

自覺運動(ㄗˋ ㄐㄩㄝˊ ㄩㄣˋ ㄉㄨㄥˋ)
a self-renewal movement; a drive to promote dedication to the nation

自掘墳墓(ㄗˋ ㄐㄩㄝˊ ㄈㄣˊ ㄇㄨˋ)
to dig one's own grave

自欺(ㄗˋ ㄑㄧ)
to deceive oneself; self-deceit

自欺欺人(ㄗˋ ㄑㄧ ㄑㄧ ㄖㄣˊ)
to deceive oneself and others as well

自謙(ㄗˋ ㄑㄧㄢ)
self-debasement (as a gesture of politeness); to be modest: 那英雄對他的豐功偉業很自謙。The hero was very modest about his great deeds.

自遣(ㄗˋ ㄑㄧㄢˇ)
to comfort, console or cheer oneself; to amuse oneself: 我讀偵探小說自遣。I amused myself by reading detective stories.

自戕(ㄗˋ ㄑㄧㄤˊ)
to harm or abuse oneself; to inflict injuries on oneself

自強(ㄗˋ ㄑㄧㄤˊ)
to goad oneself; to drive oneself hard; to strive for improvement or progress

自強不息(ㄗˋ ㄑㄧㄤˊ ㄅㄨˋ ㄒㄧ)
to exert and strive hard without stop; continuous self-renewal

自強運動(ㄗˋ ㄑㄧㄤˊ ㄩㄣˋ ㄉㄨㄥˋ)
a movement of self-improvement, self-strengthening and self-renewal

自取(ㄗˋ ㄑㄩˇ)
of one's own doing

自取滅亡(ㄗˋ ㄑㄩˇ ㄇㄧㄝˋ ㄨㄤˊ)
to court destruction upon oneself; to take the road to one's doom

自取其咎(ㄗˋ ㄑㄩˇ ㄑㄧˊ ㄐㄧㄡˋ)
to receive punishment, censure, etc. through one's own fault

自取其辱(ㄗˋ ㄑㄩˇ ㄑㄧˊ ㄖㄨˇ)
to ask for an insult; to invite humiliation

自習(ㄗˋ ㄒㄧˊ)
to learn and practice by oneself

自修(ㄗˋ ㄒㄧㄡ)
to learn and practice by oneself; to educate oneself; to discipline oneself

自新(ㄗˋ ㄒㄧㄣ)
to make a new person out of oneself; self-renewal

自信(ㄗˋ ㄒㄧㄣˋ)
self-confidence

自相矛盾(ㄗˋ ㄒㄧㄤ ㄇㄠˊ ㄉㄨㄣˋ)
inconsistent; inconsistency; self-contradictory

自相殘殺(ㄗˋ ㄒㄧㄤ ㄘㄢˊ ㄕㄚ)
to engage in an intramural fight

自行(ㄗˋ ㄒㄧㄥˊ)
individually; personally; by oneself

自行辦理(ㄗˋ ㄒㄧㄥˊ ㄅㄢˋ ㄌㄧˇ)
to manage something individually

自行其是(ㄗˋ ㄒㄧㄥˊ ㄑㄧˊ ㄕˋ)
to act as one thinks proper; to go one's own way

自行車(ㄗˋ ㄒㄧㄥˊ ㄔㄜ)

a bicycle; a bike
自省(ㄗˋ ㄒㄧㄥˇ)
to examine oneself; self-examination; introspection
自詡(ㄗˋ ㄒㄩˇ)
to brag; to boast
自許(ㄗˋ ㄒㄩˇ)
to regard oneself as; conceited; pretentious: 他以聰明自許。He is wise in his own conceit.
自序(ㄗˋ ㄒㄩˋ)
the author's preface or foreword
自衒(ㄗˋ ㄒㄩㄢˋ)
to show off
自尋煩惱(ㄗˋ ㄒㄩㄣˊ ㄈㄢˊ ㄋㄠˇ)
to look for trouble
自知理缺(ㄗˋ ㄓ ㄌㄧˇ ㄑㄩㄝ)
to realize that one is on the wrong side
自知之明(ㄗˋ ㄓ ㄓ ㄇㄧㄥˊ)
to know oneself; a correct self-assessment
自制(ㄗˋ ㄓˋ)
self-restraint; self-discipline
自製(ㄗˋ ㄓˋ)
self-made; self-manufactured; to manufacture locally or by the plant concerned
自治(ㄗˋ ㄓˋ)
① self-government; autonomy ② self-discipline
自治領(ㄗˋ ㄓˋ ㄌㄧㄥˇ)
a dominion; an autonomous region
自治會(ㄗˋ ㄓˋ ㄏㄨㄟˋ)
① the student government of a school ② a public welfare organization operated by the citizens of a community
自治區(ㄗˋ ㄓˋ ㄑㄩ)
an autonomous region
自治行政(ㄗˋ ㄓˋ ㄒㄧㄥˊ ㄓㄥˋ)
(said of villages, counties, cities, etc.) self-government
自招(ㄗˋ ㄓㄠ)
to confess; confession: 我自招做了這件事。I confess to doing it.
自找麻煩(ㄗˋ ㄓㄠˇ ㄇㄚˊ ·ㄈㄢ)
to look for trouble
自主(ㄗˋ ㄓㄨˇ)
independent; independence; autonomy
自主權(ㄗˋ ㄓㄨˇ ㄑㄩㄢˊ)
sovereignty (of a state)
自助(ㄗˋ ㄓㄨˋ)
self-help; to help oneself
自助洗衣店(ㄗˋ ㄓㄨˋ ㄒㄧˇ ㄧ ㄉㄧㄢˋ)
a launderette
自助人助(ㄗˋ ㄓㄨˋ ㄖㄣˊ ㄓㄨˋ)
People help those who help themselves.
自助餐(ㄗˋ ㄓㄨˋ ㄘㄢ)
a buffet lunch or supper
自助餐廳(ㄗˋ ㄓㄨˋ ㄘㄢ ㄊㄧㄥ)
a cafeteria
自專(ㄗˋ ㄓㄨㄢ)
dictatorial; arbitrary; having implicit faith in oneself
自轉(ㄗˋ ㄓㄨㄢˇ)or(ㄗˋ ㄓㄨㄢˋ)
(astronomy) rotation; to revolve on its own axis
自轉週期(ㄗˋ ㄓㄨㄢˇ ㄓㄡ ㄑㄧˊ)
a period of rotation
自傳(ㄗˋ ㄓㄨㄢˋ)
an autobiography
自重(ㄗˋ ㄓㄨㄥˋ)
self-respect; self-discipline; self-esteem
自持(ㄗˋ ㄔˊ)
① to restrain or discipline oneself; self-discipline ② to keep oneself arrogantly aloof
自察(ㄗˋ ㄔㄚˊ)
to make self-examination; to be aware of one's own behavior
自陳(ㄗˋ ㄔㄣˊ)
to state personally
自稱(ㄗˋ ㄔㄥ)
to call oneself; to style oneself; to claim
自乘(ㄗˋ ㄔㄥˊ)
(said of a figure) to multiply itself
自成一家(ㄗˋ ㄔㄥˊ ㄧˊ ㄐㄧㄚ)
(said of a creative writer, painter, etc.) to create a school or style of one's own
自出機杼(ㄗˋ ㄔㄨ ㄐㄧ ㄓㄨˋ)
to be original in writing
自處(ㄗˋ ㄔㄨˇ)
one's own position, situation or predicament; where to place oneself
自吹自擂(ㄗˋ ㄔㄨㄟ ㄗˋ ㄌㄟˊ)
to brag; to boast
自食其力(ㄗˋ ㄕˊ ㄑㄧˊ ㄌㄧˋ)
to live by one's own exertion: 他以自食其力爲榮。He takes pride in living by his own exertion.
自食其果(ㄗˋ ㄕˊ ㄑㄧˊ ㄍㄨㄛˇ)
to reap the fruit of what one has sown; to suffer the consequences of one's own doing
自始至終(ㄗˋ ㄕˇ ㄓˋ ㄓㄨㄥ)
from beginning to end; all the way through: 他們自始至終友善。They were on good terms from beginning to end.
自是(ㄗˋ ㄕˋ)
① to consider oneself as right ② from then on; since then
自恃(ㄗˋ ㄕˋ)
to presume on one's (talent, wealth, influential connections, etc.)
自視(ㄗˋ ㄕˋ)
to consider, to think or to imagine oneself: 其人自視甚高。That person thinks highly of himself.
自視欿然(ㄗˋ ㄕˋ ㄎㄢˇ ㄖㄢˊ)
to be dissatisfied with oneself
自殺(ㄗˋ ㄕㄚ)
to commit suicide; suicide
自殺未遂(ㄗˋ ㄕㄚ ㄨㄟˋ ㄙㄨㄟˋ)
an attempted suicide
自首(ㄗˋ ㄕㄡˇ)
to give oneself up to the law; to surrender oneself to the authorities
自身(ㄗˋ ㄕㄣ)
oneself: 人將爲此種方法而自身受害。One hurts oneself by such methods.
自身難保(ㄗˋ ㄕㄣ ㄋㄢˊ ㄅㄠˇ)
unable even to protect oneself
自傷(ㄗˋ ㄕㄤ)
①(law) to inflict injury on oneself ② to feel sorrow for oneself; to pity oneself: 他因失敗而自傷。He felt much sorrow for his failure.
自生自滅(ㄗˋ ㄕㄥ ㄗˋ ㄇㄧㄝˋ)
to grow and die without outside interference
自贖(ㄗˋ ㄕㄨˊ)
to redeem oneself; to atone for one's crime

〔自部〕

自述(ㄗˋ ㄕㄨˋ)
to narrate one's own story or experience
自署(ㄗˋ ㄕㄨˋ)
to sign one's name
自說自話(ㄗˋ ㄕㄨㄛ ㄗˋ ㄏㄨㄚˋ)
to make an arrangement without consulting those who are involved and who are in a position to disagree
自燃(ㄗˋ ㄖㄢˊ)
(chemistry) spontaneous combustion (or ignition)
自然(ㄗˋ ㄖㄢˊ)
①nature; natural world ② at ease; natural; naturally:這次演出很自然。It was a very natural piece of acting. ③a matter of course; certainly; surely; of course: 他自然會失敗。Of course he will fail. ④ (in primary school) a subject or course of study concerning natural sciences
自然美(ㄗˋ ㄖㄢˊ ㄇㄟˇ)
natural beauty; beauty of nature
自然法(ㄗˋ ㄖㄢˊ ㄈㄚˇ)
natural law
自然淘汰(ㄗˋ ㄖㄢˊ ㄊㄠˊ ㄊㄞˋ)
evolution; the survival of the fittest; natural selection
自然力(ㄗˋ ㄖㄢˊ ㄌㄧˋ)
the forces of nature
自然療法(ㄗˋ ㄖㄢˊ ㄌㄧㄠˊ ㄈㄚˇ)
naturopathy; natural ways of healing—without drugs
自然律(ㄗˋ ㄖㄢˊ ㄌㄩˋ)
the laws of nature; natural law
自然科學(ㄗˋ ㄖㄢˊ ㄎㄜ ㄒㄩㄝˊ)
natural sciences: 他決定研究自然科學。He decided to study natural sciences.
自然界(ㄗˋ ㄖㄢˊ ㄐㄧㄝˋ)
the natural world, including animals, plants and minerals
自然趨勢(ㄗˋ ㄖㄢˊ ㄑㄩ ㄕˋ)
the natural trend
自然現象(ㄗˋ ㄖㄢˊ ㄒㄧㄢˋ ㄒㄧㄤˋ)
a natural phenomenon
自然主義(ㄗˋ ㄖㄢˊ ㄓㄨˇ ㄧˋ)
naturalism
自然人(ㄗˋ ㄖㄢˊ ㄖㄣˊ)
(law) a natural person
自然而然(ㄗˋ ㄖㄢˊ ㄦˊ ㄖㄢˊ)
a matter of course; natural consequences
自任(ㄗˋ ㄖㄣˋ)
to appoint oneself to the key post; to take personal command; to assume control personally; to assume responsibility voluntarily
自認(ㄗˋ ㄖㄣˋ)
①to believe: 他自認他是對的。He believed that he was right. ②to accept adversity with resignation
自如(ㄗˋ ㄖㄨˊ)or 自若(ㄗˋ ㄖㄨㄛˋ)
①unperturbed ②freely; unhindered
自茲(ㄗˋ ㄗ)
①from now on; henceforth ②from here
自責(ㄗˋ ㄗㄜˊ)
to blame oneself; self-reproach
自在(ㄗˋ ㄗㄞˋ)
①comfortable; at ease (with oneself and the world): 她過着自在的生活。She lives a comfortable life. ②freely; at will ③(Buddhism) free from resistance; the mind free from delusion; independent
自贊(ㄗˋ ㄗㄢˋ)
①to praise oneself: 大多數人喜歡自贊。Most people like to praise themselves. ②to introduce or recommend oneself
自足(ㄗˋ ㄗㄨˊ)
self-sufficient
自足經濟(ㄗˋ ㄗㄨˊ ㄐㄧㄥ ㄐㄧˋ)
self-sufficient or self-sustaining economy within a family, clan, etc.
自足社會(ㄗˋ ㄗㄨˊ ㄕㄜˋ ㄏㄨㄟˋ)
society with self-sufficient or self-sustaining economy
自作多情(ㄗˋ ㄗㄨㄛˋ ㄉㄨㄛ ㄑㄧㄥˊ)
to imagine oneself as the favorite of one of the opposite sex; to be under the hallucination that the other party is willing
自作孽(ㄗˋ ㄗㄨㄛˋ ㄋㄧㄝˋ)
to bring disaster to oneself
自作主張(ㄗˋ ㄗㄨㄛˋ ㄓㄨˇ ㄓㄤ)
to reach a decision one is not in a position to make; to take liberties; to decide for oneself
自作自受(ㄗˋ ㄗㄨㄛˋ ㄗˋ ㄕㄡˋ)
One reaps what he sows. 或 to suffer the consequences of one's own doing
自作聰明(ㄗˋ ㄗㄨㄛˋ ㄘㄨㄥ ㄇㄧㄥˊ)
to act as if one were an expert; presumptuous; pretentious
自尊(ㄗˋ ㄗㄨㄣ)
①self-respect; self-esteem ② egotistic
自尊心(ㄗˋ ㄗㄨㄣ ㄒㄧㄣ)
a sense of self-respect; one's feelings; self-esteem
自此(ㄗˋ ㄘˇ)
from then on; henceforth
自裁(ㄗˋ ㄘㄞˊ)
to commit suicide
自慚鳩拙(ㄗˋ ㄘㄢˊ ㄐㄧㄡ ㄓㄨㄛˊ)
to feel ashamed of one's lack of creative talent
自慚形穢(ㄗˋ ㄘㄢˊ ㄒㄧㄥˊ ㄏㄨㄟˋ)
to feel inferior to others
自從(ㄗˋ ㄘㄨㄥˊ)
from (a certain period of time); since then; ever since
自私(ㄗˋ ㄙ)or 自私自利(ㄗˋ ㄙ ㄗˋ ㄌㄧˋ)
selfish; selfishness: 他相當自私。He is rather selfish.
自訴(ㄗˋ ㄙㄨˋ)
private prosecution
自訴人(ㄗˋ ㄙㄨˋ ㄖㄣˊ)
a self-complainant
自訟(ㄗˋ ㄙㄨㄥˋ)
to blame oneself; self-censure
自愛(ㄗˋ ㄞˋ)
self-respect; to behave like a gentleman: 他雖窮但很自愛。He is poor but has self-respect.
自以爲是(ㄗˋ ㄧˇ ㄨㄟˊ ㄕˋ)
to regard oneself as correct or right, in total disregard of others' or public opinion; self-approbation
自縊(ㄗˋ ㄧˋ)
to hang oneself
自由(ㄗˋ ㄧㄡˊ)
①freedom; liberty; free: 言論自由 freedom of speech ② at ease; (to feel) at home ③ of one's own free will
自由貿易(ㄗˋ ㄧㄡˊ ㄇㄠˋ ㄧˋ)

free trade
自由黨(ㄗˋ ㄧㄡˊ ㄉㄤˇ)
British Liberal Party
自由女神像(ㄗˋ ㄧㄡˊ ㄋㄩˇ ㄕㄣˊ ㄒㄧㄤˋ)
the Statue of Liberty in New York harbor
自由戀愛(ㄗˋ ㄧㄡˊ ㄌㄧㄢˋ ㄞˋ)
free love (between a man and a woman) as distinct from the old-fashioned idea of marriage
自由港(ㄗˋ ㄧㄡˊ ㄍㄤˇ)
a free port
自由教育(ㄗˋ ㄧㄡˊ ㄐㄧㄠˋ ㄩˋ)
liberal education, whose objective is the seeking of knowledge, not preparation for jobs or occupations
自由競爭(ㄗˋ ㄧㄡˊ ㄐㄧㄥˋ ㄓㄥ)
free competition
自由權(ㄗˋ ㄧㄡˊ ㄑㄩㄢˊ)
rights of freedom of the people guaranteed by the constitution
自由行動(ㄗˋ ㄧㄡˊ ㄒㄧㄥˊ ㄉㄨㄥˋ)
free movements; a free hand; free action
自由職業(ㄗˋ ㄧㄡˊ ㄓˊ ㄧㄝˋ)
professions that do not require fixed office hours, such as doctors, writers, lawyers, etc.
自由主義(ㄗˋ ㄧㄡˊ ㄓㄨˇ ㄧˋ)
liberalism; the principle of liberty 參看「放任政策」
自由鐘(ㄗˋ ㄧㄡˊ ㄓㄨㄥ)
the Liberty Bell
自由城(ㄗˋ ㄧㄡˊ ㄔㄥˊ)
Freetown, the capital of Sierra Leone in W Africa
自由城市(ㄗˋ ㄧㄡˊ ㄔㄥˊ ㄕˋ)
(in Europe, after the Industrial Revolution) a self-governing free city after shaking off the bondage of feudalism
自由詩(ㄗˋ ㄧㄡˊ ㄕ)
free verse; *vers libre*: 他擅於寫自由詩。He is good at writing free verse.
自由式(ㄗˋ ㄧㄡˊ ㄕˋ)
(swimming) freestyle
自由自在(ㄗˋ ㄧㄡˊ ㄗˋ ㄗㄞˋ)
comfortable and at ease; carefree
自由思想(ㄗˋ ㄧㄡˊ ㄙ ㄒㄧㄤˇ)
liberal ideas or thoughts
自由意志(ㄗˋ ㄧㄡˊ ㄧˋ ㄓˋ)
free will
自有道理(ㄗˋ ㄧㄡˇ ㄉㄠˋ ㄌㄧˇ)
There must be a reason (for it).
自有公論(ㄗˋ ㄧㄡˇ ㄍㄨㄥ ㄌㄨㄣˋ)
There is always (fair) public opinion.
自幼(ㄗˋ ㄧㄡˋ)
since childhood: 他們自幼即爲好友。They have been good friends since childhood.
自言自語(ㄗˋ ㄧㄢˊ ㄗˋ ㄩˇ)
to talk to oneself
自應(ㄗˋ ㄧㄥ)
ought to; to be obliged to; should: 你自應服從你的父母。You ought to obey your parents.
自侮(ㄗˋ ㄨˇ)
to insult oneself (through scandalous acts, shady practices, etc.)
自誤(ㄗˋ ㄨˋ)
to forfeit one's own chances; to cause damage to one's own interest
自誤誤人(ㄗˋ ㄨˋ ㄨˋ ㄖㄣˊ)
to compromise the interest of oneself and those of others
自我(ㄗˋ ㄨㄛˇ)
self; ego
自我批評(ㄗˋ ㄨㄛˇ ㄆㄧ ㄆㄧㄥˊ)
self-criticism; to criticize oneself
自我陶醉(ㄗˋ ㄨㄛˇ ㄊㄠˊ ㄗㄨㄟˋ)
to indulge in daydreaming; to be intoxicated by the joy of one's imaginary successes
自我檢討(ㄗˋ ㄨㄛˇ ㄐㄧㄢˇ ㄊㄠˇ)
self-examination; to review one's conduct, achievements, etc. objectively
自我犧牲(ㄗˋ ㄨㄛˇ ㄒㄧ ㄕㄥ)
to sacrifice oneself (for the sake of others, nation, etc.); self-sacrifice
自我作古(ㄗˋ ㄨㄛˇ ㄗㄨㄛˋ ㄍㄨˇ)
to be a pioneer or trailblazer (instead of a tradition-bound copycat)
自外生成(ㄗˋ ㄨㄞˋ ㄕㄥ ㄔㄥˊ)
to shut oneself from civilized ways
自慰(ㄗˋ ㄨㄟˋ)
① to comfort oneself; self-consolation ② onanism
自衛(ㄗˋ ㄨㄟˋ)
self-defense; to defend oneself
自衛隊(ㄗˋ ㄨㄟˋ ㄉㄨㄟˋ)
militia corps; a team of citizen-soldiers for local self-defense
自衛權(ㄗˋ ㄨㄟˋ ㄑㄩㄢˊ)
the right of self-defense
自刎(ㄗˋ ㄨㄣˇ)
to commit suicide by cutting one's own throat
自問(ㄗˋ ㄨㄣˋ)
to ask oneself; to search one's own soul
自娛(ㄗˋ ㄩˊ)
to amuse oneself
自圓其說(ㄗˋ ㄩㄢˊ ㄑㄧˊ ㄕㄨㄛ)
to explain oneself away; to make one's story sound plausible
自願(ㄗˋ ㄩㄢˋ)
voluntary; of one's own accord; of one's own free will
自怨自艾(ㄗˋ ㄩㄢˋ ㄗˋ ㄧˋ)
to blame and censure oneself; to complain about oneself
自用(ㄗˋ ㄩㄥˋ)
① to do something without consulting others; to have morbid faith in one's talent and capability ② personal or private (property); for personal or private use

四畫

【臬】 4765
ㄋㄧㄝˋ nieh niè
1. a rule; a law; an institution
2. another name of 按察使—the provincial judge in ancient China
3. a doorpost

臬司(ㄋㄧㄝˋ ㄙ)
the provincial judge in old China

【臭】 4766
1. ㄔㄡˋ chow chòu
1. stinking; smelly
2. notorious; flagrant; disreputable
3. very; much; soundly; sternly
4. (said of friendship, love, etc.) to cool off

5. foul and petty; worthless
6. an odor; a stench

臭皮囊(ㄔㄡˋ ㄆㄧˊ ㄋㄤˊ)
the human body

臭罵(ㄔㄡˋ ㄇㄚˋ)
a stern scolding; to scold soundly

臭美(ㄔㄡˋ ㄇㄟˇ)
presumptuous; smug

臭名(ㄔㄡˋ ㄇㄧㄥˊ)
a notorious reputation

臭腐(ㄔㄡˋ ㄈㄨˇ)
stinking and rotten

臭打(ㄔㄡˋ ㄉㄚˇ)
a sound thrashing or beating

臭豆腐(ㄔㄡˋ ㄉㄡˋ ˙ㄈㄨ)
the fermented bean curd (a popular Chinese food item)

臭東西(ㄔㄡˋ ㄉㄨㄥ ˙ㄒㄧ)
a stinking slut; a good-for-nothing

臭蹄子(ㄔㄡˋ ㄊㄧˊ ˙ㄗ)
a stinking whore or slut

臭爛(ㄔㄡˋ ㄌㄢˋ)
rotten and stinking

臭溝(ㄔㄡˋ ㄍㄡ)
a stinking ditch; a gutter

臭烘烘(ㄔㄡˋ ㄏㄨㄥ ㄏㄨㄥ)
to stink; stinking

臭街爛巷(ㄔㄡˋ ㄐㄧㄝ ㄌㄢˋ ㄒㄧㄤˋ)
(said of goods or commodities) plentiful and cheap

臭嚼(ㄔㄡˋ ㄐㄧㄠˊ)
to keep on jawing nonsense; to chatter on and on meaninglessly

臭氣冲天(ㄔㄡˋ ㄑㄧˋ ㄔㄨㄥ ㄊㄧㄢ)
a stinking smell assaulting one's nostrils

臭錢(ㄔㄡˋ ㄑㄧㄢˊ)
stinking money; the money of a rich miser

臭小子(ㄔㄡˋ ㄒㄧㄠˇ ˙ㄗ)
a bum; a tramp

臭喫臭喝(ㄔㄡˋ ㄔ ㄔㄡˋ ㄏㄜ)
to drink like a fish and eat like a pig

臭蟲(ㄔㄡˋ ㄔㄨㄥˊ)
the bedbug

臭事(ㄔㄡˋ ㄕˋ)
a scandal

臭揍(ㄔㄡˋ ㄗㄡˋ)
a sound thrashing; a good beating

臭鼬(ㄔㄡˋ ㄧㄡˋ)
a skunk

臭氧(ㄔㄡˋ ㄧㄤˇ)
ozone

臭氧層(ㄔㄡˋ ㄧㄤˇ ㄘㄥˊ)
the ozonosphere

臭味相投(ㄔㄡˋ ㄨㄟˋ ㄒㄧㄤ ㄊㄡˊ)or (ㄒㄧㄡˋ ㄨㄟˋ ㄒㄧㄤ ㄊㄡˊ)
to share the same rotten tastes, habits, etc.; to be two of a kind; birds of the similar feather; persons of similar (atrocious) tastes; a meeting of (dirty) minds

【臭】 4766
2. (嗅)ㄒㄧㄡˋ shiow xiù
1. scent; smells; odors
2. to smell

六畫

【皐】 4767
(皋、臯) ㄍㄠ gau gāo
1. a lake or pool
2. the bank or shore
3. to utter a long, wailing sound
4. a Chinese family name

十畫

【臲】 4768
ㄋㄧㄝˋ nieh niè
jumpy; jittery; worried

臲卼(ㄋㄧㄝˋ ㄨˋ)
jumpy; jittery; worried; anxious

至部
ㄓˋ jyh zhì

【至】 4769
ㄓˋ jyh zhì
1. to arrive at; to reach (a destination)
2. very; extremely; to indicate the superlative degree—the most

至寶(ㄓˋ ㄅㄠˇ)
the most precious treasure

至大(ㄓˋ ㄉㄚˋ)
the greatest; extremely large

至大至剛(ㄓˋ ㄉㄚˋ ㄓˋ ㄍㄤ)
the greatest and most unbending

至德(ㄓˋ ㄉㄜˊ)
the highest virtue

至當不移(ㄓˋ ㄉㄤˋ ㄅㄨˋ ㄧˊ)
most suitable and not subject to change

至多(ㄓˋ ㄉㄨㄛ)
at (the) most

至樂(ㄓˋ ㄌㄜˋ)
extremely happy and jubilant

至理名言(ㄓˋ ㄌㄧˇ ㄇㄧㄥˊ ㄧㄢˊ)
a proverb of lasting value; a truthful remark; a quotable quote

至高無上(ㄓˋ ㄍㄠ ㄨˊ ㄕㄤˋ)
the highest; the most exalted; above everything else; the supreme

至關緊要(ㄓˋ ㄍㄨㄢ ㄐㄧㄣˇ ㄧㄠˋ)
of utmost importance

至公(ㄓˋ ㄍㄨㄥ)
absolutely just or unbiased: 這法官至公無私。The judge was absolutely just.

至靠(ㄓˋ ㄎㄠˋ)
a most dependable or faithful (friend)

至好(ㄓˋ ㄏㄠˇ)
① the best; simply wonderful and fabulous ② the closest friend; a great friend: 我們是至好。We are great friends.

至急(ㄓˋ ㄐㄧˊ)
most or extremely urgent

至極(ㄓˋ ㄐㄧˊ)
extremely; the most; to the utmost degree

至交(ㄓˋ ㄐㄧㄠ)
one's closest friend

至今(ㄓˋ ㄐㄧㄣ)
until now; so far; up to the present time

至親(ㄓˋ ㄑㄧㄣ)
the closest relative

至親好友(ㄓˋ ㄑㄧㄣ ㄏㄠˇ ㄧㄡˇ)
close relatives and dear friends

至親無文(ㄓˋ ㄑㄧㄣ ㄨˊ ㄨㄣˊ)
One does not have to stand on ceremony in dealing with close relatives and friends.

至情(ㄓˋ ㄑㄧㄥˊ)
(said of friendship, kinship, etc.) the most genuine feeling

至孝(ㄓˋ ㄒㄧㄠˋ)

extremely filial
至心(ㄓˋ ㄒㄧㄣ)
①the most sincere heart or thought ②(Buddhism) with the utmost mind, or a perfect mind
至行(ㄓˋ ㄒㄧㄥˋ)
the most virtuous conduct
至性(ㄓˋ ㄒㄧㄥˋ)
the natural disposition to love one's parents, brothers and sisters; a great capacity for love
至囑(ㄓˋ ㄓㄨˇ)
instructions of the utmost importance or urgency; to instruct or exhort most earnestly
至誠(ㄓˋ ㄔㄥˊ)
sincere; the greatest sincerity
至誠感神(ㄓˋ ㄔㄥˊ ㄍㄢˇ ㄕㄣˊ)
Utmost sincerity can move even gods.
至少(ㄓˋ ㄕㄠˇ)
at least; the least
至善(ㄓˋ ㄕㄢˋ)
the highest level of virtue; the supreme good
至上(ㄓˋ ㄕㄤˋ)
the most revered
至聖(ㄓˋ ㄕㄥˋ)
the greatest sage—Confucius
至聖先師(ㄓˋ ㄕㄥˋ ㄒㄧㄢ ㄕ)
the greatest sage and teacher—Confucius
至日(ㄓˋ ㄖˋ)
the winter and the summer solstices
至仁(ㄓˋ ㄖㄣˊ)
the highest degree of kindness and magnanimity
至人(ㄓˋ ㄖㄣˊ)
①a saint; a sage; a man of virtue ②(Buddhism) the perfect man, i.e. Sakyamuni
至人無夢(ㄓˋ ㄖㄣˊ ㄨˊ ㄇㄥˋ)
A virtuous man seldom has dreams.
至人無己(ㄓˋ ㄖㄣˊ ㄨˊ ㄐㄧˇ)
A sage is selfless.
至如(ㄓˋ ㄖㄨˊ)
as to; with regard to
至若(ㄓˋ ㄖㄨㄛˋ)
to come to (that degree, etc.); as to; with regard to

至再至三(ㄓˋ ㄗㄞˋ ㄓˋ ㄙㄢ)
twice and thrice; repeatedly: 我曾至再至三地警告他。I've given him repeated warnings.
至尊(ㄓˋ ㄗㄨㄣ)
①the most august—the emperor ②(Buddhism) Sakyamuni
至此(ㄓˋ ㄘˇ)
①to come here; to arrive here ②to have come this far; to have developed to this point
至材(ㄓˋ ㄘㄞˊ)
extremely gifted or talented; extremely capable men
至死(ㄓˋ ㄙˇ)
till death; to the last; to the death: 他們將奮戰至死。They will fight to the death.
至死不變(ㄓˋ ㄙˇ ㄅㄨˋ ㄅㄧㄢˋ)
unswerving till death; consistent or unswerving (love, faith, etc.)
至死不屈(ㄓˋ ㄙˇ ㄅㄨˋ ㄑㄩ)
to stick to one's principle, faith, etc. till one breathes his last
至死不渝(ㄓˋ ㄙˇ ㄅㄨˋ ㄩˊ)
to remain faithful until death
至矣盡矣(ㄓˋ ㄧˇ ㄐㄧㄣˋ ㄧˇ)
to have done everything possible (to help, encourage, etc.)
至意(ㄓˋ ㄧˋ)
the best and sincerest intention
至要(ㄓˋ ㄧㄠˋ)
the most important; imperative
至友(ㄓˋ ㄧㄡˇ)
the closest friend; a close friend: 他是我的至友。He is my close friend.
至言(ㄓˋ ㄧㄢˊ)
①words of the utmost importance or significance ②the most virtuous or proper utterances ③(Buddhism) words of complete explanation
至於(ㄓˋ ㄩˊ)
①as to; with regard to ②to the extent of

三畫

【致】 4770
(致) ㄓˋ jyh zhì
1. to send; to present; to convey; to transmit; to extend (thanks, etc.)
2. to cause to come; to cause (injury, death, etc.)
3. to achieve; to attain; to amass (fortune)
4. one's principle, interest, hobby, etc.
5. to bring about; to occasion or result in
6. to retire; to resign

致命(ㄓˋ ㄇㄧㄥˋ)
①to sacrifice one's life ②fatal; fatality
致命處(ㄓˋ ㄇㄧㄥˋ ㄔㄨˋ)
①spots in the human body where injury can easily cause death ②key points in a plan, etc.
致命傷(ㄓˋ ㄇㄧㄥˋ ㄕㄤ)
①a mortal wound ②vulnerability; the weak point; the major cause that makes failure inevitable
致富(ㄓˋ ㄈㄨˋ)
to become rich; to acquire wealth: 他以勤儉致富。He became rich because of diligence and frugality.
致奠(ㄓˋ ㄉㄧㄢˋ)
(in old China, especially Ching Dynasty) the offering of personal condolences or sacrifices to the family of a deceased high official by a representative of the emperor; to offer sacrifices at the funeral service by the representative
致電(ㄓˋ ㄉㄧㄢˋ)
to send a telegram or cable
致力(ㄓˋ ㄌㄧˋ)
to devote or dedicate oneself to: 他畢生致力幫助盲人。He has devoted his life to helping blind people.
致果(ㄓˋ ㄍㄨㄛˇ)
to achieve victory; to attain result
致賀(ㄓˋ ㄏㄜˋ)
to extend or offer congratulations: 他的成功值得致賀。

〔至部〕

His success deserves congratulation.
致敬(ㄓˋ ㄐㄧㄥˋ)
to pay respects or homage; to salute
致謝(ㄓˋ ㄒㄧㄝˋ)
to offer thanks; to thank
致知(ㄓˋ ㄓ)
to extend one's knowledge; to pursue knowledge to the utmost
致政(ㄓˋ ㄓㄥˋ)
(said of a regent) to return the governing power to the throne; to retire from official life; to resign (from office) 參看「致仕」
致仕 or 致事(ㄓˋ ㄕˋ)
to resign from office; to retire from official life
致身(ㄓˋ ㄕㄣ)
to dedicate or give one's life to (a cause, etc.)
致書(ㄓˋ ㄕㄨ)
to send a letter: 余將致書令兄。I'll send a letter to your elder brother.
致辭(ㄓˋ ㄘˊ)
to address; to deliver a speech
致死(ㄓˋ ㄙˇ)
to cause death; to result in death
致意(ㄓˋ ㄧˋ)
to convey one's best wishes or regards
致癌物質(ㄓˋ ㄧㄢˊ ㄨˋ ㄓˊ)
(medicine) carcinogen; a carcinogenic substance
致用(ㄓˋ ㄩㄥˋ)
to attain practical use; for practical purposes

八畫

【臺】 4771
(台) ㄊㄞˊ tair tái
1. a lookout; a tower; an observatory
2. a terrace; an elevated platform; a stage; a stand
3. a title of respect
4. short for Taiwan
5. a Chinese family name

臺北市(ㄊㄞˊ ㄅㄟˇ ㄕˋ)
Taipei Special Municipality, provisional capital of the Republic of China
臺幣(ㄊㄞˊ ㄅㄧˋ)
Taiwan currency
臺風(ㄊㄞˊ ㄈㄥ)
the deportment of an actor or actress on stage
臺地(ㄊㄞˊ ㄉㄧˋ)
a tableland; a plateau
臺東(ㄊㄞˊ ㄉㄨㄥ)
① Taitung County ② Taitung City
臺南縣(ㄊㄞˊ ㄋㄢˊ ㄒㄧㄢˋ)
Tainan County
臺南市(ㄊㄞˊ ㄋㄢˊ ㄕˋ)
Tainan City: 臺南市以古蹟著名。Tainan City is noted for its historic relics.
臺閣(ㄊㄞˊ ㄍㄜˊ)
(in former times) a cabinet minister
臺階(ㄊㄞˊ ㄐㄧㄝ)
① brick or stone steps ② a means to save face or resolve a dispute
臺諫(ㄊㄞˊ ㄐㄧㄢˋ)
(in ancient China) a censor
臺下(ㄊㄞˊ ㄒㄧㄚˋ)
off the stage
臺榭(ㄊㄞˊ ㄒㄧㄝˋ)
terraces and pavilions in a garden or park
臺柱子(ㄊㄞˊ ㄓㄨˋ ·ㄗ)
(colloquial) the most important person in an organization or a group; the leading light; a pillar; a mainstay
臺中縣(ㄊㄞˊ ㄓㄨㄥ ㄒㄧㄢˋ)
Taichung County
臺中市(ㄊㄞˊ ㄓㄨㄥ ㄕˋ)
Taichung City
臺秤(ㄊㄞˊ ㄔㄥˋ)
① a platform scale ② the Taiwan standard of weight measure
臺上(ㄊㄞˊ ㄕㄤˋ)
on the stage
臺子(ㄊㄞˊ ·ㄗ)
①(colloquial) a platform; a stage; a terrace ②(dialect) a table; a desk
臺詞(ㄊㄞˊ ㄘˊ)
lines in a play a player is supposed to memorize; actor's lines
臺兒莊(ㄊㄞˊ ㄦˊ ㄓㄨㄤ)
name of a town near the Kiangsu(江蘇) and Shantung(山東) border, where one of the bloodiest battles in the eight-year Sino-Japanese War (1938-1945) was fought and won
臺灣(ㄊㄞˊ ㄨㄢ)
Taiwan (Formosa)
臺灣肥料公司(ㄊㄞˊ ㄨㄢ ㄈㄟˊ ㄌㄧㄠˋ ㄍㄨㄥ ㄙ) or 臺肥(ㄊㄞˊ ㄈㄟˊ)
Taiwan Fertilizer Company
臺灣大學(ㄊㄞˊ ㄨㄢ ㄉㄚˋ ㄒㄩㄝˊ) or 臺大(ㄊㄞˊ ㄉㄚˋ)
National Taiwan University
臺灣電力公司(ㄊㄞˊ ㄨㄢ ㄉㄧㄢˋ ㄌㄧˋ ㄍㄨㄥ ㄙ) or 臺電(ㄊㄞˊ ㄉㄧㄢˋ)
Taiwan Power Company
臺灣糖業公司(ㄊㄞˊ ㄨㄢ ㄊㄤˊ ㄧㄝˋ ㄍㄨㄥ ㄙ) or 臺糖(ㄊㄞˊ ㄊㄤˊ)
Taiwan Sugar Corporation
臺灣光復節(ㄊㄞˊ ㄨㄢ ㄍㄨㄤ ㄈㄨˋ ㄐㄧㄝˊ)
Restoration Day of Taiwan (on October 25) commemorating the restoration of the island province to Chinese sovereignty in 1945 亦作「光復節」
臺灣海峽(ㄊㄞˊ ㄨㄢ ㄏㄞˇ ㄒㄧㄚˊ)
Taiwan Strait
臺灣省(ㄊㄞˊ ㄨㄢ ㄕㄥˇ)
the province of Taiwan
臺灣省政府(ㄊㄞˊ ㄨㄢ ㄕㄥˇ ㄓㄥˋ ㄈㄨˇ)
Taiwan Provincial Government
臺灣省議會(ㄊㄞˊ ㄨㄢ ㄕㄥˇ ㄧˋ ㄏㄨㄟˋ)
Taiwan Provincial Assembly
臺灣省菸酒公賣局(ㄊㄞˊ ㄨㄢ ㄕㄥˇ ㄧㄢ ㄐㄧㄡˇ ㄍㄨㄥ ㄇㄞˋ ㄐㄩˊ)
Taiwan Tobacco and Wine Monopoly Bureau
臺灣省物資局(ㄊㄞˊ ㄨㄢ ㄕㄥˇ ㄨˋ ㄗ ㄐㄩˊ)
Taiwan Supply Bureau
臺灣水泥公司(ㄊㄞˊ ㄨㄢ ㄕㄨㄟˇ ㄋㄧˊ ㄍㄨㄥ ㄙ) or 臺泥(ㄊㄞˊ ㄋㄧˊ)

〔至部〕

Taiwan Cement Corporation
臺灣造船公司(ㄊㄞˊ ㄨㄢ ㄗㄠˋ ㄔㄨㄢˊ ㄍㄨㄥ ㄙ)
Taiwan Shipbuilding Corporation
臺灣銀行(ㄊㄞˊ ㄨㄢ ㄧㄣˊ ㄏㄤˊ)
Bank of Taiwan

〔臼部〕

十畫

【臻】 4772 ㄓㄣ jen zhēn
1. the utmost; the best
2. to arrive at; to reach

臼部
ㄐㄧㄡˋ jiow jiù

【臼】 4773 ㄐㄧㄡˋ jiow jiù
1. a mortar for unhusking rice
2. a socket at a bone joint
3. a Chinese family name
臼砲(ㄐㄧㄡˋ ㄆㄠˋ)
(weaponry) a mortar
臼齒(ㄐㄧㄡˋ ㄔˇ)
the molars

一畫

【臼】 4774 (掬) ㄐㄩ jyu ju
to hold or take in both hands

二畫

【臾】 4775 ㄩˊ yu yú
1. a moment; an instant; a little while; a short time
2. a Chinese family name

三畫

【臿】 4776 ㄔㄚ cha chā
1. a kind of farming instrument
2. same as 插—to insert; to drive in

四畫

【舁】 4777 ㄩˊ yu yú
to lift; to raise; to carry

【舀】 4778 ㄧㄠˇ yeau yǎo (讀音 ㄎㄨㄞˇ koai kuǎi)
to ladle out (water): 她舀出一碗湯來。She ladled out a bowl of soup.

五畫

【舂】 4779 ㄔㄨㄥ chong chōng
1. to thresh (grain in order to remove the husk)
2. to pound
舂米(ㄔㄨㄥ ㄇㄧˇ)
to pound rice to remove the husk; to husk rice by pounding
舂碓(ㄔㄨㄥ ㄉㄨㄟˋ)
a pestle (for husking grain)

六畫

【舄】 4780 (舃) ㄒㄧˋ shih xì
shoes; slippers

七畫

【舅】 4781 ㄐㄧㄡˋ jiow jiù
1. a maternal uncle (one's mother's brother)
2. a brother-in-law (one's wife's brother)
3. a woman's father-in-law
4. a man's father-in-law
舅媽(ㄐㄧㄡˋ ㄇㄚ)or 舅母(ㄐㄧㄡˋ ㄇㄨˇ)
a maternal aunt (one's mother's brother's wife)
舅父(ㄐㄧㄡˋ ㄈㄨˋ)or 舅舅(ㄐㄧㄡˋ ·ㄐㄧㄡ)
a maternal uncle (one's mother's brother)
舅姑(ㄐㄧㄡˋ ㄍㄨ)
a woman's parents-in-law
舅公(ㄐㄧㄡˋ ㄍㄨㄥ)
one's father's maternal uncle
舅甥(ㄐㄧㄡˋ ㄕㄥ)
the child of one's mother's brother or sister; a cousin on the mother's side
舅子(ㄐㄧㄡˋ ·ㄗ)
a brother-in-law (one's wife's brother)
舅祖(ㄐㄧㄡˋ ㄗㄨˇ)
the brother of one's paternal grandmother; a granduncle; a great-uncle
舅嫂(ㄐㄧㄡˋ ㄙㄠˇ)
a sister-in-law (the wife of one's wife's brother)
舅爺(ㄐㄧㄡˋ ·ㄧㄝ)
a maternal uncle (one's mother's brother)

【與】 4782 1. ㄩˇ yeu yǔ
1. and; with; together with
2. to give; to impart
與民更始(ㄩˇ ㄇㄧㄣˊ ㄍㄥ ㄕˇ)
(said of a ruler) to initiate political reforms and make a fresh start with the people
與黨(ㄩˇ ㄉㄤˇ)
a political party as an ally of another political party; a friendly party
與奪(ㄩˇ ㄉㄨㄛˊ)
giving and taking 亦作「予奪」
與他何干(ㄩˇ ㄊㄚ ㄏㄜˊ ㄍㄢ)
What does it have to do with him? 或 What has it to do with him?
與古爲徒(ㄩˇ ㄍㄨˇ ㄨㄟˊ ㄊㄨˊ)
to imitate ancient ways
與國(ㄩˇ ㄍㄨㄛˊ)
a state as an ally of another state; a friendly nation; an ally
與鬼爲鄰(ㄩˇ ㄍㄨㄟˇ ㄨㄟˊ ㄌㄧㄣˊ)
(literally) to be a next-door neighbor of ghosts—to be near one's death; dying
與共(ㄩˇ ㄍㄨㄥˋ)
to share...with...: 他們甘苦與共。They shared their joys and sorrows.
與噲爲伍(ㄩˇ ㄎㄨㄞˋ ㄨㄟˊ ㄨˇ)
to associate with vulgar people
與虎謀皮(ㄩˇ ㄏㄨˇ ㄇㄡˊ ㄆㄧˊ)or 與狐謀皮(ㄩˇ ㄏㄨˊ ㄇㄡˊ ㄆㄧˊ)
(literally) to negotiate with a tiger (fox) for its hide—to try to persuade someone to do what is against his interest
與其…不如(ㄩˇ ㄑㄧˊ…ㄅㄨˋ ㄖㄨˊ)
It's better to...than.... 或 rather...than...; ...rather than...

與衆不同(ㄩˇ ㄓㄨㄥˋ ㄅㄨˋ ㄊㄨㄥˊ)
different from other people; extraordinary; uncommon; unlike others
與世浮沉(ㄩˇ ㄕˋ ㄈㄨˊ ㄔㄣˊ)
to rise and sink with the rest of the world—to have no independent course of one's own
與世推移(ㄩˇ ㄕˋ ㄊㄨㄟ ㄧˊ)
to change with the times
與世長辭(ㄩˇ ㄕˋ ㄔㄤˊ ㄘˊ)
to depart from the world for good; to pass away
與世偃仰(ㄩˇ ㄕˋ ㄧㄢˇ ㄧㄤˇ)
to rise and fall with the world—to have no independent thinking or action of one's own
與世無爭(ㄩˇ ㄕˋ ㄨˊ ㄓㄥ)
to be in harmony with the rest of the world—to stand aloof from worldly success
與日俱增(ㄩˇ ㄖˋ ㄐㄩˋ ㄗㄥ)
to grow with each passing day; to be on the increase; ever increasing
與日月爭光(ㄩˇ ㄖˋ ㄩㄝˋ ㄓㄥ ㄍㄨㄤ)
(literally) to equal the sun and the moon in glory—to achieve glorious success; to die heroically for a just cause
與人方便(ㄩˇ ㄖㄣˊ ㄈㄤ ㄅㄧㄢˋ)
to give people convenience; to accommodate others
與人無忤(ㄩˇ ㄖㄣˊ ㄨˊ ㄨˇ)
to have no discord with others; to live in harmony with other people; to be at peace with others
與人爲善(ㄩˇ ㄖㄣˊ ㄨㄟˊ ㄕㄢˋ)
to help others
與物無忤(ㄩˇ ㄨˋ ㄨˊ ㄨˇ)
to have offended no one; to be at peace with the world
與我無涉(ㄩˇ ㄨㄛˇ ㄨˊ ㄕㄜˋ)
none of my business; having nothing to do with me

【與】 4782
2. ㄩˋ yuh yù
to take part in; to participate in
與聞(ㄩˋ ㄨㄣˊ)
to participate in the affair

【與】 4782
3. ㄩˊ yu yú
same as 歟—one of the interrogative particles

九畫

【興】 4783
1. ㄒㄧㄥ shing xīng
1. to rise; to thrive; to prosper; to flourish
2. to happen; to take place; to occur
3. to start; to begin; to launch; to initiate; to establish; to found; to open

興辦(ㄒㄧㄥ ㄅㄢˋ)
to establish; to found
興邦(ㄒㄧㄥ ㄅㄤ)
to rejuvenate a country
興兵(ㄒㄧㄥ ㄅㄧㄥ)
to mobilize troops; to open hostilities
興不起來(ㄒㄧㄥ ·ㄅㄨ ㄑㄧˇ ·ㄌㄞ)
unable to rise
興滅繼絕(ㄒㄧㄥ ㄇㄧㄝˋ ㄐㄧˋ ㄐㄩㄝˊ)
to restore a fallen state or dynasty
興廢(ㄒㄧㄥ ㄈㄟˋ)
rise or fall
興奮(ㄒㄧㄥ ㄈㄣˋ)
excited; stimulated; excitement: 人人爲此勝利的消息而興奮。Everybody was excited by the news of the victory.
興奮劑(ㄒㄧㄥ ㄈㄣˋ ㄐㄧˋ)
a stimulant
興風作浪(ㄒㄧㄥ ㄈㄥ ㄗㄨㄛˋ ㄌㄤˋ)
to cause unrest; to stir up trouble
興復(ㄒㄧㄥ ㄈㄨˋ)
to revive; to restore
興得起來(ㄒㄧㄥ ·ㄉㄜ ㄑㄧˇ ·ㄌㄞ)
able to rise
興騰(ㄒㄧㄥ ㄊㄥˊ)
to gain vigor; to become increasingly prosperous; to rise
興替(ㄒㄧㄥ ㄊㄧˋ)
rise and fall; waxing and waning; ups and downs; vicissitudes
興利除弊(ㄒㄧㄥ ㄌㄧˋ ㄔㄨˊ ㄅㄧˋ)
to initiate the useful and abolish the harmful
興隆(ㄒㄧㄥ ㄌㄨㄥˊ)
prosperous; thriving; vigorous
興革(ㄒㄧㄥ ㄍㄜˊ)
to initiate what is good to the people and get rid of what is harmful; to reform
興工(ㄒㄧㄥ ㄍㄨㄥ)
to start construction
興開了(ㄒㄧㄥ ㄎㄞ ·ㄌㄜ)
to have become popular
興化灣(ㄒㄧㄥ ㄏㄨㄚˋ ㄨㄢ)
a bay in the East China Sea, to the east of Fukien
興建(ㄒㄧㄥ ㄐㄧㄢˋ)
to establish; to build; to construct
興居(ㄒㄧㄥ ㄐㄩ)
one's daily life 亦作「起居」
興起(ㄒㄧㄥ ㄑㄧˇ)
to gain power; to rise
興修(ㄒㄧㄥ ㄒㄧㄡ)
to start reconstruction
興學(ㄒㄧㄥ ㄒㄩㄝˊ)
to promote learning; to build schools
興中會(ㄒㄧㄥ ㄓㄨㄥ ㄏㄨㄟˋ)
Hsing Chung Hui, the predecessor of the Kuomintang, founded by Dr. Sun Yat-sen at Honolulu in 1894
興師動衆(ㄒㄧㄥ ㄕ ㄉㄨㄥˋ ㄓㄨㄥˋ)
to mobilize troops and stir up the people
興師問罪(ㄒㄧㄥ ㄕ ㄨㄣˋ ㄗㄨㄟˋ)
to mobilize troops to chastise rebels
興盛(ㄒㄧㄥ ㄕㄥˋ)
prosperous; thriving; vigorous; flourishing: 他們的生意似乎很興盛。Their business seemed to flourish.
興衰(ㄒㄧㄥ ㄕㄨㄞ)
rise and fall; vicissitudes
興戎(ㄒㄧㄥ ㄖㄨㄥˊ)
to mobilize troops; to open hostilities
興作(ㄒㄧㄥ ㄗㄨㄛˋ)
① to gain power; to rise ② to build; to construct; to establish; to found
興訟(ㄒㄧㄥ ㄙㄨㄥˋ)
to start a lawsuit; to commence litigation
興安(ㄒㄧㄥ ㄢ)
Hsingan Province
興亡(ㄒㄧㄥ ㄨㄤˊ)
rise and fall; prosperity and adversity: 國家興亡，匹夫有責。All men share a common

responsibility for the rise and fall of their nation.

興旺(ㄒㄧㄥ ㄨㄤˋ)
prosperous; flourishing; thriving

【興】 4783
2. ㄒㄧㄥˋ shinq xìng

1. cheerful; happy; gay; merry
2. interest; enthusiasm; eagerness; willingness

興頭上(ㄒㄧㄥˋ ㄊㄡˊ ·ㄕㄤ)
at the height of one's enthusiasm or interest; to be carried away with something

興頭兒(ㄒㄧㄥˋ ㄊㄡˊㄦ)
the height of one's eagerness or interest

興高采烈(ㄒㄧㄥˋ ㄍㄠ ㄘㄞˇ ㄌㄧㄝˋ)
cheerful; in high spirits; elated; jubilant

興會(ㄒㄧㄥˋ ㄏㄨㄟˋ)
a fit of enthusiasm

興會淋漓(ㄒㄧㄥˋ ㄏㄨㄟˋ ㄌㄧㄣˊ ㄌㄧˊ)
showing much interest and enthusiasm

興起(ㄒㄧㄥˋ ㄑㄧˇ)
aroused; excited

興趣(ㄒㄧㄥˋ ㄑㄩˋ)
① interest; eagerness; enthusiasm; willingness ② enjoyability

興致(ㄒㄧㄥˋ ㄓˋ)
interest; eagerness; enthusiasm; willingness

興致勃勃(ㄒㄧㄥˋ ㄓˋ ㄅㄛˊ ㄅㄛˊ)
very much interested; full of enthusiasm

興匆匆(ㄒㄧㄥˋ ㄘㄨㄥ ㄘㄨㄥ)or 興沖沖(ㄒㄧㄥˋ ㄔㄨㄥ ㄔㄨㄥ)
cheerful; sprightly; gay; excitedly

興味(ㄒㄧㄥˋ ㄨㄟˋ)
enjoyability; interest

十畫

【舉】 4784
(擧) ㄐㄩˇ jeu jǔ

1. to lift; to raise: 舉起你的右手。Raise your right hand.
2. to recommend; to commend; to praise
3. entire; whole; all
4. manner; deportment: 我不喜歡他的舉止。I don't like his manner.
5. to give birth to a child

舉杯(ㄐㄩˇ ㄅㄟ)
to lift the cup; to propose a toast

舉辦(ㄐㄩˇ ㄅㄢˋ)
to sponsor, organize, or initiate

舉兵(ㄐㄩˇ ㄅㄧㄥ)
to mobilize troops; to start hostilities

舉步(ㄐㄩˇ ㄅㄨˋ)
to take strides

舉目無親(ㄐㄩˇ ㄇㄨˋ ㄨˊ ㄑㄧㄣ)
There is not a single friend or relative around.—to have no one to turn to (for help)

舉發(ㄐㄩˇ ㄈㄚ)
to expose (a secret or conspiracy)

舉凡(ㄐㄩˇ ㄈㄢˊ)
generally speaking

舉鼎絕臏(ㄐㄩˇ ㄉㄧㄥˇ ㄐㄩㄝˊ ㄅㄧㄣˋ)
(literally) to hurt the kneecap in trying to carry a caldron—to shoulder a heavy responsibility with limited strength

舉動(ㄐㄩˇ ㄉㄨㄥˋ)
① deportment; conduct; manner; behavior ② act; movement

舉頭三尺有神明(ㄐㄩˇ ㄊㄡˊ ㄙㄢ ㄔˇ ㄧㄡˇ ㄕㄣˊ ㄇㄧㄥˊ)
There is a witness everywhere.

舉例(ㄐㄩˇ ㄌㄧˋ)
to give examples

舉例說明(ㄐㄩˇ ㄌㄧˋ ㄕㄨㄛ ㄇㄧㄥˊ)
to illustrate; to cite an example by way of explanation

舉國(ㄐㄩˇ ㄍㄨㄛˊ)
the entire nation

舉國上下(ㄐㄩˇ ㄍㄨㄛˊ ㄕㄤˋ ㄒㄧㄚˋ)
the entire nation regardless of classes; the ruler and the ruled alike

舉劾(ㄐㄩˇ ㄏㄜˊ)
①to name and impeach ② recommendation and impeachment

舉火(ㄐㄩˇ ㄏㄨㄛˇ)
to cook

舉家(ㄐㄩˇ ㄐㄧㄚ)
the whole family

舉薦(ㄐㄩˇ ㄐㄧㄢˋ)
to recommend (a person)

舉進士(ㄐㄩˇ ㄐㄧㄣˋ ㄕˋ)
to become a successful candidate at the imperial examination

舉棋不定(ㄐㄩˇ ㄑㄧˊ ㄅㄨˋ ㄉㄧㄥˋ)
(literally) unable to decide about a move in playing chess—indecisive; irresolute

舉起(ㄐㄩˇ ㄑㄧˇ)
to lift; to raise: 把石塊舉起來。Lift up the stone.

舉鎗(ㄐㄩˇ ㄑㄧㄤ)
to present arms in salute

舉行(ㄐㄩˇ ㄒㄧㄥˊ)
to hold (examinations, rallies, parties, etc.); to take place: 宴會何時舉行? When will the party take place?

舉行典禮(ㄐㄩˇ ㄒㄧㄥˊ ㄉㄧㄢˇ ㄌㄧˇ)
to hold a ceremony

舉止(ㄐㄩˇ ㄓˇ)
deportment; conduct; manner; behavior

舉止大方(ㄐㄩˇ ㄓˇ ㄉㄚˋ ㄈㄤ)
to have a dignified air; to have poise

舉止行動(ㄐㄩˇ ㄓˇ ㄒㄧㄥˊ ㄉㄨㄥˋ)
deportment; conduct; manner

舉證(ㄐㄩˇ ㄓㄥˋ)
to give proof or evidence

舉箸(ㄐㄩˇ ㄓㄨˋ)
to raise chopsticks to eat

舉踵(ㄐㄩˇ ㄓㄨㄥˇ)
to be on tiptoe (with eager expectation)

舉重(ㄐㄩˇ ㄓㄨㄥˋ)
weightlifting

舉翅(ㄐㄩˇ ㄔˋ)
to wing; to fly

舉出(ㄐㄩˇ ㄔㄨ)
to enumerate; to itemize; to cite (as an example)

舉士(ㄐㄩˇ ㄕˋ)
to recommend learned men for public service

舉事(ㄐㄩˇ ㄕˋ)
to rise up; to start an uprising

舉世(ㄐㄩˇ ㄕˋ)
all the world

舉世風從(ㄐㄩˇ ㄕˋ ㄈㄥ ㄘㄨㄥˊ)
The whole world follows the example.

舉世無匹(ㄐㄩˇ ㄕˋ ㄨˊ ㄆㄧˇ)or 舉世無雙(ㄐㄩˇ ㄕˋ ㄨˊ ㄕㄨㄤ)
without a match in the

world—unique; peerless
舉世聞名(ㄐㄩˇ ㄕˋ ㄨㄣˊ ㄇㄧㄥˊ)
to be known to the whole world; world-renowned
舉首(ㄐㄩˇ ㄕㄡˇ)
to raise one's head
舉手(ㄐㄩˇ ㄕㄡˇ)
to raise one's hand
舉手表決(ㄐㄩˇ ㄕㄡˇ ㄅㄧㄠˇ ㄐㄩㄝˊ)
to vote by raising hands
舉手之勞(ㄐㄩˇ ㄕㄡˇ ㄓ ㄌㄠˊ)
(literally) the trouble involved in raising a hand—little effort
舉人(ㄐㄩˇ ㄖㄣˊ)
(in the former civil service examination system) a successful candidate in the provincial examination
舉子(ㄐㄩˇ ㄗˇ)
① to give birth to a son ② a candidate in the provincial civil service examination in former times
舉足輕重(ㄐㄩˇ ㄗㄨˊ ㄑㄧㄥ ㄓㄨㄥˋ)
so important is the role one plays in a matter that each step one takes may affect it in a significant way; capable of tipping the scale because of the sensitive post one holds
舉座(ㄐㄩˇ ㄗㄨㄛˋ)
all those present
舉措(ㄐㄩˇ ㄘㄨㄛˋ)
deportment; conduct; manner
舉哀(ㄐㄩˇ ㄞ)
to weep in mourning; to go into mourning
舉案齊眉(ㄐㄩˇ ㄢˋ ㄑㄧˊ ㄇㄟˊ)
(literally) to raise the tray to the height of one's eyebrows, a reference to Liang Hung (梁鴻) and Meng Kuang (孟光)—to show respect to one's spouse
舉一反三(ㄐㄩˇ ㄧ ㄈㄢˇ ㄙㄢ)
(literally) to be able to infer three from only one that has been told—to infer the rest from what is already known
舉義(ㄐㄩˇ ㄧˋ)
to take up arms in the cause of justice
舉業(ㄐㄩˇ ㄧㄝˋ)
(in the former civil service examination system) compositions of examinees

十二畫

【舊】 4785 ㄐㄧㄡˋ jiow jiù
1. old; past; former
2. ancient; antique
3. longstanding

舊邦(ㄐㄧㄡˋ ㄅㄤ)
① an ancient kingdom ② name of a tune in Wei (魏)
舊病復發(ㄐㄧㄡˋ ㄅㄧㄥˋ ㄈㄨˋ ㄈㄚ)
to have a relapse of an old ailment
舊部(ㄐㄧㄡˋ ㄅㄨˋ)
soldiers or men who used to be under one's command; former subordinates
舊瓶裝新酒(ㄐㄧㄡˋ ㄆㄧㄥˊ ㄓㄨㄤ ㄒㄧㄣ ㄐㄧㄡˇ)
(literally) new wine in an old bottle—new concepts in an old framework
舊夢重溫(ㄐㄧㄡˋ ㄇㄥˋ ㄔㄨㄥˊ ㄨㄣ)
to renew a sweet experience of bygone days
舊大陸(ㄐㄧㄡˋ ㄉㄚˋ ㄌㄨˋ)
the Old World (as distinct from the New World, America) 亦作「舊世界」
舊道德(ㄐㄧㄡˋ ㄉㄠˋ ㄉㄜˊ)or 舊德(ㄐㄧㄡˋ ㄉㄜˊ)
virtues of the forefathers
舊地(ㄐㄧㄡˋ ㄉㄧˋ)
a once visited place
舊地重遊(ㄐㄧㄡˋ ㄉㄧˋ ㄔㄨㄥˊ ㄧㄡˊ)
to revisit a place
舊調重彈(ㄐㄧㄡˋ ㄉㄧㄠˋ ㄔㄨㄥˊ ㄊㄢˊ)
(literally) to play an old tune again—to repeat an old argument or sermon
舊都(ㄐㄧㄡˋ ㄉㄨ)
a former capital; an ancient capital
舊套(ㄐㄧㄡˋ ㄊㄠˋ)
old stuff; a threadbare plan, suggestion, etc.
舊唐書(ㄐㄧㄡˋ ㄊㄤˊ ㄕㄨ)
The Old Tang History, by Liu Hsü (劉昫), etc.—one of the *Twenty-Four Histories*
舊腦筋(ㄐㄧㄡˋ ㄋㄠˇ ㄐㄧㄣ)
conservative-minded
舊年(ㄐㄧㄡˋ ㄋㄧㄢˊ)
① last year; yesteryear ② the Lunar New Year
舊禮教(ㄐㄧㄡˋ ㄌㄧˇ ㄐㄧㄠˋ)
the old concepts of propriety
舊曆(ㄐㄧㄡˋ ㄌㄧˋ)
the lunar calendar
舊曆年(ㄐㄧㄡˋ ㄌㄧˋ ㄋㄧㄢˊ)
the Lunar New Year; the Chinese New Year; the Spring Festival
舊稿(ㄐㄧㄡˋ ㄍㄠˇ)
an old manuscript draft
舊故(ㄐㄧㄡˋ ㄍㄨˋ)
an old friend
舊觀(ㄐㄧㄡˋ ㄍㄨㄢ)
the former appearance; the previous look; the former condition
舊觀念(ㄐㄧㄡˋ ㄍㄨㄢ ㄋㄧㄢˋ)
old ideas
舊管(ㄐㄧㄡˋ ㄍㄨㄢˇ)
what one used to be in charge of
舊貫(ㄐㄧㄡˋ ㄍㄨㄢˋ)
a former system
舊好(ㄐㄧㄡˋ ㄏㄠˇ)
an old friend; old friendship
舊恨新愁(ㄐㄧㄡˋ ㄏㄣˋ ㄒㄧㄣ ㄔㄡˊ)
sorrows old and new; new sorrows piled on old hatred
舊貨(ㄐㄧㄡˋ ㄏㄨㄛˋ)
secondhand goods; junk
舊貨攤(ㄐㄧㄡˋ ㄏㄨㄛˋ ㄊㄢ)
a stall selling used articles; a junk store
舊歡(ㄐㄧㄡˋ ㄏㄨㄢ)
a former sweetheart; an ex-lover; an old flame
舊籍(ㄐㄧㄡˋ ㄐㄧˊ)
old books
舊交(ㄐㄧㄡˋ ㄐㄧㄠ)
an old friend
舊金山(ㄐㄧㄡˋ ㄐㄧㄣ ㄕㄢ)
San Francisco
舊居(ㄐㄧㄡˋ ㄐㄩ)
a former residence
舊情(ㄐㄧㄡˋ ㄑㄧㄥˊ)
former friendship or affection
舊戲(ㄐㄧㄡˋ ㄒㄧˋ)
an old-style drama
舊鄉(ㄐㄧㄡˋ ㄒㄧㄤ)
one's native town
舊學(ㄐㄧㄡˋ ㄒㄩㄝˊ)
① what one learned in bygone days ② classic learning
舊址(ㄐㄧㄡˋ ㄓˇ)

a former site; a former address
舊制(ㄐㄧㄡˋ ㄓˋ)
a former system; an old system
舊債(ㄐㄧㄡˋ ㄓㄞˋ)
an old debt; an old loan
舊章(ㄐㄧㄡˋ ㄓㄤ)
old regulations
舊賬(ㄐㄧㄡˋ ㄓㄤˋ)
old debts; old bills
舊主(ㄐㄧㄡˋ ㄓㄨˇ)
one's former master
舊著(ㄐㄧㄡˋ ㄓㄨˋ)
an old work (of a writer)
舊稱(ㄐㄧㄡˋ ㄔㄥ)
a former name or designation; known formerly as …
舊詩(ㄐㄧㄡˋ ㄕ)
old-style poetry; classical Chinese poetry: 他喜歡研究舊詩。He enjoys studying old-style poetry.
舊石器時代(ㄐㄧㄡˋ ㄕˊ ㄑㄧˋ ㄕˊ ㄉㄞˋ)
(archeology) the Old Stone Age; the Paleolithic Age
舊式(ㄐㄧㄡˋ ㄕˋ)
old-style; old-type; old-fashioned; out-of-date; obsolescent
舊式婚姻(ㄐㄧㄡˋ ㄕˋ ㄏㄨㄣ ㄧㄣ)
an old-style marriage; an old-fashioned wedding
舊式家庭(ㄐㄧㄡˋ ㄕˋ ㄐㄧㄚ ㄊㄧㄥˊ)
an old-fashioned household; an old-style family
舊事(ㄐㄧㄡˋ ㄕˋ)
an old affair
舊事重提(ㄐㄧㄡˋ ㄕˋ ㄔㄨㄥˊ ㄊㄧˊ)
to refer again to something discussed before or that happened in the past
舊書(ㄐㄧㄡˋ ㄕㄨ)
① a used book: 舊書通常很便宜。Used books are usually very cheap. ② ancient books; antique books: 這本舊書已絕版。The ancient book is out of print.
舊書店(ㄐㄧㄡˋ ㄕㄨ ㄉㄧㄢˋ)
a secondhand bookstore
舊書攤(ㄐㄧㄡˋ ㄕㄨ ㄊㄢ)
a secondhand bookstand
舊屬(ㄐㄧㄡˋ ㄕㄨˇ)
former subordinates 參看「舊部」
舊日(ㄐㄧㄡˋ ㄖˋ)
bygone days; former times
舊族(ㄐㄧㄡˋ ㄗㄨˊ)
an ancient family or clan
舊思想(ㄐㄧㄡˋ ㄙ ㄒㄧㄤˇ)
old-fashioned ideas; archaic thinking
舊俗(ㄐㄧㄡˋ ㄙㄨˊ)
old custom; custom or practice no longer prevalent; traditional custom; tradition
舊惡(ㄐㄧㄡˋ ㄜˋ)
① a past feud; an old grudge ② past mistakes; former wickednesses
舊案(ㄐㄧㄡˋ ㄢˋ)
an old case
舊恩(ㄐㄧㄡˋ ㄣ)
a past kindness or favor: 他對我有舊恩。He has done me many kindnesses in the past.
舊衣服(ㄐㄧㄡˋ ㄧ ·ㄈㄨ)
used clothes; old clothes
舊業(ㄐㄧㄡˋ ㄧㄝˋ)
① a former profession ② estates inherited from ancestors
舊友(ㄐㄧㄡˋ ㄧㄡˇ)
an old friend
舊五代史(ㄐㄧㄡˋ ㄨˇ ㄉㄞˋ ㄕˇ)
The Old History of the Five Dynasties, by Hsüeh Chücheng (薛居正), etc.—one of the *Twenty-Four Histories*
舊雨新知(ㄐㄧㄡˋ ㄩˇ ㄒㄧㄣ ㄓ)
old friends and new acquaintances
舊約全書(ㄐㄧㄡˋ ㄩㄝ ㄑㄩㄢˊ ㄕㄨ)
the Old Testament

舌 部
ㄕㄜˊ sher shé

【舌】4786
ㄕㄜˊ sher shé
the tongue
舌本(ㄕㄜˊ ㄅㄣˇ)
the root of the tongue; the back of the tongue
舌敝脣焦(ㄕㄜˊ ㄅㄧˋ ㄔㄨㄣˊ ㄐㄧㄠ)
The tongue is weary and the lips are dry (from talking too much). 或 to talk oneself hoarse
舌鋒(ㄕㄜˊ ㄈㄥ)
eloquence: 她是一個舌鋒銳利的女人。She is an eloquent woman.
舌苔(ㄕㄜˊ ㄊㄞ)
(Chinese medicine) fur on the tongue; coating on the tongue
舌頭(ㄕㄜˊ ·ㄊㄡ)
the tongue
舌疳(ㄕㄜˊ ㄍㄢ)
(Chinese medicine) an ulcer on the tongue 亦作「舌癌」
舌根(ㄕㄜˊ ㄍㄣ)
the root of the tongue
舌根音(ㄕㄜˊ ㄍㄣ ㄧㄣ)
(phonetics) a dorsal sound
舌耕(ㄕㄜˊ ㄍㄥ)
(literally) to plow with the tongue—to teach for a living
舌骨(ㄕㄜˊ ㄍㄨˇ)
(anatomy) a hyoid bone
舌管(ㄕㄜˊ ㄍㄨㄢˇ)
① reeds (of certain wind instruments) ② reed pipes
舌尖(ㄕㄜˊ ㄐㄧㄢ)
the tip of the tongue
舌尖音(ㄕㄜˊ ㄐㄧㄢ ㄧㄣ)
(phonetics) an apical sound
舌劍脣槍(ㄕㄜˊ ㄐㄧㄢˋ ㄔㄨㄣˊ ㄑㄧㄤ)
acrimonious words used in a quarrel or debate
舌戰(ㄕㄜˊ ㄓㄢˋ)
to debate with verbal confrontation
舌狀花冠(ㄕㄜˊ ㄓㄨㄤˋ ㄏㄨㄚ ㄍㄨㄢ)
a ligulate corolla
舌人(ㄕㄜˊ ㄖㄣˊ)
an interpreter
舌葉(ㄕㄜˊ ㄧㄝˋ)
the tongue blade
舌音(ㄕㄜˊ ㄧㄣ)
(phonetics) lingual sounds

二畫

【舍】4787
1. ㄕㄜˋ sheh shè
1. a house
2. an inn
3. to halt; to stop; to rest
4. a self-depreciatory possessive pronoun for the first person singular in formal speech

〔舌部〕

舍妹(ㄕㄜˋ ㄇㄟˋ)
(a self-depreciatory term) my younger sister

舍弟(ㄕㄜˋ ㄉㄧˋ)
(a self-depreciatory term) my younger brother

舍匿(ㄕㄜˋ ㄋㄧˋ)
to hide (a person); to harbor (a criminal)

舍利(ㄕㄜˋ ㄌㄧˋ)
①(Buddhism) relics or ashes left after the cremation of a Buddha or saint, placed in stupas and worshiped ② a mynah

舍利塔(ㄕㄜˋ ㄌㄧˋ ㄊㄚˇ)
(Buddhism) a tower serving as a depository of holy relics

舍利子(ㄕㄜˋ ㄌㄧˋ ㄗˇ)
①(Buddhism) holy relics ② Sariputra, one of the principle disciples of Sakyamuni

舍利鹽(ㄕㄜˋ ㄌㄧˋ ㄧㄢˊ)
Epsom salt; magnesium sulfate

舍間(ㄕㄜˋ ㄐㄧㄢ)or 舍下(ㄕㄜˋ ㄒㄧㄚˋ)
my humble house; my home

舍監(ㄕㄜˋ ㄐㄧㄢ)
a dormitory superintendent

舍親(ㄕㄜˋ ㄑㄧㄣ)
(a self-depreciatory term) my relatives

舍姪(ㄕㄜˋ ㄓˊ)
(a self-depreciatory term) my niece or nephew

舍人(ㄕㄜˋ ㄖㄣˊ)
a kind of palace secretary in the Chou(周)and some later dynasties

【舍】4787 2. ㄕㄜˇ shee shě
same as 捨—to throw away

四畫

【舐】4788 ㄕˋ shyh shì
to lick

舐犢情深(ㄕˋ ㄉㄨˊ ㄑㄧㄥˊ ㄕㄣ)
very affectionate toward one's children (like a cow caressing her calves with the tongue)

舐糠及米(ㄕˋ ㄎㄤ ㄐㄧˊ ㄇㄧˇ)
(literally) to lick the bran until the tongue finally touches the rice—A country finally falls after its territory is nibbled away.

舐痔吮癰(ㄕˋ ㄓˋ ㄕㄨㄣˇ ㄩㄥ)
(literally) to lick piles and suck tumors (of VIPs)—to show sycophancy; obsequious

舐窗以窺(ㄕˋ ㄔㄨㄤ ㄧˇ ㄎㄨㄟ)
(literally) to lick a hole in a paper window and peep through it—to look stealthily

六畫

【舒】4789 ㄕㄨ shu shū
1. to unfold; to stretch; to open; to relax
2. slow; unhurried; leisurely
3. a Chinese family name

舒勃(ㄕㄨ ㄅㄛˊ)
to expand; to grow; to develop

舒眉(ㄕㄨ ㄇㄟˊ)
(literally) to relax the brows—to show pleasure

舒眉展眼(ㄕㄨ ㄇㄟˊ ㄓㄢˇ ㄧㄢˇ)
(literally) to relax the brows and stretch the eyes—to show pleasure

舒服(ㄕㄨ ˙ㄈㄨ)or 舒適(ㄕㄨ ㄕˋ)
comfortable; cosy; comfort: 他過着舒適的生活。He lives in comfort.

舒泰(ㄕㄨ ㄊㄞˋ)
happy and healthy; well

舒坦(ㄕㄨ ˙ㄊㄢ)
in good health; happy; comfortable

舒懷(ㄕㄨ ㄏㄨㄞˊ)
to free the mind from tension; to set the mind at rest

舒緩(ㄕㄨ ㄏㄨㄢˇ)
leisurely; relaxed; to relax

舒筋活血(ㄕㄨ ㄐㄧㄣ ㄏㄨㄛˊ ㄒㄩㄝˋ)
to relax the muscles and enliven the blood

舒卷 or 舒捲(ㄕㄨ ㄐㄩㄢˇ)
to roll back and forth; to fold or unfold

舒卷自如 or 舒捲自如(ㄕㄨ ㄐㄩㄢˇ ㄗˋ ㄖㄨˊ)
to fold or unfold at will; to do as one pleases

舒心(ㄕㄨ ㄒㄧㄣ)
pleasant; agreeable

舒展(ㄕㄨ ㄓㄢˇ)
to limber up; to unfold; to relax; to stretch

舒張壓(ㄕㄨ ㄓㄤ ㄧㄚ)
(medicine) diastolic pressure

舒暢(ㄕㄨ ㄔㄤˋ)
① pleasant; comfortable: 我們度了一個舒暢的假期。We spent a pleasant vacation. ② leisurely and harmonious

舒適(ㄕㄨ ㄕˋ)
comfortable; cosy; snug 參看「舒服」

舒散(ㄕㄨ ㄙㄢˋ)
relaxed; leisurely: 看一場電影舒散一下吧。Take a show and relax.

八畫

【舔】4790 ㄊㄧㄢˇ tean tiǎn
to lick; to taste: 貓在舔牛奶。The cat was licking milk.

舔乾淨(ㄊㄧㄢˇ ㄍㄢ ˙ㄐㄧㄥ)
to lick clean

舔一舔(ㄊㄧㄢˇ ˙ㄧ ˙ㄊㄧㄢ)
to taste by licking

九畫

【鋪】4791 (鋪) ㄆㄨˋ puh pù
a shop; a store

十畫

【館】4792 (館) ㄍㄨㄢˇ goan guǎn
a mansion; a building

舛部
ㄔㄨㄢˇ choan chuǎn

【舛】4793 ㄔㄨㄢˇ choan chuǎn
1. chaotic; disorderly; messy; confused; mixed up
2. to run counter to; to disobey; to oppose; to deviate from
3. mishap; sufferings; setbacks:

我的命運多舛。I suffered many a setback during my life.

舛駁(ㄔㄨㄢˇ ㄅㄛˊ)
incongruous; contradictory: 這是一個前後舛駁的故事。This is an incongruous story.

舛逆(ㄔㄨㄢˇ ㄋㄧˋ)
contrary to reason; absurd

舛互(ㄔㄨㄢˇ ㄏㄨˋ)
to interlace; to intermingle; to interlock

舛馳(ㄔㄨㄢˇ ㄔˊ)
to go in the opposite direction

舛雜(ㄔㄨㄢˇ ㄗㄚˊ)
all mixed up; chaotic

舛辭(ㄔㄨㄢˇ ㄘˊ)
irony

舛錯(ㄔㄨㄢˇ ㄘㄨㄛˋ)
① erroneous; inexact ② untidy; disorderly; unsystematic

舛午(ㄔㄨㄢˇ ㄨˇ)
to oppose each other; to bicker

舛誤(ㄔㄨㄢˇ ㄨˋ)
a mistake; an error

六畫

【舜】 4794 ㄕㄨㄣˋ shuenn shùn
Shun, a legendary ruler said to have ruled ancient China around 2200 B.C.

舜江(ㄕㄨㄣˋ ㄐㄧㄤ)or 舜水(ㄕㄨㄣˋ ㄕㄨㄟˇ)
name of a river in Chekiang

舜日堯年(ㄕㄨㄣˋ ㄖˋ ㄧㄠˊ ㄋㄧㄢˊ)
(literally) the reign of the legendary emperors Yao(堯) and Shun(舜), supposedly noted for peace and order—the golden age

七畫

【舝】 4795 (轄) ㄒㄧㄚˊ shya xiá
a linchpin

八畫

【舞】 4796 ㄨˇ wuu wǔ
1. to dance; to prance
2. to brandish; to wave
3. to stir up; to agitate

舞伴(ㄨˇ ㄅㄢˋ)
a dancing partner

舞弊(ㄨˇ ㄅㄧˋ)
misconduct, malpractice or irregularities (of an official); to bribe; to indulge in corruption

舞抃(ㄨˇ ㄅㄧㄢˋ)
to dance for joy

舞步(ㄨˇ ㄅㄨˋ)
a dance step

舞票(ㄨˇ ㄆㄧㄠˋ)
a dance hall ticket

舞刀(ㄨˇ ㄉㄠ)
to brandish a knife or sword; to perform swordplay

舞蹈(ㄨˇ ㄉㄠˋ)
① dancing ② a dance

舞蹈指揮(ㄨˇ ㄉㄠˋ ㄓˇ ㄏㄨㄟ)
a choreographer

舞動(ㄨˇ ㄉㄨㄥˋ)
① to dance; to prance ② to brandish

舞臺(ㄨˇ ㄊㄞˊ)
a stage (in a theater)

舞臺監督(ㄨˇ ㄊㄞˊ ㄐㄧㄢ ㄉㄨ)
a stage manager

舞臺劇(ㄨˇ ㄊㄞˊ ㄐㄩˋ)
a stage play

舞臺效果(ㄨˇ ㄊㄞˊ ㄒㄧㄠˋ ㄍㄨㄛˇ)
stage effects

舞臺照明(ㄨˇ ㄊㄞˊ ㄓㄠˋ ㄇㄧㄥˊ)
stage lighting

舞臺裝置(ㄨˇ ㄊㄞˊ ㄓㄨㄤ ㄓˋ)
a stage setting

舞臺設計(ㄨˇ ㄊㄞˊ ㄕㄜˋ ㄐㄧˋ)
a stage set

舞臺藝術(ㄨˇ ㄊㄞˊ ㄧˋ ㄕㄨˋ)
theatrical art; theatricalism

舞廳(ㄨˇ ㄊㄧㄥ)
a dance hall

舞孃(ㄨˇ ㄋㄧㄤˊ)
a taxi dancer

舞女(ㄨˇ ㄋㄩˇ)
a taxi dancer; a dancing girl

舞龍(ㄨˇ ㄌㄨㄥˊ)
a dragon dance (a team of men dancing with a cloth-made dragon on Chinese festivals)

舞弄(ㄨˇ ㄌㄨㄥˋ)
① to wave; to wield; to brandish ② to make fun of (a person)

舞弄文墨(ㄨˇ ㄌㄨㄥˋ ㄨㄣˊ ㄇㄛˋ)or 舞文弄墨(ㄨˇ ㄨㄣˊ ㄌㄨㄥˋ ㄇㄛˋ)
① to amuse oneself with writing ② to tamper with documents (for fraudulent purposes); to pervert the law by playing with legal phraseology

舞客(ㄨˇ ㄎㄜˋ)
a dance hall customer

舞會(ㄨˇ ㄏㄨㄟˋ)
a dancing party; a dance; a ball

舞技(ㄨˇ ㄐㄧˋ)
dancing skills

舞劍(ㄨˇ ㄐㄧㄢˋ)
to brandish a sword; to perform swordplay

舞劇(ㄨˇ ㄐㄩˋ)
ballet

舞曲(ㄨˇ ㄑㄩˇ)
dance music; a dance tune

舞榭歌臺(ㄨˇ ㄒㄧㄝˋ ㄍㄜ ㄊㄞˊ)
a place for dancing and singing; entertainment setups

舞池(ㄨˇ ㄔˊ)
a dance floor

舞場(ㄨˇ ㄔㄤˇ)or(ㄨˇ ㄔㄤˊ)
a dance house; a dance hall

舞師(ㄨˇ ㄕ)
a dancing master or mistress

舞獅(ㄨˇ ㄕ)
a lion dance (a two-man team dancing inside a cloth-made lion on Chinese festivals)

舞文弄法(ㄨˇ ㄨㄣˊ ㄌㄨㄥˋ ㄈㄚˇ)
to tamper with the language of documents or laws for illicit purposes

舟部
ㄓㄡ jou zhōu

【舟】 4797 ㄓㄡ jou zhōu
a boat; a ship; a vessel

舟楫(ㄓㄡ ㄐㄧˊ)
① ships; vessels ② a capable assistant

舟中敵國(ㄓㄡ ㄓㄨㄥ ㄉㄧˊ ㄍㄨㄛˊ)
(literally) the enemy in the same boat—treacherous close friends
舟車勞頓(ㄓㄡ ㄔㄜ ㄌㄠˊ ㄉㄨㄣˋ)
exhausted from a long travel
舟師(ㄓㄡ ㄕ)
the navy (in ancient times)
舟山羣島(ㄓㄡ ㄕㄢ ㄑㄩㄣˊ ㄉㄠˇ)
the Choushan Islands (off the Chekiang coast)
舟人(ㄓㄡ ㄖㄣˊ)or 舟子(ㄓㄡ ㄗˇ)
a boatman
舟次(ㄓㄡ ㄘˋ)
① to moor a boat ② in the way of a boat trip

二畫

【舠】 4798
ㄉㄠ dau dāo
a knife-shaped boat

三畫

【舢】 4799
ㄕㄢ shan shān
a sampan
舢板 or 舢舨(ㄕㄢ ㄅㄢˇ)
a sampan

【舡】 4800
ㄒㄧㄤ shiang xiāng
a ship; a boat

四畫

【航】 4801
ㄏㄤˊ harng háng
1. a ship; a boat; a vessel
2. to navigate

航道(ㄏㄤˊ ㄉㄠˋ)
a navigation route
航路(ㄏㄤˊ ㄌㄨˋ)
a route (of a ship or airplane)
航路標記(ㄏㄤˊ ㄌㄨˋ ㄅㄧㄠ ㄐㄧˋ)
route markers (for ships, etc.)
航空(ㄏㄤˊ ㄎㄨㄥ)
aviation; aeronautics
航空母艦(ㄏㄤˊ ㄎㄨㄥ ㄇㄨˇ ㄐㄧㄢˋ)
an aircraft carrier; a flattop
航空掛號(ㄏㄤˊ ㄎㄨㄥ ㄍㄨㄚˋ ㄏㄠˋ)
registered airmail
航空工程學(ㄏㄤˊ ㄎㄨㄥ ㄍㄨㄥ ㄔㄥˊ ㄒㄩㄝˊ)
aeronautical engineering
航空公司(ㄏㄤˊ ㄎㄨㄥ ㄍㄨㄥ ㄙ)
an airline
航空信(ㄏㄤˊ ㄎㄨㄥ ㄒㄧㄣˋ)
airmail; an airmail letter: 我寄給她一封航空信。I sent her a letter by airmail.
航空學校(ㄏㄤˊ ㄎㄨㄥ ㄒㄩㄝˊ ㄒㄧㄠˋ)
an aviation school
航空站(ㄏㄤˊ ㄎㄨㄥ ㄓㄢˋ)
an air station; an airfield
航空署(ㄏㄤˊ ㄎㄨㄥ ㄕㄨˇ)
the aviation department or bureau; the aeronautical bureau or department
航空郵件(ㄏㄤˊ ㄎㄨㄥ ㄧㄡˊ ㄐㄧㄢˋ)
airmail: 今早有航空郵件嗎? Is there any airmail this morning?
航空網(ㄏㄤˊ ㄎㄨㄥ ㄨㄤˇ)
a network of air routes
航空員(ㄏㄤˊ ㄎㄨㄥ ㄩㄢˊ)
an airman; an aviator: 那位航空員駕駛他的飛機。The aviator pilots his airplane.
航海(ㄏㄤˊ ㄏㄞˇ)
maritime navigation; a voyage; to sail on the seas
航海曆書(ㄏㄤˊ ㄏㄞˇ ㄌㄧˋ ㄕㄨ)
nautical almanacs
航海家(ㄏㄤˊ ㄏㄞˇ ㄐㄧㄚ)
a navigator; a seafarer
航海節(ㄏㄤˊ ㄏㄞˇ ㄐㄧㄝˊ)
Navigation Day (falling on July 11)
航海學(ㄏㄤˊ ㄏㄞˇ ㄒㄩㄝˊ)
maritime navigation
航海術(ㄏㄤˊ ㄏㄞˇ ㄕㄨˋ)
the art of (sea) navigation
航海日誌(ㄏㄤˊ ㄏㄞˇ ㄖˋ ㄓˋ)
a log (of a ship)
航權(ㄏㄤˊ ㄑㄩㄢˊ)
the right of navigation
航線(ㄏㄤˊ ㄒㄧㄢˋ)
routes (of an airline or shipping company)
航向(ㄏㄤˊ ㄒㄧㄤˋ)
a course (of a ship or plane)
航行(ㄏㄤˊ ㄒㄧㄥˊ)
① to sail ② to fly
航政(ㄏㄤˊ ㄓㄥˋ)
shipping administration
航程(ㄏㄤˊ ㄔㄥˊ)
the distance of an air or a sea trip; sail: 此處距香港有兩日之航程。It is two days' sail from Hongkong.
航船(ㄏㄤˊ ㄔㄨㄢˊ)
a liner
航業(ㄏㄤˊ ㄧㄝˋ)
shipping business
航業公司(ㄏㄤˊ ㄧㄝˋ ㄍㄨㄥ ㄙ)
a shipping company
航運(ㄏㄤˊ ㄩㄣˋ)
shipping: 他們從事航運業。They engage in shipping business.

【般】 4802
1. ㄅㄢ ban bān
1. kind; sort; class
2. same as 搬—to carry; to move
3. same as 班—to return; to call back

般般(ㄅㄢ ㄅㄢ)
① colorful; gorgeous 亦作「斑斑」② all kinds; every sort
般配(ㄅㄢ ㄆㄟˋ)
to match: 他的服飾與年齡般配。His clothes match his age.
般師(ㄅㄢ ㄕ)
to call back troops; to withdraw troops after a victorious campaign

【般】 4802
2. ㄆㄢˊ parn pán
1. to linger
2. comfort
3. a leather bag

般樂(ㄆㄢˊ ㄌㄜˋ)
to have fun without being conscious of time; pleasure
般遊(ㄆㄢˊ ㄧㄡˊ)
to play without being conscious of time

【般】 4802
3. ㄅㄛ bo bō
(Buddhism) intelligence
般若(ㄅㄛ ㄖㄜˇ)
(Buddhism) *prajna*, wisdom

【舫】 4803
ㄈㄤˇ faang fǎng
1. two boats lashed side by side
2. boats; ships

【舨】 4804
ㄅㄢˇ baan bǎn
as in 舢舨—a sampan

五畫

【舲】 4805 ㄌㄧㄥˊ ling líng
a small boat with portholes

【舳】 4806 ㄓㄨˊ jwu zhú
(又讀 ㄓㄡˊ jour zhóu)
the stern (of a ship)

舳艫(ㄓㄨˊ ㄌㄨˊ)
a rectangular boat

舳艫千里(ㄓㄨˊ ㄌㄨˊ ㄑㄧㄢ ㄌㄧˇ)
(literally) formation of ships extending over a thousand miles—a very large flotilla

【舴】 4807 ㄗㄜˊ tzer zé
a small boat

舴艋(ㄗㄜˊ ㄇㄥˇ)
a small boat

【舵】 4808 ㄉㄨㄛˋ duoh duò
a rudder; a helm

舵手(ㄉㄨㄛˋ ㄕㄡˇ)
a helmsman; a steersman: 首相是國家的舵手。The Prime Minister is the helmsman of the state.

【舶】 4809 ㄅㄛˊ bor bó
an ocean-going ship

舶來品(ㄅㄛˊ ㄌㄞˊ ㄆㄧㄣˇ)
imported goods; foreign goods

【舷】 4810 ㄒㄧㄢˊ shyan xián
bulwarks (of a ship); the gunwale or gunnel

【舸】 4811 ㄍㄜˇ gee gě
a large boat

【船】 4812 ㄔㄨㄢˊ chwan chuán
a ship; a boat; a vessel; a craft

船舶(ㄔㄨㄢˊ ㄅㄛˊ)
ships; vessels; boats; crafts

船板(ㄔㄨㄢˊ ㄅㄢˇ)
the deck (of a ship)

船幫(ㄔㄨㄢˊ ㄅㄤ)
sides of a ship

船埠(ㄔㄨㄢˊ ㄅㄨˋ)
a port; a harbor; a wharf

船破又遇打頭風(ㄔㄨㄢˊ ㄆㄛˋ ㄧㄡˋ ㄩˋ ㄉㄚˇ ㄊㄡˊ ㄈㄥ)
(literally) to meet unfavorable winds when the boat is broken—to meet additional difficulty

船篷(ㄔㄨㄢˊ ㄆㄥˊ)
coverings of a boat

船票(ㄔㄨㄢˊ ㄆㄧㄠˋ)
a ticket for passage by sea

船面(ㄔㄨㄢˊ ㄇㄧㄢˋ)
the deck (of a ship): 我們去船面上散步吧。Let's have a walk round the deck.

船費(ㄔㄨㄢˊ ㄈㄟˋ)
a fare for a voyage

船夫(ㄔㄨㄢˊ ㄈㄨ)
a sailor; a boatman

船到江心補漏遲(ㄔㄨㄢˊ ㄉㄠˋ ㄐㄧㄤ ㄒㄧㄣ ㄅㄨˇ ㄌㄡˋ ㄔˊ)
(literally) It will be too late to mend a boat when it has reached the middle of the river.—It's too late to take corrective measures when a crisis has already developed.

船到橋頭自然直(ㄔㄨㄢˊ ㄉㄠˋ ㄑㄧㄠˊ ㄊㄡˊ ㄗˋ ㄖㄢˊ ㄓˊ)
It will take care of itself when the time comes.或 Everything will be all right when the time comes.

船多不礙江(ㄔㄨㄢˊ ㄉㄨㄛ ㄅㄨˋ ㄞˋ ㄐㄧㄤ)
(literally) It does no harm to the river when there are many boats sailing on it.—Competition among businessmen does no harm to business prosperity.

船隊(ㄔㄨㄢˊ ㄉㄨㄟˋ)
a fleet; a flotilla

船東(ㄔㄨㄢˊ ㄉㄨㄥ)
a shipowner

船頭(ㄔㄨㄢˊ ㄊㄡˊ)
the bow or prow (of a boat)

船齡(ㄔㄨㄢˊ ㄌㄧㄥˊ)
the age of a ship

船客(ㄔㄨㄢˊ ㄎㄜˋ)
the passengers of a ship

船客名單(ㄔㄨㄢˊ ㄎㄜˋ ㄇㄧㄥˊ ㄉㄢ)
the passenger list (of a boat)

船戶(ㄔㄨㄢˊ ㄏㄨˋ)
a boatman's family

船貨(ㄔㄨㄢˊ ㄏㄨㄛˋ)
cargo

船籍(ㄔㄨㄢˊ ㄐㄧˊ)
nationality of a ship

船家(ㄔㄨㄢˊ ㄐㄧㄚ)
a boatman

船脚(ㄔㄨㄢˊ ㄐㄧㄠˇ)
① a boatman ② shipping freight

船期(ㄔㄨㄢˊ ㄑㄧˊ)
a shipping schedule

船舷(ㄔㄨㄢˊ ㄒㄧㄢˊ)
bulwarks (of a boat); the gunwale or gunnel

船隻(ㄔㄨㄢˊ ㄓ)
ships; boats; crafts; vessels

船長(ㄔㄨㄢˊ ㄓㄤˇ)
the captain or skipper (of a boat)

船主(ㄔㄨㄢˊ ㄓㄨˇ)
① the captain or skipper (of a boat) ② the owner (of a boat)

船廠(ㄔㄨㄢˊ ㄔㄤˇ)
a shipyard; a dockyard

船梢(ㄔㄨㄢˊ ㄕㄠ)
the bow or prow (of a boat)

船身(ㄔㄨㄢˊ ㄕㄣ)
a ship's hull

船身傾斜(ㄔㄨㄢˊ ㄕㄣ ㄑㄧㄥ ㄒㄧㄝˊ)
(said of a ship) listing; to list

船深(ㄔㄨㄢˊ ㄕㄣ)
draft (of a ship): 這船船深十英呎。This is a ship of 10 feet draft.

船上交貨價(ㄔㄨㄢˊ ㄕㄤˋ ㄐㄧㄠ ㄏㄨㄛˋ ㄐㄧㄚˋ)
free on board (F.O.B.)

船艙(ㄔㄨㄢˊ ㄘㄤ)
the hold or cabin (of a boat)

船隖 or 船塢(ㄔㄨㄢˊ ㄨˋ)
a dock (in a shipyard)

船桅(ㄔㄨㄢˊ ㄨㄟˊ)
the mast (of a ship)

船尾(ㄔㄨㄢˊ ㄨㄟˇ)
the stern (of a ship)

船位(ㄔㄨㄢˊ ㄨㄟˋ)
① accommodation (on a ship) ② a ship's position

船員(ㄔㄨㄢˊ ㄩㄢˊ)
the crew (of a ship)

船運(ㄔㄨㄢˊ ㄩㄣˋ)
to transport by ship

七畫

【艇】 4813 ㄊㄧㄥˇ tiing tǐng
a long, narrow boat

艇長(ㄊㄧㄥˇ ㄓㄤˇ)
the skipper of a naval boat

【艄】 4814
ㄕㄠ shau shāo
1. the stern (of a boat)
2. a rudder; a helm: 誰在掌艄? Who is at the helm?

艄婆(ㄕㄠ ㄆㄛˊ)
a boatwoman

艄公(ㄕㄠ ㄍㄨㄥ)
a helmsman; a boatman 亦作「船夫」

八畫

【艋】 4815
ㄇㄥˇ meeng měng
a small boat

十畫

【艘】 4816
ㄙㄠ sau sāo
a numerary adjunct for ships

【艙】 4817
ㄘㄤ tsang cāng
the hold or cabin (of a ship)

艙房(ㄘㄤ ㄈㄤˊ)
cabins (of a ship)

艙底(ㄘㄤ ㄉㄧˇ)
the bottom of a ship's hold

艙位(ㄘㄤ ㄨㄟˋ)
space for passengers (in a liner); a berth

十二畫

【艟】 4818
ㄊㄨㄥˊ torng tóng
as in 艨艟—an ancient warship

十三畫

【艤】 4819
ㄧˇ yii yǐ
to moor (a boat) to the bank

十四畫

【艦】 4820
ㄐㄧㄢˋ jiann jiàn
a warship; a man-of-war; a naval vessel

艦隊(ㄐㄧㄢˋ ㄉㄨㄟˋ)
a fleet; a naval task force

艦隊司令(ㄐㄧㄢˋ ㄉㄨㄟˋ ㄙ ㄌㄧㄥˋ)
a fleet commander

艦艇(ㄐㄧㄢˋ ㄊㄧㄥˇ)
naval vessels

艦橋(ㄐㄧㄢˋ ㄑㄧㄠˊ)
the bridge (of a naval ship)

艦隻(ㄐㄧㄢˋ ㄓ)
naval vessels

艦長(ㄐㄧㄢˋ ㄓㄤˇ)
the captain or skipper of a naval vessel

【艨】 4821
ㄇㄥˊ meng méng
as in 艨艟—an ancient warship

十六畫

【艫】 4822
ㄌㄨˊ lu lú
the bow or prow (of a boat)

艮部
ㄍㄣˋ genn gèn

【艮】 4823
1. ㄍㄣˋ genn gèn
one of the Eight Diagrams for divination

艮苦冰涼(ㄍㄣˋ ㄎㄨˇ ㄅㄧㄥ ㄌㄧㄤˊ)
① stark poverty; great misery ② ruthless; relentless; merciless; cold

【艮】 4823
2. ㄍㄣˇ geen gěn
1. (said of food) tough; leathery
2. straightforward; outspoken; blunt
3. (said of clothing) simple
4. (said of one's personality) honest; upright

一畫

【良】 4824
ㄌㄧㄤˊ liang liáng
1. good; fine; desirable: 她出身良好。She has a good background.
2. very
3. instinctive; inborn; innate

良伴(ㄌㄧㄤˊ ㄅㄢˋ)
a good companion

良弼(ㄌㄧㄤˊ ㄅㄧˋ)
a good assistant

良兵(ㄌㄧㄤˊ ㄅㄧㄥ)
good troops

良庖(ㄌㄧㄤˊ ㄆㄠˊ)
a good cook; a fine chef

良朋(ㄌㄧㄤˊ ㄆㄥˊ) or 良友(ㄌㄧㄤˊ ㄧㄡˇ) or 良朋益友(ㄌㄧㄤˊ ㄆㄥˊ ㄧˋ ㄧㄡˇ)
worthy friends; good friends; beneficial friends

良平之智(ㄌㄧㄤˊ ㄆㄧㄥˊ ㄓ ㄓˋ)
(literally) the wisdom of Chang Liang (張良) and Chen Ping (陳平) (who helped Liu Pang (劉邦) found the Han Dynasty)—great political sagacity

良馬(ㄌㄧㄤˊ ㄇㄚˇ)
a fine horse

良媒(ㄌㄧㄤˊ ㄇㄟˊ)
an able matchmaker

良民(ㄌㄧㄤˊ ㄇㄧㄣˊ)
law-abiding people; loyal subjects

良方(ㄌㄧㄤˊ ㄈㄤ)
① a good remedy; a good prescription: 這是治咳嗽的良方。This is a good prescription for a cough. ② a good course of action

良導體(ㄌㄧㄤˊ ㄉㄠˇ ㄊㄧˇ)
a good conductor (of heat or electricity)

良多(ㄌㄧㄤˊ ㄉㄨㄛ)
very much; numerous; a great deal

良田(ㄌㄧㄤˊ ㄊㄧㄢˊ)
fertile fields; good land

良圖(ㄌㄧㄤˊ ㄊㄨˊ)
a good plan or scheme

良能(ㄌㄧㄤˊ ㄋㄥˊ)
inborn ability; intuitive ability; instinct

良吏(ㄌㄧㄤˊ ㄌㄧˋ)
a good official; a virtuous public servant

良港(ㄌㄧㄤˊ ㄍㄤˇ)
a good harbor

良弓(ㄌㄧㄤˊ ㄍㄨㄥ)
① a good bowmaker ② a fine bow

良工心苦(ㄌㄧㄤˊ ㄍㄨㄥ ㄒㄧㄣ ㄎㄨˇ)
Expert craftsmanship is the result of long practice and hard work.

良好(ㄌㄧㄤˊ ㄏㄠˇ)
good; fine; desirable

良機(ㄌㄧㄤˊ ㄐㄧ)
a good chance

良機勿失(ㄌㄧㄤˊ ㄐㄧ ㄨˋ ㄕ)
Don't let the good chance slip.

良計(ㄌㄧㄤˊ ㄐㄧˋ)
a good plan, scheme, or strategy

良家(ㄌㄧㄤˊ ㄐㄧㄚ)
a good family; a respectable family

良家子女(ㄌㄧㄤˊ ㄐㄧㄚ ㄗˇ ㄋㄩˇ)
children of good parentage

良久(ㄌㄧㄤˊ ㄐㄧㄡˇ)
for a very long time: 我們在那邊停留良久。We stayed there for a very long time.

良賤(ㄌㄧㄤˊ ㄐㄧㄢˋ)
the different social classes; high and low

良金美玉(ㄌㄧㄤˊ ㄐㄧㄣ ㄇㄟˇ ㄩˋ)
(said of character, writing, etc.) like fine gold and fair jade

良將(ㄌㄧㄤˊ ㄐㄧㄤˋ)
a brilliant general

良禽擇木而棲(ㄌㄧㄤˊ ㄑㄧㄣˊ ㄗㄜˊ ㄇㄨˋ ㄦˊ ㄑㄧ)
(literally) Clever birds choose their trees when they nest.—Capable men choose the right leader to serve.

良宵(ㄌㄧㄤˊ ㄒㄧㄠ)
an enjoyable night: 那是一個滿天星斗的良宵。It was a starry enjoyable night.

良心(ㄌㄧㄤˊ ㄒㄧㄣ)
conscience

良心發現(ㄌㄧㄤˊ ㄒㄧㄣ ㄈㄚ ㄒㄧㄢˋ)
The conscience is moved.

良心譴責(ㄌㄧㄤˊ ㄒㄧㄣ ㄑㄧㄢˇ ㄗㄜˊ)
to feel the pricks of conscience; to have a guilty conscience

良心喪盡(ㄌㄧㄤˊ ㄒㄧㄣ ㄙㄤˋ ㄐㄧㄣˋ)
utterly conscienceless: 他已良心喪盡。He is utterly conscienceless.

良相(ㄌㄧㄤˊ ㄒㄧㄤˋ)
a wise prime minister

良知(ㄌㄧㄤˊ ㄓ)
①instinct; innate knowledge ②an understanding friend

良知良能(ㄌㄧㄤˊ ㄓ ㄌㄧㄤˊ ㄋㄥˊ)
innate knowledge and ability; instinct

良終(ㄌㄧㄤˊ ㄓㄨㄥ)
a peaceful death

良辰(ㄌㄧㄤˊ ㄔㄣˊ)or 良日(ㄌㄧㄤˊ ㄖˋ)
a pleasant day

良辰美景(ㄌㄧㄤˊ ㄔㄣˊ ㄇㄟˇ ㄐㄧㄥˇ)
a pleasant day coupled with a fine landscape

良師(ㄌㄧㄤˊ ㄕ)
a good teacher: 大自然是我們的良師。Nature is our good teacher.

良師興國(ㄌㄧㄤˊ ㄕ ㄒㄧㄥ ㄍㄨㄛˊ)
Good teachers can help bring a nation to power.

良師益友(ㄌㄧㄤˊ ㄕ ㄧˋ ㄧㄡˇ)
good teachers and helpful friends

良史(ㄌㄧㄤˊ ㄕˇ)
①a good history book ②a good historian

良士(ㄌㄧㄤˊ ㄕˋ)
a person of high moral standing

良善(ㄌㄧㄤˊ ㄕㄢˋ)
good; fine

良善風俗(ㄌㄧㄤˊ ㄕㄢˋ ㄈㄥ ㄙㄨˊ)
good custom or practice

良深(ㄌㄧㄤˊ ㄕㄣ)
deeply; very: 他感動良深。He was deeply moved.

良人(ㄌㄧㄤˊ ㄖㄣˊ)
①a good person ②one's husband

良策(ㄌㄧㄤˊ ㄘㄜˋ)
a good policy, scheme, or strategy

良材(ㄌㄧㄤˊ ㄘㄞˊ)
an able person

良死(ㄌㄧㄤˊ ㄙˇ)
to die a natural death

良醫(ㄌㄧㄤˊ ㄧ)
an able physician; a good doctor

良冶(ㄌㄧㄤˊ ㄧㄝˇ)
a fine metalist

良夜(ㄌㄧㄤˊ ㄧㄝˋ)
a pleasant night

良藥苦口(ㄌㄧㄤˊ ㄧㄠˋ ㄎㄨˇ ㄎㄡˇ)
(literally) Good medicine tastes bitter.—Good advice is never pleasant to the ear.

良莠不齊(ㄌㄧㄤˊ ㄧㄡˇ ㄅㄨˋ ㄑㄧˊ)
some good, some bad (especially said of a crowd of people)

良月(ㄌㄧㄤˊ ㄩㄝˋ)
the tenth month of the lunar calendar

良緣(ㄌㄧㄤˊ ㄩㄢˊ)
a harmonious union; a happy match

十一畫

【艱】 4825
ㄐㄧㄢ jian jiān

1. difficult; hard; trying
2. mourning for one's parents

艱難(ㄐㄧㄢ ㄋㄢˊ)
difficulty; distress; hardship

艱難困苦(ㄐㄧㄢ ㄋㄢˊ ㄎㄨㄣˋ ㄎㄨˇ)
great difficulties or hardships

艱苦(ㄐㄧㄢ ㄎㄨˇ)
trying; hard; privation

艱苦備嘗(ㄐㄧㄢ ㄎㄨˇ ㄅㄟˋ ㄔㄤˊ)
to have experienced all sorts of hardships

艱困(ㄐㄧㄢ ㄎㄨㄣˋ)
difficult

艱鉅(ㄐㄧㄢ ㄐㄩˋ)
hard; difficult; arduous; laborious; formidable

艱險(ㄐㄧㄢ ㄒㄧㄢˇ)or 艱危(ㄐㄧㄢ ㄨㄟˊ)
difficult and dangerous

艱辛(ㄐㄧㄢ ㄒㄧㄣ)
arduous; laborious; hard; difficult

艱貞(ㄐㄧㄢ ㄓㄣ)
fortitude under trying conditions

艱深(ㄐㄧㄢ ㄕㄣ)
abstruse; difficult: 這是一個艱深的問題。This is an abstruse question.

艱阻(ㄐㄧㄢ ㄗㄨˇ)
troublesome obstacles

艱澀(ㄐㄧㄢ ㄙㄜˋ)
abstruse; difficult

色部
ㄙㄜˋ seh sè

【色】 4826
ㄙㄜˋ seh sè
(語音 ㄕㄞˇ shae shǎi)

1. a color; a tinge; a tint; a hue
2. facial expression; a look; an appearance

3. sensuality; lust; lewdness; carnal pleasure
4. worldly things
5. a kind; a sort

色玻璃(ㄙㄜˋ ㄅㄛ ·ㄌㄧ)
stained glass; colored glass

色盲(ㄙㄜˋ ㄇㄤˊ)
color blindness; color-blind; achromatopsy

色迷(ㄙㄜˋ ㄇㄧˊ)
a sensualist; a Don Juan

色目(ㄙㄜˋ ㄇㄨˋ)
social status (as distinguished from the colors of clothing)

色膽包天(ㄙㄜˋ ㄉㄢˇ ㄅㄠ ㄊㄧㄢ)
extremely daring in lewdness

色調(ㄙㄜˋ ㄉㄧㄠˋ)
a shade of color; a tone

色狼(ㄙㄜˋ ㄌㄤˊ)
(slang) a wolf—a lecherous person 參看「色鬼」

色厲內荏(ㄙㄜˋ ㄌㄧˋ ㄋㄟˋ ㄖㄣˇ)
looking tough but scared at heart; fierce of mien but faint of heart

色鬼(ㄙㄜˋ ㄍㄨㄟˇ)
a satyr; a lecher: 他是個色鬼。He is a satyr.

色荒(ㄙㄜˋ ㄏㄨㄤ)
unrestrained indulgence in lust

色即是空(ㄙㄜˋ ㄐㄧˊ ㄕˋ ㄎㄨㄥ)
(a Buddhist concept) Everything visible is empty.

色覺(ㄙㄜˋ ㄐㄩㄝˊ)
sensation of color

色情(ㄙㄜˋ ㄑㄧㄥˊ)
sexual passion; lust

色情狂(ㄙㄜˋ ㄑㄧㄥˊ ㄎㄨㄤˊ)
① sexual insanity; satyriasis ② erotomania; nymphomania ③ an erotomaniac; a nymphomaniac

色喜(ㄙㄜˋ ㄒㄧˇ)
showing pleasure; looking pleased

色笑(ㄙㄜˋ ㄒㄧㄠˋ)
a benign look

色相(ㄙㄜˋ ㄒㄧㄤˋ)
①(Buddhism) the outward appearance of a thing ② feminine charm

色紙(ㄙㄜˋ ㄓˇ)
colored paper

色智(ㄙㄜˋ ㄓˋ)
looking arrogant in the belief that one is superior to others

色中餓鬼(ㄙㄜˋ ㄓㄨㄥ ㄜˋ ㄍㄨㄟˇ)
a satyr; an erotomaniac

色授神與(ㄙㄜˋ ㄕㄡˋ ㄕㄣˊ ㄩˇ)
communication between minds without use of words

色身(ㄙㄜˋ ㄕㄣ)
①(Buddhism) the physical body ② outward charm of a woman

色衰愛弛(ㄙㄜˋ ㄕㄨㄞ ㄞˋ ㄔˊ)
to lose beauty as well as affection

色澤(ㄙㄜˋ ㄗㄜˊ)
a tinge; a color; a hue; a tint

色彩(ㄙㄜˋ ㄘㄞˇ)
a color; a hue; a tint; a tinge: 紅、藍和黃都是色彩。Red, blue and yellow are colors.

色彩鮮明(ㄙㄜˋ ㄘㄞˇ ㄒㄧㄢ ㄇㄧㄥˊ)
bright-colored

色色俱全(ㄙㄜˋ ㄙㄜˋ ㄐㄩˋ ㄑㄩㄢˊ)
complete with all sorts of things

色素(ㄙㄜˋ ㄙㄨˋ)
pigment

色素細胞(ㄙㄜˋ ㄙㄨˋ ㄒㄧˋ ㄅㄠ)
a chromatophore

色藝(ㄙㄜˋ ㄧˋ)
beauty and accomplishments (of a woman)

色艷桃李(ㄙㄜˋ ㄧㄢˋ ㄊㄠˊ ㄌㄧˇ)
(said of a woman) as beautiful as a flower

色慾(ㄙㄜˋ ㄩˋ)
sexual desire; sexual passion; lust: 他縱情色慾。He indulged himself in lust.

五畫

【艴】 4827
ㄈㄨˊ fwu fú
to look angry

艴然(ㄈㄨˊ ㄖㄢˊ)
to look angry; an angry look

十八畫

【艷】 4828
(豔) ㄧㄢˋ yann yàn
beautiful: 她是一個艷婦。She is a beautiful woman.

艸部
ㄘㄠˇ tsao cǎo

【艸】 4829
ㄘㄠˇ tsao cǎo
grass; straw; weeds

二畫

【艾】 4830
ㄞˋ ay ài
1. moxa
2. fine; fair; beautiful; good
3. old
4. to end; to cease; to stop; to discontinue
5. a Chinese family name

艾老(ㄞˋ ㄌㄠˇ)
over 50 years old

艾酒(ㄞˋ ㄐㄧㄡˇ)
moxa wine

艾灸(ㄞˋ ㄐㄧㄡˇ) or 艾炷灸(ㄞˋ ㄓㄨˋ ㄐㄧㄡˇ)
moxibustion

艾森豪(ㄞˋ ㄙㄣ ㄏㄠˊ)
Dwight David Eisenhower, 1890-1969, 34th president of the United States

艾艾(ㄞˋ ㄞˋ)
stammering; stuttering

【艿】 4831
ㄋㄞˇ nae nǎi
a kind of vegetable

三畫

【芃】 4832
ㄆㄥˊ perng péng
growing luxuriantly; lush

【芄】 4833
ㄨㄢˊ wan wán
Metaplexis japonica

【芊】 4834
ㄑㄧㄢ chian qiān
(said of grass) lush; green

【芋】 4835
ㄩˋ yuh yù
a taro

芋頭(ㄩˋ ·ㄊㄡ) or 芋艿(ㄩˋ ㄋㄞˇ)
(botany) a taro

〔艸部〕

【芍】 4836 ㄕㄠˊ shaur sháo (讀音 ㄕㄨㄛˋ shuoh shuò)
Paeonia, a peony
芍藥(ㄕㄠˊ ㄧㄠˋ)
a Chinese herbaceous peony

【芎】 4837 ㄑㄩㄥ chiong qiōng (讀音 ㄑㄩㄥˊ chyong qióng)
a kind of herb (*Cnidium officinale*)

【芒】 4838 ㄇㄤˊ mang máng
1. *Miscanthus sinensis*, a kind of grass whose leaves can be used to make sandals
2. a sharp point
3. (botany) an awn; an arista; beards of wheat
4. rays (of stars)
5. a Chinese family name
芒芒(ㄇㄤˊ ㄇㄤˊ)
① tired; weary ② vast; extensive 亦作「茫茫」③ abundant
芒果(ㄇㄤˊ ㄍㄨㄛˇ)
a mango
芒鞋(ㄇㄤˊ ㄒㄧㄝˊ)
straw sandals: 僧人穿芒鞋。Monks wear straw sandals.
芒種(ㄇㄤˊ ㄓㄨㄥˋ)
one of the 24 seasonal periods into which the year is divided (occurring about June 5-7)
芒刃(ㄇㄤˊ ㄖㄣˋ)
a sharp blade
芒刺在背(ㄇㄤˊ ㄘˋ ㄗㄞˋ ㄅㄟˋ)
(literally) having prickles down the back—ill at ease; deeply worried

四畫

【芙】 4839 ㄈㄨˊ fwu fú
a hibiscus
芙蕖(ㄈㄨˊ ㄑㄩˊ)
lotus flowers
芙蓉(ㄈㄨˊ ㄖㄨㄥˊ)
a hibiscus
芙蓉面(ㄈㄨˊ ㄖㄨㄥˊ ㄇㄧㄢˋ)
a face fair as a hibiscus; a pretty face
芙蓉鳥(ㄈㄨˊ ㄖㄨㄥˊ ㄋㄧㄠˇ)
Serinus cannaria, a kind of singing bird
芙蓉帳(ㄈㄨˊ ㄖㄨㄥˊ ㄓㄤˋ)
a mosquito net dyed with the juice of hibiscus flowers
芙蓉出水(ㄈㄨˊ ㄖㄨㄥˊ ㄔㄨ ㄕㄨㄟˇ)
a hibiscus rising out of water (descriptive of the gracefulness of a piece of writing, a woman, etc.)

【芝】 4840 ㄓ jy zhī
1. a kind of purplish fungus symbolizing nobility
2. a kind of fragrant herb
3. a Chinese family name
芝麻(ㄓ ·ㄇㄚ)
sesame
芝麻稭(ㄓ ·ㄇㄚ ㄐㄧㄝ)
sesame stalks and husks after its seeds have been collected
芝麻醬(ㄓ ·ㄇㄚ ㄐㄧㄤˋ)
a pasty preparation from sesame; sesame butter
芝麻油(ㄓ ·ㄇㄚ ㄧㄡˊ)
sesame oil
芝眉(ㄓ ㄇㄟˊ)
dignified eyebrows
芝罘條約(ㄓ ㄈㄡˊ ㄊㄧㄠˊ ㄩㄝ)
a treaty signed with Great Britain in 1876, under which China opened five ports and paid 200,000 taels of silver as compensation for the death of a British citizen killed in Yunnan 亦作「煙臺條約」
芝焚蕙歎(ㄓ ㄈㄣˊ ㄏㄨㄟˋ ㄊㄢˋ)
One is saddened over the fall of a kindred spirit.
芝泥(ㄓ ㄋㄧˊ)
stamp ink 亦作「印泥」
芝蘭(ㄓ ㄌㄢˊ)
① the glossy ganoderma and the fragrant thoroughwort—both of them are fragrant herbs ②(figuratively) a virtuous behavior
芝蘭氣味(ㄓ ㄌㄢˊ ㄑㄧˋ ㄨㄟˋ)
noble friendship
芝蘭室(ㄓ ㄌㄢˊ ㄕˋ)
a morally fine environment
芝蘭玉樹(ㄓ ㄌㄢˊ ㄩˋ ㄕㄨˋ)
worthy followers or disciples
芝加哥(ㄓ ㄐㄧㄚ ㄍㄜ)
Chicago, Illinois
芝草(ㄓ ㄘㄠˇ)
a kind of parasitic fungus
芝艾俱焚(ㄓ ㄞˋ ㄐㄩˋ ㄈㄣˊ)
The noble and the lowly alike met their fate.
芝儀(ㄓ ㄧˊ)or 芝顏(ㄓ ㄧㄢˊ)or 芝宇(ㄓ ㄩˇ)
your noble face

【芟】 4841 ㄕㄢ shan shān
1. to mow; to cut down
2. to eliminate; to exterminate
3. a scythe
芟穢(ㄕㄢ ㄏㄨㄟˋ)
to weed out causes of harm
芟除(ㄕㄢ ㄔㄨˊ)
to weed out; to eliminate; to exterminate; to eradicate
芟草除根(ㄕㄢ ㄘㄠˇ ㄔㄨˊ ㄍㄣ)
to clear the ground of weeds and roots
芟夷(ㄕㄢ ㄧˊ)
to exterminate; to eliminate; to weed out

【芡】 4842 ㄑㄧㄢˋ chiann qiàn
(botany) Gorgon euryale (*Euryale ferox*)
芡粉(ㄑㄧㄢˋ ㄈㄣˇ)
a kind of starch
芡實(ㄑㄧㄢˋ ㄕˊ)
Gorgon fruit 亦作「雞頭米」

【芣】 4843 ㄈㄡˊ four fóu
a plantain
芣苢 or 芣苡(ㄈㄡˊ ㄧˇ)
a plantain

【芥】 4844 ㄐㄧㄝˋ jieh jiè
1. a mustard plant
2. tiny
芥末(ㄐㄧㄝˋ ·ㄇㄛ)
ground mustard
芥蒂 or 芥蔕(ㄐㄧㄝˋ ㄉㄧˋ)
① remorse; a grudge ② a barrier which mars friendship
芥藍菜(ㄐㄧㄝˋ ㄌㄢˊ ㄘㄞˋ)
a kind of green vegetable
芥子(ㄐㄧㄝˋ ㄗˇ)
① mustard seed ② a tiny thing
芥子瓦斯(ㄐㄧㄝˋ ㄗˇ ㄨㄚˇ ㄙ)or 芥子氣(ㄐㄧㄝˋ ㄗˇ ㄑㄧˋ)
(chemistry) mustard gas
芥菜(ㄐㄧㄝˋ ㄘㄞˋ)

a mustard plant; leaf mustard

【芧】 4845 ㄒㄩˋ shiuh xù
a kind of chestnut oak

芧栗(ㄒㄩˋ ㄌㄧˋ)
a small chestnut

【芩】 4846 ㄑㄧㄣˊ chyn qín
Phragmites japonica, a kind of herb whose root is medicinal

【芫】 4847 ㄩㄢˊ yuan yuán
Daphne genkwa, a kind of poisonous plant

芫荽(ㄩㄢˊ ㄙㄨㄟ)
parsley

【芬】 4848 ㄈㄣ fen fēn
fragrance; aroma; a sweet smell; perfume

芬菲(ㄈㄣ ㄈㄟ)
fragrance of flowers

芬芬(ㄈㄣ ㄈㄣ)
a sweet smell; fragrance; aroma

芬芳(ㄈㄣ ㄈㄤ)
fragrant; aromatic: 花園中的玫瑰很芬芳。The roses in the garden were fragrant.

芬馥(ㄈㄣ ㄈㄨˋ)
fragrant

芬蘭(ㄈㄣ ㄌㄢˊ)
Finland

芬蘭人(ㄈㄣ ㄌㄢˊ ㄖㄣˊ)
the Finns; a Finlander

芬蘭語(ㄈㄣ ㄌㄢˊ ㄩˇ)
the Finnish language; Finnish

芬烈(ㄈㄣ ㄌㄧㄝˋ)
exceedingly fragrant

芬華(ㄈㄣ ㄏㄨㄚˊ)
① glory; pomp ② luxuriant beauty

芬郁(ㄈㄣ ㄩˋ)
intense fragrance

【芚】 4849 ㄊㄨㄣˊ twen tún
a kind of vegetable

【芭】 4850 ㄅㄚ ba bā
1. a fragrant plant
2. a plantain; a palmetto

芭樂(ㄅㄚ ㄌㄜˋ)
a guava

芭蕾舞(ㄅㄚ ㄌㄟˇ ㄨˇ)
ballet

芭蕾舞迷(ㄅㄚ ㄌㄟˇ ㄨˇ ㄇㄧˊ)
a balletomane

芭蕾舞女(ㄅㄚ ㄌㄟˇ ㄨˇ ㄋㄩˇ)
a ballerina

芭蕾舞裙(ㄅㄚ ㄌㄟˇ ㄨˇ ㄑㄩㄣˊ)
a tutu

芭蕉(ㄅㄚ ㄐㄧㄠ)
a plantain

芭蕉布(ㄅㄚ ㄐㄧㄠ ㄅㄨˋ)
cloth woven from plantain fiber

芭蕉扇(ㄅㄚ ㄐㄧㄠ ㄕㄢˋ)
a palm-leaf fan

【芯】 4851 1. ㄒㄧㄣ shinn xīn
pith of rushes

【芯】 4851 2. ㄒㄧㄣˋ shinn xìn
the central part of an object

【芮】 4852 ㄖㄨㄟˋ ruey ruì
1. small; tiny
2. name of an ancient state in what is Shansi today
3. a Chinese family name

【芰】 4853 ㄐㄧˋ jih jì
a water caltrop

芰實(ㄐㄧˋ ㄕˊ)
a water caltrop

【花】 4854 ㄏㄨㄚ hua huā
1. a flower; a blossom
2. a flowering plant
3. a prostitute; prostitution
4. as in 天花—smallpox
5. varicolored
6. fireworks
7. to spend; to expend

花白(ㄏㄨㄚ ㄅㄞˊ)
(said of hair) white with black spots; gray; graying

花被(ㄏㄨㄚ ㄅㄟˋ)
a floral envelope; a perianth

花苞(ㄏㄨㄚ ㄅㄠ)
a calyx

花瓣(ㄏㄨㄚ ㄅㄢˋ)
the petal (of a flower or blossom)

花邊(ㄏㄨㄚ ㄅㄧㄢ)
① lace; an embroidered hem (of a garment) ② fancy borders (in printing)

花邊新聞(ㄏㄨㄚ ㄅㄧㄢ ㄒㄧㄣ ㄨㄣˊ)
a sidebar

花布(ㄏㄨㄚ ㄅㄨˋ)
calico; printed cotton

花炮(ㄏㄨㄚ ㄆㄠˋ)
fireworks and firecrackers

花盤(ㄏㄨㄚ ㄆㄢˊ)
(botany) a disk

花盆(ㄏㄨㄚ ㄆㄣˊ)
a flower pot

花棚(ㄏㄨㄚ ㄆㄥˊ) or 花架(ㄏㄨㄚ ㄐㄧㄚˋ)
an arbor; a flower stand; a pergola

花片(ㄏㄨㄚ ㄆㄧㄢˋ)
fallen petals

花品(ㄏㄨㄚ ㄆㄧㄣˇ)
a flower's grade of excellence

花瓶(ㄏㄨㄚ ㄆㄧㄥˊ)
a vase

花圃(ㄏㄨㄚ ㄆㄨˇ)
a flower bed

花蜜(ㄏㄨㄚ ㄇㄧˋ)
(botany) nectar

花面(ㄏㄨㄚ ㄇㄧㄢˋ)
(Chinese opera) an actor with a painted face

花名(ㄏㄨㄚ ㄇㄧㄥˊ)
one's official name (as given in the census register)

花名冊(ㄏㄨㄚ ㄇㄧㄥˊ ㄘㄜˋ)
a list of names; a roster

花名兒(ㄏㄨㄚ ㄇㄧㄥˊㄦ)
① names of flowers ② names of prostitutes

花木(ㄏㄨㄚ ㄇㄨˋ)
vegetation; flowers and trees (in parks or gardens)

花木蘭(ㄏㄨㄚ ㄇㄨˋ ㄌㄢˊ)
Hua Mu-lan, a well-known female character who went to war in place of her father

花費(ㄏㄨㄚ ㄈㄟˋ)
to spend; to expend

花販(ㄏㄨㄚ ㄈㄢˋ)
a florist

花粉(ㄏㄨㄚ ㄈㄣˇ)
pollen

花房(ㄏㄨㄚ ㄈㄤˊ)
① a greenhouse; a hothouse ② a corolla

花旦(ㄏㄨㄚ ㄉㄢˋ)
the vivacious female role in Chinese opera

花燈(ㄏㄨㄚ ㄉㄥ)
a fancy lantern (made for the Lantern Festival on the

15th of the first moon)
花彫 or 花雕(ㄏㄨㄚ ㄉㄧㄠ)
rice wine of the best quality from Shaohsing (紹興)
花店(ㄏㄨㄚ ㄉㄧㄢˋ)
a flower shop; a florist's shop
花鈿(ㄏㄨㄚ ㄉㄧㄢˋ)
women's head ornaments in ancient times
花朵(ㄏㄨㄚ ㄉㄨㄛˇ)
flowers: 你喜歡這些花朵嗎? Do you like these flowers?
花緞(ㄏㄨㄚ ㄉㄨㄢˋ)
brocade; flowered satin: 她穿着花緞製的衣服。She was dressed in flowered satin.
花頭(ㄏㄨㄚ ·ㄊㄡ)
a trick; a ruse; an artifice; a stratagem
花壇(ㄏㄨㄚ ㄊㄢˊ)
a flower bed (especially a raised one)
花罈(ㄏㄨㄚ ㄊㄢˊ)
the juggling of an earthen jar by an acrobat
花天酒地(ㄏㄨㄚ ㄊㄧㄢ ㄐㄧㄡˇ ㄉㄧˋ)
to lead a life of debauchery
花廳(ㄏㄨㄚ ㄊㄧㄥ)
a reception room; a parlor
花托(ㄏㄨㄚ ㄊㄨㄛ)
(botany) a receptacle; a torus
花團錦簇(ㄏㄨㄚ ㄊㄨㄢˊ ㄐㄧㄣˇ ㄘㄨˋ)
① a conglomeration of splendid and beautiful things ② a group of richly attired women
花童(ㄏㄨㄚ ㄊㄨㄥˊ)
a bridal page
花鳥畫(ㄏㄨㄚ ㄋㄧㄠˇ ㄏㄨㄚˋ)
paintings of flowers and birds
花娘(ㄏㄨㄚ ㄋㄧㄤˊ)
a prostitute
花農(ㄏㄨㄚ ㄋㄨㄥˊ)
a flower grower
花剌子模(ㄏㄨㄚ ㄌㄚˋ ㄗˇ ㄇㄛˊ)
Khorasm, or Khwarism, a state in the Middle East exterminated by the Mongols
花蕾(ㄏㄨㄚ ㄌㄟˇ)or 花咕朵(ㄏㄨㄚ ㄍㄨ ·ㄉㄨㄛ)
a flower bud
花籃(ㄏㄨㄚ ㄌㄢˊ)or 花籃兒(ㄏㄨㄚ ㄌㄚˊㄦ)
a basket of flowers; a flower basket
花郎(ㄏㄨㄚ ㄌㄤˊ)
a male beggar
花柳(ㄏㄨㄚ ㄌㄧㄡˇ)
① brothels ② prostitutes
花柳病(ㄏㄨㄚ ㄌㄧㄡˇ ㄅㄧㄥˋ)
a venereal disease; V.D.
花蓮縣(ㄏㄨㄚ ㄌㄧㄢˊ ㄒㄧㄢˋ)
Hualien County, Taiwan Province
花臉(ㄏㄨㄚ ㄌㄧㄢˇ)
(Chinese opera) a male role in Chinese opera with heavily painted face 亦作「淨」or「花面」
花露(ㄏㄨㄚ ㄌㄨˋ)
dew on flowers
花露水(ㄏㄨㄚ ㄌㄨˋ ㄕㄨㄟˇ)
Cologne water—a mildly perfumed toilet water
花蓋(ㄏㄨㄚ ㄍㄞˋ)
a perianth
花岡岩(ㄏㄨㄚ ㄍㄤ ㄧㄢˊ)or 花岡石(ㄏㄨㄚ ㄍㄤ ㄕˊ)
granite
花梗(ㄏㄨㄚ ㄍㄥˇ)
a flower stalk; a peduncle
花鼓戲(ㄏㄨㄚ ㄍㄨˇ ㄒㄧˋ)
the flower-drum opera, a kind of stage show featuring obscene singing to the accompaniment of drum beats
花國(ㄏㄨㄚ ㄍㄨㄛˊ)
① the world of flowers ② the world of prostitutes
花冠(ㄏㄨㄚ ㄍㄨㄢ)
① a corolla ② a gaily decorated hat or cap
花光(ㄏㄨㄚ ㄍㄨㄤ)
to spend all the money
花魁(ㄏㄨㄚ ㄎㄨㄟˊ)
① the plum flower ② a famous prostitute
花好月圓(ㄏㄨㄚ ㄏㄠˇ ㄩㄝˋ ㄩㄢˊ)
(literally) The flowers are in full bloom, and the moon is full.—perfect conjugal bliss
花花綠綠(ㄏㄨㄚ ㄏㄨㄚ ㄌㄩˋ ㄌㄩˋ)
varicolored; brightly colored; colorful
花花公子(ㄏㄨㄚ ㄏㄨㄚ ㄍㄨㄥ ㄗˇ)
a beau; a fop; a playboy
花花絮絮(ㄏㄨㄚ ㄏㄨㄚ ㄒㄩˋ ㄒㄩˋ)
variegated
花花世界(ㄏㄨㄚ ㄏㄨㄚ ㄕˋ ㄐㄧㄝˋ)
the gay and material world; the dazzling human world with its myriad temptations
花卉(ㄏㄨㄚ ㄏㄨㄟˋ)
flowering plants
花環(ㄏㄨㄚ ㄏㄨㄢˊ)
a flower wreath; a lei
花黃(ㄏㄨㄚ ㄏㄨㄤˊ)
yellow petals worn on the forehead by women for ornament in ancient times
花黃素(ㄏㄨㄚ ㄏㄨㄤˊ ㄙㄨˋ)
lipochrome
花紅(ㄏㄨㄚ ㄏㄨㄥˊ)
① a kind of apple, *Malus asiatica* ② a dividend
花紅柳綠(ㄏㄨㄚ ㄏㄨㄥˊ ㄌㄧㄡˇ ㄌㄩˋ)
(said of vegetation and other things) luxuriant and colorful
花雞(ㄏㄨㄚ ㄐㄧ)
a brambling 亦作「燕雀」
花甲(ㄏㄨㄚ ㄐㄧㄚˇ)
(said of a person) 60 years old
花街柳巷(ㄏㄨㄚ ㄐㄧㄝ ㄌㄧㄡˇ ㄒㄧㄤˋ)
streets of ill fame
花界(ㄏㄨㄚ ㄐㄧㄝˋ)
① the world of prostitution ② the Buddhist temple
花椒(ㄏㄨㄚ ㄐㄧㄠ)
Xanthoxylum, a kind of wild pepper
花嬌柳媚(ㄏㄨㄚ ㄐㄧㄠ ㄌㄧㄡˇ ㄇㄟˋ)
Flowers are charming and willows are fascinating. (a conventional phrase for describing spring landscapes)
花轎(ㄏㄨㄚ ㄐㄧㄠˋ)
a bridal sedan chair
花酒(ㄏㄨㄚ ㄐㄧㄡˇ)
a drinking party with prostitutes attending
花箋(ㄏㄨㄚ ㄐㄧㄢ)
fancy stationery
花匠(ㄏㄨㄚ ㄐㄧㄤˋ)
a gardener; a horticulturist: 那花匠以種植花木為樂。The gardener gardens for pleasure.
花莖(ㄏㄨㄚ ㄐㄧㄥ)or 花軸(ㄏㄨㄚ ㄓㄡˊ)
a floral axis
花鏡(ㄏㄨㄚ ㄐㄧㄥˋ)

〔艸部〕

spectacles, or glasses, for the aged 亦作「老花眼鏡」
花捲兒(ㄏㄨㄚ ㄐㄩㄢˇㄦ)
a steamed roll
花捐(ㄏㄨㄚ ㄐㄩㄢ)
taxes levied on a house of ill fame
花期(ㄏㄨㄚ ㄑㄧˊ)
the flower season
花旗(ㄏㄨㄚ ㄑㄧˊ)
the Stars and Stripes; the Star-Spangled Banner
花旗國(ㄏㄨㄚ ㄑㄧˊ ㄍㄨㄛˊ)
the United States of America
花旗銀行(ㄏㄨㄚ ㄑㄧˊ ㄧㄣˊ ㄏㄤˊ)
National City Bank of New York
花錢(ㄏㄨㄚ ㄑㄧㄢˊ)
to spend money: 花錢之前必須先賺錢。Earn before you spend.
花前月下(ㄏㄨㄚ ㄑㄧㄢˊ ㄩㄝˋ ㄒㄧㄚˋ)
before flowers and in the moonlight—an ideal setting for a couple in love
花槍(ㄏㄨㄚ ㄑㄧㄤ)
① a kind of spear ② a trick
花腔(ㄏㄨㄚ ㄑㄧㄤ)
fancy vocalism; *fioritura;* coloratura
花腔女高音(ㄏㄨㄚ ㄑㄧㄤ ㄋㄩˇ ㄍㄠ ㄧㄣ)
a coloratura soprano
花圈(ㄏㄨㄚ ㄑㄩㄢ)
a garland; a wreath; a lei
花拳(ㄏㄨㄚ ㄑㄩㄢˊ)
exhibition boxing
花拳繡腿(ㄏㄨㄚ ㄑㄩㄢˊ ㄒㄧㄡˋ ㄊㄨㄟˇ)
fancy boxing, dazzling to the eye but hardly devastating in combat
花信(ㄏㄨㄚ ㄒㄧㄣˋ)
① news of flowers blooming ②(said of a woman) 24 years old
花香(ㄏㄨㄚ ㄒㄧㄤ)
fragrance of a flower: 空氣中有花香。There is fragrance of flowers in the air.
花絮(ㄏㄨㄚ ㄒㄩˋ)
small episodes of human interest
花序(ㄏㄨㄚ ㄒㄩˋ)
the arrangement of flowers on a stem or axis; inflorescence
花枝(ㄏㄨㄚ ㄓ)
a flowering branch
花枝招展(ㄏㄨㄚ ㄓ ㄓㄠ ㄓㄢˇ)
(said of beautifully dressed women) like a flowering branch attracting people's attention
花枝兒(ㄏㄨㄚ ㄓㄜㄦ)
a flowering branch (a metaphor for a pretty woman)
花招兒(ㄏㄨㄚ ㄓㄠㄦ)
a sly trick: 這個老人會很多花招兒。The old fellow knows many sly tricks.
花朝(ㄏㄨㄚ ㄓㄠ)
the birthday of flowers (the 12th of the second lunar month)
花朝月夕(ㄏㄨㄚ ㄓㄠ ㄩㄝˋ ㄒㄧˋ)
a flowering morning and a moonlight evening— (figuratively) delightful circumstances or occasions
花帳(ㄏㄨㄚ ㄓㄤˋ)
padded accounts or bills; false accounts
花障(ㄏㄨㄚ ㄓㄤˋ)
a bamboo fence with flowering vines
花燭(ㄏㄨㄚ ㄓㄨˊ)
painted candles as the symbol of a wedding—(metaphorically) a wedding or honeymoon
花燭夫妻(ㄏㄨㄚ ㄓㄨˊ ㄈㄨ ㄑㄧ)
a formally married couple
花燭之夜(ㄏㄨㄚ ㄓㄨˊ ㄓ ㄧㄝˋ)
the wedding night
花柱(ㄏㄨㄚ ㄓㄨˋ)
(botany) a style
花磚(ㄏㄨㄚ ㄓㄨㄢ)
an ornamental brick
花種兒(ㄏㄨㄚ ㄓㄨㄥˇㄦ)
seeds of flowering plants
花癡(ㄏㄨㄚ ㄔ)or 花癲(ㄏㄨㄚ ㄉㄧㄢ)
a nymphomaniac
花茶(ㄏㄨㄚ ㄔㄚˊ)
jasmine tea; flower-scented tea
花車(ㄏㄨㄚ ㄔㄜ)
a float; a decorated vehicle in parade
花釵(ㄏㄨㄚ ㄔㄞ)
hair ornaments for women
花船(ㄏㄨㄚ ㄔㄨㄢˊ)
① a gaily decorated boat ② a boat carrying prostitutes to attract passengers
花市(ㄏㄨㄚ ㄕˋ)
a flower market
花事(ㄏㄨㄚ ㄕˋ)
a spring outing; a spring excursion
花式溜冰(ㄏㄨㄚ ㄕˋ ㄌㄧㄡ ㄅㄧㄥ)
figure skating
花神(ㄏㄨㄚ ㄕㄣˊ)
① Flora; deity of flowers ② the soul or spirit of a flower as captured in a painting
花生(ㄏㄨㄚ ㄕㄥ)
a peanut plant
花生米(ㄏㄨㄚ ㄕㄥ ㄇㄧˇ)or 花生仁兒(ㄏㄨㄚ ㄕㄥ ㄖㄜˊㄦ)
a peanut
花生糖(ㄏㄨㄚ ㄕㄥ ㄊㄤˊ)
peanut brittle; peanut candy
花生醬(ㄏㄨㄚ ㄕㄥ ㄐㄧㄤˋ)
peanut butter
花生油(ㄏㄨㄚ ㄕㄥ ㄧㄡˊ)
peanut oil
花束(ㄏㄨㄚ ㄕㄨˋ)
a bouquet; a bunch of flowers
花蕊(ㄏㄨㄚ ㄖㄨㄟˇ)
(botany) pistils and stamens
花容月貌(ㄏㄨㄚ ㄖㄨㄥˊ ㄩㄝˋ ㄇㄠˋ)
(said of a woman) fair as a flower and the moon
花子(ㄏㄨㄚ ˙ㄗ)
a beggar 亦作「叫化子」
花草(ㄏㄨㄚ ㄘㄠˇ)
flowers and grass
花叢(ㄏㄨㄚ ㄘㄨㄥˊ)
① flowering bushes ② the world of prostitution
花色(ㄏㄨㄚ ㄙㄜˋ)
varieties; kinds; sorts: 你沒有別的花色了嗎? Haven't you any other kind?
花案兒(ㄏㄨㄚ ㄚˋㄦ)
cases of sex crimes
花萼(ㄏㄨㄚ ㄜˋ)
(botany) a calyx
花兒(ㄏㄨㄚㄦ)
① a flower; a blossom ② a flowering plant ③ smallpox
花兒針(ㄏㄨㄚㄦ ㄓㄣ)
a fine needle for embroidery
花押(ㄏㄨㄚ ㄧㄚ)
a signature (on a document)

花椰菜(ㄏㄨㄚ ㄧㄝˊ ㄘㄞˋ)
a cauliflower
花煙館(ㄏㄨㄚ ㄧㄢ ㄍㄨㄢˇ)
a girlie opium den
花言巧語(ㄏㄨㄚ ㄧㄢˊ ㄑㄧㄠˇ ㄩˇ)
honeyed words
花眼(ㄏㄨㄚ ㄧㄢˇ)
farsightedness after middle age; presbyopia 亦作「老花眼」
花樣(ㄏㄨㄚ ㄧㄤˋ)or 花樣兒(ㄏㄨㄚ ㄧㄤˋㄦ)
a pattern; a style; a model
花樣翻新(ㄏㄨㄚ ㄧㄤˋ ㄈㄢ ㄒㄧㄣ)
to play new tricks
花影(ㄏㄨㄚ ㄧㄥˇ)
the shadow of flowers
花無百日紅(ㄏㄨㄚ ㄨˊ ㄅㄞˇ ㄖˋ ㄏㄨㄥˊ)
(literally) No flower can bloom for a hundred days. —An ideal state cannot last long.
花紋(ㄏㄨㄚ ㄨㄣˊ)
a decorative design or pattern
花王(ㄏㄨㄚ ㄨㄤˊ)
the king of flowers—the peony: 牡丹被稱爲花王。The peony is called the king of flowers.
花冤枉錢(ㄏㄨㄚ ㄩㄢ ·ㄨㄤ ㄑㄧㄢˊ)
to spend money to no avail; to throw money away
花園(ㄏㄨㄚ ㄩㄢˊ)or 花園兒(ㄏㄨㄚ ㄩㄚˊㄦ)
a flower garden; a garden

【芳】 4855
ㄈㄤ fang fang

1. sweet-smelling; fragrant; aromatic
2. your (used commonly in addressing a young lady)
3. virtuous; honorable; good; respectable: 孔子百世流芳。Confucius left a good name to posterity.

芳名(ㄈㄤ ㄇㄧㄥˊ)
① your name (used especially in speaking to a woman) ② a good reputation
芳名錄(ㄈㄤ ㄇㄧㄥˊ ㄌㄨˋ)
a roster of names (a euphemistic expression)
芳菲(ㄈㄤ ㄈㄟ)
① fragrance and beauty (of flowers) ② flowers
芳馥(ㄈㄤ ㄈㄨˋ)
fragrant
芳蘭(ㄈㄤ ㄌㄢˊ)
a fragrant orchid—(figuratively) a gentleman
芳醴(ㄈㄤ ㄌㄧˇ)
fragrant wine; excellent wine
芳林(ㄈㄤ ㄌㄧㄣˊ)
trees in spring
芳鄰(ㄈㄤ ㄌㄧㄣˊ)
one's neighbor (a polite expression): 她是我們的芳鄰。She is our neighbor.
芳齡(ㄈㄤ ㄌㄧㄥˊ)
age (of a young lady): 她芳齡二十。She is twenty years of age.
芳汗(ㄈㄤ ㄏㄢˋ)
perspiration (of a young woman)
芳華(ㄈㄤ ㄏㄨㄚˊ)
① the beautiful season or time ② youth: 她善於保養芳華。She keeps her youth well.
芳魂(ㄈㄤ ㄏㄨㄣˊ)
the spirit, or soul (of a young lady)
芳卿(ㄈㄤ ㄑㄧㄥ)
a lover; a sweetheart
芳心(ㄈㄤ ㄒㄧㄣ)
the affection, or heart (of a young lady): 這位小姐的芳心已碎。This lady's heart is broken.
芳心無主(ㄈㄤ ㄒㄧㄣ ㄨˊ ㄓㄨˇ)
(said of a lady) not knowing what to do
芳香(ㄈㄤ ㄒㄧㄤ)
fragrance; aroma
芳香族化合物(ㄈㄤ ㄒㄧㄤ ㄗㄨˊ ㄏㄨㄚˋ ㄏㄜˊ ㄨˋ)
aromatic compounds 亦作「芳族化合物」
芳訊(ㄈㄤ ㄒㄩㄣˋ)
① your esteemed letter ② news of flowers coming into bloom
芳旨(ㄈㄤ ㄓˇ)
fragrance; aroma
芳躅(ㄈㄤ ㄓㄨˊ)
tracks of a famous person of former times
芳辰(ㄈㄤ ㄔㄣˊ)or 芳序(ㄈㄤ ㄒㄩˋ)
a beautiful morning in spring
芳塵(ㄈㄤ ㄔㄣˊ)
a good reputation
芳澤(ㄈㄤ ㄗㄜˊ)
perfumed ointment (especially for the hair of a young lady)
芳踪(ㄈㄤ ㄗㄨㄥ)
your whereabouts (a respectful expression)
芳草(ㄈㄤ ㄘㄠˇ)or 芳芷(ㄈㄤ ㄓˇ)
a fragrant plant

【芷】 4856
ㄓˇ jyy jyy

angelica
芷若(ㄓˇ ㄖㄨㄛˋ)
angelica

【芸】 4857
ㄩㄣˊ yun yun

1. a strong-scented herb; rue
2. same as 耘—to weed

芸編(ㄩㄣˊ ㄅㄧㄢ)
books
芸臺(ㄩㄣˊ ㄊㄞˊ)or 芸閣(ㄩㄣˊ ㄍㄜˊ)
the imperial library
芸籤縹帶(ㄩㄣˊ ㄑㄧㄢ ㄆㄧㄠˇ ㄉㄞˋ)
(literally) perfumed book markers and silken laces —books
芸香(ㄩㄣˊ ㄒㄧㄤ)
a strong-scented herb; rue
芸香科(ㄩㄣˊ ㄒㄧㄤ ㄎㄜ)
Rutaceae
芸帙(ㄩㄣˊ ㄓˋ)
books
芸窗(ㄩㄣˊ ㄔㄨㄤ)
a study
芸省(ㄩㄣˊ ㄕㄥˇ)or 芸署(ㄩㄣˊ ㄕㄨˇ)
the imperial library
芸草(ㄩㄣˊ ㄘㄠˇ)
a strong-scented herb; rue
芸芸(ㄩㄣˊ ㄩㄣˊ)
many; numerous
芸芸衆生(ㄩㄣˊ ㄩㄣˊ ㄓㄨㄥˋ ㄕㄥ)
① people of the world ② all living things

【芹】 4858
ㄑㄧㄣˊ chyn chin

celery
芹獻(ㄑㄧㄣˊ ㄒㄧㄢˋ)
a humble gift (a self-depreciatory term referring to a gift one is presenting to another)
芹菜(ㄑㄧㄣˊ ㄘㄞˋ)
celery

【芼】 4859
ㄇㄠˋ maw mao

1. to choose; to select
2. green vegetables; greens

芼羹(ㄇㄠˋ ㄍㄥ)
the stew of meat and greens

【芽】4860 ㄧㄚˊ ya yá
a sprout; a shoot; a bud: 芽在春天萌發。Buds sprout in the spring.

芽胞(ㄧㄚˊ ㄅㄠ)
(botany) spores

芽韮(ㄧㄚˊ ㄐㄧㄡˇ)
leek shoots

芽茶(ㄧㄚˊ ㄔㄚˊ)
bud tea

芽菜(ㄧㄚˊ ㄘㄞˋ)
bean sprouts 亦作「豆芽菜」

芽兒(ㄧㄚˊㄦ)
a shoot; a sprout; a bud: 樹在發芽兒。The trees are unfolding their buds.

【芾】4861 1. ㄈㄟˋ fey fèi
small; little; tiny

【芾】4861 2. ㄈㄨˊ fwu fú
lush; luxuriant

【芻】4862 ㄔㄨˊ chwu chú
1. to cut grass; to mow
2. hay; fodder
3. to feed (livestock)
4. animals that feed on grass

芻秣(ㄔㄨˊ ㄇㄛˋ)
fodder; provender

芻牧(ㄔㄨˊ ㄇㄨˋ)
to pasture or graze livestock

芻糧(ㄔㄨˊ ㄌㄧㄤˊ)
fodder for horses and food for men

芻靈(ㄔㄨˊ ㄌㄧㄥˊ)
effigies burned with or for the deceased in ancient times

芻稾(ㄔㄨˊ ㄍㄠˇ)
hay

芻狗(ㄔㄨˊ ㄍㄡˇ)
straw dogs for sacrifice—things thrown away after use

芻豢(ㄔㄨˊ ㄏㄨㄢˋ)
animals that feed on grass or grain—cattle, sheep, dogs, etc.

芻菽(ㄔㄨˊ ㄕㄨˊ)
grass and beans

芻蕘之見(ㄔㄨˊ ㄖㄠˊ ㄓ ㄐㄧㄢˋ)
(literally) the opinion of a woodcutter—my humble opinion or view: 請聽芻蕘之見。Please listen to my humble opinion.

芻議(ㄔㄨˊ ㄧˋ)or 芻言(ㄔㄨˊ ㄧㄢˊ)
my humble views or opinions

五畫

【苑】4863 1. ㄩㄢˋ yuann yuàn
1. a garden; a park
2. a gathering place

苑囿(ㄩㄢˋ ㄧㄡˋ)
a park; a garden

【苑】4863 2. ㄩㄢˊ yuan yuán
a Chinese family name

【苒】4864 ㄖㄢˇ raan rǎn
(said of flowers and grass) lush or delicate

苒苒(ㄖㄢˇ ㄖㄢˇ)
(said of flowers and grass) luxuriant, lush or delicate

苒荏(ㄖㄢˇ ㄖㄣˇ)
time passing gradually 亦作「荏苒」: 時光苒荏。Time passes gradually.

苒弱(ㄖㄢˇ ㄖㄨㄛˋ)
drooping

【苓】4865 ㄌㄧㄥˊ ling líng
1. a variety of fungus
2. tuckahoe
3. licorice, or liquorice 亦作「甘草」

【苔】4866 1. ㄊㄞˊ tair tái
moss; lichen: 滾石不生苔。A rolling stone gathers no moss.

苔砌(ㄊㄞˊ ㄑㄧˋ)
mossy steps

苔錢(ㄊㄞˊ ㄑㄧㄢˊ)
coin-shaped lichen

苔蘚(ㄊㄞˊ ㄒㄧㄢˇ)
moss and lichen

苔癬(ㄊㄞˊ ㄒㄩㄢˇ)
lichen (a skin disease)

苔衣(ㄊㄞˊ ㄧ)
moss: 石頭生滿了苔衣。The stones are covered with moss.

【苔】4866 2. ㄊㄞ tai tāi
as in 舌苔—fur (on the tongue)

【苕】4867 ㄊㄧㄠˊ tyau tiáo
a plant much used for making brooms

苕帚(ㄊㄧㄠˊ ㄓㄡˇ)
a broom

【苗】4868 ㄇㄧㄠˊ miau miáo
1. a sprout
2. descendants; posterity
3. (said of children) peevish or disobedient
4. the Miao tribe in southwestern China
5. summer hunting
6. a Chinese family name
7. a beginning or omen

苗圃(ㄇㄧㄠˊ ㄆㄨˇ)
a seedbed; a nursery

苗頭(ㄇㄧㄠˊ ·ㄊㄡ)
the first sign of success

苗條(ㄇㄧㄠˊ ㄊㄧㄠˊ)
(said of a woman) slim

苗栗(ㄇㄧㄠˊ ㄌㄧˋ)
Miaoli, a county in central Taiwan

苗戶(ㄇㄧㄠˊ ㄏㄨˋ)
naturalized Miao (苗) people

苗牀(ㄇㄧㄠˊ ㄔㄨㄤˊ)
a seedbed; a nursery

苗子(ㄇㄧㄠˊ ·ㄗ)or 苗族(ㄇㄧㄠˊ ㄗㄨˊ)
the Miao (苗) people (in southwestern China)

苗兒(ㄇㄧㄠˊㄦ)
a sprout; a shoot; a seedling

苗而不秀(ㄇㄧㄠˊ ㄦˊ ㄅㄨˋ ㄒㄧㄡˋ)
(literally) to sprout but never to flower—to fail to fulfill one's potentialities

苗裔(ㄇㄧㄠˊ ㄧˋ)or 苗胤(ㄇㄧㄠˊ ㄧㄣˋ) or 苗嗣(ㄇㄧㄠˊ ㄙˋ)
descendants; posterity

【苛】4869 ㄎㄜ ke kē
harsh; severe; rigorous; caustic

苛法(ㄎㄜ ㄈㄚˇ)
a harsh law; a severe law

苛待(ㄎㄜ ㄉㄞˋ)
to treat harshly or severely

苛虐(ㄎㄜ ㄋㄩㄝˋ)
to treat cruelly; to maltreat

苛濫(ㄎㄜ ㄌㄢˋ)
improperly severe or lenient

苛禮(ㄎㄜ ㄌㄧˇ)
excessive ceremony or formality

苛吏(ㄎㄜ ㄌㄧˋ)
a cruel official
苛令(ㄎㄜ ㄌㄧㄥˋ)
harsh orders and regulations
苛刻(ㄎㄜ ㄎㄜˋ)
harsh; pitiless; relentless; merciless; unkind; cold-hearted
苛捐雜稅(ㄎㄜ ㄐㄩㄢ ㄗㄚˊ ㄕㄨㄟˋ)
extortive levies and miscellaneous taxes
苛求(ㄎㄜ ㄑㄧㄡˊ)
to be very exacting
苛細(ㄎㄜ ㄒㄧˋ)
(said of regulations, etc.) severe and exacting
苛性(ㄎㄜ ㄒㄧㄥˋ)
(chemistry) caustic
苛性鈉(ㄎㄜ ㄒㄧㄥˋ ㄋㄚˋ)
(chemistry) sodium hydroxide; caustic soda
苛性鉀(ㄎㄜ ㄒㄧㄥˋ ㄐㄧㄚˇ)
(chemistry) caustic potash; potassium hydroxide
苛性鹼(ㄎㄜ ㄒㄧㄥˋ ㄐㄧㄢˇ)
(chemistry) caustic alkali
苛性蘇達(ㄎㄜ ㄒㄧㄥˋ ㄙㄨ ㄉㄚˊ)
(chemistry) caustic soda; sodium hydroxide
苛性鹽(ㄎㄜ ㄒㄧㄥˋ ㄧㄢˊ)
(chemistry) caustic salt
苛政(ㄎㄜ ㄓㄥˋ)
despotic rule; despotism; tyranny
苛政猛於虎(ㄎㄜ ㄓㄥˋ ㄇㄥˇ ㄩˊ ㄏㄨˇ)
A tyrannical government is worse than a tiger.
苛察(ㄎㄜ ㄔㄚˊ)
relentless faultfinding
苛責(ㄎㄜ ㄗㄜˊ)
to criticize severely; to rebuke; to excoriate
苛俗(ㄎㄜ ㄙㄨˊ)
tasking customs
苛碎(ㄎㄜ ㄙㄨㄟˋ)
(said of regulations, etc.) rigorous and troublesome

【苜】 4870
ㄇㄨˋ muh mù
clover
苜蓿(ㄇㄨˋ ㄙㄨˋ)
Medicago hispida, clover, often grown as food for cattle

【苞】 4871
ㄅㄠ bau bāo
1. a variety of rush
2. a bract
3. to wrap
4. profuse; thick
5. seeds with the germ ready to burst; seeds bursting up
苞苴(ㄅㄠ ㄐㄩ)
① a bribe ② a gift ③ a parcel
苞筍(ㄅㄠ ㄙㄨㄣˇ)
tender bamboo shoots in winter 亦作「冬筍」
苞葉(ㄅㄠ ㄧㄝˋ)
a bract

【苡】 4872
ㄧˇ yii yǐ
Coix lacryma-jobi, a kind of plant whose grains are used as food or medicine

【若】 4873
1. ㄖㄨㄛˋ ruoh ruò
1. if; suppose; supposing; assuming; provided that
2. you
3. similar to; like
若輩(ㄖㄨㄛˋ ㄅㄟˋ)
you all; ye 亦作「若曹」
若不然(ㄖㄨㄛˋ ˙ㄅㄨ ㄖㄢˊ)
if not; otherwise
若非(ㄖㄨㄛˋ ㄈㄟ)
unless; if not: 若非疲倦了這嬰兒很少哭。This baby seldom cries unless he is tired.
若夫(ㄖㄨㄛˋ ㄈㄨˊ)
a connective often used to introduce a new passage in archaic Chinese
若大旱望雲霓(ㄖㄨㄛˋ ㄉㄚˋ ㄏㄢˋ ㄨㄤˋ ㄩㄣˊ ㄋㄧˊ)
It is like longing for clouds during a serious drought.
若干(ㄖㄨㄛˋ ㄍㄢ)
some; a few; several: 我看見若干認識的人。I saw some people I knew.
若果(ㄖㄨㄛˋ ㄍㄨㄛˇ)
if; provided that: 若果他來了，我一定告訴他。If he comes, I will tell him.
若何(ㄖㄨㄛˋ ㄏㄜˊ)
how; what now
若合符節(ㄖㄨㄛˋ ㄏㄜˊ ㄈㄨˊ ㄐㄧㄝˊ)
as similar as the two halves of a tally—to match completely; to tally perfectly; to fit exactly
若即若離(ㄖㄨㄛˋ ㄐㄧˊ ㄖㄨㄛˋ ㄌㄧˊ)
to appear to come together sometimes and apart at other times; to keep at arm's length
若許(ㄖㄨㄛˋ ㄒㄩˇ)
thus; like this
若使(ㄖㄨㄛˋ ㄕˇ)
assuming that...; supposing that...; if
若是(ㄖㄨㄛˋ ㄕˋ)
if; suppose: 若是我錯了，你也錯了。If I am wrong, you are wrong too.
若曹(ㄖㄨㄛˋ ㄘㄠˊ)
you all; ye
若要(ㄖㄨㄛˋ ㄧㄠˋ)
if...has (have) to...: 你若要做這件事，便早些做。If you have to do this, then do it earlier.
若要人不知，除非己莫爲(ㄖㄨㄛˋ ㄧㄠˋ ㄖㄣˊ ㄅㄨˋ ㄓ, ㄔㄨˊ ㄈㄟ ㄐㄧˇ ㄇㄛˋ ㄨㄟˊ)
The best way to hide a misdeed is not to commit it.
若有若無(ㄖㄨㄛˋ ㄧㄡˇ ㄖㄨㄛˋ ㄨˊ)
vague; intangible
若隱若現(ㄖㄨㄛˋ ㄧㄣˇ ㄖㄨㄛˋ ㄒㄧㄢˋ)
half-hidden; discernible at one moment and gone the next (like a will-o'-the-wisp)
若無其事(ㄖㄨㄛˋ ㄨˊ ㄑㄧˊ ㄕˋ)
as if nothing had happened; to remain calm; with perfect composure: 他雖面臨危機，卻能若無其事。He faced a crisis with perfect composure.

【若】 4873
2. ㄖㄜˇ ree rě
as in 般若(ㄅㄛ ㄖㄜˇ)—a transliteration of a Sanskrit word

【苦】 4874
ㄎㄨˇ kuu kǔ
1. bitter: 良藥苦口。Good medicines taste bitter.
2. painful; hard; difficult; laborious; miserable
3. strenuous; earnest; diligent
4. to abhor
5. to feel miserable about
苦不堪言(ㄎㄨˇ ㄅㄨˋ ㄎㄢ ㄧㄢˊ)
painful or miserable beyond description
苦買賣(ㄎㄨˇ ㄇㄞˇ ˙ㄇㄞ)
a hard business
苦悶(ㄎㄨˇ ㄇㄣˋ)
boredom; bored; distressed; low-spirited; depressed;

dejected

苦命(ㄎㄨˇ ㄇㄧㄥˋ)
a hard lot

苦命人(ㄎㄨˇ ㄇㄧㄥˋ ㄖㄣˊ)
a luckless person

苦鬥(ㄎㄨˇ ㄉㄡˋ)
①a hard fight or struggle ②to fight desperately

苦頭兒(ㄎㄨˇ ㄊㄡˊㄦ)
hardship(s)

苦土(ㄎㄨˇ ㄊㄨˇ)
magnesia

苦痛(ㄎㄨˇ ㄊㄨㄥˋ)
pain; suffering; discomfort; misery: 我害怕與他們分離的苦痛。I dreaded the pain of separation from them.

苦惱(ㄎㄨˇ ㄋㄠˇ)
misery; distress; trouble: 他因胃痛而苦惱。He is in misery with a stomachache.

苦難(ㄎㄨˇ ㄋㄢˋ)
privation; suffering; hardship; trials; adversity

苦樂(ㄎㄨˇ ㄌㄜˋ)
comfort and discomfort; joys and sorrows

苦累(ㄎㄨˇ ㄌㄟˋ)
toil; hardship; privation; trials; adversity

苦力(ㄎㄨˇ ㄌㄧˋ)
①strenuous efforts; hard work ②a coolie; a laborer

苦戀(ㄎㄨˇ ㄌㄧㄢˋ)
unrequited love 亦作「單戀」

苦楝子(ㄎㄨˇ ㄌㄧㄢˋ ㄗˇ)
Melia azedarach, the seeds of which are used as medicine

苦幹(ㄎㄨˇ ㄍㄢˋ)
①to make a strenuous effort ②to do something against great odds

苦瓜(ㄎㄨˇ ㄍㄨㄚ)
a bitter gourd (*Momordica charantia*)

苦功(ㄎㄨˇ ㄍㄨㄥ)
hard work; painstaking effort 亦作「苦工夫」

苦工(ㄎㄨˇ ㄍㄨㄥ)
toil; hard labor

苦工夫(ㄎㄨˇ ㄍㄨㄥ ˙ㄈㄨ)
painstaking effort 參看「苦功」

苦口(ㄎㄨˇ ㄎㄡˇ)
①bitter to the taste ②to exhort or admonish earnestly

苦口婆心(ㄎㄨˇ ㄎㄡˇ ㄆㄛˊ ㄒㄧㄣ)
to exhort or remonstrate with earnest words prompted by a kind heart

苦苦(ㄎㄨˇ ㄎㄨˇ)
strenuously; hard; arduously; persistently

苦況(ㄎㄨˇ ㄎㄨㄤˋ)
miserable conditions; hardship: 那些孤兒生活在苦況中。The orphans live in miserable conditions.

苦海(ㄎㄨˇ ㄏㄞˇ)
(literally) a sea of hardship —boundless hardship; a sea of bitterness

苦海無邊(ㄎㄨˇ ㄏㄞˇ ㄨˊ ㄅㄧㄢ)
(literally) a boundless sea of hardship—boundless hardship: 苦海無邊，回頭是岸。The sea of bitterness is boundless; if you repent, you will be saved.

苦活兒(ㄎㄨˇ ㄏㄨㄛˊㄦ)
jobs requiring much work but paying little; profitless jobs 亦作「苦差事」

苦節(ㄎㄨˇ ㄐㄧㄝˊ)
integrity maintained through hardships

苦酒(ㄎㄨˇ ㄐㄧㄡˇ)
bitter wine

苦諫(ㄎㄨˇ ㄐㄧㄢˋ)
an earnest admonition; to admonish earnestly

苦盡甘來(ㄎㄨˇ ㄐㄧㄣˋ ㄍㄢ ㄌㄞˊ)
The happy sunny days are coming after all the hardships endured.

苦勸(ㄎㄨˇ ㄑㄩㄢˋ)
earnest exhortation; to exhort or advise earnestly

苦戲(ㄎㄨˇ ㄒㄧˋ)
(Chinese opera) a tragedy; a tearjerker

苦笑(ㄎㄨˇ ㄒㄧㄠˋ)
to force a smile; a forced smile

苦辛(ㄎㄨˇ ㄒㄧㄣ)
hardship; suffering; adversity

苦心(ㄎㄨˇ ㄒㄧㄣ)
great pains taken for something

苦心孤詣(ㄎㄨˇ ㄒㄧㄣ ㄍㄨ ㄧˋ)
①to achieve a deep understanding through diligent studies ②to manage a business with great efforts

苦刑(ㄎㄨˇ ㄒㄧㄥˊ)
torture

苦行(ㄎㄨˇ ㄒㄧㄥˊ)
①to make strenuous effort ②to lead an ascetic life; self-mortification

苦行者(ㄎㄨˇ ㄒㄧㄥˊ ㄓㄜˇ)
an ascetic

苦學(ㄎㄨˇ ㄒㄩㄝˊ)
to study or learn under adversity

苦汁(ㄎㄨˇ ㄓ)
(chemistry) bittern

苦戰(ㄎㄨˇ ㄓㄢˋ)
to fight against heavy odds; to have a tough game or bitter struggle

苦竹(ㄎㄨˇ ㄓㄨˊ)
Phyllostachys bambusoides, a variety of bamboo

苦主(ㄎㄨˇ ㄓㄨˇ)
①a victim of robbery or theft ②the bereaved family of a murdered person

苦衷(ㄎㄨˇ ㄓㄨㄥ)
a reason for doing something not easily understood by others

苦中作樂(ㄎㄨˇ ㄓㄨㄥ ㄗㄨㄛˋ ㄌㄜˋ)
to find joy amid hardship; to enjoy in adversity

苦差事(ㄎㄨˇ ㄔㄞ ㄕˋ)
①an unpleasant task ②a profitless assignment 參看「苦活兒」

苦楚(ㄎㄨˇ ㄔㄨˇ)
pain; suffering

苦處(ㄎㄨˇ ˙ㄔㄨ)
the cause of pain; difficulty

苦上加苦(ㄎㄨˇ ㄕㄤˋ ㄐㄧㄚ ㄎㄨˇ)
to bring additional pain

苦水(ㄎㄨˇ ㄕㄨㄟˇ)
①bitter water ②gastric secretion, etc. rising to the mouth ③sufferings; grievances

苦日子(ㄎㄨˇ ㄖˋ ˙ㄗ)
days of hardship

苦肉計(ㄎㄨˇ ㄖㄡˋ ㄐㄧˋ)
a trick of securing another's faith by intentionally injuring oneself; acting the underdog to win sympathy

苦子(ㄎㄨˇ ˙ㄗ)

misery or loss

苦思(ㄎㄨˇ ㄙ)
to think hard; to cudgel one's brains

苦死(ㄎㄨˇ ㄙˇ)
extremely painful; extremely hard to bear

苦澀(ㄎㄨˇ ㄙㄜˋ)
① bitter and astringent ② pained; agonized; anguished

苦艾(ㄎㄨˇ ㄞˋ)
absinth(e)

苦艾酒(ㄎㄨˇ ㄞˋ ㄐㄧㄡˇ)
absinth(e)

苦役(ㄎㄨˇ ㄧˋ)
hard labor; drudgery

苦顏(ㄎㄨˇ ㄧㄢˊ)
a look of distress; a distressful expression

苦味(ㄎㄨˇ ㄨㄟˋ)
a bitter taste

苦味酸(ㄎㄨˇ ㄨㄟˋ ㄙㄨㄢ)
picric acid

苦於(ㄎㄨˇ ㄩˊ)
to suffer from (a disadvantage); to be handicapped: 他苦於貧窮。He is handicapped by poverty.

苦雨(ㄎㄨˇ ㄩˇ)
a distressing rain; an incessant rain

苦雨淒風(ㄎㄨˇ ㄩˇ ㄑㄧ ㄈㄥ)
distressing rains and depressing winds

【苧】 4875
ㄓㄨˋ juh zhù

ramie; China grass

苧麻(ㄓㄨˋ ㄇㄚˊ)
ramie

【苫】 4876
ㄕㄢ shan shān

to thatch

苫塊(ㄕㄢ ㄎㄨㄞˋ)
(literally) to sleep on a mat of straw and a pillow of earth—to mourn for a parent

苫次(ㄕㄢ ㄘˋ)
in mourning for one's parents

【英】 4877
ㄧㄥ ing yīng

1. a flower; a leaf; a petal
2. surpassing; outstanding; prominent; distinguished
3. fine; handsome: 他是一個英俊的男子。He is a handsome fellow.
4. English; British
5. a hero; an outstanding person
6. a Chinese family name

英拔(ㄧㄥ ㄅㄚˊ)
outstanding; distinguished; surpassing; prominent

英鎊(ㄧㄥ ㄅㄤˋ)
the pound sterling 亦作「英磅」

英鎊集團(ㄧㄥ ㄅㄤˋ ㄐㄧˊ ㄊㄨㄢˊ)
the sterling bloc

英布(ㄧㄥ ㄅㄨˋ)
General Ying Pu (?-195 B.C.), who played an important role in the fall of the Chin Dynasty and the rise of the Han Dynasty

英美(ㄧㄥ ㄇㄟˇ)
Britain and America; Anglo-American

英髦(ㄧㄥ ㄇㄠˊ)
men of ability 亦作「英旄」

英明(ㄧㄥ ㄇㄧㄥˊ)
(said of leaders) intelligent; sagacious; perspicacious

英名(ㄧㄥ ㄇㄧㄥˊ)
fame; glory; renown: 他的英名傳遍全國。His fame spread all over the country.

英名掃地(ㄧㄥ ㄇㄧㄥˊ ㄙㄠˇ ㄉㄧˋ)
to have one's great fame tarnished or soiled

英畝(ㄧㄥ ㄇㄨˇ)
(square measure) acre

英發(ㄧㄥ ㄈㄚ)
intelligent and energetic

英法聯軍(ㄧㄥ ㄈㄚˇ ㄌㄧㄢˊ ㄐㄩㄣ)
the allied troops of Britain and France that invaded Canton (廣州), Tientsin (天津) and Peking (北京) in 1856-60

英德(ㄧㄥ ㄉㄜˊ)
① name of a county in Kwangtung (廣東) ② England and Germany

英斷(ㄧㄥ ㄉㄨㄢˋ)
intelligent decision

英噸(ㄧㄥ ㄉㄨㄣˋ)
a long ton; a gross ton

英挺(ㄧㄥ ㄊㄧㄥˇ)
outstanding; prominent; distinguished 亦作「英特」

英年(ㄧㄥ ㄋㄧㄢˊ)
years of youthful vigor

英里(ㄧㄥ ㄌㄧˇ)
(linear measure) mile

英烈(ㄧㄥ ㄌㄧㄝˋ)
① heroic deeds ② a person of great achievements

英靈(ㄧㄥ ㄌㄧㄥˊ)
① noble spirit ② souls or spirits of the dead

英倫三島(ㄧㄥ ㄌㄨㄣˊ ㄙㄢ ㄉㄠˇ)
British Isles

英格蘭(ㄧㄥ ㄍㄜˊ ㄌㄢˊ)
England

英國(ㄧㄥ ㄍㄨㄛˊ)
Great Britain; Britain; the United Kingdom; England: 倫敦是英國的首都。London is the capital of England.

英國的(ㄧㄥ ㄍㄨㄛˊ ˙ㄉㄜ)
British; English: 他們居住在英國的鄉村中。They live in an English village.

英國人(ㄧㄥ ㄍㄨㄛˊ ㄖㄣˊ)
an Englishman; a Briton; the English; the British

英國文學(ㄧㄥ ㄍㄨㄛˊ ㄨㄣˊ ㄒㄩㄝˊ)
English literature

英國文學系(ㄧㄥ ㄍㄨㄛˊ ㄨㄣˊ ㄒㄩㄝˊ ㄒㄧˋ)
the department of English literature

英國文學史(ㄧㄥ ㄍㄨㄛˊ ㄨㄣˊ ㄒㄩㄝˊ ㄕˇ)
the history of English literature

英豪(ㄧㄥ ㄏㄠˊ)
heroes; outstanding persons 亦作「英傑」

英漢辭典(ㄧㄥ ㄏㄢˋ ㄘˊ ㄉㄧㄢˇ)
an English-Chinese dictionary

英華(ㄧㄥ ㄏㄨㄚˊ)
① luxuriant beauty ② honor; glory; fame

英魂(ㄧㄥ ㄏㄨㄣˊ)
(honorable) spirits, or souls, of the war dead

英吉利(ㄧㄥ ㄐㄧˊ ㄌㄧˋ)
Great Britain; Britain; the United Kingdom; the British Commonwealth; England

英吉利病(ㄧㄥ ㄐㄧˊ ㄌㄧˋ ㄅㄧㄥˋ)
rickets

英吉利海峽(ㄧㄥ ㄐㄧˊ ㄌㄧˋ ㄏㄞˇ ㄒㄧㄚˊ)
the English Channel

英傑(ㄧㄥ ㄐㄧㄝˊ)
a great man; a hero

英軍(ㄧㄥ ㄐㄩㄣ)
British troops; British forces
英俊(ㄧㄥ ㄐㄩㄣˋ)
(said of a man) handsome
英氣(ㄧㄥ ㄑㄧˋ)
noble spirit; bravery
英雄(ㄧㄥ ㄒㄩㄥˊ)
a hero; a great man
英雄末路(ㄧㄥ ㄒㄩㄥˊ ㄇㄛˋ ㄌㄨˋ)
the end of a hero
英雄美人(ㄧㄥ ㄒㄩㄥˊ ㄇㄟˇ ㄖㄣˊ)
an ideal combination of a hero and a beauty
英雄氣短(ㄧㄥ ㄒㄩㄥˊ ㄑㄧˋ ㄉㄨㄢˇ)
A hero has lost his might.
英雄主義(ㄧㄥ ㄒㄩㄥˊ ㄓㄨˇ ㄧˋ)
obsession with idea of making oneself a hero
英雄崇拜(ㄧㄥ ㄒㄩㄥˊ ㄔㄨㄥˊ ㄅㄞˋ)
hero worship
英雄無用武之地(ㄧㄥ ㄒㄩㄥˊ ㄨˊ ㄩㄥˋ ㄨˇ ㄓ ㄉㄧˋ)
A hero has no chance of using his might.
英制(ㄧㄥ ㄓˋ)
the British system (of measurement)
英尺(ㄧㄥ ㄔˇ)
foot (as a measure of length)
英屬(ㄧㄥ ㄕㄨˇ)
(said of a colony) administered by the British; under British administration
英姿(ㄧㄥ ㄗ)
a dashing appearance
英才(ㄧㄥ ㄘㄞˊ)
a person of outstanding ability or talent
英寸(ㄧㄥ ㄘㄨㄣˋ)
(linear measure) inch: 去年的雨量有多少英寸? How many inches of rain fell last year?
英俄(ㄧㄥ ㄜˊ)or 英蘇(ㄧㄥ ㄙㄨ)
Britain and Russia; Anglo-Russian
英武(ㄧㄥ ㄨˇ)
brave and strong; gallant; valiant; valorous
英偉(ㄧㄥ ㄨㄟˇ)
great
英文(ㄧㄥ ㄨㄣˊ)
the (written) English language; English
英文文法(ㄧㄥ ㄨㄣˊ ㄨㄣˊ ㄈㄚˇ)
English grammar
英語(ㄧㄥ ㄩˇ)
the (spoken) English language; English: 你會說英語嗎? Do you speak English?
英勇(ㄧㄥ ㄩㄥˇ)
brave; courageous; heroic; gallant; valiant; valorous: 他是一個英勇的士兵。He is a brave soldier.

【苴】 4878
1. ㄐㄩ jiu jū
1. to pack
2. a female plant of common hemp
苴布(ㄐㄩ ㄅㄨˋ)
sackcloth
苴麻(ㄐㄩ ㄇㄚˊ)
a female plant of common hemp
苴絰(ㄐㄩ ㄉㄧㄝˊ)
hemp for the heaviest mourning (for a parent)
苴稭(ㄐㄩ ㄐㄧㄝ)
a straw mat
苴杖(ㄐㄩ ㄓㄤˋ)
a mourner's staff

【苴】 4878
2. ㄔㄚˊ char chá
1. grass floating in the water; water plants
2. withered grass

【苶】 4879
ㄋㄧㄝˊ nie nié
exhausting; tired

【苯】 4880
ㄅㄣˇ been běn
benzene
苯胺(ㄅㄣˇ ㄢ)
aniline, or phenylamine

【苹】 4881
ㄆㄧㄥˊ pyng píng
1. a kind of herb
2. same as 萍—duckweed
3. celery
苹苹(ㄆㄧㄥˊ ㄆㄧㄥˊ)
(said of grass) luxuriant; lush
苹縈(ㄆㄧㄥˊ ㄧㄥˊ)
circling; revolving

【茈】 4882
1. ㄗˇ tzyy zǐ
a kind of herb

【茈】 4882
2. ㄔㄞˊ chair chái
Bupleurum, a kind of herb medicine 亦作「柴胡」
茈胡(ㄔㄞˊ ㄏㄨˊ)
Bupleurum, a kind of herb medicine 亦作「柴胡」

【苻】 4883
ㄈㄨˊ fwu fú
a kind of herb
苻堅(ㄈㄨˊ ㄐㄧㄢ)
Fu Chien, 338-385 A.D., the founder of 前秦 (one of the 16 kingdoms formed in North China by barbarian invaders during the Tsin Dynasty), who tried in vain to invade the south
苻秦(ㄈㄨˊ ㄑㄧㄣˊ)
same as 前秦, 351-394 A.D., one of the 16 barbarian kingdoms in North China that existed concurrently with the Tsin (晉) Dynasty

【苾】 4884
ㄅㄧˋ bih bì
fragrant
苾勃(ㄅㄧˋ ㄅㄛˊ)
fragrant
苾芬(ㄅㄧˋ ㄈㄣ)
fragrant
苾芻(ㄅㄧˋ ㄔㄨˊ)
bhiksu, a Buddhist monk 亦作「比丘」
苾芻尼(ㄅㄧˋ ㄔㄨˊ ㄋㄧˊ)
bhiksuni, a nun 亦作「比丘尼」

【茁】 4885
ㄓㄨㄛˊ jwo zhuó
1. sprouting; growing
2. vigorous; strong; sturdy
茁茁(ㄓㄨㄛˊ ㄓㄨㄛˊ)
sprouting
茁壯(ㄓㄨㄛˊ ㄓㄨㄤˋ)
vigorous; strong
茁芽(ㄓㄨㄛˊ ㄧㄚˊ)
to sprout

【茂】 4886
ㄇㄠˋ maw mào
(又讀 ㄇㄡˋ mow mòu)
1. exuberant; lush; luxuriant; flourishing; healthy; vigorous; strong
2. fine; fair; excellent
茂密(ㄇㄠˋ ㄇㄧˋ)
growing densely
茂年(ㄇㄠˋ ㄋㄧㄢˊ)
youth; the prime of life
茂林修竹(ㄇㄠˋ ㄌㄧㄣˊ ㄒㄧㄡ ㄓㄨˊ)
an exuberant growth of trees and bamboos
茂齒(ㄇㄠˋ ㄔˇ)
the prime of life

茂士(ㄇㄠˋ ㄕˋ)
a virtuous and capable man
茂盛(ㄇㄠˋ ㄕㄥˋ)
luxuriant; exuberant; lush; flourishing
茂才(ㄇㄠˋ ㄘㄞˊ)
① a talented person ② same as 秀才

【范】 4887 ㄈㄢˋ fann fàn
1. the bee
2. a Chinese family name
范蠡(ㄈㄢˋ ㄌㄧˇ)
Fan Li, a statesman in the Epoch of Spring and Autumn, who helped the state of Yüeh(越) to conquer the state of Wu(吳)
范仲淹(ㄈㄢˋ ㄓㄨㄥˋ ㄧㄢ)
Fan Chung-yen, 989-1052, a famed statesman of the Sung (宋) Dynasty
范增(ㄈㄢˋ ㄗㄥ)
Fan Tseng, 275-204 B.C., a strategist who helped Hsiang Yu (項羽) in his rise to power

【茄】 4888 ㄑㄧㄝˊ chye qié
an eggplant; an aubergine
茄袋(ㄑㄧㄝˊ ㄉㄞˋ)
an eggplant-shaped bag or pouch for cash
茄科(ㄑㄧㄝˊ ㄎㄜ)
Solanaceae
茄子(ㄑㄧㄝˊ ·ㄗ)
an eggplant
茄子茸(ㄑㄧㄝˊ ·ㄗ ㄖㄨㄥˊ)
purple-colored soft cores of the young antlers of the deer

【茅】 4889 ㄇㄠˊ mau máo
1. couch grass
2. a Chinese family name
茅棚(ㄇㄠˊ ㄆㄥˊ)
a thatched shed
茅房(ㄇㄠˊ ㄈㄤˊ)
① a thatched house ② a latrine
茅店(ㄇㄠˊ ㄉㄧㄢˋ)
a thatched shop or store
茅台酒(ㄇㄠˊ ㄊㄞˊ ㄐㄧㄡˇ)
Maotai—a strong, colorless liquor produced in Maotai, Kweichow
茅土(ㄇㄠˊ ㄊㄨˇ)
to confer land to vassals
茅利塔尼亞(ㄇㄠˊ ㄌㄧˋ ㄊㄚˇ ㄋㄧˊ ㄧㄚˋ)
Mauritania
茅廬(ㄇㄠˊ ㄌㄨˊ)
a simple dwelling: 我的茅廬在那邊。I have my simple dwelling there.
茅坑(ㄇㄠˊ ㄎㄥ)
a latrine
茅坤(ㄇㄠˊ ㄎㄨㄣ)
Mao Kun, 1512-1601, a statesman and man of letters of the Ming Dynasty
茅蕈(ㄇㄠˊ ㄒㄩㄣˋ)
(botany) a kind of edible mushroom
茅舍(ㄇㄠˊ ㄕㄜˋ)
① a straw hut; a thatched house ② my humble cottage: 歡迎光臨茅舍。Welcome to my humble cottage.
茅茨土階(ㄇㄠˊ ㄘˊ ㄊㄨˇ ㄐㄧㄝ)
a simple building
茅草(ㄇㄠˊ ㄘㄠˇ)
thatch; straw; couch grass
茅司(ㄇㄠˊ ·ㄙ)
a privy; a toilet; a water closet
茅廁(ㄇㄠˊ ·ㄙ)
a latrine; a lavatory; a water closet
茅塞(ㄇㄠˊ ㄙㄜˋ)
an obstacle in the mind to understanding
茅塞頓開(ㄇㄠˊ ㄙㄜˋ ㄉㄨㄣˋ ㄎㄞ)
to come to an understanding all of a sudden
茅簷(ㄇㄠˊ ㄧㄢˊ)
straw eaves
茅屋(ㄇㄠˊ ㄨ)
a thatched house; a straw hut: 他在鄉間有一幢茅屋。He has a thatched house in the country.

【茆】 4890 ㄇㄠˊ mau máo
1. *Brasenia schreberi*
2. same as 茅—couch grass
3. a Chinese family name

【茌】 4891 ㄔˊ chyr chí
as in 茌平—name of a county in Shantung

【苙】 4892 ㄌㄧˋ lih lì
1. a pigsty; a pigpen
2. a kind of medicinal herb

【苣】 4893 ㄐㄩˋ jiuh jù
as in 萵苣—lettuce

【苺】 4894 (莓) ㄇㄟˊ mei méi
berries 參看「莓」

【茀】 4895 ㄈㄨˊ fwu fú
1. weedy
2. a rank growth of weeds obstructing the way—a hindrance; an obstacle
3. luck; fortune
茀茀(ㄈㄨˊ ㄈㄨˊ)
①(said of plants) luxuriant; exuberant; lush ② vigorous

【茇】 4896 ㄅㄚˊ bar bá
1. a grass root
2. to halt in the open country, amid the grass

【茉】 4897 ㄇㄛˋ moh mò
white jasmine
茉莉(ㄇㄛˋ ·ㄌㄧ)
white jasmine

【苟】 4898 ㄍㄡˇ goou gǒu
1. against principle; illicit; improper
2. careless
3. if
苟免(ㄍㄡˇ ㄇㄧㄢˇ)
① to shirk; to avoid ② to escape (a disaster) luckily
苟非(ㄍㄡˇ ㄈㄟ)
had it not been
苟得(ㄍㄡˇ ㄉㄜˊ)
to acquire illicitly; to possess something by improper ways
苟同(ㄍㄡˇ ㄊㄨㄥˊ)
to agree without giving serious thought; to agree with somebody against principle
苟能(ㄍㄡˇ ㄋㄥˊ)
if possible; if... can...
苟合(ㄍㄡˇ ㄏㄜˊ)
① to join or associate against one's principle ② an illicit sexual act
苟活(ㄍㄡˇ ㄏㄨㄛˊ)
to live at the expense of one's principle or honor
苟簡(ㄍㄡˇ ㄐㄧㄢˇ)
unduly brief or simple
苟進(ㄍㄡˇ ㄐㄧㄣˋ)
to get promoted against

one's principle
苟且(ㄍㄡˇ ㄑㄧㄝˇ)
①against one's principle ②perfunctory ③illicit (sexual relations)
苟且偷生(ㄍㄡˇ ㄑㄧㄝˇ ㄊㄡ ㄕㄥ)
to drag out an ignominious existence
苟且偷安(ㄍㄡˇ ㄑㄧㄝˇ ㄊㄡ ㄢ)
to enjoy ease against one's principle or with a false sense of security
苟全(ㄍㄡˇ ㄑㄩㄢˊ)
to manage barely to survive
苟全性命(ㄍㄡˇ ㄑㄩㄢˊ ㄒㄧㄥˋ ㄇㄧㄥˋ)
to manage to survive in times of hardship or unrest at all costs
苟安(ㄍㄡˇ ㄢ)
to live in precarious peace without doing anything to avert the looming danger ahead; to live with a false sense of security
苟言(ㄍㄡˇ ㄧㄢˊ)
careless speech; rash remarks
苟延殘喘(ㄍㄡˇ ㄧㄢˊ ㄘㄢˊ ㄔㄨㄢˇ)
to prolong one's life only temporarily; to be on one's last legs; to linger on in a steadily deteriorating condition

【苤】 4899 ㄆㄧㄝˇ piee piě (讀音 ㄆㄧˇ pii pǐ)
1. a kind of plant
2. luxuriant flora or vegetation
苤藍(ㄆㄧㄝˇ ·ㄌㄚ)
a kohlrabi

【苽】 4900 (菰) ㄍㄨ gu gū
Zizania latifolia

【苢】 4901 (苡) ㄧˇ yii yǐ
Coix agrestis

六畫

【茗】 4902 ㄇㄧㄥˊ ming míng (又讀 ㄇㄧㄥˇ miing mǐng)
tea; a tea plant
茗圃(ㄇㄧㄥˊ ㄆㄨˇ)
a tea plantation
茗坊(ㄇㄧㄥˊ ㄈㄤ)or 茗肆(ㄇㄧㄥˊ ㄙˋ)
a tea shop; a teahouse
茗具(ㄇㄧㄥˊ ㄐㄩˋ)
a tea set

【荔】 4903 ㄌㄧˋ lih lì
a lichee
荔枝(ㄌㄧˋ ㄓ)
a lichee

【茼】 4904 ㄊㄨㄥˊ torng tóng
a kind of green vegetable
茼蒿(ㄊㄨㄥˊ ㄏㄠ)
Chrysanthemum coronarium, a kind of green vegetable

【茨】 4905 ㄘˊ tsyr cí
1. to thatch; a thatched house
2. *Tribulus terrestris*, a kind of thorny plant
3. to fill with earth
茨菰 or 慈姑(ㄘˊ ㄍㄨ)
(botany) an arrowhead

【茫】 4906 ㄇㄤˊ mang máng
1. vast; boundless
2. vague; uncertain
茫昧(ㄇㄤˊ ㄇㄟˋ)
unfathomably dark
茫茫(ㄇㄤˊ ㄇㄤˊ)
vast; boundless
茫茫大海(ㄇㄤˊ ㄇㄤˊ ㄉㄚˋ ㄏㄞˇ)
the boundless ocean
茫然(ㄇㄤˊ ㄖㄢˊ)
vague; uncertain; ignorant; blank
茫然不知(ㄇㄤˊ ㄖㄢˊ ㄅㄨˋ ㄓ)
helplessly ignorant; completely in the dark; completely at a loss
茫然自失(ㄇㄤˊ ㄖㄢˊ ㄗˋ ㄕ)
stupefied; dazed; bewildered; to be in bewilderment: 他茫然自失。He was in great bewilderment.
茫無頭緒(ㄇㄤˊ ㄨˊ ㄊㄡˊ ㄒㄩˋ)
①(said of things) to be all in a jumble ②not knowing where or how to start

【茯】 4907 ㄈㄨˊ fwu fú
tuckahoe
茯苓(ㄈㄨˊ ㄌㄧㄥˊ)
tuckahoe

【茱】 4908 ㄓㄨ ju zhū
a dogwood
茱萸(ㄓㄨ ㄩˊ)
a dogwood
茱萸囊(ㄓㄨ ㄩˊ ㄋㄤˊ)
a bag filled with dogwoods to be carried at a drinking party on the Double-Nine Festival (9th day of the 9th lunar month) to ward off disaster
茱萸會(ㄓㄨ ㄩˊ ㄏㄨㄟˋ)
a drinking party on the Double-Nine Festival (9th day of the 9th lunar month)

【茲】 4909 1. ㄗ tzy zī
1. this
2. now; here; at present
3. year: 今茲 this year
茲定(ㄗ ㄉㄧㄥˋ)
It is hereby decided....
茲令(ㄗ ㄌㄧㄥˋ)
(So-and-so) is hereby sent to....
茲者(ㄗ ㄓㄜˇ)
now
茲查(ㄗ ㄔㄚˊ)
(a documentary usage) It has been found that....
茲事體大(ㄗ ㄕˋ ㄊㄧˇ ㄉㄚˋ)
This is a big problem. 或 This is a serious matter.
茲有(ㄗ ㄧㄡˇ)
Now here is....
茲因(ㄗ ㄧㄣ)
now because...

【茲】 4909 2. ㄘˊ tsyr cí
a form used in"龜茲"(ㄑㄧㄡ ㄘˊ)

【茴】 4910 ㄏㄨㄟˊ hwei huí
fennel; aniseed
茴香(ㄏㄨㄟˊ ㄒㄧㄤ)
fennel; aniseed
茴香菜(ㄏㄨㄟˊ ㄒㄧㄤ ㄘㄞˋ)
fennel stalks and leaves (as a kind of vegetable)

【茵】 4911 ㄧㄣ in yīn
a cushion; a mat; a carpet
茵席(ㄧㄣ ㄒㄧˊ)
a cushion; a mat
茵陳 or 茵蔯(ㄧㄣ ㄔㄣˊ)or 茵陳蒿(ㄧㄣ ㄔㄣˊ ㄏㄠ)
(botany) *Artemisia capillaris*, a kind of medicinal herb
茵蓐 or 茵褥 or 茵縟(ㄧㄣ ㄖㄨˋ)
a mat; a cushion

〔艸部〕

【茶】 4912 ㄔㄚˊ char chá
tea
茶博士(ㄔㄚˊ ㄅㄛˊ ㄕˋ)
a tearoom keeper
茶杯(ㄔㄚˊ ㄅㄟ)
a teacup; a cup
茶焙(ㄔㄚˊ ㄅㄟˋ)
a bamboo tray used in baking tea
茶餅(ㄔㄚˊ ㄅㄧㄥˇ)
brick tea
茶盤兒(ㄔㄚˊ ㄆㄚˊㄦ)
a tea tray
茶棚(ㄔㄚˊ ㄆㄥˊ)
a tea booth
茶末(ㄔㄚˊ ㄇㄛˋ)
refuse tea; tea dust
茶飯(ㄔㄚˊ ㄈㄢˋ)
meals
茶飯無心(ㄔㄚˊ ㄈㄢˋ ㄨˊ ㄒㄧㄣ)
to have no appetite
茶坊(ㄔㄚˊ ㄈㄤ)
a tearoom; a teahouse; a tea shop
茶房(ㄔㄚˊ ㄈㄤˊ)
a waiter; an attendant
茶袋(ㄔㄚˊ ㄉㄞˋ)
a tea bag
茶道(ㄔㄚˊ ㄉㄠˋ)
the tea ceremony
茶顛(ㄔㄚˊ ㄉㄧㄢ)
"Tea Maniac," the nickname of 陸羽, a Tang Dynasty man of letters who was extremely fond of tea
茶點(ㄔㄚˊ ㄉㄧㄢˇ)
refreshments
茶點招待(ㄔㄚˊ ㄉㄧㄢˇ ㄓㄠ ㄉㄞˋ)
to entertain with refreshments
茶攤兒(ㄔㄚˊ ㄊㄚㄦ)
a tea stand (on the roadside)
茶托(ㄔㄚˊ ㄊㄨㄛ)
a tea tray
茶筒(ㄔㄚˊ ㄊㄨㄥˇ)
a tea caddy
茶農(ㄔㄚˊ ㄋㄨㄥˊ)
a tea grower (or planter)
茶樓(ㄔㄚˊ ㄌㄡˊ)
a tearoom; a teahouse
茶樓酒肆(ㄔㄚˊ ㄌㄡˊ ㄐㄧㄡˇ ㄙˋ)
tearooms and taverns
茶果(ㄔㄚˊ ㄍㄨㄛˇ)
tea and fruits
茶館(ㄔㄚˊ ㄍㄨㄢˇ)
a tearoom; a teahouse
茶罐(ㄔㄚˊ ㄍㄨㄢˋ)
a tea caddy
茶褐色(ㄔㄚˊ ㄏㄜˊ ㄙㄜˋ)
tea-brown
茶壺(ㄔㄚˊ ㄏㄨˊ)
a teapot
茶戶(ㄔㄚˊ ㄏㄨˋ)
①a tea merchant; a tea dealer ②a tea grower
茶花(ㄔㄚˊ ㄏㄨㄚ)
a camellia
茶花女(ㄔㄚˊ ㄏㄨㄚ ㄋㄩˇ)
La Dame Aux Camelias, a romantic drama by Alexandre Dumas (1824-1895)
茶話會(ㄔㄚˊ ㄏㄨㄚˋ ㄏㄨㄟˋ) or 茶會(ㄔㄚˊ ㄏㄨㄟˋ)
a tea party; a tea reception
茶几(ㄔㄚˊ ㄐㄧ) or 茶几兒(ㄔㄚˊ ㄐㄧㄜㄦ)
①a teapoy ②a small table
茶具(ㄔㄚˊ ㄐㄩˋ)
tea utensils; tea-things: 她把茶具放在桌上。She put the tea-things on the table.
茶錢(ㄔㄚˊ ˙ㄑㄧㄢ)
①tea bills ②tips (for attendants, waiters, etc.): 他給侍者茶錢。He gave the waiter a tip.
茶青(ㄔㄚˊ ㄑㄧㄥ)
dark green
茶箱(ㄔㄚˊ ㄒㄧㄤ)
a tea chest
茶磚(ㄔㄚˊ ㄓㄨㄢ)
brick tea
茶莊(ㄔㄚˊ ㄓㄨㄤ)
a tea dealer's shop
茶盅(ㄔㄚˊ ㄓㄨㄥ)
a teacup
茶匙(ㄔㄚˊ ㄔˊ)
a teaspoon
茶食(ㄔㄚˊ ㄕˊ)
cookies, cakes, etc.; tea pastry
茶市(ㄔㄚˊ ㄕˋ)
the tea market
茶室(ㄔㄚˊ ㄕˋ)
①a tearoom ②a brothel
茶商(ㄔㄚˊ ㄕㄤ)
a tea dealer; a tea merchant
茶樹(ㄔㄚˊ ㄕㄨˋ)
a tea tree
茶水(ㄔㄚˊ ㄕㄨㄟˇ)
tea or boiled water (furnished to walkers, trippers, etc.)
茶水錢(ㄔㄚˊ ㄕㄨㄟˇ ˙ㄑㄧㄢ)
tips given to hotel attendants
茶座(ㄔㄚˊ ㄗㄨㄛˋ)
seats in a tearoom
茶肆(ㄔㄚˊ ㄙˋ)
a tearoom; a teahouse
茶色(ㄔㄚˊ ㄙㄜˋ)
dark brown
茶素(ㄔㄚˊ ㄙㄨˋ)
theine
茶葉(ㄔㄚˊ ㄧㄝˋ)
tea leaves
茶業(ㄔㄚˊ ㄧㄝˋ)
the tea industry
茶油(ㄔㄚˊ ㄧㄡˊ)
tea oil
茶舞(ㄔㄚˊ ㄨˇ)
a tea dance
茶碗(ㄔㄚˊ ㄨㄢˇ)
a teacup; a tea bowl
茶園(ㄔㄚˊ ㄩㄢˊ)
①a tea plantation ②formerly, an opera theater

【茸】 4913 ㄖㄨㄥˊ rong róng
1. soft, fine hair; down
2. soft; downy; fluffy
3. untidy; messy; confused; disorderly
4. luxuriant; lush

茸茸(ㄖㄨㄥˊ ㄖㄨㄥˊ)
(said of grass, hair, etc.) fine, soft and thick; luxuriant; lush: 兩岸青草茸茸。Lush grass grows along the river banks.

【茹】 4914 ㄖㄨˊ ru rú (又讀 ㄖㄨˋ ruh rù)
1. entangled roots
2. to eat; to taste; to mouth
3. (figuratively) to experience
4. stinking

茹筆(ㄖㄨˊ ㄅㄧˇ)
to make writing brushes
茹毛飲血(ㄖㄨˊ ㄇㄠˊ ㄧㄣˇ ㄒㄧㄝˇ) or (ㄖㄨˊ ㄇㄠˊ ㄧㄣˇ ㄒㄩㄝˋ)
(said of primitive people) to eat birds and beasts uncooked
茹荼(ㄖㄨˊ ㄊㄨˊ)
to undergo hardships; to suf-

fer
茹苦含辛(ㄖㄨˊ ㄎㄨˇ ㄏㄢˊ ㄒㄧㄣ)
to undergo all possible hardships
茹柔吐剛(ㄖㄨˊ ㄖㄡˊ ㄊㄨˇ ㄍㄤ)
(literally) to eat the soft and spit the hard—to bully the good-natured and fear the atrocious
茹素(ㄖㄨˊ ㄙㄨˋ)
to abstain from meat; to be a vegetarian

【荀】 4915 ㄒㄩㄣˊ shyun xún
1. name of an ancient state
2. a kind of herb
3. a Chinese family name

荀況(ㄒㄩㄣˊ ㄎㄨㄤˋ)
Hsün Kuang, a contemporary of Mencius, known for his doctrine of man's natural wickedness
荀子(ㄒㄩㄣˊ ㄗˇ)
① Hsün-tzu or Hsün Kuang ② the works of Hsün-tzu

【荄】 4916 ㄍㄞ gai gāi
roots of grass

【草】 4917 ㄘㄠˇ tsao cǎo
1. grass; straw; a herb; a weed
2. coarse; crude
3. a draft (of writing); to draft
4. the script type of Chinese calligraphy

草包(ㄘㄠˇ ㄅㄠ)
a grass bag—a crude fellow; a good-for-nothing; a simpleton
草本(ㄘㄠˇ ㄅㄣˇ)
① a manuscript: 著作的草本已完成。The work is already complete in manuscript. ② herbaceous
草本植物(ㄘㄠˇ ㄅㄣˇ ㄓˊ ㄨˋ)
herbage
草鄙(ㄘㄠˇ ㄅㄧˇ)
unlearned; uncultured; crude
草標(ㄘㄠˇ ㄅㄧㄠ)
a straw attached to an article to indicate that it is on sale
草棚(ㄘㄠˇ ㄆㄥˊ)
a thatched shanty; a straw shed
草皮(ㄘㄠˇ ㄆㄧˊ)
a young grass cover
草坪(ㄘㄠˇ ㄆㄧㄥˊ)
a lawn; meadow; pasture
草莓(ㄘㄠˇ ㄇㄟˊ)
a strawberry
草昧(ㄘㄠˇ ㄇㄟˋ)
the chaos at the beginning of the world
草茅(ㄘㄠˇ ㄇㄠˊ)
① thatch; straw; grass ② the common people (as distinct from those in the imperial service)
草帽(ㄘㄠˇ ㄇㄠˋ)
a straw hat
草帽辮 or 草帽緶(ㄘㄠˇ ㄇㄠˋ ㄅㄧㄢˋ)
straw braids for making hats
草莽(ㄘㄠˇ ㄇㄤˇ)
the wilderness; thickets
草莽流寇(ㄘㄠˇ ㄇㄤˇ ㄌㄧㄡˊ ㄎㄡˋ)
bandits of the wilderness; bandits
草棉(ㄘㄠˇ ㄇㄧㄢˊ)
a cotton plant
草木(ㄘㄠˇ ㄇㄨˋ)
grass and trees; vegetation; flora
草木皆兵(ㄘㄠˇ ㄇㄨˋ ㄐㄧㄝ ㄅㄧㄥ)
All grass and trees are mistaken for enemy troops. (descriptive of the imaginary fears of a routed army)
草房(ㄘㄠˇ ㄈㄤˊ)
a thatched cottage
草地(ㄘㄠˇ ㄉㄧˋ)
meadow; pasture; a lawn: 我們要把草地上的草割去。We are going to mow the meadow.
草堆(ㄘㄠˇ ㄉㄨㄟ)
a haystack
草頭露(ㄘㄠˇ ㄊㄡˊ ㄌㄨˋ)
(literally) dew on the grass—ephemeral; fleeting
草堂(ㄘㄠˇ ㄊㄤˊ) or 草廬(ㄘㄠˇ ㄌㄨˊ)
a humble cottage (used by a hermit in reference to his simple dwelling)
草圖(ㄘㄠˇ ㄊㄨˊ)
a sketch map; a draft
草擬(ㄘㄠˇ ㄋㄧˇ)
to draft (documents): 他們正在草擬一份法案。They are drafting a bill.
草萊(ㄘㄠˇ ㄌㄞˊ)
① the wilderness ② fields
草蘭(ㄘㄠˇ ㄌㄢˊ)
Cymbidium virens
草料(ㄘㄠˇ ㄌㄧㄠˋ)
fodder; hay: 馬以草料爲食。The horses feed on fodder.
草履蟲(ㄘㄠˇ ㄌㄩˇ ㄔㄨㄥˊ)
a paramecium
草綠(ㄘㄠˇ ㄌㄩˋ)
green
草稿 or 草藁(ㄘㄠˇ ㄍㄠˇ)
a rough draft
草根大使(ㄘㄠˇ ㄍㄣ ㄉㄚˋ ㄕˇ)
a grass-roots ambassador; a trainee under the 4-H Club exchange program
草根樹皮(ㄘㄠˇ ㄍㄣ ㄕㄨˋ ㄆㄧˊ)
roots of grass and bark of trees (which one may eat when starving)
草菇(ㄘㄠˇ ㄍㄨ)
a mushroom
草寇(ㄘㄠˇ ㄎㄡˋ)
a bandit
草夾竹桃(ㄘㄠˇ ㄐㄧㄚˊ ㄓㄨˊ ㄊㄠˊ)
phlox
草芥(ㄘㄠˇ ㄐㄧㄝˋ)
a bundle of grass—valueless things; insignificant things
草芥小民(ㄘㄠˇ ㄐㄧㄝˋ ㄒㄧㄠˇ ㄇㄧㄣˊ)
an unimportant member of a community; the humble people
草菅人命(ㄘㄠˇ ㄐㄧㄢ ㄖㄣˊ ㄇㄧㄥˋ)
to treat human life as grass; to attach no importance to human life
草裙舞(ㄘㄠˇ ㄑㄩㄣˊ ㄨˇ)
a Hawaiian dance; a hula-hula: 夏威夷以草裙舞聞名。Hawaii is famous for its Hawaiian dance.
草蓆(ㄘㄠˇ ㄒㄧˊ)
a straw mat
草檄(ㄘㄠˇ ㄒㄧˊ)
to draft a call to arms
草蝦(ㄘㄠˇ ㄒㄧㄚ)
a prawn
草鞋(ㄘㄠˇ ㄒㄧㄝˊ)
straw sandals
草寫(ㄘㄠˇ ㄒㄧㄝˇ)
the script type of calligraphy
草紙(ㄘㄠˇ ㄓˇ)
coarse paper; toilet paper
草詔(ㄘㄠˇ ㄓㄠˋ)
to draft an imperial edict

草長鶯飛(ㄘㄠˇ ㄓㄤˇ ㄧㄥ ㄈㄟ)
The grasses are tall and the nightingales are in the air. (descriptive of landscapes in late spring)

草創(ㄘㄠˇ ㄔㄨㄤˋ)or 草制(ㄘㄠˇ ㄓˋ)
①the beginning or initial period (of a project) ②to make the rough copy

草食獸(ㄘㄠˇ ㄕˊ ㄕㄡˋ)or 草食動物(ㄘㄠˇ ㄕˊ ㄉㄨㄥˋ ㄨˋ)
herbivorous animals: 牛是草食動物。Cattle are herbivorous animals.

草繩(ㄘㄠˇ ㄕㄥˊ)
a straw rope; a grass rope: 擲給他一條草繩。Throw him a straw rope.

草聖(ㄘㄠˇ ㄕㄥˋ)
prodigies of the script type of calligraphy—referring to Chang Chih (張芝) of the Han Dynasty and Chang Hsü (張旭) of the Tang Dynasty

草書(ㄘㄠˇ ㄕㄨ)or 草字(ㄘㄠˇ ㄗˋ)
the script type of calligraphy

草率(ㄘㄠˇ ㄕㄨㄞˋ)
careless; perfunctory

草率從事(ㄘㄠˇ ㄕㄨㄞˋ ㄘㄨㄥˊ ㄕˋ)
to do a job carelessly or perfunctorily

草人(ㄘㄠˇ ㄖㄣˊ)
a scarecrow 亦作「稻草人」

草字(ㄘㄠˇ ㄗˋ)
①characters written in the script type ②my humble style (name)

草賊(ㄘㄠˇ ㄗㄟˊ)
bandits; outlaws

草澤(ㄘㄠˇ ㄗㄜˊ)
①the wilderness; thickets ②the common people (as distinct from the governing class)

草澤英雄(ㄘㄠˇ ㄗㄜˊ ㄧㄥ ㄒㄩㄥˊ)
heroes of the common people

草草(ㄘㄠˇ ㄘㄠˇ)
①roughly; carelessly; hastily 亦作「草蹙」 ②in sorrow ③(said of trees, etc.) lush; exuberant; luxuriant

草草了事(ㄘㄠˇ ㄘㄠˇ ㄌㄧㄠˇ ㄕˋ)
to dispose of a thing carelessly or hastily

草叢(ㄘㄠˇ ㄘㄨㄥˊ)
a thick growth of grass

草酸(ㄘㄠˇ ㄙㄨㄢ)
oxalic acid

草案(ㄘㄠˇ ㄢˋ)
a draft plan; a proposed plan: 草案已修訂完成。The draft has been amended.

草野(ㄘㄠˇ ㄧㄝˇ)
①the common people ②fields ③lowly; base

草藥(ㄘㄠˇ ㄧㄠˋ)
herb medicine

草藥商(ㄘㄠˇ ㄧㄠˋ ㄕㄤ)
a herbalist

草魚(ㄘㄠˇ ㄩˊ)
a grass carp

草約(ㄘㄠˇ ㄩㄝ)
a draft agreement or contract

草原(ㄘㄠˇ ㄩㄢˊ)
a prairie; grassland; a steppe

【荏】 4918
ㄖㄣˇ reen rěn

1. *Perilla frutescens*, whose seeds are birds' feed
2. soft; weak; fragile

荏苒(ㄖㄣˇ ㄖㄢˇ)
(said of time) to elapse imperceptibly; to slip by 亦作「苒荏」: 光陰荏苒，轉瞬又是一年。Time slipped by and the year was soon over.

荏弱(ㄖㄣˇ ㄖㄨㄛˋ)
soft; weak; fragile: 她愈來愈荏弱。She grew weaker and weaker.

【荑】 4919
1. ㄊㄧˊ tyi tí

sprouts

【荑】 4919
2. ㄧˊ yi yí

to weed; to mow

【荒】 4920
ㄏㄨㄤ huang huāng

1. uncultivated; desolate; wild; deserted; barren; waste
2. absurd; ridiculous
3. famine; scarcity; deficiency
4. to neglect
5. a Chinese family name

荒僻(ㄏㄨㄤ ㄆㄧˋ)
desolate and remote

荒謬(ㄏㄨㄤ ㄇㄧㄡˋ)
grossly absurd; ridiculous; preposterous: 那眞是荒謬至極! That is ridiculous!

荒謬絕倫(ㄏㄨㄤ ㄇㄧㄡˋ ㄐㄩㄝˊ ㄌㄨㄣˊ)
absurd in the extreme

荒湎(ㄏㄨㄤ ㄇㄧㄢˇ)
to abandon oneself to (drinking, etc.)

荒廢(ㄏㄨㄤ ㄈㄟˋ)
to neglect; to leave completely unattended to

荒怠(ㄏㄨㄤ ㄉㄞˋ)
negligent; neglectful

荒島(ㄏㄨㄤ ㄉㄠˇ)
an uninhabited island; a barren island

荒誕(ㄏㄨㄤ ㄉㄢˋ)
absurd; nonsensical; wild

荒誕不經(ㄏㄨㄤ ㄉㄢˋ ㄅㄨˋ ㄐㄧㄥ)
absurd and unthinkable

荒地(ㄏㄨㄤ ㄉㄧˋ)
the wilderness; waste land

荒唐(ㄏㄨㄤ ㄊㄤˊ)
absurd; wild; nonsensical; preposterous

荒唐無稽(ㄏㄨㄤ ㄊㄤˊ ㄨˊ ㄐㄧ)
flagrantly absurd or ridiculous; preposterous

荒田(ㄏㄨㄤ ㄊㄧㄢˊ)
fields left uncultivated; desolate fields

荒腆(ㄏㄨㄤ ㄊㄧㄢˇ)
addicted to alcoholic drinks

荒土(ㄏㄨㄤ ㄊㄨˇ)
uncultivated land; the wilderness; waste land

荒年(ㄏㄨㄤ ㄋㄧㄢˊ)
a year of bad crops; a year of famine

荒涼(ㄏㄨㄤ ㄌㄧㄤˊ)
desolate; deserted; wild

荒忽(ㄏㄨㄤ ㄏㄨ)
dim; vague; indistinct

荒瘠(ㄏㄨㄤ ㄐㄧˊ)
barren land

荒郊(ㄏㄨㄤ ㄐㄧㄠ)
the wilderness; a desolate area

荒饉(ㄏㄨㄤ ㄐㄧㄣˇ)
famine 亦作「飢荒」

荒歉(ㄏㄨㄤ ㄑㄧㄢˋ)
famine; deficiency

荒腔走調(ㄏㄨㄤ ㄑㄧㄤ ㄗㄡˇ ㄉㄧㄠˋ)

out of tune

荒政(ㄏㄨㄤ ㄓㄥˋ)
①measures for relief of a famine ②to neglect affairs of the state

荒塚(ㄏㄨㄤ ㄓㄨㄥˇ)
an abandoned grave; an uncared-for grave

荒山(ㄏㄨㄤ ㄕㄢ)
a desolate mountain; a lone hill

荒疏(ㄏㄨㄤ ㄕㄨ)
to neglect practice (of some skill)

荒草(ㄏㄨㄤ ㄘㄠˇ)
weeds

荒村(ㄏㄨㄤ ㄘㄨㄣ)
a deserted village

荒野(ㄏㄨㄤ ㄧㄝˇ)
the wilderness

荒煙蔓草(ㄏㄨㄤ ㄧㄢ ㄇㄢˋ ㄘㄠˇ)
deserted by men and infested with weeds

荒淫(ㄏㄨㄤ ㄧㄣˊ)
dissipated; dissolute; profligate

荒淫無度(ㄏㄨㄤ ㄧㄣˊ ㄨˊ ㄉㄨˋ)
immeasurably dissolute

荒蕪(ㄏㄨㄤ ㄨˊ)
deserted and desolate; desolation

荒外(ㄏㄨㄤ ㄨㄞˋ)
very remote

荒原(ㄏㄨㄤ ㄩㄢˊ)
wasteland; the wilderness

【茛】 4921
ㄍㄣˋ genn gèn
Rhus toxicodendron, a kind of poisonous vine

【茜】 4922
ㄑㄧㄢˋ chiann qiàn
madder

茜草(ㄑㄧㄢˋ ㄘㄠˇ)
madder

茜素(ㄑㄧㄢˋ ㄙㄨˋ)
alizarin

【茭】 4923
ㄐㄧㄠ jiau jiāo
Zizania latifolia, a kind of edible aquatic grass

茭白(ㄐㄧㄠ ㄅㄞˊ)or 茭白筍(ㄐㄧㄠ ㄅㄞˊ ㄙㄨㄣˇ)
Zizania latifolia, water oats

【荃】 4924
ㄑㄩㄢˊ chyuan quán
1. a fragrant herb
2. fine cloth

【荇】 4925
ㄒㄧㄥˋ shinq xìng
Nymphoides peltatum, a kind of vegetable

荇菜(ㄒㄧㄥˋ ㄘㄞˋ)
Nymphoides peltatum, a kind of vegetable; duckweed

【荐】 4926
(薦) ㄐㄧㄢˋ jiann jiàn
1. repeatedly; again and again
2. to offer; to recommend
3. a straw mattress

七畫

【荷】 4927
1. ㄏㄜˊ her hé
a lotus; a water lily

荷包(ㄏㄜˊ ㄅㄠ)
a pouch (carried with oneself); a purse

荷包蛋(ㄏㄜˊ ㄅㄠ ㄉㄢˋ)
fried eggs

荷馬(ㄏㄜˊ ㄇㄚˇ)
Homer, Greek poet

荷蘭(ㄏㄜˊ ㄌㄢˊ)
Holland; the Netherlands

荷蘭話(ㄏㄜˊ ㄌㄢˊ ㄏㄨㄚˋ)or 荷蘭語(ㄏㄜˊ ㄌㄢˊ ㄩˇ)
the Dutch language; Dutch

荷蘭豬(ㄏㄜˊ ㄌㄢˊ ㄓㄨ)
a guinea pig

荷蘭水(ㄏㄜˊ ㄌㄢˊ ㄕㄨㄟˇ)
aerated water; soda water

荷蘭人(ㄏㄜˊ ㄌㄢˊ ㄖㄣˊ)
a Dutchman; the Dutch people; the Dutch

荷花 or 荷華(ㄏㄜˊ ㄏㄨㄚ)
a lotus flower

荷錢(ㄏㄜˊ ㄑㄧㄢˊ)
sprouting lotus leaves

荷爾蒙(ㄏㄜˊ ㄦˇ ㄇㄥˊ)
hormone

荷葉(ㄏㄜˊ ㄧㄝˋ)
lotus leaves

荷葉肉(ㄏㄜˊ ㄧㄝˋ ㄖㄡˋ)
slices of pork seasoned and wrapped in lotus leaves and then steamed

荷月(ㄏㄜˊ ㄩㄝˋ)
the month of the lotus—the 6th lunar month

【荷】 4927
2. ㄏㄜˋ heh hè
1. a load; a burden
2. to bear; to carry; to shoulder
3. to receive

荷蒙(ㄏㄜˋ ㄇㄥˊ)
to receive (favor, etc.)

荷負(ㄏㄜˋ ㄈㄨˋ)
to carry; to bear

荷戴(ㄏㄜˋ ㄉㄞˋ)
to carry; to bear

荷鎗實彈(ㄏㄜˋ ㄑㄧㄤ ㄕˊ ㄉㄢˋ)
to carry loaded rifles—ready for emergencies

【荾】 4928
ㄙㄨㄟ suei suī
as in 芫荾—parsley

【莅】 4929
(蒞) ㄌㄧˋ lih lì
to arrive; to be present

莅臨(ㄌㄧˋ ㄌㄧㄣˊ)
to arrive; to be present

【荻】 4930
ㄉㄧˊ dyi dí
1. *Anaphalis yedoensis*
2. *Miscanthus sacchariflorus*, a kind of reed

荻筆(ㄉㄧˊ ㄅㄧˇ)
to learn to write on ash with reed stems

荻花(ㄉㄧˊ ㄏㄨㄚ)
a reed flower

荻畫(ㄉㄧˊ ㄏㄨㄚˋ)
to learn by writing on the ground with a reed stem, as Ou-Yang Hsiu(歐陽修) did in his childhood

【荼】 4931
ㄊㄨˊ twu tú
1. *Sonchus oleraceus*, a kind of bitter-tasting vegetable; sow thistle 亦作「苦菜」
2. to harm; to poison

荼毗(ㄊㄨˊ ㄆㄧˊ)
to cremate a body (transliteration from Sanskrit)

荼蘼 or 酴醾(ㄊㄨˊ ㄇㄧˊ)
brambles, a kind of shrub

荼毒(ㄊㄨˊ ㄉㄨˊ)
harm; poison; to cause injury or disaster

荼毒生靈(ㄊㄨˊ ㄉㄨˊ ㄕㄥ ㄌㄧㄥˊ)
to injure the people

荼炭(ㄊㄨˊ ㄊㄢˋ)
suffering of the common people 亦作「塗炭」

荼蓼(ㄊㄨˊ ㄌㄧㄠˇ)
①a kind of bitter weed ②(figuratively) hardship; privation

〔艸部〕

【荇】 4932 ㄒㄧㄥˋ shinq xìng
Nymphoides peltatum, a kind of water plant
荇菜(ㄒㄧㄥˋ ㄘㄞˋ)
Nymphoides peltatum, a kind of water plant

【莊】 4933 ㄓㄨㄤ juang zhuāng
1. solemn; dignified; stately; august; sober; gravity
2. a large farmhouse; a manor house
3. a village; a hamlet
4. a market; a shop; a store; a bank
5. a Chinese family name
莊票(ㄓㄨㄤ ㄆㄧㄠˋ)
a note issued by a local bank
莊頭(ㄓㄨㄤ ˙ㄊㄡ)
a supervisor of tenant farmers
莊田(ㄓㄨㄤ ㄊㄧㄢˊ)
① fields tilled by tenants ② (Ching Dynasty) fields near the capital with the levy turned to the imperial coffer directly
莊奴(ㄓㄨㄤ ㄋㄨˊ)
a tenant farmer
莊列(ㄓㄨㄤ ㄌㄧㄝˋ)
Chuang-tzu (莊子) and Lieh-tzu (列子), who preached Taoism after Lao-tzu (老子)
莊論(ㄓㄨㄤ ㄌㄨㄣˋ)or 莊語(ㄓㄨㄤ ㄩˇ)
a dignified statement
莊客(ㄓㄨㄤ ㄎㄜˋ)
tenant farmers
莊口(ㄓㄨㄤ ㄎㄡˇ)
a market
莊款(ㄓㄨㄤ ㄎㄨㄢˇ)
money exchanged between banks
莊戶(ㄓㄨㄤ ㄏㄨˋ)
a farmer
莊家(ㄓㄨㄤ ˙ㄐㄧㄚ)
①a farmhouse ②the banker (in gambling games)
莊稼(ㄓㄨㄤ ˙ㄐㄧㄚ)
① farming ② crops; harvests
莊稼地(ㄓㄨㄤ ˙ㄐㄧㄚ ㄉㄧˋ)
a farm; a field
莊稼老兒(ㄓㄨㄤ ˙ㄐㄧㄚ ㄌㄠˇㄦ)or 莊稼漢(ㄓㄨㄤ ˙ㄐㄧㄚ ㄏㄢˋ)or 莊稼人(ㄓㄨㄤ ˙ㄐㄧㄚ ㄖㄣˊ)
a farmer
莊稼活(ㄓㄨㄤ ˙ㄐㄧㄚ ㄏㄨㄛˊ)
farming; farm chores
莊諧並作(ㄓㄨㄤ ㄒㄧㄝˊ ㄅㄧㄥˋ ㄗㄨㄛˋ)
to combine sobriety with humor
莊周(ㄓㄨㄤ ㄓㄡ)
Chuang Chou, a contemporary of Mencius who advocated Taoism 亦作「莊子」
莊重(ㄓㄨㄤ ㄓㄨㄥˋ)
dignified; solemn: 他看起來很莊重。He looks very solemn.
莊子
①(ㄓㄨㄤ ㄗˇ)ⓐ Chuang Chou 參看「莊周」ⓑ the works of Chuang Chou
②(ㄓㄨㄤ ˙ㄗ) the landlord's mansion; a manor house; a farm village
莊騷(ㄓㄨㄤ ㄙㄠ)
the works of the philosopher Chuang-tzu (莊子) and the poet Chü Yüan(屈原), regarded as representatives of southern literature in the Epoch of Warring States
莊嚴(ㄓㄨㄤ ㄧㄢˊ)
① dignified; solemn; stately; august ② to adorn; to make solemn
莊園(ㄓㄨㄤ ㄩㄢˊ)
a manor

【莒】 4934 ㄐㄩˇ jeu jǔ
1. taros
2. name of an ancient state
3. name of a county in Shantung

【莓】 4935 ㄇㄟˊ mei méi
1. berries
2. moss; lichen

【莖】 4936 ㄐㄧㄥ jing jīng
a stalk; a stem
莖菜類(ㄐㄧㄥ ㄘㄞˋ ㄌㄟˋ)
stem vegetables

【莘】 4937 ㄕㄣ shen shēn
(又讀 ㄒㄧㄣ shin xīn)
1. long
2. numerous
3. *Asarum sieboldi*
4. a Chinese family name
莘莘(ㄒㄧㄣ ㄒㄧㄣ)or(ㄕㄣ ㄕㄣ)
numerous; many
莘莘學子(ㄒㄧㄣ ㄒㄧㄣ ㄒㄩㄝˊ ㄗˇ)or (ㄕㄣ ㄕㄣ ㄒㄩㄝˊ ㄗˇ)
students in large numbers

【莞】 4938 1. ㄨㄢˇ woan wǎn
smiling
莞爾(ㄨㄢˇ ㄦˇ)
smiling

【莞】 4938 2. ㄍㄨㄢˇ goan guǎn
as in 東莞 — a county in Kwangtung

【莞】 4938 3. ㄍㄨㄢ guan guān
Scirpus lacustris, a kind of aquatic herb

【莠】 4939 ㄧㄡˇ yeou yǒu
(又讀 ㄧㄡˋ yow yòu)
1. foxtail (a kind of weed) 亦作「狗尾草」
2. bad; ugly; undesirable; detestable; vicious: 良莠不齊。The good and the bad are intermingled.
莠民(ㄧㄡˇ ㄇㄧㄣˊ)
wicked people; villains; outlaws
莠言(ㄧㄡˇ ㄧㄢˊ)
dirty words; bad words: 莠言不聽。Do not listen to bad words.

【莢】 4940 ㄐㄧㄚˊ jya jiá
a pod—the shell or case in which plants like beans and peas grow their seed
莢果(ㄐㄧㄚˊ ㄍㄨㄛˇ)
(botany) a pod
莢錢(ㄐㄧㄚˊ ㄑㄧㄢˊ)
a small light coin

【莧】 4941 ㄒㄧㄢˋ shiann xiàn
an amaranth
莧科(ㄒㄧㄢˋ ㄎㄜ)
Amaranthaceae, the amaranth family
莧菜(ㄒㄧㄢˋ ㄘㄞˋ)
an amaranth

【莩】 4942 1. ㄈㄨˊ fwu fú
membrane in stems of rushes or reeds

【莩】 4942 2.(殍) ㄆㄧㄠˇ peau piǎo
the corpse of a person who was starved to death

【莪】 4943 ㄜˊ er é

Artemisia, a kind of plant; the aster-southernwood

莪蒿(ㄜˊ ㄏㄠ)
Artemisia, a kind of plant with edible leaves

【莫】 4944 1. ㄇㄛˋ moh mò

1. not: 莫蹉跎光陰。Don't waste time.
2. a Chinese family name

莫泊桑(ㄇㄛˋ ㄅㄛˊ ㄙㄤ)
Guy de Maupassant, 1850-1893, French novelist

莫不(ㄇㄛˋ ㄅㄨˋ)
there is no one that does not; there is no one that is not: 莫不爲之歡欣鼓舞。There was no one who was not very pleased.

莫不成(ㄇㄛˋ ·ㄅㄨ ㄔㄥˊ)
Can it be that...? 亦作「莫不是」

莫名(ㄇㄛˋ ㄇㄧㄥˊ)
inexpressible; indescribable

莫名其妙(ㄇㄛˋ ㄇㄧㄥˊ ㄑㄧˊ ㄇㄧㄠˋ)
① incomprehensible; mysterious; baffling ② impossible (as in "an impossible person")

莫非(ㄇㄛˋ ㄈㄟ)
① certainly; surely ② all; all-inclusive; the whole amount, quantity or extent of ③ Can it be that...?

莫大(ㄇㄛˋ ㄉㄚˋ)
greatest; utmost

莫道(ㄇㄛˋ ㄉㄠˋ)
Do not say....

莫逆之交(ㄇㄛˋ ㄋㄧˋ ㄓ ㄐㄧㄠ)
close friendship; bosom friends

莫干山(ㄇㄛˋ ㄍㄢ ㄕㄢ)
a mountain in Chekiang, known as a summer resort

莫過(ㄇㄛˋ ㄍㄨㄛˋ)or 莫過於(ㄇㄛˋ ㄍㄨㄛˋ ㄩˊ)
Nothing (or no one) is more...than....看信之樂，莫過於此。Of the pleasures of letter reading, none is more than this.

莫怪(ㄇㄛˋ ㄍㄨㄞˋ)
① No wonder that.... ② Please excuse....

莫管(ㄇㄛˋ ㄍㄨㄢˇ)
do not meddle with

莫可言狀(ㄇㄛˋ ㄎㄜˇ ㄧㄢˊ ㄓㄨㄤˋ)
indescribable; unspeakable; inexpressible

莫須有(ㄇㄛˋ ㄒㄩ ㄧㄡˇ)
(literally) Though not certain, it's likely to be true. (a phrase used by the traitorous minister Chin Kuei(秦檜)as a charge against the loyal general Yüeh Fei(岳飛) in the Southern Sung Dynasty)—a trumped-up charge; false accusation

莫札特(ㄇㄛˋ ㄓㄚˊ ㄊㄜˋ)
Wolfgang Amadeus Mozart, 1756-1791, Austrian composer

莫衷一是(ㄇㄛˋ ㄓㄨㄥ ㄧˊ ㄕˋ)
There is no agreement of opinion at all.

莫愁湖(ㄇㄛˋ ㄔㄡˊ ㄏㄨˊ)
a lake outside Nanking(南京), named after Lu Mochou(盧莫愁), a famed girl in the Six Dynasties

莫是(ㄇㄛˋ ㄕˋ)
① Can it be that....? ② no longer

莫說(ㄇㄛˋ ㄕㄨㄛ)
Do not say....或 not to mention

莫如(ㄇㄛˋ ㄖㄨˊ)or 莫若(ㄇㄛˋ ㄖㄨㄛˋ)
① had better ② Nothing is better than....或 would be better

莫此爲甚(ㄇㄛˋ ㄘˇ ㄨㄟˊ ㄕㄣˋ)
There is nothing worse than this.

莫測高深(ㄇㄛˋ ㄘㄜˋ ㄍㄠ ㄕㄣ)
unfathomable; inscrutable

莫斯科(ㄇㄛˋ ㄙ ㄎㄜ)
Moscow

莫三比克(ㄇㄛˋ ㄙㄢ ㄅㄧˇ ㄎㄜˋ)
Mozambique, a republic in SE Africa

莫索里尼(ㄇㄛˋ ㄙㄨㄛˇ ㄌㄧˇ ㄋㄧˊ)
Benito Mussolini, 1883-1945, Italian dictator

莫邪(ㄇㄛˋ ㄧㄝˊ)
name of a legendary sword

莫臥兒帝國(ㄇㄛˋ ㄨㄛˋ ㄦˊ ㄉㄧˋ ㄍㄨㄛˊ)
the Mogul Empire, 1526-1857 亦作「蒙兀兒帝國」

【莫】 4944 2.(暮) ㄇㄨˋ muh mù

evening; dusk

【莆】 4945 1. ㄈㄨˇ fuu fǔ

a kind of legendary tree with small leaves

【莆】 4945 2. ㄆㄨˊ pwu pú

as in 莆田—a county in Fukien(福建)

【莉】 4946 ㄌㄧˋ lih lì

as in 茉莉—white jasmine

【莽】 4947 (莾) ㄇㄤˇ maang mǎng

1. bushy; weedy
2. *Illicium anisatum*, a poisonous bushy plant
3. rude; uncultured; impolite; reckless

莽莽(ㄇㄤˇ ㄇㄤˇ)
① weedy; bushy ② boundless; endless

莽夫(ㄇㄤˇ ㄈㄨ)
a rude fellow

莽蕩(ㄇㄤˇ ㄉㄤˋ)
vast and wild; extensive and undeveloped

莽漢(ㄇㄤˇ ㄏㄢˋ)
a rude fellow; a rough

莽撞(ㄇㄤˇ ㄓㄨㄤˋ)
rude; rough; uncultured: 他的行爲莽撞。He has rude manners.

莽草(ㄇㄤˇ ㄘㄠˇ)
Illicium anisatum, a kind of poisonous shrub

莽蒼(ㄇㄤˇ ㄘㄤ)
verdure of the countryside

【莎】 4948 1. ㄙㄨㄛ suo suō

Cyperus rotundus, a kind of medicinal herb

莎草(ㄙㄨㄛ ㄘㄠˇ)
Cyperus rotundus, a kind of medicinal herb

【莎】 4948 2. ㄕㄚ sha shā

a kind of insect

莎士比亞(ㄕㄚ ㄕˋ ㄅㄧˇ ㄧㄚˋ)or 莎翁(ㄕㄚ ㄨㄥ)
William Shakespeare, 1564-1616, British poet and playwright

【莏】 4949 ㄙㄨㄛ suo suō (語音 ㄘㄨㄛ tsuo cuō)

to rub hands together

【荸】 4950 ㄅㄧˊ byi bí (又讀 ㄅㄛˊ bor bó)

〔艸部〕

a water chestnut

荸薺(ㄅㄧˊ ˙ㄑㄧ)
a water chestnut

【茝】 4951 ㄔㄞˇ chae chǎi
angelica 亦作「白芷」

【莝】 4952 ㄘㄨㄛˋ tsuoh cuò
1. to chop straw or hay for animals
2. chopped straw or hay

【莨】 4953 ㄌㄤˊ lang láng
Scopolia japonica, a kind of herb

莨尾(ㄌㄤˊ ㄨㄟˇ)
Chinese pennisetum, a kind of herb 亦作「狼尾草」

【荳】 4954 (豆) ㄉㄡˋ dow dòu
beans, peas, etc.; legumes

荳蔻(ㄉㄡˋ ㄎㄡˋ)
①a nutmeg亦作「豆蔻」② a virgin

荳蔻年華(ㄉㄡˋ ㄎㄡˋ ㄋㄧㄢˊ ㄏㄨㄚˊ)
(said of girls) the age of 13 or 14 in ancient China; marriageable age

八畫

【菟】 4955 ㄊㄨˋ tuh tù
(botany) a dodder

菟葵(ㄊㄨˋ ㄎㄨㄟˊ)
① *Eranthis pinnatifida*, a kind of mallow ② sea anemone, a kind of coral insect 亦作「海葵」

菟絲子(ㄊㄨˋ ㄙ ㄗˇ)
(botany) a dodder

【菀】 4956 ㄨㄢˇ woan wǎn
1. exuberant; luxuriant; lush
2. clogged; stagnant

【菅】 4957 ㄐㄧㄢ jian jiān
Themeda triandra, a coarse grass (used for making brushes, brooms, etc.)

【菊】 4958 ㄐㄩˊ jyu jú
a chrysanthemum

菊科(ㄐㄩˊ ㄎㄜ)
Compositae, the chrysanthemum family

菊花(ㄐㄩˊ ㄏㄨㄚ)
a chrysanthemum

菊花酒(ㄐㄩˊ ㄏㄨㄚ ㄐㄧㄡˇ)
chrysanthemum wine

菊花茶(ㄐㄩˊ ㄏㄨㄚ ㄔㄚˊ)
an infusion made from dried chrysanthemums

菊枕(ㄐㄩˊ ㄓㄣˇ)
a pillow stuffed with dried chrysanthemums

菊月(ㄐㄩˊ ㄩㄝˋ)
the month of the chrysanthemum—the 9th lunar month

【菌】 4959 ㄐㄩㄣˋ jiunn jùn
1. fungi; mushrooms
2. bacteria
3. a bamboo shoot

菌柄(ㄐㄩㄣˋ ㄅㄧㄥˇ)
mushroom stalks

菌類(ㄐㄩㄣˋ ㄌㄟˋ)
fungi

菌藻植物(ㄐㄩㄣˋ ㄗㄠˇ ㄓˊ ㄨˋ)
a thallophyte

菌傘(ㄐㄩㄣˋ ㄙㄢˇ)
a mushroom top

【棻】 4960 ㄈㄣ fen fēn
a kind of wood burnt for perfume

【菑】 4961 1.(甾) ㄗ tzy zī
1. land under cultivation for one year
2. to weed grass

菑畬(ㄗ ㄩˊ)
farming; husbandry

【菑】 4961 2.(甾、災) ㄗㄞ tzai zāi
misfortune; disaster; calamity

【菔】 4962 ㄈㄨˊ fwu fú
(botany) turnip

【菖】 4963 ㄔㄤ chang chāng
a sweet flag; a calamus

菖蒲(ㄔㄤ ㄆㄨˊ)
a sweet flag; a calamus

菖蒲酒(ㄔㄤ ㄆㄨˊ ㄐㄧㄡˇ)
calamus wine (served on the 5th of the 5th lunar month, the Dragon-Boat Festival)

【菜】 4964 ㄘㄞˋ tsay cài
1. vegetables; greens
2. food eaten with rice or alcoholic drinks
3. a dish; a course

菜包子(ㄘㄞˋ ㄅㄠ ˙ㄗ)
① vegetable dumpling ② (abusive) an idiot

菜圃(ㄘㄞˋ ㄆㄨˇ)
a vegetable garden (or field)

菜刀(ㄘㄞˋ ㄉㄠ)
a kitchen knife

菜豆(ㄘㄞˋ ㄉㄡˋ)
kidney beans; string beans

菜單兒(ㄘㄞˋ ㄉㄚㄦ)or 菜單子(ㄘㄞˋ ㄉㄢ ˙ㄗ)
a bill of fare; a menu: 請拿菜單兒給我看。Show me the menu, please.

菜墩子(ㄘㄞˋ ㄉㄨㄣ ˙ㄗ)
a chopping board

菜攤兒(ㄘㄞˋ ㄊㄚㄦ)or 菜攤子(ㄘㄞˋ ㄊㄢ ˙ㄗ)
a vegetable vendor's stall

菜牛(ㄘㄞˋ ㄋㄧㄡˊ)
beef cattle

菜農(ㄘㄞˋ ㄋㄨㄥˊ)
a vegetable grower

菜籃(ㄘㄞˋ ㄌㄢˊ)
a basket for carrying vegetables and other food items

菜根(ㄘㄞˋ ㄍㄣ)
the inedible root of a vegetable; cabbage stalks

菜瓜(ㄘㄞˋ ㄍㄨㄚ)
cucumber

菜館(ㄘㄞˋ ㄍㄨㄢˇ)
a restaurant 亦作「餐廳」：我們在菜館吃晚飯。We had dinner at a restaurant.

菜花(ㄘㄞˋ ㄏㄨㄚ)
①a cauliflower ②a rape flower

菜貨(ㄘㄞˋ ㄏㄨㄛˋ)
a person of little use

菜甲(ㄘㄞˋ ㄐㄧㄚˇ)
young leaves of a vegetable

菜畦(ㄘㄞˋ ㄑㄧˊ)
a vegetable garden

菜市場(ㄘㄞˋ ㄕˋ ㄔㄤˇ)
a grocery market; a vegetable market; a food market

菜蔬(ㄘㄞˋ ㄕㄨ)
vegetables 亦作「蔬菜」

菜籽 or 菜子(ㄘㄞˋ ㄗˇ)
① vegetable seeds ② rapeseed

菜籽油 or 菜子油(ㄘㄞˋ ㄗˇ ㄧㄡˊ)
rapeseed oil; rape oil; colza oil

菜色(ㄘㄞˋ ㄙㄜˋ)
pallor due to hunger; a famished or emaciated look
菜肴(ㄘㄞˋ ㄧㄠˊ)
food eaten with rice or alcoholic drinks
菜油(ㄘㄞˋ ㄧㄡˊ)
vegetable oil 亦作「植物油」
菜園(ㄘㄞˋ ㄩㄢˊ)
a vegetable garden

【菠】 4965
ㄅㄛ bo bō
spinach
菠薐菜(ㄅㄛ ㄌㄥˊ ㄘㄞˋ) or 菠菜(ㄅㄛ ㄘㄞˋ)
spinach
菠蘿(ㄅㄛ ㄌㄨㄛˊ)
a pineapple 亦作「鳳梨」
菠次坦宣言(ㄅㄛ ㄘˋ ㄊㄢˇ ㄒㄩㄢ ㄧㄢˊ)
the Potsdam Declaration in July, 1945, calling on Japan to surrender to the Allies unconditionally

【華】 4966
1. ㄏㄨㄚˊ hwa huá
1. Cathay; China
2. splendid; majestic; gorgeous; colorful; brilliant; bright; fine; beautiful; luxurious
3. prosperous; thriving
華北(ㄏㄨㄚˊ ㄅㄟˇ)
North China
華表(ㄏㄨㄚˊ ㄅㄧㄠˇ)
a monument formerly erected on the roadside as a guidepost
華美(ㄏㄨㄚˊ ㄇㄟˇ)
beautiful; splendid; luxurious 參看「華麗」
華美協進會(ㄏㄨㄚˊ ㄇㄟˇ ㄒㄧㄝˊ ㄐㄧㄣˋ ㄏㄨㄟˋ)
China Institute in the United States
華髮(ㄏㄨㄚˊ ㄈㄚˇ)
gray hair; white hair
華服(ㄏㄨㄚˊ ㄈㄨˊ)
fine clothes
華府(ㄏㄨㄚˊ ㄈㄨˇ)
Washington D.C.
華誕(ㄏㄨㄚˊ ㄉㄢˋ)
birthday (usually of an honored person)
華燈(ㄏㄨㄚˊ ㄉㄥ)
a colorful lantern
華燈初上(ㄏㄨㄚˊ ㄉㄥ ㄔㄨ ㄕㄤˋ)
(descriptive of urban scenes at dusk) Colorful lamps are beginning to light up.
華顛(ㄏㄨㄚˊ ㄉㄧㄢ)
gray hair; white hair
華甸(ㄏㄨㄚˊ ㄉㄧㄢˋ)
the capital (of a state)
華殿(ㄏㄨㄚˊ ㄉㄧㄢˋ)
a palace
華東(ㄏㄨㄚˊ ㄉㄨㄥ)
East China
華南(ㄏㄨㄚˊ ㄋㄢˊ)
South China
華年(ㄏㄨㄚˊ ㄋㄧㄢˊ)
youth
華麗(ㄏㄨㄚˊ ㄌㄧˋ)
magnificent; resplendent; gorgeous
華格納(ㄏㄨㄚˊ ㄍㄜˊ ㄋㄚˋ)
Wilhelm Richard Wagner, 1813-1883, German composer
華蓋(ㄏㄨㄚˊ ㄍㄞˋ)
a canopy over a carriage
華貴(ㄏㄨㄚˊ ㄍㄨㄟˋ)
luxurious; sumptuous; costly
華工(ㄏㄨㄚˊ ㄍㄨㄥ)
Chinese laborers abroad
華翰(ㄏㄨㄚˊ ㄏㄢˋ) or 華緘(ㄏㄨㄚˊ ㄐㄧㄢ) or 華札(ㄏㄨㄚˊ ㄓㄚˊ)
your esteemed letter
華界(ㄏㄨㄚˊ ㄐㄧㄝˋ)
the Chinese district (in Shanghai before World War II)
華僑(ㄏㄨㄚˊ ㄑㄧㄠˊ)
overseas Chinese
華僑節(ㄏㄨㄚˊ ㄑㄧㄠˊ ㄐㄧㄝˊ)
Overseas Chinese Day (falling on December 21)
華僑學校(ㄏㄨㄚˊ ㄑㄧㄠˊ ㄒㄩㄝˊ ㄒㄧㄠˋ)
a Chinese school abroad
華清宮(ㄏㄨㄚˊ ㄑㄧㄥ ㄍㄨㄥ)
name of a palace with a mineral spring in the Tang Dynasty (in today's Shensi)
華清池(ㄏㄨㄚˊ ㄑㄧㄥ ㄔˊ)
Hua Ching Pool, name of a mineral spring where 楊貴妃, a concubine of Emperor Hsüan (玄宗) of the Tang Dynasty, once bathed
華夏(ㄏㄨㄚˊ ㄒㄧㄚˋ)
Cathay
華軒(ㄏㄨㄚˊ ㄒㄩㄢ)
① the magnificent carriage of a high official ② (figuratively) worldly splendors
華胄(ㄏㄨㄚˊ ㄓㄡˋ)
① descendants of a nobleman ② Chinese people; people of Chinese ancestry
華燭(ㄏㄨㄚˊ ㄓㄨˊ)
painted candles—the symbol of a wedding
華中(ㄏㄨㄚˊ ㄓㄨㄥ)
Central China
華飾(ㄏㄨㄚˊ ㄕˋ)
beautiful decorations
華氏寒暑表(ㄏㄨㄚˊ ㄕˋ ㄏㄢˊ ㄕㄨˇ ㄅㄧㄠˇ) or 華氏溫度計(ㄏㄨㄚˊ ㄕˋ ㄨㄣ ㄉㄨˋ ㄐㄧˋ)
a Fahrenheit thermometer
華沙(ㄏㄨㄚˊ ㄕㄚ)
Warsaw
華首(ㄏㄨㄚˊ ㄕㄡˇ)
① gray hair; white hair ② a beauty's hair
華商(ㄏㄨㄚˊ ㄕㄤ)
businessmen of Chinese ancestry
華盛頓(ㄏㄨㄚˊ ㄕㄥˋ ㄉㄨㄣˋ)
① George Washington, 1732-1799, founder of the U.S.A. ② Washington D.C., capital of the U.S.A. ③ the state of Washington, U.S.A.
華人(ㄏㄨㄚˊ ㄖㄣˊ)
Chinese people (especially those living abroad)
華滋華斯(ㄏㄨㄚˊ ㄗ ㄏㄨㄚˊ ㄙ)
William Wordsworth, 1770-1850, English poet
華簪(ㄏㄨㄚˊ ·ㄗㄢ)
high officials
華族(ㄏㄨㄚˊ ㄗㄨˊ)
① the peerage; the aristocracy; the nobility ② Chinese people
華宗(ㄏㄨㄚˊ ㄗㄨㄥ)
of one's own clan
華辭(ㄏㄨㄚˊ ㄘˊ)
impressive but insincere words
華而不實(ㄏㄨㄚˊ ㄦˊ ㄅㄨˋ ㄕˊ)
(literally) to flower without bearing fruit—impressive merely in appearance
華爾街(ㄏㄨㄚˊ ㄦˇ ㄐㄧㄝ)
Wall Street, New York City
華爾姿舞 or 華爾茲舞(ㄏㄨㄚˊ ㄦˇ ㄗ ㄨˇ)
waltz
華裔(ㄏㄨㄚˊ ㄧˋ)
foreign citizens of Chinese

〔艸部〕

origin
華言(ㄏㄨㄚˊ ㄧㄢˊ)
impressive but insincere words
華嚴經(ㄏㄨㄚˊ ㄧㄢˊ ㄐㄧㄥ)
the Avatamsaka Sutra (a Buddhist scripture)
華洋雜處(ㄏㄨㄚˊ ㄧㄤˊ ㄗㄚˊ ㄔㄨˇ)
Chinese and foreigners live together.
華屋山丘(ㄏㄨㄚˊ ㄨ ㄕㄢ ㄑㄧㄡ)
(literally) A magnificent house has become a mound of earth.—(figuratively) vicissitudes; ups and downs
華文(ㄏㄨㄚˊ ㄨㄣˊ)
the Chinese language; Chinese 亦作「中文」
華文學校(ㄏㄨㄚˊ ㄨㄣˊ ㄒㄩㄝˊ ㄒㄧㄠˋ)
a Chinese school (usually run by foreigners for teaching Chinese to foreigners)
華腴(ㄏㄨㄚˊ ㄩˊ)
① food and clothing in abundance; a luxurious life ② the nobility; the peerage; the aristocracy
華語(ㄏㄨㄚˊ ㄩˇ)
the Chinese language; Chinese 亦作「中文」
華譽(ㄏㄨㄚˊ ㄩˋ)
insincere compliments; flattery

【華】 4966
2.(花) ㄏㄨㄚ hua huā
flowers

【華】 4966
3. ㄏㄨㄚˋ huah huà
1. luster; brilliancy; glory; splendor
2. a Chinese family name
華陀(ㄏㄨㄚˋ ㄊㄨㄛˊ)
Hua To, a legendary surgeon at the end of the Han Dynasty
華山(ㄏㄨㄚˋ ㄕㄢ)
Mountain Hua, a sacred mountain in Shensi Province
華陰(ㄏㄨㄚˋ ㄧㄣ)
name of a county in Shensi Province, north of Mountain Hua

【菇】 4967
ㄍㄨ gu gū
mushrooms; a fungus

【菰】 4968
ㄍㄨ gu gū
1. *Zizania latifolia*, an aquatic grass, the stalk of which is eaten as vegetable 亦作「茭白」
2. same as 菇—mushrooms

【菁】 4969
ㄐㄧㄥ jing jīng
1. the flower of the leek
2. the rape turnip
3. luxuriant; lush
菁華(ㄐㄧㄥ ㄏㄨㄚˊ)
essence 亦作「精華」
菁菁(ㄐㄧㄥ ㄐㄧㄥ)
a lush or rich growth (of vegetation); of luxuriant growth
菁莪(ㄐㄧㄥ ㄜˊ)
to educate promising talents

【菲】 4970
1. ㄈㄟˇ feei fěi
1. an edible vegetable—a kind of radish
2. thin; trifling; meager
3. frugal; sparing
菲薄(ㄈㄟˇ ㄅㄛˊ)
① to slight; to belittle; to underestimate: 你不可妄自菲薄。You should not underestimate yourself. ② thin; humble; poor ③ frugal; thrifty
菲敬(ㄈㄟˇ ㄐㄧㄥˋ)
(a polite expression) a trifling gift given as a token of my respect
菲酌(ㄈㄟˇ ㄓㄨㄛˊ)
(a polite expression) my poor feast
菲材(ㄈㄟˇ ㄘㄞˊ)
(a polite expression) my meager talent
菲儀(ㄈㄟˇ ㄧˊ)or 菲禮(ㄈㄟˇ ㄌㄧˇ)
(a polite expression) my meager gift

【菲】 4970
2. ㄈㄟ fei fēi
1. fragrant
2. the Philippines
3. luxuriant
菲菲(ㄈㄟ ㄈㄟ)
① fragrant ②(said of flowers) beautiful ③ mixed; confused ④ unstable
菲律賓(ㄈㄟ ㄌㄩˋ ㄅㄧㄣ)
the Philippines
菲律賓羣島(ㄈㄟ ㄌㄩˋ ㄅㄧㄣ ㄑㄩㄣˊ ㄉㄠˇ)
the Philippine Islands
菲律賓人(ㄈㄟ ㄌㄩˋ ㄅㄧㄣ ㄖㄣˊ)
Filipinos
菲律賓語(ㄈㄟ ㄌㄩˋ ㄅㄧㄣ ㄩˇ)
Tagalog
菲華(ㄈㄟ ㄏㄨㄚˊ)
overseas Chinese in the Philippines

【菸】 4971
ㄧㄢ ian yān
a tobacco leaf
菸酒(ㄧㄢ ㄐㄧㄡˇ)
tobacco and alcoholic drinks
菸酒稅(ㄧㄢ ㄐㄧㄡˇ ㄕㄨㄟˋ)
duties or taxes on tobacco and alcoholic drinks
菸鹼(ㄧㄢ ㄐㄧㄢˇ)
nicotine 亦作「尼古丁」
菸草(ㄧㄢ ㄘㄠˇ)or 菸絲(ㄧㄢ ㄙ)
tobacco
菸邑(ㄧㄢ ㄧˋ)
to wither
菸葉(ㄧㄢ ㄧㄝˋ)
tobacco leaves

【菹】 4972
ㄐㄩ jiu jū
1. salted or pickled vegetables
2. a pond or lake with a lot of weeds; grassy marshes
3. to mince human flesh and bones (a form of capital punishment in ancient times)
菹醢(ㄐㄩ ㄏㄞˇ)
to kill a person and mince his flesh and bones (a form of capital punishment in ancient times)

【菽】 4973
ㄕㄨˊ shwu shú
the general term for beans, peas, etc.
菽麥(ㄕㄨˊ ㄇㄞˋ)
(literally) beans and wheat —easily distinguishable; distinctly different
菽水承歡(ㄕㄨˊ ㄕㄨㄟˇ ㄔㄥˊ ㄏㄨㄢ)
to practice great filial piety even in poverty
菽粟(ㄕㄨˊ ㄙㄨˋ)
beans and grains; pulse and grain

【萁】 4974
ㄑㄧˊ chyi qí
the stalks of beans

【萃】 4975
ㄘㄨㄟˋ tsuey cuì
1. a thick or dense growth of grass
2. a group; a set
3. to gather; to meet; to con-

gregate
萃取(ㄘㄨㄟˋ ㄑㄩˇ)
(chemistry) extraction

【萄】 4976 ㄊㄠˊ taur táo
as in 葡萄—grapes

【萇】 4977 ㄔㄤˊ charng cháng
the fruit of *Averrhoa carambola*
萇楚(ㄔㄤˊ ㄔㄨˇ)
Averrhoa carambola

【菿】 4978 ㄉㄠˋ daw dào
tall grass

【萊】 4979 ㄌㄞˊ lai lái
1. fields lying fallow
2. wild weeds
3. to weed
4. a Chinese family name

萊菔(ㄌㄞˊ ㄈㄨˊ)
turnips 亦作「蘿蔔」
萊因河(ㄌㄞˊ ㄧㄣ ㄏㄜˊ)
the Rhine River
萊蕪(ㄌㄞˊ ㄨˊ)
① a field with a dense growth of wild weeds ② name of a county in Shantung Province

【萋】 4980 ㄑㄧ chi qi
1. luxuriant foliage; a dense growth of grass
2. many; crowded

萋萋(ㄑㄧ ㄑㄧ)
① a luxuriant growth of grass ② massing of clouds

【萌】 4981 ㄇㄥˊ meng méng
1. to bud; to sprout; to germinate; to shoot forth
2. to harbor (a thought)
3. the beginning; initiation; initial

萌動(ㄇㄥˊ ㄉㄨㄥˋ)
① to sprout; to bud ② to begin or start an action; to initiate
萌黎(ㄇㄥˊ ㄌㄧˊ)or 萌隸(ㄇㄥˊ ㄌㄧˋ)
the people; the masses
萌兆(ㄇㄥˊ ㄓㄠˋ)
an omen; a warning of a coming event 亦作「預兆」
萌茁(ㄇㄥˊ ㄓㄨㄛˊ)
to sprout; to bud
萌生(ㄇㄥˊ ㄕㄥ)
① to produce; to conceive (a view, idea, etc.) ② numerous
萌芽 or 萌牙(ㄇㄥˊ ㄧㄚˊ)
① the initial stage of something ② to sprout; to be in bud: 雨水使種子萌芽。Rain sprouts the seed.

【萍】 4982 ㄆㄧㄥˊ pyng píng
1. duckweed
2. moving about rootlessly; traveling or wandering

萍泊(ㄆㄧㄥˊ ㄅㄛˊ)
to wander about rootlessly like duckweed
萍蓬(草)(ㄆㄧㄥˊ ㄆㄥˊ (ㄘㄠˇ))
(botany) *Nuphar japonicum*, related with the lotus
萍浮(ㄆㄧㄥˊ ㄈㄨˊ)
to wander about like duckweed
萍梗(ㄆㄧㄥˊ ㄍㄥˇ)
to have no permanent address because of constant traveling
萍跡(ㄆㄧㄥˊ ㄐㄧ)
the whereabouts of a constant traveler
萍寄(ㄆㄧㄥˊ ㄐㄧˋ)
to stay in a place only briefly like someone constantly traveling
萍鄉(ㄆㄧㄥˊ ㄒㄧㄤ)
Pinghsiang, a county rich in coal in Kiangsi Province
萍水相逢(ㄆㄧㄥˊ ㄕㄨㄟˇ ㄒㄧㄤ ㄈㄥˊ)
to meet by accident
萍蹤(ㄆㄧㄥˊ ㄗㄨㄥ)
the whereabouts of a constant traveler
萍蹤無定(ㄆㄧㄥˊ ㄗㄨㄥ ㄨˊ ㄉㄧㄥˋ)or 萍蹤浪跡(ㄆㄧㄥˊ ㄗㄨㄥ ㄌㄤˋ ㄐㄧ)
to have no fixed abode because of constant traveling

【萎】 4983 ㄨㄟ uei wei
1. to wither
2. ill; sick
3. to fall; to decline; to weaken

萎靡(ㄨㄟ ㄇㄧˇ)
listless; dispirited
萎靡不振(ㄨㄟ ㄇㄧˇ ㄅㄨˋ ㄓㄣˋ)
unable to pick oneself up; despondent; lethargic
萎落(ㄨㄟ ㄌㄨㄛˋ)
to wither and fall; to weaken and decline
萎黃病(ㄨㄟ ㄏㄨㄤˊ ㄅㄧㄥˋ)
chlorosis
萎絕(ㄨㄟ ㄐㄩㄝˊ)
to wither
萎謝(ㄨㄟ ㄒㄧㄝˋ)
(said of flowers) to wither; to fade
萎縮(ㄨㄟ ㄙㄨㄛ)
① to dry up and shrink; to shrink back ② to atrophy
萎縮症(ㄨㄟ ㄙㄨㄛ ㄓㄥˋ)
atrophy

【菡】 4984 ㄏㄢˋ hann hàn
another name of water lily or lotus flower
菡萏(ㄏㄢˋ ㄉㄢˋ)
a water lily, or a lotus flower

【萏】 4985 ㄉㄢˋ dann dàn
as in 菡萏—another name of water lily

【菩】 4986 ㄆㄨˊ pwu pú
1. a fragrant herb
2. the sacred tree of the Buddhists

菩提(ㄆㄨˊ ㄊㄧˊ)
bodhi—knowledge ; understanding; perfect wisdom; the illuminated or enlightened mind
菩提樹(ㄆㄨˊ ㄊㄧˊ ㄕㄨˋ)
① a peepul tree ② (Buddhism) a bo tree; *Ficus religiosa*; a bodhi tree— the wisdom tree under which Sakyamuni attained his enlightenment and became Buddha
菩薩(ㄆㄨˊ ˙ㄙㄚ)
① Bodhisattva ② Buddha
菩薩低語(ㄆㄨˊ ㄙㄚˇ ㄉㄧ ㄩˇ)
kind, gentle or soothing words
菩薩心腸(ㄆㄨˊ ㄙㄚˇ ㄒㄧㄣ ㄔㄤˊ)
kind-hearted; compassionate

【菱】 4987 ㄌㄧㄥˊ ling líng
a water chestnut
菱錳礦(ㄌㄧㄥˊ ㄇㄥˇ ㄎㄨㄤˋ)
rhodochrosite
菱面體(ㄌㄧㄥˊ ㄇㄧㄢˋ ㄊㄧˇ)
a rhombohedron
菱鐵礦(ㄌㄧㄥˊ ㄊㄧㄝˇ ㄎㄨㄤˋ)
siderite

菱歌(ㄌㄧㄥˊ ㄍㄜ)
songs of the water-caltrop pickers

菱苦土礦(ㄌㄧㄥˊ ㄎㄨˇ ㄊㄨˇ ㄎㄨㄤˋ)
magnesite

菱角(ㄌㄧㄥˊ ㄐㄧㄠˇ)
a water chestnut

菱鋅礦(ㄌㄧㄥˊ ㄒㄧㄣ ㄎㄨㄤˋ)
smithsonite

菱形(ㄌㄧㄥˊ ㄒㄧㄥˊ)
a rhomb or rhombus; rhombic

【菴】 4988 1.(庵) ㄢ an ān

1. a small round hut
2. a small Buddhist nunnery or monastery; a temple

菴婪(ㄢ ㄌㄢˊ)
greedy; avaricious

菴廬(ㄢ ㄌㄨˊ)
a hut

【菴】 4988 2. ㄢˋ ann àn

luxuriant; prosperous

菴藹(ㄢˋ ㄞˋ)
luxuriant

【萆】 4989 ㄅㄧˋ bih bì

a herb with long hard roots

【菉】 4990 ㄌㄩˋ liuh lù (又讀 ㄌㄨˋ luh lù)

1. a kind of grass
2. green

菉竹(ㄌㄨˋ ㄓㄨˊ)
the green bamboo 亦作「綠竹」

菉筍(ㄌㄨˋ ㄙㄨㄣˇ)
greenish bamboo shoots

菉豆(ㄌㄨˋ ㄉㄡˋ)
the green beans; lentils 亦作「綠豆」

【菢】 4991 ㄅㄠˋ baw bào

to hatch (eggs); to incubate

菢蛋(ㄅㄠˋ ㄉㄢˋ)
to hatch eggs

菢小鷄(ㄅㄠˋ ㄒㄧㄠˇ ㄐㄧ)
(said of a hen) to hatch eggs

菢窩(ㄅㄠˋ ㄨㄛ)
to sit on the nest to hatch eggs

【菏】 4992 ㄍㄜ ge gē

name of a tributary of the Chi River in ancient times

菏澤(ㄍㄜ ㄗㄜˊ)
① name of a county in Shantung Province ② name of a lake in Shantung Province

【菫】 4993 ㄐㄧㄣˇ jiin jǐn

Viola verecunda, a violet

【荊】 4994 (荆) ㄐㄧㄥ jing jīng

1. a kind of bramble; a thorn
2. a cane for punishment used in ancient China
3. (a polite expression) my wife
4. (in ancient China) name of one of the nine political regions
5. a Chinese family name

荊布(ㄐㄧㄥ ㄅㄨˋ)
(said of women) simply adorned; in coarse clothing

荊璞(ㄐㄧㄥ ㄆㄨˊ)or 荊玉(ㄐㄧㄥ ㄩˋ)
unpolished precious jade

荊蠻(ㄐㄧㄥ ㄇㄢˊ)
① a collective name of four ancient counties in Hunan Province ② rough and primitive places

荊婦(ㄐㄧㄥ ㄈㄨˋ)or 荊人(ㄐㄧㄥ ㄖㄣˊ)
my wife (a polite expression)

荊桃(ㄐㄧㄥ ㄊㄠˊ)
a cherry

荊條(ㄐㄧㄥ ㄊㄧㄠˊ)
stems of a bramble which can be made into baskets, etc.

荊軻(ㄐㄧㄥ ㄎㄜ)
Ching Ko, a brave man of the State of Wei (衛) in the Epoch of Warring States, who was asked by the prince of Yen(燕) to assassinate the king of Chin (秦) but failed

荊棘(ㄐㄧㄥ ㄐㄧˊ)
① thorns; thorny ② a difficult situation

荊卿(ㄐㄧㄥ ㄑㄧㄥ)
another way of calling Ching Ko (荊軻)

荊州(ㄐㄧㄥ ㄓㄡ)
① Kingchow(name of one of the nine political regions in ancient China, including Hunan, Hupeh and part of today's Szechwan) ② an ancient name of Hupeh Province

荊釵布裙(ㄐㄧㄥ ㄔㄞ ㄅㄨˋ ㄑㄩㄣˊ)
thorns as hairpins and cotton cloth for skirts—a poor woman's wear

荊柴(ㄐㄧㄥ ㄔㄞˊ)
a poor family; a destitute household

荊楚(ㄐㄧㄥ ㄔㄨˇ)
the state of Chu which occupied Kingchow(荊州) in ancient China

荊室(ㄐㄧㄥ ㄕˋ)
(a polite expression) my wife

【菓】 4995 ㄍㄨㄛˇ guoo guǒ

fruits and nuts

九畫

【萬】 4996 (万) ㄨㄢˋ wann wàn

1. ten thousand
2. all; omni-
3. a very great number; myriad
4. very; extremely; absolutely
5. name of an ancient dance
6. a Chinese family name

萬把(ㄨㄢˋ ㄅㄚˇ)
a little more than 10,000

萬倍(ㄨㄢˋ ㄅㄟˋ)
ten thousandfold

萬般(ㄨㄢˋ ㄅㄢ)
① all; every; various; in many different ways ② extremely

萬般皆下品，惟有讀書高(ㄨㄢˋ ㄅㄢ ㄐㄧㄝ ㄒㄧㄚˋ ㄆㄧㄣˇ, ㄨㄟˊ ㄧㄡˇ ㄉㄨˊ ㄕㄨ ㄍㄠ)
(a Chinese saying) Learning is the noblest of human pursuits.

萬邦(ㄨㄢˋ ㄅㄤ)
all nations; nations all over the world; the myriad states

萬變不離其宗(ㄨㄢˋ ㄅㄧㄢˋ ㄅㄨˋ ㄌㄧˊ ㄑㄧˊ ㄗㄨㄥ)
The methods used may vary, but the principle is the same. 或 to undergo numerous changes without abandoning the basic position

萬不得已(ㄨㄢˋ ㄅㄨˋ ㄉㄜˊ ㄧˇ)
① if the worst comes to happen; as a last resort ② to

have no alternative; to have to do it; to be forced to do it; very reluctantly

萬馬奔騰(ㄨㄢˋ ㄇㄚˇ ㄅㄣ ㄊㄥˊ)
①(literally) ten thousand horses stampeding—a thunderous or roaring sound ②(figuratively) whirling wildly

萬民(ㄨㄢˋ ㄇㄧㄣˊ)
all the people

萬目睽睽(ㄨㄢˋ ㄇㄨˋ ㄎㄨㄟˊ ㄎㄨㄟˊ)
right before 10,000 eyes—under the glare of the public

萬分(ㄨㄢˋ ㄈㄣ)
very; extremely

萬方(ㄨㄢˋ ㄈㄤ)
①all nations; the myriad regions ②all sides ③(said of manners) graceful ④all and every way

萬方多難(ㄨㄢˋ ㄈㄤ ㄉㄨㄛ ㄋㄢˋ)
natural disasters and man-made calamities everywhere

萬夫不當(ㄨㄢˋ ㄈㄨ ㄅㄨˋ ㄉㄤ)
(literally) Even 10,000 men are not his match.—very brave

萬福(ㄨㄢˋ ㄈㄨˊ)
①boundless blessings; all blessings ②(said of women) a gesture to show politeness equivalent to a curtsy in the Western world

萬代(ㄨㄢˋ ㄉㄞˋ)
endless generations afterward; eternity

萬端(ㄨㄢˋ ㄉㄨㄢ)
very complicated; numerous leads (not knowing which one to follow)

萬難(ㄨㄢˋ ㄋㄢˊ)
extremely difficult; well-nigh impossible

萬能(ㄨㄢˋ ㄋㄥˊ)
omnipotent; almighty

萬能博士(ㄨㄢˋ ㄋㄥˊ ㄅㄛˊ ㄕˋ)
a jack-of-all-trades; a Mr. Know-all

萬年(ㄨㄢˋ ㄋㄧㄢˊ)
10,000 years—a very long time

萬年曆(ㄨㄢˋ ㄋㄧㄢˊ ㄌㄧˋ)
①a calendar system adopted briefly during the Yüan Dynasty ②a calendar designed for use in many years

萬年青(ㄨㄢˋ ㄋㄧㄢˊ ㄑㄧㄥ)
a Chinese evergreen

萬年枝(ㄨㄢˋ ㄋㄧㄢˊ ㄓ)
an ilex 亦作「冬青」

萬念俱灰(ㄨㄢˋ ㄋㄧㄢˋ ㄐㄩˋ ㄏㄨㄟ)
completely discouraged; extremely pessimistic; totally devoid of ambition and hope

萬籟俱寂(ㄨㄢˋ ㄌㄞˋ ㄐㄩˋ ㄐㄧˊ)
All is still. 或 All sounds are hushed (in the dead of the night).

萬里鵬程(ㄨㄢˋ ㄌㄧˇ ㄆㄥˊ ㄔㄥˊ)
(a congratulatory term) very promising; an unlimited future

萬里侯(ㄨㄢˋ ㄌㄧˇ ㄏㄡˊ)
a marquis with an extensive fief bestowed by the emperor in recognition of extremely meritorious services

萬里長征(ㄨㄢˋ ㄌㄧˇ ㄔㄤˊ ㄓㄥ)
①to launch a military expedition very far away; to embark on a long journey; mile after mile to battle ②(in Chinese Communist terminology) the Long March to Yenan after they were routed by government troops in the early 1930's

萬里長城(ㄨㄢˋ ㄌㄧˇ ㄔㄤˊ ㄔㄥˊ)
the Great Wall (of China)

萬里無雲(ㄨㄢˋ ㄌㄧˇ ㄨˊ ㄩㄣˊ)
cloudless

萬流赴壑(ㄨㄢˋ ㄌㄧㄡˊ ㄈㄨˋ ㄏㄨㄛˋ)
countless things converging on the same spot

萬靈藥(ㄨㄢˋ ㄌㄧㄥˊ ㄧㄠˋ) or 萬應藥(ㄨㄢˋ ㄧㄥˋ ㄧㄠˋ)
a panacea; a cure-all; a wonder drug: 這並不是萬靈藥。This is not a cure-all.

萬隆(ㄨㄢˋ ㄌㄨㄥˊ)
Bandung, Indonesia

萬綠叢中一點紅(ㄨㄢˋ ㄌㄩˋ ㄘㄨㄥˊ ㄓㄨㄥ ㄧˋ ㄉㄧㄢˇ ㄏㄨㄥˊ)
(literally) a single red flower in the midst of thick foliage—very outstanding or eye-catching

萬古(ㄨㄢˋ ㄍㄨˇ)
for a long, long time; immortal

萬古流芳(ㄨㄢˋ ㄍㄨˇ ㄌㄧㄡˊ ㄈㄤ)
a good name that will last forever (now often used in eulogizing a dead person at the funeral)

萬古流傳(ㄨㄢˋ ㄍㄨˇ ㄌㄧㄡˊ ㄔㄨㄢˊ)
(said of a legend, achievement, etc.) to be remembered forever

萬古長青(ㄨㄢˋ ㄍㄨˇ ㄔㄤˊ ㄑㄧㄥ)
to remain fresh forever; to be everlasting

萬國(ㄨㄢˋ ㄍㄨㄛˊ)
all nations; countless states; all over the world; international

萬國公法(ㄨㄢˋ ㄍㄨㄛˊ ㄍㄨㄥ ㄈㄚˇ)
international law

萬國音標(ㄨㄢˋ ㄍㄨㄛˊ ㄧㄣ ㄅㄧㄠ)
International Phonetic Alphabet (IPA) 亦作「國際音標」

萬國語(ㄨㄢˋ ㄍㄨㄛˊ ㄩˇ)
a lingua franca

萬國語音協會(ㄨㄢˋ ㄍㄨㄛˊ ㄩˇ ㄧㄣ ㄒㄧㄝˊ ㄏㄨㄟˋ)
International Phonetic Association, founded in 1886 亦作「國際語音協會」

萬貫(ㄨㄢˋ ㄍㄨㄢˋ)
very rich or wealthy: 他家財萬貫。He is very rich.

萬貫家私(ㄨㄢˋ ㄍㄨㄢˋ ㄐㄧㄚ ㄙ)
very wealthy; very rich

萬斛源泉(ㄨㄢˋ ㄏㄨˊ ㄩㄢˊ ㄑㄩㄢˊ)
full of inspirations in writing

萬戶侯(ㄨㄢˋ ㄏㄨˋ ㄏㄡˊ)
(Han Dynasty) a marquis with a fief of 10,000 families

萬花筒(ㄨㄢˋ ㄏㄨㄚ ㄊㄨㄥˇ)
a kaleidoscope: 人生猶如萬花筒。Life is like a kaleidoscope.

萬花爭豔(ㄨㄢˋ ㄏㄨㄚ ㄓㄥ ㄧㄢˋ)
all kinds of flowers in full bloom

萬化(ㄨㄢˋ ㄏㄨㄚˋ)
①all matters; all things ②too many variations or changes to recount

萬機 or 萬幾(ㄨㄢˋ ㄐㄧ)
(said of an emperor or president) 10,000 matters to be managed (in a single day)—a heavy work load

萬急(ㄨㄢˋ ㄐㄧˊ)
extremely or most urgent

萬家燈火(ㄨㄢˋ ㄐㄧㄚ ㄉㄥ ㄏㄨㄛˇ)

lights in 10,000 households—a night scene of a town or city

萬家生佛(ㄨㄢˋ ㄐㄧㄚ ㄕㄥ ㄈㄛˊ)
(literally) a living Buddha to 10,000 families—a benefactor to all

萬劫(ㄨㄢˋ ㄐㄧㄝˊ)
countless generations or ages

萬劫不復(ㄨㄢˋ ㄐㄧㄝˊ ㄅㄨˋ ㄈㄨˋ)
never to be recovered or restored

萬金油(ㄨㄢˋ ㄐㄧㄣ ㄧㄡˊ)
the Tiger Balm, a very popular Chinese ointment (with soothing effect derived mainly from its menthol or peppermint contents)

萬卷(ㄨㄢˋ ㄐㄩㄢˋ)
10,000 volumes; a countless number of books; mountains of printed matter

萬鈞(ㄨㄢˋ ㄐㄩㄣ)
300,000 catties—very heavy; very powerful; overwhelming

萬鈞之力(ㄨㄢˋ ㄐㄩㄣ ㄓ ㄌㄧˋ)
extremely powerful; great strength; overwhelming force

萬千(ㄨㄢˋ ㄑㄧㄢ)
numerous; myriads: 星辰萬千。There are myriads of stars.

萬籤插架(ㄨㄢˋ ㄑㄧㄢ ㄔㄚ ㄐㄧㄚˋ)
overflowing (book) shelves—a countless number of books

萬頃(ㄨㄢˋ ㄑㄧㄥˇ)
10,000 hectares (of land); large landholding; a vast space

萬頃碧波(ㄨㄢˋ ㄑㄧㄥˇ ㄅㄧˋ ㄅㄛ)
a vast expanse of water—as a big lake

萬全(ㄨㄢˋ ㄑㄩㄢˊ)
extremely safe or sound; failure-proof

萬全之計(ㄨㄢˋ ㄑㄩㄢˊ ㄓ ㄐㄧˋ)
an absolutely safe measure, plan, device, etc.

萬象(ㄨㄢˋ ㄒㄧㄤˋ)
the countless aspects, forms, etc. of the world and natural phenomena

萬象更新(ㄨㄢˋ ㄒㄧㄤˋ ㄍㄥ ㄒㄧㄣ)
a new year—as all things change from old to new

萬姓(ㄨㄢˋ ㄒㄧㄥˋ)
the people

萬幸(ㄨㄢˋ ㄒㄧㄥˋ)
extremely lucky; very fortunate indeed

萬丈深淵(ㄨㄢˋ ㄓㄤˋ ㄕㄣ ㄩㄢ)
an abyss of 100,000 feet—a bottomless abyss

萬狀(ㄨㄢˋ ㄓㄨㄤˋ)
① all possible shapes and forms; myriad forms ② extremely (frightened)

萬鍾(ㄨㄢˋ ㄓㄨㄥ)
rich reward or high salary for a government official

萬衆一心(ㄨㄢˋ ㄓㄨㄥˋ ㄧˋ ㄒㄧㄣ)
all for one and one for all; with one aspiration in their hearts; solidarity

萬世之後(ㄨㄢˋ ㄕˋ ㄓ ㄏㄡˋ)
down to endless posterity; after countless generations

萬世師表(ㄨㄢˋ ㄕˋ ㄕ ㄅㄧㄠˇ)
(literally) a paragon for all generations—Confucius

萬事通(ㄨㄢˋ ㄕˋ ㄊㄨㄥ)
a jack-of-all-trades

萬事休(ㄨㄢˋ ㄕˋ ㄒㄧㄡ)
All is lost.

萬事足(ㄨㄢˋ ㄕˋ ㄗㄨˊ)
well satisfied (usually referring to a man with a new born heir)

萬壽(ㄨㄢˋ ㄕㄡˋ)
①(in ancient China) the birthday of the emperor ② (modern usage) a congratulatory term wishing a person on his birthday many, many happy returns

萬壽山(ㄨㄢˋ ㄕㄡˋ ㄕㄢ)
name of a hill in Peking's old imperial park Yi-ho Garden(頤和園)

萬壽無疆(ㄨㄢˋ ㄕㄡˋ ㄨˊ ㄐㄧㄤ)
May you attain boundless longevity!

萬牲園(ㄨㄢˋ ㄕㄥ ㄩㄢˊ)
a zoo; a zoological garden

萬聖節(ㄨㄢˋ ㄕㄥˋ ㄐㄧㄝˊ)
All Saints' Day

萬乘之國(ㄨㄢˋ ㄕㄥˋ ㄓ ㄍㄨㄛˊ)
an empire; a big country

萬乘之尊(ㄨㄢˋ ㄕㄥˋ ㄓ ㄗㄨㄣ)
the emperor—with ten thousand chariots at his command

萬殊(ㄨㄢˋ ㄕㄨ)
all different; myriads of variations

萬人敵(ㄨㄢˋ ㄖㄣˊ ㄉㄧˊ)
the art of war which a field commander must master

萬人坑(ㄨㄢˋ ㄖㄣˊ ㄎㄥ)
a mass grave

萬人空巷(ㄨㄢˋ ㄖㄣˊ ㄎㄨㄥ ㄒㄧㄤˋ)
Everyone (in a city) turns out (to watch a spectacle, to welcome a hero, etc.)

萬人塚(ㄨㄢˋ ㄖㄣˊ ㄓㄨㄥˇ)
a mass burial ground; a mass grave

萬仞(ㄨㄢˋ ㄖㄣˋ)
very high and steep (hills or mountains)

萬紫千紅(ㄨㄢˋ ㄗˇ ㄑㄧㄢ ㄏㄨㄥˊ)
(said of flowers) a vast display of dazzling colors

萬死一生(ㄨㄢˋ ㄙˇ ㄧˋ ㄕㄥ)
a very slim chance of keeping oneself alive; very risky; very lucky for escaping death

萬歲(ㄨㄢˋ ㄙㄨㄟˋ)
① the emperor; Your Majesty; His Majesty ②(a slogan) Long live the....

萬歲爺(ㄨㄢˋ ㄙㄨㄟˋ ㄧㄝˊ)
the emperor

萬惡(ㄨㄢˋ ㄜˋ)
all the evils; extremely evil

萬惡淫爲首(ㄨㄢˋ ㄜˋ ㄧㄣˊ ㄨㄟˊ ㄕㄡˇ)
Lewdness is the worst of all sins.

萬一(ㄨㄢˋ ㄧ)
① one ten thousandth—a very tiny fraction ② just in case that; if by any chance ③ something not anticipated or happening accidentally

萬有(ㄨㄢˋ ㄧㄡˇ)
all matters in the world; all things under the sun; all creation

萬有引力(ㄨㄢˋ ㄧㄡˇ ㄧㄣˇ ㄌㄧˋ)
gravitation

萬言書(ㄨㄢˋ ㄧㄢˊ ㄕㄨ)
a long report, statement of views, etc. prepared by a subject for the emperor's

perusal

萬無(ㄨㄢˋ ㄨˊ)
never; not the least; absolutely not

萬無一失(ㄨㄢˋ ㄨˊ ㄧˋ ㄕ)
not the least mishap or mistake; absolutely safe or sure; certain to succeed

萬物(ㄨㄢˋ ㄨˋ)
all things under the sun; all God's creation

萬物之靈(ㄨㄢˋ ㄨˋ ㄓ ㄌㄧㄥˊ)
man—the wisest of all creatures

萬萬(ㄨㄢˋ ㄨㄢˋ)
①a great many ②(used in the negative sense) extremely; absolutely ③100 million

萬萬不可(ㄨㄢˋ ㄨㄢˋ ㄅㄨˋ ㄎㄜˇ)
absolutely forbidden; not by any means; under no circumstances; in no event

萬萬歲(ㄨㄢˋ ㄨㄢˋ ㄙㄨㄟˋ)
Long live (the emperor).

萬愚節(ㄨㄢˋ ㄩˊ ㄐㄧㄝˊ)
All Fools' Day

【萱】 4997
ㄒㄩㄢ shiuan xuān
a daylily (*Hemerocallis fulva*) whose edible dried flowers are known as 金針菜

萱堂(ㄒㄩㄢ ㄊㄤˊ)
one's mother

萱草(ㄒㄩㄢ ㄘㄠˇ)
the daylily 亦作「忘憂草」

【萵】 4998
ㄨㄛ uo wō
a lettuce

萵苣(ㄨㄛ ㄐㄩˋ)
a lettuce

萵笋(ㄨㄛ ㄙㄨㄣˇ)
a lettuce

【萼】 4999
ㄜˋ eh è
the calyx

萼片(ㄜˋ ㄆㄧㄢˋ)
(botany) sepal

【落】 5000
1. ㄌㄨㄛˋ luoh luò
1. to fall; to decline; to wither; weakened; fallen
2. to lose
3. few and far-spaced; to stand apart; loose and scattered
4. a village; a hamlet
5. to put (pen to paper)
6. to settle down
7. a pile; a heap

落泊(ㄌㄨㄛˋ ㄅㄛˊ)or 落魄(ㄌㄨㄛˋ ㄊㄨㄛˋ)
jobless and listless; down in one's luck; out of luck

落榜(ㄌㄨㄛˋ ㄅㄤˇ)
to flunk a competitive examination for a job or school admission

落筆(ㄌㄨㄛˋ ㄅㄧˇ)
①to start writing ②a pen mark

落寞 or 落莫(ㄌㄨㄛˋ ㄇㄛˋ)
desolate and scattered; lonely; left alone

落脈(ㄌㄨㄛˋ ㄇㄛˋ)
(geomancy) the "lode" of a dragon descending from the heights

落墨(ㄌㄨㄛˋ ㄇㄛˋ)
to start writing or painting

落髮(ㄌㄨㄛˋ ㄈㄚˇ)
to shave off one's hair; to tonsure—to become a monk or nun

落得(ㄌㄨㄛˋ ㄉㄜˊ)
to result in; as a result; to end in: 僞君子必然要落得可恥的下場。Hypocrites come to no good end.

落膽(ㄌㄨㄛˋ ㄉㄢˇ)
to be frightened out of one's wits; very scared

落彈(ㄌㄨㄛˋ ㄉㄢˋ)
(said of bullets or artillery shells) to land at a place; to hit an area

落第(ㄌㄨㄛˋ ㄉㄧˋ)
to fail in a competitive examination for a job or school admission

落地(ㄌㄨㄛˋ ㄉㄧˋ)or(ㄌㄠˋ ㄉㄧˋ)
①to be born ②to fall to the ground

落地燈(ㄌㄨㄛˋ ㄉㄧˋ ㄉㄥ)
a floor lamp

落地電扇(ㄌㄨㄛˋ ㄉㄧˋ ㄉㄧㄢˋ ㄕㄢˋ)
an electric fan with an adjustable stand

落地窗(ㄌㄨㄛˋ ㄉㄧˋ ㄔㄨㄤ)
a French window

落地生根(ㄌㄨㄛˋ ㄉㄧˋ ㄕㄥ ㄍㄣ)
①(botany) an air plant; a life plant ②to have one's abode in a strange place

落點(ㄌㄨㄛˋ ㄉㄧㄢˇ)
①(in tennis, badminton, handball, etc.) placement ②(military) the point of a fall

落胎(ㄌㄨㄛˋ ㄊㄞ)
to abort; to effect an abortion

落湯螃蟹(ㄌㄨㄛˋ ㄊㄤ ㄆㄤˊ ㄒㄧㄝˋ)
at a loss as to what to do (like a crab in hot water)

落湯雞(ㄌㄨㄛˋ ㄊㄤ ㄐㄧ)
(said of a person) drenched and bedraggled; soaked in rainwater; dripping wet

落體(ㄌㄨㄛˋ ㄊㄧˇ)
a falling body

落拓(ㄌㄨㄛˋ ㄊㄨㄛˋ)or 落托(ㄌㄨㄛˋ ㄊㄨㄛ)
unrestrained and unhampered; uninhibited; not tostick to conventions; Bohemian

落難(ㄌㄨㄛˋ ㄋㄢˋ)
to encounter difficulty, disaster, calamity, etc.; to suffer a misfortune; to be out of luck

落淚(ㄌㄨㄛˋ ㄌㄟˋ)
to cry or weep; to shed tears

落落穆穆(ㄌㄨㄛˋ ㄌㄨㄛˋ ㄇㄨˋ ㄇㄨˋ)
a reserved person who does not show much outside; an introvert

落落大方(ㄌㄨㄛˋ ㄌㄨㄛˋ ㄉㄚˋ ㄈㄤ)
(said of manner) natural; unaffected; easy

落落寡合(ㄌㄨㄛˋ ㄌㄨㄛˋ ㄍㄨㄚˇ ㄏㄜˊ)
aloofness that keeps others at a distance; unsociable; standoffish

落款(ㄌㄨㄛˋ ㄎㄨㄢˇ)
a calligrapher's or painter's signature, seal, dedicatory notes, etc. on a painting, etc.

落空(ㄌㄨㄛˋ ㄎㄨㄥ)
to fail in an attempt; to come to nothing

落後(ㄌㄨㄛˋ ㄏㄡˋ)
to fall behind; to lag behind

落後地區(ㄌㄨㄛˋ ㄏㄡˋ ㄉㄧˋ ㄑㄩ)
underdeveloped areas

落戶(ㄌㄨㄛˋ ㄏㄨˋ)
to take up one's residence in a place away from one's hometown; to settle down

落花(ㄌㄨㄛˋ ㄏㄨㄚ)
falling flowers; fallen petals

落花流水(ㄌㄨㄛˋ ㄏㄨㄚ ㄌㄧㄡˊ ㄕㄨㄟˇ)

① like flowers scattered in a flowing stream—the saddening state of a fallen family or country ②(said of a fight) to turn everything topsy-turvy; to be utterly routed

落花生(ㄌㄨㄛˋ ㄏㄨㄚ ㄕㄥ)
a groundnut, or peanut

落花有意，流水無情(ㄌㄨㄛˋ ㄏㄨㄚ ㄧㄡˇ ㄧˋ, ㄌㄧㄡˊ ㄕㄨㄟˇ ㄨˊ ㄑㄧㄥˊ)
(said of a man and a woman) a one-sided love; only one party willing; an unrequited love

落暉(ㄌㄨㄛˋ ㄏㄨㄟ)
the setting sun

落荒(ㄌㄨㄛˋ ㄏㄨㄤ)
to escape in a hurry after defeat

落荒而逃(ㄌㄨㄛˋ ㄏㄨㄤ ㄦˊ ㄊㄠˊ)
to take to the wilds—to be defeated and run away the battlefield; to turn tail

落紅(ㄌㄨㄛˋ ㄏㄨㄥˊ)
(said of a virgin) to bleed during the first sexual intercourse

落籍(ㄌㄨㄛˋ ㄐㄧˊ)
① to be discharged from military service ②(said of a prostitute in old China) to get married

落脚(ㄌㄨㄛˋ ㄐㄧㄠˇ)
to stay at; to stop at; to put up at: 我們在旅館落脚。We put up at an inn.

落井下石 or 落穽下石(ㄌㄨㄛˋ ㄐㄧㄥˇ ㄒㄧㄚˋ ㄕˊ)
(literally) to drop stones on a person who has fallen into a well—to beat a person when he's already down; to injure a person already in great difficulty

落圈套(ㄌㄨㄛˋ ㄑㄩㄢ ㄊㄠˋ)
to be trapped or swindled

落霞(ㄌㄨㄛˋ ㄒㄧㄚˊ)
colorful clouds at sunset

落下(ㄌㄨㄛˋ ㄒㄧㄚˋ)
to fall down; to descend; to drop

落雪(ㄌㄨㄛˋ ㄒㄩㄝˇ)
snowing: 我們預料在天明之前會落雪。We expect snow before morning.

落選(ㄌㄨㄛˋ ㄒㄩㄢˇ)
unable to make the list; to fail in an election

落照(ㄌㄨㄛˋ ㄓㄠˋ)
the setting sun; sunset

落差(ㄌㄨㄛˋ ㄔㄚ)
the drop in elevation (usually referring to the difference in elevation between two points along a stream, etc.)

落潮(ㄌㄨㄛˋ ㄔㄠˊ)
the ebb tide; a low tide

落塵(ㄌㄨㄛˋ ㄔㄣˊ)
① falling dust ② fallout

落成(ㄌㄨㄛˋ ㄔㄥˊ)
completion (of a new building, etc.)

落成典禮(ㄌㄨㄛˋ ㄔㄥˊ ㄉㄧㄢˇ ㄌㄧˇ)
the dedication ceremony of a new building or construction project

落實(ㄌㄨㄛˋ ㄕˊ)
① practicable; workable ② to fix (or to decide) in advance; to make sure ③ to carry out; to fulfill; to translate into reality; to implement; to put into effect ④ (dialect) to feel at ease: 我心裡總是不落實。I just can not set my mind at ease.

落水(ㄌㄨㄛˋ ㄕㄨㄟˇ)
to fall into water; to duck;to fall overboard

落水狗(ㄌㄨㄛˋ ㄕㄨㄟˇ ㄍㄡˇ)
a dog in the water—(figuratively) a person who is down

落日(ㄌㄨㄛˋ ㄖˋ)
the setting sun

落日餘暉(ㄌㄨㄛˋ ㄖˋ ㄩˊ ㄏㄨㄟ)
the last light of the day; the lingering light of the setting sun

落子(ㄌㄨㄛˋ ㄗˇ)
(in go game) to place a stone on the chessboard; to make a move

落草(ㄌㄨㄛˋ ㄘㄠˇ)
to become a bandit

落索(ㄌㄨㄛˋ ㄙㄨㄛˇ)
desolate and lonely; spiritless and discouraged

落葉(ㄌㄨㄛˋ ㄧㄝˋ)
fallen leaves

落葉樹(ㄌㄨㄛˋ ㄧㄝˋ ㄕㄨˋ)
a deciduous tree; trees that change foliage every year

落葉松(ㄌㄨㄛˋ ㄧㄝˋ ㄙㄨㄥ)
Larix leptolepis, a variety of deciduous pine tree with very tough timber good for building purposes

落雁(ㄌㄨㄛˋ ㄧㄢˋ)
a kind of medicinal plant

落英繽紛(ㄌㄨㄛˋ ㄧㄥ ㄅㄧㄣ ㄈㄣ)
fallen flowers scattering and flying around like snow flakes

落伍(ㄌㄨㄛˋ ㄨˇ)
backward; overconservative; anachronistic; to be behind the times; outmoded; to outdate; outdated

落伍思想(ㄌㄨㄛˋ ㄨˇ ㄙ ㄒㄧㄤˇ)
backward or anachronistic thinking or ideas

落網(ㄌㄨㄛˋ ㄨㄤˇ)
(said of a criminal) to be caught in the meshes of the law—to be caught; to be captured

落雨(ㄌㄨㄛˋ ㄩˇ)
to rain; raining: 此地六月間常落雨。It often rains here in June.

落雨天(ㄌㄨㄛˋ ㄩˇ ㄊㄧㄢ)
a rainy day: 落雨天，路很滑。In a rainy day, the road is slippery.

落月(ㄌㄨㄛˋ ㄩㄝˋ)
the setting moon

【落】 5000
2. ㄌㄠˋ law lào

1. to fall or drop (in prices, etc.)
2. (said of a bird, etc.) to land; to perch
3. to get
4. a net income; a surplus
5. to place

落價(ㄌㄠˋ ㄐㄧㄚˋ)
to come down in prices: 電視機落價了。The price of television sets has come down.

落棧(ㄌㄠˋ ㄓㄢˋ)
to take up one's lodgings in an inn or a tavern

落枕(ㄌㄠˋ ㄓㄣˇ)
① to drop the head on the pillow—to go to sleep ② (Chinese medicine) stiff neck

落子(ㄌㄠˋ ·ㄗ)
① a way to make a living; a

means of living ②a kind of singing in parts of North China 亦作「蓮花落」

【落】5000 3. ㄌㄚˋ lah là

1. to leave behind
2. to fall behind
3. to miss; to omit

落了(ㄌㄚˋ ˙ㄌㄜ)
to lose, to miss, or omit unintentionally: 這裡落了一段字。A paragraph is missing here.

落下(ㄌㄚˋ ˙ㄒㄧㄚ)
① to leave behind ② to fall behind

【葉】5001 1. ㄧㄝˋ yeh yè

1. a leaf; a petal (of a flower)
2. a leaf or two pages (of a book)
3. a period; an era or epoch
4. something light and tiny —as a small boat in a lake
5. a Chinese family name

葉柄(ㄧㄝˋ ㄅㄧㄥˇ)
(botany) the petiole; the leafstalk

葉片(ㄧㄝˋ ㄆㄧㄢˋ)
(botany) the leaf blade 亦作「葉身」

葉脈(ㄧㄝˋ ㄇㄞˋ) or 葉筋(ㄧㄝˋ ㄐㄧㄣ)
the veins (of a leaf)

葉茂(ㄧㄝˋ ㄇㄠˋ)
leafy

葉門(ㄧㄝˋ ㄇㄣˊ)
Yemen

葉落歸根(ㄧㄝˋ ㄌㄨㄛˋ ㄍㄨㄟ ㄍㄣ)
(literally) The leaves always fall toward the root. —When a person gets old, he thinks of going back home.

葉落知秋(ㄧㄝˋ ㄌㄨㄛˋ ㄓ ㄑㄧㄡ)
(literally) The falling leaves annouce the approach of autumn.—Revealing signs foretell things to come.

葉綠素(ㄧㄝˋ ㄌㄩˋ ㄙㄨˋ) or (ㄧㄝˋ ㄌㄨˋ ㄙㄨˋ)
(biochemistry) chlorophyll

葉黃素(ㄧㄝˋ ㄏㄨㄤˊ ㄙㄨˋ)
(biochemistry) xanthophyll

葉尖(ㄧㄝˋ ㄐㄧㄢ)
the apex (of a leaf)

葉鞘(ㄧㄝˋ ㄑㄧㄠˋ)
the sheath (of a leaf)

葉序(ㄧㄝˋ ㄒㄩˋ)
(botany) a cycle

葉針(ㄧㄝˋ ㄓㄣ)
(botany) leaf thorns

葉肉(ㄧㄝˋ ㄖㄡˋ)
(botany) mesophyll

葉子(ㄧㄝˋ ˙ㄗ) or 葉兒(ㄧㄜˋ ㄦ)
leaves: 他被葉子遮住。He was hidden by the leaves.

葉慈(ㄧㄝˋ ㄘˊ)
William Butler Yeats, 1865-1939, Irish poet and dramatist

葉芽(ㄧㄝˋ ㄧㄚˊ)
(botany) a leaf bud

葉緣(ㄧㄝˋ ㄩㄢˊ)
the margin (of a leaf)

【葉】5001 2. ㄕㄜˋ sheh shè

used in names of places

葉公好龍(ㄕㄜˋ ㄍㄨㄥ ㄏㄠˋ ㄌㄨㄥˊ)
One is not sure what he really likes (like 葉公 who was very fond of dragons in painting but was scared when a real dragon appeared). 或 One does not like what he pretends to like.

葉縣(ㄕㄜˋ ㄒㄧㄢˋ)
name of a county in Honan Province

【葑】5002 ㄈㄥ feng fēng

same as 蕪菁, the rape-turnip

葑菲(ㄈㄥ ㄈㄟˇ)
the mustard plant and earth melons — One has his good points as well as shortcomings. 或 Don't take part for all.

【著】5003 1. ㄓㄨˋ juh zhù

1. apparent; obvious; famous: 這是相當顯著的。It is quite obvious.
2. to write; to author
3. writings; a literary work; books
4. to set forth; to manifest; to make known

著名(ㄓㄨˋ ㄇㄧㄥˊ)
famous; renowned

著績(ㄓㄨˋ ㄐㄧ)
well-known achievements (especially administrative)

著稱(ㄓㄨˋ ㄔㄥ)
celebrated; famous

著書(ㄓㄨˋ ㄕㄨ)
to author or compile a book

著書立說(ㄓㄨˋ ㄕㄨ ㄌㄧˋ ㄕㄨㄛ)
to write books and establish one's theory

著述(ㄓㄨˋ ㄕㄨˋ)
① to write ② writings; a literary work

著作(ㄓㄨˋ ㄗㄨㄛˋ)
① to write ② writings; a literary work

著作等身(ㄓㄨˋ ㄗㄨㄛˋ ㄉㄥˇ ㄕㄣ)
(said of an author) with many works to his credit

著作郎(ㄓㄨˋ ㄗㄨㄛˋ ㄌㄤˊ)
(in old China) an official in charge of compiling and editing national history

著作權(ㄓㄨˋ ㄗㄨㄛˋ ㄑㄩㄢˊ)
copyright

著作者(ㄓㄨˋ ㄗㄨㄛˋ ㄓㄜˇ) or 著者(ㄓㄨˋ ㄓㄜˇ)
the writer or author

【著】5003 2.(着) ㄓㄨㄛˊ jwo zhuó

1. to wear (garments, etc.): 她著新衣。She is wearing a new dress.
2. a move (on the chessboard, in action, plans, etc.)
3. to apply (color, etc.); to start (an assignment, investigation, etc.)

著筆(ㄓㄨㄛˊ ㄅㄧˇ)
to put (or to set) pen to paper; to begin to write or paint

著地(ㄓㄨㄛˊ ㄉㄧˋ)
to reach the ground; to touch the ground

著力(ㄓㄨㄛˊ ㄌㄧˋ)
to apply force; to exert

著陸(ㄓㄨㄛˊ ㄌㄨˋ)
(said of an airplane) to land; to alight; to descend to the ground

著落(ㄓㄨㄛˊ ˙ㄌㄨㄛ) or (ㄓㄠˊ ˙ㄌㄠ)
whereabouts; results

著花(ㄓㄨㄛˊ ㄏㄨㄚ)
to blossom; to flower

著棋(ㄓㄨㄛˊ ㄑㄧˊ)
to play chess

著先鞭(ㄓㄨㄛˊ ㄒㄧㄢ ㄅㄧㄢ)
to make a head start; to be the first to move

著想(ㄓㄨㄛˊ ㄒㄧㄤˇ)
for the sake of

著著進逼(ㄓㄨㄛˊ ㄓㄨㄛˊ ㄐㄧㄣˋ ㄅㄧ)
to close in step by step

著著失敗(ㄓㄨㄛˊ ㄓㄨㄛˊ ㄕ ㄅㄞˋ)
to fail in every move

著重(ㄓㄨㄛˊ ㄓㄨㄥˋ)
to emphasize; emphasis

著實(ㄓㄨㄛˊ ㄕˊ)
① concrete and substantial; dependable ② really

著手(ㄓㄨㄛˊ ㄕㄡˇ)
to start doing something; to put or set one's hand to

著手成春(ㄓㄨㄛˊ ㄕㄡˇ ㄔㄥˊ ㄔㄨㄣ)
(said of a good physician) to cure every patient he treats

著色(ㄓㄨㄛˊ ㄙㄜˋ)
to apply coloring; to color: 他著色於圖畫。He colors a picture.

著衣(ㄓㄨㄛˊ ㄧ)
to wear clothing; to put on garments

著衣鏡(ㄓㄨㄛˊ ㄧ ㄐㄧㄥˋ)
a full-length dressing mirror; a cheval glass

著意(ㄓㄨㄛˊ ㄧˋ)
to pay attention to

【著】 5003
3.(着) ㄓㄠˊ jaur zháo

1. to hit the bull's-eye; right to the point; very worthwhile
2. to catch (fire, cold, etc.): 紙易著火。Paper catches fire easily.
3. to make a move or take action; to use

著魔(ㄓㄠˊ ㄇㄛˊ)
to be bewitched; to be possessed

著迷(ㄓㄠˊ ㄇㄧˊ)
to be fascinated; to be captivated: 這歌劇使觀衆著迷。The opera has captivated the audience.

著火(ㄓㄠˊ ㄏㄨㄛˇ)
to catch fire

著眼(ㄓㄠˊ ㄧㄢˇ)
to watch; to eye with attention; to direct one's attention to; to have something in mind; to see from the angle of; to aim at

著眼點(ㄓㄠˊ ㄧㄢˇ ㄉㄧㄢˇ)
the point to watch; the point of emphasis; a starting point

著用(ㄓㄠˊ ㄩㄥˋ)
useful; applicable

【著】 5003
4.(着) ㄓㄠ jau zhāo

1. to bear; to take
2. a plan; a method

著忙(ㄓㄠ ㄇㄤˊ)
anxious or nervous; panicky

著風(ㄓㄠ ㄈㄥ)
to expose to wind

著涼(ㄓㄠ ㄌㄧㄤˊ)
to catch cold: 我昨夜著涼了。I caught cold last night.

著慌(ㄓㄠ ㄏㄨㄤ)
anxious or worried; jittery: 他們對她的延遲著慌。They became anxious at her delay.

著急(ㄓㄠ ㄐㄧˊ)
anxious or worried: 他們爲後果著急。They were worried about the results.

著雨(ㄓㄠ ㄩˇ)
to get wet in the rain; to be drenched by rain

【著】 5003
5.(着) ˙ㄓㄜ ˙je zhe

an adverbial particle

【葚】 5004
ㄕㄣˋ shenn shèn

the mulberry

【葛】 5005
1. ㄍㄜˊ ger gé

dolichos (*Pueraria thunbergiana*), a creeping, edible bean whose fibers can be made into linen-like cloth and whose roots are used in herbal medicine

葛布(ㄍㄜˊ ㄅㄨˋ)
cloth made with the fiber of *Pueraria thunbergiana*; linen

葛粉(ㄍㄜˊ ㄈㄣˇ)
edible starch obtained by grinding the roots of *Pueraria thunbergiana*

葛藤(ㄍㄜˊ ㄊㄥˊ)
①(botany) *Pueraria lobata* ②(Buddhism) tangled and involved; complications or difficulty

葛巾(ㄍㄜˊ ㄐㄧㄣ)
a scarf or kerchief made with 葛布

葛屨履霜(ㄍㄜˊ ㄐㄩˋ ㄌㄩˇ ㄕㄨㄤ)
improper thrift; thrift at the expense of propriety

葛紗(ㄍㄜˊ ㄕㄚ)
fine linen cloth made with the fiber of *Pueraria thunbergiana*

葛衣(ㄍㄜˊ ㄧ)
clothing made with 葛布

【葛】 5005
2. ㄍㄜˇ gee gě

a Chinese family name

葛天氏(ㄍㄜˇ ㄊㄧㄢ ㄕˋ)
name of a legendary emperor in ancient times who governed with few words and less orders

葛天氏之民(ㄍㄜˇ ㄊㄧㄢ ㄕˋ ㄓ ㄇㄧㄣˊ)
subjects of 葛天氏—people with great freedom and joy

葛洪(ㄍㄜˇ ㄏㄨㄥˊ)
Ko Hung, a minister in the reign of Emperor Yüan(元帝) of Tsin(晉), c.290-c.370

【葡】 5006
ㄆㄨˊ pwu pú

1. a grape; a vine
2. short for Portugal

葡萄(ㄆㄨˊ ㄊㄠˊ)or(ㄆㄨˊ ˙ㄊㄠ)
grapes

葡萄糖(ㄆㄨˊ ㄊㄠˊ ㄊㄤˊ)
glucose

葡萄藤(ㄆㄨˊ ㄊㄠˊ ㄊㄥˊ)
a grapevine

葡萄乾(ㄆㄨˊ ㄊㄠˊ ㄍㄢ)
raisins

葡萄架(ㄆㄨˊ ㄊㄠˊ ㄐㄧㄚˋ)
a grapevine trellis

葡萄酒(ㄆㄨˊ ㄊㄠˊ ㄐㄧㄡˇ)
wine; grape wine; port wine; a vintage

葡萄球菌(ㄆㄨˊ ㄊㄠˊ ㄑㄧㄡˊ ㄐㄩㄣˋ)
(microbiology) a staphylococcus

葡萄汁(ㄆㄨˊ ㄊㄠˊ ㄓ)
grape juice

葡萄牙(ㄆㄨˊ ㄊㄠˊ ㄧㄚˊ)
Portugal

葡萄牙人(ㄆㄨˊ ㄊㄠˊ ㄧㄚˊ ㄖㄣˊ)
the Portuguese

葡萄牙語(ㄆㄨˊ ㄊㄠˊ ㄧㄚˊ ㄩˇ)
Portuguese (language)

葡萄柚(ㄆㄨˊ ㄊㄠˊ ㄧㄡˋ)
a grapefruit

葡萄園(ㄆㄨˊ ㄊㄠˊ ㄩㄢˊ)
a grapevine orchard or yard; a vine garden

【葠】 5007
(蔘、參) ㄕㄣ shen shēn

1. ginseng
2. one of the 28 constellations

【董】 5008 ㄉㄨㄥˇ doong dǒng
1. to supervise; to oversee; to rectify; to correct
2. short for directors (as a board of directors, etc.)
3. a Chinese family name
董狐(ㄉㄨㄥˇ ㄏㄨˊ)
Tung Hu, an official-historian of Chin (秦) in the Epoch of Spring and Autumn
董其昌(ㄉㄨㄥˇ ㄑㄧˊ ㄔㄤ)
Tung Chi-chang (1555-1636), a famous painter and calligrapher of the Ming Dynasty
董小宛(ㄉㄨㄥˇ ㄒㄧㄠˇ ㄨㄢˇ)
name of a very famous and talented courtesan toward the end of the Ming Dynasty
董卓(ㄉㄨㄥˇ ㄓㄨㄛˊ)
Tung Cho, a prime minister at the end of the Han Dynasty
董仲舒(ㄉㄨㄥˇ ㄓㄨㄥˋ ㄕㄨ)
Tung Chung-shu, a famous scholar in the Han Dynasty
董事(ㄉㄨㄥˇ ㄕˋ)
a director (on the board of a school, company, etc.); a trustee
董事會(ㄉㄨㄥˇ ㄕˋ ㄏㄨㄟˋ)
a meeting of board of directors; the board of directors
董事長(ㄉㄨㄥˇ ㄕˋ ㄓㄤˇ)
a board director; the chairman of the board of directors or of the board of trustees

【葦】 5009 ㄨㄟˇ woei wěi
a reed
葦箔(ㄨㄟˇ ㄅㄛˊ)
a reed screen
葦塘(ㄨㄟˇ ㄊㄤˊ)
a swampy or marshy ground covered with reeds
葦簾子(ㄨㄟˇ ㄌㄧㄢˊ ·ㄗ)
screens or curtains woven with reeds
葦杖(ㄨㄟˇ ㄓㄤˋ)
a birch or whip of reeds

【葼】 5010 ㄗㄨㄥ tzong zōng
1. small twigs
2. a kind of grass

【葩】 5011 ㄆㄚ pa pā
1. flowers
2. as in 奇葩—a wonderful work

【葫】 5012 ㄏㄨˊ hwu hú
the calabash or bottle gourd
葫蘆(ㄏㄨˊ ㄌㄨˊ)or(ㄏㄨˊ ·ㄌㄨ)
a bottle gourd; a calabash
葫蘆島(ㄏㄨˊ ㄌㄨˊ ㄉㄠˇ)
name of a peninsula in Liaoning Province, so called because it's shaped like a bottle gourd

【葬】 5013 ㄗㄤˋ tzanq zàng
to bury, inter or consign to a grave: 他昨天下葬。He was buried yesterday.
葬埋(ㄗㄤˋ ㄇㄞˊ)
to bury (the dead)亦作「埋葬」
葬地(ㄗㄤˋ ㄉㄧˋ)
the site of burial; a burial ground; a grave
葬禮(ㄗㄤˋ ㄌㄧˇ)
a funeral or burial service
葬身之地(ㄗㄤˋ ㄕㄣ ㄓ ㄉㄧˋ)
a burial ground
葬身魚腹(ㄗㄤˋ ㄕㄣ ㄩˊ ㄈㄨˋ)
to be drowned in a river or sea, thus to become food for fish
葬送(ㄗㄤˋ ㄙㄨㄥˋ)
to bury or waste (one's talent, future, hopes, etc.)
葬儀(ㄗㄤˋ ㄧˊ)
burial or funeral rites
葬玉埋香(ㄗㄤˋ ㄩˋ ㄇㄞˊ ㄒㄧㄤ)
① to bury a beauty ② the untimely death of a beauty

【葭】 5014 ㄐㄧㄚ jia jiā
1. a reed; a bulrush
2. a flute
葭莩(ㄐㄧㄚ ㄈㄨˊ)
distant relatives

【菙】 5015 ㄔㄨㄟˊ chwei chuí
a bramble; a thorn

【葳】 5016 ㄨㄟ uei wēi
1. luxuriant; flourishing
2. used for various plants
葳蕤(ㄨㄟ ㄖㄨㄟˊ)
① *Polygonatum cyrtonema*, a kind of herb ② luxuriant; lush

【葵】 5017 ㄎㄨㄟˊ kwei kuí
1. a sunflower (*Althaea rosea*)
葵笠(ㄎㄨㄟˊ ㄌㄧˋ)
a crude palm-leaf hat
葵花(ㄎㄨㄟˊ ㄏㄨㄚ)
a sunflower
葵花向日(ㄎㄨㄟˊ ㄏㄨㄚ ㄒㄧㄤˋ ㄖˋ)
(literally) The sunflower always turns to the sun. —The loyal always look to their master.
葵花子(ㄎㄨㄟˊ ㄏㄨㄚ ·ㄗ)or 葵瓜子(ㄎㄨㄟˊ ㄍㄨㄚ ·ㄗ)
sunflower seeds
葵花油(ㄎㄨㄟˊ ㄏㄨㄚ ㄧㄡˊ)
sunflower oil
葵傾(ㄎㄨㄟˊ ㄑㄧㄥ)or 葵向(ㄎㄨㄟˊ ㄒㄧㄤˋ)
to look to; to admire; to lean toward
葵扇(ㄎㄨㄟˊ ㄕㄢˋ)
a palm-leaf fan

【葷】 5018 1. ㄏㄨㄣ huen hūn
1. a meat and fish diet; meat-eating (as opposed to what vegetarians are practicing)
2. strong smelling foods or spices—such as onions, leeks, garlic, etc.
3. obscene or dirty language, narration, films, etc.
葷辛(ㄏㄨㄣ ㄒㄧㄣ)
strong smelling foods or spices
葷腥(ㄏㄨㄣ ㄒㄧㄥ)
a meat and fish diet
葷菜(ㄏㄨㄣ ㄘㄞˋ)
dishes containing meat or fish
葷油(ㄏㄨㄣ ㄧㄡˊ)
animal fat

【葷】 5018 2. ㄒㄩㄣ shiun xūn
name of a barbaric tribe in ancient China
葷粥 or 獯鬻(ㄒㄩㄣ ㄩˋ)or 獯允(ㄒㄩㄣ ㄩㄣˇ)
name of a barbaric tribe in ancient China

【葸】 5019 ㄒㄧˇ shii xǐ
1. scared; timid
2. not pleasant; a displeased look

【葺】 5020 ㄑㄧˋ chih qì

〔艸部〕

1. to repair; to have something put in repair
2. thatched
3. to pile up; to heap together

葺補(ㄑㄧˋ ㄅㄨˇ)
to repair and mend

葺覆(ㄑㄧˋ ㄈㄨˋ)
to cover or roof in

葺牆(ㄑㄧˋ ㄑㄧㄤˊ)
to repair a wall

葺屋(ㄑㄧˋ ㄨ)
a thatched house; to thatch a house

【葽】 5021
ㄧㄠ iau yāo
1. *Polygala japonica*, a variety of grass
2. a dense or luxuriant growth of grass or weeds

【葆】 5022
ㄅㄠˇ bao bǎo
1. reserved; hidden; not easily revealed
2. a dense or luxuriant growth of vegetation
3. to protect; protection

葆葆(ㄅㄠˇ ㄅㄠˇ)
a lush and luxuriant growth

葆光(ㄅㄠˇ ㄍㄨㄤ)
the shaded light; the precious light—(figuratively) one's wisdom; one's profound knowledge

葆眞 or 保眞(ㄅㄠˇ ㄓㄣ)
to safeguard one's divine nature—untarnished by all desires, etc.

【葒】 5023
ㄏㄨㄥˊ horng hóng
Polygonum orientale

【萸】 5024
ㄩˊ yu yú
dogwood

【萹】 5025
1. ㄆㄧㄢ pian piān
a variety of weed or grass with narrow thick blades

【萹】 5025
2.(稨) ㄅㄧㄢˇ bean biǎn
a kind of bean

【葖】 5026
ㄊㄨˊ twu tú
(botany) a turnip

【葱】 5027
(蔥) ㄘㄨㄥ tsong cōng
1. scallions; onions
2. bright green

葱白(ㄘㄨㄥ ㄅㄛˊ)
① pale green ② the white-colored section near the root of a scallion

葱頭(ㄘㄨㄥ ㄊㄡˊ)
onions 亦作「洋葱」

葱嶺(ㄘㄨㄥ ㄌㄧㄥˇ)
a mountain range in southwestern Sinkiang Province, known as the ridge of Asia

葱蘢(ㄘㄨㄥ ㄌㄨㄥˊ)
a luxuriant growth of green vegetation

葱綠(ㄘㄨㄥ ㄌㄩˋ)
a fresh, bright green: 稻苗一片葱綠。The rice shoots are a lush green.

葱鬍子(ㄘㄨㄥ ㄏㄨˊ ˙ㄗ)
the tiny roots of a scallion which look like a beard

葱花(ㄘㄨㄥ ㄏㄨㄚ)
scallions cut into tiny pieces for seasoning or dressing

葱黃(ㄘㄨㄥ ㄏㄨㄤˊ)
greenish yellow

葱心兒綠(ㄘㄨㄥ ㄒㄧㄣㄦ ㄌㄩˋ)
light bright green

葱翠(ㄘㄨㄥ ㄘㄨㄟˋ)
fresh green; luxuriantly green

【蒂】 5028
(蔕) ㄉㄧˋ dih dì
1. a peduncle or footstalk of a flower or fruit; a stem; a base
2. a (cigaret) butt

蒂芥(ㄉㄧˋ ㄐㄧㄝˋ)
resentment; ill will or unfriendly feeling

【葢】 5029
(蓋) ㄍㄞˋ gay gài
to cover, build, etc.

【葯】 5030
ㄧㄠˋ yaw yào
(讀音 ㄩㄝˋ yueh yuè)
1. (botany) an angelica
2. to wrap up 亦作「約」
3. a simplified form as 藥—medicine

葯胞(ㄧㄠˋ ㄅㄠ)
(botany) a loculus

【葅】 5031
(菹) ㄐㄩ jiu jū
1. salted or pickled vegetable or meat
2. a marshland covered with reeds

【韮】 5032
(韭) ㄐㄧㄡˇ jeou jiǔ
fragrant-flowered garlic; (Chinese) chives

韮黃(ㄐㄧㄡˇ ㄏㄨㄤˊ)
tender chives (which are yellow in color)

韮菜(ㄐㄧㄡˇ ㄘㄞˋ)
fragrant-flowered garlic; (Chinese) chives

十畫

【蒐】 5033
ㄙㄡ sou sōu
1. to gather; to collect
2. to hunt or search for; hunting
3. (botany) *Rubia cordifolia*, madder

蒐羅(ㄙㄡ ㄌㄨㄛˊ)
to search and collect

蒐集(ㄙㄡ ㄐㄧˊ)
to collect or gather 亦作「搜集」: 我的嗜好是蒐集郵票。My hobby is collecting stamps.

蒐索(ㄙㄡ ㄙㄨㄛˇ)
to search

【蒙】 5034
ㄇㄥˊ meng méng
1. to cover; to cover up; to wrap
2. naive; childish
3. ignorant; gullible; stupid
4. to cheat; to deceive; to fool
5. to bear; to take; to suffer
6. short for Mongolia
7. a Chinese family name

蒙蔽(ㄇㄥˊ ㄅㄧˋ)
to deceive; to swindle; to fool

蒙騙(ㄇㄥˊ ㄆㄧㄢˋ)
to fool with the intention to cheat

蒙昧(ㄇㄥˊ ㄇㄟˋ)
ignorant and stupid

蒙昧時代(ㄇㄥˊ ㄇㄟˋ ㄕˊ ㄉㄞˋ)
the period of ignorance; the primitive age

蒙昧無知(ㄇㄥˊ ㄇㄟˋ ㄨˊ ㄓ)
stupid and ignorant

蒙面盜(ㄇㄥˊ ㄇㄧㄢˋ ㄉㄠˋ)
a masked bandit, robber or burglar

蒙大拿(ㄇㄥˊ ㄉㄚˋ ㄋㄚˊ)
the state of Montana, U.S.A.

蒙特卡羅(ㄇㄥˊ ㄊㄜˋ ㄎㄚˇ ㄌㄨㄛˊ)

Monte Carlo, Monaco
蒙太奇(ㄇㄥˊ ㄊㄞˋ ㄑㄧˊ)
(movie) montage
蒙頭蓋臉(ㄇㄥˊ ㄊㄡˊ ㄍㄞˋ ㄌㄧㄢˇ)
to cover one's head and face
蒙恬(ㄇㄥˊ ㄊㄧㄢˊ)
Meng Tien, a famous general in the Chin (秦) Dynasty, who supervised the building of the Great Wall and was credited with the invention of the writing brush
蒙童(ㄇㄥˊ ㄊㄨㄥˊ)
innocent or ignorant children
蒙難(ㄇㄥˊ ㄋㄢˋ)
to suffer disaster; to be in distress
蒙蘢(ㄇㄥˊ ㄌㄨㄥˊ)
①nebulous ②(said of plants) luxuriant
蒙古(ㄇㄥˊ ㄍㄨˇ)
Mongolia; Mongolian
蒙古包(ㄇㄥˊ ㄍㄨˇ ㄅㄠ)
a yurt (a portable, tentlike dwelling used by nomadic Mongols)
蒙古大夫(ㄇㄥˊ ㄍㄨˇ ㄉㄞˋ ˙ㄈㄨ)or (ㄇㄥˊ ˙ㄍㄨ ㄉㄞˋ ˙ㄈㄨ)
a medical quack
蒙古利亞(ㄇㄥˊ ㄍㄨˇ ㄌㄧˋ ㄧㄚˇ)
Mongolia
蒙古症(ㄇㄥˊ ㄍㄨˇ ㄓㄥˋ)
(medicine) mongolism
蒙古人(ㄇㄥˊ ㄍㄨˇ ㄖㄣˊ)
the Mongols; the Mongolians
蒙古人種(ㄇㄥˊ ㄍㄨˇ ㄖㄣˊ ㄓㄨㄥˇ)
(anthropology) Mongolian stock
蒙古文(ㄇㄥˊ ㄍㄨˇ ㄨㄣˊ)
the Mongolian language
蒙館(ㄇㄥˊ ㄍㄨㄢˇ)
a village school for children
蒙汗藥(ㄇㄥˊ ㄏㄢˋ ㄧㄠˋ)
any drug or concoction used as an anesthetic; knockout drops
蒙混(ㄇㄥˊ ˙ㄏㄨㄣ)
to use a fake in place of a genuine article; to hoodwink; to deceive and swindle
蒙羞(ㄇㄥˊ ㄒㄧㄡ)
to suffer shame or insult; (said of a state) to be conquered by foreigners
蒙稚(ㄇㄥˊ ㄓˋ)
childish; naive; ignorant: 他不是愚笨，是蒙稚。He's not stupid, merely ignorant.
蒙塵(ㄇㄥˊ ㄔㄣˊ)
(said of the emperor) to flee the capital, or to be taken prisoner
蒙師(ㄇㄥˊ ㄕ)
a village school teacher
蒙受(ㄇㄥˊ ㄕㄡˋ)
to suffer; to sustain
蒙上(ㄇㄥˊ ˙ㄕㄤ)
to deceive one's elders; to hide the truth from superiors
蒙在鼓裡(ㄇㄥˊ ㄗㄞˋ ㄍㄨˇ ˙ㄌㄧ)
to be deceived; to be kept completely in the dark
蒙藏委員會(ㄇㄥˊ ㄗㄤˋ ㄨㄟˇ ㄩㄢˊ ㄏㄨㄟˋ)
Mongolian-Tibetan Affairs Commission (of the Executive Yüan)
蒙恩(ㄇㄥˊ ㄣ)
to receive favors; to be indebted for favors granted

【蒜】 5035 ㄙㄨㄢˋ suann suàn
garlic
蒜瓣兒(ㄙㄨㄢˋ ㄅㄚㄦˋ)
the quarters of a head of garlic
蒜苗(ㄙㄨㄢˋ ㄇㄧㄠˊ)
garlic sprouts (used as food)
蒜髮(ㄙㄨㄢˋ ㄈㄚˇ)
the premature white hair of a young person
蒜頭兒(ㄙㄨㄢˋ ㄊㄡㄦˊ)
the garlic head
蒜泥(ㄙㄨㄢˋ ㄋㄧˊ)
mashed garlic

【蒯】 5036 ㄎㄨㄞˇ koai kuǎi (又讀 ㄎㄨㄞˋ kuay kuài)
1. *Scirpus cyperinus Kunth var. concolor Makino,* a rush, from which many things are weaved
2. a Chinese family name

【蒱】 5037 ㄆㄨˊ pwu pú
an ancient dice game
蒱戲(ㄆㄨˊ ㄒㄧˋ)
an ancient dice game

【蒲】 5038 ㄆㄨˊ pwu pú
1. various kinds of rush from which mats, bags, etc. are made; vines of the rushes
2. a Chinese family name
蒲包(ㄆㄨˊ ㄅㄠ)
a rushbag (for packing)
蒲鞭(ㄆㄨˊ ㄅㄧㄢ)
(literally) a birch or whip made of rush for punishment —leniency
蒲團(ㄆㄨˊ ㄊㄨㄢˊ)
a rushy mat for kneeling (used especially in Buddhist temples)
蒲柳(ㄆㄨˊ ㄌㄧㄡˇ)
①(botany) *Salix gracilistyla* ②(said of a physical constitution) feeble; weak ③(said of a social position) humble; lowly
蒲隆地(ㄆㄨˊ ㄌㄨㄥˊ ㄉㄧˋ)
Burundi
蒲公英(ㄆㄨˊ ㄍㄨㄥ ㄧㄥ)
the dandelion
蒲葵(ㄆㄨˊ ㄎㄨㄟˊ)
the Chinese fan palm
蒲節(ㄆㄨˊ ㄐㄧㄝˊ)
the Dragon Boat Festival on the fifth day of the fifth lunar month
蒲劍(ㄆㄨˊ ㄐㄧㄢˋ)
the rush sword, hung in the doorway on the Dragon Boat Festival to ward off evil spirits
蒲式耳(ㄆㄨˊ ㄕˋ ㄦˇ)
a bushel
蒲扇(ㄆㄨˊ ㄕㄢˋ)
a rush-leaf fan
蒲草(ㄆㄨˊ ㄘㄠˇ)
the stem or leaf of a cattail
蒲松齡(ㄆㄨˊ ㄙㄨㄥ ㄌㄧㄥˊ)
Pu Sung-ling, 1640-1715, the author of *Strange Stories from a Chinese Studio* (聊齋誌異), a collection of ghost stories
蒲月(ㄆㄨˊ ㄩㄝˋ)
the fifth month in the lunar calendar

【蒸】 5039 ㄓㄥ jeng zheng
1. steam; to steam; to cook by steaming
2. to evaporate
3. twigs or slender branches as fuel

4.crowded; crowds; the masses
蒸餅(ㄓㄥ ㄅㄧㄥˇ)
steamed cake
蒸木油(ㄓㄥ ㄇㄨˋ ㄧㄡˊ)
creosote
蒸發(ㄓㄥ ㄈㄚ)
evaporation; to evaporate
蒸發熱(ㄓㄥ ㄈㄚ ㄖㄜˋ)
evaporation heat
蒸發作用(ㄓㄥ ㄈㄚ ㄗㄨㄛˋ ㄩㄥˋ)
evaporation; transpiration
蒸騰(ㄓㄥ ㄊㄥˊ)
rising vapor or steam
蒸餾(ㄓㄥ ㄌㄧㄡˊ)
distillation; to distill
蒸餾器(ㄓㄥ ㄌㄧㄡˊ ㄑㄧˋ)
a still; a distiller
蒸餾水(ㄓㄥ ㄌㄧㄡˊ ㄕㄨㄟˇ)
distilled water
蒸籠(ㄓㄥ ㄌㄨㄥˊ)
a tight basket and sieve of bamboo for steaming food
蒸餃(ㄓㄥ ㄐㄧㄠˇ)
steamed ravioli
蒸汽 or 蒸氣(ㄓㄥ ㄑㄧˋ)
steam; vapor: 蒸氣轉動機器。Steam drives machinery.
蒸汽鍋爐(ㄓㄥ ㄑㄧˋ ㄍㄨㄛ ㄌㄨˊ)
a steam boiler
蒸汽機(ㄓㄥ ㄑㄧˋ ㄐㄧ)
a steam engine
蒸汽浴(ㄓㄥ ㄑㄧˋ ㄩˋ)
a steam bath; a vapor bath; a Turkish bath
蒸蒸日上(ㄓㄥ ㄓㄥ ㄖˋ ㄕㄤˋ)
(usually said of business, etc.) rising and ascending; getting more and more prosperous
蒸食(ㄓㄥ ㄕˊ)
a general name of various kinds of steamed dumplings
蒸沙成飯(ㄓㄥ ㄕㄚ ㄔㄥˊ ㄈㄢˋ)
(literally) to cook sand with the hope of turning it into rice—a hopeless task
蒸暑(ㄓㄥ ㄕㄨˇ)
steaming heat (of summer); sultry 亦作「酷熱」
蒸溽(ㄓㄥ ㄖㄨˋ)
steaming heat of summer; sultry
蒸鬱(ㄓㄥ ㄩˋ)
the rising of steam or vapor

【蒹】 5040
ㄐㄧㄢ jian jiān

a kind of reed with a pithy stem

【蒺】 5041
ㄐㄧˊ jyi jí

the caltrop, or caltrap
蒺藜(ㄐㄧˊ ㄌㄧˊ)
the caltrop, or caltrap

【蒼】 5042
ㄘㄤ tsang cāng

1. green; deep green or blue
2. gray (hair); hoary: 他頭髮漸蒼白。His hair (or He) is growing gray.
3. old
4. the masses
5. a Chinese family name
蒼白(ㄘㄤ ㄅㄞˊ)
pale; pallid: 她臉色蒼白而且面露倦容。She is pale and tired-looking.
蒼茫(ㄘㄤ ㄇㄤˊ)
a vast expanse without a boundary
蒼民(ㄘㄤ ㄇㄧㄣˊ)
the masses; the ordinary people
蒼苔(ㄘㄤ ㄊㄞˊ)
deep green moss; dark moss
蒼頭(ㄘㄤ ㄊㄡˊ)or(ㄘㄤ ·ㄊㄡ)
①(in old China) servants (with green turbans) ②(in ancient China) green-turbaned soldiers
蒼天(ㄘㄤ ㄊㄧㄢ)
①the heavens; the sky ②springtime
蒼老(ㄘㄤ ㄌㄠˇ)
(said of people) hoary and old: 他顯得蒼老。He looks old.
蒼涼(ㄘㄤ ㄌㄧㄤˊ)
desolate; bleak
蒼狗白雲(ㄘㄤ ㄍㄡˇ ㄅㄞˊ ㄩㄣˊ)
the ephemeral world; ever-changing ways of a man
蒼黃(ㄘㄤ ㄏㄨㄤˊ)
①greenish yellow ②hurriedly; hastily
蒼頡(ㄘㄤ ㄐㄧㄝˊ)
Tsang Chieh, a legendary figure, who was supposed to be the inventor of Chinese characters
蒼勁(ㄘㄤ ㄐㄧㄥˋ)
①old and strong ②(said of calligraphy or painting) vigorous; bold
蒼穹(ㄘㄤ ㄑㄩㄥˊ)
the sky; the vault of heaven; the firmament
蒼朮(ㄘㄤ ㄓㄨˊ)
Atractylis lancea, a medicinal herb
蒼生(ㄘㄤ ㄕㄥ)
the ordinary people; the masses
蒼蒼(ㄘㄤ ㄘㄤ)
①deep green; blue ②old and hoary ③gray-headed
蒼翠(ㄘㄤ ㄘㄨㄟˋ)
green and bright—like leaves after a spring shower; emerald
蒼鷹(ㄘㄤ ㄧㄥ)
the eagle; the falcon
蒼蠅(ㄘㄤ ·ㄧㄥ)
the fly: 蒼蠅嗡嗡作響。The flies are buzzing.
蒼蠅拍子(ㄘㄤ ·ㄧㄥ ㄆㄞ ·ㄗ)
a flyswatter; a flyflap
蒼蠅紙(ㄘㄤ ·ㄧㄥ ㄓˇ)
flypaper

【蒿】 5043
ㄏㄠ hau hāo

1. the southernwood; plants of the mugwort or artemisia family
2. rising vapor
蒿目(ㄏㄠ ㄇㄨˋ)
①to look far ②to close one's eyes and worry about worldly affairs
蒿萊(ㄏㄠ ㄌㄞˊ)
①to live in the jungle ②the jungle
蒿里(ㄏㄠ ㄌㄧˇ)
①a tomb ②an elegiac song in ancient times
蒿廬(ㄏㄠ ㄌㄨˊ)
a hut
蒿子(ㄏㄠ ·ㄗ)
(botany) the mugwort or artemisia
蒿子桿兒(ㄏㄠ ·ㄗ ㄍㄚˇㄦ)
the stem of the mugwort or artemisia

【蓀】 5044
ㄙㄨㄣ suen sūn

a kind of aromatic grass

【蓁】 5045
ㄓㄣ jen zhēn

1. luxuriant
2. a wild pepper
蓁蓁(ㄓㄣ ㄓㄣ)

(艸部)

luxuriant (vegetation)

【蓄】 5046 ㄒㄩˋ shiuh xù

1. to collect; to store; to save up; to reserve
2. to cultivate (long hair or a beard); to grow
3. to raise; to rear; to breed
4. to wait; to expect

蓄謀(ㄒㄩˋ ㄇㄡˊ)
a plan which is being considered but not revealed; a secret scheme

蓄髮(ㄒㄩˋ ㄈㄚˇ)
to grow or cultivate long hair

蓄電量(ㄒㄩˋ ㄉㄧㄢˋ ㄌㄧㄤˋ)
the capacity of storing electricity; the capacity of a storage battery

蓄電池(ㄒㄩˋ ㄉㄧㄢˋ ㄔˊ)
a storage battery, cell, or accumulator

蓄念(ㄒㄩˋ ㄋㄧㄢˋ)
a long-conceived idea, plan, intention, etc.

蓄恨(ㄒㄩˋ ㄏㄣˋ)
a long pent-up hatred

蓄火(ㄒㄩˋ ㄏㄨㄛˇ)
(in ancient times) a fire in reserve

蓄洪(ㄒㄩˋ ㄏㄨㄥˊ)
to store floodwater

蓄積(ㄒㄩˋ ㄐㄧ)
to store or save up; storage or savings

蓄志(ㄒㄩˋ ㄓˋ)
a long-conceived hope, wish or aspiration; to harbor such hope, etc.

蓄水池(ㄒㄩˋ ㄕㄨㄟˇ ㄔˊ)
a reservoir

蓄銳(ㄒㄩˋ ㄖㄨㄟˋ)
to husband one's strength and store up energy (for a big undertaking)—as soldiers before a decisive engagement or a prize fighter before a bout

蓄財(ㄒㄩˋ ㄘㄞˊ)
to store up money or wealth

蓄意(ㄒㄩˋ ㄧˋ)
to harbor certain intentions or ideas; premeditated (murder, etc.): 這兇殺是蓄意的。The murder was premeditated.

蓄音器(ㄒㄩˋ ㄧㄣ ㄑㄧˋ)
a phonograph; a gramophone 亦作「留聲機」

蓄養(ㄒㄩˋ ㄧㄤˇ)
to raise (ducks, etc.)

蓄怨(ㄒㄩˋ ㄩㄢˋ)
to harbor animosity or ill will

【蓆】 5047 ㄒㄧˊ shyi xí

a mat, especially a straw mat

蓆子(ㄒㄧˊ ˙ㄗ)
a mat, especially a straw mat: 我們重新舖了蓆子。We had the mats recovered.

【蓉】 5048 ㄖㄨㄥˊ rong róng

as in 芙蓉—the hibiscus

【蓋】 5049 1.(盖、葢) ㄍㄞˋ gay gài

1. to cover; to hide
2. a lid; a covering
3. to build; to construct; to erect
4. to affix (a seal)
5. (an initial particle) now; then; but; because
6. (a particle indicating doubt) for; perhaps; possibly; about
7. to surpass; to excel
8. to brag; to boast

蓋被窩(ㄍㄞˋ ㄅㄟˋ ˙ㄨㄛ)
to cover with a quilt

蓋房子(ㄍㄞˋ ㄈㄤˊ ˙ㄗ)
to build a house

蓋頭(ㄍㄞˋ ˙ㄊㄡ)or 蓋巾(ㄍㄞˋ ㄐㄧㄣ)
(formerly) the head-cover or veil for the bride at a wedding

蓋圖章(ㄍㄞˋ ㄊㄨˊ ˙ㄓㄤ)or 蓋章(ㄍㄞˋ ㄓㄤ)or 蓋印(ㄍㄞˋ ㄧㄣˋ)
to affix the seal

蓋關防(ㄍㄞˋ ㄍㄨㄢ ㄈㄤˊ)
to affix an official seal

蓋棺論定(ㄍㄞˋ ㄍㄨㄢ ㄌㄨㄣˋ ㄉㄧㄥˋ)
When one's coffin is covered, one's deserts can be properly judged.

蓋仙(ㄍㄞˋ ㄒㄧㄢ)
a brag: 他是個蓋仙。He is a brag.

蓋戳(ㄍㄞˋ ㄔㄨㄛ)
to stamp (postmarks, etc.); to affix a seal; to chop

蓋世(ㄍㄞˋ ㄕˋ)or 蓋代(ㄍㄞˋ ㄉㄞˋ)
surpassing one's generation; without a match; to rank supreme in one's time

蓋世太保(ㄍㄞˋ ㄕˋ ㄊㄞˋ ㄅㄠˇ)
the Gestapo

蓋世之才(ㄍㄞˋ ㄕˋ ㄓ ㄘㄞˊ)
talent or capability unsurpassed or unmatched in one's generation

蓋世英雄(ㄍㄞˋ ㄕˋ ㄧㄥ ㄒㄩㄥˊ)
a hero among heroes: 他是一位蓋世英雄。He was a hero among heroes.

蓋世無雙(ㄍㄞˋ ㄕˋ ㄨˊ ㄕㄨㄤ)
unrivaled; matchless; peerless: 他是蓋世無雙的拳擊手。He is a peerless boxer.

蓋氏計算器(ㄍㄞˋ ㄕˋ ㄐㄧˋ ㄙㄨㄢˋ ㄑㄧˋ) or 蓋革計數器(ㄍㄞˋ ㄍㄜˊ ㄐㄧˋ ㄕㄨˋ ㄑㄧˋ)
a Geiger counter

蓋上(ㄍㄞˋ ˙ㄕㄤ)
to cover: 母親幫他蓋上毯子。Mother covered him with a blanket.

蓋然率(ㄍㄞˋ ㄖㄢˊ ㄌㄩˋ)or 蓋然性(ㄍㄞˋ ㄖㄢˊ ㄒㄧㄥˋ)
probability; the rate of probability

蓋子(ㄍㄞˋ ˙ㄗ)or 蓋兒(ㄍㄚˋㄦ)
① a lid; a cover: 請打開蓋子。Take off the lid, please. ② a shell (of a tortoise, etc.)

蓋藏(ㄍㄞˋ ㄘㄤˊ)
wealth or commodities stored away

蓋亞那(ㄍㄞˋ ㄧㄚˇ ㄋㄚˋ)
Guyana

【蓋】 5049 2. ㄍㄜˇ gee gě

a Chinese family name

【蓋】 5049 3.(盍) ㄏㄜˊ her hé

Why not? 或 Would it not be better to...?

【蓐】 5050 ㄖㄨˋ ruh rù

matting; a bed mat

蓐母(ㄖㄨˋ ㄇㄨˇ)or 蓐婦(ㄖㄨˋ ㄈㄨˋ)
a midwife

蓐食(ㄖㄨˋ ㄕˊ)
① to breakfast in bed; to take meals in bed ② rich food

【蓑】 5051 ㄙㄨㄛ suo suō

1. a raincoat or cloak of straw, rushes, coir, etc.

〔艸部〕

2. (now rarely) to cover with grass
蓑笠(ㄙㄨㄛ ㄌㄧˋ)
a coir raincoat and leaf hat; a bamboo cape and hat
蓑草(ㄙㄨㄛ ㄘㄠˇ)
sedge (of which a raincoat can be made)
蓑衣(ㄙㄨㄛ ㄧ)
a coir raincoat

【蓓】 5052 ㄅㄟˋ bey bèi
a flower bud; a bud
蓓蕾(ㄅㄟˋ ㄌㄟˇ)
a flower bud

【蒔】 5053 ㄕˊ shyr shí
1. to plant; to cultivate; to transplant
2. *Anethum graveolens*, a kind of spice
蒔花(ㄕˊ ㄏㄨㄚ)
to grow flowers

【蒨】 5054 ㄑㄧㄢˋ chiann qiàn
1. a luxuriant growth (of grass or vegetation)
2. red; crimson
蒨蒨(ㄑㄧㄢˋ ㄑㄧㄢˋ)
① bright and clear ② a luxuriant growth

【蒻】 5055 ㄖㄨㄛˋ ruoh ruò
1. a water plant; a wild arum
2. a rush mat
蒻席(ㄖㄨㄛˋ ㄒㄧˊ)
a rush mat made of arum

【蓊】 5056 ㄨㄥˇ woeng wěng
(said of vegetation) luxuriant; flourishing; lush
蓊勃(ㄨㄥˇ ㄅㄛˊ)
(said of vegetation) luxuriant; lush
蓊茸(ㄨㄥˇ ㄖㄨㄥˊ)
luxuriant; lush
蓊蔚(ㄨㄥˇ ㄨㄟˋ)
the luxuriant growth of vegetation
蓊蓊(ㄨㄥˇ ㄨㄥˇ)
the lush or luxuriant growth of vegetation
蓊鬱(ㄨㄥˇ ㄩˋ)
the lush or luxuriant growth of vegetation

【蓍】 5057 ㄕ shy shī
milfoil, the stalks of which were used in divination in ancient times
蓍龜(ㄕ ㄍㄨㄟ) or 蓍蔡(ㄕ ㄘㄞˋ)
① milfoil and tortoise divination ② foresight
蓍簪(ㄕ ㄗㄢ)
to treasure old things of little value for sentimental reasons
蓍草(ㄕ ㄘㄠˇ)
milfoil (used in divination in ancient times)

【菁】 5058 ㄍㄨˇ guu gǔ
a follicle
菁葖(ㄍㄨˇ ㄊㄨˊ)
a follicle

【蒓】 5059 (蓴) ㄔㄨㄣˊ chwen chún
Brasenia schreberi, water shield

【蒞】 5060 (莅) ㄌㄧˋ lih lì
to arrive

【萞】 5061 ㄅㄧˋ bih bì
(botany) the castor-oil plant
萞麻(ㄅㄧˋ ㄇㄚˊ)
(botany) the castor-oil plant
萞麻油(ㄅㄧˋ ㄇㄚˊ ㄧㄡˊ)
castor oil

【蒭】 5062 (芻) ㄔㄨˊ chwu chú
1. to cut grass
2. hay; fodder

十一畫

【蓬】 5063 ㄆㄥˊ perng péng
1. *Erigeron acer*, a species of raspberry
2. tangled
3. disheveled (hair)
4. flourishing; prospering
5. a Chinese family name
蓬勃(ㄆㄥˊ ㄅㄛˊ)
rising and flourishing; booming; vigorously
蓬蓽(ㄆㄥˊ ㄅㄧˋ)
①houses of the destitute ② my humble house
蓬蓽生輝(ㄆㄥˊ ㄅㄧˋ ㄕㄥ ㄏㄨㄟ)
(Your gracious presence) has added glitter to my humble house.
蓬蓬勃勃(ㄆㄥˊ ㄆㄥˊ ㄅㄛˊ ㄅㄛˊ)
flourishing and prospering; booming
蓬飄萍轉(ㄆㄥˊ ㄆㄧㄠ ㄆㄧㄥˊ ㄓㄨㄢˇ)
wandering about; having no fixed address
蓬門(ㄆㄥˊ ㄇㄣˊ) or 蓬門蓽戶(ㄆㄥˊ ㄇㄣˊ ㄅㄧˋ ㄏㄨˋ)
① houses of the poor ② my humble house; my thorn-wood gate
蓬髮(ㄆㄥˊ ㄈㄚˇ)
disheveled hair
蓬島(ㄆㄥˊ ㄉㄠˇ)
(Chinese legends) a fairy-tale island in the Yellow Sea
蓬頭垢面(ㄆㄥˊ ㄊㄡˊ ㄍㄡˋ ㄇㄧㄢˋ)
disheveled hair and a dirty face—very untidy in appearance
蓬萊(ㄆㄥˊ ㄌㄞˊ)
① a fairy-tale island in the Yellow Sea or name of an enchanted hill on such an island
蓬萊仙境(ㄆㄥˊ ㄌㄞˊ ㄒㄧㄢ ㄐㄧㄥˋ)
a fairyland; a paradise
蓬蒿(ㄆㄥˊ ㄏㄠ)
① a garland chrysanthemum 亦作「茼蒿」② the wilderness ③ weeds and thistles
蓬戶甕牖(ㄆㄥˊ ㄏㄨˋ ㄨㄥˋ ㄧㄡˇ)
houses of the destitute
蓬轉(ㄆㄥˊ ㄓㄨㄢˇ)
① quickly; rapidly ② to go adrift
蓬拆(ㄆㄥˊ ㄔㄞˋ)
① the beat of dance music ② to dance
蓬首(ㄆㄥˊ ㄕㄡˇ)
disheveled hair
蓬生麻中，不扶自直(ㄆㄥˊ ㄕㄥ ㄇㄚˊ ㄓㄨㄥ, ㄅㄨˋ ㄈㄨˊ ㄗˋ ㄓˊ)
(literally) When a raspberry grows among hemp, it stands erect without support.—When one is surrounded by the virtuous, he'll be assimilated.
蓬茸(ㄆㄥˊ ㄖㄨㄥˊ)
a luxuriant growth (of grass); lush
蓬鬆(ㄆㄥˊ ㄙㄨㄥ)
disheveled; very loose
蓬瀛(ㄆㄥˊ ㄧㄥˊ)
蓬萊 and 瀛洲, both legendary fairylands

【蓮】 5064
ㄌㄧㄢˊ lian lián
1. the lotus, or water lily
2. (Buddhism) the "clean" land —Buddhist Paradise

蓮邦(ㄌㄧㄢˊ ㄅㄤ)
(Buddhism) the Lotus Land, or the Pure Land, of Amitabha

蓮步(ㄌㄧㄢˊ ㄅㄨˋ)
steps of a beautiful woman; ladylike steps

蓮蓬(ㄌㄧㄢˊ ˙ㄆㄥ) or 蓮房(ㄌㄧㄢˊ ㄈㄤˊ)
the cupule of a lotus

蓮蓬頭(ㄌㄧㄢˊ ˙ㄆㄥ ㄊㄡˊ)
a finely perforated nozzle for a shower bath

蓮蓬子兒(ㄌㄧㄢˊ ˙ㄆㄥ ㄗˇㄦ)
lotus seeds

蓮斷絲牽(ㄌㄧㄢˊ ㄉㄨㄢˋ ㄙ ㄑㄧㄢ)
lingering affection or friendship after a formal break (as in the case of a divorced couple)

蓮塘(ㄌㄧㄢˊ ㄊㄤˊ)
a lotus pond

蓮鈎(ㄌㄧㄢˊ ㄍㄡ)
slender feet of a woman (especially referring to the bound feet of former days)

蓮龕(ㄌㄧㄢˊ ㄎㄢ)
a niche for the statue of Buddha

蓮花 or 蓮華(ㄌㄧㄢˊ ㄏㄨㄚ)
lotus blossoms or water lilies

蓮花燈(ㄌㄧㄢˊ ㄏㄨㄚ ㄉㄥ)
a lantern shaped like a lotus blossom

蓮花落(ㄌㄧㄢˊ ㄏㄨㄚ ㄌㄠˋ)
a kind of folk song often sung by beggars

蓮花池(ㄌㄧㄢˊ ㄏㄨㄚ ㄔˊ)
a lotus pond

蓮經(ㄌㄧㄢˊ ㄐㄧㄥ)
(Buddhism) the Lotus Sutra 亦作「法華經」

蓮炬(ㄌㄧㄢˊ ㄐㄩˋ)
ornamental candles in the shape of lotus flowers

蓮心(ㄌㄧㄢˊ ㄒㄧㄣ)
the heart of a lotus seed —my bitter heart

蓮船(ㄌㄧㄢˊ ㄔㄨㄢˊ)
① tiny boats for collecting lotus seeds ② large feet of women (an expression of sarcasm)

蓮實(ㄌㄧㄢˊ ㄕˊ)
lotus seeds

蓮社(ㄌㄧㄢˊ ㄕㄜˋ)
① a gathering of scholars —usually for extemporizing poems, etc. ② a gathering of Buddhists ③ the White Lotus sect, a quasi-religious secret society in the Yüan Dynasty

蓮子(ㄌㄧㄢˊ ㄗˇ)
lotus seeds

蓮座(ㄌㄧㄢˊ ㄗㄨㄛˋ)
the pedestal of a Buddha statue; a Buddha's seat in the form of a lotus flower

蓮宗(ㄌㄧㄢˊ ㄗㄨㄥ)
name of a Buddhist sect, founded in the Tsin (晉) Dynasty by Hui Yüan (慧遠) circa A.D. 390 亦作「淨土宗」

蓮藕(ㄌㄧㄢˊ ㄡˇ)
the lotus root

蓮霧(ㄌㄧㄢˊ ㄨˋ)
the wax apple

蓮輿(ㄌㄧㄢˊ ㄩˊ)
a sedan chair for a woman in ancient times

【蔻】 5065
ㄎㄡˋ kow kòu
cardamon seeds 參看「豆蔻」

蔻丹(ㄎㄡˋ ㄉㄢ)
red nail polish (a transliteration of the trade name "Cutex")

【蓼】 5066
1. ㄌㄧㄠˇ leau liǎo
1. the smartweed
2. name of a state in today's Honan Province in the Epoch of Spring and Autumn
3. a Chinese family name

蓼花(ㄌㄧㄠˇ ㄏㄨㄚ)
the smartweed

【蓼】 5066
2. ㄌㄨˋ luh lù
(said of vegetation) luxuriant; high

蓼蓼(ㄌㄨˋ ㄌㄨˋ)
(said of vegetation) luxuriant; long and large

蓼莪(ㄌㄨˋ ㄜˊ)
a poem in the *Book of Odes* (詩經) in memory of one's parents

【蓿】 5067
ㄙㄨˋ suh sù
(又讀 ㄒㄩ shiu xū)
clover; lucerne

【蔑】 5068
(蔑) ㄇㄧㄝˋ mieh miè
1. to disdain; to slight; to despise; to neglect; to disregard; to feel contempt for
2. without; none; no
3. to cast away
4. tiny; small

蔑蒙(ㄇㄧㄝˋ ㄇㄥˊ)
to fly past rapidly; to hurtle or catapult

蔑賤(ㄇㄧㄝˋ ㄐㄧㄢˋ)
humble; lowly

蔑棄(ㄇㄧㄝˋ ㄑㄧˋ)
to despise and cast away

蔑視(ㄇㄧㄝˋ ㄕˋ)
to disdain; to slight; to flout or disregard (rules, etc.); to defy (orders, etc.)

蔑如(ㄇㄧㄝˋ ㄖㄨˊ)
to slight; to belittle

【蔓】 5069
1. ㄇㄢˋ mann màn
plants with creeping tendrils or vines

蔓生植物(ㄇㄢˋ ㄕㄥ ㄓˊ ㄨˋ)
creeping plants

蔓說(ㄇㄢˋ ㄕㄨㄛ)
a windy talk

蔓草(ㄇㄢˋ ㄘㄠˇ)
grass that creeps and spreads fast and luxuriantly; creeping weeds

蔓延(ㄇㄢˋ ㄧㄢˊ)
to spread; to creep: 葡萄藤沿牆蔓延。The grapevine creeps along the wall.

蔓衍(ㄇㄢˋ ㄧㄢˇ)
to spread out far and wide

【蔓】 5069
2. ㄨㄢˋ wann wàn
a tendril; a creeper

【蔓】 5069
3. ㄇㄢˊ man mán
the rape turnip

蔓菁(ㄇㄢˊ ˙ㄐㄧㄥ)
the rape turnip 亦作「蕪菁」

【蔕】 5070
(蒂) ㄉㄧˋ dih dì
a peduncle or footstalk of a flower or fruit

【蔗】 5071
ㄓㄜˋ jeh zhè
sugarcane

蔗糖(ㄓㄜˋ ㄊㄤˊ)
sugar from sugarcane; cane sugar

蔗酒(ㄓㄜˋ ㄐㄧㄡˇ)
an alcoholic drink made with sugarcane juice; rum

蔗漿(ㄓㄜˋ ㄐㄧㄤ)
sugarcane pulp

蔗境(ㄓㄜˋ ㄐㄧㄥˋ)
(said of circumstances) improving; getting better and better (like eating sugarcane from the stem downward)

蔗汁(ㄓㄜˋ ㄓ)
sugarcane juice

【蔚】 5072
1. ㄨㄟˋ wey wèi

1. (said of vegetation) luxuriant; ornamental and colorful
2. *Artemisia japonica*

蔚藍(ㄨㄟˋ ㄌㄢˊ)
sky-blue

蔚然成風(ㄨㄟˋ ㄖㄢˊ ㄔㄥˊ ㄈㄥ)
to become common practice; to become the order of the day

蔚爲奇觀(ㄨㄟˋ ㄨㄟˊ ㄑㄧˊ ㄍㄨㄢ)
to present a magnificent sight; to offer a thrilling view

【蔚】 5072
2. ㄩˋ yuh yù

1. a Chinese family name
2. name of a county in Hopeh Province

【蔡】 5073
ㄘㄞˋ tsay cài

1. a large turtle or tortoise (whose shell was used in divination in ancient China)
2. name of an ancient state in the Epoch of Spring and Autumn
3. a Chinese family name

蔡倫(ㄘㄞˋ ㄌㄨㄣˊ)
Tsai Lun, an official in the Eastern Han Dynasty, credited with the invention of paper with bark and rag pulp

蔡襄(ㄘㄞˋ ㄒㄧㄤ)
Tsai Hsiang, a famed calligrapher of the Sung Dynasty

蔡鍔(ㄘㄞˋ ㄜˋ)
Tsai O, 1882-1916, a general who was the first to rise against Yüan Shih-kai's (袁世凱) plan to become an emperor

蔡文姬(ㄘㄞˋ ㄨㄣˊ ㄐㄧ)
Tsai Wen-chi, a talented woman at the end of the Han Dynasty, kidnaped by the northern barbarians for 12 years before she was ransomed

蔡元培(ㄘㄞˋ ㄩㄢˊ ㄆㄟˊ)
Tsai Yüan-pei (1867-1940), a scholar and the first president of the Academia Sinica

蔡邕(ㄘㄞˋ ㄩㄥ)
Tsai Yung, a famous scholar and father of Tsai Wen-chi (蔡文姬)

【蔣】 5074
ㄐㄧㄤˇ jeang jiǎng

a Chinese family name

蔣中正(ㄐㄧㄤˇ ㄓㄨㄥ ㄓㄥˋ) or 蔣介石(ㄐㄧㄤˇ ㄐㄧㄝˋ ㄕˊ)
Chiang Kai-shek, 1887-1975, late President of the Republic of China (1948-1975)

蔣山(ㄐㄧㄤˇ ㄕㄢ)
name of a mountain outside Nanking 亦作「紫金山」

【蔥】 5075
(葱) ㄘㄨㄥ tsong cōng

scallions; onions

【蔦】 5076
ㄋㄧㄠˇ neau niǎo

Ribes ambiguum, a kind of creeping plant; mistletoe

蔦蘿(ㄋㄧㄠˇ ㄌㄨㄛˊ)
① ivy ② dependent relatives

【蔬】 5077
ㄕㄨ shu shū

1. vegetables; greens
2. a vegetarian diet; vegetable food

蔬圃(ㄕㄨ ㄆㄨˇ)
a vegetable garden

蔬飯(ㄕㄨ ㄈㄢˋ)
vegetables and rice

蔬糲(ㄕㄨ ㄌㄧˋ)
wild vegetables and coarse rice—food of the destitute

蔬果(ㄕㄨ ㄍㄨㄛˇ)
vegetables and fruit

蔬食(ㄕㄨ ㄕˊ)
① a vegetarian diet ② simple or coarse food

蔬食主義(ㄕㄨ ㄕˊ ㄓㄨˇ ㄧˋ)
vegetarianism

蔬菜(ㄕㄨ ㄘㄞˋ)
vegetables; greens

【蓴】 5078
(蒓) ㄔㄨㄣˊ chwen chún

Brasenia schreberi, water shield

蓴鱸(ㄔㄨㄣˊ ㄌㄨˊ)
retirement from government office (蓴 and 鱸 being delicacies of a particular locality, which seekers of fortune must deny themselves)

蓴鱸之思(ㄔㄨㄣˊ ㄌㄨˊ ㄓ ㄙ)
homesickness, intention of retiring from office and going back home

蓴羹鱸膾(ㄔㄨㄣˊ ㄍㄥ ㄌㄨˊ ㄎㄨㄞˋ)
delicacies that make one think of retirement from government office in order to return home

蓴菜(ㄔㄨㄣˊ ㄘㄞˋ)
Brasenia schreberi, water shield

【蓽】 5079
(篳) ㄅㄧˋ bih bì

1. bamboo or wicker for making baskets, etc.
2. *Piper longum,* a kind of herb growing among bamboos, used in Chinese medicine

蓽茇(ㄅㄧˋ ㄅㄚˊ) or 蓽撥(ㄅㄧˋ ㄅㄛ)
(botany) *Piper longum,* long pepper

蓽門圭竇(ㄅㄧˋ ㄇㄣˊ ㄍㄨㄟ ㄉㄡˋ)
a small door of bamboo—a house of a poor man

蓽路藍縷 or 蓽路襤褸(ㄅㄧˋ ㄌㄨˋ ㄌㄢˊ ㄌㄩˇ)
firewood carts and rags—the hard life of pioneers

【蔌】 5080
ㄙㄨˋ suh sù

vegetables

蔌蔌(ㄙㄨˋ ㄙㄨˋ)
① crude and coarse ② the heaving of high winds ③ streams or fountains flowing ④ flowers falling ⑤ descriptive of mean, abject creatures

【蔔】 5081
ㄅㄛˊ bor bó
(語音 ·ㄅㄛ ·bo bo)

as in 蘿蔔—a common name for such edible roots as turnips, carrots, radishes

【蔞】5082 ㄌㄡˊ lou lóu
a kind of artemisia whose tender leaves are edible

蔞藤(ㄌㄡˊ ㄊㄥˊ)
a kind of vine

蔞蒿(ㄌㄡˊ ㄏㄠ)
Artemisia vulgaris, an edible water plant

【蔫】5083 1. ㄋㄧㄢ nhian niān
1. (said of plants) fading or withering
2. spiritless; ennui; listless
3. calm and quiet; expressionless

蔫了(ㄋㄧㄢ ·ㄌㄜ)
withered; finished

【蔫】5083 2. ㄧㄢ ian yān
stale; rotting or decaying

【蔭】5084 ㄧㄣˋ yinn yìn
1. the shade of trees; shade
2. to shelter; to protect
3. (with) the support or blessing of

蔭蔽(ㄧㄣˋ ㄅㄧˋ)
to shelter; to hide in the shade: 小木屋蔭蔽在樹林中。The log cabin lies hidden among the trees.

蔭庇(ㄧㄣˋ ㄅㄧˋ)
to protect; to patronize

蔭涼(ㄧㄣˋ ㄌㄧㄤˊ)
shady and cool

蔭生(ㄧㄣˋ ㄕㄥ)
(formerly) a student admitted to the Imperial Academy (國子監) because of the meritorious services rendered by his forefathers 亦作「廕生」

蔭翳(ㄧㄣˋ ㄧˋ)
in the shade of a luxuriant growth of trees or vegetation

【蔯】5085 ㄔㄣˊ chern chén
a variety of artemisia

【蔟】5086 ㄘㄨˋ tsuh cù
1. a cluster 亦作「簇」
2. a frame on which silkworms spin

蔟聚(ㄘㄨˋ ㄐㄩˋ)
to be crowded together

【蓰】5087 ㄒㄧˇ shii xǐ
1. a variety of grass
2. five times of anything

【蔴】5088 (麻) ㄇㄚˊ ma má
1. hemp
2. sesame; sesamum

十二畫

【蔽】5089 ㄅㄧˋ bih bì
1. to cover; to cover up
2. to hide; to conceal; to shelter
3. to screen; to separate

蔽目(ㄅㄧˋ ㄇㄨˋ)
to cover the eyes; to blindfold

蔽芾(ㄅㄧˋ ㄈㄟˋ) or 蔽茀(ㄅㄧˋ ㄈㄨˊ)
① tiny; petite ② to be umbrageous

蔽風雨(ㄅㄧˋ ㄈㄥ ㄩˇ)
to shelter from the wind and rain

蔽體(ㄅㄧˋ ㄊㄧˇ)
to cover the body

蔽匿(ㄅㄧˋ ㄋㄧˋ)
to hide; to conceal; to lie low

蔽護(ㄅㄧˋ ㄏㄨˋ)
to shelter; to take cover; to protect

蔽賢(ㄅㄧˋ ㄒㄧㄢˊ)
to keep the capable or virtuous from attaining fame or eminence

蔽形術(ㄅㄧˋ ㄒㄧㄥˊ ㄕㄨˋ)
(Taoism, etc.) a form of witchcraft supposedly capable of making a person invisible

蔽日(ㄅㄧˋ ㄖˋ)
to cover the sun from view; to dull the sunlight

蔽塞(ㄅㄧˋ ㄙㄜˋ)
① to block up ② stupid or dull; ignorance

蔽野(ㄅㄧˋ ㄧㄝˇ)
(descriptive of numerous banners or exuberant trees) to cover the whole field

蔽月羞花 or 閉月羞花(ㄅㄧˋ ㄩㄝˋ ㄒㄧㄡ ㄏㄨㄚ)
(said of a stunning beauty) that outshines the moon and puts flowers to shame

【蕃】5090 1. ㄈㄢˊ farn fán
1. (said of vegetation) luxuriant; flourishing
2. to increase; to multiply; to propagate
3. numerous; plentiful

蕃茂(ㄈㄢˊ ㄇㄠˋ)
flourishing and booming; thriving

蕃孌(ㄈㄢˊ ㄌㄩㄢˇ)
fabulous; splendid; exceedingly pretty or charming

蕃息(ㄈㄢˊ ㄒㄧˊ)
to increase and multiply; to propagate in great numbers

蕃殖(ㄈㄢˊ ㄓˊ)
to breed; to multiply; to reproduce; to propagate

蕃昌(ㄈㄢˊ ㄔㄤ)
thriving and prosperous; flourishing and booming

蕃庶(ㄈㄢˊ ㄕㄨˋ)
numerous

蕃滋 or 蕃孳(ㄈㄢˊ ㄗ)
to multiply or increase in large numbers; to reproduce rapidly

蕃衍(ㄈㄢˊ ㄧㄢˇ)
① to increase or multiply in large numbers; to propagate rapidly ② large and luxuriant

蕃廡(ㄈㄢˊ ㄨˇ)
flourishing and thriving

蕃育(ㄈㄢˊ ㄩˋ)
to increase and multiply in great numbers

【蕃】5090 2.(番) ㄈㄢ fan fān
barbarians (as opposed to native Chinese); foreign; uncivilized

蕃舶(ㄈㄢ ㄅㄛˊ)
(Tang Dynasty) a foreign boat; a boat from a distant land

蕃坊(ㄈㄢ ㄈㄤ)
(Sung Dynasty) a reservation or settlement for foreigners

蕃椒(ㄈㄢ ㄐㄧㄠ)
capsicum

蕃茄(ㄈㄢ ㄑㄧㄝˊ)
a tomato: 蕃茄可以生吃。Tomatoes can be eaten uncooked.

〔艸部〕

蕃茄醬(ㄈㄢ ㄑㄧㄝˊ ㄐㄧㄤˋ)
tomato catsup; tomato paste
蕃茄汁(ㄈㄢ ㄑㄧㄝˊ ㄓ)
tomato juice
蕃薯(ㄈㄢ ㄕㄨˇ)
a sweet potato
蕃人(ㄈㄢ ㄖㄣˊ)
barbarians; uncivilized people

【蒇】 5091 ㄔㄢˇ chaan chǎn
to complete; to finish

【蕉】 5092 ㄐㄧㄠ jiau jiāo
1. the banana
2. the plantain
蕉布(ㄐㄧㄠ ㄅㄨˋ)
cloth made from the fibers of the plantain
蕉風椰雨(ㄐㄧㄠ ㄈㄥ ㄧㄝˊ ㄩˇ)
(literally) banana winds and cocoanut rains—tropical sights
蕉農(ㄐㄧㄠ ㄋㄨㄥˊ)
banana growers
蕉葛(ㄐㄧㄠ ㄍㄜˊ)
linen made from the fibers of the plantain
蕉扇(ㄐㄧㄠ ㄕㄢˋ)
a palm-leaf fan
蕉葉(ㄐㄧㄠ ㄧㄝˋ)
① the leaf of a banana plant ② a very shallow wine-cup
蕉園(ㄐㄧㄠ ㄩㄢˊ)
a banana plantation

【蕊】 5093 ㄖㄨㄟˇ roei ruǐ
1. a flower bud; an unopened flower
2. the stamens or pistils of a flower

【蕎】 5094 ㄑㄧㄠˊ chyau qiáo
buckwheat
蕎麥(ㄑㄧㄠˊ ㄇㄞˋ)
buckwheat
蕎麥麪(ㄑㄧㄠˊ ㄇㄞˋ ㄇㄧㄢˋ)
①buckwheat flour ②noodles or vermicelli made with buckwheat flour

【蕕】 5095 ㄧㄡˊ you yóu
Caryopteris divaricata, a water plant with a foul smell that lasts very long—usually used figuratively to indicate an evil person

【蕘】 5096 ㄖㄠˊ rau ráo
1. grass or rushes, etc. used for fuel
2. *Wikstroemia japonica*, a kind of shrub about three feet tall with yellow flowers, whose bark is used for making paper
3. the turnip
4. firewood-gatherers

【蕙】 5097 ㄏㄨㄟˋ huey huì
1. a species of fragrant grass with red flowers and black seeds in early fall
2. a species of fragrant orchid
蕙蘭(ㄏㄨㄟˋ ㄌㄢˊ)
a species of fragrant orchid having seven to eight flowers to one stalk
蕙心(ㄏㄨㄟˋ ㄒㄧㄣ)
a pure heart
蕙質(ㄏㄨㄟˋ ㄓˋ)
a good and pure quality (of a person)
蕙質蘭心(ㄏㄨㄟˋ ㄓˋ ㄌㄢˊ ㄒㄧㄣ)
(said of a lady) beautiful and intelligent
蕙折蘭摧(ㄏㄨㄟˋ ㄓㄜˊ ㄌㄢˊ ㄘㄨㄟ)
The good and pure are destroyed.
蕙若(ㄏㄨㄟˋ ㄖㄨㄛˋ)
two species of fragrant grass, used figuratively in reference to good people

【蕡】 5098 ㄈㄣˊ fern fén
1. the seeds of hemp
2. (said of fruit) large and abundant
3. a Chinese family name

【蕞】 5099 ㄗㄨㄟˋ tzuey zuì
very small; tiny
蕞爾小國(ㄗㄨㄟˋ ㄦˇ ㄒㄧㄠˇ ㄍㄨㄛˊ)
a very small state

【蕢】 5100 ㄎㄨㄟˋ kuey kuì
1. a straw basket
2. a vegetable with a red stalk
3. a Chinese family name

【蕨】 5101 ㄐㄩㄝˊ jyue jué
the bracken

【蕭】 5102 ㄒㄧㄠ shiau xiāo
1. a common variety of artemisia; oxtail-southernwood
2. reverent; respectful
3. quiet; lonely; desolate
4. a Chinese family name
蕭伯納(ㄒㄧㄠ ㄅㄛˊ ㄋㄚˋ)
George Bernard Shaw (1856-1950), Irish dramatist and critic
蕭邦(ㄒㄧㄠ ㄅㄤ)
Frederic Francois Chopin (1810-1849), famous Polish pianist and composer
蕭條(ㄒㄧㄠ ㄊㄧㄠˊ)
①(said of a place or situation) deserted; desolate ②(said of business) sluggish; depressed; slack
蕭統(ㄒㄧㄠ ㄊㄨㄥˇ)
Hsiao Tung (501-531), also known as Prince Chao-ming (昭明太子), the compiler of 昭明文選, a 60-volume collection of literary works from the Chin Dynasty down to his era
蕭娘(ㄒㄧㄠ ㄋㄧㄤˊ)
a reference to girls in the poems of the Tang Dynasty
蕭郎(ㄒㄧㄠ ㄌㄤˊ)
a reference to a male-lover in the poems of the Tang Dynasty
蕭梁(ㄒㄧㄠ ㄌㄧㄤˊ)
the Liang Dynasty (502-557) founded by Hsiao Yen (蕭衍), during the South and North Dynasties (南北朝), as distinguished from the Liang Dynasty (後梁, 907-923) of the Five Dynasties (五代)
蕭規曹隨(ㄒㄧㄠ ㄍㄨㄟ ㄘㄠˊ ㄙㄨㄟˊ)
(literally) Hsiao Ho (蕭何) laid down the rules and Tsao Shen (曹參) followed them.—to follow the rules, methods, etc. of one's predecessor; to move in a rut; to follow suit
蕭何(ㄒㄧㄠ ㄏㄜˊ)
Hsiao Ho (?-193), who helped the first emperor of the Han Dynasty unify the whole nation and who authored many laws and regulations observed during the Han Dynasty
蕭牆之禍(ㄒㄧㄠ ㄑㄧㄤˊ ㄓ ㄏㄨㄛˋ)
a civil strife, disaster or trouble within

蕭蕭(ㄒㄧㄠ ㄒㄧㄠ)
①the whistling of strong winds ②the rustling sound of falling leaves ③ the neighing of a horse
蕭齋(ㄒㄧㄠ ㄓㄞ)
①a humble house ②a Buddhist temple
蕭晨(ㄒㄧㄠ ㄔㄣˊ)
the autumn morning
蕭疎(ㄒㄧㄠ ㄕㄨ)
(said of leaves) scattered and bleak
蕭然(ㄒㄧㄠ ㄖㄢˊ)
①desolate; deserted ②in commotion; disorderly
蕭寺(ㄒㄧㄠ ㄙˋ)
monasteries in the Liang Dynasty, A.D. 502-557, because Liang Wu Ti(梁武帝) built so many that they were called after his surname Hsiao(蕭)
蕭灑(ㄒㄧㄠ ㄙㄚˇ)
elegant; stately and easy (in one's appearance and manner)
蕭颯(ㄒㄧㄠ ㄙㄚˋ)
cool and soothing winds of autumn
蕭瑟(ㄒㄧㄠ ㄙㄜˋ)
①rough and stormy; chilly, desolate, deserted, lonely, etc.②rustle in the air; to rustle; to sough: 秋風蕭瑟。The autumn wind is soughing.
蕭騷(ㄒㄧㄠ ㄙㄠ)
desolate; lonely
蕭散(ㄒㄧㄠ ㄙㄢˇ)
uninhibited and carefree
蕭森(ㄒㄧㄠ ㄙㄣ)
desolate; lonely
蕭索(ㄒㄧㄠ ㄙㄨㄛˇ)
deserted; chilly; lonely
蕭艾(ㄒㄧㄠ ㄞˋ)
the worst variety of grass—evil elements

【蕤】 5103
ㄖㄨㄟˊ ruei ruí
1. drooping leaves, flowers or fruits
2. a shrub about three feet tall with narrow leaves and white flowers
蕤賓(ㄖㄨㄟˊ ㄅㄧㄣ)
a musical pitch roughly equivalent to an F-sharp

【蕩】 5104
ㄉㄤˋ danq dàng
1. a pond; a pool
2. to cleanse; to wash away
3. to shake; to oscillate; to move to and fro; unsettled; vagrant; to loaf about
4. dissipated; wanton; debauched; licentious; of loose morals
5. agitated; disturbed
6. vast; large; magnificent
蕩平(ㄉㄤˋ ㄆㄧㄥˊ)
to quell (a rebellion); to wipe out; to stamp out
蕩婦(ㄉㄤˋ ㄈㄨˋ)
a woman of loose morals; a dissolute woman
蕩蕩(ㄉㄤˋ ㄉㄤˋ)
①vast; large ②to be satisfied and composed ③spoilt or ruined
蕩蕩悠悠(ㄉㄤˋ ㄉㄤˋ ㄧㄡ ㄧㄡ)
swinging; moving to and fro; to shake and move
蕩滌(ㄉㄤˋ ㄉㄧˊ)
to cleanse; to wash out; to clean up: 他們蕩滌水溝。They cleaned up the ditch.
蕩寇(ㄉㄤˋ ㄎㄡˋ)
to eliminate bandits
蕩檢逾閑(ㄉㄤˋ ㄐㄧㄢˇ ㄩˊ ㄒㄧㄢˊ)
not restrained by propriety or rules; wanton
蕩氣迴腸(ㄉㄤˋ ㄑㄧˋ ㄏㄨㄟˊ ㄔㄤˊ)
(said of music or writing) very touching; pathetic
蕩鞦韆(ㄉㄤˋ ㄑㄧㄡ ㄑㄧㄢ)
to swing on a swing
蕩析(ㄉㄤˋ ㄒㄧ)
(said of the people in troubled times) dispersed or separated
蕩產(ㄉㄤˋ ㄔㄢˇ)
to bankrupt; to be bankrupt; to go bankrupt
蕩產傾家(ㄉㄤˋ ㄔㄢˇ ㄑㄧㄥ ㄐㄧㄚ)
to squander inherited property and ruin the family
蕩船(ㄉㄤˋ ㄔㄨㄢˊ)
to row a boat; boating
蕩然(ㄉㄤˋ ㄖㄢˊ)
all gone; entirely wasted or spent
蕩然無存(ㄉㄤˋ ㄖㄢˊ ㄨˊ ㄘㄨㄣˊ)
to have nothing left; everything ruined; completely gone; wiped out
蕩子(ㄉㄤˋ ㄗˇ)
①a vagrant; a jobless and dissipated person ②a traveler to a distant land having no thought of returning home
蕩漾(ㄉㄤˋ ㄧㄤˋ)
①moving, as in ripples: 湖水蕩漾。There were ripples on the lake. ② agitated or excited ③to rise and fall like waves; to ripple: 金黃色的稻子在微風中蕩漾。The golden rice rippled in the breeze.

【蕁】 5105
ㄒㄩㄣˊ shyun xún
as in 蕁蔴—an urtica
蕁蔴(ㄒㄩㄣˊ ㄇㄚˊ)
an urtica; a nettle
蕁蔴疹(ㄒㄩㄣˊ ㄇㄚˊ ㄓㄣˇ)
(pathology) nettle rash; urticaria 亦作「風疹」

【蕈】 5106
ㄒㄩㄣˋ shiunn xùn
1. a mushroom; fungus
2. mold, or mildew

【蕪】 5107
ㄨˊ wu wú
1. a luxuriant growth of weeds
2. decayed or rotten vegetation
3. confused; mixed-up; in disorder
4. waste; neglected, as land
蕪駁(ㄨˊ ㄅㄛˊ)
disorderly or mixed-up; confused
蕪累(ㄨˊ ㄌㄟˋ)
mixed-up and superfluous
蕪俚(ㄨˊ ㄌㄧˇ)
coarse and vulgar
蕪湖(ㄨˊ ㄏㄨˊ)
Wuhu, name of a lake and a county in Anhwei Province
蕪穢(ㄨˊ ㄏㄨㄟˋ)
the luxuriant growth of weeds in deserted fields
蕪菁(ㄨˊ ㄐㄧㄥ)
the turnip
蕪雜(ㄨˊ ㄗㄚˊ)
(usually referring to a piece of writing) disorderly and confusing; mixed-up and illogical

〔艸部〕

【蕖】 5108
ㄑㄩˊ chyu qú
1. a taro
2. as in 芙蕖 —a lotus flower

【蕝】 5109
ㄐㄩㄝˊ jyue jué
as in 茅蕝 —to designate an assigned position in practicing a court ceremony

【蕓】 5110
ㄩㄣˊ yun yún
蕓薹(ㄩㄣˊ ㄊㄞˊ)
rape 亦作「油菜」

十三畫

【薄】 5111
1. ㄅㄛˊ bor bó
(語音 ㄅㄠˊ baur báo)
1. thin; light; slight: 這是一張薄紙。This is a thin sheet of paper.
2. to despise; to slight; to disdain: 他厚此薄彼。He favored this and slighted that.
3. barren; not fertile
4. to cover; to hide or conceal; to shut
5. a screen
6. a patch of grass
7. to close in; to press near: 日薄西山。The sun is near the western hills.
8. an initial particle—ah; so; now
9. frivolous: 它是輕薄的話。It is a frivolous remark.
10. a Chinese family name

薄餅(ㄅㄛˊ ㄅㄧㄥˇ)
thin pancakes for wrapping up meat, vegetables, etc.

薄片(ㄅㄛˊ ㄆㄧㄢˋ)
a thin slice; a thin section: 他把檸檬切成薄片。 He cut a lemon into thin slices.

薄媚(ㄅㄛˊ ㄇㄟˋ)
very light make-up—that adds more to her charms

薄命(ㄅㄛˊ ㄇㄧㄥˋ)
① star-crossed; ill-fated; born unlucky (usually referring to young and beautiful girls) ② short-lived: 她是個薄命佳人。She was a short-lived beauty.

薄命女子負心漢(ㄅㄛˊ ㄇㄧㄥˋ ㄋㄩˇ ㄗˇ ㄈㄨˋ ㄒㄧㄣ ㄏㄢˋ)
an unfortunate girl and a heartless man

薄暮(ㄅㄛˊ ㄇㄨˋ)
around sunset; dusk

薄暮之年(ㄅㄛˊ ㄇㄨˋ ㄓ ㄋㄧㄢˊ)
old age; approaching one's grave; the sunset of life

薄夫(ㄅㄛˊ ㄈㄨ)
a person with little sentiment or affection

薄福(ㄅㄛˊ ㄈㄨˊ)
(a life) with little joy, happiness or bliss

薄待(ㄅㄛˊ ㄉㄞˋ)
to treat (a person) rather badly: 她一向薄待他人。She always treats others badly.

薄田(ㄅㄛˊ ㄊㄧㄢˊ)
barren or unfertile land

薄陋(ㄅㄛˊ ㄌㄡˋ)
without talent or ability

薄禮(ㄅㄛˊ ㄌㄧˇ)
a meager present; my humble gift (as a polite usage)

薄利多銷(ㄅㄛˊ ㄌㄧˋ ㄉㄨㄛ ㄒㄧㄠ)
small profits but a quick turnover; small profits and quick returns; to cut down the profit margin in order to sell more—commercial tactics

薄海騰歡(ㄅㄛˊ ㄏㄞˇ ㄊㄥˊ ㄏㄨㄢ)
cheers from all over the country

薄宦(ㄅㄛˊ ㄏㄨㄢˋ)
a low-ranking official position

薄技(ㄅㄛˊ ㄐㄧˋ)
meager skills or feats not worth mentioning; my poor skill (a polite usage)

薄酒(ㄅㄛˊ ㄐㄧㄡˇ)
(a polite expression) dilute wine

薄具(ㄅㄛˊ ㄐㄩˋ)
(a polite expression) coarse food

薄情(ㄅㄛˊ ㄑㄧㄥˊ)
heartless; ungrateful

薄情郎(ㄅㄛˊ ㄑㄧㄥˊ ㄌㄤˊ)
a heartless lover; an unfaithful husband

薄曉(ㄅㄛˊ ㄒㄧㄠˇ)
around sunrise; dawn

薄行(ㄅㄛˊ ㄒㄧㄥˋ)
unscrupulous conduct; immoral behavior

薄倖(ㄅㄛˊ ㄒㄧㄥˋ)
heartlessness (especially concerning love)

薄懲(ㄅㄛˊ ㄔㄥˊ)
a light punishment

薄生生的(ㄅㄛˊ ㄕㄥ ㄕㄥ ·ㄉㄜ)
thin and easily breakable

薄弱(ㄅㄛˊ ㄖㄨㄛˋ)
weak; fragile: 他是個意志薄弱之人。He is a man of weak character.

薄脆(ㄅㄛˊ ㄘㄨㄟˋ)
thin and brittle (biscuits)

薄俗(ㄅㄛˊ ㄙㄨˊ)
very practical customs that reflect no sense of hospitality, love, etc.

薄物細故(ㄅㄛˊ ㄨˋ ㄒㄧˋ ㄍㄨˋ)
trifles; trivial matters

【薄】 5111
2. ㄅㄛˋ boh bò
peppermint

薄荷(ㄅㄛˋ ·ㄏㄜ)
peppermint

薄荷精(ㄅㄛˋ ·ㄏㄜ ㄐㄧㄥ)or 薄荷腦(ㄅㄛˋ ·ㄏㄜ ㄋㄠˇ)
menthol

薄荷油(ㄅㄛˋ ·ㄏㄜ ㄧㄡˊ)
peppermint oil

【薅】 5112
ㄏㄠ hau hāo
to weed (rice fields, etc.); to root out; to pick off; to clear away

【蕷】 5113
ㄩˋ yuh yù
as in 薯蕷—the Chinese yam

【蕾】 5114
ㄌㄟˇ leei lěi
as in 蓓蕾—a flower bud; an unopened flower

【薆】 5115
ㄞˋ ay ài
1. a luxuriant growth of vegetation
2. to cover; to hide; to conceal; to be under cover

【薇】 5116
ㄨㄟˊ wei wéi
1. *Osmunda regalis*, a kind of fern; thorn-ferns
2. used with other characters for a variety of plants

【薈】 5117
ㄏㄨㄟˋ huey huì
1. a luxuriant growth of vegetation
2. to cover or conceal

薈萃(ㄏㄨㄟˋ ㄘㄨㄟˋ)
① flourishing or thriving ②

(said of distinguished people) to gather; to assemble

薈蔚(ㄏㄨㄟˋ ㄨㄟˋ)
a dense and luxuriant growth of vegetation

【薊】 5118 ㄐㄧˋ jih jì

1. *Cirsium*, a family of thorny plants
2. a Chinese family name

【薌】 5119 ㄒㄧㄤ shiang xiāng

1. the smell of rice grains
2. aromatic; spicy; a pleasant smell
3. incense used for fumigation

【薏】 5120 ㄧˋ yih yì

1. the heart of a lotus seed
2. the seeds of Job's tears; pearl barley, used for cooking congee with rice or in herbal medicine

薏米(ㄧˋ ㄇㄧˇ)
(Chinese medicine) the seed of Job's tears 亦作「薏仁米」

【薐】 5121 ㄌㄥˊ leng léng

old name of spinach

【薑】 5122 ㄐㄧㄤ jiang jiāng

ginger

薑餅(ㄐㄧㄤ ㄅㄧㄥˇ)
gingerbread; gingersnaps: 他喜歡吃薑餅。He likes gingerbread.

薑片蟲(ㄐㄧㄤ ㄆㄧㄢˋ ㄔㄨㄥˊ)
Fasciolopsis buski, an intestinal parasite

薑桂(ㄐㄧㄤ ㄍㄨㄟˋ)
① ginger and cinnamon ② stubborn; unyielding; unshakable

薑黃(ㄐㄧㄤ ㄏㄨㄤˊ)
curcuma; turmeric

薑黃紙(ㄐㄧㄤ ㄏㄨㄤˊ ㄓˇ)
curcuma paper; turmeric paper

薑酒(ㄐㄧㄤ ㄐㄧㄡˇ)
ginger wine

薑汁(ㄐㄧㄤ ㄓ)
ginger juice

薑汁汽水(ㄐㄧㄤ ㄓ ㄑㄧˋ ㄕㄨㄟˇ)
ginger ale

【薔】 5123 ㄑㄧㄤˊ chyang qiáng

the roses

薔薇(ㄑㄧㄤˊ ㄨㄟˊ)
the roses

薔薇科(ㄑㄧㄤˊ ㄨㄟˊ ㄎㄜ)
Rosaceae, the rose family

薔薇戰爭(ㄑㄧㄤˊ ㄨㄟˊ ㄓㄢˋ ㄓㄥ)
Britain's "War of the Roses" (1455-1485)

【薙】 5124 ㄊㄧˋ tih tì

1. to weed
2. to cut (hair); to shave (hair)

薙髮(ㄊㄧˋ ㄈㄚˇ)
to cut hair; a haircut; to shave hair

薙刀(ㄊㄧˋ ㄉㄠ)
a shaving knife or razor

【薛】 5125 ㄒㄩㄝ shiue xuē

1. a kind of marsh grass
2. name of an ancient state in today's Shantung Province
3. a Chinese family name

【薤】 5126 ㄒㄧㄝˋ shieh xiè

Allium bakeri, a vegetable roughly resembling a leek with tiny purple flowers in summer whose scaly stalks are edible when tender

薤露(ㄒㄧㄝˋ ㄌㄨˋ)
name of an ancient funeral song

【薦】 5127 ㄐㄧㄢˋ jiann jiàn

1. to recommend; to offer; to present
2. fodder for animals; grass
3. a straw mat; a mat, especially for sleeping
4. food and dishes
5. to repeat; repeatedly

薦拔(ㄐㄧㄢˋ ㄅㄚˊ)
to recommend and promote

薦酒(ㄐㄧㄢˋ ㄐㄧㄡˇ)
to offer wine

薦舉(ㄐㄧㄢˋ ㄐㄩˇ) or 薦引(ㄐㄧㄢˋ ㄧㄣˇ)
to propose; to introduce; to recommend (a competent person for a post): 他薦引同志。He introduced a comrade.

薦賢(ㄐㄧㄢˋ ㄒㄧㄢˊ)
to recommend, introduce or present a good and capable person

薦賢自代(ㄐㄧㄢˋ ㄒㄧㄢˊ ㄗˋ ㄉㄞˋ)
to recommend one's own successor upon leaving a post; to recommend a good man in place of oneself

薦枕席(ㄐㄧㄢˋ ㄓㄣˇ ㄒㄧˊ)
(said of a woman) to volunteer to sleep with a man

薦擢(ㄐㄧㄢˋ ㄓㄨㄛˊ)
to recommend and employ

薦任(ㄐㄧㄢˋ ㄖㄣˋ)
recommended appointment rank, the second of the three grades in the civil service of modern China

薦任官(ㄐㄧㄢˋ ㄖㄣˋ ㄍㄨㄢ)
an official of recommended appointment rank

薦材(ㄐㄧㄢˋ ㄘㄞˊ)
to recommend or present a talented person

【薨】 5128 ㄏㄨㄥ hong hōng

1. the death of a feudal lord
2. the loud buzzing of insects in flight

薨薨(ㄏㄨㄥ ㄏㄨㄥ)
① the loud buzzing of insects in flight ② the chattering and shouting of the people ③ numerous

【薪】 5129 ㄒㄧㄣ shin xīn

1. firewood; fuel; faggots
2. salary; pay

薪俸(ㄒㄧㄣ ㄈㄥˋ) or 薪金(ㄒㄧㄣ ㄐㄧㄣ) or 薪水(ㄒㄧㄣ ㄕㄨㄟˇ)
one's salary or pay; wages

薪桂米珠(ㄒㄧㄣ ㄍㄨㄟˋ ㄇㄧˇ ㄓㄨ)
the high cost of living (with firewood bought at the price of cinnamon and rice at the price of pearls)

薪工(ㄒㄧㄣ ㄍㄨㄥ)
wages; pay

薪火(ㄒㄧㄣ ㄏㄨㄛˇ)
① a torch ② the torch of learning passed from master to pupil

薪盡火傳(ㄒㄧㄣ ㄐㄧㄣˋ ㄏㄨㄛˇ ㄔㄨㄢˊ) or 薪傳(ㄒㄧㄣ ㄔㄨㄢˊ)
a learning, skill, etc. passing from master to pupil in endless succession

薪水階級(ㄒㄧㄣ ㄕㄨㄟˇ ㄐㄧㄝ ㄐㄧˊ)
the white-collar workers

【蕺】 5130 ㄐㄧˊ jyi jí

Houttuynia cordata, a smelly

〔艸部〕

but edible vegetable with light yellow flowers in summer 亦作「蕺菜」

【薜】 5131 1. ㄅㄛˋ boh bò
Chinese angelica; angelica radix 亦作「當歸」

【薜】 5131 2. ㄅㄧˋ bih bì
Ficus pumila, a climbing fig 參看「薜荔」

薜荔(ㄅㄧˋ ㄌㄧˋ)
Ficus pumila; a climbing fig

薜蘿(ㄅㄧˋ ㄌㄨㄛˊ)
the clothing of a hermit

十四畫

【薩】 5132 ㄙㄚˋ sah sà
1. a general name of Buddhist gods or immortals; Buddha
2. a Chinese family name

薩摩亞(ㄙㄚˋ ㄇㄛˊ ㄧㄚˇ)
Samoa

薩克遜人(ㄙㄚˋ ㄎㄜˋ ㄒㄩㄣˋ ㄖㄣˊ)
the Saxons

薩爾瓦多(ㄙㄚˋ ㄦˇ ㄨㄚˇ ㄉㄨㄛ)
El Salvador

薩伊(ㄙㄚˋ ㄧ)
Republic of Zaire

【薯】 5133 ㄕㄨˇ shuu shǔ
a yam; a potato

薯條(ㄕㄨˇ ㄊㄧㄠˊ)
French fries: 他喜歡吃薯條。He likes French fries.

薯蕷(ㄕㄨˇ ㄩˋ)
a yam 亦作「山藥」

【薰】 5134 ㄒㄩㄣ shiun xūn
1. to cauterize
2. to perfume; to embalm
3. to smoke; to fumigate
4. warm
5. *Coumarouna odorata*, a medical herb with a strong smell

薰沐(ㄒㄩㄣ ㄇㄨˋ)
to burn incense and take a bath—a gesture of great respect

薰風(ㄒㄩㄣ ㄈㄥ)
a warm wind from the south

薰腐(ㄒㄩㄣ ㄈㄨˇ)
the punishment of castration in ancient China

薰陶(ㄒㄩㄣ ㄊㄠˊ)
to mold a person's character, etc. through the influence of education, proper discipline, good examples, etc.; to edify

薰爐(ㄒㄩㄣ ㄌㄨˊ)
a brazier

薰心(ㄒㄩㄣ ㄒㄧㄣ)
to becloud the mind (with lust, greed, sexual desire, etc.): 他這人利慾薰心。His mind is beclouded by greed.

薰香(ㄒㄩㄣ ㄒㄧㄤ)
perfume; fragrance

薰蒸(ㄒㄩㄣ ㄓㄥ)
(said of the sultry heat in summer) to swelter and steam

薰然(ㄒㄩㄣ ㄖㄢˊ)
gently; amiably; warmly

薰染(ㄒㄩㄣ ㄖㄢˇ)
to be influenced and contaminated by one's surroundings

薰蕕(ㄒㄩㄣ ㄧㄡˊ)
fragrant and noisome grasses—good and evil people

【薺】 5135 1. ㄐㄧˋ jih jì
Capsella bursa-pastoris, a kind of vegetable; shepherd's-purse

薺菜(ㄐㄧˋ ㄘㄞˋ)
shepherd's-purse (*Capsella bursa-pastoris*)

【薺】 5135 2. ㄑㄧˊ chyi qí
1. the caltrop 亦作「蒺藜」
2. a water chestnut 亦作「荸薺」

【藉】 5136 1. ㄐㄧㄝˋ jieh jiè
1. a mat, pad, or cushion of grass (or straw)
2. to rely on; to lean on; on the strength of; to avail oneself of; by means of: 憑藉你自己的努力。Rely on your own efforts.
3. on the excuse or pretext of

藉端(ㄐㄧㄝˋ ㄉㄨㄢ)
on the excuse or pretext of

藉端敲詐(ㄐㄧㄝˋ ㄉㄨㄢ ㄑㄧㄠ ㄓㄚˋ)
to blackmail by taking advantage of a certain occasion or occurrence

藉端生事(ㄐㄧㄝˋ ㄉㄨㄢ ㄕㄥ ㄕˋ)
to stir up trouble on the pretext or excuse of something

藉故(ㄐㄧㄝˋ ㄍㄨˋ)
to avail oneself of a certain excuse or pretext

藉故推辭(ㄐㄧㄝˋ ㄍㄨˋ ㄊㄨㄟ ㄘˊ)
to decline or reject with an excuse or pretext

藉口(ㄐㄧㄝˋ ㄎㄡˇ)
an excuse; a pretext; to seize an excuse or pretext: 那不是一個好藉口。It is not a good excuse

藉重(ㄐㄧㄝˋ ㄓㄨㄥˋ)
(a polite expression) to rely on (your, his or her) capability

藉手(ㄐㄧㄝˋ ㄕㄡˇ)
by means of; by (another's) hand, as a murder, etc.

藉甚(ㄐㄧㄝˋ ㄕㄣˋ)
(said of reputation) exalted; great

藉資(ㄐㄧㄝˋ ㄗ)
to avail oneself of something in order to

藉詞(ㄐㄧㄝˋ ㄘˊ)
to make excuses; on the pretext of 參看「藉口」: 他藉詞卸責。He shirked his responsibility by making an excuse.

藉此(ㄐㄧㄝˋ ㄘˇ)
in order to; by means of; to take advantage of: 我們並未好好藉此機會發揮。We're not taking proper advantage of this opportunity.

【藉】 5136 2. ㄐㄧˊ jyi jí
disorder; confusion

藉藉(ㄐㄧˊ ㄐㄧˊ)
(in) disorder or confusion

【藍】 5137 ㄌㄢˊ lan lán
1. blue; indigo: 他打著一條藍領帶。He wears a blue necktie.
2. an indigo plant
3. a Chinese family name

藍寶石(ㄌㄢˊ ㄅㄠˇ ㄕˊ)
sapphire

藍本(ㄌㄢˊ ㄅㄣˇ)
the original; a blueprint

藍布(ㄌㄢˊ ㄅㄨˋ)
blue cloth

藍布大褂(ㄌㄢˊ ㄅㄨˋ ㄉㄚˋ ㄍㄨㄚˋ)
the long blue-cloth gown worn by men

藍皮書(ㄌㄢˊ ㄆㄧˊ ㄕㄨ)
the blue book

藍方石(ㄌㄢˊ ㄈㄤ ㄕˊ)
hauynite
藍靛(ㄌㄢˊ ㄉㄧㄢˋ)
indigo
藍鐵鑛(ㄌㄢˊ ㄊㄧㄝˇ ㄎㄨㄤˋ)
vivianite
藍田(ㄌㄢˊ ㄊㄧㄢˊ)
name of a county and a hill in Shensi Province, famous for producing precious jade
藍田種玉(ㄌㄢˊ ㄊㄧㄢˊ ㄓㄨㄥˋ ㄩˋ)
to make a girl or woman impregnated
藍田生玉(ㄌㄢˊ ㄊㄧㄢˊ ㄕㄥ ㄩˋ)
A good and capable father begets good and capable sons.
藍圖(ㄌㄢˊ ㄊㄨˊ)
a blueprint; an outline of a project
藍銅鑛(ㄌㄢˊ ㄊㄨㄥˊ ㄎㄨㄤˋ)
azurite
藍領階級(ㄌㄢˊ ㄌㄧㄥˇ ㄐㄧㄝ ㄐㄧˊ)
blue-collar
藍晶石(ㄌㄢˊ ㄐㄧㄥ ㄕˊ)
cyanite
藍青(ㄌㄢˊ ㄑㄧㄥ)
① indigo blue; a color that combines blue and green ② mixed (especially referring to a form of spoken Mandarin)
藍青官話(ㄌㄢˊ ㄑㄧㄥ ㄍㄨㄢ ㄏㄨㄚˋ)
spoken Mandarin with a local accent
藍試紙(ㄌㄢˊ ㄕˋ ㄓˇ)
litmus paper
藍色申報(ㄌㄢˊ ㄙㄜˋ ㄕㄣ ㄅㄠˋ)
a blue return

【藎】 5138
ㄐㄧㄣˋ jinn jìn
1. *Arthraxon hispidus*, a kind of weed whose stalk is used as a yellow dye
2. faithfulness; great loyalty and love
藎臣(ㄐㄧㄣˋ ㄔㄣˊ)
a loyal official; a loyal minister

【藏】 5139
1. ㄘㄤˊ tsarng cáng
1. to hide; to conceal
2. to store; to save; to hoard: 松鼠聚藏堅果過冬。A squirrel hoards nuts for the winter.
3. a Chinese family name
藏不住(ㄘㄤˊ ˙ㄅㄨ ㄓㄨˋ)
cannot be hidden (any longer); (said of a talkative person) cannot keep a secret: 他藏不住秘密。He can not keep a secret.
藏鋒(ㄘㄤˊ ㄈㄥ)
① hidden talent or ability (which one doesn't want to reveal unless absolutely necessary) ② a style of calligraphy
藏伏(ㄘㄤˊ ㄈㄨˊ)
to hide or conceal; to lie low
藏頭露尾(ㄘㄤˊ ㄊㄡˊ ㄌㄡˋ ㄨㄟˇ)
(literally) to hide the head but show the tail—① to try to hide something without success ② to reveal part of the truth and conceal the rest
藏匿(ㄘㄤˊ ㄋㄧˋ)
to hide; to conceal; to harbor (criminals)
藏怒(ㄘㄤˊ ㄋㄨˋ)
to harbor wrath in one's mind; to lay up anger
藏垢納污(ㄘㄤˊ ㄍㄡˋ ㄋㄚˋ ㄨ)
(said of disreputable places) to receive evil people; to harbor criminals
藏庋(ㄘㄤˊ ㄐㄧˇ)
to store or hoard
藏嬌(ㄘㄤˊ ㄐㄧㄠ)
to keep one's mistress at a secret residence; to marry a concubine
藏奸(ㄘㄤˊ ㄐㄧㄢ)
① to harbor treachery or guilt ② unwilling to help another though one has power to spare
藏器待時(ㄘㄤˊ ㄑㄧˋ ㄉㄞˋ ㄕˊ)
to wait for the right moment to demonstrate one's ability; to use one's talent or ability when the time comes
藏拙(ㄘㄤˊ ㄓㄨㄛˊ)
to hide one's weak points; to keep one's weaknesses unexposed
藏室史(ㄘㄤˊ ㄕˋ ㄕˇ)
an official librarian in ancient China
藏身(ㄘㄤˊ ㄕㄣ)
to hide oneself; to go into hiding; to conceal: 他無處藏身。He has no place to hide.
藏身之地(ㄘㄤˊ ㄕㄣ ㄓ ㄉㄧˋ)
a hiding place; a place to hide oneself; a hideout; a place to keep oneself out of sight
藏書(ㄘㄤˊ ㄕㄨ)
① to collect books ② a book collection
藏書目錄(ㄘㄤˊ ㄕㄨ ㄇㄨˋ ㄌㄨˋ)
a library catalogue
藏書樓(ㄘㄤˊ ㄕㄨ ㄌㄡˊ)
a library
藏書家(ㄘㄤˊ ㄕㄨ ㄐㄧㄚ)
a book collector; a bibliophile: 他是個藏書家。He is a bibliophile.
藏藏躲躲(ㄘㄤˊ ˙ㄘㄤ ㄉㄨㄛˇ ㄉㄨㄛˇ)
unwilling to appear before others because of social timidity, bashfulness or a secret
藏私(ㄘㄤˊ ㄙ)
to hide part of a full account of something; unwilling to reveal all
藏掖(ㄘㄤˊ ㄧㄝ)
① a hiding place; a hideout ② to conceal or hide a dishonest act, etc.

【藏】 5139
2. ㄗㄤˋ tzanq zàng
1. Tibet; Tibetans
2. a storage; a warehouse; a depository
3. a collective name for the Buddhist and Taoist scriptures
藏胞(ㄗㄤˋ ㄅㄠ)
the Tibetans (used in the sense that they form part of the Chinese race)
藏府(ㄗㄤˋ ㄈㄨˇ)
a storage; a warehouse; government coffers
藏藍(ㄗㄤˋ ㄌㄢˊ)
a reddish-blue color
藏青(ㄗㄤˋ ㄑㄧㄥ)
indigo blue
藏族(ㄗㄤˋ ㄗㄨˊ)
the Tibetans; the Tibetan people
藏文(ㄗㄤˋ ㄨㄣˊ)
the Tibetan language

【藐】 5140
ㄇㄧㄠˇ meau miǎo
1. to slight; to despise; to belit-

〔艸部〕

〔艸 部〕

tle; to treat with disdain
2. small; petite; petty; insignificant
藐藐(ㄇㄧㄠˇ ㄇㄧㄠˇ)
①descriptive of a contemptuous manner ② (said of Heaven) high and distant—mysterious ③ grand; magnificent
藐法(ㄇㄧㄠˇ ㄈㄚˇ)
to disregard the law; to treat the law with contempt
藐孤(ㄇㄧㄠˇ ㄍㄨ)
a small orphan
藐小(ㄇㄧㄠˇ ㄒㄧㄠˇ)
small; petty; insignificant
藐視(ㄇㄧㄠˇ ㄕˋ)
to treat with contempt or disdain; to disdain; to slight; to look down upon; to despise; to belittle
藐視一切(ㄇㄧㄠˇ ㄕˋ ㄧˊ ㄑㄧㄝˋ)
to treat everything lightly or carelessly; to look down upon everything; to despise everything

【蘶】 5141 ㄨㄟˇ woei woei
1. polygala, a herb
2. a Chinese family name

十五畫

【藕】 5142 ㄡˇ oou oǒu
rhizomes, or rootstocks of the lotus
藕棒兒(ㄡˇ ㄅㄤˋㄦ)
① rootstocks of the lotus ②(figuratively) woman's or child's white and fat arms
藕粉(ㄡˇ ㄈㄣˇ)
starch extracted from the rhizomes of lotuses
藕斷絲連(ㄡˇ ㄉㄨㄢˋ ㄙ ㄌㄧㄢˊ)
The rootstock is split but the fibers are still joined. —The ties are severed but not completely.
藕花(ㄡˇ ㄏㄨㄚ)
a lotus flower
藕灰(ㄡˇ ㄏㄨㄟ)
light grayish red
藕節(ㄡˇ ㄐㄧㄝˊ) or 藕節兒(ㄡˇ ㄐㄧㄝˊㄦ)
joints of the rhizome of a lotus
藕絲(ㄡˇ ㄙ)
the fibers of the rhizome of a lotus
藕色(ㄡˇ ㄙㄜˋ)
light grayish red; pale purple

【藜】 5143 ㄌㄧˊ lii lí
pigweeds; lamb's-quarters
藜羹(ㄌㄧˊ ㄍㄥ)
coarse food
藜藿(ㄌㄧˊ ㄏㄨㄛˋ)
coarse food (of commoners in ancient times)
藜藿不采(ㄌㄧˊ ㄏㄨㄛˋ ㄅㄨˋ ㄘㄞˇ)
not daring to go to the hills to pick edible grass
藜蕨(ㄌㄧˊ ㄐㄩㄝˊ)
coarse food
藜杖(ㄌㄧˊ ㄓㄤˋ)
a pigweed staff
藜牀(ㄌㄧˊ ㄔㄨㄤˊ)
a pigweed bed

【藝】 5144 ㄧˋ yih yì
art; skill; talent; craft; dexterity: 她繪畫的技藝很高。She has great skill in painting.
藝名(ㄧˋ ㄇㄧㄥˊ)
a stage name, or a screen name (of an entertainer)
藝徒(ㄧˋ ㄊㄨˊ)
an apprentice
藝能(ㄧˋ ㄋㄥˊ)
artistic skill; art; skill
藝林(ㄧˋ ㄌㄧㄣˊ)
①an artistic or literary salon ② the world of art; the artistic circles
藝林瓌寶(ㄧˋ ㄌㄧㄣˊ ㄍㄨㄟ ㄅㄠˇ)
a collection of art treasures
藝高膽大(ㄧˋ ㄍㄠ ㄉㄢˇ ㄉㄚˋ)
The talented or skilled are generally bold. 或 Boldness of execution stems from superb skill.
藝妓(ㄧˋ ㄐㄧˋ)
a geisha girl; a geisha
藝術(ㄧˋ ㄕㄨˋ)
art
藝術品(ㄧˋ ㄕㄨˋ ㄆㄧㄣˇ)
a work of art; an objet d'art
藝術天才(ㄧˋ ㄕㄨˋ ㄊㄧㄢ ㄘㄞˊ)
a gift for art; an artistic talent
藝術家(ㄧˋ ㄕㄨˋ ㄐㄧㄚ)
an artist: 他是個大藝術家。He is a great artist.
藝術界(ㄧˋ ㄕㄨˋ ㄐㄧㄝˋ)
the world of art; the artistic circles
藝術教育(ㄧˋ ㄕㄨˋ ㄐㄧㄠˋ ㄩˋ)
art education
藝術學系(ㄧˋ ㄕㄨˋ ㄒㄩㄝˊ ㄒㄧˋ)
the department of fine arts (in a college or university)
藝術之宮(ㄧˋ ㄕㄨˋ ㄓ ㄍㄨㄥ)
the Palace of Art (as coined by the poet Tennyson)
藝術至上主義(ㄧˋ ㄕㄨˋ ㄓˋ ㄕㄤˋ ㄓㄨˇ ㄧˋ)
art for art's sake
藝術字(ㄧˋ ㄕㄨˋ ㄗˋ)
(printed or written) characters in a fancy style
藝術無國境(ㄧˋ ㄕㄨˋ ㄨˊ ㄍㄨㄛˊ ㄐㄧㄥˋ)
Art knows no national boundary.
藝人(ㄧˋ ㄖㄣˊ)
an entertainer; a performing artist: 她是個出名的藝人。She is a famous entertainer.
藝文(ㄧˋ ㄨㄣˊ)
literature and fine arts
藝文志(ㄧˋ ㄨㄣˊ ㄓˋ)
a bibliographical sketch (of the kind as contained in old history books)
藝苑(ㄧˋ ㄩㄢˋ)
① places where works of art are collected; an artistic or literary salon; an art gallery ② the art and literary circles

【藟】 5145 ㄌㄟˇ leei lěi
1. a variety of climbing plant
2. to wind; to entwine
3. same as 蕾—a flower bud

【藫】 5146 ㄊㄢˊ tarn tán
algae 亦作「石衣」or「水苔」

【藤】 5147 ㄊㄥˊ terng téng
a rattan; a vine
藤鞭(ㄊㄥˊ ㄅㄧㄢ)
a rattan whip
藤牌(ㄊㄥˊ ㄆㄞˊ)
a rattan shield
藤條(ㄊㄥˊ ㄊㄧㄠˊ)
a rattan
藤蘿(ㄊㄥˊ ㄌㄨㄛˊ)
(botany) wisteria
藤黃(ㄊㄥˊ ㄏㄨㄤˊ)
gamboge
藤子(ㄊㄥˊ ·ㄗ)

a rattan

藤椅(ㄊㄥˊ ㄧˇ)
a rattan chair; a cane chair

【藥】 5148 ㄧㄠˋ yaw yào
(讀音 ㄩㄝˋ yueh yuè)

1. medicine; remedy; a drug; pharmaceuticals: 良藥苦口。A good medicine tastes bitter.
2. to kill with poison; to poison: 他們在藥老鼠。They are poisoning rats.

藥片(ㄧㄠˋ ㄆㄧㄢˋ)
a tablet of medicine

藥品(ㄧㄠˋ ㄆㄧㄣˇ)
pharmaceutical products; drugs

藥瓶(ㄧㄠˋ ㄆㄧㄥˊ)
a medicine bottle

藥舖(ㄧㄠˋ ㄆㄨˋ) or 藥店(ㄧㄠˋ ㄉㄧㄢˋ)
a druggist's store; a dispensary

藥麪兒(ㄧㄠˋ ㄇㄧㄚˋㄦ)
medicine in powder form

藥棉(ㄧㄠˋ ㄇㄧㄢˊ)
absorbent cotton; medically decontaminated cotton

藥粉(ㄧㄠˋ ㄈㄣˇ)
medicinal powder

藥方(ㄧㄠˋ ㄈㄤ)
a (medicinal) prescription

藥房(ㄧㄠˋ ㄈㄤˊ)
a druggist's shop; a dispensary; a pharmacy

藥單(ㄧㄠˋ ㄉㄢ)
a (medicinal) prescription

藥碾子(ㄧㄠˋ ㄋㄧㄢˇ ˙ㄗ)
a medicine mortar

藥理學(ㄧㄠˋ ㄌㄧˇ ㄒㄩㄝˊ)
pharmacology

藥力(ㄧㄠˋ ㄌㄧˋ)
the potency or effect of a drug: 藥力發作了。The medicine is taking effect.

藥料(ㄧㄠˋ ㄌㄧㄠˋ)
medicinal substance; material for a drug; material for a decoction

藥量(ㄧㄠˋ ㄌㄧㄤˋ)
dosage

藥膏(ㄧㄠˋ ㄍㄠ)
ointment; salve

藥罐子(ㄧㄠˋ ㄍㄨㄢˋ ˙ㄗ)
①a pottery jar for cooking medicinal decoctions; a drug boiler ②one who is perennially ill; a chronic invalid

藥劑(ㄧㄠˋ ㄐㄧˋ)
medicine; remedy; a drug

藥劑師(ㄧㄠˋ ㄐㄧˋ ㄕ)
a pharmacist; a druggist; a chemist; an apothecary

藥酒(ㄧㄠˋ ㄐㄧㄡˇ)
medicinal wine or liquor; medicated wine or liquor

藥局(ㄧㄠˋ ㄐㄩˊ)
a druggist's store; a dispensary 參看「藥房」: 他去藥局了。He went to the dispensary.

藥線(ㄧㄠˋ ㄒㄧㄢˋ)
①a fuse ②a medicated thread

藥箱(ㄧㄠˋ ㄒㄧㄤ)
a medicine chest; a medical kit

藥性(ㄧㄠˋ ㄒㄧㄥˋ)
the nature of a drug: 此藥藥性溫和。The nature of the drug is gentle.

藥學(ㄧㄠˋ ㄒㄩㄝˊ)
pharmacology: 她專攻藥學。She majors in pharmacology.

藥渣(ㄧㄠˋ ㄓㄚ)
dregs left after preparing a decoction

藥針(ㄧㄠˋ ㄓㄣ)
an injection syringe

藥廠(ㄧㄠˋ ㄔㄤˇ)
a pharmaceutical factory

藥師(ㄧㄠˋ ㄕ)
a pharmacist; a druggist; a chemist; an apothecary; a pharmaceutist

藥石(ㄧㄠˋ ㄕˊ)
① medicines ② sincere admonitions

藥石之言(ㄧㄠˋ ㄕˊ ㄓ ㄧㄢˊ)
sincere admonitions; exhortations

藥石罔效(ㄧㄠˋ ㄕˊ ㄨㄤˇ ㄒㄧㄠˋ)
All medicines have failed to effect a cure.

藥商(ㄧㄠˋ ㄕㄤ)
a drug dealer; a chemist

藥水(ㄧㄠˋ ㄕㄨㄟˇ)
liquid medicine

藥皂(ㄧㄠˋ ㄗㄠˋ)
medicated soap

藥材(ㄧㄠˋ ㄘㄞˊ)
medicinal substance; material for a drug; material for a decoction; medicine; a drug; medicinal herbs

藥草(ㄧㄠˋ ㄘㄠˇ)
medicinal herbs

藥死(ㄧㄠˋ ㄙˇ)
to poison to death

藥餌(ㄧㄠˋ ㄦˇ)
a medicine to give strength; tonics

藥衣子(ㄧㄠˋ ㄧ ˙ㄗ)
the coat of a pill medicine

藥引子(ㄧㄠˋ ㄧㄣˇ ˙ㄗ)
an auxiliary remedy or medicine; a helping ingredient added to enhance the efficacy of a medicine

藥物(ㄧㄠˋ ㄨˋ)
drug; medicine

藥物過敏(ㄧㄠˋ ㄨˋ ㄍㄨㄛˋ ㄇㄧㄣˇ)
drug allergy

藥物學(ㄧㄠˋ ㄨˋ ㄒㄩㄝˊ)
pharmacology

藥味(ㄧㄠˋ ㄨㄟˋ)
①medicine ②the taste of a drug ③a medicine-like taste 亦作「藥味兒」

藥丸(ㄧㄠˋ ㄨㄢˊ)
a pill medicine; a pill

藥用(ㄧㄠˋ ㄩㄥˋ)
for medical use

【藩】 5149 ㄈㄢˊ farn fán

a fence; a hedge; a boundary; a frontier; a barrier

藩蔽(ㄈㄢˊ ㄅㄧˋ)
a barrier

藩屏(ㄈㄢˊ ㄆㄧㄥˊ)
a protective barrier; a line of defense 亦作「屏藩」

藩附(ㄈㄢˊ ㄈㄨˋ)
a protectorate; a vassal state

藩籬(ㄈㄢˊ ㄌㄧˊ)
①a fence; a hedge: 此馬跳過了藩籬。This horse jumped over the fence. ②anything acting as a hedge ③a line of defense; a barrier

藩國(ㄈㄢˊ ㄍㄨㄛˊ)
a vassal state; a feudatory state

藩庫(ㄈㄢˊ ㄎㄨˋ)
a provincial treasury (in former times)

藩鎮(ㄈㄢˊ ㄓㄣˋ)
(Tang Dynasty) the governor of a frontier province in charge of both civil and mil-

itary affairs

藩臣(ㄈㄢ ㄔㄣˊ)
a vassal

藩屬(ㄈㄢ ㄕㄨˇ)
a vassal state; a protectorate

藩司(ㄈㄢ ㄙ)
a provincial governor (in ancient times)

藩維(ㄈㄢ ㄨㄟˊ)
vassal states and frontier posts

【藪】 5150 ㄙㄡˇ soou sǒu
1. a shallow lake overgrown with wild plants
2. an assembling place
3. same as 搜—to search

藪澤(ㄙㄡˇ ㄗㄜˊ)
a shallow lake

【藭】 5151 ㄑㄩㄥˊ chyong qióng
as in 芎藭—*Cnidium officinale,* a kind of medicinal herb

十六畫

【藺】 5152 ㄌㄧㄣˋ linn lìn
1. a variety of rush used in making mats
2. a Chinese family name

藺相如(ㄌㄧㄣˋ ㄒㄧㄤ ㄖㄨˊ)
Lin Hsiang-ju, a prime minister of the state of Chao (趙) during the Epoch of Warring States

藺石(ㄌㄧㄣˋ ㄕˊ)
rocks used as artillery shells in ancient warfare

【蘑】 5153 ㄇㄛˊ mo mó
a variety of edible mushroom

蘑菇 or 蘑菰(ㄇㄛˊ ·ㄍㄨ)
① a variety of edible mushrooms ② to dawdle; to dilly-dally ③ to pester; to worry

【蘄】 5154 ㄑㄧˊ chyi qí
1. ligusticum; levisticum 亦作「當歸」or「山蘄」
2. same as 祈—to beg; to seek

蘄竹(ㄑㄧˊ ㄓㄨˊ)
① bamboos produced in Chichow (蘄州), Hupeh Province ② bamboo mats

蘄水(ㄑㄧˊ ㄕㄨㄟˇ)
name of a tributary of the Yangtze River originating in Hupeh

蘄艾(ㄑㄧˊ ㄞˋ)
moxa from the Chi (蘄) area in Hupeh

【藹】 5155 ㄞˇ ae ǎi
1. exuberant; luxuriant; lush
2. gentle; kind; amiable; affable; friendly
3. gloomy; dim

藹然(ㄞˇ ㄖㄢˊ)
① glossy; lustrous ② amiable; affable; friendly; gentle; kind

藹然可親(ㄞˇ ㄖㄢˊ ㄎㄜˇ ㄑㄧㄣ)
kind and gentle; affable and friendly

藹彩(ㄞˇ ㄘㄞˇ)
a fresh look

藹藹(ㄞˇ ㄞˇ)
① exuberant; luxuriant; lush ② abundant; much; many ③ (said of moonlight) gloomy; dim ④ (said of the wood) shady

【藻】 5156 ㄗㄠˇ tzao zǎo
1. algae; pondweeds
2. diction; wording; language

藻類(ㄗㄠˇ ㄌㄟˋ) or 藻類植物(ㄗㄠˇ ㄌㄟˋ ㄓˊ ㄨˋ)
algae

藻麗(ㄗㄠˇ ㄌㄧˋ)
beautiful; splendid

藻翰(ㄗㄠˇ ㄏㄢˋ)
① a beautiful feather ② (figuratively) elegant writing

藻繪(ㄗㄠˇ ㄏㄨㄟˋ)
magnificence; splendor; elegance

藻井(ㄗㄠˇ ㄐㄧㄥˇ)
a plafond

藻飾(ㄗㄠˇ ㄕˋ)
① literary decorativeness; embellishment in writing ② to polish writings

藻思(ㄗㄠˇ ㄙ)
a fine or elegant inspiration (in writing)

藻雅(ㄗㄠˇ ㄧㄚˇ)
elegant; graceful; fine

藻玉(ㄗㄠˇ ㄩˋ)
multicolored jade

【藿】 5157 ㄏㄨㄛˋ huoh huò
1. leaves of a legume; bean sprouts
2. *Agastache rugosa,* a kind of medicinal herb 參看「藿香」

藿羹(ㄏㄨㄛˋ ㄍㄥ)
coarse food

藿香(ㄏㄨㄛˋ ㄒㄧㄤ)
Agastache rugosa, wrinkled giant hyssop

藿食(ㄏㄨㄛˋ ㄕˊ)
coarse food

【蘀】 5158 ㄊㄨㄛˋ tuoh tuò
fallen leaves and barks; withered leaves

【蘅】 5159 ㄏㄥˊ herng héng
Asarum blumei, a fragrant plant

蘅芷(ㄏㄥˊ ㄓˇ)
a fragrant plant

蘅蕪(ㄏㄥˊ ㄨˊ)
a kind of incense

【蘆】 5160 ㄌㄨˊ lu lú
1. reeds; rushes
2. gourds 參看「葫蘆」

蘆藩(ㄌㄨˊ ㄈㄢ)
a reed fence; a reed hedge

蘆荻(ㄌㄨˊ ㄉㄧˊ)
a variety of reed

蘆田(ㄌㄨˊ ㄊㄧㄢˊ)
sandy fields where reeds grow

蘆溝橋(ㄌㄨˊ ㄍㄡ ㄑㄧㄠˊ)
the Marco Polo Bridge (in Hopeh, where the first shot of the Sino-Japanese War, 1937-1945, was fired)

蘆溝橋事變(ㄌㄨˊ ㄍㄡ ㄑㄧㄠˊ ㄕˋ ㄅㄧㄢˋ)
The Marco Polo Bridge Incident (on July 7, 1937, which triggered the Sino-Japanese War)

蘆管(ㄌㄨˊ ㄍㄨㄢˇ)
a reed pipe

蘆花(ㄌㄨˊ ㄏㄨㄚ) or 蘆絮(ㄌㄨˊ ㄒㄩˋ)
reed flowers; reed catkins; rush flowers

蘆薈(ㄌㄨˊ ㄏㄨㄟˋ)
aloes: 蘆薈可作藥。Aloes can be used in medicine.

蘆席(ㄌㄨˊ ㄒㄧˊ)
a rush mat

蘆竹(ㄌㄨˊ ㄓㄨˊ)

①a variety of edible bamboo ② *Arundo donax*

蘆筍(ㄌㄨˊ ㄙㄨㄣˇ)
(botany) asparagus

蘆葦(ㄌㄨˊ ㄨㄟˇ)
reeds

【孽】 5161
(孼) ㄋㄧㄝˋ nieh niè

1. the son of a concubine
2. sin; evil
3. calamity

孽黨(ㄋㄧㄝˋ ㄉㄤˇ)
a traitorous faction; dissenters

孽障(ㄋㄧㄝˋ ㄓㄤˋ)
retribution for past evil

孽子(ㄋㄧㄝˋ ㄗˇ)
the son of a concubine

孽孫(ㄋㄧㄝˋ ㄙㄨㄣ)
the grandson of a concubine

【蘇】 5162
ㄙㄨ su sū

1. purple perilla 亦作「紫蘇」
2. to come back to life; to revive; to resurrect
3. to awake
4. to rest
5. short for Soviet Russia
6. short for Kiangsu Province or Soochow
7. a Chinese family name

蘇白(ㄙㄨ ㄅㄞˊ)
the Soochow dialect

蘇必略湖(ㄙㄨ ㄅㄧˋ ㄌㄩㄝˋ ㄏㄨˊ)
Lake Superior

蘇曼殊(ㄙㄨ ㄇㄢˋ ㄕㄨ)
Su Man-shu, 1884-1918, a writer, translator and artist

蘇門答臘(ㄙㄨ ㄇㄣˊ ㄉㄚˊ ㄌㄚˋ)
Sumatra

蘇打(ㄙㄨ ㄉㄚˇ)
soda 亦作「曹達」

蘇打餅(ㄙㄨ ㄉㄚˇ ㄅㄧㄥˇ)
a soda biscuit; a soda cracker

蘇丹(ㄙㄨ ㄉㄢ)
Sudan

蘇隄(ㄙㄨ ㄊㄧˊ)or(ㄙㄨ ㄉㄧ)
either of two dikes in the West Lake, Hangchow, built by the Sung Dynasty poet Su Tung-po(蘇東坡)

蘇鐵(ㄙㄨ ㄊㄧㄝˇ)
(botany) a cycad 亦作「鳳尾蕉」

蘇黎世(ㄙㄨ ㄌㄧˊ ㄕˋ)
Zurich, Switzerland

蘇利南(ㄙㄨ ㄌㄧˋ ㄋㄢˊ)
Surinam

蘇格拉底(ㄙㄨ ㄍㄜˊ ㄌㄚ ㄉㄧˇ)
Socrates, 469?-399B.C., Athenian philosopher and teacher

蘇格蘭(ㄙㄨ ㄍㄜˊ ㄌㄢˊ)
Scotland

蘇杭(ㄙㄨ ㄏㄤˊ)
Soochow and Hangchow

蘇黃米蔡(ㄙㄨ ㄏㄨㄤˊ ㄇㄧˇ ㄘㄞˋ)
the four great calligraphic masters of the North Sung Dynasty—Su Shih (蘇軾), Huang Ting-chien (黃庭堅), Mi Fei (米芾), and Tsai Hsiang (蔡襄)

蘇秦(ㄙㄨ ㄑㄧㄣˊ)
Su Chin, a strategist in the Epoch of Warring States

蘇息(ㄙㄨ ㄒㄧˊ)
①to rest ②to come back to life; to revive

蘇小妹(ㄙㄨ ㄒㄧㄠˇ ㄇㄟˋ)
Su Hsiao-mei, talented daughter of Su Hsün(蘇洵)

蘇小小(ㄙㄨ ㄒㄧㄠˇ ㄒㄧㄠˇ)
a famed 6th century courtesan whose grave is one of the tourist attractions of the West Lake in Hangchow

蘇醒(ㄙㄨ ㄒㄧㄥˇ)
to regain consciousness; to come to; to awaken; to revive: 他使那個暈厥的人蘇醒。He revived that man who had fainted.

蘇洵(ㄙㄨ ㄒㄩㄣˊ)
Su Hsün, 1009-1066, renowned man of letters in the Sung Dynasty, father of Su Shih (蘇軾), Su Che(蘇轍), and Su Hsiao-mei(蘇小妹)

蘇州(ㄙㄨ ㄓㄡ)
Soochow, Kiangsu Province

蘇轍(ㄙㄨ ㄔㄜˋ)
Su Che, 1039-1112, renowned man of letters in the Sung Dynasty, 2nd son of Su Hsün(蘇洵)and brother of Su Shih(蘇軾)

蘇軾(ㄙㄨ ㄕˋ)
Su Shih, 1036-1101, renowned man of letters in the Sung Dynasty, also known as Su Tung-po(蘇東坡), eldest son of Su Hsün (蘇洵) and brother of Su Che(蘇轍)

蘇俄(ㄙㄨ ㄜˊ)
Soviet Russia

蘇伊士運河(ㄙㄨ ㄧ ㄕˋ ㄩㄣˋ ㄏㄜˊ)
the Suez Canal

蘇武(ㄙㄨ ㄨˇ)
Su Wu, (c.143-60 B.C.), an emissary who spent 19 years in captivity among the Huns during the Han Dynasty

蘇維埃(ㄙㄨ ㄨㄟˊ ㄞ)
Soviet

蘇維埃聯邦(ㄙㄨ ㄨㄟˊ ㄞ ㄌㄧㄢˊ ㄅㄤ) or 蘇聯(ㄙㄨ ㄌㄧㄢˊ)
the Soviet Union; the Union of Soviet Socialist Republics; U.S.S.R.

【蘊】 5163
(藴) ㄩㄣˋ yunn yùn

1. to collect; to gather
2. to store; to have in store
3. deep; profound
4. sweltering; sultry

蘊釀(ㄩㄣˋ ㄋㄧㄤˋ)
(said of a storm, trouble, etc.) to brew; to foment

蘊涵(ㄩㄣˋ ㄏㄢˊ)
①to contain ②(logics) implication

蘊結(ㄩㄣˋ ㄐㄧㄝˊ)
(said of feelings) pent-up; restrained

蘊藉(ㄩㄣˋ ㄐㄧㄝˋ)
refined and cultivated; urbanely charming

蘊蓄(ㄩㄣˋ ㄒㄩˋ)
to hold, or contain, beneath the surface; to have in store

蘊藏(ㄩㄣˋ ㄘㄤˊ)
to have in store; to be rich in: 該國蘊藏豐富的石油和煤礦。The country is rich in oil and coal.

蘊藏量(ㄩㄣˋ ㄘㄤˊ ㄌㄧㄤˋ)
(said of minerals) deposit

蘊藹(ㄩㄣˋ ㄞˇ)
exuberant; luxuriant

蘊蘊(ㄩㄣˋ ㄩㄣˋ)
sweltering; sultry

【蘋】 5164
1. ㄆㄧㄣˊ pyn pín

duckweeds

【蘋】 5164
2. ㄆㄧㄥˊ pyng píng

an apple

蘋果(ㄆㄧㄥˊ ㄍㄨㄛˇ)
an apple

蘋果綠(ㄆㄧㄥˊ ㄍㄨㄛˇ ㄌㄩˋ)
a kind of ancient porcelain with a light-green color

蘋果酒(ㄆㄧㄥˊ ㄍㄨㄛˇ ㄐㄧㄡˇ)
hard cider; applejack

蘋果汁(ㄆㄧㄥˊ ㄍㄨㄛˇ ㄓ)
apple juice

蘋果酸(ㄆㄧㄥˊ ㄍㄨㄛˇ ㄙㄨㄢ)
malic acid

蘋果臉兒(ㄆㄧㄥˊ ·ㄍㄨㄛ ㄌㄧㄚˇㄦ)
rosy cheeks

【藷】 5165
(薯) ㄕㄨˇ shuu shǔ
a sweet potato

【蘢】 5166
ㄌㄨㄥˊ long lóng
a kind of tall grass

蘢葱(ㄌㄨㄥˊ ㄘㄨㄥ)
(said of vegetation) luxuriant and beautiful; verdant

十七畫

【蘧】 5167
ㄑㄩˊ chyu qú
1. pleasantly surprised
2. a Chinese family name

【蘗】 5168
ㄅㄛˋ boh bò
a cork tree (*Phellodendron*)

【蘖】 5169
(櫱) ㄋㄧㄝˋ nieh niè
sprouts and shoots from the stump of a felled tree

【蘚】 5170
ㄒㄧㄢˇ shean xiǎn
(botany) moss; lichen

蘚苔(ㄒㄧㄢˇ ㄊㄞˊ)
moss; lichen

蘚痕(ㄒㄧㄢˇ ㄏㄣˊ)
a moss scar; marks made by moss on rocks or steps

蘚徑(ㄒㄧㄢˇ ㄐㄧㄥˋ)
a mossy path

【蘩】 5171
ㄈㄢˊ farn fán
Artemisia stelleriana, a kind of herb; white southernwood 亦作「白蒿」

【蘭】 5172
ㄌㄢˊ lan lán
an orchid

蘭盆(ㄌㄢˊ ㄆㄣˊ) or 蘭盆會(ㄌㄢˊ ㄆㄣˊ ㄏㄨㄟˋ)
(Buddhism) Ullambana, the festival of masses for destitute ghosts, a Buddhist service on the 15th of the seventh lunar month 亦作「盂蘭盆會」

蘭譜(ㄌㄢˊ ㄆㄨˇ)
a testimonial of sworn brothers

蘭臺(ㄌㄢˊ ㄊㄞˊ)
① an alternative title by which the official historian was referred to in the Han Dynasty ② name of a county in Hupeh Province

蘭亭帖(ㄌㄢˊ ㄊㄧㄥˊ ㄊㄧㄝˋ)
a handwritten copy of 蘭亭序, by Wang Hsi-chih (王羲之), a 4th century writer and calligraphic master

蘭亭序(ㄌㄢˊ ㄊㄧㄥˊ ㄒㄩˋ)
the title of a literary piece by Wang Hsi-chih (王羲之), whose literary worth is dwarfed by its artistic value as a calligraphic masterpiece

蘭閨(ㄌㄢˊ ㄍㄨㄟ)
a boudoir

蘭科(ㄌㄢˊ ㄎㄜ)
the orchid family

蘭客(ㄌㄢˊ ㄎㄜˋ)
a good friend

蘭花(ㄌㄢˊ ㄏㄨㄚ)
an orchid; a cymbidium

蘭交(ㄌㄢˊ ㄐㄧㄠ)
a harmonious friendship

蘭薰桂馥(ㄌㄢˊ ㄒㄩㄣ ㄍㄨㄟˋ ㄈㄨˋ)
the fragrance of orchids and the scent of cinnamon—① prosperous descendants ② a lasting moral influence

蘭訊(ㄌㄢˊ ㄒㄩㄣˋ)
your letters

蘭芝(ㄌㄢˊ ㄓ)
① the fragrant thoroughwort and the glossy ganoderma—both of them are fragrant herbs ② (figuratively) virtue

蘭芷(ㄌㄢˊ ㄓˇ)
the fragrant thoroughwort and the angelica—both of them are fragrant herbs

蘭州(ㄌㄢˊ ㄓㄡ)
Lanchow, capital city of Kansu Province

蘭章(ㄌㄢˊ ㄓㄤ)
① beautiful writings ② (a polite expression) your letters

蘭室(ㄌㄢˊ ㄕˋ)
a Buddhist temple

蘭麝(ㄌㄢˊ ㄕㄜˋ)
① the fragrant thoroughwort and the musk—both of them are fragrant herbs ② fragrance; scent

蘭若
①(ㄌㄢˊ ㄖㄨㄛˋ) (botany) Chinese and Japanese thoroughwort
②(ㄌㄢˊ ㄖㄜˇ) Aranyaka, a Buddhist monastery 亦作「阿蘭若」

蘭藻(ㄌㄢˊ ㄗㄠˇ)
literary beauty

蘭摧玉折(ㄌㄢˊ ㄘㄨㄟ ㄩˋ ㄓㄜˊ)
(literally) The orchid has withered and the jade is broken.—The man of virtue is dead while still young.

蘭孫(ㄌㄢˊ ㄙㄨㄣ)
your fine grandchildren

蘭艾同焚(ㄌㄢˊ ㄞˋ ㄊㄨㄥˊ ㄈㄣˊ)
(literally) to burn the orchid and the moxa together—to impose the same destiny upon the noble and the mean alike

蘭因絮果(ㄌㄢˊ ㄧㄣ ㄒㄩˋ ㄍㄨㄛˇ)
(said of a man and a woman) well-predestined relationship and ill fated end, usually referring to the break-up of a marriage

蘭嶼(ㄌㄢˊ ㄩˇ)
Lanyü, an islet off the coast of Southeastern Taiwan

蘭月(ㄌㄢˊ ㄩㄝˋ)
the month of the orchid—the seventh lunar month

【蘞】 5173
ㄌㄧㄢˊ lian lián
a variety of vine; a convolvulus

十九畫

【蘸】 5174
ㄓㄢˋ jann zhàn
to dip

蘸筆(ㄓㄢˋ ㄅㄧˇ)
to dip a writing brush in ink

蘸濕(ㄓㄢˋ ㄕ)
to dip

【蘺】 5175
ㄌㄧˊ li lí
a kind of fragrant herb 亦作

「江蘺」

【蘼】 5176 ㄇㄧˊ mi mí
a kind of fragrant herb 參看「蘼蕪」

蘼藿(ㄇㄧˊ ㄏㄨㄛˋ)
coarse vegetable

蘼蕪(ㄇㄧˊ ㄨˊ)
Gracilaria confervoides, a kind of fragrant herb

【蘿】 5177 ㄌㄨㄛˊ luo luó
1. a kind of creeping plant; a wistaria
2. a radish; a turnip

蘿蔔(ㄌㄨㄛˊ ·ㄅㄛ)
a radish; a turnip

蘿蔔乾兒(ㄌㄨㄛˊ ·ㄅㄛ ㄍㄚㄦ)
a dried radish or turnip

蘿蔔糕(ㄌㄨㄛˊ ·ㄅㄛ ㄍㄠ)
turnip pudding

【虀】 5178 ㄐㄧ ji jī
minced pickles

二十一畫

【虆】 5179 ㄌㄟˊ lei léi
1. grass that creeps and spread fast and luxuriantly
2. a basket for carrying earth

虍部 ㄏㄨ hu hū

二畫

【虎】 5180 ㄏㄨˇ huu hǔ
1. a tiger
2. fierce; savage; brave; vigorous

虎背熊腰(ㄏㄨˇ ㄅㄟˋ ㄒㄩㄥˊ ㄧㄠ)
the back of a tiger and the waist of a bear—heavy and muscular build of the body

虎斑草(ㄏㄨˇ ㄅㄢ ㄘㄠˇ)
a tigerflower

虎賁(ㄏㄨˇ ㄅㄣ)
a warrior; a lifeguard—(figuratively) intrepid

虎榜(ㄏㄨˇ ㄅㄤˇ)
a bulletin announcing successful candidates in the examination for military officers in ancient times

虎步(ㄏㄨˇ ㄅㄨˋ)
a strutting gait

虎皮(ㄏㄨˇ ㄆㄧˊ)
① a tiger skin ② seeming bravery

虎符(ㄏㄨˇ ㄈㄨˊ)
a tiger-shaped tally used in wartime in ancient times

虎父無犬子(ㄏㄨˇ ㄈㄨˋ ㄨˊ ㄑㄩㄢˇ ㄗˇ)
(literally) A tiger father will not beget a dog son. —There will be no laggard among the children of a brave or talented man.

虎毒不食兒(ㄏㄨˇ ㄉㄨˊ ㄅㄨˋ ㄕˊ ㄦˊ)
(literally) Even a vicious tigress will not eat its cubs. —No one is capable of hurting his own children.

虎蹲砲(ㄏㄨˇ ㄉㄨㄣ ㄆㄠˋ)
a short-barreled artillery piece

虎頭牌(ㄏㄨˇ ㄊㄡˊ ㄆㄞˊ)
a tiger-headed tablet outside a public office warning against disorder

虎頭虎腦(ㄏㄨˇ ㄊㄡˊ ㄏㄨˇ ㄋㄠˇ)
looking dignified and strong

虎頭蛇尾(ㄏㄨˇ ㄊㄡˊ ㄕㄜˊ ㄨㄟˇ)
to start doing something with vigor but fail to see it through; impressive in the beginning but disappointing in the end

虎狼之年(ㄏㄨˇ ㄌㄤˊ ㄓ ㄋㄧㄢˊ)
the wolfish years of a woman from the early thirties to early forties when her sexual desire is the strongest

虎狼之國(ㄏㄨˇ ㄌㄤˊ ㄓ ㄍㄨㄛˊ)
a nation of greed and violence

虎列拉(ㄏㄨˇ ㄌㄧㄝˋ ㄌㄚ)
cholera 亦作「霍亂」

虎落平陽被犬欺(ㄏㄨˇ ㄌㄨㄛˋ ㄆㄧㄥˊ ㄧㄤˊ ㄅㄟˋ ㄑㄩㄢˇ ㄑㄧ)
(literally) The tiger, once out of his natural environment, may be bullied even by a dog. —A hero or brave man is bullied by a bunch of weaklings when he is down in his luck.

虎克黨(ㄏㄨˇ ㄎㄜˋ ㄉㄤˇ)
the Huks in the Philippines

虎口(ㄏㄨˇ ㄎㄡˇ)
① a tiger's mouth—a dangerous place; the jaws of death ② the part of a hand between the thumb and the index finger

虎口餘生(ㄏㄨˇ ㄎㄡˇ ㄩˊ ㄕㄥ)
(literally) to escape from the tiger's mouth—to survive a dangerous experience; to have a narrow escape

虎虎有生氣(ㄏㄨˇ ㄏㄨˇ ㄧㄡˇ ㄕㄥ ㄑㄧˋ)
lively; vigorous

虎將(ㄏㄨˇ ㄐㄧㄤˋ)
a brave general

虎踞龍蟠(ㄏㄨˇ ㄐㄩˋ ㄌㄨㄥˊ ㄆㄢˊ)
(literally) like a tiger crouching or a dragon curling—located in a strategic place

虎圈(ㄏㄨˇ ㄐㄩㄢˋ)
a tiger's cage or pen

虎嘯風生(ㄏㄨˇ ㄒㄧㄠˋ ㄈㄥ ㄕㄥ)
(literally) Tigers howl with the rise of winds.—Great men appear in response to the call of the times.

虎穴(ㄏㄨˇ ㄒㄩㄝˋ)
a tiger's cave—a dangerous place; a hazardous spot: 不入虎穴，焉得虎子。The only way to catch tiger cubs is to go into the tiger's cave.

虎鷙(ㄏㄨˇ ㄓˋ)
brave warriors

虎掌(ㄏㄨˇ ㄓㄤˇ)
(botany) a poisonous plant (*Arisaema ambiguum*)

虎帳(ㄏㄨˇ ㄓㄤˋ)
a military camp

虎政(ㄏㄨˇ ㄓㄥˋ)
tyrannical administration; misrule

虎倀(ㄏㄨˇ ㄔㄤ)
a spirit believed to lead a tiger to its human victims —a man who encourages or helps in sinful acts; an accomplice

虎士(ㄏㄨˇ ㄕˋ)
a brave warrior; a brave fighter

虎視眈眈(ㄏㄨˇ ㄕˋ ㄉㄢ ㄉㄢ)
to gaze with the cruel greed

〔虍部〕

of a tiger
虎入羊羣(ㄏㄨˇ ㄖㄨˋ ㄧㄤˊ ㄑㄩㄣˊ)
a tiger among a flock of sheep— (figuratively) With irresistable power, one does as one pleases.
虎子(ㄏㄨˇ ㄗˇ)
the cub of a tiger
虎殘(ㄏㄨˇ ㄘㄢˊ)
remains of a tiger's prey —(figuratively) to have a narrow escape
虎威(ㄏㄨˇ ㄨㄟ)
the frightful appearance of a tiger (assumed to scare others)

三畫

【虐】5181 ㄋㄩㄝˋ niueh nüè
1. cruel; ferocious; atrocious
2. to tyrannize over; to oppress
虐待(ㄋㄩㄝˋ ㄉㄞˋ)
to maltreat; to abuse; to torture; to ill-treat
虐待狂(ㄋㄩㄝˋ ㄉㄞˋ ㄎㄨㄤˊ)
① sadism ② a sadist
虐政(ㄋㄩㄝˋ ㄓㄥˋ)
tyrannical rule; tyranny

四畫

【虔】5182 ㄑㄧㄢˊ chyan qián
reverence; reverent; respectful; pious
虔婆(ㄑㄧㄢˊ ㄆㄛˊ)
① a low woman ② a procuress
虔心(ㄑㄧㄢˊ ㄒㄧㄣ)
sincere reverence; piety
虔誠(ㄑㄧㄢˊ ㄔㄥˊ)
devout; piety; sincerity; pious: 他是個虔誠的基督徒。He is a devout Christian.

五畫

【處】5183 1. ㄔㄨˋ chuh chù
1. a place; a spot; a location; a locality: 他的住處在台北。His dwelling place is in Taipei.
2. a department in a government agency
3. a special quality; a distinguishing mark; a point: 烹飪是她的長處。Cooking is her strong point.
處長(ㄔㄨˋ ㄓㄤˇ)
the head of a department in a government agency
處處(ㄔㄨˋ ㄔㄨˋ)
① everywhere: 他們處處都去。They go everywhere. ② in all respects
處所(ㄔㄨˋ ㄙㄨㄛˇ)
a place; a locality

【處】5183 2. ㄔㄨˇ chuu chǔ
1. to place oneself in; to be faced with; to live in
2. to get along: 他們不好相處。They are hard to get along with.
3. to dispose of; to deal with; to manage; to handle
4. to sentence; to punish: 他被判處死刑。He was sentenced to death.
5. to dwell; to live
處罰(ㄔㄨˇ ㄈㄚˊ)
to punish
處分(ㄔㄨˇ ·ㄈㄣ)
① to take action against; to take disciplinary action against; to punish: 學校給他警告處分。The school gave him disciplinary warning. ② to deal with (a matter)
處方(ㄔㄨˇ ㄈㄤ)
to write out a medical prescription; to prescribe
處斷(ㄔㄨˇ ㄉㄨㄢˋ)
to decide; to determine; to resolve
處女(ㄔㄨˇ ㄋㄩˇ)
a virgin
處女膜(ㄔㄨˇ ㄋㄩˇ ㄇㄛˊ)
the hymen; the maidenhead
處女地(ㄔㄨˇ ㄋㄩˇ ㄉㄧˋ)
virgin land; maiden ground
處女航(ㄔㄨˇ ㄋㄩˇ ㄏㄤˊ)
a maiden voyage of a ship; a maiden flight of a plane
處女作(ㄔㄨˇ ㄋㄩˇ ㄗㄨㄛˋ)
a maiden work
處理(ㄔㄨˇ ㄌㄧˇ)
① to dispose of; to handle; to deal with: 事務處理得很成功。The business has been disposed of successfully. ② to treat by a special process
處境(ㄔㄨˇ ㄐㄧㄥˋ)
the position or situation one is in; the circumstances one faces
處決(ㄔㄨˇ ㄐㄩㄝˊ)
① to decide; to resolve ② to execute (an offender); to put to death: 他們處決一名兇手。They executed a murderer.
處心積慮(ㄔㄨˇ ㄒㄧㄣ ㄐㄧ ㄌㄩˋ)
to have in mind for a long time; deliberately; to be bent on: 他處心積慮想當政治家。He is bent on becoming a statesman.
處刑(ㄔㄨˇ ㄒㄧㄥˊ)
to inflict punishment; to punish; to execute; to mete out a sentence
處之泰然(ㄔㄨˇ ㄓ ㄊㄞˋ ㄖㄢˊ)
to keep one's head; to be unmoved; to maintain composure
處置 or 處治(ㄔㄨˇ ㄓˋ)
① to dispose of; to deal with; to handle 亦作「處理」: 此事必須嚴加處置。The matter should be dealt with sternly. ② to punish
處斬(ㄔㄨˇ ㄓㄢˇ)
to behead; to decapitate
處士(ㄔㄨˇ ㄕˋ)
a scholar in retirement; a recluse
處世(ㄔㄨˇ ㄕˋ)
to conduct oneself in life: 他處世正直。He conducts himself honestly in life.
處事(ㄔㄨˇ ㄕˋ)
to deal with affairs; to manage business
處身(ㄔㄨˇ ㄕㄣ)
to conduct oneself in life
處暑(ㄔㄨˇ ㄕㄨˇ)
one of the 24 climatic periods of a year, falling on August 23 or 24
處子(ㄔㄨˇ ㄗˇ)
① a virgin; a young lady ② a scholar in retirement; a recluse
處死(ㄔㄨˇ ㄙˇ)
to punish with death; to put to death
處約(ㄔㄨˇ ㄩㄝ)

to be in adversity; to suffer privation; to be in a condition of poverty and hardship

【虖】 5184
ㄏㄨ hu hū
to cry; to shout; to howl; to roar

六畫

【虛】 5185
ㄒㄩ shiu xū
1. empty; hollow; void; unoccupied: 座無虛席。There was no empty seat.
2. unreal; false; deceptive; unfounded; groundless
3. weak; feeble: 他病後體虛。He weakened after his illness.
4. abstract; shapeless

虛薄(ㄒㄩ ㄅㄛˊ)
to be poor in ability

虛報(ㄒㄩ ㄅㄠˋ)
to report untruthfully

虛謗(ㄒㄩ ㄅㄤˋ)
to accuse groundlessly

虛糜(ㄒㄩ ㄇㄧˊ)or 虛費(ㄒㄩ ㄈㄟˋ)
to spend to no avail; to waste: 他虛糜光陰。He wasted his time.

虛名(ㄒㄩ ㄇㄧㄥˊ)or 虛譽(ㄒㄩ ㄩˋ)
a reputation unsupported by facts; an empty reputation; a false reputation; an undeserved reputation

虛發(ㄒㄩ ㄈㄚ)
to shoot without hitting the target

虛浮(ㄒㄩ ㄈㄨˊ)
impractical; unsubstantial; vain; empty: 那是個虛浮的計畫。That's an impractical plan.

虛誕(ㄒㄩ ㄉㄢˋ)
unreal; fantastic; preposterous

虛度(ㄒㄩ ㄉㄨˋ)
to pass (time) fruitlessly; to fritter away; to dream away: 切勿讓青春虛度。Don't let your youth slip by.

虛頭(ㄒㄩ ㄊㄡˊ)
a false statement; a lie

虛談(ㄒㄩ ㄊㄢˊ)
an empty talk; impractical suggestions

虛脫(ㄒㄩ ㄊㄨㄛ)
(medicine) collapse; prostration

虛擬(ㄒㄩ ㄋㄧˇ)
to suppose; to assume; to imagine; fictitious: 那是個虛擬的故事。That's a fictitious story.

虛構(ㄒㄩ ㄍㄡˋ)
made-up; fictitious; to trump up; to invent; to frame: 他虛構一篇故事。He trumped up a story.

虛誇(ㄒㄩ ㄎㄨㄚ)
to boast; to brag

虛空(ㄒㄩ ㄎㄨㄥ)
empty; hollow; void: 那是場虛空的勝利。It's a hollow victory.

虛喝(ㄒㄩ ㄏㄜˋ)
to give an empty scare; to intimidate by an empty scare

虛耗(ㄒㄩ ㄏㄠˋ)
to expend to no avail; to waste; to fritter away

虛話(ㄒㄩ ㄏㄨㄚˋ)
an empty talk; an unfounded statement; a lie

虛懷(ㄒㄩ ㄏㄨㄞˊ)
to be humble or open-minded (in accepting advice, instructions, etc.)

虛懷若谷(ㄒㄩ ㄏㄨㄞˊ ㄖㄨㄛˋ ㄍㄨˇ)
(literally) to open the mind wide as a valley—to be open-minded

虛幻(ㄒㄩ ㄏㄨㄢˋ)
illusory; visionary; unreal: 這只是一場虛幻的情景。 It's a mere illusion.

虛己(ㄒㄩ ㄐㄧˇ)
open-minded; humble

虛假(ㄒㄩ ㄐㄧㄚˇ)
false; unreal; dishonest: 我們認爲那個人待人有點虛假。We think that man is quite dishonest with people.

虛價(ㄒㄩ ㄐㄧㄚˋ)
overcharge; a nominal price

虛竭(ㄒㄩ ㄐㄧㄝˊ)
empty; exhausted

虛驕(ㄒㄩ ㄐㄧㄠ)
unfounded pride

虛驚(ㄒㄩ ㄐㄧㄥ)
a false alarm; a nervous fear: 我們飽受虛驚。We suffered from nervous fears.

虛靜(ㄒㄩ ㄐㄧㄥˋ)
having an open and peaceful mind

虛情假意(ㄒㄩ ㄑㄧㄥˊ ㄐㄧㄚˇ ㄧˋ)
hypocrisy; insincerity; hypocritical; insincere; pretended friendship or affection

虛線(ㄒㄩ ㄒㄧㄢˋ)
① a dotted line ② an imaginary line

虛心(ㄒㄩ ㄒㄧㄣ)
open-minded (for advice, instructions, etc.); modesty: 虛心使人進步。Modesty helps one to go forward.

虛心下氣(ㄒㄩ ㄒㄧㄣ ㄒㄧㄚˋ ㄑㄧˋ)
humble and meek

虛像(ㄒㄩ ㄒㄧㄤˋ)
(physics) a virtual image

虛虛實實(ㄒㄩ ㄒㄩ ㄕˊ ㄕˊ)
(said of military strategy, tactics, etc.) seemingly false and real at the same time; feints and ambushes

虛詐(ㄒㄩ ㄓㄚˋ)
falsehood and trickery

虛張聲勢(ㄒㄩ ㄓㄤ ㄕㄥ ㄕˋ)
to make a deceptive show of power; to bluff: 整個會議中他都是在虛張聲勢。He bluffed all through the conference.

虛沖(ㄒㄩ ㄔㄨㄥ)
modest; unassuming

虛實(ㄒㄩ ㄕˊ)
① true or false; falsehood versus reality; abstractness versus concreteness: 他不知虛實。He did not know whether it is true or false. ② the actual situation

虛室(ㄒㄩ ㄕˋ)
an unfurnished room; an empty room

虛設(ㄒㄩ ㄕㄜˋ)
to exist in name only

虛聲(ㄒㄩ ㄕㄥ)
① to make a deceptive show of power; to bluff ② empty reputation; undeserved reputation

虛聲恫喝(ㄒㄩ ㄕㄥ ㄉㄨㄥˋ ㄏㄜˋ)
to scare others by an empty threat

虛數(ㄒㄩ ㄕㄨˋ)
(mathematics) an imaginary number

虛弱(ㄒㄩ ㄖㄨㄛˋ)

〔虍部〕

debility; weak; feeble: 她愈來愈虛弱了。She grew weaker and weaker.
虛榮(ㄒㄩ ㄖㄨㄥˊ)
vanity; empty glory; vainglorious: 她愛慕虛榮。She was affected by vanity.
虛榮心(ㄒㄩ ㄖㄨㄥˊ ㄒㄧㄣ)
vainglory; vanity
虛字(ㄒㄩ ㄗˋ)
grammatical particles; grammatical formatives; function words; form words
虛造(ㄒㄩ ㄗㄠˋ)
to fabricate; to invent: 我們能虛造出什麼理由呢? What excuse can we invent?
虛左以待(ㄒㄩ ㄗㄨㄛˇ ㄧˇ ㄉㄞˋ)
to leave the seat of honor open (for a wise man)
虛歲(ㄒㄩ ㄙㄨㄟˋ)
age according to Chinese calculation (i.e. a person is one year old at birth)
虛有其表(ㄒㄩ ㄧㄡˇ ㄑㄧˊ ㄅㄧㄠˇ)
impressive only in appearance; to appear better than it is
虛言(ㄒㄩ ㄧㄢˊ)
① unfounded statements; false remarks ② an empty talk; meaningless words; a platitude
虛掩(ㄒㄩ ㄧㄢˇ)
(said of a door) half open, half closed; with the door left unlocked or unlatched
虛應故事(ㄒㄩ ㄧㄥˋ ㄍㄨˋ ㄕˋ)
to do a thing in a perfunctory manner; to go through the motions of doing something
虛無(ㄒㄩ ㄨˊ)
nothingness; emptiness; void; nil
虛無飄渺(ㄒㄩ ㄨˊ ㄆㄧㄠ ㄇㄧㄠˇ)
shapeless and elusive; floating and intangible; purely imaginary
虛無黨(ㄒㄩ ㄨˊ ㄉㄤˇ)
the Nihilists
虛無主義(ㄒㄩ ㄨˊ ㄓㄨˇ ㄧˋ)
nihilism
虛誣(ㄒㄩ ㄨˊ)
to accuse groundlessly
虛僞(ㄒㄩ ㄨㄟˋ)
false; spurious; hypocritical; insincere; hypocrisy
虛位以待(ㄒㄩ ㄨㄟˋ ㄧˇ ㄉㄞˋ)
to leave a position open to await (a wise man to fill it)
虛文(ㄒㄩ ㄨㄣˊ)
impractical formality or ceremony
虛文褥節(ㄒㄩ ㄨㄣˊ ㄖㄨˋ ㄐㄧㄝˊ)
empty forms or rituals
虛妄(ㄒㄩ ㄨㄤˋ)
showing wild imagination; preposterously fantastic
虛與委蛇(ㄒㄩ ㄩˇ ㄨㄟ ㄧˊ)
to pretend kindness; to feign civility

七畫

【虞】 5186 ㄩˊ yu yú
1. anxieties ; worries
2. to expect; to anticipate
3. to deceive; to cheat
4. name of a legendary dynasty
5. name of a state in the Epoch of Spring and Autumn
6. a Chinese family name

虞美人(ㄩˊ ㄇㄟˇ ㄖㄣˊ)
① a corn poppy ② the mistress of Hsiang Yü(項羽), also known as 虞姬
虞姬(ㄩˊ ㄐㄧ)
the mistress of Hsiang Yü (項羽), who ended the Chin (秦) Dynasty by defeating its army
虞舜(ㄩˊ ㄕㄨㄣˋ)
a legendary emperor of great wisdom, believed to have ruled around 2,200 B.C.
虞人(ㄩˊ ㄖㄣˊ)
an official in charge of forests, lakes, and imperial gardens in ancient times

【虜】 5187 ㄌㄨˇ luu lǔ (又讀 ㄌㄨㄛˇ luoo luǒ)
1. a captive; a prisoner
2. to take prisoner; to capture alive

虜獲(ㄌㄨˇ ㄏㄨㄛˋ)
① to capture ② men and arms captured

【號】 5188 1. ㄏㄠˋ haw hào
1. a designation; a title
2. sizes
3. orders; a command; a call
4. number (for identification or classification)
5. a mark; a sign; a signal: 語言是思想的符號。Words are the signs of ideas.
6. a store; a shop
7. a bugle
8. date: 今天幾號? What is the date today?

號兵(ㄏㄠˋ ㄅㄧㄥ)
a bugler in the army
號礮(ㄏㄠˋ ㄆㄠˋ)
artillery fire as a signal
號碼(ㄏㄠˋ ㄇㄚˇ)
a number (for identification): 你的電話號碼幾號? What's your telephone number?
號脈(ㄏㄠˋ ㄇㄞˋ)or(ㄏㄠˋ ㄇㄛˋ)
to feel the pulse
號房(ㄏㄠˋ ㄈㄤˊ)
① a janitor; a messenger ② the dormitory for candidates in civil service examination in the Ming Dynasty
號燈(ㄏㄠˋ ㄉㄥ)
a signal lamp
號頭(ㄏㄠˋ ㄊㄡˊ)
① a mark or number (for classification) ② a head workman; a foreman
號筒(ㄏㄠˋ ㄊㄨㄥˇ)
a bugle
號令(ㄏㄠˋ ㄌㄧㄥˋ)
a command; an order
號令如山(ㄏㄠˋ ㄌㄧㄥˋ ㄖㄨˊ ㄕㄢ)
Orders (in the army, etc.) are as inviolable as a mountain.
號角(ㄏㄠˋ ㄐㄧㄠˇ)
a bugle; a horn
號金(ㄏㄠˋ ㄐㄧㄣ)
registration fees
號旗(ㄏㄠˋ ㄑㄧˊ)
a signal flag
號誌(ㄏㄠˋ ㄓˋ)
a signal; a sign
號召(ㄏㄠˋ ㄓㄠˋ)
a call (to the public for an action); to summon (the public for a cause)
號稱(ㄏㄠˋ ㄔㄥ)
① to claim; to profess ② to be known as
號手(ㄏㄠˋ ㄕㄡˇ)

a bugler (in the army, etc.)

號聲(ㄏㄠˋ ㄕㄥ)
the sound of a bugle call

號數(ㄏㄠˋ ㄕㄨˋ)
number (for identification or classification)

號子(ㄏㄠˋ ·ㄗ)
① a work song sung to synchronize movements, with one person leading ②(slang) a stock exchange

號衣(ㄏㄠˋ ㄧ)
military uniforms

號外(ㄏㄠˋ ㄨㄞˋ)
an extra (issue of a newspaper)

【號】 5188
2. ㄏㄠˊ haur háo
to cry; to shout; to howl; to wail

號咷 or 號啕(ㄏㄠˊ ㄊㄠˊ)
to burst out crying; to weep aloud; to wail

號哭(ㄏㄠˊ ㄎㄨ)
to weep aloud; to wail

號寒啼飢(ㄏㄠˊ ㄏㄢˊ ㄊㄧˊ ㄐㄧ)
to cry and moan for cold and hunger

號叫(ㄏㄠˊ ㄐㄧㄠˋ)
to shout; to yell

八畫

【虡】 5189
ㄐㄩˋ jiuh jù
1. a post in the framework for a bell
2. a small table with long legs placed beside a bed

九畫

【虢】 5190
ㄍㄨㄛˊ gwo guó
name of an ancient feudal state

虢國夫人(ㄍㄨㄛˊ ㄍㄨㄛˊ ㄈㄨ ㄖㄣˊ)
Lady of Kuo—the title given to the elder sister of Yang Yü-huan (楊玉環), a famed beauty and concubine of Emperor Hsüan Tsung (玄宗) of the Tang Dynasty

十一畫

【虧】 5191
ㄎㄨㄟ kuei kuī
1. to lose; to damage; to have a deficit
2. to lack; to want; short; deficient
3. to treat unfairly; to be unfair to: 我們不會虧待你的。We won't treat you unfairly.
4. fortunately; luckily; thanks to
5. used in a mocking sense: 虧他做得出來! He had the nerve to do so.
6. the waning of the moon; to wane: 月亮漸虧。The moon is waning.

虧本(ㄎㄨㄟ ㄅㄣˇ) or 虧本兒(ㄎㄨㄟ ㄅㄜˇㄦ)
to suffer losses in business; to suffer a deficit

虧負(ㄎㄨㄟ ㄈㄨˋ)
① to be deficient ② to be negligent of an obligation; to fail

虧得(ㄎㄨㄟ ·ㄉㄜ)
① fortunately; luckily; thanks to ② a term used in a mocking sense: 虧得你說得出口! You had the nerve to say it.

虧待(ㄎㄨㄟ ㄉㄞˋ)
to treat (someone) shabbily; to maltreat

虧短(ㄎㄨㄟ ㄉㄨㄢˇ)
deficient; insufficient

虧累(ㄎㄨㄟ ㄌㄟˋ)
unable to make both ends meet; to spend more than one makes; to be in debt

虧空(ㄎㄨㄟ ·ㄎㄨㄥ)
① to spend more than one makes; to be in the red ② a loss; a deficit

虧耗(ㄎㄨㄟ ㄏㄠˋ)
to lose money; loss by a natural process

虧欠(ㄎㄨㄟ ㄑㄧㄢˋ)
① a deficit ② deficiency; insufficiency ③ to owe

虧心(ㄎㄨㄟ ㄒㄧㄣ)
to go against one's conscience; ungrateful; discreditable

虧心事(ㄎㄨㄟ ㄒㄧㄣ ㄕˋ)
a matter for remorse; something which gives one a guilty conscience

虧折(ㄎㄨㄟ ㄓㄜˊ)
① to lose ② a deficit

虧蝕(ㄎㄨㄟ ㄕˊ)
① an eclipse of the sun or moon ② a deficit

虧殺(ㄎㄨㄟ ㄕㄚ)
fortunately; luckily

虧損(ㄎㄨㄟ ㄙㄨㄣˇ)
① a deficit; a loss; to deplete: 我的虧損很大。My losses have been great. ② enfeebled or weakened by illness

虫部
ㄏㄨㄟˇ hoei huǐ

一畫

【虬】 5192
(虯) ㄑㄧㄡˊ chyou qiú
a young dragon

二畫

【虯】 5193
(虬) ㄑㄧㄡˊ chyou qiú
a young dragon

虯蟠(ㄑㄧㄡˊ ㄆㄢˊ)
curled up like a dragon

虯龍(ㄑㄧㄡˊ ㄌㄨㄥˊ)
a young dragon

虯髯(ㄑㄧㄡˊ ㄖㄢˊ) or 虯須(ㄑㄧㄡˊ ㄒㄩ)
whiskers twisted like the barbels of a dragon; curly whiskers

虯髯客(ㄑㄧㄡˊ ㄖㄢˊ ㄎㄜˋ)
the hero of a romance by Chang Yüeh (張說) of the Tang Dynasty

【虱】 5194
(蝨) ㄕ shy shī
a louse

虱目魚(ㄕ ㄇㄨˋ ㄩˊ)
milkfish

虱子(ㄕ ·ㄗ)
a louse

三畫

【虹】 5195
ㄏㄨㄥˊ horng hóng
(語音 ㄍㄤˋ ganq gàng)

a rainbow: 一道彩虹出現了。A rainbow appeared.

虹霓(ㄏㄨㄥˊ ㄋㄧˊ)
a rainbow and its reflection

虹橋(ㄏㄨㄥˊ ㄑㄧㄠˊ)
a rainbow-shaped bridge

虹吸管(ㄏㄨㄥˊ ㄒㄧ ㄍㄨㄢˇ)
a siphon

虹采(ㄏㄨㄥˊ ㄘㄞˇ)
banners; flags

虹彩(ㄏㄨㄥˊ ㄘㄞˇ)
① colors of a rainbow ② (anatomy) the iris

虹彩膜(ㄏㄨㄥˊ ㄘㄞˇ ㄇㄛˊ)
(anatomy) the iris

【虺】 5196 1. ㄏㄨㄟˇ hoei huǐ
a species of venomous snake

虺虺(ㄏㄨㄟˇ ㄏㄨㄟˇ)
(said of thunder) to rumble; rumbling

虺蜮(ㄏㄨㄟˇ ㄩˋ)
mean and vicious people

【虺】 5196 2. ㄏㄨㄟ huei huī
1. diseased; sick; ill
2. discouraged

虺隤(ㄏㄨㄟ ㄊㄨㄟˊ)
① diseased; ill; sick ② discouraged ③ tired

【虼】 5197 ㄍㄜˋ geh gè
a flea

虼蚤(ㄍㄜˋ ·ㄗㄠ)
a flea

【虻】 5198 ㄇㄥˊ meng méng
a gadfly

四畫

【蚌】 5199 ㄅㄤˋ banq bàng
an oyster

蚌埠(ㄅㄤˋ ㄅㄨˋ)
Pangfou, a city in Anhwei

蚌胎(ㄅㄤˋ ㄊㄞ)
the conception of an oyster—a pearl

蚌殼(ㄅㄤˋ ㄎㄜˊ)
an oyster shell

蚌線(ㄅㄤˋ ㄒㄧㄢˋ)
(mathematics) conchoid

蚌珠(ㄅㄤˋ ㄓㄨ)
a pearl

【蚊】 5200 (螡) ㄨㄣˊ wen wén
a mosquito; a gnat

蚊負蟻運(ㄨㄣˊ ㄈㄨˋ ㄧˇ ㄩㄣˋ)
(literally) mosquitoes carry and ants transport—to bear a heavy load with little strength

蚊雷(ㄨㄣˊ ㄌㄟˊ)
the buzz of a swarm of mosquitoes

蚊力(ㄨㄣˊ ㄌㄧˋ)
the strength of a mosquito—limited strength

蚊睫(ㄨㄣˊ ㄐㄧㄝˊ)
a mosquito's eyelash—a very tiny thing

蚊香(ㄨㄣˊ ㄒㄧㄤ) or 蚊煙(ㄨㄣˊ ㄧㄢ)
a. mosquito coil; mosquito incense

蚊陣(ㄨㄣˊ ㄓㄣˋ)
swarms of mosquitoes

蚊帳(ㄨㄣˊ ㄓㄤˋ)
a mosquito net; a mosquito-curtain; a mosquito bar

蚊蟲(ㄨㄣˊ ㄔㄨㄥˊ)
mosquitoes; gnats

蚊市(ㄨㄣˊ ㄕˋ)
swarms of mosquitoes found at dusk

蚊蚋(ㄨㄣˊ ㄖㄨㄟˋ)
mosquitoes and gnats

蚊子(ㄨㄣˊ ·ㄗ)
a mosquito; a gnat: 蚊子會咬人。Mosquitoes bite.

蚊子香(ㄨㄣˊ ·ㄗ ㄒㄧㄤ)
a mosquito coil; a mosquito stick

【蚪】 5201 ㄉㄡˇ doou dǒu
as in 蝌蚪—a tadpole

【蚋】 5202 (蜹) ㄖㄨㄟˋ ruey ruì
a gnat

蚋翼(ㄖㄨㄟˋ ㄧˋ)
wings of a gnat—very tiny things

【蚍】 5203 ㄆㄧˊ pyi pí
a large ant; a species of big ant

蚍蜉(ㄆㄧˊ ㄈㄨˊ)
Camponotus liquiperdus, a kind of black ant living on pines

蚍蜉撼大樹(ㄆㄧˊ ㄈㄨˊ ㄏㄢˋ ㄉㄚˋ ㄕㄨˋ)
(literally) an ant trying to shake a large tree—an attempt to do what is far beyond one's power

【蚓】 5204 ㄧㄣˇ yiin yǐn
as in 蚯蚓—an earthworm

【蚜】 5205 ㄧㄚˊ ya yá
a plant louse; an aphid

蚜蟲(ㄧㄚˊ ㄔㄨㄥˊ)
a plant louse; an aphid

【蚣】 5206 ㄍㄨㄥ gong gōng
as in 蜈蚣—a centipede

【蚤】 5207 ㄗㄠˇ tzao zǎo
a flea

【蚨】 5208 ㄈㄨˊ fwu fú
1. a kind of water beetle
2. as in 青蚨—another name of money or cash

【蚩】 5209 ㄔ chy chī
1. a kind of worm
2. ignorant; stupid
3. to laugh
4. ugly

蚩拙(ㄔ ㄓㄨㄛˊ)
stupid; ignorant

蚩蚩(ㄔ ㄔ)
ignorant; simple-looking

蚩尤(ㄔ ㄧㄡˊ)
Chih Yu, name of a legendary rebel overcome by Huang Ti (黃帝)

【蚇】 5210 ㄔˇ chyy chǐ
an inchworm; a measuring worm; a looper

蚇蠖 or 尺蠖(ㄔˇ ㄏㄨㄛˋ)
an inchworm; a measuring worm; a looper

五畫

【蚯】 5211 ㄑㄧㄡ chiou qiū
an earthworm

蚯蚓(ㄑㄧㄡ ㄧㄣˇ)
an earthworm

【蚰】 5212 ㄧㄡˊ you yóu
a millipede; a milleped

蚰蜒(ㄧㄡˊ ㄧㄢˊ)
① a millipede; a common house centipede ② (said of a road) winding; zigzag

【蚱】 5213 ㄓㄚˋ jah zhà

a locust; a grasshopper
蚱蜢(ㄓㄚˋ ㄇㄥˇ)
a grasshopper
蚱蟬(ㄓㄚˋ ㄔㄢˊ)
a variety of cicada

【蚶】 5214 ㄏㄢ han hān
Arca inflata, a kind of clam
蚶子(ㄏㄢ ·ㄗ)
(animal) a blood clam

【蛀】 5215 ㄓㄨˋ juh zhù
1. worms that eat into wood or books
2. (said of worms) to eat into; to bore: 這些書給蟲子蛀了。The books are moth-eaten.
蛀洞(ㄓㄨˋ ㄉㄨㄥˋ)
a cavity (in a decayed tooth)
蛀齒(ㄓㄨˋ ㄔˇ)or 蛀牙(ㄓㄨˋ ㄧㄚˊ)
decayed teeth; dental caries: 他常受蛀齒之苦。He often suffers from dental caries.
蛀蟲(ㄓㄨˋ ㄔㄨㄥˊ)
worms that eat into wood, books, etc.; a moth

【蛄】 5216 ㄍㄨ gu gū
a mole cricket 參見「螻蛄」

【蛆】 5217 ㄑㄩ chiu qū
a maggot

【蛇】 5218 1.(虵) ㄕㄜˊ sher shé
a snake; a serpent
蛇皮(ㄕㄜˊ ㄆㄧˊ)
a snake's skin
蛇皮癬(ㄕㄜˊ ㄆㄧˊ ㄒㄩㄢˇ)
(pathology) pityriasis, a skin disease marked by the shedding of branlike scales of epidermis
蛇蛻(ㄕㄜˊ ㄊㄨㄟˋ)
the slough of a snake
蛇吞象(ㄕㄜˊ ㄊㄨㄣ ㄒㄧㄤˋ)
very greedy (like a snake attempting to swallow an elephant)
蛇類(ㄕㄜˊ ㄌㄟˋ)
ophidia; snakes
蛇弓(ㄕㄜˊ ㄍㄨㄥ)
a kind of bow
蛇口蜂針(ㄕㄜˊ ㄎㄡˇ ㄈㄥ ㄓㄣ)
(literally) a snake's bite and a bee's sting—a very injurious thing or person
蛇蠍(ㄕㄜˊ ㄒㄧㄝ)
snakes and scorpions—things to be dreaded; vicious people: 此人毒如蛇蠍。This man was as vicious as a viper.
蛇行(ㄕㄜˊ ㄒㄧㄥˊ)
① to move like a snake; to take a zigzag course ② to creep along; to crawl
蛇神(ㄕㄜˊ ㄕㄣˊ)
① a deity in the form of a snake ② bizarre
蛇鼠橫行(ㄕㄜˊ ㄕㄨˇ ㄏㄥˊ ㄒㄧㄥˊ)
(literally) Snakes and rats are rampant.—Wicked people are rampant.
蛇足(ㄕㄜˊ ㄗㄨˊ)
feet for a snake—superfluity
蛇影杯弓(ㄕㄜˊ ㄧㄥˇ ㄅㄟ ㄍㄨㄥ)
illusion caused by suspicion
蛇無頭不行(ㄕㄜˊ ㄨˊ ㄊㄡˊ ㄅㄨˋ ㄒㄧㄥˊ)
(literally) A snake cannot move without a head.—A group of people can accomplish little without a leader.
蛇紋石(ㄕㄜˊ ㄨㄣˊ ㄕˊ)
(mining) serpentine (a dull-greenish rock)

【蛇】 5218 2. ㄧˊ yi yí
1. complacent
2. to pretend cordiality

【蛉】 5219 ㄌㄧㄥˊ ling líng
1. as in 蜻蛉—*Libellulidae,* a variety of dragonfly
2. as in 螟蛉—the larva of *Chilo simplex,* a kind of harmful insect; the mulberry insect

【蛋】 5220 ㄉㄢˋ dann dàn
1. an egg
2. a fellow
蛋白(ㄉㄢˋ ㄅㄞˊ)or 蛋清(ㄉㄢˋ ㄑㄧㄥ)
the white of an egg; egg white; albumen
蛋白質(ㄉㄢˋ ㄅㄞˊ ㄓˊ)
protein; albumen
蛋白石(ㄉㄢˋ ㄅㄞˊ ㄕˊ)
opal
蛋粉(ㄉㄢˋ ㄈㄣˇ)
powdered eggs
蛋糕(ㄉㄢˋ ㄍㄠ)
cake: 吃點蛋糕吧! Have some cake.
蛋殼(ㄉㄢˋ ㄎㄜˊ)
the eggshell
蛋戶 or 蜑戶(ㄉㄢˋ ㄏㄨˋ)
the boat people of Kwangtung (廣東)
蛋黃(ㄉㄢˋ ㄏㄨㄤˊ)
yolk
蛋酒(ㄉㄢˋ ㄐㄧㄡˇ)
egg flip; eggnog
蛋捲(ㄉㄢˋ ㄐㄩㄢˇ)
an egg roll
蛋捲冰淇淋(ㄉㄢˋ ㄐㄩㄢˇ ㄅㄧㄥ ㄑㄧˊ ㄌㄧㄣˊ)
an ice-cream cone
蛋形(ㄉㄢˋ ㄒㄧㄥˊ)
egg-shaped; oval

六畫

【蛙】 5221 ㄨㄚ ua wā
a frog
蛙鳴(ㄨㄚ ㄇㄧㄥˊ)
croaks of frogs
蛙鳴蟬噪(ㄨㄚ ㄇㄧㄥˊ ㄔㄢˊ ㄗㄠˋ)
(literally) croaks of frogs and chirps of cicadas—meaningless argument or debate
蛙市(ㄨㄚ ㄕˋ)
the noise of frogs in the evening
蛙人(ㄨㄚ ㄖㄣˊ)
a frogman
蛙泳(ㄨㄚ ㄩㄥˇ)
(swimming) the breaststroke

【蛔】 5222 ㄏㄨㄟˊ hwei huí
an ascarid; a roundworm
蛔蟲(ㄏㄨㄟˊ ㄔㄨㄥˊ)
an ascarid; a roundworm

【蛛】 5223 ㄓㄨ ju zhū
a spider
蛛絲(ㄓㄨ ㄙ)
gossamer; the thread spun by a spider
蛛絲馬跡(ㄓㄨ ㄙ ㄇㄚˇ ㄐㄧ)
① subtle organization (of a composition, etc.) ② clues; leads
蛛網(ㄓㄨ ㄨㄤˇ)
a spider's web; a cobweb

【蛟】 5224 ㄐㄧㄠ jiau jiāo
1. flood dragon, a mythical creature capable of invoking storms and floods

2. a shark
蛟龍(ㄐㄧㄠ ㄌㄨㄥˊ)
a flood dragon
蛟龍得水(ㄐㄧㄠ ㄌㄨㄥˊ ㄉㄜˊ ㄕㄨㄟˇ)
(literally) water for the flood dragon—opportunity for a great man to fulfill his ambition
蛟虯(ㄐㄧㄠ ㄑㄧㄡˊ)
curled up like a dragon
蛟篆(ㄐㄧㄠ ㄓㄨㄢˋ)
wriggly-shaped seal-type characters on bells, tripods, etc.

【蛤】 5225 1. ㄍㄜˊ ger gé
a clam
蛤蚌(ㄍㄜˊ ㄅㄤˋ) or 蛤蜊(ㄍㄜˊ ·ㄌㄧ) or 蛤蠣(ㄍㄜˊ ㄌㄧˋ)
Mactra veneriformis, a kind of bivalve
蛤灰(ㄍㄜˊ ㄏㄨㄟ)
lime obtained by burning sea shells

【蛤】 5225 2. ㄏㄚˊ har há
a toad
蛤蟆 or 蝦蟆(ㄏㄚˊ ·ㄇㄚ)
a toad

【蛩】 5226 ㄑㄩㄥˊ chyong qióng
1. a locust
2. a cricket
蛩鳴(ㄑㄩㄥˊ ㄇㄧㄥˊ)
the chirps of crickets
蛩螿(ㄑㄩㄥˊ ㄐㄧㄤ)
crickets and cicadas
蛩蛩(ㄑㄩㄥˊ ㄑㄩㄥˊ)
anxious; apprehensive
蛩唱(ㄑㄩㄥˊ ㄔㄤˋ)
the chirps of crickets
蛩吟(ㄑㄩㄥˊ ㄧㄣˊ)
the chirps of crickets

【蛭】 5227 ㄓˋ jyh zhì
a leech
蛭石(ㄓˋ ㄕˊ)
(mining) vermiculite

【蛐】 5228 1. ㄑㄩ chiu qū
a cricket
蛐蛐兒(ㄑㄩ ·ㄑㄩㄜㄦ)
a cricket

【蛐】 5228 2. ㄑㄩˊ chyu qú
an earthworm
蛐蟮(ㄑㄩˊ ·ㄕㄢ)
an earthworm

【蚰】 5229 ㄎㄨㄣ kuen kūn
insects

七畫

【蛺】 5230 ㄐㄧㄚˊ jya jiá
butterflies
蛺蝶(ㄐㄧㄚˊ ㄉㄧㄝˊ)
butterflies (harmful to crop plants); a vanessa

【蛸】 5231 1. ㄒㄧㄠ shiau xiāo
as in 螵蛸—mantis's egg capsule

【蛸】 5231 2. ㄕㄠ shau shāo
a variety of spider

【蛹】 5232 ㄩㄥˇ yeong yǒng
a chrysalis; a pupa
蛹化(ㄩㄥˇ ㄏㄨㄚˋ)
pupation
蛹臥(ㄩㄥˇ ㄨㄛˋ)
to live in seclusion (like a chrysalis in its cocoon)

【蛻】 5233 ㄕㄨㄟˋ shuey shuì (又讀 ㄊㄨㄟˋ tuey tuì)
1. to slough; to exuviate
2. exuviae; a slough
蛻變(ㄕㄨㄟˋ ㄅㄧㄢˋ)
① to undergo transformation ② decay
蛻皮(ㄕㄨㄟˋ ㄆㄧˊ)
to exuviate; to slough
蛻殼(ㄕㄨㄟˋ ㄎㄜˊ)
exuviae; to exuviate

【蛾】 5234 ㄜˊ er é
a moth
蛾眉(ㄜˊ ㄇㄟˊ)
long, slender eyebrows arched like the antennae of a moth; beautiful eyebrows of a woman
蛾眉月(ㄜˊ ㄇㄟˊ ㄩㄝˋ)
the crescent moon
蛾綠(ㄜˊ ㄌㄩˋ) or 蛾翠(ㄜˊ ㄘㄨㄟˋ)
dark-green coloring material for eyebrows formerly used by women

【蜀】 5235 ㄕㄨˇ shuu shǔ
1. Shu, an ancient kingdom in what is Szechwan today
2. an alternative name of Szechwan (四川)
蜀道難(ㄕㄨˇ ㄉㄠˋ ㄋㄢˊ)
The roads in Szechwan are difficult to walk.
蜀葵(ㄕㄨˇ ㄎㄨㄟˊ)
a hollyhock (*Althaea rosea*)
蜀漢(ㄕㄨˇ ㄏㄢˋ)
the Kingdom of Shu (221-263) established by Liu Pei (劉備), one of the Three Kingdoms that followed the Han Dynasty
蜀雞(ㄕㄨˇ ㄐㄧ)
a variety of large chicken (believed to originate in Szechwan)
蜀錦(ㄕㄨˇ ㄐㄧㄣˇ)
tapestry from Szechwan
蜀犬吠日(ㄕㄨˇ ㄑㄩㄢˇ ㄈㄟˋ ㄖˋ)
(literally) Szechwan dogs barking at the sun (which they see very rarely)—an inexperienced person feeling curious at or getting excited over something new to him
蜀窯(ㄕㄨˇ ㄧㄠˊ)
name of an ancient porcelain kiln in Szechwan

【蜂】 5236 ㄈㄥ feng fēng
a bee; a wasp: 蜜蜂釀蜜。The bee makes honey.
蜂蜜(ㄈㄥ ㄇㄧˋ)
honey: 這果汁像蜂蜜一樣的甜。The juice is (as) sweet as honey.
蜂目豺聲(ㄈㄥ ㄇㄨˋ ㄔㄞˊ ㄕㄥ)
with the eyes of a wasp and the voice of a wolf—very fierce; very cruel
蜂房(ㄈㄥ ㄈㄤˊ) or 蜂窩(ㄈㄥ ㄨㄛ) or 蜂巢(ㄈㄥ ㄔㄠˊ)
a beehive; a honeycomb
蜂鳥(ㄈㄥ ㄋㄧㄠˇ)
hermit, *Oreatus underwoodi*, a tiny tropical hummingbird
蜂蠟(ㄈㄥ ㄌㄚˋ)
beeswax
蜂聚(ㄈㄥ ㄐㄩˋ)
to swarm to a place
蜂起(ㄈㄥ ㄑㄧˇ)
to rise in a swarm
蜂餳(ㄈㄥ ㄒㄧㄥˊ)
honey 亦作「蜂蜜」
蜂準(ㄈㄥ ㄓㄨㄣˇ)

a high nose

蜂巢胃(ㄈㄥ ㄔㄠˊ ㄨㄟˋ)or 蜂窩胃(ㄈㄥ ㄨㄛ ㄨㄟˋ)
the reticulum (a digestive organ of animals); the honeycomb stomach

蜂出(ㄈㄥ ㄔㄨ)
numerous and confusing (like bees flying about in a swarm)

蜂乳(ㄈㄥ ㄖㄨˇ)
royal jelly

蜂刺(ㄈㄥ ㄘˋ)
the sting of a bee or wasp

蜂腰(ㄈㄥ ㄧㄠ)
①a slim waist (like that of a wasp) ②an error in versification, one of the eight faults in writing a poem

蜂午(ㄈㄥ ㄨˇ)
crowded and confusing

蜂王(ㄈㄥ ㄨㄤˊ)
a queen bee; a queen wasp

蜂擁(ㄈㄥ ㄩㄥˇ)
in a swarm; to swarm

蜂擁而上(ㄈㄥ ㄩㄥˇ ㄦˊ ㄕㄤˋ)
to close in a swarm

【蜃】 5237 ㄕㄣˋ shenn shèn
clams

蜃樓(ㄕㄣˋ ㄌㄡˊ)
same as 海市蜃樓—a mirage

蜃蛤(ㄕㄣˋ ㄍㄜˊ)
a clam

蜃氣(ㄕㄣˋ ㄑㄧˋ)or 蜃市(ㄕㄣˋ ㄕˋ)
a mirage

蜃車(ㄕㄣˋ ㄔㄜ)
a hearse

【蜆】 5238 ㄒㄧㄢˇ shean xiǎn
Corbicula leana, a variety of bivalve

【蜇】 5239 ㄓㄜˊ jer zhé
1. as in 海蜇—jellyfish
2. to sting

【蜊】 5240 ㄌㄧˊ li lí
as in 蛤蜊—a kind of bivalve

【蜓】 5241 ㄊㄧㄥˊ tyng tíng
as in 蜻蜓—a dragonfly

【蜒】 5242 ㄧㄢˊ yan yán
1. as in 蚰蜒—a millipede
2. as in 蜿蜒—to stretch for miles

【蜈】 5243 ㄨˊ wu wú
a centipede

蜈蚣(ㄨˊ ㄍㄨㄥ)
a centipede

【蜉】 5244 ㄈㄨˊ fwu fú
an ephemera; an ephemerid; a mayfly

蜉蝣(ㄈㄨˊ ㄧㄡˊ)
an ephemera; an ephemerid; a mayfly

【蜍】 5245 ㄔㄨˊ chwu chú
as in 蟾蜍—a toad

【蜋】 5246 1. ㄌㄤˊ lang láng
1. as in 螳蜋 or 螳螂—a mantis
2. a cicada

蜋蜩(ㄌㄤˊ ㄊㄧㄠˊ)
a cicada

【蜋】 5246 2. ㄌㄧㄤˊ liang liáng
as in 蜣蜋—the dung beetle (*Geotrupes laevistriatus*)

【蜑】 5247 ㄉㄢˋ dann dàn
the boat people in the coastal areas of Fukien (福建) and Kwangtung (廣東)

蜑戶(ㄉㄢˋ ㄏㄨˋ)or 蜑人(ㄉㄢˋ ㄖㄣˊ)
the boat people in the coastal areas of Fukien(福建) and Kwangtung(廣東)

蜑家(ㄉㄢˋ ㄐㄧㄚ)
boat houses of the boat people

八畫

【蜥】 5248 ㄒㄧ shi xī
a lizard

蜥蜴(ㄒㄧ ㄧˋ)
a lizard

蜥蜴類(ㄒㄧ ㄧˋ ㄌㄟˋ)
saurians

【蜘】 5249 ㄓ jy zhī
a spider

蜘蛛(ㄓ ㄓㄨ)
a spider: 蜘蛛織網。A spider weaves a web.

蜘蛛絲(ㄓ ㄓㄨ ㄙ)
gossamer; the thread spun by a spider

蜘蛛網(ㄓ ㄓㄨ ㄨㄤˇ)
a spider's web; a cobweb

【蜚】 5250 1. ㄈㄟˇ feei fěi
a cockroach

蜚蠊(ㄈㄟˇ ㄌㄧㄢˊ)
a cockroach 亦作「蟑螂」

【蜚】 5250 2.(飛) ㄈㄟ fei fēi
to fly

蜚短流長(ㄈㄟ ㄉㄨㄢˇ ㄌㄧㄡˊ ㄔㄤˊ)
to spread rumors; to gossip; rumors; gossips 亦作「飛短流長」

蜚聲(ㄈㄟ ㄕㄥ)
spreading fame; to make a name; to become famous

蜚聲國際(ㄈㄟ ㄕㄥ ㄍㄨㄛˊ ㄐㄧˋ)
world-renowned; internationally famous

蜚語(ㄈㄟ ㄩˇ)
rumors: 是誰散佈了流言蜚語? Who spread the rumors?

【蜜】 5251 ㄇㄧˋ mih mì
1. honey; nectar (in a flower)
2. sweet; syrupy; honeyed

蜜蜂(ㄇㄧˋ ㄈㄥ)
a honeybee; a bee: 他們像蜜蜂一樣忙。They are as busy as bees.

蜜蠟(ㄇㄧˋ ㄌㄚˋ)
beeswax

蜜裏調油(ㄇㄧˋ ·ㄌㄧ ㄊㄧㄠˊ ㄧㄡˊ)
on intimate terms

蜜柑(ㄇㄧˋ ㄍㄢ)or 蜜橘(ㄇㄧˋ ㄐㄩˊ)
a variety of sweet tangerine from South China

蜜供(ㄇㄧˋ ㄍㄨㄥˋ)
narrow strips of dough fried and sweetened (used as a sacrifice)

蜜酒(ㄇㄧˋ ㄐㄧㄡˇ)
sweetened wine or liquor

蜜餞(ㄇㄧˋ ㄐㄧㄢˋ)
preserves; sweetmeats; candied fruit

蜜餞砒霜(ㄇㄧˋ ㄐㄧㄢˋ ㄆㄧ ㄕㄨㄤ)
sweetmeats made with arsenic—sugarcoated poison

蜜漬(ㄇㄧˋ ㄗˋ)
preserves

蜜棗(ㄇㄧˋ ㄗㄠˇ)
date preserves

蜜語(ㄇㄧˋ ㄩˇ)
honeyed words; sweet talk

蜜月(ㄇㄧˋ ㄩㄝˋ)
a honeymoon: 他們在鄉間度

〔虫部〕

〔虫部〕

蜜月。They spent their honeymoon in the country.
蜜月旅行(ㄇㄧˋ ㄩㄝˋ ㄌㄩˇ ㄒㄧㄥˊ)
a honeymoon tour

【蜡】5252 ㄓㄚˋ jah zhà
year-end sacrifice of the Chou Dynasty
蜡祭(ㄓㄚˋ ㄐㄧˋ)
year-end sacrifice
蜡月(ㄓㄚˋ ㄩㄝˋ)
the 12th lunar month

【蝂】5253 ㄅㄢˇ baan bǎn
as in 蝜蝂—a kind of small insect which can move things many times its weight

【蜢】5254 ㄇㄥˇ meeng měng
as in 蚱蜢—a grasshopper

【蜣】5255 ㄑㄧㄤ chiang qiāng
a dung beetle
蜣螂(ㄑㄧㄤ ㄌㄤˊ) or 蜣蜋(ㄑㄧㄤ ㄌㄧㄤˊ)
a dung beetle

【蝄】5256 ㄨㄤˇ woang wǎng
a kind of monster
蝄蜽(ㄨㄤˇ ㄌㄧㄤˇ)
a kind of monster

【蜩】5257 ㄊㄧㄠˊ tyau tiáo
cicadas
蜩螗沸羹(ㄊㄧㄠˊ ㄊㄤˊ ㄈㄟˋ ㄍㄥ)
very noisy
蜩甲(ㄊㄧㄠˊ ㄐㄧㄚˇ)
a cicada's exuviae; the shell of the cicada

【蜮】5258 ㄩˋ yuh yù
a fabulous tortoise-like creature, the sand cast out of whose mouth is believed deadly to humans

【蜴】5259 ㄧˋ yih yì
as in 蜥蜴—a lizard

【蜷】5260 ㄑㄩㄢˊ chyuan quán
to wriggle; to be coiled; to be curled up
蜷伏(ㄑㄩㄢˊ ㄈㄨˊ)
to curl up; to huddle up; to lie with the knees drawn up
蜷局 or 蜷跼 or 踡跼(ㄑㄩㄢˊ ㄐㄩˊ)
curled up
蜷曲(ㄑㄩㄢˊ ㄑㄩ)
wriggly; twisted
蜷縮(ㄑㄩㄢˊ ㄙㄨㄛ)
not stretched; twisted; wriggly
蜷蜿(ㄑㄩㄢˊ ㄨㄢ)
to wind round and round

【蜻】5261 ㄑㄧㄥ ching qīng
a dragonfly
蜻蜓(ㄑㄧㄥ ㄊㄧㄥˊ)
a dragonfly
蜻蜓點水(ㄑㄧㄥ ㄊㄧㄥˊ ㄉㄧㄢˇ ㄕㄨㄟˇ)
a delicate touch (like that of a dragonfly upon the water surface)—to touch on something without going into it deeply
蜻蛉(ㄑㄧㄥ ㄌㄧㄥˊ)
Libellulidae, a species of dragonfly
蜻蜻(ㄑㄧㄥ ㄑㄧㄥ)
an insect resembling a cicada

【蜾】5262 ㄍㄨㄛˇ guoo guǒ
a kind of wasp; the sphex
蜾蠃(ㄍㄨㄛˇ ㄌㄨㄛˇ)
Eumenes pomiformis, a kind of wasp; the sphex

【蜿】5263 ㄨㄢ uan wān
to creep; to wriggle; to wind up: 道路蜿蜒到山丘上。The road winds up the hill.
蜿蜒(ㄨㄢ ㄧㄢˊ)
① creeping; snaky ② wriggly ③ to wriggle; to snake; to meander

【蝀】5264 ㄉㄨㄥ dong dōng (又讀 ㄉㄨㄥˋ donq dòng)
as in 蝃蝀—a rainbow

【蜨】5265 ㄉㄧㄝˊ dye dié
a butterfly

【蜺】5266 ㄋㄧˊ ni ní
the reflection of a rainbow

【蜹】5267 ㄖㄨㄟˋ ruey ruì
a gnat

九畫

【蝙】5268 ㄅㄧㄢ bian biān (又讀 ㄅㄧㄢˇ bean biǎn)
a bat
蝙蝠(ㄅㄧㄢ ㄈㄨˊ)
a bat
蝙蝠類(ㄅㄧㄢ ㄈㄨˊ ㄌㄟˋ)
Chiroptera

【蝌】5269 ㄎㄜ ke kē
a tadpole
蝌蚪(ㄎㄜ ㄉㄡˇ)
a tadpole
蝌蚪文(ㄎㄜ ㄉㄡˇ ㄨㄣˊ)
tadpole characters (of the Chou Dynasty, with strokes of characters shaped like tadpoles)

【蝕】5270 ㄕˊ shyr shí
1. to eclipse; an eclipse: 日蝕 a solar eclipse 月蝕 a lunar eclipse
2. to erode; to eat up slowly: 金屬爲酸所腐蝕。Metals are eroded by acids.
蝕本(ㄕˊ ㄅㄣˇ)
to suffer losses in business; to lose money; to lose one's capital
蝕損(ㄕˊ ㄙㄨㄣˇ)
to suffer losses in (funds, capital, etc.)

【蝗】5271 ㄏㄨㄤˊ hwang huáng
a locust
蝗蟲(ㄏㄨㄤˊ ㄔㄨㄥˊ)
a locust

【蝘】5272 ㄧㄢˇ yean yǎn
1. a variety of cicada
2. a gecko
蝘蜓(ㄧㄢˇ ㄊㄧㄥˊ)
a gecko 亦作「壁虎」

【蝎】5273 ㄒㄧㄝ shie xiē
a scorpion
蝎毒(ㄒㄧㄝ ㄉㄨˊ)
scorpion venom

【蝟】5274 ㄨㄟˋ wey wèi
a hedgehog
蝟毛(ㄨㄟˋ ㄇㄠˊ)
the spines of a hedgehog—crowded and complicated
蝟集(ㄨㄟˋ ㄐㄧˊ)
to be crowded and compli-

cated (like the spines of a hedgehog)

蝟起(ㄨㄟˋ ㄑㄧˇ)
(said of troubles, etc.) to arise in large numbers (like the spines of a hedgehog)

蝟鼠(ㄨㄟˋ ㄕㄨˇ)
a hedgehog 亦作「刺蝟」

蝟縮(ㄨㄟˋ ㄙㄨˋ)
to curl up like a hedgehog; to recoil; to wince; to shrink; scared

【蝠】 5275
ㄈㄨˊ fwu fú
as in 蝙蝠—a bat

【蝡】 5276
ㄖㄨㄢˇ roan ruǎn
to wriggle

【蝣】 5277
ㄧㄡˊ you yóu
as in 蜉蝣—an ephemera; a mayfly

【蝤】 5278
ㄑㄧㄡˊ chyou qiú
1. the chrysalis of a kind of beetle
2. an ephemera; a mayfly

蝤蠐(ㄑㄧㄡˊ ㄑㄧˊ)
the chrysalis of a kind of beetle; a tree-grub (to which a woman's neck was likened in ancient times)

【蝥】 5279
ㄇㄠˊ mau máo
a kind of noxious insect that feeds on the roots of rice plants

【蝦】 5280
1. ㄒㄧㄚ shia xiā
a shrimp

蝦米(ㄒㄧㄚ ㄇㄧˇ)
dried shrimps

蝦荒蟹亂(ㄒㄧㄚ ㄏㄨㄤ ㄒㄧㄝˋ ㄌㄨㄢˋ)
panic among shrimps and crabs—an omen of war

蝦醬(ㄒㄧㄚ ㄐㄧㄤˋ)
salty shrimp paste

蝦鬚(ㄒㄧㄚ ㄒㄩ)
① barbels of a shrimp ② a bamboo curtain

蝦仁(ㄒㄧㄚ ㄖㄣˊ)or 蝦仁兒(ㄒㄧㄚ ㄖㄜˊㄦ)
a shrimp with its shell removed

蝦夷(ㄒㄧㄚ ㄧˊ)
① a people who in ancient times inhabited northern Japan; Aino (or Ainu) ② old name of Hokkaido 亦作「北海道」

【蝦】 5280
2. ㄏㄚˊ har há
as in 蝦蟆—a toad

蝦蟆(ㄏㄚˊ ·ㄇㄚ)
a toad

【蝜】 5281
ㄈㄨˋ fuh fù
a kind of small insect which can move things many times its weight

蝜蝂(ㄈㄨˋ ㄅㄢˇ)
a kind of small insect which can move things many times its weight

【蝨】 5282
(虱) ㄕ shy shī
a louse

蝨目魚(ㄕ ㄇㄨˋ ㄩˊ)
a milkfish

蝨官(ㄕ ㄍㄨㄢ)
a corrupt official; a wicked official

蝨處褌中(ㄕ ㄔㄨˇ ㄎㄨㄣ ㄓㄨㄥ)
a louse inside the pants—lacking vision; mentally nearsighted

蝨子(ㄕ ·ㄗ)
a louse

【蝮】 5283
ㄈㄨˋ fuh fù
a viper

蝮蛇(ㄈㄨˋ ㄕㄜˊ)
a viper

【蝱】 5284
(虻) ㄇㄥˊ meng méng
a gadfly

【蝴】 5285
ㄏㄨˊ hwu hú
a butterfly

蝴蝶(ㄏㄨˊ ㄉㄧㄝˊ)
a butterfly

蝴蝶夢(ㄏㄨˊ ㄉㄧㄝˊ ㄇㄥˋ)
① a drama, by Kuan Han-ching (關漢卿) ② a play about Chuang-tzu's testing the chastity of his wife, by an anonymous author in the Ching Dynasty

蝴蝶骨(ㄏㄨˊ ㄉㄧㄝˊ ㄍㄨˇ)
(anatomy) the sphenoid bone 亦作「蝶骨」

蝴蝶花(ㄏㄨˊ ㄉㄧㄝˊ ㄏㄨㄚ)
a fringed iris; a fleur-de-lis

蝴蝶結(ㄏㄨˊ ㄉㄧㄝˊ ㄐㄧㄝˊ)
a rosette; a bow tie

蝴蝶裝(ㄏㄨˊ ㄉㄧㄝˊ ㄓㄨㄤ)
a way of binding books in former times somewhat similar to today's Western-style binding

【蝶】 5286
(蜨) ㄉㄧㄝˊ dye dié
a butterfly

蝶夢(ㄉㄧㄝˊ ㄇㄥˋ)
to dream in sleep (from the story of Chuang-tzu's once dreaming that he was a butterfly)

蝶粉(ㄉㄧㄝˊ ㄈㄣˇ)
powdery substance on the wings of a butterfly

蝶粉蜂黃(ㄉㄧㄝˊ ㄈㄣˇ ㄈㄥ ㄏㄨㄤˊ)
woman's virginity (from the observation that the colors of a butterfly or a bee fade after mating)

蝶衣(ㄉㄧㄝˊ ㄧ)
wings of a butterfly

蝶泳(ㄉㄧㄝˊ ㄩㄥˇ)
(swimming) butterfly stroke

【蝸】 5287
ㄍㄨㄚ gua guā
a snail

蝸髻(ㄍㄨㄚ ㄊㄧㄠˊ)
snaillike hair style of a child (in former times)

蝸牛(ㄍㄨㄚ ㄋㄧㄡˊ)
a snail: 車子像蝸牛似的前進。The cars moved at a snail's pace.

蝸廬(ㄍㄨㄚ ㄌㄨˊ)or 蝸舍(ㄍㄨㄚ ㄕㄜˋ)
a cottage; a simple dwelling

蝸角(ㄍㄨㄚ ㄐㄧㄠˇ)
a snail's tentacles—very tiny things

蝸居(ㄍㄨㄚ ㄐㄩ)
(my) humble house

蝸篆(ㄍㄨㄚ ㄓㄨㄢˋ)
the track of a snail

【蝍】 5288
ㄐㄧㄝˊ jye jié
1. a cricket
2. a centipede
3. a dragonfly

蝍蛉(ㄐㄧㄝˊ ㄌㄧㄥˊ)
a dragonfly

蝍蛆(ㄐㄧㄝˊ ㄐㄩ)
① a centipede ② a cricket

【蝯】 5289
(猿) ㄩㄢˊ yuan yuán
a monkey

〔虫部〕

〔虫部〕

十畫

【螗】5290 ㄊㄤˊ tarng táng
a kind of cicada

螗蜩(ㄊㄤˊ ㄊㄧㄠˊ)
a kind of cicada

【螃】5291 ㄆㄤˊ parng páng
a crab

螃蜞(ㄆㄤˊ ㄑㄧˊ)
Grapsus sp., a kind of crab

螃蟹(ㄆㄤˊ ˙ㄒㄧㄝ)
Grapsus nankin, a kind of crab

【螄】5292 ㄙ sy sī
a kind of mollusk with spiral shell

【螈】5293 ㄩㄢˊ yuan yuán
1. *Diemyctylus pyrrhogaster*, a kind of amphibious reptile; a salamander
2. a kind of silkworm

【融】5294 ㄖㄨㄥˊ rong róng
1. very bright; glowing; burning
2. to melt
3. to melt into; to blend; to harmonize: 油和水不相融。Oil and water don't blend.
4. cheerful; happy; joyful
5. a Chinese family name

融風(ㄖㄨㄥˊ ㄈㄥ)
spring breeze

融通(ㄖㄨㄥˊ ㄊㄨㄥ)
to comprehend; to bring together and understand thoroughly

融合 or 融和(ㄖㄨㄥˊ ㄏㄜˊ)
to blend; to fuse

融化(ㄖㄨㄥˊ ㄏㄨㄚˋ)
to melt; to fuse; to thaw

融會(ㄖㄨㄥˊ ㄏㄨㄟˋ)
to blend harmoniously

融會貫通(ㄖㄨㄥˊ ㄏㄨㄟˋ ㄍㄨㄢˋ ㄊㄨㄥ)
to blend harmoniously and grasp thoroughly; well digested and completely understood

融解(ㄖㄨㄥˊ ㄐㄧㄝˇ)
to melt; to thaw

融解點(ㄖㄨㄥˊ ㄐㄧㄝˇ ㄉㄧㄢˇ)
the melting point; the point of fusion

融解熱(ㄖㄨㄥˊ ㄐㄧㄝˇ ㄖㄜˋ)
the heat of fusion

融洽(ㄖㄨㄥˊ ㄒㄧㄚˋ)or(ㄖㄨㄥˊ ㄑㄧㄚˋ)
(said especially of human relations) harmonious

融融(ㄖㄨㄥˊ ㄖㄨㄥˊ)
① merry; happy; gay; joyful; cheerful ② warm; mild

融液(ㄖㄨㄥˊ ㄧㄝˋ)
a solid in a molten state

【螓】5295 ㄑㄧㄣˊ chyn qín
a kind of small cicada

螓首蛾眉(ㄑㄧㄣˊ ㄕㄡˇ ㄜˊ ㄇㄟˊ)
the beautiful look of a woman 參看「蛾眉」

【螞】5296 ㄇㄚˇ maa mǎ
1. an ant
2. a kind of leech

螞蟥(ㄇㄚˇ ㄏㄨㄤˊ)
a kind of leech

螞蟻(ㄇㄚˇ ㄧˇ)
an ant

【螟】5297 ㄇㄧㄥˊ ming míng
the larva of *Chilo simplex*, a kind of moth

螟蛉(ㄇㄧㄥˊ ㄌㄧㄥˊ)
the larva of *Chilo simplex*

螟蛉子(ㄇㄧㄥˊ ㄌㄧㄥˊ ㄗˇ)
an adopted son

螟蛉蛾(ㄇㄧㄥˊ ㄌㄧㄥˊ ㄜˊ)
Heliothis armigera, a kind of moth

螟蟲(ㄇㄧㄥˊ ㄔㄨㄥˊ)
the larva of *Chilo simplex*, a kind of moth

螟蛾(ㄇㄧㄥˊ ㄜˊ)
Chilo simplex, a kind of moth

【螢】5298 ㄧㄥˊ yng yíng
a luminous insect; a firefly; a glowworm

螢光(ㄧㄥˊ ㄍㄨㄤ)
fluorescence

螢光板(ㄧㄥˊ ㄍㄨㄤ ㄅㄢˇ)
a fluorescent screen

螢光幕(ㄧㄥˊ ㄍㄨㄤ ㄇㄨˋ)
a screen

螢光燈(ㄧㄥˊ ㄍㄨㄤ ㄉㄥ)
a fluorescent lamp 亦作「日光燈」

螢火蟲(ㄧㄥˊ ㄏㄨㄛˇ ㄔㄨㄥˊ)
a firefly; a glowworm

螢窗(ㄧㄥˊ ㄔㄨㄤ)
to study by the light of glowworms

螢石(ㄧㄥˊ ㄕˊ)
fluorite

【螡】5299 (蚊) ㄨㄣˊ wen wén
a mosquito

【螂】5300 (蜋) ㄌㄤˊ lang láng
same as 蜋

十一畫

【螫】5301 ㄓㄜ je zhē (又讀 ㄕˋ shyh shì)
1. a poisonous insect; a scorpion
2. to sting

【螬】5302 ㄘㄠˊ tsaur cáo
a grub (the larva of a beetle)

【螭】5303 ㄔ chy chī
a hornless dragon (usually represented in engravings adorning palaces, etc.)

螭陛(ㄔ ㄅㄧˋ)
steps of the imperial palace

螭魅 or 魑魅(ㄔ ㄇㄟˋ)
a man-eating goblin

螭魅罔兩(ㄔ ㄇㄟˋ ㄨㄤˇ ㄌㄧㄤˇ)
monsters and devils 亦作「魑魅魍魎」

螭首(ㄔ ㄕㄡˇ)or 螭頭(ㄔ ㄊㄡˊ)
the top of various structures adorned with a representation of the hornless dragon

【螮】5304 (蝃) ㄉㄧˋ dih dì
a rainbow

螮蝀 or 蝃蝀(ㄉㄧˋ ㄉㄨㄥ)
a rainbow

【螯】5305 ㄠˊ aur áo
nippers (of crabs, etc.)

【螳】5306 ㄊㄤˊ tarng táng
a mantis

螳臂當車(ㄊㄤˊ ㄅㄧˋ ㄉㄤ ㄐㄩ)
(literally) a mantis trying to stop a cart with its arms —brave but rash attempts to do what is far beyond one's ability

螳斧(ㄊㄤˊ ㄈㄨˇ)
ax-shaped forelegs of a man-

tis
螳螂(ㄊㄤˊ ㄌㄤˊ)
a mantis
螳螂捕蟬，黃雀在後(ㄊㄤˊ ㄌㄤˊ ㄅㄨˇ ㄔㄢˊ, ㄏㄨㄤˊ ㄑㄩㄝˋ ㄗㄞˋ ㄏㄡˋ)
(literally) the mantis seizing the cicada not knowing the oriole was just behind—recklessness of one blinded by greed; to covet gains ahead without knowing the danger behind

【螺】 5307 ㄌㄨㄛˊ luo luó
1. a spiral shell; a conch
2. an alias of wine cups
3. a spiral
螺杯(ㄌㄨㄛˊ ㄅㄟ)
a cup made of a spiral shell
螺貝(ㄌㄨㄛˊ ㄅㄟˋ)
a spiral shell
螺黛(ㄌㄨㄛˊ ㄉㄞˋ)
coloring material for the eyebrows used in former times
螺鈿(ㄌㄨㄛˊ ㄉㄧㄢˋ)
① inlay of polished conchs (on wares) ② mother-of-pearl inlay
螺髻(ㄌㄨㄛˊ ㄐㄧˋ)
a spiral headdress
螺階(ㄌㄨㄛˊ ㄐㄧㄝ)
a spiral staircase
螺距(ㄌㄨㄛˊ ㄐㄩˋ)
pitch
螺線(ㄌㄨㄛˊ ㄒㄧㄢˋ)
(mathematics) spiral
螺線管(ㄌㄨㄛˊ ㄒㄧㄢˋ ㄍㄨㄢˇ)
(physics) a solenoid
螺旋(ㄌㄨㄛˊ ㄒㄩㄢˊ)
a screw; a spiral
螺旋扳手(ㄌㄨㄛˊ ㄒㄩㄢˊ ㄅㄢ ㄕㄡˇ) or 螺旋起子(ㄌㄨㄛˊ ㄒㄩㄢˊ ㄑㄧˇ ·ㄗ)
a spanner
螺旋推進機(ㄌㄨㄛˊ ㄒㄩㄢˊ ㄊㄨㄟ ㄐㄧㄣˋ ㄐㄧ)
a screw propeller; a propeller; a screw
螺旋槳(ㄌㄨㄛˊ ㄒㄩㄢˊ ㄐㄧㄤˇ)
a propeller; a screw
螺旋菌(ㄌㄨㄛˊ ㄒㄩㄢˊ ㄐㄩㄣˋ)
spirillum
螺絲(ㄌㄨㄛˊ ·ㄙ)
a male screw; an external screw; a screw
螺絲母(ㄌㄨㄛˊ ·ㄙ ㄇㄨˇ)
a nut (to go with a screw)
螺絲刀(ㄌㄨㄛˊ ·ㄙ ㄉㄠ)
a screwdriver
螺絲釘(ㄌㄨㄛˊ ·ㄙ ㄉㄧㄥ)
a male screw; an external screw; a screw
螺絲起子(ㄌㄨㄛˊ ·ㄙ ㄑㄧˇ ·ㄗ)
a screwdriver
螺絲鉗(ㄌㄨㄛˊ ·ㄙ ㄑㄧㄢˊ)
a wrench
螺螄(ㄌㄨㄛˊ ㄙ)
a kind of mollusk with a spiral shell; a snail
螺壓機(ㄌㄨㄛˊ ㄧㄚ ㄐㄧ)
a screw press
螺縈(ㄌㄨㄛˊ ㄧㄥˊ)
rayon
螺紋(ㄌㄨㄛˊ ㄨㄣˊ)
① the spiral (at the tip of a finger, etc.) ② the screw thread

【螻】 5308 ㄌㄡˊ lou lóu
a mole cricket
螻蛄(ㄌㄡˊ ㄍㄨ) or 螻蟈(ㄌㄡˊ ㄩˊ)
a mole cricket
螻蟈(ㄌㄡˊ ㄍㄨㄛ)
another name of the frog
螻蟻(ㄌㄡˊ ㄧˇ)
mole crickets and ants—insignificant creatures

【螽】 5309 ㄓㄨㄥ jong zhōng
a katydid; a long-horned grasshopper; a locust
螽花(ㄓㄨㄥ ㄏㄨㄚ)
a spikelet 亦作「小穗」
螽斯(ㄓㄨㄥ ㄙ)
katydid (*Gompsocleis mikado*), a variety of the locust
螽斯衍慶(ㄓㄨㄥ ㄙ ㄧㄢˇ ㄑㄧㄥˋ)
May your offsprings be as numerous as a katydid's. (a congratulatory expression used when a son is born to a friend)

【螿】 5310 ㄐㄧㄤ jiang jiāng
a kind of cicada

【蟀】 5311 ㄕㄨㄞˋ shuay shuài (讀音 ㄕㄨㄛˋ shuoh shuò)
as in 蟋蟀—a cricket

【蟄】 5312 ㄓˊ jyr zhí (語音 ㄓㄜˊ jer zhé)
to hibernate; hibernation
蟄伏(ㄓˊ ㄈㄨˊ)
① to hibernate ② to lie low
蟄雷(ㄓˊ ㄌㄟˊ)
the first spring thunder (that awakes insects from dormancy)
蟄居(ㄓˊ ㄐㄩ)
to live in seclusion; to cloister (oneself in)
蟄蟲(ㄓˊ ㄔㄨㄥˊ)
torpid insects; dormant insects; hibernating insects
蟄獸(ㄓˊ ㄕㄡˋ)
a hibernating animal or beast

【蟆】 5313 ㄇㄚˊ ma má (語音 ·ㄇㄚ ·ma ma)
as in 蝦蟆—a toad

【蟈】 5314 ㄍㄨㄛ guo guō
1. a frog
2. a mole cricket
蟈蟈兒(ㄍㄨㄛ ·ㄍㄨㄛㄦ)
a large kind of green cricket; a katydid

【蟋】 5315 ㄒㄧ shi xī
a cricket (insect)
蟋蟀(ㄒㄧ ㄕㄨㄞˋ)
a cricket

【蟑】 5316 ㄓㄤ jang zhāng
a cockroach; a roach
蟑螂(ㄓㄤ ㄌㄤˊ)
a cockroach

【蟊】 5317 ㄇㄠˊ mau máo
insects that are injurious to crops—devourers of the grain
蟊賊(ㄇㄠˊ ㄗㄜˊ)
① insects that eat the roots of grain plants ② persons that are injurious to society; vermin

十二畫

【蟥】 5318 ㄏㄨㄤˊ hwang huáng
as in 螞蟥—a horseleech

【蟒】 5319 ㄇㄤˇ maang mǎng
1. a python; a boa
2. ceremonial robes worn by mandarins, or the embroi-

〔虫部〕

dered patterns on such robes
蟒袍(ㄇㄤˇ ㄆㄠˊ)
ceremonial robes worn by mandarins
蟒蛇(ㄇㄤˇ ㄕㄜˊ)
a python; a boa
蟒衣(ㄇㄤˇ ㄧ)
ceremonial robes worn by mandarins

【蟠】 5320 ㄆㄢˊ parn pán
1. to coil; to curl up
2. to occupy
蟠木(ㄆㄢˊ ㄇㄨˋ)
a twisted tree
蟠桃(ㄆㄢˊ ㄊㄠˊ)
① the flat peach; the saucer peach ② a legendary peach which enables the eater to live forever
蟠桃會(ㄆㄢˊ ㄊㄠˊ ㄏㄨㄟˋ)
the festival held on the 3rd day of the 3rd lunar month in honor of the Grand Old Lady of the West Heaven(西天王母)
蟠龍(ㄆㄢˊ ㄌㄨㄥˊ)
a curled-up dragon
蟠踞(ㄆㄢˊ ㄐㄩˋ)
to occupy
蟠虬紋(ㄆㄢˊ ㄑㄧㄡˊ ㄨㄣˊ)
the dragon patterns on the surface of pillars, bronzes, etc.

【蟢】 5321 ㄒㄧˇ shii xǐ
a kind of long-bodied and long-legged spider

【蟣】 5322 ㄐㄧˇ jii jǐ
1. larvae of lice
2. leeches

【蟪】 5323 ㄏㄨㄟˋ huey huì
Platypleura kaempferi, a kind of bright-colored cicada
蟪蛄(ㄏㄨㄟˋ ㄍㄨ)
Platypleura kaempferi, a kind of bright-colored cicada 亦作「寒蟬」
蟪蛄不知春秋(ㄏㄨㄟˋ ㄍㄨ ㄅㄨˋ ㄓ ㄔㄨㄣ ㄑㄧㄡ)
limited in experience or vision (like a cicada that is ignorant of spring and autumn)

【蟬】 5324 ㄔㄢˊ charn chán
1. a cicada
2. continuous; uninterrupted
蟬鬢(ㄔㄢˊ ㄅㄧㄣˋ)
the attractive hair on the temples (of a woman)
蟬不知雪(ㄔㄢˊ ㄅㄨˋ ㄓ ㄒㄩㄝˇ)
ignorant or inexperienced (like a cicada ignorant of snow)
蟬冕(ㄔㄢˊ ㄇㄧㄢˇ)or 蟬冠(ㄔㄢˊ ㄍㄨㄢ)
a kind of beautifully adorned cap worn by nobles in ancient times
蟬蛻(ㄔㄢˊ ㄊㄨㄟˋ)
① exuviae of the cicada ② to commit suicide in order to escape this dirty world
蟬聯(ㄔㄢˊ ㄌㄧㄢˊ)
① to keep on without interruption ② to stay on a position for another term; to continue to hold a post or title
蟬紗(ㄔㄢˊ ㄕㄚ)
a kind of very thin silk
蟬嘶(ㄔㄢˊ ㄙ)
the shrill sound of a cicada
蟬翼(ㄔㄢˊ ㄧˋ)
① wings of the cicada—very light things ② a kind of very thin silk
蟬吟(ㄔㄢˊ ㄧㄣˊ)
the shrill sound of the cicada
蟬紋(ㄔㄢˊ ㄨㄣˊ)
engraved cicada patterns

【蟲】 5325 ㄔㄨㄥˊ chorng chóng
insects; worms: 蠅、蚊、蚋皆是昆蟲。Flies, mosquitoes and gnats are insects.
蟲媒花(ㄔㄨㄥˊ ㄇㄟˊ ㄏㄨㄚ)
entomophilous flowers
蟲害(ㄔㄨㄥˊ ㄏㄞˋ)
damage to farm crops caused by pests; insect pest
蟲聚(ㄔㄨㄥˊ ㄐㄩˋ)
to swarm
蟲豸(ㄔㄨㄥˊ ㄓˋ)
insects and reptiles
蟲篆(ㄔㄨㄥˊ ㄓㄨㄢˋ)
a wriggly form of written characters (found on ancient bronzes, etc.)
蟲蟲蟻蟻(ㄔㄨㄥˊ ㄔㄨㄥˊ ㄧˇ ㄧˇ)
infested with insects and worms
蟲蝕(ㄔㄨㄥˊ ㄕˊ)
worm-eaten
蟲書(ㄔㄨㄥˊ ㄕㄨ)
① a wriggly form of characters (found usually on ancient bronzes) ② marks on worm-eaten objects (which look like the seal type character)
蟲霜水旱(ㄔㄨㄥˊ ㄕㄨㄤ ㄕㄨㄟˇ ㄏㄢˋ)
insects, frost, floods, and droughts—the four major terrors of farmers
蟲子
①(ㄔㄨㄥˊ ㄗˇ) eggs of insects
②(ㄔㄨㄥˊ ·ㄗ) worms; insects
蟲災(ㄔㄨㄥˊ ㄗㄞ)
a plague of insects
蟲兒(ㄔㄨㄥˊㄦ)
insects; worms
蟲兒眼(ㄔㄨㄥˊㄦ ㄧㄢˇ)
a worm-eaten cavity (in fruit)
蟲牙(ㄔㄨㄥˊ ㄧㄚˊ)
a decayed tooth; a carious tooth; dental caries
蟲瘿(ㄔㄨㄥˊ ㄧㄥˇ)
galls—gnarls on plants caused by injurious insects 亦作「五倍子」or「沒食子」
蟲魚之學(ㄔㄨㄥˊ ㄩˊ ㄓ ㄒㄩㄝˊ)
textual research of little value

【蟟】 5326 ㄌㄧㄠˇ leau liǎo
as in 蛁蟟—*Pomponia maculaticollis*, a kind of cicada

【蟮】 5327 ㄕㄢˋ shann shàn
an earthworm

十三畫

【蟹】 5328 (蠏) ㄒㄧㄝˋ shieh xiè
a crab
蟹杯(ㄒㄧㄝˋ ㄅㄟ)
a crab shell used as a wine cup
蟹殼黃(ㄒㄧㄝˋ ㄎㄜˊ ㄏㄨㄤˊ)
a crisp roll with sesame on the upper crust
蟹黃(ㄒㄧㄝˋ ㄏㄨㄤˊ)
crab spawn
蟹臍(ㄒㄧㄝˋ ㄑㄧˊ)
the underside of a crab

蟹箝(ㄒㄧㄝˋ ㄑㄧㄢˊ)
nippers, or pincers, of a crab
蟹行(ㄒㄧㄝˋ ㄒㄧㄥˊ)
to go sideways; to move laterally
蟹行文字(ㄒㄧㄝˋ ㄒㄧㄥˊ ㄨㄣˊ ㄗˋ)
the lateral writing system of European languages, such as English, Latin, etc.
蟹螯(ㄒㄧㄝˋ ㄠˊ)
nippers, or pincers, of a crab

【蟶】 5329 ㄔㄥ cheng chēng
a razor clam; a razor shell
蟶田(ㄔㄥ ㄊㄧㄢˊ)or 蟶埕(ㄔㄥ ㄔㄥˊ)
fields on the seashore where razor shells are cultivated
蟶乾(ㄔㄥ ㄍㄢ)
a dried razor clam
蟶子(ㄔㄥ ·ㄗ)
a razor clam; a razor shell

【蟺】 5330 (蟮) ㄕㄢˋ shann shàn
an earthworm

【蟻】 5331 ㄧˇ yii yǐ
an ant
蟻民(ㄧˇ ㄇㄧㄣˊ)
we (a term used in petitions to the government by the people in former times)
蟻慕(ㄧˇ ㄇㄨˋ)
to yearn for; to long for
蟻封(ㄧˇ ㄈㄥ)
an ant hill; a formicary
蟻附(ㄧˇ ㄈㄨˋ)
to swarm over (as ants swarm over their prey)
蟻垤(ㄧˇ ㄉㄧㄝˊ)or 蟻冢(ㄧˇ ㄓㄨㄥˇ)
an ant hill; a formicary
蟻動(ㄧˇ ㄉㄨㄥˋ)
to swarm or move like ants; to formicate
蟻寇(ㄧˇ ㄎㄡˋ)
a petty robber
蟻潰(ㄧˇ ㄎㄨㄟˋ)
to disperse like ants
蟻合(ㄧˇ ㄏㄜˊ)
to swarm to a place from all sides
蟻結(ㄧˇ ㄐㄧㄝˊ)
to band together
蟻聚(ㄧˇ ㄐㄩˋ)
to swarm to a place from all sides
蟻丘(ㄧˇ ㄑㄧㄡ)
an ant hill
蟻醛(ㄧˇ ㄑㄩㄢˊ)
formaldehyde
蟻穴(ㄧˇ ㄒㄩㄝˊ)
① an ants' nest ② small losses or nibblings which should be stopped in time to prevent a major disaster
蟻視(ㄧˇ ㄕˋ)
to despise: 不要蟻視窮人。Don't despise the poor.
蟻術(ㄧˇ ㄕㄨˋ)
the technique, or art, of the ant—diligence or industry
蟻壤(ㄧˇ ㄖㄤˇ)
an ants' nest
蟻酸(ㄧˇ ㄙㄨㄢ)
formic acid

【蟾】 5332 ㄔㄢˊ charn chán
a toad (especially the one supposed to live on the moon)
蟾魄(ㄔㄢˊ ㄆㄛˋ)
the moon
蟾兔(ㄔㄢˊ ㄊㄨˋ)
the hare supposed to live on the moon
蟾輪(ㄔㄢˊ ㄌㄨㄣˊ)
the moon
蟾桂(ㄔㄢˊ ㄍㄨㄟˋ)
the shades on the moon
蟾光(ㄔㄢˊ ㄍㄨㄤ)
moonlight
蟾宮(ㄔㄢˊ ㄍㄨㄥ)
the moon
蟾宮折桂(ㄔㄢˊ ㄍㄨㄥ ㄓㄜˊ ㄍㄨㄟˋ)
to emerge in success from a civil service examination
蟾蜍(ㄔㄢˊ ㄔㄨˊ)
a toad (especially in reference to the one supposed to live on the moon)
蟾彩(ㄔㄢˊ ㄘㄞˇ)
moonlight

【蠅】 5333 ㄧㄥˊ yng yíng
a fly
蠅拂(ㄧㄥˊ ㄈㄨˊ)
a fly brush; a swatter
蠅頭小楷(ㄧㄥˊ ㄊㄡˊ ㄒㄧㄠˇ ㄎㄞˇ)or 蠅頭小字(ㄧㄥˊ ㄊㄡˊ ㄒㄧㄠˇ ㄗˋ)
letters or characters as small as the head of a fly; very small (handwritten) characters
蠅頭微利(ㄧㄥˊ ㄊㄡˊ ㄨㄟˊ ㄌㄧˋ)or 蠅頭小利(ㄧㄥˊ ㄊㄡˊ ㄒㄧㄠˇ ㄌㄧˋ)
petty profits
蠅蠅(ㄧㄥˊ ㄧㄥˊ)
wriggling; crawling
蠅營狗苟(ㄧㄥˊ ㄧㄥˊ ㄍㄡˇ ㄍㄡˇ)
corrupt and servile practices; to seek advantage meanly

【蠆】 5334 ㄔㄞˋ chay chài
a kind of scorpion
蠆尾(ㄔㄞˋ ㄨㄟˇ)
the poisonous tail of a scorpion—a harmful thing or person

【蠍】 5335 ㄒㄧㄝ shie xiē
a scorpion
蠍虎(ㄒㄧㄝ ㄏㄨˇ)
a gecko; a house lizard
蠍子(ㄒㄧㄝ ·ㄗ)
a scorpion

【蠃】 5336 ㄌㄨㄛˇ luoo luǒ
the solitary wasp

十四畫

【蠐】 5337 ㄑㄧˊ chyi qí
a grub (a kind of larva)
蠐螬(ㄑㄧˊ ㄘㄠˊ)
a grub (a kind of larva)

【蠑】 5338 ㄖㄨㄥˊ rong róng
1. a kind of mollusk
2. a kind of reptile

【蠓】 5339 ㄇㄥˇ meeng měng
a kind of gnat; a midge; a biting midge
蠓蟲(ㄇㄥˇ ㄔㄨㄥˊ)
a kind of gnat

【蠔】 5340 ㄏㄠˊ haur háo
an oyster 亦作「牡蠣」
蠔白(ㄏㄠˊ ㄅㄞˊ)
the edible part of an oyster
蠔油(ㄏㄠˊ ㄧㄡˊ)
oyster sauce

【蠕】 5341 ㄖㄨㄢˇ roan ruǎn
to wriggle; to squirm
蠕動(ㄖㄨㄢˇ ㄉㄨㄥˋ)

to wriggle; to squirm
蠕形動物(ㄖㄨㄢˇ ㄒㄧㄥˊ ㄉㄨㄥˋ ㄨˋ)
vermicular animals; Vermes
蠕蠕(ㄖㄨㄢˇ ㄖㄨㄢˇ)
① wriggling; wriggly; vermicular ② name of an ancient Chinese tribe to the north

〔虫部〕

【蠖】 5342 ㄏㄨㄛˋ huoh huò
a measuring worm; a looper
蠖屈(ㄏㄨㄛˋ ㄑㄩ)
to humble oneself temporarily (as a looper loops itself momentarily)

十五畫

【蠟】 5343 ㄌㄚˋ lah là
1. wax
2. a candle
蠟板(ㄌㄚˋ ㄅㄢˇ)
a stencil plate
蠟筆(ㄌㄚˋ ㄅㄧˇ)
a crayon: 他用蠟筆畫肖像。He drew a portrait with crayons.
蠟梅(ㄌㄚˋ ㄇㄟˊ)
Calycanthus praecox, a kind of plum blooming in winter
蠟淚(ㄌㄚˋ ㄌㄟˋ)
wax guttering; drips from a burning candle
蠟炬(ㄌㄚˋ ㄐㄩˋ)
a candle
蠟扦(ㄌㄚˋ ㄑㄧㄢ)or 蠟扦兒(ㄌㄚˋ ㄑㄧㄚㄦ)
the top of a candlestick
蠟芯兒(ㄌㄚˋ ㄒㄧㄜㄦ)
a candlewick
蠟像(ㄌㄚˋ ㄒㄧㄤˋ)
a wax figure; a waxwork
蠟像館(ㄌㄚˋ ㄒㄧㄤˋ ㄍㄨㄢˇ)
a waxworks hall; a wax museum
蠟紙(ㄌㄚˋ ㄓˇ)
① wax paper; waxed paper ② stencil paper: 她正在刻蠟紙。She's cutting a stencil.
蠟燭(ㄌㄚˋ ㄓㄨˊ)
① a candle: 他正點著一支蠟燭。He is lighting a candle. ②(Shanghai dialect) one who bullies the weak and is easily bullied by the strong
蠟蟲(ㄌㄚˋ ㄔㄨㄥˊ)
a wax insect
蠟染(ㄌㄚˋ ㄖㄢˇ)
batik, or battik
蠟人(ㄌㄚˋ ㄖㄣˊ)
a wax figure 亦作「蠟像」
蠟油(ㄌㄚˋ ㄧㄡˊ)
melted wax
蠟丸(ㄌㄚˋ ㄨㄢˊ)
a wax-coated pill; a wax ball

【蠡】 5344 1. ㄌㄧˇ lii lǐ
1. a wood-boring insect
2. (said of insects) to bore or eat wood
3. worm-eaten

【蠡】 5344 2. ㄌㄧˊ li lí
1. a calabash
2. a calabash shell serving as a dipper; a dipper
蠡測(ㄌㄧˊ ㄘㄜˋ)
to be very naive (like one trying to measure the ocean with a calabash)

【蠢】 5345 (惷) ㄔㄨㄣˇ choen chǔn
1. to wriggle; to squirm
2. stupid; foolish; dull; silly
蠢笨(ㄔㄨㄣˇ ㄅㄣˋ)
stupid; foolish: 他犯了蠢笨的錯誤。He made a stupid mistake.
蠢笨愚頑(ㄔㄨㄣˇ ㄅㄣˋ ㄩˊ ㄨㄢˊ)
stupid and stubborn
蠢動(ㄔㄨㄣˇ ㄉㄨㄥˋ)
① to wriggle; to squirm ② (said of enemy troops, etc.) to move busily in preparation for action 參看「蠢蠢欲動」
蠢陋(ㄔㄨㄣˇ ㄌㄡˋ)
stupid and uncultured
蠢貨(ㄔㄨㄣˇ ㄏㄨㄛˋ)
a simpleton; a fool; an idiot; a blockhead; a dunce
蠢蠢欲動(ㄔㄨㄣˇ ㄔㄨㄣˇ ㄩˋ ㄉㄨㄥˋ)
(said of enemy troops, etc.) moving busily in preparation for action
蠢才 or 蠢材(ㄔㄨㄣˇ ㄘㄞˊ)
a simpleton; a fool; an idiot

【蠣】 5346 ㄌㄧˋ lih lì
an oyster 亦作「牡蠣」
蠣粉(ㄌㄧˋ ㄈㄣˇ)
lime obtained by burning oyster shells
蠣房(ㄌㄧˋ ㄈㄤˊ)
oyster shells
蠣黃(ㄌㄧˋ ㄏㄨㄤˊ)
the edible part of an oyster

十六畫

【蠨】 5347 ㄒㄧㄠ shiau xiāo
Teraguatha, a kind of spider with long legs 亦作「喜蛛」

十七畫

【蠱】 5348 ㄍㄨˇ guu gǔ
1. poison; venom; harm
2. to bewitch; to enchant
蠱敝(ㄍㄨˇ ㄅㄧˋ)
ills; evils
蠱媚(ㄍㄨˇ ㄇㄟˋ)
to bewitch or charm by sensual appeal
蠱毒(ㄍㄨˇ ㄉㄨˊ)
① to enchant and injure; to cast a harmful spell over ② to poison
蠱惑(ㄍㄨˇ ㄏㄨㄛˋ)
to confuse by magic or witchcraft; to put under a spell; to enchant
蠱疾(ㄍㄨˇ ㄐㄧˊ)
insanity; derangement

【蠲】 5349 ㄐㄩㄢ jiuan juān
1. a millipede
2. clean; pure; bright
3. to clean; to wash; to cleanse
4. to remit or remove (taxes, sentences, etc.)
蠲免(ㄐㄩㄢ ㄇㄧㄢˇ)
to remit (taxes, etc.)
蠲賦(ㄐㄩㄢ ㄈㄨˋ)
to remit levies
蠲滌(ㄐㄩㄢ ㄉㄧˊ)
to wash; to cleanse
蠲體(ㄐㄩㄢ ㄊㄧˇ)
to cleanse the body; to clean oneself
蠲苛(ㄐㄩㄢ ㄎㄜ)
to remove oppressive laws or taxes
蠲潔(ㄐㄩㄢ ㄐㄧㄝˊ)
to cleanse; to clean; to purify
蠲減(ㄐㄩㄢ ㄐㄧㄢˇ)

to remove or lighten (taxes, sentences, etc.)

蠲除(ㄐㄩㄢ ㄔㄨˊ)
to remove (oppressive laws, levies, etc.); to exempt

蠲租(ㄐㄩㄢ ㄗㄨ)
to remit rentals or taxes

【蠭】5350 (蜂)ㄈㄥ feng fēng
a bee; a wasp

十八畫

【蠶】5351 ㄘㄢˊ tsarn cán
a silkworm

蠶箔 or 蠶薄(ㄘㄢˊ ㄅㄛˊ)
an apparatus made of reeds for raising silkworms

蠶眠(ㄘㄢˊ ㄇㄧㄢˊ)
torpidity of a silkworm before casting its skin

蠶豆(ㄘㄢˊ ㄉㄡˋ)
a horse bean; a fava bean

蠶女(ㄘㄢˊ ㄋㄩˇ)or 蠶姑(ㄘㄢˊ ㄍㄨ)
a silkworm-raising woman

蠶工(ㄘㄢˊ ㄍㄨㄥ)
silkworm culture; sericulture

蠶繭(ㄘㄢˊ ㄐㄧㄢˇ)
the cocoon of the silkworm

蠶師(ㄘㄢˊ ㄕ)
a sericulturist

蠶食鯨吞(ㄘㄢˊ ㄕˊ ㄐㄧㄥ ㄊㄨㄣ)
now nibbling like a silkworm, now engulfing like a whale (said of the aggressive expansion of a nation)

蠶室(ㄘㄢˊ ㄕˋ)
① a silkworm nursery ② a prison where the punishment of castration was inflicted in ancient times

蠶事(ㄘㄢˊ ㄕˋ)
silkworm culture; sericulture

蠶沙(ㄘㄢˊ ㄕㄚ)
the black excretion of silkworms

蠶子(ㄘㄢˊ ㄗˇ)
the eggs of silkworms

蠶絲(ㄘㄢˊ ㄙ)
natural silk; silk: 這條領帶是蠶絲製成的。This tie is made of silk.

蠶桑(ㄘㄢˊ ㄙㄤ)
a silkworm mulberry

蠶蛾(ㄘㄢˊ ㄜˊ)
a silkworm moth

蠶衣(ㄘㄢˊ ㄧ)
① the cocoon of the silkworm ② silk dress ③ the dress of a woman who raises silkworms

蠶蟻(ㄘㄢˊ ㄧˇ)
newly-hatched silkworms

蠶月(ㄘㄢˊ ㄩㄝˋ)
the third lunar month; the silkworm month

蠶蛹(ㄘㄢˊ ㄩㄥˇ)
a silkworm chrysalis or pupa

【蠵】5352 ㄒㄧ shi xī
a kind of large-sized turtle

【蠹】5353 (蠧) ㄉㄨˋ duh dù
1. a moth; a kind of insect that eats into books or clothing: 書蠹 a bookworm
2. moth-eaten; worm-eaten
3. an insect that eats up the resources—(figuratively) an embezzler

蠹國害民(ㄉㄨˋ ㄍㄨㄛˊ ㄏㄞˋ ㄇㄧㄣˊ)
to rob the state and hurt the people; to eat up public funds and prey upon the people

蠹簡(ㄉㄨˋ ㄐㄧㄢˇ)
old worm-eaten books

蠹蟲(ㄉㄨˋ ㄔㄨㄥˊ)
① a moth ② a harmful person; vermin

蠹魚(ㄉㄨˋ ㄩˊ)
Lepisma saccharina, a kind of silvery worm that eats clothes, books, etc.; silverfish: 蠹魚蝕書。Silverfish eat away books.

十九畫

【蠻】5354 ㄇㄢˊ man mán
1. barbarous; savage; barbarians in the south
2. quite; pretty; very; fairly: 這本書蠻不錯的。This is quite a good book.

蠻不講理(ㄇㄢˊ ·ㄅㄨ ㄐㄧㄤˇ ㄌㄧˇ)
savage; rude; impervious to reason; brutal; unreasonable

蠻不錯(ㄇㄢˊ ·ㄅㄨ ㄘㄨㄛˋ)
not bad at all

蠻貊(ㄇㄢˊ ㄇㄛˋ)
barbarian tribes

蠻力氣(ㄇㄢˊ ㄌㄧˋ ·ㄑㄧ)
great strength

蠻幹(ㄇㄢˊ ㄍㄢˋ)
to go ahead without considering the consequences

蠻好(ㄇㄢˊ ㄏㄠˇ)
very good; fairly good

蠻橫(ㄇㄢˊ ㄏㄥˋ)
barbarous; savage; arbitrary; peremptory; unreasonable; arbitrarily: 他那蠻橫無理的要求很荒謬。His unreasonable demands are ridiculous.

蠻子(ㄇㄢˊ ·ㄗ)
barbarians (a contemptuous term applied to southerners by northerners in ancient times)

蠻族(ㄇㄢˊ ㄗㄨˊ)
barbarian tribes; savage tribes; primitive people

蠻夷戎狄(ㄇㄢˊ ㄧˊ ㄖㄨㄥˊ ㄉㄧˊ)
(collectively) the barbarians

蠻有道理(ㄇㄢˊ ㄧㄡˇ ㄉㄠˋ ·ㄌㄧ)
It sounds reasonable.

蠻有意思(ㄇㄢˊ ㄧㄡˇ ㄧˋ ·ㄙ)
very interesting; quite interesting 亦作「蠻有趣」

二十畫

【蠼】5355 ㄐㄩㄝˊ jyue jué
1. a female monkey 亦作「玃」
2. a black insect with six legs, capable of ejecting poison for self-defense

血部
ㄒㄩㄝˋ shiueh xuè

【血】5356 ㄒㄩㄝˋ shiueh xuè (語音 ㄒㄧㄝˇ shiee xiě)
1. blood; blood relationship
2. the menses

血泊(ㄒㄧㄝˇ ㄅㄛˊ)
a pool of blood

血本(ㄒㄧㄝˇ ㄅㄣˇ)
the net cost; the rock-bottom cost; the original capital

〔血部〕

血本無歸(ㄒㄧㄝˇ ㄅㄣˇ ㄨˊ ㄍㄨㄟ)
no return of hard-earned capital

血崩(ㄒㄧㄝˇ ㄅㄥ)
menorrhagia

血餅(ㄒㄧㄝˇ ㄅㄧㄥˇ)or 血塊(ㄒㄧㄝˇ ㄎㄨㄞˋ)
a cake of blood; coagulated blood

血珀(ㄒㄧㄝˇ ㄆㄛˋ)
crimson amber

血盆大口(ㄒㄧㄝˇ ㄆㄣˊ ㄉㄚˋ ㄎㄡˇ)
a large and fierce-looking mouth

血沫子(ㄒㄧㄝˇ ㄇㄛˋ ·ㄗ)
blood foam formed on the surface of a pool of blood

血脈(ㄒㄧㄝˇ ㄇㄞˋ)
① large and small blood vessels ② blood relationship; a strain

血點(ㄒㄧㄝˇ ㄉㄧㄢˇ)or 血滴(ㄒㄧㄝˇ ㄉㄧ)
bloody spots; drops of blood; blood splashes

血糖(ㄒㄧㄝˇ ㄊㄤˊ)
blood sugar; blood glucose

血統(ㄒㄧㄝˇ ㄊㄨㄥˇ)
blood-relationship; a strain; lineage; consanguinity; pedigree

血統證明書(ㄒㄧㄝˇ ㄊㄨㄥˇ ㄓㄥˋ ㄇㄧㄥˊ ㄕㄨ)
the pedigree certificate (of a pet)

血濃於水(ㄒㄧㄝˇ ㄋㄨㄥˊ ㄩˊ ㄕㄨㄟˇ)
Blood is thicker than water.

血淚(ㄒㄧㄝˇ ㄌㄟˋ)
tears and blood—extreme sorrow

血淚史(ㄒㄧㄝˇ ㄌㄟˋ ㄕˇ)
a story written in tears and blood—a very sad story; a heart-rending story

血流漂杵(ㄒㄧㄝˇ ㄌㄧㄡˊ ㄆㄧㄠ ㄔㄨˇ)
so much blood being shed as to float the pestles—descriptive of a fierce battle or a scene of big carnage

血流成河(ㄒㄧㄝˇ ㄌㄧㄡˊ ㄔㄥˊ ㄏㄜˊ)
People are bleeding so much on the battlefield that their blood flows as a river.

血流如注(ㄒㄧㄝˇ ㄌㄧㄡˊ ㄖㄨˊ ㄓㄨˋ)
blood cascading down without stop

血淋淋(ㄒㄧㄝˇ ㄌㄧㄣˊ ㄌㄧㄣˊ)
① sanguinary; blood-dripping; bloody ② the down-to-earth (truth); naked (facts)

血量(ㄒㄧㄝˇ ㄌㄧㄤˋ)
the total amount of blood in a human body; blood volume

血路(ㄒㄧㄝˇ ㄌㄨˋ)
a blood vessel

血淥淥(ㄒㄧㄝˇ ㄌㄨˋ ㄌㄨˋ)
blood dripping all around; sanguinary

血管(ㄒㄧㄝˇ ㄍㄨㄢˇ)
blood vessels

血管硬化(ㄒㄧㄝˇ ㄍㄨㄢˇ ㄧㄥˋ ㄏㄨㄚˋ)
sclerosis vascularis, the hardening or sclerosis of blood vessels

血口噴人(ㄒㄧㄝˇ ㄎㄡˇ ㄆㄣ ㄖㄣˊ)
to curse and slander; to make false accusations against others

血庫(ㄒㄧㄝˇ ㄎㄨˋ)
a blood bank

血塊子(ㄒㄧㄝˇ ㄎㄨㄞˋ ·ㄗ)
clotted blood; a clot of blood; blood clots

血虧(ㄒㄩㄝˋ ㄎㄨㄟ)
anemia or anaemia 參看「血虛」

血海深仇(ㄒㄧㄝˇ ㄏㄞˇ ㄕㄣ ㄔㄡˊ)
a blood feud; intense and deep-seated hatred

血汗(ㄒㄧㄝˇ ㄏㄢˋ)
blood and sweat—hard toil

血汗錢(ㄒㄧㄝˇ ㄏㄢˋ ㄑㄧㄢˊ)
money earned by very hard work or toil; hard-earned money

血花(ㄒㄧㄝˇ ㄏㄨㄚ)
blood splashes; bloodstains

血紅(ㄒㄧㄝˇ ㄏㄨㄥˊ)
as red as blood; scarlet

血跡(ㄒㄧㄝˇ ㄐㄧ)
bloodstained; bloodstains

血跡斑斑(ㄒㄧㄝˇ ㄐㄧ ㄅㄢ ㄅㄢ)
all covered with bloodstains; bloodstains everywhere; sanguinary

血祭(ㄒㄧㄝˇ ㄐㄧˋ)
a blood sacrifice or offering

血漿(ㄒㄧㄝˇ ㄐㄧㄤ)
blood plasma

血氣(ㄒㄧㄝˇ ㄑㄧˋ)
① one's temperament, disposition, etc. ② vigor; animal spirits or powers ③ courageous and upright: 他是個有血氣的青年。He is a courageous and upright young man. ④ blood and breath—human beings

血氣方剛(ㄒㄩㄝˋ ㄑㄧˋ ㄈㄤ ㄍㄤ)
(said of youths) hot-tempered; easily excited; full of vigor

血氣之勇(ㄒㄧㄝˇ ㄑㄧˋ ㄓ ㄩㄥˇ)
foolhardiness; courage or bravery emanating from one's emotional outbursts, not from cool judgment or the sense of righteousness; brute courage

血球(ㄒㄧㄝˇ ㄑㄧㄡˊ)or 血輪(ㄒㄧㄝˇ ㄌㄨㄣˊ)
blood corpuscles; blood cells: 紅血球 the red corpuscles

血球素(ㄒㄧㄝˇ ㄑㄧㄡˊ ㄙㄨˋ)
globin

血親(ㄒㄧㄝˇ ㄑㄧㄣ)
blood relatives; blood relation

血清(ㄒㄧㄝˇ ㄑㄧㄥ)
serum

血清療法(ㄒㄧㄝˇ ㄑㄧㄥ ㄌㄧㄠˊ ㄈㄚˇ)
serotherapy

血清學(ㄒㄧㄝˇ ㄑㄧㄥ ㄒㄩㄝˊ)
serology

血吸蟲(ㄒㄧㄝˇ ㄒㄧ ㄔㄨㄥˊ)
a blood fluke

血小板(ㄒㄧㄝˇ ㄒㄧㄠˇ ㄅㄢˇ)
blood platelets; thrombocyte

血腥(ㄒㄧㄝˇ ㄒㄧㄥ)
reeking of blood; bloody; sanguinary

血腥氣(ㄒㄧㄝˇ ㄒㄧㄥ ㄑㄧˋ)
the smell of raw flesh and blood

血型(ㄒㄧㄝˇ ㄒㄧㄥˊ)
a blood type; a blood group

血型鑑定(ㄒㄧㄝˇ ㄒㄧㄥˊ ㄐㄧㄢˋ ㄉㄧㄥˋ)
blood grouping

血性(ㄒㄧㄝˇ ㄒㄧㄥˋ)
a strong sense of righteousness

血虛(ㄒㄧㄝˇ ㄒㄩ)
anemia; blood deficiency 參看「血虧」

血債(ㄒㄧㄝˇ ㄓㄞˋ)
a blood debt; a heinous crime: 侵略者在中國血債纍纍。

The invaders had heavy blood debts in China.

血債血還(ㄒㄧㄝˇ ㄓㄞˋ ㄒㄧㄝˇ ㄏㄨㄢˊ)
Debts of blood must be paid in blood.

血詔(ㄒㄧㄝˇ ㄓㄠˋ)
an imperial decree written in the monarch's own blood

血戰(ㄒㄧㄝˇ ㄓㄢˋ)
a fierce or bloody battle

血赤素(ㄒㄧㄝˇ ㄔˋ ㄙㄨˋ)
hemoglobin

血仇(ㄒㄧㄝˇ ㄔㄡˊ)
a blood feud

血石(ㄒㄧㄝˇ ㄕˊ)or 血石髓(ㄒㄧㄝˇ ㄕˊ ㄙㄨㄟˇ)
(mineral)bloodstone

血書(ㄒㄧㄝˇ ㄕㄨ)
① to write in blood—in great desperation or extreme indignation ② a petition, letter, etc. written in blood

血屬(ㄒㄧㄝˇ ㄕㄨˇ)
blood relatives

血水(ㄒㄧㄝˇ ㄕㄨㄟˇ)
① blood ② bloodstained water

血栓症(ㄒㄧㄝˇ ㄕㄨㄢ ㄓㄥˋ)or 血塞(ㄒㄧㄝˇ ㄙㄜˋ)
thrombosis

血肉模糊(ㄒㄧㄝˇ ㄖㄡˋ ㄇㄛˊ ˙ㄏㄨ)
(said of human bodies) badly mutilated; mutilated beyond recognition

血肉橫飛(ㄒㄧㄝˇ ㄖㄡˋ ㄏㄥˊ ㄈㄟ)
flesh and blood flying in all directions—descriptive of a fierce battle or carnage

血肉之軀(ㄒㄧㄝˇ ㄖㄡˋ ㄓ ㄑㄩ)
the human body; flesh and blood

血染沙場(ㄒㄧㄝˇ ㄖㄢˇ ㄕㄚ ㄔㄤˇ)
The battlefield is stained with blood.

血刃(ㄒㄧㄝˇ ㄖㄣˋ)
to bloody one's blade—to kill

血族(ㄒㄧㄝˇ ㄗㄨˊ)
a clan with blood relationship

血絲蟲(ㄒㄧㄝˇ ㄙ ㄔㄨㄥˊ)
filaria

血絲兒(ㄒㄧㄝˇ ㄙㄜㄦ)
detectable traces of blood (in sputum, etc.) in silky or fibrous form

血祀(ㄒㄧㄝˇ ㄙˋ)
a blood sacrifice or offering 亦作「血祭」

血嗣(ㄒㄧㄝˇ ㄙˋ)or 血胤(ㄒㄧㄝˇ ㄧㄣˋ)
one's offspring or descendants

血色(ㄒㄧㄝˇ ㄙㄜˋ)
① scarlet; red ② one's complexion (rosy or pale)

血色素(ㄒㄧㄝˇ ㄙㄜˋ ㄙㄨˋ)
hematin

血案(ㄒㄧㄝˇ ㄢˋ)
a bloody incident; a murder case

血衣(ㄒㄧㄝˇ ㄧ)
bloodstained garments, dresses, etc.

血壓(ㄒㄧㄝˇ ㄧㄚ)
blood pressure

血壓低(ㄒㄧㄝˇ ㄧㄚ ㄉㄧ)
low blood pressure; hypotension 亦作「低血壓」

血壓高(ㄒㄧㄝˇ ㄧㄚ ㄍㄠ)
high blood pressure or hypertension 亦作「高血壓」

血壓計(ㄒㄧㄝˇ ㄧㄚ ㄐㄧˋ)
a sphygmomanometer; a hemadynamometer

血液(ㄒㄧㄝˇ ㄧㄝˋ)
the blood: 新鮮的血液 fresh blood

血液學(ㄒㄧㄝˇ ㄧㄝˋ ㄒㄩㄝˊ)
hematology

血液循環(ㄒㄧㄝˇ ㄧㄝˋ ㄒㄩㄣˊ ㄏㄨㄢˊ)
blood circulation

血友症(ㄒㄧㄝˇ ㄧㄡˇ ㄓㄥˋ)or 血友病(ㄒㄧㄝˇ ㄧㄡˇ ㄅㄧㄥˋ)
hemophilia, or haemophilia

血癌(ㄒㄧㄝˇ ㄧㄢˊ)
leukemia 亦作「白血病」

血印(ㄒㄧㄝˇ ㄧㄣˋ)
marks made with blood (as footprints, etc.)

血汚(ㄒㄧㄝˇ ㄨ)
bloodstained; blood-smeared

血雨腥風(ㄒㄧㄝˇ ㄩˇ ㄒㄧㄥ ㄈㄥ)
the scene of a field where a fierce battle has just been fought

血緣(ㄒㄧㄝˇ ㄩㄢˊ)
blood; blood relationship; a strain

血暈(ㄒㄩㄝˋ ㄩㄣˋ)
a coma after childbirth for the excessive loss of blood

四畫

【衄】 5357
ㄋㄩˋ niuh nǜ
(又讀 ㄋㄧㄡˋ niow niù)
1. nose bleeding; a bleeding nose
2. to be defeated or given a bloody nose

衄血(ㄋㄩˋ ㄒㄧㄝˇ)
nose bleeding; epistaxis

六畫

【衆】 5358
(眾) ㄓㄨㄥˋ jonq zhòng
1. a multitude; the crowd; the people
2. many; numerous
3. all

衆生(ㄓㄨㄥˋ ㄕㄥ)
all living creatures

十五畫

【衊】 5359
ㄇㄧㄝˋ mieh miè
1. to stain with blood
2. to slander; to trump up a charge; to smear

行部
ㄒㄧㄥˊ shyng xíng

【行】 5360
1. ㄒㄧㄥˊ shyng xíng
1.to walk; to go on foot: 我有時步行上學。I sometimes walk to school.
2.to move; to go; to travel
3.to act; to do; to work: 他照別人的忠告行事。He acted upon another's advice.
4.to publish
5.to be current; to prevail: 此種款式曾風行一時。The style prevailed for a time.
6.able; capable:他雖老但還很行。He is old but still quite able.
7.all right; O.K.; enough: 行了，我吃不下了。That's enough, I can't eat any more.

〔行部〕

8.baggage for travel: 我尚未打開行李。I have not unpacked my baggage yet.

9.a road; a path

10.ready to...; immediately; soon: 他行將出國留學。He will study abroad soon.

行百里者半九十(ㄒㄧㄥˊ ㄅㄞˇ ㄌㄧˇ ㄓㄜˇ ㄅㄢˋ ㄐㄧㄡˇ ㄕˊ)
(literally) To cover 90 per cent of one's destined distance brings one no farther than the midway point. —The last part of an endeavor is the hardest to finish (for one may lose one's patience and give up).

行不得也哥哥(ㄒㄧㄥˊ ㄅㄨˋ ㄉㄜˊ ㄧㄝˇ ㄍㄜ ㄍㄜ)
sounds imitating the cry of a partridge—(figuratively) The road is rough; we can not go ahead.

行不得(ㄒㄧㄥˊ ·ㄅㄨ ·ㄉㄜ)
① cannot or should not be done ② cannot or should not go

行不通(ㄒㄧㄥˊ ·ㄅㄨ ㄊㄨㄥ)
① to block; unable to pass ② won't do (or work) ; to get nowhere: 這個構想行不通。This idea won't work. ③ impracticable; not feasible

行不開(ㄒㄧㄥˊ ·ㄅㄨ ㄎㄞ)
confined or restricted; unable to act freely or as one sees fit

行不行(ㄒㄧㄥˊ ·ㄅㄨ ㄒㄧㄥˊ)
(a term used in requesting permission) can; may 或 Will it do? 或 Is it all right?

行不由徑(ㄒㄧㄥˊ ·ㄅㄨ ㄧㄡˊ ㄐㄧㄥˋ)
do not take shortcuts—(figuratively) to follow the proper rules

行騙(ㄒㄧㄥˊ ㄆㄧㄢˋ)
to cheat; to deceive; to swindle

行聘(ㄒㄧㄥˊ ㄆㄧㄣˋ)
to send betrothal presents to the girl's family

行販(ㄒㄧㄥˊ ㄈㄢˋ)
a vender; a hawker; a peddler; a traveling salesman

行房(ㄒㄧㄥˊ ㄈㄤˊ)
to have sexual relations with one's legal spouse

行大禮(ㄒㄧㄥˊ ㄉㄚˋ ㄌㄧˇ)
to pay the highest respect by kowtowing

行道(ㄒㄧㄥˊ ㄉㄠˋ)
① to practice what one has learned, as a doctor ② to preach or propagate one's theory, belief, etc.

行動(ㄒㄧㄥˊ ㄉㄨㄥˋ)
① to act; to move; to make a move ② to get about; to proceed ③ conduct; behavior; acts; movements; actions

行動電話(ㄒㄧㄥˊ ㄉㄨㄥˋ ㄉㄧㄢˋ ㄏㄨㄚˋ)
the cellular telephone

行動自如(ㄒㄧㄥˊ ㄉㄨㄥˋ ㄗˋ ㄖㄨˊ)
to move freely or without impairment

行動自由(ㄒㄧㄥˊ ㄉㄨㄥˋ ㄗˋ ㄧㄡˊ)
freedom of movements

行動坐臥(ㄒㄧㄥˊ ㄉㄨㄥˋ ㄗㄨㄛˋ ㄨㄛˋ)
behavior; conduct

行踏(ㄒㄧㄥˊ ㄊㄚˋ)
to walk; to frequent

行臺(ㄒㄧㄥˊ ㄊㄞˊ)
① an ancient official post in the border regions ② a temporary residence of a high-ranking official ③ a makeshift stage

行頭(ㄒㄧㄥˊ ·ㄊㄡ)
costumes, etc. for the stage

行同狗彘(ㄒㄧㄥˊ ㄊㄨㄥˊ ㄍㄡˇ ㄓˋ)
mean; bestial

行囊(ㄒㄧㄥˊ ㄋㄤˊ)
one's baggage and money for travel

行年(ㄒㄧㄥˊ ㄋㄧㄢˊ)
to be at the age of: 他行年五十。He is at the age of fifty.

行樂(ㄒㄧㄥˊ ㄌㄜˋ)
to play; to make merry

行樂須及時(ㄒㄧㄥˊ ㄌㄜˋ ㄒㄩ ㄐㄧˊ ㄕˊ)
Enjoy life before it's too late! 或 *Carpe diem*.

行禮(ㄒㄧㄥˊ ㄌㄧˇ)
① to salute; to bow curtsey or kowtow to show respect: 他向軍官行禮。He saluted an officer. ② to undergo a ceremony

行李(ㄒㄧㄥˊ ㄌㄧˇ)
baggage; luggage: 他們有五件行李。They have five pieces of luggage.

行李票(ㄒㄧㄥˊ ㄌㄧˇ ㄆㄧㄠˋ)
the ticket for baggage transportation; baggage checks

行李房(ㄒㄧㄥˊ ㄌㄧˇ ㄈㄤˊ)
a baggage room (or office)

行李車(ㄒㄧㄥˊ ㄌㄧˇ ㄔㄜ)
a baggage car on a train; a luggage van

行獵(ㄒㄧㄥˊ ㄌㄧㄝˋ)
to hunt; to go hunting

行令(ㄒㄧㄥˊ ㄌㄧㄥˋ)
to play wine-drinking games

行露(ㄒㄧㄥˊ ㄌㄨˋ)
the dew on the path—(figuratively) exposure of a lady's chastity to danger

行路(ㄒㄧㄥˊ ㄌㄨˋ)
to travel; to walk on the road

行路人(ㄒㄧㄥˊ ㄌㄨˋ ㄖㄣˊ)
① passers-by ② totally disinterested parties

行侶(ㄒㄧㄥˊ ㄌㄩˇ)
traveling companions

行旅(ㄒㄧㄥˊ ㄌㄩˇ)
travelers: 此地交通良好，行旅稱便。Traffic here is good and travelers find it convenient.

行賈(ㄒㄧㄥˊ ㄍㄨˇ)
a traveling businessman

行館(ㄒㄧㄥˊ ㄍㄨㄢˇ)
a temporary dwelling place of a high official

行宮(ㄒㄧㄥˊ ㄍㄨㄥ)
the abode of an emperor on a tour

行客(ㄒㄧㄥˊ ㄎㄜˋ)
travelers

行好(ㄒㄧㄥˊ ㄏㄠˇ)
to do good; to practice charitable deeds

行賄(ㄒㄧㄥˊ ㄏㄨㄟˋ)
to bribe; to offer a bribe: 行賄者可鄙。He who bribes is to be despised.

行劫(ㄒㄧㄥˊ ㄐㄧㄝˊ)
to loot or rob

行脚(ㄒㄧㄥˊ ㄐㄧㄠˇ)
(said of a Buddhist monk) to travel far and wide on foot in order to attain understanding of the essence of Buddhist teachings

行酒(ㄒㄧㄥˊ ㄐㄧㄡˇ)
to pour wine for a guest

行姦(ㄒㄧㄥˊ ㄐㄧㄢ)
to commit adultery

行檢(ㄒㄧㄥˊ ㄐㄧㄢˇ)

the code of conducts

行進(ㄒㄧㄥˊ ㄐㄧㄣˋ)
(military) to move forward; to march

行將(ㄒㄧㄥˊ ㄐㄧㄤ)
imminent; just going to; about to; on the verge of

行將就木(ㄒㄧㄥˊ ㄐㄧㄤ ㄐㄧㄡˋ ㄇㄨˋ)
dying; nearing death

行經(ㄒㄧㄥˊ ㄐㄧㄥ)
① to pass (a place, store, etc.); to pass through ② (said of women) in the period

行徑(ㄒㄧㄥˊ ㄐㄧㄥˋ)
① one's conduct or behavior; actions: 那眞是殘忍的行徑。That's really cruel conduct. ② a path; a trail

行軍(ㄒㄧㄥˊ ㄐㄩㄣ)
① the movement of an army; a march ② the deployment of military forces

行軍牀(ㄒㄧㄥˊ ㄐㄩㄣ ㄔㄨㄤˊ)
a cot (for sleeping)

行期(ㄒㄧㄥˊ ㄑㄧˊ)
the date of departure

行乞(ㄒㄧㄥˊ ㄑㄧˇ)
to beg; to be a beggar

行篋(ㄒㄧㄥˊ ㄑㄧㄝˋ)
a traveler's box for holding clothes, money, etc.

行竊(ㄒㄧㄥˊ ㄑㄧㄝˋ)
to steal: 此賊在行竊時被捕。The thief was caught in the act of stealing.

行銷(ㄒㄧㄥˊ ㄒㄧㄠ)
to sell; to effect sales; to be on sale: 此書行銷各地。The book sells everywhere.

行險(ㄒㄧㄥˊ ㄒㄧㄢˇ)
to take great risks; to embark on a dangerous task

行香(ㄒㄧㄥˊ ㄒㄧㄤ)
the burning and offering of incense at Buddhist temples on special national occasions by officials in ancient times

行星(ㄒㄧㄥˊ ㄒㄧㄥ)
the planets

行刑(ㄒㄧㄥˊ ㄒㄧㄥˊ)
① to execute (criminals); execution ② to torture (prisoners)

行刑場(ㄒㄧㄥˊ ㄒㄧㄥˊ ㄔㄤˇ)
an execution ground

行幸(ㄒㄧㄥˊ ㄒㄧㄥˋ)
the imperial tour away from the capital

行兇(ㄒㄧㄥˊ ㄒㄩㄥ)
to commit killing or murder

行止(ㄒㄧㄥˊ ㄓˇ)
① whereabouts of a person ② ways or methods of doing things ③ personal conduct or behavior

行詐(ㄒㄧㄥˊ ㄓㄚˋ)
to cheat, deceive or swindle

行者(ㄒㄧㄥˊ ㄓㄜˇ)
① a Buddhist monk ② a servant of a Buddhist abbot

行政(ㄒㄧㄥˊ ㄓㄥˋ)
① government; administration of public affairs ② the executive branch of a government

行政法(ㄒㄧㄥˊ ㄓㄥˋ ㄈㄚˇ)
administrative law

行政機關(ㄒㄧㄥˊ ㄓㄥˋ ㄐㄧ ㄍㄨㄢ)
administrative organizations

行政區畫(ㄒㄧㄥˊ ㄓㄥˋ ㄑㄩ ㄏㄨㄚˋ)
the political division of an area for administrative purposes

行政區域(ㄒㄧㄥˊ ㄓㄥˋ ㄑㄩ ㄩˋ)
an administrative district

行政權(ㄒㄧㄥˊ ㄓㄥˋ ㄑㄩㄢˊ)
administrative power; executive authority

行政長官(ㄒㄧㄥˊ ㄓㄥˋ ㄓㄤˇ ㄍㄨㄢ)
the top administrator (in an area, or region)

行政處分(ㄒㄧㄥˊ ㄓㄥˋ ㄔㄨˇ ㄈㄣˋ)
disciplinary measures taken against an official guilty of abuse of administrative powers (as opposed to punishment meted out by a court of law)

行政人員(ㄒㄧㄥˊ ㄓㄥˋ ㄖㄣˊ ㄩㄢˊ)
an administrator

行政院(ㄒㄧㄥˊ ㄓㄥˋ ㄩㄢˋ)
Executive Yuan

行裝(ㄒㄧㄥˊ ㄓㄨㄤ)
baggage or luggage

行裝甫卸(ㄒㄧㄥˊ ㄓㄨㄤ ㄈㄨˇ ㄒㄧㄝˋ)
to have just concluded a homeward journey

行車(ㄒㄧㄥˊ ㄔㄜ)
① the movement of vehicles ② to drive a vehicle

行車執照(ㄒㄧㄥˊ ㄔㄜ ㄓˊ ㄓㄠˋ)
a driver's license; a driving license

行車時間表(ㄒㄧㄥˊ ㄔㄜ ㄕˊ ㄐㄧㄢ ㄅㄧㄠˇ)
schedules or timetables of trains

行常(ㄒㄧㄥˊ ㄔㄤˊ)
ordinary; usual; common

行成(ㄒㄧㄥˊ ㄔㄥˊ)
to hold peace talks; to obtain peace

行程(ㄒㄧㄥˊ ㄔㄥˊ)
① a traveler's route or itinerary ② to embark on a journey ③ a march; a journey: 二十哩的行程。It's a march of twenty miles.

行船(ㄒㄧㄥˊ ㄔㄨㄢˊ)
① to sail or steer a boat ② the passing of boats

行尸走肉(ㄒㄧㄥˊ ㄕ ㄗㄡˇ ㄖㄡˋ)
a walking corpse—an absolutely useless person

行使(ㄒㄧㄥˊ ㄕˇ)
to exercise (powers, etc.); to employ: 他行使自己的權利。He exercised his rights.

行使權(ㄒㄧㄥˊ ㄕˇ ㄑㄩㄢˊ)
the right to exercise powers inherent in one's office

行駛(ㄒㄧㄥˊ ㄕˇ)
to drive (cars); to sail or steer (boats); to ride (bicycles or pedicabs); to fly (planes)

行事(ㄒㄧㄥˊ ㄕˋ)
① to proceed; to execute (usually a clandestine mission); to do something planned: 我們按計畫行事。We proceeded according to plan. ② conduct or behavior ③ to deal with people

行事曆(ㄒㄧㄥˊ ㄕˋ ㄌㄧˋ)
a calendar

行善(ㄒㄧㄥˊ ㄕㄢˋ)
to do good deeds; to do charitable work

行商(ㄒㄧㄥˊ ㄕㄤ)
a traveling salesman

行觴(ㄒㄧㄥˊ ㄕㄤ)
to pour wine for guests

行賞(ㄒㄧㄥˊ ㄕㄤˇ)
to reward (the meritorious)

行省(ㄒㄧㄥˊ ㄕㄥˇ)
a province (a political division in the Republic of

〔行部〕

China)
行書(ㄒㄧㄥˊ ㄕㄨ)
the running style of Chinese calligraphy
行水(ㄒㄧㄥˊ ㄕㄨㄟˇ)
① flowing water ② to travel by water, as on boats, to inspect flood ③ to convey away the waters
行人(ㄒㄧㄥˊ ㄖㄣˊ)
pedestrians; passers-by
行人道(ㄒㄧㄥˊ ㄖㄣˊ ㄉㄠˋ)
sidewalks of a street
行人穿越道(ㄒㄧㄥˊ ㄖㄣˊ ㄔㄨㄢ ㄩㄝˋ ㄉㄠˋ)
a pedestrian crossing
行在(ㄒㄧㄥˊ ㄗㄞˋ)
the temporary palace of the emperor on a tour
行走(ㄒㄧㄥˊ ㄗㄡˇ)
① to walk ② a part-time worker in a government office in ancient times ③ to have some connection
行蹤 or 行踪(ㄒㄧㄥˊ ㄗㄨㄥ)
tracks or whereabouts of a person:敵軍企圖隱匿他們的行踪。The enemy tried to cover their whereabouts.
行蹤不明 or 行踪不明(ㄒㄧㄥˊ ㄗㄨㄥ ㄅㄨˋ ㄇㄧㄥˊ)
whereabouts unknown: 她現在行蹤不明。Her present whereabouts is (or are) unknown.
行蹤飄忽(ㄒㄧㄥˊ ㄗㄨㄥ ㄆㄧㄠ ㄏㄨ)or 行跡飄忽(ㄒㄧㄥˊ ㄐㄧ ㄆㄧㄠ ㄏㄨ)
to travel here and there without a fixed itinerary; to have no fixed whereabouts
行蹤無定 or 行踪無定(ㄒㄧㄥˊ ㄗㄨㄥ ㄨˊ ㄉㄧㄥˋ)
to have no fixed abode; with an uncertain place of lodging; to have no fixed itinerary in traveling
行刺(ㄒㄧㄥˊ ㄘˋ)
to assassinate: 他們計劃行刺暴君。They planned to assassinate the tyrant.
行藏(ㄒㄧㄥˊ ㄘㄤˊ)
one's behavior and background
行色(ㄒㄧㄥˊ ㄙㄜˋ)
scenes, conditions, display, etc. at one's departure for a journey
行色匆匆(ㄒㄧㄥˊ ㄙㄜˋ ㄘㄨㄥ ㄘㄨㄥ)
in a hurry to leave; in a hurry to go on a trip
行所無事(ㄒㄧㄥˊ ㄙㄨㄛˇ ㄨˊ ㄕˋ)
to maintain perfect composure; to be unruffled
行醫(ㄒㄧㄥˊ ㄧ)
to practice medicine: 他已行醫多年。He has practiced medicine for many years.
行易知難(ㄒㄧㄥˊ ㄧˋ ㄓ ㄋㄢˊ)
To do is easier than to know. 或 To know how is easier than to know why.
行有餘力(ㄒㄧㄥˊ ㄧㄡˇ ㄩˊ ㄌㄧˋ)
to have extra resources (besides those needed to take care of oneself and his family)
行吟(ㄒㄧㄥˊ ㄧㄣˊ)
to wander while reciting or composing poems
行吟詩人(ㄒㄧㄥˊ ㄧㄣˊ ㄕ ㄖㄣˊ)
a minstrel
行營(ㄒㄧㄥˊ ㄧㄥˊ)
military headquarters set up at various strategic places
行爲(ㄒㄧㄥˊ ㄨㄟˊ)
① behavior; conduct ②(law) acts
行爲犯(ㄒㄧㄥˊ ㄨㄟˊ ㄈㄢˋ)
a criminal caught in the act; *flagrante delicto*
行文(ㄒㄧㄥˊ ㄨㄣˊ)
① to send a despatch (to another government office) ② the style or manner of writing
行轅(ㄒㄧㄥˊ ㄩㄢˊ)
the temporary residence of a high official on a tour
行遠自邇(ㄒㄧㄥˊ ㄩㄢˇ ㄗˋ ㄦˇ)
(literally) To go far, one must start from near.—One must start with the easy or basic things before one proceeds to deal with the difficult or profound subjects.
行雲流水(ㄒㄧㄥˊ ㄩㄣˊ ㄌㄧㄡˊ ㄕㄨㄟˇ)
(literally) moving clouds and flowing water—a natural and flowing style of writing, etc.: 她的詩有如行雲流水。She writes verses with natural and flowing style.
行運(ㄒㄧㄥˊ ㄩㄣˋ)
to be favored by good luck; to have everything going one's way

【行】 5360
2. ㄒㄧㄥˋ shinq xìng
one's conduct or behavior
行狀(ㄒㄧㄥˋ ㄓㄨㄤˋ)or 行述(ㄒㄧㄥˋ ㄕㄨˋ)
a brief biography of the deceased (usually accompanying an obituary notice)
行誼(ㄒㄧㄥˋ ㄧˋ)
conduct and virtues

【行】 5360
3. ㄏㄤˊ harng háng
1. a row; a line; a series:該詩每節有六行。There are six lines in each stanza of the poem.
2. a business firm; a company
3. a trade; a line; a profession: 那不是我的本行。That's not my line.
4. order of brothers (and sisters) according to seniority
5. a generation
行輩(ㄏㄤˊ ㄅㄟˋ)
sequence of seniority in a clan
行道(ㄏㄤˊ ˙ㄉㄠ)
(dialect) a trade; a profession; an occupation
行東(ㄏㄤˊ ㄉㄨㄥ)
a shopkeeper
行頭(ㄏㄤˊ ㄊㄡˊ)
①(in ancient China) a team leader ②(Han Dynasty) a shopkeeper
行列(ㄏㄤˊ ㄌㄧㄝˋ)
the rank and file; rows and columns: 他們排成整齊的行列。They are drawn up in orderly ranks.
行列式(ㄏㄤˊ ㄌㄧㄝˋ ㄕˋ)
(mathematics) a determinant
行規(ㄏㄤˊ ㄍㄨㄟ)
guild regulations; rules obeyed among members of a profession
行號(ㄏㄤˊ ㄏㄠˋ)
shops; stores; business establishments
行行出狀元(ㄏㄤˊ ㄏㄤˊ ㄔㄨ ㄓㄨㄤˋ ˙ㄩㄢ)
Every trade has its master. 或 One may distinguish himself in any trade.
行話(ㄏㄤˊ ㄏㄨㄚˋ)
the professional jargon of a

trade
行會(ㄏㄤˊ ㄏㄨㄟˋ)
trade unions; guilds
行家(ㄏㄤˊ ·ㄐㄧㄚ)
a professional; an expert
行間(ㄏㄤˊ ㄐㄧㄢ)
① in the army ② between the lines of a piece of writing
行情(ㄏㄤˊ ㄑㄧㄥˊ)
① market prices of certain commodities; a quotation; market: 行情上漲了。The market has risen. ② general standing of a person in terms of finance, influence, popularity, etc.
行棧(ㄏㄤˊ ㄓㄢˋ)
a warehouse, godown or depot
行市(ㄏㄤˊ ㄕˋ)
market quotations
行業(ㄏㄤˊ ㄧㄝˋ)
a trade; an occupation
行伍(ㄏㄤˊ ㄨˇ)
the army
行伍出身(ㄏㄤˊ ㄨˇ ㄔㄨ ㄕㄣ)
① to rise from the ranks (of the army): 他是行伍出身。He rose from the ranks. ② to have a regular military background
行員(ㄏㄤˊ ㄩㄢˊ)
a clerk (especially referring to one in the bank)

三畫

【衍】 5361 ㄧㄢˇ yean yǎn
1. to overflow; to spread out
2. plenty and abundant; ample
3. (said of fields or plains) level; plane and even
4. a lake; a marsh
5. a slope
6. superfluous
7. a bamboo box or chest
8. a Chinese family name
衍變(ㄧㄢˇ ㄅㄧㄢˋ)
to develop and change; to evolve
衍生(ㄧㄢˇ ㄕㄥ)
to derive from
衍聖公(ㄧㄢˇ ㄕㄥˋ ㄍㄨㄥ)
Duke of Yen, a hereditary title of the eldest male among the lineal descendants of Confucius (from 1055 A.D. until 1935), now known as 奉祀官
衍繹(ㄧㄢˇ ㄧˋ)
to expound or elaborate
衍衍(ㄧㄢˇ ㄧㄢˇ)
to walk fast
衍沃(ㄧㄢˇ ㄨㄛˋ)
fertile plains
衍文(ㄧㄢˇ ㄨㄣˊ)
interpolations; redundancies owing to misprinting or miscopying

五畫

【衒】 5362 ㄒㄩㄢˋ shiuann xuàn
1. to brag; to boast; to show off
2. to recommend oneself
衒賣(ㄒㄩㄢˋ ㄇㄞˋ) or 衒鬻(ㄒㄩㄢˋ ㄩˋ)
(said of a peddler, etc.) to brag about the high quality of his goods
衒女(ㄒㄩㄢˋ ㄋㄩˇ)
a girl who flaunts her beauty all around
衒露(ㄒㄩㄢˋ ㄌㄨˋ)
to show off one's talent
衒俏(ㄒㄩㄢˋ ㄑㄧㄠˋ)
to show off one's charms; to try to be cute
衒士(ㄒㄩㄢˋ ㄕˋ)
a boastful scholar; one who always tries to show off his learning
衒異(ㄒㄩㄢˋ ㄧˋ)
to show off one's talents
衒耀(ㄒㄩㄢˋ ㄧㄠˋ)
to show off; to flaunt; to brag or boast
衒玉賈石(ㄒㄩㄢˋ ㄩˋ ㄍㄨˇ ㄕˊ)
(literally) to advertise jade but sell rock—to preach like a saint but act like a crook
衒玉求售(ㄒㄩㄢˋ ㄩˋ ㄑㄧㄡˊ ㄕㄡˋ)
to recommend oneself to a position; to brag about one's own talent with a view to getting a job

【術】 5363 1. ㄕㄨˋ shuh shù
1. a skill; a feat
2. a way or method to do something
術科(ㄕㄨˋ ㄎㄜ)
courses offered in school for vocational training or learning of skills, as practical mechanics, etc.
術愧長房(ㄕㄨˋ ㄎㄨㄟˋ ㄓㄤˇ ㄈㄤˊ)
to regret that one cannot make the space shrink so as to meet a dear friend faraway
術智(ㄕㄨˋ ㄓˋ)
clever and skillful
術士(ㄕㄨˋ ㄕˋ)
① one who practices occult arts ② scholars
術數(ㄕㄨˋ ㄕㄨˋ)
① ways of administering or governing a nation ② magical calculation or fortunetelling
術語(ㄕㄨˋ ㄩˇ)
professional jargon terminology; technical terms
術語學(ㄕㄨˋ ㄩˇ ㄒㄩㄝˊ)
terminology

【術】 5363 2. ㄙㄨㄟˋ suey suì
an administrative district in ancient China in the suburbs of a city

六畫

【衕】 5364 ㄊㄨㄥˋ tonq tòng
a lane; an alley
【衖】 5365 ㄌㄨㄥˋ lonq lòng
a lane; an alley
衖堂(ㄌㄨㄥˋ ㄊㄤˊ)
a lane; an alley
【街】 5366 ㄐㄧㄝ jie jiē
a street; a road in a city; a thoroughfare
街門(ㄐㄧㄝ ㄇㄣˊ)
the front gate facing the street; a street entrance
街面兒(ㄐㄧㄝ ㄇㄧㄚˋㄦ)
market or street conditions
街坊(ㄐㄧㄝ ·ㄈㄤ)
① neighbors; the neighborhood ② neighborhood
街道(ㄐㄧㄝ ㄉㄠˋ)
streets; roads in a city or town
街燈(ㄐㄧㄝ ㄉㄥ)

street lights; street lamps
街頭(ㄐㄧㄝ ㄊㄡˊ)
street corners; streets
街頭巷尾(ㄐㄧㄝ ㄊㄡˊ ㄒㄧㄤˋ ㄨㄟˇ)
throughout the city; in every nook and corner of the city
街談巷議(ㄐㄧㄝ ㄊㄢˊ ㄒㄧㄤˋ ㄧˋ)
the talk of the town; street rumors
街里街坊(ㄐㄧㄝ ㄌㄧˇ ㄐㄧㄝ ㄈㄤ)
neighborliness; friendship among neighbors
街官(ㄐㄧㄝ ㄍㄨㄢ)
a police officer on the beat; a police patrolman
街衢(ㄐㄧㄝ ㄑㄩˊ)
streets, roads or lanes in a city or town
街巷(ㄐㄧㄝ ㄒㄧㄤˋ)
streets and lanes
街市(ㄐㄧㄝ ㄕˋ)
shopping streets; the downtown area
街市戰(ㄐㄧㄝ ㄕˋ ㄓㄢˋ)
street fighting
街上(ㄐㄧㄝ ˙ㄕㄤ)
on or in the street: 我碰巧在街上遇見他。I happened to meet him on the street.
街卒(ㄐㄧㄝ ㄗㄨˊ)
(in ancient China) scavengers

〔行部〕

七畫

【衙】 5367 ㄧㄚˊ ya yá
1. a government office
2. to meet; to gather; to congregate
3. (Tang Dynasty) a front hall of the palace
4. a Chinese family name
衙門(ㄧㄚˊ ˙ㄇㄣ)
"*yamen*"—a government office in feudal China
衙內(ㄧㄚˊ ㄋㄟˋ)
a reference to the sons of a high official in the Sung(宋) and Yüan (元) dynasties
衙署(ㄧㄚˊ ㄕㄨˇ)
a government office
衙役(ㄧㄚˊ ˙ㄧ)
errand men in a government office; an office boy; a public office runner

九畫

【衝】 5368 1. ㄔㄨㄥ chong chōng
1. to rush; to thrust; to forge ahead; to dash
2. to charge forward; to hit with force
3. a thoroughfare; a hub; a strategic place
4. to offend
衝破(ㄔㄨㄥ ㄆㄛˋ)
to break through; to breach; to smash
衝鋒(ㄔㄨㄥ ㄈㄥ)
(military) to charge; a charge; an assault
衝鋒隊(ㄔㄨㄥ ㄈㄥ ㄉㄨㄟˋ)
storm troops
衝鋒鎗(ㄔㄨㄥ ㄈㄥ ㄑㄧㄤ)
a Tommy gun, or a tommy gun
衝鋒陷陣(ㄔㄨㄥ ㄈㄥ ㄒㄧㄢˋ ㄓㄣˋ)
to charge ahead and take enemy positions; to charge the enemy lines; to charge forward
衝倒(ㄔㄨㄥ ㄉㄠˇ)
to knock down by the impact of a collision, etc.
衝動(ㄔㄨㄥ ㄉㄨㄥˋ)
① an impulse; a sudden urge ② to be excited; to get excited: 不要太衝動！冷靜些！Don't get excited! Keep cool!
衝突(ㄔㄨㄥ ㄊㄨˊ)
a conflict; a fight; a clash
衝浪(ㄔㄨㄥ ㄌㄤˋ)
to surf
衝力(ㄔㄨㄥ ㄌㄧˋ)
impulsive forces; momentum
衝冠(ㄔㄨㄥ ㄍㄨㄢ)
extreme anger that makes the hair stand on end and raise one's own cap
衝剋(ㄔㄨㄥ ㄎㄜˋ)
(a Chinese superstition) the contradicting and conflicting forces of nature
衝口而出(ㄔㄨㄥ ㄎㄡˇ ㄦˊ ㄔㄨ)
to blurt out without thinking
衝激(ㄔㄨㄥ ㄐㄧ)
① a fierce conflict; a powerful collision ② to offend

衝擊(ㄔㄨㄥ ㄐㄧˊ)
to strike against; to pound against; to charge
衝擊力(ㄔㄨㄥ ㄐㄧˊ ㄌㄧˋ)
the force of thrust or impact
衝勁(ㄔㄨㄥ ㄐㄧㄣˋ)
aggressiveness; enterprising spirit; drive: 她做任何事情總有一股衝勁。She is always full of enterprising spirit in doing everything.
衝進(ㄔㄨㄥ ㄐㄧㄣˋ)
to burst in; to rush in: 兵士們向前衝進。The soldiers rushed forward.
衝決(ㄔㄨㄥ ㄐㄩㄝˊ) or 衝潰(ㄔㄨㄥ ㄎㄨㄟˋ)
to burst open (an enemy siege, dike, etc.): 江水衝潰堤岸。The river burst its banks.
衝衢(ㄔㄨㄥ ㄑㄩˊ)
a thoroughfare
衝霄(ㄔㄨㄥ ㄒㄧㄠ)
to shoot up to the sky, as smoke, fire, etc.
衝陷(ㄔㄨㄥ ㄒㄧㄢˋ)
to charge and take (enemy positions)
衝撞(ㄔㄨㄥ ㄓㄨㄤˋ)
① to collide; to ram: 汽車遭到一輛卡車的衝撞。The car was rammed by a truck. ② to offend; to treat impolitely: 我有沒有什麼地方衝撞了你? Have I done anything to offend you?
衝出(ㄔㄨㄥ ㄔㄨ)
to rush out; to dash out; to fight a way out: 他們從屋裏衝出去。They rushed out of the room.
衝殺(ㄔㄨㄥ ㄕㄚ)
to charge; to rush ahead
衝刺(ㄔㄨㄥ ㄘˋ)
a spurt; a sprint; a burst of speed: 這跑者向終點線做最後衝刺。The runner put on a spurt toward the tape.
衝散(ㄔㄨㄥ ㄙㄢˋ)
to break up; to scatter; to disperse: 警察衝散群衆。The police dispersed the crowd.
衝要(ㄔㄨㄥ ㄧㄠˋ)
a strategic point; an important junction 亦作「要衝」

【衝】 5368 2. ㄔㄨㄥˋ chonq chòng

1. to head or go (south, north, etc.): 衝前走。Go straight up. 衝北走。Go north.
2. strong (smell): 這煙味很衝。This smoke has a strong smell.
3. brave and fierce
4. to take a nap
5. for (your, his, etc.) sake
6. to direct (one's attack, etc.) toward

衝盹兒(ㄔㄨㄥˋ ㄉㄨㄜˇㄦ)
to take a nap

衝著(ㄔㄨㄥˋ ˙ㄓㄜ)
① for (your, his, etc.) sake ② to direct (one's attack, etc.) toward

【衚】 5369 ㄏㄨˊ hwu hú
a lane; a sub-lane; a side street

衚衕(ㄏㄨˊ ㄊㄨㄥˋ)
a lane; an alley

【衛】 5370 (衞) ㄨㄟˋ wey wèi
to guard or protect; to stand guard over

十畫

【衞】 5371 (衛) ㄨㄟˋ wey wèi
1. to guard; to protect; to defend: 保衞國家是軍人的責任。The duty of a soldier is to defend his country.
2. a keeper; a bodyguard; a guard; a person having charge of guarding or protecting something or somebody
3. name of an ancient state in the Chou Dynasty
4. a Chinese family name

衞兵(ㄨㄟˋ ㄅㄧㄥ)
(military) guard; sentry

衞冕(ㄨㄟˋ ㄇㄧㄢˇ)
to defend a title

衞道(ㄨㄟˋ ㄉㄠˋ)
to protect or guard traditional cultural heritage, especially the code of ethics attributed to Confucius

衞隊(ㄨㄟˋ ㄉㄨㄟˋ)
bodyguards; guard units

衞國(ㄨㄟˋ ㄍㄨㄛˊ)
to defend one's country

衞國衞民(ㄨㄟˋ ㄍㄨㄛˊ ㄨㄟˋ ㄇㄧㄣˊ)
to defend the country and protect the people

衞青(ㄨㄟˋ ㄑㄧㄥ)
Wei Ching, one of the greatest generals during the reign of Emperor Wu of the Han Dynasty (漢武帝)

衞星(ㄨㄟˋ ㄒㄧㄥ)
satellites

衞星通訊(ㄨㄟˋ ㄒㄧㄥ ㄊㄨㄥ ㄒㄩㄣˋ)
communication by satellite

衞星國家(ㄨㄟˋ ㄒㄧㄥ ㄍㄨㄛˊ ㄐㄧㄚ)
satellite nations

衞星轉播站(ㄨㄟˋ ㄒㄧㄥ ㄓㄨㄢˇ ㄅㄛ ㄓㄢˋ)
a satellite earth station

衞士(ㄨㄟˋ ㄕˋ)
① a guard; a bodyguard ② a protector or guardian of (morality, etc.)

衞生(ㄨㄟˋ ㄕㄥ)
sanitation; sanitary; public health

衞生棉(ㄨㄟˋ ㄕㄥ ㄇㄧㄢˊ)
a sanitary napkin

衞生節(ㄨㄟˋ ㄕㄥ ㄐㄧㄝˊ)
Sanitation Day (on April 7)

衞生局(ㄨㄟˋ ㄕㄥ ㄐㄩˊ)
the bureau of public health; the bureau of sanitation

衞生學(ㄨㄟˋ ㄕㄥ ㄒㄩㄝˊ)
hygiene; hygienics

衞生知識(ㄨㄟˋ ㄕㄥ ㄓ ㄕˋ)
knowledge pertaining to sanitation or health

衞生紙(ㄨㄟˋ ㄕㄥ ㄓˇ)
tissue paper; toilet paper

衞生處(ㄨㄟˋ ㄕㄥ ㄔㄨˋ)
the department of public health; the department of sanitation

衞生設備(ㄨㄟˋ ㄕㄥ ㄕㄜˋ ㄅㄟˋ)
sanitary facilities; sanitary ware

衞生所(ㄨㄟˋ ㄕㄥ ㄙㄨㄛˇ)
a public health clinic

衞生衣(ㄨㄟˋ ㄕㄥ ㄧ)
a kind of tight cotton underwear

衞生院(ㄨㄟˋ ㄕㄥ ㄩㄢˋ)
a public health clinic; a hospital

衞戍(ㄨㄟˋ ㄕㄨˋ)
to garrison

衞戍部隊(ㄨㄟˋ ㄕㄨˋ ㄅㄨˋ ㄉㄨㄟˋ)
garrison troops

衞戍司令部(ㄨㄟˋ ㄕㄨˋ ㄙ ㄌㄧㄥˋ ㄅㄨˋ)
garrison headquarters

【衡】 5372 ㄏㄥˊ herng héng
1. to weigh; to measure; to assess; to consider
2. horizontal
3. railings
4. a beam
5. the beam of a steelyard
6. a Chinese family name

衡平(ㄏㄥˊ ㄆㄧㄥˊ)
to weigh and consider in order to uphold justice

衡量(ㄏㄥˊ ㄌㄧㄤˊ)
to weigh; to measure; to consider; to judge; to estimate; to assess: 勿用一般標準來衡量它。Don't measure it by common criteria.

衡廬(ㄏㄥˊ ㄌㄨˊ)
names of two famous mountains, Mt. Heng and Mt. Lu, in China

衡鑑(ㄏㄥˊ ㄐㄧㄢˋ)
a yardstick to tell right from wrong

衡情(ㄏㄥˊ ㄑㄧㄥˊ)
to consider the actual conditions or situations; to judge the circumstances of a case

衡視(ㄏㄥˊ ㄕˋ)
to look horizontally

衡山(ㄏㄥˊ ㄕㄢ) or 衡嶽(ㄏㄥˊ ㄩㄝˋ)
Mountain Heng, one of the Five Sacred Mountains

衡陽(ㄏㄥˊ ㄧㄤˊ)
Hengyang, a city in Hunan Province

衡宇(ㄏㄥˊ ㄩˇ)
the roof of a house

十八畫

【衢】 5373 ㄑㄩˊ chyu qú
a thoroughfare; a highway junction

衢道(ㄑㄩˊ ㄉㄠˋ)
a side street; crossroads

衢塗(ㄑㄩˊ ㄊㄨˊ)
a side street; crossroads

衢路(ㄑㄩˊ ㄌㄨˋ)
a thoroughfare

衢肆(ㄑㄩˊ ㄙˋ)
a store beside a thoroughfare

〔行部〕

〔衣部〕

衣部
ㄧ i yī

【衣】 5374
1. ㄧ i yī

1. clothing; dress; apparel; garments; attire
2. a coating; a covering
3. skin or peel of fruits
4. a Chinese family name

衣鉢(ㄧ ㄅㄛ)
teaching, skill, etc. handed down from a master to his pupil

衣包(ㄧ ㄅㄠ)
a canvas bag, usually for traveling

衣胞(ㄧ ㄅㄠ)
the placenta; the human afterbirth 亦作「胞衣」

衣不蔽體(ㄧ ㄅㄨˋ ㄅㄧˋ ㄊㄧˇ)
to wear rags, shabby clothes, or tatters

衣帽架(ㄧ ㄇㄠˋ ㄐㄧㄚˋ)
a hat tree; a hall tree

衣帽間(ㄧ ㄇㄠˋ ㄐㄧㄢ)
a cloakroom (in restaurants, theaters, etc.); a checkroom

衣服(ㄧ ˙ㄈㄨ)
clothes; clothing; dress

衣帶詔(ㄧ ㄉㄞˋ ㄓㄠˋ)
an imperial decree smuggled out of the palace by sewing it into robes or girdles (when the emperor was a prisoner of a powerful minister)

衣帶水(ㄧ ㄉㄞˋ ㄕㄨㄟˇ)
a narrow strip of water (such as a narrow channel)

衣來伸手，飯來張口(ㄧ ㄌㄞˊ ㄕㄣ ㄕㄡˇ, ㄈㄢˋ ㄌㄞˊ ㄓㄤ ㄎㄡˇ)
to live on the labor of others; to lead the life of a parasite

衣料(ㄧ ㄌㄧㄠˋ)
clothing material

衣領(ㄧ ㄌㄧㄥˇ)
a collar

衣履敝穿(ㄧ ㄌㄩˇ ㄅㄧˋ ㄔㄨㄢ)
in rags; ragged clothing

衣鈎(ㄧ ㄍㄡ)
a hook for hanging clothes

衣櫃(ㄧ ㄍㄨㄟˋ)
a wardrobe; a chest of drawers for clothing

衣冠(ㄧ ㄍㄨㄢ)
① clothes and caps—dress ② the appearance of a gentleman; the gentry

衣冠不整(ㄧ ㄍㄨㄢ ㄅㄨˋ ㄓㄥˇ)
sloppily dressed

衣冠禽獸(ㄧ ㄍㄨㄢ ㄑㄧㄣˊ ㄕㄡˋ)
a gentleman in appearance but a beast in conduct; a beast in human clothing; a wolf in sheep's clothing

衣冠中人(ㄧ ㄍㄨㄢ ㄓㄨㄥ ㄖㄣˊ)
the gentry

衣冠塚(ㄧ ㄍㄨㄢ ㄓㄨㄥˇ)
the grave of a hero whose body cannot be found (so called because only his clothes and hat are buried in place of his remains)

衣冠楚楚(ㄧ ㄍㄨㄢ ㄔㄨˇ ㄔㄨˇ)
in immaculate attire; dressed like a gentleman

衣冠文物(ㄧ ㄍㄨㄢ ㄨㄣˊ ㄨˋ)
civilization and culture

衣架(ㄧ ㄐㄧㄚˋ)
a rack for clothes; a clotheshorse; a coat hanger

衣襟(ㄧ ㄐㄧㄣ)
lapels of a garment

衣衾(ㄧ ㄑㄧㄣ)
the clothes and coverlet on the deceased in the coffin

衣取蔽寒(ㄧ ㄑㄩˇ ㄅㄧˋ ㄏㄢˊ)
Clothing is for keeping one warm.

衣箱(ㄧ ㄒㄧㄤ)
a box or chest for storing clothes

衣香鬢影(ㄧ ㄒㄧㄤ ㄅㄧㄣˋ ㄧㄥˇ)
women in rich attire

衣著(ㄧ ㄓㄨㄛˊ)
clothing; attire; apparel; dress

衣裝(ㄧ ㄓㄨㄤ)
clothes and traveling baggage

衣櫥(ㄧ ㄔㄨˊ)
a wardrobe; a clothespress

衣食(ㄧ ㄕˊ)
food and clothing; what one lives on

衣食不周(ㄧ ㄕˊ ㄅㄨˋ ㄓㄡ)
to be wanting in food and clothing—very poor

衣食父母(ㄧ ㄕˊ ㄈㄨˋ ㄇㄨˇ)
those, on whom one's livelihood depends (like customers to businessmen)

衣食住行(ㄧ ㄕˊ ㄓㄨˋ ㄒㄧㄥˊ)
food, clothing, housing and transportation—the four essential requirements of the people

衣食足然後知榮辱(ㄧ ㄕˊ ㄗㄨˊ ㄖㄢˊ ㄏㄡˋ ㄓ ㄖㄨㄥˊ ㄖㄨˋ)
One has a sense of shame and honor only when his livelihood is assured. 或 Human dignity is not the offspring of an empty stomach. 或 Well fed, well bred.

衣衫(ㄧ ㄕㄢ)
dress (and general appearance)

衣衫襤褸(ㄧ ㄕㄢ ㄌㄢˊ ㄌㄩˇ)
in rags; ragged clothing

衣裳(ㄧ ˙ㄕㄤ)
clothes; garments; clothing: 她有很多漂亮的衣裳。She has many beautiful clothes.

衣幘(ㄧ ㄗㄜˊ)
clothes and turbans

衣索比亞(ㄧ ㄙㄨㄛˇ ㄅㄧˇ ㄧㄚˇ)
Ethiopia, a kingdom in Africa

衣阿華(ㄧ ㄚ ㄏㄨㄚˊ)
the state of Iowa, U.S.A. 亦作「愛阿華」

衣魚(ㄧ ㄩˊ)
lepisma

【衣】 5374
2. ㄧˋ yih yì

to clothe; to wear; to dress

衣被(ㄧˋ ㄅㄟˋ)
to cover (with blankets, etc.)—(figuratively) to do someone a favor

衣錦還鄉(ㄧˋ ㄐㄧㄣˇ ㄏㄨㄢˊ ㄒㄧㄤ)
to return home in glory

衣錦夜行(ㄧˋ ㄐㄧㄣˇ ㄧㄝˋ ㄒㄧㄥˊ)
(literally) to travel at night in rich garments—glory unknown to others 亦作「衣繡夜行」

三畫

【表】 5375
ㄅㄧㄠˇ beau biǎo

1. outside; external; apparent;

appearance; exteriors; superficial
2. to announce; to manifest; to show
3. relatives on the side of one's mother's sisters or brothers; relatives on the side of one's father's sisters
4. a report to the emperor
5. a table; a schedule; a chart; a form

表白(ㄅㄧㄠˇ ㄅㄞˊ)
to express or state clearly; to explain; to clear up; to defend (one's position, etc.); to bare one's heart; to clarify: 他表白了誠意。He expressed his sincerity.

表報(ㄅㄧㄠˇ ㄅㄠˋ)
tables, charts, reports, etc. of an office

表皮(ㄅㄧㄠˇ ㄆㄧˊ)
① the epidermis ② the cuticle (of plants)

表妹(ㄅㄧㄠˇ ㄇㄟˋ)
a cousin (a daughter of one's father's sister or of one's mother's brother or sister, who is younger than oneself): 這位是我的表妹。This is my cousin.

表面(ㄅㄧㄠˇ ㄇㄧㄢˋ)
on the surface; externally; outwardly; superficial: 他的聰明僅僅是表面的。His cleverness is only on the surface.

表面化(ㄅㄧㄠˇ ㄇㄧㄢˋ ㄏㄨㄚˋ)
(said of a relationship, dispute, secret, etc.) to come to the surface; to become apparent

表面張力(ㄅㄧㄠˇ ㄇㄧㄢˋ ㄓㄤ ㄌㄧˋ)
(physics) surface tension

表面上(ㄅㄧㄠˇ ㄇㄧㄢˋ ·ㄕㄤ)
on the surface; externally; outwardly

表明(ㄅㄧㄠˇ ㄇㄧㄥˊ)
to indicate or state clearly or plainly

表達(ㄅㄧㄠˇ ㄉㄚˊ)
to convey or transmit (one's feelings, meaning, etc.); to present; to express; to make known; to voice: 我無法適當地把它表達出來。I can't express it properly.

表弟(ㄅㄧㄠˇ ㄉㄧˋ)
a cousin (a son of one's father's sister or of one's mother's brother or sister, who is younger than oneself)

表態(ㄅㄧㄠˇ ㄊㄞˋ)
to make known one's position towards an issue; to declare where one stands: 他已作明確表態。He has taken a clear-cut stand.

表土(ㄅㄧㄠˇ ㄊㄨˇ)
surface soil; topsoil

表同情(ㄅㄧㄠˇ ㄊㄨㄥˊ ㄑㄧㄥˊ)
to express one's sympathy; to commiserate

表裏(ㄅㄧㄠˇ ㄌㄧˇ)
① both sides—inside and outside; in front and behind ②(Chinese medicine) exterior and interior

表裏不一(ㄅㄧㄠˇ ㄌㄧˇ ㄅㄨˋ ㄧ)
to think in one way and behave in another

表裏受敵(ㄅㄧㄠˇ ㄌㄧˇ ㄕㄡˋ ㄉㄧˊ)
to encounter the enemy in front and behind

表裏一致(ㄅㄧㄠˇ ㄌㄧˇ ㄧˋ ㄓˋ)or 表裏如一(ㄅㄧㄠˇ ㄌㄧˇ ㄖㄨˊ ㄧ)
honest and sincere

表列(ㄅㄧㄠˇ ㄌㄧㄝˋ)
to catalogue; to list

表露(ㄅㄧㄠˇ ㄌㄨˋ)
to make plain; to express or expose; to voice: 他們表露了憤怒。They gave voice to their indignation.

表哥(ㄅㄧㄠˇ ㄍㄜ)
a cousin (a son of one's father's sister or of one's mother's brother or sister, who is older than oneself)

表格(ㄅㄧㄠˇ ㄍㄜˊ)
a form or blank (for filling); a table or chart

表記(ㄅㄧㄠˇ ㄐㄧˋ)
① a mark; a sign ② a souvenir

表姊(ㄅㄧㄠˇ ㄐㄧㄝˇ)
a cousin (a daughter of one's father's sister or of one's mother's brother or sister, who is older than oneself)

表姊妹(ㄅㄧㄠˇ ㄐㄧㄝˇ ㄇㄟˋ)
female first cousins (daughters of one's maternal uncles and aunts and of one's father's sisters)

表決(ㄅㄧㄠˇ ㄐㄩㄝˊ)
to vote; to put to the vote: 投票表決吧。Let's decide by vote.

表決權(ㄅㄧㄠˇ ㄐㄩㄝˊ ㄑㄩㄢˊ)
the right of voting: 他們行使表決權。They exercised the right of voting.

表親(ㄅㄧㄠˇ ㄑㄧㄣ)
relatives on the side of one's parents' sisters or of one's mother's brothers

表情(ㄅㄧㄠˇ ㄑㄧㄥˊ)
facial expression: 她的表情不自然。She wore an unnatural expression.

表情達意(ㄅㄧㄠˇ ㄑㄧㄥˊ ㄉㄚˊ ㄧˋ)
to communicate views; to convey one's ideas or feelings

表顯(ㄅㄧㄠˇ ㄒㄧㄢˇ)
to express; to display

表現(ㄅㄧㄠˇ ㄒㄧㄢˋ)
① to appear ② to behave ③ to distinguish oneself ④ to perform (a task); the way one does something: 他表現良好。He performs well.

表象(ㄅㄧㄠˇ ㄒㄧㄤˋ)
(psychology) presentation; idea

表兄(ㄅㄧㄠˇ ㄒㄩㄥ)
a cousin (a son of one's father's sister or of one's mother's brother or sister, who is older than oneself): 他是我的表兄。He is my cousin.

表兄弟(ㄅㄧㄠˇ ㄒㄩㄥ ㄉㄧˋ)
male first cousins (sons of one's maternal uncles and aunts and of one's father's sisters)

表姪(ㄅㄧㄠˇ ㄓˊ)
grandsons of one's paternal aunts

表章(ㄅㄧㄠˇ ㄓㄤ)
① a report to the emperor ② to honor 亦作「表彰」

表彰(ㄅㄧㄠˇ ㄓㄤ)
to honor; to cite; citation

表示(ㄅㄧㄠˇ ㄕˋ)
to express; to show; to indicate; expression; reaction: 他們對我表示厚誼。They showed me great kindness.

表示滿意(ㄅㄧㄠˇ ㄕˋ ㄇㄢˇ ㄧˋ)
to express or indicate satisfaction

表示反對(ㄅㄧㄠˇ ㄕˋ ㄈㄢˇ ㄉㄨㄟˋ)
to express or indicate one's opposition

表示同意(ㄅㄧㄠˇ ㄕˋ ㄊㄨㄥˊ ㄧˋ)
to indicate or show one's concurrence or approval

表示敬意(ㄅㄧㄠˇ ㄕˋ ㄐㄧㄥˋ ㄧˋ)
to show or pay respect

表示慶賀(ㄅㄧㄠˇ ㄕˋ ㄑㄧㄥˋ ㄏㄜˋ)
to show or express one's congratulations

表示謝意(ㄅㄧㄠˇ ㄕˋ ㄒㄧㄝˋ ㄧˋ)
to show one's thanks or appreciation; to express one's gratitude

表叔(ㄅㄧㄠˇ ㄕㄨˊ)
an uncle (a son of one's grandfather's sister, or a son of one's grandmother's sister or brother)

表率(ㄅㄧㄠˇ ㄕㄨㄞˋ)
an example; a paragon: 她給朋友們樹立了好表率。She set a good example to her friends.

表字(ㄅㄧㄠˇ ㄗˋ)
a courtesy name; a second name; an alias 亦作「別號」

表子(ㄅㄧㄠˇ ·ㄗ)
a prostitute 亦作「婊子」

表册(ㄅㄧㄠˇ ㄘㄜˋ)
tables, indexes, files, etc.

表層(ㄅㄧㄠˇ ㄘㄥˊ)
a surface layer

表錯情(ㄅㄧㄠˇ ㄘㄨㄛˋ ㄑㄧㄥˊ)
to show friendliness to or express support for someone who does not appreciate it

表儀(ㄅㄧㄠˇ ㄧˊ)
one's majestic appearance

表演(ㄅㄧㄠˇ ㄧㄢˇ)
to perform; to demonstrate; demonstration; a performance; a show: 你表演得很不錯。You performed very well.

表揚(ㄅㄧㄠˇ ㄧㄤˊ)
to praise in public; to cite for all to know: 他因那研究而受表揚。He was cited for his research work.

【衫】 5376
ㄕㄢ shan shān
a shirt; a garment; a gown

【衩】 5377
ㄔㄚˋ chah chà
slits on the lower part of a gown for freedom of movement

衩衣(ㄔㄚˋ ㄧ)
a woman's gown with slits on the sides

衩襪(ㄔㄚˋ ㄨㄚˋ)
stockings without bands

四畫

【衰】 5378
1. ㄕㄨㄞ shuai shuāi
1. to decline; weakening; failing (health, etc.); debility: 懶惰則體衰。Laziness leads to debility.
2. declining or falling (nations, etc.)

衰敗(ㄕㄨㄞ ㄅㄞˋ)
to decline and disintegrate

衰弊(ㄕㄨㄞ ㄅㄧˋ)
decadent and corrupt

衰邁(ㄕㄨㄞ ㄇㄞˋ) or 衰暮(ㄕㄨㄞ ㄇㄨˋ)
old and weak

衰頹(ㄕㄨㄞ ㄊㄨㄟˊ)
discouraged and despondent

衰退(ㄕㄨㄞ ㄊㄨㄟˋ)
failing (energy, strength, memory, etc.); weakening (as a result of old age, poor health, etc.); decline: 他的健康衰退了。He failed in his health.

衰老(ㄕㄨㄞ ㄌㄠˇ)
senile; senility: 他已相當衰老了。He has become perfectly senile.

衰陵(ㄕㄨㄞ ㄌㄧㄥˊ)
the decline and fall (of a nation, dynasty, etc.)

衰落(ㄕㄨㄞ ㄌㄨㄛˋ)
the decline and fall (of a nation, family fortune, etc.); to go into oblivion

衰耗(ㄕㄨㄞ ㄏㄠˋ)
to weaken and deteriorate

衰疾(ㄕㄨㄞ ㄐㄧˊ)
decrepit and beset by illness

衰竭(ㄕㄨㄞ ㄐㄧㄝˊ)
exhaustion; prostration

衰倦(ㄕㄨㄞ ㄐㄩㄢˋ)
enfeebled and tired

衰缺(ㄕㄨㄞ ㄑㄩㄝ)
declining and full of defects

衰息(ㄕㄨㄞ ㄒㄧˊ)
to come to a halt or stop (as a lawsuit, etc.)

衰謝(ㄕㄨㄞ ㄒㄧㄝˋ)
① old and desolate ②(said of hair) sparse

衰朽(ㄕㄨㄞ ㄒㄧㄡˇ)
old and useless

衰世(ㄕㄨㄞ ㄕˋ)
an age of decline and tumult

衰弱(ㄕㄨㄞ ㄖㄨㄛˋ)
to debilitate; weak; sickly; not healthy

衰弱症(ㄕㄨㄞ ㄖㄨㄛˋ ㄓㄥˋ)
a wasting disease

衰容(ㄕㄨㄞ ㄖㄨㄥˊ)
the face of an old person

衰草寒煙(ㄕㄨㄞ ㄘㄠˇ ㄏㄢˊ ㄧㄢ)
withering grass and chilly mists (descriptive of a desolate scene)

衰顏(ㄕㄨㄞ ㄧㄢˊ)
the face of an old person

衰微(ㄕㄨㄞ ㄨㄟˊ)
to decline; to wane; declining

衰亡(ㄕㄨㄞ ㄨㄤˊ)
the decline and fall

【衰】 5378
2. ㄘㄨㄟ tsuei cuī
1. order or series—from the top downward
2. mourning garments (of hemp, etc.)

【袂】 5379
ㄇㄟˋ mey mèi
sleeves

【衲】 5380
ㄋㄚˋ nah nà
1. to sew; to mend; to patch
2. the robe of a monk
3. a monk

衲被(ㄋㄚˋ ㄅㄟˋ)
①a quilt with patches on it ②a collection of cards on which literary allusions are copied and explained and then arranged and made use of in a piece of composition—a reference to the practice of Yang Yi (楊億) of the Sung Dynasty

衲頭(ㄋㄚˋ ㄊㄡˊ)
a monk's clothes made of rags

衲子(ㄋㄚˋ ㄗˇ)
a polite self-reference of a Buddhist monk

【衵】 5381
ㄋㄧˋ nih nì

a woman's underwear
衵服(ㄋ丨ˋ ㄈㄨˊ)
women's underwear

【衷】 5382 ㄓㄨㄥ jong zhōng
1. the bottom of one's heart; honest; sincere
2. good and virtuous; goodness
3. proper; appropriate; befitting; propriety
4. undergarments
5. a Chinese family name
衷款(ㄓㄨㄥ ㄎㄨㄢˇ)
sincerity
衷情(ㄓㄨㄥ ㄑ丨ㄥˊ)
the feelings or affection in one's heart
衷曲(ㄓㄨㄥ ㄑㄩ)
words from the bottom of one's heart; the voice of one's heart; inner feelings
衷心(ㄓㄨㄥ ㄒ丨ㄣ)
heartfelt; wholehearted; cordial
衷心感謝(ㄓㄨㄥ ㄒ丨ㄣ ㄍㄢˇ ㄒ丨ㄝˋ)
to thank sincerely; to thank from the bottom of one's heart
衷腸(ㄓㄨㄥ ㄔㄤˊ)or 衷懷(ㄓㄨㄥ ㄏㄨㄞˊ)
innermost feelings; sincere words
衷衣(ㄓㄨㄥ 丨)
underwear

【衺】 5383 (邪) ㄒ丨ㄝˊ shye xié
evil

【衽】 5384 (袵) ㄖㄣˋ renn rèn
1. the lapel or collar of a garment
2. sleeves
3. to arrange (one's lapel, etc.)
4. a sleeping mat
衽席(ㄖㄣˋ ㄒ丨ˊ)
a sleeping mat

【衾】 5385 ㄑ丨ㄣ chin qīn (又讀 ㄑ丨ㄣˊ chyn qín)
1. a large coverlet or quilt
2. garments or dress for the deceased
衾單(ㄑ丨ㄣ ㄉㄢ)
① clothes, etc. for the deceased ② sheets
衾枕(ㄑ丨ㄣ ㄓㄣˇ)
quilts and pillows
衾衽(ㄑ丨ㄣ ㄖㄣˋ)
in bed; between the sheets
衾影無慚(ㄑ丨ㄣ 丨ㄥˇ ㄨˊ ㄘㄢˊ)
to do nothing that one can be ashamed of even if there is no one watching

【衿】 5386 ㄐ丨ㄣ jin jīn
1. the front of a Chinese gown
2. the lapel of a Chinese dress—worn by the literati in former days
衿契(ㄐ丨ㄣ ㄑ丨ˋ)
a good friend, with whom one sees eye to eye about everything

【袁】 5387 ㄩㄢˊ yuan yuán
1. the graceful look of a flowing robe
2. a Chinese family name
袁大頭(ㄩㄢˊ ㄉㄚˋ ㄊㄡˊ)
silver coins minted in the early years of the Republic of China with the head of Yüan Shih-kai (袁世凱) on the obverse side
袁枚(ㄩㄢˊ ㄇㄟˊ)
Yüan Mei, a man of letters in the Ching Dynasty
袁世凱(ㄩㄢˊ ㄕˋ ㄎㄞˇ)
Yüan Shih-kai (1859-1916), the first President of the Republic of China, who died shortly after he proclaimed himself an emperor
袁紹(ㄩㄢˊ ㄕㄠˋ)
Yüan Shao (?-202), a warlord toward the end of the Han Dynasty

【衮】 5388 (袞) ㄍㄨㄣˇ goen gǔn
1. the imperial robe with embroidered dragons
2. robes of very high officials
衮冕(ㄍㄨㄣˇ ㄇ丨ㄢˇ)
a robe embroidered with dragons and a crown worn by the emperor in sacrificial ceremonies
衮命(ㄍㄨㄣˇ ㄇ丨ㄥˋ)
the office or appointment of the three highest officials (三公) in ancient China
衮服(ㄍㄨㄣˇ ㄈㄨˊ)
ceremonial dress or robe in ancient China
衮龍袍(ㄍㄨㄣˇ ㄌㄨㄥˊ ㄆㄠˊ)
the imperial robe embroidered with coiled dragons
衮衮諸公(ㄍㄨㄣˇ ㄍㄨㄣˇ ㄓㄨ ㄍㄨㄥ)
many eminent personalities; many VIPs; high-ranking officials
衮闕(ㄍㄨㄣˇ ㄑㄩㄝ)
the faults of the emperor
衮職(ㄍㄨㄣˇ ㄓˊ)
① the throne; the responsibility of an emperor ② the office of the three highest officials (三公) in ancient China
衮司(ㄍㄨㄣˇ ㄙ)
the three highest-ranking officials in the imperial court of ancient China 亦作「三公」
衮衣(ㄍㄨㄣˇ 丨)
robes embroidered with dragons worn only by the emperor

五畫

【袈】 5389 ㄐ丨ㄚ jia jiā
the cassock or robe of a Buddhist monk
袈裟(ㄐ丨ㄚ ㄕㄚ)
a kasaya or cassock, the robe of a Buddhist monk

【袖】 5390 ㄒ丨ㄡˋ shiow xiù
1. the sleeve
2. to hide or put things in sleeves
袖頭兒(ㄒ丨ㄡˋ ㄊㄡˊㄦ)
the cuff
袖筒兒(ㄒ丨ㄡˋ ㄊㄨㄥˇㄦ)
the sleeve
袖口(兒)(ㄒ丨ㄡˋ ㄎㄡˇ(ㄦ))
the cuff (of a sleeve); the far ends of sleeves; a wristband
袖扣(ㄒ丨ㄡˋ ㄎㄡˋ)
cuff links
袖箭(ㄒ丨ㄡˋ ㄐ丨ㄢˋ)
a cylindrical device hidden in the sleeve, which can launch small darts with its spring catapult
袖珍(ㄒ丨ㄡˋ ㄓㄣ)
pocket-size; pocket
袖珍本(ㄒ丨ㄡˋ ㄓㄣ ㄅㄣˇ)

〔衣部〕

a pocket edition; a pocket book

袖珍戰艦(ㄒㄧㄡˋ ㄓㄣ ㄓㄢˋ ㄐㄧㄢˋ)
a pocket battleship

袖珍字典(ㄒㄧㄡˋ ㄓㄣ ㄗˋ ㄉㄧㄢˇ)
a pocket dictionary

袖手旁觀(ㄒㄧㄡˋ ㄕㄡˇ ㄆㄤˊ ㄍㄨㄢ)
to look on without even lifting a finger (to help, etc.); to watch with folded arms

袖刃(ㄒㄧㄡˋ ㄖㄣˋ)
to hide a dagger or knife in a sleeve

袖子(ㄒㄧㄡˋ ・ㄗ)or 袖兒(ㄒㄧㄡˋㄦ)
the sleeve: 他拉著她的袖子。He pulled her by the sleeve.

袖刺(ㄒㄧㄡˋ ㄘˋ)
to put one's visiting cards in the sleeve

【袋】 5391 ㄉㄞˋ day dài

a bag; a sack; a pocket; a pouch

袋兒(ㄉㄚˇㄦ)
a purse; a pocket

袋鼠(ㄉㄞˋ ㄕㄨˇ)
the kangaroo

袋子(ㄉㄞˋ ・ㄗ)
a bag; a sack; a pocket: 他買了一個購物袋子。He bought a shopping bag.

【袍】 5392 ㄆㄠˊ paur páo

a long gown; a robe

袍褂(ㄆㄠˊ ㄍㄨㄚˋ)
a long gown topped off with a jacket, the ceremonial robe in the Ching Dynasty and among old-fashioned Chinese gentlemen of modern times, also worn as ceremonial dress

袍笏(ㄆㄠˊ ㄏㄨˋ)
an official robe and tablet, formal dress in audience with the emperor

袍笏登場(ㄆㄠˊ ㄏㄨˋ ㄉㄥ ㄔㄤˇ)
①(Chinese opera) to go on stage and perform ②(said of rebels or traitors) to establish a bogus government and claim legality

袍子(ㄆㄠˊ ・ㄗ)
a robe; a long gown: 他穿了一襲袍子。He wears a robe.

袍澤(ㄆㄠˊ ㄗㄜˊ)
one's buddies in the army; comrades in arms

【袒】 5393 ㄊㄢˇ taan tǎn

1. to bare; to strip; bared
2. to protect or screen (with an implication of prejudice); to be partial: 勿偏袒她。Do not be partial to her.

袒膊(ㄊㄢˇ ㄅㄛˊ)
to strip to the waist; bared to the waist

袒免(ㄊㄢˇ ㄇㄧㄢˇ)
to bare one's left arm and take off one's cap—a gesture of great sorrow in ancient times

袒縛(ㄊㄢˇ ㄈㄨˊ)
to bare oneself to the waist and bind one's hands at the back—an act of surrendering or submitting in ancient times; an expression used to show a submission

袒露(ㄊㄢˇ ㄌㄨˋ)
to expose

袒護(ㄊㄢˇ ㄏㄨˋ)
to shield; to protect; to screen; to side with; to be partial: 他公然袒護一方。He was partial to one side publicly.

袒裼(ㄊㄢˇ ㄒㄧˊ)
to bare one's breast and arms; with one's breast and arms bare

袒胸露臂(ㄊㄢˇ ㄒㄩㄥ ㄌㄨˋ ㄅㄧˋ)
to bare the chest and expose the arms

袒衣(ㄊㄢˇ ㄧ)
to dress in a hurry with part of flesh showing

【袜】 5394 1. ㄇㄛˋ moh mò

a stomacher

袜腹(ㄇㄛˋ ㄈㄨˋ)
a stomacher

袜肚(ㄇㄛˋ ㄉㄨˋ)
①a waistband ②a saddle girth

袜胸(ㄇㄛˋ ㄒㄩㄥ)
a stomacher

【袜】 5394 2. ㄨㄚˋ wah wà

a simplified form of 襪—stockings; socks

【袤】 5395 ㄇㄠˋ maw mào (又讀 ㄇㄡˋ mow mòu)

length; lengthwise—from north to south (as opposed to 廣)

【袪】 5396 ㄑㄩ chiu qū

1. cuffs; sleeves
2. to raise the sleeves; to lift up one's arms
3. to relieve

【被】 5397 1. ㄅㄟˋ bey bèi

1. bedding; a coverlet; a quilt
2. to cover; to shroud
3. to spread; to reach
4. placed before verbs to show a passive voice
5. because of; due to
6. a Chinese family name

被保護國(ㄅㄟˋ ㄅㄠˇ ㄏㄨˋ ㄍㄨㄛˊ)
a protectorate

被綁架(ㄅㄟˋ ㄅㄤˇ ㄐㄧㄚˋ)
to be kidnaped: 一個男孩被綁架。A boy was kidnaped.

被謗(ㄅㄟˋ ㄅㄤˋ)
to be slandered

被迫(ㄅㄟˋ ㄆㄛˋ)or 被逼(ㄅㄟˋ ㄅㄧ)
to be compelled or forced to

被迫降落(ㄅㄟˋ ㄆㄛˋ ㄐㄧㄤˋ ㄌㄨㄛˋ)
a forced landing; to be forced to land

被騙(ㄅㄟˋ ㄆㄧㄢˋ)
to be swindled; to be fooled

被面(ㄅㄟˋ ㄇㄧㄢˋ)
the cover side of a comforter

被俘(ㄅㄟˋ ㄈㄨˊ)
to be captured; to be taken prisoner

被服(ㄅㄟˋ ㄈㄨˊ)
①coverlets and clothes ②(figuratively) to receive; to benefit

被服廠(ㄅㄟˋ ㄈㄨˊ ㄔㄤˇ)
a factory that makes uniforms, tents and other textile goods for military use; a clothing factory

被單兒(ㄅㄟˋ ㄉㄚㄦ)or 被單子(ㄅㄟˋ ㄉㄢ ・ㄗ)
a bedsheet; a bedspread; a bed cover; bed linens

被底鴛鴦(ㄅㄟˋ ㄉㄧˇ ㄩㄢ ㄧㄤ)
(literally) mandarin ducks under the quilt—a devoted couple

被動(ㄅㄟˋ ㄉㄨㄥˋ)
passive; to act on order

被動式(ㄅㄟˋ ㄉㄨㄥˋ ㄕˋ)
(grammar) the passive voice
被套(ㄅㄟˋ ㄊㄠˋ)
ticking
被虐待狂(ㄅㄟˋ ㄋㄩㄝˋ ㄉㄞˋ ㄎㄨㄤˊ)
masochism
被裏(ㄅㄟˋ ㄌㄧˇ)or 被裏子(ㄅㄟˋ ㄌㄧˇ ˙ㄗ)
the underneath side of a quilt; the lining of a comforter
被告(ㄅㄟˋ ㄍㄠˋ)
the accused; the defendant
被害(ㄅㄟˋ ㄏㄞˋ)
to be killed or murdered
被害者(ㄅㄟˋ ㄏㄞˋ ㄓㄜˇ)
the injured or wronged party; a victim; an injured person
被加數(ㄅㄟˋ ㄐㄧㄚ ㄕㄨˋ)
a summand
被刼(ㄅㄟˋ ㄐㄧㄝˊ)
to be robbed; 我鄰居於上週被刼。The house next to mine was robbed last week.
被刼持(ㄅㄟˋ ㄐㄧㄝˊ ㄔˊ)
to be held as a hostage
被減數(ㄅㄟˋ ㄐㄧㄢˇ ㄕㄨˋ)
a minuend
被竊(ㄅㄟˋ ㄑㄧㄝˋ)
to be victimized by burglary
被擒(ㄅㄟˋ ㄑㄧㄣˊ)
to be captured alive; to be taken prisoner
被搶(ㄅㄟˋ ㄑㄧㄤˇ)
to be robbed: 我的錶被搶了。I was robbed of my watch.
被選學權(ㄅㄟˋ ㄒㄩㄢˇ ㄐㄩˇ ㄑㄩㄢˊ)
the right of being elected; eligibility for election
被選舉人(ㄅㄟˋ ㄒㄩㄢˇ ㄐㄩˇ ㄖㄣˊ)
the person to be elected; a candidate of an election
被乘數(ㄅㄟˋ ㄔㄥˊ ㄕㄨˋ)
a multiplicand
被除數(ㄅㄟˋ ㄔㄨˊ ㄕㄨˋ)
a dividend
被殺(ㄅㄟˋ ㄕㄚ)
to be killed or assassinated: 這熊昨天被殺了。The bear was killed yesterday.
被辱(ㄅㄟˋ ㄖㄨˇ)
to be insulted or humiliated
被褥(ㄅㄟˋ ㄖㄨˋ)
coverlets and mattresses; bedding
被子植物(ㄅㄟˋ ㄗˇ ㄓˊ ㄨˋ)
(botany) angiosperm
被子(ㄅㄟˋ ˙ㄗ)
a quilt
被刺(ㄅㄟˋ ㄘˋ)
to be assassinated
被誣(ㄅㄟˋ ㄨ)
to be falsely accused
被窩兒(ㄅㄟˋ ㄨㄛㄦ)or 被窩子(ㄅㄟˋ ㄨㄛ ˙ㄗ)
a quilt folded like a sleeve for sleeping

【被】 5397
2.(披) ㄆㄧ pi pī
1. to put on or throw on(garments, etc.) without buttoning up
2. to open
3. to disperse or spread out
4. to read desultorily or to thumb through
被髮入山(ㄆㄧ ㄈㄚˇ ㄖㄨˋ ㄕㄢ)
to go and live in the mountains with hair disheveled —to become a hermit
被髮左衽(ㄆㄧ ㄈㄚˇ ㄗㄨㄛˇ ㄖㄣˋ)
hair unbound and coats buttoned on the left side—to become a barbarian
被髮佯狂(ㄆㄧ ㄈㄚˇ ㄧㄤˊ ㄎㄨㄤˊ)
With hair disheveled, one pretends to be a lunatic.
被髮文身(ㄆㄧ ㄈㄚˇ ㄨㄣˊ ㄕㄣ)
(said of a barbarian) hair disheveled and the body tattooed
被褐懷玉(ㄆㄧ ㄏㄜˊ ㄏㄨㄞˊ ㄩˋ)
(said of a hermit) to dress shabbily in order to hide one's real worth
被堅執銳 or 披堅執銳(ㄆㄧ ㄐㄧㄢ ㄓˊ ㄖㄨㄟˋ)
to wear armor and hold sharp weapons—ready to defend the country

【衮】 5398
(袞) ㄍㄨㄣˇ goen gŭn
the ceremonial dress of the emperor or very high officials

六畫

【袴】 5399
(絝、褲) ㄎㄨˋ kuh kù
trousers; drawers; breeches; pants; panties 參看「褲」
袴襠(ㄎㄨˋ ㄉㄤ)
the crotch (of trousers)
袴腿(ㄎㄨˋ ㄊㄨㄟˇ)
legs of trousers
袴脚(ㄎㄨˋ ㄐㄧㄠˇ)
the part of trousers near or around the ankles
袴叉兒(ㄎㄨˋ ㄔㄚˇㄦ)
pants or trousers reaching just above the knees; short pants; shorts
袴子(ㄎㄨˋ ˙ㄗ)
trousers; breeches; pants
袴腰 or 褲腰(ㄎㄨˋ ㄧㄠ)
the waist of trousers
袴腰帶 or 褲腰帶(ㄎㄨˋ ㄧㄠ ㄉㄞˋ)
a waist belt or rope for fastening the trousers

【袱】 5400
ㄈㄨˊ fwu fú
as in包袱—a bundle wrapped in cloth

【袷】 5401
1. ㄐㄧㄚˊ jya jiá
garments with linings

【袷】 5401
2. ㄐㄧㄝˊ jye jié
the lapel or collar of robes, or, in former times, of ceremonial dress in imperial audience

【裁】 5402
ㄘㄞˊ tsair cái
1. to cut paper, cloth, etc. with a knife or scissors; to cut out or cut off
2. to diminish; to reduce
3. to delete
4. to consider; to discern; to decide; to judge
5. a form; a style
6. sanctions
7. to weight; to measure
8. to kill
裁兵(ㄘㄞˊ ㄅㄧㄥ)
to reduce the number of troops; disarmament
裁併(ㄘㄞˊ ㄅㄧㄥˋ)
(said of organizations) to cut down in size and merge into one
裁判(ㄘㄞˊ ㄆㄢˋ)
①a judge; a referee; an umpire ②a verdict or judgment by law
裁判書(ㄘㄞˊ ㄆㄢˋ ㄕㄨ)
a written court verdict
裁判委員(ㄘㄞˊ ㄆㄢˋ ㄨㄟˇ ㄩㄢˊ)

〔衣部〕

a member of a panel of judges, or referees

裁縫

①(ㄘㄞˊ ㄈㄥˊ)to tailor; to make dress

②(ㄘㄞˊ ˙ㄈㄥ)a tailor; a dress-maker 亦作「裁縫師」

裁縫補習班(ㄘㄞˊ ㄈㄥˊ ㄅㄨˇ ㄒㄧˊ ㄅㄢ)

a training class for tailoring

裁縫鋪(ㄘㄞˊ ㄈㄥˊ ㄆㄨˋ)

a tailor shop

裁答(ㄘㄞˊ ㄉㄚˊ)

to reply a letter

裁定(ㄘㄞˊ ㄉㄧㄥˋ)

(law) a court decision on the legality of a case, or the propriety or appropriateness of a verdict

裁奪(ㄘㄞˊ ㄉㄨㄛˊ)

to decide; decision

裁度(ㄘㄞˊ ㄉㄨㄛˊ)

to weigh, consider and decide

裁斷(ㄘㄞˊ ㄉㄨㄢˋ)

to decide; decision

裁汰(ㄘㄞˊ ㄊㄞˋ)

to reduce or eliminate (the superfluous) staff, etc.

裁量(ㄘㄞˊ ㄌㄧㄤˊ)

to consider and decide; to measure

裁可(ㄘㄞˊ ㄎㄜˇ)

to approve; to sign a bill into law

裁開(ㄘㄞˊ ㄎㄞ)

to cut apart with a knife or scissors

裁剪(ㄘㄞˊ ㄐㄧㄢˇ)

① to tailor; to cut out (a dress): 她正在裁剪衣服。She's cutting out garments. ② to delete the unimportant or superfluous part (of a piece of writing, etc.)

裁減(ㄘㄞˊ ㄐㄧㄢˇ)

① to reduce (personnel, the staff, etc.) ② reduction

裁決(ㄘㄞˊ ㄐㄩㄝˊ)

① to judge and decide ② a ruling; a judgment; a decision

裁軍(ㄘㄞˊ ㄐㄩㄣ)

disarmament

裁紙(ㄘㄞˊ ㄓˇ)

to cut paper into portions with a knife

裁制(ㄘㄞˊ ㄓˋ)

to restrain; to restrict; to limit

裁尺(ㄘㄞˊ ㄔˇ)

a tailor's measure

裁撤(ㄘㄞˊ ㄔㄜˋ)

to abolish (an organization)

裁成(ㄘㄞˊ ㄔㄥˊ)

to regulate and bring to completion; accomplishment

裁處(ㄘㄞˊ ㄔㄨˇ)

to make an arrangement or decision after due consideration

裁衣(ㄘㄞˊ ㄧ)

to cut cloth for making dress

裁彎取直(ㄘㄞˊ ㄨㄢ ㄑㄩˇ ㄓˊ)

to get rid of the unnecessary and take the most appropriate

裁員(ㄘㄞˊ ㄩㄢˊ)

to eliminate unnecessary personnel; to lay off workers

【裂】 5403 ㄌㄧㄝˋ lieh liè

1. to crack; to break; a crack: 杯上有一裂痕。There was a crack in the cup.
2. to split or divide up (profits, etc.); to rend; to sever; to rip open: 我頭痛欲裂。My head is splitting.

裂帛(ㄌㄧㄝˋ ㄅㄛˊ)

① a very crisp sound—like splitting silk ② ancient books ③ to cut silk into pieces for writing letters in ancient times

裂縫(ㄌㄧㄝˋ ㄈㄥˋ)

a crack or cleavage; a split; a breach; a crevice; a fissure

裂膚(ㄌㄧㄝˋ ㄈㄨ)

(literally) to crack up the skin—extreme cold

裂膽(ㄌㄧㄝˋ ㄉㄢˇ)

extremely scared or frightened

裂果(ㄌㄧㄝˋ ㄍㄨㄛˇ)

dehiscent fruits

裂開(ㄌㄧㄝˋ ㄎㄞ)

to split, rip or break apart: 衣縫裂開了。A seam rips.

裂口(ㄌㄧㄝˋ ㄎㄡˇ)

a crack; a chink

裂痕(ㄌㄧㄝˋ ㄏㄣˊ)

① a chasm (in friendship, etc.) ② a fissure; a split; a crack: 木頭上有一大裂痕。There was a big split in the wood.

裂罅(ㄌㄧㄝˋ ㄒㄧㄚˋ)

a crack; a crevice

裂眦(ㄌㄧㄝˋ ㄗˋ)

to open one's eyes wide in extreme anger

裂眼(ㄌㄧㄝˋ ㄧㄢˇ)

an angry look

裂紋(ㄌㄧㄝˋ ㄨㄣˊ)

a line of cleavage; crackle

【裉】 5404 ㄎㄣˋ kenn kèn

the seams below the sleeves in a garment

【袵】 5405 (衽) ㄖㄣˋ renn rèn

1. lapels; collars
2. sleeves
3. bedding

七畫

【裊】 5406 ㄋㄧㄠˇ neau niǎo

1. curling up (as smoke, etc.); wavering gently
2. around; all around, as sound of music or voices of spring

裊裊(ㄋㄧㄠˇ ㄋㄧㄠˇ)

① curling up ② continuous (sound of music, etc.)

裊裊婷婷 or 嬝嬝婷婷(ㄋㄧㄠˇ ㄋㄧㄠˇ ㄊㄧㄥˊ ㄊㄧㄥˊ)

(said of the charming figure and poise of a woman) curvaceous and soft

裊娜 or 嬝娜(ㄋㄧㄠˇ ㄋㄨㄛˊ)

① soft and slender ② charming figure and poise of a woman

【裋】 5407 ㄕㄨˋ shuh shù

cotton clothes of a boy servant

裋褐(ㄕㄨˋ ㄏㄜˊ)

the short, coarse garment of a boy servant

【裙】 5408 ㄑㄩㄣˊ chyun qún

a skirt; a petticoat; an apron

裙帶(ㄑㄩㄣˊ ㄉㄞˋ)

① connected through one's female relatives; apron strings (used figuratively in most cases) ② a girdle

裙帶官(ㄑㄩㄣˊ ㄉㄞˋ ㄍㄨㄢ)
an official appointment obtained through the influence of one's wife or her family

裙帶關係(ㄑㄩㄣˊ ㄉㄞˋ ㄍㄨㄢ ㄒㄧˋ)
apron-string influence or relationship; petticoat influence

裙帶親(ㄑㄩㄣˊ ㄉㄞˋ ㄑㄧㄣ)
(said of a man) relatives by marriage (sometimes also used figuratively and sarcastically)

裙屐少年(ㄑㄩㄣˊ ㄐㄧ ㄕㄠˋ ㄋㄧㄢˊ)
fops; dandies; coxcombs

裙襇(ㄑㄩㄣˊ ㄐㄧㄢˇ)
plaits on the sides of a petticoat

裙釵(ㄑㄩㄣˊ ㄔㄞ)
petticoats and hairpins —women

裙子(ㄑㄩㄣˊ ˙ㄗ)
a woman's skirt; a petticoat

【裎】 5409
ㄔㄥˊ cherng chéng
bare or nude; naked; to bare

【裏】 5410
(裡) ㄌㄧˇ lii lǐ
1. within; inside
2. used to indicate time of day, night, a season, etc.
3. the lining of a dress or clothes

裏邊(ㄌㄧˇ ㄅㄧㄢ)or 裏邊兒(ㄌㄧˇ ˙ㄅㄧㄚㄦ)
inside: 我們到裏邊(兒)去好嗎? Shall we go inside?

裏面兒(ㄌㄧˇ ㄇㄧㄚˋㄦ)
inside; within: 廚房裏面很清潔。It's very clean inside the kitchen.

裏封(ㄌㄧˇ ㄈㄥ)
a title page

裏帶(ㄌㄧˇ ㄉㄞˋ)
(colloquial) an inner tube (of a tire)

裏頭(ㄌㄧˇ ˙ㄊㄡ)
inside: 他走進裏頭。He went inside.

裏裏外外(ㄌㄧˇ ˙ㄌㄧ ㄨㄞˋ ㄨㄞˋ)
inside and out

裏勾外聯(ㄌㄧˇ ㄍㄡ ㄨㄞˋ ㄌㄧㄢˊ)
collusion of forces within and without; to be in collusion with the enemy

裏海(ㄌㄧˇ ㄏㄞˇ)
the Caspian Sea

裏脊肉(ㄌㄧˇ ㄐㄧˇ ㄖㄡˋ)or 裏脊(ㄌㄧˇ ㄐㄧˇ)
lean pork taken from under the spinal column of a hog; tenderloin

裏間兒(ㄌㄧˇ ㄐㄧㄚㄦ)
an inner room

裏出外進(ㄌㄧˇ ㄔㄨ ㄨㄞˋ ㄐㄧㄣˋ)
① uneven; not neat ② a motley of people coming and going

裏子(ㄌㄧˇ ˙ㄗ)or 裏兒(ㄌㄧˇㄜㄦ)
the lining of a garment, a hat or shoes

裏衣(ㄌㄧˇ ㄧ)
underwear

裏應外合(ㄌㄧˇ ㄧㄥˋ ㄨㄞˋ ㄏㄜˊ)
the joining of forces within and without; to enter into conspiracy with the dissidents within the enemy camp

裏外受敵(ㄌㄧˇ ㄨㄞˋ ㄕㄡˋ ㄉㄧˊ)
to encounter the enemy within and without; to face opposition inside and out

【裏】 5410
2. ˙ㄌㄧ ˙li li
used after 這 and 那 to mean "here" and "there" respectively: 把它放在這裏。Place it here.

【裒】 5411
ㄆㄡˊ pour póu
1. to collect; to gather; to scrape together
2. to reduce; to deduct

裒多益寡(ㄆㄡˊ ㄉㄨㄛ ㄧˋ ㄍㄨㄚˇ)
to collect from the rich and benefit the poor

裒斂(ㄆㄡˊ ㄌㄧㄢˇ)
to exploit (the people); to amass (a fortune)

裒輯(ㄆㄡˊ ㄐㄧˊ)
to collect and edit

【裔】 5412
ㄧˋ yih yì
1. descendants; posterity
2. the hem of a garment, robe, etc.
3. remote or border regions
4. (now rarely) a general name of northern barbarians
5. a Chinese family name

裔胄(ㄧˋ ㄓㄡˋ)or 裔孫(ㄧˋ ㄙㄨㄣ)
remote descendants or posterity

裔夷(ㄧˋ ㄧˊ)
frontier tribes

裔裔(ㄧˋ ㄧˋ)
① walking ② cascading down (as rain, etc.)

【裕】 5413
ㄩˋ yuh yù
1. abundance; affluent; plenty; to be abundant: 他生活得很富裕。He lived in plenty.
2. tolerant (administration, etc.); lenient (punishment, etc.)
3. generous; magnanimous
4. slowly; to take time

裕國(ㄩˋ ㄍㄨㄛˊ)
to enrich the nation

裕後光前(ㄩˋ ㄏㄡˋ ㄍㄨㄤ ㄑㄧㄢˊ)
to enrich one's posterity and honor one's ancestors

裕如(ㄩˋ ㄖㄨˊ)
① affluent; rich; well-to-do; in good circumstances; ample ② to take it easy; without hurry; with ease: 對於此事, 他應付裕如。He handled it with ease.

裕裕(ㄩˋ ㄩˋ)
to take it easy; to be at peace with the world

【裘】 5414
ㄑㄧㄡˊ chyou qiú
1. furs; any garments, robes, etc. of fur
2. a Chinese family name

裘弊金盡(ㄑㄧㄡˊ ㄅㄧˋ ㄐㄧㄣ ㄐㄧㄣˋ)
destitute; to have exhausted one's means; to go broke

裘馬(ㄑㄧㄡˊ ㄇㄚˇ)
furs and horses—the rich

裘馬輕肥(ㄑㄧㄡˊ ㄇㄚˇ ㄑㄧㄥ ㄈㄟˊ)
wealthy; affluent; well-to-do; in good circumstances

裘葛屢更(ㄑㄧㄡˊ ㄍㄜˊ ㄌㄩˇ ㄍㄥ)
(literally) many changes from furs (winter) to hemp (summer)—the lapse of many years

裘褐(ㄑㄧㄡˊ ㄏㄜˊ)
to dress economically or simply

【補】 5415
ㄅㄨˇ buu bǔ
1. to repair; to patch; to mend; to fill
2. to add to; to supplement; to supply
3. addenda; supplements; replen-

ishments; complements
4. nutritious; nutrient
5. rich foods; tonics
6. to nourish
7. to make up; to help (finance, etc.); to subsidize
8. to appoint to or fill a post
9. to be of help; benefit; use

補白(ㄅㄨˇ ㄅㄞˊ)
to fill a vacant space with a short piece of writing; a filler

補報(ㄅㄨˇ ㄅㄠˋ)
① to repay favors granted ② an additional statement, report, account, etc. to supplement the one submitted previously

補票(ㄅㄨˇ ㄆㄧㄠˋ)
to buy one's ticket after one gets on a bus, a train ,etc.

補偏救弊(ㄅㄨˇ ㄆㄧㄢ ㄐㄧㄡˋ ㄅㄧˋ)
to repair or correct defects, flaws, etc.

補品(ㄅㄨˇ ㄆㄧㄣˇ)
foods or medicines of highly nutritious value; tonics

補發(ㄅㄨˇ ㄈㄚ)
to issue or distribute behind schedule; to issue or distribute the balance, remaining portion, etc.; to reissue: 裝備丟失，不予補發。The equipment will not be reissued if lost.

補付(ㄅㄨˇ ㄈㄨˋ)
to supplement a deficit; to pay arrears

補靪 or 補釘(ㄅㄨˇ ·ㄉㄧㄥ)
patches (of a garment, etc.): 船帆上有一個補靪。There is a patch on the sail.

補短(ㄅㄨˇ ㄉㄨㄢˇ)
① to supplement a deficit ② to make up for a shortcoming or flaw

補貼(ㄅㄨˇ ㄊㄧㄝ)
to subsidize; a subsidy; an allowance

補天(ㄅㄨˇ ㄊㄧㄢ)
(a reference to the goddess 女媧氏 in Chinese mythology) to patch up or mend the sky

補天浴日(ㄅㄨˇ ㄊㄧㄢ ㄩˋ ㄖˋ)
(literally) to mend the sky and wash the sun—a peerless achievement; a great accomplishment

補鍋(ㄅㄨˇ ㄍㄨㄛ)
to tinker a pan

補過(ㄅㄨˇ ㄍㄨㄛˋ)
to make up for a mistake, fault, etc.

補課(ㄅㄨˇ ㄎㄜˋ)
(said of students or teachers) a private tutoring to supplement regular schooling; to make up for classes one missed

補考(ㄅㄨˇ ㄎㄠˇ)
a make-up test; an examination held for students who fail to take part in the regular one for legitimate reasons: 他上週參加補考。He took the make-up exam last week.

補空(ㄅㄨˇ ㄎㄨㄥˋ)
to fill up an empty space

補弧(ㄅㄨˇ ㄏㄨˊ)
(mathematics) a supplementary arc

補給(ㄅㄨˇ ㄐㄧˇ)
(military) provisions; supplies; to supply

補給品(ㄅㄨˇ ㄐㄧˇ ㄆㄧㄣˇ)
supplies

補給線(ㄅㄨˇ ㄐㄧˇ ㄒㄧㄢˋ)
a line of logistic support; a supply line

補給站(ㄅㄨˇ ㄐㄧˇ ㄓㄢˋ)
a supply depot

補角(ㄅㄨˇ ㄐㄧㄠˇ)
(mathematics) a supplementary angle

補救(ㄅㄨˇ ㄐㄧㄡˋ)
to save the situation; to rectify shortcomings ; to repair; to redress abuses; redress: 他們正在補救一項錯誤。They are repairing a mistake.

補救辦法(ㄅㄨˇ ㄐㄧㄡˋ ㄅㄢˋ ㄈㄚˇ)
means to save the situation; corrective measures; remedy

補苴(ㄅㄨˇ ㄐㄩ) or 補苴罅漏(ㄅㄨˇ ㄐㄩ ㄒㄧㄚˋ ㄌㄡˋ)
to make up for a deficiency or defect

補其不足(ㄅㄨˇ ㄑㄧˊ ㄅㄨˋ ㄗㄨˊ)
to make up a deficit or deficiency

補其所短(ㄅㄨˇ ㄑㄧˊ ㄙㄨㄛˇ ㄉㄨㄢˇ)
① to make up for one's shortcomings or defects ② to make up for a deficiency

補氣(ㄅㄨˇ ㄑㄧˋ)
to nourish or conserve one's vitality

補葺(ㄅㄨˇ ㄑㄧˋ)
to repair; to mend

補情(ㄅㄨˇ ㄑㄧㄥˊ)
to repay a favor; to repay hospitality

補缺(ㄅㄨˇ ㄑㄩㄝ)
to fill a vacancy; to fill an official post

補習(ㄅㄨˇ ㄒㄧˊ)
private tutoring to supplement regular schooling; to tutor

補習班(ㄅㄨˇ ㄒㄧˊ ㄅㄢ)
a class for supplementary schooling; a supplementary school to take care of dropouts or those who have failed in the entrance exams of regular schools; an extension school

補習教育(ㄅㄨˇ ㄒㄧˊ ㄐㄧㄠˋ ㄩˋ)
supplementary education—for preparing the students for jobs

補習學校(ㄅㄨˇ ㄒㄧˊ ㄒㄩㄝˊ ㄒㄧㄠˋ)
extension schools; continuation schools

補鞋匠(ㄅㄨˇ ㄒㄧㄝˊ ㄐㄧㄤˋ)
a cobbler

補血(ㄅㄨˇ ㄒㄧㄝˇ)
to nourish the blood; to increase the blood

補修(ㄅㄨˇ ㄒㄧㄡ)
(said of college students) to study for a second time courses one has flunked; to make up

補修學分(ㄅㄨˇ ㄒㄧㄡ ㄒㄩㄝˊ ㄈㄣ)
(said of college students) to catch up with the credit requirement; to study courses in order to get the minimum credits required for graduation

補絃 or 補弦(ㄅㄨˇ ㄒㄧㄢˊ)
(mathematics) a supplementary chord

補選(ㄅㄨˇ ㄒㄩㄢˇ)
by-election

補正(ㄅㄨˇ ㄓㄥˋ)
(said of printed materials) additions and corrections

補助(ㄅㄨˇ ㄓㄨˋ)

to subsidize; to help (finance, etc.)
補助費(ㄅㄨˇ ㄓㄨˋ ㄈㄟˋ) or 補助金(ㄅㄨˇ ㄓㄨˋ ㄐㄧㄣ)
a subsidy; subsidiary payments
補助角(ㄅㄨˇ ㄓㄨˋ ㄐㄧㄠˇ)
(mathematics) an auxiliary angle
補助金(ㄅㄨˇ ㄓㄨˋ ㄐㄧㄣ)
a grant
補助圓(ㄅㄨˇ ㄓㄨˋ ㄩㄢˊ)
(mathematics) an auxiliary circle
補注 or 補註(ㄅㄨˇ ㄓㄨˋ)
supplementary notes; to make supplementary notes
補拙(ㄅㄨˇ ㄓㄨㄛˊ)
to offset or make up for one's lack of acumen: 勤能補拙。Hard work can often make up for a lack of intelligence.
補綴(ㄅㄨˇ ㄓㄨㄟˋ)
to patch or mend (a garment, etc.); to darn: 他的襪子一再補綴。His socks has been darned again and again.
補償(ㄅㄨˇ ㄔㄤˊ)
to compensate; to make up; compensation: 他們補償她所受的損失。They compensated her for a loss.
補償損失(ㄅㄨˇ ㄔㄤˊ ㄙㄨㄣˇ ㄕ)
to compensate for damage, loss, etc.
補充(ㄅㄨˇ ㄔㄨㄥ)
to add; to supplement; to make up for a deficiency; to replenish; a supplement; supplementary: 我補充兩點意見。I have two points to add.
補充兵(ㄅㄨˇ ㄔㄨㄥ ㄅㄧㄥ)
(military) replacements
補足(ㄅㄨˇ ㄗㄨˊ)
to make up a deficit; to make complete or whole
補足語(ㄅㄨˇ ㄗㄨˊ ㄩˇ)
a complement; a supplementary clause 亦作「補語」
補色(ㄅㄨˇ ㄙㄜˋ)
complementary colors
補衣服(ㄅㄨˇ ㄧ ·ㄈㄨ)
to patch or mend a garment, dress, etc.: 她在補衣服。She is mending clothes now.
補遺(ㄅㄨˇ ㄧˊ)
addenda or appendixes to take care of omissions in a book, etc.
補益(ㄅㄨˇ ㄧˋ)
benefit; help
補牙(ㄅㄨˇ ㄧㄚˊ)
to fill a tooth cavity; to have a tooth stopped
補藥(ㄅㄨˇ ㄧㄠˋ)
tonics

【裝】 5416
ㄓㄨㄤ juang zhuāng

1. to fill in or up; to pack; to load: 裝好你的箱子。Pack your trunk.
2. to pretend; to feign: 她假裝自己是無辜的。She pretended innocence.
3. to adorn; to dress or make up; ornamental dressing; to decorate (a room, etc.)
4. to disguise
5. to store; to keep
6. to install (machines, equipment, etc.)
7. clothes and personal effects; an outfit: 全套新娘裝 an outfit for a bride

裝備(ㄓㄨㄤ ㄅㄟˋ)
equipment or an outfit (especially for a soldier, or armed forces): 這軍隊裝備很差。The army was poorly equipped.
裝扮(ㄓㄨㄤ ㄅㄢˋ)
① adornment; make-up; to dress or doll up; attire ② to disguise
裝裱(ㄓㄨㄤ ㄅㄧㄠˇ)
to mount a piece of calligraphy or a painting
裝病(ㄓㄨㄤ ㄅㄧㄥˋ)
to feign illness; to pretend illness; to malinger
裝病者(ㄓㄨㄤ ㄅㄧㄥˋ ㄓㄜˇ)
a malingerer
裝不下(ㄓㄨㄤ ·ㄅㄨ ㄒㄧㄚˋ)
no more space to cram in; cannot hold any more
裝配(ㄓㄨㄤ ㄆㄟˋ)
to assemble (a machine): 他裝配了一隻手錶。He assembled a watch.
裝配線(ㄓㄨㄤ ㄆㄟˋ ㄒㄧㄢˋ)
the assembly line (of a factory)
裝滿(ㄓㄨㄤ ㄇㄢˇ)
to fill up; to pack until no space is left
裝門面(ㄓㄨㄤ ㄇㄣˊ ㄇㄧㄢˋ)
to put up a front; to adorn or embellish for the sake of face
裝模作樣(ㄓㄨㄤ ㄇㄨˊ ㄗㄨㄛˋ ㄧㄤˋ)
to act affectedly; to be pretentious; to act with affected manners; to strike a pose
裝瘋賣傻(ㄓㄨㄤ ㄈㄥ ㄇㄞˋ ㄕㄚˇ)
to pretend to be crazy and stupid; to play the fool
裝點(ㄓㄨㄤ ㄉㄧㄢˇ)
to decorate; to dress; to deck: 大廳裏裝點着花燈。The hall was decorated with fancy lanterns.
裝訂(ㄓㄨㄤ ㄉㄧㄥˋ)
to bind pages into a volume or book; binding: 他裝訂報紙。He binds the papers together.
裝訂廠(ㄓㄨㄤ ㄉㄧㄥˋ ㄔㄤˇ)
a plant for binding books
裝老(ㄓㄨㄤ ㄌㄠˇ)
(euphemism) clothes for the dead in preparation for burial
裝殮(ㄓㄨㄤ ㄌㄧㄢˋ)
to dress up the deceased and put him into the coffin
裝聾作啞(ㄓㄨㄤ ㄌㄨㄥˊ ㄗㄨㄛˋ ㄧㄚˇ)
to pretend to hear and know nothing; to pretend ignorance; to pretend to be deaf and dumb; to play deaf
裝裹(ㄓㄨㄤ ·ㄍㄨㄛ)
to put on clothes for the dead
裝糊塗(ㄓㄨㄤ ㄏㄨˊ ·ㄊㄨ)
to pretend not to know; to feign ignorance 亦作「裝憨兒」
裝貨(ㄓㄨㄤ ㄏㄨㄛˋ)
to load or pack goods: 他裝貨於車上。He loaded the cart.
裝潢(ㄓㄨㄤ ㄏㄨㄤˊ)
① to mount a painting or a piece of calligraphy ② to decorate (a room, shop, etc.); decoration: 他花了很多錢裝潢房子。He spent quite a large sum of money for the decoration of his house. 訛作「裝璜」
裝幌子(ㄓㄨㄤ ㄏㄨㄤˇ ·ㄗ)
to put up a (false) front with a view to impressing

〔衣部〕

〔衣部〕

others
裝甲(ㄓㄨㄤ ㄐㄧㄚˇ)
①plate armor ②armored
裝甲兵團(ㄓㄨㄤ ㄐㄧㄚˇ ㄅㄧㄥ ㄊㄨㄢˊ)
an armored corps; a panzer corps
裝甲部隊(ㄓㄨㄤ ㄐㄧㄚˇ ㄅㄨˋ ㄉㄨㄟˋ)
armored troops or units
裝甲車(ㄓㄨㄤ ㄐㄧㄚˇ ㄔㄜ)
an armored vehicle; a tank
裝甲師(ㄓㄨㄤ ㄐㄧㄚˇ ㄕ)
an armored division
裝腔作勢(ㄓㄨㄤ ㄑㄧㄤ ㄗㄨㄛˋ ㄕˋ)
affected; pretentious; to strike an attitude; to affect manners; to put on airs: 他裝腔作勢令人難以忍受。His affectations are insufferable.
裝卸(ㄓㄨㄤ ㄒㄧㄝˋ)
to load and unload
裝修(ㄓㄨㄤ ㄒㄧㄡ)
to decorate and repair; to equip; to refurbish; to fit up (a house, etc.): 他們裝修一間舊房子。They refurbished an old house.
裝箱(ㄓㄨㄤ ㄒㄧㄤ)
to pack in a box or chest; to box: 他將衣服裝箱。He packed clothes into a trunk.
裝置(ㄓㄨㄤ ㄓˋ)
①to install (equipment, etc.) ②an installation; a (mechanical) device; a unit; a plant
裝池(ㄓㄨㄤ ㄔˊ)
to mount a painting or calligraphic work
裝車(ㄓㄨㄤ ㄔㄜ)
to load on a truck, vehicle, etc.
裝船(ㄓㄨㄤ ㄔㄨㄢˊ)
to load cargoes aboard a freighter
裝飾(ㄓㄨㄤ ㄕˋ)
①to doll up; to deck; to make up ②to decorate; to adorn; to embellish: 她以花裝飾頭髮。She adorned her hair with flowers.
裝飾品(ㄓㄨㄤ ㄕˋ ㄆㄧㄣˇ)
an ornamental item; an ornament; an adornment; a decorative article
裝傻(ㄓㄨㄤ ㄕㄚˇ)
to feign stupidity or ignorance
裝設(ㄓㄨㄤ ㄕㄜˋ)
to be equipped with; to install; to equip
裝束(ㄓㄨㄤ ㄕㄨˋ)
①to pack up; to do packing and get ready for travel ②to dress up; clothing or attire; dress
裝束入時(ㄓㄨㄤ ㄕㄨˋ ㄖㄨˋ ㄕˊ)
in fashionable dress or attire
裝睡(ㄓㄨㄤ ㄕㄨㄟˋ)
to feign sleep; to pretend to be asleep
裝子彈(ㄓㄨㄤ ㄗˇ ㄉㄢˋ)
to load a gun, or pistol: 裝子彈! Load your gun!
裝載(ㄓㄨㄤ ㄗㄞˋ)
(said of a truck, car, vessel, etc.) loaded with; to pack; to stow
裝醉(ㄓㄨㄤ ㄗㄨㄟˋ)
to pretend to be drunk
裝死(ㄓㄨㄤ ㄙˇ)
to play dead; to feign death; to sham death
裝蒜(ㄓㄨㄤ ㄙㄨㄢˋ)
to be pretentious or affected
裝樣子(ㄓㄨㄤ ㄧㄤˋ・ㄗ)
to put on an act; to do something for appearance sake
裝運(ㄓㄨㄤ ㄩㄣˋ)
to pack and transport; to load and ship

【裟】 5417 ㄕㄚ sha shā
a cassock or robe of a Buddhist monk 參看「袈裟」

【裛】 5418 ㄧˋ yih yì
1. to wrap and bind
2. damp; dripping; wet
3. a book bag

【裌】 5419 (袷) ㄐㄧㄚˊ jya jiá
a lined garment or dress

八畫

【裸】 5420 ㄌㄨㄛˇ luoo luǒ
bare; nude; naked
裸袒(ㄌㄨㄛˇ ㄊㄢˇ)
bare or naked
裸體(ㄌㄨㄛˇ ㄊㄧˇ) or 裸形(ㄌㄨㄛˇ ㄒㄧㄥˊ)
nude; naked; without a stitch on; in the altogether
裸體畫(ㄌㄨㄛˇ ㄊㄧˇ ㄏㄨㄚˋ)
a nude; a painting of a nude human figure (especially woman)
裸體像(ㄌㄨㄛˇ ㄊㄧˇ ㄒㄧㄤˋ)
a nude; a nude figure or statue
裸露(ㄌㄨㄛˇ ㄌㄨˋ)
uncovered; exposed
裸跣(ㄌㄨㄛˇ ㄒㄧㄢˇ)
(said of poor people) naked body and naked feet
裸線(ㄌㄨㄛˇ ㄒㄧㄢˋ)
(electricity) an uninsulated wire; a bare wire
裸裎(ㄌㄨㄛˇ ㄔㄥˊ)
naked; undressed
裸子植物(ㄌㄨㄛˇ ㄗˇ ㄓˊ ㄨˋ)
a gymnosperm, a plant with exposed seeds, e.g. a pine

【裰】 5421 ㄉㄨㄛˊ dwo duó
to darn; to mend; to patch (clothing): 她補裰他的襪子。She darned his socks.

【裨】 5422 1. ㄅㄧˋ bih bì
1. to aid; to supplement
2. to benefit; to help: 無裨於事。It will not help matters.
裨補(ㄅㄧˋ ㄅㄨˇ)
to supplement; to aid; to support
裨益(ㄅㄧˋ ㄧˋ)
to benefit; benefit: 運動裨益我們的健康。Exercise benefits our health.

【裨】 5422 2. ㄆㄧˊ pyi pí
1. small; petty
2. subordinate
3. a Chinese family name
裨販(ㄆㄧˊ ㄈㄢˋ)
a hawker or peddler
裨海(ㄆㄧˊ ㄏㄞˇ)
a small sea
裨將(ㄆㄧˊ ㄐㄧㄤˋ)
a deputy commander

【裯】 5423 ㄔㄡˊ chour chóu
a bed sheet

【裱】 5424 ㄅㄧㄠˇ beau biǎo
1. to mount (paintings, calligraphy, etc.)
2. a scarf

褾褙(ㄅㄧㄠˇ ㄅㄟˋ)
to mount (paintings, etc.): 他懂得褾褙國畫。He knows how to mount Chinese paintings.
褾店(ㄅㄧㄠˇ ㄉㄧㄢˋ)
a shop specialized in mounting paintings, calligraphy, etc.
褾工(ㄅㄧㄠˇ ㄍㄨㄥ)
① the work of mounting ② expenses for mounting ③ one who mounts paintings or calligraphic works
褾糊(ㄅㄧㄠˇ ㄏㄨˊ)
to paste; to paper (a wall, ceiling, etc.)
褾糊匠(ㄅㄧㄠˇ ㄏㄨˊ ㄐㄧㄤˋ)
a mounting craftsman; a paper hanger

【裳】 5425 ㄔㄤˊ charng cháng (語音 ·ㄕㄤ ·shang shang as in 衣裳)
1. a skirt (worn in ancient China); the lower garments
2. dress; garments; clothing

【裴】 5426 ㄆㄟˊ peir péi
1. the look of a flowing gown
2. a Chinese family name

【裹】 5427 ㄍㄨㄛˇ guoo guǒ
1. to tie up; to wrap or bind: 她頭上裹着毛巾。She had her head wrapped in a towel.
2. things wrapped, as a parcel
3. to surround; to encompass
4. to close in and force obedience
裹肚(ㄍㄨㄛˇ ㄉㄨˋ)
a cloth band worn around the midriff in ancient China
裹腿(ㄍㄨㄛˇ ㄊㄨㄟˇ)
leggings; puttees (usually used by soldiers in former days)
裹糧(ㄍㄨㄛˇ ㄌㄧㄤˊ)
bags of provisions for traveling
裹脚(ㄍㄨㄛˇ ㄐㄧㄠˇ)or 裹足(ㄍㄨㄛˇ ㄗㄨˊ)
(said of women in former times) to bind the feet
裹脚布(ㄍㄨㄛˇ ·ㄐㄧㄠ ㄅㄨˋ)or 裹脚條子(ㄍㄨㄛˇ ·ㄐㄧㄠ ㄊㄧㄠˊ ·ㄗ)
bandages for binding women's feet in old times
裹脅(ㄍㄨㄛˇ ㄒㄧㄝˊ)
duress; to force to join; to coerce
裹創(ㄍㄨㄛˇ ㄔㄨㄤ)
to dress a wound; to bind up a wound
裹尸 or 裹屍(ㄍㄨㄛˇ ㄕ)
to wrap up a corpse
裹足不前(ㄍㄨㄛˇ ㄗㄨˊ ㄅㄨˋ ㄑㄧㄢˊ)
to be afraid to move ahead; to be reluctant to go forward; to hesitate to move forward: 做那件事切勿裹足不前。Don't hesitate about doing that.

【裼】 5428 ㄒㄧˊ shyi xí
1. to take off one's top garment
2. (in ancient China) a wrapper or outer garment worn over a fur

【製】 5429 ㄓˋ jyh zhì
1. to produce; to make; to manufacture; to create: 這個娃娃是布製的。The doll is made of cloth.
2. to compose (writings, literature, etc.); literary works
3. to cut out garments and make them
4. a form; a model; a fashion; a pattern
製版(ㄓˋ ㄅㄢˇ)
to make a printing plate
製片(ㄓˋ ㄆㄧㄢˋ)or 製片人(ㄓˋ ㄆㄧㄢˋ ㄖㄣˊ)
(movie) a producer
製片廠(ㄓˋ ㄆㄧㄢˋ ㄔㄤˇ)
a movie studio
製品(ㄓˋ ㄆㄧㄣˇ)
products; manufactured items; manufactures
製法(ㄓˋ ㄈㄚˇ)
a formula, process, way or method of making something
製圖(ㄓˋ ㄊㄨˊ)
to make (or draw) maps, charts, etc.
製圖室(ㄓˋ ㄊㄨˊ ㄕˋ)
a draft or drawing room
製圖員(ㄓˋ ㄊㄨˊ ㄩㄢˊ)
a draughtsman; a draftsman; a cartographer
製革(ㄓˋ ㄍㄜˊ)
tanning
製革工廠(ㄓˋ ㄍㄜˊ ㄍㄨㄥ ㄔㄤˇ)
a tannery
製成(ㄓˋ ㄔㄥˊ)
to have completed production or making; to have produced or manufactured
製成品(ㄓˋ ㄔㄥˊ ㄆㄧㄣˇ)
finished products; manufactured goods; manufactures
製造(ㄓˋ ㄗㄠˋ)
to make; to produce; to manufacture; to create: 不要製造麻煩。Do not create a disturbance.
製造品(ㄓˋ ㄗㄠˋ ㄆㄧㄣˇ)
manufactured goods
製造過程(ㄓˋ ㄗㄠˋ ㄍㄨㄛˋ ㄔㄥˊ)
manufacturing process
製造技術(ㄓˋ ㄗㄠˋ ㄐㄧˋ ㄕㄨˋ)
manufacturing technology
製造廠(ㄓˋ ㄗㄠˋ ㄔㄤˇ)
a factory, plant or manufactory
製造商(ㄓˋ ㄗㄠˋ ㄕㄤ)
a manufacturer
製造業(ㄓˋ ㄗㄠˋ ㄧㄝˋ)
the manufacturing industry
製作(ㄓˋ ㄗㄨㄛˋ)
to make; to produce; to manufacture
製作人(ㄓˋ ㄗㄨㄛˋ ㄖㄣˊ)
a producer

【裾】 5430 ㄐㄩ jiu jū
the overlap of a robe; the hinder part of a garment; the lapel of a coat

【褂】 5431 ㄍㄨㄚˋ guah guà
an overcoat; a robe or gown; a jacket
褂子(ㄍㄨㄚˋ ·ㄗ)or 褂兒(ㄍㄨㄚˋㄦ)
an overcoat; a gown or robe

九畫

【複】 5432 ㄈㄨˋ fuh fù
1. double; overlapping
2. complex (concepts, etc.); compound (interest, etc.)
3. to repeat; to reiterate
4. a lined garment, dress, etc.
複本(ㄈㄨˋ ㄅㄣˇ)
a duplicate: 我們寄出了信，但留了複本。We mailed the let-

ter but kept a duplicate.
複比(ㄈㄨˋ ㄅㄧˇ)
compound ratio
複比例(ㄈㄨˋ ㄅㄧˇ ㄌㄧˋ)
compound proportion
複壁(ㄈㄨˋ ㄅㄧˋ)
double partition walls with secret hiding space in-between
複名數(ㄈㄨˋ ㄇㄧㄥˊ ㄕㄨˋ)
compound number
複利(ㄈㄨˋ ㄌㄧˋ)
compound interest
複合(ㄈㄨˋ ㄏㄜˊ)
compound; complex; composite
複合句(ㄈㄨˋ ㄏㄜˊ ㄐㄩˋ)
(linguistics) a compound sentence
複合詞(ㄈㄨˋ ㄏㄜˊ ㄘˊ)
nouns, phrases or idioms formed by two or more characters 亦作「複詞」
複基(ㄈㄨˋ ㄐㄧ)
(chemistry) a compound radical
複句(ㄈㄨˋ ㄐㄩˋ)or 複雜句(ㄈㄨˋ ㄗㄚˊ ㄐㄩˋ)
a complex sentence
複決權(ㄈㄨˋ ㄐㄩㄝˊ ㄑㄩㄢˊ)
a referendum
複習(ㄈㄨˋ ㄒㄧˊ)
to review; to revise 亦作「復習」: 我們在考試前複習所學過的功課。Before the examinations we reviewed the lessons we had learned.
複寫(ㄈㄨˋ ㄒㄧㄝˇ)
to duplicate or produce copies of a piece of writing, etc. with carbon paper, etc.: 他複寫了一份公文。He duplicated a document.
複寫紙(ㄈㄨˋ ㄒㄧㄝˇ ㄓˇ)
carbon paper
複姓(ㄈㄨˋ ㄒㄧㄥˋ)
a compound surname; a surname which comprises two characters, as 司馬, 歐陽, etc.
複選(ㄈㄨˋ ㄒㄩㄢˇ)
① an election by delegates; an indirect election ② a run-off (election) ③ (in beauty contests, etc.) a semifinal
複製(ㄈㄨˋ ㄓˋ)
to make a reproduction; to reproduce; to duplicate: 那幅畫複製得很好。The painting reproduced well.
複製品(ㄈㄨˋ ㄓˋ ㄆㄧㄣˇ)
a reproduction (of the original article); a replica: 這幅人像是原畫的複製品。This portrait is a replica of the original.
複查(ㄈㄨˋ ㄔㄚˊ)
to reinvestigate; to check again
複式學級(ㄈㄨˋ ㄕˋ ㄒㄩㄝˊ ㄐㄧˊ)
a class in which more than two different grades of school children are taught at the same time
複數(ㄈㄨˋ ㄕㄨˋ)
the plural number (of a noun or pronoun)
複雜(ㄈㄨˋ ㄗㄚˊ)
complex; complicated (matters, etc.): 這是個複雜的觀念。It's a complex idea.
複色(ㄈㄨˋ ㄙㄜˋ)
compound colors
複色光(ㄈㄨˋ ㄙㄜˋ ㄍㄨㄤ)
polychromatic light
複賽(ㄈㄨˋ ㄙㄞˋ)
(sports) a semifinal; a play-off; intermediary heat
複葉(ㄈㄨˋ ㄧㄝˋ)
a compound leaf
複眼(ㄈㄨˋ ㄧㄢˇ)
(biology) a compound eye
複印(ㄈㄨˋ ㄧㄣˋ)
the reproduction of the original copy by a copying machine; duplication
複印機(ㄈㄨˋ ㄧㄣˋ ㄐㄧ)
a copying machine; a duplicator; a duplicating machine

【褊】 5433
ㄅㄧㄢˇ bean biǎn

1. narrow; small; petty
2. small size clothes
3. narrow minded

褊能(ㄅㄧㄢˇ ㄋㄥˊ)
of little ability (sometimes used as a polite and self-depreciative expression)
褊陋(ㄅㄧㄢˇ ㄌㄡˋ)
cramped and crude; narrow-minded and ignorant
褊急(ㄅㄧㄢˇ ㄐㄧˊ)
easily irritated; lacking patience; short-tempered
褊淺(ㄅㄧㄢˇ ㄑㄧㄢˇ)
narrow-minded and shallow
褊狹(ㄅㄧㄢˇ ㄒㄧㄚˊ)
① small (piece of land) ② narrow(-minded)
褊小(ㄅㄧㄢˇ ㄒㄧㄠˇ)
petty; small; narrow
褊心(ㄅㄧㄢˇ ㄒㄧㄣ)
narrow-minded and impatient
褊隘(ㄅㄧㄢˇ ㄞˋ)
narrow-minded and impatient

【褌】 5434
ㄎㄨㄣ kuen kūn

trousers; drawers; short pants

【褐】 5435
ㄏㄜˊ her hé

1. coarse woolen cloth; coarse cloth; haircloth; rough cloth
2. the poor or destitute
3. brown: 這餅變成褐色了。The pie has become brown.

褐錳礦(ㄏㄜˊ ㄇㄥˇ ㄎㄨㄤˋ)
braunite
褐夫(ㄏㄜˊ ㄈㄨ)
a person dressed in cloth of hair—a person of little means; a humble person
褐炭(ㄏㄜˊ ㄊㄢˋ)
brown coal, or lignite
褐鐵礦(ㄏㄜˊ ㄊㄧㄝˇ ㄎㄨㄤˋ)
limonite; brown iron ore
褐色(ㄏㄜˊ ㄙㄜˋ)
(color) brown

【褓】 5436
ㄅㄠˇ bao bǎo

1. swaddling bands; swaddling clothes
2. as in 襁褓—infancy

褓母(ㄅㄠˇ ㄇㄨˇ)
a nurse; a baby-sitter: 她是個好褓母。She is a good nurse.

【褘】 5437
ㄏㄨㄟ huei huī

ceremonial gowns of a queen
褘衣(ㄏㄨㄟ ㄧ)
ceremonial dress of a queen

【褙】 5438
ㄅㄟˋ bey bèi

to mount (paintings, or calligraphic works)

【褚】 5439
ㄔㄨˇ chuu chǔ

1. a bag
2. to stuff a lined garment with cotton
3. to reserve; to save

4. a Chinese family name

褚幕(ㄔㄨˇ ㄇㄨˋ)
a piece of red cloth for covering the coffin

褚遂良(ㄔㄨˇ ㄙㄨㄟˋ ㄌㄧㄤˊ)
Chu Sui-liang (596-658), a famous scholar-calligrapher in the Tang Dynasty

【褕】 5440
ㄩˊ yu yú
1. beautiful or pretty (dresses, etc.)
2. a loose garment or cloak

【褒】 5441
(襃) ㄅㄠ bau bāo
1. to praise; to cite
2. big; great

十畫

【褥】 5442
ㄖㄨˋ ruh rù
bedding; quilts or coverlets; a mattress; cushion; bedclothes

褥單兒(ㄖㄨˋ ㄉㄚㄦ)
a bed sheet

褥套(ㄖㄨˋ ㄊㄠˋ)
a large bag holding cotton or other fibers used as a quilt or a mattress; ticking

褥子(ㄖㄨˋ ·ㄗ)
bedding; coverlets or quilts; a mattress

褥瘡(ㄖㄨˋ ㄔㄨㄤ)
(medicine) bedsores

【褦】 5443
1. ㄋㄞˋ nay nài
1. ignorant; stupid; naive
2. a palm-leaf hat worn in summer for shading the sun or rain

褦襶(ㄋㄞˋ ㄉㄞˋ)
① a light-weight hat of palm leaves or bamboo for shading the sun or rain ② ignorant; naive; unsophisticated

【褦】 5443
2. ㄌㄜ le lē
untidily dressed

褦襶(ㄌㄜ ·ㄌㄜ)
untidily dressed

褦襶兵(ㄌㄜ ·ㄌㄜ ㄅㄧㄥ)
a person in untidy or ill-fitting dress or overburdened with accessories

【褪】 5444
ㄊㄨㄣˋ tuenn tùn
1. to take off one's clothing; to strip; to slip out of something
2. to fall off; to fade, as color: 襯衫的顏色褪了。The color of the shirt has faded.
3. to retreat; to move backward

褪手(ㄊㄨㄣˋ ㄕㄡˇ)
to hide one's hands in sleeves

褪色(ㄊㄨㄣˋ ㄙㄜˋ)
color fading

【褫】 5445
ㄔˇ chyy chǐ
1. to strip off; to deprive of
2. to undress forcibly

褫魄(ㄔˇ ㄆㄛˋ)
to be scared out of one's wits; to be extremely frightened

褫奪(ㄔˇ ㄉㄨㄛˊ)
to deprive of; to strip off

褫奪公權(ㄔˇ ㄉㄨㄛˊ ㄍㄨㄥ ㄑㄩㄢˊ)
to strip or deprive one of one's civil rights; deprivation of civil rights

褫革(ㄔˇ ㄍㄜˊ)
to strip one of one's uniform, insignia, etc.—to strip one of one's office; to dismiss

褫職(ㄔˇ ㄓˊ)
to dismiss one from office; a dishonorable discharge

【褰】 5446
ㄑㄧㄢ chian qiān
1. to lift or raise (one's dress, skirt, etc.)
2. trousers; drawers; pants
3. to shrink

【褡】 5447
ㄉㄚ da dā
1. a kerchief hung at the waist
2. a purse; a tiny sack
3. worn clothes

褡褳(ㄉㄚ ㄌㄧㄢˊ)
a pouch worn at the girdle

【褟】 5448
ㄊㄚ ta tā
1. the lace-trimmed hem of a dress; lace of a dress
2. a singlet; a thin T-shirt as underwear

【褲】 5449
(袴) ㄎㄨˋ kuh kù
drawers; trousers; pants

褲帶(ㄎㄨˋ ㄉㄞˋ)
a trousers belt

褲襠(ㄎㄨˋ ㄉㄤ)
the crotch of a pair of trousers

褲管(ㄎㄨˋ ㄍㄨㄢˇ)
the legs of a pair of trousers

褲襪(ㄎㄨˋ ㄨㄚˋ)
pantyhose

十一畫

【褵】 5450
(縭) ㄌㄧˊ li lí
a bridal veil

【褶】 5451
1. ㄉㄧㄝˊ dye dié
a lined garment or dress

【褶】 5451
2. ㄓㄜˊ jer zhé
to fold; pleated

褶曲(ㄓㄜˊ ㄑㄩ)
(geology) folds

褶裙(ㄓㄜˊ ㄑㄩㄣˊ)
a pleated skirt

褶子(ㄓㄜˊ ·ㄗ)
① pleats ② folds ③ wrinkles (on the face)

【褸】 5452
ㄌㄩˇ leu lǚ
1. the collar or lapel of a garment
2. (said of clothes) tattered; in rags 參看「襤褸」

【褒】 5453
(襃) ㄅㄠ bau bāo
1. to praise; to cite; to commend; a citation
2. big; great
3. name of an ancient state in today's Shensi Province
4. a Chinese family name

褒貶(ㄅㄠ ㄅㄧㄢˇ)
① to praise and disparage; criticisms ② to disparage; unfavorable criticisms

褒美(ㄅㄠ ㄇㄟˇ)
to praise and cite

褒賚(ㄅㄠ ㄌㄞˋ)
to commend and reward

褒錄(ㄅㄠ ㄌㄨˋ)
to recommend (talented scholars) for government appointments

褒獎(ㄅㄠ ㄐㄧㄤˇ)
to praise and cite; to commend and award: 他褒獎你的工作嗎? Did he praise your work?

〔衣部〕

〔衣部〕

褒章(ㄅㄠ ㄓㄤ)
a medal of commendation
褒狀(ㄅㄠ ㄓㄨㄤˋ)
a citation (of a good deed, great achievement, etc.)
褒賞(ㄅㄠ ㄕㄤˇ)
a reward (for a praiseworthy act, etc.); to reward
褒讚(ㄅㄠ ㄗㄢˋ)
to praise; to commend; to extol; to acclaim
褒賜(ㄅㄠ ㄘˋ)
to reward; a reward for a praiseworthy deed, etc.
褒姒(ㄅㄠ ㄙˋ)
name of a favorite concubine of Emperor Yu(幽王) of the Chou Dynasty, who cost him his empire
褒衣(ㄅㄠ ㄧ)
to give dresses to officials or their wives as a token of imperial favor
褒衣博帶(ㄅㄠ ㄧ ㄅㄛˊ ㄉㄞˋ)
a robe with large sleeves and a broad waist band—the dress of an ancient scholar
褒揚(ㄅㄠ ㄧㄤˊ)
to cite; to commend; a citation

【襁】 5454
(繈) ㄑㄧㄤˇ cheang qiǎng
swaddling clothes for an infant; a broad bandage for carrying an infant on the back
襁褓(ㄑㄧㄤˇ ㄅㄠˇ)
① swaddling clothes or carrying band for an infant ② infancy: 這小孩仍在襁褓中。The baby is still in its infancy.
襁負(ㄑㄧㄤˇ ㄈㄨˋ)
① infancy ② to carry an infant on the back with a broad bandage

【襄】 5455
ㄒㄧㄤ shiang xiāng
1. to help; to assist
2. to achieve; to accomplish; to complete
3. to rise; to raise
4. high
5. to remove
6. a Chinese family name
襄辦(ㄒㄧㄤ ㄅㄢˋ)
to help manage, arrange, etc.
襄理(ㄒㄧㄤ ㄌㄧˇ)
① to help manage, arrange, etc. ② an assistant manager (of a bank)
襄助(ㄒㄧㄤ ㄓㄨˋ)
to help; to assist
襄贊(ㄒㄧㄤ ㄗㄢˋ)
to assist and support
襄陽(ㄒㄧㄤ ㄧㄤˊ)
Hsiangyang, a county in Hupeh Province

【褻】 5456
(亵) ㄒㄧㄝˋ shieh xiè
1. underwear; clothes worn in one's bedroom or house
2. dirty; filthy
3. intimate (sometimes denoting a degree of indecency)
4. to slight; to look down upon
5. to be familiar or acquainted with
褻服(ㄒㄧㄝˋ ㄈㄨˊ)
clothes worn at home; underclothing
褻瀆(ㄒㄧㄝˋ ㄉㄨˊ)
① to slight; to abuse; to insult; to blaspheme; to desecrate ②(a polite expression) to bother others with trifles, etc.
褻瀆神明(ㄒㄧㄝˋ ㄉㄨˊ ㄕㄣˊ ㄇㄧㄥˊ)
blasphemy; to blaspheme the gods
褻狎(ㄒㄧㄝˋ ㄒㄧㄚˊ)
to be close and unduly intimate
褻臣(ㄒㄧㄝˋ ㄔㄣˊ)
an intimate courtier
褻尊(ㄒㄧㄝˋ ㄗㄨㄣ)
to condescend; to deign to
褻玩(ㄒㄧㄝˋ ㄨㄢˊ)
to treat with disrespect because of over-intimacy
褻衣(ㄒㄧㄝˋ ㄧ)
undies; underwear

【褳】 5457
ㄌㄧㄢˊ lian lián
used in the phrase 褡褳—a pouch worn at the girdle

十二畫

【襇】 5458
ㄐㄧㄢˇ jean jiǎn
the pleats of a skirt

十三畫

【襞】 5459
ㄅㄧˋ bih bì
to fold clothes
襞積(ㄅㄧˋ ㄐㄧ)
pleats (in a skirt, etc.)
襞褶(ㄅㄧˋ ㄓㄜˊ)
lines or pleats on clothes as a result of folding

【襠】 5460
ㄉㄤ dang dāng
the crotch or bottom of a pair of trousers, drawers or panties 參看「袴襠」

【襟】 5461
ㄐㄧㄣ jin jīn
1. the lapel or collar of a garment or robe
2. aspiration; ambition; the mental outlook
3. (said of waters) to converge
4. the husbands of one's sisters
襟抱(ㄐㄧㄣ ㄅㄠˋ)
ambition; aspiration
襟帶(ㄐㄧㄣ ㄉㄞˋ)
strategic points; a place of strategic significance
襟弟(ㄐㄧㄣ ㄉㄧˋ)
the husband of one's wife's younger sister
襟度(ㄐㄧㄣ ㄉㄨˋ)
the mental outlook and capacity for tolerance
襟喉(ㄐㄧㄣ ㄏㄡˊ)
(literally) the collar and throat—very vital or strategic points
襟懷(ㄐㄧㄣ ㄏㄨㄞˊ) or 襟期(ㄐㄧㄣ ㄑㄧˊ)
one's feelings, ambitions, aspirations, bosom, (breadth of) mind, etc.
襟契(ㄐㄧㄣ ㄑㄧˋ)
one's bosom friends
襟情(ㄐㄧㄣ ㄑㄧㄥˊ)
feelings or emotions buried deep in one's heart
襟曲(ㄐㄧㄣ ㄑㄩ)
the true feelings, hopes, aspirations, etc. deep in one's heart
襟兄(ㄐㄧㄣ ㄒㄩㄥ)
the husband of one's wife's elder sister
襟山帶河(ㄐㄧㄣ ㄕㄢ ㄉㄞˋ ㄏㄜˊ)

cloaked by mountains and girded by rivers
襟韻(ㄐㄧㄣ ㄩㄣˋ)
one's aspirations and manners

【襖】 5462
ㄠˇ ao ǎo
a coat; a jacket or top garment padded with cotton or lined with fur

【襜】 5463
ㄔㄢ chan chān
1. the lower front of a robe, gown, etc.
2. (said of appearances) clean and neat
3. shaking or vibrating; flapping, as of curtains

十四畫

【襤】 5464
ㄌㄢˊ lan lán
1. ragged garments; clothes without a hem
2. shabbily dressed
襤褸(ㄌㄢˊ ㄌㄩˇ)
(said of clothes) tattered; in rags; ragged; shabby: 她衣衫襤褸。She was shabbily dressed.

【襦】 5465
ㄖㄨˊ ru rú
1. a short coat; a short top garment
2. the neckwear for babies
3. very fine silk fabric

十五畫

【襪】 5466
(袜) ㄨㄚˋ wah wà
stockings; socks
襪帶(ㄨㄚˋ ㄉㄞˋ)
garters
襪底兒(ㄨㄚˋ ㄉㄧˇㄜˇㄦ)
the soles of stockings or socks
襪套(ㄨㄚˋ ㄊㄠˋ)
wrappers either worn outside stockings or worn barefooted as a protection from chafing with shoes
襪頭兒(ㄨㄚˋ ㄊㄡˊㄦ)
socks
襪口(ㄨㄚˋ ㄎㄡˇ)
the openings of stockings
襪子(ㄨㄚˋ ·ㄗ)
stockings; socks

【襬】 5467
ㄅㄞˇ bae bǎi
the lower part of a Chinese long gown: 下襬 the hem of a long gown

十六畫

【襯】 5468
ㄔㄣˋ chenn chèn
1. inner garments; underwear
2. to provide a background; to bring to the fore; to supplement
3. a lining; a liner
4. to line; to place something underneath
5. to give alms(as to Buddhist monks, etc.)
襯托(ㄔㄣˋ ㄊㄨㄛ)
to bring into relief; to set off; to supplement; to embellish; to provide a contrast; a foil
襯裏(兒)(ㄔㄣˋ ㄌㄧˇ (ㄦ))
a lining
襯裙(ㄔㄣˋ ㄑㄩㄣˊ)
a petticoat; an underskirt
襯衫(ㄔㄣˋ ㄕㄢ)
a shirt
襯字(ㄔㄣˋ ㄗˋ)
words added to a Chinese poem (詞 or 曲), over and above the minimum number required
襯衣(ㄔㄣˋ ㄧ)
undergarments

【襲】 5469
ㄒㄧˊ shyi xí
1. to put on; to clothe in; to wear
2. a suit (of clothes); a set (of dress)
3. repeated; double
4. hereditary; to inherit
5. to attack or take by surprise; to raid; to assail
6. to plagiarize; to appropriate
7. to enter (a town, etc.)
8. to unite; to accord with
9. to conform to
10. a Chinese family name
襲封(ㄒㄧˊ ㄈㄥ)
to inherit a title from one's forefathers
襲奪(ㄒㄧˊ ㄉㄨㄛˊ)
to take or attack by surprise
襲迹(ㄒㄧˊ ㄐㄧ)
to follow in the footsteps of the predecessors
襲擊(ㄒㄧˊ ㄐㄧˊ)
a surprise attack; to attack by surprise; to make a raid
襲爵(ㄒㄧˊ ㄐㄩㄝˊ)
to inherit a hereditary title
襲人故智(ㄒㄧˊ ㄖㄣˊ ㄍㄨˋ ㄓˋ)
to copy an old trick
襲用(ㄒㄧˊ ㄩㄥˋ)
to take over (something that has long been used in the past)

十七畫

【襴】 5470
ㄌㄢˊ lan lán
a one-piece garment
襴裙(ㄌㄢˊ ㄑㄩㄣˊ)
an apron (used by women in the kitchen)

十八畫

【襶】 5471
1. ㄉㄞˋ day dài
as in 褦襶(ㄋㄞˋ ㄉㄞˋ)

【襶】 5471
2. ·ㄉㄜ ·de de
as in 褦襶(ㄉㄜ ·ㄉㄜ)

十九畫

【襻】 5472
ㄆㄢˋ pann pàn
1. a loop for a button
2. to tie or fasten with a rope, string, etc.

襾部
ㄧㄚˋ yah yà

【西】 5473
ㄒㄧ shi xī
1. west; the west; western
2. Western; the West; European; American; Occidental; foreign
3. a Chinese family name
西伯(ㄒㄧ ㄅㄛˊ)
the feudal title of King Wen before he rose in arms

〔襾部〕

against Chou(紂) the tyrant

西伯利亞(ㄒㄧ ㄅㄛˊ ㄌㄧˋ ㄧㄚˋ)
Siberia

西伯利亞鐵路(ㄒㄧ ㄅㄛˊ ㄌㄧˋ ㄧㄚˋ ㄊㄧㄝˇ ㄌㄨˋ)
the Siberia Railway

西柏林(ㄒㄧ ㄅㄛˊ ㄌㄧㄣˊ)
West Berlin

西北(ㄒㄧ ㄅㄟˇ)
northwest

西北航空公司(ㄒㄧ ㄅㄟˇ ㄏㄤˊ ㄎㄨㄥ ㄍㄨㄥ ㄙ)
the Northwest Airlines

西北西(ㄒㄧ ㄅㄟˇ ㄒㄧ)
northwest-by-west; northwest by west

西班牙(ㄒㄧ ㄅㄢ ㄧㄚˊ)
Spain

西班牙人(ㄒㄧ ㄅㄢ ㄧㄚˊ ㄖㄣˊ)
a Spaniard; the Spanish

西班牙語(ㄒㄧ ㄅㄢ ㄧㄚˊ ㄩˇ)
Spanish (language): 你會說西班牙語嗎? Do you speak Spanish?

西半球(ㄒㄧ ㄅㄢˋ ㄑㄧㄡˊ)
the Western Hemisphere

西賓(ㄒㄧ ㄅㄧㄣ)
a private tutor who lodges in the house of the employer

西部(ㄒㄧ ㄅㄨˋ)
the western part (of a territory); the West

西部武打片(ㄒㄧ ㄅㄨˋ ㄨˇ ㄉㄚˇ ㄆㄧㄢˋ) or 西部片(ㄒㄧ ㄅㄨˋ ㄆㄧㄢˋ)
cowboy pictures; a Western: 這是一部西部片。The picture is a Western.

西皮(ㄒㄧ ㄆㄧˊ)
name of a popular tune in Peking opera

西門(ㄒㄧ ㄇㄣˊ)
① the west gate in a city wall ② a Chinese double surname

西門豹(ㄒㄧ ㄇㄣˊ ㄅㄠˋ)
Hsi-Men Pao, a famous magistrate in the Epoch of Warring States, who did away with the evil custom of marrying maidens to the river god and who introduced an irrigation system

西門子(ㄒㄧ ㄇㄣˊ ㄗˇ)
Ernst Werner von Siemens (1816-1892), a famous German electrical engineer and industrialist

西米(ㄒㄧ ㄇㄧˇ)
sago 亦作「西穀米」

西法(ㄒㄧ ㄈㄚˇ)
European and American methods; Western or Occidental methods

西番蓮(ㄒㄧ ㄈㄢ ㄌㄧㄢˊ)
① a passionflower ② a dahlia

西方(ㄒㄧ ㄈㄤ)
① west; the West or Western: 日落於西方。The sun sets in the west. ② a Buddhist paradise ③ a Chinese double surname

西方極樂世界(ㄒㄧ ㄈㄤ ㄐㄧˊ ㄌㄜˋ ㄕˋ ㄐㄧㄝˋ) or 西方淨土(ㄒㄧ ㄈㄤ ㄐㄧㄥˋ ㄊㄨˇ)
a Buddhist paradise, or heaven

西風(ㄒㄧ ㄈㄥ)
① a west wind; a wester; a westerly ② influences, customs, ways, etc. of the West

西風東漸(ㄒㄧ ㄈㄥ ㄉㄨㄥ ㄐㄧㄢˋ)
the spread of Western influences to the East

西服(ㄒㄧ ㄈㄨˊ) or 西裝(ㄒㄧ ㄓㄨㄤ)
Western clothes; European or American attire

西德(ㄒㄧ ㄉㄜˊ)
West Germany (East Germany and West Germany were united in 1990.)

西點(ㄒㄧ ㄉㄧㄢˇ)
① western-style dessert ② West Point

西太后(ㄒㄧ ㄊㄞˋ ㄏㄡˋ)
Empress Dowager Tzu Hsi (慈禧), who ruled China as a regent toward the end of the 19th century

西天(ㄒㄧ ㄊㄧㄢ)
① the Buddhist paradise or heaven; Western Paradise ② India, as known to ancient Chinese Buddhists

西土(ㄒㄧ ㄊㄨˇ)
① the Western lands ② the Buddhist paradise or heaven ③ India ④ an old name of Changan, capital city of Shensi Province

西奈半島(ㄒㄧ ㄋㄞˋ ㄅㄢˋ ㄉㄠˇ)
Sinai Peninsula

西南(ㄒㄧ ㄋㄢˊ)
southwest

西南非(ㄒㄧ ㄋㄢˊ ㄈㄟ)
South West Africa

西南西(ㄒㄧ ㄋㄢˊ ㄒㄧ)
southwest-by-west; southwest by west

西南夷(ㄒㄧ ㄋㄢˊ ㄧˊ)
(Han Dynasty) a general name of the tribes in the southwestern Chinese provinces of Kweichow, Yunnan, Vietnam, Burma, etc.

西里伯島(ㄒㄧ ㄌㄧˇ ㄅㄛˊ ㄉㄠˇ)
Celebes, former name of Sulawesi, an island in central Indonesia

西曆(ㄒㄧ ㄌㄧˋ)
the Gregorian calendar

西涼(ㄒㄧ ㄌㄧㄤˊ)
one of the 16 tribal states in China during the Tsin (晉) Dynasty

西陵峽(ㄒㄧ ㄌㄧㄥˊ ㄒㄧㄚˊ)
one of the Three Gorges (三峽) on the upper Yangtze River, near Yichang (宜昌) in Hupeh Province

西羅馬帝國(ㄒㄧ ㄌㄨㄛˊ ㄇㄚˇ ㄉㄧˋ ㄍㄨㄛˊ)
the Western (Roman) Empire

西螺大橋(ㄒㄧ ㄌㄨㄛˊ ㄉㄚˋ ㄑㄧㄠˊ)
the Silo Bridge, the longest highway bridge in Taiwan

西穀椰子(ㄒㄧ ㄍㄨˇ ㄧㄝˊ ˙ㄗ)
sago palms

西瓜(ㄒㄧ ㄍㄨㄚ)
watermelons

西瓜子兒(ㄒㄧ ˙ㄍㄨㄚ ㄗㄜˇㄦ) or 西瓜子(ㄒㄧ ㄍㄨㄚ ㄗˇ)
watermelon seeds

西宮(ㄒㄧ ㄍㄨㄥ) or 西宮娘娘(ㄒㄧ ㄍㄨㄥ ㄋㄧㄤˊ ˙ㄋㄧㄤ)
the concubines of the king or emperor; the imperial concubines

西貢(ㄒㄧ ㄍㄨㄥˋ)
Saigon, the capital of former South Vietnam

西康(ㄒㄧ ㄎㄤ)
Sikang, a province on the southwest border of China

西崑體(ㄒㄧ ㄎㄨㄣ ㄊㄧˇ)
a style of Chinese poetry, deriving its name from 西崑酬唱集, authored by Yang Yi

(楊億) and others of the Sung Dynasty, featuring ornate diction and jingling rhythm

西河之痛(ㄒㄧ ㄏㄜˊ ㄓ ㄊㄨㄥˋ)
a reference to Pu Tzu-hsia (卜子夏) who lived in Hsi Ho (西河) and became blind in lamenting the loss of a son—now a condolatory expression used when a friend loses a son

西海岸(ㄒㄧ ㄏㄞˇ ㄢˋ)
① the western coast ② the West Coast of the United States

西漢(ㄒㄧ ㄏㄢˋ)
the Western Han or Earlier Han Dynasty, which lasted for 231 years from 206 B.C. to A.D. 24

西湖(ㄒㄧ ㄏㄨˊ)or 西子湖(ㄒㄧ ㄗˇ ㄏㄨˊ)
the West Lake, name of various lakes in a number of provinces, the most famous one is at Hangchow (杭州)

西紅柿(ㄒㄧ ㄏㄨㄥˊ ㄕˋ)
tomatoes 亦作「番茄」

西極(ㄒㄧ ㄐㄧˊ)
the remote regions in the west as known to ancient Chinese

西晉(ㄒㄧ ㄐㄧㄣˋ)
the Earlier Tsin Dynasty (265-316 A.D.) with capital at Loyang (洛陽)

西進(ㄒㄧ ㄐㄧㄣˋ)
(said of troops) to march westward

西江(ㄒㄧ ㄐㄧㄤ)
the West River, a tributary of the Pearl River (珠江)

西京(ㄒㄧ ㄐㄧㄥ)
the western capital (referring to different cities in different dynasties, particularly 長安 and 洛陽)

西經(ㄒㄧ ㄐㄧㄥ)
① west longitude ② to go through or past a certain place to the west

西秦(ㄒㄧ ㄑㄧㄣˊ)
one of the 16 states in China founded by northern tribes during the Tsin(晉) Dynasty

西西里(ㄒㄧ ㄒㄧ ㄌㄧˇ)
Sicily, Italy

西席(ㄒㄧ ㄒㄧˊ)
a private tutor; a teacher 參看「西賓」

西夏(ㄒㄧ ㄒㄧㄚˋ)
Hsi Hsia (1032-1227), a state in the Sung Dynasty, which occupied part of today's Inner Mongolia (內蒙) and Kansu (甘肅)

西廂記(ㄒㄧ ㄒㄧㄤ ㄐㄧˋ)
The West Chamber, one of the most famous Chinese dramas, authored by Wang Shih-fu (王實甫) in the Yüan Dynasty

西行(ㄒㄧ ㄒㄧㄥˊ)
to go west; to travel westward

西學(ㄒㄧ ㄒㄩㄝˊ)
Western learning (a late Ching Dynasty term for Western natural sciences)

西哲(ㄒㄧ ㄓㄜˊ)
European or American sages

西周(ㄒㄧ ㄓㄡ)
① the Earlier Chou Dynasty (1111-771 B.C.) ② name of a state in ancient China

西裝(ㄒㄧ ㄓㄨㄤ)
Western-style clothes; a Western suit

西川(ㄒㄧ ㄔㄨㄢ)
the western part of the Szechwan Province

西窗剪燭(ㄒㄧ ㄔㄨㄤ ㄐㄧㄢˇ ㄓㄨˊ)
(literally) to cut the candle wick under the western window—the happy reunion of friends chatting together late into the night

西施(ㄒㄧ ㄕ)or 西子(ㄒㄧ ㄗˇ)
Hsi Shih, a famed beauty in the Period of Spring and Autumn, who was offered to Fu Chai (夫差), King of Wu (吳), by Kou Chien(句踐), King of Yüeh (越)

西式(ㄒㄧ ㄕˋ)
Western-style; European or American style; Occidental style

西沙羣島(ㄒㄧ ㄕㄚ ㄑㄩㄣˊ ㄉㄠˇ)
Hsisha Chuntao (the Paracel Islands)

西曬(ㄒㄧ ㄕㄞˋ)
(said of houses, rooms, etc.) exposed to the intensive heat of the afternoon sun

西山(ㄒㄧ ㄕㄢ)
① western hills or mountains ② name of various scenic resorts, the most famous one being in Peking (北京)

西人(ㄒㄧ ㄖㄣˊ)
Westerners; Europeans or Americans; Occidentals

西戎(ㄒㄧ ㄖㄨㄥˊ)
tribesmen in the western borders in the Chou Dynasty

西崽(ㄒㄧ ㄗㄞˇ)
waiters in cabarets, nightclubs, restaurants, etc. owned by foreigners

西藏(ㄒㄧ ㄗㄤˋ)
① Tibet ② Tibetan

西餐(ㄒㄧ ㄘㄢ)
Western food; European or American meals

西薩摩亞(ㄒㄧ ㄙㄚˋ ㄇㄛˊ ㄧㄚˋ)
Western Samoa

西歐(ㄒㄧ ㄡ)
Western Europe

西安(ㄒㄧ ㄢ)
Sian, in Shensi Province 參看「長安」

西醫(ㄒㄧ ㄧ)
Western medicine; doctors practicing Western medicine (as distinct from Chinese herb doctors)

西雅圖(ㄒㄧ ㄧㄚˇ ㄊㄨˊ)
Seattle, an American port city

西藥(ㄒㄧ ㄧㄠˋ)
Western medicines or pharmaceuticals (as distinct from medical herbs)

西遊記(ㄒㄧ ㄧㄡˊ ㄐㄧˋ)
Pilgrimage to the West, one of the most popular novels, telling the adventures of a Buddhist monk and his three disciples on their way to India

西燕(ㄒㄧ ㄧㄢ)
one of the 16 tribal states in China during the Tsin Dynasty

西諺(ㄒㄧ ㄧㄢˋ)
a Western proverb; European or American aphorisms:「天助自助者」是一句西諺。"God helps those who

〔襾部〕

help themselves" is a Western proverb.

西印度羣島(ㄒㄧ ㄧㄣˋ ㄉㄨˋ ㄑㄩㄣˊ ㄉㄠˇ)
the West Indies

西洋(ㄒㄧ ㄧㄤˊ)
the West; Western; European or American nations

西洋景(ㄒㄧ ㄧㄤˊ ㄐㄧㄥˇ)or 西洋鏡(ㄒㄧ ㄧㄤˊ ㄐㄧㄥˋ)
①a peep show ②trickery; tricks; hanky-panky: 她拆穿了他的西洋鏡。She exposed his tricks.

西洋史(ㄒㄧ ㄧㄤˊ ㄕˇ)
history of Europe and America

西洋參(ㄒㄧ ㄧㄤˊ ㄕㄣ)
ginsengs produced in America

西洋人(ㄒㄧ ㄧㄤˊ ㄖㄣˊ)
Westerners

西洋菜(ㄒㄧ ㄧㄤˊ ㄘㄞˋ)
water cress

西魏(ㄒㄧ ㄨㄟˋ)
the Western Wei Dynasty (535-556), one of the Northern Dynasties

西王母(ㄒㄧ ㄨㄤˊ ㄇㄨˇ)
①name of an ancient state ②(name of a goddess) the Grand Old Lady of the West

西域(ㄒㄧ ㄩˋ)
a general name of regions west of Tunhwang (敦煌) in the Han Dynasty

西樂(ㄒㄧ ㄩㄝˋ)
Western music; European or American music: 他主修西樂。He majors in Western music.

西嶽(ㄒㄧ ㄩㄝˋ)
another name of Mountain Hua (華山) in Shensi Province, one of the Five Sacred Mountains in China

西元(ㄒㄧ ㄩㄢˊ)
the Gregorian calendar, which begins with the year in which Christ was supposedly born; A.D. 亦作「公元」

三畫

【要】 5474
1. ㄧㄠˋ yaw yào

1. necessary; important; essential; necessity: 睡眠對健康是必要的。Sleep is necessary to health.
2. must; should; ought to: 我想要早點動身。I should like to start early.
3. to want; to demand; to need; to require; to desire; to take: 我想要一輛新車。I want a new car.
4. to summarize; a summary; a generalization; a synopsis
5. will; shall—to indicate the future tense: 天快要黑了。It's going to be dark.
6. brief
7. if; in case

要不(ㄧㄠˋ ˙ㄅㄨ)or 要不然(ㄧㄠˋ ˙ㄅㄨ ㄖㄢˊ)
if not; otherwise; the other alternative being...; or

要不得(ㄧㄠˋ ˙ㄅㄨ ˙ㄉㄜ)
①(said of things) unusable; useless; extremely bad ②(said of people or acts) very bad; inappropriate; condemnable; intolerable: 這種墮落的行為要不得。Such depraved acts are intolerable.

要不是(ㄧㄠˋ ˙ㄅㄨ ㄕˋ)
If it were not for.... 或 But for.... 要不是你相助，我早已失敗。But for your help, I should have failed.

要不要(ㄧㄠˋ ˙ㄅㄨ ㄧㄠˋ)
Do you want it? 或 Do I have to...? 或 Shall (I, he, etc.)...? 或 Do you want (me, him, etc.)...?

要麼(ㄧㄠˋ ˙ㄇㄜ)
or; either...or...

要面子(ㄧㄠˋ ㄇㄧㄢˋ ˙ㄗ)
to be keen on face-saving; to be anxious to keep up honor

要命(ㄧㄠˋ ㄇㄧㄥˋ)
①very; extremely; awfully: 冷得要命。It's awfully cold. ②impossible: 你眞是要命！You are really impossible! ③too much to endure; an awful nuisance

要命鬼(ㄧㄠˋ ㄇㄧㄥˋ ㄍㄨㄟˇ)
①(an expression referring to one's children) the devils who make one work to death ②a person who imperils another

要目(ㄧㄠˋ ㄇㄨˋ)
①main items; main topics or subjects: 要目繁多。Main items are multifarious. ②(archaic) statistics

要犯(ㄧㄠˋ ㄈㄢˋ)
an important or dangerous criminal; a most-wanted criminal

要飯的(ㄧㄠˋ ㄈㄢˋ ˙ㄉㄜ)
a beggar

要得(ㄧㄠˋ ˙ㄉㄜ)
①good; well done; bravo: 這個辦法眞是要得！That's indeed a good idea! ②acceptable; okay

要道(ㄧㄠˋ ㄉㄠˋ)
①an important road or passage; a main route; a highway; an important line ②the essential points of what is good and appropriate

要地(ㄧㄠˋ ㄉㄧˋ)
an important or strategic place

要點(ㄧㄠˋ ㄉㄧㄢˇ)
the important or main points; the gist; the essential points (in an article, book, etc.): 告訴我他所說的要點。Tell me the gist of what he said.

要圖(ㄧㄠˋ ㄊㄨˊ)
an important plan or scheme; an urgent program or task

要臉(ㄧㄠˋ ㄌㄧㄢˇ)or 要臉面(ㄧㄠˋ ㄌㄧㄢˇ ˙ㄇㄧㄢ)
to be concerned with one's face or honor; to be highly sensitive about what others may think of oneself

要領(ㄧㄠˋ ㄌㄧㄥˇ)
essential points; important points; essentials

要路(ㄧㄠˋ ㄌㄨˋ)
①a thoroughfare; a main route ②eminent position

要略(ㄧㄠˋ ㄌㄩㄝˋ)
①an important plan or scheme ②a synopsis: 一週新聞要略 the synopsis of the week's news

要港(ㄧㄠˋ ㄍㄤˇ)
an important port; a key port: 高雄是一要港。Kaohsiung is an important port.

要公(ㄧㄠˋ ㄍㄨㄥ)
an urgent official business

要口(ㄧㄠˋ ㄎㄡˇ)
an important checkpoint

要害(ㄧㄠˋ ㄏㄞˋ)
① fatal points in a human body; a vital part; a crucial point ② strategic locations or points

要好(ㄧㄠˋ ㄏㄠˇ)
① to desire to excel ② to befriend; to be on good terms; to be close friends: 他們倆很要好。They are very good to each other. ③ to be in love with

要(我、你、他…)好看兒(ㄧㄠˋ (ㄨㄛˇ、ㄋㄧˇ、ㄊㄚ) ㄏㄠˇ ㄎㄢˋㄦ)
to want to embarrass (me, you, him, etc.); to want to make (me, you, him, etc.) suffer

要價兒(ㄧㄠˋ ㄐㄧㄚˋㄦ)
a price demanded by the seller; to quote a price which may be slashed by haggling

要件(ㄧㄠˋ ㄐㄧㄢˋ)
① an important document; an urgent or confidential matter, etc. ② a prerequisite; a necessary condition

要津(ㄧㄠˋ ㄐㄧㄣ)
① an important passage; a key road ② a key position; a sensitive post; an influential post ③ (Buddhism) an important turning point

要緊(ㄧㄠˋ ㄐㄧㄣˇ)
① important and urgent ② to be serious; to matter

要訣(ㄧㄠˋ ㄐㄩㄝˊ)
the secret of doing something; the key to doing something successfully

要強(ㄧㄠˋ ㄑㄧㄤˊ)
to strive to excel; aggressive; desiring to accept no second spot; eager to be at the top

要項(ㄧㄠˋ ㄒㄧㄤˋ)
key points or items

要之(ㄧㄠˋ ㄓ)
in a nutshell; in short; to sum up

要職(ㄧㄠˋ ㄓˊ)
an important post: 他曾身居要職。He used to hold an important post.

要旨(ㄧㄠˋ ㄓˇ)
key points; themes; epitomes; essential ideas: 要旨繁多。The essential ideas are numerous.

要賬(ㄧㄠˋ ㄓㄤˋ)
to demand payment of a debt, bill, etc.

要著(ㄧㄠˋ ㄓㄨㄛˊ)
an effective step; an important move; a timely measure

要衝(ㄧㄠˋ ㄔㄨㄥ)
a strategic position; a key place; a communication hub

要事(ㄧㄠˋ ㄕˋ)
an important matter; an urgent business: 它是件要事。It is an important matter.

要是(ㄧㄠˋ ˙ㄕ)
if; in case: 要是下雨，怎麼辦? What if it rains?

要甚麼(ㄧㄠˋ ㄕㄜˊ ˙ㄇㄜ)
What do you want? 或 What does he (or she) want?

要人(ㄧㄠˋ ㄖㄣˊ)
a VIP; a person in the Who's Who; a prominent figure: 要人善忘。A person of importance is forgetful of thing.

要死要活的(ㄧㄠˋ ㄙˇ ㄧㄠˋ ㄏㄨㄛˊ ˙ㄉㄜ)
to importune desperately

要塞(ㄧㄠˋ ㄙㄞˋ) or 要隘(ㄧㄠˋ ㄞˋ)
a fortress; a strategic point

要素(ㄧㄠˋ ㄙㄨˋ)
essentials; chief ingredients or elements or factors

要隘(ㄧㄠˋ ㄞˋ)
a strategic pass; a key point; a fortress 參看「要塞」

要義(ㄧㄠˋ ㄧˋ)
key points; main themes; essentials

要言不煩(ㄧㄠˋ ㄧㄢˊ ㄅㄨˋ ㄈㄢˊ)
brief and to the point

要務(ㄧㄠˋ ㄨˋ)
an important or urgent business, matter, task, etc.

要聞(ㄧㄠˋ ㄨㄣˊ)
important news items; headlines

要員(ㄧㄠˋ ㄩㄢˊ)
important officials; high-ranking officials; VIPs

【要】 5474
2. ㄧㄠ iau yāo
1. to invite; to request the presence of
2. to engage; to date; to make an agreement
3. to ask for; to demand; to claim; to make a claim; to request; requests: 她要求我留下。She requested me to stay.
4. to coerce; to force; to blackmail; to threaten
5. to stop
6. to censure; to investigate; to examine
7. the waist or midriff 亦作「腰」
8. a Chinese family name

要買人心(ㄧㄠ ㄇㄞˇ ㄖㄣˊ ㄒㄧㄣ)
to win people's hearts by statecraft

要盟(ㄧㄠ ㄇㄥˊ)
to impose an alliance, agreement, etc. on another (state, etc.) by threat of force

要擊(ㄧㄠ ㄐㄧ)
to ambush midway; to intercept (an enemy)

要求(ㄧㄠ ㄑㄧㄡˊ)
to demand; to request; a demand; a request: 我應他的要求而來。I came at his request.

要挾(ㄧㄠ ㄒㄧㄝˊ)
to blackmail; to put pressure on; to coerce; to threaten: 他們要挾對方。They put pressure on the other party.

要斬 or 腰斬(ㄧㄠ ㄓㄢˇ)
(an ancient punishment) to cut a criminal in half at the waist

要束(ㄧㄠ ㄕㄨˋ)
restriction or restraint; to restrain

要約(ㄧㄠ ㄩㄝ)
to enter into an agreement or a contract

六畫

【覃】 5475
1. ㄊㄢˊ tarn tán
1. to spread to; to involve
2. deep and vast; profound

覃第(ㄊㄢˊ ㄉㄧˋ)
① a vast or an extensive residence ② your house

覃思(ㄊㄢˊ ㄙ)
deep or profound thought; deep in thought; meditation

覃恩(ㄊㄢˊ ㄣ)
grace, favor or benefits for

〔襾部〕

〔襾部〕

all

【覃】 5475
2. ㄑㄧㄣˊ chyn qín
a Chinese family name

十二畫

【覆】 5476
ㄈㄨˋ fuh fù
1. to pour out
2. to overturn; to topple; to upset; to capsize; to put something upside down
3. a reply; to reply; to respond: 她沒有答覆。She made no reply.
4. to defeat; to destroy; to conquer
5. to investigate; to examine carefully
6. to cover; to screen
7. to repeat; a second time; again: 他反覆地勸告她。He warned her again and again.
8. to hide; to conceal

覆敗(ㄈㄨˋ ㄅㄞˋ)
to be beaten and destroyed; to topple

覆杯(ㄈㄨˋ ㄅㄟ)
① to put a wine-cup upside down—to decline to drink ② to drink to one's heart's content

覆蔽(ㄈㄨˋ ㄅㄧˋ)
to hide; to conceal; to cover up

覆瓿(ㄈㄨˋ ㄆㄡˇ)
(literally) to be used as a covering to a jar—worthless (a polite reference to one's own writing)

覆盆(ㄈㄨˋ ㄆㄣˊ)
① within the overturned bowl—dark and without justice ② a raspberry

覆盆之冤(ㄈㄨˋ ㄆㄣˊ ㄓ ㄩㄢ)
a wrong that cannot be redressed

覆盆子(ㄈㄨˋ ㄆㄣˊ ㄗˇ)
(Chinese medicine) a raspberry

覆沒(ㄈㄨˋ ㄇㄛˋ)
①(said of a boat) to wreck and sink ②(said of an army) routed; wiped out; destroyed

覆冒(ㄈㄨˋ ㄇㄠˋ)
to cover up; to hide or conceal

覆幬(ㄈㄨˋ ㄉㄠˋ)
to overshadow and curtain

覆蓋(ㄈㄨˋ ㄍㄞˋ)
to cover; to put a cover over something

覆核(ㄈㄨˋ ㄏㄜˊ)
to reexamine; to restudy

覆校(ㄈㄨˋ ㄐㄧㄠˋ)
to proofread again; the second proofreading: 他將該書覆校一遍。He proofread the book again.

覆車之戒(ㄈㄨˋ ㄐㄩ ㄓ ㄐㄧㄝˋ)
the lesson of a failure

覆軍(ㄈㄨˋ ㄐㄩㄣ)
to cause the whole army to be wiped out; to destroy the whole army

覆信(ㄈㄨˋ ㄒㄧㄣˋ)
① a letter in reply ② to reply a letter

覆選(ㄈㄨˋ ㄒㄩㄢˇ)
① an election by delegates; an indirect election ② a run-off (election)

覆舟(ㄈㄨˋ ㄓㄡ)
① to capsize ② a capsized boat

覆轍(ㄈㄨˋ ㄔㄜˋ)
(literally) the rut of an overturned cart—the lesson of a failure

覆巢之下無完卵(ㄈㄨˋ ㄔㄠˊ ㄓ ㄒㄧㄚˋ ㄨˊ ㄨㄢˊ ㄌㄨㄢˇ)
(literally) If the nest is overturned there won't be whole eggs left.—If a city falls, none of the residents will be safe. 或 If a country is beaten, all its people will suffer.

覆試(ㄈㄨˋ ㄕˋ)
① to test again ② a second test or examination

覆手(ㄈㄨˋ ㄕㄡˇ)
to turn one's palm—an easy task

覆審(ㄈㄨˋ ㄕㄣˇ)
a retrial of a case

覆書(ㄈㄨˋ ㄕㄨ)
① to reply a letter ② a letter in reply

覆水難收(ㄈㄨˋ ㄕㄨㄟˇ ㄋㄢˊ ㄕㄡ)
(literally) Spilt water can't be recovered.—① A divorced woman cannot hope to reunite with her former husband. ② There is no use crying over spilt milk. 或 What is done can't be undone.

覆染(ㄈㄨˋ ㄖㄢˇ)
to dye old clothes

覆載(ㄈㄨˋ ㄗㄞˋ)
the heaven and the earth

覆思(ㄈㄨˋ ㄙ)
a carved screen in a palace 亦作「罘罳」

覆餗(ㄈㄨˋ ㄙㄨˋ)
to fail owing to incompetence

覆按(ㄈㄨˋ ㄢˋ)
to reexamine; to reinvestigate

覆議(ㄈㄨˋ ㄧˋ)
① to discuss again ② a renewed discussion

覆文(ㄈㄨˋ ㄨㄣˊ)
an official reply in written form

覆亡(ㄈㄨˋ ㄨㄤˊ)
the downfall (of a nation, dynasty, or family); decline and fall

覆育(ㄈㄨˋ ㄩˋ)
protected by heaven and nourished by the earth

十三畫

【覈】 5477
(核) ㄏㄜˊ her hé
1. to test; to examine; to investigate
2. deep; deeply
3. the stone (of a fruit)

覈實(ㄏㄜˊ ㄕˊ)
to examine or investigate the fact or truth

覈物(ㄏㄜˊ ㄨˋ)
fruits that have stones

【覇】 5478
(霸) ㄅㄚˋ bah bà
1. the strong; the fierce ones
2. the dean or head of nobility
3. to stand out; outstanding; superior
4. hegemony

十七畫

【覊】 5479
(羈) ㄐㄧ ji jī
to travel; to be on a tour or trip

羇旅(ㄐㄧ ㄌㄩˇ)
a traveler 亦作「羈旅」

十九畫

【羈】 5480
(羈) ㄐㄧ ji ji
1. a halter
2. restriction; restraint
3. to live in another house; to stay in a place other than one's hometown

見部
ㄐㄧㄢˋ jiann jiàn

【見】 5481
ㄐㄧㄢˋ jiann jiàn
1. to see; to catch sight of; to perceive; to understand; to observe or examine: 百聞不如一見。Seeing is believing.
2. to visit; to see; to call on or at; to meet
3. to receive (visitors, etc.); to come face to face with
4. *vide*; see: 詳見註釋。For further information, see the footnotes.
5. to be used roughly as a verb *to be* in the passive voice: 即希見告。I hope to be informed immediately.
6. (said of a situation, condition, etc.) to move toward a certain direction, as getting worse, better, slimmer, etc.

見背(ㄐㄧㄢˋ ㄅㄟˋ)
(especially referring to parents) to turn their backs—dead; to pass away

見報(ㄐㄧㄢˋ ㄅㄠˋ)
to appear in the newspapers

見不得(ㄐㄧㄢˋ ·ㄅㄨ ·ㄉㄜ)
①not to be exposed to ②not fit to be seen or revealed

見不得人(ㄐㄧㄢˋ ·ㄅㄨ ·ㄉㄜ ㄖㄣˊ)
too ashamed to show up in public

見不及此(ㄐㄧㄢˋ ·ㄅㄨ ㄐㄧˊ ㄘˇ)
to have not considered this point; to have not observed or examined to such (depth, details, etc.); to fail to see this point

見不著(ㄐㄧㄢˋ ·ㄅㄨ ㄓㄠˊ)
cannot see; unable to meet

見票卽付(ㄐㄧㄢˋ ㄆㄧㄠˋ ㄐㄧˊ ㄈㄨˋ)
payable at sight; payable to the bearer

見面(ㄐㄧㄢˋ ㄇㄧㄢˋ)or 見面兒(ㄐㄧㄢˋ ㄇㄧㄚˋㄦ)
to come face to face; to see; to meet

見面禮(ㄐㄧㄢˋ ㄇㄧㄢˋ ㄌㄧˇ)
gift(s) given at one's first meeting, especially with a relative of a junior generation

見分曉(ㄐㄧㄢˋ ㄈㄣ ㄒㄧㄠˇ)
(said of results) to become known; to manifest; to tell

見方(ㄐㄧㄢˋ ㄈㄤ)
square, as a foot square

見風轉舵(ㄐㄧㄢˋ ㄈㄥ ㄓㄨㄢˇ ㄉㄨㄛˋ)
to steer by the wind—to see how the wind blows; to go with the tide

見風使船(ㄐㄧㄢˋ ㄈㄥ ㄕˇ ㄔㄨㄢˊ)or 見風使舵(ㄐㄧㄢˋ ㄈㄥ ㄕˇ ㄉㄨㄛˋ)
to trim one's sails—to act as the occasion dictates

見復 or 見覆(ㄐㄧㄢˋ ㄈㄨˋ)
to receive a reply

見到(ㄐㄧㄢˋ ㄉㄠˋ)
①to meet; to see: 很高興見到你。I'm glad to meet you. ②to perceive or think of

見地(ㄐㄧㄢˋ ㄉㄧˋ)
one's views, beliefs or ideas; insight: 他很有見地。He has keen insight.

見多識廣(ㄐㄧㄢˋ ㄉㄨㄛ ㄕˋ ㄍㄨㄤˇ)
experienced and knowledgeable

見天日(ㄐㄧㄢˋ ㄊㄧㄢ ㄖˋ)
(literally) to see the heaven and the sun—①to see justice prevail ②to emerge from misery

見兎顧犬(ㄐㄧㄢˋ ㄊㄨˋ ㄍㄨˋ ㄑㄩㄢˇ)
(literally) to signal to the hunting dog upon seeing a rabbit—to do the right thing to cope with a sudden new situation

見禮(ㄐㄧㄢˋ ㄌㄧˇ)
to salute or greet another upon meeting him

見利忘義(ㄐㄧㄢˋ ㄌㄧˋ ㄨㄤˋ ㄧˋ)
to forget one's integrity under the temptation of personal gain; to be blinded by the lust for gain

見獵心喜(ㄐㄧㄢˋ ㄌㄧㄝˋ ㄒㄧㄣ ㄒㄧˇ)
to have one's interest in an old hobby revived upon seeing someone else doing it; to thrill to see one's favorite sport and itch to have a go

見諒(ㄐㄧㄢˋ ㄌㄧㄤˋ)or 見原(ㄐㄧㄢˋ ㄩㄢˊ)
to pardon me; to forgive me; to excuse me

見高低(ㄐㄧㄢˋ ㄍㄠ ㄉㄧ)
to see who's the better one; to compete or fight it out

見告(ㄐㄧㄢˋ ㄍㄠˋ)
to tell; to inform; to notify

見過(ㄐㄧㄢˋ ㄍㄨㄛˋ)
to have seen; to have met

見過世面(ㄐㄧㄢˋ ㄍㄨㄛˋ ㄕˋ ㄇㄧㄢˋ)
to have seen much of the world; experienced; sophisticated

見怪(ㄐㄧㄢˋ ㄍㄨㄞˋ)
to take offense; to blame; to mind: 招待不周，請勿見怪。I hope you won't mind my poor reception.

見怪不怪，其怪自敗(ㄐㄧㄢˋ ㄍㄨㄞˋ ㄅㄨˊ ㄍㄨㄞˋ, ㄑㄧˊ ㄍㄨㄞˋ ㄗˋ ㄅㄞˋ)
If one remains calm upon seeing strange things, the strangeness will do no harm.

見鬼(ㄐㄧㄢˋ ㄍㄨㄟˇ)
(literally) to see the devil—Nonsense! 或 absurd: 活見鬼！Nonsense! You're daydreaming.

見慣(ㄐㄧㄢˋ ㄍㄨㄢˋ)
to be accustomed to seeing something

見客(ㄐㄧㄢˋ ㄎㄜˋ)
to receive guests

見好(ㄐㄧㄢˋ ㄏㄠˇ)
①to get better (especially said of illness); mend ②to be appreciated; to curry favor

見惠(ㄐㄧㄢˋ ㄏㄨㄟˋ)
to favor with

見幾 or 見機(ㄐㄧㄢˋ ㄐㄧ)
to perceive what is yet to take place; provident; far-sighted

見機行事(ㄐㄧㄢˋ ㄐㄧ ㄒㄧㄥˊ ㄕˋ)
to act as the circumstances

〔見部〕

dictate; to do as one sees fit
見解(ㄐㄧㄢˋ ㄐㄧㄝˇ)
one's views, ideas or observations or opinions about something: 這只是他個人的見解。This is just his own opinion.
見教(ㄐㄧㄢˋ ㄐㄧㄠˋ)
(a polite expression) your teachings or exhortations; to favor me with your advice; to instruct me: 有何見教? Is there something you want to instruct me?
見景生情(ㄐㄧㄢˋ ㄐㄧㄥˇ ㄕㄥ ㄑㄧㄥˊ)
to be touched by the scene; to have one's old emotion aroused by a sight
見棄(ㄐㄧㄢˋ ㄑㄧˋ)
to be cast away or rejected
見錢眼開(ㄐㄧㄢˋ ㄑㄧㄢˊ ㄧㄢˇ ㄎㄞ)
(literally) to keep one's eyes wide open upon seeing money—greedy; avaricious
見習(ㄐㄧㄢˋ ㄒㄧˊ)
apprenticeship; in-service training; probation
見習生(ㄐㄧㄢˋ ㄒㄧˊ ㄕㄥ)
an apprentice; an in-service trainee; a probationer
見習醫生(ㄐㄧㄢˋ ㄒㄧˊ ㄧ ㄕㄥ)
an intern
見小(ㄐㄧㄢˋ ㄒㄧㄠˇ)
① the ability to see what others are apt to neglect ② to see only the details
見效(ㄐㄧㄢˋ ㄒㄧㄠˋ)
effective; efficacious
見笑(ㄐㄧㄢˋ ㄒㄧㄠˋ)
① to be laughed at ② to incur ridicule (by one's poor performance)
見笑於大方之家(ㄐㄧㄢˋ ㄒㄧㄠˋ ㄩˊ ㄉㄚˋ ㄈㄤ ㄓ ㄐㄧㄚ)
to become a laughingstock of the learned people
見賢思齊(ㄐㄧㄢˋ ㄒㄧㄢˊ ㄙ ㄑㄧˊ)
to see the virtuous and think of equaling or emulating them
見信(ㄐㄧㄢˋ ㄒㄧㄣˋ)
upon reading the letter
見證(ㄐㄧㄢˋ ㄓㄥˋ)
① to bear witness ② (in a criminal case) an eyewitness
見黜(ㄐㄧㄢˋ ㄔㄨˋ)
to be rejected or dismissed; to be discharged or degraded
見世面(ㄐㄧㄢˋ ㄕˋ ㄇㄧㄢˋ)
to see the world; to enrich one's experience
見識(ㄐㄧㄢˋ ˙ㄕ)
① knowledge and experience; scope; sense: 他富有見識。He has plenty of sense. ② to experience (something new)
見識見識(ㄐㄧㄢˋ ˙ㄕ ㄐㄧㄢˋ ˙ㄕ)
to experience or see (something new)
見殺(ㄐㄧㄢˋ ㄕㄚ)
to be killed or murdered
見說(ㄐㄧㄢˋ ㄕㄨㄛ)
It is learned.... 或 It is heard.... 或 It is said....
見人(ㄐㄧㄢˋ ㄖㄣˊ)
to meet people; to appear in public
見仁見知 or 見仁見智(ㄐㄧㄢˋ ㄖㄣˊ ㄐㄧㄢˋ ㄓˋ)
to have different views or opinions
見字(ㄐㄧㄢˋ ㄗˋ)
upon reading this letter
見責(ㄐㄧㄢˋ ㄗㄜˊ)
to be blamed; to be reprimanded
見罪(ㄐㄧㄢˋ ㄗㄨㄟˋ)
to get the blame
見財起意(ㄐㄧㄢˋ ㄘㄞˊ ㄑㄧˇ ㄧˋ)
to have evil thoughts at the sight of riches
見死不救(ㄐㄧㄢˋ ㄙˇ ㄅㄨˋ ㄐㄧㄡˋ)
to see someone in mortal danger without lifting a finger to save him
見色不亂(ㄐㄧㄢˋ ㄙㄜˋ ㄅㄨˋ ㄌㄨㄢˋ)
to harbor no lustful thought in the presence of a beauty
見異思遷(ㄐㄧㄢˋ ㄧˋ ㄙ ㄑㄧㄢ)
easily moved by what one sees or hears; easily swinged by changing conditions; unstable; unfaithful
見義勇為(ㄐㄧㄢˋ ㄧˋ ㄩㄥˇ ㄨㄟˊ)
to have the courage to do what is right regardless of consequences; to act heroically
見外(ㄐㄧㄢˋ ㄨㄞˋ)
to treat as an outsider
見危致命(ㄐㄧㄢˋ ㄨㄟˊ ㄓˋ ㄇㄧㄥˋ) or 見危授命(ㄐㄧㄢˋ ㄨㄟˊ ㄕㄡˋ ㄇㄧㄥˋ)
to be ready to die for one's country in times of a national crisis
見聞(ㄐㄧㄢˋ ㄨㄣˊ)
what one has seen and heard—experience; knowledge; information: 他見聞不廣。He has only limited knowledge.
見聞廣博(ㄐㄧㄢˋ ㄨㄣˊ ㄍㄨㄤˇ ㄅㄛˊ)
experienced and knowledgeable; to have seen much of the world and heard of a lot of things
見聞有限(ㄐㄧㄢˋ ㄨㄣˊ ㄧㄡˇ ㄒㄧㄢˋ)
to have limited experience and knowledge

【見】 5481 2.(現) ㄒㄧㄢˋ shiann xiàn

1. to appear; to be visible
2. to introduce

四畫

【規】 5482 ㄍㄨㄟ guei guī

1. regulations; laws; rules; customs or usages: 你須遵守校規。You must obey the rules of the school.
2. a pair of compasses
3. to plan; to scheme
4. to advise so as to correct; to admonish
5. (now rarely) to copy; to imitate

規避(ㄍㄨㄟ ㄅㄧˋ)
to evade (obligations or duties); to shun or avoid: 不可規避問題的實質。Don't evade the substance of the issue.
規模(ㄍㄨㄟ ㄇㄛˊ)
① patterns; formulas ② scale; magnitude; scope; extent
規模宏大(ㄍㄨㄟ ㄇㄛˊ ㄏㄨㄥˊ ㄉㄚˋ)
on a large scale
規範(ㄍㄨㄟ ㄈㄢˋ)
a norm; a standard: 他的行為合乎規範。His behavior conforms to the standard.
規費(ㄍㄨㄟ ㄈㄟˋ)
fees paid to government agencies or court
規復(ㄍㄨㄟ ㄈㄨˋ)

to return to normalcy or former conditions
規定(ㄍㄨㄟ ㄉㄧㄥˋ)
to rule; to specify; to stipulate; to prescribe; to regulate; rules or regulations: 他以規定的速度駕駛。He drove at the regulation speed.
規條(ㄍㄨㄟ ㄊㄧㄠˊ)
items of regulation; rules
規律(ㄍㄨㄟ ㄌㄩˋ)
① laws, rules or regulations; discipline ② regular; regularity
規律性(ㄍㄨㄟ ㄌㄩˋ ㄒㄧㄥˋ)
regularity: 季節變換具規律性。The seasons come and go with regularity.
規略(ㄍㄨㄟ ㄌㄩㄝˋ)
to plan and operate
規格(ㄍㄨㄟ ㄍㄜˊ)
specifications (of a manufactured item); standards; gauges: 這些產品不合規格。These products fell short of specifications.
規規矩矩(ㄍㄨㄟ ˙ㄍㄨㄟ ㄐㄩˇ ˙ㄐㄩ)
① gentlemanlike; honest; polite ② well-behaved ③ orderly
規畫(ㄍㄨㄟ ㄏㄨㄚˋ)
① to map out or draw up (a plan) ② a plan or scheme: 他有一個長遠的規畫。He has a long-term scheme.
規誡(ㄍㄨㄟ ㄐㄧㄝˋ)
to admonish
規諫(ㄍㄨㄟ ㄐㄧㄢˋ)
to advise or admonish: 他規諫我說那是違法的事。He advised me that it was illegal.
規矩(ㄍㄨㄟ ㄐㄩˇ)
① rules; practices ② gentlemanlike; honest ③ well-behaved; well-disciplined ④ the compass and square
規矩準繩(ㄍㄨㄟ ㄐㄩˇ ㄓㄨㄣˇ ㄕㄥˊ)
a fixed rule or way
規求(ㄍㄨㄟ ㄑㄧㄡˊ)
greedy; avaricious
規勸(ㄍㄨㄟ ㄑㄩㄢˋ)
to admonish; to give friendly advice
規行矩步(ㄍㄨㄟ ㄒㄧㄥˊ ㄐㄩˇ ㄅㄨˋ)
to act strictly according to rules or accepted practices; to follow the beaten track
規箴(ㄍㄨㄟ ㄓㄣ)
admonitions
規章(ㄍㄨㄟ ㄓㄤ)
rules; regulations
規正(ㄍㄨㄟ ㄓㄥˋ)
to advise so as to correct a mistake
規程(ㄍㄨㄟ ㄔㄥˊ)
regulations and rules
規則(ㄍㄨㄟ ㄗㄜˊ)
① a rule or regulation ② regular; fixed; inflexible
規則動詞(ㄍㄨㄟ ㄗㄜˊ ㄉㄨㄥˋ ㄘˊ)
(grammar) regular verbs
規約(ㄍㄨㄟ ㄩㄝ)
a covenant or an agreement among members of an organization
規圓矩方(ㄍㄨㄟ ㄩㄢˊ ㄐㄩˇ ㄈㄤ)
to adhere to rules strictly

【覓】 5483
(覔) ㄇㄧˋ mih mì
to seek; to search or look for
覓保(ㄇㄧˋ ㄅㄠˇ)
to find a guarantor
覓得(ㄇㄧˋ ㄉㄜˊ)
to find what one has been looking for
覓句(ㄇㄧˋ ㄐㄩˋ)
to find a good line (for a poem)
覓索(ㄇㄧˋ ㄙㄨㄛˇ)
to seek or search for

五畫

【覘】 5484
ㄓㄢ jan zhān
to spy on; to see; to observe; to inspect; to investigate secretly
覘國(ㄓㄢ ㄍㄨㄛˊ)
to inspect and survey conditions within a nation
覘候(ㄓㄢ ㄏㄡˋ)
to spy on; to look out for

【視】 5485
ㄕˋ shyh shì
1. to look at; to observe; to inspect; to see; to watch
2. to consider or regard as; to take it for; to look upon as: 他視她如仇敵。He looks upon her as his enemy.
3. to compare; to be equivalent to
4. (now rarely) to show 亦作「示」
5. (now rarely) to receive (a present, etc.)
6. to take as a model; to imitate
視半徑(ㄕˋ ㄅㄢˋ ㄐㄧㄥˋ)
(astronomy) an apparent semidiameter
視民如傷(ㄕˋ ㄇㄧㄣˊ ㄖㄨˊ ㄕㄤ)
to take good care of the people as if they were patients
視端容寂(ㄕˋ ㄉㄨㄢ ㄖㄨㄥˊ ㄐㄧˊ)
to look serious and quiet
視聽(ㄕˋ ㄊㄧㄥ)
① what one saw and heard; knowledge and experience ② public opinion ③ audio-visual
視聽教具(ㄕˋ ㄊㄧㄥ ㄐㄧㄠˋ ㄐㄩˋ)
audio-visual aids
視聽教育(ㄕˋ ㄊㄧㄥ ㄐㄧㄠˋ ㄩˋ)
audio-visual education
視聽言動(ㄕˋ ㄊㄧㄥ ㄧㄢˊ ㄉㄨㄥˋ)
to see, hear, talk and move
視同路人(ㄕˋ ㄊㄨㄥˊ ㄌㄨˋ ㄖㄣˊ)
to treat as outsiders or strangers
視同具文(ㄕˋ ㄊㄨㄥˊ ㄐㄩˋ ㄨㄣˊ)
to regard as mere empty words
視同兒戲(ㄕˋ ㄊㄨㄥˊ ㄦˊ ㄒㄧˋ)
to take it lightly; to regard it as unimportant; to trifle; to treat (a serious matter) as a trifle: 你不應該把你的健康視同兒戲。You should not trifle with your health.
視同一體(ㄕˋ ㄊㄨㄥˊ ㄧˋ ㄊㄧˇ)
to make no distinction; to accord the same treatment to all; to be impartial
視力(ㄕˋ ㄌㄧˋ)
the visual faculty; eyesight; the power of vision: 他視力差。His vision is poor.
視力表(ㄕˋ ㄌㄧˋ ㄅㄧㄠˇ)
an eye chart
視力計(ㄕˋ ㄌㄧˋ ㄐㄧˋ)
an optometer
視官(ㄕˋ ㄍㄨㄢ)
the organ of vision
視界(ㄕˋ ㄐㄧㄝˋ)
the field or range of vision
視角(ㄕˋ ㄐㄧㄠˇ)

〔見部〕

(physics) the visual angle

視覺(ㄕˋ ㄐㄩㄝˊ)
the sense of sight; visual sensation; vision: 他有很敏銳的視覺。He has a keen sense of sight.

視覺器(ㄕˋ ㄐㄩㄝˊ ㄑㄧˋ)
an organ of sight

視覺型(ㄕˋ ㄐㄩㄝˊ ㄒㄧㄥˊ)
(psychology) the visual type

視覺暫留(ㄕˋ ㄐㄩㄝˊ ㄓㄢˋ ㄌㄧㄡˊ)
persistence of vision

視線(ㄕˋ ㄒㄧㄢˋ)
① the line of vision or sight—the straight line between an object and one's eyes ② eyesight: 這房子在視線以內。The house is within eyesight.

視差(ㄕˋ ㄔㄚ)
(astronomy) the parallax

視察(ㄕˋ ㄔㄚˊ)
to inspect; to observe; to see or examine: 他們在視察公共工程。They were inspecting public works.

視察團(ㄕˋ ㄔㄚˊ ㄊㄨㄢˊ)
an inspection team; a study group

視事(ㄕˋ ㄕˋ)
① to administer; to govern or rule ② to be installed or inaugurated; to be sworn in

視神經(ㄕˋ ㄕㄣˊ ㄐㄧㄥ)
the optic nerve

視如敝屣(ㄕˋ ㄖㄨˊ ㄅㄧˋ ㄒㄧˇ)
to regard as worn-out shoes; to throw away as worthless

視如己出(ㄕˋ ㄖㄨˊ ㄐㄧˇ ㄔㄨ)
to treat a child as if he (she) were one's own

視如草芥(ㄕˋ ㄖㄨˊ ㄘㄠˇ ㄐㄧㄝˋ)
to regard as worthless

視若無睹(ㄕˋ ㄖㄨㄛˋ ㄨˊ ㄉㄨˇ)
to be undisturbed by what one has seen

視死如歸(ㄕˋ ㄙˇ ㄖㄨˊ ㄍㄨㄟ)
to look upon death as going home—fearless and dauntless

視而不見(ㄕˋ ㄦˊ ㄅㄨˊ ㄐㄧㄢˋ)
(literally) to look but see nothing—absent-minded; to ignore

視野(ㄕˋ ㄧㄝˇ)
the field of vision; visual field

視爲(ㄕˋ ㄨㄟˊ)
to regard or consider as: 她把他視爲傻瓜。She regarded him as a fool.

視網膜炎(ㄕˋ ㄨㄤˇ ㄇㄛˊ ㄧㄢˊ)
retinitis

七畫

【覎】 5486
ㄒㄧˊ shyi xí
a wizard

八畫

【覥】 5487
(靦) ㄊㄧㄢˇ tean tiǎn
ashamed 參看「靦覥」

九畫

【覦】 5488
ㄩˊ yu yú
a strong desire for possession; to covet 參看「覬覦」

【覩】 5489
(睹) ㄉㄨˇ duu dǔ
to see; to gaze at; to observe; to witness

覩物思人(ㄉㄨˇ ㄨˋ ㄙ ㄖㄣˊ)
to think of someone who is dead or far away upon seeing something he left behind

【親】 5490
1. ㄑㄧㄣ chin qin

1. parents: 他的雙親都很健康。His parents are quite well.
2. relatives: 我們有很多親戚。We have many relatives.
3. to love; intimate; near to; dear
4. personally; personal; in person; self
5. to kiss: 她親這小男孩一下。She kissed the little boy.

親筆(ㄑㄧㄣ ㄅㄧˇ)
one's own handwriting; to write personally

親筆信(ㄑㄧㄣ ㄅㄧˇ ㄒㄧㄣˋ)
a letter in one's own handwriting; an autograph letter

親兵(ㄑㄧㄣ ㄅㄧㄥ)
bodyguards

親朋(ㄑㄧㄣ ㄆㄥˊ)
relatives and friends

親密(ㄑㄧㄣ ㄇㄧˋ)
intimate; intimacy; close: 我和他是極爲親密的朋友。I am on intimate terms with him.

親母(ㄑㄧㄣ ㄇㄨˇ)
① one's own mother, who is a concubine ② one's own mother (as distinct from a foster mother or stepmother)

親夫(ㄑㄧㄣ ㄈㄨ)
one's own husband

親父(ㄑㄧㄣ ㄈㄨˋ)
one's own father (as distinct from a foster father or stepfather)

親等(ㄑㄧㄣ ㄉㄥˇ)
(law) the degree of kinship

親爹(ㄑㄧㄣ ㄉㄧㄝ)
one's own father (as distinct from a stepfather)

親痛仇快(ㄑㄧㄣ ㄊㄨㄥˋ ㄔㄡˊ ㄎㄨㄞˋ)
(said of a mistake, blunder, etc.) to pain one's friends and please one's enemies

親暱(ㄑㄧㄣ ㄋㄧˋ)
intimate; very dear to; affectionate: 這是個親暱的稱呼。This is an affectionate form of address.

親娘(ㄑㄧㄣ ㄋㄧㄤˊ)
one's own mother (as distinct from a foster mother or stepmother)

親歷其境(ㄑㄧㄣ ㄌㄧˋ ㄑㄧˊ ㄐㄧㄥˋ)
to go through the whole thing personally; to be on the spot or scene in person; to experience personally

親臨(ㄑㄧㄣ ㄌㄧㄣˊ)
(said of a superior or elder) to arrive personally

親告罪(ㄑㄧㄣ ㄍㄠˋ ㄗㄨㄟˋ)
offenses that can be prosecuted only upon the complaint of the aggrieved party

親骨肉(ㄑㄧㄣ ㄍㄨˇ ㄖㄡˋ)
(literally) one's own flesh and blood—the ties between parents and children

親故(ㄑㄧㄣ ㄍㄨˋ) or 親舊(ㄑㄧㄣ ㄐㄧㄡˋ)
relatives and old friends

親供(ㄑㄧㄣ ㄍㄨㄥ)
to confess in person; a personal confession

親口(ㄑㄧㄣ ㄎㄡˇ)
(said of words, etc.) right from one's own mouth; to state or tell personally

親和力(ㄑㄧㄣ ㄏㄜˊ ㄌㄧˋ)
①(chemistry) affinity ② affability; amiability
親姊妹(ㄑㄧㄣ ㄐㄧㄝˇ ㄇㄟˋ)
sisters born of the same parents
親交(ㄑㄧㄣ ㄐㄧㄠ)
① to deliver (a letter, etc.) personally ② intimate friendship
親見(ㄑㄧㄣ ㄐㄧㄢˋ)
to have seen in person
親近(ㄑㄧㄣ ㄐㄧㄣˋ)
to be near to or intimate with; to be close to
親眷(ㄑㄧㄣ ㄐㄩㄢˋ)
family members
親啓(ㄑㄧㄣ ㄑㄧˇ)
(said of a letter) to be opened personally; confidential
親戚(ㄑㄧㄣ ·ㄑㄧ)
relatives: 他們是我的親戚。They are my relatives.
親切(ㄑㄧㄣ ㄑㄧㄝˋ)
intimately; cordially; kind: 她對我親切。She was kind to me.
親權(ㄑㄧㄣ ㄑㄩㄢˊ)
the right to assume guardianship for one's own children before they come of age; parental authority
親狎(ㄑㄧㄣ ㄒㄧㄚˊ)
close and intimate
親信(ㄑㄧㄣ ㄒㄧㄣˋ)
a confidant; an intimate; a trusted subordinate, etc.
親兄弟(ㄑㄧㄣ ㄒㄩㄥ ㄉㄧˋ)
brothers born of the same parents
親兄弟明算賬(ㄑㄧㄣ ㄒㄩㄥ ㄉㄧˋ ㄇㄧㄥˊ ㄙㄨㄢˋ ㄓㄤˋ)
Financial matters should be settled clearly even between brothers.
親炙(ㄑㄧㄣ ㄓˋ)
(a polite expression) personally receive your admonishment, instructions, etc.
親展(ㄑㄧㄣ ㄓㄢˇ)
① to meet in person ② (a confidential letter, etc.) to be opened by the recipient personally
親征(ㄑㄧㄣ ㄓㄥ)
(said of a king or an emperor) to lead an army personally to war
親政(ㄑㄧㄣ ㄓㄥˋ)
(said of a young king) to take over the administration or government from a regent upon coming of age
親事
①(ㄑㄧㄣ ㄕˋ) to attend to personally
②(ㄑㄧㄣ ·ㄕ) marriage
親手(ㄑㄧㄣ ㄕㄡˇ)
personally; with one's own hands
親善(ㄑㄧㄣ ㄕㄢˋ)
friendship or goodwill
親身(ㄑㄧㄣ ㄕㄣ)
personally; in person
親上加親(ㄑㄧㄣ ㄕㄤˋ ㄐㄧㄚ ㄑㄧㄣ)
to cement old ties by marriage, as a marriage between cousins, etc.
親生父母(ㄑㄧㄣ ㄕㄥ ㄈㄨˋ ㄇㄨˇ)
one's own parents (as distinct from foster parents or stepparents)
親生子女(ㄑㄧㄣ ㄕㄥ ㄗˇ ㄋㄩˇ)
one's own children (as distinct from adopted children)
親疎(ㄑㄧㄣ ㄕㄨ)
dear ones and indifferent persons; intimacy and remoteness
親屬(ㄑㄧㄣ ㄕㄨˇ)
relatives; family members
親率(ㄑㄧㄣ ㄕㄨㄞˋ)
to lead personally (an army, a group of welcomers, a troupe, etc.)
親熱(ㄑㄧㄣ ㄖㄜˋ)
very dear; very intimate; very much in love
親人(ㄑㄧㄣ ㄖㄣˊ)
close relatives—as one's parents, brothers, spouse, children, etc.
親任(ㄑㄧㄣ ㄖㄣˋ)
one's confidants
親子(ㄑㄧㄣ ㄗˇ)
one's own son (as distinct from an adopted son)
親自(ㄑㄧㄣ ㄗˋ)
personally; in person: 他親自拜訪。He made a personal call.
親自出馬(ㄑㄧㄣ ㄗˋ ㄔㄨ ㄇㄚˇ)
to go out and take care of something in person; to confront (the enemy, etc.) personally
親族(ㄑㄧㄣ ㄗㄨˊ)
one's kinsmen; members of the same clan
親嘴(ㄑㄧㄣ ㄗㄨㄟˇ)
to kiss
親裁(ㄑㄧㄣ ㄘㄞˊ)
to decide personally
親隨(ㄑㄧㄣ ㄙㄨㄟˊ)
aides; entourages
親愛(ㄑㄧㄣ ㄞˋ)
love; affection; dear
親愛的(ㄑㄧㄣ ㄞˋ ·ㄉㄜ)
my dear; my darling
親愛精誠(ㄑㄧㄣ ㄞˋ ㄐㄧㄥ ㄔㄥˊ)
camaraderie; *esprit de corps*
親友(ㄑㄧㄣ ㄧㄡˇ)
friends and relatives: 他有許多親友。He has many relatives and friends.
親眼看見(ㄑㄧㄣ ㄧㄢˇ ㄎㄢˋ ㄐㄧㄢˋ)
to witness; to see with one's own eyes: 他親眼看見那意外事件。He witnessed the accident.
親迎(ㄑㄧㄣ ㄧㄥˊ)
to receive or welcome (a visitor, etc.) personally
親吻(ㄑㄧㄣ ㄨㄣˇ)
to kiss
親王(ㄑㄧㄣ ㄨㄤˊ)
① members of the royal family who were conferred dukedom or dubbed in ancient times ② (a modern sense) a prince

【親】 5490
2. ㄑㄧㄥˋ chinq qing
relatives by marriage
親爹(ㄑㄧㄥˋ ㄉㄧㄝ)
a term of address by the junior members of one of the two families related by marriage for a senior male member of the other family
親家(ㄑㄧㄥˋ ·ㄐㄧㄚ)
① relatives as a result of marriage ② parents of the married couple
親家母(ㄑㄧㄥˋ ·ㄐㄧㄚ ㄇㄨˇ)
mother of one's daughter-in-law or son-in-law
親家女兒(ㄑㄧㄥˋ ·ㄐㄧㄚ ㄋㄩˇ ㄦˊ)
a term of address for sisters of one's daughter-in-law or

son-in-law
親家老爺(ㄑㄧㄥˋ・ㄐㄧㄚ ㄌㄠˇ・ㄧㄝ)
a term of address for male parents of the married couple
親家公(ㄑㄧㄥˋ・ㄐㄧㄚ ㄍㄨㄥ)
father of one's daughter-in-law or son-in-law
親家兒子(ㄑㄧㄥˋ・ㄐㄧㄚ ㄦˊ・ㄗ)
brothers of one's daughter-in-law or son-in-law

十畫

【覬】 5491
ㄐㄧˋ jih jì
to covet; to desire something belonging to others
覬覦(ㄐㄧˋ ㄩˊ)
to covet; to desire something belonging to others

【覯】 5492
ㄍㄡˋ gow gòu
to meet

十一畫

【覲】 5493
ㄐㄧㄣˇ jiin jǐn
(又讀 ㄐㄧㄣˋ jinn jìn)
to have an audience with a chief of state
覲禮(ㄐㄧㄣˇ ㄌㄧˇ)
rituals performed during audience
覲見(ㄐㄧㄣˇ ㄐㄧㄢˋ)
to have an audience with a chief of state

【覷】 5494
(覰・覻) ㄑㄩˋ chiuh qù
to spy on; to watch; to look; to gaze
覷步(ㄑㄩˋ ㄅㄨˋ)
to spy on
覷著眼(ㄑㄩˋ・ㄓㄜ ㄧㄢˇ)
to narrow one's eyes and gaze at something with great attention

十二畫

【覶】 5495
(覼) ㄌㄨㄛˊ luo luó
to see carefully
覶縷(ㄌㄨㄛˊ ㄌㄩˇ)
to present (a case, etc.) in a detailed and systematic way

十三畫

【覺】 5496
1. ㄐㄩㄝˊ jyue jué
1. to wake up from sleep
2. senses: 他有敏銳的嗅覺。He has a keen sense of smell.
3. to be conscious of; to sense
4. to awaken; to realize; to discover: 他察覺到自己的危險。He awoke to his danger.
5. to tell; to feel: 我感覺冷得很。I feel so cold.
6. high, large, and straight
覺得(ㄐㄩㄝˊ・ㄉㄜ)
①to be conscious of; to realize; to sense ②to feel ③to think; to be of the opinion
覺痛(ㄐㄩㄝˊ ㄊㄨㄥˋ)
to feel the sensation of pain
覺冷(ㄐㄩㄝˊ ㄌㄥˇ)
to feel cold
覺醒(ㄐㄩㄝˊ ㄒㄧㄥˇ)
to wake up
覺察(ㄐㄩㄝˊ ㄔㄚˊ)
to discover; to realize; to detect; to be aware; to sense
覺書(ㄐㄩㄝˊ ㄕㄨ)
(diplomacy) a memorandum
覺熱(ㄐㄩㄝˊ ㄖㄜˋ)
to feel hot
覺癢(ㄐㄩㄝˊ ㄧㄤˇ)
to feel itchy
覺悟(ㄐㄩㄝˊ ㄨˋ)
to become aware; to realize; to awake

【覺】 5496
2. ㄐㄧㄠˋ jiaw jiào
a sleep; a nap: 他熟睡了一覺。He slept a sound sleep.

十四畫

【覽】 5497
ㄌㄢˇ laan lǎn
1. to look at; to sightsee
2. to read: 他博覽群書。He reads widely.
3. to listen to (what others say)
4. a Chinese family name
覽古(ㄌㄢˇ ㄍㄨˇ)
to tour ancient relics
覽揆(ㄌㄢˇ ㄎㄨㄟˊ)
one's birthday
覽勝(ㄌㄢˇ ㄕㄥˋ)
to tour a resort; to see or visit a scenic spot

十五畫

【覿】 5498
ㄉㄧˊ dyi dí
to meet; to see each other
覿面(ㄉㄧˊ ㄇㄧㄢˋ)
to see each other; to meet
覿儀(ㄉㄧˊ ㄧˊ)
presents offered at a meeting

十八畫

【觀】 5499
1. ㄍㄨㄢ guan guān
1. to see; to observe; to behold; to view; to take a view of; to look; to inspect: 我們參觀了世界博覽會。We saw the World's Fair.
2. sights; views
3. to display
4. a point of view; a conception: 他的人生觀是錯誤的。He has a wrong conception of life.
觀兵(ㄍㄨㄢ ㄅㄧㄥ)
to review troops; to display military might
觀摩(ㄍㄨㄢ ㄇㄛˊ)
to emulate the good points of others; to compare notes
觀風(ㄍㄨㄢ ㄈㄥ)
①to look for opportunities ②to observe local customs ③to keep watch when a robbery or larceny is being committed by a confederate or confederates
觀點(ㄍㄨㄢ ㄉㄧㄢˇ)
a point of view; one's view on a certain matter; one's ideas or opinions concerning something
觀鼎(ㄍㄨㄢ ㄉㄧㄥˇ)
to covet the throne
觀臺(ㄍㄨㄢ ㄊㄞˊ)
an elevated stand or platform on which one can see far and wide
觀念(ㄍㄨㄢ ㄋㄧㄢˋ)
a conception; an idea; a view
觀念論(ㄍㄨㄢ ㄋㄧㄢˋ ㄌㄨㄣˋ)

idealism

觀禮(ㄍㄨㄢ ㄌㄧˇ)
to attend a celebration or ceremony

觀感(ㄍㄨㄢ ㄍㄢˇ)
one's feelings or emotional reactions after seeing or reading something

觀過知仁(ㄍㄨㄢ ㄍㄨㄛˋ ㄓ ㄖㄣˊ)
(originally from the *Analects*) After observing a person's faults and failings, one will understand what he really is.

觀光(ㄍㄨㄢ ㄍㄨㄤ)
sightseeing; to see the sights: 我喜歡觀光。I am fond of sightseeing.

觀光團(ㄍㄨㄢ ㄍㄨㄤ ㄊㄨㄢˊ)
a tour group; a tourist group

觀光旅館(ㄍㄨㄢ ㄍㄨㄤ ㄌㄩˇ ㄍㄨㄢˇ)
a tourist hotel

觀光客(ㄍㄨㄢ ㄍㄨㄤ ㄎㄜˋ)
a tourist

觀光事業(ㄍㄨㄢ ㄍㄨㄤ ㄕˋ ㄧㄝˋ)
tourism; the tourist industry

觀看(ㄍㄨㄢ ㄎㄢˋ)
to look at; to observe or inspect; to see

觀火(ㄍㄨㄢ ㄏㄨㄛˇ)
to see the fire—to view clearly

觀劇(ㄍㄨㄢ ㄐㄩˋ)
to see an opera; to watch a stage show

觀棋不語眞君子(ㄍㄨㄢ ㄑㄧˊ ㄅㄨˋ ㄩˇ ㄓㄣ ㄐㄩㄣ ㄗˇ)
He is truly a gentleman who watches in silence a game of chess.

觀心術(ㄍㄨㄢ ㄒㄧㄣ ㄕㄨˋ)
the art of mind reading

觀釁(ㄍㄨㄢ ㄒㄧㄣˋ)
to look for an opportunity (to take action or start something)

觀象(ㄍㄨㄢ ㄒㄧㄤˋ)
to observe heavenly bodies; to watch celestial phenomena

觀象臺(ㄍㄨㄢ ㄒㄧㄤˋ ㄊㄞˊ)
an observatory

觀相知人(ㄍㄨㄢ ㄒㄧㄤˋ ㄓ ㄖㄣˊ)
to study a man's physiognomy and know his character

觀止(ㄍㄨㄢ ㄓˇ)
(literally) What one has seen is perfect.—good beyond comparison: 歎爲觀止！What perfection! 或 What an unrivaled sight!

觀者如堵(ㄍㄨㄢ ㄓㄜˇ ㄖㄨˊ ㄉㄨˇ)
The spectators formed a solid wall of humanity.

觀瞻(ㄍㄨㄢ ㄓㄢ)
①the appearance or outward look of something ②to look at; to see; to view

觀戰(ㄍㄨㄢ ㄓㄢˋ)
to witness a battle; to observe a military operation

觀衆(ㄍㄨㄢ ㄓㄨㄥˋ)
the audience or spectators: 這場足球賽有很多觀衆。There were many spectators at the football match.

觀察(ㄍㄨㄢ ㄔㄚˊ)
to observe; to watch; to inspect; observation: 小心觀察你可以學到很多事。You can learn many things by careful observation.

觀察家(ㄍㄨㄢ ㄔㄚˊ ㄐㄧㄚ)
an observer; one who observes and makes comments on current events

觀潮(ㄍㄨㄢ ㄔㄠˊ)
to view a tide

觀賞(ㄍㄨㄢ ㄕㄤˇ)
to see and enjoy

觀賞植物(ㄍㄨㄢ ㄕㄤˇ ㄓˊ ㄨˋ)
garden plants; ornamental (or decorative) plants

觀測(ㄍㄨㄢ ㄘㄜˋ)
to observe and survey

觀測站(ㄍㄨㄢ ㄘㄜˋ ㄓㄢˋ)
an observation post

觀測員(ㄍㄨㄢ ㄘㄜˋ ㄩㄢˊ)
an observer (aboard an airplane or in an artillery unit)

觀音(ㄍㄨㄢ ㄧㄣ)or 觀世音(ㄍㄨㄢ ㄕˋ ㄧㄣ)or 觀音大士(ㄍㄨㄢ ㄧㄣ ㄉㄚˋ ㄕˋ)or 觀自在(ㄍㄨㄢ ㄗˋ ㄗㄞˋ)
the Goddess of Mercy; the feminine form of *Avalokitesvara Bodhisattva*

觀往知來(ㄍㄨㄢ ㄨㄤˇ ㄓ ㄌㄞˊ)
To review the past will enable one to predict the future.

觀望(ㄍㄨㄢ ㄨㄤˋ)
a wait-and-see attitude; to wait and see; to hesitate: 不要採取觀望態度。Don't take a wait-and-see attitude.

觀望不前(ㄍㄨㄢ ㄨㄤˋ ㄅㄨˋ ㄑㄧㄢˊ)
to hesitate and make no move

【觀】 5499
2. ㄍㄨㄢˋ guann guàn
a Taoist temple or shrine

角 部
ㄐㄩㄝˊ jyue jué

【角】 5500
1. ㄐㄧㄠˇ jeau jiǎo

1. the horn of an animal
2. a direction; a corner
3. an angle
4. a tenth of a dollar; a 10-cent piece
5. something in the shape of a horn
6. a cape; a promontory

角皮(ㄐㄧㄠˇ ㄆㄧˊ)or 角皮層(ㄐㄧㄠˇ ㄆㄧˊ ㄘㄥˊ)or 角皮質(ㄐㄧㄠˇ ㄆㄧˊ ㄓˊ)
(botany) cuticle; cutin

角膜(ㄐㄧㄠˇ ㄇㄛˊ)
(anatomy) cornea

角膜炎(ㄐㄧㄠˇ ㄇㄛˊ ㄧㄢˊ)
keratitis

角度(ㄐㄧㄠˇ ㄉㄨˋ)
①an angle ②angular measure

角立(ㄐㄧㄠˇ ㄌㄧˋ)
①to stand out (without a peer) ②to become stalemated

角鋼(ㄐㄧㄠˇ ㄍㄤ)
(metallurgy) angle steel

角距(ㄐㄧㄠˇ ㄐㄩˋ)
(astronomy) an angular distance

角質(ㄐㄧㄠˇ ㄓˊ)
horny; corneous

角柱(ㄐㄧㄠˇ ㄓㄨˋ)
(mathematics) a prism

角錐體(ㄐㄧㄠˇ ㄓㄨㄟ ㄊㄧˇ)
(mathematics) a pyramid

角兒(ㄐㄧㄠˇㄦ)
①a corner ②a direction

角岩(ㄐㄧㄠˇ ㄧㄢˊ)
hornstone

〔角部〕

【角】 5500
2. 讀音ㄐㄩㄝˊ jyue jué
1. to compete; to contest; to wrestle
2. a corner
3. an ancient, three-legged wine-cup
4. a dramatic role; a character
5. one of the five musical notes in ancient Chinese music

角觝 or 角抵(ㄐㄩㄝˊ ㄉㄧˇ)
to wrestle or wrestling—as a sport

角樓(ㄐㄩㄝˊ ㄌㄡˊ)
an attic

角力(ㄐㄩㄝˊ ㄌㄧˋ)
a contest in strength; to wrestle; wrestling

角力者(ㄐㄩㄝˊ ㄌㄧˋ ㄓㄜˇ)
a wrestler

角力場(ㄐㄩㄝˊ ㄌㄧˋ ㄔㄤˇ)
a palaestra; a ring for wrestling

角落(ㄐㄩㄝˊ ㄌㄨㄛˋ)or(ㄐㄧㄠˇ ㄌㄨㄛˋ)
a corner; a nook: 喜訊傳遍全國各個角落。The good news spread to every corner of the country.

角巾(ㄐㄩㄝˊ ㄐㄧㄣ)
clothing for the retired or hermits in ancient times

角巾私第(ㄐㄩㄝˊ ㄐㄧㄣ ㄙ ㄉㄧˋ)
to live in retirement; to lead a hermit's life

角逐(ㄐㄩㄝˊ ㄓㄨˊ)
to contest (for a post, etc.); to jockey (for position); to struggle for hegemony

角試(ㄐㄩㄝˊ ㄕˋ)
(in old China) a contest in martial arts

角色(ㄐㄩㄝˊ ㄙㄜˋ)
a role; a character

角兒(ㄐㄩㄝˊㄦ)
(Chinese Opera) a player

【角】 5500
3. ㄌㄨˋ luh lù
參看「角里」

角里(ㄌㄨˋ ㄌㄧˇ)
① name of a place southwest of Soochow, Kiangsu Province ② a Chinese family name

二畫

【觔】 5501
ㄐㄧㄣ jin jin
1. sinews or muscular strength 亦作「筋」
2. a catty, equivalent to 1.10231 pounds

觔斗(ㄐㄧㄣ ㄉㄡˇ)
a somersault: 我在草地上翻觔斗。I turned a somersault on the lawn.

四畫

【觖】 5502
ㄐㄩㄝˊ jyue jué
dissatisfied; discontented; not satisfactory

觖望(ㄐㄩㄝˊ ㄨㄤˋ)
to bear animus as a result of dissatisfaction; to harbor (or nurse) a grudge

五畫

【觚】 5503
ㄍㄨ gu gū
1. an ancient wine vessel; a beaker or goblet
2. a corner; an angle; angular
3. a rule
4. a square
5. correspondence or a file, etc.

觚牘(ㄍㄨ ㄉㄨˊ)
correspondence

觚稜(ㄍㄨ ㄌㄥˊ)
the tile ridge at the corner of a roof

【觝】 5504
ㄉㄧˇ dii dǐ
to butt; to resist; to push

觝排(ㄉㄧˇ ㄆㄞˊ)
to reject; to get rid of

六畫

【解】 5505
1. ㄐㄧㄝˇ jiee jiě
1. to unfasten; to untie; to loosen; to undo
2. to solve (difficult problems, etc.)
3. to explain; to clarify; to interpret; explanation; interpretation
4. to understand
5. ideas; views
6. to break up, separate or disperse
7. to take off; to strip; to remove (clothing, etc.); to get rid of
8. to relieve; to alleviate (pain, etc.)
9. to cut apart; to dissect
10. to dissolve
11. to discharge (water, etc.); to defecate

解剖(ㄐㄧㄝˇ ㄆㄡˇ)
① to dissect; dissection; anatomization ② to analyze; analysis

解剖刀(ㄐㄧㄝˇ ㄆㄡˇ ㄉㄠ)
a scalpel; a dissecting knife

解剖學(ㄐㄧㄝˇ ㄆㄡˇ ㄒㄩㄝˊ)
anatomy: 他在醫學院研究解剖學。He studied anatomy in medical school.

解剖室(ㄐㄧㄝˇ ㄆㄡˇ ㄕˋ)
a dissecting room

解聘(ㄐㄧㄝˇ ㄆㄧㄣˋ)
to relieve one of his duties; to dismiss or discharge a person from his post

解悶兒(ㄐㄧㄝˇ ㄇㄣˋㄦ)
to kill time; to dispel loneliness; to get rid of boredom

解民倒懸(ㄐㄧㄝˇ ㄇㄧㄣˊ ㄉㄠˋ ㄒㄩㄢˊ)
to liberate the people from tyranny

解紛(ㄐㄧㄝˇ ㄈㄣ)
to resolve a dispute; to disentangle

解放(ㄐㄧㄝˇ ㄈㄤˋ)
to untie or set free; to liberate; liberation

解放區(ㄐㄧㄝˇ ㄈㄤˋ ㄑㄩ)
a liberated area; an area liberated from enemy occupation

解答(ㄐㄧㄝˇ ㄉㄚˊ)
explanations or answers to certain questions; to answer or explain

解毒(ㄐㄧㄝˇ ㄉㄨˊ)
to detoxify; to neutralize poison; to antidote; detoxication

解毒劑(ㄐㄧㄝˇ ㄉㄨˊ ㄐㄧˋ)or 解毒藥(ㄐㄧㄝˇ ㄉㄨˊ ㄧㄠˋ)
an antidote

解凍(ㄐㄧㄝˇ ㄉㄨㄥˋ)
① to thaw: 魚已解凍了。The fish has thawed. ② to unfreeze (funds, assets, etc.)

解題(ㄐㄧㄝˇ ㄊㄧˊ)
explanation or answer to a problem or subject

解體(ㄐㄧㄝˇ ㄊㄧˇ)
disintegration; dissolution; to disintegrate; to fall apart; to take apart; to dismember

解脫(ㄐㄧㄝˇ ㄊㄨㄛ)
to free oneself from worldly worries; to get rid of shackles; to extricate

解囊(ㄐㄧㄝˇ ㄋㄤˊ)
to untie one's purse strings —to contribute money to charities

解纜(ㄐㄧㄝˇ ㄌㄢˇ)or 解維(ㄐㄧㄝˇ ㄨㄟˊ)
to weigh anchor; to leave port or set sail

解鈴繫鈴(ㄐㄧㄝˇ ㄌㄧㄥˊ ㄒㄧˋ ㄌㄧㄥˊ)
(literally) He who tied the bell on the tiger's neck is the only one to untie it.—He who caused the dispute is the only one to resolve it.

解詁(ㄐㄧㄝˇ ㄍㄨˇ)
explanatory notes for ancient classics; to explain ancient classics in modern language

解故(ㄐㄧㄝˇ ㄍㄨˋ)
① explanatory notes for ancient classics; to explain ancient classics in modern language ② to explain one's conduct, etc.

解雇(ㄐㄧㄝˇ ㄍㄨˋ)
to get fired; to fire; to dismiss; to discharge

解渴(ㄐㄧㄝˇ ㄎㄜˇ)
to quench thirst; to allay thirst

解開(ㄐㄧㄝˇ ㄎㄞ)
to untie; to unbind; to loosen; to undo

解扣兒(ㄐㄧㄝˇ ㄎㄡˋㄦ)
① to unbutton ② to resolve a dispute

解和(ㄐㄧㄝˇ ㄏㄜˊ)
to resolve a dispute; to mediate

解恨(ㄐㄧㄝˇ ㄏㄣˋ)
to feel satisfied or avenged; to slake one's hatred

解惑(ㄐㄧㄝˇ ㄏㄨㄛˋ)
to remove doubts

解甲歸田(ㄐㄧㄝˇ ㄐㄧㄚˇ ㄍㄨㄟ ㄊㄧㄢˊ)
(literally) to take off the armor and return to the farm—to quit military service and resume civilian life; to be demobilized

解酒(ㄐㄧㄝˇ ㄐㄧㄡˇ)
to neutralize the effect of alcoholic drinks; to alleviate a hangover

解救(ㄐㄧㄝˇ ㄐㄧㄡˋ)
to deliver (the people from tyranny, etc.); to rescue

解決(ㄐㄧㄝˇ ㄐㄩㄝˊ)
① to settle (a dispute, fight, etc.); to solve (a problem) ② to dispose of; to finish off

解決辦法(ㄐㄧㄝˇ ㄐㄩㄝˊ ㄅㄢˋ ㄈㄚˇ)
a solution (of a problem)

解氣(ㄐㄧㄝˇ ㄑㄧˋ)
to pacify; to placate; to ease anger

解勸(ㄐㄧㄝˇ ㄑㄩㄢˋ)
to pacify; to appease (an angry person, etc.); to mediate (a dispute, etc.); to patch up

解析(ㄐㄧㄝˇ ㄒㄧ)
to analyze; analysis

解析幾何(ㄐㄧㄝˇ ㄒㄧ ㄐㄧˇ ㄏㄜˊ)
analytic geometry

解職(ㄐㄧㄝˇ ㄓˊ)
to relieve someone of his duties; to dismiss or fire from office

解裝(ㄐㄧㄝˇ ㄓㄨㄤ)
(literally) to take off one's traveling clothes—to take a rest

解嘲(ㄐㄧㄝˇ ㄔㄠˊ)
to offer an explanation to save one's own face

解饞(ㄐㄧㄝˇ ㄔㄢˊ)
to satisfy a desire for delicious food

解酲(ㄐㄧㄝˇ ㄔㄥˊ)
to alleviate a hangover

解除(ㄐㄧㄝˇ ㄔㄨˊ)
① to annul or cancel (a contract, agreement, etc.) ② (law) to restore to the original status ③ to fire (a person); to relieve (a person of his duties, etc.) ④ to remove (restrictions); to get rid of

解除婚約(ㄐㄧㄝˇ ㄔㄨˊ ㄏㄨㄣ ㄩㄝ)
to renounce an engagement

解除警報(ㄐㄧㄝˇ ㄔㄨˊ ㄐㄧㄥˇ ㄅㄠˋ)
a siren signaling "all clear"

解除武裝(ㄐㄧㄝˇ ㄔㄨˊ ㄨˇ ㄓㄨㄤ)
to disarm

解釋(ㄐㄧㄝˇ ㄕˋ)
to explain; explanation; to analyze; to expound; to interpret; to account for

解事(ㄐㄧㄝˇ ㄕˋ)
clever and understanding

解手(ㄐㄧㄝˇ ㄕㄡˇ)
① to separate ② to relieve nature; to relieve oneself ③ to let go; to loosen one's grip on something

解手兒(ㄐㄧㄝˇ ㄕㄡˇㄦ)or 解溲(ㄐㄧㄝˇ ㄙㄡ)
to urinate or empty the bowels

解綬(ㄐㄧㄝˇ ㄕㄡˋ)
to resign from public office

解說(ㄐㄧㄝˇ ㄕㄨㄛ)
① to explain ② to appease; to resolve (a dispute, etc.)

解熱劑(ㄐㄧㄝˇ ㄖㄜˋ ㄐㄧˋ)
antipyretic; antipyrin(e)

解人(ㄐㄧㄝˇ ㄖㄣˊ)
a clever and understanding person; an intelligent person

解菜(ㄐㄧㄝˇ ㄘㄞˋ)
to resume eating animal food after a period of a vegetarian diet

解散(ㄐㄧㄝˇ ㄙㄢˋ)
① to dismiss (a group of soldiers in drill) ② to dissolve (a parliament, etc.); to disband (an organization, a gang, etc.)

解衣(ㄐㄧㄝˇ ㄧ)
to disrobe; to strip; to remove one's clothes; to undress

解衣推食(ㄐㄧㄝˇ ㄧ ㄊㄨㄟ ㄕˊ)
(literally) to give one's own clothes and food to others —compassionate; to treat others with friendship and sincerity

解頤(ㄐㄧㄝˇ ㄧˊ)or 解顏(ㄐㄧㄝˇ ㄧㄢˊ)
to laugh; to smile

解憂(ㄐㄧㄝˇ ㄧㄡ)
to alleviate sorrow; to relieve worries

解嚴(ㄐㄧㄝˇ ㄧㄢˊ)
to announce martial law ended

解悟(ㄐㄧㄝˇ ㄨˋ)

to realize; to understand

解危(ㄐㄧㄝˇ ㄨㄟˊ)
to head off danger

解圍(ㄐㄧㄝˇ ㄨㄟˊ)
①to resolve difficulties for others; to save others from embarrassment, etc. ②to force an enemy to raise a siege

解網(ㄐㄧㄝˇ ㄨㄤˇ)
to let loose one end of the net—merciful or lenient

解語花(ㄐㄧㄝˇ ㄩˇ ㄏㄨㄚ)
a beautiful woman

解約(ㄐㄧㄝˇ ㄩㄝ)
①to annul a contract or agreement ②to annul a marital engagement

【解】5505
2. ㄐㄧㄝˋ jieh jiè
to escort (prisoners, goods, etc.) from one place to another; to forward; to send someone in custody to; to dispatch

解差(ㄐㄧㄝˋ ㄔㄞ)
①to send prisoners from one place to another under escort ②guardsmen escorting prisoners from one place to another

解送(ㄐㄧㄝˋ ㄙㄨㄥˋ)
to transfer (a prisoner) under escort; to send (a criminal) under guard

解元(ㄐㄧㄝˋ ㄩㄢˊ)
the top candidate of the former civil service examination held on the provincial level

【解】5505
3. ㄒㄧㄝˋ shieh xiè
a Chinese family name

【觥】5506
ㄍㄨㄥ gong gōng
1. a wine vessel made of horn in ancient times
2. big; great

觥觥(ㄍㄨㄥ ㄍㄨㄥ)
straightforward; honest; upright

觥籌交錯(ㄍㄨㄥ ㄔㄡˊ ㄐㄧㄠ ㄘㄨㄛˋ)
to drink together noisily in a large party: 賓客觥籌交錯。The guests drank together noisily in the party.

觥船(ㄍㄨㄥ ㄔㄨㄢˊ)
a big wine vessel

觥羊(ㄍㄨㄥ ㄧㄤˊ)
a large sheep

七畫

【觫】5507
ㄙㄨˋ suh sù
to shrink and tremble in fear

八畫

【觭】5508
ㄐㄧ ji jī
1. (said of horns of an animal) one turning up and one turning down
2. to obtain; to get
3. odd (as contrasted to even) 亦作「奇」

觭夢(ㄐㄧ ㄇㄥˋ)
a strange dream; what one gets in a dream

觭輪(ㄐㄧ ㄌㄨㄣˊ)
a single wheel

觭偶(ㄐㄧ ㄡˇ)
odd and even 亦作「奇偶」

九畫

【觱】5509
ㄅㄧˋ bih bì
1. a chilly wind
2. water emerging from ground

觱發(ㄅㄧˋ ㄈㄚ)
a chilly wind

觱沸(ㄅㄧˋ ㄈㄟˋ)
spring water bubbling

觱篥 or 觱栗(ㄅㄧˋ ㄌㄧˋ)
an ancient windpipe musical instrument, shaped roughly like a trumpet

十畫

【觳】5510
1. ㄏㄨˊ hwu hú
1. a measure for volume in ancient times
2. to shrink and tremble in fear

觳觫(ㄏㄨˊ ㄙㄨˋ)
shrinking and trembling in fear; the appearance of fearing death

【觳】5510
2. ㄑㄩㄝˋ chiueh què
1. barren, unproductive (land)
2. simple and crude

觳土(ㄑㄩㄝˋ ㄊㄨˇ)
barren land

十一畫

【觴】5511
ㄕㄤ shang shāng
1. a general name of all sorts of wine vessels
2. to offer drinks to others

觴豆(ㄕㄤ ㄉㄡˋ)
wine vessels and food containers—wine and food

觴令(ㄕㄤ ㄌㄧㄥˋ) or 觴政(ㄕㄤ ㄓㄥˋ)
wine-drinking games conducted by an elected leader

觴詠(ㄕㄤ ㄩㄥˇ)
to compose or chant poems while drinking

十三畫

【觸】5512
ㄔㄨˋ chuh chù
1. to touch; to contact: 油漆未乾，請勿觸摸。Don't touch that paint; it's wet.
2. (said of an animal) to ram with the horn; to ram; to butt
3. to move or touch emotionally
4. to offend; to infuriate

觸媒(劑)(ㄔㄨˋ ㄇㄟˊ (ㄐㄧˋ))
a catalyst; a catalyzer; a catalytic agent

觸媒作用(ㄔㄨˋ ㄇㄟˊ ㄗㄨㄛˋ ㄩㄥˋ)
catalysis

觸霉頭(ㄔㄨˋ ㄇㄟˊ ㄊㄡˊ)
to have a stroke of bad luck; to be unfortunate

觸目皆是(ㄔㄨˋ ㄇㄨˋ ㄐㄧㄝ ㄕˋ)
can be seen everywhere; very common

觸目驚心(ㄔㄨˋ ㄇㄨˋ ㄐㄧㄥ ㄒㄧㄣ)
frightening; bloodcurdling; shocking; emotionally disturbed (by a sight)

觸發(ㄔㄨˋ ㄈㄚ)
①to touch off (a war, dispute, etc.) ②to move or touch (one's feelings)

觸犯(ㄔㄨˋ ㄈㄢˋ)
①to offend; to incur the displeasure of ②to violate or

infringe (regulations, rules, etc.)

觸電(ㄔㄨˋ ㄉㄧㄢˋ)
an electric shock; to get an electric shock

觸動(ㄔㄨˋ ㄉㄨㄥˋ)
① to touch something, and move it slightly ② to move one's heart

觸怒(ㄔㄨˋ ㄋㄨˋ)
to infuriate; to offend and cause anger

觸雷(ㄔㄨˋ ㄌㄟˊ)
(said of ships) to hit a floating mine; (said of foot soldiers) to step on a land mine

觸類旁通(ㄔㄨˋ ㄌㄟˋ ㄆㄤˊ ㄊㄨㄥ)
to draw an analogy; to understand by means of inference processes

觸感(ㄔㄨˋ ㄍㄢˇ)
the tactile impression

觸官(ㄔㄨˋ ㄍㄨㄢ)
the organ of touch or feeling

觸機(ㄔㄨˋ ㄐㄧ)
to inspire a stroke of genius; to have a brainstorm

觸擊(ㄔㄨˋ ㄐㄧˊ)
(baseball) a bunt

觸礁(ㄔㄨˋ ㄐㄧㄠ)
① to strike a submerged reef; to run aground ② to hit a snag; to meet unexpected difficulty: 我們的計畫已經觸礁。Our plans have hit a snag.

觸角(ㄔㄨˋ ㄐㄧㄠˇ)
feelers; tentacles; antennae

觸景生情(ㄔㄨˋ ㄐㄧㄥˇ ㄕㄥ ㄑㄧㄥˊ)
The scene or circumstance arouses a sense (of joy, sorrow, etc.).

觸覺(ㄔㄨˋ ㄐㄩㄝˊ)
the sense of touch

觸興(ㄔㄨˋ ㄒㄧㄥˋ)
to arouse enthusiasm or interest

觸鬚(ㄔㄨˋ ㄒㄩ)
a palpus; feelers; antennae; tentacles

觸處(ㄔㄨˋ ㄔㄨˋ)
everywhere; all over

觸脣(ㄔㄨˋ ㄔㄨㄣˊ)
the organ of touch in molluscs

觸殺(ㄔㄨˋ ㄕㄚ)
(baseball) to tag; tag

觸手(ㄔㄨˋ ㄕㄡˇ)
tentacles

觸眼(ㄔㄨˋ ㄧㄢˇ)
to strike the eye; eye-catching

觸網(ㄔㄨˋ ㄨㄤˇ)
to commit an offense against the law

十八畫

【觿】 5513
ㄒㄧ shi xi
a bodkin made of ivory, horn, etc. used for undoing knots

觿年(ㄒㄧ ㄋㄧㄢˊ)
childhood years

言部
ㄧㄢˊ yan yán

【言】 5514
ㄧㄢˊ yan yán

1. speech; words
2. to say; to talk; to speak; to mean; to express: 他常常自言自語。He often talks to himself.
3. a language; a dialect; a tongue
4. a Chinese family name
5. (now rarely) used as a particle, adverb, etc. in various ancient expressions without meaning

言必信，行必果(ㄧㄢˊ ㄅㄧˋ ㄒㄧㄣˋ, ㄒㄧㄥˊ ㄅㄧˋ ㄍㄨㄛˇ)
Promises must be kept and action must be resolute.

言必有中(ㄧㄢˊ ㄅㄧˋ ㄧㄡˇ ㄓㄨㄥˋ)
Whenever he (or she) speaks, his (or her) words sound convincing.

言不及義(ㄧㄢˊ ㄅㄨˋ ㄐㄧˊ ㄧˋ)
to make idle talks; to talk frivolously

言不盡意(ㄧㄢˊ ˙ㄅㄨ ㄐㄧㄣˋ ㄧˋ)
(often used at the end of letters) What I have said or written does not convey all in my mind.

言不出衆，貌不驚人(ㄧㄢˊ ˙ㄅㄨ ㄔㄨ ㄓㄨㄥˋ, ㄇㄠˋ ˙ㄅㄨ ㄐㄧㄥ ㄖㄣˊ)
neither outstanding in speech nor impressive in appearance—a mediocre person

言不由衷(ㄧㄢˊ ˙ㄅㄨ ㄧㄡˊ ㄓㄨㄥ)
not speaking one's mind; not to talk from the bottom of one's heart

言不應點(ㄧㄢˊ ˙ㄅㄨ ㄧㄥˋ ㄉㄧㄢˇ)
to give one's word which one does not keep; to break one's word

言明(ㄧㄢˊ ㄇㄧㄥˊ)
to state clearly; to make a statement; to declare

言多必失(ㄧㄢˊ ㄉㄨㄛ ㄅㄧˋ ㄕ)
One is bound to have a slip of the tongue if he talks too much.

言對(ㄧㄢˊ ㄉㄨㄟˋ)
① to meet and talk; to converse ② coupling of words

言動(ㄧㄢˊ ㄉㄨㄥˋ)
words and conduct; speech and behavior

言談(ㄧㄢˊ ㄊㄢˊ)
words and speech; conversation

言談林藪(ㄧㄢˊ ㄊㄢˊ ㄌㄧㄣˊ ㄙㄡˇ)
one gifted with a glib tongue; a good talker

言聽計從(ㄧㄢˊ ㄊㄧㄥ ㄐㄧˋ ㄘㄨㄥˊ)
to have full confidence in someone; to trust someone completely; to listen to every word someone says

言路(ㄧㄢˊ ㄌㄨˋ)
the channel by which one's words can reach the government

言論(ㄧㄢˊ ㄌㄨㄣˋ)
① open discussion ② speech

言論自由(ㄧㄢˊ ㄌㄨㄣˋ ㄗˋ ㄧㄡˊ)
freedom of speech

言過其實(ㄧㄢˊ ㄍㄨㄛˋ ㄑㄧˊ ㄕˊ)
to exaggerate; to boast or brag; to overstate

言歸正傳(ㄧㄢˊ ㄍㄨㄟ ㄓㄥˋ ㄓㄨㄢˋ)
Let's resume the narration. 或 Let's go back to the main topic.

言歸於好 or 言歸于好(ㄧㄢˊ ㄍㄨㄟ ㄩˊ ㄏㄠˇ)
to resume friendship; to be on good terms again; to reconcile; to be reconciled; to

maintain amicable relations hereafter
言官(ㄧㄢ ㄍㄨㄢ)
imperial censors
言和(ㄧㄢˊ ㄏㄜˊ)
to make peace; to become reconciled; to bury the hatchet (or tomahawk); to make it up: 我希望你們握手言和。I hope you shake hands and make it up.
言及(ㄧㄢˊ ㄐㄧˊ)
to talk about; to touch on; to mention
言教(ㄧㄢˊ ㄐㄧㄠˋ)
to teach by words, as distinct from by setting an example; to give verbal directions
言簡意賅(ㄧㄢˊ ㄐㄧㄢˇ ㄧˋ ㄍㄞ)
Few words were spoken, but none of the major points was missing. 或 brief and to the point; terse but comprehensive
言近指遠(ㄧㄢˊ ㄐㄧㄣˋ ㄓˇ ㄩㄢˇ)
words that carry a deeper meaning but are easily understood; to speak in plain language about something very profound in meaning
言盡於此(ㄧㄢˊ ㄐㄧㄣˋ ㄩˊ ㄘˇ)
to have said all; to have nothing more to say
言泉(ㄧㄢˊ ㄑㄩㄢˊ)
(literally) the spring of words—glib and talkative
言笑(ㄧㄢˊ ㄒㄧㄠˋ)
to talk and laugh
言行(ㄧㄢˊ ㄒㄧㄥˊ)
words and deeds; statements and actions
言行錄(ㄧㄢˊ ㄒㄧㄥˊ ㄌㄨˋ)
a book recording the words and deeds of a sage
言行相悖(ㄧㄢˊ ㄒㄧㄥˊ ㄒㄧㄤ ㄅㄟˋ)or 言行不符(ㄧㄢˊ ㄒㄧㄥˊ ㄅㄨˋ ㄈㄨˊ)
to practice against what one preaches
言行相顧(ㄧㄢˊ ㄒㄧㄥˊ ㄒㄧㄤ ㄍㄨˋ)or 言行一致(ㄧㄢˊ ㄒㄧㄥˊ ㄧˊ ㄓˋ)
words conforming to actions; to practice what one preaches
言之過早(ㄧㄢˊ ㄓ ㄍㄨㄛˋ ㄗㄠˇ)
still too early to say; premature to say
言之成理(ㄧㄢˊ ㄓ ㄔㄥˊ ㄌㄧˇ)
to present in a reasonable way; to talk sense; to speak on the strength of reason; to sound reasonable
言之有物(ㄧㄢˊ ㄓ ㄧㄡˇ ㄨˋ)
(said of a speech or writing) having substance; convincing
言者諄諄，聽者藐藐(ㄧㄢˊ ㄓㄜˇ ㄓㄨㄣ ㄓㄨㄣ, ㄊㄧㄥ ㄓㄜˇ ㄇㄧㄠˇ ㄇㄧㄠˇ)
The speaker talked with great earnestness, but the audience paid little attention.
言狀(ㄧㄢˊ ㄓㄨㄤˋ)
to describe; description
言重(ㄧㄢˊ ㄓㄨㄥˋ)
① to speak sincerely and carefully ② to use laudatory words that are unduly strong
言重九鼎(ㄧㄢˊ ㄓㄨㄥˋ ㄐㄧㄡˇ ㄉㄧㄥˇ)
One's word carries weight of nine tripods.—One's opinions are of great importance.
言差語錯(ㄧㄢˊ ㄔㄚ ㄩˇ ㄘㄨㄛˋ)
erroneous utterances; misunderstanding in verbal exchanges
言出法隨(ㄧㄢˊ ㄔㄨ ㄈㄚˇ ㄙㄨㄟˊ)
(said of a ruler) The orders, once given, will be strictly enforced.
言出如山(ㄧㄢˊ ㄔㄨ ㄖㄨˊ ㄕㄢ)
A promise is a promise.
言傳(ㄧㄢˊ ㄔㄨㄢˊ)
to explain in words
言人人殊(ㄧㄢˊ ㄖㄣˊ ㄖㄣˊ ㄕㄨ)
Everybody has a different story. 或 Everyone gives a different version.
言責(ㄧㄢˊ ㄗㄜˊ)
responsibility of offering advice or speaking honestly about public affairs
言詞 or 言辭(ㄧㄢˊ ㄘˊ)
words or expressions; statements; wording; diction
言詞辯論(ㄧㄢˊ ㄘˊ ㄅㄧㄢˋ ㄌㄨㄣˋ)
oral statements, verbal argument, or confrontation of litigants at a court of law
言三語四(ㄧㄢˊ ㄙㄢ ㄩˇ ㄙˋ)
to criticize without much thinking
言而有信(ㄧㄢˊ ㄦˊ ㄧㄡˇ ㄒㄧㄣˋ)
to be as good as one's word
言猶在耳(ㄧㄢˊ ㄧㄡˊ ㄗㄞˋ ㄦˇ)
The words are still ringing in the ear.
言偃(ㄧㄢˊ ㄧㄢˇ)
name of a disciple of Confucius 亦作「子游」
言外(ㄧㄢˊ ㄨㄞˋ)
beyond the words spoken; between the lines: 意在言外。The meaning is beyond the words spoken.
言外之意(ㄧㄢˊ ㄨㄞˋ ㄓ ㄧˋ)
hidden meaning between the lines; overtones
言爲心聲(ㄧㄢˊ ㄨㄟˊ ㄒㄧㄣ ㄕㄥ)
(literally) Speech is the voice of one's heart.—You know someone's real intention by his words.
言文對照(ㄧㄢˊ ㄨㄣˊ ㄉㄨㄟˋ ㄓㄠˋ)
writings in archaic Chinese printed side by side with the vernacular version for the benefit of modern readers
言文一致(ㄧㄢˊ ㄨㄣˊ ㄧˊ ㄓˋ)
the unification of spoken language and written language
言語
①(ㄧㄢˊ ㄩˇ) spoken language; words; speech
②(ㄧㄢˊ ·ㄩ) to report; to talk; to tell; to speak
言語妙天下(ㄧㄢˊ ㄩˇ ㄇㄧㄠˋ ㄊㄧㄢ ㄒㄧㄚˋ)
to have no peer in wisecracking
言語道斷(ㄧㄢˊ ㄩˇ ㄉㄠˋ ㄉㄨㄢˋ)
the highest principle or essence (appearing mostly in Buddhist scriptures) which can not be explained in words
言語學(ㄧㄢˊ ㄩˇ ㄒㄩㄝˊ)
philology; linguistics 亦作「語言學」
言語支吾(ㄧㄢˊ ㄩˇ ㄓ ㄨˊ)
to mince words; to mumble or stammer in an attempt to hide something; to prevaricate
言語無味(ㄧㄢˊ ㄩˇ ㄨˊ ㄨㄟˋ)
insipid talk; to keep on jawing

二畫

【計】 5515
ㄐㄧˋ jih jì

1. a scheme; a plot; a trick; a coup; a trap; a ruse
2. a plan; a program; to discuss or plan
3. to calculate; to count
4. a mechanical measuring device
5. a Chinese family name

計不得售(ㄐㄧˋ ˙ㄅㄨ ㄉㄜˊ ㄕㄡˋ)
to fail to attain the objective one has schemed for

計不出此(ㄐㄧˋ ˙ㄅㄨ ㄔㄨ ㄘˇ)
to fail to adopt the plan just described

計謀(ㄐㄧˋ ㄇㄡˊ)
a scheme; to scheme; a contrivance or device

計分(ㄐㄧˋ ㄈㄣ)
①to count scores or points ②divided or classified as follows

計吏(ㄐㄧˋ ㄌㄧˋ)
an official in charge of accounts in a feudal principality during the Han Dynasty

計量(ㄐㄧˋ ㄌㄧㄤˊ)
to calculate; to weigh; to estimate

計略(ㄐㄧˋ ㄌㄩㄝˋ)
to scheme; to deliberate; a scheme

計開(ㄐㄧˋ ㄎㄞ)
to list item by item as follows

計畫 or 計劃(ㄐㄧˋ ㄏㄨㄚˋ)
a plan; a program; to plan; to devise

計畫經濟 or 計劃經濟(ㄐㄧˋ ㄏㄨㄚˋ ㄐㄧㄥ ㄐㄧˋ)
planned economy

計畫中 or 計劃中(ㄐㄧˋ ㄏㄨㄚˋ ㄓㄨㄥ)
under consideration or contemplation

計畫生產 or 計劃生產(ㄐㄧˋ ㄏㄨㄚˋ ㄕㄥ ㄔㄢˇ)
planned production; production according to plan

計畫書 or 計劃書(ㄐㄧˋ ㄏㄨㄚˋ ㄕㄨ)
a prospectus (of a business setup or factory)

計較(ㄐㄧˋ ㄐㄧㄠˋ) or (ㄐㄧˋ ㄐㄧㄠˇ)
①to dispute; to haggle; to fuss about ②to discuss; to talk it over; to negotiate ③to mind; to care ④to plan

計件(ㄐㄧˋ ㄐㄧㄢˋ)
to reckon by the piece

計件工資(ㄐㄧˋ ㄐㄧㄢˋ ㄍㄨㄥ ㄗ)
wages paid on a piecework basis

計窮(ㄐㄧˋ ㄑㄩㄥˊ)
to be at the end of one's wits; to be at the end of one's rope

計程(ㄐㄧˋ ㄔㄥˊ)
to calculate according to mileage

計程車(ㄐㄧˋ ㄔㄥˊ ㄔㄜ)
a taxi

計出萬全(ㄐㄧˋ ㄔㄨ ㄨㄢˋ ㄑㄩㄢˊ)
a foolproof plan or scheme

計時(ㄐㄧˋ ㄕˊ)
to count time to see how long something lasts

計時表(ㄐㄧˋ ㄕˊ ㄅㄧㄠˇ)
a chronometer

計時工資(ㄐㄧˋ ㄕˊ ㄍㄨㄥ ㄗ)
wages paid on a time basis; time wages

計上心來(ㄐㄧˋ ㄕㄤˋ ㄒㄧㄣ ㄌㄞˊ)
to come across a scheme; to hit upon an idea

計數(ㄐㄧˋ ㄕㄨˋ)
to count

計策(ㄐㄧˋ ㄘㄜˋ)
a scheme; a device; a trick or trap

計算(ㄐㄧˋ ㄙㄨㄢˋ)
①to calculate; calculation; to count; to weigh: 他正在計算出席人數。He is counting the number of people present. ②to consider

計算機(ㄐㄧˋ ㄙㄨㄢˋ ㄐㄧ)
an adding machine; a calculating machine; a computer

計算器(ㄐㄧˋ ㄙㄨㄢˋ ㄑㄧˋ)
a calculating device (such as an abacus, a slide rule, etc.)

計算尺(ㄐㄧˋ ㄙㄨㄢˋ ㄔˇ)
a slide rule

計議(ㄐㄧˋ ㄧˋ)
to negotiate; to discuss; to talk it over; to consider; to deliberate; to consult: 這件事我們要從長計議。We'll discuss this matter in detail.

計無所出(ㄐㄧˋ ㄨˊ ㄙㄨㄛˇ ㄔㄨ)
unable to think of a way (to cope with a situation, etc.); to be at the end of one's rope

【訂】 5516
ㄉㄧㄥˋ dinq dìng

1. to draw up or conclude (a contract, treaty, agreement, etc.)
2. to subscribe to (a magazine, newspaper, etc.)
3. to edit; to collate; to revise; to make corrections
4. to arrange; to settle; to fix
5. to make reservations (in a hotel, restaurant, etc.)

訂報(ㄉㄧㄥˋ ㄅㄠˋ)
to subscribe to a newspaper

訂盟(ㄉㄧㄥˋ ㄇㄥˊ)
to conclude or sign a treaty of alliance

訂明(ㄉㄧㄥˋ ㄇㄧㄥˊ)
to specify clearly in a contract or agreement

訂房間(ㄉㄧㄥˋ ㄈㄤˊ ㄐㄧㄢ)
to make room reservations: 你訂房間沒有? Have you made your room reservations?

訂定(ㄉㄧㄥˋ ㄉㄧㄥˋ)
①to fix or arrange beforehand ②(law) specified in a contract or agreement between the two parties concerned

訂條約(ㄉㄧㄥˋ ㄊㄧㄠˊ ㄩㄝ)
to sign a treaty; to conclude a treaty

訂立(ㄉㄧㄥˋ ㄌㄧˋ)
to conclude or sign (a contract, agreement, treaty, etc.)

訂購(ㄉㄧㄥˋ ㄍㄡˋ)
to place a mail order for; to order (a product) in advance: 她訂購了一些新衣。She has ordered some new clothes.

訂戶(ㄉㄧㄥˋ ㄏㄨˋ)
①a subscriber (to a newspaper, etc.) ②a person with a standing order for milk, etc.

訂貨(ㄉㄧㄥˋ ㄏㄨㄛˋ)
to place an order for goods

訂貨單(ㄉㄧㄥˋ ㄏㄨㄛˋ ㄉㄢ) or 訂單(ㄉㄧㄥˋ ㄉㄢ)
an order form (or blank); a list of goods ordered

訂婚(ㄉㄧㄥˋ ㄏㄨㄣ)
to engage or betroth; an engagement; a betrothal

訂機票(ㄉㄧㄥˋ ㄐㄧ ㄆㄧㄠˋ)
to book for a seat aboard a passenger liner

訂交(ㄉㄧㄥˋ ㄐㄧㄠ)
to establish friendly relations with...

訂正(ㄉㄧㄥˋ ㄓㄥˋ)
to revise; to correct: 如有錯誤，請予以訂正。Correct errors, if any.

訂車票(ㄉㄧㄥˋ ㄔㄜ ㄆㄧㄠˋ)
to book for a seat aboard a bus or train

訂書(ㄉㄧㄥˋ ㄕㄨ)
to order books

訂雜誌(ㄉㄧㄥˋ ㄗㄚˊ ㄓˋ)
to subscribe to a magazine

訂座(ㄉㄧㄥˋ ㄗㄨㄛˋ)
to make reservations for seats in theaters, restaurants, etc.

訂約(ㄉㄧㄥˋ ㄩㄝ)
to conclude or sign a contract, agreement or treaty

訂閱(ㄉㄧㄥˋ ㄩㄝˋ)
to subscribe to (a publication); subscription

【訆】 5517
ㄐㄧㄠˋ jiaw jiào

1. to call in a loud voice; to yell or scream
2. to tell a falsehood; to talk wildly

【訃】 5518
ㄈㄨˋ fuh fù

a notice announcing the death of a person; an obituary

訃告(ㄈㄨˋ ㄍㄠˋ) or 訃聞(ㄈㄨˋ ㄨㄣˊ)
an obituary notice

【訇】 5519
ㄏㄨㄥ hong hōng

1. loudly; stentorian
2. a Chinese family name

訇訇(ㄏㄨㄥ ㄏㄨㄥ)
loud(ly); stentorian

訇哮(ㄏㄨㄥ ㄒㄧㄠ)
roaring (winds)

訇然(ㄏㄨㄥ ㄖㄢˊ)
loudly; stentorian

三畫

【討】 5520
ㄊㄠˇ tao tǎo

1. to quell (an uprising, or rebellion); to punish; to suppress; to put down
2. to denounce; to condemn
3. to marry (a wife or concubine)
4. to demand; to beg for; to get
5. to study; to examine into; to research
6. (now rarely) to govern; to administer

討便宜(ㄊㄠˇ ㄆㄧㄢˊ ˙ㄧ)
to seek profit or benefit in an improper way; to seek undue advantage: 不要讓他討(了)便宜。Don't let him seek undue advantage.

討沒趣(ㄊㄠˇ ㄇㄟˊ ㄑㄩˋ)
to ask for an insult; to make a request which is most likely to be rejected; to offer advice or service when it is not needed

討伐(ㄊㄠˇ ㄈㄚˊ)
to quell (an uprising, a rebellion, etc.); to punish (another nation, etc.) by force of arms

討飯(ㄊㄠˇ ㄈㄢˋ)
to beg for food; to be a beggar

討飯的(ㄊㄠˇ ㄈㄢˋ ˙ㄉㄜ)
a beggar

討亂(ㄊㄠˇ ㄌㄨㄢˋ)
to quell an uprising or a rebellion; to launch a punitive campaign against rebels

討論(ㄊㄠˇ ㄌㄨㄣˋ)
to discuss; discussion

討論會(ㄊㄠˇ ㄌㄨㄣˋ ㄏㄨㄟˋ)
a discussion meeting; a forum; a symposium

討個吉利(ㄊㄠˇ ˙ㄍㄜ ㄐㄧˊ ㄌㄧˋ)
to ask for something as a token of good omen

討愧(ㄊㄠˇ ㄎㄨㄟˋ)
to be ashamed

討海人(ㄊㄠˇ ㄏㄞˇ ㄖㄣˊ)
a fisherman

討好(ㄊㄠˇ ㄏㄠˇ)
① to curry favor; to please; to fawn on ② to be rewarded with a fruitful result

討價還價(ㄊㄠˇ ㄐㄧㄚˋ ㄏㄨㄢˊ ㄐㄧㄚˋ)
to haggle over prices; to bargain

討教(ㄊㄠˇ ㄐㄧㄠˋ)
(a polite expression) May I ask for your advice (or esteemed view)? 我來討教，不是來爭論。I come to ask for advice, not to argue.

討究(ㄊㄠˇ ㄐㄧㄡˋ)
to study and find the truth

討救兵(ㄊㄠˇ ㄐㄧㄡˋ ㄅㄧㄥ)
① to ask for relieving troops; to request for reinforcement ② to seek help

討賤(ㄊㄠˇ ㄐㄧㄢˋ)
to ask for insult, belittlement, etc. through lack of self-respect or self-restraint

討巧(ㄊㄠˇ ㄑㄧㄠˇ)
to try to gain advantage, benefit, etc. with little effort; to try to use finesse or take a snap course to attain one's end

討錢(ㄊㄠˇ ㄑㄧㄢˊ)
to ask for money; to ask for repayment

討親(ㄊㄠˇ ㄑㄧㄣ)
to take a wife

討情(ㄊㄠˇ ㄑㄧㄥˊ)
to ask for forgiveness; to plead for leniency

討取(ㄊㄠˇ ㄑㄩˇ)
to ask for something; to demand

討媳婦(ㄊㄠˇ ㄒㄧˊ ˙ㄈㄨ)
to get a wife for one's son

討嫌(ㄊㄠˇ ㄒㄧㄢˊ)
to incur dislike or disgust; disgusting; repulsive; revolting

討債(ㄊㄠˇ ㄓㄞˋ)
to demand repayment of a loan

討債鬼(ㄊㄠˇ ㄓㄞˋ ㄍㄨㄟˇ)
① (literally) devils asking for repayment—one's own children who died young ② an importunate or insistent person whom one finds it difficult to deal with

討賬(ㄊㄠˇ ㄓㄤˋ) or 討帳(ㄊㄠˇ ㄓㄤˋ)
to ask for repayment of a loan; to collect bills overdue; to demand the payment of a debt

討賞(ㄊㄠˇ ㄕㄤˇ)

to ask for a reward or gratuity

討生活(ㄊㄠˇ ㄕㄥ ㄏㄨㄛˊ)
to make a living: 爲了討生活，他不得不辛苦工作。He had to work hard to make a living.

討饒(ㄊㄠˇ ㄖㄠˊ)
to ask for mercy; to ask for leniency

討人喜歡(ㄊㄠˇ ㄖㄣˊ ㄒㄧˇ ˙ㄏㄨㄢ)
likable; cute; pretty; charming; delightful: 她是個非常討人喜歡的小女孩。She's a very likable little girl.

討人嫌(ㄊㄠˇ ㄖㄣˊ ㄒㄧㄢˊ)
to incur dislike or disgust; annoying: 你眞討人嫌。How annoying you are!

討賊(ㄊㄠˇ ㄗㄟˊ)
to punish the rebels by force

討厭(ㄊㄠˇ ㄧㄢˋ)
troublesome; disgusting; nasty; to dislike; to incur dislike or disgust

【訐】 5521 ㄐㄧㄝˊ jye jié

1. to pry into or expose another's secret
2. to accuse or charge; to defame; to malign (a person)

訐直(ㄐㄧㄝˊ ㄓˊ)
to blame someone bluntly for his faults

訐揚(ㄐㄧㄝˊ ㄧㄤˊ)
to expose or reveal the faults of another

【訊】 5522 ㄒㄩㄣˋ shiunn xùn

1. to ask; to inquire; to question
2. information; news
3. to put on trial; to question in court; to interrogate; interrogation

訊辦(ㄒㄩㄣˋ ㄅㄢˋ)
to put on trial and convict; to prosecute

訊斷(ㄒㄩㄣˋ ㄉㄨㄢˋ)
to hand down a judgment or verdict

訊聽(ㄒㄩㄣˋ ㄊㄧㄥ)
to make inquiries 亦作「打聽」

訊供(ㄒㄩㄣˋ ㄍㄨㄥ)
interrogations and confessions in a court of law

訊鞫(ㄒㄩㄣˋ ㄐㄩˊ)
to hold a trial

訊息(ㄒㄩㄣˋ ㄒㄧˊ)
news; information; tidings; messages 亦作「音訊」

訊問(ㄒㄩㄣˋ ㄨㄣˋ)
①to cross-examine; to interrogate ② correspondence

【訌】 5523 ㄏㄨㄥˊ horng hóng

confusion; discord; strife; a quarrel

【訓】 5524 ㄒㄩㄣˋ shiunn xùn

1. to lecture; to instruct; to teach; to exhort; to admonish; a lecture; a scolding: 我被他教訓了一番。I received a scolding from him.
2. (to serve as) a lesson; a model: 那不足爲訓。It is not fit to serve as a model.
3. an old proverb, motto, etc.

訓蒙(ㄒㄩㄣˋ ㄇㄥˊ)
to tutor children; to teach young boys and girls

訓勉(ㄒㄩㄣˋ ㄇㄧㄢˇ)
to exhort and encourage

訓導(ㄒㄩㄣˋ ㄉㄠˇ)
to teach and guide

訓導長(ㄒㄩㄣˋ ㄉㄠˇ ㄓㄤˇ)
the dean of students (at a university)

訓導主任(ㄒㄩㄣˋ ㄉㄠˇ ㄓㄨˇ ㄖㄣˋ)
the dean of students (at a primary school or high school)

訓導處(ㄒㄩㄣˋ ㄉㄠˇ ㄔㄨˋ)
an office of the dean of students

訓迪(ㄒㄩㄣˋ ㄉㄧˊ)
to teach and enlighten (the young)

訓典(ㄒㄩㄣˋ ㄉㄧㄢˇ)
books authored by sages and good emperors of ancient times

訓練(ㄒㄩㄣˋ ㄌㄧㄢˋ)
to drill; to train; training

訓練班(ㄒㄩㄣˋ ㄌㄧㄢˋ ㄅㄢ)
a training class

訓練所(ㄒㄩㄣˋ ㄌㄧㄢˋ ㄙㄨㄛˇ)
a training institute

訓令(ㄒㄩㄣˋ ㄌㄧㄥˋ)
instructions from a superior office

訓詁(ㄒㄩㄣˋ ㄍㄨˇ)
explanatory notes in ancient books

訓詁學(ㄒㄩㄣˋ ㄍㄨˇ ㄒㄩㄝˊ)
scholium

訓詁學者(ㄒㄩㄣˋ ㄍㄨˇ ㄒㄩㄝˊ ㄓㄜˇ)
a scholiast

訓話(ㄒㄩㄣˋ ㄏㄨㄚˋ)
a speech of exhortation; to lecture; to exhort

訓誨(ㄒㄩㄣˋ ㄏㄨㄟˋ)
to teach and exhort the younger generation; to instruct

訓誡(ㄒㄩㄣˋ ㄐㄧㄝˋ)
to exhort and warn; to admonish; exhortation and warning

訓政(ㄒㄩㄣˋ ㄓㄥˋ)
①political tutelage ②(Ching Dynasty) participation in political affairs by the abdicated emperor or the empress dowager

訓政時期(ㄒㄩㄣˋ ㄓㄥˋ ㄕˊ ㄑㄧˊ)
the period of political tutelage (in the early years of the Chinese Republic before the adoption of the Constitution in 1946)

訓斥(ㄒㄩㄣˋ ㄔˋ)
to scold a junior or subordinate severely; to reprimand; to rebuke; to dress down

訓飭(ㄒㄩㄣˋ ㄔˋ)
to admonish and censure a junior or subordinate severely

訓示(ㄒㄩㄣˋ ㄕˋ)
instructions; to admonish

訓人(ㄒㄩㄣˋ ㄖㄣˊ)
①(an old usage) the teacher, tutor or master ②to exhort people

訓詞(ㄒㄩㄣˋ ㄘˊ)
a speech of exhortation or admonition; instructions

訓誘(ㄒㄩㄣˋ ㄧㄡˋ)
to teach and lead on

訓育(ㄒㄩㄣˋ ㄩˋ)
to educate and train

訓諭(ㄒㄩㄣˋ ㄩˋ)
to instruct; instructions from a superior or elder

【訕】 5525 ㄕㄢˋ shann shàn

1. to laugh at; to sneer
2. to slander; to abuse
3. embarrassed; awkward; shame-

faced
訕謗(ㄕㄢˋ ㄅㄤˋ)
to slander; to libel; to backbite
訕臉(ㄕㄢˋ ㄌㄧㄢˇ)
brazen; shameless
訕笑(ㄕㄢˋ ㄒㄧㄠˋ)
to laugh or sneer at; to ridicule; to mock; to deride
訕上(ㄕㄢˋ ㄕㄤˋ)
to slander one's superiors

【訖】 5526 ㄑㄧˋ chih qì

1. to come to an end; to conclude; cleared or settled
2. until; up to 亦作「迄」

訖了(ㄑㄧˋ ㄌㄧㄠˇ)
to end; to conclude

【託】 5527 ㄊㄨㄛ tuo tuō

1. to commission; to entrust to; to charge with; to rely on
2. to ask; to request
3. to consign; consignment
4. to use as an excuse or pretext
5. (said of a dead person, etc.) to appear (in a dream)
6. to send (messages, etc.) indirectly

託辦(ㄊㄨㄛ ㄅㄢˋ)
to consign; to do something entrusted by others
託庇(ㄊㄨㄛ ㄅㄧˋ)
① to seek protection ② (a polite expression) Thanks for your protection.
託病(ㄊㄨㄛ ㄅㄧㄥˋ)
on the pretext of being ill; to use illness as an excuse: 他託病不去學校。He used his illness as an excuse for not going to school.
託夢(ㄊㄨㄛ ㄇㄥˋ)
(said of a dead person) to appear in one's dream
託名(ㄊㄨㄛ ㄇㄧㄥˊ)
① to acquire influence by making use of the name of a more prestigious person ② to assume another's name
託分(ㄊㄨㄛ ㄈㄣˋ)
to seek escape in doing something which has nothing to do with one's regular duties or career 亦作「託迹」
託諷(ㄊㄨㄛ ㄈㄥˋ)
to give vent to one's feelings in writing
託福(ㄊㄨㄛ ㄈㄨˊ)
(a polite expression) Thank you.
託福考試(ㄊㄨㄛ ㄈㄨˊ ㄎㄠˇ ㄕˋ)
TOEFL (Test of English as a Foreign Language) administered by the Educational Testing Service for foreign students who wish to pursue advanced studies in the U.S.亦作「托福測驗」
託付(ㄊㄨㄛ ㄈㄨˋ)
to entrust to ; to commission
託大(ㄊㄨㄛ ㄉㄚˋ)
self-important; conceited; to act arrogantly
託辣斯(ㄊㄨㄛ ㄌㄚˋ ㄙ)
(business) a trust 亦作「托辣斯」
託孤(ㄊㄨㄛ ㄍㄨ)or託孤寄命(ㄊㄨㄛ ㄍㄨ ㄐㄧˋ ㄇㄧㄥˋ)
to entrust an orphan to the care of a guardian
託故(ㄊㄨㄛ ㄍㄨˋ)
to make an excuse; to find a pretext: 他託故不來。He did not come under some pretexts.
託管(ㄊㄨㄛ ㄍㄨㄢˇ)
trusteeship; a mandate; to trust; to mandate
託管理事會(ㄊㄨㄛ ㄍㄨㄢˇ ㄌㄧˇ ㄕˋ ㄏㄨㄟˋ)
Trusteeship Council (of the United Nations)
託管領土(ㄊㄨㄛ ㄍㄨㄢˇ ㄌㄧㄥˇ ㄊㄨˇ)
trust territories; mandatory territories
託管權(ㄊㄨㄛ ㄍㄨㄢˇ ㄑㄩㄢˊ)
mandatory powers
託迹(ㄊㄨㄛ ㄐㄧ)
to seek escape in doing something which has nothing to do with one's regular duties or career
託疾(ㄊㄨㄛ ㄐㄧˊ)
to use poor health as an excuse
託交(ㄊㄨㄛ ㄐㄧㄠ)
① c/o; to deliver (something) in care of somebody ② to befriend; to make friends with
託情(ㄊㄨㄛ ㄑㄧㄥˊ)
to take advantage of personal friendship to gain a special privilege or favor
託之空言(ㄊㄨㄛ ㄓ ㄎㄨㄥ ㄧㄢˊ)
to give empty promises; to pay lip service
託處(ㄊㄨㄛ ㄔㄨˇ)
to lodge at places other than one's own home
託食(ㄊㄨㄛ ㄕˊ)
to eat meals at a friend's or relative's home
託實(ㄊㄨㄛ ㄕˊ)
to receive gifts or presents and take it for granted
託始(ㄊㄨㄛ ㄕˇ)
the beginning; the origin
託身(ㄊㄨㄛ ㄕㄣ)
to entrust oneself to; to live at a friend's or relative's place
託生(ㄊㄨㄛ ㄕㄥ)
(Chinese mythology) reincarnation of ghosts
託人(ㄊㄨㄛ ㄖㄣˊ)
to ask somebody to do something for oneself; to entrust to someone
託足(ㄊㄨㄛ ㄗㄨˊ)
to lodge at places other than one's home
託辭(ㄊㄨㄛ ㄘˊ)
to make excuses; pretexts or excuses: 他說有事，不過是託辭。He said he was busy, but that was just an excuse.
託兒所(ㄊㄨㄛ ㄦˊ ㄙㄨㄛˇ)
a public nursery
託言(ㄊㄨㄛ ㄧㄢˊ)
to make excuses
託運(ㄊㄨㄛ ㄩㄣˋ)
to consign for shipment; to check: 他將行李託運至台中。He checked his baggage to Taichung.

【記】 5528 ㄐㄧˋ jih jì

1. to remember; to call to mind; to bear or keep in mind
2. to record; to register
3. a book recording persons or things, anecdotes, etc.
4. seals or chops; a sign; a mark

記不得(ㄐㄧˋ ˙ㄅㄨ ㄉㄜˊ)
unable to remember or recall
記不清(ㄐㄧˋ ˙ㄅㄨ ㄑㄧㄥ)

unable to remember exactly

記名(ㄐㄧˋ ㄇㄧㄥˊ)
①to record the name; to sign ② registered (stock, bonds, etc.)

記名投票(ㄐㄧˋ ㄇㄧㄥˊ ㄊㄡˊ ㄆㄧㄠˋ)
to vote with signed ballot; open ballot 參看「無記名投票」

記分(ㄐㄧˋ ㄈㄣ)
①to record scores or points ②to register a student's mark

記分員(ㄐㄧˋ ㄈㄣ ㄩㄢˊ)
a scorekeeper; a scorer; a marker

記得(ㄐㄧˋ ˙ㄉㄜ)
to remember; to have not forgotten: 我還記得他的模樣兒。I still remember what he looked like.

記念(ㄐㄧˋ ㄋㄧㄢˋ)
to remember or commemorate 亦作「紀念」

記牢(ㄐㄧˋ ㄌㄠˊ)
to commit to memory firmly

記錄(ㄐㄧˋ ㄌㄨˋ)
①to record; to put on record; to note down ②a note-taker ③minutes of a meeting; a record 亦作「紀錄」

記錄片(ㄐㄧˋ ㄌㄨˋ ㄆㄧㄢˋ)
a documentary film; a documentary

記掛(ㄐㄧˋ ㄍㄨㄚˋ)
to remember and be anxious about; to be constantly on one's mind; to miss

記過(ㄐㄧˋ ㄍㄨㄛˋ)
to record a demerit

記功(ㄐㄧˋ ㄍㄨㄥ)
to record a merit

記功碑(ㄐㄧˋ ㄍㄨㄥ ㄅㄟ)
a tablet on which the merits of a person or persons are recorded

記號(ㄐㄧˋ ㄏㄠˋ)
a mark; a sign; a symbol

記恨(ㄐㄧˋ ㄏㄣˋ)
to bear a grudge: 他對我記恨。He bears me a grudge.

記取(ㄐㄧˋ ㄑㄩˇ)
to remember or bear in mind (this lesson, defeat, etc.): 你須將欲速則不達一語記取在心。You must bear in mind that haste makes waste.

記下來(ㄐㄧˋ ㄒㄧㄚˋ ˙ㄌㄞ)
to take down (dictation, etc.); to make a note of

記性(ㄐㄧˋ ˙ㄒㄧㄥ)
memory; the power of recollection

記性好(ㄐㄧˋ ˙ㄒㄧㄥ ㄏㄠˇ)
a powerful memory: 他的記性好。He has a powerful memory.

記性壞(ㄐㄧˋ ˙ㄒㄧㄥ ㄏㄨㄞˋ)
a poor memory

記敍文(ㄐㄧˋ ㄒㄩˋ ㄨㄣˊ)
a written narration; narrative writing

記者(ㄐㄧˋ ㄓㄜˇ)
a reporter; a newsman; a journalist: 一位地方記者報導這個故事。A local reporter covered the story.

記者公會(ㄐㄧˋ ㄓㄜˇ ㄍㄨㄥ ㄏㄨㄟˋ)
a newsmen's association, federation or league

記者節(ㄐㄧˋ ㄓㄜˇ ㄐㄧㄝˊ)
Journalist's Day (on September 1)

記者席(ㄐㄧˋ ㄓㄜˇ ㄒㄧˊ)
seats reserved for the press; a press gallery; a press box; a press stand

記者招待會(ㄐㄧˋ ㄓㄜˇ ㄓㄠ ㄉㄞˋ ㄏㄨㄟˋ)
a press conference

記賬(ㄐㄧˋ ㄓㄤˋ)
①to buy or sell on credit; to charge to an account ② to record buying, selling, etc. in books

記賬員(ㄐㄧˋ ㄓㄤˋ ㄩㄢˊ)
a bookkeeper

記住(ㄐㄧˋ ˙ㄓㄨ)
Remember! 或 to bear in mind: 記住我告訴你的話。Remember what I told you.

記傳體(ㄐㄧˋ ㄓㄨㄢˋ ㄊㄧˇ)
the style of writing recording historical facts

記仇(ㄐㄧˋ ㄔㄡˊ)
to bear a grudge; to harbor or nourish hatred

記室(ㄐㄧˋ ㄕˋ)
a secretary or clerk

記事(ㄐㄧˋ ㄕˋ)
to record facts; to make a memorandum of events

記事簿(ㄐㄧˋ ㄕˋ ㄅㄨˋ)
a notebook

記事牌(ㄐㄧˋ ㄕˋ ㄆㄞˊ)
a blackboard recording things to be done on certain days

記述(ㄐㄧˋ ㄕㄨˋ)
to record and narrate

記述體(ㄐㄧˋ ㄕㄨˋ ㄊㄧˇ)
the narrative style of writing

記入(ㄐㄧˋ ㄖㄨˋ)
to enter… in; to make an entry

記載(ㄐㄧˋ ㄗㄞˇ)
to record; an account: 警察詳細記載事情經過。The policeman recorded the incident in detail.

記錯(ㄐㄧˋ ㄘㄨㄛˋ)
①to remember incorrectly ②to make an incorrect entry in a book; to record or list something erroneously

記誦(ㄐㄧˋ ㄙㄨㄥˋ)
to recite; to commit to memory (by rote)

記憶(ㄐㄧˋ ㄧˋ)
memory or recollection: 這是我記憶中最熱的夏季。This is the hottest summer in my recollection.

記憶力(ㄐㄧˋ ㄧˋ ㄌㄧˋ)
the faculty of memory or recollection; a retentive faculty

記憶畫(ㄐㄧˋ ㄧˋ ㄏㄨㄚˋ)
memory drawing

記憶猶新(ㄐㄧˋ ㄧˋ ㄧㄡˊ ㄒㄧㄣ)
The memory is still fresh.

記言(ㄐㄧˋ ㄧㄢˊ)
a record of lectures, sayings, verbal teachings in writing

記問之學(ㄐㄧˋ ㄨㄣˋ ㄓ ㄒㄩㄝˊ)
learning that consists in repeating to students what one has read from ancient classics without proper reorganization or digestion

【訑】 5529
1. ㄧˊ yi yí
overbearing; assuming; self-satisfaction

【訑】 5529
2.ㄊㄨㄛˊ two tuó
to cheat

【訒】 5530
ㄖㄣˋ renn rèn
difficult to speak out; cau-

〔言部〕

tious in speech

【訏】 5531 ㄒㄩ shiu xū
1. boasts; braggings
2. big; great
3. to sigh

四畫

【訟】 5532 ㄙㄨㄥˋ song sòng
1. a lawsuit; litigation; to bring a dispute to court
2. to argue over the right and wrong of something; to dispute; to demand justice
3. publicly; in public
4. (now rarely) to accuse; to regret; to repent; to blame

訟費(ㄙㄨㄥˋ ㄈㄟˋ)
fees entailed in a lawsuit

訟牒(ㄙㄨㄥˋ ㄉㄧㄝˊ)
the plaintiff's written complaint

訟庭(ㄙㄨㄥˋ ㄊㄧㄥˊ)
a court of law

訟棍(ㄙㄨㄥˋ ㄍㄨㄣˋ)
pettifoggers; those who foment litigation; shysters: 他爲訟棍所害。He was the victim of a pettifogger.

訟事(ㄙㄨㄥˋ ㄕˋ)
a lawsuit; litigation

訟案(ㄙㄨㄥˋ ㄢˋ)
a case at law: 政府贏得那件訟案。The government won that case.

訟言(ㄙㄨㄥˋ ㄧㄢˊ)
to speak in public; to announce or declare

訟獄(ㄙㄨㄥˋ ㄩˋ)
litigation; lawsuits

【訛】 5533 ㄜˊ er é
1. rumors
2. errors; erroneous; wrong
3. to extort; to swindle; to deceive; to bluff
4. to move about
5. to change or transform
6. a Chinese family name

訛奪(ㄜˊ ㄉㄨㄛˊ)
errors or omissions in writing

訛詐(ㄜˊ ㄓㄚˋ)
to extort; to blackmail; to swindle: 他訛詐她的錢。He extorted money from her.

訛傳(ㄜˊ ㄔㄨㄢˊ)
false rumors; wrong information; erroneously reported

訛舛(ㄜˊ ㄔㄨㄢˇ)
mistakes; errors

訛字(ㄜˊ ㄗˋ)
the corrupted form of a character

訛音(ㄜˊ ㄧㄣ)
inaccurate or improper pronunciation

訛誤(ㄜˊ ㄨˋ)
errors; mistakes; inaccurate or wrong

【訝】 5534 ㄧㄚˋ yah yà
1. surprised or to express surprise; to wonder: 你的行爲使我驚訝。I'm surprised at you.
2. (now rarely) to welcome or receive 亦作「迓」

【訢】 5535 ㄒㄧㄣ shin xīn
joy; delight; happy

訢訢(ㄒㄧㄣ ㄒㄧㄣ)
joyfully

訢然(ㄒㄧㄣ ㄖㄢˊ)
very pleased; happy

【訣】 5536 ㄐㄩㄝˊ jyue jué
1. to part; to separate
2. sorcery; an esoteric or occult art
3. a way or formula of doing something; the secret or knack of doing things

訣別(ㄐㄩㄝˊ ㄅㄧㄝˊ)
① to say good-bye; to bid farewell ② to part forever

訣竅(ㄐㄩㄝˊ ㄑㄧㄠˋ)
the secret or knack of doing something: 老實說,我不懂其中之訣竅。To tell the truth, I can't get the knack of it.

訣要(ㄐㄩㄝˊ ㄧㄠˋ)
① a secret, occult art or way ② the secret or knack of doing something

【訥】 5537 ㄋㄜˋ neh nè (又讀 ㄋㄚˋ nah nà)
slow of speech; to stammer

訥口(ㄋㄜˋ ㄎㄡˇ)
slow of speech

訥澀(ㄋㄜˋ ㄙㄜˋ)
slow of speech; to stammer

【訩】 5538 ㄒㄩㄥ shiong xiōng
1. (said of a crowd) noisy; loudly arguing
2. litigation; to be engaged in a lawsuit
3. disorders; miseries

訩訩(ㄒㄩㄥ ㄒㄩㄥ)
(said of a crowd) noisy; loudly arguing

【訪】 5539 ㄈㄤˇ faang fǎng
1. to visit; to call on
2. to inquire of or to look for; to find out
3. a Chinese family name

訪古(ㄈㄤˇ ㄍㄨˇ)
to search for ancient relics

訪客(ㄈㄤˇ ㄎㄜˋ)
a visitor; a caller: 訪客只留下了名片。The caller merely left her card.

訪求(ㄈㄤˇ ㄑㄧㄡˊ)
to seek; to look for; to search for

訪親(ㄈㄤˇ ㄑㄧㄣ)
① to look for a relative ② to visit a kinsman

訪賢(ㄈㄤˇ ㄒㄧㄢˊ)
to search for or call upon men of virtue and ability; to inquire and search for worthies

訪查(ㄈㄤˇ ㄔㄚˊ)
to inquire about and investigate

訪友(ㄈㄤˇ ㄧㄡˇ)
to visit friends; to call on friends

訪問(ㄈㄤˇ ㄨㄣˋ)
to visit; visiting (missions); to call upon; to interview

訪問團(ㄈㄤˇ ㄨㄣˋ ㄊㄨㄢˊ)
a visiting mission

訪員(ㄈㄤˇ ㄩㄢˊ)
a reporter or correspondent sent by a press agency

【設】 5540 ㄕㄜˋ sheh shè
1. to lay out; to display
2. to establish; to set up; to found
3. to furnish; to provide
4. to arrange; to plan or devise
5. supposing that; what if; in case of

設備(ㄕㄜˋ ㄅㄟˋ)
① equipment; installations; facilities: 設備簡陋。Equip-

ment is simple and common. ②to get prepared militarily; defense works

設法(ㄕㄜˋ ㄈㄚˇ)
to think up a method; to devise a way; to try: 那個樂團正設法找個大提琴手。That orchestra is trying to find a cellist.

設防(ㄕㄜˋ ㄈㄤˊ)
to fortify; to set up defense installations; to garrison: 他們在該城設防抗敵。They fortify the town against the enemy.

設防城市(ㄕㄜˋ ㄈㄤˊ ㄔㄥˊ ㄕˋ)
a fortified city

設伏(ㄕㄜˋ ㄈㄨˊ)
to lay an ambush: 我們設伏待敵。We laid an ambush for the enemy.

設奠(ㄕㄜˋ ㄉㄧㄢˋ)
to offer sacrifices to the newly dead

設定(ㄕㄜˋ ㄉㄧㄥˋ)
(law) to establish legal relationship

設立(ㄕㄜˋ ㄌㄧˋ)
to establish; to set up: 我們將在此地設立一所學校。We'll set up a school here.

設或(ㄕㄜˋ ㄏㄨㄛˋ)
supposing that; what if; in case of

設計(ㄕㄜˋ ㄐㄧˋ)
①to map out a plan, scheme or coup ②to devise; to plan; to design; a design: 他正在設計一部新機器。He is designing a new machine.

設計教學法(ㄕㄜˋ ㄐㄧˋ ㄐㄧㄠˋ ㄒㄩㄝˊ ㄈㄚˇ)
the project method of teaching

設計者(ㄕㄜˋ ㄐㄧˋ ㄓㄜˇ)
the designer

設教(ㄕㄜˋ ㄐㄧㄠˋ)
to exert cultural influence; to teach

設穽(ㄕㄜˋ ㄐㄧㄥˇ)
to set a trap or pitfall

設局(ㄕㄜˋ ㄐㄩˊ)
①to set a trap (usually gambling, etc.) ②to establish a board or bureau

設下圈套(ㄕㄜˋ ˙ㄒㄧㄚ ㄑㄩㄢ ㄊㄠˋ)
to set a snare

設險(ㄕㄜˋ ㄒㄧㄢˇ)
to fortify strategic points

設想(ㄕㄜˋ ㄒㄧㄤˇ)
①an idea; a rough plan; a scheme; a tentative plan or idea ②to think; to imagine; to have consideration for: 設想看看我當時的感受如何。Just imagine how I felt then.

設置(ㄕㄜˋ ㄓˋ)
①to establish; to set up; to found ②establishment; installations

設帳(ㄕㄜˋ ㄓㄤˋ)
①to pitch a tent ②to set up a school

設帳授徒(ㄕㄜˋ ㄓㄤˋ ㄕㄡˋ ㄊㄨˊ)
to set up a school and instruct students

設施(ㄕㄜˋ ㄕ)
①to plan and execute ②(administrative) measures; installations; facilities

設使(ㄕㄜˋ ㄕˇ)
if; what if; supposing that

設身處地(ㄕㄜˋ ㄕㄣ ㄔㄨˇ ㄉㄧˋ)
to put oneself in another's position; to be considerate: 請你設身處地爲我想。Put yourself in my position.

設若(ㄕㄜˋ ㄖㄨㄛˋ)
if; suppose; provided: 設若有病，你必須請醫生診治。You must consult a doctor if you get ill.

設座(ㄕㄜˋ ㄗㄨㄛˋ)
to install seats

設辭(ㄕㄜˋ ㄘˊ)
an excuse or pretext; a subterfuge

設色(ㄕㄜˋ ㄙㄜˋ)
to apply color in painting

設宴(ㄕㄜˋ ㄧㄢˋ)
to give a dinner party; to throw a banquet

【許】 5541 ㄒㄩˇ sheu xǔ

1. to promise; to approve; to permit
2. to praise; to commend
3. (said of a young girl) to be betrothed; to promise to marry
4. to expect
5. perhaps; maybe
6. (said of a person's age) about; a little more than
7. a place
8. a final particle
9. so; this
10. a Chinese family name

許配(ㄒㄩˇ ㄆㄟˋ)or 許聘(ㄒㄩˇ ㄆㄧㄣˋ)
(said of a girl) to betroth; to affiance

許多(ㄒㄩˇ ㄉㄨㄛ)
many; numerous; much; a great deal of; a lot of: 屋子裏有許多人。There are many people in the room.

許諾(ㄒㄩˇ ㄋㄨㄛˋ)
to promise; a promise

許可(ㄒㄩˇ ㄎㄜˇ)
to approve; to permit or allow; approval

許可證(ㄒㄩˇ ㄎㄜˇ ㄓㄥˋ)
a permit; a license

許婚(ㄒㄩˇ ㄏㄨㄣ)
(said of a girl)to betroth

許嫁(ㄒㄩˇ ㄐㄧㄚˋ)
to betroth a daughter

許久(ㄒㄩˇ ㄐㄧㄡˇ)
for quite some time; for a long time; for ages: 我們許久沒有看到他了。We have not seen him for ages.

許是(ㄒㄩˇ ㄕˋ)
perhaps; maybe

許愼(ㄒㄩˇ ㄕㄣˋ)
Hsü Shen, a high official in the Eastern Han Dynasty and author of 說文解字

許字(ㄒㄩˇ ㄗˋ)
(said of a girl)to betroth; to affiance

許由(ㄒㄩˇ ㄧㄡˊ)
Hsü Yu, a legendary figure, who supposedly turned down offers to become emperor

許願(ㄒㄩˇ ㄩㄢˋ)
①to promise to a deity certain offerings in exchange for divine blessings; to make a vow(to a god) ②to promise somebody a reward

五畫

【訴】 5542 ㄙㄨˋ suh sù

1. to tell; to inform
2. to accuse; to file a complaint; to charge
3. to appeal; to petition
4. to resort to

〔言部〕

〔言部〕

訴苦(ㄙㄨˋ ㄎㄨˇ)
to complain about one's grievances; to air complaints; to vent one's grievances; to pour out one's woes

訴苦窮兒(ㄙㄨˋ ㄎㄨˇ ㄑㄩㄥˊㄦ)
to tell others of one's state of poverty or destitution

訴之武力(ㄙㄨˋ ㄓ ㄨˇ ㄌㄧˋ)or 訴諸武力(ㄙㄨˋ ㄓㄨ ㄨˇ ㄌㄧˋ)
to resort to force; to resort to violence: 如果其他手段都失敗，我們將訴諸武力。If other means fail, we shall resort to force.

訴諸公論(ㄙㄨˋ ㄓㄨ ㄍㄨㄥ ㄌㄨㄣˋ)
to appeal to public opinion

訴狀(ㄙㄨˋ ㄓㄨㄤˋ)
a plaint; a written complaint; a petition: 他向法院提出訴狀。He filed a plaint at court.

訴說(ㄙㄨˋ ㄕㄨㄛ)
to tell; to complain; to air grievances; to relate; to recount

訴訟(ㄙㄨˋ ㄙㄨㄥˋ)
a lawsuit; to go to law; litigation

訴訟法(ㄙㄨˋ ㄙㄨㄥˋ ㄈㄚˇ)
legal procedures involved in a lawsuit

訴訟費用(ㄙㄨˋ ㄙㄨㄥˋ ㄈㄟˋ ㄩㄥˋ)
fees entailed in a lawsuit; the cost of a civil action

訴訟代理人(ㄙㄨˋ ㄙㄨㄥˋ ㄉㄞˋ ㄌㄧˇ ㄖㄣˊ)
a legal counsel; an attorney; a legal representative

訴冤(ㄙㄨˋ ㄩㄢ)
to complain about grievances; to state injustice

訴願(ㄙㄨˋ ㄩㄢˋ)
to petition to a higher government agency against a decision of a lower office

【訶】 5543 ㄏㄜ he hē

to scold or blame in a loud voice

訶護(ㄏㄜ ㄏㄨˋ)
divine protection

訶求(ㄏㄜ ㄑㄧㄡˊ)
to find fault; to make a stiff demand

訶譴(ㄏㄜ ㄑㄧㄢˇ)
to scold; to blame; to reprimand; to censure

訶叱(ㄏㄜ ㄔˋ)
to scold in a loud voice; to upbraid or revile: 不要老是訶叱人家。Don't scold so much.

訶責(ㄏㄜ ㄗㄜˊ)
to scold; to berate; to vituperate; scoldings: 我們對母親的訶責已經習慣了。We were used to our mother's scoldings.

【診】 5544 ㄓㄣˇ jeen zhěn (又讀 ㄓㄣ jen zhēn)

1. to examine (diseases, ailments, etc.); to diagnose
2. to tell; to report

診病(ㄓㄣˇ ㄅㄧㄥˋ)
to examine a patient: 醫生替你診病了沒? Did the doctor examine you?

診脈(ㄓㄣˇ ㄇㄛˋ)or(ㄓㄣˇ ㄇㄞˋ)
to feel the pulse

診斷(ㄓㄣˇ ㄉㄨㄢˋ)
to diagnose (a disease); a diagnosis

診斷書(ㄓㄣˇ ㄉㄨㄢˋ ㄕㄨ)
a written diagnosis; a medical certificate

診療(ㄓㄣˇ ㄌㄧㄠˊ)
to diagnose and treat

診療室(ㄓㄣˇ ㄌㄧㄠˊ ㄕˋ)
a doctor's consultation room

診候(ㄓㄣˇ ㄏㄡˋ)
to examine and diagnose; to treat (a patient)

診治(ㄓㄣˇ ㄓˋ)
to diagnose and treat

診察(ㄓㄣˇ ㄔㄚˊ)
to examine and observe (the progress of a disease)

診視(ㄓㄣˇ ㄕˋ)
to examine (a patient): 醫生仔細診視她。The doctor examined her carefully.

診所(ㄓㄣˇ ㄙㄨㄛˇ)
a clinic; a dispensary

【註】 5545 ㄓㄨˋ juh zhù

1. an explanatory note; a footnote; a commentary or remark; annotations
2. to register; to record or list

註明(ㄓㄨˋ ㄇㄧㄥˊ)
to explain or state clearly in writing; to explain the clear indication of: 引文要註明出處。You must explain the sources of quotations clearly.

註定(ㄓㄨˋ ㄉㄧㄥˋ)
destined; predestined; doomed: 那是命中註定的。It is destined by fate.

註解(ㄓㄨˋ ㄐㄧㄝˇ)
explanatory notes or commentaries; definition; to define; to explain 亦作「注解」

註脚(ㄓㄨˋ ㄐㄧㄠˇ)
explanatory notes; footnotes

註銷(ㄓㄨˋ ㄒㄧㄠ)
to cancel; to nullify; to annul; to revoke; to write off

註失(ㄓㄨˋ ㄕ)
to report loss of documents, etc. to the authorities concerned

註釋(ㄓㄨˋ ㄕˋ)
explanatory notes

註疏(ㄓㄨˋ ㄕㄨ)or(ㄓㄨˋ ㄕㄨˋ)
① to explain ② explanatory notes or commentaries 亦作「注疏」

註册(ㄓㄨˋ ㄘㄜˋ)
to register (with authorities concerned, etc.); registration

註册費(ㄓㄨˋ ㄘㄜˋ ㄈㄟˋ)
registration fees

註册主任(ㄓㄨˋ ㄘㄜˋ ㄓㄨˇ ㄖㄣˋ)
(in schools) the chief registrar; the registrar

註册處(ㄓㄨˋ ㄘㄜˋ ㄔㄨˋ)
the register office

註册手續(ㄓㄨˋ ㄘㄜˋ ㄕㄡˇ ㄒㄩˋ)
registration procedures

註册商標(ㄓㄨˋ ㄘㄜˋ ㄕㄤ ㄅㄧㄠ)
a registered trademark; a registered brand

註册組(ㄓㄨˋ ㄘㄜˋ ㄗㄨˇ)
the registration section

【訾】 5546 (訿) ㄗˇ tzyy zǐ

1. to slander; to traduce; to attack
2. faults; blemishes
3. to measure
4. to consider
5. to estimate
6. poor (food); meager

訾病(ㄗˇ ㄅㄧㄥˋ)
to find fault with

訾厲(ㄗˇ ㄌㄧˋ)
illness; disease

訾訾(ㄗˇ ㄗˇ)
to slander; to defame
訾議(ㄗˇ ㄧˋ)
unfavorable criticism; to criticize; to impeach

【詁】 5547 ㄍㄨˇ guu gǔ
1. explanatory notes or commentaries
2. to transcribe the classics in everyday language
詁訓(ㄍㄨˇ ㄒㄩㄣˋ)
to explain classics in everyday language 參看「訓詁」

【詆】 5548 ㄉㄧˇ dii dǐ
to censure; to slander; to defame
詆謾(ㄉㄧˇ ㄇㄢˋ)
to slander and insult
詆讕(ㄉㄧˇ ㄌㄢˋ)
to cover up with lies
詆訶(ㄉㄧˇ ㄏㄜ)
to slander; to defame; to disparage
詆毀(ㄉㄧˇ ㄏㄨㄟˇ)
to defame; to slander
詆訾(ㄉㄧˇ ㄗˇ)
to slander or defame

【詈】 5549 ㄌㄧˋ lih lì
to scold; to berate; to upbraid; to revile; to vituperate
詈罵(ㄌㄧˋ ㄇㄚˋ)
to scold; to abuse; to revile
詈辱(ㄌㄧˋ ㄖㄨˇ)
to scold and insult

【詠】 5550 (咏) ㄩㄥˇ yeong yǒng
1. to sing; to chant; to hum
2. the chirping of birds
詠歎(ㄩㄥˇ ㄊㄢˋ)
to sigh (usually in admiration)
詠歎曲(ㄩㄥˇ ㄊㄢˋ ㄑㄩˇ)or 詠歎調(ㄩㄥˇ ㄊㄢˋ ㄉㄧㄠˋ)
(opera) arias
詠古(ㄩㄥˇ ㄍㄨˇ)
to write poems on ancient subjects
詠絮之才(ㄩㄥˇ ㄒㄩˋ ㄓ ㄘㄞˊ)
a female who has a ready talent in composing verses
詠詩(ㄩㄥˇ ㄕ)
to chant poems

【詎】 5551 ㄐㄩˋ jiuh jù
an interjection indicating surprise
詎非所料(ㄐㄩˋ ㄈㄟ ㄙㄨㄛˇ ㄌㄧㄠˋ)
unexpectedly; nobody has expected that...
詎料(ㄐㄩˋ ㄌㄧㄠˋ)
who could have expected that...; unexpectedly
詎知(ㄐㄩˋ ㄓ)
who could have expected that...; unexpectedly
詎意(ㄐㄩˋ ㄧˋ)
who could have expected that...; unexpectedly

【詐】 5552 ㄓㄚˋ jah zhà
1. deceitful; false; fake; fraudulent; crafty; artful; cunning
2. to deceive; to cheat; to lie; to swindle; to pretend; to feign
3. to trick into; to bluff somebody into giving information
4. sudden(ly); unexpected(ly) 亦作「乍」
詐敗(ㄓㄚˋ ㄅㄞˋ)
to feign defeat: 他常常詐敗誘敵。He often feigns defeat in order to lead on the enemy.
詐病(ㄓㄚˋ ㄅㄧㄥˋ)
to pretend to be ill
詐騙(ㄓㄚˋ ㄆㄧㄢˋ)
to swindle
詐婚(ㄓㄚˋ ㄏㄨㄣ)
to cheat by using marriage as a bait
詐欺(ㄓㄚˋ ㄑㄧ)
fraud; imposture; cheating
詐欺罪(ㄓㄚˋ ㄑㄧ ㄗㄨㄟˋ)
fraud(as a legal offense): 法官判定這人有詐欺罪。The judge found the man guilty of fraud.
詐降(ㄓㄚˋ ㄒㄧㄤˊ)
to fake surrender
詐諼(ㄓㄚˋ ㄒㄩㄢ)
dishonest; unfaithful; artful and crafty
詐稱(ㄓㄚˋ ㄔㄥ)
to tell a lie; to state falsely
詐術(ㄓㄚˋ ㄕㄨˋ)
fraud; cheating; chicanery; guile
詐財(ㄓㄚˋ ㄘㄞˊ)
to cheat for money
詐死(ㄓㄚˋ ㄙˇ)
to fake death; to feign death; to pretend to be dead; to play dead
詐僞(ㄓㄚˋ ㄨㄟˋ)
falsehood; deceitful; cunning; artful

【詒】 5553 ㄧˊ yi yí
1. words as a gift usually given on parting
2. to hand down to posterity

【詔】 5554 ㄓㄠˋ jaw zhào
1. to proclaim; to announce
2. to instruct; to teach and direct; to coach
3. an imperial decree or mandate; an edict
詔命(ㄓㄠˋ ㄇㄧㄥˋ)
an imperial decree or edict
詔令(ㄓㄠˋ ㄌㄧㄥˋ)
an imperial decree or edict
詔告(ㄓㄠˋ ㄍㄠˋ)
(said of the emperor) to proclaim
詔敕(ㄓㄠˋ ㄔˋ)
an imperial rescript
詔書(ㄓㄠˋ ㄕㄨ)
a proclamation by the emperor; an imperial decree or edict
詔諭(ㄓㄠˋ ㄩˋ)
imperial instructions

【評】 5555 ㄆㄧㄥˊ pyng píng
1. to comment; to criticize; to review
2. comments; reviews
3. to judge; a decision after comparison, etc. by a group, as judges in a beauty contest
4. a Chinese family name
評判(ㄆㄧㄥˊ ㄆㄢˋ)
to criticize; to judge or decide, as in a beauty contest, etc.
評判員(ㄆㄧㄥˊ ㄆㄢˋ ㄩㄢˊ)
a judge; an umpire; a juror
評分(ㄆㄧㄥˊ ㄈㄣ)
marks or points given by a judge
評點(ㄆㄧㄥˊ ㄉㄧㄢˇ)
to superscribe punctuation marks and running commentaries on a well-known book
評定(ㄆㄧㄥˊ ㄉㄧㄥˋ)

to examine, judge and decide; to evaluate
評斷(ㄆㄧㄥˊ ㄉㄨㄢˋ)
to decide; to arbitrate
評頭論足(ㄆㄧㄥˊ ㄊㄡˊ ㄌㄨㄣˋ ㄗㄨˊ)
(literally) to comment from head to feet—to make critical comments on the appearance of a woman
評理(ㄆㄧㄥˊ ㄌㄧˇ)
to ask a third party to judge which side is right
評量(ㄆㄧㄥˊ ㄌㄧㄤˊ)
to weigh; to evaluate
評論(ㄆㄧㄥˊ ㄌㄨㄣˋ)
to comment; to review; comments; commentary: 他在閒暇時寫評論文章。He reviews in his spare time.
評論家(ㄆㄧㄥˊ ㄌㄨㄣˋ ㄐㄧㄚ)
a commentator; a critic
評話(ㄆㄧㄥˊ ㄏㄨㄚˋ)
① professional storytelling 亦作「說書」② novels or anecdotes written in plain language 亦作「平話」
評價(ㄆㄧㄥˊ ㄐㄧㄚˋ)
① to estimate; to appraise; to assess: 他們對你的人格評價很高。They estimate your character highly. ② an objective assessment of the worth or merit of a person, a piece of writing, etc.
評註(ㄆㄧㄥˊ ㄓㄨˋ)
critical notes; commentaries; annotations
評註者(ㄆㄧㄥˊ ㄓㄨˋ ㄓㄜˇ)
a person who writes critical notes for an old book; an annotator
評傳(ㄆㄧㄥˊ ㄓㄨㄢˋ)
a critical biography
評議(ㄆㄧㄥˊ ㄧˋ)
to discuss or judge the right or wrong of something; to arbitrate
評議會(ㄆㄧㄥˊ ㄧˋ ㄏㄨㄟˋ)
an advisory or policy-making council; an arbitration board
評議員(ㄆㄧㄥˊ ㄧˋ ㄩㄢˊ)
① a member of 評議會 ② officers in an organization responsible for discussing and drafting the rules and operation of the organization
評語(ㄆㄧㄥˊ ㄩˇ)
comments; criticism
評閱(ㄆㄧㄥˊ ㄩㄝˋ)
to read and grade (student papers, etc.)

【詖】 5556 ㄅㄧˋ bih bì

1. unfair; erroneous; wrong
2. to argue; to debate

詖論(ㄅㄧˋ ㄌㄨㄣˋ)
erroneous statements in which the speaker is unable to see the error
詖行(ㄅㄧˋ ㄒㄧㄥˋ)
evil and one-sided conduct (or actions)
詖辭(ㄅㄧˋ ㄘˊ)
one-sided words; biased remarks; partial statements

【詛】 5557 ㄗㄨˇ tzuu zǔ

1. to curse; to imprecate
2. to vow; to pledge; to take an oath

詛罵(ㄗㄨˇ ㄇㄚˋ)
to curse and berate
詛盟(ㄗㄨˇ ㄇㄥˊ)
a vow; an oath
詛祝(ㄗㄨˇ ㄓㄨˋ)
to pray to a deity that the enemy be brought down by divine wrath
詛咒(ㄗㄨˇ ㄓㄡˋ)
to curse; to imprecate; to wish someone evil

【詞】 5558 ㄘˊ tsyr cí

1. words; phrases; expressions; speech; statements: 雙方各執一詞。Each sticks to his own words.
2. a part of speech in grammar
3. to talk, speak or tell
4. (Chinese literature) *tzu*, a form of poetry characterized by lines of irregular length

詞不達意(ㄘˊ ˙ㄅㄨ ㄉㄚˊ ㄧˋ)
The language cannot convey the ideas intended.
詞牌(ㄘˊ ㄆㄞˊ)
the verse form of *tzu* (詞)
詞譜(ㄘˊ ㄆㄨˇ)
① a collection of *tzu* (詞) ② name of a book edited by Wang Yi-ching (王奕清), etc. in the Ching Dynasty, including 2,300 *tzu* (詞)
詞鋒(ㄘˊ ㄈㄥ)
① the sharpness of one's tongue ② incisiveness of a piece of writing: 他的詞鋒銳利。His writings are sharp and incisive.
詞典(ㄘˊ ㄉㄧㄢˇ)
a dictionary 亦作「辭典」: 詞典是他的常伴。A dictionary is his frequent companion.
詞頭(ㄘˊ ㄊㄡˊ)
a prefix
詞類(ㄘˊ ㄌㄟˋ)
the parts of speech: 英文有八大詞類。There are eight parts of speech in English.
詞林(ㄘˊ ㄌㄧㄣˊ)
① (in old China) the Hanlin Academy (翰林院) ② a place where men of letters congregate
詞律(ㄘˊ ㄌㄩˋ)
rules of prosody
詞根(ㄘˊ ㄍㄣ)
a word root; a stem
詞翰(ㄘˊ ㄏㄢˋ)
① literary works, as poems, proses, etc. ② letters; correspondence
詞華(ㄘˊ ㄏㄨㄚˊ)
poetic diction
詞話(ㄘˊ ㄏㄨㄚˋ)
a book dealing with forms, styles or authors of *tzu* (詞)
詞彙(ㄘˊ ㄏㄨㄟˋ)
① a dictionary ② a vocabulary
詞句(ㄘˊ ㄐㄩˋ)
wording; text of a piece of writing; expressions; words and phrases
詞曲(ㄘˊ ㄑㄩˇ)
poems and songs
詞窮(ㄘˊ ㄑㄩㄥˊ)
(literally) to run short of words—unable to put up a riposte in an argument; unable to give an answer when confronted with overwhelming evidence of guilt, etc.
詞性(ㄘˊ ㄒㄧㄥˋ)
the characteristic or property of a certain word, by which one can determine which part of speech the word belongs to

詞章(ㄘ ㄓㄤ)
literary works
詞臣(ㄘ ㄔㄣˊ)
a court official who specializes in literature
詞書(ㄘ ㄕㄨ)
dictionaries
詞人(ㄘ ㄖㄣˊ)
① men of letters ② one who is well versed in *tzu*(詞)
詞藻(ㄘ ㄗㄠˇ)
ornamentation in the use of words; ornate terms or expressions; flowery language
詞宗(ㄘ ㄗㄨㄥ)
a great man of letters; a literary lion
詞意(ㄘ ㄧˋ)
meanings of phrases; the gist of a piece of writing; the drift
詞尾(ㄘ ㄨㄟˇ)
a suffix
詞語(ㄘ ㄩˇ)
words and expressions; terms

【詘】 5559
ㄑㄩ chiu qū
1. to bend; to crouch
2. to yield(to another's views, etc.); to submit
3. short
4. a Chinese family name

【訿】 5560
(訾) ㄗˇ tzyy zǐ
to defame or slander, etc.

【証】 5561
(證) ㄓㄥˋ jenq zhèng
evidence; proof; a certificate; to certify

六畫

【詣】 5562
ㄧˋ yih yì
1. to go(to a place); to arrive
2. to visit; to call on
3. achievements; attainments
詣門(ㄧˋ ㄇㄣˊ)
to visit someone
詣闕(ㄧˋ ㄑㄩㄝ)
to go to the palace—to see the emperor
詣謁(ㄧˋ ㄧㄝ)
to pay a visit to

【詡】 5563
ㄒㄩˇ sheu xǔ
1. to boast; to brag; to exaggerate
2. popular; to make widely known; common
3. (now rarely) clever and brave
4. (now rarely) harmonious
詡詡(ㄒㄩˇ ㄒㄩˇ)
① vivid; lively ② to boast; to brag ③ harmonious

【詢】 5564
ㄒㄩㄣˊ shyun xún
1. to inquire; to ask: 我探詢他來此的原因。I inquired his reason for coming.
2. to deliberate and plan
3. truely; honesty
詢察(ㄒㄩㄣˊ ㄔㄚˊ)
to investigate and inquire
詢問(ㄒㄩㄣˊ ㄨㄣˋ)
to inquire; to ask; to make inquiries
詢問處(ㄒㄩㄣˊ ㄨㄣˋ ㄔㄨˋ)
an information desk: 你可到詢問處詢問。Ask at the information office.

【試】 5565
ㄕˋ shyh shì
1. to try; to test; to experiment; a trial; a test
2. to use
3. to examine; examination
4. to sound out; to put up a trial balloon
5. to compare
6. a Chinese family name
試辦(ㄕˋ ㄅㄢˋ)
to do something on an experimental basis; to implement a pilot project
試飛(ㄕˋ ㄈㄟ)
to test a new airplane in flight; a test flight; a trial flight
試飛員(ㄕˋ ㄈㄟ ㄩㄢˊ)
a test pilot
試探(ㄕˋ ㄊㄢˋ)
to test; to sound out; to put up a trial balloon; to probe; to explore: 試探一下他對這個問題的看法。Try to sound him out about the question
試題(ㄕˋ ㄊㄧˊ)
questions in a test or examination
試帖(ㄕˋ ㄊㄧㄝˋ)
①the composition of poetry-writing in the civil service examination in the olden days ② a test in classics in the civil service examination during the Tang Dynasty
試圖(ㄕˋ ㄊㄨˊ)
to attempt; to try
試官(ㄕˋ ㄍㄨㄢ)
① the official in charge of an examination ② officials appointed on a probational basis
試管(ㄕˋ ㄍㄨㄢˇ)
a test tube
試管嬰兒(ㄕˋ ㄍㄨㄢˇ ㄧㄥ ㄦˊ)
a test-tube baby; a human embryo in the laboratory
試航(ㄕˋ ㄏㄤˊ)
① the trial run of a new ship ② the test flight of a new plane ③ a test sail or flight along a new route
試婚(ㄕˋ ㄏㄨㄣ)
trial marriage
試教(ㄕˋ ㄐㄧㄠˋ)or(ㄕˋ ㄐㄧㄠ)
to practise teaching
試劍(ㄕˋ ㄐㄧㄢˋ)
to test the sharpness of a newly made sword or blade; to try out a new sword
試金石(ㄕˋ ㄐㄧㄣ ㄕˊ)
① Lydian stone ② something which can make a person reveal his true character
試金術(ㄕˋ ㄐㄧㄣ ㄕㄨˋ)
assaying
試鏡(ㄕˋ ㄐㄧㄥˋ)
to undergo a screen test
試卷(ㄕˋ ㄐㄩㄢˋ)
a test paper; an examination paper
試銷(ㄕˋ ㄒㄧㄠ)
to put a new product on sale or to sell something in a new market on a limited scale in order to see the result; to sell a product on a trial basis; trial sale
試新(ㄕˋ ㄒㄧㄣ)
① name of a kind of tea ② to try the newly harvested rice ③ to try a new product
試想(ㄕˋ ㄒㄧㄤˇ)
to think it over; considering that...; just think
試行(ㄕˋ ㄒㄧㄥˊ)
to try out something
試紙(ㄕˋ ㄓˇ)

〔言部〕

①(chemistry) test paper: 石蕊試紙 litmus test paper ② an examination paper
試裝(ㄕˋ ㄓㄨㄤ)
to try a new suit
試車(ㄕˋ ㄔㄜ)
① a trial run of a vehicle ② a trial run of machinery in a new factory
試場(ㄕˋ ㄔㄤˇ)or(ㄕˋ ㄔㄤˊ)
an examination place; a test ground: 你知道你的試場在那裏嗎? Do you know where your examination place is?
試穿(ㄕˋ ㄔㄨㄢ)
to try on (a garment, shoes, etc.)
試晬(ㄕˋ ㄗㄨㄟˋ)
to try to find out a baby's likely career in the future by placing before him an assortment of articles on his first birthday and letting him pick one of them which may provide a clue to the observers
試思(ㄕˋ ㄙ)
just think; to think it over; considering that...
試藝(ㄕˋ ㄧˋ)
writing or composition in the civil service examination of former times
試一試(ㄕˋ ·ㄧ ·ㄕ)or 試試(ㄕˋ ·ㄕ)
to try 或 Let's give it a try (and see what happens). 來試試看。Come on; give it a try.
試藥(ㄕˋ ㄧㄠˋ)
a reagent
試演(ㄕˋ ㄧㄢˇ)
a dress rehearsal; a preview; to make a dress rehearsal; a trial performance
試驗(ㄕˋ ㄧㄢˋ)
an experiment; to experiment; to try, test or examine
試驗管(ㄕˋ ㄧㄢˋ ㄍㄨㄢˇ)
a test tube
試驗紙(ㄕˋ ㄧㄢˋ ㄓˇ)
test paper; litmus paper
試驗場(ㄕˋ ㄧㄢˋ ㄔㄤˇ)or(ㄕˋ ㄧㄢˋ ㄔㄤˊ)
an experimental station or ground
試驗室(ㄕˋ ㄧㄢˋ ㄕˋ)
a laboratory 亦作「實驗室」
試映(ㄕˋ ㄧㄥˋ)
a preview (of a movie); to give a preview
試問(ㄕˋ ㄨㄣˋ)
Let me ask....或 Let's post this question.... 或 May we ask...?
試用(ㄕˋ ㄩㄥˋ)
to use on a trial basis; to employ on a probational basis
試用人員(ㄕˋ ㄩㄥˋ ㄖㄣˊ ㄩㄢˊ)
probational personnel; probationers

【詩】 5566
ㄕ shy shī
1. poetry; poems; poetic
2. anything of quality as an offspring of pure imagination
3. short for *The Book of Odes* edited by Confucius
詩伯(ㄕ ㄅㄛˊ)or 詩豪(ㄕ ㄏㄠˊ)
a master in poetry; a great poet
詩派(ㄕ ㄆㄞˋ)
the different schools of poetry-writing
詩癖(ㄕ ㄆㄧˇ)
a deep love for poetry
詩篇(ㄕ ㄆㄧㄢ)
① poems ② the *Book of Psalms* in the *Old Testament*
詩品(ㄕ ㄆㄧㄣˇ)
the title of a book by Chung Jung (鍾嶸) of the Liang Dynasty and Ssu-Kung Tu (司空圖) of Tang Dynasty respectively
詩魔(ㄕ ㄇㄛˊ)
① an unorthodox style of poetry-writing ② one who has an obsessive love for poetry
詩謎(ㄕ ㄇㄧˊ)
① a riddle in the form of a poem ② a kind of gambling featuring the use of ancient poems
詩壇(ㄕ ㄊㄢˊ)
the circle of poets
詩體(ㄕ ㄊㄧˇ)
the style or form of poetry
詩奴(ㄕ ㄋㄨˊ)
inferior poets; poetasters
詩禮傳家(ㄕ ㄌㄧˇ ㄔㄨㄢˊ ㄐㄧㄚ)
a family of scholars
詩料(ㄕ ㄌㄧㄠˋ)
materials that inspire the composition of poems
詩律(ㄕ ㄌㄩˋ)
rules of prosody; restrictions of verse form
詩歌(ㄕ ㄍㄜ)
① poems and songs collectively ② poetry
詩格(ㄕ ㄍㄜˊ)
a style of poetry
詩稿(ㄕ ㄍㄠˇ)or 詩草(ㄕ ㄘㄠˇ)
scripts of poems; draft poems
詩虎(ㄕ ㄏㄨˇ)
riddles in poetry form
詩話(ㄕ ㄏㄨㄚˋ)
① a book containing comments on poetry or poets ② narratives written in the Sung Dynasty
詩集(ㄕ ㄐㄧˊ)
a collection of poems
詩箋(ㄕ ㄐㄧㄢ)
paper for writing poems
詩經(ㄕ ㄐㄧㄥ)
The Book of Odes or *The Book of Poetry,* one of the Chinese classics compiled and edited by Confucius
詩句(ㄕ ㄐㄩˋ)
a stanza or line in a poem
詩情畫意(ㄕ ㄑㄧㄥˊ ㄏㄨㄚˋ ㄧˋ)
(said of a landscape) idyllic
詩窮而後工(ㄕ ㄑㄩㄥˊ ㄦˊ ㄏㄡˋ ㄍㄨㄥ)
In writing poems one gains depth after suffering poverty.
詩仙(ㄕ ㄒㄧㄢ)
the Poetic God—Li Po (李白)
詩興(ㄕ ㄒㄧㄥˋ)
an urge to compose poems; in the mood or having a sudden inspiration for writing poems
詩興大發(ㄕ ㄒㄧㄥˋ ㄉㄚˋ ㄈㄚ)
to feel a strong urge to compose poems; to be in the mood for writing poems
詩序(ㄕ ㄒㄩˋ)
the forewords before every chapter of *The Book of Odes,* supposedly written by Tzu-hsia (子夏), one of Confucian disciples
詩學(ㄕ ㄒㄩㄝˊ)
poetics

詩選(ㄕ ㄒㄩㄢˇ)
a selection of poems
詩債(ㄕ ㄓㄞˋ)
(literally) a poetic debt—an unfulfilled promise to respond with a poem
詩鐘(ㄕ ㄓㄨㄥ)
a game in poem-composition—within a limited period of time poems are written on two different topics with unlikely associations
詩中有畫，畫中有詩(ㄕ ㄓㄨㄥ ㄧㄡˇ ㄏㄨㄚˋ, ㄏㄨㄚˋ ㄓㄨㄥ ㄧㄡˇ ㄕ)
(literally) There's a picture in the poem and a poem in the picture.—a poem replete with graphic descriptions or picture images and a painting having the quality of a good poem
詩讖(ㄕ ㄔㄣˋ)
a poem which portends what will happen to the poet
詩史(ㄕ ㄕˇ)
poems reflecting the troubles of the time, to which the works of Tu Fu (杜甫) of the Tang Dynasty is often referred
詩社(ㄕ ㄕㄜˋ)
a site of regular meetings of poets
詩聖(ㄕ ㄕㄥˋ)
the Poetic Sage—Tu Fu (杜甫)
詩書(ㄕ ㄕㄨ)
① *The Book of Odes* and *The Book of History* ② classics in general
詩書門第(ㄕ ㄕㄨ ㄇㄣˊ ㄉㄧˋ)
a scholarly family; a family of high academic standing: 他出身於詩書門第。He was brought up in a scholarly family.
詩人(ㄕ ㄖㄣˊ)
a poet
詩人節(ㄕ ㄖㄣˊ ㄐㄧㄝˊ)
Poets' Day, on the fifth day of the fifth month in the lunar calendar
詩詞歌賦(ㄕ ㄘˊ ㄍㄜ ㄈㄨˋ)
the four forms of Chinese poetry
詩思(ㄕ ㄙ)
poetic inspiration; poetical thoughts
詩以言志(ㄕ ㄧˇ ㄧㄢˊ ㄓˋ)
Poetry serves as a medium to convey one's aspiration or ambition.
詩意(ㄕ ㄧˋ)
the poetic quality; the romantic atmosphere
詩妖(ㄕ ㄧㄠ)
perversive poems and songs which are usually the harbinger of social unrest or moral degeneracy
詩友(ㄕ ㄧㄡˇ)
a friend in poetry
詩文(ㄕ ㄨㄣˊ)
literary works in general: 他晚年以詩文自娛。He amused himself by reading literary works in his old age.
詩翁(ㄕ ㄨㄥ)
a renowned poet at his advanced age
詩餘(ㄕ ㄩˊ)
another name of a form of 詞(a form of poetry)
詩韻(ㄕ ㄩㄣˋ)
① rhyme of verses ② a rhyme book

【詫】 5567 ㄔㄚˋ chah chà

1. surprised; to wonder
2. to brag; to boast
3. to cheat; to deceive
4. to inform

詫異(ㄔㄚˋ ㄧˋ)
to be surprised

【詬】 5568 ㄍㄡˋ gow gòu

1. to insult; to shame
2. to berate; to vituperate; to abuse
3. a Chinese family name

詬病(ㄍㄡˋ ㄅㄧㄥˋ)
to insult; to criticize; to blame: 它將爲世人所詬病。It will become an object that the public blame.
詬罵(ㄍㄡˋ ㄇㄚˋ)
to berate; to abuse
詬厲(ㄍㄡˋ ㄌㄧˋ)
to shame; ashamed
詬詈(ㄍㄡˋ ㄌㄧˋ)
to berate; to vituperate
詬辱(ㄍㄡˋ ㄖㄨˇ)
to insult; to shame; to mortify; mortification; an insult

【詭】 5569 ㄍㄨㄟˇ goei guǐ

1. to cheat; to deceive; to feign; to defraud
2. strange; rare; odd; peculiar; uncanny; weird
3. cunning; shrewd; stealthy
4. to urge oneself; to consider as one's responsibility
5. to go against; to defy; to contradict

詭辯(ㄍㄨㄟˇ ㄅㄧㄢˋ)
sophistry; sophistication; to argue one's point in a subtle, artful, clever, and sophisticated way
詭辯家(ㄍㄨㄟˇ ㄅㄧㄢˋ ㄐㄧㄚ)
a sophist or sophister
詭辯學派(ㄍㄨㄟˇ ㄅㄧㄢˋ ㄒㄩㄝˊ ㄆㄞˋ)
the sophistic school; the sophists
詭秘(ㄍㄨㄟˇ ㄇㄧˋ)
stealthy; clandestine; secret; surreptitious: 他的行踪詭秘。He is surreptitious in his movements.
詭道(ㄍㄨㄟˇ ㄉㄠˋ)
perverse ways; ways which are not normally or ordinarily followed
詭特(ㄍㄨㄟˇ ㄊㄜˋ)
strange; odd; peculiar
詭計(ㄍㄨㄟˇ ㄐㄧˋ)
a trick; an artful device or trap
詭計多端(ㄍㄨㄟˇ ㄐㄧˋ ㄉㄨㄛ ㄉㄨㄢ)
to have many tricks up one's sleeves; very tricky or crafty; cunning
詭譎(ㄍㄨㄟˇ ㄐㄩㄝˊ)
① changing; cunning; crafty; treacherous ② strange; odd; weird
詭詐(ㄍㄨㄟˇ ㄓㄚˋ)
tricky; deceptive; deceit; cunningness
詭辭(ㄍㄨㄟˇ ㄘˊ)
lies or deceptive words to cover up the truth
詭隨(ㄍㄨㄟˇ ㄙㄨㄟˊ)
the wily and obsequious persons
詭異(ㄍㄨㄟˇ ㄧˋ)
strange; odd; abnormal; weird; uncanny

【詮】 5570 ㄑㄩㄢˊ chyuan quán

1. to explain; to expound; to illustrate: 你的詮論正確。You explain accurately.
2. the truth or core of something
3. to weigh; to assess; to rate; to appraise

詮釋(ㄑㄩㄢˊ ㄕˋ)
to interpret; to explain; to expound; interpretation; explanation; annotations; explanatory notes

詮次(ㄑㄩㄢˊ ㄘˋ)
to arrange in order

【詰】 5571
ㄐㄧㄝˊ jye jié

1. to question; to interrogate; to ask
2. to punish
3. to prohibit; to restrain

詰屈 or 詰詘(ㄐㄧㄝˊ ㄑㄩ)
bent and twisting

詰屈聱牙(ㄐㄧㄝˊ ㄑㄩ ㄠˊ ㄧㄚˊ)
(said of writings) hard and difficult to read: 他的散文讀起來詰屈聱牙。His essays are difficult to read.

詰責(ㄐㄧㄝˊ ㄗㄜˊ)
to berate; to censure; to rebuke; to denounce

詰問(ㄐㄧㄝˊ ㄨㄣˋ)or(ㄑㄧˋ ㄨㄣˋ)
to demand an explanation angrily; to question closely; to cross-examine

【話】 5572
ㄏㄨㄚˋ huah huà

1. a speech, talk or conversation; words; sayings
2. to speak; to talk; to converse; to say
3. language

話靶(ㄏㄨㄚˋ ㄅㄚˇ)or 話把兒(ㄏㄨㄚˋ ㄅㄚˇㄦ)
one's words or conduct which become material for gossip by others; cause for talk

話本(ㄏㄨㄚˋ ㄅㄣˇ)
the plain-language version of an original work written in archaic language; the text of a story

話別(ㄏㄨㄚˋ ㄅㄧㄝˊ)
to bid farewell; to say good-bye

話柄(ㄏㄨㄚˋ ㄅㄧㄥˇ)
① words or behavior as material for others' gossip; the subject of ridicule: 不要留下話柄。Don't leave any subject of ridicule. ② a promise, remark, etc. made casually which is subsequently used by others as a weapon against the speaker

話不投機(ㄏㄨㄚˋ ˙ㄅㄨ ㄊㄡˊ ㄐㄧ)
not seeing eye to eye in conversation or talk; remarks not appealing to the other side

話不投機半句多(ㄏㄨㄚˋ ˙ㄅㄨ ㄊㄡˊ ㄐㄧ ㄅㄢˋ ㄐㄩˋ ㄉㄨㄛ)
When the conversation gets disagreeable, to say one word more is a waste of breath.

話頭兒(ㄏㄨㄚˋ ㄊㄡˊㄦ)or 話頭(ㄏㄨㄚˋ ㄊㄡˊ)
something to talk about; something to open a conversation

話題(ㄏㄨㄚˋ ㄊㄧˊ)
the topic of conversation or discussion

話題一轉(ㄏㄨㄚˋ ㄊㄧˊ ㄧˋ ㄓㄨㄢˇ)
to change the topic of conversation

話筒(ㄏㄨㄚˋ ㄊㄨㄥˇ)
① a microphone ② a telephone transmitter ③ a megaphone

話裏套話(ㄏㄨㄚˋ ˙ㄌㄧ ㄊㄠˋ ㄏㄨㄚˋ)
① to try to pry into or obtain the secret of the other party through apparently innocent conversation ② to touch upon other matters when a discussion is centered on one topic

話料兒(ㄏㄨㄚˋ ㄌㄧㄠˋㄦ)
material for talk, conversation or gossip

話舊(ㄏㄨㄚˋ ㄐㄧㄡˋ)
to talk over old times with a friend

話家常(ㄏㄨㄚˋ ㄐㄧㄚ ㄔㄤˊ)
to chitchat; to exchange small talk

話劇(ㄏㄨㄚˋ ㄐㄩˋ)
a play or drama (as distinct from opera); modern drama

話匣子(ㄏㄨㄚˋ ㄒㄧㄚˊ ˙ㄗ)
① a phonograph ② a chatterbox: 那女人是個話匣子。That woman is a chatterbox.

話中有話(ㄏㄨㄚˋ ㄓㄨㄥ ㄧㄡˇ ㄏㄨㄚˋ)or 話裏有話(ㄏㄨㄚˋ ˙ㄌㄧ ㄧㄡˇ ㄏㄨㄚˋ)
something more (implied) in what is said; overtones in conversation

話中有刺(ㄏㄨㄚˋ ㄓㄨㄥ ㄧㄡˇ ㄘˋ)
hidden barbs in one's words

話碴兒(ㄏㄨㄚˋ ㄔㄚˊㄦ)
① implication or real meaning in what is said ② the thread of discourse

話說(ㄏㄨㄚˋ ㄕㄨㄛ)
an expression introducing an episode in old novels

話音(ㄏㄨㄚˋ ㄧㄣ)or 話音兒(ㄏㄨㄚˋ ㄧㄜㄦ)
a hint in conversation; a tone: 聽他的話音兒，他想當科學家。His tone suggests that he wishes to be a scientist.

【該】 5573
ㄍㄞ gai gāi

1. should; ought to; obliged to: 他不該如此。He should not do this.
2. fated to; preordained
3. to owe
4. that; the said (person, place, matter, etc.)
5. to be somebody's turn to do something
6. to deserve: 他該受到懲罰。He deserves to be punished.
7. inclusive; complete

該博(ㄍㄞ ㄅㄛˊ)
erudite and well-experienced

該備(ㄍㄞ ㄅㄟˋ)
complete; nothing lacking

該班(ㄍㄞ ㄅㄢ)
① to be on duty by rotation ② that class or squad

該罵(ㄍㄞ ㄇㄚˋ)
to deserve a scolding

該犯(ㄍㄞ ㄈㄢˋ)
the said prisoner: 該犯已遭處決。The said prisoner has been executed.

該打(ㄍㄞ ㄉㄚˇ)
to deserve a flogging or spanking: 你眞該打。You deserve a spanking.

該當(ㄍㄞ ㄉㄤ)
① ought to; should; proper to ② to deserve

該地(ㄍㄞ ㄉㄧˋ)
that place; the said place

該管(ㄍㄞ ㄍㄨㄢˇ)
①the competent authorities; the official in charge ② ought to exercise control or assume responsibility; should be disciplined
該貫(ㄍㄞ ㄍㄨㄢˋ)
erudite; learned
該項(ㄍㄞ ㄒㄧㄤˋ)
that item; that matter
該賬(ㄍㄞ ㄓㄤˋ)
to owe debt or money
該處(ㄍㄞ ㄔㄨˋ)
①that place ②that department
該死(ㄍㄞ ㄙˇ)
to deserve death 或 Confounded! 或 Go to hell!
該員(ㄍㄞ ㄩㄢˊ)
the said so-and-so (a documentary expression referring to a subordinate)

【詳】 5574
ㄒㄧㄤˊ shyang xiáng
1. complete; detailed; details; particulars; minute
2. to know; to know the details
3. please see ... for details
4. to explain; to interpret
詳夢(ㄒㄧㄤˊ ㄇㄥˋ)
to interpret dreams
詳密(ㄒㄧㄤˊ ㄇㄧˋ)
detailed and comprehensive
詳明(ㄒㄧㄤˊ ㄇㄧㄥˊ)
detailed and very clear: 這本書有詳明的註解。The book has full and clear annotations.
詳談(ㄒㄧㄤˊ ㄊㄢˊ)
to speak in detail; to go into details
詳略(ㄒㄧㄤˊ ㄌㄩㄝˋ)
detailed or brief; complete or sketchy
詳解(ㄒㄧㄤˊ ㄐㄧㄝˇ)
to explain in detail
詳盡(ㄒㄧㄤˊ ㄐㄧㄣˋ)
detailed and complete
詳情(ㄒㄧㄤˊ ㄑㄧㄥˊ)
details of an event, incident, etc.: 詳情請至辦事處詢問。Please apply to the office for details.
詳細(ㄒㄧㄤˊ・ㄒㄧ)or 詳詳細細(ㄒㄧㄤˊ ㄒㄧㄤˊ ㄒㄧˋ ㄒㄧˋ)
in every detail and particular; detailed; minute; nothing omitted: 請說詳細一點。Please explain in greater detail.
詳細審計(ㄒㄧㄤˊ ㄒㄧˋ ㄕㄣˇ ㄐㄧˋ)
a detailed audit
詳徵博引(ㄒㄧㄤˊ ㄓㄥ ㄅㄛˊ ㄧㄣˇ)
to quote extensively and in detail (in order to support one's view or prove one's point)
詳註(ㄒㄧㄤˊ ㄓㄨˋ)
copious(explanatory)notes; to annotate fully
詳查(ㄒㄧㄤˊ ㄔㄚˊ)
to investigate fully; to examine every detail
詳實(ㄒㄧㄤˊ ㄕˊ)
(said of a report) detailed and accurate
詳審(ㄒㄧㄤˊ ㄕㄣˇ)
to think, consider or examine carefully; to go into details
詳述(ㄒㄧㄤˊ ㄕㄨˋ)
to narrate in complete detail; detailed narration
詳言之(ㄒㄧㄤˊ ㄧㄢˊ ㄓ)
to state in detail and particular
詳閱(ㄒㄧㄤˊ ㄩㄝˋ)
to read carefully: 請詳閱他的計畫。Please read his plan carefully.

【詹】 5575
ㄓㄢ jan jān
1. to talk too much; verbosity
2. to reach
3. a Chinese family name
4. (now rarely) to divine
5. to look up 亦作「瞻」
詹天佑(ㄓㄢ ㄊㄧㄢ ㄧㄡˋ)
Chan Tien-yu (1861-1919), a railroad engineer who invented a type of rail-car coupler still in use today
詹森(ㄓㄢ ㄙㄣ)
Lyndon B. Johnson, 1908-1973, the 36th president of the United States
詹尹(ㄓㄢ ㄧㄣˇ)
(in ancient China) an official in charge of divination

【詼】 5576
ㄏㄨㄟ huei huī
1. funny; humorous
2. to ridicule; to joke
詼俳(ㄏㄨㄟ ㄆㄞˊ)
to joke or jest; to ridicule
詼謔(ㄏㄨㄟ ㄋㄩㄝˋ)
to joke or jest; to ridicule
詼詭(ㄏㄨㄟ ㄍㄨㄟˇ)
grotesquely funny or hilarious
詼諧(ㄏㄨㄟ ㄒㄧㄝˊ)
funny; humorous; comical; to tell jokes; to make humorous remarks

【誄】 5577
ㄌㄟˇ leei lěi
1. writings eulogizing a dead person; a speech, an ode, etc. in praise of the dead
2. to eulogize in prayer
3. to confer a posthumous title
4. to pray for the dead

【誅】 5578
ㄓㄨ ju zhū
1. to kill; to execute; to execution; to put to death
2. to punish
3. to weed out; to exterminate
誅滅(ㄓㄨ ㄇㄧㄝˋ)
to eliminate; to eradicate
誅戮(ㄓㄨ ㄌㄨˋ)
to kill; to slaughter
誅奸(ㄓㄨ ㄐㄧㄢ)
to punish the traitorous
誅求(ㄓㄨ ㄑㄧㄡˊ)
to exact; to exploit; to demand greedily
誅心之論(ㄓㄨ ㄒㄧㄣ ㄓ ㄌㄨㄣˋ)
a statement condemning someone not because of what he did but because of his motive for doing it
誅除(ㄓㄨ ㄔㄨˊ)
to eliminate; to root out
誅夷(ㄓㄨ ㄧˊ)
to launch a punitive campaign against barbarians
誅意(ㄓㄨ ㄧˋ)
to criticize someone not because of what he has done but because of his motive for doing it

【誇】 5579
ㄎㄨㄚ kua kuā
1. to exaggerate; to boast; to brag
2. big; great
3. to show off; to flaunt
4. to praise
誇大(ㄎㄨㄚ ㄉㄚˋ)
①to exaggerate; exaggeration; to overstate; to magnify: 這分報告有點誇大。This

〔言部〕

report is somewhat exaggerated. ② arrogant
誇大狂(ㄎㄨㄚ ㄉㄚˋ ㄎㄨㄤˊ)
① megalomania ② a megalomaniac
誇大其詞(ㄎㄨㄚ ㄉㄚˋ ㄑㄧˊ ㄘˊ)
to make an overstatement; to exaggerate
誇誕(ㄎㄨㄚ ㄉㄢˋ)
exaggerating to an incredible extent
誇多鬥靡(ㄎㄨㄚ ㄉㄨㄛ ㄉㄡˋ ㄇㄧˇ)
to show off one's learning
誇功(ㄎㄨㄚ ㄍㄨㄥ)
to boast of one's contribution or achievement
誇口(ㄎㄨㄚ ㄎㄡˇ)
to boast; to brag; to talk big
誇獎(ㄎㄨㄚ ㄐㄧㄤˇ)
to praise; to extol; to acclaim; to commend
誇下海口(ㄎㄨㄚ ㄒㄧㄚˋ ㄏㄞˇ ㄎㄡˇ)
to have boasted; to have made the boast that...
誇詡(ㄎㄨㄚ ㄒㄩˇ)
to boast; to exaggerate
誇張(ㄎㄨㄚ ㄓㄤ)
to exaggerate; exaggeration; to overstate
誇張的語言(ㄎㄨㄚ ㄓㄤ ·ㄉㄜ ㄩˇ ㄧㄢˊ)
inflated language; exaggerations
誇張法(ㄎㄨㄚ ㄓㄤ ㄈㄚˇ)
hyperbole
誇示(ㄎㄨㄚ ㄕˋ)
to show off; to flaunt
誇飾(ㄎㄨㄚ ㄕˋ)
to exaggerate
誇讚(ㄎㄨㄚ ㄗㄢˋ)
to praise; to extol
誇嘴(ㄎㄨㄚ ㄗㄨㄟˇ)
to brag; to boast
誇耀(ㄎㄨㄚ ㄧㄠˋ)
to flaunt; to show off

【詵】 5580
ㄕㄣ shen shēn
1. to ask; to question
2. to address; to speak to
3. numerous; many; swarming
詵詵(ㄕㄣ ㄕㄣ)
① numerous ② collecting harmoniously

【誆】 5581
ㄎㄨㄤ kuang kuāng
to lie; to cheat; to deceive; to hoax
誆騙(ㄎㄨㄤ ㄆㄧㄢˋ)
to cheat; to swindle; to hoax; to dupe
誆哄(ㄎㄨㄤ ㄏㄨㄥˇ)
to lie; to cheat; to deceive

【詿】 5582
ㄍㄨㄚˋ guah guà
1. an error; a mistake
2. to cheat; to deceive
詿誤(ㄍㄨㄚˋ ㄨˋ)
to be punished for a mistake made by someone else 亦作「罣誤」

七畫

【認】 5583
ㄖㄣˋ renn rèn
1. to recognize; to understand; to know; to make out; to identify
2. to admit; to acknowledge; to own
3. to accept; to resign oneself to
4. to enter into a certain relationship with; to adopt
5. to promise to do something; to subscribe
認不得(ㄖㄣˋ ·ㄅㄨ ·ㄉㄜ)
unable to recognize; unrecognizable; not familiar
認不清(ㄖㄣˋ ·ㄅㄨ ㄑㄧㄥ)
unable to identify
認不出來(ㄖㄣˋ ·ㄅㄨ ㄔㄨ ㄌㄞˊ)
to fail to recognize; unable to recognize
認賠(ㄖㄣˋ ㄆㄟˊ)
to admit an obligation to pay (for damage, etc.)
認票不認人(ㄖㄣˋ ㄆㄧㄠˋ ㄅㄨˋ ㄖㄣˋ ㄖㄣˊ)
to consider the validity of a note, ticket, check, etc. independently of its bearer; payable to the bearer
認明(ㄖㄣˋ ㄇㄧㄥˊ)
to see clearly; to recognize: 他們認明他是合法的繼承人。They recognized him as the lawful heir.
認命(ㄖㄣˋ ㄇㄧㄥˋ)
to accept fate; to resign oneself to destiny
認罰(ㄖㄣˋ ㄈㄚˊ)
to admit that one deserves punishment
認得(ㄖㄣˋ ·ㄉㄜ)
to recognize; to know
認定(ㄖㄣˋ ㄉㄧㄥˋ)
① to conclude or decide (with or without adequate proof); to believe firmly ② to set one's mind on
認同(ㄖㄣˋ ㄊㄨㄥˊ)
to identify; identification
認了(ㄖㄣˋ ·ㄌㄜ)
① to accept; to tolerate; to resign oneself to what is inevitable ② to admit
認領(ㄖㄣˋ ㄌㄧㄥˇ)
① to identify and claim (a child, a lost article, etc.) ② (said of a man) to adopt a child born out of wedlock
認購公債(ㄖㄣˋ ㄍㄡˋ ㄍㄨㄥ ㄓㄞˋ)
to subscribe for bonds
認股(ㄖㄣˋ ㄍㄨˇ)
to become a shareholder; to subscribe to shares
認可(ㄖㄣˋ ㄎㄜˇ)
to sanction; to approve
認捐(ㄖㄣˋ ㄐㄩㄢ)
to subscribe; to donate
認親(ㄖㄣˋ ㄑㄧㄣ)
to acknowledge relationship (as the families of the bride and the bridegroom do at a wedding)
認清(ㄖㄣˋ ㄑㄧㄥ)
to see or know clearly (which is which); to identify clearly
認知(ㄖㄣˋ ㄓ)
cognition
認眞(ㄖㄣˋ ㄓㄣ)
to be serious; to be earnest
認賬 or 認帳(ㄖㄣˋ ㄓㄤˋ)
① to acknowledge a debt ② to admit a mistake; to accept responsibility for a failure; to admit what one has said or done: 他自己說的話,怎能不認賬? How can he refuse to admit what he has said?
認屍(ㄖㄣˋ ㄕ)
to identify (dead) bodies
認識(ㄖㄣˋ ㄕˋ)
① to recognize; to know ② to understand; to comprehend; to realize; understanding; knowledge ③(psychology) cognition
認識論(ㄖㄣˋ ㄕˋ ㄌㄨㄣˋ)
epistemology
認生(ㄖㄣˋ ㄕㄥ)

(said of children or pets) to be scared of strangers; to be shy in the presence of strangers
認輸(ㄖㄣˋ ㄕㄨ)
to concede defeat; to throw in the towel; to give up
認字(ㄖㄣˋ ㄗˋ)
① able to read; literate ② to learn to read individual characters
認賊作父(ㄖㄣˋ ㄗㄟˊ ㄗㄨㄛˋ ㄈㄨˋ)
(literally) to treat a thief as one's father—to give allegiance to an usurper or invader; to mistake an enemy for one's friend
認罪(ㄖㄣˋ ㄗㄨㄟˋ)
to acknowledge a fault; to plead guilty
認錯(ㄖㄣˋ ㄘㄨㄛˋ)
① to admit a fault or mistake ② to make identification incorrectly
認爲(ㄖㄣˋ ㄨㄟˊ)
to be of the opinion that...; to think that...; to consider that...; to hold; to deem: 這件事我們認爲有必要跟他說清楚。We deem it necessary to make this clear to him.

【誌】 5584 ㄓˋ jyh zhì
1. to write down; to put down; to record
2. a record
誌銘(ㄓˋ ㄇㄧㄥˊ)
an epitaph 亦作「墓誌銘」
誌悼(ㄓˋ ㄉㄠˋ)
to condole
誌慶(ㄓˋ ㄑㄧㄥˋ)
to offer congratulations
誌喜(ㄓˋ ㄒㄧˇ)
to offer congratulations
誌哀(ㄓˋ ㄞ)
to condole

【誆】 5585 ㄎㄨㄤ kwang kuāng (又讀 ㄍㄨㄤˋ guanq guàng)
to deceive; to delude: 你別誆我。Don't try to deceive me.
誆騙(ㄎㄨㄤ ㄆㄧㄢˋ)
to deceive; to cheat; to swindle; to defraud
誆誕(ㄎㄨㄤ ㄉㄢˋ)
to deceive; to delude
誆言(ㄎㄨㄤ ㄧㄢˊ) or 誆語(ㄎㄨㄤ ㄩˇ)
a lie; wild talk; a falsehood: 他常口出誆語。He often utters falsehoods.

【誓】 5586 ㄕˋ shyh shì
1. to pledge; to vow; to swear; a vow; an oath
2. to take an oath (of allegiance, office, etc.)
誓不兩立(ㄕˋ ˙ㄅㄨ ㄌㄧㄤˇ ㄌㄧˋ)
to vow to fight till oneself or the other party falls
誓不甘休(ㄕˋ ˙ㄅㄨ ㄍㄢ ㄒㄧㄡ)
to vow never to let the offender get away with it
誓師(ㄕˋ ㄕ)
to brief and rouse the troops before a military action; to give a pep talk to the troops at the start of a military expedition
誓詞(ㄕˋ ㄘˊ)
an oath; a pledge
誓死不屈(ㄕˋ ㄙˇ ㄅㄨˋ ㄑㄩ)
to vow that one would rather die than yield
誓言(ㄕˋ ㄧㄢˊ)
a solemn pledge; a vow; an oath
誓約(ㄕˋ ㄩㄝ)
a solemn pledge; a vow; an oath
誓願(ㄕˋ ㄩㄢˋ)
a vow or pledge (especially one made to oneself)

【誕】 5587 ㄉㄢˋ dann dàn
1. birth
2. preposterous; absurd
3. an initial particle
誕辰(ㄉㄢˋ ㄔㄣˊ)
birthday
誕生(ㄉㄢˋ ㄕㄥ)
birth
誕生地(ㄉㄢˋ ㄕㄥ ㄉㄧˋ)
birthplace: 新竹是我的誕生地。Hsinchu is my birthplace.
誕生日(ㄉㄢˋ ㄕㄥ ㄖˋ) or 誕日(ㄉㄢˋ ㄖˋ)
birthday
誕妄(ㄉㄢˋ ㄨㄤˋ)
to cheat with lies

【誘】 5588 ㄧㄡˋ yow yòu
1. to guide; to lead
2. to decoy; to tempt; to allure; to lure; to captivate; to entice
誘兵(ㄧㄡˋ ㄅㄧㄥ)
to pretend to flee in order to lead the enemy into an ambush: 誘兵不追。Do not press the troops that pretend to flee.
誘捕(ㄧㄡˋ ㄅㄨˇ)
to lure a criminal out of hiding and arrest him
誘騙(ㄧㄡˋ ㄆㄧㄢˋ)
to induce by deceit; to beguile; to cajole; to inveigle: 他誘騙我簽這合同。He beguiled me into signing this contract.
誘導(ㄧㄡˋ ㄉㄠˇ)
to guide; to lead to the right path; to induce; induction
誘導反應(ㄧㄡˋ ㄉㄠˇ ㄈㄢˇ ㄧㄥˋ)
(chemistry) an induced reaction
誘導圈(ㄧㄡˋ ㄉㄠˇ ㄑㄩㄢ)
(chemistry) an induction coil
誘敵(ㄧㄡˋ ㄉㄧˊ)
to induce the enemy (to make a wrong move)
誘逃(ㄧㄡˋ ㄊㄠˊ)
to induce someone to run away from home or abscond
誘良爲娼(ㄧㄡˋ ㄌㄧㄤˊ ㄨㄟˊ ㄔㄤ)
to induce innocent girls into prostitution
誘拐(ㄧㄡˋ ㄍㄨㄞˇ)
to seduce; to entice; to abduct; to kidnap: 那孩子昨天被誘拐。The child was abducted yesterday.
誘惑(ㄧㄡˋ ㄏㄨㄛˋ)
① to entice; to lure; to allure; to tempt; to beguile ② to attract; attractive: 窗外景色誘惑人。The view outside the window is attractive.
誘惑色(ㄧㄡˋ ㄏㄨㄛˋ ㄙㄜˋ)
alluring colors (of animals or insects)
誘姦(ㄧㄡˋ ㄐㄧㄢ)
to seduce (a girl, especially a minor); to entice into unlawful sexual intercourse; statutory rape
誘脅(ㄧㄡˋ ㄒㄧㄝˊ)
to tempt and threaten; to cajole and coerce alternatively
誘致(ㄧㄡˋ ㄓˋ)

〔言部〕

to attain an objective by means of temptation

誘殺(ㄧㄡˋ ㄕㄚ)

to trap and kill; to lure to destruction

誘人犯罪(ㄧㄡˋ ㄖㄣˊ ㄈㄢˋ ㄗㄨㄟˋ)

to induce others to break the law

誘餌(ㄧㄡˋ ㄦˇ)

① a bait ② a shill

誘掖(ㄧㄡˋ ㄧˋ)

to guide and encourage; to lead and help

誘因(ㄧㄡˋ ㄧㄣ)

an incentive; an inducement

【誚】 5589 ㄑㄧㄠˋ chiaw qiào

to blame; to reproach; to censure

誚讓(ㄑㄧㄠˋ ㄖㄤˋ)

to blame; to reproach

【誡】 5590 ㄐㄧㄝˋ jieh jiè

1. to warn; to admonish
2. a commandment

【語】 5591 1. ㄩˇ yeu yǔ

1. language; speech
2. a word; a sentence; an expression
3. a saying; a proverb
4. a sign; a signal
5. to speak; to say; to talk

語病(ㄩˇ ㄅㄧㄥˋ)

① illogical use of words; faulty wording or formulation ②difficulty in speaking caused by vocal defects

語妙天下(ㄩˇ ㄇㄧㄠˋ ㄊㄧㄢ ㄒㄧㄚˋ)

unequaled in making wisecracks

語法(ㄩˇ ㄈㄚˇ)

wording; grammar; syntax

語法學(ㄩˇ ㄈㄚˇ ㄒㄩㄝˊ)

syntax

語調(ㄩˇ ㄉㄧㄠˋ)

the tone of one's speech; intonation

語態(ㄩˇ ㄊㄞˋ)

(grammar) voice: 主動語態 the active voice 被動語態 the passive voice

語體文(ㄩˇ ㄊㄧˇ ㄨㄣˊ)

writings in the spoken style

語能喪失症(ㄩˇ ㄋㄥˊ ㄙㄤˋ ㄕ ㄓㄥˋ)

(pathology) aphasia

語錄(ㄩˇ ㄌㄨˋ)

written records of lectures (especially of the Sung Dynasty Confucian scholars); quotations

語錄體(ㄩˇ ㄌㄨˋ ㄊㄧˇ)

the lecture style of writing

語感(ㄩˇ ㄍㄢˇ)

the linguistic sense, feel, or intuition

語根(ㄩˇ ㄍㄣ)

an etymology: 幫我查查這幾個字的語根。Just look up the etymologies of these words for me.

語彙(ㄩˇ ㄏㄨㄟˋ)

vocabulary

語驚四座(ㄩˇ ㄐㄧㄥ ㄙˋ ㄗㄨㄛˋ)

The statement was received with raised eyebrows.

語句(ㄩˇ ㄐㄩˋ)

sentences; phrases: 這篇文章的語句冗長。The phrases of this article are miscellaneous and long.

語氣(ㄩˇ ㄑㄧˋ)

①(grammar) mood ② the tone (of one's speech); the manner of speaking

語系(ㄩˇ ㄒㄧˋ)

a family of languages; a language family; a linguistic family

語學(ㄩˇ ㄒㄩㄝˊ)

linguistics 參看「語言學」

語助詞(ㄩˇ ㄓㄨˋ ㄘˊ)

a grammatical particle; an auxiliary

語重心長(ㄩˇ ㄓㄨㄥˋ ㄒㄧㄣ ㄔㄤˊ)

One's words are serious and (one's) heart is thoughtful.

語勢(ㄩˇ ㄕˋ)

the force of an utterance or statement

語族(ㄩˇ ㄗㄨˊ)

a language family

語詞(ㄩˇ ㄘˊ)

words; phrases

語塞(ㄩˇ ㄙㄜˋ)

unable to utter a word in self-defense (when confronted with unfavorable evidence)

語意(ㄩˇ ㄧˋ)

the meaning (of a word, phrase, sentence, etc.): 這句子的語意清楚。The meaning of the sentence is clear.

語意學(ㄩˇ ㄧˋ ㄒㄩㄝˊ)

semantics

語焉不詳(ㄩˇ ㄧㄢ ㄅㄨˋ ㄒㄧㄤˊ)

The statement is too brief to be clear. 或 very sketchy; too generalized

語言(ㄩˇ ㄧㄢˊ)

a language; speech: 拉丁文是一種死語言。Latin is a dead language.

語言教學法(ㄩˇ ㄧㄢˊ ㄐㄧㄠˋ ㄒㄩㄝˊ ㄈㄚˇ)

language teaching methods

語言教室(ㄩˇ ㄧㄢˊ ㄐㄧㄠˋ ㄕˋ)

a language class

語言心理學(ㄩˇ ㄧㄢˊ ㄒㄧㄣ ㄌㄧˇ ㄒㄩㄝˊ)

linguistic psychology

語言學(ㄩˇ ㄧㄢˊ ㄒㄩㄝˊ)

linguistics; philology

語言學家(ㄩˇ ㄧㄢˊ ㄒㄩㄝˊ ㄐㄧㄚ)

a linguist; a linguistic scientist; a philologist

語言實驗室(ㄩˇ ㄧㄢˊ ㄕˊ ㄧㄢˋ ㄕˋ)

a language laboratory; a language lab

語音(ㄩˇ ㄧㄣ)

① a speech sound; a phone ② pronunciation

語音學(ㄩˇ ㄧㄣ ㄒㄩㄝˊ)

phonetics 參看「聲韻學」

語無倫次(ㄩˇ ㄨˊ ㄌㄨㄣˊ ㄘˋ)

to talk incoherently

語尾(ㄩˇ ㄨㄟˇ)

(grammar) a suffix

語文(ㄩˇ ㄨㄣˊ)

① Chinese (as a subject of study or a means of communication) ② language and literature

語文學(ㄩˇ ㄨㄣˊ ㄒㄩㄝˊ)

the study of written language

語源學(ㄩˇ ㄩㄢˊ ㄒㄩㄝˊ)

etymology

語云(ㄩˇ ㄩㄣˊ)

as the saying goes

【語】 5591 2. ㄩˋ yuh yù

to tell; to inform; to admonish

語人(ㄩˋ ㄖㄣˊ)

to tell others

【誠】 5592 ㄔㄥˊ cherng chéng

1. sincere; honest; cordial; sincerity
2. true; real; truly; indeed; actually

誠樸(ㄔㄥˊ ㄆㄨˊ)

honest and simple
誠非所料(ㄔㄥˊ ㄈㄟ ㄙㄨㄛˇ ㄌㄧㄠˋ)
It is really unexpected.
誠服(ㄔㄥˊ ㄈㄨˊ)
to obey willingly; to submit willingly
誠篤(ㄔㄥˊ ㄉㄨˇ)
honest
誠懇(ㄔㄥˊ ㄎㄣˇ)
sincere; true-hearted; cordial
誠惶誠恐(ㄔㄥˊ ㄏㄨㄤˊ ㄔㄥˊ ㄎㄨㄥˇ)
extremely afraid; very fearful (an expression usually used in a memorial to the emperor)
誠敬(ㄔㄥˊ ㄐㄧㄥˋ)
sincere and respectful
誠心(ㄔㄥˊ ㄒㄧㄣ)
sincerity; wholeheartedness
誠心誠意(ㄔㄥˊ ㄒㄧㄣ ㄔㄥˊ ㄧˋ)
earnestly and sincerely
誠摯(ㄔㄥˊ ㄓˋ)
sincere; true-hearted; cordial
誠實(ㄔㄥˊ ㄕˊ)
honest; upright; trustworthy; honesty: 誠實爲上策。Honesty is the best policy.
誠實可靠(ㄔㄥˊ ㄕˊ ㄎㄜˇ ㄎㄠˋ)
honest and reliable; trustworthy
誠屬(ㄔㄥˊ ㄕㄨˇ)
It is certainly....或 They are certainly....
誠然(ㄔㄥˊ ㄖㄢˊ)
certainly; surely; indeed; to be sure
誠如所言(ㄔㄥˊ ㄖㄨˊ ㄙㄨㄛˇ ㄧㄢˊ)
① It is exactly as you said. ② if it is exactly as you say
誠壹(ㄔㄥˊ ㄧ)
single-minded; single-hearted
誠意(ㄔㄥˊ ㄧˋ)
sincerity; good faith

【誣】 5593
ㄨˊ wu wú
(語音 ㄨ u wū)

to accuse falsely; to bring a false charge against
誣謗(ㄨˊ ㄅㄤˋ)
to slander; to libel
誣衊(ㄨˊ ㄇㄧㄝˋ)
to slander; to libel; to vilify; to calumniate; to smear
誣服(ㄨˊ ㄈㄨˊ)
to plead guilty when one is not (usually as a result of torture)
誣捏事實(ㄨˊ ㄋㄧㄝ ㄕˋ ㄕˊ)
to fabricate a false story
誣賴(ㄨˊ ㄌㄞˋ)
to slander; to accuse falsely; to incriminate falsely
誣良爲盜(ㄨˊ ㄌㄧㄤˊ ㄨㄟˊ ㄉㄠˋ)
to bring a false charge of theft against an upright man; to charge an innocent man with robbery
誣告(ㄨˊ ㄍㄠˋ)or 誣控(ㄨˊ ㄎㄨㄥˋ)
to bring a false charge against; to accuse falsely
誣告反坐(ㄨˊ ㄍㄠˋ ㄈㄢˇ ㄗㄨㄛˋ)
False charges will bring upon the accuser the same punishment which he intends to inflict upon the accused.
誣告罪(ㄨˊ ㄍㄠˋ ㄗㄨㄟˋ)
an offense of malicious accusation
誣害(ㄨˊ ㄏㄞˋ)
to accuse falsely
誣陷(ㄨˊ ㄒㄧㄢˋ)
to incriminate falsely; to frame somebody
誣證(ㄨˊ ㄓㄥˋ)
a perjury; to give false testimony
誣染(ㄨˊ ㄖㄢˇ)
to slander; to libel
誣罔(ㄨˊ ㄨㄤˇ)
to accuse falsely; to bring a false charge against: 切勿誣罔善人。Never accuse an innocent person.

【誤】 5594
ㄨˋ wuh wù

1. to err; a mistake; an error
2. to harm; to suffer; to injure
3. to delay
4. to miss
5. by mistake; by accident

誤報(ㄨˋ ㄅㄠˋ)
to report incorrectly
誤筆(ㄨˋ ㄅㄧˇ)
a slip of the pen 亦作「筆誤」
誤卯(ㄨˋ ㄇㄠˇ)
to fail to show up at the roll call
誤謬(ㄨˋ ㄇㄧㄡˋ)
a mistake; an error: 那是愚蠢的誤謬。That was a foolish mistake.
誤犯(ㄨˋ ㄈㄢˋ)
to offend or violate unintentionally
誤服(ㄨˋ ㄈㄨˊ)
to take the wrong (medicine); to take (medicine) by mistake
誤導(ㄨˋ ㄉㄠˇ)
to mislead: 有些報紙誤導輿論。Some newspapers mislead public opinion.
誤點(ㄨˋ ㄉㄧㄢˇ)
(said of trains, etc.) to be behind time; late; overdue: 火車誤點半小時。The train was half an hour late.
誤了(ㄨˋ ˙ㄌㄜ)
① to have caused an undue delay in ② to have mismanaged
誤國(ㄨˋ ㄍㄨㄛˊ)
to mismanage national affairs; to cause harm to national causes; to damage national interests
誤刊(ㄨˋ ㄎㄢ)
to publish something incorrectly
誤會(ㄨˋ ㄏㄨㄟˋ)
to misunderstand; to misinterpret; to misconstrue; a misunderstanding
誤記(ㄨˋ ㄐㄧˋ)
to record incorrectly
誤解(ㄨˋ ㄐㄧㄝˇ)
to misunderstand; to misinterpret; to misconstrue; a misunderstanding
誤盡蒼生(ㄨˋ ㄐㄧㄣˋ ㄘㄤ ㄕㄥ)
to bring calamity to humanity; to lead the masses to the road of disaster
誤期(ㄨˋ ㄑㄧˊ)
to fail to meet the deadline; to be behind schedule
誤信(ㄨˋ ㄒㄧㄣˋ)
to misplace one's confidence; to believe what is unreliable
誤差(ㄨˋ ㄔㄚ)
(mathematics) an error
誤傳(ㄨˋ ㄔㄨㄢˊ)
to transmit (facts) incorrectly
誤時(ㄨˋ ㄕˊ)
to be behind time
誤食(ㄨˋ ㄕˊ)
to eat (something poisonous or inedible) by mistake
誤事(ㄨˋ ㄕˋ)

〔言部〕

〔言部〕

to ruin a plan through mismanagement, negligence, etc.; to bungle matters
誤殺(ㄨˋ ㄕㄚ)
①unintentional homicide; manslaughter ②to kill or murder a person mistaken for the intended victim
誤傷(ㄨˋ ㄕㄤ)
to hurt by mistake
誤人子弟(ㄨˋ ㄖㄣˊ ㄗˇ ㄉㄧˋ)
(usually said of a poor teacher) to mislead the children of others
誤人誤己(ㄨˋ ㄖㄣˊ ㄨˋ ㄐㄧˇ)
to harm both others and oneself
誤認(ㄨˋ ㄖㄣˋ)
to identify incorrectly
誤入歧途(ㄨˋ ㄖㄨˋ ㄑㄧˊ ㄊㄨˊ)
to go astray (morally)
誤算(ㄨˋ ㄙㄨㄢˋ)
to miscalculate; to miscount
誤譯(ㄨˋ ㄧˋ)
to translate incorrectly
誤爲(ㄨˋ ㄨㄟˊ)
to mistake one thing for another

【誥】 5595 ㄍㄠˋ gaw gào
1. to grant; to confer; to bestow
2. to admonish
3. a written admonition; an imperial mandate
誥命(ㄍㄠˋ ㄇㄧㄥˋ)
a monarch's orders of conferment of titles; an imperial mandate
誥封(ㄍㄠˋ ㄈㄥ)
to bestow (a title upon the wife, living parents, etc. of an official); the conferment of honorary titles by an imperial mandate
誥誡(ㄍㄠˋ ㄐㄧㄝˋ)
an injunction of exhortation
誥敕(ㄍㄠˋ ㄔˋ)
a decree of conferment of titles upon officials in the Ming and Ching dynasties
誥授(ㄍㄠˋ ㄕㄡˋ)
to bestow (titles upon officials)
誥贈(ㄍㄠˋ ㄗㄥˋ)
to bestow (titles upon officials posthumously)

【誦】 5596 ㄙㄨㄥˋ sonq sòng
1. to recite; to intone; to chant
2. poetry; poems; songs
誦讀(ㄙㄨㄥˋ ㄉㄨˊ)
to read aloud; to recite; to intone
誦經(ㄙㄨㄥˋ ㄐㄧㄥ)
to recite passages from scriptures
誦習(ㄙㄨㄥˋ ㄒㄧˊ)
to learn by recitation
誦詩(ㄙㄨㄥˋ ㄕ)
to recite or intone a verse

【誨】 5597 ㄏㄨㄟˋ huey huì (又讀 ㄏㄨㄟˇ hoei huǐ)
1. to teach; to instruct
2. instructions
3. to admonish
4. to induce
誨盜誨淫(ㄏㄨㄟˋ ㄉㄠˋ ㄏㄨㄟˋ ㄧㄣˊ)
to encourage theft by being careless about one's valuables and incite lust by displaying one's physical charms
誨人不倦(ㄏㄨㄟˋ ㄖㄣˊ ㄅㄨˋ ㄐㄩㄢˋ)
to teach without weariness (often used as a complimentary expression in citation of teachers)

【說】 5598 1. ㄕㄨㄛ shuo shuō
1. to speak; to talk; to utter; to say
2. to explain; to clarify
3. a description; a narration; a statement
4. a theory
5. to scold; to talk to; a talking-to; a scolding
說白(ㄕㄨㄛ ㄅㄞˊ)
(Chinese opera) the spoken part (as distinct from the part that is sung)
說白道綠(ㄕㄨㄛ ㄅㄞˊ ㄉㄠˋ ㄌㄩˋ)
to comment on various things without restraint
說白了(ㄕㄨㄛ ㄅㄞˊ ·ㄌㄜ)
to put in plain language
說不得(ㄕㄨㄛ ·ㄅㄨ ·ㄉㄜ)
①unspeakable; indescribable ②unfit for mention; scandalous ③unavoidable
說不定(ㄕㄨㄛ ·ㄅㄨ ㄉㄧㄥˋ)
maybe; perhaps; probably: 說不定那船已經入港了。Maybe the ship has already arrived in harbor.
說不來(ㄕㄨㄛ ·ㄅㄨ ㄌㄞˊ)
①unable to speak; unable to utter ②not on friendly terms; unable to get along with each other
說不過(ㄕㄨㄛ ·ㄅㄨ ㄍㄨㄛˋ)
unable to outspeak or outdebate
說不過去(ㄕㄨㄛ ·ㄅㄨ ㄍㄨㄛˋ ·ㄑㄩ)
unacceptable to one's sense of propriety or justice; cannot be justified or explained away
說不開(ㄕㄨㄛ ·ㄅㄨ ㄎㄞ)
unable to reach a mutual understanding
說不清(ㄕㄨㄛ ·ㄅㄨ ㄑㄧㄥ)
unable to explain clearly
說不下去(ㄕㄨㄛ ·ㄅㄨ ㄒㄧㄚˋ ·ㄑㄩ)
①unable to continue one's speech ②not acceptable to one's sense of propriety
說不出口(ㄕㄨㄛ ·ㄅㄨ ㄔㄨ ㄎㄡˇ)
unutterable; unable to speak out
說不上(ㄕㄨㄛ ·ㄅㄨ ㄕㄤˋ)
①do not deserve mention; do not fit the description ②cannot say or tell
說不上來(ㄕㄨㄛ ·ㄅㄨ ㄕㄤˋ ㄌㄞˊ)
unable to get the words out
說破(ㄕㄨㄛ ㄆㄛˋ)
to unravel or expose by some remarks
說媒(ㄕㄨㄛ ㄇㄟˊ)
to propose a marriage as a matchmaker
說夢(ㄕㄨㄛ ㄇㄥˋ)
to talk nonsense
說夢話(ㄕㄨㄛ ㄇㄥˋ ㄏㄨㄚˋ)
①to talk in one's sleep ②to talk nonsense
說明(ㄕㄨㄛ ㄇㄧㄥˊ)
①to explain; to clarify; to expound ②expository writing; exposition; caption
說明書(ㄕㄨㄛ ㄇㄧㄥˊ ㄕㄨ)
a written explanation; written instructions attached to merchandise
說法(ㄕㄨㄛ ㄈㄚˇ)
①to preach Buddhism ②the way of reasoning; an argument; interpretation; a state-

ment; a version; wording: 這個意思可以有數種說法。This idea can be formulated in different ways.

說風涼話(ㄕㄨㄛ ㄈㄥ ㄌㄧㄤˊ ㄏㄨㄚˋ)
to talk like an unconcerned person; to make nonchalant statements

說大話(ㄕㄨㄛ ㄉㄚˋ ㄏㄨㄚˋ)
to brag; to boast; to talk big; to talk through one's hat

說得來(ㄕㄨㄛ ˙ㄉㄜ ㄌㄞˊ)
(said of two or more people) able to get along; to be on good terms: 他們很說得來。They are on good terms.

說得過去(ㄕㄨㄛ ˙ㄉㄜ ㄍㄨㄛˋ ˙ㄑㄩ)
acceptable; passable; excusable; pardonable

說得好(ㄕㄨㄛ ˙ㄉㄜ ㄏㄠˇ)
well said

說得好聽(ㄕㄨㄛ ˙ㄉㄜ ㄏㄠˇ ㄊㄧㄥ)
to make an unpleasant fact sound attractive

說得下去(ㄕㄨㄛ ˙ㄉㄜ ㄒㄧㄚˋ ˙ㄑㄩ)
passable

說得上(ㄕㄨㄛ ˙ㄉㄜ ㄕㄤˋ)
to deserve mention

說得有理(ㄕㄨㄛ ˙ㄉㄜ ㄧㄡˇ ㄌㄧˇ)
to sound reasonable

說到(ㄕㄨㄛ ㄉㄠˋ)
to speak of; to mention; to refer to; as to: 我希望你沒有向她說到我。I hope you did not mention my name to her.

說到做到(ㄕㄨㄛ ㄉㄠˋ ㄗㄨㄛˋ ㄉㄠˋ)
to do what one says; to live up to one's word: 我會說到做到的。I'll live up to my word.

說道(ㄕㄨㄛ ㄉㄠˋ)
to say

說地談天(ㄕㄨㄛ ㄉㄧˋ ㄊㄢˊ ㄊㄧㄢ)
① to talk about everything under the sun ② skilled in speech; eloquent 亦作「談天說地」

說定(ㄕㄨㄛ ㄉㄧㄥˋ)
to settle; to agree on: 關於價格我們尚未說定。We haven't agreed on the price yet.

說短論長(ㄕㄨㄛ ㄉㄨㄢˇ ㄌㄨㄣˋ ㄔㄤˊ)
to gossip; to criticize others

說東道西(ㄕㄨㄛ ㄉㄨㄥ ㄉㄠˋ ㄒㄧ)
to talk about all sorts of subjects without restraint

說頭兒(ㄕㄨㄛ ˙ㄊㄡㄦ)
① something worth talking about ② an excuse

說天說地(ㄕㄨㄛ ㄊㄧㄢ ㄕㄨㄛ ㄉㄧˋ)
① to brag; to boast ② skilled in speech; eloquent

說通(ㄕㄨㄛ ㄊㄨㄥ)
to succeed in reaching an understanding

說了不算(ㄕㄨㄛ ˙ㄌㄜ ㄅㄨˋ ㄙㄨㄢˋ)
to fail to keep a promise; to go back on one's word

說了算數(ㄕㄨㄛ ˙ㄌㄜ ㄙㄨㄢˋ ㄕㄨˋ)
I mean what I say.

說來話長(ㄕㄨㄛ ㄌㄞˊ ㄏㄨㄚˋ ㄔㄤˊ)
It is a long story....

說來說去(ㄕㄨㄛ ㄌㄞˊ ㄕㄨㄛ ㄑㄩˋ)
to say the same thing over and over again

說理(ㄕㄨㄛ ㄌㄧˇ)
① to give a sermon; to preach ② to be reasonable; to argue; to reason things out

說溜了嘴(ㄕㄨㄛ ㄌㄧㄡ ˙ㄌㄜ ㄗㄨㄟˇ)
to have a slip of the tongue; to blurt out something

說高說低(ㄕㄨㄛ ㄍㄠ ㄕㄨㄛ ㄉㄧ)
to criticize others thoughtlessly

說古(ㄕㄨㄛ ㄍㄨˇ)
(a derisive expression) to talk about one's pet subject

說鼓書(ㄕㄨㄛ ㄍㄨˇ ㄕㄨ)
the accompaniment of a drum when narrating stories in metrical form

說過(ㄕㄨㄛ ㄍㄨㄛˋ)
to have said or mentioned

說鬼話(ㄕㄨㄛ ㄍㄨㄟˇ ㄏㄨㄚˋ)
to tell a lie; to lie

說客(ㄕㄨㄛ ㄎㄜˋ)
one who tries to persuade or convince somebody on behalf of another

說開(ㄕㄨㄛ ㄎㄞ)
to explain

說合(ㄕㄨㄛ ㄏㄜˊ)
to help arrange a union

說和(ㄕㄨㄛ ˙ㄏㄜ)
to act as a mediator; to mediate: 我去給他們說和。I'll try to mediate between them.

說黑道白(ㄕㄨㄛ ㄏㄟ ㄉㄠˋ ㄅㄞˊ)
to criticize others thoughtlessly

說好(ㄕㄨㄛ ㄏㄠˇ)
to complete negotiations; to come to an agreement

說好說歹(ㄕㄨㄛ ㄏㄠˇ ㄕㄨㄛ ㄉㄞˇ)
to speak both well and ill in an attempt to influence or induce

說話(ㄕㄨㄛ ㄏㄨㄚˋ)
① to speak; to talk; to say ② to tell stories ③ a chat; a talk ④ gossip; talk ⑤ (colloquial) in a minute; in a moment; in a jiffy; right away

說話不當話(ㄕㄨㄛ ㄏㄨㄚˋ ㄅㄨˋ ㄉㄤˋ ㄏㄨㄚˋ)
to fail to keep a promise; to break one's word

說黃道黑(ㄕㄨㄛ ㄏㄨㄤˊ ㄉㄠˋ ㄏㄟ)
to criticize others

說謊(ㄕㄨㄛ ㄏㄨㄤˇ)
to tell a lie; to lie

說謊者(ㄕㄨㄛ ㄏㄨㄤˇ ㄓㄜˇ)
a liar

說教(ㄕㄨㄛ ㄐㄧㄠˋ)
to preach; to deliver a sermon

說起(ㄕㄨㄛ ㄑㄧˇ)
① to start talking about; to bring up (a subject) ② with reference to; as for

說起來(ㄕㄨㄛ ㄑㄧˇ ˙ㄌㄞ)
① as a matter of fact; in fact: 說起來我們還是同學。In fact, we were in the same school. ② to mention

說千說萬(ㄕㄨㄛ ㄑㄧㄢ ㄕㄨㄛ ㄨㄢˋ)
to talk thousands of times; to speak again and again

說親(ㄕㄨㄛ ㄑㄧㄣ)
to propose a marriage as a matchmaker

說親道熱(ㄕㄨㄛ ㄑㄧㄣ ㄉㄠˋ ㄖㄜˋ)
to say friendly things; to sound very friendly

說清道白(ㄕㄨㄛ ㄑㄧㄥ ㄉㄠˋ ㄅㄞˊ)
to talk clearly

說情(ㄕㄨㄛ ㄑㄧㄥˊ)
to solicit a favor or to ask for mercy on behalf of others; to intercede

說笑(ㄕㄨㄛ ㄒㄧㄠˋ) or 說說笑笑(ㄕㄨㄛ ㄕㄨㄛ ㄒㄧㄠˋ ㄒㄧㄠˋ)
to joke; to talk and laugh

說笑話(ㄕㄨㄛ ㄒㄧㄠˋ ㄏㄨㄚˋ)

〔言部〕

〔言部〕

to tell jokes

說閒話(ㄕㄨㄛ ㄒㄧㄢˊ ㄏㄨㄚˋ)
to gossip; to criticize; to make unfavorable comments; a gossip: 她太喜歡說閒話。She is too fond of gossip.

說現成話(ㄕㄨㄛ ㄒㄧㄢˋ ㄔㄥˊ ㄏㄨㄚˋ)
to make comments like an after-the-event prophet

說項(ㄕㄨㄛ ㄒㄧㄤˋ)
to speak favorably of another; to say a good word for another; to intercede for somebody 參看「說情」

說相聲(ㄕㄨㄛ ㄒㄧㄤˋ ·ㄕㄥ)
a kind of comic dialogue for entertainment

說著玩兒(ㄕㄨㄛ ·ㄓㄜ ㄨㄢˊㄦ)
to say something without seriously meaning it; to joke

說眞話(ㄕㄨㄛ ㄓㄣ ㄏㄨㄚˋ)
to tell the truth

說叉了(ㄕㄨㄛ ㄔㄚˋ ·ㄌㄜ)
to start quarreling (while having a conversation)

說長道短(ㄕㄨㄛ ㄔㄤˊ ㄉㄠˋ ㄉㄨㄢˇ)
to criticize others

說唱(ㄕㄨㄛ ㄔㄤˋ)
a kind of performance consisting mainly of talking and singing

說出(ㄕㄨㄛ ㄔㄨ)
to speak out; to reveal; to utter

說穿(ㄕㄨㄛ ㄔㄨㄢ)
to unravel or expose by some remarks; to tell what something really is; to reveal

說時容易做時難(ㄕㄨㄛ ㄕˊ ㄖㄨㄥˊ ㄧˋ ㄗㄨㄛˋ ㄕˊ ㄋㄢˊ)
Easier said than done.

說是一回事，做是另一回事(ㄕㄨㄛ ㄕˋ ㄧˋ ㄏㄨㄟˊ ㄕˋ, ㄗㄨㄛˋ ㄕˋ ㄌㄧㄥˋ ㄧˋ ㄏㄨㄟˊ ㄕˋ)
To say is one thing; to practice is another.

說書(ㄕㄨㄛ ㄕㄨ)
to tell stories (as professional storytellers do)

說書的(ㄕㄨㄛ ㄕㄨ ·ㄉㄜ)
a professional storyteller

說走就走(ㄕㄨㄛ ㄗㄡˇ ㄐㄧㄡˋ ㄗㄡˇ)
to announce the intention to leave and really mean it

說嘴(ㄕㄨㄛ ㄗㄨㄟˇ)
①to brag; to boast: 我們誰也別說嘴。Let's not make any boast. ②to argue; to quarrel: 他常常和人說嘴。He often quarrels with people.

說辭(ㄕㄨㄛ ㄘˊ)
excuses; pretexts: 我不相信他缺席的說辭。I don't believe his excuse for absence.

說曹操，曹操就到(ㄕㄨㄛ ㄘㄠˊ ·ㄘㄠ, ㄘㄠˊ ·ㄘㄠ ㄐㄧㄡˋ ㄉㄠˋ)
Talk of the devil and the devil appears.

說錯(ㄕㄨㄛ ㄘㄨㄛˋ)
to speak incorrectly

說錯了話(ㄕㄨㄛ ㄘㄨㄛˋ ·ㄌㄜ ㄏㄨㄚˋ)
to speak what shouldn't have been uttered

說三不接兩(ㄕㄨㄛ ㄙㄢ ㄅㄨˋ ㄐㄧㄝ ㄌㄧㄤˇ)
to talk incoherently

說三道四(ㄕㄨㄛ ㄙㄢ ㄉㄠˋ ㄙˋ)
to make thoughtless comments

說一不二(ㄕㄨㄛ ㄧ ㄅㄨˋ ㄦˋ)or 說一是一(ㄕㄨㄛ ㄧ ㄕˋ ㄧ)
to be a man of his word; to keep one's promise; to stand by one's word

說也奇怪(ㄕㄨㄛ ㄧㄝˇ ㄑㄧˊ ㄍㄨㄞˋ)
for a wonder

說五道六(ㄕㄨㄛ ㄨˇ ㄉㄠˋ ㄌㄧㄡˋ)
to make thoughtless comments

說完(ㄕㄨㄛ ㄨㄢˊ)
to finish speaking: 他說完話就走出去。He went out after he finished speaking.

說文解字(ㄕㄨㄛ ㄨㄣˊ ㄐㄧㄝˇ ㄗˋ)or 說文(ㄕㄨㄛ ㄨㄣˊ)
the title of an etymological dictionary authored by Hsü Shen(許愼)of the Han Dynasty

【說】 5598
2. ㄕㄨㄟˋ shuey shuì
to persuade; to influence

說服(ㄕㄨㄟˋ ㄈㄨˊ)or(ㄕㄨㄛ ㄈㄨˊ)
to persuade; to convince; to bring around (or round); to prevail on: 她的演講很有說服力。Her speech is very convincing.

說客(ㄕㄨㄟˋ ㄎㄜˋ)
a professional commissary in ancient times sent by one monarch to another with a view to convincing him 亦作「說士」

【說】 5598
3.(悅) ㄩㄝˋ yueh yuè
to delight; to please

【誒】 5599
ㄝˋ èh ê
an exclamation of affirmation

八畫

【課】 5600
ㄎㄜˋ keh kè
1. a class meeting
2. a course (of study)
3. a lesson
4. to impose; to levy; tax
5. a session at divination
6. a suboffice or bureau
7. to supervise

課本(ㄎㄜˋ ㄅㄣˇ)
a textbook

課表(ㄎㄜˋ ㄅㄧㄠˇ)
school timetable 亦作「功課表」

課目(ㄎㄜˋ ㄇㄨˋ)
a topic or subject of study

課堂(ㄎㄜˋ ㄊㄤˊ)
a classroom

課題(ㄎㄜˋ ㄊㄧˊ)
①a task or problem (for students) ②a theme; a question for study or discussion: 我們下次討論的課題是什麼? What's the theme of our discussion next time?

課卷(ㄎㄜˋ ㄐㄩㄢˋ)
students' papers

課長(ㄎㄜˋ ㄓㄤˇ)
a section chief (in an office)

課桌(ㄎㄜˋ ㄓㄨㄛ)
a classroom desk

課程(ㄎㄜˋ ㄔㄥˊ)
a curriculum: 這學期課程排得太多了。The curriculum is overloaded this semester.

課程表(ㄎㄜˋ ㄔㄥˊ ㄅㄧㄠˇ)
a school schedule; a class schedule; a school timetable

課室(ㄎㄜˋ ㄕˋ)
a classroom

課稅(ㄎㄜˋ ㄕㄨㄟˋ)
to levy taxes; to impose taxes: 政府爲了國家的開支而課稅。The government levies

taxes for national expenses.

課業(ㄎㄜˋ ㄧㄝˋ)
schoolwork; lessons

課外(ㄎㄜˋ ㄨㄞˋ)
extracurricular; outside class; after school

課外活動(ㄎㄜˋ ㄨㄞˋ ㄏㄨㄛˊ ㄉㄨㄥˋ)
extracurricular activities

課外作業(ㄎㄜˋ ㄨㄞˋ ㄗㄨㄛˋ ㄧㄝˋ)
homework (for a student): 我作完課外作業了。I have finished my homework.

課文(ㄎㄜˋ ㄨㄣˊ)
the text or contents of a lesson

課餘(ㄎㄜˋ ㄩˊ)or 課後(ㄎㄜˋ ㄏㄡˋ)
after school or class: 課後到我辦公室來。Come to my office after school.

5601
【誰】 ㄕㄟˊ sheir shéi (讀音 ㄕㄨㄟˊ shwei shuí)

1. who
2. anyone; someone

誰的(ㄕㄟˊ ˙ㄉㄜ)
Whose? 這是誰的意見? Whose idea is it?

誰能(ㄕㄟˊ ㄋㄥˊ)
Who can? 或 Who could? 誰能幫助他? Who can help him?

誰料(ㄕㄟˊ ㄌㄧㄠˋ)
Who could have known? 或 Who could have expected? 或 Who would have thought?

誰敢(ㄕㄟˊ ㄍㄢˇ)
Who dares?

誰肯(ㄕㄟˊ ㄎㄣˇ)
Who is willing? 誰肯付出他所要的價錢? Who is willing to pay the price he asked?

誰何(ㄕㄟˊ ㄏㄜˊ)
① Who? ② Who can do anything about it?

誰家(ㄕㄟˊ ㄐㄧㄚ)
① Whose home (or house)? 那是誰家? Whose house is that? ② Who?

誰想到(ㄕㄟˊ ㄒㄧㄤˇ ㄉㄠˋ)
Who would have thought?

誰知道(ㄕㄟˊ ㄓ ㄉㄠˋ)or 誰知(ㄕㄟˊ ㄓ)
① Who knows? ② Who would have thought?

誰承望(ㄕㄟˊ ㄔㄥˊ ㄨㄤˋ)
Who would have expected?

誰是誰非(ㄕㄟˊ ㄕˋ ㄕㄟˊ ㄈㄟ)
Who is right and who is wrong?

誰人(ㄕㄟˊ ㄖㄣˊ)
Who?

【誶】 5602
ㄙㄨㄟˋ suey suì

to reproach; to scold; to upbraid

誶罵(ㄙㄨㄟˋ ㄇㄚˋ)
to scold; to reproach; to upbraid

【誹】 5603
ㄈㄟˇ feei fěi

to attack; to condemn; to slander

誹謗(ㄈㄟˇ ㄅㄤˋ)
to libel; to slander; to calumniate: 他似乎以誹謗我爲樂。He seems to enjoy libeling me.

誹謗行爲(ㄈㄟˇ ㄅㄤˋ ㄒㄧㄥˊ ㄨㄟˊ)
an act of libel or slander; libel; slander

誹謗者(ㄈㄟˇ ㄅㄤˋ ㄓㄜˇ)
a libeler; a slanderer

誹謗罪(ㄈㄟˇ ㄅㄤˋ ㄗㄨㄟˋ)
libel (as a criminal offense)

【誼】 5604
ㄧˋ yih yì
(又讀 ㄧˊ yi yí)

1. friendship
2. same as 義—justice; righteousness

【調】 5605
1. ㄊㄧㄠˊ tyau tiáo

1. to mix; to blend
2. to regulate; to adjust
3. balance; regular
4. to make fun of; to tease
5. to mediate

調配(ㄊㄧㄠˊ ㄆㄟˋ)
① to prepare (a concoction); to mix; to blend ② to coordinate; to arrange

調皮(ㄊㄧㄠˊ ㄆㄧˊ)or(ㄉㄧㄠˋ ㄆㄧˊ)
① naughty ② sly; treacherous; cunning; unruly; tricky

調皮搗蛋(ㄊㄧㄠˊ ㄆㄧˊ ㄉㄠˇ ㄉㄢˋ)
ungovernable; making troubles; mischievous

調頻(ㄊㄧㄠˊ ㄆㄧㄣˊ)
(electricity) frequency modulation (FM)

調幅(ㄊㄧㄠˊ ㄈㄨˊ)
(radio) amplitude modulation (AM)

調停(ㄊㄧㄠˊ ㄊㄧㄥˊ)
to mediate

調弄(ㄊㄧㄠˊ ㄋㄨㄥˋ)
① to make fun of; to tease ② to arrange; to adjust ③ to instigate; to stir up ④ to play musical instruments

調理(ㄊㄧㄠˊ ㄌㄧˇ)
① to train; to teach ② to nurse impaired health; to recuperate ③ to take care of; to look after

調料(ㄊㄧㄠˊ ㄌㄧㄠˋ)
condiment; seasoning; flavoring

調羹(ㄊㄧㄠˊ ㄍㄥ)
a spoon

調侃(ㄊㄧㄠˊ ㄎㄢˇ)
to scoff; to mock; to jeer: 不要介意別人的調侃。Don't take to heart what was said in mock.

調和(ㄊㄧㄠˊ ㄏㄜˊ)
① to mix; to blend: 這兩種顏色不能調和。The two colors don't mix well. ② to harmonize; to bring into agreement ③ to adjust; to tune; to put in tune ④ to mediate; to reconcile

調和比例(ㄊㄧㄠˊ ㄏㄜˊ ㄅㄧˇ ㄌㄧˋ)
harmonic proportion

調和級數(ㄊㄧㄠˊ ㄏㄜˊ ㄐㄧˊ ㄕㄨˋ)
a harmonic progression

調和中項(ㄊㄧㄠˊ ㄏㄜˊ ㄓㄨㄥ ㄒㄧㄤˋ)
a harmonic mean

調護(ㄊㄧㄠˊ ㄏㄨˋ)
to attend to and protect; to take care of; to nurse

調劑(ㄊㄧㄠˊ ㄐㄧˋ)
① to prepare drugs or medicines ② to adjust; to make adjustments

調劑師(ㄊㄧㄠˊ ㄐㄧˋ ㄕ)
a druggist; a chemist; an apothecary; a pharmacist

調劑身心(ㄊㄧㄠˊ ㄐㄧˋ ㄕㄣ ㄒㄧㄣ)
to provide physical and mental relaxation

調節(ㄊㄧㄠˊ ㄐㄧㄝˊ)
① to regulate; to adjust ② to moderate

調解(ㄊㄧㄠˊ ㄐㄧㄝˇ)
to mediate; to patch up: 只有你才能調解他們的家庭糾紛。Only you can patch up their family quarrels.

調經(ㄊㄧㄠˊ ㄐㄧㄥ)
to regulate menstruation

according to the normal cycle by medical means
調情(ㄊㄧㄠˊ ㄑㄧㄥˊ)
to flirt; to play at love
調戲(ㄊㄧㄠˊ ㄒㄧˋ)
to flirt with (women); to assail (a woman) with obscenities
調笑(ㄊㄧㄠˊ ㄒㄧㄠˋ)
to poke fun at; to make fun of; to tease
調製(ㄊㄧㄠˊ ㄓˋ)
to prepare or concoct (drugs, etc.): 她喜歡調製外國菜。She enjoyed concocting foreign dishes.
調治(ㄊㄧㄠˊ ㄓˋ)
to undergo medical treatment and recuperation
調整(ㄊㄧㄠˊ ㄓㄥˇ)
to adjust; to tune up; to regulate
調處(ㄊㄧㄠˊ ㄔㄨˇ)
to mediate and settle (disputes, quarrels, etc.); to arbitrate
調攝(ㄊㄧㄠˊ ㄕㄜˋ)
to nurse impaired health
調人(ㄊㄧㄠˊ ㄖㄣˊ)
a mediator; an arbitrator: 這調人過於偏袒。The arbitrator is biased.
調色(ㄊㄧㄠˊ ㄙㄜˋ)
to mix colors; to mix paints
調色板(ㄊㄧㄠˊ ㄙㄜˋ ㄅㄢˇ)
a palette
調三斡四(ㄊㄧㄠˊ ㄙㄢ ㄨㄛˋ ㄙˋ)
to sow the seeds of discord everywhere
調音(ㄊㄧㄠˊ ㄧㄣ)
(music) tuning
調養(ㄊㄧㄠˊ ㄧㄤˇ)
to nurse one's health; to take care of oneself
調味(ㄊㄧㄠˊ ㄨㄟˋ)
to season foods; to mix flavors
調味品(ㄊㄧㄠˊ ㄨㄟˋ ㄆㄧㄣˇ)
seasoning; spice; dressing material; condiment: 鹽和胡椒是調味品。Salt and pepper are seasonings.
調勻(ㄊㄧㄠˊ ㄩㄣˊ)
to mix evenly

【調】 5605
2. ㄉㄧㄠˋ diaw diào
1. to transfer; to move; to shift; to change
2. to collect; to mobilize
3. a tune; a melody; an accent; a tone
調包(ㄉㄧㄠˋ ㄅㄠ)
to substitute an inferior thing in secret
調兵遣將(ㄉㄧㄠˋ ㄅㄧㄥ ㄑㄧㄢˇ ㄐㄧㄤˋ)
(literally) to move troops and despatch generals—to prepare for war; to deploy forces
調派(ㄉㄧㄠˋ ㄆㄞˋ)
to assign: 他被調派到第七艦隊服務。He is assigned to the Seventh Fleet.
調門兒(ㄉㄧㄠˋ ㄇㄜˊㄦ)
a melody; a tune; a pitch: 她說話調門兒高。She speaks in a high pitch.
調調兒(ㄉㄧㄠˋ ˙ㄉㄧㄠㄦ)
one's peculiar hobby, preference, fancy, etc.
調度(ㄉㄧㄠˋ ㄉㄨˋ)
① to move (available equipment or manpower) about according to needs; to dispatch; to manage; to control ② a dispatcher: 他是該運輸公司的調度。He is a dispatcher at the transportation company.
調動(ㄉㄧㄠˋ ㄉㄨㄥˋ)
to transfer; to shift; to move (troops)
調頭寸(ㄉㄧㄠˋ ㄊㄡˊ ㄘㄨㄣˋ)
to scrape up enough cash; to raise money for an immediate expenditure
調虎離山(ㄉㄧㄠˋ ㄏㄨˇ ㄌㄧˊ ㄕㄢ)
(literally) to induce the tiger out of the mountain—to use the stratagem of luring the opponent out of his citadel
調換(ㄉㄧㄠˋ ㄏㄨㄢˋ)
to exchange; to swap; to replace
調集(ㄉㄧㄠˋ ㄐㄧˊ)
to concentrate (troops, etc.) in a place: 敵人調集了六個師。Our enemy concentrated six divisions.
調遣(ㄉㄧㄠˋ ㄑㄧㄢˇ)
to transfer (officials, troops, etc.)
調職(ㄉㄧㄠˋ ㄓˊ)
to transfer to a new post
調查(ㄉㄧㄠˋ ㄔㄚˊ)
to investigate; to study; to probe; to survey; investigation; a survey
調查表(ㄉㄧㄠˋ ㄔㄚˊ ㄅㄧㄠˇ)
a questionnaire
調查法(ㄉㄧㄠˋ ㄔㄚˊ ㄈㄚˇ)
the survey method
調查戶口(ㄉㄧㄠˋ ㄔㄚˊ ㄏㄨˋ ㄎㄡˇ)
to take the census
調查員(ㄉㄧㄠˋ ㄔㄚˊ ㄩㄢˊ)
an investigator
調車場(ㄉㄧㄠˋ ㄔㄜ ㄔㄤˇ)
a marshaling yard; a switchyard
調差(ㄉㄧㄠˋ ㄔㄞ)
to transfer to a new assignment
調任(ㄉㄧㄠˋ ㄖㄣˋ)
to transfer to a new post
調子(ㄉㄧㄠˋ ˙ㄗ) or 調兒(ㄉㄧㄠˋㄦ)
a tune; a melody; a tone: 她哼的這個調子倒是挺熟的。The tune she is humming is quite familiar.
調走(ㄉㄧㄠˋ ㄗㄡˇ)
to send away; to banish
調用(ㄉㄧㄠˋ ㄩㄥˋ)
to transfer (an official) for temporary assignment in another organization

【諂】 5606
ㄔㄢˇ chaan chǎn
to flatter; to cringe; to fawn
諂媚(ㄔㄢˇ ㄇㄟˋ)
to flatter; to toady; flattery
諂佞(ㄔㄢˇ ㄋㄧㄥˋ)
to flatter; to toady
諂笑(ㄔㄢˇ ㄒㄧㄠˋ)
a fawning smile
諂諛(ㄔㄢˇ ㄩˊ)
to flatter; to curry favor

【諄】 5607
ㄓㄨㄣ juen zhūn
patient or earnest (in explaining, teaching, etc.)
諄諄(ㄓㄨㄣ ㄓㄨㄣ)
patient or earnest (in explaining, teaching, etc.)
諄諄教誨(ㄓㄨㄣ ㄓㄨㄣ ㄐㄧㄠˋ ㄏㄨㄟˋ) or 諄諄教導(ㄓㄨㄣ ㄓㄨㄣ ㄐㄧㄠˋ ㄉㄠˇ)
to teach and admonish with patience

【談】 5608 ㄊㄢˊ tarn tán

1. to talk; to converse; to chat: 我們明天好好談一談。Let's have a good chat tomorrow.
2. what is said or talked about; a talk; gossip
3. a Chinese family name

談柄(ㄊㄢˊ ㄅㄧㄥˇ)
an incident, etc. that makes an interesting topic of conversation

談判(ㄊㄢˊ ㄆㄢˋ)
negotiation; to negotiate; talks: 雙方談判中斷。The talks between two sides broke down.

談鋒(ㄊㄢˊ ㄈㄥ)
incisiveness of speech

談到(ㄊㄢˊ ㄉㄠˋ)
to speak of; to talk about; to refer to: 這是不是幾天前你談到的那本書? Is this the book you spoke of the other day?

談天(ㄊㄢˊ ㄊㄧㄢ)
to chat idly

談天說地(ㄊㄢˊ ㄊㄧㄢ ㄕㄨㄛ ㄉㄧˋ)
to chat about all sorts of subjects

談吐(ㄊㄢˊ ㄊㄨˇ)
the way a person talks; the manner of speaking: 他的談吐風雅。His talk is elegant.

談吐風生(ㄊㄢˊ ㄊㄨˇ ㄈㄥ ㄕㄥ)
fascinatingly voluble; eloquent and humorous

談論(ㄊㄢˊ ㄌㄨㄣˋ)
to discuss; to talk about

談客(ㄊㄢˊ ㄎㄜˋ)
an able talker

談空說有(ㄊㄢˊ ㄎㄨㄥ ㄕㄨㄛ ㄧㄡˇ)
to get together and chat

談何容易(ㄊㄢˊ ㄏㄜˊ ㄖㄨㄥˊ ㄧˋ)
How easy it is just to talk about it! (But it is easier said than done.) 或by no means easy: 一天完成工作, 眞是談何容易。It's by no means easy to finish the work in one day.

談虎色變(ㄊㄢˊ ㄏㄨˇ ㄙㄜˋ ㄅㄧㄢˋ)
(literally) to turn pale at the mention of a tiger—to turn pale when something horrible is mentioned

談話(ㄊㄢˊ ㄏㄨㄚˋ)
a statement; conversation; a talk; a chat; to talk; to converse

談話會(ㄊㄢˊ ㄏㄨㄚˋ ㄏㄨㄟˋ)
an informal meeting for conversation; a symposium

談起(ㄊㄢˊ ㄑㄧˇ)
to mention; to speak of

談情說愛(ㄊㄢˊ ㄑㄧㄥˊ ㄕㄨㄛ ㄞˋ)
(said of a couple in love) to chat intimately

談笑封侯(ㄊㄢˊ ㄒㄧㄠˋ ㄈㄥ ㄏㄡˊ)
(literally) to be ennobled while talking and laughing—to rise in the world with great ease

談笑風生(ㄊㄢˊ ㄒㄧㄠˋ ㄈㄥ ㄕㄥ)
to talk cheerfully and humorously

談笑自若(ㄊㄢˊ ㄒㄧㄠˋ ㄗˋ ㄖㄨㄛˋ)
cheerful and composed (in the face of great dangers, imminent disaster, etc.): 他們面對危險猶談笑自若。They are cheerful and composed in the face of great dangers.

談心(ㄊㄢˊ ㄒㄧㄣ)
to have a tête-à-tête: 他們昨天在公園談心。They had a tête-à-tête in the park yesterday.

談玄(ㄊㄢˊ ㄒㄩㄢˊ)
to discuss metaphysics

談麈(ㄊㄢˊ ㄓㄨˇ)
a hair duster which ancient scholars held while they were talking

談助(ㄊㄢˊ ㄓㄨˋ)
a matter for conversation: 足資談助。It serves as a good topic of conversation.

談宗(ㄊㄢˊ ㄗㄨㄥ)
one who is universally admired as a great talker

談叢(ㄊㄢˊ ㄘㄨㄥˊ)or 談藪(ㄊㄢˊ ㄙㄡˇ)
a collection of conversations

談言微中(ㄊㄢˊ ㄧㄢˊ ㄨㄟˊ ㄓㄨㄥˋ)
able to satirize aptly

【諉】 5609 ㄨㄟˇ woei wěi

to shirk; to evade; to pass the buck

諉過(ㄨㄟˇ ㄍㄨㄛˋ)
to lay the blame upon others: 不要諉過他人。Don't lay the blame on others.

諉爲不知(ㄨㄟˇ ㄨㄟˊ ㄅㄨˋ ㄓ)
to pretend not to know

【請】 5610 ㄑㄧㄥˇ chiing qǐng

1. to request; to ask; to beg; to beseech; to entreat: 敬請指教。I humbly request your advice.
2. please: 請坐。Please be seated.
3. to hire; to seek the service of; to engage: 她請了個新僕人。She engaged a new servant.

請便(ㄑㄧㄥˇ ㄅㄧㄢˋ)
as you please: 你想那樣就請便。You can go ahead if you want to.

請不動(ㄑㄧㄥˇ ·ㄅㄨ ㄉㄨㄥˋ)or 請不到(ㄑㄧㄥˇ ·ㄅㄨ ㄉㄠˋ)
unable to make someone come by an invitation

請不起(ㄑㄧㄥˇ ·ㄅㄨ ㄑㄧˇ)
cannot afford to hire

請命(ㄑㄧㄥˇ ㄇㄧㄥˋ)
① to beg for life; to ask for clemency ② to request for instructions or orders

請大夫(ㄑㄧㄥˇ ㄉㄞˋ ·ㄈㄨ)
to send for a doctor

請帖(ㄑㄧㄥˇ ㄊㄧㄝˇ)or 請柬(ㄑㄧㄥˇ ㄐㄧㄢˇ)
a printed invitation; an invitation card: 他已發出宴客請帖。He has sent out invitations to a dinner party.

請託(ㄑㄧㄥˇ ㄊㄨㄛ)
to ask for a favor

請客(ㄑㄧㄥˇ ㄎㄜˋ)
to invite guests; to give a party; to stand treat

請款(ㄑㄧㄥˇ ㄎㄨㄢˇ)
to request for funds or appropriation

請假(ㄑㄧㄥˇ ㄐㄧㄚˋ)
to ask for leave of absence

請教(ㄑㄧㄥˇ ㄐㄧㄠˋ)
to request instructions or advice; to consult

請救兵(ㄑㄧㄥˇ ㄐㄧㄡˋ ㄅㄧㄥ)
to ask for reinforcements

請見(ㄑㄧㄥˇ ㄐㄧㄢˋ)
to request an audience or interview

請君入甕(ㄑㄧㄥˇ ㄐㄩㄣ ㄖㄨˋ ㄨㄥˋ)
to make a person suffer from his own scheme (from the story of a man who,

言部

〔言部〕

after suggesting the placing of a jar in burning coals and standing prisoners in it, was made to step therein himself)

請求(ㄑㄧㄥˇ ㄑㄧㄡˊ)
to request; to ask; to beg; to entreat: 他請求她一同去。He requested her to go with him.

請求乃論(ㄑㄧㄥˇ ㄑㄧㄡˊ ㄋㄞˇ ㄌㄨㄣˋ)
(said of cases of civil offense, etc.) to consider only upon request

請示(ㄑㄧㄥˇ ㄕˋ)
to ask for instructions

請入席(ㄑㄧㄥˇ ㄖㄨˋ ㄒㄧˊ)
Please be seated at table.

請坐(ㄑㄧㄥˇ ㄗㄨㄛˋ)
Please have a seat. 或 Please take your seat. 或 Please sit down. 或 Please be seated.

請罪(ㄑㄧㄥˇ ㄗㄨㄟˋ)
① to ask for punishment ② to appeal for leniency

請辭(ㄑㄧㄥˇ ㄘˊ)
to request permission to resign; to tender one's resignation

請安(ㄑㄧㄥˇ ㄢ)
to pay respects; to inquire after (an elder)

請益(ㄑㄧㄥˇ ㄧˋ)
to ask for advice or instructions

請謁(ㄑㄧㄥˇ ㄧㄝˋ)
to ask for an audience

請纓(ㄑㄧㄥˇ ㄧㄥ)
to submit a request for a military assignment; to volunteer for military service

請勿(ㄑㄧㄥˇ ㄨˋ)
please don't: 請勿吸煙。No smoking.

請勿動手(ㄑㄧㄥˇ ㄨˋ ㄉㄨㄥˋ ㄕㄡˇ)
Do not touch. 或 Keep your hands off.

請問(ㄑㄧㄥˇ ㄨㄣˋ)
May I ask you...? 或 Please tell me.... 請問，到博物館怎麼走? Excuse me, but could you tell me the way to the museum?

請願(ㄑㄧㄥˇ ㄩㄢˋ)
to petition

請願書(ㄑㄧㄥˇ ㄩㄢˋ ㄕㄨ)
a written petition

【諍】 5611
ㄓㄥ jeng zhēng

1. to expostulate; to remonstrate; to criticize somebody's faults frankly; to admonish
2. to dispute; to compete; to vie 亦作「爭」

諍訟(ㄓㄥ ㄙㄨㄥˋ)
to fight a legal battle; a lawsuit

諍友(ㄓㄥ ㄧㄡˇ)
a friend who does not hesitate to remonstrate

諍言(ㄓㄥ ㄧㄢˊ)
a remonstrance; an expostulation; forthright admonition: 我的諍言無效。My expostulations had no result.

【諏】 5612
ㄗㄡ tzou zōu

1. to confer
2. to consult; to seek the advice of

諏訪(ㄗㄡ ㄈㄤˇ)
to consult; to seek the advice of

諏吉(ㄗㄡ ㄐㄧˊ)
to pick an auspicious day

【諑】 5613
ㄓㄨㄛˊ jwo zhuó

rumors

【諒】 5614
1. ㄌㄧㄤˋ liang liàng

1. honest; sincere
2. to forgive; to excuse; to understand: 原諒我來遲了。Excuse me for coming late.
3. to conjecture; to guess; to infer; to assume; to presume; to think; to expect; to suppose: 諒必如此。I think it must be so.
4. stubborn

諒必(ㄌㄧㄤˋ ㄅㄧˋ)
most likely; probably; in all probability

諒可(ㄌㄧㄤˋ ㄎㄜˇ)
to assume that something is possible

諒解(ㄌㄧㄤˋ ㄐㄧㄝˇ)
to forgive; to be understanding

諒已(ㄌㄧㄤˋ ㄧˇ)
I presume you (he, she, they) must have.... 或 Presumably it must have been....

【諒】 5614
2. ㄌㄧㄤˊ liang liáng

參見「諒陰」

諒陰(ㄌㄧㄤˊ ㄢ)
① imperial mourning ② a mourning shed 亦作「諒闇」or「涼陰」

【論】 5615
1. ㄌㄨㄣˋ luenn lùn

1. to discuss; to comment on; to appraise; to evaluate; to talk about; to discourse
2. to debate; to dispute; to argue
3. a theory; a system of thoughts; a dissertation; an essay
4. to mention; to regard; to consider
5. by; in terms of

論辨(ㄌㄨㄣˋ ㄅㄧㄢˋ)
argumentation (as distinct from "description," "narration," and "exposition")

論評(ㄌㄨㄣˋ ㄆㄧㄥˊ)
to comment; a commentary

論調(ㄌㄨㄣˋ ㄉㄧㄠˋ)
the tone or argument (of a speech, writing, etc.); views: 這種論調簡直荒謬。Such views are simply ridiculous.

論點(ㄌㄨㄣˋ ㄉㄧㄢˇ)
the point at issue; an issue; the point of discussion; an argument; a thesis

論斷(ㄌㄨㄣˋ ㄉㄨㄢˋ)
to discuss and judge

論壇(ㄌㄨㄣˋ ㄊㄢˊ)
the world of criticism; a tribune of opinions; a forum

論難(ㄌㄨㄣˋ ㄋㄢˋ)
to harass by arguing; to thrash out

論理(ㄌㄨㄣˋ ㄌㄧˇ)
① to reason ② logic: 他的說辭頗合乎論理。There is much logic in his argument. ③ normally; as things should be

論理學(ㄌㄨㄣˋ ㄌㄧˇ ㄒㄩㄝˊ)
logic

論理學家(ㄌㄨㄣˋ ㄌㄧˇ ㄒㄩㄝˊ ㄐㄧㄚ)
a logician

論列(ㄌㄨㄣˋ ㄌㄧㄝˋ)
to discuss and point out the favorable and unfavorable aspects of a matter

論功行賞(ㄌㄨㄣˋ ㄍㄨㄥ ㄒㄧㄥˊ ㄕㄤˇ)
to evaluate services and

grant rewards accordingly; to award people according to their contribution
論及(ㄌㄨㄣˋ ㄐㄧˊ)
to touch upon (in an exposition or argumentation)
論價(ㄌㄨㄣˋ ㄐㄧㄚˋ)
to negotiate prices
論件計酬(ㄌㄨㄣˋ ㄐㄧㄢˋ ㄐㄧˋ ㄔㄡˊ)
payment by the piece
論據(ㄌㄨㄣˋ ㄐㄩˋ)
grounds or bases (of an argument)
論者(ㄌㄨㄣˋ ㄓㄜˇ)
those who hold different opinions
論戰(ㄌㄨㄣˋ ㄓㄢˋ)
controversy; debate; argument; a battle of words; polemics: 他們曾激烈論戰。They had a bitter controversy.
論爭(ㄌㄨㄣˋ ㄓㄥ)
argument; debate; controversy
論政(ㄌㄨㄣˋ ㄓㄥˋ)
to discuss politics; to make comments on politics
論證(ㄌㄨㄣˋ ㄓㄥˋ)
proof; demonstration; to expound and prove: 這是無可辯駁的論證。This is irrefutable proof.
論著(ㄌㄨㄣˋ ㄓㄨˋ)
a treatise; a discourse; a work; a book
論述(ㄌㄨㄣˋ ㄕㄨˋ)
to discuss; to expound
論說(ㄌㄨㄣˋ ㄕㄨㄛ)
a theory, or thoughts (advanced in a treatise); exposition and argumentation
論說文(ㄌㄨㄣˋ ㄕㄨㄛ ㄨㄣˊ)
an argumentative treatise
論贊(ㄌㄨㄣˋ ㄗㄢˋ)
appraising remarks conventionally placed at the end of a biography in history books
論罪(ㄌㄨㄣˋ ㄗㄨㄟˋ)
to be considered as an offense: 這人以行賄論罪。The man was found guilty of bribery.
論次(ㄌㄨㄣˋ ㄘˋ)
to settle the order of priority, seniority, etc.

論文(ㄌㄨㄣˋ ㄨㄣˊ)
a treatise; a thesis; a dissertation; an essay; a discourse

【論】 5615 2. ㄌㄨㄣˊ luen lún
1. an alternative of 論(ㄌㄨㄣˋ) for some phrases
2. a Chinese family name
論語(ㄌㄨㄣˊ ㄩˇ)
The Analects of Confucius, one of the *Four Books*

【諗】 5616 ㄕㄣˇ sheen shěn
1. to think of
2. to let know; to tell; to announce
3. to remonstrate
4. to hide; to conceal

【諆】 5617 ㄑㄧ chi qī
to cheat

九畫

【謚】 5618 (諡) ㄕˋ shyh shì
a posthumous title
謚法(ㄕˋ ㄈㄚˇ)
the system of conferring posthumous titles

【諭】 5619 ㄩˋ yuh yù
1. to notify or inform by a directive, edict, etc.; to instruct; to tell
2. a decree; an edict; an instruction; a command
諭知(ㄩˋ ㄓ)
to notify or inform by a directive, edict, etc.
諭旨(ㄩˋ ㄓˇ)
an imperial edict
諭示(ㄩˋ ㄕˋ)
to notify or announce by an edict or decree: 諭示百姓 to notify the masses by proclamation

【諼】 5620 ㄒㄩㄢ shiuan xuān
1. to deceive; to fail in promise or appointment
2. to forget
諼草(ㄒㄩㄢ ㄘㄠˇ)
a day lily 亦作「萱草」

【諵】 5621 ㄋㄢˊ nan nán
to chatter; to gabble

【諛】 5622 ㄩˊ yu yú
to flatter; to toady
諛墓(ㄩˊ ㄇㄨˋ)
a flattering epitaph; to flatter the dead
諛辭 or 諛詞(ㄩˊ ㄘˊ)
flattering words; flattery
諛言(ㄩˊ ㄧㄢˊ)
flattering words; flattery: 諛言可憎。Flattering words are detestable.

【諜】 5623 ㄉㄧㄝˊ dye dié
1. glib; garrulous; voluble 亦作「喋」
2. spying; espionage
諜報(ㄉㄧㄝˊ ㄅㄠˋ)
a spy's report; information obtained through espionage
諜報員(ㄉㄧㄝˊ ㄅㄠˋ ㄩㄢˊ)
an intelligence agent; a spy

【諞】 5624 1. ㄆㄧㄢˊ pyan pián
to quibble
諞言(ㄆㄧㄢˊ ㄧㄢˊ)
to quibble

【諞】 5624 2. ㄆㄧㄢˇ pean piǎn
to boast; to show off
諞闊(ㄆㄧㄢˇ ㄎㄨㄛˋ)
to show off; to be boastful

【諠】 5625 (喧) ㄒㄩㄢ shiuan xuān
to bawl; to shout
諠呶(ㄒㄩㄢ ㄋㄠˊ)
an uproar; tumult
諠譁(ㄒㄩㄢ ㄏㄨㄚˊ)
turmoil; a hubbub; tumult; an uproar: 會議在諠譁中結束。The meeting ended in (an) uproar.

【諢】 5626 ㄏㄨㄣˋ huenn hùn
ridicule; derision; a joke; a jest
諢名(ㄏㄨㄣˋ ㄇㄧㄥˊ)
a nickname; a sobriquet

【諤】 5627 ㄜˋ eh è
honest speech; frank comments
諤諤(ㄜˋ ㄜˋ)
① outspoken; honest ②(said of a procession) magnificent

【諦】 5628 ㄉㄧˋ dih dì
1. attentive; careful
2. (Buddhism) truth; true

〔言部〕

meaning
諦聽(ㄉㄧˋ ㄊㄧㄥ)
to listen attentively
諦視(ㄉㄧˋ ㄕˋ)
to look attentively; to scrutinize

【諧】 5629
ㄒㄧㄝˊ shye xié
1. harmonious; congruous; in harmony; in accord
2. to come to an agreement; to settle
3. to joke; to jest; funny; humorous
諧比(ㄒㄧㄝˊ ㄅㄧˇ)
improperly familiar or intimate
諧附(ㄒㄧㄝˊ ㄈㄨˋ)
to compromise and follow
諧謔(ㄒㄧㄝˊ ㄋㄩㄝˋ)
to wisecrack, joke or jest; pleasantry; banter: 他說話時語帶諧謔。He speaks somewhat jokingly.
諧和(ㄒㄧㄝˊ ㄏㄜˊ)
harmony; accord; agreement; harmonious; concordant
諧價(ㄒㄧㄝˊ ㄐㄧㄚˋ)
to negotiate the price
諧劇(ㄒㄧㄝˊ ㄐㄩˋ)
a farce
諧趣(ㄒㄧㄝˊ ㄑㄩˋ)
fun; pleasantry; humor
諧戲(ㄒㄧㄝˊ ㄒㄧˋ)
to jest; to joke
諧星(ㄒㄧㄝˊ ㄒㄧㄥ)
a comedian
諧臣(ㄒㄧㄝˊ ㄔㄣˊ)
court players; court jesters
諧聲(ㄒㄧㄝˊ ㄕㄥ)
one of the six groups of Chinese characters (in which the radical gives the meaning and the other part gives the sound) 亦作「形聲」
諧易(ㄒㄧㄝˊ ㄧˋ)
humorous and easygoing
諧音(ㄒㄧㄝˊ ㄧㄣ)
①(said of characters) representing sound ②(physics) harmonics

【諫】 5630
ㄐㄧㄢˋ jiann jiàn
to admonish; to remonstrate
諫果(ㄐㄧㄢˋ ㄍㄨㄛˇ)
an olive 亦作「橄欖」
諫官(ㄐㄧㄢˋ ㄍㄨㄢ)
officials in charge of admonishing the emperor; imperial censors
諫諍(ㄐㄧㄢˋ ㄓㄥ)
to admonish or remonstrate (a superior)
諫書(ㄐㄧㄢˋ ㄕㄨ)
a written admonition to the emperor: 大臣已呈上諫書。The minister has submitted a written admonition.
諫議大夫(ㄐㄧㄢˋ ㄧˋ ㄉㄚˋ ㄈㄨ)
an official in charge of admonition and arbitration
諫言(ㄐㄧㄢˋ ㄧㄢˊ)
admonition
諫院(ㄐㄧㄢˋ ㄩㄢˋ)
the office of imperial censors

【諮】 5631
ㄗ tzy zī
1. to inquire; to confer; to consult
2. an official communication between offices of the same level
諮詢(ㄗ ㄒㄩㄣˊ)
to inquire and consult; to seek advice
諮商(ㄗ ㄕㄤ)
(psychology) counseling
諮諏(ㄗ ㄗㄡ)
to consult (especially on affairs of the state)
諮議(ㄗ ㄧˋ)
① to confer; to discuss ② government consultants or counselors
諮文(ㄗ ㄨㄣˊ)
an official communication between equals

【諱】 5632
ㄏㄨㄟˋ huey huì
1. to conceal; to hide
2. to shun; to avoid; to regard as taboo; taboo
3. name of a deceased elder member of the family
諱莫如深(ㄏㄨㄟˋ ㄇㄛˋ ㄖㄨˊ ㄕㄣ)
kept as a top secret; to avoid mentioning something completely
諱疾忌醫(ㄏㄨㄟˋ ㄐㄧˊ ㄐㄧˋ ㄧ)
(literally) to conceal one's ailment and refuse to consult the doctor—to refuse to face a harsh reality; to hide one's troubles and take no remedial measures
諱飾(ㄏㄨㄟˋ ㄕˋ)
to conceal the truth
諱言(ㄏㄨㄟˋ ㄧㄢˊ)
to avoid mentioning something; to conceal: 她毫不諱言。She makes no attempt to conceal the truth.

【諳】 5633
ㄢ an ān
familiar with; skilled in; versed in
諳練(ㄢ ㄌㄧㄢˋ)
skilled in; familiar with; versed in: 他諳練騎術。He is skilled in horsemanship.
諳習(ㄢ ㄒㄧˊ)
skilled in; familiar with; versed in
諳算(ㄢ ㄙㄨㄢˋ)
to calculate mentally
諳誦(ㄢ ㄙㄨㄥˋ)
to recite from memory

【諝】 5634
ㄒㄩˇ sheu xǔ
1. wisdom; sagacity
2. a clever idea; a stratagem

【諶】 5635
ㄔㄣˊ chern chén
1. sincere; honest; candid
2. a Chinese family name

【諷】 5636
ㄈㄥˋ fenq fèng
1. to recite; to chant
2. to satirize; to mock; to ridicule
3. to admonish in a roundabout way
諷諫(ㄈㄥˋ ㄐㄧㄢˋ)
to admonish or remonstrate in a roundabout way
諷示(ㄈㄥˋ ㄕˋ)
to admonish in a roundabout way
諷刺(ㄈㄥˋ ㄘˋ)
① to satirize; to mock ② irony
諷刺畫(ㄈㄥˋ ㄘˋ ㄏㄨㄚˋ)
a caricature; a cartoon
諷誦(ㄈㄥˋ ㄙㄨㄥˋ)
to recite; to chant; to intone
諷一勸百(ㄈㄥˋ ㄧ ㄑㄩㄢˋ ㄅㄞˇ)
to satirize one in order to admonish a hundred
諷味(ㄈㄥˋ ㄨㄟˋ)
to recite and enjoy (a verse, etc.); to repeat a remark and ponder its hidden mean-

ing
諷喻(ㄈㄥˋ ㄩˋ)
a parable; an allegory

【諸】 5637 ㄓㄨ ju zhū

1. all; various
2. a contraction of 之乎 or 之於 (as prepositions—in, to, from, etc.)
3. a Chinese family name

諸般(ㄓㄨ ㄅㄢ)
all sorts; all kinds
諸母(ㄓㄨ ㄇㄨˇ)
one's father's concubine
諸父(ㄓㄨ ㄈㄨˋ)
one's father's brothers; paternal uncles
諸娣(ㄓㄨ ㄉㄧˋ)
all the concubines
諸多(ㄓㄨ ㄉㄨㄛ)
many; numerous; a lot of: 很抱歉給你帶來諸多不便。I am sorry that I put you to a lot of inconvenience.
諸葛(ㄓㄨ ㄍㄜˇ)
a Chinese family name
諸葛亮(ㄓㄨ ㄍㄜˇ ㄌㄧㄤˋ)
Chu-Ko Liang, 181-234 A.D., prime minister of the Kingdom of Shu (蜀) during the Epoch of the Three Kingdoms, noted for great wisdom 亦作「孔明」
諸姑(ㄓㄨ ㄍㄨ)
one's father's sisters
諸姑姊妹(ㄓㄨ ㄍㄨ ㄗˇ ㄇㄟˋ)
all the ladies
諸公(ㄓㄨ ㄍㄨㄥ)
all the gentlemen
諸宮調(ㄓㄨ ㄍㄨㄥ ㄉㄧㄠˋ)
a style of songs prevalent in the 11th century
諸侯(ㄓㄨ ㄏㄡˊ)
the feudal princes; dukes or princes under an emperor
諸季(ㄓㄨ ㄐㄧˋ)
all the younger brothers
諸暨(ㄓㄨ ㄐㄧˋ)
Chuchi, a county in Chekiang(浙江)
諸舅(ㄓㄨ ㄐㄧㄡˋ)
all the maternal uncles
諸君(ㄓㄨ ㄐㄩㄣ)
you gentlemen
諸夏(ㄓㄨ ㄒㄧㄚˋ)
the various Chinese kingdoms
諸行無常(ㄓㄨ ㄒㄧㄥˊ ㄨˊ ㄔㄤˊ)
(Buddhism) Whatever is phenomenal is ephemeral.
諸生(ㄓㄨ ㄕㄥ)
① a successful candidate in the lowest level of civil service examination under the former system 亦作「秀才」② all the students
諸如(ㄓㄨ ㄖㄨˊ)
such as
諸如此類(ㄓㄨ ㄖㄨˊ ㄘˇ ㄌㄟˋ)
various things like this; such; and so on; and so forth: 諸如此類，不勝枚舉。Such instances are too numerous to mention.
諸子(ㄓㄨ ㄗˇ)
① the various schools of thinkers or their works in the late Chou Dynasty ② an official in charge of education and discipline in ancient times
諸子百家(ㄓㄨ ㄗˇ ㄅㄞˇ ㄐㄧㄚ)
the numerous schools of thinkers, or their works in the late Chou Dynasty
諸位(ㄓㄨ ㄨㄟˋ)
Ladies and Gentlemen

【諺】 5638 ㄧㄢˋ yann yàn

a proverb; an aphorism; a saying; a saw; an adage
諺文(ㄧㄢˋ ㄨㄣˊ)
the Korean alphabet
諺語(ㄧㄢˋ ㄩˇ)
a proverb; an aphorism; a saying; a saw; an adage
諺云(ㄧㄢˋ ㄩㄣˊ)
as the proverb says; as the saying goes: 諺云:「無風不起浪。」As the saying goes, "There is no smoke without fire."

【諾】 5639 ㄋㄨㄛˋ nuoh nuò

1. to assent
2. to promise; to pledge

諾貝爾(ㄋㄨㄛˋ ㄅㄟˋ ㄦˇ)
Alfred Bernhard Nobel, 1833-1896, Swedish chemist
諾貝爾獎(ㄋㄨㄛˋ ㄅㄟˋ ㄦˇ ㄐㄧㄤˇ)
Nobel prizes
諾曼(ㄋㄨㄛˋ ㄇㄢˋ)
Norman
諾曼第(ㄋㄨㄛˋ ㄇㄢˋ ㄉㄧˋ)
Normandy, France
諾諾(ㄋㄨㄛˋ ㄋㄨㄛˋ)
Yes, yes.
諾魯(ㄋㄨㄛˋ ㄌㄨˇ)
Nauru, a small island state in the Pacific
諾已(ㄋㄨㄛˋ ㄧˇ)
an interjection of disappointment
諾亞方舟(ㄋㄨㄛˋ ㄧㄚˋ ㄈㄤ ㄓㄡ)
Noah's Ark
諾言(ㄋㄨㄛˋ ㄧㄢˊ)
a promise; a pledge: 他從不守諾言。He never keeps his promises.

【謀】 5640 ㄇㄡˊ mou móu

1. to scheme; to plan; to plot; to design; to devise
2. a scheme; a stratagem; a plan; a conspiracy
3. resourceful; astute
4. to consult
5. to seek; to try to get

謀叛(ㄇㄡˊ ㄆㄢˋ)
to plot a revolt
謀面(ㄇㄡˊ ㄇㄧㄢˋ)
to meet each other; to see each other
謀反(ㄇㄡˊ ㄈㄢˇ)
to plot a revolt; to conspire against the state
謀利(ㄇㄡˊ ㄌㄧˋ)
to seek profit
謀略(ㄇㄡˊ ㄌㄩㄝˋ) or 謀策(ㄇㄡˊ ㄘㄜˋ)
① a strategy; a scheme; a plot ② (said of a person) resourceful; astute: 他頗有謀略。He is a man of resource and astuteness.
謀和(ㄇㄡˊ ㄏㄜˊ)
to sue for peace
謀害(ㄇㄡˊ ㄏㄞˋ)
① to plot against someone ② to murder
謀畫(ㄇㄡˊ ㄏㄨㄚˋ)
to scheme; to plot; to plan; to design; to devise
謀救(ㄇㄡˊ ㄐㄧㄡˋ)
to plan the deliverance, rescue or relief of
謀求(ㄇㄡˊ ㄑㄧㄡˊ)
to try to get; to seek: 我們正在謀求解決方法。We are trying to find a solution.
謀取(ㄇㄡˊ ㄑㄩˇ)
to try to gain; to seek; to

〔言部〕

〔言部〕

obtain
謀職(ㄇㄡˊ ㄓˊ)
to try to find employment; to hunt for a job
謀主(ㄇㄡˊ ㄓㄨˇ)
a planner; a designer; a plotter; a conspirator
謀臣(ㄇㄡˊ ㄔㄣˊ)
a brain truster or clever minister of the emperor or the king
謀食(ㄇㄡˊ ㄕˊ)
to seek food; to make a living
謀士(ㄇㄡˊ ㄕˋ)
a strategist; a man of ideas; a resourceful man; an adviser; a counselor
謀事(ㄇㄡˊ ㄕˋ)
①to manage business ②to scheme or plan for an affair ③to look for a job
謀事在人，成事在天(ㄇㄡˊ ㄕˋ ㄗㄞˋ ㄖㄣˊ, ㄔㄥˊ ㄕˋ ㄗㄞˋ ㄊㄧㄢ)
Man proposes, but God disposes.
謀殺(ㄇㄡˊ ㄕㄚ)
to murder
謀殺案(ㄇㄡˊ ㄕㄚ ㄢˋ)
a murder case
謀生(ㄇㄡˊ ㄕㄥ)
to make a living; to get a livelihood
謀財害命(ㄇㄡˊ ㄘㄞˊ ㄏㄞˋ ㄇㄧㄥˋ)
to commit murder out of greed; to murder somebody for his money
謀議(ㄇㄡˊ ㄧˋ)
to meet and plan; to confer
謀猷 or 謀猶(ㄇㄡˊ ㄧㄡˊ)
a strategy; a scheme; a plot

【謁】 5641 ㄧㄝˋ yeh yè
to have an audience with; to see a superior
謁陵(ㄧㄝˋ ㄌㄧㄥˊ)
to pay homage to a great leader by visiting his tomb or mausoleum
謁告(ㄧㄝˋ ㄍㄠˋ)
to ask for leave of absence
謁歸(ㄧㄝˋ ㄍㄨㄟ)
to go home on leave
謁見(ㄧㄝˋ ㄐㄧㄢˋ)
to have an audience with; to see a superior
謁禁(ㄧㄝˋ ㄐㄧㄣˋ)
a ban on visitors; a ban on audiences
謁者(ㄧㄝˋ ㄓㄜˇ)
an official in charge of receptions, etc. (prior to the Tang Dynasty)
謁舍(ㄧㄝˋ ㄕㄜˋ)
a hostel; a guest house
謁刺(ㄧㄝˋ ㄘˋ)
a visiting card; a calling card

【謂】 5642 ㄨㄟˋ wey wèi
1. to tell; to say
2. to name; to call; to designate
3. to think; to be of the opinion; to assume
4. meaning; sense
謂何(ㄨㄟˋ ㄏㄜˊ)
What can be done about...? 亦作「奈何」

【諲】 5643 ㄧㄣ in yīn
to respect; to venerate

【諰】 5644 ㄒㄧˇ shii xǐ
1. to speak frankly
2. apprehensive
諰諰(ㄒㄧˇ ㄒㄧˇ)
apprehensive

【諴】 5645 ㄒㄧㄢˊ shyan xián
1. in harmony
2. sincerity; honesty

【諟】 5646 ㄕˋ shyh shì
1. yes; to be 亦作「是」
2. to examine and correct

【謔】 5647 ㄋㄩㄝˋ niueh nüè
1. to jest; to joke; to banter; to tease
2. to ridicule; to satirize
謔謔(ㄋㄩㄝˋ ㄋㄩㄝˋ)
cheerful; happy
謔浪(ㄋㄩㄝˋ ㄌㄤˋ)
to make fun without restraint
謔而不虐(ㄋㄩㄝˋ ㄦˊ ㄅㄨˋ ㄋㄩㄝˋ)
to joke without hurting anyone

十畫

【謎】 5648 ㄇㄧˊ mi mí (又讀 ㄇㄟˋ mey mèi)
a riddle; a puzzle; a conundrum; an enigma; a mystery
謎面(ㄇㄧˊ ㄇㄧㄢˋ)
the verbal version of a riddle
謎底(ㄇㄧˊ ㄉㄧˇ)
an answer to a riddle; a truth
謎兒(ㄇㄧㄦˊ)
a riddle; a conundrum
謎語(ㄇㄧˊ ㄩˇ)
a riddle; a conundrum: 他出個謎語給我們猜。He asked us a riddle.

【謄】 5649 ㄊㄥˊ terng téng
to transcribe; to copy
謄本(ㄊㄥˊ ㄅㄣˇ)
a transcript; a copy
謄錄(ㄊㄥˊ ㄌㄨˋ)
①to copy; to transcribe ②to copy the examination papers of participants of the civil service examination of the old system before sending them to officials in charge with a view to preventing favoritism
謄清(ㄊㄥˊ ㄑㄧㄥ)
to make a clean copy: 我想謄清我的手稿。I wish to make a clean copy of my manuscript.
謄清賬(ㄊㄥˊ ㄑㄧㄥ ㄓㄤˋ)
a ledger
謄寫(ㄊㄥˊ ㄒㄧㄝˇ)
to copy; to transcribe
謄寫員(ㄊㄥˊ ㄒㄧㄝˇ ㄩㄢˊ)
a scribe
謄正(ㄊㄥˊ ㄓㄥˋ)
to make a clean copy

【謊】 5650 ㄏㄨㄤˇ hoang huǎng
a lie; to lie: 不許說謊。Do not lie.
謊報(ㄏㄨㄤˇ ㄅㄠˋ)
to report a falsehood; to lie about something; to give false information: 她謊報年齡。She lied about her age.
謊騙(ㄏㄨㄤˇ ㄆㄧㄢˋ)
to cheat; to deceive; to hoax
謊花兒(ㄏㄨㄤˇ ㄏㄨㄚㄦ)
sterile flowers
謊話(ㄏㄨㄤˇ ㄏㄨㄚˋ)
a lie
謊言(ㄏㄨㄤˇ ㄧㄢˊ)

a lie: 那都是謊言，別聽他的。It's all lies; don't believe him.

【謅】 5651 ㄗㄡ tzou zōu
to talk nonsense: 別胡謅了。Stop talking nonsense.

【謇】 5652 ㄐㄧㄢˇ jean jiǎn
1. to stutter; to stammer
2. to speak out boldly

謇謇(ㄐㄧㄢˇ ㄐㄧㄢˇ)
faithful; loyal

謇諤(ㄐㄧㄢˇ ㄜˋ)
outspoken; frank; candid

【謏】 5653 ㄒㄧㄠˇ sheau xiǎo
1. small; little
2. to induce

謏才(ㄒㄧㄠˇ ㄘㄞˊ)
a limited talent

謏聞(ㄒㄧㄠˇ ㄨㄣˊ)
known only to a small circle

【謐】 5654 ㄇㄧˋ mih mì
silent; quiet; serene; still

謐謐(ㄇㄧˋ ㄇㄧˋ)
silent; quiet; serene; still

謐靜(ㄇㄧˋ ㄐㄧㄥˋ)
quiet; tranquil; serene; silent; calm

【謗】 5655 ㄅㄤˋ banq bàng
to slander; to libel; to condemn

謗木(ㄅㄤˋ ㄇㄨˋ)
a board set up on roadside for the people to record the errors in the public administration

謗書(ㄅㄤˋ ㄕㄨ)
defamatory writing

謗議(ㄅㄤˋ ㄧˋ)
to slander; to criticize; to libel

謗言(ㄅㄤˋ ㄧㄢˊ)
a libel; a slander; defamatory remarks

【謙】 5656 ㄑㄧㄢ chian qiān
modest; humble; retiring; self-effacing

謙卑(ㄑㄧㄢ ㄅㄟ)
humble; self-depreciating; modest: 挫折與失敗使人謙卑。Defeat and failure make people humble.

謙退(ㄑㄧㄢ ㄊㄨㄟˋ)
modest and retiring; reserved

謙光(ㄑㄧㄢ ㄍㄨㄤ)
shining modesty

謙恭(ㄑㄧㄢ ㄍㄨㄥ)
respectful; unassuming; modest and courteous: 他的兒子謙恭有禮。His son is respectful and polite.

謙克(ㄑㄧㄢ ㄎㄜˋ)
humble and self-controlled

謙和(ㄑㄧㄢ ㄏㄜˊ)
modest and good-natured

謙謙君子(ㄑㄧㄢ ㄑㄧㄢ ㄐㄩㄣ ㄗˇ)
a modest gentleman

謙虛(ㄑㄧㄢ ㄒㄩ)
① modest; unassuming; self-effacing ② to make modest remarks

謙遜 or 謙巽(ㄑㄧㄢ ㄒㄩㄣˋ)
humble; modest; lowly; unassuming

謙沖(ㄑㄧㄢ ㄔㄨㄥ)
modest; unassuming

謙讓(ㄑㄧㄢ ㄖㄤˋ)
to yield from modesty

謙辭(ㄑㄧㄢ ㄘˊ)
① modest speech; a humble remark ② to decline out of humbleness

謙受益，滿招損(ㄑㄧㄢ ㄕㄡˋ ㄧˋ, ㄇㄢˇ ㄓㄠ ㄙㄨㄣˇ)
Benefit goes to the humble, while failure awaits the arrogant. 或 The modest receive benefit, while the conceited reap failure.

【講】 5657 ㄐㄧㄤˇ jeang jiǎng
1. to speak; to talk; to say
2. to pay particular attention to; to be particular about; to be elaborate about
3. to explain; to explicate
4. as far as something is concerned; when it comes to; as to; as regards
5. to have recourse to

講排場(ㄐㄧㄤˇ ㄆㄞˊ ㄔㄤˇ)
to impress others by extravagance; to display riches

講評(ㄐㄧㄤˇ ㄆㄧㄥˊ)
to review (a literary work, a game, etc., especially in speech); to make critical comments on some performance

講面子(ㄐㄧㄤˇ ㄇㄧㄢˋ ·ㄗ)
to care about reputation or face

講明(ㄐㄧㄤˇ ㄇㄧㄥˊ)
to explain; to make (a point) clear by explanation: 我們先講明我們的立場。We'll explain our stand first.

講法(ㄐㄧㄤˇ ㄈㄚˇ)
① a way of stating ideas or facts ② interpretation (of a theory, phenomenon, etc.)

講道(ㄐㄧㄤˇ ㄉㄠˋ)
to preach; to give sermons

講臺(ㄐㄧㄤˇ ㄊㄞˊ) or 講壇(ㄐㄧㄤˇ ㄊㄢˊ)
a platform; a dais; a podium; a rostrum

講堂(ㄐㄧㄤˇ ㄊㄤˊ)
a lecture hall; a lecture room; a classroom

講題(ㄐㄧㄤˇ ㄊㄧˊ)
the topic (of a speech or lecture)

講來講去(ㄐㄧㄤˇ ㄌㄞˊ ㄐㄧㄤˇ ㄑㄩˋ)
to talk repeatedly

講理(ㄐㄧㄤˇ ㄌㄧˇ)
① to have regard for reason; reasonable 亦作「講情理」 ② to argue with someone in order to convince him that he is wrong; to reason; to settle a dispute

講論(ㄐㄧㄤˇ ㄌㄨㄣˋ)
to discuss; to expound

講稿(ㄐㄧㄤˇ ㄍㄠˇ)
the manuscript of a prepared speech; lecture notes

講古(ㄐㄧㄤˇ ㄍㄨˇ)
to recount ancient tales; to tell stories of the past

講故事(ㄐㄧㄤˇ ㄍㄨˋ ·ㄕ)
to tell stories

講課(ㄐㄧㄤˇ ㄎㄜˋ)
to teach; to lecture

講和(ㄐㄧㄤˇ ㄏㄜˊ)
to make peace; to conclude peace; to settle a dispute; to become reconciled

講話(ㄐㄧㄤˇ ㄏㄨㄚˋ)
to talk; to speak; to address; a speech; a talk

講價(ㄐㄧㄤˇ ㄐㄧㄚˋ)
to haggle over prices; to bargain

講解(ㄐㄧㄤˇ ㄐㄧㄝˇ)
to discuss and explain (diffi-

〔言部〕

cult ideas, problems, etc.)

講交情(ㄐㄧㄤˇ ㄐㄧㄠ ˙ㄑㄧㄥ)
to care about friendship

講究(ㄐㄧㄤˇ ㄐㄧㄡˋ)
① to be particular or elaborate (about something); to stress; to have regard for ② (said of dress, buildings, furniture, etc.) tasteful

講經(ㄐㄧㄤˇ ㄐㄧㄥ)
to expound Buddhist sutras

講求(ㄐㄧㄤˇ ㄑㄧㄡˊ)
① to investigate; to study ② to strive for; to be particular or elaborate about

講情(ㄐㄧㄤˇ ㄑㄧㄥˊ)
to ask for leniency for someone else; to intercede; to plead for somebody

講席(ㄐㄧㄤˇ ㄒㄧˊ)
the position of a lecturer

講習(ㄐㄧㄤˇ ㄒㄧˊ)
short-term training or instruction (usually for adults)

講習班(ㄐㄧㄤˇ ㄒㄧˊ ㄅㄢ)
a short-term course of training or instruction; a seminar

講習會(ㄐㄧㄤˇ ㄒㄧˊ ㄏㄨㄟˋ)
a session (usually one of a brief series) for receiving instruction; a seminar

講習所(ㄐㄧㄤˇ ㄒㄧˊ ㄙㄨㄛˇ)
a school for short-term training or instruction

講笑話(ㄐㄧㄤˇ ㄒㄧㄠˋ ˙ㄏㄨㄚ)
to tell jokes; to crack jokes: 她講了一些很有趣的笑話。She told some very funny jokes.

講信修睦(ㄐㄧㄤˇ ㄒㄧㄣˋ ㄒㄧㄡ ㄇㄨˋ)
to cement peaceful relations by upholding good faith

講學(ㄐㄧㄤˇ ㄒㄩㄝˊ)
to lecture; to discourse on an academic subject

講師(ㄐㄧㄤˇ ㄕ)
a lecturer; an instructor

講授(ㄐㄧㄤˇ ㄕㄡˋ)
to teach; to lecture; to instruct

講書(ㄐㄧㄤˇ ㄕㄨ)
(said of a teacher in the classroom) to explain and discuss the content of the textbook

講疏(ㄐㄧㄤˇ ㄕㄨˋ)
to explain or explicate (something obscure)

講述(ㄐㄧㄤˇ ㄕㄨˋ)
to explain and discuss (subjects, problems, etc.); to tell about; to give an account of; to narrate; to relate

講座(ㄐㄧㄤˇ ㄗㄨㄛˋ)
a lectureship; a professorship; a chair

講詞(ㄐㄧㄤˇ ㄘˊ)
the text of a speech (delivered before an audience)

講兒(ㄐㄧㄤˇㄦ)
① meaning; the import ② reason

講義(ㄐㄧㄤˇ ㄧˋ)
① teacher's handouts at school; (mimeographed or printed) teaching materials ② commentaries on classics

講筵(ㄐㄧㄤˇ ㄧㄢˊ)
the teacher's seat

講演(ㄐㄧㄤˇ ㄧㄢˇ)
to speak or lecture; a speech

講武(ㄐㄧㄤˇ ㄨˇ)
to train in martial arts

【謝】 5658 ㄒㄧㄝˋ shieh xiè

1. to thank: 無需向我道謝。There's no need to thank me.
2. to decline
3. to fade; to wither: 花很快就凋謝了。The flowers soon withered.
4. a Chinese family name

謝表(ㄒㄧㄝˋ ㄅㄧㄠˇ)or謝章(ㄒㄧㄝˋ ㄓㄤ)
a letter of thanks to one's lord; a letter of thanks to the emperor for some appointment or other favor

謝病(ㄒㄧㄝˋ ㄅㄧㄥˋ)
to decline office on account of ill health

謝媒(ㄒㄧㄝˋ ㄇㄟˊ)
to reward a matchmaker

謝幕(ㄒㄧㄝˋ ㄇㄨˋ)
a curtain call; to bow to the audience on stage at the end of the show

謝道韞(ㄒㄧㄝˋ ㄉㄠˋ ㄩㄣˋ)
Hsieh Tao-yün (circa 376), a niece of Hsieh An(謝安), and a famed female talent

謝帖(ㄒㄧㄝˋ ㄊㄧㄝˇ)
a letter of thanks; a thank-you note

謝天謝地(ㄒㄧㄝˋ ㄊㄧㄢ ㄒㄧㄝˋ ㄉㄧˋ)
Thank God! 或 Thank Heaven!

謝禮(ㄒㄧㄝˋ ㄌㄧˇ)
① a gift sent as a token of gratitude; a return present ② an honorarium

謝靈運(ㄒㄧㄝˋ ㄌㄧㄥˊ ㄩㄣˋ)
Hsieh Ling-yün, 385-433, a renowned man of letters

謝領(ㄒㄧㄝˋ ㄌㄧㄥˇ)
to accept with thanks

謝客(ㄒㄧㄝˋ ㄎㄜˋ)
to decline to see visitors

謝函(ㄒㄧㄝˋ ㄏㄢˊ)
a thank-you letter

謝惠連(ㄒㄧㄝˋ ㄏㄨㄟˋ ㄌㄧㄢˊ)
Hsieh Hui-lien, 394-430, a talented man of letters and cousin of Hsieh Ling-yün(謝靈運)

謝絕(ㄒㄧㄝˋ ㄐㄩㄝˊ)
to decline (an offer, a request, etc.)

謝絕參觀(ㄒㄧㄝˋ ㄐㄩㄝˊ ㄘㄢ ㄍㄨㄢ)
No visitors allowed. 或 Not open to visitors.

謝啓(ㄒㄧㄝˋ ㄑㄧˇ)
a thank-you notice in the ad column of a newspaper

謝謝(ㄒㄧㄝˋ ˙ㄒㄧㄝ)
Thank you. 或 Thanks.

謝忱(ㄒㄧㄝˋ ㄔㄣˊ)
sincere gratitude; thankfulness

謝師宴(ㄒㄧㄝˋ ㄕ ㄧㄢˋ)
a dinner party given by graduating students in honor of their teachers

謝世(ㄒㄧㄝˋ ㄕˋ)
to pass away; to leave the world; to die: 此人已謝世經年。The man passed away a year ago.

謝神(ㄒㄧㄝˋ ㄕㄣˊ)
to thank the gods by offering sacrifices

謝罪(ㄒㄧㄝˋ ㄗㄨㄟˋ)
to apologize

謝詞(ㄒㄧㄝˋ ㄘˊ)
a thank-you speech

謝安(ㄒㄧㄝˋ ㄢ)
Hsieh An, 320-385, a general of Tsin(晉), who repulsed northern invaders in a major battle

謝恩(ㄒㄧㄝˋ ㄣ)
to express thanks for great favors
謝儀(ㄒㄧㄝˋ ㄧˊ)
a present sent as a token of gratitude; a return present
謝意(ㄒㄧㄝˋ ㄧˋ)
gratitude; appreciation

【謠】 5659 ㄧㄠˊ yau yáo
1. rumor
2. a ballad; a folk song; a song
謠諑(ㄧㄠˊ ㄓㄨㄛˊ)
rumor
謠諑紛紜(ㄧㄠˊ ㄓㄨㄛˊ ㄈㄣ ㄩㄣˊ)
There are many rumors going the rounds.
謠傳(ㄧㄠˊ ㄔㄨㄢˊ)
① unfounded report; rumor; hearsay② according to rumor; it is rumored; rumor has it that...
謠俗(ㄧㄠˊ ㄙㄨˊ)
folklore
謠言(ㄧㄠˊ ㄧㄢˊ)
unfounded report; rumor
謠言滿天飛(ㄧㄠˊ ㄧㄢˊ ㄇㄢˇ ㄊㄧㄢ ㄈㄟ)
All sorts of rumors are going the rounds.
謠言惑衆(ㄧㄠˊ ㄧㄢˊ ㄏㄨㄛˋ ㄓㄨㄥˋ)
to delude the people with rumors

【謖】 5660 ㄙㄨˋ suh sù
1. folded; closed
2. to rise; to raise

【謟】 5661 ㄊㄠ tau tāo
confusing; uncertain

【謚】 5662 ㄕˋ shyh shì
to confer posthumous titles 亦作「諡」

十一畫

【謾】 5663 1. ㄇㄢˋ mann màn
1. to scorn; to disdain
2. disrespectful; rude
謾罵(ㄇㄢˋ ㄇㄚˋ)
to revile scornfully; to fling abuse; to rail

【謾】 5663 2. ㄇㄢˊ man mán
to deceive
謾天謾地(ㄇㄢˊ ㄊㄧㄢ ㄇㄢˊ ㄉㄧˋ)
to deceive everybody

【謷】 5664 ㄠˊ aur áo
1. to slander; to revile; to abuse
2. massive and great
謷醜(ㄠˊ ㄔㄡˇ)
to slander; to abuse
謷謷(ㄠˊ ㄠˊ)
① slanderous; abusive ② sound of a mourning crowd

【謦】 5665 ㄑㄧㄥˇ chiing qǐng
to cough slightly
謦欬(ㄑㄧㄥˇ ㄎㄞˋ)
talking and laughing

【謨】 5666 ㄇㄛˊ mo mó
1. a plan; a course of action
2. to have no; without; to lack
謨罕摹德(ㄇㄛˊ ㄏㄢˇ ㄇㄛˊ ㄉㄜˊ)
Mohammed (or Mahomet or Muhammad), 570-632, founder of the Moslem religion亦作「穆罕默德」
謨信(ㄇㄛˊ ㄒㄧㄣˋ)
treacherous; not to be trusted

【謫】 5667 ㄓㄜˊ jer zhé
1. to censure; to reproach
2. to punish; to penalize
3. one's fault
4. to exile; to banish (an official) to a distant place
謫奸(ㄓㄜˊ ㄐㄧㄢ)
to punish the wicked
謫降(ㄓㄜˊ ㄐㄧㄤˋ)
① to demote and exile (an official) to the frontier: 他被謫降。He was degraded from his high rank. ②(said of immortals) to descend to the earth
謫居(ㄓㄜˊ ㄐㄩ)
to live in exile
謫仙(ㄓㄜˊ ㄒㄧㄢ)
an immortal living among mortals—a genius; a prodigy
謫戍(ㄓㄜˊ ㄕㄨˋ)
(said of officials) to be exiled to the border

【謬】 5668 ㄇㄧㄡˋ miow miù (又讀 ㄋㄧㄡˋ niow niù)
1. incorrect; wrong; erroneous; mistaken
2. absurd; unreasonable
謬耄(ㄇㄧㄡˋ ㄇㄠˋ)
feeble-minded and senile
謬戾(ㄇㄧㄡˋ ㄌㄧˋ)
stubbornly unreasonable
謬論(ㄇㄧㄡˋ ㄌㄨㄣˋ)
an absurd statement; a fallacious argument: 謬論不足以服人。The absurd statement convince nobody.
謬見(ㄇㄧㄡˋ ㄐㄧㄢˋ)
① a fallacious opinion ②(in self-depreciation) my absurd opinion
謬種流傳(ㄇㄧㄡˋ ㄓㄨㄥˇ ㄌㄧㄡˊ ㄔㄨㄢˊ)
to transmit falsehood or inaccuracies from one generation to another; the dissemination of error or fallacy
謬悠(ㄇㄧㄡˋ ㄧㄡ)
absurd and inaccurate
謬誤(ㄇㄧㄡˋ ㄨˋ)
an error; inaccuracy; fallacy: 謬誤百出。There are hundreds of errors.
謬妄(ㄇㄧㄡˋ ㄨㄤˋ)
absurd and reckless

【謳】 5669 ㄡ ou ōu
to sing; to chant
謳歌(ㄡ ㄍㄜ)
to sing in praise; to glorify; to eulogize

【謹】 5670 ㄐㄧㄣˇ jiin jǐn
1. cautious; prudent; careful; attentive
2. respectful; reverent; deferential; sincerely: 謹致謝意。Please accept my sincere thanks.
謹備菲酌(ㄐㄧㄣˇ ㄅㄟˋ ㄈㄟˇ ㄓㄨㄛˊ)
to provide some light wine respectfully (a conventional phrase on an invitation card for a dinner party or luncheon)
謹稟(ㄐㄧㄣˇ ㄅㄧㄥˇ)
reported respectfully by...(a conventional phrase in formal letters addressed to seniors or superiors)
謹防(ㄐㄧㄣˇ ㄈㄤˊ)
to guard carefully against; to take precautions against; to beware of
謹防扒手(ㄐㄧㄣˇ ㄈㄤˊ ㄆㄚˊ ㄕㄡˇ)

〔言部〕

〔言部〕

Beware of pickpockets!

謹防假冒(ㄐㄧㄣˇ ㄈㄤˊ ㄐㄧㄚˇ ㄇㄠˋ)
Beware of imitations! 或 Beware of fakes!

謹聽(ㄐㄧㄣˇ ㄊㄧㄥ)
to listen attentively

謹領(ㄐㄧㄣˇ ㄌㄧㄥˇ)
to receive with respect

謹記(ㄐㄧㄣˇ ㄐㄧˋ)
to remember with reverence

謹具(ㄐㄧㄣˇ ㄐㄩˋ)
① respectfully prepared by... ② respectfully signed by...

謹啓(ㄐㄧㄣˇ ㄑㄧˇ)
written respectfully by... (a conventional phrase placed after the writer's signature in a formal letter); humbly yours

謹誌 or 謹識(ㄐㄧㄣˇ ㄓˋ)
written respectfully by... (a conventional phrase placed after the writer's signature in a preface, commentary, etc.)

謹敕 or 謹飭(ㄐㄧㄣˇ ㄔˋ)
conducting oneself with prudence

謹呈(ㄐㄧㄣˇ ㄔㄥˊ)
presented respectfully by... (a conventional phrase placed after the writer's signature in a formal letter); respectfully yours

謹守(ㄐㄧㄣˇ ㄕㄡˇ)
① to guard with care ② to follow faithfully; strictly comply with

謹慎(ㄐㄧㄣˇ ㄕㄣˋ)
prudent; cautious

謹上(ㄐㄧㄣˇ ㄕㄤˋ)
presented respectfully by... (a conventional phrase placed after the writer's signature in a formal letter); humbly yours

謹嚴(ㄐㄧㄣˇ ㄧㄢˊ)
strict; rigorous; careful and precise: 他治學謹嚴。He is careful and precise in studying.

謹言愼行(ㄐㄧㄣˇ ㄧㄢˊ ㄕㄣˋ ㄒㄧㄥˊ)
to be prudent in making statements and careful in personal conduct

謹愿(ㄐㄧㄣˇ ㄩㄢˋ)
sincere; honest

【謰】 5671 ㄌㄧㄢˊ lian lián

1. to talk vaguely
2. the combination of two closely related characters which forms an inseparable thought unit

謰謱(ㄌㄧㄢˊ ㄌㄡˊ)
to talk vaguely and aimlessly

謰語(ㄌㄧㄢˊ ㄩˇ)
the combination of two characters closely related in pronunciation and meaning which forms an inseparable thought unit, as 澎湃, 崔嵬, etc.

十二畫

【譏】 5672 ㄐㄧ ji jī

1. to ridicule; to jeer; to sneer
2. to inspect

譏評(ㄐㄧ ㄆㄧㄥˊ)
to make jeering comments

譏諷(ㄐㄧ ㄈㄥˋ)
to ridicule; to deride; to satirize

譏誚(ㄐㄧ ㄑㄧㄠˋ)
to taunt; to mock; to jeer; to sneer at; to deride: 他常常譏誚同僚。He often jeers at his colleagues.

譏笑(ㄐㄧ ㄒㄧㄠˋ)
to laugh at; to make fun of; to deride; to ridicule; taunts; sneers

譏刺(ㄐㄧ ㄘˋ)
to taunt; to satirize

【譁】 5673 ㄏㄨㄚˊ hwa huá

noise; tumult; hubbub; clamor; uproar

譁變(ㄏㄨㄚˊ ㄅㄧㄢˋ)
tumultuous mutiny; to mutiny

譁囂(ㄏㄨㄚˊ ㄒㄧㄠ)
noisy commotion; tumult; uproar

譁笑(ㄏㄨㄚˊ ㄒㄧㄠˋ)
noisy laughter

譁衆取寵(ㄏㄨㄚˊ ㄓㄨㄥˋ ㄑㄩˇ ㄔㄨㄥˇ)
to practice demagogy; to make seditious speeches; to try to win popularity by shocking words; to please the public with claptrap

譁然(ㄏㄨㄚˊ ㄖㄢˊ)
uproarious; boisterous; tumultuous: 舉座譁然。The audience burst into an tumult.

譁噪(ㄏㄨㄚˊ ㄗㄠˋ)
noisy; hubbub

【證】 5674 ㄓㄥˋ jenq zhèng

1. to give evidence; to bear testimony; to bear witness; to prove; to testify; to confirm; to corroborate; to attest to; to certify
2. evidence; proof; testimony
3. a certificate; a card
4. a symptom; indication

證明(ㄓㄥˋ ㄇㄧㄥˊ)
to prove; to testify; to certify; to attest to; to confirm; to corroborate; proof; evidence; testimony: 我可以證明他的無辜。I can testify to his innocence.

證明書(ㄓㄥˋ ㄇㄧㄥˊ ㄕㄨ)
a certificate; a voucher

證明文件(ㄓㄥˋ ㄇㄧㄥˊ ㄨㄣˊ ㄐㄧㄢˋ)
supporting documents or papers; a certificate; a testimonial 亦作「證件」

證道(ㄓㄥˋ ㄉㄠˋ)
(Christianity) to give a testimonial; a testimonial

證果(ㄓㄥˋ ㄍㄨㄛˇ)
(Buddhism) the fruits or rewards of the various stages of attainment

證候(ㄓㄥˋ ㄏㄡˋ)
a symptom; indication; a sign: 發熱是許多疾病的證候。Fever is a symptom of many diseases.

證婚人(ㄓㄥˋ ㄏㄨㄣ ㄖㄣˊ)
a witness at a wedding

證件(ㄓㄥˋ ㄐㄧㄢˋ)
papers or documents supporting a claim; documentary proof; credentials; a certificate: 請出示證件。Please show your credentials (or papers).

證見(ㄓㄥˋ ㄐㄧㄢˋ)
evidence

證據(ㄓㄥˋ ㄐㄩˋ)
testimony; evidence; witness; proof

證券(ㄓㄥˋ ㄑㄩㄢˋ)
securities (bills, bonds, etc.);

stocks and bonds
證券交易所(ㄓㄥˋ ㄑㄩㄢˋ ㄐㄧㄠ ㄧˋ ㄙㄨㄛˇ)
the stock exchange
證券市場(ㄓㄥˋ ㄑㄩㄢˋ ㄕˋ ㄔㄤˇ)
the stock market
證章(ㄓㄥˋ ㄓㄤ)
a badge
證實(ㄓㄥˋ ㄕˊ)
to confirm; to corroborate; to prove; to verify
證書(ㄓㄥˋ ㄕㄨ)
a certificate; a diploma; credentials
證人(ㄓㄥˋ ㄖㄣˊ)or 證左(ㄓㄥˋ ㄗㄨㄛˇ)
a witness
證詞(ㄓㄥˋ ㄘˊ)
testimony given at a court of law
證言(ㄓㄥˋ ㄧㄢˊ)
testimony: 那證人的證言不實。The witness's testimony is false.
證驗(ㄓㄥˋ ㄧㄢˋ)
① to verify; to bear out ② real results; efficacy
證物(ㄓㄥˋ ㄨˋ)
physical evidence; an exhibit

【譎】 5675
ㄐㄩㄝˊ jyue jué
1. to cheat; to deceive; to swindle
2. wily; artful; crafty; cunning; tricky
譎詭(ㄐㄩㄝˊ ㄍㄨㄟˇ)
unpredictable; changing constantly
譎諫(ㄐㄩㄝˊ ㄐㄧㄢˋ)
to admonish by hints; to remonstrate with somebody in indirect ways

【譖】 5676
ㄗㄣˋ tzenn zen
to slander; to charge falsely
譖人(ㄗㄣˋ ㄖㄣˊ)
to slander others
譖言(ㄗㄣˋ ㄧㄢˊ)
slanderous remarks; slanders

【識】 5677
1. ㄕˋ shyh shì
1. to know; to recognize; to discern
2. an opinion; a view
3. knowledge
識拔(ㄕˋ ㄅㄚˊ)
to appreciate and promote (an employee or subordinate)
識別(ㄕˋ ㄅㄧㄝˊ)
① to discern; to distinguish; to identify ② identification
識別力(ㄕˋ ㄅㄧㄝˊ ㄌㄧˋ)
the power of discernment
識別證(ㄕˋ ㄅㄧㄝˊ ㄓㄥˋ)
an I.D. card
識破(ㄕˋ ㄆㄛˋ)
to see through: 你能識破他的騙局嗎? Can you see through his fraud?
識多見廣(ㄕˋ ㄉㄨㄛ ㄐㄧㄢˋ ㄍㄨㄤˇ)
learned and experienced
識途老馬(ㄕˋ ㄊㄨˊ ㄌㄠˇ ㄇㄚˇ)
an old horse which knows the way—an experienced person
識貨(ㄕˋ ㄏㄨㄛˋ)
to appreciate; able to evaluate wares correctly; able to judge the worth of an artistic work; able to tell good from bad
識見(ㄕˋ ㄐㄧㄢˋ)
knowledge; experience; insight; understanding
識荆(ㄕˋ ㄐㄧㄥ)or 識韓(ㄕˋ ㄏㄢˊ)
(a polite expression) one's first acquaintance with a person ; to have the honor of knowing you in person
識竅(ㄕˋ ㄑㄧㄠˋ)
to know how to ride the political tide; to be able to see which way the stream of time runs
識趣(ㄕˋ ㄑㄩˋ)
to have tact; tactful; to know how to behave in a delicate situation
識相(ㄕˋ ㄒㄧㄤˋ)
to know one's own limitations; to know when to yield with grace; to know how to avoid embarrassment; tactful
識者(ㄕˋ ㄓㄜˇ)
the knowledgeable; those in the know; an expert
識時務者爲俊傑(ㄕˋ ㄕˊ ㄨˋ ㄓㄜˇ ㄨㄟˊ ㄐㄩㄣˋ ㄐㄧㄝˊ)
A great man knows how to ride the tide of his times.
識人(ㄕˋ ㄖㄣˊ)
able to appraise a person's ability and character correctly
識字(ㄕˋ ㄗˋ)
able to read; literate
識字教育(ㄕˋ ㄗˋ ㄐㄧㄠˋ ㄩˋ)
education for literacy
識字運動(ㄕˋ ㄗˋ ㄩㄣˋ ㄉㄨㄥˋ)
a literacy campaign or movement

【識】 5677
2.(誌) ㄓˋ jyh zhì
1. to record; to remember, etc.
2. a mark; a sign

【譙】 5678
1. ㄑㄧㄠˊ chyau qiáo
1. a tower
2. a Chinese family name
譙門(ㄑㄧㄠˊ ㄇㄣˊ)or 譙樓(ㄑㄧㄠˊ ㄌㄡˊ)
a watchtower over the city gate
譙櫓(ㄑㄧㄠˊ ㄌㄨˇ)
a donjon; a tower built on the wall of a city for defense

【譙】 5678
2.(誚) ㄑㄧㄠˋ chiaw qiào
to scold; to blame

【譚】 5679
ㄊㄢˊ tarn tán
1. same as 談—to talk
2. a Chinese family name
譚嗣同(ㄊㄢˊ ㄙˋ ㄊㄨㄥˊ)
Tan Szu-tung, 1865-1898, a late Ching Dynasty reformer, executed by Empress Dowager Tzu Hsi(慈禧太后)

【譊】 5680
ㄋㄠˊ nau náo
to argue; to dispute; to wrangle; to clamor
譊譊(ㄋㄠˊ ㄋㄠˊ)
arguing voices

【譜】 5681
ㄆㄨˇ puu pǔ
1. a register; a record; a table; a list
2. (music) a score
3. to compose (a song)
4. a general idea; a rough picture; something to count on
5. a collection of examples for reference purpose; a manual; a guide
譜表(ㄆㄨˇ ㄅㄧㄠˇ)
(music) a score; a staff
譜第(ㄆㄨˇ ㄉㄧˋ)

〔言 部〕

〔言部〕

a genealogy
譜牒(ㄆㄨˇ ㄉㄧㄝˊ)or 譜錄(ㄆㄨˇ ㄌㄨˋ)
a genealogy
譜號(ㄆㄨˇ ㄏㄠˋ)
①musical notes ②a clef
譜曲(ㄆㄨˇ ㄑㄩˇ)
to compose a song; to write a musical composition
譜系(ㄆㄨˇ ㄒㄧˋ)
a genealogy; a family tree: 他追溯譜系到十七世紀。He traced his family tree back to the 17th century.
譜新聲(ㄆㄨˇ ㄒㄧㄣ ㄕㄥ)
to compose a new song
譜兄弟(ㄆㄨˇ ㄒㄩㄥ ㄉㄧˋ)
sworn brothers
譜子(ㄆㄨˇ ·ㄗ)or 譜兒(ㄆㄨˇㄦ)
①a list (of formulas, rules, procedures, etc.) ②a musical score

【譌】5682 (訛) ㄜˊ er é
false; erroneous

十三畫

【議】5683 ㄧˋ yih yì
1. to discuss; to argue; to debate; to negotiate; to talk over
2. an opinion; a view
3. to criticize; to comment; criticism; comment
3. argumentative writing; argumentation; an essay; a treatise
議定(ㄧˋ ㄉㄧㄥˋ)
to arrive at a decision after discussion or negotiation
議定書(ㄧˋ ㄉㄧㄥˋ ㄕㄨ)
a protocol: 他們簽訂貿易議定書。They signed a trade protocol.
議題(ㄧˋ ㄊㄧˊ)
a topic for discussion; a subject of debate
議論(ㄧˋ ㄌㄨㄣˋ)
①argument; debate ②comments ③to discuss; discussion; to talk
議論風生(ㄧˋ ㄌㄨㄣˋ ㄈㄥ ㄕㄥ)
to create a lively atmosphere by one's talk
議論文(ㄧˋ ㄌㄨㄣˋ ㄨㄣˊ)
argumentative writing; argumentation
議和(ㄧˋ ㄏㄜˊ)
to negotiate peace
議會(ㄧˋ ㄏㄨㄟˋ)
a parliament; an assembly; a council: 召開議會 to convene (or summon) a parliament
議會政治(ㄧˋ ㄏㄨㄟˋ ㄓㄥˋ ㄓˋ)
parliamentary politics; parliamentary government
議價(ㄧˋ ㄐㄧㄚˋ)
①to negotiate over the price ②the negotiated price; the price agreed upon
議決(ㄧˋ ㄐㄩㄝˊ)
to decide or resolve (at a meeting); to pass a resolution
議決案(ㄧˋ ㄐㄩㄝˊ ㄢˋ)
a resolution (at a meeting)
議親(ㄧˋ ㄑㄧㄣ)
to negotiate a marriage
議長(ㄧˋ ㄓㄤˇ)
the speaker, president, or chairman of an assembly, parliament, etc.
議場(ㄧˋ ㄔㄤˇ)or(ㄧˋ ㄔㄤˊ)
an assembly hall
議程(ㄧˋ ㄔㄥˊ)
agenda
議處(ㄧˋ ㄔㄨˇ)
to take disciplinary action against (derelict officials, etc.)
議事(ㄧˋ ㄕˋ)
to discuss official business
議事廳(ㄧˋ ㄕˋ ㄊㄧㄥ)
an assembly hall
議事規則(ㄧˋ ㄕˋ ㄍㄨㄟ ㄗㄜˊ)
rules of procedure; rules of debate
議事槌(ㄧˋ ㄕˋ ㄔㄨㄟˊ)
a gavel (used by the speaker of a legislature)
議事日程(ㄧˋ ㄕˋ ㄖˋ ㄔㄥˊ)
agenda; order of the day
議案(ㄧˋ ㄢˋ)
a bill; a proposal (for a legislative body); a motion
議而不決，決而不行(ㄧˋ ㄦˊ ㄅㄨˋ ㄐㄩㄝˊ, ㄐㄩㄝˊ ㄦˊ ㄅㄨˋ ㄒㄧㄥˊ)
Meetings produce no decisions and decisions produce no actions.
議員(ㄧˋ ㄩㄢˊ)
an assemblyman; a councilman; a councilor; a parliamentarian; a congressman
議院(ㄧˋ ㄩㄢˋ)
parliament; a legislature; a legislative assembly; congress

【譟】5684 ㄗㄠˋ tzaw zào
1. noise of a crowd; (said of a crowd) to shout noisily
2. to slander; to abuse

【警】5685 ㄐㄧㄥˇ jiing jǐng
1. to guard; to keep watch
2. to warn; to alert
3. an alarm: 火警的警報器響了。The fire alarm sounded.
4. quick; alert; agile: 他很機警。He has an alert mind.
5. the police
警備(ㄐㄧㄥˇ ㄅㄟˋ)
to be on one's guard to keep watch
警備司令部(ㄐㄧㄥˇ ㄅㄟˋ ㄙ ㄌㄧㄥˋ ㄅㄨˋ)
garrison headquarters
警報(ㄐㄧㄥˇ ㄅㄠˋ)
an alert; an alarm; a warning
警報器(ㄐㄧㄥˇ ㄅㄠˋ ㄑㄧˋ)
a siren
警蹕(ㄐㄧㄥˇ ㄅㄧˋ)
a herald who clears the emperor's road
警笛(ㄐㄧㄥˇ ㄉㄧˊ)
a police whistle; an alarm siren
警探(ㄐㄧㄥˇ ㄊㄢˋ)
a police detective
警惕(ㄐㄧㄥˇ ㄊㄧˋ)
①to be vigilant; to be wary; to be alert; to be watchful ②a warning
警廳(ㄐㄧㄥˇ ㄊㄧㄥ)
police headquarters
警鈴(ㄐㄧㄥˇ ㄌㄧㄥˊ)
a warning bell; an alarm bell
警告(ㄐㄧㄥˇ ㄍㄠˋ)
①to warn; to caution; to admonish ②a warning
警鼓(ㄐㄧㄥˇ ㄍㄨˇ)
a warning drum; an alarm drum
警官(ㄐㄧㄥˇ ㄍㄨㄢ)
a police officer
警官學校(ㄐㄧㄥˇ ㄍㄨㄢ ㄒㄩㄝˊ ㄒㄧㄠˋ)
a police academy

警棍(ㄐㄧㄥˇ ㄍㄨㄣˋ)
a policeman's baton or truncheon
警號(ㄐㄧㄥˇ ㄏㄠˋ)
a warning signal
警徽(ㄐㄧㄥˇ ㄏㄨㄟ)
a police insignia; a police badge
警誡(ㄐㄧㄥˇ ㄐㄧㄝˋ)
to warn and admonish
警戒(ㄐㄧㄥˇ ㄐㄧㄝˋ)
①to be on the alert; to be on one's guard; to be vigilant; to stand guard ②to warn and admonish
警戒部隊(ㄐㄧㄥˇ ㄐㄧㄝˋ ㄅㄨˋ ㄉㄨㄟˋ)
guarding troops; troops on alert; outpost troops
警戒線(ㄐㄧㄥˇ ㄐㄧㄝˋ ㄒㄧㄢˋ)
①a cordon (of sentinels, forts, etc.) ②a danger line or mark (on a riverbank, etc. for warning of floods)
警戒色(ㄐㄧㄥˇ ㄐㄧㄝˋ ㄙㄜˋ)
(biology) warning color
警句(ㄐㄧㄥˇ ㄐㄩˋ)or 警語(ㄐㄧㄥˇ ㄩˇ)
an epigram
警覺(ㄐㄧㄥˇ ㄐㄩㄝˊ)
vigilant; alert; watchful
警覺性(ㄐㄧㄥˇ ㄐㄩㄝˊ ㄒㄧㄥˋ)
vigilance; alertness
警犬(ㄐㄧㄥˇ ㄑㄩㄢˇ)
a police dog
警醒(ㄐㄧㄥˇ ㄒㄧㄥˇ)
①easily awakened from sleep; quick to awake ②vigilant
警長(ㄐㄧㄥˇ ㄓㄤˇ)
a police chief
警政(ㄐㄧㄥˇ ㄓㄥˋ)
police administration
警鐘(ㄐㄧㄥˇ ㄓㄨㄥ)
an alarm bell; a tocsin
警衆(ㄐㄧㄥˇ ㄓㄨㄥˋ)
to warn the people; to alert the public
警察(ㄐㄧㄥˇ ㄔㄚˊ)
cops; the police
警察派出所(ㄐㄧㄥˇ ㄔㄚˊ ㄆㄞˋ ㄔㄨ ㄙㄨㄛˇ)
a police substation; a station house
警察分局(ㄐㄧㄥˇ ㄔㄚˊ ㄈㄣ ㄐㄩˊ)
police precinct headquarters
警察局(ㄐㄧㄥˇ ㄔㄚˊ ㄐㄩˊ)
county (or city) police headquarters
警察學校(ㄐㄧㄥˇ ㄔㄚˊ ㄒㄩㄝˊ ㄒㄧㄠˋ)
a police school; a police academy
警車(ㄐㄧㄥˇ ㄔㄜ)
a squad car; a police patrol car; a police car
警世(ㄐㄧㄥˇ ㄕˋ)
to warn or caution mankind against impending disasters
警世通言(ㄐㄧㄥˇ ㄕˋ ㄊㄨㄥ ㄧㄢˊ)
the title of a forty-volume novel by Feng Meng-lung(馮夢龍)of the Ming Dynasty
警策(ㄐㄧㄥˇ ㄘㄜˋ)
a key phrase, sentence or passage in a piece of writing (which enlivens the writing as a whip enlivens a horse)
警悟(ㄐㄧㄥˇ ㄨˋ)
quick to realize or understand
警務(ㄐㄧㄥˇ ㄨˋ)
police affairs
警務處(ㄐㄧㄥˇ ㄨˋ ㄔㄨˋ)
a provincial department of the police
警衛(ㄐㄧㄥˇ ㄨㄟˋ)
①to guard ②a guard
警員(ㄐㄧㄥˇ ㄩㄢˊ)
a policeman; a cop

【譬】 5686 ㄆㄧˋ pih pì

1. to liken; to compare
2. a simile; an example
3. to tell
4. to understand

譬如(ㄆㄧˋ ㄖㄨˊ)or 譬若(ㄆㄧˋ ㄖㄨㄛˋ)
suppose; for instance; for example
譬喩(ㄆㄧˋ ㄩˋ)
a simile or metaphor

【譯】 5687 ㄧˋ yih yì

to translate; translation
譯本(ㄧˋ ㄅㄣˇ)
a translated version (of a book); a translation
譯筆(ㄧˋ ㄅㄧˇ)
(literally) a translator's pen —a translator's skill; the quality or style of a translation
譯名(ㄧˋ ㄇㄧㄥˊ)
a transliterated name
譯電(ㄧˋ ㄉㄧㄢˋ)
to decode, or encode, a telegram
譯學館(ㄧˋ ㄒㄩㄝˊ ㄍㄨㄢˇ)
the school for training students in foreign languages set up toward the end of the Ching Dynasty
譯者(ㄧˋ ㄓㄜˇ)
a translator
譯注(ㄧˋ ㄓㄨˋ)
to translate and annotate
譯述(ㄧˋ ㄕㄨˋ)
to translate freely
譯述者(ㄧˋ ㄕㄨˋ ㄓㄜˇ)
a translator who does not claim literal accuracy
譯意風(ㄧˋ ㄧˋ ㄈㄥ)
earphones (provided at each seat in a movie house whereby the spectator can hear the dialogues of foreign movies interpreted into Chinese); a simultaneous interpretation installation
譯音(ㄧˋ ㄧㄣ)
a transliteration; sound transcription
譯音符號(ㄧˋ ㄧㄣ ㄈㄨˊ ㄏㄠˋ)
the National Romanization, or Gwoyeu Romatzyh, for Mandarin Chinese 亦作「國語羅馬字」
譯文(ㄧˋ ㄨㄣˊ)
translated texts; a translation: 譯文不雅。The translation is not elegant.
譯員(ㄧˋ ㄩㄢˊ)
an interpreter; a translator

十四畫

【護】 5688 ㄏㄨˋ huh hù

1. to protect; to guard; to defend; to shield
2. to take sides; to be partial to

護庇(ㄏㄨˋ ㄅㄧˋ)
to shelter; to cover up
護兵(ㄏㄨˋ ㄅㄧㄥ)
military guards
護民官(ㄏㄨˋ ㄇㄧㄣˊ ㄍㄨㄢ)
(in ancient Rome) a tribune
護法(ㄏㄨˋ ㄈㄚˇ)
①to protect or maintain the Buddha-truth ②to uphold the constitution

〔言部〕

護法運動(ㄏㄨˋ ㄈㄚˇ ㄩㄣˋ ㄉㄨㄥˋ)
the movement to defend the Constitution led by Dr. Sun Yat-sen when the warlord Tuan Chi-jui (段祺瑞) dissolved the parliament in 1917
護符(ㄏㄨˋ ㄈㄨˊ)
an amulet; a charm for self-protection
護短(ㄏㄨˋ ㄉㄨㄢˇ)
① to conceal one's faults ② to side with a disputant who is in the wrong
護理(ㄏㄨˋ ㄌㄧˇ)
① to act for a senior official ② nursing
護理專科學校(ㄏㄨˋ ㄌㄧˇ ㄓㄨㄢ ㄎㄜ ㄒㄩㄝˊ ㄒㄧㄠˋ)
a junior college of nursing
護國軍(ㄏㄨˋ ㄍㄨㄛˊ ㄐㄩㄣ)
the troops that rallied against Yüan Shih-kai (袁世凱) when he attempted to restore monarchy in 1916
護軌(ㄏㄨˋ ㄍㄨㄟˇ)
a guardrail
護航(ㄏㄨˋ ㄏㄤˊ)
① to escort another vessel ② to help another illicitly during an examination
護花(ㄏㄨˋ ㄏㄨㄚ)
to protect women
護花使者(ㄏㄨˋ ㄏㄨㄚ ㄕˇ ㄓㄜˇ)
a protector of women; a woman's escort
護駕(ㄏㄨˋ ㄐㄧㄚˋ)
to guard the emperor; to escort the emperor
護照(ㄏㄨˋ ㄓㄠˋ)
a passport
護持(ㄏㄨˋ ㄔˊ)
to protect and maintain
護城河(ㄏㄨˋ ㄔㄥˊ ㄏㄜˊ)
a city moat
護士(ㄏㄨˋ ㄕˋ)
a nurse
護士節(ㄏㄨˋ ㄕˋ ㄐㄧㄝˊ)
Nurses' Day (May 12)
護手(ㄏㄨˋ ㄕㄡˇ)
the guard (of a sword or knife)
護身符(ㄏㄨˋ ㄕㄣ ㄈㄨˊ)
① an amulet; a charm for self-protection ② anything which one uses as a protective shield
護喪(ㄏㄨˋ ㄙㄤ)
one who presides over a funeral service (usually an elder of the clan)
護送(ㄏㄨˋ ㄙㄨㄥˋ)
to escort; to convoy
護岸(ㄏㄨˋ ㄢˋ)
a dike; a levee; an embankment
護衛(ㄏㄨˋ ㄨㄟˋ)
to guard; to escort; to convoy
護運(ㄏㄨˋ ㄩㄣˋ)
to ship or transport something under guard

【譴】 5689
ㄑㄧㄢˇ chean qiǎn
1. to reproach; to reprimand; to upbraid
2. punishment
譴訶(ㄑㄧㄢˇ ㄏㄜ)
to scold; to reproach
譴責(ㄑㄧㄢˇ ㄗㄜˊ)
to reprimand; to reproach; to upbraid; to blame

【譽】 5690
ㄩˋ yuh yù
1. fame; honor; glory
2. to praise; to eulogize
譽滿全球(ㄩˋ ㄇㄢˇ ㄑㄩㄢˊ ㄑㄧㄡˊ)
to achieve global fame; world-famous: 她是譽滿全球的鋼琴家。She is a world-famous pianist.

十五畫

【譾】 5691
ㄐㄧㄢˇ jean jiǎn
(mentally) shallow
譾陋(ㄐㄧㄢˇ ㄌㄡˋ)
(mentally) shallow

【讀】 5692
1. ㄉㄨˊ dwu dú
1. to read
2. to attend school; to go to school, college, etc.
3. to study
讀本(ㄉㄨˊ ㄅㄣˇ)
a reader (for a language course, etc.); a textbook: 讀本繁多。Textbooks are great in number.
讀畢(ㄉㄨˊ ㄅㄧˋ)
to finish reading
讀秒(ㄉㄨˊ ㄇㄧㄠˇ)
to remind a player in a chess game of how much time left when he has almost used up his alloted time
讀法(ㄉㄨˊ ㄈㄚˇ)
pronunciation (of a word)
讀卡機(ㄉㄨˊ ㄎㄚˇ ㄐㄧ)
(computers) a card reader
讀畫(ㄉㄨˊ ㄏㄨㄚˋ)
to appraise a painting
讀寫算(ㄉㄨˊ ㄒㄧㄝˇ ㄙㄨㄢˋ)
reading, writing, and arithmetic
讀者(ㄉㄨˊ ㄓㄜˇ)
the reader (as opposed to the writer): 希望讀者能原諒我。I hope my readers will excuse me.
讀者文摘(ㄉㄨˊ ㄓㄜˇ ㄨㄣˊ ㄓㄞ)
The Reader's Digest
讀書(ㄉㄨˊ ㄕㄨ)
① to read books ② to study; to receive education
讀書不求甚解(ㄉㄨˊ ㄕㄨ ㄅㄨˋ ㄑㄧㄡˊ ㄕㄣˋ ㄐㄧㄝˇ)
In reading a book, one does not care about the details too much.
讀書界(ㄉㄨˊ ㄕㄨ ㄐㄧㄝˋ)
the reading public
讀書種子(ㄉㄨˊ ㄕㄨ ㄓㄨㄥˇ ㄗˇ)
the seed of learning — the continuity of the scholarly tradition
讀書人(ㄉㄨˊ ㄕㄨ ㄖㄣˊ)
a scholar; an intellectual: 他可說是個讀書人。He is something of a scholar.
讀書三到(ㄉㄨˊ ㄕㄨ ㄙㄢ ㄉㄠˋ)
the three things to be used in reading a book—the eye, the mouth, and the mind
讀書五車(ㄉㄨˊ ㄕㄨ ㄨˇ ㄐㄩ)
having read five cartloads of books—learned; erudite; well-read
讀熟(ㄉㄨˊ ㄕㄨˊ)
to read until one can recite out of memory
讀錯(ㄉㄨˊ ㄘㄨㄛˋ)
to mispronounce (a word): 他將此字讀錯了。He mispronounced this word.
讀音(ㄉㄨˊ ㄧㄣ)
pronunciation (of a word)
讀物(ㄉㄨˊ ㄨˋ)
reading matter; reading: 課

外讀物 outside reading
讀完(ㄉㄨˊ ㄨㄢˊ)
①to finish reading (an article or a book)②to finish studying (at a school)

【讀】 5692
2. ㄉㄡˋ dow dòu
pauses in a sentence

【讅】 5693
ㄕㄣˇ sheen shěn
to know; to be aware

【讁】 5694
(謫) ㄓㄜˊ jer zhé
to punish; to blame

十六畫

【變】 5695
ㄅㄧㄢˋ biann biàn
1. to change; to alter
2. to change; to become different
3. to turn into; to become
4. extraordinary; uncommon
5. an accident; misfortune; tragedy; upheaval; disturbance; an unexpected turn of events
6. changeable

變本加厲(ㄅㄧㄢˋ ㄅㄣˇ ㄐㄧㄚ ㄌㄧˋ)
(said of tyranny, personal conduct, etc.) to get worse; worsening; to intensify one's effort to do something wrong
變賣(ㄅㄧㄢˋ ㄇㄞˋ)
to sell (possessions) to meet an immediate financial need
變法兒(ㄅㄧㄢˋ ㄈㄚˇㄦ)
by various means; to try different ways
變法(ㄅㄧㄢˋ ㄈㄚˇ)
to revise the law; to initiate political reform
變法自強(ㄅㄧㄢˋ ㄈㄚˇ ㄗˋ ㄑㄧㄤˊ)
to initiate political reform in quest for national strength
變法維新(ㄅㄧㄢˋ ㄈㄚˇ ㄨㄟˊ ㄒㄧㄣ)
the Constitutional Reform and Modernization (1898)
變得(ㄅㄧㄢˋ ˙ㄉㄜ)
to become
變調(ㄅㄧㄢˋ ㄉㄧㄠˋ)
to change a tune or melody; to change the key (of a tune); variations
變電所(ㄅㄧㄢˋ ㄉㄧㄢˋ ㄙㄨㄛˇ)
a power substation
變動(ㄅㄧㄢˋ ㄉㄨㄥˋ)
①(said of organizations, arrangements, etc.) to change; to reshuffle; to reorganize ②a change; alteration ③variation
變態(ㄅㄧㄢˋ ㄊㄞˋ)
①abnormality ②(zoology) metamorphosis
變態心理學(ㄅㄧㄢˋ ㄊㄞˋ ㄒㄧㄣ ㄌㄧˇ ㄒㄩㄝˊ)
abnormal psychology
變體(ㄅㄧㄢˋ ㄊㄧˇ)
a new style derived from the original
變天(ㄅㄧㄢˋ ㄊㄧㄢ)
①a change of weather (usually from fine to bad)②the changes of political situations
變通(ㄅㄧㄢˋ ㄊㄨㄥ)
to adapt oneself to circumstances; to be flexible
變通辦理(ㄅㄧㄢˋ ㄊㄨㄥ ㄅㄢˋ ㄌㄧˇ)
to handle something without the rigid application of rules
變弄(ㄅㄧㄢˋ ㄋㄨㄥˋ)
to get (money, articles, etc.) in some uncommon way
變了(ㄅㄧㄢˋ ˙ㄌㄜ)
to have changed
變臉(ㄅㄧㄢˋ ㄌㄧㄢˇ)
to turn hostile; to get angry
變亂(ㄅㄧㄢˋ ㄌㄨㄢˋ)
rebellion; revolt; upheaval; chaos; turmoil
變革(ㄅㄧㄢˋ ㄍㄜˊ)
(said of an institution, a system, etc.) to change or reform
變更(ㄅㄧㄢˋ ㄍㄥ)
to change (plans, methods, etc.); to alter; to modify: 我們的計畫稍有變更。We have modified our plan.
變故(ㄅㄧㄢˋ ㄍㄨˋ)
an accident; misfortune; mishap: 發生了變故。An accident has happened.
變卦(ㄅㄧㄢˋ ㄍㄨㄚˋ)
to change one's mind; to go back on one's words; to break an agreement: 你怎麼變卦了? What made you change your mind?
變好(ㄅㄧㄢˋ ㄏㄠˇ)
①(said of weather) to become fine; to clear up ②(said of a person) to reform; to become good
變化(ㄅㄧㄢˋ ㄏㄨㄚˋ)
①to transform; to metamorphose; to transmute ②to change ③a change; changeable
變化多端(ㄅㄧㄢˋ ㄏㄨㄚˋ ㄉㄨㄛ ㄉㄨㄢ)
changeable
變化氣質(ㄅㄧㄢˋ ㄏㄨㄚˋ ㄑㄧˋ ㄓˋ)
to change one's temperament: 教育可以變化氣質。Education can change one's temperament.
變化語(ㄅㄧㄢˋ ㄏㄨㄚˋ ㄩˇ)
an inflective language
變壞(ㄅㄧㄢˋ ㄏㄨㄞˋ)
①(said of illness) to get worse ②(said of weather or a person) to become bad
變換(ㄅㄧㄢˋ ㄏㄨㄢˋ)
①to convert (foreign money, etc.) ②to change; to vary; to switch
變幻(ㄅㄧㄢˋ ㄏㄨㄢˋ)
to change; to metamorphose; to fluctuate irregularly
變幻莫測(ㄅㄧㄢˋ ㄏㄨㄢˋ ㄇㄛˋ ㄘㄜˋ)
to metamorphose in an unpredictable way
變價(ㄅㄧㄢˋ ㄐㄧㄚˋ)
to appraise at the current price
變節(ㄅㄧㄢˋ ㄐㄧㄝˊ)
①to desert a cause or principle; to defect; to make a political recantation; to turn one's coat ②to reform; to abandon evil ways and return to the right path
變局(ㄅㄧㄢˋ ㄐㄩˊ)
a critical situation; a crisis
變遷(ㄅㄧㄢˋ ㄑㄧㄢ)
evolution; change; vicissitudes
變戲法兒(ㄅㄧㄢˋ ㄒㄧˋ ㄈㄚˇㄦ)
to perform sleight of hand; to manipulate by trickery; to conjure; to juggle
變心(ㄅㄧㄢˋ ㄒㄧㄣ)
①to change in faith or loyalty; to turn a traitor ②to jilt a lover; to cease to love one's spouse
變相(ㄅㄧㄢˋ ㄒㄧㄤˋ)
changed only in appearance; disguised; in disguise

〔言部〕

變相津貼(ㄅㄧㄢˋ ㄒㄧㄤ ㄐㄧㄣ ㄊㄧㄝ)
money paid legitimately, but not as a straightforward allowance, to an employee who is underpaid according to the official pay scale
變星(ㄅㄧㄢˋ ㄒㄧㄥ)
a variable star
變形(ㄅㄧㄢˋ ㄒㄧㄥˊ)
to transfigure; to transform; to change shape; to be out of shape
變形蟲(ㄅㄧㄢˋ ㄒㄧㄥˊ ㄔㄨㄥˊ)
an amoeba
變性(ㄅㄧㄢˋ ㄒㄧㄥˋ)
① to change sex by surgical means ② denaturation
變性酒精(ㄅㄧㄢˋ ㄒㄧㄥˋ ㄐㄧㄡˇ ㄐㄧㄥ)
denaturated alcohol
變質(ㄅㄧㄢˋ ㄓˋ)
① to change in quality or objectives ② to deteriorate; to go bad: 這魚肉已經變質了。 The fish has gone bad. ③ to degenerate
變種(ㄅㄧㄢˋ ㄓㄨㄥˇ)
an extraordinary variety (of something); a mutant; mutation
變成(ㄅㄧㄢˋ ㄔㄥˊ)
to become; to convert into; to change into: 毛毛蟲會變成蝴蝶。 Caterpillars change into butterflies.
變聲(ㄅㄧㄢˋ ㄕㄥ)
(said of a person at puberty) change of voice
變數(ㄅㄧㄢˋ ㄕㄨˋ)
(mathematics) a variable
變造(ㄅㄧㄢˋ ㄗㄠˋ)
(law) to make changes in value of property (checks) owing to alterations
變奏曲(ㄅㄧㄢˋ ㄗㄡˋ ㄑㄩˇ)
variations
變阻器(ㄅㄧㄢˋ ㄗㄨˇ ㄑㄧˋ)
a rheostat
變色(ㄅㄧㄢˋ ㄙㄜˋ)
①(said of a person) to turn white (from fear) or red (from anger); to change color; to change countenance ② to change in color; to stain; to fade; to discolor; to change the color of
變速(ㄅㄧㄢˋ ㄙㄨˋ)
to change in speed; gearshift

變異(ㄅㄧㄢˋ ㄧˋ)
(biology) variation; mutation
變易(ㄅㄧㄢˋ ㄧˋ)
to alter; to change
變壓器(ㄅㄧㄢˋ ㄧㄚ ㄑㄧˋ)
a transformer
變壓站(ㄅㄧㄢˋ ㄧㄚ ㄓㄢˋ)
a power substation
變音(ㄅㄧㄢˋ ㄧㄣ)
(phonetics) umlaut
變樣(ㄅㄧㄢˋ ㄧㄤˋ)
to change in design, patterns, style, appearance, etc.
變爲(ㄅㄧㄢˋ ㄨㄟˊ)
to become; to be converted or transformed into: 那習俗現已變爲成規。 The custom has now become a rule.
變味(ㄅㄧㄢˋ ㄨㄟˋ)
(said of stale food or drink) to taste unpleasant to the palate

【讌】 5696 ㄧㄢˋ yann yàn

a feast; a banquet
讌服(ㄧㄢˋ ㄈㄨˊ)
everyday dress; informal dress
讌饗(ㄧㄢˋ ㄒㄧㄤˇ)
a feast; a banquet
讌飲(ㄧㄢˋ ㄧㄣˇ)
a feast; a banquet

【讎】 5697 (讐) ㄔㄡˊ chour chóu

1. an enemy; a rival; a foe
2. to collate; to compare
3. to toast
4. an answer

讎敵(ㄔㄡˊ ㄉㄧˊ)
an enemy; a foe
讎定(ㄔㄡˊ ㄉㄧㄥˋ)
to correct or revise while proofreading
讎家(ㄔㄡˊ ㄐㄧㄚ)
a rival; an enemy; a foe
讎校(ㄔㄡˊ ㄐㄧㄠˋ)
to collate; to proofread
讎視(ㄔㄡˊ ㄕˋ)
to regard with hostility; to be hostile to
讎殺(ㄔㄡˊ ㄕㄚ)
to kill from hatred; murder committed out of a grudge
讎問(ㄔㄡˊ ㄨㄣˋ)
to ask difficult questions

十七畫

【讕】 5698 ㄌㄢˊ lan lán

to abuse; to revile; to slander; to libel
讕言(ㄌㄢˊ ㄧㄢˊ)
abusive words; slanderous remarks; calumny

【讒】 5699 ㄔㄢˊ charn chán

to misrepresent; to slander; to calumniate; to defame
讒謗(ㄔㄢˊ ㄅㄤˋ)
to defame; to slander; to calumniate
讒口交加(ㄔㄢˊ ㄎㄡˇ ㄐㄧㄠ ㄐㄧㄚ)
Slanders come from all quarters. 或 beset by slanders
讒害(ㄔㄢˊ ㄏㄞˋ) or 讒陷(ㄔㄢˊ ㄒㄧㄢˋ)
to incriminate by false charges
讒言(ㄔㄢˊ ㄧㄢˊ)
malicious, slanderous talk
讒言惹禍(ㄔㄢˊ ㄧㄢˊ ㄖㄜˇ ㄏㄨㄛˋ)
Calumny brings disaster.

【讓】 5700 ㄖㄤˋ ranq ràng

1. to give way; to make concession; to back down; to yield; to give ground
2. to allow; to let; to permit
3. to turn over; to transfer; to surrender; to cede
4. by: 我的眼鏡讓他打破了。 My glasses have been broken by him.
5. to step aside; to make way; to let by: 請讓一讓。 Please step aside. 或 Let me by, please.

讓步(ㄖㄤˋ ㄅㄨˋ)
to make a concession; to give way; to back down; to yield
讓畔(ㄖㄤˋ ㄆㄢˋ)
to be conciliatory in fixing the boundary of one's field
讓渡(ㄖㄤˋ ㄉㄨˋ)
to turn over; to transfer; to cede
讓梨(ㄖㄤˋ ㄌㄧˊ)
a reference to the story of Kung Jung (孔融), who yielded the bigger pear to his elder brother—to be con-

cessive to one's sibling; to show brotherly love

讓路(ㄖㄤˋ ㄌㄨˋ)
to make way; to get out of the way

讓開(ㄖㄤˋ ㄎㄞ)
to make way; to step aside; to get out of the way 參看「讓路」

讓價(ㄖㄤˋ ㄐㄧㄚˋ)
the reduced price after haggling

讓賢(ㄖㄤˋ ㄒㄧㄢˊ)
to yield one's position to a more talented person or a better qualified person

讓受(ㄖㄤˋ ㄕㄡˋ)
to get another's property or right through due process of law; acquisition

讓人(ㄖㄤˋ ㄖㄣˊ)
to yield to others; to be yielding; to be concessive

讓棗推梨(ㄖㄤˋ ㄗㄠˇ ㄊㄨㄟ ㄌㄧˊ)
to show brotherly love

讓座(ㄖㄤˋ ㄗㄨㄛˋ)
to yield a seat: 他讓座給一位老人。He yielded his bus seat to an old man.

讓位(ㄖㄤˋ ㄨㄟˋ)
① to yield the throne; to abdicate the throne ② to yield to; to give way to

讓王(ㄖㄤˋ ㄨㄤˊ)or 讓國(ㄖㄤˋ ㄍㄨㄛˊ)
to yield the throne to another

讓與(ㄖㄤˋ ㄩˇ)
to cede or surrender (titles, privileges, etc.)

【讖】 5701
ㄔㄣˋ chenn chèn
1. a prophecy; an omen
2. books about omens

讖緯(ㄔㄣˋ ㄨㄟˇ)
books about the occult

讖語(ㄔㄣˋ ㄩˇ)
a prophetic remark made casually which later comes true; a prophecy: 讖語靈驗。The prophecy is efficacious.

十八畫

【讙】 5702
ㄏㄨㄢ huan huān
1. to be noisy; to clamor
2. same as 歡—to rejoice

讙呼(ㄏㄨㄢ ㄏㄨ)
to give a cheer; to cheer: 萬衆讙呼。The crowd cheered uproariously.

十九畫

【讚】 5703
ㄗㄢˋ tzann zàn
1. to commend; to eulogize; to praise; to applaud; to laud
2. same as 贊

讚佩(ㄗㄢˋ ㄆㄟˋ)
to think highly of; to esteem; to admire

讚美(ㄗㄢˋ ㄇㄟˇ)
① to praise; to eulogize; to glorify; to extol; to laud ② laud; praise; eulogy

讚美詩(ㄗㄢˋ ㄇㄟˇ ㄕ)
hymns; psalms

讚歎(ㄗㄢˋ ㄊㄢˋ)
to sing the praises of; to gasp in admiration

讚賞(ㄗㄢˋ ㄕㄤˇ)
to praise; to commend; to extol; to laud; to appreciate

讚詞 or 讚辭(ㄗㄢˋ ㄘˊ)
words of praise; an encomium; phrases of eulogy: 讚詞甚美。Phrases of eulogy are extremely beautiful.

讚頌(ㄗㄢˋ ㄙㄨㄥˋ)
to eulogize; to extol; to praise

讚揚(ㄗㄢˋ ㄧㄤˊ)
① to glorify; to exalt; to uphold ② commendation; glorification

讚仰(ㄗㄢˋ ㄧㄤˇ)
to regard with admiration and respect

二十畫

【讞】 5704
ㄧㄢˋ yann yàn
to judge at a court of law

【讜】 5705
ㄉㄤˇ daang dǎng
to speak out boldly; (said of advice or comment) honest; unbiased; straightforward

讜論(ㄉㄤˇ ㄌㄨㄣˋ)
outspoken statements

讜辭(ㄉㄤˇ ㄘˊ)
outspoken words

讜言(ㄉㄤˇ ㄧㄢˊ)
outspoken remarks

谷部
ㄍㄨˇ guu gǔ

【谷】 5706
1. ㄍㄨˇ guu gǔ
1. a valley; a waterway between two mountains; a ravine
2. a hollow; a pit
3. a dilemma; a difficult situation; a predicament
4. a Chinese family name

谷盆地(ㄍㄨˇ ㄆㄣˊ ㄉㄧˋ)
a basin

谷風(ㄍㄨˇ ㄈㄥ)
① an east wind ② an updraft in a valley

谷底(ㄍㄨˇ ㄉㄧˇ)
the bottom of a valley

谷飲(ㄍㄨˇ ㄧㄣˇ)
to live like a hermit

【谷】 5706
2. ㄩˋ yuh yù
a Chinese family name

谷渾(ㄩˋ ㄏㄨㄣˊ)
a Chinese double-name

十畫

【豁】 5707
1. ㄏㄨㄛ huo huō
1. a crack; a break; a breach
2. to crack; to break open; to split
3. to give up; to sacrifice; to risk one's life for

豁命(ㄏㄨㄛ ㄇㄧㄥˋ)
at the expense of one's life; to risk one's life

豁口子(ㄏㄨㄛ ㄎㄡˇ ·ㄗ)or 豁口兒(ㄏㄨㄛ ㄎㄡˇㄦ)or 豁子(ㄏㄨㄛ ·ㄗ)
a crack of a vessel

豁出去(ㄏㄨㄛ ·ㄔㄨ ㄑㄩˋ)
to forge ahead in disregard of the consequence

豁脣子(ㄏㄨㄛ ㄔㄨㄣˊ ·ㄗ)or 豁脣(ㄏㄨㄛ ㄔㄨㄣˊ)or 豁嘴(ㄏㄨㄛ ㄗㄨㄟˇ)
a person with a harelip

【豁】 5707
2. ㄏㄨㄛˋ huoh huò
1. to open up; clear

〔谷部〕

2. to exempt from (duties, etc.)

豁免(ㄏㄨㄛ ㄇㄧㄢˇ)
to exempt from (taxes, military service, etc.); exemption; immunity

豁達(ㄏㄨㄛ ㄉㄚˊ)
①open and clear ②generous or magnanimous; open-minded

豁達大度(ㄏㄨㄛ ㄉㄚˊ ㄉㄚˋ ㄉㄨˋ)
generous; open-minded and magnanimous

豁蕩(ㄏㄨㄛ ㄉㄤˋ)
unrestrained; carefree

豁然(ㄏㄨㄛ ㄖㄢˊ)
open and clear

豁然貫通(ㄏㄨㄛ ㄖㄢˊ ㄍㄨㄢˋ ㄊㄨㄥ)
to dawn upon one suddenly; to understand all of a sudden

豁然開朗(ㄏㄨㄛ ㄖㄢˊ ㄎㄞ ㄌㄤˇ)
①to become clear or visible all of a sudden ②(said of space) to become extensive all of a sudden

豁如(ㄏㄨㄛ ㄖㄨˊ)
open and clear; thoroughly clear

【豁】 5707
3. ㄏㄜˋ heh hè
bright and spacious

豁亮(ㄏㄜˋ ·ㄌㄧㄤ)
bright and spacious

【豁】 5707
4. ㄏㄨㄚˊ hwa huá
to play a finger-guessing game

豁拳(ㄏㄨㄚˊ ㄑㄩㄢˊ)
finger-guessing game—a drinking game at feasts

【豀】 5708
ㄒㄧ shi xī
to squabble; to quarrel; to brawl

【谿】 5709
ㄒㄧ shi xī
1. a valley; a gorge
2. a stream; a creek; a brook
亦作「溪」

谿谷(ㄒㄧ ㄍㄨˇ)
a valley

谿壑(ㄒㄧ ㄏㄨㄛˋ)
a ravine

豆部
ㄉㄡˋ dow dòu

【豆】 5710
ㄉㄡˋ dow dòu
1. beans and peas collectively: 豆富於蛋白質。Beans are rich in protein.
2. a vessel of wood for containing flesh, sauces, etc. at sacrifices and feasts
3. a Chinese family name

豆瓣醬(ㄉㄡˋ ㄅㄢˋ ㄐㄧㄤˋ)
thick broad bean sauce

豆餅(ㄉㄡˋ ㄅㄧㄥˇ)
soybean cake (a kind of animal feed)

豆剖瓜分(ㄉㄡˋ ㄆㄡˇ ㄍㄨㄚ ㄈㄣ)
to divide up the territory (of a nation); to partition (land)

豆苗(ㄉㄡˋ ㄇㄧㄠˊ)
tender stalks and leaves of peas as a vegetable

豆腐(ㄉㄡˋ ·ㄈㄨ)
bean curd; tofu

豆腐皮(ㄉㄡˋ ·ㄈㄨ ㄆㄧˊ)or 豆腐皮兒(ㄉㄡˋ ·ㄈㄨ ㄆㄧㄜˊㄦ)
a semitransparent film formed on the surface of soybean milk

豆腐店(ㄉㄡˋ ·ㄈㄨ ㄉㄧㄢˋ)
a store where bean curd is made for sale

豆腐乾(ㄉㄡˋ ·ㄈㄨ ㄍㄢ)or 豆腐乾兒(ㄉㄡˋ ·ㄈㄨ ㄍㄚㄦ)
spiced and dried bean curd

豆腐乳(ㄉㄡˋ ·ㄈㄨ ㄖㄨˇ)
soybean cheese; fermented bean curd

豆綠(ㄉㄡˋ ㄌㄩˋ)
the green (color) of peas

豆科植物(ㄉㄡˋ ㄎㄜ ㄓˊ ㄨˋ)
legume; the pulse family; bean or pea family

豆蔻 or 荳蔻(ㄉㄡˋ ㄎㄡˋ)
①a cardamom; a nutmeg ②a virgin or maiden; young girls

豆蔻年華 or 荳蔻年華(ㄉㄡˋ ㄎㄡˋ ㄋㄧㄢˊ ㄏㄨㄚˊ)
(said of girls) in their teens

豆莢(ㄉㄡˋ ㄐㄧㄚˊ)
the pods of beans or peas

豆角(ㄉㄡˋ ㄐㄧㄠˇ)
string beans

豆漿(ㄉㄡˋ ㄐㄧㄤ)
soybean milk

豆醬(ㄉㄡˋ ㄐㄧㄤˋ)
fermented beans in paste form

豆萁(ㄉㄡˋ ㄑㄧˊ)
the stalks of beans

豆汁(ㄉㄡˋ ㄓ)
a beverage made from fermented mung beans

豆渣(ㄉㄡˋ ㄓㄚ)
the residue of soybeans in making bean curd

豆豉(ㄉㄡˋ ㄔˇ)or(ㄉㄡˋ ㄕˊ)
fermented and seasoned soybeans

豆石(ㄉㄡˋ ㄕˊ)
pisolite

豆沙(ㄉㄡˋ ㄕㄚ)
mashed beans (usually used as stuffing for dumplings)

豆子(ㄉㄡˋ ·ㄗ)
beans or peas

豆素(ㄉㄡˋ ㄙㄨˋ)
legumin

豆芽(ㄉㄡˋ ㄧㄚˊ)
bean sprouts as a vegetable

豆芽菜(ㄉㄡˋ ㄧㄚˊ ㄘㄞˋ)
mung bean sprouts as a vegetable dish

豆油(ㄉㄡˋ ㄧㄡˊ)
soybean oil

三畫

【豇】 5711
ㄐㄧㄤ jiang jiāng
a cowpea

豇豆(ㄐㄧㄤ ㄉㄡˋ)
cowpea, an asparagus bean

【豈】 5712
1. ㄑㄧˇ chii qǐ
an interrogative particle implying a conflicting or dissenting view or answer—how; what

豈不(ㄑㄧˇ ㄅㄨˋ)or 豈非(ㄑㄧˇ ㄈㄟ)
Wouldn't it result in...? 或 Isn't that...? 或 Wouldn't it be...? 豈不困難? Wouldn't it be difficult?

豈但(ㄑㄧˇ ㄉㄢˋ)

not only
豈能(ㄑㄧˇ ㄋㄥˊ)
How can...? 我豈能留下你孤單一人? How can I leave you alone?
豈敢(ㄑㄧˇ ㄍㄢˇ)
(a term implying humbleness or sarcasm) How dare I...? 或 would not dare...
豈可(ㄑㄧˇ ㄎㄜˇ)
How can...?
豈止(ㄑㄧˇ ㄓˇ)
not at all limited to...; much more than...
豈只(ㄑㄧˇ ㄓˇ)
not only that... (but)
豈有此理(ㄑㄧˇ ㄧㄡˇ ㄘˇ ㄌㄧˇ)
totally unreasonable 或 What kind of reasoning is that? 或 How absurd!

【豈】 5712
2. ㄎㄞˇ kae kǎi
happy; delighted; jubilant; harmonious
豈弟 or 愷悌(ㄎㄞˇ ㄊㄧˋ)
happy and courteous; easy to get along with

四畫

【豉】 5713
ㄔˇ chyy chǐ
(讀音 ㄕˋ shyh shì)
fermented beans; pickled black beans 亦作「豆豉」

六畫

【登】 5714
ㄉㄥ deng dēng
vessels for food used in ancient times

【豊】 5715
ㄌㄧˇ lii lǐ
a kind of ritual vessel in ancient times

八畫

【豌】 5716
ㄨㄢ uan wān
peas; garden peas
豌豆(ㄨㄢ ㄉㄡˋ)
garden peas (*Pisum sativum*)
豌豆泥(ㄨㄢ ㄉㄡˋ ㄋㄧˊ)
mashed peas (served as a dessert)
豌豆糕(ㄨㄢ ㄉㄡˋ ㄍㄠ)
a small sweetened cake made of mashed peas
豌豆黃兒(ㄨㄢ ㄉㄡˋ ㄏㄨㄤˊㄦ)
a cake made of garden-pea flour and sugar

【豎】 5717
ㄕㄨˋ shuh shù
1. to erect; to set up; to stand
2. upright; perpendicular; vertical
3. boys who have not come of age; a young servant
4. petty officers in the palace
5. a downward, perpendicular stroke in calligraphy
豎毛(ㄕㄨˋ ㄇㄠˊ)
the hair standing on end (for trepidation or as a response to some creeping expressions)
豎夫(ㄕㄨˋ ㄈㄨ)
a coolie; a servant
豎笛(ㄕㄨˋ ㄉㄧˊ)
a clarinet
豎立(ㄕㄨˋ ㄌㄧˋ)
to erect
豎箜篌(ㄕㄨˋ ㄎㄨㄥ ㄏㄡˊ)
an ancient musical instrument with 23 strings
豎褐(ㄕㄨˋ ㄏㄜˊ)
short garments worn by coolies
豎宦(ㄕㄨˋ ㄏㄨㄢˋ)
eunuchs
豎起大拇指(ㄕㄨˋ ㄑㄧˇ ㄉㄚˋ ㄇㄨˇ ㄓˇ)
to hold up one's thumb in approval; thumbs up
豎起脊梁(ㄕㄨˋ ㄑㄧˇ ㄐㄧˇ ㄌㄧㄤˊ)
to straighten up one's back—to get set for action, or to pull oneself together
豎琴(ㄕㄨˋ ㄑㄧㄣˊ)
the harp
豎蜻蜓(ㄕㄨˋ ㄑㄧㄥ ㄊㄧㄥˊ)
to stand erect on one's hands
豎直立(ㄕㄨˋ ㄓˊ ㄌㄧˋ)
to stand erect on one's hands
豎柱(ㄕㄨˋ ㄓㄨˋ)
to erect the pillars (of a house, etc.)
豎臣(ㄕㄨˋ ㄔㄣˊ)
(an abusive expression) a low-ranking court official
豎儒(ㄕㄨˋ ㄖㄨˊ)
①(an abusive expression used mostly in the Han Dynasty) petty pedants ②a fool
豎子(ㄕㄨˋ ㄗˇ)
①a boy; a youngster ②a good-for-nothing
豎兒(ㄕㄨˋㄦ)
(Chinese calligraphy) a downward, perpendicular stroke
豎眼(ㄕㄨˋ ㄧㄢˇ)
angry looks

十畫

【豏】 5718
ㄒㄧㄢˋ shiann xiàn
half-grown beans

十一畫

【豐】 5719
ㄈㄥ feng fēng
1. abundant; luxuriant; copious; fruitful; plentiful; plenty; thick; big
2. a crop; a harvest
3. a Chinese family name
豐沛(ㄈㄥ ㄆㄟˋ)
copious or plentiful (rainfall, etc.): 今年雨水豐沛。We have plenty of rain this year.
豐茂(ㄈㄥ ㄇㄠˋ)
luxuriant (growth, etc.); plentiful
豐滿(ㄈㄥ ㄇㄢˇ)
① rich; affluence; plentiful: 五穀豐滿。All food crops are plentiful. ② full-fledged ③ (said of a woman's figure) very full and voluptuous; plump; buxom
豐富(ㄈㄥ ㄈㄨˋ)
① abundant; copious or plentiful; rich ② to enrich
豐登(ㄈㄥ ㄉㄥ)
a bumper crop
豐年(ㄈㄥ ㄋㄧㄢˊ)
a plentiful year; a year of a good harvest
豐功偉績(ㄈㄥ ㄍㄨㄥ ㄨㄟˇ ㄐㄧ)
great achievements; significant contribution
豐鎬(ㄈㄥ ㄏㄠˋ)

〔豆部〕

the capital of the Chou people before they overthrew the Hsia Dynasty

豐厚(ㄈㄥ ㄏㄡˋ)
handsome (pay, gifts, etc.); plentiful or rich

豐肌(ㄈㄥ ㄐㄧ)
plump; fleshy

豐歉(ㄈㄥ ㄑㄧㄢˋ)
plenty and deficiency; a year of a bumper crop or famine

豐取刻與(ㄈㄥ ㄑㄩˇ ㄎㄜˋ ㄩˇ)
(literally) to take a lot and give away little—very greedy

豐熾(ㄈㄥ ㄔˋ)
rich or affluent; abundant; abundance; prosperous

豐實(ㄈㄥ ㄕˊ)
abundant; plentiful; rich

豐碩(ㄈㄥ ㄕˋ)
rich; plenty

豐殺(ㄈㄥ ㄕㄞˋ)
to increase or decrease

豐收(ㄈㄥ ㄕㄡ)
a rich harvest; a bumper crop: 今年豐收在望。A good harvest is in sight this year.

豐贍(ㄈㄥ ㄕㄢˋ)
prosperous; abundant; rich; plentiful

豐上銳下(ㄈㄥ ㄕㄤˋ ㄖㄨㄟˋ ㄒㄧㄚˋ)
(said of a face) plump in the upper part but sharp toward the chin

豐盛(ㄈㄥ ㄕㄥˋ)
flourishing; luxuriant; prosperous or abundant; sumptuous

豐饒(ㄈㄥ ㄖㄠˊ)
plentiful; abundant; abundance; fertile

豐稔(ㄈㄥ ㄖㄣˇ)
a rich harvest; a bumper crop

豐穰(ㄈㄥ ㄖㄤˊ)
a bumper crop

豐壤(ㄈㄥ ㄖㄤˇ)
fertile soil; rich earth

豐潤(ㄈㄥ ㄖㄨㄣˋ)
① abundant; affluent ② name of a county in Hopeh Province

豐容(ㄈㄥ ㄖㄨㄥˊ)
(said of a woman) regal and beautiful

豐足(ㄈㄥ ㄗㄨˊ)
affluent; wealthy; abundant

豐衣足食(ㄈㄥ ㄧ ㄗㄨˊ ㄕˊ)
good clothes and rich food; well-fed and well-clad; to eat and dress well; to live in affluence: 我們都過着豐衣足食的生活。We all live in affluence.

豐衍(ㄈㄥ ㄧㄢˇ)
plentiful; abundant

豐盈(ㄈㄥ ㄧㄥˊ)
① rich and full (figure, etc.); plump: 她有豐盈的身材。She has a rich and full figure. ② rich or wealthy ③ a good harvest

豐偉(ㄈㄥ ㄨㄟˇ)
tall and stout

豐腴(ㄈㄥ ㄩˊ)
plump; buxom and fair; fertile: 臺灣是塊豐腴之地。Taiwan is a fertile piece of land.

豐裕(ㄈㄥ ㄩˋ)
abundance; plentiful; high (pay, etc.): 他的生活豐裕。He lives in plenty. 或 He is comfortably off.

十七畫

【艷】 5720 ㄧㄢˋ yann yàn
same as 豔

二十一畫

【豔】 5721 (艷) ㄧㄢˋ yann yàn
1. plump; voluptuous
2. beautiful and captivating (literary writings, etc.)
3. gorgeous; colorful; gaudy
4. anything pertaining to love, as a love story, love song, etc.; amorous
5. a beauty
6. radiant
7. to admire or envy

豔婢(ㄧㄢˋ ㄅㄧˋ)
a beautiful maidservant

豔福(ㄧㄢˋ ㄈㄨˊ)
(said of a man) good fortune or success in love affairs

豔福不淺(ㄧㄢˋ ㄈㄨˊ ㄅㄨˋ ㄑㄧㄢˇ)
(said of a man) to have a lot of good fortune or success in love affairs; to have a beautiful girl friend or wife

豔麗(ㄧㄢˋ ㄌㄧˋ)
radiantly beautiful; magnificent; charming; captivating; gorgeous

豔歌(ㄧㄢˋ ㄍㄜ)
love songs

豔絕(ㄧㄢˋ ㄐㄩㄝˊ)
extremely or stunningly beautiful

豔羨(ㄧㄢˋ ㄒㄧㄢˋ)
to admire; to long for

豔稱(ㄧㄢˋ ㄔㄥ)
famed for her beauty

豔詩(ㄧㄢˋ ㄕ)
love poems

豔史(ㄧㄢˋ ㄕˇ)
one's love affairs; romantic adventures; amorous adventures

豔事(ㄧㄢˋ ㄕˋ)
erotic affairs; romantic adventures

豔姿(ㄧㄢˋ ㄗ)
a beautiful appearance; charming or enticing looks

豔色(ㄧㄢˋ ㄙㄜˋ)
the beauty of a woman

豔陽(ㄧㄢˋ ㄧㄤˊ)
sunny spring weather

豔陽天(ㄧㄢˋ ㄧㄤˊ ㄊㄧㄢ)
charming, bright springtime; bright sunny skies

豔舞(ㄧㄢˋ ㄨˇ)
striptease; voluptuous, enticing dances

豔遇(ㄧㄢˋ ㄩˋ)
an encounter with a beautiful woman

豕部
ㄕˇ shyy shǐ

【豕】 5722 ㄕˇ shyy shǐ
a swine; a pig; a hog

豕突(ㄕˇ ㄊㄨˊ)
to run wild

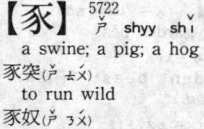

豕奴(ㄕˇ ㄋㄨˊ)
a swineherd

豕喙(ㄕˇ ㄏㄨㄟˋ)
(said of a person's mouth) shaped like that of a pig
豕交獸畜(ㄕˇ ㄐㄧㄠ ㄕㄡˋ ㄒㄩˋ)
to treat people like beasts
豕心(ㄕˇ ㄒㄧㄣ)
greedy; avaricious

四畫

【豚】 5723
ㄊㄨㄣˊ twen tún
1. a small pig
2. a Chinese family name
豚犢(ㄊㄨㄣˊ ㄉㄨˊ)
bad sons—like pigs
豚蹄穰田(ㄊㄨㄣˊ ㄊㄧˊ ㄖㄤˊ ㄊㄧㄢˊ)
to expect a tremendous return from a meager investment
豚肩(ㄊㄨㄣˊ ㄐㄧㄢ)
the pig's shoulder
豚犬(ㄊㄨㄣˊ ㄑㄩㄢˇ)
① pigs and dogs ② (self-depreciatory term) one's own sons
豚兒(ㄊㄨㄣˊ ㄦˊ)
(a self-derogative expression in polite society) my son

【豝】 5724
ㄅㄚ ba bā
a female pig; a sow

五畫

【象】 5725
ㄒㄧㄤˋ shiang xiàng
1. an elephant
2. a portrait; an image snapshot
3. a phenomenon; the outward appearance or expression of anything—especially weather, heavenly bodies, etc.; shape; an image
4. ivory
象鼻(ㄒㄧㄤˋ ㄅㄧˊ)
an elephant's trunk; a proboscis
象鼻蟲(ㄒㄧㄤˋ ㄅㄧˊ ㄔㄨㄥˊ)
a curculio; a weevil; a snout beetle
象皮病(ㄒㄧㄤˋ ㄆㄧˊ ㄅㄧㄥˋ)
elephantiasis
象皮紙(ㄒㄧㄤˋ ㄆㄧˊ ㄓˇ)
a kind of thick and strong paper for drawing
象奴(ㄒㄧㄤˋ ㄋㄨˊ)or 象夫(ㄒㄧㄤˋ ㄈㄨ)
a mahout
象管(ㄒㄧㄤˋ ㄍㄨㄢˇ)
an ivory tube for holding the Chinese writing brush
象笏(ㄒㄧㄤˋ ㄏㄨˋ)
an ivory tablet held before the breast in ceremony or audience 亦作「象簡」
象環(ㄒㄧㄤˋ ㄏㄨㄢˊ)
an ivory ring
象櫛(ㄒㄧㄤˋ ㄐㄧㄝˊ)
an ivory comb
象教(ㄒㄧㄤˋ ㄐㄧㄠˋ)
Buddhism
象棋(ㄒㄧㄤˋ ㄑㄧˊ)
Chinese chess
象限(ㄒㄧㄤˋ ㄒㄧㄢˋ)
a quadrant
象形(ㄒㄧㄤˋ ㄒㄧㄥˊ)
image shapes, or pictographs—one of the six groups into which Chinese characters are divided, which consists of greatly simplified drawings of objects the characters denote
象形文字(ㄒㄧㄤˋ ㄒㄧㄥˊ ㄨㄣˊ ㄗˋ)
hieroglyphics; a pictograph; a hieroglyph
象徵(ㄒㄧㄤˋ ㄓㄥ)
① to symbolize ② a symbol
象徵性(ㄒㄧㄤˋ ㄓㄥ ㄒㄧㄥˋ)
as a token; a token (gift, etc.); symbolic
象箸(ㄒㄧㄤˋ ㄓㄨˋ)
ivory chopsticks
象齒焚身(ㄒㄧㄤˋ ㄔˇ ㄈㄣˊ ㄕㄣ)
The elephant is killed because of its tusks.
象牀(ㄒㄧㄤˋ ㄔㄨㄤˊ)
a bed adorned with ivory
象人(ㄒㄧㄤˋ ㄖㄣˊ)
the semblances of men buried with the dead in ancient times
象牙(ㄒㄧㄤˋ ㄧㄚˊ)
ivory; elephant tusks
象牙塔(ㄒㄧㄤˋ ㄧㄚˊ ㄊㄚˇ)
the ivory tower
象牙海岸(ㄒㄧㄤˋ ㄧㄚˊ ㄏㄞˇ ㄢˋ)
the Ivory Coast
象牙婚(ㄒㄧㄤˋ ㄧㄚˊ ㄏㄨㄣ)
Ivory Wedding, the 14th wedding anniversary
象牙質(ㄒㄧㄤˋ ㄧㄚˊ ㄓˊ)
(physiology) dentine
象魏(ㄒㄧㄤˋ ㄨㄟˋ)
the palace door 亦作「象闕」

【甤】 5726
(蕤) ㄖㄨㄟˊ ruei ruí
1. hat sashes hanging down
2. luxuriant vegetation

六畫

【豢】 5727
ㄏㄨㄢˋ huann huàn
1. to feed animals with grains
2. to tempt or entice people with profit or gains
3. domesticated animals
豢養(ㄏㄨㄢˋ ㄧㄤˇ)
to feed; to rear; to raise; to keep
豢圉(ㄏㄨㄢˋ ㄩˇ)
a pen for animals; an animal barn or stable

七畫

【豪】 5728
ㄏㄠˊ haur háo
1. a person outstanding in intelligence or talent; a heroic person
2. a leader; a ringleader
3. a proclivity to the use of force, bullying ways, etc.
4. tiny; fine hair 亦作「毫」
豪邁(ㄏㄠˊ ㄇㄞˋ)
straightforward and carefree; generous and open-minded; heroic
豪門(ㄏㄠˊ ㄇㄣˊ)
a rich and powerful family; a wealthy and highly influential family
豪放(ㄏㄠˊ ㄈㄤˋ)
vigorous and unrestrained; virile; careless about details
豪放不羈(ㄏㄠˊ ㄈㄤˋ ㄅㄨˋ ㄐㄧ)
vigorous and unrestrained; virile and unconventional
豪富(ㄏㄠˊ ㄈㄨˋ)
millionaires
豪黨(ㄏㄠˊ ㄉㄤˇ)
a group of the influential local gentry who take law in their own hands
豪蕩(ㄏㄠˊ ㄉㄤˋ)
gallant, chivalrous but not behaving very properly

〔豸部〕

豪賭(ㄏㄠˊ ㄉㄨˇ)
to gamble with big stakes
豪奪(ㄏㄠˊ ㄉㄨㄛˊ)
to rob; to take by force
豪奴(ㄏㄠˊ ㄋㄨˊ)
a servant of a powerful family who bullies around
豪光(ㄏㄠˊ ㄍㄨㄤ)
a dazzling ray; flashing light
豪客(ㄏㄠˊ ㄎㄜˋ)
① robbers; burglars ② persons who spend money like water, especially in entertainment and gambling
豪橫(ㄏㄠˊ ㄏㄥˊ)
overbearing and bullying; despotic
豪華(ㄏㄠˊ ㄏㄨㄚˊ)
luxurious (hotels, theaters, etc.); swanky; plush: 他們過着豪華的生活。They led a luxurious life.
豪傑(ㄏㄠˊ ㄐㄧㄝˊ)
a man of outstanding talent, intelligence and courage; a scholar of heroism
豪舉(ㄏㄠˊ ㄐㄩˇ)
a gallant or chivalrous act; a surprisingly generous act or undertaking
豪氣(ㄏㄠˊ ㄑㄧˋ)
undaunted spirit; heroism
豪強(ㄏㄠˊ ㄑㄧㄤˊ)
bullies; those who throw their weight around
豪情(ㄏㄠˊ ㄑㄧㄥˊ)
lofty sentiments
豪俠(ㄏㄠˊ ㄒㄧㄚˊ)
a hero; chivalry; a champion of justice
豪性(ㄏㄠˊ ㄒㄧㄥˋ)
chivalry; gallantry
豪豬(ㄏㄠˊ ㄓㄨ)
a porcupine
豪士(ㄏㄠˊ ㄕˋ)
one who excels in intellectual capacity
豪爽(ㄏㄠˊ ㄕㄨㄤˇ)
bold and generous; chivalrous; straightforward
豪飲(ㄏㄠˊ ㄧㄣˇ)
to drink like a fish: 他每回豪飲必醉。Whenever he drinks like a fish, he gets drunk.
豪雨(ㄏㄠˊ ㄩˇ)
to rain cats and dogs; pouring rain; a downpour
豪語(ㄏㄠˊ ㄩˇ)
big talk; a bold promise

【豨】 5729
ㄒㄧ shi xī
a pig; a hog

九畫

【豫】 5730
ㄩˋ yuh yù
1. comfort; to be at ease
2. same as 預— to get ready or prepared; beforehand
3. to travel; to make an excursion or a trip
4. to cheat; to lie
5. one of the nine political divisions in ancient China
6. to hesitate
7. short for Honan(河南)
8. happy; delighted; pleased
9. a Chinese family name

【豭】 5731
ㄐㄧㄚ jia jiā
a male pig; a boar

【豬】 5732
ㄓㄨ ju zhū
1. a pig; a hog; a swine
2. a pigheaded person
豬八戒(ㄓㄨ ㄅㄚ ㄐㄧㄝˋ)
one of the chief characters in *Pilgrimage to the West* (西遊記), who was supposedly incarnated through the spirit of a pig, a symbol of man's cupidity
豬排(ㄓㄨ ㄆㄞˊ)
a pork chop
豬肚(ㄓㄨ ㄉㄨˇ)
pig's tripe
豬頭(ㄓㄨ ㄊㄡˊ)
pig's head (a favorite dish for drinking)
豬蹄(ㄓㄨ ㄊㄧˊ)
pigs' feet
豬腿(ㄓㄨ ㄊㄨㄟˇ)
① pig's legs ② ham; legmeat of the hog
豬欄(ㄓㄨ ㄌㄢˊ)
a pigpen; a pigsty
豬苓(ㄓㄨ ㄌㄧㄥˊ)
a kind of fungus grown on maple trees, used in herbal medicine
豬玀(ㄓㄨ ㄌㄨㄛˊ)
(a term used in reviling in Shanghai) Swine!
豬肝(ㄓㄨ ㄍㄢ)
pig's liver
豬肝麵(ㄓㄨ ㄍㄢ ㄇㄧㄢˋ)
noodles prepared with pig's liver
豬肝湯(ㄓㄨ ㄍㄢ ㄊㄤ)
pig's liver broth or soup
豬肝色(ㄓㄨ ㄍㄢ ㄙㄜˋ)
liver-colored
豬叫(ㄓㄨ ㄐㄧㄠˋ)
grunting of hogs
豬圈(ㄓㄨ ㄐㄩㄢˋ)
a pigsty; a pigpen; a hogpen
豬血(ㄓㄨ ㄒㄧㄝˇ)
coagulated pig blood used as a food item
豬肉(ㄓㄨ ㄖㄡˋ)
pork
豬仔(ㄓㄨ ㄗㄞˇ)
young pigs
豬鬃(ㄓㄨ ㄗㄨㄥ)
hog's bristles
豬腰子(ㄓㄨ ㄧㄠ ·ㄗ)
pig kidneys
豬油(ㄓㄨ ㄧㄡˊ)
lard: 她總是用豬油炒菜。She always cooks in lard.

十畫

【豳】 5733
ㄅㄧㄣ bin bīn
1. Pin, name of a state in the Chou Dynasty
2. name of a mountain in Shensi

豸部
ㄓˋ jyh zhì

【豸】 5734
ㄓˋ jyh zhì
insects without feet or legs

三畫

【豹】 5735
ㄅㄠˋ baw bào
1. a leopard; a panther
2. a Chinese family name
豹略(ㄅㄠˋ ㄌㄩㄝˋ)
① a military commander ② generalship; military strategy and tactics

豹子(ㄅㄠˋ ·ㄗ)
a leopard; a panther; a kind of wildcat
豹死留皮(ㄅㄠˋ ㄙˇ ㄌㄧㄡˊ ㄆㄧˊ)
(literally) A leopard leaves behind its skin when it dies. — A man has a reputation to leave to posterity when he dies.
豹隱(ㄅㄠˋ ㄧㄣˇ)
to live in retirement; to lead the life of a hermit

【豺】 5736 ㄔㄞˊ chair chái
1. *Canis hodophilax*, a ravenous beast, akin to the wolf
2. wickedly cunning; cruel
豺狼(ㄔㄞˊ ㄌㄤˊ)
ravenous and cruel beasts —mean and wicked persons
豺狼當道(ㄔㄞˊ ㄌㄤˊ ㄉㄤ ㄉㄠˋ)
jackals and wolves on the road—(figuratively) wicked persons in power
豺虎(ㄔㄞˊ ㄏㄨˇ)
①cruel bandits ②jackals and tigers
豺聲(ㄔㄞˊ ㄕㄥ)
to roar as fiercely as a wild beast

【豻】 5737 ㄏㄢˋ hann hàn
1. a kind of wild dog
2. a lockup

五畫

【貂】 5738 ㄉㄧㄠ diau diāo
the sable; the marten; the mink
貂皮(ㄉㄧㄠ ㄆㄧˊ)
sable skin or fur; mink
貂皮大衣(ㄉㄧㄠ ㄆㄧˊ ㄉㄚˋ ㄧ)
a mink (coat)
貂璫(ㄉㄧㄠ ㄉㄤ)
a eunuch
貂裘換酒(ㄉㄧㄠ ㄑㄧㄡˊ ㄏㄨㄢˋ ㄐㄧㄡˇ)
(literally) to trade a mink coat for wine—extravagance of the rich
貂蟬(ㄉㄧㄠ ㄔㄢˊ)
①hat ornaments of an army officer in ancient China ② Tiao Chan, wife of General Lü Pu (呂布) in the Period of Three Kingdoms

貂扇(ㄉㄧㄠ ㄕㄢˋ)
a fan made of sable tails
貂寺(ㄉㄧㄠ ㄙˋ)
a eunuch
貂羽(ㄉㄧㄠ ㄩˇ)
the fur of a sable

六畫

【貅】 5739 ㄒㄧㄡ shiou xiū
1. a kind of animal like a tiger
2. a fierce and courageous soldier

【貉】 5740 1. ㄏㄠˊ haur háo (又讀 ㄏㄜˊ her hé)
a badger; a racoon dog; a foxlike animal nocturnal in habit
貉絨(ㄏㄠˊ ㄖㄨㄥˊ)
badger skin or fur
貉子(ㄏㄠˊ ·ㄗ)
a young badger

【貉】 5740 2.(貊) ㄇㄛˋ moh mò
1. (in ancient China) the name of a northern barbarian tribe
2. quiet

七畫

【貌】 5741 ㄇㄠˋ maw mào
1. a facial appearance; features
2. a general appearance; a manner; form; bearing
3. to appear or pretend to be like
4. a ceremonious manner
貌不驚人(ㄇㄠˋ ㄅㄨˋ ㄐㄧㄥ ㄖㄣˊ)
to look mediocre
貌美(ㄇㄠˋ ㄇㄟˇ)
(said of a woman) beautiful
貌合神離(ㄇㄠˋ ㄏㄜˊ ㄕㄣˊ ㄌㄧˊ)
to appear united outwardly but divided at heart
貌侵(ㄇㄠˋ ㄑㄧㄣ)or 貌寢(ㄇㄠˋ ㄑㄧㄣˇ)
ugly; homely
貌相(ㄇㄠˋ ㄒㄧㄤˋ)
to judge someone by his appearance only
貌醜(ㄇㄠˋ ㄔㄡˇ)
ugly; ill-looking

貌似(ㄇㄠˋ ㄙˋ)
(said of a person) to look like: 他貌似忠厚。 He looks like an honest man.

【貍】 5742 ㄌㄧˊ li lí
Nyctereutus procynoides, a foxlike animal
貍貓(ㄌㄧˊ ㄇㄠ)
Paradoxurus sp., a catlike animal
貍奴(ㄌㄧˊ ㄋㄨˊ)
a cat
貍鼪(ㄌㄧˊ ㄕㄥ)
two animals which prey on rats

九畫

【貓】 5743 (猫) ㄇㄠ mhau māo
the cat
貓頭鷹(ㄇㄠ ㄊㄡˊ ㄧㄥ)
the owl
貓哭老鼠—假慈悲(ㄇㄠ ㄎㄨ ㄌㄠˇ ㄕㄨˇ—ㄐㄧㄚˇ ㄘˊ ㄅㄟ)
to shed crocodile tears (as a cat crying over the death of a rat)
貓叫(ㄇㄠ ㄐㄧㄠˋ)
the meowing of a cat
貓熊(ㄇㄠ ㄒㄩㄥˊ)
(animal) a panda
貓鼠同眠(ㄇㄠ ㄕㄨˇ ㄊㄨㄥˊ ㄇㄧㄢˊ)
(literally) The cat and the rat sleep together.—Corrupt officials collude with rascals exploiting common people.
貓眼石(ㄇㄠ ㄧㄢˇ ㄕˊ)or 貓兒眼(ㄇㄠ ㄦ ㄧㄢˇ)
(mineral) cat's-eye; cymophane

十畫

【貔】 5744 ㄆㄧˊ pyi pí
a fierce animal of the panther family
貔虎(ㄆㄧˊ ㄏㄨˇ)
fierce and courageous soldiers
貔貅(ㄆㄧˊ ㄒㄧㄡ)
①fierce and courageous soldiers ②a kind of fierce wild beast

〔貝部〕

十一畫

【貘】 5745 ㄇㄛˋ moh mò

1. the panther; the leopard
2. the tapir

十八畫

【貛】 5746 (獾) ㄏㄨㄢ huan huān

1. a he-wolf
2. a wild boar
3. a badger

貝部
ㄅㄟˋ bey bèi

【貝】 5747 ㄅㄟˋ bey bèi

1. shells; cowries (used in ancient China as currency)
2. precious; treasure; valuable
3. (physics) bel
4. a Chinese family name

貝幣(ㄅㄟˋ ㄅㄧˋ)
shells used as money in ancient times

貝編(ㄅㄟˋ ㄅㄧㄢ)
Buddhist sutras

貝母(ㄅㄟˋ ㄇㄨˇ)
(botany) fritillary, used as herbal medicine

貝多芬(ㄅㄟˋ ㄉㄨㄛ ㄈㄣ)
Ludwig van Beethoven (1770-1827), German composer

貝南(ㄅㄟˋ ㄋㄢˊ)
Benin

貝勒(ㄅㄟˋ ㄌㄜˋ)
①a rank of the Manchu nobility below that of the Prince (親王) ② shell decorations on a bridle

貝類(ㄅㄟˋ ㄌㄟˋ)
shellfish; molluscs

貝殼(ㄅㄟˋ ㄎㄜˊ)
seashells; shells: 海岸有很多貝殼。The seashore was covered with shells.

貝殼學(ㄅㄟˋ ㄎㄜˊ ㄒㄩㄝˊ)
conchology

貝殼學家(ㄅㄟˋ ㄎㄜˊ ㄒㄩㄝˊ ㄐㄧㄚ)
a conchologist

貝魯特(ㄅㄟˋ ㄌㄨˇ ㄊㄜˋ)
Beirut, the capital of Lebanon

貝貨(ㄅㄟˋ ㄏㄨㄛˋ)
cowries used as currency in ancient times

貝加爾湖(ㄅㄟˋ ㄐㄧㄚ ㄦˇ ㄏㄨˊ)
the Baikal Lake in southern Siberia

貝子(ㄅㄟˋ ˙ㄗ)
a rank of the Manchu nobility below that of 貝勒

貝葉(ㄅㄟˋ ㄧㄝˋ)
①palm leaves from the *Borassus flabelliformis* ② Buddhist sutras written on such leaves

二畫

【負】 5748 ㄈㄨˋ fuh fù

1. defeated; beaten; to lose; to fail; defeat
2. to bear; to sustain; to carry on the back; to shoulder
3. to take refuge in
4. to be proud and complacent
5. to owe
6. negative; minus
7. to turn one's back on; ungrateful
8. to let (someone) down; to disappoint
9. a Chinese family name

負負(ㄈㄨˋ ㄈㄨˋ)
ashamed or embarrassed

負德(ㄈㄨˋ ㄉㄜˊ)
against virtuous practice or morality

負戴(ㄈㄨˋ ㄉㄞˋ)
to bear and sustain (loads, etc.); the work of a laborer

負擔(ㄈㄨˋ ㄉㄢ)
① an obligation; a burden; a load; an encumbrance ② to support (a family, etc.) or pay the expenses ③ liability

負電(ㄈㄨˋ ㄉㄧㄢˋ)
negative electricity

負弩前驅(ㄈㄨˋ ㄋㄨˇ ㄑㄧㄢˊ ㄑㄩ)
① to join the army and fight at the front ② to show respect to a ranking official

負累(ㄈㄨˋ ㄌㄟˋ)
① to be defamed without grounds ② to be dragged into trouble

負固(ㄈㄨˋ ㄍㄨˋ)
to hold a strategic position

負荷(ㄈㄨˋ ㄏㄜˋ)
① to bear or sustain ② the load (of electricity, etc.)

負號(ㄈㄨˋ ㄏㄠˋ)
the negative sign(—)

負笈從師(ㄈㄨˋ ㄐㄧˊ ㄘㄨㄥˊ ㄕ)
to leave one's home in search of learned masters

負疚(ㄈㄨˋ ㄐㄧㄡˋ)
to regret; uneasy in heart; to have a guilty conscience

負荊(ㄈㄨˋ ㄐㄧㄥ)or 負荊請罪(ㄈㄨˋ ㄐㄧㄥ ㄑㄧㄥˇ ㄗㄨㄟˋ)
to proffer a birch and ask for a whipping—to offer a modest apology; to apologize

負氣(ㄈㄨˋ ㄑㄧˋ)
sullen; morose; ill-humored; stubbornly; unyielding; to do something in a fit of pique: 她負氣而去。 She went off in a fit of pique.

負險(ㄈㄨˋ ㄒㄧㄢˇ)
to hold a key position

負心(ㄈㄨˋ ㄒㄧㄣ)
ungrateful; heartless

負薪救火(ㄈㄨˋ ㄒㄧㄣ ㄐㄧㄡˋ ㄏㄨㄛˇ)
(literally) to carry firewood to put out a fire—to make things worse

負債(ㄈㄨˋ ㄓㄞˋ)
to be in debt; to owe; to incur debts: 他已負債累累。He is heavily in debt.

負重致遠(ㄈㄨˋ ㄓㄨㄥˋ ㄓˋ ㄩㄢˇ)
to bear a heavy burden and cover a long distance—to put in hard work and achieve one's goal

負重忍辱(ㄈㄨˋ ㄓㄨㄥˋ ㄖㄣˇ ㄖㄨˋ)
to bear a heavy burden and suffer disgrace with patience

負手(ㄈㄨˋ ㄕㄡˇ)
to cross one's hands behind the back

負傷(ㄈㄨˋ ㄕㄤ)
to be wounded; to sustain injuries

負數(ㄈㄨˋ ㄕㄨˋ)
a negative number

負責(ㄈㄨˋ ㄗㄜˊ)or 負責任(ㄈㄨˋ ㄗㄜˊ

ㄖㄣ)
to be responsible; to bear the responsibility; to be in charge of; conscientious: 他工作很負責。He is very conscientious in his work.
負罪(ㄈㄨˋ ㄗㄨㄟˋ)
to bear the blame
負恩(ㄈㄨˋ ㄣ)
ungrateful for favor received
負義忘恩(ㄈㄨˋ ㄧˋ ㄨㄤˋ ㄣ)
ungrateful; ingrate
負嵎頑抗(ㄈㄨˋ ㄩˊ ㄨㄢˊ ㄎㄤˋ)
to put up a stubborn resistance at a strategic position; to fight obstinately with one's back to the wall; to make a desperate struggle
負約(ㄈㄨˋ ㄩㄝ)
to break a contract, agreement, promise, etc.; to go back on one's word (or promises)

5749
【貞】 ㄓㄣ jen zhēn (又讀 ㄓㄥ jeng zhēng)
1. chastity of a woman
2. pure; virtuous
3. to be incorruptible; to be correctly firm
4. devotion; dedication
5. to divine; to inquire by divination
貞白(ㄓㄣ ㄅㄛˊ)
chastity; integrity
貞卜文字(ㄓㄣ ㄅㄨˇ ㄨㄣˊ ㄗˋ)
(in ancient China) oracle-bone characters
貞婦(ㄓㄣ ㄈㄨˋ)
a chaste woman: 她是位年輕貞婦。She was a chaste young woman.
貞德(ㄓㄣ ㄉㄜˊ)
Saint Joan of Arc (French, Jeanne d'Arc, 1412-1431), French heroine, also called the Maid of Orleans
貞女(ㄓㄣ ㄋㄩˇ)
a chaste girl; a virgin
貞女不更二夫(ㄓㄣ ㄋㄩˇ ㄅㄨˋ ㄍㄥ ㄦˋ ㄈㄨ)or 貞女不事二夫(ㄓㄣ ㄋㄩˇ ㄅㄨˋ ㄕˋ ㄦˋ ㄈㄨ)
A chaste woman never remarries.
貞烈(ㄓㄣ ㄌㄧㄝˋ)
honesty, straightforwardness, courage and virtue—which enable a person to look death in the eye without fear
貞固(ㄓㄣ ㄍㄨˋ)
to stick to righteousness and virtue
貞觀之治(ㄓㄣ ㄍㄨㄢ ㄓ ㄓˋ)
the enlightened administration of Emperor Tai Tsung of the Tang Dynasty, whose reign lasted from 627 to 649
貞潔(ㄓㄣ ㄐㄧㄝˊ)
chaste and pure; virtuous
貞節(ㄓㄣ ㄐㄧㄝˊ)
① tenacity to hold on to one's virtuous way or integrity ② (said of a woman) chastity; purity; virtue
貞節牌坊(ㄓㄣ ㄐㄧㄝˊ ㄆㄞˊ ㄈㄤ)
a stone arch erected by the government of former times in honor of a chaste woman widowed at a young age
貞士(ㄓㄣ ㄕˋ)
a man of virtue or integrity
貞淑(ㄓㄣ ㄕㄨˊ)
(said of women) pure and chaste
貞人(ㄓㄣ ㄖㄣˊ)
a person of high moral standing and integrity
貞操(ㄓㄣ ㄘㄠ)
① purity and chastity in one's conduct ② a woman's chastity or virginity

三畫

5750
【貢】 ㄍㄨㄥˋ gonq gòng
1. the tribute from a vassal state; to offer tribute
2. to recommend (a person to an office, etc.); to submit
3. (in ancient China) land tax
4. to contribute; to offer
5. a Chinese family name
貢品(ㄍㄨㄥˋ ㄆㄧㄣˇ)
items offered as tribute
貢奉(ㄍㄨㄥˋ ㄈㄥˋ)
to offer as tribute to the court
貢獻(ㄍㄨㄥˋ ㄒㄧㄢˋ)
to offer or contribute (oneself to the national cause, etc.); contribution
貢燭(ㄍㄨㄥˋ ㄓㄨˊ)
candles of the best quality
貢生(ㄍㄨㄥˋ ㄕㄥ)
(formerly) scholars recommended by local governments on the basis of their scholastic accomplishments and virtue

5751
【財】 ㄘㄞˊ tsair cái
wealth; riches; money
財帛(ㄘㄞˊ ㄅㄛˊ)
wealth; riches; valuables
財寶(ㄘㄞˊ ㄅㄠˇ)
money and jewels; valuables
財不露眼(ㄘㄞˊ ㄅㄨˋ ㄌㄨˋ ㄧㄢˇ)or 財不露白(ㄘㄞˊ ㄅㄨˋ ㄌㄨˋ ㄅㄞˊ)
Let not your wealth be exposed.
財迷(ㄘㄞˊ ㄇㄧˊ)
a person who craves for money; a moneygrubber; a miser
財迷心竅(ㄘㄞˊ ㄇㄧˊ ㄒㄧㄣ ㄑㄧㄠˋ)
to have one's head turned by greed
財命(ㄘㄞˊ ㄇㄧㄥˋ)
luck in making money
財閥(ㄘㄞˊ ㄈㄚˊ)
a financial tycoon; a plutocrat; a financier
財富(ㄘㄞˊ ㄈㄨˋ)
wealth or fortune; riches: 自然財富不同於精神財富。Natural wealth is different from spiritual wealth.
財大氣粗(ㄘㄞˊ ㄉㄚˋ ㄑㄧˋ ㄘㄨ)
(literally) He who has wealth speaks louder than others.—to presume on one's wealth and exercise undue power or authority
財團(ㄘㄞˊ ㄊㄨㄢˊ)
a consortium; a financial syndicate
財團法人(ㄘㄞˊ ㄊㄨㄢˊ ㄈㄚˇ ㄖㄣˊ)
a juridical person; a corporate body
財力(ㄘㄞˊ ㄌㄧˋ)
financial resources: 他的財力不缺。His financial resources are never exhausted.
財可通神(ㄘㄞˊ ㄎㄜˇ ㄊㄨㄥ ㄕㄣˊ)
(literally) With money one can make contacts even with gods.—(figuratively)

Money is all-powerful.

財貨(ㄘㄞˊ ㄏㄨㄛˋ)
money, currency and finances

財賄(ㄘㄞˊ ㄏㄨㄟˋ)
(in ancient China) money and grains

財盡(ㄘㄞˊ ㄐㄧㄣˋ)
money exhausted; broke

財經(ㄘㄞˊ ㄐㄧㄥ)
finance and economy

財氣(ㄘㄞˊ ㄑㄧˋ)
luck in making big money

財權(ㄘㄞˊ ㄑㄩㄢˊ)
(law) ownership of movable property

財政(ㄘㄞˊ ㄓㄥˋ)
finance; financial administration

財政部(ㄘㄞˊ ㄓㄥˋ ㄅㄨˋ)
Ministry of Finance

財政部長(ㄘㄞˊ ㄓㄥˋ ㄅㄨˋ ㄓㄤˇ)
the Minister of Finance

財政廳(ㄘㄞˊ ㄓㄥˋ ㄊㄧㄥ)
Provincial Department of Finance

財政廳長(ㄘㄞˊ ㄓㄥˋ ㄊㄧㄥ ㄓㄤˇ)
the director of the Department of Finance

財政年度(ㄘㄞˊ ㄓㄥˋ ㄋㄧㄢˊ ㄉㄨˋ)
the fiscal year

財政關稅(ㄘㄞˊ ㄓㄥˋ ㄍㄨㄢ ㄕㄨㄟˋ)
financial customs

財政困難(ㄘㄞˊ ㄓㄥˋ ㄎㄨㄣˋ ㄋㄢˊ)
financial straits or difficulties: 該項計畫有財政上的困難。The project is in financial difficulties.

財政局(ㄘㄞˊ ㄓㄥˋ ㄐㄩˊ)
Bureau of Finance

財政局長(ㄘㄞˊ ㄓㄥˋ ㄐㄩˊ ㄓㄤˇ)
the director of the Bureau of Finance

財政學(ㄘㄞˊ ㄓㄥˋ ㄒㄩㄝˊ)
the science of finance

財主(ㄘㄞˊ ㄓㄨˇ)
a wealthy man; a capitalist; a millionaire; a moneybags

財產(ㄘㄞˊ ㄔㄢˇ)
property

財產目錄(ㄘㄞˊ ㄔㄢˇ ㄇㄨˋ ㄌㄨˋ)
an inventory of property

財產權(ㄘㄞˊ ㄔㄢˇ ㄑㄩㄢˊ)
ownership of property; property right

財產稅(ㄘㄞˊ ㄔㄢˇ ㄕㄨㄟˋ)
property tax

財神(ㄘㄞˊ ㄕㄣˊ)or 財神爺(ㄘㄞˊ ㄕㄣˊ ㄧㄝˊ)
① the God of Wealth; Mammon ② a very wealthy man

財色(ㄘㄞˊ ㄙㄜˋ)
money and women: 很多人爲財色而活。Many people live for money and women.

財物(ㄘㄞˊ ㄨˋ)
property; belongings

財務(ㄘㄞˊ ㄨˋ)
finance; financial affairs

財務報告(ㄘㄞˊ ㄨˋ ㄅㄠˋ ㄍㄠˋ)
a financial report

財務地位(ㄘㄞˊ ㄨˋ ㄉㄧˋ ㄨㄟˋ)
financial position

財務管理(ㄘㄞˊ ㄨˋ ㄍㄨㄢˇ ㄌㄧˇ)
financial management

財緣兒(ㄘㄞˊ ㄩㄚˊㄦ)
opportunity of making big money

財源(ㄘㄞˊ ㄩㄢˊ)
a source of finances; financial resources

財源滾滾(ㄘㄞˊ ㄩㄢˊ ㄍㄨㄣˇ ㄍㄨㄣˇ)
profits pouring in from all sides

財運(ㄘㄞˊ ㄩㄣˋ)
luck in making money

財用(ㄘㄞˊ ㄩㄥˋ)
finances

【貤】 5752
1. ㄧˋ yih yì

1. to pile one upon another; to superimpose
2. to extend; to prolong

【貤】 5752
2. ㄧˊ yi yí

to move; to remove; to turn

貤封(ㄧˊ ㄈㄥ)
(Ching Dynasty) a request to the throne to transfer a title one was conferred upon to the most senior member of one's family

貤贈(ㄧˊ ㄗㄥˋ)
a request to the throne to transfer a title one was conferred upon to a senior member of one's family who is already dead

四畫

【貧】 5753
ㄆㄧㄣˊ pyn pín

1. poverty; poor; destitute; impoverished
2. deficiency; deficient; lack
3. (now rarely) stingy; tight-fisted
4. long, repetitious or superfluous
5. garrulous

貧病(ㄆㄧㄣˊ ㄅㄧㄥˋ)
impoverished and in poor health

貧病交迫(ㄆㄧㄣˊ ㄅㄧㄥˋ ㄐㄧㄠ ㄆㄛˋ)or 貧病交加(ㄆㄧㄣˊ ㄅㄧㄥˋ ㄐㄧㄠ ㄐㄧㄚ)
to be beset by poverty and illness

貧婆(ㄆㄧㄣˊ ㄆㄛˊ)
① a poor woman ② a nagging, old, female busybody

貧民(ㄆㄧㄣˊ ㄇㄧㄣˊ)
destitute or impoverished people; poor people; a pauper

貧民窟(ㄆㄧㄣˊ ㄇㄧㄣˊ ㄎㄨ)
a slum area; a shantytown: 他在不健全的貧民窟長大。He was brought up in an unwholesome slum.

貧民區(ㄆㄧㄣˊ ㄇㄧㄣˊ ㄑㄩ)
a slum area; a slum district

貧民學校(ㄆㄧㄣˊ ㄇㄧㄣˊ ㄒㄩㄝˊ ㄒㄧㄠˋ)
a school run by the government, charity organization, etc. for the poor with tuition and all other expenses exempted

貧民住宅(ㄆㄧㄣˊ ㄇㄧㄣˊ ㄓㄨˋ ㄓㄞˊ)
housing for poor family

貧民施醫(ㄆㄧㄣˊ ㄇㄧㄣˊ ㄕ ㄧ)
medical care for the poor

貧乏(ㄆㄧㄣˊ ㄈㄚˊ)
wanting; destitute; insufficient; deficient

貧富不均(ㄆㄧㄣˊ ㄈㄨˋ ㄅㄨˋ ㄐㄩㄣ)
the disparity between the rich and the poor; unequal distribution of wealth

貧富懸殊(ㄆㄧㄣˊ ㄈㄨˋ ㄒㄩㄢˊ ㄕㄨ)
extreme disparity between the rich and the poor

貧道(ㄆㄧㄣˊ ㄉㄠˋ)
a humble self-reference of a Taoist priest

貧農(ㄆㄧㄣˊ ㄋㄨㄥˊ)
poor peasants

貧骨頭(ㄆㄧㄣˊ ㄍㄨˇ ˙ㄊㄡ)
① a nagging and talkative person ② a stingy or tight-fisted person; a miser

貧苦(ㄆㄧㄣˊ ㄎㄨˇ)
poverty and hardship; poor; destitute; poverty-stricken

貧困(ㄆㄧㄣˊ ㄎㄨㄣˋ)
impoverished; poor; in straitened circumstances

貧寒(ㄆㄧㄣˊ ㄏㄢˊ)
poor; destitute: 他出身貧寒之家。He was born in a poor family.

貧戶(ㄆㄧㄣˊ ㄏㄨˋ)
a destitute household or family

貧瘠(ㄆㄧㄣˊ ㄐㄧˊ)
(said of land) poor and barren; wanting in natural resources

貧賤(ㄆㄧㄣˊ ㄐㄧㄢˋ)
in humble and destitute circumstances

貧賤不能移(ㄆㄧㄣˊ ㄐㄧㄢˋ ㄅㄨˋ ㄋㄥˊ ㄧˊ)
(said of one's determination, integrity, etc.) not to be shaken or modified by one's poverty or destitution

貧賤夫妻百事哀(ㄆㄧㄣˊ ㄐㄧㄢˋ ㄈㄨ ㄑㄧ ㄅㄞˇ ㄕˋ ㄞ)
To a destitute couple nothing goes well.

貧賤驕人(ㄆㄧㄣˊ ㄐㄧㄢˋ ㄐㄧㄠ ㄖㄣˊ)
Poor as one is, one does not flatter the rich.

貧賤之交(ㄆㄧㄣˊ ㄐㄧㄢˋ ㄓ ㄐㄧㄠ)
a friend of one's humble days

貧窮(ㄆㄧㄣˊ ㄑㄩㄥˊ)
poverty; impoverishment; destitution; penury; poor; needy; impoverished

貧血(ㄆㄧㄣˊ ㄒㄧㄝˇ)
anaemia; anaemic

貧血症(ㄆㄧㄣˊ ㄒㄧㄝˇ ㄓㄥˋ)
anaemia

貧相(ㄆㄧㄣˊ ㄒㄧㄤˋ)
manners of the poor

貧齒類動物(ㄆㄧㄣˊ ㄔˇ ㄌㄟˋ ㄉㄨㄥˋ ㄨˋ)
an edentate

貧士(ㄆㄧㄣˊ ㄕˋ)
a scholar with very limited means

貧嘴(ㄆㄧㄣˊ ㄗㄨㄟˇ)
talkative; garrulous

貧僧(ㄆㄧㄣˊ ㄙㄥ)
a term of self-address of a Buddhist monk

貧無所有(ㄆㄧㄣˊ ㄨˊ ㄙㄨㄛˇ ㄧㄡˇ)
abject poverty; to be as poor as a church mouse: 我年輕時貧無所有。I was as poor as a church mouse when I was young.

【貨】 5754
ㄏㄨㄛˋ huoh huò

1. commodities; goods; products; freight; cargo: 他買賣皮貨。He buys and sells leather goods.
2. money; currency; property
3. to bribe; bribery
4. to sell
5. used as a term of reviling with an abusive suffix: 我看他不是好貨。I think he is not a decent person.

貨幣(ㄏㄨㄛˋ ㄅㄧˋ)
currency; money

貨布(ㄏㄨㄛˋ ㄅㄨˋ)
the name of an ancient currency introduced by Wang Mang(王莽)

貨品(ㄏㄨㄛˋ ㄆㄧㄣˇ)
commodities; goods

貨到付款(ㄏㄨㄛˋ ㄉㄠˋ ㄈㄨˋ ㄎㄨㄢˇ)
cash on delivery (C.O.D.)

貨單(ㄏㄨㄛˋ ㄉㄢ)
a manifest; a list of goods; an invoice

貨輪(ㄏㄨㄛˋ ㄌㄨㄣˊ)
cargo tanker; cargo vessel

貨櫃(ㄏㄨㄛˋ ㄍㄨㄟˋ)
a container 亦作「貨箱」

貨櫃運輸(ㄏㄨㄛˋ ㄍㄨㄟˋ ㄩㄣˋ ㄕㄨ)
container shipment; container transport

貨款(ㄏㄨㄛˋ ㄎㄨㄢˇ)
money for buying or selling goods; payment for goods

貨價(ㄏㄨㄛˋ ㄐㄧㄚˋ)
the price of a commodity or goods

貨泉(ㄏㄨㄛˋ ㄑㄩㄢˊ)
the name of a currency introduced by Wang Mang (王莽)

貨殖(ㄏㄨㄛˋ ㄓˊ)
(in ancient China) to hoard commodities to make profit; to accumulate money in order to generate interest; to increase in wealth

貨眞價實(ㄏㄨㄛˋ ㄓㄣ ㄐㄧㄚˋ ㄕˊ)
①(a commercial slogan) goods of high quality sold at reasonable prices ② through and through; out-and-out

貨主(ㄏㄨㄛˋ ㄓㄨˇ)
the owner of a batch of commodities or goods

貨車(ㄏㄨㄛˋ ㄔㄜ)
a freight car; a cargo truck; a lorry: 我把貨物交由貨車運上。I am sending my goods by truck.

貨暢其流(ㄏㄨㄛˋ ㄔㄤˋ ㄑㄧˊ ㄌㄧㄡˊ)
to have the goods freely distributed among the consumers

貨船(ㄏㄨㄛˋ ㄔㄨㄢˊ)
a freighter; a cargo boat; a cargo vessel

貨倉(ㄏㄨㄛˋ ㄘㄤ)
a warehouse; a storehouse

貨艙(ㄏㄨㄛˋ ㄘㄤ)
the hold of a freighter; the cargo bay (of a plane)

貨色(ㄏㄨㄛˋ ㄙㄜˋ)
kinds, material or quality of goods; stock in trade; stuff: 那家商店貨色繁多。The store was rich in its variety of goods.

貨腰(ㄏㄨㄛˋ ㄧㄠ)
to work as a taxi dancer

貨腰女郎(ㄏㄨㄛˋ ㄧㄠ ㄋㄩˇ ㄌㄤˊ)
a taxi dancer

貨樣(ㄏㄨㄛˋ ㄧㄤˋ)
samples of goods

貨物(ㄏㄨㄛˋ ㄨˋ)
commodities; goods; cargo; merchandise

貨源(ㄏㄨㄛˋ ㄩㄢˊ)
the source of goods; the supply of goods

貨運(ㄏㄨㄛˋ ㄩㄣˋ)
shipment of commodities; transportation service

【販】 5755
ㄈㄢˋ fann fàn

1. to buy and sell; to deal in; to trade in
2. to carry about for sale; to peddle
3. a seller of goods; a peddler; a monger

販賣(ㄈㄢˋ ㄇㄞˋ)
to deal in; to sell; to peddle

販賣部(ㄈㄢˋ ㄇㄞˋ ㄅㄨˋ)
a commissary (in schools, barracks, etc.); a store

販賣人口(ㄈㄢˋ ㄇㄞˋ ㄖㄣˊ ㄎㄡˇ)

〔貝部〕

to deal in human beings; white slavery
販夫(ㄈㄢˋ ㄈㄨ)
a peddler; a hawker
販夫走卒(ㄈㄢˋ ㄈㄨ ㄗㄡˇ ㄗㄨˊ)
people of the lower class
販婦(ㄈㄢˋ ㄈㄨˋ)
a female peddler or hawker
販毒(ㄈㄢˋ ㄉㄨˊ)
to deal in narcotics
販土(ㄈㄢˋ ㄊㄨˇ)
to sell opium
販子(ㄈㄢˋ ·ㄗ)
a seller; a peddler; a dealer: 他是個毛皮販子。He is a dealer in furs.
販運(ㄈㄢˋ ㄩㄣˋ)
to ship goods from one place to another for sale

【貪】 5756 ㄊㄢ tan tān

1. to desire for more than one's rightful share; to covet; greedy: 貪多則無得。All covet all lose.
2. to hope or wish for; to probe or search for

貪杯(ㄊㄢ ㄅㄟ)
to indulge in drinking
貪便宜(ㄊㄢ ㄆㄧㄢˊ ·ㄧ)
to have a strong desire for (usually very small) gains (often at the expense of quality or at the price of big losses); to gain petty advantages
貪夫殉財(ㄊㄢ ㄈㄨ ㄒㄩㄣˋ ㄘㄞˊ)
The greedy die in search of wealth.
貪得無厭(ㄊㄢ ㄉㄜˊ ㄨˊ ㄧㄢˋ)
never satisfied with what one has got; to have an unlimited desire for more; insatiable covetousness
貪多嚼不爛(ㄊㄢ ㄉㄨㄛ ㄐㄧㄠˊ ㄅㄨˋ ㄌㄢˋ)
(literally) to bite more than one can chew—(figuratively) to want more than one can effectively use
貪多務得(ㄊㄢ ㄉㄨㄛ ㄨˋ ㄉㄜˊ)
insatiable covetousness
貪天之功(ㄊㄢ ㄊㄧㄢ ㄓ ㄍㄨㄥ)
to take credit for what is accomplished naturally
貪圖(ㄊㄢ ㄊㄨˊ)
to hope, wish, desire or long for; to hanker after; to covet: 他常常貪圖小利。He often covets small advantages.
貪念(ㄊㄢ ㄋㄧㄢˋ)
covetous thoughts
貪婪(ㄊㄢ ㄌㄢˊ)
covetousness; greed; cupidity; avarice: 他已經貪婪成性。His avarice has become his second nature.
貪狼(ㄊㄢ ㄌㄤˊ)
(literally) as greedy as a wolf —a very greedy person
貪戀(ㄊㄢ ㄌㄧㄢˋ)
to desire or long for (women); to hanker after; unwilling to part with something one loves
貪吝(ㄊㄢ ㄌㄧㄣˋ)
avaricious and miserly
貪官汚吏(ㄊㄢ ㄍㄨㄢ ㄨ ㄌㄧˋ)or 貪官墨吏(ㄊㄢ ㄍㄨㄢ ㄇㄛˋ ㄌㄧˋ)or 貪墨官吏(ㄊㄢ ㄇㄛˋ ㄍㄨㄢ ㄌㄧˋ)
corrupt officials; venal officials
貪花(ㄊㄢ ㄏㄨㄚ)
to indulge in carnal passion
貪求(ㄊㄢ ㄑㄧㄡˊ)
to desire or long for (usually more than one's rightful share)
貪小失大(ㄊㄢ ㄒㄧㄠˇ ㄕ ㄉㄚˋ)
to be tempted by small gains and suffer a big loss; to win battles but lose the war
貪心(ㄊㄢ ㄒㄧㄣ)
greed; cupidity; avarice; greedy; avaricious; insatiable; voracious
貪心不足(ㄊㄢ ㄒㄧㄣ ㄅㄨˋ ㄗㄨˊ)
insatiable greed or covetousness: 他這個人貪心不足。He is insatiably greedy.
貪吃(ㄊㄢ ㄔ)
gluttonous; to eat piggishly
貪生怕死(ㄊㄢ ㄕㄥ ㄆㄚˋ ㄙˇ)
cowardly; cowardice; to care for nothing but saving one's skin; to be mortally afraid of death
貪睡(ㄊㄢ ㄕㄨㄟˋ)
to be fond of sleep; lazy
貪贓(ㄊㄢ ㄗㄤ)
to take bribes; to practice graft
貪贓枉法(ㄊㄢ ㄗㄤ ㄨㄤˇ ㄈㄚˇ)
to twist the law in order to obtain bribes; corrupt
貪嘴(ㄊㄢ ㄗㄨㄟˇ)
gluttonous; piggish
貪財害命(ㄊㄢ ㄘㄞˊ ㄏㄞˋ ㄇㄧㄥˋ)
to kill for money; to commit murder for money
貪色(ㄊㄢ ㄙㄜˋ)
to have a weakness for women
貪汚(ㄊㄢ ㄨ)
corruption; graft
貪汚瀆職(ㄊㄢ ㄨ ㄉㄨˊ ㄓˊ)
(said of officials) corrupt and negligent of one's duties
貪玩(ㄊㄢ ㄨㄢˊ)
to be fond of playing or fooling around
貪慾(ㄊㄢ ㄩˋ)
greed; avarice

【貫】 5757 ㄍㄨㄢˋ guann guàn

1. a thread for stringing holed copper coins; to string on a thread
2. a string of 1,000 holed copper coins
3. to pierce through; to pass through; to see through; throughout; thorough
4. to be linked together; to follow in a continuous line
5. to hit the target
6. one's native place
7. (in Japanese) a weight measure equivalent to about 7 pounds
8. a Chinese family name

貫通(ㄍㄨㄢˋ ㄊㄨㄥ)
① to have a thorough understanding; to be well versed in ② to link up; to thread together
貫錢(ㄍㄨㄢˋ ㄑㄧㄢˊ)
to string holed copper coins
貫珠(ㄍㄨㄢˋ ㄓㄨ)
a string of pearls
貫注(ㄍㄨㄢˋ ㄓㄨˋ)
① to concentrate one's attention on; to be absorbed in: 他全神貫注於他的學業。He was absorbed in his studies. ② to be connected in meaning or feeling
貫徹(ㄍㄨㄢˋ ㄔㄜˋ)
thoroughly; from beginning

to end; to adhere to; to carry out

貫徹始終(ㄍㄨㄢˋ ㄔㄜˋ ㄕˇ ㄓㄨㄥ)
to remain consistent from the start to the very end

貫穿(ㄍㄨㄢˋ ㄔㄨㄢ)
① to penetrate or pierce through ② to run through ③ to understand thoroughly

貫串(ㄍㄨㄢˋ ㄔㄨㄢˋ)
① to string or thread together; to connect ② to run through; to permeate

貫耳(ㄍㄨㄢˋ ㄦˇ)
① to hear; to have heard: 掌聲如雷貫耳。The applause was like a thunderclap piercing through the ear. ② (in ancient China) a punishment in the military camp —to pierce the ear with an arrow

貫盈(ㄍㄨㄢˋ ㄧㄥˊ)
a long list of criminal acts; (said of iniquity) to be full

【責】 5758 ㄗㄜˊ tzer zé

1. one's duty, responsibility, obligation, etc.
2. to demand; to be strict with
3. to punish; punishment
4. to upbraid; to censure; to reprimand; to blame

責備(ㄗㄜˊ ㄅㄟˋ)
to upbraid; to reprimand; to reproach

責罵(ㄗㄜˊ ㄇㄚˋ)
to upbraid; to blame; to scold: 別老是責罵人。Don't scold so much.

責罰(ㄗㄜˊ ㄈㄚˊ)
to punish; a punishment; a penalty

責分(ㄗㄜˊ ㄈㄣˋ)
one's duty; one's share of responsibility

責打(ㄗㄜˊ ㄉㄚˇ)
to punish by beating

責難
①(ㄗㄜˊ ㄋㄢˊ) to urge someone to a difficult task; to hold high expectations for another person
②(ㄗㄜˊ ㄋㄢˋ) to demand an explanation; to upbraid; to censure

責怪(ㄗㄜˊ ㄍㄨㄞˋ)
to blame

責己(ㄗㄜˊ ㄐㄧˇ)
to blame oneself; to hold oneself responsible

責全(ㄗㄜˊ ㄑㄩㄢˊ)
to demand perfection in others; to expect others to do a flawless job

責成(ㄗㄜˊ ㄔㄥˊ)
to hold one responsible for accomplishing a task; to charge one with a duty

責善(ㄗㄜˊ ㄕㄢˋ)
to exhort or admonish someone to practice good deeds; to urge someone to virtuous deeds

責人(ㄗㄜˊ ㄖㄣˊ)
to blame others

責任(ㄗㄜˊ ㄖㄣˋ)
① duty; responsibility; an obligation ② responsibility for a fault; blame

責任保險(ㄗㄜˊ ㄖㄣˋ ㄅㄠˇ ㄒㄧㄢˇ)
liability insurance

責任內閣(ㄗㄜˊ ㄖㄣˋ ㄋㄟˋ ㄍㄜˊ)
a cabinet which is responsible to the parliament for its administrative measures

責任感(ㄗㄜˊ ㄖㄣˋ ㄍㄢˇ)or **責任心**(ㄗㄜˊ ㄖㄣˋ ㄒㄧㄣ)
a sense of responsibility

責讓(ㄗㄜˊ ㄖㄤˋ)
to upbraid

責無旁貸(ㄗㄜˊ ㄨˊ ㄆㄤˊ ㄉㄞˋ)
duty-bound 或 There is no passing the buck. 或 There's no shirking the responsibility.

責問(ㄗㄜˊ ㄨㄣˋ)
to blame and demand an explanation; to call (or bring) somebody to account

責望(ㄗㄜˊ ㄨㄤˋ)
to blame and complain when someone fails to accomplish a difficult task

五畫

【貯】 5759 ㄓㄨˇ juu zhǔ

to store up; to hoard; to save up; to deposit

貯備(ㄓㄨˇ ㄅㄟˋ)
to store up or hoard for future needs

貯備金(ㄓㄨˇ ㄅㄟˋ ㄐㄧㄣ)
reserve funds

貯積(ㄓㄨˇ ㄐㄧ)
to store up; to accumulate

貯蓄(ㄓㄨˇ ㄒㄩˋ)
to store up; to hoard

貯水(ㄓㄨˇ ㄕㄨㄟˇ)
to store water

貯水池(ㄓㄨˇ ㄕㄨㄟˇ ㄔˊ)
a pond for storing water; a reservoir

貯水組織(ㄓㄨˇ ㄕㄨㄟˇ ㄗㄨˇ ㄓ)
(botany) aqueous tissue

貯藏(ㄓㄨˇ ㄘㄤˊ)
① to store up; to hoard ② (mineral) deposits

貯藏根(ㄓㄨˇ ㄘㄤˊ ㄍㄣ)
storage roots

貯藏室(ㄓㄨˇ ㄘㄤˊ ㄕˋ)
a storage room

貯存(ㄓㄨˇ ㄘㄨㄣˊ)
to store up; to stockpile; to deposit

【貰】 5760 ㄕˋ shyh shì

1. to lend or loan; to lease
2. pardon; to pardon; to forgive
3. to sell (or buy) on credit

貰酒(ㄕˋ ㄐㄧㄡˇ)
to buy wine on credit

貰赦(ㄕˋ ㄕㄜˋ)
to pardon a criminal offense

【貲】 5761 ㄗ tzy zī

1. property; wealth; riches; money
2. to count; to measure; to estimate
3. a fine

貲郎(ㄗ ㄌㄤˊ)
one who purchases a public post

貲財(ㄗ ㄘㄞˊ)
wealth; money; valuables

【貳】 5762 ㄦˋ ell èr

1. (in ancient China) a deputy; to serve as a deputy
2. to suspect; to doubt; to distrust
3. changeable
4. an elaborate form of "two" (used in writing checks, etc. to prevent forgery)
5. to repeat
6. doubleness
7. a Chinese family name

貳車(ㄦˋ ㄐㄩ)
a carriage for a deputy or top aide

貳心(ㄦˋ ㄒㄧㄣ)
a rebellious mind

貳志(ㄦˋ ㄓˋ)
disloyalty

貳臣(ㄦˋ ㄔㄣˊ)
an official who serves under two dynasties; a turncoat official

貳室(ㄦˋ ㄕˋ)
a second palace of the emperor

貳言(ㄦˋ ㄧㄢˊ)
a different view; objection

【貴】 5763
ㄍㄨㄟˋ guey guì

1. high-placed; high-ranking; honorable; distinguished
2. expensive; costly; high-priced
3. to esteem; to treat with respect
4. to treasure; to value highly; to prize
5. valuable; precious
6. a polite expression referring to another person—you or your
7. a Chinese family name
8. short for Kweichow Province (貴州省)

貴賓(ㄍㄨㄟˋ ㄅㄧㄣ)
distinguished guests; honored guests; a VIP (a very important person)

貴賓席(ㄍㄨㄟˋ ㄅㄧㄣ ㄒㄧˊ)
seats reserved for distinguished guests

貴賓室(ㄍㄨㄟˋ ㄅㄧㄣ ㄕˋ)
a VIP room; a VIP lounge

貴嬪(ㄍㄨㄟˋ ㄆㄧㄣˊ)
women officials in the ancient Chinese court

貴妃(ㄍㄨㄟˋ ㄈㄟ)
highly honored women officials or imperial concubines in ancient China

貴府(ㄍㄨㄟˋ ㄈㄨˇ)
(a polite expression) your home; your house: 改日再到貴府拜訪。I'll call at your house some other day.

貴婦(ㄍㄨㄟˋ ㄈㄨˋ)
a noblewoman; a woman of rank

貴德(ㄍㄨㄟˋ ㄉㄜˊ)
① a distinguished and virtuous person ② to treasure virtue ③ name of a county in Tsinghai Province(青海省)

貴幹(ㄍㄨㄟˋ ㄍㄢˋ)
What can I do for you? 或 May I help you?

貴庚(ㄍㄨㄟˋ ㄍㄥ)
(a polite expression) How old are you?

貴國(ㄍㄨㄟˋ ㄍㄨㄛˊ)
(a polite expression) your country

貴官(ㄍㄨㄟˋ ㄍㄨㄢ)
honored or distinguished officials

貴客(ㄎㄨㄟˋ ㄎㄜˋ)
honored or distinguished guests; the guest of honor

貴行(ㄍㄨㄟˋ ㄏㄤˊ)
(a polite expression) your company

貴家子(ㄍㄨㄟˋ ㄐㄧㄚ ㄗˇ)
a scion of a noble family

貴介(ㄍㄨㄟˋ ㄐㄧㄝˋ)
a noble

貴价(ㄍㄨㄟˋ ㄐㄧㄝˋ)
(a polite expression) your servant

貴賤(ㄍㄨㄟˋ ㄐㄧㄢˋ)
① the eminent and the humble ② the expensive and the cheap

貴金屬(ㄍㄨㄟˋ ㄐㄧㄣ ㄕㄨˇ)
precious metals; noble metals

貴戚(ㄍㄨㄟˋ ㄑㄧ)
relatives of the emperor

貴妾(ㄍㄨㄟˋ ㄑㄧㄝˋ)
①a concubine who has given birth to a son ② the senior concubine

貴顯(ㄍㄨㄟˋ ㄒㄧㄢˇ)
highly-placed and eminent (officials, etc.)

貴幸(ㄍㄨㄟˋ ㄒㄧㄥˋ)
to earn the emperor's favor and a high position in court

貴姓(ㄍㄨㄟˋ ㄒㄧㄥˋ)
(a polite expression) May I know your distinguished name? 或 Your name, please.

貴州(ㄍㄨㄟˋ ㄓㄡ)
Kweichow, a province in Southwest China

貴胄(ㄍㄨㄟˋ ㄓㄡˋ)
offspring of the nobility

貴主(ㄍㄨㄟˋ ㄓㄨˇ)
a princess

貴重(ㄍㄨㄟˋ ㄓㄨㄥˋ)
precious; expensive; rare; valuable; highly treasured

貴處(ㄍㄨㄟˋ ㄔㄨˋ)
(a polite expression) What's your native place? 或 Where are you from?

貴寵(ㄍㄨㄟˋ ㄔㄨㄥˇ)
① to be esteemed and favored ② a favorite of the emperor

貴人(ㄍㄨㄟˋ ㄖㄣˊ)
① a distinguished, high-ranking person ② a court lady second to the queen in rank

貴人多忘事(ㄍㄨㄟˋ ㄖㄣˊ ㄉㄨㄛ ㄨㄤˋ ㄕˋ)
A highly-placed person is apt to be forgetful (because he has too many things drawing his attention).

貴族(ㄍㄨㄟˋ ㄗㄨˊ)
the nobility; the blue blood; an aristocrat

貴族政治(ㄍㄨㄟˋ ㄗㄨˊ ㄓㄥˋ ㄓˋ)
aristocracy

貴族文學(ㄍㄨㄟˋ ㄗㄨˊ ㄨㄣˊ ㄒㄩㄝˊ)
aristocratic literature (as distinct from popular literature)

貴族院(ㄍㄨㄟˋ ㄗㄨˊ ㄩㄢˋ)
the House of Lords; the House of Peers; the Upper House; the Senate

貴耳賤目(ㄍㄨㄟˋ ㄦˇ ㄐㄧㄢˋ ㄇㄨˋ)
to trust what one hears more than what one sees

貴要(ㄍㄨㄟˋ ㄧㄠˋ)
powerful and influential officials

貴陽(ㄍㄨㄟˋ ㄧㄤˊ)
Kweiyang, capital city of Kweichow Province(貴州省)

貴恙(ㄍㄨㄟˋ ㄧㄤˋ)
(a polite expression) your illness

貴爲天子(ㄍㄨㄟˋ ㄨㄟˊ ㄊㄧㄢ ㄗˇ)
as highly-placed as an emperor

【貶】 5764
ㄅㄧㄢˇ bean biǎn

1. to reduce or lower (prices, etc.); to devalue

2. to degrade; to reduce; to demote: 他被貶為平民。He was reduced to a commoner.
3. to disparage; to condemn; to censure
4. to dismiss; to send away

貶低(ㄅㄧㄢˇ ㄉㄧ)
to belittle; to depreciate; to play down: 他貶低運動的重要性。He depreciated the importance of exercise.

貶官(ㄅㄧㄢˇ ㄍㄨㄢ)
to demote an official

貶價(ㄅㄧㄢˇ ㄐㄧㄚˋ)
to reduce the price

貶值(ㄅㄧㄢˇ ㄓˊ)
to devalue or debase (especially referring to a currency); devaluation; depreciation

貶謫(ㄅㄧㄢˇ ㄓㄜˊ)
to demote and exile an official; to relegate; to banish from the court

貶斥(ㄅㄧㄢˇ ㄔˋ)
① to demote ② to denounce

貶黜(ㄅㄧㄢˇ ㄔㄨˋ)
to dismiss an official

貶黜官職(ㄅㄧㄢˇ ㄔㄨˋ ㄍㄨㄢ ㄓˊ)
to dismiss an official from office

貶詞(ㄅㄧㄢˇ ㄘˊ)
criticism; unfavorable comments; derogatory remarks

貶損(ㄅㄧㄢˇ ㄙㄨㄣˇ)
① to criticize; to speak of something unfavorably ② to derogate

貶抑(ㄅㄧㄢˇ ㄧˋ)
to debase; to devalue; to belittle; to depreciate

【買】 5765 ㄇㄞˇ mae mǎi

1. to buy; to purchase
2. to win over (usually with a promise of favors in return)

買辦(ㄇㄞˇ ㄅㄢˋ)
① a person responsible for making purchases ② a compradore (in the early days of the Republic)

買不來(ㄇㄞˇ ˙ㄅㄨ ㄌㄞˊ) or 買不了(ㄇㄞˇ ˙ㄅㄨ ㄌㄧㄠˇ)
cannot be bought with money: 金錢買不來幸福。Happiness cannot be bought with money.

買不起(ㄇㄞˇ ˙ㄅㄨ ㄑㄧˇ)
cannot afford it—too expensive

買不著(ㄇㄞˇ ˙ㄅㄨ ㄓㄠˊ) or 買不到(ㄇㄞˇ ˙ㄅㄨ ㄉㄠˋ)
cannot buy it—do not know where to buy it; sold out

買賣
①(ㄇㄞˇ ㄇㄞˋ) to buy and sell ②(ㄇㄞˇ ˙ㄇㄞ) a line of business; trade; a business transaction; a deal: 他今天做成一筆買賣。He made a deal today.

買賣人口(ㄇㄞˇ ㄇㄞˋ ㄖㄣˊ ㄎㄡˇ)
to deal in human beings; white slavery

買方(ㄇㄞˇ ㄈㄤ)
the buyer; the buying party

買得起(ㄇㄞˇ ˙ㄉㄜ ㄑㄧˇ)
able to afford it: 她買得起貂皮大衣嗎? Is she able to afford a mink?

買定(ㄇㄞˇ ㄉㄧㄥˋ)
to settle a purchase (usually with a deposit or down payment)

買櫝還珠(ㄇㄞˇ ㄉㄨˊ ㄏㄨㄢˊ ㄓㄨ)
(literally) to buy a loaded jewelry box and return its contents—to choose the wrong thing; to show lack of judgment 亦作「得匣還珠」

買斷(ㄇㄞˇ ㄉㄨㄢˋ)
to buy completely; to buy out

買通(ㄇㄞˇ ㄊㄨㄥ)
to offer bribes to facilitate one's operations; to obtain the collusion of officials with bribes; to buy off

買樂(ㄇㄞˇ ㄌㄜˋ)
to buy amusement; to spend money for entertainment

買鄰(ㄇㄞˇ ㄌㄧㄣˊ)
to select neighbors before moving to a new place

買路錢(ㄇㄞˇ ㄌㄨˋ ㄑㄧㄢˊ)
money, etc. paid to bandits for passage

買官(ㄇㄞˇ ㄍㄨㄢ)
to buy an official title with money

買客(ㄇㄞˇ ㄎㄜˋ)
a buyer; a customer

買空賣空(ㄇㄞˇ ㄎㄨㄥ ㄇㄞˋ ㄎㄨㄥ)
to speculate (on the stock, etc. markets); to buy long and sell short; speculation

買好兒(ㄇㄞˇ ㄏㄠˇㄦ)
to please; to flatter; to try to win somebody's favor; to ingratiate oneself with; to play up to

買回(ㄇㄞˇ ㄏㄨㄟˊ)
(dealing in futures) to buy a contracted commodity which one has already sold; to buy back

買價(ㄇㄞˇ ㄐㄧㄚˋ)
the buying price; the purchase price: 買價多少? What was the purchase price?

買進(ㄇㄞˇ ㄐㄧㄣˋ)
to buy

買爵(ㄇㄞˇ ㄐㄩㄝˊ)
to buy an official or a nobility title

買下來(ㄇㄞˇ ˙ㄒㄧㄚ ˙ㄌㄞ)
to settle a purchase; to contract a purchase

買笑(ㄇㄞˇ ㄒㄧㄠˋ)
to visit a whorehouse

買舟(ㄇㄞˇ ㄓㄡ) or 買棹(ㄇㄞˇ ㄓㄠˋ)
to hire a boat (for a trip)

買主(ㄇㄞˇ ㄓㄨˇ)
the buyer: 誰是這幅畫的買主? Who was the buyer of this picture?

買囑(ㄇㄞˇ ㄓㄨˇ)
to bribe another to perform something on one's behalf

買春(ㄇㄞˇ ㄔㄨㄣ)
to buy drinks

買山(ㄇㄞˇ ㄕㄢ)
to retire from public life

買入(ㄇㄞˇ ㄖㄨˋ)
to buy: 他以每個十元的價錢買入。He bought them for ten dollars each.

買醉(ㄇㄞˇ ㄗㄨㄟˋ)
to buy drinks

買一送一(ㄇㄞˇ ㄧ ㄙㄨㄥˋ ㄧ)
to buy one item with another similar item presented free (a marketing gimmick)

買宴(ㄇㄞˇ ㄧㄢˋ)
(said of an emperor) to throw a banquet and ask the guests to contribute money

【貸】 5766 ㄉㄞˋ day dài

1. to loan; to lend or borrow; a loan

〔貝部〕

〔貝部〕

2. the credit side in bookkeeping
3. to pardon; to be lenient
4. to shift (responsibility); to shirk

貸方(ㄉㄞˋ ㄈㄤ)
the credit (or creditor side) in bookkeeping or an account

貸給(ㄉㄞˋ ㄍㄟˇ)
to loan to; to lend to

貸款(ㄉㄞˋ ㄎㄨㄢˇ)
a loan (of money); credit; to provide(or grant) a loan; to extend credit to

貸借(ㄉㄞˋ ㄐㄧㄝˋ)
① credit and debit sides in bookkeeping ② to borrow

貸借對照表(ㄉㄞˋ ㄐㄧㄝˋ ㄉㄨㄟˋ ㄓㄠˋ ㄅㄧㄠˇ)
(accounting) a balance sheet; a statement of assets and liabilities

貸金(ㄉㄞˋ ㄐㄧㄣ)
money borrowed or lent

貸出(ㄉㄞˋ ㄔㄨ)
to loan to; to lend: 有些人既不貸出，亦不貸入。Some people neither borrow nor lend.

貸入(ㄉㄞˋ ㄖㄨˋ)
to borrow; to get a loan: 他向銀行貸入一筆大款。He borrowed a large sum from the bank.

貸餘(ㄉㄞˋ ㄩˊ)
credit balance

【貺】 5767
ㄎㄨㄤˋ kuanq kuàng
1. to give or bestow; to confer
2. (a polite expression) to be favored with
3. a Chinese family name

貺臨(ㄎㄨㄤˋ ㄌㄧㄣˊ)
to be honored by your presence

貺我多珍(ㄎㄨㄤˋ ㄨㄛˇ ㄉㄨㄛ ㄓㄣ)
your handsome gift

【費】 5768
1. ㄈㄟˋ fey fèi
1. expenditure; expenses; fees; dues; charges
2. to waste; to use more than is needed; wasteful; consuming too much
3. to consume; to use; to spend; to cost; to expend
4. a Chinese family name

費邊協會(ㄈㄟˋ ㄅㄧㄢ ㄒㄧㄝˊ ㄏㄨㄟˋ)
Fabian Society

費電(ㄈㄟˋ ㄉㄧㄢˋ)
to consume a lot of electricity; power-consuming

費拉得爾費亞(ㄈㄟˋ ㄌㄚ ㄉㄜˊ ㄦˇ ㄈㄟˋ ㄧㄚˋ)or 費城(ㄈㄟˋ ㄔㄥˊ)
Philadelphia, U. S. A.

費力(ㄈㄟˋ ㄌㄧˋ)
① taking a lot of exertion; to need or use great effort ② difficult (tasks)

費力不討好(ㄈㄟˋ ㄌㄧˋ ㄅㄨˋ ㄊㄠˇ ㄏㄠˇ)
to put in a lot of work without pleasing anybody; to work hard without accomplishing any good; to waste energy and come to nothing

費工(ㄈㄟˋ ㄍㄨㄥ)or 費工夫(ㄈㄟˋ ㄍㄨㄥ ·ㄈㄨ)
to take a lot of time or work; labor-consuming

費解(ㄈㄟˋ ㄐㄧㄝˇ)
difficult to understand: 他的話實在令人費解。His words are really difficult to understand.

費勁(ㄈㄟˋ ㄐㄧㄣˋ)
① labor-consuming; strenuous ② difficult (work, matters, etc.): 他毫不費勁地做完了那工作。He did the work without any difficulty.

費盡心機(ㄈㄟˋ ㄐㄧㄣˋ ㄒㄧㄣ ㄐㄧ)
to exhaust all mental efforts; to rack one's brains in scheming

費盡唇舌(ㄈㄟˋ ㄐㄧㄣˋ ㄔㄨㄣˊ ㄕㄜˊ)
to have wasted all one's breath

費錢(ㄈㄟˋ ㄑㄧㄢˊ)
to cost a great deal of money

費心(ㄈㄟˋ ㄒㄧㄣ)or 費神(ㄈㄟˋ ㄕㄣˊ)
① requiring mental exertion; to give a lot of care: 她爲她的家可費心不少。She devoted a lot of care to her family. ② Please be kind enough to.... 或 Many thanks (for doing this for me). 或 Would you mind (doing something)?

費周折(ㄈㄟˋ ㄓㄡ ㄓㄜˊ)
to take a good deal of planning, work, physical or mental exertion, etc.

費脣舌(ㄈㄟˋ ㄔㄨㄣˊ ㄕㄜˊ)
to have a lot of explaining to do; requiring a lot of talking

費時(ㄈㄟˋ ㄕˊ)
to take, need or waste a lot of time; time-consuming

費事(ㄈㄟˋ ㄕˋ)
requiring a lot of trouble to accomplish; difficult

費手脚(ㄈㄟˋ ㄕㄡˇ ㄐㄧㄠˇ)
time-consuming or troublesome; difficult

費商量(ㄈㄟˋ ㄕㄤ ·ㄌㄧㄤ)
to need a good deal of talking or negotiation

費材料(ㄈㄟˋ ㄘㄞˊ ㄌㄧㄠˋ)
to require a large quantity of material

費眼(ㄈㄟˋ ㄧㄢˇ)
to strain the eye; to waste eyesight

費用(ㄈㄟˋ ㄩㄥˋ)
expenditure; expenses; costs

【費】 5768
2. ㄅㄧˋ bih bì
name of a town in the Period of Spring and Autumn in today's 費縣, Shantung Province(山東省)

【貼】 5769
ㄊㄧㄝ tie tiē
1. to paste; to stick; to glue
2. to keep close to; to nestle closely to
3. to make up the deficiency; to subsidize; subsidies; an allowance
4. proper; appropriate; comfortable
5. attached to

貼邊(ㄊㄧㄝ ㄅㄧㄢ)
a hem; edging; trimming; lacing

貼補(ㄊㄧㄝ ㄅㄨˇ)
to make up a deficiency; to supplement; to help (out) financially; to subsidize

貼膏藥(ㄊㄧㄝ ㄍㄠ ㄧㄠˋ)
to stick on a medicated plaster

貼廣告(ㄊㄧㄝ ㄍㄨㄤˇ ㄍㄠˋ)
to paste up promotion posters; to post bills

貼己(ㄊㄧㄝ ㄐㄧˇ)
intimate; close

貼金(ㄊㄧㄝ ㄐㄧㄣ)
① to boast or brag about

oneself ② to gild; to cover with gold leaf (or gold foil)

貼近(ㄊㄧㄝ ㄐㄧㄣˋ)
nearby; close to; to press close to; to nestle up against

貼切(ㄊㄧㄝ ㄑㄧㄝˋ)
proper or appropriate; apt; suitable; very much to the point

貼錢(ㄊㄧㄝ ㄑㄧㄢˊ)
to pay out of one's own pocket—especially when one is not supposed to, as in performing an official duty

貼現(ㄊㄧㄝ ㄒㄧㄢˋ)
(banking) discount

貼現率(ㄊㄧㄝ ㄒㄧㄢˋ ㄌㄩˋ)
the discount rate 亦作「貼現利率」

貼心(ㄊㄧㄝ ㄒㄧㄣ)
intimate; close: 他對大家都很客氣，但貼心好友無幾。He was courteous to all, but intimate with few.

貼心貼意(ㄊㄧㄝ ㄒㄧㄣ ㄊㄧㄝ ㄧˋ)
① docile; amiable ② satisfying

貼身(ㄊㄧㄝ ㄕㄣ)
① personal servants ② closely attached, as children, undergarments, concubines, etc.

貼水(ㄊㄧㄝ ㄕㄨㄟˇ)
payment for the difference in changing silver dollars of lower fineness for those of higher fineness; an agio

貼耳(ㄊㄧㄝ ㄦˇ)
to be ready to listen

【貽】 5770 ㄧˊ yi yí

1. to give to; to present to
2. to hand down; to transmit; to pass on to; to bequeath; to leave behind

貽累(ㄧˊ ㄌㄟˋ)
to involve or implicate another

貽害(ㄧˊ ㄏㄞˋ)or 貽禍(ㄧˊ ㄏㄨㄛˋ)
to bring trouble or harm to another

貽笑大方(ㄧˊ ㄒㄧㄠˋ ㄉㄚˋ ㄈㄤ)
to become a laughingstock (by showing one's ignorance, etc.); to be laughed at by experts

貽羞(ㄧˊ ㄒㄧㄡ)
to cause shame or scandal

貽人口實(ㄧˊ ㄖㄣˊ ㄎㄡˇ ㄕˊ)
to give an occasion for scandal or gossip

貽贈(ㄧˊ ㄗㄥˋ)
① to present (a gift) ② to leave something to posterity

貽誤(ㄧˊ ㄨˋ)
to cause delay or hindrance; to bungle

貽誤戎機(ㄧˊ ㄨˋ ㄖㄨㄥˊ ㄐㄧ)
to hinder military operations; to cause damage to military operations; to forfeit or bungle a chance for combat

【賀】 5771 ㄏㄜˋ heh hè

1. to congratulate; to send a present in congratulation: 他的成功值得慶賀。His success deserves congratulation.
2. a Chinese family name

賀表(ㄏㄜˋ ㄅㄧㄠˇ)
a letter of congratulation and praise presented by the subjects to a king or emperor on special occasions

賀電(ㄏㄜˋ ㄉㄧㄢˋ)
a congratulatory cable or telegram

賀帖(ㄏㄜˋ ㄊㄧㄝˇ)
congratulatory cards

賀年(ㄏㄜˋ ㄋㄧㄢˊ)or 賀歲(ㄏㄜˋ ㄙㄨㄟˋ)
New Year's greetings; to offer congratulations on New Year's Day

賀年片(ㄏㄜˋ ㄋㄧㄢˊ ㄆㄧㄢˋ)
New Year's greeting cards

賀蘭山(ㄏㄜˋ ㄌㄢˊ ㄕㄢ)
Holan Shan, a mountain range in Ningsia Province

賀禮(ㄏㄜˋ ㄌㄧˇ)
a congratulatory present; a present given as a token of congratulation

賀客盈門(ㄏㄜˋ ㄎㄜˋ ㄧㄥˊ ㄇㄣˊ)
The house is crowded with well-wishers (on a happy occasion).

賀函(ㄏㄜˋ ㄏㄢˊ)or 賀柬(ㄏㄜˋ ㄐㄧㄢˇ)
a letter of congratulation; a congratulatory message

賀節(ㄏㄜˋ ㄐㄧㄝˊ)
to offer congratulations on festivals

賀喜(ㄏㄜˋ ㄒㄧˇ)
to congratulate; to felicitate: 朋友們爲他的成功賀喜。Friends congratulated him on his success.

賀正(ㄏㄜˋ ㄓㄥ)
to offer congratulations on New Year's Day 亦作「賀年」

賀忱(ㄏㄜˋ ㄔㄣˊ)or 賀悃(ㄏㄜˋ ㄎㄨㄣˇ)
sincerity in offering congratulations

賀詞(ㄏㄜˋ ㄘˊ)
messages of congratulation; congratulations; greetings

賀儀(ㄏㄜˋ ㄧˊ)
money, etc. sent as a token of one's congratulation

賀爾蒙(ㄏㄜˋ ㄦˇ ㄇㄥˊ)
hormones 亦作「荷爾蒙」

【貿】 5772 ㄇㄠˋ maw mào

1. to trade; to barter; to exchange
2. mixed
3. rashly

貿貿然(ㄇㄠˋ ㄇㄠˋ ㄖㄢˊ)
rashly; without forethought or consideration

貿名(ㄇㄠˋ ㄇㄧㄥˊ)
to purchase fame

貿然(ㄇㄠˋ ㄖㄢˊ)
rashly; blindly: 你不可貿然許諾。You should never make a rash promise. 訛作「冒然」

貿易(ㄇㄠˋ ㄧˋ)
trade; to trade: 去年貿易良好。Trade was good last year.

貿易平衡(ㄇㄠˋ ㄧˋ ㄆㄧㄥˊ ㄏㄥˊ)
the balance of trade

貿易風(ㄇㄠˋ ㄧˋ ㄈㄥ)
the trade wind

貿易逆差(ㄇㄠˋ ㄧˋ ㄋㄧˋ ㄔㄚ)
trade deficit

貿易港(ㄇㄠˋ ㄧˋ ㄍㄤˇ)
a trading port; a commercial port: 香港是一貿易港。Hong Kong is a trading port.

貿易公司(ㄇㄠˋ ㄧˋ ㄍㄨㄥ ㄙ)
a trading company or firm: 這家貿易公司專門進口玩具。The trading company imports toys exclusively.

貿易區(ㄇㄠˋ ㄧˋ ㄑㄩ)
a trade area

貿易協定(ㄇㄠˋ ㄧˋ ㄒㄧㄝˊ ㄉㄧㄥˋ)
a trade agreement

貿易中心(ㄇㄠˋ ㄧˋ ㄓㄨㄥ ㄒㄧㄣ)
a trading center

貿易商(ㄇㄠˋ ㄧˋ ㄕㄤ)
a trader; an importer; an exporter: 他是國際貿易商。He is an international trader.

貿易順差(ㄇㄠˋ ㄧˋ ㄕㄨㄣˋ ㄔㄚ)
a favorable balance of trade

貿易自由化(ㄇㄠˋ ㄧˋ ㄗˋ ㄧㄡˊ ㄏㄨㄚˋ)
liberalization of trade

貿易額 (ㄇㄠˋ ㄧˋ ㄜˊ)
a volume of trade

【賁】 5773
1. ㄅㄧˋ bih bì

1. to adorn; ornamental
2. bright; luminous

賁臨(ㄅㄧˋ ㄌㄧㄣˊ)
(a polite expression) your illustrious presence

賁然(ㄅㄧˋ ㄖㄢˊ)
bright and brilliant

賁如(ㄅㄧˋ ㄖㄨˊ)
richly adorned; brightly ornamental

【賁】 5773
2. ㄅㄣ ben bēn

1. to forge ahead
2. energetic; strenuous
3. a Chinese family name

【賁】 5773
3. ㄈㄣˊ fern fén

large; great

六畫

【賃】 5774
ㄌㄧㄣˋ linn lìn

1. to rent; to hire
2. a hireling

賃借(ㄌㄧㄣˋ ㄐㄧㄝˋ)
to hire; to borrow

賃金(ㄌㄧㄣˋ ㄐㄧㄣ)
① rent of a house ② wages of a hired hand

賃書(ㄌㄧㄣˋ ㄕㄨ)
① one who is hired to write ② to borrow books (with rental) for reading

賃租(ㄌㄧㄣˋ ㄗㄨ)
to rent

賃屋(ㄌㄧㄣˋ ㄨ)
to rent a house

【賂】 5775
ㄌㄨˋ luh lù

1. to send a gift
2. to bribe

【賄】 5776
ㄏㄨㄟˋ huey huì
(又讀 ㄏㄨㄟˇ hoei huǐ)

1. to bribe; bribery: 他被控受賄。He is charged with bribery.
2. money; wealth

賄賂(ㄏㄨㄟˋ ㄌㄨˋ)
to bribe; bribery: 他們用貴重的禮物賄賂他。They bribed him with costly presents.

賄選(ㄏㄨㄟˋ ㄒㄩㄢˇ)
to try to win in an election by means of bribery; to get elected by bribery

【資】 5777
ㄗ tzy zī

1. money; wealth; property; means; capital
2. expenses; fees; charges
3. natural endowments or gifts; one's disposition
4. to avail of
5. to aid or help; to assist; to subsidize; to support
6. to supply; to provide
7. one's qualifications, position, or record of service
8. to trust to

資本(ㄗ ㄅㄣˇ)
capital

資本逃避(ㄗ ㄅㄣˇ ㄊㄠˊ ㄅㄧˋ)
flight of capital

資本論(ㄗ ㄅㄣˇ ㄌㄨㄣˋ)
Capital (*Das Kapital*) by Karl Marx

資本集中(ㄗ ㄅㄣˇ ㄐㄧˊ ㄓㄨㄥ)
centralization of capital

資本家(ㄗ ㄅㄣˇ ㄐㄧㄚ)
a capitalist: 多餘的錢叫做資本，其所有人叫資本家。Spare money is called capital; its owner is called a capitalist.

資稟(ㄗ ㄅㄧㄥˇ)
one's natural endowments or gifts: 他兒子資稟過人。His son's natural gifts excel others.

資方(ㄗ ㄈㄤ)
the management (of a shop, factory, etc.); capital

資俸(ㄗ ㄈㄥˋ)
qualifications and duration of service of an official

資斧(ㄗ ㄈㄨˇ)
traveling expenses

資敵(ㄗ ㄉㄧˊ)
to assist the enemy; treason

資歷(ㄗ ㄌㄧˋ)
qualifications and experiences (of an applicant, etc.); professional background: 他的資歷不夠。His qualification and experience are insufficient.

資料(ㄗ ㄌㄧㄠˋ)
data: 資料已齊備，等待處理。The data is ready for processing.

資料庫(ㄗ ㄌㄧㄠˋ ㄎㄨˋ)
(computers) data base

資料處理(ㄗ ㄌㄧㄠˋ ㄔㄨˇ ㄌㄧˇ)
information processing

資格(ㄗ ㄍㄜˊ)
qualifications, requirements, or seniority of a person: 我具有必要的資格。I have the requisite qualifications.

資金(ㄗ ㄐㄧㄣ)
funds; capital

資金凍結(ㄗ ㄐㄧㄣ ㄉㄨㄥˋ ㄐㄧㄝˊ)
freezing of funds or capital

資遣(ㄗ ㄑㄧㄢˇ)
to dismiss (employees) with severance pay: 他去年被資遣。He was dismissed with severance pay last year.

資性(ㄗ ㄒㄧㄥˋ)
one's disposition; one's natural endowments: 這位學生資性忠厚。The student's natural disposition is honest.

資訊(ㄗ ㄒㄩㄣˋ)
information

資質(ㄗ ㄓˋ)
one's natural gifts or endowments; one's natural disposition: 他具有藝術方面的資質。He has a gift for art.

資治通鑑(ㄗ ㄓˋ ㄊㄨㄥ ㄐㄧㄢˋ)
the title of a 294-volume chronicle by Ssu-Ma Kuang (司馬光), covering a period of 1,362 years down to the Epoch of the Five Dynasties

資政(ㄗ ㄓㄥˋ)
a political advisor to the President of the Republic of China

資政院(ㄗ ㄓㄥˋ ㄩㄢˋ)
a nominated advisory council established toward the close of the Ching Dynasty

資助(ㄗ ㄓㄨˋ)
to help another with money; to provide financial assistance: 這位老人常常資助窮人。

The old man often helps the poor with money.
資產(ㄗ ㄔㄢˇ)
① property; real estate ② (accounting) assets
資產負債表(ㄗ ㄔㄢˇ ㄈㄨˋ ㄓㄞˋ ㄅㄧㄠˇ)
a statement of assets and liabilities; a balance sheet
資產階級(ㄗ ㄔㄢˇ ㄐㄧㄝ ㄐㄧˊ)
the bourgeoisie; the middle class 亦作「中產階級」
資深(ㄗ ㄕㄣ)
senior; seniority
資水(ㄗ ㄕㄨㄟˇ)
Tsu-shui, name of a river in Hunan Province
資財(ㄗ ㄘㄞˊ)
wealth; riches; assets
資送(ㄗ ㄙㄨㄥˋ)
① to send away with money provided ② to give a dowry to a daughter on her marriage
資優生(ㄗ ㄧㄡ ㄕㄥ)
a bright student; a student with a high IQ
資望(ㄗ ㄨㄤˋ)
qualification and prestige
資源(ㄗ ㄩㄢˊ)
resources; natural resources: 中國是資源豐富的國家。China is a resourceful country.

【賅】 5778
ㄍㄞ gai gāi
provided for; included in; all-inclusive; nothing left out

【賈】 5779
1. ㄐㄧㄚˇ jea jiǎ
a Chinese family name
賈島(ㄐㄧㄚˇ ㄉㄠˇ)
Chia Tao (779-843), a poet of the Tang Dynasty
賈誼(ㄐㄧㄚˇ ㄧˊ)
Chia Yi (200-168B.C.), a writer and political commentator of the Western Han Dynasty

【賈】 5779
2. ㄍㄨˇ guu gǔ
1. a merchant; a businessman
2. to buy; to trade
賈舶(ㄍㄨˇ ㄅㄛˊ)
merchant marine; trading vessels
賈利(ㄍㄨˇ ㄌㄧˋ)
to make a profit
賈儈(ㄍㄨˇ ㄎㄨㄞˋ)
merchants
賈禍(ㄍㄨˇ ㄏㄨㄛˋ)
to invite or bring on calamity or misfortune
賈人(ㄍㄨˇ ㄖㄣˊ)
merchants; businessmen
賈餘(ㄍㄨˇ ㄩˊ)
with courage to spare
賈怨(ㄍㄨˇ ㄩㄢˋ)
to invite complaints or grudges
賈勇(ㄍㄨˇ ㄩㄥˇ)
with courage to spare

【賊】 5780
ㄗㄟˊ tzeir zéi
(讀音 ㄗㄜˊ tzer zé)
1. a thief; a burglar; a robber; a bandit
2. rebels; traitors
3. to harm
4. to kill
5. pests on the farm
6. a term of reviling
7. clever; cunning; crafty

賊兵(ㄗㄟˊ ㄅㄧㄥ)
rebel soldiers; enemy troops
賊眉鼠眼(ㄗㄟˊ ㄇㄟˊ ㄕㄨˇ ㄧㄢˇ)
the appearance of a low, cunning person; a mean look
賊眉賊眼(ㄗㄟˊ ㄇㄟˊ ㄗㄟˊ ㄧㄢˇ)
roguish looks
賊匪(ㄗㄟˊ ㄈㄟˇ)
rebels; bandits: 這鎮爲賊匪所擾害。The town is infested with bandits.
賊黨(ㄗㄟˊ ㄉㄤˇ)
the rebel faction; a gang of bandits or rebels; a group of traitors: 賊黨已分裂爲兩派。The rebel faction has split into two factions.
賊店(ㄗㄟˊ ㄉㄧㄢˋ)
an inn operated by an evil person or persons who kill the lodgers for money, jewels, etc.
賊頭(ㄗㄟˊ ㄊㄡˊ)or 賊首(ㄗㄟˊ ㄕㄡˇ)
the leader of a band of thieves; the chief robber; a bandit leader
賊頭賊腦(ㄗㄟˊ ㄊㄡˊ ㄗㄟˊ ㄋㄠˇ)
to act suspiciously; thief-like; a mean look; acting stealthily
賊禿(ㄗㄟˊ ㄊㄨ)
an abusive term for Buddhist monks
賊徒(ㄗㄟˊ ㄊㄨˊ)
thieves
賊骨頭(ㄗㄟˊ ㄍㄨˇ ·ㄊㄡ)
depravity; meanness; wickedness
賊鬼(ㄗㄟˊ ·ㄍㄨㄟ)
cunning and crafty
賊鬼溜滑(ㄗㄟˊ ·ㄍㄨㄟ ㄌㄧㄡ ㄏㄨㄚˊ)
dishonest; crafty: 他賊鬼溜滑如狐狸。He is as crafty as a fox.
賊寇(ㄗㄟˊ ㄎㄡˋ)
rebels; bandits
賊害(ㄗㄟˊ ㄏㄞˋ)
to cause harm or injury to another
賊將(ㄗㄟˊ ㄐㄧㄤˋ)
a rebel general; a general of the enemy troops
賊心(ㄗㄟˊ ㄒㄧㄣ)
a crooked mind; a wicked and suspicious mind; evil designs
賊相(ㄗㄟˊ ㄒㄧㄤˋ)
criminal looks
賊星發旺(ㄗㄟˊ ㄒㄧㄥ ㄈㄚ ㄨㄤˋ)
(a sarcastical expression) a small-time operator hitting the jackpot
賊性(ㄗㄟˊ ㄒㄧㄥˋ)
① a crafty or cunning disposition ② an evil mind
賊性難改(ㄗㄟˊ ㄒㄧㄥˋ ㄋㄢˊ ㄍㄞˇ)
The habitual criminal is incorrigible.
賊巢(ㄗㄟˊ ㄔㄠˊ)
a den or hideout of thieves and bandits
賊出關門(ㄗㄟˊ ㄔㄨ ㄍㄨㄢ ㄇㄣˊ)
(literally) to close the door after the thieves are gone—too late
賊船(ㄗㄟˊ ㄔㄨㄢˊ)
a pirate ship; a ship owned by bandits or rebels: 賊船被燒。The pirate ship was burned.
賊人(ㄗㄟˊ ㄖㄣˊ)
a thief or robber
賊贓(ㄗㄟˊ ㄗㄤ)
stolen goods or property; loot: 賊贓起回。Stolen goods were recovered.
賊眼(ㄗㄟˊ ㄧㄢˇ)
eyes with evil twinkle; shifty eyes; a furtive glance

賊營(ㄗㄟˊ ㄧㄥˊ)
the camp of rebels, bandits, etc.: 賊營着火了。The camp of bandits caught (on) fire.
賊窩子(ㄗㄟˊ ㄨㄛ ˙ㄗ)
a den or hideout of thieves or bandits

〔貝部〕

【賉】 5781 ㄒㄩˋ shiuh xù
1. sympathy; pity
2. to give alms or compensation

【賍】 5782 ㄗㄤ tzang zāng
stolen goods or property; loot

七畫

【賑】 5783 ㄓㄣˋ jenn zhèn
1. to relieve or give aid to the distressed; to support
2. rich; wealthy; prosperous
賑田(ㄓㄣˋ ㄊㄧㄢˊ)
farmland, whose produce is used for relief or charity
賑糧(ㄓㄣˋ ㄌㄧㄤˊ)
relief food or grain
賑款(ㄓㄣˋ ㄎㄨㄢˇ)
relief funds
賑饑(ㄓㄣˋ ㄐㄧ)
to feed the hungry (refugees); to relieve famine
賑濟(ㄓㄣˋ ㄐㄧˋ) or 賑贍(ㄓㄣˋ ㄕㄢˋ)
to relieve or give aid to the distressed; to provide relief for: 政府賑濟難民。The government provided relief for refugees.
賑捐(ㄓㄣˋ ㄐㄩㄢ)
to contribute to relief funds
賑恤(ㄓㄣˋ ㄒㄩˋ)
to relieve the distressed: 這基金用於賑恤。The fund is for relieving the distressed.
賑災(ㄓㄣˋ ㄗㄞ)
to relieve the afflicted area; to relieve victims of a natural disaster

【賒】 5784 ㄕㄜ she shē
1. to buy or sell on credit
2. distant; faraway
3. slow; slowly
4. to put off or postpone
5. luxurious or extravagant
賒貸(ㄕㄜ ㄉㄞˋ)
credit
賒貨(ㄕㄜ ㄏㄨㄛˋ)
to get goods on credit
賒欠(ㄕㄜ ㄑㄧㄢˋ)
to buy on credit; such credit which has not been settled
賒賬(ㄕㄜ ㄓㄤˋ)
to buy on account or credit
賒售(ㄕㄜ ㄕㄡˋ)
sales on account

【賓】 5785 (賔) ㄅㄧㄣ bin bīn
1. a guest; a visitor
2. to treat as a guest
3. to obey; to follow instructions; to submit
4. a Chinese family name
賓白(ㄅㄧㄣ ㄅㄛˊ)
dialogue in Chinese opera
賓朋(ㄅㄧㄣ ㄆㄥˊ)
friends and guests
賓服(ㄅㄧㄣ ㄈㄨˊ)
①(said of feudal lords) to have an audience with the emperor and present him with tribute ② to pay homage
賓待(ㄅㄧㄣ ㄉㄞˋ)
to receive someone as a guest
賓禮(ㄅㄧㄣ ㄌㄧˇ)
① the courtesy or etiquette on the part of a guest ② international courtesy
賓格(ㄅㄧㄣ ㄍㄜˊ)
(grammar) the objective case
賓果(ㄅㄧㄣ ㄍㄨㄛˇ)
bingo
賓館(ㄅㄧㄣ ㄍㄨㄢˇ)
a guesthouse
賓貢(ㄅㄧㄣ ㄍㄨㄥˋ)
①(an ancient practice) to treat capable and virtuous persons in a locality as guests and recommend them to the imperial court ②(said of a small country) to pledge allegiance and offer tributes to a strong country
賓客(ㄅㄧㄣ ㄎㄜˋ)
guests and visitors
賓夕法尼亞(ㄅㄧㄣ ㄒㄧˋ ㄈㄚˇ ㄋㄧˊ ㄧㄚˋ) or 賓州(ㄅㄧㄣ ㄓㄡ)
the state of Pennsylvania, U.S.A.
賓至如歸(ㄅㄧㄣ ㄓˋ ㄖㄨˊ ㄍㄨㄟ)
Guests flock to the place like returning home.—to feel at home in a place: 在這一流的旅館，我們覺得賓至如歸。We feel at home in this first-class hotel.
賓主(ㄅㄧㄣ ㄓㄨˇ)
① the guest and the host ② secondary and principal
賓主盡歡(ㄅㄧㄣ ㄓㄨˇ ㄐㄧㄣˋ ㄏㄨㄢ)
Both the guests and the host are having a great time.
賓師(ㄅㄧㄣ ㄕ)
one who does not hold a public post but is highly respected
賓從(ㄅㄧㄣ ㄗㄨㄥˋ)
servants or retinue of a guest
賓位(ㄅㄧㄣ ㄨㄟˋ)
(grammar) the objective case
賓語(ㄅㄧㄣ ㄩˇ)
(grammar) the object of a transitive verb 亦作「受詞」

【賕】 5786 ㄑㄧㄡˊ chyou qiú
to bribe

八畫

【賚】 5787 ㄌㄞˋ lay lài
to bestow; to confer
賚品(ㄌㄞˋ ㄆㄧㄣˇ)
an article, item, gift, etc. bestowed by a superior

【賙】 5788 ㄓㄡ jou zhōu
to give; to aid; to relieve
賙濟(ㄓㄡ ㄐㄧˋ)
to relieve the needy: 我們必須賙濟貧困的家庭。We have to relieve needy families.

【賜】 5789 ㄙˋ syh sì (語音 ㄘˋ tsyh cì)
1. to bestow or confer on an inferior; to grant
2. favors; benefits
3. to order; to appoint
賜帛(ㄙˋ ㄅㄛˊ)
(in ancient China) to be bestowed silk by the emperor for hanging oneself
賜福(ㄙˋ ㄈㄨˊ)
to bless; to give blessings
賜覆(ㄙˋ ㄈㄨˋ)
Please reply. 或 to favor

with a reply: 請即賜覆。Please favor me with an early reply.
賜奠(ㄙˋ ㄉㄧㄢˋ)
(said of the emperor, especially in the Ching Dynasty) to personally offer condolences or pay last tribute to the deceased
賜給(ㄙˋ ㄍㄟˇ)
to grant; to bestow
賜告(ㄙˋ ㄍㄠˋ)
to be given official leave by the emperor
賜顧(ㄙˋ ㄍㄨˋ)
(a polite business expression) your patronage
賜函(ㄙˋ ㄏㄢˊ)
Please write me.
賜環(ㄙˋ ㄏㄨㄢˊ)
(said of an official exiled to the frontier) to be forgiven and recalled to the capital
賜假(ㄙˋ ㄐㄧㄚˋ)
to be granted a leave of absence
賜教(ㄙˋ ㄐㄧㄠˋ)
(a polite expression) your instructions; your advice: 敬請多多賜教。Please favor me with your advice.
賜爵(ㄙˋ ㄐㄩㄝˊ)
to confer titles of nobility upon the meritorious
賜姓(ㄙˋ ㄒㄧㄥˋ)
to be given the emperor's family name (in recognition of one's meritorious service)
賜示(ㄙˋ ㄕˋ)
(a polite expression) Please tell me....
賜諡(ㄙˋ ㄕˋ)
(said of a high minister) to have an honorary title conferred posthumously
賜書(ㄙˋ ㄕㄨ)
letters received from a superior or client
賜死(ㄙˋ ㄙˇ)
to be ordered by the emperor to commit suicide
賜宴(ㄙˋ ㄧㄢˋ)
to be invited to dine with the emperor
賜予 or 賜與(ㄙˋ ㄩˇ)
to bestow or confer upon; to grant (approval, etc.)

【賞】 5790 ㄕㄤˇ shaang shǎng
1. to reward; to award; to bestow; to grant; to give to an inferior
2. a reward; an award
3. to appreciate; to enjoy; to admire
4. (now rarely) to respect
5. (a polite expression) to be given the honor of...
賞罰(ㄕㄤˇ ㄈㄚˊ)
to reward and punish; reward and punishment
賞罰分明(ㄕㄤˇ ㄈㄚˊ ㄈㄣ ㄇㄧㄥˊ)
to confer reward and inflict punishment impartially
賞田(ㄕㄤˇ ㄊㄧㄢˊ)
(Chou Dynasty) land bestowed by the government
賞臉(ㄕㄤˇ ㄌㄧㄢˇ)
① to favor me with your presence or company ② to condescend to receive my humble gifts ③ to do me a favor
賞格(ㄕㄤˇ ㄍㄜˊ)
the amount of cash reward offered (for locating a person or an object)
賞光(ㄕㄤˇ ㄍㄨㄤ)
(a polite expression) to honor me with your gracious presence or company
賞花(ㄕㄤˇ ㄏㄨㄚ)
to enjoy the sight of flowers
賞金(ㄕㄤˇ ㄐㄧㄣ)
reward money; a bonus
賞錢(ㄕㄤˇ ˙ㄑㄧㄢ)
tips (for waiters, servants, etc.): 他給侍者賞錢。He gave the waiter a tip.
賞心(ㄕㄤˇ ㄒㄧㄣ)
to please the heart, as a beautiful sight, etc.
賞心樂事(ㄕㄤˇ ㄒㄧㄣ ㄌㄜˋ ㄕˋ)
pleasant things that one enjoys doing
賞心悅目(ㄕㄤˇ ㄒㄧㄣ ㄩㄝˋ ㄇㄨˋ)
to flatter the heart and please the eye—beautiful and restful
賞雪(ㄕㄤˇ ㄒㄩㄝˇ)
to enjoy snow scenes
賞識(ㄕㄤˇ ㄕˋ)
to appreciate the virtues in a person or thing; to recognize the worth of a person: 他的辛勞獲得賞識。His services were appreciated.
賞聲(ㄕㄤˇ ㄕㄥ)
the third tone in Chinese phonetics 亦作「上聲」
賞賜(ㄕㄤˇ ㄘˋ)or(ㄕㄤˇ ㄙˋ)
to bestow money or presents on an inferior or junior; gifts or money given as a reward; to award; to grant a reward
賞音(ㄕㄤˇ ㄧㄣ)
to appreciate music
賞玩(ㄕㄤˇ ㄨㄢˊ)
to enjoy or appreciate the sight of; to delight in
賞雨(ㄕㄤˇ ㄩˇ)
to enjoy rainy scenes
賞月(ㄕㄤˇ ㄩㄝˋ)
to enjoy moonlight: 他們正在賞月。They are enjoying moonlight.

【賠】 5791 ㄆㄟˊ peir péi
1. to compensate or indemnify; to make up for a loss due to one's fault; to pay for
2. to offer (an apology)
3. to lose money
賠本(ㄆㄟˊ ㄅㄣˇ)
to lose money in business; to sell at a loss: 他的貨物均賠本出售。All his goods sell at a loss.
賠本生意沒人做(ㄆㄟˊ ㄅㄣˇ ㄕㄥ ㄧˋ ㄇㄟˊ ㄖㄣˊ ㄗㄨㄛˋ)
No one will be interested in doing a losing business.
賠不是(ㄆㄟˊ ㄅㄨˊ ˙ㄕ)
to apologize
賠補(ㄆㄟˊ ㄅㄨˇ)
to compensate and make up for the deficiency
賠不起(ㄆㄟˊ ˙ㄅㄨ ㄑㄧˇ)
cannot afford to pay (for the loss); unable to pay for compensation
賠墊(ㄆㄟˊ ㄉㄧㄢˋ)
to advance money (for another) in making payment
賠了夫人又折兵(ㄆㄟˊ ˙ㄌㄜ ㄈㄨ ㄖㄣˊ ㄧㄡˋ ㄓㄜˊ ㄅㄧㄥ)
to suffer a double loss; to throw the helve after the hatchet
賠累(ㄆㄟˊ ㄌㄟˋ)

〔貝部〕

to get involved in a losing venture

賠禮(ㄆㄟˊ ㄌㄧˇ)
to offer an apology; to apologize

賠光(ㄆㄟˊ ㄍㄨㄤ)
to lose all the capital in a business adventure

賠款(ㄆㄟˊ ㄎㄨㄢˇ)
an indemnity; a compensation; reparations

賠還(ㄆㄟˊ ㄏㄨㄢˊ)
to repay: 他賠還了借款。He repaid the money he had borrowed.

賠錢(ㄆㄟˊ ㄑㄧㄢˊ)
① to make a pecuniary compensation ② to lose money in business 參看「賠本」

賠錢貨(ㄆㄟˊ ㄑㄧㄢˊ ㄏㄨㄛˋ)
daughters(who need dowries but will not bear the family name after marriage)

賠小心(ㄆㄟˊ ㄒㄧㄠˇ ˙ㄒㄧㄣ)
to make apologies; to apologize

賠笑(ㄆㄟˊ ㄒㄧㄠˋ)
to smile obsequiously or apologetically

賠償(ㄆㄟˊ ㄔㄤˊ)
reparation; compensation; indemnity; to recompense; to compensate; to indemnify; to make reparation for; to make amends for; to make good a loss due to one's own fault: 他答應賠償我的損失。He promised to indemnify me for my losses.

賠償費(ㄆㄟˊ ㄔㄤˊ ㄈㄟˋ)
damages

賠償協定(ㄆㄟˊ ㄔㄤˊ ㄒㄧㄝˊ ㄉㄧㄥˋ)
a reparations agreement

賠償損失(ㄆㄟˊ ㄔㄤˊ ㄙㄨㄣˇ ㄕ)
to indemnify; to make good a loss due to one's own fault

賠罪(ㄆㄟˊ ㄗㄨㄟˋ)
to apologize

【賡】 5792
ㄍㄥ geng gēng

to continue; to carry on

賡續(ㄍㄥ ㄒㄩˋ)
to continue

賡酬(ㄍㄥ ㄔㄡˊ)
to write poems to each other as a means of communication

賡颺 or 賡揚(ㄍㄥ ㄧㄤˊ)
to carry on; to continue

賡韻(ㄍㄥ ㄩㄣˋ)
to write a poem in response, using the same rhyme as the one received

【賢】 5793
ㄒㄧㄢˊ shyan xián

1. capable; able; versatile; talented
2. good; worthy; virtuous
3. to admire; to praise; to esteem
4. a term of respectful address to another

賢明(ㄒㄧㄢˊ ㄇㄧㄥˊ)
capable and virtuous: 他是個賢明的君主。He was a capable and virtuous king.

賢達(ㄒㄧㄢˊ ㄉㄚˊ)
wise and virtuous; the social élite

賢德(ㄒㄧㄢˊ ㄉㄜˊ)
good conduct; virtuous

賢弟(ㄒㄧㄢˊ ㄉㄧˋ)
my dear brother(a term of address to a male friend who is younger than oneself)

賢內助(ㄒㄧㄢˊ ㄋㄟˋ ㄓㄨˋ)
a good wife

賢能(ㄒㄧㄢˊ ㄋㄥˊ)
talented and virtuous

賢良(ㄒㄧㄢˊ ㄌㄧㄤˊ)
virtuous; the virtuous

賢良方正(ㄒㄧㄢˊ ㄌㄧㄤˊ ㄈㄤ ㄓㄥˋ)
the selection of proficient literary scholars from the various districts to be presented to the central government—a system started in the Han Dynasty

賢路(ㄒㄧㄢˊ ㄌㄨˋ)
a channel through which worthy men of ability can attain officialdom

賢昆仲(ㄒㄧㄢˊ ㄎㄨㄣ ㄓㄨㄥˋ)
(a polite expression) you and your brother

賢惠 or 賢慧(ㄒㄧㄢˊ ㄏㄨㄟˋ)
(usually said of women) virtuous and intelligent; good and wise

賢妻(ㄒㄧㄢˊ ㄑㄧ)
① a good wife ② my dear wife

賢妻良母(ㄒㄧㄢˊ ㄑㄧ ㄌㄧㄤˊ ㄇㄨˇ)
a dutiful wife and loving mother

賢契(ㄒㄧㄢˊ ㄑㄧˋ)
a polite term of address to one's pupils or children of one's friends

賢倩(ㄒㄧㄢˊ ㄑㄧㄢˋ)
my dear son-in-law

賢相(ㄒㄧㄢˊ ㄒㄧㄤˋ)
a capable and upright prime minister

賢哲(ㄒㄧㄢˊ ㄓㄜˊ)
a person outstanding in virtue and learning

賢者(ㄒㄧㄢˊ ㄓㄜˇ)
men of talents and virtue; the good; the virtuous

賢士(ㄒㄧㄢˊ ㄕˋ)
a person of high moral standing

賢甥(ㄒㄧㄢˊ ㄕㄥ)
my dear nephew

賢淑(ㄒㄧㄢˊ ㄕㄨˊ)
(usually said of women) virtuous and understanding

賢人(ㄒㄧㄢˊ ㄖㄣˊ)
a person of virtue and talents; a worthy man; a worthy person

賢才(ㄒㄧㄢˊ ㄘㄞˊ)
a capable and virtuous person

賢彥(ㄒㄧㄢˊ ㄧㄢˋ)
a virtuous person

賢愚(ㄒㄧㄢˊ ㄩˊ)
the wise and the stupid

【賣】 5794
ㄇㄞˋ may mài

1. to sell
2. to betray; to harm another in order to benefit oneself
3. to show off; to flaunt

賣本事(ㄇㄞˋ ㄅㄣˇ ˙ㄕ)
to show off one's feat, skill, etc.

賣卜(ㄇㄞˋ ㄅㄨˇ)
to make a living as a fortuneteller

賣不了(ㄇㄞˋ ˙ㄅㄨ ㄌㄧㄠˇ) or 賣不出去(ㄇㄞˋ ˙ㄅㄨ ㄔㄨ ㄑㄩˋ)
cannot be sold

賣面子(ㄇㄞˋ ㄇㄧㄢˋ ˙ㄗ)
to do somebody a favor for the sake of one's friendship with a third party, with whom the former is closely related or associated

賣名(ㄇㄞˋ ㄇㄧㄥˊ)or 賣名氣(ㄇㄞˋ ㄇㄧㄥˊ ㄑㄧˋ)
to capitalize on one's reputation or prestige

賣命(ㄇㄞˋ ㄇㄧㄥˋ)
①to work oneself to the bone for somebody ②to die (unworthily) for

賣方(ㄇㄞˋ ㄈㄤ)
the seller

賣風流(ㄇㄞˋ ㄈㄥ ㄌㄧㄡˊ)
to flirt; to act coquettishly

賣獃 or 賣呆(ㄇㄞˋ ㄉㄞ)or 賣傻(ㄇㄞˋ ㄕㄚˇ)
to feign stupidity; to pretend to know nothing

賣力(ㄇㄞˋ ㄌㄧˋ)or 賣力氣(ㄇㄞˋ ㄌㄧˋ ˙ㄑㄧ)
①to work as a laborer ②to work hard willingly

賣臉(ㄇㄞˋ ㄌㄧㄢˇ)
①to try to please someone obsequiously ②(said of a girl) to sell her company but not her body

賣弄(ㄇㄞˋ ㄋㄨㄥˋ)
to flaunt; to show off

賣弄風情(ㄇㄞˋ ㄋㄨㄥˋ ㄈㄥ ㄑㄧㄥˊ)
to flirt and coquet

賣弄口舌(ㄇㄞˋ ㄋㄨㄥˋ ㄎㄡˇ ㄕㄜˊ)
to show off one's glibness in speech or wits

賣膏藥(ㄇㄞˋ ㄍㄠ ㄧㄠˋ)
(literally) to be a mountebank—to make high-sounding statements without sincerity; to make propaganda亦作「賣狗皮膏藥」

賣國(ㄇㄞˋ ㄍㄨㄛˊ)
to betray one's country; sedition or treason

賣國求榮(ㄇㄞˋ ㄍㄨㄛˊ ㄑㄧㄡˊ ㄖㄨㄥˊ)
to betray one's country in exchange for a high position

賣國賊(ㄇㄞˋ ㄍㄨㄛˊ ㄗㄟˊ)
a traitor; one who collaborates with an enemy country

賣乖(ㄇㄞˋ ㄍㄨㄞ)
to show off one's cleverness

賣關子(ㄇㄞˋ ㄍㄨㄢ ˙ㄗ)
(in storytelling) to create suspense by stopping narration when it comes to the most interesting part; to withhold information that the listeners are most eager to know

賣官鬻爵(ㄇㄞˋ ㄍㄨㄢ ㄩˋ ㄐㄩㄝˊ)
to accept bribery and confer official ranks for money

賣空買空(ㄇㄞˋ ㄎㄨㄥ ㄇㄞˇ ㄎㄨㄥ)
to speculate on the stock market; speculation on the stock market

賣價(ㄇㄞˋ ㄐㄧㄚˋ)
the selling price

賣劍買牛(ㄇㄞˋ ㄐㄧㄢˋ ㄇㄞˇ ㄋㄧㄡˊ)or 賣刀買犢(ㄇㄞˋ ㄉㄠ ㄇㄞˇ ㄉㄨˊ)
(said of an official) to bring peace and diligence to a lawless area

賣勁(ㄇㄞˋ ㄐㄧㄣˋ)or 賣勁兒(ㄇㄞˋ ㄐㄧㄜˋㄦ)
to do one's utmost without complaining; to exert all one's strength

賣絕(ㄇㄞˋ ㄐㄩㄝˊ)or 賣斷(ㄇㄞˋ ㄉㄨㄢˋ)
to sell outright—without any chance of buying back

賣妻鬻子(ㄇㄞˋ ㄑㄧ ㄩˋ ㄗˇ)
to sell one's wife and sons (as in time of famine)

賣契(ㄇㄞˋ ㄑㄧˋ)
a contract for selling something; a contract of sale

賣俏(ㄇㄞˋ ㄑㄧㄠˋ)
to flirt or coquet

賣錢(ㄇㄞˋ ㄑㄧㄢˊ)
to sell for money

賣笑(ㄇㄞˋ ㄒㄧㄠˋ)
to work as a prostitute

賣招牌(ㄇㄞˋ ㄓㄠ ˙ㄆㄞ)
to sell some merchandise on the strength of its well-known brand name

賣主(ㄇㄞˋ ㄓㄨˇ)
the seller

賣唱(ㄇㄞˋ ㄔㄤˋ)
to live on singing

賣春(ㄇㄞˋ ㄔㄨㄣ)
prostitution

賣舌(ㄇㄞˋ ㄕㄜˊ)
to make sensational statements for the sake of publicity

賣身(ㄇㄞˋ ㄕㄣ)
①to sell oneself as a slave ②to become a prostitute; to prostitute

賣身投靠(ㄇㄞˋ ㄕㄣ ㄊㄡˊ ㄎㄠˋ)
to join the enemy camp for sheer profit

賣身契(ㄇㄞˋ ㄕㄣ ㄑㄧˋ)
a written contract by which one sells oneself or a member of one's family

賣人情(ㄇㄞˋ ㄖㄣˊ ㄑㄧㄥˊ)
to do someone a favor for personal consideration

賣座(ㄇㄞˋ ㄗㄨㄛˋ)
①(said of a theater, etc.) to draw large audiences ②(said of a restaurant, etc.) to attract large numbers of customers

賣恩(ㄇㄞˋ ㄣ)
to do someone a favor with a view to earning his gratitude

賣藝(ㄇㄞˋ ㄧˋ)
to earn a living by entertaining others with one's skills or stunts

賣藝人(ㄇㄞˋ ㄧˋ ㄖㄣˊ)
acrobats, jugglers, etc.

賣野人頭(ㄇㄞˋ ㄧㄝˇ ㄖㄣˊ ㄊㄡˊ)
(Shanghai dialect) to exaggerate

賣友(ㄇㄞˋ ㄧㄡˇ)
to betray a friend: 吾人不能賣友。We shouldn't betray our friends.

賣淫(ㄇㄞˋ ㄧㄣˊ)
to earn a living as a prostitute

賣完(ㄇㄞˋ ㄨㄢˊ)or 賣光(ㄇㄞˋ ㄍㄨㄤ)
sold out: 我們大號的貨品完全賣完了。We are sold out of large sizes.

賣文(ㄇㄞˋ ㄨㄣˊ)or 賣文爲生(ㄇㄞˋ ㄨㄣˊ ㄨㄟˊ ㄕㄥ)
to make a living by writing; to make a living from literary work

【賤】 5795 ㄐㄧㄢˋ jiann jiàn

1. cheap; inexpensive; low cost
2. lowly; humble; inferior in position
3. low-down; base; ignoble; despicable
4. to slight; to look down on
5. my, a self-derogatory expression
6. a Chinese family name

賤買貴賣(ㄐㄧㄢˋ ㄇㄞˇ ㄍㄨㄟˋ ㄇㄞˋ)
to buy cheap and sell high

賤買賤賣(ㄐㄧㄢˋ ㄇㄞˇ ㄐㄧㄢˋ ㄇㄞˋ)
to buy and sell at low prices

賤內(ㄐㄧㄢˋ ㄋㄟˋ)

〔貝部〕

my humble wife

賤骨頭(ㄐㄧㄢˋ ㄍㄨˇ ·ㄊㄡ)
a despicable fellow; a good-for-nothing

賤貨(ㄐㄧㄢˋ ㄏㄨㄛˋ)
①(a term of revile) a tramp; a slut ②worthless goods

賤伎(ㄐㄧㄢˋ ㄐㄧˋ)
inferior arts; lowly arts

賤價(ㄐㄧㄢˋ ㄐㄧㄚˋ)
a low price; low-priced

賤荊(ㄐㄧㄢˋ ㄐㄧㄥ)
my humble wife

賤妾(ㄐㄧㄢˋ ㄑㄧㄝˋ)
a self-reference among women of ancient times

賤軀(ㄐㄧㄢˋ ㄑㄩ)
my body; my health condition

賤息(ㄐㄧㄢˋ ㄒㄧˊ)
my humble son

賤行(ㄐㄧㄢˋ ㄒㄧㄥˋ)
evil conduct or ways

賤室(ㄐㄧㄢˋ ㄕˋ)
my humble wife

賤人(ㄐㄧㄢˋ ㄖㄣˊ)
(a term of revile used in old novels) a slut or tramp

賤儒(ㄐㄧㄢˋ ㄖㄨˊ)
a pedant

賤子(ㄐㄧㄢˋ ㄗˇ)
(archaic) a polite way of referring to oneself

賤族(ㄐㄧㄢˋ ㄗㄨˊ)
an inferior race or tribe

賤業(ㄐㄧㄢˋ ㄧㄝˋ)
a lowly or mean occupation; a low-down business (now usually referring to prostitution)

賤恙(ㄐㄧㄢˋ ㄧㄤˋ)
(a polite expression) my illness

賤物(ㄐㄧㄢˋ ㄨˋ)
a cheap and worthless thing

【賦】 5796 ㄈㄨˋ fuh fù

1. a tax; revenue
2. troops; the army; military levies
3. to bestow; to give
4. natural endowments or gifts
5. to spread; to diffuse
6. to compose or sing (especially poems)
7. one of the Chinese literary forms akin to poetry

賦稟(ㄈㄨˋ ㄅㄧㄥˇ)
natural endowments or gifts

賦斂(ㄈㄨˋ ㄌㄧㄢˋ)
to levy taxes

賦歸(ㄈㄨˋ ㄍㄨㄟ)
to return home

賦貢(ㄈㄨˋ ㄍㄨㄥˋ)
to pay tribute or levy

賦課(ㄈㄨˋ ㄎㄜˋ)
land tax, farm tax, excise tax, etc.

賦閒(ㄈㄨˋ ㄒㄧㄢˊ)
to be out of employment; jobless

賦性(ㄈㄨˋ ㄒㄧㄥˋ)
one's natural disposition or temperament

賦詩(ㄈㄨˋ ㄕ)
to compose or sing poems

賦稅(ㄈㄨˋ ㄕㄨㄟˋ)
farm tax and excise tax

賦額(ㄈㄨˋ ㄜˊ)
the prescribed amount of farm revenue

賦役(ㄈㄨˋ ㄧˋ)
a general name of all national taxes, revenues, levies, compulsory service, etc.

賦有(ㄈㄨˋ ㄧㄡˇ)
endowed or gifted with

賦予 or 賦與(ㄈㄨˋ ㄩˇ)
to give; to bestow; to endow

【質】 5797 1. ㄓˊ jyr zhí

1. matters; substances; elements
2. one's disposition or temperament; qualities
3. simple; plain
4. to question
5. to confront

質朴 or 質樸(ㄓˊ ㄆㄨˊ)
simple and unadorned

質地(ㄓˊ ㄉㄧˋ)
① quality of something ② one's disposition or endowments ③ material of piece goods

質點(ㄓˊ ㄉㄧㄢˇ)
(physics) a particle

質料(ㄓˊ ㄌㄧㄠˋ)
quality; raw materials: 這套衣服的質料很好。This suit is made of very good material.

質量(ㄓˊ ㄌㄧㄤˋ)
①(physics) mass ② quality

質量不滅律(ㄓˊ ㄌㄧㄤˋ ㄅㄨˋ ㄇㄧㄝˋ ㄌㄩˋ)
the law of conservation of mass

質詢(ㄓˊ ㄒㄩㄣˊ)
to interpellate; interpellation; to ask for an explanation

質直(ㄓˊ ㄓˊ)
simple and honest; solid and straightforward

質成(ㄓˊ ㄔㄥˊ)
to ask a third party to arbitrate a dispute, etc.

質數(ㄓˊ ㄕㄨˋ)
a prime number亦作「素數」

質讓(ㄓˊ ㄖㄤˋ)
to admonish bluntly

質子(ㄓˊ ㄗˇ)
(physics) a proton

質疑(ㄓˊ ㄧˊ)
to ask questions about something with which one is not familiar; to question; to query

質言(ㄓˊ ㄧㄢˊ)
an honest talk; a plain talk

質言之(ㄓˊ ㄧㄢˊ ㄓ)
to put it in plain language; in short; in other words

質問(ㄓˊ ㄨㄣˋ)
① to interrogate ② to raise questions in order to resolve one's doubt

【質】 5797 2. ㄓˋ jyh zhì

1. to pawn
2. a pledge; a hostage

質押(ㄓˋ ㄧㄚ)
to assign something as security under an arrangement; to mortgage

【賬】 5798 (帳) ㄓㄤˋ janq zhàng

1. accounts
2. debts
3. credits; loans; bills

賬簿(ㄓㄤˋ ㄅㄨˋ)
accounts; account books

賬目(ㄓㄤˋ ㄇㄨˋ)
accounts; details or items of accounts: 這賬目有條不紊。The accounts were perfectly in order.

賬房(ㄓㄤˋ ㄈㄤˊ)
① a cashier's office ② a cashier; a teller; a treasurer

賬單(ㄓㄤˋ ㄉㄢ)
bills; invoices: 我有許多賬單需要付款。I have many bills to pay.
賬籍(ㄓㄤˋ ㄐㄧˊ)
accounts; books
賬務(ㄓㄤˋ ㄨˋ)
affairs concerning accounts

九畫

【賭】 5799
ㄉㄨˇ duu dǔ
1. to gamble; to bet; to wager
2. to compete
3. to swear
賭博(ㄉㄨˇ ㄅㄛˊ)
to gamble; gambling: 他賭博輸去了一半財產。He has gambled away half his wealth.
賭本(ㄉㄨˇ ㄅㄣˇ)
money to gamble with
賭品(ㄉㄨˇ ㄆㄧㄣˇ)
one's manners, conduct and honesty, or the absence of it, manifested in gambling
賭命(ㄉㄨˇ ㄇㄧㄥˋ)
to gamble on one's life—to do something extremely dangerous
賭犯(ㄉㄨˇ ㄈㄢˋ)
a person guilty of gambling
賭東兒(ㄉㄨˇ ㄉㄨㄥㄦ)
to bet on something in which a loser has to pay a forfeit
賭徒(ㄉㄨˇ ㄊㄨˊ)
a gambler: 那賭徒賭掉家產。That gambler gambled away his fortune.
賭個輸贏(ㄉㄨˇ ·ㄍㄜ ㄕㄨ ㄧㄥˊ)
to bet or wager
賭鬼(ㄉㄨˇ ㄍㄨㄟˇ)
a congenital gambler
賭棍(ㄉㄨˇ ㄍㄨㄣˋ)
a person who makes a living as a gambler
賭局(ㄉㄨˇ ㄐㄩˊ)
a gambling game; a gambling gathering
賭具(ㄉㄨˇ ㄐㄩˋ)
things used in gambling—as cards, dice, mah-jong, etc.
賭氣(ㄉㄨˇ ㄑㄧˋ)
to do something out of spite (or in a rage)
賭錢(ㄉㄨˇ ㄑㄧㄢˊ)
to gamble (for money)
賭債(ㄉㄨˇ ㄓㄞˋ)or 賭賬(ㄉㄨˇ ㄓㄤˋ)
a gambling debt; a debt of honor
賭咒(ㄉㄨˇ ㄓㄡˋ)
to make an oath; to swear: 他賭咒。He swore an oath.
賭注(ㄉㄨˇ ㄓㄨˋ)
stakes: 他下很大的賭注。He played for high stakes.
賭場(ㄉㄨˇ ㄔㄤˇ)
a gambling joint; a gambling den or house
賭誓(ㄉㄨˇ ㄕˋ)
to make an oath; to vow: 他賭誓絕不再離家。He vowed never to leave home again.
賭輸(ㄉㄨˇ ㄕㄨ)
to lose in gambling; to lose a wager
賭賽(ㄉㄨˇ ㄙㄞˋ)
to compete or contest in order to determine the winner
賭友(ㄉㄨˇ ㄧㄡˇ)
gambling companions; gambling company

【賴】 5800
ㄌㄞˋ lay lài
1. to rely on; to depend on
2. to accuse without grounds or evidence; to put the blame on somebody else
3. to repudiate (a debt); to disavow; to deny something which one has said or done
4. to postpone or procrastinate intentionally
5. no good; poor; bad
6. lazy
7. a Chinese family name
賴比瑞亞(ㄌㄞˋ ㄅㄧˇ ㄖㄨㄟˋ ㄧㄚˋ)
Liberia
賴不掉(ㄌㄞˋ ·ㄅㄨ ㄉㄧㄠˋ)
cannot be denied or repudiated
賴皮(ㄌㄞˋ ㄆㄧˊ)
①a person without any sense of shame; a rogue ②shameless: 這男孩眞賴皮。The boy is thoroughly shameless.
賴得一乾二淨(ㄌㄞˋ ·ㄉㄜ ㄧˋ ㄍㄢ ㄦˋ ㄐㄧㄥˋ)
to deny or repudiate completely
賴婚(ㄌㄞˋ ㄏㄨㄣ)
to break or repudiate a marriage contract
賴學(ㄌㄞˋ ㄒㄩㄝˊ)
to play truant; to evade study at school: 他又賴學了。He played truant again.
賴債(ㄌㄞˋ ㄓㄞˋ)
to repudiate a debt: 那商人賴債。The merchant repudiated a debt.
賴賬(ㄌㄞˋ ㄓㄤˋ)
①to repudiate accounts ②to go back on one's word: 他老是賴賬。He goes back on his word all the time.
賴人(ㄌㄞˋ ㄖㄣˊ)
①to impute (a fault, etc.) to another ②to rely on somebody
賴子(ㄌㄞˋ ·ㄗ)
a rogue 亦作「無賴」
賴索托王國(ㄌㄞˋ ㄙㄨㄛˇ ㄊㄨㄛ ㄨㄤˊ ㄍㄨㄛˊ)
the Kingdom of Lesotho
賴以爲生(ㄌㄞˋ ㄧˇ ㄨㄟˊ ㄕㄥ)
to rely on something or someone for a living

十畫

【賺】 5801
ㄓㄨㄢˋ juann zhuàn
1. to earn; to make money; to gain
2. to cheat; to deceive
賺頭(兒)(ㄓㄨㄢˋ ·ㄊㄡ(ㄦ))
something to gain; a profit: 這一行生意賺頭不大。The profits in this business are not large.
賺錢(ㄓㄨㄢˋ ㄑㄧㄢˊ)
to earn money; to make a profit: 他一天賺錢五千元。He earns 5,000 dollars a day.

【賻】 5802
ㄈㄨˋ fuh fù
to help another with money in financing a funeral
賻錢(ㄈㄨˋ ㄑㄧㄢˊ)
money for helping another finance a funeral
賻贈(ㄈㄨˋ ㄗㄥˋ)
donations to another for financing a funeral
賻贈香儀(ㄈㄨˋ ㄗㄥˋ ㄒㄧㄤ ㄧˊ)
to give incense money for funeral expenses
賻儀(ㄈㄨˋ ㄧˊ)
money presented to another

〔貝部〕

〔貝部〕

for financing a funeral

【購】 5803 ㄍㄡˋ gow gòu
to buy; to purchase
購備(ㄍㄡˋ ㄅㄟˋ)
to purchase or buy beforehand (or in preparation)
購辦(ㄍㄡˋ ㄅㄢˋ)
to purchase; to buy
購買(ㄍㄡˋ ㄇㄞˇ)
to buy: 我爲她購買一頂新帽子。I bought her a new hat.
購買力(ㄍㄡˋ ㄇㄞˇ ㄌㄧˋ)
purchasing power
購買慾(ㄍㄡˋ ㄇㄞˇ ㄩˋ)
the desire to buy
購料(ㄍㄡˋ ㄌㄧㄠˋ)
to buy materials or supplies
購求(ㄍㄡˋ ㄑㄧㄡˊ)
① to offer a reward for the arrest of a person ② to offer money for something which cannot be readily bought on the market, as antiques, rare objects, etc.
購置(ㄍㄡˋ ㄓˋ)
to purchase; to buy
購物(ㄍㄡˋ ㄨˋ)
to do one's shopping; to go shopping: 他和他太太出去購物。He went out shopping with his wife.
購用(ㄍㄡˋ ㄩㄥˋ)
to buy for use

【賽】 5804 ㄙㄞˋ say sài
1. to compete; to contest; to rival; to contend for superiority
2. a race; a tournament; a match; a game
3. to surpass
4. (now rarely) an ancient sacrifice
5. a Chinese family name
賽跑(ㄙㄞˋ ㄆㄠˇ)
to run a race on foot; a foot race: 誰贏了賽跑? Who won the foot race?
賽普勒斯(ㄙㄞˋ ㄆㄨˇ ㄌㄜˋ ㄙ)
Cyprus, an island republic in the Mediterranean
賽馬(ㄙㄞˋ ㄇㄚˇ)
to race horses; a horse race
賽馬場(ㄙㄞˋ ㄇㄚˇ ㄔㄤˇ)
a race course (or ground)
賽璐珞(ㄙㄞˋ ㄌㄨˋ ㄌㄨㄛˋ)
celluloid
賽龍船(ㄙㄞˋ ㄌㄨㄥˊ ㄔㄨㄢˊ)
a dragon-boat regatta (on Poets' Day)
賽狗(ㄙㄞˋ ㄍㄡˇ)
to race dogs; a dog race
賽過(ㄙㄞˋ ·ㄍㄨㄛ)
to surpass; to be better than
賽會(ㄙㄞˋ ㄏㄨㄟˋ)
① a procession on a religious festival; a carnival ② an exhibition; a display; an exposition
賽金花(ㄙㄞˋ ㄐㄧㄣ ㄏㄨㄚ)
Sai Chin-hua, a famous patriotic courtesan (1875-1937) who allegedly saved many civilian lives when China was invaded by eight powers in the wake of the Boxer Rebellion
賽球(ㄙㄞˋ ㄑㄧㄡˊ)
a ball game
賽夏族(ㄙㄞˋ ㄒㄧㄚˋ ㄗㄨˊ)
the Saishet tribe (one of the aborigine tribes in Taiwan)
賽珍珠(ㄙㄞˋ ㄓㄣ ㄓㄨ)
Mrs. Pearl S. Buck (1892-1973), American authoress
賽車(ㄙㄞˋ ㄔㄜ)
a car race; to race cars
賽神(ㄙㄞˋ ㄕㄣˊ)
to offer sacrifices to thank gods

【賸】 5805 (剩) ㄕㄥˋ shenq shèng
1. a surplus; an overplus
2. remnants; remains; residues
3. superfluous
賸下(ㄕㄥˋ ㄒㄧㄚˋ)
to leave behind; to be left over
賸餘(ㄕㄥˋ ㄩˊ)
to leave in surplus; remnants
賸餘價值(ㄕㄥˋ ㄩˊ ㄐㄧㄚˋ ㄓˊ)
surplus value
賸餘物資(ㄕㄥˋ ㄩˊ ㄨˋ ㄗ)
a surplus; surplus goods
賸語(ㄕㄥˋ ㄩˇ)
superfluous words

十一畫

【贄】 5806 ㄓˋ jyh zhì
1. presents given at the first meeting
2. gifts to a superior
贄見(ㄓˋ ㄐㄧㄢˋ)
to bring gifts along and request an audience
贄見禮(ㄓˋ ㄐㄧㄢˋ ㄌㄧˇ)
presents offered at calling on someone
贄敬(ㄓˋ ㄐㄧㄥˋ)
money offered to a teacher or tutor
贄儀(ㄓˋ ㄧˊ)
ceremonial presents; presents of homage

【贅】 5807 ㄓㄨㄟˋ juey zhuì
1. useless; superfluous; redundant
2. repetition; to repeat; repetitious
3. to follow around, as children
4. to be burdensome
5. to pawn things for money
6. to meet; to congregate
7. a son-in-law who takes the place of a son in his wife's parental family which is lacking for an heir
贅筆(ㄓㄨㄟˋ ㄅㄧˇ)
a superfluous touch or stroke
贅瘤(ㄓㄨㄟˋ ㄌㄧㄡˊ)
① a wen; an excrescence ② something useless or superfluous
贅及(ㄓㄨㄟˋ ㄐㄧˊ)
① to add to; to append to ② a postscript
贅壻 or 贅婿(ㄓㄨㄟˋ ㄒㄩˋ)
a son-in-law who takes the place of a son and lives in his wife's home, usually an heirless family
贅述(ㄓㄨㄟˋ ㄕㄨˋ)
a repetitious or superfluous statement; verbosity; redundance: 不必贅述。It's unnecessary to make a superfluous statement.
贅子(ㄓㄨㄟˋ ㄗˇ)
(in ancient China) to sell one's son to another as a slave
贅詞(ㄓㄨㄟˋ ㄘˊ)
repetitious or superfluous words; redundance
贅疣(ㄓㄨㄟˋ ㄧㄡˊ)
a wen; an excrescence: 這只

是贅疣而已。This is merely a wen.
贅言(ㄓㄨㄟˋ ㄧㄢˊ)
verbosity; repetitious or superfluous statements, words, etc.

十二畫

【贗】 5808
(贋) ㄧㄢˋ yann yàn
a counterfeit; a sham; a fake; bogus; spurious; forged
贗本(ㄧㄢˋ ㄅㄣˇ)
(said of paintings, rare editions of a book, etc.) an imitation; a phony; a sham; a fake: 牆上的畫是贗本。The painting on the wall is an imitation.
贗品(ㄧㄢˋ ㄆㄧㄣˇ)
a counterfeit; an imitation; a phony; a sham; a fake; a forgery
贗鼎(ㄧㄢˋ ㄉㄧㄥˇ)
a counterfeit; an imitation; a sham; a phony; a fake—from the story of a fake tripod sent by a kingdom as a tribute to another kingdom

【贈】 5809
ㄗㄥˋ tzenq zèng
to send (gifts); to confer or bestow (titles); to give
贈別(ㄗㄥˋ ㄅㄧㄝˊ)
to wish (a leaving person) well with gifts or writings
贈品(ㄗㄥˋ ㄆㄧㄣˇ)
a gift; a present
贈賻(ㄗㄥˋ ㄈㄨˋ)
to contribute to funeral expenses
贈答(ㄗㄥˋ ㄉㄚˊ)
to present each other with gifts, poems, etc.
贈給(ㄗㄥˋ ㄍㄟˇ)
to present; to confer; to bestow; to give; to donate: 我贈給她一本集郵冊。I presented an album to her.
贈款(ㄗㄥˋ ㄎㄨㄢˇ)
to present money as a gift; a grant
贈金(ㄗㄥˋ ㄐㄧㄣ)
to give a cash gift; a cash gift
贈券(ㄗㄥˋ ㄑㄩㄢˋ)
a gift coupon
贈序(ㄗㄥˋ ㄒㄩˋ)
a farewell message for a departing person
贈送(ㄗㄥˋ ㄙㄨㄥˋ)
to present; to give; to donate
贈言(ㄗㄥˋ ㄧㄢˊ)
words of advice
贈遺(ㄗㄥˋ ㄨㄟˋ)
to present; to give; to donate; to bequeath
贈與(ㄗㄥˋ ㄩˇ)
to present; to give; to donate
贈閱(ㄗㄥˋ ㄩㄝˋ)
(said of publications) given free of charge; given as a compliment of the publisher or author

【賾】 5810
ㄗㄜˊ tzer zé
deep; profound; abstruse

【贊】 5811
ㄗㄢˋ tzann zàn
1. to assist; to aid; to help; to support; to back
2. to praise; to commend; to exalt; to glorify; to extol; to eulogize
贊不絕口(ㄗㄢˋ ˙ㄅㄨ ㄐㄩㄝˊ ㄎㄡˇ)
to praise profusely; to heap praises on...
贊美(ㄗㄢˋ ㄇㄟˇ)
to praise; to extol; to exalt; to glorify
贊歎(ㄗㄢˋ ㄊㄢˋ)
to exclaim in praise; to gasp with admiration
贊同(ㄗㄢˋ ㄊㄨㄥˊ)
to consent to; to approve of; to agree; to endorse: 我贊同你的看法。I agree with you.
贊理(ㄗㄢˋ ㄌㄧˇ)
to help manage
贊禮(ㄗㄢˋ ㄌㄧˇ)
① to direct the proceeding (as the master of ceremonies) ② the master of ceremonies (a government post in ancient times)
贊襄(ㄗㄢˋ ㄒㄧㄤ)
to assist; to aid: 我以金錢贊襄他。I aid him with money.
贊饗(ㄗㄢˋ ㄒㄧㄤˇ)
a message dedicated to a deity
贊許(ㄗㄢˋ ㄒㄩˇ)
to approve of: 新歌劇大受贊許。The new opera is highly approved of.
贊助(ㄗㄢˋ ㄓㄨˋ)
to sponsor; to patronize; support
贊助人(ㄗㄢˋ ㄓㄨˋ ㄖㄣˊ)
a patron; a sponsor
贊成(ㄗㄢˋ ㄔㄥˊ)
to agree to; to be in favor of; to endorse; to support: 他立刻贊成這計劃。He agreed to this plan immediately.
贊賞(ㄗㄢˋ ㄕㄤˇ)
to commend; to praise; to extol; to admire
贊翼(ㄗㄢˋ ㄧˋ)
to assist; to aid
贊揚(ㄗㄢˋ ㄧㄤˊ)
to exalt; to glorify; to extol; to praise; to commend; commendation: 他們贊揚他的勇敢。They exalted his bravery.

【贇】 5812
ㄩㄣ iun yūn
fine; pleasant; agreeable

十三畫

【贍】 5813
ㄕㄢˋ shann shàn
1. to provide; to supply
2. abundance; plenty; adequate
贍恤(ㄕㄢˋ ㄒㄩˋ)
to contribute money to charity
贍足(ㄕㄢˋ ㄗㄨˊ)
abundant; plenty
贍養(ㄕㄢˋ ㄧㄤˇ)
to provide with means of support; to support: 他工作以贍養家小。He is working to support his family.
贍養費(ㄕㄢˋ ㄧㄤˇ ㄈㄟˋ)
alimony
贍養父母(ㄕㄢˋ ㄧㄤˇ ㄈㄨˋ ㄇㄨˇ)
to support one's parents

【贏】 5814
ㄧㄥˊ yng yíng
1. to win; to beat
2. gains; profits
贏得(ㄧㄥˊ ˙ㄉㄜ)
to win (honor, a privilege, etc.)
贏利(ㄧㄥˊ ㄌㄧˋ)
profits; gains: 這一行贏利不大。The profits in this busi-

〔貝部〕

ness are not large.
贏家(ㄧㄥˊ ㄐㄧㄚ)
the winner
贏錢(ㄧㄥˊ ㄑㄧㄢˊ)
to win money by gambling

十四畫

【贓】 5815 ㄗㄤ tzang zāng
1. bribes; to bribe
2. stolen goods; loot; booty; plunder; spoils
贓品(ㄗㄤ ㄆㄧㄣˇ)
stolen goods; plunder; loot; booty: 強盜在分配贓品。The robbers share the plunder.
贓官(ㄗㄤ ㄍㄨㄢ)
a corrupt official
贓款(ㄗㄤ ㄎㄨㄢˇ)
money acquired illicitly
贓證(ㄗㄤ ㄓㄥˋ)
plunder as evidence of theft or graft
贓物(ㄗㄤ ㄨˋ)
stolen goods; plunder; booty; loot; spoils; goods obtained illicitly

【贐】 5816 ㄐㄧㄣˋ jinn jìn
a farewell present
贐儀(ㄐㄧㄣˋ ㄧˊ)
a farewell present

【贒】 5817 (賢) ㄒㄧㄢˊ shyan xián
wise; sagacious

十五畫

【贖】 5818 ㄕㄨˊ shwu shú
1. to redeem; to ransom
2. (now rarely) to buy
3. to atone for; to expiate
贖命(ㄕㄨˊ ㄇㄧㄥˋ)
to save one from death penalty by a payment
贖當(ㄕㄨˊ ㄉㄤˋ)
to redeem pawned articles
贖款(ㄕㄨˊ ㄎㄨㄢˇ)
a ransom
贖回(ㄕㄨˊ ㄏㄨㄟˊ)
to recover by paying money; to redeem; to ransom: 他贖回抵押品。He redeemed his mortgage.
贖金(ㄕㄨˊ ㄐㄧㄣ)or 贖價(ㄕㄨˊ ㄐㄧㄚˋ)
a ransom
贖刑(ㄕㄨˊ ㄒㄧㄥˊ)
to buy freedom from punishment
贖出(ㄕㄨˊ ㄔㄨ)
to get back from pawn; to redeem
贖身(ㄕㄨˊ ㄕㄣ)
to buy freedom (from slavery, prostitution, captivity, etc.)
贖罪(ㄕㄨˊ ㄗㄨㄟˋ)
① to atone for a sin; to expiate a sin ② to buy freedom from punishment ③ (Christianity) redemption
贖罪券(ㄕㄨˊ ㄗㄨㄟˋ ㄑㄩㄢˋ)
papal indulgence (proclaimed by Pope Leo X)

【贗】 5819 (贋) ㄧㄢˋ yann yàn
counterfeit; bogus

十七畫

【贛】 5820 ㄍㄢˋ gann gàn
1. an alternative name of Kiangsi Province
2. a river in Kiangsi Province
3. a county in Kiangsi Province
贛江(ㄍㄢˋ ㄐㄧㄤ)
Kan River in Kiangsi Province
贛縣(ㄍㄢˋ ㄒㄧㄢˋ)
name of a county in Kiangsi Province

赤部
ㄔˋ chyh chì

【赤】 5821 ㄔˋ chyh chì
1. red
2. bare; naked
3. sincere; loyal; single-hearted
赤膊(ㄔˋ ㄅㄛˊ)or 赤背(ㄔˋ ㄅㄟˋ)
with the upper half of the body bared; naked to the waist
赤壁(ㄔˋ ㄅㄧˋ)
the Red Cliff (name of a cliff in Hupeh over the Yangtze River made famous by a major battle during the Epoch of the Three Kingdoms, and by a number of literary works)
赤壁之戰(ㄔˋ ㄅㄧˋ ㄓ ㄓㄢˋ)
a major battle fought at the Red Cliff(赤壁) during the Epoch of the Three Kingdoms
赤貧(ㄔˋ ㄆㄧㄣˊ)
extreme poverty; abject poverty; utterly destitute
赤貧如洗(ㄔˋ ㄆㄧㄣˊ ㄖㄨˊ ㄒㄧˇ)
in extreme poverty
赤眉(ㄔˋ ㄇㄟˊ)
a party of bandits rampant toward the end of the Western Han Dynasty (206 B.C.—8 A.D.)
赤道(ㄔˋ ㄉㄠˋ)
① the equator ② (astronomy) the celestial equator
赤道儀(ㄔˋ ㄉㄠˋ ㄧˊ)
an equatorial
赤膽(ㄔˋ ㄉㄢˇ)
sincere loyalty
赤膽忠心(ㄔˋ ㄉㄢˇ ㄓㄨㄥ ㄒㄧㄣ)
utter devotion
赤黨(ㄔˋ ㄉㄤˇ)
the Communist Party 亦作「共產黨」
赤帝(ㄔˋ ㄉㄧˋ)
the god of the south
赤地千里(ㄔˋ ㄉㄧˋ ㄑㄧㄢ ㄌㄧˇ)
barren land extending over thousands of miles
赤塔(ㄔˋ ㄊㄚˇ)
Chita, a city in Siberia
赤鐵礦(ㄔˋ ㄊㄧㄝˇ ㄎㄨㄤˋ)
hematite
赤條條(ㄔˋ ㄊㄧㄠˊ ㄊㄧㄠˊ)
stark naked
赤條精光(ㄔˋ ㄊㄧㄠˊ ㄐㄧㄥ ㄍㄨㄤ)
stark naked
赤土(ㄔˋ ㄊㄨˇ)
land made barren by severe drought
赤兔(ㄔˋ ㄊㄨˋ)
name of a renowned swift horse
赤銅(ㄔˋ ㄊㄨㄥˊ)
the alloy of copper and gold
赤銅鑛(ㄔˋ ㄊㄨㄥˊ ㄎㄨㄤˋ)
cuprite
赤銅器時代(ㄔˋ ㄊㄨㄥˊ ㄑㄧˋ ㄕˊ ㄉㄞˋ)

the Bronze Age
赤痢(ㄔˋ ㄌㄧˋ)
dysentery characterized by blood in the stool
赤燐(ㄔˋ ㄌㄧㄣˊ)
red phosphorus
赤裸裸(ㄔˋ ㄌㄨㄛˇ ㄌㄨㄛˇ)
① stark naked; naked ② frank; plain; unadorned: 這事件是個赤裸裸的事實。The matter is a plain truth.
赤口白舌(ㄔˋ ㄎㄡˇ ㄅㄞˊ ㄕㄜˊ)
inauspicious remarks; unlucky words
赤口毒舌(ㄔˋ ㄎㄡˇ ㄉㄨˊ ㄕㄜˊ)
① a sharp tongue ② to slander venomously
赤崁樓(ㄔˋ ㄎㄢˇ ㄌㄡˊ)
Fort Providentia (at Tainan, Taiwan, from which the Dutch ruled Taiwan till they were ousted by Koxinga, 國姓爺 or 鄭成功, in the 17th century)
赤化(ㄔˋ ㄏㄨㄚˋ)
to sovietize; to communize: 越南被赤化了。Vietnam was communized.
赤禍(ㄔˋ ㄏㄨㄛˋ)
the calamities brought about by Communism
赤脚(ㄔˋ ㄐㄧㄠˇ)
① bare feet ② barefooted
赤脚大仙(ㄔˋ ㄐㄧㄠˇ ㄉㄚˋ ㄒㄧㄢ)
the barefooted immortal, a reference to Emperor Jen Tzung (仁宗) of the Northern Sung Dynasty
赤金(ㄔˋ ㄐㄧㄣ)
① deep-colored gold ② copper
赤經(ㄔˋ ㄐㄧㄥ)
(astronomy) right ascension
赤鉛礦(ㄔˋ ㄑㄧㄢ ㄎㄨㄤˋ)
crocoite
赤血球(ㄔˋ ㄒㄧㄝˇ ㄑㄧㄡˊ)
red blood cells; red blood corpuscles; erythrocytes
赤縣神州(ㄔˋ ㄒㄧㄢˋ ㄕㄣˊ ㄓㄡ)
China (an ancient name)
赤心(ㄔˋ ㄒㄧㄣ)
sincere loyalty
赤墀(ㄔˋ ㄔˊ)
(in a Chinese palace-style building) the yard between the main hall and the steps
赤城(ㄔˋ ㄔㄥˊ)
name of a county in Chahar Province
赤誠(ㄔˋ ㄔㄥˊ)
sincerity; loyal; upright
赤誠待人(ㄔˋ ㄔㄥˊ ㄉㄞˋ ㄖㄣˊ)
to treat people with absolute sincerity
赤舌燒城(ㄔˋ ㄕㄜˊ ㄕㄠ ㄔㄥˊ)
A slanderous tongue can burn up a city.
赤手(ㄔˋ ㄕㄡˇ)or 赤手空拳(ㄔˋ ㄕㄡˇ ㄎㄨㄥ ㄑㄩㄢˊ)
① bare hands ② barehanded
赤身露體(ㄔˋ ㄕㄣ ㄌㄨˋ ㄊㄧˇ)
stark naked
赤繩繫足(ㄔˋ ㄕㄥˊ ㄒㄧˋ ㄗㄨˊ)
to bind the feet with a red rope—to be united in wedlock
赤日(ㄔˋ ㄖˋ)
the burning sun; the scorching sun
赤子(ㄔˋ ㄗˇ)
① a newborn baby; an infant ② (figuratively) a ruler's subjects
赤子之心(ㄔˋ ㄗˇ ㄓ ㄒㄧㄣ)
(literally) a child's heart—man's natural kindness
赤字(ㄔˋ ㄗˋ)
the red (in bookkeeping); a deficit; a loss
赤幘(ㄔˋ ㄗㄜˊ)
cloth for binding the hair used by military officers in ancient times
赤足(ㄔˋ ㄗㄨˊ)
① barefooted ② bare feet 參看「赤脚」: 我看到他赤足跑步。I saw him running with bare feet.
赤色(ㄔˋ ㄙㄜˋ)
Red; Communist; Bolshevist
赤色分子(ㄔˋ ㄙㄜˋ ㄈㄣˋ ㄗˇ)
Communists; Radicals
赤色國際(ㄔˋ ㄙㄜˋ ㄍㄨㄛˊ ㄐㄧˋ)
the Third International
赤素馨(ㄔˋ ㄙㄨˋ ㄒㄧㄣ)
frangipani
赤俄(ㄔˋ ㄜˊ)or(ㄔˋ ㄜˋ)
Soviet Russia
赤楊(ㄔˋ ㄧㄤˊ)
an alder
赤外線(ㄔˋ ㄨㄞˋ ㄒㄧㄢˋ)
infrared rays
赤緯(ㄔˋ ㄨㄟˇ)
(astronomy) declination

四畫

【赦】 5822 ㄕㄜˋ sheh shè
to pardon; to excuse; to forgive; to amnesty; an amnesty
赦免(ㄕㄜˋ ㄇㄧㄢˇ)
to pardon (an offender)
赦過(ㄕㄜˋ ㄍㄨㄛˋ)
to pardon a fault
赦書(ㄕㄜˋ ㄕㄨ)
(written) orders of pardon or amnesty
赦罪(ㄕㄜˋ ㄗㄨㄟˋ)
to pardon (a criminal); to forgive (an offender)
赦宥(ㄕㄜˋ ㄧㄡˋ)
to pardon; pardon

五畫

【赧】 5823 ㄋㄢˇ naan nǎn
to turn red from shame or embarrassment; to blush
赧愧(ㄋㄢˇ ㄎㄨㄟˋ)
to blush; to be ashamed: 我深感赧愧。I feel deeply ashamed.
赧然(ㄋㄢˇ ㄖㄢˊ)
ashamed; blushing
赧顏(ㄋㄢˇ ㄧㄢˊ)
blushing; shamefaced

七畫

【赫】 5824 ㄏㄜˋ heh hè
1. bright; glowing
2. brilliant; glorious
3. angry; indignant
4. a Chinese family name
赫怒(ㄏㄜˋ ㄋㄨˋ)
angry; furious
赫赫(ㄏㄜˋ ㄏㄜˋ)
① brilliant; bright; glorious ② arid; dry ③ awe-inspiring
赫赫有名(ㄏㄜˋ ㄏㄜˋ ㄧㄡˇ ㄇㄧㄥˊ)
illustrious; far-famed
赫胥黎(ㄏㄜˋ ㄒㄩ ㄌㄧˊ)
Thomas Henry Huxley, 1825-1895, British biologist-philosopher
赫咺(ㄏㄜˋ ㄒㄩㄢˇ)or 赫烜(ㄏㄜˋ ㄒㄩㄢ)

brilliant and distinguished
赫咤(ㄏㄜˋ ㄓㄚˋ)
angry; indignant
赫哲(ㄏㄜˋ ㄓㄜˊ)or 赫哲族(ㄏㄜˋ ㄓㄜˊ ㄗㄨˊ)
name of a border tribe in Manchuria
赫然(ㄏㄜˋ ㄖㄢˊ)
①looking angry; in flaming anger: 他赫然震怒。He is in flaming anger. ②astonishing; shocking; consternation
赫爾辛基(ㄏㄜˋ ㄦˇ ㄒㄧㄣ ㄐㄧ)
Helsinki, capital of Finland
赫奕(ㄏㄜˋ ㄧˋ)
bright; glorious; magnificent

九畫

【赭】 5825 ㄓㄜˇ jee zhě
1. red
2. ocher
赭面(ㄓㄜˇ ㄇㄧㄢˋ)
to dye the face red
赭黃(ㄓㄜˇ ㄏㄨㄤˊ)
yellow ocher
赭石(ㄓㄜˇ ㄕˊ)
(mineral) ocher
赭衣(ㄓㄜˇ ㄧ)
red dress worn by convicts in ancient times

【赬】 5826 ㄔㄥ cheng chēng
red
赬尾(ㄔㄥ ㄨㄟˇ)
the toils of a gentleman

走部
ㄗㄡˇ tzoou zǒu

【走】 5827 ㄗㄡˇ tzoou zǒu
1. to walk; to go on foot
2. to run; to go swiftly
3. to go; to travel
4. to leave; to go away; to depart
5. to let out or lose (unintentionally); to leak out
6. to visit
走背運(ㄗㄡˇ ㄅㄟˋ ㄩㄣˋ)
to suffer from a spell of bad luck
走板(ㄗㄡˇ ㄅㄢˇ)
to sing out of rhythm
走筆疾書(ㄗㄡˇ ㄅㄧˇ ㄐㄧˊ ㄕㄨ)
to write swiftly
走避(ㄗㄡˇ ㄅㄧˋ)
to run away from; to evade; to shun
走邊(ㄗㄡˇ ㄅㄧㄢ)
(Peking opera) to move in supposed darkness such as stealing, peeping, etc.
走遍(ㄗㄡˇ ㄅㄧㄢˋ)
to travel all over (an area)
走不得(ㄗㄡˇ ·ㄅㄨ ·ㄉㄜ)
①(said of a way, road, path, etc.) unfit to travel; not safe to travel ②(said of a person) not entitled to leave; not allowed to leave; should not leave—indispensable
走不到(ㄗㄡˇ ·ㄅㄨ ㄉㄠˋ)
unable to walk as far as; unable to travel as far as; unable to go as far as
走不動(ㄗㄡˇ ·ㄅㄨ ㄉㄨㄥˋ)
too tired to walk
走不了(ㄗㄡˇ ·ㄅㄨ ㄌㄧㄠˇ)
not likely to leave; not able to leave
走不過去(ㄗㄡˇ ·ㄅㄨ ㄍㄨㄛˋ ·ㄑㄩ)
not able to go over
走不開(ㄗㄡˇ ·ㄅㄨ ㄎㄞ)
not able to leave; not able to get away
走馬(ㄗㄡˇ ㄇㄚˇ)
①to go swiftly on horseback; to ride swiftly ② an ambling horse
走馬燈(ㄗㄡˇ ㄇㄚˇ ㄉㄥ)
a lantern adorned with a revolving circle of paper horses
走馬看花(ㄗㄡˇ ㄇㄚˇ ㄎㄢˋ ㄏㄨㄚ)
(literally) to view flowers from the back of a galloping horse—to examine a thing hurriedly
走馬上任 (ㄗㄡˇ ㄇㄚˇ ㄕㄤˋ ㄖㄣˋ)
to travel to a place for a new post
走門路(ㄗㄡˇ ㄇㄣˊ ㄌㄨˋ)
to approach men of influence in seeking an objective
走方步(ㄗㄡˇ ㄈㄤ ㄅㄨˋ)
to exercise caution; to be prudent
走訪(ㄗㄡˇ ㄈㄤˇ)
①to interview; to have an interview with ②to visit; to go and see
走風(ㄗㄡˇ ㄈㄥ)
(said of a secret plan, etc.) to leak out; to become known
走得慢(ㄗㄡˇ ·ㄉㄜ ㄇㄢˋ)
to walk slowly; to go slowly
走得快(ㄗㄡˇ ·ㄉㄜ ㄎㄨㄞˋ)
to walk fast; to go fast
走道(ㄗㄡˇ ㄉㄠˋ)
①a pavement; a sidewalk ②a path; a footpath ③an aisle
走調兒(ㄗㄡˇ ㄉㄧㄠˋㄦ)
out of tune
走電(ㄗㄡˇ ㄉㄧㄢˋ)
electric power leakage
走讀(ㄗㄡˇ ㄉㄨˊ)
to live outside the school that one attends
走讀生(ㄗㄡˇ ㄉㄨˊ ㄕㄥ)
nonresident students (as distinct from boarding students)
走動(ㄗㄡˇ ㄉㄨㄥˋ)or 走動走動(ㄗㄡˇ ㄉㄨㄥˋ ㄗㄡˇ ㄉㄨㄥˋ)
①to take a walk; to go for a stroll ②to have intercourse; to visit
走投無路(ㄗㄡˇ ㄊㄡˊ ㄨˊ ㄌㄨˋ)
to have no one to turn to; to have no way out; to drive to the wall; in a tight corner: 他被逼得走投無路。He was driven to the wall.
走堂(ㄗㄡˇ ㄊㄤˊ)
a waiter
走內線(ㄗㄡˇ ㄋㄟˋ ㄒㄧㄢˋ)
to go through the back door (to achieve one's own goal); to curry favor with the wife of one's boss
走南闖北(ㄗㄡˇ ㄋㄢˊ ㄔㄨㄤˇ ㄅㄟˇ)
to travel everywhere
走來走去(ㄗㄡˇ ㄌㄞˊ ㄗㄡˇ ㄑㄩˋ)
to walk back and forth; to pace in anxiety
走漏(ㄗㄡˇ ㄌㄡˋ)
(said of secrets, plots, etc.) to leak
走漏消息(ㄗㄡˇ ㄌㄡˋ ㄒㄧㄠ ·ㄒㄧ)
to divulge secrets
走廊(ㄗㄡˇ ㄌㄤˊ)
a corridor; a hall; a veran-

da
走路(ㄗㄡˇ ㄌㄨˋ)
to walk; to go on foot: 我寧可走路而不搭公車。I would rather go on foot than by bus.
走狗(ㄗㄡˇ ㄍㄡˇ)
a lackey; a tool
走光(ㄗㄡˇ ㄍㄨㄤ)
①(said of a place) to be completely deserted; everyone walking away ②(said of photographic film) exposed accidentally
走開(ㄗㄡˇ ㄎㄞ)
Beat it! 或 Get out of the way!
走好運(ㄗㄡˇ ㄏㄠˇ ㄩㄣˋ)
to enjoy a spell of good luck
走候(ㄗㄡˇ ㄏㄡˋ)
to call at a person's house and inquire after him
走後門(ㄗㄡˇ ㄏㄡˋ ㄇㄣˊ)
to get in by the back door; to secure advantages through pull or influence
走話(ㄗㄡˇ ㄏㄨㄚˋ)
to divulge secrets
走火(ㄗㄡˇ ㄏㄨㄛˇ)
①(said of firearms) to go off accidentally: 手槍不慎走火。The gun went off accidentally. ②(electricity) a short circuit ③ to go too far in what one says; to put something too strongly; to overstate
走火入魔(ㄗㄡˇ ㄏㄨㄛˇ ㄖㄨˋ ㄇㄛˊ)
to be obsessed with something
走紅運(ㄗㄡˇ ㄏㄨㄥˊ ㄩㄣˋ)
to enjoy a spell of good luck 亦作「走好運」
走江湖
①(ㄗㄡˇ ㄐㄧㄤ ㄏㄨˊ) to live in seclusion
②(ㄗㄡˇ ㄐㄧㄤ ·ㄏㄨ) to wander from place to place to make a living by performing acrobatics
走氣(ㄗㄡˇ ㄑㄧˋ)
(said of spirits, perfume, etc.) to lose flavor, fragrance, etc.
走向(ㄗㄡˇ ㄒㄧㄤˋ)
① the run; the trend ②(geology) strike ③ to move toward; to head for; to be on the way to
走著瞧(ㄗㄡˇ ·ㄓㄜ ㄑㄧㄠˊ)
to wait and see
走失(ㄗㄡˇ ㄕ)
(said of persons, animals, etc.) to get lost; to be missing; to wander away
走獸(ㄗㄡˇ ㄕㄡˋ)
beasts; quadrupeds
走走(ㄗㄡˇ ·ㄗㄡ)
to take a walk; to take an airing: 我們到公園走走。Let's take a walk in the park.
走卒(ㄗㄡˇ ㄗㄨˊ)
a servant assigned exclusively to run errands
走嘴(ㄗㄡˇ ㄗㄨㄟˇ)
to let out a secret by careless speech; to make a slip of the tongue
走私(ㄗㄡˇ ㄙ)
to engage in smuggling; to smuggle; smuggling
走散(ㄗㄡˇ ㄙㄢˋ)
① to walk away in different directions ② to get separated from other travelers
走索(ㄗㄡˇ ㄙㄨㄛˇ)
to walk the rope
走一步看一步(ㄗㄡˇ ㄧˊ ㄅㄨˋ ㄎㄢˋ ㄧˊ ㄅㄨˋ)
to take one step and look around before taking another —to proceed without a plan, or with caution
走樣(ㄗㄡˇ ㄧㄤˋ)
① to get out of shape; to lose shape; to deviate from the original ② to be different from what is expected or intended
走味兒(ㄗㄡˇ ㄨㄟˋㄦ)
to turn stale; to lose flavor: 烟草已經走味兒了。The tobacco has lost its flavor.
走運(ㄗㄡˇ ㄩㄣˋ)
to be enjoying good luck; to be in luck; to have good luck

二畫

【赳】 5828 ㄐㄧㄡˇ jeou jiu (又讀 ㄐㄧㄡ jiou jiū)

valiant; gallant
赳赳(ㄐㄧㄡˇ ㄐㄧㄡˇ)
valiant; gallant; stalwart

【赴】 5829 ㄈㄨˋ fuh fù

to go to; to proceed to
赴敵(ㄈㄨˋ ㄉㄧˊ)
to go forward to fight the enemy
赴湯蹈火(ㄈㄨˋ ㄊㄤ ㄉㄠˋ ㄏㄨㄛˇ)
to go through fire and water; to defy all difficulties and dangers
赴難(ㄈㄨˋ ㄋㄢˋ)
to serve the nation in a crisis
赴考(ㄈㄨˋ ㄎㄠˇ)or 赴試(ㄈㄨˋ ㄕˋ)
to proceed to take an examination; to leave for an examination
赴會(ㄈㄨˋ ㄏㄨㄟˋ)
to go to a meeting
赴席(ㄈㄨˋ ㄒㄧˊ)
to go to a banquet
赴任(ㄈㄨˋ ㄖㄣˋ)
to proceed to one's new post
赴宴(ㄈㄨˋ ㄧㄢˋ)
to go to a banquet; to attend a banquet
赴約(ㄈㄨˋ ㄩㄝ)
to leave for an engagement

三畫

【起】 5830 ㄑㄧˇ chii qi

1. to begin; to start
2. to rise; to get up; to stand up; to go up
3. to happen; to take place
4. to unfold; to uncover
5. to build; to establish
6. a numerary adjunct for incidents

起兵(ㄑㄧˇ ㄅㄧㄥ)
to rise in arms; to start a military action
起不來(ㄑㄧˇ ·ㄅㄨ ㄌㄞˊ)
unable to get up; unable to stand up; unable to rise
起泡(ㄑㄧˇ ㄆㄠˋ)
① to get blisters ② to form bubbles
起碼(ㄑㄧˇ ㄇㄚˇ)
at least
起錨(ㄑㄧˇ ㄇㄠˊ)
to weigh anchor

〔走部〕

起錨機(ㄑㄧˇ ㄇㄠˊ ㄐㄧ)
a windlass; a capstan
起名字(ㄑㄧˇ ㄇㄧㄥˊ ㄗˋ) or 起名兒(ㄑㄧˇ ㄇㄧㄥˊㄦ)
to name; to give a name
起飛(ㄑㄧˇ ㄈㄟ)
to take off; a takeoff
起風(ㄑㄧˇ ㄈㄥ)
to get windy
起伏(ㄑㄧˇ ㄈㄨˊ)
① to undulate; undulation ② ups and downs; the rise and fall: 人生起伏良多。Life is full of ups and downs.
起點(ㄑㄧˇ ㄉㄧㄢˇ)
a starting point
起電盤(ㄑㄧˇ ㄉㄧㄢˋ ㄆㄢˊ)
an electrophorus
起電機(ㄑㄧˇ ㄉㄧㄢˋ ㄐㄧ)
an electric machine
起端(ㄑㄧˇ ㄉㄨㄢ)
the origin; the beginning; the genesis
起動(ㄑㄧˇ ㄉㄨㄥˋ)
to start (a machine, etc.): 那引擎終於起動了。The engine started at last.
起頭(ㄑㄧˇ ㄊㄡˊ) or 起頭兒(ㄑㄧˇ ㄊㄡˊㄦ)
① the origin; the beginning ② at first; in the beginning: 萬事起頭兒難。Everything is difficult in the beginning.
起跳(ㄑㄧˇ ㄊㄧㄠˋ)
(sports) to take off
起來
①(ㄑㄧˇ ㄌㄞˊ) ⓐ to stand up; to sit up; to rise: 她從椅子站起來。She rose from her chair. ⓑ to get up
②(•ㄑㄧ •ㄌㄞ) an adverbial phrase used after a verb denoting that an action is taking place: 天氣漸漸暖和起來了。The weather is getting warm.
起立(ㄑㄧˇ ㄌㄧˋ)
to stand up
起落(ㄑㄧˇ ㄌㄨㄛˋ)
rising and falling
起稿(ㄑㄧˇ ㄍㄠˇ)
to prepare a draft
起工(ㄑㄧˇ ㄍㄨㄥ)
to start work
起火(ㄑㄧˇ ㄏㄨㄛˇ)
① to catch fire; to be on fire ② to lose one's temper ③ to cook meals
起貨(ㄑㄧˇ ㄏㄨㄛˋ)
to take goods (from a warehouse)
起鬨 or 起閧(ㄑㄧˇ ㄏㄨㄥˋ)
to create disturbances; to boo; to hoot: 聽衆起鬨把演講者轟下台。The audience hooted the speaker down.
起家(ㄑㄧˇ ㄐㄧㄚ)
① the early background of a successful person ② to establish oneself in the world; to carve out a career
起價(ㄑㄧˇ ㄐㄧㄚˋ)
to raise the price; price soaring
起解(ㄑㄧˇ ㄐㄧㄝˋ)
to pack off (a captive); to transfer (a prisoner) under escort
起轎(ㄑㄧˇ ㄐㄧㄠˋ)
to set out in a sedan chair
起見(ㄑㄧˇ ㄐㄧㄢˋ)
in view of; with a view to; with the view of; for the sake of; for the purpose of; in order to
起勁(ㄑㄧˇ ㄐㄧㄣˋ)
(said of actions, performances, etc.) showing much zeal; eager; energetic; vigorous; enthusiastic; with gusto
起講(ㄑㄧˇ ㄐㄧㄤˇ)
(in the stereotyped style of compositions written in civil service examinations under the former system) the introductory passage
起敬(ㄑㄧˇ ㄐㄧㄥˋ)
to show respect
起居(ㄑㄧˇ ㄐㄩ)
rising up and sitting down—one's everyday life at home
起居注(ㄑㄧˇ ㄐㄩ ㄓㄨˋ)
① an official in charge of the emperor's daily life ② the record of the emperor's daily activities
起句(ㄑㄧˇ ㄐㄩˋ)
the opening line (of a poem)
起訖(ㄑㄧˇ ㄑㄧˋ)
the beginning and the end
起息(ㄑㄧˇ ㄒㄧˊ)
① to get up (in the morning) and retire (in the night) ② to start bearing interest
起先(ㄑㄧˇ ㄒㄧㄢ)
at first; in the beginning 參看「起初」: 起先沒人相信我。No one believes me at first.
起釁(ㄑㄧˇ ㄒㄧㄣˋ)
to start a feud; to provoke a fight
起行(ㄑㄧˇ ㄒㄧㄥˊ)
to set out; to start on a journey
起止(ㄑㄧˇ ㄓˇ)
the beginning and the end
起縐(ㄑㄧˇ ㄓㄡˋ)
to wrinkle; to crumple: 這種布容易起縐。This cloth crumples easily.
起重螺旋(ㄑㄧˇ ㄓㄨㄥˋ ㄌㄨㄛˊ ㄒㄩㄢˊ)
a jackscrew
起重機(ㄑㄧˇ ㄓㄨㄥˋ ㄐㄧ)
a crane (for lifting or moving heavy objects); a derrick
起程(ㄑㄧˇ ㄔㄥˊ)
to start on a journey; to set out
起承轉合(ㄑㄧˇ ㄔㄥˊ ㄓㄨㄢˇ ㄏㄜˊ)
the introduction, the follow-up, the transition and the conclusion (formerly accepted as the four cardinal steps of composition)
起初(ㄑㄧˇ ㄔㄨ)
at first; in the beginning; originally 參看「起先」: 那個花園起初很小。That garden was originally very small.
起牀(ㄑㄧˇ ㄔㄨㄤˊ)
to get out of bed; to get up; to rise
起牀號(ㄑㄧˇ ㄔㄨㄤˊ ㄏㄠˋ)
the reveille
起始(ㄑㄧˇ ㄕˇ)
the beginning; the start; the outset
起誓(ㄑㄧˇ ㄕˋ)
to take an oath; to swear
起事(ㄑㄧˇ ㄕˋ)
to rise in arms; to rise in revolt
起手(ㄑㄧˇ ㄕㄡˇ)
to start an action
起首(ㄑㄧˇ ㄕㄡˇ)
the beginning
起身(ㄑㄧˇ ㄕㄣ)
① to start on a journey; to

set out; to leave; to get off ②to get out of bed; to get up

起身炮(ㄑㄧˇ ㄕㄣ ㄆㄠˋ)
appointments or promotions made (by a ranking official) right before leaving a post

起子(ㄑㄧˇ ·ㄗ)
①(dialect) baking powder; leaven ②(dialect) a screwdriver ③a bottle opener

起早睡晚(ㄑㄧˇ ㄗㄠˇ ㄕㄨㄟˋ ㄨㄢˇ)
to get up early and go to bed late

起贓(ㄑㄧˇ ㄗㄤ)
to recover stolen articles

起租(ㄑㄧˇ ㄗㄨ)
(said of a lease contract) to enter into force; to start paying rent (from a date)

起坐(兒)(ㄑㄧˇ ㄗㄨㄛˋ(ㄦ))
to rise from one's seat as form of respect

起作用(ㄑㄧˇ ㄗㄨㄛˋ ㄩㄥˋ)
(said of an effect) to tell; to show effect

起草(ㄑㄧˇ ㄘㄠˇ)
to prepare a draft; to draft: 他起草議院的議案。He drafts a parliamentary bill.

起死回生(ㄑㄧˇ ㄙˇ ㄏㄨㄟˊ ㄕㄥ)
to revive the dead; to come back to life

起色(ㄑㄧˇ ㄙㄜˋ)
①a sign of improvement ②a sign of recovery; to make a quick recovery

起訴(ㄑㄧˇ ㄙㄨˋ)
(said of a prosecutor) to file a formal indictment; to indict; to sue; to prosecute

起訴人(ㄑㄧˇ ㄙㄨˋ ㄖㄣˊ)
a prosecutor

起算(ㄑㄧˇ ㄙㄨㄢˋ)
to start counting (the number of days, hours, etc., in a period or term) from a given point

起疑(ㄑㄧˇ ㄧˊ)or 起疑心(ㄑㄧˇ ㄧˊ ㄒㄧㄣ)
to begin to suspect; to become suspicious

起意(ㄑㄧˇ ㄧˋ)
to conceive a design; to have an idea (of doing something)

起義(ㄑㄧˇ ㄧˋ)
to start an uprising (in a righteous revolution); to revolt

起油(ㄑㄧˇ ㄧㄡˊ)
to remove greasy stains (from clothing, etc.)

起眼(ㄑㄧˇ ㄧㄢˇ)
to attract attention: 這些衣服不起眼。The clothes do not attract attention.

起因(ㄑㄧˇ ㄧㄣ)
a cause

起舞(ㄑㄧˇ ㄨˇ)
①to rise and dance ②to be excited with joy

起臥(ㄑㄧˇ ㄨㄛˋ)
to get up and to sleep

起源(ㄑㄧˇ ㄩㄢˊ)
the origin; the source; the beginning; the genesis

起運(ㄑㄧˇ ㄩㄣˋ)
to start shipping; to be under way

起用(ㄑㄧˇ ㄩㄥˋ)
to employ (officials previously dismissed or in retirement)

【赸】 5831
ㄕㄢˋ shann shàn
to try to conceal embarrassment

五畫

【趁】 5832
(趂) ㄔㄣˋ chenn chèn
1. to take advantage of; to avail oneself of
2. while

趁便(ㄔㄣˋ ㄅㄧㄢˋ)
to take advantage of a convenient occasion; at one's convenience: 你趁便爲我寄封信好嗎? Would you mail a letter for me at your convenience?

趁風揚帆(ㄔㄣˋ ㄈㄥ ㄧㄤˊ ㄈㄢ)
Hoist the sail when there is wind.

趁空(ㄔㄣˋ ㄎㄨㄥˋ)
to avail oneself of leisure

趁火打劫(ㄔㄣˋ ㄏㄨㄛˇ ㄉㄚˇ ㄐㄧㄝˊ)
(literally) to plunder a house when it is on fire—to try to profit from another's misfortune; to fish in troubled waters

趁機會(ㄔㄣˋ ㄐㄧ ㄏㄨㄟˋ)
to take advantage of an opportunity

趁心(ㄔㄣˋ ㄒㄧㄣ)
to have as one wishes; very gratifying and satisfactory 亦作「稱心如意」

趁虛(ㄔㄣˋ ㄒㄩ)
to take advantage of another's unwariness or absence

趁時候(ㄔㄣˋ ㄕˊ ·ㄏㄡ)
to take advantage of the chance; to act before it is too late

趁勢(ㄔㄣˋ ㄕˋ)
to take advantage of the prevailing circumstances

趁熱(ㄔㄣˋ ㄖㄜˋ)
①while it is still hot: 趁熱把這麵吃了吧。Eat the noodles while they are hot. ②to act before it is too late

趁熱打鐵(ㄔㄣˋ ㄖㄜˋ ㄉㄚˇ ㄊㄧㄝˇ)
to strike while the iron is hot

趁人之危(ㄔㄣˋ ㄖㄣˊ ㄓ ㄨㄟˊ)
to take advantage of others' perilous states; to take advantage of others' weakness

趁早(ㄔㄣˋ ㄗㄠˇ)
as early as possible; to act before it is too late

趁願(ㄔㄣˋ ㄩㄢˋ)
to feel satisfaction

【趄】 5833
ㄐㄩ jiu jū
as in 趑趄——to falter

【超】 5834
ㄔㄠ chau chāo
1. to jump over; to leap over; to fly across
2. to be more than; to exceed
3. to be better than; to excel; to surpass
4. to rise above; to transcend
5. to overtake

超拔(ㄔㄠ ㄅㄚˊ)
outstanding; surpassing

超凡入聖(ㄔㄠ ㄈㄢˊ ㄖㄨˋ ㄕㄥˋ)
to transcend worldliness and attain holiness

超等(ㄔㄠ ㄉㄥˇ)or 超級(ㄔㄠ ㄐㄧˊ)
of a special grade; of a special class

超度(ㄔㄠ ㄉㄨˋ)

〔走部〕

①to transcend; to rise above ②(Buddhism) to raise the soul from suffering in the next world

超短裙(ㄔㄠ ㄉㄨㄢˇ ㄑㄩㄣˊ)
a miniskirt 亦作「迷你裙」

超脫(ㄔㄠ ㄊㄨㄛ)
to transcend worldliness; to be detached; to detach oneself from

超齡(ㄔㄠ ㄌㄧㄥˊ)
to be over the specified age

超倫(ㄔㄠ ㄌㄨㄣˊ)
surpassing; outstanding

超格(ㄔㄠ ㄍㄜˊ)
surpassing the average; surpassing

超過(ㄔㄠ ㄍㄨㄛˋ)
①to exceed; to be more than ②to excel; to surpass; to outweigh

超級(ㄔㄠ ㄐㄧˊ)
super

超級明星(ㄔㄠ ㄐㄧˊ ㄇㄧㄥˊ ㄒㄧㄥ)
a superstar 亦作「超級巨星」

超級間諜(ㄔㄠ ㄐㄧˊ ㄐㄧㄢˋ ㄉㄧㄝˊ)
a superspy

超級強國(ㄔㄠ ㄐㄧˊ ㄑㄧㄤˊ ㄍㄨㄛˊ)
a superpower; a superstate

超級市場(ㄔㄠ ㄐㄧˊ ㄕˋ ㄔㄤˇ)
a supermarket

超絕(ㄔㄠ ㄐㄩㄝˊ)
incomparable; unsurpassed; unequaled; transcendent

超遷(ㄔㄠ ㄑㄧㄢ)
to promote, or get promoted, past one or more grades

超前(ㄔㄠ ㄑㄧㄢˊ)
①(electricity) lead ②to overtake

超群(ㄔㄠ ㄑㄩㄣˊ)
head and shoulders above all others; preeminent; surpassing: 她的美貌超群。She was of surpassing beauty.

超羣絕倫(ㄔㄠ ㄑㄩㄣˊ ㄐㄩㄝˊ ㄌㄨㄣˊ)
surpassing all others; incomparably above everything

超現實主義(ㄔㄠ ㄒㄧㄢˋ ㄕˊ ㄓㄨˇ ㄧˋ)
surrealism

超支(ㄔㄠ ㄓ)
to overspend; to overdraw

超卓(ㄔㄠ ㄓㄨㄛˊ)
transcendent; surpassing

超重(ㄔㄠ ㄓㄨㄥˋ)
①an overload ②overweight; excess

超車(ㄔㄠ ㄔㄜ)
to overtake a car: 不准超車。No overtaking!

超塵拔俗(ㄔㄠ ㄔㄣˊ ㄅㄚˊ ㄙㄨˊ)
to transcend the worldly

超出(ㄔㄠ ㄔㄨ)
to exceed; to surpass; to overtake: 他們的成功超出我們的預料之外。Their success exceeded our expectations.

超視綜合體(ㄔㄠ ㄕˋ ㄗㄨㄥˋ ㄏㄜˊ ㄊㄧˇ)
a Cinerama

超收(ㄔㄠ ㄕㄡ)
to receive more (funds) than needed; to collect more (tax revenues) than expected

超升(ㄔㄠ ㄕㄥ)
①to get promoted past one (or more) grades ②(said of the soul) to rise to Heaven upon death

超生(ㄔㄠ ㄕㄥ)
to excuse from death

超然(ㄔㄠ ㄖㄢˊ)
①transcendent ②detached; unprejudiced

超然物外(ㄔㄠ ㄖㄢˊ ㄨˋ ㄨㄞˋ)
to be above all material desires

超人(ㄔㄠ ㄖㄣˊ)
a superman

超自然(ㄔㄠ ㄗˋ ㄖㄢˊ)
supernatural: 天使和魔鬼都是超自然的存在物。Angels and devils are supernatural beings.

超載(ㄔㄠ ㄗㄞˋ)
overloading; to overload

超速(ㄔㄠ ㄙㄨˋ)
speeding

超額(ㄔㄠ ㄜˊ)
to exceed a quota or target amount

超逸(ㄔㄠ ㄧˋ)
above worldly desires; free from material desires

超音波(ㄔㄠ ㄧㄣ ㄅㄛ)
supersonic waves

超音速(ㄔㄠ ㄧㄣ ㄙㄨˋ)
supersonic speed

超越(ㄔㄠ ㄩㄝˋ)
①to excel; to surpass; to rise above; to transcend ②to fly across; to jump over

【越】 5835 ㄩㄝˋ yueh yuè

1. to go beyond; to transgress
2. to skip; to climb over; to cross over; to go across
3. even more; the more
4. name of an ancient state
5. a Chinese family name

越描越黑(ㄩㄝˋ ㄇㄧㄠˊ ㄩㄝˋ ㄏㄟ)
(informal) The more one tries to cover up a scandal, the more it stinks.

越發(ㄩㄝˋ ㄈㄚ)
even more; the more

越島進攻(ㄩㄝˋ ㄉㄠˇ ㄐㄧㄣˋ ㄍㄨㄥ)
to take enemy-held islands in a leapfrog fashion (as Gen. MacArthur did in the Pacific)

越多越好(ㄩㄝˋ ㄉㄨㄛ ㄩㄝˋ ㄏㄠˇ)
The more, the better.

越南(ㄩㄝˋ ㄋㄢˊ)
Vietnam

越年(ㄩㄝˋ ㄋㄧㄢˊ)
the following year

越來越…(ㄩㄝˋ ㄌㄞˊ ㄩㄝˋ…)
more and more; increasingly more; steadily more

越雷池一步(ㄩㄝˋ ㄌㄟˊ ㄔˊ ㄧˊ ㄅㄨˋ)
to transgress the bounds

越禮(ㄩㄝˋ ㄌㄧˇ)
to go beyond the bounds of propriety

越過(ㄩㄝˋ ㄍㄨㄛˋ)
①to exceed; to overstep ②to go across; to cross

越軌(ㄩㄝˋ ㄍㄨㄟˇ)
to go beyond what is proper

越軌行爲(ㄩㄝˋ ㄍㄨㄟˇ ㄒㄧㄥˊ ㄨㄟˊ)
impermissible behavior

越級(ㄩㄝˋ ㄐㄧˊ)
to skip grades in promotion, etc.

越界(ㄩㄝˋ ㄐㄧㄝˋ)
to go beyond the boundary; to transgress the bounds; to encroach; to trespass; to intrude

越境(ㄩㄝˋ ㄐㄧㄥˋ)
to encroach upon the territory of an adjacent country; to go beyond the national border

越劇(ㄩㄝˋ ㄐㄩˋ)
Shaohsing opera, prevalent in Chekiang(浙江) and Shanghai(上海)

越牆(ㄩㄝˋ ㄑㄧㄤˊ)
to climb over a wall; to

scale a wall: 小偷越牆而逃。The thief scaled the wall and escaped.
越權(ㄩㄝˋ ㄑㄩㄢˊ)
to act without authorization
越限(ㄩㄝˋ ㄒㄧㄢˋ)
to exceed the time limit
越日(ㄩㄝˋ ㄖˋ)
the following day
越俎代庖(ㄩㄝˋ ㄗㄨˇ ㄉㄞˋ ㄆㄠˊ)
to go beyond one's duties; to meddle with another's affairs
越次(ㄩㄝˋ ㄘˋ)
to disregard the proper order or sequence
越野賽跑(ㄩㄝˋ ㄧㄝˇ ㄙㄞˋ ㄆㄠˇ)
a cross-country race
越獄(ㄩㄝˋ ㄩˋ)
to break jail; a jailbreak: 兩名犯人越獄了。Two prisoners broke jail.
越…越好(ㄩㄝˋ…ㄩㄝˋ ㄏㄠˇ)
The..., the better. 越多越好。The more, the better.

六畫

【赼】 5836 ㄗ tzy zī
to falter
赼趄(ㄗ ㄐㄩ)
to falter; to hesitate to proceed

【趔】 5837 ㄌㄧㄝˋ lieh liè
1. falling behind; not progressing
2. unskillful; awkward
趔趄(ㄌㄧㄝˋ ·ㄐㄩ)
① falling behind; not progressing ② awkward; unskillful ③ to stagger; to reel; to stumble

七畫

【趙】 5838 ㄓㄠˋ jaw zhào
1. name of an ancient feudal state
2. a Chinese family name
趙璧(ㄓㄠˋ ㄅㄧˋ)
a famous precious stone belonging to the state of Chao (趙) during the Epoch of Warring States
趙孟頫(ㄓㄠˋ ㄇㄥˋ ㄈㄨˇ)
Chao Meng-fu, 1254-1322, a painter and calligrapher
趙飛燕(ㄓㄠˋ ㄈㄟ ㄧㄢˋ)
Chao Fei-yen, a favorite concubine of Emperor Cheng (成帝) of the Han Dynasty
趙盾(ㄓㄠˋ ㄉㄨㄣˋ)
Chao Tun, son of Chao Tsui (趙衰), a statesman of the state of Tsin (晉) during the Epoch of Spring and Autumn
趙高(ㄓㄠˋ ㄍㄠ)
Chao Kao, a powerful eunuch during the Chin (秦) Dynasty (221-206 B.C.)
趙匡胤(ㄓㄠˋ ㄎㄨㄤ ㄧㄣˋ)
Chao Kuang-yin, 927-976, founder of the Sung (宋) Dynasty (960-1279)
趙衰(ㄓㄠˋ ㄘㄨㄟ)
Chao Tsui, father of Chao Tun (趙盾), a statesman of the state of Tsin (晉) during the Epoch of Spring and Autumn
趙宋(ㄓㄠˋ ㄙㄨㄥˋ)
the Sung Dynasty (960-1279, of the House of Chao, as distinct from the Sung of the House of Liu in the 5th century A.D.)
趙雲(ㄓㄠˋ ㄩㄣˊ)
Chao Yün, ? -229, a general of the Kingdom of Shu (蜀) during the Epoch of the Three Kingdoms

【趕】 5839 ㄍㄢˇ gaan gǎn
1. to pursue; to catch up with; to overtake; to keep up with
2. to drive; to expel
3. to hurry; to rush; to hasten
4. to try to catch; to make a dash for; to rush for
趕辦(ㄍㄢˇ ㄅㄢˋ)
to hurry (work)
趕不及(ㄍㄢˇ ·ㄅㄨ ㄐㄧˊ)
unable to manage to be on time
趕不上(ㄍㄢˇ ·ㄅㄨ ㄕㄤˋ)
① unable to catch up with ② inferior to ③ to be too late for (the train, etc.) ④ to miss; unable to chance upon
趕忙(ㄍㄢˇ ㄇㄤˊ)
with haste; hurriedly
趕明兒(ㄍㄢˇ ㄇㄧㄥˊ ㄦ)
some other day; later: 我們趕明兒再討論它吧。Let's discuss it some other day.
趕得上(ㄍㄢˇ ·ㄉㄜ ㄕㄤˋ)
① able to be in time for ② able to catch up with ③ able to chance upon
趕到(ㄍㄢˇ ·ㄉㄠ)
① to arrive in haste; to come hurriedly ② by the time when...
趕牛(ㄍㄢˇ ㄋㄧㄡˊ)
to herd cattle
趕路(ㄍㄢˇ ㄌㄨˋ)
to walk hurriedly; to travel in haste; to hurry on with one's journey; to push on with one's journey
趕開(ㄍㄢˇ ㄎㄞ)
to drive away
趕考(ㄍㄢˇ ㄎㄠˇ)
to go to an examination
趕快(ㄍㄢˇ ㄎㄨㄞˋ)
to make haste; to hurry; quickly; at once
趕活(ㄍㄢˇ ㄏㄨㄛˊ)
to hurry work
趕會(ㄍㄢˇ ㄏㄨㄟˋ)
to go to a temple fair
趕回來(ㄍㄢˇ ·ㄏㄨㄟ ·ㄌㄞ)
① to come back hurriedly; to hurry back ② to chase after someone and force him to come back
趕集(ㄍㄢˇ ㄐㄧˊ)
to go to market 亦作「趁墟」
趕緊(ㄍㄢˇ ㄐㄧㄣˇ)
to hurry; quickly; with no loss of time
趕盡殺絕(ㄍㄢˇ ㄐㄧㄣˋ ㄕㄚ ㄐㄩㄝˊ)
to injure and oppress to the extreme
趕製(ㄍㄢˇ ㄓˋ)
to rush the manufacture of
趕著(ㄍㄢˇ ·ㄓㄜ)
① hurrying ② catching up; pursuing ③ to chance upon
趕車(ㄍㄢˇ ㄔㄜ)
① to drive a cart or carriage ② to catch a bus or train
趕場(ㄍㄢˇ ㄔㄤˊ)
(said of actors) after finishing a performance, to hurry

〔走部〕

to another place for a new one

趕出去(ㄍㄢˇ ㄔㄨ ·ㄑㄩ)
to drive out; to expel

趕時髦(ㄍㄢˇ ㄕˊ ㄇㄠˊ)
to follow the fashion; to try to be in the swim

趕上(ㄍㄢˇ ·ㄕㄤ)
①to catch up with; to overtake; to keep pace with ②to be in time for ③to chance upon

趕早兒(ㄍㄢˇ ㄗㄠˇㄦ)
to act before it is too late

趕三關(ㄍㄢˇ ㄙㄢ ㄍㄨㄢ)
to be in a great hurry to do one thing after another

趕鴨子上架(ㄍㄢˇ ㄧㄚ ·ㄗ ㄕㄤˋ ㄐㄧㄚˋ)
to drive a duck onto a perch —to force someone to do something against his will

趕羊(ㄍㄢˇ ㄧㄤˊ)
to herd sheep

趕羊的(ㄍㄢˇ ㄧㄤˊ ·ㄉㄜ)
a shepherd

八畫

【趣】 5840 1. ㄑㄩˋ chiuh qù
interest; fun; interesting; funny

趣話(ㄑㄩˋ ㄏㄨㄚˋ)
an amusing story; a funny story; a joke

趣向(ㄑㄩˋ ㄒㄧㄤˋ)
a personal inclination; aptitude

趣事(ㄑㄩˋ ㄕˋ)
an amusing incident; an interesting episode

趣兒(ㄑㄩˋㄦ)
fun; interest

趣味(ㄑㄩˋ ㄨㄟˋ)
fun; interest; taste: 懸疑可增加故事的趣味。Suspense can add interest to a story.

趣聞(ㄑㄩˋ ㄨㄣˊ)
an amusing report; interesting news

【趣】 5840 2.(促) ㄘㄨˋ tsuh cù
to hasten

【趟】 5841 ㄊㄤˋ tanq tàng
an auxiliary noun for verbs meaning "to walk," "to journey," etc.

趟子(ㄊㄤˋ ·ㄗ)
a round trip between two localities; commutation

十畫

【趨】 5842 ㄑㄩ chiu qū
1. to go quickly; to hasten; to hurry
2. to be inclined; to tend; to follow

趨拜(ㄑㄩ ㄅㄞˋ)
to hurry on to pay respects to

趨奉(ㄑㄩ ㄈㄥˋ)
to try to please (a notable, etc.); to hasten to please; to fawn on

趨附(ㄑㄩ ㄈㄨˋ)
to hang on (men of influence)

趨庭(ㄑㄩ ㄊㄧㄥˊ)
to receive the teachings of one's father

趨利(ㄑㄩ ㄌㄧˋ)
to go after material gain

趨候(ㄑㄩ ㄏㄡˋ)
to go to a place to pay respects to someone

趨吉避凶(ㄑㄩ ㄐㄧˊ ㄅㄧˋ ㄒㄩㄥ)
to pursue good fortune and shun the course of calamity

趨向(ㄑㄩ ㄒㄧㄤˋ)
①a tendency; a trend; a direction ②to tend to; to incline to

趨之若鶩(ㄑㄩ ㄓ ㄖㄨㄛˋ ㄨˋ)
to go after in a swarm

趨戰(ㄑㄩ ㄓㄢˋ)
to fight an enemy already firmly entrenched

趨承(ㄑㄩ ㄔㄥˊ)
to cater to someone

趨時(ㄑㄩ ㄕˊ)
to follow the trend of the times

趨勢(ㄑㄩ ㄕˋ)
①a trend; a tendency ②to go after men of power

趨走(ㄑㄩ ㄗㄡˇ)
to go in haste; to run away

趨義(ㄑㄩ ㄧˋ)
to see right and act quickly to follow it

趨謁(ㄑㄩ ㄧㄝˋ)
to go and see (a senior)

趨炎附勢(ㄑㄩ ㄧㄢˊ ㄈㄨˋ ㄕˋ)or 趨炎附熱(ㄑㄩ ㄧㄢˊ ㄈㄨˋ ㄖㄜˋ)
to hang on men of influence

趨迎(ㄑㄩ ㄧㄥˊ)or 趨而迎之(ㄑㄩ ㄦˊ ㄧㄥˊ ㄓ)
to hasten to greet or receive (a visitor)

十九畫

【趲】 5843 ㄗㄢˇ tzaan zǎn
1. to hurry; to hasten; to rush through
2. to urge
3. to save (money)

趲路(ㄗㄢˇ ㄌㄨˋ)
to hurry in a journey; to journey hurriedly

趲行(ㄗㄢˇ ㄒㄧㄥˊ)
to travel hurriedly; to hurry in a journey

趲程(ㄗㄢˇ ㄔㄥˊ)
to hurry in a journey; to journey hurriedly

足部
ㄗㄨˊ tzwu zú

【足】 5844 1. ㄗㄨˊ tzwu zú
1. the foot; the leg
2. the base (of an object)
3. sufficient; enough; adequate; full

足本(ㄗㄨˊ ㄅㄣˇ)
(said of a novel, etc.) unabridged

足不出戶(ㄗㄨˊ ·ㄅㄨ ㄔㄨ ㄏㄨˋ)
to refrain from stepping outside the house

足謀寡斷(ㄗㄨˊ ㄇㄡˊ ㄍㄨㄚˇ ㄉㄨㄢˋ)
resourceful but irresolute

足敷(ㄗㄨˊ ㄈㄨ)
enough for

足趺骨(ㄗㄨˊ ㄈㄨ ㄍㄨˇ)
the tarsal bone; the tarsus

足夠(ㄗㄨˊ ㄍㄡˋ)
enough; sufficient; full; ample

足跟(ㄗㄨˊ ㄍㄣ)
the heel: 他跌倒的時候,傷了足跟。He hurt his heel when he fell.
足迹(ㄗㄨˊ ㄐㄧ)
①footprints; footmarks; tracks ②whereabouts
足繭(ㄗㄨˊ ㄐㄧㄢˇ)
the callous skin on the feet
足見(ㄗㄨˊ ㄐㄧㄢˋ)
from this it is clear that; it serves to show
足金(ㄗㄨˊ ㄐㄧㄣ)
pure gold 亦作「足赤」
足球(ㄗㄨˊ ㄑㄧㄡˊ)
football; soccer: 你喜歡踢足球嗎? Do you like playing soccer?
足球隊(ㄗㄨˊ ㄑㄧㄡˊ ㄉㄨㄟˋ)
a football team; a soccer team
足球賽(ㄗㄨˊ ㄑㄧㄡˊ ㄙㄞˋ)
a football game; a soccer game
足球員(ㄗㄨˊ ㄑㄧㄡˊ ㄩㄢˊ)
a football player; a footballer; a soccer player
足下(ㄗㄨˊ ㄒㄧㄚˋ)
①terms of respect placed after the name when addressing another (found usually in letters): 足下意見如何? What is your opinion? ② under one's feet—a footing; a foothold
足智多謀(ㄗㄨˊ ㄓˋ ㄉㄨㄛ ㄇㄡˊ)
wise and resourceful
足吃足喝(ㄗㄨˊ ㄔ ㄗㄨˊ ㄏㄜ)
to eat and drink to one's heart's content
足赤(ㄗㄨˊ ㄔˋ)
pure gold
足食足兵(ㄗㄨˊ ㄕˊ ㄗㄨˊ ㄅㄧㄥ)
adequacy in the supply of foodstuffs and the means of defense
足資借鏡(ㄗㄨˊ ㄗ ㄐㄧㄝˋ ㄐㄧㄥˋ)
to be an object lesson
足足(ㄗㄨˊ ㄗㄨˊ)
full; no less than; as much as: 這行程足足花費四小時。The journey took fully four hours.
足色(ㄗㄨˊ ㄙㄜˋ)
(said of gold, silver, etc.) of standard purity; sterling
足歲(ㄗㄨˊ ㄙㄨㄟˋ)
to have actually reached a certain age (as distinct from the Chinese way of counting age, which makes a person one year old at the time of birth)
足額(ㄗㄨˊ ㄜˊ)
to have reached the quota or required number
足衣足食(ㄗㄨˊ ㄧ ㄗㄨˊ ㄕˊ)
to have no shortage of food and clothing
足以(ㄗㄨˊ ㄧˇ)
sufficient to; enough to: 他的話不足以影響我。What he says isn't enough to affect me.
足以自豪(ㄗㄨˊ ㄧˇ ㄗˋ ㄏㄠˊ)
enough for one to be proud of
足音跫然(ㄗㄨˊ ㄧㄣ ㄑㄩㄥˊ ㄖㄢˊ)
(literally) excited to hear footsteps—longing to have visitors
足銀(ㄗㄨˊ ㄧㄣˊ)
sterling silver
足紋(ㄗㄨˊ ㄨㄣˊ)
sterling silver

【足】5844 2. ㄐㄩˋ jiuh jù
overly modest or humble
足恭(ㄐㄩˋ ㄍㄨㄥ)
overly modest; too humble; obsequious

二畫

【趴】5845 ㄆㄚ pa pā
1. to prostrate oneself; to lie face downwards
2. to bend over
趴下(ㄆㄚ ·ㄒㄧㄚ)
①to prostrate oneself; to lie face downwards ②to fall flat on the ground
趴著(ㄆㄚ ·ㄓㄜ)
lying flat on the ground; prostrate

三畫

【趵】5846 ㄅㄠˋ baw bào
to jump; to leap
趵突泉(ㄅㄠˋ ㄊㄨ ㄑㄩㄢˊ)
a renowned spring at Tsinan, Shantung

四畫

【趾】5847 ㄓˇ jyy zhǐ
1. a toe
2. a foot
3. footprints; tracks
趾高氣揚(ㄓˇ ㄍㄠ ㄑㄧˋ ㄧㄤˊ)
(literally) to walk in a vain, swaggering manner—elated and proud; smug; to hold one's head high: 那影后趾高氣揚。The movie queen holds her head high.
趾骨(ㄓˇ ㄍㄨˇ)
the phalanx (of the foot)
趾甲(ㄓˇ ㄐㄧㄚˇ)
a toenail

【趺】5848 ㄈㄨ fu fū
1. the back of the foot
2. to sit cross-legged (as a Buddhist monk does)
趺骨(ㄈㄨ ㄍㄨˇ)
the tarsal bone; the tarsus
趺坐(ㄈㄨ ㄗㄨㄛˋ)
to sit cross-legged (as a Buddhist monk does)

【跂】5849 1. ㄑㄧˊ chyi qí
1. an extra toe
2. (said of insects) crawling

【跂】5849 2. ㄑㄧˋ chih qì
to stand on tiptoe
跂想(ㄑㄧˋ ㄒㄧㄤˇ)
to expect anxiously
跂踵(ㄑㄧˋ ㄓㄨㄥˇ)
to wait expectantly; to look forward anxiously
跂望 or 企望(ㄑㄧˋ ㄨㄤˋ)
to wait on tiptoe—to look forward with eagerness

【趿】5850 1. ㄙㄚˋ sah sà
to pick up with the foot

【趿】5850 2. ㄊㄚ ta tā
to wear (shoes) in a casual way
趿拉(ㄊㄚ ·ㄌㄚ)
to wear (shoes) in a casual way; to wear shoes with the backs turned in

五畫

〔足部〕

【跋】 5851 ㄅㄚˊ bar bá

1. to travel
2. a postscript
3. to trample

跋刺(ㄅㄚˊ ㄌㄚˋ)
the sound of fish jumping or birds flying up

跋扈(ㄅㄚˊ ㄏㄨˋ)
to be rampant in defiance of authority

跋前疐後(ㄅㄚˊ ㄑㄧㄢˊ ㄓˋ ㄏㄡˋ)
allowed to move neither forward nor backward

跋涉(ㄅㄚˊ ㄕㄜˋ)
to travel over land and water; to trudge; to trek; to wade

跋山涉水(ㄅㄚˊ ㄕㄢ ㄕㄜˋ ㄕㄨㄟˇ)
to scale mountains and ford streams; to travel across mountains and rivers

【跌】 5852 ㄉㄧㄝ dye die

1. to fall; to drop
2. to stamp
3. a fall

跌打損傷(ㄉㄧㄝ ㄉㄚˇ ㄙㄨㄣˇ ㄕㄤ)
(literally) injuries caused by a fall or beating—Chinese osteopathy

跌得倒爬得起(ㄉㄧㄝ ·ㄉㄜ ㄉㄠˇ ㄆㄚˊ ·ㄉㄜ ㄑㄧˇ)
able to rise after a fall —capable of adapting oneself to circumstances

跌倒(ㄉㄧㄝ ㄉㄠˇ)
to stumble and fall; to fall down

跌蕩 or 跌宕(ㄉㄧㄝ ㄉㄤˋ)
to behave without decorum; to act without restraint

跌跌撞撞(ㄉㄧㄝ ㄉㄧㄝ ㄓㄨㄤˋ ㄓㄨㄤˋ)
to walk unsteadily; to stagger forward

跌停板(ㄉㄧㄝ ㄊㄧㄥˊ ㄅㄢˇ)
(stock trading) to fall to the lowest point allowed for a single trading day; to hit the rock bottom

跌落(ㄉㄧㄝ ㄌㄨㄛˋ)
to go down; to fall; to drop

跌價(ㄉㄧㄝ ㄐㄧㄚˋ)
to cut a price; a price drop; to go down in price: 雞蛋跌價了。The price of eggs has gone down.

跌跤(ㄉㄧㄝ ㄐㄧㄠ)
①to have a fall; to stumble and fall; a fall: 他因跌跤而受傷了。He had been hurt by a fall. ②to make a mistake

跌進(ㄉㄧㄝ ㄐㄧㄣˋ)
①to fall into ②(said of a price) to fall below a certain level

跌傷(ㄉㄧㄝ ㄕㄤ)
to get injured by a fall; to fall and get hurt

跌足(ㄉㄧㄝ ㄗㄨˊ)
to stamp the feet

跌死(ㄉㄧㄝ ㄙˇ)
to be killed by a fall: 他跌死了。He was killed by a fall.

跌碎(ㄉㄧㄝ ㄙㄨㄟˋ)
to break into pieces upon falling on the ground

【跎】 5853 ㄊㄨㄛˊ two tuó

1. to miss one's footing; to stumble
2. to miss the opportunity; to waste time

【跑】 5854 ㄆㄠˇ pao pǎo

1. to run
2. to run away; to flee

跑冰(ㄆㄠˇ ㄅㄧㄥ)
to ice-skate; to skate on ice

跑步(ㄆㄠˇ ㄅㄨˋ)
to run; on the double

跑不掉(ㄆㄠˇ ·ㄅㄨ ㄉㄧㄠˋ)
unable to run away

跑不動(ㄆㄠˇ ·ㄅㄨ ㄉㄨㄥˋ)
too tired to run: 他疲倦得跑不動。He is too tired to run.

跑不了(ㄆㄠˇ ·ㄅㄨ ㄌㄧㄠˇ)
not likely to run away

跑跑顛顛(ㄆㄠˇ ㄆㄠˇ ㄉㄧㄢ ㄉㄧㄢ)
working in a hectic manner; to bustle about

跑馬(ㄆㄠˇ ㄇㄚˇ)
① horse racing ② to go swiftly on horseback ③ to have an involuntary emission of semen

跑馬錶(ㄆㄠˇ ㄇㄚˇ ㄅㄧㄠˇ)
a stopwatch 亦作「跑錶」

跑馬場(ㄆㄠˇ ㄇㄚˇ ㄔㄤˇ)
a racecourse (for horse racing); a racetrack

跑道(ㄆㄠˇ ㄉㄠˋ)
①a track (in a racecourse, stadium, etc.) ②a runway (in an airfield): 飛機離開跑道。The plane left the runway.

跑單幫(ㄆㄠˇ ㄉㄢ ㄅㄤ)
to smuggle goods on a small scale by a single individual

跑肚(ㄆㄠˇ ㄉㄨˋ)
to have diarrhea

跑檯子(ㄆㄠˇ ㄊㄞˊ ·ㄗ)
to steal money from the counter of a shop or bank during business hours

跑堂(ㄆㄠˇ ㄊㄤˊ)
a waiter

跑廳的(ㄆㄠˇ ㄊㄧㄥ ·ㄉㄜ)
a servant in a brothel

跑腿(ㄆㄠˇ ㄊㄨㄟˇ)
to run errands

跑來跑去(ㄆㄠˇ ㄌㄞˊ ㄆㄠˇ ㄑㄩˋ)
to run back and forth

跑壘(ㄆㄠˇ ㄌㄟˇ)
(baseball) base running

跑壘員(ㄆㄠˇ ㄌㄟˇ ㄩㄢˊ)
(baseball) a base runner

跑路(ㄆㄠˇ ㄌㄨˋ)
to travel on foot

跑龍套(ㄆㄠˇ ㄌㄨㄥˊ ㄊㄠˋ)
to play an insignificant role

跑開(ㄆㄠˇ ㄎㄞ)
①to get out of the way ② to leave; to go away; to run away

跑街(ㄆㄠˇ ㄐㄧㄝ)
to act as a traveling salesman

跑江湖(ㄆㄠˇ ㄐㄧㄤ ㄏㄨˊ)
to wander from place to place, making a living as a predictor, fortuneteller, acrobat, etc.

跑鞋(ㄆㄠˇ ㄒㄧㄝˊ)
spiked shoes (of a sprinter)

跑車(ㄆㄠˇ ㄔㄜ)
a car, bicycle, etc. for races; a racer; a sports car

【跖】 5855 ㄓˊ jyr zhí

1. the sole (of the foot)
2. name of a notorious robber

跖犬吠堯(ㄓˊ ㄑㄩㄢˇ ㄈㄟˋ ㄧㄠˊ)
to side with the wicked and hate the wise

【跗】 5856 ㄈㄨ fu fū

the instep

跗骨(ㄈㄨ ㄍㄨˇ)

the tarsus; the tarsal bone
跗蹠(ㄈㄨˊ ㄓˊ)
tarsi and metatarsi

【跚】5857 ㄕㄢ shan shān
to walk unsteadily; to stagger

【跛】5858 1. ㄅㄛˇ boo bǒ
lame; crippled
跛躄(ㄅㄛˇ ㄅㄧˋ)
lame; crippled
跛鼈千里(ㄅㄛˇ ㄅㄧㄝ ㄑㄧㄢ ㄌㄧˇ)
(literally) Even a lame turtle can travel a thousand miles.—Persistence insures success.
跛脚(ㄅㄛˇ ㄐㄧㄠˇ)
lame; crippled
跛蹇(ㄅㄛˇ ㄐㄧㄢˇ)
lame; crippled
跛蹶(ㄅㄛˇ ㄐㄩㄝˊ)
to stumble and fall
跛躓(ㄅㄛˇ ㄓˋ)
to stumble and fall
跛子(ㄅㄛˇ ˙ㄗ)
a cripple
跛足(ㄅㄛˇ ㄗㄨˊ)
lame; crippled

【跛】5858 2. ㄅㄧˋ bih bì
to lean; to be partial
跛倚(ㄅㄧˋ ㄧˇ)
partial; biased; prejudiced

【距】5859 ㄐㄩˋ jiuh jù
1. a bird's spur
2. distance
距離(ㄐㄩˋ ㄌㄧˊ)
distance
距今(ㄐㄩˋ ㄐㄧㄣ)
ago: 距今已有二十年。That was twenty years ago.

六畫

【跨】5860 ㄎㄨㄚˋ kuah kuà
1. to take a stride; to stride
2. to sit astride on; to straddle; to ride
3. to cut across; to go beyond; to extend across
跨馬(ㄎㄨㄚˋ ㄇㄚˇ)
to sit astride on a horse; to mount a horse
跨黨(ㄎㄨㄚˋ ㄉㄤˇ)
to be a member of two political parties at the same time
跨年度(ㄎㄨㄚˋ ㄋㄧㄢˊ ㄉㄨˋ)
to go beyond the year
跨鶴(ㄎㄨㄚˋ ㄏㄜˋ)
to ride the crane—to become an immortal 亦作「跨鶴西歸」
跨海(ㄎㄨㄚˋ ㄏㄞˇ)
to cross the sea; to sail across the ocean
跨竈(ㄎㄨㄚˋ ㄗㄠˋ)
to excel one's own father
跨越(ㄎㄨㄚˋ ㄩㄝˋ)
to stride over (a ditch, etc.); to leap over; to cut across: 他跨越小河。He strode over the brook.

【趼】5861 (研) ㄐㄧㄢˇ jean jiǎn
the callous skin or blisters on hands or feet

【跟】5862 ㄍㄣ gen gēn
1. the heel
2. to follow
3. to attend upon
4. and
跟包的(ㄍㄣ ㄅㄠ ˙ㄉㄜ)
the attendant of an entertainer
跟班(ㄍㄣ ㄅㄢ)
an attendant (especially of an official)
跟不上(ㄍㄣ ˙ㄅㄨ ㄕㄤˋ)
unable to keep pace with; unable to catch up with
跟定(ㄍㄣ ㄉㄧㄥˋ)
to decide to follow (a leader) for good
跟頭(ㄍㄣ ˙ㄊㄡ)
① a somersault ② failure; a frustration 亦作「栽跟頭」
跟官的(ㄍㄣ ㄍㄨㄢ ˙ㄉㄜ)
an attendant of an official
跟進(ㄍㄣ ㄐㄧㄣˋ)
to follow suit
跟前
①(ㄍㄣ ㄑㄧㄢˊ) the front, side, or presence (of a person): 在她跟前別說大話。Don't talk big in her presence.
②(ㄍㄣ ˙ㄑㄧㄢ) used with reference to children in the presence of their parents 亦作「膝下」: 您跟前有幾位公子? How many sons do you have?
跟著(ㄍㄣ ˙ㄓㄜ)
① going after; following ② soon after that
跟主兒(ㄍㄣ ㄓㄨˇㄦ)
to be a servant
跟人(ㄍㄣ ㄖㄣˊ)
an attendant; a retainer
跟踪(ㄍㄣ ㄗㄨㄥ)
to follow other's tracks or footsteps; to pursue 參看「跟蹤」
跟蹤(ㄍㄣ ㄗㄨㄥ)
to keep track of; to shadow; to tail 亦作「跟踪」: 小偷被警察跟蹤了。The thief was tailed by a policeman.
跟隨(ㄍㄣ ㄙㄨㄟˊ)
① to go closely behind; to follow: 她跟隨他進入房間。She followed him into the room. ② a retainer; an attendant
跟兒(ㄍㄜㄦ)
the heel

【跡】5863 (迹) ㄐㄧ ji jī
traces; tracks; relics; a print

【跮】5864 ㄔˋ chyh chì
to walk back and forth
跮踱(ㄔˋ ㄉㄨㄛˋ)
to walk or move back and forth

【跴】5865 (踩) ㄘㄞˇ tsae cǎi
1. to trample; to tread on
2. to chase; to pursue
跴扁(ㄘㄞˇ ㄅㄧㄢˇ)
to trample (an object) flat
跴壞(ㄘㄞˇ ㄏㄨㄞˋ)
to break or damage by trampling; to trample and break
跴著(ㄘㄞˇ ˙ㄓㄜ)
treading on; trampling
跴住(ㄘㄞˇ ㄓㄨˋ)
to keep the feet upon
跴水(ㄘㄞˇ ㄕㄨㄟˇ)
(sports) to tread water
跴三輪車(ㄘㄞˇ ㄙㄢ ㄌㄨㄣˊ ㄔㄜ)
to pedal a pedicab; to work as a pedicab driver

【跣】5866 ㄒㄧㄢˇ shean xiǎn
barefooted
跣子(ㄒㄧㄢˇ ˙ㄗ)
slippers
跣足(ㄒㄧㄢˇ ㄗㄨˊ)
barefooted

〔足部〕

【跪】 5867 ㄍㄨㄟˋ guey guì
to kneel
跪拜(ㄍㄨㄟˋ ㄅㄞˋ)
to kowtow
跪稟(ㄍㄨㄟˋ ㄅㄧㄥˇ)
to report in a kneeling position
跪門(ㄍㄨㄟˋ ㄇㄣˊ)
to kneel at another's door (and beg for forgiveness)
跪倒(ㄍㄨㄟˋ ㄉㄠˇ)
to go on one's knees; to kneel down; to prostrate oneself; to grovel
跪倒爬起(ㄍㄨㄟˋ ㄉㄠˇ ㄆㄚˊ ㄑㄧˇ)
to kowtow again and again
跪地(ㄍㄨㄟˋ ㄉㄧˋ)
to kneel on the ground
跪下(ㄍㄨㄟˋ ·ㄒㄧㄚ)
to go on one's knees; to kneel down
跪謝(ㄍㄨㄟˋ ㄒㄧㄝˋ)
to express thanks on one's knees
跪乳(ㄍㄨㄟˋ ㄖㄨˇ)
(literally) to kneel to suck (as a lamb does)—to show filial piety
跪乳之恩(ㄍㄨㄟˋ ㄖㄨˇ ㄓ ㄣ)
filial piety
跪姿(ㄍㄨㄟˋ ㄗ)
a kneeling position
跪送(ㄍㄨㄟˋ ㄙㄨㄥˋ)
to bid goodbye in a kneeling position
跪迎(ㄍㄨㄟˋ ㄧㄥˊ)
to greet or receive in a kneeling position

【跫】 5868 ㄑㄩㄥˊ chyong qióng
the sound of steps; footsteps
跫然(ㄑㄩㄥˊ ㄖㄢˊ)
the sound of footsteps
跫音(ㄑㄩㄥˊ ㄧㄣ)
the sound of steps; footsteps: 我聽到跫音。I hear footsteps.

【跬】 5869 ㄎㄨㄟˇ koei kuǐ
half a pace
跬步(ㄎㄨㄟˇ ㄅㄨˋ)
half a pace
跬步千里(ㄎㄨㄟˇ ㄅㄨˋ ㄑㄧㄢ ㄌㄧˇ)
Even small steps may carry one a thousand miles. —If you try hard, you will succeed.
跬譽(ㄎㄨㄟˇ ㄩˋ)
short-lived glory or honor

【跲】 5870 ㄐㄧㄚˊ jya jiá
to stumble

【路】 5871 ㄌㄨˋ luh lù
1. a way; a road; a path
2. a sort; a kind; a gang
3. a way; means
4. directions; courses
5. province (an administrative division during the Sung Dynasty)
6. a Chinese family name
路斃(ㄌㄨˋ ㄅㄧˋ)
to die on the roadside
路標(ㄌㄨˋ ㄅㄧㄠ)
a road sign; a signpost
路不拾遺(ㄌㄨˋ ㄅㄨˋ ㄕˊ ㄧˊ)
People do not pick up what others have left on the roadside.—efficient government administration
路旁(ㄌㄨˋ ㄆㄤˊ)
the roadside: 我們在路旁用餐。We ate our meal by the roadside.
路面(ㄌㄨˋ ㄇㄧㄢˋ)
a road surface
路費(ㄌㄨˋ ㄈㄟˋ)
traveling expenses
路德會(ㄌㄨˋ ㄉㄜˊ ㄏㄨㄟˋ)
the Lutheran Church
路道(ㄌㄨˋ ㄉㄠˋ)
① a way; a method ② a faction; a type
路燈(ㄌㄨˋ ㄉㄥ)
a street lamp
路段(ㄌㄨˋ ㄉㄨㄢˋ)
a section of a highway or railway
路透電(ㄌㄨˋ ㄊㄡˋ ㄉㄧㄢˋ)
(news) a Reuters report
路透社(ㄌㄨˋ ㄊㄡˋ ㄕㄜˋ)
Reuters; Reuter's News Agency
路條(ㄌㄨˋ ㄊㄧㄠˊ)
(communist terminology) a traveling passport; a safe-conduct
路途(ㄌㄨˋ ㄊㄨˊ)
way; a road
路柳牆花(ㄌㄨˋ ㄌㄧㄡˇ ㄑㄧㄤˊ ㄏㄨㄚ)
(euphemism) prostitutes
路路通(ㄌㄨˋ ㄌㄨˋ ㄊㄨㄥ)
(said of a person) versed in everything
路過(ㄌㄨˋ ㄍㄨㄛˋ)
to pass by or through (a place)
路軌(ㄌㄨˋ ㄍㄨㄟˇ)
railway tracks
路口(ㄌㄨˋ ㄎㄡˇ)
an entrance to a road or street; a street intersection; a street crossing
路基(ㄌㄨˋ ㄐㄧ)
a road base
路祭(ㄌㄨˋ ㄐㄧˋ)
the offering of sacrifices by friends or admirers on the roadside along the way of a funeral procession
路劫(ㄌㄨˋ ㄐㄧㄝˊ)
to commit robbery on highways; to waylay travelers
路警(ㄌㄨˋ ㄐㄧㄥˇ)
policemen patrolling railways or highways
路徑(ㄌㄨˋ ㄐㄧㄥˋ)
a way; a road; a route
路線(ㄌㄨˋ ㄒㄧㄢˋ)
a route; a road; a course; a line: 這是到歐洲最快的路線。It's the quickest route to Europe.
路障(ㄌㄨˋ ㄓㄤˋ)
a roadblock
路政(ㄌㄨˋ ㄓㄥˋ)
the administration of land transportation
路中(ㄌㄨˋ ㄓㄨㄥ)
① on the way; along the way; en route: 我在回家的路中看見他。I saw him on the way home. ② a Chinese family name
路程(ㄌㄨˋ ㄔㄥˊ)
distance to be traveled; a journey; traveling distance: 這路程長而且難行。The journey was long and difficult.
路上(ㄌㄨˋ ·ㄕㄤ)
on the way; along the way; en route: 回家路上不要耽擱。Don't waste any time on the way home.
路數(ㄌㄨˋ ㄕㄨˋ)
a method; a process; the way of doing things that is peculiar to a certain sect or group
路人(ㄌㄨˋ ㄖㄣˊ)

① a wayfarer ② a stranger: 一個路人對我說話。A stranger spoke to me.

路子(ㄌㄨˋ ·ㄗ)
a way; a method; means; an approach: 路子不對等於白費時間。A wrong method means a waste of time.

路次(ㄌㄨˋ ㄘˋ)
en route; on the way; along the way: 他路次香港。He is en route to Hong Kong.

路易十六(ㄌㄨˋ ㄧˋ ㄕˊ ㄌㄧㄡˋ)
Louis XVI, 1754-1793

路易十四(ㄌㄨˋ ㄧˋ ㄕˊ ㄙˋ)
Louis XIV, 1638-1715

路易斯安那(ㄌㄨˋ ㄧˋ ㄙ ㄢ ㄋㄚˇ)
the state of Louisiana, U.S.

路遙知馬力(ㄌㄨˋ ㄧㄠˊ ㄓ ㄇㄚˇ ㄌㄧˋ)
(literally) A horse's strength is to be known only when the road is long.—A person's true color is revealed only in the long run.

路遠(ㄌㄨˋ ㄩㄢˇ)
great distance

【跳】 5872 ㄊㄧㄠˋ tiaw tiào

1. to jump; to leap; to bounce; to spring: 他跳過泥坑。He jumped the puddle.
2. to throb; to pulsate; to beat: 我的脈搏跳動得很快。My pulse is beating fast.
3. to skip (over); to jump; to make omissions

跳白(ㄊㄧㄠˋ ㄅㄞˊ)
(Kwangtung dialect) a small fishing boat

跳班(ㄊㄧㄠˋ ㄅㄢ)
(education) to skip a grade; to be advanced two or more classes or grades at once

跳板(ㄊㄧㄠˋ ㄅㄢˇ)
① a gangplank ② a diving board; a springboard ③ a steppingstone; a staging area

跳票(ㄊㄧㄠˋ ㄆㄧㄠˋ)
a bounced check; a check that bounced 參看「空頭支票」

跳動(ㄊㄧㄠˋ ㄉㄨㄥˋ)
to throb; to pulsate; to beat

跳跳躥躥(ㄊㄧㄠˋ ㄊㄧㄠˋ ㄘㄨㄢ ㄘㄨㄢ)
to jump and skip; to gambol; to caper; to trip

跳兎(ㄊㄧㄠˋ ㄊㄨˋ)
a hare; a rabbit; a jumping hare

跳脫(ㄊㄧㄠˋ ㄊㄨㄛ)
a bracelet

跳樓自殺(ㄊㄧㄠˋ ㄌㄡˊ ㄗˋ ㄕㄚ)
to jump to death from a building

跳欄(ㄊㄧㄠˋ ㄌㄢˊ)
(sports) hurdle race; the hurdles

跳踉(ㄊㄧㄠˋ ㄌㄤˋ)
to jump about; to hop about

跳梁(ㄊㄧㄠˋ ㄌㄧㄤˊ)
① to revolt; to rebel; to defy the authorities ② to leap

跳梁小醜(ㄊㄧㄠˋ ㄌㄧㄤˊ ㄒㄧㄠˇ ㄔㄡˇ)
petty thieves; mischief-makers

跳高(ㄊㄧㄠˋ ㄍㄠ)
(sports) high jump (in track and field)

跳過(ㄊㄧㄠˋ ㄍㄨㄛˋ)
to jump over or across; to succeed in jumping over or across; to clear

跳河(ㄊㄧㄠˋ ㄏㄜˊ)
to jump into the river to drown oneself

跳海(ㄊㄧㄠˋ ㄏㄞˇ)
to jump into the sea to drown oneself

跳行(ㄊㄧㄠˋ ㄏㄤˊ)
① to skip lines in reading or copying ② to change to a new occupation

跳火坑(ㄊㄧㄠˋ ㄏㄨㄛˇ ㄎㄥ)
to plunge into a life of infamy, danger, etc.

跳級(ㄊㄧㄠˋ ㄐㄧˊ)
(education) to skip a grade; to be advanced two or more classes or grades at once

跳加官(ㄊㄧㄠˋ ㄐㄧㄚ ㄍㄨㄢ)
a ceremonial dance performed by a masked actor before the start of a Peking opera show

跳脚(ㄊㄧㄠˋ ㄐㄧㄠˇ)
to stamp one's foot: 他氣得直跳脚。He stamped his foot with rage.

跳棋(ㄊㄧㄠˋ ㄑㄧˊ)
Chinese checkers

跳牆(ㄊㄧㄠˋ ㄑㄧㄤˊ)
to jump over a fence; to jump down from a wall in desperation

跳下去(ㄊㄧㄠˋ ·ㄒㄧㄚ ·ㄑㄩ)
to jump down; to leap down: 他從岸上跳下去。He jumped down from the bank.

跳出(ㄊㄧㄠˋ ㄔㄨ)
to jump out; to leap out

跳出樊籠(ㄊㄧㄠˋ ㄔㄨ ㄈㄢˊ ㄌㄨㄥˊ)
to jump out of the cage—to gain freedom

跳出火坑(ㄊㄧㄠˋ ㄔㄨ ㄏㄨㄛˇ ㄎㄥ)
① to free oneself from a life of torture ② to free oneself from white slavery

跳神(ㄊㄧㄠˋ ㄕㄣˊ)
ceremonial dances performed by the Manchus, Tibetans and Mongolians in exorcism

跳繩(ㄊㄧㄠˋ ㄕㄥˊ)
rope skipping; rope jumping: 女孩子喜歡玩跳繩。Girls like to play rope jumping.

跳水(ㄊㄧㄠˋ ㄕㄨㄟˇ)
to dive; to jump into the water; to dive from a diving board (or a springboard)

跳水自殺(ㄊㄧㄠˋ ㄕㄨㄟˇ ㄗˋ ㄕㄚ)
to jump into the water and drown oneself

跳蚤(ㄊㄧㄠˋ ㄗㄠˇ)or 跳蝨(ㄊㄧㄠˋ ㄕ)
a flea: 小心別被跳蚤咬了。Take care not to be bitten by the fleas.

跳槽(ㄊㄧㄠˋ ㄘㄠˊ)
to abandon one occupation in favor of another; to get new employment

跳傘(ㄊㄧㄠˋ ㄙㄢˇ)
to parachute

跳舞(ㄊㄧㄠˋ ㄨˇ)
to dance; dancing

跳舞會(ㄊㄧㄠˋ ㄨˇ ㄏㄨㄟˋ)
a dancing party; a ball 亦作「舞會」

跳月(ㄊㄧㄠˋ ㄩㄝˋ)
(by the custom of the Miao people) an outdoor dancing party on a spring night at which unmarried youths select their future spouses

跳躍(ㄊㄧㄠˋ ㄩㄝˋ)
to jump; to leap; to hop: 麻雀在草地上到處跳躍。Sparrows were hopping about on the lawn.

跳遠(ㄊㄧㄠˋ ㄩㄢˇ)
(sports) the broad jump; the long jump

〔足部〕

【跺】 5873 ㄉㄨㄛˋ duoh duò
to stamp the feet
跺脚(ㄉㄨㄛˋ ㄐㄧㄠˇ)
to stamp one's foot

【跩】 5874 ㄓㄨㄞˇ joai zhuǎi
waddling

【跤】 5875 ㄐㄧㄠ jiau jiāo
a stumble; a fall

七畫

【跼】 5876 ㄐㄩˊ jyu jú
1. bent
2. contracted; cramped; confined
跼天蹐地(ㄐㄩˊ ㄊㄧㄢ ㄐㄧˊ ㄉㄧˋ)
not stretched; confined; restricted
跼蹐(ㄐㄩˊ ㄐㄧˊ)
not stretched; confined
跼躅(ㄐㄩˊ ㄓㄨˊ)
halting; faltering
跼促 or 侷促(ㄐㄩˊ ㄘㄨˋ)
① narrow-minded ② ill at ease; uneasy

【跽】 5877 ㄐㄧˋ jih jì
to kneel for a long time

【踉】 5878 1. ㄌㄤˊ lang láng (又讀 ㄌㄧㄤˊ liang liáng)
to jump about; to hop about

【踉】 5878 2. ㄌㄧㄤˋ lianq liàng
to walk unsteadily; to limp
踉蹌 or 踉蹡(ㄌㄧㄤˋ ㄑㄧㄤˋ)or 踉踉蹌蹌(ㄌㄧㄤˋ ㄌㄧㄤˋ ㄑㄧㄤˋ ㄑㄧㄤˋ)
limping; walking unsteadily

【踅】 5879 1. ㄔˋ chyh chì
to go on one leg

【踅】 5879 2. ㄒㄩㄝˊ shyue xué
to loiter around; to hang about
踅門瞭戶(ㄒㄩㄝˊ ㄇㄣˊ ㄌㄧㄠˋ ㄏㄨˋ)
to loiter and chat at friends' houses
踅探(ㄒㄩㄝˊ ㄊㄢˋ)
to spy; to peep; to watch and investigate stealthily
踅溜風(ㄒㄩㄝˊ ·ㄌㄧㄡ ㄈㄥ)
a whirlwind; a cyclone
踅轉(ㄒㄩㄝˊ ㄓㄨㄢˇ)
to whirl; to turn; to rotate

【踊】 5880 ㄩㄥˇ yeong yǒng
1. to jump; to leap
2. to rise
3. the shoes worn by the person whose feet were cut off as a form of punishment
踊貴(ㄩㄥˇ ㄍㄨㄟˋ)
the rise of a price
踊躍 or 踴躍(ㄩㄥˇ ㄩㄝˋ)
① joyful; happy ② glad to do something; eagerly

八畫

【踐】 5881 ㄐㄧㄢˋ jiann jiàn
1. to tread upon; to trample
2. to fulfill; to carry out; to perform
3. to ascend; to occupy
踐冰(ㄐㄧㄢˋ ㄅㄧㄥ)
(literally) to tread on ice —to run a risk
踐踏(ㄐㄧㄢˋ ㄊㄚˋ)
① to trample; to tread on: 不要踐踏花圃。Don't tread on the flower bed. ② to abuse
踐諾(ㄐㄧㄢˋ ㄋㄨㄛˋ)
to keep a promise; to fulfill a pledge
踐履(ㄐㄧㄢˋ ㄌㄩˇ)
① to trample ② to fulfill (pledge, etc.)
踐極(ㄐㄧㄢˋ ㄐㄧˊ)
to ascend the throne
踐阼(ㄐㄧㄢˋ ㄗㄨㄛˋ)
to succeed to the throne
踐言(ㄐㄧㄢˋ ㄧㄢˊ)
to fulfill a promise
踐位(ㄐㄧㄢˋ ㄨㄟˋ)
to ascend the throne
踐約(ㄐㄧㄢˋ ㄩㄝ)
to honor an agreement; to fulfill a promise

【踠】 5882 ㄨㄢˇ woan wǎn
a crooked leg

【踏】 5883 ㄊㄚˋ tah tà
1. to step upon; to tread upon; to trample
2. to go to the spot (to make an investigation or survey)
踏板(ㄊㄚˋ ㄅㄢˇ)
① a footboard; a footrest; a foothold; a footstool ② a pedal; a treadle
踏遍(ㄊㄚˋ ㄅㄧㄢˋ)
to traverse the length and breadth of (some place)
踏破鐵鞋(ㄊㄚˋ ㄆㄛˋ ㄊㄧㄝˇ ㄒㄧㄝˊ)
(literally) to wear out the iron shoes—to search painstakingly everywhere
踏破鐵鞋無覓處, 得來全不費功夫(ㄊㄚˋ ㄆㄛˋ ㄊㄧㄝˇ ㄒㄧㄝˊ ㄨˊ ㄇㄧˋ ㄔㄨˋ, ㄉㄜˊ ㄌㄞˊ ㄑㄩㄢˊ ㄅㄨˋ ㄈㄟˋ ㄍㄨㄥ ㄈㄨ)
to find something or somebody by chance after a painstaking search
踏伏(ㄊㄚˋ ㄈㄨˊ)
to search out hidden enemy soldiers and wipe them out
踏歌(ㄊㄚˋ ㄍㄜ)
to beat time to a song with the feet
踏看 or 踏勘(ㄊㄚˋ ㄎㄢˋ)
to make a field investigation over (an area); to survey (a construction site)
踏脚板(ㄊㄚˋ ㄐㄧㄠˇ ㄅㄢˇ)
a footboard; a footrest; a foothold
踏脚石(ㄊㄚˋ ㄐㄧㄠˇ ㄕˊ)
a steppingstone
踏蹺(ㄊㄚˋ ㄑㄧㄠ)
to walk on stilts
踏青(ㄊㄚˋ ㄑㄧㄥ)
to go hiking on a spring day; a spring outing
踏雪尋梅(ㄊㄚˋ ㄒㄩㄝˇ ㄒㄩㄣˊ ㄇㄟˊ)
(literally) to look for plum flowers on a snowy day —the behavior of a poet
踏實(ㄊㄚˋ ㄕˊ)
(said of actions, etc.) practical; realistic: 他是個踏實的人。He is a practical man.
踏月(ㄊㄚˋ ㄩㄝˋ)
to walk in the moonlight

【踝】 5884 ㄏㄨㄞˊ hwai huái
an ankle
踝子骨(ㄏㄨㄞˊ ·ㄗ ㄍㄨˇ)
an anklebone; a talus; an astragalus

【踞】 5885 ㄐㄩˋ jiuh jù
1. to squat; to crouch
2. to occupy

【踟】 5886 ㄔˊ chyr chí
to hesitate
踟躕 or 踟躇(ㄔˊ ㄔㄨˊ)
①to hesitate ②linked together ③a comb ④to be in perplexity

【踡】 5887 ㄑㄩㄢˊ chyuan quán
coiled; curled; drawn together; not stretched
踡伏(ㄑㄩㄢˊ ㄈㄨˊ)
(said of a snake, etc.) to coil up: 那蛇踡伏在樹枝上。The snake coiled itself up round the branch.
踡跼(ㄑㄩㄢˊ ㄐㄩˊ)
contracted; not stretched
踡屈(ㄑㄩㄢˊ ㄑㄩ)
curled up; not stretched

【踢】 5888 ㄊㄧ ti tī
1. to kick
2. to play (football)
踢皮球(ㄊㄧ ㄆㄧˊ ㄑㄧㄡˊ)
①to kick a ball ②to kick something back and forth like a ball—(figuratively) to shirk (responsibility, etc.)
踢飛脚(ㄊㄧ ㄈㄟ ㄐㄧㄠˇ)
a kind of acrobatic stunt involving successive kicking motions
踢達(ㄊㄧ ㄉㄚˊ)
pitapat—a succession of light, rapid pats (as of footfalls)
踢開(ㄊㄧ ㄎㄞ)
①to kick open (a door) ②to kick (something) out of the way
踢毽子(ㄊㄧ ㄐㄧㄢˋ ˙ㄗ)
the game of repeatedly bouncing a shuttlecock off a foot
踢球(ㄊㄧ ㄑㄧㄡˊ)
①to kick a ball ②to play football: 他很會踢球。He plays football well.
踢正步(ㄊㄧ ㄓㄥˋ ㄅㄨˋ)
to march in goose steps
踢出去(ㄊㄧ ㄔㄨ ˙ㄑㄩ)
to kick out
踢死(ㄊㄧ ㄙˇ)
to kick to death

【踣】 5889 ㄅㄛˊ bor bó
1. to stumble and fall
2. dead; stiff

【踥】 5890 ㄑㄧㄝˋ chieh qiè
to walk; to be in motion
踥蹀(ㄑㄧㄝˋ ㄉㄧㄝˊ)
walking; in motion
踥踥(ㄑㄧㄝˋ ㄑㄧㄝˋ)
moving back and forth

【踧】 5891 1.ㄘㄨˋ tsuh cù
reverent and nervous
踧踖(ㄘㄨˋ ㄐㄧˊ)
reverent and nervous
踧爾(ㄘㄨˋ ㄦˇ)
surprised

【踧】 5891 2.ㄉㄧˊ dyi dí
level and easy
踧踧(ㄉㄧˊ ㄉㄧˊ)
(said of roads, etc.) level and easy

【踖】 5892 ㄐㄧˊ jyi jí
to trample; to tread upon

【踔】 5893 ㄓㄨㄛˊ jwo zhuó
1. to go across; to go beyond
2. very high; very far
踔厲風發(ㄓㄨㄛˊ ㄌㄧˋ ㄈㄥ ㄈㄚ)
to talk eloquently and knowledgeably
踔絕(ㄓㄨㄛˊ ㄐㄩㄝˊ)
①very high ②prominent
踔遠(ㄓㄨㄛˊ ㄩㄢˇ)
very high; very far

【踩】 5894 (跴) ㄘㄞˇ tsae cǎi
to tread upon; to trample; to step upon
踩高蹺(ㄘㄞˇ ㄍㄠ ㄑㄧㄠ)
to walk on stilts
踩蹻(ㄘㄞˇ ㄑㄧㄠ)
(said of a vivacious lady role in Peking opera) to walk on small, artificial wooden feet tied to the ankles so that the actress sways while walking
踩三輪兒(ㄘㄞˇ ㄙㄢ ㄌㄨㄦˊ)
to paddle a pedicab

【踦】 5895 1.ㄐㄧˇ jii jǐ
1. the shin
2. to lean against

【踦】 5895 2.ㄧˇ yii yǐ
to touch; to pierce

【踪】 5896 (蹤) ㄗㄨㄥ tzong zōng
a footprint; traces; tracks

九畫

【踰】 5897 ㄩˊ yu yú
1. same as 逾—to pass over; to cross; to go beyond; to transgress; to exceed
2. excessive; overly
踰分(ㄩˊ ㄈㄣˋ)
to go beyond one's proper function or position
踰年(ㄩˊ ㄋㄧㄢˊ)
the following year
踰矩(ㄩˊ ㄐㄩˇ)
to transgress the bounds of correctness
踰閑(ㄩˊ ㄒㄧㄢˊ)
to break moral conventions; to break decorum
踰侈(ㄩˊ ㄔˇ)
too extravagant; too luxurious
踰越(ㄩˊ ㄩㄝˋ)
to go beyond; to transgress
踰垣(ㄩˊ ㄩㄢˊ)
to go over a wall—to run away; to escape

【踱】 5898 ㄉㄨㄛˋ duoh duò
to stroll; to walk slowly
踱步(ㄉㄨㄛˋ ㄅㄨˋ)
to pace; to walk slowly
踱來踱去(ㄉㄨㄛˋ ㄌㄞˊ ㄉㄨㄛˋ ㄑㄩˋ)
to stroll to and fro; to pace to and fro; to pace up and down

【踵】 5899 ㄓㄨㄥˇ joong zhǒng
1. the heel
2. to follow
3. to call personally at; to go personally to; to call in person
踵門(ㄓㄨㄥˇ ㄇㄣˊ)
to call at another's house in person
踵接(ㄓㄨㄥˇ ㄐㄧㄝ)
so crowded that the people move with their toes on the heels of others
踵見(ㄓㄨㄥˇ ㄐㄧㄢˋ)
to call repeatedly in person

〔足部〕

踵決肘見(ㄓㄨㄥˇ ㄐㄩㄝˊ ㄓㄡˇ ㄒㄧㄢˋ)
(literally) out at heels and elbows—tattered dress
踵謝(ㄓㄨㄥˇ ㄒㄧㄝˋ)
to thank in person
踵至(ㄓㄨㄥˇ ㄓˋ)
to arrive upon the heels of another; to arrive just behind
踵事增華(ㄓㄨㄥˇ ㄕˋ ㄗㄥ ㄏㄨㄚˊ)
to follow a precedent and add to its excellence
踵武(ㄓㄨㄥˇ ㄨˇ)
to carry on the work of one's predecessors

【踽】 5900 ㄐㄩˇ jeu jǔ
to walk alone
踽踽(ㄐㄩˇ ㄐㄩˇ)
walking alone

【蹀】 5901 ㄉㄧㄝˊ dye dié
to stamp one's foot
蹀躞(ㄉㄧㄝˊ ㄒㄧㄝˋ)
① ambling: 我看到他蹀躞而行。I saw him ambling along the road. ② going back and forth
蹀足(ㄉㄧㄝˊ ㄗㄨˊ)
to stamp one's foot

【蹁】 5902 ㄆㄧㄢˊ pyan pián
walking unsteadily; limping
蹁躚(ㄆㄧㄢˊ ㄒㄧㄢ)
① to walk unsteadily ② to walk with a dancing gait

【蹂】 5903 ㄖㄡˊ rou róu
1. to tread upon; to trample
2. to tread out grain
蹂躪(ㄖㄡˊ ㄌㄧㄣˋ)
① to trample ② to devastate; rapacious acts
蹂踐(ㄖㄡˊ ㄐㄧㄢˋ)
to trample

【蹄】 5904 (蹏) ㄊㄧˊ tyi tí
1. (zoology) a hoof
2. the feet of beasts
蹄膀(ㄊㄧˊ ·ㄆㄤ)
(dialect) the uppermost part of legs of pork
蹄筋(ㄊㄧˊ ㄐㄧㄣ)
the tendon of Achilles
蹄筌(ㄊㄧˊ ㄑㄩㄢˊ)
a kind of snare for game or fish
蹄形磁石(ㄊㄧˊ ㄒㄧㄥˊ ㄘˊ ㄕˊ)
a horseshoe magnet
蹄子(ㄊㄧˊ ·ㄗ)
① hoofs ② (derogatory use) a wench

【踹】 5905 ㄔㄨㄞˋ chuay chuài
1. to kick
2. to tread; to trample; to stamp: 他一脚踹進水溝裏。He stamped into a ditch.
3. to spoil: 那項計劃被人踹了。Somebody spoiled that plan.
踹踏(ㄔㄨㄞˋ ㄊㄚˋ)
to trample; to tread

【踳】 5906 ㄔㄨㄣˇ choen chǔn
incongruous; disorderly
踳駁(ㄔㄨㄣˇ ㄅㄛˊ)
incongruous; disorderly
踳踳(ㄔㄨㄣˇ ㄔㄨㄣˇ)
disappointed; frustrated; unhappy

十畫

【蹈】 5907 ㄉㄠˋ daw dào
1. to tread; to step; to stamp one's foot
2. to follow; to pursue
蹈覆轍(ㄉㄠˋ ㄈㄨˋ ㄔㄜˋ)
to repeat a mistake someone has previously made
蹈歌(ㄉㄠˋ ㄍㄜ)
to beat time to a song with the feet
蹈海(ㄉㄠˋ ㄏㄞˇ) or 蹈海而死(ㄉㄠˋ ㄏㄞˇ ㄦˊ ㄙˇ)
to kill oneself by jumping into the sea
蹈虎尾(ㄉㄠˋ ㄏㄨˇ ㄨㄟˇ)
(literally) to tread on a tiger's tail—to run a great risk
蹈火赴湯(ㄉㄠˋ ㄏㄨㄛˇ ㄈㄨˋ ㄊㄤ)
to go through fire and water; to brave all possible difficulties 亦作「赴湯蹈火」
蹈襲(ㄉㄠˋ ㄒㄧˊ)
to copy or imitate (style, practice, etc.) slavishly
蹈常襲故(ㄉㄠˋ ㄔㄤˊ ㄒㄧˊ ㄍㄨˋ)
to follow conventions blindly; to follow the beaten track
蹈義(ㄉㄠˋ ㄧˋ)
to die for a cause; to be a martyr to a cause

【蹇】 5908 ㄐㄧㄢˇ jean jiǎn
1. lame; crippled
2. slow
3. difficult; hard
4. haughty
蹇剝(ㄐㄧㄢˇ ㄅㄛ)
suffering from unfavorable times or bad luck
蹇兎(ㄐㄧㄢˇ ㄊㄨˋ)
a slow hare
蹇連(ㄐㄧㄢˇ ㄌㄧㄢˊ)
difficult to travel
蹇驢(ㄐㄧㄢˇ ㄌㄩˊ)
a lame donkey
蹇吃(ㄐㄧㄢˇ ㄐㄧˊ)
to speak indistinctly
蹇蹇(ㄐㄧㄢˇ ㄐㄧㄢˇ)
difficult; hard
蹇修(ㄐㄧㄢˇ ㄒㄧㄡ)
a matchmaker 參見「媒人」
蹇滯(ㄐㄧㄢˇ ㄓˋ)
not proceeding smoothly
蹇澀(ㄐㄧㄢˇ ㄙㄜˋ)
difficult; hard
蹇愕(ㄐㄧㄢˇ ㄜˋ)
honest; upright

【蹉】 5909 ㄘㄨㄛ tsuo cuō
a failure; a miss
蹉跌(ㄘㄨㄛ ㄉㄧㄝˊ)
a failure; a slip; a mistake
蹉跎(ㄘㄨㄛ ㄊㄨㄛˊ)
① to slip and fall ② to miss a chance; to waste time: 他一再蹉跎。He lets one opportunity after another slip away.

【蹊】 5910 ㄒㄧ shi xī
1. a path; a footpath
2. to trample; to tread
蹊徑(ㄒㄧ ㄐㄧㄥˋ)
a narrow path
蹊蹺(ㄒㄧ ㄑㄧㄠ)
extraordinary; strange; queer: 那舊閣樓有點蹊蹺。There's something strange in the old attic.

【蹋】 5911 ㄊㄚˋ tah tà
to tread on
蹋地(ㄊㄚˋ ㄉㄧˋ)
to beat time to a song with the feet 亦作「踏歌」

【蹌】 5912 1. ㄑㄧㄤ chiang qiāng
walking rapidly
蹌蹌(ㄑㄧㄤ ㄑㄧㄤ)
① walking rapidly ② dancing

【蹌】 5912 2. ㄑㄧㄤˋ chianq qiàng
walking unsteadily; limping

【蹐】 5913 ㄐㄧˊ jyi jí
to walk daintily; to walk with small steps

【蹏】 5914 ㄊㄧˊ tyi tí
same as 蹄—hoofs

十一畫

【蹣】 5915 ㄇㄢˊ man mán
1. to jump over
2. to limp
蹣跚(ㄇㄢˊ ㄕㄢ)
limping; to walk haltingly; to hobble

【蹕】 5916 ㄅㄧˋ bih bì
1. to clear (the emperor's route) of traffic
2. an imperial carriage
蹕路(ㄅㄧˋ ㄌㄨˋ)
to clear the emperor's route of traffic

【蹙】 5917 (蹴) ㄘㄨˋ tsuh cù
1. to contract; to draw together
2. urgent; imminent
3. sad; sorrowful; discomposed
蹙眉(ㄘㄨˋ ㄇㄟˊ)
to knit the brows; to frown
蹙蹐(ㄘㄨˋ ㄐㄧˊ)
to hesitate to advance
蹙金(ㄘㄨˋ ㄐㄧㄣ)
a kind of embroidery worked with golden threads
蹙蹙(ㄘㄨˋ ㄘㄨˋ)
① drawn together; wrinkled ② descriptive of general distress
蹙竦(ㄘㄨˋ ㄙㄨㄥˇ)
frightened; horrified; scared
蹙頞(ㄘㄨˋ ㄜˋ)
to knit the brows; to look distressed; to have a worried look

【蹚】 5918 ㄊㄤ tang tāng
1. to tread on; to tread
2. to walk through mud or water; to wade; to ford
蹚渾水(ㄊㄤ ㄏㄨㄣˊ ㄕㄨㄟˇ)
(literally) to tread on muddy water — to associate with wicked people
蹚水(ㄊㄤ ㄕㄨㄟˇ)
to tread or wade water

【蹤】 5919 (踪) ㄗㄨㄥ tzong zōng
1. a footprint; a track; traces; a vestige: 我找不到她的行蹤。I found no vestiges of her presence.
2. to follow the tracks of; to keep track of; to trail: 警方追蹤罪犯。The police trailed the criminal.
蹤跡(ㄗㄨㄥ ㄐㄧ)
① a track; traces; a vestige ② to keep track; to follow up clues
蹤由(ㄗㄨㄥ ㄧㄡˊ)
origin and development
蹤影(ㄗㄨㄥ ㄧㄥˇ)
traces; a vestige

【蹠】 5920 ㄓˊ jyr zhí
1. to tread on; to step on
2. the sole (of the foot)
蹠骨(ㄓˊ ㄍㄨˇ)
(anatomy) the metatarsus; metatarsal bones

【蹡】 5921 1. ㄑㄧㄤ chiang qiāng
walking; in motion
蹡蹡(ㄑㄧㄤ ㄑㄧㄤ)
walking

【蹡】 5921 2. ㄑㄧㄤˋ chianq qiàng
to limp

【蹢】 5922 1. ㄓˊ jyr zhí
to falter; to hesitate
蹢躅 or 躑躅(ㄓˊ ㄓㄨˊ)
①faltering; hesitant ②(botany) an azalea亦作「山躑躅」or「羊躑躅」

【蹢】 5922 2. ㄉㄧˊ dyi dí
a hoof

【蹦】 5923 ㄅㄥˋ benq bèng
to skip; to caper; to trip; to jump; to leap
蹦蹦跳跳(ㄅㄥˋ ㄅㄥˋ ㄊㄧㄠˋ ㄊㄧㄠˋ)
skipping; capering; tripping; romping; frolicsome
蹦蹦兒戲(ㄅㄥˋ ㄅㄥˋㄦ ㄒㄧˋ)
a form of Chinese opera enjoyed by the lower classes of Hopei Province亦作「評戲」

【蹧】 5924 ㄗㄠ tzau zāo
to spoil; to ruin
蹧蹋 or 糟蹋(ㄗㄠ ·ㄊㄚ)
to spoil; to ruin
蹧踐 or 糟踐(ㄗㄠ ·ㄐㄧㄢ)
to spoil; to ruin

【蹟】 5925 (跡) ㄐㄧ ji jī
footprints; traces

【蹔】 5926 ㄓㄢˋ jann zhàn
same as 暫—temporary; fleeting; ephemeral

【蹴】 5927 ㄘㄨˋ tsuh cù
same as 蹙—to contract or draw together

十二畫

【蹲】 5928 ㄉㄨㄣ duen dūn (讀音 ㄘㄨㄣˊ tswen cún)
1. to squat; to crouch: 他蹲了下來。He squatted (himself) down.
2. to stay
蹲不下去(ㄉㄨㄣ ·ㄅㄨ ㄒㄧㄚˋ ·ㄑㄩ)
unable to squat or crouch
蹲伏(ㄉㄨㄣ ㄈㄨˊ)
to squat; to crouch
蹲踞(ㄉㄨㄣ ㄐㄩˋ)
to squat; to crouch
蹲下去(ㄉㄨㄣ ·ㄒㄧㄚ ·ㄑㄩ) or 蹲下(ㄉㄨㄣ ㄒㄧㄚˋ)
to squat
蹲著(ㄉㄨㄣ ·ㄓㄜ)
squatting; crouching

【蹩】 5929 (蹷) ㄅㄧㄝˊ bye bié
to limp
蹩脚(ㄅㄧㄝˊ ㄐㄧㄠˇ)
① lame ② inferior in quality; poor ③ dejected

【蹬】 5930 ㄉㄥˋ denq dèng
1. to tread on; to step on

〔足部〕

2. deprived of power or influence

【蹭】 5931
ㄘㄥˋ tsenq cèng
1. deprived of power
2. to stroll
3. to protract

蹭蹬(ㄘㄥˋ ㄉㄥˋ)
deprived of power or influence; to meet with setbacks; to be down on one's luck

【蹯】 5932
ㄈㄢˊ farn fán
paws

【蹴】 5933
(蹵) ㄘㄨˋ tsuh cù
1. to tread on
2. to kick
3. respectful

蹴然(ㄘㄨˋ ㄖㄢˊ)
①respectful ②uneasy; nervous; worried

【蹶】 5934
1. ㄐㄩㄝˊ jyue jué
1. to tread
2. to stumble and fall
3. to overturn; an overthrow
4. to daunt; to frustrate; to suffer a setback

蹶躓(ㄐㄩㄝˊ ㄓˋ)
to stumble and fall

蹶然(ㄐㄩㄝˊ ㄖㄢˊ)
standing up from fright; rising suddenly from fear

【蹶】 5934
2. ㄐㄩㄝˇ jeue juě
to kick backward

蹶子(ㄐㄩㄝˇ ·ㄗ)
a horse's backward kick with its hind hoof

【蹺】 5935
ㄑㄧㄠ chiau qiāo
1. same as 蹻—to raise the feet
2. on tiptoe: 那舞者蹺著脚走路。The dancer walks on tiptoe.
3. stilts

蹺辮子(ㄑㄧㄠ ㄅㄧㄢˋ ·ㄗ)
to die

蹺課(ㄑㄧㄠ ㄎㄜˋ)
(slang) to avoid attending classes

蹺家(ㄑㄧㄠ ㄐㄧㄚ)
(slang) to run away from home

蹺捷(ㄑㄧㄠ ㄐㄧㄝˊ)
able to move quickly and easily; agile

蹺敧(ㄑㄧㄠ ㄑㄧ)
extraordinary; unusual

蹺蹺板(ㄑㄧㄠ ㄑㄧㄠ ㄅㄢˇ)
a seesaw; a teeterboard

蹺蹊(ㄑㄧㄠ ㄒㄧ)
extraordinary; queer; strange
亦作「蹊蹺」

【蹻】 5936
1. ㄑㄧㄠ chiau qiāo
1. same as 蹺—to raise feet
2. stilts (高蹻)

蹻足(ㄑㄧㄠ ㄗㄨˊ)
①to raise a foot (ready to go) ②a very brief period

【蹻】 5936
2. ㄐㄧㄠˇ jeau jiǎo
1.strong; brave
2.haughty; overbearing

蹻蹻(ㄐㄧㄠˇ ㄐㄧㄠˇ)
①strong; brave ②haughty; overbearing; to be full of pride

蹻勇(ㄐㄧㄠˇ ㄩㄥˇ)
(said of a man) strong

【蹼】 5937
ㄆㄨˊ pwu pú
webs on the feet of water fowls

【蹵】 5938
(蹴) ㄘㄨˋ tsuh cù
1. to tread
2. to kick

【蹩】 5939
ㄅㄧㄝˊ bye bié
same as 躄—to limp

【躕】 5940
ㄔㄨˊ chwu chú
same as 蹰—to hesitate to advance

十三畫

【躄】 5941
(躃) ㄅㄧˋ bih bì
having both legs disabled; crippled in both legs

躄踊(ㄅㄧˋ ㄩㄥˇ)
to stamp with grief

【躁】 5942
ㄗㄠˋ tzaw zào
1. irritable; hot-tempered
2. restless; uneasy
3. rashness

躁佻(ㄗㄠˋ ㄊㄧㄠ)
frivolous; rash

躁戾(ㄗㄠˋ ㄌㄧˋ)
irritable and cruel

躁狂(ㄗㄠˋ ㄎㄨㄤˊ)
irritable and unrestrained

躁急(ㄗㄠˋ ㄐㄧˊ)
impatient; uneasy

躁進(ㄗㄠˋ ㄐㄧㄣˋ)
impatient to rise in the world

躁競(ㄗㄠˋ ㄐㄧㄥˋ)
impatient to excel others; eager to grab power from others

躁切(ㄗㄠˋ ㄑㄧㄝˋ)
anxious or impatient

躁率(ㄗㄠˋ ㄕㄨㄞˋ)
impatient and careless

【躅】 5943
ㄓㄨˊ jwu zhú
to falter; to hesitate

【躇】 5944
ㄔㄨˊ chwu chú
to hesitate

【躉】 5945
ㄉㄨㄣˇ doen dǔn
1. a whole batch or amount
2. to buy or sell wholesale

躉批(ㄉㄨㄣˇ ㄆㄧ)
by wholesale

躉賣(ㄉㄨㄣˇ ㄇㄞˋ)
to sell wholesale

躉購(ㄉㄨㄣˇ ㄍㄡˋ)
to buy wholesale: 我們係大批躉購。We buy goods wholesale.

躉船(ㄉㄨㄣˇ ㄔㄨㄢˊ)
a lighter (for loading or unloading larger ships)

躉售(ㄉㄨㄣˇ ㄕㄡˋ)
to sell wholesale

【躂】 5946
ㄊㄚˋ tah tà
to stumble; to slip

【躃】 5947
ㄅㄧˋ bih bì
same as 躄—crippled in both legs

十四畫

【躊】 5948
ㄔㄡˊ chour chóu
1. hesitant
2. complacent; confident

躊佇(ㄔㄡˊ ㄓㄨˋ)
to falter; to hesitate

躊躇(ㄔㄡˊ ㄔㄨˊ)
①to hesitate; to waver; to falter; to vacillate; shilly-shally ②complacent; confident

〔足部〕

【躋】 5949 ㄐㄧ ji jī
to go up; to rise; to ascend

【躍】 5950 ㄩㄝ yueh yuè
(語音 ㄧㄠ yaw yào)
to jump; to leap; to bound; to spring
躍馬(ㄩㄝ ㄇㄚˇ)
to give the horse his head; to let a horse gallop
躍馬橫戈(ㄩㄝˋ ㄇㄚˇ ㄏㄥˊ ㄍㄜ)
to spur the horse and level the spear—to take a challenging position
躍動(ㄩㄝ ㄉㄨㄥˋ)
to move actively; to be in lively motion
躍進(ㄩㄝ ㄐㄧㄣˋ)or(ㄧㄠ ㄐㄧㄣˋ)
① to leap forward ② to make rapid progress: 他的功課躍進神速。He is making rapid progress in his studies.
躍起(ㄩㄝ ㄑㄧˇ)
to leap up; to jump up
躍然紙上(ㄩㄝˋ ㄖㄢˊ ㄓˇ ㄕㄤˋ)
(said of things portrayed in literature or paintings) full of life; vivid
躍躍欲試(ㄩㄝˋ ㄩㄝˋ ㄩˋ ㄕˋ)
impatient to have a try; eager to do something

十五畫

【躐】 5951 ㄌㄧㄝˋ lieh liè
to transgress; to overstep
躐等(ㄌㄧㄝˋ ㄉㄥˇ)
to skip steps; to fail to follow proper order
躐席(ㄌㄧㄝˋ ㄒㄧˊ)
to take a seat which one is not entitled to

【躑】 5952 ㄓˊ jyr zhí
to falter; to hesitate
躑躅(ㄓˊ ㄓㄨˊ)
① to falter; to hesitate; to loiter around ②(botany) an azalea

【躓】 5953 ㄓˋ jyh zhì
1. to stumble; to trip
2. to be frustrated; to suffer a setback
躓頓(ㄓˋ ㄉㄨㄣˋ)
to stumble and stop

【躕】 5954 ㄔㄨˊ chwu chú
to falter; to hesitate

十六畫

【躚】 5955 ㄒㄧㄢ shian xiān
to turn round and round
躚躚(ㄒㄧㄢ ㄒㄧㄢ)
turning round and round; twirling; dancing

十七畫

【躞】 5956 ㄒㄧㄝˋ shieh xiè
1. walking; proceeding
2. a pin or rod for rolling a scroll; an axis
躞蹀(ㄒㄧㄝˋ ㄉㄧㄝˊ)
walking; proceeding

十八畫

【躡】 5957 ㄋㄧㄝˋ nieh niè
1. to tread on; to step over
2. to follow; to pursue
3. to walk lightly; to tiptoe: 她躡著脚走出書房。She tiptoed out of the study.
躡蹀(ㄋㄧㄝˋ ㄉㄧㄝˊ)
walking with mincing steps
躡跟(ㄋㄧㄝˋ ㄍㄣ)
(said of shoes) too large or too small for the feet
躡手躡脚(ㄋㄧㄝˋ ㄕㄡˇ ㄋㄧㄝˋ ㄐㄧㄠˇ)
walking with light steps; walking stealthily: 他躡手躡脚走下樓梯。He walked downstairs stealthily.
躡足(ㄋㄧㄝˋ ㄗㄨˊ)
to step upon another's foot
躡足潛蹤(ㄋㄧㄝˋ ㄗㄨˊ ㄑㄧㄢˊ ㄗㄨㄥ)
walking with light steps; walking stealthily
躡影追蹤(ㄋㄧㄝˋ ㄧㄥˇ ㄓㄨㄟ ㄗㄨㄥ)
to trace; to look for; to locate

【躥】 5958 ㄘㄨㄢ tsuan cuān
1. to leap; to jump
2. (said of someone) to get promoted
3. to spurt out
躥房越脊(ㄘㄨㄢ ㄈㄤˊ ㄩㄝˋ ㄐㄧˇ)
to rush about on the roofs (as housebreakers)

二十畫

【躪】 5959 ㄌㄧㄣˋ linn lìn
to trample; to devastate; to overrun; to lay a place waste

〔身部〕

身部
ㄕㄣ shen shēn

【身】 5960 1. ㄕㄣ shen shēn
1. a body; a trunk
2. one's own person; oneself
3. a child in the womb
4. in person; personally
身敗名裂(ㄕㄣ ㄅㄞˋ ㄇㄧㄥˊ ㄌㄧㄝˋ)
to lose both one's fortune and honor
身邊(ㄕㄣ ㄅㄧㄢ)or 身畔(ㄕㄣ ㄆㄢˋ)
one's vicinity; one's side; one's immediate surroundings: 她坐在我身邊。She sat at my side.
身邊人(ㄕㄣ ㄅㄧㄢ ㄖㄣˊ)
① an attendant ② a concubine
身不動膀不搖(ㄕㄣ ㄅㄨˋ ㄉㄨㄥˋ ㄅㄤˇ ㄅㄨˋ ㄧㄠˊ)
not to move even the body or the arms—not to labor at all
身不由主(ㄕㄣ·ㄅㄨ ㄧㄡˊ ㄓㄨˇ)or 身不由己(ㄕㄣ·ㄅㄨ ㄧㄡˊ ㄐㄧˇ)
unable to act according to one's own will; involuntarily
身法(ㄕㄣ ㄈㄚˇ)
techniques or arts of maneuvering the body in self-defense
身分證 or 身份證(ㄕㄣ ㄈㄣˋ ㄓㄥˋ)
a citizenship card; an identity card; an ID card
身分(ㄕㄣ·ㄈㄣ)
one's status or position
身底下(ㄕㄣ ㄉㄧˇ·ㄒㄧㄚ)
① under the body ② the place where one is living
身段(ㄕㄣ ㄉㄨㄢˋ)
① physique; a figure ② postures (of a dancer, etc.)

身體(ㄕㄣ ㄊㄧˇ)
①the body ②health: 他一向身體很健康。He has always had good health.

身體力行(ㄕㄣ ㄊㄧˇ ㄌㄧˋ ㄒㄧㄥˊ)
to carry out by actual efforts; to practice personally (what one preaches)

身體檢查(ㄕㄣ ㄊㄧˇ ㄐㄧㄢˇ ㄔㄚˊ)
a physical examination; a physical checkup

身歷聲(ㄕㄣ ㄌㄧˋ ㄕㄥ)
stereophonic; high fidelity 亦作「高度傳眞」

身臨其境(ㄕㄣ ㄌㄧㄣˊ ㄑㄧˊ ㄐㄧㄥˋ)
to experience personally; to be personally on the scene

身量(ㄕㄣ ㄌㄧㄤˋ)
one's height; one's physical dimensions: 她身量不高。She is not tall.

身高(ㄕㄣ ㄍㄠ)
stature; height

身故(ㄕㄣ ㄍㄨˋ)
to die: 張先生去年身故。Mr. Chang died last year.

身後(ㄕㄣ ㄏㄡˋ)
after one's death

身後名(ㄕㄣ ㄏㄡˋ ㄇㄧㄥˊ)
posthumous fame

身後蕭條(ㄕㄣ ㄏㄡˋ ㄒㄧㄠ ㄊㄧㄠˊ)
to die without leaving property or progeny behind

身火(ㄕㄣ ㄏㄨㄛˇ)
(Buddhism) desires

身懷六甲(ㄕㄣ ㄏㄨㄞˊ ㄌㄧㄡˋ ㄐㄧㄚˇ)
to be pregnant: 她身懷六甲。She is pregnant.

身己(ㄕㄣ ㄐㄧˇ)
oneself

身家(ㄕㄣ ㄐㄧㄚ)
family background; ancestry; pedigree

身家不清(ㄕㄣ ㄐㄧㄚ ㄅㄨˋ ㄑㄧㄥ)
of mean descent or parentage (formerly said of the offspring of prostitutes, entertainers, servants, and foot soldiers, who were barred from civil service examinations)

身家調查(ㄕㄣ ㄐㄧㄚ ㄉㄧㄠˋ ㄔㄚˊ)
the investigation of one's family background

身家難保(ㄕㄣ ㄐㄧㄚ ㄋㄢˊ ㄅㄠˇ)
to live in great danger; having no safety for oneself and one's dependents

身家清白(ㄕㄣ ㄐㄧㄚ ㄑㄧㄥ ㄅㄞˊ)
of respectable descent or parentage

身家性命(ㄕㄣ ㄐㄧㄚ ㄒㄧㄥˋ ㄇㄧㄥˋ)
one's personal safety as well as that of one's family

身價(ㄕㄣ ㄐㄧㄚˋ)
one's social position or prestige

身價百倍(ㄕㄣ ㄐㄧㄚˋ ㄅㄞˇ ㄅㄟˋ)
to receive a tremendous boost in one's social position or prestige

身教(ㄕㄣ ㄐㄧㄠˋ)
to teach by personal example: 身教勝於言教。Example is better than precept.

身經百戰(ㄕㄣ ㄐㄧㄥ ㄅㄞˇ ㄓㄢˋ)
to have gone through numerous battles

身輕言微(ㄕㄣ ㄑㄧㄥ ㄧㄢˊ ㄨㄟ)
When one's position is low, one's words carry little weight.

身軀(ㄕㄣ ㄑㄩ)
one's body; one's person

身心(ㄕㄣ ㄒㄧㄣ)
body and mind: 他有健全的身心。He has a sound body and mind.

身心健康(ㄕㄣ ㄒㄧㄣ ㄐㄧㄢˋ ㄎㄤ)
sound in body and mind; physically and mentally healthy

身心愉快(ㄕㄣ ㄒㄧㄣ ㄩˊ ㄎㄨㄞˋ)
feeling well both physically and mentally

身正不怕影兒斜(ㄕㄣ ㄓㄥˋ ㄅㄨˋ ㄆㄚˋ ㄧㄥˇㄦ ㄒㄧㄝˊ)
A righteous man fears no criticisms.

身長(ㄕㄣ ㄔㄤˊ)
①the stature or height (of a person) ②the body length (of an animal)

身世(ㄕㄣ ㄕˋ)
experiences in one's lifetime; one's life

身手(ㄕㄣ ㄕㄡˇ)
agility; dexterity; artistic skill

身首(ㄕㄣ ㄕㄡˇ)
the trunk and the head

身首異處(ㄕㄣ ㄕㄡˇ ㄧˋ ㄔㄨˋ)
to be beheaded

身受(ㄕㄣ ㄕㄡˋ)
①to accept personally; to receive in person ②to experience or endure personally

身上(ㄕㄣ ˙ㄕㄤ)
①on one's body: 我身上不舒服。I'm not feeling well. ②(to have something) with one: 我身上沒帶錢。I haven't got money with me.

身子(ㄕㄣ ˙ㄗ)
①the body; the trunk ②a child in the womb; pregnancy

身在福中不知福(ㄕㄣ ㄗㄞˋ ㄈㄨˊ ㄓㄨㄥ ㄅㄨˋ ㄓ ㄈㄨˊ)
Living in happiness, one often fails to appreciate what happiness really means.

身材(ㄕㄣ ㄘㄞˊ)
physique; physical build; figure: 她身材很好。She has a nice figure.

身兒(ㄕㄜㄦ)
①a suit (of clothes) ②physical build

身影(ㄕㄣ ㄧㄥˇ)
a person's silhouette; a form; a figure

身無長物(ㄕㄣ ㄨˊ ㄓㄤˋ ㄨˋ)
to have nothing; penniless

身外之物(ㄕㄣ ㄨㄞˋ ㄓ ㄨˋ)
(literally) things that are not part of one's body — money; material wealth

身孕(ㄕㄣ ㄩㄣˋ)
a child in the womb; pregnancy

【身】 5960
2. ㄐㄩㄢ jiuan juān

參看「身毒」

身毒(ㄐㄩㄢ ㄉㄨˊ)
an ancient name of India

三畫

【躬】 5961
ㄍㄨㄥ gong gōng

1. the body; the person
2. in person; personally
3. to bend (the body)

躬逢其盛(ㄍㄨㄥ ㄈㄥˊ ㄑㄧˊ ㄕㄥˋ)
to be personally present at the gala occasion

躬臨(ㄍㄨㄥ ㄌㄧㄣˊ)
to be present personally; to attend in person

躬耕(ㄍㄨㄥ ㄍㄥ)

to plough in person (especially said of an emperor)
躬稼(ㄍㄨㄥ ㄐㄧㄚˋ)
to work on the farm personally
躬親(ㄍㄨㄥ ㄑㄧㄣ)
in person; personally
躬行(ㄍㄨㄥ ㄒㄧㄥˊ)
to take action personally; to practice a thing personally
躬身(ㄍㄨㄥ ㄕㄣ)
to bend the body in respect; to bow
躬詣(ㄍㄨㄥ ㄧˋ)
to call at (another's house) personally

四畫

【躭】5962 (耽) ㄉㄢ dan dān
to delay (unintentionally)
躭擱(ㄉㄢ ㄍㄜ)
to delay (unintentionally); to fail to complete in time
躭心(ㄉㄢ ㄒㄧㄣ)or 躭憂(ㄉㄢ ㄧㄡ)
to be worried; to be apprehensive
躭誤(ㄉㄢ ㄨˋ)
① to mismanage (a thing) by an improper delay ② to take more (time) than justified; to delay

六畫

【躲】5963 ㄉㄨㄛˇ duoo duǒ
1. to dodge; to shun; to avoid; to escape
2. to hide
躲避(ㄉㄨㄛˇ ㄅㄧˋ)
to dodge; to ward off; to shun: 她在人群中躲避他。She dodged him in the crowd.
躲避球(ㄉㄨㄛˇ ㄅㄧˋ ㄑㄧㄡˊ)
dodge ball (a kind of ball game played by children)
躲不了(ㄉㄨㄛˇ ·ㄅㄨ ㄌㄧㄠˇ)
unavoidable; inescapable
躲不開(ㄉㄨㄛˇ ·ㄅㄨ ㄎㄞ)
unable to dodge; unable to shun
躲躲閃閃(ㄉㄨㄛˇ ㄉㄨㄛˇ ㄕㄢˇ ㄕㄢˇ)
① moving carefully so as to avoid danger ② bashful; timid; shy
躲匿(ㄉㄨㄛˇ ㄋㄧˋ)
to hide oneself
躲懶(ㄉㄨㄛˇ ㄌㄢˇ)
to shun work; to shy away from work
躲開(ㄉㄨㄛˇ ·ㄎㄞ)
① to ward off; to dodge: 他躲開了這個球。He dodged the ball. ② to run away from; to shirk: 他總是躲開責任。He always shirks his duty.
躲債(ㄉㄨㄛˇ ㄓㄞˋ)
to run away from one's creditor; to avoid a creditor
躲閃(ㄉㄨㄛˇ ㄕㄢˇ)
to dodge; to ward off
躲藏(ㄉㄨㄛˇ ㄘㄤˊ)
to hide oneself; to hide: 你最好躲藏起來。You had better hide.
躲雨(ㄉㄨㄛˇ ㄩˇ)
to take shelter from the rain

八畫

【躺】5964 ㄊㄤˇ taang tǎng
to be in a lying position; to lie down
躺下(ㄊㄤˇ ·ㄒㄧㄚ)
to lie down
躺著(ㄊㄤˇ ·ㄓㄜ)
to be in a lying position
躺椅(ㄊㄤˇ ㄧˇ)
a couch; a deck chair; a divan; a reclining chair: 坐在躺椅上。Sit on the couch.

十一畫

【軀】5965 ㄑㄩ chiu qū
1. the body; the trunk
2. a child in the womb
軀體(ㄑㄩ ㄊㄧˇ)
the body
軀幹(ㄑㄩ ㄍㄢˋ)
①(anatomy) the trunk ② the body; the physical build
軀幹骨(ㄑㄩ ㄍㄢˋ ㄍㄨˇ)
the bones of the trunk
軀殼(ㄑㄩ ㄑㄧㄠˋ)or(ㄑㄩ ㄎㄜˊ)or(ㄑㄩ ㄑㄩㄝ)
the body (conceived as the shell of the soul)

車部
ㄐㄩ jiu jū

【車】5966 1. ㄐㄩ jiu jū
name of a chessman in a kind of Chinese chess known as 象棋
【車】5966 2. ㄐㄩ jiu jū (語音 ㄔㄜ che chē)
1. a vehicle
2. a wheeled machine
3. to carry in a cart
4. to shape (things) on a lathe; to lathe; to turn
5. to lift water by a waterwheel
車僕(ㄐㄩ ㄆㄨˊ)
an official in charge of vehicles in ancient times
車馬(ㄐㄩ ㄇㄚˇ)or(ㄔㄜ ㄇㄚˇ)
vehicles and horses
車馬喧闐(ㄐㄩ ㄇㄚˇ ㄒㄩㄢ ㄊㄧㄢˊ)
the hustle and bustle of a city
車馬殷闐(ㄐㄩ ㄇㄚˇ ㄧㄣ ㄊㄧㄢˊ)
crowded with carriages and horses
車服(ㄐㄩ ㄈㄨˊ)
chariots and robes (commonly used in feudal times to reward vassals)
車殆馬煩or車怠馬煩(ㄐㄩ ㄉㄞˋ ㄇㄚˇ ㄈㄢˊ)
(literally) The vehicle is worn down and the horse is weary.—the hardships of long travel
車徒(ㄐㄩ ㄊㄨˊ)
chariots and foot soldiers
車同軌(ㄐㄩ ㄊㄨㄥˊ ㄍㄨㄟˇ)
(literally) All vehicles have the same gauge.—The country is unified.
車笠之盟(ㄐㄩ ㄌㄧˋ ㄓ ㄇㄥˊ)
close friendship
車騎(ㄐㄩ ㄐㄧˋ)
groups of vehicles and horses
車騎將軍(ㄐㄩ ㄐㄧˋ ㄐㄧㄤ ㄐㄩㄣ)
an ancient title of a commanding general

〔車部〕

車駕(ㄐㄩ ㄐㄧㄚˋ)
the Emperor; His Majesty
車轍(ㄐㄩ ㄓㄜˊ)or(ㄐㄩ ㄔㄜˋ)
ruts (of vehicles)
車師(ㄐㄩ ㄕ)
name of an ancient country in what is Chinese Turkestan today
車在馬前(ㄐㄩ ㄗㄞˋ ㄇㄚˇ ㄑㄧㄢˊ)
to put the cart before the horse—preposterous
車載斗量(ㄐㄩ ㄗㄞˋ ㄉㄡˇ ㄌㄧㄤˊ)
by cartloads and bushelfuls—a great deal; available in great quantity
車右(ㄐㄩ ㄧㄡˋ)
an armed escort who proceeds on the right of the escorted carriage
車把(ㄔㄜ ㄅㄚˇ)
handle bars (on bicycles or other vehicles); the shaft (of a wheelbarrow, etc.)
車把式 or 車把勢(ㄔㄜ ㄅㄚˇ ·ㄕ)
a carrier; a carter
車牌(ㄔㄜ ㄆㄞˊ)
the license plate (on a vehicle)
車篷子(ㄔㄜ ㄆㄥˊ ·ㄗ)
the canvas tops on vehicles
車票(ㄔㄜ ㄆㄧㄠˋ)
a train or bus ticket
車馬費(ㄔㄜ ㄇㄚˇ ㄈㄟˋ)
transportation allowances
車幔(ㄔㄜ ㄇㄢˋ)
curtains on a carriage
車門(ㄔㄜ ㄇㄣˊ)
doors of a vehicle
車費(ㄔㄜ ㄈㄟˋ)
a fare
車房(ㄔㄜ ㄈㄤˊ)
a garage
車夫(ㄔㄜ ·ㄈㄨ)
a cabman; a carter; a driver; a rickshaw man; a chauffeur
車道(ㄔㄜ ㄉㄠˋ)
roads or lanes for vehicular traffic
車燈(ㄔㄜ ㄉㄥ)
the headlight (or headlamp) of an automobile or a motorcycle or bicycle
車墊子(ㄔㄜ ㄉㄧㄢˋ ·ㄗ)
a cushioned seat on a vehicle
車胎(ㄔㄜ ㄊㄞ)
tires (on vehicle wheels)
車頭(ㄔㄜ ㄊㄡˊ)
the engine or locomotive of a train
車僮(ㄔㄜ ㄊㄨㄥˊ)
boys serving passengers (on a train)
車輛(ㄔㄜ ㄌㄧㄤˋ)
vehicles; rolling stock
車輪(ㄔㄜ ㄌㄨㄣˊ)
wheels of a vehicle: 脚踏車有兩個車輪。A bicycle has two wheels.
車輪戰(ㄔㄜ ㄌㄨㄣˊ ㄓㄢˋ)
to fight an enemy by turns in order to wear him down
車轂轆(ㄔㄜ ㄍㄨ ·ㄌㄨ)
wheels of a vehicle
車轂轆話(ㄔㄜ ㄍㄨ ·ㄌㄨ ㄏㄨㄚˋ)
to keep saying the same thing
車攻(ㄔㄜ ㄍㄨㄥ)
to attack by chariots
車庫(ㄔㄜ ㄎㄨˋ)
a garage; a vehicle barn
車行(ㄔㄜ ㄏㄤˊ)
① a vehicle dealer's shop ② a taxi company
車禍(ㄔㄜ ㄏㄨㄛˋ)
an automobile or a train accident; a traffic accident: 昨天有一樁車禍。There was a motorcar accident yesterday.
車匠(ㄔㄜ ㄐㄧㄤˋ)
a wheelwright
車前子(ㄔㄜ ㄑㄧㄢˊ ㄗˇ)
(botany) plantago seeds (used as medicine)
車前草(ㄔㄜ ㄑㄧㄢˊ ㄘㄠˇ)
(botany) the plantain
車錢(ㄔㄜ ·ㄑㄧㄢ)
a taxi fare; a pedicab or rickshaw fare; a fare: 下個月車錢要漲了。Fares will be raised next month.
車繡(ㄔㄜ ㄒㄧㄡˋ)
embroidery done on a sewing machine
車廂(ㄔㄜ ㄒㄧㄤ)
cars (of a train); railway carriages; compartments
車照(ㄔㄜ ㄓㄠˋ)
the license (of a car, motorcycle, etc.)
車軸(ㄔㄜ ㄓㄡˊ)
an axle
車軸關節(ㄔㄜ ㄓㄡˊ ㄍㄨㄢ ㄐㄧㄝˊ)
a pivot joint
車站(ㄔㄜ ㄓㄢˋ)
① a railway station ② a bus station; a bus stop; a bus terminal
車長(ㄔㄜ ㄓㄤˇ)
a train master
車長室(ㄔㄜ ㄓㄤˇ ㄕˋ)
the train master's compartment
車掌(ㄔㄜ ㄓㄤˇ)
a bus conductress or conductor
車廠(ㄔㄜ ㄔㄤˇ)
a shop in which motorcars are repaired or serviced
車窗(ㄔㄜ ㄔㄨㄤ)
car windows; train windows: 誰打破車窗呢? Who broke the car window?
車牀(ㄔㄜ ㄔㄨㄤˊ)
a lathe
車身(ㄔㄜ ㄕㄣ)
the car body; the vehicle body; the automobile body
車水(ㄔㄜ ㄕㄨㄟˇ)
to lift water by means of a scoop wheel
車水馬龍(ㄔㄜ ㄕㄨㄟˇ ㄇㄚˇ ㄌㄨㄥˊ)or(ㄐㄩ ㄕㄨㄟˇ ㄇㄚˇ ㄌㄨㄥˊ)
(literally) Carts flow like a stream and horses move like a dragon.—Traffic is heavy.
車資(ㄔㄜ ㄗ)
a fare for a vehicle ride
車子(ㄔㄜ ·ㄗ)
a vehicle
車次(ㄔㄜ ㄘˋ)
① the train number ② the motor coach number (designating a schedule of departure)
車速(ㄔㄜ ㄙㄨˋ)
the speed of a motor vehicle
車帷(ㄔㄜ ㄨㄟˊ)
curtains on a carriage or car

【車】 5966
3. ㄔㄜ che chē
a Chinese family name
車胤(ㄔㄜ ㄧㄣˋ)
Che Yin, a 4th century scholar who studied under the light of glowworms in his youth

車螢孫雪(ㄔㄜ ㄧㄥˊ ㄙㄨㄣ ㄒㄩㄝˇ)
(literally) Che Yin (車胤) studied by the light of glowworms and Sun Kang (孫康) studied by the light of snow. —to study very diligently

一畫

【軋】 5967 1. ㄧㄚˋ yah yà
to crush; to grind

軋布機(ㄧㄚˋ ㄅㄨˋ ㄐㄧ)
a mangle; a calender 亦作「軋光機」

軋花機(ㄧㄚˋ ㄏㄨㄚ ㄐㄧ)or 軋棉機(ㄧㄚˋ ㄇㄧㄢˊ ㄐㄧ)
a cotton gin

軋傷(ㄧㄚˋ ㄕㄤ)
to run over and injure

軋死(ㄧㄚˋ ㄙˇ)or 軋斃(ㄧㄚˋ ㄅㄧˋ)
to run over and kill: 他被火車軋死。He was run over and killed by the train.

軋碎(ㄧㄚˋ ㄙㄨㄟˋ)
to crush to pieces

軋軋(ㄧㄚˋ ㄧㄚˋ)
the creaking sound of a machine in operation

【軋】 5967 2. ㄍㄚˊ gar gá
1. (in the Wu dialect) to crowd
2. (in the Wu dialect) to make friends
3. (in the Wu dialect) to check

軋姘頭(ㄍㄚˊ ㄆㄧㄣ ·ㄊㄡ)
(in the Wu dialect) to commit adultery

軋頭寸(ㄍㄚˊ ㄊㄡˊ ㄘㄨㄣˋ)
(informal) to scramble for cash to meet a payment 參看「調頭寸」

二畫

【軌】 5968 ㄍㄨㄟˇ goei guǐ
1. the space between the right and the left wheels of a vehicle
2. a rut; a track; a path
3. an orbit
4. a rule; a regulation
5. to follow; to comply with; to obey

軌模(ㄍㄨㄟˇ ㄇㄛˊ)
a pattern; a rule: 他是所有美德之軌模。He is a pattern of all the virtues.

軌範(ㄍㄨㄟˇ ㄈㄢˋ)
a pattern; a model; a rule

軌道(ㄍㄨㄟˇ ㄉㄠˋ)
① a railway track ② an orbit ③laws and conventions ④ a course; a track

軌度(ㄍㄨㄟˇ ㄉㄨˋ)
a rule; a regulation

軌跡(ㄍㄨㄟˇ ㄐㄧ)
①(mathematics) a locus ② (astronomy) an orbit

軌距(ㄍㄨㄟˇ ㄐㄩˋ)
(said of railroad tracks) the gauge

軌制(ㄍㄨㄟˇ ㄓˋ)
a system; a rule

軌轍(ㄍㄨㄟˇ ㄓㄜˊ)or(ㄍㄨㄟˇ ㄔㄜˋ)
a rut

軌則(ㄍㄨㄟˇ ㄗㄜˊ)
a rule; a regulation: 軌則甚嚴。The regulations are strict.

軌外行爲(ㄍㄨㄟˇ ㄨㄞˋ ㄒㄧㄥˊ ㄨㄟˊ)
transgression of rules or regulations

【軍】 5969 ㄐㄩㄣ jiun jūn
1. the military; forces; of national defense
2. corps (as a military unit)
3. an armed service

軍備(ㄐㄩㄣ ㄅㄟˋ)
armaments; arms

軍部(ㄐㄩㄣ ㄅㄨˋ)
the war ministry; the defense department

軍票(ㄐㄩㄣ ㄆㄧㄠˋ)
bank notes used by military personnel in war zones

軍帽(ㄐㄩㄣ ㄇㄠˋ)
a military cap or hat

軍門(ㄐㄩㄣ ㄇㄣˊ)
①the entrance to a military camp, fort, etc. ② (Ching Dynasty) a commander in chief

軍民(ㄐㄩㄣ ㄇㄧㄣˊ)
soldiers and civilians

軍民合作(ㄐㄩㄣ ㄇㄧㄣˊ ㄏㄜˊ ㄗㄨㄛˋ)
cooperation between soldiers and civilians

軍閥(ㄐㄩㄣ ㄈㄚˊ)
①a military clique ②the militarists ③a warlord

軍閥割據(ㄐㄩㄣ ㄈㄚˊ ㄍㄜ ㄐㄩˋ)
the rampancy of warlords; the segmentation of a country by warlords

軍法(ㄐㄩㄣ ㄈㄚˇ)
military law

軍法官(ㄐㄩㄣ ㄈㄚˇ ㄍㄨㄢ)
a judge advocate

軍法會審(ㄐㄩㄣ ㄈㄚˇ ㄏㄨㄟˋ ㄕㄣˇ)or 軍法審判(ㄐㄩㄣ ㄈㄚˇ ㄕㄣˇ ㄆㄢˋ)
courts-martial

軍法會議(ㄐㄩㄣ ㄈㄚˇ ㄏㄨㄟˋ ㄧˋ)
a court-martial sitting or session; a court-martial

軍法局長(ㄐㄩㄣ ㄈㄚˇ ㄐㄩˊ ㄓㄤˇ)
the judge advocate general

軍法裁判所(ㄐㄩㄣ ㄈㄚˇ ㄘㄞˊ ㄆㄢˋ ㄙㄨㄛˇ)
a military court; a court-martial 參看「軍事法庭」

軍法從事(ㄐㄩㄣ ㄈㄚˇ ㄘㄨㄥˊ ㄕˋ)
to be dealt with according to martial law

軍費(ㄐㄩㄣ ㄈㄟˋ)
military expenses; a defense budget: 軍費被縮減了。Military expenses were cut down.

軍方(ㄐㄩㄣ ㄈㄤ)
the military authorities

軍服(ㄐㄩㄣ ㄈㄨˊ)
(military) uniform

軍刀(ㄐㄩㄣ ㄉㄠ)
a saber

軍刀機(ㄐㄩㄣ ㄉㄠ ㄐㄧ)
Saberjet (of the U.S. Air Force in the 1950's)

軍隊(ㄐㄩㄣ ㄉㄨㄟˋ)
troops; the armed forces

軍帖(ㄐㄩㄣ ㄊㄧㄝˇ)
a military proclamation

軍團(ㄐㄩㄣ ㄊㄨㄢˊ)
①an army (a unit consisting of a number of corps) ② any large unit of troops; a legion

軍壘(ㄐㄩㄣ ㄌㄟˇ)
barriers around a fort; a fort 亦作「軍壁」

軍禮(ㄐㄩㄣ ㄌㄧˇ)
military rites; a military salute: 軍官回了一個軍禮。The officer returned a military salute.

軍力(ㄐㄩㄣ ㄌㄧˋ)
military strength (or power)

軍糧(ㄐㄩㄣ ㄌㄧㄤˊ)

food supplies for military units

軍令(ㄐㄩㄣ ㄌㄧㄥˋ)
military orders

軍令狀(ㄐㄩㄣ ㄌㄧㄥˋ ㄓㄨㄤˋ)
a written pledge to do something, the failing of which would subject one to military punishment

軍令如山(ㄐㄩㄣ ㄌㄧㄥˋ ㄖㄨˊ ㄕㄢ)
Military orders cannot be disobeyed or revoked.

軍旅(ㄐㄩㄣ ㄌㄩˇ)
troops; armies

軍律(ㄐㄩㄣ ㄌㄩˋ)
military discipline; military laws: 軍律嚴明。Military laws are peremptory.

軍略(ㄐㄩㄣ ㄌㄩㄝˋ)
military strategy

軍歌(ㄐㄩㄣ ㄍㄜ)
a war song; a martial chant: 她唱了一首軍歌。She sang a war song.

軍港(ㄐㄩㄣ ㄍㄤˇ)
a naval harbor; a naval port

軍國民教育(ㄐㄩㄣ ㄍㄨㄛˊ ㄇㄧㄣˊ ㄐㄧㄠˋ ㄩˋ)
national military education

軍國大事(ㄐㄩㄣ ㄍㄨㄛˊ ㄉㄚˋ ㄕˋ)
affairs of national defense and administration

軍國主義(ㄐㄩㄣ ㄍㄨㄛˊ ㄓㄨˇ ㄧˋ)
militarism

軍規(ㄐㄩㄣ ㄍㄨㄟ)
military discipline

軍官(ㄐㄩㄣ ㄍㄨㄢ)
(military) an officer: 他希望當軍官。He wished to be an officer.

軍官學校(ㄐㄩㄣ ㄍㄨㄢ ㄒㄩㄝˊ ㄒㄧㄠˋ)
an academy for the training of officers, such as the military academy, naval academy and air force academy

軍管區(ㄐㄩㄣ ㄍㄨㄢˇ ㄑㄩ)
a military organization on the provincial level in charge of conscription, training and mobilization of recruits and reservists, etc.

軍功(ㄐㄩㄣ ㄍㄨㄥ)
military achievements; meritorious military services; military exploits

軍號(ㄐㄩㄣ ㄏㄠˋ)
a bugle

軍火(ㄐㄩㄣ ㄏㄨㄛˇ)
arms; munitions

軍火庫(ㄐㄩㄣ ㄏㄨㄛˇ ㄎㄨˋ)
an arsenal

軍機(ㄐㄩㄣ ㄐㄧ)
① a military secret: 軍機洩露出去了。The military secret has leaked out. ② a military aircraft: 他搭軍機到高雄。He went to Kaohsiung by military aircraft.

軍機大臣(ㄐㄩㄣ ㄐㄧ ㄉㄚˋ ㄔㄣˊ)
the minister of defense (prior to the Republic)

軍機處(ㄐㄩㄣ ㄐㄧ ㄔㄨˋ)
the ministry of defense (but later expanded to deal with other affairs as well) under the Manchu government

軍籍(ㄐㄩㄣ ㄐㄧˊ)
① a military register ② military status

軍妓(ㄐㄩㄣ ㄐㄧˋ)
a military prostitute

軍紀(ㄐㄩ ㄐㄧˋ)
military discipline

軍階(ㄐㄩㄣ ㄐㄧㄝ)
(military) a rank; a grade

軍界(ㄐㄩㄣ ㄐㄧㄝˋ)
the military circles; the military

軍艦(ㄐㄩㄣ ㄐㄧㄢˋ)
a war vessel; a warship; a man-of-war

軍警(ㄐㄩㄣ ㄐㄧㄥˇ)
the military and the police

軍旗(ㄐㄩㄣ ㄑㄧˊ)
military banners, colors or flags

軍器(ㄐㄩㄣ ㄑㄧˋ)
military equipment

軍情(ㄐㄩㄣ ㄑㄧㄥˊ)
a military (or war) situation

軍權(ㄐㄩㄣ ㄑㄩㄢˊ)
the power over military or national defense matters

軍犬(ㄐㄩㄣ ㄑㄩㄢˇ)
police dogs used for military purposes

軍械(ㄐㄩㄣ ㄒㄧㄝˋ)
military equipment; ordnance; armaments

軍校(ㄐㄩㄣ ㄒㄧㄠˋ)
a military school

軍校學生(ㄐㄩㄣ ㄒㄧㄠˋ ㄒㄩㄝˊ ㄕㄥ)
a military cadet

軍校高年級生(ㄐㄩㄣ ㄒㄧㄠˋ ㄍㄠ ㄋㄧㄢˊ ㄐㄧˊ ㄕㄥ)
the upperclassmen of a military academy

軍校一年級生(ㄐㄩㄣ ㄒㄧㄠˋ ㄧˋ ㄋㄧㄢˊ ㄐㄧˊ ㄕㄥ)
a plebe

軍心(ㄐㄩㄣ ㄒㄧㄣ)
the morale of the troops: 軍心消沈。The morale of the troops is low.

軍餉(ㄐㄩㄣ ㄒㄧㄤˇ)
pay and allowances for soldiers; military payroll

軍興(ㄐㄩㄣ ㄒㄧㄥ)
① to requisition property for the army in ancient times ② the outbreak of hostilities

軍需(ㄐㄩㄣ ㄒㄩ)
① military supplies and equipment; war materials; materiel ② short for 軍需官

軍需品(ㄐㄩㄣ ㄒㄩ ㄆㄧㄣˇ)
military supplies and equipment; war materials; materiel

軍需官(ㄐㄩㄣ ㄒㄩ ㄍㄨㄢ)
an officer in charge of military supplies

軍需處(ㄐㄩㄣ ㄒㄩ ㄔㄨˋ)
the department of war materials

軍靴(ㄐㄩㄣ ㄒㄩㄝ)
combat boots

軍訓(ㄐㄩㄣ ㄒㄩㄣˋ)
military training

軍職(ㄐㄩㄣ ㄓˊ)
a military (as opposed to civilian) office or post; a military appointment

軍制(ㄐㄩㄣ ㄓˋ)
the military system

軍長(ㄐㄩㄣ ㄓㄤˇ)
a corps commander

軍政(ㄐㄩㄣ ㄓㄥˋ)
① a military government ② the administration of the armed forces

軍政部(ㄐㄩㄣ ㄓㄥˋ ㄅㄨˋ)
Ministry of War (in the early years of the Republic)

軍政部長(ㄐㄩㄣ ㄓㄥˋ ㄅㄨˋ ㄓㄤˇ)
Minister of War (in the early years of the Republic)

軍政府(ㄐㄩㄣ ㄓㄥˋ ㄈㄨˇ)

a military government
軍政大權集於一身(ㄐㄩㄣ ㄓㄥˋ ㄉㄚˋ ㄑㄩㄢˊ ㄐㄧˊ ㄩˊ ㄧˋ ㄕㄣ)
to have both civil and military powers held in the hands of a single individual
軍政權(ㄐㄩㄣ ㄓㄥˋ ㄑㄩㄢˊ)
powers for military administration
軍政時期(ㄐㄩㄣ ㄓㄥˋ ㄕˊ ㄑㄧˊ)
the Period of Military Administration (the first of the three steps of growth envisaged by Dr. Sun Yat-sen for the Republic)
軍裝(ㄐㄩㄣ ㄓㄨㄤ)
a soldier's outfit; military uniform
軍中(ㄐㄩㄣ ㄓㄨㄥ)
in the army; in the armed forces
軍中服務(ㄐㄩㄣ ㄓㄨㄥ ㄈㄨˊ ㄨˋ)
service in the army (rendered by civilians); troop-scheering activities
軍中無戲言(ㄐㄩㄣ ㄓㄨㄥ ㄨˊ ㄒㄧˋ ㄧㄢˊ)
(literally) There are no jokes in the armed forces. —A military pledge or order must be carried out.
軍種(ㄐㄩㄣ ㄓㄨㄥˇ)
the armed services; branches of the armed forces
軍車(ㄐㄩㄣ ㄔㄜ)
a military vehicle or conveyance
軍師(ㄐㄩㄣ ㄕ)
① a strategist; a tactician (a military post in ancient times roughly equivalent to the modern chief of a staff) ② an adviser; a consultant
軍使(ㄐㄩㄣ ㄕˇ)
a military envoy
軍士(ㄐㄩㄣ ㄕˋ)
a noncommissioned officer; a noncom 參看「軍曹」
軍事(ㄐㄩㄣ ㄕˋ)
military affairs
軍事犯(ㄐㄩㄣ ㄕˋ ㄈㄢˋ)
a military offender
軍事地理(ㄐㄩㄣ ㄕˋ ㄉㄧˋ ㄌㄧˇ)
military geography
軍事地區(ㄐㄩㄣ ㄕˋ ㄉㄧˋ ㄑㄩ)or 軍區(ㄐㄩㄣ ㄑㄩ)
a military area; a military scope; a military district
軍事顧問團(ㄐㄩㄣ ㄕˋ ㄍㄨˋ ㄨㄣˋ ㄊㄨㄢˊ)
a military assistance and advisory group
軍事化(ㄐㄩㄣ ㄕˋ ㄏㄨㄚˋ)
to militarize; militarization
軍事基地(ㄐㄩㄣ ㄕˋ ㄐㄧ ㄉㄧˋ)
a military base
軍事教育(ㄐㄩㄣ ㄕˋ ㄐㄧㄠˋ ㄩˋ)
military education
軍事行動(ㄐㄩㄣ ㄕˋ ㄒㄧㄥˊ ㄉㄨㄥˋ)
military action
軍事學(ㄐㄩㄣ ㄕˋ ㄒㄩㄝˊ)
military science
軍事學校(ㄐㄩㄣ ㄕˋ ㄒㄩㄝˊ ㄒㄧㄠˋ)
a military school
軍事訓練(ㄐㄩㄣ ㄕˋ ㄒㄩㄣˋ ㄌㄧㄢˋ)
military training
軍事制裁(ㄐㄩㄣ ㄕˋ ㄓˋ ㄘㄞˊ)
military sanctions
軍事占領(ㄐㄩㄣ ㄕˋ ㄓㄢˋ ㄌㄧㄥˇ)
military occupation
軍事政變(ㄐㄩㄣ ㄕˋ ㄓㄥˋ ㄅㄧㄢˋ)
a coup d'état
軍事裝備(ㄐㄩㄣ ㄕˋ ㄓㄨㄤ ㄅㄟˋ)
military equipment
軍事要塞(ㄐㄩㄣ ㄕˋ ㄧㄠˋ ㄙㄞˋ)
a military stronghold; a fortress
軍事演習(ㄐㄩㄣ ㄕˋ ㄧㄢˇ ㄒㄧˊ)
military maneuvers; military exercises; war games (or exercises)
軍事委員會(ㄐㄩㄣ ㄕˋ ㄨㄟˇ ㄩㄢˊ ㄏㄨㄟˋ)
Military Council (before and during the Second World War)
軍事委員會委員長(ㄐㄩㄣ ㄕˋ ㄨㄟˇ ㄩㄢˊ ㄏㄨㄟˋ ㄨㄟˇ ㄩㄢˊ ㄓㄤˇ)
the chairman of the Military Council; a generalissimo
軍書(ㄐㄩㄣ ㄕㄨ)
military letters; military correspondence
軍書旁午(ㄐㄩㄣ ㄕㄨ ㄅㄤˊ ㄨˇ)
(said of military commanders) very busy with directing military operations
軍人(ㄐㄩㄣ ㄖㄣˊ)
a soldier; a serviceman
軍人魂(ㄐㄩㄣ ㄖㄣˊ ㄏㄨㄣˊ)
a soldier's willingness to die for his country instead of surrendering to the enemy
軍人家屬(ㄐㄩㄣ ㄖㄣˊ ㄐㄧㄚ ㄕㄨˇ)or 軍屬(ㄐㄩㄣ ㄕㄨˇ)or 軍眷(ㄐㄩㄣ ㄐㄩㄢˋ)
a soldier's dependants
軍人節(ㄐㄩㄣ ㄖㄣˊ ㄐㄧㄝˊ)
Armed Forces Day (falling on September 3)
軍容(ㄐㄩㄣ ㄖㄨㄥˊ)
the impression which a military unit gives to a beholder; the general appearance of a military force
軍佐(ㄐㄩㄣ ㄗㄨㄛˇ)
a noncombatant member of a military unit with officer rank
軍曹(ㄐㄩㄣ ㄘㄠˊ)
a sergeant; a noncom 參看「軍士」
軍醫(ㄐㄩㄣ ㄧ)
(military) a surgeon; a medic
軍醫署長(ㄐㄩㄣ ㄧ ㄕㄨˇ ㄓㄤˇ)or 軍醫總監(ㄐㄩㄣ ㄧ ㄗㄨㄥˇ ㄐㄧㄢ)
a surgeon general
軍油(ㄐㄩㄣ ㄧㄡˊ)
military gasoline
軍郵(ㄐㄩㄣ ㄧㄡˊ)
Army Post Office (A.P.O.); military mail service
軍營(ㄐㄩㄣ ㄧㄥˊ)
a military camp
軍務(ㄐㄩㄣ ㄨˋ)
administrative matters of the armed forces
軍威(ㄐㄩㄣ ㄨㄟ)
military prestige; military prowess
軍文(ㄐㄩㄣ ㄨㄣˊ)
civilian employees in the armed forces
軍語(ㄐㄩㄣ ㄩˇ)
military terms
軍樂(ㄐㄩㄣ ㄩㄝˋ)
a martial tune
軍樂隊(ㄐㄩㄣ ㄩㄝˋ ㄉㄨㄟˋ)
a military band
軍用(ㄐㄩㄣ ㄩㄥˋ)
for military use; military
軍用品(ㄐㄩㄣ ㄩㄥˋ ㄆㄧㄣˇ)
military supplies and equipment; war materials; materiel
軍用飛機場(ㄐㄩㄣ ㄩㄥˋ ㄈㄟ ㄐㄧ ㄔㄤˇ)or(ㄐㄩㄣ ㄩㄥˋ ㄈㄟ ㄐㄧ ㄔㄤˊ)
a military airfield
軍用電話(ㄐㄩㄣ ㄩㄥˋ ㄉㄧㄢˋ ㄏㄨㄚˋ)

a military telephone

軍用車(ㄐㄩㄣ ㄩㄥˋ ㄔㄜ)
a military vehicle

軍用物資(ㄐㄩㄣ ㄩㄥˋ ㄨˋ ㄗ)
military supplies; materiel; war materials

三畫

【軒】 5970 ㄒㄩㄢ shiuan xuān

1. a carriage formerly used by high officials
2. the high front of a chariot or carriage
3. a balcony; a porch
4. a window
5. open; wide
6. high; lofty
7. smiling; laughing; delighted
8. a studio; a room

軒冕(ㄒㄩㄢ ㄇㄧㄢˇ)
① carriages and garments for high officials in former times ② eminent personages and high officials

軒朗(ㄒㄩㄢ ㄌㄤˇ)
open; wide

軒豁(ㄒㄩㄢ ㄏㄨㄛˋ)
open; wide

軒駕(ㄒㄩㄢ ㄐㄧㄚˋ)
① the emperor's carriage ② Hsüan-yüan(軒轅), a legendary ruler of virtue 亦作「黃帝」

軒檻(ㄒㄩㄢ ㄐㄧㄢˋ)
railings of a balcony

軒軒(ㄒㄩㄢ ㄒㄩㄢ)
① smug; complacent ② outstanding

軒輊(ㄒㄩㄢ ㄓˋ)
the high front and the low rear of a chariot—difference in height, rank, excellence, etc.

軒敞(ㄒㄩㄢ ㄔㄤˇ)
open; wide

軒然(ㄒㄩㄢ ㄖㄢˊ)
① smiling; delighted ② very high; towering; lofty

軒然大波(ㄒㄩㄢ ㄖㄢˊ ㄉㄚˋ ㄅㄛ)
(literally) towering waves —great repercussions; violent reactions; a great stir

軒昂(ㄒㄩㄢ ㄤˊ)
high; lofty; dignified

軒轅(ㄒㄩㄢ ㄩㄢˊ)
an alternative name of Huang Ti (黃帝), regarded as the first great ruler of China

【軔】 5971 ㄖㄣˋ renn rèn

1. a skid (for checking the motion of a vehicle)
2. to block; to obstruct
3. soft
4. idle
5. a measure of length equaling to 8 cubits

【軏】 5972 ㄩㄝˋ yueh yuè

a crossbar at the end of the poles of a cart, etc.; an arrangement for yoking the horses in a light carriage

四畫

【軛】 5973 ㄜˋ eh è

a yoke

【軟】 5974 (輭) ㄖㄨㄢˇ roan ruǎn

1. soft; pliable; tender; plastic; flexible; supple: 松木比橡木軟些。Pine wood is softer than oak.
2. soft; gentle; mild
3. weak; feeble; effeminate; cowardly
4. poor in quality, ability, etc.
5. easily moved or influenced

軟皮塞兒(ㄖㄨㄢˇ ㄆㄧˊ ㄙㄚㄦ)
a cork stopper; a cork

軟片(ㄖㄨㄢˇ ㄆㄧㄢˋ)
(photographic) film: 他需要一卷軟片。He needed a roll of film.

軟錳礦(ㄖㄨㄢˇ ㄇㄥˇ ㄎㄨㄤˋ)
pyrolusite

軟綿綿(ㄖㄨㄢˇ ㄇㄧㄢˊ ㄇㄧㄢˊ)
① soft ② (said of songs) sentimental ③ weak

軟木塞兒(ㄖㄨㄢˇ ㄇㄨˋ ㄙㄚㄦ)
a cork stopper; a cork

軟風(ㄖㄨㄢˇ ㄈㄥ)
a light wind; a gentle breeze; a zephyr

軟墊(ㄖㄨㄢˇ ㄉㄧㄢˋ)
(machinery) packing

軟糖(ㄖㄨㄢˇ ㄊㄤˊ)
a fondant; fudge

軟梯(ㄖㄨㄢˇ ㄊㄧ)
a rope ladder

軟體(ㄖㄨㄢˇ ㄊㄧˇ)
software 參看「硬體」

軟體動物(ㄖㄨㄢˇ ㄊㄧˇ ㄉㄨㄥˋ ㄨˋ)
molluscs; mollusks

軟鐵(ㄖㄨㄢˇ ㄊㄧㄝˇ)
wrought iron; soft iron

軟膿包(ㄖㄨㄢˇ ㄋㄨㄥˊ ㄅㄠ)
a coward: 他是個軟膿包。He is a coward.

軟膏(ㄖㄨㄢˇ ㄍㄠ)
ointment: 冷霜是一種軟膏。Cold cream is an ointment.

軟骨(ㄖㄨㄢˇ ㄍㄨˇ)
(anatomy) a cartilage

軟骨病(ㄖㄨㄢˇ ㄍㄨˇ ㄅㄧㄥˋ)
(medicine) rickets; rachitis 亦作「佝僂症」

軟骨組織(ㄖㄨㄢˇ ㄍㄨˇ ㄗㄨˇ ㄓ)
(anatomy) cartilaginous tissue

軟管(ㄖㄨㄢˇ ㄍㄨㄢˇ)
hose

軟工夫(ㄖㄨㄢˇ ㄍㄨㄥ ˙ㄈㄨ)
stunts performed by virtue of nimbleness or agility instead of physical strength

軟口蓋(ㄖㄨㄢˇ ㄎㄡˇ ㄍㄞˋ)
(anatomy) the soft palate; the velum

軟化(ㄖㄨㄢˇ ㄏㄨㄚˋ)
① to soften; to conciliate ② to soften: 鐵受熱即軟化。Iron softens with heat.

軟和(ㄖㄨㄢˇ ˙ㄏㄨㄛ)
① soft ② gentle; kind

軟脚病(ㄖㄨㄢˇ ㄐㄧㄠˇ ㄅㄧㄥˋ)
(medicine) beriberi 亦作「脚氣病」

軟禁(ㄖㄨㄢˇ ㄐㄧㄣˋ) or 軟監(ㄖㄨㄢˇ ㄐㄧㄢ)
to put under house arrest; to confine informally

軟席(ㄖㄨㄢˇ ㄒㄧˊ)
a soft seat or berth

軟席車廂(ㄖㄨㄢˇ ㄒㄧˊ ㄔㄜ ㄒㄧㄤ)
a railway coach with soft seats or berths

軟心腸(ㄖㄨㄢˇ ㄒㄧㄣ ㄔㄤˊ)
soft-hearted: 她是個軟心腸的女人。She is a soft-hearted woman.

軟刑(ㄖㄨㄢˇ ㄒㄧㄥˊ)
to torment or torture mentally

軟性(ㄖㄨㄢˇ ㄒㄧㄥˋ)
soft; mild; bland; gentle;

light

軟性下疳(ㄖㄨㄢˇ ㄒㄧㄥˋ ㄒㄧㄚˋ ㄍㄢ) or 軟下疳(ㄖㄨㄢˇ ㄒㄧㄚˋ ㄍㄢ)
(medicine) soft chancre; chancroid

軟性新聞(ㄖㄨㄢˇ ㄒㄧㄥˋ ㄒㄧㄣ ㄨㄣˊ)
light news; light stories; human-interest stories

軟脂(ㄖㄨㄢˇ ㄓ)
palmitin

軟脂酸(ㄖㄨㄢˇ ㄓ ㄙㄨㄢ)
(chemistry) palmitic acid

軟牀(ㄖㄨㄢˇ ㄔㄨㄤˊ)
a stretcher; a litter

軟水(ㄖㄨㄢˇ ㄕㄨㄟˇ)
(chemistry) soft water; water free from mineral contents

軟弱(ㄖㄨㄢˇ ㄖㄨㄛˋ)
① weak; feeble: 他因病而身體軟弱。He is weak from illness. ②(said of character, etc.) flabby; weak: 我不喜歡他軟弱的性格。I don't like his flabby character.

軟硬不喫(ㄖㄨㄢˇ ㄧㄥˋ ㄅㄨˋ ㄔ)
to yield to neither the carrot nor the stick; to stand pat

軟硬兼施(ㄖㄨㄢˇ ㄧㄥˋ ㄐㄧㄢ ㄕ)
to use both hard and soft tactics; to use the carrot and the stick

軟文學(ㄖㄨㄢˇ ㄨㄣˊ ㄒㄩㄝˊ)
light literature

軟語(ㄖㄨㄢˇ ㄩˇ)
gentle words

軟玉(ㄖㄨㄢˇ ㄩˋ)
① nephrite ② bean curd

軟玉溫香(ㄖㄨㄢˇ ㄩˋ ㄨㄣ ㄒㄧㄤ)
(said of a beauty's skin) as fair as jade

五畫

【軫】 5975 ㄓㄣˇ jeen zhěn

1. the wooden bumper at the rear of a cart or carriage
2. a Chinese family name

軫慕(ㄓㄣˇ ㄇㄨˋ)
to remember with deep emotion

軫悼(ㄓㄣˇ ㄉㄠˋ)
to mourn deeply

軫念(ㄓㄣˇ ㄋㄧㄢˋ)
to remember with deep emotion

軫懷(ㄓㄣˇ ㄏㄨㄞˊ)
to remember with deep emotion 亦作「軫念」

軫惜(ㄓㄣˇ ㄒㄧˊ)
to mourn with deep regret; to have pity on

軫恤(ㄓㄣˇ ㄒㄩˋ)
to pity deeply

【軨】 5976 ㄌㄧㄥˊ ling líng

1. the framework on a carriage
2. the wheels of a carriage

【軸】 5977 ㄓㄡˊ jour zhóu (讀音 ㄓㄨˊ jwu zhú)

1. an axis; a pivot; an axle: 地球繞軸自轉。The earth rotates on its own axis.
2. (said of mounted paintings or calligraphic works) a scroll

軸面(ㄓㄡˊ ㄇㄧㄢˋ)
(geology) pinacoidal faces

軸對稱(ㄓㄡˊ ㄉㄨㄟˋ ㄔㄣˋ)
(mathematics) axial symmetry

軸心(ㄓㄡˊ ㄒㄧㄣ)
an axis

軸心國(ㄓㄡˊ ㄒㄧㄣ ㄍㄨㄛˊ)
the Axis (in World War II)

軸承(ㄓㄡˊ ㄔㄥˊ)
bearings

軸子(ㄓㄡˊ ·ㄗ) or 軸兒(ㄓㄡˊㄦ)
an axis; a pivot; an axle

【軺】 5978 ㄧㄠˊ yau yáo

a kind of light carriage

【軹】 5979 ㄓˇ jyy zhǐ

the ends of an axle

軹道(ㄓˇ ㄉㄠˋ)
name of an ancient place

【軻】 5980 ㄎㄜ ke kē

1. a kind of ancient carts
2. name of Mencius

軻峨(ㄎㄜ ㄜˊ)
lofty

【軼】 5981 ㄧˋ yih yì

1. to excel; to surpass
2. to be scattered; to go loose

軼蕩(ㄧˋ ㄉㄤˋ)
unrestrained

軼倫(ㄧˋ ㄌㄨㄣˊ) or 軼群(ㄧˋ ㄑㄩㄣˊ)
to surpass one's contemporaries; to be outstanding

軼詩(ㄧˋ ㄕ)
poems not included in anthologies; scattered poems

軼事(ㄧˋ ㄕˋ)
an anecdote (not included in history)

軼材(ㄧˋ ㄘㄞˊ)
outstanding talents

軼聞(ㄧˋ ㄨㄣˊ)
an anecdote: 有很多關於他的軼聞。Many anecdotes are told about him.

【軲】 5982 ㄍㄨ gu gū

1. a wheel
2. to turn; to revolve; to rotate

軲轆(ㄍㄨ ·ㄌㄨ)
① a wheel ② to turn; to revolve

六畫

【較】 5983 ㄐㄧㄠˋ jiaw jiào (又讀 ㄐㄧㄠˇ jeau jiǎo)

1. to compare
2. in a greater or lesser degree; more or less; earlier or later
3. clear; conspicuous; obvious; marked
4. to compete; to dispute
5. fairly; quite; relatively

較炳(ㄐㄧㄠˋ ㄅㄧㄥˇ)
clear; obvious; conspicuous

較量(ㄐㄧㄠˋ ㄌㄧㄤˋ)
to compare (strength, etc.) in a contest; to contest; to have a trial (or test) of strength: 他們兩人較量高下。They contest and see who is the better (or the stronger).

較略(ㄐㄧㄠˋ ㄌㄩㄝˋ)
generally speaking; in general

較勁兒(ㄐㄧㄠˋ ㄐㄧㄣˋㄦ)
① to have a trial of strength ② to get worse; to become worse

較著(ㄐㄧㄠˋ ㄓㄨˋ)
conspicuous; obvious

較勝一籌(ㄐㄧㄠˋ ㄕㄥˋ ㄧˋ ㄔㄡˊ)
better by one degree; a little better

【軾】 5984 ㄕˋ shyh shì

the horizontal front bar on a cart or carriage

【輅】 5985 ㄌㄨˋ luh lù
1. a heavy carriage
2. the horizontal front bar on a cart or carriage
3. a state carriage

【輈】 5986 ㄓㄡ jou zhōu
the shaft or pole (of a cart or carriage)

【載】 5987 1. ㄗㄞˋ tzay zài
1. (said of vehicles, vessels, etc.) to carry (loads); to load
2. to record; to publish
3. to fill

載滿(ㄗㄞˋ ㄇㄢˇ)
to carry a full load; to be fully laden

載明(ㄗㄞˋ ㄇㄧㄥˊ)
to record clearly

載福(ㄗㄞˋ ㄈㄨˊ)
to receive blessings; to enjoy happiness

載道(ㄗㄞˋ ㄉㄠˋ)
① to fill the streets (as complaints); (said of voices) to be heard all over: 怨聲載道。Voices of complaint can be heard all over. ②(said of writings) to convey philosophical principles

載歌載舞(ㄗㄞˋ ㄍㄜ ㄗㄞˋ ㄨˇ)
to sing and dance at the same time

載客(ㄗㄞˋ ㄎㄜˋ)
to carry passengers

載貨(ㄗㄞˋ ㄏㄨㄛˋ)
to carry cargo; to carry goods: 火車及船舶可用來載貨。Trains and ships can carry goods.

載籍(ㄗㄞˋ ㄐㄧˊ)
books

載記(ㄗㄞˋ ㄐㄧˋ)
chronicles or narratives about the vicissitudes of various feudal lords (as distinct from regular dynastic histories)

載酒問字(ㄗㄞˋ ㄐㄧㄡˇ ㄨㄣˋ ㄗˋ)
studious and inquisitive

載重(ㄗㄞˋ ㄓㄨㄥˋ)
① to carry heavy loads; heavily loaded ② carrying capacity

載重量(ㄗㄞˋ ㄓㄨㄥˋ ㄌㄧㄤˋ)
loading capacity; deadweight capacity

載運(ㄗㄞˋ ㄩㄣˋ)
to transport; to carry

【載】 5987 2. ㄗㄞˇ tzae zǎi
a year

【輊】 5988 ㄓˋ jyh zhì
the low rear of a chariot, etc.

七畫

【輒】 5989 (輙) ㄓㄜˊ jer zhé
1. sides of a chariot, etc., that point downward at the front
2. arbitrary; dictatorial
3. then; in that case
4. every time; always

【輓】 5990 ㄨㄢˇ woan wǎn
1. to draw or pull (a cart)
2. to mourn
3. late 亦作「晚」

輓聯(ㄨㄢˇ ㄌㄧㄢˊ)
funeral scrolls

輓歌(ㄨㄢˇ ㄍㄜ)
a funeral hymn; a dirge; an elegy

輓近 or 晚近(ㄨㄢˇ ㄐㄧㄣˋ)
of late; lately; recently

輓詩(ㄨㄢˇ ㄕ)
a funeral ode; an elegy

【輔】 5991 ㄈㄨˇ fuu fǔ
1. human cheeks
2. protective bars on both sides of a cart or carriage
3. to assist; to help; to complement

輔弼(ㄈㄨˇ ㄅㄧˋ)
① to assist ② a prime minister

輔幣(ㄈㄨˇ ㄅㄧˋ)
coins of small denominations

輔導(ㄈㄨˇ ㄉㄠˇ)or(ㄈㄨˇ ㄉㄠˋ)
① to assist and guide ② guidance

輔導員(ㄈㄨˇ ㄉㄠˇ ㄩㄢˊ)
an assistant; an instructor

輔車相依(ㄈㄨˇ ㄐㄩ ㄒㄧㄤ ㄧ)
to depend upon each other

輔相(ㄈㄨˇ ㄒㄧㄤˋ)
① to assist ② a prime minister

輔助(ㄈㄨˇ ㄓㄨˋ)
to assist; assistance: 她輔助我工作。She assisted me in my work.

輔佐(ㄈㄨˇ ㄗㄨㄛˇ)
to assist

輔翼(ㄈㄨˇ ㄧˋ)
to assist

輔音(ㄈㄨˇ ㄧㄣ)
(phonetics) a consonant

【輕】 5992 ㄑㄧㄥ ching qīng
1. light: 油比水輕。Oil is lighter than water.
2. simple; easy; facile
3. mild; gentle; soft; tender; lightly; gently; softly
4. mean; base; lowly; unimportant
5. frivolous; flippant; fickle; rash; reckless
6. to slight; to neglect; to ignore; to underestimate; to disparage: 文人相輕。Scholars disparage one another.

輕薄(ㄑㄧㄥ ㄅㄛˊ)
① frivolous, flippant ② disrespectful; irreverent ③ to insult

輕薄少年(ㄑㄧㄥ ㄅㄛˊ ㄕㄠˋ ㄋㄧㄢˊ)
a frivolous youngster; a coxcomb

輕薄子(ㄑㄧㄥ ㄅㄛˊ ㄗˇ)or 輕薄兒(ㄑㄧㄥ ㄅㄛˊ ㄦˊ)
a frivolous youth; a fickle, callous fellow

輕便(ㄑㄧㄥ ㄅㄧㄢˋ)
handy; convenient; light; portable

輕便鐵路(ㄑㄧㄥ ㄅㄧㄢˋ ㄊㄧㄝˇ ㄌㄨˋ)
a light railway

輕拍(ㄑㄧㄥ ㄆㄞ)
to pat; to tap: 他輕拍她的肩膀。He patted her shoulder.

輕飄飄(ㄑㄧㄥ ㄆㄧㄠ ㄆㄧㄠ)
very light; lightly

輕慢(ㄑㄧㄥ ㄇㄢˋ)
disrespectful; irreverent

輕蔑(ㄑㄧㄥ ㄇㄧㄝˋ)
to despise; to disdain; to contemn; to slight: 一個偉人應該輕蔑諂媚者。A great man should disdain flatterers.

輕描淡寫(ㄑㄧㄥ ㄇㄧㄠˊ ㄉㄢˋ ㄒㄧㄝˇ)
to describe in a light, moderate tone; to play down (the importance or seriousness of

something); to water down; to touch on lightly

輕肥(ㄑㄧㄥ ㄈㄟˊ)
those who have light clothes and fat horses—the wealthy

輕放(ㄑㄧㄥ ㄈㄤˋ)
to put down gently

輕風(ㄑㄧㄥ ㄈㄥ)
a light wind; a breeze

輕浮(ㄑㄧㄥ ㄈㄨˊ)
flippant; frivolous; playful: 她是個輕浮的傻女孩。She is a frivolous, empty-headed girl.

輕敵(ㄑㄧㄥ ㄉㄧˊ)
to underestimate the enemy: 不要輕敵。Don't underestimate the enemy.

輕佻(ㄑㄧㄥ ㄊㄧㄠˊ)or 輕窕(ㄑㄧㄥ ㄊㄧㄠˊ)
frivolous; flippant; capricious; playful; sportive; skittish; giddy

輕脫(ㄑㄧㄥ ㄊㄨㄛ)
frivolous; playful

輕諾寡信(ㄑㄧㄥ ㄋㄨㄛˋ ㄍㄨㄚˇ ㄒㄧㄣˋ)
to give a promise easily and break it easily

輕利(ㄑㄧㄥ ㄌㄧˋ)
①to think little of material gain ②light and sharp

輕憐蜜愛(ㄑㄧㄥ ㄌㄧㄢˊ ㄇㄧˋ ㄞˋ)
tender affection between a couple in love

輕量級(ㄑㄧㄥ ㄌㄧㄤˋ ㄐㄧˊ)
(boxing) a lightweight, a boxer weighing between 126 and 135 pounds

輕歌曼舞(ㄑㄧㄥ ㄍㄜ ㄇㄢˋ ㄨˇ)
to sing cheerfully and dance gracefully

輕骨頭(ㄑㄧㄥ ㄍㄨˊ ˙ㄊㄡ)
①mean; base; lowly ②frivolous

輕工業(ㄑㄧㄥ ㄍㄨㄥ ㄧㄝˋ)
light industry

輕口薄舌(ㄑㄧㄥ ㄎㄡˇ ㄅㄛˊ ㄕㄜˊ)
to speak impolitely or rudely

輕快(ㄑㄧㄥ ㄎㄨㄞˋ)
①agile; sprightly; nimble; brisk; spry: 他走路輕快。He is a brisk walker. ②light-hearted ③lively: 她正在唱一首輕快的歌。She is singing a lively song.

輕狂(ㄑㄧㄥ ㄎㄨㄤˊ)
very frivolous

輕忽(ㄑㄧㄥ ㄏㄨ)
to neglect; to slight; to ignore: 他輕忽了他的健康。He neglected his health.

輕機槍(ㄑㄧㄥ ㄐㄧ ㄑㄧㄤ)
a light machine gun

輕騎(ㄑㄧㄥ ㄐㄧˋ)
①a light cavalryman; light cavalry ②a sprightly horse

輕捷(ㄑㄧㄥ ㄐㄧㄝˊ)
agile; nimble

輕賤(ㄑㄧㄥ ㄐㄧㄢˋ)
mean; base

輕金屬(ㄑㄧㄥ ㄐㄧㄣ ㄕㄨˇ)
light metals

輕車簡從(ㄑㄧㄥ ㄐㄩ ㄐㄧㄢˇ ㄗㄨㄥˋ)
(said of a high official, etc.) to travel with a minimum of pomp

輕車熟路(ㄑㄧㄥ ㄐㄩ ㄕㄨˊ ㄌㄨˋ)
as facile as traveling along a familiar road in a light carriage

輕舉妄動(ㄑㄧㄥ ㄐㄩˇ ㄨㄤˋ ㄉㄨㄥˋ)
to act rashly and blindly; to do something foolish

輕氣 or 氫氣(ㄑㄧㄥ ㄑㄧˋ)
hydrogen

輕氣球(ㄑㄧㄥ ㄑㄧˋ ㄑㄧㄡˊ)
a balloon

輕趬(ㄑㄧㄥ ㄑㄧㄠ)
agile

輕巧(ㄑㄧㄥ ㄑㄧㄠˇ)
①light and efficient; handy ②dexterous(ly)

輕裘緩帶(ㄑㄧㄥ ㄑㄧㄡˊ ㄏㄨㄢˇ ㄉㄞˋ)
(said of a general in former times) reposeful and scholarly

輕輕的(ㄑㄧㄥ ㄑㄧㄥ ˙ㄉㄜ)
lightly; gently; softly: 風從西方輕輕的吹來。The wind was blowing lightly from the west.

輕取(ㄑㄧㄥ ㄑㄩˇ)
to beat easily; to win an easy victory

輕信(ㄑㄧㄥ ㄒㄧㄣˋ)
gullible; credulous; to believe lightly: 過於猜疑,不如輕信。Better be too credulous than too skeptical.

輕刑(ㄑㄧㄥ ㄒㄧㄥˊ)
light punishment

輕巡洋艦(ㄑㄧㄥ ㄒㄩㄣˊ ㄧㄤˊ ㄐㄧㄢˋ)
a light cruiser

輕舟(ㄑㄧㄥ ㄓㄡ)
a light boat; a small boat

輕裝(ㄑㄧㄥ ㄓㄨㄤ)
light and simple luggage

輕重(ㄑㄧㄥ ㄓㄨㄥˋ)
①weight; light and heavy: 這兩個包裹輕重不一樣。The two packages do not weigh the same. ②degree of seriousness; of relative importance: 事情應分輕重緩急。Things should be done in order of importance and urgency. ③propriety

輕重倒置(ㄑㄧㄥ ㄓㄨㄥˋ ㄉㄠˋ ㄓˋ)
to neglect the important and emphasize the unimportant; to put the cart before the horse

輕脣音(ㄑㄧㄥ ㄔㄨㄣˊ ㄧㄣ)
(traditional Chinese phonology) labiodentals

輕視(ㄑㄧㄥ ㄕˋ)or 輕看(ㄑㄧㄥ ㄎㄢˋ)
to think little of; to slight; to make light of; to look down upon; to despise: 只因他家貧她便輕視他。She looks down upon him just because his family is poor.

輕手輕脚(ㄑㄧㄥ ㄕㄡˇ ㄑㄧㄥ ㄐㄧㄠˇ)
gently; softly

輕身(ㄑㄧㄥ ㄕㄣ)
①to make light of one's life ②without a burden; unmarried

輕傷(ㄑㄧㄥ ㄕㄤ)
a slight injury; a minor wound: 他的頭部受了輕傷。He received a slight injury to his head.

輕生(ㄑㄧㄥ ㄕㄥ)
to commit suicide

輕聲(ㄑㄧㄥ ㄕㄥ)
①(phonetics of Mandarin and many other Chinese dialects) a neutral tone ② in a soft voice; softly

輕聲細語(ㄑㄧㄥ ㄕㄥ ㄒㄧˋ ㄩˇ)
to speak softly; to whisper

輕率(ㄑㄧㄥ ㄕㄨㄞˋ)
①to make light of; to neglect; to slight; to ignore ②careless; reckless; rash; indiscreet; hardy: 這樣安排太輕率。It was indiscreet of you to arrange it that way.

輕爽(ㄑㄧㄥ ㄕㄨㄤˇ)

relaxed; easy; comfortable

輕柔(ㄑㄧㄥ ㄖㄡˊ)
soft; gentle: 她以輕柔的聲調回答我。She answered me in a gentle tone.

輕銳(ㄑㄧㄥ ㄖㄨㄟˋ)
light and sharp

輕財好義(ㄑㄧㄥ ㄘㄞˊ ㄏㄠˋ ㄧˋ)
generous and philanthropic

輕脆(ㄑㄧㄥ ㄘㄨㄟˋ)
light and fragile; flimsy; frail

輕鬆(ㄑㄧㄥ ㄙㄨㄥ)
① to lighten; to relax: 音樂使我們輕鬆。Music relaxes us. ② light; easy; comfortable

輕而易舉(ㄑㄧㄥ ㄦˊ ㄧˋ ㄐㄩˇ)
easy to accomplish; easy to do; to do without making an effort: 這是輕而易舉的工作。This job is easy to accomplish.

輕易(ㄑㄧㄥ ㄧˋ)
① easy; facile; effortless ② reckless; rash: 我不輕易發表意見。I do not express my viewpoint rashly.

輕油(ㄑㄧㄥ ㄧㄡˊ)
naphtha 亦作「石油精」

輕言(ㄑㄧㄥ ㄧㄢˊ)
to speak lightly; to speak without thinking

輕言細語(ㄑㄧㄥ ㄧㄢˊ ㄒㄧˋ ㄩˇ)
to speak softly; to talk in a soft voice

輕音樂(ㄑㄧㄥ ㄧㄣ ㄩㄝˋ)
light music

輕盈(ㄑㄧㄥ ㄧㄥˊ)
(said of a woman) nimble and shapely; lithe

輕侮(ㄑㄧㄥ ㄨˇ)
to insult; to contemn: 惡人輕侮上帝。The wicked contemn God.

輕微(ㄑㄧㄥ ㄨㄟˊ)
light; slight; little; unimportant; trivial; insignificant

輕微警告(ㄑㄧㄥ ㄨㄟˊ ㄐㄧㄥˇ ㄍㄠˋ)
a slap on the wrist

輕文重武(ㄑㄧㄥ ㄨㄣˊ ㄓㄨㄥˋ ㄨˇ)
to emphasize physical training at the expense of humanities; to put the sword above the pen

輕於鴻毛(ㄑㄧㄥ ㄩˊ ㄏㄨㄥˊ ㄇㄠˊ)
(literally) lighter than a feather; more trivial than a feather—without the least significance

八畫

【輜】 5993 ㄗ tzy zī
1. a curtained carriage
2. a wagon for supplies

輜重(ㄗ ㄓㄨㄥˋ)
① luggage ② military supplies

輜重兵(ㄗ ㄓㄨㄥˋ ㄅㄧㄥ)
transportation corps (as a branch of the army)

輜重隊(ㄗ ㄓㄨㄥˋ ㄉㄨㄟˋ)
transport troops; transport units; convoys of military supplies

輜重車(ㄗ ㄓㄨㄥˋ ㄔㄜ)
(military) transport vehicles

【輗】 5994 ㄋㄧˊ ni ní
the crossbar at the ends of carriage poles

【輘】 5995 ㄌㄧㄥˊ ling líng
run over by a vehicle

輘轢(ㄌㄧㄥˊ ㄌㄧˋ)
① to conflict ② to oppress

【輛】 5996 ㄌㄧㄤˋ lianq liàng
a numerary adjunct for vehicles: 我有一輛汽車。I have a car.

【輝】 5997 ㄏㄨㄟ huei huī
brightness; splendor; light; luster; luminosity; brilliance

輝沸石(ㄏㄨㄟ ㄈㄟˋ ㄕˊ)
heulandite

輝鐵礦(ㄏㄨㄟ ㄊㄧㄝˇ ㄎㄨㄤˋ)
specular iron

輝銅礦(ㄏㄨㄟ ㄊㄨㄥˊ ㄎㄨㄤˋ)
chalcocite

輝綠岩(ㄏㄨㄟ ㄌㄩˋ ㄧㄢˊ)
diabase

輝光(ㄏㄨㄟ ㄍㄨㄤ)
brightness; luminosity; brilliance

輝光燈(ㄏㄨㄟ ㄍㄨㄤ ㄉㄥ)
(physics) a glow lamp

輝赫(ㄏㄨㄟ ㄏㄜˋ)
shining; brilliant; bright; luminous

輝煌(ㄏㄨㄟ ㄏㄨㄤˊ)
magnificent; splendid; glorious; brilliant

輝石(ㄏㄨㄟ ㄕˊ)
(geology) pyroxene; augite

輝石岩(ㄏㄨㄟ ㄕˊ ㄧㄢˊ)
(geology) pyroxenite

輝耀(ㄏㄨㄟ ㄧㄠˋ)
shining; brilliant; bright; luminous

輝銀礦(ㄏㄨㄟ ㄧㄣˊ ㄎㄨㄤˋ)
argentite

輝映(ㄏㄨㄟ ㄧㄥˋ)
to emit and reflect light

【輞】 5998 ㄨㄤˇ woang wǎng
the rim of a wheel; a felly; a felloe

輞川(ㄨㄤˇ ㄔㄨㄢ)
name of a river in Shensi Province

【輟】 5999 ㄔㄨㄛˋ chuoh chuò
to stop; to halt; to suspend; to cease

輟筆(ㄔㄨㄛˋ ㄅㄧˇ)
to stop in the middle of writing or painting

輟耕(ㄔㄨㄛˋ ㄍㄥ)
to stop plowing

輟學(ㄔㄨㄛˋ ㄒㄩㄝˊ)
to drop out of school

輟朝(ㄔㄨㄛˋ ㄔㄠˊ)
to suspend business at the imperial court on account of a misfortune

【輦】 6000 ㄋㄧㄢˇ nean niǎn
1. a handcart
2. the king's carriage; the imperial carriage

輦夫(ㄋㄧㄢˇ ㄈㄨ)
a porter

輦道(ㄋㄧㄢˇ ㄉㄠˋ)or 輦路(ㄋㄧㄢˇ ㄌㄨˋ)
the emperor's road

輦轂下(ㄋㄧㄢˇ ㄍㄨˇ ㄒㄧㄚˋ)
the imperial capital

輦下(ㄋㄧㄢˇ ㄒㄧㄚˋ)
the imperial capital

【軿】 6001 ㄆㄧㄥˊ pyng píng
a curtained carriage (for women)

軿輅(ㄆㄧㄥˊ ㄌㄨˋ)
a curtained carriage for princesses

軿車(ㄆㄧㄥˊ ㄔㄜ)
a curtained carriage

【輩】 6002 ㄅㄟˋ bey bèi
1. rank; a grade
2. a generation
輩輩兒(ㄅㄟˋ ㄅㄜˋㄦ)
generation after generation; for generations
輩分(ㄅㄟˋ ·ㄈㄣ)
difference in seniority; seniority (among relatives)
輩流(ㄅㄟˋ ㄌㄧㄡˊ)
people of one's generation
輩行(ㄅㄟˋ ㄏㄤˊ)
order of seniority (among relatives, etc.)
輩出(ㄅㄟˋ ㄔㄨ)
to appear one after another; to come out in succession
輩數兒(ㄅㄟˋ ㄕㄨˇㄦ)
seniority (among relatives)
輩子(ㄅㄟˋ ·ㄗ)
① all one's life; a lifetime ② a generation
輩兒(ㄅㄜˋㄦ)
a generation

【輪】 6003 ㄌㄨㄣˊ luen lún
1. a wheel
2. to recur; to alternate
3. majestic; stately
4. to take turns; by turns; in relays
輪撥兒(ㄌㄨㄣˊ ㄅㄜㄦ)
by turns
輪暴(ㄌㄨㄣˊ ㄅㄠˋ)
to gang-rape; gang rape
輪班(ㄌㄨㄣˊ ㄅㄢ) or 輪班兒(ㄌㄨㄣˊ ㄅㄚㄦ)
to go on duty by rotation; to take turns; in shifts; in relays; in rotation
輪盤賭(ㄌㄨㄣˊ ㄆㄢˊ ㄉㄨˇ)
roulette
輪番(ㄌㄨㄣˊ ㄈㄢ)
to assume duties in turn; to take turns; in relays: 我們輪番上陣。We took turns going to battle.
輪幅(ㄌㄨㄣˊ ㄈㄨˊ)
the spokes of a wheel
輪調(ㄌㄨㄣˊ ㄉㄧㄠˋ)
to serve at a post or place for a fixed period by turns
輪渡(ㄌㄨㄣˊ ㄉㄨˋ)
a ferryboat; a steam ferry 亦作「渡輪」
輪胎(ㄌㄨㄣˊ ㄊㄞ)
the tire (of a wheel): 請給這個輪胎打氣。Please pump up this tire.
輪流(ㄌㄨㄣˊ ㄌㄧㄡˊ)
to take turns; by turns: 他們輪流划船。They rowed by turns.
輪廓(ㄌㄨㄣˊ ㄎㄨㄛˋ)
an outline; a silhouette
輪迴(ㄌㄨㄣˊ ㄏㄨㄟˊ)
① to recur successively; to move in a cycle ② transmigration (of the soul); metempsychosis; (Buddhism) *samsara*—the process of coming into existence as a differentiated, mortal creature
輪奐(ㄌㄨㄣˊ ㄏㄨㄢˋ)
(said of a building) stately; majestic
輪換(ㄌㄨㄣˊ ㄏㄨㄢˋ)
to alternate
輪機(ㄌㄨㄣˊ ㄐㄧ)
① a turbine ② a motorship engine; an engine
輪機長(ㄌㄨㄣˊ ㄐㄧ ㄓㄤˇ)
a chief engineer
輪姦(ㄌㄨㄣˊ ㄐㄧㄢ)
to gang-rape 參看「輪暴」
輪下冤鬼(ㄌㄨㄣˊ ㄒㄧㄚˋ ㄩㄢ ㄍㄨㄟˇ)
the victim of a traffic accident run over by a vehicle
輪休(ㄌㄨㄣˊ ㄒㄧㄡ)
to rest by turns; to take a day off by turns
輪形(ㄌㄨㄣˊ ㄒㄧㄥˊ)
wheel-shaped
輪軒(ㄌㄨㄣˊ ㄒㄩㄢ)
carriages of noblemen
輪值(ㄌㄨㄣˊ ㄓˊ)
to go on duty in turn; to take turns
輪軸(ㄌㄨㄣˊ ㄓㄡˊ)
wheels and axles; wheel shafts
輪轉(ㄌㄨㄣˊ ㄓㄨㄢˇ)
① to turn round; to revolve; to rotate ② to recur successively; to move in a cycle
輪轉機(ㄌㄨㄣˊ ㄓㄨㄢˇ ㄐㄧ)
(printing) a rotary press
輪種(ㄌㄨㄣˊ ㄓㄨㄥˋ)
to rotate crops; the rotation of crops
輪齒(ㄌㄨㄣˊ ㄔˇ)
gear teeth
輪掣(ㄌㄨㄣˊ ㄔㄜˋ)
brakes (of wheels)
輪唱(ㄌㄨㄣˊ ㄔㄤˋ)
① to chant Buddhist prayers ② (singing) to troll ③ a canon (a form of musical composition)
輪船(ㄌㄨㄣˊ ㄔㄨㄢˊ)
a steamship; a steamer
輪充(ㄌㄨㄣˊ ㄔㄨㄥ)
to undertake a task in turn; to take turns
輪生葉(ㄌㄨㄣˊ ㄕㄥ ㄧㄝˋ)
(botany) verticillate leaves; whorled leaves
輪子(ㄌㄨㄣˊ ·ㄗ) or 輪兒(ㄌㄨㄜˊㄦ)
a wheel
輪栽法(ㄌㄨㄣˊ ㄗㄞ ㄈㄚˇ) or 輪作法(ㄌㄨㄣˊ ㄗㄨㄛˋ ㄈㄚˇ)
crop rotation
輪繖花序(ㄌㄨㄣˊ ㄙㄢˇ ㄏㄨㄚ ㄒㄩˋ)
verticillaster
輪椅(ㄌㄨㄣˊ ㄧˇ)
a wheelchair
輪輿(ㄌㄨㄣˊ ㄩˊ) or 輪人(ㄌㄨㄣˊ ㄖㄣˊ)
a wheelwright; a carriage-wright

【輬】 6004 ㄌㄧㄤˊ liang liáng
1. a hearse
2. a sleeping carriage

【輒】 6005 ㄓㄜˊ jer zhé
same as 輙—then; in that case

九畫

【輯】 6006 ㄐㄧˊ jyi jí
1. friendly
2. to collect; to gather; to compile
輯睦 or 輯穆(ㄐㄧˊ ㄇㄨˋ)
friendliness
輯錄(ㄐㄧˊ ㄌㄨˋ)
to gather and record; to compile; to edit
輯略(ㄐㄧˊ ㄌㄩㄝˋ)
name of a bibliographical work by Liu Hsin (劉歆, ?-23 A.D.)
輯佚(ㄐㄧˊ ㄧˋ)
to gather rare and scattered writings or books
輯要(ㄐㄧˊ ㄧㄠˋ)
an outline; a summary: 他說

明了那計劃的輯要。He gave an outline of the plan.

【輳】 6007 ㄘㄡˋ tsow cou

to converge (as spokes of a wheel do at the hub)

【輶】 6008 ㄧㄡˊ you you

1. light
2. a light carriage

輶車(ㄧㄡˊ ㄐㄩ)
a light carriage

輶軒(ㄧㄡˊ ㄒㄩㄢ)
a light carriage for an imperial emissary

【輸】 6009 ㄕㄨ shu shū

1. to transport; to convey; to haul
2. to hand in; to contribute; to donate; to submit
3. to be beaten; to lose (a game, contest, etc.): 我們比賽輸了。We lost the game.

輸不起(ㄕㄨ ·ㄅㄨ ㄑㄧˇ)
①to display ill humor after losing a game, etc.; to lack sportsmanship: 他輸不起。He is a bad loser. ②cannot afford to lose

輸東道(ㄕㄨ ㄉㄨㄥ ㄉㄠˋ)or 輸東兒(ㄕㄨ ㄉㄨㄥㄦ)
the penalty (imposed upon the loser in a bet or gamble) of treating others to a dinner

輸納(ㄕㄨ ㄋㄚˋ)
to pay or submit (money, goods, etc.) to the authorities

輸尿管(ㄕㄨ ㄋㄧㄠˋ ㄍㄨㄢˇ)
(anatomy) the ureter

輸了(ㄕㄨ ·ㄌㄜ)
to be the loser; to have lost (a game, bet, etc.): 我們這隊輸了。Our team lost.

輸糧(ㄕㄨ ㄌㄧㄤˊ)
① to submit or hand in grain (as tax) ②to transport grain

輸卵管(ㄕㄨ ㄌㄨㄢˇ ㄍㄨㄢˇ)
(anatomy) the oviduct; fallopian tubes

輸攻墨守(ㄕㄨ ㄍㄨㄥ ㄇㄛˋ ㄕㄡˇ)
(literally) Kung-Shu Pan (公輸班) attacked the state of Sung (宋) with his new offensive devices but was repeatedly repelled by Motze(墨子) with his counter-devices.—Each displayed his special ability. 或 Each does his own best.

輸家(ㄕㄨ ㄐㄧㄚ)
the loser: 輸家必須付款。The loser must pay.

輸將(ㄕㄨ ㄐㄧㄤ)
①to transport; to haul ②to pay taxes or contributions to the government

輸精管(ㄕㄨ ㄐㄧㄥ ㄍㄨㄢˇ)
the deferent duct; the spermaduct

輸錢(ㄕㄨ ㄑㄧㄢˊ)
to lose money in gambling

輸情(ㄕㄨ ㄑㄧㄥˊ)
to supply secret information

輸血(ㄕㄨ ㄒㄧㄝˇ)
①(medicine) blood transfusion ②to give aid and support; to give somebody a shot in the arm

輸心服意(ㄕㄨ ㄒㄧㄣ ㄈㄨˊ ㄧˋ)
to follow or obey with sincere willingness

輸著兒(ㄕㄨ ㄓㄠㄦ)
a wrong move (in planning something)

輸誠(ㄕㄨ ㄔㄥˊ)
①to show sincerity ②to surrender: 該上尉不得不向敵人輸誠。The captain had to surrender to the enemy.

輸出(ㄕㄨ ㄔㄨ)
①export (of goods); to export: 中國輸出茶、絲到外國。China exported tea and silk to foreign countries. ②(computers) output

輸出指令(ㄕㄨ ㄔㄨ ㄓˇ ㄌㄧㄥˋ)
(computers) an output statement

輸出稅(ㄕㄨ ㄔㄨ ㄕㄨㄟˋ)
export duties

輸出額(ㄕㄨ ㄔㄨ ㄜˊ)
the amount of exports; the value of exports: 今年輸出額不如去年。The amount of exports this year is less than that of last year.

輸入(ㄕㄨ ㄖㄨˋ)
①import (of goods); to import: 美國自日本輸入生絲。America imports raw silk from Japan. ②(computers) input

輸入稅(ㄕㄨ ㄖㄨˋ ㄕㄨㄟˋ)
import duties

輸入額(ㄕㄨ ㄖㄨˋ ㄜˊ)
the amount of imports; the value of imports

輸嘴(ㄕㄨ ㄗㄨㄟˇ)
①to fail to keep promises ②to admit a mistake

輸財(ㄕㄨ ㄘㄞˊ)
to give cash donations or contributions

輸送(ㄕㄨ ㄙㄨㄥˋ)
to transport; to convey

輸送系統(ㄕㄨ ㄙㄨㄥˋ ㄒㄧˋ ㄊㄨㄥˇ)
a conveyer system

輸油管(ㄕㄨ ㄧㄡˊ ㄍㄨㄢˇ)
a pipeline (for transporting petroleum)

輸氧(ㄕㄨ ㄧㄤˇ)
(medicine) oxygen therapy

輸贏(ㄕㄨ ㄧㄥˊ)
losses and gains (in gambling, etc.); defeat or victory (in a game, etc.)

【輻】 6010 ㄈㄨˊ fwu fú

spokes (of a wheel)

輻聚(ㄈㄨˊ ㄐㄩˋ)
to gather, or converge, like spokes of a wheel

輻狀花冠(ㄈㄨˊ ㄓㄨㄤˋ ㄏㄨㄚ ㄍㄨㄢ)
the rotate corolla

輻射(ㄈㄨˊ ㄕㄜˋ)
to radiate; radiation: 這儀器產生有害的輻射。This apparatus produces harmful radiation.

輻射體(ㄈㄨˊ ㄕㄜˋ ㄊㄧˇ)
a radiant body; a radiator

輻射能(ㄈㄨˊ ㄕㄜˋ ㄋㄥˊ)
radiant energy

輻射計(ㄈㄨˊ ㄕㄜˋ ㄐㄧˋ)
a radiometer

輻射線(ㄈㄨˊ ㄕㄜˋ ㄒㄧㄢˋ)
radiant rays

輻射塵(ㄈㄨˊ ㄕㄜˋ ㄔㄣˊ)
radioactive dust; atomic fallout

輻射熱(ㄈㄨˊ ㄕㄜˋ ㄖㄜˋ)
(physics) radiant heat

輻輳 or 輻湊(ㄈㄨˊ ㄘㄡˋ)
to converge (as the spokes of a wheel do at the hub)

【輮】 6011 ㄖㄡˊ rou róu

1. the rim (of a wheel); a felly; a felloe
2. to trample

輮轢(ㄖㄡˊ ㄌㄧˋ)
trace of a wheel; a rut

【輭】 6012
ㄖㄨㄢˇ roan ruǎn
same as 軟—soft; mild; gentle

【輹】 6013
ㄈㄨˋ fuh fù
pieces of wood holding the axle underneath a cart

十畫

【輾】 6014
1. ㄓㄢˇ jaan zhǎn
to turn over; to roll over

輾轉(ㄓㄢˇ ㄓㄨㄢˇ)
①to roll about; to toss ②to take a roundabout course; to pass through many places

輾轉反側(ㄓㄢˇ ㄓㄨㄢˇ ㄈㄢˇ ㄘㄜˋ)
to toss about in bed; to turn around in bed and cannot get a sound sleep; to be sleepless

【輾】 6014
2. ㄋㄧㄢˇ nean niǎn
same as 碾—to grind; to crush; to run over

輾斃(ㄋㄧㄢˇ ㄅㄧˋ)
to be run over by a vehicle and got killed

輾鐵工場(ㄋㄧㄢˇ ㄊㄧㄝˇ ㄍㄨㄥ ㄔㄤˇ)
a rolling mill

【輿】 6015
ㄩˊ yu yú
1. a carriage; a vehicle
2. a sedan chair
3. the land; the earth
4. all; general
5. to carry; to transport

輿馬(ㄩˊ ㄇㄚˇ)
the carriage and the horse

輿夫(ㄩˊ ㄈㄨ)
sedan chair bearers

輿服(ㄩˊ ㄈㄨˊ)
one's carriage and garments

輿地(ㄩˊ ㄉㄧˋ)
the land; the earth

輿臺(ㄩˊ ㄊㄞˊ)
coolies; mean laborers

輿圖(ㄩˊ ㄊㄨˊ)
①a map ②territory (of a nation)

輿論(ㄩˊ ㄌㄨㄣˋ)
public opinion: 輿論贊成這個計劃。Public opinion is in favor of the plan.

輿論譁然(ㄩˊ ㄌㄨㄣˋ ㄏㄨㄚˊ ㄖㄢˊ)
Public opinion is seething with indignation.

輿論界(ㄩˊ ㄌㄨㄣˋ ㄐㄧㄝˋ)
the media; press circles

輿情(ㄩˊ ㄑㄧㄥˊ)
public sentiment; public feeling: 輿情激忿。Public feeling is in fury.

輿薪(ㄩˊ ㄒㄧㄣ)
a cartload of firewood—something very obvious

輿櫬(ㄩˊ ㄔㄣˋ)
to show one's determination to succeed or die by loading a coffin on one's carriage

輿師(ㄩˊ ㄕ)
a host; an army

輿人(ㄩˊ ㄖㄣˊ)
①a wheelwright ②a lowly official ③the masses; the people

輿皁(ㄩˊ ㄗㄠˋ)
a mean servant; a menial

【轂】 6016
1. ㄍㄨˇ guu gǔ
the hub (of a wheel)

轂擊肩摩(ㄍㄨˇ ㄐㄧˊ ㄐㄧㄢ ㄇㄛˊ)
(literally) Hubs hit hubs and shoulders rub shoulders.—(figuratively) a scene of a booming city

轂下(ㄍㄨˇ ㄒㄧㄚˋ)
the capital (of the empire)

【轂】 6016
2. ㄍㄨ gu gū
a wheel

轂轆(ㄍㄨ ·ㄌㄨ)
a wheel

轂轆兒(ㄍㄨ ·ㄌㄨㄦ)
①a small wheel ②a section of anything cylindric in shape (as sausage, etc.)

【轄】 6017
ㄒㄧㄚˊ shya xiá
1. a linchpin
2. to govern; to administer; administration; to manage
3. the noise of wheels

轄境(ㄒㄧㄚˊ ㄐㄧㄥˋ)or 轄地(ㄒㄧㄚˊ ㄉㄧˋ)or 轄區(ㄒㄧㄚˊ ㄑㄩ)
an area under the jurisdiction (of a magistrate, etc.); magistracy

轄下(ㄒㄧㄚˊ ㄒㄧㄚˋ)
under the command or jurisdiction of

轄治(ㄒㄧㄚˊ ㄓˋ)
to govern; to rule; to administer

【轅】 6018
ㄩㄢˊ yuan yuán
1. shafts (of a cart or carriage)
2. the magistrate's office or residence; the yamen
3. a Chinese family name

轅門(ㄩㄢˊ ㄇㄣˊ)
①an outer gate of the yamen ②an outer gate (of a commander's or an emperor's temporary residence) formed by two carriages

轅下駒(ㄩㄢˊ ㄒㄧㄚˋ ㄐㄩ)
(literally) a horse between the shafts—to be under restraint

【轀】 6019
ㄨㄣ uen wēn
1. a hearse
2. a sleeping carriage

轀輬(ㄨㄣ ㄌㄧㄤˊ)
①a hearse ②a sleeping carriage

十一畫

【轉】 6020
1. ㄓㄨㄢˇ joan zhuǎn
1. to turn: 他將車子向左轉。He turned the car to the left.
2. to take a turn; to shift; to change: 這病人的情形好轉。The sick man has taken a turn for the better.
3. to transport; to convey; to transfer; to pass on
4. indirect; roundabout
5. to roll
6. to migrate; to move

轉播(ㄓㄨㄢˇ ㄅㄛ)or(ㄓㄨㄢˇ ㄅㄛˋ)
to relay a broadcast or telecast: 這場比賽將有電視現場轉播。The race will be telecast live.

轉播站(ㄓㄨㄢˇ ㄅㄛ ㄓㄢˋ)
a relay station

轉敗爲勝(ㄓㄨㄢˇ ㄅㄞˋ ㄨㄟˊ ㄕㄥˋ)
to turn a defeat into a victory; to turn the tables (on someone)

〔車部〕

〔車部〕

轉變(ㄓㄨㄢˇ ㄅㄧㄢˋ)
①to undergo changes; to change: 熱把水轉變成蒸氣。Heat changes water into steam. ②a change or shift (of attitude, thinking, etc.)

轉盼(ㄓㄨㄢˇ ㄆㄢˋ)
to turn the eyes

轉蓬(ㄓㄨㄢˇ ㄆㄥˊ)
to wander about like stray weeds in the wind

轉賣(ㄓㄨㄢˇ ㄇㄞˋ)
to resell

轉面子(ㄓㄨㄢˇ ㄇㄧㄢˋ ·ㄗ)
to regain lost face

轉發(ㄓㄨㄢˇ ㄈㄚ)
to send (or distribute) through another person or office

轉達(ㄓㄨㄢˇ ㄉㄚˊ)
to transmit through another person or office; to convey: 請轉達我對她的問候。Please convey to her my best regards.

轉道(ㄓㄨㄢˇ ㄉㄠˋ)
①to make a detour; to go by way of ②(in ancient China) an official route of the shipping of food

轉遞(ㄓㄨㄢˇ ㄉㄧˋ)
to send through another person

轉地療養(ㄓㄨㄢˇ ㄉㄧˋ ㄌㄧㄠˊ ㄧㄤˇ)
a change of air for one's health

轉調(ㄓㄨㄢˇ ㄉㄧㄠˋ)
(music) modulation

轉動(ㄓㄨㄢˇ ㄉㄨㄥˋ)or(ㄓㄨㄢˋ ㄉㄨㄥˋ)
①to turn; to revolve; to rotate ②to budge; to move

轉頭(ㄓㄨㄢˇ ㄊㄡˊ)
to turn one's head

轉託(ㄓㄨㄢˇ ㄊㄨㄛ)
to request or entrust through another person

轉念(ㄓㄨㄢˇ ㄋㄧㄢˋ)
to change one's mind; to have second thoughts

轉捩點(ㄓㄨㄢˇ ㄌㄧㄝˋ ㄉㄧㄢˇ)
a turning point

轉令(ㄓㄨㄢˇ ㄌㄧㄥˋ)
to request a higher office to order another agency to do something

轉告(ㄓㄨㄢˇ ㄍㄠˋ)
to pass on (words); to communicate; to transmit

轉轂(ㄓㄨㄢˇ ㄍㄨˇ)
to transport by carts

轉攻爲守(ㄓㄨㄢˇ ㄍㄨㄥ ㄨㄟˊ ㄕㄡˇ)
to change from the offensive to the defensive

轉口(ㄓㄨㄢˇ ㄎㄡˇ)
transit

轉化(ㄓㄨㄢˇ ㄏㄨㄚˋ)
①to change; to transform ②to react chemically

轉禍爲福(ㄓㄨㄢˇ ㄏㄨㄛˋ ㄨㄟˊ ㄈㄨˊ)
to turn a disaster into a blessing

轉回(ㄓㄨㄢˇ ㄏㄨㄟˊ)
to turn back; to return

轉回記錄(ㄓㄨㄢˇ ㄏㄨㄟˊ ㄐㄧˋ ㄌㄨˋ)
(accounting) reversing entries

轉迴(ㄓㄨㄢˇ ㄏㄨㄟˊ)
the transmigration of souls; a metempsychosis 亦作「輪迴」

轉圜(ㄓㄨㄢˇ ㄏㄨㄢˊ)
①to intercede; to retrieve or revert an undesirable development ②to listen to counsel or advice readily

轉換(ㄓㄨㄢˇ ㄏㄨㄢˋ)
transition; to change; to switch: 我們轉換話題。We changed the topic of conversation.

轉換期(ㄓㄨㄢˇ ㄏㄨㄢˋ ㄑㄧˊ)
a transition period

轉機(ㄓㄨㄢˇ ㄐㄧ)
a turning point (usually from bad to good); a favorable turn; a turn for the better: 那女孩的病情已有了轉機。The sick girl has taken a turn for the better.

轉嫁(ㄓㄨㄢˇ ㄐㄧㄚˋ)
①(said of a woman) to remarry ②to transfer (a tax burden upon consumers, etc.); to pass (the blame, responsibility, etc. to someone else)

轉借(ㄓㄨㄢˇ ㄐㄧㄝˋ)
to lend (what has been borrowed)

轉交(ㄓㄨㄢˇ ㄐㄧㄠ)
to send or deliver through or in care of another person; to pass on to; to forward

轉角(ㄓㄨㄢˇ ㄐㄧㄠˇ)
a corner of a building; a corner of the street: 請於大街轉角處會我。Meet me at the corner of the street.

轉進(ㄓㄨㄢˇ ㄐㄧㄣˋ)
(literally) to advance backward—(euphemism) to retreat

轉去(ㄓㄨㄢˇ ㄑㄩˋ)
to turn and go; to go back

轉徙(ㄓㄨㄢˇ ㄒㄧˇ)
to migrate from place to place

轉向(ㄓㄨㄢˇ ㄒㄧㄤˋ)
(said of wind) to change directions; to turn in the direction of; to shift: 風轉向北吹。The wind shifted to the north.

轉學(ㄓㄨㄢˇ ㄒㄩㄝˊ)
to transfer to another school: 那男孩轉學到另一所學校。The boy transferred to another school.

轉學生(ㄓㄨㄢˇ ㄒㄩㄝˊ ㄕㄥ)
a transfer student: 他是個轉學生。He is a transfer student.

轉致(ㄓㄨㄢˇ ㄓˋ)
to convey or send (messages) through another person

轉折(ㄓㄨㄢˇ ㄓㄜˊ)
complications; twists and turns

轉戰(ㄓㄨㄢˇ ㄓㄢˋ)
to fight in one place after another

轉賬(ㄓㄨㄢˇ ㄓㄤˋ)
to transfer accounts (in banking)

轉注(ㄓㄨㄢˇ ㄓㄨˋ)
mutually interpretative symbols, one of the six classes of Chinese characters

轉飭(ㄓㄨㄢˇ ㄔˋ)
to order or instruct (subordinates) in accordance with orders or instructions received from one's superior

轉車(ㄓㄨㄢˇ ㄔㄜ)
to change trains or buses; to transfer to another train or bus: 我們必須在台中轉車。We have to change trains at Taichung.

轉世(ㄓㄨㄢˇ ㄕˋ)
(said of the soul) to trans-

migrate into another body; reincarnation; transmigration

轉手(ㄓㄨㄢˇ ㄕㄡˇ)
①to fall into another's hands; to change hands ②a very brief period of time

轉守爲攻(ㄓㄨㄢˇ ㄕㄡˇ ㄨㄟˊ ㄍㄨㄥ)
to change from the defensive to the offensive

轉身(ㄓㄨㄢˇ ㄕㄣ)
to turn the body; to turn round

轉瞬(ㄓㄨㄢˇ ㄕㄨㄣˋ)
①to turn the eyes ②a trice; a very brief period of time; an instant; a moment

轉讓(ㄓㄨㄢˇ ㄖㄤˋ)
to transfer (ownership, title, etc.): 這座農場已經轉讓給他了。This farm has been transferred to him.

轉入(ㄓㄨㄢˇ ㄖㄨˋ)
to change over to; to shift to; to switch over to

轉載(ㄓㄨㄢˇ ㄗㄞˇ)
to reprint (articles published in another publication)

轉側(ㄓㄨㄢˇ ㄘㄜˋ)
①to toss oneself in bed ②to shift positions; to move about

轉漕(ㄓㄨㄢˇ ㄘㄠˊ)
to transport by land and water

轉移(ㄓㄨㄢˇ ㄧˊ)
to change in position or direction; to divert; to shift; to turn; to transfer: 那狗已把它的感情轉移給新主人。The dog has transferred its affection to its new master.

轉移陣地(ㄓㄨㄢˇ ㄧˊ ㄓㄣˋ ㄉㄧˋ)
to evacuate position (in military action)

轉移視線(ㄓㄨㄢˇ ㄧˊ ㄕˋ ㄒㄧㄢˋ)
①to turn the gaze ②to divert public attention; to draw attention to some other matter

轉頁(ㄓㄨㄢˇ ㄧㄝˋ)
to turn over the leaf (in reading)

轉業(ㄓㄨㄢˇ ㄧㄝˋ)
to change one's trade; to change one's career

轉眼(ㄓㄨㄢˇ ㄧㄢˇ)or 轉眼間(ㄓㄨㄢˇ ㄧㄢˇ ㄐㄧㄢ)
a very brief period of time; in the twinkling of an eye; an instant; a moment: 小偷一轉眼就不見了。The thief disappeared in the twinkling of an eye.

轉危爲安(ㄓㄨㄢˇ ㄨㄟ ㄨㄟˊ ㄢ)
①to become safe; to avert a danger; to turn the corner ②(said of a gravely ill patient) out of danger

轉彎(ㄓㄨㄢˇ ㄨㄢ)
to take a turn; to turn in another direction; to make a turn: 這脚踏車向右轉彎兒。The bicycle made a turn to the right.

轉彎抹角(ㄓㄨㄢˇ ㄨㄢ ㄇㄛˇ ㄐㄧㄠˇ)
①to go along a zigzag course ②to talk in a roundabout way; to beat around the bush; to mince

轉彎子(ㄓㄨㄢˇ ㄨㄢ ·ㄗ)
to be roundabout (in speech)

轉文(ㄓㄨㄢˇ ㄨㄣˊ)
to quote from the classics with a view to showing off one's erudition

轉韻(ㄓㄨㄢˇ ㄩㄣˋ)
to shift to a new rhyme

轉運(ㄓㄨㄢˇ ㄩㄣˋ)
①to transport; to convey; to forward ②to be in a constant cyclic motion ③to have a turn of luck (for the better)

轉運港(ㄓㄨㄢˇ ㄩㄣˋ ㄍㄤˇ)
a transit port

轉運公司(ㄓㄨㄢˇ ㄩㄣˋ ㄍㄨㄥ ㄙ)
a forwarding company; a transportation company

轉運使(ㄓㄨㄢˇ ㄩㄣˋ ㄕˇ)
an official in charge of transportation (during the Tang and Sung Dynasties)

【轉】 6020
2. ㄓㄨㄢˋ juann zhuàn

to turn round and round; to rotate; to revolve; to gyrate: 陀螺以軸爲中心旋轉。A top rotates on its axis.

轉磨(ㄓㄨㄢˋ ㄇㄛˋ)
to be at a loss in the face of a difficulty

轉門(ㄓㄨㄢˋ ㄇㄣˊ)
a turnstile; a revolving door

轉檯(ㄓㄨㄢˋ ㄊㄞˊ)
a turntable

轉臺(ㄓㄨㄢˋ ㄊㄞˊ)
a revolving stage

轉來轉去(ㄓㄨㄢˋ ㄌㄞˊ ㄓㄨㄢˋ ㄑㄩˋ)
to walk back and forth; to hang around

轉向(ㄓㄨㄢˋ ㄒㄧㄤˋ)
①to lose one's bearings; to lose one's way ②a change in one's philosophy, beliefs, etc.

轉椅(ㄓㄨㄢˋ ㄧˇ)
a swivel chair: 我爲他買了一把轉椅。I bought him a swivel chair.

轉一轉(ㄓㄨㄢˋ ·ㄧ ㄓㄨㄢˋ)or 轉轉(ㄓㄨㄢˋ ·ㄓㄨㄢ)
to take a short walk or ride (for exercise, etc.); to take a turn

【轆】 6021
ㄌㄨˋ luh lù

1. a wheel
2. a capstan

轆轤(ㄌㄨˋ ㄌㄨˊ)
①a capstan; a windlass ②a pulley for drawing water from a well

【轇】 6022
ㄐㄧㄡ jiou jiū

1. a dispute
2. deep and vast
3. disorder

轇轕 or 轇輵(ㄐㄧㄡ ㄍㄜˊ)
①a dispute; an endless involvement 亦作「糾葛」: 他們對該問題有一場轇轕。They had a dispute over the question. ②deep and vast ③disorder

十二畫

【轍】 6023
ㄔㄜˋ cheh chè
(語音 ㄓㄜˊ jer zhé)

ruts; wheel tracks

轍鮒(ㄔㄜˋ ㄈㄨˋ)
(literally) a fish in a rut—in dire straits

轍亂旗靡(ㄔㄜˋ ㄌㄨㄢˋ ㄑㄧˊ ㄇㄧˇ)
(literally) chariots in disorder and banners dropping—(said of an army) completely routed

轍環天下(ㄔㄜˋ ㄏㄨㄢˊ ㄊㄧㄢ ㄒㄧㄚˋ)
to leave one's footprints all

over the country (or the world)

輙迹(ㄔㄜˋ ㄐㄧ)
wheel tracks; ruts

〔辛部〕

【轎】 6024 ㄐㄧㄠˋ jiaw jiào
a chair; a sedan chair; a palankeen or a palanquin

轎夫(ㄐㄧㄠˋ ㄈㄨ)
sedan chair bearers

轎車(ㄐㄧㄠˋ ㄔㄜ)
a sedan (a kind of automobile)

轎子(ㄐㄧㄠˋ ·ㄗ)
a chair; a sedan chair; a palankeen or a palanquin

【轔】 6025 ㄌㄧㄣˊ lin lín
1. noise of wheels; the rumble of vehicles
2. the threshold
3. wheels

轔轢(ㄌㄧㄣˊ ㄌㄧˋ)
①to be run over under wheels ②to oppress

轔轔(ㄌㄧㄣˊ ㄌㄧㄣˊ)
the rumble of vehicles; to rattle

十三畫

【轘】 6026 ㄏㄨㄢˋ huann huàn
to tear (an offender) asunder between vehicles (a form of ancient punishment)

轘裂(ㄏㄨㄢˋ ㄌㄧㄝˋ)
to tear (an offender) asunder between vehicles (a form of ancient punishment)

轘磔(ㄏㄨㄢˋ ㄓㄜˊ)
to tear (an offender) asunder between vehicles (a form of punishment)

轘轅(ㄏㄨㄢˋ ㄩㄢˊ)
①a topographically inaccessible place ②name of a mountain in Honan (河南)

【轕】 6027 ㄍㄜˊ ger gé
1. a dispute
2. deep and vast
3. disorder

【轙】 6028 ㄧˇ yii yǐ
1. rings on the yokes
2. to wait

【轗】 6029 ㄎㄢˇ kaan kǎn
(said of vehicles) to proceed with difficulty

轗軻(ㄎㄢˇ ㄎㄜ)
①(said of vehicles) to move with difficulty ②down in luck; frustrated; disappointed

十四畫

【轟】 6030 ㄏㄨㄥ hong hōng
1. noise of a number of vehicles
2. noise; an uproar
3. grand; magnificent
4. to bombard; to blast

轟倒(ㄏㄨㄥ ㄉㄠˇ)
to knock down by bombardment

轟動(ㄏㄨㄥ ㄉㄨㄥˋ)
①to cause an uproar; to create a sensation ②to excite (the public)

轟動一時(ㄏㄨㄥ ㄉㄨㄥˋ ㄧˋ ㄕˊ)
to create a sensation: 他們兩人的結婚轟動一時。Their marriage created a sensation.

轟隆(ㄏㄨㄥ ㄌㄨㄥˊ)
a thundering sound

轟轟(ㄏㄨㄥ ㄏㄨㄥ)
①a booming sound; a roaring sound ②in a grand fashion; with grandeur

轟轟烈烈(ㄏㄨㄥ ㄏㄨㄥ ㄌㄧㄝˋ ㄌㄧㄝˋ)
in a grand fashion; with grandeur; on a grand and spectacular scale

轟擊(ㄏㄨㄥ ㄐㄧ)
to bombard; to fire on (with artillery or rockets): 此城被敵人轟擊。The city was bombarded by the enemy.

轟炸(ㄏㄨㄥ ㄓㄚˋ)
to bomb (from an airplane)

轟炸機(ㄏㄨㄥ ㄓㄚˋ ㄐㄧ)
a bomber

轟沉(ㄏㄨㄥ ㄔㄣˊ)
to sink (a vessel) by bombardment

轟然(ㄏㄨㄥ ㄖㄢˊ)
with a deafening sound

轟走(ㄏㄨㄥ ㄗㄡˇ)
to send away unceremoniously

【轝】 6031 ㄩˊ yu yú
same as 輿—a carriage; a sedan chair

【轞】 6032 ㄒㄧㄢˋ shiann xiàn
1. noise of wheels
2. sealed carts for transporting criminals

轞車(ㄒㄧㄢˋ ㄔㄜ)
a sealed cart for transporting criminals

十五畫

【轢】 6033 ㄌㄧˋ lih lì
1. (said of a wheel) to run over
2. to oppress; to bully

【轡】 6034 ㄆㄟˋ pey pèi
reins; a bridle

轡勒(ㄆㄟˋ ㄌㄜˋ)
reins and bits

十六畫

【轤】 6035 ㄌㄨˊ lu lú
1. a pulley for drawing water
2. a windlass; a capstan

【轣】 6036 ㄌㄧˋ lih lì
1. a pulley for drawing water
2. rails for vehicles

轣轆(ㄌㄧˋ ㄌㄨˋ)
①a pulley for drawing water ②rails for vehicles

辛部
ㄒㄧㄣ shin xīn

【辛】 6037 ㄒㄧㄣ shin xīn
1. the eighth of the ten celestial stems
2. bitter; acrid
3. hard; toilsome; laborious
4. a Chinese family name

辛辣(ㄒㄧㄣ ㄌㄚˋ)
pungent; hot; bitter; peppery and acrid

辛勞(ㄒㄧㄣ ㄌㄠˊ)
great care or effort; pains

辛苦(ㄒㄧㄣ ㄎㄨˇ)

①laborious; toilsome: 捕魚這工作很辛苦。Fishing is a laborious task. ②to work hard; to go through hardships

辛亥革命(ㄒㄧㄣ ㄏㄞ ㄍㄜˊ ㄇㄧㄥˋ)
the Revolution of 1911 (the year of 辛亥), which led to the overthrow of the Ching Dynasty

辛棄疾(ㄒㄧㄣ ㄑㄧˋ ㄐㄧˊ)
Hsin Chi-chi, 1140-1207, Sung Dynasty poet

辛勤(ㄒㄧㄣ ㄑㄧㄣˊ)
hard-working; diligent; industrious: 他是我們班上最辛勤的學生。He is the most diligent student in our class.

辛辛那提(ㄒㄧㄣ ㄒㄧㄣ ㄋㄚˋ ㄊㄧˊ)
Cincinnati, U.S.A.

辛辛苦苦(ㄒㄧㄣ ㄒㄧㄣ ㄎㄨˇ ㄎㄨˇ)
laboriously; with great efforts; to take great pains

辛丑和約(ㄒㄧㄣ ㄔㄡˇ ㄏㄜˊ ㄩㄝ)
the Peace Treaty of 1901 (the year of 辛丑), signed between China and ten foreign powers in the wake of the Boxer Uprising

辛臭(ㄒㄧㄣ ㄔㄡˋ)
acrid and stinking

辛酸(ㄒㄧㄣ ㄙㄨㄢ)
hardships; the bitters of life: 他受盡各種辛酸。He suffered all kinds of hardships.

辛味(ㄒㄧㄣ ㄨㄟˋ)
an acrid taste

五畫

【辜】 6038
ㄍㄨ gu gū

1. sin; crime; guilt
2. to be negligent in an obligation or expectation; to fail
3. a Chinese family name

辜負(ㄍㄨ ㄈㄨˋ)
to fail to live up to (another's expectation, etc.); to let someone down: 我們決不辜負老師的期望。We will never let our teachers down.

辜鴻銘(ㄍㄨ ㄏㄨㄥˊ ㄇㄧㄥˊ)
Ku Hung-ming, 1847-1928, an eccentric conservative scholar who translated a number of Chinese classics into English

辜人(ㄍㄨ ㄖㄣˊ)
an executed criminal

辜月(ㄍㄨ ㄩㄝˋ)
the eleventh month of the lunar year

六畫

【辟】 6039
1.(避) ㄅㄧˋ bih bì

1. a monarch
2. to summon; to call
3. to govern; to take the law (to people)
4. to avoid; to escape

辟邪(ㄅㄧˋ ㄒㄧㄝˊ)
①to ward off evils ②a fabulous animal with two horns

辟世(ㄅㄧˋ ㄕˋ)
to withdraw (or retire) from the world; to live in seclusion

辟易(ㄅㄧˋ ㄧˋ)
to retreat or recoil (in fright)

辟言(ㄅㄧˋ ㄧㄢˊ)
①to go away because of an offensive statement ②the justest words

辟引(ㄅㄧˋ ㄧㄣˇ)
to summon to court; to appoint to office

【辟】 6039
2. ㄆㄧˋ pih pì

same as 僻—remote; inaccessible

辟匿(ㄆㄧˋ ㄋㄧˋ)
remote; out-of-the-way

辟陋(ㄆㄧˋ ㄌㄡˋ)
(said of a house) remote and crude

辟穀(ㄆㄧˋ ㄍㄨˇ)
to avoid eating cereals in order to gain immortality

辟踊(ㄆㄧˋ ㄩㄥˇ)
in extreme grief; grief-stricken

【辠】 6040
ㄗㄨㄟˋ tzuey zuì

same as 罪—sin; crime; guilt

七畫

【辣】 6041
ㄌㄚˋ lah là

1. pungent; piquant; hot
2. (said of smell or taste) to burn; to bite
3. vicious; ruthless

辣瓣兒醬(ㄌㄚˋ ㄅㄢˋㄦ ㄐㄧㄤˋ)
pungent bean paste

辣撻(ㄌㄚˋ ·ㄊㄚ)
untidy; not neat 亦作「邋遢」

辣湯(ㄌㄚˋ ㄊㄤ)
peppered soup

辣椒(ㄌㄚˋ ㄐㄧㄠ)
capsicum

辣醬(ㄌㄚˋ ㄐㄧㄤˋ)
paste of pungent condiment (especially one prepared from capsicum)

辣手(ㄌㄚˋ ㄕㄡˇ)
①cruel means; drastic means ②a ruthless person ③difficult to handle; causing much headache; a hot potato; a knotty problem (a corrupt form of 棘手 which has gained currency): 那件事眞辣手。That's really a knotty problem.

辣子(ㄌㄚˋ ·ㄗ)
capsicum

辣味(ㄌㄚˋ ㄨㄟˋ)
piquancy; pungency; peppery taste

九畫

【辦】 6042
ㄅㄢˋ bann bàn

1. to manage; to handle; to transact; to deal with; to attend to
2. to try and punish
3. to purchase

辦報(ㄅㄢˋ ㄅㄠˋ)
to publish a newspaper; to run a newspaper

辦不到(ㄅㄢˋ ·ㄅㄨ ㄉㄠˋ)
unable to accomplish or manage; impossible to accomplish or manage

辦不來(ㄅㄢˋ ·ㄅㄨ ㄌㄞˊ)
too much for one to handle

辦不了(ㄅㄢˋ ·ㄅㄨ ㄌㄧㄠˇ)
too much for one to accomplish or finish

辦不成(ㄅㄢˋ ·ㄅㄨ ㄔㄥˊ)
unable to be accomplished

辦不完(ㄅㄢˋ ·ㄅㄨ ㄨㄢˊ)
(said of work) too much for one to finish

辦法(ㄅㄢˋ ㄈㄚˇ)
means; schemes; ways;

resources: 我總有辦法說服他。 I will persuade him by some ways or other.
辦得不好(ㄅㄢˋ ·ㄉㄜ ㄅㄨˋ ㄏㄠˇ)
badly managed; poorly handled; mismanaged; bungled: 他事情辦得不好。He bungled the job.
辦得好(ㄅㄢˋ ·ㄉㄜ ㄏㄠˇ)
well-handled; well-managed; well-done
辦到(ㄅㄢˋ ㄉㄠˋ)
to get something done; to accomplish
辦妥(ㄅㄢˋ ㄊㄨㄛˇ)
to complete (procedures); to finish doing something properly
辦理(ㄅㄢˋ ㄌㄧˇ)
to take care of (some business); to handle; to manage: 這件事情你斟酌辦理。You handle this matter as you see fit.
辦理公使(ㄅㄢˋ ㄌㄧˇ ㄍㄨㄥ ㄕˇ)
a minister resident
辦稿(ㄅㄢˋ ㄍㄠˇ)
to draft a document
辦公(ㄅㄢˋ ㄍㄨㄥ)
to attend to business; to do office work
辦公費(ㄅㄢˋ ㄍㄨㄥ ㄈㄟˋ)
special administration allowances (paid to the head of an office in addition to the regular salary)
辦公廳(ㄅㄢˋ ㄍㄨㄥ ㄊㄧㄥ)
① an office building; an office: 我到他的辦公廳去拜訪他。I called on him at his office. ② the secretariat(e) of an official agency
辦公時間(ㄅㄢˋ ㄍㄨㄥ ㄕˊ ㄐㄧㄢ)
office hours
辦公室(ㄅㄢˋ ㄍㄨㄥ ㄕˋ)
an office space; an office: 他的辦公室在市中心。He has his office in the center of the city.
辦後事(ㄅㄢˋ ㄏㄡˋ ㄕˋ)
to arrange matters for the deceased
辦貨(ㄅㄢˋ ㄏㄨㄛˋ)
to handle the purchase of goods
辦酒席(ㄅㄢˋ ㄐㄧㄡˇ ㄒㄧˊ)
to prepare a banquet; to host a feast
辦交涉(ㄅㄢˋ ㄐㄧㄠ ㄕㄜˋ)
to negotiate
辦喜事(ㄅㄢˋ ㄒㄧˇ ㄕˋ)
to host a party on a joyous occasion (especially a wedding); to organize a wedding: 他們正忙着辦喜事。They were busy organizing a wedding.
辦事(ㄅㄢˋ ㄕˋ)
to handle business; to manage an affair
辦事處(ㄅㄢˋ ㄕˋ ㄔㄨˋ)
a branch office (of an organization)
辦事員(ㄅㄢˋ ㄕˋ ㄩㄢˊ)
a low-ranking staff member; a staffer
辦賊(ㄅㄢˋ ㄗㄟˊ)
to try and punish thieves or rebels
辦罪(ㄅㄢˋ ㄗㄨㄟˋ)
to try and punish an offender
辦喪事(ㄅㄢˋ ㄙㄤ ㄕˋ)
to arrange or handle funeral matters
辦案(ㄅㄢˋ ㄢˋ)
to handle a (legal or business) case

【辨】 6043
ㄅㄧㄢˋ biann biàn

1. to distinguish; to discern
2. to identify; to recognize

辨白(ㄅㄧㄢˋ ㄅㄞˊ) or 辨明(ㄅㄧㄢˋ ㄇㄧㄥˊ)
① to distinguish clearly; to identify clearly ② to account for
辨別(ㄅㄧㄢˋ ㄅㄧㄝˊ)
to distinguish between; to see the difference between; to identify
辨明是非(ㄅㄧㄢˋ ㄇㄧㄥˊ ㄕˋ ㄈㄟ)
to distinguish right from wrong; to distinguish between right and wrong: 我們應該知道如何辨明是非。We should know how to distinguish right from wrong.
辨覈(ㄅㄧㄢˋ ㄏㄜˊ)
to distinguish and evaluate
辨惑(ㄅㄧㄢˋ ㄏㄨㄛˋ)
to straighten out confusing points
辨析(ㄅㄧㄢˋ ㄒㄧ)
to analyze and distinguish
辨志(ㄅㄧㄢˋ ㄓˋ)
to analyze and identify one's intentions
辨正(ㄅㄧㄢˋ ㄓㄥˋ)
to identify and correct (errors)
辨士(ㄅㄧㄢˋ ㄕˋ)
pence
辨識(ㄅㄧㄢˋ ㄕˋ)
to recognize; to identify; recognition
辨認(ㄅㄧㄢˋ ㄖㄣˋ)
to identify; to recognize
辨色(ㄅㄧㄢˋ ㄙㄜˋ)
① to read another's facial expressions ② to distinguish colors ③ twilight

十二畫

【辭】 6044
ㄘˊ tsyr cí

1. language; words; a phrase; an expression
2. to decline; to refuse
3. to leave; to part from; to depart; to bid adieu
4. to resign; to dismiss

辭別(ㄘˊ ㄅㄧㄝˊ)
to bid farewell; to say good-bye; to take one's leave; to make one's adieus
辭不達意(ㄘˊ ·ㄅㄨ ㄉㄚˊ ㄧˋ)
The words fail to express what is meant.
辭不獲命(ㄘˊ ·ㄅㄨ ㄏㄨㄛˋ ㄇㄧㄥˋ)
to have one's resignation or declination rejected
辭費(ㄘˊ ㄈㄟˋ)
verbose; wordy
辭賦(ㄘˊ ㄈㄨˋ)
an ancient style of metrical composition
辭典(ㄘˊ ㄉㄧㄢˇ)
a dictionary; a lexicon; a thesaurus: 辭典是他的常伴。A dictionary is his frequent companion.
辭託(ㄘˊ ㄊㄨㄛ)
to decline (offers)
辭退(ㄘˊ ㄊㄨㄟˋ)
① to remove from office; to dismiss: 他被辭退了。He was dismissed (from) the service. ② to resign from office
辭令(ㄘˊ ㄌㄧㄥˋ)

diction appropriate to the occasion

辭工(ㄘˊ ㄍㄨㄥ)
to resign from manual work

辭海(ㄘˊ ㄏㄞˇ)
a collection of words

辭彙(ㄘˊ ㄏㄨㄟˋ)
vocabulary: 他的辭彙有限。His vocabulary is limited. 亦作「詞彙」

辭去(ㄘˊ ㄑㄩˋ)
to resign from (a post)

辭卻(ㄘˊ ㄑㄩㄝˋ)
to decline (offers)

辭謝(ㄘˊ ㄒㄧㄝˋ)
to decline with thanks; to ask to be excused: 他辭謝邀請。He declined the invitation with thanks.

辭行(ㄘˊ ㄒㄧㄥˊ)
to take leave of; to say good-bye to

辭職(ㄘˊ ㄓˊ)
to resign from one's post; resignation

辭章 or 詞章(ㄘˊ ㄓㄤ)
① literary compositions; poetry and prose ② the art of writing; rhetoric

辭呈(ㄘˊ ㄔㄥˊ)
a formal notice of resignation; a resignation: 他的辭呈照准了。His resignation was accepted.

辭世(ㄘˊ ㄕˋ)
to depart from the world; to die; to pass away: 他父親昨晚辭世。His father died last night.

辭讓(ㄘˊ ㄖㄤˋ)
to decline (offers)

辭藻 or 詞藻(ㄘˊ ㄗㄠˇ)
expressions in literary compositions

辭宗(ㄘˊ ㄗㄨㄥ)
a master of words; a master writer

辭色(ㄘˊ ㄙㄜˋ)
utterances and facial expressions; speech and countenance

辭歲(ㄘˊ ㄙㄨㄟˋ)
a family gathering on the Lunar New Year's Eve

辭意已決(ㄘˊ ㄧˋ ㄧˇ ㄐㄩㄝˊ)
The decision to resign has been made.

辭嚴義正(ㄘˊ ㄧㄢˊ ㄧˋ ㄓㄥˋ)
The language is stern and the reason for it is justifiable.

辭源(ㄘˊ ㄩㄢˊ)
the origin of a phrase or expression

十三畫

【辮】 6045 ㄅㄧㄢˋ biann biàn

1. to plait; to braid
2. a queue; a pigtail; a braid

辮髮(ㄅㄧㄢˋ ㄈㄚˇ)
① to braid the hair ② wearing a queue

辮子(ㄅㄧㄢˋ ˙ㄗ)
① a queue; a pigtail; a braid; a plait ② a mistake or defect that may be exploited by an opponent

十四畫

【辯】 6046 ㄅㄧㄢˋ biann biàn

1. to debate; to argue; to dispute
2. to use specious arguments

辯駁(ㄅㄧㄢˋ ㄅㄛˊ)
to defend and refute; to debate

辯白(ㄅㄧㄢˋ ㄅㄞˊ)
to defend oneself verbally; to justify

辯難(ㄅㄧㄢˋ ㄋㄢˋ)
to defend and question; to debate

辯論(ㄅㄧㄢˋ ㄌㄨㄣˋ)
to debate; a debate

辯口(ㄅㄧㄢˋ ㄎㄡˇ)
skill as a debater; eloquence

辯護(ㄅㄧㄢˋ ㄏㄨˋ)
① to speak in defense of; to defend verbally; to defend ② (law) to plead; to defend; defense: 被告人未作辯護。The accused man made no defense.

辯護士(ㄅㄧㄢˋ ㄏㄨˋ ㄕˋ)
a lawyer; a barrister 亦作「律師」

辯護人(ㄅㄧㄢˋ ㄏㄨˋ ㄖㄣˊ)
defense counsel; an advocate

辯解(ㄅㄧㄢˋ ㄐㄧㄝˇ)
to provide an explanation; to try to defend oneself.

辯證法(ㄅㄧㄢˋ ㄓㄥˋ ㄈㄚˇ)
dialectic

辯士(ㄅㄧㄢˋ ㄕˋ)
① an able speaker; a gifted debater ② a sophist

辯才(ㄅㄧㄢˋ ㄘㄞˊ)
ability as a debater; eloquence

辯才無礙(ㄅㄧㄢˋ ㄘㄞˊ ㄨˊ ㄞˋ)
very eloquent

辯誣(ㄅㄧㄢˋ ㄨ)
to defend oneself or someone falsely accused

辰部
ㄔㄣˊ chern chén

【辰】 6047 ㄔㄣˊ chern chén

1. the fifth of the twelve Terrestrial Branches (地支)
2. 7:00-9:00 in the morning; early morning
3. a time
4. fortune; luck
5. a heavenly body—the sun, the moon and stars

辰駕(ㄔㄣˊ ㄐㄧㄚˋ)
an imperial carriage

辰星(ㄔㄣˊ ㄒㄧㄥ)
① a morning star ② the planet Mercury 亦作「水星」

辰時(ㄔㄣˊ ㄕˊ)
the period of a day from 7 a.m. to 9 a.m.

辰砂(ㄔㄣˊ ㄕㄚ)
cinnabar 亦作「朱砂」

三畫

【辱】 6048 ㄖㄨˋ ruh rù (又讀 ㄖㄨˇ ruu rǔ)

1. disgrace: 他說他寧死不受辱。He says he will choose death before disgrace.
2. to disgrace; to insult; to dishonor: 他常侮辱別人。He always insults people.
3. to condescend; to deign
4. undeservingly

辱罵(ㄖㄨˋ ㄇㄚˋ)
to abuse and insult

辱沒(ㄖㄨˋ ㄇㄛˋ)
to insult; to disgrace

辱命(ㄖㄨˋ ㄇㄧㄥˋ)
to fail to live up to the expectation of one's superior; to dishonor one's commission; to fail to accomplish a mission

辱臨(ㄖㄨˋ ㄌㄧㄣˊ)
to condescend to come to such a humble place (a self-depreciatory expression in addressing a guest)

辱國(ㄖㄨˋ ㄍㄨㄛˊ)
to bring shame upon the fatherland; to disgrace the mother country

辱荷(ㄖㄨˋ ㄏㄜˋ)
(a self-depreciatory expression) to receive (a favor) undeservingly

辱教(ㄖㄨˋ ㄐㄧㄠˋ)
thanks for your instructions

辱承(ㄖㄨˋ ㄔㄥˊ)
(a self-depreciatory expression) to receive (a favor) undeservingly

辱賜(ㄖㄨˋ ㄙˋ)
thanks for your gifts

辱愛(ㄖㄨˋ ㄞˋ)
(a self-depreciatory expression) to receive a favor undeservingly

六畫

【農】 6049
ㄋㄨㄥˊ nong nóng

1. agriculture; farming
2. to farm
3. a farmer; a peasant; a husbandman

農忙(ㄋㄨㄥˊ ㄇㄤˊ)
the busy season for farmers

農民(ㄋㄨㄥˊ ㄇㄧㄣˊ)
farmers; peasants; the farming population

農民節(ㄋㄨㄥˊ ㄇㄧㄣˊ ㄐㄧㄝˊ)
Farmer's Day on February 4th

農民協會(ㄋㄨㄥˊ ㄇㄧㄣˊ ㄒㄧㄝˊ ㄏㄨㄟˋ)
a farmers' association; a farmers' cooperative

農民意識(ㄋㄨㄥˊ ㄇㄧㄣˊ ㄧˋ ㄕˋ)
peasant consciousness

農民運動(ㄋㄨㄥˊ ㄇㄧㄣˊ ㄩㄣˋ ㄉㄨㄥˋ)
a peasants' movement

農夫(ㄋㄨㄥˊ ㄈㄨ)
a farmer; a husbandman

農婦(ㄋㄨㄥˊ ㄈㄨˋ)
a farm woman

農地(ㄋㄨㄥˊ ㄉㄧˋ)
farmland; agricultural land: 他擁有很多農地。He owns a lot of farmland.

農地重劃(ㄋㄨㄥˊ ㄉㄧˋ ㄔㄨㄥˊ ㄏㄨㄚˋ)
farmland consolidation

農田(ㄋㄨㄥˊ ㄊㄧㄢˊ)
agricultural fields; farmland; agricultural land; cultivated land

農奴(ㄋㄨㄥˊ ㄋㄨˊ)
a serf

農奴制度(ㄋㄨㄥˊ ㄋㄨˊ ㄓˋ ㄉㄨˋ)
the serf system

農曆(ㄋㄨㄥˊ ㄌㄧˋ)
the traditional Chinese calendar; the lunar calendar

農林(ㄋㄨㄥˊ ㄌㄧㄣˊ)
agriculture and forestry

農林廳(ㄋㄨㄥˊ ㄌㄧㄣˊ ㄊㄧㄥ)
Department of Agriculture and Forestry (under a provincial government): 他在農林廳服務。He serves in the Department of Agriculture and Forestry.

農耕隊(ㄋㄨㄥˊ ㄍㄥ ㄉㄨㄟˋ)
an agricultural demonstration team, particularly referring to those teams dispatched to work abroad

農工(ㄋㄨㄥˊ ㄍㄨㄥ)
① agriculture and industry
② a hired farm worker

農科(ㄋㄨㄥˊ ㄎㄜ)
the department of agriculture (in college)

農戶(ㄋㄨㄥˊ ㄏㄨˋ)
a peasant family

農會(ㄋㄨㄥˊ ㄏㄨㄟˋ)
a farmers' association; a farmers' cooperative

農家(ㄋㄨㄥˊ ㄐㄧㄚ)
a farming family

農家子(ㄋㄨㄥˊ ㄐㄧㄚ ㄗˇ)
one who is brought up in a peasant family

農郊(ㄋㄨㄥˊ ㄐㄧㄠ)
countryside; the cultivated suburbs

農具(ㄋㄨㄥˊ ㄐㄩˋ)
agricultural implements; farm tools: 農夫需要農具。Farmers need farm tools.

農隙(ㄋㄨㄥˊ ㄒㄧˋ)or 農閒(ㄋㄨㄥˊ ㄒㄧㄢˊ)
the slack season for farmers

農學(ㄋㄨㄥˊ ㄒㄩㄝˊ)
science of agriculture

農學家(ㄋㄨㄥˊ ㄒㄩㄝˊ ㄐㄧㄚ)
an agriculturist

農學院(ㄋㄨㄥˊ ㄒㄩㄝˊ ㄩㄢˋ)
the faculty of agriculture

農產物(ㄋㄨㄥˊ ㄔㄢˇ ㄨˋ)or 農產品(ㄋㄨㄥˊ ㄔㄢˇ ㄆㄧㄣˇ)
farm products; agricultural products: 它主要的農產物是棉花。Its chief farm product is cotton.

農場(ㄋㄨㄥˊ ㄔㄤˊ)or(ㄋㄨㄥˊ ㄔㄤˇ)
a farm: 他在農場工作。He worked on a farm.

農時(ㄋㄨㄥˊ ㄕˊ)
the seasons for farming—spring for plowing, summer for weeding, and autumn for reaping

農事(ㄋㄨㄥˊ ㄕˋ)
farming; agricultural operations

農舍(ㄋㄨㄥˊ ㄕㄜˋ)
a farmhouse

農神火箭(ㄋㄨㄥˊ ㄕㄣˊ ㄏㄨㄛˇ ㄐㄧㄢˋ)
the Saturn rocket

農人(ㄋㄨㄥˊ ㄖㄣˊ)
a farmer; a husbandman: 農人在農田工作。Farmers work on the land.

農作物(ㄋㄨㄥˊ ㄗㄨㄛˋ ㄨˋ)
farm products; crops

農村(ㄋㄨㄥˊ ㄘㄨㄣ)
a rural community; a farm village: 他住在農村。He lives in a farm village.

農村電氣化(ㄋㄨㄥˊ ㄘㄨㄣ ㄉㄧㄢˋ ㄑㄧˋ ㄏㄨㄚˋ)
rural electrification

農桑(ㄋㄨㄥˊ ㄙㄤ)
agriculture and sericulture

農藝學(ㄋㄨㄥˊ ㄧˋ ㄒㄩㄝˊ)
agronomy: 他對農藝學感興趣。He is interested in agronomy.

農藝學家(ㄋㄨㄥˊ ㄧˋ ㄒㄩㄝˊ ㄐㄧㄚ)or 農藝師(ㄋㄨㄥˊ ㄧˋ ㄕ)
an agronomist

農業(ㄋㄨㄥˊ ㄧㄝˋ)
agriculture; farming: 農業是生產性的勞動。Farming is

productive labor.
農業土壤學(ㄋㄨㄥˊ ㄧㄝˋ ㄊㄨˇ ㄖㄤˇ ㄒㄩㄝˊ)
agrology: 他教農業土壤學。He teaches agrology.
農業國(ㄋㄨㄥˊ ㄧㄝˋ ㄍㄨㄛˊ)
an agricultural nation
農業化學(ㄋㄨㄥˊ ㄧㄝˋ ㄏㄨㄚˋ ㄒㄩㄝˊ)
agricultural chemistry
農業機械(ㄋㄨㄥˊ ㄧㄝˋ ㄐㄧ ㄒㄧㄝˋ)
farm machinery
農業學校(ㄋㄨㄥˊ ㄧㄝˋ ㄒㄩㄝˊ ㄒㄧㄠˋ)or 農校(ㄋㄨㄥˊ ㄒㄧㄠˋ)
a vocational school of agriculture
農業時代(ㄋㄨㄥˊ ㄧㄝˋ ㄕˊ ㄉㄞˋ)
the age of agriculture
農業試驗所(ㄋㄨㄥˊ ㄧㄝˋ ㄕˋ ㄧㄢˋ ㄙㄨㄛˇ)
an agricultural laboratory; an experimental farm
農業社會(ㄋㄨㄥˊ ㄧㄝˋ ㄕㄜˋ ㄏㄨㄟˋ)
agricultural society
農業生物學(ㄋㄨㄥˊ ㄧㄝˋ ㄕㄥ ㄨˋ ㄒㄩㄝˊ)
agrobiology
農藥(ㄋㄨㄥˊ ㄧㄠˋ)
pesticide; agricultural chemicals

辵部
ㄔㄨㄛˋ chuoh chuò

三畫

【迂】 6050 ㄩ iu yū
1. impractical; unrealistic; old-fashioned; trite; hackneyed; stale; pedantic
2. roundabout; indirect; circuitous; winding: 這是條迂迴小徑。It's a winding path。
3. to make a detour
4. absurd; preposterous

迂夫子(ㄩ ㄈㄨ ㄗˇ)
an impractical scholar; a pedant
迂腐(ㄩ ㄈㄨˇ)
trite; stale; hackneyed; pedantic: 不要那麼迂腐。Don't be so pedantic.
迂道(ㄩ ㄉㄠˋ)or 迂路(ㄩ ㄌㄨˋ)
to detour
迂誕(ㄩ ㄉㄢˋ)
preposterous; absurd: 多麼迂誕的建議啊! What an absurd suggestion!
迂陋(ㄩ ㄌㄡˋ)
stale; hackneyed
迂論(ㄩ ㄌㄨㄣˋ)or 迂闊之論(ㄩ ㄎㄨㄛˋ ㄓ ㄌㄨㄣˋ)
an impractical argument; an unrealistic statement; a pedantic talk
迂闊(ㄩ ㄎㄨㄛˋ)
impractical; unrealistic
迂迴(ㄩ ㄏㄨㄟˊ)
① twisty; circuitous (road) ② (military) detouring tactics; flanking tactics
迂迴曲折(ㄩ ㄏㄨㄟˊ ㄑㄩ ㄓㄜˊ)
having many turns and curves; not straightforward; circuitous; in zigzags and by roundabout ways
迂迴戰術(ㄩ ㄏㄨㄟˊ ㄓㄢˋ ㄕㄨˋ)
flanking tactics
迂緩(ㄩ ㄏㄨㄢˇ)
slow; slothful; sluggish
迂久(ㄩ ㄐㄧㄡˇ)
for a long time
迂見(ㄩ ㄐㄧㄢˋ)
an absurd view; an impractical opinion
迂氣(ㄩ ·ㄑㄧ)
indifference to reality or practicality; stubborn adherence to the absurd or the impractical; spirit of the old-fashioned
迂曲(ㄩ ㄑㄩ)
zigzag; winding; twisted: 這條小路迂曲地通往山上。The path ran zigzag up the hill.
迂直(ㄩ ㄓˊ)
impractical and artless
迂滯(ㄩ ㄓˋ)
dull; clumsy; slow
迂拙(ㄩ ㄓㄨㄛˊ)
impractical and clumsy
迂儒(ㄩ ㄖㄨˊ)
an impractical scholar; a pedant
迂叟(ㄩ ㄙㄡˇ)
an impractical old man
迂言(ㄩ ㄧㄢˊ)
an absurd statement; impractical remarks
迂遠(ㄩ ㄩㄢˇ)
① impractical; unrealistic ② long and twisty (road)

【迄】 6051 ㄑㄧˋ chih qì
up to; down to; so far; till
迄今(ㄑㄧˋ ㄐㄧㄣ)
up to now; until now; so far; to this day: 他迄今還不知道事實眞象。He doesn't know the fact up to now.
迄未(ㄑㄧˋ ㄨㄟˋ)
not until now; not yet: 這工作迄未完成。The work is not yet finished.

【迅】 6052 ㄒㄩㄣˋ shiunn xùn
swift; rapid; sudden
迅風(ㄒㄩㄣˋ ㄈㄥ)
a gale
迅雷(ㄒㄩㄣˋ ㄌㄟˊ)
a sudden clap of thunder
迅雷不及掩耳(ㄒㄩㄣˋ ㄌㄟˊ ㄅㄨˋ ㄐㄧˊ ㄧㄢˇ ㄦˇ)
as swift as a sudden clap of thunder which leaves no time for covering the ears; out of the blue
迅流(ㄒㄩㄣˋ ㄌㄧㄡˊ)
a rapid stream
迅疾(ㄒㄩㄣˋ ㄐㄧˊ)
swift; rapid; quick; speedy
迅捷(ㄒㄩㄣˋ ㄐㄧㄝˊ)
swift; quick; rapid; speedy
迅走(ㄒㄩㄣˋ ㄗㄡˇ)
to go fast; to hurry on
迅速(ㄒㄩㄣˋ ㄙㄨˋ)
by leaps and bounds; quick; swift; rapid

【巡】 6053 (廵) ㄒㄩㄣˊ shyun xún
參看「巡」, under the radical 巛 P.401

【迆】 6054 1.(迤) ㄧˇ yii yǐ
1. to extend obliquely or along a zigzag course; to proceed in a winding way
2. connected; joined
迆靡(ㄧˇ ㄇㄧˇ)
joined; connected
迆邐(ㄧˇ ㄌㄧˇ)
① joined together ② winding; meandering
迆涎(ㄧˇ ㄧㄢˊ)
to extend continuously

【迆】 6054 2. ㄧˊ yi yí

辵部

辵部

meandering; winding

四畫

【迎】 6055
1. ㄧㄥˊ yng yíng
to receive; to greet; to meet; to welcome
迎面(ㄧㄥˊ ㄇㄧㄢˋ)
right against one's face in the opposite direction; in one's face: 微風迎面向我吹來。A breeze was blowing in my face.
迎風(ㄧㄥˊ ㄈㄥ)
① facing the wind; against the wind: 小鳥迎風飛翔。The birds fly against the wind. ② down the wind; with the wind
迎風招展(ㄧㄥˊ ㄈㄥ ㄓㄠ ㄓㄢˇ)
to flutter in the wind
迎敵(ㄧㄥˊ ㄉㄧˊ)
to meet the enemy in battle; to engage the enemy forces: 士兵們開始迎敵作戰。Soldiers began to meet the enemy in battle.
迎睇(ㄧㄥˊ ㄉㄧˋ)
to meet with the eye
迎頭痛擊(ㄧㄥˊ ㄊㄡˊ ㄊㄨㄥˋ ㄐㄧˊ)
to make a frontal attack; to deal the enemy troops a stunning blow by a frontal attack; to deal a head-on blow: 他給予敵人迎頭痛擊。He dealt the enemy head-on blows.
迎頭趕上(ㄧㄥˊ ㄊㄡˊ ㄍㄢˇ ㄕㄤˋ)
to try hard to catch up
迎鑾(ㄧㄥˊ ㄌㄨㄢˊ)
to greet the imperial carriage
迎合(ㄧㄥˊ ㄏㄜˊ)
① to cater to ② to make an appointment to meet each other in the future
迎候(ㄧㄥˊ ㄏㄡˋ)
to go out to await (a visitor)
迎擊(ㄧㄥˊ ㄐㄧˊ)
to meet and attack (an advancing enemy); to intercept
迎接(ㄧㄥˊ ㄐㄧㄝ)
to receive; to greet; to welcome: 他走到門前迎接客人。He went to the door to receive his visitors.
迎親(ㄧㄥˊ ㄑㄧㄣ)or 迎娶(ㄧㄥˊ ㄑㄩˇ)
to go to meet one's bride at her home before escorting her back to one's own home for the wedding
迎新(ㄧㄥˊ ㄒㄧㄣ)
① to see the New Year in ② to welcome new arrivals
迎新送舊(ㄧㄥˊ ㄒㄧㄣ ㄙㄨㄥˋ ㄐㄧㄡˋ)
to usher in the new and send off the old; (a dinner party held) to greet a new boss, fellow students, etc. and bid good-bye to a departing boss, graduates, etc.
迎戰(ㄧㄥˊ ㄓㄢˋ)
to meet (an approaching enemy) head-on
迎粧(ㄧㄥˊ ㄓㄨㄤ)
to receive the dowry (on the eve of the wedding) by the bridegroom's family and friends
迎晨(ㄧㄥˊ ㄔㄣˊ)
at dawn or daybreak
迎春(ㄧㄥˊ ㄔㄨㄣ)or 迎年(ㄧㄥˊ ㄋㄧㄢˊ)
the ceremony of greeting the New Year; to greet the New Year
迎春典禮(ㄧㄥˊ ㄔㄨㄣ ㄉㄧㄢˇ ㄌㄧˇ)
the ceremony of welcoming spring
迎春花(ㄧㄥˊ ㄔㄨㄣ ㄏㄨㄚ)
a winter jasmine (*Jasminum nudiflorum*)
迎神賽會(ㄧㄥˊ ㄕㄣˊ ㄙㄞˋ ㄏㄨㄟˋ)
noisy processions and festivals held in honor of local deities
迎上來(ㄧㄥˊ ㄕㄤˋ ·ㄌㄞ)
to come onward
迎刃而解(ㄧㄥˊ ㄖㄣˋ ㄦˊ ㄐㄧㄝˇ)
(literally) to meet the edge of the knife blade and split in two—(said of a difficult problem) to be solved neatly; to solve itself
迎送(ㄧㄥˊ ㄙㄨㄥˋ)
to greet (new arrivals) and see off (those who are departing)
迎阿(ㄧㄥˊ ㄜ)
to flatter; to act like a sycophant
迎迓(ㄧㄥˊ ㄧㄚˋ)
to receive; to greet; to welcome
迎養(ㄧㄥˊ ㄧㄤˋ)
to support one's parents or benefactors by taking them to one's own home

【迎】 6055
2. ㄧㄥˋ yinq yìng
to go out in person to meet (a visitor)

【近】 6056
ㄐㄧㄣˋ jinn jìn
1. near or close (in space): 郵局距離這兒很近。The post office is quite near.
2. near or close (in time); immediate; recent
3. near or close (in abstract relation); intimate
4. to approach; to approximate: 這作品幾近完美。This work approximates to perfection.
近便(ㄐㄧㄣˋ ㄅㄧㄢˋ)
at a conveniently little distance; close and convenient
近傍(ㄐㄧㄣˋ ㄆㄤˊ)
adjacent to; nearby
近代(ㄐㄧㄣˋ ㄉㄞˋ)
modern times; recent times
近代史(ㄐㄧㄣˋ ㄉㄞˋ ㄕˇ)
modern history
近代思想(ㄐㄧㄣˋ ㄉㄞˋ ㄙ ㄒㄧㄤˇ)
modern thought
近地點(ㄐㄧㄣˋ ㄉㄧˋ ㄉㄧㄢˇ)
(astronomy) perigee
近東(ㄐㄧㄣˋ ㄉㄨㄥ)
the Near East
近體詩(ㄐㄧㄣˋ ㄊㄧˇ ㄕ)
"modern style" poetry, including the "regulated verse" (律詩) and "cut-short verse" (絕句), the innovations in classical poetry during the Tang Dynasty (618-907)
近年(ㄐㄧㄣˋ ㄋㄧㄢˊ)
in recent years
近來(ㄐㄧㄣˋ ㄌㄞˊ)
recently; lately: 我近來一直很累。I have been very tired recently.
近利(ㄐㄧㄣˋ ㄌㄧˋ)
immediate gain
近鄰(ㄐㄧㄣˋ ㄌㄧㄣˊ)
a close neighbor: 他是我們的近鄰。He is a close neighbor

of ours.
近路(ㄐㄧㄣˋ ㄌㄨˋ)
a shortcut
近古(ㄐㄧㄣˋ ㄍㄨˇ)
the period between now and the Middle Ages
近況(ㄐㄧㄣˋ ㄎㄨㄤˋ)
a recent situation; how things stand
近海(ㄐㄧㄣˋ ㄏㄞˇ)
(said of land) near the sea; coastal; offshore
近海漁業(ㄐㄧㄣˋ ㄏㄞˇ ㄩˊ ㄧㄝˋ)
inshore fishery
近乎(ㄐㄧㄣˋ ·ㄏㄨ)
close to; almost; nearly
近畿(ㄐㄧㄣˋ ㄐㄧ)
the outskirts of the national capital; areas around the capital
近郊(ㄐㄧㄣˋ ㄐㄧㄠ)
suburbs; outskirts: 他住在近郊。He lives in the suburbs.
近距離(ㄐㄧㄣˋ ㄐㄩˋ ㄌㄧˊ)
a little distance; a short distance; at close range
近期(ㄐㄧㄣˋ ㄑㄧˊ)
in the near future
近親(ㄐㄧㄣˋ ㄑㄧㄣ)
close relatives: 我們有很多近親。We have many close relatives.
近情(ㄐㄧㄣˋ ㄑㄧㄥˊ)or 近情近理(ㄐㄧㄣˋ ㄑㄧㄥˊ ㄐㄧㄣˋ ㄌㄧˇ)
acceptable to reason; reasonable; sensible
近頃(ㄐㄧㄣˋ ㄑㄧㄥˇ)
recently; of late
近幸(ㄐㄧㄣˋ ㄒㄧㄥˋ)
favorites at imperial court
近支(ㄐㄧㄣˋ ㄓ)
related families of clans
近戰(ㄐㄧㄣˋ ㄓㄢˋ)
a close-quarter combat; a hand-to-hand combat
近朱者赤，近墨者黑(ㄐㄧㄣˋ ㄓㄨ ㄓㄜˇ ㄔˋ, ㄐㄧㄣˋ ㄇㄛˋ ㄓㄜˇ ㄏㄟ)
(literally) He who nears vermilion becomes red; he who nears ink becomes black.—Good companions have good influence while bad ones have bad influence.
近臣(ㄐㄧㄣˋ ㄔㄣˊ)
courtiers close to the monarch; trusted courtiers; favorite courtiers; ministers belonging to a court
近程(ㄐㄧㄣˋ ㄔㄥˊ)
a short range
近處(ㄐㄧㄣˋ ㄔㄨˋ)
places nearby
近世(ㄐㄧㄣˋ ㄕˋ)
① the present era; in modern times ② the period between now and the Middle Ages
近視(ㄐㄧㄣˋ ㄕˋ)or 近視眼(ㄐㄧㄣˋ ㄕˋ ㄧㄢˇ)
nearsightedness; myopia
近視眼鏡(ㄐㄧㄣˋ ㄕˋ ㄧㄢˇ ㄐㄧㄥˋ)
glasses for myopia
近侍(ㄐㄧㄣˋ ㄕˋ)
a personal attendant
近水樓臺(ㄐㄧㄣˋ ㄕㄨㄟˇ ㄌㄡˊ ㄊㄞˊ)
a point of vantage
近水樓臺先得月(ㄐㄧㄣˋ ㄕㄨㄟˇ ㄌㄡˊ ㄊㄞˊ ㄒㄧㄢ ㄉㄜˊ ㄩㄝˋ)
A waterfront pavilion gets the moonlight first.—the advantage of being in a favorable position
近日(ㄐㄧㄣˋ ㄖˋ)
recently; lately: 我近日未曾見到他。I haven't seen him lately.
近日點(ㄐㄧㄣˋ ㄖˋ ㄉㄧㄢˇ)
(astronomy) perihelion
近在眉睫(ㄐㄧㄣˋ ㄗㄞˋ ㄇㄟˊ ㄐㄧㄝˊ)
very near as if located right before one's eyelashes
近在咫尺(ㄐㄧㄣˋ ㄗㄞˋ ㄓˇ ㄔˇ)
very near as if just a few feet away
近在眼前(ㄐㄧㄣˋ ㄗㄞˋ ㄧㄢˇ ㄑㄧㄢˊ)
very near as if located right before one's eyes; right under one's nose
近作(ㄐㄧㄣˋ ㄗㄨㄛˋ)
recent works (of a writer, an artist, etc.): 我讀過你的近作。I have read your recent works.
近村(ㄐㄧㄣˋ ㄘㄨㄣ)
a village nearby
近似(ㄐㄧㄣˋ ㄙˋ)
similar to; resembling
近似值(ㄐㄧㄣˋ ㄙˋ ㄓˊ)
(mathematics) approximate value
近歲(ㄐㄧㄣˋ ㄙㄨㄟˋ)
in recent years
近憂(ㄐㄧㄣˋ ㄧㄡ)
sorrow near at hand; an immediate cause of worry
近因(ㄐㄧㄣˋ ㄧㄣ)
an immediate cause
近悅遠來(ㄐㄧㄣˋ ㄩㄝˋ ㄩㄢˇ ㄌㄞˊ)
(said of a good government) Those who are near are made happy, and those who are far off are attracted.

【迓】 6057 ㄧㄚˋ yah yà
to go out to meet or receive

【返】 6058 ㄈㄢˇ faan fǎn
1. to go back; to come back; to return
2. to send back; to give back; to return
返轡(ㄈㄢˇ ㄆㄟˋ)
(said of a rider) to turn the horse back
返防(ㄈㄢˇ ㄈㄤˊ)
(said of a serviceman) to return to his unit on garrison duty
返老還童(ㄈㄢˇ ㄌㄠˇ ㄏㄨㄢˊ ㄊㄨㄥˊ)
to regain youth; to rejuvenate oneself
返里(ㄈㄢˇ ㄌㄧˇ)
to go home (after an extended stay elsewhere)
返國(ㄈㄢˇ ㄍㄨㄛˊ)
to return from abroad
返航(ㄈㄢˇ ㄏㄤˊ)
to return to a base or port
返回(ㄈㄢˇ ㄏㄨㄟˊ)
to return; to come or go back: 他離開辦公室，又立刻返回。He left the office and soon returned.
返魂(ㄈㄢˇ ㄏㄨㄣˊ)
to come back to life; to resurrect; to revive 亦作「復活」
返校(ㄈㄢˇ ㄒㄧㄠˋ)
to return to school; to go back to school: 他昨天返校。He returned to school yesterday.
返棹(ㄈㄢˇ ㄓㄠˋ)
(said of a boat) to take a return trip
返照(ㄈㄢˇ ㄓㄠˋ)
(said of light) to be reflected
返潮(ㄈㄢˇ ㄔㄠˊ)
to get moist; to get clammy; to get damp

返程(ㄈㄢˇ ㄔㄥˊ)
a return trip

【迕】 6059 ㄨˋ wuh wù
1. to meet
2. to oppose; to disobey

迕逆(ㄨˋ ㄋㄧˋ)
①to go against one's superiors ②delinquent in filial piety

【迍】 6060 ㄓㄨㄣ juen zhūn
a difficult position

迍邅(ㄓㄨㄣ ㄓㄢ)
to be in a difficult position 亦作「屯邅」

【迒】 6061 ㄏㄤˊ harng háng
1. animal tracks
2. a path; a way; a road

〔辵部〕

五畫

【迢】 6062 ㄊㄧㄠˊ tyau tiáo
far; distant; remote

迢遞(ㄊㄧㄠˊ ㄉㄧˋ)
far-off; faraway

迢迢(ㄊㄧㄠˊ ㄊㄧㄠˊ)
faraway; far and remote

迢遙(ㄊㄧㄠˊ ㄧㄠˊ)or 迢遠(ㄊㄧㄠˊ ㄩㄢˇ)
far; distant

【迤】 6063 ㄧˇ yii yǐ
same as 迆—connected; to proceed in a winding way

【迥】 6064 (逈) ㄐㄩㄥˇ jeong jiǒng
1. faraway
2. widely different

迥拔(ㄐㄩㄥˇ ㄅㄚˊ)
standing erect and high

迥別(ㄐㄩㄥˇ ㄅㄧㄝˊ)
a great difference; vastly different

迥非昔比(ㄐㄩㄥˇ ㄈㄟ ㄒㄧˊ ㄅㄧˇ)
so different that there is no way of comparing it with what it used to be

迥迥(ㄐㄩㄥˇ ㄐㄩㄥˇ)
faraway

迥殊(ㄐㄩㄥˇ ㄕㄨ)
vastly different; not similar at all

迥然不同(ㄐㄩㄥˇ ㄖㄢˊ ㄅㄨˋ ㄊㄨㄥˊ)
not in the least alike; diametrically different; poles apart in (nature or appearance, etc.)

迥異(ㄐㄩㄥˇ ㄧˋ)
a great difference; vastly different

迥遠(ㄐㄩㄥˇ ㄩㄢˇ)
faraway; remote

【迦】 6065 ㄐㄧㄚ jia jiā
a character used in transliterating foreign (especially Sanskrit) sounds

迦太基(ㄐㄧㄚ ㄊㄞˋ ㄐㄧ)
Carthage

迦納(ㄐㄧㄚ ㄋㄚˋ)
Ghana

【迨】 6066 ㄉㄞˋ day dài
until; up until; by the time when; to wait till

【迪】 6067 (廸) ㄉㄧˊ dyi dí
1. to advance; to progress
2. to enlighten; to teach

迪克推多(ㄉㄧˊ ㄎㄜˋ ㄊㄨㄟ ㄉㄨㄛ)
a dictator 亦作「獨裁者」

迪化(ㄉㄧˊ ㄏㄨㄚˋ)
Urumchi (or Tihwa), capital of Sinkiang Province

迪吉(ㄉㄧˊ ㄐㄧˊ)
lucky; prosperous; going well; blessed

迪斯可(ㄉㄧˊ ㄙ ㄎㄜˇ)
disco

【迫】 6068 (廹) ㄆㄛˋ poh pò
1. to press; to force; to compel; to stress: 我強迫他做此事。I forced him to do it.
2. pressing; urgent; imminent
3. pressed; distressed

迫不得已(ㄆㄛˋ ·ㄅㄨ ㄉㄜˊ ㄧˇ)
to have no alternative (but to); compelled by circumstances

迫不及待(ㄆㄛˋ ·ㄅㄨ ㄐㄧˊ ㄉㄞˋ)
so urgent that there is no time for waiting; too impatient to wait

迫令(ㄆㄛˋ ㄌㄧㄥˋ)
to order or demand forcibly

迫害(ㄆㄛˋ ㄏㄞˋ)
to persecute; to oppress cruelly: 基督徒受到嚴重迫害。Christians were terribly persecuted.

迫擊砲(ㄆㄛˋ ㄐㄧˊ ㄆㄠˋ)
a mortar (a shortbarreled cannon)

迫近(ㄆㄛˋ ㄐㄧㄣˋ)
①to press near; to close in; to draw near: 婚期迫近。The date of wedding is drawing near. ②imminent

迫降(ㄆㄛˋ ㄐㄧㄤˋ)
a forced landing; a distress landing

迫切(ㄆㄛˋ ㄑㄧㄝˋ)
pressing; urgent: 他迫切需要錢。He is urgent for money.

迫切需要(ㄆㄛˋ ㄑㄧㄝˋ ㄒㄩ ㄧㄠˋ)
an urgent need

迫脅(ㄆㄛˋ ㄒㄧㄝˊ)
to force; to coerce

迫使(ㄆㄛˋ ㄕˇ)
to force or compel (one to do a thing): 環境迫使他不顧一切。Circumstances compelled him to be desperate.

迫在眉睫(ㄆㄛˋ ㄗㄞˋ ㄇㄟˊ ㄐㄧㄝˊ)
①extremely urgent and near ②imminent

迫促(ㄆㄛˋ ㄘㄨˋ)
urgent; pressed for time

迫從(ㄆㄛˋ ㄘㄨㄥˊ)
to force to comply; to compel to submit

迫於(ㄆㄛˋ ㄩˊ)
to have no other alternative because of...

【迭】 6069 ㄉㄧㄝˊ dye dié
1. to alternate
2. repeatedly; frequently
3. as in 不迭—to stop; to cease

迭更斯(ㄉㄧㄝˊ ㄍㄥ ㄙ)
Charles Dickens, 1812-1870, English novelist

迭擊(ㄉㄧㄝˊ ㄐㄧˊ)
to attack by turns

迭興(ㄉㄧㄝˊ ㄒㄧㄥ)
to rise one after another

迭次(ㄉㄧㄝˊ ㄘˋ)
again and again; repeatedly: 我迭次警告他。I warned him again and again.

迭用(ㄉㄧㄝˊ ㄩㄥˋ)
to use alternately

【述】 6070 ㄕㄨˋ shuh shù
1. to give an account of; to explain; to expound
2. to follow (precedents); to carry forward; to continue (another's work)

述職(ㄕㄨˋ ㄓˊ)
to report in person the performance of one's official duties; to report on one's work
述聖(ㄕㄨˋ ㄕㄥˋ)
an honorary title for Tzu Szu(子思), Confucius' grandson
述說(ㄕㄨˋ ㄕㄨㄛ)
to give an account of; to narrate
述作(ㄕㄨˋ ㄗㄨㄛˋ)
to compose and create; to write; writings: 他的述作包括詩和散文。His writings include poetry and prose.
述而不作(ㄕㄨˋ ㄦˊ ㄅㄨˋ ㄗㄨㄛˋ)
to expound the theories or writings of ancient people without producing original writings oneself
述語(ㄕㄨˋ ㄩˇ)
the predicate (as distinct from the subject)

【迮】 6071
ㄗㄜˊ tzer zé
1. pressing; urgent
2. hurried; helter-skelter

六畫

【迴】 6072
(廻) ㄏㄨㄟˊ hwei huí
1. to turn; to rotate; to revolve
2. to zigzag; to wind: 峰迴路轉。The path winds along mountain ridges.
3. same as 回—to return
迴避(ㄏㄨㄟˊ ㄅㄧˋ)
①to avoid meeting (another person) ②(law) to withdraw; withdrawal ③to decline an offer, or resign from a job, in order to avoid likely suspicion of favoritism
迴風(ㄏㄨㄟˊ ㄈㄥ)
a whirlwind 亦作「旋風」
迴廊(ㄏㄨㄟˊ ㄌㄤˊ)
a winding corridor: 我走出房間到迴廊。I went out of the room into the winding corridor.
迴鑾(ㄏㄨㄟˊ ㄌㄨㄢˊ)
the return of the emperor to the capital
迴環(ㄏㄨㄟˊ ㄏㄨㄢˊ)
to recur in a cycle
迴環測試(ㄏㄨㄟˊ ㄏㄨㄢˊ ㄘㄜˋ ㄕˋ)
(computers) loop testing
迴翔(ㄏㄨㄟˊ ㄒㄧㄤˊ)
to soar round and round; to circle in the air
迴響(ㄏㄨㄟˊ ㄒㄧㄤˇ)
to echo; to resound; to reverberate
迴旋(ㄏㄨㄟˊ ㄒㄩㄢˊ)
to turn round and round; to circle
迴旋曲(ㄏㄨㄟˊ ㄒㄩㄢˊ ㄑㄩˇ)
(music) a rondo
迴轉(ㄏㄨㄟˊ ㄓㄨㄢˇ)
to turn round
迴轉爐(ㄏㄨㄟˊ ㄓㄨㄢˇ ㄌㄨˊ)
(metallurgy) a rotary furnace; a converter (for refining steel)
迴轉器(ㄏㄨㄟˊ ㄓㄨㄢˇ ㄑㄧˋ)or 迴轉儀(ㄏㄨㄟˊ ㄓㄨㄢˇ ㄧˊ)
(astronomy) a gyroscope; a gyro
迴腸(ㄏㄨㄟˊ ㄔㄤˊ)
(anatomy) the ileum
迴腸盪氣(ㄏㄨㄟˊ ㄔㄤˊ ㄉㄤˋ ㄑㄧˋ)
(said of music, poetry, etc.) to deeply affect one's emotions; very touching
迴誦(ㄏㄨㄟˊ ㄙㄨㄥˋ)
to recite, or chant repeatedly
迴文(ㄏㄨㄟˊ ㄨㄣˊ)
a palindrome
迴文錦(ㄏㄨㄟˊ ㄨㄣˊ ㄐㄧㄣˇ)
a kind of elaborately woven silk
迴紋針(ㄏㄨㄟˊ ㄨㄣˊ ㄓㄣ)or 迴形針(ㄏㄨㄟˊ ㄒㄧㄥˊ ㄓㄣ)
a paper clip
迴文詩(ㄏㄨㄟˊ ㄨㄣˊ ㄕ)
palindromic verses

【迷】 6073
ㄇㄧˊ mi mí
1. indistinct; vague; dim
2. to bewitch; to enchant; to be crazy about; to charm; to fascinate; to infatuate: 她對游泳着迷了。She was crazy about swimming.
3. a fan; a fiend: 他是個棒球迷。He is a baseball fan.
迷漫(ㄇㄧˊ ㄇㄢˋ)
vague; hazy; indistinct
迷茫(ㄇㄧˊ ㄇㄤˊ)
①vast and hazy ②confused; perplexed; dazed
迷蒙精(ㄇㄧˊ ㄇㄥˊ ㄐㄧㄥ)
(medicine) chloroform 亦作「哥羅芳」
迷蒙藥(ㄇㄧˊ ㄇㄥˊ ㄧㄠˋ)
anesthetics
迷夢(ㄇㄧˊ ㄇㄥˋ)
a delusive dream; an illusion; a delusion
迷湯(ㄇㄧˊ ㄊㄤ)
flatteries; honey words
迷途(ㄇㄧˊ ㄊㄨˊ)
①to go astray; to get lost ②a wrong path
迷途知返(ㄇㄧˊ ㄊㄨˊ ㄓ ㄈㄢˇ)
able to return to the proper path after going astray; able to correct one's own mistake
迷你(ㄇㄧˊ ㄋㄧˇ)
mini
迷你電腦(ㄇㄧˊ ㄋㄧˇ ㄉㄧㄢˋ ㄋㄠˇ)
a minicomputer
迷你裙(ㄇㄧˊ ㄋㄧˇ ㄑㄩㄣˊ)
a miniskirt
迷離(ㄇㄧˊ ㄌㄧˊ)
indistinct; vague
迷戀(ㄇㄧˊ ㄌㄧㄢˋ)
to be in blind love with; to be infatuated with; to be a slave of: 他迷戀着那個女孩。He's infatuated with that girl.
迷路(ㄇㄧˊ ㄌㄨˋ)
to go astray; to get lost: 她迷路了。She lost her way.
迷亂(ㄇㄧˊ ㄌㄨㄢˋ)
to derange; to confuse
迷宮(ㄇㄧˊ ㄍㄨㄥ)
a labyrinth; a maze
迷航(ㄇㄧˊ ㄏㄤˊ)
(said of a plane, ship, etc.) to drift off course; to lose one's course
迷忽忽(ㄇㄧˊ ㄏㄨ ㄏㄨ)
①having a confused mind; muddleheaded ②unconscious
迷糊(ㄇㄧˊ ˙ㄏㄨ)or 迷迷糊糊(ㄇㄧˊ ˙ㄇㄧ ˙ㄏㄨ ˙ㄏㄨ)
①vague; dim; indistinct ②unconscious; half awake and half asleep ③dazzled ④muddleheaded: 她這個人有點迷糊。She's somewhat muddleheaded.
迷惑(ㄇㄧˊ ㄏㄨㄛˋ)
①to misguide; to delude; to confuse; to mislead ②confused; puzzled; bewildered

迷幻藥(ㄇㄧˊ ㄏㄨㄢˋ ㄧㄠˋ)
a hallucinogenic

迷魂湯(ㄇㄧˊ ㄏㄨㄣˊ ㄊㄤ)
①the soup of infatuation; the water of oblivion ②(figuratively) flattering words

迷魂陣(ㄇㄧˊ ㄏㄨㄣˊ ㄓㄣˋ)
the charming company of beautiful women (which makes one forget everything)

迷津(ㄇㄧˊ ㄐㄧㄣ)
①a labyrinth; confusion; a puzzle ②to lose one's way ③(Buddhism) the ford of delusion, i.e. mortality

迷信(ㄇㄧˊ ㄒㄧㄣˋ)
superstition; to believe blindly

迷住(ㄇㄧˊ ·ㄓㄨ)
to bewitch; to infatuate; to charm; to captivate; to enchant; to spellbind

迷失(ㄇㄧˊ ㄕ)
to get lost; to lose (one's way, etc.)

迷人(ㄇㄧˊ ㄖㄣˊ)
charming; fascinating; enchanting; bewitching: 她是個迷人的女孩。She is a charming girl.

迷藏(ㄇㄧˊ ㄘㄤˊ)
hide-and-seek

迷岸(ㄇㄧˊ ㄢˋ)
(Buddhism) the shore of delusion

迷藥(ㄇㄧˊ ㄧㄠˋ)
knockout drops

迷霧(ㄇㄧˊ ㄨˋ)
①a dense fog ②anything that misguides people

迷罔 or 迷惘(ㄇㄧˊ ㄨㄤˇ)
bemused

迷雲(ㄇㄧˊ ㄩㄣˊ)
clouds of confusion (over the mind)

【迹】 6074
(跡) ㄐㄧ ji ji

footprints; traces; tracks

迹象(ㄐㄧ ㄒㄧㄤˋ)
signs; marks; indications: 那是一種奇怪的迹象。That is a strange indication.

【追】 6075
ㄓㄨㄟ juei zhui

1. to chase; to pursue; to follow; to trace
2. to drive; to expel
3. to demand insistently; to dun for
4. to try to recover (stolen goods, etc.); to retrieve

追奔逐北(ㄓㄨㄟ ㄅㄣ ㄓㄨˊ ㄅㄛˇ)
to chase an enemy force in full retreat

追本溯源(ㄓㄨㄟ ㄅㄣˇ ㄙㄨˋ ㄩㄢˊ)
to trace to the very source of something; to get at the root of the matter

追兵(ㄓㄨㄟ ㄅㄧㄥ)
troops in pursuit; pursuing troops

追捕(ㄓㄨㄟ ㄅㄨˇ)
to pursue and apprehend; to chase

追不到(ㄓㄨㄟ ·ㄅㄨ ㄉㄠˋ)
unable to catch up with; unable to overtake

追放(ㄓㄨㄟ ㄈㄤˋ)
to banish 亦作「放逐」

追封(ㄓㄨㄟ ㄈㄥ)
to ennoble posthumously

追到(ㄓㄨㄟ ㄉㄠˋ)
to catch up with

追悼(ㄓㄨㄟ ㄉㄠˋ)
to commemorate (the dead)

追悼會(ㄓㄨㄟ ㄉㄠˋ ㄏㄨㄟˋ)
a memorial service

追討(ㄓㄨㄟ ㄊㄠˇ)
①to dun for (debt) ②to pursue and subdue (rebels)

追念(ㄓㄨㄟ ㄋㄧㄢˋ)
to remember with nostalgia or gratitude

追趕(ㄓㄨㄟ ㄍㄢˇ)
to pursue; to chase; to try to catch up with or overtake: 獵人追趕狐狸。The hunter chased a fox.

追根問底(ㄓㄨㄟ ㄍㄣ ㄨㄣˋ ㄉㄧˇ) or 追根究底(ㄓㄨㄟ ㄍㄣ ㄐㄧㄡˋ ㄉㄧˇ)
to raise one question after another (in order to reach the bottom of a matter)

追回(ㄓㄨㄟ ㄏㄨㄟˊ)
①to recover (what has been taken away illicitly) ②to catch up with someone on the way and make him come back

追悔(ㄓㄨㄟ ㄏㄨㄟˇ)
to regret afterward; to repent

追歡(ㄓㄨㄟ ㄏㄨㄢ)
to pursue pleasure

追還(ㄓㄨㄟ ㄏㄨㄢˊ)
to recover (what has been taken away illicitly)

追擊(ㄓㄨㄟ ㄐㄧˊ)
to chase and attack; to give chase

追記(ㄓㄨㄟ ㄐㄧˋ)
a postscript; to record afterward

追加(ㄓㄨㄟ ㄐㄧㄚ)
to make an addition (to a document, etc.)

追加預算(ㄓㄨㄟ ㄐㄧㄚ ㄩˋ ㄙㄨㄢˋ)
an additional budget; a supplementary budget

追剿(ㄓㄨㄟ ㄐㄧㄠˇ)
to chase and attack retreating enemy troops

追繳(ㄓㄨㄟ ㄐㄧㄠˇ)
to demand the payment (of tax arrears, debts, etc.)

追究(ㄓㄨㄟ ㄐㄧㄡˋ)
①to try insistently to find out (the ultimate cause, etc.) ②to investigate (a fault, offense, etc.) and punish (the guilty)

追薦(ㄓㄨㄟ ㄐㄧㄢˋ)
to seek blessings for the dead; to pray for the dead

追求(ㄓㄨㄟ ㄑㄧㄡˊ)
①to seek; to pursue; to go after: 他一生都在追求眞理。He sought after the truth throughout his life. ②to court (a woman); courtship

追想(ㄓㄨㄟ ㄒㄧㄤˇ)
to remember nostalgically

追尋(ㄓㄨㄟ ㄒㄩㄣˊ)
to seek; to pursue

追逐(ㄓㄨㄟ ㄓㄨˊ)
to chase; to pursue

追查(ㄓㄨㄟ ㄔㄚˊ)
to investigate; to trace (by observing marks, tracks, bits of evidence)

追謚(ㄓㄨㄟ ㄕˋ)
to confer a posthumous title upon

追認(ㄓㄨㄟ ㄖㄣˋ)
to confirm; to ratify; to approve afterward

追贓(ㄓㄨㄟ ㄗㄤ)
to try to recover stolen articles

追贈(ㄓㄨㄟ ㄗㄥˋ)
to confer (titles or ranks)

posthumously
追尊(ㄓㄨㄟ ㄗㄨㄣ)
to bestow posthumous honors upon
追蹤(ㄓㄨㄟ ㄗㄨㄥ)
① to follow the examples of the predecessors ② to trace; to trail: 警察循跡追蹤罪犯。The police are tracing the criminal.
追思彌撒(ㄓㄨㄟ ㄙ ㄇㄧˊ ㄙㄚ)
(Catholics) Requiem Mass
追思禮拜(ㄓㄨㄟ ㄙ ㄌㄧˇ ㄅㄞˋ)
(Protestants) Requiem Service
追溯(ㄓㄨㄟ ㄙㄨˋ)
to trace the origin of; to trace back 亦作「追源」
追訴權(ㄓㄨㄟ ㄙㄨˋ ㄑㄩㄢˊ)
the right of prosecution; the right to prosecute someone for an offense committed long ago
追訴權時效法(ㄓㄨㄟ ㄙㄨˋ ㄑㄩㄢˊ ㄕˊ ㄒㄧㄠˋ ㄈㄚˇ)
(law) the statute of limitations
追訴時效(ㄓㄨㄟ ㄙㄨˋ ㄕˊ ㄒㄧㄠˋ)
the period within which a legal action may be taken; the period stipulated in a statute of limitations
追索(ㄓㄨㄟ ㄙㄨㄛˇ)
to make insistent demands for (payment)
追隨(ㄓㄨㄟ ㄙㄨㄟˊ)
to follow (a leader)
追憶(ㄓㄨㄟ ㄧˋ)
to call to memory; to remember; to look back: 事隔很久，難以追憶。It happened years ago and I can't call it to memory.
追影(ㄓㄨㄟ ㄧㄥˇ)
to paint somebody's likeness after his death
追問(ㄓㄨㄟ ㄨㄣˋ)
to question insistently
追遠(ㄓㄨㄟ ㄩㄢˇ)
to honor ancestors with sacrifices

【退】 6076
ㄊㄨㄟˋ tuey tuì

1. to retreat; to withdraw; to recede; to regress; to retrogress: 敵人已經撤退了。The enemy has retreated.
2. to recoil; to shrink
3. to bow out; to retire: 他六十歲退休。He retired at the age of sixty.
4. to send back; to give back; to return

退保(ㄊㄨㄟˋ ㄅㄠˇ)
① to return a bond; to cease to be a guarantor ② to return an insurance policy
退避(ㄊㄨㄟˋ ㄅㄧˋ)
to withdraw and avoid; to keep out of the way
退避三舍(ㄊㄨㄟˋ ㄅㄧˋ ㄙㄢ ㄕㄜˋ)
(literally) to retreat ninety *li*(里)—to retreat as far as possible in the face of a strong adversary or contestant
退兵(ㄊㄨㄟˋ ㄅㄧㄥ)
① to withdraw troops; to sound a retreat: 擊鼓退兵。The drums sounded a retreat. ② to repel enemy troops
退步(ㄊㄨㄟˋ ㄅㄨˋ)
① to fall off; to regress; to retrogress; to fall backwards; to suffer a relapse ② to retreat
退票(ㄊㄨㄟˋ ㄆㄧㄠˋ)
①(said of theaters, music halls, etc.) to refund; to return the ticket and get the money back ② (said of checks) to be dishonored; to bounce
退黨(ㄊㄨㄟˋ ㄉㄤˇ)
to withdraw from a political party
退敵(ㄊㄨㄟˋ ㄉㄧˊ)
to repel the enemy
退庭(ㄊㄨㄟˋ ㄊㄧㄥˊ)or 退堂(ㄊㄨㄟˋ ㄊㄤˊ)
to retire from the courtroom
退老(ㄊㄨㄟˋ ㄌㄠˇ)
to retire (from public life) due to old age
退路(ㄊㄨㄟˋ ㄌㄨˋ)
① a retreat ② something to fall back on
退股(ㄊㄨㄟˋ ㄍㄨˇ)
to withdraw investment in a company
退歸林下(ㄊㄨㄟˋ ㄍㄨㄟ ㄌㄧㄣˊ ㄒㄧㄚˋ)
to retire from public life
退款(ㄊㄨㄟˋ ㄎㄨㄢˇ)
to reimburse
退後(ㄊㄨㄟˋ ㄏㄡˋ)
to fall backward; to move backward
退化(ㄊㄨㄟˋ ㄏㄨㄚˋ)
to degenerate; to atrophy
退火(ㄊㄨㄟˋ ㄏㄨㄛˇ)
(metallurgy) annealing
退伙(ㄊㄨㄟˋ ㄏㄨㄛˇ)
to stop joining public mess
退貨(ㄊㄨㄟˋ ㄏㄨㄛˋ)
to return goods already purchased
退回(ㄊㄨㄟˋ ㄏㄨㄟˊ)
① to return (a gift, defective merchandise, etc.); to send back: 她的稿子已經被退回。Her manuscript has been sent back. ② to retreat; to turn back
退還(ㄊㄨㄟˋ ㄏㄨㄢˊ)
to return (a gift, defective merchandise, etc.)
退換(ㄊㄨㄟˋ ㄏㄨㄢˋ)
to return (merchandise) in exchange for another; to exchange a purchase
退婚(ㄊㄨㄟˋ ㄏㄨㄣ)
to break off a marital engagement
退居(ㄊㄨㄟˋ ㄐㄩ)
① to occupy a position less important or influential than the one held previously ② to live a retired life
退錢(ㄊㄨㄟˋ ㄑㄧㄢˊ)
to reimburse; to refund
退親(ㄊㄨㄟˋ ㄑㄧㄣ)
to break off a marital engagement
退卻(ㄊㄨㄟˋ ㄑㄩㄝˋ)
① to retreat: 敵人不得不退卻。The enemy had to retreat. ② to decline
退席(ㄊㄨㄟˋ ㄒㄧˊ)
to withdraw (from the presence of others); to retire from a banquet before it is finished; to walk out (of a meeting in protest): 他退席以示抗議。He walked out in protest.
退休(ㄊㄨㄟˋ ㄒㄧㄡ)
to retire from active life: 他自公職退休。He retired from public life.
退休年齡(ㄊㄨㄟˋ ㄒㄧㄡ ㄋㄧㄢˊ ㄌㄧㄥˊ)

〔辵部〕

retirement age
退休基金(ㄊㄨㄟˋ ㄒㄧㄡ ㄐㄧ ㄐㄧㄣ)
a superannuation fund
退休金(ㄊㄨㄟˋ ㄒㄧㄡ ㄐㄧㄣ)
a retiring allowance; a pension
退休制度(ㄊㄨㄟˋ ㄒㄧㄡ ㄓˋ ㄉㄨˋ)
a retirement system
退閒(ㄊㄨㄟˋ ㄒㄧㄢˊ)
to retire (to a life of leisure)
退省(ㄊㄨㄟˋ ㄒㄧㄥˇ)
to pause for reflection or self-examination
退學(ㄊㄨㄟˋ ㄒㄩㄝˊ)
to withdraw from a school; to drop out of a school
退職(ㄊㄨㄟˋ ㄓˊ)
to resign from office; to retire: 他退職了。He resigned from office.
退志(ㄊㄨㄟˋ ㄓˋ)
the intention to resign or retire
退朝(ㄊㄨㄟˋ ㄔㄠˊ)
to retire from the (emperor's) court
退潮(ㄊㄨㄟˋ ㄔㄠˊ)
(said of the tide) to ebb
退場(ㄊㄨㄟˋ ㄔㄤˇ)
to leave the stage; an exit
退出(ㄊㄨㄟˋ ㄔㄨ)
to withdraw or retreat (from a city or position); to renounce (membership in an organization); to step out; to bow out
退出去(ㄊㄨㄟˋ ㄔㄨ ˙ㄑㄩ)
to withdraw; to bow out
退食(ㄊㄨㄟˋ ㄕˊ)
to retire or rest for a meal
退士(ㄊㄨㄟˋ ㄕˋ)
①a recluse ②a retired official
退燒(ㄊㄨㄟˋ ㄕㄠ)or 退熱(ㄊㄨㄟˋ ㄖㄜˋ)
to reduce or remove fever; (said of a person's temperature) to come down
退燒藥(ㄊㄨㄟˋ ㄕㄠ ㄧㄠˋ)
febrifuges; antipyretics
退守(ㄊㄨㄟˋ ㄕㄡˇ)
to retreat (to a city, position, etc.) and defend it
退稅(ㄊㄨㄟˋ ㄕㄨㄟˋ)
(economics) a tax rebate
退讓(ㄊㄨㄟˋ ㄖㄤˋ)
to yield (a position, etc., especially in one's modesty); to make a concession
退走(ㄊㄨㄟˋ ㄗㄡˇ)
to retreat; to withdraw
退租(ㄊㄨㄟˋ ㄗㄨ)
to terminate a lease contract
退縮(ㄊㄨㄟˋ ㄙㄨㄛ)
to shrink; to recoil; to flinch
退而求其次(ㄊㄨㄟˋ ㄦˊ ㄑㄧㄡˊ ㄑㄧˊ ㄘˋ)
to seek what is less attractive than one's original objective
退一步想(ㄊㄨㄟˋ ㄧˊ ㄅㄨˋ ㄒㄧㄤˇ)
to consider a matter in a concessive way; to view a matter in a less favorable light; to remind oneself that things might have been worse
退役(ㄊㄨㄟˋ ㄧˋ)
to be discharged from military service
退隱(ㄊㄨㄟˋ ㄧㄣˇ)
to go into retirement; to retire from public life
退伍(ㄊㄨㄟˋ ㄨˇ)
to retire or to be discharged from military service; to leave the army
退伍軍人(ㄊㄨㄟˋ ㄨˇ ㄐㄩㄣ ㄖㄣˊ)
a retired soldier; a discharged serviceman; veterans
退位(ㄊㄨㄟˋ ㄨㄟˋ)
to abdicate the throne: 國王退位了。The king abdicated.
退約(ㄊㄨㄟˋ ㄩㄝ)
to break off a contract or agreement

【送】 6077 ㄙㄨㄥˋ sonq sòng

1. to send; to despatch; to deliver; to convey
2. to present; to give: 父親送我一本書。My father gave me a book.
3. to see someone off; to send off; to wish Godspeed to; to send away in a complimentary manner

送報(ㄙㄨㄥˋ ㄅㄠˋ)
to deliver newspapers
送報生(ㄙㄨㄥˋ ㄅㄠˋ ㄕㄥ)
a newsboy
送別(ㄙㄨㄥˋ ㄅㄧㄝˊ)
to see (a person) off; to give a send-off; to wish Godspeed to
送別會(ㄙㄨㄥˋ ㄅㄧㄝˊ ㄏㄨㄟˋ)
a farewell party; a send-off
送殯(ㄙㄨㄥˋ ㄅㄧㄣˋ)or 送喪(ㄙㄨㄥˋ ㄙㄤ)
to attend a funeral
送命(ㄙㄨㄥˋ ㄇㄧㄥˋ)
to bring death upon oneself; to lose one's life; to go to one's doom
送飯(ㄙㄨㄥˋ ㄈㄢˋ)
to bring meals (for a person)
送達(ㄙㄨㄥˋ ㄉㄚˊ)
①to deliver to; to despatch to; to send to ②(law) to serve (a writ on a person)
送到(ㄙㄨㄥˋ ㄉㄠˋ)
to send to; to deliver to
送暖偷寒(ㄙㄨㄥˋ ㄋㄨㄢˇ ㄊㄡ ㄏㄢˊ)
(said of young lovers) to have affectionate concern for each other
送老(ㄙㄨㄥˋ ㄌㄠˇ)
①to pass one's later years ②to prepare the dead for burial (especially one's parents)
送禮(ㄙㄨㄥˋ ㄌㄧˇ)
to give presents; to send gifts: 他送禮給我。He sent me gifts.
送故迎新(ㄙㄨㄥˋ ㄍㄨˋ ㄧㄥˊ ㄒㄧㄣ)or 送舊迎新(ㄙㄨㄥˋ ㄐㄧㄡˋ ㄧㄥˊ ㄒㄧㄣ)
①to bid farewell to those departing and greet the arrival of new comers ②to send off the old year and usher in the new year
送鬼(ㄙㄨㄥˋ ㄍㄨㄟˇ)
to exorcise evil spirits
送官(ㄙㄨㄥˋ ㄍㄨㄢ)
(in former times) to deliver a criminal to the yamen for punishment
送客(ㄙㄨㄥˋ ㄎㄜˋ)
①to escort a visitor on his way out ②to speed a parting guest
送寒衣(ㄙㄨㄥˋ ㄏㄢˊ ㄧ)
the ceremony of burning paper garments before a tomb on the first of the 10th lunar month
送話器(ㄙㄨㄥˋ ㄏㄨㄚˋ ㄑㄧˋ)
the transmitter (of a tele-

phone)
送貨(ㄙㄨㄥˋ ㄏㄨㄛˋ)
to deliver goods
送貨員(ㄙㄨㄥˋ ㄏㄨㄛˋ ㄩㄢˊ)
a deliveryman
送回(ㄙㄨㄥˋ ㄏㄨㄟˊ)or 送還(ㄙㄨㄥˋ ㄏㄨㄢˊ)
to send back; to return
送交(ㄙㄨㄥˋ ㄐㄧㄠ)
to hand over to; to deliver to: 請把這封信送交貴老板。Please hand over this letter to your boss.
送餞(ㄙㄨㄥˋ ㄐㄧㄢˋ)
to give a send-off party
送秋波(ㄙㄨㄥˋ ㄑㄧㄡ ㄅㄛ)
to cast an amorous glance; to make eyes at
送情(ㄙㄨㄥˋ ㄑㄧㄥˊ)
to convey one's feelings
送窮(ㄙㄨㄥˋ ㄑㄩㄥˊ)
to drive away poverty (a ceremony held on the last day of the first lunar month in the Tang Dynasty)
送信(ㄙㄨㄥˋ ㄒㄧㄣˋ)or 送信兒(ㄙㄨㄥˋ ㄒㄧㄜˋㄦ)
to carry letters; to deliver letters; to deliver a message
送香火兒的(ㄙㄨㄥˋ ㄒㄧㄤ ㄏㄨㄛˇㄦ ·ㄉㄜ)
(in Peking in former times) beggars who light pipes for smokers and get paid in return
送行(ㄙㄨㄥˋ ㄒㄧㄥˊ)
to give a send-off; to see someone off; to wish God-speed: 我到車站去爲他送行。I went to the station to see him off.
送粧(ㄙㄨㄥˋ ㄓㄨㄤ)
to deliver the dowry to the bridegroom's house
送終(ㄙㄨㄥˋ ㄓㄨㄥ)
to prepare for the burial of one's parents
送神(ㄙㄨㄥˋ ㄕㄣˊ)
to send off the gods after the offering of sacrifices
送上(ㄙㄨㄥˋ ·ㄕㄤ)
(a polite expression) to send or deliver
送人(ㄙㄨㄥˋ ㄖㄣˊ)
①to send gifts; to give presents ②to see a person off; to see someone off
送人情(ㄙㄨㄥˋ ㄖㄣˊ ㄑㄧㄥˊ)
to do another person a favor at no great cost to oneself
送子(ㄙㄨㄥˋ ㄗˇ)
(said of a goddess) to make a woman give birth to a child
送竈(ㄙㄨㄥˋ ㄗㄠˋ)
the ceremony (on the 23rd of the 12th lunar month) of sending off the kitchen god on his annual trip to Heaven with foods, drinks, etc., offered as sacrifices
送葬(ㄙㄨㄥˋ ㄗㄤˋ)or 送喪(ㄙㄨㄥˋ ㄙㄤ)
to attend a funeral; to take part in a funeral procession
送做堆(ㄙㄨㄥˋ ㄗㄨㄛˋ ㄉㄨㄟ)
(slang) to arrange a wedding for a young couple who have already lived under the same roof since their childhood
送死(ㄙㄨㄥˋ ㄙˇ)
①to prepare for the burial of one's parents ②to bring death upon oneself
送往事居(ㄙㄨㄥˋ ㄨㄤˇ ㄕˋ ㄐㄩ)
to bury the dead and support the living
送往迎來(ㄙㄨㄥˋ ㄨㄤˇ ㄧㄥˊ ㄌㄞˊ)
to escort the parting and welcome the coming—to be busy entertaining guests from afar

【适】 6078
ㄍㄨㄚ gua guā
quick; fast; swift

【逃】 6079
ㄊㄠˊ taur táo
1. to run away; to flee; to fly; to abscond; to escape: 軍隊潰逃。The troops fled in disorder.
2. to dodge; to evade; to avoid; to shirk: 他逃避我的質問。He evaded my question.
逃奔(ㄊㄠˊ ㄅㄣ)
to run away; to flee
逃避(ㄊㄠˊ ㄅㄧˋ)
to run away from; to shirk; to evade; to dodge
逃避兵役(ㄊㄠˊ ㄅㄧˋ ㄅㄧㄥ ㄧˋ)
to dodge the draft; to evade or shirk military service
逃避責任(ㄊㄠˊ ㄅㄧˋ ㄗㄜˊ ㄖㄣˋ)
to evade or shirk a responsibility
逃兵(ㄊㄠˊ ㄅㄧㄥ)
a deserter; a fugitive soldier
逃不了(ㄊㄠˊ ·ㄅㄨ ㄌㄧㄠˇ)
inescapable from; unable to escape
逃跑(ㄊㄠˊ ㄆㄠˇ)
to run away; to escape; to flee
逃名(ㄊㄠˊ ㄇㄧㄥˊ)
to avoid fame; to shun publicity
逃命(ㄊㄠˊ ㄇㄧㄥˋ)
to flee for one's life
逃反(ㄊㄠˊ ㄈㄢˇ)
to seek refuge from social unrest
逃犯(ㄊㄠˊ ㄈㄢˋ)
a fugitive from the law; a jailbreaker; a wanted criminal
逃遁(ㄊㄠˊ ㄉㄨㄣˋ)
to run away; to flee; to escape; to evade: 他受驚而逃遁。He was frightened and ran away.
逃脫(ㄊㄠˊ ㄊㄨㄛ)
to escape from; to free oneself from; to succeed in escaping from
逃難(ㄊㄠˊ ㄋㄢˋ)
to seek refuge from calamities: 難民逃難。Refugees seek refuge from calamities.
逃匿(ㄊㄠˊ ㄋㄧˋ)
to flee to a hiding place
逃祿(ㄊㄠˊ ㄌㄨˋ)
to avoid employment
逃歸(ㄊㄠˊ ㄍㄨㄟ)or 逃回(ㄊㄠˊ ㄏㄨㄟˊ)
to escape from (a dangerous place, etc.) and return home
逃婚(ㄊㄠˊ ㄏㄨㄣ)
to run away so as to avoid a marriage
逃荒(ㄊㄠˊ ㄏㄨㄤ)
to flee from a famine
逃家(ㄊㄠˊ ㄐㄧㄚ)
to run away from home
逃嫁(ㄊㄠˊ ㄐㄧㄚˋ)
①to desert a husband and remarry ②(said of a girl) to run away when reluctant to marry
逃軍(ㄊㄠˊ ㄐㄩㄣ)
①(said of a commander) to desert the troops ②a de-

serter
逃席(ㄊㄠˊ ㄒㄧˊ)
to leave a feast, etc., without permission
逃刑(ㄊㄠˊ ㄒㄧㄥˊ)
(said of a convict) to escape the sentence or punishment
逃學(ㄊㄠˊ ㄒㄩㄝˊ)
to play truant; to cut class; to truant
逃之夭夭(ㄊㄠˊ ㄓ ㄧㄠ ㄧㄠ)
to escape without leaving a single trace behind; to slip away: 他一聽到這消息就逃之夭夭。He slipped away on hearing the news.
逃債(ㄊㄠˊ ㄓㄞˋ)
to run away from the creditor
逃出虎口(ㄊㄠˊ ㄔㄨ ㄏㄨˇ ㄎㄡˇ)
(literally) to escape from a tiger's mouth—to escape from a very dangerous situation
逃出重圍(ㄊㄠˊ ㄔㄨ ㄔㄨㄥˊ ㄨㄟˊ)
to break out from a heavy siege
逃世(ㄊㄠˊ ㄕˋ)
to run away from the world; to go into seclusion
逃生(ㄊㄠˊ ㄕㄥ)
to flee for one's life
逃稅(ㄊㄠˊ ㄕㄨㄟˋ)
to avoid tax payment; tax evasion
逃走(ㄊㄠˊ ㄗㄡˇ)
to run away; to escape; to flee; to fly: 他已逃走。He has flown.
逃罪(ㄊㄠˊ ㄗㄨㄟˋ)
to escape punishment
逃竄(ㄊㄠˊ ㄘㄨㄢˋ)
to disperse and flee; to run away: 他們狼狽逃竄。They dispersed and fled helter-skelter.
逃散(ㄊㄠˊ ㄙㄢˋ)
to flee in all directions; to be separated in flight
逃逸(ㄊㄠˊ ㄧˋ)
to break loose and get away; to escape
逃隱(ㄊㄠˊ ㄧㄣˇ)
to flee into seclusion
逃亡(ㄊㄠˊ ㄨㄤˊ)
to run away; to escape; to flee; to fly; to abscond
逃亡者(ㄊㄠˊ ㄨㄤˊ ㄓㄜˇ)
a fugitive
逃往(ㄊㄠˊ ㄨㄤˇ)
to flee toward

【逅】 6080
ㄏㄡˋ how hòu
(又讀 ㄍㄡˋ gow gòu)
to meet unexpectedly; to come across; to run into

【逆】 6081
ㄋㄧˋ nih nì
1. to meet; to welcome
2. to oppose; to go against
3. beforehand; in advance
4. inverse; converse; adverse; contrary
逆叛(ㄋㄧˋ ㄆㄢˋ)
to rebel; to revolt
逆反應(ㄋㄧˋ ㄈㄢˇ ㄧㄥˋ)
an inverse reaction
逆風(ㄋㄧˋ ㄈㄥ)
① a head wind ② against the wind
逆黨(ㄋㄧˋ ㄉㄤˇ)
the rebel faction; a group of traitors
逆定理(ㄋㄧˋ ㄉㄧㄥˋ ㄌㄧˇ)
a converse theorem
逆覩(ㄋㄧˋ ㄉㄨˇ)
to see beforehand; to foresee: 我們無法逆覩未來。We cannot foresee the future.
逆來順受(ㄋㄧˋ ㄌㄞˊ ㄕㄨㄣˋ ㄕㄡˋ)
to accept adversity philosophically; to be resigned to one's fate
逆料(ㄋㄧˋ ㄌㄧㄠˋ)
to conjecture beforehand; to predict; to anticipate; to foresee
逆流(ㄋㄧˋ ㄌㄧㄡˊ)
① an adverse current ② against the current; against the stream; up the stream: 他逆流游泳。He swam against the current.
逆倫(ㄋㄧˋ ㄌㄨㄣˊ)
violation of primary relations among relatives or family members (especially referring to crimes committed against one's elders)
逆旅(ㄋㄧˋ ㄌㄩˇ)
an inn
逆跡昭彰(ㄋㄧˋ ㄐㄧ ㄓㄠ ㄓㄤ)
Signs of rebellion are evident.
逆計(ㄋㄧˋ ㄐㄧˋ)
to reckon or conjecture beforehand
逆境(ㄋㄧˋ ㄐㄧㄥˋ)
adverse circumstances; adversity
逆取順守(ㄋㄧˋ ㄑㄩˇ ㄕㄨㄣˋ ㄕㄡˇ)
to rule a country peacefully after obtaining the throne by violence
逆襲(ㄋㄧˋ ㄒㄧˊ)
a counterattack; to counterattack
逆向(ㄋㄧˋ ㄒㄧㄤˋ)
in the opposite direction
逆行(ㄋㄧˋ ㄒㄧㄥˊ)
① to proceed in the opposite direction; to go against the general trend ②(astronomy) retrograde motion
逆知(ㄋㄧˋ ㄓ)
to know beforehand; to foresee
逆折(ㄋㄧˋ ㄓㄜˊ)
to turn backward halfway
逆轉(ㄋㄧˋ ㄓㄨㄢˇ)
① to deteriorate; to turn to the worse ② a reversal
逆差(ㄋㄧˋ ㄔㄚ)
(commerce) an adverse balance of trade; a deficit
逆產(ㄋㄧˋ ㄔㄢˇ)
①(obstetrics) breech presentation, as opposed to face presentation ② the estate of a traitor
逆臣(ㄋㄧˋ ㄔㄣˊ)
a traitorous vassal; a traitor
逆事(ㄋㄧˋ ㄕˋ)
adverse affairs; misfortunes; mishaps: 他平靜地忍受逆事。He bears misfortunes calmly.
逆數(ㄋㄧˋ ㄕㄨˋ)
①(mathematics) reciprocal; a reciprocal number ② unseasonable weather
逆水行舟(ㄋㄧˋ ㄕㄨㄟˇ ㄒㄧㄥˊ ㄓㄡ)
a boat going against the stream; to sail a boat against the current: 逆水行舟，不進則退。A boat sailing against the stream must forge ahead or it will be driven back.
逆子(ㄋㄧˋ ㄗˇ)
an undutiful son; an unfilial

son
逆賊(ㄋㄧˋ ㄗㄟˊ)
a rebellious bandit; a rebel; a traitor
逆耳(ㄋㄧˋ ㄦˇ)
(said of statements) to grate on the ear; to be unpleasant to the ear: 忠言逆耳。Good advice is often grating on the ear.
逆溫層(ㄋㄧˋ ㄨㄣ ㄘㄥˊ)
(meteorology) the inversion layer

【迻】6082
ㄧˊ yi yí
to transfer; to translate
迻譯(ㄧˊ ㄧˋ)
to translate: 這本書迻譯得很好。The book translates well.

【逄】6083
ㄆㄤˊ parng páng
a Chinese family name

【逈】6084
(迥) ㄐㄩㄥˇ jeong jiǒng
far

【迺】6085
(乃) ㄋㄞˇ nae nǎi
a conjunctive and disjunctive particle with a variety of meanings

七畫

【逍】6086
ㄒㄧㄠ shiau xiāo
1. to wander in a leisurely manner; to saunter; to loiter
2. free and unfettered; to be leisurely and carefree; to take one's ease; at ease
逍遙(ㄒㄧㄠ ㄧㄠˊ)
to loiter about; to saunter about
逍遙法外(ㄒㄧㄠ ㄧㄠˊ ㄈㄚˇ ㄨㄞˋ)
to remain out of the law's reach; to get off scot-free
逍遙學派(ㄒㄧㄠ ㄧㄠˊ ㄒㄩㄝˊ ㄆㄞˋ)
the Peripatetics
逍遙自在(ㄒㄧㄠ ㄧㄠˊ ㄗˋ ㄗㄞˋ)
to enjoy leisure without restraint; to enjoy a free and leisurely life; carefree

【逝】6087
ㄕˋ shyh shì
1. to pass; to be gone; to depart
2. to pass on; to die
逝去(ㄕˋ ㄑㄩˋ)
to pass; to be gone; to depart
逝止(ㄕˋ ㄓˇ)
going and staying
逝世(ㄕˋ ㄕˋ)
to pass away; to die

【逋】6088
ㄅㄨ bu bū
1. to flee; to abscond
2. to neglect
逋慢(ㄅㄨ ㄇㄢˋ)
heedless of regulations or orders
逋負(ㄅㄨ ㄈㄨˋ)
to neglect to pay debts
逋蕩(ㄅㄨ ㄉㄤˋ)
to neglect one's duty and loaf
逋逃(ㄅㄨ ㄊㄠˊ)
to abscond; to flee (from justice)
逋留(ㄅㄨ ㄌㄧㄡˊ)
to stay; to remain; to linger: 我很匆忙，沒有時間逋留。I'm in a hurry; I've no time to stay.
逋客(ㄅㄨ ㄎㄜˋ)
① a recluse ② a fugitive
逋峭(ㄅㄨ ㄑㄧㄠˋ)
(said of a writing) containing many surprising turns; not monotonous
逋懸(ㄅㄨ ㄒㄩㄢˊ)
a long overdue rent; arrears
逋租(ㄅㄨ ㄗㄨ)
to neglect the payment of rent
逋亡(ㄅㄨ ㄨㄤˊ)
to flee; to escape; to abscond 亦作「逋逃」

【透】6089
ㄊㄡˋ tow tòu
1. to pass through; to penetrate
2. to let out; to let through
3. thorough; quite; complete: 蘋果熟透了。The apples are quite ripe.
4. to appear; to show
透闢(ㄊㄡˋ ㄆㄧˋ)
(said of statements, reasoning, etc.) revealing; penetrating
透明(ㄊㄡˋ ㄇㄧㄥˊ)
transparent: 窗戶的玻璃是透明的。Window glass is transparent.
透明體(ㄊㄡˋ ㄇㄧㄥˊ ㄊㄧˇ)
a transparent body
透風(ㄊㄡˋ ㄈㄥ)
① to let the wind through ② to divulge a secret; to let out a secret
透頂(ㄊㄡˋ ㄉㄧㄥˇ)
① in the extreme; to the utmost ② (said of syphilitic symptoms) to reach the head
透漏(ㄊㄡˋ ㄌㄡˋ)
to let out; to leak; to divulge; to reveal (secrets or news)
透亮
①(ㄊㄡˋ ㄌㄧㄤˋ) ⓐ letting light through; transparent; bright ⓑ perfectly clear
②(ㄊㄡˋ ·ㄌㄧㄤ) ⓐ (said of precious stones, etc.) brilliant; shiny ⓑ (said of statements) penetrating; incisive
透露(ㄊㄡˋ ㄌㄡˋ)
(said of something) to come to light; to divulge; to reveal; to let out: 誰透露了這個消息? Who let the news out?
透骨(ㄊㄡˋ ㄍㄨˇ)
(said of the cold) piercing; chilled to the bone
透過(ㄊㄡˋ ㄍㄨㄛˋ)
① to pass through; to penetrate ② through the intermediary of
透光(ㄊㄡˋ ㄍㄨㄤ)
① diaphaneity ② to let the light pass through
透光鏡(ㄊㄡˋ ㄍㄨㄤ ㄐㄧㄥˋ)
lenses 亦作「透鏡」
透汗(ㄊㄡˋ ㄏㄢˋ)
to perspire all over
透鏡(ㄊㄡˋ ㄐㄧㄥˋ)
lenses
透氣(ㄊㄡˋ ㄑㄧˋ)
① to let air through ② to give vent to a pent-up feeling of discontent ③ to relax from strain
透消息(ㄊㄡˋ ㄒㄧㄠ ㄒㄧˊ)
to reveal news; to let out a secret
透心涼(ㄊㄡˋ ㄒㄧㄣ ㄌㄧㄤˊ)
① penetrating coolness ② utterly disappointing

〔辵部〕

透支(ㄊㄡˋ ㄓ)
to overdraw; to spend more than the budgeted fund

透著(ㄊㄡˋ ·ㄓㄜ)
to appear to be; to seem to be

透徹(ㄊㄡˋ ㄔㄜˋ)
thorough; thoroughly; penetrating

透澈(ㄊㄡˋ ㄔㄜˋ)
clear; transparent; lucid

透濕(ㄊㄡˋ ㄕ)
dripping wet; wet through 亦作「濕透」: 我身上透濕了。I got wet to the skin.

透視(ㄊㄡˋ ㄕˋ)
①to see through; to penetrate ②to observe what is behind a solid covering (by X-ray, etc.) ③ to gain a perspective of; perspective

透視畫(ㄊㄡˋ ㄕˋ ㄏㄨㄚˋ)
a perspective drawing

透一口氣(ㄊㄡˋ ㄧ ㄎㄡˇ ㄑㄧˋ)
to catch a breath; to have a breathing spell

透味(ㄊㄡˋ ㄨㄟˋ)
(said of cooked meat, etc.) thoroughly flavored

【逐】 6090
ㄓㄨˊ jwu zhú

1. to chase; to pursue; to follow
2. to drive off; to banish; to exile; to expel: 他被放逐終身。He was exiled for life.
3. little by little; gradually

逐波而去(ㄓㄨˊ ㄅㄛ ㄦˊ ㄑㄩˋ)
to be carried away by waves; to go over the waves

逐步(ㄓㄨˊ ㄅㄨˋ)
step by step; to proceed orderly: 逐步加以解決 to settle something step by step

逐末(ㄓㄨˊ ㄇㄛˋ)
to pursue trivial things

逐條(ㄓㄨˊ ㄊㄧㄠˊ)
item by item; article by article; point by point

逐退(ㄓㄨˊ ㄊㄨㄟˋ)
to drive back; to repulse

逐年(ㄓㄨˊ ㄋㄧㄢˊ)
year by year; year after year; annually: 人口逐年增加。Population has been increasing year after year.

逐利(ㄓㄨˊ ㄌㄧˋ)
to pursue material gains

逐鹿(ㄓㄨˊ ㄌㄨˋ)
(literally) to chase the deer—to vie for the throne; to vie for power; to seek an office

逐箇 or 逐個(ㄓㄨˊ ㄍㄜˋ)
one by one: 他們逐箇調查這些問題。They investigate these questions one by one.

逐客令(ㄓㄨˊ ㄎㄜˋ ㄌㄧㄥˋ)
an announcement to a visitor that he is unwelcome

逐漸(ㄓㄨˊ ㄐㄧㄢˋ)
little by little; gradually; by degrees

逐臣(ㄓㄨˊ ㄔㄣˊ)
a banished subject; a vassal in exile

逐出(ㄓㄨˊ ㄔㄨ)
to drive out; to expel; to eject; to kick out; to oust; to chase someone (or something) out of: 他們把他逐出屋外。They chased him out of the house.

逐水(ㄓㄨˊ ㄕㄨㄟˇ)
(Chinese medicine) to eliminate the retention of fluid with powerful purgatives

逐日(ㄓㄨˊ ㄖˋ)
①day by day; day after day; daily ②(said of a horse) galloping very fast

逐字(ㄓㄨˊ ㄗˋ)
word by word; word for word: 請將此規則逐字解釋給我聽。Please explain this rule to me word by word.

逐次(ㄓㄨˊ ㄘˋ)
on each of the occasions; in succession

逐一(ㄓㄨˊ ㄧ)
one by one: 讓我們逐一上車吧。Let's get on the bus one by one.

逐月(ㄓㄨˊ ㄩㄝˋ)
month by month; monthly: 他逐月來此。He comes here monthly.

【逑】 6091
ㄑㄧㄡˊ chyou qiú

1. to pair; to match; to marry
2. to collect; to draw together; to gather together
3. a mate

【逕】 6092
ㄐㄧㄥˋ jinq jìng

1. a path
2. direct

逕庭(ㄐㄧㄥˋ ㄊㄧㄥˊ)
very unlike; quite different; poles apart

逕寄(ㄐㄧㄥˋ ㄐㄧˋ)
to mail directly to

逕啓者(ㄐㄧㄥˋ ㄑㄧˇ ㄓㄜˇ)
(a salutation in letters) Dear Sir

逕行(ㄐㄧㄥˋ ㄒㄧㄥˊ)
to do something directly; to do something on one's own initiative

【途】 6093
ㄊㄨˊ twu tú

a way; a road

途經(ㄊㄨˊ ㄐㄧㄥ)
to pass through (a place); to go by way of: 他途經上海。He came by way of Shanghai.

途徑(ㄊㄨˊ ㄐㄧㄥˋ)
a way; a road

途窮(ㄊㄨˊ ㄑㄩㄥˊ)
to come to the end of a road—at the end of one's resources

途中(ㄊㄨˊ ㄓㄨㄥ)
on the way; en route: 他在前往義大利的途中。He was en route to Italy.

途遇(ㄊㄨˊ ㄩˋ)
to encounter on the way; to meet en route

【逖】 6094
ㄊㄧˋ tih tì

far; distant

【逗】 6095
ㄉㄡˋ dow dòu

1. to stay; to linger; to remain; to pause
2. to stir; to rouse; to tickle
3. funny: 這故事眞逗! What a funny story!
4. a slight pause in reading

逗點(ㄉㄡˋ ㄉㄧㄢˇ)
a comma (,) 亦作「逗號」

逗弄(ㄉㄡˋ ·ㄋㄨㄥ)
to make fun of; to sport with; to tease; to kid: 他在逗弄那嬰兒。He's kidding that baby.

逗樂(ㄉㄡˋ ㄌㄜˋ)
to cause mirth; to rouse gaiety

逗留(ㄉㄡˋ ㄌㄧㄡˊ)
to stay; to stop over; to lin-

ger; to loiter
逗號(ㄉㄡˋ ㄏㄠˋ)
a comma(,)
逗趣(ㄉㄡˋ ㄑㄩˋ)
to amuse; to entertain(with jokes, etc.)
逗笑兒(ㄉㄡˋ ㄒㄧㄠˋㄦ)
to rouse laughter; to cause mirth
逗人(ㄉㄡˋ ㄖㄣˊ)
to tease; to tickle; to amuse
逗人喜愛(ㄉㄡˋ ㄖㄣˊ ㄒㄧˇ ㄞˋ)
(said of a child) to arouse the affection of adults

【這】 6096
1. ㄓㄜˋ jeh zhè
1. this (a pronoun)
2. this (a demonstrative adjective); such
這般(ㄓㄜˋ ㄅㄢ)
such; like this
這般光景(ㄓㄜˋ ㄅㄢ ㄍㄨㄤ ㄐㄧㄥˇ)or 這般地步(ㄓㄜˋ ㄅㄢ ㄉㄧˋ ㄅㄨˋ)
such a sad condition; such a pitiable state of affairs
這邊(ㄓㄜˋ ㄅㄧㄢ)
①this side; here: 請到這邊來。Please come over here. ② this side; our side: 勝利在我們這邊。Victory is on our side.
這步田地(ㄓㄜˋ ㄅㄨˋ ㄊㄧㄢˊ ㄉㄧˋ)
(to) such a pass; (to) such a deplorable situation
這麼(ㄓㄜˋ ·ㄇㄜ)
so; thus; (in) this way; like this: 大家都這麼說。So they say.
這麼點兒(ㄓㄜˋ ·ㄇㄜ ㄉㄧㄚˇㄦ)
such a little bit
這麼個(ㄓㄜˋ ·ㄇㄜ ·ㄍㄜ)
such a one as this
這麼著(ㄓㄜˋ ·ㄇㄜ ·ㄓㄜ)
this way (an expression to introduce a suggestion; an instruction of how to do something, etc.); like this; so
這麼一來(ㄓㄜˋ ·ㄇㄜ ㄧˊ ㄌㄞˊ)
as a result of that; as a result; in this way; consequently
這麼樣(ㄓㄜˋ ·ㄇㄜ ㄧㄤˋ)
so; thus; (in) this way; like this
這番(ㄓㄜˋ ㄈㄢ)
all this
這等(ㄓㄜˋ ㄉㄥˇ)
such; like this
這裏(ㄓㄜˋ ·ㄌㄧ)or 這兒(ㄓㄜˋㄦ)
here; this place; where we are: 她不在這裡。She is not here.
這個(ㄓㄜˋ ·ㄍㄜ)
① this; this one ② h'm, hem, or hum(an interjection indicating indecision when the sound ·ㄍㄜ is dragged too long)
這個那個的(ㄓㄜˋ ·ㄍㄜ ㄋㄚˋ ·ㄍㄜ ·ㄉㄜ)
wavering; irresolute; hesitant; to hem and haw
這還了得(ㄓㄜˋ ㄏㄞˊ ㄌㄧㄠˇ ·ㄉㄜ)
How dare! 或 How can such a thing be tolerated!
這會兒(ㄓㄜˋ ㄏㄨㄜˇㄦ)or 這會子(ㄓㄜˋ ㄏㄨㄟˋ ·ㄗ)
now; at the moment; at present: 他這會兒很忙。He is busy at the moment.
這就(ㄓㄜˋ ㄐㄧㄡˋ)
① at once; right away ② If this happens, then....或If that is the case, then....
這其間(ㄓㄜˋ ㄑㄧˊ ㄐㄧㄢ)
meanwhile; in the meantime
這些(ㄓㄜˋ ㄒㄧㄝ)
these
這種(ㄓㄜˋ ㄓㄨㄥˇ)
this kind; such kind; this type; such type
這程子(ㄓㄜˋ ㄔㄥˊ ·ㄗ)
recent; recently
這山望着那山高(ㄓㄜˋ ㄕㄢ ㄨㄤˋ ·ㄓㄜ ㄋㄚˋ ㄕㄢ ㄍㄠ)
It's always the other mountain that looks higher.—(figuratively) One is never satisfied with one's own present circumstance, position, etc.
這早晚兒(ㄓㄜˋ ·ㄗㄠ ㄨㄚˇㄦ)
as late as this; so late: 她怎麼這早晚兒才來? Why does she come so late?
這次(ㄓㄜˋ ㄘˋ)
this time; present; current
這廝(ㄓㄜˋ ㄙ)
this fellow; this guy
這兒(ㄓㄜˋㄦ)
① here: 我住在這兒。I live here. ② now; then
這一向(ㄓㄜˋ ㄧˊ ㄒㄧㄤˋ)
recently
這一陣子(ㄓㄜˋ ㄧˊ ㄓㄣˋ ·ㄗ)
recent; recently
這一回(ㄓㄜˋ ㄧˋ ㄏㄨㄟˊ)
this time
這樣那樣(ㄓㄜˋ ㄧㄤˋ ㄋㄚˋ ㄧㄤˋ)
this and that
這樣兒(ㄓㄜˋ ㄧㄤˋㄦ)or 這樣子(ㄓㄜˋ ㄧㄤˋ ·ㄗ)
so; thus; (in) this way: 別跑這樣兒快。Don't run so fast.

【這】 6096
2. ㄓㄟˋ jey zhèi
this or that (an emphatic demonstrative adjective)
這邊兒(ㄓㄟˋ ㄅㄧㄚㄦ)
over here; on this side: 到我這邊兒。Come over here.
這天(ㄓㄟˋ ㄊㄧㄢ)
(on) this (particular) day; (on) that (particular) day
這年(ㄓㄟˋ ㄋㄧㄢˊ)
(in) this (particular) year; (in) that (particular) year
這溜兒(ㄓㄟˋ ㄌㄧㄡˋㄦ)
this (particular) area; this (particular) district; this (particular) neighborhood
這個(ㄓㄟˋ ·ㄍㄜ)
this one
這塊兒(ㄓㄟˋ ㄎㄨㄚˋㄦ)
① this area; this neighborhood ② this lump
這陣兒(ㄓㄟˋ ㄓㄜˋㄦ)
this (very) moment

【通】 6097
ㄊㄨㄥ tong tōng
1. to go, move, or flow unobstructed
2. to communicate; to interchange
3. to lead to; to reach: 條條大路通羅馬。All roads lead to Rome.
4. to understand thoroughly; to be versed in
5. to let through; through
6. smooth; fluent
7. open; passable
8. all; general; overall; throughout
9. thorough
10. common; popular
11. (said of a sentence) well-constructed; containing no fallacy
通寶(ㄊㄨㄥ ㄅㄠˇ)

〔辵部〕

coins circulated in former times
通報(ㄊㄨㄥ ㄅㄠˋ)
to notify
通便(ㄊㄨㄥ ㄅㄧㄢˋ)
to facilitate bowels movement
通便劑(ㄊㄨㄥ ㄅㄧㄢˋ ㄐㄧˋ)
a laxative
通病(ㄊㄨㄥ ㄅㄧㄥˋ)
common ills; common deficiencies; common faults
通不過(ㄊㄨㄥ ˙ㄅㄨ ㄍㄨㄛˋ)
(said of a motion, law, bill, etc.) cannot be passed; cannot get the approval or consent of
通盤(ㄊㄨㄥ ㄆㄢˊ)
overall; all-round; entire
通盤考慮(ㄊㄨㄥ ㄆㄢˊ ㄎㄠˇ ㄌㄩˋ)
to consider from every possible angle; to take into consideration every aspect of a matter
通盤計畫(ㄊㄨㄥ ㄆㄢˊ ㄐㄧˋ ㄏㄨㄚˋ)
an overall plan
通判(ㄊㄨㄥ ㄆㄢˋ)
an assistant prefectural magistrate (in former times)
通票(ㄊㄨㄥ ㄆㄧㄠˋ)
a through ticket
通謀(ㄊㄨㄥ ㄇㄡˊ)
to conspire
通名(ㄊㄨㄥ ㄇㄧㄥˊ)
to introduce to each other; to identify oneself
通分(ㄊㄨㄥ ㄈㄣ)
reduction of fractions to a common denominator
通風(ㄊㄨㄥ ㄈㄥ)
① to let the wind through; ventilation: 這教室不通風。This classroom is badly ventilated. ② to let out news or secrets
通風口(ㄊㄨㄥ ㄈㄥ ㄎㄡˇ)
an opening for ventilation
通達(ㄊㄨㄥ ㄉㄚˊ)
① to understand clearly ② open to traffic; unobstructed ③ (said of a road) to lead to
通達事理(ㄊㄨㄥ ㄉㄚˊ ㄕˋ ㄌㄧˇ)
to understand ways of doing business
通道(ㄊㄨㄥ ㄉㄠˋ)
a passage; a way
通敵(ㄊㄨㄥ ㄉㄧˊ)
to collaborate with the enemy secretly
通牒(ㄊㄨㄥ ㄉㄧㄝˊ)
diplomatic communications or messages
通電(ㄊㄨㄥ ㄉㄧㄢˋ)
① to cable all concerned ② to supply electricity to; to link with the source of an electric current
通都大邑(ㄊㄨㄥ ㄉㄨ ㄉㄚˋ ㄧˋ)
a metropolis with roads leading everywhere
通透(ㄊㄨㄥ ㄊㄡˋ)
to understand thoroughly
通體(ㄊㄨㄥ ㄊㄧˇ)
① the whole ② to merge; to unite ③ sexual intercourse
通條(ㄊㄨㄥ ㄊㄧㄠˊ)
a thick iron wire used to clear blocked pipes, tubes or other small-bore objects
通天(ㄊㄨㄥ ㄊㄧㄢ)
(literally) great or high enough to reach heaven—① (said of one's abilities) the greatest; surpassing ② to have access to top leaders
通通(ㄊㄨㄥ ㄊㄨㄥ)
wholly; altogether; without exception; all: 我把所有的錢通通給他。I gave him all the money I had.
通同(ㄊㄨㄥ ㄊㄨㄥˊ)
① in common ② to maintain secret contact with (bandits, etc.)
通同作弊(ㄊㄨㄥ ㄊㄨㄥˊ ㄗㄨㄛˋ ㄅㄧˋ)
to collude in cheating or illegal activities
通例(ㄊㄨㄥ ㄌㄧˋ)
a common practice; a general rule
通力合作(ㄊㄨㄥ ㄌㄧˋ ㄏㄜˊ ㄗㄨㄛˋ)
to make a concerted effort; to join forces with; to cooperate for a common cause; to work in concert: 他們通力合作。They worked in concert.
通靈(ㄊㄨㄥ ㄌㄧㄥˊ)
(said of animals, inanimated objects, etc.) to possess supernatural powers; to have human intelligence
通令(ㄊㄨㄥ ㄌㄧㄥˋ)
to issue circular orders
通路(ㄊㄨㄥ ㄌㄨˋ)
a thoroughfare; a passageway; a route
通論(ㄊㄨㄥ ㄌㄨㄣˋ)
① a clear and logical argument ② a general discussion or exposition
通告(ㄊㄨㄥ ㄍㄠˋ)
① to notify ② an announcement; a public notice
通古斯族(ㄊㄨㄥ ㄍㄨˇ ㄙ ㄗㄨˊ)
the Tunguses
通古斯語(ㄊㄨㄥ ㄍㄨˇ ㄙ ㄩˇ)
the Tungusic; the Tungusic language
通過(ㄊㄨㄥ ㄍㄨㄛˋ)
① to pass through ② (said of a motion or bill) to be passed ③ (said of a nomination or appointment) to be confirmed or approved
通過稅(ㄊㄨㄥ ㄍㄨㄛˋ ㄕㄨㄟˋ)
a transit tax
通關(ㄊㄨㄥ ㄍㄨㄢ)
① (while drinking in a group) engaging everyone else at the table in turn in a finger game 參看「打通關」② customs clearance ③ to clear goods with the customs; to complete formalities at an immigration or customs check point at an airport or seaport
通共(ㄊㄨㄥ ㄍㄨㄥˋ)
all put together; in sum; altogether
通款曲(ㄊㄨㄥ ㄎㄨㄢˇ ㄑㄩ)
to socialize with each other; to make friendly contacts
通好(ㄊㄨㄥ ㄏㄠˇ)
(said of nations, races, etc.) to establish friendly relations
通航(ㄊㄨㄥ ㄏㄤˊ)
air or sea navigation; (said of a river) navigable, or negotiable
通話(ㄊㄨㄥ ㄏㄨㄚˋ)
to communicate by telephone or radio
通貨(ㄊㄨㄥ ㄏㄨㄛˋ)
currency 亦作「貨幣」: 這個國家的通貨穩定。The currency of this country is sound.
通貨膨脹(ㄊㄨㄥ ㄏㄨㄛˋ ㄆㄥˊ ㄓㄤˋ)

(economics) inflation
通婚(ㄊㄨㄥ ㄏㄨㄣ)
to marry (said of members of two families, tribes, etc.); to intermarry
通紅(ㄊㄨㄥ ㄏㄨㄥˊ)
red through and through; aglow; flaming red
通家之好(ㄊㄨㄥ ㄐㄧㄚ ㄓ ㄏㄠˇ)
friendship between two families which has existed for several generations
通假(ㄊㄨㄥ ㄐㄧㄚˇ)
interchangeability of words or characters
通解(ㄊㄨㄥ ㄐㄧㄝˇ)
(mathematics) a general solution
通姦(ㄊㄨㄥ ㄐㄧㄢ)
adultery; illicit intercourse; fornication
通鑑(ㄊㄨㄥ ㄐㄧㄢˋ)or 資治通鑑(ㄗ ㄓˋ ㄊㄨㄥ ㄐㄧㄢˋ)
the title of a chronological history of China, covering 1,362 years from the Epoch of Warring States to the author's time, by Ssu-Ma Kuang (司馬光) of the Sung Dynasty
通氣(ㄊㄨㄥ ㄑㄧˋ)
① sympathetic to each other ② breathing freely ③ not airtight; to aerate
通氣孔(ㄊㄨㄥ ㄑㄧˋ ㄎㄨㄥˇ)
air vents
通緝(ㄊㄨㄥ ㄑㄧˋ)
to order the arrest(of a criminal) by circular orders
通緝犯(ㄊㄨㄥ ㄑㄧˋ ㄈㄢˋ)
a criminal wanted by the law
通緝令(ㄊㄨㄥ ㄑㄧˋ ㄌㄧㄥˋ)
circular orders for the arrest of a criminal
通竅(ㄊㄨㄥ ㄑㄧㄠˋ)
to get the knack of it; to understand things
通情達理(ㄊㄨㄥ ㄑㄧㄥˊ ㄉㄚˊ ㄌㄧˇ)
sensible; reasonable: 他們是通情達理的人。They are sensible people.
通衢(ㄊㄨㄥ ㄑㄩˊ)
a highway; a thoroughfare
通權達變(ㄊㄨㄥ ㄑㄩㄢˊ ㄉㄚˊ ㄅㄧㄢˋ)
to be flexible; to act according to changes in circumstances; to exercise one's discretion: 偉大的思想家有通權達變的頭腦。Great thinkers have flexible minds.
通宵(ㄊㄨㄥ ㄒㄧㄠ)
all night; the whole night; throughout the night
通宵達旦(ㄊㄨㄥ ㄒㄧㄠ ㄉㄚˊ ㄉㄢˋ)
all night long; till daybreak
通宵值班(ㄊㄨㄥ ㄒㄧㄠ ㄓˊ ㄅㄢ)
on duty all night
通宵商店(ㄊㄨㄥ ㄒㄧㄠ ㄕㄤ ㄉㄧㄢˋ)
a shop that is open all night
通曉(ㄊㄨㄥ ㄒㄧㄠˇ)
to be familiar with; to understand
通宿(ㄊㄨㄥ ㄒㄧㄡˇ)
all night long: 我們通宿看守。We watch all night (long).
通顯(ㄊㄨㄥ ㄒㄧㄢˇ)
to achieve prominence in officialdom
通心(ㄊㄨㄥ ㄒㄧㄣ)
(said of a cylinder) hollow; tubular
通心粉(ㄊㄨㄥ ㄒㄧㄣ ㄈㄣˇ)
macaroni
通信(ㄊㄨㄥ ㄒㄧㄣˋ)
in correspondence with; communication
通信兵(ㄊㄨㄥ ㄒㄧㄣˋ ㄅㄧㄥ)
a member of the signal corps
通信鴿(ㄊㄨㄥ ㄒㄧㄣˋ ㄍㄜ)
a homing pigeon; a carrier pigeon
通信處(ㄊㄨㄥ ㄒㄧㄣˋ ㄔㄨˋ)
a mailing address: 他變更了通信處。He changed his mailing address.
通信網(ㄊㄨㄥ ㄒㄧㄣˋ ㄨㄤˇ)
a communication network
通行(ㄊㄨㄥ ㄒㄧㄥˊ)
① to travel through (a road, etc.) ② common practice
通行權(ㄊㄨㄥ ㄒㄧㄥˊ ㄑㄩㄢˊ)
the right of way
通行證(ㄊㄨㄥ ㄒㄧㄥˊ ㄓㄥˋ)
a safe-conduct; a pass
通行無阻(ㄊㄨㄥ ㄒㄧㄥˊ ㄨˊ ㄗㄨˇ)
to travel everywhere without obstruction
通性(ㄊㄨㄥ ㄒㄧㄥˋ)
common characteristics
通學(ㄊㄨㄥ ㄒㄩㄝˊ)
to attend a school by taking daily trips; to commute
通學生(ㄊㄨㄥ ㄒㄩㄝˊ ㄕㄥ)
students living outside the school (as distinct from those living in school dormitories); day students; commuters
通訊(ㄊㄨㄥ ㄒㄩㄣˋ)
correspondence; communication
通訊錄(ㄊㄨㄥ ㄒㄩㄣˋ ㄌㄨˋ)
an address book
通訊社(ㄊㄨㄥ ㄒㄩㄣˋ ㄕㄜˋ)
a news agency; a news service
通訊員(ㄊㄨㄥ ㄒㄩㄣˋ ㄩㄢˊ)or 通訊記者(ㄊㄨㄥ ㄒㄩㄣˋ ㄐㄧˋ ㄓㄜˇ)
a (press) correspondent; a reporter
通知(ㄊㄨㄥ ㄓ)
to inform; to notify; a notification
通知單(ㄊㄨㄥ ㄓ ㄉㄢ)or 通知書(ㄊㄨㄥ ㄓ ㄕㄨ)
a notification
通飭(ㄊㄨㄥ ㄔˋ)
to order or instruct (all subordinate agencies concerned)
通車(ㄊㄨㄥ ㄔㄜ)
(said of roads, etc.) to be open (to vehicular traffic)
通徹(ㄊㄨㄥ ㄔㄜˋ)
having a thorough understanding
通常(ㄊㄨㄥ ㄔㄤˊ)
normally; usually; generally; as a rule; ordinarily: 你通常在什麼地方度夏? Where do you usually spend the summer?
通暢(ㄊㄨㄥ ㄔㄤˋ)
①(said of writings) smooth; easy to read; highly readable: 他的文筆通暢。His writing is smooth. ② passing freely or smoothly
通稱(ㄊㄨㄥ ㄔㄥ)
a popular name; popularly (or generally) known as...: 汞通稱水銀。Mercury is popularly known as quicksilver.
通史(ㄊㄨㄥ ㄕˇ)
general history: 他研究中國通史。He studies general Chinese history.
通市(ㄊㄨㄥ ㄕˋ)
to have commercial rela-

〔辵部〕

tions 亦作「通商」

通事(ㄊㄨㄥ ㄕˋ)
① an interpreter ② official intercourse between two states; diplomatic affairs

通身(ㄊㄨㄥ ㄕㄣ)
all over the body

通神(ㄊㄨㄥ ㄕㄣˊ)
①(said of ability, etc.) superhuman: 他有通神的智慧。He has superhuman wisdom. ②(said of money) capable of buying even the gods

通商(ㄊㄨㄥ ㄕㄤ)
to have commercial intercourse; to trade

通商條約(ㄊㄨㄥ ㄕㄤ ㄊㄧㄠˊ ㄩㄝ)
a trade pact or treaty

通商口岸(ㄊㄨㄥ ㄕㄤ ㄎㄡˇ ㄢˋ)or 通商港 (ㄊㄨㄥ ㄕㄤ ㄍㄤˇ)
a trading port; a commercial port

通書(ㄊㄨㄥ ㄕㄨ)
an almanac; a calendar

通順(ㄊㄨㄥ ㄕㄨㄣˋ)
(said of writings) fluent; smooth: 這篇文章不通順。This article doesn't read smoothly.

通人(ㄊㄨㄥ ㄖㄣˊ)
a well-read, much experienced person

通儒(ㄊㄨㄥ ㄖㄨˊ)
a man of great learning and practical sense; an erudite scholar: 他是通儒。He is a man of great learning.

通融(ㄊㄨㄥ ㄖㄨㄥˊ)
① departure from principles for convenience; compromise; to accommodate; to compromise ② to accommodate somebody with a short-term loan

通則(ㄊㄨㄥ ㄗㄜˊ)
a general principle

通才(ㄊㄨㄥ ㄘㄞˊ)
an all-round talent; a versatile scholar

通才教育(ㄊㄨㄥ ㄘㄞˊ ㄐㄧㄠˋ ㄩˋ)
liberal education

通財(ㄊㄨㄥ ㄘㄞˊ)
to establish monetary relations

通草紙(ㄊㄨㄥ ㄘㄠˇ ㄓˇ)
rice paper

通塞(ㄊㄨㄥ ㄙㄜˋ)
① openness and cloggedness ② success and failure; satisfaction and frustration

通俗(ㄊㄨㄥ ㄙㄨˊ)
popular; common; capable of being understood or appreciated by the less educated: 這部小說通俗易懂。This novel is easy to understand.

通俗化(ㄊㄨㄥ ㄙㄨˊ ㄏㄨㄚˋ)
to popularize; popularization

通俗小說(ㄊㄨㄥ ㄙㄨˊ ㄒㄧㄠˇ ㄕㄨㄛ)
popular fiction

通俗文學(ㄊㄨㄥ ㄙㄨˊ ㄨㄣˊ ㄒㄩㄝˊ)
popular literature

通義(ㄊㄨㄥ ㄧˋ)
a constant rule or principle

通譯(ㄊㄨㄥ ㄧˋ)
① to translate ② a translator; an interpreter

通夜(ㄊㄨㄥ ㄧㄝˋ)
all night long: 他通夜不眠。He lay awake all night.

通郵(ㄊㄨㄥ ㄧㄡˊ)
postal communication

通韻(ㄊㄨㄥ ㄩㄣˋ)
interchangeable rhyme

通運(ㄊㄨㄥ ㄩㄣˋ)
to transport; to ship

通運公司(ㄊㄨㄥ ㄩㄣˋ ㄍㄨㄥ ㄙ)
a forwarding company

通用(ㄊㄨㄥ ㄩㄥˋ)
①(said of words or characters) interchangeable ② in common use ③ practicable; usable ④(said of currency) in circulation

【逛】 6098
ㄍㄨㄤˋ guanq guàng

to stroll; to roam; to ramble; to wander about

逛燈(ㄍㄨㄤˋ ㄉㄥ)
to look at the lanterns on display on the streets (on the Lantern Festival, the 15th day of the first month in the lunar calendar)

逛街(ㄍㄨㄤˋ ㄐㄧㄝ)
to stroll down the street; to go window-shopping: 我們昨天去逛街。We strolled down the streets yesterday.

逛一逛(ㄍㄨㄤˋ ·ㄧ ·ㄍㄨㄤ)or 逛逛(ㄍㄨㄤˋ ·ㄍㄨㄤ)
to take a stroll; to go for a walk

【逞】 6099
ㄔㄥˇ cheeng chěng

1. to indulge in (pleasures, etc.)
2. to use up; to exhaust
3. to display; to show off; to pose; to put up a false front: 別逞英雄。Don't pose as a hero.
4. fast; speedy
5. to presume on; presumptuous

逞能(ㄔㄥˇ ㄋㄥˊ)
to display or show off one's ability, feat, etc.; boastful

逞快一時(ㄔㄥˇ ㄎㄨㄞˋ ㄧˋ ㄕˊ)
to indulge in a moment of pleasure (implying that one is going to pay dearly for it)

逞強(ㄔㄥˇ ㄑㄧㄤˊ)
to parade one's superiority; to bully; to throw one's weight around

逞兇(ㄔㄥˇ ㄒㄩㄥ)
to resort to violence; to act like a brute

逞志(ㄔㄥˇ ㄓˋ)
to satisfy oneself; to indulge oneself

逞惡(ㄔㄥˇ ㄜˋ)
to presume on powerful connections or one's strength in doing evil

逞意(ㄔㄥˇ ㄧˋ)
to act as one pleases

逞威(ㄔㄥˇ ㄨㄟ)
to behave like a tyrant

逞勇(ㄔㄥˇ ㄩㄥˇ)
to display one's bravery

【速】 6100
ㄙㄨˋ suh sù

1. quick; speed; speedy; prompt
2. to invite: 他是不速之客。He was an uninvited guest.

速答(ㄙㄨˋ ㄉㄚˊ)
to reply promptly

速讀(ㄙㄨˋ ㄉㄨˊ)
speed-reading

速度(ㄙㄨˋ ㄉㄨˋ)
① velocity; speed ②(music) a tempo

速度計(ㄙㄨˋ ㄉㄨˋ ㄐㄧˋ)
a speedometer; a speed indicator

速度限制(ㄙㄨˋ ㄉㄨˋ ㄒㄧㄢˋ ㄓˋ)
the speed limit

速率(ㄙㄨˋ ㄌㄩˋ)
speed
速記(ㄙㄨˋ ㄐㄧˋ)
speedwriting; shorthand; stenography; to write in shorthand
速記學(ㄙㄨˋ ㄐㄧˋ ㄒㄩㄝˊ)or 速記術(ㄙㄨˋ ㄐㄧˋ ㄕㄨˋ)
stenography
速記員(ㄙㄨˋ ㄐㄧˋ ㄩㄢˊ)
a stenographer
速駕(ㄙㄨˋ ㄐㄧㄚˋ)
to request the pleasure of your early company
速寫(ㄙㄨˋ ㄒㄧㄝˇ)
(painting) to sketch; a sketch: 他畫了一張塔的速寫。He made a sketch of the tower.
速效(ㄙㄨˋ ㄒㄧㄠˋ)
speedy relief (of suffering, disease, etc.); immediate efficacy or efficiency
速戰速決(ㄙㄨˋ ㄓㄢˋ ㄙㄨˋ ㄐㄩㄝˊ)
a blitzkrieg strategy; a military strategy that calls for speedy decision by applying overwhelming forces against the enemy
速成(ㄙㄨˋ ㄔㄥˊ)
to attain goals within a short time; to complete rapidly
速成班(ㄙㄨˋ ㄔㄥˊ ㄅㄢ)
a training class for quick mastery of a subject, course; a rash course; an intensive course
速食(ㄙㄨˋ ㄕˊ)
fast food
速食麵(ㄙㄨˋ ㄕˊ ㄇㄧㄢˋ)
instant noodles
速食店(ㄙㄨˋ ㄕˊ ㄉㄧㄢˋ)
a fast food restaurant
速射炮(ㄙㄨˋ ㄕㄜˋ ㄆㄠˋ)
a rapid-fire gun; a case gun
速死(ㄙㄨˋ ㄙˇ)
to hasten one's death; to die quickly
速賜康(ㄙㄨˋ ㄙˋ ㄎㄤ)
pentazocine

【造】 6101
ㄗㄠˋ tzaw zào
1. to create; to make: 上帝創造世界。God created the world.
2. to manufacture; to make; to produce
3. to make up; to invent; to manufacture: 他揑造謠言。He invents rumors.
4. to build: 我們造房子。We built a house.
5. to arrive at; to reach
6. (law) a party concerned in the suit
7. an era; a period
8. to institute
造報表(ㄗㄠˋ ㄅㄠˋ ㄅㄧㄠˇ)
to prepare a financial report or statement
造幣權(ㄗㄠˋ ㄅㄧˋ ㄑㄩㄢˊ)
coinage (as a right)
造幣廠(ㄗㄠˋ ㄅㄧˋ ㄔㄤˇ)
a mint
造反(ㄗㄠˋ ㄈㄢˇ)
to rebel; to rise up against; revolt; uprising
造訪(ㄗㄠˋ ㄈㄤˇ)
to pay a visit to; to call on
造福(ㄗㄠˋ ㄈㄨˊ)
to bring benefit to; benefit
造福人羣(ㄗㄠˋ ㄈㄨˊ ㄖㄣˊ ㄑㄩㄣˊ)
to do good deeds to benefit mankind (as building a road, bridge, school, orphanage, etc.)
造府(ㄗㄠˋ ㄈㄨˇ)
(a polite expression) to call on someone at his home
造孽(ㄗㄠˋ ㄋㄧㄝˋ)
to do evil things
造林(ㄗㄠˋ ㄌㄧㄣˊ)
afforestation; reforestation
造花(ㄗㄠˋ ㄏㄨㄚ)
to make artificial (permanent) flowers
造化
①(ㄗㄠˋ ㄏㄨㄚˋ) Heaven; Mother Nature; the Creator
②(ㄗㄠˋ ·ㄏㄨㄚ) one's luck or fortune: 他沒有這麼好的造化。He has no such good fortune.
造化弄人(ㄗㄠˋ ㄏㄨㄚˋ ㄋㄨㄥˋ ㄖㄣˊ)or 造物弄人(ㄗㄠˋ ㄨˋ ㄋㄨㄥˋ ㄖㄣˊ)
to be a sport of fate
造價(ㄗㄠˋ ㄐㄧㄚˋ)
building cost; manufacturing cost: 這種樓房造價比較低。It costs less to build this kind of building.
造酒(ㄗㄠˋ ㄐㄧㄡˇ)
to brew alcoholic beverages: 他造酒自用。He brewed wine for home use.
造酒廠(ㄗㄠˋ ㄐㄧㄡˇ ㄔㄤˇ)
a brewery
造就(ㄗㄠˋ ㄐㄧㄡˋ)
①to educate; to bring up: 教育造就一代新人。Education brings up a new generation. ②one's achievement or accomplishment
造就人才(ㄗㄠˋ ㄐㄧㄡˋ ㄖㄣˊ ㄘㄞˊ)
to make useful citizens through education
造句(ㄗㄠˋ ㄐㄩˋ)
to make a sentence
造具(ㄗㄠˋ ㄐㄩˋ)
to prepare; to get ready (a report, etc.)
造像(ㄗㄠˋ ㄒㄧㄤˋ)
to make a statue; to make an image or a portrait
造型(ㄗㄠˋ ㄒㄧㄥˊ)
①modeling; mold-making ②a model; a mold ③(machinery) molding
造形藝術(ㄗㄠˋ ㄒㄧㄥˊ ㄧˋ ㄕㄨˋ)
formative arts; plastic arts
造紙(ㄗㄠˋ ㄓˇ)
to make paper
造紙廠(ㄗㄠˋ ㄓˇ ㄔㄤˇ)
a paper mill
造成(ㄗㄠˋ ㄔㄥˊ)
①to complete; to build up; to compose ②to result in; to cause to happen; to bring about: 火災造成重大的損害。The fire caused much damage.
造船(ㄗㄠˋ ㄔㄨㄢˊ)
to build a ship
造船公司(ㄗㄠˋ ㄔㄨㄢˊ ㄍㄨㄥ ㄙ)
a shipbuilding company
造船廠(ㄗㄠˋ ㄔㄨㄢˊ ㄔㄤˇ)
a shipbuilding yard; a dockyard
造始(ㄗㄠˋ ㄕˇ)
the beginning: 智慧造始於謙遜。Humility is the beginning of wisdom.
造勢(ㄗㄠˋ ㄕˋ)
to spin
造字(ㄗㄠˋ ㄗˋ)
to coin words
造作(ㄗㄠˋ ㄗㄨㄛˋ)
①to make ②affectations; pretentious; artificial; unnatural

〔辵 部〕

造次(ㄗㄠˋ ㄘˋ)
in a hurry; rashly; in urgency and haste; rashness
造册子(ㄗㄠˋ ㄘㄜˋ ·ㄗ)
to make an overall report; to compile a register
造詣(ㄗㄠˋ ㄧˋ)
① one's scholastic attainment, depth or profundity ② to call on; to visit
造意犯(ㄗㄠˋ ㄧˋ ㄈㄢˋ)
(law) an instigator
造謠(ㄗㄠˋ ㄧㄠˊ)or 造謠言(ㄗㄠˋ ㄧㄠˊ ·ㄧㄢ)
to start a rumor
造謠惑衆(ㄗㄠˋ ㄧㄠˊ ㄏㄨㄛˋ ㄓㄨㄥˋ)
to cheat, swindle or mislead the people with lies or rumors of one's own creation
造謠生事(ㄗㄠˋ ㄧㄠˊ ㄕㄥ ㄕˋ)
to start rumors and incite incidents; to spread rumors to cause trouble
造物(ㄗㄠˋ ㄨˋ)
Heaven; the Creator
造物主(ㄗㄠˋ ㄨˋ ㄓㄨˇ)
the Creator
造獄(ㄗㄠˋ ㄩˋ)
① to start litigation ② the extraordinary criminal code

【逡】 6102
ㄑㄩㄣ chiun qūn
to withdraw; to retreat; to move backward
逡巡 or 逡循(ㄑㄩㄣ ㄒㄩㄣˊ)
to hesitate; to waver; to shrink back
逡巡不前(ㄑㄩㄣ ㄒㄩㄣˊ ㄅㄨˋ ㄑㄧㄢˊ)
to hesitate; to waver; to be reluctant to move ahead

【逢】 6103
ㄈㄥˊ ferng féng
1. to meet; to come across: 我們久別重逢。We met again after a long separation.
2. to happen; to fall in with
3. to talk or act in order to please (a superior, etc.)
4. a Chinese family name
逢年過節(ㄈㄥˊ ㄋㄧㄢˊ ㄍㄨㄛˋ ㄐㄧㄝˊ)
on New Year's Day or other festivals
逢凶化吉(ㄈㄥˊ ㄒㄩㄥ ㄏㄨㄚˋ ㄐㄧˊ)
to turn bad luck into good fortune: 你會逢凶化吉的。You may turn ill luck into good fortune.
逢場作戲(ㄈㄥˊ ㄔㄤˇ ㄗㄨㄛˋ ㄒㄧˋ)
to participate in pleasure-seeking as a social activity without being a slave to it; to engage in merry-making occasionally; to fool around with women; to make love to a woman just for the fun of it
逢山開路(ㄈㄥˊ ㄕㄢ ㄎㄞ ㄌㄨˋ)
(literally) to open a path when faced with a mountain —to overcome a difficulty whenever it arises
逢人說項(ㄈㄥˊ ㄖㄣˊ ㄕㄨㄛ ㄒㄧㄤˋ)
to praise someone's virtue everywhere
逢迎(ㄈㄥˊ ㄧㄥˊ)
① to receive (guests, visitors, etc.) ② to talk and act in order to please; to ingratiate; to flatter: 他是在逢迎你。He is flattering you.

【連】 6104
ㄌㄧㄢˊ lian lián
1. to connect; to join; to unite: 我們的田沿河毗連。Our farms join along the river.
2. in succession
3. a company (of soldiers)
4. together with
5. even; and; including
6. a Chinese family name
連敗(ㄌㄧㄢˊ ㄅㄞˋ)
① to defeat repeatedly ② repeated defeats; to be defeated repeatedly
連本帶利(ㄌㄧㄢˊ ㄅㄣˇ ㄉㄞˋ ㄌㄧˋ)
both capital and interest
連比(ㄌㄧㄢˊ ㄅㄧˇ)
(mathematics) continued proportion
連鑣並軫(ㄌㄧㄢˊ ㄅㄧㄠ ㄅㄧㄥˋ ㄓㄣˇ)
matching; shoulder to shoulder
連不上(ㄌㄧㄢˊ ·ㄅㄨ ㄕㄤˋ)
to lack sequence—cannot be put or connected together (usually referring to two paragraphs in a piece of writing, etc.)
連篇累牘(ㄌㄧㄢˊ ㄆㄧㄢ ㄌㄟˇ ㄉㄨˊ)
(said of a piece of writing) long and repetitious; redundant; lengthy and tedious
連袂(ㄌㄧㄢˊ ㄇㄟˋ)
①(to go, visit, etc.) together ② husbands of sisters
連忙(ㄌㄧㄢˊ ㄇㄤˊ)
promptly; quickly; immediately; at once
連綿 or 連緜(ㄌㄧㄢˊ ㄇㄧㄢˊ)
continuous; unbroken; uninterrupted: 陰雨連綿。There was a continuous rain.
連緜不絕(ㄌㄧㄢˊ ㄇㄧㄢˊ ㄅㄨˋ ㄐㄩㄝˊ)
in endless succession; continuously
連名(ㄌㄧㄢˊ ㄇㄧㄥˊ)
(said of a petition, document, etc.) jointly signed
連發(ㄌㄧㄢˊ ㄈㄚ)
to fire in rapid succession
連發槍(ㄌㄧㄢˊ ㄈㄚ ㄑㄧㄤ)
a repeating rifle; a machine gun
連番(ㄌㄧㄢˊ ㄈㄢ)
repeatedly
連分數(ㄌㄧㄢˊ ㄈㄣ ㄕㄨˋ)
(mathematics) a continued fraction
連帶(ㄌㄧㄢˊ ㄉㄞˋ)
joint (responsibility, obligation, etc.); to involve; to be related: 他的行動和思想是有連帶關係的。His movement is related to his ideology.
連帶責任(ㄌㄧㄢˊ ㄉㄞˋ ㄗㄜˊ ㄖㄣˋ)
joint responsibility; responsibility incurred as a result of personal or official involvement
連…都(ㄌㄧㄢˊ …ㄉㄡ)or 連…也(ㄌㄧㄢˊ … ㄧㄝˇ)
even...can (or cannot)...: 她甚至連看也沒看他一眼。She never even took a look at him.
連偷帶扒(ㄌㄧㄢˊ ㄊㄡ ㄉㄞˋ ㄆㄚˊ)
to steal or cheat by all the means at one's command
連踢帶打(ㄌㄧㄢˊ ㄊㄧ ㄉㄞˋ ㄉㄚˇ)
to knock and kick; to beat severely with both hands and feet
連體雙生(ㄌㄧㄢˊ ㄊㄧˇ ㄕㄨㄤ ㄕㄥ)
Siamese twins
連天(ㄌㄧㄢˊ ㄊㄧㄢ)
①(said of high mountains, etc.) to stab deep into the sky ② incessantly; continuously (especially said of complaining) ③ to shake the sky (as the sound of fight-

ing in battle) ④ for several days in a row ⑤(said of the distant horizon) to merge with the sky

連同(ㄌㄧㄢˊ ㄊㄨㄥˊ)
together with; in addition to; along with

連年(ㄌㄧㄢˊ ㄋㄧㄢˊ)
for successive years; for years in a row; year after year: 人口連年上升。Population increases year after year.

連弩(ㄌㄧㄢˊ ㄋㄨˇ)
a kind of crossbow which can shoot in quick succession by means of a mechanical device

連累(ㄌㄧㄢˊ ˙ㄌㄟ)
to involve; to get someone into trouble: 我連累了你們。I got you into trouble.

連理(ㄌㄧㄢˊ ㄌㄧˇ)
① trees whose branches interlock or join together ② a couple very much in love

連連(ㄌㄧㄢˊ ㄌㄧㄢˊ)
① continuously; unceasingly; again and again: 小女孩連連點頭。The little girl nods again and again. ② one after another

連絡(ㄌㄧㄢˊ ㄌㄨㄛˋ)
liaison; to make contact with

連絡官(ㄌㄧㄢˊ ㄌㄨㄛˋ ㄍㄨㄢ)
a liaison officer

連絡站(ㄌㄧㄢˊ ㄌㄨㄛˋ ㄓㄢˋ)
a liaison office or station

連貫(ㄌㄧㄢˊ ㄍㄨㄢˋ)
① to link up; to piece together; to hang together ② coherent; consistent: 這個故事情節不連貫。The plot of the story is incoherent.

連貫性(ㄌㄧㄢˊ ㄍㄨㄢˋ ㄒㄧㄥˋ)
continuity; coherence: 字典的主題是沒有連貫性的。There is no continuity of subjects in a dictionary.

連合(ㄌㄧㄢˊ ㄏㄜˊ)
to connect or join together; to unite together

連號(ㄌㄧㄢˊ ㄏㄠˋ)
a consecutive serial number (on banknotes, tickets, etc.)

連橫 or 連衡(ㄌㄧㄢˊ ㄏㄥˊ)
a proposal advanced by Chang Yi(張儀)in the Epoch of Warring States, which called for the six other states to serve Chin

連環(ㄌㄧㄢˊ ㄏㄨㄢˊ)
interlocked rings (like those of a chain)

連環保(ㄌㄧㄢˊ ㄏㄨㄢˊ ㄅㄠˇ)
a mutual guarantee

連環圖畫(ㄌㄧㄢˊ ㄏㄨㄢˊ ㄊㄨˊ ㄏㄨㄚˋ)
a pictorial story in series; comics; a comic strip

連環計(ㄌㄧㄢˊ ㄏㄨㄢˊ ㄐㄧˋ)
a coup with coup(s) in it; a set of interlocking stratagems

連枷(ㄌㄧㄢˊ ㄐㄧㄚ)
a flail

連假帶眞(ㄌㄧㄢˊ ㄐㄧㄚˇ ㄉㄞˋ ㄓㄣ)
altogether, fake and genuine

連接(ㄌㄧㄢˊ ㄐㄧㄝ)
① continuously ② to adjoin; adjoining: 這兩幢房屋連接在一起。The two houses adjoin.

連接不斷(ㄌㄧㄢˊ ㄐㄧㄝ ㄅㄨˋ ㄉㄨㄢˋ)
successively; continuously

連接桿(ㄌㄧㄢˊ ㄐㄧㄝ ㄍㄢˇ)or 連桿(ㄌㄧㄢˊ ㄍㄢˇ)
(machinery) a connecting rod

連接詞(ㄌㄧㄢˊ ㄐㄧㄝ ㄘˊ)
(grammar) a conjunction

連結(ㄌㄧㄢˊ ㄐㄧㄝˊ)
to connect; to join: 這兩部分連結得不好。The two parts do not connect properly.

連結線(ㄌㄧㄢˊ ㄐㄧㄝˊ ㄒㄧㄢˋ)
(mathematics) a connecting line

連襟 or 連衿(ㄌㄧㄢˊ ㄐㄧㄣ)
a mutual reference among husbands of sisters

連翹(ㄌㄧㄢˊ ㄑㄧㄠˊ)
(botany) forsythia

連雀(ㄌㄧㄢˊ ㄑㄩㄝˋ)
a waxwing

連繫(ㄌㄧㄢˊ ㄒㄧˋ)
to keep in contact; contact; to keep in touch with

連線(ㄌㄧㄢˊ ㄒㄧㄢˋ)
unbroken; continuous

連心(ㄌㄧㄢˊ ㄒㄧㄣ)
the meeting of minds; bosom (friends); deeply attached to each other: 我們父子連心。We, father and son, are deeply attached to each other.

連續(ㄌㄧㄢˊ ㄒㄩˋ)
successive; continuous; incessantly

連續犯(ㄌㄧㄢˊ ㄒㄩˋ ㄈㄢˋ)
①(law) repeated offenses of the same kind ② an old (or repeated) offender

連續劇(ㄌㄧㄢˊ ㄒㄩˋ ㄐㄩˋ)
(television) a soap opera; a drama series

連選連任(ㄌㄧㄢˊ ㄒㄩㄢˇ ㄌㄧㄢˊ ㄖㄣˋ)
to hold a post for another term after being reelected

連枝(ㄌㄧㄢˊ ㄓ)
brothers; close relatives (of the same family tree)

連戰皆北(ㄌㄧㄢˊ ㄓㄢˋ ㄐㄧㄝ ㄅㄛˋ)
to suffer one defeat after another

連戰皆捷(ㄌㄧㄢˊ ㄓㄢˋ ㄐㄧㄝ ㄐㄧㄝˊ)
to win one victory after another: 我們的棒球隊連戰皆捷。Our baseball team won one victory after another.

連長(ㄌㄧㄢˊ ㄓㄤˇ)
a company commander

連珠(ㄌㄧㄢˊ ㄓㄨ)
continuous; in quick succession: 我們聽到連珠似的機槍聲。We heard a continuous rattle of machine gun fire.

連珠炮(ㄌㄧㄢˊ ㄓㄨ ㄆㄠˋ)
① a rapid-fire gun ② continuous firing; drumfire

連綴(ㄌㄧㄢˊ ㄓㄨㄟˋ)
joined or linked together

連乘積(ㄌㄧㄢˊ ㄔㄥˊ ㄐㄧ)
(mathematics) a continued product

連串(ㄌㄧㄢˊ ㄔㄨㄢˋ)
to string together; a string (of events, etc.); a series of

連史紙(ㄌㄧㄢˊ ㄕˇ ㄓˇ)
a kind of high-grade bamboo paper made in Fukien and Kiangsi provinces

連手(ㄌㄧㄢˊ ㄕㄡˇ)
① to take concerted action ②(gambling) to gang up on cheating

連聲道謝(ㄌㄧㄢˊ ㄕㄥ ㄉㄠˋ ㄒㄧㄝˋ)
to say "Thanks." repeatedly

連勝(ㄌㄧㄢˊ ㄕㄥˋ)
to win repeatedly; to score one victory after another

連署(ㄌㄧㄢˊ ㄕㄨˋ)

to sign jointly; joint signatures

連署人(ㄌㄧㄢˊ ㄕㄨˋ ㄖㄣˊ)
a joint signer

連說對不起(ㄌㄧㄢˊ ㄕㄨㄛ ㄉㄨㄟˋ ˙ㄅㄨ ㄑㄧˇ)
to say "I'm sorry." time and again

連日(ㄌㄧㄢˊ ㄖˋ)
for consecutive days; for days in a row; day after day: 連日下大雪。It snowed hard for several days running.

連任(ㄌㄧㄢˊ ㄖㄣˋ)
to continue in one's office for another term; to be reappointed or reelected: 教育部長連任。The Minister of Education was reappointed.

連字號(ㄌㄧㄢˊ ㄗˋ ㄏㄠˋ)
a hyphen"-"

連載(ㄌㄧㄢˊ ㄗㄞˇ)
to publish serially in a newspaper or magazine; to serialize: 他的小說曾在報上連載。His novel was serialized in the newspaper.

連遭敗績(ㄌㄧㄢˊ ㄗㄠ ㄅㄞˋ ㄐㄧ)
to suffer one defeat after another: 他連遭敗績。Defeats have befallen him in succession.

連坐(ㄌㄧㄢˊ ㄗㄨㄛˋ)
to share the criminal responsibility of another person without being actually guilty oneself

連詞(ㄌㄧㄢˊ ㄘˊ)
(grammar) a conjunction 亦作「連接詞」

連三帶四(ㄌㄧㄢˊ ㄙㄢ ㄉㄞˋ ㄙˋ)or 連三併四(ㄌㄧㄢˊ ㄙㄢ ㄅㄧㄥˋ ㄙˋ)
time and again; repeatedly: 我曾連三帶四地警告他。I've given him repeated warnings.

連鎖反應(ㄌㄧㄢˊ ㄙㄨㄛˇ ㄈㄢˇ ㄧㄥˋ)
a chain reaction

連鎖店(ㄌㄧㄢˊ ㄙㄨㄛˇ ㄉㄧㄢˋ)
a chain store

連夜(ㄌㄧㄢˊ ㄧㄝˋ)
all through the night

連姻(ㄌㄧㄢˊ ㄧㄣ)
(said of two families) to have a matrimonial tie

連陰雨(ㄌㄧㄢˊ ㄧㄣ ㄩˇ)
rainy days in a row

連用(ㄌㄧㄢˊ ㄩㄥˋ)
to use consecutively; to use together

【逌】6105
ㄧㄡˊ you yóu
pleased; smiling; complacent

八畫

【迸】6106
(迸) ㄅㄥˋ benq bèng
1. to scatter; to explode: 煙火亂迸。Fireworks explode in all directions.
2. to crack; to spit out; to burst forth: 你怎麼突然迸出這句話來? What made you burst out such a remark?

迸淚(ㄅㄥˋ ㄌㄟˋ)
tears pouring out

迸裂(ㄅㄥˋ ㄌㄧㄝˋ)
to crack; to split; to dash out: 他的腦漿迸裂。He has his brains dashed out.

迸流(ㄅㄥˋ ㄌㄧㄡˊ)
(said of fluid under pressure) to spit out in all directions

迸出來(ㄅㄥˋ ㄔㄨ ˙ㄌㄞ)
to squeeze out; to spit out

迸脆(ㄅㄥˋ ㄘㄨㄟˋ)
(usually said of food, etc.) crisp

【逮】6107
1. ㄉㄞˋ day dài
1. to reach; to come up to: 我力有未逮。It was beyond my reach.
2. to be after; to hunt; to chase and make arrest

逮捕(ㄉㄞˋ ㄅㄨˇ)
to make arrest: 警察逮捕那些歹徒了。The policeman arrested the evil fellows.

逮繫(ㄉㄞˋ ㄒㄧˋ)
to arrest and detain

【逮】6107
2. ㄉㄞˇ dae dǎi
to capture; to catch: 警察已逮到兇手。The policeman has caught the murderer.

逮住(ㄉㄞˇ ˙ㄓㄨ)
to catch (a thief, a ball, etc.): 我們逮住那個賊。We caught the thief.

【週】6108
ㄓㄡ jou zhōu
1. a week; a period: 上週我很忙。I was busy last week.
2. a cycle; a revolution; to revolve

週報(ㄓㄡ ㄅㄠˋ)
a weekly paper

週末(ㄓㄡ ㄇㄛˋ)
a weekend: 我們每個週末都去釣魚。We go fishing weekends.

週末旅行(ㄓㄡ ㄇㄛˋ ㄌㄩˇ ㄒㄧㄥˊ)
a weekend trip

週到(ㄓㄡ ˙ㄉㄠ)
(often said of service, etc.) thoughtful; considerate

週年(ㄓㄡ ㄋㄧㄢˊ)
a full year; an anniversary

週年紀念(ㄓㄡ ㄋㄧㄢˊ ㄐㄧˋ ㄋㄧㄢˋ)
commemoration of an anniversary: 今天是我們的結婚一週年紀念日。Today is our first wedding anniversary.

週率(ㄓㄡ ㄌㄩˋ)
a frequency

週刊(ㄓㄡ ㄎㄢ)
a weekly periodical; a weekly: 你讀什麼週刊? What weeklies do you read?

週會(ㄓㄡ ㄏㄨㄟˋ)
a weekly meeting

週期(ㄓㄡ ㄑㄧˊ)
a period; a cycle; time of a revolution or rotation

週期表(ㄓㄡ ㄑㄧˊ ㄅㄧㄠˇ)
(chemistry) a periodic table; a table of periodic law

週期律(ㄓㄡ ㄑㄧˊ ㄌㄩˋ)
(chemistry) periodic law

週期性(ㄓㄡ ㄑㄧˊ ㄒㄧㄥˋ)
periodicity; periodic; cyclic

週全(ㄓㄡ ˙ㄑㄩㄢ)
① complete and perfect; nothing left out ② to help; assistance; help

週薪(ㄓㄡ ㄒㄧㄣ)
a weekly salary: 他的週薪為三千元。His weekly salary is $3,000.

週知(ㄓㄡ ㄓ)
to make known to all; known to all

週轉(ㄓㄡ ㄓㄨㄢˇ)
① circulating or revolving (funds) ② to have enough to meet the need

週歲(ㄓㄡ ㄙㄨㄟˋ)
a full year (especially said

of a child's age)

週而復始(ㄓㄡ ㄦˊ ㄈㄨˋ ㄕˇ)
to repeat the cycle all over again

週遊世界(ㄓㄡ ㄧㄡˊ ㄕˋ ㄐㄧㄝˋ)
to go around the world; to travel all over the world

【進】 6109 ㄐㄧㄣˋ jinn jìn

1. to go ahead; to move forward; to proceed; to progress; to advance
2. to improve; improvement; progress
3. to recommend; to introduce
4. to offer (advice, presents, etc.)
5. a generation
6. income
7. rooms in a house divided by a courtyard; a courtyard
8. to enter
9. to eat; to take; to have
10. a Chinese family name

進逼(ㄐㄧㄣˋ ㄅㄧ)
to close in; to press upon: 我軍步步進逼。Our army steadily closed in.

進兵(ㄐㄧㄣˋ ㄅㄧㄥ)
to march troops forward; to lead troops onward

進步(ㄐㄧㄣˋ ㄅㄨˋ)
to improve; to progress; improvement; progress; progressive; advance: 她的發音很有進步。Her pronunciation has greatly improved.

進門(ㄐㄧㄣˋ ㄇㄣˊ)
① to enter a door ② to master the ABCs of a subject

進犯(ㄐㄧㄣˋ ㄈㄢˋ)
to intrude into; to invade: 我們打敗進犯的敵人。We beat back the invading enemy.

進度(ㄐㄧㄣˋ ㄉㄨˋ)
(said of work) degree of progress

進度表(ㄐㄧㄣˋ ㄉㄨˋ ㄅㄧㄠˇ)
a work schedule

進退(ㄐㄧㄣˋ ㄊㄨㄟˋ)
① to advance or retreat ② to stay or quit a job ③ to employ or fire a person ④ a sense of propriety: 這年青人不知進退。The young man has no sense of propriety.

進退莫決(ㄐㄧㄣˋ ㄊㄨㄟˋ ㄇㄛˋ ㄐㄩㄝˊ)
not knowing what course of action to take

進退兩難(ㄐㄧㄣˋ ㄊㄨㄟˋ ㄌㄧㄤˇ ㄋㄢˊ)
difficult either to proceed or retreat; in a dilemma; in a jam or spot; in a (tight) box

進退失據(ㄐㄧㄣˋ ㄊㄨㄟˋ ㄕ ㄐㄩˋ)
in a dilemma; in a jam or spot

進退維谷(ㄐㄧㄣˋ ㄊㄨㄟˋ ㄨㄟˊ ㄍㄨˇ)
in a dilemma; in an awkward situation

進退與共(ㄐㄧㄣˋ ㄊㄨㄟˋ ㄩˇ ㄍㄨㄥˋ)
to cast one's lot with another person

進來(ㄐㄧㄣˋ ˙ㄌㄞ)
Come in. 或 to come in; to enter

進港(ㄐㄧㄣˋ ㄍㄤˇ)
to make port; to enter a harbor

進攻(ㄐㄧㄣˋ ㄍㄨㄥ)
to attack; attack; offensive

進貢(ㄐㄧㄣˋ ㄍㄨㄥˋ)
(said of a vassal state) to offer tribute

進口(ㄐㄧㄣˋ ㄎㄡˇ)
① to import; importation ② an intake (for liquid or gaseous matters)

進口貿易(ㄐㄧㄣˋ ㄎㄡˇ ㄇㄠˋ ㄧˋ)
import trade

進口港(ㄐㄧㄣˋ ㄎㄡˇ ㄍㄤˇ)
a port of entry

進口貨(ㄐㄧㄣˋ ㄎㄡˇ ㄏㄨㄛˋ)
imported goods; imports

進口限額(ㄐㄧㄣˋ ㄎㄡˇ ㄒㄧㄢˋ ㄜˊ)
import quotas

進口許可證(ㄐㄧㄣˋ ㄎㄡˇ ㄒㄩˇ ㄎㄜˇ ㄓㄥˋ)
an import license

進口商(ㄐㄧㄣˋ ㄎㄡˇ ㄕㄤ)
an importer

進口稅(ㄐㄧㄣˋ ㄎㄡˇ ㄕㄨㄟˋ)
an import duty

進口稅率(ㄐㄧㄣˋ ㄎㄡˇ ㄕㄨㄟˋ ㄌㄩˋ)
an import tariff

進款(ㄐㄧㄣˋ ㄎㄨㄢˇ)or 進錢(ㄐㄧㄣˋ ㄑㄧㄢˊ)
income; proceeds

進化(ㄐㄧㄣˋ ㄏㄨㄚˋ)
to evolve; evolution; to progress culturally: 人是由類人猿進化而來的。Man evolved from the anthropoid ape.

進化論(ㄐㄧㄣˋ ㄏㄨㄚˋ ㄌㄨㄣˋ)
the theory of evolution

進貨(ㄐㄧㄣˋ ㄏㄨㄛˋ)
(said of a shop) to replenish the stock of merchandise

進擊(ㄐㄧㄣˋ ㄐㄧˊ)
to advance and attack: 他們進擊敵人。They advanced and attacked the enemy.

進級(ㄐㄧㄣˋ ㄐㄧˊ)
to get promoted (in ranks, grades, etc.)

進剿(ㄐㄧㄣˋ ㄐㄧㄠˇ)
to attack rebels or bandits

進酒(ㄐㄧㄣˋ ㄐㄧㄡˇ)
to fill the winecup for a guest and urge him to drink it up

進見(ㄐㄧㄣˋ ㄐㄧㄢˋ)
to call on (a superior) 亦作「晉見」

進京(ㄐㄧㄣˋ ㄐㄧㄥ)
to go to the capital 亦作「晉京」

進爵(ㄐㄧㄣˋ ㄐㄩㄝˊ)
to be promoted to the rank of nobility 亦作「晉爵」

進軍(ㄐㄧㄣˋ ㄐㄩㄣ)
to march (troops to war); to advance (with armed forces): 我們吹響了進軍的號角。We sounded the bugle to advance.

進取(ㄐㄧㄣˋ ㄑㄩˇ)
① to be aggressive, as in jockeying for position, etc. ② to forge ahead with effort; to advance: 我們應當永遠保持謙虛和進取的精神。We should always remain modest and keep forging ahead.

進取心(ㄐㄧㄣˋ ㄑㄩˇ ㄒㄧㄣ)
aggressiveness; the desire to get ahead; enterprising spirit; initiative

進去(ㄐㄧㄣˋ ˙ㄑㄩ)
to get in; to enter; to go in

進修(ㄐㄧㄣˋ ㄒㄧㄡ)
to advance in study; to engage in advanced studies

進賢(ㄐㄧㄣˋ ㄒㄧㄢˊ)
to employ the virtuous and capable

進獻(ㄐㄧㄣˋ ㄒㄧㄢˋ)
to offer as tribute; to present something (to a superior)

進香(ㄐㄧㄣˋ ㄒㄧㄤ)
to go to a Buddhist temple and offer incense to the

Buddha
進香客(ㄐㄧㄣˋ ㄒㄧㄤ ㄎㄜˋ)
a Buddhist pilgrim
進項(ㄐㄧㄣˋ ㄒㄧㄤˋ)
income; earnings; revenue
進行(ㄐㄧㄣˋ ㄒㄧㄥˊ)
①to advance; to march forward ②to proceed (with one's business, plan, etc.); to carry on; to carry out; to engage; to conduct: 我們進行科學試驗。We engage in scientific experiment.
進行曲(ㄐㄧㄣˋ ㄒㄧㄥˊ ㄑㄩˇ)
(music) a march
進行式(ㄐㄧㄣˋ ㄒㄧㄥˊ ㄕˋ)
(grammar) the progressive tense
進學(ㄐㄧㄣˋ ㄒㄩㄝˊ)
①to show marked progress in one's study or learning ②to pass the lowest level of civil service examinations of former times
進止(ㄐㄧㄣˋ ㄓˇ)
to proceed or stop; a course of action
進展(ㄐㄧㄣˋ ㄓㄢˇ)
progress; headway: 計畫進展很順利。The plan is making good progress.
進佔(ㄐㄧㄣˋ ㄓㄢˋ)
to enter and occupy (a city, position, etc.)
進賬(ㄐㄧㄣˋ ㄓㄤˋ)
income; receipts; earnings
進帳(ㄐㄧㄣˋ ㄓㄤˋ)
①to enter a tent ②income 參見「進賬」
進駐(ㄐㄧㄣˋ ㄓㄨˋ)
to march troops to a place and garrison it: 部隊已進駐該村。Troops have been garrisoned in the village.
進場(ㄐㄧㄣˋ ㄔㄤˇ)
①to get into an examination room, a theater, a sports arena, etc. ②(navigation) an approach 亦作「進近」: 飛機進場失敗。The plane missed approach.
進呈(ㄐㄧㄣˋ ㄔㄥˊ)
to offer or present (something to a superior or an elder)
進城(ㄐㄧㄣˋ ㄔㄥˊ)
to go to town; to enter a city
進程(ㄐㄧㄣˋ ㄔㄥˊ)
progress in a course of action
進出(ㄐㄧㄣˋ ㄔㄨ)or 進進出出(ㄐㄧㄣˋ ·ㄐㄧㄣ ㄔㄨ ㄔㄨ)
① to get in and out; incoming and outgoing ② (business) a turnover
進出口(ㄐㄧㄣˋ ㄔㄨ ㄎㄡˇ)
①imports and exports ② exits and entrances
進出口貿易(ㄐㄧㄣˋ ㄔㄨ ㄎㄡˇ ㄇㄠˋ ㄧˋ)
import and export trade; foreign trade
進出口行(ㄐㄧㄣˋ ㄔㄨ ㄎㄡˇ ㄏㄤˊ)
a trading company engaged in import-export business
進出口商(ㄐㄧㄣˋ ㄔㄨ ㄎㄡˇ ㄕㄤ)
an importer-exporter
進食(ㄐㄧㄣˋ ㄕˊ)
to eat; to take food: 這病人不能進食。The patient can't take food.
進士(ㄐㄧㄣˋ ㄕˋ)
a successful candidate of the national civil service examination held at the imperial capital in former times
進身之階(ㄐㄧㄣˋ ㄕㄣ ㄓ ㄐㄧㄝ)
a steppingstone for getting a post or promotion
進水(ㄐㄧㄣˋ ㄕㄨㄟˇ)
(said of a house) to get flooded; water flowing in
進水閘(ㄐㄧㄣˋ ㄕㄨㄟˇ ㄓㄚˊ)
an entry lock
進入(ㄐㄧㄣˋ ㄖㄨˋ)
to enter; to get in; to reach: 火車進入隧道。The train entered a tunnel.
進寸退尺(ㄐㄧㄣˋ ㄘㄨㄣˋ ㄊㄨㄟˋ ㄔˇ)
(literally) to advance by one inch but to retreat by a foot—to lose much more than what one gets
進而(ㄐㄧㄣˋ ㄦˊ)
to proceed to the next step
進一步(ㄐㄧㄣˋ ㄧˊ ㄅㄨˋ)
to take one step ahead; to move further ahead
進益(ㄐㄧㄣˋ ㄧˋ)
progress
進謁(ㄐㄧㄣˋ ㄧㄝˋ)
to call on (a superior)
進言(ㄐㄧㄣˋ ㄧㄢˊ)
to offer advice
進位(ㄐㄧㄣˋ ㄨㄟˋ)
(mathematics) to carry (a number, as in adding)
進用(ㄐㄧㄣˋ ㄩㄥˋ)
wealth; fortune; money

【逵】 6110
ㄎㄨㄟˊ kwei kuí
a thoroughfare; where many ways meet

【逶】 6111
ㄨㄟ uei wēi
winding; curved; tortuous (road, way)
逶迤(ㄨㄟ ㄧˊ)
①to wind; winding (river, road, etc.) ②long; distant

【逸】 6112
ㄧˋ yih yì
1. to flee; to escape; to run away
2. to go beyond; to exceed; to go to excess
3. to rusticate; to live in retirement
4. ease; idleness; leisure
5. to let loose; to let go
6. a fault; an error; a mistake
7. quick; rapid
8. lost
9. superior; outstanding

逸品(ㄧˋ ㄆㄧㄣˇ)
a superior piece of artistic work
逸民(ㄧˋ ㄇㄧㄣˊ)
a hermit; a person of virtue and ability who leads a private life
逸度(ㄧˋ ㄉㄨˋ)
an elegant air; a refined manner
逸樂(ㄧˋ ㄌㄜˋ)
enjoyment of an easy life
逸口(ㄧˋ ㄎㄡˇ)
to make an indiscreet remark
逸經(ㄧˋ ㄐㄧㄥ)
classical learning which did not originate from the orthodox classics
逸居(ㄧˋ ㄐㄩ)
to live in retirement or idleness; to be comfortably lodged
逸氣(ㄧˋ ㄑㄧˋ)
an outstanding or out-of-this-world air or disposition
逸趣橫生(ㄧˋ ㄑㄩˋ ㄏㄥˊ ㄕㄥ)
replete with humor or refined interest

逸羣(ㄧˋ ㄑㄩㄣˊ)
outstanding; head and shoulders above others
逸暇(ㄧˋ ㄒㄧㄚˊ)
leisure; spare time
逸想(ㄧˋ ㄒㄧㄤˇ)
thoughts that are not worldly; idealistic thoughts
逸興(ㄧˋ ㄒㄧㄥˋ)
refined interest or taste
逸出常軌(ㄧˋ ㄔㄨ ㄔㄤˊ ㄍㄨㄟˇ)
to run off the track; not regular or common; against the regular practice
逸詩(ㄧˋ ㄕ)
ancient poems which were not collected in the *Book of Odes* (詩經)
逸事 or 軼事(ㄧˋ ㄕˋ)
an anecdote; an episode
逸聲(ㄧˋ ㄕㄥ)
decadent music
逸書(ㄧˋ ㄕㄨ)
ancient books which have been partly lost or in private collection
逸則淫(ㄧˋ ㄗㄜˊ ㄧㄣˊ)
Ease leads to vice.
逸足(ㄧˋ ㄗㄨˊ)
walking or running very fast; fleet-footed
逸材 or 逸才(ㄧˋ ㄘㄞˊ)
outstanding talent
逸豫(ㄧˋ ㄩˋ)
to live in idleness

【逭】 6113
ㄏㄨㄢˋ huann huàn
to run away or escape from; to flee; to avoid; to evade

【逯】 6114
ㄌㄨˋ luh lù
1. to go away suddenly for no particular reason
2. a Chinese family name

九畫

【逾】 6115
ㄩˊ yu yú
1. to exceed; to pass over; more than; over: 這位老人已年逾九十。The old man is over ninety.
2. to transgress
3. added; even more: 他疼痛逾甚。His pain became even more acute.

逾邁(ㄩˊ ㄇㄞˋ)
to pass away (as time or years
逾分(ㄩˊ ㄈㄣˋ)
① to exceed propriety; to overdo something; to transgress ② exorbitant: 他沒有逾分的要求。He has no exorbitant demands.
逾格(ㄩˊ ㄍㄜˊ)
(to do something, grant a favor, etc.) as an exception
逾恆(ㄩˊ ㄏㄥˊ)
to go beyond the common or regular practice; more than usual; excessive
逾矩(ㄩˊ ㄐㄩˇ)
to transgress what is right
逾期(ㄩˊ ㄑㄧˊ)
to exceed a time limit
逾限(ㄩˊ ㄒㄧㄢˋ)
to go beyond the limits or bounds; to exceed the limit
逾越(ㄩˊ ㄩㄝˋ)
① to pass over; to scale (a wall, etc.) ② to do what one is not supposed to do; to overstep one's position; to transgress; to exceed: 你逾越權限。You exceeded your powers.

【逼】 6116
ㄅㄧ bi bī
(又讀 ㄅㄧˋ bih bì)
1. to press; to compel; to pressure; to force; to coerce
2. to close in; to draw near; to press up to: 敵軍直逼城下。The enemy pressed up to the city wall.
3. to importune; to harass; to annoy
4. narrow; strait

逼不得已(ㄅㄧ ·ㄅㄨ ㄉㄜˊ ㄧˇ)
to be compelled or forced to; can't help but; to have no alternative
逼迫(ㄅㄧ ㄆㄛˋ)
to compel; to force: 沒有任何人可以逼迫我做這件事。Nobody can compel me to do such a thing.
逼勒(ㄅㄧ ㄌㄜˋ)
to force or compel; to blackmail
逼供(ㄅㄧ ㄍㄨㄥ)
to force a confession; to exact confessions by means of torture; to obtain confessions by compulsion
逼嫁(ㄅㄧ ㄐㄧㄚˋ)
to force a woman to marry
逼姦(ㄅㄧ ㄐㄧㄢ)
to rape
逼近(ㄅㄧ ㄐㄧㄣˋ)
to close in; to draw near; to press: 敵軍已逼近運河。The enemy was pressing on towards the canal.
逼取(ㄅㄧ ㄑㄩˇ)
to extort; to blackmail; to take or get by forcible means
逼肖(ㄅㄧ ㄒㄧㄠˋ)
(said of a portrait, twins, etc.) with striking resemblance; very much alike
逼窄(ㄅㄧ ㄓㄞˇ)
very narrow; cramped
逼債(ㄅㄧ ㄓㄞˋ)
to press for payment of debts
逼眞(ㄅㄧ ㄓㄣ)
(said of acting, performances, etc.) lifelike; almost real; verisimilitude
逼視(ㄅㄧ ㄕˋ)
to stare at sternly
逼上梁山(ㄅㄧ ㄕㄤˋ ㄌㄧㄤˊ ㄕㄢ)
to be forced to do something, especially to break the law; to be forced to go to extremities
逼人(ㄅㄧ ㄖㄣˊ)
pressing; threatening: 暑氣逼人。The summer heat is very oppressive.
逼人太甚(ㄅㄧ ㄖㄣˊ ㄊㄞˋ ㄕㄣˋ)
to push someone too hard
逼走(ㄅㄧ ㄗㄡˇ)
to force to leave: 他們被逼走了。They were forced to leave.
逼死(ㄅㄧ ㄙˇ)
to be hard-pressed so that one has to commit suicide as an escape
逼問(ㄅㄧ ㄨㄣˋ)
to question closely

【遁】 6117
ㄉㄨㄣˋ duenn dùn
1. to run away; to escape
2. to conceal oneself; to retire
遁北(ㄉㄨㄣˋ ㄅㄟˇ)
to be defeated and escape

〔辵部〕

遁化(ㄉㄨㄣˋ ㄏㄨㄚˋ)
(said of a Taoist) to die

遁迹(ㄉㄨㄣˋ ㄐㄧ)
to rusticate; to retire from public life; to live like a hermit

遁迹山林(ㄉㄨㄣˋ ㄐㄧ ㄕㄢ ㄌㄧㄣˊ)
to retire to the mountains; to retire from official life: 那老人遁迹山林。The old man retired to the mountains.

遁甲(ㄉㄨㄣˋ ㄐㄧㄚˇ)
a school of ancient Chinese sorcery, supposedly based on some principles from *The Book of Changes* (易經)

遁去(ㄉㄨㄣˋ ㄑㄩˋ)
to take to one's heels; to run away: 土匪很快地遁去。Soon the bandit ran away.

遁形(ㄉㄨㄣˋ ㄒㄧㄥˊ)
to become invisible; to vanish

遁世(ㄉㄨㄣˋ ㄕˋ)
(said of a man of ability and virtue) to live incognito; to lead the life of a recluse

遁走(ㄉㄨㄣˋ ㄗㄡˇ)
to flee; to take to one's heels

遁辭(ㄉㄨㄣˋ ㄘˊ)
an excuse; a pretext; a subterfuge; a quibble; evasive words

遁藏(ㄉㄨㄣˋ ㄘㄤˊ)
to conceal oneself

【遂】 6118 ㄙㄨㄟˋ suey suì
(又讀 ㄙㄨㄟ swei suí)
1. to have one's will; to satisfy; to fulfill
2. successful; to succeed
3. to proceed to; to reach
4. then; consequently; thereupon
5. to flee; to escape

遂令(ㄙㄨㄟˋ ㄌㄧㄥˋ)
① to order thereupon ② to result in

遂即(ㄙㄨㄟˋ ㄐㄧˊ)
thereupon; forthwith; then

遂心(ㄙㄨㄟˋ ㄒㄧㄣ)
to have one's will; to have one's own way; to satisfy: 衆人皆遂心如意。All were perfectly satisfied.

遂致(ㄙㄨㄟˋ ㄓˋ)
consequently; thereupon; subsequently

遂初(ㄙㄨㄟˋ ㄔㄨ)
to retire from official life as one originally wished

遂意(ㄙㄨㄟˋ ㄧˋ)
to have everything going one's way

遂願(ㄙㄨㄟˋ ㄩㄢˋ)
to have one's wish fulfilled

【遄】 6119 ㄔㄨㄢˊ chwan chuán
1. swiftly; quickly; to hurry
2. coming and going frequently and swiftly; to and fro

遄返(ㄔㄨㄢˊ ㄈㄢˇ)
to hurry back

遄死(ㄔㄨㄢˊ ㄙˇ)
to die very quickly

【遇】 6120 ㄩˋ yuh yù
1. to meet; to run into; to come across; to encounter
2. to treat; treatment
3. opportunity; luck
4. meeting of minds; to win confidence (of a superior, king, etc.)
5. to rival; to match with
6. a Chinese family name

遇便(ㄩˋ ㄅㄧㄢˋ)
at one's convenience

遇到(ㄩˋ ㄉㄠˋ)
to run into; to meet with; to encounter; to come across: 探險隊遇到強烈的暴風雨。The expedition met with a violent storm.

遇敵(ㄩˋ ㄉㄧˊ)
to encounter the enemy

遇難(ㄩˋ ㄋㄢˋ)
① to get killed in an accident ② to be murdered by enemy troops, rebels, etc.

遇合(ㄩˋ ㄏㄜˊ)
① meeting of minds ② to enjoy the emperor's complete confidence

遇害(ㄩˋ ㄏㄞˋ)
to be murdered or assassinated

遇救(ㄩˋ ㄐㄧㄡˋ)
to be rescued; to be saved

遇見(ㄩˋ ˙ㄐㄧㄢ)
to meet with; to run into; to come across; to bump into

遇險(ㄩˋ ㄒㄧㄢˇ)
to meet with danger; to be in danger; to be in distress: 海岸外有船遇險。There was a ship in distress off the shore.

遇著(ㄩˋ ˙ㄓㄠ)
to meet; to encounter

遇時(ㄩˋ ㄕˊ)
to ride at the crest of one's fortune; to catch the right opportunity

遇事生風(ㄩˋ ㄕˋ ㄕㄥ ㄈㄥ)
to make a mountain out of a molehill; to stir up trouble

遇人不淑(ㄩˋ ㄖㄣˊ ㄅㄨˋ ㄕㄨˊ)
to marry the wrong guy; to have married a bad husband

遇刺(ㄩˋ ㄘˋ)
to be attacked by an assassin; to be assassinated: 總統遇刺身亡。The president was assassinated.

遇有(ㄩˋ ㄧㄡˇ)
in the event of; in case of

遇雨(ㄩˋ ㄩˇ)
to be caught in the rain

【遊】 6121 ㄧㄡˊ you yóu
1. to travel; to go to a distance
2. to roam; to saunter
3. to befriend; to make friends
4. freely wield (a sword), move (one's eyes), stretch (one's sight), etc.

遊伴(ㄧㄡˊ ㄅㄢˋ)
a travel companion

遊兵(ㄧㄡˊ ㄅㄧㄥ)
militiamen; soldiers who are not listed as regulars

遊民(ㄧㄡˊ ㄇㄧㄣˊ)
a vagrant; a vagabond; an idle wanderer 亦作「無業遊民」

遊牧(ㄧㄡˊ ㄇㄨˋ)
to move about to search for pasture; to rove around as a nomad

遊牧民族(ㄧㄡˊ ㄇㄨˋ ㄇㄧㄣˊ ㄗㄨˊ)
a nomadic people or tribe

遊牧時代(ㄧㄡˊ ㄇㄨˋ ㄕˊ ㄉㄞˋ)
the nomadic period or era

遊牧生活(ㄧㄡˊ ㄇㄨˋ ㄕㄥ ㄏㄨㄛˊ)
nomadic life; nomadism

遊目騁懷(ㄧㄡˊ ㄇㄨˋ ㄔㄥˇ ㄏㄨㄞˊ)
to stretch one's sight and let one's mind roam freely

遊方(ㄧㄡˊ ㄈㄤ)
(usually referring to Bud-

dhist or Taoist monks and nuns) to roam around all corners of the world

遊蕩(ㄧㄡˊ ㄉㄤˋ)
to fool around; to act like a bum or vagrant

遊惰(ㄧㄡˊ ㄉㄨㄛˋ)
to fool around and do nothing productive

遊動(ㄧㄡˊ ㄉㄨㄥˋ)
to go from place to place; to move about

遊艇(ㄧㄡˊ ㄊㄧㄥˇ)
a yacht; a pleasure boat

遊樂(ㄧㄡˊ ㄌㄜˋ) or 遊豫(ㄧㄡˊ ㄩˋ)
to make merry; to seek pleasure; entertainment

遊樂場(ㄧㄡˊ ㄌㄜˋ ㄔㄤˇ)
an amusement park; a ground where all sorts of vaudeville shows are given; a kiddie land

遊覽(ㄧㄡˊ ㄌㄢˇ)
① to visit; to tour; sightseeing: 我們大部分的時間都花在遊覽上。Most of our time was spent in sightseeing. ② to read extensively

遊覽車(ㄧㄡˊ ㄌㄢˇ ㄔㄜ)
a bus or train for tourists or sightseers; a tourist coach; a sightseeing bus

遊廊(ㄧㄡˊ ㄌㄤˊ)
corridors, etc. between pavilions, etc. in a garden; a veranda

遊歷(ㄧㄡˊ ㄌㄧˋ)
to travel abroad for study, research, inspection, etc.

遊獵(ㄧㄡˊ ㄌㄧㄝˋ)
① to travel here and there for hunting ② to dabble in (certain reading, etc.)

遊觀(ㄧㄡˊ ㄍㄨㄢ)
to travel and see the sights

遊逛(ㄧㄡˊ ㄍㄨㄤˋ)
to stroll; to roam about: 這對夫婦手牽着手遊逛。The couple strolled hand in hand.

遊客(ㄧㄡˊ ㄎㄜˋ)
a traveler; a tourist

遊客止步(ㄧㄡˊ ㄎㄜˋ ㄓˇ ㄅㄨˋ)
No trespassing.

遊魂(ㄧㄡˊ ㄏㄨㄣˊ)
(literally) a homeless spirit —somebody or something which cannot remain long in a place

遊記(ㄧㄡˊ ㄐㄧˋ)
a travelogue (in writing); a writing about one's travels; a travel sketch

遊騎(ㄧㄡˊ ㄐㄧˋ)
mounted troopers

遊騎兵(ㄧㄡˊ ㄐㄧˋ ㄅㄧㄥ)
a ranger

遊騎無歸(ㄧㄡˊ ㄐㄧˋ ㄨˊ ㄍㄨㄟ)
rootless or homeless; no place to go back to

遊街(ㄧㄡˊ ㄐㄧㄝ)
to parade a prisoner down the street as a warning to would-be offenders

遊氣(ㄧㄡˊ ㄑㄧˋ)
① fleeting clouds ② feeble breathing

遊憩(ㄧㄡˊ ㄑㄧˋ)
to play and rest

遊息(ㄧㄡˊ ㄒㄧˊ)
play and rest

遊戲(ㄧㄡˊ ㄒㄧˋ)
to play; play: 孩子們正在院子裡遊戲。The children are playing in the yard.

遊戲場(ㄧㄡˊ ㄒㄧˋ ㄔㄤˇ)
a public amusement park or ground

遊戲人間(ㄧㄡˊ ㄒㄧˋ ㄖㄣˊ ㄐㄧㄢ)
to take nothing serious in life; to live for fun

遊狎(ㄧㄡˊ ㄒㄧㄚˊ)
to befriend and be intimate with

遊俠(ㄧㄡˊ ㄒㄧㄚˊ)
a cavalier who moves about to help the poor and weak; any person who acts in this manner without asking for reward either in money or fame; a roving gallant

遊仙(ㄧㄡˊ ㄒㄧㄢ)
(said of one's mind) to roam in a fairyland and forget all worldly affairs

遊心(ㄧㄡˊ ㄒㄧㄣ)
to think deep into something

遊行(ㄧㄡˊ ㄒㄧㄥˊ)
① to parade; a parade ② to demonstrate (in protest); demonstration

遊行示威(ㄧㄡˊ ㄒㄧㄥˊ ㄕˋ ㄨㄟ)
to demonstrate (in protest); demonstration: 學生舉行遊行示威。The students held a demonstration.

遊興(ㄧㄡˊ ㄒㄧㄥˋ)
enthusiasm in merry-making, touring or sight-seeing; wanderlust

遊學(ㄧㄡˊ ㄒㄩㄝˊ)
to study abroad; to pursue advanced study far away from home

遊塵(ㄧㄡˊ ㄔㄣˊ)
fine dust floating in the air

遊春(ㄧㄡˊ ㄔㄨㄣ)
a spring outing; to roam about and enjoy the sights of spring

遊食(ㄧㄡˊ ㄕˊ)
to fool around without doing anything productive; to be a bum

遊手好閒(ㄧㄡˊ ㄕㄡˇ ㄏㄠˋ ㄒㄧㄢˊ)
to be a lazy good-for-nothing; to lead a parasitic life; to idle about: 他兒子遊手好閒，不務正業。His son idles about and does no decent work.

遊山玩水(ㄧㄡˊ ㄕㄢ ㄨㄢˊ ㄕㄨㄟˇ)
to travel high and low and enjoy the sights of mountains and rivers

遊說(ㄧㄡˊ ㄕㄨㄟˋ)
to travel around and try to talk people into accepting one's views; to lobby; to canvass 亦作「游說」：這團體試圖遊說該法案通過。The group tried to lobby the bill through.

遊人(ㄧㄡˊ ㄖㄣˊ)
a sightseer; a tourist; a visitor

遊刃有餘(ㄧㄡˊ ㄖㄣˋ ㄧㄡˇ ㄩˊ)
to handle a difficult task with great ease

遊資(ㄧㄡˊ ㄗ)
idle funds; idle money; floating capital; floating assets

遊子(ㄧㄡˊ ㄗˇ)
a traveler; a wanderer

遊蹤(ㄧㄡˊ ㄗㄨㄥ)
the whereabouts of a traveler

遊絲(ㄧㄡˊ ㄙ)
gossamer

遊藝會(ㄧㄡˊ ㄧˋ ㄏㄨㄟˋ)
public entertainment; a gathering where variety

shows are staged by sponsoring organizations and by the participants too

遊冶(ㄧㄡˊ ㄧㄝˇ)
to indulge in the pursuit of pleasure

遊玩(ㄧㄡˊ ㄨㄢˊ)
to play; to recreate; to go for a ramble: 他們經常去郊外遊玩。They often go to the suburbs to play.

遊園會(ㄧㄡˊ ㄩㄢˊ ㄏㄨㄟˋ)
a carnival; a garden party

【運】 6122
ㄩㄣˋ yunn yùn

1. to move; to revolve: 地球繞太陽運轉。The earth revolves round the sun.
2. to transport; to ship
3. to utilize; to make use of
4. one's luck or fortune: 我這個星期運氣不錯。I have had good luck this week.
5. a Chinese family name

運搬(ㄩㄣˋ ㄅㄢ)
to transport; to move

運筆(ㄩㄣˋ ㄅㄧˇ)
to wield the brush (pen) in writing or painting

運命(ㄩㄣˋ ㄇㄧㄥˋ)
fate; destiny; fortune

運費(ㄩㄣˋ ㄈㄟˋ)
a freight charge; freight

運道(ㄩㄣˋ ㄉㄠˋ)
① fortune or luck: 他的運道不佳。His fortune is not good. 或 He is out of luck. ② a road for grain transportation

運動(ㄩㄣˋ ㄉㄨㄥˋ)
① sports; physical exercises ② motion; movement ③ a social movement; a campaign; a drive ④ to lobby

運動定律(ㄩㄣˋ ㄉㄨㄥˋ ㄉㄧㄥˋ ㄌㄩˋ)
(Sir Isaac Newton's) law of motion

運動體型(ㄩㄣˋ ㄉㄨㄥˋ ㄊㄧˇ ㄒㄧㄥˊ)
sportsman's somatotype

運動力學(ㄩㄣˋ ㄉㄨㄥˋ ㄌㄧˋ ㄒㄩㄝˊ)
(physics) kinetics

運動規範(ㄩㄣˋ ㄉㄨㄥˋ ㄍㄨㄟ ㄈㄢˋ)
sports norms

運動科學(ㄩㄣˋ ㄉㄨㄥˋ ㄎㄜ ㄒㄩㄝˊ)
sports science

運動會(ㄩㄣˋ ㄉㄨㄥˋ ㄏㄨㄟˋ)
an athletic meet; a sports meeting; games: 我們今天下午開運動會。We had a sports meeting this afternoon.

運動家(ㄩㄣˋ ㄉㄨㄥˋ ㄐㄧㄚ)
a sportsman; an athlete

運動精神(ㄩㄣˋ ㄉㄨㄥˋ ㄐㄧㄥ ㄕㄣˊ)
sportsmanship: 他稱讚你的運動精神嗎? Did he praise your sportsmanship?

運動器官(ㄩㄣˋ ㄉㄨㄥˋ ㄑㄧˋ ㄍㄨㄢ)
organs of locomotion

運動器材(ㄩㄣˋ ㄉㄨㄥˋ ㄑㄧˋ ㄘㄞˊ)
sports supplies; sports equipment; sporting goods

運動信條(ㄩㄣˋ ㄉㄨㄥˋ ㄒㄧㄣˋ ㄊㄧㄠˊ)
the sports creed

運動學(ㄩㄣˋ ㄉㄨㄥˋ ㄒㄩㄝˊ)
(physics) kinematics

運動場(ㄩㄣˋ ㄉㄨㄥˋ ㄔㄤˊ)or(ㄩㄣˋ ㄉㄨㄥˋ ㄔㄤˇ)
a playground; a stadium; a gymnasium; a sports arena

運動神經(ㄩㄣˋ ㄉㄨㄥˋ ㄕㄣˊ ㄐㄧㄥ)
motor nerves

運動傷害(ㄩㄣˋ ㄉㄨㄥˋ ㄕㄤ ㄏㄞˋ)
sports injuries

運動人口(ㄩㄣˋ ㄉㄨㄥˋ ㄖㄣˊ ㄎㄡˇ)
sports population

運動資訊(ㄩㄣˋ ㄉㄨㄥˋ ㄗ ㄒㄩㄣˋ)
sports information

運動員(ㄩㄣˋ ㄉㄨㄥˋ ㄩㄢˊ)
① an athlete; a sportsman: 他是熱心的運動員。He is a keen sportsman. ② a lobbyist

運糧(ㄩㄣˋ ㄌㄧㄤˊ)
to transport food (or provisions)

運河(ㄩㄣˋ ㄏㄜˊ)
① a canal ② the Grand Canal in China

運貨(ㄩㄣˋ ㄏㄨㄛˋ)
to transport goods

運會(ㄩㄣˋ ㄏㄨㄟˋ)
trends of the time; international situations

運斤成風(ㄩㄣˋ ㄐㄧㄣ ㄔㄥˊ ㄈㄥ)
(literally) to create a gust by wielding the ax—an uncanny feat

運氣
①(ㄩㄣˋ ㄑㄧˋ) (Chinese pugilism) dynamic tension of muscles
②(ㄩㄣˋ ·ㄑㄧ) luck or fortune

運球(ㄩㄣˋ ㄑㄧㄡˊ)
to dribble balls; dribbling

運銷(ㄩㄣˋ ㄒㄧㄠ)
to ship (goods) for sales; shipping and marketing

運行(ㄩㄣˋ ㄒㄧㄥˊ)
to move in an orbit, as a planet or satellite

運轉(ㄩㄣˋ ㄓㄨㄢˇ)
① to revolve; revolution; to set in motion around a circular orbit: 地球繞着太陽運轉。The earth revolves round the sun. ② to work; to operate; to run: 機器運轉正常。The machine is working (or running) well.

運籌(ㄩㄣˋ ㄔㄡˊ)
to plan; to map out strategy

運籌帷幄(ㄩㄣˋ ㄔㄡˊ ㄨㄟˊ ㄨㄛˋ)
to map out or devise strategy in the command tent

運輸(ㄩㄣˋ ㄕㄨ)
transportation; to transport; conveyance; to convey: 該公司負責運輸。Transportation was supplied by the company.

運輸工具(ㄩㄣˋ ㄕㄨ ㄍㄨㄥ ㄐㄩˋ)
means of transportation; means of delivery

運輸機(ㄩㄣˋ ㄕㄨ ㄐㄧ)
a military transport; a cargo plane

運輸艦(ㄩㄣˋ ㄕㄨ ㄐㄧㄢˋ)
a naval supply ship; a navy transport

運數(ㄩㄣˋ ㄕㄨˋ)
fortune; fate; luck: 他不相信運數之說。He doesn't believe in fate.

運祚(ㄩㄣˋ ㄗㄨㄛˋ)
the national fortune; the fate of the world

運漕(ㄩㄣˋ ㄘㄠˊ)
to convey food by water

運算(ㄩㄣˋ ㄙㄨㄢˋ)
(mathematics) an operation

運送(ㄩㄣˋ ㄙㄨㄥˋ)
to convey; to transport; to deliver; to ship: 他用快車還是用貨車運送它? Did he ship it by express or by freight?

運用(ㄩㄣˋ ㄩㄥˋ)
to employ; to make use of; to exercise

運用資本(ㄩㄣˋ ㄩㄥˋ ㄗ ㄅㄣˇ)
working capital

6123
【遍】ㄅㄧㄢˋ biann biàn
(語音 ㄆㄧㄢˋ piann piàn)
1. a time
2. everywhere; throughout; all over
遍布(ㄅㄧㄢˋ ㄅㄨˋ)
all over; everywhere
遍地(ㄅㄧㄢˋ ㄉㄧˋ)
everywhere; throughout the land
遍體(ㄅㄧㄢˋ ㄊㄧˇ)
all over the body
遍體鱗傷(ㄅㄧㄢˋ ㄊㄧˇ ㄌㄧㄣˊ ㄕㄤ)
with wounds all over the body
遍歷(ㄅㄧㄢˋ ㄌㄧˋ)
to have experienced all sorts of...; to have traveled all (the places)
遍告(ㄅㄧㄢˋ ㄍㄠˋ)
to announce to all; to tell everyone
遍及(ㄅㄧㄢˋ ㄐㄧˊ)
to spread throughout (the world, nation, etc.): 這謠言已遍及全島。The rumor has spread throughout the whole island.
遍身(ㄅㄧㄢˋ ㄕㄣ)
all over the body: 這件羊毛衫使我遍身發癢。This wool shirt itches me all over the body.

6124
【過】1. ㄍㄨㄛˋ guoh guò
(又讀 ㄍㄨㄛ guo guō)
1. to pass; to pass through or by; to ford
2. across; past; through; over: 有一條近路橫過這片原野。There is a short cut across the field.
3. to spend or pass (time): 你的春假是怎麽過的? How did you pass the spring holidays?
4. after; past: 那個老人超過九十歲了。That old man is past ninety.
5. to go beyond the ordinary or proper limits; to surpass
6. too much; excessive
7. a mistake; a demerit; a fault; a sin: 他勇於改過。He was bold in correcting his mistakes.
8. a particle indicating the past perfect tense: 他說他曾見過她。He said that he had once met her.
9. contagious
10. to visit
11. to transfer
12. to die; death
13. to arrive; to get to
過飽和(ㄍㄨㄛˋ ㄅㄠˇ ㄏㄜˊ)
(said of a solution) supersaturated; supersaturation
過飽和溶液(ㄍㄨㄛˋ ㄅㄠˇ ㄏㄜˊ ㄖㄨㄥˊ ㄧㄝˋ)
supersaturated solution
過半(ㄍㄨㄛˋ ㄅㄢˋ)
more than half
過半數(ㄍㄨㄛˋ ㄅㄢˋ ㄕㄨˋ)
over half of the number; the majority
過磅(ㄍㄨㄛˋ ㄅㄤˋ)or(ㄍㄨㄛˋ ㄅㄥˋ)
to weigh
過不來(ㄍㄨㄛˋ ˙ㄅㄨ ㄌㄞˊ)
unable to come over
過不去(ㄍㄨㄛˋ ˙ㄅㄨ ㄑㄩˋ)
① unable to get through ② to feel sorry for ③ intentionally to make it difficult for somebody; to have a grudge against; to give someone a hard time; to be hard on
過不下去(ㄍㄨㄛˋ ˙ㄅㄨ ㄒㄧㄚˋ ˙ㄑㄩ)
unable to live on
過門兒(ㄍㄨㄛˋ ㄇㄜˊㄦ)
(Chinese opera) the musical interlude between singing parts when the string accompaniment plays alone 亦作「過板兒」
過門(ㄍㄨㄛˋ ㄇㄣˊ)
① to pass the door ②(said of girls) to get married
過門不入(ㄍㄨㄛˋ ㄇㄣˊ ㄅㄨˋ ㄖㄨˋ)
(literally) to pass one's own door without entering (because of urgent official duties)—to act beyond the call of duty
過敏(ㄍㄨㄛˋ ㄇㄧㄣˇ)
(medicine) allergy
過目(ㄍㄨㄛˋ ㄇㄨˋ)
to give a glance; to take a look; to read; to go over
過目不忘(ㄍㄨㄛˋ ㄇㄨˋ ㄅㄨˋ ㄨㄤˋ)
to have a photographic memory
過目成誦(ㄍㄨㄛˋ ㄇㄨˋ ㄔㄥˊ ㄙㄨㄥˋ)
able to recite what one has casually read only once
過分(ㄍㄨㄛˋ ㄈㄣˋ)
to go beyond the normal or proper limits; to overdo; to go too far; excessive: 不要過分謙虛。Don't carry your modesty too far.
過房(ㄍㄨㄛˋ ㄈㄤˊ)
(said of an heirless person) to adopt a son of one's brother as one's own
過訪(ㄍㄨㄛˋ ㄈㄤˇ)
to come for a visit: 今承過訪, 無任感謝。Thank you for your visit today.
過得去(ㄍㄨㄛˋ ˙ㄉㄜ ㄑㄩˋ)
①passable; not too bad; so-so; fair: 我還算過得去。I'm just so-so. ② not to embarrass another ③ to be at peace with oneself ④ passable; able to get through: 卡車從這條路過得去嗎? Can the truck get through the road?
過道兒(ㄍㄨㄛˋ ㄉㄠˋㄦ)
a narrow corridor or passageway between houses
過當(ㄍㄨㄛˋ ㄉㄤˋ)
beyond the proper limits; improper; inappropriate
過度(ㄍㄨㄛˋ ㄉㄨˋ)
① to go beyond the normal limits; to overdo ② excessive; too much: 抽煙過度對身體有害。Excessive smoking is harmful to the health.
過渡(ㄍㄨㄛˋ ㄉㄨˋ)
①(an) intermediate (state, stage, etc.); (a) transitional (period) ② to cross a river, stream, etc. by ferry
過渡時期(ㄍㄨㄛˋ ㄉㄨˋ ㄕˊ ㄑㄧˊ)
a period or stage of transition; a transitional stage or period
過多(ㄍㄨㄛˋ ㄉㄨㄛ)
too many or much; more than enough; excessive: 雨量過多引起了洪水。The excessive rainfall caused floods.
過冬(ㄍㄨㄛˋ ㄉㄨㄥ)
to pass the winter; to winter: 我們計畫到義大利過冬。We plan to winter in Italy.
過頭(ㄍㄨㄛˋ ㄊㄡˊ)
to go beyond the norm or

〔辵部〕

the set goal; to overdo; too much: 飯煮過頭了。The meal is overcooked.

過堂(ㄍㄨㄛˋ ㄊㄤˊ)
①to stand a trial in court ②(said of successful candidates of the national civil service examination in the Tang Dynasty) to call on the prime minister

過屠門而大嚼(ㄍㄨㄛˋ ㄊㄨˊ ㄇㄣˊ ㄦˊ ㄉㄚˋ ㄐㄩㄝˊ)
(literally) to do chewing actions energetically while passing by the door of a butcher—to hanker for things one cannot get

過年(ㄍㄨㄛˋ ㄋㄧㄢˊ)
①to pass the New Year: 我今年在國外過年。I'll pass the New Year holiday abroad. ②next year

過勞(ㄍㄨㄛˋ ㄌㄠˊ)
to work too hard; to overwork

過來人(ㄍㄨㄛˋ ㄌㄞˊ ㄖㄣˊ)
a person who has had the experience of something in question

過來(ㄍㄨㄛˋ ·ㄌㄞ)
Come here. 或 Come on. 或 to come up; to come over: 過來這裏你可以看得更清楚些。Come over here, you will see better.

過磷酸鈣(ㄍㄨㄛˋ ㄌㄧㄣˊ ㄙㄨㄢ ㄍㄞˋ)
calcium superphosphate

過兩天(ㄍㄨㄛˋ ㄌㄧㄤˇ ·ㄊㄧㄢ)
in the near future; in a few days; in a couple of days: 過兩天我將去拜訪你。I'll visit you in a few days.

過量(ㄍㄨㄛˋ ㄌㄧㄤˋ)
an overdose; to go beyond the limits (usually referring to drinking); to overdo: 他死於服用過量嗎啡。He died of an overdose of morphine.

過路(ㄍㄨㄛˋ ㄌㄨˋ)
to pass by; in transit

過慮(ㄍㄨㄛˋ ㄌㄩˋ)
to be worrying too much or overanxious

過濾(ㄍㄨㄛˋ ㄌㄩˋ)
to filter; to filtrate

過濾器(ㄍㄨㄛˋ ㄌㄩˋ ㄑㄧˋ)
a filter

過濾設備(ㄍㄨㄛˋ ㄌㄩˋ ㄕㄜˋ ㄅㄟˋ)
filtrating equipment

過關(ㄍㄨㄛˋ ㄍㄨㄢ)
①to go through a checkpoint ②to pass a critical test; to go through an ordeal; to weather a crisis with success ③to come up to the standard; to reach a standard

過客(ㄍㄨㄛˋ ㄎㄜˋ)
a traveler; a sojourner; a passerby

過河拆橋(ㄍㄨㄛˋ ㄏㄜˊ ㄔㄞ ㄑㄧㄠˊ)
(literally) to destroy the bridge after one has crossed the river—very ungrateful; to discard a person after he has outlasted his usefulness

過後(ㄍㄨㄛˋ ㄏㄡˋ)
later; afterward: 我們過後再討論這項計畫。Let's discuss the plan later on.

過戶(ㄍㄨㄛˋ ㄏㄨˋ)
to transfer the ownership (of bonds, stocks, or property) from one person to another: 這戶公寓不能過戶。This apartment couldn't transfer ownership.

過活(ㄍㄨㄛˋ ㄏㄨㄛˊ)
to make a living: 她父親靠捕魚過活。Her father makes a living by fishing.

過火(ㄍㄨㄛˋ ㄏㄨㄛˇ)
to go beyond the proper limits; to overdo; to go to extremes; to go too far: 別把玩笑開得太過火。Don't carry the joke too far.

過激(ㄍㄨㄛˋ ㄐㄧ)
too violent, radical or outspoken: 他的言論過激。His opinions are too radical.

過激派(ㄍㄨㄛˋ ㄐㄧ ㄆㄞˋ)
the radical faction; the radicals

過激分子(ㄍㄨㄛˋ ㄐㄧ ㄈㄣˋ ㄗˇ)
radicals; extremists

過激思想(ㄍㄨㄛˋ ㄐㄧ ㄙ ㄒㄧㄤˇ)
dangerously extreme views or thoughts

過急(ㄍㄨㄛˋ ㄐㄧˊ)
too hasty; to make haste: 勿操之過急。Don't make haste.

過繼(ㄍㄨㄛˋ ㄐㄧˋ)
①(said of an heirless person) to adopt a son of one's brother or relative as one's own ②to have one's own child adopted by a male relative as his heir: 他把兒子過繼給親戚。He has his son adopted by a relative.

過街(ㄍㄨㄛˋ ㄐㄧㄝ)
to cross the street

過節(ㄍㄨㄛˋ ㄐㄧㄝˊ)
①to pass a festival; to celebrate a festival ②a grudge: 他們之間有過節。They bear grudges against each other.

過江之鯽(ㄍㄨㄛˋ ㄐㄧㄤ ㄓ ㄐㄧˋ)
as numerous as a large school of fish migrating in a river

過獎(ㄍㄨㄛˋ ㄐㄧㄤˇ)
①to overpraise; to flatter: 你過獎了。You flatter me. ②(a polite expression) I don't deserve your praise.

過境(ㄍㄨㄛˋ ㄐㄧㄥˋ)
(said of airplanes, ships, etc.) to pass through; in transit

過境旅客(ㄍㄨㄛˋ ㄐㄧㄥˋ ㄌㄩˇ ㄎㄜˋ)
a transit visitor

過境簽証(ㄍㄨㄛˋ ㄐㄧㄥˋ ㄑㄧㄢ ㄓㄥˋ)
a transit visa

過期(ㄍㄨㄛˋ ㄑㄧˊ)
to have passed the deadline; (said of permits, etc.) to have passed the date of expiration; overdue

過期支票(ㄍㄨㄛˋ ㄑㄧˊ ㄓ ㄆㄧㄠˋ)
an out-of-date check; an overdue check

過謙(ㄍㄨㄛˋ ㄑㄧㄢ)
to be too modest: 你得獎是應該的，不必過謙了。You really deserve the prize. Don't be so modest.

過去(ㄍㄨㄛˋ ㄑㄩˋ)
①in the past; formerly; once: 她過去住在法國。She formerly lived in France. ②to go over: 我們過去對街購物吧。Let's go over to the other side of the street to go shopping. ③to pass; to pass by: 火車剛過去。The train has just passed by. ④to die; to pass away

過去分詞(ㄍㄨㄛˋ ㄑㄩˋ ㄈㄣ ㄘˊ)
(grammar) the past participle

過去了(ㄍㄨㄛˋ ㄑㄩˋ ·ㄌㄜ)
to pass away; to die: 她母親昨晚過去了。Her mother passed away last night.
過去式(ㄍㄨㄛˋ ㄑㄩˋ ㄕˋ)
(grammar) the past tense
過去完成式(ㄍㄨㄛˋ ㄑㄩˋ ㄨㄢˊ ㄔㄥˊ ㄕˋ)
(grammar) the past perfect tense
過細(ㄍㄨㄛˋ ㄒㄧˋ)
very careful or cautious; squeamish
過招(ㄍㄨㄛˋ ㄓㄠ)
(informal) to have an encounter in combat; to exchange blows
過帳(ㄍㄨㄛˋ ㄓㄤˋ)
to transfer accounts or items (from a daybook to a ledger); to post
過程(ㄍㄨㄛˋ ㄔㄥˊ)
(in) the process; (in) the course (of)
過秤(ㄍㄨㄛˋ ㄔㄥˋ)
to weigh
過處(ㄍㄨㄛˋ ㄔㄨˋ)
mistakes; errors; faults
過失(ㄍㄨㄛˋ ㄕ)
errors committed unintentionally; faults: 他懺悔過去生活中的過失。He repented the errors of a past life.
過失殺人罪(ㄍㄨㄛˋ ㄕ ㄕㄚ ㄖㄣˊ ㄗㄨㄟˋ)
manslaughter
過失傷害罪(ㄍㄨㄛˋ ㄕ ㄕㄤ ㄏㄞˋ ㄗㄨㄟˋ)
bodily injury done to others owing to negligence
過時(ㄍㄨㄛˋ ㄕˊ)
old-fashioned; anachronistic; outdated; to outdate
過時不候(ㄍㄨㄛˋ ㄕˊ ㄅㄨˋ ㄏㄡˋ)
The deadline (appointed time, or specified date) will not be extended.
過世(ㄍㄨㄛˋ ㄕˋ)
to pass away; to die; dead: 他在當晚過世。He passed away during the night.
過少(ㄍㄨㄛˋ ㄕㄠˇ)
too little; too few; far from enough: 他的薪水過少，無法維生。His salary was too little to live on.
過山砲(ㄍㄨㄛˋ ㄕㄢ ㄆㄠˋ)
a light field piece which can be easily hauled across a hill; a mountain howitzer
過生日(ㄍㄨㄛˋ ㄕㄥ ㄖˋ)
to celebrate a birthday: 他過生日請我們吃飯。He celebrated his birthday by inviting us to a dinner.
過剩(ㄍㄨㄛˋ ㄕㄥˋ)
a surplus: 巴西有很多過剩的咖啡。Brazil has a big surplus of coffee.
過剩人口(ㄍㄨㄛˋ ㄕㄥˋ ㄖㄣˊ ㄎㄡˇ)
surplus population
過水麵(ㄍㄨㄛˋ ㄕㄨㄟˇ ㄇㄧㄢˋ)
cooked noodles which have been cooled with water
過日子(ㄍㄨㄛˋ ㄖˋ ·ㄗ)
①to practice economy ②to live: 我們勤儉過日子。We lived industriously and frugally.
過人(ㄍㄨㄛˋ ㄖㄣˊ)
to surpass others (in intelligence, bravery and other attributes): 他有過人的記憶力。He surpasses others in memory.
過載(ㄍㄨㄛˋ ㄗㄞˋ)
(said of a car, ship, etc.) overloaded
過錯(ㄍㄨㄛˋ ㄘㄨㄛˋ)
mistakes; faults
過存(ㄍㄨㄛˋ ㄘㄨㄣˊ)
to give one's regards to
過從(ㄍㄨㄛˋ ㄘㄨㄥˊ)
frequency of communication or mutual visits between friends; to be associated with: 我和他們過從甚密。I am in close association with them.
過意不去(ㄍㄨㄛˋ ㄧˋ ㄅㄨˊ ㄑㄩˋ)
①very much obliged; unable to express one's thanks adequately ②to feel sorry; not knowing how to express one's regrets
過夜(ㄍㄨㄛˋ ㄧㄝˋ)
①to pass the night; to overnight ②to spend a whole night with a prostitute (as distinct from "short-time quickies")
過猶不及(ㄍㄨㄛˋ ㄧㄡˊ ㄅㄨˋ ㄐㄧˊ)
Too much is as bad as not enough.
過眼(ㄍㄨㄛˋ ㄧㄢˇ)
①to pass before the eyes ②to take a glance
過眼煙雲(ㄍㄨㄛˋ ㄧㄢˇ ㄧㄢ ㄩㄣˊ)
(literally) smoke and clouds passing before the eyes —transient; ephemeral
過癮(ㄍㄨㄛˋ ㄧㄣˇ)
①to do something to one's heart's content ②to satisfy the urge of an addiction
過氧化鈉(ㄍㄨㄛˋ ㄧㄤˇ ㄏㄨㄚˋ ㄋㄚˋ)
sodium peroxide
過氧化鉀(ㄍㄨㄛˋ ㄧㄤˇ ㄏㄨㄚˋ ㄐㄧㄚˇ)
potassium peroxide
過氧化物(ㄍㄨㄛˋ ㄧㄤˇ ㄏㄨㄚˋ ㄨˋ)
peroxide
過午(ㄍㄨㄛˋ ㄨˇ)
afternoon
過午不食(ㄍㄨㄛˋ ㄨˇ ㄅㄨˋ ㄕˊ)
(a rule for the monks) not to eat after noontime
過五關(ㄍㄨㄛˋ ㄨˇ ㄍㄨㄢ)
a kind of solitaire, played with dominoes
過問(ㄍㄨㄛˋ ㄨㄣˋ)
①to make inquiry about; to ask about: 我從不過問他們的政治活動。I never asked about their political activities. ②to interfere with: 不要過問他人的事。Don't interfere with others. ③to care; to show concern
過往(ㄍㄨㄛˋ ㄨㄤˇ)
①comings and goings: 旅客的過往 the comings and goings of tourists ②social contacts; mutual visits
過望(ㄍㄨㄛˋ ㄨㄤˋ)
beyond one's hope or expectations
過於(ㄍㄨㄛˋ ㄩˊ)
too much; excessive; over
過譽(ㄍㄨㄛˋ ㄩˋ)
excessive praise; to acclaim excessively

【過】 6124
2. ㄍㄨㄛ guo guō
a Chinese family name

【遏】 6125
ㄜˋ eh è
1. to curb; to stop; to restrain; to prevent
2. to cause one's own extinction; to extinguish; to ruin

遏捺(ㄜˋ ㄋㄚˋ)
to suppress (one's anger, etc.); to restrain
遏止(ㄜˋ ㄓˇ)

〔辵部〕

to check; to hold back; to stop
遏制(ㄜˋ ㄓˋ)
to restrain; to check; to stop; to curb
遏阻(ㄜˋ ㄗㄨˇ)
to curb; to arrest; to stop
遏惡揚善(ㄜˋ ㄜˋ ㄧㄤˊ ㄕㄢˋ)
to refrain from talking about another's evildoing but cite his good points
遏抑(ㄜˋ ㄧˋ)
to suppress; to restrain; to curb; to check

【遑】 6126 ㄏㄨㄤˊ hwang huáng
1. hurry; to hurry
2. anxious; disturbed
3. leisurely
4. not to
遑論其他(ㄏㄨㄤˊ ㄌㄨㄣˋ ㄑㄧˊ ㄊㄚ)
not to mention the others; let alone the other points
遑遑(ㄏㄨㄤˊ ㄏㄨㄤˊ)
disturbed; jittery; scared
遑急(ㄏㄨㄤˊ ㄐㄧˊ)
scared and in a hurry: 他遑急萬狀。He was in a great hurry.
遑遽(ㄏㄨㄤˊ ㄐㄩˋ)
jittery and anxious; frightened

【遐】 6127 ㄒㄧㄚˊ shya xiá
1. distant; far
2. a long time
3. advanced in years
4. to die down; to vanish
5. to abandon; to cast off
6. Why not? 或 How? 或 What?
遐布(ㄒㄧㄚˊ ㄅㄨˋ)
to spread far and wide
遐方(ㄒㄧㄚˊ ㄈㄤ)
distant places
遐福(ㄒㄧㄚˊ ㄈㄨˊ)
great happiness; lasting blessings or happiness
遐眺(ㄒㄧㄚˊ ㄊㄧㄠˋ)
to stretch one's sight as far as it can reach
遐齡(ㄒㄧㄚˊ ㄌㄧㄥˊ)
longevity; a long life; an advanced age
遐荒(ㄒㄧㄚˊ ㄏㄨㄤ)
distant and out-of-the-way places
遐迹(ㄒㄧㄚˊ ㄐㄧ)
matters and stories of ancient people
遐舉(ㄒㄧㄚˊ ㄐㄩˇ)
to go on a distant journey
遐棄(ㄒㄧㄚˊ ㄑㄧˋ)
① to cast away; to reject; to shun ② to desert one's post
遐心(ㄒㄧㄚˊ ㄒㄧㄣ)
① the thought of keeping aloof ② the wish to abandon ③ the desire to live in retirement
遐想(ㄒㄧㄚˊ ㄒㄧㄤˇ)
wild and fanciful thoughts; reverie; a daydream
遐祉(ㄒㄧㄚˊ ㄓˇ)
lasting blessings or happiness
遐志(ㄒㄧㄚˊ ㄓˋ)
lofty ambition or aspiration
遐冑(ㄒㄧㄚˊ ㄓㄡˋ)
distant descendants
遐思(ㄒㄧㄚˊ ㄙ)
wild and fanciful thoughts
遐邇(ㄒㄧㄚˊ ㄦˇ)
far and near (usually said of one's reputation): 他名聞遐邇。He was well-known far and near.
遐邇一體(ㄒㄧㄚˊ ㄦˇ ㄧˋ ㄊㄧˇ)
Both the near and the distant are treated alike.

【遒】 6128 ㄑㄧㄡˊ chyou qiú
1. strong; forceful; powerful; vigorous; sturdy
2. to come to an end; to close
3. to gather; to concentrate
遒美(ㄑㄧㄡˊ ㄇㄟˇ)
(said of the style of calligraphy) forceful and graceful
遒健(ㄑㄧㄡˊ ㄐㄧㄢˋ)
strong; vigorous
遒勁(ㄑㄧㄡˊ ㄐㄧㄥˋ)
①(said of calligraphy) forceful; vigorous ② strong; sturdy
遒逸(ㄑㄧㄡˊ ㄧˋ)
(said of a piece of writing) forceful and moving

【道】 6129 ㄉㄠˋ daw dào
1. a road; a path; a street
2. the "way" (in the metaphysical sense)
3. a way; a method: 致富沒有簡易之道。There is no easy way to wealth.
4. Taoism; a Taoist
5. to say; to speak
6. an administrative district in old China
7. a theory; a doctrine
8. to govern; to lead
9. to think; to suppose
10. a skill; an art; a craft
11. a Chinese family name
道白(ㄉㄠˋ ㄅㄞˊ)
spoken lines in Chinese opera (as distinct from the singing parts)
道不同不相爲謀(ㄉㄠˋ ㄅㄨˋ ㄊㄨㄥˊ ㄅㄨˋ ㄒㄧㄤ ㄨㄟˊ ㄇㄡˊ)
People adhering to different principles will not map their plan together. 或 Birds of different feathers will not flock together. 或 There is little common ground for understanding between persons of differing principles.
道不拾遺(ㄉㄠˋ ㄅㄨˋ ㄕˊ ㄧˊ)
(said of an orderly society) No one will pick up anything dropped by others on the road.—Honesty prevails throughout society.
道破(ㄉㄠˋ ㄆㄛˋ)
to expose or reveal some secret in utterance: 他一語道破其中奧秘。He exposed its secret with one remark.
道袍(ㄉㄠˋ ㄆㄠˊ)
a Taoist robe
道貌岸然(ㄉㄠˋ ㄇㄠˋ ㄢˋ ㄖㄢˊ)
① to maintain a serene look or dignified appearance ② to pretend to be a moralist; to look gentlemanly (but with a dirty mind)
道謀(ㄉㄠˋ ㄇㄡˊ)
to consult passers-by (and their views will certainly be different and even contradictory)
道乏(ㄉㄠˋ ㄈㄚˊ)
to thank someone for his attendance at a wedding, funeral, etc.
道德(ㄉㄠˋ ㄉㄜˊ)
morality; morals; ethics: 我們應該遵守公共道德。We should keep public morality.
道德觀念(ㄉㄠˋ ㄉㄜˊ ㄍㄨㄢ ㄋㄧㄢˋ)
moral concepts

道德經(ㄉㄠˋ ㄉㄜˊ ㄐㄧㄥ)
Tao Te Ching, another title of *Lao-tzu* (老子)

道德心(ㄉㄠˋ ㄉㄜˊ ㄒㄧㄣ)
a sense of morality

道德哲學(ㄉㄠˋ ㄉㄜˊ ㄓㄜˊ ㄒㄩㄝˊ)
moral philosophy

道德問題(ㄉㄠˋ ㄉㄜˊ ㄨㄣˋ ㄊㄧˊ)
a question of morality or ethics

道地(ㄉㄠˋ ㄉㄧˋ)
genuine; real

道臺(ㄉㄠˋ ˙ㄊㄞ)
the magistrate of a *tao,* an ancient administrative district

道體(ㄉㄠˋ ㄊㄧˇ)
①(a polite expression) your health ② the essence of the "Way"

道聽塗說(ㄉㄠˋ ㄊㄧㄥ ㄊㄨˊ ㄕㄨㄛ)
rumor; hearsay; groundless talk

道統(ㄉㄠˋ ㄊㄨㄥˇ)
orthodoxy of teachings or precepts

道里(ㄉㄠˋ ㄌㄧˇ)
① the common standard for measuring distance ② a journey

道理(ㄉㄠˋ ㄌㄧˇ)
① reason; rationality: 你的話很有道理。There is reason in what you say. ② the right way; the proper way

道林紙(ㄉㄠˋ ㄌㄧㄣˊ ㄓˇ)
Dowling paper; wood-free printing paper

道路(ㄉㄠˋ ㄌㄨˋ)
a road: 道路泥濘。The road is muddy.

道路傳聞(ㄉㄠˋ ㄌㄨˋ ㄔㄨㄢˊ ㄨㄣˊ)
news spread on roads—inaccurate and unreliable rumors

道路以目(ㄉㄠˋ ㄌㄨˋ ㄧˇ ㄇㄨˋ)
(said of the people) to be frightened (by a tyrant or ruffian) to complete silence but exchange their hatred with eyes

道籙(ㄉㄠˋ ㄌㄨˋ)
the diagrams and scriptures of Taoism

道高一尺，魔高一丈(ㄉㄠˋ ㄍㄠ ㄧˊ ㄔˇ, ㄇㄛˊ ㄍㄠ ㄧˊ ㄓㄤˋ)
(literally) If righteousness grows by a foot, the devil will grow by ten times as much.—The force of evil always manages to beat the force of law.

道姑(ㄉㄠˋ ㄍㄨ)
a woman Taoist

道故(ㄉㄠˋ ㄍㄨˋ)
to talk about old times

道觀(ㄉㄠˋ ㄍㄨㄢˋ)
a Taoist temple or shrine

道光(ㄉㄠˋ ㄍㄨㄤ)
① the glory of morality ② the reigning title of the sixth emperor, Hsüan Tzung (宣宗, 1821-1850), in the Ching Dynasty

道賀(ㄉㄠˋ ㄏㄜˋ)
to congratulate; to offer congratulations: 請接受我們的道賀。Please accept our congratulations.

道候(ㄉㄠˋ ㄏㄡˋ)
to convey one's regards to somebody

道濟(ㄉㄠˋ ㄐㄧˋ)
① name of a Buddhist monk in the Sung Dynasty 亦作「濟顛」② name of a Buddhist monk in the Ching Dynasty noted for his paintings 亦作「石濤」

道家(ㄉㄠˋ ㄐㄧㄚ)
the Taoist school

道教(ㄉㄠˋ ㄐㄧㄠˋ)
(religion) Taoism

道具(ㄉㄠˋ ㄐㄩˋ)
stage properties

道歉(ㄉㄠˋ ㄑㄧㄢˋ)
to apologize; to make an apology

道喜(ㄉㄠˋ ㄒㄧˇ)
to congratulate; to offer congratulations

道謝(ㄉㄠˋ ㄒㄧㄝˋ)
to thank; to express thanks: 無需向我道謝。There is no need to thank me.

道行(ㄉㄠˋ ㄒㄧㄥˊ)or(ㄉㄠˋ ˙ㄏㄤ)
the attainment of a Taoist

道學(ㄉㄠˋ ㄒㄩㄝˊ)
① the emphasis on rationality in learning as advocated by the Sung scholars ② the teachings of Taoism

道學先生(ㄉㄠˋ ㄒㄩㄝˊ ㄒㄧㄢ ˙ㄕㄥ)
a scholar rigidly adhering to principles; a conservative scholar

道場(ㄉㄠˋ ㄔㄤˇ)
① sites of Taoist or Buddhist rituals ② a Buddhist temple

道士(ㄉㄠˋ ㄕˋ)
a Taoist priest

道是(ㄉㄠˋ ㄕˋ)
to say so; to appear as if: 道是無情却有情。You might say someone is cold, but he isn't.

道山(ㄉㄠˋ ㄕㄢ)
① a paradise where the souls of good people dwell after death ② a cultural center

道上(ㄉㄠˋ ˙ㄕㄤ)
on the way

道術(ㄉㄠˋ ㄕㄨˋ)
Taoist magic or sorcery

道人(ㄉㄠˋ ㄖㄣˊ)
① a Buddhist ② a Taoist priest

道子(ㄉㄠˋ ˙ㄗ)
lines on the surface of something, as a piece of furniture

道藏(ㄉㄠˋ ㄗㄤˋ)
Taoist books, scriptures, etc.

道次(ㄉㄠˋ ㄘˋ)
on the way

道兒(ㄉㄠˋㄦ)
① a road; a street ② a coup; a trick; a trap

道義(ㄉㄠˋ ㄧˋ)
morals; morality; a sense of righteousness; honor

道義力量(ㄉㄠˋ ㄧˋ ㄌㄧˋ ˙ㄌㄧㄤ)
the moral force

道義之交(ㄉㄠˋ ㄧˋ ㄓ ㄐㄧㄠ)
a friendship cemented by common belief in principles or adherence to righteousness

道友(ㄉㄠˋ ㄧㄡˇ)
① friends of the same religion or belief ② friends sharing the same hobby

道院(ㄉㄠˋ ㄩㄢˋ)
a Taoist monastery

【達】 6130
1. ㄉㄚˊ dar dá

1. intelligent; smart; understanding; reasonable: 他通情達理。He is understanding and reasonable.
2. prominent; successful

〔辵部〕

〔辵部〕

3. to reach; to arrive at
4. to inform; to tell
5. open-minded
6. a Chinese family name

達摩(ㄉㄚˊ ㄇㄛˊ)
Bodhidharma, who introduced the Zen (禪) sect into China in the 6th century

達姆彈(ㄉㄚˊ ㄇㄨˇ ㄉㄢˋ)
a dumdum bullet

達達派(ㄉㄚˊ ㄉㄚˊ ㄆㄞˋ)or 達達主義(ㄉㄚˊ ㄉㄚˊ ㄓㄨˇ ㄧˋ)
Dada, or Dadaism

達達尼爾海峽(ㄉㄚˊ ㄉㄚˊ ㄋㄧˊ ㄦˇ ㄏㄞˇ ㄒㄧㄚˊ)
Dardanelles

達德(ㄉㄚˊ ㄉㄜˊ)
a virtue of all times

達到(ㄉㄚˊ ㄉㄠˋ)
to reach (a decision, or conclusion); to achieve or attain (a goal, etc.): 我希望你會達到目的。I hope you will attain your object.

達道(ㄉㄚˊ ㄉㄠˋ)
the universal path; the way everyone follows

達旦(ㄉㄚˊ ㄉㄢˋ)
(to work) until dawn or throughout the night: 我們通宵達旦地工作。We worked all through the night.

達賴喇嘛(ㄉㄚˊ ㄌㄞˋ ㄌㄚˇ ·ㄇㄚ)
Dalai Lama, the ruler and chief monk of Tibet, believed to be a reincarnation of Avalokitesvara and sought for among children after the death of the preceding Dalai Lama

達觀(ㄉㄚˊ ㄍㄨㄢ)
a kind of wisdom which enables a person to be oblivious of emotions and adversity; to take things philosophically

達官貴人(ㄉㄚˊ ㄍㄨㄢ ㄍㄨㄟˋ ㄖㄣˊ)
prominent officials and eminent personages

達卡爾(ㄉㄚˊ ㄎㄚˇ ㄦˇ)
Dakar, capital of Senegal

達荷美(ㄉㄚˊ ㄏㄜˊ ㄇㄟˇ)
Dahomey

達成(ㄉㄚˊ ㄔㄥˊ)
to succeed in (a mission, etc.); to accomplish; to reach (an agreement)

達士(ㄉㄚˊ ㄕˋ)
① a highly intelligent person; a wise man ② a reasonable and understanding man

達識(ㄉㄚˊ ㄕˋ)
intelligent, knowledgeable and well-informed

達人(ㄉㄚˊ ㄖㄣˊ)
① a very wise man ② to enlarge other's mind, knowledge, etc.

達人知命(ㄉㄚˊ ㄖㄣˊ ㄓ ㄇㄧㄥˋ)
A wise person understands the will of Heaven.

達尊(ㄉㄚˊ ㄗㄨㄣ)
the thing which is revered by all

達爾文(ㄉㄚˊ ㄦˇ ㄨㄣˊ)
Charles Robert Darwin (1809-1882), English naturalist and author

達意(ㄉㄚˊ ㄧˋ)
to make one's meaning clear

達因(ㄉㄚˊ ㄧㄣ)
(physics) dyne

【達】 6130
2. ㄊㄚˋ tah tà
loose and impudent

【違】 6131
ㄨㄟˊ wei wéi

1. to go against; to defy; to disobey; to disregard: 士兵不可違令。Soldiers must not disobey orders.
2. to be separated
3. to avoid
4. evil; fault

違背(ㄨㄟˊ ㄅㄟˋ)
to defy; to disobey; to disregard; to be contrary to

違法(ㄨㄟˊ ㄈㄚˇ)
to be against the law; to be unlawful; to violate the law; to be illegal

違法行爲(ㄨㄟˊ ㄈㄚˇ ㄒㄧㄥˊ ㄨㄟˊ)
an unlawful act

違反(ㄨㄟˊ ㄈㄢˇ)
to contradict; to disregard (the rules, etc.); to violate; to run counter to: 你違反交通規則。You violated traffic regulations.

違犯(ㄨㄟˊ ㄈㄢˋ)
to violate (a rule or law): 我並沒有違犯法律。I didn't violate the law.

違理(ㄨㄟˊ ㄌㄧˇ)
to defy good reasoning; unreasonable

違禮(ㄨㄟˊ ㄌㄧˇ)
to disregard proper rules of behavior or conduct; to go against accepted etiquette

違例(ㄨㄟˊ ㄌㄧˋ)
contrary to precedents or practices

違令(ㄨㄟˊ ㄌㄧㄥˋ)
to disobey orders

違規(ㄨㄟˊ ㄍㄨㄟ)
to be against regulations: 他違規停車。His parking was against regulations.

違抗(ㄨㄟˊ ㄎㄤˋ)
to defy and oppose; to disobey: 小孩不應違抗他的父母。No child should ever defy his parents.

違抗命令(ㄨㄟˊ ㄎㄤˋ ㄇㄧㄥˋ ㄌㄧㄥˋ)
to disobey orders

違和(ㄨㄟˊ ㄏㄜˊ)
to be indisposed; ill (a polite expression)

違禁(ㄨㄟˊ ㄐㄧㄣˋ)
to defy a prohibition

違禁品(ㄨㄟˊ ㄐㄧㄣˋ ㄆㄧㄣˇ)or 違禁物品(ㄨㄟˊ ㄐㄧㄣˋ ㄨˋ ㄆㄧㄣˇ)
forbidden goods and articles; goods prohibited by law from being imported or exported

違警(ㄨㄟˊ ㄐㄧㄥˇ)
to break a police regulation; a breach of police regulations; violation of police regulations

違警罰法(ㄨㄟˊ ㄐㄧㄥˇ ㄈㄚˊ ㄈㄚˇ)
The Law for the Punishment of Police Offenses

違警行爲(ㄨㄟˊ ㄐㄧㄥˇ ㄒㄧㄥˊ ㄨㄟˊ)
a police offense

違憲(ㄨㄟˊ ㄒㄧㄢˋ)
unconstitutional; violation of the Constitution; to violate the Constitution

違心之論(ㄨㄟˊ ㄒㄧㄣ ㄓ ㄌㄨㄣˋ)
insincere utterances, comments, etc.

違章建築(ㄨㄟˊ ㄓㄤ ㄐㄧㄢˋ ㄓㄨˊ)or 違建(ㄨㄟˊ ㄐㄧㄢˋ)
buildings erected without a license or against the provisions of the building code

違失(ㄨㄟˊ ㄕ)

faults; errors; misconduct: 她因行爲違失而被開除。She was dismissed because of misconduct.

違礙(ㄨㄟˊ ㄞˋ)
defying (orders) and going against (traditions or customs)

違拗(ㄨㄟˊ ㄠˋ)
to defy; to disobey; defiance; disobedience: 恕我違拗。Pardon me for my defying you.

違貳(ㄨㄟˊ ㄦˋ)
to harbor disloyalty

違言(ㄨㄟˊ ㄧㄢˊ)
① to be on bad terms as a result of dispute ② unreasonable talk; nonsense

違忤(ㄨㄟˊ ㄨˇ)
disobedient and unruly

違誤(ㄨㄟˊ ㄨˋ)
to disobey orders and cause delay

違約(ㄨㄟˊ ㄩㄝ)
a breach of contract; to break a contract or agreement

違約金(ㄨㄟˊ ㄩㄝ ㄐㄧㄣ)
a forfeit or penalty (imposed on for a breach of contract or agreement)

十畫

【遜】6132 ㄒㄩㄣˋ shiunn xùn (又讀 ㄙㄨㄣˋ suenn sùn)

1. respectful and compliant; obedient
2. to resign; resigning; to surrender; to abdicate; yielding
3. humble; modest
4. not as good as; inferior to
5. a Chinese family name

遜遁(ㄒㄩㄣˋ ㄉㄨㄣˋ)
① humble and resigning ② to shirk; to shun; to be cowardly

遜國(ㄒㄩㄣˋ ㄍㄨㄛˊ)
to surrender the reign of a state to another; to abdicate

遜謝(ㄒㄩㄣˋ ㄒㄧㄝˋ)
to decline humbly and modestly

遜順(ㄒㄩㄣˋ ㄕㄨㄣˋ)
respectfully obedient; humble and yielding

遜讓(ㄒㄩㄣˋ ㄖㄤˋ)
to surrender (a position) to another; to yield

遜色(ㄒㄩㄣˋ ㄙㄜˋ)
inferior to; not as good as: 這布料較眞絲遜色。This cloth is inferior to real silk.

遜位(ㄒㄩㄣˋ ㄨㄟˋ)
to abdicate; abdication

遜王(ㄒㄩㄣˋ ㄨㄤˊ)
an abdicated king

【遘】6133 ㄍㄡˋ gow gòu

to meet; to come across; to encounter

遘閔(ㄍㄡˋ ㄇㄧㄣˇ)
① to meet with distress; to suffer malicious accusations from hidden enemies ② to suffer bereavement of a parent or parents

遘患(ㄍㄡˋ ㄏㄨㄢˋ)
to meet with misfortune or bad luck; to meet with trouble

【遙】6134 ㄧㄠˊ yau yáo

distant; far; remote

遙臨(ㄧㄠˊ ㄌㄧㄣˊ)
to approach from afar

遙領(ㄧㄠˊ ㄌㄧㄥˇ)
to accept a position far away on a concurrent basis without attending to the day-to-day operations of that office in person

遙控(ㄧㄠˊ ㄎㄨㄥˋ)
remote control; telecontrol

遙控飛機(ㄧㄠˊ ㄎㄨㄥˋ ㄈㄟ ㄐㄧ)
a remote control aircraft; a telecontrolled airplane

遙控開關(ㄧㄠˊ ㄎㄨㄥˋ ㄎㄞ ㄍㄨㄢ)
a teleswitch

遙控無人機(ㄧㄠˊ ㄎㄨㄥˋ ㄨˊ ㄖㄣˊ ㄐㄧ)
remotely piloted vehicle (RPV)

遙祭(ㄧㄠˊ ㄐㄧˋ)
to offer sacrifice to the dead whose remains are buried far away

遙見(ㄧㄠˊ ㄐㄧㄢˋ)
to see at a distance

遙夜(ㄧㄠˊ ㄧㄝˋ)
a long night

遙遙領先(ㄧㄠˊ ㄧㄠˊ ㄌㄧㄥˇ ㄒㄧㄢ)
to be far ahead; to enjoy a commanding lead

遙遙相對(ㄧㄠˊ ㄧㄠˊ ㄒㄧㄤ ㄉㄨㄟˋ)
facing one another at a distance: 他們倆遙遙相對。They faced each other across a great distance.

遙遙無期(ㄧㄠˊ ㄧㄠˊ ㄨˊ ㄑㄧˊ)
in the indefinite future

遙望(ㄧㄠˊ ㄨㄤˋ)
to take a distant look; to look at a distant place

遙遠(ㄧㄠˊ ㄩㄢˇ)
far and remote: 這路途遙遠且難行。The journey was long and difficult.

【遛】6135 1. ㄌㄧㄡˊ liou liú

to hang around; to linger at a place

【遛】6135 2. ㄌㄧㄡˋ liow liù

to stroll; to walk slowly; to roam: 我想出去遛遛。I want to go for a stroll.

遛馬(ㄌㄧㄡˋ ㄇㄚˇ)
to walk a horse

遛達(ㄌㄧㄡˋ ·ㄉㄚ)
to take a walk; to stroll as an exercise 亦作「溜達」

遛遛(ㄌㄧㄡˋ ·ㄌㄧㄡ)
to take a walk

遛彎兒(ㄌㄧㄡˋ ㄨㄢㄦ)
to take a walk; to stroll

【遝】6136 ㄊㄚˋ tah tà

numerous; many; a large number of

【遞】6137 ㄉㄧˋ dih dì

1. to forward; to transmit; to hand or pass over to: 請把報紙遞給我。Hand me the paper, please.
2. to substitute; to alternate

遞補(ㄉㄧˋ ㄅㄨˇ)
to fill a vacancy: 空缺已遞補了。The vacancy has already been filled.

遞代(ㄉㄧˋ ㄉㄞˋ)
to substitute for each other; to take the place of each other

遞給(ㄉㄧˋ ㄍㄟˇ)
to hand over; to pass on: 請把牛油遞給我。Pass (me) the butter, please.

遞過來(ㄉㄧˋ ㄍㄨㄛˋ ·ㄌㄞ)
to pass (it) over here: 請把

〔辵部〕

胡椒遞過來。Pass the pepper over here, please.

遞過去(ㄉㄧˋ ㄍㄨㄛˋ ·ㄑㄩ)
to pass (it) over there

遞加(ㄉㄧˋ ㄐㄧㄚ)
progressive increase; to increase gradually

遞解(ㄉㄧˋ ㄐㄧㄝˇ)
to escort a prisoner over a long distance while the guards are changed at each stop

遞解出境(ㄉㄧˋ ㄐㄧㄝˇ ㄔㄨ ㄐㄧㄥˋ)
to deport; deportation

遞交(ㄉㄧˋ ㄐㄧㄠ)
to hand over; to deliver

遞減(ㄉㄧˋ ㄐㄧㄢˇ)
to decrease or reduce progressively

遞進(ㄉㄧˋ ㄐㄧㄣˋ)
to go forward one by one

遞降(ㄉㄧˋ ㄐㄧㄤˋ)
to decrease or reduce gradually; progressive decrease

遞降函數(ㄉㄧˋ ㄐㄧㄤˋ ㄏㄢˊ ㄕㄨˋ)
(mathematics) a descending function

遞信(ㄉㄧˋ ㄒㄧㄣˋ)
to deliver a letter

遞傳(ㄉㄧˋ ㄔㄨㄢˊ)
to hand over; to pass on

遞上(ㄉㄧˋ ·ㄕㄤ)
to forward; to present

遞昇(ㄉㄧˋ ㄕㄥ)
to rise or increase progressively

遞昇函數(ㄉㄧˋ ㄕㄥ ㄏㄢˊ ㄕㄨˋ)
(mathematics) an ascending function

遞增(ㄉㄧˋ ㄗㄥ)
to increase progressively: 汽車的數量在迅速遞增中。The number of cars is increasing rapidly.

遞送(ㄉㄧˋ ㄙㄨㄥˋ)
to deliver (a letter, etc.): 郵差是遞送信件和郵包的人。A postman is a man who delivers letters and parcels.

遞眼色(ㄉㄧˋ ㄧㄢˇ ㄙㄜˋ)
to give a signal with the eyes; to signal with the eyes; to tip somebody the wink: 我向她遞眼色。I tipped her the wink.

【遠】 6138
1. ㄩㄢˇ yeuan yuǎn

1. far; distant; remote: 石門水庫離這裏多遠? How far is the Shih-men Reservoir from here?
2. deep; profound
3. to keep at a distance; to keep away

遠播(ㄩㄢˇ ㄅㄛ)
to spread far and wide (as fame, etc.)

遠避(ㄩㄢˇ ㄅㄧˋ)
to keep far away from; to keep at a distance

遠別(ㄩㄢˇ ㄅㄧㄝˊ)
① to separate for a journey to a distant land ② to part for a long time

遠謀(ㄩㄢˇ ㄇㄡˊ)
to plan far ahead

遠方(ㄩㄢˇ ㄈㄤ)
a distant place; remote places

遠房(ㄩㄢˇ ㄈㄤˊ)
related through remote ancestry; distantly related: 他是我的遠房親戚。He is my distant relative.

遠大(ㄩㄢˇ ㄉㄚˋ)
very promising (person, etc.); (to look) far ahead; not to be limited or confined by the present

遠道(ㄩㄢˇ ㄉㄠˋ) or 遠路(ㄩㄢˇ ㄌㄨˋ)
faraway; distant; afar: 他遠道而來。He came a long way.

遠地點(ㄩㄢˇ ㄉㄧˋ ㄉㄧㄢˇ)
(astronomy) an apogee

遠遁(ㄩㄢˇ ㄉㄨㄣˋ)
to escape to a faraway place; to flee to distant places

遠東(ㄩㄢˇ ㄉㄨㄥ)
the Far East

遠眺(ㄩㄢˇ ㄊㄧㄠˋ)
to take a distant look; to view distant places: 他遠眺海洋。He took a distant view of the ocean.

遠圖(ㄩㄢˇ ㄊㄨˊ)
to plan far ahead; a plan for the future

遠念(ㄩㄢˇ ㄋㄧㄢˋ)
to show concern for a dear one during separation

遠來的和尚會念經(ㄩㄢˇ ㄌㄞˊ ·ㄉㄜ ㄏㄜˊ ·ㄕㄤ ㄏㄨㄟˋ ㄋㄧㄢˋ ㄐㄧㄥ)
(literally) Buddhist monks who come from afar are always better at reciting the scriptures.—(used sarcastically) Persons who come from distant lands are always better than local talents.

遠離(ㄩㄢˇ ㄌㄧˊ)
① to depart for a distant place ② to keep away at a great distance

遠離塵囂(ㄩㄢˇ ㄌㄧˊ ㄔㄣˊ ㄒㄧㄠ)
far from the madding crowd

遠慮(ㄩㄢˇ ㄌㄩˋ)
to worry and plan far ahead; advance planning

遠略(ㄩㄢˇ ㄌㄩㄝˋ)
① a great plan or strategy for the future ② to accomplish great achievements in a distant place

遠隔(ㄩㄢˇ ㄍㄜˊ)
far; remote; distant (in places or time)

遠古(ㄩㄢˇ ㄍㄨˇ)
ancient times; remote antiquity

遠客(ㄩㄢˇ ㄎㄜˋ)
persons coming from a distant place; a stranger; a traveler; a visitor or guest from a distant place

遠航(ㄩㄢˇ ㄏㄤˊ)
to sail to distant places

遠嫁(ㄩㄢˇ ㄐㄧㄚˋ)
(said of a girl) to marry a man who lives in a distant place

遠交近攻(ㄩㄢˇ ㄐㄧㄠ ㄐㄧㄣˋ ㄍㄨㄥ)
to make friends with distant countries and attack the neighboring ones (a stratagem adopted by the state of Chin during the Epoch of Warring States) 或 Make war on that which is near and cultivate friendship with that which is remote.

遠見(ㄩㄢˇ ㄐㄧㄢˋ)
foresight; a farsighted view; prescience

遠近(ㄩㄢˇ ㄐㄧㄣˋ)
① far and near; remote or close (relatives, etc.) ② distance

遠景(ㄩㄢˇ ㄐㄧㄥˇ)
① a vista; a distant view; a

long-range perspective ② (movies) a long shot
遠鏡(ㄩㄢˇ ㄐㄧㄥˋ)
a telescope
遠期(ㄩㄢˇ ㄑㄧˊ)
at a specified future date; forward
遠親(ㄩㄢˇ ㄑㄧㄣ)
① distant relatives ② relatives who live far away
遠親不如近鄰(ㄩㄢˇ ㄑㄧㄣ ㄅㄨˋ ㄖㄨˊ ㄐㄧㄣˋ ㄌㄧㄣˊ)
Distant relatives (or relatives who live in a distant place) are not as helpful as close neighbors. 常言說，遠親不如近鄰。As the saying goes, "Neighbors are dearer than distant relatives."
遠心力(ㄩㄢˇ ㄒㄧㄣ ㄌㄧˋ)
centrifugal force 亦作「離心力」
遠心花序(ㄩㄢˇ ㄒㄧㄣ ㄏㄨㄚ ㄒㄩˋ)
centrifugal inflorescence
遠行(ㄩㄢˇ ㄒㄧㄥˊ)
to travel to a distant place; a journey to a distant place: 他遠行在即。He will take a long journey at once.
遠支(ㄩㄢˇ ㄓ)
a remote branch of one's relatives
遠志(ㄩㄢˇ ㄓˋ)
①(a medical herb) polygala ② great ambition
遠征(ㄩㄢˇ ㄓㄥ)
to do battle in a distant land; an expedition
遠征軍(ㄩㄢˇ ㄓㄥ ㄐㄩㄣ)
an expeditionary force
遠矚(ㄩㄢˇ ㄓㄨˇ)
to look far ahead; to take a look at faraway places
遠臣(ㄩㄢˇ ㄔㄣˊ)
① officials who had very remote connection with the capital or throne ② officials from distant districts
遠程(ㄩㄢˇ ㄔㄥˊ)
long range
遠處(ㄩㄢˇ ㄔㄨˋ)
distant; distant places; located far away: 這光由遠處射來。The light came from afar.
遠識(ㄩㄢˇ ㄕˋ)
farsightedness (as a product of wisdom); forward-looking
遠視(ㄩㄢˇ ㄕˋ)
① farsightedness (as a physical defect); hypermetropia ② to look from a distance
遠視眼(ㄩㄢˇ ㄕˋ ㄧㄢˇ)
farsighted (in eye vision); hypermetropia; hyperopia
遠視眼鏡(ㄩㄢˇ ㄕˋ ㄧㄢˇ ㄐㄧㄥˋ)
spectacles for long sight
遠射(ㄩㄢˇ ㄕㄜˋ)
① to fire over a long range ②(ball games) a long shot
遠涉重洋(ㄩㄢˇ ㄕㄜˋ ㄔㄨㄥˊ ㄧㄤˊ)
to cross many seas—to go abroad
遠山近水(ㄩㄢˇ ㄕㄢ ㄐㄧㄣˋ ㄕㄨㄟˇ)
(literally) the faraway mountains and the nearby waters—beautiful scenery
遠水不救近火(ㄩㄢˇ ㄕㄨㄟˇ ㄅㄨˋ ㄐㄧㄡˋ ㄐㄧㄣˋ ㄏㄨㄛˇ)
Water from afar cannot quench a nearby fire. 或 Distant water cannot quench a fire nearby.
遠日點(ㄩㄢˇ ㄖˋ ㄉㄧㄢˇ)
(astronomy) aphelion
遠走高飛(ㄩㄢˇ ㄗㄡˇ ㄍㄠ ㄈㄟ)
to go (or flee) far away
遠足(ㄩㄢˇ ㄗㄨˊ)
an excursion; an outing: 我們全班到日月潭去遠足。Our class went on an excursion to the Sun Moon Lake.
遠族(ㄩㄢˇ ㄗㄨˊ)
a remote clan; one's distant relatives
遠祖(ㄩㄢˇ ㄗㄨˇ)
one's distant ancestors
遠裔(ㄩㄢˇ ㄧˋ)
distant descendants 亦作「遠胄」
遠遊(ㄩㄢˇ ㄧㄡˊ)
to travel far away
遠因(ㄩㄢˇ ㄧㄣ)
remote causes (of a war, etc.)
遠揚(ㄩㄢˇ ㄧㄤˊ)
(said of fame) to be known far and wide
遠颺(ㄩㄢˇ ㄧㄤˊ)
to escape or flee far away
遠洋(ㄩㄢˇ ㄧㄤˊ)
① an ocean ② of the open sea beyond the littoral zone; oceanic
遠洋航行(ㄩㄢˇ ㄧㄤˊ ㄏㄤˊ ㄒㄧㄥˊ)
an oceangoing voyage
遠洋貨輪(ㄩㄢˇ ㄧㄤˊ ㄏㄨㄛˋ ㄌㄨㄣˊ)
an oceangoing freighter
遠洋漁業(ㄩㄢˇ ㄧㄤˊ ㄩˊ ㄧㄝˋ)
deep-sea fishery; pelagic fishery
遠味(ㄩㄢˇ ㄨㄟˋ)
rare and delicious foods from distant places
遠遠兒的(ㄩㄢˇ ㄩㄚˇㄦ ˙ㄉㄜ)
from afar; a great distance away

【遠】 6138
2. ㄩㄢˋ yuann yuàn
to keep at a distance; to keep away from; to avoid; to shun
遠庖廚(ㄩㄢˋ ㄆㄠˊ ㄔㄨˊ)
to keep away from the kitchen (said of gentlemen)
遠小人(ㄩㄢˋ ㄒㄧㄠˇ ㄖㄣˊ)
to keep away from mean persons

【遡】 6139
(溯) ㄙㄨˋ suh sù
1. to trace back to a source
2. to go against a stream
遡游(ㄙㄨˋ ㄧㄡˊ)
to go down the stream; to go downstream亦作「溯游」or「泝游」

【遢】 6140
ㄊㄚˋ tah tà
untidy; slipshod; careless or negligent

【遣】 6141
ㄑㄧㄢˇ chean qiǎn
1. to dispatch; to send: 誰遣你到我這裏來的? Who sent you to me?
2. to kill (time); to forget (one's sorrow); to divert
3. to banish; to drive away
4. to release
遣悶(ㄑㄧㄢˇ ㄇㄣˋ)
to drive away melancholy; to kill time
遣返(ㄑㄧㄢˇ ㄈㄢˇ)
to send back; to send home; to deport; to repatriate; repatriation
遣歸(ㄑㄧㄢˇ ㄍㄨㄟ)
to send (a prisoner) home; to repatriate
遣懷(ㄑㄧㄢˇ ㄏㄨㄞˊ)
to dispel one's sorrow in

〔辵部〕

writing on the spur of the moment
遣价(ㄑㄧㄢˇ ㄐㄧㄝˋ)
to send a servant on an errand
遣將(ㄑㄧㄢˇ ㄐㄧㄤˋ)
to send generals or officers (to a battle, etc.)
遣刑(ㄑㄧㄢˇ ㄒㄧㄥˊ)
banishment or exile (as a form of punishment in the Ching Dynasty)
遣興(ㄑㄧㄢˇ ㄒㄧㄥˋ)
to dispel one's sad thoughts in writing on the spur of the moment 參看「遣懷」
遣使(ㄑㄧㄢˇ ㄕˇ)
to dispatch or send an envoy
遣戍(ㄑㄧㄢˇ ㄕㄨˋ)
to exile or banish prisoners to the frontier
遣詞造句(ㄑㄧㄢˇ ㄘˊ ㄗㄠˋ ㄐㄩˋ)
the choice of words and building of sentences
遣散(ㄑㄧㄢˇ ㄙㄢˋ)
to disband; to dissolve and send away; to lay off (employees)
遣散費(ㄑㄧㄢˇ ㄙㄢˋ ㄈㄟˋ)
severance pay
遣送(ㄑㄧㄢˇ ㄙㄨㄥˋ)
to send away; to deport
遣憂(ㄑㄧㄢˇ ㄧㄡ)
to dispel sadness

十一畫

【遭】 6142 ㄗㄠ tzau zāo
1. to meet with; to incur; to be victimized; to suffer: 他遭了幾次挫折。He met with several setbacks.
2. times of binding or turning around, as with a rope
3. a time; a turn
遭變(ㄗㄠ ㄅㄧㄢˋ)
to have an accident; to be hit by a great misfortune
遭逢(ㄗㄠ ㄈㄥˊ)
① to meet with: 他的家道遭逢不幸。His family met with misfortune. ② vicissitudes in one's life
遭到(ㄗㄠ ㄉㄠˋ)
to suffer; to meet with; to encounter
遭難(ㄗㄠ ㄋㄢˋ)
to meet with difficulty, misfortune, or death
遭害(ㄗㄠ ㄏㄞˋ)
to be murdered or assassinated
遭際(ㄗㄠ ㄐㄧˋ)
one's lot in life; what one has experienced in life
遭家不造(ㄗㄠ ㄐㄧㄚ ㄅㄨˋ ㄗㄠˋ)
to be bereaved of a parent or parents
遭刼(ㄗㄠ ㄐㄧㄝˊ)
to meet with disaster
遭受(ㄗㄠ ㄕㄡˋ)
to incur (losses, etc.); to be subjected to: 無禮的行爲使自己遭受同樣的對待。Rudeness subjects one to retorts in kind.
遭災(ㄗㄠ ㄗㄞ)
to encounter disaster
遭殃(ㄗㄠ ㄧㄤ)
to meet with misfortune or disaster
遭瘟(ㄗㄠ ㄨㄣ)
to meet with disaster, calamity or misfortune
遭遇(ㄗㄠ ㄩˋ)
① to meet with; to encounter: 游擊隊與敵人遭遇了。The guerilla encountered the enemy. ② vicissitudes in one's life; what one has encountered in life
遭遇戰(ㄗㄠ ㄩˋ ㄓㄢˋ)
an encounter (between opposing military forces)

【遨】 6143 ㄠˊ aur áo
to travel for pleasure; to ramble
遨嬉(ㄠˊ ㄒㄧ)
to ramble; to travel for pleasure; to make merry
遨遊(ㄠˊ ㄧㄡˊ)
to ramble; to travel: 他總是夢想遨遊太空。He always dreams of traveling through space.

【適】 6144 1. ㄕˋ shyh shì
1. to go; to arrive at; to reach
2. just right; exactly; appropriate; fit; just
3. comfortable; at ease with oneself: 我感到不適。I didn't feel comfortable.
4. (said of a girl) to marry
5. to follow; to be faithful to: 我無所適從。I don't know what course to follow.
6. only
7. by chance; accidentally
8. just now
適逢其會(ㄕˋ ㄈㄥˊ ㄑㄧˊ ㄏㄨㄟˋ)
to happen to be present at the right moment
適得其反(ㄕˋ ㄉㄜˊ ㄑㄧˊ ㄈㄢˇ)
to get exactly the opposite
適當(ㄕˋ ㄉㄤˋ)
proper; appropriate; fit: 夜晚是睡眠的適當時間。Night is the proper time to sleep.
適度(ㄕˋ ㄉㄨˋ)
appropriate; within limits; to a moderate degree: 適度的運動將有益健康。A moderate amount of physical exercise will benefit one's health.
適度人口(ㄕˋ ㄉㄨˋ ㄖㄣˊ ㄎㄡˇ)
optimal population
適來(ㄕˋ ㄌㄞˊ)
just now
適齡(ㄕˋ ㄌㄧㄥˊ)
suitable or right age; the required age (for schooling, military service, etc.)
適可而止(ㄕˋ ㄎㄜˇ ㄦˊ ㄓˇ)
to stop at the right moment or point; to exercise moderation or restraint
適口(ㄕˋ ㄎㄡˇ)
pleasant to the palate; tasty
適合(ㄕˋ ㄏㄜˊ)
suitable or suitable for; to fit; to suit
適値(ㄕˋ ㄓˊ)
to happen exactly when; coincidentally; to happen by coincidence
適者生存(ㄕˋ ㄓㄜˇ ㄕㄥ ㄘㄨㄣˊ)
the survival of the fittest
適中(ㄕˋ ㄓㄨㄥ)
proper; adequate; appropriate; propriety; just right
適時(ㄕˋ ㄕˊ)
at the right time; in the nick of time
適然(ㄕˋ ㄖㄢˊ)
① accidentally; by chance ② a matter of course
適人(ㄕˋ ㄖㄣˊ)

(said of a woman) to marry
適纔(ㄕˋ ㄘㄞˊ)
just now
適從(ㄕˋ ㄘㄨㄥˊ)
to follow; to head in a direction
適宜(ㄕˋ ㄧˊ)
fit; suitable; proper
適意(ㄕˋ ㄧˋ)
comfortable; agreeable; as desired
適有(ㄕˋ ㄧㄡˇ)
there happened to be; it just happened that; coincidentally; to happen by coincidence
適因(ㄕˋ ㄧㄣ)
because just now
適應(ㄕˋ ㄧㄥˋ)
to adapt; adaptation (to environment, etc.); to adjust; to make an adjustment: 你能適應新的工作嗎? Can you adapt yourself to a new job?
適應環境(ㄕˋ ㄧㄥˋ ㄏㄨㄢˊ ㄐㄧㄥˋ)
adaptation to environment; to adapt to circumstances
適應性(ㄕˋ ㄧㄥˋ ㄒㄧㄥˋ)
adaptability
適於(ㄕˋ ㄩˊ)
suitable for; fitting for
適用(ㄕˋ ㄩㄥˋ)
fit or suitable for use; (said of a law, rule, etc.) to apply; applicable

【適】 6144
2. (嫡)ㄉㄧˊ dyi dí
legal (wife, as opposed to concubines, etc.); sons born of one's legal wife

【遮】 6145
ㄓㄜ je zhē
1. to hide; to cover; to screen; to shade; to shield; to conceal; to shut out: 雪遮蓋着大地。Snow covered the ground.
2. to intercept; to block
遮蔽(ㄓㄜ ㄅㄧˋ)
to cover; to screen
遮蔽物(ㄓㄜ ㄅㄧˋ ㄨˋ)
a cover; a shelter
遮不了(ㄓㄜ ·ㄅㄨ ㄌㄧㄠˇ)
cannot be covered or concealed
遮不住(ㄓㄜ ·ㄅㄨ ㄓㄨˋ)
unable to cover up; cannot be concealed
遮瞞(ㄓㄜ ㄇㄢˊ)
to hide the truth; to lie in order to conceal the truth
遮面(ㄓㄜ ㄇㄧㄢˋ)
to cover the face
遮風(ㄓㄜ ㄈㄥ)
to shield from wind
遮擋(ㄓㄜ ㄉㄤˇ)
to fend
遮斷(ㄓㄜ ㄉㄨㄢˋ)
to block from view; to block off; to obstruct
遮頭蓋面(ㄓㄜ ㄊㄡˊ ㄍㄞˋ ㄇㄧㄢˋ)
(literally) to cover one's head and face—to act stealthily; to be bashful
遮攔(ㄓㄜ ㄌㄢˊ)
to fend off; to cover or screen
遮蓋(ㄓㄜ ㄍㄞˋ)
to cover; to cover up: 你的謊言遮蓋不住事實的。Your lie cannot cover up the fact.
遮光(ㄓㄜ ㄍㄨㄤ)
to block light
遮擊(ㄓㄜ ㄐㄧˊ)
to intercept; to ambush
遮架(ㄓㄜ ㄐㄧㄚˋ)
to defend; to fend off
遮截(ㄓㄜ ㄐㄧㄝˊ)
to stop; to block; to shut off
遮羞(ㄓㄜ ㄒㄧㄡ)
to hush up a scandal; to cover up one's embarrassment
遮羞費(ㄓㄜ ㄒㄧㄡ ㄈㄟˋ)
a compensation paid by a man to a woman or her family for violating her chastity with or without her consent
遮羞臉(ㄓㄜ ㄒㄧㄡ ㄌㄧㄢˇ)
(a polite expression in sending a gift) a token of one's gratitude
遮住(ㄓㄜ ·ㄓㄨ)
to cover; to block; to obstruct
遮醜(ㄓㄜ ㄔㄡˇ)
① to hide one's shame ② 亦作「遮羞臉」
遮掩(ㄓㄜ ㄧㄢˇ)
① to hide; to cover up; to conceal: 不要遮掩你的錯誤。Don't try to cover your mistakes up. ② to cover; to envelop: 太陽被雲遮掩着。The sun was enveloped in clouds.
遮蔭(ㄓㄜ ㄧㄣˋ)
to shade
遮陽(ㄓㄜ ㄧㄤˊ)
to protect from the sunlight
遮陽傘(ㄓㄜ ㄧㄤˊ ㄙㄢˇ)
a parasol

【遯】 6146
ㄉㄨㄣˋ duenn dùn
1. to escape; to run off
2. to cheat
遯世(ㄉㄨㄣˋ ㄕˋ)
to escape from the world—to retire

十二畫

【遲】 6147
1. ㄔˊ chyr chí
1. late: 現在去太遲了。It's too late to go now.
2. slow; dilatory; tardy
3. to delay
4. (said of a person) dull; stupid
5. a Chinese family name
遲暮(ㄔˊ ㄇㄨˋ)
① to be advanced in years ② slowly and unhurriedly
遲到(ㄔˊ ㄉㄠˋ)
to come or arrive late; to be late: 他去年上學遲到四次。He was late for school four times last year.
遲鈍(ㄔˊ ㄉㄨㄣˋ)
①stupid ②awkward; clumsy; ponderous; slow (in thought or action): 他反應遲鈍。He is slow in reacting.
遲留(ㄔˊ ㄌㄧㄡˊ)
to linger on; to stay
遲緩(ㄔˊ ㄏㄨㄢˇ) or 遲慢(ㄔˊ ㄇㄢˋ)
slow; tardy; tardiness
遲滯(ㄔˊ ㄓˋ)
① slow; dilatory; sluggish ② late; behindhand
遲遲不進(ㄔˊ ㄔˊ ㄅㄨˋ ㄐㄧㄣˋ)
to hesitate; to be reluctant to advance; to hesitate to push forward
遲早(ㄔˊ ㄗㄠˇ)
sooner or later: 你遲早會後悔。You will repent it sooner or later.
遲疑(ㄔˊ ㄧˊ)
to hesitate; hesitancy
遲疑不決(ㄔˊ ㄧˊ ㄅㄨˋ ㄐㄩㄝˊ)

〔辵部〕

cannot make up one's mind; to hesitate to make a decision; to be irresolute: 我對於接受那職位遲疑不決。I hesitated about taking the position.

〔辵部〕

遲延(ㄔ ㄧㄢˊ)
to delay; to procrastinate; delay

遲誤(ㄔ ㄨˋ)
to spoil a matter because of procrastination: 此事不得遲誤。This matter admitted of no procrastination.

【遲】 6147
2. ㄓˋ jyh zhì
to wait

遲明(ㄓˋ ㄇㄧㄥˊ)
dawn; daybreak 亦作「遲旦」

【遴】 6148
ㄌㄧㄣˊ lin lín
to choose or select carefully

遴派(ㄌㄧㄣˊ ㄆㄞˋ)
to dispatch or appoint a person after careful selection

遴集(ㄌㄧㄣˊ ㄐㄧˊ)
to gather together; to flock together

遴選(ㄌㄧㄣˊ ㄒㄩㄢˇ)or 遴柬(ㄌㄧㄣˊ ㄐㄧㄢˇ)
to choose or pick (a person); to select

【遵】 6149
ㄗㄨㄣ tzuen zūn
1. to follow: 病人遵醫囑。The patients follow the doctor's advice.
2 to observe (rules, regulations, etc.); to abide by (laws, etc.): 士兵們遵紀愛民。Soldiers observed discipline and cherished the people.

遵辦(ㄗㄨㄣ ㄅㄢˋ)or 遵照辦理(ㄗㄨㄣ ㄓㄠˋ ㄅㄢˋ ㄌㄧˇ)
to execute or manage according to instructions

遵命(ㄗㄨㄣ ㄇㄧㄥˋ)or 遵令(ㄗㄨㄣ ㄌㄧㄥˋ)
to obey orders; to observe instructions

遵奉(ㄗㄨㄣ ㄈㄥˋ)
to observe; to obey

遵行(ㄗㄨㄣ ㄒㄧㄥˊ)
to act in accordance with (a principle, etc.); to put into practice (an idea, or a principle)

遵循(ㄗㄨㄣ ㄒㄩㄣˊ)
① to follow; to accord with; to obey; to go by ② to hesitate 亦作「逡巡」

遵旨(ㄗㄨㄣ ㄓˇ)
to follow imperial orders or decrees

遵照(ㄗㄨㄣ ㄓㄠˋ)
to follow; to observe; to accord with; to obey

遵守(ㄗㄨㄣ ㄕㄡˇ)
to observe; to abide by; to keep (a promise): 人人遵守公共秩序。Every one observes public order.

遵從(ㄗㄨㄣ ㄘㄨㄥˊ)
to follow; to comply with; to obey (orders, etc.): 學生遵從老師的教導。Students follow the teacher's advice.

遵依(ㄗㄨㄣ ㄧ)
to follow; to comply with

遵義(ㄗㄨㄣ ㄧˋ)
① to guard or stand up for righteousness or justice ② name of a county in Kweichow Province

遵養時晦(ㄗㄨㄣ ㄧㄤˇ ㄕˊ ㄏㄨㄟˋ)or 遵時養晦(ㄗㄨㄣ ㄕˊ ㄧㄤˇ ㄏㄨㄟˋ)
to live in retirement and wait for the right time for a comeback in public life

【遶】 6150
ㄖㄠˋ raw rào
to surround

【遷】 6151
ㄑㄧㄢ chian qiān
1. to move; to remove: 他家遷往他處。His family moved to another place.
2. to change: 這件事情已經事過境遷。This matter is all over, and the situation has changed.
3. (said of officials, etc.) to get transferred
4. to be banished

遷地爲良(ㄑㄧㄢ ㄉㄧˋ ㄨㄟˊ ㄌㄧㄤˊ)
It's better to move to another place. 或A change of place is advisable.

遷調(ㄑㄧㄢ ㄉㄧㄠˋ)
to get transferred to another post

遷都(ㄑㄧㄢ ㄉㄨ)
to move the national capital

遷怒(ㄑㄧㄢ ㄋㄨˋ)
① to blame a person for one's own blunder, failure, etc. ② to shift or transfer one's anger from one person to another; to vent one's anger on (someone else): 他遷怒於他的孩子。He vented his anger on his child who was not to blame.

遷客(ㄑㄧㄢ ㄎㄜˋ)
an official banished to a minor post

遷換(ㄑㄧㄢ ㄏㄨㄢˋ)
to change

遷就(ㄑㄧㄢ ㄐㄧㄡˋ)
to compromise; to meet halfway; to accommodate: 他不能遷就於環境。He cannot accommodate himself to the circumstances.

遷居(ㄑㄧㄢ ㄐㄩ)
to move into a new residence or to a new address: 他遷居到另一個城市去了。He moved to another town.

遷徙(ㄑㄧㄢ ㄒㄧˇ)
to move; to remove: 他們遷徙鄉下。They moved to the country.

遷徙流離(ㄑㄧㄢ ㄒㄧˇ ㄌㄧㄡˊ ㄌㄧˊ)
(said of refugees) homeless and wandering from place to place

遷謫(ㄑㄧㄢ ㄓㄜˊ)
to be demoted and banished to distant places; banishment

遷善(ㄑㄧㄢ ㄕㄢˋ)
to reform one's ways

遷善改過(ㄑㄧㄢ ㄕㄢˋ ㄍㄞˇ ㄍㄨㄛˋ)
to change one's evil ways and reform

遷染(ㄑㄧㄢ ㄖㄢˇ)
to be corrupted by evil surroundings

遷移(ㄑㄧㄢ ㄧˊ)
to move (to a new address): 許多農民從農村遷移到城市。Many farmers moved from rural areas to urban areas.

遷移推理(ㄑㄧㄢ ㄧˊ ㄊㄨㄟ ㄌㄧˇ)
transferential inference

遷延(ㄑㄧㄢ ㄧㄢˊ)
to procrastinate; to delay: 他把宴會遷延一個星期。He delayed the party for a week.

【選】 6152
ㄒㄩㄢˇ sheuan xuǎn
1. to select; to choose; choice: 慎選你的朋友。Choose your friend carefully.
2. to elect; elections
選拔(ㄒㄩㄢˇ ㄅㄚˊ)
to select; to pick the better ones from a group of people
選拔賽(ㄒㄩㄢˇ ㄅㄚˊ ㄙㄞˋ)
a selective trial; a tryout (for athletes, etc.)
選派(ㄒㄩㄢˇ ㄆㄞˋ)
to nominate; to designate
選票(ㄒㄩㄢˇ ㄆㄧㄠˋ)or 選舉票(ㄒㄩㄢˇ ㄐㄩˇ ㄆㄧㄠˋ)
a ballot
選美(ㄒㄩㄢˇ ㄇㄟˇ)
a beauty contest: 他姐姐參加選美。His sister took part in a beauty contest.
選美大會(ㄒㄩㄢˇ ㄇㄟˇ ㄉㄚˋ ㄏㄨㄟˋ)
a beauty pageant
選民(ㄒㄩㄢˇ ㄇㄧㄣˊ)
the eligible voters among the citizenry; constituency
選定(ㄒㄩㄢˇ ㄉㄧㄥˋ)
to decide on a selection
選讀(ㄒㄩㄢˇ ㄉㄨˊ)
① to take an elective course in a college ② selected readings: 文學選讀 selected readings in literature
選體(ㄒㄩㄢˇ ㄊㄧˇ)
the style of poems and prose, included in the literary collection 昭明文選
選購(ㄒㄩㄢˇ ㄍㄡˋ)
to select and make purchase
選科(ㄒㄩㄢˇ ㄎㄜ)or 選修科(ㄒㄩㄢˇ ㄒㄧㄡ ㄎㄜ)
an elective course (as distinct from a required course)
選課(ㄒㄩㄢˇ ㄎㄜˋ)
to take courses in a college
選課表(ㄒㄩㄢˇ ㄎㄜˋ ㄅㄧㄠˇ)
a table of elective courses for the reference of college students
選礦(ㄒㄩㄢˇ ㄎㄨㄤˋ)
to separate the usable and unusable components of mineral ore by mechanical means
選集(ㄒㄩㄢˇ ㄐㄧˊ)
a collection of literary works
選家(ㄒㄩㄢˇ ㄐㄧㄚ)
a collector of "eight-legged" compositions for the reference of participants in the civil service examination in former times
選舉(ㄒㄩㄢˇ ㄐㄩˇ)
to elect; to vote; elections: 人民選他當總統。The people elected him President.
選舉法(ㄒㄩㄢˇ ㄐㄩˇ ㄈㄚˇ)
laws governing elections
選舉區(ㄒㄩㄢˇ ㄐㄩˇ ㄑㄩ)or 選區(ㄒㄩㄢˇ ㄑㄩ)
an electoral district; a constituency
選舉權(ㄒㄩㄢˇ ㄐㄩˇ ㄑㄩㄢˊ)
the right to vote; the elective franchise; suffrage: 他有選舉權。He has the right to vote.
選舉人(ㄒㄩㄢˇ ㄐㄩˇ ㄖㄣˊ)
a voter
選舉訴訟(ㄒㄩㄢˇ ㄐㄩˇ ㄙㄨˋ ㄙㄨㄥˋ)
lawsuits pertaining to election
選曲(ㄒㄩㄢˇ ㄑㄩˇ)
selected songs (or tunes)
選取(ㄒㄩㄢˇ ㄑㄩˇ)
to select; to choose
選修(ㄒㄩㄢˇ ㄒㄧㄡ)
to take as an elective course
選賢舉能(ㄒㄩㄢˇ ㄒㄧㄢˊ ㄐㄩˇ ㄋㄥˊ)or 選賢與能(ㄒㄩㄢˇ ㄒㄧㄢˊ ㄩˇ ㄋㄥˊ)
to pick the good and select the capable for public posts
選學(ㄒㄩㄢˇ ㄒㄩㄝˊ)
the critical study of 昭明文選
選種(ㄒㄩㄢˇ ㄓㄨㄥˇ)
seed selection
選中(ㄒㄩㄢˇ ㄓㄨㄥˋ)
① to pick out (a man) by choice or competitive examinations ② to be selected in such examinations
選出(ㄒㄩㄢˇ ㄔㄨ)
to pick out; to select; to elect
選侍(ㄒㄩㄢˇ ㄕˋ)
to select girls as maids in the imperial palace
選手(ㄒㄩㄢˇ ㄕㄡˇ)
a member of a sports team or delegation representing a school, an area or a country; a contestant
選任(ㄒㄩㄢˇ ㄖㄣˋ)
to appoint; to designate
選擇(ㄒㄩㄢˇ ㄗㄜˊ)
a choice; to choose: 我沒有選擇的餘地。I have no choice at all.
選擇題(ㄒㄩㄢˇ ㄗㄜˊ ㄊㄧˊ)
a multiple-choice question
選材(ㄒㄩㄢˇ ㄘㄞˊ)
to select the right material(s)
選樣(ㄒㄩㄢˇ ㄧㄤˋ)
sampling; a sample
選用(ㄒㄩㄢˇ ㄩㄥˋ)
to select and appoint to a post

【遹】 6153
ㄩˋ yuh yù
1. to follow; to comply with
2. to avoid; to shun
3. to be perverse; to be bad
4. a Chinese family name

【遺】 6154
1. ㄧˊ yi yí
1. to lose; lost
2. things lost: 路不拾遺。People do not pick up what others have left on the roadside.
3. to miss; an omission due to negligence
4. to forget: 我遺忘了我的帽子。I've forgotten my hat.
5. to leave over
6. remnants; leftovers
7. to abandon; to desert
8. anything left behind by the deceased; to bequeath; to hand down; a legacy
9. to urinate
10. short for nocturnal emission
遺筆(ㄧˊ ㄅㄧˇ)
writings of a deceased person
遺墨(ㄧˊ ㄇㄛˋ)
the calligraphy or paintings by a dead person
遺民(ㄧˊ ㄇㄧㄣˊ)
① people who refuse to take official jobs in a new dynasty ② descendants
遺命(ㄧˊ ㄇㄧㄥˋ)
the injunctions of a dead person
遺風(ㄧˊ ㄈㄥ)

〔辵部〕

a custom left by a preceding generation or dynasty: 昔日榮華之遺風消失了。The remains of the former glory disappeared.

遺腹子(ㄧˊ ㄈㄨˋ ㄗˇ)
an infant born after the death of its father; a posthumous child

遺大投艱(ㄧˊ ㄉㄚˋ ㄊㄡˊ ㄐㄧㄢ)
to shoulder a heavy and difficult responsibility

遺毒(ㄧˊ ㄉㄨˊ)
the evil influence or poison of some old theory, practice, etc.

遺體(ㄧˊ ㄊㄧˇ)
① the remains (of a deceased person); the corpse: 他的遺體被埋於此。His remains are buried here. ② one's body (handed down by one's parents)

遺尿(ㄧˊ ㄋㄧㄠˋ)
bed-wetting; the incontinence of urine

遺念(ㄧˊ ㄋㄧㄢˋ)
souvenirs or things left by a dead person; a legacy

遺老(ㄧˊ ㄌㄠˇ)
① ministers of the preceding emperor (father of the current emperor) ② ministers of the preceding dynasty ③ old, experienced men in the country

遺漏(ㄧˊ ㄌㄡˋ)
to omit or miss; an omission; an oversight: 我遺漏了一個字。I left out a word.

遺烈(ㄧˊ ㄌㄧㄝˋ)
the achievements of forefathers

遺留(ㄧˊ ㄌㄧㄡˊ)
to leave behind either intentionally or unintentionally: 他遺留下五千鎊。He left £5,000.

遺落(ㄧˊ ㄌㄨㄛˋ)
① to lose; lost: 我遺落了房門的鑰匙。I've lost the key of the house. ② carefree; indifferent to what's happening around

遺稿(ㄧˊ ㄍㄠˇ)
manuscripts or writings left behind by a dead person

遺孤(ㄧˊ ㄍㄨ)
orphans

遺骸(ㄧˊ ㄏㄞˊ)
one's remains; one's corpse

遺憾(ㄧˊ ㄏㄢˋ)
to regret; to feel sorry; regrettable: 我很遺憾不能幫助你。I regret that I cannot help you.

遺恨(ㄧˊ ㄏㄣˋ)
to regret; regret; to feel sorry; regrettable

遺跡(ㄧˊ ㄐㄧ)
relics; vestiges; traces: 那裡是古城的遺跡。There are vestiges of ancient cities.

遺計(ㄧˊ ㄐㄧˋ)
a mistake; a loophole; a drawback

遺教(ㄧˊ ㄐㄧㄠˋ)
① exhortation of a dying person ② teachings of a dead person

遺精(ㄧˊ ㄐㄧㄥ)
nocturnal emission; spermatorrhea

遺棄(ㄧˊ ㄑㄧˋ)
①(law) to desert, or to fail to support one's legal dependents: 他遺棄他的妻子。He deserted his wife. ② to cast away; to abandon: 我永遠不會遺棄我的朋友。I would never abandon my friends.

遺棄罪(ㄧˊ ㄑㄧˋ ㄗㄨㄟˋ)
the offense of abandonment

遺下(ㄧˊ ㄒㄧㄚˋ)
to leave behind: 他遺下一妻六子。He left a wife and six children.

遺像(ㄧˊ ㄒㄧㄤˋ)
the portrait of a dead person

遺訓(ㄧˊ ㄒㄩㄣˋ)
instructions or teachings of a dead person

遺職(ㄧˊ ㄓˊ)
① a vacated position ② a position made vacant by the departure or death of the original holder

遺址(ㄧˊ ㄓˇ)
the old site of some building or a city which no longer exists

遺志(ㄧˊ ㄓˋ)
the ideal or wish not carried out before one's death; the behest of a dying person

遺詔(ㄧˊ ㄓㄠˋ)
instructions or decrees of a dying emperor

遺珠(ㄧˊ ㄓㄨ)
a talented person out of employment

遺囑(ㄧˊ ㄓㄨˇ)
① the will of a dead person ② instructions of a dying person

遺囑執行人(ㄧˊ ㄓㄨˇ ㄓˊ ㄒㄧㄥˊ ㄖㄣˊ)
an executor

遺囑人(ㄧˊ ㄓㄨˇ ㄖㄣˊ)
a testator

遺著(ㄧˊ ㄓㄨˋ)
a posthumous book

遺臭萬年(ㄧˊ ㄔㄡˋ ㄨㄢˋ ㄋㄧㄢˊ)
(literally) The stench will persist for 10,000 years.—a bad reputation that will be long remembered

遺產(ㄧˊ ㄔㄢˇ)
① property left behind by a deceased person ② a bequest; a legacy

遺產稅(ㄧˊ ㄔㄢˇ ㄕㄨㄟˋ)
legacy tax; inheritance tax

遺臣(ㄧˊ ㄔㄣˊ)
surviving officials of a previous dynasty

遺傳(ㄧˊ ㄔㄨㄢˊ)
to inherit; hereditary; heredity

遺傳病(ㄧˊ ㄔㄨㄢˊ ㄅㄧㄥˋ)
a hereditary disease

遺傳論(ㄧˊ ㄔㄨㄢˊ ㄌㄨㄣˋ)
hereditism

遺傳性(ㄧˊ ㄔㄨㄢˊ ㄒㄧㄥˋ)
heredity; hereditary

遺傳學(ㄧˊ ㄔㄨㄢˊ ㄒㄩㄝˊ)
genetics

遺失(ㄧˊ ㄕ)
to lose; lost: 我的汽車鑰匙遺失了。I have lost the keys of my car.

遺失啓事(ㄧˊ ㄕ ㄑㄧˇ ㄕˋ)
a classified ad announcing the annulment of a lost seal, ID card, check, etc.

遺失招領(ㄧˊ ㄕ ㄓㄠ ㄌㄧㄥˇ)
lost and found

遺失聲明(ㄧˊ ㄕ ㄕㄥ ㄇㄧㄥˊ)
a lost property notice

遺世獨立(ㄧˊ ㄕˋ ㄉㄨˊ ㄌㄧˋ)

to forget all about worldly affairs

遺少(ㄧˊ ㄕㄠˋ)
youths who stick to old customs; young conservatives

遺書(ㄧˊ ㄕㄨ)
①letters written by a suicide ②ancient books scattered or lost ③manuscripts published posthumously

遺孀(ㄧˊ ㄕㄨㄤ)
a widow

遺容(ㄧˊ ㄖㄨㄥˊ)
①the portrait of a dead person ②remains (of the deceased): 我們瞻仰市長的遺容。We paid our respects to the remains of the mayor.

遺澤(ㄧˊ ㄗㄜˊ)
the benevolence left behind by a dead person

遺贈(ㄧˊ ㄗㄥˋ)
a legacy; bequest; to bequeath

遺族(ㄧˊ ㄗㄨˊ)
survivors of a deceased person's family

遺策(ㄧˊ ㄘㄜˋ)
①a mistake; a wrong move ②a plan left behind by the dead

遺才(ㄧˊ ㄘㄞˊ)
talents who failed in the civil service examinations

遺俗(ㄧˊ ㄙㄨˊ)
an old custom; traditional practices: 這是唐朝的遺俗嗎? Is this the old custom of the Tang Dynasty?

遺愛(ㄧˊ ㄞˋ)
the love or benevolence left behind by a dead person

遺業(ㄧˊ ㄧㄝˋ)
the business or career left behind by one's ancestors

遺言(ㄧˊ ㄧㄢˊ)
instructions, words, etc. of a dying person; a will; (a person's) last words: 那老人死時未留遺言。That old man died without last words.

遺物(ㄧˊ ㄨˋ)
things left behind by a dead person; relics of the deceased; personal belongings of a dead person

遺忘(ㄧˊ ㄨㄤˋ)
to forget; to neglect: 我們不應遺忘了我們的責任。We should not be forgetful of our responsibilities.

【遺】 6154 2. ㄨㄟˋ wey wei

1. to send or present as a gift
2. to be left to; to be laid upon

遺書(ㄨㄟˋ ㄕㄨ)
to send a letter

【遼】 6155 ㄌㄧㄠˊ liau liáo

1. distant; far
2. the Liao River in Manchuria
3. the Liao Dynasty (916-1125) founded by the Kitan Tartars in the greater part of northern China

遼北(ㄌㄧㄠˊ ㄅㄟˇ)
①Liaopei, a province in Manchuria ②name of an ancient political division, the northern part of the old Liaoning Province in Northeast China

遼東半島(ㄌㄧㄠˊ ㄉㄨㄥ ㄅㄢˋ ㄉㄠˇ)
the Liaotung Peninsula

遼東灣(ㄌㄧㄠˊ ㄉㄨㄥ ㄨㄢ)
the Liaotung Bay

遼寧(ㄌㄧㄠˊ ㄋㄧㄥˊ)
Liaoning Province

遼遼(ㄌㄧㄠˊ ㄌㄧㄠˊ)
distant

遼落(ㄌㄧㄠˊ ㄌㄨㄛˋ)
open and spacious

遼隔(ㄌㄧㄠˊ ㄍㄜˊ)
distantly apart

遼闊 or 遼廓(ㄌㄧㄠˊ ㄎㄨㄛˋ)
vast; distant: 沙哈拉沙漠面積遼闊。The Sahara covers a vast area.

遼河(ㄌㄧㄠˊ ㄏㄜˊ)
the Liao River in Manchuria

十三畫

【避】 6156 ㄅㄧˋ bih bì

1. to avoid; to shun; to evade; to hide: 我們盡力避免危險。We try to avoid danger.
2. to prevent; to keep away; to repel

避不見面(ㄅㄧˋ ˙ㄅㄨ ㄐㄧㄢˋ ㄇㄧㄢˋ)
to avoid meeting someone

避不作答(ㄅㄧˋ ˙ㄅㄨ ㄗㄨㄛˋ ㄉㄚˊ)
to parry a question; to decline answering a question

避免(ㄅㄧˋ ㄇㄧㄢˇ)
to avoid; to forestall; to prevent something from happening; to avert

避面(ㄅㄧˋ ㄇㄧㄢˋ)
to avoid meeting a person

避風(ㄅㄧˋ ㄈㄥ)
①to lie low; to hide from trouble ②to seek shelter against a strong wind

避難(ㄅㄧˋ ㄋㄢˋ)
to escape a calamity; to avoid disaster; to take refuge

避難港(ㄅㄧˋ ㄋㄢˋ ㄍㄤˇ)
a harbor or port of refuge; a haven

避難所(ㄅㄧˋ ㄋㄢˋ ㄙㄨㄛˇ)
a refuge; a haven; a sanctuary

避匿(ㄅㄧˋ ㄋㄧˋ)
to lie in hiding; to hide or conceal

避瘧(ㄅㄧˋ ㄋㄩㄝˋ)
to escape from malaria by hiding oneself at someone else's home during the interval of recurrent fevers (a superstitious practice dating back to the Tang Dynasty)

避雷針(ㄅㄧˋ ㄌㄟˊ ㄓㄣ)
a needle gap arrester; a lightning arrester; a lightning rod 亦作「避雷器」

避亂(ㄅㄧˋ ㄌㄨㄢˋ)
to run away from social upheavals; to find shelter against anarchy

避開(ㄅㄧˋ ㄎㄞ)
to get out of the way; to keep away from; to dodge

避坑落井(ㄅㄧˋ ㄎㄥ ㄌㄨㄛˋ ㄐㄧㄥˇ)
(literally) to avoid the pit only to fall into the well —to succeed in escaping one disaster but to be caught in the next

避害(ㄅㄧˋ ㄏㄞˋ) or 避禍(ㄅㄧˋ ㄏㄨㄛˋ)
to run away from a calamity; to escape disaster

避寒(ㄅㄧˋ ㄏㄢˊ)
to go to a winter resort; to winter; to escape the cold: 他在南方避寒。He wintered in the south.

避諱(ㄅㄧˋ ㄏㄨㄟˋ)

①(an old Chinese custom) to avoid mentioning the emperor or one's ancestors by name or using any character of it in writing except the family name ②to evade

避秦(ㄅㄧˋ ㄑㄧㄣˊ)
(literally) to seek refuge from the tyranny of Chin—to find a shelter in time of unrest

避席(ㄅㄧˋ ㄒㄧˊ)
(in ancient times) to stand up from the floor mattress to show respect

避邪(ㄅㄧˋ ㄒㄧㄝˊ)
to avoid evil spirits or influences

避嫌(ㄅㄧˋ ㄒㄧㄢˊ)
to avoid suspicion

避賢讓路(ㄅㄧˋ ㄒㄧㄢˊ ㄖㄤˋ ㄌㄨˋ)
(literally) to make room for the virtuous—to resign from a public post

避債(ㄅㄧˋ ㄓㄞˋ)
to avoid creditors

避重就輕(ㄅㄧˋ ㄓㄨㄥˋ ㄐㄧㄡˋ ㄑㄧㄥ)
①to take the easier way out; to choose the easier of the two alternatives ② to dwell on the minor points but avoid touching the core of a matter

避世(ㄅㄧˋ ㄕˋ)
to retire or withdraw from worldly affairs—to live as a recluse

避暑(ㄅㄧˋ ㄕㄨˇ)
to run away from summer heat; to take a summer vacation

避暑勝地(ㄅㄧˋ ㄕㄨˇ ㄕㄥˋ ㄉㄧˋ)
a summer resort

避稅(ㄅㄧˋ ㄕㄨㄟˋ)
to evade a tax or duty

避妊(ㄅㄧˋ ㄖㄣˋ)or 避孕(ㄅㄧˋ ㄩㄣˋ)
contraception; to avoid pregnancy

避疫(ㄅㄧˋ ㄧˋ)
to escape from epidemics

避役(ㄅㄧˋ ㄧˋ)
a chameleon (a lizard-like reptile)

避雨(ㄅㄧˋ ㄩˇ)
to find shelter against rain: 我們在一個穀倉裡避雨。We found shelter against rain in a barn.

避孕套(ㄅㄧˋ ㄩㄣˋ ㄊㄠˋ)
a condom

避孕器(ㄅㄧˋ ㄩㄣˋ ㄑㄧˋ)
contraceptive devices

避孕藥(ㄅㄧˋ ㄩㄣˋ ㄧㄠˋ)
contraceptives

避孕藥丸(ㄅㄧˋ ㄩㄣˋ ㄧㄠˋ ㄨㄢˊ)
the pill

【遽】 6157 ㄐㄩˋ jiuh jù

1. suddenly; abruptly; hastily; hurriedly: 別遽下結論。Don't pass judgment hastily.
2. scared; frightened; agitated; agitation
3. a stagecoach

遽步(ㄐㄩˋ ㄅㄨˋ)
to walk hastily or hurriedly

遽返道山(ㄐㄩˋ ㄈㄢˇ ㄉㄠˋ ㄕㄢ)
to die suddenly or unexpectedly (an expression used in condolences)

遽然(ㄐㄩˋ ㄖㄢˊ)
suddenly: 那頭牛遽然地向他衝來。Suddenly the bull rushed at him.

遽色(ㄐㄩˋ ㄙㄜˋ)
a hurried look

遽爾(ㄐㄩˋ ㄦˇ)
suddenly; unexpectedly

【邀】 6158 ㄧㄠ iau yāo

1. to invite; to ask; to request
2. to intercept
3. (now rarely) to weigh or measure

邀買人心(ㄧㄠ ㄇㄞˇ ㄖㄣˊ ㄒㄧㄣ)
to dispense favors in order to win popularity

邀天之倖(ㄧㄠ ㄊㄧㄢ ㄓ ㄒㄧㄥˋ)
to be very lucky or fortunate

邀功(ㄧㄠ ㄍㄨㄥ)
to take credit for the deeds achieved by someone else

邀功圖賞(ㄧㄠ ㄍㄨㄥ ㄊㄨˊ ㄕㄤˇ)
to strive for achievements for the sake of a reward; to seek credit for something done

邀喝 or 吆喝(ㄧㄠ ˙ㄏㄜ)
to warn people to get out the way when a ranking official of former days was passing by

邀集(ㄧㄠ ㄐㄧˊ)
to invite to a gathering

邀擊(ㄧㄠ ㄐㄧˊ)
to intercept and attack; to waylay and attack

邀截(ㄧㄠ ㄐㄧㄝˊ)
to intercept (enemy troops)

邀請(ㄧㄠ ㄑㄧㄥˇ)
to invite; invitation

邀寵(ㄧㄠ ㄔㄨㄥˇ)
①to make oneself liked by a superior ②(said of concubines) to try to win the husband's love

邀遊(ㄧㄠ ㄧㄡˊ)
to invite someone for an outing

邀宴(ㄧㄠ ㄧㄢˋ)
①to invite to a feast ②an invitation to a luncheon or dinner party

邀約(ㄧㄠ ㄩㄝ)
①an engagement; an invitation ②to invite; to make an appointment or engagement

【邁】 6159 ㄇㄞˋ may mài

1. to surpass or exceed
2. to stride; to step: 他邁著大步在街上走。He strides along the street.
3. to go on a long journey
4. old (age)
5. to pass

邁步(ㄇㄞˋ ㄅㄨˋ)
to stride; to take a step; to make a step

邁方步(ㄇㄞˋ ㄈㄤ ㄅㄨˋ)
to walk slowly

邁達(ㄇㄞˋ ㄉㄚˊ)
open-minded

邁立開江(ㄇㄞˋ ㄌㄧˋ ㄎㄞ ㄐㄧㄤ)
the Malikha River in Sikang Province

邁過去(ㄇㄞˋ ㄍㄨㄛˋ ˙ㄑㄩ)
to pass over; to stride

邁跡(ㄇㄞˋ ㄐㄧ)
to follow the examples of ancient sages

邁進(ㄇㄞˋ ㄐㄧㄣˋ)
to forge ahead

邁向(ㄇㄞˋ ㄒㄧㄤˋ)
to march toward: 軍隊邁向柏林。The soldiers marched toward Berlin.

邁往(ㄇㄞˋ ㄨㄤˇ)
to forge ahead dauntlessly

【邂】 6160 ㄒㄧㄝˋ shieh xiè
to meet without a prior engagement; to meet by chance
邂逅(ㄒㄧㄝˋ ㄍㄡˋ)or(ㄒㄧㄝˋ ㄏㄡˋ)
to meet by chance; to meet accidentally; to meet (a relative, friend, etc.) unexpectedly: 我們邂逅相遇。We met by chance.

【還】 6161 1. ㄏㄨㄢˊ hwan huán
1. to return; to come back; return: 把那本書還給圖書館。Return that book to the library.
2. to repay; to pay back; to restore; to give back: 下星期你要還我錢。You'll pay me back next week.
3. a Chinese family name
還報(ㄏㄨㄢˊ ㄅㄠˋ)
to repay; to pay back; repayment
還本(ㄏㄨㄢˊ ㄅㄣˇ)
to pay the principal (as upon the maturity of bonds, loans, etc.)
還目(ㄏㄨㄢˊ ㄇㄨˋ)
afraid to look at someone straight in the face on account of fear or respect
還禮(ㄏㄨㄢˊ ㄌㄧˇ)
① to return a salute: 他沒有還禮。He didn't return my salute. ② to send a present in return
還口(ㄏㄨㄢˊ ㄎㄡˇ)
to retort; to talk back
還魂(ㄏㄨㄢˊ ㄏㄨㄣˊ)
to come to life again; to come round
還擊(ㄏㄨㄢˊ ㄐㄧˊ)
① to fight back; to return fire; to hit back; to counterattack: 我們向敵人還擊。We hit back at the enemy. ② (fencing) a riposte
還價(ㄏㄨㄢˊ ㄐㄧㄚˋ)
to haggle over a price
還錢(ㄏㄨㄢˊ ㄑㄧㄢˊ)
to return money; to pay back a debt
還清(ㄏㄨㄢˊ ㄑㄧㄥ)
to settle an account; all paid —as an account or debt: 他還清貸款。He paid off his loans.
還情(ㄏㄨㄢˊ ㄑㄧㄥˊ)
to repay a favor
還席(ㄏㄨㄢˊ ㄒㄧˊ)
① to return a dinner ② (comically) to vomit after heavy drinking at a feast
還鄉(ㄏㄨㄢˊ ㄒㄧㄤ)
to return to one's hometown: 我的還鄉使他們驚奇。My return to the hometown surprised them.
還債(ㄏㄨㄢˊ ㄓㄞˋ)
to repay a debt; to get out of debt: 負債容易還債難。It is easier to get into debt than to get out of it.
還賬(ㄏㄨㄢˊ ㄓㄤˋ)
to pay in order to settle an account; to pay a bill or debt
還政於民(ㄏㄨㄢˊ ㄓㄥˋ ㄩˊ ㄇㄧㄣˊ)
to return the power of government to the hands of the people; to return to parliamentary rule
還手(ㄏㄨㄢˊ ㄕㄡˇ)
to hit back; to strike back; to retaliate: 他打我，因此我還手打他。He hit me, so I struck back.
還嘴(ㄏㄨㄢˊ ㄗㄨㄟˇ)
to answer (or talk) back; to retort; to answer back in abuse or self-defense
還俗(ㄏㄨㄢˊ ㄙㄨˊ)
(said of a monk or nun) to return to the laity; to return to secular life: 那和尚還俗。That Buddhist monk returned to the laity.
還言(ㄏㄨㄢˊ ㄧㄢˊ)
to retort; to swear at someone in return: 他還言說:「那不關你的事。」"It's none of your business," he retorted.
還陽(ㄏㄨㄢˊ ㄧㄤˊ)
to return to life; to come back from death
還我河山(ㄏㄨㄢˊ ㄨㄛˇ ㄏㄜˊ ㄕㄢ)
(a slogan) Let's restore our lost land!
還味(ㄏㄨㄢˊ ㄨㄟˋ)
to ponder or muse over what someone has said
還原(ㄏㄨㄢˊ ㄩㄢˊ)
① to return to normal or original status ② (chemistry) reduction
還原劑(ㄏㄨㄢˊ ㄩㄢˊ ㄐㄧˋ)
(chemistry) a reducing agent
還原作用(ㄏㄨㄢˊ ㄩㄢˊ ㄗㄨㄛˋ ㄩㄥˋ)
a reducing process
還願(ㄏㄨㄢˊ ㄩㄢˋ)
to fulfill a vow—to thank a god or goddess for answering one's prayers

【還】 6161 2.(旋) ㄒㄩㄢˊ shyuan xuán
to revolve; to turn back
還踵 or 旋踵(ㄒㄩㄢˊ ㄓㄨㄥˇ)
(literally) a turn of the heels—a brief moment

【還】 6161 3. ㄏㄞˊ hair hái
1. yet; still: 他還沒有來。He has not come yet.
2. passably; fairly; quite
3. also
4. even
5. at the same time
6. or
7. had better: 還是你自己走一趟。You'd better go yourself.
還不夠(ㄏㄞˊ ˙ㄅㄨ ㄍㄡˋ)
not enough yet; still not enough
還不錯(ㄏㄞˊ ˙ㄅㄨ ㄘㄨㄛˋ)
not bad; passable; so-so
還多(ㄏㄞˊ ㄉㄨㄛ)
① still many or much left
② even more than...
還能(ㄏㄞˊ ㄋㄥˊ)
still able to
還冷(ㄏㄞˊ ㄌㄥˇ)
still cold
還好(ㄏㄞˊ ㄏㄠˇ)
① passable; so-so; not bad ② fortunately
還是(ㄏㄞˊ ㄕˋ)
① still; nevertheless: 你還是最好的。You are still the best. ② again ③ had better ④ or (showing doubt): 你去還是我去? Are you going or am I?
還熱(ㄏㄞˊ ㄖㄜˋ)
still hot
還在(ㄏㄞˊ ㄗㄞˋ)
① still here ② still (working, gambling, etc.)
還早(ㄏㄞˊ ㄗㄠˇ)

still early

還要(ㄏㄞˊ ㄧㄠˋ)
still want to...

還有(ㄏㄞˊ ㄧㄡˇ)
① There are still some left. ② furthermore; in addition

【邅】 6162 ㄓㄢ jan zhān
very difficult to proceed

十四畫

【邇】 6163 ㄦˇ eel ěr
1. lately; recently
2. near or close to

邇來(ㄦˇ ㄌㄞˊ)
lately; recently

【邃】 6164 ㄙㄨㄟˋ suey suì
1. deep; far
2. profound; depth (of learning); abyss (of one's mind)

邃密(ㄙㄨㄟˋ ㄇㄧˋ)
abstruse and full (as thought)

邃古(ㄙㄨㄟˋ ㄍㄨˇ)
the remote past; time immemorial

邃戶(ㄙㄨㄟˋ ㄏㄨˋ)
an abysmal entrance to a large, quiet house

邃宇(ㄙㄨㄟˋ ㄩˇ)
a large house that is labyrinthic and dark

【邈】 6165 ㄇㄧㄠˇ meau miǎo
1. distant; remote
2. same as 藐—to slight; to look down upon; to show a low opinion of

邈邈(ㄇㄧㄠˇ ㄇㄧㄠˇ)
distant; remote

邈視(ㄇㄧㄠˇ ㄕˋ)
to despise; to look down upon; to underestimate

邈然(ㄇㄧㄠˇ ㄖㄢˊ)
distant; remote

十五畫

【邊】 6166 ㄅㄧㄢ bian biān
1. an edge; the end of something; a verge; a margin
2. a side
3. a hem; a decorative border
4. the border of a nation's territory; a boundary
5. limits; bounds
6. nearby; near to
7. a Chinese family name

邊鄙(ㄅㄧㄢ ㄅㄧˇ)
places near the border; borderlands

邊…邊…(ㄅㄧㄢ…ㄅㄧㄢ…)
a speech pattern indicating two actions taking place simultaneously

邊旁(ㄅㄧㄢ ㄆㄤˊ)
① nearby; close by; adjacent to ② the radical on either side of a character

邊防(ㄅㄧㄢ ㄈㄤˊ)
border defense; frontier defense

邊幅(ㄅㄧㄢ ㄈㄨˊ)
① the appearance of a person; attire: 他不修邊幅。He was careless about his attire. ② the margin (of a piece of cloth, etc.)

邊地(ㄅㄧㄢ ㄉㄧˋ)
a borderland; a frontier

邊頭風(ㄅㄧㄢ ㄊㄡˊ ㄈㄥ)
(Chinese medicine) name of an ailment roughly similar to migraine, sometimes accompanied by a swelling on either side of the head

邊關(ㄅㄧㄢ ㄍㄨㄢ)
strategic positions on the border

邊框(ㄅㄧㄢ ㄎㄨㄤ)
a frame; a rim: 她戴沒邊框的眼鏡。She wore rimless glasses.

邊患(ㄅㄧㄢ ㄏㄨㄢˋ)
trouble along the national border or frontier, as caused by foreign invasion, etc.

邊際(ㄅㄧㄢ ㄐㄧˋ)
① a boundary ② (Buddhism) the extremity of things ③ the substance of one's speech or writing: 他說話不着邊際。He talked far off the substance.

邊際利潤(ㄅㄧㄢ ㄐㄧˋ ㄌㄧˋ ㄖㄨㄣˋ)
(accounting) marginal profit

邊際效用(ㄅㄧㄢ ㄐㄧˋ ㄒㄧㄠˋ ㄩㄥˋ)
(economics) marginal utility

邊際收入(ㄅㄧㄢ ㄐㄧˋ ㄕㄡ ㄖㄨˋ)
marginal revenue

邊界(ㄅㄧㄢ ㄐㄧㄝˋ)
the national boundary: 我們政府標定邊界。Our government demarcated boundaries.

邊疆(ㄅㄧㄢ ㄐㄧㄤ)
a borderland; a frontier: 我們支援邊疆建設。We supported the construction of the borderlands.

邊疆民族(ㄅㄧㄢ ㄐㄧㄤ ㄇㄧㄣˊ ㄗㄨˊ)
tribes living on the borderland (particularly referring to the Mongolians, Tibetans and other ethnic minorities on China's borders)

邊境(ㄅㄧㄢ ㄐㄧㄥˋ)
the national boundary or border; the frontier: 我們封鎖邊境。We closed the frontiers.

邊境貿易(ㄅㄧㄢ ㄐㄧㄥˋ ㄇㄠˋ ㄧˋ)
frontier trade

邊沁(ㄅㄧㄢ ㄑㄧㄣˋ)
Jeremy Bentham (1748-1832), British philosopher and political scientist

邊沁主義(ㄅㄧㄢ ㄑㄧㄣˋ ㄓㄨˇ ㄧˋ)
Benthamism, the utilitarian philosophy of Jeremy Bentham

邊區(ㄅㄧㄢ ㄑㄩ)
a border district; the frontier

邊政(ㄅㄧㄢ ㄓㄥˋ)
frontier administration: 他主修邊政學。He majored in frontier administration.

邊陲(ㄅㄧㄢ ㄔㄨㄟˊ)
a border; a borderland; a frontier

邊塞(ㄅㄧㄢ ㄙㄞˋ)
strategic positions along the border; a border pass; a frontier fortress

邊燧(ㄅㄧㄢ ㄙㄨㄟˋ)
fire and smoke signals made by frontier guards to warn the approach of invading forces

邊隘(ㄅㄧㄢ ㄞˋ)
strategic positions along the border

邊兒(ㄅㄧㄚㄦ)
① the hem of a dress; the brim ② the edge: 一古廟矗立在崖邊兒。An old temple stood on the edge of a preci-

pice.
邊沿(ㄅㄧㄢ ㄧㄢˊ)
the edge; the fringe: 不要太走近懸崖邊沿。Don't walk too near the edge of the cliff.
邊外(ㄅㄧㄢ ㄨㄞˋ)
outside the border defense line
邊緣(ㄅㄧㄢ ㄩㄢˊ)
the edge; the verge: 他瀕於餓死之邊緣。He is on the edge of starvation.
邊遠(ㄅㄧㄢ ㄩㄢˇ)
a remote frontier or borderland
邊遠地區(ㄅㄧㄢ ㄩㄢˇ ㄉㄧˋ ㄑㄩ)
an outlying district

十九畫

【邏】 6167
ㄌㄨㄛˊ luo luó
to patrol; to inspect: 警察正在街上巡邏。The policemen are patrolling the street.
邏輯(ㄌㄨㄛˊ ㄐㄧˊ)
logic: 他的辯論既有學問又合邏輯。He argues with learning and logic.
邏輯分析(ㄌㄨㄛˊ ㄐㄧˊ ㄈㄣ ㄒㄧ)
logical analysis
邏輯符號(ㄌㄨㄛˊ ㄐㄧˊ ㄈㄨˊ ㄏㄠˋ)
a logical symbol
邏輯學(ㄌㄨㄛˊ ㄐㄧˊ ㄒㄩㄝˊ)
logic
邏輯學家(ㄌㄨㄛˊ ㄐㄧˊ ㄒㄩㄝˊ ㄐㄧㄚ)
a logician
邏卒(ㄌㄨㄛˊ ㄗㄨˊ)
a patrolman

【邐】 6168
ㄌㄧˇ lii lǐ
continuous and meandering (as mountains, roads, etc.)

邑部
ㄧˋ yih yì

【邑】 6169
ㄧˋ yih yì
1. a town
2. a political district in ancient China
3. a county
4. a state
5. a capital city
6. same as 悒—sad or melancholy
邑庠(ㄧˋ ㄒㄧㄤˊ)
a county school or its graduate in former times
邑紳(ㄧˋ ㄕㄣ)
the gentry
邑人(ㄧˋ ㄖㄣˊ)
people of the same county or district
邑宰(ㄧˋ ㄗㄞˇ)
a county magistrate (in ancient times)亦作「邑侯」

三畫

【邙】 6170
ㄇㄤˊ mang máng
name of a hill near Loyang in Honan Province

【邛】 6171
ㄑㄩㄥˊ chyong qióng
1. name of a county in the Han Dynasty in today's Shantung Province
2. a hill; the heights
3. illness; an ailment
4. a Chinese family name
邛州(ㄑㄩㄥˊ ㄓㄡ)
name of a former political division in today's Szechwan Province
邛水(ㄑㄩㄥˊ ㄕㄨㄟˇ)
①name of a county in Kweichow Province ②name of a river in Szechwan Province

【邕】 6172
ㄩㄥ iong yōng
1. harmony; peaceful; harmonious
2. (now rarely) to cultivate (plants)
3. short for 邕寧, a county in Kwangsi Province
邕江(ㄩㄥ ㄐㄧㄤ)
name of a river in Kwangsi Province
邕邕(ㄩㄥ ㄩㄥ)
harmonious; peaceful

四畫

【邠】 6173
ㄅㄧㄣ bin bīn
name of an ancient state in today's Shensi Province
邠如(ㄅㄧㄣ ㄖㄨˊ)
flourishing or booming, culturally

【那】 6174
1. ㄋㄚˋ nah nà
1. that; those: 那些書是我的。Those books are mine.
2. then; in that case: 那我就不再等了。In that case, I won't wait any longer.
那般(ㄋㄚˋ ㄅㄢ)
that way
那班人(ㄋㄚˋ ㄅㄢ ㄖㄣˊ)
those people
那不勒斯(ㄋㄚˋ ㄅㄨˋ ㄌㄜˋ ㄙ)
Naples, Italy
那麼(ㄋㄚˋ ˙ㄇㄜ)or(ㄋㄜˋ ˙ㄇㄜ)
①so; that; in that way: 我們不該那麼說。We shouldn't have said that.② then; such being the case: 那麼,我必須懲罰他。Then I've to punish him. ③ about; or so
那麼點兒(ㄋㄚˋ ˙ㄇㄜ ㄉㄧㄚˇㄦ)
so little; so few
那麼著(ㄋㄚˋ ˙ㄇㄜ ˙ㄓㄜ)or(ㄋㄜˋ ˙ㄇㄜ ˙ㄓㄜ)
① to do that; to do so; in that way or manner ② then
那麼樣(ㄋㄚˋ ˙ㄇㄜ ㄧㄤˋ)or(ㄋㄜˋ ˙ㄇㄜ ㄧㄤˋ)
that way; in that case
那裏(ㄋㄚˋ ˙ㄌㄧ)or 那兒(ㄋㄚˋㄦ)
that place; at that place; there; over there: 馬上到那裏去。Go there at once.
那個(ㄋㄚˋ ˙ㄍㄜ)
①that one ② embarrassing ③ funny ④ too much, too far, too hot, etc.
那就(ㄋㄚˋ ㄐㄧㄡˋ)
in that case; if that is the case
那其間(ㄋㄚˋ ㄑㄧˊ ㄐㄧㄢ)
at that time or moment
那些(ㄋㄚˋ ㄒㄧㄝ)
those: 那些是我的鉛筆。Those are my pencils.
那時(ㄋㄚˋ ㄕˊ)
at that time or moment; then: 到那時我會告訴你這件事。I'll tell you about it then.
那是(ㄋㄚˋ ㄕˋ)
of course: 那是他對了! Of course he's right!
那廝(ㄋㄚˋ ㄙ)

〔邑部〕

that fellow; that s. o. b.
那樣(ㄋㄚˋ ㄧㄤˋ)
①that case or manner ②that (indicating degree)

【那】 6174
2. ㄋㄟˋ ney nèi
combined form of 那一 (that+one), often used to indicate emphasis or contempt
那邊(ㄋㄟˋ ㄅㄧㄢ)or 那邊兒(ㄋㄟˋ ㄅㄧㄚㄦ)
that way or side; over there; there (often emphasizing "not here")
那步田地(ㄋㄟˋ ㄅㄨˋ ㄊㄧㄢˊ ㄉㄧˋ)
that predicament; such a pass
那批傢伙(ㄋㄟˋ ㄆㄧ ㄐㄧㄚ ·ㄏㄨㄛ)
those guys; those rascals
那天(ㄋㄟˋ ㄊㄧㄢ)
that day
那溜兒(ㄋㄟˋ ㄌㄧㄡˋㄦ)
that region or area: 孩子們常在那溜兒玩。The children often play in that region.
那個(ㄋㄟˋ ·ㄍㄜ)
①that one (sometimes emphasizing "not this one"): 這個總比那個好。This is better than that. ②embarrassing ③funny ④too much; too far
那塊兒(ㄋㄟˋ ㄎㄨㄚˋㄦ)
①that place; that region 亦作「那溜兒」 ②that piece (of land, etc., often emphasizing "not this piece"): 他擁有那塊兒地。He owns that piece of land.
那回(ㄋㄟˋ ㄏㄨㄟˊ)
that time; that occasion
那陣兒(ㄋㄟˋ ㄓㄜˋㄦ)
that period; that moment
那種(ㄋㄟˋ ㄓㄨㄥˇ)
that kind (often emphasizing "not this kind")
那宗(ㄋㄟˋ ㄗㄨㄥ)
that case
那位(ㄋㄟˋ ㄨㄟˋ)
that gentleman or lady (often emphasizing "not this gentleman or lady")

【那】 6174
3.(哪) ㄋㄚˇ naa nǎ
an interrogative particle —Who? Which? What? Where?
那般(ㄋㄚˇ ㄅㄢ)
as in 爲那般—Why?
那怕(ㄋㄚˇ ㄆㄚˋ)
①what to be afraid of ②even if
那能(ㄋㄚˇ ㄋㄥˊ)
How can one...? 或 How could one...?
那裏(ㄋㄚˇ ·ㄌㄧ)or 那兒(ㄋㄚˇㄦ)
①Where? ②a negative particle—how can: 我那裏能吃得下這麼多? How can I eat so much? ③You're being too modest, polite, etc.
那裏話(ㄋㄚˇ ·ㄌㄧ ㄏㄨㄚˋ)
You're being too modest.
那個(ㄋㄚˇ ·ㄍㄜ)
①Which one?或 Which?②Who?
那堪(ㄋㄚˇ ㄎㄢ)
How can one stand or suffer...?
那知(ㄋㄚˇ ㄓ)
Who could have known...?
那有(ㄋㄚˇ ㄧㄡˇ)
How can there be...?

【那】 6174
4. ㄋㄟˇ neei něi
an interrogative particle —which+one
那邊(ㄋㄟˇ ㄅㄧㄢ)or 那邊兒(ㄋㄟˇ ㄅㄧㄚㄦ)
which way or direction
那年(ㄋㄟˇ ㄋㄧㄢˊ)
what year; which year
那個(ㄋㄟˇ ·ㄍㄜ)
which one
那回(ㄋㄟˇ ㄏㄨㄟˊ)
which time or occasion

【那】 6174
5. ㄋㄚ nha nā
a Chinese family name
那霸(ㄋㄚ ㄅㄚˋ)
Naha, capital of the Ryukyus

【邦】 6175
ㄅㄤ bang bāng
1. a state; a country; a nation
2. a manor given to a nobleman by the emperor in feudal China
邦本(ㄅㄤ ㄅㄣˇ)
the very foundation of a nation
邦土(ㄅㄤ ㄊㄨˇ)
a nation's territory; land of a country
邦國(ㄅㄤ ㄍㄨㄛˊ)
a nation; a country; a state
邦畿(ㄅㄤ ㄐㄧ)
the territory of a nation
邦家(ㄅㄤ ㄐㄧㄚ)
one's nation; one's state; one's fatherland
邦家之光(ㄅㄤ ㄐㄧㄚ ㄓ ㄍㄨㄤ)
the glory of one's country or fatherland
邦交(ㄅㄤ ㄐㄧㄠ)
international relations; diplomatic relations or ties: 兩國建立邦交關係。Two nations established diplomatic relations.
邦禁(ㄅㄤ ㄐㄧㄣˋ)
prohibitions of a nation
邦人(ㄅㄤ ㄖㄣˊ)
fellow countrymen; compatriots; people of a nation
邦彥(ㄅㄤ ㄧㄢˋ)
capable or virtuous persons in a country
邦域(ㄅㄤ ㄩˋ)
national territory
邦媛(ㄅㄤ ㄩㄢˋ)
girls of a nation

【邪】 6176
1. ㄒㄧㄝˊ shye xié
1. evil; depraved; wicked; mean; vicious
2. pertaining to sorcery or demonism; abnormal
邪不勝正(ㄒㄧㄝˊ ·ㄅㄨ ㄕㄥˋ ㄓㄥˋ)or 邪不敵正(ㄒㄧㄝˊ ·ㄅㄨ ㄉㄧˊ ㄓㄥˋ)
The evil will not triumph over the virtuous.
邪僻(ㄒㄧㄝˊ ㄆㄧˋ)
heterodox; perverse; abnormal
邪魔(ㄒㄧㄝˊ ㄇㄛˊ)
demons; devils
邪魔外道(ㄒㄧㄝˊ ㄇㄛˊ ㄨㄞˋ ㄉㄠˋ)
①(Buddhism) demons and heretics ②unorthodox; evil and wicked
邪媚(ㄒㄧㄝˊ ㄇㄟˋ)
obsequiousness; fawning
邪謀(ㄒㄧㄝˊ ㄇㄡˊ)
an evil scheme; conspiracy
邪門兒(ㄒㄧㄝˊ ㄇㄜˊㄦ)
beyond expectation or comprehension; strange; abnormal
邪道(ㄒㄧㄝˊ ㄉㄠˋ)

evil ways; heterodoxy: 他們走邪道。They abandoned themselves to evil ways.

邪念(ㄒㄧㄝˊ ㄋㄧㄢˋ)
evil thoughts or intentions; wicked ideas: 她起了邪念。A wicked idea came into her mind.

邪佞(ㄒㄧㄝˊ ㄋㄧㄥˋ)
evil persons; mean persons

邪路(ㄒㄧㄝˊ ㄌㄨˋ)
debauchery; a wrong path; evil ways

邪計(ㄒㄧㄝˊ ㄐㄧˋ)
evil schemes; conspiracy

邪教(ㄒㄧㄝˊ ㄐㄧㄠˋ)
paganism; heathendom; perverse religious sects

邪譎(ㄒㄧㄝˊ ㄐㄩㄝˊ)
wicked and crafty; evil and dishonest

邪氣(ㄒㄧㄝˊ ㄑㄧˋ)
① an evil look; perversity ② evil influence; a perverse trend

邪曲(ㄒㄧㄝˊ ㄑㄩ)
crooked; wicked

邪心(ㄒㄧㄝˊ ㄒㄧㄣ)
evil thoughts; bad intentions

邪行
①(ㄒㄧㄝˊ ㄒㄧㄥˊ) evil ways; wicked conduct
②(ㄒㄧㄝˊ ·ㄒㄧㄥ) very strange

邪臣(ㄒㄧㄝˊ ㄔㄣˊ)
evil or wicked officials

邪術(ㄒㄧㄝˊ ㄕㄨˋ)
sorcery; voodooism; demonic magic

邪說(ㄒㄧㄝˊ ㄕㄨㄛ)
heresy; perverted views; a heretic theory: 他陷入邪說中。He fell into heresy.

邪惡(ㄒㄧㄝˊ ㄜˋ)
evil and wicked; debauchery; wickedly

邪淫(ㄒㄧㄝˊ ㄧㄣˊ)
licentiousness; lewdness; lustful

【邪】 6176
2. ㄧㄝˊ ye yé
1. to answer in unison
2. same as 耶—an ending particle

邪呼(ㄧㄝˊ ㄏㄨ)
to answer in unison

邪許(ㄧㄝˊ ㄏㄨˇ)
to yell in unison; to call out in one voice

【邢】 6177
(邢) ㄒㄧㄥˊ shyng xíng
1. name of an ancient state (during the Epoch of Spring and Autumn)
2. a Chinese family name

【邨】 6178
ㄘㄨㄣ tsuen cūn
1. same as 村—a village; the countryside
2. coarse; vulgar
3. name-calling; abusive language
4. to scold
5. to embarrass

五畫

【邵】 6179
ㄕㄠˋ shaw shào
1. advanced, as age
2. a Chinese family name

【邯】 6180
ㄏㄢˊ harn hán
1. name of a county in Hopeh Province
2. name of a river in Chinghai
3. a hill in Hopeh

邯鄲(ㄏㄢˊ ㄉㄢ)
① Hantan, name of a county in Hopeh Province ② a Chinese family name

邯鄲學步(ㄏㄢˊ ㄉㄢ ㄒㄩㄝˊ ㄅㄨˋ)
to imitate another without success and lose what used to be one's own ability (referring to an anecdote related by Chuang-tzu)

【邰】 6181
ㄊㄞˊ tair tái
1. name of an ancient state in today's Shensi Province
2. a Chinese family name

【邱】 6182
ㄑㄧㄡ chiou qiū
1. same as 丘—a hill
2. name of a county in Shantung Province
3. a Chinese family name

邱比特(ㄑㄧㄡ ㄅㄧˇ ㄊㄜˋ)
Cupid

邱吉爾(ㄑㄧㄡ ㄐㄧˊ ㄦˇ)
Winston Churchill (Sir Winston Leonard Spencer Churchill, 1874-1965), British statesman

【邲】 6183
ㄅㄧˋ bih bì
1. good-looking
2. name of an ancient place in today's Honan Province

【邳】 6184
ㄆㄟˊ peir péi
1. joyful; jubilant
2. name of an ancient place in today's Shantung Province
3. a Chinese family name

【邶】 6185
ㄅㄟˋ bey bèi
name of an ancient state in today's Honan Province

【邴】 6186
ㄅㄧㄥˇ biing bǐng
1. joyful; jubilant
2. name of a place in ancient China in today's Shantung Province
3. a Chinese family name

【邸】 6187
ㄉㄧˇ dii dǐ
1. the residence of a prince or the nobility; the residence of a high official
2. princes and noblemen
3. (now rarely) a screen
4. the bottom of something
5. a Chinese family name

邸報(ㄉㄧˇ ㄅㄠˋ)
official gazettes in ancient China

邸第(ㄉㄧˇ ㄉㄧˋ)
residences of lords and the nobility

邸舍(ㄉㄧˇ ㄕㄜˋ)
① residences of the nobility ② a shop or store ③ an inn or a tavern

六畫

【郁】 6188
ㄩˋ yuh yù
1. adorned; colorfully ornamented; beautiful; refined
2. a Chinese family name

郁穆(ㄩˋ ㄇㄨˋ)
harmonious and refined

郁馥(ㄩˋ ㄈㄨˋ)
fragrant; aromatic

郁烈(ㄩˋ ㄌㄧㄝˋ)
permeated with strong aroma

郁郁(ㄩˋ ㄩˋ)
① beautifully adorned; ornamented ② diffusing of aroma ③ flourishing; luxuriant ④ elegant; refined

〔邑部〕

【邢】6189 (邢) ㄒㄧㄥˊ shyng xíng
1. name of an ancient state in China
2. a Chinese family name

【郅】6190 ㄓˋ jyh zhì
1. very; extremely
2. a Chinese family name
郅隆(ㄓˋ ㄌㄨㄥˊ)
extremely flourishing or prosperous
郅治(ㄓˋ ㄓˋ)
extremely well-governed (nation, world, etc.)

【郇】6191 ㄒㄩㄣˊ shyun xún
1. name of an ancient state in today's Shansi Province
2. a Chinese family name
郇厨(ㄒㄩㄣˊ ㄔㄨˊ)
(literally) the cuisine of Duke Hsün 韋陟 of the Tang Dynasty—a sumptuous feast

【郊】6192 ㄐㄧㄠ jiau jiāo
1. suburbs of a city
2. a ceremony for offering sacrifices to Heaven and Earth
郊甸(ㄐㄧㄠ ㄉㄧㄢˋ)
suburbs and the regions beyond the city
郊坰(ㄐㄧㄠ ㄐㄩㄥ)
countryside; a field; open spaces
郊區(ㄐㄧㄠ ㄑㄩ)
suburban districts; suburbs; outskirts; a suburban area
郊社(ㄐㄧㄠ ㄕㄜˋ)
a sacrifice for Heaven in winter (郊) and a sacrifice for Earth in summer (社)
郊祀(ㄐㄧㄠ ㄙˋ)
to offer a sacrifice to Heaven and Earth
郊野(ㄐㄧㄠ ㄧㄝˇ)
open spaces beyond the city
郊遊(ㄐㄧㄠ ㄧㄡˊ)
an outing; an excursion
郊迎(ㄐㄧㄠ ㄧㄥˊ)
to welcome (a guest) beyond the city limit—as a gesture of profound respect
郊外(ㄐㄧㄠ ㄨㄞˋ)
suburbs
郊原(ㄐㄧㄠ ㄩㄢˊ)
plains beyond the city

【郃】6193 ㄍㄜˊ ger gé
1. name of a county in Shensi Province
2. a Chinese family name

【邽】6194 ㄍㄨㄟ guei guī
1. name of a county in the Han Dynasty, in today's Kansu Province
2. a Chinese family name

【邾】6195 ㄓㄨ ju zhū
name of an ancient state in today's Shantung Province

七畫

【郛】6196 ㄈㄨˊ fwu fú
the outer city; the suburbs
郛郭(ㄈㄨˊ ㄍㄨㄛ)
① the booming suburbs outside a city; a sturdy outer city wall ② (figuratively) shelter; a shield; protection

【郜】6197 ㄍㄠˋ gaw gào
1. name of an ancient state in today's Shantung Province
2. name of a place in the state of Tsin (晉) in the Epoch of Spring and Autumn, in today's Shansi Province
3. a Chinese family name

【郝】6198 ㄏㄠˇ hao hǎo (讀音 ㄏㄜˋ heh hè)
1. name of an ancient place in today's Shensi Province
2. a Chinese family name

【郎】6199 (郎) ㄌㄤˊ lang láng
1. an official rank in ancient times
2. a man
3. the husband; the beau
4. the master (as opposite to servants)
5. a Chinese family name
郎當(ㄌㄤˊ ㄉㄤ)
①(said of clothing) loose ② discouraged; dejected ③ shackles for prisoners
郎官(ㄌㄤˊ ㄍㄨㄢ)
an official rank in the Han Dynasty
郎舅(ㄌㄤˊ ㄐㄧㄡˋ)
brothers-in-law
郎君(ㄌㄤˊ ㄐㄩㄣ)
① a term of address for a man ② your son (a polite expression) ③ the husband
郎中(ㄌㄤˊ ㄓㄨㄥ)
① an official rank in ancient China ② a physician ③ a card shark
郎世寧(ㄌㄤˊ ㄕˋ ㄋㄧㄥˊ)
Guiseppe Castiglione (1698-1768), a naturalized Italian painter, who came to China during the early years of the Ching Dynasty
郎才女貌(ㄌㄤˊ ㄘㄞˊ ㄋㄩˇ ㄇㄠˋ)
a perfect match between a man and a woman

【郟】6200 ㄐㄧㄚˊ jya jiá
1. name of various places in China
2. a Chinese family name

【郡】6201 ㄐㄩㄣˋ jiunn jùn
a political division in ancient China; a prefecture; a county
郡國(ㄐㄩㄣˋ ㄍㄨㄛˊ)
a system of political zoning adopted by Liu Pang(劉邦), founder of the Han Dynasty, whereby he divided the empire into many prefectures under the direct jurisdiction of the throne and a number of principalities governed by the imperial princes
郡下(ㄐㄩㄣˋ ㄒㄧㄚˋ)
the capital city of a prefecture where the magistrate resides
郡縣(ㄐㄩㄣˋ ㄒㄧㄢˋ)
prefectures and counties; administrative districts smaller than a province
郡主(ㄐㄩㄣˋ ㄓㄨˇ)
a princess
郡丞(ㄐㄩㄣˋ ㄔㄥˊ)
an assistant or a deputy to the chief of a prefecture
郡城(ㄐㄩㄣˋ ㄔㄥˊ)
a prefectural city; a town
郡守(ㄐㄩㄣˋ ㄕㄡˇ)
the magistrate of a prefecture
郡王(ㄐㄩㄣˋ ㄨㄤˊ)
a rank of the nobility next

to prince

【郢】 6202
ㄧㄥˇ yiing yǐng
name of the capital of the state of Chu (楚), during the Epoch of Spring and Autumn, in today's Hupeh Province

郢書燕說(ㄧㄥˇ ㄕㄨ ㄧㄢ ㄕㄨㄛ)
distorted interpretation; to distort the meaning in order to fit one's idea

【郗】 6203
ㄔ chy chī
1. name of a town in the Chou Dynasty
2. a Chinese family name

【郤】 6204
ㄒㄧˋ shih xì
1. name of an area in the ancient state of Tsin(晉)
2. a crack
3. a Chinese family name

【郕】 6205
ㄔㄥˊ cherng chéng
name of an ancient state in today's Shantung Province

八畫

【部】 6206
ㄅㄨˋ buh bù
1. a department; a section; a division; a class; a sort; a genus
2. a cabinet ministry
3. a volume; a complete work, novel, writing, etc.
4. to lead; to head

部門(ㄅㄨˋ ㄇㄣˊ)
a class; a section; a department

部分(ㄅㄨˋ ·ㄈㄣ)
a portion; a part; partial; partly

部隊(ㄅㄨˋ ㄉㄨㄟˋ)
troops; a military unit: 那是一支野戰部隊。That is a field military unit.

部隊長(ㄅㄨˋ ㄉㄨㄟˋ ㄓㄤˇ)
the commanding officer; the C.O.

部落(ㄅㄨˋ ㄌㄨㄛˋ)
① a tribe which has not formed a nation ② the self-sustaining community of a tribe or clan; a tribal settlement

部落社會(ㄅㄨˋ ㄌㄨㄛˋ ㄕㄜˋ ㄏㄨㄟˋ)
tribal society

部會(ㄅㄨˋ ㄏㄨㄟˋ)
the ministries and commissions under the Executive Yuan of the Chinese government

部將(ㄅㄨˋ ㄐㄧㄤˋ)
military officers under one's command

部居(ㄅㄨˋ ㄐㄩ)
classification of words, etc.

部下(ㄅㄨˋ ㄒㄧㄚˋ)
subordinates: 他從不信任他的部下。He never trusts his subordinates.

部長(ㄅㄨˋ ㄓㄤˇ)
① a cabinet minister ② (in U.S.) the Secretary (of the army, the navy, the air force, the Defense Department, the Agriculture Department, etc.)

部首(ㄅㄨˋ ㄕㄡˇ)
radicals of Chinese characters

部屬(ㄅㄨˋ ㄕㄨˇ)
subordinates

部署(ㄅㄨˋ ㄕㄨˇ)
to make preparations or arrangements; to make military deployment

部位(ㄅㄨˋ ㄨㄟˋ)
location (of an injury, etc.)

部員(ㄅㄨˋ ㄩㄢˊ)
clerks or staff members in a department, section or ministry

【郫】 6207
ㄆㄧˊ pyi pí
1. name of a town in the Epoch of Spring and Autumn, in today's Honan Province
2. name of a county in Szechwan

郫筒(ㄆㄧˊ ㄊㄨㄥˇ)
a section of huge bamboo produced in Pi Hsien(郫縣), Szechwan, formerly used as a liquor container

【郭】 6208
ㄍㄨㄛ guo guō
1. as in 城郭—a town
2. the outer wall of a city
3. the outer part of anything
4. a Chinese family name

郭璞(ㄍㄨㄛ ㄆㄨˊ)
Kuo Pu (276-324), a writer of the Tsin Dynasty

郭先生(ㄍㄨㄛ ㄒㄧㄢ ·ㄕㄥ)
(slang) a dildo

郭子儀(ㄍㄨㄛ ㄗˇ ㄧˊ)
Kuo Tzu-yi (697-781), a famous general of the Tang Dynasty

郭外(ㄍㄨㄛ ㄨㄞˋ)
beyond the outer city wall; outside the city

【郯】 6209
ㄊㄢˊ tarn tán
1. name of an ancient state in today's Shantung Province
2. a Chinese family name

【郴】 6210
ㄔㄣ chen chēn
1. name of a county in Hunan Province
2. a Chinese family name

【郪】 6211
ㄑㄧ chi qī
name of a stream in Szechwan Province

【郲】 6212
ㄌㄞˊ lai lái
1. name of a place in Honan Province
2. a Chinese family name

【郵】 6213
ㄧㄡˊ you yóu
1. a post office
2. postal
3. to deliver mails, letters, etc.
4. a wayside station where couriers on government service change horses
5. a hut; a lodge in the field

郵包(ㄧㄡˊ ㄅㄠ)
a postal parcel

郵票(ㄧㄡˊ ㄆㄧㄠˋ)
postal stamps: 這是一套紀念郵票。This is a set of commemorative stamps.

郵費(ㄧㄡˊ ㄈㄟˋ)
postal charges; postage

郵費不足(ㄧㄡˊ ㄈㄟˋ ㄅㄨˋ ㄗㄨˊ)
insufficient (or short) postage

郵費免付(ㄧㄡˊ ㄈㄟˋ ㄇㄧㄢˇ ㄈㄨˋ)
post-free

郵費已付(ㄧㄡˊ ㄈㄟˋ ㄧˇ ㄈㄨˋ)
postpaid

郵費未付(ㄧㄡˊ ㄈㄟˋ ㄨㄟˋ ㄈㄨˋ)
postage unpaid

郵袋(ㄧㄡˊ ㄉㄞˋ)
a mailbag

郵遞(ㄧㄡˊ ㄉㄧˋ)
to send by mail; to deliver through postal service; mail service

郵遞區號(ㄧㄡˊ ㄉㄧˋ ㄑㄩ ㄏㄠˋ)
zip code

郵電(ㄧㄡˊ ㄉㄧㄢˋ)
postal and cable service

郵亭(ㄧㄡˊ ㄊㄧㄥˊ)
① a postal kiosk ② (in ancient China) a lodge for couriers

郵筒(ㄧㄡˊ ㄊㄨㄥˇ)
a pillar box; a postbox; a mail drop; a mailbox: 我把信投入郵筒。I took the letter to the postbox.

郵購(ㄧㄡˊ ㄍㄡˋ)
① mail order ② to buy by mail order

郵滙(ㄧㄡˊ ㄏㄨㄟˋ)
to send money by mail; to remit by post; a postal money order

郵寄(ㄧㄡˊ ㄐㄧˋ)
to send by mail; to mail: 他昨天郵寄了這封信。He mailed the letter yesterday.

郵寄名單(ㄧㄡˊ ㄐㄧˋ ㄇㄧㄥˊ ㄉㄢ)
a mailing list

郵簡(ㄧㄡˊ ㄐㄧㄢˇ)
an air letter

郵件(ㄧㄡˊ ㄐㄧㄢˋ)
mail matter; postal items; the post; mail: 郵件今早來遲了。The post came late this morning.

郵件補償(ㄧㄡˊ ㄐㄧㄢˋ ㄅㄨˇ ㄔㄤˊ)
indemnity for mail matter

郵件收集截止日(ㄧㄡˊ ㄐㄧㄢˋ ㄕㄡ ㄐㄧˊ ㄐㄧㄝˊ ㄓˇ ㄖˋ)
a mail-day

郵局(ㄧㄡˊ ㄐㄩˊ) or **郵政局**(ㄧㄡˊ ㄓㄥˋ ㄐㄩˊ)
a post office

郵區(ㄧㄡˊ ㄑㄩ)
a postal district

郵箱(ㄧㄡˊ ㄒㄧㄤ)
a postbox; a mailbox; a letter box

郵政(ㄧㄡˊ ㄓㄥˋ)
postal affairs; postal system; postal administration

郵政代辦所(ㄧㄡˊ ㄓㄥˋ ㄉㄞˋ ㄅㄢˋ ㄙㄨㄛˇ)
a postal agency

郵政滙票(ㄧㄡˊ ㄓㄥˋ ㄏㄨㄟˋ ㄆㄧㄠˋ)
a postal order

郵政滙款(ㄧㄡˊ ㄓㄥˋ ㄏㄨㄟˋ ㄎㄨㄢˇ)
postal remittance

郵政局長(ㄧㄡˊ ㄓㄥˋ ㄐㄩˊ ㄓㄤˇ)
the chief of a post office; the postmaster or postmistress

郵政信箱(ㄧㄡˊ ㄓㄥˋ ㄒㄧㄣˋ ㄒㄧㄤ)
a post-office box (P.O.B.)

郵政支局(ㄧㄡˊ ㄓㄥˋ ㄓ ㄐㄩˊ)
a (postal) suboffice

郵政儲金(ㄧㄡˊ ㄓㄥˋ ㄔㄨˇ ㄐㄧㄣ)
savings deposits in a department of the post office

郵政儲金簿(ㄧㄡˊ ㄓㄥˋ ㄔㄨˇ ㄐㄧㄣ ㄅㄨˋ)
a post savings book

郵政儲蓄存款(ㄧㄡˊ ㄓㄥˋ ㄔㄨˇ ㄒㄩˋ ㄘㄨㄣˊ ㄎㄨㄢˇ)
post office savings deposits

郵政總局(ㄧㄡˊ ㄓㄥˋ ㄗㄨㄥˇ ㄐㄩˊ)
the Directorate General of Posts (under the Ministry of Communications)

郵差(ㄧㄡˊ ㄔㄞ)
a mailman; a postman

郵車(ㄧㄡˊ ㄔㄜ)
a mail cart; a postal truck or van; postal vehicles

郵戳兒(ㄧㄡˊ ㄔㄨㄛㄦ)
a postmark; a postal dater

郵船(ㄧㄡˊ ㄔㄨㄢˊ)
① a luxurious passenger liner ② a mailboat

郵傳部(ㄧㄡˊ ㄔㄨㄢˊ ㄅㄨˋ)
the Ministry of Communications in the Ching Dynasty

郵資(ㄧㄡˊ ㄗ)
postage

郵資不足(ㄧㄡˊ ㄗ ㄅㄨˋ ㄗㄨˊ)
postage underpaid

郵資免付(ㄧㄡˊ ㄗ ㄇㄧㄢˇ ㄈㄨˋ)
post-free

郵資已付(ㄧㄡˊ ㄗ ㄧˇ ㄈㄨˋ)
postage paid

郵艙(ㄧㄡˊ ㄘㄤ)
a mail room (aboard a ship)

郵務(ㄧㄡˊ ㄨˋ)
postal administration; postal service; postal affairs

郵務生(ㄧㄡˊ ㄨˋ ㄕㄥ)
an assistant clerk in a post office

郵務佐(ㄧㄡˊ ㄨˋ ㄗㄨㄛˇ)
a junior clerk in a post office

郵務員(ㄧㄡˊ ㄨˋ ㄩㄢˊ)
a senior clerk in a post office

郵運(ㄧㄡˊ ㄩㄣˋ)
① to deliver by mail ② mail transportation

九畫

【都】 6214

1. ㄉㄨ du dū

1. a large town; a city; a metropolis
2. the capital of a nation; to make a city the national capital
3. beautiful; elegant; fine
4. (now rarely) to live or stay in
5. a Chinese family name

都伯林(ㄉㄨ ㄅㄛˊ ㄌㄧㄣˊ)
Dublin, Ireland

都鄙(ㄉㄨ ㄅㄧˇ)
manors of noblemen in ancient China

都門(ㄉㄨ ㄇㄣˊ)
the national capital

都府(ㄉㄨ ㄈㄨˇ)
① a big city ② an official rank in the Tang Dynasty

都督(ㄉㄨ ㄉㄨ)
① an army commander in ancient China ② (in the early days of the Chinese Republic) the top commanding officer in a province in charge of both military and civil administration

都會(ㄉㄨ ㄏㄨㄟˋ)
a big city; a metropolis: 他住在大都會。He lives in the metropolis.

都察院(ㄉㄨ ㄔㄚˊ ㄩㄢˋ)
the Court of Censors (in the Ming and Ching dynasties)

都城(ㄉㄨ ㄔㄥˊ)
① the national capital ② the manor for a minister in ancient China

都市(ㄉㄨ ㄕˋ)
a city; a metropolis: 台北是個繁忙的大都市。Taipei is a busy city.

都市病(ㄉㄨ ㄕˋ ㄅㄧㄥˋ)
endemic diseases among city dwellers

都市更新(ㄉㄨ ㄕˋ ㄍㄥ ㄒㄧㄣ)
urban renewal

都市規劃(ㄉㄨ ㄕˋ ㄍㄨㄟ ㄏㄨㄚˋ)
urban planning
都市工業區(ㄉㄨ ㄕˋ ㄍㄨㄥ ㄧㄝˋ ㄑㄩ)
an urban industrial area
都市化(ㄉㄨ ㄕˋ ㄏㄨㄚˋ)
to urbanize; urbanized; urbanization: 這個小鎮已經都市化了。The little town has been urbanized.
都市計畫(ㄉㄨ ㄕˋ ㄐㄧˋ ㄏㄨㄚˋ)
an urban development plan; an urban renewal plan
都市設計(ㄉㄨ ㄕˋ ㄕㄜˋ ㄐㄧˋ)
an urban design
都邑(ㄉㄨ ㄧˋ)
a metropolitan city; the national capital

【都】 6214
2. ㄉㄡ dou dōu
1. all; altogether
2. even
3. already
都不對(ㄉㄡ ˙ㄅㄨ ㄉㄨㄟˋ)
Nobody is right. 或 Everyone is wrong.
都來了(ㄉㄡ ㄌㄞˊ ˙ㄌㄜ)
All have come. 或 Everyone is present.
都可以(ㄉㄡ ㄎㄜˇ ˙ㄧ)
Anyone of them will do. 或 Either of them will do.
都是(ㄉㄡ ㄕˋ)
all; no exception
都有(ㄉㄡ ㄧㄡˇ)
all have...; to include all kinds or varieties

【郿】 6215
ㄇㄟˊ mei méi
1. Mei, a county in Shensi
2. name of a town of Lu in the Epoch of Spring and Autumn

【鄂】 6216
ㄜˋ eh è
1. the edge; the verge; the brink; the brim
2. short for Hupeh Province
3. startled; surprised
4. blunt; honest
5. a Chinese family name
鄂木斯克(ㄜˋ ㄇㄨˋ ㄙ ㄎㄜˋ)
Omsk, a Siberian city
鄂霍次克海(ㄜˋ ㄏㄨㄛˋ ㄘˋ ㄎㄜˋ ㄏㄞˇ)
the Okhotsk Sea
鄂省(ㄜˋ ㄕㄥˇ)
Hupeh Province

【鄆】 6217
ㄩㄣˋ yunn yùn
1. name of an ancient town in Shantung Province
2. a Chinese family name

【郾】 6218
ㄧㄢˇ yean yǎn
name of a county in Honan Province
郾城(ㄧㄢˇ ㄔㄥˊ)
name of a county in Honan Province

【鄄】 6219
ㄐㄩㄢˋ jiuann juàn
name of a county in Shantung Province

十畫

【鄗】 6220
ㄏㄠˋ haw hào
name of a town in ancient China in today's Hupeh Province

【鄉】 6221
1. ㄒㄧㄤ shiang xiāng
1. a village; the country, as contrasted with a city or town
2. rural
3. a small administrative unit comprising several villages
4. one's native place or birthplace; one's village; one's country: 我回到自己的家鄉。I returned to my country.
鄉巴佬(ㄒㄧㄤ ˙ㄅㄚ ㄌㄠˇ)
a country bumpkin; a hillbilly; an unsophisticated villager
鄉兵(ㄒㄧㄤ ㄅㄧㄥ)
the village militia
鄉末(ㄒㄧㄤ ㄇㄛˋ)
a modest term of self-address when talking to elders of one's own native place
鄉民(ㄒㄧㄤ ㄇㄧㄣˊ)
villagers; countryfolk
鄉黨(ㄒㄧㄤ ㄉㄤˇ)
local communities
鄉談(ㄒㄧㄤ ㄊㄢˊ)
local dialects; native dialects
鄉土(ㄒㄧㄤ ㄊㄨˇ)
① one's hometown or native place ② local geography and history
鄉土觀念(ㄒㄧㄤ ㄊㄨˇ ㄍㄨㄢ ㄋㄧㄢˋ)
provincialism; narrow-minded loyalty to one's hometown
鄉土藝術(ㄒㄧㄤ ㄊㄨˇ ㄧˋ ㄕㄨˋ)
local art; native art or handicraft
鄉老(ㄒㄧㄤ ㄌㄠˇ)
① country or village elders ② an official rank in the Chou and Han dynasties
鄉里(ㄒㄧㄤ ㄌㄧˇ)
① the village where one resides or grew up ② people from the same hometown ③ (now rarely) my wife
鄉裏鄉氣的(ㄒㄧㄤ ˙ㄌㄧ ㄒㄧㄤ ㄑㄧˋ ˙ㄉㄜ)
stupid-looking; foolish and clumsy
鄉鄰(ㄒㄧㄤ ㄌㄧㄣˊ)
persons from the same rural neighborhood
鄉國(ㄒㄧㄤ ㄍㄨㄛˊ)
one's native place or fatherland
鄉關(ㄒㄧㄤ ㄍㄨㄢ)
one's native place or hometown
鄉公所(ㄒㄧㄤ ㄍㄨㄥ ㄙㄨㄛˇ)
a public office in charge of the administration of a group of villages
鄉豪劣紳(ㄒㄧㄤ ㄏㄠˊ ㄌㄧㄝˋ ㄕㄣ)
village bullies and local tyrants
鄉間(ㄒㄧㄤ ㄐㄧㄢ)
in the countryside; in the rural area
鄉井(ㄒㄧㄤ ㄐㄧㄥˇ)
one's native place or hometown
鄉居(ㄒㄧㄤ ㄐㄩ)
to live in the countryside
鄉親(ㄒㄧㄤ ㄑㄧㄣ)
① people hailing from the same area ② local people; villagers
鄉曲(ㄒㄧㄤ ㄑㄩ)
remote and out-of-the-way rural areas
鄉下(ㄒㄧㄤ ˙ㄒㄧㄚ)
countryside; a rural area
鄉下老兒(ㄒㄧㄤ ˙ㄒㄧㄚ ㄌㄠˇㄦ)
villagers; country bumpkins
鄉下人(ㄒㄧㄤ ˙ㄒㄧㄚ ㄖㄣˊ)
villagers; countryfolk; the country people; rustics
鄉校(ㄒㄧㄤ ㄒㄧㄠˋ)
a village school
鄉先達(ㄒㄧㄤ ㄒㄧㄢ ㄉㄚˊ)

〔邑部〕

leaders of a rural community

鄉賢(ㄒㄧㄤ ㄒㄧㄢˊ)
respected village scholars

鄉學(ㄒㄧㄤ ㄒㄩㄝˊ)
a village school

鄉鎮(ㄒㄧㄤ ㄓㄣˋ)
a small town which is essentially a rural village

鄉長(ㄒㄧㄤ ㄓㄤˇ)
① elders in a village ② the chief of a group of villages

鄉愁(ㄒㄧㄤ ㄔㄡˊ)or 鄉思(ㄒㄧㄤ ㄙ)
homesickness; nostalgia

鄉試(ㄒㄧㄤ ㄕˋ)
the civil service examination held once every three years in a provincial capital in ancient times

鄉射(ㄒㄧㄤ ㄕㄜˋ)
an archery contest in villages for choosing the best archers in ancient times

鄉紳(ㄒㄧㄤ ㄕㄣ)
the country gentry; country gentlemen; squires

鄉塾(ㄒㄧㄤ ㄕㄨˊ)
a private village school

鄉人(ㄒㄧㄤ ㄖㄣˊ)
① the villagers ② persons from the same village or rural area

鄉村(ㄒㄧㄤ ㄘㄨㄣ)
a village; a country; a rural area: 他喜歡鄉村的寧靜。He likes the tranquility in the country.

鄉村教育(ㄒㄧㄤ ㄘㄨㄣ ㄐㄧㄠˋ ㄩˋ)
rural education

鄉村音樂(ㄒㄧㄤ ㄘㄨㄣ ㄧㄣ ㄩㄝˋ)
country music

鄉俗(ㄒㄧㄤ ㄙㄨˊ)
local customs of one's native place

鄉誼(ㄒㄧㄤ ㄧˊ)
friendship among people from the same area

鄉野(ㄒㄧㄤ ㄧㄝˇ)
rural; pastoral

鄉友(ㄒㄧㄤ ㄧㄡˇ)
friends from the same area

鄉音(ㄒㄧㄤ ㄧㄣ)
one's native accent; a local accent; brogue

鄉味(ㄒㄧㄤ ㄨㄟˋ)
① food from one's native place ② a way of cooking in one's native place

鄉望(ㄒㄧㄤ ㄨㄤˋ)
one's reputation or prestige in one's own town or village

鄉愚(ㄒㄧㄤ ㄩˊ)
stupid rustics

鄉愿(ㄒㄧㄤ ㄩㄢˋ)
a hypocrite or an impostor in the countryside

鄉勇(ㄒㄧㄤ ㄩㄥˇ)
village militiamen; the local militia

【鄉】 6221
2.(嚮) ㄒㄧㄤˋ shianq xiàng

1. to incline toward; to direct to
2. to guide; to approach
3. (now rarely) to advise

鄉壁虛造or向壁虛造(ㄒㄧㄤˋ ㄅㄧˋ ㄒㄩ ㄗㄠˋ)
to fabricate; to invent

鄉使 or 向使(ㄒㄧㄤˋ ㄕˇ)
if; had it been

【鄒】 6222
ㄗㄡ tzou zōu

1. name of a state in the Epoch of Warring States
2. a Chinese family name

鄒魯(ㄗㄡ ㄌㄨˇ)
native places of Mencius and Confucius respectively —where culture flourishes; a cultural center

【鄔】 6223
ㄨ u wū

1. name of various places in ancient times
2. a Chinese family name

十一畫

【鄙】 6224
ㄅㄧˇ bii bǐ
(又讀 ㄅㄧˋ bih bì)

1. mean; base; lowly; despicable
2. superficial; shallow
3. remote; out-of-the-way
4. to despise; to scorn

鄙薄(ㄅㄧˇ ㄅㄛˊ)
① mean; base ② superficial; shallow ③ to despise; to loathe: 你不應該鄙薄技術工作。You should not despise technical work.

鄙倍(ㄅㄧˇ ㄅㄟˋ)
despicably unreasonable

鄙夫(ㄅㄧˇ ㄈㄨ)
① a mean fellow; an ignorant fellow ② I (self-depreciatory)

鄙陋(ㄅㄧˇ ㄌㄡˋ)
① mean; base ② shallow (views): 他鄙陋無知。He is shallow and ignorant.

鄙俚(ㄅㄧˇ ㄌㄧˇ)
crude; coarse; vulgar

鄙吝(ㄅㄧˇ ㄌㄧㄣˋ)
stingy; niggardly; miserly

鄙賤(ㄅㄧˇ ㄐㄧㄢˋ)
lowly; mean; base

鄙棄(ㄅㄧˇ ㄑㄧˋ)
to despise; to scorn

鄙笑(ㄅㄧˇ ㄒㄧㄠˋ)
to jeer; to ridicule; to mock; to taunt

鄙詐(ㄅㄧˇ ㄓㄚˋ)
despicably untruthful; deceitful

鄙事(ㄅㄧˇ ㄕˋ)
trifles; mean matters

鄙視(ㄅㄧˇ ㄕˋ)
to despise; to disdain; to slight; to look down upon

鄙人(ㄅㄧˇ ㄖㄣˊ)
① I (a self-depreciatory way of referring to oneself); your humble servant ② a hillbilly

鄙嗇(ㄅㄧˇ ㄙㄜˋ)
① narrow-minded ② miserly; niggardly; stingy

鄙俗(ㄅㄧˇ ㄙㄨˊ)
vulgar; philistine

鄙夷(ㄅㄧˇ ㄧˊ)
to despise; to scorn

鄙意(ㄅㄧˇ ㄧˋ)or 鄙見(ㄅㄧˇ ㄐㄧㄢˋ)
my humble opinion

鄙諺(ㄅㄧˇ ㄧㄢˋ)or 鄙語(ㄅㄧˇ ㄩˇ)
a common saying; a proverb

【鄢】 6225
ㄧㄢ ian yān

1. name of an ancient state in what is today's Honan
2. a Chinese family name

【鄘】 6226
ㄩㄥ iong yōng

name of an ancient state in what is today's Honan

【鄜】 6227
ㄈㄨ fu fū

name of a county in Shensi

【鄞】 6228
ㄧㄣˊ yn yín

name of a county in Chekiang

【鄣】6229 ㄓㄤ jang zhāng
name of an ancient state in what is today's Shantung

十二畫

【鄧】6230 ㄉㄥˋ denq dèng
1. a Chinese family name
2. name of an ancient state in what is today's Honan

鄧通(ㄉㄥˋ ㄊㄨㄥ)
Teng Tung, the favorite courtier of Emperor Wen of the Han Dynasty(漢文帝), famous for his fabulous wealth

鄧石如(ㄉㄥˋ ㄕˊ ㄖㄨˊ)
Teng Shih-ju (1743-1805), a famous calligrapher

鄧艾(ㄉㄥˋ ㄞˋ)
Teng Ai (197-264), a general of the state of Wei (魏) during the Epoch of the Three Kingdoms

鄧尉(ㄉㄥˋ ㄨㄟˋ)
Tengwei, a hill near Soochow (蘇州), famous for its plum flowers

【鄭】6231 ㄓㄥˋ jenq zhèng
1. solemn; formal; serious
2. a Chinese family name
3. name of an ancient state in what is today's Honan

鄭和(ㄓㄥˋ ㄏㄜˊ)
Cheng Ho, a powerful eunuch in the early Ming Dynasty, who sailed as far as the east coast of Africa with a large fleet in a number of expeditions

鄭箋(ㄓㄥˋ ㄐㄧㄢ)
a commentary by the Han Dynasty scholar Cheng Hsüan (鄭玄) on one version of the *Book of Odes*

鄭玄(ㄓㄥˋ ㄒㄩㄢˊ)
Cheng Hsüan (127-200), a Han Dynasty scholar

鄭莊公(ㄓㄥˋ ㄓㄨㄤ ㄍㄨㄥ)
a ruler of the state of Cheng (鄭) during the Epoch of Spring and Autumn

鄭重(ㄓㄥˋ ㄓㄨㄥˋ)
① cautious; careful ② solemn; serious

鄭重其事(ㄓㄥˋ ㄓㄨㄥˋ ㄑㄧˊ ㄕˋ)
① to treat it with seriousness ② very careful or cautious

鄭成功(ㄓㄥˋ ㄔㄥˊ ㄍㄨㄥ)
Koxinga, or Cheng Cheng-kung (1624-1662), leader of an anti-Manchu resistance after the fall of the Ming Dynasty, who ousted the Dutch from Taiwan

鄭聲(ㄓㄥˋ ㄕㄥ)
the music of the state of Cheng (鄭) —decadent music

鄭衛之音(ㄓㄥˋ ㄨㄟˋ ㄓ ㄧㄣ)
the music of the states of Cheng(鄭) and Wei(衛)—decadent music

【鄯】6232 ㄕㄢˋ shann shàn
name of a region in Chinese Turkestan

【鄰】6233 (隣) ㄌㄧㄣˊ lin lín
1. neighboring; adjacent; adjoining; contiguous
2. neighborhood; a community
3. a neighbor
4. a basic community unit which consists of a number of families in the same neighborhood

鄰邦(ㄌㄧㄣˊ ㄅㄤ)
a neighboring state; a neighboring country

鄰比(ㄌㄧㄣˊ ㄅㄧˋ)
neighbors

鄰邊(ㄌㄧㄣˊ ㄅㄧㄢ)
adjacent sides (of a polygon)

鄰睦(ㄌㄧㄣˊ ㄇㄨˋ)
on friendly terms

鄰封(ㄌㄧㄣˊ ㄈㄥ)
a neighboring district

鄰敵(ㄌㄧㄣˊ ㄉㄧˊ)
a hostile neighboring country

鄰里(ㄌㄧㄣˊ ㄌㄧˇ)
neighborhood; a community

鄰里鄉黨(ㄌㄧㄣˊ ㄌㄧˇ ㄒㄧㄤ ㄉㄤˇ)
one's neighborhood and associates

鄰國(ㄌㄧㄣˊ ㄍㄨㄛˊ)
a neighboring country

鄰家(ㄌㄧㄣˊ ㄐㄧㄚ)
a close neighbor; a next-door family

鄰近(ㄌㄧㄣˊ ㄐㄧㄣˋ)
① located nearby; located in the vicinity ② neighborhood: 鄰近沒有銀行。There's no bank in the neighborhood.

鄰境(ㄌㄧㄣˊ ㄐㄧㄥˋ)
the vicinity; the neighborhood; a surrounding region

鄰居(ㄌㄧㄣˊ ㄐㄩ)
neighbors; people next-door

鄰長(ㄌㄧㄣˊ ㄓㄤˇ)
the head of a basic community unit 參看「鄰4.」

鄰舍(ㄌㄧㄣˊ ㄕㄜˋ)
a neighboring family; neighbors

鄰人(ㄌㄧㄣˊ ㄖㄣˊ)
neighbors

鄰右(ㄌㄧㄣˊ ㄧㄡˋ)
neighbors

鄰伍(ㄌㄧㄣˊ ㄨˇ)
next-door neighbors

【鄱】6234 ㄆㄛˊ por pó
Poyang, name of a county in Kiangsi

鄱陽湖(ㄆㄛˊ ㄧㄤˊ ㄏㄨˊ)
the Poyang Lake in Kiangsi Province

【鄲】6235 ㄉㄢ dan dān
used in Hantan (邯鄲)—① name of a county in Hopeh ② a Chinese family name

【鄦】6236 ㄒㄩˇ sheu xǔ
name of an ancient state in what is today's Honan

十三畫

【鄴】6237 ㄧㄝˋ yeh yè
1. an ancient name for a part of what is today's Honan
2. a Chinese family name

【鄶】6238 ㄎㄨㄞˋ kuay kuài
name of an ancient state in what is today's Honan

十四畫

【鄹】6239 ㄗㄡ tzou zōu
name of the birthplace of

Confucius in what is today's Chüfu (曲阜), Shantung

〔酉部〕

十五畫

【酇】 6240 ㄎㄨㄤˋ kuanq kuàng
a Chinese family name

十七畫

【酃】 6241 ㄌㄧㄥˊ ling líng
1. name of a lake in Hunan whose water is used to brew wine
2. name of a county in Hunan

十八畫

【酆】 6242 ㄈㄥ feng fēng
1. the capital of the Chou Dynasty under King Wen(文王)
2. a Chinese family name

酆都(ㄈㄥ ㄉㄨ)
①name of a county in Szechwan ② Hades

十九畫

【酈】 6243 ㄌㄧˋ lih lì
1. an ancient name for a part of what is Honan today
2. a Chinese family name

【酇】 6244 ㄗㄢˋ tzann zàn
1. a community of a hundred families during the Chou Dynasty
2. name of a feudal state in the Han Dynasty

酉部 ㄧㄡˇ yeou yǒu

【酉】 6245 ㄧㄡˇ yeou yǒu
1. the tenth of the Twelve Terrestrial Branches
2. 5:00-7:00 p.m.

酉時(ㄧㄡˇ ㄕˊ)
the period of the day from 5 p.m. to 7 p.m.

二畫

【酊】 6246 ㄉㄧㄥˇ diing dǐng
intoxicated; drunk

【酋】 6247 ㄑㄧㄡˊ chyou qiú
1. the chief of a clan or tribe; a chieftain
2. to end

酋矛(ㄑㄧㄡˊ ㄇㄠˊ)
a kind of long spear

酋長(ㄑㄧㄡˊ ㄓㄤˇ)
① a chieftain; the chief of a tribe ② a sheik(h); an emir

三畫

【酌】 6248 ㄓㄨㄛˊ jwo zhuó
1. to drink
2. to pour (wine)
3. to weigh and consider

酌辦(ㄓㄨㄛˊ ㄅㄢˋ)
to handle by taking actual circumstances into consideration

酌定(ㄓㄨㄛˊ ㄉㄧㄥˋ)
to decide by taking circumstances into consideration; to make a considered decision

酌奪(ㄓㄨㄛˊ ㄉㄨㄛˊ)
to make a considered decision

酌量(ㄓㄨㄛˊ ㄌㄧㄤˋ)
to weigh and consider

酌加(ㄓㄨㄛˊ ㄐㄧㄚ)
to make considered additions

酌酒(ㄓㄨㄛˊ ㄐㄧㄡˇ)
to pour wine

酌減(ㄓㄨㄛˊ ㄐㄧㄢˇ)
to make considered reductions

酌情(ㄓㄨㄛˊ ㄑㄧㄥˊ)
to take circumstances into consideration; to make allowance

酌獻(ㄓㄨㄛˊ ㄒㄧㄢˋ)
to honor a deity with wine

酌議(ㄓㄨㄛˊ ㄧˋ)
to consider and discuss

【配】 6249 ㄆㄟˋ pey pèi
1. to join in marriage
2. to mate
3. to pair; to match: 顏色配得很好。The colors match well.
4. to fit; to suit; to be a match for; to match; to equal: 我配把鑰匙。I have a key made to fit a lock.
5. to dispense (medicines); to prepare (according to a demand); to distribute (according to a plan)
6. to exile
7. a spouse; a partner
8. subordinate; supplementary; supporting; attached
9. to deserve; to be worthy of; to be qualified: 他不配當一名領導者。He is not qualified to be a leader.

配備(ㄆㄟˋ ㄅㄟˋ)
① an outfit; equipment ② to provide; to fit out

配不上(ㄆㄟˋ ·ㄅㄨ ㄕㄤˋ)
to be no match for

配發(ㄆㄟˋ ㄈㄚ)
to distribute

配方(ㄆㄟˋ ㄈㄤ)
to dispense prescriptions

配房(ㄆㄟˋ ㄈㄤˊ)
(said of a building) a wing

配搭(ㄆㄟˋ ㄉㄚ)
to accompany in a supporting position; to match

配殿(ㄆㄟˋ ㄉㄧㄢˋ)
(said of a palace building) a wing

配對(ㄆㄟˋ ㄉㄨㄟˋ)
to pair; to be a pair; to mate; to match: 那兩隻鞋子不配對。Those two shoes don't match.

配隸(ㄆㄟˋ ㄌㄧˋ)
to place in subordination to

配儷(ㄆㄟˋ ㄌㄧˋ)
a spouse

配料(ㄆㄟˋ ㄌㄧㄠˋ)
(metallurgy) burden

配合(ㄆㄟˋ ㄏㄜˊ)
to be in tune with; to be adapted to; to match; to fit; to coordinate with; to cooperate with; to synchronize with: 襯衫的顏色與上衣的顏色不配合。The color of the shirt does not match that of the coat.

配貨(ㄆㄟˋ ㄏㄨㄛˋ)

to prepare goods for delivery according to an order

配給(ㄆㄟˋ ㄐㄧˇ)
① to distribute in rations; to ration; to allocate ② allocation

配給品(ㄆㄟˋ ㄐㄧˇ ㄆㄧㄣˇ)
rationed goods; an allocation

配給證(ㄆㄟˋ ㄐㄧˇ ㄓㄥˋ)
ration cards; ration coupons

配件(ㄆㄟˋ ㄐㄧㄢˋ)
accessories: 這些是不可缺少的配件。These are indispensable accessories.

配角(ㄆㄟˋ ㄐㄩㄝˊ)
① to appear with another leading player; to costar ② a supporting role; a minor role; a supporting actor or actress

配戲(ㄆㄟˋ ㄒㄧˋ)
to play a supporting role in a play

配享(ㄆㄟˋ ㄒㄧㄤˇ)
(said of courtiers, wise men, etc.) to have the honor of being enshrined in a Confucian temple, the ancestral temple of the emperor, etc.

配享千秋(ㄆㄟˋ ㄒㄧㄤˇ ㄑㄧㄢ ㄑㄧㄡ)
to be honored in a sacred shrine for endless ages

配置(ㄆㄟˋ ㄓˋ)
to station (troops); to equip (troops with weapons); to dispose (troops); to deploy: 哨兵配置在山上站崗。The sentinel was stationed on a hill.

配製(ㄆㄟˋ ㄓˋ)
to prepare or concoct according to a recipe or prescription

配種(ㄆㄟˋ ㄓㄨㄥˇ)
(animal husbandry) breeding

配售(ㄆㄟˋ ㄕㄡˋ)
to ration merchandise for sale

配生忒(ㄆㄟˋ ㄕㄥ ㄊㄜˋ)
a transliteration of 'per cent'

配色(ㄆㄟˋ ㄙㄜˋ)
to blend colors; to match colors

配所(ㄆㄟˋ ㄙㄨㄛˇ)
a place of exile

配偶(ㄆㄟˋ ㄡˇ)
a spouse; a mate

配貳(ㄆㄟˋ ㄦˋ)
a deputy; an assistant

配藥(ㄆㄟˋ ㄧㄠˋ)
to dispense medicines; to fill a prescription: 藥劑師照藥方配藥。The druggist filled a prescription.

配鑰匙(ㄆㄟˋ ㄧㄠˋ ˙ㄕ)
to duplicate keys

配眼鏡(ㄆㄟˋ ㄧㄢˇ ˙ㄐㄧㄥ)
to get the right lenses for one's eyeglasses

配音(ㄆㄟˋ ㄧㄣ)
(movies) to dub; dubbing; to synchronize; synchronization: 我們爲外國影片配音。We dubbed foreign films in Chinese.

配樂(ㄆㄟˋ ㄩㄝˋ)
to dub in background music; incidental music

【酒】 6250
ㄐㄧㄡˇ jeou jiǔ
alcoholic drinks (brewed or distilled); wine; liquor; spirits: 酒後見眞情。In wine there is truth.

酒吧(ㄐㄧㄡˇ ㄅㄚ)
a bar (for alcoholic drinks)

酒吧女(ㄐㄧㄡˇ ㄅㄚ ㄋㄩˇ)
a bar girl; a barmaid

酒杯(ㄐㄧㄡˇ ㄅㄟ)
winecups

酒保(ㄐㄧㄡˇ ㄅㄠˇ)
a bartender; a waiter

酒癖(ㄐㄧㄡˇ ㄆㄧˇ)
dipsomania

酒瓶(ㄐㄧㄡˇ ㄆㄧㄥˊ)
a bottle for alcoholic drinks

酒鋪(ㄐㄧㄡˇ ㄆㄨˋ) or 酒店(ㄐㄧㄡˇ ㄉㄧㄢˋ)
a tavern; a saloon; a bar

酒魔(ㄐㄧㄡˇ ㄇㄛˊ)
an alcoholic; a drunkard

酒母(ㄐㄧㄡˇ ㄇㄨˇ)
distiller's grains or yeast: 酒母開始發酵。The yeast began to work.

酒坊(ㄐㄧㄡˇ ㄈㄤ)
a tavern; a bar

酒瘋(ㄐㄧㄡˇ ㄈㄥ)
the silly behavior of a drunkard; temporary mental disorder after drinking too much

酒逢知己千杯少(ㄐㄧㄡˇ ㄈㄥˊ ㄓ ㄐㄧˇ ㄑㄧㄢ ㄅㄟ ㄕㄠˇ)
(literally) When drinking with a bosom friend, a thousand cups will still be too little.—One can drink far more than usual with a bosom friend.

酒德(ㄐㄧㄡˇ ㄉㄜˊ) or 酒品(ㄐㄧㄡˇ ㄆㄧㄣˇ)
decorum in drinking

酒罈(ㄐㄧㄡˇ ㄊㄢˊ)
a large jar for wine or liquor

酒徒(ㄐㄧㄡˇ ㄊㄨˊ)
an alcoholic; a drunkard

酒桶(ㄐㄧㄡˇ ㄊㄨㄥˇ)
a wine barrel or cask

酒囊飯袋(ㄐㄧㄡˇ ㄋㄤˊ ㄈㄢˋ ㄉㄞˋ)
(literally) wine sack and rice bag—a man who can do nothing but drink and eat; a good-for-nothing

酒釀(ㄐㄧㄡˇ ㄋㄧㄤˋ)
fermented rice, barley, etc. for brewing wine or liquor

酒樓(ㄐㄧㄡˇ ㄌㄡˊ)
a tavern; a bar; a saloon; a restaurant

酒闌人散(ㄐㄧㄡˇ ㄌㄢˊ ㄖㄣˊ ㄙㄢˋ)
The wine is running out and the guests are departing.

酒力(ㄐㄧㄡˇ ㄌㄧˋ)
① the strength of an alcoholic drink ② one's capacity for drinking

酒帘(ㄐㄧㄡˇ ㄌㄧㄢˊ)
a tavern sign in the form of a streamer

酒量(ㄐㄧㄡˇ ㄌㄧㄤˋ)
one's capacity for drinking

酒令(ㄐㄧㄡˇ ㄌㄧㄥˋ)
a drinking game conducted by an elected leader

酒缸(ㄐㄧㄡˇ ㄍㄤ)
① a large jar for wine or liquor ② a tavern

酒過三巡(ㄐㄧㄡˇ ㄍㄨㄛˋ ㄙㄢ ㄒㄩㄣˊ)
after the drinking has gone through three rounds

酒鬼(ㄐㄧㄡˇ ㄍㄨㄟˇ)
① a drunkard; a sot ② a toper; a wine bibber

酒館(ㄐㄧㄡˇ ㄍㄨㄢˇ)
a tavern; a pub; a bar: 我們到酒館喝酒。We went round

to the pub for a drink.
酒客(ㄐㄧㄡˇ ㄎㄜˋ)
a drinker
酒庫(ㄐㄧㄡˇ ㄎㄨˋ)
a cellar for wine; a wine cellar
酒狂(ㄐㄧㄡˇ ㄎㄨㄤˊ)
① temporary madness caused by alcoholic intoxication ② a drunken man
酒後失態(ㄐㄧㄡˇ ㄏㄡˋ ㄕ ㄊㄞˋ)
to act ludicrously when drunk
酒後失言(ㄐㄧㄡˇ ㄏㄡˋ ㄕ ㄧㄢˊ)
to say something wrong when drunk
酒酣耳熱(ㄐㄧㄡˇ ㄏㄢ ㄦˇ ㄖㄜˋ)
The enlivening effect of alcohol is just at its height.
酒壺(ㄐㄧㄡˇ ㄏㄨˊ)
a wine pot or jar
酒話(ㄐㄧㄡˇ ㄏㄨㄚˋ)
utterances of a drunkard
酒會(ㄐㄧㄡˇ ㄏㄨㄟˋ)
a cocktail party; a cocktail reception 亦作「鷄尾酒會」
酒荒(ㄐㄧㄡˇ ㄏㄨㄤ)
① alcoholic addiction ② a shortage of alcoholic drinks
酒家(ㄐㄧㄡˇ ㄐㄧㄚ)
① a tavern; a bar; a wineshop ② the Chinese version of the geisha house in Japan; a girlie restaurant
酒家女(ㄐㄧㄡˇ ㄐㄧㄚ ㄋㄩˇ)or 酒女(ㄐㄧㄡˇ ㄋㄩˇ)
① a barmaid; a bar girl ② the Chinese counterpart of a Japanese geisha
酒窖(ㄐㄧㄡˇ ㄐㄧㄠˋ)
a wine cellar
酒禁(ㄐㄧㄡˇ ㄐㄧㄣˋ)
prohibition of alcoholic drinks
酒漿(ㄐㄧㄡˇ ㄐㄧㄤ)
wine
酒經(ㄐㄧㄡˇ ㄐㄧㄥ)
books about alcoholic drinks
酒精(ㄐㄧㄡˇ ㄐㄧㄥ)
alcohol
酒精燈(ㄐㄧㄡˇ ㄐㄧㄥ ㄉㄥ)
an alcohol burner
酒精中毒(ㄐㄧㄡˇ ㄐㄧㄥ ㄓㄨㄥˋ ㄉㄨˊ)
chronic alcoholism; alcoholism; alcohol poisoning: 酒精中毒會導致死亡。Alcoholism may result in death.
酒旗(ㄐㄧㄡˇ ㄑㄧˊ)
a tavern sign in the form of a streamer 亦作「酒帘」
酒氣噴噴(ㄐㄧㄡˇ ㄑㄧˋ ㄆㄣ ㄆㄣ)
(said of a drunkard) to smell heavily of alcohol
酒錢(ㄐㄧㄡˇ ㄑㄧㄢˊ)
tips
酒席(ㄐㄧㄡˇ ㄒㄧˊ)
a banquet; a feast
酒仙(ㄐㄧㄡˇ ㄒㄧㄢ)
"An Immortal with the Bottle"—a nickname of Li Po (李白), the famed Tang Dynasty poet, who was said to be at his inspired best in a state of drunkenness
酒興(ㄐㄧㄡˇ ㄒㄧㄥˋ)
elation from drinking
酒盅(ㄐㄧㄡˇ ㄓㄨㄥ)
winecups (especially small ones)
酒池肉林(ㄐㄧㄡˇ ㄔˊ ㄖㄡˋ ㄌㄧㄣˊ)
(literally) ponds of wine and woods of meat—debauchery on a magnificent scale; unprecedented luxury or wealth
酒廠(ㄐㄧㄡˇ ㄔㄤˇ)
a brewery; a winery; a distillery
酒食(ㄐㄧㄡˇ ㄕˊ)
food and drink
酒石(ㄐㄧㄡˇ ㄕˊ)
tartar or argol
酒石酸(ㄐㄧㄡˇ ㄕˊ ㄙㄨㄢ)
tartaric acid
酒聖(ㄐㄧㄡˇ ㄕㄥˋ)
a very strong drinker; a prodigious drinker
酒肉朋友(ㄐㄧㄡˇ ㄖㄡˋ ㄆㄥˊ ·ㄧㄡ)
friends in one's revels (not in one's need); fair-weather friends
酒肉和尙(ㄐㄧㄡˇ ㄖㄡˋ ㄏㄜˊ ·ㄕㄤ)
a drinking and nonvegetarian Buddhist monk
酒資(ㄐㄧㄡˇ ㄗ)
charges for drinks
酒滓(ㄐㄧㄡˇ ㄗˇ)or 酒糟(ㄐㄧㄡˇ ㄗㄠ)
the residue of fermented grain after the alcoholic contents have been distilled
酒糟鼻(ㄐㄧㄡˇ ㄗㄠ ㄅㄧˊ)or 酒渣鼻(ㄐㄧㄡˇ ㄓㄚ ㄅㄧˊ)
acne rosacea
酒醉(ㄐㄧㄡˇ ㄗㄨㄟˋ)
drunk; intoxicated; tipsy
酒醉飯飽(ㄐㄧㄡˇ ㄗㄨㄟˋ ㄈㄢˋ ㄅㄠˇ)
having drunk and eaten to one's heart's content
酒菜(ㄐㄧㄡˇ ㄘㄞˋ)
① relishes taken with wine ② wine and delicacies
酒肆(ㄐㄧㄡˇ ㄙˋ)
a tavern; a bar; a saloon
酒色(ㄐㄧㄡˇ ㄙㄜˋ)
wine and women—sensual pleasures
酒色過度(ㄐㄧㄡˇ ㄙㄜˋ ㄍㄨㄛˋ ㄉㄨˋ)
excessive indulgence in sensual pleasures; debauchery
酒色之徒(ㄐㄧㄡˇ ㄙㄜˋ ㄓ ㄊㄨˊ)
a libertine; a debauchee
酒色財氣(ㄐㄧㄡˇ ㄙㄜˋ ㄘㄞˊ ㄑㄧˋ)
wine, women, wealth, and power—four main temptations to a man
酒意(ㄐㄧㄡˇ ㄧˋ)
a sign of drunkenness; a tipsy feeling
酒肴(ㄐㄧㄡˇ ㄧㄠˊ)
wine and delicacies
酒友(ㄐㄧㄡˇ ㄧㄡˇ)
a bottle companion: 他被酒友引入歧途。He was led away by bottle companions.
酒言酒語(ㄐㄧㄡˇ ㄧㄢˊ ㄐㄧㄡˇ ㄩˇ)
to talk incoherently when drunk; to be unable to speak clearly when drunk
酒宴(ㄐㄧㄡˇ ㄧㄢˋ)
a feast; a banquet
酒癮(ㄐㄧㄡˇ ㄧㄣˇ)
addiction to alcohol
酒窩兒(ㄐㄧㄡˇ ㄨㄛㄦ)
dimples on one's cheeks
酒翁(ㄐㄧㄡˇ ㄨㄥ)
a brewer
酒暈(ㄐㄧㄡˇ ㄩㄣˋ)
a flush on the face as a result of drinking

四畫

【酖】6251
1. ㄉㄢ dan dān
addicted to alcoholic drinks
酖酖(ㄉㄢ ㄉㄢ)
enjoying comfort

〔酉部〕

【酖】 6251 2. ㄓㄣˋ jenn zhèn
poisonous wine
酖毒(ㄓㄣˋ ㄉㄨˊ)
poison

【酗】 6252 ㄒㄩˋ shiuh xù
to lose one's temper when drunk
酗酒(ㄒㄩˋ ㄐㄧㄡˇ)
to indulge in excessive drinking; to take to drinking: 他們酗酒滋事。They indulged in excessive drinking and created a disturbance.
酗訟(ㄒㄩˋ ㄙㄨㄥˋ)
to accuse each other because people got drunk

五畫

【酢】 6253 ㄗㄨㄛˋ tzuoh zuò
(said of a guest) to toast the host
酢漿草(ㄗㄨㄛˋ ㄐㄧㄤ ㄘㄠˇ)
(botany) the creeping oxalis (*Oxalis corniculata*)

【酣】 6254 ㄏㄢ han hān
1. to enjoy intoxicants; to drink wine
2. to one's heart's content; as much as one wants; without inhibition
酣眠(ㄏㄢ ㄇㄧㄢˊ)
to sleep soundly
酣放(ㄏㄢ ㄈㄤˋ)
①(said of writing) unrestrained ② to indulge in excessive drinking; to drink without restraint
酣謔(ㄏㄢ ㄋㄩㄝˋ)
drinking and joking
酣樂(ㄏㄢ ㄌㄜˋ)
unrestrained pleasure
酣歌(ㄏㄢ ㄍㄜ)
to sing in exhilaration from drinking
酣呼(ㄏㄢ ㄏㄨ)
to yell or shout without restraint
酣興(ㄏㄢ ㄒㄧㄥˋ)
elation or exhilaration from liquor
酣戰(ㄏㄢ ㄓㄢˋ)
① to fight a fierce battle: 兩軍正酣戰。Two armies are fighting a fierce battle. ② the fierceness of a battle
酣中客(ㄏㄢ ㄓㄨㄥ ㄎㄜˋ)
an intoxicated person
酣暢(ㄏㄢ ㄔㄤˋ)
① to drink to one's heart's content; to drink as much as one can ② with ease and verve; fully
酣賞(ㄏㄢ ㄕㄤˇ)
to enjoy without restraint
酣睡(ㄏㄢ ㄕㄨㄟˋ)
to sleep soundly
酣醉(ㄏㄢ ㄗㄨㄟˋ)
deeply intoxicated by alcoholic beverages
酣縱(ㄏㄢ ㄗㄨㄥˋ)
to indulge in excessive drinking
酣飲(ㄏㄢ ㄧㄣˇ)
to drink as much as one can; to drink like a fish
酣娛(ㄏㄢ ㄩˊ)
to enjoy oneself to one's heart's content
酣飫(ㄏㄢ ㄩˋ)
intoxicated and satiated

【酤】 6255 ㄍㄨ gu gū
to sell or buy alcoholic drinks; to sell or buy spirits
酤酒(ㄍㄨ ㄐㄧㄡˇ)
to sell or buy alcoholic drinks

【酥】 6256 ㄙㄨ su sū
1. brittle; frail; fragile
2. crisp; crunchy
3. lustrous
酥餅(ㄙㄨ ㄅㄧㄥˇ)
a kind of crisp biscuit; shortcake
酥麻(ㄙㄨ ㄇㄚˊ)
frail and numb
酥髮(ㄙㄨ ㄈㄚˇ)
lustrous hair
酥糖(ㄙㄨ ㄊㄤˊ)
crunchy candy; sugar cakes
酥酪(ㄙㄨ ㄌㄠˋ)
kumiss
酥胸(ㄙㄨ ㄒㄩㄥ)
the soft and smooth skin of a woman's bosom
酥軟(ㄙㄨ ㄖㄨㄢˇ)
lacking strength; feeble
酥脆(ㄙㄨ ㄘㄨㄟˋ)
crisp
酥脆花生(ㄙㄨ ㄘㄨㄟˋ ㄏㄨㄚ ㄕㄥ)
crisp peanuts
酥油(ㄙㄨ ㄧㄡˊ)
butter

六畫

【酩】 6257 ㄇㄧㄥˇ miing mǐng (又讀 ㄇㄧㄥˊ ming míng)
drunk; intoxicated; inebriate; inebriety; tipsy
酩酊(ㄇㄧㄥˇ ㄉㄧㄥˇ)
intoxicated; drunk; tipsy; dead drunk
酩酊大醉(ㄇㄧㄥˇ ㄉㄧㄥˇ ㄉㄚˋ ㄗㄨㄟˋ)
dead drunk

【酪】 6258 ㄌㄠˋ law lào (讀音 ㄌㄨㄛˋ luoh luò)
1. alcoholic drinks
2. animal milk
3. cheese
4. fruit jam
5. junket
6. thick fruit juice; fruit jelly
酪餅(ㄌㄠˋ ㄅㄧㄥˇ)
cheese
酪酥(ㄌㄠˋ ㄙㄨ)
cream cheese
酪酸(ㄌㄠˋ ㄙㄨㄢ)
butyric acid

【酯】 6259 ㄓˇ jyy zhǐ
esters

【酬】 6260 ㄔㄡˊ chour chóu
1. to toast; to offer or present a cup of spirits, as in 獻酬
2. to reward; to requite; to reciprocate; reward
3. to fulfill; to realize
酬報(ㄔㄡˊ ㄅㄠˋ)
to reward; to requite
酬答(ㄔㄡˊ ㄉㄚˊ)
to reward; to requite
酬對(ㄔㄡˊ ㄉㄨㄟˋ)
to deal with (guests)
酬勞(ㄔㄡˊ ㄌㄠˊ)
to reward services
酬和(ㄔㄡˊ ㄏㄜˋ)
to exchange literary works as presents
酬金(ㄔㄡˊ ㄐㄧㄣ)

a cash reward; a bounty

酬謝(ㄔㄡˊ ㄒㄧㄝˋ)
to thank or reward (with money or gifts)

酬志(ㄔㄡˊ ㄓˋ)
to fulfill one's ambition

酬唱(ㄔㄡˊ ㄔㄤˋ)
to exchange poems, etc., as presents

酬神(ㄔㄡˊ ㄕㄣˊ)
to thank the gods with sacrifices

酬酢(ㄔㄡˊ ㄗㄨㄛˋ)
① social intercourse ② to exchange toasts

酬賽(ㄔㄡˊ ㄙㄞˋ)
to thank the gods with sacrifices

酬應(ㄔㄡˊ ㄧㄥˋ)
① to deal with (guests or visitors) ② social intercourse

酬庸(ㄔㄡˊ ㄩㄥ)
to reward services

【酮】 6261 ㄊㄨㄥˊ torng tóng
ketones

七畫

【酲】 6262 ㄔㄥˊ cherng chéng
hangover after heavy drinking; to be intoxicated, stupefied by drinking

【酵】 6263 ㄒㄧㄠˋ shiaw xiào
yeast; leaven

酵母(ㄒㄧㄠˋ ㄇㄨˇ)
yeast; leaven

酵母菌(ㄒㄧㄠˋ ㄇㄨˇ ㄐㄩㄣˋ)
a yeast fungus (*Saccharomycetes*)

酵素(ㄒㄧㄠˋ ㄙㄨˋ)
an enzyme

【酷】 6264 ㄎㄨˋ kuh kù
1. (said of intoxicants) strong
2. (said of fragrance) very stimulating
3. cruel; relentless; ruthless; brutal; severe; harsh
4. exceedingly

酷吏(ㄎㄨˋ ㄌㄧˋ)
a cruel official

酷烈(ㄎㄨˋ ㄌㄧㄝˋ)
cruel; brutal; atrocious; harsh; severe

酷好(ㄎㄨˋ ㄏㄠˋ)
to be very fond of (a thing); to have a yen for

酷寒(ㄎㄨˋ ㄏㄢˊ)
severe cold

酷肖(ㄎㄨˋ ㄒㄧㄠˋ)
to resemble very closely

酷刑(ㄎㄨˋ ㄒㄧㄥˊ)
to torture; torture

酷暑(ㄎㄨˋ ㄕㄨˇ)
very hot weather

酷熱(ㄎㄨˋ ㄖㄜˋ)
torturing heat; extremely hot (weather)

酷似(ㄎㄨˋ ㄙˋ)
to resemble very closely: 她酷似她的母親。She strongly resembles her mother.

酷愛(ㄎㄨˋ ㄞˋ)
to be very fond of (a thing) 參看「酷好」: 他酷愛美術和古典音樂。He was very fond of the fine arts and classical music.

【酸】 6265 ㄙㄨㄢ suan suān
1. sour; acid; tart
2. stale; spoiled
3. sad; grieved; sorrowful
4. aching; a tingle; an ache
5. jealous; envious
6. stingy
7. (chemistry) acid

酸鼻(ㄙㄨㄢ ㄅㄧˊ)
to have an irritated sensation in the nose; to feel like crying; to be grieved

酸葡萄(ㄙㄨㄢ ㄆㄨˊ ·ㄊㄠ)
sour grapes—something scorned because it cannot be had

酸梅(ㄙㄨㄢ ㄇㄟˊ)
sour plums

酸梅湯(ㄙㄨㄢ ㄇㄟˊ ㄊㄤ)
a decoction of sour plums used as a summer drink

酸腐(ㄙㄨㄢ ㄈㄨˇ)
① stale; hackneyed; trite ② erosion caused by acid

酸疼(ㄙㄨㄢ ㄊㄥˊ) or 酸痛(ㄙㄨㄢ ㄊㄨㄥˋ)
(said of muscles) to ache from overexertion

酸甜苦辣(ㄙㄨㄢ ㄊㄧㄢˊ ㄎㄨˇ ㄌㄚˋ)
sour, sweet, bitter, and hot —the sweets and bitters (of life)

酸奶(ㄙㄨㄢ ㄋㄞˇ) or 酸牛奶(ㄙㄨㄢ ㄋㄧㄡˊ ㄋㄞˇ)
yoghurt; sour milk

酸辣湯(ㄙㄨㄢ ㄌㄚˋ ㄊㄤ)
a kind of soup seasoned with vinegar and pepper

酸類(ㄙㄨㄢ ㄌㄟˋ)
acids

酸懶(ㄙㄨㄢ ㄌㄢˇ)
indolent with aching muscles

酸梨(ㄙㄨㄢ ㄌㄧˊ)
a variety of pear (with a sour taste)

酸溜溜(ㄙㄨㄢ ㄌㄧㄡ ㄌㄧㄡ)
① sour ② sad; grievous ③ jealous; envious ④ to ache

酸根(ㄙㄨㄢ ㄍㄣ)
acid radicals

酸梗(ㄙㄨㄢ ㄍㄥˇ)
an aching void in the heart; sorrow

酸懷(ㄙㄨㄢ ㄏㄨㄞˊ)
sorrow; grief

酸基(ㄙㄨㄢ ㄐㄧ)
acid radicals 參看「酸根」

酸秀才(ㄙㄨㄢ ㄒㄧㄡˋ ㄘㄞˊ)
a pedantic scholar

酸辛(ㄙㄨㄢ ㄒㄧㄣ)
hardship: 他受盡各種艱難酸辛。He suffered all kinds of hardships.

酸心(ㄙㄨㄢ ㄒㄧㄣ)
① heartbroken; sad; grieved ② heartburn

酸性(ㄙㄨㄢ ㄒㄧㄥˋ)
acidity

酸性廢物(ㄙㄨㄢ ㄒㄧㄥˋ ㄈㄟˋ ㄨˋ)
acid waste

酸性鹽(ㄙㄨㄢ ㄒㄧㄥˋ ㄧㄢˊ)
acid salt

酸性雨(ㄙㄨㄢ ㄒㄧㄥˋ ㄩˇ)
acid rain 亦作「酸雨」

酸削(ㄙㄨㄢ ㄒㄩㄝ)
to ache

酸楚(ㄙㄨㄢ ㄔㄨˇ)
hardship

酸愴(ㄙㄨㄢ ㄔㄨㄤˋ)
grief; sorrow

酸軟(ㄙㄨㄢ ㄖㄨㄢˇ)
(said of muscles, limbs, etc.) aching and lacking strength: 他四肢酸軟無力。His limbs are aching and limp.

酸棗子(ㄙㄨㄢ ㄗㄠˇ ·ㄗ) or 酸棗兒(ㄙㄨㄢ ㄗㄠˇㄦ) or 酸棗(ㄙㄨㄢ ㄗㄠˇ)

a kind of date (with a sour taste)

酸菜(ㄙㄨㄢ ㄘㄞˋ)
pickled cabbage (which tastes sour); pickled vegetables

酸筍(ㄙㄨㄢ ㄙㄨㄣˇ)
a kind of edible bamboo shoot

酸噎(ㄙㄨㄢ ㄧㄝ)
sad; grieved; heartbroken

酸味(ㄙㄨㄢ ㄨㄟˋ)
acid; a sour taste

【酹】 6266
ㄌㄟˋ ley lèi
to make a libation

酹地(ㄌㄟˋ ㄉㄧˋ)
to make a libation; to pour wine in a libation

【酺】 6267
ㄆㄨˊ pwu pú
to drink in company

酺燕(ㄆㄨˊ ㄧㄢˋ)
to drink with one's subjects or vassals

【酴】 6268
ㄊㄨˊ twu tú
1. a distiller's grain or yeast
2. wine brewed for the second time

酴醿(ㄊㄨˊ ㄇㄧˊ)
① wine brewed for the second time ② a kind of shrub 亦作「荼蘼」

酴醿酒(ㄊㄨˊ ㄇㄧˊ ㄐㄧㄡˇ)or 酴酒(ㄊㄨˊ ㄐㄧㄡˇ)
wine brewed for the second time

酴酥(ㄊㄨˊ ㄙㄨ)
a kind of medicated wine 亦作「屠蘇酒」

八畫

【醃】 6269
ㄧㄢ ian yān
to pickle; to salt

醃肉(ㄧㄢ ㄖㄡˋ)
salted pork; salted meat

醃菜(ㄧㄢ ㄘㄞˋ)
pickled vegetables

醃魚(ㄧㄢ ㄩˊ)
salted fish

【醅】 6270
ㄆㄟ pei pēi
unstrained wine

【醇】 6271
ㄔㄨㄣˊ chwen chún
1. rich wine; strong wine
2. pure; unadulterated
3. gentle; gracious; judicious
4. ethyl alcohol

醇備(ㄔㄨㄣˊ ㄅㄟˋ)
pure and perfect

醇朴(ㄔㄨㄣˊ ㄆㄨˊ)
gentle and honest

醇美(ㄔㄨㄣˊ ㄇㄟˇ)
pure and fair

醇醲(ㄔㄨㄣˊ ㄋㄨㄥˊ)
rich wine; strong wine

醇醪(ㄔㄨㄣˊ ㄌㄠˊ)
rich wine; strong wine

醇醨(ㄔㄨㄣˊ ㄌㄧˊ)
strong wines and light wines

醇厚(ㄔㄨㄣˊ ㄏㄡˋ)
① mellow: 這種酒酒味醇厚。This kind of wine is mellow. ② gentle and kind

醇化(ㄔㄨㄣˊ ㄏㄨㄚˋ)
①(Aristotelian) catharsis ② to purify; to idealize

醇酒美人(ㄔㄨㄣˊ ㄐㄧㄡˇ ㄇㄟˇ ㄖㄣˊ)or 醇酒婦人(ㄔㄨㄣˊ ㄐㄧㄡˇ ㄈㄨˋ ㄖㄣˊ)
indulgence in wine and women—sensual pleasures

醇謹(ㄔㄨㄣˊ ㄐㄧㄣˇ)
gentle and judicious

醇精(ㄔㄨㄣˊ ㄐㄧㄥ)
diethyl ether or ethyl ether

醇儒(ㄔㄨㄣˊ ㄖㄨˊ)
a pure-minded scholar; an honest scholar

醇粹(ㄔㄨㄣˊ ㄘㄨㄟˋ)
pure; unadulterated

【醉】 6272
ㄗㄨㄟˋ tzuey zuì
1. drunk; intoxicated; tipsy
2. infatuated; charmed

醉墨(ㄗㄨㄟˋ ㄇㄛˋ)
drawings or writings done when one is drunk

醉倒(ㄗㄨㄟˋ ㄉㄠˇ)
to succumb to the effect of alcohol

醉態(ㄗㄨㄟˋ ㄊㄞˋ)
the state of being drunk

醉鬼(ㄗㄨㄟˋ ㄍㄨㄟˇ)
a drunkard: 醉鬼搗亂。A drunkard caused a disturbance.

醉客(ㄗㄨㄟˋ ㄎㄜˋ)
a drunken man

醉漢(ㄗㄨㄟˋ ㄏㄢˋ)
a drunkard; a drunken person

醉酒飽德(ㄗㄨㄟˋ ㄐㄧㄡˇ ㄅㄠˇ ㄉㄜˊ)
I am drunk with your wine and filled with your virtues. (a conventional phrase for thanking the host at the end of a banquet)

醉蟹(ㄗㄨㄟˋ ㄒㄧㄝˋ)
crabs steeped in wine (considered as a delicacy)

醉心(ㄗㄨㄟˋ ㄒㄧㄣ)
infatuated with (a pursuit); to be engrossed in; to be intoxicated with: 他醉心名譽。He was intoxicated with fame.

醉鄉(ㄗㄨㄟˋ ㄒㄧㄤ)
a paradise or utopia of drunkenness

醉醒(ㄗㄨㄟˋ ㄒㄧㄥˇ)
to regain presence of mind after getting drunk; to sober up

醉醺醺(ㄗㄨㄟˋ ㄒㄩㄣ ㄒㄩㄣ)
inebriated; sottish; drunk; tipsy; under the influence of liquor 亦作「醉薰薰」

醉生夢死(ㄗㄨㄟˋ ㄕㄥ ㄇㄥˋ ㄙˇ)
to live a befuddled life

醉聖(ㄗㄨㄟˋ ㄕㄥˋ)
① a great drinker; a prodigious drinker ② "A Sage with a Bottle"—a nickname of Li Po (李白), a famed Tang Dynasty poet who was said to write best while drinking

醉如泥(ㄗㄨㄟˋ ㄖㄨˊ ㄋㄧˊ)
dead drunk; drunk as a lord

醉意(ㄗㄨㄟˋ ㄧˋ)
slightly drunk; symptoms of drunkenness; tipsy: 你已經有幾分醉意了。You are a bit tipsy.

醉眼惺忪(ㄗㄨㄟˋ ㄧㄢˇ ㄒㄧㄥ ㄙㄨㄥ)
to have one's eyes blurred with drinking

醉臥(ㄗㄨㄟˋ ㄨㄛˋ)
to lie in a drunken stupor: 他醉臥地板上。He lay on the floor in a drunken stupor.

醉翁(ㄗㄨㄟˋ ㄨㄥ)
an old drunkard: 幾個醉翁躺在地上。Several old drunkards lay on the floor.

〔酉部〕

醉翁亭(ㄗㄨㄟˋ ㄨㄥ ㄊㄧㄥˊ)
the Pavilion of the Old Drunkard, in Anhwei, built during the Sung Dynasty and named by poet Ou-Yang Hsiu (歐陽修), who called himself the Drunken Lord

醉翁之意不在酒(ㄗㄨㄟˋ ㄨㄥ ㄓ ㄧˋ ㄅㄨˋ ㄗㄞˋ ㄐㄧㄡˇ)
(literally) The drunkard is not really interested in wine. —to be secretly interested in something while pretending to show interest in another

【餟】 6273 ㄔㄨㄛˋ chuoh chuò
to pour wine in a libation

【醋】 6274 ㄘㄨˋ tsuh cù
vinegar

醋罈子(ㄘㄨˋ ㄊㄢˊ ·ㄗ) or 醋罐子(ㄘㄨˋ ㄍㄨㄢˋ ·ㄗ)
a jealous person, especially a woman

醋海生波(ㄘㄨˋ ㄏㄞˇ ㄕㄥ ㄅㄛ) or 醋海興波(ㄘㄨˋ ㄏㄞˇ ㄒㄧㄥ ㄅㄛ)
disturbance due to jealousy; marital trouble arising from infidelity

醋勁兒(ㄘㄨˋ ㄐㄧㄣˋㄦ)
jealousy

醋酸(ㄘㄨˋ ㄙㄨㄢ)
acetic acid

醋意(ㄘㄨˋ ㄧˋ)
jealousy: 她的醋意熾熱。She is burning with jealousy.

【醁】 6275 ㄌㄨˋ luh lù
a kind of green-colored wine

九畫

【醒】 6276 ㄒㄧㄥˇ shiing xǐng
1. to recover from (drunkenness, a stupor, etc.); to sober up; to come to: 病人醒過來了。The patient has come to.
2. to awake; to wake up; to be roused: 我醒得很早。I woke up early.
3. to be clear or cool in mind: 他的頭腦清醒。He keeps a cool head.

醒脾(ㄒㄧㄥˇ ㄆㄧˊ)
①(said of plays, novels, etc.) entertaining ② to make fun of

醒木(ㄒㄧㄥˇ ㄇㄨˋ)
storyteller's wooden clappers

醒目(ㄒㄧㄥˇ ㄇㄨˋ)
① to catch the eye; eye-catching; to attract attention; refreshing ② awake; not asleep

醒來(ㄒㄧㄥˇ ㄌㄞˊ)
to wake up: 你通常在什麼時間醒來? What time do you usually wake up?

醒狂(ㄒㄧㄥˇ ㄎㄨㄤˊ)
a wild or an unrestrained person who romps without being drunk

醒豁(ㄒㄧㄥˇ ㄏㄨㄛˋ)
conspicuous; remarkable; clear; explicit: 那道理說得醒豁。That reason is clearly presented.

醒酒(ㄒㄧㄥˇ ㄐㄧㄡˇ)
to sober up from drunkenness; to dispel the effects of alcohol

醒覺(ㄒㄧㄥˇ ㄐㄩㄝˊ)
to awake; to wake

醒獅(ㄒㄧㄥˇ ㄕ)
the awakened lion

醒世(ㄒㄧㄥˇ ㄕˋ)
to rouse the public from mental slumber

醒眼(ㄒㄧㄥˇ ㄧㄢˇ)
to attract attention; to catch the eye; refreshing

醒悟(ㄒㄧㄥˇ ㄨˋ)
to awake (from errors, illusions, etc.); to come to one's senses; to come to realize: 他已醒悟了。He's come to realize the truth.

【醍】 6277 ㄊㄧˊ tyi tí
1. cream (of milk)
2. a kind of reddish wine

醍醐(ㄊㄧˊ ㄏㄨˊ)
① clarified butter (regarded as a symbol of Buddhist wisdom or truth) ② purity of a man's character

醍醐灌頂(ㄊㄧˊ ㄏㄨˊ ㄍㄨㄢˋ ㄉㄧㄥˇ)
①(Buddhism) to impart wisdom to one's mind ② to make one comfortable

【醐】 6278 ㄏㄨˊ hwu hú
as in 醍醐—clarified butter (a symbol of Buddhist truth or wisdom)

十畫

【醜】 6279 ㄔㄡˇ choou chǒu
1. ugly; homely; bad-looking: 她長得不醜。She is not bad-looking.
2. abominable; vile; bad
3. shameful; disgraceful; infamous
4. to compare

醜八怪(ㄔㄡˇ ㄅㄚ ㄍㄨㄞˋ)
a very ugly fellow; a monstrous fellow; an ugly woman 亦作「醜巴怪」

醜名(ㄔㄡˇ ㄇㄧㄥˊ)
bad reputation; dishonor; infamy; ill fame; notoriety

醜詆(ㄔㄡˇ ㄉㄧˇ)
to abuse; to revile

醜態(ㄔㄡˇ ㄊㄞˋ)
scandalous behavior; an unseemly sight; a disgraceful manner

醜態百出(ㄔㄡˇ ㄊㄞˋ ㄅㄞˇ ㄔㄨ)
to show all sorts of disgraceful behavior; to act like a buffoon

醜類(ㄔㄡˇ ㄌㄟˋ)
① the bad kind; rascals; villains ② to compare things of the same kind

醜陋(ㄔㄡˇ ㄌㄡˋ)
ugly; bad-looking

醜虜(ㄔㄡˇ ㄌㄨˇ)
(a disparaging term) the enemy

醜化(ㄔㄡˇ ㄏㄨㄚˋ)
to smear; to uglify; to defame; to vilify: 這齣戲醜化我們的形象。This play vilifies us.

醜極了(ㄔㄡˇ ㄐㄧˊ ·ㄌㄜ)
extremely ugly; monstrous; abominable

醜行(ㄔㄡˇ ㄒㄧㄥˋ)
disgraceful behavior; shameful conduct

醜事(ㄔㄡˇ ㄕˋ)
a disgraceful affair; a scandal

醜聲四溢(ㄔㄡˇ ㄕㄥ ㄙˋ ㄧˋ)
notorious 或 The ill fame has spread far and wide.

醜死了(ㄔㄡˇ ㄙˇ ·ㄌㄜ)
abominable; monstrous; extremely ugly
醜惡(ㄔㄡˇ ㄜˋ)
ugly; repulsive; hideous
醜樣(ㄔㄡˇ ㄧㄤˋ)
ugly looks
醜聞(ㄔㄡˇ ㄨㄣˊ)
scandal
醜語(ㄔㄡˇ ㄩˇ)
abusive words; vile language

【醞】 6280 ㄩㄣˋ yunn yùn
1. to brew; to ferment
2. preliminary informal discussion; to deliberate on; deliberation
3. wine
醞釀(ㄩㄣˋ ㄋㄧㄤˋ)
① to brew (wine or liquor) ② (said of a storm, disturbance, etc.) to begin to form; to brew
醞藉(ㄩㄣˋ ㄐㄧㄝˋ)
cultivated and refined 亦作「蘊藉」

【醚】 6281 ㄇㄧˊ mi mí
ether

【醛】 6282 ㄑㄩㄢˊ chyuan quán
aldehyde

【醣】 6283 ㄊㄤˊ tarng táng
carbohydrate

【醢】 6284 ㄏㄞˇ hae hǎi
1. minced and hashed meat
2. to mince a criminal as a punishment in ancient China

十一畫

【醫】 6285 ㄧ i yī
1. to cure or treat (diseases)
2. a doctor; a physician; a surgeon
3. medical science; medical service; medicine
醫病(ㄧ ㄅㄧㄥˋ)
to treat a patient; to cure a disease: 醫病是醫生的職責。The business of doctors is to cure diseases.
醫卜星相(ㄧ ㄅㄨˇ ㄒㄧㄥ ㄒㄧㄤˋ)
medicine, prophecy, astrology and physiognomy—the occult sciences or the practitioners of such
醫方(ㄧ ㄈㄤ)
a medical prescription
醫德(ㄧ ㄉㄜˊ)
medical ethics
醫道(ㄧ ㄉㄠˋ)
medical skill; medical science
醫療(ㄧ ㄌㄧㄠˊ)
to cure or treat (a disease); medical treatment
醫療用具(ㄧ ㄌㄧㄠˊ ㄩㄥˋ ㄐㄩˋ)
medical instruments
醫國(ㄧ ㄍㄨㄛˊ)
to regulate the state; to cure a country of its ills
醫科(ㄧ ㄎㄜ)
the department of medicine (at a university): 他在大學讀醫科。He is studying medicine at the university.
醫家(ㄧ ㄐㄧㄚ)
a skilled doctor
醫界(ㄧ ㄐㄧㄝˋ)
the medical circles; the medical world
醫學(ㄧ ㄒㄩㄝˊ)
medical science
醫學博士(ㄧ ㄒㄩㄝˊ ㄅㄛˊ ㄕˋ)
Doctor of Medicine; M.D.
醫學士(ㄧ ㄒㄩㄝˊ ㄕˋ)
Bachelor of Medicine; M.B.
醫學院(ㄧ ㄒㄩㄝˊ ㄩㄢˋ)
a college of medicine
醫治(ㄧ ㄓˋ)
to cure (a disease); medical treatment; to doctor: 他醫治了那老人的疔。He doctored the old man's boil.
醫師(ㄧ ㄕ)
a physician; a surgeon; a doctor: 哪位醫師替你治病? Which doctor is treating you for this trouble?
醫師公會(ㄧ ㄕ ㄍㄨㄥ ㄏㄨㄟˋ)
a medical association
醫師節(ㄧ ㄕ ㄐㄧㄝˊ)
Medical Day (November 12)
醫士(ㄧ ㄕˋ)
a herb doctor; a doctor practicing Chinese herb medicine
醫生(ㄧ ㄕㄥ)
a doctor; a physician; a surgeon
醫術(ㄧ ㄕㄨˋ)
medical skill; the art of healing
醫藥(ㄧ ㄧㄠˋ)
healing drugs; medicines
醫藥保險(ㄧ ㄧㄠˋ ㄅㄠˇ ㄒㄧㄢˇ)
medical insurance
醫藥費(ㄧ ㄧㄠˋ ㄈㄟˋ)
a hospital bill; a doctor's fee; medical expenses; a medical bill: 我有醫藥費需要付。I have the medical bill to pay.
醫藥顧問(ㄧ ㄧㄠˋ ㄍㄨˋ ㄨㄣˋ)
a medical adviser
醫藥罔效(ㄧ ㄧㄠˋ ㄨㄤˇ ㄒㄧㄠˋ)
incurable with medicine 或 Medical science has failed (to save the patient).
醫務(ㄧ ㄨˋ)
medical matters
醫院(ㄧ ㄩㄢˋ)
a hospital: 他的妹妹是醫院的護士。His younger sister is a hospital nurse.

【醨】 6286 ㄌㄧˊ li lí
1. weak wine or liquor
2. light or weak (wine, tea, etc.)

【醪】 6287 ㄌㄠˊ lau láo
1. unstrained wine or liquor
2. mellow wine
醪糟(ㄌㄠˊ ㄗㄠ)
unstrained wine

【醬】 6288 ㄐㄧㄤˋ jiang jiàng
1. soybean sauce; soy
2. food in the form of paste; jam
醬瓜(ㄐㄧㄤˋ ㄍㄨㄚ)
cucumbers, etc. pickled in soybean sauce
醬肉(ㄐㄧㄤˋ ㄖㄡˋ)
pork cooked in soy sauce; braised pork seasoned with soy sauce
醬菜(ㄐㄧㄤˋ ㄘㄞˋ)
cabbages, etc. pickled in soybean sauce
醬色(ㄐㄧㄤˋ ㄙㄜˋ)
a dark brownish color
醬油(ㄐㄧㄤˋ ㄧㄡˊ)
soybean sauce; soy; soy sauce

【醯】 6289 ㄒㄧ shi xī

〔釆部〕

vinegar; pickle; acid

十二畫

【醭】 6290
ㄅㄨˊ bwu bú
(又讀 ㄆㄨˊ pwu pú)
white specks of mildew

【醮】 6291
ㄐㄧㄠˋ jiaw jiào
1. religious service
2. wedding; marriage

醮壇(ㄐㄧㄠˋ ㄊㄢˊ)
an altar for service of offering sacrifices to gods or the deceased

【醱】 6292
ㄆㄛˋ poh pò
to brew for the second time

醱酵(ㄆㄛˋ ㄒㄧㄠˋ)
to ferment

十三畫

【醴】 6293
ㄌㄧˇ lii lǐ
1. sweet wine
2. the sweet water from a spring

醴泉(ㄌㄧˇ ㄑㄩㄢˊ)
①a sweet spring or fountain ②name of a county in Shensi (陝西省)

【醲】 6294
ㄋㄨㄥˊ nong nóng
1. strong wine; rich wine
2. thick; dense; saturated 亦作「濃」

醲郁(ㄋㄨㄥˊ ㄩˋ)
(said of wine) rich; having more body

【醵】 6295
ㄐㄩˋ jiuh jù
to pool money (for a feast, etc.)

醵金(ㄐㄩˋ ㄐㄧㄣ) or 醵資(ㄐㄩˋ ㄗ)
to pool money

十四畫

【醺】 6296
ㄒㄩㄣ shiun xūn
drunk; intoxicated; tipsy

醺酣(ㄒㄩㄣ ㄏㄢ)
(said of weather) warm; balmy

醺醺(ㄒㄩㄣ ㄒㄩㄣ)
inebriated; under the influence of liquor; tipsy

十七畫

【釀】 6297
ㄋㄧㄤˋ nianq niàng
1. to brew; to ferment
2. to take shape or form slowly
3. wine

釀蜜(ㄋㄧㄤˋ ㄇㄧˋ)
(said of bees) to make honey

釀禍(ㄋㄧㄤˋ ㄏㄨㄛˋ)
to brew mischief

釀酒(ㄋㄧㄤˋ ㄐㄧㄡˇ)
to brew wine

釀成(ㄋㄧㄤˋ ㄔㄥˊ)
to bring about slowly; to breed; to lead slowly to; to form gradually

釀造(ㄋㄧㄤˋ ㄗㄠˋ)
to brew: 這酒是用米釀造的。This wine is brewed from rice.

【醽】 6298
ㄌㄧㄥˊ ling líng
a kind of wine

醽醁(ㄌㄧㄥˊ ㄌㄨˋ)
a kind of green-colored wine

【醾】 6299
ㄇㄧˊ mi mí
as in 酴醾—wine brewed for the second time

十八畫

【釁】 6300
ㄒㄧㄣˋ shinn xìn
1. to anoint (drums, bells, etc.) with blood in worship
2. to anoint (the body)
3. a rift (between people)

釁端(ㄒㄧㄣˋ ㄉㄨㄢ)
the cause of a fight

釁鼓(ㄒㄧㄣˋ ㄍㄨˇ)
to consecrate a drum by rubbing on it the blood of a slaughtered animal (before going to a battle in ancient times)

釁隙(ㄒㄧㄣˋ ㄒㄧˋ)
a rift (between groups of people)

釁鐘(ㄒㄧㄣˋ ㄓㄨㄥ)
to consecrate a bell by rubbing on it the blood of a slaughtered animal

釁鬯(ㄒㄧㄣˋ ㄔㄤˋ)
fragrant wine for anointing a dead body

釁浴(ㄒㄧㄣˋ ㄩˋ)
to bathe and anoint with fragrant essences (before worship)

二十畫

【釅】 6301
ㄧㄢˋ yann yàn
strong (beverages)

釆部
ㄅㄧㄢˋ biann biàn

一畫

【采】 6302
1. ㄘㄞˇ tsae cǎi
1. to gather; to collect
2. to pick; to select
3. bright colors

采辦(ㄘㄞˇ ㄅㄢˋ)
to select and purchase 亦作「採辦」

采集(ㄘㄞˇ ㄐㄧˊ)
to gather or collect (materials, etc.) 亦作「採集」

采芹(ㄘㄞˇ ㄑㄧㄣˊ)
(in former times) to pass the civil service examination on the county level 亦作「採芹」

采戲(ㄘㄞˇ ㄒㄧˋ)
a kind of game played with dice

采薪之憂(ㄘㄞˇ ㄒㄧㄣ ㄓ ㄧㄡ)
(literally) to worry about gathering firewood—ill health

采摭(ㄘㄞˇ ㄓˊ)
to pick up; to collect 亦作「採摭」

采詩(ㄘㄞˇ ㄕ)
to collect popular songs (as was done by the emperor's officials in ancient times) 亦作「採詩」

采聲(ㄘㄞˇ ㄕㄥ)
applause; cheers; shouts of "Bravo!"

采衣(ㄘㄞˇ ㄧ)
colorful garments; bright

garments 亦作「彩衣」

【采】 6302
2. ㄘㄞˋ tsay cài
a fief; vassalage

采地(ㄘㄞˋ ㄉㄧˋ)
a fief; vassalage

采邑(ㄘㄞˋ ㄧˋ)
a fief; vassalage

五畫

【釉】 6303
ㄧㄡˋ yow yòu
glaze (on pottery, etc.)

釉子(ㄧㄡˋ ·ㄗ)or 釉兒(ㄧㄡˋㄦ)
glaze (on pottery, etc.)

釉藥(ㄧㄡˋ ㄧㄠˋ)or 釉灰(ㄧㄡˋ ㄏㄨㄟ)
substance used to produce glaze for pottery; glaze

十三畫

【釋】 6304
ㄕˋ shyh shì
1. to explain; to interpret
2. to set free
3. to relieve
4. to disperse; to dispel
5. of Buddha or Buddhism

釋門(ㄕˋ ㄇㄣˊ)
a gate to Buddhism—Buddhism

釋悶(ㄕˋ ㄇㄣˋ)
to disperse melancholy; to chase away gloom

釋放(ㄕˋ ㄈㄤˋ)
to set free; to release

釋道(ㄕˋ ㄉㄠˋ)or 釋老(ㄕˋ ㄌㄠˇ)
Buddhism and Taoism

釋典(ㄕˋ ㄉㄧㄢˇ)
the Buddhist scriptures

釋奠(ㄕˋ ㄉㄧㄢˋ)
to honor gods or ancestors with sacrifices of wine and foods

釋例(ㄕˋ ㄌㄧˋ)
explanatory specimens

釋憾(ㄕˋ ㄏㄢˋ)
to dispel hatred or a grudge

釋迦(ㄕˋ ㄐㄧㄚ)
Sakya, the clan or family of Buddha

釋迦牟尼(ㄕˋ ㄐㄧㄚ ㄇㄡˊ ㄋㄧˊ)
Sakyamuni (563-483 B.C.)

釋教(ㄕˋ ㄐㄧㄠˋ)
Buddhism

釋去重負(ㄕˋ ㄑㄩˋ ㄓㄨㄥˋ ㄈㄨˋ)
to be relieved of a heavy responsibility

釋嫌(ㄕˋ ㄒㄧㄢˊ)
① to dispel suspicion ② to dispel ill feeling

釋氏(ㄕˋ ㄕˋ)
① Buddha ② a follower of Buddha

釋手(ㄕˋ ㄕㄡˇ)
to relax the hold; to loosen one's grip

釋然(ㄕˋ ㄖㄢˊ)
① at ease; relaxed ② having all the misunderstandings cleared up

釋子(ㄕˋ ㄗˇ)
Buddhist priests

釋疑(ㄕˋ ㄧˊ)
to dispel doubt; to settle uncertainties

釋義(ㄕˋ ㄧˋ)
expatiation; interpretation; to explain

里部
ㄌㄧˇ lii lǐ

【里】 6305
ㄌㄧˇ lii lǐ
1. a neighborhood, or community, of 25 families (in ancient times); a neighborhood; a village
2. *li* (a unit of linear measure about one third of a mile)

里保(ㄌㄧˇ ㄅㄠˇ)
(in ancient times) the head of a neighborhood consisting of 25 families

里門(ㄌㄧˇ ㄇㄣˊ)or 里閭(ㄌㄧˇ ㄌㄩˊ)
① a village gate ② villages; rural communities

里拉(ㄌㄧˇ ㄌㄚ)
a lira

里豪(ㄌㄧˇ ㄏㄠˊ)
a village bully

里居(ㄌㄧˇ ㄐㄩ)
① to live in the country; to live in retirement ② one's address

里巷(ㄌㄧˇ ㄒㄧㄤˋ)
streets

里巷之談(ㄌㄧˇ ㄒㄧㄤˋ ㄓ ㄊㄢˊ)
idle talk in the street; gossip

里胥(ㄌㄧˇ ㄒㄩ)
the village head

里長(ㄌㄧˇ ㄓㄤˇ)
①(in ancient times) the head of a neighborhood of 25 families ② the head of a subdivision of the district, or borough, in a city or county

里程(ㄌㄧˇ ㄔㄥˊ)
① mileage ② the course of development; course

里程碑(ㄌㄧˇ ㄔㄥˊ ㄅㄟ)
a milestone; a milepost 亦作「里程標」

里程表(ㄌㄧˇ ㄔㄥˊ ㄅㄧㄠˇ)
a table of distances

里程錶(ㄌㄧˇ ㄔㄥˊ ㄅㄧㄠˇ)
an odometer; a hodometer

里社(ㄌㄧˇ ㄕㄜˋ)
a village shrine, temple, etc.

里舍(ㄌㄧˇ ㄕㄜˋ)
a residence

里斯本(ㄌㄧˇ ㄙ ㄅㄣˇ)
Lisbon, the capital of Portugal

里昂(ㄌㄧˇ ㄤˊ)
Lyons (or Lyon), a city and industrial center of east France

里諺(ㄌㄧˇ ㄧㄢˋ)
proverbs

里約熱內盧(ㄌㄧˇ ㄩㄝ ㄖㄜˋ ㄋㄟˋ ㄌㄨˊ)
Rio de Janeiro, the former capital of Brazil

二畫

【重】 6306
1. ㄓㄨㄥˋ jonq zhòng
1. heavy; weighty; much: 我的工作很重。I have a heavy work load.
2. to weigh; weight
3. difficult
4. serious; grave
5. severe
6. important; significant
7. to value; to emphasize

重寶(ㄓㄨㄥˋ ㄅㄠˇ)
treasure of much value

重辦(ㄓㄨㄥˋ ㄅㄢˋ)
to take severe action against; to punish severely

重兵(ㄓㄨㄥˋ ㄅㄧㄥ)

a large force (for military operations); massive forces
重病(ㄓㄨㄥˋ ㄅㄧㄥˋ)
a serious illness
重砲(ㄓㄨㄥˋ ㄆㄠˋ)
heavy artillery; heavy guns
重錳酸鉀(ㄓㄨㄥˋ ㄇㄥˇ ㄙㄨㄢ ㄐㄧㄚˇ)
potassium permanganate
重名(ㄓㄨㄥˋ ㄇㄧㄥˊ)
① fame ② to value fame; to attach importance to fame
重罰(ㄓㄨㄥˋ ㄈㄚˊ)
to fine heavily; to punish severely; heavy fine; severe punishment
重犯(ㄓㄨㄥˋ ㄈㄢˋ)
an important criminal; a criminal who is guilty of a serious crime
重負(ㄓㄨㄥˋ ㄈㄨˋ)
a heavy burden; a heavy load; a heavy responsibility: 他覺得如釋重負。He feels as if relieved of a heavy load.
重大(ㄓㄨㄥˋ ㄉㄚˋ)
① important; of great consequence; significant ② serious; grave
重擔(ㄓㄨㄥˋ ㄉㄢˋ)
a heavy burden; a heavy responsibility
重地(ㄓㄨㄥˋ ㄉㄧˋ)
an important place; a restricted area: 施工重地，閒人莫進。Construction Site. No Admittance.
重典(ㄓㄨㄥˋ ㄉㄧㄢˇ)
severe provisions (in the law)
重點(ㄓㄨㄥˋ ㄉㄧㄢˇ)
the point or center of emphasis
重讀(ㄓㄨㄥˋ ㄉㄨˊ)
to stress: 重讀音節 a stressed syllable
重頭戲(ㄓㄨㄥˋ ㄊㄡˊ ㄒㄧˋ)
① a play involving much singing and action: 他演重頭戲。He performed a play involving much singing and action. ② a role involving much singing and action
重碳酸鈉(ㄓㄨㄥˋ ㄊㄢˋ ㄙㄨㄢ ㄋㄚˋ)
sodium bicarbonate
重聽(ㄓㄨㄥˋ ㄊㄧㄥ)
weak in hearing; hard of hearing: 她的祖母重聽。Her grandma is hard of hearing.
重農主義(ㄓㄨㄥˋ ㄋㄨㄥˊ ㄓㄨˇ ㄧˋ)
physiocracy; the advocacy that agriculture is all important
重利(ㄓㄨㄥˋ ㄌㄧˋ)
① a high interest rate (in money lending) ② to value material gain ③ huge profit
重力(ㄓㄨㄥˋ ㄌㄧˋ)
gravity
重力擺(ㄓㄨㄥˋ ㄌㄧˋ ㄅㄞˇ)
pendulum
重利盤剝(ㄓㄨㄥˋ ㄌㄧˋ ㄆㄢˊ ㄅㄛ)
to lend money at usury; to be a loan shark
重量(ㄓㄨㄥˋ ㄌㄧㄤˋ)
weight
重量級(ㄓㄨㄥˋ ㄌㄧㄤˋ ㄐㄧˊ)
(boxing) heavyweight
重工業(ㄓㄨㄥˋ ㄍㄨㄥ ㄧㄝˋ)
heavy industry
重活(ㄓㄨㄥˋ ㄏㄨㄛˊ)
heavy work
重轟炸機(ㄓㄨㄥˋ ㄏㄨㄥ ㄓㄚˋ ㄐㄧ)
a heavy bomber
重機槍(ㄓㄨㄥˋ ㄐㄧ ㄑㄧㄤ)
a heavy machine gun
重金禮聘(ㄓㄨㄥˋ ㄐㄧㄣ ㄌㄧˇ ㄆㄧㄣˋ)
to employ with good pay
重金屬(ㄓㄨㄥˋ ㄐㄧㄣ ㄕㄨˇ)
heavy metals
重晶石(ㄓㄨㄥˋ ㄐㄧㄥ ㄕˊ)
(mineral) barite
重器(ㄓㄨㄥˋ ㄑㄧˋ)
treasured wares
重遷(ㄓㄨㄥˋ ㄑㄧㄢ)
unwilling to be moved from where one lives
重情(ㄓㄨㄥˋ ㄑㄧㄥˊ)
to attach importance to matters of emotion or affection
重心(ㄓㄨㄥˋ ㄒㄧㄣ)
the center of gravity
重刑(ㄓㄨㄥˋ ㄒㄧㄥˊ)
severe punishment; heavy penalty: 殺人的重刑是死刑。The severe punishment for murder is death.
重型(ㄓㄨㄥˋ ㄒㄧㄥˊ)
heavy-duty
重鎮(ㄓㄨㄥˋ ㄓㄣˋ)
① key positions (in military operations); an important city ② a key figure
重杖(ㄓㄨㄥˋ ㄓㄤˋ)
to flog severely
重重的(ㄓㄨㄥˋ ㄓㄨㄥˋ ˙ㄉㄜ)
heavily; severely; seriously
重酬(ㄓㄨㄥˋ ㄔㄡˊ)
a substantial reward; a handsome reward
重臣(ㄓㄨㄥˋ ㄔㄣˊ)
an important official of the emperor
重懲(ㄓㄨㄥˋ ㄔㄥˊ)
to chastise or punish severely
重脣音(ㄓㄨㄥˋ ㄔㄨㄣˊ ㄧㄣ)
(in traditional Chinese phonetics) bilabial sounds; bilabials
重創
①(ㄓㄨㄥˋ ㄔㄨㄤ) a serious wound
②(ㄓㄨㄥˋ ㄔㄨㄤˋ) to inflict a severe blow on (the enemy)
重視(ㄓㄨㄥˋ ㄕˋ)
to pay much attention to; to consider important; to take matters seriously: 我們重視這件事。We take the matter seriously.
重傷(ㄓㄨㄥˋ ㄕㄤ)
a serious injury; a severe injury
重傷風(ㄓㄨㄥˋ ㄕㄤ ㄈㄥ)
a severe cold
重商主義(ㄓㄨㄥˋ ㄕㄤ ㄓㄨˇ ㄧˋ)
mercantilism
重賞(ㄓㄨㄥˋ ㄕㄤˇ)
to reward generously
重賞之下，必有勇夫(ㄓㄨㄥˋ ㄕㄤˇ ㄓ ㄒㄧㄚˋ, ㄅㄧˋ ㄧㄡˇ ㄩㄥˇ ㄈㄨ)
Generous rewards rouse one to heroism.
重水(ㄓㄨㄥˋ ㄕㄨㄟˇ)
heavy water
重然諾(ㄓㄨㄥˋ ㄖㄢˊ ㄋㄨㄛˋ)
judicious about giving promises; to make promises only after careful consideration
重任(ㄓㄨㄥˋ ㄖㄣˋ)
an important mission; an important office or post
重責(ㄓㄨㄥˋ ㄗㄜˊ)
① important responsibility ② to scold or flog severely
重罪(ㄓㄨㄥˋ ㄗㄨㄟˋ)
a serious offense or crime; felony
重義氣(ㄓㄨㄥˋ ㄧˋ ㄑㄧˋ)

particular about loyalty to friends

重義輕利(ㄓㄨㄥˋ ㄧˋ ㄑㄧㄥ ㄌㄧˋ)
to value justice above material gains

重壓(ㄓㄨㄥˋ ㄧㄚ)
great pressure; a heavy load

重要(ㄓㄨㄥˋ ㄧㄠˋ)
important; significant; vital

重要關鍵(ㄓㄨㄥˋ ㄧㄠˋ ㄍㄨㄢ ㄐㄧㄢˋ)
a key (to a problem); a crucial point

重要人物(ㄓㄨㄥˋ ㄧㄠˋ ㄖㄣˊ ㄨˋ)
an important or great figure

重要問題(ㄓㄨㄥˋ ㄧㄠˋ ㄨㄣˋ ㄊㄧˊ)
an important question; an important issue

重油(ㄓㄨㄥˋ ㄧㄡˊ)
heavy oil

重音(ㄓㄨㄥˋ ㄧㄣ)
(phonetics) accent; stress

重文輕武(ㄓㄨㄥˋ ㄨㄣˊ ㄑㄧㄥ ㄨˇ)
to put mental or intellectual pursuits above martial arts; to put mental training above physical training; to emphasize civil administration at the expense of national defense

重於泰山(ㄓㄨㄥˋ ㄩˊ ㄊㄞˋ ㄕㄢ)
(literally) heavier than Mount Tai—very weighty; very important

重用(ㄓㄨㄥˋ ㄩㄥˋ)
to give (someone) an important assignment

【重】 6306
2. ㄔㄨㄥˊ chorng chóng

1. to pile one upon another
2. to repeat; to duplicate
3. layers
4. double; manifold
5. numerous; countless

重名兒(ㄔㄨㄥˊ ㄇㄧㄥˊㄦ)
a namesake

重返(ㄔㄨㄥˊ ㄈㄢˇ)
to go back; to return: 我們重返家園。We returned to our homeland.

重犯(ㄔㄨㄥˊ ㄈㄢˋ)
to repeat (an error or offense): 我們應避免重犯錯誤。We should avoid repeating past errors.

重逢(ㄔㄨㄥˊ ㄈㄥˊ)
to meet again; to have a reunion: 他們久別重逢。They meet again after a long separation.

重複(ㄔㄨㄥˊ ㄈㄨˋ)
① to repeat; repetition ② to duplicate

重蹈覆轍(ㄔㄨㄥˊ ㄉㄠˋ ㄈㄨˋ ㄔㄜˋ)
to follow the same old disastrous road; to fall into the same trap

重疊(ㄔㄨㄥˊ ㄉㄧㄝˊ)
to pile one upon another; to superimpose

重提(ㄔㄨㄥˊ ㄊㄧˊ)
to mention again; to bring up (a subject) again

重瞳(ㄔㄨㄥˊ ㄊㄨㄥˊ)
an eye with double pupils

重來(ㄔㄨㄥˊ ㄌㄞˊ)
to do a thing over again; to repeat from the start; to return

重卵(ㄔㄨㄥˊ ㄌㄨㄢˇ)
(literally) eggs piled up in a heap—a dangerous situation

重閨(ㄔㄨㄥˊ ㄍㄨㄟ)
chamber (of a lady) deep inside the mansion

重規疊矩(ㄔㄨㄥˊ ㄍㄨㄟ ㄉㄧㄝˊ ㄐㄩˇ)
to duplicate precedents; repetitions

重光(ㄔㄨㄥˊ ㄍㄨㄤ)
① to return to light from darkness ②(said of once lost territory, etc.) to be recovered

重婚(ㄔㄨㄥˊ ㄏㄨㄣ)
bigamy; to commit bigamy

重婚罪(ㄔㄨㄥˊ ㄏㄨㄣ ㄗㄨㄟˋ)
bigamy: 他犯重婚罪。He committed bigamy.

重九(ㄔㄨㄥˊ ㄐㄧㄡˇ)
the Double Ninth Festival (on the 9th of the 9th lunar month)

重九登高(ㄔㄨㄥˊ ㄐㄧㄡˇ ㄉㄥ ㄍㄠ)
the custom of climbing to a high place to celebrate the Double Ninth Festival (on the 9th of the 9th lunar month)

重繭(ㄔㄨㄥˊ ㄐㄧㄢˇ)
to have blistered and callous feet (from walking)

重建(ㄔㄨㄥˊ ㄐㄧㄢˋ)
to rebuild; to reconstruct; to rehabilitate

重見天日(ㄔㄨㄥˊ ㄐㄧㄢˋ ㄊㄧㄢ ㄖˋ)
to see daylight again—to regain freedom; to be liberated or emancipated

重起爐灶(ㄔㄨㄥˊ ㄑㄧˇ ㄌㄨˊ ㄗㄠˋ)
to begin all over again

重慶(ㄔㄨㄥˊ ㄑㄧㄥˋ)
Chungking, Szechwan

重修(ㄔㄨㄥˊ ㄒㄧㄡ)
① to repair again ② to take (a course at school) for the second time (because of flunking)

重修舊好(ㄔㄨㄥˊ ㄒㄧㄡ ㄐㄧㄡˋ ㄏㄠˇ)
to renew friendly relations; to patch up; to reconcile: 我倆重修舊好。We renewed our friendly relations.

重現(ㄔㄨㄥˊ ㄒㄧㄢˋ)
to appear again; to reappear

重新(ㄔㄨㄥˊ ㄒㄧㄣ)
anew; afresh

重新部署(ㄔㄨㄥˊ ㄒㄧㄣ ㄅㄨˋ ㄕㄨˋ)
redeployment

重新分配(ㄔㄨㄥˊ ㄒㄧㄣ ㄈㄣ ㄆㄟˋ)
to distribute anew; to reallocate

重新組織(ㄔㄨㄥˊ ㄒㄧㄣ ㄗㄨˇ ㄓ)or 重組(ㄔㄨㄥˊ ㄗㄨˇ)
to reorganize

重振軍威(ㄔㄨㄥˊ ㄓㄣˋ ㄐㄩㄣ ㄨㄟ)
to restore the prestige of an army

重整(ㄔㄨㄥˊ ㄓㄥˇ)
to readjust (debts or credit)

重整旗鼓(ㄔㄨㄥˊ ㄓㄥˇ ㄑㄧˊ ㄍㄨˇ)
to rearm; to make preparations for a comeback; to rally one's forces

重抄(ㄔㄨㄥˊ ㄔㄠ)
to copy again: 他重抄書中的一頁。He copied a page of a book again.

重唱(ㄔㄨㄥˊ ㄔㄤˋ)
an ensemble of two or more singers, each singing one part

重出(ㄔㄨㄥˊ ㄔㄨ)
to appear again

重創(ㄔㄨㄥˊ ㄔㄨㄤ)
to injure again

重重(ㄔㄨㄥˊ ㄔㄨㄥˊ)
ring upon ring; one after another: 我們克服重重困難。We overcame one difficulty after another.

重重疊疊(ㄔㄨㄥˊ ㄔㄨㄥˊ ㄉㄧㄝˊ ㄉㄧㄝˊ)

〔里部〕

to pile one upon another
重施故技(ㄔㄨㄥˊ ㄕ ㄍㄨˋ ㄐㄧˋ)
to play the same old trick
重申(ㄔㄨㄥˊ ㄕㄣ)
to reaffirm; to reiterate; to restate
重奏(ㄔㄨㄥˊ ㄗㄡˋ)
an ensemble of two or more instrumentalists, each playing one part
重足側目(ㄔㄨㄥˊ ㄗㄨˊ ㄘㄜˋ ㄇㄨˋ)
very much scared
重作馮婦(ㄔㄨㄥˊ ㄗㄨㄛˋ ㄈㄥˊ ㄈㄨˋ)
to do something which one has done before
重操舊業(ㄔㄨㄥˊ ㄘㄠ ㄐㄧㄡˋ ㄧㄝˋ)
to return to one's old trade
重孫(ㄔㄨㄥˊ ㄙㄨㄣ)
a great-grandchild
重譯(ㄔㄨㄥˊ ㄧˋ)
to retranslate
重遊(ㄔㄨㄥˊ ㄧㄡˊ)
to revisit: 我重遊該地。I revisited that place.
重演(ㄔㄨㄥˊ ㄧㄢˇ)
to repeat the performance of; to repeat: 歷史的錯誤不許重演。Historical mistakes should not be repeated.
重印(ㄔㄨㄥˊ ㄧㄣˋ)
to reprint
重洋(ㄔㄨㄥˊ ㄧㄤˊ)
the ocean: 她遠渡重洋。She traveled across the oceans.
重圍(ㄔㄨㄥˊ ㄨㄟˊ)
a many-layered siege; a tight encirclement: 士兵們殺出重圍。The soldiers broke through a tight encirclement.
重溫舊夢(ㄔㄨㄥˊ ㄨㄣ ㄐㄧㄡˋ ㄇㄥˋ)
to revive an old dream; to reproduce the good old days; to rekindle the old flame of love
重文(ㄔㄨㄥˊ ㄨㄣˊ)
graphic variance of a word in Chinese
重淵(ㄔㄨㄥˊ ㄩㄢ)
deep water; the deepest part of a body of water

四畫

【野】 6307
ㄧㄝˇ yee yě
1. the countryside; fields; the wilderness
2. the people (as opposed to the government)
3. wild; uncultured; undomesticated; coarse; barbarous; rude
野百合(ㄧㄝˇ ㄅㄞˇ ㄏㄜˊ)
a kind of lily (*Crotalaria sessiliflora*)
野堡(ㄧㄝˇ ㄅㄠˇ)
a fieldwork
野砲(ㄧㄝˇ ㄆㄠˋ)
a field gun; a fieldpiece; field artillery
野葡萄(ㄧㄝˇ ㄆㄨˊ ·ㄊㄠ)
a kind of bryony
野馬(ㄧㄝˇ ㄇㄚˇ)
① a wild horse; a mustang ② floating mist
野貓(ㄧㄝˇ ㄇㄠ)
① a wild cat; a serval ② a badger ③ (dialect) a hare
野蠻(ㄧㄝˇ ㄇㄢˊ)
① barbarous; savage; uncivilized ② unreasonable; rude; brutal
野蠻人(ㄧㄝˇ ㄇㄢˊ ㄖㄣˊ)
barbarians; savages
野牡丹(ㄧㄝˇ ㄇㄨˇ ㄉㄢ)
a kind of peony (*Melastoma candidum*)
野地(ㄧㄝˇ ㄉㄧˋ)
① the countryside ② the wilderness
野兔(ㄧㄝˇ ㄊㄨˋ)
a hare: 野兔跑得很快。Hares can run very fast.
野牛(ㄧㄝˇ ㄋㄧㄡˊ)
a wild ox; a bison; a buffalo: 野牛有大角。Wild buffaloes have big horns.
野老(ㄧㄝˇ ㄌㄠˇ)
an aged rustic; an old peasant; an old man
野驢(ㄧㄝˇ ㄌㄩˊ)
an onager
野狗(ㄧㄝˇ ㄍㄡˇ)
a wild dog; a stray dog; a dog without an owner
野果(ㄧㄝˇ ㄍㄨㄛˇ)
wild fruit
野合(ㄧㄝˇ ㄏㄜˊ)
illicit copulation or connection
野鶴(ㄧㄝˇ ㄏㄜˋ)
a wild crane—a recluse
野孩子(ㄧㄝˇ ㄏㄞˊ ·ㄗ)
an urchin; a street urchin
野海棠(ㄧㄝˇ ㄏㄞˇ ㄊㄤˊ)
a begonia
野漢子(ㄧㄝˇ ㄏㄢˋ ·ㄗ)
(a woman's) paramour
野狐禪(ㄧㄝˇ ㄏㄨˊ ㄔㄢˊ)
(Buddhism) wild-fox meditators, i.e. non-Buddhist ascetics; heterodoxy in general
野花(ㄧㄝˇ ㄏㄨㄚ)
① a wild flower ② a harlot
野火(ㄧㄝˇ ㄏㄨㄛˇ)
① will-o'-the-wisp ② prairie fire; bushfire; wildfire ③ farm fire (for clearing the field)
野雞(ㄧㄝˇ ㄐㄧ)
① a pheasant ② a streetwalker; an unlicensed prostitute ③ unlicensed taxicabs
野雞大學(ㄧㄝˇ ㄐㄧ ㄉㄚˋ ㄒㄩㄝˊ)
a university which is not accredited by the authorities and whose major purpose is to make money instead of educating the students
野菊花(ㄧㄝˇ ㄐㄩˊ ㄏㄨㄚ)
(botany) mother chrysanthemum
野禽(ㄧㄝˇ ㄑㄧㄣˊ)
a wild fowl
野薔薇(ㄧㄝˇ ㄑㄧㄤˊ ㄨㄟˊ)
a wild rose
野小子(ㄧㄝˇ ㄒㄧㄠˇ ·ㄗ)
a boor (an abusive term applied to an ill-mannered stranger)
野莧菜(ㄧㄝˇ ㄒㄧㄢˋ ㄘㄞˋ)
tumbleweed
野心(ㄧㄝˇ ㄒㄧㄣ)
① ambition; careerism (especially of the objectionable kind) ② greediness
野心勃勃(ㄧㄝˇ ㄒㄧㄣ ㄅㄛˊ ㄅㄛˊ)
full of ambition: 他野心勃勃。He was over-ambitious.
野心家(ㄧㄝˇ ㄒㄧㄣ ㄐㄧㄚ)
a man of ambition (especially referring to the ambition one is not supposed to have); a careerist
野性(ㄧㄝˇ ㄒㄧㄥˋ)
jungle instincts; ungovernableness; untamedness; unruliness; wild nature
野性難馴(ㄧㄝˇ ㄒㄧㄥˋ ㄋㄢˊ ㄒㄩㄣˊ)

untamable: 他的孩子野性難馴。His son was untamable.
野戰(ㄧㄝˇ ㄓㄢˋ)
(military) field operations
野戰部隊(ㄧㄝˇ ㄓㄢˋ ㄅㄨˋ ㄉㄨㄟˋ)
(military) combat troops
野戰砲(ㄧㄝˇ ㄓㄢˋ ㄆㄠˋ)
(military) a field gun; a fieldpiece; field artillery
野戰醫院(ㄧㄝˇ ㄓㄢˋ ㄧ ㄩㄢˋ)
(military) field hospitals
野豬(ㄧㄝˇ ㄓㄨ)
a boar: 這些野豬已被閹割。These boars have been castrated.
野種(ㄧㄝˇ ㄓㄨㄥˇ)
a term of abuse applied to an adopted heir, meaning "a man of wild origin"
野史(ㄧㄝˇ ㄕˇ)or 野乘(ㄧㄝˇ ㄕㄥˋ)
unofficial history
野獸(ㄧㄝˇ ㄕㄡˋ)
a wild beast; a brute
野山羊(ㄧㄝˇ ㄕㄢ ㄧㄤˊ)
a markhor
野生(ㄧㄝˇ ㄕㄥ)
wild; undomesticated: 這種玫瑰是野生的。This kind of rose grows wild.
野生動物(ㄧㄝˇ ㄕㄥ ㄉㄨㄥˋ ㄨˋ)
wildlife; undomesticated animals
野生植物(ㄧㄝˇ ㄕㄥ ㄓˊ ㄨˋ)
wild plants; undomesticated plants
野人(ㄧㄝˇ ㄖㄣˊ)
①a rustic ②a barbarian; a savage
野人獻曝(ㄧㄝˇ ㄖㄣˊ ㄒㄧㄢˋ ㄆㄨˋ)or 野人獻日(ㄧㄝˇ ㄖㄣˊ ㄒㄧㄢˋ ㄖˋ)
(literally) a rustic offering sunshine—a trivial contribution (an expression of self-depreciation)
野菜(ㄧㄝˇ ㄘㄞˋ)
edible wild vegetables
野草(ㄧㄝˇ ㄘㄠˇ)
a weed: 花園中佈滿了野草。The garden was covered with weeds.
野餐(ㄧㄝˇ ㄘㄢ)
a picnic; a barbecue: 我們到山上野餐。We went on a picnic to the hill.
野鴨子(ㄧㄝˇ ㄧㄚ ·ㄗ)
a wild duck; a mallard
野宴(ㄧㄝˇ ㄧㄢˋ)
a picnic; a barbecue
野營(ㄧㄝˇ ㄧㄥˊ)
outdoor camping: 他外出野營。He went camping.
野外(ㄧㄝˇ ㄨㄞˋ)
the outdoors; the open
野外旅行(ㄧㄝˇ ㄨㄞˋ ㄌㄩˇ ㄒㄧㄥˊ)
an outing; an excursion: 我們去野外旅行。We went for an outing.
野味(ㄧㄝˇ ㄨㄟˋ)
game as food
野鴛鴦(ㄧㄝˇ ㄩㄢ ㄧㄤ)
a couple living as husband and wife without being legally married; illicit lovers
野雲雀(ㄧㄝˇ ㄩㄣˊ ㄑㄩㄝˋ)
a meadow lark

五畫

【量】 6308
1. ㄌㄧㄤˊ liang liáng
to measure: 我們量丈這屋子。We measured the room.
量杯(ㄌㄧㄤˊ ㄅㄟ)
a graduated cylinder; a measuring glass or cup
量肺器(ㄌㄧㄤˊ ㄈㄟˋ ㄑㄧˋ)
a spirometer
量度(ㄌㄧㄤˊ ㄉㄨㄛˋ)
to measure; to estimate
量角規(ㄌㄧㄤˊ ㄐㄧㄠˇ ㄍㄨㄟ)
a graduator; a protractor
量角器(ㄌㄧㄤˊ ㄐㄧㄠˇ ㄑㄧˋ)
a protractor
量熱器(ㄌㄧㄤˊ ㄖㄜˋ ㄑㄧˋ)
a calorimeter
量一量(ㄌㄧㄤˊ ·ㄧ ㄌㄧㄤˊ)or 量量(ㄌㄧㄤˊ ·ㄌㄧㄤ)
to take a measurement; to measure: 讓我來量量他的身高。Let me measure his height.
量雨表(ㄌㄧㄤˊ ㄩˇ ㄅㄧㄠˇ)
a rain gauge

【量】 6308
2. ㄌㄧㄤˋ lianq liàng
1. quantity
2. capacity
3. to estimate
量力(ㄌㄧㄤˋ ㄌㄧˋ)
to estimate one's strength, resources or ability: 他不自量力。He overrated his ability.
量力而爲(ㄌㄧㄤˋ ㄌㄧˋ ㄦˊ ㄨㄟˊ)
to estimate one's strength or resources before acting
量入爲出(ㄌㄧㄤˋ ㄖㄨˋ ㄨㄟˊ ㄔㄨ)
to regulate one's expenses according to one's income
量子(ㄌㄧㄤˋ ㄗˇ)
(physics) quantum
量子論(ㄌㄧㄤˋ ㄗˇ ㄌㄨㄣˋ)
the quantum theory
量詞(ㄌㄧㄤˋ ㄘˊ)
a classifier (as 個, 隻, 次)
量才取用(ㄌㄧㄤˋ ㄘㄞˊ ㄑㄩˇ ㄩㄥˋ)
to employ a person on the basis of his merits

十一畫

【釐】 6309
1. ㄌㄧˊ li lí
1. a unit of linear measure equal to one thousandth of the Chinese foot
2. a unit of weight equal to one thousandth of the tael
3. to manage; to administer; to arrange
4. to revise; to reform; to correct
5. same as 嫠—a widow
釐米(ㄌㄧˊ ㄇㄧˇ)
centimeter
釐婦(ㄌㄧˊ ㄈㄨˋ)
a widow
釐定(ㄌㄧˊ ㄉㄧㄥˋ)
to formulate (rules, etc.)
釐革(ㄌㄧˊ ㄍㄜˊ)
to revise; to reform
釐金(ㄌㄧˊ ㄐㄧㄣ)
likin, transportation tax levied on traders before the Republic
釐捐(ㄌㄧˊ ㄐㄩㄢ)
transportation tax levied on traders before the Republic
釐正(ㄌㄧˊ ㄓㄥˋ)
to correct; to rectify; to reform

【釐】 6309
2. ㄒㄧ shi xī
a blessing; happiness; bliss

〔金部〕

金部
ㄐㄧㄣ jin jīn

【金】 6310 ㄐㄧㄣ jin jīn

1. gold
2. metal
3. money; wealth
4. weapons; arms
5. precious; excellent; fine
6. golden
7. durable
8. name of the Tungusic Dynasty (1115-1234), which dominated Manchuria and North China
9. a Chinese family name

金波(ㄐㄧㄣ ㄅㄛ)
golden waves—the moonlight

金箔(ㄐㄧㄣ ㄅㄛˊ)
gold foil; gold leaf; gilt

金本位制(ㄐㄧㄣ ㄅㄣˇ ㄨㄟˋ ㄓˋ)
gold monometallism

金榜(ㄐㄧㄣ ㄅㄤˇ)
(under the former civil service examination system) the billboard announcing the names of successful candidates

金榜題名(ㄐㄧㄣ ㄅㄤˇ ㄊㄧˊ ㄇㄧㄥˊ)
to emerge successful from a competitive examination

金鎊(ㄐㄧㄣ ㄅㄤˋ)
pound sterling

金筆(ㄐㄧㄣ ㄅㄧˇ)
a (quality) fountain pen

金幣(ㄐㄧㄣ ㄅㄧˋ)
gold coins

金碧輝煌(ㄐㄧㄣ ㄅㄧˋ ㄏㄨㄟ ㄏㄨㄤˊ)
(said of a building) resplendent; gorgeous; grand; splendid; magnificent

金邊眼鏡(ㄐㄧㄣ ㄅㄧㄢ ㄧㄢˇ ㄐㄧㄥˋ)
gold-rimmed spectacles

金兵(ㄐㄧㄣ ㄅㄧㄥ)
troops of the Tungusic Dynasty of Chin (金) (1115-1234) who often invaded China

金不換(ㄐㄧㄣ ˙ㄅㄨ ㄏㄨㄢˋ)
① something not to be exchanged for gold—a very precious thing ② Chinese ink ③ a Chinese medicinal herb, also known as 三七草 (*Gynura pinnatifida*)

金牌(ㄐㄧㄣ ㄆㄞˊ)
a gold medal

金瓶梅(ㄐㄧㄣ ㄆㄧㄥˊ ㄇㄟˊ)
The Golden Lotus, a title of a novel written by an anonymous author in the Ming Dynasty, commonly regarded as an obscene book

金馬(ㄐㄧㄣ ㄇㄚˇ) or 金門馬祖(ㄐㄧㄣ ㄇㄣˊ ㄇㄚˇ ㄗㄨˇ)
Kinmen (or Quemoy) and Matsu, two groups of islands off the Fukien coast remaining free from Communism

金黴素(ㄐㄧㄣ ㄇㄟˊ ㄙㄨˋ)
Aureomycin

金門(ㄐㄧㄣ ㄇㄣˊ)
① Kinmen (or Quemoy), an island opposite Amoy in Fukien ② the Gate of Gold—(figuratively) the gate of the palace

金迷紙醉(ㄐㄧㄣ ㄇㄧˊ ㄓˇ ㄗㄨㄟˋ)
a luxurious life; an extravagant life

金木水火土(ㄐㄧㄣ ㄇㄨˋ ㄕㄨㄟˇ ㄏㄨㄛˇ ㄊㄨˇ)
metal, wood, water, fire and earth—the five elements in ancient Chinese philosophy and fortunetelling

金髮女郎(ㄐㄧㄣ ㄈㄚˇ ㄋㄩˇ ㄌㄤˊ)
a blonde

金粉(ㄐㄧㄣ ㄈㄣˇ)
① women's face powder ② gold dust

金風(ㄐㄧㄣ ㄈㄥ)
an autumn breeze

金鳳花(ㄐㄧㄣ ㄈㄥˋ ㄏㄨㄚ)
the buttercup

金丹(ㄐㄧㄣ ㄉㄢ)
a pill of immortality

金貂(ㄐㄧㄣ ㄉㄧㄠ)
attendants or retainers (who in ancient times used to wear caps trimmed with golden-colored sable)

金店(ㄐㄧㄣ ㄉㄧㄢˋ)
a jeweler's shop; a goldsmith's shop

金殿(ㄐㄧㄣ ㄉㄧㄢˋ)
a magnificent palace

金鈿(ㄐㄧㄣ ㄉㄧㄢˋ)
a golden hairpin

金太祖(ㄐㄧㄣ ㄊㄞˋ ㄗㄨˇ)
the founder of the Tungusic Dynasty of Chin (金), which dominated Manchuria and much of North China during 1115-1234 A.D.

金湯(ㄐㄧㄣ ㄊㄤ)
an impregnable fortress

金條(ㄐㄧㄣ ㄊㄧㄠˊ)
a gold bar

金柝(ㄐㄧㄣ ㄊㄨㄛˋ)
a night watchman's bell

金童玉女(ㄐㄧㄣ ㄊㄨㄥˊ ㄩˋ ㄋㄩˇ)
young boys and girls attending upon an immortal

金猊(ㄐㄧㄣ ㄋㄧˊ)
an incense burner shaped like a lion's head

金牛宮(ㄐㄧㄣ ㄋㄧㄡˊ ㄍㄨㄥ) or 金牛座(ㄐㄧㄣ ㄋㄧㄡˊ ㄗㄨㄛˋ)
Taurus

金諾(ㄐㄧㄣ ㄋㄨㄛˋ)
your esteemed pledge

金蘭(ㄐㄧㄣ ㄌㄢˊ)
harmonious friendship; sworn brotherhood

金蓮(ㄐㄧㄣ ㄌㄧㄢˊ)
(euphemism) bound feet of a woman

金蓮花(ㄐㄧㄣ ㄌㄧㄢˊ ㄏㄨㄚ)
(botany) a canary-creeper

金陵(ㄐㄧㄣ ㄌㄧㄥˊ)
Nanking (a former name)

金鈴子(ㄐㄧㄣ ㄌㄧㄥˊ ˙ㄗ)
① a kind of insect, like a cricket but smaller ② fruit of *Melia azedarach* (楝樹)

金鑾殿(ㄐㄧㄣ ㄌㄨㄢˊ ㄉㄧㄢˋ)
the main building of the imperial palace

金輪(ㄐㄧㄣ ㄌㄨㄣˊ)
the golden disk—the moon

金縷衣(ㄐㄧㄣ ㄌㄩˇ ㄧ)
a gold-threaded robe

金戈鐵馬(ㄐㄧㄣ ㄍㄜ ㄊㄧㄝˇ ㄇㄚˇ)
① weapons; arms; military hardware ② warfare

金革(ㄐㄧㄣ ㄍㄜˊ)
military hardware; arms

金剛(ㄐㄧㄣ ㄍㄤ)
① hard metal ② a Buddhist god sometimes identified with Indra

金剛怒目(ㄐㄧㄣ ㄍㄤ ㄋㄨˋ ㄇㄨˋ)

an awful look
金剛經(ㄐㄧㄣ ㄍㄤ ㄐㄧㄥ)
The Diamond Sutra, also known as *Prajna-Paramita Sutra* (般若波羅蜜經)
金剛石(ㄐㄧㄣ ㄍㄤ ㄕˊ)
diamond
金剛砂(ㄐㄧㄣ ㄍㄤ ㄕㄚ)
emery
金剛鑽(ㄐㄧㄣ ㄍㄤ ㄗㄨㄢ)
a diamond drill
金箍棒(ㄐㄧㄣ ㄍㄨ ㄅㄤˋ)
a magic cudgel—a weapon used by the Monkey King in the novel *Pilgrimage to the West* (西遊記)
金瓜(ㄐㄧㄣ ㄍㄨㄚ)
pumpkin
金閨(ㄐㄧㄣ ㄍㄨㄟ)
① a boudoir ② the imperial court
金龜(ㄐㄧㄣ ㄍㄨㄟ)
emblems worn by officials during the Tang Dynasty
金龜壻(ㄐㄧㄥ ㄍㄨㄟ ㄒㄩˋ)
a fine son-in-law; a rich son-in-law
金龜子(ㄐㄧㄣ ㄍㄨㄟ ˙ㄗ)
a tumblebug
金匱(ㄐㄧㄣ ㄍㄨㄟˋ)
a metal bookcase
金櫃(ㄐㄧㄣ ㄍㄨㄟˋ)
a strongbox; a safe
金棺(ㄐㄧㄣ ㄍㄨㄢ)
① a gilded coffin ②(euphemism) a coffin; a casket
金光黨(ㄐㄧㄣ ㄍㄨㄤ ㄉㄤˇ)
swindlers; racketeers
金光閃閃(ㄐㄧㄣ ㄍㄨㄤ ㄕㄢˇ ㄕㄢˇ)
glittering; glistening
金工(ㄐㄧㄣ ㄍㄨㄥ)
① metalwork ② a metal craftsman
金科玉律(ㄐㄧㄣ ㄎㄜ ㄩˋ ㄌㄩˋ)
the golden rule; an immutable law
金口(ㄐㄧㄣ ㄎㄡˇ)
① the Buddha's mouth ② utterances that carry weight
金口木舌(ㄐㄧㄣ ㄎㄡˇ ㄇㄨˋ ㄕㄜˊ)
a metal bell with a wooden clapper 亦作「木鐸」
金庫(ㄐㄧㄣ ㄎㄨˋ)
coffers; a treasury
金塊(ㄐㄧㄣ ㄎㄨㄞˋ)
gold bullion; a gold ingot
金礦(ㄐㄧㄣ ㄎㄨㄤˋ)
a gold mine
金華火腿(ㄐㄧㄣ ㄏㄨㄚˊ ㄏㄨㄛˇ ㄊㄨㄟˇ)
(a noted product) salted ham from Chinhua (金華), Chekiang 亦作「金腿」
金環蝕(ㄐㄧㄣ ㄏㄨㄢˊ ㄕˊ)
an annular eclipse of the sun
金婚(ㄐㄧㄣ ㄏㄨㄣ)
a golden wedding; the 50th wedding anniversary
金黃色(ㄐㄧㄣ ㄏㄨㄤˊ ㄙㄜˋ)
bright yellow; golden
金紅(色)(ㄐㄧㄣ ㄏㄨㄥˊ(ㄙㄜˋ))
reddish yellow; orange; golden-red
金紅石(ㄐㄧㄣ ㄏㄨㄥˊ ㄕˊ)
(mineral) rutile
金雞納(ㄐㄧㄣ ㄐㄧ ㄋㄚˋ)
(botany) cinchona
金雞納霜(ㄐㄧㄣ ㄐㄧ ㄋㄚˋ ㄕㄨㄤ)
quinine
金甲(ㄐㄧㄣ ㄐㄧㄚˇ)
armor (worn by a warrior)
金甲蟲(ㄐㄧㄣ ㄐㄧㄚˇ ㄔㄨㄥˊ)
a golden beetle
金價(ㄐㄧㄣ ㄐㄧㄚˋ)
the price of gold: 金價多少? What is the price of gold?
金盡交絕(ㄐㄧㄣ ㄐㄧㄣˋ ㄐㄧㄠ ㄐㄩㄝˊ)
Friendship lasts as long as money does.
金漿玉醴(ㄐㄧㄣ ㄐㄧㄤ ㄩˋ ㄌㄧˇ)
① good wine ② marvelous medicine; a panacea
金匠(ㄐㄧㄣ ㄐㄧㄤˋ)
a goldsmith
金橘(ㄐㄧㄣ ㄐㄩˊ)
(botany) a cumquat
金橘餅(ㄐㄧㄣ ㄐㄩˊ ㄅㄧㄥˇ)
a crushed cumquat preserved with sugar
金器(ㄐㄧㄣ ㄑㄧˋ)
a gold vessel
金錢(ㄐㄧㄣ ㄑㄧㄢˊ)
money; cash; riches; wealth: 時間即是金錢。Time is money.
金錢豹(ㄐㄧㄣ ㄑㄧㄢˊ ㄅㄠˋ)
a spotted leopard
金錢花(ㄐㄧㄣ ㄑㄧㄢˊ ㄏㄨㄚ)
Pentapetes phoenicea
金錢主義(ㄐㄧㄣ ㄑㄧㄢˊ ㄓㄨˇ ㄧˋ)
mercenariness
金錢萬能(ㄐㄧㄣ ㄑㄧㄢˊ ㄨㄢˋ ㄋㄥˊ)
Money is almighty.
金鎗魚(ㄐㄧㄣ ㄑㄧㄤ ㄩˊ)
the tunny
金闕(ㄐㄧㄣ ㄑㄩㄝ)
an imperial palace; an imperial abode
金雀花(ㄐㄧㄣ ㄑㄩㄝˋ ㄏㄨㄚ)
the furze
金像獎(ㄐㄧㄣ ㄒㄧㄤˋ ㄐㄧㄤˇ)
an Oscar award
金相玉質(ㄐㄧㄣ ㄒㄧㄤˋ ㄩˋ ㄓˋ)
① of very fine and durable material ② immortal literary works
金星(ㄐㄧㄣ ㄒㄧㄥ)
(astronomy) Venus
金枝玉葉(ㄐㄧㄣ ㄓ ㄩˋ ㄧㄝˋ)
a term referring to the members of the royal family
金針度人(ㄐㄧㄣ ㄓㄣ ㄉㄨˋ ㄖㄣˊ)
to teach others a knack of the trade
金針菜(ㄐㄧㄣ ㄓㄣ ㄘㄞˋ)
a day lily
金鐲(ㄐㄧㄣ ㄓㄨㄛˊ)
a gold bracelet
金鐘罩(ㄐㄧㄣ ㄓㄨㄥ ㄓㄠˋ)
(Chinese pugilism) the ability to sustain the thrusts of sharp weapons on one's bare skin
金翅雀(ㄐㄧㄣ ㄔˋ ㄑㄩㄝˋ)
a goldfinch
金釵(ㄐㄧㄣ ㄔㄞ)
a gold hairpin
金釵十二(ㄐㄧㄣ ㄔㄞ ㄕˊ ㄦˋ)
having many concubines
金蟬脫殼(ㄐㄧㄣ ㄔㄢˊ ㄊㄨㄛ ㄎㄜˊ)
to break loose and get away; to escape by a cunning maneuver
金城湯池(ㄐㄧㄣ ㄔㄥˊ ㄊㄤ ㄔˊ)
(literally) a city wall built with gold and a moat filled with boiling water—an impregnable fortress
金創 or 金瘡(ㄐㄧㄣ ㄔㄨㄤ)
wounds inflicted by sharp weapons; knife wounds 亦作「金瘍」
金石(ㄐㄧㄣ ㄕˊ)
① metal and stone—a symbol of durability ② gold and precious stones ③ weapons; arms ④ bronze and stone inscriptions

〔金部〕

〔金部〕

金石交(ㄐㄧㄣ ㄕˊ ㄐㄧㄠ)
durable friendship
金石學(ㄐㄧㄣ ㄕˊ ㄒㄩㄝˊ)
the study of bronze and stone inscriptions
金石聲(ㄐㄧㄣ ㄕˊ ㄕㄥ)
the sound of metal and stone (said of a piece of good writing)
金石絲竹(ㄐㄧㄣ ㄕˊ ㄙ ㄓㄨˊ)
various musical instruments made of metals, stone, strings, and bamboo
金石爲開(ㄐㄧㄣ ㄕˊ ㄨㄟˊ ㄎㄞ)
Sincerity can make metal and stone crack.
金史(ㄐㄧㄣ ㄕˇ)
History of the Chin Dynasty (a Tungusic Dynasty 1115-1234), one of the *Twenty-Four Histories*
金沙江(ㄐㄧㄣ ㄕㄚ ㄐㄧㄤ)
the Kinsha River, the headwaters of the Yangtze
金身(ㄐㄧㄣ ㄕㄣ)
the Buddha's gilded image
金聲玉振(ㄐㄧㄣ ㄕㄥ ㄩˋ ㄓㄣˋ)
(literally) ringing the bells as an overture and striking the stone chimes at the close; making use of various instruments in one musical performance—to gather the best of various schools of thought and form a complete whole
金屬(ㄐㄧㄣ ㄕㄨˇ)
metals
金屬器皿(ㄐㄧㄣ ㄕㄨˇ ㄑㄧˋ ㄇㄧㄣˇ)
metalware
金屬原素(ㄐㄧㄣ ㄕㄨˇ ㄩㄢˊ ㄙㄨˋ)
metallic elements
金人(ㄐㄧㄣ ㄖㄣˊ)
a metal image
金人三緘其口(ㄐㄧㄣ ㄖㄣˊ ㄙㄢ ㄐㄧㄢ ㄑㄧˊ ㄎㄡˇ)
to remain tight-lipped; to say nothing
金融(ㄐㄧㄣ ㄖㄨㄥˊ)
finance; banking; a monetary situation
金融卡(ㄐㄧㄣ ㄖㄨㄥˊ ㄎㄚˇ)
a fiscard
金融恐慌(ㄐㄧㄣ ㄖㄨㄥˊ ㄎㄨㄥˇ ㄏㄨㄤ)
a monetary crisis; a financial panic
金融機關(ㄐㄧㄣ ㄖㄨㄥˊ ㄐㄧ ㄍㄨㄢ)
a financial organization; a banking agency
金融界(ㄐㄧㄣ ㄖㄨㄥˊ ㄐㄧㄝˋ)
the financial world; financial circles
金融中心(ㄐㄧㄣ ㄖㄨㄥˊ ㄓㄨㄥ ㄒㄧㄣ)
a financial center
金融市場(ㄐㄧㄣ ㄖㄨㄥˊ ㄕˋ ㄔㄤˇ)
the money market
金融資本(ㄐㄧㄣ ㄖㄨㄥˊ ㄗ ㄅㄣˇ)
financial capital
金字塔(ㄐㄧㄣ ㄗˋ ㄊㄚˇ)
a pyramid
金字招牌(ㄐㄧㄣ ㄗˋ ㄓㄠ ㄆㄞˊ)
(literally) a signboard with gilded inscriptions—a good reputation; high prestige
金子(ㄐㄧㄣ ˙ㄗ)
gold: 在岩石及溪流中發現金子。Gold is found in rock and streams.
金絲雀(ㄐㄧㄣ ㄙ ㄑㄩㄝˋ)
a canary bird; a canary: 她有一隻金絲雀。She has a canary.
金絲燕(ㄐㄧㄣ ㄙ ㄧㄢˋ)
Collocalia esculenta
金色(ㄐㄧㄣ ㄙㄜˋ)
golden
金額(ㄐㄧㄣ ㄜˊ)
the amount of money
金甌無缺(ㄐㄧㄣ ㄡ ㄨˊ ㄑㄩㄝ)
(literally) The golden goblet is intact.—The integrity of the national territory is unaffected.
金牙(ㄐㄧㄣ ㄧㄚˊ)
gold-capped teeth
金曜日(ㄐㄧㄣ ㄧㄠˋ ㄖˋ)
Friday
金言(ㄐㄧㄣ ㄧㄢˊ)
a maxim; an adage; a wise saying; sage advice: 「三思而後行」是一句金言。"Look before you leap" is a maxim.
金銀花(ㄐㄧㄣ ㄧㄣˊ ㄏㄨㄚ)
the flower of honeysuckle; honeysuckle
金銀財寶(ㄐㄧㄣ ㄧㄣˊ ㄘㄞˊ ㄅㄠˇ)
treasures; wealth; riches
金印紫綬(ㄐㄧㄣ ㄧㄣˋ ㄗˇ ㄕㄡˋ)
the gold seal and the purple sash—high government posts 亦作「金紫」
金鶯(ㄐㄧㄣ ㄧㄥ)
an oriole
金烏(ㄐㄧㄣ ㄨ)
(literally) the golden crow—the sun: 金烏西墜。The sun is sinking in the west.
金烏玉兔(ㄐㄧㄣ ㄨ ㄩˋ ㄊㄨˋ)
(literally) the crow of gold and the hare of jade—the sun and the moon
金屋藏嬌(ㄐㄧㄣ ㄨ ㄘㄤˊ ㄐㄧㄠ)
to build a magnificent house for a beloved woman (especially a concubine or mistress)
金文(ㄐㄧㄣ ㄨㄣˊ)
ancient inscriptions on bronze
金魚(ㄐㄧㄣ ㄩˊ)
goldfish
金魚缸(ㄐㄧㄣ ㄩˊ ㄍㄤ)
a goldfish basin; a globe
金魚藻(ㄐㄧㄣ ㄩˊ ㄗㄠˇ)
(botany) hornwort
金魚草(ㄐㄧㄣ ㄩˊ ㄘㄠˇ)
(botany) snapdragon
金玉滿堂(ㄐㄧㄣ ㄩˋ ㄇㄢˇ ㄊㄤˊ)
to have one's house filled with riches
金玉良言(ㄐㄧㄣ ㄩˋ ㄌㄧㄤˊ ㄧㄢˊ)
a wise saying; good counsel: 對於這事，他給我金玉良言。He gave me good counsel on this matter.
金玉其外，敗絮其中(ㄐㄧㄣ ㄩˋ ㄑㄧˊ ㄨㄞˋ, ㄅㄞˋ ㄒㄩˋ ㄑㄧˊ ㄓㄨㄥ)
a rotten interior beneath a fine exterior
金元外交(ㄐㄧㄣ ㄩㄢˊ ㄨㄞˋ ㄐㄧㄠ)
checkbook diplomacy; diplomacy of bribery
金元王國(ㄐㄧㄣ ㄩㄢˊ ㄨㄤˊ ㄍㄨㄛˊ)
(literally) the kingdom of golden dollars—the United States

一畫

【釔】 6311
ㄧˇ yii yǐ
yttrium

【釓】 6312
ㄍㄚˊ gar gá
gadolinium

二畫

【釘】 6313
1. ㄉㄧㄥ ding dīng

1. nails (for fastening things): 這釘已鬆動了。The nail has started.
2. to look steadily

釘鞋(ㄉㄧㄥ ㄒㄧㄝˊ)
boots with nailed soles (for wet weather); track shoes; shoes with spikes

釘錘(ㄉㄧㄥ ㄔㄨㄟˊ)
a hammer

釘梢(ㄉㄧㄥ ㄕㄠ)
to tail; to shadow; to trail: 賊被警察釘梢。The thief was tailed by a policeman.

釘子(ㄉㄧㄥ ·ㄗ)
nails (for fastening): 只一下他就把釘子釘進去了。With one blow he drove the nail home.

釘問(ㄉㄧㄥ ·ㄨㄣ)
to question persistently

【釘】 6313
2. ㄉㄧㄥˋ dinq dìng
to fasten (with nails, etc.)

釘馬掌(ㄉㄧㄥˋ ㄇㄚˇ ㄓㄤˇ)
to shoe a horse; to nail on horseshoes

釘釘子(ㄉㄧㄥˋ ㄉㄧㄥ ·ㄗ)
to drive a nail

釘鈕扣(ㄉㄧㄥˋ ㄋㄧㄡˇ ㄎㄡˋ)
to sew buttons on: 她在我的外套上釘鈕扣。She sewed buttons on my coat.

釘住(ㄉㄧㄥˋ ·ㄓㄨ)
to nail securely

釘書(ㄉㄧㄥˋ ㄕㄨ)
to bind books

釘書機(ㄉㄧㄥˋ ㄕㄨ ㄐㄧ)
a stapler

釘死(ㄉㄧㄥˋ ㄙˇ)
①to nail securely; to nail up: 他把窗子釘死。He nailed up a window. ②to nail to death; to crucify

【釜】 6314
ㄈㄨˇ fuu fǔ
1. a cauldron; a kettle
2. an ancient unit of capacity

釜底抽薪(ㄈㄨˇ ㄉㄧˇ ㄔㄡ ㄒㄧㄣ)
(literally) to make water stop boiling by pulling firewood from under the kettle —to remove the ultimate cause of trouble

釜中魚(ㄈㄨˇ ㄓㄨㄥ ㄩˊ)
fish in a kettle—doomed

釜山(ㄈㄨˇ ㄕㄢ)
Pusan, Korea

【釗】 6315
ㄓㄠ jau zhāo
to encourage

【針】 6316
(鍼) ㄓㄣ jen zhēn
1. a needle; a pin; a probe: 針是用來縫紉的。Needles are used for sewing.
2. a stitch

針鼻兒(ㄓㄣ ㄅㄧˊㄦ)
the eye of a needle

針砭(ㄓㄣ ㄅㄧㄢ)
①acupuncture ②remonstrance; to point out someone's errors and offer salutary advice; admonition

針鋒(ㄓㄣ ㄈㄥ)or 針芒(ㄓㄣ ㄇㄤˊ)
the point of a needle

針鋒相對(ㄓㄣ ㄈㄥ ㄒㄧㄤ ㄉㄨㄟˋ)
(literally) two needles pointed against each other —to oppose each other with equal harshness; to attack each other in equally sharp language; to match point by point: 兩邊針鋒相對。Two sides of the argument match point by point.

針對(ㄓㄣ ㄉㄨㄟˋ)
①to aim directly at; to focus on ②in accordance with

針頭(ㄓㄣ ㄊㄡˊ)
(medicine) a syringe needle

針盒(ㄓㄣ ㄏㄜˊ)
a sewing kit

針脚(ㄓㄣ ㄐㄧㄠˇ)
stitches

針灸(ㄓㄣ ㄐㄧㄡˇ)
acupuncture and moxibustion; acupuncture and cauterization

針灸麻醉(ㄓㄣ ㄐㄧㄡˇ ㄇㄚˊ ㄗㄨㄟˋ)
acupuncture anesthesia

針線(ㄓㄣ ㄒㄧㄢˋ)
①a needle and thread ②needlework

針線包(ㄓㄣ ㄒㄧㄢˋ ㄅㄠ)
a sewing kit

針織(ㄓㄣ ㄓ)
knitting

針織品(ㄓㄣ ㄓ ㄆㄧㄣˇ)
knit goods; knitwear; knitting

針織廠(ㄓㄣ ㄓ ㄔㄤˇ)
a knitting mill

針黹(ㄓㄣ ㄓˇ)
fine needlework; embroidery

針車(ㄓㄣ ㄔㄜ)
a sewing machine

針樅(ㄓㄣ ㄘㄨㄥ)
(botany) a spruce

針葉樹(ㄓㄣ ㄧㄝˋ ㄕㄨˋ)
conifers; coniferous trees: 松樹和樅樹是針葉樹。The pine and fir are conifers.

針眼(ㄓㄣ ㄧㄢˇ)
①(pathology) hordeolum; sty(e) ②perforation made with a needle

針魚(ㄓㄣ ㄩˊ)
the saury

【釙】 6317
ㄆㄨˊ pwu pú
polonium

【釕】 6318
ㄌㄧㄠˇ leau liǎo
ruthenium

三畫

【釩】 6319
ㄈㄢˊ farn fán
vanadium

【釣】 6320
ㄉㄧㄠˋ diaw diào
1. to fish (with a hook and line); to angle
2. to lure; to tempt
3. a fishhook

釣名(ㄉㄧㄠˋ ㄇㄧㄥˊ)or 釣譽(ㄉㄧㄠˋ ㄩˋ)
to angle for fame; to seek publicity

釣臺(ㄉㄧㄠˋ ㄊㄞˊ)
a platform to fish from

釣鉤(ㄉㄧㄠˋ ㄍㄡ)
a fishhook

釣竿(ㄉㄧㄠˋ ㄍㄢ)
a fishing rod; a fish pole

釣線(ㄉㄧㄠˋ ㄒㄧㄢˋ)
a fish twine; a fishing line

釣餌(ㄉㄧㄠˋ ㄦˇ)
a bait

釣魚(ㄉㄧㄠˋ ㄩˊ)
to fish; to angle: 我到河中釣魚。I went fishing in the river.

釣魚用具(ㄉㄧㄠˋ ㄩˊ ㄩㄥˋ ㄐㄩˋ)
fishing gear

【釷】 6321
ㄊㄨˇ tuu tǔ
thorium

釷石(ㄊㄨˇ ㄕˊ)

〔金部〕

(mineral) thorite

【釹】6322 ㄋㄩˇ neu nǚ
neodymium, a rare-earth metallic chemical element found in cerite and various other rare minerals

【釦】6323 ㄎㄡˋ kow kòu
buttons (on garments)

釦子(ㄎㄡˋ ·ㄗ)or 釦兒(ㄎㄡˋㄦ)
buttons (on garments)

【釧】6324 ㄔㄨㄢˋ chuann chuàn
a bracelet; an armlet

【釵】6325 ㄔㄞ chai chāi
a kind of hairpin

釵光鬢影(ㄔㄞ ㄍㄨㄤ ㄅㄧㄣˋ ㄧㄥˇ)
gathering of richly dressed women

釵橫鬢亂(ㄔㄞ ㄏㄥˊ ㄅㄧㄣˋ ㄌㄨㄢˋ)
pins awry and hair in disorder

【釤】6326 ㄕㄢ shan shān
samarium

四畫

【鈧】6327 ㄎㄤˋ kanq kàng
scandium

【鈥】6328 ㄏㄨㄛˇ huoo huǒ
holmium

【鈀】6329 ㄅㄚˇ baa bǎ
palladium

【鈦】6330 ㄊㄞˋ tay tài
titanium

【鈔】6331 ㄔㄠ chau chāo
("鈔票"又讀 ㄔㄠˋ chaw chào)
1. to copy; to transcribe
2. bank notes

鈔票(ㄔㄠ ㄆㄧㄠˋ)or(ㄔㄠˋ ㄆㄧㄠˋ)
bank notes; paper money; a bill

鈔錄 or 抄錄(ㄔㄠ ㄌㄨˋ)
to copy; to transcribe

鈔寫 or 抄寫(ㄔㄠ ㄒㄧㄝˇ)
to copy or transcribe by hand: 鈔寫這一頁。Copy this page.

【鈇】6332 ㄈㄨ fu fū
an ax; a hatchet

鈇鑕(ㄈㄨ ㄓˋ)
a kind of ax (for chopping the body of a convict in two)

鈇鉞(ㄈㄨ ㄩㄝˋ)
punishment of crimes

【鈉】6333 ㄋㄚˋ nah nà
sodium; natrium: 鹽和汽水含有鈉。Salt and soda contain sodium.

鈉玻璃(ㄋㄚˋ ㄅㄛ ·ㄌㄧ)
soda glass

【鈍】6334 ㄉㄨㄣˋ duenn dùn
1. blunt; dull; obtuse: 這把刀鈍了。This knife is blunt.
2. dull; obtuse

鈍兵(ㄉㄨㄣˋ ㄅㄧㄥ)
① blunt weapons ② soldiers low in morale

鈍根(ㄉㄨㄣˋ ㄍㄣ)
(Buddhism) of dull capacity, unable to receive Buddha's truth

鈍漢(ㄉㄨㄣˋ ㄏㄢˋ)
a stupid fellow; a dullard

鈍角(ㄉㄨㄣˋ ㄐㄧㄠˇ)
an obtuse angle

鈍角三角形(ㄉㄨㄣˋ ㄐㄧㄠˇ ㄙㄢ ㄐㄧㄠˇ ㄒㄧㄥˊ)
an obtuse-angled triangle

鈍舌(ㄉㄨㄣˋ ㄕㄜˊ)
ineloquence

【鈐】6335 ㄑㄧㄢˊ chyan qián
1. a latch; a lock
2. a seal; a stamp; a chop

鈐記(ㄑㄧㄢˊ ㄐㄧˋ)
an official seal; a chop

鈐鍵(ㄑㄧㄢˊ ㄐㄧㄢˋ)
the key; the crucial point

鈐印(ㄑㄧㄢˊ ㄧㄣˋ)
to put a stamp

【鈕】6336 ㄋㄧㄡˇ neou niǔ
1. buttons: 我按鈕等電梯。I pushed the button for the elevator.
2. a Chinese family name

鈕扣(ㄋㄧㄡˇ ㄎㄡˋ)
buttons: 有一個鈕釦脫落了。One of the buttons is missing.

鈕孔(ㄋㄧㄡˇ ㄎㄨㄥˇ)
a buttonhole

鈕子(ㄋㄧㄡˇ ·ㄗ)
buttons

【鈞】6337 ㄐㄩㄣ jiun jūn
1. a unit of weight (equal to 30 catties) in former times
2. (in addressing a superior in a letter) you; your

鈞命(ㄐㄩㄣ ㄇㄧㄥˋ)
your esteemed instructions (used in formally addressing a superior)

鈞衡(ㄐㄩㄣ ㄏㄥˊ)
to evaluate a person's abilities

鈞鑒(ㄐㄩㄣ ㄐㄧㄢˋ)
a conventional phrase used in the salutation in formal letters addressed to a superior

鈞啓(ㄐㄩㄣ ㄑㄧˇ)
a conventional phrase used in the envelope address of a letter to a superior

鈞座(ㄐㄩㄣ ㄗㄨㄛˋ)
your good self; your excellency; your honor

鈞安(ㄐㄩㄣ ㄢ)
May you enjoy peace. —a form of complimentary close in a letter to a superior

鈞諭(ㄐㄩㄣ ㄩˋ)
your esteemed instructions (used in formally addressing a superior)

【鈣】6338 ㄍㄞˋ gay gài
calcium

鈣片(ㄍㄞˋ ㄆㄧㄢˋ)
a calcium tablet

鈣質(ㄍㄞˋ ㄓˊ)
calcium content

【鈎】6339 (鉤) ㄍㄡ gou gōu
a hook; to hook: 請將我的衣服掛到鈎上。Please hook my dress for me.

五畫

【鈸】6340 ㄅㄚˊ bar bá
(又讀 ㄅㄛˊ bor bó)
cymbals

【鈴】6341 ㄌㄧㄥˊ ling líng

〔金部〕

(jingling) bells: 小鈴叮噹地響。The small bell sounded with a jingle.

鈴鐺(ㄌㄧㄥˊ ˙ㄉㄤ)
(jingling) bells

鈴鐸(ㄌㄧㄥˊ ㄉㄨㄛˊ)
bells under palace eaves; wind bells

鈴閣(ㄌㄧㄥˊ ㄍㄜˊ)
a general's abode

鈴下(ㄌㄧㄥˊ ㄒㄧㄚˋ)
① sir (in addressing a general) ② bodyguards

鈴聲(ㄌㄧㄥˊ ㄕㄥ)
the tinkle of bells

【鈿】 6342 ㄉㄧㄢˋ diann diàn (又讀 ㄊㄧㄢˊ tyan tián)
filigree

鈿合(ㄉㄧㄢˋ ㄏㄜˊ)
a filigree case

【鉀】 6343 ㄐㄧㄚˇ jea jiǎ
potassium

鉀肥(ㄐㄧㄚˇ ㄈㄟˊ)
potash fertilizer

鉀鹽(ㄐㄧㄚˇ ㄧㄢˊ)
sylvite

【鉧】 6344 ㄇㄨˇ muu mǔ
an iron

【鉅】 6345 ㄐㄩˋ jiuh jù
1. great 亦作「巨」
2. steel

鉅富(ㄐㄩˋ ㄈㄨˋ)
a very rich man; a millionaire; a plutocrat

鉅公(ㄐㄩˋ ㄍㄨㄥ)
① the Emperor; His Majesty ② venerable sir; sir

鉅款(ㄐㄩˋ ㄎㄨㄢˇ)
a large sum of money

鉅子(ㄐㄩˋ ㄗˇ)
a great man; a tycoon; a magnate: 他是化學工業界的鉅子。He is a tycoon of the chemical industry.

鉅萬(ㄐㄩˋ ㄨㄢˋ)
great wealth

【鉉】 6346 ㄒㄩㄢˋ shiuann xuàn
a device for carrying a tripod

【鉋】 6347 (鑤) ㄅㄠˋ baw bào
1. to plane (wood)
2. a plane (for carpentry)

鉋凳(ㄅㄠˋ ㄉㄥˋ)
a stool on which the carpenter sits as he planes wood

鉋花(ㄅㄠˋ ˙ㄏㄨㄚ)
shavings

鉋牀(ㄅㄠˋ ㄔㄨㄤˊ)
a lathe for planing; a planing machine

鉋子(ㄅㄠˋ ˙ㄗ)
a plane (for carpentry): 他用鉋子把木材鉋平。He smoothed the wood with a plane.

【鉏】 6348 1. ㄔㄨˊ chwu chú
1. a hoe
2. to hoe
3. to eliminate; to uproot
4. a Chinese family name

【鉏】 6348 2. ㄐㄩˇ jeu jǔ
discordant; disharmonious

鉏鋙 or 齟齬(ㄐㄩˇ ㄩˇ)
discordant; disharmonious

【鉑】 6349 ㄅㄛˊ bor bó
1. a thin sheet of metal; foil 亦作「箔」
2. platinum

【鉗】 6350 ㄑㄧㄢˊ chyan qián
1. pincers; forceps; tweezers; tongs; pliers; clamps
2. chains put around a prisoner's neck
3. to hold with tongs, etc.

鉗徒(ㄑㄧㄢˊ ㄊㄨˊ)
a pilloried prisoner

鉗工(ㄑㄧㄢˊ ㄍㄨㄥ)
① bench work ② a fitter

鉗口結舌(ㄑㄧㄢˊ ㄎㄡˇ ㄐㄧㄝˊ ㄕㄜˊ)
① to silence a person with a gag; to silence a person with threats ② to remain silent; to keep one's mouth shut

鉗噤(ㄑㄧㄢˊ ㄐㄧㄣˋ)
to keep one's mouth shut; to keep quiet

鉗形攻勢(ㄑㄧㄢˊ ㄒㄧㄥˊ ㄍㄨㄥ ㄕˋ)
a two-pronged offensive; a pincers movement

鉗制 or 箝制(ㄑㄧㄢˊ ㄓˋ)
to keep under control with force; to tie down or pin down (enemy forces)

鉗制輿論(ㄑㄧㄢˊ ㄓˋ ㄩˊ ㄌㄨㄣˋ)
to muzzle public opinion

鉗子(ㄑㄧㄢˊ ˙ㄗ)
① tongs; pincers; forceps; tweezers ② a convict; a prisoner ③ earrings

【鉛】 6351 ㄑㄧㄢ chian qiān
lead (a metal): 鉛是重金屬。Lead is a heavy metal.

鉛板(ㄑㄧㄢ ㄅㄢˇ)
① sheet iron ② a lead plate (in printing)

鉛版(ㄑㄧㄢ ㄅㄢˇ)
a lead plate (in printing)

鉛筆(ㄑㄧㄢ ㄅㄧˇ)
a pencil; a lead pencil

鉛筆畫(ㄑㄧㄢ ㄅㄧˇ ㄏㄨㄚˋ)
pencil drawings

鉛粉(ㄑㄧㄢ ㄈㄣˇ) or 鉛白(ㄑㄧㄢ ㄅㄛˊ)
① white lead; ceruse ② cosmetic powder; face powder: 她買了些鉛粉。She bought some face powder.

鉛黛(ㄑㄧㄢ ㄉㄞˋ)
face powder and eyebrow paint; cosmetics

鉛刀駑馬(ㄑㄧㄢ ㄉㄠ ㄋㄨˊ ㄇㄚˇ) or 鉛駑(ㄑㄧㄢ ㄋㄨˊ)
(literally) a lead knife and old horse—a man of little use

鉛丹(ㄑㄧㄢ ㄉㄢ)
red lead; minium

鉛彈(ㄑㄧㄢ ㄉㄢˋ)
a lead bullet; a dumdum bullet

鉛毒(ㄑㄧㄢ ㄉㄨˊ)
lead poisoning; plumbism

鉛條(ㄑㄧㄢ ㄊㄧㄠˊ)
① the graphite stick of a pencil ② slender pieces of lead ③ wire

鉛管(ㄑㄧㄢ ㄍㄨㄢˇ)
a lead pipe; a leaden pipe

鉛塊(ㄑㄧㄢ ㄎㄨㄞˋ)
a block of lead; a piece of lead

鉛礦(ㄑㄧㄢ ㄎㄨㄤˋ)
lead ore

鉛華(ㄑㄧㄢ ㄏㄨㄚˊ)
cosmetics; face powder

鉛黃(ㄑㄧㄢ ㄏㄨㄤˊ)
① proofreading ② lead oxide; litharge

鉛球(ㄑㄧㄢ ㄑㄧㄡˊ)
a shot (thrown in the shotput)

〔金部〕

鉛槧(ㄑㄧㄢ ㄑㄧㄢˋ)
lead and tablets—materials used in recording and printing
鉛字(ㄑㄧㄢ ㄗˋ)
lead type (in printing)
鉛絲(ㄑㄧㄢ ㄙ)
zinc-coated wire
鉛印(ㄑㄧㄢ ㄧㄣˋ)
printing by lead plates

【鉞】 6352 ㄩㄝˋ yueh yuè
a large ax

【鉢】 6353 (缽、盋) ㄅㄛ bo bō
1. an earthenware basin or bowl
2. a Buddhist priest's rice bowl
鉢盂(ㄅㄛ ㄩˊ)
an earthenware basin or bowl

【鉤】 6354 (鈎) ㄍㄡ gou gōu
1. a hook
2. to hook
3. to probe; to investigate
4. to entice; to lure
鉤毛衣(ㄍㄡ ㄇㄠˊ ㄧ)
to crochet a wool sweater
鉤搭 or 勾搭(ㄍㄡ ·ㄉㄚ)
① to seduce; to inveigle ② to make a secret alliance; a secret alliance
鉤黨(ㄍㄡ ㄉㄤˇ)
to draw one another to form a clique
鉤梯(ㄍㄡ ㄊㄧ)
a scaling ladder 亦作「雲梯」
鉤勒法 or 勾勒法(ㄍㄡ ㄌㄜˋ ㄈㄚˇ)
drawing or writing in outline
鉤稽(ㄍㄡ ㄐㄧ)
to audit (accounts)
鉤肩搭背(ㄍㄡ ㄐㄧㄢ ㄉㄚ ㄅㄟˋ)
to hold each other's arms while walking side by side
鉤距(ㄍㄡ ㄐㄩˋ)
to probe or investigate in a circuitous manner
鉤心鬥角(ㄍㄡ ㄒㄧㄣ ㄉㄡˋ ㄐㄩㄝˊ)
to strain the wits of each other (in a contest, etc.); to engage in a battle of wits; to intrigue against each other: 他們鉤心鬥角。They in-trigued against each other.
鉤玄(ㄍㄡ ㄒㄩㄢˊ)
to probe the depth of something abstract
鉤摭(ㄍㄡ ㄓˊ)
to audit (accounts)
鉤爪(ㄍㄡ ㄓㄠˇ)
talons
鉤針(ㄍㄡ ㄓㄣ)
a crochet hook; a crochet needle
鉤章棘句(ㄍㄡ ㄓㄤ ㄐㄧˊ ㄐㄩˋ)
difficult sentences and phrases (in a piece of writing); abstruse language
鉤住(ㄍㄡ ·ㄓㄨ)
to hold on a hook; to seize with a hook; to hook
鉤出來(ㄍㄡ ㄔㄨ ·ㄌㄞ)
to pull out with a hook; to hook out
鉤蟲(ㄍㄡ ㄔㄨㄥˊ)
a hookworm
鉤繩(ㄍㄡ ㄕㄥˊ)
a straightened line or string used as a marker in construction
鉤子(ㄍㄡ ·ㄗ) or 鉤兒(ㄍㄡㄦ)
a hook: 把衣服掛在鉤子上。Hang your coat on the hook.
鉤引 or 勾引(ㄍㄡ ㄧㄣˇ)
to entice; to ensnare; to lure

【鉦】 6355 ㄓㄥ jeng zhēng
a kind of gong (used by marching troops in ancient times)

【鈺】 6356 ㄩˋ yuh yù
a hard variety of gold

【鈾】 6357 ㄧㄡˊ you yóu
uranium

【鈷】 6358 1. ㄍㄨ gu gū
cobalt

【鈷】 6358 2. ㄍㄨˇ guu gǔ
an iron

【鉈】 6359 ㄊㄚ ta tā
thallium

【鈰】 6360 ㄕˋ shyh shì
cerium

【鉍】 6361 ㄅㄧˋ bih bì
bismuth

【鈹】 6362 ㄆㄧˊ pyi pí
beryllium

【鉬】 6363 ㄇㄨˋ muh mù
molybdenum

【鉭】 6364 ㄉㄢˋ dann dàn
tantalum

【鈳】 6365 ㄎㄜ ke kē
columbium

【鉯】 6366 ㄧˇ yii yǐ
illinium

【鉮】 6367 ㄕㄣ shen shēn
arsonium

六畫

【銀】 6368 ㄧㄣˊ yn yín
1. silver: 言語似銀，沉默似金。Speech is silver, but silence is golden.
2. money; wealth
3. silvery
銀杯(ㄧㄣˊ ㄅㄟ)
a silver cup (especially one used as a trophy)
銀本位(ㄧㄣˊ ㄅㄣˇ ㄨㄟˋ)
the silver standard (a monetary standard)
銀幣(ㄧㄣˊ ㄅㄧˋ)
a silver coin; silver
銀牌(ㄧㄣˊ ㄆㄞˊ)
a silver medal
銀票(ㄧㄣˊ ㄆㄧㄠˋ)
a bank note (in former times)
銀瓶(ㄧㄣˊ ㄆㄧㄥˊ)
a silver pot; a silver vase
銀幕(ㄧㄣˊ ㄇㄨˋ)
① screen (for motion pictures) ② the screen
銀粉(ㄧㄣˊ ㄈㄣˇ)
silvery powder
銀錠(ㄧㄣˊ ㄉㄧㄥˋ)
silver ingots
銀盾(ㄧㄣˊ ㄉㄨㄣˋ)
a silver plaque
銀條(ㄧㄣˊ ㄊㄧㄠˊ)
a silver bar
銀樓(ㄧㄣˊ ㄌㄡˊ)
a jeweler's shop
銀兩(ㄧㄣˊ ㄌㄧㄤˇ)

silver (as one of valuables)
銀鉤(ㄧㄣˊ ㄍㄡ)
①a fine stroke (in calligraphy) ②hooks for bamboo blinds, etc.
銀根(ㄧㄣˊ ㄍㄣ)
money supply; the money market; money
銀櫃(ㄧㄣˊ ㄍㄨㄟˋ)
a safe
銀庫(ㄧㄣˊ ㄎㄨˋ)
a treasury
銀礦(ㄧㄣˊ ㄎㄨㄤˋ)
silver ore; a silver mine
銀河(ㄧㄣˊ ㄏㄜˊ) or 銀漢(ㄧㄣˊ ㄏㄢˋ) or 銀潢(ㄧㄣˊ ㄏㄨㄤˊ)
the Milky Way
銀河倒瀉(ㄧㄣˊ ㄏㄜˊ ㄉㄠˋ ㄒㄧㄝˋ)
a silvery stream cascading downward (descriptive of a waterfall)
銀河系(ㄧㄣˊ ㄏㄜˊ ㄒㄧˋ)
the Galaxy
銀海(ㄧㄣˊ ㄏㄞˇ)
moviedom; filmdom
銀號(ㄧㄣˊ ㄏㄠˋ)
a banking house
銀行(ㄧㄣˊ ㄏㄤˊ)
a bank
銀行本票(ㄧㄣˊ ㄏㄤˊ ㄅㄣˇ ㄆㄧㄠˋ)
promissory notes
銀行電匯(ㄧㄣˊ ㄏㄤˊ ㄉㄧㄢˋ ㄏㄨㄟˋ)
bank cable transfer
銀行透支(ㄧㄣˊ ㄏㄤˊ ㄊㄡˋ ㄓ)
bank overdraft
銀行團(ㄧㄣˊ ㄏㄤˊ ㄊㄨㄢˊ)
a banking consortium; a consortium
銀行利率(ㄧㄣˊ ㄏㄤˊ ㄌㄧˋ ㄌㄩˋ)
the bank rate
銀行利息(ㄧㄣˊ ㄏㄤˊ ㄌㄧˋ ㄒㄧˊ)
bank interest
銀行公會(ㄧㄣˊ ㄏㄤˊ ㄍㄨㄥ ㄏㄨㄟˋ)
a banker's association
銀行行員(ㄧㄣˊ ㄏㄤˊ ㄏㄤˊ ㄩㄢˊ)
a bank employee
銀行匯票(ㄧㄣˊ ㄏㄤˊ ㄏㄨㄟˋ ㄆㄧㄠˋ)
a bank draft; a bank bill
銀行家(ㄧㄣˊ ㄏㄤˊ ㄐㄧㄚ)
a banker
銀行界(ㄧㄣˊ ㄏㄤˊ ㄐㄧㄝˋ)
the banking circle
銀行借款(ㄧㄣˊ ㄏㄤˊ ㄐㄧㄝˋ ㄎㄨㄢˇ)
bank loans
銀行經理(ㄧㄣˊ ㄏㄤˊ ㄐㄧㄥ ㄌㄧˇ)
the manager of a bank
銀行支票(ㄧㄣˊ ㄏㄤˊ ㄓ ㄆㄧㄠˋ)
a bank check: 請給我這個數額的銀行支票。Please give me a bank check for this amount.
銀行手續費(ㄧㄣˊ ㄏㄤˊ ㄕㄡˇ ㄒㄩˋ ㄈㄟˋ)
bank charges
銀行存款(ㄧㄣˊ ㄏㄤˊ ㄘㄨㄣˊ ㄎㄨㄢˇ)
a bank deposit
銀行存摺(ㄧㄣˊ ㄏㄤˊ ㄘㄨㄣˊ ㄓㄜˊ)
a bankbook; a passbook
銀貨兩清(ㄧㄣˊ ㄏㄨㄛˋ ㄌㄧㄤˇ ㄑㄧㄥ)
completion of a business transaction with goods delivered and payment made
銀灰色(ㄧㄣˊ ㄏㄨㄟ ㄙㄜˋ)
silver-gray
銀婚(ㄧㄣˊ ㄏㄨㄣ)
a silver wedding; the 25th wedding anniversary
銀價(ㄧㄣˊ ㄐㄧㄚˋ)
the price of silver
銀角(ㄧㄣˊ ㄐㄧㄠˇ)
silver coins of small denominations
銀匠(ㄧㄣˊ ㄐㄧㄤˋ)
a silversmith
銀器(ㄧㄣˊ ㄑㄧˋ)
silverware
銀錢(ㄧㄣˊ ㄑㄧㄢˊ)
money; wealth
銀杏(ㄧㄣˊ ㄒㄧㄥˋ)
(botany) gingko; ginkgo
銀朱 or 銀硃(ㄧㄣˊ ㄓㄨ)
vermilion
銀鼠(ㄧㄣˊ ㄕㄨˇ)
an ermine; a snow weasel
銀座(ㄧㄣˊ ㄗㄨㄛˋ)
Ginza (a shopping center of Tokyo)
銀子(ㄧㄣˊ ˙ㄗ)
silver (as one of valuables): 我付他五千兩銀子。I paid him 5,000 taels of silver.
銀色(ㄧㄣˊ ㄙㄜˋ)
silvery
銀筍 or 銀笋(ㄧㄣˊ ㄙㄨㄣˇ)
icicles
銀耳(ㄧㄣˊ ㄦˇ)
a kind of semitransparent white fungus (*Tremella fuciformis*) believed to be highly nutritious
銀洋(ㄧㄣˊ ㄧㄤˊ)
silver dollar (a major silver coin in circulation formerly)
銀魚(ㄧㄣˊ ㄩˊ)
silverfish 亦作「蠹魚」
銀元 or 銀圓(ㄧㄣˊ ㄩㄢˊ)
①silver dollar (a major silver coin formerly in circulation) ②*yuan*, an arbitrarily fixed monetary unit worth NT$3 now used as a standard in fines only

【鉸】 6369 ㄐㄧㄠˇ jeau jiǎo

1. scissors; shears
2. hinges
3. to shear

鉸刀(ㄐㄧㄠˇ ㄉㄠ)
scissors; shears
鉸鏈(ㄐㄧㄠˇ ㄌㄧㄢˋ)
hinges

【銃】 6370 ㄔㄨㄥˋ chonq chòng

1. firearms
2. a joint of the metal head to the handle of an ax

【銅】 6371 ㄊㄨㄥˊ torng tóng

copper; bronze; brass: 銅是一種甚爲有用的金屬。Copper is a very useful metal.
銅板(ㄊㄨㄥˊ ㄅㄢˇ)
a copper coin 參看「銅幣」
銅版(ㄊㄨㄥˊ ㄅㄢˇ)
copperplate (in printing)
銅版畫(ㄊㄨㄥˊ ㄅㄢˇ ㄏㄨㄚˋ)
copperplate etching (or engraving)
銅版紙(ㄊㄨㄥˊ ㄅㄢˇ ㄓˇ)
art printing paper
銅幣(ㄊㄨㄥˊ ㄅㄧˋ)
a copper coin
銅琶鐵板(ㄊㄨㄥˊ ㄆㄚˊ ㄊㄧㄝˇ ㄅㄢˇ)
bold and vehement language (in writing)
銅牌(ㄊㄨㄥˊ ㄆㄞˊ)
a bronze medal
銅模(ㄊㄨㄥˊ ㄇㄨˊ)
a copper mold
銅頭鐵額(ㄊㄨㄥˊ ㄊㄡˊ ㄊㄧㄝˇ ㄜˊ)
audacious; fearless; intrepid
銅駝荊棘(ㄊㄨㄥˊ ㄊㄨㄛˊ ㄐㄧㄥ ㄐㄧˊ)
devastation of palaces as a result of war
銅鑼(ㄊㄨㄥˊ ㄌㄨㄛˊ)
a copper gong 參看「銅鉦」
銅綠(ㄊㄨㄥˊ ㄌㄩˋ) or 銅青(ㄊㄨㄥˊ ㄑㄧㄥ)
patina; verdigris

銅礦(ㄊㄨㄥˊ ㄎㄨㄤˋ)
①copper ore ②copper mine
銅壺(ㄊㄨㄥˊ ㄏㄨˊ)
①a copper pot; a copper urn ②a clepsydra; a water clock
銅壺滴漏(ㄊㄨㄥˊ ㄏㄨˊ ㄉㄧ ㄌㄡˋ)
a clepsydra; a water clock
銅筋鐵骨(ㄊㄨㄥˊ ㄐㄧㄣ ㄊㄧㄝˇ ㄍㄨˇ)
(said of a man's physique) strongly built; sturdy
銅匠(ㄊㄨㄥˊ ㄐㄧㄤˋ)
a coppersmith
銅鏡(ㄊㄨㄥˊ ㄐㄧㄥˋ)
a copper mirror
銅器(ㄊㄨㄥˊ ㄑㄧˋ)
bronze utensils
銅器時代(ㄊㄨㄥˊ ㄑㄧˋ ㄕˊ ㄉㄞˋ)
the Copper Age
銅錢(ㄊㄨㄥˊ ㄑㄧㄢˊ)
copper coins
銅牆鐵壁(ㄊㄨㄥˊ ㄑㄧㄤˊ ㄊㄧㄝˇ ㄅㄧˋ)
an extremely sturdy structure; tight (siege); strong (fortress, defense, etc.); impregnable like walls of brass and iron
銅雀臺(ㄊㄨㄥˊ ㄑㄩㄝˋ ㄊㄞˊ)
a tower built by Tsao Tsao (曹操) in what is Honan today
銅像(ㄊㄨㄥˊ ㄒㄧㄤˋ)
a bronze image; a bronze statue
銅鉦(ㄊㄨㄥˊ ㄓㄥ)
a brass gong
銅臭(ㄊㄨㄥˊ ㄔㄡˋ)
a smell of copper (a term of derision applied to wealthy but mean people); the stink of money; stinking with money: 他滿身銅臭。He was stinking with money.
銅人(ㄊㄨㄥˊ ㄖㄣˊ)
a bronze image; a bronze statue 亦作「銅狄」
銅子兒(ㄊㄨㄥˊ ㄗˇㄦ)
(colloquial) copper coins; coppers
銅絲(ㄊㄨㄥˊ ㄙ)
copper wire
銅印(ㄊㄨㄥˊ ㄧㄣˋ)
a copper seal
銅元(ㄊㄨㄥˊ ㄩㄢˊ)
copper coins

【銑】 6372
ㄒㄧㄢˇ shean xiǎn
1. shiny metal
2. pig iron
銑鐵(ㄒㄧㄢˇ ㄊㄧㄝˇ)
pig iron; cast iron

【銓】 6373
ㄑㄩㄢˊ chyuan quán
1. to weigh
2. to evaluate qualifications in selecting officials
3. a Chinese family name
銓衡(ㄑㄩㄢˊ ㄏㄥˊ)
to measure and select talents
銓敍 or 銓序(ㄑㄩㄢˊ ㄒㄩˋ)
to select and appoint officials
銓敍部(ㄑㄩㄢˊ ㄒㄩˋ ㄅㄨˋ)
Ministry of Personnel (under the Examination Yuan)
銓選(ㄑㄩㄢˊ ㄒㄩㄢˇ)
to select (officials) after evaluating qualifications
銓擇(ㄑㄩㄢˊ ㄗㄜˊ)
to evaluate and select
銓次(ㄑㄩㄢˊ ㄘˋ)
procedures for selecting officials

【銖】 6374
ㄓㄨ ju zhū
1. an ancient unit of weight (equal to 1/48th, or by other interpretations 1/24th, of a tael); the ancient coinage of Han
2. blunt; dull; obtuse
3. a Chinese family name
銖鈍(ㄓㄨ ㄉㄨㄣˋ)
dull knives and spears
銖兩(ㄓㄨ ㄌㄧㄤˇ)
very small; tiny; minute
銖兩悉稱(ㄓㄨ ㄌㄧㄤˇ ㄒㄧ ㄔㄥˋ)
to match in every small detail; to have the same weight
銖積寸累(ㄓㄨ ㄐㄧ ㄘㄨㄣˋ ㄌㄟˇ)
Trifles amount to much when accumulated. 或 to build up bit by bit
銖衣(ㄓㄨ ㄧ)
an extremely light-weight garment

【銘】 6375
ㄇㄧㄥˊ ming míng
1. to engrave; to inscribe; to imprint
2. inscriptions
銘佩(ㄇㄧㄥˊ ㄆㄟˋ)
to remember with admiration
銘感(ㄇㄧㄥˊ ㄍㄢˇ)
to remember with gratitude
銘刻(ㄇㄧㄥˊ ㄎㄜˋ)
to engrave; to imprint
銘肌鏤骨(ㄇㄧㄥˊ ㄐㄧ ㄌㄡˋ ㄍㄨˇ)
to feel deep gratitude
銘記在心(ㄇㄧㄥˊ ㄐㄧˋ ㄗㄞˋ ㄒㄧㄣ)
to imprint on one's mind
銘旌 or 明旌(ㄇㄧㄥˊ ㄐㄧㄥ)
a funeral streamer bearing the titles of the deceased
銘謝(ㄇㄧㄥˊ ㄒㄧㄝˋ)
to show gratefulness
銘心(ㄇㄧㄥˊ ㄒㄧㄣ)
to imprint on one's mind
銘誌(ㄇㄧㄥˊ ㄓˋ)
to record, or commemorate, with an engraved inscription
銘篆(ㄇㄧㄥˊ ㄓㄨㄢˋ)
to remember with deep gratitude
銘文(ㄇㄧㄥˊ ㄨㄣˊ)
an inscription; an epigraph

【銚】 6376
1. ㄧㄠˊ yau yáo
1. a kind of farm tool
2. a Chinese family name

【銚】 6376
2. ㄉㄧㄠˋ diaw diào
1. a small pot with a handle
2. a brass cymbal

【銛】 6377
ㄒㄧㄢ shian xiān
sharp; keen-edged
銛利(ㄒㄧㄢ ㄌㄧˋ)
sharp; keen-edged

【銜】 6378
ㄒㄧㄢˊ shyan xián
1. a bit (in a horse's mouth)
2. the title (of an official)
3. to hold in the mouth
4. to harbor; to cherish
5. to follow (orders)
銜璧(ㄒㄧㄢˊ ㄅㄧˋ)
to surrender with one's hands bound and with a piece of jade held in one's mouth
銜轡(ㄒㄧㄢˊ ㄆㄟˋ)
a bit (in a horse's mouth)
銜枚疾走(ㄒㄧㄢˊ ㄇㄟˊ ㄐㄧˊ ㄗㄡˇ)
to march swiftly with a gag in the mouth (to prevent unnecessary noise which may

alert the enemy)

銜命(ㄒㄧㄢˊ ㄇㄧㄥˋ)or 銜令(ㄒㄧㄢˊ ㄌㄧㄥˋ)
to follow an order; to act according to a directive

銜勒(ㄒㄧㄢˊ ㄌㄜˋ)
a bit (in a horse's mouth)

銜恨(ㄒㄧㄢˊ ㄏㄣˋ)
to harbor grudges: 他銜恨以終。He harbored grudges for the rest of his life.

銜華佩實(ㄒㄧㄢˊ ㄏㄨㄚˊ ㄆㄟˋ ㄕˊ)
(said of a piece of writing) rich in substance and graceful in style

銜環(ㄒㄧㄢˊ ㄏㄨㄢˊ)
A bird returns with rings in its mouth thanking its owner for freedom.—to repay with gratitude

銜環結草(ㄒㄧㄢˊ ㄏㄨㄢˊ ㄐㄧㄝˊ ㄘㄠˇ)
to repay a kindness 參看「銜環」

銜接(ㄒㄧㄢˊ ㄐㄧㄝ)
to adjoin; to lie next to; to connect; to dovetail; to link up: 這運河把兩城鎮銜接起來。This canal links up the two towns.

銜尾相隨(ㄒㄧㄢˊ ㄨㄟˇ ㄒㄧㄤ ㄙㄨㄟˊ)
one close behind another

銜冤(ㄒㄧㄢˊ ㄩㄢ)
to have no chance of airing one's grievances; to have a simmering sense of injustice

【銍】 6379 ㄓˋ jyh zhì
a sickle

【銬】 6380 ㄎㄠˋ kaw kào
manacles; handcuffs

【銥】 6381 ㄧˇ yii yǐ
iridium

【鉺】 6382 ㄦˇ eel ěr
erbium

【銠】 6383 ㄌㄠˇ lao lǎo
rhodium

【銪】 6384 ㄧㄡˇ yeou yǒu
europium

【鉿】 6385 ㄏㄜˊ her hé
hafnium

【銦】 6386 ㄧㄣ in yīn
indium

【銫】 6387 ㄙㄜˋ seh sè
caesium

【銩】 6388 ㄉㄧㄡ diou diū
thulium

【鉻】 6389 ㄍㄜˋ geh gè
chromium

【銣】 6390 ㄖㄨˊ ruh rú
rubidium

七畫

【銳】 6391 ㄖㄨㄟˋ ruey ruì
1. sharp; acute; keen
2. quick-witted; intelligent; clever
3. energetic; vigorous

銳不可當(ㄖㄨㄟˋ ˙ㄅㄨ ㄎㄜˇ ㄉㄤ)
too sharp to resist; too powerful to stop

銳敏(ㄖㄨㄟˋ ㄇㄧㄣˇ)
quick-witted; acute; keen; sharp: 狗的嗅覺銳敏。Dogs have a keen sense of smell.

銳髮(ㄖㄨㄟˋ ㄈㄚˇ)
stray hair before the ear

銳利(ㄖㄨㄟˋ ㄌㄧˋ)
sharp; pointed: 他用銳利的刀子切斷繩子。He cut the rope with a sharp knife.

銳角(ㄖㄨㄟˋ ㄐㄧㄠˇ)
an acute angle

銳角三角形(ㄖㄨㄟˋ ㄐㄧㄠˇ ㄙㄢ ㄐㄧㄠˇ ㄒㄧㄥˊ)
an acute-angled triangle

銳減(ㄖㄨㄟˋ ㄐㄧㄢˇ)
to decline sharply; to drop markedly

銳氣(ㄖㄨㄟˋ ㄑㄧˋ)
dash; mettle; vigor; virility; aggressiveness

銳志(ㄖㄨㄟˋ ㄓˋ)
sharp will; earnest intention; determination; spirit of enterprise

銳士(ㄖㄨㄟˋ ㄕˋ)
①a man of intelligence; a man of energy ②brave soldiers of the state of Chin (秦)during the Epoch of Warring States

銳意(ㄖㄨㄟˋ ㄧˋ)
sharp will; eager intention; determination 參看「銳志」

銳眼(ㄖㄨㄟˋ ㄧㄢˇ)
sharp eyes; vision; insight

【銷】 6392 ㄒㄧㄠ shiau xiāo
1. to melt
2. to be marketed; to be circulated; to sell
3. to vanish; to dispel; to cancel 亦作「消」
4. pig iron; crude iron

銷路(ㄒㄧㄠ ㄌㄨˋ)
a sale; a market; a circulation (of publications, commodities, etc.); a market demand: 這本書銷路很廣。The book has a large circulation.

銷耗(ㄒㄧㄠ ㄏㄠˋ)
① expenditure ② to spend; to cost: 我們爲它銷耗很多勞力。We spent so much labor on it.

銷貨部(ㄒㄧㄠ ㄏㄨㄛˋ ㄅㄨˋ)
a sales department

銷貨發票(ㄒㄧㄠ ㄏㄨㄛˋ ㄈㄚ ㄆㄧㄠˋ)
(accounting) the invoice for sales; a sales invoice; sales tickets

銷貨點(ㄒㄧㄠ ㄏㄨㄛˋ ㄉㄧㄢˇ)
points of sale

銷貨折扣(ㄒㄧㄠ ㄏㄨㄛˋ ㄓㄜˊ ㄎㄡˋ)
(accounting) sales discount

銷毀(ㄒㄧㄠ ㄏㄨㄟˇ)
to destroy: 這嫌疑犯銷毀罪證。The suspect destroyed incriminating evidence.

銷魂(ㄒㄧㄠ ㄏㄨㄣˊ)
enraptured; transported; carried away

銷假(ㄒㄧㄠ ㄐㄧㄚˋ)
to begin work anew after a leave of absence or vacation: 他銷假了。He reported back after leave of absence.

銷金(ㄒㄧㄠ ㄐㄧㄣ)
① to lavish wealth ② decorated with gold; gilt

銷金窟(ㄒㄧㄠ ㄐㄧㄣ ㄎㄨ)
a brothel

銷金紙(ㄒㄧㄠ ㄐㄧㄣ ㄓˇ)
gilt paper

銷金帳(ㄒㄧㄠ ㄐㄧㄣ ㄓㄤˋ)
a gilt curtain

銷行(ㄒㄧㄠ ㄒㄧㄥˊ)
(said of goods) to be marketed; to be sold; to sell

〔金部〕

銷賬(ㄒㄧㄠ ㄓㄤˋ)
to cancel debts
銷差(ㄒㄧㄠ ㄔㄞ)
to report mission accomplished
銷場(ㄒㄧㄠ ㄔㄤˇ)
demand (for goods, services, etc.)
銷售(ㄒㄧㄠ ㄕㄡˋ)
to sell (goods): 這書銷售得非常多。The book is selling remarkably well.
銷售部門(ㄒㄧㄠ ㄕㄡˋ ㄅㄨˋ ㄇㄣˊ)
a marketing department
銷售方法(ㄒㄧㄠ ㄕㄡˋ ㄈㄤ ㄈㄚˇ)
the marketing method
銷售服務(ㄒㄧㄠ ㄕㄡˋ ㄈㄨˊ ㄨˋ)
marketing service
銷售地區(ㄒㄧㄠ ㄕㄡˋ ㄉㄧˋ ㄑㄩ)
sales territory
銷售量(ㄒㄧㄠ ㄕㄡˋ ㄌㄧㄤˋ)
sales volume
銷售活動(ㄒㄧㄠ ㄕㄡˋ ㄏㄨㄛˊ ㄉㄨㄥˋ)
marketing activity
銷售計畫(ㄒㄧㄠ ㄕㄡˋ ㄐㄧˋ ㄏㄨㄚˋ)
a marketing plan
銷售折扣(ㄒㄧㄠ ㄕㄡˋ ㄓㄜˊ ㄎㄡˋ)
(accounting) discount on sales
銷售狀況(ㄒㄧㄠ ㄕㄡˋ ㄓㄨㄤˋ ㄎㄨㄤˋ)
sales status
銷聲匿跡(ㄒㄧㄠ ㄕㄥ ㄋㄧˋ ㄐㄧ)
to vanish without leaving any trace behind; to go into hiding
銷鎔(ㄒㄧㄠ ㄖㄨㄥˊ)
to melt
銷贓(ㄒㄧㄠ ㄗㄤ)
(law) the disposal of stolen goods
銷案(ㄒㄧㄠ ㄢˋ)
to close a case

【銻】 6393 ㄊㄧˋ tih tì
antimony

【鋱】 6394 ㄊㄜˋ teh tè
terbium

【鋇】 6395 ㄅㄟˋ bey bèi
barium

【鋰】 6396 ㄌㄧˇ lii lǐ
lithium

【鋯】 6397 ㄍㄠˋ gaw gào
zirconium

【鋨】 6398 ㄜˊ er é
osmium

【鋁】 6399 ㄌㄩˇ leu lǚ
aluminium; aluminum
鋁箔(ㄌㄩˇ ㄅㄛˊ)
aluminium foil
鋁錠(ㄌㄩˇ ㄉㄧㄥˋ)
aluminium ingot
鋁合金(ㄌㄩˇ ㄏㄜˊ ㄐㄧㄣ)
aluminium alloy
鋁廠(ㄌㄩˇ ㄔㄤˇ)
an aluminium plant

【鋃】 6400 ㄌㄤˊ lang láng
1. chains for prisoners
2. the tolling of a bell
鋃鐺(ㄌㄤˊ ㄉㄤ)
chains for prisoners
鋃鐺入獄(ㄌㄤˊ ㄉㄤ ㄖㄨˋ ㄩˋ)
to be shackled and imprisoned; to be jailed

【鋅】 6401 ㄒㄧㄣ shin xīn
zinc
鋅版(ㄒㄧㄣ ㄅㄢˇ)
zincotype; zincograph
鋅鐵礦(ㄒㄧㄣ ㄊㄧㄝˇ ㄎㄨㄤˋ)
franklinite
鋅華(ㄒㄧㄣ ㄏㄨㄚˊ) or 鋅白(ㄒㄧㄣ ㄅㄞˊ)
zinc white

【鋌】 6402 ㄊㄧㄥˇ tiing tǐng
to rush
鋌而走險(ㄊㄧㄥˇ ㄦˊ ㄗㄡˇ ㄒㄧㄢˇ)
to be forced to break the law; to risk danger in desperation: 他鋌而走險。He risked danger in desperation.

【鋏】 6403 ㄐㄧㄚˊ jya jiá
1. pincers; tongs
2. a sword
3. a hilt

【鋒】 6404 ㄈㄥ feng fēng
1. sharp point (as the tip of a lance, pencil, etc.)
2. the vanguard; the van
鋒芒(ㄈㄥ ㄇㄤˊ)
① sharp point (as of a lance, etc.) ② dash; mettle; vigor
鋒芒畢露(ㄈㄥ ㄇㄤˊ ㄅㄧˋ ㄌㄨˋ)
to show one's intelligence, ability, knowledge, etc. to the full extent
鋒面(ㄈㄥ ㄇㄧㄢˋ)
(meteorology) frontal surface; a front
鋒發韻流(ㄈㄥ ㄈㄚ ㄩㄣˋ ㄌㄧㄡˊ)
fluent and overpowering (said of a literary style)
鋒鏑(ㄈㄥ ㄉㄧˊ)
sharp-pointed weapons
鋒利(ㄈㄥ ㄌㄧˋ)
① sharp-pointed; sharp: 用一把鋒利的小刀吧。Use a sharp knife. ② vigorous; energetic; keen; sharp; incisive: 他的文章富有鋒利尖刻的筆調。His essay has a sharp and pungent style.
鋒起(ㄈㄥ ㄑㄧˇ)
to rise with irresistible force or suddenness
鋒出(ㄈㄥ ㄔㄨ)
to occur suddenly; to come as a surprise
鋒刃(ㄈㄥ ㄖㄣˋ)
sharp points and edges of weapons
鋒銳(ㄈㄥ ㄖㄨㄟˋ)
sharp; keen; acute; spirited; vigorous
鋒鍔(ㄈㄥ ㄜˋ)
the point and edge of a knife

【鋦】 6405 ㄐㄩ jiu jū
1. a kind of nail for mending crockery
2. curium 亦作「鋸」
鋦碗(ㄐㄩ ㄨㄢˇ)
to mend crockery

【鋙】 6406 ㄩˇ yeu yǔ
1. discordant; disharmonious
2. a kind of musical instrument

【鋤】 6407 ㄔㄨˊ chwu chú
1. a hoe 亦作「鉏」
2. to hoe: 他正在鋤田。He is hoeing the fields.
鋤頭(ㄔㄨˊ ·ㄊㄡ)
a hoe
鋤骨(ㄔㄨˊ ㄍㄨˇ)
the vomer bone 亦作「犂骨」
鋤奸(ㄔㄨˊ ㄐㄧㄢ)
to wipe out the wicked elements
鋤強扶弱(ㄔㄨˊ ㄑㄧㄤˊ ㄈㄨˊ ㄖㄨㄛˋ)

to eliminate the bullies and help the downtrodden

【鋩】 6408
ㄇㄤˊ mang máng
the point of a knife

【銼】 6409
ㄘㄨㄛˋ tsuoh cuò
1. a kind of widemouthed cauldron used in ancient China
2. a file (a steel tool)
3. to make smooth with a file; to file

銼刀(ㄘㄨㄛˋ ㄉㄠ)
a file (a steel tool)

【鋪】 6410
1. ㄆㄨ pu pū
to lay in order; to spread; to arrange; to pave: 這條路鋪上了瀝青。The street is paved with asphalt.

鋪排(ㄆㄨ ˙ㄆㄞ)
①to arrange; to lay in order; arrangement ②to handle things with pomp; pomp

鋪平(ㄆㄨ ㄆㄧㄥˊ)
to smooth out; to spread out and make smooth

鋪地磚(ㄆㄨ ㄉㄧˋ ㄓㄨㄢ)
a floor tile; a paving tile

鋪墊(ㄆㄨ ㄉㄧㄢˋ)
①a cushion ②to spread a cushion ③to foreshadow

鋪路(ㄆㄨ ㄌㄨˋ)
to surface a road; to pave a road; to pave the way: 他小心地工作以便替我鋪路。He paved the way for me by doing careful work.

鋪蓋(ㄆㄨ ˙ㄍㄞ)
bedding

鋪蓋捲兒(ㄆㄨ ˙ㄍㄞ ㄐㄩㄚˇㄦ)
bedding rolled up for transportation during travel

鋪敍(ㄆㄨ ㄒㄩˋ)
to state in detail; to give a detailed account of

鋪展(ㄆㄨ ㄓㄢˇ)
①to arrange; to lay in order: 把報紙鋪展在桌面上。Arrange the papers on the table. ②to handle things with pomp

鋪張(ㄆㄨ ㄓㄤ)
①to arrange; to lay in order ②to make an ostentatious or vain show; to be pompous

鋪張浪費(ㄆㄨ ㄓㄤ ㄌㄤˋ ㄈㄟˋ)
extravagant and wasteful

鋪張揚厲(ㄆㄨ ㄓㄤ ㄧㄤˊ ㄌㄧˋ)
①to praise profusely; to eulogize ②to exaggerate; to make a big show

鋪陳(ㄆㄨ ㄔㄣˊ)
①to state in detail; to elaborate ②to arrange for display

鋪牀(ㄆㄨ ㄔㄨㄤˊ)
to make the bed

鋪設(ㄆㄨ ㄕㄜˋ)
to lay in order; to arrange

【鋪】 6410
2.(舖) ㄆㄨˋ puh pù
a store; a shop; a grocery: 我在雜貨鋪購買砂糖。I bought sugar at the grocery.

鋪保(ㄆㄨˋ ㄅㄠˇ)
a guarantee (for a person's reliability) given by a shopkeeper

鋪面(ㄆㄨˋ ㄇㄧㄢˋ)
the shop front; the facade of a store: 這鋪面面向公園。The front of this shop faces the park.

鋪面房(ㄆㄨˋ ㄇㄧㄢˋ ㄈㄤˊ)
a shop building

鋪底(ㄆㄨˋ ㄉㄧˇ)
shop fixtures

鋪規(ㄆㄨˋ ㄍㄨㄟ)
rules of a shop or store

鋪戶(ㄆㄨˋ ㄏㄨˋ)
shops; stores

鋪子(ㄆㄨˋ ˙ㄗ)
shops; stores: 她去鋪子買麵包。She went to the store to buy bread.

【銲】 6411
(釬) ㄏㄢˋ hann hàn
to solder; to weld

銲工(ㄏㄢˋ ㄍㄨㄥ)
①welding; soldering ②a welder; a solderer

銲接(ㄏㄢˋ ㄐㄧㄝ)
to join with solder; to weld; to solder: 這接頭處易於銲接。The joint solders easily.

銲錫(ㄏㄢˋ ㄒㄧˊ)
solder

銲住(ㄏㄢˋ ˙ㄓㄨ)
to fix with solder

【銹】 6412
(鏽) ㄒㄧㄡˋ shiow xiù
rust

銹斑(ㄒㄧㄡˋ ㄅㄢ)
rust stains

八畫

【鋸】 6413
1. ㄐㄩˋ jiuh jù
1. a saw
2. to saw; to cut with a saw: 軟質的木材容易鋸。Soft wood saws easily.
3. to amputate: 醫生鋸掉這士兵的腿。The doctor amputated the soldier's leg.

鋸木(ㄐㄩˋ ㄇㄨˋ)
to saw wood

鋸木廠(ㄐㄩˋ ㄇㄨˋ ㄔㄤˇ)
a sawmill

鋸腿(ㄐㄩˋ ㄊㄨㄟˇ)
to amputate a leg

鋸開(ㄐㄩˋ ㄎㄞ)
to saw asunder

鋸屑(ㄐㄩˋ ㄒㄧㄝˋ)
sawdust

鋸齒(ㄐㄩˋ ㄔˇ) or 鋸牙(ㄐㄩˋ ㄧㄚˊ)
teeth of a saw

鋸齒狀(ㄐㄩˋ ㄔˇ ㄓㄨㄤˋ)
serrated

鋸子(ㄐㄩˋ ˙ㄗ)
a saw: 我用鋸子鋸開木頭。I cut through the wood with a saw.

【鋸】 6413
2. ㄐㄩ jiu jū
1. a kind of nail for mending crockery
2. to mend (crockery)
3. curium 亦作「鋦」

鋸碗(ㄐㄩ ㄨㄢˇ)
to mend crockery

【鋼】 6414
ㄍㄤ gang gāng
steel: 許多工具是鋼製的。Many tools are made of steel.

鋼板(ㄍㄤ ㄅㄢˇ)
a steel plate

鋼筆(ㄍㄤ ㄅㄧˇ)
a fountain pen: 用鋼筆和墨水寫。Write with a fountain pen and ink.

鋼筆頭兒(ㄍㄤ ㄅㄧˇ ㄊㄡˊㄦ)
the point of a fountain pen

鋼鐵(ㄍㄤ ㄊㄧㄝˇ)
steel; steel and iron: 我有鋼鐵般的意志。I have an iron will.

〔金部〕

鋼鐵公司(ㄍㄤ ㄊㄧㄝˇ ㄍㄨㄥ ㄙ)
a steel company: 他在鋼鐵公司上班。He is working in a steel company.

鋼鐵廠(ㄍㄤ ㄊㄧㄝˇ ㄔㄤˇ)
a steelworks; a steel mill

鋼條(ㄍㄤ ㄊㄧㄠˊ)
a steel wire

鋼骨混凝土(ㄍㄤ ㄍㄨˇ ㄏㄨㄣˋ ㄋㄧㄥˊ ㄊㄨˇ)
reinforced concrete 亦作「鋼骨水泥」or「鋼筋水泥」

鋼管(ㄍㄤ ㄍㄨㄢˇ)
a steel pipe

鋼盔(ㄍㄤ ㄎㄨㄟ)
a steel helmet; a helmet

鋼筋(ㄍㄤ ㄐㄧㄣ)
steel bars; steel rods; wire mesh

鋼筋水泥(ㄍㄤ ㄐㄧㄣ ㄕㄨㄟˇ ㄋㄧˊ)
reinforced concrete

鋼琴(ㄍㄤ ㄑㄧㄣˊ)
a piano: 她鋼琴彈得很好。She plays the piano very well.

鋼琴伴奏(ㄍㄤ ㄑㄧㄣˊ ㄅㄢˋ ㄗㄡˋ)
the piano accompaniment

鋼琴家(ㄍㄤ ㄑㄧㄣˊ ㄐㄧㄚ)
a pianist

鋼琴協奏曲(ㄍㄤ ㄑㄧㄣˊ ㄒㄧㄝˊ ㄗㄡˋ ㄑㄩˇ)
a piano concerto

鋼琴演奏會(ㄍㄤ ㄑㄧㄣˊ ㄧㄢˇ ㄗㄡˋ ㄏㄨㄟˋ)
a piano concert; a piano recital

鋼珠(ㄍㄤ ㄓㄨ)or 鋼球(ㄍㄤ ㄑㄧㄡˊ)
a steel ball (in a ball bearing)

鋼尺(ㄍㄤ ㄔˇ)
a steel ruler

鋼絲(ㄍㄤ ㄙ)
steel wire: 這條鋼絲太長。This steel wire is too long.

鋼絲絨(ㄍㄤ ㄙ ㄖㄨㄥˊ)
steel wool

鋼玉(ㄍㄤ ㄩˋ)
corundum; corundumite

【釓】 6415 ㄍㄚˊ gar gá
gadolinium

【錸】 6416 ㄌㄞˊ lai lái
rhenium

【錒】 6417 ㄚ̀ ah à
actinium

【錄】 6418 ㄌㄨˋ luh lù
1. to take down; to copy; to record
2. to accept (applicants)
3. a record: 他保持跳高的最高紀錄。He holds the record for the high jump.

錄放影機(ㄌㄨˋ ㄈㄤˋ ㄧㄥˇ ㄐㄧ)
a videocassette recorder (VCR)

錄供(ㄌㄨˋ ㄍㄨㄥ)
to take down testimony

錄取(ㄌㄨˋ ㄑㄩˇ)
to accept (applicants after screening, examinations, etc.)

錄下(ㄌㄨˋ ·ㄒㄧㄚ)
to record

錄製(ㄌㄨˋ ㄓˋ)
to record

錄事(ㄌㄨˋ ㄕˋ)
a clerk whose job is to record or copy documents

錄音(ㄌㄨˋ ㄧㄣ)
① to record (songs, music, etc.) ②(songs, music, etc.) recording

錄音帶(ㄌㄨˋ ㄧㄣ ㄉㄞˋ)
a recording tape

錄音機(ㄌㄨˋ ㄧㄣ ㄐㄧ)
a tape recorder; a recorder

錄音室(ㄌㄨˋ ㄧㄣ ㄕˋ)
a recording room

錄影帶(ㄌㄨˋ ㄧㄥˇ ㄉㄞˋ)
a videotape

錄影機(ㄌㄨˋ ㄧㄥˇ ㄐㄧ)
a videorecorder

錄用(ㄌㄨˋ ㄩㄥˋ)
to accept for employment

【鉶】 6419 ㄒㄧㄥˊ shyng xíng
a kind of receptacle for food in ancient times

【錐】 6420 ㄓㄨㄟ juei zhuī
1. an awl
2. to pierce; to bore; to drill; to make a hole
3. conical

錐面(ㄓㄨㄟ ㄇㄧㄢˋ)
①(mathematics) conical surface ②(mineralogy) pyramidal faces

錐刀之末(ㄓㄨㄟ ㄉㄠ ㄓ ㄇㄛˋ)
small gains; negligible profits

錐股(ㄓㄨㄟ ㄍㄨˇ)
(literally) to prick the thigh with an awl (as 蘇秦 did in order to stay awake when studying)—to study with great determination and diligence

錐形(ㄓㄨㄟ ㄒㄧㄥˊ)
a taper; a cone: 鋸屑堆成大錐形物。Sawdust piled up in a great cone.

錐指(ㄓㄨㄟ ㄓˇ)
a very limited outlook

錐處囊中(ㄓㄨㄟ ㄔㄨˇ ㄋㄤˊ ㄓㄨㄥ)
(literally) an awl in a bag (which may be temporarily hidden but will eventually pierce the bag and show itself)—A talented person will sooner or later distinguish himself despite temporary adversity. 或 Real talent will be discovered.

錐子(ㄓㄨㄟ ·ㄗ)
an awl

【錘】 6421 ㄔㄨㄟˊ chwei chuí
1. a weight on a steelyard: 平衡錘 a balance weight
2. an ancient unit of weight
3. a kind of ancient weapon
4. to hammer; to pound
5. a hammer

錘鍊(ㄔㄨㄟˊ ㄌㄧㄢˋ)
① to forge (metal); to temper ② to polish

錘子(ㄔㄨㄟˊ ·ㄗ)
a hammer

【錙】 6422 ㄗ tzy zī
an ancient unit of weight (said to equal 8 taels)

錙銖(ㄗ ㄓㄨ)
a very small quantity; a trifle

錙銖必較(ㄗ ㄓㄨ ㄅㄧˋ ㄐㄧㄠˋ)
to be particular even about a trifling amount

【錚】 6423 ㄓㄥ jeng zhēng
1. a clang of metal
2. gongs

錚錚(ㄓㄥ ㄓㄥ)
① a clang of metal ② righteous; incorruptible; upright

錚鏦(ㄓㄥ ㄘㄨㄥ)
a clang of metal; to clang

【錠】 6424 ㄉㄧㄥˋ dinq dìng
1. a kind of ancient utensil
2. ingots of gold or silver
3. a spindle
4. a (medical) tablet
錠劑(ㄉㄧㄥˋ ㄐㄧˋ)
medicine in tablet form

【錡】 6425 ㄑㄧˊ chyi qí
1. a tripod
2. a kind of chisel

【錢】 6426 ㄑㄧㄢˊ chyan qián
1. money; cash: 時間即是金錢。Time is money.
2. a unit of weight (equal to 1/10th of a tael)
3. a Chinese family name
錢包(ㄑㄧㄢˊ ㄅㄠ)
a wallet; a purse
錢幣(ㄑㄧㄢˊ ㄅㄧˋ)
① coin ② currency; money
錢癖(ㄑㄧㄢˊ ㄆㄧˇ)
inveterate love of money
錢票(ㄑㄧㄢˊ ㄆㄧㄠˋ)
paper money; bank notes
錢鋪(ㄑㄧㄢˊ ㄆㄨˋ)
a banking house (in former times)
錢褡褳(ㄑㄧㄢˊ ㄉㄚ ·ㄌㄧㄢ)or 錢褡子(ㄑㄧㄢˊ ㄉㄚ ·ㄗ)
a moneybag
錢袋(ㄑㄧㄢˊ ㄉㄞˋ)
a moneybag; a money purse: 你看到我的小錢袋嗎? Have you seen my little money purse?
錢塘江(ㄑㄧㄢˊ ㄊㄤˊ ㄐㄧㄤ)
the Chientang River, in Chekiang
錢糧(ㄑㄧㄢˊ ㄌㄧㄤˊ)
taxes on farmland
錢穀(ㄑㄧㄢˊ ㄍㄨˇ)
taxes on farmland
錢櫃(ㄑㄧㄢˊ ㄍㄨㄟˋ)
a cash box
錢滾錢(ㄑㄧㄢˊ ㄍㄨㄣˇ ㄑㄧㄢˊ)
Money begets money.
錢可通神(ㄑㄧㄢˊ ㄎㄜˇ ㄊㄨㄥ ㄕㄣˊ)or 錢能通神(ㄑㄧㄢˊ ㄋㄥˊ ㄊㄨㄥ ㄕㄣˊ)
Money can move the gods. 或Money makes the mare go. 或 Money talks.
錢可使鬼(ㄑㄧㄢˊ ㄎㄜˇ ㄕˇ ㄍㄨㄟˇ)
Money can make the devil work for you. 或 Money makes the mare go. 亦作「有錢能使鬼推磨」
錢荒(ㄑㄧㄢˊ ㄏㄨㄤ)
scarcity of money
錢債(ㄑㄧㄢˊ ㄓㄞˋ)
debts
錢莊(ㄑㄧㄢˊ ㄓㄨㄤ)
a banking house (in former times)
錢財(ㄑㄧㄢˊ ㄘㄞˊ)
wealth; riches
錢財身外物(ㄑㄧㄢˊ ㄘㄞˊ ㄕㄣ ㄨㄞˋ ㄨˋ)
Money is not an inherent part of the human being (and therefore is not worth so much of one's efforts to get and to keep it).

【錦】 6427 ㄐㄧㄣˇ jiin jǐn
1. brocade; tapestry
2. brilliant and beautiful
3. glorious
錦標(ㄐㄧㄣˇ ㄅㄧㄠ)
① a championship (in a tournament) ② a trophy (for a sports champion); a cup: 他贏得錦標。He won the cup.
錦標賽(ㄐㄧㄣˇ ㄅㄧㄠ ㄙㄞˋ)
a sports tournament; championship contests; championships: 世界田徑錦標賽 the World Track and Field Championships
錦緞(ㄐㄧㄣˇ ㄉㄨㄢˋ)
brocade
錦堂(ㄐㄧㄣˇ ㄊㄤˊ)
a richly decorated hall
錦囊(ㄐㄧㄣˇ ㄋㄤˊ)
a bag made of brocade (used to hold manuscripts for poetry in ancient times)
錦囊妙計(ㄐㄧㄣˇ ㄋㄤˊ ㄇㄧㄠˋ ㄐㄧˋ)
a clever scheme yet to be revealed
錦葵(ㄐㄧㄣˇ ㄎㄨㄟˊ)
(botany) a mallow
錦還(ㄐㄧㄣˇ ㄏㄨㄢˊ)
to return home with glory
錦雞(ㄐㄧㄣˇ ㄐㄧ)
Phasianus pictus, a golden pheasant
錦牋(ㄐㄧㄣˇ ㄐㄧㄢ)
fancy stationery
錦旗(ㄐㄧㄣˇ ㄑㄧˊ)
an embroidered flag; a pennant; a silk banner (as an award or a gift)
錦繡河山(ㄐㄧㄣˇ ㄒㄧㄡˋ ㄏㄜˊ ㄕㄢ)
land of splendor—one's fatherland
錦繡前程(ㄐㄧㄣˇ ㄒㄧㄡˋ ㄑㄧㄢˊ ㄔㄥˊ)
a glorious or promising future; a bright or rosy future: 他有着錦繡前程。He has a bright future ahead.
錦心繡口(ㄐㄧㄣˇ ㄒㄧㄣ ㄒㄧㄡˋ ㄎㄡˇ)
exquisite thoughts and elegant language (said of a piece of writing)
錦注(ㄐㄧㄣˇ ㄓㄨˋ)
(a polite expression) your concern, or the interest you have shown (in the matter, etc.) 亦作「錦念」
錦上添花(ㄐㄧㄣˇ ㄕㄤˋ ㄊㄧㄢ ㄏㄨㄚ)
to give something or someone additional splendor; to cap it all
錦字(ㄐㄧㄣˇ ㄗˋ)
characters embroidered on brocade or tapestry
錦瑟(ㄐㄧㄣˇ ㄙㄜˋ)
a kind of Chinese musical instrument with 50 strings
錦衣衞(ㄐㄧㄣˇ ㄧ ㄨㄟˋ)
imperial guards of the Ming Dynasty which eventually became a sort of SS Troops
錦衣玉食(ㄐㄧㄣˇ ㄧ ㄩˋ ㄕˊ)
to lead a luxurious life; to live in luxury

【錫】 6428 ㄒㄧˊ shyi xí
1. tin
2. to bestow...on; to confer... on
錫箔(ㄒㄧˊ ㄅㄛˊ)
tinfoil; tinfoil paper
錫命(ㄒㄧˊ ㄇㄧㄥˋ)
the emperor's edict conferring the degree of nobility on his feudal princes
錫福(ㄒㄧˊ ㄈㄨˊ)
to bestow happiness; to bless
錫鑞(ㄒㄧˊ ㄌㄚˋ)
pewter; solder; tin
錫蘭(ㄒㄧˊ ㄌㄢˊ)
Ceylon, former name of Sri Lanka (斯里蘭卡)
錫蘭人(ㄒㄧˊ ㄌㄢˊ ㄖㄣˊ)
a Ceylonese; the Ceylonese
錫蘭語(ㄒㄧˊ ㄌㄢˊ ㄩˇ)
the Ceylonese language;

〔金部〕

Ceylonese
錫罐(ㄒㄧˊ ㄍㄨㄢˋ)
a can; a tin; a tin can
錫礦(ㄒㄧˊ ㄎㄨㄤˋ)
① tin ore ② tin mine
錫金(ㄒㄧˊ ㄐㄧㄣ)
Sikkim
錫匠(ㄒㄧˊ ㄐㄧㄤˋ)
a tinsmith
錫器(ㄒㄧˊ ㄑㄧˋ)
tinware
錫紙(ㄒㄧˊ ㄓˇ)
silver paper; tinfoil
錫杖(ㄒㄧˊ ㄓㄤˋ)
a Buddhist monk's walking stick 亦作「禪杖」
錫石(ㄒㄧˊ ㄕˊ)
cassiterite; tinstone
錫砂(ㄒㄧˊ ㄕㄚ)
stream tin
錫人(ㄒㄧˊ ㄖㄣˊ)
a tin figure buried together with a dead person
錫酸(ㄒㄧˊ ㄙㄨㄢ)
stannic acid
錫恩(ㄒㄧˊ ㄣ)
to do a favor

【錕】 6429
ㄎㄨㄣ kuen kūn
used in "錕鋙", name of a precious sword

【錮】 6430
ㄍㄨˋ guh gù
1. to run metal into cracks
2. to confine; to keep in custody; to imprison: 禁錮 to throw into a prison
3. sturdy; secure
錮蔽(ㄍㄨˋ ㄅㄧˋ)
stopped up; clogged
錮疾 or 痼疾(ㄍㄨˋ ㄐㄧˊ)
a chronic complaint, disease or ailment
錮寢(ㄍㄨˋ ㄑㄧㄣˇ)
(said of members of an imperial harem) to have the emperor's exclusive affection
錮身(ㄍㄨˋ ㄕㄣ)
to fetter a person

【錯】 6431
ㄘㄨㄛˋ tsuoh cuò
1. wrong; mistaken; erroneous: 你答錯了。You answered wrong.
2. a mistake; an error; a fault: 絕對沒錯。There's no mistake about it.
3. disorderly; untidy; irregular; uneven; complicated; intricate
4. a grindstone
5. prudent; cautious
錯別字(ㄘㄨㄛˋ ㄅㄧㄝˊ ㄗˋ)
characters wrongly written or mispronounced
錯不了(ㄘㄨㄛˋ ˙ㄅㄨ ㄌㄧㄠˇ)
unlikely to go wrong; to be good: 今年小麥的收成錯不了。This year's wheat harvest is sure to be good.
錯翻眼皮(ㄘㄨㄛˋ ㄈㄢ ㄧㄢˇ ㄆㄧˊ)
to turn a wrong eyelid—to misjudge a person
錯刀(ㄘㄨㄛˋ ㄉㄠ)
① the knife for dressing and polishing jade ② a kind of coin introduced by 王莽
錯落(ㄘㄨㄛˋ ㄌㄨㄛˋ)
disorderly; untidy; irregular; uneven
錯亂(ㄘㄨㄛˋ ㄌㄨㄢˋ)
disorderly; confused; abnormal; deranged: 他有點兒精神錯亂。He is somewhat mentally deranged.
錯過(ㄘㄨㄛˋ ㄍㄨㄛˋ)
to let (a chance) slip by; to miss: 你錯過了大好機會。You missed out on a great chance.
錯過機會(ㄘㄨㄛˋ ㄍㄨㄛˋ ㄐㄧ ㄏㄨㄟˋ)
loss of opportunity
錯怪(ㄘㄨㄛˋ ㄍㄨㄞˋ)
to blame unjustly or wrongly
錯開(ㄘㄨㄛˋ ㄎㄞ)
to stagger: 他們把交通的擁擠時間錯開了。They staggered the rush hour.
錯話(ㄘㄨㄛˋ ㄏㄨㄚˋ)
improper remarks
錯角(ㄘㄨㄛˋ ㄐㄧㄠˇ)
(mathematics) an alternate angle
錯簡(ㄘㄨㄛˋ ㄐㄧㄢˇ)
misplaced leaves, phrases, etc. in a book
錯覺(ㄘㄨㄛˋ ㄐㄩㄝˊ)
hallucination; illusion; a false impression: 這會給我們造成錯覺。This will give us a false impression.
錯處(ㄘㄨㄛˋ ㄔㄨˋ)
an error; a mistake; a fault: 你的報告上有許多錯處。There are a lot of faults in your paper.
錯失(ㄘㄨㄛˋ ㄕ)
an error; a mistake; a fault: 我知道是我的錯失。I know I am at fault.
錯認(ㄘㄨㄛˋ ㄖㄣˋ)
to misidentify
錯字(ㄘㄨㄛˋ ㄗˋ)
misspelling; a misprint
錯雜(ㄘㄨㄛˋ ㄗㄚˊ)
intermixed; confused; irregular; intricate
錯綜(ㄘㄨㄛˋ ㄗㄨㄥˋ)
intermixed; confused; irregular; intricate
錯綜複雜(ㄘㄨㄛˋ ㄗㄨㄥˋ ㄈㄨˋ ㄗㄚˊ)
very complicated; intricate
錯彩鏤金(ㄘㄨㄛˋ ㄘㄞˇ ㄌㄡˋ ㄐㄧㄣ)
gorgeously wrought; colorfully and dazzlingly embellished
錯愕(ㄘㄨㄛˋ ㄜˋ)
startled; astonished
錯愛(ㄘㄨㄛˋ ㄞˋ)
your misplaced favor; your favor which I do not deserve
錯兒(ㄘㄨㄛˋㄦ)
an error; a mistake; a fault: 那是我的錯兒。It was my fault.
錯誤(ㄘㄨㄛˋ ㄨˋ)
① an error; a mistake; a fault: 這書中有許多錯誤。There are many faults in the book. ② erroneous; wrong: 它是個錯誤的答案。It is a wrong answer.
錯誤百出(ㄘㄨㄛˋ ㄨˋ ㄅㄞˇ ㄔㄨ)
full of mistakes; riddled with errors

【錳】 6432
ㄇㄥˇ meeng měng
manganese

【錶】 6433
ㄅㄧㄠˇ beau biǎo
a watch (a timepiece): 他把錶對準。He set his watch.
錶帶(ㄅㄧㄠˇ ㄉㄞˋ)
the band of a wrist watch; a watchband
錶鏈(ㄅㄧㄠˇ ㄌㄧㄢˋ)
a watch chain
錶殼(ㄅㄧㄠˇ ㄎㄜˊ)

a watchcase

【錛】 6434 ㄅㄣ ben bēn

an adz; an adze

錛子(ㄅㄣ ·ㄗ)

an adz; an adze

九畫

【鍊】 6435 ㄌㄧㄢˋ liann liàn

1. to smelt; to refine; to forge; to temper
2. to polish: 他的文詞缺乏洗鍊。His speech needs polishing.
3. a chain 參看「鏈」

鍊丹(ㄌㄧㄢˋ ㄉㄢ)

to make pills of wonder; to practice alchemy 亦作「煉丹」

鍊丹家(ㄌㄧㄢˋ ㄉㄢ ㄐㄧㄚ)

an alchemist

鍊鐵(ㄌㄧㄢˋ ㄊㄧㄝˇ)

to smelt iron; to refine iron

鍊鋼(ㄌㄧㄢˋ ㄍㄤ)

to refine steel

鍊鋼廠(ㄌㄧㄢˋ ㄍㄤ ㄔㄤˇ)

a steel mill; a steelworks

鍊金術(ㄌㄧㄢˋ ㄐㄧㄣ ㄕㄨˋ)

alchemy 亦作「煉金術」

鍊句(ㄌㄧㄢˋ ㄐㄩˋ)

to remove the superfluous words and reduce the sentence to its simplest and most effective form; to polish and repolish a sentence

鍊石補天(ㄌㄧㄢˋ ㄕˊ ㄅㄨˇ ㄊㄧㄢ)

to smelt stone to mend the sky (a feat performed by 女媧氏, a mythological character)

鍊乳(ㄌㄧㄢˋ ㄖㄨˇ)

condensed milk

鍊字(ㄌㄧㄢˋ ㄗˋ)

to try hard to find the fittest words or expressions (to be used in a composition)

鍊子(ㄌㄧㄢˋ ·ㄗ)or 鍊兒(ㄌㄧㄚˋㄦ)or 鍊條(ㄌㄧㄢˋ ㄊㄧㄠˊ)

a chain

【錨】 6436 ㄇㄠˊ mau máo

to anchor; an anchor: 拋錨 to cast(or drop) anchor 起錨 to weigh anchor

【鍋】 6437 ㄍㄨㄛ guo guō

1. a cooking pot; a pan; a boiler; a caldron: 火鍋 a chafing dish 飯鍋 a rice pot
2. (said of a pipe, etc.) a bowl: 煙袋鍋兒 the bowl of a pipe

鍋巴(ㄍㄨㄛ ㄅㄚ)

burnt rice that sticks to the bottom and sides of the cooking pot

鍋餅(ㄍㄨㄛ ·ㄅㄧㄥ)

a kind of large cake made of dough

鍋貼兒(ㄍㄨㄛ ㄊㄧㄝㄦ)

a common Chinese delicacy in the form of minced meat wrapped in a skin of dough and lightly fried; lightly fried dumpling

鍋爐(ㄍㄨㄛ ㄌㄨˊ)

a boiler (especially of a steam engine)

鍋蓋(ㄍㄨㄛ ㄍㄞˋ)

the cover of a cooking pot; a pot cover

鍋戶(ㄍㄨㄛ ㄏㄨˋ)

families which make a living on evaporating seawater to make salt

鍋子(ㄍㄨㄛ ·ㄗ)or 鍋兒(ㄍㄨㄛㄦ)

a cooking pot; a pan: 他昨兒買了一口鍋子。He bought a cooking pot yesterday.

鍋煙子(ㄍㄨㄛ ㄧㄢ ·ㄗ)

soot on the underside of a cooking pot, pan, etc.

【鍍】 6438 ㄉㄨˋ duh dù

to plate; to gilt: 電鍍 electroplating

鍍銅(ㄉㄨˋ ㄊㄨㄥˊ)

plated copper

鍍金(ㄉㄨˋ ㄐㄧㄣ)

① to plate with gold ② to spend some time abroad to add to the impressiveness of one's background

鍍銀(ㄉㄨˋ ㄧㄣˊ)

to plate with silver; silverplating

【鍔】 6439 ㄜˋ eh è

1. the edge of a knife
2. lofty; towering

鍔鍔(ㄜˋ ㄜˋ)

towering; lofty

【鍘】 6440 ㄓㄚˊ jar zhá

1. a long knife hinged at one end for cutting hay
2. to cut up with a hay cutter

鍘刀(ㄓㄚˊ ㄉㄠ)

a long knife hinged at one end for cutting hay; a fodder chopper

鍘刀開關(ㄓㄚˊ ㄉㄠ ㄎㄞ ㄍㄨㄢ)

a knife switch

【鍛】 6441 (煅) ㄉㄨㄢˋ duann duàn

1. to smelt; to refine
2. to forge (iron, etc.)

鍛鐵(ㄉㄨㄢˋ ㄊㄧㄝˇ)

wrought iron

鍛鐵爐(ㄉㄨㄢˋ ㄊㄧㄝˇ ㄌㄨˊ)

a forge

鍛鍊(ㄉㄨㄢˋ ㄌㄧㄢˋ)

① to forge (metal); to temper ② to train (oneself); to discipline; to (take) exercise

鍛工(ㄉㄨㄢˋ ㄍㄨㄥ)

a smith; a metal worker

【鍥】 6442 ㄑㄧㄝˋ chieh qiè

to carve

鍥薄(ㄑㄧㄝˋ ㄅㄛˊ)

merciless; unsympathetic; pitiless

鍥而不舍(ㄑㄧㄝˋ ㄦˊ ㄅㄨˋ ㄕㄜˇ)

to carve without rest—to make steady efforts

【鍪】 6443 ㄇㄡˊ mou móu

1. a kind of cooking pot
2. a kind of metal helmet: 兜鍪 a helmet

【鍫】 6444 (鍬) ㄑㄧㄠ chiau qiāo

a shovel; a spade

【鍰】 6445 ㄏㄨㄢˊ hwan huán

1. an ancient unit of weight
2. money; cash: 罰鍰 to fine or be fined cash

【鍵】 6446 ㄐㄧㄢˋ jiann jiàn

key (to a door or on a musical instrument, etc.): 關鍵 key to situation

鍵盤(ㄐㄧㄢˋ ㄆㄢˊ)

a keyboard (on a piano, typewriter, etc.)

鍵盤樂器(ㄐㄧㄢˋ ㄆㄢˊ ㄩㄝˋ ㄑㄧˋ)

a keyed instrument

【鍼】 6447 ㄓㄣ jen zhēn

a needle; a pin; a probe 亦作

〔金部〕

〔金部〕

「針」
鍼言 or 箴言(ㄓㄣ ㄧㄢˊ)
① maxims ② *Proverbs* (a book of the Bible)

【鍾】 6448
ㄓㄨㄥ jong zhōng
1. a kind of wine container
2. to concentrate; to accumulate
3. a Chinese family name
鍾靈毓秀(ㄓㄨㄥ ㄌㄧㄥˊ ㄩˋ ㄒㄧㄡˋ)
The subtle spirit of Nature converges to nurture geniuses.
鍾馗(ㄓㄨㄥ ㄎㄨㄟˊ)
a deity who supposedly protects man from evil spirits
鍾情(ㄓㄨㄥ ㄑㄧㄥˊ)
to fall in love: 我對她一見鍾情。I fell in love with her at first sight.
鍾嶸(ㄓㄨㄥ ㄖㄨㄥˊ)
Chung Jung, a sixth century literary critic
鍾子期(ㄓㄨㄥ ㄗˇ ㄑㄧˊ)
Chung Tzu-chi, a musician of the state of 楚 during the Epoch of Spring and Autumn
鍾愛(ㄓㄨㄥ ㄞˋ)
to cherish; to dote on; to love deeply (especially children)

【鎂】 6449
ㄇㄟˇ meei měi
magnesium: 硫酸鎂 magnesium sulphate
鎂光燈(ㄇㄟˇ ㄍㄨㄤ ㄉㄥ)
a magnesium light

【鍺】 6450
ㄓㄜˇ jee zhě
germanium

【鍶】 6451
ㄙ sy sī
strontium

【鎃】 6452
ㄆㄞˋ pay pài
protoactinium

【鍇】 6453
ㄎㄞˇ kae kǎi
refined iron

【鍬】 6454
ㄑㄧㄠ chiau qiāo
a spade; a shovel 亦作「鍫」

十畫

【鎖】 6455
(鏁) ㄙㄨㄛˇ suoo suǒ
1. a lock: 她用鑰匙把鎖打開。She opened the lock with a key.
2. fetters; chains
3. to lock
4. to confine
5. to lockstitch
鎖不住(ㄙㄨㄛˇ ·ㄅㄨ ㄓㄨˋ)
(said of a captive) cannot be locked up or kept in confinement
鎖不上(ㄙㄨㄛˇ ·ㄅㄨ ㄕㄤˋ)
(said of a door, etc.) incapable of locking; failing to become locked; failing to lock
鎖眉(ㄙㄨㄛˇ ㄇㄟˊ)
to knit one's brows; to frown
鎖門(ㄙㄨㄛˇ ㄇㄣˊ)
to lock a door; to lock a gate
鎖頭(ㄙㄨㄛˇ ·ㄊㄡ)
a lock
鎖吶(ㄙㄨㄛˇ ㄋㄚˋ)
a Turkish flute 亦作「嗩吶」
鎖鐐(ㄙㄨㄛˇ ㄌㄧㄠˋ)
fetters; manacles
鎖鏈(ㄙㄨㄛˇ ㄌㄧㄢˋ)
chains
鎖骨(ㄙㄨㄛˇ ㄍㄨˇ)
(anatomy) the collarbone
鎖簧(ㄙㄨㄛˇ ㄏㄨㄤˊ)
the spring of a lock
鎖匠(ㄙㄨㄛˇ ㄐㄧㄤˋ)
a locksmith
鎖起來(ㄙㄨㄛˇ ㄑㄧˇ ·ㄌㄞ)
to lock or lock up (a house, a door, a person or an animal): 請將房子鎖起來好嗎? Will you lock up the house, please?
鎖住(ㄙㄨㄛˇ ·ㄓㄨ)
to lock up (a captive)
鎖上(ㄙㄨㄛˇ ㄕㄤˋ)
to lock (a door, etc.)
鎖鑰(ㄙㄨㄛˇ ㄧㄠˋ)
a key (to a door)
鎖陰(ㄙㄨㄛˇ ㄧㄣ)
gynatresia, a physical defect characterized by vaginal constriction, which makes sexual intercourse impossible

【鎡】 6456
ㄗ tzy zī
a hoe; a mattock

【鎊】 6457
ㄅㄤˋ banq bàng
pound sterling: 英幣五鎊 five pounds sterling

【鎋】 6458
(轄) ㄒㄧㄚˊ shya xiá
a linchpin

【鎔】 6459
(熔) ㄖㄨㄥˊ rong róng
1. to melt; to smelt; to fuse
2. a mold
3. a kind of spear
鎔點(ㄖㄨㄥˊ ㄉㄧㄢˇ)
the melting point
鎔度(ㄖㄨㄥˊ ㄉㄨˋ)
fusibility (of a mineral, etc.)
鎔爐(ㄖㄨㄥˊ ㄌㄨˊ)
a smelting furnace; a cupola
鎔化(ㄖㄨㄥˊ ㄏㄨㄚˋ)
to melt; to fuse: 熱使鐵鎔化。Heat will melt iron.
鎔化爐(ㄖㄨㄥˊ ㄏㄨㄚˋ ㄌㄨˊ)
a melting furnace
鎔劑(ㄖㄨㄥˊ ㄐㄧˋ)
fusing mixture; flux
鎔解(ㄖㄨㄥˊ ㄐㄧㄝˇ)
to melt; to fuse: 鐵在高溫下鎔解。The iron was melted by great heat.
鎔解熱(ㄖㄨㄥˊ ㄐㄧㄝˇ ㄖㄜˋ)
heat of fusion
鎔銷(ㄖㄨㄥˊ ㄒㄧㄠ)
to melt; to smelt
鎔鑄(ㄖㄨㄥˊ ㄓㄨˋ)
to cast (metal)
鎔融(ㄖㄨㄥˊ ㄖㄨㄥˊ)
to melt; to fuse
鎔冶(ㄖㄨㄥˊ ㄧㄝˇ)
to smelt
鎔岩(ㄖㄨㄥˊ ㄧㄢˊ)
molten rock; lava; magma

【鎗】 6460
(槍) ㄑㄧㄤ chiang qiāng
firearms; small arms; guns; pistols; rifles: 那強盜持有手鎗。The robber had a pistol.
鎗把(ㄑㄧㄤ ㄅㄚˇ)
a rifle butt
鎗靶(ㄑㄧㄤ ㄅㄚˇ)
the target for shooting
鎗斃(ㄑㄧㄤ ㄅㄧˋ)
execution by a firing squad; execution by shooting
鎗礮(ㄑㄧㄤ ㄆㄠˋ)
rifles and artillery pieces
鎗彈(ㄑㄧㄤ ㄉㄢˋ)

bullets
鎗膛(ㄑㄧㄤ ㄊㄤˊ)
the barrel (of a rifle, pistol, etc.)亦作「鎗身」or「鎗管」
鎗托(ㄑㄧㄤ ㄊㄨㄛ)
a gunstock; a rifle butt
鎗筒(ㄑㄧㄤ ㄊㄨㄥˇ)
the barrel (of a rifle, etc.)
鎗林彈雨(ㄑㄧㄤ ㄌㄧㄣˊ ㄉㄢˋ ㄩˇ)
a hail of bullets; heavy gunfire
鎗桿(ㄑㄧㄤ ㄍㄢˇ)or 鎗桿兒(ㄑㄧㄤ ㄍㄚˇㄦ)
rifles; firearms
鎗口(ㄑㄧㄤ ㄎㄡˇ)
the muzzle of a gun
鎗架(ㄑㄧㄤ ㄐㄧㄚˋ)
a rifle rack
鎗決(ㄑㄧㄤ ㄐㄩㄝˊ)
to execute by shooting
鎗戰(ㄑㄧㄤ ㄓㄢˋ)
gun battle; exchange of rifle or pistol fire
鎗手(ㄑㄧㄤ ㄕㄡˇ)
① a gunman ② a substitute writer in an examination
鎗眼(ㄑㄧㄤ ㄧㄢˇ)
an embrasure (in a parapet); a crenel

【鎚】 6461 ㄔㄨㄟˊ chwei chuí
1. to hammer: 我把釘子鎚入木板中。I hammered a nail into the board.
2. a hammer
3. an ancient weapon
鎚子(ㄔㄨㄟˊ ·ㄗ)or 鎚兒(ㄔㄨㄜˊㄦ)
a hammer

【鎛】 6462 ㄅㄛˊ bor bó
1. a kind of ancient bell
2. a variety of hoe

【鎧】 6463 ㄎㄞˇ kae kǎi
armor (worn by a warrior)
鎧馬(ㄎㄞˇ ㄇㄚˇ)
① armor and war-horses ② a horse protected by a coat of mail
鎧甲(ㄎㄞˇ ㄐㄧㄚˇ)
armor; a coat of mail

【鎬】 6464 1. ㄏㄠˋ haw hào
1. bright
2. an ancient place name (the first capital of the Chou Dynasty)
鎬鎬(ㄏㄠˋ ㄏㄠˋ)
bright; brilliant
鎬京(ㄏㄠˋ ㄐㄧㄥ)
the first capital of the Chou Dynasty (in what is Shensi today)

【鎬】 6464 2. ㄍㄠ gao gāo
a kind of hoe

【鎮】 6465 ㄓㄣˋ jenn zhèn
1. to subdue; to suppress; to quell; to put down
2. to cool with water or ice
3. weight (for pressing down)
4. whole
5. a town; a township: 我住在小鎮上。I live in a small town.
6. a garrison post
鎮暴(ㄓㄣˋ ㄅㄠˋ)
riot control
鎮服(ㄓㄣˋ ㄈㄨˊ)
to subdue; to conquer: 他終於鎮服敵人。He finally subdued his enemies.
鎮撫(ㄓㄣˋ ㄈㄨˇ)
to suppress and pacify
鎮定(ㄓㄣˋ ㄉㄧㄥˋ)
self-composed; calm; cool: 你應保持鎮定。You should keep cool.
鎮痛劑(ㄓㄣˋ ㄊㄨㄥˋ ㄐㄧˋ)
an anodyne; a painkiller
鎮南關(ㄓㄣˋ ㄋㄢˊ ㄍㄨㄢ)
name of a place in Kwangsi (the location of a former border checkpoint)
鎮公所(ㄓㄣˋ ㄍㄨㄥ ㄙㄨㄛˇ)
a town hall; a townhouse
鎮江(ㄓㄣˋ ㄐㄧㄤ)
Chenchiang, capital city of Kiangsu Province
鎮靜(ㄓㄣˋ ㄐㄧㄥˋ)
self-composed; calm; cool: 他故作鎮靜地如此說。He said so with forced calm.
鎮靜劑(ㄓㄣˋ ㄐㄧㄥˋ ㄐㄧˋ)or 鎮定劑(ㄓㄣˋ ㄉㄧㄥˋ ㄐㄧˋ)
a sedative; a tranquilizer
鎮紙(ㄓㄣˋ ㄓˇ)
a paperweight
鎮長(ㄓㄣˋ ㄓㄤˇ)
the town master; the head of a town
鎮守(ㄓㄣˋ ㄕㄡˇ)
to garrison: 他令軍隊鎮守此城。He garrisoned troops in the city.
鎮守使(ㄓㄣˋ ㄕㄡˇ ㄕˇ)
a provincial garrison commander (in the early years of the Republic)
鎮日(ㄓㄣˋ ㄖˋ)
the whole day; all day long: 他鎮日無所事事。He does nothing the whole day.
鎮遏(ㄓㄣˋ ㄜˋ)
to curb; to quell
鎮壓(ㄓㄣˋ ㄧㄚ)
to suppress; to put down; suppression: 他們採取鎮壓政策。They took a policy of suppression.

【鎰】 6466 ㄧˋ yih yì
an ancient unit of weight

【鎳】 6467 ㄋㄧㄝˋ nieh niè
nickel
鎳幣(ㄋㄧㄝˋ ㄅㄧˋ)
nickel coins

【鎢】 6468 ㄨˋ wuh wù
tungsten; wolfram
鎢錳鐵礦(ㄨˋ ㄇㄥˇ ㄊㄧㄝˇ ㄎㄨㄤˋ)
wolframite
鎢鋼(ㄨˋ ㄍㄤ)
wolfram steel; tungsten steel
鎢絲(ㄨˋ ㄙ)
a tungsten filament

【鎉】 6469 ㄊㄚˋ tah tà
thallium

【鎌】 6470 (鐮) ㄌㄧㄢˊ lian lián
a sickle
鎌倉(ㄌㄧㄢˊ ㄘㄤ)
Kamakura, Japan

【鎷】 6471 ㄇㄚˇ maa mǎ
masurium

【鎘】 6472 ㄍㄜˊ ger gé
cadmium

【鎵】 6473 ㄐㄧㄚ jia jiā
gallium

十一畫

【鏃】 6474 ㄗㄨˊ tzwu zú
as in 箭鏃—an arrowhead

〔金部〕

【鏇】 6475 ㄒㄩㄢˋ shiuann xuàn
1. a kind of wine heater
2. a kind of metal tray
3. to pare with a knife

鏇牀(ㄒㄩㄢˋ ㄔㄨㄤˊ)
a lathe

【鎩】 6476 ㄕㄚ sha shā
1. a lance
2. to shed (feathers)

鎩羽(ㄕㄚ ㄩˇ)
① having shed feathers ② discouraged; crestfallen; disheartened; defeated

【鏦】 6477 ㄘㄨㄥ tsong cōng
1. a spear
2. to pierce with a spear
3. the clang of metal

鏦鏦(ㄘㄨㄥ ㄘㄨㄥ)
the clang of metal

【鏈】 6478 ㄌㄧㄢˋ liann liàn
a chain: 他將狗用鏈繫住。He fastened the dog with a chain.

鏈黴素(ㄌㄧㄢˋ ㄇㄟˊ ㄙㄨˋ)
streptomycin

鏈條(ㄌㄧㄢˋ ㄊㄧㄠˊ)
a chain

鏈螺菌屬(ㄌㄧㄢˋ ㄌㄨㄛˊ ㄐㄩㄣˋ ㄕㄨˇ)
streptospirillum

鏈球(ㄌㄧㄢˋ ㄑㄧㄡˊ)
(sports) ① a hammer ② hammer throw

鏈球菌(ㄌㄧㄢˋ ㄑㄧㄡˊ ㄐㄩㄣˋ)
streptococcus

鏈著(ㄌㄧㄢˋ ·ㄓㄜ)
chained; in chains

鏈子(ㄌㄧㄢˋ ·ㄗ) or 鏈兒(ㄌㄧㄚˋㄦ)
a chain: 用鏈子將那隻狗栓起來。Keep the dog on a chain.

鏈絲菌屬(ㄌㄧㄢˋ ㄙ ㄐㄩㄣˋ ㄕㄨˇ)
streptomyces

鏈鎖反應(ㄌㄧㄢˋ ㄙㄨㄛˇ ㄈㄢˇ ㄧㄥˋ)
a chain reaction

【鏊】 6479 ㄠˊ aur áo
a kind of round, flat plate for baking; a griddle

【鏑】 6480 ㄉㄧˊ dyi dí
1. an arrowhead
2. dysprosium

【鏖】 6481 ㄠˊ aur áo
to fight hard

鏖兵(ㄠˊ ㄅㄧㄥ)
to engage in hard fighting

鏖戰(ㄠˊ ㄓㄢˋ)
to engage in hard fighting (or a bloody battle)

鏖糟(ㄠˊ ㄗㄠ)
① to fight a fierce battle ② filthy; dirty ③ to be stubborn and unpleasant

【鏗】 6482 ㄎㄥ keng kēng
1. the clang of metal; clatter
2. the twang of a string
3. to strike; to smash

鏗鏗(ㄎㄥ ㄎㄥ)
a tinkle; a clang; clatter

鏗鏘(ㄎㄥ ㄑㄧㄤ)
① a tinkle; a clang ② (figuratively) sonorous and forceful: 這首詩讀起來鏗鏘有力。This poem is sonorous and forceful.

【鏘】 6483 ㄑㄧㄤ chiang qiāng
a tinkle; a clang

鏘鏘(ㄑㄧㄤ ㄑㄧㄤ)
① a tinkle; a clang ② lofty; high

【鏹】 6484 1. ㄑㄧㄤˇ cheang qiǎng
money; wealth

【鏹】 6484 2. ㄑㄧㄤ chiang qiāng
corrosive

鏹水(ㄑㄧㄤ ㄕㄨㄟˇ)
corrosive acid (such as sulfuric acid)亦作「硫酸」

【鏜】 6485 1. ㄊㄤ tang tāng
1. the noise of drums or gongs
2. a small gong

【鏜】 6485 2. ㄊㄤˊ tarng táng
(machinery) boring

【鏝】 6486 (墁) ㄇㄢˋ mann màn
a trowel

【鏟】 6487 ㄔㄢˇ chaan chǎn
1. a shovel; a scoop
2. to shovel; to scoop

鏟幣(ㄔㄢˇ ㄅㄧˋ)
a shovel-shaped coin minted before the time of Confucius

鏟除(ㄔㄢˇ ㄔㄨˊ)
to eliminate; to uproot; to clear off

鏟子(ㄔㄢˇ ·ㄗ) or 鏟兒(ㄔㄚˇㄦ)
a shovel; a scoop

【鏡】 6488 ㄐㄧㄥˋ jinq jìng
1. a mirror
2. lenses; spectacles; glasses: 他有兩副眼鏡。He has two pairs of glasses.
3. to mirror
4. to take warning (from a past failure)

鏡片(ㄐㄧㄥˋ ㄆㄧㄢˋ)
a lens

鏡臺(ㄐㄧㄥˋ ㄊㄞˊ)
a mirror stand; a dressing stand

鏡頭(ㄐㄧㄥˋ ㄊㄡˊ)
① the lens of a camera ② a scene captured by the camera

鏡鸞(ㄐㄧㄥˋ ㄌㄨㄢˊ)
to lose one's spouse

鏡框(ㄐㄧㄥˋ ㄎㄨㄤˋ)
a picture frame

鏡花水月(ㄐㄧㄥˋ ㄏㄨㄚ ㄕㄨㄟˇ ㄩㄝˋ)
(literally) flowers in a mirror and the moon in water —things appealing but unreal

鏡花緣(ㄐㄧㄥˋ ㄏㄨㄚ ㄩㄢˊ)
the title of a Ching Dynasty novel by Li Ju-chen (李汝珍)

鏡戒(ㄐㄧㄥˋ ㄐㄧㄝˋ) or 鏡鑒(ㄐㄧㄥˋ ㄐㄧㄢˋ)
a lesson; a warning

鏡匣(ㄐㄧㄥˋ ㄒㄧㄚˊ)
a vanity case; a vanity box; a dressing case

鏡子(ㄐㄧㄥˋ ·ㄗ) or 鏡兒(ㄐㄧㄥˋㄦ)
① a mirror ② a mirror (in a non-material sense): 小說是反映時代的一面鏡子。Novels are a mirror of the times. ③ a lens; glasses

【鏢】 6489 ㄅㄧㄠ biau biāo
1. a javelin; a dart; a harpoon; a dartlike weapon
2. an escort; a guard; a bodyguard

鏢客(ㄅㄧㄠ ㄎㄜˋ)
(in former times) hired escorts for traveling merchants, etc.

鏢局(ㄅㄧㄠ ㄐㄩˊ)
(in former times) an establishment which provides escorts or bodyguards for

fees
鏢鎗 or 鏢槍(ㄅㄧㄠ ㄑㄧㄤ)
a javelin

【鏤】 6490 ㄌㄡˋ low lòu
to engrave; to carve
鏤版(ㄌㄡˋ ㄅㄢˇ)
an engraved plate
鏤冰(ㄌㄡˋ ㄅㄧㄥ)
(literally) to carve on ice—(figuratively) to labor in vain
鏤骨銘心(ㄌㄡˋ ㄍㄨˇ ㄇㄧㄥˊ ㄒㄧㄣ)
(literally) to engrave on the bones and imprint on the heart—the memory of a favor received; to remember forever with gratitude
鏤刻(ㄌㄡˋ ㄎㄜˋ)
to engrave; to carve
鏤空(ㄌㄡˋ ㄎㄨㄥ)
to hollow out; hollowed-out
鏤花(ㄌㄡˋ ㄏㄨㄚ)
①to engrave a design of flowers ②ornamental engraving
鏤金錯彩(ㄌㄡˋ ㄐㄧㄣ ㄘㄨㄛˋ ㄘㄞˇ)
(said of works of art) exquisitely wrought
鏤塵吹影(ㄌㄡˋ ㄔㄣˊ ㄔㄨㄟ ㄧㄥˇ)
(literally) to carve dust and blow shadows—to make futile efforts
鏤身(ㄌㄡˋ ㄕㄣ)
to tattoo the body 亦作「紋身」
鏤月裁雲(ㄌㄡˋ ㄩㄝˋ ㄘㄞˊ ㄩㄣˊ)
(said of works of art) ingeniously wrought

【鏨】 6491 ㄗㄢˋ tzann zàn
1. a chisel
2. to chisel; to engrave; to carve
鏨刀(ㄗㄢˋ ㄉㄠ)
a chisel; a graver
鏨子(ㄗㄢˋ ·ㄗ)
a chisel

【鏁】 6492 (鎖) ㄙㄨㄛˇ suoo suǒ
a lock; to lock

十二畫

【鐘】 6493 ㄓㄨㄥ jong zhōng
1. a bell (which tolls as distinct from that which jingles)
2. a clock: 這鐘走得太快了。The clock gains.
3. time as measured in hours and minutes: 現在正好兩點鐘。It's exactly two o'clock.
4. a Chinese family name
鐘擺(ㄓㄨㄥ ㄅㄞˇ)
a pendulum
鐘錶 or 鐘表(ㄓㄨㄥ ㄅㄧㄠˇ)
timepieces; clocks and watches
鐘錶鋪(ㄓㄨㄥ ㄅㄧㄠˇ ㄆㄨˋ) or 鐘錶店(ㄓㄨㄥ ㄅㄧㄠˇ ㄉㄧㄢˋ) or 鐘錶行(ㄓㄨㄥ ㄅㄧㄠˇ ㄏㄤˊ)
a watchmaker's shop
鐘鳴鼎食(ㄓㄨㄥ ㄇㄧㄥˊ ㄉㄧㄥˇ ㄕˊ)
to enjoy affluence
鐘鳴鼎食之家(ㄓㄨㄥ ㄇㄧㄥˊ ㄉㄧㄥˇ ㄕˊ ㄓ ㄐㄧㄚ)
a family of great wealth
鐘鳴漏盡(ㄓㄨㄥ ㄇㄧㄥˊ ㄌㄡˋ ㄐㄧㄣˋ)
to be in one's declining years
鐘點(ㄓㄨㄥ ㄉㄧㄢˇ)
①hours ②a time for something to be done or to happen: 到鐘點兒了，我們快走吧! It's time; let's go.
鐘點費(ㄓㄨㄥ ㄉㄧㄢˇ ㄈㄟˋ)
remuneration for teaching paid by the hour
鐘鼎文(ㄓㄨㄥ ㄉㄧㄥˇ ㄨㄣˊ)
ancient inscriptions on bronzes; bronze inscriptions
鐘頭(ㄓㄨㄥ ㄊㄡˊ)
an hour
鐘樓(ㄓㄨㄥ ㄌㄡˊ)
a bell tower; a belfry
鐘形花植物(ㄓㄨㄥ ㄒㄧㄥˊ ㄏㄨㄚ ㄓˊ ㄨˋ)
(botany) bluebells
鐘狀花冠(ㄓㄨㄥ ㄓㄨㄤˋ ㄏㄨㄚ ㄍㄨㄢ)
(botany) campanulate corolla
鐘聲(ㄓㄨㄥ ㄕㄥ)
the toll of a bell
鐘乳石(ㄓㄨㄥ ㄖㄨˇ ㄕˊ)
a stalactite
鐘兒(ㄓㄨㄥㄦ)
a bell: 教堂的鐘兒正在響。The church bells are ringing.

【鐃】 6494 ㄋㄠˊ nau náo
1. a kind of bell used in the army in ancient times
2. cymbals
鐃鈸(ㄋㄠˊ ㄅㄚˊ)
cymbals
鐃歌(ㄋㄠˊ ㄍㄜ) or 鐃吹(ㄋㄠˊ ㄔㄨㄟ)
military music; martial strains
鐃鼓(ㄋㄠˊ ㄍㄨˇ)
a kind of drum

【鐐】 6495 ㄌㄧㄠˊ liau liáo (又讀 ㄌㄧㄠˋ liaw liào)
shackles; fetters
鐐銬(ㄌㄧㄠˊ ㄎㄠˋ)
fetters; manacles: 囚犯上了鐐銬。The prisoners are in fetters.

【鐙】 6496 1. ㄉㄥˋ denq dèng
a stirrup
鐙骨(ㄉㄥˋ ㄍㄨˇ)
(anatomy) stapes

【鐙】 6496 2. ㄉㄥ deng dēng
1. same as 燈—a lamp
2. a kind of cooking vessel in ancient times

【鏽】 6497 (銹) ㄒㄧㄡˋ shiow xiù
rust; to rust

【鐧】 6498 1. ㄐㄧㄢˇ jean jiǎn
a kind of ancient weapon; a mace

【鐧】 6498 2. ㄐㄧㄢˋ jiann jiàn
protective metal on the axis of a wheel

【鐠】 6499 ㄆㄨˇ puu pǔ
praseodymium

【鐂】 6500 ㄌㄧㄡˊ liou liú
lutecium

十三畫

【鐲】 6501 ㄓㄨㄛˊ jwo zhuó
1. a kind of bell used in the army in ancient times
2. a bracelet; an armlet
鐲子(ㄓㄨㄛˊ ·ㄗ)
a bracelet; an armlet: 她買了一個金鐲子。She bought a gold bracelet.

【鐫】 6502 ㄐㄩㄢ jiuan juān
1. to carve; to engrave

〔金部〕

〔金部〕

2. (said of an official) to be demoted
鐫刻(ㄐㄩㄢ ㄎㄜˋ)
to engrave; to carve: 他用石頭鐫刻了一個人像。He carved a figure in stone.

【鐮】6503
ㄌㄧㄢˊ lian lián
a sickle
鐮刀(ㄌㄧㄢˊ ㄉㄠ)
a sickle

【鐵】6504
ㄊㄧㄝˇ tiee tiě
1. iron: 這東西堅硬似鐵。This is as hard as iron.
2. firm; indisputable; unyielding (like iron)
3. cruel; merciless; unfeeling
4. arms; weapons
鐵板(ㄊㄧㄝˇ ㄅㄢˇ)
① an iron plate; sheet iron ② a kind of percussion instrument
鐵板大鼓(ㄊㄧㄝˇ ㄅㄢˇ ㄉㄚˋ ㄍㄨˇ)
a kind of singing performance in which the singer beats time with a drum on the right and with semicircular metal pieces on the left
鐵板牛扒(ㄊㄧㄝˇ ㄅㄢˇ ㄋㄧㄡˊ ㄆㄚˊ)
broiled steak
鐵棒(ㄊㄧㄝˇ ㄅㄤˋ)
an iron club
鐵筆(ㄊㄧㄝˇ ㄅㄧˇ)
① a burin ② a stylus
鐵餅(ㄊㄧㄝˇ ㄅㄧㄥˇ)
a discus
鐵布衫(ㄊㄧㄝˇ ㄅㄨˋ ㄕㄢ)
(Chinese pugilism) the ability to sustain the thrusts of sharp weapons on one's bare skin
鐵皮(ㄊㄧㄝˇ ㄆㄧˊ)
iron sheet
鐵馬(ㄊㄧㄝˇ ㄇㄚˇ)
① strong cavalry ② (colloquial) a bicycle ③ armored horses
鐵門(ㄊㄧㄝˇ ㄇㄣˊ)
① a metal security door ② name of a county in Honan
鐵面無私(ㄊㄧㄝˇ ㄇㄧㄢˋ ㄨˊ ㄙ)
inflexibly just and fair; Rhadamanthine: 他是個鐵面無私的判官。He was a just judge.
鐵幕(ㄊㄧㄝˇ ㄇㄨˋ)
the Iron Curtain
鐵木眞(ㄊㄧㄝˇ ㄇㄨˋ ㄓㄣ)
name of Genghis Khan, 1162-1227, Mongol conqueror of central Asia
鐵肺(ㄊㄧㄝˇ ㄈㄟˋ)
an iron lung
鐵礬土(ㄊㄧㄝˇ ㄈㄢˊ ㄊㄨˇ)
bauxite
鐵飯碗(ㄊㄧㄝˇ ㄈㄢˋ ㄨㄢˇ)
(literally) an iron rice bowl —a very secure job
鐵道(ㄊㄧㄝˇ ㄉㄠˋ) or 鐵路(ㄊㄧㄝˇ ㄌㄨˋ)
a railway; a railroad
鐵釘(ㄊㄧㄝˇ ㄉㄧㄥ)
iron nails
鐵定(ㄊㄧㄝˇ ㄉㄧㄥˋ)
definitely; ironclad; unalterable; not subject to change
鐵塔(ㄊㄧㄝˇ ㄊㄚˇ)
an iron or steel tower
鐵蹄(ㄊㄧㄝˇ ㄊㄧˊ)
① (literally) iron hoofs—(figuratively) devastation by invading troops ② fine horses
鐵桶(ㄊㄧㄝˇ ㄊㄨㄥˇ)
(literally) an iron bucket —(figuratively) impregnable defense
鐵牛(ㄊㄧㄝˇ ㄋㄧㄡˊ)
an iron ox (thrown into rivers in ancient times as a ritual for warding off floods)
鐵欄(ㄊㄧㄝˇ ㄌㄢˊ)
an iron barrier
鐵鏈(ㄊㄧㄝˇ ㄌㄧㄢˋ)
an iron chain
鐵路(ㄊㄧㄝˇ ㄌㄨˋ)
a railroad; a railway
鐵路局(ㄊㄧㄝˇ ㄌㄨˋ ㄐㄩˊ)
Railway Administration
鐵路局長(ㄊㄧㄝˇ ㄌㄨˋ ㄐㄩˊ ㄓㄤˇ)
the director of the Railway Administration
鐵路網(ㄊㄧㄝˇ ㄌㄨˋ ㄨㄤˇ)
a railway network; a network of railroads
鐵籠子(ㄊㄧㄝˇ ㄌㄨㄥˊ ·ㄗ)
an iron cage
鐵拐李(ㄊㄧㄝˇ ㄍㄨㄞˇ ㄌㄧˇ)
one of the Eight Immortals of Taoism who limps with an iron walking stick
鐵軌(ㄊㄧㄝˇ ㄍㄨㄟˇ)
iron rails (of a railway): 火車出了鐵軌。The train went off the rails.
鐵櫃(ㄊㄧㄝˇ ㄍㄨㄟˋ)
a safe
鐵觀音(ㄊㄧㄝˇ ㄍㄨㄢ ㄧㄣ)
a variety of oolong tea
鐵棍(ㄊㄧㄝˇ ㄍㄨㄣˋ)
an iron club
鐵工(ㄊㄧㄝˇ ㄍㄨㄥ)
① ironwork ② an ironworker; a blacksmith
鐵工場(ㄊㄧㄝˇ ㄍㄨㄥ ㄔㄤˇ) or 鐵工廠(ㄊㄧㄝˇ ㄍㄨㄥ ㄔㄤˇ)
ironworks
鐵公鷄(ㄊㄧㄝˇ ㄍㄨㄥ ㄐㄧ)
an iron cock—a stingy person
鐵礦(ㄊㄧㄝˇ ㄎㄨㄤˋ)
① iron ore ② an iron mine
鐵漢(ㄊㄧㄝˇ ㄏㄢˋ)
① a strong fellow ② a man of firm principle; a strong determined person
鐵畫銀鉤(ㄊㄧㄝˇ ㄏㄨㄚˋ ㄧㄣˊ ㄍㄡ)
vigorous touches and fine strokes (in calligraphy)
鐵蒺藜(ㄊㄧㄝˇ ㄐㄧˊ ㄌㄧˊ)
barbed-wire barricades; caltrop
鐵騎(ㄊㄧㄝˇ ㄐㄧˋ)
strong cavalry
鐵甲(ㄊㄧㄝˇ ㄐㄧㄚˇ)
steel armor
鐵甲車(ㄊㄧㄝˇ ㄐㄧㄚˇ ㄔㄜ)
an armored car; an armored vehicle
鐵甲船(ㄊㄧㄝˇ ㄐㄧㄚˇ ㄔㄨㄢˊ)
an ironclad
鐵匠(ㄊㄧㄝˇ ·ㄐㄧㄤ)
an ironsmith; a blacksmith
鐵軍(ㄊㄧㄝˇ ㄐㄩㄣ)
① an invincible army ② the Ironsides of Oliver Cromwell, 1599-1658
鐵器(ㄊㄧㄝˇ ㄑㄧˋ)
ironware
鐵器時代(ㄊㄧㄝˇ ㄑㄧˋ ㄕˊ ㄉㄞˋ)
the Iron Age
鐵鍬(ㄊㄧㄝˇ ㄑㄧㄠ)
an iron spade; a spade
鐵橋(ㄊㄧㄝˇ ㄑㄧㄠˊ)
① an iron bridge ② a railway bridge
鐵球(ㄊㄧㄝˇ ㄑㄧㄡˊ)
a shot (thrown in shot put)

鐵青(ㄊㄧㄝˇ ㄑㄧㄥ)
livid; bluish black: 他氣得臉色鐵青。His face was livid with anger.
鐵血主義(ㄊㄧㄝˇ ㄒㄧㄝˇ ㄓㄨˇ ㄧˋ)
blood and iron policy
鐵血宰相(ㄊㄧㄝˇ ㄒㄧㄝˇ ㄗㄞˇ ㄒㄧㄤˋ)
the Iron Chancellor (Otto von Bismarck, 1815-1898)
鐵銹(ㄊㄧㄝˇ ㄒㄧㄡˋ)
rust: 這把刀長滿了鐵銹。The knife was covered with rust.
鐵掀(ㄊㄧㄝˇ ㄒㄧㄢ)
a shovel; a spade
鐵線蓮(ㄊㄧㄝˇ ㄒㄧㄢˋ ㄌㄧㄢˊ)
(botany) cream clematis
鐵線草(ㄊㄧㄝˇ ㄒㄧㄢˋ ㄘㄠˇ)
(botany) adiantum
鐵心(ㄊㄧㄝˇ ㄒㄧㄣ)
① an iron heart; ruthlessness ② a strong will; firm determination ③ (iron) core
鐵箱(ㄊㄧㄝˇ ㄒㄧㄤ)
a safe
鐵柵(ㄊㄧㄝˇ ㄓㄚˋ)
an iron fence; an iron barrier
鐵證(ㄊㄧㄝˇ ㄓㄥˋ)
proof strong as iron; irrefutable evidence; ironclad evidence
鐵證如山(ㄊㄧㄝˇ ㄓㄥˋ ㄖㄨˊ ㄕㄢ)
irrefutable, decisive evidence
鐵尺(ㄊㄧㄝˇ ㄔˇ)
① a short iron staff (used as a weapon) ② an iron ruler
鐵廠(ㄊㄧㄝˇ ㄔㄤˇ)
ironworks
鐵杵磨針(ㄊㄧㄝˇ ㄔㄨˇ ㄇㄛˊ ㄓㄣ)
(literally) An iron pestle can be ground into a needle. —Steady efforts can work miracles.
鐵鎚(ㄊㄧㄝˇ ㄔㄨㄟˊ)
an iron hammer; a hammer
鐵窗(ㄊㄧㄝˇ ㄔㄨㄤ)
① a window with metal gratings ② a prison
鐵窗風味(ㄊㄧㄝˇ ㄔㄨㄤ ㄈㄥ ㄨㄟˋ)
(literally) the flavor of iron-barred windows—life in prison of a convict
鐵牀(ㄊㄧㄝˇ ㄔㄨㄤˊ)
steel beds
鐵石骨子(ㄊㄧㄝˇ ㄕˊ ㄍㄨˇ ·ㄗ)
a very strong body; great physical strength
鐵石心腸(ㄊㄧㄝˇ ㄕˊ ㄒㄧㄣ ㄔㄤˊ)
a cold heart; an unfeeling heart; iron-hearted; hard-hearted
鐵石人(ㄊㄧㄝˇ ㄕˊ ㄖㄣˊ)
an iron-hearted person; an unfeeling person; a cruel person
鐵石英(ㄊㄧㄝˇ ㄕˊ ㄧㄥ)
ferruginous quartz
鐵砂(ㄊㄧㄝˇ ㄕㄚ)
iron ore; iron sand
鐵沙掌(ㄊㄧㄝˇ ㄕㄚ ㄓㄤˇ)
a Chinese version of karate
鐵杉(ㄊㄧㄝˇ ㄕㄢ)
hemlock spruces
鐵樹(ㄊㄧㄝˇ ㄕㄨˋ)
a cycad 亦作「鳳尾蕉」
鐵樹開花(ㄊㄧㄝˇ ㄕㄨˋ ㄎㄞ ㄏㄨㄚ)
(literally) the blooming of an iron tree—an impossibility; something that very rarely happens
鐵人(ㄊㄧㄝˇ ㄖㄣˊ)
(literally) an iron man—(figuratively) a man of great physical strength
鐵則(ㄊㄧㄝˇ ㄗㄜˊ)
unalterable rules; iron rules
鐵嘴(ㄊㄧㄝˇ ㄗㄨㄟˇ)
accurate judgment or prediction
鐵絲(ㄊㄧㄝˇ ㄙ) or 鐵線(ㄊㄧㄝˇ ㄒㄧㄢˋ)
iron wire
鐵絲網(ㄊㄧㄝˇ ㄙ ㄨㄤˇ)
① barbed-wire entanglements ② wire netting; wire meshes
鐵索(ㄊㄧㄝˇ ㄙㄨㄛˇ)
iron cable; cable
鐵算盤(ㄊㄧㄝˇ ㄙㄨㄢˋ ·ㄆㄢ)
the iron abacus—the trick, or spell, by which wandering sorcerers were believed to swindle people out of their money
鐵案如山(ㄊㄧㄝˇ ㄢˋ ㄖㄨˊ ㄕㄢ)
facts as irrevocable as a mountain
鐵衣(ㄊㄧㄝˇ ㄧ)
① armor ② iron rust
鐵硯磨穿(ㄊㄧㄝˇ ㄧㄢˋ ㄇㄛˊ ㄔㄨㄢ)
to rub through an iron ink slab—to study with uncommon diligence
鐵腕(ㄊㄧㄝˇ ㄨㄢˋ)
iron hand; iron fist

【鐶】 6505 ㄏㄨㄢˊ hwan huan
a ring

【鐸】 6506 ㄉㄨㄛˊ dwo duó
1. a large bell
2. a Chinese family name

【鐺】 6507 1. ㄉㄤ dang dāng
1. the sound of striking a gong
2. shackles 參看「鋃鐺」
鐺鐺(ㄉㄤ ㄉㄤ)
the sound of striking a gong

【鐺】 6507 2. ㄔㄥ cheng chēng
1. a kind of wine heater
2. a cauldron-like vessel with legs
3. a pan for frying; a shallow pot

【鐳】 6508 ㄌㄟˊ lei léi
1. radium
2. a pot; a jar
鐳錠(ㄌㄟˊ ㄉㄧㄥˋ)
radium (Ra)

【鐿】 6509 ㄧˋ yih yì
ytterbium

十四畫

【鑊】 6510 ㄏㄨㄛˋ huoh huò
a cauldron for cooking (used mostly in ancient times)
鑊烹(ㄏㄨㄛˋ ㄆㄥ)
(an ancient punishment) to cook a criminal in a cauldron

【鑄】 6511 ㄓㄨˋ juh zhù
1. to melt or cast metal; to coin; to mint
2. to make or commit (blunders, etc.)
3. to educate and influence (a person)
4. a Chinese family name
鑄幣(ㄓㄨˋ ㄅㄧˋ)
to mint (coins)
鑄幣廠(ㄓㄨˋ ㄅㄧˋ ㄔㄤˇ)
a mint
鑄鐵(ㄓㄨˋ ㄊㄧㄝˇ)
① cast iron ② iron casting
鑄像(ㄓㄨˋ ㄒㄧㄤˋ)

〔金部〕

to erect a metal statue
鑄成大錯(ㄓㄨˋ ㄔㄥˊ ㄉㄚˋ ㄘㄨㄛˋ)
to commit a serious mistake; to make a gross error
鑄山煑海(ㄓㄨˋ ㄕㄢ ㄓㄨˇ ㄏㄞˇ)
(literally) to excavate copper from mountain mine for coining and cook seawater for salt—to develop natural resources
鑄人(ㄓㄨˋ ㄖㄣˊ)
to educate and influence people
鑄字(ㄓㄨˋ ㄗˋ)
type founding; typecasting
鑄造(ㄓㄨˋ ㄗㄠˋ)
① to educate ② to melt or cast (metal) ③ to mint (coins)
鑄錯(ㄓㄨˋ ㄘㄨㄛˋ)
to commit blunders

【鑑】 6512 ㄐㄧㄢˋ jiann jiàn
1. a mirror
2. to mirror; to reflect; to shine
3. to study or examine; to scrutinize
4. an example serving as a rule or warning
鑑別(ㄐㄧㄢˋ ㄅㄧㄝˊ)
to distinguish (the genuine from an imitation); to judge or identify something by carefully examining it; to discriminate; to make an appraisal of something: 她善於鑑別文物。She is good at making an appraisal of a cultural relic.
鑑定(ㄐㄧㄢˋ ㄉㄧㄥˋ)
to examine and determine; to judge; to make an appraisal
鑑定書(ㄐㄧㄢˋ ㄉㄧㄥˋ ㄕㄨ)
the appraisal of an expert in written form
鑑定人(ㄐㄧㄢˋ ㄉㄧㄥˋ ㄖㄣˊ)
(law) an appraiser; an expert examiner
鑑戒(ㄐㄧㄢˋ ㄐㄧㄝˋ)
a warning example; to take warning from a past failure
鑑識(ㄐㄧㄢˋ ㄕˋ)
to tell; to judge; to distinguish; to discern
鑑賞(ㄐㄧㄢˋ ㄕㄤˇ)
to examine and appreciate: 她具有鑑賞音樂的能力。She has the ability to appreciate music.
鑑賞家(ㄐㄧㄢˋ ㄕㄤˇ ㄐㄧㄚ)
a connoisseur
鑑往知來(ㄐㄧㄢˋ ㄨㄤˇ ㄓ ㄌㄞˊ)
to foresee the future by reviewing the past

【鑒】 6513 (鑑) ㄐㄧㄢˋ jiann jiàn
to examine, etc.
鑒諒(ㄐㄧㄢˋ ㄌㄧㄤˋ)
to study and forgive (my fault, etc.)
鑒核(ㄐㄧㄢˋ ㄏㄜˊ)
to examine (a case, etc.) and make a decision: 請鑒核。Please examine.
鑒察(ㄐㄧㄢˋ ㄔㄚˊ)
to examine and study

十五畫

【鑠】 6514 ㄕㄨㄛˋ shuoh shuò
1. to melt metals with fire or heat; to smelt
2. to wear off
3. shining; lustrous
4. powerful
鑠石流金(ㄕㄨㄛˋ ㄕˊ ㄌㄧㄡˊ ㄐㄧㄣ)
(literally) to melt stone and turn metal into fluid —extreme heat
鑠鑠(ㄕㄨㄛˋ ㄕㄨㄛˋ)
brilliant; lustrous

【鑕】 6515 ㄓˋ jyh zhì
an ancient Chinese version of a guillotine

【鑛】 6516 (礦) ㄎㄨㄤˋ kuanq kuàng
a mine or mineral
鑛山(ㄎㄨㄤˋ ㄕㄢ)
a mine

【鑞】 6517 ㄌㄚˋ lah là
an alloy of tin and lead for welding

【鑣】 6518 ㄅㄧㄠ biau biāo
1. a bit for a horse
2. said of a horse
3. a dart-like projectile thrown by hand as a weapon 亦作「鏢」

十六畫

【鑪】 6519 ㄌㄨˊ lu lú
1. a stove, an oven, a furnace, etc. 亦作「爐」
2. (chemistry) rutherfordium

【鑫】 6520 ㄒㄧㄣ shin xīn
a word of no definite meaning, used only in names, with a connotation of prosperity or good profit

十七畫

【鑰】 6521 ㄧㄠˋ yaw yào (讀音 ㄩㄝˋ yueh yuè)
1. a key
2. a lock
鑰匙(ㄧㄠˋ ·ㄕ)
a key: 他轉動鑰匙。He turned the key in the lock.
鑰匙圈(ㄧㄠˋ ·ㄕ ㄑㄩㄢ)
a key ring
鑰匙兒(ㄧㄠˋ ·ㄕㄦ)
a latchkey child

【鑲】 6522 ㄒㄧㄤ shiang xiāng
1. to fill in (a tooth, etc.); to mount; to inlay; to set (jewels, etc.)
2. to edge; to border; to hem; bordered
3. name of an ancient weapon
鑲邊(ㄒㄧㄤ ㄅㄧㄢ)
to edge or hem (handkerchief, dress, etc.)
鑲嵌(ㄒㄧㄤ ㄑㄧㄢ)
to inlay; to set (jewels, etc.)
鑲住了(ㄒㄧㄤ ·ㄓㄨ ·ㄌㄜ)
to be constrained by common practice, courtesy, etc. so that one can not do anything otherwise
鑲牙(ㄒㄧㄤ ㄧㄚˊ)
to fill in an artificial tooth; to crown a tooth

十八畫

【鑷】 6523 ㄋㄧㄝˋ nieh niè
1. tweezers; pincers; forceps
2. to pull out; to nip
鑷子(ㄋㄧㄝˋ ·ㄗ)

a pair of tweezers

十九畫

【鑼】 6524 ㄌㄨㄛˊ luo luó

a gong: 他正在那兒敲鑼。He is striking a gong there.

鑼鼓(ㄌㄨㄛˊ ㄍㄨˇ)
①gongs and drums ②traditional percussion instruments ③ensemble of such instruments with gongs and drums playing the main part

鑼鼓喧天(ㄌㄨㄛˊ ㄍㄨˇ ㄒㄩㄢ ㄊㄧㄢ)
(literally) the sound of gongs and drums shakes the sky—noisy celebration of a festival or carnival

【鑽】 6525 1. ㄗㄨㄢ tzuan zuān

1. to pierce; to drill; to bore; to dig through; to penetrate: 這木頭不容易鑽。The wood bores hard.
2. to go through; to make one's way into
3. to gain (profit, a position, etc.) through special favor, contact, relations, etc.
4. to study intensively; to dig into; to bury oneself in

鑽門子(ㄗㄨㄢ ㄇㄣˊ ·ㄗ)
to try to gain profit, a position, etc. by exploiting personal connections in a devious way

鑽頭覓縫兒(ㄗㄨㄢ ㄊㄡˊ ㄇㄧˋ ㄈㄥˋㄦ) or 鑽天入地(ㄗㄨㄢ ㄊㄧㄢ ㄖㄨˋ ㄉㄧˋ)
to look for profit, a position by hook or by crook

鑽探(ㄗㄨㄢ ㄊㄢˋ)
to prospect; to investigate; to explore; (exploration) drilling

鑽牛犄角(ㄗㄨㄢ ㄋㄧㄡˊ ㄐㄧ ·ㄐㄧㄠ) or 鑽牛角尖(ㄗㄨㄢ ㄋㄧㄡˊ ㄐㄧㄠˇ ㄐㄧㄢ)
(literally) to worm oneself into the horn's point—to get oneself into a dead-end alley through sheer stubbornness

鑽狗洞(ㄗㄨㄢ ㄍㄡˇ ㄉㄨㄥˋ)
to do evil

鑽故紙(ㄗㄨㄢ ㄍㄨˋ ㄓˇ)
to be wrapped up in the study of ancient books, like a pedant

鑽過去(ㄗㄨㄢ ·ㄍㄨㄛ ·ㄑㄩ)
①to bore through ②to squeeze through: 他從人羣中鑽過去。He squeezed through the crowd.

鑽研(ㄗㄨㄢ ㄧㄢˊ)
to study or scrutinize thoroughly; to dig into

鑽營(ㄗㄨㄢ ㄧㄥˊ)
①to seek advantage for oneself by all means ②to study and scrutinize thoroughly

【鑽】 6525 2. ㄗㄨㄢˇ tzoan zuǎn (又讀ㄗㄨㄢ tzuan zuān)

to bore or pierce a hole

鑽木取火(ㄗㄨㄢˇ ㄇㄨˋ ㄑㄩˇ ㄏㄨㄛˇ)
to bore wood and get fire by friction

鑽孔(ㄗㄨㄢˇ ㄎㄨㄥˇ)
to make a hole; to perforate

鑽孔機(ㄗㄨㄢˇ ㄎㄨㄥˇ ㄐㄧ)
a drilling machine 亦作「鑽探機」

鑽井(ㄗㄨㄢˇ ㄐㄧㄥˇ)
①to drill a well ②well drilling

鑽牀(ㄗㄨㄢˇ ㄔㄨㄤˊ)
a drill; a drilling machine

【鑽】 6525 3. ㄗㄨㄢˋ tzuann zuàn

1. a gimlet; an awl or auger; a borer; a drill
2. a diamond; a jewel

鑽頭(ㄗㄨㄢˋ ·ㄊㄡ)
(geophysical exploration) the point of an awl; a bit of a drill

鑽戒(ㄗㄨㄢˋ ㄐㄧㄝˋ)
a diamond ring: 她戴着一顆鑽戒。She wears a diamond ring.

鑽石(ㄗㄨㄢˋ ㄕˊ)
a diamond: 她有一顆10克拉的鑽石。She has a diamond of 10 carats.

鑽石婚(ㄗㄨㄢˋ ㄕˊ ㄏㄨㄣ)
diamond wedding

鑽子(ㄗㄨㄢˋ ·ㄗ)
an awl; a drill, etc.

【鑾】 6526 ㄌㄨㄢˊ luan luán

1. bells around the neck of a horse; bells hung on the imperial chariot
2. the imperial carriage

鑾鈴(ㄌㄨㄢˊ ㄌㄧㄥˊ)
bells hung on the imperial chariot or carriage

鑾駕(ㄌㄨㄢˊ ㄐㄧㄚˋ)
①carriages or chariots used by the emperor ②the emperor

鑾輿(ㄌㄨㄢˊ ㄩˊ)
①the imperial carriage ②the emperor

二十畫

【鑿】 6527 1. ㄗㄨㄛˋ tzuoh zuò

1. an instrument for boring wood
2. to bore or pierce through; to chisel
3. real; true; actual; indisputable; authentic; conclusive
4. to polish rice
5. to make a forced interpretation of text

鑿壁偷光(ㄗㄨㄛˋ ㄅㄧˋ ㄊㄡ ㄍㄨㄤ)
(literally) to bore a hole on the wall in order to get some light from the neighbor's house—very studious

鑿枘(ㄗㄨㄛˋ ㄖㄨㄟˋ)
(literally) a square peg for a round hole—not at all fit or suitable

鑿鑿(ㄗㄨㄛˋ ㄗㄨㄛˋ)
①real; indisputable ②with certainty

鑿鑿可據(ㄗㄨㄛˋ ㄗㄨㄛˋ ㄎㄜˇ ㄐㄩˋ)
certain and reliable

【鑿】 6527 2. ㄗㄠˊ tzaur záo

1. to chisel or dig; to bore or pierce through
2. to scuttle
3. a chisel

鑿洞(ㄗㄠˊ ㄉㄨㄥˋ)
to bore or drill a hole

鑿開(ㄗㄠˊ ㄎㄞ)
to bore through; to cut open

鑿井(ㄗㄠˊ ㄐㄧㄥˇ)
①to dig or drill a well ②(mining) shaft sinking; pit sinking

鑿子(ㄗㄠˊ ·ㄗ)
a chisel

長部
ㄔㄤˊ charng cháng

【長】 6528
1. ㄔㄤˊ charng cháng

1. long; length: 她有一頭長髮。She has long hair.
2. a forte; strong points: 舞蹈是她的特長。Dancing is her forte.
3. to be good at; to excel: 他長於數字計算。He is good at figures.
4. a Chinese family name

長波(ㄔㄤˊ ㄅㄛ)
long wave

長白山(ㄔㄤˊ ㄅㄞˊ ㄕㄢ)
Chang Pai Shan, a mountain range in Manchuria

長鼻類(ㄔㄤˊ ㄅㄧˊ ㄌㄟˋ)
(zoology) proboscidian

長臂猿(ㄔㄤˊ ㄅㄧˋ ㄩㄢˊ)
the gibbon: 動物園裡有兩隻長臂猿。There are two gibbons in the zoo.

長編(ㄔㄤˊ ㄅㄧㄢ)
(said of a history, biography, etc.) the collection of data, materials arranged in chronological order

長袍(ㄔㄤˊ ㄆㄠˊ)
a long gown; a robe

長袍兒短褂兒(ㄔㄤˊ ㄆㄠˊㄦ ㄉㄨㄢˇ ㄍㄨㄚˋㄦ)
long gown and short jacket, the ceremonial dress of a Chinese gentleman

長跑(ㄔㄤˊ ㄆㄠˇ)
a long-distance foot race

長篇(ㄔㄤˊ ㄆㄧㄢ)
a long (literary) piece

長篇大論(ㄔㄤˊ ㄆㄧㄢ ㄉㄚˋ ㄌㄨㄣˋ)
a harangue or tirade; a lengthy comment; a ponderous talk; a long speech

長篇小說(ㄔㄤˊ ㄆㄧㄢ ㄒㄧㄠˇ ㄕㄨㄛ)
a novel: 這部長篇小說充滿了冒險的故事。This novel is full of adventures.

長矛(ㄔㄤˊ ㄇㄠˊ)
a long spear

長毛(ㄔㄤˊ ㄇㄠˊ)
the Taiping rebel troops in the mid-19th century

長眠不醒(ㄔㄤˊ ㄇㄧㄢˊ ㄅㄨˋ ㄒㄧㄥˇ)
to die

長明燈(ㄔㄤˊ ㄇㄧㄥˊ ㄉㄥ)
an oil lamp lit day and night before a Buddha statue

長命(ㄔㄤˊ ㄇㄧㄥˋ)
a long life; longevity: 長命者少知交。To live long is to outlive many.

長命百歲(ㄔㄤˊ ㄇㄧㄥˋ ㄅㄞˇ ㄙㄨㄟˋ)
May you live a hundred years! (an expression of congratulations for a month-old baby)

長命富貴(ㄔㄤˊ ㄇㄧㄥˋ ㄈㄨˋ ㄍㄨㄟˋ)
May you live long and be successful! (a congratulatory expression in celebrating a baby's first month)

長方體(ㄔㄤˊ ㄈㄤ ㄊㄧˇ)
a cuboid; a rectangular parallelepiped

長方形(ㄔㄤˊ ㄈㄤ ㄒㄧㄥˊ)
a rectangle; an oblong

長島(ㄔㄤˊ ㄉㄠˇ)
the Long Island, an island in SE New York

長等短等(ㄔㄤˊ ㄉㄥˇ ㄉㄨㄢˇ ㄉㄥˇ)
to wait for a long time

長櫈(ㄔㄤˊ ㄉㄥˋ)
a bench

長笛(ㄔㄤˊ ㄉㄧˊ)
a flute: 他吹長笛。He plays (on) the flute.

長調(ㄔㄤˊ ㄉㄧㄠˋ)
① a Chinese poem of irregular lines, which exceeds 91 characters in length ② (music) major

長度(ㄔㄤˊ ㄉㄨˋ)
length: 他們在量田的長度。They were measuring the length of a field.

長短(ㄔㄤˊ ㄉㄨㄢˇ)
① long or short ② length ③ mishaps or accidents which may endanger one's life ④ good or bad; malicious criticism

長短不齊(ㄔㄤˊ ㄉㄨㄢˇ ㄅㄨˋ ㄑㄧˊ)
not uniform in length

長短句(ㄔㄤˊ ㄉㄨㄢˇ ㄐㄩˋ)
another name of *tsu* (詞)

長談(ㄔㄤˊ ㄊㄢˊ)
a long talk or chat; a long conversation or discussion

長歎(ㄔㄤˊ ㄊㄢˋ)
to sigh deeply

長堤(ㄔㄤˊ ㄊㄧˊ)
① a long dike ② Long Beach, U.S.A.

長堤選美(ㄔㄤˊ ㄊㄧˊ ㄒㄩㄢˇ ㄇㄟˇ)
Miss International Contest at Long Beach

長條兒(ㄔㄤˊ ㄊㄧㄠˊㄦ)
a long and narrow strip

長亭(ㄔㄤˊ ㄊㄧㄥˊ)
a small pavilion to rest a traveler's weary feet (in ancient China, one was built every 10 *li*)

長途(ㄔㄤˊ ㄊㄨˊ)
a long distance; a long journey

長途跋涉(ㄔㄤˊ ㄊㄨˊ ㄅㄚˊ ㄕㄜˋ)
to travel a long distance; to make a long, arduous journey

長途飛行(ㄔㄤˊ ㄊㄨˊ ㄈㄟ ㄒㄧㄥˊ)
a long-distance flight

長途電話(ㄔㄤˊ ㄊㄨˊ ㄉㄧㄢˋ ㄏㄨㄚˋ)
a long-distance (telephone) call

長途旅行(ㄔㄤˊ ㄊㄨˊ ㄌㄩˇ ㄒㄧㄥˊ)
a long journey; a long-distance travel: 他們上個月作了一次長途旅行。They made a long journey last month.

長途汽車(ㄔㄤˊ ㄊㄨˊ ㄑㄧˋ ㄔㄜ)
a long-distance bus; a coach

長途運輸(ㄔㄤˊ ㄊㄨˊ ㄩㄣˋ ㄕㄨ)
long-distance transport

長統靴(ㄔㄤˊ ㄊㄨㄥˇ ㄒㄩㄝ)
jackboots

長統襪(ㄔㄤˊ ㄊㄨㄥˇ ㄨㄚˋ)
stockings

長年(ㄔㄤˊ ㄋㄧㄢˊ)
yearlong; all the year round

長年累月(ㄔㄤˊ ㄋㄧㄢˊ ㄌㄟˇ ㄩㄝˋ)
year in, year out; over the years

長樂未央(ㄔㄤˊ ㄌㄜˋ ㄨㄟˋ ㄧㄤ)
endless joy; to be happy to no end

長廊(ㄔㄤˊ ㄌㄤˊ)
① a roofed corridor or passage; a gallery ② the Long Corridor (of the Summer Palace in Peking)

長林豐草(ㄔㄤˊ ㄌㄧㄣˊ ㄈㄥ ㄘㄠˇ)
a field with luxuriant vege-

tation—a seclusion for a hermit to live in

長龍(ㄔㄤˊ ㄌㄨㄥˊ)
a long line; a long queue

長庚(ㄔㄤˊ ㄍㄥ)or 長庚星(ㄔㄤˊ ㄍㄥ ㄒㄧㄥ)
(astronomy) Hesperus; an ancient Chinese name for Venus

長跪(ㄔㄤˊ ㄍㄨㄟˋ)
to kneel upright

長工(ㄔㄤˊ ㄍㄨㄥ)
a regular laborer on a farm; a farm hand; a long-term hired hand

長褲(ㄔㄤˊ ㄎㄨˋ)
a pair of trousers (as distinct from panties or shorts)

長號
①(ㄔㄤˊ ㄏㄠˊ) to cry aloud
②(ㄔㄤˊ ㄏㄠˋ) (music) a trombone

長恨歌(ㄔㄤˊ ㄏㄣˋ ㄍㄜ)
the "Song of Eternal Sorrow," by the poet Pai Chü-i (白居易), a long poem describing the rise and downfall of the famed beauty Yang Kuei-fei(楊貴妃)

長話短說(ㄔㄤˊ ㄏㄨㄚˋ ㄉㄨㄢˇ ㄕㄨㄛ)
to make a long story short

長假(ㄔㄤˊ ㄐㄧㄚˋ)
① to retire or resign from office ② a long leave of absence

長久(ㄔㄤˊ ㄐㄧㄡˇ)
permanent; a very long time: 這不是個長久之計。This is not a permanent solution.

長江(ㄔㄤˊ ㄐㄧㄤ)
the Yangtze River

長江天塹(ㄔㄤˊ ㄐㄧㄤ ㄊㄧㄢ ㄑㄧㄢˋ)
The Yangtze River is a natural barrier (to invaders).

長頸鹿(ㄔㄤˊ ㄐㄧㄥˇ ㄌㄨˋ)
a giraffe

長頸烏喙(ㄔㄤˊ ㄐㄧㄥˇ ㄨ ㄏㄨㄟˋ)
the look of a mean fellow

長徑(ㄔㄤˊ ㄐㄧㄥˋ)
(mathematics) major axis

長局(ㄔㄤˊ ㄐㄩˊ)
a permanent or long-term arrangement

長崎(ㄔㄤˊ ㄑㄧˊ)
Nagasaki, Japan

長期(ㄔㄤˊ ㄑㄧˊ)
① a long time ② long-term; long-range; long-standing: 他們作了長期打算。They made long-term plans.

長期目標(ㄔㄤˊ ㄑㄧˊ ㄇㄨˋ ㄅㄧㄠ)
long-term objectives

長期貸款(ㄔㄤˊ ㄑㄧˊ ㄉㄞˋ ㄎㄨㄢˇ)
long-term loans

長期抗戰(ㄔㄤˊ ㄑㄧˊ ㄎㄤˋ ㄓㄢˋ)
a long-term war of resistance, as the Sino-Japanese War of 1937-1945

長期合同(ㄔㄤˊ ㄑㄧˊ ㄏㄜˊ ㄊㄨㄥˊ)
a long-term contract

長期計劃(ㄔㄤˊ ㄑㄧˊ ㄐㄧˋ ㄏㄨㄚˋ)
a long-term plan

長期證券(ㄔㄤˊ ㄑㄧˊ ㄓㄥˋ ㄑㄩㄢˋ)
long-term securities

長期資本(ㄔㄤˊ ㄑㄧˊ ㄗ ㄅㄣˇ)
(accounting) a long-term capital

長期租賃(ㄔㄤˊ ㄑㄧˊ ㄗㄨ ㄌㄧㄣˋ)
a long-term lease

長槍(ㄔㄤˊ ㄑㄧㄤ)
①a spear ②a long-barreled gun

長驅直入(ㄔㄤˊ ㄑㄩ ㄓˊ ㄖㄨˋ)
(said of an advancing army) to march in without opposition

長嘯(ㄔㄤˊ ㄒㄧㄠˋ)
to cry or yell loud and long; a long and loud cry

長袖善舞(ㄔㄤˊ ㄒㄧㄡˋ ㄕㄢˋ ㄨˇ)
①(literally) One who has long sleeves dances best. —One will succeed much easier if he has something to rely upon. ② to be resourceful, especially in a dishonest way

長相廝守(ㄔㄤˊ ㄒㄧㄤ ㄙ ㄕㄡˇ)
to stay married forever; to keep each other company for life

長吁(ㄔㄤˊ ㄒㄩ)
to heave a deep sigh

長吁短歎(ㄔㄤˊ ㄒㄩ ㄉㄨㄢˇ ㄊㄢˋ)
to sigh incessantly; to sigh and groan

長支(ㄔㄤˊ ㄓ)
to overdraw; to spend more than the budgeted fund

長治久安(ㄔㄤˊ ㄓˋ ㄐㄧㄡˇ ㄢ)
a lengthy peaceful reign

長齋(ㄔㄤˊ ㄓㄞ)
(said of a Buddhist in secular life) to be a vegetarian throughout the year

長針(ㄔㄤˊ ㄓㄣ)
the minute hand; the long hand

長枕大被(ㄔㄤˊ ㄓㄣˇ ㄉㄚˋ ㄅㄟˋ)
(literally) to share a long pillow and a large bed cover —brotherly love or fraternity

長征(ㄔㄤˊ ㄓㄥ)
an expedition (usually military); to take a long journey to a distant place

長住(ㄔㄤˊ ㄓㄨˋ)
to stay long; to live at a place for a long time

長長短短(ㄔㄤˊ ㄔㄤˊ ㄉㄨㄢˇ ㄉㄨㄢˇ)
not uniform in length

長城(ㄔㄤˊ ㄔㄥˊ)
① the Great Wall ② someone who can be trusted

長程(ㄔㄤˊ ㄔㄥˊ)
long-range; long-distance

長處(ㄔㄤˊ ㄔㄨˋ)
merits; good points; advantages: 她有許多長處。She has many merits.

長川(ㄔㄤˊ ㄔㄨㄢ)
① continuous or incessant ② a long river

長春(ㄔㄤˊ ㄔㄨㄣ)
① Changchun, a city in Kirin Province ② ilex ③ the monthly rose

長蟲(ㄔㄤˊ ㄔㄨㄥˊ)
the long worm—the snake

長石(ㄔㄤˊ ㄕˊ)
feldspar

長時間(ㄔㄤˊ ㄕˊ ㄐㄧㄢ)
a long time

長逝(ㄔㄤˊ ㄕˋ)
to die

長沙(ㄔㄤˊ ㄕㄚ)
Changsha, capital city of Hunan Province

長舌(ㄔㄤˊ ㄕㄜˊ)
to be fond of gossip; long-tongued

長舌婦(ㄔㄤˊ ㄕㄜˊ ㄈㄨˋ)
a loquacious woman of the vicious type

長蛇陣(ㄔㄤˊ ㄕㄜˊ ㄓㄣˋ)
military formations in a row like a long snake

長射程(ㄔㄤˊ ㄕㄜˋ ㄔㄥˊ)
(said of artillery pieces)

〔長部〕

long-range
長壽(ㄔㄤˊ ㄕㄡˋ)
longevity; a long life
長壽麵(ㄔㄤˊ ㄕㄡˋ ㄇㄧㄢˋ)
noodles eaten on one's birthday
長衫(ㄔㄤˊ ㄕㄢ)
a Chinese long gown for man
長生(ㄔㄤˊ ㄕㄥ)
to live long; a long life; longevity
長生不老(ㄔㄤˊ ㄕㄥ ㄅㄨˋ ㄌㄠˇ)
(especially in Taoism) immortality
長生不老藥(ㄔㄤˊ ㄕㄥ ㄅㄨˋ ㄌㄠˇ ㄧㄠˋ)
an elixir to prolong life indefinitely; the elixir of life
長生殿(ㄔㄤˊ ㄕㄥ ㄉㄧㄢˋ)
name of a palace in the Tang Dynasty, which was made the subject of a drama about Emperor Hsüan Tsung (唐玄宗) and his favorite concubine Lady Yang (楊貴妃)
長生果(ㄔㄤˊ ㄕㄥ ㄍㄨㄛˇ)
a groundnut, or a peanut
長人(ㄔㄤˊ ㄖㄣˊ)
an extremely tall man
長足進步(ㄔㄤˊ ㄗㄨˊ ㄐㄧㄣˋ ㄅㄨˋ)
marked progress; to come a long way
長此以往(ㄔㄤˊ ㄘˇ ㄧˇ ㄨㄤˇ)
continuously for a long time hence
長策(ㄔㄤˊ ㄘㄜˋ)
a sound plan; a good scheme
長存(ㄔㄤˊ ㄘㄨㄣˊ)
to exist forever; to last forever
長安(ㄔㄤˊ ㄢ)
Changan, an ancient name of Sian (西安), capital of the Chinese empire during several dynasties
長安道上(ㄔㄤˊ ㄢ ㄉㄠˋ ㄕㄤˋ)
(literally) the road to Changan—an arena where people struggle for fame or wealth
長揖(ㄔㄤˊ ㄧ)
to fold one's hands and make a deep bow
長揖不拜(ㄔㄤˊ ㄧ ㄅㄨˋ ㄅㄞˋ)
to make a deep bow but refuse to kneel down
長夜(ㄔㄤˊ ㄧㄝˋ)
① the long night ② the grave
長夜漫漫(ㄔㄤˊ ㄧㄝˋ ㄇㄢˋ ㄇㄢˋ)
the long, long night
長音(ㄔㄤˊ ㄧㄣ)
a prolonged sound; a long vowel
長音階(ㄔㄤˊ ㄧㄣ ㄐㄧㄝ)
(music) a major scale
長音程(ㄔㄤˊ ㄧㄣ ㄔㄥˊ)
(music) a major interval
長襪(ㄔㄤˊ ㄨㄚˋ)
stockings
長尾鷄(ㄔㄤˊ ㄨㄟˇ ㄐㄧ)
a phoenix cock; a paradise flycatcher
長尾猴(ㄔㄤˊ ㄨㄟˇ ㄏㄡˊ)or 長尾猿(ㄔㄤˊ ㄨㄟˇ ㄩㄢˊ)
a kind of long-tailed monkey in Africa (*Cercopithecus aethiops*)
長圓(ㄔㄤˊ ㄩㄢˊ)
an ellipse; a regular oval
長遠(ㄔㄤˊ ㄩㄢˇ)
for a long time; long-range; long-term
長遠之計(ㄔㄤˊ ㄩㄢˇ ㄓ ㄐㄧˋ)
a long-range plan (for the future)

【長】 6528
2. ㄓㄤˇ jaang zhǎng
1. senior; old: 她比我年長。She is older than I.
2. the eldest: 他是張先生的長子。He is Mr. Chang's eldest son.
3. a head; a chief; a leader; a commander; a chairman: 他是警察局長。He is the chief of a police station.
4. to grow: 這城市快速成長。The city is growing rapidly.
5. to increase; to advance: 旅行增長了他的知識。Traveling increases his knowledge.
6. to look; to appear; to become
長輩(ㄓㄤˇ ㄅㄟˋ)
the senior generation; the older member of a family; an elder
長胖(ㄓㄤˇ ㄆㄤˋ)
to become fat; to gain weight
長黴(ㄓㄤˇ ㄇㄟˊ)
to mildew; to become mildewy
長毛(ㄓㄤˇ ㄇㄠˊ)
to grow hair; to get hairy; to grow feather
長房(ㄓㄤˇ ㄈㄤˊ)
the branch of the family tree from the first-born male
長大(ㄓㄤˇ ㄉㄚˋ)
to grow up; to attain manhood; to mature
長得(ㄓㄤˇ ˙ㄉㄜ)
to look (beautiful, handsome, etc.): 她長得眞漂亮。She looks very pretty.
長男(ㄓㄤˇ ㄋㄢˊ)
the eldest son
長女(ㄓㄤˇ ㄋㄩˇ)
the eldest daughter
長老(ㄓㄤˇ ㄌㄠˇ)
① seniors or oldsters ② a presbyter ③reverent address for a monk
長老會(ㄓㄤˇ ㄌㄠˇ ㄏㄨㄟˋ)
the Presbyterian Church
長吏(ㄓㄤˇ ㄌㄧˋ)
① officials of higher seniority ② superiors
長瘤(ㄓㄤˇ ㄌㄧㄡˊ)
to have a tumor
長官(ㄓㄤˇ ㄍㄨㄢ)
one's superior in office, etc.; (a polite expression) officers or officials; a commanding officer
長公主(ㄓㄤˇ ㄍㄨㄥ ㄓㄨˇ)
sisters of the emperor
長行市(ㄓㄤˇ ㄏㄤˊ ˙ㄕ)
to hike prices
長機(ㄓㄤˇ ㄐㄧ)
the command plane; the plane piloted by the commanding officer in a group of attacking aircraft; the leading aircraft
長見識(ㄓㄤˇ ㄐㄧㄢˋ ˙ㄕ)
to increase one's knowledge or to gain experience
長進(ㄓㄤˇ ㄐㄧㄣˋ)
to make progress (especially in scholastic pursuit, etc.)
長媳(ㄓㄤˇ ㄒㄧˊ)
the wife of one's eldest son
長相兒(ㄓㄤˇ ㄒㄧㄤˋㄦ)
one's looks or appearances: 她長相兒好。She is good-looking.
長兄(ㄓㄤˇ ㄒㄩㄥ)

one's eldest brother

長者(ㄓㄤˇ ㄓㄜˇ)
a senior; an elder; a person of virtue

長成(ㄓㄤˇ ㄔㄥˊ)
① to grow to manhood ② to grow into: 她已長成漂亮的女孩。She has grown into a pretty girl.

長瘡(ㄓㄤˇ ㄔㄨㄤ)
to be affected by scabies; to ulcerate

長上(ㄓㄤˇ ㄕㄤˋ)
elders and superiors

長子(ㄓㄤˇ ㄗˇ)
the eldest son: 他是林先生的長子。He is Mr. Lin's eldest son.

長子繼承權(ㄓㄤˇ ㄗˇ ㄐㄧˋ ㄔㄥˊ ㄑㄩㄢˊ)
the right of primogeniture

長子繼承制(ㄓㄤˇ ㄗˇ ㄐㄧˋ ㄔㄥˊ ㄓˋ)
primogeniture

長嫂比母(ㄓㄤˇ ㄙㄠˇ ㄅㄧˇ ㄇㄨˇ)
One should treat his eldest brother's wife with the same respect as that accorded to his mother.

長孫(ㄓㄤˇ ㄙㄨㄣ)
① the eldest of one's grandsons ② a Chinese double-name

長牙(ㄓㄤˇ ㄧㄚˊ)
(said of babies or young animals) to grow teeth

長幼(ㄓㄤˇ ㄧㄡˋ)
young and old; seniority among family members

長幼有序(ㄓㄤˇ ㄧㄡˋ ㄧㄡˇ ㄒㄩˋ)
respect for seniority; an order, system, institution, etc. arranged according to seniority in age or generation; precedence maintained between seniors and juniors

【長】 6528
3. ㄓㄤˋ janq zhàng
a surplus; a remainder

長物(ㄓㄤˋ ㄨˋ)
property; belongings

門 部
ㄇㄣˊ men mén

【門】 6529
ㄇㄣˊ men mén
1. a door; a gateway; an opening: 門口有人。There is someone at the door.
2. a family; a clan
3. a sect; a school; a gang
4. a class; a category
5. the key; the turning point
6. a piece of (artillery); a (cannon)
7. gate-keeping
8. a Chinese family name

門兒(ㄇㄜˊㄦ)
① the door ② the family ③ a branch of study: 你專攻那一門兒? What branch of study do you major in?

門把(ㄇㄣˊ ㄅㄚˇ)
a doorknob; a door handle

門板(ㄇㄣˊ ㄅㄢˇ)
the plank(s) of a door

門牓 or 門榜(ㄇㄣˊ ㄅㄤˇ)
a notice hung at the gateway

門牌(ㄇㄣˊ ㄆㄞˊ)
a doorplate, indicating the exact address of a residence

門派(ㄇㄣˊ ㄆㄞˋ)
a sect

門票(ㄇㄣˊ ㄆㄧㄠˋ)
an admission ticket; an entrance ticket

門脈(ㄇㄣˊ ㄇㄞˋ)
① the portal system; the portal vein 亦作「門靜脈」② outpatient service

門楣(ㄇㄣˊ ㄇㄟˊ)
① a beam over a doorway
② family standing

門面(ㄇㄣˊ ㄇㄧㄢˋ)
①the front of a store ②the outward appearance; a facade

門面話(ㄇㄣˊ ·ㄇㄧㄢ ㄏㄨㄚˋ)
insincere talk; lip service; formal and insincere remarks

門閥(ㄇㄣˊ ㄈㄚˊ)
high family standing

門法(ㄇㄣˊ ㄈㄚˇ)
a family code of conduct

門房(ㄇㄣˊ ㄈㄤˊ)
① a gatekeeper; a janitor; a doorman ② a room for a janitor or doorman; a gatehouse ③ distant relatives of the same clan

門風(ㄇㄣˊ ㄈㄥ)
moral standing of a family; family reputation

門縫(ㄇㄣˊ ㄈㄥˋ)
crevices or cracks in the door

門道
①(ㄇㄣˊ ·ㄉㄠ) means of approach, influence or contacts; intellectual resources 亦作「門路」
②(ㄇㄣˊ ㄉㄠˋ) a doorway; a gateway 亦作「門洞兒」

門當戶對(ㄇㄣˊ ㄉㄤ ㄏㄨˋ ㄉㄨㄟˋ)
families of equal standing (usually referring to those of a married couple); well matched

門第(ㄇㄣˊ ㄉㄧˋ)
family standing or reputation; family status: 這兩家門第相稱。The two families are equal in social status.

門丁(ㄇㄣˊ ㄉㄧㄥ)
a doorkeeper; a janitor

門庭若市(ㄇㄣˊ ㄊㄧㄥˊ ㄖㄨㄛˋ ㄕˋ)
①(said of a store, etc.) doing booming business ② (said of a household) swarmed with visitors; much visited

門徒(ㄇㄣˊ ㄊㄨˊ)
one's students, pupils, followers, or disciples

門類(ㄇㄣˊ ㄌㄟˋ)
a category, division, or classification

門樓(ㄇㄣˊ ㄌㄡˊ)
① the tower above a gate (usually a city gate) ② an arch over a gateway

門吏(ㄇㄣˊ ㄌㄧˋ)
① a gatekeeper ② a person working for a large family, as a secretary, etc.

門聯(ㄇㄣˊ ㄌㄧㄢˊ) or 門對(ㄇㄣˊ ㄉㄨㄟˋ)
couplets pasted on doors or doorposts (usually at the lunar new year)

門簾 or 門帘(ㄇㄣˊ ㄌㄧㄢˊ)
a door curtain or screen

門鈴(ㄇㄣˊ ㄌㄧㄥˊ)
the doorbell: 請按門鈴。Ring the doorbell, please.

門路(ㄇㄣˊ ㄌㄨˋ)
① one's means of approach, contacts, connections, etc. ② a key or tip to a beginner in

the pursuit of a certain skill; a knack

門羅主義(ㄇㄣˊ ㄌㄨㄛˊ ㄓㄨˇ ㄧˋ)
the Monroe Doctrine

門崗(ㄇㄣˊ ㄍㄤˇ)
guards posted at the door or gateway

門可羅雀(ㄇㄣˊ ㄎㄜˇ ㄌㄨㄛˊ ㄑㄩㄝˋ)
You can catch sparrows on the doorstep.—(said of a store, fallen family, etc.) where visitors are few and far between; deserted

門客(ㄇㄣˊ ㄎㄜˋ)
①(in ancient China) mentor-advisors fed by an influential person at his residence ②(Sung Dynasty) a family tutor

門口(ㄇㄣˊ ㄎㄡˇ)
a gate; a doorway; an entrance

門檻(ㄇㄣˊ ㄎㄢˇ)or 門限(ㄇㄣˊ ㄒㄧㄢˋ)
a threshold; a doorsill

門框(ㄇㄣˊ ㄎㄨㄤˋ)
a doorframe; a doorcase

門戶(ㄇㄣˊ ㄏㄨˋ)
①a family ②a strategic position ③a sect; a bloc; a gang ④a door

門戶開放(ㄇㄣˊ ㄏㄨˋ ㄎㄞ ㄈㄤˋ)
an open-door policy

門戶之見(ㄇㄣˊ ㄏㄨˋ ㄓ ㄐㄧㄢˋ)
prejudiced or biased views of a particular sect, bloc, gang, etc.; factional views; sectarianism

門環(ㄇㄣˊ ㄏㄨㄢˊ)
rings on the doors used as knockers

門戟(ㄇㄣˊ ㄐㄧˇ)
spears displayed at the door of a powerful family in ancient China

門階(ㄇㄣˊ ㄐㄧㄝ)
a doorstep

門臼(ㄇㄣˊ ㄐㄧㄡˋ)
a door socket

門禁(ㄇㄣˊ ㄐㄧㄣˋ)
a checkpoint at the gate

門禁森嚴(ㄇㄣˊ ㄐㄧㄣˋ ㄙㄣ ㄧㄢˊ)
The gate is strictly guarded.

門警(ㄇㄣˊ ㄐㄧㄥˇ)
a police guard at an entrance

門牆(ㄇㄣˊ ㄑㄧㄤˊ)
the invisible boundaries of a school or sect founded by the master

門下(ㄇㄣˊ ㄒㄧㄚˋ)
pupils or disciples

門診(ㄇㄣˊ ㄓㄣˇ)
to treat patients at the OPD; the outpatient service

門診部(ㄇㄣˊ ㄓㄣˇ ㄅㄨˋ)
the outpatient department (OPD)

門齒(ㄇㄣˊ ㄔˇ)or 門牙(ㄇㄣˊ ㄧㄚˊ)
front teeth; incisors

門窗(ㄇㄣˊ ㄔㄨㄤ)
doors and windows: 將門窗閂上。Latch the doors and windows.

門市(ㄇㄣˊ ㄕˋ)
to sell by retail; to sell over the counter

門市部(ㄇㄣˊ ㄕˋ ㄅㄨˋ)
a retail department; a sales department

門首(ㄇㄣˊ ㄕㄡˇ)
in front of the door

門扇(ㄇㄣˊ ㄕㄢˋ)
the wing of a door; a door leaf

門神(ㄇㄣˊ ㄕㄣˊ)
the door-god—said to guard the household against evil spirits

門生(ㄇㄣˊ ㄕㄥ)
pupils or disciples

門生故吏(ㄇㄣˊ ㄕㄥ ㄍㄨˋ ㄌㄧˋ)
pupils and former subordinates

門塾(ㄇㄣˊ ㄕㄨˊ)
a family school

門閂 or 門栓(ㄇㄣˊ ㄕㄨㄢ)or 門插管兒(ㄇㄣˊ ㄔㄚ ㄍㄨㄢˇㄦ)
a latch; a door bolt

門人(ㄇㄣˊ ㄖㄣˊ)
①pupils or disciples ②doorkeepers ③advisors and protégés of a family

門司(ㄇㄣˊ ㄙ)
Moji, a port city in Japan

門鎖(ㄇㄣˊ ㄙㄨㄛˇ)
a door catch; a door lock; a door latch

門外(ㄇㄣˊ ㄨㄞˋ)
outside the door: 他正站在門外。He was standing just outside the door.

門外漢(ㄇㄣˊ ㄨㄞˋ ㄏㄢˋ)
an outsider; the laity; a layman

門衛(ㄇㄣˊ ㄨㄟˋ)
guards posted at the door or gateway

門望(ㄇㄣˊ ㄨㄤˋ)
family reputation or prestige

一畫

【閂】 6530 ㄕㄨㄢ shuan shuān

1. to fasten with a bolt or latch: 請把門閂好。Please bolt the door.
2. the latch of a door: 此門已上了門閂。The door is on the latch.

二畫

【閃】 6531 ㄕㄢˇ shaan shǎn

1. to flash; a flash, as of lightning; a very brief glimpse: 閃電閃過天空。The lightning flashed across the sky.
2. to dodge; to evade; to avoid
3. to twist, strain or sprain (one's back, etc.): 他閃了腰。He sprained his back.
4. to cast away; to leave behind

閃避(ㄕㄢˇ ㄅㄧˋ)
to dodge quickly: 他很靈巧地閃避車子。He dodged the car cleverly.

閃電(ㄕㄢˇ ㄉㄧㄢˋ)
①to lighten: 遠方閃電又打雷。It thundered and lightened in the distance. ②lightning: 閃電之後常有打雷聲。Lightning is usually followed by thunder. ③with lightning speed

閃電攻擊(ㄕㄢˇ ㄉㄧㄢˋ ㄍㄨㄥ ㄐㄧˊ)
a lightning attack

閃電戰(ㄕㄢˇ ㄉㄧㄢˋ ㄓㄢˋ)
a blitzkrieg; a blitz; a lightning war

閃躲(ㄕㄢˇ ㄉㄨㄛˇ)
to dodge; to evade

閃動(ㄕㄢˇ ㄉㄨㄥˋ)
to move fast; to shine off and on; to scintillate; to flash; to twinkle; to glisten: 他們的眼裏閃動着興奮的光芒。Their eyes glistened with

excitement.

閃亮兒(ㄕㄢˇ ㄌㄧㄤˋㄦ)
(dialect) dawn

閃光(ㄕㄢˇ ㄍㄨㄤ)
① sparks; a flash ② to flash; to sparkle

閃光燈(ㄕㄢˇ ㄍㄨㄤ ㄉㄥ)
a flashlight; a blinker

閃開(ㄕㄢˇ ㄎㄞ)
to dodge quickly; to avoid (a hit, collision, etc.)

閃景(ㄕㄢˇ ㄐㄧㄥˇ)
(movie) a flash

閃現(ㄕㄢˇ ㄒㄧㄢˋ)
a flicker; a flash; to flash before one: 我突然間靈感閃現。Suddenly I felt a flash of inspiration.

閃失(ㄕㄢˇ ㄕ)
① errors or mistakes ② an accident

閃閃(ㄕㄢˇ ㄕㄢˇ)
flickering; scintillating; to glint; to flash: 天空中電光閃閃。Lightning flashed in the sky.

閃閃發光(ㄕㄢˇ ㄕㄢˇ ㄈㄚ ㄍㄨㄤ)
sparkling; twinkling; scintillating

閃身(ㄕㄢˇ ㄕㄣ)
① to dodge ② sideways: 他閃身進門。He walked sideways through the door.

閃爍(ㄕㄢˇ ㄕㄨㄛˋ)
① to twinkle; twinkling; to scintillate: 燦爛的星斗在天空中閃爍。Brilliant stars glitter the sky. ② vague; evasive

閃爍其詞(ㄕㄢˇ ㄕㄨㄛˋ ㄑㄧˊ ㄘˊ)
to speak evasively; to use many evasions in one's speech; to make an ambiguous speech

閃族(ㄕㄢˇ ㄗㄨˊ)
the Semites, any of a group of peoples of southern Asia chiefly represented now by the Jews and the Arabs

閃腰(ㄕㄢˇ ㄧㄠ)
to strain a muscle on the waist

閃耀(ㄕㄢˇ ㄧㄠˋ)
to glint; to twinkle; to sparkle: 他的眼睛閃耀著光采。His eyes twinkled.

三畫

【閉】 6532 ㄅㄧˋ bih bì

1. to close; to shut: 他閉上眼睛。He closed his eyes.
2. (said of a conference, etc.) to conclude; to end
3. to block up; to stop; to obstruct: 他突然閉住氣。He suddenly stopped his breath.
4. to restrain

閉門不納(ㄅㄧˋ ㄇㄣˊ ㄅㄨˋ ㄋㄚˋ)
to refuse to admit a caller

閉門天子(ㄅㄧˋ ㄇㄣˊ ㄊㄧㄢ ㄗˇ)
(literally) a monarch behind closed doors—authority narrowly confined

閉門羹(ㄅㄧˋ ㄇㄣˊ ㄍㄥ)
to treat someone to a closed door; to close the door on; to turn a cold shoulder on; to refuse to see (a visitor): 她當面使他吃閉門羹。She shut the door in his face.

閉門却掃(ㄅㄧˋ ㄇㄣˊ ㄑㄩㄝˋ ㄙㄠˇ)
to cut off communication with the outside world

閉門謝客(ㄅㄧˋ ㄇㄣˊ ㄒㄧㄝˋ ㄎㄜˋ)
to refuse visitors; to lead a retiring life

閉門造車(ㄅㄧˋ ㄇㄣˊ ㄗㄠˋ ㄐㄩ)
(literally) to make a cart in one's room (that won't go on the road)—to do something impractical, useless, or out of one's pure imagination

閉門思過(ㄅㄧˋ ㄇㄣˊ ㄙ ㄍㄨㄛˋ)
to reflect on one's faults or misdeeds in private

閉門塞竇(ㄅㄧˋ ㄇㄣˊ ㄙㄜˋ ㄉㄡˋ)
strongly guarded

閉幕(ㄅㄧˋ ㄇㄨˋ)
(said of shows, meetings, etc.) to close or conclude: 大會已順利閉幕。The conference has closed successfully.

閉目養神(ㄅㄧˋ ㄇㄨˋ ㄧㄤˇ ㄕㄣˊ)
to close the eyes and give the mind a brief rest

閉路電視(ㄅㄧˋ ㄌㄨˋ ㄉㄧㄢˋ ㄕˋ)
closed-circuit television

閉果(ㄅㄧˋ ㄍㄨㄛˇ)
indehiscent fruit

閉關時代(ㄅㄧˋ ㄍㄨㄢ ㄕˊ ㄉㄞˋ)
the period of isolationism

閉關自守(ㄅㄧˋ ㄍㄨㄢ ㄗˋ ㄕㄡˇ)
to adopt a policy of exclusion or isolation

閉口無言(ㄅㄧˋ ㄎㄡˇ ㄨˊ ㄧㄢˊ)
to remain silent (in the face of overwhelming evidence pointing to one's guilt): 人贓俱獲使他閉口無言。He was caught together with the loot so he remained silent.

閉會(ㄅㄧˋ ㄏㄨㄟˋ)
to close a meeting: 大會將在下月閉會。The conference will be closed next month.

閉結(ㄅㄧˋ ㄐㄧㄝˊ)
constipation 亦作「便秘」: 此類食物會引起閉結。This kind of food is constipating.

閉經(ㄅㄧˋ ㄐㄧㄥ)
an irregular stoppage of menses; amenorrhea

閉氣(ㄅㄧˋ ㄑㄧˋ)
① to feel suffocated; unable to breathe ② to stop breathing—to die

閉歇(ㄅㄧˋ ㄒㄧㄝ)
to close shop

閉蟄(ㄅㄧˋ ㄓˊ)
the hibernation of animals or insects

閉塞(ㄅㄧˋ ㄙㄜˋ)
① to block up; to obstruct ② backward ③ hard to get to; inaccessible: 那個地區交通閉塞。That district was very hard to get to.

閉戹(ㄅㄧˋ ㄜˋ)
in a fix or spot; in a difficult position; in straits

閉月羞花(ㄅㄧˋ ㄩㄝˋ ㄒㄧㄡ ㄏㄨㄚ)
(descriptive of a woman's beauty) that causes the moon to hide and put the blossoms to shame

四畫

【開】 6533 ㄎㄞ kai kāi

1. to open: 門打不開。The door won't open.
2. to drive: 他在學開車。He is learning to drive.
3. to begin; to start: 火車準時開了。The train started on time.
4. to reveal; to disclose
5. to state; to explain
6. to found; to expand

門部

7. to eliminate
8. to divide into
9. to write down; to list
10. to undo; to unfold; to wind off: 張開你的雙臂。Unfold your arms.
11. a carat: 二十四開金 24-carat gold
12. to run (a shop or business)

開拔(ㄎㄞ ㄅㄚˊ)
(troops) to move; to set out

開包 or 開苞(ㄎㄞ ㄅㄠ)
(slang) to have sexual intercourse with a virgin

開辦(ㄎㄞ ㄅㄢˋ)
to start or open (a shop, school, business, etc.)

開辦費(ㄎㄞ ㄅㄢˋ ㄈㄟˋ)
funds needed for starting a school, new organization, etc.; organization cost

開本(ㄎㄞ ㄅㄣˇ)
a format; a book size: 四開本 a quarto 八開本 an octavo

開筆(ㄎㄞ ㄅㄧˇ)
(said of a learner) to begin to write the first composition, poem, etc.

開標(ㄎㄞ ㄅㄧㄠ)
to announce the result of bidding in an open tender; to open sealed tenders

開埠(ㄎㄞ ㄅㄨˋ)
to build a city; the founding of a city

開步走(ㄎㄞ ㄅㄨˋ ㄗㄡˇ)
Forward march!

開不動(ㄎㄞ ·ㄅㄨ ㄉㄨㄥˋ)
①(said of a door, lock, etc.) cannot be opened ②(said of a machine, car, etc.) cannot be started

開不開(ㄎㄞ ·ㄅㄨ ㄎㄞ)
①cannot be opened: 我開不開這扇門。I cannot open the door. ② Will you open it or not?

開砲(ㄎㄞ ㄆㄠˋ)
①(said of a fieldpiece, battery, or artillery) to open fire ②to launch a verbal attack

開盤(ㄎㄞ ㄆㄢˊ)
(said of a market) the opening quotation

開闢(ㄎㄞ ㄆㄧˋ)
to open up or develop (a new market, farm plot, etc.); to start: 他們開闢了一條航線。They opened an air route.

開闢市場(ㄎㄞ ㄆㄧˋ ㄕˋ ㄔㄤˇ)
to open up or develop a market

開票(ㄎㄞ ㄆㄧㄠˋ)
① to count ballots or votes ② to make out an invoice

開票所(ㄎㄞ ㄆㄧㄠˋ ㄙㄨㄛˇ)
a place for counting ballots

開瓶(ㄎㄞ ㄆㄧㄥˊ)
to open or uncork a bottle

開平方(ㄎㄞ ㄆㄧㄥˊ ㄈㄤ)
extraction of the square root

開普敦(ㄎㄞ ㄆㄨˇ ㄉㄨㄣ)
Capetown, South Africa

開麥拉(ㄎㄞ ㄇㄞˋ ㄌㄚ)
① a camera ② (a movie director's command) Camera!

開門(ㄎㄞ ㄇㄣˊ)
to open the door

開門見山(ㄎㄞ ㄇㄣˊ ㄐㄧㄢˋ ㄕㄢ)
to talk or write right to the point; to come straight to the point

開門七件事(ㄎㄞ ㄇㄣˊ ㄑㄧ ㄐㄧㄢˋ ㄕˋ)
daily necessities—fuel, rice, oil or fat, salt, sauce, vinegar, and tea

開門揖盜(ㄎㄞ ㄇㄣˊ ㄧ ㄉㄠˋ)
(literally) to open the door to a thief—to befriend a bad fellow and suffer the consequences

開蒙(ㄎㄞ ㄇㄥˊ)
to teach the beginner

開廟(ㄎㄞ ㄇㄧㄠˋ)
the date of a fair held in a Buddhist temple

開明(ㄎㄞ ㄇㄧㄥˊ)
enlightened; enlightenment; open-minded: 他是個思想開明的人。He is an open-minded man.

開幕(ㄎㄞ ㄇㄨˋ)
① to raise the curtain: 這齣戲已經開幕了。The curtain rose on the play. ② to open; to begin a meeting: 展覽會將於星期天開幕。The exhibition will open on Sunday.

開幕典禮(ㄎㄞ ㄇㄨˋ ㄉㄧㄢˇ ㄌㄧˇ)
inauguration; the opening ceremony 亦作「開幕式」

開發(ㄎㄞ ㄈㄚ)
to develop; developed; development (of natural resources, industry, etc.)

開發票(ㄎㄞ ㄈㄚ ㄆㄧㄠˋ)
to write an invoice

開發條(ㄎㄞ ㄈㄚ ㄊㄧㄠˊ)
to wind a spring

開發中國家(ㄎㄞ ㄈㄚ ㄓㄨㄥ ㄍㄨㄛˊ ㄐㄧㄚ)
a developing country

開飛機(ㄎㄞ ㄈㄟ ㄐㄧ)
to pilot a plane

開飯(ㄎㄞ ㄈㄢˋ)
to prepare food for a meal; to serve a meal: 開飯了！The meal's ready!

開方(ㄎㄞ ㄈㄤ)
①(mathematics) evolution ② name of a prince in the Epoch of Spring and Autumn

開方子(ㄎㄞ ㄈㄤ ·ㄗ)
to write a prescription; to prescribe for

開放(ㄎㄞ ㄈㄤˋ)
① to open (to trade, traffic, etc.); to be open ② to liberalize or hand over a government monopoly to private operations ③ to lift a ban ④ to come into bloom: 花都開放了。The flowers were all open.

開封(ㄎㄞ ㄈㄥ)
① Kaifeng, capital city of Honan Province ② to break or open a seal

開赴(ㄎㄞ ㄈㄨˋ)
to march to; to be bound for

開刀(ㄎㄞ ㄉㄠ)
① to operate on (a patient); an operation 亦作「手術」: 醫生爲傷者開刀。The doctor operated on the injured man. ② to punish: 先拿他開刀。He is the first to be punished. ③ to behead

開導(ㄎㄞ ㄉㄠˇ)
to educate and enlighten; to explain and make (someone) understand

開道(ㄎㄞ ㄉㄠˋ)
(in ancient China) to clear the way for an important official

開倒車(ㄎㄞ ㄉㄠˋ ㄔㄜ)
① to back a car, train, etc.

②to be old-fashioned or anachronistic; to turn back the clock; to retrograde

開單子(ㄎㄞ ㄉㄢ ·ㄗ)
①to write a bill, etc. ②to list expenditures or items needed

開襠褲(ㄎㄞ ㄉㄤ ㄎㄨˋ)
a pair of bottomless trousers for babies; a pair of open-bottomed pants for children

開燈(ㄎㄞ ㄉㄥ)
to turn on the light

開弔(ㄎㄞ ㄉㄧㄠˋ)
to hold a memorial service or funeral rites

開店(ㄎㄞ ㄉㄧㄢˋ)
to open a shop; to run a store

開端(ㄎㄞ ㄉㄨㄢ)
the beginning or start: 萬物皆有開端。Everything has a beginning.

開冬(ㄎㄞ ㄉㄨㄥ)
early winter

開動(ㄎㄞ ㄉㄨㄥˋ)
①to start; to set in motion: 他開動引擎。He started the engine. ②to be on the move

開頭(ㄎㄞ ㄊㄡˊ)
in the beginning; from the start

開談判(ㄎㄞ ㄊㄢˊ ㄆㄢˋ)
to negotiate; to start negotiations

開天闢地(ㄎㄞ ㄊㄧㄢ ㄆㄧˋ ㄉㄧˋ)
①creation of the world ②to open or develop

開天窗(ㄎㄞ ㄊㄧㄢ ㄔㄨㄤ)
①to open up a skylight ②open space in a newspaper (as when the original story has been censored by the authorities) ③ (comically) inflammation or erosion of the nosebone due to syphilitic infection

開庭(ㄎㄞ ㄊㄧㄥˊ)
to start a court trial; to hold a court session

開脫(ㄎㄞ ㄊㄨㄛ)
to extricate a person from certain involvements (usually criminal); to vindicate

開拓(ㄎㄞ ㄊㄨㄛˋ)
to open up, enlarge or expand (new frontiers, territory, etc.): 他們爲定居開拓新土地。They opened new land for settlement.

開通(ㄎㄞ ㄊㄨㄥ)
①open-minded; modern-minded; liberal; enlightened; progressive ②to do away with all obstructions; to be opened; to be dredged

開年(ㄎㄞ ㄋㄧㄢˊ)or 開歲(ㄎㄞ ㄙㄨㄟˋ)
at the beginning of a year

開朗(ㄎㄞ ㄌㄤˇ)
①to clear up, as weather ②open and clear ③broad-minded and outspoken: 她的性情開朗。She is of a broad-minded and outspoken disposition.

開例(ㄎㄞ ㄌㄧˋ)
to set a precedent

開立方(ㄎㄞ ㄌㄧˋ ㄈㄤ)
extraction of a cubic root

開列(ㄎㄞ ㄌㄧㄝˋ)
to list; to make a list of

開臉(ㄎㄞ ㄌㄧㄢˇ)
(said of a girl on the eve of marriage) to remove the fine hair on the face and neck

開路(ㄎㄞ ㄌㄨˋ)
to pioneer; to cut the way, as in a jungle

開路先鋒(ㄎㄞ ㄌㄨˋ ㄒㄧㄢ ㄈㄥ)
a pioneer; a trailblazer; to blaze a trail

開鑼(ㄎㄞ ㄌㄨㄛˊ)
(in Chinese opera) to begin a performance

開羅(ㄎㄞ ㄌㄨㄛˊ)
Cairo, capital of Egypt

開羅宣言(ㄎㄞ ㄌㄨㄛˊ ㄒㄩㄢ ㄧㄢˊ)
the Cairo Declaration, signed by China, Great Britain and the United States in 1943

開革(ㄎㄞ ㄍㄜˊ)
to dismiss; to fire; dismissal

開國(ㄎㄞ ㄍㄨㄛˊ)
to found a country or state

開國紀念日(ㄎㄞ ㄍㄨㄛˊ ㄐㄧˋ ㄋㄧㄢˋ ㄖˋ)
the founding anniversary of a nation; the national day

開國元勳(ㄎㄞ ㄍㄨㄛˊ ㄩㄢˊ ㄒㄩㄣ)
elder statesmen or generals who participated in the founding of a new nation or dynasty

開關(ㄎㄞ ㄍㄨㄢ)
①a switch or similar device to put on or shut off an electric current, etc. ②to open the city gate ③to open and close

開棺驗屍(ㄎㄞ ㄍㄨㄢ ㄧㄢˋ ㄕ)
to open the coffin and examine the corpse therein

開館子(ㄎㄞ ㄍㄨㄢˇ ·ㄗ)
to run a restaurant

開罐器(ㄎㄞ ㄍㄨㄢˋ ㄑㄧˋ)
a can opener

開光(ㄎㄞ ㄍㄨㄤ)
to enshrine a Buddha statue

開弓(ㄎㄞ ㄍㄨㄥ)
to pull or draw a bow

開工(ㄎㄞ ㄍㄨㄥ)
to go into operation; to start work; to begin a building project

開科取士(ㄎㄞ ㄎㄜ ㄑㄩˇ ㄕˋ)
to enlist talents through the old civil service examination system

開課(ㄎㄞ ㄎㄜˋ)
①to lecture on a new subject in the curriculum ②to start a class at the beginning of a new semester

開開玩笑(ㄎㄞ ㄎㄞ ㄨㄢˊ ㄒㄧㄠˋ)
to have a little fun at someone; to make fun of

開口(ㄎㄞ ㄎㄡˇ)
①to open one's mouth; to speak: 他覺得此事難以開口。He found it difficult to speak of the matter. ②to laugh ③to sharpen the edge of a new blade—to get it ready for cutting ④to cut an opening

開口閉口(ㄎㄞ ㄎㄡˇ ㄅㄧˋ ㄎㄡˇ)
to say the same thing again and again

開墾(ㄎㄞ ㄎㄣˇ)
to open up wasteland for farming

開闊(ㄎㄞ ㄎㄨㄛˋ)
①spacious; open; wide ②tolerant; broad-minded: 他的心胸開闊。He is broad-minded. ③to widen; to broaden: 旅行開闊了他的眼界。Travel broadened his outlook.

開快車(ㄎㄞ ㄎㄨㄞˋ ㄔㄜ)

〔門部〕

①(said of a car, etc.) to speed; speeding: 他因開快車而被捕。He was arrested for speeding. ②to hasten up with one's work; to catch up with one's working schedule

開礦(ㄎㄞ ㄎㄨㄤˋ)
to mine; to excavate a mine

開航(ㄎㄞ ㄏㄤˊ)
①to open up for navigation: 這條運河已經開航了。The canal is open for navigation. ②to set sail

開戶(ㄎㄞ ㄏㄨˋ)
to open a bank account

開花(ㄎㄞ ㄏㄨㄚ)
①to flower; to blossom: 有些玫瑰早開花。Some roses flower early. ②(said of shells) to burst: 炸彈開花。The bomb burst.

開花彈(ㄎㄞ ㄏㄨㄚ ㄉㄢˋ)
a fragmentation bomb; an artillery shell

開花結果(ㄎㄞ ㄏㄨㄚ ㄐㄧㄝˊ ㄍㄨㄛˇ)
to blossom and bear fruit—to yield positive results

開花賬(ㄎㄞ ㄏㄨㄚ ㄓㄤˋ)
to make a false report on (an) expenditure

開化(ㄎㄞ ㄏㄨㄚˋ)
civilized

開化史(ㄎㄞ ㄏㄨㄚˋ ㄕˇ)
a history recording the development of human civilization in its proper sequence

開話匣子(ㄎㄞ ㄏㄨㄚˋ ㄒㄧㄚˊ ˙ㄗ)
to keep on talking without stop, like starting a talking machine

開火(ㄎㄞ ㄏㄨㄛˇ)
to open fire; to engage in battle

開伙(ㄎㄞ ㄏㄨㄛˇ)
to cook a meal

開豁(ㄎㄞ ㄏㄨㄛˋ)
①carefree; without a worry ②straightforward; frank

開懷(ㄎㄞ ㄏㄨㄞˊ)
joyful; jubilant; happy; to one's heart's content: 他開懷暢飲。He drinks to his heart's content.

開會(ㄎㄞ ㄏㄨㄟˋ)
to hold a meeting; to attend a meeting or conference: 他在開會嗎? Is he at the meeting?

開葷(ㄎㄞ ㄏㄨㄣ)
(said of vegetarians or people fasting) to shift to meat-eating

開荒(ㄎㄞ ㄏㄨㄤ)
to cultivate virgin land

開黃腔(ㄎㄞ ㄏㄨㄤˊ ㄑㄧㄤ)
(informal) to lace one's utterance with reference to sex; to make lewd utterances

開架(ㄎㄞ ㄐㄧㄚˋ)
open-shelf

開價(ㄎㄞ ㄐㄧㄚˋ)
to ask for a price; to quote; the price quoted

開解(ㄎㄞ ㄐㄧㄝˇ)
to advise and persuade; to explain and make (someone) understand

開戒(ㄎㄞ ㄐㄧㄝˋ)
to break one's resolution; to break one's abstinence (from smoking, drinking, etc.)

開交(ㄎㄞ ㄐㄧㄠ)
an end or solution; to settle dispute: 他們鬧得不可開交。They got into a hot dispute.

開禁(ㄎㄞ ㄐㄧㄣˋ)
to rescind a prohibition

開疆(ㄎㄞ ㄐㄧㄤ)
to expand national boundaries

開獎(ㄎㄞ ㄐㄧㄤˇ)
to draw the winning numbers of a lottery

開講(ㄎㄞ ㄐㄧㄤˇ)
to begin a speech or lecture; to begin telling a story

開井(ㄎㄞ ㄐㄧㄥˇ)
to dig or drill a well

開卷有益(ㄎㄞ ㄐㄩㄢˋ ㄧㄡˇ ㄧˋ)
(literally) Whenever you open a book, you'll be benefited.—Reading is always beneficial (or profitable).

開濬(ㄎㄞ ㄐㄩㄣˋ)
to open up, dig or dredge a waterway

開啓(ㄎㄞ ㄑㄧˇ)
to open: 這門可以自動開啓。This door can open automatically.

開竅(ㄎㄞ ㄑㄧㄠˋ)
①to open one's eyes to; to have one's ideas straightened out; to understand ②(said of a girl) to start getting sex-conscious; to reach puberty

開球(ㄎㄞ ㄑㄧㄡˊ)
to kick, throw or toss the ball to start a game

開腔(ㄎㄞ ㄑㄧㄤ)
to talk; to speak out; to open one's mouth

開槍(ㄎㄞ ㄑㄧㄤ)
to shoot; to fire: 他朝著目標開槍射擊。He shot at a target.

開缺(ㄎㄞ ㄑㄩㄝ)
to suspend an official from his post because of his faults or death, etc.

開小差(ㄎㄞ ㄒㄧㄠˇ ㄔㄞ)
to desert one's unit or post; desertion

開銷 or 開消(ㄎㄞ ˙ㄒㄧㄠ)
①expenses; (an) expenditure; an account of expenses: 你必須節省開銷。You must cut down your expenses. ②to pay expenses

開心(ㄎㄞ ㄒㄧㄣ)
①happy; to have a grand time ②to play a joke on; to amuse oneself at somebody's expense; to make fun of someone: 別尋他開心了。Do not amuse yourself at his expense. ③to be sincere to others ④to enlighten

開心果(ㄎㄞ ㄒㄧㄣ ㄍㄨㄛˇ)
a pistachio

開釁(ㄎㄞ ㄒㄧㄣˋ)
to start a trouble; to provoke

開學(ㄎㄞ ㄒㄩㄝˊ)
The school starts. 學校甚麼時候開學? When does the school start?

開學典禮(ㄎㄞ ㄒㄩㄝˊ ㄉㄧㄢˇ ㄌㄧˇ)
a ceremony held to signal the beginning of a school semester

開支(ㄎㄞ ㄓ)
expenses; (an) expenditure: 他們節省開支。They retrench their expenses.

開支票(ㄎㄞ ㄓ ㄆㄧㄠˋ)
to write a check

開齋(ㄎㄞ ㄓㄞ)
(said of a Buddhist follower) to discontinue a vegetarian diet; to break the fast
開展(ㄎㄞ ㄓㄢˇ)
to expand; to spread out; to develop: 他正努力開展業務。He is trying to expand his business.
開戰(ㄎㄞ ㄓㄢˋ)
to declare war; to do battle
開張(ㄎㄞ ㄓㄤ)
①(said of a store) to open a shop; to start doing a business ② to expand, spread out or develop
開張大吉(ㄎㄞ ㄓㄤ ㄉㄚˋ ㄐㄧˊ)
the auspicious beginning of a new enterprise (an expression used when one opens a new shop or factory)
開賬(ㄎㄞ ㄓㄤˋ)
to bill (one) for things purchased, etc.
開徵 or 開征(ㄎㄞ ㄓㄥ)
to start collecting taxes
開茶館(ㄎㄞ ㄔㄚˊ ㄍㄨㄢˇ)
to run a tea shop
開衩(ㄎㄞ ㄔㄚˋ)
to open a slit in a dress
開車(ㄎㄞ ㄔㄜ)
to drive a car, or start a train: 我開車送你去車站。I drive you to the station.
開場(ㄎㄞ ㄔㄤˇ)
the beginning of a show or anything
開場白(ㄎㄞ ㄔㄤˇ ㄅㄞˊ)
a prologue; a speech that opens a show or a meeting; the opening words; a preface, foreword, preamble in the first issue of a magazine, paper, report, etc.
開城(ㄎㄞ ㄔㄥˊ)
to open the city gates
開誠布公(ㄎㄞ ㄔㄥˊ ㄅㄨˋ ㄍㄨㄥ)
to wear one's heart on one's sleeve; to be honest, frank, sincere and just; to speak frankly and sincerely
開除(ㄎㄞ ㄔㄨˊ)
to dismiss; to fire; to expel; dishonorable discharge: 他被學校開除了。He was expelled from school.
開船(ㄎㄞ ㄔㄨㄢˊ)
to set sail; to weigh anchor
開春(ㄎㄞ ㄔㄨㄣ)
in early spring
開創(ㄎㄞ ㄔㄨㄤˋ)
to found (a nation, big business, etc.); to start; to initiate: 他們開創一項新事業。They founded a new business.
開始(ㄎㄞ ㄕˇ)
to begin; to commence; to start; the beginning; the outset; the start: 學校九點開始上課。School begins (or starts) at nine.
開市(ㄎㄞ ㄕˋ)
to start trading; to open the market
開釋(ㄎㄞ ㄕˋ)
to release (a prisoner, etc.); to set free
開設(ㄎㄞ ㄕㄜˋ)
to establish; to set up: 他最近開設了一家新店舖。He has set up a new store recently.
開山祖師(ㄎㄞ ㄕㄢ ㄗㄨˇ ㄕ)
the founder of a religion or a sect of religion (now used figuratively in most cases)
開曙(ㄎㄞ ㄕㄨˇ)
to dawn; the beginning of a new day
開水(ㄎㄞ ㄕㄨㄟˇ)
boiled water
開鑿(ㄎㄞ ㄗㄠˊ)
to dig (a well, canal, etc.); to drill
開足馬力(ㄎㄞ ㄗㄨˊ ㄇㄚˇ ㄌㄧˋ)
to put into high gear; to go full steam ahead; to go forward at full speed; to open the throttle
開罪(ㄎㄞ ㄗㄨㄟˋ)
to offend another with what one says, writes or does: 我又怎麼開罪人了? In what way have I offended?
開宗明義(ㄎㄞ ㄗㄨㄥ ㄇㄧㄥˊ ㄧˋ)
an outline delineating the purpose, objectives, means of achievement, etc. of an undertaking or an endeavor (originally, the title of the first chapter of the *Canon of Filial Piety* 孝經)
開採(ㄎㄞ ㄘㄞˇ)
to excavate; to mine
開鎖(ㄎㄞ ㄙㄨㄛˇ)
to pick a lock; to unlock
開恩(ㄎㄞ ㄣ)
to have mercy on; to grant special favor to
開業(ㄎㄞ ㄧㄝˋ)
to start doing business; to start practicing (law, medicine, etc.): 他已經開業行醫了。He has practiced medicine.
開夜車(ㄎㄞ ㄧㄝˋ ㄔㄜ)
to burn the midnight oil; to work late into the night; to sit up late at night
開誘(ㄎㄞ ㄧㄡˋ)
to teach step by step; to teach by stimulating the learner's interest in the subject taught
開言(ㄎㄞ ㄧㄢˊ)
to speak; to talk
開筵(ㄎㄞ ㄧㄢˊ)
to give a feast; to throw a banquet
開顏(ㄎㄞ ㄧㄢˊ)
to smile; to laugh; to beam
開演(ㄎㄞ ㄧㄢˇ)
to start showing (a picture, etc.); (said of a play, movie, etc.) to begin; to start performing
開眼(ㄎㄞ ㄧㄢˇ)
to add to one's experience; to see new things; to extend the mental horizon
開眼界(ㄎㄞ ㄧㄢˇ ㄐㄧㄝˋ)
to expand one's experience and horizon
開印(ㄎㄞ ㄧㄣˋ)
(Ching Dynasty) to resume using the official seal after the New Year holidays (around the 15th of the first month)
開陽(ㄎㄞ ㄧㄤˊ)
① dried shrimp meat ② (astronomy) Mizar
開洋葷(ㄎㄞ ㄧㄤˊ ㄏㄨㄣ)
(informal) to have a delightful new experience; to see, eat or do something delightful for the first time
開映(ㄎㄞ ㄧㄥˋ)
to show motion pictures
開挖(ㄎㄞ ㄨㄚ)
to excavate
開外(ㄎㄞ ㄨㄞˋ)

〔門部〕

upwards of; over or more than: 她看起來四十開外。She looks over forty.

開胃(ㄎㄞ ㄨㄟˋ)
①appetizing; to whet or stimulate one's appetite ②to make fun of; to tease: 別拿他開胃。Do not make fun of him.

開玩笑(ㄎㄞ ㄨㄢˊ ㄒㄧㄠˋ)
to play a joke; to joke: 你一定是開玩笑的。You must be joking (or kidding).

開往(ㄎㄞ ㄨㄤˇ)
①(said of a train, ship, etc.) to leave for; to be bound for ②(said of troops, etc.) to move; to set out

開源節流(ㄎㄞ ㄩㄢˊ ㄐㄧㄝˊ ㄌㄧㄡˊ)
to open more sources of income and cut down expenses

開雲見日(ㄎㄞ ㄩㄣˊ ㄐㄧㄢˋ ㄖˋ)
from dark to light; from obscurity to clarity

【間】 6534
1. ㄐㄧㄢ jian jiān

1. between two things; the space between; among
2. a numerical adjunct for rooms
3. within a definite time or space

間關(ㄐㄧㄢ ㄍㄨㄢ)
①the sound of rolling carts ②the sound of birds chirping ③(said of roads or writings) full of twists and turns

間架(ㄐㄧㄢ ㄐㄧㄚˋ)
the framework of a house

【間】 6534
2.(閒) ㄐㄧㄢˋ jiann jiàn

1. a crevice; a leak; space in between
2. to divide; a division of a house; to separate
3. to put a space between; to drive a wedge between; to part friends
4. to change; to substitute
5. to block up
6. (said of illness) to get a little better
7. occasionally

間壁(ㄐㄧㄢˋ ㄅㄧˋ)
on the other side of the wall; next door; the neighbor

間不容髮(ㄐㄧㄢˋ ·ㄅㄨ ㄖㄨㄥˊ ㄈㄚˇ)
①very close; imminent ②precarious; by a hair's breadth; not a hair's breadth in between—The situation is extremely critical.

間不容息(ㄐㄧㄢˋ ·ㄅㄨ ㄖㄨㄥˊ ㄒㄧˊ)
a very short while; imminent

間道(ㄐㄧㄢˋ ㄉㄠˋ)
a trail; an out-of-the-way path; a short cut

間諜(ㄐㄧㄢˋ ㄉㄧㄝˊ)
a spy; a secret agent

間斷(ㄐㄧㄢˋ ㄉㄨㄢˋ)
suspended; interrupted

間隔(ㄐㄧㄢˋ ㄍㄜˊ)
①separated; spaced at intervals ②distance; intervals; space in between: 這一行字間隔勻整。The words on this line are evenly spaced.

間闊(ㄐㄧㄢˋ ㄎㄨㄛˋ)
to have been separated for a long time

間或(ㄐㄧㄢˋ ㄏㄨㄛˋ)
occasional(ly): 他間或寫寫信。He writes occasionally.

間接(ㄐㄧㄢˋ ㄐㄧㄝ)
indirect; indirectly; vicariously: 那是間接答覆。It's an indirect answer.

間接貿易(ㄐㄧㄢˋ ㄐㄧㄝ ㄇㄠˋ ㄧˋ)
indirect trade

間接民權(ㄐㄧㄢˋ ㄐㄧㄝ ㄇㄧㄣˊ ㄑㄩㄢˊ)
civil rights that are exercised through representatives

間接滙兌(ㄐㄧㄢˋ ㄐㄧㄝ ㄏㄨㄟˋ ㄉㄨㄟˋ)
(accounting) indirect exchange

間接侵略(ㄐㄧㄢˋ ㄐㄧㄝ ㄑㄧㄣ ㄌㄩㄝˋ)
indirect aggression

間接行動(ㄐㄧㄢˋ ㄐㄧㄝ ㄒㄧㄥˊ ㄉㄨㄥˋ)
indirect action

間接選舉(ㄐㄧㄢˋ ㄐㄧㄝ ㄒㄩㄢˇ ㄐㄩˇ)
indirect election; election by delegates

間接證據(ㄐㄧㄢˋ ㄐㄧㄝ ㄓㄥˋ ㄐㄩˋ)
indirect evidence

間接稅(ㄐㄧㄢˋ ㄐㄧㄝ ㄕㄨㄟˋ)
indirect tax or taxation (as commodity tax)

間隙(ㄐㄧㄢˋ ㄒㄧˋ)
①a crevice; a space between; an interval ②animosity; a grudge; discord ③(machinery) clearance

間歇(ㄐㄧㄢˋ ㄒㄧㄝ)
①intermittent; sporadic; intermittently; sporadically: 熱病間歇地發生。The fever intermits. ②short intervals or stops; a pause

間歇泉(ㄐㄧㄢˋ ㄒㄧㄝ ㄑㄩㄢˊ)
an intermittent spring; a geyser

間歇熱(ㄐㄧㄢˋ ㄒㄧㄝ ㄖㄜˋ)
intermittent fever, as in the case of malaria

間歇遺傳(ㄐㄧㄢˋ ㄒㄧㄝ ㄧˊ ㄔㄨㄢˊ)
heredity occurring in every other generation; atavism

間出(ㄐㄧㄢˋ ㄔㄨ)
to find time for a private visit; to take a personal tour

間日(ㄐㄧㄢˋ ㄖˋ)
every other day

間雜(ㄐㄧㄢˋ ㄗㄚˊ)
to mix; not continuous

間奏曲(ㄐㄧㄢˋ ㄗㄡˋ ㄑㄩˇ)
(music) an intermezzo

間作(ㄐㄧㄢˋ ㄗㄨㄛˋ)
intercropping

間色(ㄐㄧㄢˋ ㄙㄜˋ)
assorted colors; multicolored

【閎】 6535
ㄏㄨㄥˊ horng hóng

1. a gate or barrier across a lane
2. big; large
3. spacious inside
4. a Chinese family name

閎達 or 宏達(ㄏㄨㄥˊ ㄉㄚˊ)
intelligent and broad-minded

閎中肆外(ㄏㄨㄥˊ ㄓㄨㄥ ㄙˋ ㄨㄞˋ)
(said of a piece of writing) rich in substance and graceful in style

閎澤(ㄏㄨㄥˊ ㄗㄜˊ)
a big lake

閎衍(ㄏㄨㄥˊ ㄧㄢˇ)
a beautiful writing style

【閏】 6536
ㄖㄨㄣˋ ruenn rùn

1. with surplus or leftover
2. usurped; deputy or substitute
3. extra, inserted between others, as a day, or a month; to intercalate

閏年(ㄖㄨㄣˋ ㄋㄧㄢˊ)
a leap year; an intercalary year: 一九八四年是個閏年。

1984 was a leap year.

閏日(ㄖㄨㄣˋ ㄖˋ)
February 29, the intercalary day; the leap day

閏音(ㄖㄨㄣˋ ㄧㄣ)
sounds in local dialects not found in the Mandarin pronunciation

閏音字母(ㄖㄨㄣˋ ㄧㄣ ㄗˋ ㄇㄨˇ)
a vowel used in pronouncing certain words peculiar to a local dialect

閏位(ㄖㄨㄣˋ ㄨㄟˋ)
an imperial reign not in the direct or conventional line of succession, as in the case of usurpation

閏月(ㄖㄨㄣˋ ㄩㄝˋ)
an intercalary moon or month—an extra month inserted seven times in 19 years to make for the difference between the solar and the lunar years

【閑】 6537 ㄒㄧㄢˊ shyan xián

1. a fence; a bar; a barrier
2. to defend
3. big
4. familiar with; accustomed to; well-versed in
5. same as 閒—leisure
6. laws or regulations
7. a stable

閑媚(ㄒㄧㄢˊ ㄇㄟˋ)
(said of a woman) quiet and charming

閑磕牙(ㄒㄧㄢˊ ㄎㄜ ㄧㄚˊ)
leisure talks or conversation about nothing in particular

閑漢 or 閒漢(ㄒㄧㄢˊ ㄏㄢˋ)
a bum; a vagrant; an idler

閑花野草(ㄒㄧㄢˊ ㄏㄨㄚ ㄧㄝˇ ㄘㄠˇ)
disreputable women; promiscuous women

閑靜(ㄒㄧㄢˊ ㄐㄧㄥˋ)
peaceful and calm in mind—without desires

閑居(ㄒㄧㄢˊ ㄐㄩ)
to lead a quiet life; to lead a retired life

閑習(ㄒㄧㄢˊ ㄒㄧˊ)
to be well versed in or familiar with

閑暇 or 閒暇(ㄒㄧㄢˊ ㄒㄧㄚˊ)
leisure; spare time

閑常(ㄒㄧㄢˊ ㄔㄤˊ)
ordinary; usually

閑書 or 閒書(ㄒㄧㄢˊ ㄕㄨ)
books for killing time, as novels, etc.

閑耍(ㄒㄧㄢˊ ㄕㄨㄚˇ) or 閑玩(ㄒㄧㄢˊ ㄨㄢˊ)
to kill time; to amuse oneself

【閒】 6538 1. ㄒㄧㄢˊ shyan xián

1. quiet; tranquil; calm; placid
2. leisure; spare time

閒步(ㄒㄧㄢˊ ㄅㄨˋ)
to stroll without a destination; to roam at leisure: 他在街上閒步。He was roaming about the streets.

閒不住(ㄒㄧㄢˊ ˙ㄅㄨ ㄓㄨˋ)
① to have to keep oneself busy; unable to remain idle: 我閒不住。I always kept myself busy. ② to have no worry about unemployment

閒篇兒(ㄒㄧㄢˊ ㄆㄧㄚㄦ)
random talk or conversation; idle talk

閒民(ㄒㄧㄢˊ ㄇㄧㄣˊ)
the unemployed

閒房(ㄒㄧㄢˊ ㄈㄤˊ)
a vacant house or room

閒蕩(ㄒㄧㄢˊ ㄉㄤˋ)
to saunter; to stroll; to loaf

閒地(ㄒㄧㄢˊ ㄉㄧˋ)
① retirement; a position without responsibility; a sinecure ② vacant land; idle land

閒談(ㄒㄧㄢˊ ㄊㄢˊ)
idle talk; to chat: 他與父親閒談。He chatted with his father.

閒聊(ㄒㄧㄢˊ ㄌㄧㄠˊ)
① to chat; to gossip ② a gossip; a chat

閒官(ㄒㄧㄢˊ ㄍㄨㄢ)
an official with very light duties; one who holds a sinecure position

閒逛(ㄒㄧㄢˊ ㄍㄨㄤˋ)
to saunter; to stroll: 他在市街上閒逛。He strolled about the streets.

閒工夫(ㄒㄧㄢˊ ㄍㄨㄥ ˙ㄈㄨ)
leisure; spare time

閒磕打牙(ㄒㄧㄢˊ ㄎㄜ ㄉㄚˇ ㄧㄚˊ) or 閒磕牙(ㄒㄧㄢˊ ㄎㄜ ㄧㄚˊ)
to chat without a purpose

閒空兒(ㄒㄧㄢˊ ㄎㄨㄥˋㄦ)
spare time; leisure: 我閒空兒時作畫。I paint at my leisure.

閒漢(ㄒㄧㄢˊ ㄏㄢˋ)
a bum; a vagrant; a jobless person

閒話(ㄒㄧㄢˊ ㄏㄨㄚˋ)
① random or idle talk; gossip:他愛說人閒話。He's fond of gossip. ② complaint ③ to talk casually about; to chat about

閒居(ㄒㄧㄢˊ ㄐㄩ)
to lead an idle, leisure, quiet or placid life: 她喜歡閒居獨處。She enjoys living idly and alone.

閒氣(ㄒㄧㄢˊ ㄑㄧˋ)
anger caused by something insignificant; needless anger

閒錢(ㄒㄧㄢˊ ㄑㄧㄢˊ)
spare money; idle money

閒情逸致(ㄒㄧㄢˊ ㄑㄧㄥˊ ㄧˋ ㄓˋ)
a peaceful and comfortable mood

閒暇(ㄒㄧㄢˊ ㄒㄧㄚˊ)
unoccupied; leisure

閒心(ㄒㄧㄢˊ ㄒㄧㄣ)
a peaceful or easy mood

閒置(ㄒㄧㄢˊ ㄓˋ)
to leave unused; to let something lie idle; to set aside

閒扯(ㄒㄧㄢˊ ㄔㄜˇ)
to chat; to engage in chitchat

閒時(ㄒㄧㄢˊ ㄕˊ)
spare time; leisure

閒事(ㄒㄧㄢˊ ㄕˋ)
matters not of one's concern; others' business; matters one has nothing to do with: 別管閒事! Mind your own business.

閒適(ㄒㄧㄢˊ ㄕˋ)
quiet and comfortable

閒書(ㄒㄧㄢˊ ㄕㄨ)
books for killing time, as novels

閒人(ㄒㄧㄢˊ ㄖㄣˊ)
① idlers; persons with nothing to do ② persons not concerned

閒人免進(ㄒㄧㄢˊ ㄖㄣˊ ㄇㄧㄢˇ ㄐㄧㄣˋ)
Out of bounds to non-authorized personnel! 或 No admittance! 或 Admittance

門部

〔門部〕

to staff only.
閒宂(ㄒㄧㄢ ㄖㄨㄥˇ)
officials with light duties; supernumeraries
閒雜(ㄒㄧㄢ ㄗㄚˊ)
without fixed duties
閒雜人等(ㄒㄧㄢ ㄗㄚˊ ㄖㄣˊ ㄉㄥˇ)
① loafers; idlers ② unconcerned persons
閒在(ㄒㄧㄢ ·ㄗㄞ)
quiet and comfortable; idle
閒坐(ㄒㄧㄢ ㄗㄨㄛˋ)
to sit idle: 他閒坐在椅子上。He sat idle on a chair.
閒散(ㄒㄧㄢ ㄙㄢˋ)
with no important tasks or duties at hand; with nothing to do; unoccupied
閒言(ㄒㄧㄢ ㄧㄢˊ)
① gossip; idle talk ② balderdash
閒言閒語(ㄒㄧㄢ ㄧㄢˊ ㄒㄧㄢ ㄧㄢˊ ㄒㄧㄢ ㄩˇ)
sarcastic remarks or complaints; gossips
閒言少敍(ㄒㄧㄢ ㄧㄢˊ ㄕㄠˇ ㄒㄩˋ)
to leave out the nonessentials in narration; to make a long story short
閒宴 or 閒燕(ㄒㄧㄢ ㄧㄢˋ)
peace and quiet
閒屋子(ㄒㄧㄢ ㄨ ·ㄗ)
an unoccupied house
閒語(ㄒㄧㄢ ㄩˇ)
① a personal or confidential talk ② sarcastic remarks or complaints; gossips
閒月(ㄒㄧㄢ ㄩㄝˋ)
(in a rural community) the leisure months; the time when farmers have little to do; the period between harvest and sowing
閒雲野鶴(ㄒㄧㄢ ㄩㄣˊ ㄧㄝˇ ㄏㄜˋ)
① as free as a bird; carefree ② the quietness and comfortableness of a secluded life

【閒】 6538
2. ㄐㄧㄢ jian jiān

same as 間(ㄐㄧㄢ)

【閒】 6538
3. ㄐㄧㄢˋ jiann jiàn

same as 間 (ㄐㄧㄢˋ)—to separate
閒隔(ㄐㄧㄢˋ ㄍㄜˊ)
to be separated in time and space

【閔】 6539
ㄇㄧㄣˇ miin mǐn

1. to mourn; to pity; to commiserate or be sympathetic with; to condole
2. to urge; to encourage
3. trouble; distress
4. to be grieved
5. a Chinese family name

閔閔(ㄇㄧㄣˇ ㄇㄧㄣˇ)
① worried and scared ② grieved; sad
閔凶(ㄇㄧㄣˇ ㄒㄩㄥ)
① sorrow; affliction ② the death of one's parents

五畫

【閘】 6540
ㄓㄚˊ jar zhá

1. a floodgate; a lock; a sluice
2. a brake; a device on a vehicle for halting its motion
3. a switch or similar devices

閘北(ㄓㄚˊ ㄅㄟˇ)
the northwest portion of Shanghai, bordering on the former international settlement
閘板(ㄓㄚˊ ㄅㄢˇ)
a sluice
閘門(ㄓㄚˊ ㄇㄣˊ)
a floodgate
閘口(ㄓㄚˊ ㄎㄡˇ)
a floodgate; a sluice

【閟】 6541
ㄅㄧˋ bih bì

1. to close the door
2. to shut; to repress
3. deep; obscure; solemn

六畫

【閣】 6542
ㄍㄜˊ ger gé

1. a room; a chamber; a pavilion
2. an attic; a place for storing something not frequently in use
3. a cabinet: 他們正在組閣當中。They're forming a cabinet.
4. a boudoir
5. a Chinese family name

閣道(ㄍㄜˊ ㄉㄠˋ)
① a path paved with timber or planks on which vehicles can move smoothly ② name of a constellation
閣老(ㄍㄜˊ ㄌㄠˇ)
elder officials of different ranks in various dynasties
閣樓(ㄍㄜˊ ㄌㄡˊ)
an attic; a garret
閣閣(ㄍㄜˊ ㄍㄜˊ)
neat and properly placed
閣揆(ㄍㄜˊ ㄎㄨㄟˊ)
the premier; the prime minister
閣下(ㄍㄜˊ ㄒㄧㄚˋ)
Your Excellency; you (a polite expression)
閣臣(ㄍㄜˊ ㄔㄣˊ)
a deputy premier in the Ming and Ching dynasties
閣子(ㄍㄜˊ ·ㄗ)or 閣兒(ㄍㄜˊㄦ)
a cabin; a small room
閣議(ㄍㄜˊ ㄧˋ)
a cabinet meeting or conference
閣員(ㄍㄜˊ ㄩㄢˊ)
cabinet ministers; members of the cabinet

【閡】 6543
ㄏㄜˊ her hé

1. to block or separate; to obstruct
2. to prevent; to shut out

【閤】 6544
1. ㄍㄜˊ ger gé

1. a small side door
2. same as 閣—a chamber, pavilion, etc.

閤中(ㄍㄜˊ ㄓㄨㄥ)
your wife (a polite expression)

【閤】 6544
2. (闔) ㄏㄜˊ her hé

1. to close (doors)
2. whole; all

閤第(ㄏㄜˊ ㄉㄧˋ)or 閤府(ㄏㄜˊ ㄈㄨˇ)
your whole family

【閥】 6545
ㄈㄚˊ far fá

1. a threshold; a doorsill
2. an influential person, family, or clique; a bloc: 門閥 a powerful family
3. a valve: 安全閥 a safety valve

閥閱之家(ㄈㄚˊ ㄩㄝˋ ㄓ ㄐㄧㄚ)
an influential or powerful family

【閨】 6546
ㄍㄨㄟ guei guī

1. a small door
2. the women's apartment

3. feminine
閨門(ㄍㄨㄟ ㄇㄣˊ)
①the door of an inner chamber ②a small door or gate in a palace or city wall
閨範(ㄍㄨㄟ ㄈㄢˋ)
①the code of conduct for women ②a paragon of feminine virtue
閨房(ㄍㄨㄟ ㄈㄤˊ)
the private quarters of a house where women live; a boudoir
閨房之樂(ㄍㄨㄟ ㄈㄤˊ ㄓ ㄌㄜˋ)
marital bliss; the happiness of a married couple
閨闥(ㄍㄨㄟ ㄊㄚˋ)
①apartments for ladies ②a small palace door
閨女(ㄍㄨㄟ ˙ㄋㄩ)
a maiden; a virgin; an unmarried girl
閨閣(ㄍㄨㄟ ㄍㄜˊ)
women's quarters
閨閫(ㄍㄨㄟ ㄎㄨㄣˇ)
women's quarters
閨秀(ㄍㄨㄟ ㄒㄧㄡˋ)
a well-educated girl brought up in a good family: 她們是大家閨秀。They are girls from respectable families.
閨怨(ㄍㄨㄟ ㄩㄢˋ)
writings, or verses that reflect and reveal sorrow and woe in a girl's heart

【閩】 6547 ㄇㄧㄣˇ miin mǐn (又讀 ㄇㄧㄣˊ min mín)
1. another name for Fukien Province
2. name of a river and an ancient tribe in today's Fukien Province
3. a Chinese family name
閩南(ㄇㄧㄣˇ ㄋㄢˊ)
the southern part of Fukien Province
閩南語(ㄇㄧㄣˇ ㄋㄢˊ ㄩˇ)or 閩南話(ㄇㄧㄣˇ ㄋㄢˊ ㄏㄨㄚˋ)
the southern Fukien dialect
閩江(ㄇㄧㄣˇ ㄐㄧㄤ)
the Min River in Fukien Province

七畫

【閫】 6548 ㄎㄨㄣˇ koen kǔn
1. same as 梱—a threshold
2. apartments or quarters for ladies
3. feminine
閫範(ㄎㄨㄣˇ ㄈㄢˋ)
①a paragon of feminine virtue ②the code of conduct for women
閫德(ㄎㄨㄣˇ ㄉㄜˊ)
feminine virtues
閫令(ㄎㄨㄣˇ ㄌㄧㄥˋ)
a woman's orders to her henpecked husband; one's wife's commands
閫寄(ㄎㄨㄣˇ ㄐㄧˋ)
to appoint a commanding officer with full authority to act according to his discretion
閫奧(ㄎㄨㄣˇ ㄠˋ)
①the inner part of a large building ②the essence of learning
閫外之任(ㄎㄨㄣˇ ㄨㄞˋ ㄓ ㄖㄣˋ)
the full authority given to a commanding general
閫威(ㄎㄨㄣˇ ㄨㄟ)
the overwhelming authority of a henpecked man's wife
閫闈(ㄎㄨㄣˇ ㄨㄟˊ)
a boudoir; women's quarters

【閬】 6549 ㄌㄤˇ laang lǎng (又讀 ㄌㄤˋ lanq làng)
1. a high door
2. high; tall; big
3. clear; lucid; bright
4. open and spacious
閬中(ㄌㄤˇ ㄓㄨㄥ)
name of a county and a mountain in Szechwan Province
閬苑(ㄌㄤˇ ㄩㄢˋ)
land where immortals dwell; a paradise

【閭】 6550 ㄌㄩˊ liu lǘ
1. a community of 25 families in ancient China—a community or neighborhood
2. the gate of a village
3. to meet; to gather together
4. a Chinese family name
閭里(ㄌㄩˊ ㄌㄧˇ)or 閭巷(ㄌㄩˊ ㄒㄧㄤˋ)
alleys or lanes—①one's neighbors; one's neighborhood ②one's native village; one's hometown
閭丘(ㄌㄩˊ ㄑㄧㄡ)
①name of an ancient county in today's Shantung Province ②a Chinese compound surname
閭閻(ㄌㄩˊ ㄧㄢˊ)
①the gate of a village ②the people; the rural community
閭伍(ㄌㄩˊ ㄨˇ)
neighbors; neighborhood

【閱】 6551 ㄩㄝˋ yueh yuè
1. to read; to go over (examination papers)
2. to review; to inspect; to examine; to observe
3. to experience
4. to pass
5. (now rarely) to gather; to collect
6. (now rarely) appearance; looks
閱報(ㄩㄝˋ ㄅㄠˋ)
to read newspapers
閱報室(ㄩㄝˋ ㄅㄠˋ ㄕˋ)
a room for reading newspapers and magazines, etc.
閱兵(ㄩㄝˋ ㄅㄧㄥ)
to inspect or review troops
閱兵臺(ㄩㄝˋ ㄅㄧㄥ ㄊㄞˊ)
a stand for reviewing troops
閱兵式(ㄩㄝˋ ㄅㄧㄥ ㄕˋ)
a military parade before the commander in chief or commanding officer; a military review
閱讀(ㄩㄝˋ ㄉㄨˊ)
to read
閱覽(ㄩㄝˋ ㄌㄢˇ)
to read
閱覽室(ㄩㄝˋ ㄌㄢˇ ㄕˋ)
a reading room
閱歷(ㄩㄝˋ ㄌㄧˋ)
①to see, hear, or do for oneself: 他已閱歷過許多事。He has seen much of the world. ②experience; background: 她的閱歷頗淺。She has little experience.
閱卷(ㄩㄝˋ ㄐㄩㄢˋ)
to grade examination papers; to go over examination papers
閱時(ㄩㄝˋ ㄕˊ)

to last a period of time

閱世(ㄩㄝˋ ㄕˋ)
to experience the ways of life; one's experience

閱人多矣(ㄩㄝˋ ㄖㄣˊ ㄉㄨㄛ ㄧˇ)
to have a great deal of experience about men

閱操(ㄩㄝˋ ㄘㄠ)
to watch a military drill

八畫

【閻】 6552 ㄧㄢˊ yan yán

1. a village gate; the gate of a lane
2. a Chinese family name

閻羅王(ㄧㄢˊ ㄌㄨㄛˊ ㄨㄤˊ)or 閻王(ㄧㄢˊ ㄨㄤˊ)or 閻王爺(ㄧㄢˊ ㄨㄤˊ ㄧㄝˊ)
① the Ruler of Hades; the King of Hell; the Chinese Pluto ② one who is feared by all others; a tyrant

閻王賬(ㄧㄢˊ ㄨㄤˊ ㄓㄤˋ)
a loan with exorbitantly high interest rate; a usurious loan; a shark's loan

【閶】 6553 ㄔㄤ chang chāng

1. the gate of heaven
2. the front gate of a palace

閶風(ㄔㄤ ㄈㄥ)
autumn winds

閶闔(ㄔㄤ ㄏㄜˊ)
① the gate of heaven ② the front gate of a palace

【閼】 6554 1. ㄜˋ eh è

1. to block up; to stop up
2. anything used to block up a flow

閼塞(ㄜˋ ㄙㄜˋ)
to block up; to stop up

【閼】 6554 2. ㄧㄢ ian yān

the formal wife of the chieftain of the Huns (匈奴) in the Han Dynasty

閼氏(ㄧㄢ ㄓ)
參看「閼 2.」

【閹】 6555 ㄧㄢ ian yān

1. to castrate
2. a eunuch

閹黨(ㄧㄢ ㄉㄤˇ)
the clique faithful to the powerful eunuch, Wei Chung-hsien (魏忠賢), in the closing years of the Ming Dynasty

閹割(ㄧㄢ ㄍㄜ)
① to castrate or spay; to emasculate ② to deprive theory, etc. of its essence

閹鷄(ㄧㄢ ㄐㄧ)
a capon

閹人(ㄧㄢ ㄖㄣˊ)
a castrated person; a eunuch

閹寺(ㄧㄢ ㄙˋ)
a eunuch

【閽】 6556 ㄏㄨㄣ huen hūn

1. a door or gate; a palace gate
2. a gatekeeper

閽人(ㄏㄨㄣ ㄖㄣˊ)
a doorman; a gatekeeper

【閾】 6557 ㄩˋ yuh yù

1. a doorsill; a threshold
2. separated
3. confined

九畫

【闃】 6558 ㄑㄩˋ chiuh qù

quiet; without people around

闃寂(ㄑㄩˋ ㄐㄧˊ)
still; quiet

闃然(ㄑㄩˋ ㄖㄢˊ)
quiet

【闇】 6559 ㄢˋ ann àn

1. to shut the door
2. dark; obscure; obscurity
3. evening; night
4. lunar or solar eclipses
5. stupid and dull; ignorant and foolish

闇昧(ㄢˋ ㄇㄟˋ)
① ignorant and stupid ② clandestine dealings

闇暝(ㄢˋ ㄇㄧㄥˊ)
getting dark

闇劣(ㄢˋ ㄌㄧㄝˋ)
stupid and incompetent

闇練(ㄢˋ ㄌㄧㄢˋ)
to be familiar with; to be proficient in 亦作「諳練」

闇淺(ㄢˋ ㄑㄧㄢˇ)
shallow, ignorant and stupid

闇室(ㄢˋ ㄕˋ)
a dark room 亦作「暗室」

闇然(ㄢˋ ㄖㄢˊ)
obscure; concealed

闇弱(ㄢˋ ㄖㄨㄛˋ)
ignorant, stupid and cowardly; irresolute

闇誦(ㄢˋ ㄙㄨㄥˋ)
to commit to memory; to recite in silence

闇藹(ㄢˋ ㄞˇ)
luxuriant; numerous; flourishing 亦作「暗藹」

闇闇(ㄢˋ ㄢˋ)
dark and obscure 亦作「暗暗」

【闈】 6560 ㄨㄟˊ wei wéi

1. the side doors of a palace
2. the living quarters of the queen and the imperial concubines
3. ladies' living quarters; private quarters
4. (formerly) a hall where the civil service examination took place

闈墨(ㄨㄟˊ ㄇㄛˋ)
compositions of the successful candidates in the civil service examination in ancient China

【闉】 6561 ㄧㄣ in yīn

1. curved; bent
2. the gate of the city wall

【闊】 6562 ㄎㄨㄛˋ kuoh kuò

1. broad; wide; width
2. separated; widely apart
3. rich; wealthy; extravagant; loaded
4. (now rarely) to ease

闊別(ㄎㄨㄛˋ ㄅㄧㄝˊ)
separated for a long time: 我們是闊別多年的友人。We are long-separated friends.

闊步(ㄎㄨㄛˋ ㄅㄨˋ)
to walk with big strides; to stride: 他在街上闊步行走。He strode along the street.

闊達(ㄎㄨㄛˋ ㄉㄚˊ)
broad-minded; not caring for trifles

闊大(ㄎㄨㄛˋ ㄉㄚˋ)
capacious; spacious

闊大爺(ㄎㄨㄛˋ ㄉㄚˋ ㄧㄝˊ)
a wealthy man who lives a very luxurious life

闊得很(ㄎㄨㄛˋ ˙ㄉㄜ ㄏㄣˇ)
loaded; very rich

闊老 or 闊佬(ㄎㄨㄛˋ ㄌㄠˇ)

a rich man: 他是個闊佬。He's a rich man.
闊落(ㄎㄨㄛˋ ㄌㄨㄛˋ)
not fine
闊氣(ㄎㄨㄛˋ ˙ㄑㄧ)
extravagant in spending; lavish
闊綽(ㄎㄨㄛˋ ㄔㄨㄛˋ)
extravagant; throwing money around; lavish
闊少(ㄎㄨㄛˋ ㄕㄠˋ)
sons of a wealthy family
闊人(ㄎㄨㄛˋ ㄖㄣˊ)
the rich
闊葉樹(ㄎㄨㄛˋ ㄧㄝˋ ㄕㄨˋ)
broad-leaved trees

【闋】 6563
ㄑㄩㄝˋ chiueh què
1. to close or shut the door after finishing something
2. to be at rest
3. to end
4. the expiry of the period of mourning
5. a numerical adjunct for songs
6. empty; blank

【闌】 6564
ㄌㄢˊ lan lán
1. a door curtain or screen
2. a fence
3. to block up; to cut off
4. the end of (a year, etc.); late (in the night, etc.): 夜闌人靜。All is quiet in the dead of night.
5. weakened; withered
闌風(ㄌㄢˊ ㄈㄥ)
the continuous blowing of wind
闌殫(ㄌㄢˊ ㄉㄢ)
tired and exhausted
闌干(ㄌㄢˊ ㄍㄢ)
① a fence; banisters; a balustrade; railings ② the eye sockets ③ a crisscross
闌檻(ㄌㄢˊ ㄐㄧㄢˋ)
railings or fences
闌出(ㄌㄢˊ ㄔㄨ)
to go out wantonly
闌珊(ㄌㄢˊ ㄕㄢ)
withered; declining; waning: 春意闌珊。The spring is waning.
闌入(ㄌㄢˊ ㄖㄨˋ)
① to barge in; to intrude; to trespass ② to put in something where it does not belong
闌尾(ㄌㄢˊ ㄨㄟˇ)
(anatomy) the appendix 亦作「盲腸」
闌尾炎(ㄌㄢˊ ㄨㄟˇ ㄧㄢˊ)
appendicitis 亦作「盲腸炎」

【闆】 6565
ㄅㄢˇ baan bǎn
the boss; the owner: 他被老闆開除。He is fired by his boss.

【闍】 6566
1. ㄉㄨ du dū
a tower over a city wall

【闍】 6566
2. ㄕㄜˊ sher shé
as in 阿闍梨—a Buddhist high priest

十畫

【闐】 6567
ㄊㄧㄢˊ tyan tián
to fill; to fill to the brim; to be full of
闐闐(ㄊㄧㄢˊ ㄊㄧㄢˊ)
① brimming; full; flourishing ② the sound of drums
闐池(ㄊㄧㄢˊ ㄔˊ)
Issiq Köl, or Issyk-Kul, a lake in Soviet Central Asia
闐溢(ㄊㄧㄢˊ ㄧˋ)
to fill to the brim

【闑】 6568
ㄋㄧㄝˋ nieh niè
the wood bars on both sides of the central door

【闒】 6569
ㄊㄚˋ tah tà
1. the upstairs door
2. the sound of bells and drums
3. mean

【闓】 6570
ㄎㄞˇ kae kǎi
1. to open
2. peaceful; harmonious

【闔】 6571
ㄏㄜˊ her hé
1. a leaf of a door
2. to shut or close
3. all; the whole
4. Why? 或 Why not?
闔府(ㄏㄜˊ ㄈㄨˇ)or 闔第(ㄏㄜˊ ㄉㄧˋ)
your whole family
闔府平安(ㄏㄜˊ ㄈㄨˇ ㄆㄧㄥˊ ㄢ)
Hope your whole family is doing well.
闔第光臨(ㄏㄜˊ ㄉㄧˋ ㄍㄨㄤ ㄌㄧㄣˊ)
(a conventional term used in Chinese invitation cards) Please come with your whole family. 或 The whole family is invited.
闔廬(ㄏㄜˊ ㄌㄨˊ)or 闔閭(ㄏㄜˊ ㄌㄩˊ)
① one's house ② name of the king of Wu in the Epoch of Spring and Autumn
闔國(ㄏㄜˊ ㄍㄨㄛˊ)
the whole country
闔家(ㄏㄜˊ ㄐㄧㄚ)
the whole family
闔城(ㄏㄜˊ ㄔㄥˊ)
the whole city; the whole town
闔扇(ㄏㄜˊ ㄕㄢˋ)
a door panel; a wing of a door

【闕】 6572
1. ㄑㄩㄝˋ chiueh què
1. a watchtower outside the palace gate in ancient China
2. a palace: 宮闕 the imperial palace
3. a Chinese family name
闕下(ㄑㄩㄝˋ ㄒㄧㄚˋ)
① the imperial palace ② Your (or His) Majesty

【闕】 6572
2. ㄑㄩㄝ chiue quē
1. faults; errors; mistakes; defects
2. to lack; deficient; deficiency
闕失(ㄑㄩㄝ ㄕ)
a mistake; an error
闕如(ㄑㄩㄝ ㄖㄨˊ)
lacking; wanting; deficient
闕字(ㄑㄩㄝ ㄗˋ)
an omission in an article, writing, etc.; a hiatus
闕疑(ㄑㄩㄝ ㄧˊ)
to lay aside something doubtful and try to verify later; to leave the question open; an unsettled point
闕文(ㄑㄩㄝ ㄨㄣˊ)
omissions or missing parts in writings or books; a hiatus in the text

【闖】 6573
1. ㄔㄨㄤˇ choang chuǎng
1. to rush in all of a sudden; to intrude into: 他闖了進來。

He rushed in.
2. to be trained by experience; to hew out one's way
3. to cause (a disaster, etc.)

闖大運(ㄔㄨㄤˇ ㄉㄚˋ ㄩㄣˋ)
to rush ahead for a try without much planning beforehand

闖關(ㄔㄨㄤˇ ㄍㄨㄢ)
to run a blockade; to try to break into a guarded point

闖空門(ㄔㄨㄤˇ ㄎㄨㄥ ㄇㄣˊ)
to break into a home or building when the occupants are absent

闖禍(ㄔㄨㄤˇ ㄏㄨㄛˋ)
to cause a disaster or misfortune; to get into trouble

闖紅燈(ㄔㄨㄤˇ ㄏㄨㄥˊ ㄉㄥ)
to continue walking or driving when the red light is on; to run through a red light

闖江湖(ㄔㄨㄤˇ ㄐㄧㄤ ·ㄏㄨ)
to roam about to make a living

闖將(ㄔㄨㄤˇ ㄐㄧㄤˋ)
①the title that the rebel leader Li Tzu-cheng (李自成) gave himself in the closing years of the Ming Dynasty ②a rogue; a rascal ③a pathbreaker

闖子(ㄔㄨㄤˇ ㄗˇ)
a rash and bold person; a fearless and rude person

闖座(ㄔㄨㄤˇ ㄗㄨㄛˋ)or 闖席(ㄔㄨㄤˇ ㄒㄧˊ)
to attend a feast without being invited

闖王(ㄔㄨㄤˇ ㄨㄤˊ)
the title assumed by the rebel leader Kao Ying-hsiang (高迎祥) and later passed to Li Tzu-cheng(李自成)in their uprisings during the closing years of the Ming Dynasty

【闖】 6573 2. ㄔㄨㄤˋ chuanq chuàng
1. to cause (a disaster)
2. to hit

十一畫

【關】 6574 ㄍㄨㄢ guan guān
1. to shut; to close: 請將門關上。Will you shut the door?
2. a frontier pass or checkpoint: 我們今晚把關。We guard the pass tonight.
3. the bar across the door
4. a customs house; a customs barrier
5. a key point; a turning point
6. related; relationship; to involve; to concern
7. to negotiate; to go between
8. to draw (money, or pay)
9. a Chinese family name

關閉(ㄍㄨㄢ ㄅㄧˋ)
①to close ②to close down; to shut down (a store, plant, etc.): 該公司因財務困難而關閉工廠。The company shut down the factory because of financial difficulties.

關不住(ㄍㄨㄢ ·ㄅㄨ ㄓㄨˋ)
cannot be shut out, as the charming sight of spring; cannot be shut in, as the restless spirit of a child

關門(ㄍㄨㄢ ㄇㄣˊ)
①to close the door ②to close a shop ③to close its door—to go bankrupt

關門大吉(ㄍㄨㄢ ㄇㄣˊ ㄉㄚˋ ㄐㄧˊ)
to close down for good

關防(ㄍㄨㄢ ㄈㄤˊ)
①the seal of a government agency ②a military position at a strategic point on the border

關夫子(ㄍㄨㄢ ㄈㄨ ㄗˇ)or 關羽(ㄍㄨㄢ ㄩˇ)or 關帝(ㄍㄨㄢ ㄉㄧˋ)or 關公(ㄍㄨㄢ ㄍㄨㄥ)
Kuan Yü (關羽, ?—219), a general in the Epoch of the Three Kingdoms, deified in later generations as China's god of war

關刀(ㄍㄨㄢ ㄉㄠ)
a knife with a long handle for fighting on horseback, so called for it's believed to be the weapon used by Kuan Yü(關羽)

關島(ㄍㄨㄢ ㄉㄠˇ)
Guam

關帝廟(ㄍㄨㄢ ㄉㄧˋ ㄇㄧㄠˋ)
a shrine dedicated to General Kuan Yü(關羽)

關東(ㄍㄨㄢ ㄉㄨㄥ)
①the old name for the area east of the Han Ku Pass (函谷關), including today's Honan and Shantung Provinces ②the land east of the Shan Hai Pass(山海關); northeast China

關頭(ㄍㄨㄢ ㄊㄡˊ)
a key point; a crucial period; a crux

關內(ㄍㄨㄢ ㄋㄟˋ)or 關裏(ㄍㄨㄢ ㄌㄧˇ)
within the Han Ku Pass(函谷關) or Shan Hai Pass(山海關)

關聯(ㄍㄨㄢ ㄌㄧㄢˊ)
related; connected; involved; involvement; connection

關關(ㄍㄨㄢ ㄍㄨㄢ)
the sound of birds chirping

關卡(ㄍㄨㄢ ㄎㄚˇ)
a customs station or barrier

關口(ㄍㄨㄢ ㄎㄡˇ)
①a checkpoint; a strategic point ②a key point; a turning point

關懷(ㄍㄨㄢ ㄏㄨㄞˊ)
to be concerned about; to show concern; concern: 我們十分關懷父母的健康。We pay great attention to our parents' health.

關節(ㄍㄨㄢ ㄐㄧㄝˊ)
①joints in the human body ②to bribe; a bribe ③illegal transactions between the examiner and the examinee ④key links; crucial links

關節炎(ㄍㄨㄢ ㄐㄧㄝˊ ㄧㄢˊ)
(pathology) arthritis

關鍵(ㄍㄨㄢ ㄐㄧㄢˋ)
a key point; a key (to a problem); an important turning point; a hinge; a pivotal point; a crux: 它是個關鍵字。It's a key word.

關鍵字(ㄍㄨㄢ ㄐㄧㄢˋ ㄗˋ)
a key word

關津(ㄍㄨㄢ ㄐㄧㄣ)
a hub or key point for both land and water transportation

關禁閉(ㄍㄨㄢ ㄐㄧㄣˋ ㄅㄧˋ)
(military) to be put in a dark cell as a form of punishment

關起來(ㄍㄨㄢ ㄑㄧˇ ·ㄌㄞ)
①to close; to shut ②to imprison

關切(ㄍㄨㄢ ㄑㄧㄝˋ)

to be concerned about; to show concern; concern: 他們極爲關切此一消息。They are deeply concerned at the news.

關西(ㄍㄨㄢ ㄒㄧ)
the land west of the Han Ku Pass(函谷關), including Shensi and Kansu provinces

關係(ㄍㄨㄢ ㄒㄧˋ)
①relation; relationship; connection; ties: 她跟你是什麼關係? What relation is she to you? ②to matter: 有何關係? What does it matter?

關係密切(ㄍㄨㄢ ㄒㄧˋ ㄇㄧˋ ㄑㄧㄝˋ)
close relationship; intimate contact or connection: 他與那件事關係密切。He had a close relationship to the incident.

關係代名詞(ㄍㄨㄢ ㄒㄧˋ ㄉㄞˋ ㄇㄧㄥˊ ㄘˊ)
relative pronouns

關係斷絕(ㄍㄨㄢ ㄒㄧˋ ㄉㄨㄢˋ ㄐㄩㄝˊ)
(diplomacy, etc.) severance of relations; relations severed

關係人(ㄍㄨㄢ ㄒㄧˋ ㄖㄣˊ)
(law) persons or parties concerned

關係詞(ㄍㄨㄢ ㄒㄧˋ ㄘˊ)
(English grammar) a relative pronoun, adverb, etc. (such as who, which, what, etc.)

關心(ㄍㄨㄢ ㄒㄧㄣ)
to be concerned about; to show concern; concern: 我很關心她。I was much concerned about her.

關心民瘼(ㄍㄨㄢ ㄒㄧㄣ ㄇㄧㄣˊ ㄇㄛˋ)
to be concerned about the afflictions of the people

關照(ㄍㄨㄢ ㄓㄠˋ)
①to notify; to inform: 他來的話,請關照一聲。Please inform me if he comes. ②to take care of; to look after: 這裡的工作請多關照了。Please look after the work here.

關注(ㄍㄨㄢ ㄓㄨˋ)
to be concerned about; to show concern

關中(ㄍㄨㄢ ㄓㄨㄥ)
① the old name of Shensi Province ② the central Shensi plain

關窗(ㄍㄨㄢ ㄔㄨㄤ)
to close the window: 晚上要關窗。Close the windows at night.

關涉(ㄍㄨㄢ ㄕㄜˋ)
to involve; to concern; to be related to; relations

關山迢遞(ㄍㄨㄢ ㄕㄢ ㄊㄧㄠˊ ㄉㄧˋ)
to be separated far apart

關說(ㄍㄨㄢ ㄕㄨㄛ)
to lobby illegally, usually by pedaling one's influence; to ask a favor of someone for a friend

關稅(ㄍㄨㄢ ㄕㄨㄟˋ)
customs duty

關稅率(ㄍㄨㄢ ㄕㄨㄟˋ ㄌㄩˋ)
customs tariffs

關稅及貿易總協定(ㄍㄨㄢ ㄕㄨㄟˋ ㄐㄧˊ ㄇㄠˋ ㄧˋ ㄗㄨㄥˇ ㄒㄧㄝˊ ㄉㄧㄥˋ)
the General Agreement on Tariffs and Trade (GATT)

關稅自主(ㄍㄨㄢ ㄕㄨㄟˋ ㄗˋ ㄓㄨˇ)
tariff autonomy

關稅優惠(ㄍㄨㄢ ㄕㄨㄟˋ ㄧㄡ ㄏㄨㄟˋ)
tariff preference

關塞(ㄍㄨㄢ ㄙㄞˋ)
strategic positions or passes on the border

關隘(ㄍㄨㄢ ㄞˋ)
strategic positions or passes on the border

關愛(ㄍㄨㄢ ㄞˋ)
to express solicitude for the well-being of someone

關礙(ㄍㄨㄢ ㄞˋ)
to hinder; to obstruct

關外(ㄍㄨㄢ ㄨㄞˋ)
outside the Han Ku Pass(函谷關) or the Shan Hai Pass (山海關)

關於(ㄍㄨㄢ ㄩˊ)
concerning; with regard to; regarding: 那末關於錢的方面,怎麼辦呢? Now, regarding money, what is to be done?

【闚】 6575
ㄎㄨㄟ kuei kuī

1. same as 窺—to steal a glance; to peep; to spy: 他從牆頭闚視。He peeped over a wall.
2. to tempt with material gain

十二畫

【闞】 6576
1. ㄎㄢˋ kann kàn
(又讀 ㄎㄢˇ kaan kǎn)

1. to steal a glance; to peep; to spy; to watch secretly
2. a Chinese family name

【闞】 6576
2. ㄏㄢˇ haan hǎn

1. roaring (of a tiger); growling
2. brave

【闠】 6577
ㄏㄨㄟˋ huey huì

the gate of a market

【闡】 6578
ㄔㄢˇ chaan chǎn

1. to make clear; to elaborate; to elucidate; to expound
2. evident; clear

闡明(ㄔㄢˇ ㄇㄧㄥˊ)
to elucidate; to clarify; to make clear: 他闡明了自己的理念。He clarified his own concept.

闡發(ㄔㄢˇ ㄈㄚ)
to expound and promote

闡究(ㄔㄢˇ ㄐㄧㄡˋ)
to study and expound

闡士(ㄔㄢˇ ㄕˋ)
a learned monk; a Buddhist high priest

闡釋(ㄔㄢˇ ㄕˋ)
to explain; to expound; to interpret

闡述(ㄔㄢˇ ㄕㄨˋ)
to expound; to elaborate; to set forth: 他對浪漫主義作了有系統的闡述。He made a systematic exposition of romanticism.

闡幽(ㄔㄢˇ ㄧㄡ)
to expound the hidden points or meanings

闡揚(ㄔㄢˇ ㄧㄤˊ)
to expound and propagate; to expound and advocate (an ideology, theory, principle, etc.)

十三畫

【闢】 6579
ㄆㄧˋ pih pì

1. to open up; to develop
2. to rid; to do away with
3. to refute

闢謬(ㄆㄧˋ ㄇㄧㄡˋ)
to refute absurdities

闢佛(ㄆㄧˋ ㄈㄛˊ)
to argue against Buddhism

闢地(ㄆㄧˋ ㄉㄧˋ)
to open up land for cultivation

闢田(ㄆㄧˋ ㄊㄧˊ ㄢ)
to open up land for farming; to develop farmland

闢墾(ㄆㄧˋ ㄎㄣˇ)
to open up land for farming

闢邪(ㄆㄧˋ ㄒㄧˊ ㄝ)
to refute heresy

闢謠(ㄆㄧˋ ㄧˊ ㄠ)
to refute rumors; to clarify rumored reports

【闤】 6580 ㄏㄨㄢˊ hwan huán
a wall around a marketplace

【闥】 6581 ㄊㄚˋ tah tà
1. a door; a small door; a wicket gate
2. the space between the door and the screen; inside the door
3. fast

阜部
ㄈㄨˋ fuh fù

【阜】 6582 ㄈㄨˋ fuh fù
1. a mound; a small hill
2. the continent; the mainland
3. abundant; flourishing; numerous: 物阜民豐。Products abound and the people live in plenty.

阜陵(ㄈㄨˋ ㄌㄧˊ ㄥ)
a mound; a small hill

三畫

【阡】 6583 ㄑㄧ ㄢ chian qiān
1. paths on farms; a footpath between fields, running north and south
2. the path leading to a grave

阡表(ㄑㄧ ㄢ ㄅㄧˇ ㄠ)
a tomb tablet; a grave stone

阡陌(ㄑㄧ ㄢ ㄇㄛˋ)
paths on farmland; crisscross footpaths between fields

阡陌縱橫(ㄑㄧ ㄢ ㄇㄛˋ ㄗㄨㄥˋ ㄏㄥˊ)
crisscross paths on farmland

【阢】 6584 ㄨˋ wuh wù
uneasy; apprehensive

阢隉(ㄨˋ ㄋㄧˋ ㄝ)
uneasy; jittery

四畫

【阬】 6585 (坑) ㄎㄥ keng kēng
a pit; a shaft

【阨】 6586 ㄜˋ eh è
1. a strategic position
2. a precarious position
3. to block up or obstruct
4. destitute; poverty-stricken; difficulty

阨窮(ㄜˋ ㄑㄩㄥˊ)
destitute; difficulty; poverty-stricken

阨塞(ㄜˋ ㄙㄞˋ)
a strategic place or position

【阪】 6587 ㄅㄢˇ baan bǎn
1. the slope of a hill; a hillside
2. a hillside farm field

阪田(ㄅㄢˇ ㄊㄧˊ ㄢ)
① a hillside farm field ② a rugged and stony field

阪上走丸(ㄅㄢˇ ㄕㄤˋ ㄗㄡˇ ㄨㄢˊ)
(literally) to roll a ball down the slope—to become irresistible because of natural advantages

【阮】 6588 ㄖㄨㄢˇ roan ruǎn
1. name of an ancient state in today's Kansu Province
2. an ancient musical instrument
3. a Chinese family name

阮囊羞澀(ㄖㄨㄢˇ ㄋㄤˊ ㄒㄧㄡ ㄙㄜˋ)
having an empty pocket; short of cash; poor

阮籍(ㄖㄨㄢˇ ㄐㄧˊ)
Juan Chi (210-263), an eccentric scholar in the Epoch of the Three Kingdoms

阮咸(ㄖㄨㄢˇ ㄒㄧˊ ㄢ)
① Juan Hsien, nephew of Juan Chi(阮籍), who was well versed in music ② name of an ancient Chinese guitar; a plucked stringed instrument 亦作「阮」

【阱】 6589 ㄐㄧˇ ㄥ jiing jǐng
a trap; a snare

【防】 6590 ㄈㄤˊ farng fáng
1. to defend; defense
2. to prepare for; to take precautions; to prevent; prevention: 預防勝於治療。Prevention is better than cure.
3. a Chinese family name

防波堤(ㄈㄤˊ ㄅㄛ ㄊㄧˊ)
a breakwater; a mole

防備(ㄈㄤˊ ㄅㄟˋ)
to get ready or prepared (for an incident, etc.); to guard against

防不勝防(ㄈㄤˊ ·ㄅㄨ ㄕㄥ ㄈㄤˊ)
There's no way of preventing it. 或 It's impossible to guard against (such things).

防範(ㄈㄤˊ ㄈㄢˋ)
to be alert against; to take precautions; to guard against

防風(ㄈㄤˊ ㄈㄥ)
① *Siler divaricatum*, a herbal weed ② protection against wind

防風林(ㄈㄤˊ ㄈㄥ ㄌㄧˊ ㄣ)
a windbreak; a forest shelter belt

防腐(ㄈㄤˊ ㄈㄨˇ)
to preserve (food, timber, etc.) from chemical decomposition; to prevent decay

防腐劑(ㄈㄤˊ ㄈㄨˇ ㄐㄧˋ)
antiseptic; preservative

防盜(ㄈㄤˊ ㄉㄠˋ)
prevention of burglary; to guard against burglary

防彈(ㄈㄤˊ ㄉㄢˋ)
bulletproof; to protect against bullets

防彈玻璃(ㄈㄤˊ ㄉㄢˋ ㄅㄛ ·ㄌㄧ)
bulletproof glass

防彈背心(ㄈㄤˊ ㄉㄢˋ ㄅㄟˋ ㄒㄧ ㄣ)
a bulletproof vest; a flak jacket

防地(ㄈㄤˊ ㄉㄧˋ)
an area where troops are stationed for defense

防諜(ㄈㄤˊ ㄉㄧˊ ㄝ)
anti-espionage; to prevent espionage

防毒(ㄈㄤˊ ㄉㄨˊ)
anti-poison; gas defense

防毒面具(ㄈㄤˊ ㄉㄨˊ ㄇㄧㄢˋ ㄐㄩˋ)
a gas mask; a protective mask
防癆(ㄈㄤˊ ㄌㄠˊ)
tuberculosis prevention; TB control
防老(ㄈㄤˊ ㄌㄠˇ)
to make provision for one's old age
防空(ㄈㄤˊ ㄎㄨㄥ)
air defense; antiaircraft
防空洞(ㄈㄤˊ ㄎㄨㄥ ㄉㄨㄥˋ)
an air-raid or bomb shelter
防空壕(ㄈㄤˊ ㄎㄨㄥ ㄏㄠˊ)
a ditch serving as an air-raid shelter
防空警報(ㄈㄤˊ ㄎㄨㄥ ㄐㄧㄥˇ ㄅㄠˋ)
an air defense warning
防空演習(ㄈㄤˊ ㄎㄨㄥ ㄧㄢˇ ㄒㄧˊ)
air defense exercises; an air-raid drill
防旱(ㄈㄤˊ ㄏㄢˋ)
prevention of drought
防護(ㄈㄤˊ ㄏㄨˋ)
① to protect or safeguard ② first aid
防護團(ㄈㄤˊ ㄏㄨˋ ㄊㄨㄢˊ)
civil defense corps
防護林(ㄈㄤˊ ㄏㄨˋ ㄌㄧㄣˊ)
a shelter forest
防護裝置(ㄈㄤˊ ㄏㄨˋ ㄓㄨㄤ ㄓˋ)
protective equipment
防護油(ㄈㄤˊ ㄏㄨˋ ㄧㄡˊ)
preservative oil
防火(ㄈㄤˊ ㄏㄨㄛˇ)
to guard against fire hazards; fire prevention; fireproof
防火板(ㄈㄤˊ ㄏㄨㄛˇ ㄅㄢˇ)
an anti-firing plate
防火牆(ㄈㄤˊ ㄏㄨㄛˇ ㄑㄧㄤˊ)
a fire wall
防火設備(ㄈㄤˊ ㄏㄨㄛˇ ㄕㄜˋ ㄅㄟˋ)
fire-fighting facilities; facilities to guard against fire hazards
防患未然(ㄈㄤˊ ㄏㄨㄢˋ ㄨㄟˋ ㄖㄢˊ)
to take precautions against a calamity
防洪(ㄈㄤˊ ㄏㄨㄥˊ)
flood control
防洪措施(ㄈㄤˊ ㄏㄨㄥˊ ㄘㄨㄛˋ ㄕ)
flood control measures
防飢(ㄈㄤˊ ㄐㄧ)
to guard against famine or hunger
防銹(ㄈㄤˊ ㄒㄧㄡˋ)
antirust
防線(ㄈㄤˊ ㄒㄧㄢˋ)
a line of defense
防止(ㄈㄤˊ ㄓˇ)
to prevent; to guard against; to prohibit: 他們竭力防止戰爭。They tried hard to prevent the war.
防治(ㄈㄤˊ ㄓˋ)
prevention and treatment (of diseases)
防震(ㄈㄤˊ ㄓㄣˋ)
shock-resistant; quakeproof
防潮(ㄈㄤˊ ㄔㄠˊ)
① dampproof; moistureproof ② protection against the tide
防臭劑(ㄈㄤˊ ㄔㄡˋ ㄐㄧˋ)
a deodorizer; a deodorant
防塵(ㄈㄤˊ ㄔㄣˊ)
dustproof
防蟲(ㄈㄤˊ ㄔㄨㄥˊ)
pest control; pest prevention; to guard against harmful insects
防蝕劑(ㄈㄤˊ ㄕˊ ㄐㄧˋ)
an anticorrosive
防守(ㄈㄤˊ ㄕㄡˇ)
to defend; to guard: 他們防守此城以禦敵。They defended the city against the enemy.
防身(ㄈㄤˊ ㄕㄣ)
to guard personal safety; self-protection
防身術(ㄈㄤˊ ㄕㄣ ㄕㄨˋ)
the science (or art) of self-defense
防水(ㄈㄤˊ ㄕㄨㄟˇ)
① waterproof; watertight ② to guard against flood; anti-flood
防水布(ㄈㄤˊ ㄕㄨㄟˇ ㄅㄨˋ)
mackintosh; waterproof canvas
防水劑(ㄈㄤˊ ㄕㄨㄟˇ ㄐㄧˋ)
a waterproofing agent
防水水泥(ㄈㄤˊ ㄕㄨㄟˇ ㄕㄨㄟˇ ㄋㄧˊ)
waterproof cement
防災(ㄈㄤˊ ㄗㄞ)
to take precautions against natural calamities
防疫(ㄈㄤˊ ㄧˋ)
to guard against or prevent an epidemic
防疫所(ㄈㄤˊ ㄧˋ ㄙㄨㄛˇ)
a quarantine office
防意如城(ㄈㄤˊ ㄧˋ ㄖㄨˊ ㄔㄥˊ)
to guard against one's desire as if to guard a city against the enemy
防務(ㄈㄤˊ ㄨˋ)
defense; defense measures
防微杜漸(ㄈㄤˊ ㄨㄟ ㄉㄨˋ ㄐㄧㄢˋ)
to take every precaution at the beginning; to nip trouble in the bud
防衞(ㄈㄤˊ ㄨㄟˋ) or 防禦(ㄈㄤˊ ㄩˋ)
to defend; to guard; defense
防雨布(ㄈㄤˊ ㄩˇ ㄅㄨˋ)
waterproof cloth; tarpaulin
防禦力(ㄈㄤˊ ㄩˋ ㄌㄧˋ)
the defensive force or strength
防禦工事(ㄈㄤˊ ㄩˋ ㄍㄨㄥ ㄕˋ)
defense works
防禦戰(ㄈㄤˊ ㄩˋ ㄓㄢˋ)
the defensive war

【阯】 6591
(址) ㄓˇ jyy zhǐ
a site; an address

五畫

【阻】 6592
ㄗㄨˇ tzuu zǔ
1. to prevent; to stop; to prohibit or proscribe
2. to separate; separated
3. to hinder; to obstruct; to oppose; to impede; to detain; to blockade
4. difficulty; to suffer
5. to rely on
6. a strategic pass

阻擋(ㄗㄨˇ ㄉㄤˇ)
to stop; to be in the way; to block the way; to hinder: 任何事也阻擋不了我們到那裏去。Nothing will stop us from going there.
阻斷交通(ㄗㄨˇ ㄉㄨㄢˋ ㄐㄧㄠ ㄊㄨㄥ)
to obstruct traffic
阻撓(ㄗㄨˇ ㄋㄠˊ)
to obstruct; to thwart; obstruction: 他們設法阻撓敵人的計畫。They tried to thwart the enemy's plans.
阻難(ㄗㄨˇ ㄋㄢˋ)
to obstruct; to make it difficult
阻攔(ㄗㄨˇ ㄌㄢˊ)
to stop; to prevent; to retard

〔阜部〕

〔阜部〕

阻力(ㄗㄨˇ ㄌㄧˋ)
the force of resistance
阻隔(ㄗㄨˇ ㄍㄜˊ)
① to be separated; to be isolated ②to cut off: 濃霧阻隔了我們的視線。A thick fog cut off our view.
阻隔活門(ㄗㄨˇ ㄍㄜˊ ㄏㄨㄛˊ ㄇㄣˊ)
a check valve
阻梗(ㄗㄨˇ ㄍㄥˇ)
to obstruct or hinder; to impede
阻擊(ㄗㄨˇ ㄐㄧˊ)
to block; to check
阻絕(ㄗㄨˇ ㄐㄩㄝˊ)
to stop up; to obstruct, hinder or impede
阻修(ㄗㄨˇ ㄒㄧㄡ)
(referring to a road) obstructed and distant
阻止(ㄗㄨˇ ㄓˇ)
to stop or prevent; to prohibit or proscribe; to block: 他們想阻止事態惡化。They tried to prevent the situation from getting worse.
阻滯(ㄗㄨˇ ㄓˋ)
impeded; obstructed; blocked
阻深(ㄗㄨˇ ㄕㄣ)
(said of a place) far away beyond many mountains and streams
阻塞(ㄗㄨˇ ㄙㄜˋ)
① to block up; to clog; to obstruct: 落石阻塞了交通。Fallen rocks obstructed the traffic. ② a jam; a block: 交通阻塞使車輛無法通行。A block in the traffic keeps cars from moving on.
阻遏(ㄗㄨˇ ㄜˋ)
to stop; to hinder; to check
阻礙(ㄗㄨˇ ㄞˋ)
an obstacle or hindrance; obstruction; to obstruct; to impede; to prevent; to bar; to retard: 健康不佳阻礙了他成功的機會。Poor health barred his chances of success.

【阼】 6593
ㄗㄨㄛˋ tzuoh zuò

1. the main steps
2. the throne

阼階(ㄗㄨㄛˋ ㄐㄧㄝ)
the eastern steps where the host stood to welcome his guests in old and ancient China

【阿】 6594
1. ㄜ e ē

1. to favor; to toady; to assent; to pander to; to play up to
2. to rely on
3. a riverbank
4. the corner or edge
5. a pillar
6. slender and beautiful
7. to discharge (night soil, urine, etc.)
8. a Chinese family name

阿媚(ㄜ ㄇㄟˋ)
to flatter or toady
阿彌陀佛(ㄜ ㄇㄧˊ ㄊㄨㄛˊ ㄈㄛˊ)
Amitabha, the Buddha of infinite qualities (an imaginary being unknown to ancient Buddhism, possibly of Persian or Iranian origin, who has eclipsed the historical Buddha in becoming the most popular divinity in the Mahayana Pantheon)
阿房宮(ㄜ ㄈㄤˊ ㄍㄨㄥ)
name of a fabulous palace in the Chin Dynasty, which was later destroyed by Hsiang Yü (項羽)
阿芙蓉(ㄜ ㄈㄨˊ ㄖㄨㄥˊ)
a poppy; opium
阿附(ㄜ ㄈㄨˋ)
to toady and support; to flock to; to curry favor with; to jump on the bandwagon (of someone in power)
阿黨(ㄜ ㄉㄤˇ)
to twist law for private purposes
阿尿(ㄜ ㄋㄧㄠˋ)
to urinate
阿羅漢(ㄜ ㄌㄨㄛˊ ㄏㄢˋ)
Arhat or *Lohan* (羅漢) (from Sanskrit *arhat*)
阿好(ㄜ ㄏㄠˋ)or 阿其所好(ㄜ ㄑㄧˊ ㄙㄨㄛˇ ㄏㄠˋ)
to flatter whom one likes; to practice favoritism
阿修羅(ㄜ ㄒㄧㄡ ㄌㄨㄛˊ)
(Buddhism) a frightful demon (from Sanskrit *asura*)
阿諂(ㄜ ㄔㄢˇ)
to flatter; to toady; to fawn upon: 許多親戚阿諂那位老富翁。Many relatives fawned on the rich old man.
阿屎(ㄜ ㄕˇ)
to move the bowels
阿順(ㄜ ㄕㄨㄣˋ)
to flatter and be obsequious
阿私(ㄜ ㄙ)
to be biased or partial
阿諛(ㄜ ㄩˊ)
to flatter

【阿】 6594
2. ㄚˋ ah à
(又讀 ㄚ a ā)

1. an initial particle; a prefix to a name or a term of address
2. a word often used in transliterations
3. an exclamation of unpleasant surprise

阿比西尼亞(ㄚˋ ㄅㄧˇ ㄒㄧ ㄋㄧˊ ㄧㄚˋ)
Abyssinia; Ethiopia
阿坡羅(ㄚˋ ㄆㄛ ㄌㄨㄛˊ)
Apollo 亦作「阿波羅」
阿片(ㄚˋ ㄆㄧㄢˋ)
opium 亦作「鴉片」
阿摩尼亞(ㄚˋ ㄇㄛˊ ㄋㄧˊ ㄧㄚˋ)
ammonia
阿眉(ㄚˋ ㄇㄟˊ)or 阿美族(ㄚˋ ㄇㄟˇ ㄗㄨˊ)
the Ami tribe among the aborigines in Taiwan
阿曼(ㄚˋ ㄇㄢˋ)
①Amman, capital of Jordan ② Oman
阿們(ㄚˋ ㄇㄣˊ)
Amen
阿米巴(ㄚˋ ㄇㄧˇ ㄅㄚ)
ameba, or amoeba 亦作「變形蟲」
阿姆斯特丹(ㄚˋ ㄇㄨˇ ㄙ ㄊㄜˋ ㄉㄢ)
Amsterdam, Holland
阿飛(ㄚˋ ㄈㄟ)
a young man who combines the characteristics of a hippie and a juvenile delinquent; a Teddy boy
阿非利加(ㄚˋ ㄈㄟ ㄌㄧˋ ㄐㄧㄚ)
Africa 亦作「非洲」
阿富汗(ㄚˋ ㄈㄨˋ ㄏㄢˋ)
Afghanistan
阿富汗人(ㄚˋ ㄈㄨˋ ㄏㄢˋ ㄖㄣˊ)
an Afghan
阿斗(ㄚˋ ㄉㄡˇ)
①the pet name of Liu Chan (劉禪), lackluster son of Liu Pei (劉備) in the Epoch of the Three Kingdoms ② a name that has become a synonym of a good-for-nothing:

他眞是個扶不起的阿斗。He is indeed a good-for-nothing person.

阿堵物(ㄚ ㄉㄨˇ ㄨˋ)
money (used in a contemptuous sense); pelf; wealth

阿拉(ㄚ ㄌㄚ)
①(Mohammedan) Allah ②(Ningpo dialect) me; I

阿拉巴馬(ㄚ ㄌㄚ ㄅㄚ ㄇㄚˇ)
the state of Alabama, U. S. A.

阿拉斯加(ㄚ ㄌㄚ ㄙ ㄐㄧㄚ)
the state of Alaska, U. S. A.

阿剌伯(ㄚ ㄌㄚˋ ㄅㄛˊ)
①Arabia②Arab 亦作「阿拉伯」

阿剌伯半島(ㄚ ㄌㄚˋ ㄅㄛˊ ㄅㄢˋ ㄉㄠˇ)
the Arabian Peninsula 亦作「阿拉伯半島」

阿剌伯聯合大公國(ㄚ ㄌㄚˋ ㄅㄛˊ ㄌㄧㄢˊ ㄏㄜˊ ㄉㄚˋ ㄍㄨㄥ ㄍㄨㄛˊ)
United Arab Emirates (UAE)亦作「阿拉伯聯合大公國」

阿剌伯聯合共和國(ㄚ ㄌㄚˋ ㄅㄛˊ ㄌㄧㄢˊ ㄏㄜˊ ㄍㄨㄥˋ ㄏㄜˊ ㄍㄨㄛˊ)
the United Arab Republic (UAR) 亦作「阿拉伯聯合共和國」

阿剌伯數字(ㄚ ㄌㄚˋ ㄅㄛˊ ㄕㄨˋ ㄗˋ)
Arabic numerals 亦作「阿拉伯數字」

阿剌伯人(ㄚ ㄌㄚˋ ㄅㄛˊ ㄖㄣˊ)
an Arab 亦作「阿拉伯人」

阿剌伯文(ㄚ ㄌㄚˋ ㄅㄛˊ ㄨㄣˊ)
Arabic (language) 亦作「阿拉伯文」

阿里山(ㄚ ㄌㄧˇ ㄕㄢ)
Mt. Ali, Taiwan

阿留申群島(ㄚ ㄌㄧㄡˊ ㄕㄣ ㄑㄩㄣˊ ㄉㄠˇ)
the Aleutian Islands

阿聯(ㄚ ㄌㄧㄢˊ)
short for the United Arab Republic (UAR)

阿根廷(ㄚ ㄍㄣ ㄊㄧㄥˊ)
Argentina; the Argentine

阿肯色(ㄚ ㄎㄣˇ ㄙㄜˋ)
the state of Arkansas, U. S. A.

阿基米德(ㄚ ㄐㄧ ㄇㄧˇ ㄉㄜˊ)
Archimedes (287-212 B.C.), Greek physicist, mathematician and inventor

阿基米德原理(ㄚ ㄐㄧ ㄇㄧˇ ㄉㄜˊ ㄩㄢˊ ㄌㄧˇ)
the Archimedean principle (of the lever and of specific gravity)

阿司匹靈or阿斯匹靈(ㄚ ㄙ ㄆㄧˇ ㄌㄧㄥˊ)
aspirin

阿薩姆(ㄚ ㄙㄚˋ ㄇㄨˇ)
Assam, India

阿爾巴尼亞(ㄚ ㄦˇ ㄅㄚ ㄋㄧˊ ㄧㄚˋ)
Albania

阿爾卑斯山(ㄚ ㄦˇ ㄅㄟ ㄙ ㄕㄢ)
the Alps

阿爾泰山(ㄚ ㄦˇ ㄊㄞˋ ㄕㄢ)
the Altai Mountains

阿爾及利亞(ㄚ ㄦˇ ㄐㄧˊ ㄌㄧˋ ㄧㄚˋ)
Algeria

阿爾薩斯(ㄚ ㄦˇ ㄙㄚˋ ㄙ)
Alsace

阿姨(ㄚ ㄧˊ)
①an aunt, one's mother's sister: 這位是我阿姨。This is my aunt. ②one's wife's sister ③a stepmother

【陀】 6595
ㄊㄨㄛˊ two tuó

craggy; rugged terrain

陀螺(ㄊㄨㄛˊ ㄌㄨㄛˊ)
a top: 我小時候喜歡玩陀螺。I liked to spin (or whip) a top in my boyhood.

陀羅尼(ㄊㄨㄛˊ ㄌㄨㄛˊ ㄋㄧˊ)
(Buddhism) *Dharani,* complete in all virtues; able to lay hold of the good so that it cannot be lost, and likewise of the evil so that it cannot arise; magical formulas, or mystic forms of prayer, or spells of the Tantric Order, often in Sanskrit, found in China as early as the third century A. D.

【陂】 6596
1. ㄆㄧˊ pyi pí

1. a reservoir; a water pond
2. a hillside

陂塘(ㄆㄧˊ ㄊㄤˊ)
a pond; a small lake

陂池(ㄆㄧˊ ㄔˊ)
a pond; a small lake; a reservoir

【陂】 6596
2. ㄆㄛ po po

steep and craggy

陂陀(ㄆㄛ ㄊㄨㄛˊ)
(said of dikes, hill lines, etc.) craggy; steep; winding; with ups and downs

【附】 6597
ㄈㄨˋ fuh fù

1. to rely on; to be dependent on; to attach to; to adhere to
2. to attach; to enclose; to send along with; to append; enclosed
3. near or close to
4. to add to; to increase
5. (said of an evil spirit) to be possessed by; to possess

附表(ㄈㄨˋ ㄅㄧㄠˇ)
supporting schedules (or statements)

附匪(ㄈㄨˋ ㄈㄟˇ)
to adhere to the bandits

附帶(ㄈㄨˋ ㄉㄞˋ)
①supplementary②to attach ③in passing

附帶民事訴訟(ㄈㄨˋ ㄉㄞˋ ㄇㄧㄣˊ ㄕˋ ㄙㄨˋ ㄙㄨㄥˋ)
a supplementary civil action (in a criminal lawsuit)

附帶條件(ㄈㄨˋ ㄉㄞˋ ㄊㄧㄠˊ ㄐㄧㄢˋ)
conditions attached to a pledge, promise, etc.

附圖(ㄈㄨˋ ㄊㄨˊ)
an attached map or drawing; a figure

附麗(ㄈㄨˋ ㄌㄧˋ)
to adhere to; to submit to; to follow 亦作「附離」

附錄(ㄈㄨˋ ㄌㄨˋ)
an appendix or annex

附郭(ㄈㄨˋ ㄍㄨㄛ)
near the outer wall of a city

附款(ㄈㄨˋ ㄎㄨㄢˇ)
appendant provisions in a legal document

附和(ㄈㄨˋ ㄏㄜˋ)
to agree without conviction; to repeat what others say; to echo; to chime in: 他附和我的意見。He echoed my views.

附化(ㄈㄨˋ ㄏㄨㄚˋ)
to be assimilated or naturalized

附會(ㄈㄨˋ ㄏㄨㄟˋ)
to twist in making an explanation; to make a forced interpretation; to make a far-fetched comparison

附記(ㄈㄨˋ ㄐㄧˋ)

①to add to; to append to ②a supplement; an appendix
附驥(ㄈㄨˋ ㄐㄧˋ)
(a modest expression) to ride on the coattails of a famed person to success
附加(ㄈㄨˋ ㄐㄧㄚ)
①to add to; to add...to...; to append...to; to attach...to...: 這個合約附加了一項說明。The contract has an explanatory note attached to it. ②supplementary
附加稅(ㄈㄨˋ ㄐㄧㄚ ㄕㄨㄟˋ)
a surtax; additional tax
附加語(ㄈㄨˋ ㄐㄧㄚ ㄩˇ)
an adjunct
附交(ㄈㄨˋ ㄐㄧㄠ)
to hand in or deliver as an attachment
附件(ㄈㄨˋ ㄐㄧㄢˋ)
an enclosure; an accessory; an attachment (of a letter, etc.): 這些是不可缺少的附件。These are indispensable accessories.
附近(ㄈㄨˋ ㄐㄧㄣˋ)
around; nearby; the vicinity: 他來自附近的鄉村。He came from a nearby village.
附註(ㄈㄨˋ ㄓㄨˋ)
remarks; notes
附著(ㄈㄨˋ ㄓㄨㄛˊ)
to adhere to; to stick together: 整日下雨，我們的鞋子附著了汚泥。It had rained all day and the mud adhered to our shoes.
附著力(ㄈㄨˋ ㄓㄨㄛˊ ㄌㄧˋ)
adhesion; adhesive force
附贅懸疣(ㄈㄨˋ ㄓㄨㄟˋ ㄒㄩㄢˊ ㄧㄡˊ)
a superfluity
附設(ㄈㄨˋ ㄕㄜˋ)
to have as an attached institution: 這個大學附設一所中學。There is a middle school attached to the university.
附上(ㄈㄨˋ ㄕㄤˋ)
enclosed herewith: 隨信附上相片一張。A photograph is enclosed herewith.
附屬(ㄈㄨˋ ㄕㄨˇ)
accessory; subordinate; to affiliate with; to be attached to: 這是個附屬子句。It is a subordinate clause.
附屬品(ㄈㄨˋ ㄕㄨˇ ㄆㄧㄣˇ)
accessory items or articles; an adjunct; an accompaniment
附屬公司(ㄈㄨˋ ㄕㄨˇ ㄍㄨㄥ ㄙ)
a sub-company; a subsidiary company
附屬小學(ㄈㄨˋ ㄕㄨˇ ㄒㄧㄠˇ ㄒㄩㄝˊ)or 附小(ㄈㄨˋ ㄒㄧㄠˇ)
a primary school affiliated with an educational institution of higher level; an affiliated elementary school
附屬中學(ㄈㄨˋ ㄕㄨˇ ㄓㄨㄥ ㄒㄩㄝˊ)or 附中(ㄈㄨˋ ㄓㄨㄥ)
a middle (or high) school affiliated with a college or university; an affiliated middle school
附屬幼稚園(ㄈㄨˋ ㄕㄨˇ ㄧㄡˋ ㄓˋ ㄩㄢˊ)
a kindergarten attached to a primary school
附則(ㄈㄨˋ ㄗㄜˊ)
supplementary or additional rules
附耳(ㄈㄨˋ ㄦˇ)
to whisper: 她對我附耳說了些話。She whispered something in my ear.
附益(ㄈㄨˋ ㄧˋ)
added benefit
附議(ㄈㄨˋ ㄧˋ)
to second a motion; to support a proposal
附言(ㄈㄨˋ ㄧㄢˊ)
a postscript (P.S.)
附庸(ㄈㄨˋ ㄩㄥ)
a vassal state; subordinate; a puppet
附庸風雅(ㄈㄨˋ ㄩㄥ ㄈㄥ ㄧㄚˇ)
to try to act or speak like a refined, elegant or sophisticated person when one is not
附庸國(ㄈㄨˋ ㄩㄥ ㄍㄨㄛˊ)
a satellite state; a vassal state or dependant state

【阨】 6598
(阨) ㄜˋ eh è
difficulty

六畫

【陋】 6599
ㄌㄡˋ low lòu
1. narrow and small
2. ugly
3. vile; low; mean; humble
4. ignorant; crude; simple-minded
5. poor (performances, knowledge, etc.); inferior; superficial; shallow
6. stingy; tight-fisted
陋規(ㄌㄡˋ ㄍㄨㄟ)
bad practices
陋見(ㄌㄡˋ ㄐㄧㄢˋ)
vulgar views; shallow views
陋習(ㄌㄡˋ ㄒㄧˊ)
bad habits; corrupt practices
陋巷(ㄌㄡˋ ㄒㄧㄤˋ)
a narrow, dirty alley; slums
陋室(ㄌㄡˋ ㄕˋ)
a crude abode; a humble room; a room totally without decoration
陋儒(ㄌㄡˋ ㄖㄨˊ)
an ignorant scholar; a scholar with little learning
陋俗(ㄌㄡˋ ㄙㄨˊ)
vile customs; vulgar customs

【陌】 6600
ㄇㄛˋ moh mò
1. paths in the rice field: 阡陌縱橫。The paths crisscrossed on a farmland.
2. a road; a street
陌頭(ㄇㄛˋ ㄊㄡˊ)
①a handkerchief used to tie a man's hair in ancient China ②the roadside
陌路(ㄇㄛˋ ㄌㄨˋ)
①paths in the rice field ②a stranger: 我們對他視如陌路。We treat him as a stranger.
陌生(ㄇㄛˋ ㄕㄥ)
unfamiliar; strange; inexperienced
陌生人(ㄇㄛˋ ㄕㄥ ㄖㄣˊ)
a stranger

【降】 6601
1. ㄐㄧㄤˋ jianq jiàng
1. to descend
2. to lower
3. to condescend; to deign
4. to drop; to decline
5. to surrender
降凡(ㄐㄧㄤˋ ㄈㄢˊ)
to come into the world, as in the incarnation of the divine
降福(ㄐㄧㄤˋ ㄈㄨˊ)
to bless; blessings from Heaven: 願上帝降福予你。God bless you!

降低(ㄐㄧㄤˋ ㄉㄧ)
to lower; to fall; to drop: 他降低了聲音說話。He lowered his voice.
降低價格(ㄐㄧㄤˋ ㄉㄧ ㄐㄧㄚˋ ㄍㄜˊ)
marking down prices
降低身分(ㄐㄧㄤˋ ㄉㄧ ㄕㄣ ㄈㄣˋ)
to lower one's social status or standing
降低生產成本(ㄐㄧㄤˋ ㄉㄧ ㄕㄥ ㄔㄢˇ ㄔㄥˊ ㄅㄣˇ)
to reduce the production costs
降臨(ㄐㄧㄤˋ ㄌㄧㄣˊ)
①to come down; to fall: 黑夜漸漸降臨。Night is falling. ②to condescend (to visit)
降落(ㄐㄧㄤˋ ㄌㄨㄛˋ)
①to land; landing; descent; to descend: 該飛機安全降落了。The airplane made a safe landing. ② to drop; to rain down ③as in 跳傘降落—to parachute
降落傘(ㄐㄧㄤˋ ㄌㄨㄛˋ ㄙㄢˇ)
a parachute
降落傘部隊(ㄐㄧㄤˋ ㄌㄨㄛˋ ㄙㄢˇ ㄅㄨˋ ㄉㄨㄟˋ)
paratroopers; paratroop units
降格(ㄐㄧㄤˋ ㄍㄜˊ)
to lower the scale, standard, standing or status
降格以求(ㄐㄧㄤˋ ㄍㄜˊ ㄧˇ ㄑㄧㄡˊ)
to lower the standard and to be satisfied with the next best or less qualified
降級(ㄐㄧㄤˋ ㄐㄧˊ)
to degrade; to demote; to downgrade
降級數(ㄐㄧㄤˋ ㄐㄧˊ ㄕㄨˋ)
a descending series
降價銷售(ㄐㄧㄤˋ ㄐㄧㄚˋ ㄒㄧㄠ ㄕㄡˋ)
mark-down sale
降咎(ㄐㄧㄤˋ ㄐㄧㄡˋ)
to send down disaster or calamity from Heaven
降旗(ㄐㄧㄤˋ ㄑㄧˊ)
to lower the flag
降心相從(ㄐㄧㄤˋ ㄒㄧㄣ ㄒㄧㄤ ㄘㄨㄥˊ)
to subject one's own will to the dictates of others
降祥(ㄐㄧㄤˋ ㄒㄧㄤˊ)or 降祉(ㄐㄧㄤˋ ㄓˇ)
to send down blessings from Heaven; a godsend
降旨(ㄐㄧㄤˋ ㄓˇ)
to issue an imperial decree
降志辱身(ㄐㄧㄤˋ ㄓˋ ㄖㄨˇ ㄕㄣ)
to lower one's aspiration and denigrate oneself
降世(ㄐㄧㄤˋ ㄕˋ)
to come down to the world, as Jesus Christ
降神(ㄐㄧㄤˋ ㄕㄣˊ)
to invite the visit of spirits
降生(ㄐㄧㄤˋ ㄕㄥ)
to be born into the world
降溫(ㄐㄧㄤˋ ㄨㄣ)
①to lower the temperature (as in a workshop) ②to drop in temperature
降雨量(ㄐㄧㄤˋ ㄩˇ ㄌㄧㄤˋ)
rainfall

【降】 6601 2. ㄒㄧㄤˊ shyang xiáng

1. to surrender; to submit to
2. to bring to terms; to conquer; to subjugate

降表(ㄒㄧㄤˊ ㄅㄧㄠˇ)
a letter of surrender or capitulation
降伏(ㄒㄧㄤˊ ㄈㄨˊ)
① to bring to terms; to conquer; to subjugate ② to break in; to tame: 他降伏了一頭野牛。He broke in a wild ox.
降服(ㄒㄧㄤˊ ㄈㄨˊ)or 降附(ㄒㄧㄤˊ ㄈㄨˋ)
① to surrender and give allegiance to the new master ②to bring to terms; to subdue: 他降服了敵人。He subdued his enemies.
降龍伏虎(ㄒㄧㄤˊ ㄌㄨㄥˊ ㄈㄨˊ ㄏㄨˇ)
①to subjugate dragons and tigers with magic—to overcome powerful adversaries ②(Taoism) to conquer one's passions
降將(ㄒㄧㄤˊ ㄐㄧㄤˋ)
a general who has come over from the enemy camp; a general who has surrendered
降旗(ㄒㄧㄤˊ ㄑㄧˊ)
the white flag signifying surrender
降妖(ㄒㄧㄤˊ ㄧㄠ)
to subjugate evil spirits

【限】 6602 ㄒㄧㄢˋ shiann xiàn

1. a boundary; a line
2. a doorsill or threshold
3. limits; restriction; to limit or restrict: 我的能力有限。My powers are limited.
4. to specify; to fix

限定(ㄒㄧㄢˋ ㄉㄧㄥˋ)
to fix (a deadline, time limit, etc.); to specify (qualifications of a person or merchandise); to limit
限度(ㄒㄧㄢˋ ㄉㄨˋ)
limits; limitation; degree (of what one can take): 一個人的忍耐是有限度的。There is a limit to one's patience.
限量(ㄒㄧㄢˋ ㄌㄧㄤˋ)
limits; limitation; a boundary; to restrict or measure
限令(ㄒㄧㄢˋ ㄌㄧㄥˋ)
to order somebody to do something within a certain time
限價(ㄒㄧㄢˋ ㄐㄧㄚˋ)
price control; a price fixed under a government specified ceiling
限交本人(ㄒㄧㄢˋ ㄐㄧㄠ ㄅㄣˇ ㄖㄣˊ)
delivery to the addressee in person
限期(ㄒㄧㄢˋ ㄑㄧˊ)
①a time limit; a deadline: 限期已屆。The time limit has been reached. ② within a definite time
限制(ㄒㄧㄢˋ ㄓˋ)
limits; limitations; to restrict; restrictions; to confine something within certain limits: 車子進口設有限制。There is a limitation on car imports.
限制行爲能力人(ㄒㄧㄢˋ ㄓˋ ㄒㄧㄥˊ ㄨㄟˊ ㄋㄥˊ ㄌㄧˋ ㄖㄣˊ)
(law) a person with a limited disposing capacity
限制性(ㄒㄧㄢˋ ㄓˋ ㄒㄧㄥˋ)
restricted; restrictive
限制生產(ㄒㄧㄢˋ ㄓˋ ㄕㄥ ㄔㄢˇ)
to control production; controlled production
限時(ㄒㄧㄢˋ ㄕˊ)
to fix or set the time; to set a time limit or deadline
限時專送(ㄒㄧㄢˋ ㄕˊ ㄓㄨㄢ ㄙㄨㄥˋ)
(Chinese postal service) prompt delivery
限額(ㄒㄧㄢˋ ㄜˊ)

a quota; the maximum number or amount allowed

限外(ㄒㄧㄢˋ ㄨㄞˋ)
beyond the specified limit (as the issuance of bank notes, etc.)

限於(ㄒㄧㄢˋ ㄩˊ)
(in writing, etc.) owing to the limitation of; due to (regulations, etc.): 他的活動限於教育界。He confined his activities in educational circles.

【陔】 6603
ㄍㄞ gai gāi
1. steps; grades
2. ridges between plots of farm land

七畫

【陘】 6604
ㄒㄧㄥˊ shyng xíng
a defile; a gorge; a deep valley

【陛】 6605
ㄅㄧˋ bih bì
wide and high steps in the palace; the steps to the throne

陛戟(ㄅㄧˋ ㄐㄧˇ)
imperial guards armed with spears

陛見(ㄅㄧˋ ㄐㄧㄢˋ)
to have an audience with the emperor

陛下(ㄅㄧˋ ㄒㄧㄚˋ)
Your Majesty; His or Her Majesty

陛辭(ㄅㄧˋ ㄘˊ)
to leave the capital after bidding the emperor goodbye in audience

陛衞(ㄅㄧˋ ㄨㄟˋ)
the imperial guard

【陞】 6606
ㄕㄥ sheng shēng
1. to ascend; to promote; to hoist; to rise; to elevate
2. a Chinese family name

【陟】 6607
ㄓˋ jyh zhì
1. to mount; to ascend
2. to advance; to elevate; to promote

陟罰(ㄓˋ ㄈㄚˊ)
to promote and demote; to reward and punish

陟降(ㄓˋ ㄐㄧㄤˋ)
to promote and demote

陟黜(ㄓˋ ㄔㄨˋ)
to promote or demote; to promote or dismiss

【陡】 6608
ㄉㄡˇ doou dǒu
1. suddenly; abruptly
2. steep; precipitous: 這坡很陡。The slope is very steep.

陡壁(ㄉㄡˇ ㄅㄧˋ)
a steep bank; a precipitous cliff

陡坡(ㄉㄡˇ ㄆㄛ)
a steep slope

陡頓(ㄉㄡˇ ㄉㄨㄣˋ)
suddenly; abruptly

陡覺(ㄉㄡˇ ㄐㄩㄝˊ)
to feel all of a sudden

陡峭(ㄉㄡˇ ㄑㄧㄠˋ)
steep; precipitous

陡然(ㄉㄡˇ ㄖㄢˊ)
suddenly; abruptly: 橋陡然塌下。The bridge fell suddenly.

【院】 6609
ㄩㄢˋ yuann yuàn
1. a courtyard; a yard
2. a designation for certain government offices and public places
3. short for the Executive Yuan, Legislative Yuan, Examination Yuan, Judicial Yuan, or Control Yuan

院本(ㄩㄢˋ ㄅㄣˇ)
the plays staged at brothels during the Mongol and Tungusic era

院落(ㄩㄢˋ ㄌㄨㄛˋ)
a courtyard; a compound

院際比賽(ㄩㄢˋ ㄐㄧˋ ㄅㄧˇ ㄙㄞˋ)
a competition between colleges; an intercollegiate competition

院牆(ㄩㄢˋ ㄑㄧㄤˊ)
the wall that surrounds a house

院轄市(ㄩㄢˋ ㄒㄧㄚˊ ㄕˋ)
a municipality under the direct jurisdiction of the Executive Yuan; a special municipality

院長(ㄩㄢˋ ㄓㄤˇ)
the dean of a college or court of law; the director of a hospital, museum, etc.; the president of Academia Sinica or one of the five Yuan under the Chinese government system (including the premier)

院士(ㄩㄢˋ ㄕˋ)
a member of Academia Sinica, or an academician

院子(ㄩㄢˋ ·ㄗ) or 院兒 (ㄩㄚˋㄦ)
a yard; a courtyard: 院子裡種了一些玫瑰。There are some roses in the courtyard.

院宇(ㄩㄢˋ ㄩˇ)
the house and the yard

【陣】 6610
ㄓㄣˋ jenn zhèn
1. a column or row of troops; the army; the rank and file
2. to battle; to go to war; to fight at the front; the battlefield; battle array (or formation)
3. anything that occurs in a certain duration or spell of time (as rain, wind, business, etc.): 他感到一陣劇痛。He felt a gust of pain.

陣歿(ㄓㄣˋ ㄇㄛˋ)
to die on the battlefield; to be killed in action 亦作「陣亡」

陣法(ㄓㄣˋ ㄈㄚˇ)
tactical deployment of troops; the plan of a campaign

陣地(ㄓㄣˋ ㄉㄧˋ)
a (military) position: 他們潛入陣地。They slipped into the position.

陣地戰(ㄓㄣˋ ㄉㄧˋ ㄓㄢˋ)
trench warfare; position warfare

陣圖(ㄓㄣˋ ㄊㄨˊ)
a map showing the deployment of troops

陣痛(ㄓㄣˋ ㄊㄨㄥˋ)
labor pangs; pangs of childbirth; throes; pains that occur at intervals

陣脚(ㄓㄣˋ ㄐㄧㄠˇ)
① a front line ② position; situation; circumstances: 我們必須穩住陣脚。We have to secure our position.

陣前(ㄓㄣˋ ㄑㄧㄢˊ)
on the battlefield: 他死在陣前。He died on the battlefield.

陣前起義(ㄓㄣˋ ㄑㄧㄢˊ ㄑㄧˇ ㄧˋ)

(said of enemy troops) to defect in the course of a battle
陣線(ㄓㄣˋ ㄒㄧㄢˋ)
line of battle
陣陣(ㄓㄣˋ ㄓㄣˋ)
intermittently; intermittent (rains, winds, pain, etc.); now and again; at intervals; repeatedly; by fits and starts; gusts: 風陣陣吹。The wind blew in gusts.
陣勢(ㄓㄣˋ ㄕˋ)
order of battle; battle array (or formation)
陣首(ㄓㄣˋ ㄕㄡˇ)
the forward echelons of combat troops in battle
陣容(ㄓㄣˋ ㄖㄨㄥˊ)
① the appearance of a military deployment; the layout of troops ② the lineup of a cabinet; the composition of a sports team, an organization, etc. ③ the cast of a movie
陣容整齊(ㄓㄣˋ ㄖㄨㄥˊ ㄓㄥˇ ㄑㄧˊ)
① a neat or appropriate layout of troops; a flawless deployment ② (said of a movie cast, sports team, etc.) Everyone is a top choice. 或 There is no second-rater among them.
陣子(ㄓㄣˋ ·ㄗ)
a spell of
陣營(ㄓㄣˋ ㄧㄥˊ)
a camp; an encampment; a barracks
陣亡(ㄓㄣˋ ㄨㄤˊ)
to be killed in action
陣亡將士紀念碑(ㄓㄣˋ ㄨㄤˊ ㄐㄧㄤˋ ㄕˋ ㄐㄧˋ ㄋㄧㄢˋ ㄅㄟ)
a monument in honor of servicemen killed in action
陣雨(ㄓㄣˋ ㄩˇ)
occasional drizzle; showers (especially in summer)
陣雲(ㄓㄣˋ ㄩㄣˊ)
dense clouds

【除】 6611
ㄔㄨˊ chwu chú
1. (mathematics) to divide; division; divisible
2. to remove; to rid of; to wipe out: 他們消除了疑慮。They removed all doubts.
3. to be appointed to an official rank or office
4. to subtract; to deduct
5. aside from; besides; except; unless: 除了李小姐，我們都去了。We all went except Miss Lee.
6. to change or turn, as a new year
除拜(ㄔㄨˊ ㄅㄞˋ)
to be appointed to an office
除暴安良(ㄔㄨˊ ㄅㄠˋ ㄢ ㄌㄧㄤˊ)
to get rid of lawless elements and protect the good
除弊(ㄔㄨˊ ㄅㄧˋ)
to remove evil practices or abuses
除病(ㄔㄨˊ ㄅㄧㄥˋ)
① to get rid of a disease ② to get rid of a bad habit, practice, etc.
除不盡(ㄔㄨˊ ·ㄅㄨ ㄐㄧㄣˋ)
indivisible
除刨淨剩(ㄔㄨˊ ㄆㄠˊ ㄐㄧㄥˋ ㄕㄥˋ)
leftovers; remnants
除貧(ㄔㄨˊ ㄆㄧㄣˊ)
to save the poor; to get rid of poverty
除名(ㄔㄨˊ ㄇㄧㄥˊ)
to dismiss; to strike one's name off the list; to expel
除目(ㄔㄨˊ ㄇㄨˋ)
written order of appointment
除法(ㄔㄨˊ ㄈㄚˇ)
(mathematics) division
除非(ㄔㄨˊ ㄈㄟ)
unless: 若欲人不知，除非己莫爲。If you don't want people to know, you'd better not do it.
除服(ㄔㄨˊ ㄈㄨˊ)
to take off the mourning garment at the end of the mourning period
除道(ㄔㄨˊ ㄉㄠˋ)
to start building a road
除掉(ㄔㄨˊ ㄉㄧㄠˋ)
to remove; to get rid of (prejudices, obstacles, etc.)
除汰(ㄔㄨˊ ㄊㄞˋ)
to remove; to get rid of
除了(ㄔㄨˊ ·ㄌㄜ)
① except that; except ② aside from; besides
除靈(ㄔㄨˊ ㄌㄧㄥˊ)
to burn the spirit tablet after completing the mass for the deceased
除根(ㄔㄨˊ ㄍㄣ)
to root out; to uproot; to dig up the roots; to cure once and for all
除官(ㄔㄨˊ ㄍㄨㄢ)
to be formally appointed to an office
除害(ㄔㄨˊ ㄏㄞˋ)
to get rid of evils, bad habits or practices or evil persons
除號(ㄔㄨˊ ㄏㄠˋ)
(mathematics) the sign of division "÷"
除籍(ㄔㄨˊ ㄐㄧˊ)
to strike one's name off the list; to disenroll; to dismiss; to expel
除舊布新(ㄔㄨˊ ㄐㄧㄡˋ ㄅㄨˋ ㄒㄧㄣ)
to remove the old and introduce the new; to replace the old with the new
除菊(ㄔㄨˊ ㄐㄩˊ)
the pyrethrum
除清(ㄔㄨˊ ㄑㄧㄥ)
to clear up
除去(ㄔㄨˊ ㄑㄩˋ)
to remove; to get rid of; to except: 他們將他從名單上除去。They excepted him from the list.
除却(ㄔㄨˊ ㄑㄩㄝˋ)
① to remove or root out ② unless
除夕(ㄔㄨˊ ㄒㄧˋ) or 除夜(ㄔㄨˊ ㄧㄝˋ)
Lunar New Year's Eve
除邪(ㄔㄨˊ ㄒㄧㄝˊ)
to do away with evil (spirits, or influences); to exorcise
除臭劑(ㄔㄨˊ ㄔㄡˋ ㄐㄧˋ)
deodorants
除塵器(ㄔㄨˊ ㄔㄣˊ ㄑㄧˋ)
a dust remover
除濕機(ㄔㄨˊ ㄕ ㄐㄧ)
a dehumidifier
除數(ㄔㄨˊ ㄕㄨˋ)
a divisor
除災(ㄔㄨˊ ㄗㄞ)
to save from misfortune or disaster
除罪(ㄔㄨˊ ㄗㄨㄟˋ)
to remit sin or punishment
除此之外(ㄔㄨˊ ㄘˇ ㄓ ㄨㄞˋ)

besides this (or these); in addition: 除此之外，我什麼都不要。I want nothing besides this.

除草(ㄔㄨˊ ㄘㄠˇ)
to weed (in farming); to mow grass or cut weeds: 他用除草機除草。He mowed the grass with the lawn mower.

〔阜部〕

除喪(ㄔㄨˊ ㄙㄤ)
to remove the mourning garments at the end of the mourning period

除惡務盡(ㄔㄨˊ ㄜˋ ㄨˋ ㄐㄧㄣˋ)
Evil must be completely eradicated. 或 One must be thorough in exterminating an evil.

除以(ㄔㄨˊ ㄧˇ)
(a number) to be divided by

除役(ㄔㄨˊ ㄧˋ)
to have one's name struck off the reserve list when he reaches the specified age

除外(ㄔㄨˊ ㄨㄞˋ)
except; to except: 我當然把你除外。Of course I except you.

除月(ㄔㄨˊ ㄩㄝˋ)
the last (12th) moon of the lunar year

【陝】 6612
ㄕㄢˇ shaan shǎn

1. short for Shensi Province
2. a Chinese family name

陝西(ㄕㄢˇ ㄒㄧ)
Shensi Province

八畫

【陪】 6613
ㄆㄟˊ peir péi

1. to accompany; to keep company: 請陪我散步。Please accompany me on my walk.
2. same as 賠—to make up for; to compensate
3. to assist

陪拜(ㄆㄟˊ ㄅㄞˋ)
to accompany or follow another in making bows or kneeling

陪伴(ㄆㄟˊ ㄅㄢˋ)
to keep company; to accompany: 他陪伴我。He kept me company.

陪不是(ㄆㄟˊ ㄅㄨˋ ·ㄕ)
to apologize; to ask forgiveness

陪房(ㄆㄟˊ ㄈㄤˊ)
(in former times) maids that accompanied the bride to her husband's house and stayed there to serve her

陪都(ㄆㄟˊ ㄉㄨ)
an alternate capital; a secondary capital; a provisional capital 亦作「陪京」

陪同(ㄆㄟˊ ㄊㄨㄥˊ)
to accompany

陪禮(ㄆㄟˊ ㄌㄧˇ)
to ask forgiveness; to apologize

陪客
①(ㄆㄟˊ ·ㄎㄜ) guests invited to keep the guest of honor company
②(ㄆㄟˊ ㄎㄜˋ) ⓐ to receive guests; to keep guests company ⓑ (said of girls in gay establishments) to attend on patrons

陪話(ㄆㄟˊ ㄏㄨㄚˋ)
to apologize

陪嫁(ㄆㄟˊ ㄐㄧㄚˋ)
the dowry given to a daughter on her marriage

陪酒(ㄆㄟˊ ㄐㄧㄡˇ)
(said of a bar girl, etc.) to accompany a patron in drinking

陪京(ㄆㄟˊ ㄐㄧㄥ)
a secondary capital; a provisional capital; an alternate capital 亦作「陪都」

陪小心(ㄆㄟˊ ㄒㄧㄠˇ ㄒㄧㄣ)
to talk and act obsequiously in order to placate or please another

陪笑(ㄆㄟˊ ㄒㄧㄠˋ)or陪笑臉(ㄆㄟˊ ㄒㄧㄠˋ ㄌㄧㄢˇ)
to put up a smiling face in order to please or placate someone

陪襯(ㄆㄟˊ ㄔㄣˋ)
to serve as a background in order to bring out the subject with greater brilliance; to serve as a prop (as in photography)

陪侍(ㄆㄟˊ ㄕˋ)
to assist in attendance

陪審(ㄆㄟˊ ㄕㄣˇ)
① to act (or serve) as an assessor (in a law case) ② to serve on a jury

陪審團(ㄆㄟˊ ㄕㄣˇ ㄊㄨㄢˊ)
the jury

陪審制度(ㄆㄟˊ ㄕㄣˇ ㄓˋ ㄉㄨˋ)
the jury system

陪審員(ㄆㄟˊ ㄕㄣˇ ㄩㄢˊ)
a juror member of the jury; a juror; a juryman; a jurywoman

陪葬(ㄆㄟˊ ㄗㄤˋ)
to bury (a person or things) along with the deceased

陪罪(ㄆㄟˊ ㄗㄨㄟˋ)
to ask forgiveness; to apologize

陪送(ㄆㄟˊ ㄙㄨㄥˋ)
the dowry given to a daughter on her marriage

陪位(ㄆㄟˊ ㄨㄟˋ)
to be seated beside the emperor

【陬】 6614
ㄗㄡ tzou zōu

1. a corner; a nook
2. foothills
3. a frontier village where people live together
4. the first month of the lunar year

陬落(ㄗㄡ ㄌㄨㄛˋ)
a frontier village where people live together

陬月(ㄗㄡ ㄩㄝˋ)
the first month of the lunar year

【陰】 6615
1. ㄧㄣ in yīn

1. negative (as opposite to positive, as electricity)
2. feminine; female
3. cloudy; dark
4. shady
5. secret
6. the back side
7. the north side of a mountain
8. the south side of a stream
9. reproductive organs of both sexes
10. Hades; hell
11. cunning and crafty
12. to injure another in a clandestine manner
13. time
14. a Chinese family name

陰部(ㄧㄣ ㄅㄨˋ)
(said of the human body) the private part

陰平(ㄧㄣ ㄆㄧㄥˊ)
①(Chinese phonetics) the first tone ② name of an ancient place in Kansu Province (甘肅省)

陰霾(ㄧㄣ ㄇㄞˊ)
haze; thin mist

陰毛(ㄧㄣ ㄇㄠˊ)
the hair at the private part; pubes

陰謀(ㄧㄣ ㄇㄡˊ)
a conspiracy; a plot; a secret scheme

陰謀詭計(ㄧㄣ ㄇㄡˊ ㄍㄨㄟˇ ㄐㄧˋ)
dark schemes and tricks; schemes and intrigues

陰風(ㄧㄣ ㄈㄥ)
① chilly winds ② winds that often precede the appearance of a ghost

陰伏(ㄧㄣ ㄈㄨˊ)
① one's sins unknown to others ② to ambush secretly

陰府(ㄧㄣ ㄈㄨˇ)
the nether world; Hades

陰阜(ㄧㄣ ㄈㄨˋ)
the mound of the vulva

陰德(ㄧㄣ ㄉㄜˊ)
one's unpublicized good deeds

陰道(ㄧㄣ ㄉㄠˋ)
① the vagina ② a shaded road ③ the "subordinate ways"—the ways of subjects to the king, of children to parents and of wife to husband

陰地(ㄧㄣ ㄉㄧˋ)
① a graveyard ② a place where sunshine cannot reach

陰電(ㄧㄣ ㄉㄧㄢˋ)
negative electricity

陰毒(ㄧㄣ ㄉㄨˊ)
mean, cunning, etc. in a clandestine way

陰天(ㄧㄣ ㄊㄧㄢ)
a cloudy day

陰囊(ㄧㄣ ㄋㄤˊ)
the scrotum

陰冷(ㄧㄣ ㄌㄥˇ)
①(said of weather) gloomy and cold; raw ②(said of a person's look) somber; glum

陰離子(ㄧㄣ ㄌㄧˊ ˙ㄗ)
a negative ion

陰曆(ㄧㄣ ㄌㄧˋ)
the lunar calendar

陰涼處(ㄧㄣ ㄌㄧㄤˊ ㄔㄨˋ)
a shaded, cool place: 我們找個陰涼處歇歇吧！Let's have a rest in the shade.

陰靈(ㄧㄣ ㄌㄧㄥˊ)
the spirits of the deceased

陰溝(ㄧㄣ ㄍㄡ)
① a covered drain; a sewer ② the vagina

陰乾(ㄧㄣ ㄍㄢ)
to be placed in the shade to dry; to dry in the shade

陰官(ㄧㄣ ㄍㄨㄢ)
① reigning authorities in Hades ② the rain god

陰功(ㄧㄣ ㄍㄨㄥ)
one's unpublicized good deeds or virtues

陰核(ㄧㄣ ㄏㄜˊ)
the clitoris

陰戶(ㄧㄣ ㄏㄨˋ)
the female reproductive organ; the vagina

陰晦(ㄧㄣ ㄏㄨㄟˋ)
shady; dark; dismal

陰魂(ㄧㄣ ㄏㄨㄣˊ)
the spirits of the dead

陰魂不散(ㄧㄣ ㄏㄨㄣˊ ㄅㄨˋ ㄙㄢˋ)
The soul (or spirit) refuses to leave.

陰極(ㄧㄣ ㄐㄧˊ)
the cathode; the negative pole

陰間(ㄧㄣ ㄐㄧㄢ)
Hades; the shades; the underworld

陰莖(ㄧㄣ ㄐㄧㄥ)
the penis

陰譴(ㄧㄣ ㄑㄧㄢˇ)
punishment meted out by the hands of God

陰險(ㄧㄣ ㄒㄧㄢˇ)
cunning; crafty; deceitful; sinister: 他爲人陰險毒辣。He was sinister and ruthless.

陰性(ㄧㄣ ㄒㄧㄥˋ)
① negative ② female

陰性反應(ㄧㄣ ㄒㄧㄥˋ ㄈㄢˇ ㄧㄥˋ)
negative reaction

陰宅(ㄧㄣ ㄓㄞˊ)
a graveyard 參看「陽宅」

陰著兒(ㄧㄣ ㄓㄠ ㄦ)
a clandestine and vicious move

陰沈(ㄧㄣ ㄔㄣˊ)
① gloomy (sky); overcast; somber; cloudy; clouded: 整個下午天都是陰沈的。The sky was cloudy all afternoon. ② quiet and designing (persons)

陰脣(ㄧㄣ ㄔㄨㄣˊ)
the labia

陰事(ㄧㄣ ㄕˋ)
① secrets ② the affairs between the emperor and his concubines

陰室(ㄧㄣ ㄕˋ)
①one's private quarter; one's bedroom ② an underground cellar for storage of ice

陰山(ㄧㄣ ㄕㄢ)
the Yin Mountains

陰曹地府(ㄧㄣ ㄘㄠˊ ㄉㄧˋ ㄈㄨˇ)
Hades

陰錯陽差(ㄧㄣ ㄘㄨㄛˋ ㄧㄤˊ ㄔㄚ)
due to all sorts of accidental mishaps

陰司(ㄧㄣ ㄙ)
officials in Hades

陰私(ㄧㄣ ㄙ)
personal secrets

陰森(ㄧㄣ ㄙㄣ)
gloomy; gruesome; ghastly: 那是個陰森的樹林。That is a gloomy forest.

陰森森(ㄧㄣ ㄙㄣ ㄙㄣ)
gloomy; weird; ominous

陰惡(ㄧㄣ ㄜˋ)
undiscovered evil deeds

陰暗(ㄧㄣ ㄢˋ)
dim; dark; gloomy; overcast

陰翳(ㄧㄣ ㄧˋ)
shady; dark; gloomy

陰陰沈沈(ㄧㄣ ㄧㄣ ㄔㄣˊ ㄔㄣˊ)
gloomy; dusky; dreary: 天空陰陰沈沈地。It's a gloomy sky.

陰陽(ㄧㄣ ㄧㄤˊ)
(Chinese philosophy, medicine, etc.) *yin* (shade) and *yang* (light), the two opposing principles in nature, the former feminine and negative, the latter masculine and positive

陰陽怪氣(ㄧㄣ ㄧㄤˊ ㄍㄨㄞˋ ㄑㄧˋ)
① to act or speak in an odd or queer manner ② eccentric; queer

陰陽家(ㄧㄣ ㄧㄤˊ ㄐㄧㄚ)
① a geomancer; a sorcerer; an astrologer ② the Yin-

〔阜部〕

Yang School (in the Epoch of Warring States, 475-221B.C.)

陰陽人(ㄧㄣ ㄧㄤˊ ㄖㄣˊ)
a hermaphrodite

陰影(ㄧㄣ ㄧㄥˇ)
shades; shadows

陰文(ㄧㄣ ㄨㄣˊ)
incised inscriptions 亦作「陰識」

陰紋(ㄧㄣ ㄨㄣˊ)
an internal or female screw

陰雨(ㄧㄣ ㄩˇ)
cloudy and rainy; overcast and rainy: 連日陰雨不斷。It has been cloudy and drizzly day after day.

陰鬱(ㄧㄣ ㄩˋ)
gloomy; dismal; depressed: 他心情陰鬱。He felt depressed.

陰雲(ㄧㄣ ㄩㄣˊ)
dark clouds; rain clouds

【陰】 6615
2.(蔭) ㄧㄣˋ yinn yìn
shaded by trees

【陲】 6616
ㄔㄨㄟˊ chwei chuí
a border; a frontier

【陳】 6617
1. ㄔㄣˊ chern chén

1. a Chinese family name
2. to arrange; to display; to spread out
3. to tell, state, or narrate; to explain
4. old; stale; preserved for a long time
5. name of a state in the Epoch of Spring and Autumn
6. name of a dynasty (557-589)
7. to make public

陳編(ㄔㄣˊ ㄅㄧㄢ)
books authored by ancient writers

陳兵(ㄔㄣˊ ㄅㄧㄥ)
to mass troops; to deploy troops: 他們陳兵邊境。They are massing troops along the border.

陳病(ㄔㄣˊ ㄅㄧㄥˋ)
an old or chronic disease

陳皮梅(ㄔㄣˊ ㄆㄧˊ ㄇㄟˊ)
sugar preserved prunes

陳平(ㄔㄣˊ ㄆㄧㄥˊ)
Chen Ping, a strategist who helped Liu Pang (劉邦) found the Han Dynasty

陳墨(ㄔㄣˊ ㄇㄛˋ)
an old inkstick—considered to be precious

陳米(ㄔㄣˊ ㄇㄧˇ)
old rice

陳明(ㄔㄣˊ ㄇㄧㄥˊ)
to state clearly: 證人將事實陳明了。The witness stated the facts very clearly.

陳腐(ㄔㄣˊ ㄈㄨˇ)
old or hackneyed (expressions, etc.); stale (food or fruit): "潔白似雪"是個陳腐的比喻。"White as snow" is a hackneyed comparison.

陳那(ㄔㄣˊ ㄋㄚˋ)
Dignaga, circa A. D. 500 or 550, a great Buddhist logician and founder of the new logic

陳年(ㄔㄣˊ ㄋㄧㄢˊ)
(wine, etc.) of many years' standing

陳年老酒(ㄔㄣˊ ㄋㄧㄢˊ ㄌㄠˇ ㄐㄧㄡˇ)
alcoholic drinks that have been preserved for a long time; aged wine

陳列(ㄔㄣˊ ㄌㄧㄝˋ)
to arrange and display; to set out; to exhibit: 她們在陳列出售的貨物。They're displaying goods for sale.

陳列品(ㄔㄣˊ ㄌㄧㄝˋ ㄆㄧㄣˇ)
articles on display; exhibits

陳列所(ㄔㄣˊ ㄌㄧㄝˋ ㄙㄨㄛˇ)
an exhibition hall; a display room

陳琳(ㄔㄣˊ ㄌㄧㄣˊ)
Chen Lin, a writer of the Eastern Han Dynasty

陳糧(ㄔㄣˊ ㄌㄧㄤˊ)
old grain

陳穀(ㄔㄣˊ ㄍㄨˇ)
rice harvested in the previous year

陳穀子爛芝蔴(ㄔㄣˊ ㄍㄨˇ ·ㄗ ㄌㄢˋ ㄓ ·ㄇㄚ)
(figuratively) petty and stale gossip

陳規(ㄔㄣˊ ㄍㄨㄟ)
out-of-date conventions

陳後主(ㄔㄣˊ ㄏㄡˋ ㄓㄨˇ)
Chen Shu-pao (陳叔寶), 553-604, the last monarch of the Chen Dynasty, noted for his poems and debauchery

陳貨(ㄔㄣˊ ㄏㄨㄛˋ)
old goods; goods from old stock

陳迹(ㄔㄣˊ ㄐㄧ)
relics; vestiges; things of the past; an old trace

陳酒(ㄔㄣˊ ㄐㄧㄡˇ)
old wine: 陳酒香醇。Old wine is fragrant and good.

陳舊(ㄔㄣˊ ㄐㄧㄡˋ)
old; worn-out; outmoded; obsolete; shabby: 它是個陳舊的觀念。It is an outmoded idea.

陳腔濫調(ㄔㄣˊ ㄑㄧㄤ ㄌㄢˋ ㄉㄧㄠˋ)
hackneyed expressions; clichés; corny statements

陳情(ㄔㄣˊ ㄑㄧㄥˊ)
to give a full statement or account of a situation, etc.

陳請(ㄔㄣˊ ㄑㄧㄥˇ)
to state and plead

陳寫(ㄔㄣˊ ㄒㄧㄝˇ)
to narrate; to describe

陳陳相因(ㄔㄣˊ ㄔㄣˊ ㄒㄧㄤ ㄧㄣ)
writing without new ideas; to copy or follow precedents, old practices, etc.

陳誠(ㄔㄣˊ ㄔㄥˊ)
Chen Cheng, 1897-1965, architect of land reform in Taiwan

陳屍(ㄔㄣˊ ㄕ)
to exhibit or expose a corpse

陳事(ㄔㄣˊ ㄕˋ)
things or happenings of the past; old affairs

陳設(ㄔㄣˊ ㄕㄜˋ)
to display; to decorate; to exhibit; to set out; to furnish (especially interior)

陳紹(ㄔㄣˊ ㄕㄠˋ)
the old Shaohsing wine (紹興酒)

陳壽(ㄔㄣˊ ㄕㄡˋ)
Chen Shou, a scholar of the Tsin Dynasty and author of *The History of the Three Kingdoms* (三國志)

陳述(ㄔㄣˊ ㄕㄨˋ)
to tell; to narrate; to state: 請陳述你的見解。Please state your views.

陳說(ㄔㄣˊ ㄕㄨㄛ)or 陳詞(ㄔㄣˊ ㄘˊ)
to state; to explain

陳訴(ㄔㄣˊ ㄙㄨˋ)
to state; to plead

陳義甚高(ㄔㄣˋ ㄧˋ ㄕㄣˋ ㄍㄠ)
with lofty ideals
陳言(ㄔㄣˊ ㄧㄢˊ)
hackneyed or stale expressions
陳圓圓(ㄔㄣˊ ㄩㄢˊ ㄩㄢˊ)
a concubine of General Wu San-kuei (吳三桂) of the Ming Dynasty, popularly considered a traitor who asked for military assistance from Ching troops to fight rebel troops

【陳】 6617
2.(陣) ㄓㄣˋ jenn zhèn
tactical deployment of troops

【陴】 6618
ㄆㄧˊ pyi pí
a parapet on a city wall

【陵】 6619
ㄌㄧㄥˊ ling líng
1. a high mound
2. the tomb of an emperor; a mausoleum
3. to offend; to insult; to outrage; to abuse
4. to usurp
5. to climb; to scale
6. a Chinese family name
陵廟(ㄌㄧㄥˊ ㄇㄧㄠˋ)
the tomb and ancestral shrine
陵墓(ㄌㄧㄥˊ ㄇㄨˋ)
a tomb; a grave; a mausoleum
陵替(ㄌㄧㄥˊ ㄊㄧˋ)
to deteriorate; to fall into decadence (usually said of law and order, or moral standards)
陵轢(ㄌㄧㄥˊ ㄌㄧˋ)
①to encroach upon each other; to infringe ②to jockey for position
陵谷(ㄌㄧㄥˊ ㄍㄨˇ)
high banks and deep valleys—changes of worldly affairs; ups and downs; vicissitudes
陵居(ㄌㄧㄥˊ ㄐㄩ)
to live on the highland
陵丘(ㄌㄧㄥˊ ㄑㄧㄡ)
a grave or tomb as big as a high mound
陵寢(ㄌㄧㄥˊ ㄑㄧㄣˇ)
the tomb of an emperor or king; a mausoleum
陵遲 or 凌遲(ㄌㄧㄥˊ ㄔˊ)
①to deteriorate; to fall into decadence ②(in ancient China) to execute a criminal after cutting off his limbs
陵夷(ㄌㄧㄥˊ ㄧˊ)
to deteriorate; to decay
陵雨(ㄌㄧㄥˊ ㄩˇ)
storms; torrential rains
陵園(ㄌㄧㄥˊ ㄩㄢˊ)
the tomb of an emperor; an imperial mausoleum; a tomb surrounded by a park; a cemetery

【陶】 6620
1. ㄊㄠˊ taur táo
1. to make pottery or earthenware; pottery or earthenware
2. happy; joyful
3. to move and influence a person
4. a Chinese family name
陶唐氏(ㄊㄠˊ ㄊㄤˊ ㄕˋ)
another name of Yao the Great (堯)
陶土(ㄊㄠˊ ㄊㄨˇ)
pot earth; pottery clay; potter's clay; kaolin
陶侃(ㄊㄠˊ ㄎㄢˇ)
Tao Kan (259-334), a great minister of the Tsin Dynasty
陶化(ㄊㄠˊ ㄏㄨㄚˋ)
to move, influence and mold (a person)
陶匠(ㄊㄠˊ ㄐㄧㄤˋ)
a pottery maker; a potter 亦作「陶人」
陶器(ㄊㄠˊ ㄑㄧˋ)
pottery; earthenware
陶潛(ㄊㄠˊ ㄑㄧㄢˊ)
Tao Chien (365-427), one of China's great poets 亦作「陶令」 or「陶淵明」
陶情(ㄊㄠˊ ㄑㄧㄥˊ)
to feel pleased and at ease with the world
陶犬瓦雞(ㄊㄠˊ ㄑㄩㄢˇ ㄨㄚˇ ㄐㄧ)
(literally) pottery dogs and chickens—useless things
陶朱公(ㄊㄠˊ ㄓㄨ ㄍㄨㄥ)
another name of Fan Li (范蠡), one of the richest men in Chinese history
陶鑄(ㄊㄠˊ ㄓㄨˋ)
to educate and mold persons of talent 亦作「陶甄」or「陶鎔」
陶然(ㄊㄠˊ ㄖㄢˊ)
happy; cheerful; joyous
陶染(ㄊㄠˊ ㄖㄢˇ)
to move, influence and mold (people)
陶醉(ㄊㄠˊ ㄗㄨㄟˋ)
to be intoxicated (with success, etc.); very happy; highly gratified; greatly pleased
陶瓷(ㄊㄠˊ ㄘˊ)
pottery and porcelain
陶瓷業(ㄊㄠˊ ㄘˊ ㄧㄝˋ)
ceramics; the ceramic industry
陶猗(ㄊㄠˊ ㄧ)
rich men
陶冶(ㄊㄠˊ ㄧㄝˇ)
①to mold (pottery) and smelt (metals) ②to cultivate or shape (taste, character, etc.)
陶冶性情(ㄊㄠˊ ㄧㄝˇ ㄒㄧㄥˋ ㄑㄧㄥˊ)
to shape or cleanse one's spirit
陶硯(ㄊㄠˊ ㄧㄢˋ)
an inkstone made of pottery

【陶】 6620
2. ㄧㄠˊ yau yáo
as in 皋陶—name of a person in ancient China

【陷】 6621
ㄒㄧㄢˋ shiann xiàn
1. to sink; to fall; to submerge; to stick; to bog: 我們的車子陷在泥裏。Our car stuck in the mud.
2. to frame (up); to harm another with trumped-up charges
3. to entrap; to beguile: 他陷她於絕境。He entrapped her to destruction.
4. to crush (the enemy position); to fall; to capture (a city, etc.): 他死於城陷之日。He died on the day the city fell.
5. a defect; a deficiency
陷沒(ㄒㄧㄢˋ ㄇㄛˋ)
①to sink; to submerge ②to be captured by the enemy
陷敵(ㄒㄧㄢˋ ㄉㄧˊ)
①to crash into the enemy position (and take it) ②to fall into the enemy's hands; to be captured by the enemy
陷溺(ㄒㄧㄢˋ ㄋㄧˋ)
to sink; to submerge; to be drowned

〔阜部〕

陷落(ㄒㄧㄢˋ ㄌㄨㄛˋ)
①to sink; to submerge ② (said of a city, position,etc.) to be lost to the enemy
陷坑(ㄒㄧㄢˋ ㄎㄥ)
①a trap; a snare ②a hollow; a cave
陷害(ㄒㄧㄢˋ ㄏㄞˋ)
to frame; to snare; to harm another with a trumped-up charge, slander, etc.
陷阱(ㄒㄧㄢˋ ㄐㄧㄥˇ)
a trap; a snare; a booby trap
陷陣(ㄒㄧㄢˋ ㄓㄣˋ)
to take an enemy position
陷入(ㄒㄧㄢˋ ㄖㄨˋ)
to sink into; to fall into; to be entrapped: 他陷入沈睡中。He sank into a deep sleep.
陷入絕境(ㄒㄧㄢˋ ㄖㄨˋ ㄐㄩㄝˊ ㄐㄧㄥˋ)
to get into extreme difficulty; to be drawn into a hopeless situation

【陸】 6622
ㄌㄨˋ luh lù
1. land; the shore; a continent: 我們看見遠處的陸地了。We sighted land in the distance.
2. by way of land; land transportation: 水陸交通 land and water communications
3. an elaborate form of 六 (six) used in documents or checks to prevent forgery
4. a Chinese family name
陸半球(ㄌㄨˋ ㄅㄢˋ ㄑㄧㄡˊ)
(geography) the Northern Hemisphere, where land constitutes a greater proportion than that of the Southern Hemisphere
陸稻(ㄌㄨˋ ㄉㄠˋ)
(botany) upland rice; dryland rice 亦作「旱稻」or「旱禾」
陸地(ㄌㄨˋ ㄉㄧˋ)
land (as distinct from the water of oceans and seas): 我們望見了陸地。We came in sight of land.
陸田(ㄌㄨˋ ㄊㄧㄢˊ)
dry field (as distinct from the rice field which is submerged in water during a large part of the rice growing period) 亦作「旱田」
陸離(ㄌㄨˋ ㄌㄧˊ)
①varied and numerous ②a kind of fine jade
陸路(ㄌㄨˋ ㄌㄨˋ)
by land; a highway or railway; by way of land: 他們走陸路。They traveled by land.
陸海空(ㄌㄨˋ ㄏㄞˇ ㄎㄨㄥ)
land, sea and air
陸海空三軍(ㄌㄨˋ ㄏㄞˇ ㄎㄨㄥ ㄙㄢ ㄐㄩㄣ)
the army, navy and air force; the armed forces
陸九淵(ㄌㄨˋ ㄐㄧㄡˇ ㄩㄢ)
Lu Chiu-yüan (1139-1192), one of the leading philosophers of the Sung Dynasty 亦作「象山先生」
陸軍(ㄌㄨˋ ㄐㄩㄣ)
the army; the land force
陸軍大學(ㄌㄨˋ ㄐㄩㄣ ㄉㄚˋ ㄒㄩㄝˊ)
Army Command and Staff College
陸軍軍官學校(ㄌㄨˋ ㄐㄩㄣ ㄐㄩㄣ ㄍㄨㄢ ㄒㄩㄝˊ ㄒㄧㄠˋ)
Military Academy
陸軍中將(ㄌㄨˋ ㄐㄩㄣ ㄓㄨㄥ ㄐㄧㄤˋ)
lieutenant general
陸軍中校(ㄌㄨˋ ㄐㄩㄣ ㄓㄨㄥ ㄒㄧㄠˋ)
lieutenant colonel
陸軍中尉(ㄌㄨˋ ㄐㄩㄣ ㄓㄨㄥ ㄨㄟˋ)
first lieutenant
陸軍少將(ㄌㄨˋ ㄐㄩㄣ ㄕㄠˋ ㄐㄧㄤˋ)
major general
陸軍少校(ㄌㄨˋ ㄐㄩㄣ ㄕㄠˋ ㄒㄧㄠˋ)
major
陸軍少尉(ㄌㄨˋ ㄐㄩㄣ ㄕㄠˋ ㄨㄟˋ)
second lieutenant
陸軍上將(ㄌㄨˋ ㄐㄩㄣ ㄕㄤˋ ㄐㄧㄤˋ)
(full) general
陸軍上校(ㄌㄨˋ ㄐㄩㄣ ㄕㄤˋ ㄒㄧㄠˋ)
colonel
陸軍上尉(ㄌㄨˋ ㄐㄩㄣ ㄕㄤˋ ㄨㄟˋ)
captain
陸軍總司令(ㄌㄨˋ ㄐㄩㄣ ㄗㄨㄥˇ ㄙ ㄌㄧㄥˋ)
the commander in chief of the army; (in the U. S. Army) the Chief of Staff
陸橋(ㄌㄨˋ ㄑㄧㄠˊ)
①an overpass 亦作「天橋」② a land bridge
陸續(ㄌㄨˋ ㄒㄩˋ)
continuous; one by one; one after another: 賓客陸續到來。The guests arrived one after another.
陸贄(ㄌㄨˋ ㄓˋ)
Lu Chih, a courtier in the Tang Dynasty, famous for his literary prowess
陸戰隊(ㄌㄨˋ ㄓㄢˋ ㄉㄨㄟˋ)
the marines; the Marine Corps
陸戰隊司令(ㄌㄨˋ ㄓㄢˋ ㄉㄨㄟˋ ㄙ ㄌㄧㄥˋ)
the commandant of the Marine Corps; the marine commandant
陸沈(ㄌㄨˋ ㄔㄣˊ)
①sinking of land ②upheavals; social chaos
陸上(ㄌㄨˋ ㄕㄤˋ)
on land
陸游(ㄌㄨˋ ㄧㄡˊ)
Lu Yu (1125-1210), a prominent poet in the Sung Dynasty 亦作「陸放翁」
陸運(ㄌㄨˋ ㄩㄣˋ)
land transportation

九畫

【陽】 6623
ㄧㄤˊ yang yáng
1. positive (electricity, etc.)
2. male; masculine
3. the sun; solar; sunlight
4. the north of a stream
5. the south of a hill
6. bright; brilliant
7. the male genitals
8. pertaining to this world, as opposed to Hades
9. a Chinese family name
陽平(ㄧㄤˊ ㄆㄧㄥˊ)
(Chinese phonetics) the second tone
陽明學派(ㄧㄤˊ ㄇㄧㄥˊ ㄒㄩㄝˊ ㄆㄞˋ)
the School of Wang Yangming which centers on identity of reason and mind and the theory that action must go hand in hand with knowledge
陽明山(ㄧㄤˊ ㄇㄧㄥˊ ㄕㄢ)
Yangmingshan, a mountain resort in suburban Taipei, Taiwan
陽明山管理局(ㄧㄤˊ ㄇㄧㄥˊ ㄕㄢ ㄍㄨㄢˇ ㄌㄧˇ ㄐㄩˊ)
the Yangmingshan Administration, a special district in the Taipei Special Municipality

陽奉陰違(ㄧㄤˊ ㄈㄥˋ ㄧㄣ ㄨㄟˊ)
to observe rules or obey orders ostensibly; to pretend to obey
陽道(ㄧㄤˊ ㄉㄠˋ)
①the ways or virtues of man ②external affairs (outside the household) ③the male reproductive organ
陽電(ㄧㄤˊ ㄉㄧㄢˋ)
positive electricity
陽臺(ㄧㄤˊ ㄊㄞˊ)
①a veranda or balcony ②a trysting place; a tryst
陽離子(ㄧㄤˊ ㄌㄧˊ ㄗˇ)
a positive ion; a cation
陽曆(ㄧㄤˊ ㄌㄧˋ)
the solar calendar; the Gregorian calendar
陽螺絲(ㄧㄤˊ ㄌㄨㄛˊ ·ㄙ)
a bolt (as distinct from a nut)
陽溝(ㄧㄤˊ ㄍㄡ)
an open ditch or drainage 亦作「羊溝」
陽剛(ㄧㄤˊ ㄍㄤ)
tough, strong, positive, stern, etc. in character
陽關(ㄧㄤˊ ㄍㄨㄢ)
Yang Pass, name of a border gate in the Han Dynasty in Kansu (甘肅)
陽關大道(ㄧㄤˊ ㄍㄨㄢ ㄉㄚˋ ㄉㄠˋ)
a wide street, especially a thoroughfare
陽關三疊(ㄧㄤˊ ㄍㄨㄢ ㄙㄢ ㄉㄧㄝˊ)
a parting tune with a thrice repeated refrain
陽光(ㄧㄤˊ ㄍㄨㄤ)
sunshine; sunlight; sunbeams
陽和(ㄧㄤˊ ㄏㄜˊ)
warm; balmy
陽極(ㄧㄤˊ ㄐㄧˊ)
the anode; the positive pole
陽間(ㄧㄤˊ ㄐㄧㄢ)
the world of the living (as distinct from Hades)
陽具(ㄧㄤˊ ㄐㄩˋ)
the male reproductive organ
陽起石(ㄧㄤˊ ㄑㄧˇ ㄕˊ)
actinolite
陽性(ㄧㄤˊ ㄒㄧㄥˋ)
①positive (electricity, etc.) ②the male sex; masculinity
陽性反應(ㄧㄤˊ ㄒㄧㄥˋ ㄈㄢˇ ㄧㄥˋ)
positive reaction
陽宅(ㄧㄤˊ ㄓㄞˊ)
a human habitation; a house; the residence of the living
陽春(ㄧㄤˊ ㄔㄨㄣ)
①springtime ②the title of an ancient tune ③enlightened rule—as peaceful and delightful as springtime ④name of a county in Kwangtung Province(廣東省)
陽春白雪(ㄧㄤˊ ㄔㄨㄣ ㄅㄛˊ ㄒㄩㄝˇ)
songs that appeal to the highbrows only
陽春麪(ㄧㄤˊ ㄔㄨㄣ ㄇㄧㄢˋ)
cooked noodles without any dressing
陽世(ㄧㄤˊ ㄕˋ)
the world of the living
陽壽(ㄧㄤˊ ㄕㄡˋ)
one's predestined life span
陽傘(ㄧㄤˊ ㄙㄢˇ)
a parasol; an umbrella
陽物(ㄧㄤˊ ㄨˋ)
the penis
陽痿(ㄧㄤˊ ㄨㄟˇ)
impotence
陽文(ㄧㄤˊ ㄨㄣˊ)
characters cut in relief 亦作「陽識」
陽紋(ㄧㄤˊ ㄨㄣˊ)
the external screw; the male screw 亦作「外螺紋」
陽月(ㄧㄤˊ ㄩㄝˋ)
the 10th month in the lunar calendar

【陻】 6624
(堙) ㄧㄣ in yin
1. a mound
2. to bury
3. to dam (a stream); to block up

【隃】 6625
ㄩˊ yu yú
1. to exceed 亦作「逾」
2. name of a county in Shensi (陝西) Province during the Han Dynasty, famous for producing ink-sticks

【隄】 6626
(堤) ㄊㄧˊ tyi tí
(又讀 ㄉㄧ di dī)
a dike, levee or embankment
隄壩(ㄊㄧˊ ㄅㄚˋ)
dikes and dams
隄邊(ㄊㄧˊ ㄅㄧㄢ)
the side of a dike; by the side of a levee
隄防(ㄊㄧˊ ㄈㄤˊ)
①a dike or levee ②to remain alert; to be watchful 亦作「提防」
隄岸(ㄊㄧˊ ㄢˋ)
a dike, levee or embankment
隄堰(ㄊㄧˊ ㄧㄢˋ)
an embankment, dike or levee

【隅】 6627
ㄩˊ yu yú
1. a corner; a nook
2. an angle
3. an out-of-the-way place; a recess
隅目(ㄩˊ ㄇㄨˋ)
①angry eyes ②furious
隅反(ㄩˊ ㄈㄢˇ)
to assess, understand or visualize by inference
隅角(ㄩˊ ㄐㄧㄠˇ)
(geometry) a solid angle
隅中(ㄩˊ ㄓㄨㄥ)
approaching noontime

【隆】 6628
ㄌㄨㄥˊ long lóng
1. prosperous; flourishing; brisk (business, etc.); booming
2. lofty; eminent; glorious
3. abundant; ample; generous
4. the rumble (of thunder, vehicles, artillery fire, etc.)
5. a Chinese family name
隆冬(ㄌㄨㄥˊ ㄉㄨㄥ)
(in) the depth of winter; winter at its coldest
隆替(ㄌㄨㄥˊ ㄊㄧˋ)
the rise and fall (of a reign, regime, nation, etc.)
隆頹(ㄌㄨㄥˊ ㄊㄨㄟˊ)
craggy; not even
隆隆(ㄌㄨㄥˊ ㄌㄨㄥˊ)
①flourishing; booming ②(said of sound) roaring, booming or rumbling
隆古(ㄌㄨㄥˊ ㄍㄨˇ)
prosperous reign in ancient times
隆貴(ㄌㄨㄥˊ ㄍㄨㄟˋ)
very noble; lofty in position
隆厚(ㄌㄨㄥˊ ㄏㄡˋ)
(said of friendship or sentiments) profound; deep; generous
隆寒(ㄌㄨㄥˊ ㄏㄢˊ)

winter at its coldest; the severe cold
隆極(ㄌㄨㄥˊ ㄐㄧˊ)
the highest position or status

隆起(ㄌㄨㄥˊ ㄑㄧˇ)
to rise up; to swell up; to bulge: 山漸漸從平原隆起。Hills swell gradually from the plain.
隆情厚誼(ㄌㄨㄥˊ ㄑㄧㄥˊ ㄏㄡˋ ㄧˋ)
great kindness, hospitality and friendship; profound sentiments of friendship
隆穹(ㄌㄨㄥˊ ㄑㄩㄥˊ)
① high; soaring ② canvas top on a vehicle
隆刑(ㄌㄨㄥˊ ㄒㄧㄥˊ)
strict or severe punishment
隆準(ㄌㄨㄥˊ ㄓㄨㄣˇ)
a prominent nose
隆重(ㄌㄨㄥˊ ㄓㄨㄥˋ)
(said of ceremony, rites, etc.) impressive, grand and solemn: 他受到隆重的接待。He was accorded a grand reception.
隆盛(ㄌㄨㄥˊ ㄕㄥˋ)
abundant; booming; flourishing; prosperous
隆暑(ㄌㄨㄥˊ ㄕㄨˇ)
summer at its hottest
隆乳(ㄌㄨㄥˊ ㄖㄨˇ)
to raise the breasts of a flat-chested woman by means of plastic surgery
隆恩(ㄌㄨㄥˊ ㄣ)
great kindness, favor or grace
隆顏(ㄌㄨㄥˊ ㄧㄢˊ)
the imperial countenance

【隈】 6629
ㄨㄟ uei wei
1. a river bend
2. a mountain recess

【隉】 6630
ㄋㄧㄝ nieh nie
as in 阢隉—precarious; dangerous

【隋】 6631
ㄙㄨㄟˊ swei suí
1.name of a dynasty (581-618)
2. a Chinese family name
隋隄(ㄙㄨㄟˊ ㄊㄧˊ)
embankments along the Grand Canal dug by order of Emperor Yang(煬帝) of the Sui Dynasty
隋書(ㄙㄨㄟˊ ㄕㄨ)
a history of the Sui Dynasty
隋煬帝(ㄙㄨㄟˊ ㄧㄤˋ ㄉㄧˋ)
Emperor Yang (580-618), one of the most debauched and vainglorious rulers in ancient China
隋文帝(ㄙㄨㄟˊ ㄨㄣˊ ㄉㄧˋ)
Emperor Wen (541-604), father of Emperor Yang (隋煬帝), the founding monarch of the Sui Dynasty

【隊】 6632
ㄉㄨㄟˋ duey duì
1. a group; a team; a batch
2. the troops
隊旗(ㄉㄨㄟˋ ㄑㄧˊ)
the flag of a team; the team pennant: 他們互贈隊旗。They exchanged team pennants.
隊形(ㄉㄨㄟˋ ㄒㄧㄥˊ)
formation (of airplanes in flight or soldiers drilling)
隊長(ㄉㄨㄟˋ ㄓㄤˇ)
the team leader; the captain of a sports team; the commanding officer of a small military unit
隊伍(ㄉㄨㄟˋ ㄨˇ)
① troops in ranks and files ② a line of (people)
隊員(ㄉㄨㄟˋ ㄩㄢˊ)
members of a team or group: 我不是任何隊的隊員。I am not on (or in) any team.

【階】 6633
ㄐㄧㄝ jie jie
1. a way leading to the main hall
2. a flight of steps or stairs
3. a grade or a rank
4. to rely on
階陛(ㄐㄧㄝ ㄅㄧˋ)
a flight of steps leading to the throne 亦作「階墀」
階段(ㄐㄧㄝ ㄉㄨㄢˋ)
a stage or phase (in a development process)
階梯(ㄐㄧㄝ ㄊㄧ)
① a flight of stairs or steps ②(figuratively) a way, ladder or step leading to success
階級(ㄐㄧㄝ ㄐㄧˊ)
a rank; a class (of people): 他們屬於中等階級。They belong to the middle class(es).
階級偏見(ㄐㄧㄝ ㄐㄧˊ ㄆㄧㄢ ㄐㄧㄢˋ)
(sociology) class bias
階級鬥爭(ㄐㄧㄝ ㄐㄧˊ ㄉㄡˋ ㄓㄥ)
a class struggle
階級利益(ㄐㄧㄝ ㄐㄧˊ ㄌㄧˋ ㄧˋ)
class interests
階級衝突(ㄐㄧㄝ ㄐㄧˊ ㄔㄨㄥ ㄊㄨˊ)
(sociology) a class conflict
階級意識(ㄐㄧㄝ ㄐㄧˊ ㄧˋ ㄕˋ)
(sociology) class consciousness
階前萬里(ㄐㄧㄝ ㄑㄧㄢˊ ㄨㄢˋ ㄌㄧˇ)
It's 10,000 miles away, and it's near at hand as well.
階下漢(ㄐㄧㄝ ㄒㄧㄚˋ ㄏㄢˋ)
a beginner; an apprentice; a novice
階下囚(ㄐㄧㄝ ㄒㄧㄚˋ ㄑㄧㄡˊ)
a prisoner; a captive: 他後來成了階下囚。He finally became a prisoner.
階墀(ㄐㄧㄝ ㄔˊ)
a flight of steps leading to the throne
階除(ㄐㄧㄝ ㄔㄨˊ)
steps in the yard
階次(ㄐㄧㄝ ㄘˋ)
grades or ranks in officialdom
階層(ㄐㄧㄝ ㄘㄥˊ)
subdivisions within a class of people; a class of people; a social stratum; a walk of life
階緣(ㄐㄧㄝ ㄩㄢˊ)
to climb by riding on the coattails of a powerful person

十畫

【隔】 6634
ㄍㄜˊ ger gé
1. to separate; to divide; to partition
2. blocked; to obstruct; to be veiled
3. at a distance from; at an interval of
隔壁(ㄍㄜˊ ㄅㄧˋ)
next door: 她住在隔壁。She lives next door now.
隔別(ㄍㄜˊ ㄅㄧㄝˊ)
separated (for a long time, etc.)
隔膜(ㄍㄜˊ ㄇㄛˊ)
① the diaphragm ② to have

no communication or contact with; to be out of touch with; not familiar with ③ the absence of the meeting of minds; to be estranged

隔膜炎(ㄍㄜˊ ㄇㄛˊ ㄧㄢˊ)
diaphragmatitis

隔代遺傳(ㄍㄜˊ ㄉㄞˋ ㄧˊ ㄔㄨㄢˊ)
atavism

隔斷(ㄍㄜˊ ㄉㄨㄢˋ)
blocked or obstructed; to separate; to cut off: 我們被潮水所隔斷。We were cut off by the tide.

隔年(ㄍㄜˊ ㄋㄧㄢˊ)
in the following year; in the year following

隔離(ㄍㄜˊ ㄌㄧˊ)
to separate; to isolate; to segregate; to quarantine

隔離病房(ㄍㄜˊ ㄌㄧˊ ㄅㄧㄥˋ ㄈㄤˊ)
an isolation ward

隔開(ㄍㄜˊ ㄎㄞ)
to separate; to set apart; to partition

隔閡(ㄍㄜˊ ㄏㄜˊ)
no meeting of minds; a mental barrier

隔間(ㄍㄜˊ ㄐㄧㄢ)
a partition

隔絕(ㄍㄜˊ ㄐㄩㄝˊ)
blocked or obstructed; separated; to cut off; to isolate

隔牆有耳(ㄍㄜˊ ㄑㄧㄤˊ ㄧㄡˇ ㄦˇ)
(literally) There are ears on the other side of the wall. —It's difficult to keep a secret. 或 Beware of eavesdroppers.

隔靴搔癢(ㄍㄜˊ ㄒㄩㄝ ㄙㄠ ㄧㄤˇ)
(literally) to scratch an itching foot with the boot on —not to the point; having no effect; to attempt an ineffective solution

隔肢(ㄍㄜˊ ˙ㄓ)
① to titillate ② to give someone a hard time

隔肢窩(ㄍㄜˊ ˙ㄓ ㄨㄛ)
the armpit

隔山(ㄍㄜˊ ㄕㄢ)
the relationship between half brothers and sisters by the same father

隔扇(ㄍㄜˊ ㄕㄢˋ)
a paper or wooden partition

隔日(ㄍㄜˊ ㄖˋ)
① the next day or the day after next ② every other day

隔熱(ㄍㄜˊ ㄖㄜˋ)
(construction) heat insulation

隔宿(ㄍㄜˊ ㄙㄨˋ)
after a night; overnight

隔岸(ㄍㄜˊ ㄢˋ)
on the other side of the river, sea, etc.

隔岸觀火(ㄍㄜˊ ㄢˋ ㄍㄨㄢ ㄏㄨㄛˇ)
(literally) to watch a fire on the other side of the river —to be indifferent; to show no concern

隔夜(ㄍㄜˊ ㄧㄝˋ)
after a night; last night

隔音(ㄍㄜˊ ㄧㄣ)
soundproof: 這是一間隔音室。This is a soundproof room.

隔音板(ㄍㄜˊ ㄧㄣ ㄅㄢˇ)
an acoustic tile; an acoustic board

【隕】 6635
ㄩㄣˇ yeun yǔn

1. to fall
2. to die

隕滅(ㄩㄣˇ ㄇㄧㄝˋ)
① to fall from outer space and burn up ② to meet one's death; to perish

隕命(ㄩㄣˇ ㄇㄧㄥˋ)
to die 亦作「殞命」

隕涕(ㄩㄣˇ ㄊㄧˋ)
tears falling

隕鐵(ㄩㄣˇ ㄊㄧㄝˇ)
meteoric iron

隕落(ㄩㄣˇ ㄌㄨㄛˋ)
① (said of a meteorite, etc.) to fall from the sky or outer space ② (said of a famous or influential person) to pass away; to die

隕星(ㄩㄣˇ ㄒㄧㄥ)
(astronomy) a meteor; a meteoroid that has entered the earth's atmosphere

隕石(ㄩㄣˇ ㄕˊ)
a meteorite; a fallen meteoroid; a mass of stone or metal that has reached the earth from outer space

隕泗(ㄩㄣˇ ㄙˋ)
to shed tears

隕越(ㄩㄣˇ ㄩㄝˋ)
① to topple and fall down ② to fulfill one's duties improperly or erroneously

【隖】 6636
ㄨˋ wuh wù

1. a parapet; a low wall
2. a structure sloping toward the middle on all sides, as a dock

【隘】 6637
ㄞˋ ay ài

1. a strategic pass; a strategic point
2. narrow
3. urgent
4. destitute

隘路(ㄞˋ ㄌㄨˋ)
a narrow road; a road flanked by water or streams

隘口(ㄞˋ ㄎㄡˇ)
a (mountain) pass

隘害(ㄞˋ ㄏㄞˋ)
a strategic pass or point

隘險(ㄞˋ ㄒㄧㄢˇ)
of great strategic value

【隙】 6638
(隟) ㄒㄧˋ shih xì

1. a crack; a fissure; a crevice
2. a grudge; a dislike; a dispute; a quarrel; a complaint
3. spare time; leisure
4. an opportunity; a loophole
5. an important passageway or corridor, as the Berlin Corridor

隙地(ㄒㄧˋ ㄉㄧˋ)
a vacant lot or space; an uncultivated land or tract

隙駒(ㄒㄧˋ ㄐㄩ)
How time flies!

隙罅(ㄒㄧˋ ㄒㄧㄚˋ)
a crack, crevice, or fissure: 杯子上有一條隙罅。There was a crack in the cup.

【隗】 6639
ㄨㄟˇ woei wěi

1. high; lofty
2. a Chinese family name

十一畫

【際】 6640
ㄐㄧˋ jih jì

1. (to occur) at the time or on the occasion of
2. a border or boundary; an edge
3. by the side of; beside
4. in the middle; between; among

〔阜部〕

5. opportunity; fortune or luck

際畔(ㄐㄧˋ ㄆㄢˋ)
along the border; bordering on

際會(ㄐㄧˋ ㄏㄨㄟˋ)
① to meet; to encounter ② a happenstance

際此(ㄐㄧˋ ㄘˇ)
at a time like this; on such an occasion: 際此佳期特向你祝賀。I send you my best wishes on this happy occasion.

際遇(ㄐㄧˋ ㄩˋ)
① opportunity; chance ② what one has experienced or encountered in one's life

際涯(ㄐㄧˋ ㄧㄚˊ)
a margin; an outer limit

【障】 6641
ㄓㄤˋ jang zhàng

1. to separate; to screen; a barrier; a screen
2. a dike; an embankment
3. to defend; to guard; to shield
4. to guarantee
5. to hinder; to obstruct

障蔽(ㄓㄤˋ ㄅㄧˋ)
to screen; to obstruct

障礙(ㄓㄤˋ ㄞˋ)
① obstacles; barriers; obstructions: 有勇氣就無障礙。Courage knows no obstacle. ② a malfunction; a handicap: 視力不好是學生的障礙。Poor eyesight is a handicap to a student.

障礙競走(ㄓㄤˋ ㄞˋ ㄐㄧㄥˋ ㄗㄡˇ)
the game of walking over a prepared course with artificial obstructions

障礙物(ㄓㄤˋ ㄞˋ ㄨˋ)
an obstacle; an obstruction; anything that hinders

障翳(ㄓㄤˋ ㄧˋ)
① a wooden fan carried in procession ② to conceal or screen

障眼法(ㄓㄤˋ ㄧㄢˇ ㄈㄚˇ)
① legerdemain ② a cover-up; camouflage

十二畫

【隤】 6642
(穨) ㄊㄨㄟˊ twei tuí

1. to fall in ruins; to collapse
2. (said of horses) tired and jaded

【隣】 6643
(鄰) ㄌㄧㄣˊ lin lín

1. a neighbor: 愛你的隣居像愛自己一樣。Love your neighbors as yourself.
2. neighboring; nearby: 他住在隣近村內。He lives in the neighboring village.

十三畫

【隨】 6644
ㄙㄨㄟˊ swei suí

1. to follow; to trace; to come after
2. to listen to; to submit to; to comply with
3. to let (it go, it be, etc.)
4. to accompany: 雷隨閃電而來。Thunder accompanies lightning.
5. to resemble; to look like
6. a Chinese family name

隨波逐流(ㄙㄨㄟˊ ㄅㄛ ㄓㄨˊ ㄌㄧㄡˊ)
① to follow the currents in sailing ② to speak and behave as others do without views of his own

隨報附送(ㄙㄨㄟˊ ㄅㄠˋ ㄈㄨˋ ㄙㄨㄥˋ)
to be distributed gratis along with the newspaper

隨筆(ㄙㄨㄟˊ ㄅㄧˇ)
to write as one's thought rambles; literary rambles; miscellaneous writings; jottings

隨便(ㄙㄨㄟˊ ㄅㄧㄢˋ)
① as you like; as you see fit; as you please: 隨便你去做。You can do as you like. ② casual; careless: 他待人很隨便。He is very casual with other people.

隨票附送(ㄙㄨㄟˊ ㄆㄧㄠˋ ㄈㄨˋ ㄙㄨㄥˋ)
to be distributed gratis along with the ticket

隨片登臺(ㄙㄨㄟˊ ㄆㄧㄢˋ ㄉㄥ ㄊㄞˊ)
(said of a leading actor or actress) to appear on stage in person on the premiere of a movie

隨分(ㄙㄨㄟˊ ㄈㄣˋ)
① to be content with one's lot ② (to do things) within the limits of one's strength or resources ③ to contribute one's share as part of a present

隨方就圓(ㄙㄨㄟˊ ㄈㄤ ㄐㄧㄡˋ ㄩㄢˊ)
easygoing; adaptable; accommodating; easy to get along with

隨風轉舵(ㄙㄨㄟˊ ㄈㄥ ㄓㄨㄢˇ ㄉㄨㄛˋ) or 隨風倒舵(ㄙㄨㄟˊ ㄈㄥ ㄉㄠˇ ㄉㄨㄛˋ)
① to take action as opportunity arises ② irresolution

隨風兒倒(ㄙㄨㄟˊ ㄈㄥㄦ ㄉㄠˇ)
(literally) to turn with the wind—without any views or ideas of one's own

隨帶(ㄙㄨㄟˊ ㄉㄞˋ)
to carry about; to take along: 除信以外隨帶書籍兩包。Accompanying the letter are two parcels of books.

隨到隨考(ㄙㄨㄟˊ ㄉㄠˋ ㄙㄨㄟˊ ㄎㄠˇ)
to undergo a test as soon as one arrives

隨地(ㄙㄨㄟˊ ㄉㄧˋ)
any place

隨地吐痰(ㄙㄨㄟˊ ㄉㄧˋ ㄊㄨˇ ㄊㄢˊ)
to spit freely at any place

隨地小便(ㄙㄨㄟˊ ㄉㄧˋ ㄒㄧㄠˇ ㄅㄧㄢˋ)
to urinate freely at any place

隨同(ㄙㄨㄟˊ ㄊㄨㄥˊ)
to follow or accompany; together with

隨來隨走(ㄙㄨㄟˊ ㄌㄞˊ ㄙㄨㄟˊ ㄗㄡˇ)
Some people are arriving, and others are leaving.

隨高就低(ㄙㄨㄟˊ ㄍㄠ ㄐㄧㄡˋ ㄉㄧ)
to adapt to circumstances

隨口(ㄙㄨㄟˊ ㄎㄡˇ)
to slip out of one's tongue without much thought: 他隨口答覆了她。He gave her a casual answer.

隨和
①(ㄙㄨㄟˊ ㄏㄜˊ) priceless treasures (隨侯珠 and 卞和璧)
②(ㄙㄨㄟˊ ㄏㄜˋ) to repeat what others are saying
③(ㄙㄨㄟˊ ˙ㄏㄜ) easygoing; amiable: 她是個隨和的女孩。She is an amiable girl.

隨後(ㄙㄨㄟˊ ㄏㄡˋ)
immediately afterward; right off; in no time at all; right after

隨宦(ㄙㄨㄟˊ ㄏㄨㄢˋ)
to follow one's father or elder brother on a tour of

official duty
隨機教學(ㄙㄨㄟˊ ㄐㄧ ㄐㄧㄠˋ ㄒㄩㄝˊ)
to teach whenever and wherever opportunity presents itself (as teaching names of animals in a zoo)
隨機應變(ㄙㄨㄟˊ ㄐㄧ ㄧㄥˋ ㄅㄧㄢˋ)
to adapt oneself quickly to the changing circumstances
隨即(ㄙㄨㄟˊ ㄐㄧˊ)
right away; promptly; immediately; soon afterward: 她說完隨即離去。She left right away after saying something.
隨叫隨到(ㄙㄨㄟˊ ㄐㄧㄠˋ ㄙㄨㄟˊ ㄉㄠˋ)
(said of goods or service) to arrive as soon as it is ordered by telephone call; to be on call at any hour
隨軍記者(ㄙㄨㄟˊ ㄐㄩㄣ ㄐㄧˋ ㄓㄜˇ)
a war correspondent
隨喜(ㄙㄨㄟˊ ㄒㄧˇ)
① to visit temples or shrines ②(Buddhism) to feel happy when one sees others doing good
隨心所欲(ㄙㄨㄟˊ ㄒㄧㄣ ㄙㄨㄛˇ ㄩˋ)
to do anything one's heart dictates
隨鄉入鄉(ㄙㄨㄟˊ ㄒㄧㄤ ㄖㄨˋ ㄒㄧㄤ)
In a strange land, do as the natives do. 或 When in Rome, do as the Romans do.
隨想曲(ㄙㄨㄟˊ ㄒㄧㄤˇ ㄑㄩˇ)
(music) caprice; *capriccio*
隨行(ㄙㄨㄟˊ ㄒㄧㄥˊ)
to follow or accompany someone on a trip
隨行人員(ㄙㄨㄟˊ ㄒㄧㄥˊ ㄖㄣˊ ㄩㄢˊ)
an entourage; a suite; attendants or aides accompanying a VIP on a tour; retinues
隨着(ㄙㄨㄟˊ ˙ㄓㄜ)
along with; in the wake of; in pace with: 我願隨着你去。I'll go along with you.
隨珠彈雀(ㄙㄨㄟˊ ㄓㄨ ㄊㄢˊ ㄑㄩㄝˋ)
(literally) to kill a bird with a precious pearl—to gain a trifle at great cost
隨衆(ㄙㄨㄟˊ ㄓㄨㄥˋ)
to follow the crowd
隨處(ㄙㄨㄟˊ ㄔㄨˋ)
everywhere; at all places: 他們隨處都去。They go everywhere.
隨時(ㄙㄨㄟˊ ㄕˊ)
at all times; anytime
隨時制宜(ㄙㄨㄟˊ ㄕˊ ㄓˋ ㄧˊ)
to change tactics as a situation demands; to act according to circumstances
隨時隨地(ㄙㄨㄟˊ ㄕˊ ㄙㄨㄟˊ ㄉㄧˋ)
at all times and places; anytime and anyplace; wherever and whenever
隨侍(ㄙㄨㄟˊ ㄕˋ)
① to wait upon ② an orderly; a personal attendant
隨侍在側(ㄙㄨㄟˊ ㄕˋ ㄗㄞˋ ㄘㄜˋ)
to be by the side (of a sick elder, usually one's parent) —an expression usually appearing in a funeral notice
隨手(ㄙㄨㄟˊ ㄕㄡˇ)
at hand; readily; immediately: 請隨手關門。Please shut the door after you.
隨身(ㄙㄨㄟˊ ㄕㄣ)
to carry something with one; to take something with one; to carry about: 警察可以隨身帶槍。The policemen can take guns with them.
隨身東西(ㄙㄨㄟˊ ㄕㄣ ㄉㄨㄥ ˙ㄒㄧ)
things that one carries with him
隨身聽(ㄙㄨㄟˊ ㄕㄣ ㄊㄧㄥ)
a walkman
隨身衣服(ㄙㄨㄟˊ ㄕㄣ ㄧ ˙ㄈㄨ)
clothes for change one takes along during a trip
隨聲附和(ㄙㄨㄟˊ ㄕㄥ ㄈㄨˋ ㄏㄜˋ)
to echo another's utterances without ideas or views of one's own; to chime in with others
隨順(ㄙㄨㄟˊ ㄕㄨㄣˋ)
to accord or comply with
隨從(ㄙㄨㄟˊ ㄗㄨㄥˋ)
an entourage; aides; attendants
隨從武官(ㄙㄨㄟˊ ㄘㄨㄥˊ ㄨˇ ㄍㄨㄢ)
an aide-de-camp
隨俗(ㄙㄨㄟˊ ㄙㄨˊ)
to act according to the prevailing customs or practices: 入境隨俗。When in Rome, do as the Romans do.
隨俗浮沈(ㄙㄨㄟˊ ㄙㄨˊ ㄈㄨˊ ㄔㄣˊ)
(literally) to drift along with the world—without ideas or ambition of one's own
隨隨便便(ㄙㄨㄟˊ ㄙㄨㄟˊ ㄅㄧㄢˋ ㄅㄧㄢˋ)
easygoing; casual; sloppy
隨宜(ㄙㄨㄟˊ ㄧˊ)
to comply with propriety
隨意(ㄙㄨㄟˊ ㄧˋ)
according to your wish; as you like it; as you please; to have no restraint; to act as one pleases 參看「隨便①」: 隨意拿吧! Take as many as you please.
隨意畫(ㄙㄨㄟˊ ㄧˋ ㄏㄨㄚˋ)
freehand drawing
隨意肌(ㄙㄨㄟˊ ㄧˋ ㄐㄧ)
voluntary muscles
隨遇平衡(ㄙㄨㄟˊ ㄩˋ ㄆㄧㄥˊ ㄏㄥˊ)
(physics) indifferent or neutral equilibrium
隨遇而安(ㄙㄨㄟˊ ㄩˋ ㄦˊ ㄢ)
to feel at ease under all circumstances: 他隨遇而安。He feels at ease under all circumstances.
隨員(ㄙㄨㄟˊ ㄩㄢˊ)
an entourage; a retinue; aides on a tour 亦作「隨行人員」
隨緣(ㄙㄨㄟˊ ㄩㄢˊ)
(Buddhism) ① one's activities resulting from the outer circumstances ② to do things in accordance with one's situation

【隧】 6645 ㄙㄨㄟˋ suey suì
1. an underground passage; a tunnel
2. to go round and round
3. (in ancient China) a tower on the wall to watch signal fires
隧道(ㄙㄨㄟˋ ㄉㄠˋ)
a tunnel: 這火車通過隧道。The train passed through a tunnel.

【隩】 6646 ㄩˋ yuh yù (又讀 ㄠˋ aw ào)
1. a bend of a stream; a cove
2. warm
3. inhabitable land

【險】 6647 ㄒㄧㄢˇ shean xiǎn
1. dangerous; danger
2. obstructed; difficult
3. a strategic pass

阜部

4. cunning; mean and crafty; sinister
5. nearly; almost; within an ace of: 他險遭不幸。He came within an ace of death.

險詖(ㄒㄧㄢˇ ㄅㄧˋ)
①vile; mean ②fawning; obsequiousness

險灘(ㄒㄧㄢˇ ㄊㄢ)
a dangerous shoal; rapids

險固(ㄒㄧㄢˇ ㄍㄨˋ)
strategic and impregnable

險棘(ㄒㄧㄢˇ ㄐㄧˊ)
(said of terrain, roads, etc.) difficult; hazardous

險境(ㄒㄧㄢˇ ㄐㄧㄥˋ)
a dangerous situation

險句(ㄒㄧㄢˇ ㄐㄩˋ)
a sentence whose construction is out of the ordinary or peculiar

險譎(ㄒㄧㄢˇ ㄐㄩㄝˊ)
cunning and vicious; crafty and mean

險峻(ㄒㄧㄢˇ ㄐㄩㄣˋ)
(said of terrain) of highly strategic significance; (said of hills, etc.) precipitous

險戲(ㄒㄧㄢˇ ㄒㄧˋ) or 險巇(ㄒㄧㄢˇ ㄒㄧ)
dangerous; danger(s)

險些(ㄒㄧㄢˇ ㄒㄧㄝ) or 險些兒(ㄒㄧㄢˇ ㄒㄧㄜㄦ)
nearly; almost: 他險些兒死了。He was almost dead.

險象環生(ㄒㄧㄢˇ ㄒㄧㄤˋ ㄏㄨㄢˊ ㄕㄥ)
dangers lurking on all sides; to be beset with danger; signs of danger appearing everywhere

險詐(ㄒㄧㄢˇ ㄓㄚˋ)
treacherous; treachery; sinister and crafty

險症(ㄒㄧㄢˇ ㄓㄥˋ)
a serious disease; a severe illness

險勝(ㄒㄧㄢˇ ㄕㄥˋ)
to win by a narrow margin

險遭不測(ㄒㄧㄢˇ ㄗㄠ ㄅㄨˊ ㄘㄜˋ)
to escape death by a hair's breadth

險遭毒手(ㄒㄧㄢˇ ㄗㄠ ㄉㄨˊ ㄕㄡˇ)
to have a narrow escape from assassination, murder, attack, etc.

險阻(ㄒㄧㄢˇ ㄗㄨˇ) or 險澀(ㄒㄧㄢˇ ㄙㄜˋ)
hazardous; dangerous (mountain passes, etc.); precarious (situations, etc.); difficult (terrain)

險惡(ㄒㄧㄢˇ ㄜˋ)
①dangerous; perilous; ominous; precarious ②devious; diabolic; mean; sinister: 他居心險惡。He had sinister intentions.

險隘(ㄒㄧㄢˇ ㄞˋ)
dangerous; strategic

險易(ㄒㄧㄢˇ ㄧˋ)
①difficult and easy ②disturbance and peace

險要(ㄒㄧㄢˇ ㄧㄠˋ)
(said of a place) strategic and capable of being easily defended

險語(ㄒㄧㄢˇ ㄩˇ)
sensational remarks

險韻(ㄒㄧㄢˇ ㄩㄣˋ)
to rhyme with obscure words; difficult rhyme

十四畫

【隱】 6648
ㄧㄣˇ yiin yǐn

1. hidden; concealed; secret; mysterious
2. dark; obscure; not evident or obvious
3. to retire; to reject public life; to live like a hermit
4. painful; grievous
5. a riddle
6. destitute; poor
7. to examine and study
8. a low wall
9. a Chinese family name

隱比(ㄧㄣˇ ㄅㄧˇ)
metaphor 亦作「暗喻」

隱蔽(ㄧㄣˇ ㄅㄧˋ)
to conceal; to take cover; to cover up

隱沒(ㄧㄣˇ ㄇㄛˋ)
①to pass unnoticed by the public ②to fade; to disappear: 他的身影隱沒在黑暗中。His figure faded into the darkness.

隱瞞(ㄧㄣˇ ㄇㄢˊ)
to hide the truth; to cover up: 我沒什麼好隱瞞的。I have nothing to hide.

隱秘(ㄧㄣˇ ㄇㄧˋ)
①to conceal; to hide ②a secret

隱名(ㄧㄣˇ ㄇㄧㄥˊ)
to remain anonymous; to conceal one's name

隱伏(ㄧㄣˇ ㄈㄨˊ)
to lie concealed (or hidden); to lie low

隱遁(ㄧㄣˇ ㄉㄨㄣˋ)
to retire from public life; to live in reclusion

隱慝(ㄧㄣˇ ㄊㄜˋ)
a hidden crime; unrevealed guilt; some secret wickedness

隱聽(ㄧㄣˇ ㄊㄧㄥ)
to keep quiet and listen; to eavesdrop

隱退(ㄧㄣˇ ㄊㄨㄟˋ)
to retire; retirement: 他已隱退了。He has retired from the world.

隱痛(ㄧㄣˇ ㄊㄨㄥˋ)
hidden sorrow or pain

隱匿(ㄧㄣˇ ㄋㄧˋ)
to conceal; to hide: 他隱匿在山中。His hideaway is in the mountains.

隱宮(ㄧㄣˇ ㄍㄨㄥ)
castration (as a form of punishment in ancient times)

隱花果(ㄧㄣˇ ㄏㄨㄚ ㄍㄨㄛˇ)
syconium, such as a fig

隱花植物(ㄧㄣˇ ㄏㄨㄚ ㄓˊ ㄨˋ)
the cryptogam

隱諱(ㄧㄣˇ ㄏㄨㄟˋ)
①taboo (on the parent's or emperor's personal name) ②to avoid mentioning; to cover up

隱晦(ㄧㄣˇ ㄏㄨㄟˋ)
obscure; ambiguous

隱患(ㄧㄣˇ ㄏㄨㄢˋ)
hidden dangers; latent dangers; lurking perils

隱疾(ㄧㄣˇ ㄐㄧˊ)
①ailments beneath one's garment ②ailments one wants to keep to oneself, as syphilis, impotence, etc.

隱居(ㄧㄣˇ ㄐㄩ)
to retire from public life; to live in seclusion

隱君子(ㄧㄣˇ ㄐㄩㄣ ㄗˇ)
a retired scholar

隱情(ㄧㄣˇ ㄑㄧㄥˊ)
secrets; things which cannot be revealed to others; facts one wishes to hide

隱修(ㄧㄣˇ ㄒㄧㄡ)
an anchorite
隱顯墨水(ㄧㄣˇ ㄒㄧㄢˇ ㄇㄛˋ ㄕㄨㄟˇ)
invisible ink; sympathetic ink
隱形人(ㄧㄣˇ ㄒㄧㄥˊ ㄖㄣˊ)
an invisible man
隱形眼鏡(ㄧㄣˇ ㄒㄧㄥˊ ㄧㄢˇ ㄐㄧㄥˋ)
contact lenses
隱性(ㄧㄣˇ ㄒㄧㄥˋ)
(genetics) recessive
隱姓埋名(ㄧㄣˇ ㄒㄧㄥˋ ㄇㄞˊ ㄇㄧㄥˊ)
to live incognito; to live in obscurity; to live as a hermit
隱者(ㄧㄣˇ ㄓㄜˇ)
a recluse; a hermit
隱士(ㄧㄣˇ ㄕˋ)
a retired scholar; a recluse
隱身術(ㄧㄣˇ ㄕㄣ ㄕㄨˋ) or 隱身法(ㄧㄣˇ ㄕㄣ ㄈㄚˇ)
the magic of making oneself invisible
隱忍(ㄧㄣˇ ㄖㄣˇ)
to bear insults, effrontery, grievances, etc. with patience; to forbear; to bottle up one's resentment
隱惻(ㄧㄣˇ ㄘㄜˋ)
commiseration or sympathy
隱藏(ㄧㄣˇ ㄘㄤˊ)
to hide; to conceal
隱私(ㄧㄣˇ ㄙ)
one's secrets; private matters one wants to hide
隱私權(ㄧㄣˇ ㄙ ㄑㄩㄢˊ)
privacy
隱惡揚善(ㄧㄣˇ ㄜˋ ㄧㄤˊ ㄕㄢˋ)
to cover up another's bad deeds and praise his virtues
隱逸(ㄧㄣˇ ㄧˋ)
a recluse; a retired person
隱憂(ㄧㄣˇ ㄧㄡ)
hidden or latent worries; lurking dangers
隱隱作痛(ㄧㄣˇ ㄧㄣˇ ㄗㄨㄛˋ ㄊㄨㄥˋ)
to feel dull pain
隱語(ㄧㄣˇ ㄩˇ)
parables; riddles
隱喻(ㄧㄣˇ ㄩˋ)
a metaphor
隱約(ㄧㄣˇ ㄩㄝ) or 隱隱約約(ㄧㄣˇ ㄧㄣˇ ㄩㄝ ㄩㄝ)
indistinct; obscure; ambiguous; abstruse

【隰】 6649 ㄒㄧˊ shyi xí
1. low, marshy land
2. newly opened farmland
3. a Chinese family name

【隮】 6650 ㄐㄧ ji jī
1. to rise up; to ascend
2. a rainbow
3. to fall; to topple

十五畫

【隳】 6651 ㄏㄨㄟ huei huī
to destroy; to ruin; to break

十六畫

【隴】 6652 ㄌㄨㄥˇ loong lǒng
1. another name of Kansu (甘肅) Province
2. a mound 亦作「壟」
3. prosperous
4. a Chinese family name
隴畝(ㄌㄨㄥˇ ㄇㄨˇ)
a rural community; the farm
隴海鐵路(ㄌㄨㄥˇ ㄏㄞˇ ㄊㄧㄝˇ ㄌㄨˋ)
the Lung-Hai Railway, from Lanchow, Kansu (甘肅蘭州), to Lienyünkang, Kiangsu (江蘇連雲港, formerly known as 海州)

隶部
ㄉㄞˋ day dài

九畫

【隸】 6653 ㄌㄧˋ lih lì
1. to be subordinate to; inferior; to belong or attach to
2. servants; slaves; underlings
3. a type of Chinese calligraphy
4. to practice; to learn
5. a Chinese family name
隸書(ㄌㄧˋ ㄕㄨ) or 隸字(ㄌㄧˋ ㄗˋ)
a clerical style of Chinese calligraphy; official script, an ancient style of calligraphy current in the Han Dynasty (206 B.C.—A.D. 220), simplified from *Hsiao-chuan* (小篆)
隸屬(ㄌㄧˋ ㄕㄨˇ)
to be attached to; subordinate to; under the jurisdiction or command of
隸人(ㄌㄧˋ ㄖㄣˊ)
① convicts ② petty officials
隸圉(ㄌㄧˋ ㄩˇ)
servants; underlings

隹部
ㄓㄨㄟ juei zhuī

【隹】 6654 ㄓㄨㄟ juei zhuī
a general name of short-tailed birds, such as pigeons

二畫

【隻】 6655 ㄓ jy zhī
1. a numerary adjunct for a hen, pigeon, bird, ox, goat, hand, foot, etc.: 她買了一隻鷄。She bought a chicken.
2. single; alone; one of a pair: 他隻身前來。He came alone.
3. odd (number)
隻立(ㄓ ㄌㄧˋ)
to stand alone
隻輪不反(ㄓ ㄌㄨㄣˊ ㄅㄨˋ ㄈㄢˇ)
(literally) not a single chariot returned—routed
隻鷄絮酒(ㄓ ㄐㄧ ㄒㄩˋ ㄐㄧㄡˇ)
(an expression used in writing mourning for the death of a friend) sacrifice offered to the dead
隻句(ㄓ ㄐㄩˋ)
a single sentence; a brief note
隻手(ㄓ ㄕㄡˇ)
single-handed
隻身(ㄓ ㄕㄣ)
alone; all by oneself: 他隻身到台北。He went to Taipei alone. 他隻身在外。He was away from home all by himself.
隻日(ㄓ ㄖˋ)
odd days of a lunar month

〔隹部〕

隻字(ㄓ ㄗˋ)
a single word or character; a very brief note: 隻字無誤。 Not a single character is wrong.
隻字片紙(ㄓ ㄗˋ ㄆㄧㄢˋ ㄓˇ)
a very brief note or letter
隻言片語(ㄓ ㄧㄢˊ ㄆㄧㄢˋ ㄩˇ)
a few words: 她未留下隻言片語。She left behind not even a few words.
隻眼(ㄓ ㄧㄢˇ)
① one-eyed—(figuratively) a discerning viewpoint ② an original idea; a fresh view
隻影(ㄓ ㄧㄥˇ)
all alone; all by oneself

【隼】 6656 ㄓㄨㄣˇ joen zhǔn (又讀 ㄙㄨㄣˇ soen sǔn)
1. an aquiline nose
2. a hawk; a falcon

三畫

【雀】 6657 ㄑㄩㄝˋ chiueh què (語音 ㄑㄧㄠˇ cheau qiǎo)
1. a general name of small birds, as sparrows, chickadees, etc.
2. freckled
雀斑(ㄑㄩㄝˋ ㄅㄢ)
freckles: 她的臉上有雀斑。She has a freckled face.
雀屏中選(ㄑㄩㄝˋ ㄆㄧㄥˊ ㄓㄨㄥˋ ㄒㄩㄢˇ) or 雀屏中目(ㄑㄩㄝˋ ㄆㄧㄥˊ ㄓㄨㄥˋ ㄇㄨˋ)
to be selected as someone's son-in-law (a reference to the founding emperor of the Tang Dynasty who won the hand of his queen by hitting the eyes of two peacocks painted on screen doors in an archery contest)
雀麥(ㄑㄩㄝˋ ㄇㄞˋ)
Bromus japonicus, a variety of oats
雀盲(ㄑㄩㄝˋ ㄇㄤˊ) or 雀瞀(ㄑㄩㄝˋ ㄇㄠˋ)
night blindness; nyctalopia
雀立(ㄑㄩㄝˋ ㄌㄧˋ)
to hop around
雀羅(ㄑㄩㄝˋ ㄌㄨㄛˊ)
a net for catching birds
雀息(ㄑㄩㄝˋ ㄒㄧˊ)
to remain quiet; to remain silent
雀戰(ㄑㄩㄝˋ ㄓㄢˋ)
to play a game of mah-jong
雀巢鳩佔(ㄑㄩㄝˋ ㄔㄠˊ ㄐㄧㄡ ㄓㄢˋ)
(literally) The sparrow's nest is occupied by a pigeon. —to usurp other's position, property, etc.
雀舌(ㄑㄩㄝˋ ㄕㄜˊ)
name of a kind of tender tea leaves
雀鼠之爭(ㄑㄩㄝˋ ㄕㄨˇ ㄓ ㄓㄥ)
a lawsuit; a dispute
雀噪(ㄑㄩㄝˋ ㄗㄠˋ)
noisy and vociferous
雀躍(ㄑㄩㄝˋ ㄩㄝˋ)
to jump up with joy; greatly excited with joy: 他們聽到這個消息雀躍不已。They jumped for joy at the news.

四畫

【雄】 6658 ㄒㄩㄥˊ shyong xióng
1. male; masculine; virile
2. a person or state having great power and influence
3. heroic; brave; strong; martial; ambitious
4. to win; to triumph; victory
5. to scold others with insulting words
6. a Chinese family name
雄霸一方(ㄒㄩㄥˊ ㄅㄚˋ ㄧˋ ㄈㄤ) or 雄據一方(ㄒㄩㄥˊ ㄐㄩˋ ㄧˋ ㄈㄤ)
(said of warlords, contending princes, etc.) to hold a part of the country and to exercise undisputed authority
雄辯(ㄒㄩㄥˊ ㄅㄧㄢˋ)
a forceful presentation of one's points in a debate; eloquence: 事實勝於雄辯。Facts speak louder than eloquent words.
雄辯滔滔(ㄒㄩㄥˊ ㄅㄧㄢˋ ㄊㄠ ㄊㄠ)
to argue eloquently
雄兵(ㄒㄩㄥˊ ㄅㄧㄥ)
crack troops; powerful armies
雄飛(ㄒㄩㄥˊ ㄈㄟ)
to strive for bigger and better things
雄風(ㄒㄩㄥˊ ㄈㄥ)
an awe-inspiring air; a gallant and stately manner
雄圖(ㄒㄩㄥˊ ㄊㄨˊ) or 雄略(ㄒㄩㄥˊ ㄌㄩㄝˋ)
an ambitious scheme; a great aspiration
雄豪(ㄒㄩㄥˊ ㄏㄠˊ)
① heroes or powerful persons ② ambitious and warlike; martial
雄厚(ㄒㄩㄥˊ ㄏㄡˋ)
ample; plentiful; rich; abundant; substantial or very considerable (strength, wealth, etc.): 他的資金雄厚。He has abundant funds.
雄花(ㄒㄩㄥˊ ㄏㄨㄚ)
(botany) a male flower; a staminate flower
雄渾(ㄒㄩㄥˊ ㄏㄨㄣˊ)
powerful; grand; grandiose
雄黃(ㄒㄩㄥˊ ㄏㄨㄤˊ)
realgar
雄黃酒(ㄒㄩㄥˊ ㄏㄨㄤˊ ㄐㄧㄡˇ)
liquor with a small amount of realgar to be drunk on the Dragon Boat Festival so that one can avoid snake and insect poisoning the year round
雄雞(ㄒㄩㄥˊ ㄐㄧ)
a cock; a male chicken
雄赳赳(ㄒㄩㄥˊ ㄐㄧㄡ ㄐㄧㄡ)
imposing; looking brave and resolute; valiantly
雄劍(ㄒㄩㄥˊ ㄐㄧㄢˋ)
one of a pair of famous swords in ancient China
雄健(ㄒㄩㄥˊ ㄐㄧㄢˋ)
powerful; vigorous; strapping; very healthy, virile and energetic
雄將(ㄒㄩㄥˊ ㄐㄧㄤˋ)
a top-notch soldier or general; a man of great physical strength
雄氣(ㄒㄩㄥˊ ㄑㄧˋ)
a gallant or heroic disposition
雄器(ㄒㄩㄥˊ ㄑㄧˋ)
(botany) antheridia
雄心(ㄒㄩㄥˊ ㄒㄧㄣ)
ambition; great expectations
雄心勃勃(ㄒㄩㄥˊ ㄒㄧㄣ ㄅㄛˊ ㄅㄛˊ)
very ambitious
雄心壯志(ㄒㄩㄥˊ ㄒㄧㄣ ㄓㄨㄤˋ ㄓˋ)

high hopes and great ambition; lofty ideals and high goals; lofty aspirations and great ideals
雄心未死(ㄒㄩㄥˊ ㄒㄧㄣ ㄨㄟˋ ㄙˇ)
undying ambition; not to give up yet
雄雄(ㄒㄩㄥˊ ㄒㄩㄥˊ)
imposing and overpowering
雄峙(ㄒㄩㄥˊ ㄓˋ)
to stand imposingly
雄鎭(ㄒㄩㄥˊ ㄓㄣˋ)
a strategic city which can be easily defended
雄長(ㄒㄩㄥˊ ㄓㄤˇ)
hegemony
雄壯(ㄒㄩㄥˊ ㄓㄨㄤˋ)
majestic; virile; powerful; strong
雄師(ㄒㄩㄥˊ ㄕ)
crack troops; a powerful army 亦作「雄兵」
雄視(ㄒㄩㄥˊ ㄕˋ)
to dominate (in a certain field of achievement)
雄勝(ㄒㄩㄥˊ ㄕㄥˋ)
a strategic pass, position, etc.
雄蕊(ㄒㄩㄥˊ ㄖㄨㄟˇ)
(botany) the stamen
雄姿(ㄒㄩㄥˊ ㄗ)
a dashing look; a manly form; a brave appearance; the look of audacity and prowess
雄才大略(ㄒㄩㄥˊ ㄘㄞˊ ㄉㄚˋ ㄌㄩㄝˋ)
(said of a ruler) extremely capable
雄兒(ㄒㄩㄥˊ ㄦˊ)
a man among men; a hero
雄偉(ㄒㄩㄥˊ ㄨㄟˇ)
grandeur; majestic; stately; imposing; magnificent

【雁】 6659
(鴈) ㄧㄢˋ yann yàn
the wild goose
雁帛(ㄧㄢˋ ㄅㄛˊ)
letters; correspondence
雁門(ㄧㄢˋ ㄇㄣˊ)
name of several places in Shansi, Shensi, Honan and Kiangsu
雁杳魚沈(ㄧㄢˋ ㄇㄧㄠˇ ㄩˊ ㄔㄣˊ)
without news or letters; to have lost contact
雁來紅(ㄧㄢˋ ㄌㄞˊ ㄏㄨㄥˊ)
the Chinese amaranth
雁行(ㄧㄢˋ ㄏㄤˊ)
① to walk like flying wild geese, one after another ② brothers
雁行折翼(ㄧㄢˋ ㄏㄤˊ ㄓㄜˊ ㄧˋ)
the death of a brother
雁戶(ㄧㄢˋ ㄏㄨˋ)
a transient resident
雁序(ㄧㄢˋ ㄒㄩˋ)
brothers
雁陣(ㄧㄢˋ ㄓㄣˋ)
wild geese flying in good order, like a military deployment
雁齒(ㄧㄢˋ ㄔˇ)
things laid out in a neat row or in good order
雁字(ㄧㄢˋ ㄗˋ)
characters formed by flying wild geese (as "一" or "人")
雁足傳書(ㄧㄢˋ ㄗㄨˊ ㄔㄨㄢˊ ㄕㄨ)
to bring a message or letter

【雅】 6660
ㄧㄚˇ yea yǎ
1. refined; polished; sophisticated; not common or vulgar
2. elegant; graceful
3. usually; often; frequently; much
4. name of an ancient musical instrument
5. friendship; acquaintance
6. (now rarely) a wine vessel
7. (a polite term) your
8. a Chinese family name
雅步(ㄧㄚˇ ㄅㄨˋ)
leisurely and graceful steps
雅痞(ㄧㄚˇ ㄆㄧˇ)
Yuppie or Yuppy (a young, ambitious, and well-educated city-dweller who has a professional career and an affluent lifestyle)
雅美族(ㄧㄚˇ ㄇㄟˇ ㄗㄨˊ)
the Yamis, an aborigine tribe on Orchid Island (Lanyü) off the eastern coast of Taiwan
雅典(ㄧㄚˇ ㄉㄧㄢˇ)
Athens, capital of Greece
雅典那(ㄧㄚˇ ㄉㄧㄢˇ ㄋㄚˋ)
Athena
雅典主義(ㄧㄚˇ ㄉㄧㄢˇ ㄓㄨˇ ㄧˋ)
Atticism, or atticism
雅利安族(ㄧㄚˇ ㄌㄧˋ ㄢ ㄗㄨˊ)
the Aryans
雅量(ㄧㄚˇ ㄌㄧㄤˋ)
① magnanimity; generous; broad-mindedness ② a great capacity for drinking
雅魯藏布江(ㄧㄚˇ ㄌㄨˇ ㄗㄤˋ ㄅㄨˋ ㄐㄧㄤ)
the Brahmaputra River
雅歌(ㄧㄚˇ ㄍㄜ)
① to sing highbrow songs ② (in the Bible) the Song of Solomon
雅故(ㄧㄚˇ ㄍㄨˋ)
① an old friend ② usually
雅觀(ㄧㄚˇ ㄍㄨㄢ)
graceful and elegant in appearance; propriety in conduct
雅庫特人(ㄧㄚˇ ㄎㄨˋ ㄊㄜˋ ㄖㄣˊ)
the Yakuts
雅庫次克(ㄧㄚˇ ㄎㄨˋ ㄘˋ ㄎㄜˋ)
Yakutsk, U.S.S.R.
雅號(ㄧㄚˇ ㄏㄠˋ)
(a polite expression) your name
雅懷(ㄧㄚˇ ㄏㄨㄞˊ)
a generous heart; refined taste and disposition
雅誨(ㄧㄚˇ ㄏㄨㄟˋ) or 雅教(ㄧㄚˇ ㄐㄧㄠˋ)
(a polite expression used in letters) your instruction or advice; your esteemed opinion
雅集(ㄧㄚˇ ㄐㄧˊ)
a gathering of men of letters
雅鑒(ㄧㄚˇ ㄐㄧㄢˋ)
(a polite expression) for your perusal
雅趣(ㄧㄚˇ ㄑㄩˋ)
refined tastes
雅興(ㄧㄚˇ ㄒㄧㄥˋ)
enthusiasm in refined pursuits
雅馴(ㄧㄚˇ ㄒㄩㄣˋ)
(said of writing or remarks) polished, refined or elegant
雅致(ㄧㄚˇ ㄓˋ)
① refined tastes; refinement ② fine; delicate; elegant; tasteful
雅正(ㄧㄚˇ ㄓㄥˋ)
① graceful and upright ② (a polite expression written on one's own calligraphic work presented to a friend as a gift) Please point out my shortcomings.

雅囑(ㄧㄚˇ ㄓㄨˇ)
(a polite expression) your orders or advice
雅士(ㄧㄚˇ ㄕˋ) or 雅人(ㄧㄚˇ ㄖㄣˊ)
a refined scholar; a person of refined tastes
雅事(ㄧㄚˇ ㄕˋ)
refined activities of the intelligentsia
雅人深致(ㄧㄚˇ ㄖㄣˊ ㄕㄣ ㄓˋ)
a sophisticated person with profound thoughts
雅賊(ㄧㄚˇ ㄗㄟˊ)
a thief who steals only books and works of art
雅座(ㄧㄚˇ ㄗㄨㄛˋ)
a nicely fixed chamber or room in a restaurant for customers who desire privacy
雅俗(ㄧㄚˇ ㄙㄨˊ)
the refined and the vulgar; the sophisticated and the simple-minded
雅俗共賞(ㄧㄚˇ ㄙㄨˊ ㄍㄨㄥˋ ㄕㄤˇ)
(said of art, performances, etc.) to appeal to both the sophisticated and the simple-minded
雅素(ㄧㄚˇ ㄙㄨˋ)
① personal background ② old friendship ③ virtue in simplicity
雅愛(ㄧㄚˇ ㄞˋ)
(a polite expression) your patronage; your help: 多謝雅愛。Thanks for your patronage (or help).
雅爾達會議(ㄧㄚˇ ㄦˇ ㄉㄚˊ ㄏㄨㄟˋ ㄧˋ)
the Yalta Conference among Roosevelt, Churchill and Stalin, held on February 4, 1945
雅意(ㄧㄚˇ ㄧˋ)
your ideas or views
雅游(ㄧㄚˇ ㄧㄡˊ)
very sociable; easy to get along with people
雅言(ㄧㄚˇ ㄧㄢˊ)
① well-intentioned criticism; honest advice ② things one often talks about
雅玩(ㄧㄚˇ ㄨㄢˊ)
① refined pastimes of the intelligentsia ② a polite expression in presenting a curio, etc. to a friend
雅望(ㄧㄚˇ ㄨㄤˋ)
your spotless fame
雅樂(ㄧㄚˇ ㄩㄝˋ)
①(in ancient China) ceremonial music ② Chinese classical music
雅韻(ㄧㄚˇ ㄩㄣˋ)
refined or sophisticated taste

【集】 6661 ㄐㄧˊ jyi jí

1. to assemble; to collect; to gather together; to concentrate
2. a collection of works by one or more authors; to compile; to edit
3. achievements
4. a fair; a periodical market

集部(ㄐㄧˊ ㄅㄨˋ)
the fourth section of *Encyclopedia Sinica,* which contains literary works
集大成(ㄐㄧˊ ㄉㄚˋ ㄔㄥˊ)
a theory, etc. representing a generalization of many views or ideas; eclectic
集體(ㄐㄧˊ ㄊㄧˇ)
collective
集體農場(ㄐㄧˊ ㄊㄧˇ ㄋㄨㄥˊ ㄔㄤˊ)
a collective farm
集體領導(ㄐㄧˊ ㄊㄧˇ ㄌㄧㄥˇ ㄉㄠˇ)
collective leadership
集體管理(ㄐㄧˊ ㄊㄧˇ ㄍㄨㄢˇ ㄌㄧˇ)
mass management
集體經濟(ㄐㄧˊ ㄊㄧˇ ㄐㄧㄥ ㄐㄧˋ)
collective economy
集體決定(ㄐㄧˊ ㄊㄧˇ ㄐㄩㄝˊ ㄉㄧㄥˋ)
group decision
集體創作(ㄐㄧˊ ㄊㄧˇ ㄔㄨㄤˋ ㄗㄨㄛˋ)
a collective (literary or artistic) work; collective creation
集體安全(ㄐㄧˊ ㄊㄧˇ ㄢ ㄑㄩㄢˊ)
collective security
集體研究(ㄐㄧˊ ㄊㄧˇ ㄧㄢˊ ㄐㄧㄡˋ)
team research
集團(ㄐㄧˊ ㄊㄨㄢˊ)
an organization; a body of people; a bloc; a faction; a clique
集團結婚(ㄐㄧˊ ㄊㄨㄢˊ ㄐㄧㄝˊ ㄏㄨㄣ)
a mass wedding; a wedding ceremony either held at a court of law or under the sponsorship of a civic or military organization, in which many couples are joined in wedlock
集團軍(ㄐㄧˊ ㄊㄨㄢˊ ㄐㄩㄣ)
an army (a military outfit which consists of more than two corps)
集股(ㄐㄧˊ ㄍㄨˇ)
to collect capital (in order to establish a business)
集刊(ㄐㄧˊ ㄎㄢ)
collected papers (of an academic institution)
集合(ㄐㄧˊ ㄏㄜˊ)
to assemble; to gather together; to muster
集合名詞(ㄐㄧˊ ㄏㄜˊ ㄇㄧㄥˊ ㄘˊ)
a collective noun
集合體(ㄐㄧˊ ㄏㄜˊ ㄊㄧˇ)
(said of minerals) an aggregate
集會(ㄐㄧˊ ㄏㄨㄟˋ)
a meeting; a conference; an assemblage; an assembly
集會結社(ㄐㄧˊ ㄏㄨㄟˋ ㄐㄧㄝˊ ㄕㄜˋ)
to assemble and form an organization, society, etc.
集會自由(ㄐㄧˊ ㄏㄨㄟˋ ㄗˋ ㄧㄡˊ)
freedom of assembly
集結(ㄐㄧˊ ㄐㄧㄝˊ)
to concentrate (troops)
集錦(ㄐㄧˊ ㄐㄧㄣˇ)
a collection of homogeneous passages from various literary pieces; a hodgepodge
集句(ㄐㄧˊ ㄐㄩˋ)
to cull lines here and there from a poet's work and piece them together into a new poem
集聚(ㄐㄧˊ ㄐㄩˋ)
to collect or gather together: 一群人集聚在街角。A crowd gathered on the corner.
集權(ㄐㄧˊ ㄑㄩㄢˊ)
centralization of authority; concentration of power
集訓(ㄐㄧˊ ㄒㄩㄣˋ)
to train many people at the same place and same time; a camp training
集注(ㄐㄧˊ ㄓㄨˋ)
① to focus ② variorum
集中(ㄐㄧˊ ㄓㄨㄥ)
① to concentrate; to center; to centralize: 他集中心力在工作上。He concentrated his mind on his work. ② to gather

集中營(ㄐㄧˊ ㄓㄨㄥ ㄧㄥˊ)
a concentration camp
集產主義(ㄐㄧˊ ㄔㄢˇ ㄓㄨˇ ㄧˋ)
collectivism
集市(ㄐㄧˊ ㄕˋ)
a periodic market
集少成多(ㄐㄧˊ ㄕㄠˇ ㄔㄥˊ ㄉㄨㄛ)
Many a little makes a mickle.
集上(ㄐㄧˊ ・ㄕㄤ)
on the market
集資(ㄐㄧˊ ㄗ)
to raise funds; to collect money; to pool resources
集子(ㄐㄧˊ ・ㄗ)
a collection; collected works; an anthology: 這本集子很不錯。This collection is very good.
集思廣益(ㄐㄧˊ ㄙ ㄍㄨㄤˇ ㄧˋ)
to canvass various opinions and benefit from them
集散地(ㄐㄧˊ ㄙㄢˋ ㄉㄧˋ)
a commercial center; a commercial port
集議(ㄐㄧˊ ㄧˋ)
to meet and discuss; to hold a conference
集腋成裘(ㄐㄧˊ ㄧㄝˋ ㄔㄥˊ ㄑㄧㄡˊ)
Small resources pooled together can accomplish big things. 或 Many a little makes a mickle.
集郵(ㄐㄧˊ ㄧㄡˊ)
philately; stamp collection
集郵簿(ㄐㄧˊ ㄧㄡˊ ㄅㄨˋ)
a stamp album
集郵家(ㄐㄧˊ ㄧㄡˊ ㄐㄧㄚ)
a philatelist or stamp collector
集於一身(ㄐㄧˊ ㄩˊ ㄧˋ ㄕㄣ)
to center on one person, as powers, etc.

【雇】 6662
ㄍㄨˋ guh gù
to employ or hire
雇不到(ㄍㄨˋ ・ㄅㄨ ㄉㄠˋ)
unable to hire or employ —either because of low pay or shortage of labor supply
雇不起(ㄍㄨˋ ・ㄅㄨ ㄑㄧˇ)
cannot afford to hire: 他雇不起佣人。He couldn't afford to hire a servant.
雇農(ㄍㄨˋ ㄋㄨㄥˊ)
hired laborers on the farm; a hired farm hand
雇工(ㄍㄨˋ ㄍㄨㄥ)
① a hired laborer: 他做臨時雇工。He worked for hire. ② to hire a laborer
雇主(ㄍㄨˋ ㄓㄨˇ)
the employer
雇車(ㄍㄨˋ ㄔㄜ)
to hire a cab, truck, etc. together with its driver
雇船(ㄍㄨˋ ㄔㄨㄢˊ)
to charter or hire a boat
雇員(ㄍㄨˋ ㄩㄢˊ)
an auxiliary employee of very low rank in a government office
雇傭(ㄍㄨˋ ㄩㄥ)
hired or employed

五畫

【雍】 6663
ㄩㄥ iong yōng
1. harmonious; harmony; peaceful; union
2. name of various places or states throughout the dynasties
3. to block up; to obstruct
4. a Chinese family name
雍睦(ㄩㄥ ㄇㄨˋ)
harmonious or friendly
雍和(ㄩㄥ ㄏㄜˊ)
harmony
雍正(ㄩㄥ ㄓㄥˋ)
the reigning title of the third emperor of the Ching Dynasty
雍容(ㄩㄥ ㄖㄨㄥˊ)
a majestic, stately or imposing appearance
雍容華貴(ㄩㄥ ㄖㄨㄥˊ ㄏㄨㄚˊ ㄍㄨㄟˋ)
(said of a woman) graceful and poised; regal
雍容自得(ㄩㄥ ㄖㄨㄥˊ ㄗˋ ㄉㄜˊ)
poised; in the peace of mind
雍閼(ㄩㄥ ㄜˋ)
to block or stop up; to obstruct
雍雍(ㄩㄥ ㄩㄥ)
harmonious; peaceful

【雉】 6664
ㄓˋ jyh zhì
1. a pheasant
2. a unit of volume measure in ancient China (about 30' square by 10')
雉媒(ㄓˋ ㄇㄟˊ)
a domesticated pheasant used as a decoy in pheasant hunting
雉堞(ㄓˋ ㄉㄧㄝˊ)
a parapet with embrasures; crenelation
雉雞(ㄓˋ ㄐㄧ)
a pheasant; a tartar pheasant
雉經(ㄓˋ ㄐㄧㄥ)
to commit suicide by hanging

【雊】 6665
ㄍㄡˋ gow gòu
the crow of a male pheasant

【雌】 6666
ㄘ tsy cī
1. female; feminine; womanlike; soft (voice, etc.)
2. weak; retiring
3. the vanquished; defeated
4. to scold
5. to expose or show (the teeth) 亦作「齜」
雌風(ㄘ ㄈㄥ)
① evil practice or custom ② the tantrum of a virago or shrew
雌伏(ㄘ ㄈㄨˊ)
to lie low; not ambitious; retiring; withdrawing; not aggressive
雌懦(ㄘ ㄋㄨㄛˋ)
weak-minded; cowardly
雌老虎(ㄘ ㄌㄠˇ ・ㄏㄨ)
① a tigress ② (colloquial) a loud-mouthed shrew, fishwife or virago 亦作「母老虎」
雌花(ㄘ ㄏㄨㄚ)
a pistillate flower
雌黃(ㄘ ㄏㄨㄤˊ)
① orpiment (As_2S_3) ② to make changes in writing ③ to criticize without grounds; to malign 參看「信口雌黃」
雌性(ㄘ ㄒㄧㄥˋ)
female
雌雄(ㄘ ㄒㄩㄥˊ)
① the female and the male ② the victor and the loser: 讓我們決一雌雄。Let's have a showdown. 或 Let's fight a decisive battle. ③ things that form a pair—as precious swords in ancient China
雌雄莫辨(ㄘ ㄒㄩㄥˊ ㄇㄛˋ ㄅㄧㄢˋ)
unable to distinguish the sex

隹部

identity
雌雄淘汰(ㄘ ㄒㄩㄥˊ ㄊㄠˊ ㄊㄞˋ)
sexual selection
雌雄同體(ㄘ ㄒㄩㄥˊ ㄊㄨㄥˊ ㄊㄧˇ)
hermaphrodite
雌雄同株(ㄘ ㄒㄩㄥˊ ㄊㄨㄥˊ ㄓㄨ)
monoecious; monoecism
雌雄劍(ㄘ ㄒㄩㄥˊ ㄐㄧㄢˋ)
the name of a pair of precious swords in ancient China
雌雄異體(ㄘ ㄒㄩㄥˊ ㄧˋ ㄊㄧˇ)
gonochorism
雌雄異株(ㄘ ㄒㄩㄥˊ ㄧˋ ㄓㄨ)
dioecious
雌蕊(ㄘ ㄖㄨㄟˇ)
a pistil
雌威(ㄘ ㄨㄟ)
the tantrum of a shrew

【雋】 6667
1. ㄐㄩㄣˋ jiunn jùn
1. good-looking
2. talented; outstanding; extraordinary
雋拔(ㄐㄩㄣˋ ㄅㄚˊ)
outstandingly talented
雋楚(ㄐㄩㄣˋ ㄔㄨˇ)
outstanding; extraordinary; preeminence
雋譽(ㄐㄩㄣˋ ㄩˋ)
high fame or good reputation

【雋】 6667
2. ㄐㄩㄢˋ jiuann juàn
1. fat meat
2. meaningful
3. a Chinese family name
雋永(ㄐㄩㄢˋ ㄩㄥˇ)
(said of remarks or writings) very interesting or intriguing; meaningful

【雎】 6668
ㄐㄩ jiu jū
1. a kind of waterfowl (雎鳩) which observes fidelity in sex life, probably the osprey
2. (now rarely) to hesitate; to avoid

六畫

【雒】 6669
ㄌㄨㄛˋ luoh luò
1. a black horse with white mane
2. to brand
3. name of a river
4. an owl

八畫

【雕】 6670
ㄉㄧㄠ diau diāo
1. to engrave; to carve or cut, as in sculpture
2. an eagle; a hawk
3. to exhaust; to weaken
雕板(ㄉㄧㄠ ㄅㄢˇ)
to cut blocks of wood for printing (first started in the Sui (隋) Dynasty)
雕梁畫棟(ㄉㄧㄠ ㄌㄧㄤˊ ㄏㄨㄚˋ ㄉㄨㄥˋ)
carved beams and painted rafters—a richly ornamented building
雕龍(ㄉㄧㄠ ㄌㄨㄥˊ)
(literally) the carving of dragons—a highly embellished literary style
雕戈(ㄉㄧㄠ ㄍㄜ)
a carved lance or engraved spear
雕肝琢腎(ㄉㄧㄠ ㄍㄢ ㄓㄨㄛˊ ㄕㄣˋ)
to exhaust physical and mental energy
雕弓(ㄉㄧㄠ ㄍㄨㄥ)
a painted or ornamented bow
雕刻(ㄉㄧㄠ ㄎㄜˋ)
①sculpture ② to engrave
雕花(ㄉㄧㄠ ㄏㄨㄚ)
to engrave figures or pictures
雕漆(ㄉㄧㄠ ㄑㄧ)
to engrave or carve on lacquer ware
雕像(ㄉㄧㄠ ㄒㄧㄤˋ)
① a sculptured statue ② portrayal of a person
雕琢(ㄉㄧㄠ ㄓㄨㄛˊ)
① to cut and polish (gems) ② to polish a piece of writing; to write in an ornate style
雕蟲小技(ㄉㄧㄠ ㄔㄨㄥˊ ㄒㄧㄠˇ ㄐㄧˋ)
a petty skill or craft; a skill which has no significant value
雕蟲篆(ㄉㄧㄠ ㄔㄨㄥˊ ㄓㄨㄢˋ)
a type of calligraphy featuring characters twisting and turning like worms
雕蟲篆刻(ㄉㄧㄠ ㄔㄨㄥˊ ㄓㄨㄢˋ ㄎㄜˋ)
(a self-derogatory expression) skill in writing poetic prose
雕塑(ㄉㄧㄠ ㄙㄨˋ)
① sculpture; to cut wood or clay for a statue or idol ② (figuratively) to paint a picture (of something or somebody)
雕雲(ㄉㄧㄠ ㄩㄣˊ)
propitious clouds; clouds portending good fortune

【雔】 6671
ㄔㄡˊ chour chóu
a pair of birds

九畫

【雖】 6672
ㄙㄨㄟ suei suī
(又讀 ㄙㄨㄟˊ swei suí)
1. although; even though; even if; supposing
2. to push away; to dismiss
3. only
4. (now rarely) a lizard-like reptile
雖敗猶榮(ㄙㄨㄟ ㄅㄞˋ ㄧㄡˊ ㄖㄨㄥˊ)
to feel proud even in defeat
雖說(ㄙㄨㄟ ㄕㄨㄛ)
even though; although
雖然(ㄙㄨㄟ ㄖㄢˊ)
even though; although; in spite of; even if
雖則(ㄙㄨㄟ ㄗㄜˊ)
although; even if; still: 雖則他不來，我也不介意。I won't mind even if he doesn't come.

十畫

【雙】 6673
ㄕㄨㄤ shuang shuāng
1. a pair; a brace; a couple; persons or things that come in pairs: 他有一雙新襪子。He has a new pair of socks.
2. two; both; even (as distinct from odd)
雙倍(ㄕㄨㄤ ㄅㄟˋ)
double; twofold; twice the amount or number: 十為五之雙倍。Ten is the double of five.
雙胞胎(ㄕㄨㄤ ㄅㄠ ㄊㄞ)
twins
雙邊貿易(ㄕㄨㄤ ㄅㄧㄢ ㄇㄠˋ ㄧˋ)
bilateral trade; two-way

trade

雙面(ㄕㄨㄤ ㄇㄧㄢˋ)
two-sided; double-edged; double-faced; reversible

雙名(ㄕㄨㄤ ㄇㄧㄥˊ)
a given name consists of two characters

雙目失明(ㄕㄨㄤ ㄇㄨˋ ㄕ ㄇㄧㄥˊ)
to be blind in both eyes

雙分兒(ㄕㄨㄤ ㄈㄜˋㄦ)
double shares; double the amount; twice as much

雙飛(ㄕㄨㄤ ㄈㄟ)
flying in pairs—close union as man and wife who are very much in love

雙方(ㄕㄨㄤ ㄈㄤ)
both parties or sides (in a dispute, an agreement, etc.)

雙方同意(ㄕㄨㄤ ㄈㄤ ㄊㄨㄥˊ ㄧˋ)
mutual consent

雙峯駝(ㄕㄨㄤ ㄈㄥ ㄊㄨㄛˊ)
a double-humped camel; the Bactrian camel

雙幅(ㄕㄨㄤ ㄈㄨˊ)
(said of fabrics or piece goods) of double standard width

雙打(ㄕㄨㄤ ㄉㄚˇ)
to play in doubles (as tennis); doubles: 男女混合雙打 mixed doubles

雙瞳翦水(ㄕㄨㄤ ㄊㄨㄥˊ ㄐㄧㄢˇ ㄕㄨㄟˇ)
clear, beautiful eyes of a pretty girl

雙鯉(ㄕㄨㄤ ㄌㄧˇ)
letters

雙料(ㄕㄨㄤ ㄌㄧㄠˋ)
articles, products built with added strength, durability, etc. by using better and more raw materials

雙掛號(ㄕㄨㄤ ㄍㄨㄚˋ ㄏㄠˋ)
registered mail with return receipt

雙軌(ㄕㄨㄤ ㄍㄨㄟˇ)
double-tracked (railway); double tracks: 雙軌鐵路 a railway with a double track

雙軌制(ㄕㄨㄤ ㄍㄨㄟˇ ㄓˋ)
(education) the double-track system

雙關(ㄕㄨㄤ ㄍㄨㄢ)
ambiguous; subject to two different interpretations: 一語雙關 a phrase with a double meaning

雙關語(ㄕㄨㄤ ㄍㄨㄢ ㄩˇ)
a double entendre; a pun

雙管齊下(ㄕㄨㄤ ㄍㄨㄢˇ ㄑㄧˊ ㄒㄧㄚˋ)
① to do two things simultaneously in order to attain an objective; a double-barreled move ② ambiguous; subject to two different interpretations

雙款(ㄕㄨㄤ ㄎㄨㄢˇ)
(said of paintings, calligraphy, etc.) with both "upper" and "lower" inscriptions (i.e. both the names of the recipient and the artist)

雙號(ㄕㄨㄤ ㄏㄠˋ)
(said of tickets, seats, etc.) an even number

雙簧(ㄕㄨㄤ ㄏㄨㄤˊ)
a kind of variety show featuring two performers, one of whom speaks while the other acts out the gestures at the same time; a two-man comic show

雙簧管(ㄕㄨㄤ ㄏㄨㄤˊ ㄍㄨㄢˇ)
(music) an oboe

雙頰(ㄕㄨㄤ ㄐㄧㄚˊ)
both cheeks: 這小孩雙頰通紅。The boy has rosy cheeks.

雙脚(ㄕㄨㄤ ㄐㄧㄠˇ)
both feet; the two feet

雙肩(ㄕㄨㄤ ㄐㄧㄢ)
both shoulders; the two shoulders

雙棲(ㄕㄨㄤ ㄑㄧ)
to live together as man and wife

雙親(ㄕㄨㄤ ㄑㄧㄣ)
one's parents: 他的雙親很富有。His parents are very rich.

雙曲線(ㄕㄨㄤ ㄑㄩ ㄒㄧㄢˋ)
(mathematics) a hyperbola

雙全(ㄕㄨㄤ ㄑㄩㄢˊ)
① both (parents) alive ② both intact; possessing both: 他智勇雙全。He possesses both intelligence and bravery.

雙喜臨門(ㄕㄨㄤ ㄒㄧˇ ㄌㄧㄣˊ ㄇㄣˊ)
to have simultaneously two happy events in a family (such as a son getting married on the father's birthday)或 A double blessing has descended upon the house.

雙下巴(ㄕㄨㄤ ㄒㄧㄚˋ ㄅㄚ)
a double chin

雙薪家庭(ㄕㄨㄤ ㄒㄧㄣ ㄐㄧㄚ ㄊㄧㄥˊ)
two-paycheck families

雙響(ㄕㄨㄤ ㄒㄧㄤˇ)
name of a kind of firecracker which soars like a rocket and explodes with two blasts 亦作「二踢腳」

雙餉(ㄕㄨㄤ ㄒㄧㄤˇ)
double pay for soldiers

雙向溝通(ㄕㄨㄤ ㄒㄧㄤˋ ㄍㄡ ㄊㄨㄥ)
two-way communication

雙向交通(ㄕㄨㄤ ㄒㄧㄤˋ ㄐㄧㄠ ㄊㄨㄥ)
two-way traffic

雙姓(ㄕㄨㄤ ㄒㄧㄥˋ)
a family name which consists of two characters

雙週刊(ㄕㄨㄤ ㄓㄡ ㄎㄢ)
a fortnightly; a biweekly

雙翅類(ㄕㄨㄤ ㄔˋ ㄌㄟˋ)
(zoology) the Diptera

雙城記(ㄕㄨㄤ ㄔㄥˊ ㄐㄧˋ)
A Tale of Two Cities, by Charles Dickens

雙唇音(ㄕㄨㄤ ㄔㄨㄣˊ ㄧㄣ)
bilabial consonants

雙重(ㄕㄨㄤ ㄔㄨㄥˊ)
double; dual; twofold: 它起雙重作用。It served a dual purpose.

雙重標準(ㄕㄨㄤ ㄔㄨㄥˊ ㄅㄧㄠ ㄓㄨㄣˇ)
double standard

雙重國籍(ㄕㄨㄤ ㄔㄨㄥˊ ㄍㄨㄛˊ ㄐㄧˊ)
dual nationality

雙重人格(ㄕㄨㄤ ㄔㄨㄥˊ ㄖㄣˊ ㄍㄜˊ)
(psychology) a dual personality; a split personality; a dual nature

雙十節(ㄕㄨㄤ ㄕˊ ㄐㄧㄝˊ)
the "Double Tenth", October 10, the National Day of the Republic of China

雙殺(ㄕㄨㄤ ㄕㄚ)
(baseball) double play

雙手(ㄕㄨㄤ ㄕㄡˇ)
the two hands; both hands

雙手萬能(ㄕㄨㄤ ㄕㄡˇ ㄨㄢˋ ㄋㄥˊ)
With two hands, one can work miracles.

雙身子(ㄕㄨㄤ ㄕㄣ ˙ㄗ)
a pregnant woman

雙生(ㄕㄨㄤ ㄕㄥ)
twin; twins: 這兩個學生是雙生兄弟。The two students are

twin brothers.

雙聲叠韻(ㄕㄨㄤ ㄕㄥ ㄉㄧㄝˊ ㄩㄣˋ)
alliteration and repetition in rhyme, such as 祈求 and 叮嚀

雙數(ㄕㄨㄤ ㄕㄨˋ)
an even number 亦作「偶數」

雙雙對對(ㄕㄨㄤ ㄕㄨㄤ ㄉㄨㄟˋ ㄉㄨㄟˋ)
in pairs and couples: 他們雙雙對對地進來。They came in in pairs.

雙日(ㄕㄨㄤ ㄖˋ)
even days

雙人房(ㄕㄨㄤ ㄖㄣˊ ㄈㄤˊ)
a double room; a twin room

雙人牀(ㄕㄨㄤ ㄖㄣˊ ㄔㄨㄤˊ)
a double bed

雙人舞(ㄕㄨㄤ ㄖㄣˊ ㄨˇ)
a dance for two people; *pas de deux*

雙子星(ㄕㄨㄤ ㄗˇ ㄒㄧㄥ) or 雙子宮(ㄕㄨㄤ ㄗˇ ㄍㄨㄥ) or 雙子座(ㄕㄨㄤ ㄗˇ ㄗㄨㄛˋ)
(astronomy) Gemini

雙子葉植物(ㄕㄨㄤ ㄗˇ ㄧㄝˋ ㄓˊ ㄨˋ)
(botany) a dicotyledon

雙層(ㄕㄨㄤ ㄘㄥˊ)
double layers; double decks

雙層牀(ㄕㄨㄤ ㄘㄥˊ ㄔㄨㄤˊ)
a double-decked bunk

雙宿雙飛(ㄕㄨㄤ ㄙㄨˋ ㄕㄨㄤ ㄈㄟ)
to live like man and wife; to sleep and move together

雙蛾(ㄕㄨㄤ ㄜˊ)
eyebrows of a woman

雙翼飛機(ㄕㄨㄤ ㄧˋ ㄈㄟ ㄐㄧ)
a biplane

雙眼皮兒(ㄕㄨㄤ ㄧㄢˇ ㄆㄧˊㄦ)
the upper eyelid which has a double fold at the lower edge, a common feature among Occidentals

雙氧水(ㄕㄨㄤ ㄧㄤˇ ㄕㄨㄟˇ)
hydrogen peroxide

雙亡(ㄕㄨㄤ ㄨㄤˊ)
(said of one's parents or of a couple) Both are dead.

雙魚座(ㄕㄨㄤ ㄩˊ ㄗㄨㄛˋ)
(astronomy) Pisces

雙月刊(ㄕㄨㄤ ㄩㄝˋ ㄎㄢ)
a bimonthly

【雛】 6674
ㄔㄨˊ chwu chú

1. a chick
2. a very young bird—a fledgling
3. a small kid or toddler

雛鳳(ㄔㄨˊ ㄈㄥˋ)
bright and promising children

雛鳥(ㄔㄨˊ ㄋㄧㄠˇ)
a very young bird—a fledgling

雛鷄(ㄔㄨˊ ㄐㄧ)
a chick; a chicken

雛妓(ㄔㄨˊ ㄐㄧˋ)
a very young prostitute

雛菊(ㄔㄨˊ ㄐㄩˊ)
a daisy

雛形(ㄔㄨˊ ㄒㄧㄥˊ)
a miniature form; a scaled-down model of anything; an embryonic form

雛兒(ㄔㄨˊㄦ)
① a very young prostitute ② an inexperienced young man; a novice ③ a young girl

雛鴨(ㄔㄨˊ ㄧㄚ)
a duckling

【雜】 6675
ㄗㄚˊ tzar zá

1. to mix; to blend; mixed; blended
2. miscellaneous
3. motley; medley
4. petty and numerous

雜拌兒(ㄗㄚˊ ㄅㄚˋㄦ)
mixed nuts; sweetmeats and sundries (served in New Year holidays)

雜八湊兒(ㄗㄚˊ ˙ㄅㄚ ㄘㄡˋㄦ)
a motley of different things; a collection of varied things

雜牌(ㄗㄚˊ ㄆㄞˊ)
a less known and inferior brand

雜評(ㄗㄚˊ ㄆㄧㄥˊ)
(journals, newspapers, etc.) a short commentary; a leaderette

雜麪(ㄗㄚˊ ㄇㄧㄢˋ)
noodles made of flour of mixed grains

雜費(ㄗㄚˊ ㄈㄟˋ)
miscellaneous expenses; sundry charges

雜沓(ㄗㄚˊ ㄊㄚˋ)
confused or disorderly

雜遝(ㄗㄚˊ ㄊㄚˋ)
numerous; many

雜談(ㄗㄚˊ ㄊㄢˊ)
a chat; a rambling talk; a random talk

雜念(ㄗㄚˊ ㄋㄧㄢˋ)
distracting thoughts

雜流(ㄗㄚˊ ㄌㄧㄡˊ)
①(formerly) petty officials ②(formerly) people dealing in commerce and trade

雜糧(ㄗㄚˊ ㄌㄧㄤˊ)
miscellaneous grain crops, as oat, millet, etc. (as opposed to rice and wheat which are staple foods)

雜亂(ㄗㄚˊ ㄌㄨㄢˋ)
confused and disorderly; to be jumbled

雜亂無章(ㄗㄚˊ ㄌㄨㄢˋ ㄨˊ ㄓㄤ)
motley; disorderly; in utter confusion; in a great mess

雜感(ㄗㄚˊ ㄍㄢˇ)
rambling observations; random thoughts

雜合菜(ㄗㄚˊ ˙ㄏㄜ ㄘㄞˋ)
a dish prepared by mixing or cooking the leftovers of a previous dinner or feast

雜貨(ㄗㄚˊ ㄏㄨㄛˋ)
groceries; sundry goods

雜貨店(ㄗㄚˊ ㄏㄨㄛˋ ㄉㄧㄢˋ)
a sundry store; a grocery; a corner drugstore

雜貨商(ㄗㄚˊ ㄏㄨㄛˋ ㄕㄤ)
a sundriesman

雜燴(ㄗㄚˊ ㄏㄨㄟˋ)
a dish of mixed food items

雜婚(ㄗㄚˊ ㄏㄨㄣ)
intermarriage

雜記(ㄗㄚˊ ㄐㄧˋ)
a miscellany; miscellaneous notes; random notes; jottings

雜技(ㄗㄚˊ ㄐㄧˋ)
a variety of juggling skills; a vaudeville; an acrobatic feat

雜技團(ㄗㄚˊ ㄐㄧˋ ㄊㄨㄢˊ)
an acrobatic troupe

雜家(ㄗㄚˊ ㄐㄧㄚ)
one of the nine schools of learning in ancient China, which combined the various schools of thoughts

雜交(ㄗㄚˊ ㄐㄧㄠ)
① (biology) to hybridize; to cross ② hybridization; crossbreed; a cross; interbreeding ③ promiscuity

雜居(ㄗㄚˊ ㄐㄩ) or 雜處(ㄗㄚˊ ㄔㄨˇ)
the living together of differ-

ent races or classes of people

雜劇(ㄗㄚˊ ㄐㄩˋ)
a variety show; a comedy or farce

雜七雜八(ㄗㄚˊ ㄑㄧ ㄗㄚˊ ㄅㄚ)or 雜七八拉(ㄗㄚˊ ㄑㄧ ㄅㄚ ㄌㄚ)
a motley; a jumble of various things; odds and ends

雜項(ㄗㄚˊ ㄒㄧㄤˋ)
miscellaneous items; (said of people) of different backgrounds and occupations

雜性花(ㄗㄚˊ ㄒㄧㄥˋ ㄏㄨㄚ)
a polygamous flower

雜學(ㄗㄚˊ ㄒㄩㄝˊ)
miscellaneous learning —unorthodox or unconventional learning

雜質(ㄗㄚˊ ㄓˊ)
impurities

雜誌(ㄗㄚˊ ㄓˋ)
a magazine; a periodical; a journal

雜種(ㄗㄚˊ ㄓㄨㄥˇ)
①a mixed breed; a hybrid ②(in ancient China) a foreign race or tribe ③a bastard; son of a bitch

雜史(ㄗㄚˊ ㄕˇ)
a personal recording of a single incident or of happenings during a given period

雜耍(ㄗㄚˊ ㄕㄨㄚˇ)
juggler's feats; a vaudeville or variety show

雜稅(ㄗㄚˊ ㄕㄨㄟˋ)
miscellaneous taxes; irregular taxes

雜糅(ㄗㄚˊ ㄖㄡˇ)
the mixing or blending together of a variety of things

雜然(ㄗㄚˊ ㄖㄢˊ)
all; unanimously

雜纂(ㄗㄚˊ ㄗㄨㄢˇ)
notes or records of miscellaneous and petty incidents, episodes, etc.

雜廁(ㄗㄚˊ ㄘˋ)
disorderly and confused; motley

雜草(ㄗㄚˊ ㄘㄠˇ)
weeds: 這花園雜草叢生。The garden was covered with weeds.

雜湊(ㄗㄚˊ ㄘㄡˋ)
the mixing or assorting (especially impromptu) of miscellaneous things together which usually don't have a central theme

雜錯(ㄗㄚˊ ㄘㄨㄛˋ)
mixed 亦作「雜厝」

雜爨(ㄗㄚˊ ㄘㄨㄢˋ)
feats displayed in a vaudeville or variety show

雜色(ㄗㄚˊ ㄙㄜˋ)
variegated; parti-colored; motley

雜碎(ㄗㄚˊ ·ㄙㄨㄟ)
① complicated and trifling ② the internal organs of cattle or lambs as a dish ③ chop suey, or chop sooy ④ conscience; the true nature of a person

雜役(ㄗㄚˊ ㄧˋ)
odd jobs; chores

雜音(ㄗㄚˊ ㄧㄣ)
noises; (recording) humming or other unwanted sounds

雜樣(ㄗㄚˊ ㄧㄤˋ)
to mix together different types of things

雜務(ㄗㄚˊ ㄨˋ)
chores; miscellaneous duties

雜物(ㄗㄚˊ ㄨˋ)
miscellaneous articles or objects; odds and ends

雜文學(ㄗㄚˊ ㄨㄣˊ ㄒㄩㄝˊ)
(literally) miscellaneous literature, as narratives, commentaries, etc.

雜院兒(ㄗㄚˊ ㄩㄢˋㄦ)
a cluster of houses sharing a common courtyard and inhabited by a number of families

【巂】 6676
ㄙㄨㄟˇ soei suĭ
name of an old town in today's Szechwan Province

【雞】 6677
(鷄) ㄐㄧ ji jī
a chicken; a hen; a cock; a fowl

雞巴(ㄐㄧ ·ㄅㄚ)
(colloquial) the penis

雞皮(ㄐㄧ ㄆㄧˊ)
(figuratively) the shriveled skin of the aged

雞皮疙瘩(ㄐㄧ ㄆㄧˊ ㄍㄜ ·ㄉㄚ)
goose pimples; goose flesh

雞皮鶴髮(ㄐㄧ ㄆㄧˊ ㄏㄜˋ ㄈㄚˇ)
(said of the aged) with shriveled skin and hoary-headed

雞毛帚(ㄐㄧ ㄇㄠˊ ㄓㄡˇ)
a chicken-feather duster 亦作「雞毛撣子」

雞毛蒜皮(ㄐㄧ ㄇㄠˊ ㄙㄨㄢˋ ㄆㄧˊ)
(literally) chicken feathers and pieces of garlic skin —petty or trifling things

雞鳴狗盜(ㄐㄧ ㄇㄧㄥˊ ㄍㄡˇ ㄉㄠˋ)
(ability to) crow like a cock and snatch like a dog — small tricks; various kinds of talent or skill useful in emergency

雞飛蛋打(ㄐㄧ ㄈㄟ ㄉㄢˋ ㄉㄚˇ)
(literally) The hen has flown away and the eggs have been broken.—Everything's lost.

雞坊(ㄐㄧ ㄈㄤ)
a chicken farm; a pen for raising chickens; a chicken coop

雞蛋(ㄐㄧ ㄉㄢˋ)or 雞卵(ㄐㄧ ㄌㄨㄢˇ)
a hen's egg

雞蛋碰石頭(ㄐㄧ ㄉㄢˋ ㄆㄥˋ ㄕˊ ·ㄊㄡ)
like an egg hitting a rock —to attack someone much stronger than oneself

雞蛋裏挑骨頭(ㄐㄧ ㄉㄢˋ ㄌㄧˇ ㄊㄧㄠ ㄍㄨˊ ·ㄊㄡ)
to look for a bone in an egg —to look for a flaw where there is none; to find fault on purpose; to nitpick

雞蛋糕(ㄐㄧ ㄉㄢˋ ㄍㄠ)
sponge cake

雞蛋黃(ㄐㄧ ㄉㄢˋ ㄏㄨㄤˊ)
the yolk of a hen's egg

雞蛋青(ㄐㄧ ㄉㄢˋ ㄑㄧㄥ)
the white of a hen's egg

雞頭(ㄐㄧ ㄊㄡˊ)
(botany) a popular name of seeds of euryale ferox (芡實)

雞頭肉(ㄐㄧ ㄊㄡˊ ㄖㄡˋ)
a young woman's breasts

雞湯(ㄐㄧ ㄊㄤ)
chicken soup

雞啼(ㄐㄧ ㄊㄧˊ)
the crowing of cocks; cockcrow: 他雞啼即起。He was up at cockcrow.

雞腿(ㄐㄧ ㄊㄨㄟˇ)
drumsticks (chicken's legs)

〔隹部〕

〔隹部〕

雞肋(ㄐㄧ ㄌㄜˋ)
① tasteless; meaningless; something one is reluctant to give up although it's both tasteless and meaningless ② to be weak physically

雞零狗碎(ㄐㄧ ㄌㄧㄥˊ ㄍㄡˇ ㄙㄨㄟˋ)
pieces and bits; piecemeal

雞籠(ㄐㄧ ㄌㄨㄥˊ)
a basket for fowls; a fowl coop

雞冠(ㄐㄧ ㄍㄨㄢ)
the cockscomb

雞冠花(ㄐㄧ ㄍㄨㄢ ㄏㄨㄚ)
(botany) a cockscomb

雞冠石(ㄐㄧ ㄍㄨㄢ ㄕˊ)
(mineral) realgar

雞口牛後(ㄐㄧ ㄎㄡˇ ㄋㄧㄡˊ ㄏㄡˋ)
(literally) It's better to be the bill of a chicken than the anus of an ox.—The king of a small country is preferable to a prime minister of an empire. 或 It's better to be the boss of a small group than the top lieutenant in a large organization. 或 It is better to reign in hell than serve in heaven.

雞叫(ㄐㄧ ㄐㄧㄠˋ)
(said of a cock) to crow; (said of a hen) to cackle

雞姦(ㄐㄧ ㄐㄧㄢ)
sodomy; to bugger

雞棲(ㄐㄧ ㄑㄧ)
the place where chickens are raised

雞犬不寧(ㄐㄧ ㄑㄩㄢˇ ㄅㄨˋ ㄋㄧㄥˊ)
(literally) Not even the chickens and dogs are left in peace.—great disturbance; a pandemonium

雞犬不留(ㄐㄧ ㄑㄩㄢˇ ㄅㄨˋ ㄌㄧㄡˊ)
(literally) Not even a chicken or dog is left alive.—to give no quarter; to kill all

雞犬不驚(ㄐㄧ ㄑㄩㄢˇ ㄅㄨˋ ㄐㄧㄥ)
(literally) Not even a single chicken or dog is being disturbed.—peaceful and quiet

雞犬相聞(ㄐㄧ ㄑㄩㄢˇ ㄒㄧㄤ ㄨㄣˊ)
to live nearby or in the neighborhood

雞犬升天(ㄐㄧ ㄑㄩㄢˇ ㄕㄥ ㄊㄧㄢ)or 雞犬皆仙(ㄐㄧ ㄑㄩㄢˇ ㄐㄧㄝ ㄒㄧㄢ)
(literally) Even chickens and dogs ascended to the heaven after their master became an immortal.—the rise of a powerful person's underlings

雞心(ㄐㄧ ㄒㄧㄣ)
a jewel shaped like a chicken's heart

雞胸(ㄐㄧ ㄒㄩㄥ)or 雞胸脯兒(ㄐㄧ ㄒㄩㄥ ㄆㄨˊㄦ)
human chest shaped like a chicken's

雞汁(ㄐㄧ ㄓ)
broth prepared by steaming chicken

雞肫(ㄐㄧ ㄓㄨㄣ)
the gizzard of a chicken

雞吵鵝鬥(ㄐㄧ ㄔㄠˇ ㄜˊ ㄉㄡˋ)
to fight noisily and incessantly

雞尸牛從(ㄐㄧ ㄕ ㄋㄧㄡˊ ㄗㄨㄥˋ)
better to be a dog's head than a lion's tail—better to lead in a small position than to take a back seat under a great leader 參看「雞口牛後」

雞肉(ㄐㄧ ㄖㄡˋ)
chicken (as food)

雞子(ㄐㄧ ㄗˇ)
a chick

雞子兒(ㄐㄧ ㄗㄜˇㄦ)
the hen's egg

雞兒(ㄐㄧㄜㄦ)
a chicken

雞眼(ㄐㄧ ˙ㄧㄢ)
corns (on the feet)

雞窩(ㄐㄧ ㄨㄛ)
a chicken coop

雞尾酒(ㄐㄧ ㄨㄟˇ ㄐㄧㄡˇ)
cocktail

雞尾酒會(ㄐㄧ ㄨㄟˇ ㄐㄧㄡˇ ㄏㄨㄟˋ)
a cocktail party

雞瘟(ㄐㄧ ㄨㄣ)
chicken plague

【雝】 6678 ㄩㄥ iong yōng
harmonious; peaceful

十一畫

【離】 6679 ㄌㄧˊ li lí

1. to leave; to depart; to separate; separation: 他離開巴黎到紐約去。He left Paris for New York.
2. to defy; to go against
3. distant from; apart from: 月球與地球距離甚遠。The moon is distant from the earth.
4. to run into; to meet with
5. to act in pair
6. (said of light) bright
7. a Chinese family name

離別(ㄌㄧˊ ㄅㄧㄝˊ)
to say good-bye; to leave; to separate; separation; parting

離不開(ㄌㄧˊ ˙ㄅㄨ ㄎㄞ)
① cannot do without; unable to separate from ② cannot get away—too busy

離不開手兒(ㄌㄧˊ ˙ㄅㄨ ㄎㄞ ㄕㄡˇㄦ)or 離不開身兒(ㄌㄧˊ ˙ㄅㄨ ㄎㄞ ㄕㄜㄦ)
not having a free hand—very busy

離叛(ㄌㄧˊ ㄆㄢˋ)
to rebel; to turn one's back to; to walk out on

離披(ㄌㄧˊ ㄆㄧ)
scattered; dispersed

離譜(ㄌㄧˊ ㄆㄨˇ)
too far away from what is normal or acceptable; far off the beam

離得了(ㄌㄧˊ ˙ㄉㄜ ㄌㄧㄠˇ)or 離得開(ㄌㄧˊ ˙ㄉㄜ ㄎㄞ)
① able to do without ② can leave

離地(ㄌㄧˊ ㄉㄧˋ)
① to leave the ground; to rise from the ground; to soar into the air ② above the ground

離題(ㄌㄧˊ ㄊㄧˊ)
to depart from the topic; to digress; digression

離離(ㄌㄧˊ ㄌㄧˊ)
① lushly; luxuriantly; in rich clusters ② not to attend personally

離宮(ㄌㄧˊ ㄍㄨㄥ)
① a temporary abode for an emperor on a tour ② name of a constellation

離開(ㄌㄧˊ ㄎㄞ)
to separate from; to leave; to depart; to keep away from; to deviate from

離合(ㄌㄧˊ ㄏㄜˊ)
separation and reunion

離合器(ㄌㄧˊ ㄏㄜˊ ㄑㄧˋ)
the clutch (of a motorcycle)

離恨(ㄌㄧˊ ㄏㄣˋ)
parting grief

離婚(ㄌㄧˊ ㄏㄨㄣ)
to divorce; a divorce
離婚者(ㄌㄧˊ ㄏㄨㄣ ㄓㄜˇ)
(said of a woman) a divorcée; (said of a man) a divorcé
離婚書(ㄌㄧˊ ㄏㄨㄣ ㄕㄨ)
a certificate of divorce
離家(ㄌㄧˊ ㄐㄧㄚ)
to leave home; to be away from home; to depart from home
離間(ㄌㄧˊ ㄐㄧㄢˋ)
to drive a wedge between; to alienate (allies, etc.); to sow discord
離經叛道(ㄌㄧˊ ㄐㄧㄥ ㄆㄢˋ ㄉㄠˋ)
to rebel against orthodox teachings
離境(ㄌㄧˊ ㄐㄧㄥˋ)
to leave a country or place
離境簽證(ㄌㄧˊ ㄐㄧㄥˋ ㄑㄧㄢ ㄓㄥˋ)
an exit visa
離奇(ㄌㄧˊ ㄑㄧˊ)
odd; fantastic; strange; intriguing: 這是件很離奇的事兒。It's a very odd business.
離棄(ㄌㄧˊ ㄑㄧˋ)
to abandon; to desert: 他離棄了他的妻兒。He abandoned his wife and children.
離情別緒(ㄌㄧˊ ㄑㄧㄥˊ ㄅㄧㄝˊ ㄒㄩˋ)
the sad feelings at separation; parting sorrows
離去(ㄌㄧˊ ㄑㄩˋ)
to leave; to go away; to depart: 我的打字員已離去。My typist has left me.
離羣索居(ㄌㄧˊ ㄑㄩㄣˊ ㄙㄨㄛˇ ㄐㄩ)
to leave one's friends and live alone
離析(ㄌㄧˊ ㄒㄧ)
to disintegrate (as a regime, etc.)
離席(ㄌㄧˊ ㄒㄧˊ)
to leave or withdraw a dinner party, conference, etc.
離心離德(ㄌㄧˊ ㄒㄧㄣ ㄌㄧˊ ㄉㄜˊ)
(said of many people) each going his own way; lacking unity
離心力(ㄌㄧˊ ㄒㄧㄣ ㄌㄧˋ)
① centrifugal force ② factors which give rise to disloyalty
離心角(ㄌㄧˊ ㄒㄧㄣ ㄐㄧㄠˇ)
an eccentric angle
離心器(ㄌㄧˊ ㄒㄧㄣ ㄑㄧˋ)
a centrifuge; a centrifugal machine 亦作「離心機」
離鄉背井(ㄌㄧˊ ㄒㄧㄤ ㄅㄟˋ ㄐㄧㄥˇ)
to travel to a distant land; to stay far away from home 亦作「背井離鄉」
離職(ㄌㄧˊ ㄓˊ)
① to leave or resign from one's office ② to retire from one's office
離愁(ㄌㄧˊ ㄔㄡˊ)
parting sorrow or grief; sadness at separation
離任(ㄌㄧˊ ㄖㄣˋ)
to leave one's post
離子(ㄌㄧˊ ㄗˇ)
an ion
離座(ㄌㄧˊ ㄗㄨㄛˋ)
to leave one's seat
離騷(ㄌㄧˊ ㄙㄠ)
the title of a long poem authored by Chü Yüan (屈原) of the state of Chu (楚) during the Epoch of Warring States in which Chü Yüan vented his grievances for being disparaged and discarded by the king
離散(ㄌㄧˊ ㄙㄢˋ)
separated and scattered; dispersed
離貳(ㄌㄧˊ ㄦˋ)
to harbor a rebellious heart
離異(ㄌㄧˊ ㄧˋ)
to separate; to divorce: 他們已經離異。They have been divorced.

【難】 6680
1. ㄋㄢˊ nan nán

1. difficult; not easy; hard
2. unable; not in a position to
3. unpleasant; not good

難保(ㄋㄢˊ ㄅㄠˇ)
① difficult to judge; hard to say; unable to guarantee: 今天難保不下雨。It's hard to say that it won't rain today. ② difficult to hold (a city, position, etc.); hard to guard or keep
難辦(ㄋㄢˊ ㄅㄢˋ)
difficult to manage or operate
難憑(ㄋㄢˊ ㄆㄧㄥˊ)
cannot be relied upon; unreliable; cannot be accepted as evidence; cannot be taken as truth
難買難賣(ㄋㄢˊ ㄇㄞˇ ㄋㄢˊ ㄇㄞˋ)
to make things difficult for somebody; to give someone a hard time
難免(ㄋㄢˊ ㄇㄧㄢˇ)
can hardly avoid; inescapable; inevitable: 犯錯是難免的。Mistakes can hardly be avoided.
難分難捨(ㄋㄢˊ ㄈㄣ ㄋㄢˊ ㄕㄜˇ)
(said of a couple in love) very reluctant to separate 亦作「難捨難分」
難打交道(ㄋㄢˊ ㄉㄚˇ ㄐㄧㄠ ˙ㄉㄠ)
hard to deal wih; difficult to get along with
難得(ㄋㄢˊ ㄉㄜˊ)
① rare; hard to get; hard to come by: 它是本難得的書。It's a rare book. ② fortunate; lucky ③ rarely; seldom: 我難得碰見他。I rarely met him.
難倒(ㄋㄢˊ ㄉㄠˇ)
to confound; to daunt; to baffle; to beat
難道(ㄋㄢˊ ㄉㄠˋ) or 難道說(ㄋㄢˊ ㄉㄠˋ ㄕㄨㄛ)
Is it possible…? 或 Do you really mean to say…?
難當(ㄋㄢˊ ㄉㄤ)
① hard to shoulder (such a responsibility, etc.) ② hard to endure; unbearable
難度(ㄋㄢˊ ㄉㄨˋ)
degree of difficulty; difficulty: 這種動作難度很大。This action is extremely difficult.
難懂(ㄋㄢˊ ㄉㄨㄥˇ)
hard to understand; difficult to comprehend
難逃法網(ㄋㄢˊ ㄊㄠˊ ㄈㄚˇ ㄨㄤˇ)
It's hard to escape the dragnet of law. 或 Crime does not pay.
難題(ㄋㄢˊ ㄊㄧˊ)
a hard nut to crack; a tough problem; a puzzle
難聽(ㄋㄢˊ ㄊㄧㄥ)
① unpleasant to hear (often referring to vulgar or abusive expressions, etc.); to grate on the ear ② offensive; coarse ③ scandalous
難耐(ㄋㄢˊ ㄋㄞˋ)
unable to endure; unbearable

〔隹部〕

難能可貴(ㄋㄢˊ ㄋㄥˊ ㄎㄜˇ ㄍㄨㄟˋ)
rare and commendable (merits, achievements, etc.)
難過(ㄋㄢˊ ㄍㄨㄛˋ)
①to feel uneasy; to feel bad; to feel sorry: 我對她的不幸感到難過。I felt sorry about her misfortune.② hard to endure or bear; uncomfortable ③ difficult; hard
難怪(ㄋㄢˊ ㄍㄨㄞˋ)
①cannot hold responsible for ②no wonder that; it's understandable that: 難怪他做了此事。No wonder he should have done it.
難關(ㄋㄢˊ ㄍㄨㄢ)or(ㄋㄢˋ ㄍㄨㄢ)
an impasse; an obstacle or obstruction difficult to overcome; a difficult situation; a crisis; a juncture of great difficulty; straits: 他們終於度過難關。They finally tided over a crisis.
難管(ㄋㄢˊ ㄍㄨㄢˇ)
difficult to govern; hard to rule or restrain
難堪(ㄋㄢˊ ㄎㄢ)
①to embarrass; embarrassment ②intolerable; unbearable
難看(ㄋㄢˊ ㄎㄢˋ)
①bad-looking; not pleasant to the eye; ugly; offensive; repulsive ② embarrassing; awkward
難解(ㄋㄢˊ ㄐㄧㄝˇ)
difficult to understand; incomprehensible; hard to solve
難解難分(ㄋㄢˊ ㄐㄧㄝˇ ㄋㄢˊ ㄈㄣ)
①difficult to separate ②to be locked together (in a struggle)
難講(ㄋㄢˊ ㄐㄧㄤˇ)
hard to say; difficult to predict: 很難講那一個比較好。It's hard to say which is better.
難兄難弟(ㄋㄢˊ ㄒㄩㄥ ㄋㄢˊ ㄉㄧˋ)
brothers who are equally talented
難治(ㄋㄢˊ ㄓˋ)
difficult to cure
難吃(ㄋㄢˊ ㄔ)
unbearable to palate; unpalatable; tasting bad
難纏(ㄋㄢˊ ㄔㄢˊ)
hard to deal with
難產(ㄋㄢˊ ㄔㄢˇ)
①(medicine) difficult labor; dystocia ②hard to come into being or materialize
難成(ㄋㄢˊ ㄔㄥˊ)
difficult to accomplish or succeed
難處
①(ㄋㄢˊ ㄔㄨˇ) hard to get along with
②(ㄋㄢˊ ·ㄔㄨ) difficult points; problems: 她有她的難處。She has her problems.
難事(ㄋㄢˊ ㄕˋ)
a difficult task; something not easy to manage; a difficult matter
難受(ㄋㄢˊ ㄕㄡˋ)
①to feel bad; to feel sorry ②unbearable; intolerable ③ to suffer pain; to feel unwell
難上加難(ㄋㄢˊ ㄕㄤˋ ㄐㄧㄚ ㄋㄢˊ)or 難上難(ㄋㄢˊ ㄕㄤˋ ㄋㄢˊ)
most difficult; almost impossible
難說(ㄋㄢˊ ㄕㄨㄛ)
①hard to say or predict ② difficult to speak out (for fear of embarrassing or paining others, etc.) ③not easy to express with words
難說話(ㄋㄢˊ ㄕㄨㄛ ㄏㄨㄚˋ)
(said of a person) hard to deal with; very strict with subordinates
難字(ㄋㄢˊ ㄗˋ)
a difficult word; a big word; hard words
難走(ㄋㄢˊ ㄗㄡˇ)
(said of a road) tortuous; difficult to negotiate
難色(ㄋㄢˊ ㄙㄜˋ)
an expression of reluctance or unwillingness: 他面有難色。He showed an expression of reluctance.
難以(ㄋㄢˊ ㄧˇ)
difficult; hard to: 她很難以取悅。She is hard to please.
難以逆料(ㄋㄢˊ ㄧˇ ㄋㄧˋ ㄌㄧㄠˋ)
hard to predict
難以相信(ㄋㄢˊ ㄧˇ ㄒㄧㄤ ㄒㄧㄣˋ)or 難信(ㄋㄢˊ ㄒㄧㄣˋ)
incredible; difficult to believe; hard to believe 亦作「難以置信」
難以相處(ㄋㄢˊ ㄧˇ ㄒㄧㄤ ㄔㄨˇ)
hard to get along with
難以形容(ㄋㄢˊ ㄧˇ ㄒㄧㄥˊ ㄖㄨㄥˊ)
indescribable; beyond description
難以出口(ㄋㄢˊ ㄧˇ ㄔㄨ ㄎㄡˇ)
difficult to speak out one's mind (for various reasons)
難以爲繼(ㄋㄢˊ ㄧˇ ㄨㄟˊ ㄐㄧˋ)
hard to carry on; difficult to continue
難言之隱(ㄋㄢˊ ㄧㄢˊ ㄓ ㄧㄣˇ)
secrets or problems one doesn't want to reveal
難爲
①(ㄋㄢˊ ㄨㄟˊ) difficult to perform or manage
②(ㄋㄢˊ ·ㄨㄟ) ⓐ to put (someone) in a spot; to make matters difficult for someone; to press ⓑ Thanks for the trouble you have taken.ⓒ an expression to comfort someone who has had some very unpleasant experience
難爲情(ㄋㄢˊ ㄨㄟˊ ㄑㄧㄥˊ)
to feel ashamed, uneasy or embarrassed; bashful: 她好難爲情。She is rather bashful.
難聞(ㄋㄢˊ ㄨㄣˊ)
stinking; malodorous
難忘(ㄋㄢˊ ㄨㄤˋ)
difficult to forget; unforgettable

【難】 6680
2. ㄋㄢˋ nann nàn

1. disaster; calamity; misfortune
2. to rebuke; to reprove; to reprimand
3. to discountenance

難不倒(ㄋㄢˊ ·ㄅㄨ ㄉㄠˇ)or 難不住(ㄋㄢˊ ·ㄅㄨ ㄓㄨˋ)
will not be beaten (by a problem or question); cannot beat or corner someone (with a question or task)
難民(ㄋㄢˋ ㄇㄧㄣˊ)
refugees
難民收容所(ㄋㄢˋ ㄇㄧㄣˊ ㄕㄡ ㄖㄨㄥˊ ㄙㄨㄛˇ)
a haven or shelter for refugees; a refugee camp or center 亦作「難民營」
難童(ㄋㄢˋ ㄊㄨㄥˊ)
a refugee child

難兄難弟(ㄋㄢ ㄒㄩㄥ ㄋㄢ ㄉㄧˋ)
fellow sufferers

難住了(ㄋㄢ ·ㄓㄨ ·ㄌㄜ)
to be unable to answer a question or to do a task that is too difficult

難友(ㄋㄢ ㄧㄡˇ)
a fellow sufferer

雨 部
ㄩˇ yeu yǔ

【雨】 6681
1. ㄩˇ yeu yǔ

rain; rainy

雨布(ㄩˇ ㄅㄨˋ)
waterproof cloth

雨棚(ㄩˇ ㄆㄥˊ)
a rainshed

雨帽(ㄩˇ ㄇㄠˋ)
a rain hat; a rain cap

雨沐風餐(ㄩˇ ㄇㄨˋ ㄈㄥ ㄘㄢ)
(literally) to bathe in the rain and eat meals in the wind—to toil rain or shine

雨滴(ㄩˇ ㄉㄧ)or 雨點兒(ㄩˇ ㄉㄧㄚˇㄦ)
raindrops

雨天(ㄩˇ ㄊㄧㄢ)
a rainy day: 那天是雨天。It was rainy that day.

雨立(ㄩˇ ㄌㄧˋ)
to stand in the rain

雨林(ㄩˇ ㄌㄧㄣˊ)
rain trees; a rainforest

雨淋日曬(ㄩˇ ㄌㄧㄣˊ ㄖˋ ㄕㄞˋ)
wear and tear of the weather; exposure to the elements

雨量(ㄩˇ ㄌㄧㄤˋ)
(meteorology) rainfall; the amount of rainfall or precipitation

雨量計(ㄩˇ ㄌㄧㄤˋ ㄐㄧˋ)
a rain gauge; a udometer

雨露(ㄩˇ ㄌㄨˋ)
favors and kindness; benevolence

雨果(ㄩˇ ㄍㄨㄛˇ)
Victor Marie Hugo (1802-1885), French poet, novelist and dramatist

雨過天青(ㄩˇ ㄍㄨㄛˋ ㄊㄧㄢ ㄑㄧㄥ)or 雨過天晴(ㄩˇ ㄍㄨㄛˋ ㄊㄧㄢ ㄑㄧㄥˊ)
(literally) When the rain is over, the sky clears up. 或 After a storm comes a calm. —When the incident (or confusion) is over, everything goes back to normal.

雨後春筍(ㄩˇ ㄏㄡˋ ㄔㄨㄣ ㄙㄨㄣˇ)
to mushroom like bamboo shoots after rain

雨後送傘(ㄩˇ ㄏㄡˋ ㄙㄨㄥˋ ㄙㄢˇ)
(literally) to give someone an umbrella after the rain is over—to give untimely help

雨花臺(ㄩˇ ㄏㄨㄚ ㄊㄞˊ)
name of a spot in suburban Nanking, noted for its colorful pebbles

雨季(ㄩˇ ㄐㄧˋ)
the rainy season; the monsoon

雨脚(ㄩˇ ㄐㄧㄠˇ)
dense raindrops

雨具(ㄩˇ ㄐㄩˋ)
things for wet weather—umbrellas, raincoats, galoshes, etc.

雨泣(ㄩˇ ㄑㄧˋ)
tears falling down like rain

雨鞋(ㄩˇ ㄒㄧㄝˊ)
rainshoes; galoshes

雨靴(ㄩˇ ㄒㄩㄝ)
oiled or rubber boots for wet weather; galoshes

雨珠(ㄩˇ ㄓㄨ)
raindrops

雨師(ㄩˇ ㄕ)
the rain god

雨水(ㄩˇ ㄕㄨㄟˇ)
①rain water ②one of the 24 climatic periods in the solar calendar, which falls on February 19 or 20

雨字頭兒(ㄩˇ ㄗˋ ㄊㄡˊㄦ)
a Chinese character topped by the radical 雨, as 霖, 電, 雷, etc.

雨傘(ㄩˇ ㄙㄢˇ)
an umbrella

雨散雲收(ㄩˇ ㄙㄢˋ ㄩㄣˊ ㄕㄡ)
① (literally) The rain stops and the sky clears up. ② to separate, as friends ③ afterwards (after sexual intercourse)

雨衣(ㄩˇ ㄧ)
a raincoat

雨意(ㄩˇ ㄧˋ)
signs indicating rain; signs which is about to rain: 現在頗有雨意。Now it looks like rain.

雨雲(ㄩˇ ㄩㄣˊ)
rain clouds

【雨】 6681
2. ㄩˋ yuh yù

to rain down; to pour down

雨淚(ㄩˇ ㄌㄟˋ)
tears pouring down like rain

三畫

【雩】 6682
1. ㄩˊ yu yú

to pray for rain; the sacrifice for the rain god

雩壇(ㄩˊ ㄊㄢˊ)
a stand or platform where praying for rain is conducted

雩祭(ㄩˊ ㄐㄧˋ)
a sacrifice or ritual in praying for rain

【雩】 6682
2. ㄩˋ yuh yù

the rainbow

【雪】 6683
1. ㄒㄩㄝˇ sheue xuě

1. snow: 山上積雪很深。The mountains are deep in snow.
2. to clean; to wash or wipe away

雪崩(ㄒㄩㄝˇ ㄅㄥ)
a snowslide; an avalanche of snow

雪片(ㄒㄩㄝˇ ㄆㄧㄢˋ)
① snowflakes ② to come in like an avalanche

雪盲(ㄒㄩㄝˇ ㄇㄤˊ)
snow blindness

雪膚(ㄒㄩㄝˇ ㄈㄨ)
a snow-white skin

雪地冰天(ㄒㄩㄝˇ ㄉㄧˋ ㄅㄧㄥ ㄊㄧㄢ)
a land of snow and ice; a frozen land

雪堆(ㄒㄩㄝˇ ㄉㄨㄟ)
a snowbank; a snowdrift

雪泥鴻爪(ㄒㄩㄝˇ ㄋㄧˊ ㄏㄨㄥˊ ㄓㄠˇ)
(literally) talon marks on the snow—traces of past events

雪虐風饕(ㄒㄩㄝˇ ㄋㄩㄝˋ ㄈㄥ ㄊㄠ)
heavy snows and high winds —extreme cold

雪萊(ㄒㄩㄝˇ ㄌㄞˊ)
Percy Bysshe Shelley (1792-1822), British poet

雪梨(ㄒㄩㄝˇ ㄌㄧˊ)
① Sydney, Australia ② a kind of pear

雪裏紅(ㄒㄩㄝˇ ㄌㄧˇ ㄏㄨㄥˊ)or 雪裏蕻(ㄒㄩㄝˇ ㄌㄧˇ ㄏㄨㄥˋ)
(botany) *Brassica juncea,* potherb mustard

雪裏青(ㄒㄩㄝˇ ㄌㄧˇ ㄑㄧㄥ)
an ilex 亦作「冬青」

雪花(ㄒㄩㄝˇ ㄏㄨㄚ)
snowflakes

雪花膏(ㄒㄩㄝˇ ㄏㄨㄚ ㄍㄠ)
any kind of vanishing face-cream 亦作「面霜」

雪花石膏(ㄒㄩㄝˇ ㄏㄨㄚ ㄕˊ ㄍㄠ)
(mineral) alabaster 亦作「純百生石膏」

雪肌(ㄒㄩㄝˇ ㄐㄧ)
a snow-white skin 參看「雪膚」

雪茄(ㄒㄩㄝˇ ㄐㄧㄚ)
cigars

雪窖冰天(ㄒㄩㄝˇ ㄐㄧㄠˋ ㄅㄧㄥ ㄊㄧㄢ)
a snow-and-ice-locked land

雪景(ㄒㄩㄝˇ ㄐㄧㄥˇ)
a landscape of snow; a snow scene

雪橇(ㄒㄩㄝˇ ㄑㄧㄠ)
a sled; a toboggan; a sledge; a sleigh (a transportation vehicle on the snow-covered ground)

雪球(ㄒㄩㄝˇ ㄑㄧㄡˊ)
① a snowball ② as in 擲雪球—to snowball

雪青(ㄒㄩㄝˇ ㄑㄧㄥ)
lilac 亦作「淡紫色」

雪鞋(ㄒㄩㄝˇ ㄒㄧㄝˊ)
snowshoes

雪線(ㄒㄩㄝˇ ㄒㄧㄢˋ)
the snow line

雪中高士(ㄒㄩㄝˇ ㄓㄨㄥ ㄍㄠ ㄕˋ)or 雪中君子(ㄒㄩㄝˇ ㄓㄨㄥ ㄐㄩㄣ ㄗˇ)
a poetic name of plum blossoms (梅花)

雪中送炭(ㄒㄩㄝˇ ㄓㄨㄥ ㄙㄨㄥˋ ㄊㄢˋ)
to give timely assistance; to send things which are in urgent need, as food for hungry refugees

雪車(ㄒㄩㄝˇ ㄔㄜ)or 雪橇(ㄒㄩㄝˇ ㄑㄧㄠ)
a sledge; a sled; a sleigh

雪鋤(ㄒㄩㄝˇ ㄔㄨˊ)
a snowplow

雪窗(ㄒㄩㄝˇ ㄔㄨㄤ)
(literally) to study by the window lighted by reflection of snow—very diligent in study

雪山(ㄒㄩㄝˇ ㄕㄢ)
① a snow-capped mountain ② the Snow Mountains, in New Guinea

雪上加霜(ㄒㄩㄝˇ ㄕㄤˋ ㄐㄧㄚ ㄕㄨㄤ)
(literally) to add frost to snow—disasters coming one after another in succession

雪人(ㄒㄩㄝˇ ㄖㄣˊ)
① Abominable Snowman, the legendary snowman in the Himalayas; the yeti ② a human figure made out of snow

雪壓霜欺(ㄒㄩㄝˇ ㄧㄚ ㄕㄨㄤ ㄑㄧ)
to be slighted and insulted by all

雪鵐(ㄒㄩㄝˇ ㄨˊ)
a snowbird

6683
【雪】 2. ㄒㄩㄝˋ shiueh xuè
(又讀 ㄒㄩㄝˇ sheue xuě)

1. snow-white; snowy
2. to avenge; to wipe out grievances

雪白(ㄒㄩㄝˋ ㄅㄞˊ)
snow-white; snowy

雪亮(ㄒㄩㄝˋ ㄌㄧㄤˋ)
bright as snow; shiny: 人民的眼睛是雪亮的。People's eyes are as bright as snow.

雪恨(ㄒㄩㄝˋ ㄏㄣˋ)or(ㄒㄩㄝˇ ㄏㄣˋ)
to avenge one's grudge; to avenge wrongs done to one; to avenge oneself on; to avenge

雪恥(ㄒㄩㄝˋ ㄔˇ)or(ㄒㄩㄝˇ ㄔˇ)
to wipe out a shame; to avenge an insult or humiliation

雪恥復國(ㄒㄩㄝˋ ㄔˇ ㄈㄨˋ ㄍㄨㄛˊ)
to wipe out national shame and recover the fatherland

雪寃(ㄒㄩㄝˋ ㄩㄢ)or(ㄒㄩㄝˇ ㄩㄢ)
to wipe out grievances; to vindicate oneself; to clear oneself of a false charge; to redress a wrong

四畫

【雯】 6684
ㄨㄣˊ wen wén
the coloring on the clouds

【雰】 6685
ㄈㄣ fen fēn
mist; fog

【雱】 6686
ㄆㄤˊ parng páng
snowing heavily

【雲】 6687
ㄩㄣˊ yun yún
1. clouds
2. a cloud of; a large number of
3. short for Yunnan Province
4. a Chinese family name

雲豹(ㄩㄣˊ ㄅㄠˋ)
a clouded leopard

雲鬢(ㄩㄣˊ ㄅㄧㄣˋ)
the hairdo of a beautiful woman—like floating clouds

雲片糕(ㄩㄣˊ ㄆㄧㄢˋ ㄍㄠ)
a kind of Chinese dessert made of rice in the shape of rectangular thin strips

雲杪(ㄩㄣˊ ㄇㄧㄠˇ)
distant and high

雲母(ㄩㄣˊ ㄇㄨˇ)
mica

雲房(ㄩㄣˊ ㄈㄤˊ)
chambers or cabins where Buddhist monks live

雲端(ㄩㄣˊ ㄉㄨㄢ)
in the clouds

雲梯(ㄩㄣˊ ㄊㄧ)
a scaling ladder

雲天(ㄩㄣˊ ㄊㄧㄢ)
clouds and sky—high above

雲天高誼(ㄩㄣˊ ㄊㄧㄢ ㄍㄠ ㄧˋ)
(your) great kindness and friendship (used mostly in correspondence)

雲吞(ㄩㄣˊ ㄊㄨㄣ)
Chinese ravioli; stuffed dumplings with delicate flour wrapping 亦作「餛飩」

雲南(ㄩㄣˊ ㄋㄢˊ)
Yunnan Province, Southwestern China

雲南起義(ㄩㄣˊ ㄋㄢˊ ㄑㄧˇ ㄧˋ)
the military uprising against Yüan Shih-kai (袁世凱) in 1915 led by General Tsai O (蔡鍔) in Yunnan

雲霓(ㄩㄣˊ ㄋㄧˊ)
clouds and rainbows—which give promise of rain in a

drought

雲泥(ㄩㄣˊ ㄋㄧˊ)
clouds and mud—great difference in social standing

雲量(ㄩㄣˊ ㄌㄧㄤˋ)
(meteorology) cloudiness; cloud amount; cloud cover

雲羅(ㄩㄣˊ ㄌㄨㄛˊ)
dense clouds

雲龍風虎(ㄩㄣˊ ㄌㄨㄥˊ ㄈㄥ ㄏㄨˇ)
A great leader attracts capable followers.

雲岡石窟(ㄩㄣˊ ㄍㄤ ㄕˊ ㄎㄨ)
a number of grottos stretching about half a kilometer long at Yunkang, Shansi Province, containing thousands of Buddha statues of various sizes carved over a period of about 100 years between the 4th and the 5th centuries

雲貴(ㄩㄣˊ ㄍㄨㄟˋ)
Yunnan and Kweichow provinces

雲貴高原(ㄩㄣˊ ㄍㄨㄟˋ ㄍㄠ ㄩㄢˊ)
the Yunnan-Kweichow Plateau

雲開見日(ㄩㄣˊ ㄎㄞ ㄐㄧㄢˋ ㄖˋ)
(literally) When the clouds part, one sees the sun.—a turn of fortune for the better

雲海(ㄩㄣˊ ㄏㄞˇ)
a sea of clouds

雲漢(ㄩㄣˊ ㄏㄢˋ)
the Milky Way

雲鬟(ㄩㄣˊ ㄏㄨㄢˊ)
the beautiful hairdo of an attractive woman

雲集(ㄩㄣˊ ㄐㄧˊ)
to congregate; to gather; to flock together; to come together in crowds

雲際(ㄩㄣˊ ㄐㄧˋ)
in the clouds

雲髻(ㄩㄣˊ ㄐㄧˋ)
women's hair; a lady's hair-coil

雲譎波詭(ㄩㄣˊ ㄐㄩㄝˊ ㄅㄛ ㄍㄨㄟˇ)
the unpredictable, ever-changing nature of things

雲起龍驤(ㄩㄣˊ ㄑㄧˇ ㄌㄨㄥˊ ㄒㄧㄤ)
(said of heroes, rebels, etc.) rising up in time of social upheavals

雲氣(ㄩㄣˊ ㄑㄧˋ)
thin, floating clouds

雲衢(ㄩㄣˊ ㄑㄩˊ) or 雲路(ㄩㄣˊ ㄌㄨˋ)
high official ranks

雲雀(ㄩㄣˊ ㄑㄩㄝˋ)
a skylark; a meadow lark

雲霞(ㄩㄣˊ ㄒㄧㄚˊ)
① clouds ② one who is unmoved by monetary gains or high positions; a person of high virtue

雲簫(ㄩㄣˊ ㄒㄧㄠ)
a kind of panpipe

雲霄(ㄩㄣˊ ㄒㄧㄠ)
① the sky—very high: 爆竹聲響徹雲霄。The cracking noise of firecracker resounded to the skies. ② name of a county in Fukien

雲霄飛車(ㄩㄣˊ ㄒㄧㄠ ㄈㄟ ㄔㄜ)
a roller coaster

雲消霧散(ㄩㄣˊ ㄒㄧㄠ ㄨˋ ㄙㄢˋ)
(literally) clouds dissipating and fog melting away—The troubles are over.

雲行雨施(ㄩㄣˊ ㄒㄧㄥˊ ㄩˇ ㄕ)
(said of a ruler) to be benevolent to the people

雲蒸霞蔚(ㄩㄣˊ ㄓㄥ ㄒㄧㄚˊ ㄨㄟˋ)
radiant, colorful and flourishing

雲中白鶴(ㄩㄣˊ ㄓㄨㄥ ㄅㄞˊ ㄏㄜˋ)
a man of unimpeachable integrity

雲收雨散(ㄩㄣˊ ㄕㄡ ㄩˇ ㄙㄢˋ)
① separation; dispersion ② the end of sexual intercourse

雲杉(ㄩㄣˊ ㄕㄢ)
a spruce fir

雲彩(ㄩㄣˊ ˙ㄘㄞ)
clouds illuminated by the rising or setting sun

雲層(ㄩㄣˊ ㄘㄥˊ)
layers of clouds

雲遊(ㄩㄣˊ ㄧㄡˊ)
to travel without a destination; to wander about

雲煙(ㄩㄣˊ ㄧㄢ)
clouds and smog

雲煙過眼(ㄩㄣˊ ㄧㄢ ㄍㄨㄛˋ ㄧㄢˇ)
(literally) clouds and smoke that float past the eyes—transient glories; things having no lasting value

雲霧(ㄩㄣˊ ㄨˋ)
clouds and fog—obscure places

雲雨(ㄩㄣˊ ㄩˇ)
① grace and favor ② sexual intercourse; making love

雲雨巫山(ㄩㄣˊ ㄩˇ ㄨ ㄕㄢ)
(figuratively) The couple are enraptured with love.

五畫

【零】 6688
ㄌㄧㄥˊ ling líng

1. zero; nil; nought
2. a fraction; fractional; remainder
3. to flow down
4. a light rain; drizzle

零賣(ㄌㄧㄥˊ ㄇㄞˋ)
① retail sales ② to sell by the piece or in small quantities

零分(ㄌㄧㄥˊ ㄈㄣ)
① (grading examination papers) zero; no marks ② (sports) scoreless

零丁(ㄌㄧㄥˊ ㄉㄧㄥ)
left alone without company; solitary; lonely 亦作「伶仃」

零丁孤苦(ㄌㄧㄥˊ ㄉㄧㄥ ㄍㄨ ㄎㄨˇ)
solitary; lonely; without friends or relatives

零度(ㄌㄧㄥˊ ㄉㄨˋ)
zero; nought degrees: 昨晚氣溫降到零度。The temperature fell to zero last night.

零頭(ㄌㄧㄥˊ ㄊㄡˊ)
① oddments (a sum which together with a much larger round figure makes the whole) ② small bits of cloth good only for patching clothes, etc.

零零碎碎(ㄌㄧㄥˊ ㄌㄧㄥˊ ㄙㄨㄟˋ ㄙㄨㄟˋ)
fragmented; piecemeal

零落(ㄌㄧㄥˊ ㄌㄨㄛˋ) or 零零落落(ㄌㄧㄥˊ ㄌㄧㄥˊ ㄌㄨㄛˋ ㄌㄨㄛˋ)
① desolate and scattered; dilapidated; run-down ② withered and fallen

零亂(ㄌㄧㄥˊ ㄌㄨㄢˋ)
disorderly; in confusion; in disorder: 桌子很零亂。The table was in disorder.

零股(ㄌㄧㄥˊ ㄍㄨˇ)
(stock exchange) ① odd lot ② a small band of (stragglers or guerrillas separated

〔雨部〕

from the main force)
零工(ㄌㄧㄥˊ ㄍㄨㄥ)
①odd jobs; short-term hired labor ②an odd-job man; a casual laborer
零花(ㄌㄧㄥˊ ㄏㄨㄚ)
(said of money) for everyday expenses, such as buying a bus ticket or a pack of cigarettes, etc.; incidental expenses
零件(ㄌㄧㄥˊ ㄐㄧㄢˋ)
(said of machines) component parts; spare parts
零錢(ㄌㄧㄥˊ ㄑㄧㄢˊ)
small change; petty cash; odd change
零星(ㄌㄧㄥˊ ㄒㄧㄥ)
①fragmented; fractional; not as a whole ②scattered
零食(ㄌㄧㄥˊ ㄕˊ)
snacks; refreshments: 他一直吃零食，所以他老是超重。He's forever snacking and will always be overweight.
零時(ㄌㄧㄥˊ ㄕˊ)
zero hour
零售(ㄌㄧㄥˊ ㄕㄡˋ)
retail sales; to sell by retail
零售店(ㄌㄧㄥˊ ㄕㄡˋ ㄉㄧㄢˋ)
a retail shop; a sundry store
零售商(ㄌㄧㄥˊ ㄕㄡˋ ㄕㄤ)
a retailer
零數(ㄌㄧㄥˊ ㄕㄨˋ)
oddments
零嘴(ㄌㄧㄥˊ ㄗㄨㄟˇ)
snacks 參看「零食」
零存整付(ㄌㄧㄥˊ ㄘㄨㄣˊ ㄓㄥˇ ㄈㄨˋ)
(banking) to deposit small sums of money every day, week, or month and to draw out both principal and interest in a lump sum when the specified time comes up
零散(ㄌㄧㄥˊ ㄙㄢˇ)
scattered: 農舍零散分佈在各處。Farmhouses are scattered here and there.
零碎(ㄌㄧㄥˊ ·ㄙㄨㄟ)
fragments; fragmentary; fractions; fractional; odds and ends
零兒(ㄌㄧㄥˊㄦ)
oddments
零用(ㄌㄧㄥˊ ㄩㄥˋ)
①(said of money) for everyday expenses of a nondescript nature ②pocket money
零用錢(ㄌㄧㄥˊ ㄩㄥˋ ㄑㄧㄢˊ)
pocket money

【雷】 6689
ㄌㄟˊ lei léi

1. thunder: 遠處在打雷。It's thundering in the distance.
2. a mine (an explosive): 車子觸爆地雷。The car struck a mine.
3. a Chinese family name

雷劈(ㄌㄟˊ ㄆㄧ)
to be struck by lightning (or thunder)
雷鳴(ㄌㄟˊ ㄇㄧㄥˊ)
①roars of thunder; thunderpeal ②very loud sounds; thunderous: 他們的表演受到雷鳴般的掌聲。Their performance met with thunderous applause.
雷達(ㄌㄟˊ ㄉㄚˊ)
a radar
雷達網(ㄌㄟˊ ㄉㄚˊ ㄨㄤˇ)
a radar network
雷電(ㄌㄟˊ ㄉㄧㄢˋ)
lightning and thunder
雷電交加(ㄌㄟˊ ㄉㄧㄢˋ ㄐㄧㄠ ㄐㄧㄚ)
It's thundering and lightening.
雷動(ㄌㄟˊ ㄉㄨㄥˋ)
(said of cheers, applause, etc.) thunderous: 運動場上歡聲雷動。There are thunderous cheers in the playground.
雷頭風(ㄌㄟˊ ㄊㄡˊ ㄈㄥ)
the initial severity of a new boss, which often tapers off as time goes by
雷霆(ㄌㄟˊ ㄊㄧㄥˊ)
①great wrath; a great fury; a rage ②overwhelming or overpowering
雷霆萬鈞(ㄌㄟˊ ㄊㄧㄥˊ ㄨㄢˋ ㄐㄩㄣ)
overwhelming or overpowering (power, strength, etc.); extremely powerful
雷同(ㄌㄟˊ ㄊㄨㄥˊ)
similar; identical; exactly the same: 金子的顏色和黃銅雷同。Gold is similar to brass in color.
雷鳥(ㄌㄟˊ ㄋㄧㄠˇ)
a thunderbird (in the mythology of some North America Indians)
雷厲風行(ㄌㄟˊ ㄌㄧˋ ㄈㄥ ㄒㄧㄥˊ)
to enforce a law or rule with speed and great determination; to take drastic measures
雷管(ㄌㄟˊ ㄍㄨㄢˇ)
a percussion cap; a detonator
雷公(ㄌㄟˊ ㄍㄨㄥ)
the thunder god
雷汞(ㄌㄟˊ ㄍㄨㄥˇ)or 雷酸汞(ㄌㄟˊ ㄙㄨㄢ ㄍㄨㄥˇ)
fulminating mercury
雷虎小組(ㄌㄟˊ ㄏㄨˇ ㄒㄧㄠˇ ㄗㄨˇ)
the Thunder Tigers, a daredevil aerobatic team of the Chinese Air Force
雷擊(ㄌㄟˊ ㄐㄧˊ)
to be electrocuted by lightning accidentally; to be struck by lightning
雷州半島(ㄌㄟˊ ㄓㄡ ㄅㄢˋ ㄉㄠˇ)
the Leichou Peninsula in southwest Kwangtung
雷震(ㄌㄟˊ ㄓㄣˋ)
thunderclaps
雷陣(ㄌㄟˊ ㄓㄣˋ)
a continuous peal of rolling thunder
雷陣雨(ㄌㄟˊ ㄓㄣˋ ㄩˇ)
a thundershower
雷池(ㄌㄟˊ ㄔˊ)
①name of a lake in Anhwei Province ②(figuratively) the utmost limit: 他不敢越雷池一步。He doesn't dare to transgress the utmost limit.
雷師(ㄌㄟˊ ㄕ)
the thunder god
雷射(ㄌㄟˊ ㄕㄜˋ)
a laser
雷射唱片(ㄌㄟˊ ㄕㄜˋ ㄔㄤˋ ㄆㄧㄢˋ)
a compact disc (CD)
雷射唱機(ㄌㄟˊ ㄕㄜˋ ㄔㄤˋ ㄐㄧ)
a CD player
雷聲(ㄌㄟˊ ㄕㄥ)
a thunderclap; thunder: 閃電過後，就是雷聲。After the lightning came the thunder.
雷聲大，雨點小(ㄌㄟˊ ㄕㄥ ㄉㄚˋ, ㄩˇ ㄉㄧㄢˇ ㄒㄧㄠˇ)
to talk a great deal about something with little or no follow-up action
雷雨(ㄌㄟˊ ㄩˇ)

a thunderstorm

【電】 6690
ㄉㄧㄢˋ diann diàn
1. electricity; power
2. short for cable or telegram
電波(ㄉㄧㄢˋ ㄅㄛ)
electric waves
電報(ㄉㄧㄢˋ ㄅㄠˋ)
a cable; a telegram; to wire: 我發一通電報給他。I sent a telegram to him.
電報費(ㄉㄧㄢˋ ㄅㄠˋ ㄈㄟˋ)
a cable charge; a telegram fee
電報掛號(ㄉㄧㄢˋ ㄅㄠˋ ㄍㄨㄚˋ ㄏㄠˋ)
a cable address
電報機(ㄉㄧㄢˋ ㄅㄠˋ ㄐㄧ)
a telegraph transmitter or receiver: 誰發明電報機? Who invented the telegraph transmitter?
電報局(ㄉㄧㄢˋ ㄅㄠˋ ㄐㄩˊ)
a telegraph office
電報轉發機(ㄉㄧㄢˋ ㄅㄠˋ ㄓㄨㄢˇ ㄈㄚ ㄐㄧ)
a telegraph repeater
電表(ㄉㄧㄢˋ ㄅㄧㄠˇ)
① any meter for measuring electricity, such as an ammeter or a voltmeter ② a kilowatt-hour meter
電冰箱(ㄉㄧㄢˋ ㄅㄧㄥ ㄒㄧㄤ) or 電氣冰箱(ㄉㄧㄢˋ ㄑㄧˋ ㄅㄧㄥ ㄒㄧㄤ)
a refrigerator; an ice box 亦作「冰箱」
電瓶(ㄉㄧㄢˋ ㄆㄧㄥˊ)
a storage battery; an accumulator
電碼(ㄉㄧㄢˋ ㄇㄚˇ)
the code (of a cable); a cipher
電碼簿(ㄉㄧㄢˋ ㄇㄚˇ ㄅㄨˋ) or 電碼本(ㄉㄧㄢˋ ㄇㄚˇ ㄅㄣˇ)
a code book
電鰻(ㄉㄧㄢˋ ㄇㄢˊ)
Gymnotus electricus, an electric eel
電門(ㄉㄧㄢˋ ㄇㄣˊ)
a switch for electric current; a switch 亦作「開關」: 電門發生故障。The switch was out of order.
電木(ㄉㄧㄢˋ ㄇㄨˋ)
(chemistry) bakelite
電費(ㄉㄧㄢˋ ㄈㄟˋ)
a power rate; a power bill
電赴(ㄉㄧㄝ ㄈㄨˋ)
to rush to a place like a flash
電覆(ㄉㄧㄢˋ ㄈㄨˋ)
to cable a reply
電導(ㄉㄧㄢˋ ㄉㄠˇ)
conductivity
電導體(ㄉㄧㄢˋ ㄉㄠˇ ㄊㄧˇ)
an electric conductor
電燈(ㄉㄧㄢˋ ㄉㄥ)
electric lights or lamps
電燈泡(ㄉㄧㄢˋ ㄉㄥ ㄆㄠˋ)
①an electric bulb ②(colloquial) an unwanted third party who accompanies a courting pair
電鍍(ㄉㄧㄢˋ ㄉㄨˋ)
electroplate
電動(ㄉㄧㄢˋ ㄉㄨㄥˋ)
powered by electricity
電動刮鬍刀(ㄉㄧㄢˋ ㄉㄨㄥˋ ㄍㄨㄚ ㄏㄨˊ ㄉㄠ)
a shaver; an electric shaver
電動機(ㄉㄧㄢˋ ㄉㄨㄥˋ ㄐㄧ)
an electric motor; an induction motor
電動車(ㄉㄧㄢˋ ㄉㄨㄥˋ ㄔㄜ)
an electric motor car; an electric driven vehicle
電動玩具(ㄉㄧㄢˋ ㄉㄨㄥˋ ㄨㄢˊ ㄐㄩˋ)
① a battery-powered toy ② a video game; a TV game; a computer game
電臺(ㄉㄧㄢˋ ㄊㄞˊ)
a radio station
電毯(ㄉㄧㄢˋ ㄊㄢˇ)
an electric blanket
電燙(ㄉㄧㄢˋ ㄊㄤˋ)
to wave or curl hair by electricity
電梯(ㄉㄧㄢˋ ㄊㄧ)
an electric lift; an elevator
電筒(ㄉㄧㄢˋ ㄊㄨㄥˇ)
a flashlight
電腦(ㄉㄧㄢˋ ㄋㄠˇ)
a computer; an electronic computer; an electronic brain
電腦指令(ㄉㄧㄢˋ ㄋㄠˇ ㄓˇ ㄌㄧㄥˋ)
computer instructions
電腦製圖(ㄉㄧㄢˋ ㄋㄠˇ ㄓˋ ㄊㄨˊ)
computer cartography
電腦終端機(ㄉㄧㄢˋ ㄋㄠˇ ㄓㄨㄥ ㄉㄨㄢ ㄐㄧ)
a computer terminal
電腦程式(ㄉㄧㄢˋ ㄋㄠˇ ㄔㄥˊ ㄕˋ)
a computer program
電腦設備(ㄉㄧㄢˋ ㄋㄠˇ ㄕㄜˋ ㄅㄟˋ)
computer installation
電腦擇偶(ㄉㄧㄢˋ ㄋㄠˇ ㄗㄜˊ ㄡˇ)
computer dating
電腦印表機(ㄉㄧㄢˋ ㄋㄠˇ ㄧㄣˋ ㄅㄧㄠˇ ㄐㄧ)
a computer printer
電腦語言(ㄉㄧㄢˋ ㄋㄠˇ ㄩˇ ㄧㄢˊ)
computer language
電能(ㄉㄧㄢˋ ㄋㄥˊ)
electric energy
電鈕(ㄉㄧㄢˋ ㄋㄧㄡˇ)
a button that controls electric currents
電纜(ㄉㄧㄢˋ ㄌㄢˇ)
a cable (usually submarine)
電離(ㄉㄧㄢˋ ㄌㄧˊ)
electrolytic dissociation
電力(ㄉㄧㄢˋ ㄌㄧˋ)
electric power
電力公司(ㄉㄧㄢˋ ㄌㄧˋ ㄍㄨㄥ ㄙ)
a power company
電力學(ㄉㄧㄢˋ ㄌㄧˋ ㄒㄩㄝˊ)
electrodynamics
電療法(ㄉㄧㄢˋ ㄌㄧㄠˊ ㄈㄚˇ)
electrotherapy
電料行(ㄉㄧㄢˋ ㄌㄧㄠˋ ㄏㄤˊ)
a store selling electric appliances or accessories
電流(ㄉㄧㄢˋ ㄌㄧㄡˊ)
an electric current
電流計(ㄉㄧㄢˋ ㄌㄧㄡˊ ㄐㄧˋ)
a galvanometer
電聯車(ㄉㄧㄢˋ ㄌㄧㄢˊ ㄔㄜ)
an electric multiple unit railcar (EMUR)
電鈴(ㄉㄧㄢˋ ㄌㄧㄥˊ)
an electric bell; a buzzer
電令(ㄉㄧㄢˋ ㄌㄧㄥˋ)
to transmit orders by cable or telegram
電爐(ㄉㄧㄢˋ ㄌㄨˊ)
an electric stove; a hot plate
電路(ㄉㄧㄢˋ ㄌㄨˋ)
an electric circuit
電杆(ㄉㄧㄢˋ ㄍㄢ)
poles for electric wires
電感應(ㄉㄧㄢˋ ㄍㄢˇ ㄧㄥˋ)
electric induction
電鍋(ㄉㄧㄢˋ ㄍㄨㄛ)
an electric rice cooker
電光(ㄉㄧㄢˋ ㄍㄨㄤ)
electric light; a flash of lightning
電光石火(ㄉㄧㄢˋ ㄍㄨㄤ ㄕˊ ㄏㄨㄛˇ)
anything that vanishes in a flash

〔雨部〕

電工(ㄉㄧㄢˋ ㄍㄨㄥ)
① an electrician ② electric engineering

電工技術(ㄉㄧㄢˋ ㄍㄨㄥ ㄐㄧˋ ㄕㄨˋ)
electrotechnics

電烤箱(ㄉㄧㄢˋ ㄎㄠˇ ㄒㄧㄤ)
an electric oven

電賀(ㄉㄧㄢˋ ㄏㄜˋ)
to congratulate by cable

電荷(ㄉㄧㄢˋ ㄏㄜˋ)
an electric charge

電銲 or 電焊(ㄉㄧㄢˋ ㄏㄢˋ)
electric welding; electric soldering

電焊棒(ㄉㄧㄢˋ ㄏㄢˋ ㄅㄤˋ)
a soldering iron

電弧(ㄉㄧㄢˋ ㄏㄨˊ)
an electric arc

電花(ㄉㄧㄢˋ ㄏㄨㄚ)
electric sparks

電話(ㄉㄧㄢˋ ㄏㄨㄚˋ)
telephone; phone

電話簿(ㄉㄧㄢˋ ㄏㄨㄚˋ ㄅㄨˋ)
a telephone directory; a telephone book

電話分機(ㄉㄧㄢˋ ㄏㄨㄚˋ ㄈㄣ ㄐㄧ)
a telephone extension

電話亭(ㄉㄧㄢˋ ㄏㄨㄚˋ ㄊㄧㄥˊ)
a telephone booth

電話號碼(ㄉㄧㄢˋ ㄏㄨㄚˋ ㄏㄠˋ ㄇㄚˇ)
a telephone number

電話會議(ㄉㄧㄢˋ ㄏㄨㄚˋ ㄏㄨㄟˋ ㄧˋ)
a telecon

電話機(ㄉㄧㄢˋ ㄏㄨㄚˋ ㄐㄧ)
a telephone set

電話接線生(ㄉㄧㄢˋ ㄏㄨㄚˋ ㄐㄧㄝ ㄒㄧㄢˋ ㄕㄥ)
a telephone operator

電話交換機(ㄉㄧㄢˋ ㄏㄨㄚˋ ㄐㄧㄠ ㄏㄨㄢˋ ㄐㄧ)
a telephone switchboard

電話局(ㄉㄧㄢˋ ㄏㄨㄚˋ ㄐㄩˊ)
a telephone office

電話用戶(ㄉㄧㄢˋ ㄏㄨㄚˋ ㄩㄥˋ ㄏㄨˋ)
a telephone subscriber

電化教育(ㄉㄧㄢˋ ㄏㄨㄚˋ ㄐㄧㄠˋ ㄩˋ)
audio-visual education

電匯(ㄉㄧㄢˋ ㄏㄨㄟˋ)
T/T (telegraphic transfer)

電機(ㄉㄧㄢˋ ㄐㄧ)
electrical machinery

電機工程(ㄉㄧㄢˋ ㄐㄧ ㄍㄨㄥ ㄔㄥˊ)
electrical engineering: 他主修電機工程。He majors in electrical engineering.

電機系(ㄉㄧㄢˋ ㄐㄧ ㄒㄧˋ)
the department of electrical engineering in a college

電極(ㄉㄧㄢˋ ㄐㄧˊ)
an electrode

電擊(ㄉㄧㄢˋ ㄐㄧˊ)
an electric shock; struck by lightning

電吉他(ㄉㄧㄢˋ ㄐㄧˊ ㄊㄚ)
an electric guitar

電解(ㄉㄧㄢˋ ㄐㄧㄝˇ)
electrolysis

電解質(ㄉㄧㄢˋ ㄐㄧㄝˇ ㄓˊ) or 電解液(ㄉㄧㄢˋ ㄐㄧㄝˇ ㄧㄝˋ)
an electrolyte

電鍵(ㄉㄧㄢˋ ㄐㄧㄢˋ)
a switch (for connecting or shutting off electric current)

電晶體(ㄉㄧㄢˋ ㄐㄧㄥ ㄊㄧˇ)
a transistor

電晶體收音機(ㄉㄧㄢˋ ㄐㄧㄥ ㄊㄧˇ ㄕㄡ ㄧㄣ ㄐㄧ)
a transistor radio

電鋸(ㄉㄧㄢˋ ㄐㄩˋ)
an electric saw

電氣(ㄉㄧㄢˋ ㄑㄧˋ)
electric

電氣化(ㄉㄧㄢˋ ㄑㄧˋ ㄏㄨㄚˋ)
electrification; to electrify

電氣設備(ㄉㄧㄢˋ ㄑㄧˋ ㄕㄜˋ ㄅㄟˋ)
electrical equipment

電氣用品(ㄉㄧㄢˋ ㄑㄧˋ ㄩㄥˋ ㄆㄧㄣˇ) or 電器(ㄉㄧㄢˋ ㄑㄧˋ)
electric appliances

電請(ㄉㄧㄢˋ ㄑㄧㄥˇ)
to invite by telegram

電線(ㄉㄧㄢˋ ㄒㄧㄢˋ)
electric wires: 電線能輸送電流。Electric wires carry electricity.

電線走火(ㄉㄧㄢˋ ㄒㄧㄢˋ ㄗㄡˇ ㄏㄨㄛˇ)
a short circuit

電信(ㄉㄧㄢˋ ㄒㄧㄣˋ)
telecommunications

電信局(ㄉㄧㄢˋ ㄒㄧㄣˋ ㄐㄩˊ)
① a telephone and telegraph office ② Directorate General of Telecommunications under the Ministry of Communications

電信業務(ㄉㄧㄢˋ ㄒㄧㄣˋ ㄧㄝˋ ㄨˋ)
telecommunication service

電刑(ㄉㄧㄢˋ ㄒㄧㄥˊ)
electrocution (of criminals); death by electric chair

電訊(ㄉㄧㄢˋ ㄒㄩㄣˋ)
telecommunications; wire communications

電訊局(ㄉㄧㄢˋ ㄒㄩㄣˋ ㄐㄩˊ)
the office of telecommunications

電鐘(ㄉㄧㄢˋ ㄓㄨㄥ)
an electric clock

電池(ㄉㄧㄢˋ ㄔˊ)
an electric battery; a dry cell

電插頭(ㄉㄧㄢˋ ㄔㄚ ㄊㄡˊ)
a wire plug

電插座(ㄉㄧㄢˋ ㄔㄚ ㄗㄨㄛˋ)
a wire socket

電車(ㄉㄧㄢˋ ㄔㄜ)
a tramcar; a streetcar; a trolley car: 他乘電車上下班。He rides on a streetcar to and from work.

電掣(ㄉㄧㄢˋ ㄔㄜˋ)
with great speed, like lightning

電場(ㄉㄧㄢˋ ㄔㄤˇ)
an electric field

電廠(ㄉㄧㄢˋ ㄔㄤˇ)
a power plant

電唱頭(ㄉㄧㄢˋ ㄔㄤˋ ㄊㄡˊ)
a pickup

電唱機(ㄉㄧㄢˋ ㄔㄤˋ ㄐㄧ)
an electric phonograph; a record player

電傳打字電報機(ㄉㄧㄢˋ ㄔㄨㄢˊ ㄉㄚˇ ㄗˋ ㄉㄧㄢˋ ㄅㄠˋ ㄐㄧ)
a teletypewriter

電石(ㄉㄧㄢˋ ㄕˊ)
calcium carbide or carbide

電石氣(ㄉㄧㄢˋ ㄕˊ ㄑㄧˋ)
acetylene

電示(ㄉㄧㄢˋ ㄕˋ)
to instruct by cable or telegram

電勢(ㄉㄧㄢˋ ㄕˋ)
electric potential 亦作「電位」

電視(ㄉㄧㄢˋ ㄕˋ)
television; TV: 你看了電視上的賽船節目嗎? Did you see the boat race on (the) television?

電視播送機(ㄉㄧㄢˋ ㄕˋ ㄅㄛ ㄙㄨㄥˋ ㄐㄧ)
a television transmitter

電視頻道(ㄉㄧㄢˋ ㄕˋ ㄆㄧㄣˊ ㄉㄠˋ)
television channel

電視臺(ㄉㄧㄢˋ ㄕˋ ㄊㄞˊ)
a television station

電視連續劇(ㄉㄧㄢˋ ㄕˋ ㄌㄧㄢˊ ㄒㄩˋ ㄐㄩˋ)
a soap opera

電視錄影(ㄉㄧㄢˋ ㄕˋ ㄌㄨˋ ㄧㄥˇ)
video recording
電視廣播(ㄉㄧㄢˋ ㄕˋ ㄍㄨㄤˇ ㄅㄛ)
a videocast
電視機(ㄉㄧㄢˋ ㄕˋ ㄐㄧ)
a TV set; a television receiving set: 黑白電視機比彩色的便宜。A black-and-white TV is cheaper than a color set.
電視節目(ㄉㄧㄢˋ ㄕˋ ㄐㄧㄝˊ ㄇㄨˋ)
a TV program
電視劇(ㄉㄧㄢˋ ㄕˋ ㄐㄩˋ)
a teleplay
電視轉播(ㄉㄧㄢˋ ㄕˋ ㄓㄨㄢˇ ㄅㄛ)
a television relay
電視採訪(ㄉㄧㄢˋ ㄕˋ ㄘㄞˇ ㄈㄤˇ)
a televised interview
電視遊樂器(ㄉㄧㄢˋ ㄕˋ ㄧㄡˊ ㄌㄜˋ ㄑㄧˋ)
a video game
電視演説(ㄉㄧㄢˋ ㄕˋ ㄧㄢˇ ㄕㄨㄛ)
a televised speech
電視影片(ㄉㄧㄢˋ ㄕˋ ㄧㄥˇ ㄆㄧㄢˋ)
a telefilm
電視網(ㄉㄧㄢˋ ㄕˋ ㄨㄤˇ)
a television network
電扇(ㄉㄧㄢˋ ㄕㄢˋ) or 電風扇(ㄉㄧㄢˋ ㄈㄥ ㄕㄢˋ)
an electric fan: 他想買的是冷氣，不是電扇。What he wants to buy is an air conditioner, not an electric fan.
電熱(ㄉㄧㄢˋ ㄖㄜˋ)
electric heat
電熱器(ㄉㄧㄢˋ ㄖㄜˋ ㄑㄧˋ)
an electric heater or radiator
電容器(ㄉㄧㄢˋ ㄖㄨㄥˊ ㄑㄧˋ)
a capacitor
電子(ㄉㄧㄢˋ ㄗˇ)
an electron
電子翻譯機(ㄉㄧㄢˋ ㄗˇ ㄈㄢ ㄧˋ ㄐㄧ)
an electronic translator
電子計算機(ㄉㄧㄢˋ ㄗˇ ㄐㄧˋ ㄙㄨㄢˋ ㄐㄧ)
an electronic computer
電子計算中心(ㄉㄧㄢˋ ㄗˇ ㄐㄧˋ ㄙㄨㄢˋ ㄓㄨㄥ ㄒㄧㄣ)
a computing center
電子琴(ㄉㄧㄢˋ ㄗˇ ㄑㄧㄣˊ)
an electronic organ
電子顯微鏡(ㄉㄧㄢˋ ㄗˇ ㄒㄧㄢˇ ㄨㄟˊ ㄐㄧㄥˋ)
an electron microscope; an electronic microscope
電子音樂(ㄉㄧㄢˋ ㄗˇ ㄧㄣ ㄩㄝˋ)
electron music
電阻(ㄉㄧㄢˋ ㄗㄨˇ)
(electricity) resistance
電磁(ㄉㄧㄢˋ ㄘˊ)
electromagnetism
電磁鐵(ㄉㄧㄢˋ ㄘˊ ㄊㄧㄝˇ)
electromagnetic steel
電磁爐(ㄉㄧㄢˋ ㄘˊ ㄌㄨˊ)
an induction cooker
電磁學(ㄉㄧㄢˋ ㄘˊ ㄒㄩㄝˊ)
electromagnetics
電磁石(ㄉㄧㄢˋ ㄘˊ ㄕˊ)
an electromagnet
電椅(ㄉㄧㄢˋ ㄧˇ)
the electric chair
電壓(ㄉㄧㄢˋ ㄧㄚ)
voltage
電壓計(ㄉㄧㄢˋ ㄧㄚ ㄐㄧˋ)
a voltmeter
電邀(ㄉㄧㄢˋ ㄧㄠ)
to invite by cable or telegram
電眼(ㄉㄧㄢˋ ㄧㄢˇ)
an electric eye; a magic eye
電影(ㄉㄧㄢˋ ㄧㄥˇ)
movies; motion pictures: 下午看電影去吧。Let's go to the movies this afternoon.
電影明星(ㄉㄧㄢˋ ㄧㄥˇ ㄇㄧㄥˊ ㄒㄧㄥ)
a movie star
電影圖書館(ㄉㄧㄢˋ ㄧㄥˇ ㄊㄨˊ ㄕㄨ ㄍㄨㄢˇ)
a film library
電影界(ㄉㄧㄢˋ ㄧㄥˇ ㄐㄧㄝˋ)
the moviedom; the filmdom
電影劇本(ㄉㄧㄢˋ ㄧㄥˇ ㄐㄩˋ ㄅㄣˇ)
a screenplay
電影製片廠(ㄉㄧㄢˋ ㄧㄥˇ ㄓˋ ㄆㄧㄢˋ ㄔㄤˇ)
a movie studio
電影製片人(ㄉㄧㄢˋ ㄧㄥˇ ㄓˋ ㄆㄧㄢˋ ㄖㄣˊ)
a movie producer
電影字幕(ㄉㄧㄢˋ ㄧㄥˇ ㄗˋ ㄇㄨˋ)
a film caption
電影演員(ㄉㄧㄢˋ ㄧㄥˇ ㄧㄢˇ ㄩㄢˊ)
a movie actor or actress; a cinemactor or cinemactress
電影音樂(ㄉㄧㄢˋ ㄧㄥˇ ㄧㄣ ㄩㄝˋ)
film music
電影院(ㄉㄧㄢˋ ㄧㄥˇ ㄩㄢˋ)
a movie theater; a cinema
電位(ㄉㄧㄢˋ ㄨㄟˋ)
electric potential
電位器(ㄉㄧㄢˋ ㄨㄟˋ ㄑㄧˋ)
a potentiometer
電網(ㄉㄧㄢˋ ㄨㄤˇ)
a net or fence connected with electric current
電魚(ㄉㄧㄢˋ ㄩˊ)
① to fish by electricity ② *Narke japonica,* a flatfish
電源(ㄉㄧㄢˋ ㄩㄢˊ)
the source of electricity
電熨斗(ㄉㄧㄢˋ ㄩㄣˋ ㄉㄡˇ)
an electric iron

【雹】 6691
ㄅㄠˊ baur báo
(讀音 ㄅㄛˊ bor bó)
hail; a hailstone
雹子(ㄅㄠˊ ˙ㄗ)
hail; a hailstone

六畫

【需】 6692
ㄒㄩ shiu xū
1. to need; to require; to demand
2. expenses; provisions; needs; necessaries
3. hesitation; delay
需款(ㄒㄩ ㄎㄨㄢˇ)
to need money; in need of money
需求(ㄒㄩ ㄑㄧㄡˊ)
to need; to require; needs; demands: 他的需求不多。He does not need much.
需次(ㄒㄩ ㄘˋ)
to wait for an official appointment
需才孔亟(ㄒㄩ ㄘㄞˊ ㄎㄨㄥˇ ㄐㄧˊ)
to urgently need persons of ability or talent
需要(ㄒㄩ ㄧㄠˋ)
to need or require; needs or requirements
需要品(ㄒㄩ ㄧㄠˋ ㄆㄧㄣˇ)
necessities; essentials
需要額(ㄒㄩ ㄧㄠˋ ㄜˊ)
the amount needed

七畫

【震】 6693
ㄓㄣˋ jenn zhèn
1. to shake; to tremble, as an earthquake
2. to excite; to shock
3. scared; terrified
4. (now rarely) thunder; a thunderclap
5. the 4th of the Eight Diagrams

〔雨部〕

震幅(ㄓㄣˋ ㄈㄨˊ)
the amplitude of an earthquake
震悼(ㄓㄣˋ ㄉㄠˋ)
to be shocked and grieved
震旦(ㄓㄣˋ ㄉㄢˋ)
the ancient Indian name of China
震動(ㄓㄣˋ ㄉㄨㄥˋ)or 震蕩(ㄓㄣˋ ㄉㄤˋ)
①to vibrate; to shake; to move: 雷聲震動山谷。The thunder shook the valley. ②to be shocked or shaken
震天駭地(ㄓㄣˋ ㄊㄧㄢ ㄏㄞˋ ㄉㄧˋ)
terrifying; tremendously shocking; world-shaking
震霆(ㄓㄣˋ ㄊㄧㄥˊ)
a loud thunderclap; a sudden peal of thunder
震怒(ㄓㄣˋ ㄋㄨˋ)
greatly infuriated; wrath; rage
震慄(ㄓㄣˋ ㄌㄧˋ)
trembling from fear
震古鑠今(ㄓㄣˋ ㄍㄨˇ ㄕㄨㄛˋ ㄐㄧㄣ)
(said of a great achievement, etc.) unprecedented; peerless
震宮(ㄓㄣˋ ㄍㄨㄥ)
the palace of a prince
震恐(ㄓㄣˋ ㄎㄨㄥˇ)
to be shocked
震駭(ㄓㄣˋ ㄏㄞˋ)
greatly terrified or shocked; stunned
震撼(ㄓㄣˋ ㄏㄢˋ)
to shake; shaken
震悸(ㄓㄣˋ ㄐㄧˋ)
terrified; shocked
震驚(ㄓㄣˋ ㄐㄧㄥ)
greatly surprised
震懼(ㄓㄣˋ ㄐㄩˋ)
terrified; in trepidation
震懾(ㄓㄣˋ ㄓㄜˊ)
to awe; to frighten
震災(ㄓㄣˋ ㄗㄞ)
a disaster caused by an earthquake
震耳欲聾(ㄓㄣˋ ㄦˇ ㄩˋ ㄌㄨㄥˊ)
deafening; ear-splitting (sound, voice, etc.)
震央(ㄓㄣˋ ㄧㄤ)or 震源(ㄓㄣˋ ㄩㄢˊ)
an epicenter; a focus

【霄】6694
ㄒㄧㄠ shiau xiāo
1. the sky
2. night
3. to exhaust; to dissolve
4. clouds or mist
霄漢(ㄒㄧㄠ ㄏㄢˋ)
the sky; the firmament
霄壤(ㄒㄧㄠ ㄖㄤˇ)
heaven and earth
霄壤之分(ㄒㄧㄠ ㄖㄤˇ ㄓ ㄈㄣ)or 霄壤之別(ㄒㄧㄠ ㄖㄤˇ ㄓ ㄅㄧㄝˊ)
as far apart as heaven and earth; poles apart
霄外(ㄒㄧㄠ ㄨㄞˋ)
beyond the sky or clouds

【霆】6695
ㄊㄧㄥˊ tyng tíng
a sudden peal of thunder; a thunderbolt
霆擊(ㄊㄧㄥˊ ㄐㄧˊ)
as quickly as lightning

【霈】6696
ㄆㄟˋ pey pèi
1. rains; torrential rains
2. favors; good graces
霈然(ㄆㄟˋ ㄖㄢˊ)
copious; plentiful

【霉】6697
ㄇㄟˊ mei méi
musty; moldy; mold; mildewed; mildew
霉天(ㄇㄟˊ ㄊㄧㄢ)
the rainy season
霉爛(ㄇㄟˊ ㄌㄢˋ)
moldy and rotten
霉菌(ㄇㄟˊ ㄐㄩㄣˋ)
mold; mildew
霉氣(ㄇㄟˊ ㄑㄧˋ)
①a moldy smell; musty ②bad luck or fortune: 我一星期來霉氣不斷。I've had bad luck all week.

八畫

【霍】6698
ㄏㄨㄛˋ huoh huò
1. very rapidly; in a flash; suddenly
2. a Chinese family name
霍地(ㄏㄨㄛˋ ㄉㄧˋ)
suddenly; very quickly: 他霍地立起身來。He suddenly stood up.
霍亂(ㄏㄨㄛˋ ㄌㄨㄢˋ)
cholera
霍光(ㄏㄨㄛˋ ㄍㄨㄤ)
Huo Kuang, one of the greatest generals in the Western Han Dynasty
霍霍(ㄏㄨㄛˋ ㄏㄨㄛˋ)
① rapidly ② the sound of grinding or sharpening knives, etc. ③ bright; brilliant; sparkling
霍去病(ㄏㄨㄛˋ ㄑㄩˋ ㄅㄧㄥˋ)
Huo Chü-ping, a famous general in the Western Han Dynasty
霍閃(ㄏㄨㄛˋ ㄕㄢˇ)
①lightning ②at lightning speed
霍然(ㄏㄨㄛˋ ㄖㄢˊ)
①rapidly; suddenly ②(said of an illness) to be cured quickly

【霎】6699
ㄕㄚˋ shah shà
1. an instant; in the twinkle of an eye—a very short time
2. a slight rain; drizzle
霎時(ㄕㄚˋ ㄕˊ)or 霎時間(ㄕㄚˋ ㄕˊ ㄐㄧㄢ)
in a very short while or moment; in a split second; in a jiffy
霎霎(ㄕㄚˋ ㄕㄚˋ)
①the sound of falling rain ②chilly air; cold winds
霎眼(ㄕㄚˋ ㄧㄢˇ)
to wink

【霏】6700
ㄈㄟ fei fēi
the falling of snow and rain
霏霏(ㄈㄟ ㄈㄟ)
to whirl around in confusion; to fly all over

【霑】6701
ㄓㄢ jan zhān
1. soaked; to become wet or damp; to moisten
2. to receive (benefits, etc.)
霑沐(ㄓㄢ ㄇㄨˋ)
to receive favors
霑染(ㄓㄢ ㄖㄢˇ)
①to get affected by a communicable disease ②to gain a small advantage
霑醉(ㄓㄢ ㄗㄨㄟˋ)
dead drunk
霑恩(ㄓㄢ ㄣ)
to be granted special favors; to be indebted to

【霓】6702
ㄋㄧˊ ni ní
a rainbow; a colored cloud

霓虹燈(ㄋㄧˊ ㄏㄨㄥˊ ㄉㄥ)
the neon light
霓裳舞(ㄋㄧˊ ㄔㄤˊ ㄨˇ)
name of a dance in the Tang Dynasty; a dance in which the female dancers wear colorful costumes
霓裳羽衣曲(ㄋㄧˊ ㄔㄤˊ ㄩˇ ㄧ ㄑㄩ)
name of a tune composed by Emperor Ming of the Tang Dynasty

【霖】 6703 ㄌㄧㄣˊ lin lín
a copious rain falling continuously; a continuous heavy rain
霖霖(ㄌㄧㄣˊ ㄌㄧㄣˊ)
incessant raining
霖雨(ㄌㄧㄣˊ ㄩˇ)
① a pouring rain ② graces; favors; benevolence

九畫

【霜】 6704 ㄕㄨㄤ shuang shuāng
1. frost; hoarfrost
2. white and powdery—like hoarfrost
3. coolness; indifference; grave
4. virtuous; pure and clean
霜鬢(ㄕㄨㄤ ㄅㄧㄣˋ)
hoary hair on the temples
霜毛(ㄕㄨㄤ ㄇㄠˊ)
pure, white feathers
霜鋒(ㄕㄨㄤ ㄈㄥ)
sharp, gleaming blades
霜刀(ㄕㄨㄤ ㄉㄠ)
a sharp, shining knife
霜臺(ㄕㄨㄤ ㄊㄞˊ)
a respectful reference to an imperial censor 亦作「御史臺」
霜天(ㄕㄨㄤ ㄊㄧㄢ)
a bleak sky (in cold weather)
霜害(ㄕㄨㄤ ㄏㄞˋ)
damage to farm crops caused by frost; frostbite; frost injury: 受霜害的農作物 frostbitten crops
霜降(ㄕㄨㄤ ㄐㄧㄤˋ)
one of the 24 climatic periods in the lunar calendar, which begins from October 23 or 24
霜期(ㄕㄨㄤ ㄑㄧˊ)
(meteorology) the frost season
霜淇淋(ㄕㄨㄤ ㄑㄧˊ ㄌㄧㄣˊ)
soft ice cream
霜雪(ㄕㄨㄤ ㄒㄩㄝˇ)
① frost and snow ② snow-white
霜準(ㄕㄨㄤ ㄓㄨㄣˇ)
severe laws or regulations
霜刃(ㄕㄨㄤ ㄖㄣˋ)
a sharp edged sword or knife
霜操(ㄕㄨㄤ ㄘㄠ)
moral uprightness; incorruptibility
霜草(ㄕㄨㄤ ㄘㄠˇ)
white grass
霜葉(ㄕㄨㄤ ㄧㄝˋ)
leaves turning white
霜威(ㄕㄨㄤ ㄨㄟ)
gravity and severity; awe
霜月(ㄕㄨㄤ ㄩㄝˋ)
the seventh moon in the lunar calendar

【霞】 6705 ㄒㄧㄚˊ shya xiá
colored, low-hanging clouds; rosy clouds
霞帔(ㄒㄧㄚˊ ㄆㄟˋ)
① an embroidered scarf or cape for a woman of noble rank in ancient times ② robes, etc. of a Taoist monk ③ a beautiful dancing dress
霞片(ㄒㄧㄚˊ ㄆㄧㄢˋ)
multicolored glaze of porcelain
霞光(ㄒㄧㄚˊ ㄍㄨㄤ)
rays of morning or evening sunlight
霞蔚(ㄒㄧㄚˊ ㄨㄟˋ)
splendid; magnificent

【霝】 6706 ㄌㄧㄥˊ ling líng
1. to rain; rainfall
2. to fall

十一畫

【霧】 6707 ㄨˋ wuh wù
fog; mist; vapor
霧豹(ㄨˋ ㄅㄠˋ)
to retire from public life; to live as a recluse
霧鬢風鬟(ㄨˋ ㄅㄧㄣˋ ㄈㄥ ㄏㄨㄢˊ)
beautiful tresses of a woman
霧裏看花(ㄨˋ ㄌㄧˇ ㄎㄢˋ ㄏㄨㄚ)
(literally) to look at flowers in a fog—failing eyesight of the aged
霧縠(ㄨˋ ㄏㄨˊ)
gossamer; a piece of extremely thin silk
霧氣(ㄨˋ ·ㄑㄧ)
fog or mist
霧塞(ㄨˋ ㄙㄜˋ)
obscured; mentally blinded
霧散(ㄨˋ ㄙㄢˋ)
to disperse like mist or fog

【霪】 6708 ㄧㄣˊ yn yín
to rain for a long time
霪雨(ㄧㄣˊ ㄩˇ)
an incessant rain: 霪雨爲災。An incessant rain becomes disastrous.

十二畫

【霰】 6709 ㄒㄧㄢˋ shiann xiàn
sleet; snow and rain
霰彈(ㄒㄧㄢˋ ㄉㄢˋ)
a case shot; a canister shot
霰石(ㄒㄧㄢˋ ㄕˊ)
aragonite

【霤】 6710 (霤) ㄌㄧㄡˋ liow liù
1. the dripping of water (rain, etc.) from the eaves
2. eaves

【露】 6711 1. ㄌㄨˋ luh lù
1. dew
2. uncovered; exposed; to show; to reveal; to betray
3. a cold, soothing and aromatic drink; beverages distilled from flowers, fruit or leaves
4. a Chinese family name
露布(ㄌㄨˋ ㄅㄨˋ) or 露板(ㄌㄨˋ ㄅㄢˇ) or 露版(ㄌㄨˋ ㄅㄢˇ)
① an unsealed letter or imperial edict ② a message reporting a military victory
露封(ㄌㄨˋ ㄈㄥ)
an unsealed letter
露地(ㄌㄨˋ ㄉㄧˋ)
an open field
露點(ㄌㄨˋ ㄉㄧㄢˇ)
(meteorology) the dew point
露臺(ㄌㄨˋ ㄊㄞˊ)
a topless balcony or terrace where emperors observed

〔雨部〕

heavenly phenomena in ancient times

露頭(ㄌㄨˋ ㄊㄡˊ)
①to take off a hat and lay bare the top of a head ② (mineralogy) an outcrop 亦作「礦苗」

露頭角(ㄌㄨˋ ㄊㄡˊ ㄐㄧㄠˇ)or(ㄌㄡˋ ㄊㄡˊ ㄐㄧㄠˇ)
(said of a young person) beginning to show ability or talent; budding

露袒(ㄌㄨˋ ㄊㄢˇ)
(said of the human body) exposed or uncovered; naked

露體(ㄌㄨˋ ㄊㄧˇ)
naked; in the nude; in the altogether

露天(ㄌㄨˋ ㄊㄧㄢ)
open air; outdoor

露天電影院(ㄌㄨˋ ㄊㄧㄢ ㄉㄧㄢˋ ㄧㄥˇ ㄩㄢˋ)
an open-air cinema (or movie theater)

露天學校(ㄌㄨˋ ㄊㄧㄢ ㄒㄩㄝˊ ㄒㄧㄠˋ)
an open-air school

露立(ㄌㄨˋ ㄌㄧˋ)
①to stand outdoors ② with no place to live in

露骨(ㄌㄨˋ ㄍㄨˇ)
(said of remarks, etc.) without reserve or tact; candid; outspoken; thinly veiled; undisguised

露井(ㄌㄨˋ ㄐㄧㄥˇ)
an uncovered well

露禽(ㄌㄨˋ ㄑㄧㄣˊ)
a crane (a kind of bird)

露止(ㄌㄨˋ ㄓˇ)
to sleep outdoors 亦作「露宿」

露珠(ㄌㄨˋ ㄓㄨ)
dewdrops: 樹葉上有露珠。There were dewdrops on the leaves.

露車(ㄌㄨˋ ㄔㄜ)
a topless cart

露水(ㄌㄨˋ ㄕㄨㄟˇ)
dew: 草爲露水所沾溼。The grass was wet with dew.

露水夫妻(ㄌㄨˋ ㄕㄨㄟˇ ㄈㄨ ㄑㄧ)
a couple living together without being married

露水珠兒(ㄌㄨˋ ㄕㄨㄟˇ ㄓㄨㄦ)
dewdrops 亦作「露珠」

露次(ㄌㄨˋ ㄘˋ)
to station (troops, etc.) in the open air 亦作「露宿」

露宿(ㄌㄨˋ ㄙㄨˋ)
to stay overnight in an open field

露宿風餐(ㄌㄨˋ ㄙㄨˋ ㄈㄥ ㄘㄢ)
(literally) to sleep in the open air and eat in the wind —the hardships of a traveler

露營(ㄌㄨˋ ㄧㄥˊ)
to camp; to bivouac; an open-air camping; a jamboree; a camporee

露尾藏頭(ㄌㄨˋ ㄨㄟˇ ㄘㄤˊ ㄊㄡˊ)
①to act clandestinely ② The more one tries to cover, the more one reveals.

【露】 6711
2. ㄌㄡˋ low lòu

to appear; to emerge; to show: 他的臉上露出怒容。Anger showed in his face.

露白(ㄌㄡˋ ㄅㄞˊ)or(ㄌㄨˋ ㄅㄞˊ)
to show money, valuables, etc. one carries unintentionally

露苗兒(ㄌㄡˋ ㄇㄧㄠˊㄦ)
①to sprout; to put forth ② imminent (occurrence of something)

露面(ㄌㄡˋ ㄇㄧㄢˋ)
to show up; to appear in public; to show one's face; to make an appearance

露風(ㄌㄡˋ ㄈㄥ)
to divulge; to become known

露鋒芒(ㄌㄡˋ ㄈㄥ ㄇㄤˊ)
to make one's aggressiveness or talent felt

露頭(兒)(ㄌㄡˋ ㄊㄡˊ(ㄦ))
to appear

露臉(ㄌㄡˋ ㄌㄧㄢˇ)
① successful; with flying colors ② to show one's face; to appear

露怯(ㄌㄡˋ ㄑㄧㄝˋ)
to appear clumsy (in manners); (usually said of the country people) to show one's ignorance

露相(ㄌㄡˋ ㄒㄧㄤˋ)
to show one's true form or colors

露齒(ㄌㄡˋ ㄔˇ)
to show one's teeth

露出破綻(ㄌㄡˋ ㄔㄨ ㄆㄛˋ ㄓㄢˋ)
to show one's slip; to belie

露出馬脚(ㄌㄡˋ ㄔㄨ ㄇㄚˇ ·ㄐㄧㄠ)or 露馬脚(ㄌㄡˋ ㄇㄚˇ ㄐㄧㄠˇ)
to reveal one's true form or character; to show the cloven hoof; to reveal slips or leave loopholes in one's story

露出眞相(ㄌㄡˋ ㄔㄨ ㄓㄣ ㄒㄧㄤˋ)
to give one away

露才(ㄌㄡˋ ㄘㄞˊ)
to display one's talent or knowledge

露財(ㄌㄡˋ ㄘㄞˊ)
to show wealth unintentionally

露一手(ㄌㄡˋ ㄧˋ ㄕㄡˇ)
to make an exhibition of one's skills; to show off; to display one's skills or cleverness

十三畫

【霹】 6712
ㄆㄧ pi pī

thunders; a sudden peal of thunder

霹雷(ㄆㄧ ㄌㄟˊ)
a sudden peal of thunder

霹靂(ㄆㄧ ㄌㄧˋ)
a sudden peal of thunder; a thunderclap; a thunderbolt

霹靂火(ㄆㄧ ㄌㄧˋ ㄏㄨㄛˇ)
a person with a very low boiling point; a rash and impatient person; a hotspur

霹靂車(ㄆㄧ ㄌㄧˋ ㄔㄜ)
carts equipped with rock-throwing catapults for attacking fortresses in ancient times

霹靂手(ㄆㄧ ㄌㄧˋ ㄕㄡˇ)
a judge capable of making fast decisions and judgments

霹靂舞(ㄆㄧ ㄌㄧˋ ㄨˇ)
break dance

【霸】 6713
(覇)ㄅㄚˋ bah bà

1. to dominate; to rule by might rather than right
2. a feudal lord; a chief or leader; an oppressor
3. something in which one is specially talented or gifted; outstanding

霸道
①(ㄅㄚˋ ㄉㄠˋ) to rule by might and tact instead of right and

virtue; to throw one's weight or to bully around; overbearing; high-handed
②(ㄅㄚˋ·ㄉㄠ) a strong or heavy dosage (of medicine)
霸略(ㄅㄚˋ ㄌㄩㄝˋ)
the strategy or scheme of a tyrant
霸功(ㄅㄚˋ ㄍㄨㄥ)
hegemony; hegemonic achievements
霸據(ㄅㄚˋ ㄐㄩˋ)
to occupy by force
霸氣(ㄅㄚˋ ㄑㄧˋ)
aggressiveness
霸權(ㄅㄚˋ ㄑㄩㄢˊ)
the authority of a powerful feudal prince; hegemony
霸者(ㄅㄚˋ ㄓㄜˇ)
an oppressor; a tyrant
霸佔(ㄅㄚˋ ㄓㄢˋ)
to occupy or take by force
霸主(ㄅㄚˋ ㄓㄨˇ)
① a powerful chief of the princes of the Epoch of Spring and Autumn (722-484 B.C.) ② an overlord; a hegemon
霸術(ㄅㄚˋ ㄕㄨˋ)
Machiavellianism
霸業(ㄅㄚˋ ㄧㄝˋ)
the achievement, career, etc. of a powerful head of feudal lords
霸王(ㄅㄚˋ ㄨㄤˊ)
① the leader of feudal lords ② the supreme chief or leader

【霶】 6714
(滂) ㄆㄤ pang pāng
to rain cats and dogs
霶霈(ㄆㄤ ㄆㄟˋ)
to rain hard; a heavy rain

十四畫

【霽】 6715
ㄐㄧˋ jih jì
1. to stop raining; to clear up after rain or snow: 雨霽。The rain is over.
2. to stop being angry
霽範(ㄐㄧˋ ㄈㄢˋ)
a mild and moderate manner
霽色(ㄐㄧˋ ㄙㄜˋ)
① mild and pleasant expression ②(said of the sky after rain) clear and blue
霽威(ㄐㄧˋ ㄨㄟ)
to stop being angry; to stop anger
霽月(ㄐㄧˋ ㄩㄝˋ)
① a clear moon after rain; an unclouded moon ② open-minded

【霾】 6716
ㄇㄞˊ mai mái
1. cloudy; misty or foggy; haze: 他在一個陰霾的日子離去。He left on a cloudy day.
2. a duststorm

十六畫

【靂】 6717
ㄌㄧˋ lih lì
as in 霹靂—a sudden peal of thunder

【靄】 6718
ㄞˇ ae ǎi
1. mild; amiable; peaceful; kind; amicable; friendly
2. cloudy; haze; mist
3. a Chinese family name
靄靄(ㄞˇ ㄞˇ)
① luxuriant growth ② numerous ③cloudy—thick and dusky

【靆】 6719
ㄉㄞˋ day dài
as in 靉靆，參看「靉」

【靈】 6720
ㄌㄧㄥˊ ling líng
1. the spirit; the soul
2. a fairy; an elf
3. anything pertaining to the deceased
4. wonderful; a wonder
5. mysterious; supernatural; divine
6. clever; nimble; sharp; with quick reflexes: 他的耳朵很靈。He has sharp ears.
7. good; excellent; efficacious; effective; to work: 這藥靈不靈? Does this medicine work?
8. witchcraft
9. a Chinese family name
靈便(ㄌㄧㄥˊ ㄅㄧㄢˋ)
① nimble; adroit; dexterous ② convenient; easy to handle; handy
靈牌(ㄌㄧㄥˊ ㄆㄞˊ)
a spirit tablet; an ancestral tablet
靈媒(ㄌㄧㄥˊ ㄇㄟˊ)
spirit mediumship
靈敏(ㄌㄧㄥˊ ㄇㄧㄣˇ)
adroitness; dexterity; sensitive; clever; skillful; active; acute; nimble
靈妃(ㄌㄧㄥˊ ㄈㄟ)
a woman immortal
靈旛(ㄌㄧㄥˊ ㄈㄢ)
a streamer borne by the eldest son of the deceased at a funeral
靈府(ㄌㄧㄥˊ ㄈㄨˇ)
① the source of one's spirit —the mind, or brain ② one of the five sage emperors in ancient times ③ the earth
靈丹(ㄌㄧㄥˊ ㄉㄢ) or 靈丹妙藥(ㄌㄧㄥˊ ㄉㄢ ㄇㄧㄠˋ ㄧㄠˋ)
a wonder drug; a panacea; a drug with high efficacy
靈臺(ㄌㄧㄥˊ ㄊㄞˊ)
① the source of one's spirit —the mind or brain ② a balcony or terrace where ancient emperors watched heavenly phenomena ③ name of a county in Kansu Province
靈透(ㄌㄧㄥˊ ·ㄊㄡ)
clever and bright; active, energetic and lovable 亦作「伶透」
靈堂(ㄌㄧㄥˊ ㄊㄤˊ)
a hall where the body of the deceased is placed during the funeral service; a mourning hall
靈通(ㄌㄧㄥˊ ㄊㄨㄥ)
①(said of news, messages, etc.) to spread fast; to pass with great speed ② having quick access to information; well-informed
靈童(ㄌㄧㄥˊ ㄊㄨㄥˊ)
(Taoism) an immortal who appears in the form of a boy; an immortal boy
靈感(ㄌㄧㄥˊ ㄍㄢˇ)
① inspiration ② the faculty of telepathy
靈根(ㄌㄧㄥˊ ㄍㄣ)
① morality; virtue ② the body ③ the tongue
靈骨塔(ㄌㄧㄥˊ ㄍㄨˇ ㄊㄚˇ)
a pagoda-shaped ossuary or ossuarium

〔雨部〕

靈光(ㄌㄧㄥˊ ㄍㄨㄤ)
①(Buddhism) the natural inclination or goodness in a person ②strange light; divine light ③(Shanghai dialect) wonderful; good; excellent

靈光殿(ㄌㄧㄥˊ ㄍㄨㄤ ㄉㄧㄢˋ)
①name of an imperial hall in the Han Dynasty which survived many calamities ②a person or thing which survives continuous disasters

靈龕(ㄌㄧㄥˊ ㄎㄢ)
a niche, jar or shrine where the remains of a deceased person are contained

靈活(ㄌㄧㄥˊ ㄏㄨㄛˊ)
energetic, active and clever; quick-witted; quick-minded; flexible; nimble: 這位學生腦筋靈活。The student is quick-witted.

靈魂(ㄌㄧㄥˊ ㄏㄨㄣˊ)
the soul; the spirit

靈魂論(ㄌㄧㄥˊ ㄏㄨㄣˊ ㄌㄨㄣˋ)
animism

靈機一動(ㄌㄧㄥˊ ㄐㄧ ㄧˊ ㄉㄨㄥˋ)
to have a brainstorm; to have a brain wave; to dawn on one suddenly

靈界(ㄌㄧㄥˊ ㄐㄧㄝˋ)
(Buddhism) the realm of departed spirits

靈柩(ㄌㄧㄥˊ ㄐㄧㄡˋ)
a coffin containing a corpse; a bier

靈均(ㄌㄧㄥˊ ㄐㄩㄣ)
another name of Chü Yüan (屈原), an aggrieved poet-official of Chu in ancient China

靈祇(ㄌㄧㄥˊ ㄑㄧˊ)
gods; deities

靈氣(ㄌㄧㄥˊ ㄑㄧˋ)
(said of beautiful mountains) spiritual influence

靈巧(ㄌㄧㄥˊ ㄑㄧㄠˇ)
①clever; ingenious; nimble: 她有一雙靈巧的手。She has a pair of clever hands. ②cute; lovable: 她眞是個靈巧可愛的女孩子。She is such a cute girl.

靈前(ㄌㄧㄥˊ ㄑㄧㄢˊ)
before the spirit of the deceased; in front of the tablet honoring the deceased

靈犀一點通(ㄌㄧㄥˊ ㄒㄧ ㄧˋ ㄉㄧㄢˇ ㄊㄨㄥ)
a meeting of minds; mental rapport

靈效(ㄌㄧㄥˊ ㄒㄧㄠˋ)
(usually said of drugs, etc.) with unbelievable efficacy or curing power

靈脩(ㄌㄧㄥˊ ㄒㄧㄡ)
the king

靈秀(ㄌㄧㄥˊ ㄒㄧㄡˋ)
refined, elegant and exquisite

靈心慧性(ㄌㄧㄥˊ ㄒㄧㄣ ㄏㄨㄟˋ ㄒㄧㄥˋ)
intelligent and talented

靈性(ㄌㄧㄥˊ ㄒㄧㄥˋ)
intelligence, or a natural gift

靈芝(ㄌㄧㄥˊ ㄓ)
Ganoderma lucidum, a kind of dark brownish and hard fungus, which is supposed to possess supernatural powers

靈車(ㄌㄧㄥˊ ㄔㄜ)
a hearse; a funeral carriage

靈櫬(ㄌㄧㄥˊ ㄔㄣˋ)
a coffin

靈牀(ㄌㄧㄥˊ ㄔㄨㄤˊ)
a bier; a spirit bed

靈爽(ㄌㄧㄥˊ ㄕㄨㄤˇ)
gods and deities

靈肉(ㄌㄧㄥˊ ㄖㄡˋ)
the soul and the flesh; the soul and the body

靈人(ㄌㄧㄥˊ ㄖㄣˊ)
an immortal being

靈草(ㄌㄧㄥˊ ㄘㄠˇ)
a kind of fungus regarded as an elixir of life in ancient times

靈異(ㄌㄧㄥˊ ㄧˋ)
strange; mysterious; occult: 靈魂論是靈異之學。Animism is an occult science.

靈藥(ㄌㄧㄥˊ ㄧㄠˋ)
wonderful drugs; magic draughts

靈驗(ㄌㄧㄥˊ ㄧㄢˋ)
①(said of a prediction, or prophecy) to come true; with unbelievable accuracy ②(said of a drug, etc.) with uncanny or unbelievable efficacy

靈位(ㄌㄧㄥˊ ㄨㄟˋ)
a tablet inscribed with the name of the deceased (for worshiping, etc.)

靈雨(ㄌㄧㄥˊ ㄩˇ)
a timely rain

十七畫

【靉】 6721
ㄞˋ ay ài
參看「靉靆」

靉靆(ㄞˋ ㄉㄞˋ)
①cloudy ②glasses or spectacles ③unclear; obscure; indistinct

青 部
ㄑㄧㄥ ching qīng

【青】 6722
ㄑㄧㄥ ching qīng
1. green; blue; black
2. green grass
3. not ripe
4. young; youth; youthful
5. the skin of bamboo
6. as in 蛋青—the white of an egg
7. short for Tsinghai Province or Tsingtao
8. a Chinese family name

青白眼(ㄑㄧㄥ ㄅㄞˊ ㄧㄢˇ)
to esteem or look down

青幫(ㄑㄧㄥ ㄅㄤ)
a secret society founded by Chen Yüan(陳園) toward the last years of the Ching Dynasty

青萍(ㄑㄧㄥ ㄆㄧㄥˊ)
①green duckweeds ②name of a treasured sword

青梅(ㄑㄧㄥ ㄇㄟˊ)
green plums; unripened plums

青梅竹馬(ㄑㄧㄥ ㄇㄟˊ ㄓㄨˊ ㄇㄚˇ)
green plums and a bamboo horse—the innocent affection between a boy and a girl in their childhood

青黴素(ㄑㄧㄥ ㄇㄟˊ ㄙㄨˋ)
penicillin 亦作「盤尼西林」

青盲(ㄑㄧㄥ ㄇㄤˊ)
①green-blindness; eyesight which cannot recognize green color ②glaucoma

青苗(ㄑㄧㄥ ㄇㄧㄠˊ)

rice seedlings: 這些青苗長得很好。The rice seedlings grow well.

青苗法(ㄑㄧㄥ ㄇㄧㄠˊ ㄈㄚˇ)
a loan program introduced by Prime Minister Wang An-shih(王安石) of the northern Sung Dynasty, under which farmers would get the government loan when they planted rice seedlings and would make repayment after a harvest, plus a 20 percent interest

青面獠牙(ㄑㄧㄥ ㄇㄧㄢˋ ㄌㄧㄠˊ ㄧㄚˊ)
green-faced and long-toothed —to have a fierce look on one's face

青黛(ㄑㄧㄥ ㄉㄞˋ)or 青靛(ㄑㄧㄥ ㄉㄧㄢˋ)
name of a Chinese medicine, mostly for external use

青島(ㄑㄧㄥ ㄉㄠˇ)
Tsingtao, a port-and-resort city in Shantung Province

青燈(ㄑㄧㄥ ㄉㄥ)
oil lamps

青苔(ㄑㄧㄥ ㄊㄞˊ)
green moss (lichen): 石頭長滿了青苔。The stones are covered with moss.

青天(ㄑㄧㄥ ㄊㄧㄢ)
①the blue sky ②(in old China) an incorruptible and wise judge; an upright official

青天白日(ㄑㄧㄥ ㄊㄧㄢ ㄅㄞˊ ㄖˋ)
blue sky and white sun—a fine day; in broad daylight

青天白日滿地紅旗(ㄑㄧㄥ ㄊㄧㄢ ㄅㄞˊ ㄖˋ ㄇㄢˇ ㄉㄧˋ ㄏㄨㄥˊ ㄑㄧˊ)
the national flag of the Republic of China

青天白日旗(ㄑㄧㄥ ㄊㄧㄢ ㄅㄞˊ ㄖˋ ㄑㄧˊ)
the flag of blue sky and white sun—the flag of the Kuomintang

青天霹靂(ㄑㄧㄥ ㄊㄧㄢ ㄆㄧ ㄌㄧˋ)
a bolt from the blue

青銅(ㄑㄧㄥ ㄊㄨㄥˊ)
bronze

青銅時代(ㄑㄧㄥ ㄊㄨㄥˊ ㄕˊ ㄉㄞˋ)
the Bronze Age

青內障(ㄑㄧㄥ ㄋㄟˋ ㄓㄤˋ)
glaucoma 亦作「青光眼」or「青盲」

青囊(ㄑㄧㄥ ㄋㄤˊ)
medical practice

青鳥(ㄑㄧㄥ ㄋㄧㄠˇ)
①a bird messenger of Fairy God-Mother(西王母)—a messenger ②*The Blue Bird* by Maurice Maeterlinck

青年(ㄑㄧㄥ ㄋㄧㄢˊ)
youthful people; youths; young people; young men or women

青年團(ㄑㄧㄥ ㄋㄧㄢˊ ㄊㄨㄢˊ)
①a youth corps ②China Youth Corps

青年會(ㄑㄧㄥ ㄋㄧㄢˊ ㄏㄨㄟˋ)
YMCA (Young Men's Christian Association)參看「女青年會」

青年軍(ㄑㄧㄥ ㄋㄧㄢˊ ㄐㄩㄣ)
military units formed by student volunteers toward the end of the Sino-Japanese War of 1937-1945

青睞(ㄑㄧㄥ ㄌㄞˋ)
a look of joy; favor; preference; high regard

青樓(ㄑㄧㄥ ㄌㄡˊ)
①a brothel—(figuratively) prostitutes ②a mansion in ancient times ③the abode of a beauty

青驪(ㄑㄧㄥ ㄌㄧˊ)
a dark horse; a black horse

青帘(ㄑㄧㄥ ㄌㄧㄢˊ)
the streamer of a wineshop

青蓮(ㄑㄧㄥ ㄌㄧㄢˊ)
utpala, the blue lotus, to the shape of whose leaves Buddha's eyes are likened

青蓮居士(ㄑㄧㄥ ㄌㄧㄢˊ ㄐㄩ ㄕˋ)
another name of Li Po(李白), a great Chinese poet

青果(ㄑㄧㄥ ㄍㄨㄛˇ)
①fresh fruits ②an olive

青光眼(ㄑㄧㄥ ㄍㄨㄤ ㄧㄢˇ)
glaucoma 參看「青內障」

青宮(ㄑㄧㄥ ㄍㄨㄥ)
the palace of a prince 亦作「東宮」

青海(ㄑㄧㄥ ㄏㄞˇ)
①Tsinghai (or Chinghai) Province, China ②Koko Nor, a lake in Tsinghai

青蒿(ㄑㄧㄥ ㄏㄠ)
Artemisia apiacea, a grassy plant of the chrysanthemum family with pale yellow and aromatic blossoms in autumn

青黃不接(ㄑㄧㄥ ㄏㄨㄤˊ ㄅㄨˋ ㄐㄧㄝ)
(literally) The old grain is used up before the harvest of the new crop.—a period of insufficiency to tide over; temporary shortage

青紅皂白(ㄑㄧㄥ ㄏㄨㄥˊ ㄗㄠˋ ㄅㄞˊ)
(literally) different colors —right and wrong; the truth about an event

青及(ㄑㄧㄥ ㄐㄧˊ)
to be honored by your perusal (a conventional phrase used in correspondence)亦作「青覽」

青椒(ㄑㄧㄥ ㄐㄧㄠ)
green cayenne pepper

青簡(ㄑㄧㄥ ㄐㄧㄢˇ)
books

青衿 or 青襟(ㄑㄧㄥ ㄐㄧㄣ)
①the blue collar of a student's dress in ancient China —(figuratively) a student ②a young man

青筋(ㄑㄧㄥ ㄐㄧㄣ)
blue veins

青青(ㄑㄧㄥ ㄑㄧㄥ)
green; blue

青杏(ㄑㄧㄥ ㄒㄧㄥˋ)
a green apricot—not ripe yet

青州從事(ㄑㄧㄥ ㄓㄡ ㄘㄨㄥˊ ㄕˋ)
fine wine

青竹絲(ㄑㄧㄥ ㄓㄨˊ ㄙ)
Trimeresurus gramineus, a kind of very venomous snake

青冢(ㄑㄧㄥ ㄓㄨㄥˇ)
the tomb of Wang Chao-chün(王昭君), a famed beauty of the Han Dynasty, in present Inner Mongolia (Suiyüan)

青出於藍(ㄑㄧㄥ ㄔㄨ ㄩˊ ㄌㄢˊ)
to surpass one's master or teacher in learning

青春(ㄑㄧㄥ ㄔㄨㄣ)
①one's youth; young adulthood: 他們充滿青春活力。They are bursting with youthful vigor. ②age (in asking a youth): 她青春幾何? How young (or old) is she?

青春痘(ㄑㄧㄥ ㄔㄨㄣ ㄉㄡˋ)or 青春痣(ㄑㄧㄥ ㄔㄨㄣ ㄓˋ)
acne

青春期(ㄑㄧㄥ ㄔㄨㄣ ㄑㄧˊ)
adolescence; puberty; teens

青春腺(ㄑㄧㄥ ㄔㄨㄣ ㄒㄧㄢˋ)
reproductive glands

青史(ㄑㄧㄥ ㄕˇ)
①history: 他的名字將永垂青史。His name will go down in the annals of history. ②a Chinese double name

青少年(ㄑㄧㄥ ㄕㄠˋ ㄋㄧㄢˊ)
teenagers; youngsters

青少年問題(ㄑㄧㄥ ㄕㄠˋ ㄋㄧㄢˊ ㄨㄣˋ ㄊㄧˊ)
the problems of adolescent

青衫(ㄑㄧㄥ ㄕㄢ)
①clothes worn by low-rank officials ②(Chinese opera) a leading female role

青山(ㄑㄧㄥ ㄕㄢ)
a green hill: 留得青山在，不愁沒柴燒。While there is a life, there is a hope.

青山綠水(ㄑㄧㄥ ㄕㄢ ㄌㄩˋ ㄕㄨㄟˇ)
blue mountains and green water—a charming natural scene

青紫(ㄑㄧㄥ ㄗˇ)
①purple and blue (bruises) ②the purple silk ribbons and blue silk ribbons attached to an official seal; (figuratively) officials of high rank

青菜(ㄑㄧㄥ ㄘㄞˋ)
vegetables; the greens

青草(ㄑㄧㄥ ㄘㄠˇ)
green grass

青翠(ㄑㄧㄥ ㄘㄨㄟˋ)
fresh green; verdant

青葱(ㄑㄧㄥ ㄘㄨㄥ)
verdant; fresh green

青絲(ㄑㄧㄥ ㄙ)
①black hair (of a woman or girl) ②sliced preserved plums used as dressing on food (usually sweet)

青娥(ㄑㄧㄥ ㄜˊ)
young girls

青蛾(ㄑㄧㄥ ㄜˊ)
eyebrows

青衣(ㄑㄧㄥ ㄧ)
①clothes of the poor in ancient China ②everyday clothes ③(Chinese opera) a leading female role

青衣祭酒(ㄑㄧㄥ ㄧ ㄐㄧˋ ㄐㄧㄡˇ)
(Chinese opera) the most accomplished female role player

青眼(ㄑㄧㄥ ㄧㄢˇ)
preference; high regard; favor

青烏術(ㄑㄧㄥ ㄨ ㄕㄨˋ)
geomancy

青蛙(ㄑㄧㄥ ㄨㄚ)
a frog

青魚(ㄑㄧㄥ ㄩˊ)
a mackerel

青玉(ㄑㄧㄥ ㄩˋ)
a sapphire

青雲(ㄑㄧㄥ ㄩㄣˊ)
①high in virtue or position ②retirement ③the sky

青雲直上(ㄑㄧㄥ ㄩㄣˊ ㄓˊ ㄕㄤˋ)
to soar higher and higher in one's career

青雲志(ㄑㄧㄥ ㄩㄣˊ ㄓˋ)
great ambition; high and noble ambition or aspiration: 願君能遂青雲志。May you realize your great ambition.

五畫

【靖】 6723
ㄐㄧㄥˋ jinq jìng

1. peaceful; still; tranquil; quiet
2. to pacify; to quell (an uprising, etc.); to tranquilize
3. to order
4. to praise in public
5. a Chinese family name

靖邊(ㄐㄧㄥˋ ㄅㄧㄢ)
①to pacify or safeguard the border ②name of a county in Shensi Province

靖難(ㄐㄧㄥˋ ㄋㄢˋ)
①to stabilize a dangerous situation, etc.; to pacify ②a historical episode during the reign of Emperor 建文 of the Ming Dynasty when the capital was taken by the emperor's uncle who later on usurped the throne

靖亂(ㄐㄧㄥˋ ㄌㄨㄢˋ)
to quell uprisings; to put down a rebellion

靖國(ㄐㄧㄥˋ ㄍㄨㄛˊ)
to pacify the nation; to restore order in the country

靖言(ㄐㄧㄥˋ ㄧㄢˊ)
insincere words; sweet talk; flattery

七畫

【靚】 6724
ㄐㄧㄥˋ jinq jìng

1. to ornament; to doll up
2. still; quiet; tranquil

靚妝 or 靚粧 or 靚糚(ㄐㄧㄥˋ ㄓㄨㄤ)
(said of a woman) fully dressed and ornamented

靚衣(ㄐㄧㄥˋ ㄧ)
beautiful dresses, jewels, etc.

八畫

【靜】 6725
ㄐㄧㄥˋ jinq jìng

1. still; motionless; quiet(ly); calm; tranquility; silent: 請安靜。Please be quiet.
2. peaceful; harmonious; serene
3. virtuous; chaste

靜僻(ㄐㄧㄥˋ ㄆㄧˋ)
quiet or out-of-the-way (spots, places, etc.)

靜默(ㄐㄧㄥˋ ㄇㄛˋ)
①silence; to become silent: 他是一位靜默寡言的人。He is a man of silence. ②to mourn in silence

靜脈(ㄐㄧㄥˋ ㄇㄞˋ)
veins

靜脈曲張(ㄐㄧㄥˋ ㄇㄞˋ ㄑㄩ ㄓㄤ)
varix; varicosity

靜脈注射(ㄐㄧㄥˋ ㄇㄞˋ ㄓㄨˋ ㄕㄜˋ)
intravenous injection

靜美(ㄐㄧㄥˋ ㄇㄟˇ)
(art) static beauty

靜謐(ㄐㄧㄥˋ ㄇㄧˋ)
quiet; still; tranquil

靜穆(ㄐㄧㄥˋ ㄇㄨˋ)
solemn and quiet

靜電(ㄐㄧㄥˋ ㄉㄧㄢˋ)
static electricity

靜電感應(ㄐㄧㄥˋ ㄉㄧㄢˋ ㄍㄢˇ ㄧㄥˋ)
electrostatic induction

靜電場(ㄐㄧㄥˋ ㄉㄧㄢˋ ㄔㄤˇ)
an electrostatic field

靜態(ㄐㄧㄥˋ ㄊㄞˋ)
a motionless state; the state of stillness; a stationary state

靜聽(ㄐㄧㄥˋ ㄊㄧㄥ)
to listen quietly

靜力學(ㄐㄧㄥˋ ㄌㄧˋ ㄒㄩㄝˊ)
statics
靜觀(ㄐㄧㄥˋ ㄍㄨㄢ)
to observe quietly
靜觀自得(ㄐㄧㄥˋ ㄍㄨㄢ ㄗˋ ㄉㄜˊ)
Everything comes to one who waits.
靜候(ㄐㄧㄥˋ ㄏㄡˋ)
to await quietly
靜寂(ㄐㄧㄥˋ ㄐㄧˊ)
calm; quiet; tranquility
靜極思動(ㄐㄧㄥˋ ㄐㄧˊ ㄙ ㄉㄨㄥˋ)
When one remains idle for too long, he thinks of taking an active role in life.
靜靜地(ㄐㄧㄥˋ ㄐㄧㄥˋ ·ㄉㄜ)
quietly; calmly; silently
靜靜兒(ㄐㄧㄥˋ ㄐㄧㄥˋㄦ)
quiet; silent
靜居思過(ㄐㄧㄥˋ ㄐㄩ ㄙ ㄍㄨㄛˋ)
to live in seclusion and make self-examination
靜悄悄(ㄐㄧㄥˋ ㄑㄧㄠˇ ㄑㄧㄠˇ)
quietly; stealthily; very quiet: 教室靜悄悄的。It was very quiet in the classroom.
靜修(ㄐㄧㄥˋ ㄒㄧㄡ)
to study, train, or discipline (oneself) without being disturbed by what's going on outside
靜心(ㄐㄧㄥˋ ㄒㄧㄣ)
to calm one's mind; a peaceful mind
靜止(ㄐㄧㄥˋ ㄓˇ)
motionless; static; rest; at a standstill: 光陰不是永遠靜止的。Time is never at a standstill.
靜舍(ㄐㄧㄥˋ ㄕㄜˋ)
① a Buddhist temple ② a quiet house
靜水(ㄐㄧㄥˋ ㄕㄨㄟˇ)
still water; stagnant water
靜若處女，動若脫兎(ㄐㄧㄥˋ ㄖㄨㄛˋ ㄔㄨˇ ㄋㄩˇ, ㄉㄨㄥˋ ㄖㄨㄛˋ ㄊㄨㄛ ㄊㄨˋ)
Deliberate in counsel, prompt in action.
靜字(ㄐㄧㄥˋ ㄗˋ)
an adjective
靜坐(ㄐㄧㄥˋ ㄗㄨㄛˋ)
to sit still with a peaceful mind; to sit still as a form of therapy
靜坐示威(ㄐㄧㄥˋ ㄗㄨㄛˋ ㄕˋ ㄨㄟ)or 靜坐抗議(ㄐㄧㄥˋ ㄗㄨㄛˋ ㄎㄤˋ ㄧˋ)
to sit in; a sit-in demonstration; a sit-in protest
靜思(ㄐㄧㄥˋ ㄙ)
to think or contemplate quietly; to meditate
靜以制動(ㄐㄧㄥˋ ㄧˇ ㄓˋ ㄉㄨㄥˋ)
to beat action by inaction
靜夜(ㄐㄧㄥˋ ㄧㄝˋ)
a silent night; in the still of the night: 我喜歡在靜夜沈思。I like to meditate in the still of the night.
靜養(ㄐㄧㄥˋ ㄧㄤˇ)
to rest or convalesce without disturbance; to recuperate in quiet surroundings
靜物畫(ㄐㄧㄥˋ ㄨˋ ㄏㄨㄚˋ)
(painting) still life

【靛】 6726
ㄉㄧㄢˋ diann diàn
indigo; any blue dyes; indigo color
靛白(ㄉㄧㄢˋ ㄅㄞˊ)
indigo white
靛藍(ㄉㄧㄢˋ ㄌㄢˊ)
indigo blue
靛精(ㄉㄧㄢˋ ㄐㄧㄥ)
indigotin
靛青(ㄉㄧㄢˋ ㄑㄧㄥ)
indigo—a blue dye obtained from various plants
靛油(ㄉㄧㄢˋ ㄧㄡˊ)
aniline oil

十畫

【靝】 6727
ㄊㄧㄢ tian tian
(Taoism) the heaven

非 部
ㄈㄟ fei fēi

【非】 6728
ㄈㄟ fei fēi
1. negative; not; not to be; non-: 細菌非肉眼所能見。Germs cannot be seen by the naked eye.
2. faults; mistakes; evils; wrong: 他想要文過飾非。He tries to cover up his mistakes.
3. to object; to refute; to consider as wrong; to censure; to blame
4. short for Africa
非賣品(ㄈㄟ ㄇㄞˋ ㄆㄧㄣˇ)
items not for sale: 所有物品都是非賣品。All these items are not for sale.
非美活動委員會(ㄈㄟ ㄇㄟˇ ㄏㄨㄛˊ ㄉㄨㄥˋ ㄨㄟˇ ㄩㄢˊ ㄏㄨㄟˋ)
House Committee on Un-American Activities
非命(ㄈㄟ ㄇㄧㄥˋ)
① death by accident or violence: 他死於非命。He died a violent death. ② a refutation on fatalism
非法(ㄈㄟ ㄈㄚˇ)
illegal; unlawful; illicit
非法罷工(ㄈㄟ ㄈㄚˇ ㄅㄚˋ ㄍㄨㄥ)
an illegal strike
非法翻印(ㄈㄟ ㄈㄚˇ ㄈㄢ ㄧㄣˋ)
to pirate
非法集會(ㄈㄟ ㄈㄚˇ ㄐㄧˊ ㄏㄨㄟˋ)
an illegal assembly
非法拘留(ㄈㄟ ㄈㄚˇ ㄐㄩ ㄌㄧㄡˊ)
illegal detention
非法行爲(ㄈㄟ ㄈㄚˇ ㄒㄧㄥˊ ㄨㄟˊ)
illegal acts
非法佔領(ㄈㄟ ㄈㄚˇ ㄓㄢˋ ㄌㄧㄥˇ)
illegal occupation
非法持有(ㄈㄟ ㄈㄚˇ ㄔˊ ㄧㄡˇ)
illegal possession
非法收入(ㄈㄟ ㄈㄚˇ ㄕㄡ ㄖㄨˋ)
illicit income
非法遊行示威(ㄈㄟ ㄈㄚˇ ㄧㄡˊ ㄒㄧㄥˊ ㄕˋ ㄨㄟ)
an illegal demonstration
非非之想(ㄈㄟ ㄈㄟ ㄓ ㄒㄧㄤˇ)
wishful thinking
非肥皂(ㄈㄟ ㄈㄟˊ ㄗㄠˋ)
detergent
非凡(ㄈㄟ ㄈㄢˊ)
extraordinary; remarkable; uncommon; outstanding: 他最後獲得非凡的成功。He finally achieved extraordinary success.
非分(ㄈㄟ ㄈㄣˋ)
undeserved; beyond the scope of duty or position; presumptuous: 我不想知道他的非分要求。I do not want to know his presumptuous demands.
非分之想(ㄈㄟ ㄈㄣˋ ㄓ ㄒㄧㄤˇ)
a thought or desire entirely

〔非部〕

not on a par with or within one's ability, position, duty, etc. to harbor; an improper thought or desire

非得(ㄈㄟ ㄉㄟˇ)
must; to have to; to have no other alternative but to...: 做這種事非得仔細才行。You must be careful when you do this job.

非導體(ㄈㄟ ㄉㄠˇ ㄊㄧˇ)
nonconductors

非但(ㄈㄟ ㄉㄢˋ)or 非止(ㄈㄟ ㄓˇ)
not only

非獨(ㄈㄟ ㄉㄨˊ)
not only; not merely

非同小可(ㄈㄟ ㄊㄨㄥˊ ㄒㄧㄠˇ ㄎㄜˇ)
tremendously important; no small matter; very serious; having grave consequences

非難(ㄈㄟ ㄋㄢˋ)
to blame; to dispute; to censure; to criticize; to reproach

非類(ㄈㄟ ㄌㄟˋ)
① gangsters; robbers; bandits ② people not of the same race

非禮(ㄈㄟ ㄌㄧˇ)
① improper ② to assault a woman sexually

非驢非馬(ㄈㄟ ㄌㄩˊ ㄈㄟ ㄇㄚˇ)
neither an ass nor a horse —grotesque; unlike anything; to imitate unsuccessfully

非官方(ㄈㄟ ㄍㄨㄢ ㄈㄤ)or 非官式(ㄈㄟ ㄍㄨㄢ ㄕˋ)
unofficial

非婚生子女(ㄈㄟ ㄏㄨㄣ ㄕㄥ ㄗˇ ㄋㄩˇ)
illegitimate children

非計(ㄈㄟ ㄐㄧˋ)
not a good idea; a poor plan

非冀(ㄈㄟ ㄐㄧˋ)
a hope beyond one's reach; a wild hope

非交戰國(ㄈㄟ ㄐㄧㄠ ㄓㄢˋ ㄍㄨㄛˊ)
a nonbelligerent

非金屬(ㄈㄟ ㄐㄧㄣ ㄕㄨˇ)
nonmetals

非晶體(ㄈㄟ ㄐㄧㄥ ㄊㄧˇ)
amorphous

非君莫屬(ㄈㄟ ㄐㄩㄣ ㄇㄛˋ ㄕㄨˇ)
Only you can fill the post.

非軍事化(ㄈㄟ ㄐㄩㄣ ㄕˋ ㄏㄨㄚˋ)
to demilitarize

非軍事區(ㄈㄟ ㄐㄩㄣ ㄕˋ ㄑㄩ)
a demilitarized zone

非軍事人員(ㄈㄟ ㄐㄩㄣ ㄕˋ ㄖㄣˊ ㄩㄢˊ)
civilian personnel

非笑(ㄈㄟ ㄒㄧㄠˋ)
to ridicule; to laugh at

非刑(ㄈㄟ ㄒㄧㄥˊ)
torture; punishment not specified in the law: 獄卒非刑拷打囚犯。The jailer tortured the prisoner brutally.

非支群島(ㄈㄟ ㄓ ㄑㄩㄣˊ ㄉㄠˇ)
the Fiji Islands 亦作「飛枝群島」

非洲(ㄈㄟ ㄓㄡ)
Africa

非戰鬪員(ㄈㄟ ㄓㄢˋ ㄉㄡˋ ㄩㄢˊ)
noncombatants

非戰公約(ㄈㄟ ㄓㄢˋ ㄍㄨㄥ ㄩㄝ)
① an antiwar pact; a treaty renouncing the use of force ② the General Treaty of the Renunciation of War signed in 1928

非正式(ㄈㄟ ㄓㄥˋ ㄕˋ)
informal; unofficial: 宴會要穿什麼衣服—正式或非正式的? What dress should we wear —formal or informal?

非正式訪問(ㄈㄟ ㄓㄥˋ ㄕˋ ㄈㄤˇ ㄨㄣˋ)
an informal (or unofficial) visit

非池中物(ㄈㄟ ㄔˊ ㄓㄨㄥ ㄨˋ)
one who has a promising future

非常(ㄈㄟ ㄔㄤˊ)
① extraordinary; emergency; unusual ② very; highly; terribly; simply: 他的表演非常精彩。His performance was simply wonderful.

非常時期(ㄈㄟ ㄔㄤˊ ㄕˊ ㄑㄧˊ)
time of emergency

非常識(ㄈㄟ ㄔㄤˊ ㄕˋ)
silly; absurd; nonsensical; lack of common sense

非常手段(ㄈㄟ ㄔㄤˊ ㄕㄡˇ ㄉㄨㄢˋ)or 非常方式(ㄈㄟ ㄔㄤˊ ㄈㄤ ㄕˋ)
emergency measures

非常上訴(ㄈㄟ ㄔㄤˊ ㄕㄤˋ ㄙㄨˋ)
an extraordinary appeal (initiated by the procurator general of the Supreme Court)

非常人(ㄈㄟ ㄔㄤˊ ㄖㄣˊ)
an extraordinary person; an outstanding person

非時(ㄈㄟ ㄕˊ)
wrong timing; not the proper time

非人(ㄈㄟ ㄖㄣˊ)
① a bad man; a ruffian; a villain ② not the right man ③ inhuman

非人待遇(ㄈㄟ ㄖㄣˊ ㄉㄞˋ ㄩˋ)
inhuman treatment

非人生活(ㄈㄟ ㄖㄣˊ ㄕㄥ ㄏㄨㄛˊ)
a miserable life; the life of beasts of burden: 那裏的難民過着非人生活。The fugitives there live a miserable life.

非此不可(ㄈㄟ ㄘˇ ㄅㄨˋ ㄎㄜˇ)
Nothing else will do. 或 There's no alternative. 或 This is the only way.

非議(ㄈㄟ ㄧˋ)
to censure; to dispute; to reproach

非也(ㄈㄟ ㄧㄝˇ)
This is not so.

非楊即墨(ㄈㄟ ㄧㄤˊ ㄐㄧˊ ㄇㄛˋ)
to have to be either this or that

非我莫屬(ㄈㄟ ㄨㄛˇ ㄇㄛˋ ㄕㄨˇ)
I, and I alone, am qualified for, or deserve, (the position).

非我族類(ㄈㄟ ㄨㄛˇ ㄗㄨˊ ㄌㄟˋ)
not one among us—aliens

非望(ㄈㄟ ㄨㄤˋ)
a wild hope or desire

七畫

【靠】 6729
ㄎㄠˋ kaw kào

1. to rely on; to depend on
2. to lean on: 把梯子靠在牆上。Lean the ladder against the wall.
3. near to; bordering on; to keep to (the left or the right), as in driving: 所有的行人一律靠右走。All pedestrians should keep to the right.
4. (Chinese opera) make-believe armor worn by actors

靠背(ㄎㄠˋ ㄅㄟˋ)
the back of a chair

靠背椅(ㄎㄠˋ ㄅㄟˋ ㄧˇ)
a chair with a high back

靠邊兒(ㄎㄠˋ ㄅㄧㄚㄦ)or 靠邊(ㄎㄠˋ

ㄅㄧㄢ)
①to keep to the right or left side (of the road): 請靠邊兒站。Please stand aside. 行人靠邊走。Pedestrians keep to the side of the road. ② reasonable; near the truth

靠不住(ㄎㄠˋ ·ㄅㄨ ㄓㄨˋ)
not dependable; not to be trusted; not reliable

靠得住(ㄎㄠˋ ·ㄉㄜ ㄓㄨˋ)
dependable; can be trusted; reliable

靠墊(ㄎㄠˋ ㄉㄧㄢˋ)
a (back) cushion

靠天吃飯(ㄎㄠˋ ㄊㄧㄢ ㄔ ㄈㄢˋ)
to depend on heaven for food—to leave everything to fate

靠攏(ㄎㄠˋ ㄌㄨㄥˇ)
①to shorten the distance; to sit or stand closer: 向前靠攏! Close ranks! ②to shift allegiance to a new master; to tergiversate

靠攏分子(ㄎㄠˋ ㄌㄨㄥˇ ㄈㄣˋ ㄗˇ)
a turncoat; a tergiversator: 我們鄙視靠攏分子。We despise tergiversators.

靠近(ㄎㄠˋ ㄐㄧㄣˋ)
①near to; in the neighborhood ②to approach; to draw nearer

靠枕(ㄎㄠˋ ㄓㄣˇ)
a pillow; a cushion

靠山(ㄎㄠˋ ㄕㄢ)
a person from whom one draws his influence; a supporter in high position; someone to lean on; a backer; a patron; a helper; a protector

靠山吃山，靠水吃水(ㄎㄠˋ ㄕㄢ ㄔ ㄕㄢ, ㄎㄠˋ ㄕㄨㄟˇ ㄔ ㄕㄨㄟˇ)
to make a living in one's given circumstances

靠自己(ㄎㄠˋ ㄗˋ ㄐㄧˇ)
to rely on oneself; independent

靠子(ㄎㄠˋ ·ㄗ)
①something to lean on ② embroidered make-believe armor worn by warriors in Chinese opera

靠岸(ㄎㄠˋ ㄢˋ)
to draw alongside the shore, quay or pier; to pull in to the shore

靠椅(ㄎㄠˋ ㄧˇ)
an easy chair; a lounge chair

十一畫

【靡】 6730
1. ㄇㄧˇ mii mǐ
1. to disperse; to scatter; to divide; blown away by the wind
2. to lean with pressure
3. not; no; negative
4. tiny; petty; small
5. wonderful; good; excellent

靡敝(ㄇㄧˇ ㄅㄧˋ)
decline; to get weak; emaciated

靡靡(ㄇㄧˇ ㄇㄧˇ)
① lewd; licentious ② delayed; procrastinating ③ slowly

靡靡之音(ㄇㄧˇ ㄇㄧˇ ㄓ ㄧㄣ)
lewd music or songs; decadent music

靡麗(ㄇㄧˇ ㄌㄧˋ)
extravagant

靡有孑遺(ㄇㄧˇ ㄧㄡˇ ㄐㄧㄝˊ ㄧˊ)
not a person left; all have died off; no survivor

靡顏膩理(ㄇㄧˇ ㄧㄢˊ ㄋㄧˋ ㄌㄧˇ)
beautiful and fair-skinned

【靡】 6730
2. ㄇㄧˊ mi mí
1. to waste; extravagant: 他過著奢靡的生活。He lived an extravagant life.
2. to rot

靡費(ㄇㄧˊ ㄈㄟˋ)
to waste; extravagant; wasteful 亦作「糜費」

面 部
ㄇㄧㄢˋ miann miàn

【面】 6731
ㄇㄧㄢˋ miann miàn
1. the face of a person
2. the surface; the top; the face
3. a side; a direction; an aspect
4. extent; range; scale; scope
5. to face or confront; to look
6. face-to-face; in or to one's face; personally; directly
7. (mathematics) a plane
8. to indicate something flat

面壁(ㄇㄧㄢˋ ㄅㄧˋ)
①to face the wall ②to do nothing; to waste time ③ (Zen Buddhism) to face the wall and meditate

面稟(ㄇㄧㄢˋ ㄅㄧㄥˇ)
to report to a superior or an elder in person

面部(ㄇㄧㄢˋ ㄅㄨˋ)
the face; facial

面不改色(ㄇㄧㄢˋ ㄅㄨˋ ㄍㄞˇ ㄙㄜˋ)
not to change color; to remain composed; without batting an eyelid

面皰(ㄇㄧㄢˋ ㄆㄠˋ)
pimples; acne; comedos

面盆(ㄇㄧㄢˋ ㄆㄣˊ)
a wash basin

面龐(ㄇㄧㄢˋ ㄆㄤˊ)
facial appearance; facial features: 我弟弟有圓圓的面龐。My younger brother has a round face.

面皮(ㄇㄧㄢˋ ㄆㄧˊ)
① face-skin; face ② fine leather covering the exterior of a bag, case, etc.

面皮薄(ㄇㄧㄢˋ ㄆㄧˊ ㄅㄠˊ)
sensitive; with a sharp sense of shame

面皮厚(ㄇㄧㄢˋ ㄆㄧˊ ㄏㄡˋ)
shameless; brazen; thick-skinned

面貌(ㄇㄧㄢˋ ㄇㄠˋ)
appearance; features of a person; face; looks

面面(ㄇㄧㄢˋ ㄇㄧㄢˋ)
(from) all sides or angles

面面觀(ㄇㄧㄢˋ ㄇㄧㄢˋ ㄍㄨㄢ)
a comprehensive analysis; an exhaustive description

面面俱到(ㄇㄧㄢˋ ㄇㄧㄢˋ ㄐㄩˋ ㄉㄠˋ)
well considered in every respect

面面相覷(ㄇㄧㄢˋ ㄇㄧㄢˋ ㄒㄧㄤ ㄑㄩˋ)
to look at each other in fear, not knowing what to do; to gaze at each other in speechless despair

面命(ㄇㄧㄢˋ ㄇㄧㄥˋ)
to instruct or charge someone face to face

面目(ㄇㄧㄢˋ ㄇㄨˋ)
face; features; looks; appear-

〔面部〕

ance; countenance: 這小女孩面目清秀。The little girl has a delicate appearance.

面目可憎(ㄇㄧㄢˋ ㄇㄨˋ ㄎㄜˇ ㄗㄥ)
abominable (in looks); ugly; repulsive in appearance

面目全非(ㄇㄧㄢˋ ㄇㄨˋ ㄑㄩㄢˊ ㄈㄟ)
Everything's changed beyond recognition.

面目猙獰(ㄇㄧㄢˋ ㄇㄨˋ ㄓㄥ ㄋㄧㄥˊ)
sinister in appearance

面目一新(ㄇㄧㄢˋ ㄇㄨˋ ㄧˋ ㄒㄧㄣ)
a brand-new look; to present a completely new appearance; to assume a new aspect

面縛(ㄇㄧㄢˋ ㄈㄨˊ)
to tie hands behind the back

面帶病容(ㄇㄧㄢˋ ㄉㄞˋ ㄅㄧㄥˋ ㄖㄨㄥˊ)
One's face shows a sickly countenance.

面帶愁容(ㄇㄧㄢˋ ㄉㄞˋ ㄔㄡˊ ㄖㄨㄥˊ)
sad-faced; a woeful look

面豆(ㄇㄧㄢˋ ㄉㄡˋ)
smallpox 亦作「天花」

面對(ㄇㄧㄢˋ ㄉㄨㄟˋ)
to face (a person, situation, direction or object); to confront; opposite; facing: 我們要面對現實。We must face reality.

面對面(ㄇㄧㄢˋ ㄉㄨㄟˋ ㄇㄧㄢˋ)
face-to-face; vis-à-vis

面談(ㄇㄧㄢˋ ㄊㄢˊ)
to talk face-to-face; to take up a matter with somebody personally; to interview

面託(ㄇㄧㄢˋ ㄊㄨㄛ)
to ask someone to do something in person

面團團(ㄇㄧㄢˋ ㄊㄨㄢˊ ㄊㄨㄢˊ)
a full round face

面嫩(ㄇㄧㄢˋ ㄋㄣˋ)
timid; sensitive

面臨(ㄇㄧㄢˋ ㄌㄧㄣˊ)
to be faced with; to be confronted with; to be up against: 我們面臨了一個新的問題。A new problem confronted us.

面告(ㄇㄧㄢˋ ㄍㄠˋ)
to tell in person

面寬(ㄇㄧㄢˋ ˙ㄎㄨㄢ)
latitude; width; breadth

面孔(ㄇㄧㄢˋ ㄎㄨㄥˇ)
the face (of a person)

面和心不和(ㄇㄧㄢˋ ㄏㄜˊ ㄒㄧㄣ ㄅㄨˋ ㄏㄜˊ)
to remain friendly in appearance but estranged at heart

面會(ㄇㄧㄢˋ ㄏㄨㄟˋ)
to meet

面黃肌瘦(ㄇㄧㄢˋ ㄏㄨㄤˊ ㄐㄧ ㄕㄡˋ)
thin and sickly in appearance; an emaciated look; sallow and emaciated

面紅(ㄇㄧㄢˋ ㄏㄨㄥˊ)
to blush

面紅耳赤(ㄇㄧㄢˋ ㄏㄨㄥˊ ㄦˇ ㄔˋ)
to blush; to flush (either because of shame or anger): 她因爲羞愧而面紅耳赤。She flushed with shame.

面積(ㄇㄧㄢˋ ㄐㄧ)
area

面頰(ㄇㄧㄢˋ ㄐㄧㄚˊ)
cheeks

面交(ㄇㄧㄢˋ ㄐㄧㄠ)
① to deliver (something) to the recipient in person ② an acquaintance

面巾(ㄇㄧㄢˋ ㄐㄧㄣ)
① a face towel ② a piece of cloth covering the face of the dead

面巾紙(ㄇㄧㄢˋ ㄐㄧㄣ ㄓˇ)or 面紙(ㄇㄧㄢˋ ㄓˇ)
face tissues

面具(ㄇㄧㄢˋ ㄐㄩˋ)
a mask; a face: 這位警察戴着防毒面具。The policeman is wearing a gas mask.

面前(ㄇㄧㄢˋ ㄑㄧㄢˊ)
in front of; in the presence of; before

面牆(ㄇㄧㄢˋ ㄑㄧㄤˊ)
to face a wall (and see nothing)—unlearned

面請(ㄇㄧㄢˋ ㄑㄧㄥˇ)
to request in person

面洽(ㄇㄧㄢˋ ㄒㄧㄚˊ)or(ㄇㄧㄢˋ ㄑㄧㄚˋ)
to meet and talk it over; to take up a matter with someone personally

面謝(ㄇㄧㄢˋ ㄒㄧㄝˋ)
to thank in person

面向(ㄇㄧㄢˋ ㄒㄧㄤˋ)
to face (a certain direction, a person or object): 那房子面向街道。The house faces the street.

面相學(ㄇㄧㄢˋ ㄒㄧㄤˋ ㄒㄩㄝˊ)
physiognomy

面值(ㄇㄧㄢˋ ㄓˊ)
① par value; face value; nominal value ② denomination

面折(ㄇㄧㄢˋ ㄓㄜˊ)or 面斥(ㄇㄧㄢˋ ㄔˋ)or 面責(ㄇㄧㄢˋ ㄗㄜˊ)
to scold a person to his face

面罩(ㄇㄧㄢˋ ㄓㄠˋ)
a face guard

面囑(ㄇㄧㄢˋ ㄓㄨˇ)
to tell a subordinate or junior in person

面陳(ㄇㄧㄢˋ ㄔㄣˊ)
to report in person; to deliver something to a superior in person

面試(ㄇㄧㄢˋ ㄕˋ)
an oral quiz; an audition; an interview

面紗(ㄇㄧㄢˋ ㄕㄚ)
a veil (for women)

面首(ㄇㄧㄢˋ ㄕㄡˇ)
a catamite

面授機宜(ㄇㄧㄢˋ ㄕㄡˋ ㄐㄧ ㄧˊ)
personally instruct somebody on the line of action to pursue; personally tell someone how to do something; to give confidential briefing

面善(ㄇㄧㄢˋ ㄕㄢˋ)
① to look familiar: 她很面善。Her face seems familiar. ② to look kind-hearted

面善心險(ㄇㄧㄢˋ ㄕㄢˋ ㄒㄧㄣ ㄒㄧㄢˇ)or 面善心惡(ㄇㄧㄢˋ ㄕㄢˋ ㄒㄧㄣ ㄜˋ)
a wolf in sheep's clothing

面商(ㄇㄧㄢˋ ㄕㄤ)
to meet in person and talk it over; to consult personally

面上無光(ㄇㄧㄢˋ ㄕㄤˋ ㄨˊ ㄍㄨㄤ)
loss of prestige

面生(ㄇㄧㄢˋ ㄕㄥ)
(said of a person) unfamiliar; to have not met before: 這女人面生得很。I don't think I've seen this woman before.

面熟(ㄇㄧㄢˋ ㄕㄨˊ)
to look familiar

面霜(ㄇㄧㄢˋ ㄕㄨㄤ)
cream

面如土色(ㄇㄧㄢˋ ㄖㄨˊ ㄊㄨˇ ㄙㄜˋ)
to look ashen; to look pale: 小男孩嚇得面如土色。The little boy turned pale with fright.

面容(ㄇㄧㄢˋ ㄖㄨㄥˊ)
countenance; face
面子(ㄇㄧㄢˋ ˙ㄗ)
① honor; one's face (in the figurative sense): 他不給我面子。He won't do me the honor. ② the outside or facing of a garment
面奏(ㄇㄧㄢˋ ㄗㄡˋ)
to report to the emperor in person
面辭(ㄇㄧㄢˋ ㄘˊ)
① to decline in person ② to go to say good-bye to somebody; to take leave of somebody
面從(ㄇㄧㄢˋ ㄘㄨㄥˊ)
to feign obedience
面色(ㄇㄧㄢˋ ㄙㄜˋ)
① one's facial complexion: 她的面色紅潤。She is ruddy-cheeked. ② facial expression
面色蒼白(ㄇㄧㄢˋ ㄙㄜˋ ㄘㄤ ㄅㄞˊ)
to look pale
面額(ㄇㄧㄢˋ ㄜˊ)
(economics) denomination
面議(ㄇㄧㄢˋ ㄧˋ)
face-to-face negotiations; to negotiate face to face
面謁(ㄇㄧㄢˋ ㄧㄝˋ)
to call on a superior or an elder
面邀(ㄇㄧㄢˋ ㄧㄠ)
to invite in person
面有難色(ㄇㄧㄢˋ ㄧㄡˇ ㄋㄢˊ ㄙㄜˋ)
to look reluctant
面有菜色(ㄇㄧㄢˋ ㄧㄡˇ ㄘㄞˋ ㄙㄜˋ)
to look pale or pallid
面無人色(ㄇㄧㄢˋ ㄨˊ ㄖㄣˊ ㄙㄜˋ)
to look extremely scared; to look ghastly pale
面晤(ㄇㄧㄢˋ ㄨˋ)
to meet in person
面諭(ㄇㄧㄢˋ ㄩˋ)
instructions or exhortations given in person; to give orders in person
面譽(ㄇㄧㄢˋ ㄩˋ)
to praise a person in his presence

七畫

【靦】6732
1. ㄊㄧㄢˇ tean tiǎn
ashamed and embarrassed
靦冒(ㄊㄧㄢˇ ㄇㄠˋ)
ashamed and embarrassed
靦臉(ㄊㄧㄢˇ ㄌㄧㄢˇ)
shameless; to brazen it out
靦然(ㄊㄧㄢˇ ㄖㄢˊ)
to blush for shame; to come to blush with shame
靦顏(ㄊㄧㄢˇ ㄧㄢˊ)
shameless

【靦】6732
2. ㄇㄧㄢˇ mean miǎn
shy; timid
靦覥(ㄇㄧㄢˇ ㄊㄧㄢˇ)
shy; timid; bashful: 她在生人面前顯得靦覥。She's shy with strangers.

十二畫

【靧】6733
ㄏㄨㄟˋ huey huì
to wash one's face

十四畫

【靨】6734
ㄧㄝˋ yeh yè
dimples in the face
靨酺 or 靨輔(ㄧㄝˋ ㄈㄨˇ)
dimples in the face

革部
ㄍㄜˊ ger gé

【革】6735
1. ㄍㄜˊ ger gé
1. hides stripped of hair; skin; leather
2. to get rid of; to eliminate
3. to change; to reform; to renovate
4. (now rarely) human skin
5. Chinese percussion musical instruments
6. armor
7. soldiers
8. one of the Eight Diagrams
9. a Chinese family name

革面革心(ㄍㄜˊ ㄇㄧㄢˋ ㄍㄜˊ ㄒㄧㄣ)
to repent and reform oneself inside out
革命(ㄍㄜˊ ㄇㄧㄥˋ)
a revolution (political, economic, etc.)
革命黨(ㄍㄜˊ ㄇㄧㄥˋ ㄉㄤˇ)
a revolutionary political party
革命軍(ㄍㄜˊ ㄇㄧㄥˋ ㄐㄩㄣ)
the revolutionary army; the revolutionary forces
革命先烈紀念日(ㄍㄜˊ ㄇㄧㄥˋ ㄒㄧㄢ ㄌㄧㄝˋ ㄐㄧˋ ㄋㄧㄢˋ ㄖˋ)
Revolutionary Martyrs' Day on March 29
革退(ㄍㄜˊ ㄊㄨㄟˋ)
to dismiss; to fire; dishonorable discharge
革囊(ㄍㄜˊ ㄋㄤˊ)
① a leather bag ② the human body
革履(ㄍㄜˊ ㄌㄩˇ)
leather shoes
革故鼎新(ㄍㄜˊ ㄍㄨˋ ㄉㄧㄥˇ ㄒㄧㄣ)
to rid the old bane and reform
革心(ㄍㄜˊ ㄒㄧㄣ)
to repent
革新(ㄍㄜˊ ㄒㄧㄣ)
to reform; to renovate; innovation
革新運動(ㄍㄜˊ ㄒㄧㄣ ㄩㄣˋ ㄉㄨㄥˋ)
a reformation movement
革職(ㄍㄜˊ ㄓˊ)
to fire; a dishonorable discharge; to dismiss
革除(ㄍㄜˊ ㄔㄨˊ)
① to rid; to eliminate (ills, etc.); to abolish ② to expel; to dismiss

【革】6735
2. ㄐㄧˊ jyi jí
urgent; dangerous

二畫

【靪】6736
ㄉㄧㄥ ding ding
1. to mend the soles of shoes
2. a patch

四畫

【靳】6737
ㄐㄧㄣˋ jinn jìn
1. ornamental trappings under the neck of a horse
2. stingy
3. a Chinese family name

【靴】6738
ㄒㄩㄝ shiue xuē
boots

〔革部〕

靴底(ㄒㄩㄝ ㄉㄧˇ)
soles of boots
靴子(ㄒㄩㄝ ˙ㄗ)
boots: 他的靴子是用橡膠做的。His boots are made of rubber.

【靶】6739 ㄅㄚˇ baa bǎ
1. the target
2. the splashboard of a chariot
靶機(ㄅㄚˇ ㄐㄧ)
a drone (a pilotless plane for target shooting)
靶心(ㄅㄚˇ ㄒㄧㄣ)
bull's-eye
靶場(ㄅㄚˇ ㄔㄤˇ)
a firing range; a shooting range
靶子(ㄅㄚˇ ˙ㄗ)
a target: 他的箭沒有射中靶子。His arrow missed the target.

【靷】6740 ㄧㄣˇ yiin yǐn
the leather belts that connect a cart with the horse, etc.

【靸】6741 1. ㄙㄚˇ saa sǎ
a child's shoes
靸鞋(ㄙㄚˇ ㄒㄧㄝ)
slippers

【靸】6741 2. ㄊㄚ ta tā
to wear (shoes) in a casual way

五畫

【鞅】6742 ㄧㄤˇ yeang yǎng (又讀 ㄧㄤ iang yāng)
1.a martingale; a halter
2.a horse
鞅掌(ㄧㄤˇ ㄓㄤˇ)
weariness; all-bustled; to be overburdened
鞅鞅(ㄧㄤˇ ㄧㄤˇ)
discontentedly 亦作「怏怏」

【韎】6743 ㄇㄛˋ moh mò
1. stockings
2. the Tungusic tribe
韎鞨(ㄇㄛˋ ㄏㄜˊ)
①the Tungusic tribe in ancient China ②name of a precious stone

【靼】6744 ㄉㄚˊ dar dá
1. as in 韃靼—the Tartars
2. soft leather

六畫

【鞍】6745 ㄢ an ān
a saddle; a saddle-like terrain or thing
鞍轡(ㄢ ㄆㄟˋ)
saddles and reins
鞍馬(ㄢ ㄇㄚˇ)
①(gymnastics) a pommel horse; a side horse ②saddle and horse
鞍馬勞頓(ㄢ ㄇㄚˇ ㄌㄠˊ ㄉㄨㄣˋ)
tired because of long travel on horseback; travel-worn
鞍子(ㄢ ˙ㄗ)
a saddle

【鞋】6746 ㄒㄧㄝˊ shye xié
shoes; footwear
鞋拔子(ㄒㄧㄝˊ ㄅㄚˊ ˙ㄗ)
a shoehorn; a shoe lifter: 我穿鞋要用鞋拔子。I have to use a shoe lifter to put on my shoes.
鞋幫(ㄒㄧㄝˊ ㄅㄤ)
the sides of a shoe
鞋面(ㄒㄧㄝˊ ㄇㄧㄢˋ)
the vamp
鞋帶(ㄒㄧㄝˊ ㄉㄞˋ)
a shoestring; a shoelace
鞋底(ㄒㄧㄝˊ ㄉㄧˇ)or 鞋底子(ㄒㄧㄝˊ ㄉㄧˇ ˙ㄗ)or 鞋底兒(ㄒㄧㄝˊ ㄉㄧㄜˇㄦ)
the sole of a shoe: 這隻鞋的鞋底有一個洞。There is a hole in the sole of this shoe.
鞋店(ㄒㄧㄝˊ ㄉㄧㄢˋ)
a shoeshop
鞋童(ㄒㄧㄝˊ ㄊㄨㄥˊ)
a shoeshine boy
鞋墊(ㄒㄧㄝˊ ㄉㄧㄢˋ)
a shoepad; an insole
鞋跟(ㄒㄧㄝˊ ㄍㄣ)
the heel of a shoe
鞋扣子(ㄒㄧㄝˊ ㄎㄡˋ ˙ㄗ)
shoe buckle
鞋匠(ㄒㄧㄝˊ ㄐㄧㄤˋ)
a shoemaker; a cobbler: 這位作家當過鞋匠。The writer had been a shoemaker.
鞋楦子(ㄒㄧㄝˊ ㄒㄩㄢˋ ˙ㄗ)
a last; a shoe tree
鞋刷子(ㄒㄧㄝˊ ㄕㄨㄚ ˙ㄗ)
a shoebrush
鞋油(ㄒㄧㄝˊ ㄧㄡˊ)
shoe polish
鞋襪(ㄒㄧㄝˊ ㄨㄚˋ)
shoes and socks

【鞏】6747 ㄍㄨㄥˇ goong gǒng
1. to tie or bind with thongs
2. secure; firm; strong; to guard; to secure; to strengthen
3. a Chinese family name
鞏膜(ㄍㄨㄥˇ ㄇㄛˊ)
(anatomy) sclera
鞏固(ㄍㄨㄥˇ ㄍㄨˋ)
①strong; secure; well-guarded ②to consolidate (one's position, strength, etc.)

七畫

【鞘】6748 ㄑㄧㄠˋ chiaw qiào
a scabbard; a sheath

八畫

【鞠】6749 ㄐㄩ jyu jū
1. to bow; a bow (as a gesture of respect)
2. a ball; a leather ball
3. to nourish; to raise or rear
4. young; tender
5. high
6. to exhaust
7. to admonish; to warn; to caution
8. to make judicial investigation
9. a Chinese family name
鞠躬(ㄐㄩ ㄍㄨㄥ)
to bow; a bow (as a gesture of respect): 主人鞠躬迎客。The host bowed his guest in.
鞠躬盡瘁，死而後已(ㄐㄩˊ ㄍㄨㄥ ㄐㄧㄣˋ ㄘㄨㄟˋ, ㄙˇ ㄦˊ ㄏㄡˋ ㄧˇ)
to devote oneself to the task until one's death; to concentrate on one's task till one's heart stops beating
鞠子(ㄐㄩˊ ㄗˇ)
a little child
鞠養(ㄐㄩˊ ㄧㄤˇ)or 鞠育(ㄐㄩˊ ㄩˋ)
to raise or rear kids

九畫

【鞭】6750
ㄅㄧㄢ bian biān
1. a whip; a lash; to whip or lash; to flagellate; to flog
2. an ancient weapon shaped like a whip
3. a string of firecrackers
鞭背(ㄅㄧㄢ ㄅㄟˋ)
to whip the back as a form of punishment in ancient times
鞭辟(ㄅㄧㄢ ㄅㄧˋ)
to urge and encourage
鞭辟入裏(ㄅㄧㄢ ㄅㄧˋ ㄖㄨˋ ㄌㄧˇ)
deep-cutting; incisive; penetrating; trenchant
鞭炮(ㄅㄧㄢ ㄆㄠˋ)
(a long string of) firecrackers: 孩子們在燃放鞭炮。The children are letting off firecrackers.
鞭扑(ㄅㄧㄢ ㄆㄨ)
to whip; to lash or chastise
鞭毛(ㄅㄧㄢ ㄇㄠˊ)
(biology) flagellum
鞭打(ㄅㄧㄢ ㄉㄚˇ)
to flog with a whip; to flagellate: 他屢次鞭打這個男孩。He gave the boy repeated floggings.
鞭撻(ㄅㄧㄢ ㄊㄚˋ)
to flog with a whip; to flagellate; to castigate
鞭刑(ㄅㄧㄢ ㄒㄧㄥˊ)
flogging
鞭笞(ㄅㄧㄢ ㄔ)
① to flog with a whip: 他毫無怨言地接受了鞭笞。He took the whipping without a murmur. ② to urge or goad along
鞭長莫及(ㄅㄧㄢ ㄔㄤˊ ㄇㄛˋ ㄐㄧˊ)
beyond one's influence; beyond one's reach; out of range
鞭楚(ㄅㄧㄢ ㄔㄨˇ)
to whip; to flog; to flagellate
鞭箠 or 鞭捶(ㄅㄧㄢ ㄔㄨㄟˊ)
to flog with a whip
鞭尸(ㄅㄧㄢ ㄕ)
to give vent to one's hatred by whipping the body of a dead enemy or tyrant
鞭子(ㄅㄧㄢ ·ㄗ)
a whip; a lash: 該拿鞭子抽他一頓。He wants the whiplash.
鞭策(ㄅㄧㄢ ㄘㄜˋ)
① a horsewhip ② to urge or goad on; to encourage: 我們應該經常鞭策自己，努力讀書。We should constantly urge ourselves on to study hard.

【鞦】6751
ㄑㄧㄡ chiou qiū
1. a swing
2. a crupper
3. traces
鞦韆(ㄑㄧㄡ ㄑㄧㄢ)
a swing: 小孩子在盪鞦韆。The children were playing on the swings.

【鞧】6752
ㄑㄧㄡ chiou qiū
a crupper

【鞨】6753
ㄏㄜˊ her hé
as in 靺鞨—the Tungusic tribe in ancient China
鞨巾(ㄏㄜˊ ㄐㄧㄣ)
a turban

【鞫】6754
ㄐㄩˊ jyu jú
1. to question criminals
2. extreme poverty

【鞬】6755
ㄐㄧㄢ jian jiān
1. a quiver (for arrows) on a horse
2. to store; to keep and collect

十畫

【韝】6756
ㄍㄡ gou gōu
the armlet and glove of a falconer
韝韛(ㄍㄡ ㄅㄟˋ)
a piston

【鞳】6757
ㄊㄚˋ tah tà
the sound of bells and drums

【韛】6758
ㄅㄟˋ bey bèi
as in 韝韛—a piston
韛馬(ㄅㄟˋ ㄇㄚˇ)
to ride a horse

【鞶】6759
ㄆㄢˊ parn pán
a large belt

十一畫

【鞺】6760
ㄊㄤˊ tarng táng
the sound of drums
鞺鞳(ㄊㄤˊ ㄊㄚˋ)
the sound of bells and drums

十三畫

【韃】6761
ㄉㄚˊ dar dá
Tartars
韃靼(ㄉㄚˊ ㄉㄚˊ)
Tartars
韃靼海峽(ㄉㄚˊ ㄉㄚˊ ㄏㄞˇ ㄒㄧㄚˊ)
Tatar Strait

【韁】6762
ㄐㄧㄤ jiang jiāng
same as 繮—reins

十五畫

【韆】6763
ㄑㄧㄢ chian qiān
as in 鞦韆—a swing

十七畫

【韉】6764
ㄐㄧㄢ jian jiān
saddle cloth

韋部
ㄨㄟˊ wei wéi

【韋】6765
ㄨㄟˊ wei wéi
1. tanned leather; leather
2. a Chinese family name
韋伯斯特(ㄨㄟˊ ㄅㄛˊ ㄙ ㄊㄜˋ)
Noah Webster, 1758-1843, American lexicographer and essayist
韋編(ㄨㄟˊ ㄅㄧㄢ)
(before the invention of paper in China) a book consisting of bamboo slabs strung together with leather strings
韋編三絕(ㄨㄟˊ ㄅㄧㄢ ㄙㄢ ㄐㄩㄝˊ)
to study diligently
韋布(ㄨㄟˊ ㄅㄨˋ)
leather girdles and coarse cloth—the dress of com-

moners

韋帶(ㄨㄟˊ ㄉㄞˋ)
a leather girdle worn by a commoner

韋馱(ㄨㄟˊ ㄊㄨㄛˊ)
a Buddhist god whose job is to keep evils away and to guard the temple; Skanda

韋氏音標(ㄨㄟˊ ㄕˋ ㄧㄣ ㄅㄧㄠ)
phonetic symbols adopted in Webster's dictionaries

韋衣(ㄨㄟˊ ㄧ)
①hunting clothes ②simple clothes

三畫

【韌】 6766
ㄖㄣˋ renn rèn
soft but tough; elastic; pliable but strong; tenacious

韌皮(ㄖㄣˋ ㄆㄧˊ)
the bast (of a tree)

韌帶(ㄖㄣˋ ㄉㄞˋ)
(physiology) ligaments

韌度(ㄖㄣˋ ㄉㄨˋ)
resilience

韌性(ㄖㄣˋ ㄒㄧㄥˋ)
tenacity

五畫

【韍】 6767
ㄈㄨˊ fwu fú
a leather garment worn during sacrificial rituals in ancient times

八畫

【韓】 6768
ㄏㄢˊ harn hán
1. a fence
2. name of two feudal states in the late Chou Dynasty
3. short for the Republic of Korea
4. a Chinese family name

韓非(ㄏㄢˊ ㄈㄟ)
Han Fei, a famous legalist (? -234 B.C.) during the Epoch of Warring States

韓非子(ㄏㄢˊ ㄈㄟ ㄗˇ)
title of a 20-volume work by Han Fei(韓非)

韓柳(ㄏㄢˊ ㄌㄧㄡˇ)
Han Yü(韓愈) and Liu Tzung-yüan(柳宗元), two leading writers of the Tang Dynasty

韓國(ㄏㄢˊ ㄍㄨㄛˊ)
①the Republic of Korea ②the state of Han in the Epoch of Spring and Autumn ③the state of Han in the Epoch of Warring States

韓信(ㄏㄢˊ ㄒㄧㄣˋ)
Han Hsin, a famous general who helped found the Western Han Dynasty

韓戰(ㄏㄢˊ ㄓㄢˋ)
the Korean War (1950-1953)

韓世忠(ㄏㄢˊ ㄕˋ ㄓㄨㄥ)
Han Shih-chung (1089-1151), a famous general of the Sung Dynasty

韓愈(ㄏㄢˊ ㄩˋ)
Han Yü (768-824), a literary giant in the Tang Dynasty

【韔】 6769
ㄔㄤˋ chanq chàng
1. a wrapper or case for bow
2. to sheathe a bow; to put a bow in its case

九畫

【韙】 6770
ㄨㄟˇ woei wěi
right; proper; propriety

十畫

【韜】 6771
ㄊㄠ tau tāo
1. scabbards or sheaths for blades or swords
2. military strategy; tactics
3. to conceal
4. to idle

韜筆(ㄊㄠ ㄅㄧˇ)
to let the pen idle—to write no more

韜略(ㄊㄠ ㄌㄩㄝˋ)
military strategy or tactics

韜光(ㄊㄠ ㄍㄨㄤ)
①to conceal one's talents, gifts, etc. ②name of a learned Buddhist monk in the Tang Dynasty

韜光養晦(ㄊㄠ ㄍㄨㄤ ㄧㄤˇ ㄏㄨㄟˋ)
to conceal one's ability and bide one's time

韜弓(ㄊㄠ ㄍㄨㄥ)
to sheathe a bow; to put a bow in its case

韜晦(ㄊㄠ ㄏㄨㄟˋ)
to obscure; oblivion; to hide one's true capacities or intentions

【韞】 6772
ㄩㄣˋ yunn yùn
to conceal; to hide (one's talents, etc.)

韞櫝 or 韞匵(ㄩㄣˋ ㄉㄨˊ)
(said of a talented person) to live like a recluse; to prefer to be a commoner

韭部
ㄐㄧㄡˇ jeou jiǔ

【韭】 6773
(韮) ㄐㄧㄡˇ jeou jiǔ
scallions; leeks; Chinese chives

韭花(ㄐㄧㄡˇ ㄏㄨㄚ)or 韭菜花(ㄐㄧㄡˇ ㄘㄞˋ ㄏㄨㄚ)
blossoms of leeks or scallions, edible when tender

韭黃(ㄐㄧㄡˇ ㄏㄨㄤˊ)
yellow, tender leeks or scallions

韭菜(ㄐㄧㄡˇ ㄘㄞˋ)
leeks or scallions

音部
ㄧㄣ in yin

【音】 6774
ㄧㄣ in yin
1. sound; voice
2. tone; accent; timbre
3. a musical note
4. (usually used in correspondence) news; information; tidings: 他帶來佳音。He brought welcome news.

音波(ㄧㄣ ㄅㄛ)
sound waves 亦作「聲波」

音爆(ㄧㄣ ㄅㄠˋ)
a sonic boom: 我早上聽到了音爆。I heard the sonic boom this morning.

音標(ㄧㄣ ㄅㄧㄠ)

phonetic signs (or symbols)
音標文字(ㄧㄣ ㄅㄧㄠ ㄨㄣˊ ㄗˋ)
phonetic transcription; phonography
音變(ㄧㄣ ㄅㄧㄢˋ)
change of intonation of words in a sentence for emphasis, etc.
音符(ㄧㄣ ㄈㄨˊ)
(music) notes: 高音符我唱不來。I can't sing the high notes.
音帶(ㄧㄣ ㄉㄞˋ)
the vocal cords
音調(ㄧㄣ ㄉㄧㄠˋ)
① the pitch of a sound; tone: 她用高音調唱歌。She sings at a high pitch. ② musical pitch according to the standard of ancient pitch pipes
音量(ㄧㄣ ㄌㄧㄤˋ)
the volume (of sound)
音律(ㄧㄣ ㄌㄩˋ)
temperament
音高(ㄧㄣ ㄍㄠ)
(music) pitch
音階(ㄧㄣ ㄐㄧㄝ)
musical scale
音節(ㄧㄣ ㄐㄧㄝˊ)
a syllable: "China" 是個兩音節的字。"China" is a word of two syllables.
音強(ㄧㄣ ㄑㄧㄤˊ)
the loudness of a sound
音信(ㄧㄣ ㄒㄧㄣˋ)or 音訊(ㄧㄣ ㄒㄩㄣˋ)
news; information; tidings; messages: 我一直沒有他的音信。I have had no news from him.
音響(ㄧㄣ ㄒㄧㄤˇ)
① audio ② sound; acoustics
音響電子琴(ㄧㄣ ㄒㄧㄤˇ ㄉㄧㄢˋ ㄗˇ ㄑㄧㄣˊ)
a synthesizer
音響效果(ㄧㄣ ㄒㄧㄤˇ ㄒㄧㄠˋ ㄍㄨㄛˇ)
sound effect
音訊(ㄧㄣ ㄒㄩㄣˋ)
letters; news
音訓(ㄧㄣ ㄒㄩㄣˋ)
to teach the pronunciation of a word and explain its meaning
音質(ㄧㄣ ㄓˊ)
tonality; tone quality
音叉(ㄧㄣ ㄔㄚ)
a tuning fork
音塵(ㄧㄣ ㄔㄣˊ)
traces; whereabouts
音長(ㄧㄣ ㄔㄤˊ)
(phonetics) length
音程(ㄧㄣ ㄔㄥˊ)
(music) interval
音書(ㄧㄣ ㄕㄨ)
letters; correspondence; information or news
音容(ㄧㄣ ㄖㄨㄥˊ)
voice and countenance
音容宛在(ㄧㄣ ㄖㄨㄥˊ ㄨㄢˇ ㄗㄞˋ)
(a conventional written expression referring to the deceased in a funeral rite) His or her voice and appearance seem to be still with us.
音色(ㄧㄣ ㄙㄜˋ)or 音品(ㄧㄣ ㄆㄧㄣˇ)
timbre (of a sound or voice); tone color
音速(ㄧㄣ ㄙㄨˋ)
the speed of sound (about 1,087 ft. per second or 738 miles per hour)
音素(ㄧㄣ ㄙㄨˋ)
sound elements; phonemes
音義(ㄧㄣ ㄧˋ)
pronunciation and meaning
音譯(ㄧㄣ ㄧˋ)
transliteration by sound rather than meaning (as 布爾喬亞 for "bourgeois")
音問(ㄧㄣ ㄨㄣˋ)
news or information; letter or correspondence
音域(ㄧㄣ ㄩˋ)
(music) the range; the compass; the register
音樂(ㄧㄣ ㄩㄝˋ)
music: 他們隨音樂跳舞。They danced to the music.
音樂比賽(ㄧㄣ ㄩㄝˋ ㄅㄧˇ ㄙㄞˋ)
a musical competition
音樂電視(節目)(ㄧㄣ ㄩㄝˋ ㄉㄧㄢˋ ㄕˋ (ㄐㄧㄝˊ ㄇㄨˋ))
MTV (Music Television)
音樂會(ㄧㄣ ㄩㄝˋ ㄏㄨㄟˋ)
a concert; a musical recital
音樂家(ㄧㄣ ㄩㄝˋ ㄐㄧㄚ)
a musician
音樂節(ㄧㄣ ㄩㄝˋ ㄐㄧㄝˊ)
Music Day on April 5
音樂系(ㄧㄣ ㄩㄝˋ ㄒㄧˋ)
the department of music in college
音樂演奏(ㄧㄣ ㄩㄝˋ ㄧㄢˇ ㄗㄡˋ)
a musical performance
音樂院(ㄧㄣ ㄩㄝˋ ㄩㄢˋ)or 音樂學院(ㄧㄣ ㄩㄝˋ ㄒㄩㄝˊ ㄩㄢˋ)
a conservatory of music; the academy of music
音韻(ㄧㄣ ㄩㄣˋ)
a rhyme
音韻學(ㄧㄣ ㄩㄣˋ ㄒㄩㄝˊ)
phonology

四畫

【韵】 6775 (韻)ㄩㄣˋ yunn yùn
1. rhyme
2. harmony

【歆】 6776 ㄒㄧㄣ shin xin
1. to inhale; to smell
2. to envy
3. sacrificial food
4. to move; to touch
5. to admire

歆羨(ㄒㄧㄣ ㄒㄧㄢˋ)
to envy

五畫

【韶】 6777 ㄕㄠˊ shaur sháo
1. the music during the time of the sage emperor Shun (舜)
2. beautiful; excellent; harmonious
3. continuous

韶光(ㄕㄠˊ ㄍㄨㄤ)or 韶華(ㄕㄠˊ ㄏㄨㄚˊ)
① beautiful scenes in the spring: 韶華不再。Springtime waits for no man. ② best years of one's life—youth
韶秀(ㄕㄠˊ ㄒㄧㄡˋ)
good-looking and handsome
韶山(ㄕㄠˊ ㄕㄢ)
Shaoshan, a mountain in Hunan Province

十畫

【韻】 6778 ㄩㄣˋ yunn yùn
1. rhymes
2. harmony of sound
3. refined; sophisticated; polished; elegant
4. vowels

韻母(ㄩㄣˋ ㄇㄨˇ)
vowel—an open sound

produced by the voice
韻符(ㄩㄣˋ ㄈㄨˊ)
vowel—a symbol representing an open sound produced by the voice
韻律(ㄩㄣˋ ㄌㄩˋ)
meter; rhythm; rhyme scheme
韻律舞(ㄩㄣˋ ㄌㄩˋ ㄨˇ)
an aerobic dance
韻脚(ㄩㄣˋ ㄐㄧㄠˇ)
rhyme at the end of a line of poetry
韻致(ㄩㄣˋ ㄓˋ)
a manner; a poise; a style
韻事(ㄩㄣˋ ㄕˋ)
a romantic incident of an intellectual which smacks of refined taste and elegant style; a romantic affair: 張先生的韻事極多。Mr. Chang's romantic affairs are numerous.
韻書(ㄩㄣˋ ㄕㄨ)
books listing characters grouped under various rhymes; a dictionary of rhymes
韻味(ㄩㄣˋ ㄨㄟˋ)
refined and sophisticated taste; lingering charm; lasting appeal
韻文(ㄩㄣˋ ㄨㄣˊ)
a rhymed composition; verse: 韻文不一定就是好詩。Not all verse is great poetry.
韻語(ㄩㄣˋ ㄩˇ)
① rhymed sentences or phrases ② a refined remark

十三畫

【響】 6779
ㄒㄧㄤˇ sheang xiǎng

1. a report; a sound; an echo; a noise: 我聽到一聲炮響。I heard a report of a cannon.
2. (said of sound) loud or high: 馬達聲太響了。The motor's too loud (or noisy).
3. to make a sound; to sound; to ring: 門鈴響了。The doorbell rang.

響馬(ㄒㄧㄤˇ ㄇㄚˇ)
mounted highwaymen in North China—so called for shooting a sounding arrow as a signal for action
響動(ㄒㄧㄤˇ ㄉㄨㄥˋ)
sound of something tumultuous
響亮(ㄒㄧㄤˇ ㄌㄧㄤˋ)
① sonorous; loud and clear; stentorian: 別用空洞而響亮的文句。Don't use phrases of empty sonorousness. ② straightforward
響鈴(兒)(ㄒㄧㄤˇ ㄌㄧㄥˊ(ㄦ))
a bell
響箭(ㄒㄧㄤˇ ㄐㄧㄢˋ)
sounding arrows, used in old days as signals
響徹(ㄒㄧㄤˇ ㄔㄜˋ)
to resound through; to reverberate through: 勝利的歌聲響徹雲霄。Songs of victory resound through the skies.
響聲(ㄒㄧㄤˇ ㄕㄥ)
a sound; an echo; a noise: 聽不見響聲了。No more sound was heard.
響應(ㄒㄧㄤˇ ㄧㄥˋ)
to echo in support; to respond favorably; to rise in support
響尾蛇(ㄒㄧㄤˇ ㄨㄟˇ ㄕㄜˊ)
the rattlesnake; the sidewinder
響尾蛇飛彈(ㄒㄧㄤˇ ㄨㄟˇ ㄕㄜˊ ㄈㄟ ㄉㄢˋ)
(military) a sidewinder

頁 部
ㄧㄝˋ yeh yè

【頁】 6780
ㄧㄝˋ yeh yè

a page (in books, etc.); a sheet (of paper, etc): 他撕下一頁。He tore one of the pages.

頁邊(ㄧㄝˋ ㄅㄧㄢ)
the margin
頁碼(ㄧㄝˋ ㄇㄚˇ)
the page number
頁次(ㄧㄝˋ ㄘˋ)
the page number
頁岩(ㄧㄝˋ ㄧㄢˊ)
shale

二畫

【頂】 6781
ㄉㄧㄥˇ diing dǐng

1.the top of anything
2.the crown of the head
3.topmost; extremely; very: 這本手册頂有用的。The handbook is very useful.
4.to carry (a weight) on one's head; to push the head against; to wear on the head
5.to gore; to butt: 這牛不頂人。This bull does not gore people.
6.to push up; to prop up
7.to cope with; to stand up to
8.to substitute: 教練叫我頂替那投手。The coach told me to substitute for that pitcher.
9.to equal; to be equivalent to
10.to offend intentionally; to retort; to turn down: 他頂了他的母親幾句。He said a few words to his mother in retort.
11.used as a unit

頂拜(ㄉㄧㄥˇ ㄅㄞˋ)
to kneel down and kowtow
頂盤(ㄉㄧㄥˇ ㄆㄢˊ)
to buy a shop from another person after it has been liquidated
頂批(ㄉㄧㄥˇ ㄆㄧ)
running commentaries on the upper margin of the pages in a Chinese book
頂名(ㄉㄧㄥˇ ㄇㄧㄥˊ)
to assume someone's name with the intent to cheat
頂風(ㄉㄧㄥˇ ㄈㄥ)
① to move against the wind: 他們頂風而行。They walked against the wind. ② a head wind
頂峰(ㄉㄧㄥˇ ㄈㄥ)
the peak; the summit; the pinnacle
頂大(ㄉㄧㄥˇ ㄉㄚˋ)
the largest
頂戴(ㄉㄧㄥˇ ㄉㄞˋ)
① to salute or pay respects to ② (Ching Dynasty) the color and quality of the bead on the ceremonial hat of an official, which indicates the wearer's rank ③ to wear on one's head
頂點(ㄉㄧㄥˇ ㄉㄧㄢˇ)
the pinnacle; the topmost;

the top (of a hill); the utmost; the apex; the zenith; the acme: 他曾經達到了名氣的頂點。He was once on the pinnacle of fame.
頂多(ㄉㄧㄥˇ ㄉㄨㄛ)
at (the) most; at best
頂端(ㄉㄧㄥˇ ㄉㄨㄢ)
the top; the peak; the apex
頂頭(ㄉㄧㄥˇ ㄊㄡˊ)
① the top; a superior officer ② the opposite; the end
頂頭上司(ㄉㄧㄥˇ ㄊㄡˊ ㄕㄤˋ ㄙ)
the immediate boss
頂替(ㄉㄧㄥˇ ㄊㄧˋ)
① to assume someone's name with the intent to cheat ② to represent someone; to take someone's place: 主席走了誰來頂替他? Who's going to take the chairman's place after he leaves?
頂天立地(ㄉㄧㄥˇ ㄊㄧㄢ ㄌㄧˋ ㄉㄧˋ)
(literally) with one's feet planted on the ground and head supporting the sky—independent and indomitable
頂禮膜拜(ㄉㄧㄥˇ ㄌㄧˇ ㄇㄛˊ ㄅㄞˋ)
to bow and kneel in worship; to pay homage to
頂缸(ㄉㄧㄥˇ ㄍㄤ)
to take the blame for someone else
頂骨(ㄉㄧㄥˇ ㄍㄨˇ)
parietal bones
頂瓜瓜 or 頂呱呱(ㄉㄧㄥˇ ㄍㄨㄚ ㄍㄨㄚ)
topmost; the top; the best; excellent; first-rate: 他的英文眞是頂呱呱。His English is indeed excellent.
頂好(ㄉㄧㄥˇ ㄏㄠˇ)
the best; the first; the topmost; good; excellent; wonderful: 近來天氣頂好的。The weather has been wonderful.
頂角(ㄉㄧㄥˇ ㄐㄧㄠˇ)
(mathematics) a vertical angle; a vertex angle
頂尖(ㄉㄧㄥˇ ㄐㄧㄢ)
the peak; the highest point; the top; the best: 他在班上的成績是頂尖的。He is at the top of his class.
頂針(ㄉㄧㄥˇ ㄓㄣ)
a thimble
頂眞(ㄉㄧㄥˇ ㄓㄣ)
to do something in a serious manner; to take something seriously: 我只是在開玩笑, 別太頂眞了。I am only joking; don't take it too seriously.
頂住(ㄉㄧㄥˇ ㄓㄨˋ)
to support with the head; to brace or strengthen something with a support
頂撞(ㄉㄧㄥˇ ㄓㄨㄤˋ)
to offend or dispute with words; to talk back; to contradict (one's elder or superior): 他公然頂撞我。He contradicted me openly.
頂踵(ㄉㄧㄥˇ ㄓㄨㄥˇ)
from head to heel
頂少(ㄉㄧㄥˇ ㄕㄠˇ)
at least
頂上(ㄉㄧㄥˇ ㄕㄤˋ)
① on the top; the highest point ② the best; top-grade
頂上功夫(ㄉㄧㄥˇ ㄕㄤˋ ㄍㄨㄥ ·ㄈㄨ)
the work at the top of the head—the work of the barber
頂嘴(ㄉㄧㄥˇ ㄗㄨㄟˇ)
① to quarrel ② to argue with a superior or an elder; to reply defiantly; to answer (or talk) back: 不要頂嘴, 否則我就處罰你。Don't answer (me) back, or I'll punish you.
頂罪(ㄉㄧㄥˇ ㄗㄨㄟˋ)
to act as a fall guy; to be a scapegoat; to receive punishment for another person
頂罪者(ㄉㄧㄥˇ ㄗㄨㄟˋ ㄓㄜˇ)
a whipping boy 亦作「代人受過者」
頂喪駕靈(ㄉㄧㄥˇ ㄙㄤ ㄐㄧㄚˋ ㄌㄧㄥˊ)
(said of the sons of the deceased) to carry streamers and protect the spirit of their father or mother beside the coffin in a funeral procession
頂芽(ㄉㄧㄥˇ ㄧㄚˊ)
(botany) a terminal bud

【頃】 6782 ㄑㄧㄥˇ chiing qǐng
1. a moment; an instant; just; just now
2. a hundred *mu* (畝)—10,000 square meters
3. to lean toward one side; to incline
頃步(ㄑㄧㄥˇ ㄅㄨˋ)
half a step
頃刻(ㄑㄧㄥˇ ㄎㄜˋ)
in a short moment: 他頃刻就來。He will be here in less than a moment.
頃刻之間(ㄑㄧㄥˇ ㄎㄜˋ ㄓ ㄐㄧㄢ)
in a twinkling; in an instant
頃者(ㄑㄧㄥˇ ㄓㄜˇ)
just now; a short while ago

三畫

【項】 6783 ㄒㄧㄤˋ shianq xiàng
1. the back of the neck; the nape
2. the back of a cap or crown
3. an item; an article; a matter; a kind; a class
4. funds; a sum of money
5. (mathematics) a term
6. a Chinese family name
項背相望(ㄒㄧㄤˋ ㄅㄟˋ ㄒㄧㄤ ㄨㄤˋ)
to walk in an unbroken procession; one after another in close succession
項目(ㄒㄧㄤˋ ㄇㄨˋ)
an item; an article (in an agreement, etc.)
項鍊(ㄒㄧㄤˋ ㄌㄧㄢˋ)
a necklace
項領(ㄒㄧㄤˋ ㄌㄧㄥˇ)
① the large neck ② strategic positions or places
項圈(ㄒㄧㄤˋ ㄑㄩㄢ)
a collar; a necklace
項下(ㄒㄧㄤˋ ㄒㄧㄚˋ)
under a certain article or item
項莊舞劍, 意在沛公(ㄒㄧㄤˋ ㄓㄨㄤ ㄨˇ ㄐㄧㄢˋ, ㄧˋ ㄗㄞˋ ㄆㄟˋ ㄍㄨㄥ)
Hsiang Chuang performed the sword dance as a cover for his attempt on Liu Pang's life.—to act with a hidden motive
項羽(ㄒㄧㄤˋ ㄩˇ) or 項籍(ㄒㄧㄤˋ ㄐㄧˊ)
Hsiang Yü, a great warrior who contested the throne with the founding emperor of the Western Han Dynasty and lost

【順】 6784 ㄕㄨㄣˋ shuenn shùn
1. to follow; to submit to; obe-

〔頁部〕

dient; to cause to surrender; to fall in with: 他順從了多數的決定。He submitted to the majority decision
2. in the same direction as; with; along: 船順流而下。The ship went downstream.
3. agreeable; favorable; comfortable; happy: 她的聲音很順耳。Her voice is agreeable on the ear.
4. to arrange; to put in order
5. convenient; smooth
6. to take the opportunity to

順便(ㄕㄨㄣˋ ㄅㄧㄢˋ)
at one's convenience; (to do something) while on one's way to perform a major work; without taking extra trouble: 我可以順便做完它。I can finish doing it without taking extra trouble.

順民(ㄕㄨㄣˋ ㄇㄧㄣˊ)
① the people who surrender to their new lord ② people who leave their fate to heaven

順命(ㄕㄨㄣˋ ㄇㄧㄥˋ)
①to obey orders ② to leave one's fate to heaven; resigned to one's fate

順風(ㄕㄨㄣˋ ㄈㄥ)
① to move with the wind: 祝你一路順風。May you have a pleasant journey. 或 *Bon voyage*. ② good luck ③ a favorable wind; a tail wind

順風轉舵(ㄕㄨㄣˋ ㄈㄥ ㄓㄨㄢˇ ㄉㄨㄛˋ)
to trim one's sails; to take one's cue from changing conditions

順風扯旗(ㄕㄨㄣˋ ㄈㄥ ㄔㄜˇ ㄑㄧˊ)
to do an undertaking at an opportune moment

順風吹火(ㄕㄨㄣˋ ㄈㄥ ㄔㄨㄟ ㄏㄨㄛˇ)
to do a job made easy by outside help

順風而呼(ㄕㄨㄣˋ ㄈㄥ ㄦˊ ㄏㄨ)
to promote a public cause; to champion a cause that enjoys popular support

順風耳(ㄕㄨㄣˋ ㄈㄥ ㄦˇ)
① an old-fashioned loudspeaker ② (in Chinese mythology) ears that could hear sounds miles away; a clairaudient ③ a well-informed person: 他是我們這個社區的順風耳。He is a well-informed man in our community.

順道(ㄕㄨㄣˋ ㄉㄠˋ)
① to obey good reasons ② to do something on the way to a place, which requires no additional travel

順當(ㄕㄨㄣˋ ·ㄉㄤ)
without a hitch; easy and smooth: 一切進行順當。Everything went off without a hitch.

順條順理(ㄕㄨㄣˋ ㄊㄧㄠˊ ㄕㄨㄣˋ ㄌㄧˇ)
pliant; obedient; to go along; to comply

順天者昌，逆天者亡(ㄕㄨㄣˋ ㄊㄧㄢ ㄓㄜˇ ㄔㄤ, ㄋㄧˋ ㄊㄧㄢ ㄓㄜˇ ㄨㄤˊ)
(said of rulers) Those who obey the mandate of heaven will prosper, while those who defy it will perish.

順天應人(ㄕㄨㄣˋ ㄊㄧㄢ ㄧㄥˋ ㄖㄣˊ)
(said of a monarch) to follow the mandate of heaven and comply with the wishes of the people

順理(ㄕㄨㄣˋ ㄌㄧˇ)
reasonable; logical

順理成章(ㄕㄨㄣˋ ㄌㄧˇ ㄔㄥˊ ㄓㄤ)
logical; as a matter of course

順利(ㄕㄨㄣˋ ㄌㄧˋ)
(going) smoothly; easy (going); having no trouble; encountering no difficulties; without a hitch: 會議正順利進行。The meeting is going on smoothly.

順流(ㄕㄨㄣˋ ㄌㄧㄡˊ)
① going with the (water) current: 他順流游泳。He swimmed with the current. ② to do things properly or according to reason

順溜(ㄕㄨㄣˋ ·ㄌㄧㄡ)
① easy and amiable ② kind and peaceful ③ without any hindrance; smooth

順路(ㄕㄨㄣˋ ㄌㄨˋ)
in passing; while on the way; direct route: 到學校這麼走不順路。This is not the direct route to school.

順竿兒爬(ㄕㄨㄣˋ ㄍㄚㄦ ㄆㄚˊ)
to fawn; to act as a yesman; to fall readily in with other people's wishes

順口(ㄕㄨㄣˋ ㄎㄡˇ)
① to speak without much thought; to slip out of one's tongue; to talk casually: 他也不想想就順口說了。He spoke without thinking. ② easy to speak, read or sing ③ to suit one's taste: 這些點心我吃得很順口。I like the taste of these desserts.

順口溜(ㄕㄨㄣˋ ㄎㄡˇ ㄌㄧㄡ)
doggerel; a jingle

順候(ㄕㄨㄣˋ ㄏㄡˋ)
(used in the conclusion of a letter, roughly equivalent to) with best wishes or regards

順化(ㄕㄨㄣˋ ㄏㄨㄚˋ)
① to obey the law of nature ② Hue, old capital of Vietnam

順境(ㄕㄨㄣˋ ㄐㄧㄥˋ)
in easy circumstances; in favorable circumstances: 處順境之人不可志得意滿。One should not be complacent in easy circumstances.

順其自然(ㄕㄨㄣˋ ㄑㄧˊ ㄗˋ ㄖㄢˊ)
to let nature take its course; in accordance with its natural tendency

順情順理(ㄕㄨㄣˋ ㄑㄧㄥˊ ㄕㄨㄣˋ ㄌㄧˇ)
in accordance with propriety and reason

順心(ㄕㄨㄣˋ ㄒㄧㄣ)
satisfactorily; gratifying: 他最近過得很順心。He spent his life satisfactorily recently.

順序(ㄕㄨㄣˋ ㄒㄩˋ)
according to right order; sequence

順治(ㄕㄨㄣˋ ㄓˋ)
the reigning title of the first emperor of the Ching Dynasty

順差(ㄕㄨㄣˋ ㄔㄚ)
favorable balance; surplus

順暢(ㄕㄨㄣˋ ㄔㄤˋ)
smooth; unhindered

順時(ㄕㄨㄣˋ ㄕˊ)
① on time ② to be in luck

順事(ㄕㄨㄣˋ ㄕˋ)
matters that one is happy to talk about; matters that make one leap with joy

順適(ㄕㄨㄣˋ ㄕˋ)
(said of one's manner) casual, composed, or natural

順勢(ㄕㄨㄣˋ ㄕˋ)
to take advantage of an opportunity (as provided by an opponent's reckless move)
順手(ㄕㄨㄣˋ ㄕㄡˇ)
① smooth (operation); easy (going): 事情辦得相當順手。It was done quite smoothly. ② to do something without extra trouble ③ handy; conveniently
順手牽羊(ㄕㄨㄣˋ ㄕㄡˇ ㄑㄧㄢ ㄧㄤˊ)
to steal something in passing; to steal something without premeditation because the article in question happens to be conveniently located when one chances to see it; to pick up something on the sly
順守(ㄕㄨㄣˋ ㄕㄡˇ)
just to carry on according to former practices
順水(ㄕㄨㄣˋ ㄕㄨㄟˇ)
(to sail) with the stream or current; downstream: 順水游泳或划船都不難。It is easy to swim or row downstream.
順水推舟(ㄕㄨㄣˋ ㄕㄨㄟˇ ㄊㄨㄟ ㄓㄡ)
to approve something that is sure to succeed; to render help where it is scarcely needed; to make use of an opportunity to gain one's end
順水人情(ㄕㄨㄣˋ ㄕㄨㄟˇ ㄖㄣˊ ㄑㄧㄥˊ)
to do someone a favor without causing oneself any trouble; a favor done at little cost to oneself
順嘴兒(ㄕㄨㄣˋ ㄗㄨㄟˇㄦ)
to speak casually without much thought; to slip out of one's tongue
順從(ㄕㄨㄣˋ ㄘㄨㄥˊ)
① to obey; obedient; to comply ②(psychology) submission
順俗(ㄕㄨㄣˋ ㄙㄨˊ)
to act according to the customs; to go with the crowd
順遂(ㄕㄨㄣˋ ㄙㄨㄟˋ)
without a hitch or obstruction; very smooth or easy going; in satisfactory circumstances
順耳(ㄕㄨㄣˋ ㄦˇ)
pleasant to the ear
順延(ㄕㄨㄣˋ ㄧㄢˊ)
to postpone for one day, and another day, and so on, in case of necessity (as in the case of poor weather upsetting a games schedule); to put off until another time: 他們把遠足順延到下個月。They put off the outing till next month.
順眼(ㄕㄨㄣˋ ㄧㄢˇ)
to please the eye; pleasant to the eye: 他看起來挺順眼的。He pleases the eye.
順應(ㄕㄨㄣˋ ㄧㄥˋ)
to adjust (to changes)
順應潮流(ㄕㄨㄣˋ ㄧㄥˋ ㄔㄠˊ ㄌㄧㄡˊ)
to conform to modern trends
順應時代(ㄕㄨㄣˋ ㄧㄥˋ ㄕˊ ㄉㄞˋ)
to conform to the times

【頇】 6785
ㄏㄢ han hān
as in 顢頇—stupid and incompetent; foolish and slow

【須】 6786
ㄒㄩ shiu xū
1. to have to; must; to need: 他必須很努力。He has to make a great effort.
2. necessary; proper
3. probably
4. a beard
5. a moment; a while
6. to wait for
7. to stop at
8. a Chinese family name
須得(ㄒㄩ ㄉㄜˊ)
must have; should have
須待(ㄒㄩ ㄉㄞˋ)
① to have to wait until… ② to expect; to look forward to
須當(ㄒㄩ ㄉㄤ)
must: 此事須當如此。You must do it like this.
須知(ㄒㄩ ㄓ)
① to have to know; should know ② that which is essential to know—common knowledge; to note
須要(ㄒㄩ ㄧㄠˋ)
to have to; must: 你須要趕快去。You must go quickly.
須臾(ㄒㄩ ㄩˊ)
in an instant; a short while or moment: 他們須臾不可分離。They cannot do without each other even for a short moment.

四畫

【頌】 6787
ㄙㄨㄥˋ sonq sòng
1. to praise; to acclaim; an accolade; to extol; to eulogize; to laud
2. a hymn to something; a composition in praise of some achievements, etc.; an ode; a eulogy; a paean
3. a section in *The Book of Poetry* 詩經
頌美(ㄙㄨㄥˋ ㄇㄟˇ)
to praise the achievements of others; to acclaim
頌德碑(ㄙㄨㄥˋ ㄉㄜˊ ㄅㄟ)
a stone tablet with inscriptions in praise of the achievements in the administration of an official
頌歌(ㄙㄨㄥˋ ㄍㄜ)
hymns; odes
頌聲載道(ㄙㄨㄥˋ ㄕㄥ ㄗㄞˋ ㄉㄠˋ)
praises all along the way—popular support
頌讚(ㄙㄨㄥˋ ㄗㄢˋ)
to praise; acclaim; an accolade
頌詞(ㄙㄨㄥˋ ㄘˊ)
a message of praise, congratulations or felicitations; a eulogy; a complimentary address; a speech delivered by an ambassador on presentation of his credentials
頌揚(ㄙㄨㄥˋ ㄧㄤˊ)
to praise; to acclaim; to eulogize; to laud; to extol: 無私是值得頌揚的。Unselfishness is laudable.

【頎】 6788
ㄑㄧˊ chyi qí
tall (physical build)
頎然(ㄑㄧˊ ㄖㄢˊ)
tall

【頏】 6789
ㄏㄤˊ harng háng
as in 頡頏-to match; to contest; birds flying up and down; well-matched

【預】 6790
(豫) ㄩˋ yuh yù
1. beforehand; previously; in advance: 我們預先商量一下。

〔頁部〕

Let's have a talk about it in advance.
2. to prepare; to make ready; reserve (funds, troops, etc.)
3. to take part in

預備(ㄩˋ ㄅㄟˋ)
to prepare; to get ready beforehand; preparatory: 你們預備好了嗎? Are you all ready?

預備兵(ㄩˋ ㄅㄟˋ ㄅㄧㄥ)
reservists

預備會議(ㄩˋ ㄅㄟˋ ㄏㄨㄟˋ ㄧˋ)
a preparatory meeting or conference

預備金(ㄩˋ ㄅㄟˋ ㄐㄧㄣ)
reserve funds; budget allowance

預備軍官(ㄩˋ ㄅㄟˋ ㄐㄩㄣ ㄍㄨㄢ)
a reserve officer; an officer on the reserve list

預備役(ㄩˋ ㄅㄟˋ ㄧˋ)
reserve service

預報(ㄩˋ ㄅㄠˋ)
a forecast; an advance notice or announcement: 根據天氣預報, 明天是晴天。According to the weather forecast tomorrow will be fine.

預卜(ㄩˋ ㄅㄨˇ)
to augur; to foretell; to predict: 這件事情的結果如何尚難預卜。The consequence of this thing is hard to predict.

預謀(ㄩˋ ㄇㄡˊ)
to scheme or plan beforehand; premeditated (manslaughter, etc.)

預防(ㄩˋ ㄈㄤˊ)
to prevent beforehand; to nip in the bud; to prepare against; to forestall; prevention: 預防勝於治療。Prevention is better than cure.

預防注射(ㄩˋ ㄈㄤˊ ㄓㄨˋ ㄕㄜˋ)
preventive inoculation

預防醫學(ㄩˋ ㄈㄤˊ ㄧ ㄒㄩㄝˊ)
preventive medicine

預付(ㄩˋ ㄈㄨˋ)
to pay in advance

預付費用(ㄩˋ ㄈㄨˋ ㄈㄟˋ ㄩㄥˋ)
prepaid expenses

預付利息(ㄩˋ ㄈㄨˋ ㄌㄧˋ ㄒㄧˊ)
prepaid interest

預定(ㄩˋ ㄉㄧㄥˋ)
①to reserve (seats, rooms, etc.) 參看「預訂」②to set (a date, etc.); to be scheduled

預訂(ㄩˋ ㄉㄧㄥˋ)
to subscribe or order in advance; to place an order; to book; to reserve: 房間已被預訂一空。All rooms are reserved.

預力混凝土(ㄩˋ ㄌㄧˋ ㄏㄨㄣˋ ㄋㄧㄥˊ ㄊㄨˇ)
prestressed concrete

預料(ㄩˋ ㄌㄧㄠˋ)
to predict; to surmise; to anticipate; to expect: 沒有人預料到會有驟雨。Nobody expected the shower.

預留(ㄩˋ ㄌㄧㄡˊ)
to put aside for later use; to keep something in reserve

預告(ㄩˋ ㄍㄠˋ)
to inform or notify beforehand; advance notice; to herald; to preannounce

預告片(ㄩˋ ㄍㄠˋ ㄆㄧㄢˋ)
(motion picture) a trailer

預購(ㄩˋ ㄍㄡˋ)
to purchase in advance

預感(ㄩˋ ㄍㄢˇ)
① a premonition; a presentiment: 我有不祥的預感。I have a bad presentiment. ②to have a premonition

預科(ㄩˋ ㄎㄜ)
a preparatory course

預計(ㄩˋ ㄐㄧˋ)
to estimate; to surmise; estimates; to calculate in advance

預計成本(ㄩˋ ㄐㄧˋ ㄔㄥˊ ㄅㄣˇ)
predetermined costs

預計收入(ㄩˋ ㄐㄧˋ ㄕㄡ ㄖㄨˋ)
anticipated revenue

預借(ㄩˋ ㄐㄧㄝˋ)
to borrow or draw money (or one's salary) in advance

預繳(ㄩˋ ㄐㄧㄠˇ)
to pay (taxes, etc.) in advance

預見(ㄩˋ ㄐㄧㄢˋ)
to anticipate; to envision; to foresee; foresight; prevision: 這結果是可以預見的。This result can be predicted.

預期(ㄩˋ ㄑㄧˊ)
to expect; to estimate; to anticipate: 結果和預期的相符。The results are consistent with expectations.

預習(ㄩˋ ㄒㄧˊ)
①(said of students) to prepare lessons before class ②to rehearse or drill; a rehearsal or drill

預先(ㄩˋ ㄒㄧㄢ)
beforehand; in advance: 你最好預先聲明。You'd better state it explicitly beforehand.

預想(ㄩˋ ㄒㄧㄤˇ)
to anticipate; to expect

預選(ㄩˋ ㄒㄩㄢˇ)
① a preliminary selection or contest ②primaries (in the U.S. presidential election etc.)

預支(ㄩˋ ㄓ)
to draw (salary) in advance

預支費用(ㄩˋ ㄓ ㄈㄟˋ ㄩㄥˋ)
prepaid expenses

預知(ㄩˋ ㄓ)
to know beforehand or in advance; a fore-knowledge

預兆(ㄩˋ ㄓㄠˋ)
an omen; premonition; a presage; a sign; a harbinger: 這是吉祥的預兆。It is an auspicious omen.

預展(ㄩˋ ㄓㄢˇ)
a preview (of an exhibition)

預政(ㄩˋ ㄓㄥˋ)
to take an active part in politics

預鑄混凝土(ㄩˋ ㄓㄨˋ ㄏㄨㄣˋ ㄋㄧㄥˊ ㄊㄨˇ)
precast concrete

預鑄式房屋(ㄩˋ ㄓㄨˋ ㄕˋ ㄈㄤˊ ㄨ)
a prefabricated house; a prefab

預祝(ㄩˋ ㄓㄨˋ)
to congratulate (victory or success) beforehand

預產期(ㄩˋ ㄔㄢˇ ㄑㄧˊ)
(medicine) the estimated date of childbirth (E.D.C.)

預示(ㄩˋ ㄕˋ)
to betoken; to indicate

預審(ㄩˋ ㄕㄣˇ)
a preliminary trial; an inquest

預測(ㄩˋ ㄘㄜˋ)
to predict; to make a forecast; prediction: 並非所有的天氣預測都準確。Not all the predictions about the weather will come true.

預賽(ㄩˋ ㄙㄞˋ)

a preliminary competition; an elimination contest; a trial match

預算(ㄩˋ ㄙㄨㄢˋ)

an estimate; a budget; to calculate in advance: 每人都應該有自己的預算。Everybody must have a budget of his own.

預算案(ㄩˋ ㄙㄨㄢˋ ㄢˋ)

the budget as a bill in the assembly

預言(ㄩˋ ㄧㄢˊ)

① prophecy; a prediction; a forecast: 有些人自稱有預言的本領。Some people claim to have natural powers of prediction. ② to predict; to foretell

預言家(ㄩˋ ㄧㄢˊ ㄐㄧㄚ)

a prophet; a fortuneteller

預演(ㄩˋ ㄧㄢˇ)

a preview; a rehearsal: 我們預演之後見面。We'll meet after rehearsal.

預聞(ㄩˋ ㄨㄣˊ)

to participate in; to interfere with

預約(ㄩˋ ㄩㄝ)

a preliminary agreement; to preengage; to subscribe for a book that is to be published; to make an appointment

預約掛號(ㄩˋ ㄩㄝ ㄍㄨㄚˋ ㄏㄠˋ)

to have an appointment with a doctor

【頑】 6791 ㄨㄢˊ wan wán

1. stupid; dull; ignorant
2. obstinate; stubborn
3. recalcitrant; unruly; defiant
4. to play
5. naughty or impish

頑皮(ㄨㄢˊ ㄆㄧˊ)

naughty or impish (children)

頑民(ㄨㄢˊ ㄇㄧㄣˊ)

unruly or ungovernable people; refractory people

頑鈍(ㄨㄢˊ ㄉㄨㄣˋ)

① foolish; stupid; dull ② a person without principles; a shameless person

頑童(ㄨㄢˊ ㄊㄨㄥˊ)

naughty or unruly children; an urchin

頑劣(ㄨㄢˊ ㄌㄧㄝˋ)

stubborn and stupid; good-for-nothing

頑廉懦立(ㄨㄢˊ ㄌㄧㄢˊ ㄋㄨㄛˋ ㄌㄧˋ)

to lead the people toward virtuous ways

頑梗(ㄨㄢˊ ㄍㄥˇ)

foolishly stubborn or obstinate; perverse; pigheaded

頑固(ㄨㄢˊ ㄍㄨˋ)

① stubborn; obstinate; headstrong: 他像騾子一樣頑固。He is as stubborn as a mule. ② ultraconservative

頑固份子(ㄨㄢˊ ㄍㄨˋ ㄈㄣˋ ㄗˇ)

die-hards

頑抗(ㄨㄢˊ ㄎㄤˋ)

to resist stubbornly; stubborn resistance

頑健(ㄨㄢˊ ㄐㄧㄢˋ)

(I'm) still healthy and strong—a polite expression: 頑健如故。I am in good health as usual.

頑強(ㄨㄢˊ ㄑㄧㄤˊ)

stubborn; obstinacy; tenacious

頑癬(ㄨㄢˊ ㄒㄧㄢˇ)

ringworm that is difficult to cure; stubborn dermatitis

頑石(ㄨㄢˊ ㄕˊ)

unpolished stones or coarse rocks

頑石點頭(ㄨㄢˊ ㄕˊ ㄉㄧㄢˇ ㄊㄡˊ)

(said of statements or teachings) so persuasive and moving that even the rocks nod in agreement

頑耍(ㄨㄢˊ ㄕㄨㄚˇ)

to play; to romp about: 他們正在院子裡頑耍。They are romping about in the yard.

【頒】 6792 ㄅㄢ ban ban

1. to bestow on; to grant; to confer on
2. to proclaim; to make public; to promulgate
3. to distribute; to send out

頒布(ㄅㄢ ㄅㄨˋ)

to proclaim or promulgate (laws or regulations, orders, etc.): 國王頒布了一項命令。The king promulgated a decree.

頒發(ㄅㄢ ㄈㄚ)

to bestow; to award or distribute (prizes, etc.)

頒獎(ㄅㄢ ㄐㄧㄤˇ)

to hand out an award or prize

頒行(ㄅㄢ ㄒㄧㄥˊ)

to promulgate and enforce; to make public and put into practice

頒贈(ㄅㄢ ㄗㄥˋ)

to confer (honors or degrees) on someone

【頓】 6793 1. ㄉㄨㄣˋ duenn dùn

1. to stop or halt; to pause
2. to kowtow
3. to stamp (the foot)
4. to arrange; to put in order
5. a time; a turn
6. immediately; promptly
7. to be tired; to fall apart
8. to be broken
9. a Chinese family name

頓巴敦橡園(ㄉㄨㄣˋ ㄅㄚ ㄉㄨㄣ ㄒㄧㄤˋ ㄩㄢˊ)

the Dumbarton Oaks, an estate in the District of Columbia

頓巴敦橡園會議(ㄉㄨㄣˋ ㄅㄚ ㄉㄨㄣ ㄒㄧㄤˋ ㄩㄢˊ ㄏㄨㄟˋ ㄧˋ)

the Dumbarton Oaks Conference—It was held at the Dumbarton Oaks to discuss proposals for creation of the United Nations, August—October, 1944.

頓筆(ㄉㄨㄣˋ ㄅㄧˇ)

①to stop writing②to pause in writing

頓開茅塞(ㄉㄨㄣˋ ㄎㄞ ㄇㄠˊ ㄙㄜˋ)

suddenly see the light; suddenly come to an understanding

頓口無言(ㄉㄨㄣˋ ㄎㄡˇ ㄨˊ ㄧㄢˊ)

to have nothing to say in reply; to be completely silenced

頓河(ㄉㄨㄣˋ ㄏㄜˊ)

the Don River, in European U.S.S.R.

頓號(ㄉㄨㄣˋ ㄏㄠˋ)

a punctuation mark "、" indicating a very brief pause in reading

頓躓(ㄉㄨㄣˋ ㄓˋ)

① to trip over something and fall ② in dire straits

頓時(ㄉㄨㄣˋ ㄕˊ)

immediately; promptly.
頓首(ㄉㄨㄣˋ ㄕㄡˇ)
to make a ceremonious nod; to kowtow
頓足(ㄉㄨㄣˋ ㄗㄨˊ)or 頓脚(ㄉㄨㄣˋ ㄐㄧㄠˇ)
to stamp one's foot
頓足捶胸(ㄉㄨㄣˋ ㄗㄨˊ ㄔㄨㄟˊ ㄒㄩㄥ)
to stamp one's foot and hit one's breast
頓挫(ㄉㄨㄣˋ ㄘㄨㄛˋ)
①to encounter failure; to receive a setback ②(said of musical notes) rising and falling
頓悟(ㄉㄨㄣˋ ㄨˋ)
to realize suddenly; to come to a sudden realization

【頓】 6793
2. ㄉㄨˊ dwu dú
as in 冒頓(ㄇㄛˋ ㄉㄨˊ)—name of a Tartar chieftain in the early Western Han Dynasty

【頍】 6794
ㄎㄨㄟˇ koei kuǐ
to raise one's head

五畫

【領】 6795
ㄌㄧㄥˇ liing lǐng
1. the neck
2. the collar; the neckband: 他抓住我的衣領。He took me by the collar.
3. a piece of clothing
4. to lead; to head; to guide; to usher: 把客人領到大廳去。Usher the guests into the hall.
5. to receive; to get: 他已經領了養老金。He has received his pension.
6. to understand
7. (now rarely) to manage; to operate
領班(ㄌㄧㄥˇ ㄅㄢ)
the leader of a team; a headman; a foreman
領兵(ㄌㄧㄥˇ ㄅㄧㄥ)
①to lead troops ②a military officer
領帶(ㄌㄧㄥˇ ㄉㄞˋ)
①a necktie ②to lead
領帶夾(ㄌㄧㄥˇ ㄉㄞˋ ㄐㄧㄚˊ)
a tie clip
領導(ㄌㄧㄥˇ ㄉㄠˇ)
①to lead; leadership: 誰將領導這個班? Who is going to lead this class? ②a guide
領導有方(ㄌㄧㄥˇ ㄉㄠˇ ㄧㄡˇ ㄈㄤ)
to lead correctly; wise leadership
領道(ㄌㄧㄥˇ ㄉㄠˋ)
to lead the way
領單(ㄌㄧㄥˇ ㄉㄢ)
a slip of paper which entitles the bearer to get something
領隊(ㄌㄧㄥˇ ㄉㄨㄟˋ)
the leader of a team or group; to lead a group: 這支探險隊由周先生領隊。The expedition was led by Mr. Chou.
領頭(ㄌㄧㄥˇ ㄊㄡˊ)
to initiate; to start; to begin; to lead; to make a beginning; to be the first to do something: 我領頭，大家跟着唱吧! I'll lead off, please join in.
領土(ㄌㄧㄥˇ ㄊㄨˇ)or 領地(ㄌㄧㄥˇ ㄉㄧˋ)
territory
領土完整(ㄌㄧㄥˇ ㄊㄨˇ ㄨㄢˊ ㄓㄥˇ)
territorial integrity: 我們要保衛國家的領土完整。We'll safeguard our country's territorial integrity.
領路(ㄌㄧㄥˇ ㄌㄨˋ)
to lead the way
領略(ㄌㄧㄥˇ ㄌㄩㄝˋ)
to understand; to taste; to experience; to appreciate
領港(ㄌㄧㄥˇ ㄍㄤˇ)
a pilot(in a port)
領口(ㄌㄧㄥˇ ㄎㄡˇ)
the collar of a garment; the neckband
領款(ㄌㄧㄥˇ ㄎㄨㄢˇ)
to receive funds; to draw money
領空(ㄌㄧㄥˇ ㄎㄨㄥ)
territorial air; an aerial domain
領海(ㄌㄧㄥˇ ㄏㄞˇ)
territorial waters or seas
領航(ㄌㄧㄥˇ ㄏㄤˊ)
to navigate; navigation; to pilot
領航員(ㄌㄧㄥˇ ㄏㄤˊ ㄩㄢˊ)
a navigator; a pilot
領回(ㄌㄧㄥˇ ㄏㄨㄟˊ)
to get back; to take back
領會(ㄌㄧㄥˇ ㄏㄨㄟˋ)
to understand; to appreciate: 我還沒有領會你的意思。I still don't understand what you mean.
領結(ㄌㄧㄥˇ ㄐㄧㄝˊ)
the loop of a necktie; a bow tie
領教(ㄌㄧㄥˇ ㄐㄧㄠˋ)
① to be taught; to get instruction ②(a polite expression) to have received your reply ③ thanks; much obliged ④ (sarcastically) to experience or encounter ⑤ to ask advice
領巾(ㄌㄧㄥˇ ㄐㄧㄣ)
a scarf
領獎(ㄌㄧㄥˇ ㄐㄧㄤˇ)
to receive an award or prize
領情(ㄌㄧㄥˇ ㄑㄧㄥˊ)
to appreciate favors given; to feel grateful to somebody: 你的好意我十分領情。I feel very grateful to you for your kindness.
領取(ㄌㄧㄥˇ ㄑㄩˇ)
to get; to receive
領悉(ㄌㄧㄥˇ ㄒㄧ)
to have learned(an expression used in letters)
領洗(ㄌㄧㄥˇ ㄒㄧˇ)
to be baptized; to receive baptism: 他領洗成爲羅馬天主教徒。He was baptized a Roman Catholic.
領謝(ㄌㄧㄥˇ ㄒㄧㄝˋ)
to receive with thanks
領袖(ㄌㄧㄥˇ ㄒㄧㄡˋ)
a leader; the leading figure
領袖慾(ㄌㄧㄥˇ ㄒㄧㄡˋ ㄩˋ)
the desire or drive to be a leader
領先(ㄌㄧㄥˇ ㄒㄧㄢ)
①to lead; to walk ahead ② the lead; the first place or position: 他在賽跑中領先。He took the lead in the race.
領銜(ㄌㄧㄥˇ ㄒㄧㄢˊ)
①the first to sign in a list of signatures ② to be the first on a name list ③ to play the lead in a film: 這部電影由他領銜主演。He played the lead in this film.
領薪水(ㄌㄧㄥˇ ㄒㄧㄣ ㄕㄨㄟˇ)
to receive pay; to get salary; to get the pay check

領章(ㄌㄧㄥˇ ㄓㄤ)
insignia on the collars of military uniforms; collar badges

領事(ㄌㄧㄥˇ ㄕˋ)
(diplomacy)a consul

領事館(ㄌㄧㄥˇ ㄕˋ ㄍㄨㄢˇ)
a consulate

領事裁判權(ㄌㄧㄥˇ ㄕˋ ㄘㄞˊ ㄆㄢˋ ㄑㄩㄢˊ)
consular jurisdiction

領受(ㄌㄧㄥˇ ㄕㄡˋ)
to receive; to enjoy (your favors, etc.)

領賞(ㄌㄧㄥˇ ㄕㄤˇ)
to receive a reward

領水(ㄌㄧㄥˇ ㄕㄨㄟˇ)
① inland waters ② territorial waters; territorial sea

領子(ㄌㄧㄥˇ ˙ㄗ)
the collar or neck of a garment

領座員(ㄌㄧㄥˇ ㄗㄨㄛˋ ㄩㄢˊ)
an usher in a theater or concert hall

領罪(ㄌㄧㄥˇ ㄗㄨㄟˋ)
to admit guilt; to plead guilty

領養(ㄌㄧㄥˇ ㄧㄤˇ)
to adopt(a child)

領悟(ㄌㄧㄥˇ ㄨˋ)
to understand; to comprehend

領域(ㄌㄧㄥˇ ㄩˋ)
① a domain; a realm; the territory of a nation: 領域廣大。The domain is vast. ② a realm; a field; a sphere; a domain

【頗】 6796
1. ㄆㄛˇ poo pǒ

1. somewhat
2. quite; very; fairly; considerably; rather
3. a Chinese family name

頗表同情(ㄆㄛˇ ㄅㄧㄠˇ ㄊㄨㄥˊ ㄑㄧㄥˊ)
rather sympathetic; to sympathize considerably

頗多(ㄆㄛˇ ㄉㄨㄛ)
rather many; many

頗好(ㄆㄛˇ ㄏㄠˇ)
rather good; good

頗佳(ㄆㄛˇ ㄐㄧㄚ)
rather good; fairly good

頗久(ㄆㄛˇ ㄐㄧㄡˇ)
for quite a while

頗想(ㄆㄛˇ ㄒㄧㄤˇ)
to be rather inclined to do something

頗知一二(ㄆㄛˇ ㄓ ㄧ ㄦˋ)
(literally)to know one or two things (about it) —to know it rather well: 他對歌劇頗知一二。He knows opera rather well.

頗重(ㄆㄛˇ ㄓㄨㄥˋ)
rather heavy; fairly heavy: 這本書頗重。The book is rather heavy.

頗有(ㄆㄛˇ ㄧㄡˇ)
to have a lot of (dough, etc.); to be very much like (his father's ways, etc.); a lot of: 我頗有同感。I feel the same way as you do.

頗爲滿意(ㄆㄛˇ ㄨㄟˊ ㄇㄢˇ ㄧˋ)
rather or much satisfied; very contented: 我對你的解釋頗爲滿意。I am much satisfied with your explanation.

頗欲(ㄆㄛˇ ㄩˋ)
rather intend to do something

【頗】 6796
2. ㄆㄛ po pō

inclined to one side; unjustly

六畫

【頡】 6797
1. ㄐㄧㄚˊ jya jiá

to deduct; to omit

【頡】 6797
2. ㄒㄧㄝˊ shye xié
(又讀 ㄐㄧㄝˊ jye jié)

to fly up

頡頏(ㄒㄧㄝˊ ㄏㄤˊ)
① to match; to contest: 從未有人能跟他頡頏。He never met his match. ②(said of birds)to fly high and low ③ haughty; conceited

【頦】 6798
ㄏㄞˊ hair hái
(又讀 ㄎㄜ ke kē
ㄎㄜˊ ker ké)

the chin

【頫】 6799
ㄈㄨˇ fuu fǔ

with one's chin down; to bow one's head

【頠】 6800
ㄨㄟˇ woei wěi

quiet; tranquil

【嬃】 6801
ㄒㄩ shiu xū

a term of address for elder sisters in the state of Chu (楚) in ancient China

〔頁部〕

七畫

【頤】 6802
ㄧˊ yi yí

1. the cheeks
2. to nourish; to rear; to take care of oneself
3. a Chinese family name

頤和園(ㄧˊ ㄏㄜˊ ㄩㄢˊ)
the Yi-ho Garden (or the Summer Palace) built by Empress Dowager Tzu Hsi (慈禧) at the end of the Ching Dynasty, where the summer palace was located: 頤和園是著名的觀光勝地。The Yi-ho Garden is a famous tourist resort.

頤指(ㄧˊ ㄓˇ)
to signify one's intentions to servants or subordinates by merely twisting the cheeks

頤指氣使(ㄧˊ ㄓˇ ㄑㄧˋ ㄕˇ)
to order about; to be extremely bossy: 他的妻子喜歡頤指氣使。He has a very bossy wife.

頤神(ㄧˊ ㄕㄣˊ)
to rest one's mind; to have a mental relaxation

頤養(ㄧˊ ㄧㄤˇ)
to nourish; to keep fit; to take care of oneself; to recuperate

【頭】 6803
1. ㄊㄡˊ tour tóu

1. the head: 他打我的頭。He hit me on the head.
2. the top; the first; first; the beginning
3. the chief; the boss; the leader; the head (of a group)
4. the two ends (of anything); a side; an aspect
5. a head(of cattle, etc.)
6. an auxiliary, as a suffix

頭版(ㄊㄡˊ ㄅㄢˇ)
①the front page (of a newspaper) ② the first edition

頭部(ㄊㄡˊ ㄅㄨˋ)
the head

頭破血流(ㄊㄡˊ ㄆㄛˋ ㄒㄧㄝˇ ㄌㄧㄡˊ)

with one's head broken and bleeding (as a result of a savage beating)
頭皮(ㄊㄡˊ ㄆㄧˊ)
the scalp
頭皮屑(ㄊㄡˊ ㄆㄧˊ ㄒㄧㄝˋ)
dandruff
頭毛(ㄊㄡˊ ㄇㄠˊ)
the hair
頭名(ㄊㄡˊ ㄇㄧㄥˊ)
the first (in an examination, contest, etc.)
頭目(ㄊㄡˊ ㄇㄨˋ)
a chief; a leader; a ringleader; a chieftain; the head of a group
頭髮(ㄊㄡˊ ·ㄈㄚ)
hair on the head: 她留頭髮。She is letting her hair grow.
頭風(ㄊㄡˊ ㄈㄥ)
a headache
頭戴式耳機(ㄊㄡˊ ㄉㄞˋ ㄕˋ ㄦˇ ㄐㄧ)
a headband receiver
頭道(ㄊㄡˊ ㄉㄠˋ)
① the first time ② the first (course or dish in a feast)
頭燈(ㄊㄡˊ ㄉㄥ)
(mining) a head lamp
頭等(ㄊㄡˊ ㄉㄥˇ)
first class; the best quality
頭等艙(ㄊㄡˊ ㄉㄥˇ ㄘㄤ)
a first-class cabin
頭頂(ㄊㄡˊ ㄉㄧㄥˇ)
① the top of one's head ② to wear or support with one's head
頭胎(ㄊㄡˊ ㄊㄞ)
the firstborn
頭套(ㄊㄡˊ ㄊㄠˋ)
an actor's headgear
頭頭是道(ㄊㄡˊ ㄊㄡˊ ㄕˋ ㄉㄠˋ)
logically (arranged and narrated); systematically and orderly (stated); clearly and reasonably (presented)
頭疼(ㄊㄡˊ ㄊㄥˊ)
(to have a) headache
頭挑(ㄊㄡˊ ㄊㄧㄠ)
the choicest; the best choice
頭童齒豁(ㄊㄡˊ ㄊㄨㄥˊ ㄔˇ ㄏㄨㄛˋ)
bald head and teeth gone—old
頭痛(ㄊㄡˊ ㄊㄨㄥˋ)
a headache: 這孩子眞讓我頭痛。This boy is a headache for me.
頭痛醫頭，脚痛醫脚(ㄊㄡˊ ㄊㄨㄥˋ ㄧ ㄊㄡˊ, ㄐㄧㄠˇ ㄊㄨㄥˋ ㄧ ㄐㄧㄠˇ)
to treat only where the pain is—not to find the source of a disease; a superficial way of doing things; to deal with problems on an ad hoc basis
頭腦(ㄊㄡˊ ㄋㄠˇ)
①brains; mind: 他頭腦簡單。He is simple-minded. ② main threads; clues: 他的話讓我摸不着頭腦。I cannot grasp the main threads of his words. ③ the chief or boss
頭腦不淸(ㄊㄡˊ ㄋㄠˇ ㄅㄨˋ ㄑㄧㄥ)
mixed-up; muddleheaded
頭腦淸楚(ㄊㄡˊ ㄋㄠˇ ㄑㄧㄥ ㄔㄨˇ)
clearheaded; with an alert mind
頭裏(ㄊㄡˊ ·ㄌㄧ)
① earlier; before (with reference to time) ② in front; ahead: 請頭裏走，我馬上就來。Please go ahead. I will be there soon.
頭臉(ㄊㄡˊ ㄌㄧㄢˇ)
one's appearance or features
頭領(ㄊㄡˊ ㄌㄧㄥˇ)
the leader
頭顱(ㄊㄡˊ ㄌㄨˊ)
the head
頭路(ㄊㄡˊ ㄌㄨˋ)
① a clue; a main thread ② one's occupation; one's job ③ access
頭蓋骨(ㄊㄡˊ ㄍㄞˋ ㄍㄨˇ) or 頭骨(ㄊㄡˊ ㄍㄨˇ)
(anatomy) the skull; the cranium
頭會箕斂(ㄊㄡˊ ㄎㄨㄞˋ ㄐㄧ ㄌㄧㄢˋ)
heavy taxation
頭盔(ㄊㄡˊ ㄎㄨㄟ)
a helmet: 消防隊員戴皮製頭盔。Firemen wear leather helmets.
頭號(ㄊㄡˊ ㄏㄠˋ)
① number one; principal; leading; arch (enemy) ② the best ③ the largest
頭號新聞(ㄊㄡˊ ㄏㄠˋ ㄒㄧㄣ ㄨㄣˊ)
headline news; the leading story in a paper
頭昏(ㄊㄡˊ ㄏㄨㄣ)
dizzy; giddy: 他突然感到頭昏。He felt dizzy suddenly.
頭昏腦脹(ㄊㄡˊ ㄏㄨㄣ ㄋㄠˇ ㄓㄤˋ)
to feel dizzy and have a headache
頭昏眼花(ㄊㄡˊ ㄏㄨㄣ ㄧㄢˇ ㄏㄨㄚ)
dizzy
頭家(ㄊㄡˊ ㄐㄧㄚ)
the operator of a gambling joint
頭巾(ㄊㄡˊ ㄐㄧㄣ)
a turban; a kerchief
頭獎(ㄊㄡˊ ㄐㄧㄤˇ)
the first prize
頭角(ㄊㄡˊ ㄐㄩㄝˊ)
① a lead or clue ② looks of a promising youth; brilliance (of a young person); talent
頭角崢嶸(ㄊㄡˊ ㄐㄩㄝˊ ㄓㄥ ㄖㄨㄥˊ)
outstanding
頭屑(ㄊㄡˊ ㄒㄧㄝˋ)
dandruff
頭銜(ㄊㄡˊ ㄒㄧㄢˊ)
the official title of a person
頭緖(ㄊㄡˊ ㄒㄩˋ)
① leads or clues; main clues (said of a complicated affair) ② ways or means ③ systematical; sequence
頭緖繁多(ㄊㄡˊ ㄒㄩˋ ㄈㄢˊ ㄉㄨㄛ)
numerous leads and clues; confusing
頭陣(ㄊㄡˊ ㄓㄣˋ)
① the first battle ② the beginning of anything
頭脹(ㄊㄡˊ ㄓㄤˋ)
to feel heavy in the head
頭重脚輕(ㄊㄡˊ ㄓㄨㄥˋ ㄐㄧㄠˇ ㄑㄧㄥ)
top-heavy
頭蝨(ㄊㄡˊ ㄕ)
head lice; *Pediculus humanus capitis*
頭上(ㄊㄡˊ ·ㄕㄤ)
on the head; on top
頭生兒(ㄊㄡˊ ·ㄕㄥㄦ)
the firstborn
頭水貨(ㄊㄡˊ ㄕㄨㄟˇ ㄏㄨㄛˋ)
goods of the best quality
頭子(ㄊㄡˊ ·ㄗ)
① the best; the winner ② the leader (of bandits, rebels, etc.) 參看「頭目」: 土匪頭子已被絞死。The bandit chief has been hanged.
頭遭(ㄊㄡˊ ㄗㄠ) or 頭一遭(ㄊㄡˊ ㄧˋ ㄗㄠ)
the first time: 我頭一遭受騙時非常生氣。I was very angry when I was cheated the first

time.
頭足異處(ㄊㄡˊ ㄗㄨˊ ㄧˋ ㄔㄨˋ)
(literally) with one's head and feet in different places —beheaded
頭彩(ㄊㄡˊ ㄘㄞˇ)
the first prize in a lottery
頭寸(ㄊㄡˊ ㄘㄨㄣˋ)
cash; money supply
頭兒(ㄊㄡˊㄦ)
① the head: 他是我們這隊的頭兒。He is the head of our team. ② the boss ③ the ends ④ extremes
頭一回(ㄊㄡˊ ㄧˋ ㄏㄨㄟˊ)
for the first time: 他生平頭一回看到海。He saw the sea for the first time in his life.
頭油(ㄊㄡˊ ㄧㄡˊ)
hair tonic or oil
頭尾(ㄊㄡˊ ㄨㄟˇ)
① head and tail—beginning and end ② a Chinese dish with the head and tail of a fish cooked in soybean sauce and sugar
頭暈(ㄊㄡˊ ㄩㄣˊ)
dizzy; giddy; dizziness
頭暈眼花(ㄊㄡˊ ㄩㄣˊ ㄧㄢˇ ㄏㄨㄚ)
dizzy of head and dim of eyes

【頭】 6803
2. ·ㄊㄡ ·tou tou
1. a suffix indicating positions or directions
2. as a suffix to certain verbs to indicate the worthiness

【頰】 6804
ㄐㄧㄚˊ jya jiá
the cheeks: 這小孩雙頰緋紅。The boy has rosy cheeks.
頰輔(ㄐㄧㄚˊ ㄈㄨˇ)
flesh on the cheeks
頰骨(ㄐㄧㄚˊ ㄍㄨˇ)
the cheekbone
頰上添毫(ㄐㄧㄚˊ ㄕㄤˋ ㄊㄧㄢ ㄏㄠˊ)
(literally) to make a portrait come alive by adding some hair on the cheeks—to give a magic touch to a literary piece; to add the punch line

【頷】 6805
ㄏㄢˋ hann hàn
1. the chin; the jaws
2. a slight nod of the head
頷聯(ㄏㄢˋ ㄌㄧㄢˊ)
(in a poem of eight lines) the third and fourth lines which form a couplet
頷首(ㄏㄢˋ ㄕㄡˇ)
to nod the head—a sign of approval: 他頷首表示贊成。He nodded approval (or in approval or approvingly).
頷首示意(ㄏㄢˋ ㄕㄡˇ ㄕˋ ㄧˋ)
to give a nod as a signal

【頵】 6806
ㄐㄩㄣ jiun jūn
large-headed; top-heavy

【頸】 6807
ㄐㄧㄥˇ jiing jǐng
the neck; the throat: 她的頸子戴着金鍊。She wore a gold chain around the neck.
頸聯(ㄐㄧㄥˇ ㄌㄧㄢˊ)
(in a poem of eight lines) the fifth and sixth lines of a poem which form a couplet
頸項(ㄐㄧㄥˇ ㄒㄧㄤˋ)
the front and back of the neck
頸枕(ㄐㄧㄥˇ ㄓㄣˇ)
(machinery) bearing

【頹】 6808
ㄊㄨㄟˊ twei tuí
1. to crumble; disintegrated; ruined; dilapidated; to collapse
2. weakened; withered; emaciated; declining; decadent
3. bald
4. to descend; to cascade down
5. a Chinese family name
頹波(ㄊㄨㄟˊ ㄅㄛ)
water cascading—declining; worsening; deteriorating
頹敗(ㄊㄨㄟˊ ㄅㄞˋ)
degenerating; decadent; depraved
頹圮(ㄊㄨㄟˊ ㄆㄧˇ)
to sink and become ruined; dilapidated
頹廢(ㄊㄨㄟˊ ㄈㄟˋ)
① ruined; weakened; decadent ② low-spirited; depressed
頹廢派(ㄊㄨㄟˊ ㄈㄟˋ ㄆㄞˋ)
the decadents
頹廢主義(ㄊㄨㄟˊ ㄈㄟˋ ㄓㄨˇ ㄧˋ)
decadentism
頹放(ㄊㄨㄟˊ ㄈㄤˋ)
slovenly; unconventional; bohemian; cynical
頹風(ㄊㄨㄟˊ ㄈㄥ)
depraved or decadent customs; corruptive practices; moral degeneracy
頹唐(ㄊㄨㄟˊ ㄊㄤˊ)
dispirited; decrepit; failing
頹替(ㄊㄨㄟˊ ㄊㄧˋ)
falling apart; ruined; to disintegrate or deteriorate
頹齡(ㄊㄨㄟˊ ㄌㄧㄥˊ)
closing years of one's life; the declining years
頹勢(ㄊㄨㄟˊ ㄕˋ)
a declining tendency: 他試著去挽回頹勢。He tried to turn the tide in his favor.
頹然(ㄊㄨㄟˊ ㄖㄢˊ)
submissive; pliant
頹喪(ㄊㄨㄟˊ ㄙㄤˋ)
beaten; ruined; discouraged: 勿因一次失敗而頹喪，再試試看。Don't let one failure discourage you. Try again.
頹陽(ㄊㄨㄟˊ ㄧㄤˊ)
the setting sun
頹運(ㄊㄨㄟˊ ㄩㄣˋ)
declining fortune

【頻】 6809
ㄆㄧㄣˊ pyn pín
1. incessant; successive; continuous; frequently or repeatedly
2. urgent; precarious
3. same as 顰—to knit the brows
4. frequency
頻頻(ㄆㄧㄣˊ ㄆㄧㄣˊ)
incessantly; repeatedly; continuously; frequently: 她對他頻頻招手。She waved her hand to him again and again.
頻煩 or 頻繁(ㄆㄧㄣˊ ㄈㄢˊ)
frequent; incessant; busy
頻道(ㄆㄧㄣˊ ㄉㄠˋ)
(television) a channel
頻年(ㄆㄧㄣˊ ㄋㄧㄢˊ)
years in a row; successive years; year after year
頻率(ㄆㄧㄣˊ ㄌㄩˋ)
frequency
頻數(ㄆㄧㄣˊ ㄕㄨㄛˋ)
repeatedly; incessantly; frequently
頻仍(ㄆㄧㄣˊ ㄖㄥˊ)
frequently; often: 中國過去外患頻仍。China was subject to repeated foreign aggression.
頻蹙(ㄆㄧㄣˊ ㄘㄨˋ)

〔頁部〕

a woebegone look; looking sad

八畫

【顆】 6810 ㄎㄜ ke kē
a drop or droplet; a grain; a pill; a numerary adjunct (for bombs, bullets, etc.)：天上有幾顆星。There are a few stars in the sky.
顆粒(ㄎㄜ ㄌㄧˋ)
a drop; a grain; a bead

【顇】 6811 ㄘㄨㄟˋ tsuey cuì
as in 顦顇—haggard (from grief or anxiety)

九畫

【額】 6812 ㄜˊ er é
1. the forehead
2. a fixed amount, value, number, etc.; a quota
3. a horizontal tablet
4. a Chinese family name
額面(ㄜˊ ㄇㄧㄢˋ)
face value (of a banknote, bond, etc.)
額面價格(ㄜˊ ㄇㄧㄢˋ ㄐㄧㄚˋ ㄍㄜˊ)
face value
額非爾士峯(ㄜˊ ㄈㄟ ㄦˇ ㄕˋ ㄈㄥ)
Mt. Everest
額定(ㄜˊ ㄉㄧㄥˋ)
specified (numbers or amounts); rated
額定人數(ㄜˊ ㄉㄧㄥˋ ㄖㄣˊ ㄕㄨˋ)
the maximum number of persons allowed; the stipulated number of personnel
額頭(ㄜˊ ㄊㄡˊ)
the forehead
額骨(ㄜˊ ㄍㄨˇ)
the frontal bone
額黃(ㄜˊ ㄏㄨㄤˊ)
(said of women in ancient times) to paint the forehead yellow as makeup
額角(ㄜˊ ㄐㄩㄝˊ)
the temples
額手(ㄜˊ ㄕㄡˇ)
to raise the hand to the forehead—a gesture of respect or congratulations
額手稱慶(ㄜˊ ㄕㄡˇ ㄔㄥ ㄑㄧㄥˋ)
to put one's hand on one's forehead in jubilation; to be overjoyed
額數(ㄜˊ ㄕㄨˋ)
the fixed figure, amount, number, etc.
額外(ㄜˊ ㄨㄞˋ)
extra; beyond the set amount, figure, number or quota
額外費用(ㄜˊ ㄨㄞˋ ㄈㄟˋ ㄩㄥˋ)
extraneous expenses
額外收入(ㄜˊ ㄨㄞˋ ㄕㄡ ㄖㄨˋ)
extra income: 我去年都沒有額外收入。I did not have any extra income last year.

【顋】 6813 (腮) ㄙㄞ sai sāi
the cheeks
顋幫子(ㄙㄞ ㄅㄤ ·ㄗ) or 顋頰(ㄙㄞ ㄐㄧㄚˊ)
the cheeks

【題】 6814 ㄊㄧˊ tyi tí
1. the forehead
2. a sign; a signal
3. a subject; the title of a composition or speech
4. commentaries; notes
5. to sign; to write; to inscribe
6. the end; the top
7. the ornamental woodwork under the eaves of public buildings
8. a Chinese family name
題跋(ㄊㄧˊ ㄅㄚˊ)
a colophon; notes or commentaries in a book, painting or calligraphy; prefaces and postscripts
題筆(ㄊㄧˊ ㄅㄧˇ)
to write: 他很早便開始靠題筆爲生。He began to earn his living by writing early.
題壁(ㄊㄧˊ ㄅㄧˋ)
to write on the wall
題品(ㄊㄧˊ ㄆㄧㄣˇ) or 題評(ㄊㄧˊ ㄆㄧㄥˊ)
to comment on; to criticize
題名(ㄊㄧˊ ㄇㄧㄥˊ)
①to inscribe one's name; to autograph ②to name a work; to entitle
題名錄(ㄊㄧˊ ㄇㄧㄥˊ ㄌㄨˋ)
①a roster of successful candidates who participated in the same civil service examination in former times ②a book for recording names
題目(ㄊㄧˊ ㄇㄨˋ)
① the subject or title of a composition or speech; a theme or heading ② a question or problem (especially in a test)
題款(ㄊㄧˊ ㄎㄨㄢˇ)
(on a scroll) the date and the name of a writer and the person it is dedicated to
題畫(ㄊㄧˊ ㄏㄨㄚˋ)
to write on a painting
題解(ㄊㄧˊ ㄐㄧㄝˇ)
① explanatory notes on the title or background of a book ② keys to exercises or problems
題簽(ㄊㄧˊ ㄑㄧㄢ)
to write the title on a book
題詩(ㄊㄧˊ ㄕ)
to write verses on something
題署(ㄊㄧˊ ㄕㄨˋ)
to write on scrolls of couplets or horizontal tablets
題字(ㄊㄧˊ ㄗˋ)
to write on something; an inscription; an autograph
題辭 or 題詞(ㄊㄧˊ ㄘˊ)
① complimentary verses or prose inserted at the beginning of a book by a person other than the author; a foreword ② an inscription; a dedication ③ to write a few words of encouragement, appreciation or commemoration; to inscribe
題材(ㄊㄧˊ ㄘㄞˊ)
material constituting the main theme of an article, composition, etc.: 這是寫劇本的好題材。This is good material for a play.
題額(ㄊㄧˊ ㄜˊ)
to write on a horizontal tablet
題外(ㄊㄧˊ ㄨㄞˋ)
beyond the subject being discussed

【顎】 6815 ㄜˋ eh è
1. the jowl; the cheek bones; jaws
2. high-cheekboned
3. reverence
顎骨(ㄜˋ ㄍㄨˇ)

the jawbones; maxillary bones
顎下腺(ㄜˋ ㄒㄧㄚˋ ㄒㄧㄢˋ)
the submaxillary gland

【顏】 6816 ㄧㄢˊ yan yán
1. face (physically); countenance; features
2. reputation; prestige; face (figuratively): 他竟厚顏說出此話。He has the face to say that.
3. dyes; colors: 他用明亮的顏色來畫它。He painted it with bright colors.
4. a Chinese family name
顏面(ㄧㄢˊ ㄇㄧㄢˋ)
①face; honor: 他必須顧全顏面。He has to save face. ②countenance; face
顏料(ㄧㄢˊ ㄌㄧㄠˋ)
dyestuffs; pigments
顏厚(ㄧㄢˊ ㄏㄡˋ)
①thick-skinned; unblushing; brazen ②(figuratively) face thickened because of feeling shame—shame-faced
顏回(ㄧㄢˊ ㄏㄨㄟˊ)
Yen Hui (521-490B.C.), one of the most respected disciples of Confucius
顏筋柳骨(ㄧㄢˊ ㄐㄧㄣ ㄌㄧㄡˇ ㄍㄨˇ)
the sinews of Yen Chen-ching (顏眞卿) and the bones of Liu Kung-chüan (柳公權), (Yen and Liu were both famous calligraphers in the Tang Dynasty)—calligraphy of the highest order
顏之推(ㄧㄢˊ ㄓ ㄊㄨㄟ)
Yen Chih-tui (531-?), a famous writer-official
顏眞卿(ㄧㄢˊ ㄓㄣ ㄑㄧㄥ)
Yen Chen-ching (708-784), a famous general-calligrapher in the Tang Dynasty
顏氏家訓(ㄧㄢˊ ㄕˋ ㄐㄧㄚ ㄒㄩㄣˋ)
a work by Yen Chih-tui (顏之推) dealing with the discipline of one's own mind and the family
顏色(ㄧㄢˊ ㄙㄜˋ)or(ㄧㄢˊ ·ㄕㄞ)
①color; hue; pigment ②countenance; facial expression ③a lesson: 給他一點顏色看看。Teach him a lesson.
顏色自若(ㄧㄢˊ ㄙㄜˋ ㄗˋ ㄖㄨㄛˋ)
to be composed with the face unchanged

【顒】 6817 ㄩㄥˊ yong yóng
1. severe
2. great; large
3. large-headed

【顓】 6818 ㄓㄨㄢ juan zhuān
1. cautious
2. stupid; dull; ignorant
3. a Chinese family name
顓頊(ㄓㄨㄢ ㄒㄩˋ)
name of an emperor in ancient China, a grandson of the Yellow Emperor (黃帝)

十畫

【顗】 6819 ㄧˇ yii yǐ
quiet; tranquil; solemn

【願】 6820 ㄩㄢˋ yuann yuàn
1. to be willing; to be desirous of; to hope; to wish
2. anything one wishes or desires; an ambition or aspiration: 他終於如願以償。Finally he had his wishes fulfilled.
3. a vow
4. to think
願天下有情人皆成眷屬(ㄩㄢˋ ㄊㄧㄢ ㄒㄧㄚˋ ㄧㄡˇ ㄑㄧㄥˊ ㄖㄣˊ ㄐㄧㄝ ㄔㄥˊ ㄐㄩㄢˋ ㄕㄨˇ)
May all lovers unite in marriage!
願海(ㄩㄢˋ ㄏㄞˇ)
a profound wish
願心(ㄩㄢˋ ㄒㄧㄣ)
①the wish of Buddha to save all people and the wish of all the faithful to become Buddha ②a vow
願意(ㄩㄢˋ ㄧˋ)
①to be willing ②to like; to want ③to approve of
願望(ㄩㄢˋ ㄨㄤˋ)
one's wish, aspiration; what one's heart desires: 和平是全世界人類的共同願望。Peace is the common aspirations of the world's people.

【顙】 6821 ㄙㄤˇ saang sǎng
1. the forehead
2. to kowtow

【顛】 6822 ㄉㄧㄢ dian diān
1. the top; the highest spot; the head
2. to fall; to topple; to upset
3. to jolt; to bump
4. upside down
5. mad; lunatic
顛簸(ㄉㄧㄢ ㄅㄛˇ)
to shake; to joggle or jolt; to bump; to toss
顛沛(ㄉㄧㄢ ㄆㄟˋ)or 顛頓(ㄉㄧㄢ ㄉㄨㄣˋ)
①to fall ②(figuratively) to be desperate; to fail in one's attempt
顛沛流離(ㄉㄧㄢ ㄆㄟˋ ㄌㄧㄡˊ ㄌㄧˊ)or 顛連(ㄉㄧㄢ ㄌㄧㄢˊ)
(said of refugees) suffering deprivations and hardships; running around without a roof over one's head; to lead a vagrant life
顛仆(ㄉㄧㄢ ㄆㄨ)
to fall down
顛撲不破(ㄉㄧㄢ ㄆㄨ ㄅㄨˊ ㄆㄛˋ)
(said of theories) irrefutable; absolutely right: 世界上沒有顛撲不破的眞理。There is no irrefutable truth in the world.
顛末(ㄉㄧㄢ ㄇㄛˋ)
from the beginning to the end
顛毛(ㄉㄧㄢ ㄇㄠˊ)
hair on top of head
顛覆(ㄉㄧㄢ ㄈㄨˋ)
to topple; to subvert; subversion
顛倒(ㄉㄧㄢ ㄉㄠˇ)or 顛顛倒倒(ㄉㄧㄢ ㄉㄧㄢ ㄉㄠˇ ㄉㄠˇ)
①upside down; to reverse; to transpose; to invert: 他把圖畫掛顛倒了。He hung the picture upside down. ②mentally deranged; infatuated; lunatic; confused; disordered: 我爲我表妹神魂顛倒。I was infatuated with my cousin.
顛倒是非(ㄉㄧㄢ ㄉㄠˇ ㄕˋ ㄈㄟ)or 顛倒黑白(ㄉㄧㄢ ㄉㄠˇ ㄏㄟ ㄅㄞˊ)
to confuse justice and injustice; to distort truth; to twist facts
顛來倒去(ㄉㄧㄢ ㄌㄞˊ ㄉㄠˇ ㄑㄩˋ)
①to lack orderliness or cohesion of thought; all jumbled up ②over and over
顛鸞倒鳳(ㄉㄧㄢ ㄌㄨㄢˊ ㄉㄠˇ ㄈㄥˋ)

〔頁部〕

the ecstasy of a couple in the act of making love

顛狂 or 癲狂(ㄉㄧㄢ ㄎㄨㄤˊ)
mad; lunatic; crazy

顛躓(ㄉㄧㄢ ㄓˋ)
to fall down

顛三倒四(ㄉㄧㄢ ㄙㄢ ㄉㄠˇ ㄙˋ)
①in total disorder; topsy-turvy; all in confusion ② lunatic; insane

【類】 6823 ㄌㄟˋ ley lèi
1. a species; a kind; a class; a race; a group; a category
2. similar; alike
3. (now rarely) good; virtue
4. a kind of wildcat
5. (now rarely) biased; prejudiced
6. a Chinese family name

類比(ㄌㄟˋ ㄅㄧˇ)
(logic) analogy

類別(ㄌㄟˋ ㄅㄧㄝˊ)
classification; categorization

類篇(ㄌㄟˋ ㄆㄧㄢ)
one of the oldest and largest dictionaries in China compiled by Szu-Ma Kuang (司馬光) and others, containing 53,165 characters

類推(ㄌㄟˋ ㄊㄨㄟ)
to reason by analogy; to draw analogies

類同(ㄌㄟˋ ㄊㄨㄥˊ)
similar to; alike

類固醇(ㄌㄟˋ ㄍㄨˋ ㄔㄨㄣˊ)
steroid

類化(ㄌㄟˋ ㄏㄨㄚˋ)
(psychology) apprehension

類皆如此(ㄌㄟˋ ㄐㄧㄝ ㄖㄨˊ ㄘˇ)
similar in kind; in like way

類聚(ㄌㄟˋ ㄐㄩˋ)
Birds of the same feather flock together.

類型(ㄌㄟˋ ㄒㄧㄥˊ)
a type; a category: 像他那一類型的人不可信賴。Men of his type are not to be trusted.

類書(ㄌㄟˋ ㄕㄨ)
any reference book with entries arranged in the form of a dictionary or according to subjects

類人猿(ㄌㄟˋ ㄖㄣˊ ㄩㄢˊ)
an anthropoid

類似(ㄌㄟˋ ㄙˋ)
to resemble; similar to; like; to be analogous to: 人的心臟類似喞筒。The human heart is analogous to a pump.

類似點(ㄌㄟˋ ㄙˋ ㄉㄧㄢˇ)
similarities

【顖】 6824 ㄒㄧㄣˋ shinn xìn
the part of the human head from the top to the forehead

十一畫

【顢】 6825 ㄇㄢˊ man mán
careless, ignorant and stupid

顢頇(ㄇㄢˊ ㄏㄢ)
① careless ② ignorant and stupid

十二畫

【顧】 6826 ㄍㄨˋ guh gù
1. to look at; to gaze
2. to turn the head around and look
3. to attend to; to mind; to care for; to concern oneself about; to regard; to look after
4. to visit; to call on
5. however; but; nevertheless
6. indeed; really
7. a Chinese family name

顧不得(ㄍㄨˋ ˙ㄅㄨ ㄉㄜˊ)
unable to take care of; to have to disregard

顧不了(ㄍㄨˋ ˙ㄅㄨ ㄌㄧㄠˇ)
unable to look after

顧不過來(ㄍㄨˋ ˙ㄅㄨ ㄍㄨㄛˋ ㄌㄞˊ)
unable to take care of (so many things)

顧盼(ㄍㄨˋ ㄆㄢˋ)
to look around

顧盼生姿(ㄍㄨˋ ㄆㄢˋ ㄕㄥ ㄗ)
to look around charmingly

顧盼自雄(ㄍㄨˋ ㄆㄢˋ ㄗˋ ㄒㄩㄥˊ)
complacent; proud and satisfied; to look down upon the world

顧面子(ㄍㄨˋ ㄇㄧㄢˋ ˙ㄗ)
① to care for one's face or reputation ②to value friendship; unwilling to embarrass others

顧名思義(ㄍㄨˋ ㄇㄧㄥˊ ㄙ ㄧˋ)
(literally) to see the name and think of the meaning; as a term suggests—self-explanatory; self-evident

顧得過來(ㄍㄨˋ ˙ㄉㄜ ㄍㄨㄛˋ ㄌㄞˊ)
able to take care of

顧到(ㄍㄨˋ ㄉㄠˋ)
to take something into consideration: 失敗的可能性已經被顧到。The possibility of failure has been taken into consideration.

顧念(ㄍㄨˋ ㄋㄧㄢˋ)
①to care for; to be worried about ②to think of with affection

顧臉面(ㄍㄨˋ ㄌㄧㄢˇ ˙ㄇㄧㄢ)
to have regard for one's face, reputation or respectability

顧慮(ㄍㄨˋ ㄌㄩˋ)
to show concern about; misgivings; concern; scruple: 我們對他的教學能力有所顧慮。We had misgivings about his ability to teach.

顧客(ㄍㄨˋ ㄎㄜˋ) or 顧主(ㄍㄨˋ ㄓㄨˇ)
customers; patrons; clients: 顧客至上。The customer is king.

顧愷之(ㄍㄨˋ ㄎㄞˇ ㄓ)
Ku Kai-chih, circa 345-411, a famous painter in the Tsin (晉) Dynasty

顧及(ㄍㄨˋ ㄐㄧˊ)
in consideration of; in view of; to care about; to attend to; to take something into consideration: 他無暇顧及此事。He has no time to attend to the matter.

顧忌(ㄍㄨˋ ㄐㄧˋ)
misgivings; scruple; fear: 他做此事毫無顧忌。He did it without scruple.

顧前不顧後(ㄍㄨˋ ㄑㄧㄢˊ ㄅㄨˋ ㄍㄨˋ ㄏㄡˋ)
to act with no regard for the consequences; to see only one aspect of a matter; to act rashly

顧曲周郎(ㄍㄨˋ ㄑㄩˇ ㄓㄡ ㄌㄤˊ)
a music connoisseur

顧全(ㄍㄨˋ ㄑㄩㄢˊ)
to have consideration for and take care to preserve

顧全面子(ㄍㄨˋ ㄑㄩㄢˊ ㄇㄧㄢˋ ˙ㄗ)
to save somebody's face; to spare somebody's feelings

顧全大局(ㄍㄨˋ ㄑㄩㄢˊ ㄉㄚˋ ㄐㄩˊ)
in the interest of the whole; for the sake of the country, organization, etc.; to take the situation as a whole into consideration
顧惜(ㄍㄨˋ ㄒㄧˊ)
to value; to care for
顧恤(ㄍㄨˋ ㄒㄩˋ)
to care for; to sympathize with
顧主(ㄍㄨˋ ㄓㄨˇ)
a customer; a patron; a client; clientele: 我們設法讓顧主完全滿意。We try to give our clients complete satisfaction.
顧左右而言他(ㄍㄨˋ ㄗㄨㄛˇ ㄧㄡˋ ㄦˊ ㄧㄢˊ ㄊㄚ)
to fudge a question
顧此失彼(ㄍㄨˋ ㄘˇ ㄕ ㄅㄧˇ)
to take care of one thing and miss the other
顧炎武(ㄍㄨˋ ㄧㄢˊ ㄨˇ)
Ku Yen-wu, 1613-1682, a famous scholar in the closing years of the Ming Dynasty, also known as Ku Ting-lin(顧亭林)
顧影(ㄍㄨˋ ㄧㄥˇ)
complacent
顧影自憐(ㄍㄨˋ ㄧㄥˇ ㄗˋ ㄌㄧㄢˊ)
(literally) to look at one's shadow and fall in love with oneself — narcissism; self-glorification; to look at one's shadow and lament one's lot
顧問(ㄍㄨˋ ㄨㄣˋ)
an advisor; a consultant; a counsellor

【頪】 6827
ㄌㄟˋ ley lèi
1. blemish
2. fierce; recalcitrant

【顥】 6828
ㄏㄠˋ haw hào
1. bright; luminous
2. (said of hair) hoary or white
3. very great; very large

【顦】 6829
(憔) ㄑㄧㄠˊ chyau qiáo
haggard
顦顇(ㄑㄧㄠˊ ㄘㄨㄟˋ)
haggard as a result of grief, etc.

十三畫

【顫】 6830
ㄔㄢˋ chann chàn
(又讀 ㄓㄢˋ jann zhàn)
to tremble; to shake; to shiver; to quiver; to vibrate
顫筆(ㄔㄢˋ ㄅㄧˇ)
(Chinese calligraphy) to write with the hand shaking in order to gain forcefulness in the strokes
顫抖(ㄔㄢˋ ㄉㄡˇ)
to tremble; to shiver; to shake; to quiver
顫動(ㄔㄢˋ ㄉㄨㄥˋ)
to shake; to tremble; to quiver; to shiver; to vibrate: 樹葉在微風中顫動。The leaves quivered in the breeze.
顫悠悠(ㄔㄢˋ ㄧㄡ ㄧㄡ)
trembling; shaky; flickering
顫巍巍(ㄔㄢˋ ㄨㄟˊ ㄨㄟˊ) or 顫顫巍巍(ㄔㄢˋ ·ㄔㄢ ㄨㄟˊ ㄨㄟˊ)
shaking; shivering; tottering; faltering

十四畫

【顯】 6831
ㄒㄧㄢˇ shean xiǎn
1. evident; manifest; clear
2. high-positioned; eminent; prominent
3. well-known; renowned; famed; reputed
4. to expose; to make known; to display; to show; to manifest
5. a prefix referring to one's forebears
顯妣(ㄒㄧㄢˇ ㄅㄧˇ)
my late mother
顯明(ㄒㄧㄢˇ ㄇㄧㄥˊ)
evident; clear; remarkable
顯達(ㄒㄧㄢˇ ㄉㄚˊ)
to attain high office; to achieve prominence in officialdom
顯得(ㄒㄧㄢˇ ·ㄉㄜ)
to look; to seem; to appear: 他顯得有點不舒服。He seems a bit unwell.
顯靈(ㄒㄧㄢˇ ㄌㄧㄥˊ)
omens, etc. given by the soul of a dead person; a divine manifestation; an epiphany
顯露(ㄒㄧㄢˇ ㄌㄨˋ)
to appear; to show; to manifest; to unveil: 她臉上顯露出輕蔑的笑容。A contemptuous smile appeared on her face.
顯露頭角(ㄒㄧㄢˇ ㄌㄨˋ ㄊㄡˊ ㄐㄧㄠˇ)
to show one's promise
顯貴(ㄒㄧㄢˇ ㄍㄨㄟˋ)
bigwigs; eminent personages: 他專門結交顯貴。He associated with eminent personages exclusively.
顯官(ㄒㄧㄢˇ ㄍㄨㄢ)
a ranking or high official
顯考(ㄒㄧㄢˇ ㄎㄠˇ)
my late father
顯赫(ㄒㄧㄢˇ ㄏㄜˋ)
outstanding; illustrious; powerful; mighty; prominent; renowned; glorious: 他的聲勢顯赫。He has a powerful influence.
顯花植物(ㄒㄧㄢˇ ㄏㄨㄚ ㄓˊ ㄨˋ)
a flowering plant; a phanerogam
顯豁(ㄒㄧㄢˇ ㄏㄨㄛˋ)
evident; clear; conspicuous
顯懷(ㄒㄧㄢˇ ㄏㄨㄞˊ)
a state of pregnancy which is already visible
顯晦(ㄒㄧㄢˇ ㄏㄨㄟˋ)
the luminous and the obscure; brightness and darkness
顯宦(ㄒㄧㄢˇ ㄏㄨㄢˋ)
a ranking or high official
顯見(ㄒㄧㄢˇ ㄐㄧㄢˋ)
It is evident that....
顯爵(ㄒㄧㄢˇ ㄐㄩㄝˊ)
a high government position
顯親(ㄒㄧㄢˇ ㄑㄧㄣ)
① to glorify one's parents ② powerful relatives
顯顯(ㄒㄧㄢˇ ㄒㄧㄢˇ)
bright and brilliant; illustrious
顯現(ㄒㄧㄢˇ ㄒㄧㄢˋ)
to appear; to reveal
顯像(ㄒㄧㄢˇ ㄒㄧㄤˋ)
(photography) to develop
顯像電話(ㄒㄧㄢˇ ㄒㄧㄤˋ ㄉㄧㄢˋ ㄏㄨㄚˋ)
a video phone
顯像液(ㄒㄧㄢˇ ㄒㄧㄤˋ ㄧㄝˋ)
(photography) developer
顯形兒(ㄒㄧㄢˇ ㄒㄧㄥˊㄦ)
(said of apparitions or spirits) to appear in human form; to show one's true

form or colors

顯性(ㄒㄧㄢˇ ㄒㄧㄥˋ)
(biology) dominance

顯性基因(ㄒㄧㄢˇ ㄒㄧㄥˋ ㄐㄧ ㄧㄣ)
a dominant gene

顯學(ㄒㄧㄢˇ ㄒㄩㄝˊ)
practical learning (referring to Confucianism and Mohism)

顯者(ㄒㄧㄢˇ ㄓㄜˇ)
a dignitary; the eminent ones

顯着(ㄒㄧㄢˇ ˙ㄓㄜ)
① to appear; to seem ② to feel; to cause to feel

顯章(ㄒㄧㄢˇ ㄓㄤ)
to make clear; to clarify; to state with honesty

顯著(ㄒㄧㄢˇ ㄓㄨˋ)
evident; clear; notable; eye-catching; marked; remarkable; outstanding: 學生進步顯著。The students have made marked progress.

顯著特徵(ㄒㄧㄢˇ ㄓㄨˋ ㄊㄜˋ ㄓㄥ)
a marked feature

顯敞(ㄒㄧㄢˇ ㄔㄤˇ)
spacious

顯出(ㄒㄧㄢˇ ㄔㄨ)
to appear; to show (in contrast)

顯示(ㄒㄧㄢˇ ㄕˋ)
to indicate; to show; to reveal; to demonstrate

顯身手(ㄒㄧㄢˇ ㄕㄣ ㄕㄡˇ)
to show one's talent or skill

顯聖(ㄒㄧㄢˇ ㄕㄥˋ)
to make evident a divine presence or power

顯然(ㄒㄧㄢˇ ㄖㄢˊ)
evident; clearly visible; obvious; apparent: 顯然他已改變意向。Apparently he has changed his mind.

顯祖(ㄒㄧㄢˇ ㄗㄨˇ)
one's forebears

顯而易見(ㄒㄧㄢˇ ㄦˊ ㄧˋ ㄐㄧㄢˋ)
evidently; apparently

顯要(ㄒㄧㄢˇ ㄧㄠˋ)
bigwigs; notables; VIPs (very important persons)

顯眼(ㄒㄧㄢˇ ㄧㄢˇ)
conspicuous; striking; eye-catching: 把它放在顯眼的地方。Put it in a conspicuous place.

顯揚(ㄒㄧㄢˇ ㄧㄤˊ)
to cite; to commend; to praise; to acclaim

顯影(ㄒㄧㄢˇ ㄧㄥˇ)
(cinematography) to develop

顯微膠片(ㄒㄧㄢˇ ㄨㄟˊ ㄐㄧㄠ ㄆㄧㄢˋ)
microfilm

顯微鏡(ㄒㄧㄢˇ ㄨㄟˊ ㄐㄧㄥˋ)
a microscope

顯微外科(ㄒㄧㄢˇ ㄨㄟˊ ㄨㄞˋ ㄎㄜ)
microsurgery

【顬】 6832
ㄖㄨˊ ru rú
參看「顳顬」

十五畫

【顰】 6833
ㄆㄧㄣˊ pyn pín
to frown; to knit one's brows

顰眉(ㄆㄧㄣˊ ㄇㄟˊ)
to knit the brows

顰蹙(ㄆㄧㄣˊ ㄘㄨˋ)
a look of grief, sorrow or anxiety; a glum look

十六畫

【顱】 6834
ㄌㄨˊ lu lú
1. the skull
2. the head
3. the forehead

顱骨(ㄌㄨˊ ㄍㄨˇ)
the skull; the parietal bone

十八畫

【顴】 6835
ㄑㄩㄢˊ chyuan quán
the cheekbone

顴骨(ㄑㄩㄢˊ ㄍㄨˇ)
the cheekbone; the malar bone; the malar: 她的顴骨突起。She has prominent cheekbones.

【顳】 6836
ㄋㄧㄝˋ nieh niè
the temple

顳顬(ㄋㄧㄝˋ ㄖㄨˊ)
(physiology) the temple

風部
ㄈㄥ feng fēng

【風】 6837
1. ㄈㄥ feng fēng
1. wind; a gust; breeze; a gale
2. education; influence
3. customs; practices; a fad; fashion; fashionable
4. a scene
5. a style; a manner; deportment; taste
6. fame; reputation
7. rumor
8. ailments supposedly caused by wind and dampness 參看「風濕」

風波(ㄈㄥ ㄅㄛ)
disputes; quarrels; disturbances; restlessness

風伯(ㄈㄥ ㄅㄛˊ) or 風師(ㄈㄥ ㄕ)
the god of wind

風暴(ㄈㄥ ㄅㄠˋ)
a storm; a windstorm

風標(ㄈㄥ ㄅㄧㄠ)
① a wind sock or wind cone; a weathercock ② a typical personal style

風平浪靜(ㄈㄥ ㄆㄧㄥˊ ㄌㄤˋ ㄐㄧㄥˋ)
a calm and unruffled sea; calm and tranquil: 暴風雨過後，海上風平浪靜。After the storm the sea was calm.

風馬牛不相及(ㄈㄥ ㄇㄚˇ ㄋㄧㄡˊ ㄅㄨˋ ㄒㄧㄤ ㄐㄧˊ)
things entirely not related; irrelevant

風媒花(ㄈㄥ ㄇㄟˊ ㄏㄨㄚ)
an anemophilous flower

風貌(ㄈㄥ ㄇㄠˋ)
① style and features ② a view; a scene

風帽(ㄈㄥ ㄇㄠˋ)
a hood; a cowl-like hat worn in winter

風靡一時(ㄈㄥ ㄇㄧˇ ㄧˋ ㄕˊ)
to become a fad or vogue of the time; to become fashionable for a time

風木(ㄈㄥ ㄇㄨˋ) or 風樹(ㄈㄥ ㄕㄨˋ)
to regret that one failed to take good care of his parents while they were alive

風帆(ㄈㄥ ㄈㄢ)
a sailboat
風範(ㄈㄥ ㄈㄢˋ)
① appearance; an air; a manner ② a model; a paragon
風風雨雨(ㄈㄥ ㄈㄥ ㄩˇ ㄩˇ)
① storms; winds and rains ② rumors being rife; gossips going the rounds
風德(ㄈㄥ ㄉㄜˊ)
to exert moral influence
風度(ㄈㄥ ㄉㄨˋ)
a manner; poise; bearing; carriage
風度翩翩(ㄈㄥ ㄉㄨˋ ㄆㄧㄢ ㄆㄧㄢ)
(said of a young man) graceful bearing or carriage
風動(ㄈㄥ ㄉㄨㄥˋ)
to receive popular response or wide support
風頭(ㄈㄥ ˙ㄊㄡ)
① a situation; circumstances; the trend of events (as affecting a person) ② the way the wind blows ③ popularity, distinction or prominence (of a person of accomplishment); the limelight: 她似乎很愛出風頭。She seems fond of the limelight.
風頭甚健(ㄈㄥ ˙ㄊㄡ ㄕㄣˋ ㄐㄧㄢˋ)
very popular; enjoying great distinction
風調雨順(ㄈㄥ ㄊㄧㄠˊ ㄩˇ ㄕㄨㄣˋ)
favorable weather (for raising crops); a timely wind and rain
風土誌(ㄈㄥ ㄊㄨˇ ㄓˋ)
a record of local customs, tradition, etc.
風土人情(ㄈㄥ ㄊㄨˇ ㄖㄣˊ ㄑㄧㄥˊ)
local customs and practices
風浪(ㄈㄥ ㄌㄤˋ)
① wind and waves at sea ② a storm (in the figurative sense): 他是個久經風浪的人。He has weathered many a storm.
風裏來，雨裏去(ㄈㄥ ㄌㄧˇ ㄌㄞˊ, ㄩˇ ㄌㄧˇ ㄑㄩˋ)
to come in the wind and go in the rain—to accomplish one's task even in the teeth of wind and rain
風力(ㄈㄥ ㄌㄧˋ)
the force of the wind; wind power
風力表(ㄈㄥ ㄌㄧˋ ㄅㄧㄠˇ)
a wind gauge; an anemometer
風流(ㄈㄥ ㄌㄧㄡˊ)
① elegant style; a refined taste; intellectually sophisticated ② to have a weakness for women
風流倜儻(ㄈㄥ ㄌㄧㄡˊ ㄊㄧˋ ㄊㄤˇ)
casual and elegant bearing; charming; dashing
風流債(ㄈㄥ ㄌㄧㄡˊ ㄓㄞˋ)
predestined romantic ties between a man and a woman
風流事(ㄈㄥ ㄌㄧㄡˊ ㄕˋ)
① an affair; a romance; a romantic episode ② poetic pursuits
風流罪過(ㄈㄥ ㄌㄧㄡˊ ㄗㄨㄟˋ ㄍㄨㄛˋ)
blemishes; small defects
風流雲散(ㄈㄥ ㄌㄧㄡˊ ㄩㄣˊ ㄙㄢˋ)
① to dissipate to nothing; to vanish without a trace ② (said of old companions) separated and dispersed
風流韻事(ㄈㄥ ㄌㄧㄡˊ ㄩㄣˋ ㄕˋ)
a romantic affair; gaieties
風涼(ㄈㄥ ㄌㄧㄤˊ)
cool
風涼話(ㄈㄥ ㄌㄧㄤˊ ㄏㄨㄚˋ)
irresponsible and satiric remarks; sarcastic comments: 我討厭他的風涼話。I hate his sarcastic comments.
風鈴(ㄈㄥ ㄌㄧㄥˊ)
aeolian bells (hung on the eaves of pagodas or temple buildings)
風鈴草(ㄈㄥ ㄌㄧㄥˊ ㄘㄠˇ)
Canterbury bells; bellflowers
風格(ㄈㄥ ㄍㄜˊ)
a style: 風格即其人。The style is the man.
風概(ㄈㄥ ㄍㄞˋ)
bearing and magnanimity
風乾(ㄈㄥ ㄍㄢ)
to dry in the shade by air or wind; to air-dry
風骨(ㄈㄥ ㄍㄨˇ)
① incorruptibility; moral fortitude; the strength of character ② the vigor of style
風光(ㄈㄥ ㄍㄨㄤ)
① scenery ② elegant style or taste ③ glory; good reputation
風口(ㄈㄥ ㄎㄡˇ)
a place where there is a draught
風和日暖(ㄈㄥ ㄏㄜˊ ㄖˋ ㄋㄨㄢˇ) or 風和日麗(ㄈㄥ ㄏㄜˊ ㄖˋ ㄌㄧˋ)
the bright sunshine and gentle breezes; warm and sunny weather
風寒(ㄈㄥ ㄏㄢˊ)
a cold; flu; a chill: 大夫說她是受了風寒。The doctor said that she has caught a chill.
風花雪月(ㄈㄥ ㄏㄨㄚ ㄒㄩㄝˇ ㄩㄝˋ)
wind, flowers, snow and the moon—all ingredients for a gay life; love affairs
風華(ㄈㄥ ㄏㄨㄚˊ)
elegance and talent; grace
風華絕代(ㄈㄥ ㄏㄨㄚˊ ㄐㄩㄝˊ ㄉㄞˋ)
unsurpassed elegance and intellectual brilliance
風化(ㄈㄥ ㄏㄨㄚˋ)
① customs and cultural influence; decency ② (chemistry) efflorescence ③ erosion by the elements
風化區(ㄈㄥ ㄏㄨㄚˋ ㄑㄩ)
a district of loose women
風化作用(ㄈㄥ ㄏㄨㄚˋ ㄗㄨㄛˋ ㄩㄥˋ)
(chemistry) efflorescence
風化罪(ㄈㄥ ㄏㄨㄚˋ ㄗㄨㄟˋ)
an offense against public morals
風紀(ㄈㄥ ㄐㄧˋ)
discipline (of students, troops, etc.); general moral standards
風節(ㄈㄥ ㄐㄧㄝˊ)
moral fortitude
風教(ㄈㄥ ㄐㄧㄠˋ)
customs and cultural influence
風景(ㄈㄥ ㄐㄧㄥˇ)
scenery; a landscape
風景畫(ㄈㄥ ㄐㄧㄥˇ ㄏㄨㄚˋ)
a landscape
風景區(ㄈㄥ ㄐㄧㄥˇ ㄑㄩ)
scenic spots
風鏡(ㄈㄥ ㄐㄧㄥˋ)
goggles
風捲殘雲(ㄈㄥ ㄐㄩㄢˇ ㄘㄢˊ ㄩㄣˊ)
like wind sweeping away clouds—to make a clean sweep of something
風起雲湧(ㄈㄥ ㄑㄧˇ ㄩㄣˊ ㄩㄥˇ)

〔風部〕

like rising winds and surging clouds—popular support; an enthusiastic response

風氣(ㄈㄥ ㄑ丨ˋ)
①customs; a general mood; common practices; general environment or circumstances; traditions ②air; manner; bearing

風氣未開(ㄈㄥ ㄑ丨ˋ ㄨㄟˋ ㄎㄞ)
comparatively primitive or simple in customs; uncivilized; culturally backward

風琴(ㄈㄥ ㄑ丨ㄣˊ)
(a musical instrument) an organ

風情(ㄈㄥ ㄑ丨ㄥˊ)
①romantic feelings ②flirtatious expressions; coquetry: 她善於賣弄風情。She is good at playing the coquetry. ③fine taste; refined feelings

風趣(ㄈㄥ ㄑㄩˋ)
interesting; funny; humorous; witty; wit; a sense of humor: 他說話很風趣。He is a witty talker.

風險(ㄈㄥ ㄒ丨ㄢˇ)
risk; danger: 從事探險的人必須不怕風險。Those who take exploration must fear no dangers.

風信(ㄈㄥ ㄒ丨ㄣˋ)
the season and direction of wind

風信器(ㄈㄥ ㄒ丨ㄣˋ ㄑ丨ˋ)
a wind cone

風信子(ㄈㄥ ㄒ丨ㄣˋ ㄗˇ)
(botany) a hyacinth 亦作「洋水仙」

風箱(ㄈㄥ ㄒ丨ㄤ)
bellows; a wind chest

風向(ㄈㄥ ㄒ丨ㄤˋ)
the direction of wind

風行(ㄈㄥ ㄒ丨ㄥˊ)
to become fashionable; to be popular: 這首歌曾經風行一時。The song had a great vogue at one time.

風行草偃(ㄈㄥ ㄒ丨ㄥˊ ㄘㄠˇ 丨ㄢˇ)
(literally) When the wind blows, the grass bends.—the influence of moral teaching

風行一時(ㄈㄥ ㄒ丨ㄥˊ 丨ˋ ㄕˊ)
to be fashionable for a certain duration; to become a fad of the time

風穴(ㄈㄥ ㄒㄩㄝˋ)
where the wind comes from

風致(ㄈㄥ ㄓˋ)
appearance; manner and bearing; poise: 風致極佳。One's appearance and bearing are excellent.

風疹(ㄈㄥ ㄓㄣˇ)
rubeola; rubella; German measles; urticaria

風箏(ㄈㄥ ㄓㄥ)
a kite: 那些孩子們在廣場上放風箏。Those children were flying kites in the square.

風燭(ㄈㄥ ㄓㄨˊ) or 風中殘燭(ㄈㄥ ㄓㄨㄥ ㄘㄢˊ ㄓㄨˊ)
a lighted candle in the wind—old and ailing

風燭殘年(ㄈㄥ ㄓㄨˊ ㄘㄢˊ ㄋ丨ㄢˊ)
old and ailing like a candle guttering in the wind—old age; in the closing years of one's life

風馳電掣(ㄈㄥ ㄔˊ ㄉ丨ㄢˋ ㄔㄜˋ)
to whip along as fast as wind and lightning

風車(ㄈㄥ ㄔㄜ)
①a windmill ②a kind of toy wheel which turns by the power of wind ③a winnower

風車花(ㄈㄥ ㄔㄜ ㄏㄨㄚ)
a passionflower 亦作「西番蓮」

風潮(ㄈㄥ ㄔㄠˊ)
①directions of wind and tide ②disturbance, upheaval; a storm; unrest

風塵(ㄈㄥ ㄔㄣˊ)
①hardships of traveling around ②confusion of the world ③the world of prostitution

風塵僕僕(ㄈㄥ ㄔㄣˊ ㄆㄨˊ ㄆㄨˊ)
dust-covered and tired from traveling; to be travel-worn and weary

風塵女郎(ㄈㄥ ㄔㄣˊ ㄋㄩˇ ㄌㄤˊ)
a prostitute; a call girl

風成岩(ㄈㄥ ㄔㄥˊ 丨ㄢˊ)
(geology) aeolian rocks

風吹草動(ㄈㄥ ㄔㄨㄟ ㄘㄠˇ ㄉㄨㄥˋ)
the rustle of leaves in the wind—slight commotion; disquiet; slight disturbance

風傳(ㄈㄥ ㄔㄨㄢˊ)
①It is said that.... 或It is rumored that.... ②hearsay; rumor

風濕(ㄈㄥ ㄕ)
rheumatism

風沙(ㄈㄥ ㄕㄚ)
a sandy wind; a sandstorm

風扇(ㄈㄥ ㄕㄢˋ)
①a fan ②an electric fan

風神(ㄈㄥ ㄕㄣˊ)
①the god of wind; Aeolus ②poise; bearing; manner

風尚(ㄈㄥ ㄕㄤˋ)
fashion; a custom; a vogue; a fad; taste of the time

風聲(ㄈㄥ ㄕㄥ)
①news; rumor; information: 你聽到戰爭的風聲沒有? Have you got news of the war? ②(now rarely) teaching

風聲鶴唳(ㄈㄥ ㄕㄥ ㄏㄜˋ ㄌ丨ˋ)
to sense danger everywhere; very scared and jittery; to be afraid of one's own shadow

風水(ㄈㄥ ·ㄕㄨㄟ)
fengshui—the direction and surroundings of a house or tomb, supposed to have an influence on the fortune of a family and their offsprings; a geomantic omen: 他很會看風水。He is good at practicing geomancy.

風水先生(ㄈㄥ ·ㄕㄨㄟ ㄒ丨ㄢ ·ㄕㄥ)
a geomancer

風霜(ㄈㄥ ㄕㄨㄤ)
①wind and frost—hardships; suffering (usually referring to traveling) ②severe; severity ③time-honored

風姿(ㄈㄥ ㄗ)
looks; graceful bearing

風姿綽約(ㄈㄥ ㄗ ㄔㄨㄛˋ ㄩㄝ)
(said of a woman) charming poise and graceful bearing

風災(ㄈㄥ ㄗㄞ)
disaster caused by strong winds, typhoons, etc.

風采(ㄈㄥ ㄘㄞˇ)
an elegant manner and appearance; fine deportment; graceful bearing

風操(ㄈㄥ ㄘㄠ)
style, character and behavior

風餐露宿(ㄈㄥ ㄘㄢ ㄌㄨˋ ㄙㄨˋ)

(literally) to eat in the wind and sleep in the open air —the hardships of traveling or fieldwork
風從(ㄈㄥ ㄘㄨㄥˊ)
to follow or obey (a popular leader) willingly
風絲(ㄈㄥ ㄙ)
slight breezes; zephyrs
風騷(ㄈㄥ ㄙㄠ)
①(said of women) seductive; flirtatious; coquettish ②refinement in literary works; literary excellence
風掃落葉(ㄈㄥ ㄙㄠˇ ㄌㄨㄛˋ ㄧㄝˋ)
(literally) like wind sweeping away the fallen leaves —irresistible
風俗(ㄈㄥ ㄙㄨˊ)
customs; accepted practices
風俗習慣(ㄈㄥ ㄙㄨˊ ㄒㄧˊ ㄍㄨㄢˋ)
customs and habits
風速(ㄈㄥ ㄙㄨˋ)
wind velocity (or speed)
風衣(ㄈㄥ ㄧ)
a thin, usually waterproof, overcoat for warding off wind and rain
風雅(ㄈㄥ ㄧㄚˇ)
①matters pertaining to writing of poems or other literary works; refinement ②graceful; tasteful; refined: 他的舉止風雅。He has refined manners.
風謠(ㄈㄥ ㄧㄠˊ)
customs and ditties
風言風語(ㄈㄥ ㄧㄢˊ ㄈㄥ ㄩˇ)or 風言霧語(ㄈㄥ ㄧㄢˊ ㄨˋ ㄩˇ)
groundless, satiric remarks; gossips; slanderous gossips: 風言風語，不聽也罷。You might as well not listen to the slanderous gossips.
風物(ㄈㄥ ㄨˋ)
sights; scenes; scenery
風味(ㄈㄥ ㄨㄟˋ)
①the bearing and taste of a person ②elegance ③the taste and style of food
風聞(ㄈㄥ ㄨㄣˊ)
rumored; according to unconfirmed reports; to get wind of
風雨(ㄈㄥ ㄩˇ)
wind and rain; the elements —trials and hardships
風雨表(ㄈㄥ ㄩˇ ㄅㄧㄠˇ)
a barometer 亦作「氣壓計」
風雨飄搖(ㄈㄥ ㄩˇ ㄆㄧㄠ ㄧㄠˊ)
precarious; critical (times)
風雨同舟(ㄈㄥ ㄩˇ ㄊㄨㄥˊ ㄓㄡ)
to be in the same boat; sharing a common fate
風雨淒其(ㄈㄥ ㄩˇ ㄑㄧ ㄑㄧˊ)
dejection or gloom one feels in time of incessant wind and rain
風雨如晦，雞鳴不已(ㄈㄥ ㄩˇ ㄖㄨˊ ㄏㄨㄟˋ, ㄐㄧ ㄇㄧㄥˊ ㄅㄨˋ ㄧˇ)
(figuratively) to remain sober when the rest of the world is in confusion; to think of the just in times of stress (詩經・國風・風雨)
風雨無阻(ㄈㄥ ㄩˇ ㄨˊ ㄗㄨˇ)
to take place on schedule regardless of weather changes; rain or shine: 我們明天一定到那裏，風雨無阻。We will be there tomorrow, rain or shine.
風月(ㄈㄥ ㄩㄝˋ)
①matters concerning love; seductive arts of a woman ②easy and random (talks, etc.)
風月場中(ㄈㄥ ㄩㄝˋ ㄔㄤˇ ㄓㄨㄥ)
places of debauchery or sensuality; the world of carnal pleasure
風月無邊(ㄈㄥ ㄩㄝˋ ㄨˊ ㄅㄧㄢ)
①The wonders of natural beauty are boundless. ②An amorous affair knows no limits.
風雲(ㄈㄥ ㄩㄣˊ)
①wind and clouds ②unpredictable changes ③high-positioned; high and exalted; imposing
風雲變色(ㄈㄥ ㄩㄣˊ ㄅㄧㄢˋ ㄙㄜˋ)
(said of a disaster) catastrophic; drastic change of a political situation
風雲際會(ㄈㄥ ㄩㄣˊ ㄐㄧˋ ㄏㄨㄟˋ)
the gathering of heroes or talented persons
風雲人物(ㄈㄥ ㄩㄣˊ ㄖㄣˊ ㄨˋ)
a heroic figure; a famed personage; one who is constantly in the news; a man of the hour
風韻(ㄈㄥ ㄩㄣˋ)
charms; poise and bearing
風韻猶存(ㄈㄥ ㄩㄣˋ ㄧㄡˊ ㄘㄨㄣˊ)
(said of a middle-aged woman) to look still attractive

【風】 6837
2. ㄈㄥˋ fenq fèng
1. to announce; to make known
2. to ridicule; to satirize
3. to blow

五畫

【颯】 6838
ㄙㄚˋ sah sà
1. the sound of wind; rustling
2. weakened; failing; declining
颯沓(ㄙㄚˋ ㄊㄚˋ)
①crowded; numerous; abundant ②flying in a flock
颯遝(ㄙㄚˋ ㄊㄚˋ)
(said of sound) roaring and reverberating
颯然(ㄙㄚˋ ㄖㄢˊ)
the sound of wind
颯颯(ㄙㄚˋ ㄙㄚˋ)
①the swishing sound of wind ②the pattering sound of rain

【颱】 6839
ㄊㄞˊ tair tái
a typhoon; a hurricane
颱風(ㄊㄞˊ ㄈㄥ)
a typhoon; a hurricane
颱風警報(ㄊㄞˊ ㄈㄥ ㄐㄧㄥˇ ㄅㄠˋ)
a typhoon warning
颱風眼(ㄊㄞˊ ㄈㄥ ㄧㄢˇ)
a typhoon eye

六畫

【颳】 6840
ㄍㄨㄚ gua guā
wind blowing; to blow
颳風(ㄍㄨㄚ ㄈㄥ)
wind blowing

八畫

【颶】 6841
ㄐㄩˋ jiuh jù
a hurricane; a gale; strong gusts at sea; a cyclone
颶風(ㄐㄩˋ ㄈㄥ)
a hurricane; a gale; a cyclone

〔飛部〕

九畫

【颺】6842 ㄧㄤˊ yang yáng
1. blown or tossed about by the wind; to float
2. to fly or blow away
3. to scatter; to spread

颺帆 or 揚帆(ㄧㄤˊ ㄈㄢ) to set sail

十畫

【颼】6843 ㄙㄡ sou sōu
1. blown about by wind
2. the swishing sound of a fast-flying object, as an arrow

【颻】6844 ㄧㄠˊ yaw yáo
waving and drifting with the wind

十一畫

【飄】6845 ㄆㄧㄠ piau piāo
1. to blow; to float (in the air); to waft; to move with the wind: 風飄葉落。The wind blows and the leaves fall from the trees.
2. a cyclone; a whirling wind
3. to float; to drift (on the water) 亦作「漂」: 樹葉在水上飄流著。Leaves were floating on the water.

飄泊 or 飄薄(ㄆㄧㄠ ㄅㄛˊ) to drift about—with no fixed lodging place; to wander: 他在異鄉飄泊了三年。He wandered aimlessly in a strange land for three years.

飄布(ㄆㄧㄠ ㄅㄨˋ) an identification badge made of cloth issued by secret societies to their members

飄蓬(ㄆㄧㄠ ㄆㄥˊ) ① scattered; dispersed ② to drift about alone

飄飄(ㄆㄧㄠ ㄆㄧㄠ) ① lightly; airily ② wind blowing ③ to be driven; to wander

飄飄然(ㄆㄧㄠ ㄆㄧㄠ ㄖㄢˊ) feeling slightly comfortably dizzy, as after a light drink; complacent; self-satisfaction; having a feeling of euphoria or elation; light-footed

飄飄欲仙(ㄆㄧㄠ ㄆㄧㄠ ㄩˋ ㄒㄧㄢ) light, airy, comfortable, complacent

飄風(ㄆㄧㄠ ㄈㄥ) ① a violent wind ② a whirlwind; a cyclone

飄帶(ㄆㄧㄠ ㄉㄞˋ) long bands or ribbons attached to clothes, hats, etc.

飄蕩 or 漂蕩(ㄆㄧㄠ ㄉㄤˋ) to drift along without fixed lodging; to float: 小船隨波飄蕩。The boat floated off with the tide.

飄流 or 漂流(ㄆㄧㄠ ㄌㄧㄡˊ) ① to drift; to float ② to knock about; to wander aimlessly

飄零(ㄆㄧㄠ ㄌㄧㄥˊ) ①(said of leaves and plants) falling and withering ② to drift about alone; wandering; homeless

飄落(ㄆㄧㄠ ㄌㄨㄛˋ) to fall down slowly in the air

飄忽(ㄆㄧㄠ ㄏㄨ) ① to float in the air hither and thither ② to have no fixed address ③ light and speedy

飄忽不定(ㄆㄧㄠ ㄏㄨ ㄅㄨˋ ㄉㄧㄥˋ) to drift from place to place: 他的行踪飄忽不定。He drifted from place to place.

飄疾(ㄆㄧㄠ ㄐㄧˊ) quickly; rapidly

飄蕭(ㄆㄧㄠ ㄒㄧㄠ) withering and dilapidated

飄雪(ㄆㄧㄠ ㄒㄩㄝˇ) snowflakes falling

飄然(ㄆㄧㄠ ㄖㄢˊ) gracefully; airily; flying

飄散(ㄆㄧㄠ ㄙㄢˋ) dispersed and flying about

飄逸(ㄆㄧㄠ ㄧˋ) elegant; high, stately and graceful: 他的神采飄逸。He has an elegant bearing.

飄搖(ㄆㄧㄠ ㄧㄠˊ) ① to dance and toss about in the wind ② precarious; unsteady

飄洋(ㄆㄧㄠ ㄧㄤˊ) to take a sea voyage

飄揚(ㄆㄧㄠ ㄧㄤˊ) to be blown about in the wind; to flutter

十二畫

【飆】6846 (飇) ㄅㄧㄠ biau biāo
violent winds; gales

飆車(ㄅㄧㄠ ㄔㄜ) to speed a car or a motorcycle

飛部
ㄈㄟ fei fēi

【飛】6847 ㄈㄟ fei fēi
1. to fly; to flit: 我們自倫敦飛抵巴黎。We flew from London to Paris.
2. quickly; rapidly
3. high, as a bridge
4. to hang in the air; in the air

飛報(ㄈㄟ ㄅㄠˋ) to report by a fleet messenger; an express message; an urgent dispatch

飛奔(ㄈㄟ ㄅㄣ) or 飛跑(ㄈㄟ ㄆㄠˇ) to run very fast; to fly: 他沿路飛奔。He flew down the road.

飛盤(ㄈㄟ ㄆㄢˊ) a Frisbee

飛蓬(ㄈㄟ ㄆㄥˊ) ① *Erigeron acris*, a species of raspberry ② to drift or toss about in the wind—uncertain or unsteady ③(said of hair) disheveled

飛瀑(ㄈㄟ ㄆㄨˋ) a waterfall; a cascade; a cataract

飛沫(ㄈㄟ ㄇㄛˋ) droplets (of a waterfall or from other sputtering sources)

飛毛腿(ㄈㄟ ㄇㄠˊ ㄊㄨㄟˇ) a fast runner; fleet-footed

飛刀(ㄈㄟ ㄉㄠ)

①to wield the knife ②a flying knife

飛彈(ㄈㄟ ㄉㄢˋ)
①a stray bullet or shell ②a missile

飛碟(ㄈㄟ ㄉㄧㄝˊ)
a flying saucer; an unidentified flying object (UFO)

飛短流長(ㄈㄟ ㄉㄨㄢˇ ㄌㄧㄡˊ ㄔㄤˊ)
rumors; malicious gossips: 她太喜歡飛短流長了。She is too fond of gossip.

飛騰(ㄈㄟ ㄊㄥˊ)
①to fly high (as one's fortune) ②to soar (as prices)

飛梯(ㄈㄟ ㄊㄧ)
a kind of ladder used in ancient times for attacking the enemy by scaling the city wall

飛艇(ㄈㄟ ㄊㄧㄥˇ)
an airship; a flying boat

飛鳥(ㄈㄟ ㄋㄧㄠˇ)
flying birds

飛來橫禍(ㄈㄟ ㄌㄞˊ ㄏㄥˊ ㄏㄨㄛˋ)or 飛禍(ㄈㄟ ㄏㄨㄛˋ)
sudden, unexpected calamity or misfortune

飛來豔福(ㄈㄟ ㄌㄞˊ ㄧㄢˋ ㄈㄨˊ)
an unexpected romance or affair with a beauty

飛梁(ㄈㄟ ㄌㄧㄤˊ)
a single-span bridge

飛輪(ㄈㄟ ㄌㄨㄣˊ)
①a balance wheel; a flywheel ②a sprocket wheel

飛快(ㄈㄟ ㄎㄨㄞˋ)
①fast; rapidly; with lightning speed; at full speed ②extremely sharp

飛黃騰達(ㄈㄟ ㄏㄨㄤˊ ㄊㄥˊ ㄉㄚˊ)
to make rapid advances in one's career; to ride on the crest of one's success

飛機(ㄈㄟ ㄐㄧ)
an airplane; a plane: 他們搭飛機去香港。They went to Hong Kong by plane.

飛機棚(ㄈㄟ ㄐㄧ ㄆㄥˊ)or 飛機庫(ㄈㄟ ㄐㄧ ㄎㄨˋ)
a hangar

飛機場(ㄈㄟ ㄐㄧ ㄔㄤˇ)
an airport; an airfield; an airdrome

飛機失事(ㄈㄟ ㄐㄧ ㄕ ㄕˋ)
an air accident; a plane crash

飛騎(ㄈㄟ ㄐㄧˋ)
light cavalry

飛劍(ㄈㄟ ㄐㄧㄢˋ)
(in Chinese legend) a sword which can take the life of a person miles away; a flying sword

飛濺(ㄈㄟ ㄐㄧㄢˋ)
to sputter; to splash: 浪花飛濺到岩石上。The waves splashed on the rock.

飛將軍(ㄈㄟ ㄐㄧㄤ ㄐㄩㄣ)or 飛將(ㄈㄟ ㄐㄧㄤˋ)
①the nickname of Li Kuang (李廣), one of the greatest generals in the Han Dynasty ②an ace pilot

飛禽(ㄈㄟ ㄑㄧㄣˊ)
birds

飛禽走獸(ㄈㄟ ㄑㄧㄣˊ ㄗㄡˇ ㄕㄡˋ)
birds and beasts

飛泉(ㄈㄟ ㄑㄩㄢˊ)
leaping fountains; a geyser; a cliffside spring

飛檄(ㄈㄟ ㄒㄧˊ)
to issue a manifesto

飛翔(ㄈㄟ ㄒㄧㄤˊ)
to fly; to glide in the air; to hover in the air

飛行(ㄈㄟ ㄒㄧㄥˊ)
to fly, as a plane; flight; flying: 飛行是鳥類天生的能力。Flight is natural to birds.

飛行家(ㄈㄟ ㄒㄧㄥˊ ㄐㄧㄚ)
a flyer

飛行甲板(ㄈㄟ ㄒㄧㄥˊ ㄐㄧㄚˇ ㄅㄢˇ)
a flight deck

飛行員(ㄈㄟ ㄒㄧㄥˊ ㄩㄢˊ)
the pilot of a plane

飛雪(ㄈㄟ ㄒㄩㄝˇ)
the falling snow

飛針走線(ㄈㄟ ㄓㄣ ㄗㄡˇ ㄒㄧㄢˋ)
to sew quickly

飛漲(ㄈㄟ ㄓㄤˇ)
(said of prices) to soar rapidly; to skyrocket

飛馳(ㄈㄟ ㄔˊ)
to speed along: 時間飛馳而過。The time sped quickly by.

飛船(ㄈㄟ ㄔㄨㄢˊ)
an airship

飛蟲(ㄈㄟ ㄔㄨㄥˊ)
flying insects

飛石(ㄈㄟ ㄕˊ)
stone missiles used in ancient warfare

飛矢(ㄈㄟ ㄕˇ)
a flying arrow

飛砂走石(ㄈㄟ ㄕㄚ ㄗㄡˇ ㄕˊ)
sand and stones flying all about—a very strong wind

飛昇(ㄈㄟ ㄕㄥ)
to soar; to ascend

飛聲騰實(ㄈㄟ ㄕㄥ ㄊㄥˊ ㄕˊ)
excellent in fame as in substance

飛鼠(ㄈㄟ ㄕㄨˇ)
①a bat ②a squirrel glider

飛賊(ㄈㄟ ㄗㄟˊ)
①a thief capable of acrobatic feats; a nimble-footed burglar; a cat burglar ②an intruding enemy airman; an air marauder

飛走(ㄈㄟ ㄗㄡˇ)
①birds and beasts ②to fly away

飛速(ㄈㄟ ㄙㄨˋ)
urgent; quickly; at full speed: 我們的重工業正飛速發展。Our heavy industry is progressing quickly.

飛送(ㄈㄟ ㄙㄨㄥˋ)
to send by an express courier

飛蛾(ㄈㄟ ㄜˊ)
the flying moth; the moth

飛蛾赴火(ㄈㄟ ㄜˊ ㄈㄨˋ ㄏㄨㄛˇ)or 飛蛾投火(ㄈㄟ ㄜˊ ㄊㄡˊ ㄏㄨㄛˇ)or 飛蛾撲火(ㄈㄟ ㄜˊ ㄆㄨ ㄏㄨㄛˇ)
(literally) The flying moth is forever attracted by the flame.—to dig one's own grave; to flirt with death

飛檐(ㄈㄟ ㄧㄢˊ)
the up-turned eaves on the corners of a roof

飛簷走壁(ㄈㄟ ㄧㄢˊ ㄗㄡˇ ㄅㄧˋ)
(said of swordsmen, etc. in old Chinese novels) to leap onto roofs and vault over walls; to fly on eaves and walk on walls—acrobatic feats

飛眼(ㄈㄟ ㄧㄢˇ)
to speak with the eyes; to make eyes; to ogle

飛燕(ㄈㄟ ㄧㄢˋ)
①nimble and quick ②Flying Swallow—name of a queen in the Han Dynasty, a

famous skinny beauty

飛揚(ㄈㄟ ㄧㄤˊ)
to rise up and flutter, as a flag; to float in the air, as music; to fly about, as dust: 到處飛揚着歡樂的笑聲。Laughter was floating in the air.

飛揚跋扈(ㄈㄟ ㄧㄤˊ ㄅㄚˊ ㄏㄨˋ)
unruly and haughty

飛鷹走狗(ㄈㄟ ㄧㄥ ㄗㄡˇ ㄍㄡˇ)
to release falcons and unleash dogs—hunting

飛舞(ㄈㄟ ㄨˇ)
① to dance in the wind: 雪花在空中飛舞。 Snowflakes are dancing in the air. ② to flutter: 蝴蝶在花叢中翩然飛舞。 Butterflies fluttered from flower to flower.

飛吻(ㄈㄟ ㄨㄣˇ)
to throw someone a kiss

飛魚(ㄈㄟ ㄩˊ)
a flying fish; a skipjack

飛魚飛彈(ㄈㄟ ㄩˊ ㄈㄟ ㄉㄢˋ)
(military) an Exocet

飛語(ㄈㄟ ㄩˇ)
groundless words; rumors

飛躍(ㄈㄟ ㄩㄝˋ)
by leaps and bounds; advancing rapidly

十二畫

【飜】 6848
(翻) ㄈㄢ fan fān
to turn over

食部
ㄕˊ shyr shí

【食】 6849
1. ㄕˊ shyr shí

1. to eat
2. food; meal
3. livelihood; living
4. (an old usage) salary; pay
5. same as 蝕—eclipse

食不甘味(ㄕˊ ˙ㄅㄨ ㄍㄢ ㄨㄟˋ)or 食不知味(ㄕˊ ˙ㄅㄨ ㄓ ㄨㄟˋ)
to eat food but without knowing its taste—deep anxiety, grief, etc.

食不果腹(ㄕˊ ˙ㄅㄨ ㄍㄨㄛˇ ㄈㄨˋ)
to have not enough to eat

食不厭精(ㄕˊ ˙ㄅㄨ ㄧㄢˋ ㄐㄧㄥ)
to be meticulous about fine food

食品(ㄕˊ ㄆㄧㄣˇ)
foods; food items; foodstuffs: 穀類和肉都是食品。Grain and meat are foodstuffs.

食品防腐劑(ㄕˊ ㄆㄧㄣˇ ㄈㄤˊ ㄈㄨˇ ㄐㄧˋ)
food disinfectant

食品店(ㄕˊ ㄆㄧㄣˇ ㄉㄧㄢˋ)
a store for selling food items; a food store; a confectionary; a bakery

食品加工(ㄕˊ ㄆㄧㄣˇ ㄐㄧㄚ ㄍㄨㄥ)
food processing

食譜(ㄕˊ ㄆㄨˇ)
a cookbook; a collection of recipes: 請把食譜借給我。 Please lend me your cookbook.

食毛踐土(ㄕˊ ㄇㄠˊ ㄐㄧㄢˋ ㄊㄨˇ)
to live on the land and eat what it produces

食米(ㄕˊ ㄇㄧˇ)
rice (husked): 大部分中國人以食米爲生。Most Chinese live on rice.

食俸(ㄕˊ ㄈㄥˋ)
① the salary of a public official ② to be in government service

食道(ㄕˊ ㄉㄠˋ)
① the ways of eating; table manners ② the route for transporting foodstuffs ③ the gullet; the esophagus

食道癌(ㄕˊ ㄉㄠˋ ㄧㄢˊ)
esophageal cancer; carcinoma esophagi

食道炎(ㄕˊ ㄉㄠˋ ㄧㄢˊ)
esophagitis

食堂(ㄕˊ ㄊㄤˊ)
a mess hall; the restaurant

食糖(ㄕˊ ㄊㄤˊ)
sugar

食料(ㄕˊ ㄌㄧㄠˋ)
edibles; foodstuffs; eatables

食糧(ㄕˊ ㄌㄧㄤˊ)
foodstuffs; food grain; provisions: 我們冬季的食糧夠嗎? Have we enough provisions for the winter?

食量(ㄕˊ ㄌㄧㄤˋ)
the quantity of food one consumes; appetite

食祿(ㄕˊ ㄌㄨˋ)
① to draw government pay; to be in public service ② the salary of an official

食古不化(ㄕˊ ㄍㄨˇ ㄅㄨˋ ㄏㄨㄚˋ)
to read a lot of classics without digestion; to be pedantic

食管(ㄕˊ ㄍㄨㄢˇ)
the esophagus 亦作「食道」

食客(ㄕˊ ㄎㄜˋ)
dependent-advisors under a leader in ancient times, especially during the Epoch of Warring States; a person sponging on an aristocrat

食後(ㄕˊ ㄏㄡˋ)
after meal

食火鷄(ㄕˊ ㄏㄨㄛˇ ㄐㄧ)
the cassowary

食具(ㄕˊ ㄐㄩˋ)
a table service (such as bowls, etc.)

食前(ㄕˊ ㄑㄧㄢˊ)
before meal

食指(ㄕˊ ㄓˇ)
the index finger

食指浩繁(ㄕˊ ㄓˇ ㄏㄠˋ ㄈㄢˊ)
many mouths to feed

食蟲動物(ㄕˊ ㄔㄨㄥˊ ㄉㄨㄥˋ ㄨˋ)
an insectivore; insectivorous animals

食蟲類(ㄕˊ ㄔㄨㄥˊ ㄌㄟˋ)
the insectivora

食蟲植物(ㄕˊ ㄔㄨㄥˊ ㄓˊ ㄨˋ)
an insectivore; insectivorous plants

食少事繁(ㄕˊ ㄕㄠˇ ㄕˋ ㄈㄢˊ)
to eat little and work a lot—won't be able to last long

食肉動物 (ㄕˊ ㄖㄡˋ ㄉㄨㄥˋ ㄨˋ)
the carnivore

食肉類(ㄕˊ ㄖㄡˋ ㄌㄟˋ)
the carnivora

食肉寢皮(ㄕˊ ㄖㄡˋ ㄑㄧㄣˇ ㄆㄧˊ)
(literally) to eat an enemy's flesh and sleep on his hide—deep hatred for an enemy

食肉獸(ㄕˊ ㄖㄡˋ ㄕㄡˋ)
carnivorous animals

食草動物(ㄕˊ ㄘㄠˇ ㄉㄨㄥˋ ㄨˋ)
herbivorous animals; herbivores

食草獸(ㄕˊ ㄘㄠˇ ㄕㄡˋ)
herbivorous animals

食色性也(ㄕˊ ㄙㄜˋ ㄒㄧㄥˋ ㄧㄝˇ)
The desire for food and sex is part of human nature.

食宿(ㄕˊ ㄙㄨˋ)
board and lodging; bed and board

食而不化(ㄕˊ ㄦˊ ㄅㄨˋ ㄏㄨㄚˋ)
to eat without digesting—to read without real comprehension

食蟻獸(ㄕˊ ㄧˇ ㄕㄡˋ)
the anteater; the Ameisenbär

食邑(ㄕˊ ㄧˋ)
a fief granted to a meritorious person in ancient times

食油(ㄕˊ ㄧㄡˊ)
edible oil

食鹽(ㄕˊ ㄧㄢˊ)
kitchen salt; table salt

食言(ㄕˊ ㄧㄢˊ)
to break one's words or promise

食言而肥(ㄕˊ ㄧㄢˊ ㄦˊ ㄈㄟˊ)
to grow fat by eating one's words—to break a promise

食無求飽(ㄕˊ ㄨˊ ㄑㄧㄡˊ ㄅㄠˇ)
to practice pertinence in eating habits

食物(ㄕˊ ㄨˋ)
eatables; provisions; foodstuffs: 牛奶是有價值的食物。Milk is a valuable food.

食物配給(ㄕˊ ㄨˋ ㄆㄟˋ ㄐㄧˇ)
a ration of foodstuffs; food rationing

食物療法(ㄕˊ ㄨˋ ㄌㄧㄠˊ ㄈㄚˇ)
dietotherapy

食物鏈(ㄕˊ ㄨˋ ㄌㄧㄢˋ)
a food chain

食物過敏(ㄕˊ ㄨˋ ㄍㄨㄛˋ ㄇㄧㄣˇ)
food allergy

食物中毒(ㄕˊ ㄨˋ ㄓㄨㄥˋ ㄉㄨˊ)
food poisoning

食慾(ㄕˊ ㄩˋ)
appetite: 這盤菜能促進你的食慾。The dish will whet your appetite.

食慾不振(ㄕˊ ㄩˋ ㄅㄨˋ ㄓㄣˋ)
a poor appetite; lack of appetite: 他今天食慾不振。He has a poor appetite today.

食玉炊桂(ㄕˊ ㄩˋ ㄔㄨㄟ ㄍㄨㄟˋ)
the high living costs

食用(ㄕˊ ㄩㄥˋ)
① edible ② living expenses

食用動物(ㄕˊ ㄩㄥˋ ㄉㄨㄥˋ ㄨˋ)
meat animals

食用植物(ㄕˊ ㄩㄥˋ ㄓˊ ㄨˋ)
edible plants; vegetables

【食】 6849
2. (飼) ㄙˋ syh sì
to feed

二畫

【飢】 6850
ㄐㄧ ji jī
1. hungry; hunger; starving; famine
2. a Chinese family name

飢不擇食(ㄐㄧ ㄅㄨˋ ㄗㄜˊ ㄕˊ)
(both literally and figuratively) When one is hungry, one is not particular about what he is going to eat. 或 Hunger is the best sauce.

飢民(ㄐㄧ ㄇㄧㄣˊ)
starved people; famished people

飢渴(ㄐㄧ ㄎㄜˇ)
hungry and thirsty: 她覺得飢渴。She was feeling hungry and thirsty.

飢困(ㄐㄧ ㄎㄨㄣˋ)
to be beset by hunger and poverty

飢寒交迫(ㄐㄧ ㄏㄢˊ ㄐㄧㄠ ㄆㄛˋ)
to suffer from hunger and cold

飢荒(ㄐㄧ ㄏㄨㄤ)
famine: 千萬人死於飢荒。Thousands died of famine.

飢饉(ㄐㄧ ㄐㄧㄣˇ)
famine

飢驅(ㄐㄧ ㄑㄩ)
driven by hunger—to toil for a living

飢者易為食(ㄐㄧ ㄓㄜˇ ㄧˋ ㄨㄟˊ ㄕˊ)
A hungry person would eat whatever food that is available.

飢腸轆轆(ㄐㄧ ㄔㄤˊ ㄌㄨˋ ㄌㄨˋ)
to feel very hungry

飢色(ㄐㄧ ㄙㄜˋ)
a hungry look

飢餓(ㄐㄧ ㄜˋ)
hunger; hungry; starvation: 所有人都感到飢餓。All the people felt hungry.

【飣】 6851
ㄉㄧㄥˋ dinq dìng
1. food items for the display purpose only
2. flowery language without substance

【飡】 6852
(餐) ㄘㄢ tsan cān
a meal; to eat

三畫

【飧】 6853
(飱) ㄙㄨㄣ suen sūn
1. cooked food
2. supper
3. to mix cooked rice with water

四畫

【飩】 6854
ㄊㄨㄣˊ twen tún
as in 餛飩—stuffed dumplings

【飪】 6855
(餁) ㄖㄣˋ renn rèn
to cook

【飭】 6856
ㄔˋ chyh chì
1. severe
2. reverent; respectful; careful
3. to manage; to make ready; to keep in order
4. to order; to instruct or direct

飭辦(ㄔˋ ㄅㄢˋ)
to instruct a subordinate to do something

飭拿(ㄔˋ ㄋㄚˊ)
to give orders for the arrest of: 警方飭拿刼匪。The police warrant the arrest of robbers.

飭厲(ㄔˋ ㄌㄧˋ)
to exhort; to instruct and encourage 亦作「敕厲」

飭令(ㄔˋ ㄌㄧㄥˋ)
to order; to instruct or direct

飭交(ㄔˋ ㄐㄧㄠ)
to order someone to dispatch forward; to deliver

飭知(ㄔˋ ㄓ)
to inform or notify a subordinate or a lower agency: 他已飭知下屬。He has made orders known to all the subordinates.

飭查(ㄔˋ ㄔㄚˊ)
to order an investigation: 警長已飭查此案。The sheriff ordered an investigation of the case.

飭屬(ㄔˋ ㄕㄨˇ)
to order subordinates (to do

something)
飭遵(ㄔˋ ㄗㄨㄣ)
(said of orders) to be obeyed

【飲】 6857
1. ㄧㄣˇ yiin yǐn
1. to drink
2. drinks: 冷飲 cold drinks 熱飲 hot drinks
3. to swallow (insult, anger, etc.)
4. to be hit (by a bullet, an arrow, etc.)

飲彈(ㄧㄣˇ ㄉㄢˋ)
to be hit by bullets: 他飲彈身亡。He was killed by a bullet.
飲料(ㄧㄣˇ ㄌㄧㄠˋ)
beverages; drinks (usually referring to soft drinks)
飲恨(ㄧㄣˇ ㄏㄣˋ)
① to swallow grievances; to harbor a grudge: 他飲恨而終。He died with a grievance in his heart. ②to be defeated in a competition or contest
飲酒(ㄧㄣˇ ㄐㄧㄡˇ)
to drink wine or liquor
飲泣(ㄧㄣˇ ㄑㄧˋ)
to weep in deep sorrow
飲血(ㄧㄣˇ ㄒㄧㄝˇ)
① to weep in deep sorrow ② to drink blood, as savages do
飲鴆止渴(ㄧㄣˇ ㄓㄣˋ ㄓˇ ㄎㄜˇ)
(literally) to drink poison in order to quench one's thirst —shortsightedness 或 A moment's relief or pleasure can bring endless sufferings to come.
飲茶(ㄧㄣˇ ㄔㄚˊ)
①to drink tea ②(in Kwangtung) to drink tea along with refreshments
飲醇自醉(ㄧㄣˇ ㄔㄨㄣˊ ㄗˋ ㄗㄨㄟˋ)
to win other's support or heart with one's virtue
飲食(ㄧㄣˇ ㄕˊ)
to drink and eat; drink and food: 醫生給病人規定飲食。The doctor put the patient on a diet.
飲食店(ㄧㄣˇ ㄕˊ ㄉㄧㄢˋ)
a small restaurant; an eatery
飲食男女(ㄧㄣˇ ㄕˊ ㄋㄢˊ ㄋㄩˇ)
food and drink and sex —man's major desire
飲食業(ㄧㄣˇ ㄕˊ ㄧㄝˋ)
the catering trade; the restaurant business
飲食無味(ㄧㄣˇ ㄕˊ ㄨˊ ㄨㄟˋ)
to have no appetite for food or drink
飲食衛生(ㄧㄣˇ ㄕˊ ㄨㄟˋ ㄕㄥ)
dietetic hygiene
飲水(ㄧㄣˇ ㄕㄨㄟˇ)
① drinking water ② to drink water
飲水機(ㄧㄣˇ ㄕㄨㄟˇ ㄐㄧ)
a water fountain; a drinking fountain
飲水思源(ㄧㄣˇ ㄕㄨㄟˇ ㄙ ㄩㄢˊ)
(literally) When one drinks water, one thinks of its source.—grateful for favors received; not to forget one's origin
飲醉(ㄧㄣˇ ㄗㄨㄟˋ)
to get drunk
飲用(ㄧㄣˇ ㄩㄥˋ)
to drink: 此水不可飲用。The water is not drinkable.

【飲】 6857
2. ㄧㄣˋ yinn yìn
to make animals drink

飲馬(ㄧㄣˋ ㄇㄚˇ)
to water a horse

【飫】 6858
ㄩˋ yuh yù
1. surfeited; glutted
2. to grant; to confer
3. to feast
4. to eat or drink to repletion

飫聞(ㄩˋ ㄨㄣˊ)
to have heard enough—not again

【飯】 6859
ㄈㄢˋ fann fàn
1. cooked rice; cooked grain for food
2. a meal: 飯前洗手。Wash your hands before you have a meal.
3. to feed
4. a profession; a means of living: 這口飯不容易吃。It is difficult to earn this kind of a living.

飯票(ㄈㄢˋ ㄆㄧㄠˋ)
①a food coupon ②(slang) a husband
飯鋪(ㄈㄢˋ ㄆㄨˋ)
a restaurant; a store selling cooked rice only
飯店(ㄈㄢˋ ㄉㄧㄢˋ)
① a restaurant ② a hotel
飯攤(ㄈㄢˋ ㄊㄢ)
a food stall; a food stand
飯廳(ㄈㄢˋ ㄊㄧㄥ)
a dining room; a mess hall
飯桶(ㄈㄢˋ ㄊㄨㄥˇ)
① a tub for storing cooked rice ② a good-for-nothing; a stupid or clumsy fellow
飯來開口(ㄈㄢˋ ㄌㄞˊ ㄎㄞ ㄎㄡˇ)or 飯來張口(ㄈㄢˋ ㄌㄞˊ ㄓㄤ ㄎㄡˇ)
to eat but not to work; to live like a parasite; to have only to open one's mouth to be fed—to live an easy life, with everything provided
飯粒(ㄈㄢˋ ㄌㄧˋ)
a grain of cooked rice
飯量(ㄈㄢˋ ㄌㄧㄤˋ)
an appetite; capacity for eating: 他的飯量比你小。He eats less than you do.
飯落兒(ㄈㄢˋ ㄌㄨㄛˋㄦ)
a means of living
飯鍋(ㄈㄢˋ ㄍㄨㄛ)
a pot for cooking rice
飯館(ㄈㄢˋ ㄍㄨㄢˇ)
a restaurant
飯盒(ㄈㄢˋ ㄏㄜˊ)
a lunch box; a rice container; a mess tin
飯後(ㄈㄢˋ ㄏㄡˋ)
after meals: 飯後要刷牙。Brush your teeth after meals.
飯局(ㄈㄢˋ ㄐㄩˊ)
a luncheon or dinner party; a feast: 他下星期有兩個飯局。He has two dinner parties next week.
飯前(ㄈㄢˋ ㄑㄧㄢˊ)
before meals: 我們在飯前洗手。We wash our hands before meals.
飯桌(ㄈㄢˋ ㄓㄨㄛ)
a dining table
飯匙倩(ㄈㄢˋ ㄔˊ ㄑㄧㄢˋ)
a trimerous snake, a very venomous snake, found in the mountains of Taiwan
飯食(ㄈㄢˋ ㄕˊ)
① food and meals: 那兒的飯食挺不錯的。I got fine food there. ② to eat rice as staple food

飯菜(ㄈㄢˋ ㄘㄞˋ)
① dishes to go with rice ② a meal; a repast; food
飯碗(ㄈㄢˋ ㄨㄢˇ)
① a rice bowl ②(slang) one's job: 他上個月丢了飯碗。He lost his job last month.

五畫

【飼】6860 ㄙˋ syh sì
to feed; to raise (domesticated animals): 他飼養許多羊。He raises a large number of sheep.
飼兎(ㄙˋ ㄊㄨˋ)
① domesticated rabbits ② to feed rabbits
飼料(ㄙˋ ㄌㄧㄠˋ)
animal feed; fodder; forage: 放些飼料到倉裏。Put some fodder in the bins.
飼養(ㄙˋ ㄧㄤˇ)
to raise; to breed: 你用什麼飼養家禽? What do you feed your poultry on?

【飴】6861 ㄧˊ yi yí
1. syrup; jellylike sugar made from grains
2. delicious; tasty
3. delicacies
4. to give as a gift; to present

【飽】6862 ㄅㄠˇ bao bǎo
1. to eat to the full; surfeited
2. satisfied
3. full; plump
4. fully; to the full
飽飽的(ㄅㄠˇ ㄅㄠˇ ˙ㄉㄜ)
stuffed with food; glutted; surfeited
飽滿(ㄅㄠˇ ㄇㄢˇ)
well-stacked (figures, etc.); full; plump: 他給我看顆粒飽滿的小麥。He showed me the plump wheat.
飽暖(ㄅㄠˇ ㄋㄨㄢˇ)
well-fed and well-clad; more than enough to eat and wear
飽暖思淫慾(ㄅㄠˇ ㄋㄨㄢˇ ㄙ ㄧㄣˊ ㄩˋ)
Debauchery is a common vice among the wealthy.
飽嗝兒(ㄅㄠˇ ㄍㄜˊㄦ)
flatulence after a solid meal; a hiccup
飽看(ㄅㄠˇ ㄎㄢˋ)
to read or look at to one's heart's content; to feast one's eyes on
飽和(ㄅㄠˇ ㄏㄜˊ)
saturation; saturated: 舊車買賣的市場已趨飽和。The market for used cars is saturated.
飽和點(ㄅㄠˇ ㄏㄜˊ ㄉㄧㄢˇ)
the saturation point
飽和脂肪酸(ㄅㄠˇ ㄏㄜˊ ㄓ ㄈㄤˊ ㄙㄨㄢ)
saturated fatty acid
飽經風霜(ㄅㄠˇ ㄐㄧㄥ ㄈㄥ ㄕㄨㄤ)
① weather-beaten ② to have experienced the vicissitudes of life or have experienced the hardships of life
飽經世故(ㄅㄠˇ ㄐㄧㄥ ㄕˋ ㄍㄨˋ)
well-experienced in the ways of the world
飽學(ㄅㄠˇ ㄒㄩㄝˊ)
well-versed; well-learned or widely-read: 他父親是個飽學鴻儒之士。His father is a well-read, learned literate.
飽學之士(ㄅㄠˇ ㄒㄩㄝˊ ㄓ ㄕˋ)
a learned scholar; an erudite person
飽脹(ㄅㄠˇ ㄓㄤˋ)
glutted; surfeited to the bursting point
飽吃(ㄅㄠˇ ㄔ) or 飽餐(ㄅㄠˇ ㄘㄢ)
to eat to one's heart's content; to glut
飽嘗(ㄅㄠˇ ㄔㄤˊ)
to experience or taste (bitterness, hardships, etc.) to the fullest extent: 他飽嘗人生的苦樂。He fully tasted all the sweets and bitters of life.
飽食煖衣(ㄅㄠˇ ㄕˊ ㄋㄨㄢˇ ㄧ)
well-fed and well-clad
飽食終日(ㄅㄠˇ ㄕˊ ㄓㄨㄥ ㄖˋ)
well-fed all day (without doing anything worthwhile)
飽受(ㄅㄠˇ ㄕㄡˋ)
to suffer (insult, grievances, etc.) to the fullest extent: 在車禍中,她飽受虛驚。She suffered from nervous fears in the car accident.
飽人不知餓人饑(ㄅㄠˇ ㄖㄣˊ ㄅㄨˋ ㄓ ㄜˋ ㄖㄣˊ ㄐㄧ) or 飽漢不知餓漢饑(ㄅㄠˇ ㄏㄢˋ ㄅㄨˋ ㄓ ㄜˋ ㄏㄢˋ ㄐㄧ)
(literally) He who is well-fed does not know what hunger is like.—He who is in comfortable circumstances does not know the bitterness of misfortune.
飽入私囊(ㄅㄠˇ ㄖㄨˋ ㄙ ㄋㄤˊ)
to embezzle public funds
飽以老拳(ㄅㄠˇ ㄧˇ ㄌㄠˇ ㄑㄩㄢˊ)
to give someone a sound beating or slugging

【飾】6863 ㄕˋ shyh shì
1. to ornament; to decorate; to polish (writing); to adorn: 他的言語需要潤飾。His speech needs polishing.
2. ornamentation; decorations
3. to excuse oneself on a pretext, etc.; to fake
4. clothing and dresses
5. to whitewash; to deceive; to cover up
6. to play the role of; to act the part of
飾非(ㄕˋ ㄈㄟ)
to hide and gloss over one's faults
飾過(ㄕˋ ㄍㄨㄛˋ)
to hide and gloss over one's mistakes; to whitewash: 報告書極力爲他飾過。The report whitewashed him.
飾終(ㄕˋ ㄓㄨㄥ)
funeral rites
飾詞 or 飾辭(ㄕˋ ㄘˊ)
① an excuse; a pretext ② to polish a piece of writing
飾物(ㄕˋ ㄨˋ)
adornments; decorations; ornaments: 她的房間滿是飾物。Her room is crowded with ornaments.
飾僞(ㄕˋ ㄨㄟˋ)
to fake; to make or copy something in order to deceive

六畫

【餂】6864 ㄊㄧㄢˇ tean tiǎn
to obtain by hook—to entice or bait with flatteries

【餃】6865 ㄐㄧㄠˇ jeau jiǎo
stuffed dumplings; ravioli
餃子(ㄐㄧㄠˇ ˙ㄗ)
stuffed dumplings; ravioli

〔食部〕

〔食部〕

【餈】 6866 (粢) ㄘˊ tsyr cí

rice cakes

【餉】 6867 ㄒㄧㄤˇ sheang xiǎng

1. pay, provisions, rations, etc. for the military or the police
2. to entertain with food; to feast; to present food as a gift

餉賓(ㄒㄧㄤˇ ㄅㄧㄣ)or 餉客(ㄒㄧㄤˇ ㄎㄜˋ)
to entertain guests with food

餉錢(ㄒㄧㄤˇ ㄑㄧㄢˊ)
a soldier's pay

餉銀(ㄒㄧㄤˇ ㄧㄣˊ)
military expenditure; a serviceman's pay

【養】 6868 1. ㄧㄤˇ yeang yǎng

1. to grow; to raise; to breed; to rear; to bring up
2. to support or keep (a family, etc.)
3. to give birth to: 她養了一個女兒。She gave birth to a girl.
4. to nourish; to cultivate (one's mind, etc.)
5. to educate
6. to nurse (a wound or illness)
7. oxygen 亦作「氧」
8. a Chinese family name

養兵(ㄧㄤˇ ㄅㄧㄥ)
to maintain and train soldiers (in preparation for war)

養兵千日，用在一朝(ㄧㄤˇ ㄅㄧㄥ ㄑㄧㄢ ㄖˋ, ㄩㄥˋ ㄗㄞˋ ㄧˋ ㄓㄠ)
(literally) to maintain an army for a thousand days to use it for a moment

養病(ㄧㄤˇ ㄅㄧㄥˋ)
① to convalesce; to recuperate; to nurse a disease: 他的父親在家養病。His father is recuperating at home. ② convalescence; recuperation

養母(ㄧㄤˇ ㄇㄨˇ)
a foster mother

養分(ㄧㄤˇ ㄈㄣˋ)
the amount of nutritious substance in a given food item; nutrition

養蜂(ㄧㄤˇ ㄈㄥ)
to raise or keep bees; to engage in apiculture

養蜂場(ㄧㄤˇ ㄈㄥ ㄔㄤˇ)
an apiary; a bee yard

養蜂業(ㄧㄤˇ ㄈㄥ ㄧㄝˋ)
apiculture business

養父(ㄧㄤˇ ㄈㄨˋ)
a foster father

養父母(ㄧㄤˇ ㄈㄨˋ ㄇㄨˇ)
foster parents

養鳥室(ㄧㄤˇ ㄋㄧㄠˇ ㄕˋ)
an aviary 亦作「鳥舍」

養女(ㄧㄤˇ ㄋㄩˇ)
an adopted daughter; a foster daughter

養樂多(ㄧㄤˇ ㄌㄜˋ ㄉㄨㄛ)
the trademark of a yogurt preparation

養老(ㄧㄤˇ ㄌㄠˇ)
①(said of persons) to retire and enjoy the fruit of one's work in the past ② to provide for the aged

養老保險(ㄧㄤˇ ㄌㄠˇ ㄅㄠˇ ㄒㄧㄢˇ)
endowment insurance

養老費(ㄧㄤˇ ㄌㄠˇ ㄈㄟˋ)
money saved up for old age

養老金(ㄧㄤˇ ㄌㄠˇ ㄐㄧㄣ)
an old age pension: 他退休後靠養老金過活。He lived on a pension after his retirement.

養老院(ㄧㄤˇ ㄌㄠˇ ㄩㄢˋ)
a home for destitute old people

養料(ㄧㄤˇ ㄌㄧㄠˋ)
nutrition; nutritious value

養廉(ㄧㄤˇ ㄌㄧㄢˊ)
① an old name of salary for public officials ② expenses for supporting or maintaining a living

養路(ㄧㄤˇ ㄌㄨˋ)
highway or railroad maintenance

養路隊(ㄧㄤˇ ㄌㄨˋ ㄉㄨㄟˋ)
a road gang; a road maintenance crew

養路稅(ㄧㄤˇ ㄌㄨˋ ㄕㄨㄟˋ)
highway maintenance tax

養漢(ㄧㄤˇ ㄏㄢˋ)
(said of a woman) to have extramarital affairs

養虎傷身(ㄧㄤˇ ㄏㄨˇ ㄕㄤ ㄕㄣ)
(literally) to raise a tiger which will injure its feeder later on—to keep a bad subordinate who will one day bring ruin to his protector

養虎遺患(ㄧㄤˇ ㄏㄨˇ ㄧˊ ㄏㄨㄢˋ)
To keep a tiger is to invite calamity.—Appeasement brings disaster.

養護(ㄧㄤˇ ㄏㄨˋ)
① to rear and educate kids ② to maintain; to conserve

養活(ㄧㄤˇ ˙ㄏㄨㄛ)
① to support or keep (a family or somebody): 他獨力養活一個大家庭。He alone supports a big family. ② to rear; to bring up

養晦(ㄧㄤˇ ㄏㄨㄟˋ)
to live in retirement and wait for the opportune moment to stage a comeback

養鷄(ㄧㄤˇ ㄐㄧ)
to raise chickens

養鷄場(ㄧㄤˇ ㄐㄧ ㄔㄤˇ)
a chicken farm

養家(ㄧㄤˇ ㄐㄧㄚ)
to support one's family

養家費(ㄧㄤˇ ㄐㄧㄚ ㄈㄟˋ)
a family support allowance given to an employee sent away for an assignment which calls for his long absence from home

養家活口(ㄧㄤˇ ㄐㄧㄚ ㄏㄨㄛˊ ㄎㄡˇ)
to support one's family

養精蓄銳(ㄧㄡˇ ㄐㄧㄥ ㄒㄩˋ ㄖㄨㄟˋ)
to nourish and discipline one's stamina; to nurse one's strength (in preparation for a challenging task ahead)

養氣(ㄧㄤˇ ㄑㄧˋ)
① oxygen ② to cultivate and discipline one's capacity for greatness

養媳(ㄧㄤˇ ㄒㄧˊ)
a daughter-in-law who is brought up in her future husband's home until she comes of age and formally gets married

養心(ㄧㄤˇ ㄒㄧㄣ)
to cultivate mental calm; to nourish the mind

養性(ㄧㄤˇ ㄒㄧㄥˋ)
to discipline one's temperament

養殖(ㄧㄤˇ ㄓˊ)
to breed (aquatics)

養殖漁業(ㄧㄤˇ ㄓˊ ㄩˊ ㄧㄝˋ)

pisciculture

養志(ㄧㄤˇ ㄓˋ)
①to ennoble one's aspirations ②to be obedient to one's parents; to be a dutiful son

養眞(ㄧㄤˇ ㄓㄣ)
to discipline one's temperament

養珠(ㄧㄤˇ ㄓㄨ)
cultured pearls

養豬(ㄧㄤˇ ㄓㄨ)
to raise hogs or pigs

養豬場(ㄧㄤˇ ㄓㄨ ㄔㄤˇ)
a pig farm

養成(ㄧㄤˇ ㄔㄥˊ)
to discipline and train; to cultivate (good habits, etc.); to develop (bad habits, etc.): 我們要養成良好的習慣。We should cultivate good habits.

養成所(ㄧㄤˇ ㄔㄥˊ ㄙㄨㄛˇ)
a training school; a training seminar

養贍(ㄧㄤˇ ㄕㄢˋ)
to support (parents or a family)

養神(ㄧㄤˇ ㄕㄣˊ)
to have mental relaxation; to give one's mental faculty a rest: 他正在閉目養神呢！He is sitting in repose with his eyes closed.

養傷(ㄧㄤˇ ㄕㄤ)
to nurse one's injuries or wounds

養生(ㄧㄤˇ ㄕㄥ)
to preserve one's health; to keep in good condition

養生之道(ㄧㄤˇ ㄕㄥ ㄓ ㄉㄠˋ)
a regimen; the formula of healthy living

養生送死(ㄧㄤˇ ㄕㄥ ㄙㄨㄥˋ ㄙˇ)or(ㄧㄤˇ ㄕㄥ ㄙㄨㄥˋ ㄙˇ)
to support one's parents when they are alive and to look after their funeral arrangement upon their death (which is the duty of a son)

養子(ㄧㄤˇ ㄗˇ)
①a foster or an adopted son ②to bring up children

養尊處優(ㄧㄤˇ ㄗㄨㄣ ㄔㄨˇ ㄧㄡ)
to live in luxury (or clover); to enjoy high rank and live at ease and in comfort

養蠶(ㄧㄤˇ ㄘㄢˊ)
to engage in sericulture

養疴 or 養痾(ㄧㄤˇ ㄜ)
to undergo a period of recuperation or convalescence 參看「養病」

養而不教(ㄧㄤˇ ㄦˊ ㄅㄨˋ ㄐㄧㄠˋ)
to bear children without educating them

養兒防老(ㄧㄤˇ ㄦˊ ㄈㄤˊ ㄌㄠˇ)
to raise sons as insurance against the insecurity of old age

養魚(ㄧㄤˇ ㄩˊ)
to breed fish; to engage in pisciculture

養魚池(ㄧㄤˇ ㄩˊ ㄔˊ)
a fishpond

養育(ㄧㄤˇ ㄩˋ)
to rear; to raise and educate: 養育兒女並非易事。It is not easy to rear children.

養癰遺患(ㄧㄤˇ ㄩㄥ ㄧˊ ㄏㄨㄢˋ)
(literally) A wound not treated in time will cause great trouble afterwards. —Appeasement will bring greater disasters afterwards.

【養】 6868
2. ㄧㄤˋ yanq yàng

to support one's parents

【餌】 6869
ㄦˇ eel ěr

1. to bait; to entice; bait
2. cakes
3. food
4. to eat

餌敵(ㄦˇ ㄉㄧˊ)
to set up a trap for the enemy

【餁】 6870
ㄖㄣˋ renn rèn

same as 飪—to cook

【餅】 6871
(餠) ㄅㄧㄥˇ biing bǐng

1. cakes; biscuits; pastry
2. anything round and flat, as a disc

七畫

【餐】 6872
(湌) ㄘㄢ tsan cān

1. a meal: 我們一日吃三餐。We take three meals a day.
2. to eat
3. food

餐費(ㄘㄢ ㄈㄟˋ)
boarding expense; a food bill

餐風宿露(ㄘㄢ ㄈㄥ ㄙㄨˋ ㄌㄨˋ)
(literally) to eat in the wind and sleep in the dew—hardships of traveling in old times 參看「風餐露宿」

餐廳(ㄘㄢ ㄊㄧㄥ)
a restaurant; a dining hall; a mess hall

餐後演說(ㄘㄢ ㄏㄡˋ ㄧㄢˇ ㄕㄨㄛ)
an after-dinner speech

餐巾(ㄘㄢ ㄐㄧㄣ)
a napkin

餐具(ㄘㄢ ㄐㄩˋ)
a dinner set; tableware; a dinner-service

餐券(ㄘㄢ ㄑㄩㄢˋ)
a meal coupon; a meal ticket

餐車(ㄘㄢ ㄔㄜ)
a diner; a dining car

餐飲業(ㄘㄢ ㄧㄣˇ ㄧㄝˋ)
restaurants, bars, coffee houses and tearooms

【餑】 6873
ㄅㄛ bo bō

cakes; fancy baked foods

餑餑(ㄅㄛ ˙ㄅㄛ)
cakes; pies, tarts, and other pastry foods

【餒】 6874
ㄋㄟˇ neei něi

1. to starve; hungry
2. decay or decomposition of fish
3. lacking in confidence, courage, etc.; disheartened; dispirited

【餓】 6875
ㄜˋ eh è

1. hungry; hunger
2. greedy; covetous
3. to starve

餓不死(ㄜˋ ˙ㄅㄨ ㄙˇ)
won't starve; cannot be starved to death

餓莩 or 餓殍(ㄜˋ ㄆㄧㄠˇ)
persons starved to death; bodies of famine victims

餓倒(ㄜˋ ㄉㄠˇ)
to collapse from hunger

餓了(ㄜˋ ˙ㄌㄜ)
hungry: 她覺得餓了。She was feeling hungry.

餓狼(ㄜˋ ㄌㄤˊ)
a greedy and covetous per-

〔食部〕

son
餓鬼(ㄜˋ ㄍㄨㄟˇ)
①a person who is always hungry ②a person who eats piggishly
餓漢(ㄜˋ ㄏㄢˋ)
a starving or hungry man
餓虎撲食(ㄜˋ ㄏㄨˇ ㄆㄨ ㄕˊ)
to seize fiercely—like a hungry tiger
餓壞了(ㄜˋ ㄏㄨㄞˋ ·ㄌㄜ)
to be starving: 我餓壞了！何時進餐? I'm starving. What time is dinner?
餓死(ㄜˋ ㄙˇ) or 餓殺(ㄜˋ ㄕㄚ)
to die of hunger; to be starved to death: 很多人餓死了。A lot of people were starved to death.

【餔】 6876
ㄅㄨ bu bū
1. to eat
2. time for supper
3. sunset
餔啜(ㄅㄨ ㄔㄨㄛˋ)
to eat and drink
餔時(ㄅㄨ ㄕˊ)
evening; late afternoon; suppertime 亦作「晡時」

【餖】 6877
ㄉㄡˋ dow dòu
food items set out for show, not to be eaten
餖飣(ㄉㄡˋ ㄉㄧㄥˋ)
①food items set out for show ②showy and flashy expressions in writings

【餗】 6878
ㄙㄨˋ suh sù
food in a caldron or tripod

【餘】 6879
ㄩˊ yu yú
1. remaining; the remnant or remainder; the rest
2. a surplus; an overplus; an excess
3. a balance
4. a complement of a number or figure; odd
5. after
餘波(ㄩˊ ㄅㄛ)
aftermaths; the swell after a storm; a postlude
餘波蕩漾(ㄩˊ ㄅㄛ ㄉㄤˋ ㄧㄤˋ)
The effect (of a major event) is still being felt.
餘黨(ㄩˊ ㄉㄤˇ)
remnants of an outlawed faction or disbanded gang
餘地(ㄩˊ ㄉㄧˋ)
a spare space; an alternative; elbowroom; leeway: 還有改進的餘地。There is some room for improvement.
餘桃(ㄩˊ ㄊㄠˊ)
male homosexuality
餘孽(ㄩˊ ㄋㄧㄝˋ)
remnants of rebel groups, secret societies, etc.; surviving supporters of an evil cause
餘年(ㄩˊ ㄋㄧㄢˊ)
the remaining years of one's life: 餘年可數。One's failing years are numbered.
餘利(ㄩˊ ㄌㄧˋ)
a profit; net profit
餘力(ㄩˊ ㄌㄧˋ)
strength or energy to spare
餘糧(ㄩˊ ㄌㄧㄤˊ)
surplus grain
餘論(ㄩˊ ㄌㄨㄣˋ)
①unfinished comments ②an epilogue, etc.
餘割(ㄩˊ ㄍㄜ)
(mathematics) a cosecant
餘可類推(ㄩˊ ㄎㄜˇ ㄌㄟˋ ㄊㄨㄟ)
The rest may be inferred by analogy.
餘款(ㄩˊ ㄎㄨㄢˇ)
remaining funds; a favorable balance; surplus funds
餘暉 or 餘輝(ㄩˊ ㄏㄨㄟ)
twilight at sunset
餘悸(ㄩˊ ㄐㄧˋ)
a lingering shock or fear: 她至今仍心有餘悸。She still has a lingering fear until now.
餘角(ㄩˊ ㄐㄧㄠˇ)
(mathematics) a complement of an angle; a complementary angle
餘燼(ㄩˊ ㄐㄧㄣˋ)
①ashes; embers ②defeated and dispersed troops
餘切(ㄩˊ ㄑㄧㄝ)
(mathematics) a cotangent
餘錢(ㄩˊ ㄑㄧㄢˊ)
spare money; surplus funds: 你有沒有餘錢可借? Do you have any spare money to lend?
餘慶(ㄩˊ ㄑㄧㄥˋ)
①blessings left to one's children ②the name of counties in Kweichow (貴州) and Heilungkiang (黑龍江) provinces
餘暇(ㄩˊ ㄒㄧㄚˊ)
spare time; leisure; free time: 我沒有餘暇。I have no spare time.
餘下的(ㄩˊ ㄒㄧㄚˋ ·ㄉㄜ)
the remainder; the remaining; the rest
餘閒(ㄩˊ ㄒㄧㄢˊ)
spare time; leisure
餘弦(ㄩˊ ㄒㄧㄢˊ)
(mathematics) a cosine
餘羨(ㄩˊ ㄒㄧㄢˋ)
a surplus; an overplus; a profit
餘香(ㄩˊ ㄒㄧㄤ)
lingering fragrance
餘興(ㄩˊ ㄒㄧㄥˋ)
①an entertainment program arranged for a gathering ②a lingering interest; a wish to prolong a pleasant amusement
餘震(ㄩˊ ㄓㄣˋ)
aftershocks in the wake of a strong earthquake
餘喘(ㄩˊ ㄔㄨㄢˇ)
①the last breath of a dying person ②the last days of one's life
餘事(ㄩˊ ㄕˋ)
①unfinished tasks ②extra tasks or matters ③matters of secondary importance
餘生(ㄩˊ ㄕㄥ)
①the remaining years of one's life; old age ②a survival (after a disaster)
餘剩(ㄩˊ ㄕㄥˋ)
the remainder; the residue
餘數(ㄩˊ ㄕㄨˋ)
①the balance ②(mathematics) the complement of a number ③(mathematics) the residue; the remainder
餘熱(ㄩˊ ㄖㄜˋ)
decay heat
餘子(ㄩˊ ㄗˇ)
①the others; the rest: 餘子碌碌。The rest are commonplace. ②children by a concubine
餘存(ㄩˊ ㄘㄨㄣˊ)
a balance; the remainder
餘額(ㄩˊ ㄜˊ)

①a surplus amount; a remaining sum; a balance: 餘額不多。The balance is not much. ②vacancies to be filled

餘音嫋嫋(ㄩˊ ㄧㄣ ㄋㄧㄠˇ ㄋㄧㄠˇ)
The enchanting notes persist long after the musicians bowed out.

餘音繞梁(ㄩˊ ㄧㄣ ㄖㄠˋ ㄌㄧㄤˊ)
The thrilling voice keeps reverberating in the air after the vocalist has stopped singing.

餘蔭(ㄩˊ ㄧㄣˋ)
blessings left to one's children

餘殃(ㄩˊ ㄧㄤ)
calamity or misfortune which makes itself felt long after the seed was sown

餘外(ㄩˊ ㄨㄞˋ)
over and above; in addition

餘威(ㄩˊ ㄨㄟ)
the influence or power of someone that remains after his death

餘味(ㄩˊ ㄨㄟˋ)
pleasant memories; delicious taste one feels afterward; an aftertaste

餘裕(ㄩˊ ㄩˋ)
①more than enough; abundant; very well-to-do; ample; plenty②(said of action) freely and without any constraint

餘勇可賈(ㄩˊ ㄩㄥˇ ㄎㄜˇ ㄍㄨˇ)
with courage to spare; very courageous or brave

八畫

【餅】 6880
(餠) ㄅㄧㄥˇ biing bǐng
1. cakes; cookies; biscuits; pastries; pies; dumplings: 吃一點水果餅吧! Have some fruit pies.
2. anything roundish, as a disc

餅乾(ㄅㄧㄥˇ ㄍㄢ)
biscuits or crackers

餅餡(ㄅㄧㄥˇ ㄒㄧㄢˋ)
the filling of a pie

餅餌(ㄅㄧㄥˇ ㄦˇ)
steamed cakes of rice or wheat flour

【餚】 6881
ㄧㄠˊ yau yáo
dishes and foods

【餛】 6882
ㄏㄨㄣˊ hwen hún
stuffed dumplings with delicate flour wrapping; ravioli

餛飩(ㄏㄨㄣˊ ·ㄊㄨㄣ)
stuffed dumplings with delicate flour wrapping; ravioli

【餞】 6883
ㄐㄧㄢˋ jiann jiàn
1. a farewell dinner or luncheon
2. to send off; to convoy
3. to present as a gift
4. preserves; jam: 她很喜歡吃蜜餞。She likes to eat preserves very much.

餞別(ㄐㄧㄢˋ ㄅㄧㄝˊ) or 餞行(ㄐㄧㄢˋ ㄒㄧㄥˊ)
to entertain a parting friend with a feast or a farewell dinner: 我們下週要爲朋友餞行。We'll give our friend a farewell dinner next week.

餞春(ㄐㄧㄢˋ ㄔㄨㄣ)
(a Chinese custom) a feast to bid farewell to spring toward the end of the season

【餡】 6884
ㄒㄧㄢˋ shiann xiàn
anything serving as stuffing for dumplings, etc.

餡兒(ㄒㄧㄚˋㄦ)
stuffing: 這些餃子餡兒聞起來好香。The stuffing of these dumplings smells good.

餡兒餅(ㄒㄧㄚˋㄦ ㄅㄧㄥˇ)
a kind of broiled-and-baked meat pie; a pasty

【餧】 6885
ㄨㄟˋ wey wèi
same as 餵—to feed

【館】 6886
(舘) ㄍㄨㄢˇ goan guǎn
1. a house; a guesthouse; a hotel
2. to stay or lodge
3. an official residence
4. an embassy; a legation; a consulate
5. a place for cultural activities
6. premises
7. a school (in former times)
8. a suffix for a library, teahouse, restaurant, theater, etc.

館兒(ㄍㄨㄚˇㄦ)
a restaurant; a teahouse; a wineshop

館閣(ㄍㄨㄢˇ ㄍㄜˊ)
another name of 翰林, an official in charge of academic affairs in former times

館閣氣(ㄍㄨㄢˇ ㄍㄜˊ ㄑㄧˋ)
flowery, ornamental but a little stale literary style

館長(ㄍㄨㄢˇ ㄓㄤˇ)
a superintendent; a curator; the head of a library or an institute, etc.: 這個圖書館的館長工作很努力。The head of the library works very hard.

館舍(ㄍㄨㄢˇ ㄕㄜˋ)
a guesthouse: 館舍幽雅。The guesthouse is quiet and tasteful.

館子(ㄍㄨㄢˇ ·ㄗ)
①a restaurant: 我們常上館子。We often dine in a restaurant. ②a theater

【餜】 6887
ㄍㄨㄛˇ guoo guǒ
cakes, dumplings, etc.

餜子(ㄍㄨㄛˇ ·ㄗ)
twisted fritters 亦作「油條」

【餟】 6888
ㄓㄨㄟˋ juey zhuì
a libation

九畫

【餮】 6889
ㄊㄧㄝˋ tieh tiè
as in 饕餮
1. a legendary fierce animal
2. a greedy and gluttonous person

【餱】 6890
ㄏㄡˊ hour hóu
dry provisions

餱糧(ㄏㄡˊ ㄌㄧㄤˊ)
dry provisions

【餬】 6891
ㄏㄨˊ hwu hú
1. congee; porridge; gruel
2. paste

餬口(ㄏㄨˊ ㄎㄡˇ)
just to make ends meet; to make a bare living; to eke out one's livelihood

餬紙(ㄏㄨˊ ㄓˇ)
①to paste paper ②paper

〔食部〕

for pasting

【餳】 6892
ㄒㄧㄥˊ shyng xíng
1. malt sugar or syrup
2. sticky
3. poor or dull (eyesight)

〔食部〕

【餵】 6893
(餧) ㄨㄟˋ wey wèi
to feed; to raise
餵奶(ㄨㄟˋ ㄋㄞˇ)
to feed a baby with milk; to breast-feed: 她堅持要自己餵奶。She insisted on breast-feeding her own child.
餵牲口(ㄨㄟˋ ㄕㄥ ㄎㄡˇ)
to raise or feed domestic animals
餵養(ㄨㄟˋ ㄧㄤˇ)
to raise; to rear; to keep

十畫

【餿】 6894
ㄙㄡ sou sōu
1. decayed; rotten; stale; rancid; spoiled: 菜餿了。The dish has spoiled.
2. lousy; foul
餿腿(ㄙㄡ ㄊㄨㄟˇ)
to do a lot of legwork in vain
餿主意(ㄙㄡ ㄓㄨˇ ㄧˋ)
a lousy idea: 這是誰的餿主意? Whose rotten (or lousy) idea is this?
餿臭(ㄙㄡ ㄔㄡˋ)
rotten and smelly
餿酸(ㄙㄡ ㄙㄨㄢ)
stale

【餼】 6895
ㄒㄧˋ shih xì
1. to present as a gift
2. animals; animals for sacrifices
3. grains; rice
4. animal feed; fodder
餼牢(ㄒㄧˋ ㄌㄠˊ)
animals; animals for sacrifices
餼廩(ㄒㄧˋ ㄌㄧㄣˇ)
(in ancient China) grain allowances for salaried graduates
餼羊(ㄒㄧˋ ㄧㄤˊ)
sheep for sacrifices

【餾】 6896
ㄌㄧㄡˋ liow liù
1. to steam
2. distilled (water)

【餻】 6897
(糕) ㄍㄠ gau gāo
cakes; dumplings

【餽】 6898
(饋) ㄎㄨㄟˋ kuey kuì
1. to offer food to a superior
2. to present as a gift

十一畫

【饅】 6899
ㄇㄢˊ man mán
stuffed or unstuffed dumplings; steamed buns; steamed bread
饅頭(ㄇㄢˊ ·ㄊㄡ)
steamed dumplings

【饈】 6900
ㄒㄧㄡ shiou xiū
1. to eat; a meal
2. to offer; to offer as tribute
3. delicious food; a delicacy; a dainty

【饉】 6901
ㄐㄧㄣˇ jiin jǐn
as in 饑饉—famine; hunger

十二畫

【饋】 6902
(餽) ㄎㄨㄟˋ kuey kuì
1. to offer food to a superior
2. to send someone a present; to present as a gift
饋貧糧(ㄎㄨㄟˋ ㄆㄧㄣˊ ㄌㄧㄤˊ)
①food for the poor② (figuratively) knowledge for the ignorant
饋糧(ㄎㄨㄟˋ ㄌㄧㄤˊ)
to send provisions
饋路(ㄎㄨㄟˋ ㄌㄨˋ)
a route for military supplies
饋食(ㄎㄨㄟˋ ㄕˊ)
(in ancient China) to offer cooked food as sacrifices
饋人(ㄎㄨㄟˋ ㄖㄣˊ)
a cook
饋贈(ㄎㄨㄟˋ ㄗㄥˋ)
to present (a gift); to make a present of something

【饌】 6903
ㄓㄨㄢˋ juann zhuàn
1. to prepare food
2. food and drink; dainties
3. to eat and drink
饌具(ㄓㄨㄢˋ ㄐㄩˋ)
food vessels: 饌具齊備。Food vessels are complete.

【饑】 6904
ㄐㄧ ji jī
1. a year of famine
2. hunger; hungry
饑溺(ㄐㄧ ㄋㄧˋ)
extreme sufferings among the masses
饑寒交迫(ㄐㄧ ㄏㄢˊ ㄐㄧㄠ ㄆㄛˋ)
to suffer from both the cold and hunger
饑荒(ㄐㄧ ㄏㄨㄤ)
famine
饑饉(ㄐㄧ ㄐㄧㄣˇ)
starvation; famine
饑歉(ㄐㄧ ㄑㄧㄢˋ)
famine; scarcity
饑驅(ㄐㄧ ㄑㄩ)
driven by hunger or famine

【饒】 6905
ㄖㄠˊ rau ráo
1. abundant; plentiful; full of; fertile
2. to give something extra as a gift; to let somebody have something into the bargain
3. to forgive; to spare; to have mercy; to let somebody off
4. lenient; liberal
5. (now rarely) even though; in spite of the fact that; whatever
6. a Chinese family name
饒命(ㄖㄠˊ ㄇㄧㄥˋ)
to spare a life
饒富(ㄖㄠˊ ㄈㄨˋ)
affluence; abundant; plentiful
饒侈(ㄖㄠˊ ㄔˇ)
affluence
饒舌(ㄖㄠˊ ㄕㄜˊ)
loquacious; talkative; garrulous; voluble
饒恕(ㄖㄠˊ ㄕㄨˋ)
to forgive; to pardon: 他偷錢已被饒恕。He was forgiven for stealing the money.
饒人(ㄖㄠˊ ㄖㄣˊ)
①to forgive another person: 他不輕易饒人。He is not a man who forgives easily. ②to give the other guy a way out
饒讓(ㄖㄠˊ ㄖㄤˋ)
to forgive; to be tolerant or lenient
饒益(ㄖㄠˊ ㄧˋ)

abundance; wealthy; a surplus

饒沃(ㄖㄠˊ ㄨㄛˋ)
fertile: 臺灣是饒沃之地。Taiwan is a piece of fertile land.

饒裕(ㄖㄠˊ ㄩˋ)
abundance; affluence

【饍】 6906
(膳) ㄕㄢˋ shann shàn
1. a meal
2. to eat; to board

【餾】 6907
(餾) ㄌㄧㄡˋ liow liù
1. to steam
2. to distill

十三畫

【饗】 6908
ㄒㄧㄤˇ sheang xiǎng
1. to dine and wine guests; to give a big party or a banquet
2. a sacrificial ceremony

饗宴(ㄒㄧㄤˇ ㄧㄢˋ)
a feast

【饔】 6909
ㄩㄥ iong yōng
1. cooked food
2. breakfast
3. slaughtered animals

饔餼(ㄩㄥ ㄒㄧˋ)
to present slaughtered or live animals to another

饔飧(ㄩㄥ ㄙㄨㄣ)
breakfast and supper

饔飧不繼(ㄩㄥ ㄙㄨㄣ ㄅㄨˋ ㄐㄧˋ)
discontinuation of supper after breakfast—poverty-stricken

【饕】 6910
ㄊㄠ tau tāo
1. name of a legendary ferocious animal
2. a fierce person
3. a greedy and gluttonous person

饕餮(ㄊㄠ ㄊㄧㄝˋ) or 饕餮之徒(ㄊㄠ ㄊㄧㄝˋ ㄓ ㄊㄨˊ)
① gluttons; greedy persons ②
name of ancient barbarian tribes

【饘】 6911
ㄓㄢ jan zhān
thick congee or porridge

饘粥(ㄓㄢ ㄓㄡˋ) or (ㄓㄢ ㄓㄡ)
congee; porridge

十四畫

【饜】 6912
ㄧㄢˋ yann yàn
1. full-stomached; sufficient; surfeited; satiated
2. to partake plentifully of

饜食(ㄧㄢˋ ㄕˊ)
to eat to repletion

饜事(ㄧㄢˋ ㄕˋ)
plenty to do; busy

饜足(ㄧㄢˋ ㄗㄨˊ)
surfeited; satiated

饜飫(ㄧㄢˋ ㄩˋ)
to eat to repletion; to glut

十六畫

【饝】 6913
(饃) ㄇㄛˊ mo mó
steamed dumplings

饝饝(ㄇㄛˊ ·ㄇㄛ)
steamed dumplings

十七畫

【饞】 6914
ㄔㄢˊ charn chán
piggish; gluttonous; greedy

饞癆(ㄔㄢˊ ㄌㄠˊ)
① to be piggish about good food ② lecherous; lewd

饞涎欲滴(ㄔㄢˊ ㄒㄧㄢˊ ㄩˋ ㄉㄧ)
(said of mouth) to water; to drool over; to covet

饞嘴(ㄔㄢˊ ㄗㄨㄟˇ)
gluttonous

首部
ㄕㄡˇ shoou shǒu

【首】 6915
ㄕㄡˇ shoou shǒu
1. the head
2. the king; the emperor; the chief; the leader
3. the first; the beginning: 他搭首班車去台中。He took the first bus to Taichung.
4. a (poem, song, etc.): 請爲我們唱一首歌。Sing a song for us.

首謀(ㄕㄡˇ ㄇㄡˊ)
the first and chief planner; the mastermind; the ringleader

首犯(ㄕㄡˇ ㄈㄢˋ)
the ringleader; the principal criminal

首逢(ㄕㄡˇ ㄈㄥˊ)
(said of a sports team) to meet another team for the first game

首府(ㄕㄡˇ ㄈㄨˇ)
the capital city: 倫敦是英國的首府。London is the capital city of England.

首當其衝(ㄕㄡˇ ㄉㄤ ㄑㄧˊ ㄔㄨㄥ)
the first to bear the brunt of

首都(ㄕㄡˇ ㄉㄨ)
the (national) capital: 華盛頓爲美國首都。Washington, D. C. is the capital of the U.S.

首塗 or 首途(ㄕㄡˇ ㄊㄨˊ)
to start on one's way; to embark on a journey

首推(ㄕㄡˇ ㄊㄨㄟ)
to consider (a person) first

首腦(ㄕㄡˇ ㄋㄠˇ) or 首腦人物(ㄕㄡˇ ㄋㄠˇ ㄖㄣˊ ㄨˋ)
the chief; the boss; the key member; the mastermind

首難(ㄕㄡˇ ㄋㄢˋ)
the first to start an uprising

首領(ㄕㄡˇ ㄌㄧㄥˇ)
① the leader; the chief: 他是我的首領。He is my chief. ② head and neck

首輪放映(ㄕㄡˇ ㄌㄨㄣˊ ㄈㄤˋ ㄧㄥˋ)
first runs

首告(ㄕㄡˇ ㄍㄠˋ)
① the informer; the squeaker ② the first to

首功(ㄕㄡˇ ㄍㄨㄥ)
① merit for the number of enemy soldiers one has beheaded ② the first merit; the most merited

首肯(ㄕㄡˇ ㄎㄣˇ)
to nod one's head in approval; to approve

首揆(ㄕㄡˇ ㄎㄨㄟˊ) or 首相(ㄕㄡˇ ㄒㄧㄤˋ)
the premier; the prime minister: 大家向首相歡呼。The people cheered the premier.

首級(ㄕㄡˇ ㄐㄧˊ)
the human head

首屆(ㄕㄡˇ ㄐㄧㄝˋ)

〔首部〕

the first (conference, assembly, etc.)

首七(ㄕㄡˇ ㄑㄧ)
the 7th day after a person's death

〔香部〕

首妻(ㄕㄡˇ ㄑㄧ)
one's first wife; one's legal wife (as distinct from concubines)

首屈一指(ㄕㄡˇ ㄑㄩ ㄧˋ ㄓˇ)
the foremost; second to none; the best: 他是我國首屈一指的詩人。He is our foremost poet.

首席(ㄕㄡˇ ㄒㄧˊ)
the highest-ranking; the highest-positioned; the senior

首席代表(ㄕㄡˇ ㄒㄧˊ ㄉㄞˋ ㄅㄧㄠˇ)
the chief delegate

首席女高音(ㄕㄡˇ ㄒㄧˊ ㄋㄩˇ ㄍㄠ ㄧㄣ)
the chief soprano

首席女主角(ㄕㄡˇ ㄒㄧˊ ㄋㄩˇ ㄓㄨˇ ㄐㄧㄠˇ)
the premiere (the leading lady in an opera)

首席檢察官(ㄕㄡˇ ㄒㄧˊ ㄐㄧㄢˇ ㄔㄚˊ ㄍㄨㄢ)
the chief procurator

首席小提琴手(ㄕㄡˇ ㄒㄧˊ ㄒㄧㄠˇ ㄊㄧˊ ㄑㄧㄣˊ ㄕㄡˇ)
the concertmaster

首先(ㄕㄡˇ ㄒㄧㄢ)
the very first; at first; first of all: 首先要盡你自己的義務。Do your own duty first of all.

首選(ㄕㄡˇ ㄒㄩㄢˇ)
① the best among the successful candidates under the old civil service examination system ② preliminary elections

首長(ㄕㄡˇ ㄓㄤˇ)
the chief (of a tribe, bureau, department, ministry, etc.); the leading cadre; the senior officer

首倡(ㄕㄡˇ ㄔㄤˋ)
the first to advocate; to initiate; to pioneer; to originate: 這計劃是誰首倡的? With whom did the scheme originate?

首唱(ㄕㄡˇ ㄔㄤˋ)
① the first to advocate ② (in a poem-composing contest) the first to complete a poem

首創(ㄕㄡˇ ㄔㄨㄤˋ)
to found; to start; to initiate

首飾(ㄕㄡˇ ㄕˋ)
jewelry; ornaments; trinkets

首善之區(ㄕㄡˇ ㄕㄢˋ ㄓ ㄑㄩ)
the national capital

首鼠兩端(ㄕㄡˇ ㄕㄨˇ ㄌㄧㄤˇ ㄉㄨㄢ)
procrastinating; vacillating; hesitating

首任(ㄕㄡˇ ㄖㄣˋ)
the first to be appointed to an office

首如飛蓬(ㄕㄡˇ ㄖㄨˊ ㄈㄟ ㄆㄥˊ)
disheveled hair; hair like the flying artemisia; hair like a rebellious floor-mopper

首遭敗績(ㄕㄡˇ ㄗㄠ ㄅㄞˋ ㄐㄧ)
to suffer the first defeat

首座(ㄕㄡˇ ㄗㄨㄛˋ)
① the first seat; the highest ranking or positioned ② the senior monk in a Buddhist sanctuary

首從(ㄕㄡˇ ㄗㄨㄥˋ)or(ㄕㄡˇ ㄘㄨㄥˊ)
the ringleader and the followers; the principal and the accessory

首次(ㄕㄡˇ ㄘˋ)
the first time: 我首次見到她是五年以前。I first met her five years ago.

首惡(ㄕㄡˇ ㄜˋ)
the principal (criminal); the ringleader

首義(ㄕㄡˇ ㄧˋ)
the first to rise up against tyranny, etc.

首頁(ㄕㄡˇ ㄧㄝˋ)
the first page; page number one; the title page

首要(ㄕㄡˇ ㄧㄠˋ)
of the first importance; first of all; chief

首要條件(ㄕㄡˇ ㄧㄠˋ ㄊㄧㄠˊ ㄐㄧㄢˋ)
the number one condition; a prerequisite; the most important

首映(ㄕㄡˇ ㄧㄥˋ)
the premiere (of a movie)

首尾(ㄕㄡˇ ㄨㄟˇ)
① the head and the tail; the beginning and the end ② from beginning to end

首尾相應(ㄕㄡˇ ㄨㄟˇ ㄒㄧㄤ ㄧㄥˋ)
head and tail (or beginning and end) corresponding with each other

首位(ㄕㄡˇ ㄨㄟˋ)
① the place of honor ② the first place

二畫

【馗】 6916
ㄎㄨㄟ kwei kuí

1. a road; a path
2. as in 鍾馗—the name of a Taoist immortal, famous for catching evil spirits

八畫

【馘】 6917
(聝) ㄍㄨㄛˊ gwo guó

to count the number of enemy troops one killed by the number of the left ears cut from the bodies

香部
ㄒㄧㄤ shiang xiāng

【香】 6918
ㄒㄧㄤ shiang xiāng

1. sweet-smelling; fragrant; aromatic; balmy
2. tasty; delicious
3. fair; beautiful
4. incense; spice; balm

香餑餑兒(ㄒㄧㄤ ㄅㄛ ˙ㄅㄛㄦ)
① a beloved person ② a welcome thing

香檳 or 香賓(ㄒㄧㄤ ㄅㄧㄣ)
champagne

香噴噴的(ㄒㄧㄤ ㄆㄣ ㄆㄣ ˙ㄉㄜ)
smelling very good; sweet-smelling

香片(ㄒㄧㄤ ㄆㄧㄢˋ)
jasmine tea: 我喜歡香片甚於紅茶。I like jasmine tea better than black tea.

香妃(ㄒㄧㄤ ㄈㄟ)
a Muslim concubine of Emperor Kao Tsung of the Ching Dynasty

香粉(ㄒㄧㄤ ㄈㄣˇ)
cosmetic powder

香楓(ㄒㄧㄤ ㄈㄥ)
a kind of liquidambar; a sweet gum

香馥馥(ㄒㄧㄤ ㄈㄨˋ ㄈㄨˋ)

sweet-smelling; fragrant

香袋(ㄒㄧㄤ ㄉㄞˋ)
a sachet; a small perfumed bag

香稻(ㄒㄧㄤ ㄉㄠˋ)
rice (a poetic term)

香燈(ㄒㄧㄤ ㄉㄥ)
incense sticks and lamps burning on an altar

香甜(ㄒㄧㄤ ·ㄊㄧㄢ)
①sweet; delicious ②(to sleep) soundly

香囊(ㄒㄧㄤ ㄋㄤˊ)
a sachet

香蠟紙馬(ㄒㄧㄤ ㄌㄚˋ ㄓˇ ㄇㄚˇ)or 香燭帋馬(ㄒㄧㄤ ㄓㄨˊ ㄓˇ ㄇㄚˇ)
incense, candles and paper horses—materials for worship and sacrifices for the dead

香料(ㄒㄧㄤ ㄌㄧㄠˋ)
spice; balm: 她在小甜餅上加香料。She adds spice to cookies.

香奩(ㄒㄧㄤ ㄌㄧㄢˊ)
women's toiletries

香爐(ㄒㄧㄤ ㄌㄨˊ)
a thurible; a censer

香港(ㄒㄧㄤ ㄍㄤˇ)
Hong Kong, or Hongkong: 香港是遠東的貿易中心。Hong Kong is the commercial center of the Far East.

香港脚(ㄒㄧㄤ ㄍㄤˇ ㄐㄧㄠˇ)
Hongkong foot; athlete's foot

香菇(ㄒㄧㄤ ㄍㄨ)
a kind of edible mushroom grown on wooden logs

香瓜(ㄒㄧㄤ ㄍㄨㄚ)
a muskmelon; a cantaloupe: 這香瓜味道甚美。This cantaloupe is delicious.

香閨(ㄒㄧㄤ ㄍㄨㄟ)
a lady's chamber

香客(ㄒㄧㄤ ㄎㄜˋ)
visitors to temples; pilgrims: 很多香客去耶路撒冷。Many pilgrims went to Jerusalem.

香荷包(ㄒㄧㄤ ㄏㄜˊ ·ㄅㄠ)
a kind of sachet

香花(ㄒㄧㄤ ㄏㄨㄚ)
fragrant flowers

香火(ㄒㄧㄤ ㄏㄨㄛˇ)
①incense burned and candles lighted in honor of a deity, an ancestor, etc. ②an oath; a vow

香火因緣(ㄒㄧㄤ ㄏㄨㄛˇ ㄧㄣ ㄩㄢˊ)
brotherhood based on an oath made in one's previous life; deep mental accord between friends

香灰(ㄒㄧㄤ ㄏㄨㄟ)
ashes of incense

香會(ㄒㄧㄤ ㄏㄨㄟˋ)
a group of pilgrims from various walks of people such as acrobats, stilts-walkers, tailors, food vendors, etc.

香蕉(ㄒㄧㄤ ㄐㄧㄠ)
a banana

香蕉皮(ㄒㄧㄤ ㄐㄧㄠ ㄆㄧˊ)
banana peelings

香精(ㄒㄧㄤ ㄐㄧㄥ)
essence

香氣(ㄒㄧㄤ ㄑㄧˋ)
a sweet smell; a pleasant odor; fragrance; aroma: 玫瑰花香氣宜人。These roses have delightful fragrance.

香錢(ㄒㄧㄤ ㄑㄧㄢˊ)
cash contributions by visitors to a temple

香消玉殞(ㄒㄧㄤ ㄒㄧㄠ ㄩˋ ㄩㄣˇ)
(literally) The fragrance is gone and the jade is fallen. —The beauty is dead.

香燭(ㄒㄧㄤ ㄓㄨˊ)
incense and candles—materials for the altar

香巢(ㄒㄧㄤ ㄔㄠˊ)
a brothel; a house of ill fame

香腸(ㄒㄧㄤ ㄔㄤˊ)
sausage

香串(ㄒㄧㄤ ㄔㄨㄢˋ)
a rosary made of fragrant material

香椿頭(ㄒㄧㄤ ㄔㄨㄣ ㄊㄡˊ)
cedar shoots

香山居士(ㄒㄧㄤ ㄕㄢ ㄐㄩ ㄕˋ)
a nickname of the Tang Dynasty poet Pai Chü-i(白居易)

香水(ㄒㄧㄤ ㄕㄨㄟˇ)
perfume; scent: 她用了過多的香水。She uses too much scent.

香肉(ㄒㄧㄤ ㄖㄡˋ)
(euphemism) dog meat

香澤(ㄒㄧㄤ ㄗㄜˊ)
perfumed hair oil

香皂(ㄒㄧㄤ ㄗㄠˋ)
perfumed soap; toilet soap: 我買了一塊香皂。I bought a cake of toilet soap.

香菜(ㄒㄧㄤ ㄘㄞˋ)
parsley

香草(ㄒㄧㄤ ㄘㄠˇ)
①vanilla ②a fragrant herb

香草美人(ㄒㄧㄤ ㄘㄠˇ ㄇㄟˇ ㄖㄣˊ)
a loyal vassal and his lord (from a metaphor in 離騷)

香酥雞(ㄒㄧㄤ ㄙㄨ ㄐㄧ)
crisp fried chicken

香案(ㄒㄧㄤ ㄢˋ)
a long altar on which incense burners are placed; an incense table

香油(ㄒㄧㄤ ㄧㄡˊ)
①perfumed oil; aromatic oil ②sesame oil

香煙(ㄒㄧㄤ ㄧㄢ)
①cigarettes ②continuity of the family line: 他家香煙絕了。His family line died out. ③smoke of burning incense

香豔(ㄒㄧㄤ ㄧㄢˋ)
full of glamor; glamorous; amorous

香豔故事(ㄒㄧㄤ ㄧㄢˋ ㄍㄨˋ ·ㄕ)or 香豔小說(ㄒㄧㄤ ㄧㄢˋ ㄒㄧㄠˇ ㄕㄨㄛ)
a love story

香味(ㄒㄧㄤ ㄨㄟˋ)
spicy taste; aromatic flavor

香櫞(ㄒㄧㄤ ㄩㄢˊ)
a kind of fragrant but inedible citron 亦作「佛手柑」

香雲紗(ㄒㄧㄤ ㄩㄣˊ ㄕㄚ)
silk fabric with a thin film of lacquer on the surface, manufactured in Kwangtung and used as summer dress material

九畫

【馥】 6919
ㄈㄨˋ fuh fù
fragrance; aroma

馥郁(ㄈㄨˋ ㄩˋ)
powerfully fragrant

十一畫

6920
【馨】 ㄒㄧㄣ shin xīn (又讀 ㄒㄧㄥ shing xīng)

〔馬部〕

fragrance or aroma (especially that which comes from afar)

馨香(ㄒㄧㄣ ㄒㄧㄤ)
fragrance; aroma

馬 部
ㄇㄚˇ maa mǎ

【馬】 6921 ㄇㄚˇ maa mǎ

1. a horse: 人有失錯，馬有漏蹄。Men all make mistakes; horses all stumble.
2. a Chinese family name

馬背(ㄇㄚˇ ㄅㄟˋ)
horseback: 他騎在馬背上。He is on horseback.

馬寶(ㄇㄚˇ ㄅㄠˇ)
bezoar of a horse (used as medicine)

馬棒(ㄇㄚˇ ㄅㄤˋ)
a short club for driving a horse

馬錶 or 馬表(ㄇㄚˇ ㄅㄧㄠˇ)
a pocket watch; a stopwatch: 馬錶壞了。The stopwatch will not work.

馬鞭子(ㄇㄚˇ ㄅㄧㄢ ˙ㄗ)
a horsewhip

馬弁(ㄇㄚˇ ㄅㄧㄢˋ)
bodyguards or orderlies of ranking officers in former times

馬不停蹄(ㄇㄚˇ ㄅㄨˋ ㄊㄧㄥˊ ㄊㄧˊ)
to travel on horseback without stop—to do something without stop or a single halt

馬棚(ㄇㄚˇ ㄆㄥˊ)
a stable

馬匹(ㄇㄚˇ ㄆㄧ)
horses; horseflesh: 他是個鑑別馬匹的行家。He's a good judge of horseflesh.

馬屁大王(ㄇㄚˇ ㄆㄧˋ ㄉㄚˋ ㄨㄤˊ)
a sycophant; a flatterer

馬屁精(ㄇㄚˇ ㄆㄧˋ ㄐㄧㄥ)
a flatterer; a toady

馬屁之用大矣哉(ㄇㄚˇ ㄆㄧˋ ㄓ ㄩㄥˋ ㄉㄚˋ ㄧˇ ㄗㄞ)
Flattery is everything.

馬票(ㄇㄚˇ ㄆㄧㄠˋ)
a pari-mutuel ticket

馬馬虎虎(ㄇㄚˇ ˙ㄇㄚ ㄏㄨ ㄏㄨ) or 馬虎(ㄇㄚˇ ˙ㄏㄨ)
① perfunctory; careless; sloppy; slovenly ② not very good; so-so

馬販子(ㄇㄚˇ ㄈㄢˋ ˙ㄗ)
a horse dealer; a horse-coper

馬糞(ㄇㄚˇ ㄈㄣˋ)
horse dung

馬糞紙(ㄇㄚˇ ㄈㄣˋ ㄓˇ)
a kind of coarse cardboard; strawboard

馬房(ㄇㄚˇ ㄈㄤˊ)
a stable

馬夫(ㄇㄚˇ ˙ㄈㄨ)
a groom: 馬夫餵食廐中的馬。The groom fed the horses in the stable.

馬達(ㄇㄚˇ ㄉㄚˊ)
a motor

馬達加斯加(ㄇㄚˇ ㄉㄚˊ ㄐㄧㄚ ㄙ ㄐㄧㄚ)
Madagascar

馬德拉斯(ㄇㄚˇ ㄉㄜˊ ㄌㄚ ㄙ)
Madras, an Indian port

馬德里(ㄇㄚˇ ㄉㄜˊ ㄌㄧˇ)
Madrid, the capital of Spain

馬刀(ㄇㄚˇ ㄉㄠ)
a saber

馬到成功(ㄇㄚˇ ㄉㄠˋ ㄔㄥˊ ㄍㄨㄥ)
to be accomplished quickly and easily; with immediate success

馬燈(ㄇㄚˇ ㄉㄥ)
a barn lantern

馬蹬(ㄇㄚˇ ㄉㄥˋ)
a stirrup

馬丁路得(ㄇㄚˇ ㄉㄧㄥ ㄌㄨˋ ㄉㄜˊ)
Martin Luther, 1483-1546, the founder of the Protestant movement

馬隊(ㄇㄚˇ ㄉㄨㄟˋ)
mounted troops; cavalry troops

馬太福音(ㄇㄚˇ ㄊㄞˋ ㄈㄨˊ ㄧㄣ)
the Gospel of Matthew

馬蹄(ㄇㄚˇ ㄊㄧˊ)
①hoofs of a horse②a horseshoe

馬蹄表(ㄇㄚˇ ㄊㄧˊ ㄅㄧㄠˇ)
a desk clock; a table clock

馬蹄鐵(ㄇㄚˇ ㄊㄧˊ ㄊㄧㄝˇ)
a horseshoe

馬蹄袖(ㄇㄚˇ ㄊㄧˊ ㄒㄧㄡˋ)
sleeves with a flapper for the protection of a horse rider's hand holding the rein against cold

馬蹄形(ㄇㄚˇ ㄊㄧˊ ㄒㄧㄥˊ)
the shape of a hoof; U-shaped

馬蹄銀(ㄇㄚˇ ㄊㄧˊ ㄧㄣˊ)
silver ingots in the shape of a horseshoe

馬桶(ㄇㄚˇ ㄊㄨㄥˇ)
a chamber pot; a close-stool; a nightstool

馬尼拉(ㄇㄚˇ ㄋㄧˊ ㄌㄚ)
Manila, the capital of Philippines 亦作「馬尼剌」

馬拉加西共和國(ㄇㄚˇ ㄌㄚ ㄐㄧㄚ ㄒㄧ ㄍㄨㄥˋ ㄏㄜˊ ㄍㄨㄛˊ)
the Malagasy Republic

馬拉松(ㄇㄚˇ ㄌㄚ ㄙㄨㄥ)
① marathon ② Marathon

馬拉威共和國(ㄇㄚˇ ㄌㄚ ㄨㄟ ㄍㄨㄥˋ ㄏㄜˊ ㄍㄨㄛˊ)
the Republic of Malawi

馬勒(ㄇㄚˇ ㄌㄜˋ)
the bit of a horse

馬來半島(ㄇㄚˇ ㄌㄞˊ ㄅㄢˋ ㄉㄠˇ)
the Malay Peninsula

馬來羣島(ㄇㄚˇ ㄌㄞˊ ㄑㄩㄣˊ ㄉㄠˇ)
the Malay Archipelago

馬來西亞(ㄇㄚˇ ㄌㄞˊ ㄒㄧ ㄧㄚˋ)
Malaysia; Malaysian: 他太太是馬來西亞人。His wife comes from Malaysia.

馬來人(ㄇㄚˇ ㄌㄞˊ ㄖㄣˊ)
a Malay; the Malays

馬來亞(ㄇㄚˇ ㄌㄞˊ ㄧㄚˋ)
Malaya, a state of Malaysia

馬來語(ㄇㄚˇ ㄌㄞˊ ㄩˇ)
the Malay language; Malay: 他說馬來語。He speaks Malay.

馬力(ㄇㄚˇ ㄌㄧˋ)
horsepower

馬利蘭(ㄇㄚˇ ㄌㄧˋ ㄌㄢˊ)
the state of Maryland, U.S.A.

馬利共和國(ㄇㄚˇ ㄌㄧˋ ㄍㄨㄥˋ ㄏㄜˊ ㄍㄨㄛˊ)
the Republic of Mali

馬利亞(ㄇㄚˇ ㄌㄧˋ ㄧㄚˋ)
Mary; the Virgin Mary 亦作「瑪利亞」

馬鬣(ㄇㄚˇ ㄌㄧㄝˋ)
a mane: 那匹馬的馬鬣稀少。That horse has a thin mane.

馬列主義(ㄇㄚˇ ㄌㄧㄝˋ ㄓㄨˇ ㄧˋ) or 馬克斯列寧主義(ㄇㄚˇ ㄎㄜˋ ㄙ ㄌㄧㄝˋ

ㄋㄧㄥˊ ㄓㄨˇ ㄧˋ)
Marxism-Leninism

馬六甲海峽(ㄇㄚˇ ㄌㄧㄡˋ ㄐㄧㄚˇ ㄏㄞˇ ㄒㄧㄚˊ)
the Strait of Malacca 亦作「麻六甲海峽」

馬鈴薯(ㄇㄚˇ ㄌㄧㄥˊ ㄕㄨˇ)
a potato: 馬鈴薯長在地下。Potatoes grow under the ground.

馬路(ㄇㄚˇ ㄌㄨˋ)
a street; a highway; a road: 你穿越馬路時要小心。Be careful when you cross streets.

馬路如虎口(ㄇㄚˇ ㄌㄨˋ ㄖㄨˊ ㄏㄨˇ ㄎㄡˇ)
The street is as dangerous as a tiger.— Beware of traffic accidents.

馬絡頭(ㄇㄚˇ ㄌㄨㄛˋ ㄊㄡˊ)
a halter

馬哥孛羅(ㄇㄚˇ ㄍㄜ ㄅㄛˊ ㄌㄨㄛˊ)
Marco Polo, C. 1254-1324, Italian traveler who stayed in China for 23 years

馬革裹屍(ㄇㄚˇ ㄍㄜˊ ㄍㄨㄛˇ ㄕ)
to have the corpse wrapped in horsehide—to die in battle

馬褂(ㄇㄚˇ ㄍㄨㄚˋ)
the ceremonial jacket of a mandarin

馬關條約(ㄇㄚˇ ㄍㄨㄢ ㄊㄧㄠˊ ㄩㄝ)
the Treaty of Shimonoseki, 1895, under which Taiwan and the Pescadores were ceded to Japan by the Manchu government

馬公(ㄇㄚˇ ㄍㄨㄥ)
Makung, a harbor of the Pescadores: 我們在早晨到達馬公。We arrived at Makung in the morning.

馬可尼(ㄇㄚˇ ㄎㄜˇ ㄋㄧˊ)
Marchese Guglielmo Marconi, 1874-1937, Italian inventor

馬克(ㄇㄚˇ ㄎㄜˋ)
a Deutsche mark; an ostmark; a mark

馬克白(ㄇㄚˇ ㄎㄜˋ ㄅㄞˊ)
Macbeth, a tragedy

馬克吐溫(ㄇㄚˇ ㄎㄜˋ ㄊㄨˇ ㄨㄣ)
Mark Twain, 1835-1910, American writer

馬克斯(ㄇㄚˇ ㄎㄜˋ ㄙ)
Karl Marx, 1818-1883, German philosopher

馬克斯主義(ㄇㄚˇ ㄎㄜˋ ㄙ ㄓㄨˇ ㄧˋ)
Marxism, the system of economic and political thought developed by Karl Marx

馬口鐵(ㄇㄚˇ ㄎㄡˇ ㄊㄧㄝˇ)
tinplate 亦作「洋鐵」

馬褲(ㄇㄚˇ ㄎㄨˋ)
riding breeches

馬後砲(ㄇㄚˇ ㄏㄡˋ ㄆㄠˋ)
① belated action: 我這個建議也許是馬後砲。My suggestion may already be too late. ② I-told-you-so remarks

馬虎(ㄇㄚˇ ·ㄏㄨ)
careless; casual: 這個年輕人做事較馬虎。This young man is a rather careless fellow.

馬蟥(ㄇㄚˇ ㄏㄨㄤˊ)
a horseleech

馬甲(ㄇㄚˇ ㄐㄧㄚˇ)
① armor for a horse ② (Shanghai dialect) a vest

馬脚(ㄇㄚˇ ㄐㄧㄠˇ)
one's concealed true character

馬廄(ㄇㄚˇ ㄐㄧㄡˋ)
a stable

馬具(ㄇㄚˇ ㄐㄩˋ)
horse gear; riding gear

馬其頓(ㄇㄚˇ ㄑㄧˊ ㄉㄨㄣˋ)
Macedonia

馬球(ㄇㄚˇ ㄑㄧㄡˊ)
polo: 你會玩馬球嗎? Do you know how to play polo?

馬戲(ㄇㄚˇ ㄒㄧˋ)
a circus show; a circus

馬戲團(ㄇㄚˇ ㄒㄧˋ ㄊㄨㄢˊ)
a circus troupe; a circus

馬歇爾計劃(ㄇㄚˇ ㄒㄧㄝ ㄦˇ ㄐㄧˋ ㄏㄨㄚˋ)
the Marshall Plan

馬靴(ㄇㄚˇ ㄒㄩㄝ)
jackboots; riding boots: 他買了一雙新馬靴。He bought a pair of new jackboots.

馬掌(ㄇㄚˇ ㄓㄤˇ)
a horseshoe

馬齒徒增(ㄇㄚˇ ㄔˇ ㄊㄨˊ ㄗㄥ)
(literally) like a horse that grows only in the number of teeth—having accomplished nothing despite one's advanced age (usually a polite expression)

馬車(ㄇㄚˇ ㄔㄜ)
a carriage; a coach; a landau: 汽車已取代了四輪馬車。Automobiles have taken the place of carriages.

馬氏文通(ㄇㄚˇ ㄕˋ ㄨㄣˊ ㄊㄨㄥ)
title of a book by Ma Chien-chung (馬建中) in the late 19th century, in which Chinese grammar was discussed for the first time

馬首是瞻(ㄇㄚˇ ㄕㄡˇ ㄕˋ ㄓㄢ)
to follow someone; to look on someone as an example

馬上(ㄇㄚˇ ㄕㄤˋ)
① on horseback ② right away; at once; immediately; without delay: 我離開之後,他馬上就到。He arrived immediately after I left.

馬術(ㄇㄚˇ ㄕㄨˋ)
horsemanship

馬祖(ㄇㄚˇ ㄗㄨˇ)
① the goddess of the sea much worshiped in Taiwan and the southern China coast 亦作「媽祖」② the Matsu Islands (off the Fukien coast)

馬鬃(ㄇㄚˇ ㄗㄨㄥ)
a mane; horsehair

馬槽(ㄇㄚˇ ㄘㄠˊ)
a manger

馬嘶(ㄇㄚˇ ㄙ)
to neigh; a neigh

馬賽(ㄇㄚˇ ㄙㄞˋ)
Marseilles, a French port: 馬賽是法國第二大城市。Marseilles is the second largest city in France.

馬賽克(ㄇㄚˇ ㄙㄞˋ ㄎㄜˋ)
(architecture) mosaic

馬鞍子(ㄇㄚˇ ㄢ ·ㄗ)
a saddle

馬爾地夫(ㄇㄚˇ ㄦˇ ㄉㄧˋ ㄈㄨ)
the Maldive Islands

馬爾他(ㄇㄚˇ ㄦˇ ㄊㄚ)
Malta, an island in the Mediterranean between Sicily and Africa

馬爾薩斯(ㄇㄚˇ ㄦˇ ㄙㄚˋ ㄙ)
Thomas Robert Malthus, 1766-1834, English economist: 馬爾薩斯以人口論聞名。Malthus was famous for his *Essay on Population.*

馬醫(ㄇㄚˇ ㄧ)
a horse doctor; a veterinarian

馬衣(ㄇㄚˇ ㄧ)

〔馬部〕

〔馬部〕

horsecloth

馬雅文化(ㄇㄚˇ ㄧㄚˇ ㄨㄣˊ ㄏㄨㄚˋ)
Maya civilization

馬仰人翻(ㄇㄚˇ ㄧㄤˇ ㄖㄣˊ ㄈㄢ)
The rider falls as the horse rears in fright.—There is panic.

馬尾(ㄇㄚˇ ㄨㄟˇ)
①a horsetail ②name of a harbor in Fukien

馬援(ㄇㄚˇ ㄩㄢˊ)
Ma Yüan, 14 B.C.—49 A.D., a famous general of the Han Dynasty

二畫

【馭】 6922
ㄩˋ yuh yù
1. to drive (a carriage, chariot, etc.)
2. to govern; to rule; to control
3. a driver

【馮】 6923
1. ㄈㄥˊ ferng féng
a Chinese family name

馮婦(ㄈㄥˊ ㄈㄨˋ)
①Feng Fu, a man in Tsin, famous for his skill in seizing tigers ②as in 重作馮婦—a role one has played before; something one is called upon to do again

馮夷(ㄈㄥˊ ㄧˊ)
the water god in charge of the Yellow River 亦作「河伯」

【馮】 6923
2. ㄆㄧㄥˊ pyng píng
1. to gallop
2. by dint of; on the strength of 亦作「憑」

馮河(ㄆㄧㄥˊ ㄏㄜˊ)
(literally) to cross a river without a boat—to be reckless

馮虛御風(ㄆㄧㄥˊ ㄒㄩ ㄩˋ ㄈㄥ)
to tread thin air and sail by wind (a feat attributed to immortals)

三畫

【馱】 6924
1. ㄊㄨㄛˊ two tuó
to carry (a load) on the back

馱不動(ㄊㄨㄛˊ ·ㄅㄨ ㄉㄨㄥˋ)
too heavy to carry on the back

馱著(ㄊㄨㄛˊ ·ㄓㄜ)
carrying (a load) on the back

【馱】 6924
2. ㄉㄨㄛˋ duoh duò
a load carried by a pack animal

【馳】 6925
ㄔˊ chyr chí
1. to go swiftly; to fleet; to rush; to speed: 一架飛機由天空飛馳而過。A plane fleeted across the sky.
2. to exert; to exercise
3. to spread; to propagate

馳辯(ㄔˊ ㄅㄧㄢˋ)
to exert the gift of speech; to exercise one's eloquence

馳馬(ㄔˊ ㄇㄚˇ)
to go swiftly on horseback

馳名(ㄔˊ ㄇㄧㄥˊ)
① to spread one's fame ② famous; well-known; renowned: 一大群人向那馳名的英雄歡呼。A great crowd of people greeted the famous hero.

馳名中外(ㄔˊ ㄇㄧㄥˊ ㄓㄨㄥ ㄨㄞˋ)
renowned at home and abroad

馳年(ㄔˊ ㄋㄧㄢˊ)
the fleeting years

馳念(ㄔˊ ㄋㄧㄢˋ)or 馳思(ㄔˊ ㄙ)or 馳系(ㄔˊ ㄒㄧˋ)
to let one's thoughts run to (somebody or something missed)

馳驅(ㄔˊ ㄑㄩ)
①to move swiftly; to fleet; to rush; to speed ②to run errands; to serve others ③ to race horses and whip them

馳檄(ㄔˊ ㄒㄧˊ)
to speed the mobilization order

馳騁(ㄔˊ ㄔㄥˇ)
①to rush about on horseback ②to play an active part in

馳驛(ㄔˊ ㄧˋ)
(said of government officials on official tour in ancient times) to travel speedily from post to post along a designated route

馳騖(ㄔˊ ㄨˋ)
to move swiftly; to speed; to run after (empty fame, power, money, etc.)

【馴】 6926
ㄒㄩㄣˊ shyun xún
(又讀ㄒㄩㄣˋ shiunn xùn)
1. tame
2. mild; docile; obedient; well-bred
3. gradual
4. to tame; to put under control; to break (an animal)

馴服(ㄒㄩㄣˊ ㄈㄨˊ)
to tame; to subdue; to break in; subdued; obedient: 這隻老虎終被馴服了。The tiger was finally broken in.

馴良(ㄒㄩㄣˊ ㄌㄧㄤˊ)
docile; obedient; tractable; gentle

馴鹿(ㄒㄩㄣˊ ㄌㄨˋ)
a reindeer

馴和(ㄒㄩㄣˊ ㄏㄜˊ)
mild; good-natured; gentle: 這男孩有馴和的性情。The boy has a gentle spirit (or nature).

馴行(ㄒㄩㄣˊ ㄒㄧㄥˊ)
good deeds

馴至(ㄒㄩㄣˊ ㄓˋ)
(said of a situation) to develop gradually; to come by degrees

馴獅人(ㄒㄩㄣˊ ㄕ ㄖㄣˊ)
a lion tamer

馴獸者(ㄒㄩㄣˊ ㄕㄡˋ ㄓㄜˇ)
an animal tamer

馴善(ㄒㄩㄣˊ ㄕㄢˋ)
good-natured; mild; gentle

馴順(ㄒㄩㄣˊ ㄕㄨㄣˋ)
obedient; docile; tractable: 她騎著一匹馴順的馬。She rides a docile horse.

馴養(ㄒㄩㄣˊ ㄧㄤˇ)
to raise (animals); to domesticate (animals); to tame: 象可以馴養以供表演之用。Elephants can be tamed for show.

【馵】 6927
ㄓㄨˋ juh zhù
a horse with the hind left leg white

四畫

【駁】 6928
ㄅㄛˊ bor bó

1. variegated; parti-colored
2. mixed; impure; jumbled
3. to rebut; to dispute; to refute; to disprove: 眞理不怕人駁。Truth fears no refutation.
4. to transport; to ship; to load and unload

駁辯(ㄅㄛˊ ㄅㄧㄢˋ)
to argue; to dispute; to debate

駁倒(ㄅㄛˊ ㄉㄠˇ)
to defeat in a debate

駁回(ㄅㄛˊ ㄏㄨㄟˊ)
to reject; to turn down; to overrule (an appeal, request, etc.): 他駁回這項控告。He rejected the accusation.

駁回上訴(ㄅㄛˊ ㄏㄨㄟˊ ㄕㄤˋ ㄙㄨˋ)
to reject an appeal

駁詰(ㄅㄛˊ ㄐㄧㄝˊ)
to question persistently

駁正(ㄅㄛˊ ㄓㄥˋ)
to correct by argument

駁斥(ㄅㄛˊ ㄔˋ)
① to refute; to rebut; to disprove; to contradict ② to reject (an appeal)

駁船(ㄅㄛˊ ㄔㄨㄢˊ)
a lighter (in a harbor, etc.) 亦作「搬運船」

駁雜(ㄅㄛˊ ㄗㄚˊ) or 駁錯(ㄅㄛˊ ㄘㄨㄛˋ)
mixed; impure

駁色(ㄅㄛˊ ㄙㄜˋ)
variegated; parti-colored

駁議(ㄅㄛˊ ㄧˋ)
to dispute; to refute

駁運(ㄅㄛˊ ㄩㄣˋ)
to transport; to ship

【駃】 6929
ㄐㄩㄝˊ jyue jué

a hybrid horse

駃騠(ㄐㄩㄝˊ ㄊㄧˊ)
a hybrid horse (the product of a donkey after mating a stallion)

五畫

【駐】 6930
ㄓㄨˋ juh zhù

1. to halt
2. to remain temporarily; to station (troops, diplomatic representatives, etc.)

駐蹕(ㄓㄨˋ ㄅㄧˋ)
the emperor's lodging when traveling

駐兵(ㄓㄨˋ ㄅㄧㄥ)
to station troops

駐防(ㄓㄨˋ ㄈㄤˊ)
to garrison (a place)

駐地(ㄓㄨˋ ㄉㄧˋ)
a place where a particular military unit is stationed

駐屯(ㄓㄨˋ ㄊㄨㄣˊ)
(said of troops) to be stationed at

駐華大使(ㄓㄨˋ ㄏㄨㄚˊ ㄉㄚˋ ㄕˇ)
an ambassador to China: 他奉派爲駐華大使。He was appointed ambassador to China.

駐華大使館(ㄓㄨˋ ㄏㄨㄚˊ ㄉㄚˋ ㄕˇ ㄍㄨㄢˇ)
an embassy in China

駐節(ㄓㄨˋ ㄐㄧㄝˊ)
(said of diplomats) to be stationed in a country

駐軍(ㄓㄨˋ ㄐㄩㄣ)
① to station troops ② an occupation force ③ a garrison; garrison troops

駐紮(ㄓㄨˋ ㄓㄚˊ)
(said of troops) to be stationed at

駐守(ㄓㄨˋ ㄕㄡˇ)
to station troops at a place for defense purpose: 他們被派駐守臺南。They were stationed at Tainan.

駐顏(ㄓㄨˋ ㄧㄢˊ)
to preserve a youthful complexion

駐顏有術(ㄓㄨˋ ㄧㄢˊ ㄧㄡˇ ㄕㄨˋ)
(said of a woman) to possess the secret of preserving a youthful complexion

【駑】 6931
ㄋㄨˊ nu nú

1. an old, worn-out horse; a jade; a hack
2. incompetent; stupid; good-for-nothing

駑馬(ㄋㄨˊ ㄇㄚˇ)
an old, worn-out horse; a jade; a hack

駑馬戀棧豆(ㄋㄨˊ ㄇㄚˇ ㄌㄧㄢˋ ㄓㄢˋ ㄉㄡˋ)
(literally) a jaded horse hankering after its stall—an incompetent man clinging to a good position

駑鈍(ㄋㄨˊ ㄉㄨㄣˋ)
incompetent; incapable

駑駘(ㄋㄨˊ ㄊㄞˊ)
an old, worn-out horse; a jade; a hack

駑鉛(ㄋㄨˊ ㄑㄧㄢ)
mediocre

駑下(ㄋㄨˊ ㄒㄧㄚˋ)
inferior

駑散(ㄋㄨˊ ㄙㄢˇ)
inferior; mediocre

【駒】 6932
ㄐㄩ jiu jū

1. a young and fleet-footed horse; a foal; a colt
2. (figuratively) the sun

駒光(ㄐㄩ ㄍㄨㄤ)
fleeting time

駒隙(ㄐㄩ ㄒㄧˋ)
fleeting time

駒齒(ㄐㄩ ㄔˇ)
milk teeth—youth

駒影(ㄐㄩ ㄧㄥˇ)
fleeting time

【駔】 6933
1. ㄗㄤˇ tzaang zǎng

1. a strong horse
2. a horse broker

【駔】 6933
2. ㄗㄨˋ tzuh zù

a swift horse; a fine horse

【駔】 6933
3. ㄘㄤˇ tsaang cǎng

參看「駔子」

駔子(ㄘㄤˇ ·ㄗ)
a rascal; a ruffian; a mean person

【駕】 6934
ㄐㄧㄚˋ jiah jià

1. to ride; to drive; to pilot: 你會駕車嗎? Can you drive a car?
2. to excel; to surpass
3. to yoke; to put the horses to the carriage
4. vehicles
5. an honorific epithet
6. to control; to reign or rule
7. the emperor

駕崩(ㄐㄧㄚˋ ㄅㄥ)
(said of the emperor) to pass away

駕臨(ㄐㄧㄚˋ ㄌㄧㄣˊ)
to give (our humble place) the honor of your visit

駕機(ㄐㄧㄚˋ ㄐㄧ)
to pilot a plane

駕輕就熟(ㄐㄧㄚˋ ㄑㄧㄥ ㄐㄧㄡˋ ㄕㄨˊ)
(literally) to drive a light

〔馬部〕

carriage through a familiar road—to do a task with ease
駕車(ㄐㄧㄚˋ ㄔㄜ)
to drive a vehicle
駕駛(ㄐㄧㄚˋ ㄕˇ)
①to drive (automobiles); to pilot (aircraft); to steer (boats): 小心駕駛。Drive with caution. ②a driver: 他是個莽撞的駕駛。He is a reckless driver.
駕駛執照(ㄐㄧㄚˋ ㄕˇ ㄓˊ ㄓㄠˋ)
a driver's license
駕駛員(ㄐㄧㄚˋ ㄕˇ ㄩㄢˊ)
a driver; a pilot: 駕駛員降下飛機。The pilot landed the airplane.
駕霧騰雲(ㄐㄧㄚˋ ㄨˋ ㄊㄥˊ ㄩㄣˊ)
to ride mist and float on clouds (as immortals do)
駕馭(ㄐㄧㄚˋ ㄩˋ)
①to drive (horse-drawn vehicles) ②to control; to tame; to maneuver; to direct: 這些馬不好駕馭。These horses are hard to control.
駕御(ㄐㄧㄚˋ ㄩˋ)
to exercise control; to be at the helm

【駘】 6935 ㄊㄞˊ tair tái
1. a worn-out horse; a jade
2. weary; exhausted; jaded
3. incompetent

【駙】 6936 ㄈㄨˋ fuh fù
1. extra horses harnessed by the side of the team
2. swift
駙馬(ㄈㄨˋ ㄇㄚˇ)
① an ancient official title ② imperial son-in-law

【駛】 6937 ㄕˇ shyy shǐ
1. (said of vehicles) to run; (said of vessels) to sail: 你會駕駛船嗎? Can you sail a boat?
2. fast; fleeting
駛回(ㄕˇ ㄏㄨㄟˊ)
(said of vessels or vehicles) to return; to sail back; to go back
駛近(ㄕˇ ㄐㄧㄣˋ)
(said of vehicles or vessels) to approach
駛行(ㄕˇ ㄒㄧㄥˊ)
(said of vessels or vehicles) to go; to run; to sail: 該船順風駛行。The ship ran before the wind.
駛船(ㄕˇ ㄔㄨㄢˊ)
to sail a ship: 孩子們正在學習駛船。The boys are learning to sail.

【駝】 6938 ㄊㄨㄛˊ two tuó
1. a camel: 駱駝被人稱爲沙漠之舟。A camel is called a ship of the desert.
2. hunchbacked
3. to carry on the back
4. to pay
駝背(ㄊㄨㄛˊ ㄅㄟˋ)
hunchbacked; humpbacked
駝峯(ㄊㄨㄛˊ ㄈㄥ)
the hump of a camel
駝鳥(ㄊㄨㄛˊ ㄋㄧㄠˇ)
an ostrich: 駝鳥不會飛。Ostriches cannot fly.
駝絨(ㄊㄨㄛˊ ㄖㄨㄥˊ)
①camel's hair ②fabric made of camel's hair
駝子(ㄊㄨㄛˊ ·ㄗ)
a humpbacked person; a humpback; a hunchback

【駟】 6939 ㄙˋ syh sì
1. a team of four horses
2. horses
3. four
4. name of a star
駟不及舌(ㄙˋ ㄅㄨˋ ㄐㄧˊ ㄕㄜˊ)
Even a team of four horses cannot overtake and recover what is already said.
駟馬難追(ㄙˋ ㄇㄚˇ ㄋㄢˊ ㄓㄨㄟ)
Even with a team of four horses, it is difficult to overtake carelessly uttered words. 一言既出，駟馬難追。When a word has once left the lips, the swiftest horse cannot overtake it.
駟馬高車(ㄙˋ ㄇㄚˇ ㄍㄠ ㄐㄩ)
a high carriage drawn by a team of four horses—(figuratively) vehicles of the rich

六畫

【駭】 6940 ㄏㄞˋ hay hài
1. to terrify; to frighten; to startle; to scare; to amaze; to surprise: 這消息使我們大爲驚駭。The news greatly surprised us.
2. to marvel; to wonder
駭怕(ㄏㄞˋ ㄆㄚˋ)
scared; frightened: 此次地震你駭怕嗎? Were you frightened by the earthquake?
駭浪(ㄏㄞˋ ㄌㄤˋ)
awful waves; fearful billows
駭怪(ㄏㄞˋ ㄍㄨㄞˋ)
to be shocked; to be astonished; to marvel and wonder
駭汗(ㄏㄞˋ ㄏㄢˋ)
to perspire as a result of fright
駭人聽聞(ㄏㄞˋ ㄖㄣˊ ㄊㄧㄥ ㄨㄣˊ)
(said of atrocities, crimes, etc.) frightening; blood-curdling; shocking (news)
駭愕(ㄏㄞˋ ㄜˋ)
to be amazed; to be flabbergasted: 我對他的行爲感到駭愕。I was amazed at his conduct.
駭異(ㄏㄞˋ ㄧˋ)
surprised; amazed
駭惋(ㄏㄞˋ ㄨㄢˋ)
to marvel

【駱】 6941 ㄌㄨㄛˋ luoh luò
1. a white horse (or steed) with black mane
2. a camel
3. a Chinese family name
駱賓王(ㄌㄨㄛˋ ㄅㄧㄣ ㄨㄤˊ)
Lo Pin-wang, ?-684, an early Tang Dynasty man of letters, noted for his denunciation of Empress Wu in a manifesto
駱馬(ㄌㄨㄛˋ ㄇㄚˇ)
(zoology) a llama
駱駝(ㄌㄨㄛˋ ·ㄊㄨㄛ)
a camel
駱駝隊(ㄌㄨㄛˋ ·ㄊㄨㄛ ㄉㄨㄟˋ)
a camel train; a caravan of camels
駱駝絨(ㄌㄨㄛˋ ·ㄊㄨㄛ ㄖㄨㄥˊ)
①camel's hair ②fabric made of camel's hair

【駬】 6942 ㄦˇ eel ěr
name of a legendary swift horse

【駮】 6943 ㄅㄛˊ bor bó
1. a kind of fierce animal
2. mixed; impure

3. to refute 亦作「駁」

【駢】 6944
ㄆㄧㄢ pyan pián
1. a pair of horses
2. to stand or lie side by side
參看「駢」

七畫

【騁】 6945
ㄔㄥˇ cheeng chěng
1. to go swiftly; to speed
2. to exert; to unfold; to develop
3. to give free play to; to lend wings to

騁步(ㄔㄥˇ ㄅㄨˋ)
to rush; to speed

騁目(ㄔㄥˇ ㄇㄨˋ)
to look as far as the eyes can see

騁能(ㄔㄥˇ ㄋㄥˊ)
to give full display to one's abilities

騁懷(ㄔㄥˇ ㄏㄨㄞˊ)
to feel elated; to feel brimming happiness; to have one's heart filled with joy

騁志(ㄔㄥˇ ㄓˋ)
to lend wings to one's ambition

騁馳(ㄔㄥˇ ㄔˊ)
(said of a person or animal) to go at full speed

騁望(ㄔㄥˇ ㄨㄤˋ)
to look as far as one can see

【駿】 6946
ㄐㄩㄣˋ jiunn jùn
1. a fine horse; a swift horse
2. great; large
3. swift; speedy
4. rigorous; stringent 亦作「峻」
5. outstanding

駿奔(ㄐㄩㄣˋ ㄅㄣ)
to speed; to rush

駿馬(ㄐㄩㄣˋ ㄇㄚˇ)
a fine horse

駿命(ㄐㄩㄣˋ ㄇㄧㄥˋ)
the great appointment—Heaven's will

駿發(ㄐㄩㄣˋ ㄈㄚ)
swift success in life

駿骨(ㄐㄩㄣˋ ㄍㄨˇ)
① a talented person ② a fine horse

駿驥(ㄐㄩㄣˋ ㄐㄧˋ)
a fine horse

駿足(ㄐㄩㄣˋ ㄗㄨˊ)
① a fine horse ② a talented person

駿逸(ㄐㄩㄣˋ ㄧˋ)
distinguished; outstanding; surpassing 亦作「俊逸」

【騂】 6947
ㄒㄧㄥ shing xīng
red

【騃】 6948
ㄞˊ air ái
stupid; foolish

【駸】 6949
ㄑㄧㄣ chin qīn
galloping; speeding

【騅】 6950
ㄏㄢˋ hann hàn
1. wild (horses); fierce
2. a saddle

騅馬(ㄏㄢˋ ㄇㄚˇ)
an untamed horse; a fierce-tempered horse

八畫

【騎】 6951
ㄑㄧˊ chyi qí
(名詞讀音 ㄐㄧˋ jih jì)
to ride (a horse, etc.); to sit astride on: 你會騎馬嗎? Can you ride?

騎兵(ㄑㄧˊ ㄅㄧㄥ) or (ㄐㄧˋ ㄅㄧㄥ)
cavalry; mounted troops

騎馬(ㄑㄧˊ ㄇㄚˇ)
to ride a horse: 他每天早晨騎馬。He rides every morning.

騎馬布(ㄑㄧˊ ㄇㄚˇ ㄅㄨˋ)
a hygienic band

騎馬找馬(ㄑㄧˊ ㄇㄚˇ ㄓㄠˇ ㄇㄚˇ)
(literally) to ride a horse while looking for another one—to hold a temporary position while seeking a better job

騎縫(ㄑㄧˊ ㄈㄥˋ)
the edges of two separate sheets of a document (on which a seal is to be stamped with part of the impression on each of the two sheets)

騎樓(ㄑㄧˊ ㄌㄡˊ)
an arcade (a covered avenue)

騎驢(ㄑㄧˊ ㄌㄩˊ)
① to ride a donkey ② intermediary exploitation

騎驢覓驢(ㄑㄧˊ ㄌㄩˊ ㄇㄧˋ ㄌㄩˊ)
(literally) to seek a donkey while riding one—to forget what one already has

騎驢找馬(ㄑㄧˊ ㄌㄩˊ ㄓㄠˇ ㄇㄚˇ)
(literally) to ride a donkey as one seeks a horse—to maintain a job while looking for a better one

騎寇(ㄑㄧˊ ㄎㄡˋ)
mounted bandits; invading enemy cavalry

騎虎難下(ㄑㄧˊ ㄏㄨˇ ㄋㄢˊ ㄒㄧㄚˋ)
(literally) unable to get down from the tiger's back—in a position from which there is no easy retreat; unable to stop or quit; to have no way to back down

騎虎之勢(ㄑㄧˊ ㄏㄨˇ ㄓ ㄕˋ)
an awkward position from which there is no retreat

騎牆(ㄑㄧˊ ㄑㄧㄤˊ)
to sit on the fence; uncommitted between two opposing forces

騎牆派(ㄑㄧˊ ㄑㄧㄤˊ ㄆㄞˋ)
fence-sitters; a timeserver; an opportunist

騎師(ㄑㄧˊ ㄕ)
a jockey

騎士(ㄑㄧˊ ㄕˋ)
① a knight ② a horseback rider

騎射(ㄑㄧˊ ㄕㄜˋ)
horsemanship and archery

騎術(ㄑㄧˊ ㄕㄨˋ)
equitation; horsemanship

騎從(ㄐㄧˋ ㄗㄨㄥˋ)
aides and servants on horseback

【駢】 6952
(駢) ㄆㄧㄢ pyan pián
1. a pair of horses
2. to stand, lie, or go side by side

駢比(ㄆㄧㄢ ㄅㄧˋ)
contiguous

駢拇枝指(ㄆㄧㄢ ㄇㄨˇ ㄑㄧˊ ㄓˇ)
a superfluity; a redundancy

駢體文(ㄆㄧㄢ ㄊㄧˇ ㄨㄣˊ) or 駢文(ㄆㄧㄢ ㄨㄣˊ)
a euphuistically antithetic style of writing prevalent in the 6th and 7th centuries A.D.

駢儷(ㄆㄧㄢ ㄌㄧˋ)

the antithesis of four-word and six-word clauses or sentences which was in vogue in the 6th and 7th centuries A. D.

駢鄰(ㄆㄧㄢˊ ㄌㄧㄣˊ)
a next-door neighbor; side by side

駢肩(ㄆㄧㄢˊ ㄐㄧㄢ)
shoulders beside shoulders —crowded

駢四儷六(ㄆㄧㄢˊ ㄙˋ ㄌㄧˋ ㄌㄧㄡˋ)
antithesis of four-word and six-word sentences prevalent in the 6th and 7th centuries A.D.

【騏】 6953 ㄑㄧˊ chyi qí
1. a dark-blue horse
2. a fine horse
3. dark blue

騏驎 or 麒麟(ㄑㄧˊ ㄌㄧㄣˊ)
name of a fabulous animal

騏驥(ㄑㄧˊ ㄐㄧˋ)
a legendary fine horse (said capable of covering 1,000 *li* in a day)

【騄】 6954 ㄌㄨˋ luh lù
name of a legendary swift horse

騄駬 or 綠耳(ㄌㄨˋ ㄦˇ)
name of a legendary swift horse

【騅】 6955 ㄓㄨㄟ juei zhuī
a piebald horse

【騐】 6956 (驗) ㄧㄢˋ yann yàn
to test

九畫

【騖】 6957 ㄨˋ wuh wù
1. to rush; to speed
2. unrestrained; uninhibited

騖外(ㄨˋ ㄨㄞˋ)
to depart from one's proper role

騖遠(ㄨˋ ㄩㄢˇ)
impractically ambitious; overambitious

【騙】 6958 ㄆㄧㄢˋ piann piàn
1. to cheat; to defraud; to swindle; to deceive
2. to get by fraud

騙局(ㄆㄧㄢˋ ㄐㄩˊ)
a fraud; a swindle; a trick; a chicanery; a deception; a hoax; a racket: 這只是個騙局，別太認眞。It is only a hoax. Don't take it seriously.

騙錢(ㄆㄧㄢˋ ㄑㄧㄢˊ)
to cheat a person out of money; to get money by fraud

騙取(ㄆㄧㄢˋ ㄑㄩˇ)
to obtain by fraud; to cheat: 他騙取我的錢。He cheated me out of money.

騙取選票(ㄆㄧㄢˋ ㄑㄩˇ ㄒㄩㄢˇ ㄆㄧㄠˋ)
to wangle votes

騙術(ㄆㄧㄢˋ ㄕㄨˋ)
a trick; a ruse; a stratagem; wiles

騙人(ㄆㄧㄢˋ ㄖㄣˊ)
to cheat others; to defraud others; to swindle others; to lie

騙子(ㄆㄧㄢˋ ·ㄗ)
a swindler; a cheat; a confidence man; a racketeer; an impostor; a fraud

騙嘴(ㄆㄧㄢˋ ㄗㄨㄟˇ) or 騙吃(ㄆㄧㄢˋ ㄔ)
to get food by fraud or trickery

騙財(ㄆㄧㄢˋ ㄘㄞˊ)
to get money by fraud or trickery

騙案(ㄆㄧㄢˋ ㄢˋ)
a case of fraud

【騣】 6959 (鬃) ㄗㄨㄥ tzong zōng
a mane

【騤】 6960 ㄎㄨㄟˊ kwei kuí
(said of a horse) lively; vigorous; strong

【騠】 6961 ㄊㄧˊ tyi tí
a hybrid horse produced by mating a donkey with a stallion

【騞】 6962 ㄏㄨㄛˋ huoh huò
the sound of a knife cutting something

十畫

【騫】 6963 ㄑㄧㄢ chian qiān
1. to raise high; to uplift
2. to soar; to fly; to rise
3. to pull up
4. frightened

騫騰(ㄑㄧㄢ ㄊㄥˊ)
to soar high or go up (especially in officialdom)

騫舉(ㄑㄧㄢ ㄐㄩˇ)
to soar

騫旗斬將(ㄑㄧㄢ ㄑㄧˊ ㄓㄢˇ ㄐㄧㄤˋ)
to pull up enemy flags and behead enemy generals on the battlefield

【騭】 6964 ㄓˋ jyh zhì
1. a stallion
2. to go up; to rise
3. predestined

【騰】 6965 ㄊㄥˊ terng téng
1. to prance; to rear; to leap; to jump
2. to go up; to rise; to fly; to soar
3. to turn over; to surrender; to transfer

騰馬(ㄊㄥˊ ㄇㄚˇ)
a stallion

騰達(ㄊㄥˊ ㄉㄚˊ)
to prosper; to thrive

騰騰(ㄊㄥˊ ㄊㄥˊ)
① soaring; rising ② drunk; asleep ③ slowly

騰挪(ㄊㄥˊ ㄋㄨㄛˊ)
① to transfer ② to move something to make room

騰貴(ㄊㄥˊ ㄍㄨㄟˋ)
(said of prices) to skyrocket

騰空(ㄊㄥˊ ㄎㄨㄥ)
to fly in the sky; to soar

騰捷(ㄊㄥˊ ㄐㄧㄝˊ)
to fly swiftly; to flit

騰蛟起鳳(ㄊㄥˊ ㄐㄧㄠ ㄑㄧˇ ㄈㄥˋ)
(literally) a flying dragon and soaring phoenix—(figuratively) genius

騰笑(ㄊㄥˊ ㄒㄧㄠˋ)
to arouse laughter

騰驤(ㄊㄥˊ ㄒㄧㄤ)
to leap high; to prance

騰閃(ㄊㄥˊ ㄕㄢˇ)
to dodge; to ward off; to evade

騰躍(ㄊㄥˊ ㄧㄠˋ)
① to prance; to be lively; to be active ② (said of prices) to skyrocket

騰雲駕霧(ㄊㄥˊ ㄩㄣˊ ㄐㄧㄚˋ ㄨˋ)

①to sail clouds and ride mist (as immortals do) ② fast; quick

【騷】 6966 ㄙㄠ sau sāo

1. to disturb; to agitate
2. to worry; to feel concerned
3. ill-smelling; stinking
4. (colloquial) amorous; erotic

騷動(ㄙㄠ ㄉㄨㄥˋ)
disturbance; unrest; upheaval; commotion; tumult: 群衆騷動起來。The crowd was in unrest.

騷體(ㄙㄠ ㄊㄧˇ)
poetic style in the tradition of 離騷 by Chü Yüan(屈原)

騷女人(ㄙㄠ ㄋㄩˇ ㄖㄣˊ)
a woman of loose morals; an erotic woman

騷老頭兒(ㄙㄠ ㄌㄠˇ ㄊㄡˊㄦ)
(colloquial) an old man with strong sexual desire; an old wolf

騷亂(ㄙㄠ ㄌㄨㄢˋ)
disturbance; unrest; upheaval; agitation; tumult

騷客(ㄙㄠ ㄎㄜˋ)or 騷人(ㄙㄠ ㄖㄣˊ)or 騷人墨客(ㄙㄠ ㄖㄣˊ ㄇㄛˋ ㄎㄜˋ)
a poet; a bard

騷屑(ㄙㄠ ㄒㄧㄝˋ)
the whistling sound of wind

騷擾(ㄙㄠ ㄖㄠˇ)
to disturb; to harass; to agitate

騷然(ㄙㄠ ㄖㄢˊ)
disturbed; tumultuous; agitated; in commotion; an uproar: 天下騷然。The whole country was thrown into an uproar.

【騶】 6967 ㄗㄡ tzou zōu

1. an official in charge of driving carriages
2. a mounted escort

騶卒(ㄗㄡ ㄗㄨˊ)
①a servant ②a groom

騶從(ㄗㄡ ㄗㄨㄥˋ)
the escort of a nobleman

【騮】 6968 ㄌㄧㄡˊ liou liú

a legendary fine horse

十一畫

【騾】 6969 ㄌㄨㄛˊ luo luó

a mule

騾馬(ㄌㄨㄛˊ ㄇㄚˇ)
a mule

騾夫(ㄌㄨㄛˊ ㄈㄨ)
a muleteer; a muleman

騾車(ㄌㄨㄛˊ ㄔㄜ)
a mule cart

騾子(ㄌㄨㄛˊ ·ㄗ)
①a mule ②a stubborn person

【驁】 6970 ㄠˊ aur áo

1. a fine horse
2. an untamed horse
3. proud; haughty; arrogant

驁放(ㄠˊ ㄈㄤˋ)
very haughty and unrestrained

【驀】 6971 ㄇㄛˋ moh mò

1. sudden; abrupt
2. to mount the horse

驀地(ㄇㄛˋ ㄉㄧˋ)
suddenly; all of a sudden

驀忽(ㄇㄛˋ ㄏㄨ)
suddenly; all of a sudden

驀然(ㄇㄛˋ ㄖㄢˊ)
suddenly; all of a sudden

【驂】 6972 ㄘㄢ tsan cān

the two outside horses of a team of three

驂乘(ㄘㄢ ㄕㄥˋ)
(in ancient China) three persons sat in one chariot, the driver sat between the other two, the first one sitting by his left was a senior or the director, the third one sitting in his right was called 驂乘 (the third one in the chariot) 亦作「陪乘」

【驃】 6973 ㄆㄧㄠˋ piaw piào

1. a horse with a yellowish white color
2. valiant
3. galloping

驃騎(ㄆㄧㄠˋ ㄐㄧˋ)
an ancient title of general rank

【驄】 6974 ㄘㄨㄥ tsong cōng

a horse with a bluish white color

【驅】 6975 ㄑㄩ chiu qū

1. to go before others
2. to drive; to urge
3. to expel
4. to command

驅鬼(ㄑㄩ ㄍㄨㄟˇ)
to exorcise evil spirits

驅遣(ㄑㄩ ㄑㄧㄢˇ)
①to send away (a person so as to get rid of him)②to order (a person) about

驅邪(ㄑㄩ ㄒㄧㄝˊ)
to expel evil; to keep evil spirits away

驅逐(ㄑㄩ ㄓㄨˊ)
to drive out; to get rid of; to expel: 敵人被驅逐出城。The enemy were driven out of the city.

驅逐機(ㄑㄩ ㄓㄨˊ ㄐㄧ)
a pursuit plane

驅逐艦(ㄑㄩ ㄓㄨˊ ㄐㄧㄢˋ)
a destroyer

驅馳(ㄑㄩ ㄔˊ)
to run about busily (for others)

驅車(ㄑㄩ ㄔㄜ)
to drive a carriage or car

驅除(ㄑㄩ ㄔㄨˊ)
to drive out; to get rid of; to eliminate

驅蟲劑(ㄑㄩ ㄔㄨㄥˊ ㄐㄧˋ)or 驅蟲藥(ㄑㄩ ㄔㄨㄥˊ ㄧㄠˋ)
a helminthic; an anthelmintic; an insect repellent; vermifuge

驅使(ㄑㄩ ㄕˇ)
to order (a person) about: 你沒有權力驅使我。You have no right to order me about.

驅策(ㄑㄩ ㄘㄜˋ)
①to urge; to spur: 他驅策同仁們更加努力。He urged (on) the crew to greater efforts. ②to order (a person) about

驅散(ㄑㄩ ㄙㄢˋ)
to disperse by force; to scatter; to dispel: 陽光驅散了薄霧。The sun dispelled the mist.

十二畫

【驕】 6976 ㄐㄧㄠ jiau jiāo

1. untamed; intractable; disobedient
2. proud; haughty; arrogant; overbearing

〔馬部〕

3. severe; harsh; intense
驕兵必敗(ㄐㄧㄠ ㄅㄧㄥ ㄅㄧˋ ㄅㄞˋ)
An army which is cocksure about its invincibility is doomed to defeat.
驕敵(ㄐㄧㄠ ㄉㄧˊ)
①to underestimate the enemy ②an enemy who is excessively self-confident
驕態(ㄐㄧㄠ ㄊㄞˋ)
proud bearing; a haughty manner; an overbearing attitude
驕橫(ㄐㄧㄠ ㄏㄥˋ)
arrogant and high-handed
驕驕(ㄐㄧㄠ ㄐㄧㄠ)
(said of grass, weeds, etc.) luxuriant and tall
驕蹇(ㄐㄧㄠ ㄐㄧㄢˇ)
proud and disrespectful
驕矜(ㄐㄧㄠ ㄐㄧㄣ)
(literary language) puffed up; conceited; self-important; proud; haughty
驕狎(ㄐㄧㄠ ㄒㄧㄚˊ)
to treat with haughty disrespect
驕者必敗(ㄐㄧㄠ ㄓㄜˇ ㄅㄧˋ ㄅㄞˋ)
Pride goes before a fall.
驕戰(ㄐㄧㄠ ㄓㄢˋ)
Relying on one's own force, one fights fiercely.
驕奢(ㄐㄧㄠ ㄕㄜ)
pride and extravagance
驕奢淫佚(ㄐㄧㄠ ㄕㄜ ㄧㄣˊ ㄧˋ)
pride, luxury, dissolute and self-indulgence—characteristics that tend to mark the life of the wealthy or the powerful
驕人(ㄐㄧㄠ ㄖㄣˊ)
①a successful flatterer ②to try to impress people; to show off ③the proud
驕子(ㄐㄧㄠ ㄗˇ)
a proud favorite (of Heaven, etc.)
驕恣(ㄐㄧㄠ ㄗˋ)
proud and unruly
驕縱(ㄐㄧㄠ ㄗㄨㄥˋ)
disregardful of all authority; proud and unruly
驕色(ㄐㄧㄠ ㄙㄜˋ)
a haughty expression; a proud look
驕傲(ㄐㄧㄠ ㄠˋ)
proud; haughty; disdainful; pride: 不要驕傲自滿。Don't be full of pride and conceit.
驕兒(ㄐㄧㄠ ㄦˊ)
a beloved son
驕易(ㄐㄧㄠ ㄧˋ)
to treat with disrespect
驕陽(ㄐㄧㄠ ㄧㄤˊ)
the intense sunshine; the hot sunshine
驕盈(ㄐㄧㄠ ㄧㄥˊ)
proud and self-complacent

【驊】 6977
ㄏㄨㄚˊ hwa huá
name of a legendary fine horse
驊騮(ㄏㄨㄚˊ ㄌㄧㄡˊ)
name of a legendary fine horse

【驍】 6978
ㄒㄧㄠ shiau xiāo
1. having courage and agility; brave; valiant
2. a fine horse
驍悍(ㄒㄧㄠ ㄏㄢˋ)
brave and fierce
驍騎(ㄒㄧㄠ ㄐㄧˋ)
brave and fierce cavalry
驍將(ㄒㄧㄠ ㄐㄧㄤˋ)
a valiant general
驍雄(ㄒㄧㄠ ㄒㄩㄥˊ)
capable and ambitious
驍衛(ㄒㄧㄠ ㄨㄟˋ)
the imperial guards
驍勇(ㄒㄧㄠ ㄩㄥˇ)
brave and skillful in fighting

【驎】 6979
ㄌㄧㄣˊ lin lín
(said of horses) piebald

【驑】 6980
(騮) ㄌㄧㄡˊ liou liú
name of a legendary fine horse

十三畫

【驗】 6981
(驗) ㄧㄢˋ yann yàn
1. to test; to examine; to analyze
2. to produce an effect: 這藥效靈驗。The medicine has produced an effect.
3. to verify; to prove
驗明(ㄧㄢˋ ㄇㄧㄥˊ)
to ascertain by a test or examination
驗明正身(ㄧㄢˋ ㄇㄧㄥˊ ㄓㄥˋ ㄕㄣ)
to make a positive identification of a criminal before execution
驗方(ㄧㄢˋ ㄈㄤ)
effective medical prescriptions
驗放(ㄧㄢˋ ㄈㄤˋ)
(said of a customs office or checkpoint) to allow shipment of goods to pass after checking the contents
驗電器(ㄧㄢˋ ㄉㄧㄢˋ ㄑㄧˋ)
an electroscope
驗痰(ㄧㄢˋ ㄊㄢˊ)
to examine sputum under the microscope
驗尿(ㄧㄢˋ ㄋㄧㄠˋ)
a urine test; a urinalysis
驗光(ㄧㄢˋ ㄍㄨㄤ)
optometry
驗看(ㄧㄢˋ ㄎㄢˋ)
to examine; to take a close look
驗勘(ㄧㄢˋ ㄎㄢ)
to investigate; to inspect
驗訖(ㄧㄢˋ ㄑㄧˋ)
"examined" (a note stamped on or attached to finished products)
驗槍(ㄧㄢˋ ㄑㄧㄤ)
(military) to inspect arms
驗血(ㄧㄢˋ ㄒㄧㄝˇ)
a blood test
驗屍(ㄧㄢˋ ㄕ)
a post-mortem examination; an autopsy
驗屍官(ㄧㄢˋ ㄕ ㄍㄨㄢ)
a coroner
驗濕器(ㄧㄢˋ ㄕ ㄑㄧˋ)
a hygroscope
驗收(ㄧㄢˋ ㄕㄡ)
to accept (goods, buildings, etc.) after ascertaining that the quality or quantity meets requirements
驗傷(ㄧㄢˋ ㄕㄤ)
to examine an injury by competent authorities of law
驗算(ㄧㄢˋ ㄙㄨㄢˋ)
to check computations

【驚】 6982
ㄐㄧㄥ jing jīng
1. to startle; to surprise; to amaze; to astound; to alarm; to flabbergast; to dumbfound; to terrify; to frighten
2. afraid; frightened; scared;

fearful; terrified
3. to marvel; to be surprised; to be amazed
驚怕(ㄐㄧㄥ ㄆㄚˋ)
scared; afraid; fearful
驚風(ㄐㄧㄥ ㄈㄥ)
(Chinese medicine) convulsions or spasms suffered by a convalescent child
驚風駭浪(ㄐㄧㄥ ㄈㄥ ㄏㄞˋ ㄌㄤˋ)
fearful winds and terrific billows
驚服(ㄐㄧㄥ ㄈㄨˊ)
to marvel at and acknowledge the superiority of someone
驚倒(ㄐㄧㄥ ㄉㄠˇ)
to collapse from fright
驚動(ㄐㄧㄥ ㄉㄨㄥˋ)
① to astonish; to startle; to stir up; to alarm ② to bother; to disturb; to trouble
驚濤駭浪(ㄐㄧㄥ ㄊㄠ ㄏㄞˋ ㄌㄤˋ)
(said of the sea) churning; furious; choppy; mountainous waves
驚歎(ㄐㄧㄥ ㄊㄢˋ)
to marvel; to exclaim
驚歎號(ㄐㄧㄥ ㄊㄢˋ ㄏㄠˋ)
an exclamation mark; an exclamation point
驚堂木(ㄐㄧㄥ ㄊㄤˊ ㄇㄨˋ)
a wooden block used by a judge in former times to maintain order in the court
驚天地，泣鬼神(ㄐㄧㄥ ㄊㄧㄢ ㄉㄧˋ, ㄑㄧˋ ㄍㄨㄟˇ ㄕㄣˊ)
(said of heroism, etc.) to startle the universe and move the gods
驚天動地(ㄐㄧㄥ ㄊㄧㄢ ㄉㄨㄥˋ ㄉㄧˋ)
to startle even the universe; earthshaking; world-shaking
驚怪(ㄐㄧㄥ ㄍㄨㄞˋ)
to marvel; to be amazed and puzzled
驚弓之鳥(ㄐㄧㄥ ㄍㄨㄥ ㄓ ㄋㄧㄠˇ)
(literally) a bird frightened by the bow—a person seized with fear because of some frightening experience encountered in the past; scared as a rabbit
驚恐(ㄐㄧㄥ ㄎㄨㄥˇ)
scared; afraid; fearful
驚駭(ㄐㄧㄥ ㄏㄞˋ)
frightened; terrified; terror-stricken: 這受驚駭的孩子跑回家。The terrified child ran home.
驚汗(ㄐㄧㄥ ㄏㄢˋ)
perspiration of fear; cold perspiration
驚魂(ㄐㄧㄥ ㄏㄨㄣˊ)
a frightened mind
驚魂未定(ㄐㄧㄥ ㄏㄨㄣˊ ㄨㄟˋ ㄉㄧㄥˋ)
not yet become calm or normal from a fright; not yet recovered from astonishment; still badly shaken: 我還驚魂未定。I haven't yet recovered from my astonishment.
驚慌(ㄐㄧㄥ ㄏㄨㄤ)
to lose one's head from terror; to be frightened and confused; to panic
驚惶失措(ㄐㄧㄥ ㄏㄨㄤˊ ㄕ ㄘㄨㄛˋ)
to lose one's head from fear; terrified and not knowing what to do; to panic
驚鴻(ㄐㄧㄥ ㄏㄨㄥˊ)
a woman with an amazing grace
驚鴻一瞥(ㄐㄧㄥ ㄏㄨㄥˊ ㄧˋ ㄆㄧㄝ)
to have a fleeting glimpse of a beauty
驚悸(ㄐㄧㄥ ㄐㄧˋ)
quickened heartbeat due to fear
驚叫(ㄐㄧㄥ ㄐㄧㄠˋ)
to cry in fear; to scream
驚懼(ㄐㄧㄥ ㄐㄩˋ)
scared; afraid; fearful
驚奇(ㄐㄧㄥ ㄑㄧˊ)
to be surprised; to marvel
驚喜(ㄐㄧㄥ ㄒㄧˇ)
pleasantly surprised
驚嚇(ㄐㄧㄥ ㄒㄧㄚˋ)
to frighten; to scare; to alarm suddenly
驚險(ㄐㄧㄥ ㄒㄧㄢˇ)
alarmingly dangerous; breathtaking; thrilling: 那眞是一個驚險的場面。That's really a thrilling scene.
驚心(ㄐㄧㄥ ㄒㄧㄣ)
to be shaken; to be frightened
驚心動魄(ㄐㄧㄥ ㄒㄧㄣ ㄉㄨㄥˋ ㄆㄛˋ)
heart-shaking; soul-stirring; horrifying
驚醒(ㄐㄧㄥ ㄒㄧㄥˇ)
to cause to wake up with a startle
驚蟄(ㄐㄧㄥ ㄓㄜˊ)or(ㄐㄧㄥ ㄓˊ)
one of the 24 climatic periods into which the solar year is divided (beginning from March 5 or 6)
驚視(ㄐㄧㄥ ㄕˋ)
to look at in surprise
驚世駭俗(ㄐㄧㄥ ㄕˋ ㄏㄞˋ ㄙㄨˊ)
to astound the world with an extraordinary idea, etc.
驚擾(ㄐㄧㄥ ㄖㄠˇ)
to disturb; to cause trouble to others
驚人(ㄐㄧㄥ ㄖㄣˊ)
surprising; astonishing; astounding; startling; amazing; sensational: 多麼驚人的消息！What startling news!
驚走(ㄐㄧㄥ ㄗㄡˇ)
① to run away in a fright ② to scare away: 狗把賊驚走。The dog scared the thief away.
驚座(ㄐㄧㄥ ㄗㄨㄛˋ)
to amaze fellow guests; to cause raised eyebrows among those present
驚愕(ㄐㄧㄥ ㄜˋ)
to be astonished; to be astounded; to be dumbfounded; to be flabbergasted
驚疑(ㄐㄧㄥ ㄧˊ)
fearful and apprehensive; afraid and anxious; suspicious from fear
驚異(ㄐㄧㄥ ㄧˋ)
to be surprised; to be amazed; to marvel: 我們對他的成功都感到驚異。We are marveled at his success.
驚訝(ㄐㄧㄥ ㄧㄚˋ)
to be surprised; to be amazed; to marvel

【驛】 6983 ㄧˋ yih yì
a station where couriers rested in former times; a courier station
驛馬車(ㄧˋ ㄇㄚˇ ㄔㄜ)
a stagecoach
驛亭(ㄧˋ ㄊㄧㄥˊ)
a station where couriers rested in former times; a courier station; a post house
驛吏(ㄧˋ ㄌㄧˋ)
officers in charge of a

courier station 亦作「驛丞」

驛館(ㄧˋ ㄍㄨㄢˇ)
a post house

驛騎(ㄧˋ ㄐㄧˋ)
horses kept at a courier station in former times

驛站(ㄧˋ ㄓㄢˋ)
a courier station; a post (where formerly couriers changed horses or rested)

驛車(ㄧˋ ㄔㄜ)
courier carts at a post house in former times

驛丞(ㄧˋ ㄔㄥˊ)
an official in charge of a courier station

驛使(ㄧˋ ㄕˇ)
a courier

十四畫

【驟】 6984 ㄗㄡˋ tzow zòu

1. to gallop
2. swift; sudden: 狂風驟起。A strong wind struck all of a sudden.
3. frequent

驟降(ㄗㄡˋ ㄐㄧㄤˋ)
a rapid fall (of snow)

驟至(ㄗㄡˋ ㄓˋ)
to arrive suddenly; to come without warning

驟然(ㄗㄡˋ ㄖㄢˊ)
suddenly: 驟然下起雨來了。All of a sudden it began to rain.

驟雨(ㄗㄡˋ ㄩˇ)
a sudden rainstorm

十六畫

【驢】 6985 ㄌㄩˊ liu lǘ

an ass; a donkey

驢蒙虎皮(ㄌㄩˊ ㄇㄥˊ ㄏㄨˇ ㄆㄧˊ)
a donkey in a tiger's skin—an empty show of strength

驢鳴狗吠(ㄌㄩˊ ㄇㄧㄥˊ ㄍㄡˇ ㄈㄟˋ)
asses braying and dogs barking—a poor style of writing

驢年馬月(ㄌㄩˊ ㄋㄧㄢˊ ㄇㄚˇ ㄩㄝˋ)
a time that will never come

驢輦(ㄌㄩˊ ㄋㄧㄢˇ)
donkeys as draft animals

驢臉(ㄌㄩˊ ㄌㄧㄢˇ)
a donkey's face—a long face

驢叫(ㄌㄩˊ ㄐㄧㄠˋ)
a donkey's bray—a loud, unpleasant voice

驢駒子(ㄌㄩˊ ㄐㄩ ·ㄗ)
a young donkey; the foal of a donkey

驢車(ㄌㄩˊ ㄔㄜ)
a donkey cart

驢脣不對馬嘴(ㄌㄩˊ ㄔㄨㄣˊ ㄅㄨˊ ㄉㄨㄟˋ ㄇㄚˇ ㄗㄨㄟˇ)
(literally) A donkey's lips do not match a horse's mouth.— incongruous; irrelevant

驢子(ㄌㄩˊ ·ㄗ) or 驢兒(ㄌㄩㄦˊ)
a donkey; an ass

【驥】 6986 ㄐㄧˋ jih jì

1. a very fast horse
2. a man of outstanding ability; a great man

驥子龍文(ㄐㄧˋ ㄗˇ ㄌㄨㄥˊ ㄨㄣˊ)
outstanding children of a family

驥足(ㄐㄧˋ ㄗㄨˊ)
a great talent

驥尾(ㄐㄧˋ ㄨㄟˇ)
on the coattails of a great man

十七畫

【驤】 6987 ㄒㄧㄤ shiang xiāng

1. a horse with the right hind leg white
2. to uplift
3. galloping with a raised head

驤騰(ㄒㄧㄤ ㄊㄥˊ)
to gallop forward; to advance with determination

驤首(ㄒㄧㄤ ㄕㄡˇ)
to raise the head proudly

十八畫

【驩】 6988 (歡) ㄏㄨㄢ huan huān

to have joy

十九畫

【驪】 6989 ㄌㄧˊ li lí

1. a black horse
2. to drive a carriage drawn by two horses

驪龍(ㄌㄧˊ ㄌㄨㄥˊ)
a black dragon

驪歌(ㄌㄧˊ ㄍㄜ)
a song of farewell (from a farewell poem entitled 驪駒)

驪姬(ㄌㄧˊ ㄐㄧ)
name of a princess during the Epoch of Spring and Autumn

驪駕(ㄌㄧˊ ㄐㄧㄚˋ)
to drive a carriage drawn by two horses

驪駒(ㄌㄧˊ ㄐㄩ)
① a black horse ② the title of a farewell poem

驪珠(ㄌㄧˊ ㄓㄨ)
a pearl supposedly held under the jaw of a black dragon

驪山老母(ㄌㄧˊ ㄕㄢ ㄌㄠˇ ㄇㄨˇ)
name of a female immortal

骨 部
ㄍㄨˇ guu gǔ

【骨】 6990 1. ㄍㄨˇ guu gǔ

1. a bone: 他跌斷了肋骨。He broke his rib bone.
2. a framework; a frame; a skeleton: 研究一下房子的骨架。Study the frame of a house.

骨牌(ㄍㄨˇ ㄆㄞˊ)
dominoes or similar pieces used in mahjong, etc.

骨牌理論(ㄍㄨˇ ㄆㄞˊ ㄌㄧˇ ㄌㄨㄣˋ)
the domino theory—the theory that if one act or event is allowed to take place a succession of similar acts or events will follow

骨盤(ㄍㄨˇ ㄆㄢˊ) or 骨盆(ㄍㄨˇ ㄆㄣˊ)
(anatomy) the pelvis

骨膜炎(ㄍㄨˇ ㄇㄛˋ ㄧㄢˊ)
periostitis

骨法(ㄍㄨˇ ㄈㄚˇ)
① a frame (of the body) ② phrenological features ③ (calligraphy) forcefulness of strokes

骨肥(ㄍㄨˇ ㄈㄟˊ)
fertilizer made from animal

bones; bone meal
骨董(ㄍㄨˇ ㄉㄨㄥˇ)
curios; antique objects
骨炭(ㄍㄨˇ ㄊㄢˋ)
boneblack; animal charcoal
骨痛(ㄍㄨˇ ㄊㄨㄥˋ)
osteocope
骨力(ㄍㄨˇ ㄌㄧˋ)
forcefulness of calligraphic strokes
骨立(ㄍㄨˇ ㄌㄧˋ)
skinny; bony
骨瘤(ㄍㄨˇ ㄌㄧㄡˊ)
an osteoma
骨骼 or 骨格(ㄍㄨˇ ㄍㄜˊ)
a frame of the body; a skeleton
骨幹(ㄍㄨˇ ㄍㄢˋ)
①(anatomy) a diaphysis ② the backbone; a mainstay: 這種人是國家的骨幹。Such men are the backbone of the country.
骨鯁 or 骨骾(ㄍㄨˇ ㄍㄥˇ)
honest; upright; outspoken
骨鯁在喉(ㄍㄨˇ ㄍㄥˇ ㄗㄞˋ ㄏㄡˊ)
to have a fishbone caught in one's throat—to have opinions one cannot but express
骨科(ㄍㄨˇ ㄎㄜ)
osteopathy
骨科醫生(ㄍㄨˇ ㄎㄜ ㄧ ㄕㄥ)
an osteopath
骨灰(ㄍㄨˇ ㄏㄨㄟ)
bone ashes
骨架(ㄍㄨˇ ㄐㄧㄚˋ)
a framework; a frame; a skeleton
骨節(ㄍㄨˇ ㄐㄧㄝˊ)or 骨關節(ㄍㄨˇ ㄍㄨㄢ ㄐㄧㄝˊ)
joints (of bones)
骨節痛(ㄍㄨˇ ㄐㄧㄝˊ ㄊㄨㄥˋ)
gout
骨節炎(ㄍㄨˇ ㄐㄧㄝˊ ㄧㄢˊ)
osteoarthritis
骨氣(ㄍㄨˇ ㄑㄧˋ)
fortitude; backbone; pluck; guts; grit; spirit; courage: 他是一個有骨氣的人。He is a man of backbone.
骨相學(ㄍㄨˇ ㄒㄧㄤˋ ㄒㄩㄝˊ)
phrenology
骨學(ㄍㄨˇ ㄒㄩㄝˊ)
osteology
骨質(ㄍㄨˇ ㄓˊ)
osseous tissue

骨折(ㄍㄨˇ ㄓㄜˊ)
a bone fracture
骨瘦如柴(ㄍㄨˇ ㄕㄡˋ ㄖㄨˊ ㄔㄞˊ)
thin and emaciated; very skinny; as thin as a stick; all bone and skin; to be reduced to a skeleton
骨肉(ㄍㄨˇ ㄖㄡˋ)or(ㄍㄨˊ ㄖㄡˋ)
one's own flesh and blood—blood relations
骨肉之情(ㄍㄨˇ ㄖㄡˋ ㄓ ㄑㄧㄥˊ)
love of one's own flesh and blood
骨肉至親(ㄍㄨˇ ㄖㄡˋ ㄓˋ ㄑㄧㄣ)
blood relations
骨軟筋酥(ㄍㄨˇ ㄖㄨㄢˇ ㄐㄧㄣ ㄙㄨ)
unnerved; enervated; unmanned
骨子(ㄍㄨˇ ˙ㄗ)
a framework; a frame; a skeleton
骨子裏頭(ㄍㄨˇ ˙ㄗ ㄌㄧˇ ˙ㄊㄡ)
① in one's innermost nature; at heart ② in substance; fundamentally
骨刺(ㄍㄨˇ ㄘˋ)
(pathology) a bony spur; a bony projection or exostosis
骨髓(ㄍㄨˇ ㄙㄨㄟˇ)
marrow: 他被凍得透到骨髓。He was frozen to the marrow.
骨髓炎(ㄍㄨˇ ㄙㄨㄟˇ ㄧㄢˊ)
osteomyelitis
骨炎(ㄍㄨˇ ㄧㄢˊ)
osteitis
骨癌(ㄍㄨˇ ㄧㄢˊ)
cancer in the bone: 他死於骨癌。He died of the cancer in the bone.

【骨】 6990
2. ㄍㄨˊ gwu gú
a bone (in some colloquial phrases)
骨頭(ㄍㄨˊ ˙ㄊㄡ)
①bone: 骨頭鯁住了我的喉嚨。A bone stuck in my throat. ② a contemptible person ③ strong character, fortitude; guts
骨頭架子(ㄍㄨˊ ˙ㄊㄡ ㄐㄧㄚˋ ˙ㄗ)
① a frame (of the body); a skeleton ② a skinny person; a bag of bones 亦作「瘦皮猴」
骨碌(ㄍㄨˇ ˙ㄌㄨ)
rolling; to turn round and round: 他從床上一骨碌爬起來。He rolls out of bed.

【骨】 6990
3. ㄍㄨ gu gū
an alternative pronunciation of 骨(ㄍㄨˇ) used in some phrases
骨朵兒(ㄍㄨ ˙ㄉㄨㄛㄦ)
a bud

三畫

【骭】 6991
ㄍㄢˋ gann gàn
the shinbone

【骫】 6992
ㄨㄟˇ woei wěi
to bend; to twist

四畫

【骰】 6993
1. ㄕㄞˇ shae shǎi
dice; to dice
骰花兒(ㄕㄞˇ ㄏㄨㄚㄦ)
spots on a dice
骰子(ㄕㄞˇ ˙ㄗ)or 骰兒(ㄕㄚˇㄦ)
dice

【骰】 6993
2. ㄊㄡˊ tour tóu
a literary pronunciation of 骰(ㄕㄞˇ)
骰子令(ㄊㄡˊ ˙ㄗ ㄌㄧㄥˋ)
(at a banquet) obligation to drink imposed on someone by throwing dice
骰子選(ㄊㄡˊ ˙ㄗ ㄒㄩㄢˇ)
a game basically similar to backgammon

【骯】 6994
ㄤ ang āng
dirty; filthy; foul
骯髒(ㄤ ㄗㄤ)
dirty; filthy

五畫

【骷】 6995
ㄎㄨ ku kū
a human skeleton
骷髏(ㄎㄨ ㄌㄡˊ)
a human skeleton

六畫

【骻】 6996
ㄎㄨㄚˋ kuah kuà
the waist bone

〔骨部〕

【骸】 6997 ㄏㄞˊ hair hái
1. the shinbone
2. a skeleton
骸骨(ㄏㄞˊ ㄍㄨˇ)
a skeleton

【骼】 6998 ㄍㄜˊ ger gé
a bone; a skeleton

七畫

【骾】 6999 ㄍㄥˇ geeng gěng
a fishbone, etc., stuck in the throat 亦作「鯁」

八畫

【髀】 7000 ㄅㄧˋ bih bì
1. buttocks
2. the hipbone; the innominate bone
髀骨(ㄅㄧˋ ㄍㄨˇ)
the hipbone; the innominate bone
髀肉復生(ㄅㄧˋ ㄖㄡˋ ㄈㄨˋ ㄕㄥ)
having put on flesh again at the buttocks (an expression of regret at a long absence from horseback, where a soldier is supposed to belong)

【髁】 7001 ㄎㄜ ke kē
1. the hipbone; the innominate bone
2. the kneecap; the kneepan

十一畫

【髏】 7002 ㄌㄡˊ lou lóu
as in 骷髏—a human skeleton

十三畫

【髒】 7003 ㄗㄤ tzang zāng
dirty; filthy: 軟布易髒。Soft clothes dirty easily.
髒東西(ㄗㄤ ㄉㄨㄥ ·ㄒㄧ)
a dirty thing; filth
髒土(ㄗㄤ ㄊㄨˇ)
dirty soil
髒兮兮的(ㄗㄤ ㄒㄧ ㄒㄧ ·ㄉㄜ)
very much soiled; very dirty: 把你髒兮兮的臉洗一洗。Wash your dirty face.
髒心(ㄗㄤ ㄒㄧㄣ)
an impure heart; a dirty mind
髒症(ㄗㄤ ㄓㄥˋ)
venereal disease
髒瘡(ㄗㄤ ㄔㄨㄤ)
syphilitic lesions of the skin
髒字(ㄗㄤ ㄗˋ) or 髒字眼兒(ㄗㄤ ㄗˋ ㄧㄚˇㄦ)
an obscene word; a swear-word; a profane word

【髓】 7004 ㄙㄨㄟˇ soei suǐ
marrow; pith; essence: 簡潔乃機智之精髓。Brevity is the marrow and pith of wit.

【體】 7005 ㄊㄧˇ tii tǐ
1. the body
2. shape; form
3. an entity; a unit
4. a style; a fashion; a system
5. substance; essence
6. theory (as opposed to practice)
體魄(ㄊㄧˇ ㄆㄛˋ)
the human body as the source of strength: 他的體魄強壯結實。His physical form is strong and stout.
體貌(ㄊㄧˇ ㄇㄠˋ)
① a figure and face ② decorum; propriety
體面(ㄊㄧˇ ㄇㄧㄢˋ)
①honor; dignity; face: 東方人很講體面。Face is very important to Oriental peoples. ②appearing good; looking elegant
體罰(ㄊㄧˇ ㄈㄚˊ)
corporal punishment
體法(ㄊㄧˇ ㄈㄚˇ)
an established mode or style
體範(ㄊㄧˇ ㄈㄢˋ)
a model; a pattern: 這學生是勤勉的體範。This student is a model of diligence.
體大思精(ㄊㄧˇ ㄉㄚˋ ㄙ ㄐㄧㄥ)
(said of a book) extensive in scope and penetrating in thought
體態(ㄊㄧˇ ㄊㄞˋ)
① outward form; an exterior look ② a manner, deportment, or a carriage (of a woman): 她體態優雅。She has a graceful carriage.
體態輕盈(ㄊㄧˇ ㄊㄞˋ ㄑㄧㄥ ㄧㄥˊ)
(said of a woman) with a charming sprightly carriage
體貼(ㄊㄧˇ ㄊㄧㄝ)
kind; considerate; thoughtful
體統(ㄊㄧˇ ㄊㄨㄥˇ)
① a system; an organized whole ② propriety in conduct
體能(ㄊㄧˇ ㄋㄥˊ)
physical agility; stamina
體念(ㄊㄧˇ ㄋㄧㄢˋ)
to be understanding; to make allowance for; to be sympathetic toward
體力(ㄊㄧˇ ㄌㄧˋ)
physical strength; stamina: 這年輕人缺乏體力。The youth lacks stamina.
體力勞動(ㄊㄧˇ ㄌㄧˋ ㄌㄠˊ ㄉㄨㄥˋ)
physical or manual labor
體例(ㄊㄧˇ ㄌㄧˋ)
general form
體諒(ㄊㄧˇ ·ㄌㄧㄤ)
to be understanding or sympathetic toward; to be considerate of: 我的父親是很體諒人的。My father is quite understanding.
體格(ㄊㄧˇ ㄍㄜˊ)
physique: 他是一個體格強壯的男人。He is a man of strong physique.
體格檢查(ㄊㄧˇ ㄍㄜˊ ㄐㄧㄢˇ ㄔㄚˊ)
a physical examination
體高(ㄊㄧˇ ㄍㄠ)
height (of a person)
體會(ㄊㄧˇ ㄏㄨㄟˋ)
to understand through something beyond the intellect; to comprehend intuitively
體積(ㄊㄧˇ ㄐㄧ)
volume (of a solid)
體己(ㄊㄧˇ ·ㄐㄧ)
① private; personal ② confidential
體系(ㄊㄧˇ ㄒㄧˋ)
a system (of thoughts, etc.); orderliness
體現(ㄊㄧˇ ㄒㄧㄢˋ)
to embody; to incarnate; to reflect; to express
體行(ㄊㄧˇ ㄒㄧㄥˊ)
to embody in one's own

actions
體刑(ㄊㄧˇ ㄒㄧㄥˊ)
corporal punishment meted out by a court of law in former times
體型(ㄊㄧˇ ㄒㄧㄥˊ)
an external physical appearance; (physical) build
體恤(ㄊㄧˇ ㄒㄩˋ)
to be considerate of and sympathize with
體質(ㄊㄧˇ ㄓˋ)
a bodily constitution; a physical make-up
體制(ㄊㄧˇ ㄓˋ)
a system of rules; a system
體製(ㄊㄧˇ ㄓˋ)
a style in art; a layout
體脹係數(ㄊㄧˇ ㄓㄤˋ ㄒㄧˋ ㄕㄨˋ)
a coefficient of cubical expansion
體重(ㄊㄧˇ ㄓㄨㄥˋ)
body weight
體察(ㄊㄧˇ ㄔㄚˊ)
①to examine or investigate with intensive personal attention ②to be understanding or sympathetic toward
體式(ㄊㄧˇ ㄕˋ)
a mode; a style
體認(ㄊㄧˇ ㄖㄣˋ)
to perceive intuitively
體裁(ㄊㄧˇ ㄘㄞˊ)
a form or a style (of writing): 那個作家用簡潔的體裁寫作。The author writes in a concise style.
體操(ㄊㄧˇ ㄘㄠ)
gymnastics; calisthenics
體操選手(ㄊㄧˇ ㄘㄠ ㄒㄩㄢˇ ㄕㄡˇ)
a gymnast
體要(ㄊㄧˇ ㄧㄠˋ)
① an outline; a summary; the gist: 體要鮮明。The substance and outline are clear. ② concise; terse; succinct
體驗(ㄊㄧˇ ㄧㄢˋ)
to experience firsthand; firsthand experience
體無完膚(ㄊㄧˇ ㄨˊ ㄨㄢˊ ㄈㄨ)
injured all over the body (often used figuratively for damage inflicted by verbal attacks): 這男孩被打得體無完膚。The boy was injured all over the body.
體外受精(ㄊㄧˇ ㄨㄞˋ ㄕㄡˋ ㄐㄧㄥ)
(anatomy) external fertilization
體位(ㄊㄧˇ ㄨㄟˋ)
the grade of a draftee's physical fitness
體味(ㄊㄧˇ ㄨㄟˋ)
to appreciate; to savor
體溫(ㄊㄧˇ ㄨㄣ)
body temperature: 他的體溫在上升。His temperature is going up.
體溫計(ㄊㄧˇ ㄨㄣ ㄐㄧˋ)
a clinical thermometer
體育(ㄊㄧˇ ㄩˋ)
① physical education ② athletics: 他擅長體育。He is good at athletics.
體育道德(ㄊㄧˇ ㄩˋ ㄉㄠˋ ㄉㄜˊ)
sportsmanship
體育舘(ㄊㄧˇ ㄩˋ ㄍㄨㄢˇ)
a gymnasium; an indoor stadium
體育會(ㄊㄧˇ ㄩˋ ㄏㄨㄟˋ)
an athletic club
體育記者(ㄊㄧˇ ㄩˋ ㄐㄧˋ ㄓㄜˇ)
a sportswriter
體育家(ㄊㄧˇ ㄩˋ ㄐㄧㄚ)
a physical educator
體育節(ㄊㄧˇ ㄩˋ ㄐㄧㄝˊ)
Athletics Day (September 9)
體育系(ㄊㄧˇ ㄩˋ ㄒㄧˋ)
the department of physical education (in a college)
體育場(ㄊㄧˇ ㄩˋ ㄔㄤˇ)
a stadium; a play ground
體育用具(ㄊㄧˇ ㄩˋ ㄩㄥˋ ㄐㄩˋ)
sports goods; sports requisites 亦作「體育用品」
體用(ㄊㄧˇ ㄩㄥˋ)
theory and practice

【髑】 7006
ㄉㄨˊ dwu dú
the human skull
髑髏(ㄉㄨˊ ㄌㄡˊ)
the human skull

十四畫

【髕】 7007
ㄅㄧㄣˋ binn bìn
the kneecap; the kneepan
髕脚(ㄅㄧㄣˋ ㄐㄧㄠˇ)
an ancient punishment of cutting off the kneecap

高部
ㄍㄠ gau gāo

〔高部〕

【高】 7008
ㄍㄠ gau gāo
1. high; tall: 那是一座很高的塔。That's a very high tower.
2. of a high level or degree; above the average
3. lofty
4. a Chinese family name
高不可攀(ㄍㄠ ·ㄅㄨ ㄎㄜˇ ㄆㄢ)
too high to be reached (both literally and figuratively)
高不成低不就(ㄍㄠ ·ㄅㄨ ㄔㄥˊ ㄉㄧ ·ㄅㄨ ㄐㄧㄡˋ)
unable to find a mate or employment because the object available is either beyond one's reach or below one's minimum expectations
高攀(ㄍㄠ ㄆㄢ)
① to climb high ② to cultivate friendship with the socially elevated
高朋滿座(ㄍㄠ ㄆㄥˊ ㄇㄢˇ ㄗㄨㄛˋ)
All the seats are occupied by distinguished guests.
高帽(ㄍㄠ ㄇㄠˋ) or 高帽子(ㄍㄠ ㄇㄠˋ ·ㄗ)
flattery; soft soap: 別被她的高帽所騙。Don't be deceived by her flattery.
高門(ㄍㄠ ㄇㄣˊ)
an illustrious family
高錳酸鉀(ㄍㄠ ㄇㄥˇ ㄙㄨㄢ ㄐㄧㄚˇ)
potassium permanganate
高妙(ㄍㄠ ㄇㄧㄠˋ)
exquisite; excellent
高棉(ㄍㄠ ㄇㄧㄢˊ)
Cambodia
高明(ㄍㄠ ㄇㄧㄥˊ)
① clever; wise; superior: 這個方法一點也不高明。This method is not clever at all. ② an expert; a master; a qualified person
高名(ㄍㄠ ㄇㄧㄥˊ)
fame; renown; great reputation
高發(ㄍㄠ ㄈㄚ)
(in former times) to pass the civil service examination

高飛球(ㄍㄠ ㄈㄟ ㄑㄧㄡˊ)
(baseball) fly

高飛遠走(ㄍㄠ ㄈㄟ ㄩㄢˇ ㄗㄡˇ)
to abscond

高峯(ㄍㄠ ㄈㄥ)
the peak; the summit; the culmination; the climax: 他現在人緣達最高峯。He is at the climax of his popularity.

高風(ㄍㄠ ㄈㄥ)
noble character

高風亮節(ㄍㄠ ㄈㄥ ㄌㄧㄤˋ ㄐㄧㄝˊ)
noble character and incorruptible principle

高大(ㄍㄠ ㄉㄚˋ)
tall and big; colossal

高蹈(ㄍㄠ ㄉㄠˋ)
① to go on a long journey ② to be aloof from the world

高蹈派(ㄍㄠ ㄉㄠˋ ㄆㄞˋ)
the Parnassians (in French literature)

高蛋白(ㄍㄠ ㄉㄢˋ ㄅㄞˊ)
high protein

高檔(ㄍㄠ ㄉㄤˋ)
(dialect) the top grade; superior quality

高等(ㄍㄠ ㄉㄥˇ)
high or advanced (in the grade)

高等法院(ㄍㄠ ㄉㄥˇ ㄈㄚˇ ㄩㄢˋ)
the High Court: 囚犯被帶到高等法院候審。The prisoner was brought to the High Court for trial.

高等代數(ㄍㄠ ㄉㄥˇ ㄉㄞˋ ㄕㄨˋ)
higher algebra

高等動物(ㄍㄠ ㄉㄥˇ ㄉㄨㄥˋ ㄨˋ)
higher animals

高等考試(ㄍㄠ ㄉㄥˇ ㄎㄠˇ ㄕˋ)
the Higher Civil Service Examination in the country

高等教育(ㄍㄠ ㄉㄥˇ ㄐㄧㄠˋ ㄩˋ)
higher education

高等小學(ㄍㄠ ㄉㄥˇ ㄒㄧㄠˇ ㄒㄩㄝˊ)or **高小**(ㄍㄠ ㄒㄧㄠˇ)
senior primary school which consists of the fifth and sixth grades

高等植物(ㄍㄠ ㄉㄥˇ ㄓˊ ㄨˋ)
higher plants

高等文官(ㄍㄠ ㄉㄥˇ ㄨㄣˊ ㄍㄨㄢ)
a high civil official

高低(ㄍㄠ ㄉㄧ)
① height ② a sense of propriety; discretion ③(dialect) on any account; simply ④(dialect) at last; after all ⑤ relative superiority or inferiority

高低不平(ㄍㄠ ㄉㄧ ㄅㄨˋ ㄆㄧㄥˊ)
uneven; rugged; irregular

高地(ㄍㄠ ㄉㄧˋ)
high ground; uplands

高第(ㄍㄠ ㄉㄧˋ)
a high place on the list of successful examinees

高調(ㄍㄠ ㄉㄧㄠˋ)
① a high-pitched note ② high-sounding (but impractical) assertions

高度(ㄍㄠ ㄉㄨˋ)
① an altitude; a height; an elevation: 這座山的高度是多少? What is the height of the mountain? ② highly; great

高度表(ㄍㄠ ㄉㄨˋ ㄅㄧㄠˇ)
an altimeter

高段(ㄍㄠ ㄉㄨㄢˋ)
(said of chess masters, judo experts, etc.) top-grade

高塔(ㄍㄠ ㄊㄚˇ)
a high tower; a high steeple

高擡貴手(ㄍㄠ ㄊㄞˊ ㄍㄨㄟˋ ㄕㄡˇ)
(literally) Raise your noble hands.—Please be merciful.

高擡身價(ㄍㄠ ㄊㄞˊ ㄕㄣ ㄐㄧㄚˋ)
to put a high price on oneself

高談闊論(ㄍㄠ ㄊㄢˊ ㄎㄨㄛˋ ㄌㄨㄣˋ)
to talk freely; to talk in a lively atmosphere

高湯(ㄍㄠ ㄊㄤ)
① consommé ② thin soup

高堂(ㄍㄠ ㄊㄤˊ)
① a hall with a high ceiling ② parents

高徒(ㄍㄠ ㄊㄨˊ)
(your) esteemed student

高能(ㄍㄠ ㄋㄥˊ)
having outstanding competence; very capable

高年(ㄍㄠ ㄋㄧㄢˊ)
advanced in age; aged

高樓大廈(ㄍㄠ ㄌㄡˊ ㄉㄚˋ ㄒㄧㄚˋ)or (ㄍㄠ ㄌㄡˊ ㄉㄚˋ ㄕㄚˋ)
tall buildings; skyscrapers

高欄(ㄍㄠ ㄌㄢˊ)
the high hurdles

高麗(ㄍㄠ ㄌㄧˊ)
a former name of Korea

高麗棒子(ㄍㄠ ㄌㄧˊ ㄅㄤˋ ·ㄗ)
(offensive) a Korean

高麗參(ㄍㄠ ㄌㄧˊ ㄕㄣ)
ginseng 亦作「人參」: 高麗參很貴。The ginseng is very expensive.

高麗人(ㄍㄠ ㄌㄧˊ ㄖㄣˊ)
a Korean

高利貸(ㄍㄠ ㄌㄧˋ ㄉㄞˋ)
usury: 那商人放高利貸。That merchant lent money at usury.

高利率政策(ㄍㄠ ㄌㄧˋ ㄌㄩˋ ㄓㄥˋ ㄘㄜˋ)
high interest policy

高硫酸(ㄍㄠ ㄌㄧㄡˊ ㄙㄨㄢ)
persulfuric acid

高粱(ㄍㄠ ㄌㄧㄤˊ)
kaoliang; sorghum; kafir

高粱酒(ㄍㄠ ㄌㄧㄤˊ ㄐㄧㄡˇ)
kaoliang wine

高齡(ㄍㄠ ㄌㄧㄥˊ)
advanced age; great age; old age

高盧(ㄍㄠ ㄌㄨˊ)
Gaul

高論(ㄍㄠ ㄌㄨㄣˋ)
an outstanding statement; original remarks; brilliant ideas

高歌(ㄍㄠ ㄍㄜ)
to sing aloud

高箇子 or **高個子**(ㄍㄠ ㄍㄜˋ ·ㄗ)or **高箇兒**(ㄍㄠ ㄍㄜˋㄦ)
a tall person: 他是個高箇子。He is a tall man.

高高低低(ㄍㄠ ㄍㄠ ㄉㄧ ㄉㄧ)
uneven; rugged

高高在上(ㄍㄠ ㄍㄠ ㄗㄞˋ ㄕㄤˋ)
(literally) situated high above—(figuratively) lofty; aloof

高跟鞋(ㄍㄠ ㄍㄣ ㄒㄧㄝˊ)
high-heeled shoes

高崗(ㄍㄠ ㄍㄤ)
the peak or summit; a high mountain

高掛(ㄍㄠ ㄍㄨㄚˋ)
hanging high; suspended high

高貴(ㄍㄠ ㄍㄨㄟˋ)
noble; exalted

高官厚祿(ㄍㄠ ㄍㄨㄢ ㄏㄡˋ ㄌㄨˋ)
a high position and a good salary

高功能(ㄍㄠ ㄍㄨㄥ ㄋㄥˊ)

high-performance; high performance
高科技產品(ㄍㄠ ㄎㄜ ㄐㄧˋ ㄔㄢˇ ㄆㄧㄣˇ)
a high-tech product
高亢(ㄍㄠ ㄎㄤˋ)
proud and indomitable
高空(ㄍㄠ ㄎㄨㄥ)
high altitude; upper air
高呼(ㄍㄠ ㄏㄨ)
to shout; to call out aloud
高級(ㄍㄠ ㄐㄧˊ)
①a high grade; a high class; superior ②advanced (courses)
高級中學(ㄍㄠ ㄐㄧˊ ㄓㄨㄥ ㄒㄩㄝˊ)or 高中(ㄍㄠ ㄓㄨㄥ)
a senior middle school; a senior high school
高級參謀(ㄍㄠ ㄐㄧˊ ㄘㄢ ㄇㄡˊ)
a high staff officer; a top-grade counselor
高寄(ㄍㄠ ㄐㄧˋ)
exalted ideals
高髻(ㄍㄠ ㄐㄧˋ)
a kind of tall coiffure
高加索(ㄍㄠ ㄐㄧㄚ ㄙㄨㄛˇ)
Caucasus; Caucasia
高價(ㄍㄠ ㄐㄧㄚˋ)
a high price; an exorbitant price: 他以高價售出他的房子。He has sold his house at a high price.
高價收購(ㄍㄠ ㄐㄧㄚˋ ㄕㄡ ㄍㄡˋ)
to buy (usually from private individuals) for a high price
高架鐵路(ㄍㄠ ㄐㄧㄚˋ ㄊㄧㄝˇ ㄌㄨˋ)
an elevated railroad
高架橋(ㄍㄠ ㄐㄧㄚˋ ㄑㄧㄠˊ)
a viaduct
高階層(ㄍㄠ ㄐㄧㄝ ㄘㄥˊ)
high rank; top rank
高階層人物(ㄍㄠ ㄐㄧㄝ ㄘㄥˊ ㄖㄣˊ ㄨˋ)
persons of high rank
高節(ㄍㄠ ㄐㄧㄝˊ)
great moral fortitude; incorruptibility
高潔(ㄍㄠ ㄐㄧㄝˊ)
noble and pure; exalted and immaculate
高就(ㄍㄠ ㄐㄧㄡˋ)
opportunity for a high or higher position, a good or better employment, etc.
高見(ㄍㄠ ㄐㄧㄢˋ)
your esteemed opinion or advice: 對於此事您有何高見? What is your esteemed opinion of this matter?
高車(ㄍㄠ ㄐㄩ)
①name of an ancient tribe in what is Mongolia today ②a high-canopied chariot of ancient times
高舉(ㄍㄠ ㄐㄩˇ)
①to raise high; to uplift ②to become a hermit
高峻(ㄍㄠ ㄐㄩㄣˋ)
precipitous; steep: 此山高峻。This mountain is steep.
高氣壓(ㄍㄠ ㄑㄧˋ ㄧㄚ)
high atmospheric pressure
高峭(ㄍㄠ ㄑㄧㄠˋ)
precipitous; high and steep
高蹺(ㄍㄠ ˙ㄑㄧㄠ)
stilts
高強(ㄍㄠ ㄑㄧㄤˊ)
surpassing; outstanding; superior
高情(ㄍㄠ ㄑㄧㄥˊ)
your kindness; your thoughtfulness
高下(ㄍㄠ ㄒㄧㄚˋ)
superiority and inferiority
高效率(ㄍㄠ ㄒㄧㄠˋ ㄌㄩˋ)
high-efficiency
高薪(ㄍㄠ ㄒㄧㄣ)
high pay; a handsome salary: 他支領高薪。He receives a high salary.
高行(ㄍㄠ ㄒㄧㄥˋ)
noble conduct
高興(ㄍㄠ ㄒㄧㄥˋ)or 高高興興(ㄍㄠ ㄍㄠ ㄒㄧㄥˋ ㄒㄧㄥˋ)
glad; elated; delighted: 很高興看到你。I am delighted to see you.
高血糖症(ㄍㄠ ㄒㄩㄝˋ ㄊㄤˊ ㄓㄥˋ)
(pathology) hyperglycemia
高血壓(ㄍㄠ ㄒㄩㄝˋ ㄧㄚ)
high blood pressure; hypertension
高軒(ㄍㄠ ㄒㄩㄢ)
a large, spacious vehicle
高懸(ㄍㄠ ㄒㄩㄢˊ)
to hang high
高雄(ㄍㄠ ㄒㄩㄥˊ)
Kaohsiung, a port city in southern Taiwan
高著兒(ㄍㄠ ㄓㄠㄦ)
a very clever sort of stratagem or scheme; a clever move 亦作「高招」
高瞻遠矚(ㄍㄠ ㄓㄢ ㄩㄢˇ ㄓㄨˇ)
farseeing; provident; far-sighted
高枕無憂(ㄍㄠ ㄓㄣˇ ㄨˊ ㄧㄡ)
to sleep in peace; to be free from worries
高漲(ㄍㄠ ㄓㄤˇ)
(said of a price or the water level) to rise
高掌遠蹠(ㄍㄠ ㄓㄤˇ ㄩㄢˇ ㄓˊ)
①wide open ②having great ambitions
高躅(ㄍㄠ ㄓㄨˊ)
noble conduct
高中
①(ㄍㄠ ㄓㄨㄥ) a senior high school
②(ㄍㄠ ㄓㄨㄥˋ) to pass an examination
高超(ㄍㄠ ㄔㄠ)
surpassing; outstanding; exalted; superior; superb
高潮(ㄍㄠ ㄔㄠˊ)
①a high tide ②a climax: 劇情漸入高潮。The plot is reaching a dramatic climax.
高敞(ㄍㄠ ㄔㄤˇ)
(said of buildings, etc.) tall and spacious: 這些建築物很高敞。These buildings were tall and spacious.
高唱入雲(ㄍㄠ ㄔㄤˋ ㄖㄨˋ ㄩㄣˊ)
(literally) to sing in a very high pitch or with very great intensity—to be very much talked about; on everybody's lips
高處(ㄍㄠ ㄔㄨˋ)
a high place; altitudes
高士(ㄍㄠ ㄕˋ)
a man with a noble character
高視闊步(ㄍㄠ ㄕˋ ㄎㄨㄛˋ ㄅㄨˋ)
①having uncommon dignity ②proud; disdainful; to stalk: 一個年輕人高視闊步走出房來。A young man stalks out of the room.
高射砲(ㄍㄠ ㄕㄜˋ ㄆㄠˋ)
an antiaircraft gun; an ack-ack
高燒(ㄍㄠ ㄕㄠ)
a high fever: 他發高燒。He has a high fever.
高手(ㄍㄠ ㄕㄡˇ)
a master (in a skill, trade, etc.); an expert: 他是下棋的

高手。He is a master of chess.

高壽(ㄍㄠ ㄕㄡˋ)
①advanced age; old age; great age ②your age (in addressing an aged person)

高山病(ㄍㄠ ㄕㄢ ㄅㄧㄥˋ)
mountain sickness; altitude sickness

高山流水(ㄍㄠ ㄕㄢ ㄌㄧㄡˊ ㄕㄨㄟˇ)
(literally) high mountains and flowing waters—sympathetic interaction between two minds, from the story of the musician Po Ya (伯牙) and his friend Chung Tzu-chi (鍾子期) who knew his mind was on high mountains and flowing waters merely by listening to his music

高山景行(ㄍㄠ ㄕㄢ ㄐㄧㄥˇ ㄒㄧㄥˊ)
to admire great virtue

高山植物(ㄍㄠ ㄕㄢ ㄓˊ ㄨˋ)
an alpine plant

高山族(ㄍㄠ ㄕㄢ ㄗㄨˊ)
the aborigines of Taiwan

高山仰止(ㄍㄠ ㄕㄢ ㄧㄤˇ ㄓˇ)
The mountain is so high that one looks up to it with awe.—(figuratively) A man of virtue is so great that one looks up to him awfully.

高深(ㄍㄠ ㄕㄣ)
recondite; abstruse; profound; deep; advanced; lofty

高尚(ㄍㄠ ㄕㄤˋ)
①noble; exalted ②(said of pursuits, entertainments, etc.) high-class; refined; respectable

高陞(ㄍㄠ ㄕㄥ)
to get a promotion; to be promoted

高聲大笑(ㄍㄠ ㄕㄥ ㄉㄚˋ ㄒㄧㄠˋ)
to roar with laughter

高聲朗誦(ㄍㄠ ㄕㄥ ㄌㄤˇ ㄙㄨㄥˋ)
to recite aloud: 他高聲朗誦這首長詩。He recited the long poem aloud.

高熱(ㄍㄠ ㄖㄜˋ)
a high temperature; a high fever: 她發高熱。She has a high fever.

高人(ㄍㄠ ㄖㄣˊ)
①a man of lofty character 亦作「高士」②an expert; a person of superior talent or ability; a master

高人一等(ㄍㄠ ㄖㄣˊ ㄧˊ ㄉㄥˇ)
a cut above other people

高人一籌(ㄍㄠ ㄖㄣˊ ㄧˋ ㄔㄡˊ)
a notch better than average people

高姿態(ㄍㄠ ㄗ ㄊㄞˋ)
a lofty stance

高足(ㄍㄠ ㄗㄨˊ)or 高足弟子(ㄍㄠ ㄗㄨˊ ㄉㄧˋ ㄗˇ)or 高弟(ㄍㄠ ㄉㄧˋ)
(an honorific term) your capable student; your brilliant disciple

高祖(ㄍㄠ ㄗㄨˇ)
①one's great-great-grandfather ②one's ancestor ③the founder of a dynasty

高祖母(ㄍㄠ ㄗㄨˇ ㄇㄨˇ)
one's great-great-grandmother

高祖父(ㄍㄠ ㄗㄨˇ ㄈㄨˋ)
one's great-great-grandfather

高蹤(ㄍㄠ ㄗㄨㄥ)
noble deeds

高才生(ㄍㄠ ㄘㄞˊ ㄕㄥ)
a bright and excellent student

高僧(ㄍㄠ ㄙㄥ)
a high-ranking monk; a prelate; a learned monk

高速(ㄍㄠ ㄙㄨˋ)
high speed

高速公路(ㄍㄠ ㄙㄨˋ ㄍㄨㄥ ㄌㄨˋ)
an expressway; a freeway; a motorway

高聳(ㄍㄠ ㄙㄨㄥˇ)
to tower; to rise high

高額(ㄍㄠ ㄜˊ)
a large sum; a large amount (of money)亦作「鉅額」

高矮(ㄍㄠ ㄞˇ)
stature; height; high and low

高傲(ㄍㄠ ㄠˋ)
proud; overbearing; haughty

高昂(ㄍㄠ ㄤˊ)
(said of prices, morale, etc.) rising high

高爾夫球(ㄍㄠ ㄦˇ ㄈㄨ ㄑㄧㄡˊ)
golf

高爾夫球棒(ㄍㄠ ㄦˇ ㄈㄨ ㄑㄧㄡˊ ㄅㄤˋ)
golf clubs

高爾夫球僮(ㄍㄠ ㄦˇ ㄈㄨ ㄑㄧㄡˊ ㄊㄨㄥˊ)
a caddie

高爾夫球場(ㄍㄠ ㄦˇ ㄈㄨ ㄑㄧㄡˊ ㄔㄤˇ)
a golf course; a golf links

高爾基(ㄍㄠ ㄦˇ ㄐㄧ)
Maxim Gorki, 1868-1936, Russian writer

高義 or 高誼(ㄍㄠ ㄧˋ)
a great friendship; a great kindness

高壓電線(ㄍㄠ ㄧㄚ ㄉㄧㄢˋ ㄒㄧㄢˋ)or 高壓線(ㄍㄠ ㄧㄚ ㄒㄧㄢˋ)
a high-tension wire

高壓政策(ㄍㄠ ㄧㄚ ㄓㄥˋ ㄘㄜˋ)
a high-handed policy

高壓手段(ㄍㄠ ㄧㄚ ㄕㄡˇ ㄉㄨㄢˋ)
high-handed measures; tyrannical measures

高牙大纛(ㄍㄠ ㄧㄚˊ ㄉㄚˋ ㄉㄠˋ)
flags and emblems of a high official

高雅(ㄍㄠ ㄧㄚˇ)
elegant; noble and graceful; refined

高眼(ㄍㄠ ㄧㄢˇ)
keen foresight; vision

高音(ㄍㄠ ㄧㄣ)
①high tones; treble ②a soprano or tenor

高臥(ㄍㄠ ㄨㄛˋ)
to live in peace and ease; to be free from anxiety; to sleep soundly

高位(ㄍㄠ ㄨㄟˋ)
a high position: 他在銀行裡位居高位。He holds a high position in a bank.

高溫(ㄍㄠ ㄨㄣ)
a high temperature

高溫計(ㄍㄠ ㄨㄣ ㄐㄧˋ)
a pyrometer

高文典册(ㄍㄠ ㄨㄣˊ ㄉㄧㄢˇ ㄘㄜˋ)
major administrative documents of the imperial court

高原(ㄍㄠ ㄩㄢˊ)
highlands; plateaus

髟 部

ㄅㄧㄠ biau biāo

三畫

【髡】 7009
ㄎㄨㄣ kuen kūn

1. an ancient punishment of shaving the hair

2. to shear trees
髡鉗(ㄎㄨㄣ ㄑㄧㄢˊ)
ancient punishments of shaving the hair and chaining the neck

【髢】 7010 ㄊㄧˋ tih tì
wearing false hair

四畫

【髣】 7011 ㄈㄤˇ faang fǎng
like; similar
髣髴 or 彷彿(ㄈㄤˇ ㄈㄨˊ)
① like; similar ② seem; as if

【髥】 7012 (髯) ㄖㄢˊ ran rán
1. whiskers
2. a heavily bearded man
髥奴(ㄖㄢˊ ㄋㄨˊ)
a heavily bearded fellow
髥口(ㄖㄢˊ ㄎㄡˇ)
artificial whiskers worn by actors in Peiking opera
髥叟(ㄖㄢˊ ㄙㄡˇ)
a bearded old man; an old man
髥蘇(ㄖㄢˊ ㄙㄨ)
a nickname of the Sung Dynasty poet Su Shih (蘇軾), who was heavily bearded

【髦】 7013 ㄇㄠˊ mau máo
1. a children's hair style with front hair covering the forehead
2. the mane
3. a man of talent
髦俊(ㄇㄠˊ ㄐㄩㄣˋ)
a man of talent
髦士(ㄇㄠˊ ㄕˋ)
a man of talent; a man of superior character

五畫

【髫】 7014 ㄊㄧㄠˊ tyau tiáo
1. a children's hair style with hair hanging down the forehead
2. a youngster; a child
髫辮(ㄊㄧㄠˊ ㄅㄧㄢˋ)
childhood; youth
髫年(ㄊㄧㄠˊ ㄋㄧㄢˊ)
childhood; youth
髫齔(ㄊㄧㄠˊ ㄔㄣˋ)
childhood; youth

【髮】 7015 ㄈㄚˇ faa fǎ
1. hair (covering human heads)
2. a hairbreadth; a hair's breadth
髮匪(ㄈㄚˇ ㄈㄟˇ)
the Taiping rebels of the late Ching Dynasty who grew long hair
髮膚(ㄈㄚˇ ㄈㄨ)
one's hair and skin
髮短心長(ㄈㄚˇ ㄉㄨㄢˇ ㄒㄧㄣ ㄔㄤˊ)
(literally) to have sparse hair and an intelligent mind—old and wise
髮蠟(ㄈㄚˇ ㄌㄚˋ)
pomade
髮際(ㄈㄚˇ ㄐㄧˋ)
hairline
髮髻(ㄈㄚˇ ㄐㄧˋ)
hair tied in a knot
髮夾(ㄈㄚˇ ㄐㄧㄚˊ)
a hairpin; a bobby pin
髮膠(ㄈㄚˇ ㄐㄧㄠ)
hair spray; fixture for hair
髮妻(ㄈㄚˇ ㄑㄧ)
one's first wife
髮型(ㄈㄚˇ ㄒㄧㄥˊ) or 髮式(ㄈㄚˇ ㄕˋ)
a hair style; a hairdo; a coiffure
髮指(ㄈㄚˇ ㄓˇ)
so angry that the hair rises; to boil with anger: 他的暴行令人髮指。His atrocities made one boil with anger.
髮針(ㄈㄚˇ ㄓㄣ)
a hairpin
髮刷(ㄈㄚˇ ㄕㄨㄚ)
a hairbrush
髮油(ㄈㄚˇ ㄧㄡˊ)
hair oil; pomade: 他塗髮油。He puts pomade on the hair.
髮網(ㄈㄚˇ ㄨㄤˇ)
a hair net

【髴】 7016 ㄈㄨˊ fwu fú
as in 髣髴—like; similar

【髯】 7017 ㄖㄢˊ ran rán
same as 髥—whiskers

【髭】 7018 ㄗ tzy zī
moustaches
髭鬚(ㄗ ㄒㄩ)
moustaches and beards

六畫

【髻】 7019 ㄐㄧˋ jih jì
a coiffure with a topknot

【髹】 7020 ㄒㄧㄡ shiou xiū
1. a kind of dark-red paint
2. to paint or lacquer (articles)

七畫

【鬁】 7021 ㄌㄧˋ lih lì
as in 鬎鬁—favus

【髽】 7022 ㄓㄨㄚ jua zhuā
women's headdresses in mourning
髽髻(ㄓㄨㄚ ·ㄐㄧ)
a kind of hairdo worn by young girls and maid servants in former times

八畫

【鬆】 7023 ㄙㄨㄥ song sōng
1. loose; lax; slack
2. to relax: 放鬆你的肌肉。Relax your muscles.
3. to loosen: 螺絲釘鬆了。The screw has loosened.
4. soft; light
鬆綁(ㄙㄨㄥ ㄅㄤˇ)
to untie, undo, or unfasten someone or something tied
鬆動(ㄙㄨㄥ ·ㄉㄨㄥ) or 鬆通(ㄙㄨㄥ ·ㄊㄨㄥ)
① to become less crowded ② not hard up; well-off ③ to become relaxed or flexible
鬆土機(ㄙㄨㄥ ㄊㄨˇ ㄐㄧ)
a scarifier
鬆口氣(ㄙㄨㄥ ㄎㄡˇ ㄑㄧˋ)
to relax for a while; to get a breathing spell
鬆開(ㄙㄨㄥ ㄎㄞ)
to loosen
鬆緊(ㄙㄨㄥ ㄐㄧㄣˇ)
tension and relaxation
鬆緊帶(ㄙㄨㄥ ㄐㄧㄣˇ ㄉㄞˋ)
an elastic cord, string, band, etc.
鬆勁(ㄙㄨㄥ ㄐㄧㄣˋ) or 鬆勁兒(ㄙㄨㄥ

〔髟部〕

ㄐㄧㄝˇㄦ
to slack; to loose strength
鬆懈(ㄙㄨㄥ ㄒㄧㄝˋ)
to relax efforts, attention, etc.: 你不能鬆懈，要繼續努力。You must not relax in your efforts.
鬆心(ㄙㄨㄥ ㄒㄧㄣ)
carefree
鬆性(ㄙㄨㄥ ㄒㄧㄥˋ)
(physics) porosity
鬆弛(ㄙㄨㄥ ㄔˊ)
① relaxed; flabby ② lax; slack: 繩子鬆弛了。The rope was slack.
鬆手(ㄙㄨㄥ ㄕㄡˇ)
to let go the hands; to relax the hold
鬆輭(ㄙㄨㄥ ㄖㄨㄢˇ)
loose and soft
鬆脆(ㄙㄨㄥ ㄘㄨㄟˋ)
(said of food) crisp and soft
鬆散(ㄙㄨㄥ ㄙㄢˇ)
incompact; not solid; loosely arranged: 文章結構鬆散。The article is loosely organized.
鬆鬆垮垮(ㄙㄨㄥ ㄙㄨㄥ ㄎㄨㄚˇ ㄎㄨㄚˇ)
to behave in a lax way; to be slack and perfunctory

【鬈】 7024 ㄑㄩㄢˊ chyuan quán
1. fine hair
2. curled hair
鬈髮(ㄑㄩㄢˊ ㄈㄚˇ)
crimps
鬈曲(ㄑㄩㄢˊ ㄑㄩ)
to crinkle; to curl 亦作「捲曲」

【鬃】 7025 ㄗㄨㄥ tzong zōng
1. the topknot of a lady's headdress
2. the mane: 那匹馬鬃稀。That horse has a thin mane.
3. a bristle
鬃毛(ㄗㄨㄥ ㄇㄠˊ)
a horse mane

九畫

【鬎】 7026 ㄌㄚˋ lah là
favus
鬎鬁(ㄌㄚˋ ㄌㄧˋ)
favus
鬎鬁頭(ㄌㄚˋ ㄌㄧˋ ㄊㄡˊ)
a scalp affected with favus

【鬍】 7027 ㄏㄨˊ hwu hú
beard
鬍鬚(ㄏㄨˊ ㄒㄩ)
beard
鬍子(ㄏㄨˊ ˙ㄗ)
beard

十畫

【鬑】 7028 ㄌㄧㄢˊ lian lián
hair hanging down the temples
鬑鬑(ㄌㄧㄢˊ ㄌㄧㄢˊ)
having sparse hair on the temples

【鬐】 7029 ㄑㄧˊ chyi qí
1. the mane
2. fins 亦作「鰭」

【鬒】 7030 ㄓㄣˇ jeen zhěn
having dark, glossy hair

十一畫

【鬘】 7031 ㄇㄢˊ man mán
(said of hair) fair

十二畫

【鬚】 7032 ㄒㄩ shiu xū
1. beard; whiskers
2. whiskers (of a cat, etc.)
3. an awn
鬚眉(ㄒㄩ ㄇㄟˊ)
① beard and eyebrows ② men
鬚髮(ㄒㄩ ㄈㄚˇ)
beard and hair
鬚根(ㄒㄩ ㄍㄣ)
fine rootlets of plants; fibrous roots
鬚生(ㄒㄩ ㄕㄥ)
a bearded character (in Chinese opera)
鬚髯如戟(ㄒㄩ ㄖㄢˊ ㄖㄨˊ ㄐㄧˇ)
beard bristling like halberds

十三畫

【鬟】 7033 ㄏㄨㄢˊ hwan huán
1. to dress the hair in a coiled knot
2. a female servant; a maid
鬟髻(ㄏㄨㄢˊ ㄐㄧˋ)
a woman's coiffure with a topknot

十四畫

【鬢】 7034 ㄅㄧㄣˋ binn bìn
hair on the temples
鬢斑(ㄅㄧㄣˋ ㄅㄢ)
hair turning gray at the temples
鬢邊(ㄅㄧㄣˋ ㄅㄧㄢ)
temples (behind the forehead)
鬢毛(ㄅㄧㄣˋ ㄇㄠˊ)
hair on the temples
鬢髮(ㄅㄧㄣˋ ㄈㄚˇ)
hair on the temples
鬢亂釵橫(ㄅㄧㄣˋ ㄌㄨㄢˋ ㄔㄞ ㄏㄥˊ)
hair in disorder and hairpins out of place (said of women upon getting out of bed)
鬢角 or 鬢脚(ㄅㄧㄣˋ ㄐㄧㄠˇ)
temples (beside the ears)
鬢霜(ㄅㄧㄣˋ ㄕㄨㄤ)
temples covered with white hair

十五畫

【鬣】 7035 ㄌㄧㄝˋ lieh liè
1. long beard; long whiskers
2. the mane
3. fins
鬣狗(ㄌㄧㄝˋ ㄍㄡˇ)
a hyena or a hyaena 亦作「土狼」

鬥部
ㄉㄡˋ dow dòu

【鬥】 7036 ㄉㄡˋ dow dòu
same as 鬭—to struggle

四畫

【鬦】 7037 ㄉㄡˋ dow dòu
same as 鬭—to struggle

鬥部

五畫

【鬧】 7038 ㄋㄠˋ naw nào

1. to disturb; to agitate; to trouble
2. to have or experience (disasters, sickness, etc.)
3. noisy; uproarious; stormy; clamorous

鬧彆扭(ㄋㄠˋ ㄅㄧㄝ ·ㄋㄧㄡ)
to act peevishly; to show resentment; to be dissatisfied; to bicker; to be at odds: 他們又在鬧彆扭。They are bickering again.

鬧病(ㄋㄠˋ ㄅㄧㄥˋ)
to get sick; to fall ill

鬧不清(ㄋㄠˋ ·ㄅㄨ ㄑㄧㄥ)
unable to tell apart; unable to distinguish

鬧脾氣(ㄋㄠˋ ㄆㄧˊ ·ㄑㄧ)
to show temper; to get into a temper

鬧翻(ㄋㄠˋ ㄈㄢ)
to fall out with somebody: 那兩個人鬧翻了。The two men fell out.

鬧翻天(ㄋㄠˋ ㄈㄢ ㄊㄧㄢ)
to raise a hell of a noise; to raise a rumpus

鬧房(ㄋㄠˋ ㄈㄤˊ)
rough horseplay at weddings; to play practical jokes on the newlyweds on the wedding night 參看「鬧新房」

鬧風潮(ㄋㄠˋ ㄈㄥ ·ㄔㄠ)
to stir up a public commotion

鬧肚子(ㄋㄠˋ ㄉㄨˋ ·ㄗ)
to have loose bowels: 他鬧肚子。He has loose bowels.

鬧亂子(ㄋㄠˋ ㄌㄨㄢˋ ·ㄗ)
to start trouble; to create disturbances

鬧革命(ㄋㄠˋ ㄍㄜˊ ㄇㄧㄥˋ)
to make revolution; to rise in revolution

鬧個不休(ㄋㄠˋ ·ㄍㄜ ㄅㄨˋ ㄒㄧㄡ)
to have a ceaseless storm or dispute; to cause trouble or harass persistently

鬧鬼(ㄋㄠˋ ㄍㄨㄟˇ)
①(said of a house, etc.) haunted ②to play tricks behind somebody's back; to use underhand means

鬧耗子(ㄋㄠˋ ㄏㄠˋ ·ㄗ)
infested with rats

鬧轟轟(ㄋㄠˋ ㄏㄨㄥ ㄏㄨㄥ)
① arousing intense excitement; sensational; very exciting ② uproarious; clamorous; noisy

鬧饑荒(ㄋㄠˋ ㄐㄧ ·ㄏㄨㄤ)
to have a famine

鬧家務(ㄋㄠˋ ㄐㄧㄚ ·ㄨ)
to have a domestic disturbance

鬧酒(ㄋㄠˋ ㄐㄧㄡˇ)
to start a drinking bout; to engage in a drunken brawl; to behave ridiculously when drunk

鬧情緒(ㄋㄠˋ ㄑㄧㄥˊ ㄒㄩˋ)
to be in a bad mood; to be in low spirits

鬧窮(ㄋㄠˋ ㄑㄩㄥˊ)
to be poor; to be in lack of money or funds

鬧戲(ㄋㄠˋ ㄒㄧˋ)
a farce 亦作「鬧劇」

鬧笑話(ㄋㄠˋ ㄒㄧㄠˋ ㄏㄨㄚˋ)
to arouse ridicule; to make oneself a laughing stock

鬧新房(ㄋㄠˋ ㄒㄧㄣ ㄈㄤˊ)
rough horseplay at a wedding; to play practical jokes on the newlyweds in the bridal chamber

鬧性子(ㄋㄠˋ ㄒㄧㄥˋ ·ㄗ)
to go into a temper

鬧學潮(ㄋㄠˋ ㄒㄩㄝˊ ·ㄔㄠ)
to incite the student riot or demonstration on or outside the school campus

鬧著玩兒(ㄋㄠˋ ·ㄓㄜ ㄨㄚˊㄦ)
to raise hell just for fun or joke

鬧鐘(ㄋㄠˋ ㄓㄨㄥ)
an alarm clock: 鬧鐘壞了。The alarm clock is out of order.

鬧事(ㄋㄠˋ ㄕˋ)
to cause trouble or uproar; to raise hell

鬧市(ㄋㄠˋ ㄕˋ)
a busy shopping district

鬧熱(ㄋㄠˋ ㄖㄜˋ)
full of noisy bustle

鬧嚷嚷(ㄋㄠˋ ㄖㄤ ㄖㄤ)
noisy; clamorous

鬧賊(ㄋㄠˋ ㄗㄟˊ)
to be visited by burglars

鬧意見(ㄋㄠˋ ㄧˋ ㄐㄧㄢˋ)
to have differences of opinion; to have disputes

六畫

【鬨】 7039 ㄏㄨㄥˋ honq hòng

1. to be boisterous or uproarious; uproar; clamor; noise
2. a dispute; a quarrel

鬨堂(ㄏㄨㄥˋ ㄊㄤˊ)
to fill a room with roars of laughter; to bring the house down

八畫

【鬩】 7040 ㄒㄧˋ shih xì
to quarrel; to conflict

鬩牆(ㄒㄧˋ ㄑㄧㄤˊ)
to quarrel within the family; an intramural fight

十畫

【鬪】 7041 (鬭) ㄉㄡˋ dow dòu
to struggle

十四畫

【鬭】 7042 ㄉㄡˋ dow dòu
to struggle; to fight; to contend; to conflict; to vie; to compete; quarrelsomeness

鬭不過(ㄉㄡˋ ·ㄅㄨ ㄍㄨㄛˋ)
unable to win in the struggle; can't be able to fight against

鬭牌(ㄉㄡˋ ㄆㄞˊ)
to play cards: 來鬭牌吧。Let's play cards.

鬭富(ㄉㄡˋ ㄈㄨˋ)
to vie in wealth

鬭牛(ㄉㄡˋ ㄋㄧㄡˊ)
a bullfight

鬭牛者(ㄉㄡˋ ㄋㄧㄡˊ ㄓㄜˇ)or 鬭牛士(ㄉㄡˋ ㄋㄧㄡˊ ㄕˋ)
a bullfighter; a matador

鬭牛場(ㄉㄡˋ ㄋㄧㄡˊ ㄔㄤˇ)
a bullring

鬭弄(ㄉㄡˋ ·ㄋㄨㄥ)

①to seduce; to flirt with ② to play jokes; to make fun of

鬪狠 or 鬪很(ㄉㄡˋ ㄏㄣˇ)
to compete in ferocities

鬪話(ㄉㄡˋ ㄏㄨㄚˋ)
to argue; to debate

鬪雞(ㄉㄡˋ ㄐㄧ)
a cockfight; cockfighting

鬪雞眼(ㄉㄡˋ ㄐㄧ ㄧㄢˇ)
crossed eyes; convergent strabismus

鬪勁(ㄉㄡˋ ㄐㄧㄣˋ)
to compete in strength

鬪氣(ㄉㄡˋ ㄑㄧˋ)
to quarrel on emotional grounds

鬪巧(ㄉㄡˋ ㄑㄧㄠˇ)
①by chance; by coincidence; accidentally 亦作「碰巧」: 我鬪巧遇到他。I met him by chance. ②to compete in skill or ingenuity

鬪趣(ㄉㄡˋ ㄑㄩˋ)
to joke

鬪拳(ㄉㄡˋ ㄑㄩㄢˊ)
boxing: 你喜歡鬪拳嗎? Do you like boxing?

鬪蟋蟀(ㄉㄡˋ ㄒㄧ ㄕㄨㄞˋ)or 鬪促織(ㄉㄡˋ ㄘㄨˋ ㄓ)
a cricketfight

鬪閑氣(ㄉㄡˋ ㄒㄧㄢˊ ㄑㄧˋ)
to quarrel about trifles

鬪志(ㄉㄡˋ ㄓˋ)
pugnacious spirit; fighting spirit; the determination to compete or fight

鬪智(ㄉㄡˋ ㄓˋ)
a battle of wits; a contest of wits

鬪智不鬪力(ㄉㄡˋ ㄓˋ ㄅㄨˋ ㄉㄡˋ ㄌㄧˋ)
to fight a battle of wits, not of limbs

鬪爭(ㄉㄡˋ ㄓㄥ)
struggle; conflict; strife

鬪嘴(ㄉㄡˋ ㄗㄨㄟˇ)or 鬪口(ㄉㄡˋ ㄎㄡˇ)
to quarrel; to wrangle; to squabble

鬪毆(ㄉㄡˋ ㄡ)
to have a fight; to fight; to brawl: 孩子們在鬪毆。The boys are fighting.

鬪鵪鶉(ㄉㄡˋ ㄢ ㄔㄨㄣˊ)
a quailfight

鬪鴨(ㄉㄡˋ ㄧㄚ)
a duckfight

十六畫

【鬮】 7043 ㄐㄧㄡ jiou jiū
lots (to be drawn)

鬮兒(ㄐㄧㄡㄦ)
lots (to be drawn)

鬯部
ㄔㄤˋ chanq chàng

【鬯】 7044 ㄔㄤˋ chanq chàng
1. sacrificial spirits; herb-flavored spirits
2. same as 暢—unobstructed

鬯酒(ㄔㄤˋ ㄐㄧㄡˇ)
sacrificial spirits

十九畫

【鬱】 7045 ㄩˋ yuh yù
1. a tulip
2. a plum (*Prunus japonica*)
3. held in check; pent-up; stagnant
4. luxuriant; lush

鬱悶(ㄩˋ ㄇㄣˋ)
to have pent-up emotions or thoughts

鬱陶(ㄩˋ ㄊㄠˊ)
melancholy; pensive; sad; anxiously

鬱積(ㄩˋ ㄐㄧ)
pent-up (feelings); to smolder: 仇恨鬱積在他心頭。Hatred smolders in his bosom.

鬱結(ㄩˋ ㄐㄧㄝˊ)or 鬱塞(ㄩˋ ㄙㄜˋ)
to suffer from pent-up feelings

鬱金(ㄩˋ ㄐㄧㄣ)
Curcuma longa, a kind of fragrant herb

鬱金香(ㄩˋ ㄐㄧㄣ ㄒㄧㄤ)
a tulip: 這裏的鬱金香在五月開花。Tulips bloom here in May.

鬱沈沈(ㄩˋ ㄔㄣˊ ㄔㄣˊ)
depressed; despondent; dejected; low-spirited

鬱伊(ㄩˋ ㄧ)
melancholy; pensive; sad

鬱蓊(ㄩˋ ㄨㄥˇ)
luxuriant; lush

鬱郁(ㄩˋ ㄩˋ)
fragrant; sweet-smelling

鬱鬱不樂(ㄩˋ ㄩˋ ㄅㄨˋ ㄌㄜˋ)
despondent; dejected; depressed; low-spirited

鬱鬱寡歡(ㄩˋ ㄩˋ ㄍㄨㄚˇ ㄏㄨㄢ)
to mope; to feel low; one's spirits droop

鬲部
ㄌㄧˋ lih lì

【鬲】 7046 1. ㄍㄜˊ ger gé
1. name of an ancient state
2. name of an ancient sage
3. same as 隔

【鬲】 7046 2. ㄌㄧˋ lih lì
a kind of caldron

十二畫

【鬻】 7047 ㄩˋ yuh yù
1. to sell
2. to bring up
3. young; childish

鬻子(ㄩˋ ㄗˇ)
① a merchant; a trader ② a young child ③to sell one's own children

鬻文(ㄩˋ ㄨㄣˊ)
to write for pay: 他鬻文爲生。He makes a living by writing.

鬻獄(ㄩˋ ㄩˋ)
to accept bribes from litigants

鬼部
ㄍㄨㄟˇ goei guǐ

【鬼】 7048 ㄍㄨㄟˇ goei guǐ
1. spirits; ghosts; demons; devils
2. cunning; crafty; wily; deceitful

3. sinister; dark; evil; a dirty trick, work, etc.

鬼魔(ㄍㄨㄟˇ ㄇㄛˊ)
evil spirits; demons

鬼魅(ㄍㄨㄟˇ ㄇㄟˋ)
bogies; goblins; monsters

鬼門關(ㄍㄨㄟˇ ㄇㄣˊ ㄍㄨㄢ)
the gate to the land of ghosts; the gate of hell

鬼迷心竅(ㄍㄨㄟˇ ㄇㄧˊ ㄒㄧㄣ ㄑㄧㄠˋ)
to be possessed; to be obsessed

鬼斧神工(ㄍㄨㄟˇ ㄈㄨˇ ㄕㄣˊ ㄍㄨㄥ)
prodigious workmanship

鬼道(ㄍㄨㄟˇ ㄉㄠˋ)
magic; wizardry; sorcery

鬼點子(ㄍㄨㄟˇ ㄉㄧㄢˇ ˙ㄗ)
wicked ideas; tricks

鬼胎(ㄍㄨㄟˇ ㄊㄞ)
an evil plot; a dark scheme: 他心懷鬼胎。He harbored sinister designs.

鬼頭風(ㄍㄨㄟˇ ㄊㄡˊ ㄈㄥ)
a tornado; a twister; a whirlwind

鬼頭鬼腦(ㄍㄨㄟˇ ㄊㄡˊ ㄍㄨㄟˇ ㄋㄠˇ)
①crafty and sinister; evil and shrewd; secretive ②hiding and peeping

鬼剃頭(ㄍㄨㄟˇ ㄊㄧˋ ㄊㄡˊ)
a kind of balding disease

鬼臉(ㄍㄨㄟˇ ㄌㄧㄢˇ)
a grimace; to grimace: 小丑向孩子們做鬼臉。The clown grimaced at the children.

鬼錄(ㄍㄨㄟˇ ㄌㄨˋ)
a register or roll of the dead

鬼怪(ㄍㄨㄟˇ ㄍㄨㄞˋ)
monsters; goblins; bogies; ghosts

鬼鬼祟祟(ㄍㄨㄟˇ ㄍㄨㄟˇ ㄙㄨㄟˋ ㄙㄨㄟˋ)
stealthy; furtive; sneaky; clandestine; surreptitious; secretive

鬼工(ㄍㄨㄟˇ ㄍㄨㄥ)
prodigious skill; marvelous workmanship

鬼哭狼號(ㄍㄨㄟˇ ㄎㄨ ㄌㄤˊ ㄏㄠˊ)or 鬼哭神號(ㄍㄨㄟˇ ㄎㄨ ㄕㄣˊ ㄏㄠˊ)
to give dreary cries and screams

鬼話(ㄍㄨㄟˇ ㄏㄨㄚˋ)
false words; lies; nonsense

鬼話連篇(ㄍㄨㄟˇ ㄏㄨㄚˋ ㄌㄧㄢˊ ㄆㄧㄢ)
to tell a whole series of lies; to lie from start to finish; to talk nonsense throughout

鬼畫符(ㄍㄨㄟˇ ㄏㄨㄚˋ ㄈㄨˊ)
①a very poor work of calligraphy; awful calligraphy ②a hypocritical talk

鬼火(ㄍㄨㄟˇ ㄏㄨㄛˇ)
a jack-o'-lantern; a will-o'-the-wisp

鬼魂(ㄍㄨㄟˇ ㄏㄨㄣˊ)
ghosts; spirits of the dead; apparitions

鬼混(ㄍㄨㄟˇ ㄏㄨㄣˋ)
to spend days in an idle, slovenly way; to hang around; to fool around

鬼機伶兒(ㄍㄨㄟˇ ㄐㄧ ˙ㄌㄧㄥㄦ)
cleverness; sly

鬼節(ㄍㄨㄟˇ ㄐㄧㄝˊ)
the Ghosts' Festival (the 15th of the 7th lunar month)

鬼黠(ㄍㄨㄟˇ ㄒㄧㄚˊ)
cunning; crafty; shrewd; wily; sly: 那孩子可鬼黠了。The kid is very shrewd.

鬼主意(ㄍㄨㄟˇ ㄓㄨˇ ㄧˋ)
a crafty idea; a dark scheme

鬼出電入(ㄍㄨㄟˇ ㄔㄨ ㄉㄧㄢˋ ㄖㄨˋ)
to move in and out with lightning speed and wizardly elusiveness

鬼使神差(ㄍㄨㄟˇ ㄕˇ ㄕㄣˊ ㄔㄞ)
to do something inexplicably as if manipulated by supernatural beings

鬼市(ㄍㄨㄟˇ ㄕˋ)
a secret market with business done after dark

鬼神(ㄍㄨㄟˇ ㄕㄣˊ)
ghosts and deities; spirits and gods; spiritual beings

鬼子(ㄍㄨㄟˇ ˙ㄗ)
a devil or monster (a term of abuse for foreigners)

鬼才(ㄍㄨㄟˇ ㄘㄞˊ)
a genius in an unorthodox way

鬼聰明(ㄍㄨㄟˇ ㄘㄨㄥ ˙ㄇㄧㄥ)
petty cleverness

鬼祟(ㄍㄨㄟˇ ㄙㄨㄟˋ)
①misfortunes brought by evil spirits ②stealthy; clandestine

鬼物(ㄍㄨㄟˇ ㄨˋ)
evil spirits; devils; demons; ghosts

鬼蜮伎倆(ㄍㄨㄟˇ ㄩˋ ㄐㄧˋ ㄌㄧㄤˇ)
dirty underhand tricks

四畫

【魁】 7049
ㄎㄨㄟˊ kwei kuí

1. the chief; the head; the leader
2. tall; big; great

魁北克(ㄎㄨㄟˊ ㄅㄟˇ ㄎㄜˋ)
Quebec, a province in Canada

魁杓(ㄎㄨㄟˊ ㄅㄧㄠ)
the second star of the Dipper

魁柄(ㄎㄨㄟˊ ㄅㄧㄥˇ)
the reins of government

魁甲(ㄎㄨㄟˊ ㄐㄧㄚˇ)
the top candidate in the national civil service examination in former times

魁星(ㄎㄨㄟˊ ㄒㄧㄥ)
the god of literature

魁士(ㄎㄨㄟˊ ㄕˋ)
an eminent scholar

魁首(ㄎㄨㄟˊ ㄕㄡˇ)
①the first on the list of successful candidates in the former civil service examination ②the leader; the chief; the head

魁梧(ㄎㄨㄟˊ ㄨˊ)or 魁岸(ㄎㄨㄟˊ ㄢˋ)or 魁偉(ㄎㄨㄟˊ ㄨㄟˇ)
tall and robust; husky

【魂】 7050
ㄏㄨㄣˊ hwen hún

a soul; a spirit

魂不附體(ㄏㄨㄣˊ ˙ㄅㄨ ㄈㄨˋ ㄊㄧˇ)
frightened out of one's wits

魂魄(ㄏㄨㄣˊ ㄆㄛˋ)
a soul

魂飛魄散(ㄏㄨㄣˊ ㄈㄟ ㄆㄛˋ ㄙㄢˋ)
①frightened out of one's senses; frightened out of one's wits ②as good as dead

魂飛天外(ㄏㄨㄣˊ ㄈㄟ ㄊㄧㄢ ㄨㄞˋ)
①frightened out of one's senses; frightened out of one's wits ②completely carried away by passion; infatuated

魂靈(ㄏㄨㄣˊ ㄌㄧㄥˊ)
a soul 亦作「靈魂」

魂銷(ㄏㄨㄣˊ ㄒㄧㄠ)
spellbound; infatuated; bewitched

五畫

【魄】 7051
1. ㄆㄛˋ poh pò

1. (Taoism) vigor; animation; life
2. form; shape; body
3. the dark part of the moon

魄力(ㄆㄛˋ ㄌㄧˋ)
guts; decisiveness; the ability to make major decisions promptly; courage to plunge ahead in big things: 他沒有魄力。He has no guts.

魄散(ㄆㄛˋ ㄙㄢˋ)
unnerved; unmanned

【魄】 7051
2. ㄊㄨㄛˋ tuoh tuò

used in the phrase 落魄—dispirited; out of luck

【魅】 7052
ㄇㄟˋ mey mèi

1. a mischievous spirit; a goblin; an elf
2. to charm; to mislead

魅力(ㄇㄟˋ ㄌㄧˋ)
glamor; sexiness; attractiveness; spell; charm; charisma

魅惑(ㄇㄟˋ ㄏㄨㄛˋ)
to bedevil; to bewitch; to captivate

八畫

【魍】 7053
ㄨㄤˇ woang wǎng

a kind of monster

魍魎(ㄨㄤˇ ㄌㄧㄤˇ)
a kind of monster

【魎】 7054
ㄌㄧㄤˇ leang liǎng

a kind of monster

【魏】 7055
ㄨㄟˋ wey wèi

1. lofty; stately; magnificent
2. name of a kingdom during the Epoch of Warring States, and another in the 3rd century A.D.
3. a Chinese family name

魏碑(ㄨㄟˋ ㄅㄟ)
stone tablets of the Northern Wei Dynasty, noted for the vigorous calligraphy carved on them, the rubbings of which are used as models among calligraphers

魏闕(ㄨㄟˋ ㄑㄩㄝˋ)
the gate of the imperial palace

魏徵(ㄨㄟˋ ㄓㄥ)
Wei Cheng, 580-643, a famous statesman during the heyday of the Tang Dynasty

魏武帝(ㄨㄟˋ ㄨˇ ㄉㄧˋ)
the title of Tsao Tsao (曹操) as emperor

魏文帝(ㄨㄟˋ ㄨㄣˊ ㄉㄧˋ)
the title of Tsao Pi (曹丕), eldest son of Tsao Tsao (曹操) as emperor

【魊】 7056
(蜮) ㄩˋ yuh yù

a fabulous creature which supposedly hurts human beings by casting sand out of its mouth

十一畫

【魑】 7057
ㄔ chy chī

a mountain demon resembling a tiger

魑魅(ㄔ ㄇㄟˋ)
evil spirits; demons

魑魅魍魎(ㄔ ㄇㄟˋ ㄨㄤˇ ㄌㄧㄤˇ)
all sorts of monsters and goblins

【魔】 7058
ㄇㄛˊ mo mó

a wizard; a witch; a demon; a devil

魔法(ㄇㄛˊ ㄈㄚˇ)
magic; wizardry; sorcery; witchcraft

魔道(ㄇㄛˊ ㄉㄠˋ)
evil principles of courses

魔力(ㄇㄛˊ ㄌㄧˋ)
magic power; wizardly ability; charm; spell

魔鬼(ㄇㄛˊ ㄍㄨㄟˇ)
devils; demons; evil spirits

魔掌(ㄇㄛˊ ㄓㄤˇ)
devil's clutches; evil hands

魔障(ㄇㄛˊ ㄓㄤˋ)
(Buddhism) evil obstacles on the way to truth

魔術(ㄇㄛˊ ㄕㄨˋ)
magic; wizardry; witchcraft; sorcery

魔術方塊(ㄇㄛˊ ㄕㄨˋ ㄈㄤ ㄎㄨㄞˋ)
a magic square

魔術家(ㄇㄛˊ ㄕㄨˋ ㄐㄧㄚ)
a magician

魔王(ㄇㄛˊ ㄨㄤˊ)
the Devil; Satan; Prince of Darkness

十四畫

【魘】 7059
ㄧㄢˇ yean yǎn

a nightmare: 我昨夜夢魘。I had a nightmare last night.

魘魅(ㄧㄢˇ ㄇㄟˋ)
to kill by magic, witchcraft or voodoo

魚 部
ㄩˊ yu yú

【魚】 7060
ㄩˊ yu yú

fish

魚白色(ㄩˊ ㄅㄞˊ ㄙㄜˋ)
silver-gray (like the belly of a fish)

魚鰾(ㄩˊ ㄅㄧㄠˋ)
the air bladder of a fish; a swimming bladder

魚片(ㄩˊ ㄆㄧㄢˋ) or 魚片兒(ㄩˊ ㄆㄧㄚˋㄦ)
slices of fish meat; a fish fillet

魚米之鄉(ㄩˊ ㄇㄧˇ ㄓ ㄒㄧㄤ)
land of agriculture and fishery; land of plenty

魚苗(ㄩˊ ㄇㄧㄠˊ)
fry (of fish)

魚目混珠(ㄩˊ ㄇㄨˋ ㄏㄨㄣˋ ㄓㄨ)
(literally) to pass fish eyes as pearls—① to masquerade ② to offer something bogus

魚販(ㄩˊ ㄈㄢˋ)
a fishmonger

魚封(ㄩˊ ㄈㄥ)
letters; epistles

魚肚(ㄩˊ ㄉㄨˇ)
fish maws used as food

魚肚白(ㄩˊ ㄉㄨˇ ㄅㄞˊ)
silver-gray (like the belly of a fish)—gray dawn

魚塘(ㄩˊ ㄊㄤˊ)
a fishpond

魚雷(ㄩˊ ㄌㄟˊ)
a torpedo

魚雷艇(ㄩˊ ㄌㄟˊ ㄊㄧㄥˇ)

a torpedo boat
魚類(ㄩˊ ㄌㄟˋ)
fishes; Pisces
魚類學(ㄩˊ ㄌㄟˋ ㄒㄩㄝˊ)
ichthyology
魚爛而亡(ㄩˊ ㄌㄢˋ ㄦˊ ㄨㄤˊ)
(said of a country) to fall because of internal strife
魚鱗(ㄩˊ ㄌㄧㄣˊ)
scales (of fish)
魚鱗天兒(ㄩˊ ㄌㄧㄣˊ ㄊㄧㄚㄦ)
a mackerel sky
魚鱗癬(ㄩˊ ㄌㄧㄣˊ ㄒㄧㄢˇ)
ichthyosis
魚卵(ㄩˊ ㄌㄨㄢˇ)
roe; spawn
魚卵石(ㄩˊ ㄌㄨㄢˇ ㄕˊ)
oolite
魚龍(ㄩˊ ㄌㄨㄥˊ)
an ichthyosaur
魚龍混雜(ㄩˊ ㄌㄨㄥˊ ㄏㄨㄣˋ ㄗㄚˊ)
Fish and dragons jumbled together. —various kinds of people mixed up; a mixed lot
魚鈎(ㄩˊ ㄍㄡ)
a fishhook
魚狗(ㄩˊ ㄍㄡˇ)or 魚虎(ㄩˊ ㄏㄨˇ)
Alcedo bengalensis, a species of kingfisher
魚竿(ㄩˊ ㄍㄢ)
a fishing rod; a fish pole
魚肝油(ㄩˊ ㄍㄢ ㄧㄡˊ)
cod-liver oil
魚缸(ㄩˊ ㄍㄤ)
a fish globe
魚罟(ㄩˊ ㄍㄨˇ)
a fishnet; a fishing net
魚骨(ㄩˊ ㄍㄨˇ)
fishbones
魚鼓(ㄩˊ ㄍㄨˇ)
a wooden drum (in a Buddhist temple, etc.)
魚貫(ㄩˊ ㄍㄨㄢˋ)
in a column; in procession; to proceed one by one
魚口(ㄩˊ ㄎㄡˇ)or 魚口疔(ㄩˊ ㄎㄡˇ ㄉㄧㄥ)
bubo
魚膾(ㄩˊ ㄎㄨㄞˋ)
a dish prepared from slices of fish
魚化石(ㄩˊ ㄏㄨㄚˋ ㄕˊ)
ichthyolite
魚箋(ㄩˊ ㄐㄧㄢ)
letter paper; stationery
魚鰭(ㄩˊ ㄑㄧˊ)
fins
魚群(ㄩˊ ㄑㄩㄣˊ)
a shoal of fish
魚蝦(ㄩˊ ㄒㄧㄚ)
fish and shrimps
魚腥味(ㄩˊ ㄒㄧㄥ ㄨㄟˋ)
a fishy smell
魚玄機(ㄩˊ ㄒㄩㄢˊ ㄐㄧ)
a talented woman of the Tang Dynasty whose poems are famous
魚質龍文(ㄩˊ ㄓˋ ㄌㄨㄥˊ ㄨㄣˊ)
(literally) a dragon in outward marks but a fish in essence—an inferior thing with an impressive appearance
魚池(ㄩˊ ㄔˊ)
a fishpond: 一隻青蛙跳入魚池。A frog jumped into the fishpond.
魚翅(ㄩˊ ㄔˋ)
shark's fins, a delicacy on a Chinese menu
魚叉(ㄩˊ ㄔㄚ)
a harpoon; a gaff; a fish spear
魚沈雁杳(ㄩˊ ㄔㄣˊ ㄧㄢˋ ㄇㄧㄠˇ)
heard of no more (like a fish that dives and never surfaces or a wild duck that departs and never returns)
魚市(ㄩˊ ㄕˋ)
a fish market: 他上魚市買魚去。He went to the fish market to buy fish.
魚生(ㄩˊ ㄕㄥ)
raw fish in fine cuts
魚水和諧(ㄩˊ ㄕㄨㄟˇ ㄏㄜˊ ㄒㄧㄝˊ)
(said of a married couple) to live in harmony like fish and water
魚肉(ㄩˊ ㄖㄡˋ)
① fish and meat ② victims of oppression ③ to oppress; to bully: 好的統治者不會魚肉貧民。A good ruler will not oppress the poor.
魚肉鄉民(ㄩˊ ㄖㄡˋ ㄒㄧㄤ ㄇㄧㄣˊ)
to oppress the people
魚子(ㄩˊ ㄗˇ)
spawn; roe
魚子醬(ㄩˊ ㄗˇ ㄐㄧㄤˋ)
caviar
魚刺(ㄩˊ ㄘˋ)
fishbones
魚鬆(ㄩˊ ㄙㄨㄥ)
dried fish floss
魚餌(ㄩˊ ㄦˇ)
fish bait
魚游釜中(ㄩˊ ㄧㄡˊ ㄈㄨˇ ㄓㄨㄥ)
(literally) to be a fish swimming in the cooking pot—to have one's days numbered; to be doomed
魚鹽(ㄩˊ ㄧㄢˊ)
fish and salt—marine resources
魚鹽之利(ㄩˊ ㄧㄢˊ ㄓ ㄌㄧˋ)
gain from marine resources
魚眼石(ㄩˊ ㄧㄢˇ ㄕˊ)
apophyllite
魚雁(ㄩˊ ㄧㄢˋ)
letters; epistles
魚雁鮮通(ㄩˊ ㄧㄢˋ ㄒㄧㄢˇ ㄊㄨㄥ)
hardly write to one another
魚秧(ㄩˊ ㄧㄤ)
fry (of fish)亦作「魚栽」
魚鷹(ㄩˊ ㄧㄥ)
a kind of sea bird
魚尾板(ㄩˊ ㄨㄟˇ ㄅㄢˇ)
a fishplate
魚尾紋(ㄩˊ ㄨㄟˇ ㄨㄣˊ)
crow's-feet
魚丸子(ㄩˊ ㄨㄢˊ ˙ㄗ)
a fish ball; a fish cake
魚塭(ㄩˊ ㄨㄣ)
a fish farm
魚網(ㄩˊ ㄨㄤˇ)
a fishnet; a fishing net: 他們用魚網捕魚。They caught fish with a fishing net.
魚與熊掌(ㄩˊ ㄩˇ ㄒㄩㄥˊ ㄓㄤˇ)
unable to make up one's mind as to which of two desirable things to choose

三畫

【魟】 7061 ㄏㄨㄥ hong hōng
rays
魟魚(ㄏㄨㄥ ㄩˊ)
a skate

四畫

【魷】 7062 ㄧㄡˊ you yóu
a cuttlefish
魷魚(ㄧㄡˊ ㄩˊ)
a cuttlefish

〔魚部〕

【魯】 7063 ㄌㄨˇ luu lŭ
1. stupid; dull
2. vulgar
3. name of an ancient kingdom in what is today's Shantung; an alternative name of Shantung
4. a Chinese family name

魯般 or 魯班(ㄌㄨˇ ㄅㄢ)
another name of Kung-Shu Pan (公輸班), a master carpenter in the kingdom of Lu (魯) during the Epoch of Spring and Autumn

魯般尺 or 魯班尺(ㄌㄨˇ ㄅㄢ ㄔˇ)
a carpenter's square

魯壁(ㄌㄨˇ ㄅㄧˋ)
the walls of Confucius' home (from which a number of classics were later discovered)

魯濱遜飄流記(ㄌㄨˇ ㄅㄧㄣ ㄒㄩㄣˋ ㄆㄧㄠ ㄌㄧㄡˊ ㄐㄧˋ)
Robinson Crusoe, by Daniel Defoe, 1659?-1731

魯莽(ㄌㄨˇ ㄇㄤˇ)
① rude; disrespectful; ill-mannered; uncivil; discourteous ② rash; careless

魯殿靈光(ㄌㄨˇ ㄉㄧㄢˋ ㄌㄧㄥˊ ㄍㄨㄤ)
① the only remaining embodiment of past glory ② the sole survivor among elder scholars of virtue or among statesmen commanding respect

魯鈍(ㄌㄨˇ ㄉㄨㄣˋ)
dull; slow-witted

魯男子(ㄌㄨˇ ㄋㄢˊ ㄗˇ)
men unmoved by feminine charms

魯凱(ㄌㄨˇ ㄎㄞˇ)
the Rukai tribe among the aborigines in Taiwan

魯仲連(ㄌㄨˇ ㄓㄨㄥˋ ㄌㄧㄢˊ)
① Lu Chung-lien, a person in the Epoch of Warring States, skilled in mediating ② a mediator

魯人(ㄌㄨˇ ㄖㄣˊ)
① a slow-witted person; a dullard ② a native of the kingdom of Lu(魯); a native of Shantung

魯衛之政(ㄌㄨˇ ㄨㄟˋ ㄓ ㄓㄥˋ)
things very much alike

魯魚亥豕(ㄌㄨˇ ㄩˊ ㄏㄞˋ ㄕˇ)
(literally) the confusion of 魯 with 魚 and of 亥 with 豕 —copying or typographical errors

【魴】 7064 ㄈㄤˊ farng fáng
the freshwater bream

五畫

【鮎】 7065 ㄋㄧㄢˊ nian nián
Parasilurus asotus, a kind of slippery long fish

【鮑】 7066 ㄅㄠˋ baw bào
1. an abalone
2. salted fish
3. a Chinese family name

鮑叔牙(ㄅㄠˋ ㄕㄨ ㄧㄚˊ)
Pao Shu-ya, a statesman in the Epoch of Spring and Autumn, known for his great friendship for Kuan Chung(管仲)

鮑魚(ㄅㄠˋ ㄩˊ)
① an abalone 亦作「石決明」 ② salted fish

鮑魚之肆(ㄅㄠˋ ㄩˊ ㄓ ㄙˋ)
a market for salted fish—an objectionable environment

【鮒】 7067 ㄈㄨˋ fuh fù
a gold carp; a crucian carp

六畫

【鮫】 7068 ㄐㄧㄠ jiau jiāo
a shark

鮫魚(ㄐㄧㄠ ㄩˊ)
a shark

【鮪】 7069 ㄨㄟˇ woei wěi
a tuna

鮪釣(ㄨㄟˇ ㄉㄧㄠˋ)
a tuna liner

【鮭】 7070 ㄍㄨㄟ guei guī
a salmon

【鮮】 7071 1. ㄒㄧㄢ shian xiān
1. fresh; new: 這肉不太新鮮。This meat is not very fresh.
2. delicious; tasty
3. bright; attractive: 這件裙子顏色太鮮豔。This skirt is too bright.

鮮卑(ㄒㄧㄢ ㄅㄟ)
a tribe of the Tungusic people in Manchuria and eastern Mongolia from 2nd to 7th century A.D.

鮮眉亮眼(ㄒㄧㄢ ㄇㄟˊ ㄌㄧㄤˋ ㄧㄢˇ)
distinct eyebrows and bright eyes—a good-looking face

鮮美(ㄒㄧㄢ ㄇㄟˇ)
fresh and delicious

鮮明(ㄒㄧㄢ ㄇㄧㄥˊ)
① sharp; distinct ② bright-colored

鮮嫩(ㄒㄧㄢ ㄋㄣˋ)
fresh and tender

鮮果(ㄒㄧㄢ ㄍㄨㄛˇ)
fresh fruit: 你喜歡吃鮮果嗎? Do you like fresh fruit?

鮮花(ㄒㄧㄢ ㄏㄨㄚ)
fresh flowers: 李小姐喜歡鮮花。Miss Lee likes fresh flowers.

鮮活(ㄒㄧㄢ ㄏㄨㄛˊ)
fresh and lively

鮮貨(ㄒㄧㄢ ㄏㄨㄛˋ)
fresh batches of fruit or vegetables

鮮紅(ㄒㄧㄢ ㄏㄨㄥˊ)
bright red

鮮血(ㄒㄧㄢ ㄒㄧㄝˇ)
fresh blood; blood

鮮血淋漓(ㄒㄧㄢ ㄒㄧㄝˇ ㄌㄧㄣˊ ㄌㄧˊ)
drenched with blood; blood dripping

鮮食(ㄒㄧㄢ ㄕˊ)
① fresh food ② to eat fresh food

鮮肉(ㄒㄧㄢ ㄖㄡˋ)
fresh meat

鮮豔(ㄒㄧㄢ ㄧㄢˋ)
bright-colored; resplendent

鮮豔奪目(ㄒㄧㄢ ㄧㄢˋ ㄉㄨㄛˊ ㄇㄨˋ)
attractively bright-colored; resplendent

鮮味(ㄒㄧㄢ ㄨㄟˋ)
fresh flavor

鮮于(ㄒㄧㄢ ㄩˊ)
a double Chinese family name

鮮魚(ㄒㄧㄢ ㄩˊ)
fish fresh from water; fresh fish

【鮮】 7071 2. ㄒㄧㄢˇ shean xiăn
rare; few; seldom

鮮民(ㄒㄧㄢˇ ㄇㄧㄣˊ)
① an orphan ② underprivileged people
鮮少(ㄒㄧㄢˇ ㄕㄠˇ)
rare; few
鮮有(ㄒㄧㄢˇ ㄧㄡˇ)
seldom to have; rare

【鯗】 7072 ㄒㄧㄤˇ sheang xiǎng
dried and salted fish

七畫

【鯀】 7073 ㄍㄨㄣˇ goen gǔn
1. name of a kind of fish
2. father of the legendary ruler, Yü(禹)

【鯇】 7074 ㄏㄨㄣˋ huenn hùn
a grass carp

【鯁】 7075 ㄍㄥˇ geeng gěng
1. a fishbone stuck in the throat
2. honest; straightforward
鯁直(ㄍㄥˇ ㄓˊ)
honest; straightforward; outspoken

【鯉】 7076 ㄌㄧˇ lii lǐ
1. a carp
2. letters; epistles
鯉庭(ㄌㄧˇ ㄊㄧㄥˊ)
receiving instructions from one's father
鯉素(ㄌㄧˇ ㄙㄨˋ)
letters
鯉魚(ㄌㄧˇ ㄩˊ)
a common carp: 在日本鯉魚象徵勇氣。In Japan a carp symbolizes courage.
鯉魚跳龍門(ㄌㄧˇ ㄩˊ ㄊㄧㄠˋ ㄌㄨㄥˊ ㄇㄣˊ)
to succeed in the civil service examination in former times

【鯊】 7077 ㄕㄚ sha shā
a shark
鯊魚(ㄕㄚ ㄩˊ)
a shark 亦作「沙魚」
鯊魚皮(ㄕㄚ ㄩˊ ㄆㄧˊ)
sharkskin

八畫

【鯤】 7078 ㄎㄨㄣ kuen kūn
1. a kind of legendary fish said to be thousands of miles long
2. spawn; roe

【鯡】 7079 ㄈㄟ fei fēi
a herring

【鯖】 7080 ㄑㄧㄥ ching qīng
a mackerel

【鯛】 7081 ㄉㄧㄠ diau diāo
a sea bream; a porgy; a scup

【鯨】 7082 ㄐㄧㄥ jing jīng
a whale
鯨波(ㄐㄧㄥ ㄅㄛ)
huge waves in the ocean
鯨吞蠶食(ㄐㄧㄥ ㄊㄨㄣ ㄘㄢˊ ㄕˊ)
aggression by engulfing and nibbling processes
鯨類(ㄐㄧㄥ ㄌㄟˋ)
whales
鯨油(ㄐㄧㄥ ㄧㄡˊ)
whale oil
鯨魚(ㄐㄧㄥ ㄩˊ)
a whale

【鯪】 7083 ㄌㄧㄥˊ ling líng
1. a legendary fish
2. a dace

【鯫】 7084 ㄗㄡ tzou zōu
1. a small fish
2. small

九畫

【鯽】 7085 ㄐㄧˋ jih jì
a gold carp
鯽魚(ㄐㄧˋ ㄩˊ)
a gold carp

【鰈】 7086 ㄉㄧㄝˊ dye dié
a sole (fish)

【鯿】 7087 ㄅㄧㄢ bian biān
a freshwater bream

【鰌】 7088 (鰍) ㄑㄧㄡ chiou qiū
a loach

【鰒】 7089 ㄈㄨˋ fuh fù
an abalone 亦作「鮑魚」or「石決明」

【鰍】 7090 ㄑㄧㄡ chiou qiū
a loach

【鰓】 7091 ㄙㄞ sai sāi
gills (of fish): 魚和蝌蚪有鰓。Fish and tadpoles have gills.

十畫

【鰥】 7092 ㄍㄨㄢ guan guān
1. a kind of huge predatory fish
2. a widower
3. a bachelor
鰥夫(ㄍㄨㄢ ㄈㄨ)
① a widower ② a bachelor
鰥寡(ㄍㄨㄢ ㄍㄨㄚˇ)
① old widowers and widows ② old bachelors and spinsters
鰥寡孤獨(ㄍㄨㄢ ㄍㄨㄚˇ ㄍㄨ ㄉㄨˊ)
those who have no wives, husbands, parents or children
鰥棍兒(ㄍㄨㄢ ㄍㄨㄣˋㄦ)
a bachelor

【鰜】 7093 ㄐㄧㄢ jian jiān
a sole (fish)
鰜鰈(ㄐㄧㄢ ㄉㄧㄝˊ)
a couple in love

【鰛】 7094 ㄨㄣ uen wēn
a sardine

【鰭】 7095 ㄑㄧˊ chyi qí
fins

【鰣】 7096 ㄕˊ shyr shí
a reeves shad; a hilsa herring

【鰩】 7097 ㄧㄠˊ yau yáo
the nautilus; the ray

十一畫

【鰻】 7098 ㄇㄢˊ man mán
an eel

【鱈】 7099 ㄒㄩㄝˇ sheue xuě
a cod: 鱈魚是主要的食用魚之一。Cod is one of the chief food fishes.

【鰲】 7100 (鼇) ㄠˊ aur áo
a sea-tortoise
鰲頭(ㄠˊ ㄊㄡˊ)

the top successful candidate in the civil service examination in former times

【鰱】 7101
ㄌㄧㄢˊ lian lián
a silver carp

【鰾】 7102
ㄅㄧㄠˋ biaw biào
1. the maw of a fish; the air bladder; the swimming bladder
2. fish glue

鰾膠(ㄅㄧㄠˋ ㄐㄧㄠ)
fish glue

【鱅】 7103
ㄩㄥˊ yong yóng
a bighead

【鰹】 7104
ㄐㄧㄢ jian jiān
a bonito

十二畫

【鱔】 7105
ㄕㄢˋ shann shàn
an eel; a moray eel: 鱔魚看起來像蛇。An eel looks like a snake.

【鱖】 7106
ㄐㄩㄝˊ jyue jué
(又讀 ㄍㄨㄟˋ guey guì)
Mandarinfish

【鱗】 7107
ㄌㄧㄣˊ lin lín
scales (of fish)

鱗苞(ㄌㄧㄣˊ ㄅㄠ)
(botany) a scale

鱗片(ㄌㄧㄣˊ ㄆㄧㄢˋ)
① scales (of fish, etc.) ② a bud scale

鱗鱗(ㄌㄧㄣˊ ㄌㄧㄣˊ)
ripples

鱗淪(ㄌㄧㄣˊ ㄌㄨㄣˊ)
ripple-like

鱗鴻(ㄌㄧㄣˊ ㄏㄨㄥˊ)
letters; epistles

鱗集(ㄌㄧㄣˊ ㄐㄧˊ)
to flock together; to assemble

鱗甲(ㄌㄧㄣˊ ㄐㄧㄚˇ)
hard scales (of crocodiles, etc.)

鱗介(ㄌㄧㄣˊ ㄐㄧㄝˋ)
fishes and mollusks; fishery products

鱗莖(ㄌㄧㄣˊ ㄐㄧㄥ)
(botany) a bulb 亦作「球莖」

鱗屑癬(ㄌㄧㄣˊ ㄒㄧㄝˋ ㄒㄧㄢˇ)
ringworm

鱗爪(ㄌㄧㄣˊ ㄓㄠˇ)
(literally) scales and claws—minutiae; trifles

鱗傷(ㄌㄧㄣˊ ㄕㄤ)
wounds or injuries all over the body

鱗次櫛比(ㄌㄧㄣˊ ㄘˋ ㄐㄧㄝˊ ㄅㄧˋ)
(said of houses or buildings) systematically arranged like scales of a fish or teeth of a comb; row upon row

鱗萃(ㄌㄧㄣˊ ㄘㄨㄟˋ)
to herd together; to flock together

【鱘】 7108
ㄒㄩㄣˊ shyun xún
a sturgeon

十三畫

【鱟】 7109
ㄏㄡˋ how hòu
a king crab

【鱣】 7110
1. ㄓㄢ jan zhān
Acipenser mikadoi, a kind of sturgeon

【鱣】 7110
2. ㄕㄢˋ shann shàn
an eel

十五畫

【鱵】 7111
ㄓㄣ jen zhēn
a saury

十六畫

【鱸】 7112
ㄌㄨˊ lu lú
perch; bass

鱸魚(ㄌㄨˊ ㄩˊ)
the sea bass

【鱷】 7113
ㄜˋ eh è
a crocodile; an alligator

鱷魚(ㄜˋ ㄩˊ)
a crocodile; an alligator

二十二畫

【鱻】 7114
(鮮) ㄒㄧㄢ shian xiān
fresh; tasty

鳥部
ㄋㄧㄠˇ neau niǎo

【鳥】 7115
ㄋㄧㄠˇ neau niǎo
a bird

鳥媒花(ㄋㄧㄠˇ ㄇㄟˊ ㄏㄨㄚ)
ornithophilous flowers

鳥面鵠形(ㄋㄧㄠˇ ㄇㄧㄢˋ ㄏㄨˊ ㄒㄧㄥˊ)
gaunt and emaciated from hunger

鳥糞(ㄋㄧㄠˇ ㄈㄣˋ)
bird droppings

鳥道(ㄋㄧㄠˇ ㄉㄠˋ)
a path wide enough only for a bird to pass—a precipitous path

鳥蛋(ㄋㄧㄠˇ ㄉㄢˋ)or 鳥卵(ㄋㄧㄠˇ ㄌㄨㄢˇ)
bird's eggs

鳥類(ㄋㄧㄠˇ ㄌㄟˋ)
birds

鳥類學(ㄋㄧㄠˇ ㄌㄟˋ ㄒㄩㄝˊ)
ornithology

鳥類學家(ㄋㄧㄠˇ ㄌㄟˋ ㄒㄩㄝˊ ㄐㄧㄚ)
an ornithologist

鳥籠(ㄋㄧㄠˇ ㄌㄨㄥˊ)
a birdcage

鳥革翬飛(ㄋㄧㄠˇ ㄍㄜˊ ㄏㄨㄟ ㄈㄟ)
(said of buildings) graceful and handsome like a bird spreading its wings or a pheasant showing off its resplendent feathers in flight

鳥瞰(ㄋㄧㄠˇ ㄎㄢˋ)
① to have a bird's-eye view ② an aerial view; a bird's-eye view

鳥喙(ㄋㄧㄠˇ ㄏㄨㄟˋ)
a beak

鳥集鱗萃(ㄋㄧㄠˇ ㄐㄧˊ ㄌㄧㄣˊ ㄘㄨㄟˋ)
to gather in large numbers like birds or fishes; to flock together

鳥盡弓藏(ㄋㄧㄠˇ ㄐㄧㄣˋ ㄍㄨㄥ ㄘㄤˊ)
(literally) to put away the bow when the birds are gone—to discharge a worthy official in times of peace

鳥舉(ㄋㄧㄠˇ ㄐㄩˇ)
to act as quickly as a bird takes off

鳥槍(ㄋㄧㄠˇ ㄑㄧㄤ)
a fowling piece
鳥之將死，其鳴也悲(ㄋㄧㄠˇ ㄓ ㄐㄧㄤ ㄙˇ, ㄑㄧˊ ㄇㄧㄥˊ ㄧㄝˇ ㄅㄟ)
(literally) When a bird is about to die, its songs are pathetic.—A man's last words are sincere.
鳥爪(ㄋㄧㄠˇ ㄓㄠˇ)
① bird's talons ② fine, delicate human finger tips
鳥篆(ㄋㄧㄠˇ ㄓㄨㄢˋ)or 鳥籀(ㄋㄧㄠˇ ㄓㄡˋ)
an ancient form of Chinese characters shaped like bird tracks
鳥巢(ㄋㄧㄠˇ ㄔㄠˊ)or 鳥窠(ㄋㄧㄠˇ ㄎㄜ)
a bird's nest
鳥蟲書(ㄋㄧㄠˇ ㄔㄨㄥˊ ㄕㄨ)
one of the six forms of Chinese characters established by Wang Mang(王莽)
鳥銃(ㄋㄧㄠˇ ㄔㄨㄥˋ)
a fowling piece
鳥獸(ㄋㄧㄠˇ ㄕㄡˋ)
birds and beasts
鳥獸行(ㄋㄧㄠˇ ㄕㄡˋ ㄒㄧㄥˋ)
beastly conduct; incestuous scandal
鳥獸散(ㄋㄧㄠˇ ㄕㄡˋ ㄙㄢˋ)
to disperse in confusion like birds or beasts
鳥葬(ㄋㄧㄠˇ ㄗㄤˋ)
exposure of a corpse to birds of prey
鳥嘴(ㄋㄧㄠˇ ㄗㄨㄟˇ)
a beak; a bill
鳥彝(ㄋㄧㄠˇ ㄧˊ)
cups engraved with designs of birds
鳥窩(ㄋㄧㄠˇ ㄨㄛ)
a bird's nest
鳥胃(ㄋㄧㄠˇ ㄨㄟˋ)
a gizzard
鳥爲食亡，人爲財死(ㄋㄧㄠˇ ㄨㄟˋ ㄕˊ ㄨㄤˊ, ㄖㄣˊ ㄨㄟˋ ㄘㄞˊ ㄙˇ)
(a Chinese proverb) Birds die in pursuit of food, and human beings die in pursuit of wealth. 亦作「人爲財死，鳥爲食亡」
鳥王(ㄋㄧㄠˇ ㄨㄤˊ)
the king of birds—phoenix
鳥語(ㄋㄧㄠˇ ㄩˇ)or 鳥言(ㄋㄧㄠˇ ㄧㄢˊ)
① birds' songs or chirps ② foreign languages
鳥語花香(ㄋㄧㄠˇ ㄩˇ ㄏㄨㄚ ㄒㄧㄤ)
birds singing and flowers radiating fragrance—the joyous scene in spring
鳥園(ㄋㄧㄠˇ ㄩㄢˊ)
an aviary

二畫

【鳧】 7116 ㄈㄨˊ fwu fú
a wild duck
鳧脛雖短(ㄈㄨˊ ㄐㄧㄥˋ ㄋㄢˊ ㄐㄧㄚ)
(literally) It is hard to lengthen a duck's legs.—One should be contented with what one has.
鳧趨雀躍(ㄈㄨˊ ㄑㄩ ㄑㄩㄝˋ ㄩㄝˋ)
to dance with excitement; to jump about for joy
鳧水(ㄈㄨˊ ㄕㄨㄟˇ)
to swim 亦作「游泳」: 他鳧水過河。He swam across the river.
鳧藻之士(ㄈㄨˊ ㄗㄠˇ ㄓ ㄕˋ)
a man in a right environment (like wild ducks among duckweed)
鳧燕難明(ㄈㄨˊ ㄧㄢˋ ㄋㄢˊ ㄇㄧㄥˊ)or 鳧乙(ㄈㄨˊ ㄧˇ)or 鳧燕(ㄈㄨˊ ㄧㄢˋ)
(literally) It's hard to distinguish between high-flying wild ducks and swallows.—things easily confused

【鳩】 7117 ㄐㄧㄡ jiou jiū
1. a pigeon; a dove
2. to collect; to assemble
鳩摩羅什(ㄐㄧㄡ ㄇㄛˊ ㄌㄨㄛˊ ㄕˊ)
Kumarajiva, name of a Buddhist monk from Central Asia who translated a number of Buddhist scriptures into Chinese in the 5th century
鳩民(ㄐㄧㄡ ㄇㄧㄣˊ)
to assemble people peacefully
鳩斂(ㄐㄧㄡ ㄌㄧㄢˋ)
to collect taxes
鳩工(ㄐㄧㄡ ㄍㄨㄥ)
to assemble workmen
鳩工庀材(ㄐㄧㄡ ㄍㄨㄥ ㄆㄧˇ ㄘㄞˊ)
to assemble workmen and procure materials (in preparation for a construction job)
鳩合(ㄐㄧㄡ ㄏㄜˊ)
to gather together; to assemble
鳩集(ㄐㄧㄡ ㄐㄧˊ)or 鳩聚(ㄐㄧㄡ ㄐㄩˋ)
to assemble; to gather
鳩居(ㄐㄧㄡ ㄐㄩ)
my humble house
鳩形鵠面(ㄐㄧㄡ ㄒㄧㄥˊ ㄏㄨˊ ㄇㄧㄢˋ)
gaunt and emaciated from malnutrition
鳩胸(ㄐㄧㄡ ㄒㄩㄥ)
a pigeon breast; pigeon-breasted
鳩占鵲巢(ㄐㄧㄡ ㄓㄢˋ ㄑㄩㄝˋ ㄔㄠˊ)
(literally) a pigeon in a magpie's nest—enjoying the fruits of others' without having worked hard; to usurp what is another's
鳩杖(ㄐㄧㄡ ㄓㄤˋ)
a staff with a pigeon-like handle (presented to the aged as a token of respect)
鳩拙(ㄐㄧㄡ ㄓㄨㄛˊ)
(a self-depreciatory term) stupid as a pigeon
鳩衆(ㄐㄧㄡ ㄓㄨㄥˋ)
to assemble a big crowd
鳩率(ㄐㄧㄡ ㄕㄨㄞˋ)
to assemble and lead

三畫

【鳲】 7118 ㄕ shy shī
a cuckoo
鳲鳩(ㄕ ㄐㄧㄡ)
① a cuckoo; a turtledove ② a poem in *The Book of Odes* (詩經)

【鳳】 7119 ㄈㄥˋ fenq fèng
Feng—a male phoenix
鳳毛(ㄈㄥˋ ㄇㄠˊ)
a fine son taking after his father
鳳毛麟角(ㄈㄥˋ ㄇㄠˊ ㄌㄧㄣˊ ㄐㄧㄠˇ)
the feathers of a phoenix and the horn of a unicorn—rare treasures or talents; something extremely rare
鳳鳴朝陽(ㄈㄥˋ ㄇㄧㄥˊ ㄓㄠ ㄧㄤˊ)
(literally) the phoenix singing to the sun—capable men born in the right time (whose talents are employed by a wise ruler instead of

being buried)

鳳邸(ㄈㄥˋ ㄉㄧˇ)
the emperor's abode where he lived before his accession to the throne

鳳蝶(ㄈㄥˋ ㄉㄧㄝˊ)
Papilio xuthus, a kind of butterfly

鳳頭鞋(ㄈㄥˋ ㄊㄡˊ ㄒㄧㄝˊ)
shoes with the tip adorned with the image of a phoenix (formerly worn by women)

鳳鳥不至(ㄈㄥˋ ㄋㄧㄠˇ ㄅㄨˋ ㄓˋ)
(literally) The Feng bird does not come.—There are no wise men in the government. 或 There is no wise king or emperor in the court.

鳳輦(ㄈㄥˋ ㄋㄧㄢˇ)
① the imperial carriage ② the carriage of an immortal

鳳梨(ㄈㄥˋ ㄌㄧˊ)
a pineapple

鳳閣龍樓(ㄈㄥˋ ㄍㄜˊ ㄌㄨㄥˊ ㄌㄡˊ)
the imperial palace

鳳冠(ㄈㄥˋ ㄍㄨㄢ)
a kind of headgear for a lady (especially for a bride) in former times

鳳冠霞帔(ㄈㄥˋ ㄍㄨㄢ ㄒㄧㄚˊ ㄆㄟˋ)
the headgear and dress of a lady or bride in former times

鳳凰(ㄈㄥˋ ㄏㄨㄤˊ)
Feng-huang—phoenixes (鳳 being male and 凰 being female)

鳳凰木(ㄈㄥˋ ㄏㄨㄤˊ ㄇㄨˋ)
Delonix regia, a flame tree

鳳凰來儀(ㄈㄥˋ ㄏㄨㄤˊ ㄌㄞˊ ㄧˊ)
the phoenix coming and showing a gentle air—a good omen

鳳凰于飛(ㄈㄥˋ ㄏㄨㄤˊ ㄩˊ ㄈㄟ)
a couple of phoenixes on the wing—happy marriage

鳳駕(ㄈㄥˋ ㄐㄧㄚˋ)
the imperial carriage

鳳舉(ㄈㄥˋ ㄐㄩˇ)
① to soar high; to rise to a high position ② the travel of a courtier on an imperial assignment ③ the flight of an immortal

鳳旗(ㄈㄥˋ ㄑㄧˊ)
the imperial flag

鳳翹(ㄈㄥˋ ㄑㄧㄠˊ)
① a kind of headgear for women ② formerly, women's shoes adorned with the embroidered images of phoenixes

鳳求凰(ㄈㄥˋ ㄑㄧㄡˊ ㄏㄨㄤˊ)
courtship

鳳闕(ㄈㄥˋ ㄑㄩㄝˋ)
the gate of the imperial palace

鳳仙花(ㄈㄥˋ ㄒㄧㄢ ㄏㄨㄚ)
a balsam; a garden balsam

鳳穴(ㄈㄥˋ ㄒㄩㄝˋ)
a cultural center

鳳詔(ㄈㄥˋ ㄓㄠˋ)
the imperial mandate; the imperial decree

鳳池(ㄈㄥˋ ㄔˊ)or 鳳沼(ㄈㄥˋ ㄓㄠˇ)
① a position enjoying the trust of the emperor ② an ancient government agency vested with broad powers

鳳雛(ㄈㄥˋ ㄔㄨˊ)
(literally) a young phoenix —a capable young man; a talented person

鳳山(ㄈㄥˋ ㄕㄢ)
Fengshan, a city in Taiwan

鳳生鳳兒(ㄈㄥˋ ㄕㄥ ㄈㄥˋ ㄦˊ)
a fine son born of a fine father

鳳藻(ㄈㄥˋ ㄗㄠˇ)
beautiful expressions

鳳髓龍肝(ㄈㄥˋ ㄙㄨㄟˇ ㄌㄨㄥˊ ㄍㄢ)
(figuratively) rare delicacies

鳳尾蕉(ㄈㄥˋ ㄨㄟˇ ㄐㄧㄠ)or 鳳尾松(ㄈㄥˋ ㄨㄟˇ ㄙㄨㄥ)
a cycad

鳳尾草(ㄈㄥˋ ㄨㄟˇ ㄘㄠˇ)
ferns

鳳尾魚(ㄈㄥˋ ㄨㄟˇ ㄩˊ)
a long-tailed anchovy

【鳴】 7120
ㄇㄧㄥˊ ming míng

1. (said of birds) to sing; to chirp; to warble; (said of cocks) to crow
2. the notes of birds
3. to make sounds; to sound

鳴不平(ㄇㄧㄥˊ ㄅㄨˋ ㄆㄧㄥˊ)
to voice grievances; to complain against injustice

鳴砲示敬(ㄇㄧㄥˊ ㄆㄠˋ ㄕˋ ㄐㄧㄥˋ)
to salute by setting off firecrackers or by firing cannons

鳴放(ㄇㄧㄥˊ ㄈㄤˋ)
the airing of views (through posters, meetings or other media)

鳴鳳(ㄇㄧㄥˊ ㄈㄥˋ)
(literally) a singing phoenix —something of rare beauty or value

鳴笛(ㄇㄧㄥˊ ㄉㄧˊ)
to blow a whistle; to signal with a siren

鳴鏑(ㄇㄧㄥˊ ㄉㄧˊ)
arrows that give a particular sound when shot (used to signal commands to an army in ancient times)

鳴蜩(ㄇㄧㄥˊ ㄊㄧㄠˊ)
Graptopsaltria corolata, a kind of cicada

鳴鑼聚衆(ㄇㄧㄥˊ ㄌㄨㄛˊ ㄐㄩˋ ㄓㄨㄥˋ)
to beat the gong to assemble people

鳴鑾(ㄇㄧㄥˊ ㄌㄨㄢˊ)
the emperor's journey

鳴鼓(ㄇㄧㄥˊ ㄍㄨˇ)
to beat the drum

鳴鼓而攻(ㄇㄧㄥˊ ㄍㄨˇ ㄦˊ ㄍㄨㄥ)
to attack while beating the drum; to stage an open attack or condemnation

鳴管(ㄇㄧㄥˊ ㄍㄨㄢˇ)
(said of birds) syrinxes

鳴鳩(ㄇㄧㄥˊ ㄐㄧㄡ)
a pigeon; a dove

鳴金收兵(ㄇㄧㄥˊ ㄐㄧㄣ ㄕㄡ ㄅㄧㄥ)
to beat the gong to call back the troops; to withdraw the troops from the battle

鳴禽類(ㄇㄧㄥˊ ㄑㄧㄣˊ ㄌㄟˋ)
the oscines

鳴琴而治(ㄇㄧㄥˊ ㄑㄧㄣˊ ㄦˊ ㄓˋ)
to rule by enlightenment; to rule by minimum interference with the people

鳴槍(ㄇㄧㄥˊ ㄑㄧㄤ)
to fire rifles into the air (as a warning to a mob, rioters, etc.)

鳴謝(ㄇㄧㄥˊ ㄒㄧㄝˋ)
to express gratitude

鳴冤(ㄇㄧㄥˊ ㄩㄢ)
to complain of unfairness; to air grievances

【鳶】 7121
ㄩㄢ iuan yuan

1. a kite; a hawk

2. a kite (a toy)
鳶飛魚躍(ㄩㄢ ㄈㄟ ㄩˊ ㄩㄝˋ)
kites flying and fishes jumping—natural freedom of things in the universe
鳶尾科(ㄩㄢ ㄨㄟˇ ㄎㄜ)
(botany) the iris family

四畫

【鴆】 7122 ㄓㄣˋ jenn zhèn
1. a kind of venomous bird
2. poisoned wine
鴆媒(ㄓㄣˋ ㄇㄟˊ)
to slander; to libel
鴆毒(ㄓㄣˋ ㄉㄨˊ)
① poison; venom ② to slander; to harm by devious means
鴆酒(ㄓㄣˋ ㄐㄧㄡˇ)
poisoned wine

【鴇】 7123 ㄅㄠˇ bao bǎo
1. *Otis dybowskii*, a bird resembling the wild goose
2. a prostitute
3. a procuress
鴇母(ㄅㄠˇ ㄇㄨˇ)
a procuress
鴇兒(ㄅㄠˇ ㄦˊ)
① a prostitute ② a procuress

【鴉】 7124 ㄧㄚ ia yā
a crow; a raven: 天下烏鴉一般黑。Crows are black the whole world over.
鴉鬢(ㄧㄚ ㄅㄧㄣˋ)
the raven black hair of a woman
鴉片(ㄧㄚ ㄆㄧㄢˋ)
opium
鴉片戰爭(ㄧㄚ ㄆㄧㄢˋ ㄓㄢˋ ㄓㄥ)
the Opium War (1839-1842)
鴉片煙(ㄧㄚ ㄆㄧㄢˋ ㄧㄢ)
opium (to be smoked)
鴉片煙鬼(ㄧㄚ ㄆㄧㄢˋ ㄧㄢ ㄍㄨㄟˇ)
an addict to opium smoking; an opium addict
鴉片煙館(ㄧㄚ ㄆㄧㄢˋ ㄧㄢ ㄍㄨㄢˇ)
an opium den
鴉片煙癮(ㄧㄚ ㄆㄧㄢˋ ㄧㄢ ㄧㄣˇ)
addiction to opium smoking; opium addiction
鴉默雀靜兒的(ㄧㄚ ·ㄇㄛ ㄑㄩㄝˋ ㄐㄧㄥˋㄦ ·ㄉㄜ)
so quiet that not a voice can be heard
鴉鳴鵲噪(ㄧㄚ ㄇㄧㄥˊ ㄑㄩㄝˋ ㄗㄠˋ)
full of confused voices
鴉飛雀亂(ㄧㄚ ㄈㄟ ㄑㄩㄝˋ ㄌㄨㄢˋ)
utter disorder
鴉鬟(ㄧㄚ ·ㄏㄨㄢ)or 鴉頭(ㄧㄚ ·ㄊㄡ)
a female servant; a maid 亦作「丫鬟」or「丫頭」
鴉髻(ㄧㄚ ㄐㄧˋ)
a glossy headdress of a woman
鴉雀無聲(ㄧㄚ ㄑㄩㄝˋ ㄨˊ ㄕㄥ)or 鴉雀無聞(ㄧㄚ ㄑㄩㄝˋ ㄨˊ ㄨㄣˊ)
so quiet that not a single voice can be heard
鴉巢生鳳(ㄧㄚ ㄔㄠˊ ㄕㄥ ㄈㄥˋ)
(literally) a phoenix born in a crow's nest—a distinguished man from a humble family
鴉嘴鋤(ㄧㄚ ㄗㄨㄟˇ ㄔㄨˊ)
a mattock
鴉色(ㄧㄚ ㄙㄜˋ)
reddish blue

【鴂】 7125 (鴃) ㄐㄩㄝˊ jyue jué
a shrike; a butcherbird
鴂舌(ㄐㄩㄝˊ ㄕㄜˊ)
languages of barbarians

【鴈】 7126 ㄧㄢˋ yann yàn
1. same as 雁—a wild goose
2. same as 贗—bogus; forged, etc.

五畫

【鴒】 7127 ㄌㄧㄥˊ ling líng
a wagtail

【鴕】 7128 ㄊㄨㄛˊ two tuó
an ostrich
鴕鳥(ㄊㄨㄛˊ ㄋㄧㄠˇ)
an ostrich

【鴛】 7129 ㄩㄢ iuan yuān
the male mandarin duck
鴛夢重溫(ㄩㄢ ㄇㄥˋ ㄔㄨㄥˊ ㄨㄣ)
reunion of the old lovers after a long separation; to rekindle old flame of love
鴛侶(ㄩㄢ ㄌㄩˇ)
a spouse
鴛機(ㄩㄢ ㄐㄧ)
an embroidery kit
鴛綺(ㄩㄢ ㄑㄧˇ)
magnificent fabrics
鴛釵(ㄩㄢ ㄔㄞ)
a kind of hairpin for women
鴛鴦(ㄩㄢ ㄧㄤ)
mandarin ducks, which always live in pairs—a symbol of lovers
鴛鴦被(ㄩㄢ ㄧㄤ ㄅㄟˋ)or 鴛被(ㄩㄢ ㄅㄟˋ)
bedding for a couple; double bedding
鴛鴦梅(ㄩㄢ ㄧㄤ ㄇㄟˊ)
plums hanging in pairs from the same footstalks
鴛鴦桃(ㄩㄢ ㄧㄤ ㄊㄠˊ)
a kind of peach
鴛鴦蝴蝶派(ㄩㄢ ㄧㄤ ㄏㄨˊ ㄉㄧㄝˊ ㄆㄞˋ)
literature characterized by shallow love stories
鴛鴦劍(ㄩㄢ ㄧㄤ ㄐㄧㄢˋ)
swords made in pairs
鴛鴦戲水(ㄩㄢ ㄧㄤ ㄒㄧˋ ㄕㄨㄟˇ)
(literally) mandarin ducks playing in the water—lovemaking
鴛鴦枕(ㄩㄢ ㄧㄤ ㄓㄣˇ)
a double pillow (for the newly married)
鴛鴦草(ㄩㄢ ㄧㄤ ㄘㄠˇ)
a kind of herb
鴛鴦瓦(ㄩㄢ ㄧㄤ ㄨㄚˇ)
mandarin duck roof-tiles—roof-tiles in pairs

【鴞】 7130 ㄒㄧㄠ shiau xiāo
an owl
鴞科(ㄒㄧㄠ ㄎㄜ)
the owl family
鴞炙(ㄒㄧㄠ ㄓˋ)
to expect a roast owl—to count the chickens before they are hatched

【鴟】 7131 ㄔ chy chī
1. a kite
2. an owl
3. winecups
鴟甍(ㄔ ㄇㄥˊ)
a kind of roof ornament
鴟目虎吻(ㄔ ㄇㄨˋ ㄏㄨˇ ㄨㄣˇ)
(literally) an owl's eyes and a tiger's lips—a very fierce-looking face
鴟顧(ㄔ ㄍㄨˋ)
to look back without moving the body like an owl
鴟梟(ㄔ ㄒㄧㄠ)

〔鳥部〕

an owl
鴟鴞(ㄔ ㄒㄧㄠ)
①an owl ②a canto in *The Book of Odes* (詩經)
鴟峙(ㄔ ㄓˋ)
to form an abominable or brutal opposition
鴟張(ㄔ ㄓㄤ)
stretched wings of an owl —brutal oppressors
鴟視(ㄔ ㄕˋ)
to watch with greed or avarice
鴟蹲(ㄔ ㄘㄨㄣˊ)
to squat like an owl
鴟夷(ㄔ ㄧˊ)
a leather bag
鴟尾(ㄔ ㄨㄟˇ)or 鴟吻(ㄔ ㄨㄣˇ)
a kind of ornament on the roof ridge

【鴣】 7132 ㄍㄨ gu gū
a kind of pigeon, as in 鷓鴣—a partridge; a francolin
鴣鴿(ㄍㄨ ㄍㄜ)
a kind of pigeon

【鴦】 7133 ㄧㄤ iang yāng
the female mandarin duck
參看「鴛」

【鴨】 7134 ㄧㄚ ia yā
a duck
鴨蛋(ㄧㄚ ㄉㄢˋ)
①a duck's egg ②(slang) scoreless; zero
鴨蛋臉兒(ㄧㄚ ㄉㄢˋ ㄌㄧㄢˇㄦ)
an oval face (regarded as an ideal shape for a woman's face)
鴨蛋圓兒(ㄧㄚ ㄉㄢˋ ㄩㄢˊㄦ)
egg-shaped; oval
鴨爐(ㄧㄚ ㄌㄨˊ)
a censer or thurible (so named because they were often shaped like ducks)
鴨綠江(ㄧㄚ ㄌㄨˋ ㄐㄧㄤ)
the Yalu River
鴨黃(ㄧㄚ ㄏㄨㄤˊ)
a duckling 亦作「小鴨」
鴨脚(ㄧㄚ ㄐㄧㄠˇ)
①a duck's feet ②gingko or ginkgo (so named because the tree leaf looks like the duck's webbed foot)
鴨叫(ㄧㄚ ㄐㄧㄠˋ)
quacks of the duck
鴨掌(ㄧㄚ ㄓㄤˇ)
webs on duck's feet
鴨翅席(ㄧㄚ ㄔˋ ㄒㄧˊ)
a banquet featuring ducks and fish fins
鴨舌帽(ㄧㄚ ㄕㄜˊ ㄇㄠˋ)
a cap with a visor
鴨絨(ㄧㄚ ㄖㄨㄥˊ)
down on a duck's abdomen
鴨子(ㄧㄚ ˙ㄗ)
a duck
鴨子房兒(ㄧㄚ ˙ㄗ ㄈㄤˊㄦ)
a duckhouse
鴨子兒(ㄧㄚ ㄗㄜˇㄦ)
a duck's egg
鴨嘴筆(ㄧㄚ ㄗㄨㄟˇ ㄅㄧˇ)
a drawing pen; a ruling pen
鴨嘴獸(ㄧㄚ ㄗㄨㄟˇ ㄕㄡˋ)
an ornithorhynchus; a duckbill; a platypus
鴨兒梨(ㄧㄚㄦ ㄌㄧˊ)
a kind of pear

【鴥】 7135 ㄩˋ yuh yù
flying rapidly; flitting

【鴝】 7136 ㄑㄩˊ chyu qú
a species of myna (or mynah, minah)
鴝鵒(ㄑㄩˊ ㄩˋ)
a species of myna (or mynah, minah)

六畫

【鴿】 7137 ㄍㄜ ge gē
a pigeon; a dove
鴿派(ㄍㄜ ㄆㄞˋ)
the doves (persons who support a peaceful policy)
鴿棚(ㄍㄜ ㄆㄥˊ)or 鴿籠(ㄍㄜ ㄌㄨㄥˊ)
a pigeon house
鴿雛兒(ㄍㄜ ㄔㄨˊㄦ)
a young pigeon
鴿子(ㄍㄜ ˙ㄗ)
a pigeon
鴿子傳書(ㄍㄜ ˙ㄗ ㄔㄨㄢˊ ㄕㄨ)
transmission of messages by homing pigeons

【鵁】 7138 ㄐㄧㄠ jiau jiāo
Nycticorax prasinosceles, a kind of water bird
鵁鶄(ㄐㄧㄠ ㄐㄧㄥ)
Nycticorax prasinosceles, a kind of water bird

【鴻】 7139 ㄏㄨㄥˊ horng hóng
1. a wild swan; a wild goose
2. great; huge; large
鴻博(ㄏㄨㄥˊ ㄅㄛˊ)
marked by extensive learning; erudite
鴻寶(ㄏㄨㄥˊ ㄅㄠˇ)
a secret collection of rare books
鴻筆(ㄏㄨㄥˊ ㄅㄧˇ)
a great pen—(figuratively) a great literary style
鴻毛(ㄏㄨㄥˊ ㄇㄠˊ)
swan's down—something very light or insignificant
鴻門宴(ㄏㄨㄥˊ ㄇㄣˊ ㄧㄢˋ)
a banquet held by Hsiang Yü (項羽) for his rival Liu Pang (劉邦) at Hung-men (鴻門) in which attempt was made on the guest's life but foiled, an event often referred to in describing similar situations
鴻名(ㄏㄨㄥˊ ㄇㄧㄥˊ)
great reputation; great fame
鴻飛冥冥(ㄏㄨㄥˊ ㄈㄟ ㄇㄧㄥˊ ㄇㄧㄥˊ)
to run away without leaving any trace behind
鴻範(ㄏㄨㄥˊ ㄈㄢˋ)
a great plan or enterprise
鴻福齊天(ㄏㄨㄥˊ ㄈㄨˊ ㄑㄧˊ ㄊㄧㄢ)
One's vast happiness is as high as the heaven.
鴻都(ㄏㄨㄥˊ ㄉㄨ)
a library (in the Han Dynasty)
鴻洞(ㄏㄨㄥˊ ㄉㄨㄥˋ)
①profound; deep ②joined together; blended; to merge with
鴻圖(ㄏㄨㄥˊ ㄊㄨˊ)
①a great plan; a great enterprise; a great undertaking ②a great domain
鴻烈(ㄏㄨㄥˊ ㄌㄧㄝˋ)
great exploits
鴻臚(ㄏㄨㄥˊ ㄌㄨˊ)
an ancient official title
鴻溝(ㄏㄨㄥˊ ㄍㄡ)
①the river that separated the domain of Hsiang Yü (項羽) from that of Liu Pang(劉邦) ②a border; a boundary ③a gulf

鴻鵠(ㄏㄨㄥˊ ㄏㄨˊ)
a wild swan
鴻鵠之志(ㄏㄨㄥˊ ㄏㄨˊ ㄓ ㄓˋ)
great ambition
鴻基(ㄏㄨㄥˊ ㄐㄧ)
foundation of a great undertaking
鴻漸(ㄏㄨㄥˊ ㄐㄧㄢˋ)
gradual promotion on the ladder of officialdom; gradual rise in one's career
鴻禧(ㄏㄨㄥˊ ㄒㄧˇ)
great felicity
鴻緒(ㄏㄨㄥˊ ㄒㄩˋ)
the throne; imperial succession
鴻志(ㄏㄨㄥˊ ㄓˋ)
great ambition
鴻爪(ㄏㄨㄥˊ ㄓㄠˇ)
traces that one leaves behind
鴻鐘(ㄏㄨㄥˊ ㄓㄨㄥ)
a great bell
鴻儒(ㄏㄨㄥˊ ㄖㄨˊ) or 鴻生(ㄏㄨㄥˊ ㄕㄥ)
a man of great scholarship; a man of extensive learning
鴻藻(ㄏㄨㄥˊ ㄗㄠˇ)
great writing
鴻材(ㄏㄨㄥˊ ㄘㄞˊ)
a great literary style
鴻嗷(ㄏㄨㄥˊ ㄠˊ)
moans of a starving crowd
鴻案(ㄏㄨㄥˊ ㄢˋ)
mutual respect between husband and wife, from the story of Liang Hung(梁鴻), whose wife, when attending on him, always held the tray as high as the eyebrows
鴻恩(ㄏㄨㄥˊ ㄣ)
great favor or kindness
鴻儀(ㄏㄨㄥˊ ㄧˊ)
① your valued present ② your honorable appearance
鴻業(ㄏㄨㄥˊ ㄧㄝˋ)
achievements of a ruler
鴻猷(ㄏㄨㄥˊ ㄧㄡˊ)
great plans
鴻雁 or 鴻鴈(ㄏㄨㄥˊ ㄧㄢˋ)
wild swans and geese—refugees
鴻雁傳書(ㄏㄨㄥˊ ㄧㄢˋ ㄔㄨㄢˊ ㄕㄨ)
to deliver messages by wild swans
鴻雁哀鳴(ㄏㄨㄥˊ ㄧㄢˋ ㄞ ㄇㄧㄥˊ)
The refugees are moaning sorrowfully.
鴻文(ㄏㄨㄥˊ ㄨㄣˊ)
great writing

【鴳】 7140
ㄧㄢˋ yann yàn
a species of quail
鴳雀(ㄧㄢˋ ㄑㄩㄝˋ)
a species of quail

【鵃】 7141
ㄓㄡ jou zhōu
as in 鶻鵃—*Treron permagna*, a kind of pigeon

【鴽】 7142
ㄖㄨˊ ru rú
Trunix blakistoni, a kind of quail

【鴷】 7143
ㄌㄧㄝˋ lieh liè
a woodpecker

【鴰】 7144
ㄍㄨㄚ gua guā
as in 老鴰—the crow

【鵂】 7145
ㄒㄧㄡ shiou xiū
an owl
鵂鶹(ㄒㄧㄡ ㄌㄧㄡˊ)
an owl

七畫

【鵒】 7146
ㄩˋ yuh yù
as in 鸜鵒 —myna (or mynah)

【鵑】 7147
ㄐㄩㄢ jiuan juān
as in 杜鵑—① the cuckoo ② an azalea

【鵚】 7148
ㄊㄨ tu tū
a kind of water bird
鵚鶖(ㄊㄨ ㄑㄧㄡ)
a kind of water bird

【鵓】 7149
ㄅㄛˊ bor bó
a kind of pigeon
鵓鴿(ㄅㄛˊ ㄍㄜ)
a pigeon
鵓鴣(ㄅㄛˊ ㄍㄨ)
a kind of pigeon

【鵌】 7150
ㄊㄨˊ twu tú
a kind of bird which shares its nest with rats

【鵜】 7151
ㄊㄧˊ tyi tí
a pelican
鵜鶘(ㄊㄧˊ ㄏㄨˊ)
a pelican
鵜鴂(ㄊㄧˊ ㄐㄩㄝˊ)
a cuckoo

【鵝】 7152
(鵞、䳘) ㄜˊ er é
a goose; a gander
鵝毛(ㄜˊ ㄇㄠˊ)
goose feathers
鵝毛被(ㄜˊ ㄇㄠˊ ㄅㄟˋ)
bedding stuffed with goose down
鵝毛筆(ㄜˊ ㄇㄠˊ ㄅㄧˇ)
a quill pen
鵝毛管(ㄜˊ ㄇㄠˊ ㄍㄨㄢˇ)
a goose quill
鵝毛雪(ㄜˊ ㄇㄠˊ ㄒㄩㄝˇ)
heavy snow
鵝蛋臉兒(ㄜˊ ㄉㄢˋ ㄌㄧㄚˇㄦ)
an egg-shaped face; an oval face
鵝梨(ㄜˊ ㄌㄧˊ)
a kind of pear grown in Hsüan City (宣城), Anhwei Province
鵝翎扇(ㄜˊ ㄌㄧㄥˊ ㄕㄢˋ)
a goose-feather fan
鵝鑾鼻(ㄜˊ ㄌㄨㄢˊ ㄅㄧˊ)
name of the southernmost cape of Taiwan
鵝卵石(ㄜˊ ㄌㄨㄢˇ ㄕˊ)
pebbles
鵝湖之會(ㄜˊ ㄏㄨˊ ㄓ ㄏㄨㄟˋ)
a meeting between Sung Dynasty Confucian scholars Chu Hsi (朱熹) and Lu Chiu-yüan (陸九淵) at O-hu (鵝湖), a hill in Kiangsi, to discuss their differences
鵝黃(ㄜˊ ㄏㄨㄤˊ)
the fine yellow of the gosling
鵝叫(ㄜˊ ㄐㄧㄠˋ)
cackles of geese
鵝行鴨步(ㄜˊ ㄒㄧㄥˊ ㄧㄚ ㄅㄨˋ)
to walk at the slow pace of geese or ducks
鵝掌(ㄜˊ ㄓㄤˇ)
webbed feet of the goose
鵝準(ㄜˊ ㄓㄨㄣˇ)
the crest of a gander
鵝絨(ㄜˊ ㄖㄨㄥˊ)
down of a goose

【鵠】 7153
1. ㄏㄨˊ hwu hú
1. a swan
2. standing erect; standing quietly
鵠面鳩形(ㄏㄨˊ ㄇㄧㄢˋ ㄐㄧㄡ ㄒㄧㄥˊ)
emaciated from hunger

〔鳥部〕

鵠髮(ㄏㄨˊ ㄈㄚˇ)
gray hair; white hair
鵠立(ㄏㄨˊ ㄌㄧˋ)
to stand on the lookout
鵠候(ㄏㄨˊ ㄏㄡˋ)
to await eagerly
鵠企(ㄏㄨˊ ㄑㄧˋ)or 鵠望(ㄏㄨˊ ㄨㄤˋ)
to expect, or anticipate, eagerly
鵠侍(ㄏㄨˊ ㄕˋ)
to attend upon respectfully

【鵠】 7153
2. ㄍㄨˇ guu gǔ
a target
鵠的(ㄍㄨˇ ㄉㄧˋ)or 鵠子(ㄍㄨˇ ·ㄗ)
the target; the bull's-eye

【鵡】 7154
ㄨˇ wuu wǔ
as in 鸚鵡—a parrot

八畫

【鵬】 7155
ㄆㄥˊ perng péng
Peng, a fabulous bird supposed to be the greatest of all kinds, comparable to the roc
鵬圖(ㄆㄥˊ ㄊㄨˊ)
great ambition
鵬摶(ㄆㄥˊ ㄊㄨㄢˊ)
to strive for greatness
鵬鯤(ㄆㄥˊ ㄎㄨㄣ)
① the greatest thing ② a very great personage
鵬舉(ㄆㄥˊ ㄐㄩˇ)
① to push ahead toward an objective ② another name of Yüeh Fei (岳飛) of the Sung Dynasty
鵬程萬里(ㄆㄥˊ ㄔㄥˊ ㄨㄢˋ ㄌㄧˇ)
(literally) a journey of 10,000 miles faced by the roc —of great promise
鵬鷃(ㄆㄥˊ ㄧㄢˋ)
as different in size as the roc is from the quail

【鵩】 7156
ㄈㄨˊ fwu fú
a buzzard; a vulture
鵩鳥(ㄈㄨˊ ㄋㄧㄠˇ)
a buzzard; a vulture

【鵪】 7157
ㄢ an ān
a quail
鵪鶉(ㄢ ㄔㄨㄣˊ)
a quail

【鵰】 7158
ㄉㄧㄠ diau diāo
a bird of prey; a vulture 亦作「鷲」

【鵾】 7159
ㄎㄨㄣ kuen kūn
a bird resembling the crane
鵾雞(ㄎㄨㄣ ㄐㄧ)
① a bird resembling the crane ② a phoenix

【鵲】 7160
ㄑㄩㄝˋ chiueh què
(又讀 ㄑㄧㄠˇ cheau qiǎo)
a magpie
鵲報(ㄑㄩㄝˋ ㄅㄠˋ)or 鵲報喜(ㄑㄩㄝˋ ㄅㄠˋ ㄒㄧˇ)
the magpie's lucky chirp—a good omen
鵲起(ㄑㄩㄝˋ ㄑㄧˇ)
to rise at an opportune time
鵲橋(ㄑㄩㄝˋ ㄑㄧㄠˊ)
(in folklore) the bridge of magpies, which Weaving Maid (織女) supposedly crosses to meet Cowherd (牛郎) on the 7th of the 7th lunar month
鵲笑鳩舞(ㄑㄩㄝˋ ㄒㄧㄠˋ ㄐㄧㄡ ㄨˇ)
(literally) Magpies laugh and pigeons dance.—All are happy and merry.
鵲巢鳩占 or 鵲巢鳩佔(ㄑㄩㄝˋ ㄔㄠˊ ㄐㄧㄡ ㄓㄢˋ)
(literally) The magpie's nest is occupied by the pigeon. —illegal occupation of another's place
鵲噪(ㄑㄩㄝˋ ㄗㄠˋ)
the chattering of magpies

【鵷】 7161
ㄩㄢ iuan yuān
參看「鵷雛」
鵷行(ㄩㄢ ㄏㄤˊ)
courtiers as a collective body
鵷雛(ㄩㄢ ㄔㄨˊ)
a bird resembling the legendary phoenix

【鵮】 7162
ㄑㄧㄢ chian qiān
1. to peck
2. to ridicule; to deride

【鶉】 7163
ㄔㄨㄣˊ chwen chún
a quail
鶉雞類(ㄔㄨㄣˊ ㄐㄧ ㄌㄟˋ)
Gallinaceae
鶉居(ㄔㄨㄣˊ ㄐㄩ)
to be without a fixed home
鶉衣百結(ㄔㄨㄣˊ ㄧ ㄅㄞˇ ㄐㄧㄝˊ)
coarse clothes with many patches

【鶄】 7164
ㄐㄧㄥ jing jīng
Mycticorax prasinosceles, a kind of water bird

【鶊】 7165
ㄍㄥ geng gēng
as in 鶬鶊—an oriole

九畫

【鶘】 7166
ㄏㄨˊ hwu hú
as in 鵜鶘—a pelican

【鶖】 7167
ㄑㄧㄡ chiou qiū
a marabou, a kind of water bird

【鶚】 7168
ㄜˋ eh è
an osprey; a water hawk
鶚表(ㄜˋ ㄅㄧㄠˇ)
a letter of recommendation
鶚薦(ㄜˋ ㄐㄧㄢˋ)
to recommend (a person)
鶚眙(ㄜˋ ㄔˋ)
frightened; scared
鶚視(ㄜˋ ㄕˋ)
to look fiercely
鶚書(ㄜˋ ㄕㄨ)
a letter of recommendation

【鶡】 7169
ㄏㄜˊ her hé
1. a sort of nightingale
2. a sort of pheasant
鶡旦(ㄏㄜˊ ㄉㄢˋ)
Pteropus pselaphon
鶡冠(ㄏㄜˊ ㄍㄨㄢ)
a kind of cap worn by ancient warriors or by hermits
鶡雞(ㄏㄜˊ ㄐㄧ)
a sort of pheasant

【鶩】 7170
ㄨˋ wuh wù
ducks
鶩舲(ㄨˋ ㄌㄧㄥˊ)
a small boat

【鶒】 7171
ㄔˋ chyh chì
a kind of water bird

【鶗】 7172
ㄊㄧˊ tyi tí
a cuckoo

鵜鴃(ㄊㄧˊ ㄐㄩㄝˊ)
a cuckoo

十畫

【鶴】 7173 ㄏㄜˋ heh hè (語音 ㄏㄠˊ haur háo)
a crane
鶴板(ㄏㄜˋ ㄅㄢˇ)
an imperial edict calling on the capable to volunteer for government service
鶴鳴之士(ㄏㄜˋ ㄇㄧㄥˊ ㄓ ㄕˋ)
a scholar widely admired for both virtue and learning
鶴髮(ㄏㄜˋ ㄈㄚˇ)
white hair
鶴髮童顏(ㄏㄜˋ ㄈㄚˇ ㄊㄨㄥˊ ㄧㄢˊ)
a hoary head with a youthful face
鶴髮雞皮(ㄏㄜˋ ㄈㄚˇ ㄐㄧ ㄆㄧˊ)
a hoary head with wrinkled skin
鶴頂紅(ㄏㄜˋ ㄉㄧㄥˇ ㄏㄨㄥˊ)
a fleshy knob on the head of a crane (said to be poisonous)
鶴立(ㄏㄜˋ ㄌㄧˋ)or 鶴望(ㄏㄜˋ ㄨㄤˋ)
to expect, or await, eagerly
鶴立雞羣(ㄏㄜˋ ㄌㄧˋ ㄐㄧ ㄑㄩㄣˊ)
(literally) a crane standing among chickens — far surpassing the others; to stand head and shoulders over others
鶴唳(ㄏㄜˋ ㄌㄧˋ)
the cries of cranes
鶴列(ㄏㄜˋ ㄌㄧㄝˋ)
to array troops in orderly formations
鶴林(ㄏㄜˋ ㄌㄧㄣˊ)
Buddhist or Taoist temples
鶴宮(ㄏㄜˋ ㄍㄨㄥ)
the palace of the crown prince
鶴駕(ㄏㄜˋ ㄐㄧㄚˋ)
①the carriage of the crown prince ②the whereabouts of an immortal
鶴金梅(ㄏㄜˋ ㄐㄧㄣ ㄇㄟˊ)
(botany) silverweed
鶴禁(ㄏㄜˋ ㄐㄧㄣˋ)
the palace of the crown prince
鶴警(ㄏㄜˋ ㄐㄧㄥˇ)
a warning of danger
鶴企(ㄏㄜˋ ㄑㄧˇ)
waiting for or looking forward in eagerness
鶴膝(ㄏㄜˋ ㄒㄧ)
①a slender spear ②(in poetic composition) the defect of an identical sound occurring in the 5th and the 15th words
鶴軒(ㄏㄜˋ ㄒㄩㄢ)
(a polite expression referring to oneself) an incompetent person holding a high position
鶴氅(ㄏㄜˋ ㄔㄤˇ)
a coat made of feathers
鶴壽(ㄏㄜˋ ㄕㄡˋ)or 鶴算(ㄏㄜˋ ㄙㄨㄢˋ)
longevity
鶴觴(ㄏㄜˋ ㄕㄤ)
good wine from a distant source
鶴書(ㄏㄜˋ ㄕㄨ)
an imperial summons for a hermit
鶴嘴鋤(ㄏㄜˋ ㄗㄨㄟˇ ㄔㄨˊ)
a mattock; a pickaxe
鶴尊(ㄏㄜˋ ㄗㄨㄣ)
a kind of wine container
鶴馭(ㄏㄜˋ ㄩˋ)
the carriage of an immortal

【鶬】 7174 ㄘㄤ tsang cāng
an oriole
鶬鶊(ㄘㄤ ㄍㄥ)
an oriole

【鶯】 7175 ㄧㄥ ing yīng
a greenfinch; a Chinese oriole
鶯啼燕語(ㄧㄥ ㄊㄧˊ ㄧㄢˋ ㄩˇ)
Orioles sing and swallows chatter. (a phrase descriptive of a fine spring day)
鶯歌(ㄧㄥ ㄍㄜ)
songs of the oriole
鶯谷(ㄧㄥ ㄍㄨˇ)
talented but remaining in obscurity (like an oriole hidden in a valley)
鶯簧(ㄧㄥ ㄏㄨㄤˊ)or 鶯舌(ㄧㄥ ㄕㄜˊ)
the melodious warble of the oriole
鶯遷(ㄧㄥ ㄑㄧㄢ)
to be promoted, or move into a new residence (an expression of congratulation)
鶯聲燕語(ㄧㄥ ㄕㄥ ㄧㄢˋ ㄩˇ)
(literally) like an oriole singing and a swallow talking—the pleasant effect of a woman's speech
鶯梭(ㄧㄥ ㄙㄨㄛ)
orioles flitting
鶯鶯燕燕(ㄧㄥ ㄧㄥ ㄧㄢˋ ㄧㄢˋ)
a crowd of women chattering together pleasantly

【鶿】 7176 (鷀) ㄘˊ tsyr cí
as in 鸕鶿—a cormorant

【鶺】 7177 ㄐㄧˊ jyi jí
a wagtail
鶺鴒 or 脊令(ㄐㄧˊ ㄌㄧㄥˊ)
a wagtail

【鶻】 7178 1. ㄍㄨˇ guu gǔ
Treron permagna, a kind of pigeon
鶻鷉(ㄍㄨˇ ㄊㄧˊ)
a wild duck
鶻鵃(ㄍㄨˇ ㄓㄡ)or 鶻鳩(ㄍㄨˇ ㄐㄧㄡ)
Treron pe8magna, a kind of pigeon

【鶻】 7178 2. ㄏㄨˊ hwu hú
a kind of bird of prey
鶻突(ㄏㄨˊ ㄊㄨˊ)
muddleheaded; confused
鶻淪(ㄏㄨˊ ㄌㄨㄣˊ)
whole 亦作「囫圇」
鶻軍(ㄏㄨˊ ㄐㄩㄣ)
a swift army

【鶼】 7179 ㄐㄧㄢ jian jiān
a fabulous bird having only one wing so that a pair must unite in order to fly
鶼鰈(ㄐㄧㄢ ㄉㄧㄝˊ)
birds and fishes that move in pairs—a devoted couple

【鷁】 7180 ㄧˋ yih yì
a fabulous sea bird
鷁首(ㄧˋ ㄕㄡˇ)
the bow of a boat

【鶹】 7181 ㄌㄧㄡ liou liū
as in 鵂鶹—the owl

【鷂】 7182 ㄧㄠˋ yaw yào
a hawk; a sparrow hawk
鷂子(ㄧㄠˋ ·ㄗ)

【鳥部】

①a sparrow hawk ②a kite (a toy)
鷂子翻身(ㄧㄠˋ ˙ㄗ ㄈㄢ ㄕㄣ)
a hawk's turn (a fast bodily motion in Chinese pugilism)
鷂鷹(ㄧㄠˋ ㄧㄥ)
a hawk; a sparrow hawk

【鷃】 7183 ㄧㄢˋ yann yàn
a quail
鷃雀(ㄧㄢˋ ㄑㄩㄝˋ)
quails and sparrows; small birds

【鷇】 7184 ㄎㄡˋ kow kòu
fledglings
鷇食(ㄎㄡˋ ㄕˊ)
to live on the help of others (like fledglings)
鷇音(ㄎㄡˋ ㄧㄣ)
(literally) the chirping of fledglings—divergent opinions

【鷄】 7185 (雞) ㄐㄧ ji jī
fowls

十一畫

【鷓】 7186 ㄓㄜˋ jeh zhè
a partridge
鷓鴣(ㄓㄜˋ ㄍㄨ)
a partridge; a francolin
鷓鴣菜(ㄓㄜˋ ㄍㄨ ㄘㄞˋ)
①digenea simplex ②Chinese medicine made from this sea plant as a parasiticide for children

【鷖】 7187 ㄧ i yī
1. a gull
2. dark blue
3. a phoenix

【鷗】 7188 ㄡ ou ōu
a gull
鷗波(ㄡ ㄅㄛ)
to lead the free and leisurely life of a hermit (like that of a gull among the waves)
鷗盟(ㄡ ㄇㄥˊ)
(literally) to live with gulls as if they were one's sworn companions—to live a hermit's life
鷗鷺忘機(ㄡ ㄌㄨˋ ㄨㄤˋ ㄐㄧ)
(said of a hermit) so much in harmony with nature that the water birds are not frightened away by his presence

【鷙】 7189 ㄓˋ jyh zhì
1. birds of prey
2. fierce; cruel; violent
鷙猛(ㄓˋ ㄇㄥˇ)
fierce; cruel; ruthless
鷙鳥(ㄓˋ ㄋㄧㄠˇ)
birds of prey
鷙勇(ㄓˋ ㄩㄥˇ)
fierce and brave

【鷟】 7190 ㄓㄨㄛˊ jwo zhuó
a kind of water bird

十二畫

【鷥】 7191 ㄙ sy sī
an egret

【鷦】 7192 ㄐㄧㄠ jiau jiāo
a wren
鷦鷯(ㄐㄧㄠ ㄌㄧㄠˊ)
a wren; the tailorbird
鷦鷯一枝(ㄐㄧㄠ ㄌㄧㄠˊ ㄧˋ ㄓ)
(literally) just one twig for the wren to perch on—any humble position

【鷯】 7193 ㄌㄧㄠˊ liau liáo
as in 鷦鷯—a wren

【鷩】 7194 ㄅㄧˋ bih bì
a kind of pheasant
鷩雉(ㄅㄧˋ ㄓˋ)
a kind of pheasant

【鷫】 7195 ㄙㄨˋ suh sù
a kind of wild swan

【鷲】 7196 ㄐㄧㄡˋ jiow jiù
a vulture

【鷸】 7197 ㄩˋ yuh yù
a snipe
鷸蚌相爭(ㄩˋ ㄅㄤˋ ㄒㄧㄤ ㄓㄥ)
(literally) the fight between the snipe and the clam (with both ending up as captives of the fisherman)—a quarrel which benefits only a third party
鷸冠(ㄩˋ ㄍㄨㄢ)
a kind of ancient cap adorned with snipe feathers

【鷺】 7198 ㄌㄨˋ luh lù
Egretta garzetta, an egret
鷺序(ㄌㄨˋ ㄒㄩˋ)
orderly formation of egrets flying—distinct order of seniority in officialdom
鷺鷥(ㄌㄨˋ ㄙ)
an egret

十三畫

【鷽】 7199 ㄒㄩㄝˊ shyue xué
a tanager
鷽鳩(ㄒㄩㄝˊ ㄐㄧㄡ)
a kind of pigeon
鷽鳩笑鵬(ㄒㄩㄝˊ ㄐㄧㄡ ㄒㄧㄠˋ ㄆㄥˊ)
(literally) the pigeon laughing at the roc—ignorance of one's own limitations

【鸀】 7200 ㄕㄨˇ shuu shǔ
a blackbird

【鸂】 7201 ㄒㄧ shi xī
a kind of water bird resembling the mandarin duck
鸂鶒(ㄒㄧ ㄔˋ)
a kind of water bird resembling the mandarin duck

【鸇】 7202 ㄓㄢ jan zhān
a kind of bird of prey

【鷹】 7203 ㄧㄥ ing yīng
a hawk; an eagle; a falcon
鷹鼻鷂眼(ㄧㄥ ㄅㄧˊ ㄧㄠˋ ㄧㄢˇ)
the nose and eyes of a hawk—an avaricious look
鷹瞵鶚視(ㄧㄥ ㄌㄧㄣˊ ㄜˋ ㄕˋ)
to look at something or someone fiercely
鷹鉤鼻子(ㄧㄥ ㄍㄡ ㄅㄧˊ ˙ㄗ)
an aquiline nose
鷹架(ㄧㄥ ㄐㄧㄚˋ)
a scaffold (for supporting workmen and building materials)
鷹犬(ㄧㄥ ㄑㄩㄢˇ)
①falcons and dogs used in hunting ②hired ruffians; rapacious underlings
鷹爪(ㄧㄥ ㄓㄠˇ)
①talons (or claws) of a falcon, hawk, etc. ②a kind of young tea leaves

鷹鸇(ㄧㄥ ㄓㄢ)
powerful men
鷹師(ㄧㄥ ㄕ)
a falconer
鷹視(ㄧㄥ ㄕˋ)
a fierce look
鷹式飛彈(ㄧㄥ ㄕˋ ㄈㄟ ㄉㄢˋ)
the Hawk missiles
鷹隼(ㄧㄥ ㄙㄨㄣˇ)or(ㄧㄥ ㄓㄨㄣˇ)
hawks and falcons—cruel or fierce people
鷹洋(ㄧㄥ ㄧㄤˊ)
a Mexican silver dollar
鷹揚(ㄧㄥ ㄧㄤˊ)
powerful, or outstanding (like a soaring falcon)
鷹揚宴(ㄧㄥ ㄧㄤˊ ㄧㄢˋ)
a banquet for celebration following announcement of the results of a local examination under the military service examination system of the Ching Dynasty

十六畫

【鸕】 7204 ㄌㄨˊ lu lú
a cormorant
鸕鷀(ㄌㄨˊ ㄘˊ)
a cormorant

十七畫

【鸚】 7205 ㄧㄥ ing ying
a parrot
鸚哥(ㄧㄥ ㄍㄜ)
a parrot
鸚哥鼻(ㄧㄥ ㄍㄜ ㄅㄧˊ)
a hooked nose
鸚哥綠(ㄧㄥ ㄍㄜ ㄌㄩˋ)or 鸚綠(ㄧㄥ ㄌㄩˋ)
green of the parrot
鸚鵡(ㄧㄥ ㄨˇ)
a parrot
鸚鵡杯(ㄧㄥ ㄨˇ ㄅㄟ)
a cup made of a kind of spiral shell
鸚鵡螺(ㄧㄥ ㄨˇ ㄌㄨㄛˊ)
a nautilus (a kind of mollusk)
鸚鵡學舌(ㄧㄥ ㄨˇ ㄒㄩㄝˊ ㄕㄜˊ)
to parrot another's statement, theory, etc.

十八畫

【鸛】 7206 ㄍㄨㄢˋ guann guàn
a stork
鸛雀(ㄍㄨㄢˋ ㄑㄩㄝˋ)
a stork

【鸜】 7207 ㄑㄩˊ chyu qú
a species of myna (or mynah)
鸜鵒(ㄑㄩˊ ㄩˋ)
Aethiopsar cristatellus, a species of myna (or mynah)

十九畫

【鸝】 7208 ㄌㄧˊ li lí
as in 黃鸝—a Chinese oriole

【鸞】 7209 ㄌㄨㄢˊ luan luán
1. a *luan* (a fabulous bird related to the phoenix)
2. the bells at horses' bits
鸞飄鳳泊(ㄌㄨㄢˊ ㄆㄧㄠ ㄈㄥˋ ㄅㄛˊ)
① fine calligraphy ② separation of husband and wife
鸞鳳(ㄌㄨㄢˊ ㄈㄥˋ)
① a married couple ② a *luan* (a fabulous bird) and a phoenix—(figuratively) good beings ③ handsome; gallant
鸞鳳和鳴(ㄌㄨㄢˊ ㄈㄥˋ ㄏㄜˊ ㄇㄧㄥˊ)
harmony in marriage
鸞帶(ㄌㄨㄢˊ ㄉㄞˋ)
a kind of dressing band worn by players in Chinese opera
鸞刀(ㄌㄨㄢˊ ㄉㄠ)
a sword adorned with bells
鸞鶴(ㄌㄨㄢˊ ㄏㄜˋ)
a *luan* (a fabulous bird) and a crane which immortals supposedly ride about
鸞交鳳友(ㄌㄨㄢˊ ㄐㄧㄠ ㄈㄥˋ ㄧㄡˇ)
a couple deeply in love
鸞箋(ㄌㄨㄢˊ ㄐㄧㄢ)
tinted letter paper
鸞車(ㄌㄨㄢˊ ㄐㄩ)
an imperial carriage
鸞旗(ㄌㄨㄢˊ ㄑㄧˊ)
an imperial flag
鸞翔鳳集(ㄌㄨㄢˊ ㄒㄧㄤˊ ㄈㄥˋ ㄐㄧˊ)
gathering together of talented men
鸞翔鳳翥(ㄌㄨㄢˊ ㄒㄧㄤˊ ㄈㄥˋ ㄓㄨˋ)
fine calligraphy
鸞帚(ㄌㄨㄢˊ ㄓㄡˇ)
a kind of broom
鸞躅(ㄌㄨㄢˊ ㄓㄨˊ)
an itinerary of the emperor on tour
鸞輿(ㄌㄨㄢˊ ㄩˊ)
an imperial sedan chair

鹵部
ㄌㄨˇ luu lǔ

【鹵】 7210 ㄌㄨˇ luu lǔ
1. alkaline or saline soil
2. natural salt
3. rude; unrefined 亦作「魯」
4. to capture; to seize 亦作「擄」
鹵莽(ㄌㄨˇ ㄇㄤˇ)
rude; rash; foolhardy: 他是個鹵莽的傢伙。He is a rude fellow.
鹵莽滅裂(ㄌㄨˇ ㄇㄤˇ ㄇㄧㄝˋ ㄌㄧㄝˋ)
careless and haphazard; crude; coarse
鹵掠 or 擄掠(ㄌㄨˇ ㄌㄩㄝˋ)
to plunder; to seize; to capture
鹵鹼(ㄌㄨˇ ㄐㄧㄢˇ)or 鹵鹽(ㄌㄨˇ ㄧㄢˊ)
alkali
鹵水(ㄌㄨˇ ㄕㄨㄟˇ)
alkaline, or saline ground water
鹵素(ㄌㄨˇ ㄙㄨˋ)
halogen
鹵味(ㄌㄨˇ ㄨㄟˋ)
① pot-stewed fowl, meat, etc. served cold ② a salty taste; saltiness

九畫

【鹹】 7211 ㄒㄧㄢˊ shyan xián
saltish; salty; briny; salted: 這湯太鹹了。The soup is too salty.
鹹蛋(ㄒㄧㄢˊ ㄉㄢˋ)
salted eggs
鹹海(ㄒㄧㄢˊ ㄏㄞˇ)
Lake Aral

鹹湖(ㄒㄧㄢˊ ㄏㄨˊ)or 鹹水湖(ㄒㄧㄢˊ ㄕㄨㄟˇ ㄏㄨˊ)
salt lakes
鹹鷄子兒(ㄒㄧㄢˊ ㄐㄧ ㄗㄜˇㄦ)
brined hen's eggs
鹹津(ㄒㄧㄢˊ ㄐㄧㄣ)
a salty taste; saltiness
鹹津津兒(ㄒㄧㄢˊ ㄐㄧㄣ ㄐㄧㄜㄦ)or 鹹津津的(ㄒㄧㄢˊ ㄐㄧㄣ ㄐㄧㄣ ·ㄉㄜ)
salty
鹹潟(ㄒㄧㄢˊ ㄒㄧˋ)
salt land
鹹水(ㄒㄧㄢˊ ㄕㄨㄟˇ)
saline water; salt water
鹹水妹(ㄒㄧㄢˊ ㄕㄨㄟˇ ㄇㄟˋ)
(Cantonese dialect) prostitutes who do business exclusively with foreigners
鹹水魚(ㄒㄧㄢˊ ㄕㄨㄟˇ ㄩˊ)
salt-water fish
鹹肉(ㄒㄧㄢˊ ㄖㄡˋ)
salted meat
鹹肉莊(ㄒㄧㄢˊ ㄖㄡˋ ㄓㄨㄤ)
(Shanghai dialect) an unlicensed brothel
鹹菜(ㄒㄧㄢˊ ㄘㄞˋ)
pickled vegetables; pickles
鹹酸(ㄒㄧㄢˊ ㄙㄨㄢ)
salty and sour at the same time
鹹鴨蛋(ㄒㄧㄢˊ ㄧㄚ ㄉㄢˋ)
salted duck's eggs
鹹味(ㄒㄧㄢˊ ㄨㄟˋ)
a salty taste; saltiness
鹹魚(ㄒㄧㄢˊ ㄩˊ)
salted fish

十畫

【鹺】 7212 ㄘㄨㄛˊ tswo cuó
1. briny; salty
2. salt
鹺使(ㄘㄨㄛˊ ㄕˇ)
(Ching Dynasty) an official in charge of the salt industry in a given area; a salt commissioner 亦作「鹽運使」

【鹻】 7213 (鹼) ㄐㄧㄢˇ jean jiǎn
alkali

十三畫

【鹼】 7214 (鹻) ㄐㄧㄢˇ jean jiǎn
lye; alkali
鹼地(ㄐㄧㄢˇ ㄉㄧˋ)
alkaline soil
鹼度(ㄐㄧㄢˇ ㄉㄨˋ)
basicity
鹼化(ㄐㄧㄢˇ ㄏㄨㄚˋ)
saponification
鹼金屬(ㄐㄧㄢˇ ㄐㄧㄣ ㄕㄨˇ)
alkali metal
鹼性(ㄐㄧㄢˇ ㄒㄧㄥˋ)
alkalinity
鹼性反應(ㄐㄧㄢˇ ㄒㄧㄥˋ ㄈㄢˇ ㄧㄥˋ)
alkaline reaction
鹼性鹽(ㄐㄧㄢˇ ㄒㄧㄥˋ ㄧㄢˊ)
basic salt
鹼石灰(ㄐㄧㄢˇ ㄕˊ ㄏㄨㄟ)
soda-lime

十四畫

【鹽】 7215 1. ㄧㄢˊ yan yán
common salt; salt: 請把鹽遞給我。Pass me the salt, please.
鹽巴(ㄧㄢˊ ㄅㄚ)
(dialect) salt; common salt
鹽民(ㄧㄢˊ ㄇㄧㄣˊ)
the population engaged in the salt industry
鹽法(ㄧㄢˊ ㄈㄚˇ)
laws governing the salt industry; salt laws
鹽鐵(ㄧㄢˊ ㄊㄧㄝˇ)
manufacture of salt and iron (a basic industry in ancient times)
鹽田(ㄧㄢˊ ㄊㄧㄢˊ)
a salt garden; a salt pond
鹽類(ㄧㄢˊ ㄌㄟˋ)
(chemistry) salt
鹽滷(ㄧㄢˊ ㄌㄨˇ)
a kind of thick brine; bittern
鹽湖(ㄧㄢˊ ㄏㄨˊ)
salt lakes
鹽花(ㄧㄢˊ ㄏㄨㄚ)
fine grains of salt
鹽基(ㄧㄢˊ ㄐㄧ)
(chemistry) a base; a hydroxyl radical
鹽價(ㄧㄢˊ ㄐㄧㄚˋ)
the price of salt
鹽井(ㄧㄢˊ ㄐㄧㄥˇ)
a salt well
鹽區(ㄧㄢˊ ㄑㄩ)
districts for administration of the salt industry
鹽泉(ㄧㄢˊ ㄑㄩㄢˊ)
a brine spring
鹽梟(ㄧㄢˊ ㄒㄧㄠ)
an illegal salt dealer
鹽政(ㄧㄢˊ ㄓㄥˋ)
administration of the salt industry; salt administration
鹽池(ㄧㄢˊ ㄔˊ)
a salt pond
鹽場(ㄧㄢˊ ㄔㄤˊ)or(ㄧㄢˊ ㄔㄤˇ)
a salt farm; a salt field; a saltworks
鹽場公署(ㄧㄢˊ ㄔㄤˊ ㄍㄨㄥ ㄕㄨˇ)
the saltworks administration (a government agency in charge of salt manufacture in a given district in the early years of the Republic)
鹽商(ㄧㄢˊ ㄕㄤ)
salt merchants; salt dealers
鹽水(ㄧㄢˊ ㄕㄨㄟˇ)
salt solution; salt water; brine
鹽水灌腸(ㄧㄢˊ ㄕㄨㄟˇ ㄍㄨㄢˋ ㄔㄤˊ)
salt enema
鹽水注射(ㄧㄢˊ ㄕㄨㄟˇ ㄓㄨˋ ㄕㄜˋ)
a salt injection
鹽稅(ㄧㄢˊ ㄕㄨㄟˋ)
salt tax; salt gabelle
鹽竈(ㄧㄢˊ ㄗㄠˋ)
a stove for boiling brine (in salt manufacture)
鹽酸(ㄧㄢˊ ㄙㄨㄢ)
hydrochloric acid
鹽務(ㄧㄢˊ ㄨˋ)
administration of the salt industry
鹽務管理局(ㄧㄢˊ ㄨˋ ㄍㄨㄢˇ ㄌㄧˇ ㄐㄩˊ)
Salt Administration
鹽味(ㄧㄢˊ ㄨㄟˋ)
a salty taste; saltiness
鹽運使(ㄧㄢˊ ㄩㄣˋ ㄕˇ)
(in former times) an official in charge of the salt industry in given area; a salt commissioner

【鹽】 7215 2. ㄧㄢˋ yann yàn
1. to salt
2. to envy

鹿部
ㄌㄨˋ luh lù

【鹿】 7216 ㄌㄨˋ luh lù
a deer; a stag; a doe
鹿皮(ㄌㄨˋ ㄆㄧˊ)
deerskin
鹿皮冠(ㄌㄨˋ ㄆㄧˊ ㄍㄨㄢ)or 鹿巾(ㄌㄨˋ ㄐㄧㄣ)
the costume customarily worn by a hermit
鹿鳴宴(ㄌㄨˋ ㄇㄧㄥˊ ㄧㄢˋ)
a celebration party following success in the local examination under the former civil service examination system
鹿特丹(ㄌㄨˋ ㄊㄜˋ ㄉㄢ)
Rotterdam, Holland
鹿駭(ㄌㄨˋ ㄏㄞˋ)
frightened like a deer
鹿角(ㄌㄨˋ ㄐㄧㄠˇ)
antlers
鹿筋(ㄌㄨˋ ㄐㄧㄣ)
deer's sinews (regarded as a delicacy)
鹿肉(ㄌㄨˋ ㄖㄡˋ)
venison
鹿茸(ㄌㄨˋ ㄖㄨㄥˊ)
young antlers (regarded as a very valuable medicine)
鹿死不擇音(蔭)(ㄌㄨˋ ㄙˇ ㄅㄨˋ ㄗㄜˊ ㄧㄣ)
A dying deer does not choose a shade.—A desperate man will resort to anything.
鹿死誰手(ㄌㄨˋ ㄙˇ ㄕㄟˊ ㄕㄡˇ)
(literally) Who is to kill the deer?—Who will win?
鹿兒島(ㄌㄨˋ ㄦˊ ㄉㄠˇ)
Kagoshima, a Japanese island
鹿尾(ㄌㄨˋ ㄨㄟˇ)
a deer's tail (a rare delicacy)
鹿苑(ㄌㄨˋ ㄩㄢˋ)
a deer garden

二畫

【麀】 7217 ㄧㄡ iou yōu
a female deer; a doe
麀鹿(ㄧㄡ ㄌㄨˋ)
a female deer; a doe

【麂】 7218 ㄐㄧˇ jii jǐ
Moschus chinensis, an animal resembling the deer but without antlers

四畫

【麃】 7219 1. ㄅㄧㄠ biau biāo
to till the land; to weed
麃麃(ㄅㄧㄠ ㄅㄧㄠ)
having a martial appearance

【麃】 7219 2. (麅) ㄆㄠˊ paur páo
a species of roe

五畫

【麈】 7220 ㄓㄨˇ juu zhǔ
1. a kind of deer
2. to whisk; to dust
麈談(ㄓㄨˇ ㄊㄢˊ)
to converse or talk leisurely while holding a duster
麈尾(ㄓㄨˇ ㄨㄟˇ)
a duster

【麅】 7221 ㄆㄠˊ paur páo
a species of roe

六畫

【麋】 7222 ㄇㄧˊ mi mí
Alces machlis, a kind of deer
麋沸(ㄇㄧˊ ㄈㄟˋ)
disturbance; chaos; unrest
麋黎(ㄇㄧˊ ㄌㄧˊ)
old; aged
麋鹿(ㄇㄧˊ ㄌㄨˋ)
①(animal) the elk and the deer ②(figuratively) a rude person

七畫

【麐】 7223 (麟) ㄌㄧㄣˊ lin lín
the female of a fabulous animal resembling a deer

【麕】 7224 (麏) ㄐㄩㄣ jiun jūn
a species of roe deer

八畫

【麑】 7225 ㄋㄧˊ ni ní
a young deer; a fawn
麑鹿(ㄋㄧˊ ㄌㄨˋ)
a young deer; a fawn
麑裘(ㄋㄧˊ ㄑㄧㄡˊ)
fawn's furs

【麒】 7226 ㄑㄧˊ chyi qí
the male of a fabulous animal resembling the deer
麒麟(ㄑㄧˊ ㄌㄧㄣˊ)
Chi-lin, a fabulous animal resembling the deer said to appear only in time of peace and prosperity
麒麟楦(ㄑㄧˊ ㄌㄧㄣˊ ㄒㄩㄢˋ)
something impressive in appearance only
麒麟座(ㄑㄧˊ ㄌㄧㄣˊ ㄗㄨㄛˋ)
(astronomy) Monoceros
麒麟兒(ㄑㄧˊ ㄌㄧㄣˊ ㄦˊ)
a wonder child; an infant prodigy

【麓】 7227 ㄌㄨˋ luh lù
the foot of a hill or mountain

【麗】 7228 ㄌㄧˋ lih lì
1. beautiful; elegant; fine; magnificent
2. to hang
3. same as 儷—dual; double
麗風(ㄌㄧˋ ㄈㄥ)
a northwest wind
麗服(ㄌㄧˋ ㄈㄨˊ)
beautiful dress
麗都(ㄌㄧˋ ㄉㄨ)
beautiful; fine
麗譙(ㄌㄧˋ ㄑㄧㄠˊ)
a magnificent tower
麗質(ㄌㄧˋ ㄓˋ)
beauty (especially feminine)
麗矚(ㄌㄧˋ ㄓㄨˇ)
pleasing in appearance; good-looking
麗日光天(ㄌㄧˋ ㄖˋ ㄍㄨㄤ ㄊㄧㄢ)
a beautiful, bright day
麗人(ㄌㄧˋ ㄖㄣˊ)
a beautiful woman; a beauty;

a belle 亦作「美人」

麗澤(ㄌㄧˋ ㄗㄜˊ)
benefits derivable from mutual contact between friends

麗藻(ㄌㄧˋ ㄗㄠˇ)
fine language; flowery words

麗辭(ㄌㄧˋ ㄘˊ)
flowery language; elegant phrases

麗文(ㄌㄧˋ ㄨㄣˊ)
elegant writing

麗月(ㄌㄧˋ ㄩㄝˋ)
the second lunar month

【麕】 7229 ㄐㄩㄣ jiun jūn
a species of roe

麕集(ㄐㄩㄣ ㄐㄧˊ)
to herd together; to flock together; to gather

十畫

【麝】 7230 ㄕㄜˋ sheh shè
a musk deer

麝墨(ㄕㄜˋ ㄇㄛˋ)
sweet-smelling ink

麝牛(ㄕㄜˋ ㄋㄧㄡˊ)
a musk ox

麝香(ㄕㄜˋ ㄒㄧㄤ)
musk

麝月(ㄕㄜˋ ㄩㄝˋ)
the moon

十一畫

【麞】 7231 ㄓㄤ jang zhāng
Moschus chinloo, a deer-like animal

麞頭鼠目(ㄓㄤ ㄊㄡˊ ㄕㄨˇ ㄇㄨˋ)
a roe's head and a mouse's eyes—a mean physiognomy

十二畫

【麟】 7232 ㄌㄧㄣˊ lin lín
the female of a fabulous animal resembling the deer

麟鳳(ㄌㄧㄣˊ ㄈㄥˋ)
① rare treasures ② persons of rare virtue

麟牒(ㄌㄧㄣˊ ㄉㄧㄝˊ)
the genealogy of the royal household

麟臺(ㄌㄧㄣˊ ㄊㄞˊ)
the imperial secretariat of the Tang Dynasty

麟麟(ㄌㄧㄣˊ ㄌㄧㄣˊ)
bright; brilliant

麟閣(ㄌㄧㄣˊ ㄍㄜˊ)
the place where images of meritorious subjects were displayed during the Han Dynasty 亦作「麒麟閣」

麟角(ㄌㄧㄣˊ ㄐㄧㄠˇ)or 麟角鳳毛(ㄌㄧㄣˊ ㄐㄧㄠˇ ㄈㄥˋ ㄇㄠˊ)
rare things

麟經(ㄌㄧㄣˊ ㄐㄧㄥ)or 麟史(ㄌㄧㄣˊ ㄕˇ)
the *Spring and Autumn Annals* by Confucius

麟趾(ㄌㄧㄣˊ ㄓˇ)
accomplished children

麟兒(ㄌㄧㄣˊ ㄦˊ)
a fine son

二十二畫

【麤】 7233 ㄘㄨ (粗) tsu cū
coarse; rough

麥部
ㄇㄛˋ moh mò

【麥】 7234 ㄇㄞˋ may mài (讀音 ㄇㄛˋ moh mò)
1. wheat; barley; oats
2. a Chinese family name

麥餅(ㄇㄞˋ ㄅㄧㄥˇ)
wheaten cake

麥片(ㄇㄞˋ ㄆㄧㄢˋ)
oatmeal

麥芒(ㄇㄞˋ ㄇㄤˊ)
beards or awns of barley, oats, etc.

麥苗(ㄇㄞˋ ㄇㄧㄠˊ)
young wheat, barley, etc.

麥飯豆羹(ㄇㄞˋ ㄈㄢˋ ㄉㄡˋ ㄍㄥ)
coarse meals of a farming family

麥粉(ㄇㄞˋ ㄈㄣˇ)
flour

麥麩(ㄇㄞˋ ㄈㄨ)
wheat bran

麥地那(ㄇㄞˋ ㄉㄧˋ ㄋㄚˋ)
Medina, Saudi Arabia

麥冬(ㄇㄞˋ ㄉㄨㄥ)or 麥門冬(ㄇㄞˋ ㄇㄣˊ ㄉㄨㄥ)
Liriope graminifolia, a medicinal herb

麥田(ㄇㄞˋ ㄊㄧㄢˊ)
wheatland; a wheat field

麥浪(ㄇㄞˋ ㄌㄤˋ)
the wavy motion of wheat, etc., in the field when winds blow

麥卡圖(ㄇㄞˋ ㄎㄚˇ ㄊㄨˊ)
Gerhardus Mercator, 1512-1594, Flemish geographer

麥克風(ㄇㄞˋ ㄎㄜˋ ㄈㄥ)
a microphone: 他正在試麥克風。He is testing the microphone.

麥克阿瑟(ㄇㄞˋ ㄎㄜˋ ㄚ ㄙㄜˋ)
Douglas MacArthur, 1880-1964, American general

麥加(ㄇㄞˋ ㄐㄧㄚ)
Mecca, Saudi Arabia

麥稭(ㄇㄞˋ ㄐㄧㄝ)
wheat straw; stalks of wheat, etc.

麥角病(ㄇㄞˋ ㄐㄧㄠˇ ㄅㄧㄥˋ)
ergot—a disease of rye and other cereals in which the grains are replaced by blackish fungous growths

麥角菌(ㄇㄞˋ ㄐㄧㄠˇ ㄐㄩㄣˋ)
ergot—any fungus producing 麥角病

麥酒(ㄇㄞˋ ㄐㄧㄡˇ)
beer 亦作「啤酒」: 喝麥酒要連泡沫喝。Drink beer with the froth.

麥秀黍油(ㄇㄞˋ ㄒㄧㄡˋ ㄕㄨˇ ㄧㄡˊ)
The wheat and corn grow but the fatherland is no more.

麥哲倫(ㄇㄞˋ ㄓㄜˊ ㄌㄨㄣˊ)
Ferdinand Magellan (c. 1480-1521), Portuguese navigator

麥哲倫海峽(ㄇㄞˋ ㄓㄜˊ ㄌㄨㄣˊ ㄏㄞˇ ㄒㄧㄚˊ)
Strait of Magellan, a strait near the south tip of South America

麥場(ㄇㄞˋ ㄔㄤˊ)
a wheat-thrashing floor

麥子(ㄇㄞˋ ˙ㄗ)
wheat; barley

麥穗(ㄇㄞˋ ㄙㄨㄟˋ)
ears of wheat, etc.

麥芽(ㄇㄞˋ ㄧㄚˊ)
malt
麥芽糖(ㄇㄞˋ ㄧㄚˊ ㄊㄤˊ)
malt sugar; maltose
麥芽酵素(ㄇㄞˋ ㄧㄚˊ ㄒㄧㄠˋ ㄙㄨˋ)
maltase

四畫

【麩】7235 ㄈㄨ fu fū
bran
麩素(ㄈㄨ ㄙㄨˋ)
gluten
麩酸(ㄈㄨ ㄙㄨㄢ)
glutamic acid

【麪】7236 (麵) ㄇㄧㄢˋ miann miàn
1. flour
2. dough
3. noodles
麪包(ㄇㄧㄢˋ ㄅㄠ)
bread
麪包店(ㄇㄧㄢˋ ㄅㄠ ㄉㄧㄢˋ)
a bakery
麪包屑(ㄇㄧㄢˋ ㄅㄠ ㄒㄧㄝˋ)
crumbs of bread
麪包師(ㄇㄧㄢˋ ㄅㄠ ㄕ)
a baker
麪包樹(ㄇㄧㄢˋ ㄅㄠ ㄕㄨˋ)
a breadfruit tree
麪粉(ㄇㄧㄢˋ ㄈㄣˇ)
flour: 我們用麪粉做成麪包。We make flour into bread.
麪粉廠(ㄇㄧㄢˋ ㄈㄣˇ ㄔㄤˇ)
a flour mill
麪條(ㄇㄧㄢˋ ㄊㄧㄠˊ)
noodles; spaghetti; vermicelli
麪糰(ㄇㄧㄢˋ ㄊㄨㄢˊ)
dough
麪糊(ㄇㄧㄢˋ ㄏㄨˊ)
flour paste
麪筋(ㄇㄧㄢˋ ㄐㄧㄣ)
gluten of flour
麪杖(ㄇㄧㄢˋ ㄓㄤˋ)
a rolling pin 亦作「擀麪杖」
麪茶(ㄇㄧㄢˋ ㄔㄚˊ)
porridge made by mixing roasted flour in boiling water
麪食(ㄇㄧㄢˋ ㄕˊ)
wheaten foods; pastry

六畫

【麯】7237 (麴) ㄑㄩˊ chyu qú
a ferment for brewing

【麰】7238 ㄇㄡˊ mou móu
barley: 啤酒是麰製成的。Beer is made from barley.

八畫

【麴】7239 (麯) ㄑㄩˊ chyu qú
yeast; a ferment for brewing: 麴是一種發酵劑。Yeast is a ferment.
麴黴(ㄑㄩˊ ㄇㄟˊ)or 麴菌 (ㄑㄩˊ ㄐㄩㄣˋ)
aspergilli (especially those with enzymes capable of effecting fermentation)
麴糵(ㄑㄩˊ ㄋㄧㄝˋ)
① the yeast and the malt—a ferment for brewing ② brewed spirits
麴監(ㄑㄩˊ ㄐㄧㄢˋ)
an official in charge of wines and liquors
麴錢(ㄑㄩˊ ㄑㄧㄢˊ)
the tax paid by brewers
麴秀才(ㄑㄩˊ ㄒㄧㄡˋ ㄘㄞˊ)or 麴生 (ㄑㄩˊ ㄕㄥ) or 麴君 (ㄑㄩˊ ㄐㄩㄣ)
wine; liquor
麴院(ㄑㄩˊ ㄩㄢˋ)
a brewery

九畫

【麵】7240 (麪) ㄇㄧㄢˋ miann miàn
flour; noodles

麻部 ㄇㄚˊ ma má

【麻】7241 ㄇㄚˊ ma má
1. hemp; jute; ramie; sisal; flax
2. sesame
3. numb; torpid
4. a tingle; to tingle
5. pockmarked
6. rough
7. pitted; spotty
麻痺 (ㄇㄚˊ ㄅㄧˋ)
paralysis; palsy; numbness: 他的左脚麻痺了。His left leg is paralyzed.
麻布 (ㄇㄚˊ ㄅㄨˋ)
hempen fabrics; gunny; linen
麻面 (ㄇㄚˊ ㄇㄧㄢˋ)
a pockmarked face
麻木 (ㄇㄚˊ ㄇㄨˋ)
paralyzed; numbed; palsied
麻木不仁 (ㄇㄚˊ ㄇㄨˋ ㄅㄨˋ ㄖㄣˊ)
numbed; paralyzed; unsympathetic; unfeeling
麻煩 (ㄇㄚˊ ·ㄈㄢ)
① troublesome: 這事眞麻煩。This thing is really troublesome. ② trouble ③ to bother: 這點小事不要去麻煩老師了。Don't bother our teacher with such trifles.
麻袋 (ㄇㄚˊ ㄉㄞˋ)
a jute bag; a hemp bag; a gunny-bag
麻刀(ㄇㄚˊ ·ㄉㄠ)or 麻擣 (ㄇㄚˊ ㄉㄠˇ)
hemp chopped up for strengthening mortar
麻俐 (ㄇㄚˊ ·ㄌㄧ)
quick; swift; agile
麻六甲 (ㄇㄚˊ ㄌㄧㄡˋ ㄐㄧㄚˇ)
Malacca
麻六甲海峽 (ㄇㄚˊ ㄌㄧㄡˋ ㄐㄧㄚˇ ㄏㄞˇ ㄒㄧㄚˊ)
Strait of Malacca, a strait between Sumatra and the Malay Peninsula
麻臉 (ㄇㄚˊ ㄌㄧㄢˇ)
a pockmarked face
麻姑 (ㄇㄚˊ ㄍㄨ)
① name of a mountain in Kiangsi ② name of a female immortal
麻胡 (ㄇㄚˊ ㄏㄨˊ)
① a pockmarked, bearded man ②參看「麻虎子」
麻虎子 (ㄇㄚˊ ㄏㄨˇ ·ㄗ)
a goblin often mentioned to scare children
麻黃 (ㄇㄚˊ ㄏㄨㄤˊ)
Ephedra sinica, a medical herb; a horsetail
麻稭 (ㄇㄚˊ ㄐㄧㄝ)
hemp stalks
麻醬 (ㄇㄚˊ ㄐㄧㄤˋ)
sesame paste
麻將牌 (ㄇㄚˊ ㄐㄧㄤˋ ㄆㄞˊ)
mah-jong pieces
麻雀 (ㄇㄚˊ ㄑㄩㄝˋ)

〔黃部〕

①a sparrow ②mah-jong
麻雀雖小，五臟俱全 (ㄇㄚˊ ㄑㄩㄝˋ ㄙㄨㄟ ㄒㄧㄠˇ, ㄨˇ ㄗㄤˋ ㄐㄩˋ ㄑㄩㄢˊ)
Although the sparrow is small, it has all the vital organs.—small but complete
麻鞋 (ㄇㄚˊ ㄒㄧㄝˊ)
hempen sandals
麻線 (ㄇㄚˊ ㄒㄧㄢˋ)
linen threads
麻織品 (ㄇㄚˊ ㄓ ㄆㄧㄣˇ)
linen fabrics
麻疹 (ㄇㄚˊ ㄓㄣˇ)
(medicine) measles: 麻疹是小孩子生的病。Measles is a children's disease.
麻繩 (ㄇㄚˊ ㄕㄥˊ)
hemp cordage; hemp rope: 他抓住麻繩。He grasps the hemp rope.
麻省理工學院 (ㄇㄚˊ ㄕㄥˇ ㄌㄧˇ ㄍㄨㄥ ㄒㄩㄝˊ ㄩㄢˋ)
Massachusetts Institute of Technology (MIT)
麻子 (ㄇㄚˊ ·ㄗ)
①a pockmarked person ②pockmarks
麻醉 (ㄇㄚˊ ㄗㄨㄟˋ)
①to anesthetize ②to dope; to drug
麻醉劑 (ㄇㄚˊ ㄗㄨㄟˋ ㄐㄧˋ) or 麻藥 (ㄇㄚˊ ㄧㄠˋ)
①an anesthetic ②narcotics; drugs; dopes
麻醉藥品 (ㄇㄚˊ ㄗㄨㄟˋ ㄧㄠˋ ㄆㄧㄣˇ)
narcotics
麻薩諸塞州 (ㄇㄚˊ ㄙㄚˋ ㄓㄨ ㄙㄜˋ ㄓㄡ)
the state of Massachusetts, U. S. A.
麻衣 (ㄇㄚˊ ㄧ)
①hemp mourning garments; gunny garments worn as mourning dress by the children and wife of the deceased ②a robe of hemp
麻衣相法 (ㄇㄚˊ ㄧ ㄒㄧㄤˋ ㄈㄚˇ)
a system of physiognomy said to originate from a Taoist in the Sung Dynasty
麻油 (ㄇㄚˊ ㄧㄡˊ)
sesame oil

三畫

【麼】 7242
1. ㄇㄛˊ mo mó
1. tiny
2. a special particle found in dramatic dialogues

【麼】 7242
2. (麼・嗎) ·ㄇㄚ ·ma ma
a final interrogative particle

【麼】 7242
3. ㄇㄚˊ ma má
a particle used in the phrase 「幹麼」(why): 你來此幹麼? Why are you coming here?

【麼】 7242
4. ·ㄇㄜ ·me me
a particle used in the interrogative phrase 「甚麼」(what): 甚麼事情? What is the matter?

四畫

【麾】 7243
ㄏㄨㄟ huei hui
1. a flag; a banner; a standard
2. to command; to lead
麾節 (ㄏㄨㄟ ㄐㄧㄝˊ)
flags; banners
麾軍 (ㄏㄨㄟ ㄐㄩㄣ)
to lead an army
麾下 (ㄏㄨㄟ ㄒㄧㄚˋ)
①under a general's command ②sir (in addressing a general)

黃部
ㄏㄨㄤˊ hwang huáng

【黃】 7244
ㄏㄨㄤˊ hwang huáng
1. yellow
2. a Chinese family name
黃白花兒 (ㄏㄨㄤˊ ㄅㄞˊ ㄏㄨㄚㄦ)
(usually said of cats, dogs, etc.) white with yellow spots
黃柏 (ㄏㄨㄤˊ ㄅㄞˇ) or 黃檗 (ㄏㄨㄤˊ ㄅㄛˋ)
Phellodendron amurense, a kind of oak, whose bark is used in Chinese medicine
黃包車 (ㄏㄨㄤˊ ㄅㄠ ㄔㄜ)
a ricksha
黃榜 (ㄏㄨㄤˊ ㄅㄤˇ)
an imperial edict
黃埔軍官學校 (ㄏㄨㄤˊ ㄅㄨˋ ㄐㄩㄣ ㄍㄨㄢ ㄒㄩㄝˊ ㄒㄧㄠˋ)
Whampoa Military Academy (the cradle of the military leaders of China)
黃袍 (ㄏㄨㄤˊ ㄆㄠˊ)
①high-ranking Buddhist monks (marked by their yellow robes) ②the imperial robe
黃袍加身 (ㄏㄨㄤˊ ㄆㄠˊ ㄐㄧㄚ ㄕㄣ)
to be made emperor (a reference to Chao Kuang-yin (趙匡胤), who was put to the throne by the rebellious troops under his command)
黃皮書 (ㄏㄨㄤˊ ㄆㄧˊ ㄕㄨ)
a yellow book
黃浦灘 (ㄏㄨㄤˊ ㄆㄨˇ ㄊㄢ)
Shanghai (an alternative name): 她在黃浦灘長大。She grew up in Shanghai.
黃麻 (ㄏㄨㄤˊ ㄇㄚˊ)
jute
黃馬褂 (ㄏㄨㄤˊ ㄇㄚˇ ㄍㄨㄚˋ)
a costume of the mandarins, often bestowed by the emperor as a special favor
黃梅 (ㄏㄨㄤˊ ㄇㄟˊ)
①ripe plums ②name of a county in Hupeh Province
黃梅調 (ㄏㄨㄤˊ ㄇㄟˊ ㄉㄧㄠˋ)
a popular folk melody originated from 黃梅 (revived by Hong Kong film makers)
黃梅天氣 (ㄏㄨㄤˊ ㄇㄟˊ ㄊㄧㄢ ㄑㄧˋ)
the weather when plums ripen; early summer weather, usually rainy
黃梅雨 (ㄏㄨㄤˊ ㄇㄟˊ ㄩˇ)
early summer rain
黃毛丫頭 (ㄏㄨㄤˊ ㄇㄠˊ ㄧㄚ ·ㄊㄡ)
a fledgling little girl
黃門 (ㄏㄨㄤˊ ㄇㄣˊ)
①a yellow palace gate ②a eunuch
黃米 (ㄏㄨㄤˊ ㄇㄧˇ)
①coarse rice ②millet: 黃米粥很美味。Millet porridge is delicious.
黃米麪 (ㄏㄨㄤˊ ㄇㄧˇ ㄇㄧㄢˋ)
millet flour
黃髮垂髫 (ㄏㄨㄤˊ ㄈㄚˇ ㄔㄨㄟˊ ㄊㄧㄠˊ)
the aged and the young
黃扉 (ㄏㄨㄤˊ ㄈㄟ)
the prime minister's abode
黃蜂 (ㄏㄨㄤˊ ㄈㄥ)
wasps
黃道吉日 (ㄏㄨㄤˊ ㄉㄠˋ ㄐㄧˊ ㄖˋ)
a lucky day

黃豆(ㄏㄨㄤˊ ㄉㄡˋ)
soybean: 醬油是用黃豆製造的。Sauce is made from soybeans.
黃豆芽(ㄏㄨㄤˊ ㄉㄡˋ ㄧㄚˊ)
soybean sprouts
黃膽病(ㄏㄨㄤˊ ㄉㄢˇ ㄅㄧㄥˋ)or 黃疸(ㄏㄨㄤˊ ㄉㄢˇ)
jaundice; icterus: 她患了黃膽病。She suffers from jaundice.
黃帝(ㄏㄨㄤˊ ㄉㄧˋ)
Huang Ti, or the Yellow Emperor, a legendary ruler
黃湯(ㄏㄨㄤˊ ㄊㄤ)
wine: 他灌了不少黃湯。He has taken a lot of wine.
黃鐵鑛(ㄏㄨㄤˊ ㄊㄧㄝˇ ㄎㄨㄤˋ)
pyrites
黃天(ㄏㄨㄤˊ ㄊㄧㄢ)
the name assumed by Chang Chiao (張角), the leader of the Yellow Turban Rebels (黃巾賊) at the close of the Eastern Han Dynasty
黃庭堅(ㄏㄨㄤˊ ㄊㄧㄥˊ ㄐㄧㄢ)
Huang Ting-chien (1045–1105), a famed poet and calligrapher
黃土(ㄏㄨㄤˊ ㄊㄨˇ)
loess
黃土泥(ㄏㄨㄤˊ ㄊㄨˇ ㄋㄧˊ)
muddy loess
黃童(ㄏㄨㄤˊ ㄊㄨㄥˊ)
a child; a youngster
黃銅(ㄏㄨㄤˊ ㄊㄨㄥˊ)
brass
黃銅鑛(ㄏㄨㄤˊ ㄊㄨㄥˊ ㄎㄨㄤˋ)
chalcopyrite
黃牛(ㄏㄨㄤˊ ㄋㄧㄡˊ)
① a common Chinese ox ② a scalper of tickets, etc. ③ (slang) to fail to appear on an appointment; to fail to show up; to break a promise: 他今天又黃牛了。He fails to show up again today.
黃牛票(ㄏㄨㄤˊ ㄋㄧㄡˊ ㄆㄧㄠˋ)
scalped tickets
黃蠟(ㄏㄨㄤˊ ㄌㄚˋ)
beeswax
黃老(ㄏㄨㄤˊ ㄌㄠˇ)
①Huang Ti (黃帝) and Laotzu (老子) ② Taoism
黃鸝(ㄏㄨㄤˊ ㄌㄧˊ)
the oriole
黃曆(ㄏㄨㄤˊ ㄌㄧˋ)
(colloquial) an almanac
黃連(ㄏㄨㄤˊ ㄌㄧㄢˊ)
Coptis chinensis, whose bitter seeds are used in Chinese medicine
黃連樹下彈琴(ㄏㄨㄤˊ ㄌㄧㄢˊ ㄕㄨˋ ㄒㄧㄚˋ ㄊㄢˊ ㄑㄧㄣˊ)
(figuratively) to seek pleasure under adverse circumstances
黃臉婆(ㄏㄨㄤˊ ㄌㄧㄢˇ ㄆㄛˊ)
the yellow-faced woman—my wife
黃燐(ㄏㄨㄤˊ ㄌㄧㄣˊ)
yellow phosphorus
黃粱(ㄏㄨㄤˊ ㄌㄧㄤˊ)
a variety of millet
黃粱夢(ㄏㄨㄤˊ ㄌㄧㄤˊ ㄇㄥˋ)
an evanescent dream(from the story of a man who had all sorts of wonderful experiences in a dream only to discover that he had just dozed off briefly while having his millet cooked)
黃落(ㄏㄨㄤˊ ㄌㄨㄛˋ)
(said of vegetation in autumn) yellow and bare
黃龍府(ㄏㄨㄤˊ ㄌㄨㄥˊ ㄈㄨˇ)
an administrative district set up in part of what is today's Inner Mongolia and Manchuria by the Tungusic invaders in the 11th and 12th centuries
黃瓜(ㄏㄨㄤˊ ㄍㄨㄚ)
a cucumber
黃冠(ㄏㄨㄤˊ ㄍㄨㄢ)
① a Taoist priest ② costumes of farmers
黃口孺子(ㄏㄨㄤˊ ㄎㄡˇ ㄖㄨˊ ㄗˇ)
a sucking child; a baby
黃河(ㄏㄨㄤˊ ㄏㄜˊ)
the Yellow River
黃河流域(ㄏㄨㄤˊ ㄏㄜˊ ㄌㄧㄡˊ ㄩˋ)
the Yellow River Valley
黃河水澄清(ㄏㄨㄤˊ ㄏㄜˊ ㄕㄨㄟˇ ㄔㄥˊ ㄑㄧㄥ)
the clearing of the Yellow River—an impossibility (because the turbulent water carries large amount of sands from the upperstream)
黃海(ㄏㄨㄤˊ ㄏㄞˇ)
the Yellow Sea
黃花(ㄏㄨㄤˊ ㄏㄨㄚ)
a chrysanthemum: 她很喜歡黃花。She is very fond of chrysanthemums.
黃花崗(ㄏㄨㄤˊ ㄏㄨㄚ ㄍㄤ)
Huanghuakang, a knoll outside Canton
黃花岡七十二烈士(ㄏㄨㄤˊ ㄏㄨㄚ ㄍㄤ ㄑㄧ ㄕˊ ㄦˋ ㄌㄧㄝˋ ㄕˋ)
the 72 Revolutionary Martyrs of Huanghuakang (who lost their lives on March 29, 1911, in an attempt to capture Canton and were buried at 黃花岡)
黃花閨女(ㄏㄨㄤˊ ㄏㄨㄚ ㄍㄨㄟ ㄋㄩˇ)
a virgin
黃花九輪草(ㄏㄨㄤˊ ㄏㄨㄚ ㄐㄧㄡˇ ㄌㄨㄣˊ ㄘㄠˇ)
polyanthus
黃花魚(ㄏㄨㄤˊ ㄏㄨㄚ ㄩˊ)
a labrus
黃禍(ㄏㄨㄤˊ ㄏㄨㄛˋ)
the yellow peril
黃昏(ㄏㄨㄤˊ ㄏㄨㄣ)
dusk: 在黃昏時燈光亮了起來。The lights go on at dusk.
黃酒(ㄏㄨㄤˊ ㄐㄧㄡˇ)
① same as 紹興酒—wine from Shaohsing (紹興) ② a kind of yellowish rice wine brewed in Taiwan
黃巾(ㄏㄨㄤˊ ㄐㄧㄣ)
the Yellow Turban Rebels at the close of the Eastern Han Dynasty
黃金(ㄏㄨㄤˊ ㄐㄧㄣ)
gold: 過去人們常以黃金付帳。People used to pay in gold.
黃金海岸(ㄏㄨㄤˊ ㄐㄧㄣ ㄏㄞˇ ㄢˋ)
Gold Coast, Africa
黃金時代(ㄏㄨㄤˊ ㄐㄧㄣ ㄕˊ ㄉㄞˋ)
the golden age
黃卷青燈(ㄏㄨㄤˊ ㄐㄩㄢˋ ㄑㄧㄥ ㄉㄥ)
the Buddhist scriptures and lamps for the Buddhist altar—the life or abode of a Buddhist
黃絹幼婦(ㄏㄨㄤˊ ㄐㄩㄢˋ ㄧㄡˋ ㄈㄨˋ)
a popular code for the phrase 絕妙 (extremely exquisite)
黃旗紫蓋(ㄏㄨㄤˊ ㄑㄧˊ ㄗˇ ㄍㄞˋ)
a symbol, or spirit, of the emperor
黃鉛鑛(ㄏㄨㄤˊ ㄑㄧㄢ ㄎㄨㄤˋ)
mimetite
黃麴毒素(ㄏㄨㄤˊ ㄑㄩ ㄉㄨˊ ㄙㄨˋ)
aflatoxin

〔黃部〕

黃雀(ㄏㄨㄤˊ ㄑㄩㄝˋ)
a titmouse
黃泉(ㄏㄨㄤˊ ㄑㄩㄢˊ)
Hades
黃錫鑛(ㄏㄨㄤˊ ㄒㄧˊ ㄎㄨㄤˋ)
stannite
黃癬(ㄏㄨㄤˊ ㄒㄧㄢˇ)
favus
黃興(ㄏㄨㄤˊ ㄒㄧㄥ)
Huang Hsing, 1872-1916, a leader of the Chinese National Revolution
黃鐘(ㄏㄨㄤˊ ㄓㄨㄥ)
one of the notes in traditional Chinese music
黃種人(ㄏㄨㄤˊ ㄓㄨㄥˇ ㄖㄣˊ)
the yellow race; the Mongolian race
黃巢(ㄏㄨㄤˊ ㄔㄠˊ)
Huang Chao, the bloodthirsty leader of a rebellion at the time of Hsi Tzung (僖宗) during the Tang Dynasty
黃澄澄(ㄏㄨㄤˊ ㄔㄥˊ ㄔㄥˊ)
glistening yellow; golden
黃石公園(ㄏㄨㄤˊ ㄕˊ ㄍㄨㄥ ㄩㄢˊ)
Yellowstone National Park, U.S.A.
黃砂(ㄏㄨㄤˊ ㄕㄚ)
yellow soil; loess
黃鼠(ㄏㄨㄤˊ ㄕㄨˇ)
a kind of desert gopher
黃鼠狼(ㄏㄨㄤˊ ㄕㄨˇ ㄌㄤˊ)
a weasel 亦作「鼬」
黃水瘡(ㄏㄨㄤˊ ㄕㄨㄟˇ ㄔㄨㄤ)
eczema
黃熱病(ㄏㄨㄤˊ ㄖㄜˋ ㄅㄧㄥˋ)
yellow fever
黃色(ㄏㄨㄤˊ ㄙㄜˋ)
①yellow②decadent; obscene; pornographic
黃色小說(ㄏㄨㄤˊ ㄙㄜˋ ㄒㄧㄠˇ ㄕㄨㄛ)
a sex novel; a pornographic novel
黃色新聞(ㄏㄨㄤˊ ㄙㄜˋ ㄒㄧㄣ ㄨㄣˊ)
① yellow journalism ② sex news
黃色炸藥(ㄏㄨㄤˊ ㄙㄜˋ ㄓㄚˋ ㄧㄠˋ)
trinitrotoluene (TNT)
黃色書刊(ㄏㄨㄤˊ ㄙㄜˋ ㄕㄨ ㄎㄢ)
pornographic books and periodicals
黃芽菜(ㄏㄨㄤˊ ㄧㄚˊ ㄘㄞˋ)
a celery cabbage
黃油(ㄏㄨㄤˊ ㄧㄡˊ)
① butter oil ② tallow
黃楊木(ㄏㄨㄤˊ ㄧㄤˊ ㄇㄨˋ)
boxwood
黃鶯(ㄏㄨㄤˊ ㄧㄥ)
an oriole
黃魚(ㄏㄨㄤˊ ㄩˊ)
a yellow croaker
黃玉(ㄏㄨㄤˊ ㄩˋ)
topaz

五畫

【黈】 7245 ㄊㄡˇ toou tǒu
1. yellow
2. to increase

十三畫

【黌】 7246 ㄏㄨㄥˊ horng hóng
a school
黌門(ㄏㄨㄥˊ ㄇㄣˊ)
a school
黌教(ㄏㄨㄥˊ ㄐㄧㄠˋ)
schooling
黌舍(ㄏㄨㄥˊ ㄕㄜˋ)or 黌宇(ㄏㄨㄥˊ ㄩˇ)
a school building

黍部 ㄕㄨˇ shuu shǔ

【黍】 7247 ㄕㄨˇ shuu shǔ
a variety of millet
黍米(ㄕㄨˇ ㄇㄧˇ)
grain of 黍 (a variety of millet); millet grain
黍谷生春(ㄕㄨˇ ㄍㄨˇ ㄕㄥ ㄔㄨㄣ)
the advent of spring in the cold Shu-ku Hills—a change for the better of a needy life
黍稷(ㄕㄨˇ ㄐㄧˋ)
a variety of millet
黍子(ㄕㄨˇ ·ㄗ)
a variety of millet
黍油麥秀(ㄕㄨˇ ㄧㄡˊ ㄇㄞˋ ㄒㄧㄡˋ)
The grains grow luxuriantly among the ruins of the former capital.

三畫

【黎】 7248 ㄌㄧˊ li lí
1. many; numerous
2. black; dark
3. the aborigines of Hainan
4. a Chinese family name
黎巴嫩(ㄌㄧˊ ㄅㄚ ㄋㄣˋ)
Lebanon
黎苗(ㄌㄧˊ ㄇㄧㄠˊ)
the people; the common people
黎民(ㄌㄧˊ ㄇㄧㄣˊ)or 黎首(ㄌㄧˊ ㄕㄡˇ)or 黎庶(ㄌㄧˊ ㄕㄨˋ)
the multitude; the common people
黎明(ㄌㄧˊ ㄇㄧㄥˊ)
dawn; daybreak: 他黎明卽起。He got up at dawn.
黎老(ㄌㄧˊ ㄌㄠˇ)
an aged person
黎黑(ㄌㄧˊ ㄏㄟ)
black; dark
黎元洪(ㄌㄧˊ ㄩㄢˊ ㄏㄨㄥˊ)
Li Yüan-hung, 1864-1928, a general serving under the Manchu rulers, who joined the National Revolution and was later made president of the Republic

五畫

【黏】 7249 ㄋㄧㄢˊ nian nián
1. to stick
2. sticky; glutinous; gluey; adhesive; clammy; viscid
黏不住(ㄋㄧㄢˊ ·ㄅㄨ ㄓㄨˋ)
to fail to stick or adhere: 這郵票黏不住。The stamp won't stick.
黏膜(ㄋㄧㄢˊ ㄇㄛˊ)
the mucous membrane
黏米(ㄋㄧㄢˊ ㄇㄧˇ)
glutinous rice
黏度(ㄋㄧㄢˊ ㄉㄨˋ)
(chemistry) viscosity
黏貼(ㄋㄧㄢˊ ㄊㄧㄝ)
to glue; to paste; to stick: 這些郵票都黏貼在一起。These stamps have stuck together.
黏土(ㄋㄧㄢˊ ㄊㄨˇ)
clay: 磚是用黏土做的。Bricks are made of clay.
黏土細工(ㄋㄧㄢˊ ㄊㄨˇ ㄒㄧˋ ㄍㄨㄥ)
clay work
黏力(ㄋㄧㄢˊ ㄌㄧˋ)

adhesive power; viscosity
黏合劑(ㄋㄧㄢˊ ㄏㄜˊ ㄐㄧˋ)
adhesives
黏糊糊兒的(ㄋㄧㄢˊ ·ㄏㄨ ·ㄏㄨㄦ ·ㄉㄜ)
pasty; sticky; glutinous
黏涎子(ㄋㄧㄢˊ ㄒㄧㄢˊ ·ㄗ)
slaver; slobber
黏性(ㄋㄧㄢˊ ㄒㄧㄥˋ)
viscosity
黏住(ㄋㄧㄢˊ ·ㄓㄨ)
to stick; to adhere: 黏膠黏住那男孩的頭髮。Gum adhered to the boy's hair.
黏着(ㄋㄧㄢˊ ㄓㄨㄛˊ)
to stick together; to adhere
黏液(ㄋㄧㄢˊ ㄧㄝˋ)
viscous liquid; mucus; mucilage
黏油(ㄋㄧㄢˊ ㄧㄡˊ)
sticky oil; heavy oil

黑 部
ㄏㄜˋ heh hè

【黑】 7250 ㄏㄟ hei hēi
(讀音 ㄏㄜˋ heh hè)
1. black; dark: 這是個黑夜。It is a black night.
2. evil; sinister; gloomy: 未來似乎充滿了黑暗。The future seemed filled with gloom.

黑白(ㄏㄟ ㄅㄞˊ)
black and white—right and wrong, good and bad, etc.
黑白片(ㄏㄟ ㄅㄞˊ ㄆㄧㄢˋ)
black-and-white photos or films
黑白分明(ㄏㄟ ㄅㄞˊ ㄈㄣ ㄇㄧㄥˊ)
① right and wrong clearly distinguished ② the sharp contrast between black and white
黑白花兒(ㄏㄟ ㄅㄞˊ ㄏㄨㄚㄦ)
(said of animals) covered with spots of white and black; white with black spots; piebald
黑斑(ㄏㄟ ㄅㄢ)
dark spots; black specks
黑板(ㄏㄟ ㄅㄢˇ)
a blackboard
黑板刷(ㄏㄟ ㄅㄢˇ ㄕㄨㄚ)
an eraser; a wiper 亦作「黑板擦」
黑不溜偢(ㄏㄟ ·ㄅㄨ ㄌㄧㄡ ㄑㄧㄡ)
swarthy; dark; black
黑煤(ㄏㄟ ㄇㄟˊ)
coal: 我們缺黑煤。We are short of coal.
黑莓(ㄏㄟ ㄇㄟˊ)
a blackberry
黑眉烏嘴(ㄏㄟ ㄇㄟˊ ㄨ ㄗㄨㄟˇ)
dark or filthy (said of a face or anything that is dirty looking)
黑眸(ㄏㄟ ㄇㄡˊ)
the black pupil of the eye
黑麵包(ㄏㄟ ㄇㄧㄢˋ ㄅㄠ)
black bread; rye bread
黑名單(ㄏㄟ ㄇㄧㄥˊ ㄉㄢ)
a blacklist
黑幕(ㄏㄟ ㄇㄨˋ)
what is done under cover; a dark secret
黑道日(ㄏㄟ ㄉㄠˋ ㄖˋ)
an unlucky day
黑道人物(ㄏㄟ ㄉㄠˋ ㄖㄣˊ ㄨˋ)
a gangster; an underworld figure
黑店(ㄏㄟ ㄉㄧㄢˋ)
an inn that kills and robs lodgers
黑洞(ㄏㄟ ㄉㄨㄥˋ)
(astronomy) a black hole
黑洞洞(ㄏㄟ ㄉㄨㄥˋ ㄉㄨㄥˋ)
very dark
黑陶文化(ㄏㄟ ㄊㄠˊ ㄨㄣˊ ㄏㄨㄚˋ)
Black-Pottery Culture
黑炭(ㄏㄟ ㄊㄢˋ)
charcoal
黑體字(ㄏㄟ ㄊㄧˇ ㄗˋ)
boldface type
黑尿病(ㄏㄟ ㄋㄧㄠˋ ㄅㄧㄥˋ)
blackwater fever
黑奴(ㄏㄟ ㄋㄨˊ)
Negro slaves
黑龍江(ㄏㄟ ㄌㄨㄥˊ ㄐㄧㄤ)
①the Amur River ②Heilungkiang (a province in Manchuria)
黑格爾(ㄏㄟ ㄍㄜˊ ㄦˇ)
Georg Wilhelm Friedrich Hegel, 1770-1831, German philosopher
黑咕隆咚(ㄏㄟ ·ㄍㄨ ㄌㄨㄥ ㄉㄨㄥ)
very dark; gloomy; pitch-dark
黑寡婦(ㄏㄟ ㄍㄨㄚˇ ㄈㄨˋ)
a black widow (a poisonous spider)
黑鍋(ㄏㄟ ㄍㄨㄛ)
a blackened pot—(figuratively) a wrong; an injustice 參看「背黑鍋」
黑口(ㄏㄟ ㄎㄡˇ)
the black croaker
黑盒子(ㄏㄟ ㄏㄜˊ ·ㄗ)
a cockpit voice recorder
黑海(ㄏㄟ ㄏㄞˇ)
the Black Sea
黑話(ㄏㄟ ㄏㄨㄚˋ)
argot; secret jargon of thieves, etc.
黑貨(ㄏㄟ ㄏㄨㄛˋ)
① stolen goods; smugglers' goods: 他們如何得到黑貨? How did they get the stolen goods? ② opium
黑錢(ㄏㄟ ㄑㄧㄢˊ)
(slang) underhand payment; bribery
黑漆漆(ㄏㄟ ㄑㄩ ㄑㄩ)
pitch-dark; very dark: 屋子裏黑漆漆的。The room was pitch-dark.
黑心(ㄏㄟ ㄒㄧㄣ)
a black heart; an evil heart
黑心肝(ㄏㄟ ㄒㄧㄣ ㄍㄢ)
an ungrateful person
黑猩猩(ㄏㄟ ㄒㄧㄥ ·ㄒㄧㄥ)
a chimpanzee
黑熊(ㄏㄟ ㄒㄩㄥˊ)
a black bear
黑痣(ㄏㄟ ㄓˋ)
a mole (on the skin)
黑種(ㄏㄟ ㄓㄨㄥˇ)or 黑種人(ㄏㄟ ㄓㄨㄥˇ ㄖㄣˊ)
the black race
黑船(ㄏㄟ ㄔㄨㄢˊ)
a pirate ship
黑市(ㄏㄟ ㄕˋ)
a black market
黑社會(ㄏㄟ ㄕㄜˋ ㄏㄨㄟˋ)
underworld society; the underworld; gangsterdom: 黑社會中鮮有善終者。Natural death is a rarity in gangsterdom.
黑手(ㄏㄟ ㄕㄡˇ)
a vicious backstage manipulator
黑手黨(ㄏㄟ ㄕㄡˇ ㄉㄤˇ)
the Black Hand; the Mafia

〔黑部〕

黑人(ㄏㄟ ㄖㄣˊ)
a Negro; a black: 他是個黑人。He is a Negro.
黑棗(ㄏㄟ ㄗㄠˇ)
dateplum persimmon (*Diospyros lotus*)
黑死病(ㄏㄟ ㄙˇ ㄅㄧㄥˋ)
the Black Death
黑色(ㄏㄟ ㄙㄜˋ)
black
黑色火藥(ㄏㄟ ㄙㄜˋ ㄏㄨㄛˇ ㄧㄠˋ)
black powder; gunpowder
黑色素(ㄏㄟ ㄙㄜˋ ㄙㄨˋ)
melanin
黑暗(ㄏㄟ ㄢˋ)
darkness; dark: 不要讓小孩獨自在黑暗裏。Don't leave the child alone in the dark.
黑暗時代(ㄏㄟ ㄢˋ ㄕˊ ㄉㄞˋ)
the dark ages
黑暗世界(ㄏㄟ ㄢˋ ㄕˋ ㄐㄧㄝˋ)
a dark world—a world without justice
黑壓壓(ㄏㄟ ㄧㄚ ·ㄧㄚ)
extremely crowded; a dense or dark mass of
黑夜(ㄏㄟ ㄧㄝˋ)
a dark night; night
黑黝黝(ㄏㄟ ㄧㄡˇ ㄧㄡˇ)
① shiny black ② dim; dark: 這房間黑黝黝的。This room is dark.
黑煙(ㄏㄟ ㄧㄢ)
① black smoke ② opium
黑影(ㄏㄟ ㄧㄥˇ)
a dark shadow; a shadow
黑五類(ㄏㄟ ㄨˇ ㄌㄟˋ)
The five black categories of the Mao era—landlords, rich farmers, counter revolutionaries, rightists and criminals

三畫

【黓】 7251
ㄧˋ yih yì
black

四畫

【黔】 7252
ㄑㄧㄢˊ chyan qián
1. black
2. Kweichow (an alternative name)
黔黎(ㄑㄧㄢˊ ㄌㄧˊ)
the common people
黔驢技窮(ㄑㄧㄢˊ ㄌㄩˊ ㄐㄧˋ ㄑㄩㄥˊ)
the Kweichow donkey at the end of its resourcefulness—a person who has exposed his limited ability (from the story of a donkey brought to Kweichow which the tiger first feared but soon overpowered after discovering that it could only bray and kick)
黔首(ㄑㄧㄢˊ ㄕㄡˇ)
the people; the multitude

【默】 7253
ㄇㄛˋ moh mò
1. speechless; silent
2. quiet; still
默不作聲(ㄇㄛˋ ·ㄅㄨ ㄗㄨㄛˋ ㄕㄥ)
to keep silence; to keep quiet; to refuse to speak
默片(ㄇㄛˋ ㄆㄧㄢˋ)
a silent movie
默默(ㄇㄛˋ ㄇㄛˋ)
① quietly; silently ② secretly; in one's heart
默默無言(ㄇㄛˋ ㄇㄛˋ ㄨˊ ㄧㄢˊ)
wordless; speechless; silent; in silence: 他默默無言地走了。He silently went away.
默默無聞(ㄇㄛˋ ㄇㄛˋ ㄨˊ ㄨㄣˊ)
obscure; unknown to the public; without getting public attention: 他一生默默無聞。He remains obscure all his life.
默禱(ㄇㄛˋ ㄉㄠˇ)
to pray silently: 她默禱上帝賜助。She prayed silently to God for help.
默讀(ㄇㄛˋ ㄉㄨˊ)
to read silently
默念(ㄇㄛˋ ㄋㄧㄢˋ)
① to repeat (a passage, etc.) silently inside the mind ② to ponder or think
默記(ㄇㄛˋ ㄐㄧˋ)
silently remember
默劇(ㄇㄛˋ ㄐㄩˋ)
pantomime 亦作「啞劇」
默契(ㄇㄛˋ ㄑㄧˋ)
a tacit understanding; an implicit agreement; a secret agreement
默寫(ㄇㄛˋ ㄒㄧㄝˇ)or 默書(ㄇㄛˋ ㄕㄨ)
to write from memory
默許(ㄇㄛˋ ㄒㄩˇ)
tacit permission
默識(ㄇㄛˋ ㄓˋ)
to memorize silently
默然(ㄇㄛˋ ㄖㄢˊ)
silently; in silence: 我們數分鐘默然無語。We passed several minutes in silence.
默認(ㄇㄛˋ ㄖㄣˋ)
tacit consent, confession or approval; to pass over something in silence: 他默認此事。He passed over the matter in silence.
默坐(ㄇㄛˋ ㄗㄨㄛˋ)
to sit in silence: 她默坐。She sits in silence.
默誦(ㄇㄛˋ ㄙㄨㄥˋ)
① to read silently ② to repeat (a passage, etc.) silently
默哀(ㄇㄛˋ ㄞ)
to stand in silent tribute

五畫

【點】 7254
ㄉㄧㄢˇ dean diǎn
1.a dot; a spot; a speck
2.a point: 請說要點! Come to the point, please.
3.a drop; a small amount; a little: 請給我一點點。Please give me a little.
4.snacks; refreshments
5.hours
6.to dot; to mark
7.to instruct; to teach
8.to check; to examine; to investigate; to review
9.to light; to ignite: 請將火點着。Light the fire, please.
10.to select; to pick out
11.to nod (the head): 他走過時向我點頭。He nodded to me as he passed.
12.to touch; to point at
點撥(ㄉㄧㄢˇ ㄅㄛ)
① to teach; to instruct ② to instigate
點播(ㄉㄧㄢˇ ㄅㄛ)
(agriculture) dibble seeding; dibbling
點兵(ㄉㄧㄢˇ ㄅㄧㄥ)
(in the army) to gather men for a roll call
點不著(ㄉㄧㄢˇ ·ㄅㄨ ㄓㄠˊ)
incapable of being lighted; incapable of igniting

點破(ㄉㄧㄢˇ ㄆㄛˋ)
to unravel (a mystery, etc.); to point out
點卯(ㄉㄧㄢˇ ㄇㄠˇ)
to call the roll (of officials in former times)
點名(ㄉㄧㄢˇ ㄇㄧㄥˊ)
①to call the roll; to make a roll call ②to mention somebody by name
點名簿(ㄉㄧㄢˇ ㄇㄧㄥˊ ㄅㄨˋ)or 點名册(ㄉㄧㄢˇ ㄇㄧㄥˊ ㄘㄜˋ)
a roll (of names)
點到爲止(ㄉㄧㄢˇ ㄉㄠˋ ㄨㄟˊ ㄓˇ)
to go through the motions
點燈(ㄉㄧㄢˇ ㄉㄥ)
to light lamps: 需要我點燈嗎? Shall I light the lamp?
點滴(ㄉㄧㄢˇ ㄉㄧ)
①drops; small amounts; a bit ②(medicine) an intravenous drip
點滴歸公(ㄉㄧㄢˇ ㄉㄧ ㄍㄨㄟ ㄍㄨㄥ)
Every particle of the revenues goes into the state coffers.—very honest
點點(ㄉㄧㄢˇ ㄉㄧㄢˇ)
①small and numerous ②to have a snack ③to supply punctuation marks
點定(ㄉㄧㄢˇ ㄉㄧㄥˋ)
to make corrections in writings
點頭(ㄉㄧㄢˇ ㄊㄡˊ)or 點點頭(ㄉㄧㄢˇ ㄉㄧㄢˇ ㄊㄡˊ)
to nod: 她點頭並微笑。She nodded and smiled.
點頭哈腰(ㄉㄧㄢˇ ㄊㄡˊ ㄏㄚ ㄧㄠ)
to say hello
點鐵成金(ㄉㄧㄢˇ ㄊㄧㄝˇ ㄔㄥˊ ㄐㄧㄣ)
to transform common metal into gold—to make a poor writing into a literary masterpiece by skillful retouching
點鬼簿(ㄉㄧㄢˇ ㄍㄨㄟˇ ㄅㄨˋ)
a roll of ghosts (a term derisively applied to the writings of the Tang Dynasty writer Yang Chiung (楊炯), which abounded in names of ancients)
點勘(ㄉㄧㄢˇ ㄎㄢ)
to collate
點號(ㄉㄧㄢˇ ㄏㄠˋ)
a comma and the pause mark "、"
點翰林(ㄉㄧㄢˇ ㄏㄢˋ ㄌㄧㄣˊ)
to be chosen as a member of 翰林院
點化(ㄉㄧㄢˇ ㄏㄨㄚˋ)
to enlighten; to point out the correct path
點火(ㄉㄧㄢˇ ㄏㄨㄛˇ)
to light a fire: 請點火。Light the fire, please.
點交(ㄉㄧㄢˇ ㄐㄧㄠ)
to hand over (articles) after a checkup
點檢(ㄉㄧㄢˇ ㄐㄧㄢˇ)
to check or inspect (articles) one by one: 他點檢所有物品。He checked all articles one by one.
點金成鐵(ㄉㄧㄢˇ ㄐㄧㄣ ㄔㄥˊ ㄊㄧㄝˇ)
to damage the beauty of the original work (through ill-advised changes or corrections)
點將(ㄉㄧㄢˇ ㄐㄧㄤˋ)
to make a roll call of officers
點睛(ㄉㄧㄢˇ ㄐㄧㄥ)
(said of writing) to provide striking key points; to write the punch line
點清(ㄉㄧㄢˇ ㄑㄧㄥ)
to count accurately
點戲(ㄉㄧㄢˇ ㄒㄧˋ)
(Peking opera) to select from a list the performances one desires to see
點心(ㄉㄧㄢˇ ㄒㄧㄣ)
snacks; refreshments: 我們在那兒吃點心。We had a snack there.
點醒(ㄉㄧㄢˇ ㄒㄧㄥˇ)
to point out someone's errors and make him realize them
點穴(ㄉㄧㄢˇ ㄒㄩㄝˋ)
①(Chinese boxing) to attack a vital point ②to select the site of a grave through geomancy, etc.
點著(ㄉㄧㄢˇ ㄓㄠˊ)
to have lighted or ignited
點綴(ㄉㄧㄢˇ ㄓㄨㄟˋ)
to provide decorative accessories; to embellish
點鐘(ㄉㄧㄢˇ ㄓㄨㄥ)
hours; o'clock
點唱(ㄉㄧㄢˇ ㄔㄤˋ)
(said of a music audience, etc.) to select one's desired numbers or songs for the performers to sing or play
點穿(ㄉㄧㄢˇ ㄔㄨㄢ)
to unravel (a mystery, etc.)
點石成金(ㄉㄧㄢˇ ㄕˊ ㄔㄥˊ ㄐㄧㄣ)
①to turn stone into gold (by merely touching it) ②(figuratively) to make sentences or a composition perfect
點收(ㄉㄧㄢˇ ㄕㄡ)
to check and accept (articles that are delivered or handed over)
點首(ㄉㄧㄢˇ ㄕㄡˇ)
to nod: 他點首表示同意。He nodded in agreement.
點數
①(ㄉㄧㄢˇ ㄕㄨˋ) the number of points; a score
②(ㄉㄧㄢˇ ㄕㄨˇ) to count the number of articles or the amount of money
點燃(ㄉㄧㄢˇ ㄖㄢˊ)
to light; to kindle; to ignite
點字(ㄉㄧㄢˇ ㄗˋ)
Braille
點子(ㄉㄧㄢˇ ·ㄗ)
①a dot; a spot; a speck ②a little; a bit ③a key point ④ideas: 這男孩點子很多。The boy is full of ideas.
點菜(ㄉㄧㄢˇ ㄘㄞˋ)
to order favorite dishes at a restaurant
點竄(ㄉㄧㄢˇ ㄘㄨㄢˋ)
to alter phrases in (a composition)
點兒(ㄉㄧㄚˇㄦ)
①a little; a bit ②a dot; a spot ③a punctuation point ④a drop
點眼藥(ㄉㄧㄢˇ ㄧㄢˇ ㄧㄠˋ)
to apply eye lotion

【黛】 7255 ㄉㄞˋ day dài

1. a bluish-black material used by ancient women to blacken their eyebrows
2. a beauty

黛眉(ㄉㄞˋ ㄇㄟˊ)
①to blacken the eyebrows ②blackened eyebrows of women
黛螺(ㄉㄞˋ ㄌㄨㄛˊ)
①a kind of green paint in

〔黑部〕

Chinese painting ② a woman's blackened eyebrows and spiral headdress
黛綠(ㄉㄞˋ ㄌㄩˋ)
① a beauty in full dress ② dark green
黛鬟(ㄉㄞˋ ㄏㄨㄢˊ)
glossy dark hair of women
黛蛾(ㄉㄞˋ ㄜˊ)
beautiful eyebrows of a woman
黛奧辛 or 戴奧辛(ㄉㄞˋ ㄠˋ ㄒㄧㄣ)
dioxin

〔黑部〕

【黜】 7256 ㄔㄨˋ chuh chù
1. to reject; to dispel
2. to dismiss; to degrade; to demote
黜免(ㄔㄨˋ ㄇㄧㄢˇ)
to dismiss from office; to remove from office
黜退(ㄔㄨˋ ㄊㄨㄟˋ)
to dismiss; to send away
黜華崇實(ㄔㄨˋ ㄏㄨㄚˊ ㄔㄨㄥˊ ㄕˊ)
to reject luxury and uphold simplicity
黜陟(ㄔㄨˋ ㄓˋ)
demotion and promotion
黜斥(ㄔㄨˋ ㄔˋ)
to dispel; to reject; to keep away
黜升(ㄔㄨˋ ㄕㄥ)
demotion and promotion

【黝】 7257 ㄧㄡˇ yeou yǒu
bluish black
黝黑(ㄧㄡˇ ㄏㄟ)
(said of a complexion) dark; swarthy
黝堊(ㄧㄡˇ ㄜˋ)
① black pillars and white walls ② to decorate with both white paint and black paint
黝黝(ㄧㄡˇ ㄧㄡˇ)
gloomy; dark

六畫

【黠】 7258 ㄒㄧㄚˊ shya xiá
1. smart; clever; shrewd
2. crafty; cunning; artful; wily
黠吏(ㄒㄧㄚˊ ㄌㄧˋ)
a crafty evil official
黠慧(ㄒㄧㄚˊ ㄏㄨㄟˋ)
clever; smart; shrewd: 她是個黠慧的女孩子。She is a very clever girl.
黠智(ㄒㄧㄚˊ ㄓˋ)
clever; smart; shrewd; crafty
黠鼠(ㄒㄧㄚˊ ㄕㄨˇ)
① a cunning rat ② a cunning person

【黟】 7259 ㄧ i yī
1. ebony
2. dark; black

八畫

【黥】 7260 ㄑㄧㄥˊ chyng qíng
ancient punishment of tattooing the face; branding
黥面(ㄑㄧㄥˊ ㄇㄧㄢˋ) or 黥首(ㄑㄧㄥˊ ㄕㄡˇ)
ancient punishment of tattooing the face

【黧】 7261 ㄌㄧˊ li lí
dark yellow; sallow
黧黑(ㄌㄧˊ ㄏㄟ)
(said of a complexion) dark: 他的膚色黧黑。He has a dark complexion.
黧黃(ㄌㄧˊ ㄏㄨㄤˊ)
① dark yellow; sallow ② an oriole
黧雞(ㄌㄧˊ ㄐㄧ)
the look of worry, cunning, jealousy, or hatred revealed through one's eyes
黧鶯(ㄌㄧˊ ㄧㄥ)
a kind of oriole

【黨】 7262 ㄉㄤˇ daang dǎng
1. a party; a faction; a clique; a gang; an association
2. relatives
3. a community of 500 families (in ancient times)
4. to take sides; to associate; to be a partizan
5. as in 鄉黨—village
黨部(ㄉㄤˇ ㄅㄨˋ)
the headquarters of a political party
黨派(ㄉㄤˇ ㄆㄞˋ)
factions; parties; cliques: 這個國家有許多黨派。There are many parties in this country.
黨派政治(ㄉㄤˇ ㄆㄞˋ ㄓㄥˋ ㄓˋ)
party politics
黨費(ㄉㄤˇ ㄈㄟˋ)
membership dues paid to a political party
黨代表(ㄉㄤˇ ㄉㄞˋ ㄅㄧㄠˇ)
a party representative
黨徒(ㄉㄤˇ ㄊㄨˊ)
followers; parties and their members (a derogatory expression)
黨同伐異(ㄉㄤˇ ㄊㄨㄥˊ ㄈㄚˊ ㄧˋ)
to unite with those who agree and fight those who differ
黨歌(ㄉㄤˇ ㄍㄜ)
the song of a political party
黨綱(ㄉㄤˇ ㄍㄤ)
the platform of a political party
黨錮(ㄉㄤˇ ㄍㄨˋ)
interdiction of party activities by confinement of partisans, etc.
黨國(ㄉㄤˇ ㄍㄨㄛˊ)
the party and the nation: 他忠於黨國。He is royal to the party and the nation.
黨國元老(ㄉㄤˇ ㄍㄨㄛˊ ㄩㄢˊ ㄌㄠˇ)
an elder statesman of the party and the nation
黨棍(ㄉㄤˇ ㄍㄨㄣˋ)
a dirty politician who uses his party membership as a means of promoting self-interest
黨魁(ㄉㄤˇ ㄎㄨㄟˊ)
a party boss; a party chieftain: 他是共和黨的黨魁。He is the boss of the Republican Party.
黨禍(ㄉㄤˇ ㄏㄨㄛˋ)
disasters resulting from partisanship
黨徽(ㄉㄤˇ ㄏㄨㄟ)
the emblem of a political party
黨籍(ㄉㄤˇ ㄐㄧˊ)
a party affiliation
黨紀(ㄉㄤˇ ㄐㄧˋ)
party discipline
黨見(ㄉㄤˇ ㄐㄧㄢˋ)
sentiments of a party, clique, etc.
黨禁(ㄉㄤˇ ㄐㄧㄣˋ)
interdiction of party activities by confinement of partisans, etc.
黨旗(ㄉㄤˇ ㄑㄧˊ)
the flag of a political party

黨性(ㄉㄤˇ ㄒㄧㄥˋ)
loyalty to the party
黨章(ㄉㄤˇ ㄓㄤ)
the constitution of a political party
黨爭(ㄉㄤˇ ㄓㄥ)
a factional fight; a partisan war
黨政(ㄉㄤˇ ㄓㄥˋ)
the party and the government administration
黨證(ㄉㄤˇ ㄓㄥˋ)
a membership card of a political party
黨人(ㄉㄤˇ ㄖㄣˊ)
partisans
黨義(ㄉㄤˇ ㄧˋ)
principles of a party
黨務(ㄉㄤˇ ㄨˋ)
party affairs
黨外(ㄉㄤˇ ㄨㄞˋ)
outside the party
黨羽(ㄉㄤˇ ㄩˇ)
adherents or followers (especially of a condemned leader); members of a clique
黨與(ㄉㄤˇ ㄩˇ)
fellow partisans
黨員(ㄉㄤˇ ㄩㄢˊ)
a party member; a partisan

【黦】 7263
ㄩˋ yuh yù
yellowish black

【黤】 7264
ㄧㄢˇ yean yǎn
bluish black

九畫

【黯】 7265
ㄢˋ ann àn
1. very dark; pitch-dark: 這房間太黯。This room is too dark.
2. miserable; dismal
黯淡無光(ㄢˋ ㄉㄢˋ ㄨˊ ㄍㄨㄤ)
gloomy; somber; dismal
黯然消魂(ㄢˋ ㄖㄢˊ ㄒㄧㄠ ㄏㄨㄣˊ)
deeply affected (as by the sorrow of parting)
黯然失色(ㄢˋ ㄖㄢˊ ㄕ ㄙㄜˋ)
to appear very dull or poor in comparison; to be outshone; to be eclipsed
黯然神傷(ㄢˋ ㄖㄢˊ ㄕㄣˊ ㄕㄤ)
to feel dejected; to feel depressed
黯慘(ㄢˋ ㄘㄢˇ)
gloomy; dismal
黯黯(ㄢˋ ㄢˋ)
gloomy; somber; sad

【黮】 7266
1. ㄊㄢˇ taan tǎn
pitch-dark; pitch-black

【黮】 7266
2. ㄕㄣˋ shenn shèn
a mulberry

十一畫

【黲】 7267
ㄘㄢˇ tsaan cǎn
light bluish dark
黲白(ㄘㄢˇ ㄅㄞˊ)
gray
黲淡(ㄘㄢˇ ㄉㄢˋ)
gloomy; dull

【黴】 7268
ㄇㄟˊ mei méi
1. mold; mildew; must
2. germs; bacteria
3. fungi
4. dirty; dingy
黴毒(ㄇㄟˊ ㄉㄨˊ)
syphilis 亦作「梅毒」
黴爛(ㄇㄟˊ ㄌㄢˋ)
decaying and mildew-covered
黴菌(ㄇㄟˊ ㄐㄩㄣˋ)
①fungi; mold fungi ②germs; bacteria

十三畫

【黵】 7269
ㄉㄢˇ daan dǎn
to tattoo the face
黵面(ㄉㄢˇ ㄇㄧㄢˋ)
an ancient punishment of tattooing a criminal's face

十四畫

【黶】 7270
ㄧㄢˇ yean yǎn
black moles (on the skin)

十五畫

【黷】 7271
ㄉㄨˊ dwu dú
1. to tarnish
2. to be rash about
3. to corrupt
黷武(ㄉㄨˊ ㄨˇ)
to use military might rashly; to be trigger-happy

黹部
ㄓˇ jyy zhǐ

【黹】 7272
ㄓˇ jyy zhǐ
embroidery; needlework

五畫

【黻】 7273
ㄈㄨˊ fwu fú
a kind of embroidered design on ancient sacrificial robes; a kind of sacrificial robes

七畫

【黼】 7274
ㄈㄨˇ fuu fǔ
a kind of ancient sacrificial robes embroidered with hatchets
黼黻(ㄈㄨˇ ㄈㄨˊ)
axes embroidered on an official's robe as a symbol of distinction

黽部
ㄇㄧㄣˇ miin mǐn

【黽】 7275
ㄇㄧㄣˇ miin mǐn
to strive; to endeavor
黽勉(ㄇㄧㄣˇ ㄇㄧㄢˇ)
to strive; to endeavor; to exert oneself

四畫

【黿】 7276
ㄩㄢˊ yuan yuán
a kind of large turtle
黿鳴鼈應(ㄩㄢˊ ㄇㄧㄥˊ ㄅㄧㄝ ㄧㄥˋ)
(literally) The small turtle responds as the large turtle calls.—The lord and his vassals get along quite well.

〔鼎部〕

五畫

【鼂】 7277
ㄔㄠˊ chaur cháo
1. a kind of sea turtle
2. a Chinese family name

六畫

【鼃】 7278
(蛙) ㄨㄚ ua wā
a frog

八畫

【鼅】 7279
(蜘) ㄓ jy zhī
a spider

十一畫

【鼇】 7280
ㄠˊ aur áo
a huge sea turtle
鼇背負山(ㄠˊ ㄅㄟˋ ㄈㄨˋ ㄕㄢ)
My indebtedness to you is as great as the load of a mountain to a turtle. 參看「鼇戴」
鼇抃(ㄠˊ ㄅㄧㄢˋ)
to clap and dance with joy
鼇峯(ㄠˊ ㄈㄥ)or 鼇禁(ㄠˊ ㄐㄧㄣˋ)or 鼇署(ㄠˊ ㄕㄨˇ)or 鼇掖(ㄠˊ ㄧㄝˋ)
the highly revered center for men of letters 亦作「翰苑」
鼇戴(ㄠˊ ㄉㄞˋ)
to feel indebted (used in expressing one's gratitude)
鼇頭 or 鰲頭(ㄠˊ ㄊㄡˊ)
the top successful candidate in a civil service examination under the former system

十二畫

【鼈】 7281
(鱉) ㄅㄧㄝ bie biē
Trionyx sinenis, a kind of fresh-water turtle 亦作「甲魚」
鼈縮頭(ㄅㄧㄝ ㄙㄨㄛ ㄊㄡˊ)
to hide oneself from danger (as a turtle withdraws its head under its shell); to behave cowardly

【鼉】 7282
ㄊㄨㄛˊ two tuó
a kind of water lizard (whose skin was often used to make drums)
鼉更(ㄊㄨㄛˊ ㄍㄥ)
to beat the watches (with drums)
鼉鼓(ㄊㄨㄛˊ ㄍㄨˇ)
① drums made of the skins of large water lizards; lizard-skin drums ② to beat the watches with drums

鼎部
ㄉㄧㄥˇ diing dǐng

【鼎】 7283
ㄉㄧㄥˇ diing dǐng
1. a huge tripod of bronze with two ears; a heavy three-legged caldron or sacrificial vessel
2. vigorous; thriving; flourishing
3. involving three parts or things; triangular
鼎沸(ㄉㄧㄥˇ ㄈㄟˋ)
tumultuous; boiling; hubbub; noisy and confused
鼎輔(ㄉㄧㄥˇ ㄈㄨˇ)
the three chief ministers of the state (in ancient times)
鼎鼎大名(ㄉㄧㄥˇ ㄉㄧㄥˇ ㄉㄚˋ ㄇㄧㄥˊ)
renowned; famous; illustrious; celebrated; a great reputation
鼎鼐(ㄉㄧㄥˇ ㄋㄞˋ)
the office of the prime minister; premiership
鼎力(ㄉㄧㄥˇ ㄌㄧˋ)
① great strength; herculean strength ② your kind effort
鼎力玉成(ㄉㄧㄥˇ ㄌㄧˋ ㄩˋ ㄔㄥˊ)
to help accomplish this small task with your great power (in complimenting another for a help sought or rendered)
鼎立(ㄉㄧㄥˇ ㄌㄧˋ)
(said of rival groups, etc.) to develop a triangular balance of power
鼎革(ㄉㄧㄥˇ ㄍㄜˊ)
(said of dynastic changes) replacement of the old by the new
鼎湖(ㄉㄧㄥˇ ㄏㄨˊ)
an emperor's death
鼎鑊(ㄉㄧㄥˇ ㄏㄨㄛˋ)
① a caldron used as a cooking vessel in ancient times ② to cook an offending minister in a caldron, one of the severest punishments in ancient times
鼎甲(ㄉㄧㄥˇ ㄐㄧㄚˇ)
the three top candidates in the imperial examination under the former civil service examination system
鼎席(ㄉㄧㄥˇ ㄒㄧˊ)
the office of a minister
鼎新(ㄉㄧㄥˇ ㄒㄧㄣ)
to renew
鼎姓(ㄉㄧㄥˇ ㄒㄧㄥˋ)
a great clan
鼎峙(ㄉㄧㄥˇ ㄓˋ)
to form a triangular balance of power
鼎折足(ㄉㄧㄥˇ ㄓㄜˊ ㄗㄨˊ)
a tripod with a broken leg —a minister who ruins the state
鼎鐘(ㄉㄧㄥˇ ㄓㄨㄥ)
bells or vessels engraved with inscriptions honoring worthy men
鼎臣(ㄉㄧㄥˇ ㄔㄣˊ)
important courtiers; high ministers
鼎食(ㄉㄧㄥˇ ㄕˊ)
food of the nobility
鼎士(ㄉㄧㄥˇ ㄕˋ)
a strong man; a man of great strength
鼎盛(ㄉㄧㄥˇ ㄕㄥˋ)
in a period of great prosperity; prosperous; thriving; vigorous; flourishing
鼎足(ㄉㄧㄥˇ ㄗㄨˊ)
① a triangular situation; a triangular balance of power ② the three top ministers of a state in ancient times
鼎足而三(ㄉㄧㄥˇ ㄗㄨˊ ㄦˊ ㄙㄢ)
divided into three rival groups; developing into a triangular balance of power
鼎族(ㄉㄧㄥˇ ㄗㄨˊ)
a great clan 亦作「鼎姓」
鼎俎(ㄉㄧㄥˇ ㄗㄨˇ)
① a prime minister; a pre-

mier ② vessels holding sacrificial animals; cooking vessels
鼎彝(ㄉㄧㄥˇ ㄧˊ)
sacrificial vessels engraved with inscriptions in honor of worthy men
鼎業(ㄉㄧㄥˇ ㄧㄝˋ)
a ruler's achievements
鼎言(ㄉㄧㄥˇ ㄧㄢˊ)
words of importance; important statements
鼎位(ㄉㄧㄥˇ ㄨㄟˋ)
the office of the prime minister; premiership
鼎運(ㄉㄧㄥˇ ㄩㄣˋ)or 鼎祚(ㄉㄧㄥˇ ㄗㄨㄛˋ)
the destiny of the nation

二畫

【鼐】 7284 ㄋㄞˋ nay nài
a huge tripod caldron
【鼏】 7285 ㄇㄧˋ mih mì
the cover of a tripod caldron

三畫

【鼒】 7286 ㄗ tzy zi
a tripod with a small opening on the top

鼓部 ㄍㄨˇ guu gǔ

【鼓】 7287 ㄍㄨˇ guu gǔ
1. drums
2. to drum; to beat a drum
3. to vibrate; to quiver
4. to rouse; to stir up; to instigate
鼓盆(ㄍㄨˇ ㄆㄣˊ)or 鼓盆之戚(ㄍㄨˇ ㄆㄣˊ ㄓ ㄑㄧ)
to pound on a tub—to be bereaved of one's wife
鼓鼙(ㄍㄨˇ ㄆㄧˊ)
a kind of military drum
鼓膜(ㄍㄨˇ ㄇㄛˊ)
the eardrum; the tympanic membrane
鼓風爐(ㄍㄨˇ ㄈㄥ ㄌㄨˊ)
a blast furnace
鼓腹(ㄍㄨˇ ㄈㄨˋ)
① well-fed and unoccupied; eating well and living well ② to beat one's belly as a drum
鼓刀(ㄍㄨˇ ㄉㄠ)
to manipulate the knife—to slaughter animals
鼓動(ㄍㄨˇ ㄉㄨㄥˋ)
to instigate; to rouse; to incite; to stir up; to excite
鼓樓(ㄍㄨˇ ㄌㄡˊ)
a drum tower
鼓浪嶼(ㄍㄨˇ ㄌㄤˋ ㄩˇ)
Kulangyu, an islet facing Amoy, Fukien
鼓勵(ㄍㄨˇ ㄌㄧˋ)
to encourage; to hearten: 英文老師講很多話鼓勵我們。Our English teacher said a lot to encourage us.
鼓號樂隊(ㄍㄨˇ ㄏㄠˋ ㄩㄝˋ ㄉㄨㄟˋ)
a drum and bugle band
鼓惑(ㄍㄨˇ ㄏㄨㄛˋ)
to instigate; to induce to go astray
鼓角(ㄍㄨˇ ㄐㄩㄝˊ)
drums and horns (especially in the army)
鼓起勇氣(ㄍㄨˇ ㄑㄧˇ ㄩㄥˇ ㄑㄧˋ)
to pluck up courage
鼓掌(ㄍㄨˇ ㄓㄤˇ)
to clap the hands; to give applause: 他們鼓掌歡迎他。They clapped their hands to welcome him.
鼓脹(ㄍㄨˇ ㄓㄤˋ)
bloating (of the abdomen, etc.); tympanites; to bloat
鼓吹
①(ㄍㄨˇ ㄔㄨㄟ) to advocate; to uphold; to promote; to propagate: 他鼓吹多建學校。He advocates building more schools.
②(ㄍㄨˇ ㄔㄨㄟˋ)a kind of ancient court music
鼓舌如簧(ㄍㄨˇ ㄕㄜˊ ㄖㄨˊ ㄏㄨㄤˊ)
to wag one's tongue (for honeyed words, malicious gossip, etc.)
鼓手(ㄍㄨˇ ·ㄕㄡ)
a drum player; a drummer: 少年鼓手擊鼓。The boy drummer beat a drum.
鼓聲(ㄍㄨˇ ㄕㄥ)
drumbeats
鼓譟 or 鼓噪(ㄍㄨˇ ㄗㄠˋ)
to raise an uproar; to be uproarious: 聽衆鼓譟起來。The audience are uproarious.
鼓兒詞(ㄍㄨˇ ㄦ ㄘˊ)
a form of folk entertainment with singing accompanied by drums
鼓翼(ㄍㄨˇ ㄧˋ)
to flap the wings: 鳥正鼓翼飛翔。The bird was flapping its wings.
鼓舞(ㄍㄨˇ ㄨˇ)
① to rouse; to inspire; to stir up; to excite; to spur on: 成功鼓舞我們做出更大的努力。Success inspires us to geater efforts. ② to dance for joy; to rejoice
鼓舞士氣(ㄍㄨˇ ㄨˇ ㄕˋ ㄑㄧˋ)
to enhance troop morale; to cheer up troops: 他們唱歌鼓舞士氣。They sing to cheer up troops.
鼓樂喧天(ㄍㄨˇ ㄩㄝˋ ㄒㄩㄢ ㄊㄧㄢ)
Loud music fills the air.

五畫

【鼕】 7288 ㄉㄨㄥ dong dōng
the rattle of drums

六畫

【鼗】 7289 ㄊㄠˊ taur táo
a kind of small hand-drum with two swinging knobs (that can strike the face of the drum being twirled)

八畫

【鼙】 7290 ㄆㄧˊ pyi pí
a kind of war drum
鼙鼓(ㄆㄧˊ ㄍㄨˇ)
a kind of war drum

〔鼓部〕

鼠部
ㄕㄨˇ shuu shǔ

【鼠】 7291 ㄕㄨˇ shuu shǔ
a mouse; a rat: 老鼠吱吱叫。A mouse squeaks.

鼠輩(ㄕㄨˇ ㄅㄟˋ)
a mean fellow

鼠目(ㄕㄨˇ ㄇㄨˋ)
① small, protruding eyes ② lacking foresight; short-sighted

鼠目寸光(ㄕㄨˇ ㄇㄨˋ ㄘㄨㄣˋ ㄍㄨㄤ)
lacking foresight; short-sighted

鼠膽(ㄕㄨˇ ㄉㄢˇ)
cowardice

鼠肚雞腸(ㄕㄨˇ ㄉㄨˋ ㄐㄧ ㄔㄤˊ)
(literally) a rat's stomach and a chicken's bowels—narrow-mindedness

鼠遁(ㄕㄨˇ ㄉㄨㄣˋ)
to flee helter-skelter like a rat

鼠狼(ㄕㄨˇ ㄌㄤˊ)
a weasel 亦作「鼬鼠」

鼠肝蟲臂(ㄕㄨˇ ㄍㄢ ㄔㄨㄥˊ ㄅㄧˋ)
(literally) a rat's liver and an insect's limbs—things of very little value

鼠口不出象牙(ㄕㄨˇ ㄎㄡˇ ㄅㄨˋ ㄔㄨ ㄒㄧㄤˋ ㄧㄚˊ)
(figuratively) to utter nothing but dirty words

鼠窟(ㄕㄨˇ ㄎㄨ)or 鼠穴(ㄕㄨˇ ㄒㄩㄝˋ)
a rat hole

鼠灰色(ㄕㄨˇ ㄏㄨㄟ ㄙㄜˋ)
dark gray

鼠技(ㄕㄨˇ ㄐㄧˋ)
(literally) a rat's ability—limited talents; versatile but not impressive 或 Jack of all trades but master of none.

鼠竊狗盜(ㄕㄨˇ ㄑㄧㄝˋ ㄍㄡˇ ㄉㄠˋ)
(figuratively) petty thieves and small-time robbers

鼠蹊(ㄕㄨˇ ㄒㄧ)
the groin

鼠子(ㄕㄨˇ ㄗˇ)
a mean fellow

鼠攛狼奔(ㄕㄨˇ ㄘㄨㄢ ㄌㄤˊ ㄅㄣ)
to run away in all directions

鼠竄(ㄕㄨˇ ㄘㄨㄢˋ)
to run away like frightened rats: 敵軍抱頭鼠竄。Our enemies run away like frightened rats.

鼠思(ㄕㄨˇ ㄙ)
to be pensive

鼠疫(ㄕㄨˇ ㄧˋ)
a bubonic plague; a pestilence

鼠疫菌(ㄕㄨˇ ㄧˋ ㄐㄩㄣˋ)
plague bacilli

鼠牙雀角(ㄕㄨˇ ㄧㄚˊ ㄑㄩㄝˋ ㄐㄩㄝˊ)
(figuratively) to carry on a lawsuit; to litigate

鼠眼(ㄕㄨˇ ㄧㄢˇ)
① small, protruding eyes ② lack of foresight

鼠尾草(ㄕㄨˇ ㄨㄟˇ ㄘㄠˇ)
Salvia japonica, a kind of medical herb

五畫

【鼬】 7292 ㄧㄡˋ yow yòu
a weasel

鼬鼠(ㄧㄡˋ ㄕㄨˇ)
a weasel

【鼪】 7293 ㄕㄥ sheng shēng
a weasel

七畫

【鼯】 7294 ㄨˊ wu wú
a flying squirrel

鼯鼠(ㄨˊ ㄕㄨˇ)
a flying squirrel

鼯鼠技窮 or 梧鼠技窮(ㄨˊ ㄕㄨˇ ㄐㄧˋ ㄑㄩㄥˊ)
at one's wit's end: 他幾乎鼯鼠技窮。He was almost at his wit's end.

九畫

【鼴】 7295 ㄧㄢˇ yean yǎn
a mole (a burrowing animal)

十畫

【鼷】 7296 ㄒㄧ shi xi
a mouse

【鼹】 7297 ㄧㄢˇ yean yǎn
Mogera wogura wogura, a kind of insectivorous rodent

鼻部
ㄅㄧˊ byi bí

【鼻】 7298 ㄅㄧˊ byi bí
1. a nose
2. before any others; first

鼻峯(ㄅㄧˊ ㄈㄥ)
the bridge of the (human) nose

鼻竇炎(ㄅㄧˊ ㄉㄡˋ ㄧㄢˊ)
sinusitis

鼻塌嘴歪(ㄅㄧˊ ㄊㄚ ㄗㄨㄟˇ ㄨㄞ)
(literally) a snub nose and a wry mouth—a very ugly face

鼻頭(ㄅㄧˊ ㄊㄡˊ)
a nose

鼻涕(ㄅㄧˊ ㄊㄧˋ)
nasal mucus; snivel; nasal drips

鼻牛兒(ㄅㄧˊ ㄋㄧㄡˊㄦ)
nose wax; nose dirt

鼻梁兒(ㄅㄧˊ ㄌㄧㄤˊㄦ)
the bridge of the nose

鼻孔(ㄅㄧˊ ㄎㄨㄥˇ)
nostrils

鼻尖(ㄅㄧˊ ㄐㄧㄢ)
the tip of the nose

鼻腔(ㄅㄧˊ ㄑㄧㄤ)
the nasal cavity

鼻青臉腫(ㄅㄧˊ ㄑㄧㄥ ㄌㄧㄢˇ ㄓㄨㄥˇ)
a bloody nose and a swollen face—bruised in the face: 他摔得鼻青臉腫。He fell and bruised his face.

鼻息(ㄅㄧˊ ㄒㄧˊ)
the breath

鼻息如雷(ㄅㄧˊ ㄒㄧˊ ㄖㄨˊ ㄌㄟˊ)
to snort or snore terribly

鼻血(ㄅㄧˊ ㄒㄧㄝˇ)
nosebleed; nasal hemorrhage

鼻準(ㄅㄧˊ ㄓㄨㄣˇ)
the tip of the nose

鼻子(ㄅㄧˊ ˙ㄗ)
a nose

鼻子眼兒(ㄅㄧˊ ·ㄗ ㄧㄚˇㄦ)
nostrils
鼻祖(ㄅㄧˊ ㄗㄨˇ)
a founder; an originator
鼻塞(ㄅㄧˊ ㄙㄞ)
to have a stuffy nose; nasal congestion
鼻煙(ㄅㄧˊ ㄧㄢ)
snuff (a kind of tobacco); to snuff
鼻煙壺(ㄅㄧˊ ㄧㄢ ㄏㄨˊ)
a snuff bottle
鼻咽癌(ㄅㄧˊ ㄧㄢ ㄧㄢˊ)
nasopharyngeal carcinoma
鼻炎(ㄅㄧˊ ㄧㄢˊ)
nasal catarrh: 他能治好你的鼻炎。He can cure your nasal catarrh.
鼻癌(ㄅㄧˊ ㄧㄢˊ)
nasopharyngeal cancer
鼻音(ㄅㄧˊ ㄧㄣ)
(phonetics) nasal sounds; nasals

三畫

【鼾】 7299
ㄏㄢ han hān
to snore
鼾聲如雷(ㄏㄢ ㄕㄥ ㄖㄨˊ ㄌㄟˊ)
to snore terribly
鼾睡(ㄏㄢ ㄕㄨㄟˋ)
a heavy sleep with snoring

五畫

【齁】 7300
ㄏㄡ hou hōu
1. snoring; snorting
2. (sickeningly) sweet or salty

十畫

【齅】 7301
(嗅) ㄒㄧㄡˋ shiow xiù
to smell

十三畫

【齈】 7302
ㄋㄨㄥˊ nong nóng
a kind of nasal ailment characterized by abundance of snivel

齊部
ㄑㄧˊ chyi qí

【齊】 7303
1. ㄑㄧˊ chyi qí
1. equal; uniform; to be on a level
2. name of an ancient feudal state
3. name of a dynasty
4. to set in order
5. a Chinese family name
齊備(ㄑㄧˊ ㄅㄟˋ)
everything complete; everything ready
齊步(ㄑㄧˊ ㄅㄨˋ)
in step; uniform steps
齊眉(ㄑㄧˊ ㄇㄟˊ)
respect between husband and wife—referring to the story of Liang Hung (梁鴻) and Meng Kuang(孟光)
齊民(ㄑㄧˊ ㄇㄧㄣˊ)
the masses; the multitude; the common people; the ordinary people
齊名(ㄑㄧˊ ㄇㄧㄥˊ)
equally well-known; equal in fame
齊大非偶(ㄑㄧˊ ㄉㄚˋ ㄈㄟ ㄡˇ)
(said of a family as possible future in-laws) too rich to be a good match
齊東野語(ㄑㄧˊ ㄉㄨㄥ ㄧㄝˇ ㄩˇ)
unreliable talk
齊頭並進(ㄑㄧˊ ㄊㄡˊ ㄅㄧㄥˋ ㄐㄧㄣˋ)
to go ahead together; to march together; to do something simultaneously; to do two or more things at once
齊年(ㄑㄧˊ ㄋㄧㄢˊ)
of the same age: 他們齊年。They are of the same age.
齊國(ㄑㄧˊ ㄍㄨㄛˊ)
the ancient state of Chi in what is today's Shantung
齊桓公(ㄑㄧˊ ㄏㄨㄢˊ ㄍㄨㄥ)or 齊桓(ㄑㄧˊ ㄏㄨㄢˊ)
a powerful ruler till 643 B.C. of the ancient state of Chi (齊) during the Epoch of Warring States
齊集(ㄑㄧˊ ㄐㄧˊ)
all assembled: 學生們在禮堂齊集。The students were all assembled in the school hall.
齊家(ㄑㄧˊ ㄐㄧㄚ)
to govern one's family; to regulate one's family
齊齊哈爾(ㄑㄧˊ ㄑㄧˊ ㄏㄚ ㄦˇ)
Tsitsihar (or Lungkiang), Manchuria
齊驅(ㄑㄧˊ ㄑㄩ)
to advance abreast—to be equal in ability
齊全(ㄑㄧˊ ㄑㄩㄢˊ)
everything complete; nothing missing; all in readiness: 我希望一切齊全。I hope nothing is missing.
齊心(ㄑㄧˊ ㄒㄧㄣ)
of one mind: 如果我們齊心,一切事情就好辦了。When we are of one mind, everything becomes easy.
齊整(ㄑㄧˊ ㄓㄥˇ)
orderly; tidy; neat
齊齒(ㄑㄧˊ ㄔˇ)
① of the same age ②(traditional Chinese phonetics) a final beginning with an unrounded high front vowel (*ia, ian*, etc.)
齊楚(ㄑㄧˊ ㄔㄨˇ)
① orderly; tidy ② Chi and Chu, two important feudal states in the Epoch of Warring States
齊聲(ㄑㄧˊ ㄕㄥ)
in unison; with one voice
齊人之福(ㄑㄧˊ ㄖㄣˊ ㄓ ㄈㄨˊ)
to have more than one wife; to have a concubine: 那商人享齊人之福。The merchant has more than one wife.
齊一(ㄑㄧˊ ㄧ)
uniform; equal

【齊】 7303
2.(齋) ㄓㄞ jai zhāi
pious; respectful; chaste
齊莊(ㄓㄞ ㄓㄨㄤ)
respectful; sober; serious
齊宿(ㄓㄞ ㄙㄨˋ)
to show piety by passing the night in fasting
齊肅(ㄓㄞ ㄙㄨˋ)
grave and respectful

【齊】 7303
3. ㄗ tzy zī
1. the lower edge of a garment

2. same as 粢—sacrificial grain
齊盛(ㄗ ㄔㄥˊ)
sacrifices offered
齊衰(ㄗ ㄘㄨㄟ)
dress worn for the second degree of mourning

〔齒部〕

三畫

【齋】7304
(斎) ㄓㄞ jai zhāi
1. pious; respectful; chaste; pure
2. to abstain from meat; to fast
3. to purify oneself
4. to provide Buddhist monks with meals
5. a room for study; a study; a school
6. a vegetarian meal
齋飯(ㄓㄞ ㄈㄢˋ)
a vegetarian meal for a Buddhist monk
齋壇(ㄓㄞ ㄊㄢˊ)
an altar for Buddhist worship
齋堂(ㄓㄞ ㄊㄤˊ)
a dining room in a Buddhist temple
齋戒(ㄓㄞ ㄐㄧㄝˋ)
to abstain from meat, wine, etc. (when offering sacrifices to gods); to fast
齋戒沐浴(ㄓㄞ ㄐㄧㄝˋ ㄇㄨˋ ㄩˋ)
to purify oneself by observing abstinent rules and bathing
齋醮(ㄓㄞ ㄐㄧㄠˋ)
to perform a Buddhist service
齋心(ㄓㄞ ㄒㄧㄣ)
to purify the mind
齋主(ㄓㄞ ㄓㄨˇ)
the host at a Buddhist vegetarian dinner
齋舍(ㄓㄞ ㄕㄜˋ)or 齋屋(ㄓㄞ ㄨ)
①a room for fasting ②a study ③a school
齋僧(ㄓㄞ ㄙㄥ)
to provide Buddhist monks with meals
齋月(ㄓㄞ ㄩㄝˋ)
①(Buddhism) the first, fifth and ninth lunar months ②(Islam) Ramadan; the month of fast

七畫

【齎】7305
1.(賫、賷) ㄐㄧ ji jī
1. to present; to offer
2. to harbor; to have in one's mind; to entertain
齎盜糧(ㄐㄧ ㄉㄠˋ ㄌㄧㄤˊ)
(figuratively) to become the unwitting tool of the enemy
齎恨(ㄐㄧ ㄏㄣˋ)
to harbor hatred; to entertain a grudge
齎志(ㄐㄧ ㄓˋ)
to cherish unfulfilled ambitions
齎咨(ㄐㄧ ㄗ)
an exclamation
齎送(ㄐㄧ ㄙㄨㄥˋ)
to present; to offer

【齎】7305
2. ㄗ tzy zī
same as 資—wealth; estates

九畫

【齏】7306
ㄐㄧ ji jī
1. pulverized; powdered
2. seasonings in powdered form
齏粉(ㄐㄧ ㄈㄣˇ)
①fine powder; powdered; pulverized ②to be completely annihilated; to run the greatest risk; to raze to the ground
齏糟(ㄐㄧ ㄗㄠ)
minute and complicated

齒 部
ㄔˇ chyy chǐ

【齒】7307
ㄔˇ chyy chǐ
1. teeth: 他拔掉兩顆牙齒。He had two teeth pulled.
2. age
3. to speak of; to mention: 不足掛齒。Don't mention it.
4. a tooth-like part of anything
齒髮(ㄔˇ ㄈㄚˇ)
one's tooth and hair—one's age
齒蠹(ㄔˇ ㄉㄨˋ)
tooth decay
齒痛(ㄔˇ ㄊㄨㄥˋ)
toothache
齒冷(ㄔˇ ㄌㄥˇ)
to scorn; to ridicule; to jeer
齒輪(ㄔˇ ㄌㄨㄣˊ)
a cogwheel; a gear wheel; a gear
齒垢(ㄔˇ ㄍㄡˋ)
tartar (on the teeth)
齒根(ㄔˇ ㄍㄣ)
the root of a tooth
齒軌(ㄔˇ ㄍㄨㄟˇ)
a rack railway
齒冠(ㄔˇ ㄍㄨㄢ)
the crown of a tooth
齒科(ㄔˇ ㄎㄜ)
dentistry: 他主修齒科。He is a dentistry major.
齒寒(ㄔˇ ㄏㄢˊ)
(said of either of two interdependent beings) to suffer due to failure of the other
齒及(ㄔˇ ㄐㄧˊ)
to mention (something not worth mentioning)
齒擊(ㄔˇ ㄐㄧˊ)
to clatter the teeth in trembling
齒決(ㄔˇ ㄐㄩㄝˊ)
to bite off with the teeth
齒腔(ㄔˇ ㄑㄧㄤ)
the gum of the tooth
齒齲(ㄔˇ ㄑㄩˇ)
tooth decay
齒質(ㄔˇ ㄓˊ)
dentine
齒讓(ㄔˇ ㄖㄤˋ)
to yield to seniors
齒如編貝(ㄔˇ ㄖㄨˊ ㄅㄧㄢ ㄅㄟˋ)or 齒如齊貝(ㄔˇ ㄖㄨˊ ㄑㄧˊ ㄅㄟˋ)
very beautiful teeth
齒次(ㄔˇ ㄘˋ)
order of seniority
齒髓(ㄔˇ ㄙㄨㄟˇ)
pulp of the tooth
齒兒(ㄔˇㄜˊㄦ)
teeth (of a comb, a saw, etc.)
齒牙餘論(ㄔˇ ㄧㄚˊ ㄩˊ ㄌㄨㄣˋ)
to praise others
齒音(ㄔˇ ㄧㄣ)

(phonetics) dental sounds; dentals
齒齦(ㄔˇ ㄧㄣˊ)
gums (of the teeth)
齒危(ㄔˇ ㄨㄟˊ)
very old age (with teeth about to fall out)
齒吻(ㄔˇ ㄨㄣˇ)
teeth and lips
齒亡舌存(ㄔˇ ㄨㄤˊ ㄕㄜˊ ㄘㄨㄣˊ)
(literally) After the teeth have fallen out, the tongue remains.—The strong is more likely to fall than the weak.

二畫

【齔】 7308 ㄔㄣˋ chenn chèn
1. to have milk teeth replaced with permanent teeth
2. children

三畫

【齕】 7309 ㄏㄜˊ her hé
to gnaw; to munch
齕吞(ㄏㄜˊ ㄊㄨㄣ)
to swallow without mastication

四畫

【齗】 7310 ㄧㄣˊ yn yín
1. gums (of the teeth)
2. to dispute
齗齗(ㄧㄣˊ ㄧㄣˊ)
disputing

五畫

【齟】 7311 ㄐㄩˇ jeu jǔ
irregular teeth
齟齬(ㄐㄩˇ ㄩˇ)
① irregular teeth ② to have discord; to disagree
【齠】 7312 ㄊㄧㄠˊ tyau tiáo
to shed the milk teeth
齠年(ㄊㄧㄠˊ ㄋㄧㄢˊ) or 齠齡(ㄊㄧㄠˊ ㄌㄧㄥˊ)
the age of shedding the milk teeth—childhood
齠齔(ㄊㄧㄠˊ ㄔㄣˋ)
to shed the milk teeth
齠容(ㄊㄧㄠˊ ㄖㄨㄥˊ)
a youthful look
【齡】 7313 ㄌㄧㄥˊ ling líng
age; years: 他們是學齡兒童。They are school-age children.
【齣】 7314 ㄔㄨ chu chū
1. a chapter (of old-style novels)
2. a numerary adjunct for plays
【齜】 7315 ㄗ tzy zī
1. to open the mouth and show the teeth
2. uneven teeth
齜牙(ㄗ ㄧㄚˊ)
to open the mouth and show the teeth

六畫

【齦】 7316 ㄧㄣˊ yn yín
gums (of the teeth)
【齧】 7317 (嚙、囓) ㄋㄧㄝˋ nieh niè
to gnaw; to bite
齧臂(ㄋㄧㄝˋ ㄅㄧˋ)
to bite one's arm as a sign of determination (as in taking the oath of brotherhood, etc.)
齧斷(ㄋㄧㄝˋ ㄉㄨㄢˋ)
to bite off
齧齒類(ㄋㄧㄝˋ ㄔˇ ㄌㄟˋ)
rodents
齧噬(ㄋㄧㄝˋ ㄕˋ)
to bite; to gnaw: 恐懼齧噬他的心靈。Fear is gnawing his heart.
【齩】 7318 (咬) ㄧㄠˇ yeau yǎo
to bite: 這狗齩他一口。The dog bit him.

七畫

【齪】 7319 ㄔㄨㄛˋ chuoh chuò
as in 齷齪—① narrow; small ② dirty
【齬】 7320 ㄩˇ yeu yǔ
as in 齟齬—① uneven teeth ② to disagree; to have discord

九畫

【齷】 7321 ㄨㄛˋ woh wò
參看「齷齪」
齷齪(ㄨㄛˋ ㄔㄨㄛˋ)
① narrow; small ② dirty
【齲】 7322 ㄑㄩˇ cheu qǔ
tooth decay
齲齒(ㄑㄩˇ ㄔˇ)
a decayed tooth; a carious tooth
【齶】 7323 ㄜˋ eh è
the roof of the mouth; the palate

十畫

【齹】 7324 (齒差) ㄔˊ chy chī
irregular teeth; uneven teeth

龍部
ㄌㄨㄥˊ long lóng

【龍】 7325 ㄌㄨㄥˊ long lóng
1. a dragon
2. of the emperor; imperial
3. a huge extinct reptile
4. a Chinese family name
龍幣(ㄌㄨㄥˊ ㄅㄧˋ)
the silver dollar coin, 8 taels in weight, minted by Emperor Wu in the Han Dynasty
龍牌(ㄌㄨㄥˊ ㄆㄞˊ)
an imperial tablet (kept in schools, government offices, etc., during the Ching Dynasty, to which students or officials were required to pay their respect)
龍袍(ㄌㄨㄥˊ ㄆㄠˊ)
an imperial robe
龍蟠鳳逸(ㄌㄨㄥˊ ㄆㄢˊ ㄈㄥˋ ㄧˋ)
exceedingly talented (persons)

〔龍部〕

〔龍部〕

龍蟠虎踞(ㄌㄨㄥˊ ㄆㄢˊ ㄏㄨˇ ㄐㄩˋ)
like a dragon that coils and a tiger that crouches—impressive terrain
龍馬(ㄌㄨㄥˊ ㄇㄚˇ)
(figuratively) aged but vigorous; old but strong
龍脈(ㄌㄨㄥˊ ㄇㄞˋ)
a winding mountain range
龍門(ㄌㄨㄥˊ ㄇㄣˊ)
fame; success; glory
龍門造像(ㄌㄨㄥˊ ㄇㄣˊ ㄗㄠˋ ㄒㄧㄤˋ)
stones images of Buddha cut into the cliff at Lungmen (龍門), Honan, during the 6th century
龍目(ㄌㄨㄥˊ ㄇㄨˋ)
① the emperor's eyes ②(botany) longan
龍飛(ㄌㄨㄥˊ ㄈㄟ)
to ascend the throne
龍飛榜(ㄌㄨㄥˊ ㄈㄟ ㄅㄤˇ)
the first list of officials selected after an emperor's accession
龍飛鳳舞(ㄌㄨㄥˊ ㄈㄟ ㄈㄥˋ ㄨˇ)
(literally) like dragons flying and phoenixes dancing—vivid and vigorous flourishes in calligraphy
龍鳳(ㄌㄨㄥˊ ㄈㄥˋ)
① fine offspring; excellent children ② men of wisdom ③ a noble look④man and woman ⑤ dragon and phoenix
龍鳳餅(ㄌㄨㄥˊ ㄈㄥˋ ㄅㄧㄥˇ)
cake presented to the bride's family by the bridegroom's
龍鳳帖(ㄌㄨㄥˊ ㄈㄥˋ ㄊㄧㄝˇ)
betrothal cards亦作「結婚證書」
龍鳳相配(ㄌㄨㄥˊ ㄈㄥˋ ㄒㄧㄤ ㄆㄟˋ)
union of a dragon and a phoenix (a congratulatory phrase on the occasion of a wedding)
龍鳳呈祥(ㄌㄨㄥˊ ㄈㄥˋ ㄔㄥˊ ㄒㄧㄤˊ)
prosperity brought by the dragon and the phoenix—in extremely good fortune
龍膽紫(ㄌㄨㄥˊ ㄉㄢˇ ㄗˇ)
gentian violet
龍燈(ㄌㄨㄥˊ ㄉㄥ)
a lantern shaped like a dragon
龍邸(ㄌㄨㄥˊ ㄉㄧˇ)
the emperor's abode prior to his accession
龍套(ㄌㄨㄥˊ ㄊㄠˋ)
① a kind of costume in Chinese opera ② a character in such a costume in Chinese opera—a role that requires neither acting nor singing ③ a very insignificant role: 他只是個跑龍套的。He plays an insignificant role.
龍頭(ㄌㄨㄥˊ ㄊㄡˊ)
① a faucet; a tap; a cock ② the top successful candidate in the imperial examination under the former civil service examination system ③ the leader of a sect, secret society, etc.
龍頭蛇尾(ㄌㄨㄥˊ ㄊㄡˊ ㄕㄜˊ ㄨㄟˇ)
(literally) to have a dragon's head and a snake's tail—to dwindle away to nothing after an initial display of strength
龍潭虎穴(ㄌㄨㄥˊ ㄊㄢˊ ㄏㄨˇ ㄒㄩㄝˋ)
(literally) the dragon's lake and the tiger's den—places of extreme danger
龍騰虎躍(ㄌㄨㄥˊ ㄊㄥˊ ㄏㄨˇ ㄩㄝˋ)
dragons rising and tigers leaping—a scene of bustling activity
龍跳虎臥(ㄌㄨㄥˊ ㄊㄧㄠˋ ㄏㄨˇ ㄨㄛˋ)
(literally) the dragon dancing and the tiger lurking—a free and vigorous style of writing
龍庭(ㄌㄨㄥˊ ㄊㄧㄥˊ)
① the imperial court ② the facial features of a noble man
龍腦(ㄌㄨㄥˊ ㄋㄠˇ)
Borneo camphor; borneol
龍樓鳳閣(ㄌㄨㄥˊ ㄌㄡˊ ㄈㄥˋ ㄍㄜˊ)
the emperor's abode; the imperial palace
龍鱗(ㄌㄨㄥˊ ㄌㄧㄣˊ)
① neatly arranged ②(figuratively) the grandeur of the king
龍肝鳳髓(ㄌㄨㄥˊ ㄍㄢ ㄈㄥˋ ㄙㄨㄟˇ)
rare delicacies
龍骨(ㄌㄨㄥˊ ㄍㄨˇ)
① a keel (of a boat) ② fossiles of animals supposed to be dragons' bones
龍袞(ㄌㄨㄥˊ ㄍㄨㄣˇ)
an imperial emblem
龍宮(ㄌㄨㄥˊ ㄍㄨㄥ)
the palace of the sea god
龍葵(ㄌㄨㄥˊ ㄎㄨㄟˊ)
(botany) black nightshade
龍虎山(ㄌㄨㄥˊ ㄏㄨˇ ㄕㄢ)
name of a mountain in Kiangsi, the holy land of Taoists
龍江(ㄌㄨㄥˊ ㄐㄧㄤ)
Lungkiang (or Tsitsihar), Manchuria
龍井茶(ㄌㄨㄥˊ ㄐㄧㄥˇ ㄔㄚˊ)
a kind of green tea produced at Hangchow, Chekiang
龍駒(ㄌㄨㄥˊ ㄐㄩ)
① a fine horse ② talented youth
龍捲風(ㄌㄨㄥˊ ㄐㄩㄢˇ ㄈㄥ)
a tornado; a cyclone; a twister
龍潛(ㄌㄨㄥˊ ㄑㄧㄢˊ)
(said of a prospective emperor) to wait for accession
龍蝦(ㄌㄨㄥˊ ㄒㄧㄚ)
a lobster
龍涎(ㄌㄨㄥˊ ㄒㄧㄢˊ)or 龍涎香(ㄌㄨㄥˊ ㄒㄧㄢˊ ㄒㄧㄤ)
ambergris, found in sperm whales, used in perfumes
龍驤虎步(ㄌㄨㄥˊ ㄒㄧㄤ ㄏㄨˇ ㄅㄨˋ)
(literally) to prance in a dragon-like manner and pace in a tiger-like manner—an imposing air; a dignified manner; an awe-inspiring carriage
龍驤虎視(ㄌㄨㄥˊ ㄒㄧㄤ ㄏㄨˇ ㄕˋ)
(literally) to prance like the dragon and glance like the tiger—to cherish great ambitions
龍行虎步(ㄌㄨㄥˊ ㄒㄧㄥˊ ㄏㄨˇ ㄅㄨˋ)
the dignified manner of an emperor
龍性(ㄌㄨㄥˊ ㄒㄧㄥˋ)
recalcitrance; unmanageability; intractability
龍鬚菜(ㄌㄨㄥˊ ㄒㄩ ㄘㄞˋ)
Asparagus schoberioides
龍穴(ㄌㄨㄥˊ ㄒㄩㄝˊ)
(geomancy) an ideal site for a grave
龍舟(ㄌㄨㄥˊ ㄓㄡ)or 龍船(ㄌㄨㄥˊ ㄔㄨㄢˊ)
a dragon-shaped racing boat

(for use on the Dragon-Boat Festival); a dragon boat
龍舟競渡(ㄌㄨㄥˊ ㄓㄡ ㄐㄧㄥˋ ㄉㄨˋ)
a dragon-boat race (the major event on the Dragon-Boat Festival on the 5th of the 5th lunar month)
龍章(ㄌㄨㄥˊ ㄓㄤ)
① an imperial emblem ② the emperor's calligraphy
龍章鳳姿(ㄌㄨㄥˊ ㄓㄤ ㄈㄥˋ ㄗ)
a noble and handsome appearance
龍爭虎鬥(ㄌㄨㄥˊ ㄓㄥ ㄏㄨˇ ㄉㄡˋ)
a fierce battle between giants
龍種(ㄌㄨㄥˊ ㄓㄨㄥˇ)
the dragon's seed—descendants of an emperor
龍牀(ㄌㄨㄥˊ ㄔㄨㄤˊ)
the emperor's bed
龍蛇(ㄌㄨㄥˊ ㄕㄜˊ)
① men of extraordinary talent ② strokes in cursive calligraphy ③ weapons
龍蛇混雜(ㄌㄨㄥˊ ㄕㄜˊ ㄏㄨㄣˋ ㄗㄚˊ)
the wise and the unwise huddled together
龍山寺(ㄌㄨㄥˊ ㄕㄢ ㄙˋ)
Lung Shan Temple, an old temple in Taipei, Taiwan
龍生龍，鳳生鳳(ㄌㄨㄥˊ ㄕㄥ ㄌㄨㄥˊ, ㄈㄥˋ ㄕㄥ ㄈㄥˋ)
Like father, like son.
龍牙草(ㄌㄨㄥˊ ㄧㄚˊ ㄘㄠˇ)
(botany) an agrimony
龍顏(ㄌㄨㄥˊ ㄧㄢˊ)
the noble face of the emperor
龍顏大悅(ㄌㄨㄥˊ ㄧㄢˊ ㄉㄚˋ ㄩㄝˋ)
The emperor looks greatly pleased. 或The imperial countenance shows great pleasure.
龍眼(ㄌㄨㄥˊ ㄧㄢˇ)
longan
龍吟虎嘯(ㄌㄨㄥˊ ㄧㄣˊ ㄏㄨˇ ㄒㄧㄠˋ)
the howl of dragons mingled with the roar of tigers; awe-inspiring roars (as of winds, waves, etc.)
龍洋(ㄌㄨㄥˊ ㄧㄤˊ)
a kind of silver coin minted toward the close of the Ching Dynasty
龍陽君(ㄌㄨㄥˊ ㄧㄤˊ ㄐㄩㄣ)
a catamite
龍文(ㄌㄨㄥˊ ㄨㄣˊ)
① a fine horse ② fine writing ③ a fine son
龍王(ㄌㄨㄥˊ ㄨㄤˊ)or 龍王爺(ㄌㄨㄥˊ ㄨㄤˊ ㄧㄝˊ)
the sea god
龍馭上賓(ㄌㄨㄥˊ ㄩˋ ㄕㄤˋ ㄅㄧㄣ)
The emperor has passed away.
龍躍鳳鳴(ㄌㄨㄥˊ ㄩㄝˋ ㄈㄥˋ ㄇㄧㄥˊ)
(said of the intellect) bright; brilliant

六畫

【龔】 7326
ㄍㄨㄥ gong gōng
1. reverential 亦作「恭」
2. a Chinese family name

【龕】 7327
ㄎㄢ kan kān
a niche for an idol

龜 部
ㄍㄨㄟ guei guī

【龜】 7328
1. ㄍㄨㄟ guei guī
a tortoise; a turtle
龜貝(ㄍㄨㄟ ㄅㄟˋ)
tortoise shell used as money in ancient times
龜版(ㄍㄨㄟ ㄅㄢˇ)
tortoiseshell
龜頭(ㄍㄨㄟ ㄊㄡˊ)
the glans penis; the glans
龜奴(ㄍㄨㄟ ㄋㄨˊ)
a servant in a brothel
龜鶴(ㄍㄨㄟ ㄏㄜˋ)
very old age
龜甲(ㄍㄨㄟ ㄐㄧㄚˇ)
tortoiseshell
龜甲獸骨文字(ㄍㄨㄟ ㄐㄧㄚˇ ㄕㄡˋ ㄍㄨˇ ㄨㄣˊ ㄗˋ)
the oracle-bone characters
龜鑑(ㄍㄨㄟ ㄐㄧㄢˋ)or 龜鏡(ㄍㄨㄟ ㄐㄧㄥˋ)
divination and retrospection
龜兆(ㄍㄨㄟ ㄓㄠˋ)
① marks on seared tortoise shell used for divination in ancient times ② omens
龜坼(ㄍㄨㄟ ㄔㄜˋ)
cracks in the soil due to drought
龜筮(ㄍㄨㄟ ㄕˋ)
divination
龜玉(ㄍㄨㄟ ㄩˋ)
a treasure

【龜】 7328
2. ㄐㄩㄣ jiun jūn
chapped; cracked
龜裂(ㄐㄩㄣ ㄌㄧㄝˋ)
chapped; cracked: 花瓶掉落而龜裂。A vase fell and cracked.

【龜】 7328
3. ㄑㄧㄡ chiou qiū
used in 龜茲
龜茲(ㄑㄧㄡ ㄘˊ)
a country in Central Asia during the Han Dynasty

龠 部
ㄩㄝˋ yueh yuè

【龠】 7329
ㄩㄝˋ yueh yuè
1. a kind of flute
2. a kind of measuring vessel

五畫

【龢】 7330
(和) ㄏㄜˊ her hé
harmonious; peaceful

九畫

【龥】 7331
(籲) ㄩˋ yuh yù
to call for; to make an appeal for

〔龜·龠部〕

國語注音符號索引

編　法：本索引係照單字讀音，按國語注音符號順序編列，其讀音相同者，再按部首順序。單字後註明單字編號。

用　法：遇有僅知讀音不悉字形之單字，可按國語注音符號，查出索引中單字，再根據單字編號，查出書內單字及這一單字爲首所組成的詞語。

MANDARIN PHONETIC SYMBOL INDEX

In this index the characters are arranged according to their respective MPS transcriptions. Characters with the same pronunciation are arranged according to their respective radicals. The figure to the right of each character is its identification number under which the character can be found in the body of the dictionary.

If the dictionary user knows the pronunciation of the character he is looking for but is unfamiliar with its strokes, he can find it in the index according to its MPS transcription. Using the identification number as a guide, he can locate in the dictionary the character and the entries beneath it.

ㄅ

	彼	1461
	比	2731
	秕	3986
	筆	4109
	鄙	6224
ㄅㄧˋ	俾	187
	嗶	723
	壁	882
	婢	1023
	嬖	1059
	幣	1343
	庇	1361
	弊	1414
	弼	1435
	必	1497
	愎	1639
	愊	1642
	拂	1834
	敝	2133
	斃	2148
	比	2731
	毖	2732
	泌	2829
	湢	2994
	狴	3355
	璧	3503
	畀	3559
	畢	3573
	痺	3636
	皕	3704
	睥	3782
	碧	3887
	祕	3936
	秘	3936
	(祕)	
	箅	4146
	篦	4173
	篳	4181
	臂	4740
	苾	4884
	萆	4989
	蓖	5061
	蓽	5079
	蔽	5089
	薜	5131
	裨	5422
	襞	5459
	觱	5509
	詖	5556
	費	5768
	賁	5773
	跛	5858
	蹕	5916
	躄	5941
	躃	5947
	辟	6039
	逼	6116
	避	6156
	邲	6183
	鄙	6224
	鉍	6361
	閉	6532
	閟	6541
	陛	6605
	髀	7000
	鷩	7194
ㄅㄧㄝ	憋	1711
	鼈	7281
	鱉	7281
	(鼈)	
ㄅㄧㄝˊ	別	372
	蹩	5929
	蹩	5939
ㄅㄧㄝˇ	癟	3675
	癟	3675
	(癟)	
ㄅㄧㄝˋ	彆	1438
ㄅㄧㄠ	彪	1454
	摽	2018
	杓	2345
	標	2581
	熛	3248
	猋	3370
	臕	4751
	膘	4751
	(臕)	
	鏢	6489
	鑣	6518
	飆	6846
	颷	6846
	(飆)	
	麃	7219
ㄅㄧㄠˇ	婊	1028
	表	5375
	裱	5424
	錶	6433
ㄅㄧㄠˋ	鰾	7102
ㄅㄧㄢ	砭	3851
	箯	4156
	籩	4229
	編	4389
	蝙	5268
	邊	6166
	鞭	6750
	鯿	7087
ㄅㄧㄢˇ	匾	471
	扁	1783
	稨	4017
	窆	4049
	萹	5025
	蝙	5268
	褊	5433
	貶	5764
ㄅㄧㄢˋ	便	164
	卞	489
	弁	1410
	徧	1483
	忭	1512
	抃	1810
	昪	2236
	汴	2788
	緶	4398
	辮	4455
	變	5695
	辨	6043
	辦	6045
	辯	6046
	遍	6123
ㄅㄧㄣ	儐	277
	彬	1453
	攽	2120
	斌	2151
	檳	2626
	濱	3131
	瀕	3146
	繽	4458
	豳	5733
	賓	5785
	賔	5785
	(賓)	
	邠	6173
ㄅㄧㄣˋ	儐	277
	擯	2077
	殯	2713
	臏	4748
	髕	7007
	鬢	7034
ㄅㄧㄥ	兵	316
	冰	335
	幷	1351
ㄅㄧㄥˇ	丙	16
	屏	1198
	昺	2237
	昞	2237
	(昺)	
	柄	2393
	炳	3187
	秉	3982
	稟	4007
	邴	6186
	餅	6871
	餠	6880
ㄅㄧㄥˋ	並	19
	併	189
	倂	189
	(併)	
	幷	1351
	摒	2008
	柄	2393
	病	3607
	竝	4076
ㄅㄨ	晡	2249
	逋	6088
	餔	6876
ㄅㄨˊ	不	8
	醭	6290
ㄅㄨˇ	卜	488
	哺	637
	捕	1892
	補	5415
ㄅㄨˋ	不	8
	佈	125
	埠	841
	布	1307
	怖	1525
	步	2684
	篰	4194
	簿	4214
	部	6206

ㄆ

注音	單字	字號
ㄆㄚ	葩	5011
	趴	5845
ㄆㄚˊ	扒	1793
	爬	3285
	琶	3458
	耙	4581
ㄆㄚˋ	帕	1312
	怕	1526
•ㄆㄚ	杷	2363
	琶	3458
ㄆㄛ	坡	820
	波	2839
	潑	3072
	陂	6596
	頗	6796
ㄆㄛˊ	婆	1015
	皤	3708
	繁	4428
	鄱	6234
ㄆㄛˇ	叵	544
	頗	6796
ㄆㄛˋ	拍	1844
	朴	2337
	泊	2827
	珀	3427
	破	3854
	粕	4238
	迫	6068
	廹	6068
	(迫)	
	醱	6292
	魄	7051
ㄆㄞ	拍	1844
ㄆㄞˊ	俳	183
	徘	1477
	排	1921
	牌	3303
	簰	4196
ㄆㄞˋ	派	2874
	湃	2971
	鎃	6452
ㄆㄟ	披	1828
	肧	4651
	醅	6270
ㄆㄟˊ	培	839
	裴	5426
	賠	5791

	邳	6184		磐	3903		硼	3872		陂	6596		片	3301		瓶	3526
	陪	6613		胖	4648	ㄆㄥˊ	彭	1455		陴	6618		篇	4162		甁	3526
ㄆㄟˋ	佩	141		般	4802		朋	2316		鼙	7290		翩	4554		(瓶)	
	帔	1310		蟠	5320		棚	2486	ㄆㄧˇ	仳	98		萹	5025		秤	3992
	旆	2181		鞶	6759		澎	3090		劈	411	ㄆㄧㄢˊ	便	164		缾	4479
	沛	2807	ㄆㄢˋ	判	371		硼	3872		匹	470		楩	2537		苹	4881
	珮	3437		叛	524		篷	4184		否	566		胼	4689		萍	4982
	轡	6034		拌	1841		膨	4731		庀	1359		胼	4689		蘋	5164
	配	6249		拚	1853		芃	4832		疋	3587		(胼)			評	5555
	霈	6696		泮	2843		蓬	5063		痞	3630		諞	5624		軿	6001
ㄆㄠ	抛	1840		畔	3564		鵬	7155		癖	3672		蹁	5902		馮	6923
	拋	1840		盼	3745	ㄆㄥˇ	捧	1898		苤	4899		駢	6944	ㄆㄧㄥˋ	聘	4601
	(抛)			襻	5472	ㄆㄥˋ	碰	3879	ㄆㄧˋ	僻	268		騈	6952	ㄆㄨ	仆	77
	泡	2841	ㄆㄣ	噴	761		掽	3879		屁	1187	ㄆㄧㄢˇ	諞	5624		扑	1792
	脬	4681		歕	2675		(碰)			擗	2064	ㄆㄧㄢˋ	徧	1483		撲	2046
ㄆㄠˊ	刨	373	ㄆㄣˊ	湓	2980	ㄆㄧ	丕	13		澼	3109		片	3301		痡	3629
	匏	454		盆	3717		劈	411		甓	3534		遍	6123		鋪	6410
	咆	602	ㄆㄤ	乓	27		匹	470		譬	5686		騙	6958	ㄆㄨˊ	僕	256
	庖	1365		滂	3018		批	1808		辟	6039	ㄆㄧㄣ	姘	1018		匍	453
	炮	3185		磅	3898		披	1828		闢	6579		姘	1018		幞	1340
	袍	5392		霶	6714		砒	3848	ㄆㄧㄝ	撇	2034		(姘)			朴	2337
	麃	7219	ㄆㄤˊ	徬	235		紕	4292		瞥	3815		拼	1924		樸	2587
	麅	7221		厖	507		被	5397	ㄆㄧㄝˇ	撇	2034		拼	1924		濮	3128
ㄆㄠˇ	跑	5854		尨	1175		霹	6712		苤	4899		(拼)			璞	3498
ㄆㄠˋ	泡	2841		龐	1403	ㄆㄧˊ	啤	658	ㄆㄧㄠ	漂	3041	ㄆㄧㄣˊ	嬪	1068		脯	4680
	炮	3185		彷	1459		埤	842		飄	6845		蘋	5164		莆	4945
	疱	3612		徬	1487		枇	2362	ㄆㄧㄠˊ	嫖	1048		貧	5753		菩	4986
	皰	3710		旁	2178		毗	2733		瓢	3519		頻	6809		葡	5006
	砲	3859		㫄	2178		琵	3457	ㄆㄧㄠˇ	摽	2018		顰	6833		蒱	5037
	礮	3920		(旁)			疲	3599		殍	2701	ㄆㄧㄣˇ	品	621		蒲	5038
ㄆㄡˊ	抔	1817		膀	4718		皮	3709		漂	3041	ㄆㄧㄣˋ	牝	3311		蹼	5937
	掊	1919		螃	5291		紕	4292		瞟	3803		聘	4601		酺	6267
	裒	5411		逄	6083		罷	4505		縹	4424	ㄆㄧㄥ	乒	34		醭	6290
ㄆㄡˇ	剖	394		雱	6686		羆	4508		莩	4942		娉	1003		釙	6317
	掊	1919	ㄆㄤˋ	胖	4648		脾	4699	ㄆㄧㄠˋ	剽	407	ㄆㄧㄥˊ	坪	828	ㄆㄨˇ	圃	795
	瓿	3525	ㄆㄥ	怦	1529		蚍	5203		漂	3041		屏	1198		埔	838
ㄆㄢ	攀	2093		抨	1827		裨	5422		票	3948		平	1349		普	2255
	潘	3074		澎	3090		貔	5744		驃	6973		憑	1710		浦	2885
	番	3575		烹	3202		郫	6207	ㄆㄧㄢ	偏	221		枰	2419		溥	3006
ㄆㄢˊ	槃	2552		砰	3852		鈹	6362		扁	1783		洴	2919		譜	5681
	盤	3732															

注音	單字	字號
	棻	2490
	氛	2751
	紛	4299
	芬	4848
	棻	4960
	雰	6685
ㄈㄣˊ	墳	881
	枌	2369
	棼	2492
	汾	2789
	焚	3211
	羒	4521
	蕡	5098
	豶	5773
ㄈㄣˇ	粉	4235
ㄈㄣˋ	分	359
	份	359
	(分)	
	噴	761
	奮	948
	忿	1520
	憤	1719
	糞	4260
ㄈㄤ	坊	811
	妨	969
	方	2174
	枋	2370
	肪	4635
	芳	4855
ㄈㄤˊ	妨	969
	房	1781
	肪	4635
	防	6590
	魴	7064
ㄈㄤˇ	仿	102
	倣	102
	(仿)	
	彷	1459
	昉	2214
	紡	4300
	舫	4803
	訪	5539
	髣	7011
ㄈㄤˋ	放	2119
ㄈㄥ	丰	22
	封	1159
	峯	1230
	楓	2515
	灃	3161
	烽	3201
	瘋	3643
	葑	5002
	蜂	5236
	蠭	5350
	豐	5719
	酆	6242
	鋒	6404
	風	6837
ㄈㄥˊ	縫	4416
	逢	6103
	馮	6923
ㄈㄥˇ	唪	668
ㄈㄥˋ	俸	185
	奉	931
	縫	4416
	諷	5636
	風	6837
	鳳	7119
ㄈㄨ	夫	919
	孵	1093
	敷	2142
	枹	2389
	柎	2392
	膚	4724
	趺	5848
	跗	5856
	鄜	6227
	鈇	6332
	麩	7235
ㄈㄨˊ	伏	109
	俘	174
	匐	455
	夫	919
	孚	1080
	帗	1314
	幅	1328
	弗	1421
	彿	1465
	怫	1533
	扶	1804
	拂	1834
	服	2317
	枹	2389
	桴	2451
	氟	2752
	洑	2852
	浮	2890
	涪	2910
	祓	3934
	福	3956
	符	4101
	箙	4151
	紱	4310
	紼	4313
	縛	4408
	罘	4493
	艴	4827
	芙	4839
	芾	4861
	苻	4883
	茀	4895
	茯	4907
	莩	4942
	菔	4962
	蚨	5208
	蜉	5244
	蝠	5275
	袱	5400
	輻	6010
	郛	6196
	韍	6767
	髴	7016
	鳧	7116
	鵩	7156
	黻	7273
ㄈㄨˇ	俯	181
	府	1368
	拊	1839
	撫	2042
	斧	2166
	父	3290
	甫	3547
	簠	4203
	脯	4680
	腐	4695
	腑	4696
	莆	4945
	輔	5991
	釜	6314
	頫	6799
	黼	7274
ㄈㄨˋ	仆	77
	付	86
	傅	234
	副	399
	咐	606
	婦	1024
	富	1136
	復	1485
	服	2317
	父	3290
	祔	3935
	腹	4711
	蝜	5281
	蝮	5283
	複	5432
	覆	5476
	訃	5518
	負	5748
	賦	5796
	賻	5802
	赴	5829
	輹	6013
	阜	6582
	附	6597
	馥	6919
	駙	6936
	鮒	7067
	鰒	7089

ㄉ

注音	單字	字號
ㄉㄚ	搭	1988
	答	4119
	耷	4592
	褡	5447
ㄉㄚˊ	妲	970
	怛	1528
	打	1794
	瘩	3656
	答	4119
	繨	4450
	達	6130
	靼	6744
	韃	6761
ㄉㄚˇ	打	1794
ㄉㄚˋ	大	916
˙ㄉㄚ	瘩	3656
	繨	4450
ㄉㄜˊ	得	1476
	德	1493
˙ㄉㄜ	得	1476
	的	3696
	襶	5471
ㄉㄞ	呆	584
	待	1466
	獃	3383
ㄉㄞˇ	歹	2691
	逮	6107
ㄉㄞˋ	代	91
	大	916
	岱	1220
	帶	1325
	待	1466
	怠	1545
	戴	1775
	殆	2695
	玳	3420
	袋	5391
	襶	5471
	貸	5766
	迨	6066
	逮	6107
	靆	6719
	黛	7255
ㄉㄟˇ	得	1476
ㄉㄠ	刀	356
	叨	528
	忉	1498
	舠	4798
ㄉㄠˇ	倒	199
	導	1167
	島	1232
	搗	1982
	擣	2075
	禱	3972
ㄉㄠˋ	倒	199
	到	377
	導	1167
	幬	1344
	悼	1602
	燾	3274
	盜	3727
	稻	4022
	纛	4473
	翿	4566
	菿	4978
	蹈	5907
	道	6129
ㄉㄡ	兜	304

	笣	4182
	都	6214
ㄉㄡˇ	抖	1821
	斗	2156
	蚪	5201
	陡	6608
ㄉㄡˋ	痘	3623
	竇	4070
	脰	4682
	荳	4954
	讀	5692
	豆	5710
	逗	6095
	餖	6877
	鬥	7036
	鬦	7037
	鬪	7041
	鬭	7042
ㄉㄢ	丹	25
	儋	275
	單	701
	擔	2059
	担	2059
	(擔)	
	殫	2710
	眈	3749
	簞	4198
	耽	4593
	聃	4595
	耼	4595
	(聃)	
	躭	5962
	鄲	6235
	酖	6251
ㄉㄢˇ	撢	2050
	撣	2050
	(撢)	
	疸	3601
	膽	4736
	胆	4736
	(膽)	
	黵	7269
ㄉㄢˋ	但	123
	啖	661
	噉	661
	(啖)	
	彈	1437
	憚	1701
	憺	1722
	擔	2059
	旦	2199
	氮	2759
	淡	2931
	澹	3110
	癉	3670
	石	3841
	萏	4985
	蛋	5220
	蜑	5247
	誕	5587
	鉭	6364
ㄉㄤ	噹	760
	璫	3506
	當	3582
	襠	5460
	鐺	6507
ㄉㄤˇ	擋	2061
	攩	2107
	檔	2610
	當	3582
	讜	5705
	黨	7262
ㄉㄤˋ	宕	1109
	擋	2061
	檔	2610
	當	3582
	盪	3737
	蕩	5104
ㄉㄥ	燈	3250
	登	3689
	簦	4202
	豋	5714
	鐙	6496
ㄉㄥˇ	戥	1768
	等	4113
ㄉㄥˋ	凳	350
	櫈	350
	(凳)	
	嶝	1271
	澄	3088
	凳	3691
	櫈	3691
	(凳)	
	瞪	3810
	磴	3909
	蹬	5930
	鄧	6230
	鐙	6496
ㄉㄧ	低	127
	提	1951
	氐	2747
	滴	3033
	羝	4522
	隄	6626
	堤	6626
	(隄)	
ㄉㄧˊ	嫡	1051
	敵	2141
	滌	3030
	狄	3344
	的	3696
	笛	4096
	糴	4272
	翟	4547
	荻	4930
	覿	5498
	踧	5891
	蹢	5922
	迪	6067
	廸	6067
	(迪)	
	適	6144
	鏑	6480
ㄉㄧˇ	底	1364
	抵	1829
	柢	2406
	氐	2747
	牴	3320
	砥	3849
	觝	5504
	詆	5548
	邸	6187
ㄉㄧˋ	地	810
	娣	1012
	帝	1320
	弟	1424
	棣	2487
	的	3696
	睇	3774
	禘	3962
	第	4102
	締	4385
	蔕	5028
	蒂	5070
	螮	5304
	蝃	5304
	(螮)	
	諦	5628
	遞	6137
ㄉㄧㄝ	爹	3292
ㄉㄧㄝˊ	喋	685
	惵	1628
	昳	2234
	牒	3304
	瓞	3517
	疊	3586
	叠	3586
	(疊)	
	眣	3757
	碟	3892
	絰	4336
	耋	4574
	蜨	5265
	蝶	5286
	褶	5451
	諜	5623
	跌	5852
	蹀	5901
	迭	6069
	鰈	7086
ㄉㄧㄠ	凋	341
	刁	357
	叼	529
	彫	1451
	碉	3876
	貂	5738
	雕	6670
	鯛	7081
	鵰	7158
ㄉㄧㄠˋ	弔	1420
	吊	1420
	(弔)	
	掉	1920
	調	5605
	釣	6320
	銚	6376
ㄉㄧㄡ	丟	18
	銩	6388
ㄉㄧㄢ	巔	1286
	掂	1910
	攧	2105
	滇	3021
	癲	3686
	顛	6822
ㄉㄧㄢˇ	典	319
	碘	3881
	點	7254
ㄉㄧㄢˋ	佃	122
	墊	873
	奠	942
	店	1366
	惦	1616
	殿	2721
	淀	2914
	澱	3107
	玷	3419
	甸	3556
	痁	3613
	簟	4199
	鈿	6342
	電	6690
	靛	6726
ㄉㄧㄥ	丁	2
	仃	75
	叮	538
	玎	3410
	町	3557
	疔	3591
	盯	3740
	釘	6313
	靪	6736
ㄉㄧㄥˇ	酊	6246
	頂	6781
	鼎	7283
ㄉㄧㄥˋ	定	1114
	碇	3878
	訂	5516
	釘	6313
	錠	6424
	飣	6851
ㄉㄨ	督	3787
	都	6214
	闍	6566
ㄉㄨˊ	櫝	2632
	毒	2729
	瀆	3136
	牘	3307
	犢	3335
	獨	3391
	碡	3883

	纛	4473
	讀	5692
	頓	6793
	髑	7006
	黷	7271
ㄉㄨˇ	堵	854
	睹	3790
	篤	4170
	肚	4626
	覩	5489
	賭	5799
ㄉㄨˋ	妒	961
	妬	961
	(妒)	
	度	1369
	斁	2146
	杜	2349
	渡	2960
	肚	4626
	蠹	5353
	蠧	5353
	(蠹)	
	鍍	6438
ㄉㄨㄛ	哆	624
	多	909
ㄉㄨㄛˊ	多	909
	奪	945
	掇	1914
	敠	2135
	裰	5421
	鐸	6506
ㄉㄨㄛˇ	朶	2339
	朵	2339
	(朶)	
	躱	5963
ㄉㄨㄛˋ	剁	380
	咄	601
	墮	880
	度	1369
	惰	1625

	柮	2415
	柁	2418
	舵	4808
	跺	5873
	踱	5898
	馱	6924
ㄉㄨㄟ	堆	847
ㄉㄨㄟˋ	兌	298
	對	1166
	憝	1715
	懟	1737
	敦	2138
	碓	3877
	隊	6632
ㄉㄨㄢ	端	4083
	耑	4578
ㄉㄨㄢˇ	短	3836
ㄉㄨㄢˋ	斷	2173
	段	2716
	緞	4382
	鍛	6441
	煅	6441
	(鍛)	
ㄉㄨㄣ	墩	879
	惇	1607
	敦	2138
	燉	3253
	蹲	5928
ㄉㄨㄣˇ	盹	3751
	躉	5945
ㄉㄨㄣˋ	噸	757
	沌	2797
	炖	3179
	燉	3253
	盾	3752
	遁	6117
	遯	6146
	鈍	6334
	頓	6793
ㄉㄨㄥ	冬	334

	咚	596
	東	2360
	蝀	5264
	鼕	7288
ㄉㄨㄥˇ	懂	1723
	董	5008
ㄉㄨㄥˋ	凍	343
	動	433
	峒	1226
	恫	1561
	棟	2485
	洞	2859
	胴	4663
	蝀	5264

ㄊ

注音	單字	字號
ㄊㄚ	他	84
	塌	857
	她	953
	它	1099
	牠	3314
	禢	5448
	趿	5850
	鉈	6359
	靸	6741
ㄊㄚˇ	塔	860
ㄊㄚˋ	嗒	710
	拓	1847
	搨	1992
	撻	2051
	榻	2549
	沓	2806
	漯	3056
	獺	3401
	踏	5883
	蹋	5911
	躂	5946
	達	6130
	遝	6136

	溻	6140
	鍚	6469
	闒	6569
	闥	6581
	鞳	6757
ㄊㄜ	忒	1501
	牠	3314
ㄊㄜˋ	忒	1501
	忑	1503
	慝	1685
	特	3321
	鋱	6394
ㄊㄞ	胎	4647
	苔	4866
ㄊㄞˊ	台	540
	擡	2073
	抬	2073
	(擡)	
	枱	2420
	檯	2625
	臺	4771
	苔	4866
	邰	6181
	颱	6839
	駘	6935
ㄊㄞˋ	太	918
	態	1668
	汰	2783
	泰	2849
	鈦	6330
ㄊㄠ	叨	528
	慆	1664
	挑	1868
	掏	1917
	搯	1996
	滔	3024
	濤	3124
	絛	4342
	縧	4435
	謟	5661

	韜	6771
	饕	6910
ㄊㄠˊ	桃	2440
	檮	2622
	洮	2869
	淘	2925
	濤	3124
	燾	3274
	翿	4566
	萄	4976
	逃	6079
	陶	6620
	鼗	7289
ㄊㄠˇ	討	5520
ㄊㄠˋ	套	939
ㄊㄡ	偷	231
ㄊㄡˊ	投	1819
	頭	6803
	骰	6993
ㄊㄡˇ	黈	7245
ㄊㄡˋ	透	6089
˙ㄊㄡ	頭	6803
ㄊㄢ	坍	816
	怹	1548
	探	1930
	攤	2103
	灘	3164
	癱	3687
	貪	5756
ㄊㄢˊ	壇	885
	彈	1437
	曇	2280
	檀	2607
	潭	3081
	澹	3110
	痰	3632
	罈	4484
	罎	4488
	藫	5146
	覃	5475

	談	5608
	譚	5679
	郯	6209
ㄊㄢˇ	坦	822
	忐	1502
	毯	2739
	袒	5393
	黮	7266
ㄊㄢˋ	探	1930
	歎	2668
	嘆	2668
	(歎)	
	炭	3190
	碳	3890
ㄊㄤ	湯	2989
	蹚	5918
	鏜	6485
ㄊㄤˊ	唐	644
	堂	845
	塘	862
	搪	1994
	棠	2488
	糖	4258
	膛	4729
	螗	5290
	螳	5306
	醣	6283
	鏜	6485
	鞺	6760
ㄊㄤˇ	倘	202
	帑	1311
	惝	1615
	淌	2920
	躺	5964
ㄊㄤˋ	燙	3259
	趟	5841
ㄊㄥˊ	滕	3028
	疼	3605
	籐	4220
	縢	4414

	耐	4576
	褦	5443
	鼐	7284
ㄋㄟˇ	那	6174
	餒	6874
ㄋㄟˋ	內	307
	那	6174
ㄋㄠˊ	怓	1539
	撓	2035
	橈	2597
	猱	3375
	譊	5680
	鐃	6494
ㄋㄠˇ	惱	1626
	瑙	3468
	腦	4704
ㄋㄠˋ	淖	2921
	鬧	7038
ㄋㄡˋ	耨	4588
ㄋㄢˊ	南	486
	喃	678
	枏	2367
	楠	2367
	(枏)	
	男	3555
	諵	5621
	難	6680
ㄋㄢˇ	腩	4712
	赧	5823
ㄋㄢˋ	難	6680
ㄋㄣˋ	嫩	1054
ㄋㄤˊ	囊	780
ㄋㄤˇ	攮	2112
	曩	2299
ㄋㄥˊ	能	4666
ㄋㄥˋ	濘	3119
ㄋㄧˊ	倪	212
	呢	587
	妮	971
	尼	1183

	怩	1532
	泥	2842
	猊	3364
	鶃	4758
	蜺	5266
	輗	5994
	霓	6702
	麑	7225
ㄋㄧˇ	你	115
	妳	985
	擬	2076
	旎	2186
	禰	3971
ㄋㄧˋ	匿	472
	惄	1620
	暱	2278
	昵	2278
	(暱)	
	泥	2842
	溺	3013
	睨	3783
	膩	4732
	衵	5381
	逆	6081
ㄋㄧㄝ	捏	1895
	揑	1895
	(捏)	
	捻	1908
ㄋㄧㄝˊ	苶	4879
ㄋㄧㄝˋ	乜	38
	囁	776
	孽	1096
	孼	1096
	(孽)	
	槷	2638
	涅	2895
	湼	2895
	(涅)	
	蘖	4273
	櫱	4273

	(蘖)	
	聶	4611
	臬	4765
	臲	4768
	孽	5161
	孼	5161
	(孽)	
	蘖	5169
	躡	5957
	鎳	6467
	鑷	6523
	闑	6568
	隉	6630
	顳	6836
	齧	7317
	嚙	7317
	(齧)	
	囓	7317
	(齧)	
ㄋㄧㄠˇ	嬝	1065
	嫋	1065
	(嬝)	
	嬲	1067
	蔦	5076
	裊	5406
	鳥	7115
ㄋㄧㄠˋ	尿	1185
	溺	3013
ㄋㄧㄡ	妞	963
ㄋㄧㄡˊ	牛	3310
ㄋㄧㄡˇ	忸	1514
	扭	1802
	狃	3346
	紐	4289
	鈕	6336
ㄋㄧㄡˋ	拗	1849
	衄	5357
	謬	5668
ㄋㄧㄢ	蔫	5083
ㄋㄧㄢˊ	年	1350

	拈	1836
	粘	4239
	鮎	7065
	黏	7249
ㄋㄧㄢˇ	捻	1908
	撚	2037
	攆	2092
	碾	3894
	輦	6000
	輾	6014
ㄋㄧㄢˋ	唸	669
	廿	1409
	念	1518
ㄋㄧㄣˊ	您	1596
ㄋㄧㄤˊ	娘	1007
	孃	1007
	(娘)	
ㄋㄧㄤˋ	釀	6297
ㄋㄧㄥˊ	凝	345
	嚀	765
	寧	1143
	擰	2082
	檸	2620
	獰	3397
	甯	3550
ㄋㄧㄥˇ	擰	2082
ㄋㄧㄥˋ	佞	139
	擰	2082
	濘	3119
	甯	3550
ㄋㄨˊ	奴	950
	孥	1086
	笯	4104
	駑	6931
ㄋㄨˇ	努	422
	弩	1428
	砮	3857
ㄋㄨˋ	怒	1543
ㄋㄨㄛˊ	娜	1009
	挪	1877

	挼	1881
ㄋㄨㄛˇ	娜	1009
ㄋㄨㄛˋ	喏	686
	懦	1734
	搦	1990
	糯	4269
	粫	4269
	(糯)	
	穤	4269
	(糯)	
	諾	5639
ㄋㄨㄢˇ	暖	2270
	煖	3220
ㄋㄨㄥˊ	儂	270
	濃	3115
	穠	4034
	膿	4735
	農	6049
	醲	6294
	齈	7302
ㄋㄨㄥˋ	弄	1411
ㄋㄩˇ	女	949
	釹	6322
ㄋㄩˋ	忸	1514
	恧	1574
	衄	5357
ㄋㄩㄝˋ	瘧	3648
	虐	5181
	謔	5647

ㄌ

注音	單字	字號
ㄌㄚ	喇	681
	拉	1838
ㄌㄚˊ	剌	391
	拉	1838
	旯	2205
ㄌㄚˇ	喇	681
ㄌㄚˋ	剌	391
	瘌	3646

	腊	4700
	臘	4750
	落	5000
	蠟	5343
	辣	6041
	鑞	6517
	鬎	7026
•ㄌㄚ	啦	664
•ㄌㄛ	咯	614
ㄌㄜ	褦	5443
ㄌㄜˋ	仂	74
	勒	432
	垃	827
	捋	1887
	樂	2571
	泐	2826
	肋	4621
•ㄌㄜ	了	46
ㄌㄞˊ	來	149
	崍	1248
	徠	1481
	淶	2944
	萊	4979
	郲	6212
	錸	6416
ㄌㄞˋ	瀨	3151
	癩	3680
	睞	3778
	籟	4223
	賚	5787
	賴	5800
ㄌㄟ	勒	432
ㄌㄟˊ	擂	2054
	累	4307
	縲	4421
	纍	4466
	罍	4487
	羸	4534
	蘲	5179
	鐳	6508

	雷	6689	ㄌㄡˊ	僂	250	ㄌㄤˊ	廊	1385		罹	4506		吏	560	ㄌㄧㄝˋ	冽	338
ㄌㄟˇ	儡	283		嘍	729		榔	2539		藜	5143		唳	650		列	368
	壘	891		婁	1019		浪	2887		蘺	5175		慄	1660		劣	420
	磊	3901		摟	2007		狼	3356		蜊	5240		戾	1779		捩	1899
	累	4307		樓	2580		琅	3442		蠡	5344		曆	2282		洌	2853
	耒	4579		蔞	5082		瑯	3479		褵	5450		栗	2426		烈	3194
	蕾	5114		螻	5308		稂	4004		貍	5742		櫟	2629		獵	3398
	藟	5145		髏	7002		莨	4953		醨	6286		櫪	2634		裂	5403
	誄	5577	ㄌㄡˇ	摟	2007		蜋	5246		釐	6309		歷	2689		趔	5837
ㄌㄟˋ	擂	2054		簍	4193		螂	5300		離	6679		沴	2813		躐	5951
	淚	2926	ㄌㄡˋ	漏	3043		踉	5878		驪	6989		涖	2904		鬣	7035
	泪	2926		瘻	3662		郎	6199		鸝	7208		溧	3007		鴷	7143
	(淚)			鏤	6490		鋃	6400		黎	7248		瀝	3148	ㄌㄧㄠ	撩	2044
	累	4307		陋	6599	ㄌㄤˇ	朗	2322		黧	7261		痢	3625	ㄌㄧㄠˊ	僚	258
	纇	4467		露	6711		烺	3205	ㄌㄧˇ	俚	175		癘	3673		嘹	743
	肋	4621	˙ㄌㄡ	嘍	729		閬	6549		哩	633		礫	3916		寥	1147
	酹	6266	ㄌㄢˊ	婪	1025	ㄌㄤˋ	浪	2887		娌	1004		礪	3917		寮	1153
	類	6823		嵐	1258		閬	6549		悝	1591		立	4073		竂	1172
	類	6827		攔	2095	ㄌㄥˊ	楞	2520		李	2340		笠	4095		憀	1684
ㄌㄠ	撈	2028		斕	2155		稜	4010		浬	2886		粒	4237		憭	1707
ㄌㄠˊ	勞	438		欄	2641		薐	5121		澧	3103		糲	4271		撩	2044
	嘮	736		瀾	3158	ㄌㄥˇ	冷	337		理	3441		苙	4892		漻	3069
	撈	2028		籃	4217	ㄌㄥˋ	愣	1634		禮	3970		荔	4903		潦	3079
	牢	3315		藍	5137		楞	2520		蠡	5344		莅	4929		獠	3388
	癆	3668		蘭	5172	ㄌㄧ	哩	633		裏	5410		莉	4946		療	3665
	醪	6287		襤	5464	ㄌㄧˊ	嫠	1047		裡	5410		蒞	5060		繚	4439
ㄌㄠˇ	佬	158		襴	5470		棃	2475		(裏)			蠣	5346		聊	4598
	姥	991		讕	5698		梨	2475		豊	5715		詈	5549		遼	6155
	潦	3079		闌	6564		(棃)			邐	6168		轢	6033		鐐	6495
	老	4568	ㄌㄢˇ	懶	1740		氂	2742		醴	6293		轣	6036		鷯	7193
	銠	6383		攬	2111		漓	3044		里	6305		酈	6243	ㄌㄧㄠˇ	了	46
ㄌㄠˋ	勞	438		擥	2111		漦	3066		鋰	6396		隸	6653		憭	1707
	憦	1708		(攬)			犂	3326		鯉	7076		靂	6717		燎	3252
	潦	3079		欖	2649		犁	3326	ㄌㄧˋ	例	151		鬁	7021		瞭	3811
	澇	3094		纜	4475		(犂)			俐	171		鬲	7046		蓼	5066
	烙	3200		覽	5497		犛	3334		儷	286		麗	7228		蟟	5326
	絡	4331	ㄌㄢˋ	濫	3126		狸	3359		利	374	˙ㄌㄧ	裏	5410		釕	6318
	落	5000		瀾	3158		璃	3490		力	417	ㄌㄧㄚˇ	倆	190	ㄌㄧㄠˋ	廖	1388
	酪	6258		爛	3281		籬	4230		勵	445	ㄌㄧㄝˊ	咧	607		撂	2021
ㄌㄡ	摟	2007		纜	4475		縭	4417		厲	513	ㄌㄧㄝˇ	咧	607		料	2157

注音	單字	字號
ㄌㄨㄢˊ	巒	1285
	欒	2648
	灤	3168
	臠	4756
	鑾	6526
	鸞	7209
ㄌㄨㄢˇ	卵	498
ㄌㄨㄢˋ	亂	45
ㄌㄨㄣ	掄	1915
ㄌㄨㄣˊ	倫	213
	圇	798
	崙	1242
	掄	1915
	淪	2936
	綸	4365
	論	5615
	輪	6003
ㄌㄨㄣˋ	論	5615
ㄌㄨㄥˊ	嚨	771
	攏	2094
	曨	2298
	朧	2329
	櫳	2637
	槞	2637
	(櫳)	
	瀧	3152
	瓏	3513
	癃	3666
	矓	3822
	礱	3921
	窿	4067
	籠	4224
	聾	4613
	蘢	5166
	隆	6628
	龍	7325
ㄌㄨㄥˇ	壟	892
	攏	2094
	籠	4224
	隴	6652
ㄌㄨㄥˋ	弄	1411
	衖	5365
ㄌㄩˊ	婁	1019
	櫚	2628
	瘻	3662
	閭	6550
	驢	6985
ㄌㄩˇ	侶	161
	呂	583
	婁	1019
	屢	1202
	履	1205
	捋	1887
	旅	2183
	梠	2469
	縷	4423
	膂	4719
	褸	5452
	鋁	6399
ㄌㄩˋ	律	1471
	慮	1695
	氯	2758
	濾	3137
	率	3407
	綠	4354
	菉	4990
ㄌㄩㄝˋ	掠	1927
	略	3572
	畧	3572
	(略)	
ㄌㄩㄢˊ	孿	1097
	攣	2106
ㄌㄩㄢˇ	孌	1072

ㄍ

注音	單字	字號
ㄍㄚ	咖	605
	旮	2204
ㄍㄚˊ	軋	5967
	釓	6312
	[illegible]	6415
ㄍㄚˋ	尬	1176
ㄍㄜ	割	402
	咯	614
	哥	630
	戈	1751
	擱	2079
	歌	2667
	牁	3298
	疙	3592
	紇	4284
	肐	4629
	胳	4674
	菏	4992
	鴿	7137
ㄍㄜˊ	咯	614
	嗝	715
	格	2433
	槅	2564
	膈	4720
	葛	5005
	蛤	5225
	轕	6027
	郃	6193
	鎘	6472
	閣	6542
	閤	6544
	隔	6634
	革	6735
	骼	6998
	鬲	7046
ㄍㄜˇ	哿	4105
	舸	4811
	葛	5005
	蓋	5049
ㄍㄜˋ	個	192
	各	550
	硌	3861
	箇	4152
	虼	5197
	鉻	6389
ㄍㄞ	垓	830
	荄	4916
	該	5573
	賅	5778
	陔	6603
ㄍㄞˇ	改	2117
ㄍㄞˋ	丐	10
	概	2568
	槩	2568
	(概)	
	漑	3045
	葢	5029
	蓋	5049
	盖	5049
	(蓋)	
	鈣	6338
ㄍㄟˇ	給	4333
ㄍㄠ	槹	2543
	皋	3700
	臯	3700
	(皋)	
	睪	3788
	睾	3788
	(睪)	
	篙	4171
	糕	4257
	羔	4518
	膏	4721
	臯	4767
	餻	6897
	高	7008
ㄍㄠˇ	搞	2003
	攪	2108
	杲	2358
	槁	2554
	槀	2554
	(槁)	
	稿	4019
	稾	4019
	(稿)	
	縞	4411
	鎬	6464
ㄍㄠˋ	告	580
	膏	4721
	誥	5595
	郜	6197
	鋯	6397
ㄍㄡ	勾	449
	句	531
	枸	2388
	溝	3002
	篝	4167
	緱	4394
	鈎	6339
	鉤	6354
	韝	6756
ㄍㄡˇ	枸	2388
	狗	3348
	耇	4573
	耉	4573
	(耇)	
	苟	4898
ㄍㄡˋ	冓	327
	勾	449
	垢	831
	夠	912
	够	912
	(夠)	
	姤	990
	媾	1044
	彀	1436
	搆	1976
	構	2555
	覯	5492
	詬	5568
	購	5803
	逅	6080
	遘	6133
	雊	6665
ㄍㄢ	乾	44
	(乾)	
	尷	1178
	干	1348
	杆	2353
	柑	2398
	泔	2830
	玕	3411
	甘	3536
	疳	3600
	竿	4088
	肝	4628
ㄍㄢˇ	感	1652
	擀	2065
	敢	2136
	桿	2474
	橄	2591
	澉	3097
	稈	4003
	簳	4215
	趕	5839
ㄍㄢˋ	幹	1353
	旰	2206
	榦	2541
	淦	2933
	灨	3169
	紺	4317
	贛	5820
	骭	6991
ㄍㄣ	根	2431
	跟	5862
ㄍㄣˇ	艮	4823
ㄍㄣˋ	亙	56
	艮	4823
	茛	4921
ㄍㄤ	剛	396
	岡	1216
	崗	1241
	杠	2352
	綱	4360

	繮	4447
	缸	4477
	罡	4494
	肛	4627
	鋼	6414
ㄍㄤˇ	岡	1216
	崗	1241
	港	2967
ㄍㄤˋ	槓	2560
	虹	5195
ㄍㄥ	庚	1367
	更	2304
	浭	2888
	秔	3988
	稉	3988
	(秔)	
	粳	4248
	羹	4533
	耕	4582
	賡	5792
	鶊	7165
ㄍㄥˇ	哽	639
	埂	836
	梗	2462
	綆	4348
	耿	4594
	骾	6999
	鯁	7075
ㄍㄥˋ	亙	56
	更	2304
ㄍㄨ	估	114
	呱	591
	咕	594
	姑	981
	孤	1087
	沽	2818
	箍	4141
	苽	4900
	菇	4967
	菰	4968

	蛄	5216
	觚	5503
	軲	5982
	轂	6016
	辜	6038
	酤	6255
	鈷	6358
	骨	6990
	鴣	7132
ㄍㄨˊ	骨	6990
ㄍㄨˇ	古	530
	嘏	730
	榖	2542
	榾	2563
	汩	2781
	牯	3318
	盬	3738
	瞽	3818
	穀	4018
	罟	4495
	羖	4519
	股	4631
	臌	4745
	蓇	5058
	蠱	5348
	詁	5547
	谷	5706
	賈	5779
	轂	6016
	鈷	6358
	骨	6990
	鵠	7153
	鶻	7178
	鼓	7287
ㄍㄨˋ	估	114
	僱	265
	固	793
	故	2122
	梏	2460
	痼	3637

	錮	6430
	雇	6662
	顧	6826
ㄍㄨㄚ	刮	375
	括	1860
	栝	2424
	瓜	3516
	筈	4120
	聒	4599
	蝸	5287
	适	6078
	颳	6840
	鴰	7144
ㄍㄨㄚˇ	寡	1144
ㄍㄨㄚˋ	卦	493
	掛	1928
	挂	1928
	(掛)	
	絓	4327
	罣	4497
	褂	5431
	詿	5582
ㄍㄨㄛ	渦	2965
	蟈	5314
	過	6124
	郭	6208
	鍋	6437
ㄍㄨㄛˊ	國	797
	幗	1336
	摑	2005
	虢	5190
	馘	6917
	聝	6917
	(馘)	
ㄍㄨㄛˇ	果	2377
	椁	2504
	槨	2504
	(椁)	
	猓	3368
	菓	4995

	蜾	5262
	裹	5427
	餜	6887
ㄍㄨㄛˋ	過	6124
ㄍㄨㄞ	乖	35
ㄍㄨㄞˇ	拐	1842
	枴	2382
ㄍㄨㄞˋ	夬	920
	怪	1535
ㄍㄨㄟ	傀	233
	圭	808
	歸	2690
	潙	3095
	珪	3435
	瑰	3480
	瓌	3514
	皈	3699
	規	5482
	邽	6194
	閨	6546
	鮭	7070
	龜	7328
ㄍㄨㄟˇ	匭	466
	宄	1098
	晷	2261
	癸	3688
	簋	4190
	詭	5569
	軌	5968
	鬼	7048
ㄍㄨㄟˋ	劊	413
	會	2312
	桂	2439
	檜	2612
	櫃	2624
	溎	3027
	瞶	3812
	貴	5763
	跪	5867
	鱖	7106

ㄍㄨㄢ	倌	193
	冠	329
	官	1112
	棺	2498
	瘝	3649
	矜	3827
	綸	4365
	莞	4938
	觀	5499
	關	6574
	鰥	7092
ㄍㄨㄢˇ	琯	3461
	筦	4126
	管	4149
	脘	4675
	舘	4792
	莞	4938
	館	6886
ㄍㄨㄢˋ	冠	329
	慣	1675
	摜	2006
	灌	3162
	盥	3733
	祼	3953
	罐	4490
	觀	5499
	貫	5757
	鸛	7206
ㄍㄨㄣˇ	滾	3036
	滚	3036
	(滾)	
	衮	5388
	袞	5398
	鯀	7073
ㄍㄨㄣˋ	棍	2479
ㄍㄨㄤ	光	296
	洸	2877
	胱	4662
ㄍㄨㄤˇ	廣	1399
	獷	3399

ㄍㄨㄤˋ	桄	2441
	誑	5585
	逛	6098
ㄍㄨㄥ	供	156
	公	312
	功	418
	宮	1122
	工	1293
	弓	1418
	恭	1576
	攻	2118
	紅	4283
	肱	4638
	蚣	5206
	觥	5506
	躬	5961
	龔	7326
ㄍㄨㄥˇ	拱	1861
	栱	2450
	汞	2778
	珙	3429
	鞏	6747
ㄍㄨㄥˋ	供	156
	共	315
	貢	5750

ㄎ

注音	單字	字號
ㄎㄚ	咖	605
ㄎㄚˇ	卡	491
	咳	616
ㄎㄚˋ	喀	675
ㄎㄜ	剋	384
	柯	2408
	棵	2499
	珂	3422
	疴	3602
	痾	3602
	(疴)	
	瞌	3800

ㄏ

	蝦	5280
ㄏㄚˇ	哈	626
ㄏㄜ	呵	593
	喝	693
	訶	5543
ㄏㄜˊ	何	132
	劾	426
	合	547
	和	604
	曷	2305
	核	2428
	河	2816
	涸	2912
	盍	3721
	盒	3724
	禾	3978
	紇	4284
	翮	4557
	荷	4927
	蓋	5049
	褐	5435
	覈	5477
	貉	5740
	鉿	6385
	閡	6543
	閤	6544
	闔	6571
	鞨	6753
	鶡	7169
	齕	7309
	龢	7330
ㄏㄜˋ	和	604
	喝	693
	嚇	766
	奭	947
	荷	4927
	豁	5707
	賀	5771
	赫	5824
	郝	6198
	鶴	7173
	黑	7250
ㄏㄞˊ	孩	1088
	還	6161
	頦	6798
	骸	6997
ㄏㄞˇ	海	2891
	醢	6284
ㄏㄞˋ	亥	63
	咳	616
	害	1124
	氦	2756
	駭	6940
ㄏㄟ	嘿	747
	黑	7250
ㄏㄠ	嚆	764
	蒿	5043
	薅	5112
ㄏㄠˊ	嗥	742
	嚎	762
	壕	889
	毫	2737
	濠	3122
	號	5188
	蠔	5340
	豪	5728
	貉	5740
	鶴	7173
ㄏㄠˇ	好	954
	郝	6198
ㄏㄠˋ	好	954
	昊	2215
	晧	2252
	浩	2883
	涸	2912
	澔	3098
	灝	3165
	皓	3702
	皜	3707
	耗	4584
	號	5188
	鄗	6220
	鎬	6464
	顥	6828
ㄏㄡ	齁	7300
ㄏㄡˊ	侯	160
	喉	683
	猴	3376
	瘊	3833
	篌	4165
	餱	6890
ㄏㄡˇ	吼	577
ㄏㄡˋ	候	203
	厚	508
	后	557
	後	1472
	逅	6080
	鱟	7109
ㄏㄢ	憨	1717
	蚶	5214
	酣	6254
	頇	6785
	鼾	7299
ㄏㄢˊ	函	355
	含	568
	寒	1138
	嵅	1250
	榦	2541
	汗	2772
	涵	2911
	邯	6180
	韓	6768
ㄏㄢˇ	喊	684
	罕	4492
	闞	6576
ㄏㄢˋ	悍	1586
	憾	1721
	扞	1796
	捍	1890
	撼	2052
	旱	2207
	暵	2277
	汗	2772
	漢	3053
	瀚	3147
	翰	4558
	菡	4984
	豻	5737
	銲	6411
	銲	6411
	(銲)	
	頷	6805
	駻	6950
ㄏㄣˊ	痕	3620
ㄏㄣˇ	很	1468
	狠	3352
ㄏㄣˋ	恨	1558
ㄏㄤ	夯	924
ㄏㄤˊ	杭	2356
	桁	2432
	沆	2796
	航	4801
	行	5360
	迒	6061
	頏	6789
ㄏㄤˋ	桁	2432
	沆	2796
ㄏㄥ	亨	65
	哼	638
ㄏㄥˊ	恆	1551
	恒	1551
	(恆)	
	桁	2432
	横	2606
	珩	3433
	蘅	5159
	衡	5372
ㄏㄥˋ	横	2606
ㄏㄨ	乎	32
	呼	598
	忽	1519
	惚	1612
	戲	1774
	欻	2660
	歑	2670
	淴	2953
	滹	3034
	虖	5184
ㄏㄨˊ	囫	790
	壺	901
	弧	1426
	斛	2158
	槲	2572
	湖	2984
	狐	3349
	猢	3371
	瑚	3472
	糊	4252
	縠	4403
	胡	4654
	葫	5012
	蝴	5285
	衚	5369
	觳	5510
	醐	6278
	餬	6891
	鬍	7027
	鵠	7153
	鶘	7166
	鶻	7178
ㄏㄨˇ	唬	667
	滸	3035
	琥	3452
	虎	5180
ㄏㄨˋ	互	53
	怙	1527
	戶	1777
	戽	1780
	扈	1787
	楛	2519
	滬	3029
	瓠	3518
	祜	3939
	笏	4091
	護	5688
ㄏㄨㄚ	嘩	734
	花	4854
	華	4966
ㄏㄨㄚˊ	划	365
	劃	409
	嘩	734
	滑	3023
	猾	3381
	華	4966
	譁	5673
	豁	5707
	驊	6977
ㄏㄨㄚˋ	劃	409
	化	457
	樺	2589
	畫	3578
	華	4966
	話	5572
ㄏㄨㄛ	豁	5707
ㄏㄨㄛˊ	活	2873
ㄏㄨㄛˇ	伙	112
	夥	915
	火	3171
	鈥	6328
ㄏㄨㄛˋ	和	604
	壑	888
	惑	1621
	或	1760
	擭	2080
	濩	3132
	獲	3394
	矱	3840

	砉	3844
	禍	3955
	穫	4036
	藿	5157
	蠖	5342
	豁	5707
	貨	5754
	鑊	6510
	霍	6698
	騞	6962
ㄏㄨㄞˊ	徊	1470
	懷	1739
	槐	2558
	淮	2939
	踝	5884
ㄏㄨㄞˋ	壞	893
ㄏㄨㄟ	徽	1495
	恢	1557
	揮	1963
	撝	2049
	暉	2266
	灰	3172
	翬	4553
	虺	5196
	褘	5437
	詼	5576
	輝	5997
	隳	6651
	麾	7243
ㄏㄨㄟˊ	回	784
	徊	1470
	洄	2850
	茴	4910
	蛔	5222
	迴	6072
	廻	6072
	(迴)	
ㄏㄨㄟˇ	悔	1584
	會	2312
	毀	2722
	燬	3268
	虺	5196
	誨	5597
	賄	5776
ㄏㄨㄟˋ	匯	467
	卉	481
	芔	481
	(卉)	
	喙	690
	彗	1443
	彙	1445
	恚	1569
	惠	1623
	慧	1689
	晦	2251
	會	2312
	槥	2565
	濊	3116
	燴	3270
	穢	4033
	篲	4197
	繢	4443
	繪	4446
	翽	4565
	蕙	5097
	薈	5117
	蟪	5323
	誨	5597
	諱	5632
	賄	5776
	闠	6577
	靧	6733
ㄏㄨㄢ	懽	1747
	歡	2680
	讙	5702
	貛	5746
	獾	5746
	(貛)	
	驩	6988
ㄏㄨㄢˊ	寰	1154
	桓	2446
	環	3504
	繯	4448
	還	6161
	鍰	6445
	鐶	6505
	闤	6580
	鬟	7033
ㄏㄨㄢˇ	浣	2882
	澣	3118
	緩	4390
ㄏㄨㄢˋ	喚	691
	奐	935
	宦	1121
	幻	1355
	患	1594
	換	1958
	擐	2066
	渙	2955
	漶	3063
	煥	3224
	瘓	3644
	豢	5727
	轘	6026
	逭	6113
ㄏㄨㄣ	婚	1022
	惛	1614
	昏	2218
	葷	5018
	閽	6556
ㄏㄨㄣˊ	混	2945
	渾	2975
	琿	3473
	餛	6882
	魂	7050
ㄏㄨㄣˇ	混	2945
ㄏㄨㄣˋ	恩	1670
	慁	1670
	(恩)	
	混	2945
	渾	2975
	溷	3012
	諢	5626
	鯇	7074
ㄏㄨㄤ	慌	1663
	肓	4625
	荒	4920
ㄏㄨㄤˊ	凰	348
	徨	1484
	惶	1630
	湟	2990
	潢	3077
	煌	3217
	璜	3497
	皇	3698
	磺	3911
	篁	4160
	簧	4206
	蝗	5271
	蟥	5318
	遑	6126
	黃	7244
ㄏㄨㄤˇ	幌	1333
	怳	1536
	恍	1555
	晃	2242
	謊	5650
ㄏㄨㄤˋ	晃	2242
ㄏㄨㄥ	哄	623
	烘	3197
	薨	5128
	訇	5519
	轟	6030
	魟	7061
ㄏㄨㄥˊ	宏	1108
	弘	1422
	泓	2831
	洪	2865
	紅	4283
	紘	4293
	翃	4540
	葒	5023
	虹	5195
	訌	5523
	閎	6535
	鴻	7139
	黌	7246
ㄏㄨㄥˇ	哄	623
ㄏㄨㄥˋ	汞	2778
	閧	7039

ㄐ

注音	單字	字號
ㄐㄧ	乩	42
	几	346
	唧	694
	喞	694
	(唧)	
	嘰	738
	基	844
	奇	929
	姬	1005
	屐	1196
	嵇	1255
	幾	1358
	期	2325
	朞	2325
	(期)	
	機	2605
	激	3112
	犄	3328
	璣	3499
	畸	3581
	畿	3583
	磯	3908
	禨	3969
	稽	4023
	積	4029
	笄	4121
	筓	4121
	(笄)	
	箕	4143
	績	4431
	羈	4510
	覊	4511
	肌	4622
	虀	5178
	羇	5479
	覉	5480
	觭	5508
	譏	5672
	跡	5863
	蹟	5925
	躋	5949
	迹	6074
	隮	6650
	雞	6677
	飢	6850
	饑	6904
	鷄	7185
	齎	7305
	賫	7305
	(齎)	
	賷	7305
	(齎)	
	齏	7306
ㄐㄧˊ	亟	59
	伋	106
	卽	504
	即	504
	(卽)	
	及	518
	吃	549
	吉	551
	唧	694
	喞	694
	(唧)	
	嫉	1045
	寂	1132
	岌	1213

	急	1546		冀	321		嘉	728		架	2385		結	4326		跤	5875
	戢	1767		劑	415		夾	927		稼	4021		絜	4341		郊	6192
	擊	2069		妓	959		家	1127		駕	6934		羯	4529		驕	6976
	棘	2482		季	1085		枷	2386	ㄐㄧㄝ	偕	223		蜐	5288		鮫	7068
	楫	2529		寄	1133		珈	3428		喈	682		袷	5401		鵁	7138
	極	2531		忌	1499		痂	3611		嗟	717		訐	5521		鷦	7192
	檝	2619		悸	1599		笳	4103		接	1932		詰	5571	ㄐㄧㄠˊ	嚼	774
	殛	2704		技	1811		葭	5014		揭	1964		頡	6797	ㄐㄧㄠˇ	佼	145
	汲	2785		旡	2196		袈	5389		癤	3678	ㄐㄧㄝˇ	姊	977		僥	260
	疾	3606		既	2197		豭	5731		皆	3697		姉	977		剿	405
	瘠	3653		旣	2197		迦	6065		稭	4016		(姊)			勦	405
	笈	4092		(既)			鎵	6473		結	4326		姐	980		(剿)	
	籍	4219		暨	2281	ㄐㄧㄚˊ	夾	927		街	5366		解	5505		徼	1494
	級	4298		洎	2851		恝	1570		階	6633	ㄐㄧㄝˋ	介	80		撟	2040
	脊	4672		漈	3039		戛	1764	ㄐㄧㄝˊ	偈	217		借	206		攪	2108
	蒺	5041		濟	3123		戞	1764		傑	236		屆	1189		湫	2988
	蕺	5130		祭	3949		(戛)			刦	423		戒	1758		狡	3353
	藉	5136		稷	4020		筴	4132		刧	423		械	2467		皎	3701
	踖	5892		穄	4030		莢	4940		(刦)			玠	3417		矯	3838
	蹐	5913		紀	4278		蛺	5230		婕	1021		界	3560		筊	4123
	輯	6006		繫	4452		袷	5401		孑	1074		疥	3596		絞	4330
	集	6661		繼	4459		裌	5419		嵑	1253		芥	4844		繳	4449
	革	6735		罽	4507		跲	5870		截	1770		藉	5136		脚	4687
	鶺	7177		芰	4853		郟	6200		拮	1858		解	5505		腳	4707
ㄐㄧˇ	几	346		薊	5118		鋏	6403		捷	1909		誡	5590		角	5500
	己	1299		薺	5135		頡	6797		㨗	1909	ㄐㄧㄠ	交	62		蹻	5936
	幾	1358		覬	5491		頰	6804		(捷)			噍	748		較	5983
	庋	1362		計	5515	ㄐㄧㄚˇ	假	216		擷	2085		姣	989		鉸	6369
	戟	1765		記	5528		夏	904		杰	2379		嬌	1058		餃	6865
	戟	1765		跽	5877		岬	1218		桀	2434		憍	1697	ㄐㄧㄠˋ	叫	535
	(戟)			際	6640		斝	2160		桔	2447		敎	2126		噍	748
	掎	1916		霽	6715		檟	2614		楬	2530		椒	2494		嶠	1272
	擠	2072		騎	6951		甲	3553		櫛	2631		澆	3092		徼	1494
	濟	3123		驥	6986		胛	4650		潔	3071		焦	3213		撟	2040
	給	4333		髻	7019		賈	5779		癤	3678		燋	3261		教	2126
	脊	4672		鯽	7085		鉀	6343		睫	3785		礁	3913		斠	2163
	蟣	5322	ㄐㄧㄚ	伽	121	ㄐㄧㄚˋ	假	216		碣	3888		膠	4728		校	2429
	踦	5895		佳	143		價	267		竭	4082		茭	4923		窖	4052
	麂	7218		傢	232		夾	927		箑	4140		蕉	5092		覺	5496
ㄐㄧˋ	伎	108		加	419		嫁	1037		節	4159		蛟	5224		訆	5517

	較	5983		鷲	7196		簡	4200		間	6534		藎	5138		涇	2894
	轎	6024	ㄐㄧㄢ	兼	320		簡	4200		閒	6538		覲	5493		睛	3777
	醮	6291		堅	846		(簡)			餞	6883		贐	5816		秔	3988
ㄐㄧㄡ	啾	674		奸	952		繭	4453	ㄐㄧㄣ	今	79		近	6056		稉	3988
	噍	748		姦	992		翦	4551		巾	1305		進	6109		(秔)	
	揪	1962		尖	1170		襇	5458		斤	2164		靳	6737		粳	4248
	揫	1962		戔	1762		謇	5652		津	2861	ㄐㄧㄤ	僵	266		精	4249
	(揪)			椷	2510		譾	5691		矜	3827		姜	987		經	4350
	摎	2015		殲	2714		趼	5861		祲	3950		將	1162		耕	4582
	樛	2582		湔	2981		跰	5861		禁	3954		殭	2711		莖	4936
	湫	2988		漸	3062		(趼)			筋	4118		江	2776		菁	4969
	究	4039		煎	3229		蹇	5908		衿	5386		漿	3067		荊	4994
	糺	4276		犍	3331		鐧	6498		襟	5461		疆	3584		荆	4994
	糾	4277		監	3731		鹻	7213		觔	5501		繮	4447		(荊)	
	赳	5828		箋	4138		鹼	7214		金	6310		薑	5122		驚	6982
	轇	6022		牋	4138	ㄐㄧㄢˋ	件	100	ㄐㄧㄣˇ	僅	251		螿	5310		鯨	7082
	鬮	7043		(箋)			健	226		儘	281		豇	5711		鶄	7164
	鳩	7117		緘	4380		僭	263		卺	502		韁	6762	ㄐㄧㄥˇ	井	55
ㄐㄧㄡˇ	久	29		縑	4406		儉	274		廑	1389	ㄐㄧㄤˇ	獎	946		儆	272
	九	39		肩	4634		劍	414		槿	2573		槳	2570		剄	387
	灸	3173		艱	4825		建	1408		殣	2706		蔣	5074		憬	1703
	玖	3412		菅	4957		檻	2623		瑾	3487		講	5657		景	2256
	糺	4276		蒹	5040		毽	2741		緊	4375	ㄐㄧㄤˋ	匠	462		璟	3495
	糾	4277		間	6534		漸	3062		菫	4993		將	1162		警	5685
	韭	5032		閒	6538		澗	3078		覲	5493		強	1434		阱	6589
	赳	5828		韉	6755		濺	3134		謹	5670		强	1434		頸	6807
	酒	6250		韀	6764		監	3731		錦	6427		(強)		ㄐㄧㄥˋ	倞	195
	韮	6773		鰜	7093		箭	4155		饉	6901		彊	1434		凊	340
ㄐㄧㄡˋ	僦	261		鰹	7104		腱	4708	ㄐㄧㄣˋ	勁	427		(強)			勁	427
	咎	590		鶼	7179		艦	4820		噤	750		洚	2903		境	870
	就	1177	ㄐㄧㄢˇ	儉	274		荐	4926		搢	1984		糨	4266		徑	1474
	廄	1387		剪	400		薦	5127		晉	2241		糡	4266		敬	2139
	救	2128		戩	1769		見	5481		晋	2241		(糨)			淨	2937
	柩	2407		揀	1944		諫	5630		(晉)			絳	4338		痙	3624
	桕	2449		撿	2067		賤	5795		浸	2892		醬	6288		竟	4077
	疚	3593		柬	2410		踐	5881		燼	3275		降	6601		競	4084
	究	4039		檢	2615		鍵	6446		瑨	3485	ㄐㄧㄥ	京	67		脛	4676
	臼	4773		減	2959		鐧	6498		盡	3730		兢	305		逕	6092
	舅	4781		瞼	3817		鑑	6512		禁	3954		旌	2185		鏡	6488
	舊	4785		筧	4137		鑒	6513		縉	4409		晶	2260		靖	6723

ㄑ

	啟	660
	(啓)	
	屺	1211
	杞	2350
	棨	2489
	稽	4023
	綺	4366
	綮	4374
	豈	5712
	起	5830
ㄑㄧˋ	企	103
	器	751
	契	936
	妻	974
	憩	1713
	憇	1713
	(憩)	
	棄	2476
	弃	2476
	(棄)	
	氣	2753
	汽	2794
	泣	2840
	砌	3846
	磧	3906
	緝	4383
	葺	5020
	訖	5526
	跂	5849
	迄	6051
˙ㄑㄧ	唭	659
ㄑㄧㄚ	掐	1918
ㄑㄧㄚˊ	卡	491
ㄑㄧㄚˇ	卡	491
ㄑㄧㄚˋ	恰	1564
	洽	2872
ㄑㄧㄝ	切	360
ㄑㄧㄝˊ	伽	121
	茄	4888
ㄑㄧㄝˇ	且	12
ㄑㄧㄝˋ	切	360
	契	936
	妾	975
	怯	1534
	愜	1643
	慊	1662
	挈	1875
	朅	2313
	竊	4072
	篋	4164
	踥	5890
	鍥	6442
ㄑㄧㄠ	撬	2045
	敲	2140
	橇	2596
	磽	3912
	蹺	5935
	蹻	5936
	鍫	6444
	鍬	6454
ㄑㄧㄠˊ	僑	255
	喬	700
	嶠	1272
	憔	1700
	樵	2588
	橋	2598
	燋	3261
	瞧	3813
	翹	4561
	蕎	5094
	譙	5678
	顦	6829
ㄑㄧㄠˇ	巧	1295
	悄	1581
	愀	1637
	雀	6657
	鵲	7160
ㄑㄧㄠˋ	俏	170
	峭	1229
	撬	2045
	殼	2719
	㱿	2719
	(殼)	
	壳	2719
	(殼)	
	竅	4069
	翹	4561
	誚	5589
	譙	5678
	鞘	6748
ㄑㄧㄡ	丘	15
	楸	2534
	秋	3983
	秌	3983
	(秋)	
	蚯	5211
	邱	6182
	鞦	6751
	鞧	6752
	鰌	7088
	鰍	7090
	鶖	7167
	龜	7328
ㄑㄧㄡˊ	仇	78
	囚	782
	毬	2738
	求	2767
	泅	2828
	球	3440
	虬	5192
	虯	5193
	蝤	5278
	裘	5414
	賕	5786
	逑	6091
	遒	6128
	酋	6247
ㄑㄧㄡˇ	糗	4255
ㄑㄧㄢ	仟	89
	僉	252
	千	475
	嵌	1257
	愆	1648
	慳	1680
	扦	1800
	掔	1943
	搴	2002
	攐	2019
	牽	3324
	簽	4211
	籤	4226
	籖	4226
	(籤)	
	芊	4834
	褰	5446
	謙	5656
	遷	6151
	鉛	6351
	阡	6583
	韆	6763
	騫	6963
	鵮	7162
ㄑㄧㄢˊ	乾	44
	前	392
	拑	1843
	掮	1936
	潛	3073
	箝	4148
	虔	5182
	鈐	6335
	鉗	6350
	錢	6426
	黔	7252
ㄑㄧㄢˇ	淺	2947
	繾	4460
	譴	5689
	遣	6141
ㄑㄧㄢˋ	倩	211
	塹	868
	慊	1662
	槧	2569
	欠	2650
	歉	2666
	縴	4422
	芡	4842
	茜	4922
	蒨	5054
ㄑㄧㄣ	侵	162
	嶔	1274
	欽	2658
	衾	5385
	親	5490
	駸	6949
ㄑㄧㄣˊ	勤	441
	懃	1730
	擒	2062
	檎	2613
	琴	3456
	禽	3977
	秦	3989
	芩	4846
	芹	4858
	螓	5295
	衾	5385
	覃	5475
ㄑㄧㄣˇ	寢	1145
ㄑㄧㄣˋ	撳	2032
	沁	2790
ㄑㄧㄤ	嗆	705
	戧	1771
	搶	1989
	槍	2557
	瑲	3484
	羌	4514
	羗	4514
	(羌)	
	羫	4517
	腔	4697
	蜣	5255
	蹌	5912
	蹡	5921
	鎗	6460
	鏘	6483
	鏹	6484
ㄑㄧㄤˊ	嬙	1061
	強	1434
	强	1434
	(強)	
	彊	1434
	(強)	
	戕	1761
	檣	2616
	牆	3300
	墻	3300
	(牆)	
	薔	5123
ㄑㄧㄤˇ	強	1434
	强	1434
	(強)	
	彊	1434
	(強)	
	搶	1989
	襁	5454
	繦	5454
	(襁)	
	鏹	6484
ㄑㄧㄤˋ	嗆	705
	戧	1771
	熗	3238
	蹌	5912
	蹡	5921
ㄑㄧㄥ	傾	249
	卿	505
	氫	2757
	清	2946
	蜻	5261
	輕	5992
	青	6722
	鯖	7080
ㄑㄧㄥˊ	情	1606

	擎	2070
	晴	2259
	黥	7260
ㄑㄧㄥˇ	請	5610
	頃	6782
ㄑㄧㄥˋ	慶	1696
	磬	3905
	綮	4374
	罄	4481
	親	5490
	謦	5665
ㄑㄩ	區	473
	屈	1190
	嶇	1265
	毆	2144
	曲	2302
	沏	2805
	瞿	3819
	祛	3940
	胠	4653
	蛆	5217
	蛐	5228
	袪	5396
	詘	5559
	趨	5842
	軀	5965
	驅	6975
ㄑㄩˊ	劬	424
	渠	2962
	璩	3507
	癯	3685
	瞿	3819
	籧	4228
	絇	4305
	朐	4656
	蕖	5108
	蘧	5167
	蛐	5228
	衢	5373
	鴝	7136
	鸜	7207
	麯	7237
	麴	7239
ㄑㄩˇ	取	522
	娶	1017
	曲	2302
	齲	7322
ㄑㄩˋ	去	514
	淶	3042
	覰	5494
	覷	5494
	(覰)	
	覻	5494
	(覰)	
	趣	5840
	闃	6558
ㄑㄩㄝ	缺	4478
	闕	6572
ㄑㄩㄝˊ	瘸	3663
ㄑㄩㄝˋ	卻	503
	却	503
	(卻)	
	怯	1534
	恪	1560
	愨	1686
	搉	1972
	榷	2561
	殼	2719
	殻	2719
	(殼)	
	壳	2719
	(殼)	
	确	3870
	碏	3882
	確	3893
	觳	5510
	闋	6563
	闕	6572
	雀	6657
	鵲	7160
ㄑㄩㄢ	圈	799
	弮	1430
	悛	1588
	棬	2496
ㄑㄩㄢˊ	全	308
	卷	499
	惓	1610
	拳	1873
	權	2647
	泉	2848
	牷	3322
	痊	3618
	筌	4111
	荃	4924
	蜷	5260
	詮	5570
	踡	5887
	醛	6282
	銓	6373
	顴	6835
	鬈	7024
ㄑㄩㄢˇ	犬	3338
	畎	3563
	綣	4356
ㄑㄩㄢˋ	券	376
	勸	446
ㄑㄩㄣ	逡	6102
ㄑㄩㄣˊ	羣	4526
	群	4526
	(羣)	
	裙	5408
ㄑㄩㄥ	穹	4041
	芎	4837
ㄑㄩㄥˊ	嬛	1062
	惸	1635
	煢	3233
	瓊	3512
	穹	4041
	窮	4061
	筇	4110
	䓖	4837
	藭	5151
	蛩	5226
	跫	5868
	邛	6171

ㄒ

注音	單字	字號
ㄒㄧ	僖	257
	兮	314
	吸	574
	唏	643
	嘻	744
	奚	941
	嬉	1055
	巇	1281
	希	1309
	徯	1489
	恓	1554
	悉	1593
	扱	1807
	攜	2100
	携	2100
	(攜)	
	擕	2100
	(攜)	
	攜	2100
	(攜)	
	晞	2248
	晰	2257
	晳	2258
	曦	2297
	析	2371
	栖	2423
	棲	2497
	樨	2590
	欷	2656
	淅	2917
	溪	3009
	烯	3207
	熙	3234
	熹	3257
	熺	3257
	(熹)	
	犀	3327
	犧	3336
	畦	3570
	晳	3705
	硒	3862
	禧	3967
	稀	4000
	羲	4530
	膝	4726
	蜥	5248
	蟋	5315
	蠵	5352
	西	5473
	觿	5513
	谿	5708
	豀	5709
	豨	5729
	蹊	5910
	醯	6289
	釐	6309
	鸂	7201
	鼷	7296
ㄒㄧˊ	媳	1039
	席	1323
	息	1575
	惜	1617
	昔	2220
	檄	2608
	熄	3237
	習	4544
	腊	4700
	蓆	5047
	裼	5428
	襲	5469
	覡	5486
	錫	6428
	隰	6649
ㄒㄧˇ	喜	692
	屣	1203
	徙	1479
	憙	1714
	枲	2384
	洒	2855
	洗	2856
	璽	3508
	禧	3967
	葸	5019
	蓰	5087
	蟢	5321
	諰	5644
ㄒㄧˋ	係	165
	卌	480
	夕	907
	戲	1774
	戯	1774
	(戲)	
	歙	2672
	汐	2771
	潟	3075
	盻	3745
	矽	3842
	禊	3958
	穸	4040
	系	4275
	細	4309
	繫	4452
	翕	4546
	肸	4641
	舄	4780
	舃	4780
	(舄)	
	郤	6204
	隙	6638
	隟	6638
	(隙)	
	餼	6895

注音	單字	字號
	箱	4154
	緗	4384
	纕	4471
	舡	4800
	薌	5119
	襄	5455
	鄉	6221
	鑲	6522
	香	6918
	驤	6987
ㄒㄧㄤˊ	庠	1370
	祥	3946
	翔	4545
	詳	5574
	降	6601
ㄒㄧㄤˇ	享	66
	想	1644
	響	6779
	餉	6867
	饗	6908
	鮝	7072
ㄒㄧㄤˋ	像	254
	向	559
	嚮	769
	巷	1303
	曏	2290
	橡	2601
	相	3744
	象	5725
	鄉	6221
	項	6783
ㄒㄧㄥ	惺	1636
	星	2223
	猩	3374
	腥	4703
	興	4783
	馨	6920
	騂	6947
ㄒㄧㄥˊ	刑	364
	型	832
	形	1448
	形	1448
	(形)	
	硎	3871
	行	5360
	邢	6177
	郉	6189
	鈃	6419
	陘	6604
	餳	6892
ㄒㄧㄥˇ	惺	1636
	擤	2081
	省	3753
	醒	6276
ㄒㄧㄥˋ	倖	201
	姓	983
	幸	1352
	性	1531
	悻	1600
	杏	2344
	興	4783
	荇	4925
	莕	4932
	行	5360
ㄒㄩ	吁	548
	噓	735
	墟	874
	戌	1754
	歔	2673
	盱	3741
	繻	4457
	胥	4643
	蓿	5067
	虛	5185
	訏	5531
	需	6692
	須	6786
	嬃	6801
	鬚	7032
ㄒㄩˊ	徐	1473
ㄒㄩˇ	呴	2233
	栩	2425
	湑	2993
	煦	3231
	許	5541
	詡	5563
	諝	5634
	鄦	6236
ㄒㄩˋ	勗	434
	勖	434
	(勗)	
	卹	501
	壻	899
	婿	899
	(壻)	
	序	1363
	恤	1559
	慉	1665
	敍	2125
	敘	2125
	(敍)	
	叙	2125
	(敍)	
	旭	2203
	洫	2863
	漵	3058
	畜	3567
	絮	4340
	緒	4379
	續	4464
	芧	4845
	蓄	5046
	賉	5781
	酗	6252
ㄒㄩㄝ	噱	756
	薛	5125
	靴	6738
ㄒㄩㄝˊ	學	1094
	尋	1165
	踅	5879
	鷽	7199
ㄒㄩㄝˇ	雪	6683
	鱈	7099
ㄒㄩㄝˋ	削	389
	穴	4038
	血	5356
	雪	6683
ㄒㄩㄢ	喧	696
	嬛	1062
	宣	1118
	揎	1971
	暄	2264
	瑄	3465
	翾	4564
	萱	4997
	諼	5620
	諠	5625
	軒	5970
ㄒㄩㄢˊ	懸	1742
	旋	2184
	漩	3052
	玄	3406
	璇	3489
	璿	3510
	縣	4402
	還	6161
ㄒㄩㄢˇ	癬	3683
	選	6152
ㄒㄩㄢˋ	旋	2184
	渲	2968
	漩	3052
	炫	3183
	眩	3760
	絢	4332
	衒	5362
	鉉	6346
	鏇	6475
ㄒㄩㄣ	勳	444
	壎	887
	曛	2294
	焄	3203
	熏	3236
	燻	3236
	(熏)	
	獯	3396
	窨	4059
	纁	4461
	葷	5018
	薰	5134
	醺	6296
ㄒㄩㄣˊ	尋	1165
	峋	1225
	巡	1291
	廵	1291
	(巡)	
	徇	1467
	循	1486
	恂	1550
	撏	2033
	旬	2202
	洵	2870
	潯	3083
	珣	3436
	紃	4280
	荀	4915
	蕁	5105
	詢	5564
	巡	6053
	廵	6053
	(巡)	
	郇	6191
	馴	6926
	鱘	7108
ㄒㄩㄣˋ	巽	1304
	徇	1467
	殉	2699
	汛	2777
	蕈	5106
	訊	5522
	訓	5524
	迅	6052
	遜	6132
	馴	6926
ㄒㄩㄥ	兄	291
	兇	294
	凶	351
	匈	452
	恟	1556
	洶	2871
	胸	4664
	胷	4664
	(胸)	
	詾	5538
ㄒㄩㄥˊ	熊	3235
	雄	6658
ㄒㄩㄥˋ	夐	905

ㄓ

注音	單字	字號
ㄓ	之	30
	卮	494
	指	1867
	搘	1985
	支	2113
	枝	2376
	梔	2461
	栀	2461
	(梔)	
	氏	2746
	汁	2765
	知	3831
	祇	3930
	祗	3938
	織	4437
	肢	4632
	胝	4658
	脂	4668
	芝	4840
	蜘	5249
	隻	6655

	韜	7279		寘	1140		輊	5988		螫	5301		瘵	3661		軸	5977
ㄓˊ	値	208		峙	1227		遲	6147		遮	6145		砦	3858	ㄓㄡˇ	帚	1317
	執	843		帙	1316		郅	6190	ㄓㄜˊ	哲	636	ㄓㄟˋ	這	6096		肘	4624
	姪	994		幟	1339		銍	6379		慴	1682	ㄓㄠ	招	1855	ㄓㄡˋ	冑	326
	指	1867		彘	1444		鑕	6515		懾	1745		昭	2228		呪	589
	摭	2011		志	1504		陟	6607		折	1822		朝	2324		宙	1113
	擲	2084		忮	1511		雉	6664		摘	2004		着	3776		晝	2247
	植	2500		懥	1733		騭	6964		摺	2016		著	5003		甃	3528
	殖	2702		摯	2024		鷙	7189		磔	3899		釗	6315		皺	3713
	直	3743		智	2262	ㄓㄚ	扎	1791		翟	4547	ㄓㄠˊ	着	3776		籀	4216
	縶	4426		桎	2444		挓	1872		蜇	5239		著	5003		籒	4216
	職	4609		治	2819		揸	1967		蟄	5312	ㄓㄠˇ	找	1809		(籀)	
	蟄	5312		滯	3031		査	2411		褶	5451		沼	2817		紂	4279
	質	5797		炙	3181		楂	2514		謫	5667		爪	3284		縐	4405
	跖	5855		畤	3571		渣	2961		讁	5694	ㄓㄠˋ	兆	293		胄	4645
	蹠	5920		疐	3590	ㄓㄚˊ	劄	408		輒	5989		召	536	ㄓㄢ	占	490
	蹢	5922		痔	3621		扎	1791		輙	6005		旐	2188		旃	2180
	躑	5952		痣	3627		札	2334		轍	6023		曌	2287		氈	2745
ㄓˇ	只	534		知	3831		炸	3189	ㄓㄜˇ	者	4572		棹	2502		毡	2745
	咫	612		秩	3993		箚	4150		赭	5825		櫂	2627		(氈)	
	址	813		稚	4009		紮	4304		鍺	6450		炤	3191		氊	2745
	徵	1491		穉	4009		紥	4304	ㄓㄜˋ	宅	1102		照	3232		(氈)	
	恉	1578		(稚)			(紮)			柘	2400		笊	4090		沾	2820
	指	1867		窒	4050		鍘	6440		浙	2878		罩	4498		瞻	3816
	旨	2200		紩	4324		閘	6540		蔗	5071		肇	4618		覘	5484
	枳	2381		緻	4397	ㄓㄚˇ	眨	3761		這	6096		詔	5554		詹	5575
	止	2681		置	4500	ㄓㄚˋ	乍	31		鷓	7186		趙	5838		邅	6162
	沚	2804		膣	4730		吒	555	•ㄓㄜ	着	3776	ㄓㄡ	周	588		霑	6701
	砥	3849		至	4769		咋	603		著	5003		啁	653		饘	6911
	祇	3930		致	4770		咤	608	ㄓㄞ	摘	2004		州	1290		鱣	7110
	祉	3932		致	4770		搾	1979		齊	7303		洲	2868		鸇	7202
	紙	4295		(致)			柵	2416		齋	7304		盩	3736	ㄓㄢˇ	展	1195
	耆	4571		蛭	5227		榨	2546		斎	7304		粥	4242		嶄	1267
	芷	4856		製	5429		炸	3189		(齋)			舟	4797		搌	2001
	趾	5847		誌	5584		痄	3614	ㄓㄞˊ	宅	1102		賙	5788		斬	2168
	軹	5979		識	5677		笮	4107		擇	2060		輈	5986		琖	3444
	酯	6259		豸	5734		蚱	5213		翟	4547		週	6108		盞	3728
	阯	6591		質	5797		蜡	5252	ㄓㄞˇ	窄	4048		鵃	7141		輾	6014
	黹	7272		贄	5806		詐	5552	ㄓㄞˋ	債	246	ㄓㄡˊ	妯	972	ㄓㄢˋ	佔	131
ㄓˋ	制	381		躓	5953	ㄓㄜ	折	1822		寨	1149		舳	4806		占	490

	戰	1773		軫	5975		崢	1244		豬	5732		苧	4875		鷟	7190
	暫	2275		鬒	7030		征	1463		邾	6195		著	5003	ㄓㄨㄞ	拽	1869
	棧	2484	ㄓㄣˋ	振	1880		徵	1491		銖	6374		蛀	5215	ㄓㄨㄞˇ	跩	5874
	湛	2986		揕	1952		怔	1537	ㄓㄨˊ	朮	2335		註	5545	ㄓㄨㄞˋ	拽	1869
	站	4074		朕	2320		掙	1925		燭	3271		鑄	6511	ㄓㄨㄟ	椎	2501
	綻	4367		枕	2373		楨	2528		竹	4085		馵	6927		追	6075
	蘸	5174		瑱	3481		正	2682		竺	4086		駐	6930		錐	6420
	蹔	5926		賑	5783		烝	3195		筑	4115	ㄓㄨㄚ	抓	1816		隹	6654
	顫	6830		酖	6251		爭	3286		築	4166		撾	2053		騅	6955
ㄓㄣ	偵	229		鎮	6465		猙	3365		舳	4806		髽	7022	ㄓㄨㄟˋ	墜	876
	振	1880		陣	6610		癥	3679		躅	5943	ㄓㄨㄚˇ	爪	3284		惴	1627
	斟	2161		陳	6617		睜	3781		軸	5977	ㄓㄨㄛ	捉	1888		綴	4362
	椹	2508		震	6693		箏	4139		逐	6090		桌	2436		縋	4404
	楨	2528		鴆	7122		蒸	5039	ㄓㄨˇ	主	26		棹	2502		贅	5807
	榛	2540	ㄓㄤ	張	1433		諍	5611		囑	781		涿	2913		餟	6888
	珍	3425		彰	1456		貞	5749		屬	1207	ㄓㄨㄛˊ	卓	484	ㄓㄨㄢ	專	1161
	甄	3527		樟	2577		鉦	6355		拄	1833		啄	654		甎	3530
	眞	3762		漳	3059		錚	6423		渚	2956		拙	1851		塼	3530
	真	3762		獐	3387	ㄓㄥˇ	拯	1859		煮	3228		擢	2074		(甎)	
	(眞)			璋	3493		整	2145		煑	3228		斫	2167		磚	3907
	砧	3850		章	4078	ㄓㄥˋ	幀	1330		(煮)			斮	2169		耑	4578
	禎	3960		蟑	5316		掙	1925		矚	3825		斲	2172		顓	6818
	禛	3964		鄣	6229		政	2121		貯	5759		斵	2172	ㄓㄨㄢˇ	囀	775
	箴	4158		麞	7231		正	2682		麈	7220		(斲)			轉	6020
	胗	4657	ㄓㄤˇ	掌	1940		症	3608	ㄓㄨˋ	佇	124		梲	2468	ㄓㄨㄢˋ	傳	244
	臻	4772		漲	3060		証	5561		住	128		椓	2506		撰	2047
	蓁	5045		長	6528		證	5674		助	421		浞	2905		瑑	3466
	診	5544	ㄓㄤˋ	丈	4		鄭	6231		宁	1100		濁	3113		篆	4163
	貞	5749		仗	85	ㄓㄨ	侏	153		杼	2364		濯	3127		篹	4192
	針	6316		嶂	1266		朱	2336		柱	2409		灼	3174		賺	5801
	鍼	6447		帳	1324		株	2427		柷	2414		焯	3210		轉	6020
	鱵	7111		幛	1338		櫫	2639		注	2845		琢	3446		饌	6903
ㄓㄣˇ	枕	2373		杖	2348		洙	2857		炷	3188		着	3776	ㄓㄨㄣ	窀	4045
	畛	3565		漲	3060		瀦	3154		祝	3942		繳	4449		肫	4636
	疹	3603		瘴	3659		珠	3432		竚	4075		茁	4885		諄	5607
	稹	4024		脹	4688		硃	3860		筯	4129		著	5003		迍	6060
	紾	4314		賬	5798		茱	4908		箸	4157		諑	5613	ㄓㄨㄣˇ	准	339
	縝	4412		長	6528		蛛	5223		粥	4242		踔	5893		準	3004
	胗	4657		障	6641		誅	5578		紵	4316		酌	6248		隼	6656
	診	5544	ㄓㄥ	丁	2		諸	5637		翥	4552		鐲	6501	ㄓㄨㄤ	妝	965

注音	單字	字號
	庄	1360
	樁	2575
	粧	4244
	莊	4933
	裝	5416
ㄓㄨㄤˋ	僮	264
	壯	898
	戇	1750
	撞	2039
	狀	3342
ㄓㄨㄥ	中	21
	忪	1516
	忠	1517
	盅	3716
	終	4319
	螽	5309
	衷	5382
	鍾	6448
	鐘	6493
ㄓㄨㄥˇ	冢	332
	塚	858
	種	4014
	腫	4705
	踵	5899
ㄓㄨㄥˋ	中	21
	仲	97
	眾	3772
	種	4014
	衆	5358
	重	6306

ㄔ

注音	單字	字號
ㄔ	吃	549
	喫	549
	(吃)	
	嗤	719
	媸	1041
	摛	2009
	痴	3641
	癡	3676
	眵	3771
	笞	4098
	絺	4344
	蚩	5209
	螭	5303
	郗	6203
	魑	7057
	鴟	7131
	鸁	7324
ㄔˊ	匙	459
	墀	875
	尺	1180
	弛	1423
	持	1865
	池	2773
	治	2819
	箎	4174
	篪	4174
	(箎)	
	茌	4891
	踟	5886
	遲	6147
	馳	6925
ㄔˇ	侈	150
	呎	585
	尺	1180
	恥	1577
	耻	4596
	蚇	5210
	褫	5445
	豉	5713
	齒	7307
ㄔˋ	傺	248
	勅	429
	叱	541
	啻	672
	彳	1458
	敕	2129
	斥	2165
	熾	3249
	眙	3756
	翅	4539
	赤	5821
	跮	5864
	趩	5879
	飭	6856
	鶒	7171
ㄔㄚ	叉	517
	喳	702
	差	1298
	扠	1801
	扱	1807
	插	1954
	挿	1954
	(插)	
	杈	2342
	臿	4776
ㄔㄚˊ	察	1142
	搽	1981
	查	2411
	槎	2559
	碴	3891
	苴	4878
	茶	4912
ㄔㄚˇ	叉	517
ㄔㄚˋ	侘	155
	刹	379
	剎	379
	(刹)	
	姹	997
	奼	997
	(姹)	
	岔	1212
	差	1298
	杈	2342
	汊	2768
	衩	5377
	詫	5567
ㄔㄜ	車	5966
ㄔㄜˇ	尺	1180
	扯	1805
	撦	2041
ㄔㄜˋ	坼	824
	徹	1492
	拆	1837
	掣	1941
	撤	2030
	澈	3089
	轍	6023
ㄔㄞ	差	1298
	拆	1837
	釵	6325
ㄔㄞˊ	儕	280
	柴	2413
	茈	4882
	豺	5736
ㄔㄞˇ	茝	4951
ㄔㄞˋ	瘥	3655
	蠆	5334
ㄔㄠ	弨	1427
	抄	1812
	超	5834
	鈔	6331
ㄔㄠˊ	嘲	739
	巢	1292
	晁	2243
	朝	2324
	潮	3082
	鼂	7277
ㄔㄠˇ	吵	572
	炒	3182
ㄔㄠˋ	鈔	6331
ㄔㄡ	抽	1831
	搊	1973
	犨	3337
	瘳	3660
	篘	4177
	紬	4308
ㄔㄡˊ	仇	78
	儔	279
	幬	1344
	惆	1605
	愁	1646
	疇	3585
	稠	4012
	籌	4218
	紬	4308
	綢	4355
	裯	5423
	讎	5697
	讐	5697
	(讎)	
	躊	5948
	酬	6260
	雔	6671
ㄔㄡˇ	丑	11
	瞅	3792
	醜	6279
ㄔㄡˋ	臭	4766
ㄔㄢ	攙	2098
	襜	5463
ㄔㄢˊ	單	701
	嬋	1057
	孱	1091
	巉	1282
	廛	1393
	欃	2644
	毚	2734
	潺	3085
	澶	3111
	瀍	3143
	禪	3968
	纏	4465
	蟬	5324
	蟾	5332
	讒	5699
	饞	6914
ㄔㄢˇ	剷	406
	產	3541
	蕆	5091
	諂	5606
	鏟	6487
	闡	6578
ㄔㄢˋ	懺	1743
	羼	4535
	顫	6830
ㄔㄣ	嗔	712
	抻	1904
	琛	3445
	瞋	3796
	郴	6210
ㄔㄣˊ	塵	867
	宸	1128
	忱	1513
	晨	2253
	橙	2599
	沈	2798
	沉	2798
	(沈)	
	臣	4759
	蔯	5085
	諶	5635
	辰	6047
	陳	6617
ㄔㄣˋ	櫬	2635
	稱	4015
	襯	5468
	讖	5701
	趁	5832
	趂	5832
	(趁)	
	齔	7308
ㄔㄤ	倀	188
	倡	207
	娼	1026
	昌	2216
	猖	3362
	菖	4963
	閶	6553

ㄔㄤˊ	償	282
	嘗	733
	場	853
	嫦	1053
	常	1327
	徜	1478
	腸	4710
	萇	4977
	裳	5425
	長	6528
ㄔㄤˇ	場	853
	廠	1396
	敞	2134
	昶	2232
	氅	2743
ㄔㄤˋ	倡	207
	唱	649
	悵	1598
	暢	2273
	韔	6769
	鬯	7044
ㄔㄥ	撐	2027
	撑	2027
	(撐)	
	檉	2611
	牚	3309
	琤	3448
	瞠	3804
	稱	4015
	蟶	5329
	赬	5826
	鐺	6507
ㄔㄥˊ	丞	17
	乘	36
	呈	570
	城	835
	懲	1738
	成	1757
	承	1825
	晟	2245
	棖	2483
	橙	2599
	澄	3088
	瀓	3099
	盛	3726
	程	4005
	裎	5409
	誠	5592
	郕	6205
	酲	6262
ㄔㄥˇ	懲	1738
	逞	6099
	騁	6945
ㄔㄥˋ	秤	3992
	稱	4015
ㄔㄨ	出	354
	初	369
	齣	7314
ㄔㄨˊ	儲	285
	幮	1347
	廚	1392
	櫥	2633
	橱	2633
	(櫥)	
	滁	3016
	篨	4175
	耡	4586
	芻	4862
	蒭	5062
	蜍	5245
	蹰	5940
	躇	5944
	躕	5954
	鉏	6348
	鋤	6407
	除	6611
	雛	6674
ㄔㄨˇ	儲	285
	杵	2361
	楚	2525
	楮	2532
	礎	3914
	處	5183
	褚	5439
ㄔㄨˋ	亍	50
	俶	184
	怵	1541
	搐	1995
	歜	2676
	畜	3567
	矗	3823
	絀	4315
	處	5183
	觸	5512
	黜	7256
ㄔㄨㄚ	欻	2660
ㄔㄨㄛ	戳	1776
ㄔㄨㄛˋ	啜	671
	惙	1613
	歠	2679
	綽	4368
	輟	5999
	醊	6273
	齪	7319
ㄔㄨㄞ	搋	1974
ㄔㄨㄞˇ	揣	1960
ㄔㄨㄞˋ	嘬	749
	踹	5905
ㄔㄨㄟ	吹	575
	炊	3177
ㄔㄨㄟˊ	倕	197
	垂	826
	捶	1938
	搥	1986
	椎	2501
	槌	2556
	箠	4145
	菙	5015
	錘	6421
	鎚	6461
	陲	6616
ㄔㄨㄢ	川	1289
	穿	4043
ㄔㄨㄢˊ	傳	244
	椽	2511
	船	4812
	遄	6119
ㄔㄨㄢˇ	喘	689
	舛	4793
ㄔㄨㄢˋ	串	23
	釧	6324
ㄔㄨㄣ	春	2225
	椿	2513
ㄔㄨㄣˊ	淳	2941
	純	4290
	脣	4677
	唇	4677
	(脣)	
	蒓	5059
	蓴	5078
	醇	6271
	鶉	7163
ㄔㄨㄣˇ	蠢	5345
	惷	5345
	(蠢)	
	踳	5906
ㄔㄨㄤ	創	404
	瘡	3651
	窗	4053
	牕	4053
	(窗)	
	窓	4053
	(窗)	
	窻	4053
	(窗)	
ㄔㄨㄤˊ	幢	1342
	牀	3297
	床	3297
	(牀)	
ㄔㄨㄤˇ	闖	6573
ㄔㄨㄤˋ	創	404
	愴	1655
	闖	6573
ㄔㄨㄥ	充	292
	充	292
	(充)	
	忡	1508
	憧	1702
	沖	2801
	冲	2801
	(沖)	
	舂	4779
	衝	5368
ㄔㄨㄥˊ	崇	1236
	种	3987
	蟲	5325
	重	6306
ㄔㄨㄥˇ	寵	1155
ㄔㄨㄥˋ	衝	5368
	銃	6370

ㄕ

注音	單字	字號
ㄕ	失	922
	尸	1179
	屍	1193
	師	1322
	拾	1864
	施	2176
	濕	3133
	溼	3133
	(濕)	
	獅	3380
	絁	4325
	蓍	5057
	虱	5194
	蝨	5282
	詩	5566
	鳲	7118
ㄕˊ	什	72
	十	474
	實	1148
	射	1160
	拾	1864
	時	2240
	旹	2240
	(時)	
	湜	2982
	石	3841
	碩	3889
	蒔	5053
	蝕	5270
	食	6849
	鰣	7096
ㄕˇ	使	147
	史	542
	始	978
	屎	1194
	弛	1423
	矢	3829
	豕	5722
	駛	6937
ㄕˋ	世	14
	事	48
	仕	83
	使	147
	侍	152
	勢	439
	嗜	714
	噬	755
	士	896
	奭	947
	室	1119
	市	1306
	式	1416
	弒	1417
	恃	1552
	拭	1857
	是	2229
	柹	2387

	栻	2422		廈	1383	ㄕㄠ	弰	1431		杉	2341		燊	3260	ㄕㄥ	勝	437
	氏	2746		歃	2665		捎	1894		潸	3086		甡	3540		升	476
	澨	3105		煞	3230		梢	2470		煽	3239		申	3554		昇	2213
	示	3923		箑	4140		燒	3254		珊	3424		砷	3855		牲	3319
	筮	4128		翣	4549		稍	3999		羴	4531		紳	4311		生	3539
	耆	4571		霎	6699		筲	4131		羶	4532		莘	4937		甥	3542
	舐	4788	ㄕㄜ	奢	943		箾	4176		膻	4747		葠	5007		笙	4094
	螫	5301		畬	3577		䈰	4195		舢	4799		蓡	5007		聲	4606
	視	5485		賒	5784		艄	4814		芟	4841		(葠)			陞	6606
	試	5565	ㄕㄜˊ	什	72		蛸	5231		苫	4876		詵	5580		鼪	7293
	誓	5586		佘	134	ㄕㄠˊ	勺	447		衫	5376		身	5960	ㄕㄥˊ	澠	3100
	諡	5618		折	1822		杓	2345		跚	5857		鉮	6367		繩	4445
	諟	5646		揲	1966		芍	4836		釤	6326	ㄕㄣˊ	神	3943	ㄕㄥˇ	省	3753
	謚	5662		甚	3537		韶	6777	ㄕㄢˇ	閃	6531	ㄕㄣˇ	哂	622		眚	3763
	識	5677		舌	4786	ㄕㄠˇ	少	1169		陝	6612		嬸	1069	ㄕㄥˋ	乘	36
	豉	5713		蛇	5218	ㄕㄠˋ	劭	425	ㄕㄢˋ	善	679		審	1150		剩	401
	貰	5760		虵	5218		哨	632		單	701		沈	2798		勝	437
	軾	5984		(蛇)			少	1169		嬗	1060		瀋	3140		嵊	1263
	逝	6087		闍	6566		捎	1894		扇	1786		矧	3832		晟	2245
	適	6144	ㄕㄜˇ	捨	1897		潲	3093		掞	1926		諗	5616		盛	3726
	釋	6304		舍	4787		紹	4312		擅	2057		讅	5693		聖	4600
	鈰	6360	ㄕㄜˋ	射	1160		邵	6179		汕	2770	ㄕㄣˋ	愼	1661		膡	4746
	飾	6863		拾	1864	ㄕㄡ	收	2115		疝	3594		滲	3032		賸	5805
·ㄕ	匙	459		攝	2101	ㄕㄡˊ	熟	3243		禪	3968		甚	3537	ㄕㄨ	姝	988
ㄕㄚ	挱	1878		歙	2672	ㄕㄡˇ	守	1104		繕	4438		脤	4684		抒	1815
	殺	2718		涉	2896		手	1789		膳	4733		腎	4694		摴	2020
	沙	2802		社	3925		首	6915		蟮	5327		葚	5004		攄	2091
	煞	3230		舍	4787	ㄕㄡˋ	受	523		蟺	5330		蜃	5237		書	2306
	痧	3626		葉	5001		售	647		訕	5525		黮	7266		梳	2473
	砂	3845		設	5540		壽	903		贍	5813	ㄕㄤ	傷	247		梳	2473
	紗	4294		赦	5822		授	1913		赸	5831		商	655		(梳)	
	莎	4948		麝	7230		狩	3354		鄯	6232		殤	2707		樗	2578
	裟	5417	ㄕㄞ	篩	4172		獸	3400		饍	6906		湯	2989		樞	2583
	鎩	6476	ㄕㄞˇ	色	4826		瘦	3652		鱔	7105		觴	5511		殊	2700
	鯊	7077		骰	6993		綬	4357		鱣	7110	ㄕㄤˇ	上	6		殳	2715
ㄕㄚˊ	啥	670	ㄕㄞˋ	曬	2300	ㄕㄢ	刪	370	ㄕㄣ	伸	118		晌	2244		洙	2857
ㄕㄚˇ	傻	276		晒	2300		姍	979		參	515		賞	5790		疏	3588
	儍	276		(曬)			山	1209		呻	597	ㄕㄤˋ	上	6		疎	3588
	(傻)			殺	2718		扇	1786		娠	1011		尙	1171		(疏)	
ㄕㄚˋ	嗄	703	ㄕㄟˊ	誰	5601		搧	1991		深	2943	·ㄕㄤ	裳	5425		疏	3588

	(疏)	
	紓	4291
	舒	4789
	蔬	5077
	輸	6009
ㄕㄨˊ	叔	521
	塾	869
	孰	1090
	淑	2922
	熟	3243
	秫	3997
	菽	4973
	贖	5818
ㄕㄨˇ	屬	1207
	數	2143
	暑	2268
	署	4502
	薯	5133
	藷	5165
	蜀	5235
	鸀	7200
	黍	7247
	鼠	7291
ㄕㄨˋ	倏	196
	墅	871
	庶	1376
	恕	1568
	戍	1755
	數	2143
	曙	2291
	束	2351
	樹	2595
	沭	2811
	漱	3057
	澍	3091
	疏	3588
	署	4502
	術	5363
	裋	5407
	豎	5717

	述	6070
ㄕㄨㄚ	刷	382
ㄕㄨㄚˇ	耍	4577
ㄕㄨㄚˋ	刷	382
ㄕㄨㄛ	說	5598
ㄕㄨㄛˋ	妁	955
	帥	1319
	搠	1999
	數	2143
	朔	2319
	槊	2553
	爍	3278
	碩	3889
	芍	4836
	蟀	5311
	鑠	6514
ㄕㄨㄞ	摔	2010
	衰	5378
ㄕㄨㄞˇ	甩	3546
ㄕㄨㄞˋ	帥	1319
	率	3407
	蟀	5311
ㄕㄨㄟˊ	誰	5601
ㄕㄨㄟˇ	水	2761
ㄕㄨㄟˋ	帨	1321
	睡	3779
	稅	4001
	蛻	5233
	說	5598
ㄕㄨㄢ	拴	1862
	栓	2421
	閂	6530
ㄕㄨㄢˋ	涮	2952
ㄕㄨㄣˇ	吮	569
	楯	2536
	盾	3752
ㄕㄨㄣˋ	瞬	3807
	舜	4794
	順	6784
ㄕㄨㄤ	孀	1070

	瀧	3152
	雙	6673
	霜	6704
ㄕㄨㄤˇ	爽	3295

ㄖ

注音	單字	字號
ㄖˋ	日	2198
ㄖㄜˇ	喏	686
	惹	1645
	若	4873
ㄖㄜˋ	熱	3245
	爇	3279
ㄖㄠˊ	蕘	5096
	饒	6905
ㄖㄠˇ	擾	2088
ㄖㄠˋ	繞	4442
	遶	6150
ㄖㄡˊ	揉	1948
	柔	2397
	蹂	5903
	輮	6011
ㄖㄡˇ	糅	4254
ㄖㄡˋ	肉	4619
ㄖㄢˊ	然	3215
	燃	3251
	髥	7012
	髯	7017
ㄖㄢˇ	冉	322
	染	2396
	苒	4864
ㄖㄣˊ	人	71
	仁	73
	任	101
	壬	897
	紝	4297
	絍	4297
	(紝)	
ㄖㄣˇ	忍	1500
	稔	4008

注音	單字	字號
	荏	4918
ㄖㄣˋ	仞	88
	任	101
	刃	358
	妊	960
	恁	1566
	紉	4286
	紝	4297
	絍	4297
	(紝)	
	衽	5384
	袵	5405
	訒	5530
	認	5583
	軔	5971
	韌	6766
	飪	6855
	餁	6870
ㄖㄤ	嚷	773
ㄖㄤˊ	攘	2097
	瓤	3521
	禳	3973
	穰	4037
	纕	4471
ㄖㄤˇ	嚷	773
	壤	894
	攘	2097
ㄖㄤˋ	讓	5700
ㄖㄥ	扔	1795
ㄖㄥˊ	仍	81
	礽	3924
ㄖㄨˊ	儒	278
	嚅	763
	如	956
	孺	1095
	濡	3125
	茹	4914
	襦	5465
	銣	6390
	顬	6832

注音	單字	字號
	鴽	7142
ㄖㄨˇ	乳	43
	汝	2775
	辱	6048
ㄖㄨˋ	入	306
	洳	2867
	溽	3015
	縟	4413
	肉	4619
	茹	4914
	蓐	5050
	褥	5442
	辱	6048
ㄖㄨㄛˊ	挼	1881
ㄖㄨㄛˋ	偌	219
	弱	1432
	爇	3279
	箬	4153
	篛	4178
	若	4873
	蒻	5055
ㄖㄨㄟˊ	甤	3544
	緌	4377
	蕤	5103
	甤	5726
ㄖㄨㄟˇ	蕊	5093
ㄖㄨㄟˋ	枘	2374
	汭	2782
	瑞	3471
	睿	3794
	芮	4852
	蚋	5202
	蜹	5267
	銳	6391
ㄖㄨㄢˇ	蝡	5276
	蠕	5341
	軟	5974
	輭	6012
	阮	6588
ㄖㄨㄣˊ	犉	3329

注音	單字	字號
ㄖㄨㄣˋ	潤	3080
	閏	6536
ㄖㄨㄥˊ	容	1129
	嶸	1277
	戎	1756
	榕	2538
	榮	2551
	毧	2736
	溶	3014
	熔	3240
	絨	4334
	羢	4525
	肜	4630
	茸	4913
	蓉	5048
	融	5294
	蠑	5338
	鎔	6459
ㄖㄨㄥˇ	冗	1101
	氄	2744

ㄗ

注音	單字	字號
ㄗ	吱	578
	咨	610
	姿	999
	孜	1082
	孳	1092
	淄	2915
	滋	3022
	粢	4241
	緇	4370
	茲	4909
	菑	4961
	菑	4961
	(菑)	
	諮	5631
	貲	5761
	資	5777
	趑	5836

注音	單字	字號
	輜	5993
	錙	6422
	鎡	6456
	髭	7020
	鼒	7286
	齊	7303
	齎	7305
	齜	7315
ㄗˇ	仔	82
	姊	977
	姉	977
	(姊)	
	子	1073
	梓	2459
	滓	3025
	秭	3995
	笫	4100
	耔	4234
	紫	4306
	秄	4580
	茈	4882
	訾	5546
	訿	5560
ㄗˋ	剚	395
	字	1078
	恣	1572
	漬	3055
	牸	3323
	眥	3764
	眦	3764
	(眥)	
	胾	4667
	自	4764
ㄗㄚ	匝	460
	咂	595
	紮	4304
	紥	4304
	(紮)	
	臢	4757
ㄗㄚˊ	拶	1863
	桚	2448
	砸	3856
	雜	6675
ㄗㄜˊ	則	385
	咋	603
	嘖	732
	幘	1337
	擇	2060
	澤	3106
	窄	4048
	笮	4107
	簀	4189
	舴	4807
	責	5758
	賊	5780
	賾	5810
	迮	6071
ㄗㄜˇ	怎	1542
ㄗㄜˋ	仄	76
	昃	2211
ㄗㄞ	哉	627
	栽	2438
	災	3175
	灾	3175
	(災)	
	烖	3175
	(災)	
	菑	4961
	葘	4961
	(菑)	
ㄗㄞˇ	仔	82
	宰	1123
	崽	1254
	載	5987
ㄗㄞˋ	再	324
	在	806
	載	5987
ㄗㄟˊ	賊	5780
ㄗㄠ	糟	4263
	蹧	5924
	遭	6142
ㄗㄠˊ	鑿	6527
ㄗㄠˇ	早	2201
	棗	2481
	澡	3102
	繰	4454
	藻	5156
	蚤	5207
ㄗㄠˋ	噪	753
	慥	1676
	燥	3269
	皁	3694
	皂	3695
	竈	4071
	灶	4071
	(竈)	
	簉	4191
	譟	5684
	躁	5942
	造	6101
ㄗㄡ	掫	1939
	緅	4371
	諏	5612
	謅	5651
	鄒	6222
	鄹	6239
	陬	6614
	騶	6967
	鯫	7084
ㄗㄡˇ	走	5827
ㄗㄡˋ	奏	934
	揍	1950
	驟	6984
ㄗㄢ	簪	4205
ㄗㄢˊ	咱	615
ㄗㄢˇ	拶	1863
	揝	1969
	攢	2102
	昝	2235
	桚	2448
	趲	5843
ㄗㄢˋ	暫	2275
	讚	5703
	贊	5811
	酇	6244
	鏨	6491
ㄗㄣ	簪	4205
ㄗㄣˇ	怎	1542
ㄗㄣˋ	譖	5676
ㄗㄤ	牂	3299
	臢	4757
	臧	4762
	賍	5782
	贓	5815
	髒	7003
ㄗㄤˇ	駔	6933
ㄗㄤˋ	奘	938
	臟	4755
	葬	5013
	藏	5139
ㄗㄥ	增	877
	憎	1699
	曾	2309
	橧	3839
	繒	4436
ㄗㄥˋ	甑	3532
	繒	4436
	贈	5809
ㄗㄨ	租	3990
ㄗㄨˊ	卒	483
	捽	1906
	族	2187
	椊	2566
	足	5844
	鏃	6474
ㄗㄨˇ	俎	169
	祖	3937
	組	4320
	詛	5557
	阻	6592
ㄗㄨˋ	駔	6933
ㄗㄨㄛ	作	138
	嘬	749
ㄗㄨㄛˊ	作	138
	捽	1906
	昨	2227
ㄗㄨㄛˇ	佐	129
	左	1294
	撮	2048
ㄗㄨㄛˋ	作	138
	做	224
	坐	818
	座	1372
	怍	1523
	柞	2404
	祚	3941
	胙	4649
	酢	6253
	鑿	6527
	阼	6593
ㄗㄨㄟˇ	嘴	740
ㄗㄨㄟˋ	晬	2254
	最	2311
	罪	4499
	蕞	5099
	辠	6040
	醉	6272
ㄗㄨㄢ	鑽	6525
ㄗㄨㄢˇ	篹	4192
	纂	4456
	纘	4474
	鑽	6525
ㄗㄨㄢˋ	揝	1969
	攥	2110
	鑽	6525
ㄗㄨㄣ	尊	1164
	樽	2593
	罇	4483
	遵	6149
ㄗㄨㄣˇ	撙	2036
ㄗㄨㄥ	宗	1111
	從	1480
	棕	2507
	椶	2507
	(棕)	
	縱	4418
	葼	5010
	踪	5896
	蹤	5919
	騣	6959
	鬃	7025
ㄗㄨㄥˇ	偬	227
	總	4425
ㄗㄨㄥˋ	從	1480
	从	1480
	(從)	
	糉	4253
	粽	4253
	(糉)	
	綜	4353
	縱	4418

ㄘ

注音	單字	字號
ㄘ	差	1298
	恣	1572
	疵	3615
	雌	6666
ㄘˊ	慈	1666
	瓷	3524
	疵	3615
	磁	3896
	祠	3944
	粢	4241
	茨	4905
	茲	4909
	詞	5558
	辭	6044
	餈	6866
	鷀	7176

	鶿	7176
	(鴜)	
ㄘˇ	此	2683
	泚	2835
	玼	3423
ㄘˋ	伺	119
	刺	383
	廁	1381
	次	2651
	賜	5789
ㄘㄚ	擦	2078
ㄘㄜˋ	側	228
	册	323
	廁	1381
	惻	1638
	測	2969
	策	4122
	筴	4132
ㄘㄞ	猜	3367
ㄘㄞˊ	才	1790
	材	2346
	纔	4469
	裁	5402
	財	5751
ㄘㄞˇ	彩	1452
	採	1929
	睬	3786
	綵	4363
	跴	5865
	踩	5894
	采	6302
ㄘㄞˋ	菜	4964
	蔡	5073
	采	6302
ㄘㄠ	操	2058
	糙	4261
ㄘㄠˊ	嘈	727
	曹	2307
	槽	2574
	漕	3048

	螬	5302
ㄘㄠˇ	懆	1724
	艸	4829
	草	4917
ㄘㄠˋ	慥	1676
ㄘㄡˋ	湊	2977
	凑	2977
	(湊)	
	腠	4702
	輳	6007
ㄘㄢ	參	515
	飡	6852
	餐	6872
	驂	6972
ㄘㄢˊ	慚	1688
	慙	1688
	(慚)	
	殘	2703
	蠶	5351
ㄘㄢˇ	慘	1673
	憯	1709
	黲	7267
ㄘㄢˋ	燦	3267
	璨	3505
	粲	4245
ㄘㄣ	參	515
ㄘㄣˊ	岑	1215
	涔	2901
ㄘㄤ	倉	191
	傖	237
	滄	3019
	艙	4817
	蒼	5042
	鶬	7174
ㄘㄤˊ	藏	5139
ㄘㄤˇ	駔	6933
ㄘㄥˊ	層	1204
	嶒	1269
	曾	2309
ㄘㄥˋ	蹭	5931

ㄘㄨ	粗	4236
	麤	7233
ㄘㄨˊ	徂	1464
	殂	2698
ㄘㄨˋ	促	166
	卒	483
	猝	3369
	簇	4187
	蔟	5086
	趣	5840
	踧	5891
	蹙	5917
	⿰足戚	5927
	蹴	5933
	蹵	5938
	醋	6274
ㄘㄨㄛ	搓	1980
	撮	2048
	磋	3897
	莏	4949
	蹉	5909
ㄘㄨㄛˊ	嵯	1264
	痤	3631
	瘥	3655
	矬	3835
	鹺	7212
ㄘㄨㄛˇ	瑳	3483
	脞	4683
ㄘㄨㄛˋ	剉	388
	厝	510
	挫	1879
	措	1934
	撮	2048
	莝	4952
	銼	6409
	錯	6431
ㄘㄨㄟ	催	241
	崔	1239
	摧	2012
	榱	2548

	縗	4407
	衰	5378
ㄘㄨㄟˇ	璀	3488
ㄘㄨㄟˋ	啐	659
	悴	1601
	橇	2596
	毳	2740
	淬	2938
	瘁	3640
	粹	4250
	翠	4548
	脆	4669
	脃	4669
	(脆)	
	脺	4693
	膵	4693
	(脺)	
	萃	4975
	顇	6811
ㄘㄨㄢ	攛	2099
	汆	2763
	躥	5958
ㄘㄨㄢˊ	攢	2102
ㄘㄨㄢˋ	爨	3283
	竄	4068
	篡	4169
ㄘㄨㄣ	村	2347
	皴	3711
	邨	6178
ㄘㄨㄣˊ	存	1079
	蹲	5928
ㄘㄨㄣˇ	忖	1507
ㄘㄨㄣˋ	吋	552
	寸	1157
ㄘㄨㄥ	囪	789
	從	1480
	怱	1549
	匆	1549
	(怱)	
	悤	1595

	樅	1576
	瑽	3486
	璁	3494
	聰	4605
	葱	5027
	蔥	5075
	鏦	6477
	驄	6974
ㄘㄨㄥˊ	叢	526
	從	1480
	从	1480
	(從)	
	淙	2928
	琮	3455

ㄙ

注音	單字	字號
ㄙ	司	546
	嘶	741
	廝	1394
	思	1544
	撕	2038
	斯	2170
	澌	3096
	私	3981
	絲	4339
	緦	4387
	罳	4503
	螄	5292
	鍶	6451
	鷥	7191
ㄙˇ	死	2692
ㄙˋ	伺	119
	似	120
	俟	177
	兕	302
	嗣	718
	四	783
	姒	982
	寺	1158

	巳	1301
	廁	1381
	柶	2417
	汜	2774
	泗	2833
	祀	3927
	禩	3966
	笥	4099
	耜	4585
	肆	4616
	賜	5789
	食	6849
	飼	6860
	駟	6939
ㄙㄚ	仨	94
	撒	2029
ㄙㄚˇ	撒	2029
	洒	2855
	灑	3163
	靸	6741
ㄙㄚˋ	卅	478
	薩	5132
	趿	5850
	颯	6838
ㄙㄜˋ	嗇	706
	圾	812
	塞	863
	澀	3121
	澁	3121
	(澀)	
	瑟	3462
	穡	4032
	色	4826
	銫	6387
ㄙㄞ	塞	863
	腮	4716
	顋	6813
	鰓	7091
ㄙㄞˋ	塞	863

	賽	5804
ㄙㄠ	搔	1978
	繅	4432
	繰	4454
	臊	4744
	艘	4816
	騷	6966
ㄙㄠˇ	嫂	1038
	掃	1912
	埽	1912
	(掃)	
ㄙㄠˋ	掃	1912
	埽	1912
	(掃)	
	臊	4744
ㄙㄡ	嗖	680
	廋	1386
	搜	1987
	溲	3010
	蒐	5033
	颼	6843
	餿	6894
ㄙㄡˇ	叟	525
	嗾	725
	擻	2090
	瞍	3798
	藪	5150
ㄙㄡˋ	嗽	724
	漱	3057
ㄙㄢ	三	5
	參	515
ㄙㄢˇ	傘	238
	散	2137
	糝	4262
	繖	4440
ㄙㄢˋ	散	2137
ㄙㄣ	森	2493
ㄙㄤ	喪	699
	桑	2437
ㄙㄤˇ	嗓	711

	顙	6821
ㄙㄤˋ	喪	699
ㄙㄥ	僧	262
ㄙㄨ	甦	3543
	穌	4026
	蘇	5162
	酥	6256
ㄙㄨˊ	俗	173
ㄙㄨˋ	嗉	707
	塑	859
	夙	910
	宿	1131
	愫	1656
	愬	1671
	泝	2836
	涑	2898
	溯	3008
	簌	4185
	粟	4240
	素	4302
	縮	4419
	肅	4617
	膆	4722
	蓿	5067
	蔌	5080
	觫	5507
	訴	5542
	謖	5660
	速	6100
	遡	6139
	餗	6878
	鷫	7195
ㄙㄨㄛ	唆	641
	娑	1006
	挱	1878
	桫	2452
	梭	2471
	簑	4179
	縮	4419
	莎	4948

	莎	4949
	蓑	5051
ㄙㄨㄛˊ	索	4303
ㄙㄨㄛˇ	嗩	708
	所	1782
	瑣	3478
	索	4303
	鎖	6455
	鏁	6492
ㄙㄨㄟ	睢	3780
	綏	4349
	荽	4928
	雖	6672
ㄙㄨㄟˊ	綏	4349
	遂	6118
	隋	6631
	隨	6644
	雖	6672
ㄙㄨㄟˇ	巂	6676
	髓	7004
ㄙㄨㄟˋ	歲	2688
	燧	3265
	碎	3875
	祟	3945
	穗	4031
	術	5363
	誶	5602
	遂	6118
	邃	6164
	隧	6645
ㄙㄨㄢ	痠	3628
	酸	6265
ㄙㄨㄢˇ	篹	4192
ㄙㄨㄢˋ	筭	4135
	算	4144
	蒜	5035
ㄙㄨㄣ	孫	1089
	猻	3382
	蓀	5044
	飧	6853

	飱	6853
	(飧)	
ㄙㄨㄣˇ	損	1975
	榫	2545
	筍	4112
	笋	4112
	(筍)	
	簨	4204
	隼	6656
ㄙㄨㄣˋ	遜	6132
ㄙㄨㄥ	崧	1246
	嵩	1261
	忪	1516
	松	2366
	淞	2930
	鬆	7023
ㄙㄨㄥˇ	悚	1587
	慫	1687
	竦	4081
	聳	4607
ㄙㄨㄥˋ	宋	1106
	訟	5532
	誦	5596
	送	6077
	頌	6787

ㄚ

注音	單字	字號
ㄚ	啊	657
	腌	4692
	阿	6594
ㄚˊ	嗄	703
ㄚˋ	錒	6417
	阿	6594
˙ㄚ	啊	657

ㄛ

注音	單字	字號
ㄛ	喔	688
ㄛˊ	哦	631
˙ㄛ	呵	593

ㄜ

注音	單字	字號
ㄜ	婀	1016
	屙	1200
	痾	3602
	疴	3602
	(痾)	
	阿	6594
ㄜˊ	俄	167
	哦	631
	娥	1013
	峨	1228
	莪	4943
	蛾	5234
	訛	5533
	譌	5682
	鋨	6398
	額	6812
	鵝	7152
	鵞	7152
	(鵝)	
	鵝	7152
	(鵝)	
ㄜˇ	惡	1624
	我	1759
	猗	3363
ㄜˋ	俄	167
	厄	506
	呃	582
	噩	752
	崿	1260
	惡	1624
	愕	1633
	戹	1778
	扼	1824
	搤	1824
	(扼)	
	歹	2691
	歺	2691
	(歹)	
	腭	4715
	萼	4999
	諤	5627
	軛	5973
	遏	6125
	鄂	6216
	鍔	6439
	閼	6554
	阨	6586
	阸	6598
	顎	6815
	餓	6875
	鱷	7113
	鶚	7168
	齶	7323

ㄝ

注音	單字	字號
ㄝˋ	誒	5599

ㄞ

注音	單字	字號
ㄞ	哀	620
	哎	628
	唉	642
	埃	837
	挨	1876
ㄞˊ	呆	584
	挨	1876
	捱	1903
	敱	3383
	癌	3667
	皚	3706
	騃	6948
ㄞˇ	噯	759
	欸	2655
	毒	2728
	矮	3837

	異	3574		押	1832		曳	2303		繇	4430		楢	2523		莠	4939
	(異)			椏	2505		業	2526		肴	4640		油	2815		誘	5588
	疫	3597		鴉	7124		液	2909		謠	5659		游	2974		釉	6303
	瘞	3657		鴨	7134		燁	3263		軺	5978		猶	3373		鼬	7292
	益	3720	ㄧㄚˊ	枒	2372		腋	4691		遙	6134		猷	3377	ㄧㄢ	咽	618
	瞖	3806		涯	2908		葉	5001		銚	6376		由	3552		奄	928
	縊	4415		牙	3308		謁	5641		陶	6620		疣	3598		嫣	1052
	繹	4451		芽	4860		鄴	6237		餚	6881		繇	4430		崦	1251
	義	4528		蚜	5205		靨	6734		鰩	7097		蕕	5095		懕	1735
	羿	4537		衙	5367		頁	6780	ㄧㄠˇ	咬	613		蚰	5212		懨	1735
	翊	4541	ㄧㄚˇ	亞	58	ㄧㄞˊ	崖	1240		夭	921		蝣	5277		(懕)	
	翌	4543		啞	665	ㄧㄠ	吆	554		杳	2359		輶	6008		殷	2717
	翳	4559		雅	6660		夭	921		殀	2694		逌	6105		淹	2948
	翼	4560	ㄧㄚˋ	亞	58		妖	962		窅	4046		遊	6121		烟	3199
	肄	4615		婭	1027		幺	1354		窈	4047		郵	6213		焉	3204
	肊	4620		揠	1957		么	1354		舀	4778		鈾	6357		煙	3222
	腋	4691		訝	5534		(幺)			齩	7318		魷	7062		燕	3258
	臆	4742		軋	5967		徼	1494	ㄧㄠˋ	拗	1849	ㄧㄡˇ	卣	492		胭	4659
	薏	5120		迓	6057		祅	3929		曜	2293		友	519		腌	4692
	藝	5144	·ㄧㄚ	呀	581		腰	4706		樂	2571		有	2315		臙	4753
	蜴	5259	ㄧㄛ	唷	663		葽	5021		燿	3276		槱	2567		菸	4971
	衣	5374	ㄧㄝ	噎	746		要	5474		耀	4567		[illegible]	3246		蔫	5083
	裔	5412		掖	1923		邀	6158		葯	5030		[illegible]	3246		鄢	6225
	裛	5418		耶	4591	ㄧㄠˊ	堯	851		藥	5148		([illegible])			醃	6269
	詣	5562	ㄧㄝˊ	揶	1968		姚	986		要	5474		牖	3306		閼	6554
	誼	5604		椰	2512		崤	1245		躍	5950		羑	4516		閹	6555
	議	5683		爺	3293		嶢	1273		鑰	6521		莠	4939	ㄧㄢˊ	嚴	772
	譯	5687		琊	3443		徭	1488		颻	6844		酉	6245		姸	996
	貤	5752		耶	4591		搖	1983		鷂	7182		銪	6384		妍	996
	軼	5981		邪	6176		殽	2720	ㄧㄡ	優	284		黝	7257		(姸)	
	逸	6112	ㄧㄝˇ	也	41		洮	2869		幽	1357	ㄧㄡˋ	佑	130		岩	1224
	邑	6169		冶	336		淆	2918		悠	1592		侑	154		巖	1287
	鎰	6466		野	6307		爻	3294		憂	1694		又	516		延	1406
	鐿	6509	ㄧㄝˋ	咽	618		猺	3378		攸	2116		右	543		掔	2025
	驛	6983		夜	911		傜	3378		滺	3065		囿	794		檐	2609
	鷁	7180		射	1160		(猺)			燠	3266		宥	1120		沿	2823
	黓	7251		拽	1869		瑤	3477		耰	4589		幼	1356		炎	3176
ㄧㄚ	丫	20		掖	1923		窰	4062		麀	7217		有	2315		焰	3216
	呀	581		擪	2083	ㄧㄡ	窯	4062	ㄧㄡˊ	尤	1174		柚	2402		燄	3216
	壓	886		曄	2283		(窰)			斿	2177		祐	3933		(焰)	

	癌	3667
	研	3864
	硏	3864
	(研)	
	筵	4134
	簷	4209
	綖	4352
	蜒	5242
	言	5514
	閻	6552
	顏	6816
	鹽	7215
ㄧㄢˇ	偃	215
	儼	287
	兗	303
	奄	928
	巘	1288
	弇	1412
	掩	1935
	揜	1956
	沇	2795
	渰	2996
	演	3047
	琰	3460
	甗	3535
	眼	3769
	蝘	5272
	衍	5361
	郾	6218
	魘	7059
	黤	7264
	黶	7270
	鼴	7295
	鼹	7297
ㄧㄢˋ	厭	512
	咽	618
	唁	640
	嚥	770
	堰	852
	宴	1125
	彥	1449
	晏	2239
	沿	2823
	灎	3170
	灩	3170
	(灎)	
	焱	3212
	焰	3216
	燄	3216
	(焰)	
	燕	3258
	硯	3868
	艷	4828
	諺	5638
	讌	5696
	讞	5704
	豔	5720
	豓	5721
	贗	5808
	贋	5819
	釅	6301
	雁	6659
	饜	6912
	騐	6956
	驗	6981
	鴈	7126
	鴳	7140
	鷃	7183
	鹽	7215
ㄧㄣ	喑	687
	因	786
	姻	998
	愔	1641
	慇	1669
	殷	2717
	氤	2754
	湮	2987
	瘖	3645
	禋	3957
	絪	4335
	茵	4911
	諲	5643
	銦	6386
	闉	6561
	陰	6615
	陻	6624
	堙	6624
	(陻)	
	音	6774
ㄧㄣˊ	吟	564
	垠	829
	夤	914
	寅	1134
	淫	2940
	狺	3361
	鄞	6228
	銀	6368
	霪	6708
	齗	7310
	齦	7316
ㄧㄣˇ	尹	1181
	引	1419
	檃	2646
	㱃	2671
	癮	3682
	蚓	5204
	隱	6648
	靷	6740
	飲	6857
ㄧㄣˋ	印	496
	廕	1391
	憖	1716
	窨	4059
	胤	4655
	蔭	5084
	陰	6615
	飲	6857
ㄧㄤ	央	923
	殃	2697
	泱	2846
	秧	3991
	鞅	6742
	鴦	7133
ㄧㄤˊ	佯	142
	徉	1469
	揚	1955
	暘	2238
	楊	2516
	洋	2854
	烊	3196
	煬	3227
	瘍	3642
	羊	4512
	陽	6623
	颺	6842
ㄧㄤˇ	仰	96
	氧	2755
	瀁	3144
	癢	3677
	痒	3677
	(癢)	
	鞅	6742
	養	6868
ㄧㄤˋ	怏	1524
	恙	1571
	樣	2585
	漾	3061
	煬	3227
	養	6868
ㄧㄥ	媖	1036
	嬰	1066
	應	1729
	攖	2096
	櫻	2642
	瑛	3469
	瓔	3515
	纓	4470
	罃	4480
	罌	4486
	膺	4738
	英	4877
	鶯	7175
	鷹	7203
	鸚	7205
ㄧㄥˊ	塋	856
	嬴	1064
	楹	2535
	滎	3026
	瀅	3142
	瀛	3150
	瀠	3155
	熒	3241
	營	3264
	瑩	3476
	盈	3718
	縈	4401
	螢	5298
	蠅	5333
	贏	5814
	迎	6055
ㄧㄥˇ	影	1457
	景	2256
	潁	3068
	癭	3681
	穎	4027
	頴	4027
	(穎)	
	郢	6202
ㄧㄥˋ	媵	1040
	應	1729
	映	2224
	硬	3866
	迎	6055

ㄨ

注音	單字	字號
ㄨ	嗚	713
	圬	807
	屋	1192
	巫	1297
	惡	1624
	於	2175
	汚	2779
	污	2779
	(汚)	
	汙	2779
	(汚)	
	烏	3193
	誣	5593
	鄔	6223
ㄨˊ	吳	571
	吾	579
	巫	1297
	无	2195
	梧	2453
	毋	2725
	浯	2906
	無	3214
	蕪	5107
	蜈	5243
	誣	5593
	鼯	7294
ㄨˇ	五	54
	仵	99
	伍	107
	侮	159
	午	477
	嘸	745
	娬	1029
	嫵	1029
	(娬)	
	廡	1397
	忤	1509
	憮	1706
	摀	2000
	武	2686
	牾	3325
	舞	4796
	鵡	7154
ㄨˋ	兀	288

	畬	3576		域	840		谷	5706		說	5598		怨	1547		韻	6778
	盂	3715		嫗	1049		豫	5730		越	5835		愿	1672	ㄩㄥ	傭	242
	禺	3976		寓	1139		遇	6120		躍	5950		掾	1947		墉	872
	窬	4060		尉	1163		遹	6153		軏	5972		瑗	3474		壅	884
	竽	4087		峪	1235		郁	6188		鉞	6352		苑	4863		庸	1378
	腴	4709		彧	1450		鈺	6356		鑰	6521		遠	6138		廱	1404
	臾	4775		御	1482		閾	6557		閱	6551		院	6609		慵	1681
	舁	4777		愈	1649		隩	6646		龠	7329		願	6820		擁	2056
	與	4782		慾	1692		雨	6681	ㄩㄢ	冤	330	ㄩㄣ	暈	2267		灉	3160
	萸	5024		拗	1849		雩	6682		寃	330		氳	2760		癰	3684
	虞	5186		昱	2230		預	6790		(寃)			贇	5812		臃	4741
	褕	5440		棫	2495		飫	6858		嬽	1050	ㄩㄣˊ	云	52		邕	6172
	覦	5488		欲	2654		馭	6922		淵	2942		勻	448		鄘	6226
	諛	5622		毓	2730		鬱	7045		鳶	7121		昀	2222		雍	6663
	踰	5897		汩	2781		鬻	7047		鴛	7129		筠	4124		雝	6678
	輿	6015		浴	2889		魊	7056		鵷	7161		紜	4296		饔	6909
	轝	6031		煜	3221		鴥	7135	ㄩㄢˊ	元	290		耘	4583	ㄩㄥˊ	傭	242
	逾	6115		熨	3247		鵒	7146		原	509		芸	4857		喁	676
	隃	6625		燠	3266		鷸	7197		員	629		蕓	5110		墉	872
	隅	6627		獄	3384		黦	7263		園	801		雲	6687		庸	1378
	雩	6682		玉	3408		龥	7331		圓	802	ㄩㄣˇ	允	289		慵	1681
	餘	6879		瘉	3647	ㄩㄝ	曰	2301		援	1965		殞	2705		顒	6817
	魚	7060		癒	3674		約	4282		沅	2792		狁	3345		鱅	7103
ㄩˇ	予	47		矞	3828	ㄩㄝˋ	刖	367		湲	2992		磒	3902	ㄩㄥˇ	俑	172
	傴	245		禦	3965		岳	1221		源	2999		隕	6635		勇	430
	圄	796		禺	3976		嶽	1280		爰	3287	ㄩㄣˋ	孕	1077		壅	884
	宇	1103		籞	4225		悅	1582		猿	3379		惲	1629		慂	1667
	嶼	1279		籲	4232		戉	1753		猨	3379		慍	1657		擁	2056
	庾	1380		聿	4614		曜	2293		(猿)			暈	2267		永	2762
	敔	2132		育	4639		月	2314		緣	4388		熨	3247		泳	2847
	瑀	3475		與	4782		樂	2571		芫	4847		縕	4410		涌	2907
	禹	3975		芋	4835		樾	2592		苑	4863		蘊	5163		湧	2983
	窳	4063		蔚	5072		瀹	3157		蝯	5289		藴	5163		甬	3548
	羽	4536		蕷	5113		禴	3974		螈	5293		(蘊)			臃	4741
	與	4782		蜮	5258		籥	4227		袁	5387		運	6122		蛹	5232
	語	5591		裕	5413		粵	4243		轅	6018		鄆	6217		詠	5550
	鋙	6406		語	5591		耀	4567		黿	7276		醞	6280		咏	5550
	雨	6681		諭	5619		葯	5030	ㄩㄢˇ	遠	6138		韞	6772		(詠)	
	齬	7320		譽	5690		藥	5148	ㄩㄢˋ	媛	1034		韻	6775		踊	5880
ㄩˋ	喻	698													ㄩㄥˋ	用	3545

國語羅馬字索引

編　法：本索引係照單字讀音，按國語羅馬字字母順序編列。其讀音相同者，再按部首順序。單字後註明單字編號。

用　法：遇有僅知讀音不悉字形之單字，可按國語羅馬字字母查出索引中單字，再根據單字編號，查出書內單字及這一單字爲首所組成的詞語。

GWOYEU ROMATZYH INDEX

In this index the characters are arranged according to the alphabetical order of Gwoyeu Romatzyh. Characters with the same pronunciation are arranged according to their respective radicals. The figure to the right of each character is its identification number under which the character can be found in the body of the dictionary.

If the dictionary user knows the pronunciation of the character he is looking for but is unfamiliar with its strokes, he can find it in the index according to the alphabetical order of Gwoyeu Romatzyh. Using the identification number as a guide, he can locate in the dictionary the character and the entries beneath it.

	箔	4142
	篺	4207
	檗	4268
	脖	4685
	膊	4723
	舶	4809
	荸	4950
	蔔	5081
	薄	5111
	踣	5889
	鈸	6340
	鉑	6349
	鎛	6462
	雹	6691
	駁	6928
	駮	6943
	鵓	7149
bu	晡	2249
	逋	6088
	餔	6876
buh	不	8
	佈	125
	埠	841
	布	1307
	怖	1525
	步	2684
	篰	4194
	簿	4214
	部	6206
buu	卜	488
	哺	637
	捕	1892
	補	5415
bwu	不	8
	醭	6290
bye	別	372
	蹩	5929
	蹴	5939
byi	荸	4950
	鼻	7298

C

注音	單字	字號
•ch	啐	659
cha	叉	517
	喳	702
	差	1298
	扠	1801
	扱	1807
	插	1954
	揷	1954
	(插)	
	杈	2342
	臿	4776
chaa	叉	517
chaan	剷	406
	產	3541
	蕆	5091
	諂	5606
	鏟	6487
	闡	6578
chaang	場	853
	廠	1396
	惝	1615
	敞	2134
	昶	2232
	氅	2743
chae	茝	4951
chah	侘	155
	剎	379
	刹	379
	(剎)	
	姹	997
	奼	997
	(姹)	
	岔	1212
	差	1298
	杈	2342
	汊	2768
	衩	5377

注音	單字	字號
	詫	5567
chai	差	1298
	拆	1837
	釵	6325
chair	儕	280
	柴	2413
	茈	4882
	豺	5736
chan	攙	2098
	襜	5463
chang	倀	188
	倡	207
	娼	1026
	昌	2216
	猖	3362
	菖	4963
	閶	6553
chann	懺	1743
	羼	4535
	顫	6830
chanq	倡	207
	唱	649
	悵	1598
	暢	2273
	韔	6769
	鬯	7044
chao	吵	572
	炒	3182
char	察	1142
	搽	1981
	査	2411
	槎	2559
	碴	3891
	苴	4878
	茶	4912
charn	單	701
	嬋	1057
	孱	1091
	巉	1282
	廛	1393

注音	單字	字號
	欃	2644
	毚	2734
	潺	3085
	澶	3111
	瀍	3143
	禪	3968
	纏	4465
	蟬	5324
	蟾	5332
	讒	5699
	饞	6914
charng	償	282
	嘗	733
	場	853
	嫦	1053
	常	1327
	徜	1478
	腸	4710
	萇	4977
	裳	5425
	長	6528
chau	弨	1427
	抄	1812
	超	5834
	鈔	6331
chaur	嘲	739
	巢	1292
	晁	2243
	朝	2324
	潮	3082
	鼂	7277
chaw	鈔	6331
chay	瘥	3655
	蠆	5334
che	車	5966
chea	卡	491
chean	淺	2947
	繾	4460
	譴	5689
	遣	6141

注音	單字	字號
cheang	強	1434
	强	1434
	(強)	
	彊	1434
	(強)	
	搶	1989
	襁	5454
	繈	5454
	(襁)	
	鏹	6484
cheau	巧	1295
	悄	1581
	愀	1637
	雀	6657
	鵲	7160
chee	尺	1180
	扯	1805
	撦	2041
cheeng	懲	1738
	逞	6099
	騁	6945
cheh	坼	824
	徹	1492
	拆	1837
	掣	1941
	撤	2030
	澈	3089
	轍	6023
chen	嗔	712
	抻	1904
	琛	3445
	瞋	3796
	郴	6210
cheng	撐	2027
	撑	2027
	(撐)	
	檉	2611
	瞠	3309
	琤	3448
	瞠	3804

注音	單字	字號
	稱	4015
	蟶	5329
	赬	5826
	鐺	6507
chenn	櫬	2635
	稱	4015
	襯	5468
	讖	5701
	趁	5832
	趂	5832
	(趁)	
	齔	7308
chenq	秤	3992
	稱	4015
cheou	糗	4255
chern	塵	867
	宸	1128
	忱	1513
	晨	2253
	橙	2599
	沈	2798
	沉	2798
	(沈)	
	臣	4759
	蔯	5085
	諶	5635
	辰	6047
	陳	6617
cherng	丞	17
	乘	36
	呈	570
	城	835
	懲	1738
	成	1757
	承	1825
	晟	2245
	棖	2483
	橙	2599
	澄	3088
	澂	3099

盜	3727		嶝	1271		靛	6726		砥	3849	doong	懂	1723		炖	3179
	稻	4022		澄	3088	diau	凋	341		舾	5504		董	5008		燉	3253
	纛	4473		凳	3691		刁	357		詆	5548	doou	抖	1821		盾	3752
	翿	4566		櫈	3691		叼	529		邸	6187		斗	2156		遁	6117
	菿	4978		(櫈)			彫	1451	diing	酊	6246		蚪	5201		鈍	6334
	蹈	5907		瞪	3810		碉	3876		頂	6781		陡	6608		頓	6793
	道	6129		磴	3909		貂	5738		鼎	7283	dou	兜	304	duey	兌	298
day	代	91		蹬	5930		雕	6670	ding	丁	2		篼	4182		對	1166
	大	916		鄧	6230		鯛	7081		仃	75		都	6214		憝	1715
	岱	1220		鐙	6496		鵰	7158		叮	538	dow	痘	3623		憝	1737
	帶	1325	der	得	1476	diaw	弔	1420		玎	3410		竇	4070		敦	2138
	待	1466		德	1493		吊	1420		町	3557		脰	4682		碓	3877
	怠	1545	di	低	127		(弔)			疔	3591		荳	4954		隊	6632
	戴	1775		提	1951		掉	1920		盯	3740		讀	5692	duh	妒	961
	殆	2695		氐	2747		調	5605		釘	6313		豆	5710		妒	961
	玳	3420		滴	3033		釣	6320		靪	6736		逗	6095		(妒)	
	袋	5391		甋	4522		銚	6376	dinq	定	1114		餖	6877		度	1369
	襶	5471		隄	6626	die	爹	3292		碇	3878		鬥	7036		敦	2146
	貸	5766		堤	6626	dih	地	810		訂	5516		鬦	7037		杜	2349
	迨	6066		(隄)			娣	1012		釘	6313		鬪	7041		渡	2960
	逮	6107	dian	顛	1286		帝	1320		錠	6424		鬭	7042		肚	4626
	靆	6719		掂	1910		弟	1424		釘	6851	du	督	3787		蠹	5353
	黛	7255		攧	2105		棣	2487	diou	丟	18		都	6214		蠹	5353
•de	得	1476		滇	3021		的	3696		銩	6388		闍	6566		(蠹)	
	的	3696		顛	3686		睇	3774	doan	短	3836	duan	端	4083		鍍	6438
	襶	5471		顛	6822		禘	3962	doen	盹	3751		耑	4578	duo	哆	624
dean	典	319	diann	佃	122		第	4102		躉	5945	duann	斷	2173		多	909
	碘	3881		墊	873		締	4385	dong	冬	334		段	2716	duoh	剁	380
	點	7254		奠	942		蒂	5028		咚	596		緞	4382		咄	601
deei	得	1476		店	1366		蔕	5070		東	2360		鍛	6441		墮	880
deeng	戥	1768		惦	1616		螮	5304		蝀	5264		煅	6441		度	1369
	等	4113		殿	2721		蝶	5304		鶇	7288		(鍛)			惰	1625
deng	燈	3250		淀	2914		(螮)		donq	凍	343	duei	堆	847		柚	2415
	登	3689		澱	3107		諦	5628		動	433	duen	墩	879		桗	2418
	簦	4202		玷	3419		遞	6137		峒	1226		惇	1607		舵	4808
	登	5714		甸	3556	dii	底	1364		恫	1561		敦	2138		跺	5873
	鐙	6496		坫	3613		抵	1829		棟	2485		燉	3253		躱	5898
denq	凳	350		簟	4199		柢	2406		洞	2859		蹲	5928		馱	6924
	櫈	350		鈿	6342		氐	2747		胴	4663	duenn	噸	757	duoo	朵	2339
	(凳)			電	6690		牴	3320		蝀	5264		沌	2797

	朵	2339
	(朶)	
	躲	5963
duu	堵	854
	睹	3790
	篤	4170
	肚	4626
	覩	5489
	賭	5799
dwo	多	909
	奪	945
	掇	1914
	敠	2135
	裰	5421
	鐸	6506
dwu	櫝	2632
	毒	2729
	瀆	3136
	牘	3307
	犢	3335
	獨	3391
	碡	3883
	纛	4473
	讀	5692
	韥	6793
	髑	7006
	黷	7271
dye	喋	685
	惵	1628
	昳	2234
	牒	3304
	瓞	3517
	疊	3586
	疂	3586
	(疊)	
	眣	3757
	碟	3892
	絰	4336
	耋	4574
	蜨	5265
	蝶	5286
	褶	5451
	諜	5623
	跌	5852
	蹀	5901
	迭	6069
	鰈	7086
dyi	嫡	1051
	敵	2141
	滌	3030
	狄	3344
	的	3696
	笛	4096
	糴	4272
	翟	4547
	荻	4930
	覿	5498
	踧	5891
	蹢	5922
	迪	6067
	廸	6067
	(迪)	
	適	6144
	鏑	6480

E

注音	單字	字號
e	婀	1016
	屙	1200
	疴	3602
	痾	3602
	(疴)	
	阿	6594
ee	惡	1624
	我	1759
	猗	3363
eel	洱	2866
	爾	3296
	珥	3430
	耳	4590
	邇	6163
	鉺	6382
	餌	6869
	駬	6942
een	嗯	716
eh	俄	167
	厄	506
	呃	582
	噩	752
	崿	1260
	惡	1624
	愕	1633
	戹	1778
	扼	1824
	扼	1824
	(扼)	
	歹	2691
	歺	2691
	(歹)	
	腭	4715
	蕚	4999
	諤	5627
	軛	5973
	遏	6125
	鄂	6216
	鍔	6439
	閼	6554
	阨	6586
	阸	6598
	顎	6815
	餓	6875
	鱷	7113
	鶚	7168
	齶	7323
êh	誒	5599
ell	二	49
	貳	5762
en	恩	1573
enn	嗯	716
	摁	1997
er	俄	167
	哦	631
	娥	1013
	峨	1228
	莪	4943
	蛾	5234
	訛	5533
	譌	5682
	鋨	6398
	額	6812
	鵝	7152
	鵞	7152
	(鵝)	
	䳘	7152
	(鵝)	
erl	兒	300
	洏	2876
	而	4575
	胹	4673
ern	嗯	716
ey	欸	2655

F

注音	單字	字號
fa	伐	110
	法	2832
	發	3690
faa	法	2832
	灋	2832
	(法)	
	髮	7015
faan	反	520
	返	6058
faang	仿	102
	倣	102
	(仿)	
	彷	1459
	昉	2214
	紡	4300
	舫	4803
	訪	5539
	髣	7011
fah	法	2832
	琺	3453
fan	帆	1308
	帆	1308
	(帆)	
	幡	1341
	旛	2192
	番	3575
	繙	4441
	翻	4562
	蕃	5090
	飜	6848
fang	坊	811
	妨	969
	方	2174
	枋	2370
	肪	4635
	芳	4855
fann	梵	2465
	氾	2764
	汎	2769
	泛	2838
	犯	3340
	笵	4108
	範	4161
	范	4887
	販	5755
	飯	6859
fanq	放	2119
far	乏	33
	伐	110
	法	2832
	砝	3853
	筏	4114
	罰	4501
	閥	6545
farn	凡	347
	帆	1308
	帆	1308
	(帆)	
	樊	2579
	煩	3226
	燔	3256
	璠	3500
	礬	3918
	繁	4428
	緐	4428
	(繁)	
	膰	4734
	蕃	5090
	藩	5149
	蘩	5171
	蹯	5932
	釩	6319
farng	妨	969
	房	1781
	肪	4635
	防	6590
	魴	7064
feei	匪	465
	悱	1597
	斐	2152
	朏	2318
	棐	2491
	榧	2562
	篚	4168
	翡	4550
	菲	4970
	蜚	5250
	誹	5603
feen	粉	4235
feeng	唪	668
fei	啡	652
	妃	957
	扉	1788
	緋	4376
	菲	4970
	蜚	5250

	霏	6700
	非	6728
	飛	6847
	鯡	7079
feir	淝	2927
	肥	4633
	腓	4701
fen	分	359
	吩	567
	棻	2490
	氛	2751
	紛	4299
	芬	4848
	棻	4960
	雰	6685
feng	丰	22
	封	1159
	夆	1230
	楓	2515
	灃	3161
	烽	3201
	瘋	3643
	葑	5002
	蜂	5236
	蠭	5350
	豐	5719
	酆	6242
	鋒	6404
	風	6837
fenn	分	359
	份	359
	(分)	
	噴	761
	奮	948
	忿	1520
	憤	1719
	糞	4260
fenq	俸	185
	奉	931
	縫	4416
	諷	5636
	風	6837
	鳳	7119
fern	墳	881
	粉	2369
	棼	2492
	汾	2789
	焚	3211
	羒	4521
	蕡	5098
	賁	5773
ferng	縫	4416
	逢	6103
	馮	6923
fey	吠	565
	廢	1398
	佛	1533
	沸	2814
	狒	3350
	痱	3633
	疿	3633
	(痱)	
	肺	4642
	芾	4861
	費	5768
foou	否	566
	缶	4476
for	佛	137
four	浮	2890
	罘	4493
	芣	4843
fu	夫	919
	孵	1093
	敷	2142
	枹	2389
	柎	2392
	膚	4724
	趺	5848
	跗	5856
	鄜	6227
	鈇	6332
	麩	7235
fuh	仆	77
	付	86
	傅	234
	副	399
	咐	606
	婦	1024
	富	1136
	復	1485
	服	2317
	父	3290
	祔	3935
	腹	4711
	蝜	5281
	蝮	5283
	複	5432
	覆	5476
	訃	5518
	負	5748
	賦	5796
	賻	5802
	赴	5829
	輹	6013
	阜	6582
	附	6597
	馥	6919
	駙	6936
	鮒	7067
	鰒	7089
fuu	俯	181
	府	1368
	拊	1839
	撫	2042
	斧	2166
	父	3290
	甫	3547
	簠	4203
	脯	4680
	腐	4695
	腑	4696
	莆	4945
	輔	5991
	釜	6314
	頫	6799
	黼	7274
fwu	伏	109
	俘	174
	匐	455
	夫	919
	孚	1080
	帗	1314
	幅	1328
	弗	1421
	彿	1465
	怫	1533
	扶	1804
	拂	1834
	服	2317
	枹	2389
	桴	2451
	氟	2752
	洑	2852
	浮	2890
	涪	2910
	祓	3934
	福	3956
	符	4101
	箙	4151
	紱	4310
	紼	4313
	縛	4408
	罘	4493
	艴	4827
	芙	4839
	芾	4861
	苻	4883
	茀	4895
	茯	4907
	莩	4942
	菔	4962
	蚨	5208
	蜉	5244
	蝠	5275
	袱	5400
	輻	6010
	郛	6196
	韍	6767
	髴	7016
	鳧	7116
	鵩	7156
	黻	7273

G

注音	單字	字號
ga	咖	605
	旮	2204
gaan	感	1652
	擀	2065
	敢	2136
	桿	2474
	橄	2591
	澉	3097
	稈	4003
	簳	4215
	趕	5839
gaang	岡	1216
	崗	1241
	港	2967
gae	改	2117
gah	尬	1176
gai	垓	830
	荄	4916
	該	5573
	賅	5778
	陔	6603
gan	乾	44
	乾	44
	(乾)	
	尷	1178
	干	1348
	杆	2353
	柑	2398
	泔	2830
	玕	3411
	甘	3536
	疳	3600
	竿	4088
	肝	4628
gang	剛	396
	岡	1216
	崗	1241
	杠	2352
	綱	4360
	繮	4447
	缸	4477
	罡	4494
	肛	4627
	鋼	6414
gann	幹	1353
	旰	2206
	榦	2541
	淦	2933
	灨	3169
	紺	4317
	贛	5820
	骭	6991
ganq	槓	2560
	虹	5195
gao	搞	2003
	攪	2108
	杲	2358
	槁	2554
	槀	2554
	(槁)	
	稿	4019
	稾	4019
	(稿)	
	縞	4411
	鎬	6464

guanq	桄	2441
	誑	5585
	逛	6098
guay	夬	920
	怪	1535
guei	傀	233
	圭	808
	歸	2690
	潙	3095
	珪	3435
	瑰	3480
	瓌	3514
	皈	3699
	規	5482
	邽	6194
	閨	6546
	鮭	7070
	龜	7328
guenn	棍	2479
guey	劊	413
	會	2312
	桂	2439
	檜	2612
	櫃	2624
	溎	3027
	瞶	3812
	貴	5763
	跪	5867
	鱖	7106
guh	估	114
	僱	265
	固	793
	故	2122
	梏	2460
	痼	3637
	錮	6430
	雇	6662
	顧	6826
guo	渦	2965
	蟈	5314
	過	6124
	郭	6208
	鍋	6437
guoh	過	6124
guoo	果	2377
	椁	2504
	槨	2504
	(椁)	
	猓	3368
	菓	4995
	蜾	5262
	裹	5427
	餜	6887
guu	古	530
	嘏	730
	穀	2542
	榾	2563
	汩	2781
	牯	3318
	盬	3738
	瞽	3818
	縠	4018
	罟	4495
	羖	4519
	股	4631
	臌	4745
	蓇	5058
	蠱	5348
	詁	5547
	谷	5706
	賈	5779
	轂	6016
	鈷	6358
	骨	6990
	鴣	7153
	鶻	7178
	鼓	7287
gwo	國	797
	幗	1336
	摑	2005
	虢	5190
	馘	6917
	聝	6917
	(馘)	
gwu	骨	6990

H

注音	單字	字號
ha	哈	626
haa	哈	626
haan	喊	684
	罕	4492
	闞	6576
hae	海	2891
	醢	6284
hair	孩	1088
	還	6161
	頦	6798
	骸	6997
han	憨	1717
	蚶	5214
	酣	6254
	頇	6785
	鼾	7299
hang	夯	924
hann	悍	1586
	憾	1721
	扞	1796
	捍	1890
	撼	2052
	旱	2207
	暵	2277
	汗	2772
	漢	3053
	瀚	3147
	翰	4558
	菡	4984
	豻	5737
	銲	6411
	釬	6411
	(銲)	
	頷	6805
	馯	6950
hanq	桁	2432
	沆	2796
hao	好	954
	郝	6198
har	蛤	5225
	蝦	5280
harn	函	355
	含	568
	寒	1138
	嵅	1250
	榦	2541
	汗	2772
	涵	2911
	邯	6180
	韓	6768
harng	杭	2356
	桁	2432
	沆	2796
	航	4801
	行	5360
	迒	6061
	頏	6789
hau	嚆	764
	蒿	5043
	薅	5112
haur	嗥	742
	嚎	762
	壕	889
	毫	2737
	濠	3122
	號	5188
	蠔	5340
	豪	5728
	貉	5740
	鶴	7173
haw	好	954
	昊	2215
	晧	2252
	浩	2883
	滈	2912
	澔	3098
	灝	3165
	皓	3702
	皜	3707
	耗	4584
	號	5188
	鄗	6220
	鎬	6464
	顥	6828
hay	亥	63
	咳	616
	害	1124
	氦	2756
	駭	6940
he	呵	593
	喝	693
	訶	5543
heen	很	1468
	狠	3352
heh	和	604
	喝	693
	嚇	766
	奭	947
	荷	4927
	豁	5707
	賀	5771
	赫	5824
	郝	6198
	鶴	7173
	黑	7250
hei	嘿	747
	黑	7250
heng	亨	65
	哼	638
henn	恨	1558
henq	橫	2606
her	何	132
	劾	426
	合	547
	和	604
	曷	2305
	核	2428
	河	2816
	涸	2912
	盍	3721
	盒	3724
	禾	3978
	紇	4284
	翮	4557
	荷	4927
	蓋	5049
	褐	5435
	覈	5477
	貉	5740
	鉿	6385
	閡	6543
	閤	6544
	闔	6571
	鞨	6753
	鶡	7169
	齕	7309
	龢	7330
hern	痕	3620
herng	恆	1551
	恒	1551
	(恆)	
	桁	2432
	橫	2606
	珩	3433
	蘅	5159
	衡	5372
hm	噷	758
hoan	浣	2882
	澣	3118
	緩	4390
hoang	幌	1333
	恍	1536

	湛	2986
	站	4074
	綻	4367
	蘸	5174
	蹔	5926
	顫	6830
janq	丈	4
	仗	85
	嶂	1266
	帳	1324
	幛	1338
	杖	2348
	漲	3060
	瘴	3659
	脹	4688
	賬	5798
	長	6528
	障	6641
jao	找	1809
	沼	2817
	爪	3284
jar	劄	408
	扎	1791
	札	2334
	炸	3189
	箚	4150
	紮	4304
	紥	4304
	(紮)	
	鍘	6440
	閘	6540
jau	招	1855
	昭	2228
	朝	2324
	着	3776
	著	5003
	釗	6315
jaur	着	3776
	著	5003
jaw	兆	293
	召	536
	旐	2188
	曌	2287
	棹	2502
	櫂	2627
	炤	3191
	照	3232
	笊	4090
	罩	4498
	肇	4618
	詔	5554
	趙	5838
jay	債	246
	寨	1149
	瘵	3661
	砦	3858
je	折	1822
	螫	5301
	遮	6145
·je	着	3776
	著	5003
jea	假	216
	夏	904
	岬	1218
	斝	2160
	檟	2614
	甲	3553
	胛	4650
	賈	5779
	鉀	6343
jean	儉	274
	剪	400
	戩	1769
	揀	1944
	撿	2067
	柬	2410
	檢	2615
	減	2959
	瞼	3817
	筧	4137
	簡	4200
	簡	4200
	(簡)	
	繭	4453
	翦	4551
	襇	5458
	謇	5652
	譾	5691
	趼	5861
	跰	5861
	(趼)	
	蹇	5908
	鐧	6498
	鹻	7213
	鹼	7214
jeang	獎	946
	槳	2570
	蔣	5074
	講	5657
jeau	佼	145
	僥	260
	剿	405
	勦	405
	(剿)	
	徼	1494
	撟	2040
	攪	2108
	湫	2988
	狡	3353
	皎	3701
	矯	3838
	筊	4123
	絞	4330
	繳	4449
	脚	4687
	腳	4707
	角	5500
	蹻	5936
	較	5983
	鉸	6369
	餃	6865
jee	者	4572
	赭	5825
	鍺	6450
jeen	枕	2373
	畛	3565
	疹	3603
	稹	4024
	紾	4314
	縝	4412
	胗	4657
	診	5544
	軫	5975
	鬒	7030
jeeng	拯	1859
	整	2145
jeh	宅	1102
	柘	2400
	浙	2878
	蔗	5071
	這	6096
	鷓	7186
jen	偵	229
	振	1880
	斟	2161
	椹	2508
	楨	2528
	榛	2540
	珍	3425
	甄	3527
	眞	3762
	真	3762
	(眞)	
	砧	3850
	禎	3960
	禛	3964
	箴	4158
	胗	4657
	臻	4772
	蓁	5045
	診	5544
	貞	5749
	針	6316
	鍼	6447
	鱵	7111
jeng	丁	2
	崢	1244
	征	1463
	徵	1491
	怔	1537
	掙	1925
	楨	2528
	正	2682
	烝	3195
	爭	3286
	狰	3365
	癥	3679
	睜	3781
	箏	4139
	蒸	5039
	諍	5611
	貞	5749
	鉦	6355
	錚	6423
jenn	振	1880
	揕	1952
	朕	2320
	枕	2373
	瑱	3481
	賑	5783
	酖	6251
	鎮	6465
	陣	6610
	陳	6617
	震	6693
	鴆	7122
jenq	幀	1330
	掙	1925
	政	2121
	正	2682
	症	3608
	証	5561
	證	5674
	鄭	6231
jeong	扃	1784
	泂	2822
	炯	3186
	烱	3186
	(炯)	
	窘	4054
	絅	4322
	迥	6064
	逈	6084
jeou	久	29
	九	39
	灸	3173
	玖	3412
	糺	4276
	糾	4277
	韮	5032
	赳	5828
	酒	6250
	韭	6773
jer	哲	636
	慴	1682
	懾	1745
	折	1822
	摘	2004
	摺	2016
	磔	3899
	翟	4547
	蜇	5239
	蟄	5312
	褶	5451
	謫	5667
	讁	5694
	輒	5989
	輙	6005
	轍	6023
jeu	咀	600

K

	愷	1658
	慨	1678
	楷	2533
	豈	5712
	鍇	6453
	鎧	6463
	闓	6570
kah	喀	675
kai	揩	1961
	開	6533
kan	刊	362
	勘	435
	堪	850
	戡	1766
	看	3755
	龕	7327
kang	康	1377
	慷	1679
	糠	4264
kann	勘	435
	看	3755
	瞰	3808
	矙	3824
	闞	6576
kanq	亢	61
	伉	104
	抗	1820
	炕	3178
	鈧	6327
kao	拷	1871
	栲	2430
	烤	3198
	考	4569
	攷	4569
	(考)	
karng	扛	1798
kau	尻	1182
kaw	犒	3332
	銬	6380
	靠	6729
kay	愒	1631
	愾	1659
	慨	1678
	欬	2653
ke	刻	384
	柯	2408
	棵	2499
	珂	3422
	痾	3602
	疴	3602
	(痾)	
	瞌	3800
	磕	3900
	科	3984
	稞	4013
	窠	4056
	苛	4869
	蝌	5269
	軻	5980
	鈳	6365
	頦	6798
	顆	6810
	髁	7001
kee	可	539
	坷	823
	渴	2970
keen	啃	666
	墾	883
	懇	1731
	肯	4637
	肎	4637
	(肯)	
	肻	4637
	(肯)	
keeng	肯	4637
	肎	4637
	(肯)	
	肻	4637
	(肯)	
keh	克	297
	刻	384
	剋	390
	可	539
	嗑	721
	客	1117
	恪	1560
	溘	3000
	緙	4399
	課	5600
keng	傾	249
	坑	819
	硜	3865
	鏗	6482
	阬	6585
kenn	裉	5404
ker	咳	616
	欬	2653
	殼	2719
	㱿	2719
	(殼)	
	壳	2719
	(殼)	
	頦	6798
koa	垮	833
koai	擓	2068
	舀	4778
	蒯	5036
koan	款	2657
	欵	2657
	(款)	
	窾	4066
koei	傀	233
	跬	5869
	頍	6794
koen	壼	902
	悃	1579
	捆	1886
	綑	4351
	閫	6548
kong	悾	1603
	空	4042
	箜	4147
konq	控	1931
	空	4042
koong	孔	1076
	恐	1567
koou	口	527
kou	摳	2014
kow	叩	533
	寇	1135
	扣	1797
	蔻	5065
	釦	6323
	鷇	7184
ku	刳	378
	哭	634
	枯	2380
	窟	4055
	骷	6995
kua	夸	926
	姱	995
	誇	5579
kuah	胯	4660
	跨	5860
	髂	6996
kuan	寬	1152
kuang	匡	463
	恇	1562
	框	2443
	筐	4116
	誆	5581
kuanq	壙	890
	曠	2295
	框	2443
	況	2821
	况	2821
	(況)	
	眶	3767
	礦	3919
	纊	4463
	貺	5767
	鄺	6240
	鑛	6516
kuay	儈	273
	劊	413
	塊	855
	快	1510
	旝	2193
	會	2312
	檜	2612
	澮	3104
	獪	3392
	筷	4136
	膾	4737
	蒯	5036
	鄶	6238
kuei	巋	1283
	悝	1591
	盔	3725
	窺	4064
	虧	5191
	闚	6575
kuen	坤	821
	崑	1238
	昆	2212
	琨	3450
	蚰	5229
	褌	5434
	錕	6429
	髡	7009
	鯤	7078
	鵾	7159
kuenn	困	787
	睏	3775
kuey	匱	468
	喟	695
	愧	1654
	媿	1654
	(愧)	
	憒	1704
	潰	3087
	簣	4201
	聵	4610
	蕢	5100
	餽	6898
	饋	6902
kuh	庫	1373
	矻	3843
	袴	5399
	絝	5399
	(袴)	
	褲	5449
	酷	6264
kuoh	廓	1390
	括	1860
	擴	2086
	闊	6562
kuu	楛	2519
	苦	4874
kwang	狂	3343
	誑	5585
kwei	夔	906
	奎	933
	揆	1946
	暌	2271
	睽	3791
	葵	5017
	逵	6110
	馗	6916
	騤	6960
	魁	7049

L

注音	單字	字號
la	剌	391
	拉	1838
	旯	2205
·la	啦	664
laa	喇	681
laan	懶	1740

	晾	2263		鬣	7035		隸	6653		臨	4763		齡	7313		閭	6550
	諒	5614		鴷	7143		靂	6717		轔	6025	linn	吝	562		驢	6985
	踉	5878	lih	例	151		鬁	7021		遴	6148		淋	2924	liuan	孌	1097
	輛	5996		俐	171		鬲	7046		鄰	6233		磷	3910		攣	2106
	量	6308		儷	286		麗	7228		隣	6643		藺	5152	liueh	掠	1927
liau	僚	258		利	374	lii	俚	175		霖	6703		賃	5774		略	3572
	嘹	743		力	417		哩	633		驎	6979		躪	5959		畧	3572
	寥	1147		勵	445		娌	1004		鱗	7107	linq	令	92		(略)	
	寮	1153		厲	513		悝	1591		麐	7223		另	532	liuh	律	1471
	寮	1172		吏	560		李	2340		麟	7232	liou	劉	412		慮	1695
	憀	1684		唳	650		浬	2886	ling	令	92		旒	2189		氯	2758
	憭	1707		慄	1660		澧	3103		伶	117		榴	2550		濾	3137
	撩	2044		戾	1779		理	3441		凌	342		流	2875		率	3407
	漻	3069		曆	2282		禮	3970		囹	792		瀏	3141		綠	4354
	潦	3079		栗	2426		蠡	5344		岭	1219		琉	3438		葎	4990
	獠	3388		櫟	2629		裏	5410		怜	1538		留	3569	·lo	咯	614
	療	3665		櫪	2634		裡	5410		櫺	2640		畱	3569	loan	卵	498
	繚	4439		歷	2689		(裏)			泠	2837		(留)		long	嚨	771
	聊	4598		沴	2813		豊	5715		淩	2935		瘤	3658		攏	2094
	遼	6155		涖	2904		邐	6168		玲	3418		癅	3658		曨	2298
	鐐	6495		溧	3007		醴	6293		瓴	3523		(瘤)			朧	2329
	鷯	7193		瀝	3148		里	6305		綾	4369		硫	3863		櫳	2637
liaw	廖	1388		痢	3625		鋰	6396		羚	4523		硫	3863		櫳	2637
	撂	2021		癘	3673		鯉	7076		翎	4542		(硫)			(櫳)	
	料	2157		礫	3916	liin	凜	344		聆	4597		遛	6135		瀧	3152
	燎	3252		礪	3917		廩	1401		舲	4805		鎦	6500		瓏	3513
	瞭	3811		立	4073		懍	1727		苓	4865		騮	6968		癃	3666
	鐐	6495		笠	4095		檁	2617		菱	4987		驑	6980		矓	3822
lie	咧	607		粒	4237		澟	3117		蛉	5219		鷚	7181		礱	3921
liee	咧	607		糲	4271	liing	嶺	1278		軨	5976	liow	六	313		窿	4067
lieh	冽	338		苙	4892		領	6795		輘	5995		溜	3003		籠	4224
	列	368		荔	4903	lin	嶙	1268		酃	6241		遛	6135		聾	4613
	劣	420		莅	4929		林	2375		醽	6298		霤	6710		蘢	5166
	捩	1899		莉	4946		淋	2924		鈴	6341		霤	6710		隆	6628
	洌	2853		蒞	5060		燐	3255		陵	6619		(霤)			龍	7325
	烈	3194		蠣	5346		琳	3459		零	6688		餾	6896	lonq	弄	1411
	獵	3398		詈	5549		璘	3496		霝	6706		䭷	6907		衖	5365
	裂	5403		轢	6033		痳	3634		靈	6720	liu	婁	1019	loong	壟	892
	趔	5837		轣	6036		瞵	3814		鯪	7083		櫚	2628		攏	2094
	躐	5951		酈	6243		磷	3910		鴒	7127		瘻	3662		籠	4224

	隴	6652		圇	798		籮	4231		麻	7241		盲	3742		茂	4886
loou	摟	2007		崙	1242		羅	4509		麼	7242		硭	3869		袤	5395
	簍	4193		掄	1915		蘿	5177	·ma	嗎	709		芒	4838		貌	5741
lou	僂	250		淪	2936		螺	5307		蟆	5313		茫	4906		貿	5772
	嘍	729		綸	4365		覶	5495		麼	7242		邙	6170	may	脈	4671
	婁	1019		論	5615		覼	5495		麼	7242		鋩	6408		衇	4671
	摟	2007		輪	6003		(覶)			(麼)		mann	嫚	1050		(脈)	
	樓	2580	luenn	論	5615		邏	6167	maa	嗎	709		幔	1334		脉	4671
	蔞	5082	luh	僇	253		鑼	6524		瑪	3482		慢	1674		(脈)	
	螻	5308		六	313		騾	6969		碼	3895		曼	2308		賣	5794
	髏	7002		勠	442	luoh	咯	614		螞	5296		漫	3054		邁	6159
·lou	嘍	729		彔	1441		洛	2860		鎷	6471		縵	4420		麥	7234
low	漏	3043		戮	1772		濼	3135		馬	6921		蔓	5069	·me	麼	7242
	瘻	3662		淥	2934		烙	3200	maan	滿	3037		謾	5663	mean	丏	9
	鏤	6490		漉	3040		犖	3333	maang	[illegible]	2604		鏝	6486		免	299
	陋	6599		潞	3076		珞	3431		漭	3070		墁	6486		免	299
	露	6711		璐	3501		絡	4331		莽	4947		(鏝)			(免)	
lu	廬	1402		碌	3873		落	5000		莾	4947	mao	卯	495		冕	328
	櫨	2636		祿	3952		酪	6258		(莽)			昴	2231		勉	431
	瀘	3145		簏	4186		雒	6669		蟒	5319		泖	2834		娩	1014
	爐	3280		籙	4221		駱	6941	mae	買	5765	mau	旄	2182		愐	1632
	盧	3735		綠	4354	luoo	擄	2055	mah	禡	3963		毛	2735		沔	2800
	纑	4468		菉	4990		蠃	4754		罵	4504		氂	2742		湎	2978
	罏	4489		蓼	5066		虜	5187	mai	埋	834		矛	3826		眄	3747
	臚	4752		角	5500		蠃	5336		霾	6716		茅	4889		緬	4392
	艫	4822		賂	5775		裸	5420	man	埋	834		茆	4890		腼	4714
	蘆	5160		路	5871	luu	擄	2055		樠	2586		蝥	5279		靦	6732
	轤	6035		輅	5985		櫓	2630		漫	3054		蟊	5317	meau	杪	2355
	鑪	6519		轆	6021		樐	2630		瞞	3802		錨	6436		淼	2954
	顱	6834		逯	6114		(櫓)			蔓	5069		髦	7013		渺	2973
	鱸	7112		醁	6275		滷	3064		蠻	5354	maw	冒	325		眇	3748
	鸕	7204		錄	6418		虜	5187		謾	5663		帽	1329		秒	3985
luan	巒	1285		陸	6622		魯	7063		蹣	5915		懋	1732		緲	4391
	欒	2648		露	6711		鹵	7210		顢	6825		旄	2182		藐	5140
	灤	3168		騄	6954					饅	6899		楙	2518		邈	6165
	臠	4756		鷺	7198		M			鬘	7031		瑁	3463	meei	每	2727
	鑾	6526		鹿	7216	注音	單字	字號		鰻	7098		眊	3750		浼	2893
	鸞	7209		麓	7227	ma	痲	3635	mang	厖	507		瞀	3795		美	4515
luann	亂	45	luo	囉	779		蔴	5088		忙	1506		耄	4570		鎂	6449
luen	倫	213		玀	3404		蟆	5313		氓	2749		芼	4859	meeng	懵	1741

	猛	3366		艨	4821		蘼	5176		(覓)			螟	5297		膜	4725
	艋	4815		萌	4981		謎	5648		謐	5654		酩	6257		茉	4897
	蜢	5254		蒙	5034		迷	6073		鼏	7285		銘	6375		莫	4944
	蠓	5339		虻	5198		醚	6281	mii	弭	1429		鳴	7120		袜	5394
	錳	6432		蝱	5284		醾	6299		敉	2124	minq	命	599		貉	5740
mei	媒	1032	menn	悶	1619		靡	6730		眯	3765		暝	2272		貊	5740
	嵋	1256		懣	1736		麋	7222		米	4233	miow	繆	4434		(貉)	
	枚	2378		燜	3262	mian	棉	2477		芈	4513		謬	5668		貘	5745
	梅	2458	menq	夢	913		眠	3759		靡	6730	mo	摩	2022		陌	6600
	楣	2527		孟	1084		綿	4372	miin	愍	1647		摹	2023		靺	6743
	沒	2803	mey	妹	973		緜	4400		憫	1705		模	2584		驀	6971
	湄	2976		媚	1033	miann	瞑	3799		抿	1854		磨	3904		麥	7234
	煤	3223		寐	1137		面	6731		敏	2127		糢	4265		默	7253
	玫	3413		昧	2226		麪	7236		泯	2844		膜	4725	moo	抹	1830
	眉	3754		沫	2809		麵	7240		湣	2972		蘑	5153	moou	某	2395
	苺	4894		瑁	3463	miau	描	1949		澠	3100		謨	5666		牡	3313
	莓	4935		眛	3758		瞄	3793		皿	3714		饝	6913	mou	牟	3312
	郿	6215		袂	5379		苗	4868		閔	6539		饃	6913		眸	3768
	霉	6697		謎	5648	miaw	妙	964		閩	6547		(饝)			繆	4434
	黴	7268		魅	7052		廟	1395		黽	7275		魔	7058		謀	5640
men	們	198	mha	媽	1043		繆	4434	miing	皿	3714		麼	7242		鍪	6443
	捫	1901	mhau	摸	2017	mieh	滅	3020		瞑	3799	moh	嘿	747		麰	7238
	穈	4025		貓	5743		篾	4183		茗	4902		墨	878	mow	瞀	3795
	門	6529		猫	5743		篾	4183		酩	6257		寞	1141		茂	4886
·men	們	198		(貓)			(篾)		min	岷	1222		抹	1830		袤	5395
meng	尨	1175	mhen	悶	1619		蔑	5068		忞	1521		末	2332	mu	模	2584
	幪	1346		燜	3262		蔑	5068		旻	2209		歿	2693		獏	3386
	懵	1741	mheng	矇	3820		(蔑)			民	2748		殁	2693	muh	募	440
	懞	1741	mhi	咪	611		蠛	5359		珉	3421		(歿)			墓	866
	(懵)			瞇	3801	mih	冪	333		緡	4386		沒	2803		幕	1335
	曚	2292	mhie	乜	38		宓	1110		緍	4386		沫	2808		慕	1693
	朦	2328		哶	646		密	1130		(緡)			漠	3049		暮	2274
	檬	2621		芈	4513		汨	2780		閩	6547		瘼	3664		木	2330
	氓	2749	mho	摸	2017		泌	2829	ming	冥	331		磨	3904		沐	2799
	濛	3120	mi	彌	1439		祕	3936		名	556		秣	3994		牧	3316
	甍	3531		瀰	3156		秘	3936		明	2217		脈	4671		目	3739
	甿	3558		獼	3403		(祕)			暝	2272		衇	4671		睦	3784
	盟	3729		禰	3971		蜜	5251		溟	3001		(脈)			穆	4028
	瞢	3805		糜	4259		覓	5483		瞑	3799		脉	4671		繆	4434
	矇	3820		縻	4427		覔	5483		茗	4902		(脈)			苜	4870

注音	單字	字號
	莫	4944
	鉬	6363
muu	姆	976
	拇	1835
	母	2726
	牡	3313
	畝	3568
	鉧	6344

N

注音	單字	字號
na	南	486
	拿	1874
	拏	1874
	(拿)	
·na	哪	645
naa	哪	645
	那	6174
naan	腩	4712
	赧	5823
naang	攮	2112
	曩	2299
nae	乃	28
	奶	951
	氖	2750
	艿	4831
	迺	6085
nah	吶	573
	娜	1009
	捺	1905
	納	4288
	衲	5380
	訥	5537
	那	6174
	鈉	6333
nan	南	486
	喃	678
	枏	2367
	楠	2367
	(枏)	
	男	3555
	諵	5621
	難	6680
nang	囊	780
nann	難	6680
nao	惱	1626
	瑙	3468
	腦	4704
nau	呶	1539
	撓	2035
	橈	2597
	猱	3375
	譊	5680
	鐃	6494
naw	淖	2921
	鬧	7038
nay	奈	930
	柰	2412
	耐	4576
	褦	5443
	鼐	7284
·ne	呢	587
nean	捻	1908
	撚	2037
	攆	2092
	碾	3894
	輦	6000
	輾	6014
neau	嬝	1065
	嫋	1065
	(嬝)	
	嬲	1067
	蔦	5076
	裊	5406
	鳥	7115
neei	那	6174
	餒	6874
neh	訥	5537
neng	能	4666
nenn	嫩	1054
nenq	濘	3119
neou	忸	1514
	扭	1802
	狃	3346
	紐	4289
	鈕	6336
neu	女	949
	釹	6322
ney	內	307
	那	6174
nha	那	6174
nhian	蔫	5083
nhie	捏	1895
	揑	1895
	(捏)	
	捻	1908
nhiou	妞	963
ni	倪	212
	呢	587
	妮	971
	尼	1183
	怩	1532
	泥	2842
	猊	3364
	臡	4758
	蜺	5266
	輗	5994
	霓	6702
	麑	7225
nian	年	1350
	拈	1836
	粘	4239
	鮎	7065
	黏	7249
niang	娘	1007
	孃	1007
	(娘)	
niann	唸	669
	廿	1409
	念	1518
nianq	釀	6297
niaw	尿	1185
	溺	3013
nie	苶	4879
nieh	乜	38
	囁	776
	孽	1096
	孼	1096
	(孽)	
	櫱	2638
	涅	2895
	湼	2895
	(涅)	
	糵	4273
	糱	4273
	(糵)	
	聶	4611
	臬	4765
	臲	4768
	孽	5161
	孼	5161
	(孽)	
	蘖	5169
	躡	5957
	鎳	6467
	鑷	6523
	闑	6568
	隉	6630
	顳	6836
	齧	7317
	嚙	7317
	(齧)	
	囓	7317
	(齧)	
nih	匿	472
	惄	1620
	暱	2278
	昵	2278
	(暱)	
	泥	2842
	溺	3013
	睨	3783
	膩	4732
	衵	5381
	逆	6081
nii	你	115
	妳	985
	擬	2076
	旎	2186
	禰	3971
niing	擰	2082
nin	您	1596
ning	凝	345
	嚀	765
	寧	1143
	擰	2082
	檸	2620
	獰	3397
	甯	3550
ninq	佞	139
	擰	2082
	濘	3119
	甯	3550
niou	牛	3310
niow	拗	1849
	衄	5357
	謬	5668
niueh	瘧	3648
	虐	5181
	謔	5647
niuh	忸	1514
	恧	1574
	衄	5357
noan	暖	2270
	煖	3220
nong	儂	270
	濃	3115
	穠	4034
	膿	4735
	農	6049
	醲	6294
	齈	7302
nonq	弄	1411
now	耨	4588
nu	奴	950
	孥	1086
	笯	4104
	駑	6931
nuh	怒	1543
nuo	娜	1009
	挪	1877
	挼	1881
nuoh	喏	686
	懦	1734
	搦	1990
	糯	4269
	稬	4269
	(糯)	
	穤	4269
	(糯)	
	諾	5639
nuoo	娜	1009
nuu	努	422
	弩	1428
	砮	3857

O

注音	單字	字號
o	喔	688
·o	呵	593
oou	偶	230
	嘔	731
	耦	4587
	藕	5142
or	哦	631
ou	敺	2144
	歐	2669
	毆	2724
	漚	3046
	甌	3529

	謳	5669
	鷗	7188
ow	嘔	731
	慪	1683
	漚	3046

P

注音	單字	字號
pa	葩	5011
	趴	5845
·pa	杷	2363
	琶	3458
pah	帕	1312
	怕	1526
pai	拍	1844
pair	俳	183
	徘	1477
	排	1921
	牌	3303
	簰	4196
pan	攀	2093
	潘	3074
	番	3575
pang	乓	27
	滂	3018
	磅	3898
	霶	6714
pann	判	371
	叛	524
	拌	1841
	拚	1853
	泮	2843
	畔	3564
	盼	3746
	襻	5472
panq	胖	4648
pao	跑	5854
par	扒	1793
	爬	3285
	琶	3458
	耙	4581
parn	槃	2552
	盤	3732
	磐	3903
	胖	4648
	般	4802
	蟠	5320
	鞶	6759
parng	傍	235
	厐	507
	尨	1175
	龐	1403
	彷	1459
	徬	1487
	旁	2178
	㫄	2178
	(旁)	
	膀	4718
	螃	5291
	逄	6083
	雱	6686
pau	拋	1840
	抛	1840
	(拋)	
	泡	2841
	脬	4681
paur	刨	373
	匏	454
	咆	602
	庖	1365
	炮	3185
	袍	5392
	麃	7219
	麅	7221
paw	泡	2841
	炮	3185
	疱	3612
	皰	3710
	砲	3859
	礮	3920
pay	派	2874
	湃	2971
	鎃	6452
pean	諞	5624
peau	摽	2018
	殍	2701
	漂	3041
	瞟	3803
	縹	4424
	莩	4942
peeng	捧	1898
pei	披	1828
	胚	4651
	醅	6270
peir	培	839
	裴	5426
	賠	5791
	邳	6184
	陪	6613
pen	噴	761
	歕	2675
peng	怦	1529
	抨	1827
	澎	3090
	烹	3202
	砰	3852
	硼	3872
penq	碰	3879
	掽	3879
	(碰)	
pern	湓	2980
	盆	3717
perng	彭	1455
	朋	2316
	棚	2486
	澎	3090
	硼	3872
	篷	4184
	膨	4731
	芃	4832
	蓬	5063
	鵬	7155
pey	佩	141
	帔	1310
	旆	2181
	沛	2807
	珮	3437
	轡	6034
	配	6249
	霈	6696
pi	丕	13
	劈	411
	匹	470
	批	1808
	披	1828
	砒	3848
	紕	4292
	被	5397
	霹	6712
pian	偏	221
	扁	1783
	片	3301
	篇	4162
	翩	4554
	萹	5025
piann	徧	1483
	片	3301
	遍	6123
	騙	6958
piau	漂	3041
	飄	6845
piaw	剽	407
	漂	3041
	票	3948
	驃	6973
pie	撇	2034
	瞥	3815
piee	撇	2034
	苤	4899
pih	僻	268
	屁	1187
	擗	2064
	澼	3019
	甓	3534
	譬	5686
	辟	6039
	闢	6579
pii	仳	98
	劈	411
	匹	470
	否	566
	庀	1359
	疋	3587
	痞	3630
	癖	3672
	苤	4899
piin	品	621
pin	姘	1018
	姘	1018
	(姘)	
	拼	1924
	拼	1924
	(拼)	
ping	乒	34
	娉	1003
pinn	牝	3311
	聘	4601
pinq	聘	4601
po	坡	820
	波	2839
	潑	3072
	陂	6596
	頗	6796
poh	拍	1844
	朴	2337
	泊	2827
	珀	3427
	破	3854
	粕	4238
	迫	6068
	廹	6068
	(迫)	
	醱	6292
	魄	7051
poo	叵	544
	頗	6796
poou	剖	394
	掊	1919
	瓿	3525
por	婆	1015
	皤	3708
	繁	4428
	鄱	6234
pour	抔	1817
	掊	1919
	裒	5411
pu	仆	77
	扑	1792
	撲	2046
	痡	3629
	鋪	6410
puh	暴	2276
	曝	2296
	瀑	3138
	舖	4791
	鋪	6410
puu	圃	795
	埔	838
	普	2255
	浦	2885
	溥	3006
	譜	5681
	鐠	6499
pwu	僕	256
	匍	453
	幞	1340
	朴	2337
	樸	2587
	濮	3128
	璞	3498

注音	單字	字號
	脯	4680
	莆	4945
	菩	4986
	葡	5006
	蒱	5037
	蒲	5038
	蹼	5937
	酺	6267
	醭	6290
	釙	6317
pyan	便	164
	楩	2537
	胼	4689
	胼	4689
	(胼)	
	諞	5624
	蹁	5902
	駢	6944
	骿	6952
pyau	嫖	1048
	瓢	3519
pyi	啤	658
	埤	842
	枇	2362
	毗	2733
	琵	3457
	疲	3599
	皮	3709
	紕	4292
	羆	4505
	羆	4508
	脾	4699
	蚍	5203
	裨	5422
	貔	5744
	郫	6207
	鈹	6362
	陂	6596
	陴	6618
	鼙	7290
pyn	嬪	1068
	蘋	5164
	貧	5753
	頻	6809
	顰	6833
pyng	坪	828
	屏	1198
	平	1349
	憑	1710
	枰	2419
	洴	2919
	瓶	3526
	甁	3526
	(瓶)	
	秤	3992
	缾	4479
	苹	4881
	萍	4982
	蘋	5164
	評	5555
	軿	6001
	馮	6923
	R	
注音	單字	字號
raan	冉	322
	染	2396
	苒	4864
raang	嚷	773
	壤	894
	攘	2097
ran	然	3215
	燃	3251
	髯	7012
	髥	7017
rang	攘	2097
	瓤	3521
	禳	3973
	穰	4037
	纕	4471
ranq	讓	5700
rao	擾	2088
rau	蕘	5096
	饒	6905
raw	繞	4442
	遶	6150
ree	喏	686
	惹	1645
	若	4873
reen	忍	1500
	稔	4008
	紝	4297
	紝	4297
	(紝)	
	荏	4918
reh	熱	3245
	爇	3279
ren	人	71
	仁	73
	任	101
	壬	897
	紝	4297
	紝	4297
	(紝)	
reng	仍	81
	礽	3924
renn	仭	88
	任	101
	刃	358
	妊	960
	恁	1566
	紉	4286
	衽	5384
	袵	5405
	訒	5530
	認	5583
	軔	5971
	韌	6766
	飪	6855
	餁	6870
rhang	嚷	773
rheng	扔	1795
roan	蝡	5276
	蠕	5341
	軟	5974
	輭	6012
	阮	6588
roei	蕊	5093
rong	容	1129
	嶸	1277
	戎	1756
	榕	2538
	榮	2551
	毧	2736
	溶	3014
	熔	3240
	絨	4334
	羢	4525
	肜	4630
	茸	4913
	蓉	5048
	融	5294
	蠑	5338
	鎔	6459
roong	宂	1101
	氄	2744
roou	糅	4254
rou	揉	1948
	柔	2397
	蹂	5903
	輮	6011
row	肉	4619
ru	儒	278
	嚅	763
	如	956
	孺	1095
	濡	3125
	茹	4914
	襦	5465
	顬	6832
	鴽	7142
ruei	甤	3544
	緌	4377
	蕤	5103
	甤	5726
ruen	犉	3329
ruenn	潤	3080
	閏	6536
ruey	枘	2374
	汭	2782
	瑞	3471
	睿	3794
	芮	4852
	蚋	5202
	蜹	5267
	銳	6391
ruh	入	306
	洳	2867
	溽	3015
	縟	4413
	肉	4619
	茹	4914
	蓐	5050
	褥	5442
	辱	6048
	鉫	6390
ruo	挼	1881
ruoh	偌	219
	弱	1432
	爇	3279
	箬	4153
	篛	4178
	若	4873
	蒻	5055
ruu	乳	43
	汝	2775
	辱	6048
ryh	日	2198
	S	
注音	單字	字號
sa	仨	94
	撒	2029
saa	撒	2029
	洒	2855
	灑	3163
	靸	6741
saan	傘	238
	散	2137
	糝	4262
	繖	4440
saang	嗓	711
	顙	6821
sah	卅	478
	薩	5132
	趿	5850
	颯	6838
sai	塞	863
	腮	4716
	顋	6813
	鰓	7091
san	三	5
	參	515
sang	喪	699
	桑	2437
sann	散	2137
sanq	喪	699
sao	嫂	1038
	掃	1912
	埽	1912
	(掃)	
sau	搔	1978
	繅	4432
	繰	4454
	臊	4744
	艘	4816
	騷	6966
saw	掃	1912
	埽	1912

	(掃)			煞	3230		蟮	5327		賒	5784		讅	5693		陞	6606
	臊	4744		箑	4140		蟺	5330	shean	尠	1173	sheeng	省	3753		鼪	7293
say	塞	863		翣	4549		訕	5525		尟	1173		眚	3763	shenn	慎	1661
	賽	5804		霎	6699		贍	5813		(尠)		sheh	射	1160		滲	3032
seh	嗇	706	shai	篩	4172		赸	5831		嶮	1276		拾	1864		甚	3537
	圾	812	shan	刪	370		鄯	6232		洒	2855		攝	2101		脤	4684
	塞	863		姍	979		饍	6906		洗	2856		歙	2672		腎	4694
	澀	3121		山	1209		鱔	7105		燹	3273		涉	2896		葚	5004
	澁	3121		扇	1786		鱣	7110		獮	3395		社	3925		蜃	5237
	(澀)			搧	1991	shanq	上	6		玁	3405		舍	4787		黮	7266
	瑟	3462		杉	2341		尙	1171		獫	3405		葉	5001	shenq	乘	36
	穡	4032		潸	3086	shao	少	1169		(玁)			設	5540		剩	401
	色	4826		煽	3239	shar	啥	670		癬	3683		赦	5822		勝	437
	銫	6387		珊	3424	shau	弰	1431		蘚	5170		麝	7230		嵊	1263
sen	森	2493		羴	4531		捎	1894		蜆	5238	sheir	誰	5601		晟	2245
seng	僧	262		羶	4532		梢	2470		跣	5866	shen	伸	118		盛	3726
sha	抄	1878		膻	4747		燒	3254		銑	6372		參	515		聖	4600
	殺	2718		舢	4799		稍	3999		險	6647		呻	597		膡	4746
	沙	2802		芟	4841		筲	4131		顯	6831		娠	1011		賸	5805
	煞	3230		苫	4876		箾	4176		鮮	7071		深	2943	sheou	宿	1131
	痧	3626		衫	5376		𥳓	4195	sheang	享	66		燊	3260		朽	2338
	砂	3845		跚	5857		艄	4814		想	1644		甡	3540	sher	什	72
	紗	4294		釤	6326		蛸	5231		響	6779		申	3554		佘	134
	莎	4948	shang	傷	247	shaur	勺	447		餉	6867		砷	3855		折	1822
	裟	5417		商	655		杓	2345		饗	6908		紳	4311		揲	1966
	鎩	6476		殤	2707		芍	4836		鯗	7072		莘	4937		甚	3537
	鯊	7077		湯	2989		韶	6777	sheau	小	1168		蓡	5007		舌	4786
shaa	傻	276		觴	5511	shaw	劭	425		曉	2285		蔘	5007		蛇	5218
	儍	276	·shang	裳	5425		哨	632		筱	4130		(蓡)			虵	5218
	(傻)		shann	善	679		少	1169		篠	4180		詵	5580		(蛇)	
shaan	閃	6531		單	701		捎	1894		謏	5653		身	5960		闍	6566
	陝	6612		嬗	1060		潲	3093	shee	捨	1897		鉮	6367	shern	神	3943
shaang	上	6		扇	1786		紹	4312		舍	4787	sheng	勝	437	sherng	澠	3100
	晌	2244		掞	1926		邵	6179	sheen	哂	622		升	476		繩	4445
	賞	5790		擅	2057	shay	曬	2300		嬸	1069		昇	2213	sheu	昫	2233
shae	色	4826		汕	2770		晒	2300		審	1150		牲	3319		栩	2425
	骰	6993		疝	3594		(曬)			沈	2798		生	3539		湑	2993
shah	嗄	703		禪	3967		殺	2718		瀋	3140		甥	3542		煦	3231
	廈	1383		繕	4438	she	奢	943		矧	3832		笙	4094		許	5541
	歃	2665		膳	4733		畬	3577		諗	5616		聲	4606		詡	5563

	諝	5634		熺	3257		銛	6377		象	5725	shieh	卸	500		矽	3842
	鄦	6236		(熹)			鮮	7071		鄉	6221		寫	1151		禊	3958
sheuan	癬	3683		犀	3327		鱻	7114		項	6783		屑	1197		穸	4040
	選	6152		犧	3336	shiang	廂	1382	shiau	削	389		廨	1400		系	4275
sheue	雪	6683		畦	3570		湘	2985		哮	635		懈	1725		細	4309
	鱈	7099		皙	3705		相	3744		囂	777		械	2467		繫	4452
shi	僖	257		硒	3862		箱	4154		宵	1126		楔	2517		翕	4546
	兮	314		禧	3966		緗	4384		枵	2383		榭	2544		肸	4641
	吸	574		稀	4000		纕	4471		梟	2464		泄	2824		舄	4780
	唏	643		羲	4530		舡	4800		消	2897		洩	2864		舃	4780
	嘻	744		膝	4726		薌	5119		瀟	3149		渫	2991		(舄)	
	奚	941		蜥	5248		襄	5455		硝	3867		澥	3101		郤	6204
	嬉	1055		蟋	5315		鄉	6221		簫	4208		瀉	3139		隙	6638
	巇	1281		蠵	5352		鑲	6522		綃	4346		瀣	3153		隟	6638
	希	1309		西	5473		香	6918		蕭	5102		燮	3272		(隙)	
	徯	1489		觿	5513		驤	6987		蛸	5231		獬	3393		餼	6895
	恓	1554		豀	5708	shiann	峴	1231		蟰	5347		絏	4329		鬩	7040
	悉	1593		谿	5709		憲	1718		逍	6086		紲	4329	shii	喜	692
	扱	1807		豨	5729		獻	3402		銷	6392		(絏)			屣	1203
	攜	2100		蹊	5910		現	3439		霄	6694		薤	5126		徙	1479
	携	2100		醯	6289		綫	4378		驍	6978		蟹	5328		憙	1714
	(攜)			釐	6309		線	4381		鴞	7130		蠏	5328		枲	2384
	擕	2100		鸂	7201		縣	4402		哮	635		(蟹)			洒	2855
	(攜)			鼷	7296		羨	4527		嘯	737		褻	5456		洗	2856
	擕	2100	shia	瞎	3797		腺	4713		孝	1083		褻	5456		璽	3508
	(攜)			蝦	5280		莧	4941		效	2123		(褻)			禧	3967
	晞	2248	shiah	下	7		見	5481		効	2123		解	5505		葸	5019
	晰	2257		嚇	766		蹮	5718		(效)			謝	5658		蓰	5087
	晳	2258		夏	904		轞	6032		斅	2149		躞	5956		蟢	5321
	曦	2297		廈	1383		限	6602		校	2429		邂	6160		諰	5644
	析	2371		暇	2265		陷	6621		歊	2674	shih	係	165	shiing	惺	1636
	栖	2423		罅	4482		霰	6709		笑	4093		卌	481		擤	2081
	棲	2497	shian	仙	87		餡	6884		肖	4623		夕	907		省	3753
	樨	2590		先	295	shianq	像	254		酵	6263		戱	1774		醒	6276
	欷	2656		孅	1071		向	559	shie	些	57		戲	1774	shin	心	1496
	淅	2917		掀	1911		嚮	769		歇	2663		(戲)			忻	1515
	溪	3009		暹	2279		巷	1303		蝎	5273		歙	2672		新	2171
	烯	3207		祆	3928		曏	2290		蠍	5335		汐	2771		昕	2221
	熙	3234		纖	4472		橡	2601	shiee	寫	1151		潟	3075		欣	2652
	熹	3257		躚	5955		相	3744		血	5356		盻	3745		歆	2664

	炘	3180		胷	4664		鬚	7032		(敍)		shoei	水	2761	shuah	刷	382
	芯	4851		(胸)		shiuan	喧	696		敘	2125	shoen	吮	569	shuai	摔	2010
	莘	4937		詾	5538		嬛	1062		(敍)			楯	2536		衰	5378
	薪	5129	shionq	敻	905		宣	1118		旭	2203		盾	3752	shuan	拴	1862
	訢	5535	shiou	休	111		揎	1971		洫	2863	shoou	守	1104		栓	2421
	辛	6037		修	180		暄	2264		漵	3058		手	1789		閂	6530
	鋅	6401		庥	1371		瑄	3465		畜	3567		首	6915	shuang	孀	1070
	鑫	6520		羞	4524		翾	4564		絮	4340	shou	收	2115		瀧	3152
	歆	6776		脩	4678		萱	4997		緒	4379	shour	熟	3243		雙	6673
	馨	6920		貅	5739		諼	5620		續	4464	show	受	523		霜	6704
shing	惺	1636		饈	6900		諠	5625		芧	4845		售	647	shuann	涮	2952
	星	2223		髹	7020		軒	5970		蓄	5046		壽	903	shuay	帥	1319
	猩	3374		鵂	7145	shiuann	旋	2184		賉	5781		授	1913		率	3407
	腥	4703	shiow	嗅	704		渲	2968		酗	6252		狩	3354		蟀	5311
	興	4783		宿	1131		漩	3052	shiun	勳	444		獸	3400	shuenn	瞬	3807
	馨	6920		岫	1217		炫	3183		壎	887		瘦	3652		舜	4794
	騂	6947		溴	3011		眩	3760		曛	2294		綬	4357		順	6784
shinn	信	179		秀	3980		絢	4332		焄	3203	shu	姝	988	shuey	帨	1321
	囟	785		繡	4444		衒	5362		熏	3236		抒	1815		睡	3779
	焮	3209		綉	4444		鉉	6346		燻	3236		摴	2020		稅	4001
	芯	4851		(繡)			鏇	6475		(熏)			攄	2091		蛻	5233
	釁	6300		臭	4766	shiue	噱	756		獯	3396		書	2306		說	5598
	顖	6824		袖	5390		薛	5125		窨	4059		梳	2473	shuh	倏	196
shinq	倖	201		銹	6412		靴	6738		纁	4461		梳	2473		墅	871
	姓	983		鏽	6497	shiueh	削	389		葷	5018		(梳)			庶	1376
	幸	1352		齅	7301		穴	4038		薰	5134		樗	2578		恕	1568
	性	1531	shiu	吁	548		血	5356		醺	6296		樞	2583		戍	1755
	悻	1600		噓	735		雪	6683	shiunn	巽	1304		殊	2700		數	2143
	杏	2344		墟	874	shiuh	勗	434		徇	1467		殳	2715		曙	2291
	興	4783		戌	1754		勖	434		殉	2699		洙	2857		束	2351
	荇	4925		歔	2673		(勗)			汛	2777		疏	3588		樹	2595
	莕	4932		盱	3741		卹	501		蕈	5106		疎	3588		沭	2811
	行	5360		繻	4457		壻	899		訊	5522		(疏)			漱	3057
shiong	兄	291		胥	4643		婿	899		訓	5524		疏	3588		澍	3091
	兇	294		蓿	5067		(壻)			迅	6052		(疏)			疏	3588
	凶	351		虛	5185		序	1363		遜	6132		紓	4291		署	4502
	匈	452		訏	5531		恤	1559		馴	6926		舒	4789		術	5363
	恟	1556		需	6692		慉	1665	shoa	耍	4577		蔬	5077		裋	5407
	洶	2871		須	6786		敍	2125	shoai	甩	3546		輸	6009		豎	5717
	胸	4664		嬃	6801		叙	2125	shoang	爽	3295	shua	刷	382		述	6070

shuo	說	5598		獅	3380		銜	6378		嗜	714		檄	2608	shyu	徐	1473
shuoh	妁	955		絁	4325		閑	6537		噬	755		熄	3237	shyuan	懸	1742
	帥	1319		蓍	5057		閒	6538		士	896		習	4544		旋	2184
	搠	1999		虱	5194		鹹	7211		奭	947		腊	4700		漩	3052
	數	2143		蝨	5282	shyang	庠	1370		室	1119		蓆	5047		玄	3406
	朔	2319		詩	5566		祥	3946		市	1306		裼	5428		璇	3489
	槊	2553		鳲	7118		翔	4545		式	1416		襲	5469		璿	3510
	爍	3278	·shy	匙	459		詳	5574		弑	1417		覡	5486		縣	4402
	碩	3889	shya	俠	178		降	6601		恃	1552		錫	6428		還	6161
	芍	4836		匣	464	shyau	學	1094		拭	1857		隰	6649	shyue	學	1094
	蟀	5311		峽	1234		爻	3294		是	2229	shyn	尋	1165		尋	1165
	鑠	6514		挾	1889	shye	偕	223		柿	2387	shyng	刑	364		踅	5879
shuu	屬	1207		暇	2265		勰	443		栻	2422		型	832		鷽	7199
	數	2143		柙	2401		協	485		氏	2746		形	1448	shyun	尋	1165
	暑	2268		洽	2872		叶	545		澨	3105		形	1448		峋	1225
	署	4502		狎	3347		恊	1565		示	3923		(形)			巡	1291
	薯	5133		狹	3360		挾	1889		筮	4128		硎	3871		廵	1291
	藷	5165		瑕	3467		擷	2085		耆	4571		行	5360		(巡)	
	蜀	5235		舝	4795		攜	2100		舐	4788		邢	6177		徇	1467
	鸀	7200		轄	6017		擕	2100		螫	5301		郉	6189		循	1486
	黍	7247		遐	6127		(攜)			視	5485		鉶	6419		恂	1550
	鼠	7291		鎋	6458		㩗	2100		試	5565		陘	6604		撏	2033
shwei	誰	5601		霞	6705		(攜)			誓	5586		餳	6892		旬	2202
shwu	叔	521		黠	7258		携	2100		諡	5618	shyong	熊	3235		洵	2870
	塾	869	shyan	咸	617		(攜)			諟	5646		雄	6658		潯	3083
	孰	1090		啣	662		斜	2159		謚	5662	shyr	什	72		珣	3436
	淑	2922		嫌	1046		絜	4341		識	5677		十	474		紃	4280
	熟	3243		嫺	1056		纈	4462		豉	5713		實	1148		荀	4915
	秫	3997		嫻	1056		脅	4670		貰	5760		射	1160		蕁	5105
	菽	4973		(嫺)			衺	5383		軾	5984		拾	1864		詢	5564
	贖	5818		弦	1425		諧	5629		逝	6087		時	2240		巡	6053
shy	失	922		椷	2510		邪	6176		適	6144		旹	2240		廵	6053
	尸	1179		涎	2900		鞋	6746		釋	6304		(時)			(巡)	
	屍	1193		痃	3609		頡	6797		鈰	6360		湜	2982		郇	6191
	師	1322		癇	3669	shyh	世	14		飾	6863		石	3841		馴	6926
	拾	1864		絃	4318		事	48	shyi	媳	1039		碩	3889		鱘	7108
	施	2176		舷	4810		仕	83		席	1323		蒔	5053	shyy	使	147
	濕	3133		諴	5645		使	147		息	1575		蝕	5270		史	542
	溼	3133		賢	5793		侍	152		惜	1617		食	6849		始	978
	(濕)			賢	5817		勢	439		昔	2220		鰣	7096		屎	1194

	從	1480		脺	4693	tswu	徂	1464	tuh	兎	301		沱	2812		提	1951
	从	1480		膵	4693		殂	2698		兔	301		紽	4323		禔	3959
	(從)			(脺)		tsy	差	1298		(兎)			詑	5529		稊	4002
	淙	2928		萃	4975		恣	1572		吐	558		跎	5853		綈	4347
	琮	3455		顇	6811		疵	3615		菟	4955		陀	6595		緹	4396
tsow	湊	2977	tsuh	促	166		雌	6666	tuo	佗	133		馱	6924		荑	4919
	凑	2977		卒	483	tsyh	伺	119		它	1099		駝	6938		蹄	5904
	(湊)			猝	3369		刺	383		托	1799		鮀	7128		蹏	5914
	腠	4702		簇	4187		廁	1381		拖	1850		鼉	7282		醍	6277
	輳	6007		蔟	5086		次	2651		拕	1850	twu	凸	352		隄	6626
tsu	粗	4236		趣	5840		賜	5789		(拖)			圖	803		堤	6626
	麤	7233		踧	5891	tsyr	慈	1666		牠	3314		塗	861		(隄)	
tsuan	攛	2099		蹙	5917		瓷	3524		脫	4679		屠	1201		題	6814
	汆	2763		蹙	5927		疵	3615		託	5527		徒	1475		騠	6961
	躥	5958		蹴	5933		磁	3896	tuoh	唾	651		稌	4006		鵜	7151
tsuann	爨	3283		蹵	5938		祠	3944		拓	1847		突	4044		鶗	7172
	竄	4068		醋	6274		粢	4241		柝	2405		荼	4931	tyng	亭	68
	篡	4169	tsuo	搓	1980		茨	4905		籜	4222		葖	5026		停	225
tsuei	催	241		撮	2048		茲	4909		蘀	5158		途	6093		婷	1030
	崔	1239		磋	3897		詞	5558		魄	7051		酴	6268		庭	1374
	摧	2012		莎	4949		辭	6044	tuoo	妥	968		駼	7150		廷	1407
	榱	2548		蹉	5909		餈	6866		庹	1379	tyan	塡	864		渟	2957
	縗	4407	tsuoh	剉	388		鷀	7176		橢	2602		恬	1563		筳	4133
	衰	5378		厝	510		鶿	7176	tuu	吐	558		湉	2997		蜓	5241
tsuen	村	2347		挫	1879		(鷀)			土	805		滇	3021		霆	6695
	皴	3711		措	1934	tsyy	此	2683		釷	6321		甜	3538	tza	匝	460
	邨	6178		撮	2048		泚	2835	twan	團	804		田	3551		咂	595
tsuenn	吋	522		莝	4952		玼	3423		摶	2013		畋	3562		紮	4304
	寸	1157		銼	6409	tu	禿	3979		糰	4270		鈿	6342		紥	4304
tsuey	啐	659		錯	6431		秃	3979	twei	隤	6642		闐	6567		(紮)	
	悴	1601	tsuoo	瑳	3483		(禿)			頹	6808	tyau	佻	144		臢	4757
	橇	2596		脞	4683		鵚	7148	twen	囤	788		條	2463	tzaan	拶	1863
	毳	2740	tswan	攢	2102	tuan	湍	2979		屯	1208		笤	4106		揝	1969
	淬	2938	tswen	存	1079	tuann	彖	1442		臀	4739		苕	4867		攢	2102
	瘁	3640		蹲	5928	tuei	推	1933		芚	4849		蜩	5257		昝	2235
	粹	4250	tswo	嵯	1264	tuen	吞	563		豚	5723		調	5605		桚	2448
	翠	4548		痤	3631		暾	2288		飩	6854		迢	6062		趲	5843
	脆	4669		瘥	3655	tuenn	褪	5444	two	佗	133		髫	7014	tzaang	駔	6933
	脃	4669		矬	3835	tuey	蛻	5233		柁	2418		齠	7312	tzae	仔	82
	(脆)			鹺	7212		退	6076		橐	2594	tyi	啼	673		宰	1123

	崽	1254
	載	5987
tzai	哉	627
	栽	2438
	災	3175
	灾	3175
	(災)	
	烖	3175
	(災)	
	菑	4961
	葘	4961
	(菑)	
tzan	簪	4205
tzang	牂	3299
	臢	4757
	臧	4762
	賍	5782
	贓	5815
	髒	7003
tzann	暫	2275
	讚	5703
	贊	5811
	酇	6244
	鏨	6491
tzanq	奘	938
	臟	4755
	葬	5013
	藏	5139
tzao	早	2201
	棗	2481
	澡	3102
	繰	4454
	藻	5156
	蚤	5207
tzar	拶	1863
	桚	2448
	砸	3856
	雜	6675
tzarn	咱	615
tzau	糟	4263
	蹧	5924
	遭	6142
tzaur	鑿	6527
tzaw	噪	753
	慥	1676
	燥	3269
	皁	3694
	皂	3695
	竈	4071
	灶	4071
	(竈)	
	簉	4191
	譟	5684
	躁	5942
	造	6101
tzay	再	324
	在	806
	載	5987
tzee	怎	1542
tzeen	怎	1542
tzeh	仄	76
	昃	2211
tzeir	賊	5780
tzen	簪	4205
tzeng	增	877
	憎	1699
	曾	2309
	矰	3839
	繒	4436
tzenn	譖	5676
tzenq	甑	3532
	繒	4436
	贈	5809
tzer	則	385
	咋	603
	嘖	732
	幘	1337
	擇	2060
	澤	3106
	窄	4048
	笮	4107
	簀	4189
	舴	4807
	責	5758
	賊	5780
	賾	5810
	迮	6071
tzoan	篹	4192
	纂	4456
	纘	4474
	鑽	6525
tzoei	嘴	740
tzoen	撙	2036
tzong	宗	1111
	從	1480
	棕	2507
	椶	2507
	(棕)	
	縱	4418
	葼	5010
	踪	5896
	蹤	5919
	騣	6959
	鬃	7025
tzonq	從	1480
	从	1480
	(從)	
	糉	4253
	粽	4253
	(糉)	
	綜	4353
	縱	4418
tzoong	傯	227
	總	4425
tzoou	走	5827
tzou	掫	1939
	緅	4371
	諏	5612
	謅	5651
	鄒	6222
	鄹	6239
	陬	6614
	騶	6967
	鯫	7084
tzow	奏	934
	揍	1950
	驟	6984
tzu	租	3990
tzuan	鑽	6525
tzuann	揝	1969
	攥	2110
	鑽	6525
tzuen	尊	1164
	樽	2593
	罇	4483
	遵	6149
tzuey	晬	2254
	最	2311
	罪	4499
	蕞	5099
	辠	6040
	醉	6272
tzuh	駔	6933
tzuo	作	138
	嘬	749
tzuoh	作	138
	做	224
	坐	818
	座	1372
	怍	1523
	柞	2404
	祚	3941
	胙	4649
	酢	6253
	鑿	6527
	阼	6593
tzuoo	佐	129
	左	1294
	撮	2048
tzuu	俎	169
	祖	3937
	組	4320
	詛	5557
	阻	6592
tzwo	作	138
	捽	1906
	昨	2227
tzwu	卒	483
	捽	1906
	族	2187
	槭	2566
	足	5844
	鏃	6474
tzy	吱	578
	咨	610
	姿	999
	孜	1082
	孳	1092
	淄	2915
	滋	3022
	粢	4241
	緇	4370
	茲	4909
	菑	4961
	葘	4961
	(菑)	
	諮	5631
	貲	5761
	資	5777
	趑	5836
	輜	5993
	錙	6422
	鎡	6456
	髭	7018
	鼒	7286
	齊	7303
	齋	7305
	齜	7315
tzyh	剚	395
	字	1078
	恣	1572
	漬	3055
	牸	3323
	眥	3764
	眦	3764
	(眥)	
	胾	4667
	自	4764
tzyy	仔	82
	姊	977
	姉	977
	(姊)	
	子	1073
	梓	2459
	滓	3025
	秭	3995
	笫	4100
	籽	4234
	紫	4306
	耔	4580
	茈	4882
	訾	5546
	訿	5560

U

注音	單字	字號
u	嗚	713
	圬	807
	屋	1192
	巫	1297
	惡	1624
	於	2175
	汚	2779
	污	2779
	(汚)	
	汙	2779
	(汚)	
	烏	3193
	誣	5593

	鄔	6223
ua	呱	591
	哇	625
	媧	1035
	挖	1870
	窪	4058
	蛙	5221
	鼃	7278
·ua	哇	625
uai	歪	2687
uan	剜	397
	彎	1440
	灣	3167
	蜿	5263
	豌	5716
uang	汪	2784
uei	倭	214
	偎	220
	委	984
	威	1000
	崴	1252
	微	1490
	椳	2509
	渨	2995
	煨	3225
	萎	4983
	葳	5016
	逶	6111
	隈	6629
uen	溫	2998
	温	2998
	(溫)	
	瘟	3650
	轀	6019
	鰮	7094
ueng	嗡	720
	翁	4538
uo	倭	214
	渦	2965
	窩	4057
	萵	4998

W

注音	單字	字號
wa	娃	1001
wah	瓦	3522
	袜	5394
	襪	5466
wan	丸	24
	刓	366
	完	1107
	烷	3206
	玩	3415
	紈	4285
	芄	4833
	頑	6791
wang	亡	60
	忘	1505
	王	3409
wann	惋	1608
	曼	2308
	玩	3415
	翫	4555
	腕	4698
	萬	4996
	万	4996
	(萬)	
	蔓	5069
wanq	妄	958
	往	1462
	忘	1505
	旺	2208
	望	2323
	朢	2326
	王	3409
way	外	908
wei	危	497
	唯	648
	圍	800
	嵬	1262
	巍	1284
	帷	1326
	幃	1331
	微	1490
	惟	1618
	桅	2442
	濰	3130
	為	3192
	爲	3288
	維	4358
	薇	5116
	違	6131
	闈	6560
	韋	6765
wen	文	2150
	紋	4287
	聞	4603
	蚊	5200
	蟁	5299
	雯	6684
wenn	問	656
	抆	1814
	揾	1998
	文	2150
	汶	2787
	璺	3511
	紊	4301
	聞	4603
wenq	甕	3533
	罋	4485
wey	位	126
	僞	259
	味	592
	喂	677
	尉	1163
	慰	1690
	未	2331
	渭	2966
	濊	3116
	為	3192
	爲	3288
	畏	3561
	胃	4644
	蔚	5072
	蝟	5274
	衛	5370
	衞	5371
	謂	5642
	遺	6154
	餧	6885
	餵	6893
	魏	7055
woa	瓦	3522
woan	娩	1014
	婉	1020
	宛	1115
	挽	1883
	晚	2246
	浣	2882
	澣	3118
	琬	3454
	畹	3580
	皖	3703
	盌	3723
	碗	3886
	椀	3886
	(碗)	
	綰	4359
	莞	4938
	菀	4956
	踠	5882
	輓	5990
woang	往	1462
	惘	1611
	枉	2368
	網	4361
	罔	4491
	蛧	5256
	輞	5998
	魍	7053
woei	偉	218
	僞	259
	唯	648
	委	984
	娓	1002
	尾	1184
	洧	2862
	煒	3219
	猥	3372
	瑋	3464
	痏	3619
	痿	3639
	緯	4393
	葦	5009
	蓶	5141
	諉	5609
	隗	6639
	韙	6770
	頠	6800
	骪	6992
	鮪	7069
woen	刎	363
	吻	576
	穩	4035
	脗	4686
woeng	滃	3017
	蓊	5056
woh	偓	222
	喔	688
	幄	1332
	握	1959
	斡	2162
	沃	2793
	涴	2950
	渥	2964
	臥	4761
	齷	7321
woo	我	1759
wu	吳	571
	吾	579
	巫	1297
	无	2195
	梧	2453
	毋	2725
	浯	2906
	無	3214
	蕪	5107
	蜈	5243
	誣	5593
	鼯	7294
wuh	兀	288
	務	436
	勿	450
	塢	865
	婺	1031
	寤	1146
	悟	1590
	惡	1624
	戊	1752
	晤	2250
	杌	2343
	物	3317
	誤	5594
	迕	6059
	鋈	6468
	阢	6584
	隖	6636
	霧	6707
	騖	6957
	鶩	7170
wuu	五	54
	仵	99
	伍	107
	侮	159
	午	477
	嘸	745
	娬	1029
	嫵	1029
	(娬)	

	圄	796
	宇	1103
	嶼	1279
	庾	1380
	敔	2132
	瑀	3475
	禹	3975
	窳	4063
	羽	4536
	與	4782
	語	5591
	鋙	6406
	雨	6681
	齬	7320
yeuan	遠	6138
yeun	允	289
	殞	2705
	狁	3345
	磒	3902
	隕	6635
yi	一	1
	儀	269
	匜	461
	咦	609
	圯	809
	夷	925
	姨	993
	宜	1116
	彝	1446
	彜	1446
	(彛)	
	怡	1530
	沂	2791
	洟	2858
	疑	3589
	痍	3617
	眙	3756
	眱	3766
	移	3998
	簃	4188
	胰	4661
	𦣞	4760
	荑	4919
	蛇	5218
	訑	5529
	詒	5553
	誼	5604
	貤	5752
	貽	5770
	迆	6054
	迻	6082
	遺	6154
	頤	6802
	飴	6861
yih	一	1
	亦	64
	仡	90
	佚	136
	佾	146
	億	271
	刈	361
	劓	416
	囈	778
	奕	937
	射	1160
	屹	1210
	嶧	1275
	弈	1413
	弋	1415
	役	1460
	悒	1585
	意	1650
	憶	1720
	懌	1728
	懿	1746
	懿	1746
	(懿)	
	抑	1823
	拽	1869
	挹	1882
	掖	1923
	斁	2146
	易	2219
	昳	2234
	曀	2286
	曳	2303
	杙	2354
	枻	2391
	殪	2709
	毅	2723
	泄	2824
	泆	2825
	浥	2884
	液	2909
	溢	3005
	熠	3242
	異	3574
	異	3574
	(異)	
	疫	3597
	瘞	3657
	益	3720
	瞖	3806
	縊	4415
	繹	4451
	義	4528
	羿	4537
	翊	4541
	翌	4543
	翳	4559
	翼	4560
	肄	4615
	肊	4620
	腋	4691
	臆	4742
	薏	5120
	藝	5144
	蜴	5259
	衣	5374
	裔	5412
	裛	5418
	詣	5562
	誼	5604
	議	5683
	譯	5687
	貤	5752
	軼	5981
	逸	6112
	邑	6169
	鎰	6466
	鐿	6509
	驛	6983
	鷁	7180
	黓	7251
yii	乙	37
	以	93
	倚	204
	已	1300
	扆	1785
	旖	2191
	椅	2503
	檥	2618
	矣	3830
	艤	4819
	苡	4872
	苢	4901
	蟻	5331
	踦	5895
	轙	6028
	迆	6054
	迤	6063
	釔	6311
	鉯	6366
	銥	6381
	顗	6819
yiin	尹	1181
	引	1419
	檃	2646
	㱃	2671
	癮	3682
	蚓	5204
	隱	6648
	靷	6740
	飲	6857
yiing	影	1457
	景	2256
	潁	3068
	癭	3681
	穎	4027
	頴	4027
	(穎)	
	郢	6202
yinn	印	496
	廕	1391
	憖	1716
	窨	4059
	胤	4655
	蔭	5084
	陰	6615
	飲	6857
yinq	媵	1040
	應	1729
	映	2224
	硬	3866
	迎	6055
yn	吟	564
	垠	829
	夤	914
	寅	1134
	淫	2940
	狺	3361
	鄞	6228
	銀	6368
	霪	6708
	齗	7310
	齦	7316
yng	塋	856
	嬴	1064
	楹	2535
	滎	3026
	瀅	3142
	瀛	3150
	瀠	3155
	熒	3241
	營	3264
	瑩	3476
	盈	3718
	縈	4401
	螢	5298
	蠅	5333
	贏	5814
	迎	6055
yong	傭	242
	喁	676
	墉	872
	庸	1378
	慵	1681
	顒	6817
	鱅	7103
yonq	用	3545
you	尤	1174
	斿	2177
	楢	2523
	油	2815
	游	2974
	猶	3373
	猷	3377
	由	3552
	疣	3598
	繇	4430
	蕕	5095
	蚰	5212
	蝣	5277
	輶	6008
	逌	6105
	遊	6121
	郵	6213
	鈾	6357
	魷	7062
yow	佑	130

	侑	154		盂	3715		猨	3379		耀	4567		玉	3408		鬱	7045
	又	516		禺	3976		(猿)			葯	5030		瘉	3647		鬻	7047
	右	543		窬	4060		緣	4388		藥	5148		癒	3674		魊	7056
	囿	794		竽	4087		芫	4847		說	5598		矞	3828		鴥	7135
	宥	1120		腴	4709		苑	4863		越	5835		禦	3965		鵒	7146
	幼	1356		臾	4775		蝯	5289		躍	5950		禺	3976		鷸	7197
	有	2315		舁	4777		螈	5293		軏	5972		籞	4225		黦	7263
	柚	2402		與	4782		袁	5387		鉞	6352		籲	4232		龥	7331
	祐	3933		萸	5024		轅	6018		鑰	6521		聿	4614	yun	云	52
	莠	4939		虞	5186		黿	7276		閱	6551		育	4639		勻	448
	誘	5588		褕	5440	yuann	媛	1034		龠	7329		與	4782		昀	2222
	釉	6303		覦	5488		怨	1547	yuh	喻	698		芋	4835		筠	4124
	鼬	7292		諛	5622		愿	1672		域	840		蔚	5072		紜	4296
yu	予	47		踰	5897		掾	1947		嫗	1049		蕷	5113		耘	4583
	于	51		輿	6015		瑗	3474		寓	1139		蜮	5258		芸	4857
	余	135		轝	6031		苑	4863		尉	1163		裕	5413		蕓	5110
	俞	310		逾	6115		遠	6138		峪	1235		語	5591		雲	6687
	妤	967		隃	6625		院	6609		彧	1450		諭	5619	yunn	孕	1077
	娛	1008		隅	6627		願	6820		御	1482		譽	5690		惲	1629
	嵎	1259		雩	6682	yueh	刖	367		愈	1649		谷	5706		慍	1657
	愉	1640		餘	6879		岳	1221		慾	1692		豫	5730		暈	2267
	愚	1651		魚	7060		嶽	1280		拗	1849		遇	6120		熨	3247
	揄	1945	yuan	元	290		悅	1582		昱	2230		遹	6153		縕	4410
	於	2175		原	509		戉	1753		棫	2495		郁	6188		蘊	5163
	旟	2194		員	629		曜	2293		欲	2654		鈺	6356		藴	5163
	榆	2521		園	801		月	2314		毓	2730		閾	6557		(蘊)	
	楰	2524		圓	802		樂	2571		汩	2781		隩	6646		運	6122
	歟	2678		援	1965		樾	2592		浴	2889		雨	6681		鄆	6217
	渝	2958		沅	2792		瀹	3157		煜	3221		雩	6682		醞	6280
	漁	3038		湲	2992		禴	3974		熨	3247		預	6790		韞	6772
	瑜	3470		源	2999		籥	4227		燠	3266		飫	6858		韵	6775
	璵	3509		爰	3287		粵	4243		獄	3384		馭	6922		韻	6778
	畬	3576		猿	3379												

聯合國華語注音符號索引

編　法：本索引係照單字讀音，按聯合國華語注音符號順序編列。其讀音相同者，再按部首順序。單字後註明單字編號。

用　法：遇有僅知讀音不悉字形之單字，可按聯合國華語注音查出索引中單字，再根據單字編號，查出書內單字及這一單字爲首所組成的詞語。

U. N. MANDARIN PHONETIC SYMBOL INDEX

In this index the characters are arranged according to the alphabetical order of U. N. MPS. Characters with the same pronunciation are arranged according to their respective radicals. The figure to the right of each character is its identification number under which the character can be found in the body of the dictionary.

If the dictionary user knows the pronunciation of the character he is looking for but is unfamiliar with its strokes, he can find it in the index according to the alphabetical order of U.N.MPS. Using the identification number as a guide, he can locate in the dictionary the character and the entries beneath it.

A

注音	單字	字號
ā	啊	657
	腌	4692
	阿	6594
á	嗄	703
à	錒	6417
	阿	6594
a	啊	657
āi	哀	620
	哎	628
	唉	642
	埃	837
	挨	1876
ái	呆	584
	挨	1876
	捱	1903
	獃	3383
	癌	3667
	皚	3706
	騃	6948
ǎi	噯	759
	欸	2655
	毐	2728
	矮	3837
	藹	5155
	靄	6718
ài	噯	759
	嬡	1063
	愛	1653
	曖	2289
	瑷	3502
	碍	3885
	礙	3915
	艾	4830
	薆	5115
	隘	6637
	靉	6721
ān	安	1105
	庵	1375
	盦	3734
	菴	4988
	諳	5633
	鞍	6745
	鵪	7157
ǎn	俺	186
àn	岸	1223
	按	1866
	暗	2269
	案	2435
	犴	3341
	菴	4988
	闇	6559
	黯	7265
āng	腌	4692
	骯	6994
áng	昂	2210
àng	盎	3722
āo	凹	353
	熬	3244
áo	嗷	722
	嗸	722
	(嗷)	
	敖	2130
	熬	3244
	獒	3385
	璈	3492
	翱	4556
	翶	4563
	聱	4608
	螯	5305
	謷	5664
	遨	6143
	鏊	6479
	鏖	6481
	驁	6970
	鰲	7100
	鼇	7280
ǎo	媼	1042
	拗	1849
	襖	5462
ào	傲	243
	坳	825
	奧	944
	懊	1726
	拗	1849
	敖	2130
	澳	3108
	燠	3266
	隩	6646

B

注音	單字	字號
bā	八	311
	叭	537
	吧	586
	巴	1302
	扒	1793
	捌	1891
	疤	3595
	笆	4089
	粑	4520
	芭	4850
	豝	5724
bá	八	311
	拔	1848
	茇	4896
	跋	5851
	鈸	6340
bǎ	把	1818
	鈀	6329
	靶	6739
bà	壩	895
	把	1818
	灞	3166
	爸	3291
	罷	4505
	耙	4581
	覇	5478
	霸	6713
ba	吧	586
	罷	4505
bāi	掰	1942
bái	白	3692
bǎi	伯	113
	捭	1900
	擺	2087
	柏	2394
	百	3693
	襬	5467
bài	拜	1856
	敗	2131
	稗	4011
	粺	4251
bān	扳	1806
	搬	1993
	斑	2153
	斒	2154
	班	3434
	瘢	3654
	癍	3671
	般	4802
	頒	6792
bǎn	坂	814
	板	2365
	版	3302
	舨	4804
	蝂	5253
	闆	6565
	阪	6587
bàn	伴	116
	半	479
	扮	1803
	拌	1841
	瓣	3520
	絆	4321
	辦	6042
bāng	傍	235
	幫	1345
	帮	1345
	(幫)	
	梆	2472
	浜	2880
	邦	6175
bǎng	榜	2547
	牓	3305
	綁	4345
	膀	4718
bàng	傍	235
	旁	2178
	棒	2480
	磅	3898
	膀	4718
	蚌	5199
	謗	5655
	鎊	6457
bāo	剝	398
	包	451
	炮	3185
	炰	3185
	(炮)	
	胞	4652
	苞	4871
	褒	5441
	襃	5453
báo	薄	5111
	雹	6691
bǎo	保	176
	堡	849
	寶	1156
	寳	1156
	(寶)	
	葆	5022
	褓	5436
	飽	6862
	鴇	7123
bào	報	848
	抱	1826
	暴	2276
	瀑	3138
	爆	3277
	菢	4991
	豹	5735
	趵	5846
	鉋	6347
	鑤	6347
	(鉋)	
	鮑	7066
bēi	卑	482
	埤	842
	悲	1622
	揹	1970
	杯	2357
	盃	3719
	碑	3874
	背	4646
běi	北	458
bèi	倍	194
	備	239
	孛	1081
	悖	1589
	憊	1712
	焙	3208
	狽	3357
	碚	3880
	糒	4256
	背	4646
	臂	4740
	蓓	5052
	被	5397
	褙	5438
	貝	5747
	輩	6002
	邶	6185
	鋇	6395
	鞴	6758

bēn	奔	932
	奔	932
	(奔)	
	犇	3330
	賁	5773
	錛	6434
běn	畚	940
	本	2333
	畚	3566
	苯	4880
bèn	奔	932
	奔	932
	(奔)	
	笨	4097
bēng	崩	1247
	繃	4433
	綳	4433
	(繃)	
béng	甭	3549
běng	繃	4433
	綳	4433
	(繃)	
bèng	榜	2547
	繃	4433
	綳	4433
	(繃)	
	蹦	5923
	迸	6106
	进	6106
	(迸)	
bī	屄	1191
	逼	6116
bí	荸	4950
	鼻	7298
bǐ	匕	456
	妣	966
	彼	1461
	比	2731
	秕	3986
	筆	4109
	鄙	6224
bì	俾	187
	嗶	723
	壁	882
	婢	1023
	嬖	1059
	幣	1343
	庇	1361
	弊	1414
	弼	1435
	必	1497
	愎	1639
	愊	1642
	拂	1834
	敝	2133
	斃	2148
	比	2731
	毖	2732
	泌	2829
	湢	2994
	狴	3355
	璧	3503
	畀	3559
	畢	3573
	痹	3636
	皕	3704
	睥	3782
	碧	3887
	祕	3936
	秘	3936
	(祕)	
	箅	4146
	篦	4173
	篳	4181
	臂	4740
	苾	4884
	萆	4989
	蓖	5061
	蓽	5079
	蔽	5089
	薜	5131
	裨	5422
	襞	5459
	觱	5509
	詖	5556
	費	5768
	賁	5773
	跛	5858
	蹕	5916
	躄	5941
	躃	5947
	辟	6039
	逼	6116
	避	6156
	邲	6183
	鄙	6224
	鉍	6361
	閉	6532
	閟	6541
	陛	6605
	髀	7000
	鷩	7194
biān	砭	3851
	箯	4156
	籩	4229
	編	4389
	蝙	5268
	邊	6166
	鞭	6750
	鯿	7087
biǎn	匾	471
	扁	1783
	稨	4017
	窆	4049
	萹	5025
	蝙	5268
	褊	5433
	貶	5764
biàn	便	164
	卞	489
	弁	1410
	徧	1483
	忭	1512
	抃	1810
	昪	2236
	汴	2788
	緶	4398
	辮	4455
	變	5695
	辨	6043
	辦	6045
	辯	6046
	遍	6123
biāo	彪	1454
	摽	2018
	杓	2345
	標	2581
	熛	3248
	猋	3370
	膔	4751
	膘	4751
	(膔)	
	鏢	6489
	鑣	6518
	飆	6846
	飇	6846
	(飆)	
	麃	7219
biǎo	婊	1028
	表	5375
	裱	5424
	錶	6433
biào	鰾	7102
biē	憋	1711
	鼈	7281
	鱉	7281
	(鼈)	
bié	別	372
	蹩	5929
	蹷	5939
biě	癟	3675
	癟	3675
	(癟)	
biè	彆	1438
bīn	儐	277
	彬	1453
	攽	2120
	斌	2151
	檳	2626
	濱	3131
	瀕	3146
	繽	4458
	豳	5733
	賓	5785
	賔	5785
	(賓)	
	邠	6173
bìn	儐	277
	擯	2077
	殯	2713
	臏	4748
	髕	7007
	鬢	7034
bīng	兵	316
	冰	335
	并	1351
bǐng	丙	16
	屏	1198
	昺	2237
	昞	2237
	(昺)	
	柄	2393
	炳	3187
	秉	3982
	稟	4007
	邴	6186
	餅	6871
	餠	6880
bìng	並	19
	併	189
	倂	189
	(併)	
	并	1351
	摒	2008
	柄	2393
	病	3607
	竝	4076
bō	剝	398
	嶓	1270
	撥	2031
	播	2043
	波	2839
	玻	3426
	番	3575
	般	4802
	菠	4965
	鉢	6353
	盋	6353
	(鉢)	
	缽	6353
	(鉢)	
	餑	6873
bó	伯	113
	勃	428
	博	487
	帛	1318
	搏	1977
	柏	2394
	欂	2645
	泊	2827
	浡	2881
	渤	2963
	濼	3135
	犮	3339
	白	3692
	百	3693
	礴	3922
	箔	4142
	簙	4207
	檗	4268
	脖	4685

	膊	4723
	舶	4809
	荸	4950
	蔔	5081
	薄	5111
	踣	5889
	鈸	6340
	鉑	6349
	鎛	6462
	雹	6691
	駁	6928
	駮	6943
	鵓	7149
bǒ	簸	4210
	跛	5858
bò	亳	70
	北	458
	播	2043
	擘	2071
	簸	4210
	薄	5111
	薜	5131
	蘗	5168
bo	蔔	5081
bū	晡	2249
	逋	6088
	餔	6876
bú	不	8
	醭	6290
bǔ	卜	488
	哺	637
	捕	1892
	補	5415
bù	不	8
	佈	125
	埠	841
	布	1307
	怖	1525
	步	2684
	部	4194
	簿	4214
	部	6206

C

注音	單字	字號
cā	擦	2078
cāi	猜	3367
cái	才	1790
	材	2346
	纔	4469
	裁	5402
	財	5751
cǎi	彩	1452
	採	1929
	睬	3786
	綵	4363
	跴	5865
	踩	5894
	采	6302
cài	菜	4964
	蔡	5073
	采	6302
cān	參	515
	飡	6852
	餐	6872
	驂	6972
cán	慚	1688
	慙	1688
	(慚)	
	殘	2703
	蠶	5351
cǎn	慘	1673
	憯	1709
	黲	7267
càn	燦	3267
	璨	3505
	粲	4245
cāng	倉	191
	傖	237
	滄	3019
	艙	4817
	蒼	5042
	鶬	7174
cáng	藏	5139
cǎng	駔	6933
cāo	操	2058
	糙	4261
cáo	嘈	727
	曹	2307
	槽	2574
	漕	3048
	螬	5302
cǎo	懆	1724
	艸	4829
	草	4917
cào	慥	1676
cè	側	228
	冊	323
	廁	1381
	惻	1638
	測	2969
	策	4122
	筴	4132
cēn	參	515
cén	岑	1215
	涔	2901
céng	層	1204
	嶒	1269
	曾	2309
cèng	蹭	5931
chā	叉	517
	喳	702
	差	1298
	扠	1801
	扱	1807
	插	1954
	揷	1954
	(插)	
	杈	2342
	臿	4776
chá	察	1142
	搽	1981
	查	2411
	槎	2559
	碴	3891
	茬	4878
	茶	4912
chǎ	叉	517
chà	侘	155
	刹	379
	剎	379
	(刹)	
	姹	997
	奼	997
	(姹)	
	岔	1212
	差	1298
	杈	2342
	汊	2768
	衩	5377
	詫	5567
chāi	差	1298
	拆	1837
	釵	6325
chái	儕	280
	柴	2413
	茈	4882
	豺	5736
chǎi	茝	4951
chài	瘥	3655
	蠆	5334
chān	攙	2098
	襜	5463
chán	單	701
	嬋	1057
	孱	1091
	巉	1282
	廛	1393
	欃	2644
	毚	2734
	潺	3085
	澶	3111
	瀍	3143
	禪	3968
	纏	4465
	蟬	5324
	蟾	5332
	讒	5699
	饞	6914
chǎn	剷	406
	產	3541
	蕆	5091
	諂	5606
	鏟	6487
	闡	6578
chàn	懺	1743
	羼	4535
	顫	6830
chāng	倀	188
	倡	207
	娼	1026
	昌	2216
	猖	3362
	菖	4963
	閶	6553
cháng	償	282
	嘗	733
	場	853
	嫦	1053
	常	1327
	徜	1478
	腸	4710
	萇	4977
	裳	5425
	長	6528
chǎng	場	853
	廠	1396
	惝	1615
	敞	2134
	昶	2232
	氅	2743
chàng	倡	207
	唱	649
	悵	1598
	暢	2273
	韔	6769
	鬯	7044
chāo	弨	1427
	抄	1812
	超	5834
	鈔	6331
cháo	嘲	739
	巢	1292
	晁	2243
	朝	2324
	潮	3082
	鼂	7277
chǎo	吵	572
	炒	3182
chào	鈔	6331
chē	車	5966
chě	尺	1180
	扯	1805
	撦	2041
chè	坼	824
	徹	1492
	拆	1837
	掣	1941
	撤	2030
	澈	3089
	轍	6023
chēn	嗔	712
	抻	1904
	琛	3445
	瞋	3796
	郴	6210
chén	塵	867
	宸	1128
	忱	1513
	晨	2253

	橙	2599		盛	3726		遲	6147	chǒng	寵	1155		篨	4175		遄	6119
	沈	2798		程	4005		馳	6925	chòng	衝	5368		耡	4586	chuǎn	喘	689
	沉	2798		裎	5409	chǐ	侈	150		銃	6370		芻	4862		舛	4793
	(沈)			誠	5592		呎	585	chōu	抽	1831		蒢	5062	chuàn	串	23
	臣	4759		郕	6205		尺	1180		搊	1973		蜍	5245		釧	6324
	蔯	5085		酲	6262		恥	1577		犨	3337		蹰	5940	chuāng	創	404
	諶	5635	chěng	懲	1738		耻	4596		瘳	3660		躇	5944		瘡	3651
	辰	6047		逞	6099		蚇	5210		篘	4177		躕	5954		窗	4053
	陳	6617		騁	6945		褫	5445		紬	4308		鉏	6348		窻	4053
chèn	櫬	2635	chèng	秤	3992		豉	5713	chóu	仇	78		鋤	6407		(窗)	
	稱	4015		稱	4015		齒	7307		儔	279		除	6611		牕	4053
	襯	5468	chī	吃	549	chì	傺	248		幬	1344		雛	6674		(窗)	
	讖	5701		喫	549		勅	429		惆	1605	chǔ	儲	285		窓	4053
	趁	5832		(吃)			叱	541		愁	1646		杵	2361		(窗)	
	趂	5832		嗤	719		啻	672		疇	3585		楚	2525	chuáng	幢	1342
	(趁)			媸	1041		彳	1458		稠	4012		楮	2532		牀	3297
	齔	7308		摛	2009		敕	2129		籌	4218		礎	3914		床	3297
chēng	撐	2027		痴	3641		斥	2165		紬	4308		處	5183		(牀)	
	撑	2027		癡	3676		熾	3249		綢	4355		褚	5439	chuǎng	闖	6573
	(撐)			眵	3771		眙	3756		裯	5423	chù	亍	50	chuàng	創	404
	檉	2611		笞	4098		翅	4539		讎	5697		俶	184		愴	1655
	牚	3309		絺	4344		赤	5821		讐	5697		怵	1541		闖	6573
	琤	3448		蚩	5209		跮	5864		(讎)			搐	1995	chuī	吹	575
	瞠	3804		螭	5303		踅	5879		躊	5948		歜	2676		炊	3177
	稱	4015		郗	6203		飭	6856		酬	6260		畜	3567	chuí	倕	197
	蟶	5329		魑	7057		鶒	7171		雔	6671		矗	3823		垂	826
	赬	5826		鴟	7131	chōng	充	292	chǒu	丑	11		絀	4315		捶	1938
	鐺	6507		[illegible]	7324		充	292		瞅	3792		處	5183		搥	1986
chéng	丞	17	chí	匙	459		(充)			醜	6279		觸	5512		椎	2501
	乘	36		墀	875		忡	1508	chòu	臭	4766		黜	7256		槌	2556
	呈	570		尺	1180		憧	1702	chū	出	354	chuā	欻	2660		箠	4145
	城	835		弛	1423		沖	2801		初	369	chuāi	搋	1974		菙	5015
	懲	1738		持	1865		冲	2801		齣	7314	chuǎi	揣	1960		錘	6421
	成	1757		池	2773		(沖)		chú	儲	285	chuài	嘬	749		鎚	6461
	承	1825		治	2819		舂	4779		幮	1347		踹	5905		陲	6616
	晟	2245		箎	4174		衝	5368		廚	1392	chuān	川	1289	chūn	春	2225
	棖	2483		篪	4174	chóng	崇	1236		櫥	2633		穿	4043		椿	2513
	橙	2599		(箎)			种	3987		橱	2633	chuán	傳	244	chún	淳	2941
	澄	3088		茌	4891		蟲	5325		(櫥)			椽	2511		純	4290
	瀓	3099		踟	5886		重	6306		滁	3016		船	4812		脣	4677

	唇	4677
	(脣)	
	蒓	5059
	蓴	5078
	醇	6271
	鶉	7163
chǔn	蠢	5345
	惷	5345
	(蠢)	
	踳	5906
chuō	戳	1776
chuò	啜	671
	惙	1613
	歠	2679
	綽	4368
	輟	5999
	醊	6273
	齪	7319
cī	差	1298
	恣	1572
	疵	3615
	雌	6666
cí	慈	1666
	瓷	3524
	疵	3615
	磁	3896
	祠	3944
	茨	4905
	茲	4909
	詞	5558
	辭	6044
	餈	6866
	粢	4241
	(餈)	
	鷀	7176
	鶿	7176
	(鷀)	
cǐ	此	2683
	泚	2835
	玼	3423
cì	伺	119
	刺	383
	廁	1381
	次	2651
	賜	5789
cōng	囪	789
	從	1480
	怱	1549
	匆	1549
	(怱)	
	悤	1595
	樅	2576
	瑽	3486
	璁	3494
	聰	4605
	葱	5027
	蔥	5075
	鏦	6477
	驄	6974
cóng	叢	526
	從	1480
	从	1480
	(從)	
	淙	2928
	琮	3455
còu	湊	2977
	凑	2977
	(湊)	
	腠	4702
	輳	6007
cū	粗	4236
	麤	7233
cú	徂	1464
	殂	2698
cù	促	166
	卒	483
	猝	3369
	簇	4187
	蔟	5086
	趣	5840
	踧	5891
	蹙	5917
	䠞	5927
	蹴	5933
	蹵	5938
	醋	6274
cuān	攛	2099
	汆	2763
	躥	5958
cuán	攢	2102
cuàn	爨	3283
	竄	4068
	篡	4169
cuī	催	241
	崔	1239
	摧	2012
	榱	2548
	縗	4407
	衰	5378
cuǐ	璀	3488
cuì	啐	659
	悴	1601
	橇	2596
	毳	2740
	淬	2938
	瘁	3640
	粹	4250
	翠	4548
	脆	4669
	脃	4669
	(脆)	
	脺	4693
	膵	4693
	(脺)	
	萃	4975
	顇	6811
cūn	村	2347
	皴	3711
	邨	6178
cún	存	1079
	蹲	5928
cǔn	忖	1507
cùn	吋	552
	寸	1157
cuō	搓	1980
	撮	2048
	磋	3897
	莎	4949
	蹉	5909
cuó	嵯	1264
	痤	3631
	瘥	3655
	矬	3835
	鹺	7212
cuǒ	瑳	3483
	脞	4683
cuò	剉	388
	厝	510
	挫	1879
	措	1934
	撮	2048
	莝	4952
	銼	6409
	錯	6431

D

注音	單字	字號
dā	搭	1988
	答	4119
	耷	4592
	褡	5447
dá	妲	970
	怛	1528
	打	1794
	瘩	3656
	答	4119
	繨	4450
	達	6130
	靼	6744
	韃	6761
dǎ	打	1794
dà	大	916
da	瘩	3656
	繨	4450
dāi	呆	584
	待	1466
	獃	3383
dǎi	歹	2691
	逮	6107
dài	代	91
	大	916
	岱	1220
	帶	1325
	待	1466
	怠	1545
	戴	1775
	殆	2695
	玳	3420
	袋	5391
	襶	5471
	貸	5766
	迨	6066
	逮	6107
	靆	6719
	黛	7255
dān	丹	25
	儋	275
	單	701
	擔	2059
	担	2059
	(擔)	
	殫	2710
	眈	3749
	簞	4198
	耽	4593
	聃	4595
	耼	4595
	(聃)	
	躭	5962
	鄲	6235
	酖	6251
dǎn	撢	2050
	撣	2050
	(撢)	
	疸	3601
	膽	4736
	胆	4736
	(膽)	
	黵	7269
dàn	但	123
	啖	661
	噉	661
	(啖)	
	彈	1437
	憚	1701
	憺	1722
	擔	2059
	旦	2199
	氮	2759
	淡	2931
	澹	3110
	癉	3670
	石	3841
	萏	4985
	蛋	5220
	蜑	5247
	誕	5587
	鉭	6364
dāng	噹	760
	璫	3506
	當	3582
	襠	5460
	鐺	6507
dǎng	擋	2061
	攩	2107
	檔	2610
	當	3582
	讜	5705
	黨	7262

E

F

	腓	4701
fěi	匪	465
	悱	1597
	斐	2152
	朏	2318
	棐	2491
	榧	2562
	篚	4168
	翡	4550
	菲	4970
	蜚	5250
	誹	5603
fèi	吠	565
	廢	1398
	怫	1533
	沸	2814
	狒	3350
	疿	3633
	痱	3633
	(疿)	
	肺	4642
	芾	4861
	費	5768
fēn	分	359
	吩	567
	棻	2490
	氛	2751
	紛	4299
	芬	4848
	棻	4960
	雰	6685
fén	墳	881
	枌	2369
	棼	2492
	汾	2789
	焚	3211
	羒	4521
	蕡	5098
	賁	5773
fěn	粉	4235
fèn	分	359
	份	359
	(分)	
	噴	761
	奮	948
	忿	1520
	憤	1719
	糞	4260
fēng	丰	22
	封	1159
	峯	1230
	楓	2515
	灃	3161
	烽	3201
	瘋	3643
	葑	5002
	蜂	5236
	蠭	5350
	豐	5719
	酆	6242
	鋒	6404
	風	6837
féng	縫	4416
	逢	6103
	馮	6923
fěng	唪	668
fèng	俸	185
	奉	931
	縫	4416
	諷	5636
	風	6837
	鳳	7119
fó	佛	137
fóu	浮	2890
	罘	4493
	芣	4843
fǒu	否	566
	缶	4476
fū	夫	919
	孵	1093
	敷	2142
	枹	2389
	柎	2392
	膚	4724
	趺	5848
	跗	5856
	鄜	6227
	鈇	6332
	麩	7235
fú	伏	109
	俘	174
	匐	455
	夫	919
	孚	1080
	帗	1314
	幅	1328
	弗	1421
	彿	1465
	怫	1533
	扶	1804
	拂	1834
	服	2317
	枹	2389
	桴	2451
	氟	2752
	洑	2852
	浮	2890
	涪	2910
	祓	3934
	福	3956
	符	4101
	箙	4151
	紱	4310
	紼	4313
	縛	4408
	罘	4493
	艴	4827
	芙	4839
	芾	4861
	苻	4883
	茀	4895
	茯	4907
	莩	4942
	菔	4962
	蚨	5208
	蜉	5244
	蝠	5275
	袱	5400
	輻	6010
	郛	6196
	韍	6767
	髴	7016
	鳧	7116
	鵩	7156
	黻	7273
fǔ	俯	181
	府	1368
	拊	1839
	撫	2042
	斧	2166
	父	3290
	甫	3547
	簠	4203
	脯	4680
	腐	4695
	腑	4696
	莆	4945
	輔	5991
	釜	6314
	頫	6799
	黼	7274
fù	仆	77
	付	86
	傅	234
	副	399
	咐	606
	婦	1024
	富	1136
	復	1485
	服	2317
	父	3290
	祔	3935
	腹	4711
	蝜	5281
	蝮	5283
	複	5432
	覆	5476
	訃	5518
	負	5748
	賦	5796
	賻	5802
	赴	5829
	輹	6013
	阜	6582
	附	6597
	馥	6919
	駙	6936
	鮒	7067
	鰒	7089

G

注音	單字	字號
gā	咖	605
	旮	2204
gá	軋	5967
	釓	6312
	錷	6415
gà	尬	1176
gāi	垓	830
	荄	4916
	該	5573
	賅	5778
	陔	6603
gǎi	改	2117
gài	丐	10
	概	2568
	槩	2568
	(概)	
	漑	3045
	葢	5029
	蓋	5049
	盖	5049
	(蓋)	
	鈣	6338
gān	乾	44
	乹	44
	(乾)	
	尷	1178
	干	1348
	杆	2353
	柑	2398
	泔	2830
	玕	3411
	甘	3536
	疳	3600
	竿	4088
	肝	4628
gǎn	感	1652
	擀	2065
	敢	2136
	桿	2474
	橄	2591
	澉	3097
	稈	4003
	簳	4215
	趕	5839
gàn	幹	1353
	旰	2206
	榦	2541
	淦	2933
	灨	3169
	紺	4317
	贛	5820
	骭	6991
gāng	剛	396
	岡	1216
	崗	1241
	杠	2352
	綱	4360

注音	單字	字號
	棺	2498
	瘝	3649
	矜	3827
	綸	4365
	莞	4938
	觀	5499
	關	6574
	鰥	7092
guǎn	琯	3461
	筦	4126
	管	4149
	脘	4675
	舘	4792
	莞	4938
	館	6886
guàn	冠	329
	慣	1675
	摜	2006
	灌	3162
	盥	3733
	祼	3953
	罐	4490
	觀	5499
	貫	5757
	鸛	7206
guāng	光	296
	洸	2877
	胱	4662
guǎng	廣	1399
	獷	3399
guàng	桄	2441
	誑	5585
	逛	6098
guī	傀	233
	圭	808
	歸	2690
	潙	3095
	珪	3435
	瑰	3480
	瓌	3514
	皈	3699
	規	5482
	邽	6194
	閨	6546
	鮭	7070
	龜	7328
guǐ	匭	466
	宄	1098
	晷	2261
	癸	3688
	簋	4190
	詭	5569
	軌	5968
	鬼	7048
guì	劊	413
	會	2312
	桂	2439
	檜	2612
	櫃	2624
	溎	3027
	瞶	3812
	貴	5763
	跪	5867
	鱖	7106
gǔn	滾	3036
	滚	3036
	(滾)	
	袞	5388
	衮	5398
	鯀	7073
gùn	棍	2479
guō	渦	2965
	蟈	5314
	過	6124
	郭	6208
	鍋	6437
guó	國	797
	幗	1336
	摑	2005
	虢	5190
	馘	6917
	聝	6917
	(馘)	
guǒ	果	2377
	椁	2504
	槨	2504
	(椁)	
	猓	3368
	菓	4995
	蜾	5262
	裹	5427
	餜	6887
guò	過	6124

H

注音	單字	字號
hā	哈	626
há	蛤	5225
	蝦	5280
hǎ	哈	626
hái	孩	1088
	還	6161
	頦	6798
	骸	6997
hǎi	海	2891
	醢	6284
hài	亥	63
	咳	616
	害	1124
	氦	2756
	駭	6940
hān	憨	1717
	蚶	5214
	酣	6254
	頇	6785
	鼾	7299
hán	函	355
	含	568
	寒	1138
	崡	1250
	榦	2541
	汗	2772
	涵	2911
	邯	6180
	韓	6768
hǎn	喊	684
	罕	4492
	闞	6576
hàn	悍	1586
	憾	1721
	扞	1796
	捍	1890
	撼	2052
	旱	2207
	暵	2277
	汗	2772
	漢	3053
	瀚	3147
	翰	4558
	菡	4984
	豻	5737
	銲	6411
	釬	6411
	(銲)	
	頷	6805
	馯	6950
hāng	夯	924
háng	杭	2356
	桁	2432
	沆	2796
	航	4801
	行	5360
	迒	6061
	頏	6789
hàng	桁	2432
	沆	2796
hāo	嚆	764
	蒿	5043
	薅	5112
háo	嗥	742
	嚎	762
	壕	889
	毫	2737
	濠	3122
	號	5188
	蠔	5340
	豪	5728
	貉	5740
	鶴	7173
hǎo	好	954
	郝	6198
hào	好	954
	昊	2215
	晧	2252
	浩	2883
	涸	2912
	澔	3098
	灝	3165
	皓	3702
	皜	3707
	耗	4584
	號	5188
	鄗	6220
	鎬	6464
	顥	6828
hē	呵	593
	喝	693
	訶	5543
hé	何	132
	劾	426
	合	547
	和	604
	曷	2305
	核	2428
	河	2816
	涸	2912
	盍	3721
	盒	3724
	禾	3978
	紇	4284
	翮	4557
	荷	4927
	蓋	5049
	褐	5435
	覈	5477
	貉	5740
	鉿	6385
	閡	6543
	閤	6544
	闔	6571
	鞨	6753
	鶡	7169
	齕	7309
	龢	7330
hè	和	604
	喝	693
	嚇	766
	奭	947
	荷	4927
	豁	5707
	賀	5771
	赫	5824
	郝	6198
	鶴	7173
	黑	7250
hēi	嘿	747
	黑	7250
hén	痕	3620
hěn	很	1468
	狠	3352
hèn	恨	1558
hēng	亨	65
	哼	638
héng	恆	1551
	恒	1551
	(恆)	
	桁	2432
	横	2606
	珩	3433

	蘅	5159	hū	乎	32		扈	1787		環	3504		遑	6126		喙	690
	衡	5372		呼	598		楛	2519		繯	4448		黃	7244		彗	1443
hèng	橫	2606		忽	1519		滬	3029		還	6161	huǎng	幌	1333		彙	1445
hm̄	噷	758		惚	1612		瓠	3518		鍰	6445		悅	1536		恚	1569
hōng	哄	623		戲	1774		祜	3939		鐶	6505		恍	1555		惠	1623
	烘	3197		欻	2660		笏	4091		闤	6580		晃	2242		慧	1689
	薨	5128		歑	2670		護	5688		鬟	7033		謊	5650		晦	2251
	訇	5519		淴	2953	huā	嘩	734	huǎn	浣	2882	huàng	晃	2242		會	2312
	轟	6030		滹	3034		花	4854		澣	3118	huī	徽	1495		槥	2565
	魟	7061		虖	5184		華	4966		緩	4390		恢	1557		濊	3116
hóng	宏	1108	hú	囫	790	huá	划	365	huàn	喚	691		揮	1963		燴	3270
	弘	1422		壺	901		劃	409		奐	935		撝	2049		穢	4033
	泓	2831		弧	1426		嘩	734		宦	1121		暉	2266		篲	4197
	洪	2865		斛	2158		滑	3023		幻	1355		灰	3172		繢	4443
	紅	4283		楜	2572		猾	3381		患	1594		翬	4553		繪	4446
	紘	4293		湖	2984		華	4966		換	1958		虺	5196		翽	4565
	翃	4540		狐	3349		譁	5673		擐	2066		褘	5437		蕙	5097
	葒	5023		猢	3371		豁	5707		渙	2955		詼	5576		薈	5117
	虹	5195		瑚	3472		驊	6977		漶	3063		輝	5997		蟪	5323
	訌	5523		糊	4252	huà	劃	409		煥	3224		隳	6651		誨	5597
	閎	6535		縠	4403		化	457		瘓	3644		麾	7243		諱	5632
	鴻	7139		胡	4654		樺	2589		豢	5727	huí	回	784		賄	5776
	黌	7246		葫	5012		畫	3578		轘	6026		徊	1470		闠	6577
hǒng	哄	623		蝴	5285		華	4966		逭	6113		洄	2850		靧	6733
hòng	汞	2778		衚	5369		話	5572	huāng	慌	1663		茴	4910	hūn	婚	1022
	鬨	7039		觳	5510	huái	徊	1470		肓	4625		蛔	5222		惛	1614
hōu	齁	7300		醐	6278		懷	1739		荒	4920		迴	6072		昏	2218
hóu	侯	160		餬	6891		槐	2558	huáng	凰	348		廻	6072		葷	5018
	喉	683		鬍	7027		淮	2939		徨	1484		(迴)			閽	6556
	猴	3376		鵠	7153		踝	5884		惶	1630	huǐ	悔	1584	hún	混	2945
	瘊	3833		鶘	7166	huài	壞	893		湟	2990		會	2312		渾	2975
	篌	4165		鶻	7178	huān	懽	1747		潢	3077		毀	2722		琿	3473
	餱	6890	hǔ	唬	667		歡	2680		煌	3217		燬	3268		餛	6882
hǒu	吼	577		滸	3035		讙	5702		璜	3497		虺	5196		魂	7050
hòu	候	203		琥	3452		貛	5746		皇	3698		誨	5597	hǔn	混	2945
	厚	508		虎	5180		獾	5746		磺	3911		賄	5776	hùn	慁	1670
	后	557	hù	互	53		(貛)			篁	4160	huì	匯	467		㥵	1670
	後	1472		怙	1527		驩	6988		簧	4206		卉	480		(慁)	
	逅	6080		戶	1777	huán	寰	1154		蝗	5271		卉	480		混	2945
	鱟	7109		戽	1780		桓	2446		蟥	5318		(卉)			渾	2975

注音	單字	字號
	溷	3012
	諢	5626
	鯇	7074
huō	豁	5707
huó	活	2873
huǒ	伙	112
	夥	915
	火	3171
	鈥	6328
huò	和	604
	壑	888
	惑	1621
	或	1760
	擭	2080
	濩	3132
	獲	3394
	矱	3840
	砉	3844
	禍	3955
	穫	4036
	藿	5157
	蠖	5342
	豁	5707
	貨	5754
	鑊	6510
	霍	6698
	騞	6962

J

注音	單字	字號
jī	乩	42
	几	346
	唧	694
	喞	694
	(唧)	
	嘰	738
	基	844
	奇	929
	姬	1005
	屐	1196
	嵇	1255
	幾	1358
	期	2325
	朞	2325
	(期)	
	機	2605
	激	3112
	犄	3328
	璣	3499
	畸	3581
	畿	3583
	磯	3908
	禨	3969
	稽	4023
	積	4029
	笄	4121
	筓	4121
	(笄)	
	箕	4143
	績	4431
	羈	4510
	羇	4511
	肌	4622
	虀	5178
	覊	5479
	覉	5480
	觭	5508
	譏	5672
	跡	5863
	蹟	5925
	躋	5949
	迹	6074
	隮	6650
	雞	6677
	飢	6850
	饑	6904
	鷄	7185
	齎	7305
	賫	7305
	(齎)	
	賷	7305
	(齎)	
	齏	7306
jí	亟	59
	伋	106
	卽	504
	即	504
	(卽)	
	及	518
	吃	549
	吉	551
	唧	694
	喞	694
	(唧)	
	嫉	1045
	寂	1132
	岌	1213
	急	1546
	戢	1767
	擊	2069
	棘	2482
	楫	2529
	極	2531
	檝	2619
	殛	2704
	汲	2785
	疾	3606
	瘠	3653
	笈	4092
	籍	4219
	級	4298
	脊	4672
	蒺	5041
	蕺	5130
	藉	5136
	踖	5892
	蹐	5913
	輯	6006
	集	6661
	革	6735
	鶺	7177
jǐ	几	346
	己	1299
	幾	1358
	庋	1362
	戟	1765
	戟	1765
	(戟)	
	掎	1916
	擠	2072
	濟	3123
	給	4333
	脊	4672
	蟣	5322
	踦	5895
	麂	7218
jì	伎	108
	冀	321
	劑	415
	妓	959
	季	1085
	寄	1133
	忌	1499
	悸	1599
	技	1811
	旡	2196
	既	2197
	旣	2197
	(既)	
	暨	2281
	洎	2851
	漈	3039
	濟	3123
	祭	3949
	稷	4020
	穄	4030
	紀	4278
	繫	4452
	繼	4459
	罽	4507
	芰	4853
	薊	5118
	薺	5135
	覬	5491
	計	5515
	記	5528
	跽	5877
	際	6640
	霽	6715
	騎	6951
	驥	6986
	髻	7018
	鯽	7085
jiā	伽	121
	佳	143
	傢	232
	加	419
	嘉	728
	夾	927
	家	1127
	枷	2386
	珈	3428
	痂	3611
	笳	4103
	葭	5014
	袈	5389
	豭	5731
	迦	6065
	鎵	6473
jiá	夾	927
	恝	1570
	戞	1764
	戛	1764
	(戞)	
	筴	4132
	莢	4940
	蛺	5230
	袷	5401
	裌	5419
	跲	5870
	郟	6200
	鋏	6403
	頡	6797
	頰	6804
jiǎ	假	216
	夏	904
	岬	1218
	斝	2160
	檟	2614
	甲	3553
	胛	4650
	賈	5779
	鉀	6343
jià	假	216
	價	267
	夾	927
	嫁	1037
	架	2385
	稼	4021
	駕	6934
jiān	兼	320
	堅	846
	奸	952
	姦	992
	尖	1170
	戔	1762
	椷	2510
	殲	2714
	湔	2981
	漸	3062
	煎	3229
	犍	3331
	監	3731
	箋	4138
	牋	4138
	(箋)	
	緘	4380
	縑	4406
	肩	4634

艱 4825	建 1408	將 1162	徼 1494	街 5366	解 5505
菅 4957	檻 2623	強 1434	撟 2040	階 6633　**jiè**	介 80
蘮 5040	毽 2741	強 1434	攪 2108　**jié**	偈 217	借 206
間 6534	漸 3062	(強) 1434	湫 2988	傑 236	屆 1189
閒 6538	澗 3078	彊 1434	狡 3353	劫 423	戒 1758
鞬 6755	濺 3134	(彊) 1434	皎 3701	刦 423	械 2467
韉 6764	監 3731	洚 2903	矯 3838	(刦)	玠 3417
鰜 7093	箭 4155	糨 4266	筊 4123	婕 1021	界 3560
鰹 7104	腱 4708	糡 4266	絞 4330	孑 1074	疥 3596
鵳 7179	艦 4820	(糡)	繳 4449	竭 1253	芥 4844
jiǎn 儉 274	荐 4926	絳 4338	脚 4687	截 1770	藉 5136
剪 400	薦 5127	醬 6288	腳 4707	拮 1858	解 5505
戩 1769	見 5481	降 6601	角 5500	捷 1909	誡 5590
揀 1944	諫 5630	**jiāo** 交 62	蹻 5936	捷 1909　**jīn**	今 79
撿 2067	賤 5795	噍 748	較 5983	(捷)	巾 1305
柬 2410	踐 5881	姣 989	鉸 6369	擷 2085	斤 2164
檢 2615	鍵 6446	嬌 1058	餃 6865	杰 2379	津 2861
減 2959	鐧 6498	憍 1697	**jiào** 叫 535	桀 2434	矜 3827
瞼 3817	鑑 6512	教 2126	噍 748	桔 2447	祲 3950
筧 4137	鑒 6513	椒 2494	嶠 1272	楬 2530	禁 3954
簡 4200	間 6534	澆 3092	徼 1494	櫛 2631	筋 4118
簡 4200	閒 6538	焦 3213	撟 2040	潔 3071	衿 5386
(簡)	餞 6883	燋 3261	教 2126	癤 3678	襟 5461
繭 4453	**jiāng** 僵 266	礁 3913	斠 2163	睫 3785	觔 5501
翦 4551	姜 987	膠 4728	校 2429	碣 3888	金 6310
襉 5458	將 1162	茭 4923	窖 4052	竭 4082　**jǐn**	僅 251
謇 5652	殭 2711	蕉 5092	覺 5496	莭 4140	儘 281
謭 5691	江 2776	蛟 5224	訓 5517	節 4159	卺 502
趼 5861	漿 3067	跤 5875	較 5983	結 4326	廑 1389
趼 5861	疆 3584	郊 6192	轎 6024	絜 4341	槿 2573
(趼)	繮 4447	驕 6976	醮 6291	羯 4529	殣 2706
蹇 5908	薑 5122	鮫 7068	**jiē** 偕 223	蜐 5288	瑾 3487
鐧 6498	螿 5310	鷦 7138	喈 682	袷 5401	緊 4375
鹸 7213	豇 5711	鷮 7192	嗟 717	訐 5521	菫 4993
鹻 7214	韁 6762	**jiáo** 嚼 774	接 1932	詰 5571	覲 5493
jiàn 件 100	**jiǎng** 獎 946	**jiǎo** 佼 145	揭 1964	頡 6797	謹 5670
健 226	槳 2570	僥 260	癤 3678　**jié**	**jiě** 姊 977	錦 6427
僭 263	蔣 5074	剿 405	皆 3697	姐 977	饉 6901
儉 274	講 5657	勦 405	稭 4016	(姊)	**jìn** 勁 427
劍 414	**jiàng** 匠 462	(勦)	結 4326	姐 980	噤 750

	搢	1984
	晉	2241
	晋	2241
	(晉)	
	浸	2892
	燼	3275
	瑨	3485
	盡	3730
	禁	3954
	縉	4409
	藎	5138
	覲	5493
	贐	5816
	近	6056
	進	6109
	靳	6737
jīng	京	67
	兢	305
	旌	2185
	晶	2260
	涇	2894
	睛	3777
	秔	3988
	稉	3988
	(秔)	
	粳	4248
	精	4249
	經	4350
	耕	4582
	莖	4936
	菁	4969
	荊	4994
	荆	4994
	(荊)	
	驚	6982
	鯨	7082
	鶄	7164
jǐng	井	55
	儆	272
	剄	387

	憬	1703
	景	2256
	璟	3495
	警	5685
	阱	6589
	頸	6807
jìng	倞	195
	凊	340
	勁	427
	境	870
	徑	1474
	敬	2139
	淨	2937
	痙	3624
	竟	4077
	競	4084
	脛	4676
	逕	6092
	鏡	6488
	婧	6723
	靚	6724
	靜	6725
jiōng	扃	1784
jiǒng	扄	1784
	泂	2822
	炯	3186
	烱	3186
	(炯)	
	窘	4054
	絅	4322
	迥	6064
	逈	6084
jiū	啾	674
	噍	748
	揪	1962
	揫	1962
	(揪)	
	摎	2015
	樛	2582
	湫	2988

	究	4039
	糺	4276
	糾	4277
	赳	5828
	轇	6022
	鬮	7043
	鳩	7117
jiǔ	久	29
	九	39
	灸	3173
	玖	3412
	糺	4276
	糾	4277
	韮	5032
	赳	5828
	酒	6250
	韭	6773
jiù	僦	261
	咎	590
	就	1177
	廄	1387
	救	2128
	柩	2407
	桕	2449
	疚	3593
	究	4039
	臼	4773
	舅	4781
	舊	4785
	鷲	7196
jū	俱	182
	居	1188
	崌	1249
	拘	1852
	据	1902
	沮	2810
	狙	3351
	琚	3447
	疽	3604
	痀	3610

	罝	4496
	苴	4878
	菹	4972
	葅	5031
	裾	5430
	趄	5833
	車	5966
	鋦	6405
	鋸	6413
	雎	6668
	駒	6932
jú	侷	163
	局	1186
	挶	1896
	掬	1937
	桔	2447
	橘	2600
	臼	4774
	菊	4958
	跼	5876
	鞠	6749
	鞫	6754
jǔ	咀	600
	枸	2388
	柜	2403
	櫸	2643
	沮	2810
	矩	3834
	筥	4125
	籧	4228
	舉	4784
	擧	4784
	(舉)	
	莒	4934
	踽	5900
	鉏	6348
	齟	7311
jù	俱	182
	倨	210
	具	318

	劇	410
	句	531
	屨	1206
	巨	1296
	懼	1744
	拒	1846
	据	1902
	據	2063
	沮	2810
	炬	3184
	瞿	3819
	秬	3996
	窶	4065
	簴	4213
	聚	4602
	苣	4893
	虡	5189
	詎	5551
	足	5844
	距	5859
	踞	5885
	遽	6157
	醵	6295
	鉅	6345
	鋸	6413
	颶	6841
juān	圈	799
	娟	1010
	悁	1580
	捐	1893
	涓	2899
	蠲	5349
	身	5960
	鐫	6502
	鵑	7147
juǎn	卷	499
	捲	1907
juàn	倦	209
	卷	499
	圈	799

	悁	1580
	狷	3358
	眷	3773
	睠	3789
	絹	4343
	鄄	6219
	雋	6667
juē	撅	2026
jué	倔	200
	厥	511
	噱	756
	嚼	774
	孓	1075
	崛	1243
	憰	1749
	抉	1813
	掘	1922
	攫	2109
	桷	2455
	梏	2460
	決	2786
	决	2786
	(決)	
	爝	3282
	爵	3289
	獗	3390
	玦	3414
	珏	3416
	玨	3416
	(珏)	
	矍	3821
	絕	4328
	脚	4687
	腳	4707
	蕨	5101
	蕝	5109
	蠼	5355
	覺	5496
	角	5500
	觖	5502

注音	單字	字號
	訣	5536
	譎	5675
	蹶	5934
	駃	6929
	鱖	7106
	鴂	7125
	鴃	7125
	(鴂)	
juě	蹶	5934
juè	倔	200
jūn	君	561
	困	791
	均	815
	皸	3712
	軍	5969
	鈞	6337
	頵	6806
	麏	7224
	麕	7229
	龜	7328
jùn	俊	168
	峻	1233
	捃	1885
	浚	2879
	濬	3129
	畯	3579
	竣	4080
	菌	4959
	郡	6201
	雋	6667
	駿	6946

K

注音	單字	字號
kā	咖	605
kǎ	卡	491
	咳	616
kà	喀	675
kāi	揩	1961

注音	單字	字號
	開	6533
kǎi	凱	349
	剴	403
	嘅	726
	嘅	726
	(嘅)	
	愷	1658
	慨	1678
	楷	2533
	豈	5712
	鍇	6453
	鎧	6463
	闓	6570
kài	愒	1631
	愾	1659
	慨	1678
	欬	2653
kān	刊	362
	勘	435
	堪	850
	戡	1766
	看	3755
	龕	7327
kǎn	侃	148
	坎	817
	檻	2623
	欿	2661
	砍	3847
	轗	6029
	闞	6576
kàn	勘	435
	看	3755
	瞰	3808
	矙	3824
	闞	6576
kāng	康	1377
	慷	1679
	糠	4264
káng	扛	1798
kǎng	慷	1679

注音	單字	字號
kàng	亢	61
	伉	104
	抗	1820
	炕	3178
	鈧	6327
kāo	尻	1182
kǎo	拷	1871
	栲	2430
	烤	3198
	考	4569
	攷	4569
	(考)	
kào	犒	3332
	銬	6380
	靠	6729
kē	刻	384
	柯	2408
	棵	2499
	珂	3422
	疴	3602
	痾	3602
	(疴)	
	瞌	3800
	磕	3900
	科	3984
	稞	4013
	窠	4056
	苛	4869
	蝌	5269
	軻	5980
	鈳	6365
	頦	6798
	顆	6810
	髁	7001
ké	咳	616
	欬	2653
	殼	2719
	壳	2719
	(殼)	
	殸	2719

注音	單字	字號
	(殼)	
	頦	6798
kě	可	539
	坷	823
	渴	2970
kè	克	297
	刻	384
	剋	390
	可	539
	嗑	721
	客	1117
	恪	1560
	溘	3000
	緙	4399
	課	5600
kěn	啃	666
	墾	883
	懇	1731
	肯	4637
	肎	4637
	(肯)	
	肻	4637
	(肯)	
kèn	裉	5404
kēng	傾	249
	坑	819
	硜	3865
	鏗	6482
	阬	6585
kěng	肯	4637
	肎	4637
	(肯)	
	肻	4637
	(肯)	
kōng	悾	1603
	空	4042
	箜	4147
kǒng	孔	1076
	恐	1567
kòng	控	1931

注音	單字	字號
	空	4042
kōu	摳	2014
kǒu	口	527
kòu	叩	533
	寇	1135
	扣	1797
	蔻	5065
	釦	6323
	㲄	7184
kū	刳	378
	哭	634
	枯	2380
	窟	4055
	骷	6995
kǔ	楛	2519
	苦	4874
kù	庫	1373
	矻	3843
	袴	5399
	絝	5399
	(袴)	
	褲	5449
	酷	6264
kuā	夸	926
	姱	995
	誇	5579
kuǎ	垮	833
kuà	胯	4660
	跨	5860
	骻	6996
kuǎi	擓	2068
	舀	4778
	蒯	5036
kuài	儈	273
	劊	413
	塊	855
	快	1510
	旝	2193
	會	2312
	檜	2612

注音	單字	字號
	澮	3104
	獪	3392
	筷	4136
	膾	4737
	蒯	5036
	鄶	6238
kuān	寬	1152
kuǎn	款	2657
	欵	2657
	(款)	
	窾	4066
kuāng	匡	463
	恇	1562
	框	2443
	筐	4116
	誆	5581
kuáng	狂	3343
	誑	5585
kuàng	壙	890
	曠	2295
	框	2443
	況	2821
	况	2821
	(況)	
	眶	3767
	礦	3919
	纊	4463
	貺	5767
	鄺	6240
	鑛	6516
kuī	巋	1283
	悝	1591
	盔	3725
	窺	4064
	虧	5191
	闚	6575
kuí	夔	906
	奎	933
	揆	1946
	睽	2271

注音	單字	字號
	暌	3791
	葵	5017
	逵	6110
	馗	6916
	騤	6960
	魁	7049
kuǐ	傀	233
	跬	5869
	頍	6794
kuì	匱	468
	喟	695
	愧	1654
	媿	1654
	(愧)	
	憒	1704
	潰	3087
	簣	4201
	聵	4610
	蕢	5100
	餽	6898
	饋	6902
kūn	坤	821
	崑	1238
	昆	2212
	琨	3450
	蚰	5229
	褌	5434
	鋸	6429
	髡	7009
	鯤	7078
	鵾	7159
kǔn	壼	902
	悃	1579
	捆	1886
	綑	4351
	閫	6548
kùn	困	787
	睏	3775

注音	單字	字號
kuò	廓	1390
	括	1860
	擴	2086
	闊	6562

L

注音	單字	字號
lā	喇	681
	拉	1838
lá	剌	391
	拉	1838
	旯	2205
lǎ	喇	681
là	剌	391
	瘌	3646
	腊	4700
	臘	4750
	落	5000
	蠟	5343
	辣	6041
	鑞	6517
	鬎	7026
la	啦	664
lái	來	149
	崍	1248
	徠	1481
	淶	2944
	萊	4979
	郲	6212
	錸	6416
lài	瀨	3151
	癩	3680
	睞	3778
	籟	4223
	賚	5787
	賴	5800
lán	婪	1025
	嵐	1258
	攔	2095
	欄	2155
	欗	2641
	瀾	3158
	籃	4217
	藍	5137
	蘭	5172
	襤	5464
	襴	5470
	讕	5698
	闌	6564
lǎn	懶	1740
	攬	2111
	擥	2111
	(攬)	
	欖	2649
	纜	4475
	覽	5497
làn	濫	3126
	瀾	3158
	爛	3281
	纜	4475
láng	廊	1385
	榔	2539
	浪	2887
	狼	3356
	琅	3442
	瑯	3479
	稂	4004
	莨	4953
	蜋	5246
	螂	5300
	踉	5878
	郎	6199
	鋃	6400
lǎng	朗	2322
	烺	3205
	閬	6549
làng	浪	2887
	閬	6549
lāo	撈	2028
láo	勞	438
	嘮	736
	撈	2028
	牢	3315
	癆	3668
	醪	6287
lǎo	佬	158
	姥	991
	潦	3079
	老	4568
	銠	6383
lào	勞	438
	憦	1708
	潦	3079
	澇	3094
	烙	3200
	絡	4331
	落	5000
	酪	6258
lē	褦	5443
lè	仂	74
	勒	432
	垃	827
	捋	1887
	樂	2571
	泐	2826
	肋	4621
le	了	46
lēi	勒	432
léi	擂	2054
	累	4307
	縲	4421
	纍	4466
	罍	4487
	羸	4534
	蘲	5179
	鐳	6508
	雷	6689
lěi	儡	283
	壘	891
	磊	3901
	累	4307
	耒	4579
	蕾	5114
	藟	5145
	誄	5577
lèi	擂	2054
	淚	2926
	泪	2926
	(淚)	
	累	4307
	纇	4467
	肋	4621
	酹	6266
	頪	6823
	類	6827
léng	楞	2520
	稜	4010
	薐	5121
lěng	冷	337
lèng	愣	1634
	楞	2520
lī	哩	633
lí	嫠	1047
	棃	2475
	梨	2475
	(棃)	
	氂	2742
	漓	3044
	漦	3066
	犂	3326
	犁	3326
	(犂)	
	犛	3334
	狸	3359
	璃	3490
	籬	4230
	縭	4417
	罹	4506
	藜	5143
	蘺	5175
	蜊	5240
	蠡	5344
	褵	5450
	貍	5742
	醨	6286
	釐	6309
	離	6679
	驪	6989
	鸝	7208
	黎	7248
	黧	7261
lǐ	俚	175
	哩	633
	娌	1004
	悝	1591
	李	2340
	浬	2886
	澧	3103
	理	3441
	禮	3970
	蠡	5344
	裏	5410
	裡	5410
	(裏)	
	豊	5715
	邐	6168
	醴	6293
	里	6305
	鋰	6396
	鯉	7076
lì	例	151
	俐	171
	儷	286
	利	374
	力	417
	勵	445
	厲	513
	吏	560
	唳	650
	慄	1660

M

注音	單字	字號
	沒	2803
	沫	2808
	漠	3049
	瘼	3664
	磨	3904
	秣	3994
	脈	4671
	衇	4671
	(脈)	
	脉	4671
	(脈)	
	膜	4725
	茉	4897
	莫	4944
	袜	5394
	貉	5740
	貊	5740
	(貉)	
	貘	5745
	陌	6600
	靺	6743
	驀	6971
	麥	7234
	默	7253
móu	牟	3312
	眸	3768
	繆	4434
	謀	5640
	鍪	6443
	麰	7238
mǒu	某	2395
	牡	3313
mòu	瞀	3795
	茂	4886
	袤	5395
mú	模	2584
	獏	3386
mǔ	姆	976
	拇	1835
	母	2726
	牡	3313
	畝	3568
	鉧	6344
mù	募	440
	墓	866
	幕	1335
	慕	1693
	暮	2274
	木	2330
	沐	2799
	牧	3316
	目	3739
	睦	3784
	穆	4028
	繆	4434
	苜	4870
	莫	4944
	鉬	6363

N

注音	單字	字號
nā	那	6174
ná	南	486
	拿	1874
	拏	1874
	(拿)	
nǎ	哪	645
	那	6174
nà	吶	573
	娜	1009
	捺	1905
	納	4288
	衲	5380
	訥	5537
	那	6174
	鈉	6333
na	哪	645
nǎi	乃	28
	奶	951
	氖	2750
	艿	4831
	迺	6085
nài	奈	930
	柰	2412
	耐	4576
	褦	5443
	鼐	7284
nán	南	486
	喃	678
	枬	2367
	楠	2367
	(枬)	
	男	3555
	諵	5621
	難	6680
nǎn	腩	4712
	赧	5823
nàn	難	6680
náng	囊	780
nǎng	攮	2112
	曩	2299
náo	怓	1539
	撓	2035
	橈	2597
	猱	3375
	譊	5680
	鐃	6494
nǎo	惱	1626
	瑙	3468
	腦	4704
nào	淖	2921
	鬧	7038
nè	訥	5537
ne	呢	587
něi	那	6174
	餒	6874
nèi	內	307
	那	6174
nèn	嫩	1054
néng	能	4666
nèng	濘	3119
ní	倪	212
	呢	587
	妮	971
	尼	1183
	怩	1532
	泥	2842
	猊	3364
	麑	4758
	蜺	5266
	輗	5994
	霓	6702
	麑	7225
nǐ	你	115
	妳	985
	擬	2076
	旎	2186
	禰	3971
nì	匿	472
	惄	1620
	暱	2278
	昵	2278
	(暱)	
	泥	2842
	溺	3013
	睨	3783
	膩	4732
	衵	5381
	逆	6081
niān	蔫	5083
nián	年	1350
	拈	1836
	粘	4239
	鮎	7065
	黏	7249
niǎn	捻	1908
	撚	2037
	攆	2092
	碾	3894
	輦	6000
	輾	6014
niàn	唸	669
	廿	1409
	念	1518
niáng	娘	1007
	孃	1007
	(娘)	
niàng	釀	6297
niǎo	嫋	1065
	嬝	1065
	(嫋)	
	嬲	1067
	蔦	5076
	裊	5406
	鳥	7115
niào	尿	1185
	溺	3013
niē	捏	1895
	揑	1895
	(捏)	
	捻	1908
nié	苶	4879
niè	乜	38
	囁	776
	孽	1096
	孼	1096
	(孽)	
	櫱	2638
	涅	2895
	湼	2895
	(涅)	
	糵	4273
	糱	4273
	(糵)	
	聶	4611
	臬	4765
	臲	4768
	蘗	5161
	蘖	5161
	(蘗)	
	蘗	5169
	躡	5957
	鎳	6467
	鑷	6523
	闑	6568
	隉	6630
	顳	6836
	齧	7317
	嚙	7317
	(齧)	
	囓	7317
	(齧)	
nín	您	1596
níng	凝	345
	嚀	765
	寧	1143
	擰	2082
	檸	2620
	獰	3397
	甯	3550
nǐng	擰	2082
nìng	佞	139
	擰	2082
	濘	3119
	甯	3550
niū	妞	963
niú	牛	3310
niǔ	忸	1514
	扭	1802
	狃	3346
	紐	4289
	鈕	6336
niù	拗	1849
	衄	5357
	謬	5668
nóng	儂	270
	濃	3115
	穠	4034
	膿	4735

	農	6049
	醲	6294
	齈	7302
nòng	弄	1411
nòu	耨	4588
nú	奴	950
	孥	1086
	笯	4104
	駑	6931
nǔ	努	422
	弩	1428
	砮	3857
nù	怒	1543
nǚ	女	949
	釹	6322
nǜ	忸	1514
	恧	1574
	衄	5357
nuǎn	暖	2270
	煖	3220
nüè	瘧	3648
	虐	5181
	謔	5647
nuó	娜	1009
	挪	1877
	挼	1881
nuǒ	娜	1009
nuò	喏	686
	懦	1734
	搦	1990
	糯	4269
	稬	4269
	(糯)	
	穤	4269
	(糯)	
	諾	5639

O

注音	單字	字號
ō	喔	688
ó	哦	631
o	呵	593
ōu	敺	2144
	歐	2669
	毆	2724
	漚	3046
	甌	3529
	謳	5669
	鷗	7188
ǒu	偶	230
	嘔	731
	耦	4587
	藕	5142
òu	嘔	731
	慪	1683
	漚	3046

P

注音	單字	字號
pā	葩	5011
	趴	5845
pá	扒	1793
	爬	3285
	琶	3458
	耙	4581
pà	帕	1312
	怕	1526
pa	杷	2363
	琶	3458
pāi	拍	1844
pái	俳	183
	徘	1477
	排	1921
	牌	3303
	簰	4196
pài	派	2874
	湃	2971
	鎃	6452
pān	攀	2093
	潘	3074
	番	3575
pán	槃	2552
	盤	3732
	磐	3903
	胖	4648
	般	4802
	蟠	5320
	鞶	6759
pàn	判	371
	叛	524
	拌	1841
	拚	1853
	泮	2843
	畔	3564
	盼	3746
	襻	5472
pāng	乓	27
	滂	3018
	磅	3898
	雱	6714
páng	傍	235
	厖	507
	尨	1175
	龐	1403
	彷	1459
	徬	1487
	旁	2178
	㫄	2178
	(旁)	
	膀	4718
	螃	5291
	逄	6083
	雱	6686
pàng	胖	4648
pāo	拋	1840
	抛	1840
	(拋)	
	泡	2841
	脬	4681
páo	刨	373
	匏	454
	咆	602
	庖	1365
	炮	3185
	袍	5392
	麃	7219
	麅	7221
pǎo	跑	5854
pào	泡	2841
	炮	3185
	疱	3612
	皰	3710
	砲	3859
	礮	3920
pēi	披	1828
	胚	4651
	醅	6270
péi	培	839
	裴	5426
	賠	5791
	邳	6184
	陪	6613
pèi	佩	141
	帔	1310
	旆	2181
	沛	2807
	珮	3437
	轡	6034
	配	6249
	霈	6696
pēn	噴	761
	歕	2675
pén	湓	2980
	盆	3717
pēng	怦	1529
	抨	1827
	澎	3090
	烹	3202
	砰	3852
	硼	3872
péng	彭	1455
	朋	2316
	棚	2486
	澎	3090
	硼	3872
	篷	4184
	膨	4731
	芃	4832
	蓬	5063
	鵬	7155
pěng	捧	1898
pèng	碰	3879
	掽	3879
	(碰)	
pī	丕	13
	劈	411
	匹	470
	批	1808
	披	1828
	砒	3848
	紕	4292
	被	5397
	霹	6712
pí	啤	658
	埤	842
	枇	2362
	毗	2733
	琵	3457
	疲	3599
	皮	3709
	紕	4292
	罷	4505
	羆	4508
	脾	4699
	蚍	5203
	裨	5422
	貔	5744
	郫	6207
	鈹	6362
	陂	6596
	陴	6618
	鼙	7290
pǐ	仳	98
	劈	411
	匹	470
	否	566
	庀	1359
	疋	3587
	痞	3630
	癖	3672
	苤	4899
pì	僻	268
	屁	1187
	擗	2064
	澼	3109
	甓	3534
	譬	5686
	辟	6039
	闢	6579
piān	偏	221
	扁	1783
	片	3301
	篇	4162
	翩	4554
	萹	5025
pián	便	164
	楩	2537
	胼	4689
	骿	4689
	(胼)	
	諞	5624
	蹁	5902
	駢	6944
	騈	6952
piǎn	諞	5624
piàn	徧	1483
	片	3301
	遍	6123

Q

piàn	騗	6958		洴	2919		瓿	3525		妻	974		祁	3926		弃	2476
piāo	漂	3041		瓶	3526	pū	仆	77		崎	1237		祇	3930		(棄)	
	飄	6845		瓶	3526		扑	1792		悽	1604		祈	3931		氣	2753
piáo	嫖	1048		(瓶)			撲	2046		慽	1691		祺	3951		汽	2794
piáo	瓢	3519		秤	3992		痡	3629		憾	1691		綦	4373		泣	2840
piǎo	摽	2018		缾	4479		鋪	6410		(慽)			耆	4571		砌	3846
	殍	2701		萃	4881	pú	僕	256		戚	1763		臍	4749		磧	3906
	漂	3041		萍	4982		匍	453		敧	2114		其	4974		緝	4383
	瞟	3803		蘋	5164		幞	1340		期	2325		薺	5135		葺	5020
	縹	4424		評	5555		朴	2337		柒	2390		蕲	5154		訖	5526
	荸	4942		軿	6001		樸	2587		栖	2423		蜞	5337		跂	5849
piào	剽	407		馮	6923		濮	3128		棲	2497		跂	5849		迄	6051
	漂	3041	pìng	聘	4601		璞	3498		欺	2659		錡	6425	qì	唭	659
	票	3948	pō	坡	820		脯	4680		沏	2805		頎	6788	qiā	掐	1918
	驃	6973		波	2839		莆	4945		凄	2923		騎	6951	qiǎ	卡	491
piě	撇	2034		潑	3072		菩	4986		溪	3009		騏	6953	qiǎ	卡	491
	瞥	3815		陂	6596		葡	5006		漆	3042		鬐	7029	qià	恰	1564
piè	撇	2034		頗	6796		蒲	5037		緝	4383		鰭	7095		洽	2872
	苤	4899	pó	婆	1015		蒲	5038		萋	4980		麒	7226	qiān	仟	89
pīn	姘	1018		墦	3708		蹼	5937		諆	5617		齊	7303		僉	252
	姘	1018		繁	4428		醭	6267		郪	6211	qǐ	乞	40		千	475
	(姘)			鄱	6234		醱	6290	qī	七	3		啓	660		嵌	1257
	拼	1924	pǒ	叵	544		釙	6317		其	317		啟	660		慳	1648
	拼	1924		頗	6796	pǔ	圃	795		奇	929		(啓)			掔	1680
	(拼)		pò	拍	1844		埔	838		岐	1214		屺	1211		扦	1800
pín	嬪	1068		朴	2337		普	2255		崎	1237		杞	2350		掔	1943
	蘋	5164		泊	2827		浦	2885		旂	2179		棨	2489		搴	2002
	貧	5753		珀	3427		溥	3006		旗	2190		稽	4023		摼	2019
	頻	6809		破	3854		譜	5681		期	2325		綺	4366		牽	3324
	顰	6833		粕	4238		錯	6499		枝	2376		綮	4374		簽	4211
pǐn	品	621		迫	6068	pù	暴	2276		棋	2478		豈	5712		籤	4226
pìn	牝	3311		廹	6068		曝	2296		基	2478		起	5830		籤	4226
	聘	4601		(迫)			瀑	3138		(棋)		qì	企	103		(籤)	
pīng	乒	34		酸	6292		舖	4791		歧	2685		器	751		芊	4834
	娉	1003		魄	7051		鋪	6410		淇	2951		契	936		褰	5446
píng	坪	828	póu	抔	1817					琦	3449		妻	974		謙	5656
	屏	1198		掊	1919					琪	3451		憩	1713		遷	6151
	平	1349		裒	5411					畦	3570		憩	1713		鉛	6351
	憑	1710	pǒu	剖	394					畿	3583		(憩)			阡	6583
	枰	2419		掊	1919					碁	3884		棄	2476		韆	6763

注音	單字	字號
q	唭	659
qī	七	3

	騫	6963		鎗	6460		嶠	1272		篋	4164		綮	4374		裘	5414
	鵮	7162		鏘	6483		憔	1700		踥	5890		罄	4481		賕	5786
qián	乾	44		鏹	6484		樵	2588		鍥	6442		親	5490		逑	6091
	前	392	qiáng	嬙	1061		橋	2598	qīn	侵	162		謦	5665		遒	6128
	拑	1843		強	1434		瞧	3813		嶔	1274	qiōng	穹	4041		酋	6247
	掮	1936		强	1434		翹	4561		欽	2658		芎	4837	qiǔ	糗	4255
	潛	3073		(強)			蕎	5094		衾	5385	qióng	嬛	1062	qū	區	473
	箝	4148		彊	1434		譙	5678		親	5490		惸	1635		屈	1190
	虔	5182		(強)			顦	6829		駸	6949		煢	3233		嶇	1265
	鈐	6335		戕	1761	qiǎo	巧	1295	qín	勤	441		瓊	3512		毆	2144
	鉗	6350		檣	2616		悄	1581		懃	1730		穹	4041		曲	2302
	錢	6426		牆	3300		愀	1637		擒	2062		窮	4061		沏	2805
	黔	7252		墻	3300		雀	6657		檎	2613		筇	4110		瞿	3819
qiǎn	淺	2947		(牆)			鵲	7160		琴	3456		芎	4837		祛	3940
	繾	4460		薔	5123	qiào	俏	170		禽	3977		藭	5151		胠	4653
	譴	5689	qiǎng	強	1434		峭	1229		秦	3989		蛩	5226		蛆	5217
	遣	6141		强	1434		撬	2045		芩	4846		跫	5868		蛐	5228
qiàn	倩	211		(強)			殼	2719		芹	4858		邛	6171		袪	5396
	塹	868		彊	1434		壳	2719		螓	5295	qiū	丘	15		詘	5559
	慊	1662		(強)			(殼)			衾	5385		楸	2534		趨	5842
	槧	2569		搶	1989		㱿	2719		覃	5475		秋	3983		軀	5965
	欠	2650		襁	5454		(殼)		qǐn	寢	1145		秌	3983		驅	6975
	歉	2666		繦	5454		竅	4069	qìn	撳	2032		(秋)		qú	劬	424
	縴	4422		(襁)			翹	4561		沁	2790		蚯	5211		渠	2962
	芡	4842		鏹	6484		誚	5589	qīng	傾	249		邱	6182		璩	3507
	茜	4922	qiàng	嗆	705		譙	5678		卿	505		鞦	6751		癯	3685
	蒨	5054		戧	1771		鞘	6748		氫	2757		鞧	6752		瞿	3819
qiāng	嗆	705		熗	3238	qiē	切	360		清	2946		鰌	7088		籧	4228
	戧	1771		蹌	5912	qié	伽	121		蜻	5261		鰍	7090		絇	4305
	搶	1989		蹡	5921		茄	4888		輕	5992		鶖	7167		朐	4656
	槍	2557	qiāo	撬	2045	qiě	且	12		青	6722		龜	7328		蕖	5108
	瑲	3484		敲	2140	qiè	切	360		鯖	7080	qiú	仇	78		蘧	5167
	羌	4514		橇	2596		契	936	qíng	情	1606		囚	782		蛐	5228
	羗	4514		磽	3912		妾	975		擎	2070		毬	2738		衢	5373
	(羌)			蹺	5935		怯	1534		晴	2259		求	2767		鴝	7136
	羌	4517		蹻	5936		愜	1643		黥	7260		泅	2828		鸜	7207
	腔	4697		鍫	6444		慊	1662	qǐng	請	5610		球	3440		麴	7237
	蜣	5255		鍬	6454		挈	1875		頃	6782		虬	5192		麯	7239
	蹌	5912	qiáo	僑	255		朅	2313	qìng	慶	1696		虯	5193	qǔ	取	522
	蹡	5921		喬	700		竊	4072		磬	3905		蝤	5278		娶	1017

注音	單字	字號
	曲	2302
	麴	7322
qù	去	514
	漆	3042
	覰	5494
	覷	5494
	(覰)	
	覷	5494
	(覻)	
	趣	5840
	闃	6558
quān	圈	799
	弮	1430
	悛	1588
	棬	2496
quán	全	308
	卷	499
	惓	1610
	拳	1873
	權	2647
	泉	2848
	牷	3322
	痊	3618
	筌	4111
	荃	4924
	蜷	5260
	詮	5570
	踡	5887
	醛	6282
	銓	6373
	顴	6835
	鬈	7024
quǎn	犬	3338
	畎	3563
	綣	4356
quàn	券	376
	勸	446
quē	缺	4478
	闕	6572
qué	瘸	3663
què	卻	503
	却	503
	(卻)	
	怯	1534
	恪	1560
	愨	1686
	搉	1972
	榷	2561
	殼	2719
	壳	2719
	(殼)	
	㱿	2719
	(殼)	
	确	3870
	碏	3882
	確	3893
	觳	5510
	闋	6563
	闕	6572
	雀	6657
	鵲	7160
qūn	逡	6102
qún	羣	4526
	群	4526
	(羣)	
	裙	5408

R

注音	單字	字號
rán	然	3215
	燃	3251
	髯	7012
	髥	7017
rǎn	冉	322
	染	2396
	苒	4864
rāng	嚷	773
ráng	攘	2097
	瓤	3521
	禳	3973
	穰	4037
	纕	4471
rǎng	嚷	773
	壤	894
	攘	2097
ràng	讓	5700
ráo	蕘	5096
	饒	6905
rǎo	擾	2088
rào	繞	4442
	遶	6150
rě	喏	686
	惹	1645
	若	4873
rè	熱	3245
	爇	3279
rén	人	71
	仁	73
	任	101
	壬	897
	紝	4297
	絍	4297
	(紝)	
rěn	忍	1500
	稔	4008
	荏	4918
rèn	仞	88
	任	101
	刃	358
	妊	960
	恁	1566
	紉	4286
	紝	4297
	絍	4297
	(紝)	
	衽	5384
	袵	5405
	訒	5530
	認	5583
	軔	5971
	靭	6766
	飪	6855
	餁	6870
rēng	扔	1795
réng	仍	81
	礽	3924
rì	日	2198
róng	容	1129
	嶸	1277
	戎	1756
	榕	2538
	榮	2551
	毧	2736
	溶	3014
	熔	3240
	絨	4334
	羢	4525
	肜	4630
	茸	4913
	蓉	5048
	融	5294
	蠑	5338
	鎔	6459
rǒng	冗	1101
	氄	2744
róu	揉	1948
	柔	2397
	蹂	5903
	鞣	6011
rǒu	糅	4254
ròu	肉	4619
rú	儒	278
	嚅	763
	如	956
	孺	1095
	濡	3125
	茹	4914
	襦	5465
	顬	6832
	鴽	7142
rǔ	乳	43
	汝	2775
	辱	6048
rù	入	306
	洳	2867
	溽	3015
	縟	4413
	肉	4619
	茹	4914
	蓐	5050
	褥	5442
	辱	6048
	鉫	6390
ruǎn	蝡	5276
	蠕	5341
	軟	5974
	輭	6012
	阮	6588
ruí	甤	3544
	緌	4377
	蕤	5103
	甤	5726
ruǐ	蕊	5093
ruì	枘	2374
	汭	2782
	瑞	3471
	睿	3794
	芮	4852
	蚋	5202
	蜹	5267
	銳	6391
rún	犉	3329
rùn	潤	3080
	閏	6536
ruó	挼	1881
ruò	偌	219
	弱	1432
	爇	3279
	箬	4153
	篛	4178
	若	4873
	蒻	5050

S

注音	單字	字號
sā	仨	94
	撒	2029
sǎ	撒	2029
	洒	2855
	灑	3163
	靸	6741
sà	卅	478
	薩	5132
	趿	5850
	颯	6838
sāi	塞	863
	腮	4716
	顋	6813
	鰓	7091
sài	塞	863
	賽	5804
sān	三	5
	參	515
sǎn	傘	238
	散	2137
	糝	4262
	繖	4440
sàn	散	2137
sāng	喪	699
	桑	2437
sǎng	嗓	711
	顙	6821
sàng	喪	699
sāo	搔	1978
	繅	4432
	繰	4454
	臊	4744
	艘	4816
	騷	6966
sǎo	嫂	1038

	掃	1912
	埽	1912
	(掃)	
sào	掃	1912
	埽	1912
	(掃)	
	臊	4744
sè	嗇	706
	圾	812
	塞	863
	澀	3121
	澁	3121
	(澀)	
	瑟	3462
	穡	4032
	色	4826
	銫	6387
sēn	森	2493
sēng	僧	262
shā	挱	1878
	殺	2718
	沙	2802
	煞	3230
	痧	3626
	砂	3845
	紗	4294
	莎	4948
	裟	5417
	鎩	6476
	鯊	7077
shá	啥	670
shǎ	傻	276
	儍	276
	(傻)	
shà	嗄	703
	廈	1383
	歃	2665
	煞	3230
	箑	4140
	翣	4549
	霎	6699
shāi	篩	4172
shǎi	色	4826
	骰	6993
shài	曬	2300
	晒	2300
	(曬)	
	殺	2718
shān	刪	370
	姍	979
	山	1209
	扇	1786
	搧	1991
	杉	2341
	潸	3086
	煽	3239
	珊	3424
	羴	4531
	羶	4532
	膻	4747
	舢	4799
	芟	4841
	苫	4876
	衫	5376
	跚	5857
	釤	6326
shǎn	閃	6531
	陝	6612
shàn	善	679
	單	701
	嬗	1060
	扇	1786
	掞	1926
	擅	2057
	汕	2770
	疝	3594
	禪	3968
	繕	4438
	膳	4733
	蟮	5327
	蟺	5330
	訕	5525
	贍	5813
	赸	5831
	鄯	6232
	鐥	6906
	鱔	7105
	鱣	7110
shāng	傷	247
	商	655
	殤	2707
	湯	2989
	觴	5511
shǎng	上	6
	晌	2244
	賞	5790
shàng	上	6
	尚	1171
shang	裳	5425
shāo	弰	1431
	捎	1894
	梢	2470
	燒	3254
	稍	3999
	筲	4131
	箾	4176
	篍	4195
	艄	4814
	蛸	5231
sháo	勺	447
	杓	2345
	芍	4836
	韶	6777
shǎo	少	1169
shào	劭	425
	哨	632
	少	1169
	捎	1894
	潲	3093
	紹	4312
	邵	6179
shē	奢	943
	畬	3577
	賒	5784
shé	什	72
	佘	134
	折	1822
	揲	1966
	甚	3537
	舌	4786
	蛇	5218
	虵	5218
	(蛇)	
	闍	6566
shě	捨	1897
	舍	4787
shè	射	1160
	拾	1864
	攝	2101
	歙	2672
	涉	2896
	社	3925
	舍	4787
	葉	5001
	設	5540
	赦	5822
	麝	7230
shéi	誰	5601
shēn	伸	118
	參	515
	呻	597
	娠	1011
	深	2943
	燊	3260
	甡	3540
	申	3554
	砷	3855
	紳	4311
	莘	4937
	蓡	5007
	蓡	5007
	(葠)	
	詵	5580
	身	5960
	鉮	6367
shén	神	3943
shěn	哂	622
	嬸	1069
	審	1150
	沈	2798
	瀋	3140
	矧	3832
	諗	5616
	讅	5693
shèn	慎	1661
	滲	3032
	甚	3537
	脤	4684
	腎	4694
	葚	5004
	蜃	5237
	黮	7266
shēng	勝	437
	升	476
	昇	2213
	牲	3319
	生	3539
	甥	3542
	笙	4094
	聲	4606
	陞	6606
	鼪	7293
shéng	澠	3100
	繩	4445
shěng	省	3753
	眚	3763
shèng	乘	36
	剩	401
	勝	437
	嵊	1263
	晟	2245
	盛	3726
	聖	4600
	膡	4746
	賸	5805
shī	失	922
	尸	1179
	屍	1193
	師	1322
	拾	1864
	施	2176
	濕	3133
	溼	3133
	(濕)	
	獅	3380
	絁	4325
	蓍	5057
	虱	5194
	蝨	5282
	詩	5566
	鳲	7118
shí	什	72
	十	474
	實	1148
	射	1160
	拾	1864
	時	2240
	旹	2240
	(時)	
	湜	2982
	石	3841
	碩	3889
	蒔	5053
	蝕	5270
	食	6849
	鰣	7096
shǐ	使	147
	史	542
	始	978
	屎	1194

	弛	1423		逝	6087		輸	6009	shuāi	摔	2010	sī	司	546		松	2366
	矢	3829		適	6144	shú	叔	521		衰	5378		嘶	741		淞	2930
	豕	5722		釋	6304		塾	869	shuǎi	甩	3546		廝	1394		鬆	7023
	駛	6937		鈰	6360		孰	1090	shuài	帥	1319		思	1544	sǒng	悚	1587
shì	世	14		飾	6863		淑	2922		率	3407		撕	2038		慫	1687
	事	48	shi	匙	459		熟	3243		蟀	5311		斯	2170		竦	4081
	仕	83	shōu	收	2115		秫	3997	shuān	拴	1862		澌	3096		聳	4607
	使	147	shóu	熟	3243		菽	4973		栓	2421		私	3981	sòng	宋	1106
	侍	152	shǒu	守	1104		贖	5818		閂	6530		絲	4339		訟	5532
	勢	439		手	1789	shǔ	屬	1207	shuàn	涮	2952		緦	4387		誦	5596
	嗜	714		首	6915		數	2143	shuāng	孀	1070		罳	4503		送	6077
	噬	755	shòu	受	523		暑	2268		瀧	3152		螄	5292		頌	6787
	士	896		售	647		署	4502		雙	6673		鍶	6451	sōu	嗖	680
	奭	947		壽	903		薯	5133		霜	6704		鷥	7191		廋	1386
	室	1119		授	1913		藷	5165	shuǎng	爽	3295	sǐ	死	2692		搜	1987
	市	1306		狩	3354		蜀	5235	shuí	誰	5601	sì	伺	119		溲	3010
	式	1416		獸	3400		鸀	7200	shuǐ	水	2761		似	120		蒐	5033
	弒	1417		瘦	3652		黍	7247	shuì	帨	1321		俟	177		颼	6843
	恃	1552		綬	4357		鼠	7291		睡	3779		兕	302		餿	6894
	拭	1857	shū	姝	988	shù	倏	196		稅	4001		嗣	718	sǒu	叟	525
	是	2229		抒	1815		墅	871		蛻	5233		四	783		嗾	725
	柿	2387		摴	2020		庶	1376		說	5598		姒	982		擻	2090
	栻	2422		攄	2091		恕	1568	shǔn	吮	569		寺	1158		瞍	3798
	氏	2746		書	2306		戍	1755		楯	2536		巳	1301		藪	5150
	澨	3105		梳	2473		數	2143		盾	3752		廁	1381	sòu	嗽	724
	示	3923		梳	2473		曙	2291	shùn	瞬	3807		柶	2417		漱	3057
	筮	4128		(梳)			束	2351		舜	4794		汜	2774	sū	甦	3543
	耆	4571		樗	2578		樹	2595		順	6784		泗	2833		穌	4026
	舐	4788		樞	2583		沭	2811	shuō	說	5598		祀	3927		蘇	5162
	螫	5301		殊	2700		漱	3057	shuò	妁	955		禩	3966		酥	6256
	視	5485		殳	2715		澍	3091		帥	1319		笥	4099	sú	俗	173
	試	5565		洙	2857		疏	3588		搠	1999		耜	4585	sù	嗉	707
	誓	5586		疏	3588		署	4502		數	2143		肆	4616		塑	859
	諡	5618		疏	3588		術	5363		朔	2319		賜	5789		夙	910
	諟	5646		(疏)			裋	5407		槊	2553		食	6849		宿	1131
	謚	5662		踈	3588		豎	5717		爍	3278		飼	6860		愫	1656
	識	5677		(疏)			述	6070		碩	3889		駟	6939		愬	1671
	豉	5713		紓	4291	shuā	刷	382		芍	4836	sōng	崧	1246		泝	2836
	貰	5760		舒	4789	shuǎ	耍	4577		蟀	5311		嵩	1261		涑	2898
	軾	5984		蔬	5077	shuà	刷	382		鑠	6514		忪	1516		溯	3008

T

W

注音	單字	字號
	踠	5882
	輓	5990
wàn	惋	1608
	曼	2308
	玩	3415
	翫	4555
	腕	4698
	萬	4996
	万	4996
	(萬)	
	蔓	5069
wāng	汪	2784
wáng	亡	60
	忘	1505
	王	3409
wǎng	往	1462
	惘	1611
	枉	2368
	網	4361
	罔	4491
	蛧	5256
	輞	5998
	魍	7053
wàng	妄	958
	往	1462
	忘	1505
	旺	2208
	望	2323
	朢	2326
	王	3409
wēi	倭	214
	偎	220
	委	984
	威	1000
	崴	1252
	微	1490
	椳	2509
	渨	2995
	煨	3225
	萎	4983
	葳	5016
	逶	6111
	隈	6629
wéi	危	497
	唯	648
	圍	800
	嵬	1262
	巍	1284
	帷	1326
	幃	1331
	微	1490
	惟	1618
	桅	2442
	濰	3130
	為	3192
	爲	3288
	維	4358
	薇	5116
	違	6131
	闈	6560
	韋	6765
wěi	偉	218
	僞	259
	唯	648
	委	984
	娓	1002
	尾	1184
	洧	2862
	煒	3219
	猥	3372
	瑋	3464
	痏	3619
	痿	3639
	緯	4393
	葦	5009
	薳	5141
	諉	5609
	隗	6639
	韙	6770
	頠	6800
	骫	6992
	鮪	7069
wèi	位	126
	僞	259
	味	592
	喂	677
	尉	1163
	慰	1690
	未	2331
	渭	2966
	濊	3116
	為	3192
	爲	3288
	畏	3561
	胃	4644
	蔚	5072
	蝟	5274
	衛	5370
	衞	5371
	謂	5642
	遺	6154
	餧	6885
	餵	6893
	魏	7055
wēn	溫	2998
	温	2998
	(溫)	
	瘟	3650
	轀	6019
	鰮	7094
wén	文	2150
	紋	4287
	聞	4603
	蚊	5200
	蟁	5299
	雯	6684
wěn	刎	363
	吻	576
	穩	4035
	脗	4686
wèn	問	656
	抆	1814
	搵	1998
	文	2150
	汶	2787
	璺	3511
	紊	4301
	聞	4603
wēng	嗡	720
	翁	4538
wěng	滃	3017
	蓊	5056
wèng	甕	3533
	罋	4485
wō	倭	214
	渦	2965
	窩	4057
	萵	4998
wǒ	我	1759
wò	偓	222
	喔	688
	幄	1332
	握	1959
	斡	2162
	沃	2793
	涴	2950
	渥	2964
	臥	4761
	齷	7321
wū	嗚	713
	圬	807
	屋	1192
	巫	1297
	惡	1624
	於	2175
	汚	2779
	汙	2779
	(汚)	
	污	2779
	(汚)	
	烏	3193
	誣	5593
	鄔	6223
wú	吳	571
	吾	579
	巫	1297
	无	2195
	梧	2453
	毋	2725
	浯	2906
	無	3214
	蕪	5107
	蜈	5243
	誣	5593
	鼯	7294
wǔ	五	54
	仵	99
	伍	107
	侮	159
	午	477
	嘸	745
	娬	1029
	嫵	1029
	(娬)	
	廡	1397
	忤	1509
	憮	1706
	摀	2000
	武	2686
	牾	3325
	舞	4796
	鵡	7154
wù	兀	288
	務	436
	勿	450
	塢	865
	婺	1031
	寤	1146
	悟	1590
	惡	1624
	戊	1752
	晤	2250
	杌	2343
	物	3317
	誤	5594
	迕	6059
	鋈	6468
	阢	6584
	隖	6636
	霧	6707
	騖	6957
	鶩	7170

X

注音	單字	字號
xī	僖	257
	兮	314
	吸	574
	唏	643
	嘻	744
	奚	941
	嬉	1055
	巇	1281
	希	1309
	徯	1489
	恓	1554
	悉	1593
	扱	1807
	攜	2100
	携	2100
	(攜)	
	擕	2100
	(攜)	
	携	2100
	(攜)	
	晞	2248
	晰	2257
	晳	2258
	曦	2297
	析	2371

	絢	4332
	衒	5362
	鉉	6346
	鏇	6475
xuē	噱	756
	薛	5125
	靴	6738
xué	學	1094
	尋	1165
	踅	5879
	鷽	7199
xuě	雪	6683
	鱈	7099
xuè	削	389
	穴	4038
	血	5356
	雪	6683
xūn	勳	444
	壎	887
	曛	2294
	焄	3203
	熏	3236
	燻	3236
	(熏)	
	獯	3396
	窨	4059
	纁	4461
	葷	5018
	薰	5134
	醺	6296
xún	尋	1165
	峋	1225
	巡	1291
	廵	1291
	(巡)	
	徇	1467
	循	1486
	恂	1550
	撏	2033
	旬	2202
	洵	2870
	潯	3083
	珣	3436
	紃	4280
	荀	4915
	蕁	5105
	詢	5564
	巡	6053
	廵	6053
	(巡)	
	郇	6191
	馴	6926
	鱘	7108
xùn	巽	1304
	徇	1467
	殉	2699
	汛	2777
	蕈	5106
	訊	5522
	訓	5524
	迅	6052
	遜	6132
	馴	6926

Y

注音	單字	字號
yā	丫	20
	呀	581
	壓	886
	押	1832
	椏	2505
	鴉	7124
	鴨	7134
yá	枒	2372
	涯	2908
	牙	3308
	芽	4860
	蚜	5205
	衙	5367
yǎ	亞	58
	啞	665
	雅	6660
yà	亞	58
	娅	1027
	揠	1957
	訝	5534
	軋	5967
	迓	6057
ya	呀	581
yái	崖	1240
yān	咽	618
	奄	928
	嫣	1052
	崦	1251
	懨	1735
	懕	1735
	(懨)	
	殷	2717
	淹	2948
	烟	3199
	焉	3204
	煙	3222
	燕	3258
	胭	4659
	腌	4692
	臙	4753
	菸	4971
	蔫	5083
	鄢	6225
	醃	6269
	閼	6554
	閹	6555
yán	嚴	772
	姸	996
	妍	996
	(姸)	
	岩	1224
	巖	1287
	延	1406
	揅	2025
	檐	2609
	沿	2823
	炎	3176
	焰	3216
	燄	3216
	(焰)	
	癌	3667
	研	3864
	硏	3864
	(研)	
	筵	4134
	簷	4209
	綖	4352
	蜒	5242
	言	5514
	閻	6552
	顏	6816
	鹽	7215
yǎn	偃	215
	儼	287
	兗	303
	奄	928
	巘	1288
	弇	1412
	掩	1935
	揜	1956
	沇	2795
	渰	2996
	演	3047
	琰	3460
	甗	3535
	眼	3769
	蝘	5272
	衍	5361
	郾	6218
	魘	7059
	黤	7264
	黶	7270
	鼴	7295
	鼹	7297
yàn	厭	512
	咽	618
	唁	640
	嚥	770
	堰	852
	宴	1125
	彥	1449
	晏	2239
	沿	2823
	灩	3170
	灧	3170
	(灩)	
	焱	3212
	焰	3216
	燄	3216
	(焰)	
	燕	3258
	硯	3868
	艷	4828
	諺	5638
	讌	5696
	讞	5704
	豔	5720
	豓	5721
	贗	5808
	贋	5819
	釅	6301
	雁	6659
	饜	6912
	驗	6956
	驗	6981
	鴈	7126
	鴳	7140
	鷃	7183
	鹽	7215
yāng	央	923
	殃	2697
	泱	2846
	秧	3991
	鞅	6742
	鴦	7133
yáng	佯	142
	徉	1469
	揚	1955
	易	2238
	楊	2516
	洋	2854
	烊	3196
	煬	3227
	瘍	3642
	羊	4512
	陽	6623
	颺	6842
yǎng	仰	96
	氧	2755
	瀁	3144
	癢	3677
	痒	3677
	(癢)	
	鞅	6742
	養	6868
yàng	怏	1524
	恙	1571
	樣	2585
	漾	3061
	煬	3227
	養	6868
yāo	吆	554
	夭	921
	妖	962
	幺	1354
	么	1354
	(幺)	
	徼	1494
	祅	3929
	腰	4706
	葽	5021
	要	5474
	邀	6158

	銦	6386
	闉	6561
	陰	6615
	陻	6624
	堙	6624
	(陻)	
	音	6774
yín	吟	564
	垠	829
	夤	914
	寅	1134
	淫	2940
	狺	3361
	鄞	6228
	銀	6368
	霪	6708
	齗	7310
	齦	7316
yǐn	尹	1181
	引	1419
	檃	2646
	㱃	2671
	癮	3682
	蚓	5204
	隱	6648
	靷	6740
	飲	6857
yìn	印	496
	廕	1391
	憖	1716
	窨	4059
	胤	4655
	蔭	5084
	陰	6615
	飲	6857
yīng	媖	1036
	嬰	1066
	應	1729
	攖	2096
	櫻	2642
	瑛	3469
	瓔	3515
	纓	4470
	罃	4480
	罌	4486
	膺	4738
	英	4877
	鶯	7175
	鷹	7203
	鸚	7205
yíng	塋	856
	嬴	1064
	楹	2535
	滎	3026
	瀅	3142
	瀛	3150
	瀠	3155
	熒	3241
	營	3264
	瑩	3476
	盈	3718
	縈	4401
	螢	5298
	蠅	5333
	贏	5814
	迎	6055
yǐng	影	1457
	景	2256
	潁	3068
	癭	3681
	穎	4027
	頴	4027
	(穎)	
	郢	6202
yìng	媵	1040
	應	1729
	映	2224
	硬	3866
	迎	6055
yō	喲	663
yōng	傭	242
	墉	872
	壅	884
	庸	1378
	廱	1404
	慵	1681
	擁	2056
	灉	3160
	癰	3684
	臃	4741
	邕	6172
	鄘	6226
	雍	6663
	雝	6678
	饔	6909
yóng	傭	242
	喁	676
	墉	872
	庸	1378
	慵	1681
	顒	6817
	鱅	7103
yǒng	俑	172
	勇	430
	壅	884
	慂	1667
	擁	2056
	永	2762
	泳	2847
	涌	2907
	湧	2983
	甬	3548
	臃	4741
	蛹	5232
	詠	5550
	咏	5550
	(詠)	
	踊	5880
yòng	用	3545
yōu	優	284
	幽	1357
	悠	1592
	憂	1694
	攸	2116
	滺	3065
	燠	3266
	耰	4589
	麀	7217
yóu	尤	1174
	斿	2177
	楢	2523
	油	2815
	游	2974
	猶	3373
	猷	3377
	由	3552
	疣	3598
	繇	4430
	蕕	5095
	蚰	5212
	蝣	5277
	輶	6008
	逌	6105
	遊	6121
	郵	6213
	鈾	6357
	魷	7062
yǒu	卣	492
	友	519
	有	2315
	槱	2567
	槱	3246
	櫌	3246
	(槱)	
	牖	3306
	羑	4516
	莠	4939
	酉	6245
	銪	6384
	黝	7257
yòu	佑	130
	侑	154
	又	516
	右	543
	囿	794
	宥	1120
	幼	1356
	有	2315
	柚	2402
	祐	3933
	莠	4939
	誘	5588
	釉	6303
	鼬	7292
yū	淤	2932
	瘀	3638
	紆	4281
	迂	6050
yú	予	47
	于	51
	余	135
	俞	310
	妤	967
	娛	1008
	嵎	1259
	愉	1640
	愚	1651
	揄	1945
	於	2175
	旟	2194
	榆	2521
	楰	2524
	歟	2678
	渝	2958
	漁	3038
	瑜	3470
	璵	3509
	畬	3576
	盂	3715
	禺	3976
	窬	4060
	竽	4087
	腴	4709
	臾	4775
	舁	4777
	與	4782
	萸	5024
	虞	5186
	褕	5440
	覦	5488
	諛	5622
	踰	5897
	輿	6015
	轝	6031
	逾	6115
	隃	6625
	隅	6627
	雩	6682
	餘	6879
	魚	7060
yǔ	予	47
	傴	245
	圄	796
	宇	1103
	嶼	1279
	庾	1380
	敔	2132
	瑀	3475
	禹	3975
	窳	4063
	羽	4536
	與	4782
	語	5591
	鋙	6406
	雨	6681
	齬	7320
yù	喻	698
	域	840
	嫗	1049
	寓	1139

Z

附錄㈠國語注音符號與各式羅馬拼音對照表

一、聲母

國語注音符號 Mandarin Phonetic Symbols	威妥瑪式 Wade System	國語羅馬字 Gwoyeu Romatzyh	聯合國華語注音符號 U.N. Mandarin Phonetic Symbols	國語注音符號 Mandarin Phonetic Symbols	威妥瑪式 Wade System	國語羅馬字 Gwoyeu Romatzyh	聯合國華語注音符號 U.N. Mandarin Phonetic Symbols
ㄅ	p	b	b	ㄏ	h	h	h
ㄆ	p'	p	p	ㄐ	ch(i)	j(i)	j
ㄇ	m	m	m	ㄑ	ch'(i)	ch(i)	q
ㄈ	f	f	f	(ㄬ)		(gn)	
(ㄪ)		(v)		ㄒ	hs	sh(i)	x
ㄉ	t	d	d	ㄓ	ch	j	zh
ㄊ	t'	t	t	ㄔ	ch'	ch	ch
ㄋ	n	n	n	ㄕ	sh	sh	sh
ㄌ	l	l	l	ㄖ	j	r	r
ㄍ	k	g	g	ㄗ	tz, ts-	tz	z
ㄎ	k'	k	k	ㄘ	tz', ts'-	ts	c
(ㄫ)		(ng)		ㄙ	sz, ss, s-	s	s

二、韻母

國語注音符號 Mandarin Phonetic Symbols	威妥瑪式 Wade System	國語羅馬字 Gwoyeu Romatzyh	聯合國華語注音符號 U.N. Mandarin Phonetic Symbols	國語注音符號 Mandarin Phonetic Symbols	威妥瑪式 Wade System	國語羅馬字 Gwoyeu Romatzyh	聯合國華語注音符號 U.N. Mandarin Phonetic Symbols
(ㄭ)	-u, -ih	y		ㄧㄡ	yu, -iu	iou	iou
ㄚ	a	a	ɑ	ㄧㄢ	yen, -ien	ian	iɑn
ㄛ	o	o	o	ㄧㄣ	yin, -in	in	in
ㄜ	o(ê)	e	e	ㄧㄤ	yang, -iang	iang	iɑng
ㄝ		è	ê	ㄧㄥ	ying, -ing	ing	ing
ㄞ	ai	ai	ɑi				
ㄟ	ei	ei	ei	ㄨ	wu, -u	u	u
ㄠ	ao	au	ɑo	ㄨㄚ	wa, -ua	ua	uɑ
ㄡ	ou	ou	ou	ㄨㄛ	wo, -uo	uo	uo
ㄢ	an	an	ɑn	ㄨㄞ	wai, -uai	uai	uɑi
ㄣ	ên	en	en	ㄨㄟ	wei, -ui(-uei)	uei	uei
ㄤ	ang	ang	ɑng	ㄨㄢ	wan, -uan	uan	uɑn
ㄥ	êng	eng	eng	ㄨㄣ	wên, -un	uen	uen
ㄦ	êrh	el	er	ㄨㄤ	wang, -uang	uang	uɑng
				ㄨㄥ	wêng, -ung	ueng, -ong	ueng, -ong
ㄧ	i	i	i				
ㄧㄚ	ya, -ia	ia	iɑ	ㄩ	yü, -ü	iu	ü
ㄧㄛ		io		ㄩㄝ	yüeh, -üeh	iue	üe
ㄧㄝ	yeh, -ieh	ie	ie	ㄩㄢ	yüan, -üan	iuan	üɑn
ㄧㄞ	yai	iai	iɑi	ㄩㄣ	yün, -ün	iun	ün
ㄧㄠ	yao, -iao	iau	iɑo	ㄩㄥ	yung, -iung	iong	iong

三、聲調

式名 / 調類	國語注音符號 Mandarin Phonetic Symbols	威妥瑪式 Wade System	聯合國華語注音符號 U. N. Mandarin Phonetic Symbols	註：國語羅馬字條例複雜，於附錄㈢說明。
陰平	無號(可用"-"代表)	1	ˉ	
陽平	ˊ	2	ˊ	
上聲	ˇ	3	ˇ	
去聲	ˋ	4	ˋ	
輕聲	˙	5	無號	

附錄(二)國語羅馬字聲調

(1)陰　平

		ㄧ	i	ㄨ	u	ㄩ	iu
(帀)	-y						
ㄚ	a	ㄧㄚ	ia	ㄨㄚ	ua		
ㄛ	o	ㄧㄛ	io	ㄨㄛ	uo		
ㄜ	e						
ㄝ	è	ㄧㄝ	iè			ㄩㄝ	iue
ㄞ	ai	ㄧㄞ	iai	ㄨㄞ	uai		
ㄟ	ei			ㄨㄟ	uei		
ㄠ	au	ㄧㄠ	iau				
ㄡ	ou	ㄧㄡ	iou				
ㄢ	an	ㄧㄢ	ian	ㄨㄢ	uan	ㄩㄢ	iuan
ㄣ	en	ㄧㄣ	in	ㄨㄣ	uen	ㄩㄣ	iun
ㄤ	ang	ㄧㄤ	iang	ㄨㄤ	uang		
ㄥ	eng	ㄧㄥ	ing	ㄨㄥ	ueng		
ㄨㄥ	-ong	ㄩㄥ	iong				
ㄦ(-ㄦ)	el(-l)						

註：聲母如果是 m, n, l, r 等濁音就在聲母後加 h，如 mhau(貓)，nhiou(妞)，lhiou(溜)，rheng(扔)。

(2)陽　平

		ㄧˊ	yi	ㄨˊ	wu	ㄩˊ	yu
(帀ˊ)	-yr						
ㄚˊ	ar	ㄧㄚˊ	ya	ㄨㄚˊ	wa		
ㄛˊ	or			ㄨㄛˊ	wo		
ㄜˊ	er						
ㄝˊ	èr	ㄧㄝˊ	ye			ㄩㄝˊ	yue
ㄞˊ	air	ㄧㄞˊ	yai	ㄨㄞˊ	wai		
ㄟˊ	eir			ㄨㄟˊ	wei		
ㄠˊ	aur	ㄧㄠˊ	yau				
ㄡˊ	our	ㄧㄡˊ	you				
ㄢˊ	arn	ㄧㄢˊ	yan	ㄨㄢˊ	wan	ㄩㄢˊ	yuan
ㄣˊ	ern	ㄧㄣˊ	yn	ㄨㄣˊ	wen	ㄩㄣˊ	yun
ㄤˊ	arng	ㄧㄤˊ	yang	ㄨㄤˊ	wang		
ㄥˊ	erng	ㄧㄥˊ	yng				
-ㄨㄥˊ	-orng	ㄩㄥˊ	yong				
ㄦˊ(-ㄦ)	erl(-r)						

註：聲母如果是 m, n, l, r 就用基本形式，如 mau(毛)，niou(牛)，liou(流)，ren(人)。

(3)上　聲

		ㄧˇ	yii,-ii	ㄨˇ	wuu,-uu	ㄩˇ	yeu,-eu
(帀ˇ)	-yy						
ㄚˇ	aa	ㄧㄚˇ	yea,-ea	ㄨㄚˇ	woa,-oa		
ㄛˇ	oo			ㄨㄛˇ	woo,-uoo		
ㄜˇ	ee						
ㄝˇ	èè	ㄧㄝˇ	yee,-iee			ㄩㄝˇ	eue
ㄞˇ	ae			ㄨㄞˇ	woai,-oai		
ㄟˇ	eei			ㄨㄟˇ	woei,-oei		
ㄠˇ	ao	ㄧㄠˇ	yeau,-eau				
ㄡˇ	oou	ㄧㄡˇ	yeou,-eou				
ㄢˇ	aan	ㄧㄢˇ	yean,-ean	ㄨㄢˇ	woan,-oan	ㄩㄢˇ	yeuan,-euan
ㄣˇ	een	ㄧㄣˇ	yiin,-iin	ㄨㄣˇ	woen,-oen	ㄩㄣˇ	yeun,-eun
ㄤˇ	aang	ㄧㄤˇ	yeang,-eang	ㄨㄤˇ	woang,-oang		
ㄥˇ	eeng	ㄧㄥˇ	yiing,-iing	ㄨㄥˇ	woeng		
-ㄨㄥˇ	-oong	ㄩㄥˇ	yeong,-eong				
ㄦˇ(-ㄦ)	eel(-l)						

(4)去　聲

		ㄧˋ	yih,-ih	ㄨˋ	wuh,-uh	ㄩˋ	yuh,-iuh
(帀ˋ)	-yh						
ㄚˋ	ah	ㄧㄚˋ	yah,-iah	ㄨㄚˋ	wah,-uah		
ㄛˋ	oh			ㄨㄛˋ	woh,-woh		
ㄜˋ	eh						
ㄝˋ	èh	ㄧㄝˋ	yeh,-ieh			ㄩㄝˋ	yueh,-iueh
ㄞˋ	ay			ㄨㄞˋ	way,-uay		
ㄟˋ	ey			ㄨㄟˋ	wey,-uey		
ㄠˋ	aw	ㄧㄠˋ	yaw,-iaw				
ㄡˋ	ow	ㄧㄡˋ	yow,-iow				
ㄢˋ	ann	ㄧㄢˋ	yann,-iann	ㄨㄢˋ	wann,-uann	ㄩㄢˋ	yuann,-iuann
ㄣˋ	enn	ㄧㄣˋ	yinn,-inn	ㄨㄣˋ	wenn,-uenn	ㄩㄣˋ	yunn,-iunn
ㄤˋ	anq	ㄧㄤˋ	yanq,-ianq	ㄨㄤˋ	wanq,-uanq		
ㄥˋ	enq	ㄧㄥˋ	yinq,-inq	ㄨㄥˋ	wenq		
-ㄨㄥˋ	onq	ㄩㄥˋ	yonq,-ionq				
ㄦˋ(-ㄦ)	ell(-l)						

(5)輕聲

國語羅馬字的輕聲，以用基本形式爲原則。如果是會話教科書，要確切標出輕聲，可以在字前點上“•”。

附錄㈢國語注音符號第一式與第二式對照表

	國語注音符號第一式				國語注音符號第二式			
				一、聲母				
唇　　音	ㄅ	ㄆ	ㄇ	ㄈ	b	p	m	f
舌 尖 音	ㄉ	ㄊ	ㄋ	ㄌ	d	t	n	l
舌 根 音	ㄍ	ㄎ	ㄏ		g	k	h	
舌 面 音	ㄐ	ㄑ	ㄒ		j(i)	ch(i)	sh(i)	
翹 舌 音	ㄓ	ㄔ	ㄕ	ㄖ	j	ch	sh	r
舌 齒 音	ㄗ	ㄘ	ㄙ		tz	ts	s	
				二、韻母				
單 韻 ①	(ㄭ)				r, z			
單 韻 ②	ㄧ	ㄨ	ㄩ		i, yi,	u, wu	iu, yu	
單 韻 ③	ㄚ	ㄛ	ㄜ	ㄝ	a	o	e	ê
複　　韻	ㄞ	ㄟ	ㄠ	ㄡ	ai	ei	au	ou
聲 隨 韻	ㄢ	ㄣ、	ㄤ	ㄥ	an	en	ang	eng
捲 舌 韻	ㄦ				er			
				三、結合韻母(前有聲母時用)				
齊 齒 呼	ㄧㄚ ㄧㄞ ㄧㄢ	ㄧㄛ ㄧㄠ ㄧㄣ	ㄧㄝ ㄧㄡ ㄧㄤ	 ㄧㄥ	ia iai ian	io iau in	ie iou iang	 ing
合 口 呼	ㄨㄚ ㄨㄢ	ㄨㄛ ㄨㄣ	ㄨㄞ ㄨㄤ	ㄨㄟ ㄨㄥ	ua uan	uo uen	uai uang	uei ung
撮 口 呼	ㄩㄝ	ㄩㄢ	ㄩㄣ	ㄩㄥ	iue	iuan	iun	iung
				四、聲　調				
陰 平 聲	(不加)				¯			
陽 平 聲	ˊ				ˊ			
上　　聲	ˇ				ˇ			
去　　聲	ˋ				ˋ			
輕　　聲	˙				(不加)			

附錄㈣國音儿化韻表

中華新韻六兒附韻目	韻內所含等呼				併入之韻	變入之韻	略例			
一蝦兒	ㄚㄦ						法兒(ㄈㄚㄦ)	雜兒(ㄗㄚˊㄦ)	塔兒(ㄊㄚˇㄦ)	那兒(ㄋㄚˋㄦ)
(ㄚㄦ)					ㄞㄦ		呆兒(ㄉㄞㄦ)	孩兒(ㄏㄞˊㄦ)	矮兒(ㄞˇㄦ)	菜兒(ㄘㄞˋㄦ)
					ㄢㄦ		竿兒(ㄍㄢㄦ)	盤兒(ㄆㄢˊㄦ)	桿兒(ㄍㄢˇㄦ)	瓣兒(ㄅㄢˋㄦ)
		ㄧㄚㄦ					蝦兒(ㄒㄧㄚㄦ)	芽兒(ㄧㄚˊㄦ)	倆兒(ㄌㄧㄚˇㄦ)	價兒(ㄐㄧㄚˋㄦ)
					ㄧㄞㄦ					
					ㄧㄢㄦ		烟兒(ㄧㄢㄦ)	錢兒(ㄑㄧㄢˊㄦ)	碾兒(ㄋㄧㄢˇㄦ)	辮兒(ㄅㄧㄢˋㄦ)
			ㄨㄚㄦ				窪兒(ㄨㄚㄦ)	滑兒(ㄏㄨㄚˊㄦ)	爪兒(ㄓㄨㄚˇㄦ)	話兒(ㄏㄨㄚˋㄦ)
					ㄨㄞㄦ		快兒(ㄎㄨㄞㄦ)	懷兒(ㄏㄨㄞˊㄦ)	枴兒(ㄍㄨㄞˇㄦ)	塊兒(ㄎㄨㄞˋㄦ)
					ㄨㄢㄦ		灣兒(ㄨㄢㄦ)	丸兒(ㄨㄢˊㄦ)	碗兒(ㄨㄢˇㄦ)	段兒(ㄉㄨㄢˋㄦ)
				ㄩㄚㄦ		ㄩㄢㄦ	圈兒(ㄑㄩㄢㄦ)	園兒(ㄩㄢˊㄦ)	遠兒(ㄩㄢˇㄦ)	院兒(ㄩㄢˋㄦ)
二蟈兒	ㄛㄦ						坡兒(ㄆㄛㄦ)	脖兒(ㄅㄛˊㄦ)	抹兒(ㄇㄛˇㄦ)	破兒(ㄆㄛˋㄦ)
(ㄛㄦ)			ㄨㄛㄦ				蟈兒(ㄍㄨㄛㄦ)	鐲兒(ㄓㄨㄛˊㄦ)	夥兒(ㄏㄨㄛˇㄦ)	座兒(ㄗㄨㄛˋㄦ)
三鴿兒	ㄜㄦ						鴿兒(ㄍㄜㄦ)	盒兒(ㄏㄜˊㄦ)		個兒(ㄍㄜˋㄦ)
(ㄜㄦ)							枝兒(ㄓㄦ)	姪兒(ㄓˊㄦ)	紙兒(ㄓˇㄦ)	翅兒(ㄔˋㄦ)
					ㄓㄦ		絲兒(ㄙㄦ)	詞兒(ㄘˊㄦ)	子兒(ㄗˇㄦ)	字兒(ㄗˋㄦ)
					ㄟㄦ		碑兒(ㄅㄟㄦ)			輩兒(ㄅㄟˋㄦ)
					ㄣㄦ		根兒(ㄍㄣㄦ)	門兒(ㄇㄣˊㄦ)	本兒(ㄅㄣˇㄦ)	悶兒(ㄇㄣˋㄦ)
		ㄧㄜㄦ				ㄧㄝㄦ	些兒(ㄒㄧㄝㄦ)	茶兒(ㄋㄧㄝˊㄦ)	帖兒(ㄊㄧㄝˇㄦ)	葉兒(ㄧㄝˋㄦ)
					ㄧㄦ		滴兒(ㄉㄧㄦ)	鼻兒(ㄅㄧˊㄦ)	底兒(ㄉㄧˇㄦ)	氣兒(ㄑㄧˋㄦ)
					ㄧㄣㄦ		今兒(ㄐㄧㄣㄦ)		緊兒(ㄐㄧㄣˇㄦ)	信兒(ㄒㄧㄣˋㄦ)
			ㄨㄜㄦ			ㄨㄟㄦ	堆兒(ㄗㄨㄟㄦ)	回兒(ㄏㄨㄟˊㄦ)	鬼兒(ㄍㄨㄟˇㄦ)	味兒(ㄨㄟˋㄦ)
					ㄨㄣㄦ		村兒(ㄘㄨㄣㄦ)	唇兒(ㄔㄨㄣˊㄦ)	盹兒(ㄉㄨㄣˇㄦ)	棍兒(ㄍㄨㄣˋㄦ)
				ㄩㄜㄦ		ㄩㄝㄦ				月兒(ㄩㄝˋㄦ)
					ㄩㄦ		駒兒(ㄐㄩㄦ)	菊兒(ㄐㄩˊㄦ	曲兒(ㄑㄩˇㄦ)	句兒(ㄐㄩˋㄦ)
					ㄩㄣㄦ					運兒(ㄩㄣˋㄦ)
四鵰兒	ㄠㄦ						羔兒(ㄍㄠㄦ)	桃兒(ㄊㄠˊㄦ)	棗兒(ㄗㄠˇㄦ)	道兒(ㄉㄠˋㄦ)
(ㄠㄦ)		ㄧㄠㄦ					鵰兒(ㄉㄧㄠㄦ)	橋兒(ㄑㄧㄠˊㄦ)	鳥兒(ㄋㄧㄠˇㄦ)	票兒(ㄆㄧㄠˋㄦ)
五牛兒	ㄡㄦ						鉤兒(ㄍㄡㄦ)	頭兒(ㄊㄡˊㄦ)	口兒(ㄎㄡˇㄦ)	豆兒(ㄉㄡˋㄦ)
(ㄡㄦ)		ㄧㄡㄦ					妞兒(ㄋㄧㄡㄦ)	牛兒(ㄋㄧㄡˊㄦ)	酒兒(ㄐㄧㄡˇㄦ)	袖兒(ㄒㄧㄡˋㄦ)
六羊兒	ㄤㄦ						缸兒(ㄍㄤㄦ)	忙兒(ㄇㄤˊㄦ)	膀兒(ㄅㄤˇㄦ)	杖兒(ㄓㄤˋㄦ)
(ㄤㄦ)		ㄧㄤㄦ					箱兒(ㄒㄧㄤㄦ)	羊兒(ㄧㄤˊㄦ)	響兒(ㄒㄧㄤˇㄦ)	亮兒(ㄌㄧㄤˋㄦ)
			ㄨㄤㄦ				樁兒(ㄓㄨㄤㄦ)	黃兒(ㄏㄨㄤˊㄦ)	網兒(ㄨㄤˇㄦ)	框兒(ㄎㄨㄤˋㄦ)
七蜂兒	ㄥㄦ						蜂兒(ㄈㄥㄦ)	繩兒(ㄕㄥˊㄦ)	捧兒(ㄆㄥˇㄦ)	凳兒(ㄉㄥˋㄦ)
(ㄥㄦ)		ㄧㄥㄦ					釘兒(ㄉㄧㄥㄦ)	明兒(ㄇㄧㄥˊㄦ)	井兒(ㄐㄧㄥˇㄦ)	杏兒(ㄒㄧㄥˋㄦ)
			ㄨㄥㄦ				翁兒(ㄨㄥㄦ)			
八蟲兒 一ㄨㄥㄦ (ㄩㄥㄦ)	一ㄨ ㄥㄦ						盅兒(ㄓㄨㄥㄦ)	蟲兒(ㄔㄨㄥˊㄦ)	孔兒(ㄎㄨㄥˇㄦ)	洞兒(ㄉㄨㄥˋㄦ)
		ㄩㄥㄦ							蛹兒(ㄩㄥˇㄦ)	
九蛛兒 (ㄨㄦ)			ㄨㄦ				珠兒(ㄓㄨㄦ)	雛兒(ㄔㄨˊㄦ)	鼓兒(ㄍㄨˇㄦ)	兔兒(ㄊㄨˋㄦ)
	開口	齊齒	合口	撮口						

附錄(五)國語注音符號與聯合國華語注音符號對照表

	國語注音符號第一式				聯合國華語注音			
一、聲母								
唇音	ㄅ	ㄆ	ㄇ	ㄈ	b	p	m	f
舌尖音	ㄉ	ㄊ	ㄋ	ㄌ	d	t	n	l
舌根音	ㄍ	ㄎ	ㄏ		g	k	h	
舌面音	ㄐ	ㄑ	ㄒ		j	q	x	
翹舌音	ㄓ	ㄔ	ㄕ	ㄖ	zh	ch	sh	r
舌齒音	ㄗ	ㄘ	ㄙ		z	c	s	
二、韻母								
單韻①	(ㄭ)							
單韻②	ㄧ	ㄨ	ㄩ		i	u	ü	
單韻③	ㄚ	ㄛ	ㄜ	ㄝ	a	o	e	
複韻	ㄞ	ㄟ	ㄠ	ㄡ	ai	ei	ao	ou
聲隨韻	ㄢ	ㄣ	ㄤ	ㄥ	an	en	ang	eng
捲舌韻	ㄦ				er			
三、結合韻母(前有聲母時用)								
齊齒呼	ㄧㄚ	ㄧㄛ	ㄧㄝ		ia		ie	
	ㄧㄞ	ㄧㄠ	ㄧㄡ			iao	iou	
	ㄧㄢ	ㄧㄣ	ㄧㄤ	ㄧㄥ	ian	in	iang	ing
合口呼	ㄨㄚ	ㄨㄛ	ㄨㄞ	ㄨㄟ	ua	uo	uai	uei
	ㄨㄢ	ㄨㄣ	ㄨㄤ	ㄨㄥ	uan	uen	uang	ueng
撮口呼	ㄩㄝ	ㄩㄢ	ㄩㄣ	ㄩㄥ	üe	üan	ün	iong
四、聲調								
陰平聲	(不加)				¯			
陽平聲	ˊ				ˊ			
上聲	ˇ				ˇ			
去聲	ˋ				ˋ			
輕聲	•				•(或不加)			

※聯合國華語注音(漢語注音)補充說明

(1)「ㄓ(知)、ㄔ(蚩)、ㄕ(詩)、ㄖ(日)、ㄗ(資)、ㄘ(雌)、ㄙ(思)」等七個音節的韻母用i，即：知、蚩、詩、日、資、雌、思等字拼作 zhi, chi, shi, ri, zi, ci, si。

(2)韻母ㄦ寫成 er，用做韻尾的時候寫成 r。例如：「兒童」拼作 ertong，「花兒」拼作 huar。

(3)韻母ㄝ單用的時候寫成 ê。

(4) i, ia, ie, iao, iou, ian, in, iang, ing, iong 等韻母，前面沒有聲母的時候，寫成：yi(衣)，ya(呀)，ye(耶)，yao(腰)，you(憂)，yan(烟)，yin(因)，yang(央)，ying(英)，yong(雍)。

(5) u, ua, uo, uai, uei, uan, uen, uang, ueng 等韻母，前面沒有聲母的時候，寫成：wu(烏)，wa(蛙)，wo(窩)，wai(歪)，wei(威)，wan(彎)，wen(溫)，wang(汪)，weng(翁)。

(6) ü, üe, üan, ün 等韻母，前面沒有聲母的時候，寫成：yu(迂)，yue(約)，yuan(冤)，yun(暈)；ü 上兩點省略。若跟聲母 j,q, x 拼的時候，寫成：ju(居)，qu(區)，xu(虛)，ü 上兩點也省略；但是跟聲母 n, l 拼的時候，仍然寫成：nü(女)，lü(呂)。

(7) iou, uei, uen 前面加聲母的時候，寫成：iu, ui, un。例如：niu(牛)，gui(歸)，lun(論)。

(8)在給華語注音的時候，爲了使拼式簡短，ng 可以省作 ŋ。

附錄(六)　二十四節氣

The Twenty-four Solar Terms

APPROXIMATE DATES		THE SOLAR TERMS		ZODIACAL POSITION OF THE SUN
Feb.	5	立　春	Spring begins	Aquarius
〃	19	雨　水	Rain water	Pisces
Mar.	5	驚　蟄	Excited insects	〃
〃	20	春　分	Vernal equinox	Aries
Apr.	5	清　明	Clear and bright	〃
〃	20	穀　雨	Grain rains	Taurus
May	5	立　夏	Summer begins	〃
〃	21	小　滿	Grain fills	Gemini
June	6	芒　種	Grain in ear	〃
〃	21	夏　至	Summer solstice	Cancer
July	7	小　暑	Slight heat	〃
〃	23	大　暑	Great heat	Leo
Aug.	7	立　秋	Autumn begins	〃
〃	23	處　暑	Limit of heat	Virgo
Sep.	8	白　露	White dew	〃
〃	23	秋　分	Autumnal equinox	Libra
Oct.	8	寒　露	Cold dew	〃
〃	23	霜　降	Hoar frost descends	Scorpio
Nov.	7	立　多	Winter begins	〃
〃	22	小　雪	Little snow	Sagittarius
Dec.	7	大　雪	Heavy snow	〃
〃	21	多　至	Winter solstice	Capricorn
Jan.	6	小　寒	Little cold	〃
〃	21	大　寒	Severe cold	Aquarius

附錄(七)　中國月分名

Ordinary and Literary Names for the Months

1	正　月	春王,		元月,	青陽,	三陽, 孟陽,
2	二　月	中和,		杏月,		如月, 花朝,
3	三　月	桃月,		上巳,		寒食,
4	四　月	清和,		麥秋,	槐月,	梅月,
5	五　月	榴月,	蒲月,	天中,		滿月, 端月,
6	六　月	荷月,	伏月,	天眖,		
7	七　月	桐月,		巧月,	中元,	蘭月,
8	八　月	桂月,		中秋,		
9	九　月	菊秋,		菊月,		重陽,
10	十　月	陽春,		小陽春,		
11	十一月	葭月,	多月,	多仲月,	長至,	
12	十二月	臘月,		嘉平,		淸祀,

The literary names follow those used colloquially, which are given in the second column.

附錄（八）專有名詞漢語拼音與本典拼音對照表

漢語拼音	本典拼音	中文	漢語拼音	本典拼音	中文
Achang nationality	Achang nationality	阿昌族	Bodao	Po-tao	伯道
(Altai) Mountains	Altai Mountains	阿爾泰山	Bohai	Pohai	渤海
Ai Hui	Ai Hui	璦琿	Boniu	Po-niu	伯牛
Mt. Ali	Mt. Ali	阿里山	Bo Ya	Po Ya	伯牙
Amei tribe	Ami tribe	阿眉族	Boyi	Po-yi	伯夷
Anhui	Anhwei	安徽	Bu Zixia	Pu Tzu-hsia	卜子夏
An Lushan	An Lu-shan	安祿山	Cai	Tsai	蔡
Anqing	Anching	安慶	Cai E	Tsai O	蔡鍔
Ao	Ao	奡	Cai Lun	Tsai Lun	蔡倫
Ba	Pa	巴	Cai Wenji	Tsai Wen-chi	蔡文姬
Ba Gorge	Pa Gorge	巴峽	Cai Xiang	Tsai Hsiang	蔡襄
Bai Juyi	Pai Chü-i	白居易	Cai Yong	Tsai Yung	蔡邕
Bai Li Xi	Pai-Li Hsi	百里溪	Cai Yuanpei	Tsai Yüan-pei	蔡元培
Bai nationality	Bai(Pai)nationality	白族	Cang Jie	Tsang Chieh	倉頡
Bai Suzhen	Pai Su-chen	白素貞	the earl of Cao	the earl of Tsao	曹伯
Ban Chao	Pan Ch'ao	班超	Cao Cao	Tsao Tsao	曹操
Ban Gu	Pan Ku	班固	Cao Kun	Tsao Kun	曹錕
Ban Zhao	Pan Chao	班昭	Cao Pi	Tsao Pi	曹丕
Duke of Bao	Duke of Pao	褒公	Cao Shen	Tsao Shen	曹參
Bao Shuya	Pao Shu-ya	鮑叔牙	Cao Xueqin	Tsao Hsüeh-chin	曹雪芹
Bao Zheng	Pao Cheng	包拯	Cao Zhan	Tsao Zhan	曹霑
Ba valley	Pa valley	灞原	Cao Zhi	Tsao Chih	曹植
Beigang	Peikang	北港	Cao Zijian	Tsao Tzu-chien	曹子建
Beijing	Peking	北京	Changan	Changan	長安
Beiping	Peiping	北平	Mt. Changbai	Mt. Changpai	長白山
Beitou	Peitou	北投	Changchun	Changchun	長春
Bengbu	Pangfou	蚌埠	Chang'e	Chang-o	嫦娥
Bian Que	Pien Chüeh	扁鵲	Changgan	Chang-kan	長干
Bian River	Pien River	汴水	Chang Hong	Chang Hung	萇弘
Bigan	Pi-kan	比干	Changjiang River	Yangtze River	長江
Bin	Pin	邠	Changju	Chang-chü	長沮
Bingwu	Ping-wu	丙午	Changsha	Changsha	長沙
Bingzhou	Pingchow	幷州	Changyang	Changyang	長陽
Bi River	Pi River	泌水	Changzhou	Changchow	常州
Bi Sheng	Pi Sheng	畢昇	Chan River	Chan River	瀍水
Bo	Po	亳	Chao Cuo	Chao Tso	鼂錯

漢語拼音	本典拼音	中文	漢語拼音	本典拼音	中文
Chaozhou	Chaochow	潮州	De Zong of the Qing	Te Tsung of the Ching	清德宗
Chen	Chen	陳	Dian Lake	Tien Lake	滇池
Emperor Cheng	Emperor Cheng	成帝(漢)	Diao Chan	Tiao Chan	貂蟬
Cheng and Kang	Cheng and Kang	成康	Dihua	Tihwa	迪化
Chengdu	Chengtu	成都	Dinghai	Tinghai	定海
Cheng Hao	Cheng Hao	程顥	Dingzhou	Tingchou	定州
Cheng Miao	Cheng Miao	程邈	Dongguo	Tungkuo	東郭
Cheng Yi	Cheng Yi	程頤	Dong Hu	Tung Hu	董狐
Cheng Zu of the Ming	Cheng Tsu of the Ming	明成祖	Dong Lin faction	Tung Lin faction	東林黨
Chen Lin	Chen Lin	陳琳	Dong Qichang	Tung Chi-chang	董其昌
Chen Ping	Chen Ping	陳平	Dong Shi	Tung Shih	東施
Chen Sheng	Chen Sheng	陳勝	Dongting (Lake)	Tungting (Lake)	洞庭(湖)
Chen Shou	Chen Shou	陳壽	Dongxiang	Tunghsiang	東鄉
Chen Shubao	Chen Shu-pao	陳叔寶	Dong Zhongshu	Tung Chung-shu	董仲舒
Chen Zhongzi	Chen Chung-tzu	陳仲子	Dong Zhuo	Tung Cho	董卓
Che Yin	Che Yin	車胤	Duan Qirui	Tuan Chi-jui	段祺瑞
Chi	Chih	赤	Duanxi	Tuanhsi	端溪
Chih You	Chih Yu	蚩尤	Du Fu	Tu Fu	杜甫
Chi Zhongyu	Chih Chung-yü	池仲魚	Du Kang	Tu Kang	杜康
Chong	Chung	崇(國)	Du Mu	Tu Mu	杜牧
Chongqing	Chungking	重慶	Dunhuang	Tunhwang	敦煌
Chu	Chu	楚	Duke of E	Duke of O	鄂公
Chu Suiliang	Chu Sui-liang	褚遂良	Eastern Han	Eastern Han	東漢
Ci Xi	Tzu Hsi	慈禧	Eastern Jin	Eastern Tsin	東晉
Count of Wu	Count of Wu	武侯	Ehu	Ohu	鵝湖
Cuiheng	Tsuiheng	翠亨	Emei	Omei	峨嵋
Mt. Dai	Mt. Tai	岱山	Fan Chi	Fan Chih	樊遲
Danjiang	Tamkang	淡江	Fang Bao	Fang Pao	方苞
Danshui	Tamsui	淡水	Fang Shu	Fang Shu	方叔
Dao De Jing	Tao Te Ching	道德經	Fang Xiaoru	Fang Hsiao-ju	方孝孺
Da Qing River	Ta Ching River	大清(河)	Fang Xuanling	Fang Hsüan-ling	房玄齡
Daren	Ta-jen	大任	Fan Li	Fan Li	范蠡
Dasi	Ta-szu	大姒	Fan Rongqi	Fan Jung-chi	范榮期
Deng Ai	Teng Ai	鄧艾	Fan Ye	Fan Yeh	范曄
Deng Shiru	Teng Shih-ju	鄧石如	Fan Zeng	Fan Tseng	范增
Deng Tong	Teng Tung	鄧通	Fan Zhongyan	Fan Chung-yen	范仲淹
Dengwei	Tengwei	鄧尉	Fei River	Fei River	淝水

漢語拼音	本典拼音	中文	漢語拼音	本典拼音	中文
Feng	Feng	封	Guangdong	Kwangtung	廣東
Feng Fu	Feng Fu	馮婦	Guan Gong	Kuan Kung	關公
Fenghuang	Feng-huang	鳳凰	Emperor Guang Wu	Emperor Kuang Wu	光武帝
Feng Menglong	Feng Meng-lung	馮夢龍	Guangxi	Kwangsi	廣西
Fengshan	Fengshan	鳳山	Guang Xu	Kuang Hsü	光緒
Feng Zicai	Feng Tzu-tsai	馮子才	Guangzhou	Kwangchow; Canton	廣州
Fen River	Fen River	汾水	Guan Hanqing	Kuan Han-ching	關漢卿
Fen River	Fen River	汾河	Guan Yu	Kuan Yü	關羽
Fuchai	Fu-chai	夫差	Guan Zhong	Kuan Chung	管仲
Fuguan	Fu-kuan	復關	Guanzhong	Kuan-chung	關中
Fu Jian	Fu Chien	苻堅	Guazhou	Kua-chou	瓜洲
Fujian	Fukien	福建	Gu-cheng County	Ku-cheng County	穀城縣
Fushan	Pusan	釜山	Gu Hongming	Ku Hung-ming	辜鴻銘
Fuxi	Fu-hsi	伏羲	Guiji	Kueichi	會稽
Fuzhou	Foochow	福州	Guilin	Kweilin	桂林
Gan Luo	Kan Lo	甘羅	Guisui	Kweisui	歸綏
Gan River	Kan River	贛江	Guiyang	Kweiyang	貴陽
Gansu	Kansu	甘肅	Guizhou	Kweichow	貴州
Gantang	Kantang	甘棠	Gu Liang Chi	Ku-Liang Chih	穀梁赤
Gao	Kao	高(子)	Gun	Kun	鯀
Gao	Kaou	郜	Guo	Kuo	虢
Emperor Gao	Emperor Kao	高帝	Guo Jujing	Kuo Chü-ching	郭居敬
Gaoxiong	Kaohsiung	高雄	(Kuomintang)	Kuomintang	國民黨
Gao Yingxiang	Kao Ying-hsiang	高迎祥	Guo Pu	Kuo Pu	郭璞
Gao Zong	Kao Tsung	高宗(南宋)	Guo She	Kuo She	虢射
Gao Zong	Kao Tsung	高宗(清)	Guoxingye	Koxinga	國姓爺
Gebi	Gobi	戈壁	Guo Ziyi	Kuo Tzu-yi	郭子儀
Geng Zhongming	Keng Chung-ming	耿仲明	Gusou	Ku-sou	瞽瞍
Gongfu	Kung fu	功夫	Gu Tinglin	Ku Ting-lin	顧亭林
Gongguan	Kungkung	公館	Gu Yan	Ku Yen	顧彥
Gongshu Ban	Kung-Shu Pan	公輸班	(Harbin)	Harbin	哈爾濱
Gongshu Zi	Kung-Shu Tzu	公輸子	Hainan Island	Hainan Island	海南島
Gongsun Baoxu	Kung-Sun Pao-hsü	公孫包胥	Haizhou	Haichow	海州
Gongsun Long	Kung-Sun Lung	公孫龍	Hami	Hami	哈密
Gongyang Gao	Kung-Yang Kao	公羊高	Mountain Han	Mountain Han	旱麓
Gong Yu	Kung Yü	貢禹	Han	Han	漢
Gou Jian	Kou Chien	句踐			

漢語拼音	本典拼音	中文	漢語拼音	本典拼音	中文
Han	Han	韓	Hu	Hu	虎
Han Boyu	Han Po-yü	韓伯兪	Mt. Hua	Mt. Hwa	華山
Handan	Hantan	邯鄲	Huai (River)	Huai (River)	淮(水)
Han Fei	Han Fei	韓非	Huai River	Huai River	淮河
Hangai Mountain	Hangai Mountain	杭愛山	Huai Yin	Huai Yin	淮陰
Han Gan	Han Kan	韓幹	Hualian	Hualien	花蓮
Han Gu Pass	Han Ku Pass	函谷關	Huamen	Huamen	花門
Hangzhou	Hangchow	杭州	Hua Mulan	Hua Mu-lan	花木蘭
Hankou	Hankow	漢口	Duke Huan	Duke Huan	桓公
Hanlin Academy	Hanlin Academy	翰林院	Huang Di	Huang Ti	黃帝
Han River	Han River	漢水	Huangfu	Huang-fu	皇父
Hanshan	Hanshan	寒山	Huanggang	Huanggang	黃崗
Han Shizhong	Han Shih-chung	韓世忠	Huang Longshi	Huang Lung-shih	黃龍士
Han Xin	Han Hsin	韓信	Huangpi	Huangpi	黃陂
Hanyang	Hanyang	漢陽	Huangpu	Whampoa	黃埔
Han Yu	Han Yü	韓愈	Huangpu River	Huangpu River	黃浦江
Hao	Hao	鎬	Huang Shigong	Huang Shih-kung	黃石公
He	Ho	和	Huang Tingjian	Huang Ting-chien	黃庭堅
He	Ho	河	Huang Valley	Huang Valley	皇澗
Hebei	Hopeh; Hopei	河北	Huang Xie	Huang Hsieh	黃歇
Hefei	Hofei	合肥	Huan Wen	Huan Wen	桓溫
Heilongjiang	Heilungkiang	黑龍江	Hua Qing Pool	Hua Ching Pool	華清池
Helan Shan	Holan Shan	賀蘭山	Huating	Huating	華亭
Henan	Honan	河南	Hubei	Hupeh	湖北
Mt. Heng	Mt. Heng	衡山	Hu Hanmin	Hu Han-min	胡漢民
Mt. Heng	Mt. Heng	恒山	Hui	Hui	回(顏回)
Hengyang	Hengyang	衡陽	Hui nationality	Hui nationality	回族
He Xiangu	Ho Hsien-ku	何仙姑	Hui Neng	Hui Neng	慧能
Historian Zhou	Historian Chou	史籀	Hui of Liuxia	Hui of Liu-hsia	柳下惠
Honggan	Hungkan	鴻干	Hui Yuan	Hui Yüan	慧遠
Hongmen	Hung-men	鴻門	Huizhou	Huichow	徽州
Hong Xiuquan	Hung Hsiu-chüan	洪秀全	Huizi	Hui-tzu	惠子
Hou	Hou	侯	Hui Zong	Hui Tsung	徽宗
Houji	Hou-chi	后稷	Hunan	Hunan	湖南
the House of Tuoba	the House of Toba	托跋氏	Huo Guang	Huo Kuang	霍光
Hu	Hu	鵠	Huo Qubing	Huo Chü-ping	霍去病

漢語拼音	本典拼音	中文	漢語拼音	本典拼音	中文
Hu Shi	Hu Shih	胡適	Jing Gang	Ching Kang	井岡
Huzhou	Huchow	湖州	Jing Gong	Ching Kung	景公
Ji	Chi	稷	Jing Ke	Ching Ko	荆軻
Jia Dao	Chia Tao	賈島	Jing River	Ching River	涇河
Jiafu	Chia-fu	家父	Jingwei	Ching-wei	精衛
Jialing	Chialing	嘉陵	Jinhua	Chinhua	金華
Jia Nan	Chia Nan	嘉南	Jinmen	Kinmen	金門
Jian An Period	Chien An Period	建安時期	Jinsha River	Kinsha River	金沙江
Jiang	Chiang	姜	Jin Wuzhu	Jin Wu-chu	金兀朮
Jiang	Chiang	江	Ji (River)	Chi (River)	沛(水)
Jiangnan	Chiang-nan	江南	Ji River	Chi River	濟水
Jiangning	Kiangning	江寧	Ji Sun	Chi-Sun	季孫
Jiang Qing	Chiang Ching	江青	Jiujiang	Chiuchiang	九江
Jiangsu	Kiangsu	江蘇	Jiulong	Kowloon	九龍
Jiang Tai Gong	Chiang Tai Kung	姜太公	Jiumoloshi	Kumarajiva	鳩摩羅什
			Jiuyi	Chiu-yi	九疑
Jiangxi	Kiangsi	江西	Ji Zi	Chi Tzu	箕子
Jiang Yan	Chiang Yen	江淹	Ju	Chü	沮
Jiang Ziya	Chiang Tzu-ya	姜子牙	Mount Ju	Mount Chü	崌山
Jiao Tong University	Chiao Tung University	交通大學	Mt. Julai	Mt. Chülai	崌崍山
			Jun	Chün	浚
Jiaozhi	Cochin	交趾	Ju Song	Chü Sung	沮誦
Jiaozhou	Chiaochow	膠州	Kaifeng	Kaifeng	開封
Jiasa	Gaza	加薩	Kan	Kan	坎
Jia Yi	Chia Yi	賈誼	Kangding	Kangting	康定
Jiayu	Chiayü	嘉裕	Kang Sengyuan	Kang Seng-yüan	康僧淵
Jie	Chieh	桀	Kang Xi	Kang Hsi	康熙
Jieni	Chieh-ni	桀溺	Kang Youwei	Kang Yu-wei	康有為
Jieyu	Chieh-yü	接輿	Kehan	Khan	可汗
Ji Kang	Chi Kang	嵇康	Kending	Kenting	墾丁
Jilin	Kirin	吉林	Ke Shaomin	Ko Shao-min	柯劭忞
Jilong	Keelung	基隆	King Dai	King Tai	大王
Jilu	Chi-lu	季路	King of Huai Nan	King of Huai Nan	淮南王
Jin	Tsin	晉			
Jin	Jin	金	King Xuan of Qi	King Hsüan of Chi	齊宣王
Duke Wen of Jin	Duke Wen of Tsin	晉文公			
			King Wen	King Wen	文王
Jinan	Tsinan	濟南	King Wu	King Wu	武王
Jing Bo	Ching Po	井伯	Kong Rong	Kung Jung	孔融

漢語拼音	本典拼音	中文
Mt. Kongtong	Mt. Kungtung	崆峒山
(Confucius)	Confucius	孔子
Kulun	Kulun	庫倫
Kun	Kun	鯤
Kunlun	Kunlun	崑崙
the Kunlun Mountains	the Kunlun Mountains	崑崙山
Kunming	Kunming	昆明
Kunshan	Kunshan	崑山
Lady Xi	Lady Hsi	西子
Lady Xu	Lady Hsü	徐娘
Mt. Lai	Mt. Lai	崍山
Lancang River	Lantsang River	瀾滄江
Lanyu	Lanyü	蘭嶼
Lanzhou	Lanchow	蘭州
Lao Laizi	Lao Lai-tse; Lao Lai-tzu	老萊子
Lao Naixuan	Lao Nai-hsüan	勞乃宣
(Lao-tzu)	Lao-tzu	老子
(Lhasa)	Lhasa	拉薩
Lashu	Lashio	臘戌
Later Han	Later Han	後漢
Later Liang	Later Liang	後梁
Later Zhou	Later Chou	後周
Leizhou	Leichou	雷州
Liang	Liang	梁
Liang Hong	Liang Hung	梁鴻
Liang Hongyu	Liang Hung-yü	梁紅玉
Mt. Liang	Mt. Liang	梁山
Liang Qichao	Liang Chi-chao	梁啓超
Liangshan	Liangshan	梁山
Liang Wu Di	Liang Wu Ti	梁武帝
Lian Po	Lien Po	廉頗
Lian xi	Lienhsi	濂溪
Lianyungang	Lienyünkang	連雲港
Liao	Liao	遼
Liaodong	Liaotung	遼東
Liao Hua	Liao Hua	廖化
Liaoning	Liaoning	遼寧

漢語拼音	本典拼音	中文
Liao River	Liao River	遼河
Li Baojia	Li Pao-chia	李寶嘉
Li Bo	Li Po	李白
Li Chunfeng	Li Chun-feng	李淳風
Lie Yukou	Lieh Yü-kou	列禦寇
Liezi	Lieh-tzu	列子
Li Guang	Li Kuang	李廣
Li Hongzhang	Li Hung-chang	李鴻章
Li Lou	Li Lou	離婁
Lin Bu	Lin Pu	林逋
Lin Fang	Lin Fang	林放
Lin Shu	Lin Shu	林紓
Lin Xiangru	Lin Hsiang-ju	藺相如
Lin Zexu	Lin Tse-hsü	林則徐
Li Qingzhao	Li Ching-chao	李清照
Li Ruzhen	Li Ju-chen	李汝珍
Lisao	Li-sao	離騷
Li Shizhen	Li Shih-chen	李時珍
Li Si	Li Ssu	李斯
Little Qiao	Little Chiao	小喬
Little Tong	Little Tung	通子
Liu	Liu	劉
Duke Liu	Duke Lew	公劉
Liu An	Liu An	劉安
Liu Bang	Liu Pang	劉邦
Liu Bei	Liu Pei	劉備
Liu Chan	Liu Chan	劉禪
Liu E	Liu O	劉鶚
Liu Gongquan	Liu Kung-chüan	柳公權
Liujiang	Liuchiang	柳江
Liu Kezhuang	Liu Ke-chuang	劉克莊
Liu Xiang	Liu Hsiang	劉向
Liu Xie	Liu Hsieh	劉勰
Liu Xin	Liu Hsin	劉歆
Liu Xu	Liu Hsü	劉昫
Liu Yong	Liu Yung	柳永
Liu Zongyuan	Liu Tzung-yüan	柳宗元
Li Yu	Li Yü	李煜

漢語拼音	本典拼音	中文	漢語拼音	本典拼音	中文
Li Yuan	Li Yüan	李淵	Mao Kun	Mao Kun	茅坤
Li Zicheng	Li Tzu-cheng	李自成	Mao Qiang	Mao Chiang	毛嬙
Longmen	Lungmen	龍門	Mao Sui	Mao Sui	毛遂
Lord Wenhui	Lord Wen-hui	文惠君	Maotai	Maotai	茅台
Lu	Lu	魯	Mao Zedong	Mao Zedong	毛澤東
Lu Ban	Lu Pan	魯班	Ma Qiancheng	Ma Chieh-cheng	馬千乘
the Marquis of Lu	the Marquis of Lu	魯侯	Ma Wei	Ma Wei	馬嵬
			Ma Yuan	Ma Yüan	馬援
Lu E	Lu O	蓼莪	Mazu	Matsu	馬祖
Lugang	Lukang	鹿港	Mei	Mei	郿
Lu Jiuyuan	Lu Chiu-yüan	陸九淵	Menba nationality	Menba nationality	門巴族
the Lukai tribe	the Rukai tribe	魯凱族			
Lu Mochou	Lu Mo-chou	盧莫愁	(Mongolia)	Mongolia	蒙古
Mt. Lu	Mt. Lu	廬山	Meng Guang	Meng Kuang	孟光
Luo	Lo	洛	Meng Tian	Meng Tien	蒙恬
Luo Binwang	Lo Pin-wang	駱賓王	(Mencius)	Mencius	孟子
Luo Fu	Lo Fu	羅敷	Meng Zong	Meng Tzung	孟宗
Luo Guanzhong	Lo Kuan-chung	羅貫中	Mianchi	Minchih	澠池
Luo River	Lo River	洛河	Mian River	Mien River	沔水
Luoyang	Loyang	洛陽	Miao	Miao	苗
Lushan	Lushan	廬山	Miaoli	Miaoli	苗栗
Lu Xiufu	Lu Hsiu-fu	陸秀夫	Mi Fu	Mi Fu	米芾
Lu Xun	Lu Hsün	魯迅	Mile	Maitreya	彌勒
Lu You	Lu Yu	陸游	Min	Min	閩
Lu Yu	Lu Yü	陸羽	Mt. Min	Mt. Min	岷山
Lu Zhi	Lu Chih	陸贄	Ming	Ming	明
Lu Zhonglian	Lu Chung-lien	魯仲連	Min River	Min River	閩江
Lü	Lü	呂	Moao	Mo-ao	莫敖
Lü Bu	Lü Pu	呂布	Mo Di	Mo Ti	墨翟
Lü Dongbin	Lü Tung-pin	呂洞賓	Mozi	Mo-tze	墨子
Lüshun	Lüshun	旅順	Muji	Mu-chi	穆姬
Magong	Makung	馬公	Mujianlian	Moginlin	目犍連
Mailikai River	Malikha River	邁立開江	Muzha	Mucha	木柵
Ma Jianzhong	Ma Chien-chung	馬建中	Nanchang	Nanchang	南昌
Manzhou	Manchu; Manchuria	滿洲	Nangang	Nankang	南港
			Nanjing	Nanking	南京
Manzhouguo	Manchukuo	滿洲國	Nanke	Nanko	南柯
Mao Heng	Mao Heng	毛亨	Nan Tian	Nan Tien	南田
Mao Jin	Mao Chin	毛晉			

漢語拼音	本典拼音	中文
Nanzhao	Nanchao	南詔
Nen River	Nen River	嫩江
Nian	Nien	捻
Nian Gengyao	Nien Keng-yao	年羹堯
Ningxia	Ningsia	寧夏
Ni (River)	Ni (River)	禰(水)
Northern Song	Northern Sung	北宋
(Nurhachi)	Nurhachu	努爾哈赤
Nü Wa	Nü Wa	女媧
Nüzhen	Nüchen	女眞
Ou-Yang Xiu	Ou-Yang Hsiu	歐陽修
Ou-Yang Xun	Ou-Yang Hsün	歐陽詢
Paiwan	Paiwan	排灣
(Pamirs)	Pamirs	帕米爾
Pang Meng	Pang Meng	逄蒙
Pan Gu	Pan Ku	盤古
Pan Jinlian	Pan Chin-lien	潘金蓮
Pan Yue	Pan Yüeh	潘岳
Peak Huile	Peak Hui-le	回樂峰
Penghu	Penghu	澎湖
Peng Ze	Peng Tse	彭澤
Pengzu	Pengtsu	彭祖
Pichen	Pi-chen	裨諶
Pingdong	Pingtung	屏東
Pi Xian	Pi Hsien	郫縣
Posterior Han	Posterior Han	後漢
Posterior Jin	Posterior Tsin	後晉
Posterior Liang	Posterior Liang	後梁
Posterior Tang	Posterior Tang	後唐
Posterior Zhou	Posterior Chou	後周
Poyang Lake	Poyang Lake	鄱陽湖
Prince Zhaoming	Prince Chao-ming	昭明太子
Pu Songling	Pu Sung-ling	蒲松齡
Mt. Putuo	Mt. Puto	普陀山
Puyi	Pu-yi	溥儀
Qi	Chi	齊
Qi	Chi	杞

漢語拼音	本典拼音	中文
Qi	Chi	啓
Qi (River)	Chi (River)	漆水
Mt. Qi	Mt. Chi	岐山
Duke Huan of Qi	Duke Huan of Chi	齊桓公
Duke Jing of Qi	Duke Ching of Chi	齊景公
Qiang nationality	Chiang nationality	羌(族)
Qian Liu	Chien Liu	錢鏐
Qiantang River	Chientang River	錢塘江
Qi Bo	Chi Po	歧伯
Qi Jiguang	Chi Chi-kuang	戚繼光
Qilin	Chi-lin	麒麟
Qin	Chin	秦
Mt. Qin	Mt. Chin	秦山
Qing	Ching	清
Qingdao	Tsingtao	青島
Qing Feng County	Ching Feng County	清豐縣
Qing Fu	Ching Fu	慶父
Qinghai	Chinghai	青海
Qing Hua University	Qing Hua University	清華大學
Qin Guan	Chin Kuan	秦觀
Qinhuai	Chin-huai	秦淮
Qinhuai River	Chinhuai River	秦淮河
Qinhuangdao	Chinhuangtao	秦皇島
Qin Hui	Chin Kuei	秦檜
Qin Liangyu	Chin Liang-yü	秦良玉
Qin Pass	Chin Pass	秦關
Qin Shaoyou	Chin Shao-yu	秦少游
Qin Shi Huang	Chin Shih Huang	秦始皇
Qiong Hua Islet	Chiung Hua Islet	瓊華島
Qi (River)	Chi (River)	淇(水)
Qiu Jin	Chiu Chin	秋瑾
Qiuniang	Chiu-niang	秋娘
Qizhou	Chichow	蘄州
Quanzhou	Chuanchow	泉州

漢語拼音	本典拼音	中文
Qufu	Chüfu	曲阜
Qu Tang Gorge	Chü Tang Gorge	瞿唐峽
Qu Yuan	Chü Yüan	屈原
Ran	Jan	冉
Ran You	Jan Yu	冉有
Ren Xu	Jen Hsü	壬戌
Ren Zong	Jen Tzung	仁宗(北宋)
River Li	River Li	荔江
Rong Lu	Jung Lu	榮祿
Rongxian	Junghsien	容縣
Ruan	Juan	阮
Ruan Ji	Juan Chi	阮籍
Ruan Xian	Juan Hsien	阮咸
Ruan Zhan	Juan Chan	阮瞻
Ruo River	Jo River	弱水
Ru (River)	Ju (River)	汝(水)
Ruzhou	Juchou	汝州
Sai Jinhua	Sai Chin-hua	賽金花
Sangzhong	San-chung	桑中
Sanmiao	San-miao	三苗
Sanwei	San-wei	三危
Shamian	Shamien	沙面
Shandong	Shantung	山東
Shang	Shang	商
Shangcai	Shangtsiai	上蔡
Shanghai	Shanghai	上海
Shang Kexi	Shang Ke-hsi	尙可喜
Shangqiu	Shangchiu	商邱
Shanhaiguan	Shanhaikuan	山海關
Shanhai Pass	Shanhai Pass	山海關
Shantou	Swatow	汕頭
Shanxi	Shansi	山西
(Shaanxi)	Shensi	陝西
Shao	Shao	韶
Shaoshan	Shaoshan	韶山
Shaoxing	Shaohsing	紹興
Shen	Shen	申
Shen	Shen	參
She nationality	She nationality	畬族
Shen Baoxu	Shen Pao-hsü	申包胥
Shen Nong	Shen Nung	神農
Shen Sanbai	Shen San-pai	沈三白
Shenyang	Mukden (Shenyang)	瀋陽
Shen Yue	Shen Yüeh	沈約
Shen Zhou	Shen Chou	沈周
Shen Zong	Shen Tzung	神宗
Shi	Shih	石
Shi Dakai	Shih Ta-kai	石達開
Shi Huang	Shih Huang	始皇
Shi Huang Di	Shih Huang Ti	始皇帝
Shi Jingtang	Shih Ching-tang	石敬瑭
Shi Kefa	Shih Ko-fa	史可法
Shimen	Shih-men	石門
Shi Naian	Shih Nai-an	施耐庵
Shishu	Shih-shu	世叔
Shi Siming	Shih Szu-ming	史思明
Shouyang	Shouyang	首陽
Shu	Shu	叔
Shu	Shu	蜀
Shun	Shun	舜
Shunzhi	Shunchih	順治
Shuqi	Shu-chi	叔齊
Si	Szu	賜
Sichuan	Szechwan	四川
Sikong Tu	Ssu-Kung Tu	司空圖
Sima Guang	Ssu-Ma Kuang	司馬光
Sima Qian	Ssu-Ma Chien	司馬遷
Sima Tan	Ssu-Ma Tan	司馬談
Sima Xiangru	Ssu-Ma Hsiang-ju	司馬相如
Sima Yan	Ssu-Ma Yen	司馬炎
Sima Zhao	Ssu-Ma Chao	司馬昭
Si River	Ssu River	泗水
Song	Sung	宋
Songhua River	Sungari River	松花江

漢語拼音	本典拼音	中文	漢語拼音	本典拼音	中文
Mt. Song	Mt. Sung	嵩山	Tang	Tang	唐
Song Qi	Sung Chi	宋祁	Tangnuwuliang-hai	Tannu Tuva	唐努烏梁海
Song River	Sung River	淞江	Tang Shunzhi	Tang Shun-chih	唐順之
Su	Su	蘇	Tang Xianzu	Tang Hsien-tsu	湯顯祖
the elder Su	the elder Su	老蘇	Tang Yao	Tang Yao	唐堯
Su Che	Su Che	蘇轍	Tan Sitong	Tan Szu-tung	譚嗣同
Su Dongpo	Su Tung-po	蘇東坡	Tao Kan	Tao Kan	陶侃
Sui	Sui	穗	Taolin	Tao-lin	桃林
Sui	Sui	隋	Tao Qian	Tao Chien	陶潛
Su Manshu	Su Man-shu	蘇曼殊	Taoyuan	Taoyuan	桃園
Sun Bin	Sun Pin	孫臏	Tao Yuanming	Tao Yüan-ming	陶淵明
Sun Chu	Sun Chu	孫楚	Teng	Teng	滕
Sun Kang	Sun Kang	孫康	Tian An Men	Tien An Men	天安門
Sun Quan	Sun Chüan	孫權	Tian Dan	Tien Tan	田單
Sun Wu Kong	Sun Wu Kung	孫悟空	Tianjin	Tientsin	天津
Sun Xing	Sun Hsing	孫興	Tianshan	Tienshan	天山
(Sun Yat-sen)	Sun Yat-sen	孫逸仙	Tiantai	Tien-tai	天台
Sun Zi	Sun Tzu	孫子	Tiemuer	Timur	帖木兒
Sun Zijing	Sun Tzu-ching	孫子荆	Ti Ying	Ti Ying	緹縈
Su Qin	Su Chin	蘇秦	(Tungusic)	Tungusic	通古斯
Su Shi	Su Shih	蘇軾	Tong Meng Hui	Tung Meng Hui	同盟會
Su Wu	Su Wu	蘇武	Tongzhou	Tungchow	通州
Su Xiaomei	Su Hsiao-mei	蘇小妹	the tribes of the Huai	the tribes of the Huai	淮夷
Su Xun	Su Hsün	蘇洵	Tuoba	Toba	拓跋
Su Yuanchun	Su Yüan-chun	蘇元春	Tuqiu	Tuchiu	菟裘
Suzhou	Soochow	蘇州	Wang Anshi	Wang An-shih	王安石
Taibei	Taipei	台北	Wang Bo	Wang Po	王勃
Taidong	Taitung	臺東	Wang Dao	Wang Tao	王導
Tai Lake	Tai Lake	太湖	Wang Hongwen	Wang Hung-wen	王洪文
Mt. Tai	Mt. Tai	泰山	Wang Ji	Wang Chi	王濟
Tainan	Tainan	台南	Wang Jingwei	Wang Ching-wei	汪精衛
Taiping rebels	Taiping rebels	太平軍	Wang Mang	Wang Mang	王莽
Taiwan	Taiwan	台灣	Wang Qiang	Wang Chiang	王嬙
Taizhong	Taichung	台中	Wang Shifu	Wang Shih-fu	王實甫
Tai Zong	Tai Tsung	太宗(唐)	Wang Shouren	Wang Shou-jen	王守仁
Tai Zu	Tai Tsu	太祖	Wang Wei	Wang Wei	王維
Tanfu	Tan-fu	亶父	Wang Wuzi	Wang Wu-tzu	王武子
Tang	Tang	湯			

漢語拼音	本典拼音	中文	漢語拼音	本典拼音	中文
Wang Xiang	Wang Hsiang	王祥	Wu Jingzi	Wu Ching-tze	吳敬梓
Wang Xizhi	Wang Hsi-chih	王羲之	Wulianghai	Uriankhai	烏梁海
Wang Yangming	Wang Yang-ming	王陽明	Wuling	Wu-ling	武陵
			Wuling	Wu-ling	於陵
Wang Yifu	Wang Yi-fu	王夷甫	(Urumqi)	Urumchi	烏魯木齊
Wang Yiqing	Wang Yi-ching	王奕清	Mt. Wu	Mt. Wu	巫山
Wang Zhaojun	Wang Chao-chün	王昭君	Wu Qi	Wu Chi	吳起
the Wan Li reign	the Wan Li reign	萬曆年間	Wu Sangui	Wu San-kuei	吳三桂
			Wu Shen	Wu-shen	戊申
Wei	Wei	魏	Wuxi	Wuhsi	無錫
Wei	Wei	衛	Wu Xu	Wu Hsü	戊戌
Duke Xuan of Wei	Duke Hsüan of Wei	衛宣公	Wu Xun	Wu Hsün	武訓
			Wu Yi	Wu Yi	武夷
Weihaiwei	Weihaiwei	威海衛	Wu Yong	Wu Yung	吳用
Wei Jie	Wei Chieh	衛玠	Wu Zixu	Wu Tzu-hsü	伍子胥
Wei Mou	Wei Mou	魏牟	Xia	Hsia	夏
Wei Qing	Wei Ching	衛青	Xiamen	Amoy	廈門
Wei River	Wei River	濰水	Xi'an	Sian	西安
Wei River	Wei River	渭河	Emperor Xian	Emperor Hsien	獻帝
Wei Zhi	Wei Chih	韋陟	Xianbei	Hsien-pei	鮮卑
Wei Zhongxian	Wei Chung-hsien	魏忠賢	Xiang	Hsiang	湘
Emperor Wen	Emperor Wen	文帝(漢)	Xiang River	Hsiang River	湘水
Wen and Jing	Wen and Ching	文景	Xiang River	Hsiang River	湘江
Wen and Wu	Wen and Wu	文武	Xiangyang	Hsiangyang	襄陽
Weng Tonghe	Weng Tung-ho	翁同龢	Xiang Yu	Hsiang Yü	項羽
Wen Tianxiang	Wen Tien-hsiang	文天祥	Xiang Zhuang	Hsiang Chuang	項莊
Wu	Wu	吳	Xianyang	Hsienyang	咸陽
Wu	Wu	武	Xianyun	Hsien-yün	玁狁
Emperor Wu	Emperor Wu	武帝	Xiao	Hsiao	蕭
Empress Wu	Empress Wu	武后	Xiao He	Hsiao Ho	蕭何
Wuchang	Wuchang	武昌	Xiao River	Hsiao River	瀟水
Wu Chengen	Wu Cheng-en	吳承恩	Xiao Tong	Hsiao Tung	蕭統
Wudang	Wutang	武當	Xiao Yen	Hsiao Yen	蕭衍
Wu Daozi	Wu Tao-tzu	吳道子	Xibo nationality	Sibo nationality	錫伯族
Wu Feng	Wu Feng	吳鳳	Xie	Hsieh	謝
Wu Gorge	Wu Gorge	巫峽	Xie An	Hsieh An	謝安
Wu Guang	Wu Kuang	吳廣	Xie Daoyun	Hsieh Tao-yün	謝道韞
Wuhan	Wuhan	武漢	Xie Huilian	Hsieh Hui-lien	謝惠連
Wuhu	Wuhu	蕪湖			

漢語拼音	本典拼音	中文	漢語拼音	本典拼音	中文
Xie Lingyun	Hsieh Ling-yün	謝靈運	Yan	Yen	燕
			Yan'an	Yenan	延安
Xie Xuan	Hsieh Hsüan	謝玄	Yan Di	Yen Ti	炎帝
Xi He	Hsi Ho	西河	Yan Fu	Yen Fu	嚴復
Xikang	Sikang	西康	Yang and Mo	Yang and Mo	楊墨
Xiluo	Silo	西螺	Emperor Yang	Emperor Yang	煬帝
Xi Men Bao	Hsi-Men Pao	西門豹	Yang Hu	Yang Hu	羊祜
Xin	Hsin	新(朝)	Yang Jiong	Yang Chiung	楊炯
Xingan	Hsingan	興安	Yangmingshan	Yangmingshan	陽明山
Xing Zhong Hui	Hsing Chung Hui	興中會	Yangshao	Yang-shao	仰韶
			Yang Shi	Yang Shih	楊時
Xining	Hsining	西寧	Yang Xiong	Yang Hsiung	揚雄
Xinjiang	Shinkiang	新疆	Yang Yi	Yang Yi	楊億
Xin Qiji	Hsin Chi-chi	辛棄疾	Yang Yuhuan	Yang Yü-huan	楊玉環
Xinzhu	Hsinchu	新竹	Yangzhou	Yangchow	揚州
Xiongnu	Hun	匈奴	Yang Zhu	Yang Chu	楊朱
Xi Shi	Hsi Shih	西施	Yang Ziju	Yang Tzu-chü	陽子居
Xiu	Hsiu	秀	Yangzi River	Yangtze River	揚子江
(Tibet)	Sitsang (Tibet)	西藏	Yan Hui	Yen Hui	顏回
Xu	Hsü	許子	Yanjing University	Yenching University	燕京大學
Xuancheng	Hsüancheng	宣城			
Xuanyuan	Hsüan-yüan	軒轅	Mt. Yan	Mt. Yen	崦山
Xuan Zang	Hsüan Tsang	玄奘	Yan River	Yen River	沇水
Xuan Zong	Hsüan Tzung	宣宗(清)	Yan Ying	Yen Ying	晏嬰
Xuan Zong	Hsüan Tsung	玄宗	Yan Yuan	Yen Yüan	顏淵
Xue Juzheng	Hsüeh Cü-cheng	薛居正	Yan Zhenqing	Yen Chen-ching	顏眞卿
Xu Guangqi	Hsü Kuang-chi	徐光啓	Yan Zhi	Yen Chih	閻職
Duke Xun	Duke Hsün	郇公	Yanzi	Yen-tzu	顏子
Xun Kuang	Hsün Kuang	荀況	Yao	Yao	堯
Xun Yan	Hsün Yen	荀偃	Mt. Yao	Mt. Yao	嶢山
Xunyang	Hsünyang	潯陽	Yao Nai	Yao Nai	姚鼐
Xu Shen	Hsü Shen	許愼	Yao nationality	Yao nationality	瑤族(猺族)
Xu Xian	Hsü Hsien	許仙	Yao Wenyuan	Yao Wen-yüan	姚文元
Xu Xing	Hsü Hsing	許行	Yelang	Yahlang	夜郎
Xuzhou	Hsüchow	徐州	Yi	Yi	益
Xu Ziping	Hsü Tzu-ping	徐子平	Yi	Yi	羿
Yalü River	Yalü River	鴨綠江	Yichang	Yichang	宜昌
Yan	Yen	偃	Yihe Garden	Yi-ho Garden	頤和園

漢語拼音	本典拼音	中文	漢語拼音	本典拼音	中文
Yin	Yin	殷	Yunnan	Yunnan; Yünnan	雲南
Ying Bu	Ying Pu	英布	Yun Shouping	Yün Shou-ping	惲壽平
Ying River	Ying River	穎川	Yu the Great	Yü the Great	大禹
Yingying	Ying-ying	鶯鶯	Yu Xin	Yü Hsin	庾信
Yin Mountains	Yin Mountains	陰山	Yuyang	Yüyang	漁陽
Yinshang	Yin-shang	殷商	Zai Lai Rice	Tsai Lai Rice	在來米
Yin Yang	Yin-Yang	陰陽	Zai Wo	Tsai Wo	宰我
Yi River	I River	易水	Zai Yu	Tsai Yü	宰予
Yi (River)	Yi (River)	沂(水)	Zang Cang	Tsang Ts'ang	臧倉
Yixing	Yihsing	宜興	Zang Wenzhong	Tsang Wen-chung	臧文仲
Yi Ya	I Yah	易牙			
Yi Yin	Yi Yin	伊尹	Zeng	Tseng	曾
Yong feng County	Yung feng County	永豐縣	Zeng Gong	Tseng Kung	曾鞏
			Zeng Shen	Tseng Shen	曾參
Yongji County	Yung-chi County	永濟縣	Zeng Xi	Tseng Hsi	曾西
You	Yu	由	Zengzi	Tseng-tzu	曾子
You	Yu	幽	Zhan	Chan	展(氏)
Emperor You	Emperor Yu	幽王	Zhang Chunqiao	Chang Chun-chiao	張春橋
Youzhou	Yuchow	幽州			
You Zuo	Yu Tso	游酢	Zhang Daoling	Chang Tao-lin	張道陵
Yu	Yü	虞	Zhang Fei	Chang Fei	張飛
Yu	Yü	禹	Zhang Heng	Chang Heng	張衡
Mountain Yu	Mountain Yü	羽山	Zhanghua	Changhua	彰化
Yuan	Yüan	元	Zhangjiakou	Changchiakou	張家口
Yuan Mei	Yüan Mei	袁枚	Zhang Jiao	Chang Chiao	張角
Yuanmou	Yüanmou	元謀	Zhang Liang	Chang Liang	張良
Yuanshan	Yüanshan	圓山	Zhang Qian	Chang Chien	張騫
Yuan Shao	Yüan Shao	袁紹	Zhang Tingyu	Chang Ting-yü	張廷玉
Yuan Shikai	Yüan Shih-kai	袁世凱	Zhang Xian-zhong	Chang Hsien-chung	張獻忠
Yuan Tiangang	Yüan Tien-kang	袁天綱			
Yue	Yüeh	越	Zhang Xu	Chang Hsü	張旭
Yue Fei	Yüeh Fei	岳飛	Zhang Xun	Chang Hsün	張巡
Yueyang Tower	Yüeyang Tower	岳陽樓	Zhang Yi	Chang Yi	張儀
			Zhang Yue	Chang Yüeh	張說
Yu Gong	Yü Kung	愚公	Zhang Zai	Chang Tsai	張載
Yugu	Yüku	裕固	Zhang Zhi	Chang Chih	張芝
Yulin	Yülin	榆林	Zhang Zhidong.	Chang Chih-tung	張之洞
Yumen Pass	Yü-men Pass	玉門關	Zhang Zhong	Chang Chung	張仲
Yungang	Yünkang	雲岡	Zhangzhou	Changchow	漳州

漢語拼音	本典拼音	中文	漢語拼音	本典拼音	中文
Zhang Zuolin	Chang Tso-lin	張作霖	Zhuang Zhou	Chuang Chou	莊周
Zhan Qin	Chan Chin	展禽	Zhuangzi	Chuang-tzu	莊子
Zhao	Chao	趙	Zhuanxu	Chuan-hsü	顓頊
Zhao	Chao	召	Zhuanyu	Chuan-yü	顓臾
Zhao Cui	Chao Tsui	趙衰	Zhu Da	Chu Ta	朱耷
Zhao Dun	Chao Tun	趙盾	Zhu Di	Chu Ti	朱棣
Zhao Feiyan	Chao Fei-yen	趙飛燕	Zhu Dunru	Chu Tun-ju	朱敦儒
Zhao Gao	Chao Kao	趙高	Zhuge Kong-ming	Chu-Ko Kung-ming	諸葛孔明
Zhao Kuangyin	Chao Kuang-yin	趙匡胤	Zhuge Liang	Chu-Ko Liang	諸葛亮
Zhao Mengfu	Chao Meng-fu	趙孟頫	Zhuji	Chuchi	諸暨
Zhao Yun	Chao Yün	趙雲	Zhu Maichen	Chu Mai-chen	朱買臣
Zhejiang	Chekiang	浙江	Zhuo County	Cho County	涿縣
Zhen	Chen	溱	Zhuo Wenjun	Cho Wen-chün	卓文君
Zheng	Cheng	鄭	Zhu Song	Chu Sung	朱松
Zheng Cheng-gong	Cheng Cheng-kung	鄭成功	Zhu Wen	Chu Wen	朱溫
Zheng He	Cheng Ho	鄭和	Zhu Xi	Chu Hsi	朱熹
Zheng Xuan	Cheng Hsüan	鄭玄	Zhu Yuanzhang	Chu Yüan-chang	朱元璋
Zhi	Chih	摯	Zhuzhou	Chuchow	株洲
Zhong Kui	Chung Kuei	鍾馗	Zidu	Tzu-tu	子都
Zhong Nan Mountain	Chung-Nan Mountain	終南山	Zigong	Tzu-kung	子貢
Zhongni	Chung-ni	仲尼	Zihe	Tzu-he	子貉
Zhong Rong	Chung Jung	鍾嶸	Zijin City	Forbidden City	紫禁城
Zhong Shanfu	Chung Shan-fu	仲山甫	Zilu	Tzu-lu	子路
Zhongyun	Chung-yün	仲允	Zishui	Tsu-shui	資水
Zhong Ziqi	Chung Tzu-chi	鍾子期	Zisi	Tzu-szu	子思
Zhou	Chou	紂	Zixia	Tzu-hsia	子夏
Zhou	Chou	周	Ziyou	Tzu-yu	子游
Zhou Dunyi	Chou Tun-yi	周敦頤	Zizhang	Tzu-chang	子張
Zhou Gong	Chou Kung	周公	Zizhong	Tzu-chung	子仲
Zhoukoudian	Choukoutien	周口店	Zu Chongzhi	Tsu Chung-chih	祖沖之
Zhou Mi	Chou Mi	周密	Zuo Qiuming	Tso Chiu-ming	左丘明
Zhoushan	Choushan	舟山	Zuo Zongtang	Tso Chung-tang	左宗棠
Zhou Shuren	Chou Shu-jen	周樹人	Zu Ti	Tsu Ti	祖逖
Zhou Xin	Chou Hsin	紂王辛			
Zhou Xingsi	Chou Hsing-szu	周興嗣			
Zhou Yu	Chou Yü	周瑜			

編輯經過

一九八五年春，遠東編審委員會決定將梁實秋先生主編之最新實用漢英辭典擴充增編，並成立擴編小組，立即著手籌備。擴編人員除原 遠東編審委員當然參加外，同時另行邀請各大專院校教授及百餘位優秀同學參加查證、校訂等工作。

一九八七年秋，擴編小組完成初稿，爲愼重審核初稿起見，另行設立編審小組，分三班制，日夜加班，假日亦然，期能於最短時間內完成。

一九八七年十一月三日，梁實秋先生逝世，吾等痛失導師，惟編審方針依舊，同仁更加全力以赴，務期擴編工作按原定計畫完成。遇有疑難，統由編審委員會及主編張芳杰先生及總審定朱良箴先生會同詳加審核訂正。

擴編期間，路瑞教授就原典提諸多建議，彌足珍貴。陳如一先生提「師丈」一詞，經梁實秋教授指示收入本典。其他專家學者亦相繼提供寶貴意見，吾等獲益良多，至爲感謝。意見既多，爭議之處在所難免。其中最引起爭議者，則爲冠詞。部分英語教師力主在英文「可數名詞」前加 a, 在機關名稱前加 the, 如公共汽車 a bus；父親 a father；台灣銀行 the Bank of Taiwan。部分專家認爲加冠詞誤導讀者，如：他坐公共汽車上學。He goes to school by bus. 讀者不能在 bus 前加 a；兒子叫父親Father, 絕不會在Father前加a；台灣銀行大門上方的英文名稱Bank of Taiwan, 不是The Bank of Taiwan, 至於在英文句子中該加冠詞或不加冠詞，乃屬英文法領域。擴編小組同仁斟酌各方意見，決定在英文「可數名詞」前加 a, 在機關名稱前不加 the。定義說明部分及例句，則依據文法及習慣用法加冠詞或不加冠詞。至於人名、地名，有主張用威妥瑪氏拼音法，有主張用國語羅馬拼音法，有主張用聯合國華語拼音法。我們愼重研究後，決定保留現有拼法，不加更改；爲便於讀者查閱，在附錄部分增列「專有名詞拼音對照表」。

爲適應一般讀者及大、中學生攜帶輕便需要，編審會將遠東漢英大辭典加以精簡，縮小版本，酌量刪除部分詞條、例句及附錄。謹此說明。

惟編校工作浩繁，疏漏之處在所難免，尙祈　海內外專家學者不吝指教爲幸。

遠東編審委員會

新字新詞補充

新字新詞補充

新字新詞補充

新字新詞補充

新字新詞補充

新字新詞補充

新字新詞補充

國家圖書館出版品預行編目資料

遠東漢英大辭典(簡明本) : Far East Chinese-English dictionary / 張芳杰主編. -- 初版. -- 臺北市；遠東，1993 [民82] 印刷
面； 公分
含索引
ISBN 957-612-229-5 (32K精裝聖經)
ISBN 957-612-230-9 (32K精裝道林)
ISBN 957-612-231-7 (50K精裝聖經)
ISBN 957-612-232-5 (50K精裝道林)
1.中國語言－字典，辭典－英國語言
805.133 81005853

FAR EAST CHINESE-ENGLISH DICTIONARY
遠東漢英大辭典
(簡明本)

32開道林紙本定價新台幣720元 (外埠酌加運匯費)

主編者／張芳杰
總審定／朱良箴
總編輯／鄧樂然
發行人／浦永強
出版者／遠東圖書公司
印刷者／遠東圖書公司
發行所／遠東圖書公司
地址／台北市重慶南路一段66號
www.fareast.com.tw
電話／(02)23118740 傳真／(02)23114184
郵政劃撥／00056691
美國發行所／U.S. 國際出版公司
U.S. International Publishing Inc.
www.usipusa.com
登記證／局版台業字第0820號